LONGMAN

DICTIONARY OF
AMERICAN
ENGLISH

롱맨
영영한사전

KB118160

금성출판사

Table of Contents (차례)

Preface

This new edition of the *Longman Dictionary of American English*, the foremost ESL dictionary, has been specially researched and written to meet the real needs of students of English as a second or foreign language.

Real Language

The new edition of the *Dictionary* is based on the authentic language data in the Longman Corpus Network. Longman's unique computerized language database contains over 328 million words from all types of written texts, and from real conversations recorded across the US.

The Corpus tells us how frequently words and phrases are used, so there's no guesswork in deciding what words and phrases students need to know most.
The Corpus shows which grammar patterns are the most important to illustrate.
It shows important new words and idioms that people use every day, and words that are frequently used together (called *collocations*). We take our example sentences from the Corpus, and this makes the language come alive as never before.

Real Clarity

The definitions in the *Dictionary* are written using only the 2000 most common English words — the Longman Defining Vocabulary. Longman pioneered the use of a limited vocabulary as the best way to guarantee that definitions are clear and easy to understand.

The comprehensive grammatical information in the *Dictionary* is easy to understand and use. Important patterns are highlighted in the example sentences, so that you can see at a glance how to use a word in a sentence.

The meaning you want is easy to find in the *Dictionary*. Words that have a large number of meanings have short, clear *Signposts* to guide you to the right meaning quickly.

Real Help

The new edition of the *Dictionary* is the result of extensive research into student needs and abilities, and has been tested in schools and colleges all over the US.

The writers have also used their knowledge from years of ESL teaching to analyze the Longman Learner's Corpus, which is a computerized collection of over 8 million words of writing in English by learners of the language. By Studying the errors students make in essays and exams, the writers were able to give clear, helpful usage information throughout the *Dictionary* — in the definitions, example sentences, study notes, and usage notes — to help students avoid common errors.

Use the exercises in the Dictionary Skills Workbook on pages xiii-xxvi to learn how to get the most from your *Dictionary*. The grammar codes and labels are inside the front cover, and the IPA (International Phonetic Alphabet) pronunciation table is on page iii, so they are always easy to find and use.

Whether you are writing a report, sending an e-mail, or chatting with friends, the *Longman Dictionary of American English* will help you choose the right words, understand them clearly, and use them correctly.

제2판 머리말

Longman Dictionary of American English는 롱맨사가 특별히 영어를 외국어로 학습하는 사람들을 대상으로 하여 간행한 사전이다. 롱맨사는 이 사전을 개발하기 위해 두 가지 코퍼스(언어 텍스트를 컴퓨터로 입력한 데이터베이스)를 구축해 활용하였는데, 그 하나는 미국의 실생활에서 쓰이고 있는 말과 글을 모은 3억 2,800만 단어의 코퍼스이고, 다른 하나는 영어 학습자의 영어 작문을 모은 800만 단어의 코퍼스이다. 전자는 미국 영어를 생생하게 보여주는 자료로서 활용되었고, 후자는 영어 학습자가 작문이나 시험에서 범하기 쉬운 오류를 찾아내는 자료로 활용되었다. 롱맨 사전의 이와 같은 첨단적이고 독보적인 노력은 다음과 같은 특장 속에 구석구석 녹아 있다.

첫째, 단어 풀이는 2,000개의 기본어만을 사용함으로써 초급 학습자도 쉽게 이해할 수 있게 하였다.

둘째, 방대한 코퍼스에서 뽑아 낸 예문은 현대 미국 영어를 생생하게 보여주고 있다.

셋째, 구어체 어구(spoken phrases)는 즉각 활용이 가능한 것으로 알아보기 쉽게 박스로 처리하였다.

넷째, 어법 노트(USAGE NOTE)를 통해 외국인 영어 학습자가 자주 범하는 오류를 정확히 꼬집어 낸 뒤 그것을 바로잡아 주었다.

다섯째, 학습 노트(STUDY NOTE)를 통해 전치사, 조동사, 구동사 등 문법 사항을 일목 요연하게 정리하였다.

여섯째, 빈도가 높은 연어(collocation) 정보는 예문을 통해 보여 주었다.

일곱째, 뜻갈래가 여럿 있을 때 빨리 찾을 수 있도록 팻말어(signpost)를 두었다.

여덟째, blog, botox, e-book, MP3 등 최신 용어를 다량 수록하였다.

아홉째, 다양한 삽화로 입체적 시각 정보를 제공하였다.

한편, 번역을 맡은 금성출판사에서는 뜻풀이 원문을 축소해서 번역하거나 대역어로 대체하는 기존의 영영한사전의 폐단을 지양하여, 전문을 하나도 빠짐없이 치밀하게 번역하였다.

Acknowledgments (인사말)

- *Editorial Directors*　　　　Della Summers
　　　　　　　　　　　　　　Adam Gadsby

- *Editorial Manager*　　　　　Wendalyn Nichols

- *Senior Editor*　　　　　　　Karen Stern

- *Lexicographers*　　　　　　Rebecca Campbell
　　　　　　　　　　　　　　Robert Clevenger
　　　　　　　　　　　　　　Dewayne Crawford
　　　　　　　　　　　　　　Dileri Borunda Johnston
　　　　　　　　　　　　　　Carol Pomeroy Zhong

- *Publishing Management*　　Joanne Dresner
　　　　　　　　　　　　　　Allen Ascher

- *Design*　　　　　　　　　　Jenny Fleet
　　　　　　　　　　　　　　Carolyn Viola John

- *Project Manager*　　　　　　Alan Savill

- *Administrative Assistant*　　Sandra Rootsey

- *Senior Lexicographer*　　　　Karen Cleveland Marwick

- *Associate Lexicographer*　　Sue Engineer

- *Pronunciation Editor*　　　　Rebecca Dauer, PhD

- *Corpus development*　　　　Steve Crowdy
　　　　　　　　　　　　　　Denise Denney

- *Production*　　　　　　　　Clive McKeough
　　　　　　　　　　　　　　Patrice Fraccio

- *Illustrator*　　　　　　　　　Len Shalansky

- *Production Editor*　　　　　Claire Parkyns

- *Keyboarder*　　　　　　　　Pauline Savill

The Publishers Would like to thank:

- Professor Jack du Bois of the University of California at Santa Barbara, for the development of the Longman Corpus of Spoken American English. This unique corpus, developed especially for the Longman Dictionary of American English, consists of 5 million words of everyday conversation by US speakers of English. The corpus was designed to provide a representative sample of the US population, by age, sex, region, educational attainment and ethnic origin. Volunteers were selected to wear a digital cassette recorder and record their conversations over a two-week period. The tapes were then transcribed and built into a computer system so that the lexicographic team could analyze exactly how native speakers use the language.

- the thousands of teachers and students from around the world who have contributed scripts for the Longman Learner's Corpus. This corpus consists of 8 million words of writing in English by learners, and helps lexicographers to analyze what students know and where they have difficulty.

- the Linguistic Data Consortium for texts included in the 80-million-word Longman Corpus of Written American English.

- the many teachers and students who have taken part in the development of the new edition of the dictionary. This has included focus groups, questionnaires, student vocabulary notebooks (in which students kept a record of which words they looked up), classroom piloting of material, and written feedback on text by teachers.

Nancy Ackles, University of Washington Extension, Seattle. **Thomas W. Adams**, University of Pennsylvania. **Monica Alcarez-Snow**, California State University, Fullerton. **Isabella Anikst**, American Language Center, University of California, Los Angeles Extension. **Cathrine Berg**, Drexel University, Philadelphia. **Gretchen Bitterlin**, San Diego Community College. **Donna Brinton**, University of California, Los Angeles. **Arlene Bublick**, William Rainey Harper College, Palatine, Illinois. **Christine Bunn**, City College of San Francisco. **Dorothy Burak**, University of California, San Diego. **Rand Burger**, California State Polytechnic University, Pomona University. **Laura Cameron**, A.C.E. Language Institute, Seattle Pacific University. **Sarah Canady**, Bellevue Community College, Seattle. **Jane Cater**, A.C.E. Language Institute, Seattle Pacific University. **Rick Chapman**, California State University, Fullerton. **Martha Compton**, University of California, Irvine. **Jan Copeland**, Long Beach City College, Long Beach, California. **Patrick Cox**, Houston Community College. **Nick Crump**, Merritt College, Oakland. **Catherine Crystal**, Laney College, Oakland. **Kevin G. Curry**, Wichita State University, Kansas. **Susan Davis**, EF International. **Carlos C. Delgado**, North Valley Occupational Center, Mission Hills, California. **Carolyn Dupaquier**, California State University, Fullerton. **Nancy Dyer**, A.C.E. Language Institute, Seattle Pacific University. **Julie Easton**, Adult Education Center, Santa Monica. **Gerry Eldred**, Long Beach City College, Long Beach, California. **Rita Esquivel**, Adult Education Center, Santa Monica. **Mary Fitzpatrick**, College of Marin, Novato. **Annette Fruehan**, Orange Coast College, California. **Caroline Gibbs**, College of Marin, Novato. **Janet Goodwin**, University of California, Los Angeles. **Lisa Hale**, St Giles College, London. **James Harris**, Rancho Santiago College, Santa Ana. **Tamara Hefter**, Truman College, Chicago. **Patti Heiser**, University of Washington Extension. **Julie Herrmann**, A.C.E. Language Institute, Seattle Pacific University. **Wayne Heuple**, A.C.E. Language Institute, Seattle Pacific University. **Kathi Holper**, William Rainey Harper College, Palatine, Illinois. **Barbara Howard**, Daley College ALSP, Chicago. **Kathryn Howard**, **Leann Howard**, San Diego Community College. **Stephanie Howard**, American Language Center, University of California, Los Angeles Extension. **Gail Hutchins**, East San Jose College. **Susan Jamieson**, Bellevue Community College. **Jeff Janulis**, Daley College, Chicago. **Linda Jensen**, University of California, Los Angeles. **Winston Joffrion**, Bellevue Community College, Bellevue. **Deborah Jonas**, California State University, Long Beach. **Kathryn Curry Keesler**, Orange Coast College. **Barbara Logan**, A.C.E. Language Institute, Seattle Pacific University. **Walter Lowe**, Bellevue Community College, Bellevue. **Lynne Lucas**, Daley College ALSP, Chicago. **Robyn Mann**, William Rainey Harper College, Palatine, Illinois. **Anne McGinley**, San Diego State University. **Elaine McVey**, San Diego State University. **Amy Meepoe**, University of California, Los Angeles. **Andy Muller**, A.C.E.Language Institute, Seattle Pacific University. **Jill Neely**, Merritt College, Oakland. **Maura Newberry**, University of California, Los Angeles. **Yvonne Nishio**, Evans Community Adult School, Los Angeles. **Roxanne Nuhaily**, University of California, San Diego. **Carla Nyssen**, California State University, Long Beach. **David Olsher**, University of California, Los Angeles. **Jorge Perez**, Southwestern College, San Diego. **Ellen Pentkowski**, Truman College, Chicago. **Eileen Prince Lou**, Northeastern University, Boston. **Nancy Quinn**, Truman College, Chicago. **Ralph Radell**, Bunker Hill Community College, Boston. **Eva Ramirez**, Laney College, Oakland. **Alison Rice**, Hunter College. **Lenore Richmond**, California State University, Fullerton. **Jane Rinaldi**, California State Polytechnic University, Pomona. **Bruce Rindler**, CELOP, Boston University. **Shirley Roberts**, Long Beach City College, Long Beach. **William Robertson**, Northeastern University, Boston. **Bonnie Rose**, University of Denver. **Teresa Ross**, California State University, Long Beach. **Paul Safstrom** South Seattle Community College. **Karen Santiago**, American Language Academy, Philadelphia. **Irene Schoenberg**, Hunter College, New York. **Esther Sunde**, South Seattle Community College, Seattle. **Barbara Swartz**, Northeastern University, Boston. **Priscilla Taylor**, California State University, Los Angeles. **Elizabeth Terplan**, College of Marin, Novato, California. **Bill Trimble**, Modesto Junior College. **Wendy Walsh**, College of Marin, Novato, California. **Colleen Weldele**, Palomar College, San Marcos, California. **Sabella Wells**, A.C.E. Language Instiute, Seattle Pacific University. **Madeleine Youmans**, Long Beach City College, Long Beach. **Christine Zilkow**, California State University, Fullerton. **Janet Zinner**, Northeastern University, Boston. **Jean Zukowski-Faust**, Northern Arizona University.

Yuri Komuro, for assistance in compiling the results of teacher questionnaires and student word diaries

Norma A. Register, PhD, for advice on coverage of socially sensitive langue

Key to the Dictionary (일러두기)

이 일러두기는 이 사전에 제시된 정보에 신속히 접근하게 하는 안내자이다. 보다 자세한 설명과 연습은 xi-xxiv 페이지의 Dictionary Skills Workbook에 있는 각 내용을 참고하라.

철자 및 검색 – workbook pages xi-xii

철자가 다른 것

gan·gling /ˈgæŋglɪŋ/, **gan·gly** /ˈgæŋgli/ *adj* unusually tall and thin and unable to move gracefully: *a gangly teenager*

철자가 다른 것은 이와 같이 표시하였다 — xi 참조

불규칙 복수형

medium² *n* **1** *plural* **media** a way of communicating or expressing something: *The Internet is a powerful advertising medium.* **2** *plural* **media** the material, paints etc. that an artist uses: *This sculptor's favorite medium is wood.* **3** *plural* **mediums** someone who claims to speak to dead people and receive

복수형이 media인가, medium인가? 정확한 철자를 이와 같이 표시하였다 — xii 참조

불규칙 동사와 그 철자

sing /sɪŋ/ *v* **sang, sung, singing 1** [I, T] to make musical sounds, songs etc. with your voice: *Do you like singing folk*

철자가 달라지나? 철자가 달라지는 것은 이와 같이 표시하였다 — xii 참조

불규칙 비교급과 최상급

bad¹ /bæd/ *adj* **worse, worst 1** not good and unpleasant: *I'm afraid I have some*

단어 형태가 달라지나? 형태가 달라지는 것은 이와 같이 표시하였다 — xii 참조

발음 및 강세 – workbook pages xiii-xiv

발음

air·plane /ˈɛrpleɪn/ *n* a vehicle that flies by using wings and one or more engines;

각 단어의 발음을 이와 같이 표시하였다 — xiii 참조

강세

e·lec·tion /ɪˈlɛkʃən/ *n* an occasion when you vote in order to choose someone for an official position: *The election results*

eléction이라고 하나 élection이라고 하나? — xiii 참조

어의 검색 및 이해 – workbook pages xiv-xvi

간단 명료한 설명

kay·ak /ˈkaɪæk/ *n* a CANOE (=type of boat) usually for one person, that is enclosed

어의(語義)는 간단히 설명하여 이해하기가 쉽다. 알지 못할 가능성이 있는 어휘는 이와 같이 소대자(小大字)로 표시하였다. 소대자로 나타낸 단어는 이 사전에서 찾아볼 수 있다 — xiv 참조

어의가 둘 이상인 경우

favorite² *n* **1** someone or something that you like more than any other one of its kind: *I like all her books, but this one is my favorite.* **2** someone who receives more attention and approval than is fair: *Teachers shouldn't have favorites.*

많은 단어들이 두 가지 이상의 어의를 갖고 있다. 첫째 의미가 가장 일반적인 것이지만 다른 어의들도 점검하는 것을 잊지 않기를 바란다. — xv 참조

관용적 표현

calm³ *n* **1** [singular, U] a time that is quiet and peaceful **2 the calm before the storm** a peaceful situation just

특별한 뜻이 있는 어구들은 이와 같이 표시하였다 — xv 참조

팻말어

school¹ /skul/ *n*
1 ▶BUILDING◀ [C, U] a place where children are taught: *Which school did*

이 팻말어들은 찾고 싶은 어의를 빨리 찾도록 도움을 준다 — xvi 참조

문법 설명 – workbook pages xvi-xviii

품사

o·ver·night² /ˈouvəˌnaɪt/ *adj* continuing all night: *an overnight flight to*

이 문자들은 명사·동사·형용사 등의 품사를 나타낸다 — xvi 참조

파생어

street lights **3** unkind, cruel, or strict: *harsh criticism / harsh unfair laws* – **harshly** *adv* – **harshness** *n* [U]

파생어는 이와 같이 표시하였다 — xvi 참조

명사

pit·y¹ /ˈpɪti/ *n* **1** [U] sympathy for someone who is suffering or unhappy: *I don't need your pity!* **2** [singular] a sad

이 기호들은 명사의 사용법을 나타낸다. [U]와 [singular]는 이 의미로는 복수형을 쓸 수 없다는 것을 뜻한다 — xvii 참조

동사

cheat¹ /tʃit/ *v* **1** [I] to behave in a dishonest way in order to win or gain something: *He always cheats when we play cards.* **2** [T] to trick or deceive

이 기호들은 동사의 목적어 수반 여부를 나타낸다. [I]는 목적어와 함께 쓸 수 없다는 것을 뜻하며 [T]는 목적어와 함께 써야 한다는 것을 뜻한다 — xvii 참조

구동사

check on sb/sth *phr v* [T] to make sure that someone or something is doing

이 문자들은 구동사의 목적어가 사람 또는 사물이 될 수 있다는 것을 나타낸다 — xviii 참조

dawn on sb *phr v* [T] to realize something: *It suddenly dawned on me*

이 문자들은 dawn on을 쓸 때 목적어가 전치사 뒤에만 올 수 있다는 것을 나타낸다 — xviii 참조

rinse sth ↔ **out** *phr v* [T] to wash something with clean water but not soap: *Please rinse out your bottles*

이 문자들은 rinse something out 또는 rinse out something을 쓸 수 있다는 것을 나타낸다 — xviii 참조

어휘의 올바른 사용 – workbook pages xviii-xix

용례

adj **1** completely sure and without any doubts: *I'm not certain (that) he's telling me the truth. / No one was certain what to expect. / Are you certain about that?* **2 know/say for**

많은 유익한 예문들이 어휘의 용법을 알려 준다. 문형은 굵은 글씨로 나타냈다 — xviii 참조

Key to the Dictionary

상용어구

2 ▶MAIN IDEA 주된 생각◀ the main meaning or idea in something that is said or done: *Get to the point!* (=say your idea directly)

이와 같은 분명한 설명은 단어가 사용된 상용어구의 이해에 도움을 준다 — xviii 참조

용법 해설

USAGE NOTE gain, earn, and win

Use **gain** to talk about gradually getting more of something, such as an ability or quality: *You'll gain a lot of experience working here.* Use **earn** to

용법 해설은 단어 이용시 흔히 저지르는 실수를 하지 않도록 도움을 준다. 유의어들의 뜻과 용법을 설명해 주는가 하면 특정 단어의 난해한 문법을 설명해 주기도 하고 어떤 것은 미국 영어에서 특이하게 쓰이는 단어에 대한 설명을 해 준다 — xix 참조

용법 지시

you speak any foreign languages?" "Yes, I speak French." ✗DON'T SAY "I speak French language."✗

용법 지시는 특정 단어에 관련하여 흔히 저지르는 실수를 하지 않도록 도움을 준다 — xix 참조

정확한 단어 선택 – workbook pages xx-xxi

격식어, 비격식어, 구어 등의 용법 분류

guy /gaɪ/ *n* **1** INFORMAL a man: *I'm going out with a few guys from work tonight. / Some guy wanted to talk to you.* **2 you guys/those guys** SPOKEN said when

이 단어를 작문에 사용하는 것이 옳은 것일까? — xx 참조

유의어

elementary school /..'.. ,./ *n* a school in the US for the first six or eight years of a child's education; GRADE SCHOOL

이것은 동일하게 쓸 수 있는 유사한 뜻을 지닌 다른 단어를 나타낸다

fac·sim·i·le /fæk'sɪməli/ *n* **1** an exact copy of a picture, piece of writing etc. **2** ⇨ FAX

이것은 훨씬 잘 쓰이는 동일한 것을 의미하는 단어를 나타낸다 — xx 참조

반의어

large /lɑrdʒ/ *adj* **1** big, or bigger than usual in size, number, or amount: *I'd like a large pepperoni pizza, please. / What's the largest city in Canada?* —opposite SMALL —see usage note

이것은 반대의 뜻을 지닌 단어를 나타낸다 — xxi 참조

참조

mint¹ /mɪnt/ *n* **1** a candy with a sweet hot taste: *an after dinner mint* **2** [U] a plant with sweet hot-tasting leaves used in cooking and making medicine —see also PEPPERMINT, SPEARMINT **3 a mint**

이것은 표제어 mint와 관련된 단어를 나타낸다

비교

in·ter·pret·er /ɪn'tɜprətɚ/ *n* someone who changes the spoken words of one language into another —compare TRANSLATOR

이것은 표제어 interpreter와 혼동을 일으킬 수 있는 단어를 나타낸다 — xxi 참조

Pronunciation (발음)

미국 영어

이 사전은 가장 널리 통용되는 미국식 영어를 사용하는 사람들이 쓰는 발음을 보여 주고 있으며 때때로 하나 이상의 발음이 표기되어 있다.

예를 들어 다수의 미국인들은 data의 첫 모음을 /eɪ/로 발음하지만 또 다른 다수는 /æ/로도 발음하므로 이 사전은 data /ˈdeɪṱə, ˈdæṱə/로 표기하고 있다. 이것은 두 발음이 모두 가능하며 교육을 받은 영어 사용자들이 일반적으로 사용하고 있다는 것을 뜻한다.

그러나 미국 내의 온갖 방언과 가능한 발음 전부를 실은 것은 아니다. 예컨대 news를 소수의 미국인들이 /nyuz/로 발음하고 있더라도 이곳에서는 /nuz/만을 보여 주고 있다.

또 많은 미국인들이 /ɔ/ 발음을 사용하지 않고 /ɔ/ 대신에 /ɑ/를 사용해서 caught와 cot를 둘 다 /kɑt/로 발음하지만 이곳에서는 모음 /ɔ/와 /ɑ/ 둘 다를 보여 주고 있다.

하이픈(hyphen)의 사용

한 단어에 두 가지 이상의 발음이 주어질 때는 보통 첫 발음 기호와 다른 부분만을 표기하고 동일한 부분은 하이픈으로 대신했다: economics /ˌɛkəˈnɑmɪks, ˌi-/. 하이픈은 또한 명확하지 않은 음절 간의 구분을 표시하는 데에도 사용한다: boyish /ˈbɔɪ-ɪʃ/, drawing /ˈdrɔ-ɪŋ/, clockwise /ˈklɑk-waɪz/.

발음 기호

이 사전에 사용된 발음 기호들은 국제 음성 기호(IPA ; International Phonetic Alphabet)를 기초로 몇 가지만 바꾼 것이다. 발음 기호 /y/는 IPA에서 사용하는 /j/보다 영어 철자에 더 가까운 것으로 you/yu/의 첫 음에 쓰인다. 다른 차이점들은 미국 영어 발음란에 상세히 다뤄져 있다.

외래어

외래어에 대해서는 일부 사용자들이 원어에 더 가깝게 발음을 할지라도 영어식 발음으로 표기했다.

약어

대다수의 약어에는 발음 기호를 표기하지 않았다. 이것은 약어들이 written abbreviation(문어체 약어)로 규정되어 구어에는 쓰지 않거나, 제1강세는 마지막 글자에, 제2강세는 첫 글자에 두어 각 철자명을 읽는 형태로 발음되기 때문이다: VCR /ˌviˈsiˈɑr/. 그러나 약어가 일반 단어처럼 별도의 발음이 있을 때에는 발음 기호를 표기했다: RAM /ræm/.

표제어 관련 언어군

표제어의 다른 품사형은 그 단어의 설명 끝에 표시했다. 표제어의 동족어가 표제어에 접미사(1908페이지 표 참조)만 추가해서 발음되는 경우는 별도의 발음 기호는 표기하지 않았지만 접미사 추가로 표제어의 발음이 변하는 경우는 발음 기호를 모두 표기했다: impossible /ɪmˈpɑsəbəl/, impossibility /ɪmˌpɑsəˈbɪləṱi/.

그러나 일부 발음 변화는 규칙적인 형식을 따르기 때문에 이 범주에는 포함시키지 않았다.
1) 어미 -ly나 -er가 /-bəl/, /-kəl/, /-pəl/, /-gəl/, /-dəl/로 끝나는 표제어에 추가될 때 /ə/는 대개 생략된다: practical /ˈpræktɪkəl/로 발음된 -ly가 추가되면 practically /ˈpræktɪkli/가 되지만 이 발음 변화는 표시하지 않았다.
2) -y/i/로 끝나는 단어에 -ly나 -ity가 추가되면 /i/는 /ə/가 된다: angry /ˈæŋgri/는 angrily /ˈæŋgrəli/가 되지만 이 역시 표시하지 않았다.

강세

2음절 단어들은 최소한 한 음절은 다른 음절들보다 강하게 발음하는데 /ˈ/ 기호는 제1강세로 부르며 가장 강한 음절 앞에 놓인다 : person /ˈpəsən/, percent /pəˈsɛnt/.

일부 단어들은 다른 음절에 제1강세보다 약한 강세를 갖는데 제2강세로 부르며 /ˌ/ 기호가 그 음절 앞에 놓인다: personality /ˌpəsəˈnæləṱi/, personify /pəˈsɑnəˌfaɪ/.

즉 두 번째 음절이 starlet /ˈstɑrlət/과 비교하여 starlit /ˈstɑrˌlɪt/에서처럼 반드시 짧게 발음하면 안 된다는 것을 보일 필요가 있지 않는 한 제2강세가 2음절어의 두 번째 음절에 항상 표시되는 것은 아니다.

무강세 모음

/ə/와 /ɪ/ 미국식 영어에서 /ə/와 /ɪ/는 여러 강세 없는 음절 속에서 매우 짧고 불분명하게 발음이 된다. 이들은 일상적으로 이어나가는 대화에서는 그 차이가 거의 없다. 예컨대 affect /əˈfɛkt/와 effect /ɪˈfɛkt/는 보통 발음이 같고 rabbit의 발음 기호는 /ˈræbɪt/이지만 /ˈræbət/으로도 발음될 수 있다.

/ə/와 /ʌ/ 이 두 발음은 매우 유사한데 /ə/는 무강세 음절에 사용되고 /ʌ/는 더 길게 발음되며 제1강세와 제2강세 음절에 쓰인다. 그러나 빠르게 발음하면 제2강세는 강세가 없어져 /ʌ/는 /ə/로 발음된다. 예컨대 difficult /ˈdɪfɪˌkʌlt/와 coconut /ˈkoʊkəˌnʌt/은 각각 /ˈdɪfɪkəlt/와 /ˈkoʊkənət/으로 발음될 수 있지만 이 사전은 /ʌ/만을 나타냈다.

분리 복합어와 하이픈 복합어

많은 복합어들은 성분이 되는 단어들 사이가 띄어져 있거나 하이픈으로 연결된 형태로 되어 있다. 성분이 되는 단어들이 모두 별도의 표제어로 실린 경우에 전체 발음 기호는 표기하지 않고 강세 형태만을 나타냈다. 각 음절을 점 /./로 표시하여 강세 음절을 나타내는 점 /./ 앞에 강세 기호를 두었다: bus stop /ˈ. ./, town hall /ˌ. ˈ./.

때때로 복합어가 이 사전에 실린 표제어와 흔히 쓰이는 접미사로 이루어진 경우에도 단지 강세 형태만 나타냈다: washing machine /ˈ...ˌ.ˈ./. 이 경우 washing은 표제어가 아니지만 wash는 표제어로 이 사전에 실려 있고 접미사 -ing는 흔히 쓰이는 것이므로 단지 강세 형태만 표시되어 있다.

그러나 어느 한쪽이라도 독립 표제어가 아닌 경우는 전체 발음 기호를 표기했다 : **helter-skelter**/ˌhɛltəˈskɛltə/.

강세 변화
많은 복합어들은 어떤 명사 앞에 쓰일 때 강세의 위치가 변할 수 있다. 예컨대 복합어 plate glass는 단독으로 쓰이거나 "The window was made of plate glass." 등의 문장에 쓰일 때는 /ˌ.ˈ./ 형태를 취하지만 plate glass window라는 구에서는 보통 /ˌ.ˈ../ 형태를 취한다. 기호/./는 이러한 강세 변화를 나타낸다: **plate glass**/ˌ.ˈ./.

강세 변화는 단일어들에서도 나타난다 : **artificial**/ˌartəˈfɪʃəl/, **independent**/ˌɪndɪˈpɛndənt/.

성절(成節) 자음
/n/과 /l/ 발음은 성절(成節)적이어서 특히 단어의 끝(그리고 특정 자음 특히 /t/와 /d/ 뒤)에서 자체로 음절을 이룰 수 있다. 예컨대 **sudden**/ˈsʌdn/에서 /n/은 성절 자음이고 /d/와 /n/ 사이에 모음이 없으므로 발음 기호에도 모음이 나타나지 않는다. 단어 중간에, /n/이나 /l/ 다음의 하이픈이나 강세 부호는 그것이 성절음이라는 것을 나타낸다: **botanist**/ˈbɑtn-ɪst/와 **catalog**/ˈkætl̩ˌɔg/는 3음절로 된 단어들이다.

발음 기호 자음 /r/이나 모음 /ɚ/ 어느 쪽으로도 발음될 수 있다. 즉 /ɚ/에 무강세 모음이 뒤따르면 /ɚ/와 다음의 모음이 합해져 연속 모음처럼 발음될 수 있거나 /r/로 시작되는 음절 앞의 /ə/처럼 발음될 수 있다. 예컨대 단어 coloring은 /ˈkʌlərɪŋ/ 대신에 /ˈkʌlərɪŋ/으로

발음될 수 있지만 이곳에서는 발음 기호 /ˈkʌlərɪŋ/만을 나타냈다.

미국 영어 발음
/t/ tap 또는 sat의 /t/는 무성음이다. 그러나 많은 미국인들은 latter, party, little 등의 단어에 있는 t를 속음(速音) /d/처럼 유성음으로 발음한다. 이 사전에 /t/로 표기된 이와 같은 단어들의 t는 ladder, hardy, middle에서의 d처럼 발음한다. 이 소리는 보통 모음들 사이(특히 강세가 없는 모음 앞), r과 모음 사이, 또는 성절음 /l/ 앞에서 나타난다.

/tˀ/ 이 기호는 많은 사람들이 /t/ 대신 또는 /t/와 동일하게 발음하는 성문 폐쇄음을 나타낸다. 성문 폐쇄음은 uh oh의 중간 소리를 말한다. 일례로 **button**/ˈbʌtˀn/과 **football** /ˈfʊtˀbɔl/에서의 t는 ton/tʌn/에서의 t와 똑같은 소리가 나지 않는다. 오히려 소리가 잠시 나지 않는 것처럼 들린다. 성문 폐쇄음은 보통 성절음 /n/ 앞이나 다음 음절이 시작되는 자음 앞에서 일어난다.

/t/, /d/ 이 기호들은 이 자음들의 발음을 해도 좋고 생략해도 좋다는 것을 뜻한다. 예컨대 **restless**/ˈrɛstlɪs/의 t와 **grandfather** /ˈgrænˌfɑðəˀ/의 d는 신중하게 천천히 말할 때는 발음할지라도 정상적으로 연속해서 말할 때는 보통 발음이 생략된다.

/nʃ/ 많은 사람들이 연속음 /nʃ/를 /ntʃ/로 발음한다. 예컨대 **attention**/əˌtɛnʃən/, **conscious** /ˈkɑnʃəs/를 /əˈtɛntʃən/, /ˈkɑntʃəs/로 발음하기도 하지만 이곳에서는 /nʃ/만을 나타냈다.

PRONUNCIATION TABLE (발음기호표)

VOWELS (모음)

Symbol	Key Word
i	beat, feed
ɪ	bit, did
eɪ	date, paid
ɛ	bet, bed
æ	bat, bad
ɑ	box, odd, father
ɔ	bought, dog
oʊ	boat, road
ʊ	book, good
u	boot, food, student
ʌ	but, mud, mother
ə	banana, among
ɚ	shirt, murder
aɪ	bite, cry, buy, eye
aʊ	about, how
ɔɪ	voice, boy
ɪr	beer
ɛr	bare
ɑr	bar
ɔr	door
ʊr	tour

CONSONANTS (자음)

Symbol	Key Word		
p	pack, happy	w	wet, white
b	back, rubber	l	light, long
t	tie	r	right, wrong
d	die	y	yes, use, music
k	came, key, quick	ţ	butter, bottle
g	game, guest	tˀ	button
tʃ	church, nature, watch		
dʒ	judge, general, major		
f	fan, photograph		
v	van	/t/	means that/t/ may be dropped. 생략 가능
θ	thing, breath		
ð	then, breathe		
s	sip, city, psychology	/d/	means that/d/ may be dropped. 생략 가능
z	zip, please, goes		
ʃ	ship, machine, special	/ˈ/	shows main stress. 제1 강세
ʒ	measure, vision	/ˌ/	shows secondary stress. 제2 강세
h	hot, who		
m	men, some	/·/	shows stress shift. 강세 변동
n	sun, know, pneumonia		
ŋ	sung, ringing		

Dictionary Skills Workbook

This dictionary is full of information that makes spoken and written English easier to understand and use correctly. Use the exercises in this workbook to learn how to find and use the information you want.

SPELLING AND FINDING WORDS

The alphabet

The words in this dictionary are listed in alphabetical order. Here is the English alphabet:

Lowercase letters   a b c d e f g h i j k l m n o p q r s t u v w x y z

Uppercase or capital letters   A B C D E F G H I J K L M N O P Q R S T U V W X Y Z

Compounds

Sometimes two words have a special meaning when they are used together. They can be written as two words, like **ice cream**, or with a HYPHEN, like **role-play**. In this dictionary, words like these are listed alphabetically as though they were just one word, like this:

> **forward⁴** *n* in basketball, one of two

> **for·ward·ing ad·dress** /ˌ... ˈ.., ˌ... .ˈ./ *n* an

> **forward-look·ing** /ˈ.. ˌ../, **forward-thinking**

> **fos·sil** /ˈfɑsəl/ *n* part of an animal or

Phrasal verbs

Two- and three-word verbs that are related to the main verb are listed separately, under the main verb, like this:

> **chime²** *v* [I, T] to make a ringing (RING) sound, especially in order to show what time it is: *The clock chimed six.*
>
> **chime in** *phr v* [I] to agree with what someone has just said, often by

Abbreviations

Abbreviations are also listed alphabetically:

> **ba·zaar** /bəˈzɑr/ *n* **1** an occasion when

> **BB gun** /ˈbibi ˌɡʌn/ *n* a gun that uses

> **BBQ** /ˈbɑrbɪˌkyu/ a written abbreviation

EXERCISE 1   **Put these words in the order that you can find them in the dictionary.**

pay   _pawn_

pay-TV   _____

pay off   _____

payroll   _____

pea   _____

PE   _____

pay dirt   _____

pay up   _____

pawn   _____

Different spellings

If you look up the word **ambiance** in the dictionary, you will see that there are two different spellings for this word. Both of them are correct, but **ambiance** is the more common one, so it is written first:

> **am·bi·ance, ambience** /ˈæmbiəns, ˈɑmbiɑns/ *n* [U] the way a place makes

Dictionary Skills Workbook

Irregular plurals

Most nouns form their plural by adding **-s** or **-es**. However, some nouns have special plural forms. When the plural of a noun is not formed by adding **-s** or **-es**, this dictionary shows the irregular plural form:

> **child** /tʃaɪld/ *n, plural* **children** /'tʃɪldrən/
> **1** a young person who is not yet fully grown

Irregular verbs and verb spellings

Most verbs form the past tense and PAST PARTICIPLE by adding **-ed** and the PRESENT PARTICIPLE by adding **-ing**, such as **helped**, **have helped**, **be helping**. However, some verbs have special forms. When a verb is irregular, this dictionary shows the irregular verb form:

> **grow** /groʊ/ *v* **grew, grown, growing**
> [I] **1** ▶ DEVELOP ◀ to develop and become bigger or longer over time, or to

Sometimes only the spelling is irregular in the past tense and past participle. This shows that the spelling of **spot** changes when you add **-ed** or **-ing**:

> **spot²** *v* **-tted, -tting** [T] **1** to notice or recognize something that is difficult to

Irregular comparatives and superlatives

Most adjectives and adverbs form the COMPARATIVE by adding **-er** and the SUPERLATIVE by adding **-est**, for example **mild**, **milder**, **mildest**. However, some of these have special forms. When the comparative or superlative of an adjective or adverb is irregular, this dictionary shows the irregular form:

> **good¹** /gʊd/ *adj* **better, best**
> **1** ▶ HIGH IN QUALITY ◀ of a high standard: *His score on the test was very good. / Thanks, Maria, you did a good job.* ✗DON'T SAY "You did good."

Common spelling changes

Many spelling changes are the result of regular rules, and are therefore not shown in this dictionary as irregular forms. For example:

"Drop the **-y** and add **-ies**": **party**, *plural* **parties**
"Drop the **-y** and add **-ied**": **study**, *past tense* **studied**
"Drop the **-e** and add **-ing**": **amaze**, *present participle* **amazing**
"Drop the **-e** and add **-er** or **-est**": **sane**, *comparative* **saner**, *superlative* **sanest**

EXERCISE 2 Write the correct form of each word in the correct column. (Irregular spelling patterns are shown in the dictionary, and regular ones are not.)

verb	past tense	past participle	present participle
take	*took*		
make			*making*
eat			
lag		*lagged*	
carry			

adjective	comparative	superlative
mad	*madder*	
tiny		
bad		
crazy		*craziest*
funny		

noun	plural
domino	
knife	
candy	*candies*
axis	
aircraft	

SOUNDS AND STRESS

Vowels and consonants

The pronunciation of a word is shown between sloping lines, like this: /....../

phone¹ /fəʊn/ *n* **1** a piece of equipment that you use in order to talk with

On page iii of this dictionary is a list of the special alphabet in PHONETIC letters that we have used for showing pronunciation. Next to each SYMBOL(=special letter) is a common word that shows what the sound is like. Because many different letters can have the same sound in English, the list also shows different ways of spelling the same sounds:

vowels		consonants	
Symbol	Key Word	Symbol	Key Word
aʊ	ab**out**, h**ow**	m	**m**en, so**m**e
eɪ	d**a**te, p**ai**d	f	**f**an, **ph**otograph

EXERCISE 3A **VOWELS: Use this exercise to learn some of the most common symbols.**

Put the words below under the correct vowel symbol, by looking in the dictionary to see which sound each word uses.

**said   need   awful   glue   new   bet   field   thought   boot   even   seed   soft
clean   dead   mood   true   do   ever   next   taught   went   malt**

/i/	/ɛ/	/ɔ/	/u/
need	said	awful	glue

EXERCISE 3B **CONSONANTS: Use this exercise to learn how some common sounds can be spelled.**

Put the words below under the consonant symbol, by looking in the dictionary to see which sound each word starts with.

**kite   night   city   cool   noon   knead   pneumatic   key   science   psyche
cyberspace   cream   color   seal**

/s/	/k/	/n/
city	kite	night

STRESS

Many words contain more than one SYLLABLE(=part that has a vowel sound). The words **agree**, **announce**, and **around** all have two syllables. If you look at the pronunciation guides for these words, you will see that they have a sign /'/ in front of their second syllables. This means that when we say these words, we put more STRESS(=force) on the syllable with the sign in front of it:

agree/ə'gri/ **announce**/ə'naʊns/ **around**/ə'raʊnd/

Look at the pronunciation guides for the words **airfare**, **bookstore**, and **forty**. When we say these words, the stress is on the first syllable of these words, so the sign is at the beginning:

airfare /ˈɛrfɛr/   **bookstore** /ˈbʊkstɔr/   **forty** /ˈfɔrt̬i/

For more information on stress, see page ix.

EXERCISE 4   **Look up the pronunciation guides for the words listed below. All of them have more than one syllable, so look for the sign / ˈ/. Underline the part of the word that has the stress put on it:**

gazebo   horizon   mercury   successfully

Words with the same spelling, but different sounds or stress

When two words are spelled the same but have different sounds or stress patterns, this dictionary shows them like this:

de·fense¹ /dɪˈfɛns/ *n* **1** [U] the act of

de·fense² /ˈdifɛns/ *n* [U] the players in

EXERCISE 5   **Use your dictionary to check the stress and pronunciation of *record*, *increase*, *permit*, and *upset* in the sentences below. Underline the syllable where the stress should be put on these words in each sentence.**

*We keep a careful **record** of our household expenses.*   *You need a special **permit** to park here.*
*We carefully **record** all our household expenses.*   *They only **permit** employees to park here.*
*The Governor does not want a tax **increase**.*   *Sorry, I didn't mean to **upset** you.*
*The Governor does not want taxes to **increase**.*   *Sorry, I didn't mean to cause a big **upset**.*

Syllables and hyphenation

It helps to learn the pronunciation of a long word if you start by saying it one syllable at a time. This dictionary uses DOTS(=small round marks) between the syllables of words to show where the syllables are:

in·her·i·tance /ɪnˈhɛrɪt̬əns/ *n*

Say each syllable slowly:
  in her i tance
  ɪnˈhɛr ɪ t̬əns
Now say the word quickly. Remember to put the stress on /hɛr/: **inheritance**
The dots also show you where you can break a word at the end of a line of writing:

*Milton's aunt left him a large **inher-***   *Milton's aunt left him a large **inheri-***
***itance** when she died.*   ***tance** when she died.*

✗Do not break a word after only one letter, and do not leave just one letter on the new line, after the hyphen.✗

FINDING AND UNDERSTANDING MEANINGS

The defining vocabulary

This dictionary makes it easy for you to understand the meanings of words – their DEFINITIONS – because the definitions have been written using a defining vocabulary of only 2000 common words.

For example, look at the entry for **ice cream**. Because there are no difficult words used in the definition, you do not have to look up other words to understand what it means.

ice cream /ˈ. ./ *n* [U] a frozen sweet food made of milk or cream and sugar, usually with

If it is impossible to avoid using a more difficult word in a definition, that word is shown in CAPITAL LETTERS like this. You can find this word in the dictionary, and many words like this have short explanations after them.

tom·a·hawk /ˈtɑmə,hɔk/ *n* a HATCHET (=type of weapon) used by some Native

EXERCISE 6 Use your dictionary to answer these questions by looking up the words shown in dark letters and reading their definitions.

1. What type of things would use a **beacon** to guide them? *Answer: boats, planes, etc.*
2. If you **stride**, how do you walk?
3. How would you play a **cymbal**?
4. If two things are **diametrically** opposed, are they similar or different?
5. When might you say "good **riddance**"?
6. How many quarts make up a **gallon**?
7. Does a **plaintive** sound seem happy or sad?
8. What might make you **wince**?

More than one meaning
Many words have more than one meaning. When this is true, you should read through all the meanings until you find the one that correctly explains the use of the word you are looking for. To help you find the meaning you want quickly, this dictionary puts the most frequent meaning first, the second most frequent meaning second, and so on.

For example, at the noun **rap**, the first meaning listed is the musical meaning, because people use that meaning the most. The second meaning listed is the noise, because that is the next most frequent meaning.

> **rap**¹ /ræp/ *n* **1** [C, U] a type of popular music in which the words are not sung, but spoken in time to music with a steady beat **2** a quick light hit or knock: *a rap at the door*

EXERCISE 7A Look up these words in the dictionary. How many meanings does each one have?

| setting | _3_ | beaker | _____ | poach | _____ |
| dizzy | _____ | language | _____ | gloom | _____ |

EXERCISE 7B In the sentences below, the words in dark letters all have more than one meaning. Look them up in the dictionary and decide which meaning correctly explains the use of the word in these sentences. Then, write the number of that meaning next to the sentence.

1. Polish the tiles with an **abrasive** cleaner. _2_
2. She won a scholarship to a **ballet** school in Vienna. _____
3. The camping equipment is out in the **garage**. _____
4. The pills come in childproof **packaging**. _____
5. Cut the dough into **diamonds** and place on a cookie sheet. _____

Idomatic expressions
Some meanings in this dictionary start with a phrase in **dark letters**. This shows that the phrase is a very common expression, which has its own meaning.

For example, look at the entry for the verb **jog**. The expression **jog sb's memory** is listed as a separate meaning, because you cannot guess the meaning of this phrase, even if you know all the words in it.

> **jog**¹ /dʒɑg/ *v* **-gged, -gging 1** [I] to run slowly and in a steady way, especially for exercise: *Julie jogs every morning.* **2 jog sb's memory** to make someone remember something: *This picture*

These phrases are all shown at the first important word in the phrase, so for example **join the club!** is at the main word **join**, and **you name it** is at the main word **name**. In some phrases, you have a choice of words to use, for example **keep/lose your head**. This phrase is shown at the word **head**. (Words such as prepositions and verbs like *make, get,* and *go* are usually not the most important word in the phrase.)

EXERCISE 8 Look up the phrases below in the dictionary. Next to each phrase, write the main word where the phrase is shown.

phrase	main word	phrase	main word
go against the grain	*grain*	hit the sack	
take sb for granted		for sale	
kick/break the habit		ulterior motive/reason	
early bird		under the weather	

Signposts

Some words have so many meanings that it can be difficult to find the one you are looking for. In this dictionary, words with many meanings that are clearly different from each other have special, short words called *signposts* at the beginning of each meaning. These help you find the meaning you want more quickly.

For example, the noun **school** has several very different meanings. Some meanings are special phrases, and the other meanings have signposts.

school¹ /skul/ *n*
1 ▶BUILDING◀ [C, U] a place where
2 ▶TIME AT SCHOOL◀ [U] the time
3 ▶TEACHERS/STUDENTS◀ the students
4 **in school** attending a school: *Are your*

UNDERSTANDING THE GRAMMAR

This dictionary makes it easier to understand the grammar of words.

Parts of speech

The first thing this dictionary tells you is whether a word is a noun, a verb, an adjective etc. Some of the parts of speech are written as complete words. The most common parts of speech are written as short forms; look at the list on the inside front cover for these.

EXERCISE 9 Look up the words in the first column in the dictionary. Write the part of speech next to each one, in the second column. If the part of speech has a short form, write it in the third column.

word	part of speech	short form	word	part of speech	short form
also	*adverb*	*adv*	excellent		
although			you		
may			several		
aluminum			hundred		
consider			run into		
a/an			do¹		
the			at		
every			wow		

Word families

Many words in English have several different forms, which are often made by adding a group of letters to the end of a word. For example, you can add **-ly** to the adjective **sweet** to make the adverb **sweetly**, or you can add **-ness** to make the noun **sweetness**.

Sometimes, a word like **sweetly** does not change very much in meaning from the main word **sweet**. It only means "in a sweet way." Related words like this are shown at the end of the entry for the main word:

sweet /swit/ *adj* 1 having a taste like

to eat sweet foods 5 making you feel pleased and satisfied: *Revenge is sweet!*
– **sweetly** *adv* – **sweetness** *n* [U]

Related words are only shown if they are frequent, and they are put in frequency order so you can tell which one is more common.

mil·i·tant¹ /ˈmɪlətənt/ *adj* willing to use force or violence: *Militant groups were still protesting against the new law.* – **militancy** *n* [U]

Some related words are so common that they are shown as main words. Words like this may have several meanings, or special usage that you need to know about.

un·for·tu·nate /ʌnˈfɔrtʃənɪt/ *adj* **1** hap

un·for·tu·nate·ly /ʌnˈfɔrtʃənɪtli/ *adv*

There is a list of word endings at the back of this dictionary on page 1908. This list tells you what the endings mean, and gives you examples of words that are made with them.

EXERCISE 10 Look up the words in the first column in the dictionary. At the end of the entry for the main word, you will find words that are related to it. Write the different forms of the word in the columns on the right. Not every word will have related words in every column.

word	adj	adv	n	n	v
barbarian	barbarous				
respectable					
eccentric					
takeout					
perplex					
babysit					
careless					
magnet					
permanent					

Nouns

If the word you look up is a noun, this dictionary shows you whether it has a plural form or not.

Nouns that have a plural form are COUNTABLE nouns, and do not have a grammar sign.

Nouns that do not have a plural form are UN-COUNTABLE nouns, and are shown with the sign [U].

car /kɑr/ *n* **1** a vehicle with four wheels and an engine, used for traveling from

air¹ /ɛr/ *n* **1** [U] the mixture of gases

Some nouns can be both countable and uncountable, and are shown with the sign [C,U].

fash·ion¹ /ˈfæʃən/ *n* **1** [C, U] the

Other nouns are only [singular] or [plural].

past³ *n* [singular] **1** the time that existed before now: *People travel more now*

See the Study Notes on page 940 for more information about nouns.

re·sour·ces /ˈriˌsɔrsɪz/ *n* [plural] all

Verbs

If the word you look up is a verb, this dictionary tells you what kind of a verb it is.

Verbs that are not followed by an object are INTRANSITIVE verbs, and are shown with the sign [I].

daw·dle /ˈdɔdl/ *v* [I] INFORMAL to waste time by doing things too slowly: *Stop*

Verbs that must be followed by an object are TRANSITIVE verbs, and are shown with the sign [T].

needle² *v* [T] INFORMAL to deliberately

Some verbs can be both intransitive and transitive, and are shown with the sign [I,T].

fin·ish¹ /ˈfɪnɪʃ/ *v* **1** [I, T] to come to the

LINKING verbs are shown with the sign [linking verb].

seem /sim/ *v* [linking verb] **1** to appear to be a particular thing or to have a

See the Study Notes on page 942 for more information about verbs.

Dictionary Skills Workbook

Phrasal verbs

This dictionary helps you to put the object in the correct position when you are using a phrasal verb. The short forms **sb** and **sth** tell you whether the object can be only a person (**sb**), only a thing (**sth**), or either a person or a thing (**sb/sth**).

Sometimes the object can only follow the phrasal verb:

> **take after** sb *phr v* [T] to look or behave like another member of your family: *Jenny takes after her dad.*

Sometimes the object can only come between the parts of the phrasal verb:

> **cheer** sb **on** *phr v* [T] to encourage someone by cheering for him/her: *Hansen's family was there cheering him on.*

Sometimes a phrasal verb has more than one object:

> **read** sth **into** sth *phr v* [T] to think that a situation, action etc. means more than it

Sometimes the object can either come between the parts of the phrasal verb, or follow it. The sign (↔) tells you that the object is not fixed:

> **pick** sth ↔ **over** *phr v* [T] to carefully examine a group of things in order to

See the Study Note on page 936 for more information about phrasal verbs.

EXERCISE 11 Read each sentence below and look up the word in dark letters in the dictionary. If the word is used correctly in the sentence, put a check (√) next to the sentence. If it is used incorrectly, write a new, correct sentence on a sheet of paper.

1. It's only $3.50 – that's a **chickenfeed**. _____
2. Tell him that Melanie sends her **regard**. _____
3. He's just trying to **protect** his little sister. _____
4. We decided it was best not to **interfere** their affairs. _____
5. We can eat as soon as **I heat up** the tortillas. _____
6. Stand on the corner so you can **flag** the bus **down**. _____
7. I need a new car – mine is **falling apart**. _____
8. It was her personality that **endeared to** the students. _____

USING THE WORDS CORRECTLY

This dictionary makes it easier to use words correctly in speech and writing.

Examples of use

Example sentences show you how a word is typically used. Grammar patterns and frequent phrases are shown in **dark letters** so you can see clearly what the patterns are.

> **half·way** /ˌhæfˈweɪ/ *adj, adv* **1** at the middle point between two places or two points: *Their boat was halfway across the lake when it started to rain.*

Example sentences can show typical prepositions that a word is used with:

> **sip²** *n* a very small amount of a drink: *He took a sip of coffee.*

They can also show verbs, nouns, adjectives etc. That are usually used with the main word:

> **dam·age¹** : *The tests show some brain/ liver damage. / Was there any damage to your car? / The earthquake caused serious/severe damage to the*

Frequent phrases

Some common phrases that are used with main words are not very easy to understand. This dictionary gives clear explanations next to these phrases so that it is easier to understand the usage.

> **date¹** /deɪt/ *n* **1** a particular day of the month or of the year, shown by a number: *"What's today's date?" "It's August 11th." / Have you set a date* (=chosen a day) *for the wedding?* **2** an

EXERCISE 12 **Look up the words in dark letters in the dictionary and answer the questions.**

1. Does someone do a **crime** or <u>commit</u> a crime? *Answer: someone commits a crime.*
2. Draw a line under the most common prepositions that are used with the verb **work**:
   on   by   with   for   to   along   at
3. Does something <u>have</u> an **effect** or <u>give</u> an effect?
4. Does an object have **sentimental** <u>worth</u> or sentimental <u>value</u>?
5. Do we say "**prevent** someone to do something" or "prevent someone from doing something"?

Usage notes and culture notes

The usage notes in this dictionary help you avoid the most common mistakes that are made in using words, by giving longer explanations when this is important.

Some sets of words are very easy to confuse with each other.

> **USAGE NOTE affect** and **effect**
>
> Use the verb **affect** to talk about

Some words have very difficult grammar that needs more explanation.

> **USAGE NOTE all**
>
> **All** is used with a singular verb with uncountable nouns: *All the money is*

Some words are used in a special way in American English.

> **CULTURE NOTE soda, soda pop, pop,** and **soft drink**
>
> All of these words mean the same

Culture notes tell you useful things to know about North American culture, such as how people expect you to behave:

> **CULTURE NOTE getting attention in a restaurant**
>
> In the US and Canada, when you are

Usage hints

In this dictionary, many words also have short hints about common mistakes.

The following usage hint means that it is wrong to say *Butter wasn't in the shopping list.*

remember them: *Make a list of the equipment you'll need. / Butter wasn't on the shopping list.* ✗DON'T SAY "in the list."✗

EXERCISE 13 **Read each sentence below and look up the usage note for the word in dark letters in the dictionary. If the word is used correctly in the sentence, put a check (√) next to the sentence. If it is used incorrectly, write a new, correct sentence below the incorrect sentence.**

1. I'm **gonna** the movies tomorrow night.   _____

_____

2. Please **remember** me to mail this letter.   _____

_____

3. Renata always tries **hard** to do her best.   _____

_____

4. My new **pair** of jeans are dirty.   _____

_____

CHOOSING THE RIGHT WORD

SPOKEN, INFORMAL AND FORMAL

It is not always easy to know which words are acceptable to use in essays, formal letters etc. This dictionary helps you choose the right word for the right situation.

The label SPOKEN tells you that this word or phrase is not written very often at all, and cannot be used in an essay.

> **4 [T]** SPOKEN to like something or someone: *You really dig her, don't you?*

The label INFORMAL tells you that this word or phrase may be written, but that is still not good to use it in an essay.

> *clicked.* **3 [I]** INFORMAL to like someone and share his/her ideas, opinions etc.: *We clicked the first time we met.*

The label FORMAL tells you that this word is used in official documents or in formal writing. You can usually use these words in essays, but be careful not to use too many of them.

> **re·vere** /rɪˈvɪr/ *v* [T] FORMAL to greatly respect and admire someone: *He was revered as a*

Most words and phrases have no label, and are the best ones to use in essays, because they are neither too informal nor too formal.

> *happy?* **8 think well/highly of** to admire or approve of someone or his/her work: *People had always thought highly of her*

EXERCISE 14   **Look up the words and phrases below in the dictionary. put a check (√) next to each one that would be acceptable to use in an essay. If you are not sure about whether a formal word is acceptable or not, ask your teacher.**

mess up	noteworthy
ruin	noticeable
spoil	negate
wreck	stop
merit	desist
deserve	knock it off
be worth it	quit

Synonyms

Words that are very similar in meaning are called SYNONYMS. Many words have synonyms, but the words are usually used in very different ways. To help you avoid choosing the wrong word, this dictionary shows synonyms only when they are used in similar ways.

For example, the only difference between **wing it** and **improvise** is that **wing it** is an INFORMAL phrase. The entry for **wing it** is labeled INFORMAL, so the synonym IMPROVISE is shown. The word **improvise** can be used in exactly the same way: *"just improvise, you'll be fine!"*

> **wing²** *v* **1 wing it** INFORMAL to do or say something without any planning or preparation; IMPROVISE: *"I can't give a speech!" "Just wing it, you'll be fine!"* **2 [I]** LITERARY to fly

Sometimes there is a synonym that is much less common than a main word, although the two words mean exactly the same thing. This dictionary shows the synonym, but tells you which main word to look up in order to find the definition.

For example, the word **pool** is much more common than the phrase **swimming pool**. So, the entry for **swimming pool** tells you that you can find the definition at **pool**.

> **swimming pool** /ˈ.. ./ *n* ⇨ POOL¹

You can find much more information in the Usage Notes about special groups of synonyms.

Opposites

This dictionary shows whether an opposite is formed with common prefixes such as **un-** and **non-**, or with more unusual prefixes such as **ir-** and **il-**

An opposite is usually shown at the end of an entry.

> **leg·i·ble** /ˈlɛdʒəbəl/ *adj* written or printed clearly enough for you to read: *His writing was barely legible.* – **legibly** *adv* —opposite ILLEGIBLE

An opposite is shown at a particular meaning if the opposites for different meanings are different, or if the opposite is not used very often with the other meanings.

> **hard¹** /hɑrd/ *adj*
> **1** ▶FIRM TO TOUCH◀ firm and stiff, and difficult to cut, press down, or break: *I can't sleep on a hard mattress. / hard candy / The plums are still too hard to eat.* —opposite SOFT
> **2** ▶DIFFICULT◀ difficult to do or understand: *It was the hardest class he'd ever had. / It is* **hard** *for me to understand why this happened.* —opposite EASY¹

"See also" cross-references

Sometimes the word or meaning you are looking for may not be shown at the main word you looked up. This dictionary tells you where to look for these words and meanings.

Many nouns have a plural form that has its own meaning. These nouns are shown as main words. If you look up the singular form first, the dictionary will tell you where to find the plural form.

> **flu·id¹** /ˈfluɪd/ *n* [C, U] a liquid ‖ 액체: *It is a clear fluid that smells of alcohol.* —see also FLUIDS

Sometimes a phrase is at another entry. If you look up one word in the phrase, the dictionary tells you where to find that phrase.

> **grind·stone** /ˈɡraɪndstoʊn/ *n* a large round stone that is turned like a wheel and is used for making tools sharp —see also **keep your nose to the grindstone** (NOSE¹)

The dictionary also tells you where to look for a word with a similar spelling, or an entry that includes the word you are looking up.

> **kar·at** /ˈkærət/ *n* a unit for measuring how pure a piece of gold is —see also CARAT

> **lag²** *n* a delay between two events —see also JET LAG

"Compare" cross-references

Sometimes the word or meaning you are looking up is related in a special way to another word or meaning. This dictionary makes it easy for you to compare these words and meanings, and to choose the right one.

Some words are used in similar ways, but mean slightly different things.

> **Jun·ior** /ˈdʒunyɚ/, *written abbreviation* **Jr.** *adj* used after the name of a man who has the same name as his father: *William Jones Jr.* —compare SENIOR

Some words are not exact opposites, but their meanings are different from another word in a special way.

> **in·tran·si·tive verb** /ˌ.... ˈ./ *n* TECHNICAL in grammar, an intransitive verb has a subject but no object. In the sentence, "They arrived early," "arrive" is an intransitive verb —compare TRANSITIVE VERB

Some words are easily confused with each other.

> **im·ply** /ɪmˈplaɪ/ *v* [T] to suggest that something is true without saying or showing it directly: *He implied that the money hadn't been lost, but was stolen.* —compare INFER

Dictionary Skills Workbook: Answers

ANSWERS TO THE WORKBOOK EXERCISES

EXERCISE 1

pay	*pawn*
pay-TV	*pay*
pay off	*pay off*
payroll	*pay up*
pea	*pay dirt*
PE	*payroll*
pay dirt	*pay-TV*
pay up	*PE*
pawn	*pea*

EXERCISE 2

verb	past tense	past participle	present participle
take	*took*	*taken*	*taking*
make	*made*	*made*	*making*
eat	*ate*	*eaten*	*eating*
lag	*lagged*	*lagged*	*lagging*
carry	*carried*	*carried*	*carrying*

adjective	comparative	superlative
mad	*madder*	*maddest*
tiny	*tinier*	*tiniest*
bad	*worse*	*worst*
crazy	*crazier*	*craziest*
funny	*funnier*	*funniest*

noun	plural
domino	*dominos*
knife	*knives*
candy	*candies*
axis	*axes*
aircraft	*aircraft*

EXERCISE 3A

/i/	/ɛ/	/ɔ/	/u/
need	*said*	*awful*	*glue*
field	*bet*	*thought*	*new*
even	*dead*	*soft*	*boot*
seed	*ever*	*taught*	*wood*
clean	*next*	*walt*	*true*
	went		*do*

EXERCISE 3B

/s/	/k/	/n/
city	*kite*	*night*
science	*cool*	*noon*
psyche	*key*	*knead*
cyberspace	*cream*	*pneumatic*
seal	*color*	

EXERCISE 4   ga<u>z</u>ebo ho<u>r</u>izon <u>mercury</u> <u>successfully</u>

EXERCISE 5   <u>record</u> re<u>cord</u>; <u>increase</u> in<u>crease</u>; <u>permit</u> per<u>mit</u>; up<u>set</u> upset

EXERCISE 6

1. **boats, planes, etc.**
2. **with quick long steps**
3. **by hitting it with a stick or hitting two of them together**
4. **different**
5. **when you are glad someone or something has gone away**
6. **four**
7. **sad**
8. **pain or embarrassment**

EXERCISE 7A

setting	_3_	beaker	_1_	poach	_2_
dizzy	_2_	language	_5_	gloom	_2_

EXERCISE 7B

1. Polish the tiles with an **abrasive** cleaner.   _2_
2. She won a scholarship to a **ballet** school in Vienna.   _2_
3. The camping equipment is out in the **garage**.   _1_
4. The pills come in childproof **packaging**.   _1_
5. Cut the dough into **diamonds** and place on a cookie sheet.   _2_

EXERCISE 8

phrase	main word	phrase	main word
go against the grain	grain	hit the sack	hit
take sb for granted	grant	for sale	sale
kick/break the habit	habit	ulterior motive/reason	ulterior
early bird	early	under the weather	weather

EXERCISE 9

word	part of speech	short form	word	part of speech	short form
also	adverb	adv	excellent	adjective	adj
although	conjunction		you	pronoun	pron
may	modal verb		several	quantifier	
aluminum	noun	n	hundred	number	
consider	verb	v	run into	phrasal verb	phr v
a/an	indefinite article determiner		do¹	auxiliary verb	
the	definite article determiner		at	preposition	prep
every	determiner		wow	interjection	

EXERCISE 10

word	adj	adv	n	n	v
barbarian	barbarous				
respectable		respectably	respectability		
eccentric			eccentricity		
takeout	take-out				
perplex	perplexed		perplexity		
babysit			babysitter	babysitting	
careless		carelessly	carelessness		
magnet					magnetize
permanent			permanence		

Dictionary Skills Workbook: Answers

EXERCISE 11

The wrong sentences are **1**, **2**, **4**, and **8**. They should look like this:
1. It's only $3.50 – that's chickenfeed.
2. Tell him that Melanie sends her regards.
4. We decided it was best not to interfere in their affairs.
8. It was her personality that endeared her to the students.

EXERCISE 12

1. someone commits a crime
2. for, at, and with
3. something has an effect
4. sentimental value
5. prevent someone from doing something

EXERCISE 13

The wrong sentences are **1**, **2**, and **4**. They should look like this:
1. I'm going to the movies tomorrow night.
2. Please remind me to mail this letter.
4. My new pair of jeans is dirty.

EXERCISE 14

The acceptable words are:

ruin, spoil, merit, deserve, be worth it, noticeable, negate, stop

The formal words that may be acceptable are:

noteworthy, desist

Aa

A, a /eɪ/ the first letter of the English alphabet ‖ 영어 알파벳의 첫째 자

A /eɪ/ *n* **1** the best grade that can be given to a student's work ‖ 학업에 주어지는 최고의 성적. 에이(A): *I got an "A" on my math test!* 나는 수학 시험에서 "A"를 받았어! / *Rick was an A student* (=always received the best grades) *in high school.* 릭은 고등 학교에서 우등생이었다. **2** the sixth note in the musical SCALE of C, or the musical KEY based on this note ‖ 다 음계의 여섯째 음이나 이 음을 기초로 한 조(調). 가 음. 가 조.

a /ə; *strong* eɪ/ *also* **an** (BEFORE A VOWEL SOUND 모음 앞에서) *indefinite article, determiner* **1** used before a noun to show that you are talking about a general type of thing, not a specific thing ‖ 특정의 것이 아니라 일반적인 것을 나타내는 명사 앞에 쓰여: *Do you have a car?* 차가 있습니까? / *I'll find you a pencil.* 내가 연필을 찾아줄게. —compare THE¹ **2 a)** one ‖ 하나: *a thousand dollars* 1천 달러 / *a dozen eggs* 계란 한 다스 **b)** used before some words that show how much of something there is ‖ 사물의 양을 나타내는 말 앞에 쓰여: *a few weeks from now* 지금부터 몇 주간 / *a little water* 약간의 물 / *a lot of people* 많은 사람들 **3** used before a noun that is one of many similar things, people, events, times etc ‖ 유사한 여러 사물·사람·일·회(回) 등에서 하나를 나타내는 명사 앞에 쓰여: *I'd like to be a teacher.* 나는 선생님이 되고 싶다. / *This is a very good wine.* 이것은 아주 좋은 포도주이다. **4** every or each ‖ 모두, 각각: *A square has 4 sides.* 정사각형은 네 변이 있다. **5 once a week/$100 a day etc.** one time each week, $100 a day etc.; per ‖ 한 주에 한 번, 하루에 100달러 등; …당 **6** used before two nouns that are frequently mentioned together ‖ 자주 함께 언급되는 두 명사 앞에 쓰여: *a cup and saucer* 찻잔과 받침접시 / *a knife and fork* (한 벌의) 나이프와 포크 **7 a)** used before the -ing form of some verbs when they are used as nouns ‖ 명사로 쓰이는 동사의 -ing형 앞에 쓰여: *a loud screeching of brakes* 브레이크의 시끄러운 끽 하는 소리 **b)** used before some singular nouns that are actions ‖ 행위를 나타내는 단수 명사 앞에 쓰여: *Take a look at that!* 저것 봐!

AA *n* Associate of Arts; a college degree given after two years of study, usually at a COMMUNITY COLLEGE ‖ Associate of Arts(준(準)문학사)의 약어; 보통 지역 사회 대학에서 2년 과정 수료 후에 주는 단기 대학 졸업 학위

a·back /əˈbæk/ *adv* **be taken aback** to be very surprised, often in an unpleasant way ‖ 종종 기분 나쁘게, 매우 놀라다. 당황하다: *I was taken aback by Linda's anger.* 나는 린다가 화를 내어 당황했다.

ab·a·cus /ˈæbəkəs/ *n* a frame with balls that slide along BARs to help you count, add etc. ‖ 막대를 따라 움직이는 알이 달린, 셈·합산 등을 도와주는 기구. 수판

a·ban·don /əˈbændən/ *v* [T] **1** to leave someone or something you are responsible for; DESERT ‖ 책임져야 할 사람이나 사물을 버리다. 유기하다; ⌐ desert: *She just abandoned her family!* 그녀는 그냥 가족을 버렸어! **2** to stop doing or using something because of problems ‖ 문제가 있어서 어떤 것의 수행이나 사용을 그만두다. 단념[포기]하다: *The policy had to be abandoned.* 그 정책은 포기해야만 했다. – **abandonment** *n* [U]

a·ban·doned /əˈbændənd/ *adj* not being used or taken care of any longer ‖ 더 이상 쓰이지 않거나 돌봐지지 않는. 유기된. 버림받은: *an abandoned* *building/child* 버려진 건물[버림받은 아이]]

a·bashed /ə'bæʃt/ *adj* feeling or looking shy or ashamed ‖ 수줍게 또는 창피하게 느끼거나 보이는. 겸연쩍은. 당혹한: *an abashed grin* 겸연쩍은 웃음 — opposite UNABASHED

a·bate /ə'beɪt/ *v* [I] FORMAL to become less loud, strong, painful etc. ‖ 소리·강도·통증 등이 덜해지다. 줄다. 약해지다: *Public anger does not appear to be abating.* 대중의 분노는 가라앉지 않는 것 같다. —compare UNABATED

ab·bey /'æbi/ *n* a building in which NUNS or MONKs lived, especially in past times ‖ 특히 예전에 수녀나 수사들이 살았던 건물. 수녀원. 수도원

ab·bre·vi·ate /ə'brivi‚eɪt/ *v* [T] FORMAL to make a word, story etc. shorter ‖ 어구·이야기 등을 줄이다. 단축하다

ab·bre·vi·a·tion /ə‚brivi'eɪʃən/ *n* the short form of a word used in writing. For example, Mr. is the abbreviation of Mister ‖ 글에 쓰이는 어구의 단축형. 약어. 예를 들면 Mr.는 Mister의 약어이다.

ABC *n* [U] American Broadcasting Company; one of the national companies that broadcasts television and radio programs in the US ‖ American Broadcasting Company(아메리칸 방송사)의 약어; 텔레비전·라디오 프로그램을 전국적으로 방송하는 미국 방송사의 하나

ABC's /‚eɪbi'siz/ *n* [plural] the letters of the English alphabet ‖ 영어의 알파벳: *a three-year old learning her ABC's* 세 살배기의 알파벳 학습

ab·di·cate /'æbdɪ‚keɪt/ *v* [I, T] to give up a high position, or refuse responsibility for something ‖ 높은 직위를 포기하거나 어떤 것에 대한 책임을 거부하다. 버리다 – **abdication** /‚æbdɪ'keɪʃən/ *n* [C, U]

ab·do·men /'æbdəmən/ *n* TECHNICAL the part of your body between your chest and your legs ‖ 가슴과 다리 사이의 신체 부위. 배. 복부 – **abdominal** /æb'dɑmənəl, əb-/ *adj*

ab·duct /əb'dʌkt, æb-/ *v* [T] to take someone away illegally and by force; KIDNAP ‖ 사람을 불법적·강제적으로 데려가다. 납치하다; ⑩ kidnap – **abduction** /-'dʌkʃən/ *n* [U]

ab·er·ra·tion /‚æbə'reɪʃən/ *n* [C, U] a situation or action that is different from what you expect or what is normal ‖ 예상한 것이나 정상적인 것에서 벗어나는 상황이나 행동. 탈선: *a minor aberration in*

the plan 계획상의 사소한 차질

a·bet /ə'bɛt/ *v* **-tted, -tting** [T] ⇨ **aid and abet** (AID²)

ab·hor /əb'hɔr, æb-/ *v* **-rred, -rring** [T] FORMAL to hate something ‖ 어떤 것을 싫어하다. 질색[혐오]하다: *Smith abhorred slavery for moral reasons.* 스미스는 도덕적인 이유로 노예 제도를 혐오했다.

ab·hor·rent /əb'hɔrənt, -'hɑr-, æb-/ *adj* FORMAL an idea that is abhorrent is one you hate ‖ 생각이 혐오감을 일으키는. 질색인 – **abhorrence** *n* [U]

a·bide /ə'baɪd/ *v* [T] **sb can't abide sth** used in order to say that someone does not like someone or something at all ‖ 사람이나 사물을 아주 싫어하는 것을 말하는 데 쓰여. …을 참을 수 없다: *I can't abide his stupid jokes.* 그의 어리석은 농담을 참을 수 없다.

abide by sth *phr v* [T] to obey a law, agreement etc. ‖ 법률·협정 등을 지키다. 따르다: *If you're going to live here, you will abide by my rules!* 네가 여기에 살려면 내 규칙을 따라야 한다!

a·bid·ing /ə'baɪdɪŋ/ *adj* LITERARY continuing for a long time ‖ 오랫동안 계속하는. 지속적인

a·bil·i·ty /ə'bɪləti/ *n* [C, U] the mental skill or physical power to do something ‖ 어떤 것을 할 지력이나 체력. 능력: *A manager must have the ability to communicate well.* 매니저는 의사 소통을 잘 하는 능력이 있어야 한다. / *a young girl with great musical ability* 뛰어난 음악적 재능이 있는 어린 소녀

USAGE NOTE ability, skill, talent, knack

Use these words to talk about how well someone does something. An **ability** is what you can do with your mind or your body: *artistic ability / athletic ability.* You can lose your **ability** to do something: *Ryan lost the ability to walk after his skiing accident.* A **skill** is something that you do very well because you have learned and practiced it: *I'm taking this class to improve my writing skills.* **Talent** is a natural ability to do something well: *Joan has a real talent for music.* **Knack** is a more informal word than **talent**: *Kate has a knack for decorating.* 이 단어들은 사람이 어떤 것을 잘하는 정도를 언급하는 데 쓴다. **ability**는 정신적 또는 신체적 능력을 말한다: 예술

적 능력/운동 능력. 사람은 무엇을 할 **ability**를 잃을 수 있다: 라이언은 스키 사고 후에 보행력을 잃었다. **skill**은 배워 익혀서 잘 할 수 있는 것을 뜻한다: 나는 작문력을 향상시키기 위해 이 수업을 듣고 있다. **talent**는 어떤 것을 잘 할 수 있는 타고난 능력을 말한다: 조안은 음악에 진짜 천부적 재능이 있다. **knack**은 **talent**에 비하여 비격식적인 말이다: 케이트는 장식에 재주가 있다.

ab·ject /ˈæbdʒɛkt, æbˈdʒɛkt/ *adj* **1** abject conditions are severe or extreme ∥ 상태가 심하거나 극한적인. 극도의: *abject poverty* 극빈. **2** abject behavior shows that you do not respect yourself ∥ 행동이 스스로를 존중하지 않음을 보여주는. 비열한. 굴욕적인: *an abject apology* 치사한 변명 **– abjectly** *adv*

a·blaze /əˈbleɪz/ *adj* **1 be ablaze** to be burning ∥ 불타고 있다: *The old house was quickly ablaze.* 그 낡은 집은 순식간에 불탔다. **2 be ablaze with** to be very bright with color or light ∥ 빛깔이나 불빛으로 매우 빛나다: *a garden ablaze with summer flowers* 여름 꽃으로 빛나는 정원

a·ble /ˈeɪbəl/ *adj* **1 able to do sth** having the power, skill, or time to do something ∥ 어떤 것을 할 힘이나 재능, 또는 시간이 있는. …(할) 수 있는: *Will you be able to come tonight?* 오늘밤에 오실 수 있습니까? / *I was just able to reach the handle.* 나는 겨우 손잡이를 잡을 수 있었다. **— opposite** UNABLE **2** intelligent or skilled ∥ 유능한, 재능 있는: *an able student* 유능한 학생 **—see study note on page 932**

ab·nor·mal /æbˈnɔrməl/ *adj* different from what usually happens or what ought to be ∥ 보통 일어나는 것이나 그래야 마땅한 것과는 다른. 비정상적인: *abnormal levels of chemicals in the water* 물속의 비정상적인 수준의 화학 성분 **– abnormally** *adv* **– abnormality** /ˌæbnɔrˈmæləti, -nə-/ *n* [C, U]

a·board /əˈbɔrd/ *adv, prep* on or onto a ship, plane, or train ∥ 배나 비행기, 또는 열차 등에[을 타고]: *A reporter aboard the President's plane asked the question.* 대통령 전용기에 탄 한 기자가 질문을 했다.

a·bode /əˈboʊd/ *n* FORMAL the place where you live ∥ 사는 곳. 주거. 거처

a·bol·ish /əˈbɑlɪʃ/ *v* [T] to officially end a law, system etc ∥ 법률·제도 등을 공식적으로 끝내다. 폐지하다: *Welfare programs cannot be abolished that quickly.* 사회 복지 프로그램은 그렇게 빨리 폐지될 수가 없다. **– abolition** /ˌæbəˈlɪʃən/ *n* [U]: *the abolition of slavery* 노예제도의 폐지 **– abolitionist** *n*

a·bom·i·na·ble /əˈbɑmənəbəl/ *adj* extremely unpleasant, or of very bad quality ∥ 매우 불쾌하거나 질이 매우 형편없는

ab·o·rig·i·nal /ˌæbəˈrɪdʒənəl/ *adj* relating to the people or animals that have lived in a place from the earliest times ∥ 예로부터 한 지역에서 살아온 사람이나 동물의. 토착의

ab·o·rig·i·ne /ˌæbəˈrɪdʒəni/ *n* a member of the people who have lived in Australia from the earliest times ∥ 예로부터 호주에서 살아온 국민의 한 사람. 호주 원주민

a·bort /əˈbɔrt/ *v* [T] **1** to end an activity because it would be too difficult or dangerous to continue ∥ 계속하기에 너무 어렵거나 위험하여 활동을 중단시키다: *The Reagan administration had to abort plans to sell public lands.* 레이건 정부는 국유지 매각 계획을 중단해야만 했다. **2** to deliberately end a PREGNANCY when the baby is still too young to live ∥ 태아가 아직 살기에는 너무 어릴 때 고의로 임신을 중절하다. 낙태[유산]시키다 **— compare** MISCARRY

a·bor·tion /əˈbɔrʃən/ *n* [C, U] the act of ABORTing a baby ∥ 임신 중절. 낙태. 유산: *She was told about the dangers of having an abortion.* 그녀는 낙태의 위험성에 대한 말을 들었다.

a·bor·tive /əˈbɔrtɪv/ *adj* an abortive action or plan is not successful ∥ 행위나 계획이 성공하지 못한. 무위[실패]로 끝난

a·bound /əˈbaʊnd/ *v* [I] LITERARY to exist in large numbers ∥ 많이 있다. 풍부하다: *Images of African life abound in her books.* 그녀의 책에는 아프리카 생활상이 많이 들어 있다.

a·bout¹ /əˈbaʊt/ *prep* **1** on or dealing with a particular subject ∥ 특정 주제에 관한. 특정 주제를 다루는. …에 대하여: *I'll call you and tell you all about it later.* 나중에 네게 전화해서 그에 대해 모두 알려줄게. / *a book about how the universe began* 우주의 생성에 관한 책. **2** in the nature or character of a person or thing ∥ 사람이나 사물의 속성 또는 특성에: *There's something weird about that guy.* 그 놈은 어딘지 기이한 데가 있다. **3 what about/how about** SPOKEN **a)** used in order to make a suggestion ∥ 제안하는 데에 쓰여: *How about coming to my house after we're done here?* 여기

서 끝난 후 우리 집 가는 게 어때? / *What about bringing a potato salad?* 감자 샐러드를 가져오는 게 어떨까? **b)** used in order to ask for news, or for a suggestion ‖ 정보나 제안의 요청에 쓰여: *What about Jack? We can't just leave him here.* 잭은 어떻게 하지? 그를 여기에 그냥 남겨 둘 수는 없잖아. **4** SPOKEN used in order to introduce a subject ‖ 주제를 도입하는 데에 쓰여: *About those tickets, I do want to buy one.* 그 표 말인데, 한 장 사고 싶어.

about² *adv* **1** a little more or less than a particular number or amount; APPROXIMATELY ‖ 특정의 수나 양보다 다소 많거나 적게. 대략. 약: ㉴ approximately: *I live about 10 miles from here.* 나는 여기서 약 10마일 떨어진 곳에 산다. **2** almost ‖ 거의: *Dinner's about ready. Come and sit down.* 식사가 거의 준비되었다. 와서 앉아라.

about³ *adj* **1 be about to do sth** to be just ready to start doing something ‖ 막 무엇을 하려고 하다: *We were about to leave, when Jerry arrived.* 우리가 막 떠나려고 할 때에 제리가 도착했다. **2 not be about to do sth** to be very unwilling to do something ‖ 무엇을 하고 싶은 마음이 들지 않다: *I'm not about to give him any more money!* 그에게 더 이상 돈을 주고 싶지 않아!

above

The picture is above / over the mantlepiece.

The dog jumped over the wall.

a·bove¹ /əˈbʌv/ *prep* **1** in or to a higher position than something else ‖ 어떤 것보다 위에 또는 높게: *Raise your arm above your head.* 머리 위로 팔을 올려라. **2** at or to a higher number, amount, or level than something else ‖ 수나 양 또는 정도가 어떤 것보다 위인, 또는 위로: *Temperatures rose above freezing today.* 온도가 오늘 영상으로 올랐다. / *50 feet above ground* 지상 50피트 **3** louder

or higher in PITCH than other sounds ‖ 다른 소리보다 크거나 높게: *He couldn't hear her voice above the noise.* 그는 소음에 묻혀 그녀의 목소리를 들을 수 없었다. **4 above all** FORMAL most importantly ‖ 가장 중요하게. 무엇보다도: *Above all, I would like to thank my parents.* 무엇보다도 부모님께 감사드리고 싶다. **5 above suspicion/criticism etc.** so honest or good that no one can doubt you ‖ 아무도 의심할 수 없을 만큼 정직하거나 착한. 의심의/비판의 여지가 없는

above² *adv* **1** more or higher than a particular number, amount, or level ‖ 특정한 수나 양, 또는 수준 이상으로: *Males aged 18 and above could be drafted.* 18세 이상의 남자는 징집이 가능하다. **2** in an earlier part of something you are reading ‖ 읽고 있는 것의 앞부분에: *The graph above shows the growth in pollution levels.* 위 그래프는 오염 수준의 증가를 보여준다. **3** in a higher place than something else ‖ 다른 것보다 상위에: *The sound came from the room above.* 그 소리는 윗방에서 흘러나왔다.

above·board /əˈbʌvˌbɔrd/ *adj* honest and legal ‖ 정직하고 합법적인. 공명정대한: *The agreement seems to be aboveboard.* 협정은 공명정대해 보인다.

a·bra·sive /əˈbreɪsɪv, -zɪv/ *adj* **1** rude and annoying ‖ 무례하고 신경질 나게 하는. 거슬리는: *an abrasive personality* 거슬리는 성격 **2** having a rough surface that can be used for rubbing things off other surfaces ‖ 다른 표면을 문질러 없애는 데 쓰일 수 있는 거친 표면의. 닳게 하는. 연마용의 **– abrasively** *adv*

a·breast /əˈbrɛst/ *adv* **1 keep abreast of** to know the most recent facts about a subject ‖ 주제에 관한 가장 최근의 사실들을 알다: *I assume you will keep us abreast of his progress.* 나는 네가 그의 진행 사항을 우리에게 알려줄 것으로 여긴다. **2** next to someone or something, usually in a line, and facing the same direction ‖ 보통 같은 줄에서 같은 방향을 보고 있는 사람이나 사물의 옆에. 나란히: *Patrol cars were lined up four abreast.* 경찰차 네 대가 나란히 늘어서 있었다.

a·bridge /əˈbrɪdʒ/ *v* [T] to make a book, play etc. shorter, keeping the general meaning the same ‖ 책·연극 등을 전체적인 뜻은 유지하면서 줄이다. 약하다: *the abridged version of the dictionary* 사전의 축약판 —compare UNABRIDGED

a·broad /əˈbrɔd/ *adv* in or to a foreign country ‖ 외국에서, 외국으로: *He* *suggested that his son go abroad for a year.* 그는 아들에게 1년 동안 외국에 나가 있을 것을 제안했다.

a·brupt /əˈbrʌpt/ *adj* **1** sudden and unexpected ‖ 갑작스럽고 예기치 않은. 돌연한. 뜻밖의: *an abrupt change in the attitudes of voters* 유권자들의 돌연한 태도 변화 **2** not polite or friendly, especially because you do not want to waste time ‖ 특히 시간을 낭비하고 싶지 않아서 정중하거나 다정하지 않은. 통명스러운. 무뚝뚝한: *She was abrupt on the phone the first time we talked.* 처음으로 우리가 전화로 이야기를 나눌 때 그녀는 통명스러웠다. – **abruptly** *adv*

ab·scess /ˈæbsɛs/ *n* a place on your body that is swollen and contains a poisonous liquid ‖ 독액이 들어 있는 신체의 부어 오른 곳. 농양(膿瘍). 종양

ab·scond /əbˈskɑnd, æb-/ *v* [I] FORMAL to leave a place secretly because you have done something wrong ‖ 나쁜 짓을 저질러서 어떤 곳을 몰래 떠나다. 몰래 도주하다

ab·sence /ˈæbsəns/ *n* **1** [C, U] the state of being away from a place, or the time you are away ‖ 어떤 장소에 없는 상태 또는 시간. 결석[부재] (기간): *The vice president will handle things in my absence.* 내가 부재시 부사장이 일을 처리할 것이다. / *frequent absences from work* 잦은 업무 이탈. **2** [U] the lack of something ‖ 무엇의 결여. 부족: *the absence of evidence of murder* 살인에 대한 증거 부족

ab·sent /ˈæbsənt/ *adj* **1** not here ‖ 이곳에 없는. 결석한: *Most of the class was absent with flu today.* 오늘 그 반의 대부분의 학생들은 감기로 결석했다. **2** **absent look/smile/expression** a look etc. that shows you are not thinking about what is happening ‖ 일어나는 일에 대하여 생각하지 않음을 나타내는 얼굴 등. 멍한 얼굴/웃음/표정

ab·sen·tee /ˌæbsənˈti/ *n* FORMAL someone who is supposed to be in a place but is absent ‖ 어떤 장소에 있기로 되어 있지만 결석한 사람. 결석[결근]자

absentee bal·lot /ˌ... ˈ.../ *n* a process by which people can send their votes by mail because they will be away during an election ‖ 선거 기간 동안 유권자의 부재로 인하여 우편으로 행하는 투표 방법. 부재자 투표

ab·sen·tee·ism /ˌæbsənˈtiɪzəm/ *n* [U] regular absence from work or school without a good reason ‖ 정당한 사유가 없는 통상적인 결근이나 결석

ab·sent·ly /ˈæbsəntˌli/ *adv* in a way that shows you are not interested in or not thinking about what is happening ‖ 무슨 일이 일어나는지에 대해 관심이나 생각 없다는 듯이. 멍하게. 방심하여: *Jason patted his son absently.* 제이슨은 무심히 아들을 쓰다듬었다.

absent-mind·ed /ˌ... ˈ.../ *adj* often forgetting or not noticing things because you are thinking of something else ‖ 다른 일을 생각하느라 종종 잊거나 알아채지 못하는. 멍한. 얼 빠진 – **absent-mindedly** *adv*

ab·so·lute /ˈæbsəˌlut, ˌæbsəˈlut/ *adj* **1** complete or total ‖ 완전한. 전적인: *The show was an absolute disaster the first night.* 그 쇼는 첫날 밤 공연에서 완전히 실패했다. / *absolute authority* 절대 권력 **2** definite and not likely to change ‖ 명확하고 바뀌지 않을 듯한. 확고한. 확실한: *I can't give you any absolute promises.* 나는 네게 어떤 확고한 약속도 할 수 없다.

ab·so·lute·ly /ˌæbsəˈlutli, ˈæbsəˌlutli/ *adv* **1** completely or totally ‖ 완전히. 전부: *Are you absolutely sure?* 전적으로 확신합니까? / *The two women had absolutely nothing* (=nothing at all) *in common.* 그 두 여자는 공통점이 전혀 없었다. —compare RELATIVELY **2 Absolutely!** SPOKEN said when you agree completely, or used in order to emphasize the answer "yes" ‖ 완전히 동의할 때나 "예"라는 대답의 강조에 쓰여. 물론이지!: *"I wondered if I could talk to you?" "Absolutely, come in!"* "당신과 이야기를 좀 나누고 싶은데 괜찮은지 모르겠습니다." "물론이죠, 들어오세요!" **3 Absolutely not!** SPOKEN said when you disagree completely, or used in order to add emphasis when you say "no" ‖ 절대 동의하지 않을 때나 "아니오"라는 대답의 강조에 쓰여. 절대 안돼!

ab·solve /əbˈzɑlv, -ˈsɑlv/ *v* [T] FORMAL to formally forgive someone or say that s/he is not guilty ‖ 사람을 정식으로 용서하거나 무죄라고 말하다. 면책하다

ab·sorb /əbˈsɔrb, -ˈzɔrb/ *v* [T] **1** if something absorbs a liquid, it takes in the liquid through its surface ‖ 액체를 표면을 통해 받아들이다. 빨아들이다 ‖ 흡수하다: *The towel absorbed most of the water.* 수건은 대부분의 물을 흡수했다. **2** to interest

absorb

absorbent cloth

someone very much ∥ 사람을 대단히 흥미를 갖게 하다. 열중하게 하다: *I was completely absorbed in the book.* 나는 완전히 그 책에 빠져 있었다. **3** to understand something ∥ 어떤 것을 이해하다: *She's a good student who absorbs ideas quickly.* 그녀는 개념을 금방 이해하는 우수한 학생이다. **– absorption** /-ˈɔrpʃən/ *n* [U]

ab·sorb·ent /əbˈsɔrbənt, -ˈzɔr-/ *adj* something that is absorbent can take in liquid through its surface ∥ 액체를 표면을 통해 받아들일 수 있는. 흡수할 수 있는: *absorbent diapers* 흡수력이 있는 기저귀

ab·sorb·ing /əbˈsɔrbɪŋ, -ˈzɔr-/ *adj* so interesting that you do not notice or think about other things ∥ 다른 것을 알아차리거나 생각하지 못할 정도로 매우 흥미있는. 마음을 빼앗는: *an absorbing article* 마음을 사로잡는 기사

ab·stain /əbˈsteɪn/ *v* [I] **1** to not vote ∥ 투표를 하지 않다. 기권하다: *Three members of the committee abstained.* 위원 세 명이 기권했다. **2** to not allow yourself to do something ∥ 스스로 어떤 것을 하는 것을 삼가다. 자제하다 **– abstention** /əbˈstɛnʃən/ *n* [C, U]

ab·sti·nence /ˈæbstənəns/ *n* [U] the practice of not doing something you enjoy, or the length of time you do this ∥ 즐기는 일을 끊음, 또는 끊는 기간. 절제 (기간) **– abstinent** *adj*

ab·stract[1] /əbˈstrækt, æb-, ˈæbstrækt/ *adj* **1** existing as a general idea, or based on general ideas rather than a specific example or real event ∥ 구체적인 예나 실제의 일이 아니라 관념으로 존재하는, 또는 관념에 기초를 둔. 관념적인: *Beauty is an abstract idea.* 미는 관념적인 개념이다. / *an abstract argument about justice* 정의에 관한 관념적인 논쟁 **2** abstract art is made of shapes and patterns that do not look like real things or people ∥ 예술이 실체 또는 실물과는 다른 형태나 모양으로 된. 추상적인 **– abstraction** /əbˈstrækʃən/ *n* [C, U]

abstract[2] *n* a short written statement of the most important ideas in a long piece of writing ∥ 긴 글의 핵심 개념에 대한 간략한 진술. 요약

ab·surd /əbˈsɚd, -ˈzɚd/ *adj* seeming completely unreasonable or silly ∥ 아주 불합리하거나 어리석어 보이는. 부조리한. 터무니없는: *an absurd situation* 불합리한 상황 / *an absurd hat* 우스꽝스러운 모자 **– absurdly** *adv* **– absurdity** *n* [C, U]

a·bun·dance /əˈbʌndəns/ *n* [singular, U] FORMAL a large quantity of something ∥ 많은 양의 것. 풍부. 다량: *an abundance of wavy red hair* 웨이브가 진 풍성한 붉은색 머리 / *Wild flowers grow in abundance on the hillsides.* 야생화가 언덕 비탈에 군락을 이루고 있다.

a·bun·dant /əˈbʌndənt/ *adj* more than enough in quantity ∥ 양적으로 충분한 이상의. 남아도는. 풍부한: *an abundant supply of fresh fruit* 신선한 과일의 풍부한 공급

a·bun·dant·ly /əˈbʌndəntli/ *adv* completely, or in large amounts ∥ 충분히 또는 풍부하게. 매우. 많이: *Kaplan made it abundantly clear that we weren't welcome.* 카플란은 우리가 환영받지 못했다는 점을 아주 분명히 밝혔다.

a·buse[1] /əˈbyus/ *n* **1** [C, U] the use of something in a way it should not be used ∥ 사용 금지된 방법으로 무엇을 사용함. 오용. 악용. 남용: *The newspapers are calling the President's action an abuse of power.* 신문들은 대통령의 행위를 권력의 남용이라고 말하고 있다. / *There has been a decrease in the amount of drug abuse in schools.* 학교에서의 마약 남용은 양적으로 감소했다. **2** [U] cruel or violent treatment of someone, usually by someone in a position of authority ∥ 보통 권력자에 의한 사람에 대한 잔인하거나 폭력적인 취급. 학대. 폭행: *statistics on child abuse in middle class homes* 중산층 가정에서의 아동 학대에 대한 통계 / *sexual abuse* (=using sex in a way that is unacceptable or violent) 성적 학대 **3** [U] unkind or cruel things someone says to another person ∥ 남에게 하는 고약하거나 잔인한 말. 욕설. 폭언

a·buse[2] /əˈbyuz/ *v* [T] **1** to do cruel or violent things to someone ∥ 누군가에게 잔인하거나 난폭한 짓을 하다. 학대하다: *He used to get drunk and abuse his wife.* 그는 술에 취해서 아내를 학대하곤 했다. **2** to use something too much or in the wrong way ∥ 어떤 것을 지나치게 쓰거나 그릇되게 사용하다. 남용[오용, 악용]하다: *The laws are meant to prevent people from abusing the tax system.* 그 법안은 사람들이 세금 제도를 악용하는 것을 막기 위하여 제정되었다. / *He had been abusing drugs since the age of 12.* 그는 12살 이후부터 약물을 남용해 오고 있었다. **3** to say cruel or unkind things to someone ∥ 누군가에게 잔인하거나 고약한 말을 하다. 폭언하다. 욕하다

a·bu·sive /əˈbyusɪv/ *adj* using cruel

words or physical violence ‖ 잔인한 말이
나 신체적 폭력을 쓰는. 욕하는. 폭력적
인: *an abusive husband* 폭력적인 남편

a·bys·mal /ə'bɪzməl/ *adj* very bad ‖ 매
우 나쁜. 최저[최악]의: *The food at
school was abysmal.* 학교에서 제공되는
음식은 형편없었다.

a·byss /ə'bɪs/ *n* 1 a deep space that
seems to have no bottom, usually in the
ocean or mountains ‖ 보통 바다나 산의,
바닥이 보이지 않는 깊은 곳. 심연. 심해
2 LITERARY a very dangerous,
frightening, sad etc. situation ‖ 매우 위
험한·두려운·슬픈 상태: *an abyss of
loneliness* 한없는 고독

AC *n* [U] alternating current; the type of
electric current used in buildings for
electrical equipment ‖ alternating
current(교류)의 약어; 건물의 전기 기구
에 쓰이는 전류 형태 —compare DC

ac·a·dem·ic[1] /ˌækə'dɛmɪk/ *adj* relating
to teaching or studying subjects such as
science, English, mathematics etc.,
especially in a college or university ‖ 특
히 대학에서의 과학·영어·수학 등의 교육
이나 연구에 관련된. 학문의[에 관한]:
*The academic year starts September
3rd.* 학년도는 9월 3일에 시작한다.

academic[2] *n* a teacher in a college or
university ‖ 대학 교수

a·cad·e·my /ə'kædəmi/ *n* 1 a school,
especially one that trains students in a
special art or skill ‖ 특히 학생들에게 특
수 기술이나 기능을 훈련시키는 (전문) 학
교 2 an organization of people who
want to encourage the progress of art,
science, literature etc. ‖ 예술·과학·문화
등의 발전을 촉진하려는 사람들의 단체.
학회. 협회

ac·cel·er·ate /ək'sɛləˌreɪt/ *v* 1 [I] if a
vehicle or its driver accelerates, it
moves faster ‖ 차량이나 그 운전자가 속
도를 내다. 가속하다: *Mel accelerated as
she drove onto the highway.* 멜은 고속도
로로 진입하자 가속을 했다. / *a plane
accelerating rapidly towards take-off* 이
륙 지점을 향해 급속하게 가속하는 비행기
2 [I, T] to happen at a faster rate than
usual, or to make something do this ‖ 평
상시보다 빨라지거나 무엇을 빨라지게 하
다: *We tried to accelerate the process by
heating the chemicals.* 우리는 화학 물질
을 가열하여 반응을 촉진시키려 했다. –
acceleration /əkˌsɛlə'reɪʃən/ *n* [U]

ac·cel·er·a·tor /ək'sɛləˌreɪtə/ *n* the
PEDAL in a car that you push to increase
its speed ‖ 차의 속력을 내기 위하여 밟는
페달. 액셀러레이터. 가속 페달 —see

picture on page 943

ac·cent[1] /'æksɛnt/ *n* 1 a way of
speaking that someone has because of
where s/he was born or lives ‖ 태어나거
나 사는 장소 탓으로 습득한 말투. 사투리:
a strong southern accent 강한 남부 억양
2 the part of a word that you emphasize
when you say it ‖ 말할 때 강조하는 부분.
악센트. 강세: *The accent in the word
"important" is on the second syllable.*
"important"라는 단어의 강세는 제2음절
에 있다. 3 a mark written above some
letters (such as à or ê) that shows what
type of sound to make when you say it ‖
말할 때의 소리의 형태를 나타내는 (à나
ê 등의) 글자 위에 표시한 부호. 악센트 부
호

ac·cent[2] /'æksɛnt, æk'sɛnt/ *v* [T] to
emphasize a word or part of a word ‖ 단
어나 음절을 강하게 발음하다: *In the
word "baby" you accent the first
syllable.* "baby"라는 단어는 제1음절을
강하게 발음한다.

ac·cent·ed /'æksɛntɪd/ *adj* a language
that is accented is spoken with an
ACCENT from another country ‖ 언어가 다
른 지역의 억양이 있는: *heavily accented
English* 타지의 억양이 심한 영어

ac·cen·tu·ate /ək'sɛntʃuˌeɪt, æk-/ *v* [T]
to make something easier to notice ‖ 무
엇을 알아보기 쉽게 하다. 두드러지게[돋
보이게] 하다: *Her scarf accentuated the
blue of her eyes.* 그녀의 스카프는 그녀의
파란 눈을 돋보이게 했다.

ac·cept /ək'sɛpt/ *v* 1 [I, T] to take
something that someone offers you ‖ 누
군가가 제공하는 것을 받다. 받아들이다:
*Mr. Ryan wouldn't accept any money
from us.* 라이언 씨는 우리가 제공하는 어
떤 돈도 받지 않으려고 했다. / *The
company offered him the job, but he
decided not to accept.* 그 회사는 그에게
일자리를 제공했지만, 그는 받아들이지 않
기로 결정했다. 2 [I, T] to agree to do
something or to allow a plan to happen
‖ 어떤 것을 하기로 동의하거나 계획대로
일어나게 하다. 수락하다: *You shouldn't
have accepted when he offered you a
ride home.* 너는 그가 집까지 태워 준다고
제의했을 때 받아들이지 말았어야 했다. /
*Will the City Council accept the changes
in the rules?* 시의회가 규칙의 변경을 수
용할까? 3 [I, T] to agree, admit, or
believe that something, often something
unpleasant, is true ‖ 종종 못마땅한 것을
사실로 여기거나 인정하거나, 또는 믿다: *I
accept that we've made mistakes, but
it's nothing we can't fix.* 우리가 실수한

것은 인정하지만, 그것을 바로잡을 수 없는 것은 아니다. / *Barbara wouldn't accept her husband's death for months afterwards.* 바바라는 남편이 죽은 후 몇 달 동안 그 사실을 믿으려 하지 않았다. **4** [T] to let someone join an organization, university etc. ‖ 누군가를 조직·대학 등에 입회[입학]시키다: *I've been accepted at Harvard.* 나는 하버드 대학에 입학했다 **5** [T] to let someone new become part of a group or society and to treat him/her in the same way as other members ‖ 새로운 사람을 단체나 사회의 일원이 되게 하고 다른 회원과 동일한 방식으로 대우하다. 받아들이다: *It was a long time before the other kids at school accepted him.* 오랜 시간이 지나서야 학교의 다른 아이들이 그를 받아들였다. **6** [T] to let customers use a particular type of money to pay for something ‖ 고객에게 특정한 종류의 화폐로 물건값을 내게 하다. 받다. 인수하다: *We don't accept credit cards.* 저희는 신용 카드를 받지 않습니다. **7 accept responsibility** FORMAL to agree that you are responsible for something ‖ 어떤 것에 대한 책임을 인정하다. 책임지다: *I won't accept responsibility for something I didn't do!* 내가 하지도 않은 것에 대해서는 책임지지 않겠다!

ac·cept·a·ble /ək'sɛptəbəl/ *adj* **1** good enough for a particular purpose ‖ 특정 목적에 적합한. 만족스러운: *The paper was acceptable, but it wasn't her best work.* 그 보고서는 만족스럽기는 하지만 그녀가 최선을 다한 작품은 아니었다. **2** acceptable behavior is considered to be morally or socially good enough ‖ 행동이 도덕적으로나 사회적으로 적합한 것으로 간주되는. 받아들일[용인할]만한: *Smoking isn't acceptable any more in many places in America.* 미국 곳곳에서 흡연은 더 이상 허용되지 않는다. – **acceptability** /ək,sɛptə'bɪləti/ *n* [U] — opposite UNACCEPTABLE

ac·cept·ance /ək'sɛptəns/ *n* [U] **1** the act of agreeing that an idea, statement, explanation etc. is right or true ‖ 생각·진술·설명 등이 맞거나 사실이라는 것에 대한 동의. 찬성. 승인: *the White House's acceptance of a new bill from the Senate* 상원이 제출한 새 법안에 대한 백악관의 승인 **2** the act of agreeing to do, use, or take something ‖ 무엇을 하거나 사용하거나, 또는 가져도 좋다는 동의. 허용. 수락: *I was surprised at her acceptance of my offer to help her.* 그녀를 돕겠다는 내 제안을 그녀가 받아들여서 놀랐다. **3** the process of allowing someone to become part of a group or society ‖ 누군가를 단체나 사회의 일원이 되도록 허락함. 수용: *the immigrants' gradual acceptance into the community* 이민자들에 대한 지역 공동체로의 점진적인 수용 **4 gain/find acceptance** to become popular or liked ‖ 일반화되다, 인정받다: *Home computers first gained wide acceptance in the 1980s.* 가정용 컴퓨터는 1980년대에 처음으로 널리 일반화되었다. **5** the state of accepting an unpleasant situation, without getting angry or upset about it ‖ 화내거나 속상해 하지 않고 마음이 내키지 않는 상황을 받아들임. 묵인

ac·cess¹ /'æksɛs/ *n* [U] **1** the ability, chance, or right to use something ‖ 사물을 이용할 능력이나 기회나, 또는 권리: *Students need to have access to a computer system.* 학생들은 컴퓨터 시스템을 이용할 기회가 필요하다. **2** the way in which you can enter a building or get to a place ‖ 건물이나 장소에 들어가거나 도달하는 방법 —see also **gain access** (GAIN)

access² *v* [T] to find and use information, especially on a computer ‖ 특히 컴퓨터로 정보를 입수하여 이용하다. 접근하다: *I couldn't access the file.* 나는 그 파일에 접근할 수 없었다.

ac·ces·si·ble /ək'sɛsəbəl/ *adj* **1** able to be easily opened, used, traveled to etc. ‖ 열기·쓰기·여행하기 쉬운: *The national park is not accessible by road.* 그 국립 공원은 도로로 여행하기가 쉽지 않다. / *A college education wasn't accessible to women until the 1920s.* 1920년대까지 여자들은 대학 교육을 받기가 쉽지 않았다. **2** easy to understand and enjoy ‖ 이해하며 즐기기 쉬운: *I thought his first book was more accessible than the second.* 나는 그의 첫 번째 책이 두 번째 책보다 더 이해하기 쉽다고 생각했다. – **accessibility** /ək,sɛsə'bɪləti/ *n* [U] —opposite INACCESSIBLE

ac·ces·so·ry /ək'sɛsəri/ *n* **1** [C usually plural] something such as a belt, jewelry etc. that you wear or carry because it is attractive ‖ 매력적으로 보여서 착용하거나 갖고 다니는 허리띠·보석 등의 것. 장신구. 액세서리: *a dress with matching accessories* 어울리는 액세서리가 달린 옷 **2** something that you add to a machine, tool, car etc. to make it more useful ‖ 보다 유용하도록 기계·도구·자동차 등에 덧붙이는 것. 부속품. 장식품 **3** LAW someone who helps a criminal

‖ 범인을 돕는 사람. 종범(從犯)

access pro·vid·er /'.. .,../ *n* a company that provides the technical services that allow people to use the Internet, usually in exchange for a monthly payment ‖ 다달이 돈을 내는 대신에 사람들에게 인터넷을 이용하도록 기술적 서비스를 제공하는 회사. 인터넷 서비스 업체

ac·ci·dent /'æksədənt, -,dɛnt/ *n* 1 a situation in which someone is hurt or something is damaged without anyone intending it to happen ‖ 아무도 그러려는 의도가 없는데 사람이 다치거나 사물이 손상되는 상황. 우연한 사고: *She didn't do it on purpose, it was an accident.* 그녀는 그것을 고의로 하지는 않았다. 그것은 우연한 사고였다. / *I was in an accident* (=involved in a car accident) *on the way home from work.* 나는 직장에서 집으로 오는 중에 차 사고를 당했다. 2 **by accident** in a way that is not intended or planned ‖ 의도하거나 계획하지 않은 형태로. 우연히: *I discovered by accident that he'd lied to me.* 그가 나에게 거짓말을 했다는 것을 우연히 알았다.

ac·ci·den·tal /,æksə'dɛntəl/ *adj* not intended to happen ‖ 뜻하지 않게 일어나는. 우연한. 뜻밖의: *Most accidental deaths occur at work.* 대부분의 횡사[뜻하지 않은 죽음]는 일하는 중에 일어난다. **– accidentally** *adv*

accident-prone /'... ,./ *adj* likely to have accidents ‖ 사고를 당하기 쉬운: *an accident-prone child* 사고를 잘 일으키는 아이

ac·claim¹ /ə'kleɪm/ *v* [T] **be acclaimed (as)** to be praised very much, especially for particular qualities ‖ 특히 특정한 자질에 대해 격찬 받다: *Landry was being acclaimed as the best coach around.* 랜드리는 주위에서 최고의 코치로 격찬을 받고 있었다.

acclaim² *n* [U] strong praise for a person, idea, book etc. ‖ 사람·생각·책 등에 대한 격찬. 갈채. 환호

ac·claimed /ə'kleɪmd/ *adj* praised by a lot of people ‖ 많은 사람들에게 칭찬받는: *Rodzinki's latest film has been highly/widely acclaimed.* 로드진키의 최근의 영화는 대단한 격찬을 받았다.

ac·cli·mate /'æklə,meɪt/, **ac·cli·ma·tize** /ə'klaɪmə,taɪz/ *v* [I, T] to become used to the weather, way of living etc. in a new place, or to make someone do this ‖ 새로운 곳의 날씨·생활 방식 등에 익숙해지다, 또는 누군가를 익숙해지게 하다: *It takes the astronauts a day to get acclimated to conditions in space.* 우주 비행사들이 우주 상태에 익숙해지는 데는 하루가 걸린다. **– acclimatization** /ə,klaɪmətɪ'zeɪʃən/ *n* [U]

ac·co·lade /'ækə,leɪd/ *n* [C usually plural] FORMAL strong praise and approval ‖ 열렬한 칭찬 및 승인. 격찬

ac·com·mo·date /ə'kɑmə,deɪt/ *v* [T] 1 to have enough space for a particular number of people or things ‖ 특정수의 사람이나 사물용의 충분한 공간이 있다. …의 수용력이 있다: *The auditorium can accommodate 300 people.* 그 강당은 300명을 수용할 수 있다. 2 to give someone a place to stay, live, or work ‖ 누군가에게 머물거나 쉴, 또는 일할 곳을 제공하다: *A new dorm was built to accommodate graduate students.* 대학원생들에게 숙소를 제공하기 위해 새 기숙사가 건립되었다. 3 to do what someone wants or needs in order to help him/her or satisfy him/her ‖ 도와주거나 만족시키기 위해 어떤 사람이 원하는 것이나 필요한 것을 해 주다. 편의를 도모하다: *If you need more time, we'll try to accommodate you.* 만일 당신이 시간이 더 필요하다면 우리는 편의를 봐 주도록 하겠다.

ac·com·mo·dat·ing /ə'kɑmə,deɪtɪŋ/ *adj* helpful and willing to do what someone else wants ‖ 타인이 원하는 것을 하도록 기꺼이 잘 도와 주는. 편의를 잘 봐주는

ac·com·mo·da·tion /ə,kɑmə'deɪʃən/ *n* [U] 1 also **accommodations** a place to live, stay, or work in ‖ 살[머물, 일할] 곳. 숙박시설: *Accommodation will be provided for all new students.* 숙박 시설은 모든 신입생들에게 제공될 것이다. 2 a way of solving a problem between two people or groups so that both are satisfied ‖ 양쪽이 모두 만족하도록 두 사람이나 집단간의 문제를 해결하는 방식. 조정

ac·com·pa·ni·ment /ə'kʌmpənimənt/ *n* 1 music played along with someone while s/he sings or plays an instrument ‖ 노래나 악기 연주에 맞춰 연주되는 음악. 반주: *a tune with a simple guitar accompaniment* 기타 하나의 반주로 된 곡 2 something that is served or used with something else ‖ 다른 것과 함께 제공되거나 사용되는 것. 딸린 것. 부속물: *This wine makes a nice accompaniment to fish.* 이 포도주는 생선 요리에 잘 어울리는 곁들이가 된다.

ac·com·pa·nist /ə'kʌmpənɪst/ *n* someone who plays a musical instrument while another person sings or plays the main tune ‖ 남이 노래를 하거나 주선율을 연주하는 동안 반주를 하는 사람. 반주자

ac·com·pa·ny /əˈkʌmpəni/ v [T] **1** FORMAL to go somewhere with someone, especially in order to help or take care of him/her ‖ 특히 도와주거나 돌봐 주기 위해 누군가와 함께 어떤 곳에 가다. …을 동반[동행]하다: *Children under 12 must be accompanied by an adult.* 12세 미만의 어린이들은 성인을 동반해야 한다. **2** to happen or exist at the same time ‖ 동시에 일어나거나 존재하다. 수반하다: *Tonight, heavy rains accompanied by high winds will make driving difficult.* 오늘 밤 강한 바람을 동반한 폭우로 운전이 어려울 것으로 보입니다. **3** to play music along with someone who is playing or singing the main tune ‖ 주선율을 연주하거나 노래하는 사람에 맞춰 연주하다. 반주하다

ac·com·plice /əˈkʌmplɪs/ n someone who helps someone do something wrong or illegal ‖ 그릇되거나 불법적인 일을 하는 사람을 돕는 사람. 공모자. 공범

ac·com·plish /əˈkʌmplɪʃ/ v [T] to succeed in doing something, especially after trying hard to do it; achieve ‖ 특히 열심히 애쓴 뒤에 무엇을 하는 데에 성공하다. …을 성취하다. 이룩하다; 달성하다: *We've accomplished our goal of raising $45,000.* 우리는 45,000달러 모금 목표를 달성했다.

ac·com·plished /əˈkʌmplɪʃt/ adj very skillful ‖ 아주 능란한. 노련한: *an accomplished musician* 노련한 음악가

ac·com·plish·ment /əˈkʌmplɪʃmənt/ n **1** something you achieve or are able to do well, especially after a lot of effort ‖ 많은 노력을 하여 성취하거나 잘 할 수 있게 되는 것. 기예: *Playing the piano is one of her many accomplishments.* 피아노 연주는 그녀의 많은 기예 중 하나이다. **2** [U] the act of accomplishing something ‖ 무엇을 이룩하는 행위. 성취. 완수: *I'm looking for a job that gives me more of a sense of accomplishment.* (=a feeling that you have achieved something) 나는 내게 보다 많은 성취감을 주는 일을 찾고 있다.

ac·cord¹ /əˈkɔrd/ n FORMAL **1 of sb's own accord** without being asked; willingly ‖ 요청을 받지 않고. 자발적으로; 자진하여: *I didn't say anything. He left of his own accord.* 나는 어떤 말도 하지 않았어. 그가 자진해서 떠난 거야. **2** [C, U] the state of agreeing about

something, or a particular agreement ‖ 무엇에 대해 동의하는 상태나 특정한 합의. 일치. 협정: *The committee's report is completely in accord with our suggestions.* 위원회의 보고서는 우리의 제안과 완전히 일치한다.

ac·cord² v FORMAL [T] to treat someone or something in a particular way, or to give someone a prize, reward etc. ‖ 사람이나 사물을 특정하게 취급하거나 누군가에게 시상·보상 등을 하다: *He was accorded the honor in 1972.* 그는 1972년에 훈장을 받았다.

ac·cord·ance /əˈkɔrdns/ n [U] the state of agreeing about something ‖ 무엇에 대해 동의하는 상태. 일치. 조화: *The amount of money varies in accordance with what each family needs.* 금액은 각 가정의 필요에 따라 다르다.

ac·cord·ing·ly /əˈkɔrdɪŋli/ adv **1** in a way that is suitable for a particular situation ‖ 특정 상황에 알맞게. 그에 맞게. 적절히: *If you break the rules, you will be punished accordingly.* 만일 당신이 규칙을 어긴다면 응분의 벌을 받을 것이다. **2** as a result of something; therefore ‖ 무엇의 결과로서. 따라서; 그러므로: *He knows how the Democrats like to work. Accordingly, he can help the Republicans defeat them.* 그는 민주당이 일을 해 나가는 방식을 안다. 그러므로, 그는 공화당이 민주당을 이기도록 도울 수 있다.

according to /.ˈ.. ./ prep **1** as shown by something or said by someone ‖ 사물이 나타내거나 사람이 말한 대로. …에 의하면: *According to our records, you still have six of our books.* 우리의 기록에 의하면 당신은 아직까지 우리의 책 여섯 권을 가지고 있다. / *According to Angel, she's a great teacher.* 엔젤의 말에 의하면 그녀는 훌륭한 교사이다. **2** in a way that is suitable to a particular situation ‖ 특정한 상황에 적합하게. …에 따라서 [맞춰서]: *You will be paid according to the amount of work you do.* 당신이 하는 작업량에 따라 돈은 지불됩니다.

ac·cor·di·on /əˈkɔrdiən/ n a musical instrument that you pull in and out while pushing buttons to produce different notes ‖ 각각의 음을 내기 위해 건반을 누르면서 접었다 펼쳤다 하는 악기. 손풍금. 아코디언

ac·cost /əˈkɔst, əˈkɑst/ v [T] to go up to someone you do not know and speak to him/her in a threatening way ‖ 모르는 사람에게 다가가 위협적으로 말을 건네다: *I was accosted by a man asking for* *money.* 한 남자가 내게 다가와 위협적으로 돈을 요구했다.

ac·count[1] /əˈkaʊnt/ *n* **1** a sum of money you keep in a bank, that you can add to or take from ‖ 증액하거나 인출할 수 있도록 은행에 저금해 둔 돈의 총액. 예금액. 예금 계좌: *I don't have much money in my account.* 내 예금 계좌에는 많은 돈이 들어 있지는 않다. / *He couldn't remember his account number.* 그는 자기의 예금 계좌 번호를 기억할 수 없었다. / *checking account* (=one that you can take money out of at anytime) 당좌 예금 계좌 / *savings account* (=one in which you save money so that the amount increases) 보통 예금 계좌 **2** a written or spoken description of an event or situation ‖ 사건이나 상황에 대한 서면 또는 구두 묘사. 설명. 기술: *Can you give us an account of what happened?* 일어난 일을 우리에게 말해 줄 수 있니? / *By/from all accounts* (=according to what everyone says), *Frank was once a great player.* 모든 사람들의 이야기에 따르면, 프랭크는 한때 훌륭한 선수였다. **3** [C, U] an agreement that allows you to buy goods and pay for them later ‖ 상품을 구입하고 후불할 수 있도록 한 계약. 신용 거래: *buying a dishwasher on account* 식기 세척기의 외상 구입 / *Please settle your account* (=pay all you owe) *as soon as possible.* 가능한 한 빨리 빚진 것을 모두 갚으세요. **4 take sth into account/take account of sth** to consider particular facts when you make a judgment or decision about something ‖ 무엇에 대한 판단이나 결정을 할 때 특정한 사실을 고려하다: *The tax is unfair because it does not take account of people's ability to pay.* 그 세금은 낼 사람들의 능력을 고려하지 않았기 때문에 불공평하다. **5** an agreement to sell goods or services to someone over a period of time ‖ 일정 기간 동안 상품이나 용역을 판매하는 계약: *Our sales manager won five new accounts this year.* 우리 영업부장은 올해 다섯 건의 새 계약을 따냈다. **6 not on my/his etc. account** SPOKEN said when you do not want someone to do something for you unless s/he really wants to ‖ 누군가가 진정 하고 싶지 않으면서 상대를 위해 무엇을 하는 것을 원하지 않을 때 쓰여. …을 위해서 …하지 않다: *Don't stay up late on my account.* 나 때문에 일부러 늦게까지 자지 않고 있지는 마라. **7 on no account** FORMAL used in order to say that someone must not do something for

any reason ‖ 어떠한 이유로든 무엇을 하지 말아야 한다고 말하는 데에 쓰여. 무슨 일이 있어도 …해서는 안 된다: *On no account should anyone go near the building.* 아무도 절대로 그 건물 근처에 가서는 안 된다. —see also ACCOUNTS

account[2] *v* [T]

account for sth *phr v* [T] to give a reason for something that has happened ‖ 어떤 일이 일어난 이유를 밝히다. 설명하다: *How do you account for the $20 that's missing?* 20달러가 비는 것을 어떻게 설명할거니?

ac·count·a·bil·i·ty /əˌkaʊntəˈbɪləti/ *n* [U] a system that allows you to know who is responsible for a particular action ‖ 특정한 행위에 대해 누가 책임을 져야 하는지 알도록 한 체계. 책임: *There is no accountability in our department.* 우리 부서는 아무런 책임이 없다.

ac·count·a·ble /əˈkaʊntəbəl/ *adj* responsible for the effects of your actions and willing to explain them ‖ 행동의 결과에 책임을 지며 그것을 기꺼이 해명하는. 책임이 있는. 해명할 의무가 있는: *If anything happens to Max, I'll hold you accountable!* (=consider you responsible) 만일 맥스에게 무슨 일이 있으면 네게 책임을 물을 거야! —opposite UNACCOUNTABLE

ac·count·ant /əˈkaʊntənt, əˈkaʊntʰnt/ *n* someone whose job is to take care of financial accounts ‖ 재무 회계를 맡아보는 직업인. 회계사

ac·count·ing /əˈkaʊntɪŋ/ *n* [U] the profession of being an ACCOUNTANT, or the activity of dealing with financial accounts ‖ 회계사의 직업이나 재무 회계를 취급하는 활동. 회계직. 회계

ac·counts /əˈkaʊnts/ *n* [plural] a record of the money that a company has received and the money it has spent ‖ 한 회사의 자금의 입출금에 대한 기록. 장부. 출납부: *last year's accounts* 작년 출납부

ac·cred·i·ta·tion /əˌkrɛdəˈteɪʃən/ *n* [U] official approval for a person or organization ‖ 사람이나 기구에 대한 공식적인 승인. 인가

ac·cred·it·ed /əˈkrɛdɪtɪd/ *adj* having official approval as being of a high standard ‖ 높은 수준임을 공식적으로 승인 받은. 공인된: *an accredited journalist/school* 공인된 언론인[인가된 학교]

ac·crue /əˈkru/ *v* [I, T] to increase over a period of time ‖ 일정 기간에 걸쳐 증가하다. 자연증가로 생기다: *tax benefits that accrue to investors* 투자자가 얻는

세금 혜택

ac·cu·mu·late /əˈkyumyəˌleɪt/ v [I, T] to gradually increase in quantity or size, or to make something do this ‖ 점진적으로 양이나 크기가 늘거나 무엇을 이렇게 되게 하다. 쌓이다. 쌓다: *Dirt and dust had accumulated in the corners of the room.* 티끌과 먼지가 방구석에 쌓였다. / *Myers accumulated a huge debt from gambling.* 마이어스는 노름으로 거액의 빚을 졌다. - **accumulation** /əˌkyu-myəˈleɪʃən/ n [C, U]

ac·cu·ra·cy /ˈækyərəsi/ n [U] the quality of being accurate ‖ 정확성. 정밀성: *The bombs can be aimed with amazing accuracy.* 그 폭탄은 놀라울 정도로 정확하게 목표물을 명중시킬 수 있다. —opposite INACCURACY

ac·cu·rate /ˈækyərɪt/ adj exactly correct ‖ 정확한: *an accurate report of what happened* 일어난 일에 대한 정확한 보고 - **accurately** adv —opposite INACCURATE

ac·cu·sa·tion /ˌækyəˈzeɪʃən/ n a statement saying that someone has done something wrong or illegal ‖ 남이 비행이나 불법을 저질렀다는 진술. 비난. 고발. 고소: *Serious accusations have been made against the Attorney General.* 법무 장관에 대한 중대한 고발이 있었다.

ac·cuse /əˈkyuz/ v [T] to make a statement saying that someone has done something wrong or illegal ‖ 남이 비행이나 불법을 저질렀다고 언명하다. 비난[고발, 고소]하다: *Norton was accused of murder.* 노턴은 살인죄로 기소되었다. / *Are you accusing me of cheating?* 너 내가 속인다고 비난하는거니? - **accuser** n

ac·cused /əˈkyuzd/ n LAW the accused the person or people who are being tried (TRY) for a crime in a court of law ‖ 법정에서 범죄에 대한 재판을 받고 있는 사람이나 사람들. 피의자. 피고인

ac·cus·tom /əˈkʌstəm/ v [T] to make yourself or another person become used to something ‖ 자신이나 남을 어떤 것에 익숙해지게 하다. 습관을 들이다: *They'll have to accustom themselves to working harder.* 그들은 더 열심히 일하는 것에 익숙해져야 할 것이다.

ac·cus·tomed /əˈkʌstəmd/ adj FORMAL **be accustomed to (doing) sth** to be used to something ‖ 어떤 것에 익숙해지다: *Ed's eyes quickly became/got/grew accustomed to the dark room.* 에드의 눈은 어두운 방에 곧 익숙해졌다. —

opposite UNACCUSTOMED

ace¹ /eɪs/ n **1** a playing card with one mark on it, that has the highest or lowest value in a game ‖ 게임에서 가장 높거나 낮은 점수가 되는 문양이 한 개만 있는 카드. 에이스: *the ace of spades* (카드의) 스페이드 에이스 **2** a first hit in tennis or VOLLEYBALL that is hit so well that your opponent cannot hit it back ‖ 테니스나 배구에서 상대가 받아 넘길 수 없게 잘 쳐넣은 서브. 서비스 에이스 **ace in the hole** a secret advantage ‖ 비장의 카드: *Money was Brown's ace in the hole; he could afford an expensive campaign.* 브라운의 비장의 무기는 돈이어서 비용이 많이 드는 선거 운동도 할 수 있었다.

ace² adj INFORMAL **ace pilot/player etc.** someone who has a lot of skill as a pilot, player etc. ‖ 대단한 솜씨를 가진 조종사·선수 등. 최우수 조종사/선수

ace³ v [T] INFORMAL to get the best grade possible on a test, piece of written work etc. ‖ 시험·작문 등에서 최고의 성적을 받다: *Danny aced the spelling test.* 대니는 철자 시험에서 A를 받았다.

a·cer·bic /əˈsɜbɪk/ adj criticizing in a smart but unkind way ‖ 날카롭고 매정하게 비판하는. 신랄한: *Simon was known for his acerbic theater reviews.* 사이먼은 연극에 대한 비평이 신랄하기로 유명했다.

ache¹ /eɪk/ n **1** headache/backache/toothache a continuous pain in your head, back etc. ‖ 머리·등의 계속적인 통증. 두통/등의 통증/치통 **2** a continuous dull pain ‖ 지속적인 무지근한 아픔. 통증: *an ache in the knee* 무릎의 통증 - **achy** adj: *My arm feels all achy.* 팔이 굉장히 아프다.

ache² v [I] **1** to feel a continuous dull pain ‖ 계속되는 무지근한 통증을 느끼다. 아프다: *I ache all over.* 나는 온몸이 아프다. **2** ache to do sth to want to do something very much ‖ 몹시 무엇을 하고 싶어하다: *Jenny was aching to go home.* 제니는 몹시 집에 가고 싶어하고 있었다.

a·chieve /əˈtʃiv/ v [T] to succeed in doing or getting something as a result of your actions ‖ 행동의 결과로 무엇을 하거나 얻는 데 성공하다. 성취하다: *You'll never achieve anything if you don't work harder.* 일을 더 열심히 하지 않으면 어떠한 것도 이룰 수 없을 것이다. / *We've achieved excellent sales this year.* 우리는 올해 눈부신 매출을 올렸다. - **achiever** n : *a high achiever* 성취도가 높은 사람 - **achievable** adj

a·chieve·ment /ə'tʃivmənt/ *n* **1** something important that you succeed in doing through skill and hard work ‖ 기술과 노력을 통해 이룩한 중요한 것. 위업: *Winning the championship is quite an achievement.* 선수권을 획득하는 것은 대단한 위업이다. **2** [U] the act of achieving something ‖ 어떤 것을 성취하는 행위. 획득: *the achievement of a goal* 목표 성취

ac·id¹ /'æsɪd/ *n* **1** [C, U] a chemical substance that can produce salts or burn holes in the things it touches ‖ 염기(鹽基)를 생성하거나 사물에 닿으면 타서 구멍이 생기게 하는 화학 물질. 산(酸): *hydrochloric/citric acid* 염산[시트르산] **2 acid test** a situation that proves whether something is true or is as good as it is supposed to be ‖ 어떤 것이 사실인지 또는 예상대로 좋은지를 시험하는 경우. 시금(試金). **3** [U] SLANG the drug LSD ‖ 환각제 LSD

acid² *adj* **1** having a very sour or bitter taste ‖ 매우 시거나 쓴맛이 나는. **2 acid remark/comment** something you say that uses humor in an unkind way ‖ 짓궂게 익살을 써서 하는 말. 신랄한 말/비평 – **acidity** /ə'sɪdəti/ *n* [U]

acid rain /ˌ.. './ *n* [U] rain that damages the environment because it contains acid, especially from factory smoke ‖ 산이 들어 있어서 환경을 파괴하는, 특히 공장 연기에서 나오는 비. 산성비

ac·knowl·edge /ək'nɑlɪdʒ/ *v* [T] **1** to accept or admit that something is true or that a situation exists ‖ 무엇이 사실이거나 상황이 존재하는 것으로 받아들이거나 시인하다. 인정하다: *Angie acknowledged that she had made a mistake.* 앤지는 자기가 실수했다는 것을 인정했다. **2** to officially accept that a government, court, leader etc. has legal authority ‖ 법적인 권한을 가진 정부·법정·지도자 등을 정식으로 인정하다. 승인하다: *They are refusing to acknowledge the court's decision.* 그들은 법원의 판결을 인정하기를 거부하고 있다. **3** to publicly announce that you are grateful for the help that someone has given you ‖ 누군가가 베푼 도움에 대하여 감사의 뜻을 공표하다. 사의를 표하다: *The author wishes to acknowledge the help of the Art Museum.* 그 작가는 미술관의 도움을 받은 것에 대하여 사의를 표하고 싶어한다. **4** to show someone that you have seen him/her or heard what s/he has said ‖ 어떤 사람에게 자기가 상대방을 보거나 상대방이 말한 것을 들어 이미 알고

있음을 나타내다: *Tina didn't even acknowledge me.* 티나는 나에게 안다는 내색조차도 하지 않았다.

ac·knowl·edg·ment /ək'nɑlɪdʒmənt/ *n* something given, done, or said to thank someone or to show that something has been received ‖ 어떤 사람에게 감사나 어떤 것을 받았음을 표시하기 위해 준[한, 말한] 것. 회답. 사례물: *I haven't received an acknowledgment of my letter yet.* 나는 아직 내가 보낸 편지의 답장을 받지 않았다.

ac·ne /'ækni/ *n* [U] a skin disease that causes small red spots to appear, especially on someone's face ‖ 특히 얼굴에 작은 붉은 점이 생기게 하는 피부병. 여드름

a·corn /'eɪkɔrn/ *n* the nut of the OAK tree ‖ 오크나무의 견과. 도토리

a·cous·tic /ə'kustɪk/ *adj* **1** relating to sound and the way people hear things ‖ 소리와 듣는 방법에 관련된. 음향의 **2** an acoustic musical instrument does not have its sound made louder electronically ‖ 악기가 소리를 전자 증폭시키지 않은. 전자 장치를 쓰지 않은

a·cous·tics /ə'kustɪks/ *n* [plural] **1** the scientific study of sound ‖ 소리에 대한 과학적 연구. 음향학 **2** the qualities of a room, such as its shape and size, that affect the way sound is heard in it ‖ 방의 모양이나 크기 등의, 소리가 들리는 데에 영향을 미치는 실내의 특성. 음향 효과

ac·quaint /ə'kweɪnt/ *v* [T] to know about something, because you have read about it, used it etc. ‖ 읽거나 사용해 본 까닭에 무엇을 알다: *We have already acquainted ourselves with the facts.* 우리는 이미 그 사실을 알고 있다.

ac·quaint·ance /ə'kweɪnt'ns/ *n* someone you know, but not very well ‖ 잘 몰라도 아는 사람: *an acquaintance of mine* 내가 아는 사람

ac·quaint·ed /ə'kweɪntɪd/ *adj* **1 get acquainted** to meet someone and start to know more about him/her ‖ 어떤 사람을 만나 상대에 대하여 보다 많이 알게 되다. 사귀게 되다: *How did you two get acquainted?* 두 분은 어떻게 알게 되었죠? **2 be acquainted (with sb)** to know someone, but not well ‖ 잘은 몰라도 어떤 사람을 알다: *Yes, I'm acquainted with Roger.* 그래, 나는 로저를 알고 있어.

ac·qui·esce /ˌækwi'ɛs/ *v* [I] FORMAL to agree with someone without arguing or complaining, often when you do not want to ‖ 흔히 원하지는 않지만 논쟁이나 불평없이 동의하다. 묵묵히[마지못해] 따

르다 - **acquiescence** *n* [U]

ac·quire /əˈkwaɪə/ *v* [T] **1** to get something, either by buying it or through hard work ‖ 사거나 열심히 일해서 무엇을 얻다. 입수[획득]하다 : *Think about the skills you have acquired, and how you can use them.* 당신이 취득한 기술들과 그 기술들을 이용할 방법을 생각해 봐라. **2 an acquired taste** something that you only begin to like after you have tried it a few times ‖ 몇 차례 해 본 뒤에야 좋아하게 되는 것: *Whiskey is often an acquired taste.* 위스키는 대개 몸에 익어야 맛을 알게 된다.

ac·qui·si·tion /ˌækwəˈzɪʃən/ *n* FORMAL **1** [U] the act of getting something ‖ 사물을 얻음. 취득. 획득: *the acquisition of new companies* 새 회사의 인수 **2** something that you have gotten ‖ 입수한 것. 취득물: *a recent acquisition* 최근의 취득물

ac·quit /əˈkwɪt/ *v* [T] to decide in a court of law that someone is not guilty of a crime ‖ 법정에서 사람이 무죄라는 판결을 내리다. 무죄를 선고하다: *Simmons was acquitted of murder.* 사이먼은 살인죄에 대한 무죄 선고를 받았다. —opposite CONVICT

ac·quit·tal /əˈkwɪtl/ *n* [C, U] an official announcement in a court of law that someone is not guilty ‖ 죄가 없다는 법정에서의 공식 발표. 무죄 선고 —opposite CONVICTION

a·cre /ˈeɪkə/ *n* a unit for measuring an area of land, equal to 4,840 square yards or about 4,047 square meters ‖ 4,840 평방야드나 약 4,047 평방미터에 해당하는 토지 측량 단위. 에이커

a·cre·age /ˈeɪkərɪdʒ/ *n* [U] the area of a piece of land measured in ACRES ‖ 에이커로 잰 토지의 면적. 평수

ac·rid /ˈækrɪd/ *adj* having a very strong and unpleasant smell or taste that hurts your nose or throat ‖ 코나 목을 자극하는 강하고 불쾌한 냄새나 맛이 나는. 얼얼한. 메케한: *a cloud of acrid smoke* 자욱하게 퍼진 메케한 연기

ac·ri·mo·ni·ous /ˌækrəˈmoʊniəs/ *adj* if an argument, meeting etc. is acrimonious, the people involved are extremely angry and not kind to each other ‖ 논쟁·모임 등에서 관련자들이 서로 몹시 화가 나 있어서 서로 친절하지 못한. 톡 쏘는. 독살스러운: *an acrimonious divorce* 독기가 어린 이혼

ac·ri·mo·ny /ˈækrəˌmoʊni/ *n* [U] FORMAL very angry feelings between people, often strongly expressed ‖ 흔히 격렬하게 표현되는 사람들 간의 매우 화난 감정. 독살[표독]스러움

ac·ro·bat /ˈækrəˌbæt/ *n* someone who does difficult physical actions such as walking on his/her hands or balancing on a high rope ‖ 높은 줄 위에서 손으로 걷거나 몸의 균형을 잡는 등의 어려운 동작을 하는 사람. 곡예사 — **acrobatic** /ˌækrəˈbætɪk/ *adj*

ac·ro·bat·ics /ˌækrəˈbætɪks/ *n* [plural] the skill or tricks of an ACROBAT ‖ 곡예사의 기술이나 재주. 곡예

ac·ro·nym /ˈækrənɪm/ *n* a word that is made from the first letters of a group of words. For example, NATO is an acronym for the North Atlantic Treaty Organization ‖ 일단의 단어들의 첫 번째 글자에서 조성된 단어. 두문자어. 예를 들면 NATO는 North Atlantic Treaty Organization의 두문자어이다.

a·cross¹ /əˈkrɔs/ *prep* **1** going, looking, moving etc. from one side of something to the other side ‖ 어떤 것의 한 쪽에서 다른 쪽으로 가거나 보거나, 또는 움직이는. …을 가로질러: *Vince stared across the canyon.* 빈스는 계곡 건너편을 응시했다. / *flying across the Atlantic* 대서양을 횡단하는 비행 —see picture at OVER¹ **2** on or toward the opposite side of something ‖ 무엇의 반대쪽에, 반대쪽을 향하여: *Andy lives across the street from us.* 앤디는 우리집 길 맞은편에 살고 있다. **3** reaching or spreading from one side of an area to the other ‖ 한 지역에서 다른 쪽까지 이르거나 퍼져 있는: *There was only one bridge across the bay.* 그 만을 가로지르는 유일한 다리가 하나 있었다. **4** in every part of an organization or government ‖ 기관이나 정부의 모든 부문에: *Changes will have to be made across the board.* (=affecting everyone) 전면적인 변화가 일어나야 한다.

across² *adv* **1** from one side of something to the other ‖ 한 쪽에서 다른 쪽으로. 가로질러서. 건너서: *The road's too busy to walk across.* 그 길은 너무 붐벼 걸어서 건너갈 수가 없다. **2 10 feet/5 miles etc. across** measuring 10 feet, 5 miles etc. from one side to the other ‖ 한 쪽에서 다른 쪽까지 10 피트·5 마일 등의 측정치. 직경 10피트/5마일: *At its widest point, the river is 2 miles across.* 그 강의 가장 넓은 지점은 폭이 2 마일이다. **3 across from** opposite something or someone ‖ 사물이나 사람의 바로 맞은편에: *One kid sitting across from me was really noisy.* 내 바로 맞은

편에 앉아 있는 아이는 정말로 시끄러웠다.

a·cryl·ic /ə'krılık/ *adj* acrylic paints, cloth etc. are made from a chemical substance ‖ 그림·천 등이 화학 물질로 만든. 아크릴성(性)의

act¹ /ækt/ *v* **1** [I] to behave in a particular way ‖ 특정하게 행동하다: *She always acts shy when she's on the phone.* 그녀는 통화 중에는 항상 수줍어한다. / *Pam's just acting like a baby.* 팸은 꼭 아기처럼 굴고 있다. **2** [I] to do something ‖ 무엇을 하다: *They think doctors can't act as managers.* 그들은 의사가 경영자 노릇을 할 수 없다고 생각한다. / *We're acting on the advice of our lawyer.* (=doing what s/he says) 우리는 변호사의 조언에 따라 행동하고 있다. **3** [I, T] to perform as a character in a play or movie ‖ 연극이나 영화에서 등장인물로 공연을 하다. 연기하다: *She acts very well.* 그녀는 연기를 아주 잘한다. **4** [I] to produce a particular effect ‖ 특정한 효과를 내다: *Salt acts as a preservative.* 소금은 방부제 역할을 한다.

act sth ↔ **out** *phr v* [T] to show how an event happened by performing it like a play ‖ 연극처럼 연기를 하여 사건이 어떻게 일어났는지 보여 주다. 실연하다: *The third graders acted out the story of the first Thanksgiving.* 3학년 학생들은 첫 번째 추수 감사절 이야기를 실연했다.

act up *phr v* [I] INFORMAL to behave badly or not work correctly ‖ 못되게 굴다, 제대로 작동하지 않다: *The car's acting up again.* 그 차는 또 고장났다.

act² *n* **1** a particular type of action ‖ 특정한 유형의 행동: *an act of cruelty* 잔인한 행위 **2** also **Act** a law that has been officially passed by the government ‖ 정부에 의해 공식으로 통과된 법률: *the Civil Rights Act* 공민권법, 시민의 권리에 관한 법률 **3** also **Act** one of the main parts into which a play, OPERA etc. is divided ‖ 연극·오페라 등에서 구획이 그어지는 주요 부분의 하나. 막: *Hamlet kills the king in Act 5.* 햄릿은 5막에서 왕을 죽인다. **4** the performance of one of the singers, groups of musicians etc. in a show ‖ 쇼에서 가수·악단 등의 공연: *a comedy act* 촌극 **5** [singular] insincere behavior that is meant to have a particular effect ‖ 특별한 효과를 보려는 의도가 담긴 불성실한 행동. 연극조의 행동: *He doesn't care, Laura – it's just an act.* 그는 신경도 안 쓴다니까 로라야. 그건 그저 연극일 뿐이야. **6 get your act together** INFORMAL to do things in a more

organized or effective way ‖ 보다 조직적이거나 효율적으로 일을 하다. 정신차리다. 마음을 다잡다: *If Julie doesn't get her act together, she'll never graduate.* 만일 줄리가 정신차리지 않으면 결코 졸업하지 못할 게다. **7 get in on the act** INFORMAL to try to get advantages from an activity that someone else has started, especially when s/he does not want you to ‖ 특히 남이 원하지 않는데도 남이 시작한 활동에서 이익을 보려 하다. 한몫 끼다

USAGE NOTE act and action

Use **action** as a countable noun when it means the same as **act**: *a kind act / a kind action.* Use **act** in some fixed phrases when it means a particular type of action: *an act of friendship / an act of war / He was caught in the act of stealing.* **Act** is always countable, but **action** can be uncountable: *What we need now is quick action.*
action이 가산 명사로 쓰일 때는 **act**와 의미가 같다: 친절한 행위/친절한 행위. **act**는 특정한 유형의 행동을 의미하는 관용구에 쓰인다: 우정의 행동/전쟁 행위/그는 절도 현장에서 체포되었다. **act**는 항상 가산 명사이지만 **action**은 불가산 명사가 될 수 있다: 우리에게 지금 필요한 것은 재빠른 행동이다.

---

act·ing¹ /'æktıŋ/ *adj* **acting manager/director etc.** someone who replaces the manager etc. for a short time ‖ 잠시 동안 지배인 등을 대리하는 사람. 지배인/국장 대리

acting² *n* [U] the job or skill of representing a character, especially in a play or movie ‖ 특히 연극이나 영화에서 배역을 실연하는 일이나 기예. 연기

ac·tion /'ækʃən/ *n* **1** something that you do ‖ 하는 것. 행위: *His quick actions probably saved my life.* 아마도 그의 재빠른 행동이 나를 구했을 것이다. **2** [U] the process of doing things for a particular purpose ‖ 특정한 목적을 위하여 일을 하는 과정. 행동: *We must take action* (=start doing something) *before it's too late.* 우리는 너무 늦기 전에 행동을 취해야만 한다. / *It's time to put the plan into action.* (=do things to make it happen) 계획을 실행에 옮길 때다. —opposite INACTION **3** [singular, U] the way in which something moves, works, or has an effect on something else ‖ 사물이 움직이거나 작동하는, 또는 다른 것에 영향

을 주는 방식. 작용. 영향: *The rock is worn down by the action of the falling water.* 그 바위는 떨어지는 물의 작용으로 마모되었다. **4 out of action** INFORMAL not working because of damage or injury ‖ 손상되거나 다쳐서 움직이지 않는: *My car's out of action.* 내 차는 고장 났다. / *Jim will be out of action for two weeks.* 짐은 2주 동안 활동하지 못할 것이다. **5 the action** INFORMAL exciting and important things that are happening ‖ 일어나고 있는 자극적이며 중요한 일. 활동. 활기: *New York's where the action is.* 뉴욕은 활기가 넘치는 곳이다. **6 in action** doing a particular job or activity ‖ 특정한 일이나 활동을 하고 있는: *a chance to see ski jumpers in action* 경기 중인 스키 점프 선수를 볼 수 있는 기회 **7** [C, U] fighting during a war ‖ 전투. 교전: *Ann's husband was killed in action.* 앤의 남편은 전사했다. —see usage note at ACT²

ac·ti·vate /'æktə‚veɪt/ *v* [T] FORMAL to make something start working ‖ 무엇을 작동하게 하다: *This switch activates the radar.* 이 스위치는 레이더를 작동시킨다. **– activation** /‚æktə'veɪʃən/ *n* [U]

ac·tive¹ /'æktɪv/ *adj* **1** always doing things, or always ready and able to do something ‖ 항상 무엇을 하고 있는, 또는 늘 준비가 되어 무엇을 할 수 있는. 활동 중인. 활동력이 있는: *Grandpa's active for his age.* 할아버지는 나이에 비해 활동적이다. / *an active volcano* 활화산 **2** TECHNICAL able or ready to operate ‖ 작동 가능하거나 작동 준비된: *The alarm is now active.* 경보기는 지금 작동 중이다.

active² *n* **the active (voice)** TECHNICAL in grammar, in the active voice, the subject of the sentence does the action of the verb. In the sentence, "They grow oranges in California," the verb is in the active voice ‖ 문법에서 문장의 주어가 스스로 동사가 나타내는 동작을 하는 능동태. "They grow oranges in California."라는 문장에서 동사 grow는 능동형이다. —compare PASSIVE²

ac·tiv·ist /'æktəvɪst/ *n* someone who works to achieve social or political change ‖ 사회적이거나 정치적인 변화를 이루기 위해 일하는 사람. 행동주의자. 운동가 **– activism** *n* [U]

ac·tiv·i·ty /æk'tɪvəti/ *n* **1** [U] movement and action ‖ 움직임 및 행동. 활기: *the noise and activity of the city* 도시의 시끌벅적하고 활기참 / *a day full of activity* 활기찬 하루 **2** [C, U] things that

you do for pleasure, or because you want to achieve something ‖ 즐거움을 위해 또는 어떤 것을 이루고 싶어서 하는 일. 활동: *after-school activities* 방과 후 활동 / *an increase in terrorist activity* 테러범들의 활동의 증가

ac·tor /'æktɚ/ *n* someone who performs in a play, movie etc. ‖ 연극·영화 등에서 연기하는 사람. 배우

ac·tress /'æktrɪs/ *n* a woman who performs in a play, movie etc. ‖ 연극·영화 등에서 연기하는 여성. 여배우

ac·tu·al /'æktʃuəl, 'ækʃuəl/ *adj* real, especially when compared with what is believed, expected, or intended ‖ 특히 믿거나 예상하거나, 또는 의도된 것과 비교하여 실제의. 사실상의: *Were those his actual words?* 그것들이 그가 실제로 한 말이냐? / *Well, the actual cost is a lot higher than they say.* 그런데, 실제 비용은 그들이 말한 것보다 훨씬 더 높다.

ac·tu·al·i·ty /‚ækʃu'æləti/ *n* **in actuality** really ‖ 실제로: *I always thought that making wine was complicated, when in actuality it's simple.* 나는 늘 포도주 만드는 것이 복잡하다고 생각했는데 실제로는 간단했다.

ac·tu·al·ly /'æktʃuəli, -tʃəli, 'ækʃuəli, -ʃəli/ *adv* **1** used in order to emphasize an opinion or give new information ‖ 의견을 강조하거나 새 정보를 주는 데에 쓰여. 실은. 실제로: *I do actually think that things have improved.* 나는 정말 상황이 개선됐다고 생각한다. / *Actually, a lot of Vancouver's restaurants are non-smoking.* 실제로, 밴쿠버의 많은 식당에서 담배를 피울 수 없다. **2** used when you are telling or asking someone what the truth about something is ‖ 어떤 것에 관한 진실이 무엇인지 사람에게 말하거나 물을 때 쓰여: *Is George actually 65?* 조지가 정말 65세야? / *Actually, I forgot to get the milk.* 사실, 나는 우유 사는 것을 잊어버렸다. **3** although it may seem strange ‖ 이상하게 보일지 모르나. 정말로: *Pete was actually polite for once!* 피트는 한때 정말 예의 발랐다.

a·cu·men /ə'kyumən, 'ækyəmən/ *n* [U] the ability to think quickly and make good judgments ‖ 재빨리 생각하여 적절한 판단을 내리는 능력. 총명. 통찰력: *business acumen* 상재(商才)

ac·u·punc·ture /'ækyə‚pʌŋktʃɚ/ *n* [U] a method used in Chinese medicine in which needles are put into someone's body in order to treat pain or illness ‖ 통증이나 병을 치료하기 위해 남의 몸에 바

늘을 꽂는 한의학에서 사용하는 방법. 침
술(요법)

a·cute /ə'kyut/ *adj* **1** very serious or
severe ‖ 매우 심각한, 격심한: *acute pain*
격심한 통증 **2** showing an ability to
clearly understand things ‖ 일을 명확히
이해하는 능력을 나타내는. 명민한: *an
acute observation* 예리한 관찰 **3**
showing an ability to notice small
differences in sound, taste etc. ‖ 소리·맛
등의 조그만 차이까지 알아차리는 능력을
보여 주는. 예민한. 민감한: *acute
hearing* 예민한 청력 **4** TECHNICAL a
disease or illness that is acute quickly
becomes dangerous ‖ 질병이 갑작스럽게
위험해지는. 급성인: *acute tuberculosis*
급성 폐결핵 —compare CHRONIC **5**
TECHNICAL an acute angle is less than 90
degrees ‖ 각도가 90도보다 작은. 예각(銳
角)의 　 **– acutely** *adv* : *acutely
embarrassed* 몹시 당황한

A.D. Anno Domini; used in order to
show that a date is a particular number
of years after the birth of Christ ‖ Anno
Domini (서력 기원)의 약어; 예수의 탄생
후의 특정한 연도를 나타내는 데에 쓰여:
in the first century A.D. A.D. 1세기에 —
compare B.C.

ad /æd/ *n* INFORMAL ⇨ ADVERTISEMENT

ad·age /'ædɪdʒ/ *n* a well-known phrase
that says something wise; PROVERB ‖ 지
혜를 알려 주는 잘 알려진 어구. 금언. 격
언; Ⓕ proverb

ad·a·mant /'ædəmənt/ *adj* FORMAL
determined not to change your opinion,
decision etc. ‖ 의견·결정 등을 바꾸지 않
기로 결정한. 단호한. 요지부동의: *Ann
was adamant (that) she would not go
with us.* 앤이 우리와 같이 가지 않겠다는
생각은 단호했다. **– adamantly** *adv*

Ad·am's ap·ple /'ædəmz ˌæpəl/ *n* the
part of your body at the front of your
neck that sticks out slightly and moves
when you talk or swallow ‖ 말하거나 음
식을 삼킬 때 움직이는 살짝 튀어나온 목
의 앞쪽에 있는 신체 부위. 후골(喉骨)

a·dapt /ə'dæpt/ *v* **1** [I] to change your
behavior or ideas to fit a new situation
‖ 행동이나 생각을 새로운 상황에 맞춰 바
꾸다. 적응하다: *The kids are having
trouble adapting to their new school.* 그
아이들은 새 학교에 적응하느라 고생하고
있다. **2** [T] to change something so that
it is suitable for a new need or purpose
‖ 새로운 요구나 목적에 맞도록 무엇을 바
꾸다. 개조[개작]하다: *Mom's chili recipe
is adapted from my Grandma's.* 엄마의
칠리 조리법은 내 할머니의 조리법을 바꾼

것이다. **– adaptation** /ˌædəp'teɪʃən,
ˌædæp-/ *n* [C, U]: *a film adaptation of
"Huckleberry Finn"* "허클베리 핀"을 각
색한 영화

a·dapt·a·ble /ə'dæptəbəl/ *adj* able to
change in order to be suitable or
successful in new or different situations
‖ 새롭거나 달라진 상황에 적합하거나 성
공적이 되도록 변화할 수 있는. 적응[순
응]할 수 있는 **– adaptability** /əˌdæ-
ptə'bɪləti/ *n* [U]

a·dapt·er /ə'dæptə/ *n* something that is
used for connecting two pieces of
equipment, especially if they are
different sizes or power levels ‖ 특히 서
로 크기나 전력의 수준이 다를 때 두 기구
를 연결하는 데에 사용되는 것. 어댑터

add /æd/ *v* [T] **1** to put something
together with something else or with a
group of other things ‖ 무엇을 다른 것과
또는 일단의 다른 것들과 함께 놓다. 추가
하다: *Do you want to add your name to
the mailing list?* 우편물 수취인 명부에
당신의 이름을 추가하기를 원합니까? /
Add one egg to the flour mixture. 계란
하나를 밀가루 반죽에다 넣으세요. **2** to
put numbers or amounts together and
then calculate the total ‖ 수나 양을 합하
여 총계를 내다. 더하다. 합계하다: *If you
add 5 and 3 you get 8.* 5에다 3을 더하면
8이 된다. **3** to say more about
something when you are speaking ‖ 말하
면서 무엇을 덧붙여 말하다. 부연하다:
*The Judge added that this case was one
of the worst she had ever tried.* 그 판사
는 이 사건이 지금까지 재판했던 것 중에
최악의 하나라고 덧붙였다. **4 add insult
to injury** to make a situation even more
upsetting for someone who has been
badly or unfairly treated ‖ 좋지 않게 또
는 불공정하게 대우를 받아온 사람에게 상
황을 더욱 심란하게 만들다. 설상가상이
되게 하다

add to sth *phr v* [T] to increase
something ‖ 무엇을 증가시키다: *The
change of plans only added to our
confusion.* 계획의 변경은 우리를 더욱 혼
란스럽게만 했다.

add up *phr v* **1** [I,T **add** sth ↔ **up**] to
put numbers or amounts together and
then calculate the total ‖ 수나 양을 합하
여 총계를 내다. 합계하다: *We're now
adding up the latest figures.* 지금 우리
는 가장 최근의 수치를 합계하고 있다. **2
not add up** to not seem true or
reasonable ‖ 사실이 아니거나 이치에 맞
지 않는 듯하다: *Her story just doesn't
add up.* 그녀의 이야기는 앞뒤가 안 맞는

다.

ad·dict /'ædɪkt/ *n* someone who is unable to stop a harmful habit, such as taking drugs ‖ 마약 복용 등의 해로운 습관을 끊을 수 없는 사람. (마약) 중독자: *a heroin/cocaine addict* 헤로인[코카인] 중독자

ad·dict·ed /ə'dɪktɪd/ *adj* unable to stop taking drugs or doing something harmful ‖ 마약 복용이나 해로운 일을 하는 것을 끊을 수 없는. 중독된: *Marvin was addicted to sleeping pills.* 마빈은 수면제에 중독되었다.

ad·dic·tion /ə'dɪkʃən/ *n* [C, U] the need to have something regularly because you are ADDICTED to it ‖ 중독되어 있어서 정기적으로 어떤 것을 필요로 함. 중독: *drug addiction* 마약 중독 / *his addiction to alcohol* 그의 알코올 중독

ad·dic·tive /ə'dɪktɪv/ *adj* making you ADDICTED to something ‖ 무엇에 중독되게 하는. 중독성의: *a highly addictive drug* 중독성이 강한 약물

ad·di·tion /ə'dɪʃən/ *n* **1 in addition** used in order to add another fact to what has already been mentioned ‖ 이미 언급한 것에 다른 사실을 추가하는 데에 쓰여. 게다가. …에 더하여: *In addition to his job, Harvey also coaches Little League.* 하비는 그의 직업 외에 소년 야구 리그의 코치도 맡고 있다. / *In addition, you need a driver's license.* 추가로, 운전 면허증도 필요하다. **2** [U] the adding together of several numbers or amounts ‖ 몇몇의 수나 양을 함께 더함. 덧셈 **3** something added ‖ 덧붙인 것. 부가[첨가]물: *She was an important addition to our group.* 그녀는 우리 단체의 중요한 추가 인원이었다.

ad·di·tion·al /ə'dɪʃənəl/ *adj* more than what was agreed or expected ‖ 동의하거나 예상한 것 이상의. 부가의. 추가의: *We were charged an additional $50 in late fees.* 우리는 추가로 50달러의 연체료를 부과받았다.

ad·di·tive /'ædətɪv/ *n* a substance, especially a chemical, added to a food or drink in order to improve it, add color, preserve it etc. ‖ 질을 높이거나 색깔을 내거나 보존하기 위해 음식이나 음료수에 첨가하는, 특히 화학적인 첨가물

ad·dress¹ /ə'drɛs, 'ædrɛs/ *n* the details of where someone lives or works, including the number of a building, name of the street and town etc. ‖ 건물의 호수(號數)·거리명·도시명 등을 포함한 주거지나 근무처에 대한 상세한 기술. 주

소: *I forgot to give Damien my new address.* 데미엔에게 내 새 주소를 주는 것을 잊어 버렸다.

address² *v* [T] **1 address a problem/question/issue etc.** to try to find a way to solve a problem, answer a difficult question etc. ‖ 문제를 해결하거나 어려운 질문에 대답하는 법 등을 모색하려고 애쓰다. 문제/질문/쟁점과 씨름하다: *Special meetings address the concerns of new members.* 특별 회의에서는 신입 회원 문제를 놓고 토론을 벌인다. **2** FORMAL to speak directly to a person or a group ‖ 어떤 사람이나 집단에 직접 말하다. 연설하다: *A guest speaker then addressed the audience.* 그때 초청 연사가 청중에게 연설했다. **3** to write a name and address on an envelope, package etc. ‖ 봉투·소포 등에 성명·주소를 쓰다. 겉봉을 쓰다: *There's a letter here addressed to you.* 여기 당신에게 온 편지가 있다. **4** to use a particular name or title when speaking or writing to someone ‖ 누군가에게 말하거나 글을 쓸 때 특정한 이름이나 직함을 사용하다. …이라고 부르다: *The President should be addressed as "Mr. President."* 대통령은 "대통령 각하"라고 불러야 한다.

address³ /ə'drɛs/ *n* a formal speech ‖ 공식적인 연설: *the Gettysburg Address* 게티스버그 연설

a·dept /ə'dɛpt/ *adj* good at doing something that needs care or skill ‖ 주의나 기술이 필요한 일을 잘하는. 숙련된: *Melissa was quickly becoming an adept skier.* 멜리사는 빠르게 스키의 명수가 되어 가고 있었다. / *He is adept at cooking Polish dishes.* 그는 폴란드 요리를 하는 데 능숙하다. **- adeptly** *adv*

ad·e·quate /'ædɪkwɪt/ *adj* **1** enough for a particular purpose ‖ 특정한 목적을 충족시키는. 충분한: *We have not been given adequate information.* 우리에겐 충분한 정보가 주어지지 않았다. / *Her income is hardly adequate to pay the bills.* 그녀의 수입은 이런저런 요금들을 치르기에도 충분히 못하다. **2** fairly good, but not excellent ‖ 뛰어나지는 않지만 꽤 좋은. 괜찮은: *an adequate performance* 그런대로 괜찮은 공연 **- adequately** *adv* —opposite INADEQUATE

ad·here /əd'hɪr/ *v* [I] to stick firmly to something ‖ 어떤 것에 꽉 들러붙다. 부착하다

adhere to *sth phr v* [I] to continue to behave according to a particular rule, agreement, or belief ‖ 계속 특정한 규칙이나 협정 또는 신념에 따라서 행동하다.

고수하다. 집착하다: *Not all the states adhered to the treaty.* 모든 국가들이 그 조약을 준수한 것은 아니었다.

ad·her·ence /əd'hɪrəns/ *n* [U] the act of behaving according to particular rules, ideas, or beliefs ‖ 특정한 규칙이나 사상 또는 신념에 따라 하는 행위. 집착. 고집: *a strict adherence to religious beliefs* 종교적 신념에 대한 철저한 신봉

ad·her·ent /əd'hɪrənt/ *n* someone who agrees with and supports a particular idea, opinion, or political party ‖ 특정한 사상이나 견해 또는 정당을 찬성하여 지지하는 사람. 지지자. 추종자

ad·he·sion /əd'hiʒən/ *n* [U] the ability of one thing to stick to another thing ‖ 한 사물이 다른 것에 붙는 힘. 점착력

ad·he·sive /əd'hisɪv, -zɪv/ *n* a substance that can stick things together, such as glue ‖ 물건을 붙일 수 있는 아교 등의 물질. 접착제 – **adhesive** *adj* : *adhesive tape* 접착 테이프

ad hoc /ˌæd 'hɑk/ *adj* done or arranged only when a situation makes something necessary, and without any previous planning ‖ 사전 계획 없이 필요한 상황에만 이루어지거나 마련되는. 임시의: *an ad hoc committee* 임시 위원회 – **ad hoc** *adv*

ad·ja·cent /ə'dʒeɪsənt/ *adj* very close to something, or next to it ‖ 무엇에 아주 가깝거나 인접한. 부근의. 인근의: *A fire broke out in the building adjacent to the police station.* 경찰서에 인접한 빌딩에서 화재가 발생했다.

ad·jec·tive /'ædʒɪktɪv, 'ædʒətɪv/ *n* TECHNICAL in grammar, a word that describes a noun or pronoun. In the sentence "I bought a new car," "new" is an adjective ‖ 문법에서 명사나 대명사를 묘사하는 단어. 형용사."I bought a new car." 라는 문장에서 "new"는 형용사이다

ad·join·ing /ə'dʒɔɪnɪŋ/ *adj* next to something, and connected to it ‖ 어떤 것에 이웃하여 연결된. 접해[붙어] 있는: *a bedroom with an adjoining bathroom* 욕실이 딸린 침실 – **adjoin** *v* [T]

ad·journ /ə'dʒɚn/ *v* [I, T] to stop a meeting for a short time ‖ 잠시 동안 회의를 중지하다. 휴회되다. 휴회시키다: *This court is adjourned until 2:30 p.m. tomorrow.* 이 법정은 내일 오후 2시 30분까지 휴정합니다. / *The assembly adjourned for an hour.* 회의는 1시간 동안 휴회했다. – **adjournment** *n* [C, U]

ad·ju·di·cate /ə'dʒudɪˌkeɪt/ *v* [I, T] FORMAL to judge something such as a competition, or to make an official decision ‖ 경기 등을 심판하거나 공식 결정을 내리다. 판결하다 – **adjudicator** *n*

ad·junct /'ædʒʌŋkt/ *n* **1** someone such as a doctor or teacher who works at a hospital, university etc. for a few hours a week, in addition to having another job ‖ 다른 직업을 가지고 있으면서 병원·대학 등에서 주당 몇 시간씩 일하는 의사나 교수 등의 사람. 겸직자 **2 an adjunct to sth** something that is added or joined to something else, but is not part of it. ‖ 그 일부는 아니지만 다른 것에 추가되거나 연결된 것. 부속물 – **adjunct** *adj*: *an adjunct professor* 겸임 교수

ad·just /ə'dʒʌst/ *v* **1** [T] to make small changes to the position of something in order to improve it ‖ 개선하기 위해 무엇의 위치를 약간 변화시키다. 조정하다: *Where's the thing for adjusting the car seat?* 차 좌석을 조정하는 것이 어디 있지? **2** [I] to make small changes to the way you do things in order to feel more comfortable in a new situation or condition ‖ 새로운 상황이나 여건에서 보다 편안함을 느낄 수 있도록 일하는 방식에 약간의 변화를 주다. 적응하다: *We're finally getting adjusted to all the heat.* 우리는 마침내 찌는 더위에 적응해 가고 있다. – **adjustable** *adj*

ad·just·ment /ə'dʒʌstmənt/ *n* [C, U] **1** a small change made to a machine or system ‖ 기계나 시스템에 가해지는 조그만 변화. 조정. 정비: *We've made some adjustments to our original calculations.* 우리는 원래의 계산을 다소 조정했다. **2** a change in the way you behave or think, made when your situation changes ‖ 상황이 바뀌어 생긴 행동이나 사고방식상의 변화. 적응. 순응: *It hasn't been an easy adjustment to his new job.* 그는 새로운 직업에 적응하기가 쉽지 않았다.

ad-lib /ˌæd'lɪb/ *v* [I, T] to say something in a speech or a performance without preparing or planning it ‖ 연설이나 연기에서 준비나 계획 없이 말하다. 즉흥적으로 연설[연기]하다 – **ad lib** *adj, adv*

ad·min·is·ter /əd'mɪnəstɚ/ *v* [T] **1** to manage and organize the affairs of a company, government etc. ‖ 회사·정부 등의 일을 관리·운영하다 **2** FORMAL to give someone a medicine or drug ‖ 누군가에게 약을 주다. 복용시키다. 투여하다

ad·min·is·tra·tion /ədˌmɪnə'streɪʃən/ *n* [U] **1** the management or organization of the affairs of a company, government etc. ‖ 기업·정부 등의 일의 관리나 조직화. 경영. 행정 **2 the Administration** the part of the national, state, or city government that is controlled by the president, GOVERNOR, or MAYOR ‖ 대통령 [주지사, 시장]이 관리하는 국가[주, 시] 의 행정부: *the Kennedy Administration* 케네디 정부 – **administrative** /əd'mɪnə,streɪtɪv, -strə-/ *adj*

ad·min·is·tra·tor /əd'mɪnə,streɪt̬ə/ *n* someone who manages or organizes the affairs of a company, government etc. ‖ 기업·정부 등의 일을 관리 또는 조직화하는 사람. 관리자. 행정관

ad·mi·ra·ble /'ædmərəbəl/ *adj* having a good quality that you respect and admire ‖ 존경스럽고 탄복할 만한 좋은 특성을 지닌. 훌륭한: *an admirable achievement* 감탄할 만한 업적 / *She never bragged, which was admirable of her.* 그녀는 감탄할 정도로 결코 자만하지 않았다.

ad·mi·ral, Ad·mi·ral /'ædmərəl/ *n* an officer who has the second highest rank in the Navy ‖ 제2위의 고위직 해군 장교. 해군 대장

ad·mi·ra·tion /,ædmə'reɪʃən/ *n* [U] a feeling of approval and respect for something or someone ‖ 사물이나 사람을 인정하고 존경하는 감정. 감탄. 탄복: *Dylan had a deep admiration for Auden's later work.* 딜런은 오든의 후기 작품에 깊이 감탄했다.

ad·mire /əd'maɪɚ/ *v* [T] **1** to approve of and respect someone or something ‖ 사람이나 사물을 인정하고 존경하다. 감탄하다: *Mark Twain is often admired for his humor.* 마크 트웨인은 종종 그의 유머로 존경을 받고 있다. **2** to look at someone or something because you think it is beautiful or impressive ‖ 사람이나 사물을 아름답거나 인상적이라 여겨서 바라보다: *We stopped halfway up the hill to admire the view.* 우리는 경치를 보기 위해 언덕을 오르는 도중에 멈췄다. – **admirer** *n* : *I'm a great admirer of Melville.* 나는 멜빌의 열렬한 팬이다.

ad·mis·si·ble /əd'mɪsəbəl/ *adj* FORMAL acceptable or allowed, especially in a court of law ‖ 특히 법정에서 받아들여질 수 있거나 허용되는: *admissible evidence* 법정이 채택하는 증거 —opposite INADMISSIBLE

ad·mis·sion /əd'mɪʃən/ *n* **1** a statement saying that something bad or slightly unpleasant is true ‖ 나쁘거나 다소 불쾌한 일이 사실임을 밝히는 진술. 시인. 자백: *If he resigns, it will be an admission of guilt.* 그가 사임한다면 죄를 시인하는 것이 된다. **2** [U] permission that is given to someone to study at a college, be treated in a hospital, join a club etc. ‖ 대학에서의 학업·병원에서의 치료·클럽에의 가입 등을 하도록 허락하는 허가. 입학[입원, 입회] 허가: *Tom has applied for admission to the graduate program at Northwestern.* 톰은 노스웨스턴 대학의 대학원 과정에 입학 허가 신청을 했다. **3** the price charged when you go to a movie, sports event, concert etc. ‖ 영화·스포츠 경기·콘서트 등에 입장 할 때 부과되는 요금. 입장료: *Admission $6.50* 입장료 6달러 50센트 —compare ADMITTANCE

ad·mis·sions /əd'mɪʃənz/ *n* [plural] the process of letting people study at a college, be treated at a hospital, join a club etc., or the number of people who do this ‖ 대학에서의 학업·병원에서의 치료·클럽에의 가입 등을 허가함, 또는 허가를 받은 사람들의 숫자. 입학[입원, 입회] 허가 [허가자 수]: *Admissions dropped by 13% last year.* 입학자 수가 작년에 13퍼센트 감소했다.

ad·mit /əd'mɪt/ *v* **-tted, -tting** [T] **1** to agree or say that something is true, although you do not want to ‖ 그러고 싶지는 않지만 무엇을 사실이라고 동의하거나 말하다. 인정[시인]하다: *You have to admit that Sheila has a good point.* 당신은 쉴라가 장점을 가지고 있다는 것을 인정해야 한다. / *He was wrong, but he won't admit it.* 그는 잘못했지만 그걸 인정하지 않을 거야. / *They said how hard it was to admit to being an alcoholic.* 그

들은 알코올 중독자임을 인정하기가 얼마나 어려운지 말했다. **2** to say that you did something wrong or are guilty of a crime; CONFESS ‖ 잘못했거나 유죄라고 말하다. 시인하다; 命 confess: *He'll never admit to the murder.* 그는 절대 살인을 했다고 시인하지 않을 것이다. **3** to let someone enter a place, study at a college, be treated in a hospital, join a club etc. ‖ 장소에의 입장·대학에서의 공부·병원에서의 치료·클럽에의 가입 등을 하게 하다. 허가하다: *Only ticket holders will be admitted into the stadium.* 표를 가진 사람에게만 경기장에 들어가는 것이 허용된다.

ad·mit·tance /əd'mɪtˈns/ *n* [U] permission to enter a place ‖ 장소에의 입장 허가: *Most journalists were unable to gain admittance backstage.* 대부분의 기자들은 무대 뒤편 출입을 할 수 없었다. —compare ADMISSION —see usage note at ADMISSION

ad·mit·ted·ly /əd'mɪtɪdli/ *adv* used when admitting that something is true ‖ 무엇을 사실이라고 인정할 때에 쓰여. 자인하듯이. 명백히: *Our net profit this year is admittedly much smaller than we had expected.* 우리의 올해 순이익은 명백히 우리가 예상했던 것보다도 훨씬 적다.

ad·mon·ish /əd'manɪʃ/ *v* [T] LITERARY to warn someone, or to tell him/her that s/he has done something wrong ‖ 남에게 잘못했다고 경고하거나 말하다. 타이르다. 훈계하다 – **admonition** /ˌædmə'nɪʃən/ **admonishment** /əd'manɪʃmənt/ *n* [C, U]

a·do·be /ə'doʊbi/ *n* [U] a material made of clay and STRAW, used for building houses ‖ 집을 짓는 데에 사용되는 진흙과 짚으로 만든 재료. 아도비 벽돌

a·do·les·cence /ˌædl'ɛsəns/ *n* the period of time, from about 13 to 17 years of age, when a young person is developing into an adult ‖ 청소년이 성인으로 되어 가는 약 13세에서 17세까지의 기간. 청춘기. 사춘기

ad·o·les·cent /ˌædl'ɛsənt/ *n* a young person who is developing into an adult ‖ 성인으로 성장해 가고 있는 사람. 사춘기의 사람. 청소년 – **adolescent** *adj*

a·dopt /ə'dapt/ *v* [T] **1** to legally have someone else's child become a part of your family ‖ 남의 아이를 법률상의 가족의 일원이 되게 하다. 양자로 삼다: *Melissa was adopted when she was only two.* 멜리사는 겨우 2살 때 양녀가 되었다. **2** to begin to have or use an idea, plan, or way of doing something ‖

어떤 생각[계획, 행동방식]을 가지거나 사용하기 시작하다. 채택[채용]하다: *They've been forced to adopt stricter rules.* 그들은 보다 엄격한 규칙을 받아들이도록 강요당했다. **3** to formally approve and accept something ‖ 무엇을 승인하여 받아들이다: *A "no smoking" policy has recently been adopted at work.* "흡연 금지" 정책이 최근에 직장에서 공인되었다. – **adoption** /ə'dapʃən/ *n* [C, U]: *She's put her baby up for adoption.* 그녀는 자기의 아기를 양자로 보냈다. – **adopted** *adj* : *their adopted daughter* 그들의 양녀

a·dop·tive /ə'daptɪv/ *adj* having adopted a child ‖ 아이를 양자로 삼고 있는. 양자 관계의: *an adoptive parent* 양부[양모]

a·dor·a·ble /ə'dɔrəbəl/ *adj* a word meaning very attractive and pleasant, used especially to describe young children and pets ‖ 특히 어린애나 애완동물을 묘사할 때 사용되는 말로 매우 매력적이고 호감이 가는. 사랑스러운. 귀여운: *What an adorable little puppy!* 정말 귀엽고 작은 강아지군!

ad·o·ra·tion /ˌædə'reɪʃən/ *n* [U] great love and admiration ‖ 대단한 사랑과 감탄. 숭배. 경애

a·dore /ə'dɔr/ *v* [T] **1** to love and admire someone very much ‖ 누군가를 매우 사랑하고 감탄하다. 숭배[경애]하다: *Tim absolutely adores his older brother.* 팀은 그의 형을 굉장히 경애한다. **2** to like something very much ‖ 어떤 것을 매우 좋아하다: *I adore the place. It has such a great atmosphere.* 나는 그곳이 매우 멋진 분위기여서 매우 좋아한다.

a·dorn /ə'dɔrn/ *v* [T] FORMAL to decorate something ‖ 어떤 것을 장식하다: *carvings that adorn the church walls* 교회 벽에 장식된 조각물

a·dorn·ment /ə'dɔrnmənt/ *n* **1** something that is used as jewelry or to decorate a thing or place ‖ 보석처럼 또는 물건이나 장소를 장식하기 위해 사용되는 것. 장식품 **2** [U] the act of adorning something ‖ 무엇을 장식하는 행위. 장식

a·dren·a·line /ə'drɛnl-ɪn/ *n* [U] a chemical produced by your body that makes your heart beat faster and gives you extra strength when you are afraid, excited, or angry ‖ 두려움을 느끼거나 흥분하거나 또는 화났을 때 심장 박동을 빠르게 하며, 가외의 힘을 주는, 몸에서 생성되는 화학 물질. 아드레날린

a·drift /ə'drɪft/ *adv* **1** not tied to anything, and moved around by the ocean or wind ‖ 묶여 있지 않고 바다나 바람에 의해 이리저리 움직여. 표류하여 **2** not having any aims, or not following an earlier plan ‖ 아무런 목표 없이, 또는 이전의 계획을 쫓지 않고. 헤매어: *The schedule has gone adrift.* 그 계획은 흐지부지되어 버렸다. – **adrift** *adj*

a·droit /ə'drɔɪt/ *adj* able to use your hands skillfully, or to think and use words quickly ‖ 손을 능숙하게, 또는 말을 금방 생각해서 사용할 수 있는. 솜씨있는. 능숙한: *an adroit negotiator* 능숙한 협상자 – **adroitly** *adv*

ADSL *n* [U] asymmetric digital subscriber line; a system that makes it possible for information, such as VIDEO images, to be sent to computers through telephone wires at a very high speed ‖ 비대칭 디지털 가입자 회선)의 약어; 비디오 영상 등의 정보를 아주 빠른 속도로 전화선을 통해 컴퓨터에 전송 가능하게 하는 시스템

ad·u·la·tion /ˌædʒə'leɪʃən/ *n* [U] praise and admiration that is more than what someone deserves ‖ 사람이 받아야 할 이상의 지나친 찬사. 과찬

a·dult¹ /ə'dʌlt, 'ædʌlt/ *n* a person or animal that has finished growing ‖ 성장을 끝낸 사람이나 동물. 성인. 성체

adult² *adj* **1** completely grown ‖ 완전히 다 자란: *an adult male frog* 다 자란 수컷 개구리 **2** typical of an adult, or suitable for an adult ‖ 성인 특유의, 성인에게 적합한: *Children should take half the adult dose.* 아이들은 어른 복용량의 반을 먹어야 한다. / *an adult view of the world* 성인의 세계관

a·dul·ter·ate /ə'dʌltəˌreɪt/ *v* [T] to make something less pure by adding a substance of a lower quality to it ‖ 저질인 물질을 넣어 순수함이 덜하게 하다. 질을 떨어뜨리다 – **adulteration** /əˌdʌltə'reɪʃən/ *n* [U] —compare UNADULTERATED

a·dul·ter·y /ə'dʌltəri/ *n* [U] a sexual relationship between someone who is married and someone who is not that person's husband or wife ‖ 기혼자와 그 사람의 남편이나 아내가 아닌 사람과의 성교. 간통 – **adulterous** *adj*

ad·vance¹ /əd'væns/ *n* **1 in advance** before something happens or is expected to happen ‖ 무엇이 일어나거나 일어나리라는 예상에 앞서서. 미리: *The quiche can be made in advance.* 그 파이는 미리 만들어 놓을 수 있다. **2** [C, U] a change, discovery, or invention that makes something develop or improve ‖ 무엇을 발전시키거나 향상시키는 변화[발견, 발명]. 진보. 발전: *advances in medicine* 의학의 발전 **3** movement forward to a new position ‖ 새로운 위치로의 진출. 전진. 진격: *the army's advance into enemy territory* 적진으로의 군대의 진격 **4** [C usually singular] money paid to someone before the usual time ‖ 평소보다 앞서 지불된 돈. 선금: *I asked for an advance on my salary.* 나는 가불을 요청했다.

advance² *v* **1** [I] to move forward to a new position ‖ 새로운 위치를 향해 나아가다. 전진하다: *Troops advanced on* (=moved forward while attacking) *the rebel forces.* 군대는 반란군을 공격하며 전진했다. / *Stanford advanced to the playoffs.* 스탠포드 대학팀은 플레이오프에 진출했다. **2** [I, T] to improve, help, or develop ‖ 향상하다[시키다], 촉진하다[시키다], 발전하다[시키다]: *research to advance our understanding of genetics* 유전학의 이해를 촉진시키기 위한 연구 **3** [T] to suggest a plan or idea so that people can consider it ‖ 사람들이 고려해 보도록 계획이나 생각을 제안하다: *arguments advanced by the Libertarians* 자유론자에 의해 제기된 토론 – **advancement** *n* [U]

advance³ *adj* happening before something else ‖ 다른 일 전에 일어나는. 사전의: *advance warning of a hurricane* 허리케인에 대한 사전 경보

ad·vanced /əd'vænst/ *adj* **1** using the most modern ideas, equipment, and methods ‖ 가장 현대적인 사상·기구·방법을 사용한. 최신의: *the most advanced computer on the market* 시판 중인 최신형 컴퓨터 **2** studying or relating to a school subject at a difficult level ‖ 어려운 수준의 과목을 공부하거나 그와 관련된. 고등의: *an advanced student* 상급 학생 / *advanced physics* 고등 물리학

ad·van·ces /əd'vænsɪz/ *n* [plural] efforts to start a sexual relationship with someone ‖ 남과 성관계를 시작하려는 노력. 유혹. 접근

ad·van·tage /əd'væntɪdʒ/ *n* **1** something that helps you to be better or more successful than others ‖ 남보다 더 낫거나 성공적이 되도록 돕는 것. 유리한 점. 이점: *Her education gave her an advantage over the other applicants.* 그녀의 교육은 다른 지원자들을 능가하는 이점이 되었다. **2 take advantage of sth** to use a situation or thing to help you do or get something you want ‖ 원하는 것을

하거나 얻는 데 유리하도록 상황이나 사물을 이용하다: *You should definitely take advantage of a chance to study abroad.* 너는 유학의 기회를 확실히 이용해야 한다. **3** [C, U] a good or useful quality that something has ‖ 사물이 가지는 좋거나 유용한 특성. 편의. 이익: *the advantages of living in a big city* 대도시 생활의 이로움 **4 take advantage of sb** to treat someone unfairly or to control a particular situation in order to get what you want ‖ 원하는 것을 얻기 위해 남을 부당하게 이용하거나 특정한 상황을 조정하다: *I don't mind helping, but I resent being taken advantage of.* 도와 주는 것은 상관없지만 이용당하는 것은 불쾌하다. **5 to your advantage** useful or helpful to you ‖ 자신에게 유용하거나 도움이 되는. …에게 유리한: *It's to your advantage to arrive early.* 일찍 도착하는 것이 너에게 유리하다. – **advantageous** /ˌædvən'teɪdʒəs, -vən-/ *adj* — opposite DISADVANTAGE

ad·vent /'ædvɛnt/ *n* the start of an important event or period, or the first time an invention is used ‖ 중요한 사건이나 시기의 시작, 또는 발명품이 사용된 첫 시기. 도래. 출현: *the advent of television* 텔레비전의 등장

ad·ven·ture /əd'vɛntʃɚ/ *n* [C, U] an exciting experience in which dangerous or unusual things happen, or the act of having these experiences ‖ 위험하거나 예사롭지 않은 일이 일어나는 짜릿한 경험, 또는 그것을 체험하기. 모험

ad·ven·tur·er /əd'vɛntʃərɚ/ *n* someone who enjoys traveling and doing exciting things ‖ 여행과 짜릿한 일을 하는 것을 즐기는 사람. 모험가

ad·ven·ture·some /əd'vɛntʃɚsəm/ *adj* enjoying exciting and slightly dangerous activities ‖ 짜릿하고 다소 위험한 활동을 즐기는. 모험을 즐기는

ad·ven·tur·ous /əd'vɛntʃərəs/ *adj* exciting and slightly dangerous ‖ 흥분되고 약간 위험한: *an adventurous expedition up the Amazon* 아마존 강으로의 위험한 탐험

ad·verb /'ædvɚb/ *n* TECHNICAL in grammar, a word or a group of words that describes or adds to the meaning of a verb, an adjective, another adverb, or a sentence. For example, "slowly" in "He walked slowly" and "very" in "It was a very nice day" are adverbs ‖ 문법에서 동사[형용사, 다른 부사, 문장]의 의미를 수식하거나 더해주는 단어나 어구. 부사. 예를 들면 "He walked slowly"에서의 slowly와 "It was a very nice day"의 very는 부사이다. – **adverbial** /əd'vɚbiəl/ *adj*

ad·ver·sar·y /'ædvɚˌsɛri/ *n* FORMAL a country or person you are fighting or competing with ‖ 싸우거나 경쟁하는 상대국이나 상대자. 적국. 적수

ad·verse /əd'vɚs, æd-, 'ædvɚs/ *adj* FORMAL not favorable ‖ 호의적이지 않은. 적의를 품은: *adverse publicity* 적대적인 평판

ad·ver·si·ty /əd'vɚsəti, æd-/ *n* [C, U] difficulties or problems that seem to be caused by bad luck ‖ 운이 나빠서 생긴 것처럼 보이는 어려움이나 문제. 역경

ad·ver·tise /'ædvɚˌtaɪz/ *v* **1** [I, T] to use an advertisement to tell people about a product, event, or service in order to persuade them to buy or use it ‖ 제품이나 행사, 또는 서비스를 구매하거나 이용하도록 설득하기 위해 광고를 이용하다. 선전하다: *a new shampoo being advertised on TV* 텔레비전으로 광고되고 있는 새로운 샴푸 **2** [I] to make an announcement in a newspaper asking for someone to work for you, or for something that you need ‖ 신문에 일할 사람이나 필요한 사물을 구하는 광고를 하다: *They're advertising for an accountant.* 그들은 회계사 구인 광고를 내고 있다. – **advertiser** *n*

ad·ver·tise·ment /ˌædvɚ'taɪzmənt/ *n* a set of words or pictures in a newspaper, magazine etc. that gives information about a product, event, or service in order to persuade people to buy or use it ‖ 제품이나 행사, 또는 서비스를 구매하거나 이용하도록 설득하기 위한 정보를 제공하는 신문·잡지 등의 일련의 문구나 사진. 광고 —compare COMMERCIAL²

ad·ver·tis·ing /'ædvɚˌtaɪzɪŋ/ *n* [U] the activity or business of advertising things on television, in newspapers etc. ‖ 텔레비전·신문 등으로 어떤 것을 광고하는 활동이나 사업. 광고하기. 광고업

ad·vice /əd'vaɪs/ *n* [U] an opinion you give someone about what s/he should do ‖ 해야 하는 것에 대하여 남에게 주는 의견. 충고. 조언: *Did you follow/take your father's advice?* 너는 아버지의 충고에 따랐니? / *If you want my advice, I think you should move.* 내가 조언을 하자면, 너는 이사해야 한다고 생각한다. / *Let me give you some advice.* 너에게 몇 가지 충고 좀 할게. / *He offered them one piece of advice: Don't panic.* 그는 그들에게 "허둥대지 마"라고 한 마디 충고를

했다.

ad·vise /əd'vaɪz/ v **1** [I, T] to tell someone what you think s/he should do ‖ 남에게 해야 한다고 여기는 것을 말하다. 충고[조언]하다: *Doctors advised her to have the operation.* 의사는 그녀에게 수술하기를 권했다. / *Franklin advises us on financial matters.* 프랭클린은 우리에게 재정적인 문제에 대해 조언해 준다. **2** [T] to inform someone of something ‖ 누군가에게 무엇을 알리다: *You will be advised when the shipment arrives.* 뱃짐이 도착하면 알려 주겠다.

ad·vis·er /əd'vaɪzɚ/, **advisor** n someone whose job is to give advice about a particular subject ‖ 특정한 문제에 대해 조언해 주는 직업인. 상담가. 고문: *our adviser on foreign affairs* 외교 문제에 대한 고문 / *an academic advisor* 학문적 조언자

ad·vi·so·ry /əd'vaɪzəri/ adj having the purpose of giving advice ‖ 충고의 목적을 띤. 충고의. 자문의: *an advisory committee* 자문 위원회.

ad·vo·cate¹ /'ædvə,keɪt/ v [T] to strongly support a particular way of doing things ‖ 무엇을 하는 특정한 방법을 강력하게 지지하다: *Buchanan advocates tougher trade policies.* 뷰캐넌은 좀 더 강경한 무역 정책을 지지한다. **- advocacy** /'ædvəkəsi/ n [U]

ad·vo·cate² /'ædvəkət, -keɪt/ n **1** someone who strongly supports a particular way of doing things ‖ 무엇을 하는 특정한 방법을 강력하게 지지하는 사람. 지지자: *an advocate of prison reform* 교도소 개혁의 지지자. **2** LAW a lawyer who speaks in a court of law ‖ 법정 변호사.

aer·i·al /'ɛriəl/ adj from the air or happening in the air ‖ 공중으로부터 또는 공중에서 일어나는. 공중의: *aerial photographs* 항공 사진 / *aerial stunts* 공중 곡예.

ae·ro·bic /ə'roʊbɪk, ɛ-/ adj relating to exercises that strengthen your heart and lungs ‖ 심장과 폐를 강화하는 운동과 관련된. 유산소 운동의

ae·ro·bics /ə'roʊbɪks, ɛ-/ n [U] a very active type of physical exercise done to music, usually in a class ‖ 보통 교실에서 음악에 맞춰서 하는 격렬한 육체 운동의 일종. 에어로빅

aer·o·dy·nam·ics /,ɛroʊdaɪ'næmɪks/ n [U] the scientific study of how objects move through the air ‖ 공기를 통한 물체의 이동 방법에 대한 과학적 연구. 공기 역학 **- aerodynamic** adj

aer·o·sol /'ɛrə,sɔl, -,sɑl/ n [U] a small metal container from which a liquid can be forced out using high pressure ‖ 고압을 이용하여 액체가 밀려 나오게 된 금속제의 작은 용기. 에어러졸. 분무기: *an aerosol hairspray* 분무 헤어스프레이

aer·o·space /'ɛroʊ,speɪs/ adj involving the designing and building of aircraft and space vehicles ‖ 항공기와 우주선의 설계와 건조에 관련된. 항공 우주의: *the aerospace industry* 항공 우주 산업

aes·thet·ic /ɛs'θɛtɪk, ɪs-/ adj ⇨ ESTHETIC

aes·thet·ics /ɛs'θɛtɪks, ɪs-/ n [U] ⇨ ESTHETICS

a·far /ə'fɑr/ adv LITERARY **from afar** from a long distance away ‖ 멀리 떨어진 거리에서. 멀리서

AFC American Football Conference; a group of teams that is part of the NFL ‖ American Football Conference (미식 축구 협회) 의 약어 ; NFL의 일부인 팀들의 단체

af·fa·ble /'æfəbəl/ adj friendly and easy to talk to ‖ 다정해서 말을 걸기 쉬운. 붙임성 있는: *an affable guy* 붙임성 있는 사내 **- affably** adv

af·fair /ə'fɛr/ n **1** an event or a set of related events, especially unpleasant ones ‖ 사건, 또는 특히 불쾌한 일련의 사건: *The Watergate affair brought down the Nixon administration.* 워터게이트 사건은 닉슨 정부를 전복시켰다. **2** a secret sexual relationship between two people, when at least one of them is married to someone else ‖ 적어도 한 사람은 기혼인, 두 사람 사이의 비밀스러운 성적 관계. 불륜 관계. 정사(情事): *I heard that Ed is having an affair.* 에드가 불륜 관계에 있다는 얘기를 들었다.

af·fairs /ə'fɛrz/ n [plural] events or activities relating to a particular subject that a person, business, government etc. deals with ‖ 사람·회사·정부 등이 다루는 특정한 주제에 관련된 일이나 활동. 사무. 업무: *affairs of state* (=government business) 국정 / *I've never been good at dealing with financial affairs.* 나는 재정적인 업무를 능숙하게 처리해 본 적이 없다.

af·fect /ə'fɛkt/ v [T] **1** to do something that produces a change in someone or something ‖ 사람이나 사물에 변화를 주는 일을 하다. 영향을 미치다: *The disease affected his breathing.* 그 병은 그의 호흡에 영향을 미쳤다. **2** to make someone feel strong emotions ‖ 누군가를 격한 감정을 느끼게 하다. …을 감동시키다: *I was* *deeply affected by the news of Paul's death.* 폴이 죽었다는 소식을 듣고 나는 크게 상심했다. —compare EFFECT²

USAGE NOTE affect and effect

Use the verb **affect** to talk about making changes, and the noun **effect** to talk about the results of changes: *Do you think the changes in the law will* **affect** *us?* / *I don't know what* **effect** *they will have.* **Effect** can be used as a verb, but only in very formal English.
변화를 일으키는 것에 대해 말할 때는 동사 **affect**를 쓰고, 변화의 결과에 대해 말할 때는 명사 **effect**를 쓴다: 법 개정이 우리에게 영향을 미칠 것으로 생각하니?/ 그들이 어떤 영향을 받을지 모르겠다. **effect**는 매우 격식적인 영어에서만 동사로 쓸 수 있다.

---

af·fec·ta·tion /ˌæfɛkˈteɪʃən/ *n* [C, U] an action or type of behavior that is not sincere || 솔직하지 못한 행동이나 행위. 꾸미기. 가장 —compare UNAFFECTED

af·fect·ed /əˈfɛktɪd/ *adj* not sincere || 솔직하지 못한. 거짓의: *an affected laugh* 거짓된 웃음.

af·fec·tion /əˈfɛkʃən/ *n* [C, U] a feeling of gentle love and caring || 온화한 사랑과 염려. 애정. 애착: *Bart felt great affection for/towards the old woman.* 바트는 노부인에 대해서 깊은 애정을 느꼈다. / *He doesn't show affection easily.* 그는 애정을 쉽게 드러내지 않는다.

af·fec·tion·ate /əˈfɛkʃənɪt/ *adj* showing gentle love toward people || 사람들에게 따뜻한 애정을 보이는. 애정 깊은: *an affectionate child* 애정이 넘치는 아이. **- affectionately** *adv*

af·fi·da·vit /ˌæfəˈdeɪvɪt/ *n* LAW a written statement about something that you swear is true and that can be used in a court of law || 맹세하는 것이 사실이며 법정에서 쓰일 수 있다는 진술서. 선서 진술서

af·fil·i·ate¹ /əˈfɪliˌeɪt/ *v* **be affiliated with/to** to be a member of or closely related to a larger organization || 더 큰 조직의 구성원이 되거나 밀접히 관련되다. 제휴하다: *a TV station affiliated to CBS* CBS와 제휴하는 TV 방송국 **- affiliation** /əˌfɪliˈeɪʃən/ *n* [C, U]: *What are Jean's political affiliations?* 진의 소속 정당은 어디니?

affiliate² *n* a small company or organization that is controlled by a larger one || 더 큰 회사나 조직의 통제를

받는 작은 회사나 조직. 계열 회사. 지점

af·fin·i·ty /əˈfɪnəti/ *n* [C, U] **1** a strong feeling that you like and understand someone or something, especially because you have similar qualities, interests, or ideas || 특히 특징이나 관심, 또는 생각이 비슷하기 때문에 사람이나 사물을 좋아하고 이해하는 강한 감정. 애호. 좋아함: *The two men have an affinity for hiking and mountain biking.* 그 두 남자는 하이킹과 산악 자전거타기를 좋아한다. **2** a close similarity or relationship between two things || 두 사물 사이의 밀접한 유사성이나 관계

af·firm /əˈfɚm/ *v* [T] FORMAL to state publicly that something is true || 무엇이 사실이라고 공적으로 말하다. 공언하다: *The President affirmed his intention to reduce taxes.* 대통령은 조세를 삭감할 계획이라고 공언했다. **- affirmation** /ˌæfɚˈmeɪʃən/ *n* [C, U]

af·firm·a·tive /əˈfɚmətɪv/ *adj* FORMAL a word, sign etc. that is affirmative means "yes" || 말·신호 등이 찬성을 의미하는. 긍정적인 **- affirmatively** *adv*

affirmative ac·tion /.ˌ... ˈ../ *n* [U] the practice of choosing people for jobs, education etc. who have been treated unfairly because of their race, sex etc. || 인종·성 등의 문제로 불공정한 처우를 받아 온 사람들에 대한 고용·교육상의 선발의 시행. 차별 철폐 조치

af·fix /əˈfɪks/ *v* [T] FORMAL to fasten or stick something to something else || 무엇을 다른 것에 고정시키거나 붙이다

af·flict /əˈflɪkt/ *v* [T usually passive] FORMAL to make someone have serious problems || 남에게 심각한 문제를 갖게 하다. 괴롭히다: *a child afflicted by/with blindness* 실명으로 고통받는 아이

af·flic·tion /əˈflɪkʃən/ *n* [C, U] FORMAL something that causes pain or makes you unhappy || 고통을 주거나 불행하게 만드는 것. 고통[고민] 거리

af·flu·ent /ˈæfluənt/ *adj* having plenty of money, or other possessions || 다른 재산이 많은. 부유한. 풍부한: *an affluent suburb of Baltimore* 부유한 볼티모어의 근교 **- affluence** *n* [U]

af·ford /əˈfɔrd/ *v* [T] **can afford a)** to have enough money to buy something || 무엇을 살 충분한 돈이 있다: *I can't afford to buy a new car.* 새 차를 구입할 여유가 없다. / *Do you think we can afford a computer now?* 너는 지금 우리에게 컴퓨터를 살 여유가 있다고 생각하니? **b)** to be able to do something or let something happen without risk or

damage to yourself ‖ 무엇을 할 수 있거
나 위험이나 손실 없이 어떤 것이 일어나
게 하다: *I can't afford any more time
away from work.* 더 이상 일을 하지 않고
쉴 수 없다. / *We can't afford to offend
regular customers.* 우리는 단골 고객의
기분을 상하게 해서는 안 된다.

af·ford·a·ble /ə'fɔrdəbəl/ *adj* not
expensive ‖ 비싸지 않은. 싼: *We had
trouble finding an affordable hotel.* 우리
는 싼 호텔을 찾느라고 고생했다.

af·front /ə'frʌnt/ *n* [C usually singular]
a remark or action that offends or
insults someone ‖ 남의 기분을 상하게 하
거나 모욕하는 언동: *Borrowing money
was an affront to his pride.* 돈을 꾸는
것은 그의 자존심을 다치는 것이었다.

a·float /ə'floʊt/ *adj* **1** having enough
money to stay out of debt ‖ 빚을 지지 않
을 만큼 충분한 돈이 있는 : *Smaller
companies can barely stay afloat in
this market.* 더 작은 회사들은 이 시장에
서 간신히 파산을 면할 수 있다. **2**
floating on water ‖ 물 위에 뜬

AFN Armed Forces Network; a network
that broadcasts American radio and
television programs all over the world ‖
Armed Forces Network (미군 방송)의 약
어 ; 전 세계에 미국의 라디오·텔레비전
프로그램을 방송하는 방송망

a·fraid /ə'freɪd/ *adj* **1** very frightened
about something, because you think
something bad may happen ‖ 나쁜 일이
일어날지도 모른다고 생각하여 무엇을 매
우 두려워하는: *Small children are often
afraid of the dark.* 어린아이들은 종종 어
둠을 무서워한다. / *Mary's afraid to
walk home alone.* 메리는 집에 혼자 걸어
가는 것을 무서워한다. / *A lot of people
there are afraid for their lives.* (=afraid
they will be killed) 많은 사람들이 살해될
까봐 두려워한다. —opposite UNAFRAID **2**
very worried about what might happen
‖ 일어날지도 모를 일에 대해 매우 걱정하
는: *A lot of workers are afraid of losing
their jobs.* 많은 근로자들이 실직을 염려한
다. / *I didn't say anything because I was
afraid (that) the other kids would
laugh at me.* 다른 아이들이 나를 비웃을
까봐 걱정되어 아무 말도 하지 않았다. **3
I'm afraid** SPOKEN used in order to
politely tell someone something that
may annoy, upset, or disappoint
him/her ‖ 남을 화나게 하거나 심란하게
하거나 실망시킬지도 모를 일에 대해 정중
하게 말하는 데에 쓰여. 유감입니다만: *I'm
afraid (that) this is a "no smoking"
area.* 말씀드리기 안됐습니다만 여기는

"금연" 구역입니다. / *"Are we late?" "I'm
afraid so"* (=yes) "우리 늦었니?" "유감
이지만 그런 것 같아."/"*Are there any
tickets left?" "I'm afraid not."* (=no) "표
가 좀 남았습니까?" "유감스럽게도 남은
게 없습니다."

a·fresh /ə'frɛʃ/ *adv* FORMAL done again
from the beginning, especially in a new
way ‖ 특히 새로운 방식으로 처음부터 다
시 하여. 새로: *We decided to move to
Texas and start afresh.* 우리는 텍사스로
이사해서 새로 시작하기로 결정했다.

Africa /'æfrɪkə/ *n* one of the seven
CONTINENTs, that includes land south of
Europe and west of the Indian Ocean ‖
남유럽과 인도양 서부를 포함하는 일곱 대
륙의 하나. 아프리카

Af·ri·can[1] /'æfrɪkən/ *adj* relating to or
coming from Africa ‖ 아프리카에 관한,
아프리카 출신의. 아프리카(산(産))의

African[2] *n* someone from Africa ‖ 아프
리카인

Af·ro-A·mer·i·can /,æfroʊ-ə'mɛrɪkən/
n an American whose family originally
came from Africa ‖ 원래 아프리카 출신의
미국인. 아프리카계 미국인 – **Afro-
American** *adj*

af·ter[1] /'æftɚ/ *prep* **1** when a particular
time or event has happened ‖ 특정한 시
간이나 사건이 생기고 나서. …후에:
We're going out after the soccer game.
우리는 축구 경기 후에 외출할 생각이다.
/ *A month/year after the fire, the
house was rebuilt.* 불이 나고 나서 한 달
[일년] 후에 그 집은 새로 지어졌다. **2**
following someone or something in a
series of things ‖ 연이은 사람이나 사물의
뒤를 따라. …의 뒤에: *Whose name is
after mine on the list?* 목록에 내 이름 뒤
에 누구의 이름이 있니? **3 after 10
minutes/3 hours etc.** when a
particular amount of time has passed ‖
특정 시간의 경과 후에. 10분 후/3시간
후: *After a while, the woman returned.*
잠시 후에 그 여자는 돌아왔다. **4** used
when telling time to say how many
minutes past the hour it is ‖ 몇 시에서
몇 분이 지났는지 시각을 말하는 데에 쓰
여: *It's ten after five.* 5시 10분이다. **5
day after day/year after year etc.**
continuing for a very long time ‖ 매우 오
랫동안 계속해서. 나날이/몇 년이고: *Day
after day we waited, hoping she'd call.*
우리는 그녀가 전화하기를 바라며 날마다
기다렸다. **6 one after the other**
following just behind or a short amount
of time later than the one before ‖ 바로
뒤따르거나 그 전보다 약간의 시간 뒤에.

잇따라서: *We led the horses one after the other out of the barn.* 우리는 마구간에서 잇따라 나오는 말들을 끌고 갔다. **7 because of** ‖ …때문에. …므로: *After his insults, I don't see why I should be nice to him!* 나는 그에게 모욕을 당했기 때문에 내가 왜 그에게 친절해야만 하는지 알 수 없어! **8 in spite of** ‖ …에도 불구하고: *After all the trouble I had, Reese didn't even say thank you.* 내가 겪은 많은 어려움에도 불구하고 레시는 나에게 고맙다는 말조차 하지 않았다. **9 be after sb** to be looking for someone or something ‖ 사람이나 사물을 찾고 있다: *The FBI is after him for fraud.* FBI는 그를 사기죄로 쫓고 있다. **10 be after sth** to be trying to get something that belongs to someone else ‖ 남의 것을 얻으려고 하다. 가로채려고 하다: *You're just after my money!* 너는 내 돈을 가로채려고만 하는구나! **11 after all a)** in spite of what you think, or what you thought was true ‖ 진실이라고 여기거나 생각한 것에도 불구하고. 결국: *Rita didn't have my pictures after all. Jake did.* 결국 리타는 내 사진을 가지고 있지 않았다. 제이크가 가지고 있었다. / *Don't worry too much. After all, it's not your problem.* 너무 걱정하지 마. 결국 그건 네 문제가 아니야. **b)** in spite of what you expected ‖ 예상했던 것에도 불구하고. 어찌되었건: *It didn't rain after all.* 어찌됐건 비가 오지 않았다. —compare BEFORE¹, SINCE²

USAGE NOTE after an hour and in an hour

Use these phrases to talk about the time when you plan to do something. However, compare the sentences: *We'll leave after an hour and We'll leave in an hour.* In the first sentence the speaker is planning how long to stay in a place before going there. In the second sentence, the speaker is already at a place and is deciding how much longer to stay there.
이런 구들은 어떤 일을 하려고 하는 시간을 말할 때 쓴다. 다음 두 문장을 비교해 보자: 둘 다 「우리는 한 시간 후에 떠날 것이다」라는 표현이다. 그러나 첫 번째 문장에서 화자는 거기로 가기 전에 어떤 장소에서 얼마나 머물 것인지를 계획하고 있다. 두 번째 문장에서 화자는 이미 어떤 장소에 있고 거기에서 얼마나 더 머물 것인지를 결정하고 있다.

---

after² *conjunction* when a particular time has passed, or an event has happened ‖ 특정 시간이 지나거나 사건이 일어난 후에. …한 뒤에. 나중에: *Regan changed his name after he left Poland.* 리건은 폴란드를 떠난 후에 이름을 바꿨다. / *He discovered the jewel was fake 10 days/3 weeks after he bought it.* 그는 보석을 사고 10일[3주]이 지나서 그것이 가짜라는 것을 알았다.

after³ *adv* later than someone or something else ‖ 어떤 사람이나 사물보다 나중에: *Gina came on Monday, and I got here the day after.* 지나는 여기에 월요일에 왔고, 나는 하루 뒤에 왔다.

af·ter·ef·fect /ˈæftəˌfɛkt/ *n* [C usually plural] an unpleasant effect that remains after the condition or event that caused it ‖ 상태나 사건이 생긴 후에 남아 있는 불유쾌한 효과. 여파: *the aftereffects of the drought last summer* 지난 여름 가뭄의 여파

af·ter·life /ˈæftəˌlaɪf/ *n* [singular] the life that some people believe you have after death ‖ 일부의 사람들이 죽은 뒤에 맞는다고 믿는 삶. 내세

af·ter·math /ˈæftəˌmæθ/ *n* [singular] the period of time after something bad has happened ‖ 좋지 않은 일이 생긴 뒤의 일정 기간. 직후의 시기: *the danger of fire in the aftermath of the earthquake* 지진 직후의 화재의 위험

af·ter·noon /ˌæftəˈnun/ *n* [C, U] the period of time between 12 o'clock and the evening ‖ 정오에서 저녁 사이의 시간. 오후: *a class on Friday afternoon* 금요일 오후 수업 / *We should get there about 3 in the afternoon.* 우리는 대략 오후 3시에 거기에 도착해야 한다. / *Can you go swimming this afternoon?* (=today in the afternoon) 오늘 오후에 수영하러 갈 수 있어요? ✗DON'T SAY "next/last afternoon"✗ "next/last afternoon"이라고는 하지 않는다. – **afternoon** *adj* : *an afternoon snack* 오후 간식

af·ter·shave /ˈæftəˌʃeɪv/ *n* [C, U] a liquid with a pleasant smell that a man puts on his face after he SHAVEs ‖ 면도 후에 얼굴에 바르는 상쾌한 향이 나는 남성용 용액. 애프터셰이브 로션

af·ter·taste /ˈæftəˌteɪst/ *n* [C usually singular] a taste that stays in your mouth after you eat or drink something ‖ 무엇을 먹거나 마신 후 입안에 남아 있는 맛. 뒷맛: *a drink with a sour aftertaste* 뒷맛이 시큼한 음료

af·ter·thought /ˈæftəˌθɔt/ *n* something thought of, mentioned, or added later, especially something that was not part of an original plan ‖ 원래 계획했던 부분이 아니라 나중에 생각하거나 언급하거나, 또는 추가한 것: *The bar was only added as an afterthought.* 그 술집은 재고하여 추가됐을 뿐이었다.

af·ter·ward /'æftəwəd/, **afterwards** *adv* after something else has happened; later ‖ 다른 일이 일어난 후에 ; 나중에: *We met at school but didn't get married until two years afterward.* 우리는 학교에서 만났지만 그 후 2년이 지나도록 결혼을 하지 않았다.

a·gain /ə'gɛn/ *adv* **1** one more time ‖ 한 번 더: *Could you say that again? I couldn't hear you.* 한 번 더 말씀해 주시겠습니까? 못 들었거든요. **2** at another time ‖ 또, 다시: *Thanks for coming! Please come again.* 와 주셔서 감사합니다. 또 오세요. **3** in the same way, situation, or place as before ‖ 이전과 같은 방법이나 상황, 또는 장소로: *Is it already time to do taxes again?* 벌써 또 세금 낼 때니? / *Susan's home again, after studying in Europe.* 수잔은 유럽에서 공부한 후 다시 집에 있다. **4 again and again** repeating many times ‖ 몇 번이고 되풀이해서: *I've tried again and again to contact her.* 나는 그녀에게 거듭거듭 연락을 해 봤다. —see also **but then (again)** (BUT¹)

a·gainst /ə'gɛnst/ *prep* **1** touching, pushing on, hitting etc. another surface ‖ 다른 표면에 갖다 대어·기대어·부딪쳐: *The cat's fur felt soft against her face.* 고양이의 털이 그녀의 얼굴에 부드럽게 느껴졌다. / *waves slapping against the boat* 배에 철썩 부딪치는 파도 / *Sheldon leaned lazily against the wall.* 셸던은 나른한 듯이 벽에 기댔다. **2** opposed to or disagreeing with an idea, belief etc. ‖ 생각·신념 등에 대항하거나 반대하여: *Everyone was against closing the factory.* 모든 사람이 공장 폐쇄에 반대했다. / *against the law* (=illegal) 불법[위법]적인 **3** in a way that has a bad or unfair effect ‖ 나쁘거나 부당한 영향을 띤 방법으로: *discrimination against racial minorities* 소수 민족에 대한 차별 **4** fighting or competing with someone or something ‖ 사람이나 사물과 싸우거나 경쟁하여. …에 대항하여: *He was injured in the game against the Cowboys.* 그는 카우보이 대항 경기에서 다쳤다. / *the battle against inflation* 인플레이션과의 전쟁 **5** in the opposite direction from something ‖ 어떤 것과 반대 방향에: *At least my drive to work is against the traffic.* 최소한 내 출근길은 교통 혼잡과는

거리가 멀다. **6 have sth against sb/sth** to dislike or disapprove of someone or something ‖ 사람이나 사물을 싫어하거나 반대하다: *I have nothing against people making money, but they ought to pay taxes on it.* 사람들이 돈을 버는 것에 대해서는 전혀 반대하지 않지만, 그 수입에 대한 세금은 꼭 내야 한다.

age¹ /eɪdʒ/ *n* **1** [C, U] the period of time that someone has lived or that something has existed, usually expressed as a number of years ‖ 보통 햇수로 나타내는 사람이 산 기간이나 사물이 존재한 기간. 나이: *Patrick is my age.* (=the same age as me) 패트릭은 나와 나이가 같다. / *Jamie won his first tournament at the age of 15.* 제이미는 15살 때 첫 토너먼트에서 우승했다. / *Most kids start kindergarten at age 5.* 대부분의 아이들은 5세 때 유치원을 다니기 시작한다. / *girls who become mothers at an early age* (=very young) 매우 어린 나이에 엄마가 되는 소녀들 / *Stop messing around and act your age!* (=behave in a way that is suitable for how old you are) 어지럽히지 좀 말고 나이에 맞게 행동해! / *Judy's very smart for her age.* (=compared to others of the same age) 주디는 나이에 비해 매우 영리하다. **2** [C, U] one of the particular periods of someone's life ‖ 사람의 생애 중의 특정한 한 시기: *Who will look after you in old age?* 노년에는 누가 당신을 돌봐 줄니까? / *voting/drinking/retirement age* (=when you can legally vote, drink alcohol, etc.) 투표[음주, 퇴직] 연령 / *I'm sorry, but you're under age.* (=too young to be legally allowed to do something) 미안하지만 당신은 법률상 미성년자입니다. **3** [C usually singular] a particular period of history ‖ 역사상의 특정한 시기. 시대: *the computer age* 컴퓨터 시대 **4 be/come of age** to be or become old enough that you are considered to be a responsible adult ‖ 책임감 있는 어른이 되었다고 여겨질 정도의 나이이다[나이가 되다]. 성년이다[성년이 되다] **5** [U] the state of being old ‖ 오래된 상태. 고령. 노령: *a letter that was brown with age* 오래 되어 누레진 편지 **6 age group/bracket** the people between two particular ages, considered as a group ‖ 한 집단으로 여겨지는 특정한 두 연령 사이에 속하는 사람들. 동일 연령 집단: *a book for children in the 8-12 age group* 8세에서 12세까지의 어린이를 위한 책 —see also AGES

age² *v* **1** [I, T] to become older and weaker, or to make someone seem this way ‖ 더 늙고 약해지다, 또는 더 늙어 보이게 하거나 약해지게 하다: *After his wife's death, he aged quickly.* 아내가 죽은 후 그는 급속도로 쇠약해졌다. **2** to improve or develop in quality and taste over a period of time ‖ 시간이 지남에 따라 질과 맛이 향상되다. 익(힉)다: *a wine that has aged well* 잘 숙성된 와인 –
aging *adj* : *an aging movie star* 나이 든 영화 배우

aged¹ /eɪdʒd/ *adj* **aged 5/15/50 etc.** 5, 15 etc. years old ‖ 5/15/50살의: *a game for children aged 12 and over* 12세 이상의 어린이용 게임

aged² /'eɪdʒɪd/ *adj* **1** very old ‖ 상당히 나이가 든. 늙은. 고령의: *an aged man* 노인 **2 the aged** old people ‖ 노인들

age·less /'eɪdʒlɪs/ *adj* never seeming old or old-fashioned ‖ 결코 늙거나 낡아 보이지 않는. 늘 변함없는: *an ageless song* 언제나 변함없이 불리는 노래

a·gen·cy /'eɪdʒənsi/ *n* **1** a business that provides a particular service ‖ 특정한 서비스를 제공해 주는 회사. 대리점: *an employment agency* 직업 소개소 **2** an organization or department, especially within a government, that does a specific job ‖ 특히 정부 내에서, 특정한 업무를 담당하는 기구나 부서. …국: *the UN agency responsible for helping refugees* 난민 구제를 담당하는 유엔 기구

a·gen·da /ə'dʒɛndə/ *n* **1** a list of the subjects to be discussed at a meeting ‖ 회의에서 논의될 주제들의 목록. 의제. 협의 사항: *Let's move on to item five on the agenda.* 계속해서 다섯 번째 의제로 넘어 갑시다. **2 on the agenda** being considered and discussed as something to do ‖ 해야 할 사항으로 고려·논의되어: *Health care reforms are on top of the agenda/high on the agenda.* (=very important) 의료 서비스 개혁은 매우 중요한 논의 대상이다.

a·gent /'eɪdʒənt/ *n* **1** a person or company that helps another person or company deal with business problems, finding work etc. ‖ 다른 사람이나 회사를 도와 업무나 구직 문제 등의 조치를 취해 주는 사람이나 회사. 대리인. 대행사: *I got a call from my agent about a job.* 나는 직장 문제로 대행사로부터 전화 한 통을 받았다. / *We're acting as agents for Mr. Rogers.* 우리는 로저스 씨의 대리인으로서 활동하고 있다. **2** someone who works for a government or police department in order to get secret information about another country or an organization ‖ 다른 나라나 조직의 비밀 정보를 입수하기 위해 정부나 경찰에 소속되어 일하는 사람. 스파이. 첩보원 **3** something that makes something else happen ‖ 다른 일을 일어나게 하는 것. 매개물. 작용물: *an agent for change* 변화 요인 / *bleaching agent* 표백제

ag·es /'eɪdʒɪz/ *n* [plural] a long time ‖ 오랜 시간. 장시간: *It's been ages since I played volleyball.* 배구를 한 지 정말 오래 되었다.

ag·gra·vate /'æɡrə,veɪt/ *v* [T] **1** to make a bad situation worse ‖ 나쁜 상황을 더 나쁘게 만들다. 악화시키다: *The doctors say her condition is aggravated by stress.* 의사들은 그녀의 상태가 스트레스로 인해 더욱 악화된다고 말한다. **2** to annoy someone ‖ 남을 화나게 하다: *Jerry really aggravates me sometimes.* 제리는 때때로 나를 정말 화나게 한다. –
aggravating *adj* – **aggravation** /,æɡrə'veɪʃən/ *n* [C, U]

USAGE NOTE aggravate

We often use **aggravate** to mean "annoy." However, many teachers think this is incorrect. A problem or situation is **aggravated**, but a person is **annoyed** or **irritated**.
우리는 종종 "화나게 하다"라는 의미로 **aggravate**를 쓴다. 하지만 많은 교사들이 이것을 그릇된 용법으로 생각한다. 어떤 문제나 상황이 악화되는 경우에는 **aggravated**를 쓰지만, 사람이 화나게 되는 경우에는 **annoyed**나 **irritated**를 쓴다.

---

ag·gres·sion /ə'ɡrɛʃən/ *n* [U] angry or threatening behavior, especially in which you attack someone ‖ 특히 남을 공격하는, 화내거나 위협하는 행동. 침략: *bombings and other acts of aggression* 폭격과 다른 침략 행위

ag·gres·sive /ə'ɡrɛsɪv/ *adj* **1** forceful and showing that you are determined to succeed ‖ 힘이 넘치고 성공하기로 작정한 것을 보여 주는. 적극적인: *Borland's aggressive sales tactics* 보어랜드의 적극적인 판매 전략 **2** always ready to argue with people or attack them ‖ 언제나 사람들과 논쟁하거나 그들을 공격할 준비가 되어 있는. 시비조의. 공격적인: *Ricky's aggressive behavior on the playground is causing problems.* 경기장에서의 리키의 공격적인 행동은 문제를 일으키고 있다. – **aggressively** *adv* – **aggressiveness** *n* [U]

A

ag·gres·sor /ə'grɛsə/ *n* [U] a person or country that begins a fight or war with another person or country ‖ 타인이나 타국과의 싸움이나 전쟁을 거는 사람이나 국가. 공격자. 침략국

ag·grieved /ə'grivd/ *adj* feeling angry or unhappy because you think you have been unfairly treated ‖ 부당한 대우를 받았다는 생각에 화가 나거나 불행하다고 느끼는. 기분이 상한

a·ghast /ə'gæst/ *adj* suddenly feeling or looking shocked ‖ 갑자기 충격을 느끼거나 충격받은 듯한. 대경실색한

ag·ile /'ædʒəl, 'ædʒaɪl/ *adj* **1** able to move quickly and easily ‖ 빠르고 쉽게 움직일 수 있는. 민첩한 **2** able to think quickly and intelligently ‖ 빠르고 총명하게 생각할 수 있는. 명민한: *She's 92, but still mentally agile.* 그녀는 92세지만 여전히 정신적으로는 명민하다. **– agility** /ə'dʒɪləti/ *n* [U]

ag·i·tate /'ædʒə,teɪt/ *v* **1** [I] to argue strongly in public for social or political changes ‖ 사회적 또는 정치적 변화를 위해 사람들 앞에서 강하게 주장하다. 선동하다: *workers agitating for higher pay* 더 높은 임금을 요구하며 선동하는 노동자들 **2** [T] to make someone feel anxious, nervous, or upset ‖ 남을 걱정시키거나 신경질나거나 혼란스럽게 하다. 동요시키다 **– agitation** /,ædʒə'teɪʃən/ *n* [U]

ag·i·tat·ed /'ædʒə,teɪtɪd/ *adj* very anxious, nervous, or upset ‖ 매우 걱정하거나 신경질 나거나 화난

ag·i·ta·tor /'ædʒə,teɪtə/ *n* DISAPPROVING someone who does things to make people pay attention to and change social or political problems ‖ 사람들의 관심을 불러일으켜 사회적이거나 정치적인 문제를 변화시키는 일을 하는 사람. 선동가. 운동가

ag·nos·tic /æg'nɑstɪk, əg-/ *n* someone who believes that people cannot know whether God exists or not ‖ 신의 존재 여부를 알 수 없다고 여기는 사람. 불가지론자 **– agnostic** *adj* **– agnosticism** /æg'nɑstə,sɪzəm, əg-/ *n* [U]

a·go /ə'goʊ/ *adj* used in order to show how far back in the past something happened ‖ 과거지사가 얼마나 되었는지 나타내는 데에 쓰여. …전에: *Jeff left for work 10 minutes/2 hours ago.* 제프는 10분[2시간] 전에 일하러 갔다. / *We went to Maine once, but it was a long time ago.* 우리는 메인에 한 번 갔었지만 매우 오래 전이었다. / *I had the tickets a minute ago!* 나는 방금 전에야 표를 샀어! / *Scott's dad called a little while ago.* 스콧의 아빠는 조금 전에 전화를 했다.

USAGE NOTE ago, for, since

Use **ago** to show how far back in the past something happened. Always use it with verbs in the simple past: *I came here a year ago.* Use **for** and **since** with the present perfect to talk about a situation that began in the past and continues now. **Since** is used with dates: *I have lived here since 1992.* **For** is used with periods of time: *I have lived here for six years.*

ago는 과거에 일어난 일이 얼마나 지났는지를 나타낼 때 쓴다. **ago**는 항상 단순 과거 형태의 동사와 함께 쓴다: 나는 1년 전에 이곳에 왔다. **for**와 **since**는 과거에 시작되어 현재도 계속되는 상황을 나타내는 현재 완료형과 함께 쓴다. **since**는 시점과 함께 쓰인다: 나는 1992년 이후로 여기에서 살았다. **for**는 기간과 함께 쓰인다: 나는 6년 동안 여기에서 살았다.

a·gon·ize /'ægə,naɪz/ *v* [I] to think about a decision very carefully and with a lot of effort ‖ 결정에 대해서 매우 신중하고 많이 애써서 생각하다. 번민하다: *Will has been agonizing about/over whether to get married.* 윌은 결혼을 할지 말지에 대해서 고민해오고 있다.

a·gon·iz·ing /'ægə,naɪzɪŋ/ *adj* extremely painful or difficult ‖ 극도로 고통스럽거나 힘든. 괴로운: *It was an agonizing decision to disconnect their son's life support system.* 아들의 생명 유지 장치를 떼내는 것은 너무나 고통스러운 결정이었다. **– agonizingly** *adv*

ag·o·ny /'ægəni/ *n* [C, U] very severe pain or suffering ‖ 극심한 통증이나 고통. 괴로움: *The poor guy was in agony.* 그 가난한 남자는 괴로워하고 있었다.

a·gree /ə'gri/ *v* **1** [I, T] to have the same opinion about something ‖ 무엇에 대해 같은 의견을 가지다. 동의하다: *Oh, I agree with you on that.* 오, 그것에 대해서는 너에게 동의해. / *Most experts agree that global warming is a serious problem.* 많은 전문가들이 지구 온난화가 심각한 문제라는 데 의견을 같이한다. / *Mike and I certainly don't agree on/about everything.* 마이크와 나는 모든 것에 대해 반드시 의견을 같이 하지는 않는다. ✗DON'T SAY "I am agree"✗ "I am agree."라고는 하지 않는다. —opposite DISAGREE **2** [I, T] to make a decision with someone or say yes to someone after a discussion with him/her ‖ 남과 토론 후에 결정을 내리거나 찬성하다. 합의하다: *She agreed to stay home with Charles.* 그녀는 집에 있기로 찰스와 합의했다. / *We agreed on a price for the car.* 우리는 차의 가격 흥정에서 합의를 보았다. / *You know Dad won't agree to getting you a motorbike.* 알다시피 아빠는 네게 오토바이 사주는 것에 동의하지 않으신다. **3** [I] if two pieces of information agree, they say the same thing ‖ 두 가지 정보가 일치하다: *Your story doesn't agree with what the police have said.* 너의 이야기는 경찰이 말한 것과 일치하지 않는다.

agree with *phr v* [T] **1** to believe that something is right ‖ 무엇을 옳다고 믿다: *I don't agree with spanking children.* 손으로 아이들을 때리는 것은 옳지 않다고 생각한다. **2 not agree with sb** to make you feel sick ‖ 몸이 좋지 않은 느낌이 들게 하다. 맞지 않다: *Some dairy products don't agree with me.* 어떤 유제품은 나에게는 맞지 않는다.

a·gree·a·ble /əˈgriəbəl/ *adj* **1** nice, acceptable, or enjoyable ‖ 기분 좋은[받아들일] 만한, 즐거운: *agreeable weather* 좋은 날씨 —opposite DISAGREEABLE **2 be agreeable to sth** to be willing to do or accept something ‖ 기꺼이 무엇을 하거나 받아들이다: *Are you sure Johnson is agreeable to the idea?* 존슨이 그 생각에 흔쾌히 동의할 것이라고 확신하니? – **agreeably** *adv*

a·greed /əˈgrid/ *adj* having been discussed and accepted ‖ 토론하여 받아들인. 합의된: *an agreed price* 협정가

a·gree·ment /əˈgrimənt/ *n* **1** an arrangement or promise to do something, made by two or more people, countries, organizations etc. ‖ 둘 이상의 사람[나라, 조직 등]에 의해 맺어진 어떤 것을 하자는 협정이나 약속. 합의: *Lawyers on both sides finally reached an agreement.* 양측 변호사는 마침내 합의에 도달했다. **2** [U] a situation in which two or more people have the same opinion as each other ‖ 둘 이상의 사람들이 서로 같은 의견을 지닌 상황. 동의: *Not all scholars are in agreement on this point.* 이 점에 있어서는 모든 학자들이 동감하는 것은 아니다. —opposite DISAGREEMENT

ag·ri·cul·ture /ˈægrɪˌkʌltʃəʳ/ *n* [U] the science or practice of farming, especially of growing crops ‖ 특히 작물을 재배하는 농사에 대한 학문이나 그 실제. 농학. 농업 – **agricultural** /ˌægrə-

ˈkʌltʃərəl/ *adj*

ah /ɑ/ *interjection* said in order to express surprise, pity, dislike, pleasure etc. ‖ 놀람·동정·싫어함·기쁨 등을 나타내는 데에 쓰여. 아: *Ah, what a cute kid!* 아, 귀여운 아이군요!

a·ha /ɑˈhɑ/ *interjection* said in order to express surprise, satisfaction, or understanding ‖ 놀람[만족, 이해]을 나타내는 데에 쓰여. 아하: *Aha! So that's where you've been hiding!* 아하! 그래서 네가 거기에 숨어 있었구나!

a·head /əˈhɛd/ *adv* **1** in front of someone or something ‖ 사람이나 사물의 앞쪽에: *Do you see that red convertible ahead of us?* 우리 앞쪽에 빨간색 오픈카 보이니? / *Just up ahead and to the right is my old school.* 조금만 앞쪽으로 올라가면 오른쪽에 오래 된 나의 모교가 있다. **2** before an event or a particular time ‖ 사건이나 특정한 시간 전에. 앞서서: *You can make the pie crust ahead of time.* 너는 시간 전에 페이스트리를 만들 수 있다. / *At this point we're ahead of schedule.* 현재 우리는 일정보다 앞서 있다. **3** into the future ‖ 장차. 앞으로: *Eddy never looks/plans ahead.* 에디는 결코 장래를 생각하지[장래 계획을 세우지] 않는다. **4 go ahead a)** SPOKEN used in order to tell someone s/he can do something ‖ 어떤 사람에게 무엇을 하라는 권유에 쓰여. …하세요: *Go ahead and help yourself to some punch.* 자, 펀치 좀 드세요. **b)** used in order to say you are going to start doing something ‖ 어떤 일을 시작하겠다고 말하는 데에 쓰여: *I'll go ahead and start the coffee.* 나는 어서 가서 커피 좀 마셔야겠다. **5** more advanced, developed, successful etc. than someone or something else ‖ 다른 사람이나 사물보다 더 진보[발달, 성공]하여: *Jane is ahead of the rest of her class.* 제인은 반에서 다른 학생들보다 뛰어나다. **6 get/keep ahead** to succeed or to continue to succeed ‖ 성공하거나 또는 성공을 유지하다: *Stick with me if you want to get ahead in the world, kid.* 얘야, 세상에서 성공하고 싶으면 내 곁을 떠나지 마라.

aid¹ /eɪd/ *n* **1** [U] money, food, or services that are given by an organization to help people ‖ 사람들을 돕기 위해 단체가 제공하는 돈[음식, 각종 서비스]. 원조. 보조: *sending aid to the earthquake victims* 지진 희생자들에게 보내는 원조 **2** [U] help or support given to someone ‖ 남에게 주어진 도움이나 지지: *financial aid* 금전적인 도움 **3** [C, U] a thing that helps you do something ‖ 무엇을 하는 데 도움이 되는 것: *notebooks and study aids* 공책과 학습 용품 / *bacteria viewed with the aid of a microscope* 현미경의 도움을 받아 검사된 박테리아 **4 in aid of** intended to help ‖ 돕기로 되어 있는. …을 돕기 위한[위하여]: *a fundraiser in aid of the Red Cross* 적십자를 돕기 위한 기금 조성자 **5 come/go to sb's aid** FORMAL to help someone ‖ 남을 돕다

aid² *v* [T] **1** FORMAL to help or give support to someone ‖ 남을 돕거나 지지하다 **2 aid and abet** LAW to help someone do something illegal ‖ 남이 불법적인 일을 하도록 돕다. 범행을 방조하다

aide /eɪd/ *n* someone whose job is to help someone in a more important position ‖ 더 중요한 위치에 있는 사람을 돕는 직업인. 조수. 보좌관: *a nurse's aide* 보조 간호사

AIDS /eɪdz/ *n* [U] Acquired Immune Deficiency Syndrome; a very serious disease that stops your body from defending itself against infection ‖ Acquired Immune Deficiency Syndrome(에이즈. 후천성 면역 결핍증)의 약어;몸이 감염에 대하여 스스로를 방어하지 못하는 심각한 질병

ail·ing /ˈeɪlɪŋ/ *adj* weak or sick, and not getting stronger or better ‖ 약하거나 아프며 강해지지나 나아지지 않는. 허약한: *the country's ailing economy* 허약한 그 나라의 경제

ail·ment /ˈeɪlmənt/ *n* an illness that is not very serious ‖ 심각하지 않은 질병. 가벼운 병

aim¹ /eɪm/ *v* **1** [I] to plan or intend to achieve something ‖ 무엇을 이루기 위해 계획을 세우거나 작정하다. 겨누다. 노리다: *a program aimed at creating more jobs* 더 많은 직업 창출을 노린 프로그램 / *We're aiming to qualify for the summer Olympics.* 우리는 하계 올림픽에 참가할 작정이다. **2** [I] to do or say something to a particular person or group, in order to influence them, annoy them etc. ‖ 특정한 사람이나 집단에 영향을 주고 곤혹스럽게 하려고 무엇을 하거나 말하다. 목표삼다: *a TV commercial aimed at teenagers* 십대들을 겨냥한 TV 광고 **3** [I, T] to point a weapon at a person or thing you want to hit ‖ 맞히고 싶은 사람이나 물체에 무기를 겨냥하다. 조준하다: *A gun was aimed at his head.* 그 총은 그의 머리에 조준되었다.

aim² *n* **1** something you are trying to do or get ‖ 하거나 얻으려는 것. 의도. 목적:

I flew to California with the aim of finding a job. 나는 일자리를 구하려 캘리포니아로 날아갔다. **2 take aim** to point a weapon at someone or something ‖ 무기를 사람이나 물건에 겨냥하다. **3** someone's ability to hit something by throwing or shooting something at it ‖ 어떤 것을 던지거나 쏴서 맞히는 능력. 적중력: *Mabel's aim has improved.* 마벨의 적중력은 향상되었다.

aim·less /ˈeɪmlɪs/ *adj* without a clear purpose or reason ‖ 명백한 목적이나 이유가 없는 **– aimlessly** *adv*

ain't /eɪnt/ *v* SPOKEN NONSTANDARD a short form of "am not," "is not," "are not," "has not," or "have not" ‖ "am not", "is not", "are not", "has not", "have not"의 단축형: *Ain't that the truth!* 그건 사실이 아니야!

air¹ /ɛr/ *n* **1** [U] the mixture of gases that we breathe and that surrounds the Earth ‖ 우리가 호흡하며 지구를 둘러싸고 있는 기체의 혼합물. 공기: *Let's go outside and get some fresh air.* 밖에 나가서 신선한 공기 좀 마시자. **2** [U] the space above the ground or around things ‖ 땅 위나 물체 주변의 공간. 공중: *tossing a ball into the air* 공중으로 공을 던져 올리기 **3 by air** traveling by or using a plane ‖ 비행기로 이동하는, 비행기를 이용하는. 비행기로. 항공편으로: *Are you shipping that box by air or by land?* 그 상자를 항공편으로 보내실 겁니까, 육로로 보내실 겁니까? **4** [singular] a general appearance or feeling ‖ 일반적인 모습이나 느낌. 외견. 분위기: *an air of mystery about her* 그녀에게서 풍기는 신비로운 분위기 **5 it's up in the air** SPOKEN used to say that something has not been decided yet ‖ 아직 결정되지 않은 것을 말하는 데에 쓰여. 그건 아직 미결정 상태이다 **6 be on/off the air** to be broadcasting or to stop broadcasting ‖ 방송되고 있다, 방송을 중단하다. **7** SPOKEN ⇨ AIR CONDITIONING

air² *v* **1** [T] to broadcast a program on television or radio ‖ 텔레비전이나 라디오로 프로그램을 방송하다: *Star Trek was first aired in 1966.* 스타 트렉은 1966년에 처음 방송되었다. **2** [T] to make your opinions, ideas, complaints etc. known to other people ‖ 남에게 의견·생각·불만 등을 알리다: *You will all get a chance to air your views.* 여러분은 모두 견해를 말할 기회를 가지게 될 것이다. **3** [I, T] also **air sth ↔ out** to make a room, clothes, BLANKETs etc. smell fresh by letting air, especially from outdoors, go through

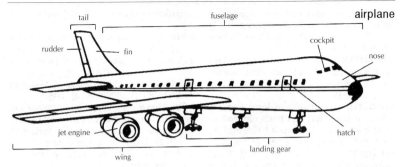

airplane

tail / fuselage / rudder / fin / cockpit / nose / jet engine / wing / landing gear / hatch

them ‖ 특히 문을 열어 방·옷·담요 등에 공기를 쐬어 상쾌하게 하다. 환기하다 –

airing *n* [U]

air·bag /'ɛrbæg/ *n* a bag in a car that fills with air to protect people in an accident ‖ 사고시에 사람을 보호하기 위해 공기가 들어차는 차 안의 주머니. 에어백

air·borne /'ɛrbɔrn/ *adj* flying or floating in the air ‖ 비행 중이거나 공중에 떠 있는: *They'll serve drinks once we're airborne.* 우리의 비행 중 그들은 음료를 한 차례 제공할 것이다.

air con·di·tion·er /'. .,../ *n* a machine that makes the air in a room, car etc. stay cool ‖ 방이나 차 안의 공기를 시원하게 유지해 주는 기계. 에어컨(디셔너). 냉방 장치

air con·di·tion·ing /'. .,../ *n* [U] a system of machines that makes the air in a room, building etc. stay cool ‖ 방이나 건물 안의 공기를 시원하게 유지하는 기계 시스템. 냉방 – **air conditioned** *adj*

aircraft /'ɛrkræft/ *n, plural* **aircraft** a plane or any vehicle that can fly ‖ 비행기나 날 수 있는 운송 수단. 항공기

aircraft car·ri·er /'.. ,.../ *n* a type of ship that has a large flat surface that planes fly from ‖ 비행기가 이륙할 수 있는 너른 평면을 갖춘 배의 일종. 항공 모함

air·fare /'ɛrfɛr/ *n* [U] the price of a plane trip ‖ 항공 요금

air·field /'ɛrfild/ *n* a place where military planes or small planes fly from ‖ 군용기나 경비행기가 이륙하는 장소. 비행장

Air Force /'. ,./ *n* **the Air Force** the military organization of the US that uses planes when fighting a war ‖ 전쟁시 비행기를 이용해서 싸우는 미국의 군사 조직. 미국 공군

air·head /'ɛr,hɛd/ *n* SLANG someone who is stupid ‖ 어리석은 사람. 멍청이. 바보

air·i·ly /'ɛrəli/ *adv* in a way that shows that you are not serious or do not care very much ‖ 심각하지 않다거나 그다지 신경쓰지 않는다는 것을 나타내는 투로. 가볍게: *"Oh, just do whatever you want,"* she said airily. "오, 그냥 네가 하고 싶은 대로 해."라며 그녀는 대수롭지 않게 말했다.

air·less /'ɛrlɪs/ *adj* without fresh air ‖ 신선한 공기가 없는. 답답한: *a hot airless room* 덥고 답답한 방

air·line /'ɛrlaɪn/ *n* a business that regularly flies passengers to different places by plane ‖ 승객들을 비행기로 다른 장소로 정기적으로 수송하는 회사. 정기 항공사

air·lin·er /'ɛr,laɪnɚ/ *n* a large plane for passengers ‖ 승객용의 대형 비행기. 대형 여객기

air·mail /'ɛrmeɪl/ *n* [U] letters, packages etc. that are sent to another country by plane, or the system of doing this ‖ 비행기로 다른 나라에 우송되는 편지나 소포, 또는 그 시스템. 항공 우편물. 항공편 – **airmail** *adj, adv*

air·plane /'ɛrpleɪn/ *n* a vehicle that flies by using wings and one or more engines; plane ‖ 날개 및 한 개 이상의 엔진을 이용하여 나는 운송 수단. 항공기; 비행기

air·port /'ɛrpɔrt/ *n* a place where planes fly from ‖ 비행기가 이륙하는 곳. 공항

air raid /'. ,./ *n* an attack by military planes ‖ 군용기에 의한 공격. 공습

airs /ɛrz/ *n* [plural] the things someone does and says in order to seem more important than s/he really is ‖ 실제보다 더 중요하게 보이게 하려고 하는 것이나 말하는 것. 뽐내기: *Monica has been putting on airs ever since she moved to Beverly Hills.* 모니카는 비벌리힐스로 이사간 이후 줄곧 잘난 체하고 있다.

air·space /'ɛrspeɪs/ *n* [U] the sky

above a particular country, considered to be controlled by that country ‖ 특정한 국가에 의해 통제된다고 여겨지는 그 나라의 상공. 영공

air strike /'. ./ n an attack on a place in which military aircraft drop bombs on it ‖ 군용기로 어떤 곳에 폭탄을 투하하는 공격. 공습

air·strip /'ɛrstrɪp/ n a long narrow piece of land that has been cleared so that planes can fly from it ‖ 비행기가 날 수 있도록 정비된 좁고 긴 땅. 활주로

air·tight /'ɛr,taɪt, ˌɛr'taɪt/ adj 1 not allowing air to get in or out ‖ 공기가 들어오거나 나가지 못하는. 밀폐된: airtight containers 밀폐 용기 2 having no mistakes or weaknesses ‖ 실수나 약점이 없는. 빈틈없는: an airtight argument/excuse 빈틈없는 논거[변명]

air time /'. ./ n [U] the period of time or the amount of time during a day that a radio or television station broadcasts its programs ‖ 하루 동안 라디오나 텔레비전 방송국에서 프로그램을 방송하는 시간. 방송 시간: Thirty seconds of air time will cost $1500. 방송 시간 30초당 1,500 달러가 들 것이다.

air·waves /'ɛrweɪvz/ n [plural] INFORMAL all the programs that are broadcast on radio and television ‖ 라디오나 텔레비전에서 방송되는 모든 프로그램. 방송 (전파)

air·y /'ɛri/ adj an airy room, building etc. has a lot of space and fresh air ‖ 방이나 건물 등이 공간이 넓고 공기가 신선한. 바람이 잘 통하는

aisle /aɪl/ n a long passage between rows of seats in a theater, church, bus, plane etc. ‖ 극장·교회·버스·비행기 등의 좌석열 간의 긴 통로

a·jar /ə'dʒɑr/ adj a door or window that is ajar is not completely closed ‖ 문이나 창문이 완전히 닫히지 않은. 조금 열린

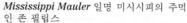
ajar

AK the written abbreviation of Alaska ‖ Alaska (알래스카 주)의 약어

a.k.a. adv the abbreviation of "also known as"; used when giving someone's real name together with the name s/he is known by ‖ "also known as"(일명[별명])의 약어; 누군가의 본명을 말하면서 이미 잘 알려진(다른) 이름을 말할 때에 쓰여 : John Phillips, a.k.a. The

Mississippi Mauler 일명 미시시피의 주먹인 존 필립스

a·kin /ə'kɪn/ adj FORMAL **akin to** similar to something ‖ 무엇과 유사한: His music is much more akin to jazz than rock. 그의 음악은 록보다 재즈에 훨씬 더 가깝다.

AL the written abbreviation of Alabama ‖ Alabama (앨라배마 주)의 약어

à la carte /ˌɑlə'kɑrt, ˌælə-, ˌɑlɑ-/ adj food in a restaurant that is **à la carte** has its own separate price for each dish ‖ 식당의 음식이 각 요리마다 따로 가격이 매겨진. 알라카르트의. 일품 요리의 **–à la carte** adv

a·lac·ri·ty /ə'lækrəti/ n [U] FORMAL eager willingness to do something ‖ 선뜻 어떤 것을 함: Thomas agreed with alacrity. 토마스는 흔쾌히 동의했다.

à la mode /ˌɑlə'moud, ˌælə-, ˌɑlɑ-/ adj served with ice cream ‖ 아이스크림이 함께 제공되는

a·larm¹ /ə'lɑrm/ n [U] 1 something such as a bell, loud noise, or light that warns people of danger ‖ 사람들에게 위험을 경고하는 벨·큰 소리·빛 등의 것. 경보 (장치): a fire/burglar alarm 화재 [도난] 경보기 / a car alarm (=one attached to your car) 자동차 경보기 2 INFORMAL ⇨ ALARM CLOCK 3 a feeling of fear or anxiety because something dangerous might happen ‖ 위험한 일이 일어날지도 모른다는 두려움이나 걱정. 불안: Calm down! There's no cause for alarm. 침착해! 불안할 이유가 전혀 없어. 4 **raise/sound the alarm** to warn everyone about something bad or dangerous that is happening ‖ 나쁘거나 위험한 일이 일어나고 있다고 모든 사람에게 경고하다. 경보를 발하다: They first sounded the alarm about the problem of nuclear waste in 1955. 그들은 1955년에 핵폐기물 문제에 대해 처음으로 경고했다.

alarm² v [T] to make someone feel very worried or anxious ‖ 남을 매우 걱정시키거나 초조하게 하다. …을 놀라게[불안하게] 하다: Local residents have been alarmed by the recent police activity. 지역 주민들은 최근의 경찰 활동으로 인해 불안해 했다. **– alarmed** adj

alarm clock /.'. ˌ./ n a clock that will make a noise at a particular time to wake you up ‖ 잠에서 깨울 특정한 시간에 소리를 내게 되어 있는 시계. 자명종

a·larm·ing /ə'lɑrmɪŋ/ adj very frightening or worrying ‖ 매우 놀라거나 걱정하는. 놀라운. 놀랄 만한: an alarming increase in violent crime 흉악한 범죄의 놀랄 만한 증가

a·larm·ist /ə'lɑrmɪst/ *adj* making people unnecessarily worried about dangers that do not exist ‖ 존재하지도 않는 위험에 대해서 쓸데없이 걱정하게 하는. 군걱정을 하게 하는 - **alarmist** *n*

a·las /ə'læs/ *interjection* LITERARY said in order to express sadness ‖ 슬픔을 나타내는 데에 쓰여. 아아

al·be·it /ɔl'biːɪt, æl-/ *conj* FORMAL although ‖ 비록 …이라 할지라도

al·bi·no /æl'baɪnoʊ/ *n* a person or animal with a GENETIC condition that makes the skin and hair extremely pale or white ‖ 피부와 털이 지나치게 창백해지거나 하얘지는 유전적 현상을 지닌 사람이나 동물. 알비노

al·bum /'ælbəm/ *n* **1** a group of songs or pieces of music recorded by a particular performer or group on a record, CD or tape ‖ 특정 연주자나 그룹이 음반[CD, 테이프]에 녹음한 노래나 연주 모음. 앨범: *Do you have Neil Young's new album?* 널 영의 새 앨범 가지고 있니? **2** a book in which you put photographs, stamps etc. that you want to keep ‖ 간직하고 싶은 사진·우표 등을 끼워 넣는 책. 앨범

al·co·hol /'ælkə,hɔl, -,hɑl/ *n* **1** [U] drinks such as beer, wine, WHISKEY etc. that contain a substance that can make you drunk ‖ 맥주·와인·위스키 등의 취하게 하는 성분이 함유된 음료. 알코올성 음료. 술: *We do not serve alcohol to people under age 21.* 21세 미만인 사람에게는 술을 팔지 않습니다. **2** [C, U] a chemical substance that can be used for cleaning medical or industrial equipment ‖ 의료나 공업 장비를 닦는 데에 쓰이는 화학 물질. 알코올

al·co·hol·ic /,ælkə'hɔlɪk, -'hɑ-/ *n* someone who cannot stop the habit of drinking too much alcohol ‖ 알코올성 음료를 너무 많이 마시는 습관을 끊을 수 없는 사람. 알코올 중독자: *His father was an alcoholic.* 그의 아버지는 알코올 중독자였다.

alcoholic² *adj* containing alcohol or relating to alcohol ‖ 알코올이 든, 알코올에 관련된: *an alcoholic beverage* 알코올성 음료 —opposite NONALCOHOLIC

al·co·hol·is·m /'ælkəhə,lɪzəm, -hɑ-/ *n* [U] the medical condition of being an alcoholic ‖ 의학적으로 알코올 중독자인 상태. 알코올 중독

al·cove /'ælkoʊv/ *n* a small place in a wall of a room that is built further back than the rest of the wall ‖ 방의 벽의 한쪽을 다른 벽들보다 쑥 들어가게 만든 작은 공간. 벽감.

al·der·man /'ɔldə-mən/, **al·der·wo·man** /'ɔldə-,wʊmən/ *n* a low level city or town government official who is elected ‖ 대도시나 소도시의 선출직 관료. 시의회 의원

ale /eɪl/ *n* [U] a type of beer with a slightly bitter taste ‖ 약간 쓴맛이 나는 맥주의 일종. 에일

a·lert¹ /ə'lɚt/ *adj* **1** always watching and ready to notice anything strange, unusual, dangerous etc. ‖ 이상한 것·특이한 것·위험한 것 등을 알아차리기 위해 항상 살피고 준비하는. 주의깊은: *Cyclists must always be alert to the dangers on a busy road.* 자전거를 타는 사람들은 붐비는 도로에서는 항상 위험에 깊이 주의해야 한다. **2** able to think quickly and clearly ‖ 빠르고 명확하게 생각할 수 있는. 기민한: *I didn't feel alert enough to do any more work.* 나는 일을 더 할 수 있을 정도로 기민하지 못했다.

alert² *v* [T] **1** to officially warn someone of a problem or of possible danger ‖ 남에게 문제나 위험 가능성에 대해 공식적으로 경고하다. 경보를 발하다: *An unnamed woman alerted the police about the bomb.* 익명의 한 여자가 폭탄에 대해 경찰에 경고했다. **2** to make someone notice something important, dangerous etc. ‖ 남에게 중요한 것·위험한 것 등을 알려 주다. 주의를 환기시키다: *A large sign alerts drivers to bad road conditions.* 커다란 표지판은 운전자들에게 좋지 않은 도로 상태에 주의를 환기시킨다.

alert³ *n* **1 be on the alert** to be ready to notice and deal with a problem ‖ 문제를 알아차리고 대처할 준비가 되다. 경계하다: *Police are on the alert for trouble.* 경찰은 분쟁 사태에 경계하고 있다. **2** a warning to be ready for possible danger ‖ 일어날지 모를 위험에 대비하는 경고. 경보: *The FBI put out an alert for a man seen near the crime.* FBI는 범죄 현장 근처에서 목격된 남자에 대해 경계를 발령했다.

al·fal·fa sprout /æl'fælfə spraʊt/ *n* a very small plant, eaten raw as a vegetable in SALADs ‖ 샐러드로 만들어 날로 먹는 야채인 작은 식물. 자주개자리

al·gae /'ældʒi/ *n* [U] a very simple plant without stems or leaves that lives in or near water ‖ 바다 속이나 근처에서 자라는 가지나 잎이 없는 매우 단순한 식물. 말. 조류(藻類)

al·ge·bra /'ældʒəbrə/ *n* [U] a type of mathematics that uses letters and signs

algorithm 36

to represent numbers and values ‖ 숫자와 값을 표시하기 위해 문자와 기호를 사용하는 수학의 일종. 대수학 - **algebraic** /ˌældʒəˈbreɪ-ɪk/ *adj*

al·go·rithm /ˈælgəˌrɪðəm/ *n* a set of mathematical instructions that are done in a particular order ‖ 특정한 순서에 의해 작성된 수학적 지시표. 알고리듬

a·li·as¹ /ˈeɪliəs, ˈeɪlyəs/ *prep* used when giving a criminal's real name together with the name s/he uses ‖ 범죄자 자신이 쓰는 이름과 함께 본명을 말할 때에 쓰여. 일명[별명]은…: *the spy Margaret Zelle, alias Mata Hari* 스파이 마가렛 젤르, 일명 마타 하리

alias² *n* a false name, usually used by a criminal ‖ 보통 범죄자가 쓰는 가명. 별명

al·i·bi /ˈæləˌbaɪ/ *n* proof that someone was not where a crime happened and is therefore not guilty of the crime ‖ 사람이 범죄 현장에 없었으므로 무죄라는 증거. 알리바이. 현장 부재 증명

a·li·en¹ /ˈeɪliən, ˈeɪlyən/ *adj* **1** very different or strange ‖ 매우 다르거나 이상한. 이질적인: *Her way of life is totally alien to me.* 그녀의 생활 방식은 나와 전적으로 다르다. **2** relating to creatures from other worlds ‖ 다른 세계에서 온 생물에 관한. 지구상의 것이 아닌. 외계 (생명체)의

alien² *n* **1** someone who lives or works in a country but is not a citizen ‖ 어떤 나라에서 살거나 일하지만 그 나라의 국민은 아닌 사람. 외국인: *State authorities are not dealing well with the problem of illegal aliens.* 주 당국은 불법 체류자 문제를 제대로 처리하지 못하고 있다. **2** a creature that comes from another world ‖ 다른 세계에서 온 생물. 외계인. 우주인

a·li·en·ate /ˈeɪliəˌneɪt, ˈeɪlyə-/ *v* [T] to make someone stop feeling friendly or stop feeling like s/he belongs in a group ‖ 남을 우호적이거나 동아리에 속한 느낌이 들지 못하게 하다. 소외시키다: *We don't want to alienate kids who already have problems at school.* 우리는 학교에서 이미 문제를 가지고 있는 아이들을 소외시키고 싶지 않다. - **alienation** /ˌeɪliəˈneɪʃən, -ˌeɪlyə-/ *n* [U]

a·light¹ /əˈlaɪt/ *adj* **1** burning ‖ 불타는: *Several cars were set alight by rioters.* 폭도들에 의해 몇몇 자동차에 불이 붙었다. **2** someone whose face or eyes are alight is happy or excited ‖ 사람의 얼굴이나 눈이 행복이나 흥분으로 밝아진. 빛나는

alight² *v* [I] FORMAL **1 alight on/upon sth** if a bird, insect etc. alights on

something, it stops flying in order to stand on a surface ‖ 새·곤충 등이 표면 위에 서려고 비행을 중단하다. …에 내려앉다 **2 alight from** to step out of a vehicle at the end of a trip ‖ 여행이 끝나 차에서 내리다. 하차[착륙]하다

a·lign /əˈlaɪn/ *v* [I, T] **1** to work together with another person or group because you have the same aims ‖ 같은 목적을 지니고 있어서 다른 사람이나 집단과 함께 일하다. 제휴하다: *Five Democrats have aligned themselves with the Republicans on this vote.* 다섯 명의 민주당원들은 이번 투표에 공화당원들과 손을 잡았다. **2** to arrange something so that it is in the same line as something else ‖ 다른 것과 일직선이 되도록 물건을 배열하다. 정렬하다: *It looks like your wheels need aligning.* 당신의 차바퀴를 일직선으로 맞춰야 할 것 같아요. - **alignment** *n* [C, U]: *a close alignment between Syria and Egypt* 시리아와 이집트 사이의 긴밀한 협력

a·like¹ /əˈlaɪk/ *adj* almost exactly the same; similar ‖ 거의 똑같은; 유사한: *All the new cars look alike to me.* 모든 새 차가 똑같아 보인다.

alike² *adv* **1** in a similar way, or in the same way ‖ 유사하거나 동일한 방식으로. 비슷하게. 똑같게: *When we were younger, we dressed alike.* 우리가 젊었을 때는 똑같이 입었다. **2** equally ‖ 동등하게: *The new rule was criticized by teachers and students alike.* 새 규칙은 교사들과 학생들로부터 똑같이 비난을 받았다.

al·i·mo·ny /ˈæləˌmoʊni/ *n* [singular] money that someone has to pay regularly to his/her former wife or husband after a DIVORCE ‖ 이혼 후에 전 부인이나 전 남편에게 정기적으로 지불해야 하는 돈. 부양금. 별거[이혼] 수당

a·live /əˈlaɪv/ *adj* **1** living and not dead ‖ 죽지 않고 살아 있는. 생존하는: *They didn't expect to find anyone alive after the explosion.* 그들은 폭발 후에 살아 있는 사람을 발견하리라 기대하지 않았다. / *I'm amazed my plants have stayed alive in this weather.* 이런 날씨에 내 식물이 살아 남아 있다니 놀랍다. **2** continuing to exist ‖ 계속 존재하는. 존속하는: *Let's keep the traditions of the Inuit alive.* 이뉴잇족의 전통을 존속시킵시다. **3** full of activity or interest ‖ 활동이나 흥미로 가득한. 활동적인. 생동하는: *The streets come alive after ten o'clock.* 10시 이후에 거리는 활기를 띤다. / *The stadium was alive with excitement.* 그

경기장은 흥분으로 생기가 넘쳤다. **4 be alive and well** healthy or successful ‖ 건강하거나 성공적인. 건재한: *Grandpa is alive and well at the age of 85.* 할아버지는 85세로 건재하시다.

al·ka·li /ˈælkəˌlaɪ/ *n* [C, U] a substance that forms a chemical salt when combined with an acid ‖ 산과 결합할 때 화학염을 만드는 물질. 알칼리. 염기성 물질 - **alkaline** *adj*

all¹ /ɔl/ *determiner* **1** the whole of an amount or time ‖ 양이나 시간의 전체: *All the money is gone.* 모든 돈을 다 써 버렸다. / *We've spent it all.* 우리는 그것을 모두 써 버렸다. / *I've been waiting all day/week.* 나는 하루 종일[일주일 내내] 기다리고 있다. / *Bill talks about work all the time.* (=very often or too much) 빌은 항상 업무에 관해 이야기한다. **2** every one of a group of things or people ‖ 일단의 사물이나 사람 하나하나 전부. 모든: *Answer all twenty questions.* 20가지 질문에 모두 대답하시오. / *Nearly/almost all my teachers are married.* 거의 모든 선생님들이 결혼했다. / *Have you told them all?* 당신은 그들에게 모든 것을 말했습니까? —see usage note at EACH¹ **3 all kinds of/all sorts of** very many different types of things, people, or places ‖ 온갖 종류의 것[사람, 곳]. 온갖 종류의…: *We saw all kinds of animals on our field trip.* 우리는 견학 여행 때 온갖 종류의 동물을 보았다. **4 for all…** in spite of a particular fact or situation ‖ 특정 사실이나 상황에도 불구하고: *For all his faults, he's a good father.* 그의 결점에도 불구하고 그는 좋은 아버지다. **5 go all out** to do all you can to succeed ‖ 성공하기 위하여 할 수 있는 모든 것을 다하다. 전력을 다하다: *To win the race, you have to go all out from the very start.* 경기에 이기기 위하여 맨 처음부터 온 힘을 다해야 한다. —see study note on page 940

USAGE NOTE all

All is used with a singular verb with uncountable nouns: *All the money is gone.* It is used with a plural verb with countable nouns: *All the people have gone.*

all은 불가산 명사와 함께 쓰여 단수 동사를 취한다: 돈을 다 써 버렸다. **all**은 가산 명사와 함께 쓰여 복수 동사를 취한다: 모든 사람들이 가 버렸다.

---

all² *adv* **1** completely, entirely ‖ 완전히, 전적으로: *I walked all alone in the*

woods. 나는 숲속을 홀로 걸었다. / *The judges were dressed all in black.* 판사들은 검은 복장 일색이었다. **2 all over a)** everywhere on a surface or in a place ‖ 어떤 장소의 표면이나 안 어느 곳이나. 도처에. 사방에: *The grave was decorated all over with flowers.* 그 무덤은 온통 꽃으로 장식되었다. / *We looked all over the place for it.* 우리는 그것을 사방으로 찾았다. **b)** finished ‖ 끝나서: *I used to travel a lot, but that's all over now.* 나는 여행을 많이 다니곤 했는데 지금은 끝났다. **3 be all over sb** to be kissing or touching someone a lot in a sexual way ‖ 누군가를 성적으로 여러 차례 키스를 하거나 만지다. …에게 반하다: *He was all over Pam last night in the bar.* 그는 어젯밤 바에서 팸에게 홀딱 빠져 있었다. **4** used in order to say that both sides have the same number of points in a game ‖ 경기에서 양측이 동점임을 말하는 데에 쓰여. 쌍방[양팀] 모두: *The score was 10-all at half time.* 하프 타임 때 점수는 양쪽 다 10점 동점이었다. **5 all but** almost completely ‖ 거의 완전히: *The wine left a stain that was all but impossible to get rid of.* 포도주가 얼룩을 남겼는데 지우기가 거의 불가능했다. **6 all along** the whole time ‖ 내내. 줄곧: *I knew all along that I couldn't trust him.* 나는 그를 신뢰할 수 없다는 것을 줄곧 알고 있었다. **7 all of a sudden** in a very quick and surprising way ‖ 빠르고 놀랍게. 갑자기: *All of a sudden I realized that the car in front of me was stopped.* 갑자기 차가 내 앞에서 멈춰 선 것을 알았다. —see also **after all** (AFTER¹) —see usage notes at ALREADY, ALTOGETHER

all³ *pron* **1** everyone; everything ‖ 모든 사람; 모든 것: *Mandy thinks she knows it all.* 맨디는 그녀가 그것을 모두 안다고 생각한다. / *All of the books were overdue.* 모든 책이 반납 기한이 넘었다. —see usage note at EACH¹ **2 not at all** not in any way ‖ 조금도 아닌: *The snow didn't affect us at all.* 눈은 우리에게 전혀 영향을 미치지 않았다. / *He's not at all happy.* 그는 조금도 행복하지 않다. **3 at all** used in questions to mean "in any way" ‖ "어떤 식으로든"을 뜻하는 질문에 쓰여. 적어도. 조금이라도: *Did the new drugs help her at all?* 그 신약이 어떤 식으로든 그녀에게 도움이 되었습니까? **4 all in all** considering everything ‖ 모든 것을 고려하여. 전반적으로. 대체로: *It wasn't funny, but all in all it was a good movie.* 재미는 없었지만 대체로 좋은 영화였다.

Al·lah /'ælə, 'ɑlə/ *n* the name used in Islam for God ‖ 이슬람교에서 쓰이는 신에 대한 명칭. 알라신

all-A·mer·i·can /,. .'..../ *adj* typical of America or Americans ‖ 미국이나 미국인에게 전형적인: *an all-American girl* 전형적인 미국 소녀

all-a·round /,. .'../ *adj* good at doing many different things, especially in sports ‖ 특히 스포츠에서 여러 다양한 것을 잘 하는. 다재다능한: *the best all-around player* 최고의 만능 선수

al·lay /ə'leɪ/ *v* [T] to make the effect of an unpleasant feeling or situation less strong ‖ 불쾌한 감정이나 상황의 영향을 약화시키다. 가라앉히다. 누그러뜨리다: *The report allayed fears/worries etc. about the economy.* 그 기사는 경제에 대한 공포[불안]을 진정시켰다.

all-clear /,. '.'/ *n* permission to begin doing something ‖ 무엇을 시작하기 위한 허가: *We have to wait for the all-clear from the safety committee before we can start.* 우리는 시작하기 전에 안전 위원회로부터 허가를 기다려야 한다.

al·le·ga·tion /,ælə'geɪʃən/ *n* a statement that someone has done something illegal, which is not supported by proof ‖ 남이 불법적인 일을 했다는, 증거의 뒷받침이 없는 진술. 주장: *allegations of child abuse* 아동 학대에 대한 진술

al·lege /ə'lɛdʒ/ *v* [T] to say that something is true without showing proof ‖ 증거의 제시 없이 무엇을 사실이라고 말하다. …을 주장하다: *Baldwin is alleged to have killed two people.* 볼드윈은 두 사람을 죽인 혐의를 받고 있다.

al·leged /ə'lɛdʒd/ *adj* supposed to be true, but not proven ‖ 사실로 가정되지만 입증되지 않는. 추정의: *the group's alleged connections with organized crime* 그 그룹의 조직 범죄와의 의심스러운[추정된] 연관성

al·leg·ed·ly /ə'lɛdʒɪdli/ *adv* used when repeating what other people say is true, when it has not been proven to be true ‖ 사실로 입증되지 않았는데 남들이 말하는 바를 사실이라고 인용할 때에 쓰여. 전언[사람들의 말]에 따르면: *He was arrested for allegedly raping a woman.* 전해지는 바에 의하면 그는 한 여성을 강간하여 체포되었다.

al·le·giance /ə'lidʒəns/ *n* loyalty to or support for a leader, country, belief etc. ‖ 지도자·국가·신념 등에 대한 충성이나 지지. 충성. 옹호

al·le·go·ry /'ælə,gɔri/ *n* [C, U] a story, poem, painting etc. in which the events and characters represent good and bad qualities ‖ 사건·등장 인물이 나타내는 선·악의 속성을 담은 소설·시·그림 등. 풍유(소설·시·그림) **– allegorical** /,ælə'gɔrɪkəl/ *adj*

al·ler·gic /ə'lədʒɪk/ *adj* 1 having an ALLERGY ‖ 알레르기가 있는: *Are you allergic to anything?* 당신은 어떠한 알레르기가 있나요? 2 caused by an ALLERGY ‖ 알레르기에 의해 야기된. 알레르기성의: *an allergic reaction to the bee sting* 벌침에 대한 알레르기 반응

al·ler·gy /'ælədʒi/ *n* a condition that makes you ill when you eat, touch, or breathe a particular thing ‖ 특정한 것을 먹으면[만지면, 호흡하면] 병이 나는 현상. 알레르기: *an allergy to cats* 고양이 알레르기

al·le·vi·ate /ə'livi,eɪt/ *v* [T] to make something less bad or severe ‖ 어떤 것의 나쁘거나 심한 정도를 약화시키다. 경감하다: *Aspirin should alleviate the pain.* 아스피린은 고통을 완화한다. / *The road was built to alleviate traffic problems.* 그 도로는 교통 문제를 완화하려고 건설되었다.

al·ley /'æli/ *n* a narrow street between buildings ‖ 건물 사이의 좁은 길. 골목길

al·li·ance /ə'laɪəns/ *n* a close agreement or connection between people, countries etc. ‖ 국민·국가 간의 긴밀한 협정이나 유대. 동맹. 연합: *the NATO alliance* 나토 연합

al·lied /ə'laɪd, 'ælaɪd/ *adj* joined or closely related, especially by a political or military agreement ‖ 특히 정치적 또는 군사적 협정에 의해 동맹을 맺거나 긴밀히 관련된. 연합한: *allied forces* 연합군 / *The two leaders were closely allied during the Gulf War.* 두 지도자는 걸프 전쟁 동안 긴밀히 협력했다.

al·li·ga·tor /'ælə,geɪtə/ *n* a large REPTILE (=type of animal) with a long body, a long mouth, and sharp teeth, that lives in hot wet areas of the US and China ‖ 긴 몸통·긴 입·날카로운 이빨을 가지고 있고 미국과 중국의 덥고 습한 지역에 사는 큰 파충류. 엘리게이터. 악어

all-in·clu·sive /,. .'..../ *adj* including everything ‖ 모든 것을 포함한. 포괄적인: *The price is all-inclusive – it covers your hotel, flight, and food.* 그 가격은 일괄적이어서 호텔비, 항공료와 식사비가 포함된다.

al·lo·cate /'ælə,keɪt/ *v* [T] to decide to allow a particular amount of money, time etc. to be used for a particular purpose ‖ 특정한 목적에 쓰기 위하여 특정한 양의 돈·시간 등을 허용하기로 하다. 떼어 놓다. 할당[배당]하다: *The hospital has allocated $500,000 for cancer research.* 그 병원은 암 연구에 50만 달러를 할당했다.

al·lo·ca·tion /ˌæləˈkeɪʃən/ *n* [C, U] the amount of something that is ALLOCATED, or the decision to allocate ‖ 할당된 무엇의 양이나 할당하기로 한 결정. 배당: *the allocation of state funds to the university* 대학교에 대한 주 기금의 할당

al·lot /əˈlɑt/ *v* -tted, -tting [T] to ALLOCATE something ‖ 무엇을 할당하다: *Each person was allotted nine tickets.* 각 사람에게 표를 9장씩 주었다. / *He allotted 20 minutes a day to his exercises.* 그는 운동하는 데에 매일 20분을 할애했다. – **allotment** *n* [C, U]: *a decrease in the allotment of funds* 기금 할당액의 감소

al·low /əˈlaʊ/ *v* [T] 1 to give someone permission to do something or have something ‖ 누군가에게 무엇을 하거나 갖도록 허락하다: *Smoking is not allowed.* 흡연은 허용되지 않는다. / *You're allowed one candy bar after lunch.* 너는 점심 식사 후에 막대 사탕 한 개를 먹어도 좋다. 2 to let someone go somewhere ‖ 남이 어디에 가도록 내버려 두다: *You're not allowed in here.* 너는 이곳에 있어서는 안 된다. 3 to make it possible for something to happen ‖ 어떤 일이 일어나도록 하다: *I can't allow the situation to get any worse.* 상황이 더 악화되게 할 수는 없다. 4 to let someone have an amount of time or money for a particular purpose ‖ 누군가에게 특정한 목적을 위한 일정 시간이나 돈을 갖도록 하다. 시간[돈]을 주다: *Allow ten days for delivery.* 배달하는 데에 10일을 주시오. / *Allow yourself enough time to shop.* 쇼핑하는 데에 충분한 시간을 가져라.

allow for sb/sth *phr v* [T] to consider the possible effects of something and make plans to deal with it ‖ 있을 수 있는 어떤 것의 영향을 고려하여 대처 방안을 수립하다. 참작하다: *Even allowing for delays, we should finish early.* 지연을 고려해서라도 우리는 일찍 끝내야 한다.

al·low·a·ble /əˈlaʊəbəl/ *adj* acceptable according to particular rules ‖ 특정 규율에 따라 받아들일 수 있는. 허용되는: *allowable vacation time* 허용되는 휴가 기간

al·low·ance /əˈlaʊəns/ *n* 1 [C, U] money you are given regularly or for a special reason ‖ 정기적으로 또는 특별한 이유로 받은 돈. 용돈: *How much allowance do your parents give you?* 부모님은 당신에게 용돈을 얼마나 줍니까? / *a travel allowance* 여행비 2 **make allowances for** to consider the facts about someone or something when making judgments or decisions ‖ 판단이나 결정을 할 때 사람이나 사물에 대한 사실을 고려하다. …을 참작하다: *He's so tired I'll make allowances for him.* 그가 매우 피곤하다는 것을 참작하겠다.

al·loy /ˈælɔɪ/ *n* a metal made by mixing two or more different metals ‖ 둘 이상의 다른 금속을 혼합하여 만든 금속. 합금

all right /ˌ ˈ / *adj, adv* SPOKEN 1 acceptable, but not excellent ‖ 수용할 만하지만 뛰어나지는 않은. 괜찮은. 양호한: *"How's the food?" "It's all right, but I've had better."* "음식이 어떻습니까?" "괜찮지만 더 나아졌으면 해요." 2 not hurt, not upset, or not having problems ‖ 다치거나 심란하지 않거나, 또는 문제 없는. 무사한. 괜찮은: *Sue, are you all right?* 수, 너 괜찮니? / *Did everything go all right* (=happen without any problems) *with your test?* 시험 괜찮게 봤니? 3 used in order to say you agree with a plan, suggestion etc. ‖ 계획·제안 등에 동의하는 데에 쓰여: *"Let's go now." "All right."* "지금 갑시다." "좋아요." 4 **that's all right** a) used in order to reply when someone thanks you ‖ 남이 감사하다고 할 때 대답하는 데에 쓰여. 그래 알았어: *"Thanks for your help!" "That's all right."* "도와 주셔서 감사해요!" "네, 알겠어요." b) used in order to tell someone you are not angry when s/he says s/he is sorry ‖ 남이 미안하다고 말할 때 화나지 않았다고 말하는 데에 쓰여. 괜찮아: *"Sorry I'm late!" "That's all right."* "늦어서 미안해요." "괜찮아요." 5 used in order to say or ask whether something is convenient for you ‖ 어떤 것의 편리함의 여부를 말하거나 묻는 데에 쓰여: *Would that bar on Front Street be all right to meet in?* 프론트가의 술집에서 만나는 것이 괜찮겠습니까? 6 **is it all right if**… used in order to ask for someone's permission to do something ‖ 무엇을 하기 위한 남의 허락을 받는 데에 쓰여. …해도 괜찮을까요?: *Is it all right if I close the window?* 창문 닫아도 되니? 7 used in order to ask if someone has understood something ‖ 남에게 무엇을 이해하는지 묻는 데에 쓰여. 알겠지?: *You should do this exercise by yourself, all right?* 혼자서 이 운동을 해야 한다. 알았지? 8 used in order to say you are happy about something ‖ 무엇에 대한 만족을 말하는 데에 쓰여. 잘 됐다!: *"I got the job!" "All right!"* "직장을 잡았어!" "잘 됐네!" **9 be doing all right** to be successful in your job or life ‖ 직업이나 인생에 성공하다.

USAGE NOTE all right and alright

All right is the usual way we spell this phrase: *Don't worry. I'm all right. / All right, let's go!* Many teachers think that **alright** is incorrect in formal writing.
all right가 일반적으로 철자하는 방식이다: 걱정 마라. 난 괜찮아./좋아, 가자! 많은 교사들은 격식적인 문장에서 **alright**를 쓰는 것을 틀린 용법으로 간주한다.

---

al·lude /ə'lud/ *v*
allude to sb/sth *phr v* [T] FORMAL to talk about something in an indirect way ‖ 어떤 것을 간접적으로 말하다. 넌지시 말하다. 암시하다.

al·lure¹ /ə'lʊr/ *n* [singular, U] a pleasant or exciting quality that attracts people ‖ 사람들을 끄는 즐겁거나 신나는 특성. 매력. 매혹: *the allure of travel* 여행의 매력

allure² *v* [T] to attract someone by seeming to offer something pleasant or exciting ‖ 즐겁거나 신나는 것을 제공하는 듯이 보이게 하여 남을 끌다. 매혹하다 – **alluring** *adj* : *an alluring smile* 매혹적인 미소

al·lu·sion /ə'luʒən/ *n* [C, U] FORMAL the act of speaking or writing in an indirect way about something ‖ 무엇에 대해 간접적으로 말하거나 쓰기. 빗댐. 암시: *His poetry is full of allusions to other literature.* 그의 시에는 다른 문학에 대한 암시가 많이 있다. – **allusive** *adj*

al·ly¹ /ə'laɪ, 'ælaɪ/ *n* a person or country that helps another, especially in war ‖ 특히 전시에 남을 돕는 사람이나 국가. 동맹자. 동맹국: *the US and its European allies* 미국 및 그 유럽 동맹국

ally² *v* [I, T] **ally yourself to/with** to join with other people or countries to help each other ‖ 서로 돕기 위하여 다른 사람들이나 국가들과 결연하다. 동맹[제휴]하다

al·ma ma·ter /ˌælmə 'mɑtɚ, ˌɑl-/ *n* [singular, U] FORMAL **1** the school, college, or university where you used to study ‖ 전에 공부했던 학교[단과 대학, 종합 대학]. 모교. 출신교: *He returned to his alma mater to teach.* 그는 가르치기 위하여 모교로 돌아갔다. **2** the official song of a school, college, or university ‖ 학교[단과 대학, 종합 대학]의 공식적인 노래. 교가

al·ma·nac /'ɔlmə,næk/ *n* **1** a book giving a list of the days of a year, times the sun rises and sets, changes in the moon etc. ‖ 날짜·일출 및 일몰 시간·달의 변화 등을 열거한 책. 역서. 책력 **2** a book giving information about a particular subject or activity ‖ 특정한 주제나 활동에 관한 정보를 제공하는 책. 연감: *a farmers' almanac* 농업 경영자 연감

al·might·y /ɔl'maɪti/ *adj* **1** having the power to do anything ‖ 어떤 일이든 할 능력이 있는. 전능한: *Almighty God* 전능한 하나님 **2** very important or powerful ‖ 매우 중요하거나 강력한. 막강한: *the almighty dollar* 막강한 달러

al·mond /'ɑmənd, 'æm-/ *n* a flat white nut with a slightly sweet taste, or the tree on which these nuts grow ‖ 약간 단맛이 나는 납작한 흰 견과나 이 견과가 자라는 나무. 아몬드(나무)

al·most /'ɔlmoʊst, ɔl'moʊst/ *adv* nearly but not quite ‖ 완전히는 아니지만 아주 가깝게. 거의: *Are we almost there?* 우리 그곳에 거의 다 왔나요? / *Almost all children like to read.* 거의 모든 아이들이 책 읽기를 좋아한다.

alms /ɑmz/ *n* [plural] OLD-FASHIONED money, food etc. given to poor people ‖ 가난한 사람들에게 주는 돈·음식 등. 빈민 구호금[구호품]

a·loft /ə'lɔft/ *adv* LITERARY high up in the air ‖ 공중에 높이. 하늘 높이

a·lo·ha /ə'loʊhɑ/ *interjection* used in order to say hello or goodbye in Hawaii ‖ 하와이에서 안부나 작별의 말을 하는 데에 쓰여. 안녕

a·lone /ə'loʊn/ *adj* **1** away from other people ‖ 남과 떨어져. 홀로. 단독으로: *She lives alone.* 그녀는 혼자 산다. **2** only ‖ 단지 …뿐인. …만인: *He alone can do the job.* (=he is the only one who can do it) 그 사람만이 그 일을 할 수 있다. **3 leave sb alone** to stop annoying someone ‖ 남을 귀찮게 하는 것을 멈추다. …을 내버려 두다: *Go away and leave me alone.* 저리 가고 나 좀 내버려 둬. **4 leave sth alone** to not touch something ‖ 물건을 건드리지 않다. …을 내버려 두다: *Leave that alone! It's mine.* 그거 내버려 둬! 내 거야.

along¹ /ə'lɔŋ/ *prep* **1** by the side of something and from one part of it to another part of it ‖ 무엇의 옆으로 한 쪽

에서 다른 쪽까지. …을 끼고 죽: *We took a walk along the river.* 우리는 강을 끼고 죽 걸었다. / *She looked anxiously along the line of faces.* 그녀는 근심스레 늘어선 얼굴들을 죽 바라보았다. **2** in a line next to or on something ‖ 무엇의 옆에 한 줄로. …을 따라: *They've put up a fence along the road.* 그들은 도로를 따라 울타리를 설치했다. / *photographs arranged along the wall* 벽을 따라 배열된 사진들 **3** at a particular place on something, usually something long ‖ 특히 긴 사물의 특정한 지점에. … 사이에, …의 도중에: *The house is somewhere along this road.* 그 집은 이 길 중간의 어딘가에 있다.

along² *adv* **1** going forward in time or direction ‖ 시간이나 방향상으로 전진하여. 앞으로. 계속: *I was driving along, listening to the radio.* 나는 라디오를 들으면서 계속 운전하고 있었다. **2** **go/come/be along** to go to, come to, or be in the place where something is happening ‖ 일이 일어난 곳에 가다[오다, 있다]: *We're going out – you're welcome to come along!* 우리 외출할 거야. 네가 오면 환영이지! **3** **along with** in addition to and at the same time ‖ …에다가 동시에. …과 함께. 아울러: *There has been a sudden rise in the number of rapes, along with other forms of violence.* 강간 건수는 다른 형태의 폭력과 더불어 갑자기 증가했다. —see also **all along** (ALL²), **get along** (GET)

a·long·side /ə,lɔŋˈsaɪd/ *adv, prep* close to and in line with the edge of something ‖ 무엇의 가장자리에 가깝고 나란하게: *a boat tied up alongside the dock* 부두 곁에 나란히 매어 놓은 배

a·loof¹ /əˈluf/ *adv* apart from other people, not doing things with them ‖ 남들과 함께 일을 하지 않고 멀리 떨어져: *She keeps aloof from us.* 그녀는 우리와는 거리를 둔다.

aloof² *adj* staying apart from other people, especially because you think you are better than they are ‖ 남들보다 낫다고 생각하여 남들과 떨어져 지내는. 초연한: *Your friend Jack seems pretty aloof.* 당신 친구 잭은 꽤 초연한 것 같다.

a·loud /əˈlaʊd/ *adv* **1** in a voice that you can hear ‖ 들을 수 있는 소리로. 소리 내어: *Will you please read the poem aloud?* 시를 낭독해 주시겠습니까? **2** in a loud voice ‖ 큰 소리로. 소리 높이: *James cried aloud with pain.* 제임스는 아파서 크게 소리질렀다.

al·pha·bet /ˈælfə,bɛt/ *n* a set of letters in a particular order, used in writing a language ‖ 한 언어의 표기에 쓰이는 특정 순서로 이루어진 일련의 문자. 알파벳: *the Greek alphabet* 그리스 문자

al·pha·bet·i·cal /,ælfəˈbɛtɪkəl/ *adj* arranged according to the letters of the alphabet ‖ 알파벳에 따라 배열된. 알파벳 순의: *The dictionary is in alphabetical order.* 그 사전은 알파벳순으로 되어 있다. **– alphabetically** *adv*

al·pine /ˈælpaɪn/ *adj* being in or related to the Alps or other high mountains ‖ 알프스 산맥 또는 고산(高山)에 있거나 관련된: *alpine flowers* 고산 꽃

al·read·y /ɔlˈrɛdi/ *adv* **1** before a particular time ‖ 특정한 시간 전에. 이미: *By the time he arrived, the room was already crowded.* 그가 도착했을 때 그 방은 이미 만원이었다. **2** before ‖ 이전에: *We've been there already.* 우리는 이전에 그곳에 가 봤다. **3** sooner than expected ‖ 예상했던 것보다 빨리. 벌써: *I've forgotten the number already.* 나는 벌써 그 숫자를 잊어 버렸다. / *Is he leaving already?* 그 사람 벌써 떠납니까? **4** SPOKEN said in order to emphasize that you are annoyed ‖ 짜증나 있다는 것을 강조하는 데에 쓰여: *"Cindy, come on!" "All right already! Stop rushing me!"* "신디야, 서둘러!" "그래, 알았다니까! 재촉하지 마!" —see usage note at JUST¹

USAGE NOTE all ready and already

Use **all ready** as an adjective phrase to say that someone is ready to do something, or that something is completely prepared: *We're all ready to go now.* / *Dinner is all ready.* Use **already** as an adverb to talk about something that has happened: *John has already seen the movie.*

all ready는 사람이 일을 할 준비가 되거나 일이 완전히 준비된 것을 나타내기 위한 형용사 구로 쓰인다: 우리는 모두 지금 갈 준비가 되어 있다./식사가 완전히 준비되어 있다. **already**는 일어난 일을 말하기 위한 부사로 쓰인다: 존은 이미 그 영화를 보았다.

---

al·right /ɔlˈraɪt/ *adv* ⇨ ALL RIGHT —see usage note at ALL RIGHT

al·so /ˈɔlsoʊ/ *adv* **1** in addition; too ‖ 추가로; 또한: *We specialize in shoes, but we also sell accessories.* 우리는 구두를 전문적으로 취급하지만 액세서리도 판다. **2** used in order to say that one thing or fact is the same as another one ‖ 하나의 사물이나 사실이 다른 것과 같다고 말하는

데에 쓰여. 역시: *My father also died of a heart attack.* 내 아버지 역시 심장 마비로 돌아가셨다.

al·tar /ˈɔltɚ/ n a table or raised structure used in a religious ceremony ‖ 종교적 의식에 쓰이는 탁자 또는 높인 구조물. 제단. 성찬대

al·ter /ˈɔltɚ/ v [I, T] to change in some way ‖ 어떤 식으로 바뀌다. 변하다. 변경하다: *The design has been altered slightly.* 그 디자인은 약간 변경되었다.

al·ter·a·tion /ˌɔltɚˈreɪʃən/ n [C, U] a change in something, or the act of changing it ‖ 무엇의 변화, 무엇을 변화시킴. 변경. 개조: *Alterations to clothes can be expensive.* 옷 수선은 비용이 많이 들 수 있다.

al·ter·ca·tion /ˌɔltɚˈkeɪʃən/ n FORMAL a noisy argument ‖ 소란한 논쟁. 언쟁. 말다툼

al·ter·nate¹ /ˈɔltɚˌneɪt/ v 1 [I] to follow regularly, first one thing and then the other thing happening ‖ 하나가 먼저 일어나고 다음에 다른 것이 일어나는 식으로 규칙적으로 뒤따르다. 번갈아 일어나다. 교대하다: *Jenny kept alternating between leaving and staying.* 제니는 번갈아 떠났다가 머물렀다가 해오고 있었다. 2 [T] to do or use first one thing and then the other ‖ 먼저 하나를 그 다음 다른 것을 하거나 사용하다. …을 교대로 하다[사용하다]: *Alternate the layers of pasta and meat sauce.* 파스타와 고기 소스 층을 번갈아 바꾸어라. – **alternation** /ˌɔltɚˈneɪʃən/ n [C, U]

alternate² adj 1 happening in a regular way, first one thing and then the other thing ‖ 처음에 한 가지가, 그리고 나서 다른 일이 규칙적으로 일어나는. 번갈아 일어나는: *alternate rain and sunshine* 번갈아 비가 왔다 개었다 함 2 able to be used instead of something or someone else ‖ 사물이나 다른 사람 대신에 사용될 수 있는. 대체의: *an alternate method of payment* 대체 지급 방법

alternative¹ /ɔlˈtɚnətɪv/ adj 1 an alternative plan, idea etc. can be used instead of another one ‖ 계획·생각 등이 다른 것 대신 사용될 수 있는. 대신[대체]의: *an alternative way home* 집으로 가는 다른 방법 2 an alternative system or solution is considered to be simpler or more natural than the old one ‖ 체제나 해결책이 옛 것보다 더 단순하거나 자연적인. 대체의. 새로운: *alternative sources of energy* 대체 에너지원 3 different from what is usual or accepted ‖ 일상적인 것이나 용인된 것과 다른: *alternative*

medicine 대체 의학 – **alternatively** adv

alternative² n something you can choose to do or use instead of something else ‖ 다른 것 대신에 선택해서 하거나 사용할 수 있는 것. 양자택일: *He has the alternative of living at home or renting an apartment.* 그는 집에서 사느냐 아파트를 빌리느냐의 선택 방안이 있다. / *There's no alternative to your plan.* 너의 계획에 대안은 없다. / *I have no alternative but to report you to the police.* 나는 너를 경찰에 신고하는 수밖에 없다.

USAGE NOTE alternative

Use **alternative** to talk about a choice between two things: *If we don't drive, what's the alternative?* We sometimes say "What are the alternatives?" when there are several choices, but many teachers think that this is incorrect.

alternative는 두 가지 것 중의 선택에 대하여 쓰인다: 우리가 차로 가지 않는다면 대안은 뭔데? 몇 가지 선택의 여지가 있을 때 때때로 우리는 "What are the alternatives?"라고 말하는데 많은 교사들은 이 표현을 (alternatives가 양자 택일을 뜻하므로) 그릇된 것으로 간주한다.

---

al·though /ɔlˈðoʊ/ conjunction 1 in spite of the fact that; though ‖ …이라는 사실임에도 불구하고; 비록 …일지라도: *Although the car's old, it still runs well.* 그 차는 오래되었지만 아직 잘 달린다. 2 but; HOWEVER ‖ 그러나; 🇺🇸 however: *Patty might have left, although I'm not sure.* 확신할 수는 없지만 패티가 떠났는지도 모른다. –see also THOUGH¹

al·ti·tude /ˈæltəˌtud/ n the height of something above sea level ‖ 해수면 위의 높이. 고도: *flying at high/low altitude* 높은[낮은] 고도로의 비행

alto /ˈæltoʊ/ n [C, U] a female singer with a low voice, or the line of a piece of music that this person sings ‖ 낮은 목소리를 지닌 여성 가수, 또는 저음 여성 가수가 노래하는 악곡부. 알토[저음 여성 가수](부)

al·to·geth·er /ˌɔltəˈgɛðɚ, ˈɔltəˌgɛðɚ/ adv 1 a word meaning "completely", used in order to emphasize what you are saying ‖ 말하고자 하는 바를 강조하는 데에 쓰이는 "완전히"라는 뜻의 단어: *Bradley seems to have disappeared altogether.* 브래들리는 완전히 자취를 감

춘 것 같다. **2** considering everything or the whole amount ‖ 전부 또는 전체의 양을 고려하여. 전부 합해서. 대체로: *There were five people altogether.* 전부 다섯 명이 있었다. / *It did rain a lot, but altogether it was a good trip.* 비가 많이 왔으나 대체로 좋은 여행이었다.

USAGE NOTE altogether and **all together**

Use **altogether** as an adverb to talk about the total amount or number of something: *There were 50 guests altogether at the wedding.* Use **all together** as an adjective phrase to say that things or people are together in a group: *Try to keep the pieces of the puzzle all together.*
altogether는 무엇의 총량이나 총수를 나타내는 부사로 쓰인다: 결혼식에는 통틀어 50명의 손님이 있었다. **all together**는 사물이나 사람이 떼를 지어 함께 있는 것을 말하는 형용사구로 쓰인다: 조각을 모두 합쳐서 퍼즐을 맞춰 보아라.

al·tru·ism /'æltru,ɪzəm/ *n* [U] the practice of thinking of the needs of other people before thinking of your own ‖ 자기 자신을 생각하기 전에 다른 사람들의 욕구를 생각하는 습관. 이타(利他)주의 **– altruist** *n* **– altruistic** /,æltru'ɪstɪk/ *adj*

a·lu·mi·num /ə'lumənəm/ *n* [U] a silver-white metal that is an ELEMENT, and that is light and easily bent ‖ 가볍고 잘 휘는 은백색의 금속 원소. 알루미늄

al·ways /'ɔlweɪz, -wiz, -wɪz/ *adv* **1** at all times, or each time ‖ 모든 경우에, 매번. 언제나. 항상: *Always lock the car doors at night in the city.* 도시에서는 밤에 항상 차 문을 잠그라. **2** for a very long time, or as long as you can remember ‖ 아주 오랫동안, 기억할 수 있는 한 오래. 줄곧. 영원히: *He said he'd always love her.* 그는 영원히 그녀를 사랑할 거라고 말했다. / *I've always wanted to go to China.* 나는 줄곧 중국에 가고 싶었다. **3** happening continuously, especially in an annoying way ‖ 특히 짜증스럽게 끊임없이 일어나는. 노상. 시종: *The stupid car is always breaking down!* 이 시시껄렁한 차는 노상 고장난단 말이야! **4 you could always**... SPOKEN said in order to make a polite suggestion ‖ 정중한 제안을 하는 데에 쓰여. 언제라도 …하다: *You could always try calling her.* 언제든지 그녀에게 전화를 걸어 보세요.

USAGE NOTE always

Use **always** between the auxiliary or modal verb and the main verb: *I can always tell when he's lying.* ✗DON'T SAY "I always can tell."✗ Use **always** after the verb "to be" when it is the main verb in a sentence: *The twins are always together.* ✗DON'T SAY "They always are together."✗
always는 조동사 또는 상태 동사와 본동사 사이에 쓰인다: 나는 그가 거짓말할 때면 항상 그것을 알 수 있다. (순서를 바꿔) "I always can tell."이라고는 하지 않는다. "be"가 문장의 본동사일 때 **always**는 "be" 다음에 쓰인다: 그 쌍둥이는 항상 함께 있다. (순서를 바꿔) "They always are together."라고는 하지 않는다.

AM /,eɪ 'ɛm·/ amplitude modulation; a system of broadcasting radio programs in which the strength of the radio waves varies ‖ amplitude modulation(진폭 변조)의 약어; 전파의 세기가 변화하는 라디오 프로그램의 방송 시스템 **—compare** FM

a.m. /,eɪ 'ɛm/ LATIN the abbreviation of "ante meridiem"; used after numbers to show times from MIDNIGHT until just before NOON ‖ ante meridiem(오전)의 약어; 자정부터 정오 바로 전까지의 시간을 나타내는 숫자 뒤에 쓰여: *I start work at 9:00 a.m.* 나는 오전 9시에 일을 시작한다. **—see also** P.M.

am /m, əm; *strong* æm/ the first person singular and present tense of the verb BE ‖ be동사의 1인칭 단수 현재 시제

a·mal·gam·ate /ə'mælgə,meɪt/ *v* [I, T] to join to form a bigger organization ‖ 결합하여 큰 조직이 되다. 합병하다[합병시키다] **– amalgamation** /ə,mælgə'meɪʃən/ *n* [C, U]

a·mass /ə'mæs/ *v* [T] to gather together or collect money or information in large amounts ‖ 돈이나 정보를 상당히 그러모으거나 수집하다. 축적하다: *amassing evidence for the case* 그 사건에 대한 축적된 증거

amateur¹ /'æmətʃə/ *adj* doing something for enjoyment, but not for money ‖ 돈 때문이 아니라 즐거움을 위하여 무엇을 하는. 아마추어의. 비전문가의: *an amateur boxer/musician* 아마추어 권투 선수[음악가]

amateur² *n* **1** someone who does something because they enjoy it, but not for money ‖ 돈 때문이 아니라 즐기기 때

문에 무엇을 하는 사람. 아마추어. 비전문가—compare PROFESSIONAL² **2** someone who does not have experience or skill in a particular activity‖특정 활동에 경험이나 기술이 없는 사람. 아마추어. 미숙자: *Don't have your tattoo done by an amateur.* 아마추어에게 네 문신을 맡기지 마라. – **amateurish** *adj*

a·maze /əˈmeɪz/ *v* [T] to make someone feel great surprise‖남을 깜짝 놀라게 하다. 대경실색케 하다: *The variety of food at the cafe never ceases to amaze me.* (=always surprises me) 카페에 있는 다양한 음식은 끊임없이 나를 놀라게 한다.

a·mazed /əˈmeɪzd/ *adj* **be amazed** to be very surprised‖몹시 놀라다. 대경실색하다: *We were amazed at how quickly the kids learned.* 우리는 그 아이들이 얼마나 빨리 배우는지 몹시 놀랐다. / *I'm amazed (that) you remember him.* 당신이 그를 기억한다니 놀랍다. / *We were amazed to hear/see that he was alive.* 우리는 그가 살아 있다는 것을 듣고[보고] 놀랐다.

a·maze·ment /əˈmeɪzmənt/ *n* [U] the state or feeling of being AMAZED‖놀란 상태나 느낌. 놀람. 대경실색: *We watched the dancers in/with amazement.* 우리는 깜짝 놀라서 그 무용가들을 지켜보았다.

a·maz·ing /əˈmeɪzɪŋ/ *adj* making someone feel very surprised‖사람을 매우 놀라게 하는. 놀라운: *The computers are absolutely amazing!* 그 컴퓨터들은 아주 놀랍군요!

a·maz·ing·ly /əˈmeɪzɪŋli/ *adv* in an AMAZING way‖놀랍게도. 기가 막히게: *an amazingly skilled athlete* 기가 막히게 숙련된 운동 선수 / *Amazingly enough, he lived to tell his story.* 아주 놀랍게도 그는 오래 살아 자신의 이야기를 들려 줬다.

am·bas·sa·dor /æmˈbæsədə, əm-/ *n* an important official who represents his/her country in another country‖타국에서 자기 나라를 대표하는 중요한 관리. 대사: *the Mexican ambassador to Canada* 주캐나다 멕시코 대사 – **ambassadorial** /æmˌbæsəˈdɔriəl/ *adj*

am·bi·ance, ambience /ˈæmbiəns, ˈɑmbiəns/ *n* [U] the way a place makes you feel‖느낌을 갖게 하는 장소의 형세. 분위기: *the restaurant's friendly ambiance* 그 레스토랑의 친근한 분위기

am·bi·dex·trous /ˌæmbɪˈdɛkstrəs/ *adj* able to use both hands with equal skill‖두 손을 같은 기량으로 쓸 수 있는. 양손잡이인

am·bi·gu·i·ty /ˌæmbəˈgyuɪti/ *n* [C, U]

the state of being AMBIGUOUS‖애매모호한 상태. 불명확함: *There were some ambiguities in the letter.* 그 편지에는 약간 애매모호한 것이 있었다. / *the ambiguity of her words* 그녀 말의 모호함

am·big·u·ous /æmˈbɪgyuəs/ *adj* an ambiguous remark, word etc. is not clear because it could have more than one meaning‖말·단어 등이 한 가지 이상의 뜻이 있어서 의미가 명확하지 않은. 모호한. 애매한 —opposite UNAMBIGUOUS

am·bi·tion /æmˈbɪʃən/ *n* **1** [U] the quality of being determined to succeed‖성공하기로 결심한 상태. 야망: *Saul has no ambition at all.* 사울은 야망이 전혀 없다. **2** a strong desire to do or achieve something‖무엇을 하거나 성취하려는 강한 욕구. 의욕. 열망: *Her ambition is to climb Mount Everest.* 그녀가 열망하는 것은 에베레스트 산을 등반하는 일이다.

am·bi·tious /æmˈbɪʃəs/ *adj* **1** needing a lot of skill and effort to achieve something‖일을 성취하기 위해 많은 기술과 노력을 필요로 하는. 야심적인. 의욕적인: *The goals we set were too ambitious.* 우리가 세운 목표는 너무 야심적이었다. **2** having a strong desire to be successful or powerful‖성공하거나 강하게 되고자 하는 강한 욕구가 있는. 야망이 있는: *He is young and very ambitious.* 그는 젊고 매우 야망에 차 있다. – **ambitiously** *adv*

am·biv·a·lent /æmˈbɪvələnt/ *adj* not sure whether you like something or not‖어떤 것이 좋은지 싫은지 확신이 서지 않는. 갈등을 느끼는. 양면 가치의: *I think Carla's ambivalent about getting married.* 나는 칼라가 결혼에 대해 갈등을 느끼고 있다고 나는 생각한다. – **ambivalence** *n* [U]

am·ble /ˈæmbəl/ *v* [I] to walk slowly in a relaxed way‖한가롭게 천천히 걷다: *He ambled down the street, smoking a cigarette.* 그는 담배를 피우면서 거리를 천천히 걸었다.

am·bu·lance /ˈæmbyələns/ *n* a special vehicle for taking sick or injured people to the hospital‖환자나 부상자를 병원으로 나르는 특수 차량. 앰뷸런스. 구급차

am·bush¹ /ˈæmbʊʃ/ *n* an attack against someone, in which the attackers have been hiding‖공격자가 숨어서 하는 남에 대한 공격. 매복 공격: *Two soldiers were killed in an ambush near the border.* 두 병사가 국경 부근에서 매복 공격으로 살해되었다.

ambush² *v* [T] to attack someone from

a place where you have been hiding ‖ 숨어 있는 곳에서 남을 공격하다. 매복하여 공격하다

a·me·lio·rate /ə'miːljəˌreɪt/ v [T] FORMAL to make something better ‖ 무엇을 더 낫게 만들다. 개선[개량]하다 – **amelioration** /əˌmiːljə'reɪʃən/ n [U]

a·men /ˌeɪ'mɛn, ˌɑ-/ interjection said at the end of a prayer to express agreement or the hope that it will be true ‖ 동의나 그렇게 되기를 바라는 희망을 나타내어 기도문 뒤에 쓰여. 아멘

a·me·na·ble /ə'miːnəbəl, ə'mɛ-/ adj willing to listen to or do something ‖ 기꺼이 무엇을 듣거나 하려고 하는. 기꺼이 따르는: *I'm sure they'll be amenable to your suggestions.* 그들이 너의 제안을 따를 것이라고 확신한다.

a·mend /ə'mɛnd/ v [T] to make small changes or improvements, especially in the words of a law ‖ 특히 법문(法文)을 약간 변경하거나 개선하다. 수정[개정]하다: *The statute has been amended several times.* 그 법령은 여러 번 개정되었다.

a·mend·ment /ə'mɛndmənt/ n [C, U] a change, especially in the words of a law ‖ 특히 법문(法文)의 개정. 수정(안): *an amendment to the new banking bill* 새 은행 법안의 수정

a·mends /ə'mɛndz/ n **make amends** to do something that shows you are sorry for something ‖ 어떤 것에 대하여 미안함을 보여 주는 일을 하다. 보상하다: *I tried to make amends by inviting him to lunch.* 나는 그를 점심 식사에 초대함으로써 보상하려 했다.

a·men·i·ty /ə'mɛnəti, ə'miː-/ n [C usually plural] something in a place that makes living there enjoyable and pleasant ‖ 생활을 즐겁고 유쾌하게 하는 장소에 있는 것. 위락 시설: *The hotel's amenities include a pool and two bars.* 호텔의 위락 시설에는 수영장과 두 개의 술집이 있다.

A·mer·i·can¹ /ə'mɛrɪkən/ n someone from the US ‖ 미국 출신의 사람. 미국인

American² adj relating to or coming from the US ‖ 미국에 관련된, 미국 출신의. 미국(산)의: *American cars* 미제 차

A·mer·i·ca·na /əˌmɛrə'kɑːnə/ n [U] objects, styles, stories etc. that are typical of America ‖ 미국을 대표하는 사물·양식·이야기 등. 미국에 관한 풍물[자료, 문헌]

American dream /ˌ.ˌ... '.ˌ/ n [singular] **the American Dream** belief that everyone in the US has the opportunity

to be successful if s/he works hard ‖ 미국에 있는 모든 사람이 열심히 일하면 성공할 기회가 있다는 신념. 아메리칸 드림

American In·di·an /ˌ.ˌ... '...ˌ/ n ⇨ NATIVE AMERICAN

A·mer·i·can·ism /ə'mɛrɪkəˌnɪzəm/ n an English word or phrase that is used in the US ‖ 미국에서 사용되는 영어 단어나 어구. 미국식 어법

A·mer·i·can·i·za·tion /əˌmɛrɪkənɪ'zeɪʃən/ n [U] change in a foreign society that is influenced by American values ‖ 미국의 가치에 의해 영향을 받는 외국 사회의 변화. 미국화: *They don't like the Americanization of European culture.* 그들은 유럽 문화의 미국화를 좋아하지 않는다.

A·mer·i·cas /ə'mɛrɪkəz/ n [plural] **the Americas** North, Central, and South America considered together as a whole ‖ 전체로 본 북·중앙·남아메리카

a·mi·a·ble /'eɪmiəbəl/ adj friendly and pleasant ‖ 우호적이며 유쾌한. 붙임성 있는: *an amiable child* 붙임성 있는 아이 – **amiably** adv

am·i·ca·ble /'æmɪkəbəl/ adj done without arguments ‖ 논쟁 없이 이루어진: *an amicable divorce* 원만한 이혼

a·mid /ə'mɪd/, **a·midst** /ə'mɪdst/ prep FORMAL among or in the middle of ‖ … 사이에, …의 한복판에: *surviving amid the horrors of World War I* 제1차 세계 대전의 공포 속에서의 생존

amiss /ə'mɪs/ adj **be amiss** FORMAL to be a problem or to be wrong ‖ 문제가 되다, 잘못되다: *She sensed something was amiss.* 그녀는 뭔가가 잘못되었다는 것을 감지했다.

am·mo /'æmoʊ/ n [U] INFORMAL ammunition ‖ 탄약

am·mo·nia /ə'moʊnjə/ n [U] a gas or liquid with a strong unpleasant smell, used in cleaning ‖ 세정용의 지독히 불쾌한 냄새가 나는 가스나 액체. 암모니아

am·mu·ni·tion /ˌæmjə'nɪʃən/ n [U] **1** things such as bullets, bombs etc. that are fired from guns ‖ 대포에서 발사되는 총탄·포탄 등. 탄약 **2** information that can be used in order to criticize someone ‖ 남을 비판하는 데에 쓰일 수 있는 정보: *The press has lots of ammunition to use against Ramirez.* 그 신문은 라미레즈를 반대하여 사용할 많은 정보가 있다.

am·ne·sia /æm'niːʒə/ n [U] the medical condition of not being able to remember anything ‖ 아무것도 기억할 수 없는 의학적 상태. 기억 상실

am·ne·si·ac /æm'nizi,æk, -ʒi-/ *n* someone with AMNESIA ‖ 기억 상실증 환자

am·nes·ty /'æmnəsti/ *n* [C, U] an official order forgiving criminals or freeing prisoners, especially people who have opposed the government ‖ 특히 정부에 반대한 범죄자를 용서하거나 죄수를 석방하는 공식적인 명령. 사면

a·moe·ba /ə'mibə/ *n* a very small creature that has only one cell ‖ 단 하나의 세포만 있는 아주 작은 생물. 아메바

a·mok /ə'mʌk, ə'mɑk/ *adv* **run amok** to behave or happen in an uncontrolled way ‖ 통제할 수 없게 행동하거나 발생하다. 날뛰다. 자제심을 잃다

a·mong /ə'mʌŋ/, **amongst** /ə'mʌŋst/ *prep* **1** in a particular group of people or things ‖ 사람이나 사물의 특정한 집단에서: *rising unemployment among men under 25* 25세 미만의 남성들 사이에 증가하는 실업 / *Relax, you're among friends here.* 마음 놓아, 친구들이 여기 함께 있으니까. / *They were talking amongst themselves.* (=a group of people were talking) 그들은 저희들끼리 이야기하고 있었다. **2** in the middle of, through, or between ‖ …의 한가운데에, …을 뚫고, …사이에: *We looked for the watch among the bushes.* 우리는 덤불 속에서 시계를 찾았다. / *He stood among the huge piles of papers, frowning.* 그는 눈살을 찌푸리며 거대한 종이 더미 사이에 서 있었다. **3** used when mentioning one or two people or things from a larger group ‖ 큰 그룹에서 한두 사람이나 물건을 언급할 때에 쓰여. …중에서: *Swimming and diving are among the most popular Olympic events.* 수영과 다이빙은 가장 인기 있는 올림픽 종목 중의 하나이다. / *We discussed, among other things, ways to raise money.* 우리는 특히 돈을 마련하는 방법을 토의했다.

a·mor·al /eɪ'mɔrəl, -'mɑr-/ *adj* not moral ‖ 도덕적이지 않은. 도덕 관념이 없는: *amoral actions/behavior* 도덕 관념이 없는 행동[행실]

a·mor·ous /'æmərəs/ *adj* full of sexual desire or feelings of love ‖ 성적 욕구나 사랑에 대한 감정으로 가득한. 호색적인. 사랑[애정]을 느끼는

a·mor·phous /ə'mɔrfəs/ *adj* FORMAL without a fixed form or shape, or without clear organization ‖ 일정한 형태[모양, 뚜렷한 조직]가 없는. 무정형(無定形)의. 무조직의

a·mount[1] /ə'maʊnt/ *n* how much of something there is, or how much is needed ‖ 사물이 있거나 필요한 정도. 양. 액수: *I was surprised at the large amount of trash on the streets.* 나는 거리의 엄청난 쓰레기의 양에 놀랐다. / *Please pay the full amount.* 전액을 지불하세요.

USAGE NOTE amount and number

Use **amount** with uncountable nouns: *a large amount of money*. Use **number** with countable nouns: *a number of cities*
amount는 불가산 명사와 함께 쓰인다: 많은 양의 돈. **number**는 가산 명사와 함께 쓰인다: 수많은 도시

---

amount[2] *v*

amount to sth *phr v* [T] **1 amount to sth** to mean something without saying it directly ‖ 직접적으로 말하지 않고 어떤 것을 나타내다. …과 마찬가지다: *What he said amounted to an apology.* 그가 한 말은 사과나 다름없다. **2** to add up to a total of a particular amount ‖ 특정 양의 합계에 추가하다. 총계가 …에 이르다: *Jenny's debts amount to over $1000.* 제니의 빚은 1,000달러 이상에 달한다.

amp /æmp/, **ampere** *n* a unit for measuring an electric current ‖ 전류를 측정하는 단위. 암페어(ampere)

am·per·sand /'æmpəsænd/ *n* [C] the sign '&'; a short way of writing 'and' ‖ &의 기호; 'and' 표기의 단축형

am·phet·a·mine /æm'fɛtə,min, -mɪn/ *n* [C, U] a drug that gives people more energy and makes them feel excited ‖ 사람에게 활력을 주고 흥분시키는 약물. 각성제

am·phib·i·an /æm'fɪbiən/ *n* an animal such as a FROG that can live on land and in water ‖ 땅 위에서도 물속에서도 살 수 있는 개구리 등의 동물. 양서류

am·phib·i·ous /æm'fɪbiəs/ *adj* **1** an amphibious vehicle can travel on land and water ‖ 차량이 육지와 수상에서 다닐 수 있는. 수륙 양용의 **2** an amphibious animal can live on land and in water ‖ 동물이 육상과 수중에서 살 수 있는. 양서류의

am·phi·the·a·ter /'æmfə,θiətə/ *n* a large structure with rows of seats that curve partly around a central space, used for performances ‖ 중앙의 공간 주위로 약간 곡선을 그리며 좌석이 배열된 공연용 대형 건축물. 원형극장[경기장]

am·ple /'æmpəl/ *adj* **1** more than enough ‖ 충분함 이상의. 넉넉한. 풍부한:

There's ample room in here for everyone. 여기에 모두를 수용할 수 있는 큰 방이 있다. **2 ample belly/bosom etc.** an expression meaning that a part of someone's body is large, used in order to be polite ‖ 신체 부위가 큰 것을 뜻하는 완곡한 표현. 풍만한 배/가슴 – **amply** *adv*

am·pli·fi·er /'æmplə,faɪərə/ *n* a piece of electronic equipment that makes an electrical sound signal stronger, so that it is loud enough to hear ‖ 전자음 신호를 강화시켜 크게 들리게 하는 전자 장비. 증폭기. 앰프

am·pli·fy /'æmplə,faɪ/ *v* [T] **1** to make something louder or stronger ‖ 무엇을 더 크거나 강하게 하다. 증대[강화]하다: *We may need to amplify your voice on the tape.* 테이프상의 당신 목소리를 키울 필요가 있을 것 같습니다. **2** FORMAL to explain something in more detail ‖ 무엇을 더 상세히 설명하다 – **amplification** /,æmpləfə'keɪʃən/ *n* [singular, U]

am·pu·tate /'æmpyə,teɪt/ *v* [I, T] to cut off a part of someone's body for medical reasons ‖ 의학적인 이유로 신체의 일부를 잘라내다. 절단하다 – **amputation** /,æmpyə'teɪʃən/ *n* [C, U]

am·pu·tee /,æmpyə'ti/ *n* someone who has a part of his/her body cut off for medical reasons ‖ 의학적인 이유로 신체 일부분을 잘라낸 사람

a·muck /ə'mʌk/ *adv* ⇨ AMOK

a·muse /ə'myuz/ *v* [T] **1** to make someone laugh or smile ‖ 누군가를 웃거나 미소짓게 하다. 유쾌하게 하다: *Harry's jokes always amused me.* 해리의 농담은 나를 항상 웃긴다. **2** to make the time pass in an enjoyable way for someone ‖ 누군가를 즐겁게 시간을 보내게 하다. 즐겁게 하다: *I've been trying to find ways to keep the kids amused.* 나는 아이들을 즐겁게 하는 방법을 찾기 위해 노력해 오고 있다.

a·muse·ment /ə'myuzmənt/ *n* **1** [U] the feeling you get when something makes you laugh or smile ‖ 어떤 것이 자신을 웃게 하거나 미소짓게 할 때 느끼는 감정. 즐거움: *"You're not asking me for help, are you?" she said with amusement.* "제게 도움을 청하는 게 아니죠, 그렇죠?"라고 그녀는 흥겹게 물었다. **2** [C, U] something such as a movie or a sports game that makes the time pass in an enjoyable way ‖ 즐겁게 시간을 보내게 하는 영화나 스포츠 경기 등의 것. 오락(물): *What do you do for amusement in this town?* 이 마을에서 당

신은 오락으로 뭘 합니까?

amusement park /.'.. ,./ *n* a large park where people can play games of skill, go on large rides, and see performances ‖ 솜씨 겨루기·대형 놀이 기구 타기·공연 관람을 할 수 있는 공원. 놀이동산. 유원지

a·mus·ing /ə'myuzɪŋ/ *adj* funny and entertaining ‖ 웃기고 재미있는. 즐거운: *I didn't find your comment amusing.* (=did not think it was funny) 저는 당신의 말이 재미있지 않았습니다.

an /ən; *strong* æn/ *determiner* a word meaning "a," used when the following word begins with a vowel sound ‖ 다음 단어가 모음으로 시작될 때 쓰이는 "a"를 의미하는 단어: *an orange* 오렌지 한 개 / *an X-ray of her chest* 그녀의 흉부 엑스레이 / *an hour before the movie* 영화 상영 한 시간 전 —see usage note at A

a·nach·ro·nism /ə'nækrə,nɪzəm/ *n* someone or something that is or seems to be in the wrong historical time ‖ 부적당한 역사적 시간에 있거나 있는 듯한 사람이나 사물. 시대 착오적인 사람[사물]: *Tourists in their modern clothes seem an anachronism in the tiny old town.* 그 작고 오래된 읍에서는 현대적인 옷을 입은 여행객들이 시대 착오적으로 보인다. – **anachronistic** /ə,nækrə'nɪstɪk/ *adj*

an·a·gram /'ænə,græm/ *n* a word or phrase made by changing the order of the letters in another word or phrase ‖ 철자의 순서를 바꾸어 다른 어구로 만든 어구. 전철(轉綴) 어구. 애너그램: *"Silent" is an anagram of "listen."* "silent"는 "listen"의 전철 어구이다.

a·nal /'eɪnl/ *n* relating to the ANUS ‖ 항문과 관련된. 항문의

an·al·ge·sic /,ænl'dʒizɪk/ *n* TECHNICAL a drug that reduces pain ‖ 통증을 줄이는 약. 진통제

a·nal·o·gous /ə'næləgəs/ *adj* FORMAL similar to another situation or thing ‖ 다른 상황이나 사물과 흡사한. 닮은. 유사한: *The system works in a way that is analogous to a large clock.* 그 시스템은 대형 시계와 유사한 방식으로 작동된다.

a·nal·o·gy /ə'nælədʒi/ *n* [C, U] a comparison between two situations, processes etc. that seem similar ‖ 비슷해 보이는 두 가지 상황·절차 사이의 비교. 유사(점): *We can **draw an analogy***

between the brain and a computer. 우리 는 뇌와 컴퓨터의 유사점을 유추할 수 있 다.

a·nal·y·sis /ə'næləsɪs/ *n* [C, U] **1** the careful examination of something in order to understand it better or explain what it consists of ‖ 어떤 것의 구성을 보 다 잘 이해하거나 설명하기 위한 주의깊은 조사. 분석: *an analysis of the test results* 테스트 결과의 분석 **2** ⇨ PSYCHOANALYSIS

analyst /'ænl-ɪst/ *n* **1** someone whose job is to ANALYZE things ‖ 사물을 분석하 는 직업인. 분석가: *a financial analyst* 재 정[금융] 분석가 **2** ⇨ PSYCHOANALYST

an·a·ly·tic·al /,ænl'ɪtɪkəl/, **analytic** *adj* using methods that help you examine things carefully ‖ 사물을 면밀히 조사하는 데에 도움이 되는 방법을 이용하 는. 분석적인: *an analytical mind* 분석력 / *an analytic method* 분석적 방법

an·al·yze /'ænl,aɪz/ *v* [T] **1** to examine or think about something carefully in order to understand it ‖ 어떤 것을 이해 하려고 면밀히 조사하거나 생각하다. 분석 하다: *We're trying to analyze what went wrong.* 우리는 무엇이 잘못되었는지를 분 석하려고 애쓰고 있다. / *The patient's blood is then tested and analyzed.* 환자 의 혈액은 곧 검사·분석되었다. **2** to examine someone's mental or emotional problems by using PSYCHOANALYSIS ‖ 정신 분석을 이용하여 정신적인 또는 정서적 문 제를 검사하다. 정신 분석하다

an·ar·chy /'ænəki/ *n* [U] **1** a situation in which no one obeys rules or laws ‖ 아 무도 규칙이나 법률을 지키지 않는 상태. 무법 상태: *Officials are worried that the fighting in the city could lead to anarchy.* 관리들은 도시에서의 싸움이 무 법 상태로 번지지 않을까 노심초사한다. **2** a situation in which there is no government in a country ‖ 국가에 정부가 없는 상태. 무정부 상태 – **anarchic** /æ'narkɪk/ *adj*

a·nath·e·ma /ə'næθəmə/ *n* [singular, U] FORMAL a thing or an idea which you hate because it is the opposite of what you believe ‖ 믿는 것과 반대되기 때문에 싫어하는 것 또는 생각. 증오[혐오]하는 사람[것]: *liberal values that were anathema to conservative voters* 보수적 인 유권자들에게 혐오스러웠던 자유주의 적 가치

a·nat·o·my /ə'nætəmi/ *n* **1** [U] the scientific study of the structure of the body ‖ 신체 구조에 대한 과학적인 연구. 해부학 **2** [C usually singular] the

structure of a living thing, organization, or social group, and how it works ‖ 생물 체[조직, 사회 집단]의 구조 및 작동 원리: *the anatomy of modern society* 현대 사 회의 구조 – **anatomical** /,ænə'tɑmɪkəl/ *adj*

an·ces·tor /'æn,sɛstə/ *n* a member of your family who lived in past times ‖ 과 거에 살았던 가족 구성원. 조상. 선조: *My ancestors were Italian.* 우리 조상은 이탈 리아인이었다. – **ancestral** /æn'sɛstrəl/ *adj* —compare DESCENDANT

an·ces·try /'æn,sɛstri/ *n* [U] the members of your family who lived in past times ‖ 과거에 살았던 가족 구성원 들. 조상. 선조: *people of Scottish ancestry* 스코틀랜드가(家) 사람들

an·chor[1] /'æŋkə/ *n* **1** someone who reads the news on television or radio and is in charge of the program ‖ 텔레비 전이나 라디오 뉴스를 읽어 주고 그 프로 그램을 책임지는 사람. 진행자. 앵커: *the local evening news anchor* 지역 저녁 뉴 스 진행자 **2** a heavy metal object that is lowered into the water to prevent a ship or boat from moving ‖ 배가 움직이는 것 을 막기 위해 물속에 가라앉히는 무거운 금속 물체. 닻

anchor[2] *v* [I, T] **1** to lower the anchor on a ship or boat to keep it from moving ‖ 배가 움직이지 못하게 배 위의 닻을 내 리다. 정박하다[시키다]: *Three tankers were anchored in the harbor.* 세 척의 유 조선이 항구에 정박해 있었다. **2** to fasten something firmly to something so that it cannot move ‖ 움직일 수 없도록 무엇을 단단히 고정하다: *The main rope anchors the tent to the ground.* 큰 밧줄이 천막을 땅에 고정시킨다.

an·chor·man /'æŋkəmən/, **an·chor·wom·an** /'æŋkə,wʊmən/ *n* ⇨ ANCHOR[1]

an·cho·vy /'æn,tʃoʊvi, -tʃə-, æn'tʃoʊvi/ *n* [C, U] a very small ocean fish that tastes very salty ‖ 매우 짠 맛이 나는 아 주 작은 바다 물고기. 멸치속(屬)의 작은 물고기

an·cient /'eɪnʃənt/ *adj* **1** happening or existing very far back in history ‖ 역사상 아주 오래 전에 일어났거나 존재한. 고대 의: *ancient Rome* 고대 로마 **2** HUMOROUS very old ‖ 매우 오래된. 낡은: *I parked my ancient little car next to a big new Jaguar.* 나는 내 작은 고물차를 큰 신형 재규어 옆에 주차시켰다. —compare ANTIQUE —see also OLD

and /ən, n, ənd; *strong* ænd/ *conjunction* **1** used in order to join two words or parts of sentences ‖ 두 개의 단어나 문구

를 이어주는 데에 쓰여. 그리고. …과: *a peanut butter and jelly sandwich* 땅콩 버터와 젤리 샌드위치 / *They have two kids, a boy and a girl.* 그들은 아이가 둘 인데 한 명은 아들이고 한 명은 딸이다. / *Martha is going to cook, and Tom is going to help her.* 마사가 요리하고 톰은 그녀를 도울 것이다. **2** used in order to say that one thing happens after another ‖ 어떤 일이 다른 일 다음에 일어 나는 것을 말하는 데에 쓰여: *Grant knocked and went in.* 할머니는 노크를 하고 안으로 들어갔다. **3** SPOKEN used instead of "to" after "come," "go," "try," and some other verbs ‖ "come," "go," "try" 등의 동사 뒤에서 to를 대신해 쓰여: *Try and finish your homework before dinner, okay?* 저녁 먹기 전에 숙 제를 끝내도록 노력해 보아라, 알겠니? / *A guy comes every Sunday and cuts my grass for me.* 한 남자가 나를 위해 잔디를 깎아 주려고 일요일마다 온다. **4** used when adding numbers ‖ 숫자를 더할 때 에 쓰여: *Six and four make ten.* 6 더하기 4는 10이다. / *a hundred and thirty dollars* 100달러 30센트 **5** used in order to say that one thing is caused by something else ‖ 어떤 일이 다른 일에 의 해 야기된 것임을 말하는 데에 쓰여: *I missed supper and I'm starving!* 저녁을 못 먹었더니 배가 고파 죽겠어!

an·dro·gyn·ous /æn'drɑdʒənəs/ *adj* **1** someone who is androgynous looks both female and male ‖ 사람이 남녀의 외형적 특성을 모두 가진. 남녀 양성의 **2** an androgynous plant or animal has both male and female parts ‖ 식물이나 동물이 암·수의 요소를 모두 가진. 자웅 동화(同花)[양성]의

an·droid /'ændrɔɪd/ *n* a ROBOT that looks completely human ‖ 인간과 똑같이 생긴 로봇

an·ec·dot·al /ˌænɪk'doʊtl/ *adj* consisting of stories based on someone's personal experience ‖ 개인적 경험에 기 초한 이야기로 구성된. 일화의. 일화적인: *The report is based on anecdotal evidence. It can't be called scientific!* 그 보고서는 일화적인 증거에 바탕을 두고 있 으니 과학적이라고 말할 수 없어!

an·ec·dote /'ænɪkˌdoʊt/ *n* a short interesting story about a particular person or event ‖ 특정 인물이나 사건에 관한 짧고 흥미로운 이야기. 일화

a·ne·mi·a /ə'nimiə/ *n* [U] the unhealthy condition of not having enough red cells in your blood ‖ 혈액 중의 적혈구 부족으 로 생기는 건강하지 않은 상태. 빈혈 –

anemic *adj*

an·es·the·sia /ˌænəs'θiʒə/ *n* [U] the use of ANESTHETICS in medicine ‖ 의학상 의 마취제의 사용. 마취

an·es·thet·ic /ˌænəs'θɛtɪk/ *n* [C, U] a drug that stops feelings of pain, used during a medical operation ‖ 수술할 때 에 쓰는 통증을 멈추게 하는 약물. 마취제: *local anesthetic* (=affecting part of your body) 국소[국부] 마취제 / *general anesthetic* (=affecting all of your body) 전신 마취제

an·es·thet·ist /ə'nɛsθəˌtɪst/ *n* someone whose job is to give ANESTHETIC to people in hospitals ‖ 병원에서 사람들에 게 마취제를 투여하는 직업인. 마취사

a·nes·the·tize /ə'nɛsθəˌtaɪz/ *v* [T] to make someone unable to feel pain or strong emotions ‖ 고통이나 강렬한 감정 을 느끼지 못하게 하다. …의 감각을 잃게 하다. 마취시키다

a·new /ə'nu/ *adv* LITERARY in a new or different way; again ‖ 새롭거나 다른 방 식으로; 다시: *She started life anew in New York.* 그녀는 뉴욕에서 새롭게 인생 을 시작했다.

an·gel /'eɪndʒəl/ *n* **1** a spirit who lives with God in heaven, usually represented as a person with wings and dressed in white ‖ 천상에서 신과 더불어 살며 보통 날개가 있고 흰 옷을 입은 사람의 형상을 한 영혼. 천사 **2** SPOKEN someone who is very kind or helpful ‖ 매우 친절한 도움을 주는 사람. 천사 같은 사람: *Oh, thanks! You're an angel!* 어머나, 고마워! 정말 친 절하네! – **angelic** /æn'dʒɛlɪk/ *adj*

an·ger¹ /'æŋgɚ/ *n* [U] a strong feeling of wanting to hurt or criticize someone because s/he has done something bad to you or been unkind to you ‖ 누군가가 자 신에게 나쁜 짓을 했거나 불친절하게 굴어 서 해를 끼치거나 비난하고 싶은 격한 느 낌. 화. 노여움: *Paul had punched the wall in anger.* 폴은 화가 나서 벽을 쳤다. / *I try not to react to her with anger.* 나 는 화난 상태로 그녀에게 응수하지 않으려 고 애쓴다.

anger² *v* [T] to make someone feel angry ‖ 누군가를 화나게 하다. 격노시키 다: *The court's decision angered environmentalists.* 법원의 판결은 환경론 자들을 격노시켰다.

an·gle¹ /'æŋgəl/ *n* **1** the space between two lines or surfaces that meet or cross each other, measured in degrees ‖ 서로 접하거나 교차하는 두 개의 선이나 면 사 이의 공간. 각(도): *an angle of 90 degrees* 90도 각도 / *a 45-degree angle*

45도 각도 —see also RIGHT ANGLE **2 at an angle** not upright or straight ‖ 곧거나 똑바르지 않은. 비스듬한: *The plant was growing at an angle.* 그 식물은 비스듬히 자라고 있었다. **3 a way of** considering a problem or situation ‖ 문제나 상황을 생각하는 방법. 관점. 견지: *We need to look at this from a new angle.* 우리는 이것을 새로운 각도에서 바라볼 필요가 있다.

angle² *v* [T] to turn or move something so that it is at an angle ‖ 무엇을 비스듬하게 돌리거나 움직이다. …의 각도로 맞추다: *You could angle the table away from the wall.* 테이블을 벽에서 떼어 비스듬하게 할 수 있다.

angle for sth *phr v* [T] to try to get something without asking for it directly ‖ 직접 요구하지 않으면서 무엇을 얻으려고 하다: *I think she's angling for an invitation to the party.* 내 생각에 그녀는 파티에 초대받으려고 술책을 쓰고 있다.

An·gli·can /'æŋglɪkən/ *adj* relating to the church of England a branch of the Christian religion ‖ 기독교의 한 분파인 영국 국교회와 관련된. 영국 국교회의 - **Anglican** *n*

an·gling /'æŋglɪŋ/ *n* [U] fishing with a hook and a line ‖ 낚싯바늘과 낚싯줄을 이용한 낚시질 - **angle** *v* [I] - **angler** *n*

an·go·ra /æŋ'gɔrə/ *n* [U] wool or thread made from the fur of some goats or rabbits ‖ 염소나 토끼의 털로 만든 모직이나 실

an·gry /'æŋgri/ *adj* feeling or showing anger ‖ 화를 느끼거나 드러내는. 성난. 화난: *I'm so angry with/at her!* 난 그녀에게 너무 화가 나! / *My parents were really angry about my bad grades.* 우리 부모님은 내 형편없는 성적 때문에 정말로 화가 나셨다. - **angrily** *adv*

angst /ɑŋst, 'æŋst/ *n* [U] strong feelings of anxiety and sadness because you are worried about your life ‖ 삶에 대한 걱정 때문에 생기는 근심이나 슬픔의 강한 느낌. 불안. 고민

an·guish /'æŋgwɪʃ/ *n* [U] very great pain or worry ‖ 심한 고통이나 걱정. 괴로움. 고뇌: *the anguish of the hostages' families* 인질들의 가족이 당하는 심한 고통 - **anguished** *adj* : *anguished cries for help* 도와 달라는 고통스러운 외침

an·gu·lar /'æŋgyələr/ *adj* **1** having sharp corners ‖ 날카로운 모서리를 지닌. 모가 나 있는. 뾰족한: *an angular shape* 모난 형태 **2** very thin, and without much flesh on your bones ‖ 매우 야위고 뼈에 살이 많지 않은. 깡마른: *a tall*

angular young man 키 크고 깡마른 청년

an·i·mal¹ /'ænəməl/ *n* **1** any living creature like a cow or dog, that is not a bird, insect, fish, or person ‖ 조류, 곤충류, 어류, 사람이 아닌 소나 개 같은 생물체. 동물. 포유류: *farm animals* 농장 동물 / *wild animals* 야생 동물 **2** any living creature that can move around ‖ 움직일 수 있는 생명체: *Humans are highly intelligent animals.* 인간은 매우 지적인 고등 동물이다. **3** INFORMAL someone who behaves in a cruel, violent, or rude way ‖ 잔인한[폭력적인, 무례한] 태도로 행동하는 사람. 비인간. 짐승: *Stay away from that crowd - they're a bunch of animals.* 저 군중에서 떨어져 있어. 그들은 한 무리의 짐승 같은 족속이야. —see also **party animal** (PARTY)

animal² *adj* **1** relating to or made from animals ‖ 동물과 관계된, 또는 동물에서 생겨난. 동물성의: *animal fats* 동물성 지방 **2 animal urges/instincts etc.** human feelings, desires etc. that relate to sex, food, and other basic needs ‖ 성·음식·다른 기본 욕구에 관련된 인간의 감정·욕망 등. 동물적 충동/본능

an·i·mate¹ /'ænə,meɪt/ *v* [T] to make something seem to have more life or energy ‖ 무엇을 더 많은 활기나 기운을 지닌 것처럼 보이게 하다. …을 생기 넘치게 하다: *Laughter animated his face.* 웃음은 그의 얼굴을 생기 있게 만들었다.

animate² /'ænəmɪt/ *adj* FORMAL living ‖ 살아 있는 —opposite INANIMATE

an·i·mat·ed /'ænə,meɪtɪd/ *adj* **1** full of interest and energy ‖ 흥미와 활기로 가득 찬. 활발한: *an animated debate* 활기찬 논쟁 **2 animated cartoon/film etc.** a movie in which pictures, clay models etc. seem to move and talk ‖ 그림·점토 모형 등이 움직이고 말하는 것처럼 보이는 영화. 애니메이션. 만화 영화 - **animatedly** *adv*

an·i·ma·tion /,ænə'meɪʃən/ *n* [U] **1** energy and excitement ‖ 활력 및 열기. 생기. 활기: *talking with animation* 활기찬 대담 **2** the process of making ANIMATED movies ‖ 애니메이션 제작 과정

an·i·mos·i·ty /,ænə'mɑsəti/ *n* [C, U] FORMAL strong dislike or hatred ‖ 강한 반감이나 증오. 적개심

an·kle /'æŋkəl/ *n* the joint between your foot and your leg ‖ 발과 다리의 연결 부분. 발목 —see picture at BODY

an·nals /'ænlz/ *n* [plural] **in the annals of** sth in the whole history of a particular subject ‖ 특정 주제에 관한 전체 역사에서. …의 역사상으로

an·nex¹ /ə'nɛks, 'ænɛks/ v [T] to take control of a country or area next to your own, especially by using force ‖ 특히 무력을 사용하여 한 국가나 인접 지역을 통제 하 다 . 병 합 하 다 **– annexation** /ˌænɪk'seɪʃən, ˌænɛk-/ n [C, U]

annex² n a separate building that has been added to a larger one ‖ 더 큰 건물에 부속된 별도의 건물. 증축물. 별관

an·ni·hi·late /ə'naɪəˌleɪt/ v [T] to destroy something or defeat someone completely ‖ 사물을 철저히 파괴시키다, 사람을 완전히 패배시키다. 전멸[절멸]시키 다 : *Both forts were nearly annihilated.* 양쪽 요새가 거의 전멸되었다. **– annihilation** /əˌnaɪə'leɪʃən/ n [U]

an·ni·ver·sa·ry /ˌænə'vəsəri/ n a date on which something important or special happened in an earlier year ‖ 예년에 중요하거나 특별한 일이 일어난 날. 기념일: *our wedding anniversary* 우리의 결혼 기념일 —compare BIRTHDAY

an·nounce /ə'naʊns/ v [T] 1 to officially and publicly tell people about something ‖ 사람들에게 공식적 및 공개적으로 무엇을 알리다. 발표[공지, 공표]하다: *The police announced that an arrest would be made within 24 hours.* 경찰은 24시간 이내에 검거할 것이라고 발표했다. 2 to say something in a loud or angry way ‖ 크거나 성난 소리로 무엇을 말하다: *Randy suddenly announced (that) he was leaving.* 랜디는 갑자기 떠나겠다고 말했다.

an·nounce·ment /ə'naʊnsmənt/ n 1 an official public statement ‖ 공식적이고 공개적인 진술: *We all waited for the captain to make an announcement.* 우리 모두는 선장이 공표하기를 기다렸다. / *I didn't hear the announcement that the store was closing.* 나는 그 가게가 문을 닫는다는 발표를 듣지 못했다. 2 [U] the act of telling people something publicly ‖ 사람들에게 무엇을 공개적으로 알리는 행위. 발표: *the announcement of the winners* 우승자 발표

an·nounc·er /ə'naʊnsɚ/ n someone who gives people news or tells them what is happening at an event, during a broadcast etc. ‖ 방송 등으로 사람들에게 뉴스를 제공하거나 일어나는 사건을 알리는 사람. 아나운서. 안내 방송자

an·noy /ə'nɔɪ/ v [T] to make someone feel slightly angry about something; IRRITATE ‖ 남을 무엇에 대해 약간 화나게 하다. 귀찮게 하다; 逮 irritate : *You're beginning to annoy me!* 당신은 날 성가시게 굴기 시작하는군요!

an·noy·ance /ə'nɔɪəns/ n 1 [U] the feeling of being slightly angry; IRRITATION ‖ 약간 화 난 느낌. 짜증; 逮 irritation : *Mia's annoyance never showed.* 미아는 결코 짜증을 내지 않았다. 2 something that makes you slightly angry ‖ 약간 화나게 하는 일: *The kids next door are a constant annoyance.* 옆집 아이들 때문에 계속 짜증이 난다.

an·noyed /ə'nɔɪd/ adj slightly angry ‖ 약간 화가 난: *I'm getting annoyed with her.* 나는 그녀 때문에 점점 짜증이 난다. / *Ben was annoyed at his mother.* 벤은 엄마에게 짜증이 났다. / *Joel is really annoyed about the mess we left.* 우리가 엉망으로 해 놓고 가서 조엘은 진짜 화가 났다. / *My sister's annoyed (that) we didn't call.* 우리가 전화하지 않아서 누이는 약간 화가 났다.

an·noy·ing /ə'nɔɪ-ɪŋ/ adj making you feel slightly angry; IRRITATING ‖ 약간 화나게 하는. 곤혹스럽게 하는; 逮 irritating: *an annoying habit* 짜증나는 습관 / *It's annoying that we didn't know about this before.* 우리가 전에 이를 몰랐다는 사실이 곤혹스럽다. **– annoyingly** adv

an·nu·al¹ /'ænyuəl/ adj 1 happening once a year ‖ 일년에 한 번 일어나는. 연간[연례]의: *the annual conference* 연례 회의 2 calculated over a period of one year ‖ 일년을 단위로 계산[산출]한: *my annual income* 나의 연간 수입 **– annually** adv

annual² n 1 a plant that lives for one year or season ‖ 1년이나 한 계절 동안 사는 식물 2 a book that is produced once a year with the same title but with different stories, pictures etc. that relate to that year ‖ 제목은 같으나 이야기·사진 등은 그 해에 관련된 것을 실은, 해마다 한 번 발간하는 책. 연감

an·nu·i·ty /ə'nuəti/ n an amount of money that is paid each year to someone, usually until they die ‖ 어떤 사람에게 죽을 때까지 매해 지급되는 금액. 연금

annul /ə'nʌl/ v -lled, -lling [T] TECHNICAL to officially state that a marriage or legal agreement no longer exists ‖ 결혼이나 법적 합의가 더 이상 존재하지 않는다는 것을 공식적으로 언명하다. 결혼·법률 등을 무효로 하다 **– annulment** n [C, U]

a·noint /ə'nɔɪnt/ v [T] to put oil or water on someone's head or body during a religious ceremony ‖ 종교 의식에서 사람의 머리나 몸에 기름이나 물을

바르다 - **anointment** n [C, U]

a·nom·a·ly /ə'nɑməli/ n [C, U] FORMAL something that is very noticeable because it is so different from what is usual ‖ 보통의 것과는 달라서 매우 눈에 띄는 것. 이례적인 것 : *Women firefighters are still an anomaly in a largely male profession.* 대개 남자들의 직업인 소방관 사이에 여자 소방관은 여전히 이례적이다.

a·non /ə'nɑn/ the written abbreviation of ANONYMOUS ‖ anonymous의 약어

a·non·ymi·ty /,ænə'nɪmɪti/ n [U] **1** the state of not having your name known ‖ 이름이 알려지지 않은 상태. 익명: *The author prefers anonymity.* 그 저자는 익명을 좋아한다. **2** the state of not having any unusual or interesting features ‖ 특이하거나 흥미로운 특징을 갖지 않은 상태. 평범한 상태: *the drab anonymity of the city* 도시의 단조로운 평범함

a·non·y·mous /ə'nɑnəməs/ adj **1** not known by name ‖ 이름이 알려지지 않은. 무명의: *an anonymous writer* 무명 작가 **2** done, made, or given by someone whose name is not known ‖ 이름을 모르는 사람이 행한[만든, 제공한]: *an anonymous letter* 익명의 편지 **3** without interesting features or qualities ‖ 흥미로운 특징이나 속성이 없는. 개성 없는: *an anonymous black car* 개성 없는 검정색 차 - **anonymously** adv

a·no·rex·i·a /,ænə'rɛksiə/ n [U] a mental illness that makes people stop eating ‖ 먹는 것을 중단하게 하는 정신병. 신경성 식욕 결핍증. 식욕 부진

a·no·rex·ic /,ænə'rɛksɪk/ adj having ANOREXIA, or relating to anorexia ‖ 식욕 결여증이 있는, 식욕 결여증에 관계된. 식욕 감퇴[부진]의 - **anorexic** n

an·oth·er /ə'nʌðɚ/ determiner, pron **1** one more person or thing of the same kind ‖ 같은 종류에서 또 한 사람이나 또 하나: *Do you want another beer?* 맥주 한 잔 더 드실래요? / *I'll cancel that check and send you another.* 그 수표는 취소하고 다른 수표를 보내겠습니다. **2** a different person or thing ‖ 다른 사람이나 사물: *Is there another room we could use?* 우리가 사용할 수 있는 또 다른 방이 있습니까? / *You'll just have to find another job.* 너는 다른 직업을 구해야 할 거야. **3** something in addition to a particular amount, distance, period of time etc. ‖ 일정한 양·거리·기간 등에 덧붙여지는 것: *We'll wait another ten minutes.* 우리는 10분 더 기다릴 것이다. —see also **one after the other/one**

after another (ONE²), ONE ANOTHER — see usage note at OTHER¹

an·swer¹ /'ænsɚ/ v **1** [I, T] to reply to something that someone has asked or written ‖ 질문이나 편지에 답하다. 대답하다: *I can't really answer your question.* 당신의 질문에 정말 대답할 수가 없습니다. / *Why don't you answer me?* 왜 제게 대답을 하지 않으시죠? / *He answered that he did not know.* 그는 몰랐다고 대답했다. **2** to reply to a question in a test, competition etc. ‖ 시험·시합 등에서 문제에 답하다: *Please answer questions 1-20.* 문제 1번에서 20번까지 답하시오. **3** **answer the telephone/door** to pick up the telephone when it rings or go to the door when someone knocks or rings a bell ‖ 전화벨이 울릴 때 수화기를 들거나 누군가가 노크하거나 초인종을 울릴 때에 문쪽으로 가다. **4** to react to something that someone else has done ‖ 다른 사람이 한 일에 대해 반응하다. …으로 보답하다: *The army answered by firing into the crowd.* 군대는 군중을 향해 발포하는 것으로 응수했다.

answer back phr v [I, T] to reply to someone in a rude way ‖ 무례하게 대답하다. 말대꾸하다: *Don't answer back, young man!* 말대꾸하지 말게, 젊은이!

answer for sth phr v [T] **1** to explain why you did something or why something happened, and be punished if necessary ‖ 어떤 일을 한 이유나 일이 일어난 이유를 설명하고 필요하다면 처벌받다. 해명[보상]하다. 책임지다: *One day you'll have to answer for this.* 언젠가는 이 일에 대해 해명해야 할 것입니다. / *That sister of yours has a lot to answer for.* 당신의 저 누이는 해명해야 할 것이 많습니다. **2** **answer for sb/sth** to say you are sure that someone will do something or that s/he has particular qualities ‖ 어떤 사람이 무엇을 할 것이라고 또는 특정한 자질이 있다고 확신하여 말하다. 보증[확증]하다: *I can answer for his honesty.* 저는 그가 정직하다는 것을 보장할 수 있습니다.

answer to sb phr v to be judged by someone, especially someone you work for ‖ 특히 상사로부터 평가받다: *Wharton doesn't answer to anyone.* 와튼은 누구에게도 평가받지 않는다.

USAGE NOTE answer, reply, respond

When you are asked a question you can **answer** or **reply**: *"Are you coming?" "Yes," he replied. / She* *reluctantly answered his question.* ✗DON'T SAY "answered to his question."✗ **Respond** means the same thing, but it is more formal: *We would like to thank everyone who responded to our survey.* 질문을 받으면 대답(**answer**나 **reply**) 할 수 있다: "올 거니?" "그래." 하고 그 는 대답했다. / 그녀는 그의 질문에 머뭇 거리며 대답했다. "answerd to his question"이 라고는 하지 않는다. **respond**도 같은 뜻이지만 보다 격식 적이다: 우리의 설문에 응해 주신 여러 분께 감사의 말씀을 드립니다.

answer[2] *n* **1** [C, U] a reply to what someone asks or writes ‖ 질문이나 편지 에 대한 대답. 응답. 답변: *Give me an answer as soon as possible.* 가능한 한 빨리 대답해 주세요. / *I told you before, the answer is no!* 저번에 아니라고 대답 했잖아요! / *In answer to your question, I think Paul's right.* 당신의 질문에 답하 자면, 저는 폴이 맞다고 생각해요. **2** a reply to a question in a test, competition etc. ‖ 시험·시합 등에서의 문제에 대한 대 답: *What was the answer to question 7?* 7번 문제의 답이 무엇이었습니까? **3** something that you get as a result of thinking or calculating with numbers ‖ 숫자를 암산하거나 계산하여 얻어진 결과. 답: *The answer is 255.* 답은 255이다. **4** something that solves a problem ‖ 문제 를 해결하는 것. 해결책: *A new car would be the answer to all our problems.* 새 차 가 우리의 모든 문제를 해결해 줄 것이다. **5** a reaction to something ‖ 무엇에 대한 반응: *Jim's answer to their threat was to run.* 그들의 위협에 대한 짐의 반응은 도망가는 것이다.

an·swer·a·ble /ˈænsərəbəl/ *adj* **be answerable (to sb) for sth** to have to explain your actions to someone ‖ 남에 게 자신의 행동을 해명해야 하다: *You're all answerable for anything that goes wrong.* 당신은 잘못된 일에 대해 모두 해 명해야 한다.

an·swer·ing ma·chine /ˈ... .,./ *n* a machine that records your telephone calls when you cannot answer them ‖ 전 화를 받을 수 없을 때 걸려온 전화를 녹음 하는 기계. 자동 응답기

ant /ænt/ *n* a common small black or red insect that lives in groups ‖ 떼지어 사는 검은색 또는 붉은색의 작고 흔한 곤 충. 개미

an·tac·id /ˌæntˈæsɪd/ *n* a drug that gets rid of the burning feeling in your stomach when you have eaten too much, drunk too much alcohol etc. ‖ 과 식·과음했을 때 위의 쓰라린 느낌을 없애 주는 약물. 산중화제. 제산제

an·tag·o·nism /ænˈtægə,nɪzəm/ *n* [U] strong opposition to or hatred of someone else ‖ 남에 대한 강한 반감이나 적 대 감 . 적 개 심 . 반 목: *Polucci's antagonism towards the press is obvious.* 폴루치는 언론에 대한 적대감을 갖고 있는 것이 분명하다. / *There has always been antagonism between the two groups.* 그 두 집단 사이에는 항상 반 목이 있어 왔다.

an·tag·o·nist /ænˈtægə,nɪst/ *n* your opponent in an argument, fight etc. ‖ 논 쟁·싸움 등에서의 반대자. 적대자

an·tag·o·nis·tic /æn,tægəˈnɪstɪk/ *adj* showing opposition to or hatred of someone or something ‖ 무엇에 대한 반 감이나 적의를 드러내는. 대립하는. 적대 적인: *His reactions to the teacher's questions were always antagonistic.* 선 생님의 질문에 대한 그의 반응은 항상 적 대적이다. – **antagonistically** *adv*

an·tag·o·nize /ænˈtægə,naɪz/ *v* [T] to make someone feel angry with you ‖ 남 을 화나게 하다. 적의를 품게 하다. 반감 을 사다: *Don't try to antagonize me.* 나 에게 반감을 갖게 하지 마라.

Ant·arc·tic /æntˈɑrktɪk, æntˈɑrtɪk/ *n* **the Antarctic** the very cold, most southern part of the world ‖ 매우 추운 지구의 최남단. 남극 – **antarctic** *adj*

Ant·arc·ti·ca /æntˈɑrktɪkə, -ˈɑrtɪkə/ *n* one of the seven CONTINENTs, that is the most southern area of land on earth ‖ 지 구 최남단의, 7대륙 중 하나. 남극 대륙

an·te /ˈænti/ *n* **up/raise the ante** to increase your demands or try to get more things from a situation ‖ 요구 사항 을 늘리거나 어떠한 상황에서 더 많은 것 을 얻으려 하다: *They've upped the ante by making a $120 million bid to buy the company.* 그들은 그 회사의 매입에 1억 2 천만 달러의 값을 입찰금을 올렸다.

ant·eat·er /ˈæntitɚ/ *n* an animal that has a very long nose and eats small insects ‖ 코가 아주 길며, 작은 곤충들을 잡아 먹는 동물. 개미핥기

an·te·lope /ˈæntəl,oʊp/ *n* an animal that has long horns, can run very fast, and is very graceful ‖ 긴 뿔이 있고, 매우 빨리 달리며, 기품이 있는 동물. 영양

an·ten·na /ænˈtɛnə/ *n* **1** a piece of equipment on a television, car, roof etc. for receiving or sending radio or television signals ‖ 라디오나 텔레비전의

전파를 수신 또는 송신하기 위해 텔레비전·차·지붕 등에 설치하는 장치. 안테나 **2** *plural* **antennae** one of two long thin things like hairs on an insect's head, that it uses to feel things ∥ 물체를 감지하는 데에 쓰는 머리카락처럼 생긴 곤충의 두 개의 길고 가는 것 중 하나. 더듬이

an·them /'ænθəm/ *n* **1** a formal or religious song ∥ 격식적 또는 종교적 노래. 성가 **2** a song that a particular group of people consider to be very important to them ∥ 특정 집단의 사람들이 자신들에게 매우 중요하다고 여기는 노래. 송가: *an anthem for our generation* 우리 세대의 송가

ant·hill /'ænt,hɪl/ *n* a small pile of dirt on the ground over the place where ANTs live ∥ 개미가 사는 땅 위의 작은 흙더미. 개미총. 개미탑

an·thol·o·gy /æn'θɑlədʒi/ *n* a set of stories, poems etc. by different people collected together in one book ∥ 여러 사람들이 쓴 소설·시 등을 한 권에 모아 놓은 것. 문집. 선집

an·thro·pol·o·gy /,ænθrə'pɑlədʒi/ *n* [U] the scientific study of people, their societies, beliefs etc. ∥ 사람·사회·신념 등에 대한 과학적인 연구. 인류학 – **anthropologist** *n* – **anthropological** /,ænθrəpə'lɑdʒɪkəl/ *adj*

an·ti·air·craft /,ænti'ɛrkræft/ *adj* able to be used against enemy aircraft ∥ 적기에 대항해 사용할 수 있는. 대공(對空)의: *antiaircraft missiles* 대공 미사일

an·ti·bi·ot·ic /,æntibaɪ'ɑtɪk, ,æntaɪ-/ *n* [C usually plural] a drug that is used in order to kill BACTERIA and cure infections ∥ 박테리아를 죽이고 감염의 치료에 쓰이는 약물. 항생 물질 – **antibiotic** *adj*

an·ti·bod·y /'ænti,bɑdi/ *n* a substance produced by your body to fight disease ∥ 질병과 싸우기 위해 몸에서 만들어지는 물질. 항체

an·tic·i·pate /æn'tɪsə,peɪt/ *v* [T] **1** to expect something to happen ∥ 어떤 것이 일어나리라고 예상하다: *They anticipate trouble when the factory opens up again.* 그들은 공장이 다시 가동될 때 발생할 문제를 예상하고 있다. / *It's anticipated that grain prices will fall.* 곡물 가격의 하락이 예상된다. **2** to expect that something will happen and do something to prepare for it or prevent it ∥ 무엇이 일어날 것을 예상하고 그것을 대비하거나 방지하다. 대책을 세우다: *We're trying to anticipate what questions we'll be asked.* 우리는 예상되

는 질문을 미리 준비하려 하고 있다. / *Anticipating that the enemy would cross the river, they destroyed the bridge.* 그들은 적이 다리를 건널 것을 예상하고, 다리를 파괴했다.

an·tic·i·pa·tion /æn,tɪsə'peɪʃən/ *n* [U] the act of expecting something to happen ∥ 무엇이 일어나리라는 예상. 예견 : *Roy bought a new car in anticipation of his promotion.* 로이는 승진될 것을 예상하고 새 차를 구입했다.

an·ti·cli·max /,ænti'klaɪmæks/ *n* [C, U] something that seems disappointing because it happens after something that was much better ∥ 훨씬 나은 일 다음에 일어나 실망스럽게 느껴지는 것. 맥빠지는 것: *After all the advertising, the concert itself was kind of an anticlimax.* 온갖 광고에도 불구하고 콘서트 자체는 실망스러웠다 – **anticlimactic** /,æntɪklaɪ'mæktɪk/ *adj*

antics /'æntɪks/ *n* [plural] behavior that seems strange, funny, silly, or annoying ∥ 이상하게[우스꽝스럽게, 엉뚱하게, 짜증나게] 보이는 행동. 기이한 행동: *Larry's antics last night really annoyed me.* 나는 지난 밤 래리의 이상한 행동 때문에 정말 화가 치솟았다.

an·ti·de·pres·sant /,æntidɪ'prɛsənt, ,æntaɪ-/ *n* [C, U] a drug used for treating DEPRESSION (=a mental illness that makes people very unhappy) ∥ 우울증을 치료하는 데에 쓰이는 약물. 항우울제 – **antidepressant** *adj*

an·ti·dote /'ænti,dout/ *n* **1** a substance that stops the effects of a poison ∥ 독의 작용을 멈추게 하는 물질. 해독제: *There's no antidote to these chemical weapons.* 이 화학 무기에 대한 해독제는 없다. **2** something that makes an unpleasant situation better ∥ 불쾌한 상황을 호전시키는 것. 방어[대항] 수단: *Laughter is one of the best antidotes to stress.* 웃음은 최고의 스트레스 해소법 중 하나이다.

an·ti·freeze /'ænti,friz/ *n* [U] a substance that is put in the water in car engines to stop it from freezing ∥ 자동차 엔진의 냉각수가 얼지 않도록 냉각수 안에 넣는 물질. 부동액

an·ti·his·ta·mine /,ænti'hɪstəmin, -mɪn/ *n* [C, U] a drug that is used for treating an ALLERGY or COLD (=common illness) ∥ 알레르기성 질환이나 감기 치료에 쓰이는 약물. 항히스타민제 – **antihistamine** *adj*

an·tip·a·thy /æn'tɪpəθi/ *n* [U] FORMAL a feeling of strong dislike or opposition ∥ 몹시 싫거나 반대하는 감정. 혐오. 반감

an·ti·per·spi·rant /ˌæntɪˈpɚspərənt/ n [U] a substance that prevents you from sweating (SWEAT) ‖ 땀흘림을 억제하는 물질. 발한 억제제

an·ti·quat·ed /ˈæntɪˌkweɪtɪd/ adj old-fashioned and not suitable for modern needs or conditions ‖ 구식이라 현대의 요구나 여건에 적합지 않은. 시대에 뒤진. 한물 간: antiquated laws 시대에 뒤진 법

an·tique /ænˈtik/ n a piece of furniture, jewelry etc. that is old and usually valuable ‖ 오래되어 보통 값이 비싼 가구·보석 등. 골동품: priceless antiques 아주 값비싼 골동품 – **antique** adj : an antique table 골동품 테이블 — compare ANCIENT

an·tiq·ui·ty /ænˈtɪkwəti/ n **1** [U] ancient times ‖ 고대의 시기. 아득한 옛날. 태고: a tradition that stretches back into antiquity 태고적으로 거슬러 올라가는 전통 **2** [U] the state of being very old ‖ 아주 오래된 상태: a building of great antiquity 아주 오래된 건물 **3** [C usually plural] a building or object made in ancient times ‖ 고대에 만들어진 건물이나 물건. 유적: a collection of Roman antiquities 로마 유적 모음[컬렉션]

an·ti-Sem·i·tism /ˌæntiˈsɛməˌtɪzəm, ˌæntaɪ-/ n [U] hatred of Jewish people ‖ 유대인들에 대한 증오. 반유대주의 – **anti-Semitic** /ˌæntisəˈmɪtɪk, ˌæntaɪ-/ adj

an·ti·sep·tic /ˌæntəˈsɛptɪk/ n a chemical substance that prevents a wound from becoming infected ‖ 상처의 감염을 막는 화학 물질. 소독[방부]제 – **antiseptic** adj : antiseptic lotion 살균 로션

an·ti·so·cial /ˌæntiˈsoʊʃəl, ˌæntaɪ-/ adj **1** unwilling to meet people and talk to them ‖ 사람을 만나고 대화하는 것을 꺼리는. 비사교적인: Jane's friendly, but her husband's a little antisocial. 제인은 친화적이지만, 그녀의 남편은 약간 비사교적이다. **2** not caring if you cause problems for other people ‖ 타인에게 문제를 야기시키는지에 신경쓰지 않는. 비우호적인. 반사회적인: Some people think smoking in public is antisocial. 공공 장소에서의 흡연이 반사회적이라 생각하는 사람들도 있다.

an·tith·e·sis /ænˈtɪθəsɪs/ n FORMAL the exact opposite of something ‖ 어떤 것의 정반대: Her style of writing is the antithesis of Dickens'. 그녀의 문체는 디킨스의 문체와 정반대이다.

an·ti·trust /ˌæntɪˈtrʌst, ˌæntaɪ-/ adj preventing one company from unfairly controlling prices ‖ 한 회사가 불공정하게 가격을 통제하는 것을 금지하는. 독점 금지의. 트러스트 반대의: antitrust laws 독점 금지법

ant·ler /ˈæntˡɚ/ n one of the two horns that look like tree branches on the head of animals such as DEER ‖ 수사슴 등의 동물의 머리에 난 나뭇가지처럼 생긴 두 개의 뿔 중 하나. 가지진 뿔

an·to·nym /ˈæntəˌnɪm/ n TECHNICAL a word that means the opposite of another word. For example, "war" is the antonym of "peace". ‖ 다른 단어와 정반대의 의미를 지닌 단어. 반의어. 예를 들어, "전쟁"은 "평화"의 반의어이다. — opposite SYNONYM

a·nus /ˈeɪnəs/ n the hole in your body through which solid waste leaves your BOWELs ‖ 고형 노폐물이 장(腸)에서 빠져나갈 때 통과하는 몸의 구멍. 항문

an·vil /ˈænvɪl/ n a heavy iron block on which pieces of metal are shaped using a hammer ‖ 망치로 금속의 모양을 만들 때 쓰는 무거운 철제 받침대. 모루

anx·i·e·ty /æŋˈzaɪəti/ n **1** [C, U] a strong feeling of worry about something ‖ 무엇에 대해 걱정하는 강한 느낌. 근심. 염려: fears and anxieties 두려움과 근심 / The public's anxiety about job security is increasing. 직업 안정에 대한 대중들의 근심이 커지고 있다. **2** [U] a feeling of wanting to do something very much, but being worried that you will not succeed ‖ 무엇을 몹시 하고 싶어하나 성공하지 못할 것을 걱정하는 마음. 갈망: In her anxiety to make us comfortable, she managed to make us nervous. 우리를 편하게 해 주겠다는 그녀의 갈망이 본의 아니게 우리를 초조하게 만들었다.

anx·ious /ˈæŋkʃəs, ˈæŋʃəs/ adj **1** very worried about something, or showing that you are worried ‖ 무엇에 대해서 매우 걱정하거나 걱정하는 모습을 보이는. 염려하는: June's anxious about the results of her blood test. 준은 자신의 혈액 검사 결과를 걱정하고 있다. / an anxious look 근심어린 표정 **2** feeling strongly that you want something to happen, especially in order to improve a bad situation ‖ 특히 나쁜 상황을 개선시키기 위해 어떤 일이 일어나기를 갈망하는: Ralph is anxious to prove that he can do the job. 랠프는 자신이 그 일을 할 수 있다는 것을 증명하고 싶어한다. / His parents were anxious that he be given another chance. 그의 부모님은 그가 한번 더 기회를 얻기를 갈망했다. —see usage note at NERVOUS

an·y¹ /'ɛni/ *quantifier, pron* **1** a word meaning "some," used in negative statements and questions ‖ 부정문·의문문에서 "some"을 의미하는 단어. 무슨. 어떤. 어느. 누군가. 약간. 아무것도. 아무도. 조금도: *Is there any coffee left?* 남은 커피 좀 있습니까? / *Do you want any?* 원하는 거라도 있니? / *I don't think that will make any difference.* 저는 그것이 어떤 영향도 미치지 않을 것이라고 생각합니다. / *Are any of Norm's relatives coming for Christmas?* 놈의 친척 중에 누군가 크리스마스에 옵니까? **2** used in order to say that it does not matter which person or thing you choose from a group ‖ 특정 그룹에서 어떤 사람이나 사물을 선택하든 상관없다고 말하는 데에 쓰여: *Any of the restaurants in Chinatown would be fine.* 차이나타운에 있는 어떤 식당이든 괜찮다. / *There are bad things about any job.* 어떤 직업에도 나쁜 점은 있다. —see also **in any case** (CASE¹), **at any rate** (RATE¹) —see usage notes at EITHER², SOME¹ —see study note on page 940

an·y² *adv* used in negative statements to mean "at all" ‖ 부정문에서 "at all"을 의하는 데에 쓰여. 전혀. 조금도: *I don't see how things could be any worse.* 나는 상황이 얼마나 더 악화될지 모르겠다. / *Sandra couldn't walk any farther without a rest.* 산드라는 휴식을 취하지 않고서는 조금도 더 걸을 수 없었다.

an·y·bod·y /'ɛni,bɑdi, -,bʌdi, -bədi/ *pron* INFORMAL ⇨ ANYONE —see usage notes at ANYONE, SOME¹

an·y·how /'ɛni,haʊ/ *adv* INFORMAL ⇨ ANYWAY

an·y·more /,ɛni'mɔr/ *adv* **not anymore** used in order to say that something happened or was true before, but is not now ‖ 예전에 일어났거나 사실이었던 것이 현재는 아니라고 말하는 데에 쓰여. 더 이상 ⋯아닌: *Frank doesn't live here anymore.* 프랭크는 이제는 여기에 살지 않는다.

an·y·one /'ɛni,wʌn, -wən/ *pron* **1** a word meaning "any person" or "any people," used when it does not matter exactly who ‖ 정확히 누구인지는 중요하지 않고 "어떤 사람"이나 "어떤 사람들"을 의미하는 단어. 누구나[라도]: *Anyone can learn to swim in just a few lessons.* 누구라도 몇 번만 교습을 받으면 수영을 배울 수 있다. / *Why would anyone want to do that?* 누가 왜 그것을 하고 싶겠는가? **2** used in questions and negative statements to mean "a person" ‖ 의문문·부정문에서 "a person"을 의미하는 데에 쓰여. 누군가. 아무도: *Is anyone home?* 집에 누구 있습니까? / *She'd just moved and didn't know anyone.* 그녀는 막 이사해서 아무도 몰랐다. —see usage note at PRONOUN

USAGE NOTE anyone and **anybody**

Use **anyone, someone, no one, anywhere, somewhere** and **nowhere** in all types of writing and in speech. We often use **anybody, somebody, nobody, anyplace, someplace** and **no place** in speech. They can also be used in informal writing, but not in formal writing.

anyone·someone·no one·anywhere·somewhere·nowhere는 모든 형태의 글과 말에서 사용할 수 있다. 말할 때는 종종 **anybody·somebody·nobody·anyplace·someplace·no place**를 사용하기도 한다. 이 단어들은 격식을 갖추지 않는 글에서도 사용할 수 있지만, 격식을 갖춘 글에서는 사용하지 않는다.

---

an·y·place /'ɛni,pleɪs/ *adv* INFORMAL ⇨ ANYWHERE —see usage note at ANYONE

an·y·thing /'ɛni,θɪŋ/ *pron* **1** used in questions and negative statements to mean "something" ‖ 의문문·부정문에서 "something"을 의미하는 데에 쓰여. 무언가. 아무것도: *Do you need anything from the store?* 가게에서 무엇인가 살 것이 있습니까? / *Her dad didn't know anything about it.* 그녀의 아버지는 그것에 대해 아무것도 몰랐다. **2** any thing, event, situation etc., when it does not matter exactly which ‖ 정확히 어떤 것인지 중요하지 않을 때, 어떤 것·사건·상황 등. 무엇이든: *That cat will eat anything.* 저 고양이는 아무거나 먹을 것이다. / *I could have told him almost anything, and he would have believed me.* 내가 그에게 무슨 말이든 거의 하기만 했더라면 그가 나를 믿었을 텐데. **3 or anything** SPOKEN said when there are several things or ideas that are possible ‖ 가능한 여러 가지 사물이나 생각이 있을 때에 쓰여. ⋯나 그 밖에 뭔가: *Do you want a Coke or anything?* 콜라든 뭐든 마실래? / *It wasn't like we were going steady or anything.* 우리는 서로 사귀거나 그런 사이는 아니었다. **4 anything like** used in questions and negative statements to mean "similar to" ‖ 의문문·부정문에서 "similar to"를 뜻하는 데에 쓰여. ⋯과 비

숫한. 유사한: *Carrie doesn't look anything like her sister.* 캐리는 자기 여동생과 전혀 닮지 않았다. **5 anything goes** used in order to say that anything is possible ‖ 무엇이든 가능하다는 것을 말하는 데에 쓰여: *Don't worry about what to wear – anything goes at Ben's parties.* 무엇을 입을지 걱정하지 마. 벤의 파티에는 아무 옷이나 괜찮아.

an·y·way /'ɛni,weɪ/ *adv* in spite of something ‖ 무엇에도 불구하고: *The bride's mother was sick, but they had the wedding anyway.* 신부의 어머니가 아픈데도 불구하고 그들은 결혼식을 했다.

SPOKEN PHRASES

1 used in order to continue a story or change the subject of a conversation ‖ 이야기를 계속하거나 화제를 바꾸는 데에 쓰여. 어쨌든. 아무튼: *I think she's Lori's age, but anyway, she just had a baby.* 나는 그녀가 로리 나이 정도 된다고 생각하지만 어쨌든 그녀는 아이를 가졌다. / *Anyway, where do you want to go for lunch?* 아무튼 점심 먹으러 어디 가고 싶니? **2** used when you are saying something to support what you have just said ‖ 방금 말한 것을 뒷받침할 말을 할 때에 쓰여: *We decided to sell it because nobody uses it anyway.* 아무도 그것을 쓰지 않아서 우리는 팔기로 결정했다. **3** used in order to find out the real reason for something ‖ 어떤 것에 대한 진짜 이유를 알아내는 데에 쓰여. 도대체: *What were you doing at his house anyway?* 그의 집에서 정말 뭘 하고 있었니?

an·y·where /'ɛni,wɛr/ *adv* **1** in or to any place, when it does not matter exactly where ‖ 정확히 어디인지는 중요하지 않을 때, 어디에서든[어디로든]: *Fly anywhere in the US for only $170 with this special offer.* 특별가 170달러만으로 미국 어디든 항공 여행 하세요. **2** used in questions and negative sentences to mean "somewhere" or "nowhere" ‖ 의문문·부정문에서 "somewhere"나 "nowhere"를 뜻하는 데에 쓰여. 어딘가에. 아무 데도: *I can't find my keys anywhere.* 나는 어디에서도 내 열쇠를 찾을 수가 없다. / *Are you going anywhere exciting on vacation this year?* 올 휴가 때는 어디 신나는 곳에 가십니까? **3 not anywhere near** not at all similar to something else ‖ 다른 것과 전혀 비슷하지 않은: *The new car doesn't have anywhere near the power our last one*

had. 새 차는 지난번 차의 동력에 전혀 미치지 못한다. **4 not get anywhere** SPOKEN to not be successful at something ‖ 무엇에 성공적이지 못하다: *I'm trying to set up a meeting, but I don't seem to be getting anywhere.* 나는 회의 준비를 하려고 하는데 잘 안되는 것 같다. —see usage note at ANYONE

a·part /ə'pɑrt/ *adv* **1** separated by distance or time ‖ 거리나 시간이 떨어져: *The two towns are 15 miles apart.* 두 마을은 15마일 떨어져 있다. / *Our birthdays are only two days apart.* 우리 생일은 불과 이틀 차이이다. / *We try to keep the cats apart as much as possible because they fight.* 고양이들이 싸워서 가능한 한 따로 떼어 놓으려 한다. **2** separated into many pieces ‖ 많은 조각으로 나뉘어져. 산산이: *He had to take the camera apart to fix it.* 그는 카메라를 수리하기 위해 낱낱이 분해해야 했다. —see also fall apart (FALL¹) **3 apart from a)** except for ‖ 제외하고: *Apart from a couple of spelling mistakes, your paper looks fine.* 몇 가지 틀린 철자만 제외하고 네 보고서는 괜찮아 보인다. **b)** in addition to ‖ …에 추가로. …이외에: *What do you do for fun? Apart from volleyball, I mean.* 놀이로 뭘 하시죠? 제 말은 배구 이외에 말이에요.

a·part·heid /ə'pɑrtaɪt, -teɪt, -taɪd/ *n* [U] a system in which the different races in a country are separated from each other ‖ 한 나라에서 다른 인종을 분리하는 제도. 아파르트헤이트

a·part·ment /ə'pɑrt'mənt/ *n* a place to live that consists of a set of rooms in a large building ‖ 큰 건물 내에 일련의 방들로 이뤄진 주거지. 아파트

apartment build·ing /.'.. ,./ *n* **apartment house** /.'.. ,./ a building that is divided into separate apartments ‖ 각각 분리된 아파트로 나뉘어진 건물 — see picture on page 945

apartment com·plex /.'.. ,./ *n* a group of apartment buildings built at the same time in the same area ‖ 같은 지역에 동시에 지어진 일단의 아파트 건물들. 아파트 단지

ap·a·thet·ic /,æpə'θɛtɪk/ *adj* not interested in something ‖ 어떤 것에 흥미가 없는. 무관심한: *Too many of our students are apathetic about learning.* 너무 많은 학생들이 학습에 무관심하다.

ap·a·thy /'æpəθi/ *n* [U] the feeling of not being interested in something or not caring about life ‖ 어떤 것에 흥미가 없거나 삶에 대해 신경쓰지 않는 마음 상태. 무

관심: *public apathy about the coming election* 다가오는 선거에 대한 대중의 무관심

ape /eɪp/ *n* **1** a large monkey without a tail or with a very short tail, such as a GORILLA ‖ 꼬리가 없거나 아주 짧은 꼬리가 달린 고릴라 등의 큰 원숭이. 유인원 **2 go ape/apeshit** SLANG to become very angry or excited ‖ 매우 화나거나 흥분하다

a·per·i·tif /ə,pɛrə'tif, ɑ-/ *n* a small alcoholic drink that you have before a meal ‖ 식전에 마시는 적은 양의 술. 아페리티프. 반주

ap·er·ture /'æpətʃə/ *n* a small opening, especially one that lets light into a camera ‖ 특히 카메라에 빛을 들여보내는 작은 구멍. 조리개

a·pex /'eɪpɛks/ *n* **1** the top or highest part of something ‖ 무엇의 꼭대기나 가장 높은 부분. 정점. 정상: *the apex of the pyramid* 피라미드의 꼭대기 **2** the most successful part of something ‖ 무엇의 최고로 잘된 부분. 극치. 절정: *the apex of her career* 그녀의 경력의 절정

aph·o·rism /'æfə,rɪzəm/ *n* a short expression that says something true ‖ 진실을 이야기하는 짤막한 표현. 금언. 경구

aph·ro·dis·i·ac /,æfrə'dizi,æk, -'dɪ-/ *n* a food or drug that makes someone feel sexual excitement ‖ 성적 흥분을 일으키는 음식이나 약물. 최음제 – **aphrodisiac** *adj*

a·piece /ə'pis/ *adv* each ‖ 각각: *Oranges are 20¢* apiece. (=for each one) 오렌지는 하나에 20센트이다. / *We gave $10 apiece for the gift.* (=each of us gave $10) 우리는 각자 선물값으로 10달러씩 냈다.

a·plomb /ə'plɑm, ə'plʌm/ *n* [U] FORMAL **with aplomb** in a confident or skillful way, especially in a difficult situation ‖ 특히 어려운 상황에서 자신있거나 노련하게: *She answered all their questions with great aplomb.* 그녀는 그들의 모든 질문에 아주 노련하게 답변했다.

a·po·ca·lypse /ə'pɑkəlɪps/ *n* [U] **1** a dangerous situation that results in great destruction, death, or harm ‖ 크나큰 파괴[죽음, 피해]를 일으키는 위험한 상황. 대참사 **2 the Apocalypse** the religious idea of the destruction and end of the world ‖ 세계의 파멸과 종말에 대한 종교적 사상. 요한 계시록 – **apocalyptic** /ə,pɑkə'lɪptɪk/ *adj*

a·po·lit·i·cal /,eɪpə'lɪtɪkəl/ *adj* not having any interest in or connection with politics ‖ 정치에 전혀 관심이나 관련

이 없는

a·pol·o·get·ic /ə,pɑlə'dʒɛtɪk/ *adj* showing or saying that you are sorry about something ‖ 무엇에 대한 미안함을 나타내거나 말하는. 미안해하는: *He was really apologetic about forgetting my birthday.* 그는 내 생일을 잊어버린 것에 대해 정말 미안해했다. – **apologetically** *adv*

a·pol·o·gize /ə'pɑlə,dʒaɪz/ *v* [I] to say that you are sorry about something that you have done, said etc. ‖ 자기가 한 행동·말 등에 대하여 미안하다고 말하다. 사과하다: *Shawn apologized for being mean.* 숀은 못되게 군 것에 대해 사과했다. / *Apologize to your sister now!* 지금 네 누나에게 사과해라!

USAGE NOTE apologizing

Say **I'm sorry** or **excuse me** when you make a small mistake: *I'm sorry – I didn't mean to step on your foot.* / *"You're blocking the entrance." "Oh, excuse me."* Use **I'm sorry** to apologize when you have done something wrong or upset someone: *I'm sorry about all the mess.* If you are late, say **I'm sorry** and give a reason: *I'm sorry I'm late. The traffic was bad.* In formal speech and writing, use **I apologize**: *I apologize for the inconvenience.*
사소한 실수를 한 경우에 **I'm sorry** 또는 **excuse me**라고 말한다: 미안합니다, 일부러 발을 밟으려고 한 것은 아니었습니다./"출입구를 막고 계시는군요." "아, 미안합니다." 잘못을 저지르거나 남을 화나게 한 경우, "**I'm sorry**"를 사용한다: 사방이 엉망진창이라 미안합니다. 지각한 경우 먼저 "**I'm sorry**"라고 말하고 나서 사유를 댄다: 늦어서 죄송합니다. 교통 사정이 안 좋았어요. 격식을 차린 말과 글에서는 **I apologize**를 쓴다: 불편을 드려 사과드립니다.

---

a·pol·o·gy /ə'pɑlədʒi/ *n, plural* **-ies** something that you say or write to show that you are sorry ‖ 미안함을 나타내는 말이나 글. 사과. 사죄: *I owe you an apology for snapping at you.* 불쑥 달려들어 죄송합니다. / *I hope you will accept my apology for missing our appointment.* 약속을 못 지킨 점에 대한 사과를 받아 주시기 바랍니다.

ap·o·plec·tic /,æpə'plɛktɪk/ *adj* **1** so angry you cannot control yourself ‖ 자제할 수 없을 정도로 화가 난. 성난 **2** seeming to have had a STROKE ‖ 발작이

있었던 것으로 보이는. 뇌졸중의. 중풍의

ap·o·plex·y /ˈæpəˌplɛksi/ *n* [U] ⇨ STROKE¹

a·pos·tle /əˈpɑsəl/ *n* **1** one of the 12 men chosen by Christ to teach his message ‖ 복음을 전파하도록 그리스도에게 선택된 12제자 중의 한 사람. 사도(使徒) **2** someone who believes strongly in a new idea and tries to persuade other people to believe it ‖ 새 사상을 열심히 믿고 타인에게 그것을 믿게 설득하는 사람. 전도자 – **apostolic** /ˌæpəˈstɑlɪk/ *adj*

a·pos·tro·phe /əˈpɑstrəfi/ *n* **1** the mark (') used in writing to show that one or more letters or figures are missing, such as don't (=do not)) or '96 (=1896/1996 etc.) ‖ don't나 '96 등에서와 같이 한 자 이상의 문자나 숫자가 생략되어 있음을 나타내는 문장 부호('). 생략 기호. 아포스트로피 **2** the same mark used before or after the letter "s" to show that something belongs or relates to someone ‖ "s" 앞이나 뒤에서 사물이 어떤 사람에게 소속되거나 연관된 것을 나타내는 데에 쓰이는 기호. 소유격 기호: *Mandy's coat* 맨디의 코트 / *the workers' strike* 근로자의 파업 **3** the same sign used before "s" to show the plural of letters and numbers ‖ "s" 앞에서 문자와 숫자의 복수를 나타내는 데에 쓰이는 기호. 복수 기호: *4 A's and 2 B's on my report card* 내 성적 통지표에 있는 A 학점 4개와 B 학점 2개

ap·pall /əˈpɔl/ *v* [T] to shock someone greatly ‖ 어떤 사람을 매우 놀라게 하다. 오싹하게 하다: *We were appalled at/by the treatment of the refugees.* 우리는 난민에 대한 대우에 경악했다.

ap·pall·ing /əˈpɔlɪŋ/ *adj* **1** shocking or terrible ‖ 놀랍거나 무서운. 오싹해지는: *animals kept in appalling conditions* 끔찍한 환경에 갇혀 있는 동물 **2** INFORMAL very bad ‖ 아주 나쁜. 지독한: *an appalling movie* 형편없는 영화 – **appallingly** *adv*

ap·pa·rat·us /ˌæpəˈrætəs, -ˈreɪtəs/ *n*, *plural* **apparatus** *or* **apparatuses** [C, U] a set of instruments, tools, machines etc. used for a particular purpose ‖ 특정한 목적에 쓰이는 한 벌의 기구·도구·기계 등. 장치. 설비: *an apparatus for breathing under water* 수중 호흡 장치

ap·par·el /əˈpærəl/ *n* [U] a word meaning clothing, used in stores ‖ 옷을 뜻하는, 가게에서 쓰는 용어. 의복: *men's/children's apparel* 남성[아동]복

ap·par·ent /əˈpærənt, əˈpɛr-/ *adj* **1** easily seen or understood ‖ 쉽게 보이거나 이해할 수 있는. 명백한. 흔히 알 수 있는: *Her embarrassment was apparent to everyone in the room.* 그녀가 당황하는 것을 그 방의 모든 사람들이 훤히 알 수 있었다. / *Suddenly for no apparent reason* (=without a clear reason) *he began to shout at her.* 갑자기 뚜렷한 이유도 없이 그는 그녀에게 소리치기 시작했다. **2** seeming to be true or real, although it may not really be ‖ 실제로는 아닐지도 모르지만 겉으로는 진실이나 사실인 듯한. 표면상의: *We were fooled by his apparent lack of fear.* 우리는 두려움을 모르는 그의 겉모습에 속았다.

ap·par·ent·ly /əˈpærəntˈli, əˈpɛr-/ *adv* **1** according to what you have heard is true, although you are not completely sure about it ‖ 완전히 확신할 수는 없지만 들은 사실에 따르면. 듣자니: *She apparently caught him in bed with another woman.* 듣기로는 그는 다른 여자와 동침하다가 그녀에게 들켰다. / *Apparently, Susan's living in Madrid now.* 듣자니 수잔은 지금 마드리드에 살고 있다. **2** according to the way something appears or someone looks, although it may not really be ‖ 사실이 아닐지는 몰라도 사물이나 사람이 겉으로 보이는 것에 따르면. 외관상으로: *We waited in apparently endless lines at the airport.* 우리는 공항에서 끝없이 보이는 줄을 기다렸다.

ap·pa·ri·tion /ˌæpəˈrɪʃən/ *n* ⇨ GHOST

ap·peal¹ /əˈpil/ *v* [I] **1** to make an urgent public request for money, information etc. ‖ 금전·정보 등에 대한 급한 공적 요구를 하다. 간청하다. 호소하다: *Police are appealing to the public for information.* 경찰은 일반 시민에게 제보해 달라고 호소하고 있다. / *The water company appealed to everyone to save water.* 수도 회사는 물을 아껴 쓰라고 모든 사람에게 호소했다. **2 appeal to sb** to seem attractive or interesting to someone ‖ 누군가에게 끌리거나 흥미있어 보이다: *The program should appeal to older viewers.* 그 프로그램은 노인 시청자들의 흥미를 끌 것이다. / *The clothes don't appeal to me.* 그 옷은 내 마음에 들지 않는다. **3** to make a request to a higher court to change the decision of a lower court ‖ 하급 법원 판결의 변경을 상급 법원에 요구하다. 상소하다: *The defense is certain to appeal against the conviction.* 피고측은 유죄 판결에 불복해서 상소할 것이 확실하다.

appeal² *n* **1** an urgent public request for money, information etc. ‖ 금전, 정보

등에 대한 긴급한 공적인 요구. 탄원. 호소: *UNICEF is launching* (=starting) *an appeal for the flood victims.* 유니세프 [유엔 아동 기금]는 수재민 돕기 호소에 나서고 있다. **2** [U] the quality that makes you like or want something ‖ 무엇을 좋아하거나 원하게 하는 속성. 매력: *sex appeal* 성적 매력 **3** [C, U] a request to a higher court to change the decision of a lower court ‖ 상급 법원에의 하급 법원의 판결 변경에 대한 요구. 상소: *an appeal to the Supreme Court* 대법원에의 상고

ap·peal·ing /əˈpiliŋ/ *adj* attractive or interesting ‖ 매력적인, 흥미있는: *I found his smile very appealing.* 나는 그의 미소가 아주 매력적으로 보였다. / *The package should make it more appealing to kids.* 포장은 아이들의 흥미를 더 자극해야 한다. **— appealingly** *adv —* opposite UNAPPEALING

ap·pear /əˈpɪr/ *v* [I] **1** to begin to be seen ‖ 눈에 띄기 시작하다. 나타나다: *Suddenly, clouds began to appear in the sky.* 갑자기 하늘에 구름이 끼기 시작했다. / *A face appeared at the window.* 어떤 얼굴이 창문가에 나타났다. **2** to seem ‖ …으로 보이다. …인 듯하다. …인 것 같다: *The man appeared to be dead.* 그 남자는 죽은 것 같았다. / *The noise appeared to come from the closet.* 그 소음은 벽장에서 나는 것 같았다. **3** to take part in a movie, television program, play etc. ‖ 영화·텔레비전 프로그램·연극 등에 참가하다. 출연하다: *He'll be appearing in a new Broadway musical this fall.* 그는 이번 가을에 새로운 브로드웨이 뮤지컬에 출연할 예정이다. **4** to happen, exist, or become available for the first time ‖ 세상에 처음 일어나거나 존재하거나 쓰이다: *Irving's novel is soon to appear in paperback.* 어빙의 소설이 곧 보급판으로 출간된다. **5** to be present officially, especially in a court of law ‖ 공무상 특히 법정에 나가다: *Foster had to appear before the Senate subcommittee to testify.* 포스터는 상원 소위원회에 증언하기 위해 출석해야 했다.

ap·pear·ance /əˈpɪrəns/ *n* **1** the way someone or something looks or seems to other people ‖ 사람이나 사물이 타인에게 보여지는 방식. 외관. 용모: *Here are six ways to improve your personal appearance.* 여기 개인의 외모를 향상시키는 여섯 가지 방법이 있다. / *The Christmas lights gave the house a festive appearance.* 크리스마스 조명은 집에 축제 분위기를 자아냈다. **2** an

arrival by someone or something ‖ 사람이나 사물의 도착. 출석. 출현: *the sudden appearance of several reporters at the hospital* 몇몇 기자들이 갑작스레 병원에 출현함 **3** the point at which something begins to exist or starts being used ‖ 어떤 것이 존재하거나 사용되기 시작하는 시점. 등장. 출현: *Viewing has increased since the appearance of cable TV.* 케이블 텔레비전의 등장 이래로 시청률이 증가했다. **4** a public performance in a film, play, concert etc. ‖ 영화·연극·콘서트 등의 공개적인 공연. 출연: *his first appearance on stage* 그의 첫 무대 출연 **5** the act of arriving at or attending an event because you think you should ‖ 해야 한다는 생각 때문에 행사에 도착하거나 참가하는 행위. 참석: *I put in an appearance at the wedding but did not stay long.* 결혼식에 참석했으나 오래 있지는 않았다.

ap·pease /əˈpiz/ *v* [T] to do something or give someone something to make him/her less angry ‖ 화를 덜 내게 남에게 무엇을 하거나 어떤 것을 주다. 진정시키다. 달래다: *We changed the title to appease the critics.* 우리는 비평가들을 진정시키려고 제목을 변경했다. **— appeasement** *n*

ap·pel·late /əˈpɛlɪt/ *adj* LAW able to change a decision that was made earlier in a court of law ‖ 이미 법원에서 선고한 판결을 변경할 수 있는. 항소[상고]의: *the appellate court* 항소[상고] 법원 / *an appellate judge* 항소[상고]심 판사

ap·pend /əˈpɛnd/ *v* [T] FORMAL to add something to a piece of writing ‖ 글[문서]에 무엇을 추가하다. 첨부하다: *Please see the conditions appended to this contract.* 이 계약서에 첨부된 조건을 참조하세요

ap·pend·age /əˈpɛndɪdʒ/ *n* something that is added or attached to something larger or more important ‖ 보다 크거나 중요한 것에 부가하거나 첨부하는 것. 첨가물. 부가물

ap·pen·di·ci·tis /əˌpɛndəˈsaɪtɪs/ *n* [U] an illness in which your APPENDIX swells and becomes painful ‖ 맹장이 부어 고통스러워지는 질병. 맹장염

ap·pen·dix /əˈpɛndɪks/ *n, plural* **appendixes** or **appendices** **1** a small organ in your body that has little or no use ‖ 쓸모가 적거나 없는 신체의 작은 기관. 맹장 **2** a part at the end of a book that has additional information ‖ 추가 정보가 들어 있는 책의 맨 끝 부분. 부록

ap·pe·tite /ˈæpəˌtaɪt/ *n* [C, U] a strong

desire or liking for something, especially food || 특히 음식에 대한 강렬한 욕구나 선호. 식욕: *Don't eat now, you'll ruin/spoil your appetite.* 지금은 먹지 마라, 네 식욕을 망친다[버린다]. / *Marcy seems to have lost her appetite for travel.* 마시는 여행을 하고픈 욕구를 잃어 버린 듯하다.

ap·pe·tiz·er /ˈæpə,taɪzɚ/ *n* a small dish of food served at the beginning of a meal || 식사 처음에 제공되는 적은 음식. 전채

ap·pe·tiz·ing /ˈæpə,taɪzɪŋ/ *adj* food that is appetizing looks or smells very good || 음식이 맛있어 보이거나 좋은 냄새가 나는. 식욕을 돋우는. 구미가 당기는

ap·plaud /əˈplɔd/ *v* [T] **1** to hit your open hands together to show that you have enjoyed a play, concert, speaker etc.; CLAP || 연극·콘서트·연사에게 즐거움을 표시하기 위해 손뼉을 치다. 박수 갈채하다; 윤 clap **2** FORMAL to express strong approval of an idea, plan etc. || 생각·계획 등에 대한 강력한 승인을 표현하다. 박수 갈채하다: *We applaud the company's efforts to improve safety.* 우리는 안전을 개선하려는 회사의 노력에 갈채를 보낸다.

ap·plause /əˈplɔz/ *n* [U] the sound of people hitting their hands together in order to show that they enjoy or approve of something || 어떤 것을 즐기거나 인정하는 것을 나타내기 위해 손뼉 치는 소리. 박수 갈채: *There was whistling and applause as the band got ready to play.* 악단이 연주를 시작하려 하자 휘파람과 박수 갈채가 터져 나왔다. / *Let's give Rodney a big round of applause!* 로드니에게 큰 박수 갈채를 보냅시다!

ap·ple /ˈæpəl/ *n* a hard round red or green fruit that is white inside, or the tree this fruit grows on || 속은 희며, 단단하고 둥근 붉거나 푸른 과일, 또는 이 과일이 자라는 나무. 사과. 사과나무 —see picture on page 944

ap·ple·sauce /ˈæpəl,sɔs/ *n* [U] a food made from crushed cooked apples || 사과를 으깨어 요리한 음식. 사과 소스

ap·pli·ance /əˈplaɪəns/ *n* a piece of electrical equipment such as a REFRIGERATOR or a DISHWASHER, used in people's homes || 가정용 냉장고나 식기 세척기 등의 전기 기구. 장치 —see usage note at MACHINE¹

ap·pli·ca·ble /ˈæplɪkəbəl, əˈplɪkəbəl/ *adj* **1** affecting a particular person, group, or situation || 특정한 사람[집단, 상황]에 영향을 주는. 적용할 수 있는:

*These tax laws are not **applicable to** foreigners.* 이 세법은 외국인들에게는 적용되지 않는다. **2** suitable for a particular situation || 특정 상황에 적합한: *That argument is not applicable here.* 그 논쟁은 이곳에서는 부적절하다.

ap·pli·cant /ˈæplɪkənt/ *n* someone who has formally asked for a job, place at a college etc., especially by writing a letter || 특히 문서를 작성하여, 일자리·대학 입학 등을 공식적으로 요청하는 사람. 지원자. 신청자

ap·pli·ca·tion /ˌæplɪˈkeɪʃən/ *n* **1** a formal, usually written, request for a job, place at a college etc. || 일자리·대학 입학 등을 위해 대개 문서로 작성한 공식 신청. 지원: *It took me three hours to fill in my Stanford application form.* 나는 스탠포드 대학 입학 지원서를 기재하는 데 3시간이 걸렸다. **2** a piece of SOFTWARE || 각각의 소프트웨어 **3** [C, U] the use of a machine, idea etc. for a practical purpose || 실용적 목적을 위한 기계·생각 등의 사용. 적용: *There are limits to the application of his theory.* 그의 이론을 적용하는 데는 한계가 있다. **4** [C, U] the act of putting something like paint, medicine etc. on to a surface || 페인트·약품 등을 표면에 바르기. 도포. 도장

application soft·ware /ˌ..ˈ.. ,../ *n* [U] TECHNICAL COMPUTER software that is designed for a particular use or user || 특정한 용도나 사용자용으로 설계된 컴퓨터 소프트웨어. 응용 프로그램

ap·pli·ca·tor /ˈæplɪ,keɪtɚ/ *n* a special brush or tool used for putting paint, glue, medicine etc. on something || 페인트·접착제·의약품 등을 바르는 데에 사용되는, 특수한 솔이나 도구. 도포구(塗布具): *It comes with its own special applicator.* 그것은 자체의 특수 도포 도구를 갖추고 있다.

ap·plied /əˈplaɪd/ *adj* a subject such as applied mathematics or applied science is studied for a practical purpose || 수학이나 과학 등의 과목이 실용적인 목적을 위해 연구되는. 응용의

ap·ply /əˈplaɪ/ *v* **1** [I] to make a formal, especially written, request for a job, place at a college etc. || 일자리·대학 입학 등을 공식적인 서면으로 신청하다. 지원하다: *Good luck applying for that job!* 그 일자리 지원에 행운이 있기를! **2** [I, T] to affect or be suitable for a particular person, group, or situation || 특정한 사람[집단, 상황]에 영향을 주거나 적합하다. 적용되다[하다]: *The 20% discount only applies to club members.* 20% 할인

은 클럽 회원들에게만 적용된다. **3** [T] to use a method, idea etc. in a particular situation, activity, or process ‖ 특정 상황[활동, 과정]에 방법·생각 등을 이용하다. 적용[응용]하다: *I should be able to apply what I'm learning now in my job.* 내가 지금 배우고 있는 것을 내 업무에 활용할 수 있을 것이다. **4** [T] to put something such as paint, medicine etc. on a surface ‖ 페인트·의약품 등을 표면에 바르다. 붙이다: *Be careful not to apply too much glue.* 아교를 너무 많이 바르지 않도록 조심하세요. **5** [T] **apply yourself (to sth)** to work very hard and very carefully, especially for a long time ‖ 특히 장시간 동안 매우 열심히 주의깊게 일하다. 전념[몰두]하다: *I wish John would apply himself a little more!* 나는 존이 좀 더 전념했으면 좋겠다!

ap·point /əˈpɔɪnt/ *v* [T] **1** to choose someone for a job, position, etc. ‖ 일자리·직위 등에 사람을 선발하다. 임용[임명]하다: *They've appointed a new principal at Ralston Elementary.* 그들은 랠스턴 초등학교의 새 교장을 임명했다. **2** FORMAL to arrange or decide a time or place for something to happen ‖ 일어날 일에 대한 시간이나 장소를 배정하거나 결정하다. 정하다: *Judge Bailey appointed a new time for the trial.* 베일리 판사는 새 공판 기일을 지정했다. – **appointed** *adj* : *We met at the appointed time.* 우리는 정해진 시간에 만났다.

ap·point·ee /ə̩pɔɪnˈti/ *n* someone who is chosen to do a particular job ‖ 특정 직무 수행을 위해 선택된 사람. 임명받은 사람. 피임명자: *a Presidential appointee* 대통령으로 임명된 자

ap·point·ment /əˈpɔɪntˈmənt/ *n* **1** a meeting that has been arranged for a particular time and place ‖ 특정한 시간·장소가 지정된 만남. 약속. 예약: *I'd like to make an appointment with Dr. Hanson.* (=arrange to see the doctor) 핸슨 의사와 진료 예약을 하고 싶습니다. / *I'm sorry I missed our appointment.* 약속을 지키지 못해서 미안합니다. (=did not go to meet someone) / *Roy is bad at keeping appointments.* (=remembering to meet people as arranged) 로이는 약속을 잘 안 지킨다. / *She had to call a client to cancel an appointment.* (=say she could not come) 약속을 취소하기 위해 그녀는 고객에게 전화를 해야 했다. **2** [C, U] the act of choosing someone for a job, position etc. ‖ 일자리·직위 등에 사람을 선발하는 행위. 임용: *the appointment of a new Supreme Court*

Justice 새 대법관의 임명 **3 by appointment** after arranging to meet at a particular time ‖ 특정 시간에 만나기로 정하고 나서. 약속을 하고: *Dr. Sutton will only see you by appointment.* 서턴 박사는 약속을 미리 해야만 만날 수 있다.

appointment book /.ˈ.. ͺ./ *n* a book you keep at work with a CALENDAR in it, in which you write meetings, events, and other things you plan to do ‖ 회의·행사·그 밖의 계획하고 있는 일들을 기재하는 달력이 붙어 있는 업무용 메모장. 스케줄 관리 수첩

ap·por·tion /əˈpɔrʃən/ *v* [T] FORMAL to decide how something should be divided between various people ‖ 여러 사람에게 어떻게 분배해야 하는가를 결정하다. 배분[할당]하다: *The district has to find a better way to apportion funds among schools.* 그 지역은 학교 간의 더 나은 기금 분배 방식을 찾아야 한다.

ap·prais·al /əˈpreɪzəl/ *n* [C, U] an official judgment about how valuable, effective, or successful someone or something is ‖ 사람이나 사물이 얼마나 가치 있는[능률적인, 성공적인]가에 대한 공식적인 판단. 감정. 평가: *You should get an appraisal of Grandma's watch.* (=find out how much it is worth) 너는 할머니의 시계 가격을 감정 받아야 한다.

ap·praise /əˈpreɪz/ *v* [T] to make an APPRAISAL of someone or something ‖ 사람이나 사물의 평가를 하다. 감정하다: *The furniture was appraised at $14,000.* 그 가구의 감정가는 14,000달러로 나왔다. / *We're waiting for the report before appraising the situation.* 우리는 상황 평가에 앞서 보고서를 기다리고 있다.

ap·pre·ci·a·ble /əˈpriʃəbəl/ *adj* large enough to be noticed, felt, or considered important ‖ 인식할[느낄, 중요하게 여길] 만큼 충분히 큰. 뚜렷한. 상당한: *There's been no appreciable change in the patient's condition.* 환자의 상태에 뚜렷한 변화가 없다.

ap·pre·ci·ate /əˈpriʃiˌeɪt/ *v* **1** [T] to be grateful for something ‖ 무엇에 대해 감사하다. 고맙게 여기다: *Mom really appreciated the flowers you sent.* 엄마는 네가 보낸 꽃을 정말로 고맙게 생각했다. **2** [T] to understand and enjoy the good qualities or value of something ‖ 어떤 것의 좋은 자질이나 가치를 이해하며 즐기다. …의 진가를 인정[감상]하다: *All the bad weather here makes me appreciate home.* 이곳의 온갖 나쁜 날씨로 인해 나는 가정의 소중함을 깨닫는다. **3 I would appreciate it if** used in order to politely ask for something ‖ 어떤 것을 정중하게 요청하는 데에 쓰여. …이라면 감사하겠습니다: *I'd really appreciate it if you could drive Kathy to school today.* 오늘 캐시를 학교에 태워다 주시면 정말 감사하겠습니다. **4** [T] to understand a difficult situation or problem ‖ 어려운 상황이나 문제점을 이해하다. 인식하다: *You don't seem to appreciate how hard this is for us.* 너는 이것이 우리에게 얼마나 어려운 일인지 인식하지 못하는 것 같다. **5** [I] to gradually increase in value ‖ 가치가 점차로 오르다: *Your investment should appreciate by 10% over the next five years.* 당신의 투자는 향후 5년 동안 그 가치가 10% 증가할 것이다. —opposite DEPRECIATE

ap·pre·ci·a·tion /ə͵priʃiˈeɪʃən, ə͵pri-/ *n* [singular, U] **1** something you say or do to thank someone or show you are grateful ‖ 남에게 감사하거나 감사 표시를 위한 말이나 행동. 감사. 사의: *I'd like to show/express my appreciation for everything you've done.* 당신이 한 모든 것에 대해 감사를 표하고 싶습니다. **2** an understanding of a difficult situation or problem ‖ 곤란한 상황이나 문제에 대한 이해. 인식: *I've gained a new appreciation of the problems Ellen has faced.* 나는 엘렌이 직면한 문제점들을 새롭게 인식했다. **3** the enjoyment you feel when you recognize the good qualities of something ‖ 무엇의 우수성에 대해서 인식할 때 느끼는 기쁨. 음미. 감상: *As he grew older, his appreciation for his home town grew.* 그는 나이가 듦에 따라 고향의 진가를 더욱 인식해 갔다. **4** a rise in the value of something ‖ 무엇의 가치 상승: *the appreciation of the dollar against the yen* 엔화에 대한 달러화(貨)의 가치 상승

ap·pre·cia·tive /əˈpriʃətɪv/ *adj* feeling or showing admiration or thanks ‖ 감탄이나 감사를 느끼거나 나타내는. 진가를 인정하는. 감사하는 - **appreciatively** *adv*

ap·pre·hend /͵æpriˈhɛnd/ *v* [T] FORMAL to find a criminal and take him/her to prison; ARREST ‖ 범법자를 찾아서 교도소에 보내다. 체포하다; 웬 arrest

ap·pre·hen·sion /͵æpriˈhɛnʃən/ *n* [U] **1** anxiety or fear, especially about the future ‖ 특히 미래에 대한 걱정이나 두려움: *News of the plane crash increased Tim's apprehension about flying.* 비행기 추락 뉴스는 항공기 여행에 대한 팀의 불안을 가중시켰다. **2** [C, U] FORMAL the act

of catching a criminal ‖ 범인을 붙잡는 행위. 체포

ap·pre·hen·sive /͵æpriˈhɛnsɪv/ *adj* worried or anxious, especially about the future ‖ 특히 미래에 대해 걱정하거나 우려하는. 불안한. 두려워하는: *She felt apprehensive at the thought of Mark's reaction.* 그녀는 마크의 반응을 생각만 해도 걱정이 앞섰다. - **apprehensively** *adv*

ap·pren·tice /əˈprɛntɪs/ *n* someone who works for an employer for an agreed amount of time, usually for low pay, in order to learn a particular skill ‖ 특정한 기술을 습득하기 위해 보통 저임금으로 합의된 시간 동안 고용주를 위해 일하는 사람. 견습공.

ap·pren·tice·ship /əˈprɛntɪ͵ʃɪp/ *n* [C, U] the job of being an APPRENTICE, or the time spent as one ‖ 견습공의 직분이나 견습공으로 보내는 시간. 견습공 신분 [기간]

ap·prise /əˈpraɪz/ *v* [T] FORMAL to formally or officially tell someone about something ‖ 남에게 무엇에 대해 격식을 갖추거나 공식적으로 말하다. 통지하다: *Mrs. Bellamy has been apprised of the situation.* 벨라미 여사는 그 상황에 대해 통고받았다.

ap·proach¹ /əˈproʊtʃ/ *v* **1** [I, T] to move closer to someone or something ‖ 사람이나 사물에 더 가까이 이동하다. 접근하다: *We watched as their car approached.* 우리는 그들의 차가 접근하는 것을 지켜보았다. / *A man approached me, asking if I'd seen a little girl.* 한 남자가 나에게 다가와서 작은 소녀를 보았는지 물었다. **2** [T] to ask someone for something when you are not sure if s/he will do what you want ‖ 자신이 원하는 것을 상대가 해줄지 확실치 않을 때 그에 대해 청하다: *She's been approached by two schools about teaching jobs.* 그녀는 두 학교에서 교직에 대한 제안을 받았다. **3** [I, T] to almost be a particular time, age, amount, temperature etc. ‖ 특정 시간·나이·양·온도 등에 가까워지다: *It's now approaching seven o'clock.* 이제 7시가 다 되었다. **4** [T] to begin to deal with something ‖ 어떤 것을 처리하기 시작하다. 다루다: *What's the best way to approach the problem?* 그 문제를 다루는 가장 좋은 방법은 무엇인가?

approach² *n* **1** a way of doing something or dealing with a problem ‖ 어떤 일을 하거나 문제를 처리하는 방법. 접근법: *a creative approach to teaching science* 과학 교육에 대한 창의적인 접근

법 **2** [U] the act of coming closer in time or distance ‖ 시간이나 거리상 더 가까워짐. 접근. 근접: *The air got colder with the approach of winter.* 겨울이 다가옴에 따라 공기가 더욱 차가워졌다. **3** a road or path leading to a place ‖ 어떤 장소로 가는 도로나 작은 길: *The easiest approach to the beach is from down here.* 해변에 이르는 가장 쉬운 길은 여기서 내려가는 것이다.

ap·proach·a·ble /ə'proʊtʃəbəl/ *adj* **1** friendly and easy to talk to ‖ 친밀하고 말붙이기 쉬운. 가까이하기 쉬운: *Dr. Grieg seems very approachable.* 그리그 박사는 사귀기가 아주 쉬운 것 같다. **2** able to be reached ‖ 접근할 수 있는: *The castle was only approachable via a bridge.* 그 성은 다리를 통해서만 접근 할 수 있었다.

ap·pro·ba·tion /ˌæprə'beɪʃən/ *n* [U] FORMAL praise or approval ‖ 칭찬, 찬성 —opposite DISAPPROBATION

ap·pro·pri·ate¹ /ə'proʊpriɪt/ *adj* suitable for a particular time, situation, or purpose ‖ 특정한 시간[상황, 목적]에 적합한. 어울리는. 타당한: *My mother didn't think my shoes were appropriate for church.* 어머니는 내 구두가 교회에는 어울리지 않는다고 생각하셨다. – **appropriately** *adv* – **appropriateness** *n* [U] —opposite INAPPROPRIATE

USAGE NOTE appropriate, suitable, suited

Use these words to talk about things or people that are right or acceptable for a particular situation. Use **appropriate** to talk about a person's clothes or behavior: *an appropriate dress for the party.* Use **suitable** to say that something has the right qualities for a particular person or purpose: *a suitable school for the children.* Use **suited** to say that a person has the right qualities to do something: *He'd be well suited to the job.*
이 단어들은 특정 상황에 적절하거나 받아들일 만한 사물이나 사람을 언급하는 데에 쓰인다. 사람의 옷이나 행동에 관해서 말할 때는 **appropriate**를 쓴다: 파티에 적합한 의상. 특정한 사람이나 목적에 맞는 성질을 지닌 사물을 말할 때는 **suitable**을 쓴다: 어린이에 적당한 학교. 어떤 사람이 어떤 일을 하는 데 적합한 성질을 가졌다고 말할 때 **suited**를 쓴다: 그는 그 직무에 아주 적합하다.

---

ap·pro·pri·ate² /ə'proʊpriˌeɪt/ *v* [T] FORMAL **1** to keep something such as money separate to be used for a particular purpose ‖ 특정한 목적에 사용하기 위해 돈 등을 따로 보관하다. 충당하다. … 을 책정하다: *Congress appropriated funds for new laboratories in Hawaii.* 의회는 하와이 주의 새로운 연구소들을 위한 기금을 책정했다. **2** a word meaning to steal something, used in order to avoid saying this directly ‖ 어떤 것을 훔치는 것을 의미하는 말로서 직접적으로 말하는 것을 피하는 데에 쓰여. …을 도용하다

ap·prov·al /ə'pruvəl/ *n* [U] **1** the belief that someone or something is good or doing something right ‖ 사람이나 사물이 좋거나 어떤 일을 제대로 하고 있다는 믿음. 찬성. 승인: *It took three years to win/earn my father-in-law's approval.* 내 장인의 인정을 받는 데 3년이 걸렸다. **2** official permission ‖ 공식적 허가. 승인. 인가: *We have to get approval from the council.* 우리는 의회 승인을 받아야 한다.

ap·prove /ə'pruv/ *v* **1** [I] to believe that someone or something is good or acceptable ‖ 사람이나 사물이 좋거나 받아들일 수 있다고 믿다. 인정하다. 찬성하다: *I don't approve of drunk drivers.* 나는 음주 운전자를 좋아하지 않는다. **2** [T] to officially agree to something ‖ 어떤 일에 공식적으로 동의하다. 인가하다. 승인하다: *Congress approved an amendment to the Social Security Act.* 의회는 사회 보장법의 개정을 승인했다.

ap·prox. *adv* the written abbreviation of APPROXIMATELY ‖ approximately의 약어

ap·prox·i·mate¹ /ə'praksəmɪt/ *adj* an approximate number, amount, or time is not exact ‖ 숫자[수량, 시간]이 정확하지 않은. 대략적인. 근사한: *What is the approximate cost of the materials?* 그 재료의 어림 가격은 얼마인가?

ap·prox·i·mate² /ə'praksəˌmeɪt/ *v* FORMAL **approximate sth** to become similar to but not exactly the same as something else ‖ 다른 것과 비슷하지만 똑같지는 않다. …에 가깝다: *We try to give the animals food that approximates what they would eat in the wild.* 우리는 동물들이 야생에서 먹을 수 있는 것과 거의 비슷한 음식물을 동물들에게 주려고 한다. – **approximation** /əˌpraksə'meɪʃən/ *n* [C, U]

ap·prox·i·mate·ly /ə'praksəmɪtˈli/ *adv* a little bit more or less than an exact number, amount etc.; about ‖ 정확한 숫

자·수량보다 약간 많거나 적은. 대략. 대 강; 약: *Approximately 35% of the students come from Japan.* 대략 35%의 학생들이 일본 출신이다.

ap·ri·cot /'eɪprɪˌkɑt, 'æ-/ *n* a small soft yellow-orange fruit with a single large seed ‖ 큰 씨가 하나 있는 연한 주황색의 작은 과일. 살구(나무)

A·pril /'eɪprəl/, *written abbreviation* **Apr.** *n* the fourth month of the year ‖ 그 해의 네 번째 달. 4월 —see usage note at JANUARY

April Fool's Day /ˌ·· '· ˌ·/ *n* April 1 in the US and Canada, a day for playing funny tricks on people ‖ 사람들에게 재미 있는 속임수를 쓰는 날로 미국·캐나다에서 4월 1일. 만우절

a·pron /'eɪprən/ *n* a piece of clothing you wear to protect your clothes when you cook ‖ 요리할 때 옷을 보호하기 위해 입는 옷. 앞치마

apt /æpt/ *adj* **1 apt to** likely to do something ‖ 어떤 일을 하기 쉬운. …하는 경향이 있는: *If your camp is clean, you're less apt to attract bears.* 야영지 가 깨끗하면 곰의 접근을 줄일 수 있다. **2** exactly right for a particular situation or purpose ‖ 특정 상황이나 목적에 꼭 맞는. 적절한. 적당한: *an apt remark* 적절한 언 급[발언] **3** able to learn or understand things quickly ‖ 사물을 빨리 배우거나 이 해할 수 있는. 영리한: *an apt pupil* 영리 한 학생 – **aptly** *adv*

apt. *n* the written abbreviation of APARTMENT ‖ apartment의 약어

ap·ti·tude /'æptəˌtud/ *n* [C, U] a natural ability or skill, especially in learning ‖ 특히 학습상의 타고난 능력이나 기술. 재능. 소질. 적성: *Ginny seems to have a real aptitude for painting.* 지니는 그림에 대단한 소질을 갖고 있는 듯하다.

aptitude test /'·· ˌ·/ *n* a test used for finding out what someone's best skills are ‖ 사람의 최상의 소질을 발견해 내는 데에 쓰는 시험. 적성 검사: *the Scholastic Aptitude Test* 수학 능력 시험

a·quar·i·um /ə'kwɛriəm/ *n* **1** a clear glass or plastic container for fish or other water animals to live in ‖ 물고기나 다른 수생(水生) 동물이 살 수 있는 투명 한 유리나 플라스틱 용기. 어항. 수조(水 槽) **2** a building with many large aquariums where people go to look at fish or other water animals ‖ 사람들이 어류나 해양 동물을 구경하러 가는 대형 수조가 많은 건물. 수족관(水族館)

A·quar·i·us /ə'kwɛriəs/ *n* **1** [singular] the eleventh sign of the ZODIAC, represented by a person pouring water ‖ 물을 붓고 있는 사람으로 상징되는 황도 12궁의 열한째 별자리. 물병자리 **2** someone born between January 20 and February 18 ‖ 1월 20일에서 2월 18일 사이에 태어난 사람. 물병좌 태생자

a·quat·ic /ə'kwætɪk, ə'kwɑtɪk/ *adj* living or happening in water ‖ 물에서 살 거나 생기는. 수생(水生)의: *aquatic plants* 수생 식물 / *aquatic sports* 수중 스 포츠

aq·ue·duct /'ækwəˌdʌkt/ *n* a structure like a bridge for carrying water across a valley ‖ 계곡을 가로질러 물을 전달하기 위한 다리 같은 구조(물). 수로교. 송수관

AR the written abbreviation of Arkansas ‖ Arkansas(아칸소 주)의 약어

Ar·a·bic numeral /ˌærəbɪk 'numərəl/ *n* the sign 1, 2, 3, 4, 5, 6, 7, 8, 9, or 0, or a combination of these signs, used as a number ‖ 숫자로 쓰이는 1,2,3,4,5, 6,7,8,9,0의 기호나 이 기호들의 조합. 아 라비아 숫자 —see also ROMAN NUMERAL

ar·a·ble /'ærəbəl/ *adj* arable land is suitable for growing crops ‖ 토양이 작물 이 자라는 데 적합한. 경작에 알맞은

ar·bi·ter /'ɑrbətə/ *n* **1** a person or organization that settles an argument between two groups or people ‖ 두 집단 이나 사람 사이의 다툼을 해결하는 사람이 나 조직. 중재[조정]자 **2** an arbiter of style, fashion, taste etc. influences society's opinions about what is fashionable ‖ 스타일·패션·취향 등의 유 행에 대해 사회 여론에 영향을 주는 사람. 선도[주도]자

ar·bi·trar·y /'ɑrbəˌtrɛri/ *adj* based on personal opinions rather than having good reasons ‖ 합당한 이유보다는 개인적 의견에 기초한. 독단적인. 임의의: *Their reasons for firing Mr. Casey seemed arbitrary.* 그들이 케이지 씨를 해고한 사 유는 전횡적으로 보였다 – **arbitrarily** /ˌɑrbə'trɛrəli/ *adv* – **arbitrariness** /ˌɑrbə'trɛrinɪs/ *n* [U]

ar·bi·trate /'ɑrbəˌtreɪt/ *v* [I, T] to be a judge in an argument because both sides have asked for this ‖ 논쟁에서 양측 요청으로 중재인이 되다. 중재하다. 조정 하다 – **arbitrator** *n*

ar·bi·tra·tion /ˌɑrbə'treɪʃən/ *n* the process in which someone tries to help two opposing sides settle an argument ‖ 양 당사자가 분쟁을 해결하도록 돕는 과 정. 중재. 조정

arc /ɑrk/ *n* part of a circle or any curved line ‖ 원이나 굽은 선의 일부분. 호 (弧). 원호(圓弧)

ar·cade /ɑrˈkeɪd/ *n* **1** a special room or small building where people go to play VIDEO GAMEs ‖ 사람들이 비디오 게임을 하기 위해 가는 특별한 방이나 작은 건물. 전자 오락실 **2** a passage or side of a building that has small stores next to it and is covered with an ARCHed roof ‖ 옆에 작은 가게가 있고 아치형의 지붕이 덮힌 건물의 통로나 측면. 아케이드

arch¹ /ɑrtʃ/ *n, plural* **arches 1** a curved structure at the top of a door, window, bridge etc., or something that has this curved shape ‖ 문·창·다리 등의 꼭대기가 굽은 구조물이나 이런 굽은 형태를 지닌 것. 아치. 궁형(의 것) **2** the curved middle part of the bottom of your foot ‖ 발바닥 가운데의 오목한 부위. 장심 – **arched** *adj* : *an arched doorway* 아치형의 출입구

arch² *v* [I, T] to make something form an ARCH, or be in the shape of an arch ‖ 무엇을 궁형으로 만들다, 또는 아치 모양이 되다: *The cat arched her back and hissed.* 그 고양이는 등을 아치 모양으로 구부리고 위협적인 소리를 냈다.

ar·chae·ol·o·gy, archeology /ˌɑrkiˈɑlədʒi/ *n* [U] the study of ancient societies by examining what remains of their buildings, graves, tools etc. ‖ 고대의 건축물·무덤·도구 등 유물을 조사하여 고대 사회를 연구하는 학문. 고고학 – **archaeological** /ˌɑrkiəˈlɑdʒɪkəl/ *adj* – **archaeologist** /ˌɑrkiˈɑlədʒɪst/ *n*

ar·cha·ic /ɑrˈkeɪ-ɪk/ *adj* belonging to the past, or OLD-FASHIONED and no longer used ‖ 과거에 속하는, 또는 구식이어서 더 이상 쓰이지 않는. 구식의. 낡은

arch·bish·op /ˌɑrtʃˈbɪʃəp-/ *n* a priest with a very high rank ‖ 고위직의 성직자. 대주교(大主敎). 대감독(大監督)

ar·chi·pel·a·go /ˌɑrkəˈpɛləˌgoʊ/ *n* a group of small islands ‖ 일단의 작은 섬. 군도(群島). 열도(列島)

ar·chi·tect /ˈɑrkəˌtɛkt/ *n* someone whose job is to design buildings ‖ 건물을 설계하는 직업인. 건축가. 건축 설계사

ar·chi·tec·ture /ˈɑrkəˌtɛktʃər/ *n* [U] **1** the style and design of a building or buildings ‖ 건물(들)의 방식과 디자인. 건축 양식: *medieval architecture* 중세 건축 양식 / *the architecture of Venice* 베니스의 건축 양식 **2** the art and practice of planning and designing buildings ‖ 건축물의 고안·설계에 관한 기술과 실제. 건축. 건축학. 건축술 – **architectural** /ˌɑrkəˈtɛktʃərəl/ *adj*

ar·chives /ˈɑrkaɪvz/ *n* [plural] a large number of records, reports, letters etc. relating to the history of a country, organization, family etc., or the place where these records are stored ‖ 국가·조직·가계 등의 역사에 관한 수많은 기록·보고서·서신 등, 또는 그 보관소. 고문서 (보관소)

arch·way /ˈɑrtʃweɪ/ *n* a passage or entrance under an ARCH or arches ‖ 아치 밑의 통로나 입구. 아치 길

Arc·tic /ˈɑrktɪk, -tɪk/ *n* **the Arctic** the most northern part of the earth, including parts of Alaska and Greenland, and the sea called the Arctic Ocean ‖ 알래스카·그린랜드·북극해 등의 지역을 포함하는 지구의 최북단. 북극(권) – **arctic** *adj*

ar·dent /ˈɑrdnt/ *adj* having very strong feelings of admiration or determination about someone or something ‖ 사람이나 사물에 대한 강한 숭배나 결의의 감정을 지닌. 열렬한. 격렬한: *He's an ardent supporter of his son's baseball team.* 그는 자기 아들 야구팀의 열렬한 후원자다. – **ardently** *adv*

ar·dor /ˈɑrdər/ *n* [U] very strong feelings of admiration, excitement, or love ‖ 감탄[흥분, 사랑]의 강한 감정. 열정. 열의: *He pursued her with surprising ardor.* 그는 놀랍도록 정열적으로 그녀를 쫓아다녔다.

ar·du·ous /ˈɑrdʒuəs/ *adj* needing a lot of hard and continuous effort ‖ 상당히 힘들고 지속적인 노력을 요하는. 고생스러운. 험난한: *an arduous task* 몹시 힘든 작업 / *an arduous climb* 험난한 등반

are /ər; *strong* ɑr/ the present tense plural of BE ‖ be의 복수형 현재 시제

ar·e·a /ˈɛriə/ *n* **1** a particular part of a place, city, country etc. ‖ 장소·도시·국가 등의 특정한 구역. 지역: *Mom grew up in the Portland area.* 어머니는 포틀랜드 지역에서 자랐다. **2** a part of a house, office, park etc. that is used for a particular purpose ‖ 특정 목적으로 사용되는 집·사무실·공원 등의 일정 부분. 구역: *Their apartment has a large dining area.* 그들의 아파트에는 큰 식당 공간이 있다 **3** a particular subject or type of activity ‖ 특정 활동의 주제나 유형. 분야: *She talked about literary theory – her area of study.* 그녀는 연구 분야인 문학 이론에 대해 말했다. **4** the size of a flat surface, calculated by multiplying its length by its width ‖ 길이와 폭을 곱해 계산된 평면의 크기. 면적

area code /ˈ... ˌ./ *n* the three numbers before a telephone number when you telephone someone outside your local area in the US ‖ 미국내에서 해당 지역 외의 사람에게 전화할 때 쓰는 전화 번호 앞의 세 자리 번호. 지역 번호

a·re·na /əˈriːnə/ *n* **1** a building with a large flat central area surrounded by raised seats, used for sports or entertainment ‖ 넓고 평평한 중앙부가 높여 쌓은 좌석에 둘러싸인 스포츠나 오락에 쓰이는 건물. 경기장 **2 the political/public/national arena** all the people and activities relating to politics or public life ‖ 정치·공적 생활에 관련된 모든 사람 및 활동. 정치/공인/국민 생활: *Our mayor has been in the political arena for over 12 years.* 우리 시장은 12년 이상 정계에 몸담아 왔다.

aren't /ˈɑrənt/ **1** the short form of "are not" ‖ "are not"의 단축형: *Things aren't the same since you left.* 네가 떠난 후로 상황이 전과 같지 않다. **2** the short form of "am not", used in asking questions ‖ 의문문에 쓰이는 "am not"의 단축형: *I'm in big trouble, aren't I?* 내가 굉장히 곤경에 처한 것 맞죠?

ar·gu·a·ble /ˈɑrgyuəbəl/ *adj* **1** not at all certain, and therefore easy to doubt ‖ 전혀 확실치 않아 의심하기 쉬운. 논란[논쟁]의 여지가 있는: *Some of the paintings in the gallery are of arguable value.* 그 화랑의 몇몇 그림들은 가치가 의문스럽다. **2 it is arguable that**... used in order to give good reasons why something might be true ‖ 어떤 것이 사실일거라는 정당한 이유를 제시하는 데에 쓰여. …을 논증할 수 있다: *It's arguable that the new law will make things worse.* 새 법이 사태를 악화시킬 거라는 것은 불을 보듯 뻔하다.

ar·gu·a·bly /ˈɑrgyuəbli/ *adv* able to be argued or proven true ‖ 사실로 논증되거나 입증될 수 있게. 틀림없이: *Wagner is arguably the best athlete in the school.* 와그너는 분명히 교내 최고의 운동 선수다.

ar·gue /ˈɑrgyu/ *v* **1** [I] to disagree with someone, usually by talking or shouting in an angry way, or getting upset ‖ 보통 화난 투로 말하거나 소리를 치거나 화를 내며 남과 의견을 달리하다. 논쟁[언쟁]하다: *Mom and Dad always seem to be arguing over/about the bills.* 엄마와 아빠는 항상 청구서를 놓고 논란을 벌이는 것 같다. **2** [I, T] to clearly explain or prove why you think something is true or should be done ‖ 어떤 것이 사실이거나 당연히 행해져야 한다고 생각하는 이유를 분명히 설명하거나 증명하다: *It can be argued that most teachers are*

underpaid. 대부분의 교사가 박봉을 받는 것은 분명한 사실이다. / *I couldn't argue the point because I didn't know anything about it.* 나는 그것에 대해 아무것도 몰라서 뭐라고 말할 수 없었다.

ar·gu·ment /ˈɑrgyəmənt/ *n* **1** a disagreement, especially one in which people talk loudly ‖ 특히 큰 소리로 말하는 의견 차이. 논쟁. 언쟁: *Jodie and I had a really big argument last night.* 조디와 나는 어젯밤 크게 다퉜다. **2** a set of explanations you use to try to prove that something is right or wrong, true or false etc. ‖ 어떤 일의 옳고 그름이나 진위를 증명하려고 사용하는 일련의 설명. 논리. 주장: *the arguments for/against becoming a vegetarian* 채식주의자가 되는 데 대한 찬성론[반대론]

ar·gu·men·ta·tive /ˌɑrgyəˈmɛntətɪv/ *adj* liking to argue ‖ 논쟁하기를 좋아하는. 논쟁적인

a·ri·a /ˈɑriə/ *n* a song that is sung by only one person in an OPERA ‖ 오페라에서 독창하는 노래. 아리아. 영창(詠唱)

ar·id /ˈærɪd/ *adj* **1** getting very little rain, and therefore very dry ‖ 비가 거의 내리지 않아 매우 건조한. 메마른. 불모의: *arid land* 메마른 땅 / *an arid climate* 건조 기후 **2** unable to produce anything new, exciting, or useful ‖ 새로운[자극적인, 유용한] 것을 생산할 수 없는. 무미 건조한: *arid discussions* 비생산적인 토론

Ar·ies /ˈɛriz/ *n* **1** [singular] the first sign of the ZODIAC, represented by a RAM ‖ 양으로 상징되는 황도 12궁의 첫째 별자리. 양자리 **2** someone born between March 21 and April 19 ‖ 3월 21일부터 4월 19일 사이에 태어난 사람. 양좌 태생자

a·rise /əˈraɪz/ *v* [I] **1** to happen or appear ‖ 일어나다, 나타나다. 생기다. 발생하다: *the problems that arise from losing a job* 실업으로 발생하는 문제들 **2** LITERARY to get up ‖ 일어나다. 기상하다

ar·is·toc·ra·cy /ˌærəˈstɑkrəsi/ *n* the people in the highest social class, who traditionally have a lot of land, money, and power ‖ 대대로 많은 땅·돈·권력을 가진 최상위 사회 계급 사람들. 상류 계층. 귀족 계급

ar·is·to·crat /əˈrɪstəˌkræt/ *n* someone who belongs to the highest social class ‖ 최상위 사회 계급에 속하는 사람들. 특권 계급의 사람. 귀족 – **aristocratic** /əˌrɪstəˈkrætɪk/ *adj*

a·rith·me·tic¹ /əˈrɪθməˌtɪk/ *n* [U] the science of numbers involving adding, dividing, multiplying etc. ‖ 덧셈·나눗셈·곱셈을 포함한 수에 관한 학문. 산술

—compare MATHEMATICS

ar·ith·me·tic² /,ærɪθ'mɛtɪk/ *adj* involving or relating to ARITHMETIC ‖ 산술을 포함하거나 산술에 관련된. 산술의. 계산상의 **- arithmetically** *adv*

arm¹ /ɑrm/ *n* **1** one of the two long parts of your body between your shoulders and your hands ‖ 어깨와 손 사이에 있는 인체의 두 긴 부분 중 하나. 팔: *a broken arm* 골절된 팔 / *I had a pile of books in my arms.* 나는 한 무더기의 책을 팔로 감싸 안았다. / *John and Marsha walked away arm in arm.* (=with their arms bent around each other's) 존과 마샤는 팔짱을 끼고 걸어갔다 / *She took him by the arm* (=led him by holding his arm) *and pushed him out the door.* 그녀는 그의 팔을 잡아 문 밖으로 밀어냈다. **2** a part of something that is shaped like or moves like an arm ‖ 팔처럼 생겼거나 움직이는 사물의 부분: *the arm of a chair* 의자의 팔걸이 **3** ⇨ SLEEVE **be up in arms** INFORMAL to be very angry and ready to argue or fight ‖ 매우 화가 나서 다투거나 싸울 태세이다. 분개하다: *The whole town is up in arms about the decision to build a new highway.* 마을 전체가 새 고속도로 건설 결정에 대해 격분하고 있다. **5** a particular part of a group ‖ 한 집단의 특정 부문: *the political arm of the terrorist organization* 테러 조직의 정치부

arm² *v* [T] to give someone the weapons or information s/he needs ‖ 어떤 사람에게 필요한 무기나 정보를 주다. 무장시키다: *arming the local people with rifles* 지역 주민들을 소총으로 무장시킴 / *Jess armed himself with all the facts he needed to prove his case.* 제스는 자신의 사건을 입증하는 데 필요한 모든 사실을 스스로 갖추었다.

ar·ma·dil·lo /,ɑrmə'dɪloʊ/ *n* a small animal with a pointed nose and a hard shell that lives in hot dry parts of North and South America ‖ 북·남미의 고온 건조 지역에 사는, 뾰족한 코와 단단한 껍질을 가진 작은 동물. 아르마딜로

ar·ma·ments /'ɑrməmənts/ *n* [plural] weapons and military equipment ‖ 무기류와 군사 장비. 군비: *nuclear armaments* 핵무기

arm·band /'ɑrmbænd/ *n* a band of material that you wear around your arm, for example to show that someone you love has died ‖ 예컨대 사랑하는 사람이 죽은 것을 표시하기 위해 팔에 두르는 띠. 상장(喪章). 완장

arm·chair /'ɑrmtʃɛr/ *n* a chair with

sides that you can rest your arms on ‖ 팔을 올려 놓을 수 있는 옆부분이 있는 의자. 팔걸이 의자

armed /ɑrmd/ *adj* **1** carrying one or more weapons ‖ 하나 이상의 무기를 소지하고 있는. 무장한: *an armed guard* 무장한 경비원 / *The suspect is armed with a shotgun.* 용의자는 엽총으로 무장하고 있다. / *armed robbery* (=stealing using guns) 무장 강도 / *The fort was heavily armed.* (=had a lot of weapons) 그 요새는 중무장되었다. **2** having or knowing something useful ‖ 유용한 것을 갖추거나 알고 있는. …을 갖춘: *I went to the meeting armed with all the facts I could find.* 나는 찾아낼 수 있는 모든 사실을 갖추어 그 회의에 갔다.

armed forc·es /,. '../ *n* [plural] **the armed forces** a country's military organizations ‖ 한 나라의 군사 조직. 군(軍). 군대

arm·ful /'ɑrmfʊl/ *n* the amount of something that you can hold in one or both arms ‖ 한 팔이나 두 팔로 안을 수 있는 물건의 양. 한 아름: *an armful of books* 한 아름의 책

arm·hole /'ɑrm,hoʊl/ *n* a hole in a shirt, coat etc. that you put your arm through ‖ 셔츠·코트 등의 팔을 집어 넣는 구멍. (옷의)진동 둘레

ar·mi·stice /'ɑrməstɪs/ *n* an agreement to stop fighting, usually for a specific period of time ‖ 보통 특정 기간 동안 전쟁을 중단하는 협정. 정전[휴전] 협정

ar·mor /'ɑrmɚ/ *n* [U] **1** metal or leather clothing worn in past times by men and horses in battle ‖ 과거에 전쟁터에서 사람·말에 입힌 금속이나 가죽 옷. 갑옷. 갑주: *a suit of armor* 한 벌의 갑옷. **2** a strong layer of metal that protects vehicles, ships, and aircraft ‖ 차량·선박·항공기를 보호하는 강력한 금속층. 장갑용 강철판

ar·mored /'ɑrmɚd/ *adj* protected against bullets or other weapons by a strong layer of metal ‖ 강한 금속층에 의해 총탄이나 기타 무기류로부터 보호된. 갑옷을 입은. 장갑을 갖춘: *an armored car* 장갑차

ar·mor·y /'ɑrməri/ *n* a place where weapons are stored ‖ 무기가 보관되어 있는 곳. 무기고. 병기창

arm·pit /'ɑrm,pɪt/ *n* **1** the hollow place under your arm where it joins your body ‖ 팔이 몸통에 연결되는 팔밑의 우묵한 곳. 겨드랑이 **2** SLANG a very unpleasant or ugly place ‖ 매우 불쾌하거나 추악한 곳. 치부: *This town is the armpit of the state.* 이 시는 주내(州內)의

치부이다.

arms /ɑrmz/ *n* [plural] weapons used for fighting wars ‖ 전쟁에 쓰이는 무기. 병기

arms con·trol /'. .,./ *n* [U] the attempt by powerful countries to limit the number of war weapons that exist ‖ 보유하는 전쟁 무기 수량을 제한하려는 강대국들의 시도. 무기[군비] 제한

arms race /'. ,./ *n* a struggle between two or more unfriendly countries to produce more and better weapons than the others ‖ 다른 나라보다 더 많고 좋은 무기를 생산하려는 둘 이상의 비우호 국가 간의 경쟁. 군비(확장) 경쟁

ar·my /'ɑrmi/ *n* **1** the part of a country's military force that is trained to fight on land ‖ 육상에서 싸우도록 훈련된 한 나라 군대의 일부. 육군. 군: *Our son is in the army.* 우리 아들은 육군 복무중이다. / *The two armies advanced across Europe.* 2개 군이 유럽을 가로질러 진격했다. **2** a large group of people or animals involved in the same activity ‖ 동일 활동에 관련된 사람이나 동물의 대규모 집단. 떼: *an army of ants* 개미떼

a·ro·ma /ə'roumə/ *n* a strong pleasant smell ‖ 강하고 기분 좋은 향기. 방향. 아로마: *the aroma of fresh coffee* 신선한 커피향 – **aromatic** /,ærə'mætɪk/ *adj* : *aromatic oils* 방향유(芳香油) —see usage note at SMELL²

a·ro·ma·ther·a·py /ə,roumə'θɛrəpi/ *n* [U] the use of pleasant-smelling oils to help you feel more healthy ‖ 보다 건강함을 느낄 수 있도록 쾌적한 향을 내는 오일을 사용하는 것. 아로마테라피. 향기 요법 – **aromatherapist** *n*

a·rose /ə'rouz/ *v* the past tense of ARISE ‖ arise의 과거형

a·round /ə'raund/ *adv, prep* **1** on all sides of something, so that it is surrounded ‖ 어떤 것의 사방으로 둘러싸여: *We put a fence around the yard.* 우리는 마당 주위에 빙 둘러 울타리를 쳤다. / *Mario put his arms around her.* 마리오는 자신의 팔로 그녀를 감쌌다. **2** to or in many parts of a place, room etc. ‖ 장소·방 등의 곳곳으로, 또는 곳곳에. 도처에: *Stan showed me around the office.* 스탠은 나에게 사무실 곳곳을 보여 주었다. / *an international company with offices all around* (=in all parts of) *the world* 세계 도처에 사무실을 두고 있는 국제 기업 **3** in or near a particular place ‖ 특정 장소나 근처에. 주변에: *Is there a bank around here?* 이 근처에 은행이 있습니까? **4 around 10/6/200 etc.** used when you do not know an exact number, to give a number that is close to it; APPROXIMATELY ‖ 정확한 수치를 모르고 거기에 가까운 수치를 제시할 때에 쓰여. 약 10/6/200; ㉿ approximately: *Dodger Stadium seats around 50,000 people.* 다저 경기장은 약 5만명의 사람들을 수용할 수 있다. **5 in a circular movement** ‖ 회전하여. 빙글 돌아서: *Water pushes the wheel around.* 물이 수차를 (밀어)돌린다. **6 along the outside of a place, instead of through it** ‖ 한 장소를 통과하는 대신에 바깥쪽을 따라서. 주위를 따라. 빙 돌아 둘레에: *We had to go around to the back of the house.* 우리는 집 뒤로 빙 돌아가야 했다. **7 so as to be turned in the opposite direction** ‖ 반대 방향으로 돌려서. 반대로: *I'll turn the car around and pick you up at the door.* 차를 돌려서 현관에서 태워 줄게. **8 be around a)** to be present in the same place as you ‖ 동일 장소에 있다. 참석하다: *It was 11:30 at night, and nobody was around.* 밤 11시 30분이었고 주변에 아무도 없었다. **b)** to exist or be available to use ‖ 존재하거나 사용할 수 있다: *That joke's been around for years.* 그 농담은 수년 묵은 것이다. / *I think the B52's were the best band around at the time.* 나는 B52가 그 무렵에는 최고의 밴드였다고 생각한다. **9 10 feet/3 inches etc. around** measuring a particular distance on the outside of a round object ‖ 둥근 물체의 바깥쪽 특정 거리의 측정치. 둘레 10피트/3인치: *Redwood trees can measure 30 or 40 feet around.* 레드우드 나무는 둘레 30 내지 40피트까지 자란다. **10 around and around** continuing to move in circles ‖ 계속해서 둥글게 움직여. 빙글빙글. 돌고 돌아: *We drove around and around the block, looking for the house.* 우리는 그 집을 찾아서 그 구역을 돌고돌아 운전했다. —see also **around the clock** (CLOCK¹)

a·rou·sal /ə'rauzəl/ *n* [U] excitement, especially sexual excitement ‖ 자극, 특히 성적 흥분

a·rouse /ə'rauz/ *v* [T] **1** to make someone have a particular feeling ‖ 남에게 특정한 감정을 갖게 하다. 유발하다: *Her behavior aroused the suspicions of the police.* 그녀의 행동은 경찰의 의심을 불러일으켰다. **2** to make someone feel sexually excited ‖ 남을 성적으로 흥분되게 하다. 자극하다 **3** FORMAL to wake someone up ‖ 남을 깨우다

ar·raign /ə'reɪn/ *v* [T] LAW to make

someone come to a court of law to hear what the court says his/her crime is ‖ 법정이 밝히는 죄에 대해 들려주기 위해 어떤 사람을 법정 소환하다. …을 법정에 출두시키다 - **arraignment** *n* [C, U]

ar·range /ə'reɪndʒ/ *v* **1** [I, T] to make plans for something to happen ‖ 어떤 일이 일어나게 계획을 세우다. 준비하다. 마련하다: *Jeff will arrange our flights.* 제프가 우리 항공편을 마련할 것이다. / *We've arranged to go to the cabin this weekend.* 우리는 이번 주말에 오두막에 가기로 되어 있다. / *I've arranged for Mark to join us.* 나는 마크가 우리와 합류하도록 주선했다. / *We still have to arrange where to meet.* 우리는 여전히 만날 장소를 정해야 한다. **2** [T] to put a group of things or people in a particular order or position ‖ 사물이나 사람 집단을 특정한 순서나 위치별로 놓다. 배열[배치]하다. 정리[정돈]하다: *The file is arranged alphabetically.* 그 파일은 알파벳 순으로 정리돼 있다. **3** [T] to write or change a piece of music so that it is suitable for a particular instrument ‖ 음악 작품을 특정 악기에 맞도록 쓰거나 바꾸다. 편곡하다

ar·range·ment /ə'reɪndʒmənt/ *n* **1** [C usually plural] the things that you must organize for something to happen ‖ 어떤 일이 일어나도록 조직화해야 하는 일. 사전 준비[조정]. 예정된 계획: *travel arrangements* 여행 (사전)준비 / *making arrangements for the wedding* 결혼 준비하기 **2** [C, U] something that has been agreed on ‖ 어떤 것에 동의함. 협정. 타협. 합의: *We have a special arrangement with the bank.* 우리는 은행측과 특별한 약정을 맺고 있다. / *I'm sure we can come to some arrangement.* 나는 우리가 어느 정도 합의에 도달할 것으로 믿는다. **3** [C, U] a group of things in a particular order or position, or the activity of arranging things in this way ‖ 특정 순서나 위치로 된 사물군, 또는 사물을 이렇게 배열하는 행위. 배열. 배치. 정리[정돈](하기): *a flower arrangement* 꽃꽂이 **4** [C, U] a piece of music that has been written or changed for a particular instrument ‖ 특정 악기용으로 작곡되거나 변경된 악곡. 편곡(한 것)

ar·ray¹ /ə'reɪ/ *n* **1** an attractive collection or group ‖ 이목을 끄는 수집물이나 집단. 배열. 정열. 대열: *a dazzling array of acting talent* 화려한 출연진 **2** [C, U] LITERARY clothes worn for a special occasion ‖ 특별한 경우에 입는 의

상. 치장

ar·ray² *v* [T] FORMAL **1** to arrange something in an attractive way ‖ 사물을 멋있게 배열하다. 진열하다 **2** to dress someone in a particular type of clothes ‖ 남에게 특정 유형의 옷을 입히다. 치장시키다

ar·rears /ə'rɪrz/ *n* [plural] **1 be in arrears** to owe someone more money that you should because your payment is late ‖ 지불이 늦어서 지불해야 할 돈보다 더 많은 돈을 남에게 빚지다. 연체[체납]되다. 밀리다: *We're six weeks in arrears with the rent.* 우리 집세가 6주나 밀려 있다. **2** money that is owed and should have been paid ‖ 빚져서 지불되어야 할 돈. 상환금. 지불금: *mortgage arrears* 주택 융자 상환금

ar·rest¹ /ə'rest/ *v* [T] **1** to catch someone and take him/her away because s/he is believed to be guilty of a crime ‖ 범죄에 대해 유죄로 생각되는 자를 붙잡아 격리하다. 체포[검거]하다. 구금[투옥]하다: *The police arrested Eric for shoplifting.* 경찰은 가게 물건을 훔친 혐의로 에릭을 체포했다. **2** FORMAL to stop something happening or make it happen more slowly ‖ 어떤 일이 발생하는 것을 막거나 천천히 일어나게 하다. 방해하다. 억제하다. 막다: *The drug is used to arrest the spread of the disease.* 그 약은 질병의 확산을 막는 데에 쓰인다.

arrest² *n* [C, U] the act of taking someone away and guarding him/her because s/he is believed to be guilty of a crime ‖ 범죄 혐의자를 잡아가서 감시하는 행위. 체포. 구금. 검거: *The police expect to make an arrest soon.* 경찰은 곧 체포할 것으로 기대한다. / *Don't move, you're under arrest!* 꼼짝마, 체포한다!

ar·riv·al /ə'raɪvəl/ *n* **1** [U] the act of arriving somewhere ‖ 어딘가에 도착하는 행위: *The arrival of our flight was delayed.* 우리 비행기의 도착이 지연되었다. / *Shortly after our arrival in Toronto, Lisa got sick.* 우리가 토론토에 도착한 직후 리사가 아팠다. **2 the arrival of** the time when a new idea, method, product etc. is first used or discovered ‖ 새로운 사상·방법·제품 등이 처음 사용되거나 발견되는 시기. 도래. 출현: *The arrival of the personal computer changed the way we work.* PC의 출현은 우리의 일하는 방식을 바꾸어 놓았다. **3** a person or thing that has arrived ‖ 도착한 사람이나 사물. 신제품 (출현). 탄생: *Congratulations on your new arrival!* (=new baby) 당신의 출산을 축하합니다!

ar·rive /ə'raɪv/ *v* [I] **1** to get to a place ‖ 장소에 닿다. 도착[도달]하다. 이르다: *Your letter arrived last week.* 지난 주에 네 편지가 도착했다. / *What time does the plane arrive in New York?* 그 비행기는 뉴욕에 몇 시에 도착합니까? / *We arrived at Mom's two hours late.* 우리는 2시간 늦게 어머니 집에 도착했다. **2** to happen ‖ 일어나다. 오다. 시작되다: *At last the big day arrived!* 마침내 그 날이 왔어! **3 arrive at a conclusion/ decision** to decide what to do about something after a lot of effort ‖ 많은 노력 끝에 어떤 것을 하기로 결정하다. 결론/결정을 내리다[에 도달하다] **4** to begin to exist, or start being used ‖ 존재하거나 사용되기 시작하다. 출현하다. 도래하다: *Our toy sales have doubled since computer games arrived.* 우리 장난감의 매출이 컴퓨터 게임 출현 이후 두 배로 뛰었다. / *It was just past midnight when the baby arrived.* (=was born) 자정이 막 지나자 아이가 태어났다. **5** INFORMAL to succeed ‖ 성공하다. 출세하다: *Moving into my new office, I knew I'd finally arrived.* 새 사무실로 이사하면서 나는 마침내 성공했음을 실감했다

ar·ro·gance /'ærəgəns/ *n* [U] the quality of being ARROGANT ‖ 오만한 성질. 거만: *I can't stand her arrogance.* 나는 그녀의 오만함을 참을 수 없다.

ar·ro·gant /'ærəgənt/ *adj* believing that you are more important than anyone else, or showing this quality ‖ 다른 사람보다 더 중요하다고 믿는, 또는 이런 특성을 보이는. 오만[거만]한. 건방진: *an arrogant selfish man* 무례하고 이기적인 남자 / *an arrogant smile* 오만한 웃음 – **arrogantly** *adv*

ar·row /'ærou/ *n* **1** a weapon like a thin straight stick with a point at one end and feathers at the other that you shoot with a BOW ‖ 가늘고 곧은 막대의 한쪽 끝은 촉을, 다른 쪽 끝에는 깃털을 달아 활로 쏘는 무기. 화살 **2** a sign (→), used in order to show the direction or position of something ‖ 사물의 방향이나 위치를 나타내는 데에 쓰이는 기호(→). 화살표

ar·se·nal /'ɑrsnl/ *n* a large number of weapons, or the building where they are stored ‖ 대량의 무기 또는 그것들이 저장된 건물. 무기고. 군수품 창고

ar·se·nic /'ɑrsənɪk, 'ɑrsnɪk/ *n* [U] a very poisonous chemical that is often used for killing rats ‖ 종종 쥐를 잡기 위해 쓰이는 맹독성 화학 물질. 비소

ar·son /'ɑrsən/ *n* [U] the crime of deliberately making something burn,

especially a building ‖ 고의로, 특히 건물에 불을 지르는 범죄. 방화(放) – **arsonist** *n*

art /ɑrt/ *n* **1** [U] the use of drawing, painting etc. to represent things or express ideas ‖ 사물을 나타내거나 생각을 표현하기 위해 소묘·채색 등을 사용하는 것. 미술. 예술: *Steve's studying art at college.* 스티브는 대학에서 미술을 공부하고 있다. **2** [U] things that are produced by art, such as drawings, paintings etc. ‖ 소묘화·채색화 등과 같은 미술의 산출물. 미술품. 예술 작품: *modern art* 현대 미술 / *an art exhibition* 미술(품) 전시회 / *Several famous works of art were stolen from the museum.* 몇몇 유명한 미술 작품이 박물관에서 도난당했다. **3** [C, U] the skill involved in making or doing something ‖ 어떤 것을 만들거나 하는 것과 관련된 기술. 기교: *the art of writing* 작문 기술

ar·ter·y /'ɑrtəri/ *n* **1** one of the tubes that carries blood from your heart to the rest of your body ‖ 심장에서 신체의 다른 부분으로 피를 운반하는 관의 하나. 동맥 —compare VEIN **2** a main road, railroad line, or river, considered as a way to carry people, goods etc. ‖ 사람·물자 등을 운반하는 통로로 여겨지는 주요 도로[철로, 강]. 간선도로[수로] – **arterial** /ɑr'tɪriəl/ *adj*

ar·thri·tis /ɑr'θraɪtɪs/ *n* [U] a disease that causes pain and swelling in the joints of your body ‖ 인체의 관절 부위에 통증과 부기를 일으키는 질병. 관절염 – **arthritic** /ɑr'θrɪtɪk/ *adj* : *arthritic fingers* 관절염에 걸린 손가락

ar·ti·choke /'ɑrtɪ,tʃouk/ *n* a green round vegetable with thick pointed leaves and a firm base ‖ 두껍고 뾰족한 잎과 단단한 속을 가진 녹색의 둥근 채소. 아티초크 —see picture on page 944

ar·ti·cle /'ɑrtɪkəl/ *n* **1** a piece of writing in a newspaper, magazine etc. ‖ 신문·잡지 등의 글. 기사. 논설: *Did you read that article on the space shuttle?* 당신은 우주 왕복선에 대한 기사를 읽어 보셨습니까? **2** a thing, especially one of a group of things ‖ 특히 일단의 물건 중의 하나. 한 가지. 한 개[점]: *an article of clothing* 의류 한 점 **3** TECHNICAL in grammar, a word used before a noun to show whether the noun is a particular example of something (definite article) or a general example (indefinite article). In the sentence "I saw the woman", the word "the" is a definite article. In the sentence "I saw a woman," the word "a" is an indefinite article ‖ 문법에서 명사가 사물의 특별한 예(정관사)인지 일반적인 예(부정관사)인지를 나타내기 위해 명사 앞에 쓰는 단어. 관사. "I saw the woman"라는 문장에서 "the"는 정관사다. 문장 "I saw a woman" 의 단어 "a"는 부정관사이다.

ar·tic·u·late¹ /ɑrˈtɪkyəlɪt/ *adj* expressing or able to express thoughts and feelings clearly ‖ 생각과 감정을 분명히 표현하거나 표현할 수 있는. 똑똑히[분명히] 표현된. 명확한: *a bright and articulate child* 영리하고 똑똑한 아이 – **articulately** *adv*

ar·tic·u·late² /ɑrˈtɪkyəˌleɪt/ *v* [I, T] to express something very clearly ‖ 어떤 것을 매우 분명하게 표현하다. 똑똑히 말하다: *It's hard to articulate what I'm feeling.* 내가 느끼고 있는 것을 분명히 말하기는 어렵다. / *You have to articulate* (=speak clearly) *if you want to be heard.* 다른 사람들이 네 말을 듣게 하려면 분명히 표현해야 한다 – **articulation** /ɑrˌtɪkyəˈleɪʃən/ *n* [U]

ar·ti·fact /ˈɑrtɪˌfækt/ *n* a small object that was made and used a long time ago, especially one that is studied by scientists ‖ 오래 전에 제작되어 사용되었던, 과학자들이 연구하는 작은 물건. 옛 기물: *Egyptian artifacts* 이집트의 유물

ar·ti·fi·cial /ˌɑrtəˈfɪʃəl/ *adj* **1** not natural, but made by people ‖ 천연적이 아니라 인간에 의해 만들어진. 인공의. 인조의: *artificial sweeteners* 인공 감미료 / *an artificial leg* 의족 **2** not natural or sincere ‖ 자연산이나 진짜가 아닌. 모조의. 가식의: *an artificial smile* 억지웃음 – **artificially** *adv* : *artificially colored* 인공적으로 색을 입힌

artificial in·tel·li·gence /ˌ.... .ˈ.../ *n* [U] the study of how to make computers do things that people can do, such as make decisions or see things ‖ 의사 결정이나 사물 인식 등의, 사람이 할 수 있는 일을 컴퓨터에게 하게 하는 방법에 관한 연구. 인공 지능(학)

artificial res·pi·ra·tion /ˌ.... ..ˈ.., ..,.. ..ˈ../ *n* [U] a method of helping someone who is nearly dead breathe again by blowing air into his/her mouth ‖ 거의 죽어 있는 사람의 입속으로 공기를 불어넣어 다시 숨을 쉴 수 있게 도와 주는 방법. 인공 호흡(법)

ar·til·ler·y /ɑrˈtɪləri/ *n* [U] large guns, either on wheels or fixed in one place ‖ 이동할 수 있거나 한 장소에 고정된 큰 포(砲). 대포

ar·ti·san /ˈɑrtəzən, -sən/ *n* someone who does work with his/her hands that needs skill; CRAFTSMAN ‖ 기술을 필요로 하는 수작업을 하는 사람. 장인(匠人). 기능공; ⓢ craftsman

art·ist /ˈɑrtɪst/ *n* someone who produces or performs any type of art, including painting, drawing, music, dance etc. ‖ 채색·소묘·음악·무용을 포함하여 어떤 형태의 예술을 창작하거나 공연하는 사람. 예술가. 미술가

ar·tis·tic /ɑrˈtɪstɪk/ *adj* **1** showing skill or imagination in an art ‖ 예술에서 기교나 창의력을 보이는. 예술적인. 예술성이 뛰어난: *I never knew you were so artistic.* 나는 네가 그렇게 예술적 재능이 있는지 몰랐다. **2** relating to art or with the practice of being an artist ‖ 예술이나 예술가로서의 활동에 관련된. 예술[미술]의: *artistic freedom* 예술의 자유 – **artistically** *adv*

art·ist·ry /ˈɑrtəstri/ *n* [U] skill in a particular ARTISTIC activity ‖ 특정 예술 활동의 재능. 예술성: *an example of the painter's artistry* 그 화가의 예술성을 보여주는 예

arts /ɑrts/ *n* [plural] **1 the arts** painting, music, literature etc. all considered together ‖ 미술·음악·문학 등을 모두 망라한 것. 예술(분야): *government funding for the arts* 예술(분야)에 대한 정부의 자금 지원 **2** subjects of study that are not considered scientific, such as history, languages etc. ‖ 역사·언어 등의 과학적이 아닌 것으로 여겨지는 학문 과목. 인문 과학. 교양 과목: *an arts degree* 인문 과학 학위

art·sy /ˈɑrtsi/ *adj* INFORMAL interested in art, or seeming to know a lot about art ‖ 예술에 관심이 있는, 또는 예술에 대해 많이 아는 듯한. 예술가인 체하는. 예술가처럼 보이는: *He's not a businessman – he's sort of artsy.* 그는 사업가가 아니다. 그는 예술가인 체하는 부류이다.

art·work /ˈɑrtwɜrk/ *n* **1** [U] the pictures or decorations that are included in a book, a magazine etc. ‖ 책·잡지 등에 포함되어 있는 사진이나 장식. 삽화. 도판: *The artwork is the best thing in this book.* 이 책에서는 삽화가 최고로 좋다. **2** [C, U] paintings and other pieces of art ‖ 미술품 및 기타 예술 작품들: *damaged paintings and other artwork* 훼손된 미술 작품과 기타 예술품 / *His private collection includes artworks by Dufy and Miro.* 그의 개인 소장품에는 뒤피와 미로의 예술 작품들이 들어 있다.

as¹ /əz; *strong* æz/ *adv, prep* **1** used

when comparing things, or saying that they are like each other in some way ‖ 사물을 비교할 때, 또는 그것들이 어떤 면에서 서로 유사하다고 말할 때 쓰여. …만큼. …과 마찬가지로. …처럼: *These houses aren't as old as the ones downtown.* 이 집들은 상업 지구의 집들만큼 낡지 않았다. / *He was as surprised as anyone when they offered him the job.* 그들이 그에게 일자리를 제안하자 그도 남들처럼 놀랐다. / *You can use cherries instead of plums – they work just as well.* 당신은 자두 대신에 체리를 사용해도 됩니다. 그것들은 동일한 효과를 냅니다. **2** used when describing what someone's job, duty, or position is ‖ 사람의 직업[임무, 지위]를 기술할 때 쓰여. …으로(서). …의 신분[조건]으로서: *In the past, women were mainly employed as secretaries or teachers.* 과거에는 여성들이 주로 비서나 교사로서 채용되었다. / *The kids dressed up as animals for Halloween.* 아이들은 할로윈에 동물로 가장했다. **3** used when describing the way something is being used or considered ‖ 사물이 현재 사용되거나 고려되는 방식을 기술할 때 쓰여. …(대)용으로. …으로(서). …한 것으로: *John used an old blanket as a tent.* 존은 낡은 담요를 텐트 대용으로 썼다. / *Settlers saw the wilderness as dangerous rather than beautiful.* 개척자들은 자연을 아름답다기보다 위험한 것으로 보았다. —see also **as long as** (LONG²), **as a matter of fact** (MATTER¹), **such as** (SUCH), **as well as** (WELL¹)

USAGE NOTE as, like and so

Use **as** and **like** to make comparisons: *He's as good as a professional golfer.* / *He plays golf like a professional.* ✗DON'T SAY "He's so good as a professional."✗ The sentence "He plays golf as a professional." means that he is a professional golfer.

as와 **like**는 비교할 때 쓴다: 그는 프로 골프 선수만큼 골프를 잘 친다. / 그는 프로 골프 선수처럼 골프를 친다: "He's so good as a professional."이라고는 하지 않는다. 문장 "He plays golf as a professional"은 그가 프로 골프 선수임을 의미한다.

---

as² *conjunction* **1** used when comparing things, or saying that they are like each other in some way ‖ 사물을 비교할 때, 또는 그들이 어떤 면에서 서로 비슷하다는 것을 말할 때 쓰여. …만큼[…처럼]. …과 같게. …과 마찬가지로: *I can't run nearly as fast as I used to.* 나는 옛날만큼 그렇게 빨리 달릴 수 없다. / *I'll be there as soon as I can.* 가능한 한 빨리 그곳에 갈게. **2** in the way or manner mentioned ‖ 이미 언급된 방법이나 방식으로. …과 같이. …처럼. …한 대로: *Leave things as they are until the police come.* 경찰이 올 때까지 물건을 그대로 두세요. / *As I said earlier, this research has just started.* 내가 전에 말한 대로 이 연구는 이제 시작되었다. **3** while something is happening ‖ 어떤 일이 일어나는 동안. …하면서. …하고 있을 때: *Be patient with your puppy as he adjusts to his new home.* 강아지가 새 집에 적응하는 동안 참고 기다려라. / *The phone rang just as I was leaving.* 자리를 뜨려는 순간 전화벨이 울렸다. **4** as if/though in a way that suggests that something is true ‖ 어떤 것이 사실임을 암시하는 식으로. …인 것처럼: *They all looked as if they were scared.* 그들은 모두 겁먹은 것처럼 보였다. **5** as to concerning or regarding a particular thing ‖ 특정 사물에 대한, 또는 관련된: *The President asked for opinions as to the likelihood of war.* 대통령은 전쟁의 가능성에 대한 견해를 물었다. / *She offered no explanation as to why she'd left so suddenly.* 그녀는 왜 그렇게 갑자기 떠났는지에 대해 아무런 설명도 해주지 않았다. **6** as of today/December 12th/next spring etc. starting at a particular time and continuing from that time ‖ 특정 시간에 시작하여 그때부터 계속되는. 오늘/12월 12일/내년 봄을 기점으로 하여: *The pay raise will come into effect as of January.* 급여 인상은 1월을 기점으로 하여 실행될 것이다. **7** as for sb/sth concerning a person or subject that is connected with what you were talking about before ‖ 이전에 말했던 것과 관련된 사람이나 주제에 관해서. …에 대해서는. …은 어떤가 하면: *As for racism, much progress has been made, but there is still much to do.* 인종 차별에 대해서는 많이 개선되었지만 아직도 시정할 점이 많다. **8** as it is according to the situation that exists ‖ 현재의 상황에 따라. 사실은. 실제로(는): *We were saving money to go to Hawaii, but as it is we can only afford a camping trip.* 우리는 하와이에 가려고 돈을 저축해 왔지만 실제로 그 돈으로는 겨우 캠핑 여행만 할 수 있다. **9** because ‖ …해서, …하므로: *James decided not to go out as he was* *still really tired.* 제임스는 아직도 너무 피곤해서 외출하지 않기로 했다. —see also **as well** (WELL¹), **so as (not) to do sth** (SO¹)

a.s.a.p. *n* the abbreviation of "as soon as possible" ‖ "as soon as possible(가능 한 한 빨리)"의 약어: *Please reply a.s.a.p.* 조속히 회답 바람

as·bes·tos /æsˈbɛstəs, æz-, əs-, əz-/ *n* [U] a substance that does not burn easily, which was used in some clothing and building material ‖ 불에 잘 타지 않아서 옷이나 건자재로 쓰는 물질. 석면

as·cend /əˈsɛnd/ *v* [I, T] FORMAL to move up or move to the top of something ‖ 상승하다, 또는 어떤 것의 위로 움직이다. 올라가다: *The plane ascended rapidly.* 비행기가 급격하게 상승했다. —opposite DESCEND

as·cen·dan·cy /əˈsɛndənsi/, **ascendency** *n* [U] a position of power, influence, or control ‖ 권력[영향력, 통제력]이 있는 위치. 지배력. 우위: *the ascendancy of Japanese industry* 일본 산업의 지배력

as·cent /əˈsɛnt, ˈæsɛnt/ *n* **1** the act of moving or climbing up ‖ 상승하거나 올라가는 행위. 상승. 오르기: *a successful ascent of the mountain* 성공적인 산악 등반 **2** [U] the process of becoming more important or successful ‖ 더 중요해지거나 성공적으로 되는 과정. 승진. 향상: *Jerry's quick ascent into management surprised no one.* 제리가 경영진으로 빨리 승진한 것에 아무도 놀라지 않았다. **3** a path or road that goes gradually up ‖ 점차적으로 위로 올라가는 길이나 도로. 오르막. 비탈길: *a steep ascent* 가파른 비탈길 —opposite DESCENT

as·cer·tain /ˌæsərˈteɪn/ *v* [T] FORMAL to discover or find out something ‖ 어떤 것을 발견하거나 찾아내다. …을 밝혀내다. …을 확인하다: *School officials are trying to ascertain the facts.* 학교 관계자들은 사실을 밝혀내려고 노력중이다.

as·cet·ic /əˈsɛtɪk/ *adj* living a simple strict life, usually for religious reasons ‖ 보통 종교적인 이유에서 단순하고 엄격한 삶을 사는. 금욕적인. 금욕 생활을 하는 **- ascetic** *n* **- asceticism** /əˈsɛtəˌsɪzəm/ *n* [U]

as·cribe /əˈskraɪb/ *v* [T] FORMAL **ascribe sth to** sb/sth *phr v* [T] FORMAL to believe that something happens or exists because of someone or something else ‖ 어떤 것이 다른 사람이나 사물 때문에 일어나거나 존재한다고 믿다. …을 다른 사람[사물] 탓으로 돌리다: *Carter*

ascribed his problems to a lack of money. 카터는 자신의 문제를 자금 부족 탓으로 돌렸다. **- ascribable** *adj*

a·sex·u·al /eɪˈsɛkʃuəl/ *adj* without sex, sex organs, or sexual activity ‖ 성[성기, 성행위]이 없는. 무성의. 무성생식의

ash /æʃ/ *n, plural* **ashes** [C, U] **1** the soft gray powder that remains after something has been burned ‖ 사물이 타고 난 뒤에 남는 부드러운 회색의 가루. 재: *cigarette ash* 담뱃재. **2** a type of forest tree, or the hard wood of this tree —see also ASHES ‖ 산림수의 일종, 또는 그 나무의 단단한 목재. 양물푸레나무

a·shamed /əˈʃeɪmd/ *adj* **1** feeling embarrassed or guilty about something ‖ 어떤 것에 대해 당혹스러워하거나 떳떳치 못하다고 느끼는. 부끄러워하는: *Mike felt ashamed of his old clothes.* 마이크는 그의 낡은 옷을 부끄럽게 여겼다. / *You should be ashamed of yourself, acting like that!* 그와 같이 행동을 하다니 부끄러운 줄 알아라! / *Fred was ashamed to admit his mistake.* 프레드는 실수를 인정하는 것을 수치스럽게 여겼다. **2 be ashamed of sb** feeling upset because someone embarrasses you ‖ 남이 난처하게 만들어서 당황스러워하다. 부끄럽게 여기다: *Helen felt ashamed of her parents.* 헬렌은 그녀의 부모님을 창피하게 여겼다. —see usage note at GUILTY

ash·en /ˈæʃən/ *adj* very pale because of shock or fear ‖ 충격이나 공포로 인하여 매우 창백한. 핏기가 없는: *her ashen face* 그녀의 창백한 얼굴

ash·es /ˈæʃɪz/ *n* [plural] the ASH that remains after the body of a dead person has been burned ‖ 죽은 사람의 시신이 화장(火葬)되고 난 뒤에 남는 재. 유해: *We scattered my father's ashes over the lake.* 우리는 아버지의 유해를 호수 위에 뿌렸다.

a·shore /əˈʃɔr/ *adv* onto or toward the shore of a lake, river, sea, or ocean ‖ 호수[강, 바다, 대양]의 기슭에 또는 기슭으로: *Brian pulled the boat ashore.* 브라이언은 해변으로 보트를 끌었다.

ash·tray /ˈæʃtreɪ/ *n* a small dish for cigarette ASHes ‖ 담뱃재용 작은 접시. 재떨이

A·sia /ˈeɪʒə/ *n* one of the seven CONTINENTs, that includes land between the Ural mountains and the Pacific Ocean ‖ 우랄 산맥과 태평양 사이에 있는 육지를 포함하는 7대륙의 하나. 아시아

A·sian /ˈeɪʒən/ *adj* relating to or coming from Asia ‖ 아시아와 관련되거나 아시아

출신의. 아시아(산)의

A·sian-A·mer·i·can /ˌ.. .ˈ.../ *n* an American whose family originally came from Asia ‖ 본래 가족이 아시아 출신인 미국인. 아시아계 미국인 - **Asian- American** *adj*

a·side¹ /əˈsaɪd/ *adv* **1** to the side ‖ 옆으로: *Jim stepped aside to let me pass.* 짐은 내가 지나가도록 비켜섰다. **2 put/set sth aside** to not use something, especially money, so that it can be used for a particular purpose later ‖ 어떤 것을, 특히 돈을 나중에 특별한 용도에 사용할 수 있도록 쓰지 않다. 별도로 떼어 두다. 비축하다: *I try to set aside $30 a week for my vacation.* 나는 휴가 때 쓰려고 일주일에 30달러를 따로 떼어 놓으려고 애쓰고 있다. / *A room was set aside for the tests.* 방 하나는 시험을 위해 따로 남겨 놓았다. **3 aside from** ⇨ **apart from** (APART)

aside² *n* a remark you make in a quiet voice so that only a few people can hear ‖ 사람들이 거의 들을 수 없도록 조용한 목소리로 하는 말. 귀엣[귓속]말

ask /æsk/ *v* [I, T] **1** to make a request for someone to tell you something ‖ 남에게 어떤 것을 알려 달라고 요청하다. 묻다. 질문하다: *"What's your name?" she asked.* "이름이 무엇입니까?"라고 그녀는 물었다. / *Can I ask a question?* 질문 하나 해도 괜찮겠습니까? / *He asked how this could have happened.* 그는 이것이 어떻게 해서 발생할 수 있었는지를 질문했다. / *Visitors often ask about the place.* 방문객들은 자주 그 장소에 관해 질문한다. / *You should ask around* (=ask a lot of people) *before deciding.* 너는 결정을 하기 전에 많은 사람들에게 물어봐야 한다. **2** to make a request for help, advice, information etc. ‖ 도움·충고·정보 등을 요청하다. 부탁하다: *If you need anything, just ask.* 무엇이든 필요하면 즉시 요청해라. / *Ask Paula to mail the letters.* 편지들을 부쳐달라고 폴라에게 부탁해라. / *Some people don't like to ask for help.* 어떤 사람들은 도움을 요청하는 것을 꺼린다. / *Ask your Dad if we can borrow his car.* 우리가 차를 빌릴 수 있는지 네 아버지께 여쭈어 보아라. / *All I ask is that you be faithful to me.* 내가 바라는 것이라고는 네가 나에게 충실하라는 것뿐이다. **3** to invite someone to go somewhere ‖ 어떤 장소로 사람을 초대하다. 초청하다: *Jerry would like to ask her out.* 제리는 그녀를 불러내고 싶어한다. / *Why don't you ask them over for dinner?* 그들을 만찬에 초대하는 것이 어

때? **4** to want a particular amount of money for something you are selling ‖ 판매하고 있는 물건에 대한 특정의 금액을 원하다. …에 대하여 대금을 청구[요구]하다: *He's asking $2000 for that old car!* 그가 그 낡은 찻값으로 2천달러나 요구하네! **5 If you ask me** used in order to emphasize your own opinion ‖ 자신의 의견을 강조하는 데에 쓰여. 내 생각으로는: *If you ask me, he's crazy.* 내 생각에 그는 미쳤어. **6 Don't ask me!** SPOKEN said when you do not know the answer to a question and are annoyed that someone has asked ‖ 누군가가 물은 질문에 대한 해답을 모르고 질문이 귀찮을 때 쓰여. 난 몰라! 묻지마!: *"When will Vicky get home?" "Don't ask me!"* "비키는 언제 집에 오니?" "난 몰라!" **7 be asking for trouble** to be behaving in a way that will probably cause trouble ‖ 말썽을 일으키게끔 처신하다. 화를 자초하다: *Allowing campus police to have guns is just asking for trouble.* 대학 캠퍼스 경비원에게 무기 소지를 허용하는 것은 바로 화를 자초하는 일이다. —see usage note at RECOMMEND

USAGE NOTE ask, inquire, demand, request

Ask is the usual verb that we use for questions: *You should ask Dave. / Would anyone like to ask any questions?* **Inquire** is more formal than **ask**: *I would like to inquire about job openings.* When you **demand** something, you expect to get what you want: *The principal demanded to know why we were late.* Use **request** to ask for something formally: *I'd like to request permission to leave.*

ask는 질문에 쓰이는 가장 일반적인 동사이다: 너는 데이브에게 물어봐야 한다./누구든지 질문할 것 있어요? **inquire**는 **ask**보다 격식을 갖춘 말이다: 저는 취직 자리에 관해 문의하고 싶습니다. **demand**는 바라는 것의 획득을 예상하고 무엇인가를 요구할 때에 쓴다: 교장은 우리가 늦은 이유를 해명하라고 했다. **request**는 공식적으로 어떤 것을 요청하는 데에 쓴다: (이만) 물러가도록 허락받고 싶습니다.

---

a·skance /əˈskæns/ *adv* **look askance (at)** to look at or consider something in a way that shows you do not believe it or approve of it ‖ 믿거나 인정하지 않음을 나타내는 투로 어떤 것을 보거나 생각하

다. 불신하는[의심어린] 태도로 보다

a·skew /əˈskyu/ *adv* not exactly straight or level ‖ 정확하게 수직적이거나 수평적이지 않은. 비스듬히: *His coat was wrinkled and his hat was askew.* 그의 코트는 구겨지고 모자는 삐딱해 있었다.

a·sleep /əˈslip/ *adj* **1** sleeping ‖ 잠든: *Be quiet. The baby is asleep.* 조용해라. 아기가 잠들어 있다. / *Look at Jerry. He's fast/sound asleep.* 제리를 봐라. 잠이 푹 들었네. (=sleeping very deeply) **2 fall asleep** to begin to sleep ‖ 잠들기 시작하다. 잠 들다: *I always fall asleep watching TV.* 나는 항상 TV를 보다가 잠들어 버린다. **3** if your arm or leg is asleep, it has been in one position too long so that you cannot feel anything ‖ 한 자세로 너무 오랫동안 있어서 팔이나 다리가 아무것도 느낄 수 없는. 저려

as·par·a·gus /əˈspærəgəs/ *n* [U] a slightly bitter green vegetable shaped like a small stick with a point on one end ‖ 한쪽 끝에 점이 있는 작은 막대기 같이 생긴 약간 쓴 녹색 채소. 아스파라거스 —see picture on page 944

as·pect /ˈæspɛkt/ *n* one of the parts or features of a situation, idea, problem etc. ‖ 상황·생각·문제 등의 일부나 특징. 양상: *The committee discussed several aspects of the traffic problem.* 위원회는 교통 문제의 여러 양상을 논의했다.

as·pen /ˈæspən/ *n* a tall thin straight tree that grows in the western US, with leaves that make a pleasant noise in the wind ‖ 미국 서부에서 자라며 잎이 바람에 유쾌한 소리를 내는, 가늘고 곧게 뻗은 큰 나무. 사시나무

as·per·sion /əˈspɚʒən, -ʃən/ *n* FORMAL **cast aspersions on** to suggest that someone is not very good at something ‖ 남이 어떤 것에 뛰어나지 못하다고 말하다. …을 비방하다

as·phalt /ˈæsfɔlt/ *n* [U] a black sticky substance that gets hard when it dries, used for making the surface of roads ‖ 도로 포장용으로 쓰이며, 마르면 굳는 검고 끈적끈적한 물질. 아스팔트

as·phyx·i·ate /əˈsfɪksiˌeɪt, æ-/ *v* [I, T] FORMAL to be unable to breathe or to make someone unable to breathe, often resulting in death; SUFFOCATE ‖ 숨을 쉴 수 없거나 사람이 숨을 쉴 수 없게 하여 종종 사망을 초래하다. 질식하다. 질식 (사)시키다 ; ⟲ suffocate – **asphyxiation** /əˌsfɪksiˈeɪʃən/ *n* [U]

as·pi·ra·tion /ˌæspəˈreɪʃən/ *n* a strong desire to have or achieve something ‖ 어떤 것을 소유하거나 달성하려는 강한 욕망. 소망. 야망: *Annette has aspirations to become a writer.* 아네트는 작가가 되려는 대망이 있다.

as·pire /əˈspaɪɚ/ *v* [I] to have a strong desire to do something important ‖ 중요한 일을 하려는 강한 욕망을 가지다. 갈망하다. 열망하다: *Milligan aspires to be Governor of the state.* 밀리건은 주지사가 되기를 열망하고 있다.

as·pi·rin /ˈæsprɪn/ *n, plural* **aspirins** or **aspirin** [C, U] a drug that reduces pain and fever ‖ 통증과 열을 완화시키는 약품. 아스피린

as·pir·ing /əˈspaɪrɪŋ/ *adj* an aspiring actor, politician etc. is trying to become an actor, politician etc. ‖ 배우·정치인 등이 되려고 애쓰는. 포부[야심]가 있는

ass /æs/ *n* **1** ⇨ DONKEY

SPOKEN PHRASES

2 an impolite word for the part of your body that you sit on ‖ 앉는 신체 부위를 이르는 점잖치 못한 단어. 궁둥이: *Jamie fell right on his ass.* 제이미는 바로 엉덩방아를 찧었다. **3 your ass/his ass etc.** used in many impolite phrases as a way of talking to or about someone ‖ 남에게 말하거나 남에 관해 말하는 방법으로서 여러 점잖치 못한 어구에 쓰여: *Get your ass in gear!* (=hurry up) 서둘러! **4** SLANG used in order to emphasize an adjective ‖ 형용사를 강조하는 데에 쓰여: *That's one big ass car!* 저 차 진짜 크다!

---

as·sail /əˈseɪl/ *v* [T] **1** to strongly criticize someone or something ‖ 사람이나 사물을 강하게 비판하다 **2** to attack someone physically ‖ 사람의 신체를 공격하다.

as·sail·ant /əˈseɪlənt/ *n* FORMAL someone who attacks someone else ‖ 타인을 공격하는 사람. 공격자. 가해자

as·sas·sin /əˈsæsən/ *n* someone who murders a ruler or politician, usually for political reasons ‖ 정치적 동기로 통치자나 정치가를 살해하는 사람. 암살자

as·sas·si·nate /əˈsæsəˌneɪt/ *v* [T] to murder a ruler or politician, usually for political reasons ‖ 정치적 동기로 통치자나 정치가를 살해하다. 암살하다 – **assassination** /əˌsæsəˈneɪʃən/ *n* [C, U]

as·sault¹ /əˈsɔlt/ *n* [C, U] a violent attack on someone ‖ 사람에 대한 맹렬한 공격. 맹공격. 폭행: *He served three years in prison for assault.* 그는 폭행으로 3년간 복역했다. / *an increase in* *sexual assaults* 성폭행의 증가

assault² *v* [T] to attack someone violently ‖ 남을 맹렬히 공격하다: *Demonstrators assaulted some of the policemen.* 시위대는 몇몇 경찰관을 맹렬히 공격했다.

as·sem·bly /ə'sɛmbli/ *n* [C, U] **1** a meeting of a group of people for a particular purpose ‖ 특정 목적을 위한 일단의 사람들의 모임. 회합. 집회: *The school assembly begins at 9 o'clock.* 학교 조회는 9시에 시작한다. **2** the name of the group of people who are elected to make laws in some states ‖ 일부 국가에서 입법을 위해 선출된 사람들의 집단 이름. 의회: *the New York State Assembly* 뉴욕 주의회

as·sem·bly·man /ə'sɛmblimən/, **as·sem·bly·woman** /ə'sɛmbli-,wʊmən/ *n* a member of a state assembly ‖ 국가 의회의 구성원. 의원

as·sent /ə'sɛnt/ *v* [I] FORMAL to agree to a suggestion, idea etc ‖ 제안·의견 등에 동의하다. 찬성하다. – **assent** *n* [U] —opposite DISSENT²

as·sert /ə'sɚt/ *v* **1** [T] to state an opinion or belief firmly ‖ 의견이나 신념을 강력히 말하다. 단언하다. 주장하다: *Professor Ross asserts that American schools are not strict enough.* 로스 교수는 미국 학교는 별로 엄격하지 않다고 주장한다. **2** [T] to behave in a way that shows your right to do or have something ‖ 어떤 것을 하거나 가질 권리를 나타내는 투로 행동하다. 강력히 주장하다: *The president tried to assert his power over the military.* 대통령은 군부에 자신의 권력을 강력히 주장하려고 했다. **3** **assert yourself** to behave in a determined way so that no one makes you do things you do not want to do ‖ 원하지 않는 일을 아무도 시키지 못하도록 단호하게 행동하다. 제 주장을 내세우다: *Don't be afraid to assert yourself in the interview.* 인터뷰할 때에는 자기 자신의 주장을 내세우는 것을 두려워하지 마라.

as·ser·tion /ə'sɚʃən/ *n* [C, U] something that you say or write that you strongly believe ‖ 자신이 강하게 믿는 것을 말하거나 쓰는 일. 주장. 단언: *He repeated his assertion that he was innocent.* 그는 자신이 결백하다는 주장을 되풀이했다.

as·ser·tive /ə'sɚtɪv/ *adj* behaving confidently so that people pay attention to what you say ‖ 다른 사람들이 자신이 말하는 것에 주의를 기울이도록 자신있게 행동하는. 단언[단정]적인: *Kramer's*

more assertive than I am. 크래머는 나보다 더 단정적이다. – **assertively** *adv* – **assertiveness** *n* [U]

as·sess /ə'sɛs/ *v* [T] **1** to make a judgment about a person or situation after thinking carefully about it ‖ 주의깊게 고려한 뒤에 사람이나 상황에 대해 판단하다. 평가하다: *Psychologists will assess the child's behavior.* 심리학자들이 그 아동의 행동을 평가할 것이다. / *We're trying to assess what went wrong.* 우리는 무엇이 잘못되었는지를 판단하려고 노력하고 있다. **2** to judge the quality, amount, or value of something ‖ 어떤 것의 질[양, 가치]을 판단하다. 사정[평가]하다: *They assessed the house at $90,000.* 그들은 그 집을 9만 달러로 평가했다. – **assessment** *n* [C, U]

as·set /'æsɛt/ *n* **1** something that a company owns, that can be sold to pay debts ‖ 채무 변제를 위해 팔 수 있는 회사의 소유물. 재산. 자산 **2** someone or something that is useful in helping you succeed or deal with problems ‖ 성공하거나 문제를 처리하는 데 유용하게 도움이 되는 사람이나 물건. 가치있는 사람[것]: *A sense of humor is a real asset.* 유머 감각은 진짜로 유용한 자질이다. / *You're an asset to the company, George.* 조지, 너는 그 회사의 보배[인재]야. —compare LIABILITY

as·sign /ə'saɪn/ *v* [T] **1** to give someone a job to do ‖ 사람에게 해야 할 직무를 부여하다. 선임하다. 배정하다: *Guards were assigned to the President.* 경호원들이 대통령에게 배속되었다. **2** to give something to someone so s/he can use it for a particular purpose ‖ 특정 목적을 위해 사용하도록 어떤 것을 사람에게 주다. 할당하다: *They assigned me a small room.* 그들은 나에게 작은 방 하나를 할당했다.

as·sign·ment /ə'saɪnmənt/ *n* **1** a job or piece of work that you are given to do ‖ 하도록 부여된 직무나 업무. 임무: *The newspaper is sending her on a special assignment to China.* 그 신문사는 특별 임무를 위해 그녀를 중국에 파견하려 한다. / *a homework assignment* 숙제 **2** the act of giving people particular jobs to do ‖ 사람에게 특정한 업무를 부여하는 행위. 임명: *the assignment of chores* 잡일을 맡김

as·sim·i·late /ə'sɪmə,leɪt/ *v* **1** [I, T] to accept someone completely as a member of a group, or to become an accepted member of a group ‖ 사람을 단체의 구성원으로 완전히 받아들이거나 단

체의 구성원이 되다. 동화되다[시키다]: *As the immigrants were assimilated into the US, they stopped speaking their languages.* 이민자들이 미국에 동화되었을 때 그들은 자신의 모국어로 말하지 않았다. **2** [T] to completely understand new facts and information, and be able to use them ‖ 새 사실과 정보를 완전히 이해하며 그 활용이 가능하다. 흡수 · 소화하다: *The person we need for the job must be able to assimilate new ideas quickly.* 그 업무에 우리가 필요로 하는 사람은 새로운 개념들을 신속히 받아들일 수 있어야만 한다. – **assimilation** /ə,sɪmə'leɪʃən/ *n* [U]

as·sist /ə'sɪst/ *v* [I, T] to help someone do something that needs special skills ‖ 특별한 기술을 요하는 일을 하는 사람을 돕다. 도와주다: *Two nurses assisted Dr. Bernard in performing the operation.* 두 명의 간호사가 버나드 박사의 수술을 도왔다. —see usage note at HELP[1]

as·sist·ance /ə'sɪstəns/ *n* [U] help or support ‖ 도움, 지원: *The company provides assistance for new computer users.* 그 회사는 새로운 컴퓨터 사용자들을 지원한다. / *Can I be of any assistance?* 제가 뭘 좀 도와 드릴 수 있겠습니까? (=a formal phrase meaning "Can I help you?")

as·sist·ant /ə'sɪstənt/ *n* someone who helps someone else who has a higher rank ‖ 상급자를 돕는 사람. 조수. 보조자: *a sales assistant* 판매 보조원 / *the assistant manager* 부지배인

as·so·ci·ate[1] /ə'soʊʃi,eɪt, -si,eɪt/ *v* **1** [I, T] to make a connection in your mind between one thing or person and another ‖ 한 가지 일이나 사람과 다른 것이나 사람과의 사이를 마음속으로 연결짓다. 연상하다: *I always associate summer with travel.* 나는 항상 여름하면 여행을 연상한다. **2 be associated with** to be connected with a particular subject, activity, group etc ‖ 특정한 주제 · 활동 · 단체 등과 연관되다: *health problems associated with tobacco* 담배와 연관되어 있는 건강 문제 **3 associated with sb** to spend time with or work with someone ‖ 남과 함께 시간을 보내거나 일을 하다. 제휴하다. 협동[협력]하다: *She had been associated with the Paris fashion designers for years.* 그녀는 수년 동안 파리의 패션 디자이너들과 제휴하여 일했었다.

as·so·ci·ate[2] /ə'soʊʃiɪt, -siɪt/ *n* someone whom you work or do business with ‖ 함께 일이나 사업을 하는 사람. 제

휴자. 공동 경영자: *a business associate* 사업상 동료

Associate of Arts /.......... './, **Associate degree** *n* a college degree given after two years of study, usually at a COMMUNITY COLLEGE ‖ 보통 지역 사회 대학에서 2년 수료 후에 주는 학사 학위. 준문학사 학위

as·so·ci·a·tion /ə,soʊsi'eɪʃən, -ʃi'eɪ-/ *n* **1** an organization that consists of people who have the same aims or interests ‖ 동일한 목적이나 이익을 가진 사람들로 구성된 조직. 협회. 회: *an association for librarians* 사서(司書)를 위한 단체 **2 in association with** together with someone or something else ‖ 다른 사람이나 사물과 함께 . …과 공동으로: *Community groups are working in association with the schools.* 지역 사회 단체는 학교와 공동으로 일하고 있다. **3** a connection in your mind between two things ‖ 두 가지 것 사이에서 마음에 연관지어지는 것. 연상되는 것: *Los Angeles has happy associations for me.* 로스앤젤레스 하면 내게는 즐거운 것이 연상된다.

as·sort·ed /ə'sɔrtɪd/ *adj* of various different types ‖ 갖가지 다른 형태의. 잡다한: *a box of assorted cookies* 한 상자의 종합 과자

as·sort·ment /ə'sɔrt ̚mənt/ *n* a mixture of various things or of different types of the same thing ‖ 여러 가지 사물이나 다른 형태의 동일 사물의 혼합물: *an assortment of chocolates* 각종 초콜릿

as·sume /ə'sum/ *v* [T] **1** to think that something is true although you have no proof ‖ 증거는 없지만 무엇을 사실로 여기다. 당연한 것으로 여기다. 가정하다: *Your light wasn't on so I assumed (that) you were out.* 네 방의 불이 꺼져 있어서 외출한 줄 알았다. / *Assuming (that) Dad agrees, when do you want to shop for cars?* 아빠가 동의해 주신다면 넌 언제 자동차를 사러 가겠느냐? **2** to start to do a job, sometimes when you do not have the right to ‖ 때로는 권한 없이 직무를 하기 시작하다. 수행하다: *Stalin assumed power/control in 1941.* 스탈린은 1941년에 집권했다. **3 assume an air/expression of** to pretend to have a particular quality ‖ 특정한 성질을 가진 듯이 가장하다. …의 태도를/…의 표정을 가장하다: *Andy assumed an air of innocence when the teacher walked by.* 앤디는 선생님이 지나갈 때 결백한 척했다. **4** to start having a particular quality or appearance ‖ 특정한 성질이나 양상을 띠기 시작하다. …을 띠다[지니다]: *Her* *family life assumed more importance after the accident.* 그녀에게 가정 생활은 그 사고 후에 더욱 소중하게 되었다.

as·sumed /ə'sumd/ *adj* **an assumed name/identity** a false name ‖ 가짜 이름. 가명/가짜 신원

as·sump·tion /ə'sʌmpʃən/ *n* something that you think is true although you have no proof ‖ 증거는 없지만 생각하기에 사실로 여김. 상정(想定). 억측: *How could you make an assumption about her without meeting her!* 그녀를 만나 보지도 않고 그녀에 대해 억측을 하다니!

as·sur·ance /ə'ʃʊrəns/ *n* **1** a promise that you give to someone to make him/her feel less worried ‖ 남이 덜 불안하도록 제시하는 약속. 확언. 보증: *We need an assurance that you can pay off your loan.* 우리는 네가 채무를 상환할 수 있도록 보증이 필요하다. **2** [U] confidence in your own abilities ‖ 자신의 능력에 대한 확신: *Cindy answered their questions with quiet assurance.* 신디는 그들의 질문에 자신만만하게 답변했다.

as·sure /ə'ʃʊr/ *v* [T] **1** to make someone feel less worried by promising that something is definitely true ‖ 어떤 것이 틀림없는 사실이라고 약속을 하여 남을 덜 불안하게 하다. 보증하다. 장담하다: *The doctors assured me that her life was not in danger.* 의사들은 그녀의 목숨이 위험하지 않다고 나에게 장담했다. / *The concert won't be canceled, I can assure you.* 음악회는 취소되지 않을 거야, 틀림없어. **2** to make something certain to happen or be achieved ‖ 어떤 것이 발생하거나 달성되는 것을 확실하게 하다: *The new contract means that the future of the company is assured.* 새 계약은 회사 장래가 확실하다는 것을 뜻한다.

as·sured /ə'ʃʊrd/ *adj* certain to be achieved ‖ 달성되는 것이 확실한: *an assured victory* 확실한 승리 — **assuredly** /ə'ʃʊrɪdli/ *adv*

as·ter·isk /'æstərɪsk/ *n* a mark like a star (*) used in order to show something interesting or important ‖ 관심이 있거나 중요한 것을 나타내기 위해 사용되는 별 모양의 마크. 별표

as·ter·oid /'æstə,rɔɪd/ *n* one of the many small PLANETs between Jupiter and Mars ‖ 목성과 화성 사이에 있는 수많은 작은 행성 중의 하나. 소행성

asth·ma /'æzmə/ *n* [U] an illness that causes difficulties in breathing ‖ 호흡 곤란을 일으키는 질병. 천식 — **asthmatic** /æz'mætɪk/ *adj*

as·ton·ish /ə'stanɪʃ/ *v* [T] to surprise someone very much ‖ 사람을 크게 놀라게 하다: *Grandma was astonished by how much Hal could eat.* 할머니는 핼이 얼마나 먹어대는지 아연했다. / *I was astonished to learn that she was only 22.* 나는 그녀가 겨우 22세라는 것을 알고 깜짝 놀랐다.

as·ton·ished /ə'stanɪʃt/ *adj* very surprised about something ‖ 어떤 것에 깜짝 놀란: *Parker seemed astonished that someone wanted to buy the house.* 파커는 누군가가 그 집을 구입하고 싶어한다는 것에 크게 놀란 듯했다.

as·ton·ish·ing /ə'stanɪʃɪŋ/ *adj* so surprising that it is difficult to believe ‖ 믿기 어려울 정도로 너무 놀라운. 뜻밖의: *astonishing news* 놀라운 뉴스 — **astonishingly** *adv*

as·ton·ish·ment /ə'stanɪʃmənt/ *n* [U] great surprise ‖ 몹시 놀람. 경악: *To our astonishment, Sue won the race.* 놀랍게도 수는 경주에서 우승했다.

as·tound /ə'staʊnd/ *adj* to make someone feel very surprised or shocked ‖ 사람을 크게 놀라거나 충격받게 하다. 대경실색케 하다: *My brother's decision astounded us all.* 내 동생의 결정은 우리 모두를 경악케 했다.

as·tound·ing /ə'staʊndɪŋ/ *adj* so surprising or shocking that it is difficult to believe ‖ 믿기 어려울 정도로 놀랍거나 충격적인. 대경실색케 하는: *his astounding success* 그의 놀라운 성공 — **astoundingly** *adv*

a·stray /ə'streɪ/ *adv* **1 go astray** to become lost ‖ 잃어버리다. 행방불명되다: *One of the documents we sent them has gone astray.* 우리가 그들에게 보낸 문서 중 하나가 분실됐다. **2 lead sb astray** OFTEN HUMOROUS to persuade someone to believe something that is not true or to do something wrong ‖ 사람에게 진실이 아닌 것을 믿거나 나쁜 짓을 하도록 설득하다. 남을 타락시키다: *I think Mom's worried I'll be led astray if I live alone!* 내가 혼자 살면 타락할까봐 어머니께서 걱정하신다는 생각이 들어!

a·stride /ə'straɪd/ *adv* having one leg on each side of something ‖ 어떤 것의 양쪽으로 각각 다리 하나씩을 놓아. 두 다리를 벌려: *sitting astride a horse* 두 다리를 벌려서 말에 올라타기

astride

as·trin·gent /ə'strɪndʒənt/ *adj* **1** criticizing someone very severely ‖ 사람을 아주 심하게 비판하는. 준엄한. 가혹한. 엄격한: *astringent remarks* 신랄한 논평 **2** TECHNICAL able to make your skin less oily or stop a wound from bleeding ‖ 피부에 기름기를 적게 하거나 출혈을 막는. 수렴성의: *an astringent cream* 수렴성 크림

as·trol·o·gy /ə'strɑlədʒi/ *n* [U] the study of the movements of the stars and their influence on people or events ‖ 별의 움직임과 사람이나 사건에 대한 별의 영향력에 관한 연구. 점성학(占星學). 점성술 – **astrological** /ˌæstrə'lɑdʒɪkəl/ *adj* – **astrologist** /ə'strɑlədʒɪst/ *n*

as·tro·naut /'æstrə,nɔt, -,nɑt/ *n* someone who travels and works in a SPACECRAFT ‖ 우주선으로 여행하거나 일하는 사람. 우주 비행사

as·tro·nom·i·cal /ˌæstrə'nɑmɪkəl/ *adj* **1** extremely large in amount ‖ 양이 아주 많은. 천문학적인. 어마어마한: *astronomical prices* 엄청난 가격 **2** relating to the study of the stars ‖ 별에 관한 연구에 관련된. 천문학(상)의

as·tron·o·my /ə'strɑnəmi/ *n* [U] the scientific study of the stars ‖ 별에 대한 과학적인 연구. 천문학 – **astronomer** *n*

As·tro·Turf /'æstroʊ,tɚf/ *n* [U] TRADEMARK a type of artificial grass that people play sports on ‖ 그 위에서 사람들이 운동을 하는 인공 잔디의 일종

as·tute /ə'stut/ *adj* very good at using your knowledge in order to become successful ‖ 성공적이 되도록 지식을 대단히 잘 활용하는. 기민한. 통찰력 있는: *an astute journalist* 통찰력 있는 언론인 – **astutely** *adv*

a·sy·lum /ə'saɪləm/ *n* **1** [U] protection that a government gives to someone who escapes from a country for political reasons ‖ 정치적 이유로 어떤 나라로부터 도망하는 자에게 다른 나라 정부가 제공하는 보호. 정치범 비호. 망명 **2** OLD-FASHIONED a hospital for people with mental illnesses ‖ 정신 질환자를 위한 병원. 정신 병원

at /ət; *strong* æt/ *prep* **1** used in order to show the position of someone or something, or where something is happening ‖ 사람이나 사물의 위치 또는 일이 일어나고 있는 장소를 나타내는 데 쓰여. …에(서), …에 있어서: *Meet me at my house.* 우리 집에서 봐. / *There was a long line at the bank.* 은행에 사람들이 길게 늘어서 있었다. / *A lot of people were at the funeral.* 장례식에는 많은 사람들이

있었다. **2** when it is a particular time ‖ 특정한 시간에: *The movie starts at 8:00.* 그 영화는 8시에 시작한다. / *Alison gets lonely at Christmas.* 앨리슨은 크리스마스 때 외로워진다. **3** toward someone or something ‖ 사람이나 사물을 향하여: *Jake shot at the deer but missed.* 제이크는 사슴을 향해 쏘았으나 빗나갔다. / *Stop shouting at me!* 나에게 고함지르지 마라! **4** because of someone or something ‖ 사람이나 사물 때문에: *None of the kids laughed at his joke.* 아이들 가운데 아무도 그의 농담을 듣고 웃지 않았다. / *Jenny, I'm surprised at you!* 제니, 너 때문에 놀랐어! **5** used in order to show what you are considering when making a judgment about someone's ability ‖ 사람의 능력에 관한 판단을 할 때 고려하고 있는 것을 나타내는 데 쓰여. …의 점에서: *How's Brian doing at his new job?* 브라이언은 새 업무를 어떻게 하고 있지? / *Debbie is good/bad at math.* 데비는 수학을 잘[잘 못] 한다. **6** used in order to show what someone is doing or the state someone or something is in ‖ 사람이 하는 일이나 사람이나 물건이 처해 있는 상태를 나타내는 데 쓰여. …에 종사[열중]하여. …의 상태[입장]에: *I'm sorry, Mr. Rivers is at lunch* (=eating lunch). 죄송합니다. 리버스 씨는 점심 식사중입니다. / *Many children are still at risk of disease.* 많은 어린이들이 아직 질병의 위험에 처해 있다. **7** used in order to show a price, rate, speed, level, age etc. ‖ 값·비율·속도·수준·나이 등을 나타내는 데 쓰여: *Gas is selling at about $1.25 a gallon.* 휘발유는 1갤런에 약 1달러 25센트에 팔린다. / *I started school at age five.* 나는 다섯 살에 입학했다. —see also **at all** (ALL²), **at first** (FIRST¹), **at least** (LEAST¹)

ate /eɪt/ the past tense of EAT ‖ eat의 과거형

a·the·ist /'eɪθiɪst/ *n* someone who does not believe in the existence of God ‖ 신의 존재를 믿지 않는 사람. 무신론자 – **atheism** *n* [U]

ath·lete /'æθlit/ *n* someone who is good at sports ‖ 스포츠를 잘 하는 사람. 스포츠맨. 운동 선수

ath·let·ic /æθ'lɛtɪk/ *adj* **1** able to play a particular sport or a lot of sports very well ‖ 특정 스포츠나 여러 스포츠를 잘 할 수 있는 **2** having a healthy body with very strong muscles ‖ 아주 튼튼한 근육으로 된 건강한 몸을 가진. 강건한

ath·let·ics /æθ'lɛtɪks/ *n* [U] physical activities such as sports and exercises ‖

스포츠와 운동 등의 신체 활동. 운동 경기. 체육: *high school athletics* 고교 체육

At·lan·tic O·cean /ət˺ˌlæntɪk ˈoʊʃən/ *n* **the Atlantic** the large ocean between North and South America in the west, and Europe and Africa in the east ‖ 서쪽으로는 북미와 남미 사이, 동쪽으로는 유럽과 아프리카 사이에 있는 대양. 대서양

at·las /ˈæt˺ləs/ *n* a book of maps ‖ 지도책: *a world atlas* 세계 지도책

ATM *n* Automated Teller Machine; a machine outside of a bank that you use to get money out of your account ‖ Automated Teller Machine(현금 자동 인출기)의 약어; 계좌에서 돈을 인출하는 데에 쓰이는 은행 점포 밖에 있는 기계

at·mos·phere /ˈæt˺məsˌfɪr/ *n* [C, U] **1** the feeling that an event, situation, or place gives you ‖ 사건[상황, 장소]이 빚어내는 느낌. 분위기: *The atmosphere at home's been really depressing since you left.* 네가 떠나고 나서 집안 분위기는 정말 침울했다. **2 the atmosphere** the mixture of gases that surrounds the Earth ‖ 지구를 둘러싼 기체의 혼합물. 대기 **3** the air inside a room ‖ 실내의 공기: *a smoky atmosphere* 담배 연기가 자욱한 실내 공기 **- atmospheric** /ˌæt˺məsˈfɪrɪk/ *adj*

at·om /ˈætəm/ *n* one of the smallest parts that any substance can be divided into, that combines with other atoms to make a MOLECULE ‖ 물질이 나뉠 수 있는 가장 작은 요소의 하나로 다른 원자와 결합하여 분자를 이룸. 원자 **- atomic** /əˈtɑmɪk/ *adj*

a·tom·ic bomb /.ˌ.. ˈ./ *n* a very powerful bomb that causes an explosion by splitting ATOMs ‖ 원자의 분열로 폭발을 일으키는 매우 강력한 폭탄. 원자탄

a·tomic en·er·gy /.ˌ.. ˈ.../ *n* [U] the power that comes from splitting atoms, often used in making electricity ‖ 종종 발전에 이용되기도 하는, 원자 분열에서 발생하는 힘. 원자력

a·tone /əˈtoʊn/ *v* [I] FORMAL to do something to show that you are sorry for doing something wrong ‖ 잘못한 것에 대한 유감을 나타내는 일을 하다. 속죄하다. 보상하다 **- atonement** *n* [U]

a·tro·cious /əˈtroʊʃəs/ *adj* extremely bad ‖ 지극히 나쁜. 극악(무도)한. 지독한: *atrocious weather/behavior* 지독한 날씨[잔학한 행동] **- atrociously** *adv*

a·troc·i·ty /əˈtrɑsəti/ *n* [C, U] an extremely cruel or violent action ‖ 아주 잔인하거나 난폭한 행동. 극악무도함. 잔학 행위: *the atrocities of war* 전쟁의 잔

인성

at·tach /əˈtætʃ/ *v* **1** [T] to make something stick to or be connected with something else ‖ 무엇을 다른 것에 붙이거나 연결시키다. 붙이다. 첨부하다: *Please attach a photograph to your application form.* 신청서에 사진을 붙이세요. **2 get attached to** to like someone or something, especially more than you should ‖ 해야 할 정도 이상으로 사람이나 사물을 좋아하다. 사랑하다. 애착을 느끼다: *As a doctor I cannot get too attached to my patients.* 의사로서 나는 환자들에게 지나친 애착을 가질 수는 없다. **3 attach importance/blame etc.** to believe that someone or something is important, valuable, guilty etc. ‖ 사람이나 사물이 소중하다[가치 있다, 죄가 있다]고 여기다. 중요성을 부여하다/허물을 두 다 : *They seem to attach more importance to money than to happiness.* 그들은 행복보다는 돈을 더 중시하는 것 같다.

attach

at·tach·é /ˌætæˈʃeɪ, ˌætə-/ *n* someone who works in an EMBASSY, and deals with a particular area of knowledge ‖ 대사관에 근무하면서 정통한 특정 분야에 관계하는 사람. 대[공]사관원: *a military attaché* 무관(武官)

at·tach·ment /əˈtætʃmənt/ *n* **1** [U] a strong feeling of loyalty, love, or friendship for someone or something ‖ 사람이나 사물에 대한 충성[사랑, 우정]의 강한 감정. 애착: *a mother's deep attachment to her baby* 아기에 대한 어머니의 깊은 사랑 **-opposite** DETACHMENT **2** a piece of equipment that you attach to a machine to make it do different things ‖ 다른 일을 하도록 기계에 부착하는 장비의 부품. 부속품: *attachments for the food processor* 만능 조리 기구 부속품

at·tack¹ /əˈtæk/ *n* **1** [C, U] a violent action that is intended to damage someone or something ‖ 사람이나 사물을 해치려는 난폭 행위. 공격. 습격: *There have been several attacks on foreigners recently.* 최근에 여러 차례 외국인들에 대한 습격이 있었다. / *The city is under attack.* (=being attacked) 그 도시는 공격을 받고 있다. **2** [C, U] strong criticism ‖ 강한 비난. 비방: *an attack on the government's welfare policy* 정부의 복지

정책에 대한 비난 **3** a sudden short period of time when you suffer from an illness, or feel frightened or worried ‖ 급작스레 질병으로 고통을 받거나, 또는 두려움이나 불안을 느끼게 되는 순간. 발병. 발작: *an attack of asthma* 천식의 발병 / *panic attacks* 공포의 엄습 – **attacker** *n* —see also HEART ATTACK

attack² *v* **1** [I, T] to try to hurt someone physically, especially by using a weapon ‖ 특히 무기를 사용하여 남의 신체를 해치려고 하다. 공격하다: *Dan was attacked as he got into his car.* 댄은 자동차에 타자마자 바로 공격 당했다. **2** [T] to severely criticize someone or something ‖ 사람이나 사물을 심하게 비평하다. 비난하다: *Newspapers attacked the President for failing to cut taxes.* 신문들은 조세 삭감의 실패에 대하여 대통령을 비난했다. **3** [T] if an illness attacks a part of your body, it damages it ‖ 질병이 침범하여 몸의 일부 부위를 해치다: *The AIDS virus attacks the body's immune system.* AIDS 바이러스는 신체의 면역 체계를 파괴한다.

at·tain /ə'teɪn/ *v* [T] to succeed in getting something you want, especially after trying for a long time ‖ 장시간 노력 끝에 원하는 것을 달성하다. 성공하다. 도달하다: *More women are attaining high positions in business.* 많은 여성들이 재계에서 고위직을 획득하고 있다. – **attainable** *adj* – **attainment** *n* [C, U]

at·tempt¹ /ə'tɛmpt/ *v* [T] to try to do something ‖ 어떤 것을 하려고 애쓰다. 시도하다. 꾀하다: *I never would have attempted to climb that mountain!* 나는 그 산을 오르려고 시도해 본 적도 없어!

attempt² *n* **1** an act of trying to do something ‖ 어떤 것을 해 보려는 행위. 시도. 기도: *Can't you make an attempt to be nice to your sister?* 네 누이에게 다정하게 대해 보지 않겠니? **2 an attempt on sb's life** an action intended to kill someone, especially someone important ‖ 특히 중요한 인물을 살해하려는 행위. …을 죽이려 함

at·tend /ə'tɛnd/ *v* [T] **1** to go to an event, such as a meeting, wedding etc. ‖ 회의·결혼식 등의 행사에 가다. 참석[출석]하다: *Most of the people who attended the concert were teenagers.* 콘서트에 온 사람들은 대부분 10대였다. **2** to regularly go to an institution, such as a school or church ‖ 학교나 교회 등의 기관에 정기적으로 가다. 다니다: *All students must attend classes regularly.* 모든 학생들은 꼬박꼬박 수업에 출석해야

한다. **3** to take care of someone ‖ 사람을 돌보다. 시중들다: *a doctor attending one of her patients* 그녀의 환자 중 한 명을 돌보고 있는 의사

attend to sb/sth *phr v* [T] to deal with someone or something ‖ 사람이나 사물에 대처하다: *Do our public schools attend to our children's needs?* 우리 공립 학교는 아이들의 욕구에 대처하고 있습니까?

at·tend·ance /ə'tɛndəns/ *n* **1** [C, U] the act of regularly going to an institution, such as a school or church ‖ 학교나 교회 등의 기관에 정기적으로 가는 행위. 출석. 참석: *A child's attendance at school is required by law.* 아동의 취학은 법적으로 요구된다. **2** [singular] the number of people who attend an event, such as a meeting, concert etc. ‖ 회의·음악회 등의 행사에 참석하는 사람의 숫자. 출석[참석]자(수): *Be quiet while I take attendance.* (=count how many students are in class today) 내가 출석자를 세고 있는 동안에 조용히 해라.

at·tend·ant /ə'tɛndənt/ *n* someone whose job is to take care of someone or something ‖ 사람이나 사물을 돌보는 직업인. 시중드는 사람. 종업원: *a parking lot attendant* 주차장 관리인

at·ten·tion /ə'tɛnʃən/ *n* [U] **1** the state of watching, listening to, noticing, or thinking about something ‖ 어떤 것에 대해 보거나 듣거나 인식하거나 생각하는 상태. 주의(력). 주목: *Sorry, what did you say? I wasn't paying attention.* 죄송하지만 무슨 말씀을 하셨지요? 주의를 기울이지 못했습니다. / *Charlie tried to catch/get/attract our attention.* (=make us notice him) 찰리는 우리의 주의를 끌려고 했다. **2** the special care or interest you give to someone or something ‖ 사람이나 사물에 대한 특별한 배려나 관심: *Johnny always has to be the center of attention.* (=the person everyone notices) 조니는 항상 모든 사람에 배려해 주어야 한다. / *The back yard really needs some attention – it's full of weeds.* 뒤뜰에 정말 관심을 좀 가져야 돼, 잡초투성이야. **3 (could I have your) attention, please** SPOKEN used in order to ask people to be quiet and to listen to what you are going to say ‖ 남에게 조용히 하고 말하려는 것을 경청해 달라고 부탁하는 데에 쓰여. 주목해 주세요 **4 stand at/to attention** used in order to tell a soldier to stand up straight and stay still ‖ 군인에게 똑바로 서서 가만히 있으라고 말하는 데에 쓰여. 차려

at·ten·tive /ə'tɛntɪv/ *adj* carefully

listening to or watching someone because you are interested in what s/he is doing ‖ 남이 하는 일에 관심이 있어 주의깊게 듣거나 보는. 주의 깊은. 주의[주목]하고 있는: *an attentive audience* 경청하는 관중 **– attentively** *adv* **– attentiveness** *n* [U]

at·test /ə'tɛst/ *v* [I, T] **1** to prove something or show that something is true ‖ 어떤 것을 증명하거나 어떤 것이 진실이라는 것을 보이다. 입증하다: *The crowd of people waiting outside his door attests to this young star's popularity.* 그의 집 문 밖에서 기다리고 있는 군중들이 젊은 스타의 인기를 증명해 준다. **2** to say officially that something is true, especially in a court of law ‖ 특히 법정에서 어떤 것이 사실이라고 공식적으로 말하다. 증언하다

at·tic /'ætɪk/ *n* a space or room at the top of a house, usually used for storing things ‖ 물건 보관에 쓰이는 집 꼭대기의 공간이나 방. 더그매. 다락

attic

attic

second floor

first floor / ground floor

at·tire /ə'taɪə/ *n* [U] FORMAL clothes ‖ 옷. 의상

at·ti·tude /'ætə,tud/ *n* **1** [C, U] the opinions and feelings that you usually have about a particular thing, idea, or person ‖ 특정한 사물[생각, 사람]에 대해 갖는 견해와 느낌. 태도: *Pete has a really negative attitude toward/about work.* 피트는 업무에 대한 매우 부정적인 태도를 취한다. **2** [C, U] the way that you behave towards someone or in a situation ‖ 사람에 대한 또는 어떤 상황에서의 행동 방식. 자세. 거동: *Their whole attitude changed once they found out Ron was rich.* 론이 부자라는 것을 알고서는 그들의 자세는 전적으로 바뀌었다. / *Cathy has a real attitude problem.* (=she is not helpful or pleasant to be with) 캐시는 정말로 자세에 문제가 있다. **3** INFORMAL the confidence to do unusual and exciting things without caring what other people think ‖ 남이 어떻게 생각하는지는 개의치 않고 유별나고 자극적인 일을 하는 자신감: *a young singer with attitude* 자신만만한 젊은 가수

at·tor·ney /ə'təni/ *n* ⇨ LAWYER

attorney gen·er·al /,... '.../ *n* the chief lawyer in a state, or of the government in the US ‖ 미국 주 또는 정부의 법무장관

at·tract /ə'trækt/ *v* **1** [T] to make someone interested in something, or to make him/her want to be involved in something ‖ 사람이 어떤 것에 흥미를 갖게 하거나 열중하고 싶은 마음이 들게 하다. 끌다. 매혹하다: *Disneyland attracts millions of tourists each year.* 디즈니랜드는 매년 수백만 명의 관광객을 끌어들인다. / *The story attracted a lot of attention from the media.* 그 이야기는 매스컴의 많은 관심을 끌었다. **2 be attracted to sb** to like someone and want to have a romantic or sexual relationship with him/her ‖ 사람을 좋아해서 연애나 성적 관계를 가지고 싶어하다. …에게 매혹[매료]되다: *I was immediately attracted to him.* 나는 곧바로 그에게 매료되었다. **3** [T] to make something move toward another thing ‖ 어떤 것을 다른 사물 쪽으로 움직이게 하다. …을 끌어들이다. 유인하다: *Your perfume is attracting the bees.* 너의 향수가 벌들을 끌어들이고 있다.

at·trac·tion /ə'trækʃən/ *n* **1** [U] the feeling of liking someone or something very much ‖ 사람이나 사물을 매우 좋아하는 감정. 매력: *I can't understand Beth's attraction to Stan.* 베스가 스탠에게 느끼는 매력을 나는 이해할 수 없다. **2** something interesting or fun to see or do ‖ 보거나 하는 것이 흥미있거나 재미있는 것. 인기물. 인기거리: *hundreds of attractions at the county fair* 군 박람회의 수백 가지 인기 물건들 **3** [U] the ability to make things move toward each other ‖ 물체가 서로 끌어당기는 힘. 인력: *magnetic attraction* 자력

at·trac·tive /ə'træktɪv/ *adj* **1** pretty or beautiful, especially in a sexual way ‖ 특히 성적으로 예쁘거나 아름다운. 매력적인: *an attractive young woman/man* 매력적인 젊은 여자[남자] **2** pleasant to look at ‖ 보기에 즐거운: *an attractive location for a wedding* 매력적인 결혼식 장소 **3** good enough to make people interested ‖ 사람들의 관심을 불러일으킬 정도로 좋은: *an attractive salary/offer* 구미가 당기는 급료[제안] **—opposite** UNATTRACTIVE

at·trib·ut·a·ble /ə'trɪbyətəbəl/ *adj* **attributable to sth** likely to be caused by something ‖ 어떤 것으로 인해 일어날 수 있는. …에 기인하는

at·trib·ute¹ /ə'trɪbyut/ *v*

attribute sth **to** sb/sth *phr v* [T] to say that someone or something is responsible for something ‖ 사람이나 사물이 어떤 것에 대하여 책임이 있다고 말

하다. …을 …의 결과[탓]로 보다: *Many diseases can be attributed to stress.* 많은 질병은 스트레스 탓이라고 할 수 있다. / *a painting attributed to Rembrandt* 렘브란트의 작품으로 추정되는 그림 – **attribution** /ˌætrəˈbyuʃən/ *n* [U]

at·tri·bute² /ˈætrəˌbyut/ *n* a good or useful quality that someone or something has ‖ 사람이나 사물이 가지고 있는 좋거나 유용한 성질. 특성. 속성

at·trib·u·tive /əˈtrɪbyətɪv/ *adj* TECHNICAL in grammar, an attributive adjective or noun comes before the noun or phrase it describes. In the sentence "I heard a funny story," the word "funny" is attributive ‖ 문법에서 형용사나 명사가 그것이 묘사하는 명사나 구(句)의 앞에 오는. 한정적인. "I heard a funny story"라는 문장에서 "funny"는 한정적이다.

at·tuned /əˈtund/ *adj* so familiar with someone or something that you know how to deal with him, her, or it ‖ 사람이나 사물과 친숙하여 어떻게 다루어야 되는지를 아는. 익숙한: *It took me a while to become attuned to the strong southern accent.* 나는 강한 남부 억양에 익숙해지는 데 시간이 약간 걸렸다.

au·burn /ˈɔbən/ *n* [U] a red-brown color ‖ 적갈색 – **auburn** *adj* : *auburn hair* 적갈색 머리카락

auc·tion /ˈɔkʃən/ *n* a public meeting where art, furniture, land etc. is sold to the person who offers the most money ‖ 최고액을 제시하는 사람에게 미술 작품·가구·땅 등이 판매되는 공개 모임. 경매 – **auction** *v* [T]

auc·tion·eer /ˌɔkʃəˈnɪr/ *n* someone who is in charge of an auction ‖ 경매를 담당하는 사람. 경매인

au·da·cious /ɔˈdeɪʃəs/ *adj* brave and shocking ‖ 용감하고 충격적인. 대담한: *audacious behavior* 저돌적인 행동 – **audaciously** *adv*

au·dac·i·ty /ɔˈdæsəti/ *n* [U] the courage to take risks and do things that are shocking or rude ‖ 위험을 무릅쓰고 충격적이거나 무례한 일을 하는 용기. 대담. 과감. 무례함: *I can't believe he had the audacity to call your father at 3 a.m.* 그가 새벽 3시에 네 아버지에게 전화를 걸 만큼 무례한 사람이라고 생각할 수가 없다.

au·di·ble /ˈɔdəbəl/ *adj* able to be heard ‖ 목소리가 들리는: *Her voice was barely audible.* 그녀의 목소리는 겨우 알아들을 수 있을 정도로 작았다. – **audibly** *adj* —opposite INAUDIBLE

au·di·ence /ˈɔdiəns/ *n* **1** the people watching or listening to a concert, speech, movie etc. ‖ 음악회·연설·영화 등을 보거나 듣는 사람들. 청중. 관객: *There were over 500 people in the audience.* 청중이 500명을 넘었다. **2** the number or the type of people in an audience ‖ 청중의 수나 유형: *Cartoons usually attract a younger audience.* 만화는 대체로 젊은 독자를 끌어들인다. **3** a formal meeting with someone who is very important ‖ 아주 중요한 인물과의 공식적인 모임. 접견. 알현: *an audience with the Pope* 교황의 알현

au·di·o /ˈɔdioʊ/ *adj* relating to recording and broadcasting sound ‖ 녹음 및 방송 소리에 관한. 음성의 — compare VIDEO²

au·di·o·vis·u·al /ˌɔdioʊˈvɪʒuəl/ *adj* involving the use of recorded pictures and sound ‖ 녹화된 그림과 소리를 이용하는. 시청각의: *audiovisual materials for use in the language lab* 어학 실습용 시청각 교재

au·dit /ˈɔdɪt/ *v* [T] **1** to check that a company's financial records are correct ‖ 회사의 재무 기록의 정확성을 검사하다. 회계를 감사하다 **2** to study a subject at college without getting a grade for it ‖ 학점 취득 없이 대학에서 과목을 수강하다. 청강하다 – **audit** *n* – **auditor** *n*

au·di·tion¹ /ɔˈdɪʃən/ *n* a short performance by an actor, singer etc. that is judged in order to decide if s/he should act in a play, sing in a concert etc. ‖ 연극 무대에 설 수 있는지 또는 음악회에서 노래를 부를 수 있는지를 결정하는 판단을 위한 배우·가수 등의 간단한 공연. 오디션. 시연(試演)

audition² *v* [I, T] to perform in an AUDITION or judge someone in an audition ‖ 오디션을 받거나 오디션에서 사람을 심사하다

au·di·to·ri·um /ˌɔdɪˈtɔriəm/ *n* a large room, especially in a school or in a movie theater, where people sit to watch a performance ‖ 특히 학교나 영화관 등의 사람들이 앉아서 공연을 관람하는 큰 실내 공간. 강당. 회관

aug·ment /ɔgˈmɛnt/ *v* [T] FORMAL to increase the amount of something ‖ 사물의 분량을 늘리다. 증대시키다

Au·gust /ˈɔgəst/, *written abbreviation* **Aug.** *n* the eighth month of the year ‖ 그 해의 여덟 번째 달. 8월 —see usage note at JANUARY

aunt /ænt, ɑnt/ *n* the sister of your mother or father, or the wife of your

UNCLE ‖ 어머니나 아버지의 여형제, 또는 (외)숙부의 부인. 이모. 고모. 백모. (외)숙모

au·ra /'ɔrə/ n a quality or feeling that seems to come from a person or place ‖ 사람이나 장소에서 풍기는 듯한 특성이나 느낌. 분위기: *There's an aura of mystery around the castle.* 그 성 주변에는 신비스러운 분위기가 감돈다.

au·ral /'ɔrəl/ adj related to the ear or the sense of hearing ‖ 귀나 청각에 관련된. 귀의. 청각의: *aural skills* 청취 기술

aus·pi·ces /'ɔspəsɪz, -,sɪz/ n [plural] FORMAL help and support, especially from an organization ‖ 특히 조직으로부터의 도움과 원조. 찬조. 후원: *The research was done under the auspices of Harvard Medical School.* 그 연구는 하버드 의과 대학의 후원으로 이뤄졌다.

aus·pi·cious /ɔ'spɪʃəs/ adj showing that something is likely to be successful ‖ 어떤 것이 성공의 가능성을 보이는. 길조의. 상서로운: *an auspicious beginning to her career* 그녀의 출세로의 순조로운 출발 —opposite INAUSPICIOUS

aus·tere /ɔ'stɪr/ adj **1** very strict and very serious ‖ 매우 엄격하고 진지한. 준엄한: *a cold austere woman* 냉정하고 준엄한 여성 **2** plain and simple and without any decoration ‖ 아무 장식 없이 수수하고 간소한. 꾸밈 없는. 간결한: *an austere style of painting* 간결한 회화 양식 **3** without a lot of comfort or enjoyment ‖ 큰 위안이나 즐거움이 없는. 금욕적인. 절도 있는: *They lived an austere life.* 그들은 금욕 생활을 했다.

aus·ter·i·ty /ɔ'stɛrəṭi/ n [U] **1** bad economic conditions in which people do not have enough money to live ‖ 사람이 생활을 할 돈이 없는 나쁜 경제 상황. 내핍. 긴축 재정 **2** the quality of being AUSTERE ‖ 엄격한[간결한] 성질. 엄격(함). 간결(함): *She spoke with austerity.* 그녀는 엄숙하게 말했다. / *the austerity of the church's architecture* 교회 건축의 간결성

Aus·tra·li·a /ɑs'treɪliə/ n one of the seven CONTINENTS, that is also its own country ‖ 7대륙의 하나이자 하나의 국가. 오스트레일리아. 호주

Aus·tra·li·an /ɑs'treɪliən/ adj relating to or coming from Australia ‖ 호주와 관련되거나 호주에서 온. 호주(산(產))의

au·then·tic /ɔ'θɛntɪk/ adj **1** done or made in a traditional way ‖ 전통적인 방식으로 시행되거나 만들어진. 진짜의. 진정한: *authentic Indian food* 정통 인디언 음식 **2** proven to be made by a

particular person; GENUINE ‖ 특정인에 의하여 만들어진 것으로 입증된. 진짜의. 진품의; ㉤ genuine: *an authentic Renoir painting* 진짜 르누아르 그림 – **authentically** adv

au·then·ti·cate /ɔ'θɛntɪ,keɪt/ v [T] to prove that something is real and not a copy ‖ 사물이 복제가 아닌 진짜임을 증명하다

au·then·ti·ci·ty /,ɔθən'tɪsəṭi/ n [U] the quality of being real or true and not a copy ‖ 진짜나 사실이며 복제가 아닌 특성. 진짜임. 신빙성: *Tests confirmed the book's authenticity.* 여러 가지 조사로 그 책이 진본이라는 것이 확인되었다.

au·thor /'ɔθə/ n someone who writes a book, story, article, play etc. ‖ 책·이야기·기사·희곡 등을 집필하는 사람. 작가

au·thor·i·tar·i·an /ə,θɔrə'tɛriən, ə,θɑr-/ adj forcing people to obey rules and laws that are often wrong or unfair ‖ 종종 그릇되거나 불공평한 규칙과 법을 준수하도록 강요하는. 권위주의적인. 독재적인: *an authoritarian government* 독재 정부 – **authoritarian** n : *Papa was a strict authoritarian.* 아빠는 엄격한 권위주의자였다.

au·thor·i·ta·tive /ə'θɔrə,teɪṭɪv, ə'θɑr-/ adj respected and trusted as being true, or making people respect and obey you ‖ 진실한 것으로 존경과 신뢰를 받거나 사람들에게 존경과 복종을 하게 하는. 권위 있는. 신뢰할 만한: *an authoritative account of the country's history* 그 나라의 역사에 대한 권위 있는 서술 / *an authoritative voice* 고압적인 목소리 – **authoritatively** adv

au·thor·i·ty /ə'θɔrəṭi, ə'θɑr-/ n **1** [U] the power or right to control and command people ‖ 사람을 통제·명령하는 힘이나 권리. 권위. 권한: *You have no authority over me!* 당신은 내게 지시할 권한이 없어요! / *Who's in authority here?* 여기 책임자는 누구입니까? **2 the authorities** the people or organizations that are in charge of a particular place ‖ 특정한 곳의 책임을 맡고 있는 사람이나 기관. 당국(자) —see usage note at OFFICER

au·thor·i·za·tion /,ɔθərə'zeɪʃən/ n [C, U] official permission to do something ‖ 어떤 일을 하기 위한 공식적인 허가. 인가. 공인: *You'll need authorization from the Director to do that.* 그 일을 하려면 너는 국장의 결재가 필요하다.

au·thor·ize /'ɔθə,raɪz/ v **1 be authorized to** to have the power to give official permission for something ‖ 어떤

것에 대한 공식적인 허가를 할 힘이 있다. 권한이 있다: *I'm not authorized to sign this.* 나는 여기에 서명할 권한이 없다. **2** [T] to give official permission for something ‖ 어떤 것에 대하여 공식적 허가를 하다: *Can you authorize my expenses?* 제 경비를 승인해 주시겠습니까?

au·to /'ɔtoʊ/ *adj* relating to cars ‖ 자동차에 관한: *auto parts* 자동차 부품

au·to·bi·og·ra·phy /ˌɔtəbaɪ'ɑgrəfi/ *n* a book about your life, written by yourself ‖ 자신의 인생에 관하여 직접 쓴 책. 자서전 – **autobiographical** /ˌɔtəˌbaɪə'græfɪkəl/ *adj*

au·toc·ra·cy /ɔ'tɑkrəsi/ *n* [C, U] a system of government in which one person or group has unlimited power, or a country governed in this way ‖ 한 사람이나 집단이 무한한 권력을 지니는 정치 체제, 또는 그런 국가. 독재[전제] 정치 [국가]

au·to·crat·ic /ˌɔtə'krætɪk/ *adj* **1** giving orders to people without considering their opinions ‖ 국민의 의견을 무시하고 명령을 내리는. 전제의. 독재적인: *an autocratic style of management* 독재적인 경영 방식 **2** having unlimited control over a country, or showing this quality ‖ 국가에 대해 무한한 통제력을 가지거나 이런 특성을 나타내는. 독재[전제] 정치의: *an autocratic government* 독재 정부 – **autocrat** /'ɔtəˌkræt/ *n*

au·to·graph /'ɔtəgræf/ *n* a famous person's name, written in his/her own writing ‖ 유명한 사람의 자필 서명. 사인: *I have Keanu Reeves' autograph!* 나는 키아누 리브스의 사인이 있다!

autograph *v* [T] if a famous person autographs something, s/he writes his/her name on it ‖ 유명 인사가 자신의 이름을 사물 위에 쓰다. 자필 서명하다. 사인하다: *Please, will you autograph my baseball?* 제 야구공에 사인 좀 해 주시겠습니까?

au·to·mate /'ɔtəˌmeɪt/ *v* [T] to change to a system in which work is done by machines instead of people ‖ 사람 대신 기계에 의해 작업을 수행하는 체제로 변경하다. 자동화하다: *They automated the factory ten years ago.* 그들은 공장을 십년 전에 자동화했다. – **automation** /ˌɔtə'meɪʃən/ *n* [U]

au·to·mat·ic /ˌɔtə'mætɪk/ *adj* **1** an automatic machine is designed to operate by itself after you start it ‖ 기계가 작동시킨 후 스스로 작동되도록 고안된. 자동의: *an automatic timer* 자동 타이

머 **2** certain to happen ‖ 반드시 생기는. 자동적인: *We get an automatic pay increase every year.* 우리는 매년 자동적으로 봉급이 인상된다. **3** done without thinking ‖ 생각 없이 행해지는. 무의식적인: *At first, driving is hard, but then it just becomes automatic.* 운전은 처음에는 어렵지만 나중에는 무의식적으로 하게 된다. – **automatically** *adv*

automatic *n* **1** a car with a system of GEARs that operate themselves ‖ 자동 변속 장치가 달린 자동차 **2** a gun that can shoot bullets continuously ‖ 연속적으로 총알을 발사시킬 수 있는 총. 자동(소)총. 자동 권총

au·to·mo·bile /ˌɔtəmə'bil, 'ɔtəməˌbil/ *n* a car ‖ 자동차

au·to·mo·tive /ˌɔtə'moʊtɪv/ *adj* relating to cars ‖ 자동차와 관련된: *the automotive industry* 자동차 업계

au·ton·o·mous /ɔ'tɑnəməs/ *adj* having the power or freedom to do what you want, especially to govern your own country ‖ 자신이 원하는 것을 할, 특히 자기 나라를 통치할 권력이나 자유를 갖는. 자율의. 자치권이 있는: *an autonomous nation* 자치 국가 – **autonomously** *adv*

au·ton·o·my /ɔ'tɑnəmi/ *n* [U] the freedom or power to do what you want ‖ 원하는 것을 할 자유나 권력. 자치(권)

au·top·sy /'ɔˌtɑpsi/ *n* an examination of a dead body to discover the cause of death ‖ 죽음의 원인을 밝히기 위한 사체에 대한 조사. 검시(檢屍). 부검

au·to·work·er /'ɔtoʊˌwɚkɚ/ *n* someone whose job is to make cars ‖ 자동차를 만드는 직업인. 자동차 제조 노동자

au·tumn /'ɔtəm/ *n* ⇨ FALL² – **autumnal** /ɔ'tʌmnəl/ *adj*

aux·il·ia·ry /ɔg'zɪləri, -'zɪlyəri/ *adj* ready to be used in an urgent situation ‖ 긴급한 상황에 쓰이도록 예비된. 보조적인: *The factory has an auxiliary power supply.* 그 공장은 보조 전력 공급원이 있다. – **auxiliary** *n*

auxiliary verb /.'... ˌ./ *n* TECHNICAL in grammar, verbs such as "be," "do," "have," and the MODAL VERBs that are used with another verb to show the tense, person, mood etc. ‖ 문법에서 "be"·"do"·"have" 등의 동사와 시제·인칭·법 등을 나타내기 위해 다른 동사와 함께 사용되는 법(法) 동사. 조동사

AV the abbreviation of AUDIOVISUAL ‖ audiovisual의 약어: *the company's AV department* 회사의 시청각 부문

a·vail /ə'veɪl/ *n* **to no avail** without

success ‖ 성공 없이. 무익하게. 보람도 없이: *We searched everywhere to no avail.* 우리는 곳곳을 찾아 보았지만 허사였다.

avail² *v* **avail yourself of sth** FORMAL to accept an offer or use an opportunity to do something ‖ 어떤 것을 할 제의를 받아들이거나 기회를 이용하다: *Avail yourself of every chance to improve your English.* 당신의 영어 실력을 향상시키기 위해 모든 기회를 이용해라.

a·vail·a·ble /əˈveɪləbəl/ *adj* **1** able to be used or obtained ‖ 이용하거나 획득할 수 있는: *The database in the library is available to anyone.* 그 도서관의 데이터베이스는 누구라도 이용할 수 있다. / *When will the video be available?* 그 비디오는 언제 볼 수 있냐? **2** free to see or talk to someone ‖ 남을 만나거나 남과 말하기가 자유로운. 여가가[틈이] 있는: *I'm available after lunch.* 나는 점심 식사 후에는 시간이 난다. **3** free to start a romantic relationship with someone new ‖ 새롭게 누군가와 연애 관계를 시작하기에 자유로운. 애인이 없는: *I'd ask her for a date if I thought she was available.* 그녀가 혼자라고 생각했다면 그녀에게 데이트를 신청했을 것이다. – **availability** /əˌveɪləˈbɪləti/ *n* [U] – opposite UNAVAILABLE

av·a·lanche /ˈævəˌlæntʃ, -ˌlɑntʃ/ *n* **1** a large amount of snow, ice, and rocks that fall down the side of a mountain ‖ 산비탈로 떨어지는 대량의 눈·얼음·바위. 눈[산]사태 **2 an avalanche of** a very large number of things that happen or arrive at the same time ‖ 동시에 발생하거나 도착하는 매우 많은 수의 것. 쇄도: *An avalanche of letters came in from 101 FM listeners.* FM 101 청취자들로부터 편지가 쇄도했다.

a·vant-garde /ˌævɑntˈɡɑrd, ˌɑ-/ *adj* extremely modern and often strange or shocking ‖ 대단히 현대적이며 종종 이상하거나 충격적인. 전위적인. 아방가르드의: *avant-garde music/art* 전위 음악[예술]

av·a·rice /ˈævərɪs/ *n* [U] FORMAL an extreme desire for wealth; GREED ‖ 부에 대한 과도한 욕망. 탐욕; 逾 greed – **avaricious** /ˌævəˈrɪʃəs/ *adj*

Ave. the written abbreviation of AVENUE ‖ Avenue의 약어

a·venge /əˈvɛndʒ/ *v* [T] LITERARY to do something to hurt or punish someone because s/he has harmed or offended you ‖ 자신이 해를 입거나 공격을 받아서 남을 다치게 하거나 벌주다. 원수를 갚다. 복수[앙갚음]하다 – **avenger** *n*

av·e·nue /ˈævəˌnu/ *n* **1** also **Avenue** a street in a town or city ‖ 읍내나 도시의 도로. 큰거리. 가(街): *Fifth Avenue* 5번가(街) **2** a possible way of achieving something ‖ 무엇을 성취하는 가능한 방식. 수단. 방법: *We explored every avenue, but couldn't find a solution.* 우리는 모든 수단을 강구했지만 해결책을 찾지 못했다.

av·er·age¹ /ˈævrɪdʒ/ *adj* **1** calculated by adding several quantities together and then dividing by the number of quantities ‖ 여러 수를 함께 더한 다음 그 개수로 나누어 계산된. 평균의: *What's the average rainfall for May?* 5월의 평균 강수량은 얼마입니까? **2** having qualities that are typical ‖ 전형적인 성질을 가진. 보통의: *"How tall is he?" "Oh, average."* "그의 키는 얼마나 돼?" "응, 보통이야." **3** not special or unusual in any way ‖ 어떤 점에서도 특별하거나 비범하지 않은. 평범한: *It wasn't a great book–just average.* 그 책은 대단한 것이 아니고 그저 평범했다.

average² *n* **1** the amount calculated by adding several quantities together and then dividing by the number of quantities ‖ 여러 수를 함께 더한 다음 그 개수로 나눈 계산치. 평균치. 산술 평균: *The average of 3, 8, and 10 is 7.* 3과 8 그리고 10의 산술 평균은 7이다. **2 on average** based on a calculation that shows what usually happens ‖ 일반적으로 일어난 것을 보여주는 계산에 근거한. 평균적으로. 대체로: *On average, women live longer than men.* 대체로 여자가 남자보다 더 오래 산다. **3** [C, U] the usual level or amount ‖ 보통의 수준이나 양. 평균(치): *Annette is an above average student.* (=better than the average) 아네트는 보통 수준 이상의 학생이다.

average³ *v* [T] **1** to do or have something usually ‖ 어떤 것을 일반적으로 하거나 가지다: *I average about 10 cigarettes a day.* 나는 보통 하루에 약 10개피의 담배를 피운다. **2** to calculate the average of quantities ‖ 평균치를 계산하다. 평균하다

average out *phr v* [I] to result in a particular average amount ‖ 특정한 평균량을 얻다. 평균 …에 달하다: *Our weekly profits average out at about $750.* 우리의 주당 수익은 평균 약 750달러이다.

a·verse /əˈvɜrs/ *adj* **not be averse to** used in order to say that you do not mind doing something ‖ 어떤 것을 하는 것을 꺼리지 않는다고 말하는 데에 쓰여. 마다하지[꺼려하지] 않다: *I don't drink* *much, but I'm not averse to the occasional glass of wine.* 나는 술을 많이 마시지는 않지만 이따금 마시는 포도주는 싫어하지 않는다.

a·ver·sion /əˈvɜːʒən/ *n* [singular, U] a strong dislike of something or someone ‖ 사물이나 사람을 몹시 싫어함. 혐오: *Mary has an aversion to cats.* 메리는 고양이를 몹시 싫어한다.

a·vert /əˈvɜːt/ *v* [T] **1** to prevent something from happening ‖ 어떤 일이 발생하는 것을 막다. 피하다: *The whole thing could've been averted if you'd listened to us.* 당신이 우리말을 들었다면 모든 것을 피할 수도 있었다. **2 avert your eyes/gaze** to look away from something you do not want to see ‖ 보고 싶지 않은 것을 피하다. 눈길/시선을 피하다

a·vi·a·tion /ˌeɪviˈeɪʃən/ *n* [U] the science or practice of flying or making aircraft ‖ 항공기의 비행과 제작에 관한 학문이나 기술. 비행술. 항공학

a·vi·a·tor /ˈeɪvieɪtər/ *n* OLD-FASHIONED the pilot of an aircraft ‖ 항공기 조종사

av·id /ˈævɪd/ *adj* **avid reader/collector/fan etc.** someone who does something a lot because s/he enjoys it ‖ 어떤 것을 즐기기 때문에 그것을 많이 하는 사람. 열광적인 독자/수집가/팬: *an avid collector of coins* 열광적인 동전 수집가

av·o·ca·do /ˌævəˈkɑːdoʊ, ˌɑː-/ *n* [C, U] a firm green fruit, eaten as a vegetable ‖ 야채로 먹는 단단하고 푸른 과일. 아보카도

a·void /əˈvɔɪd/ *v* [T] **1** to make an effort not to do something or to stop something from happening ‖ 어떤 일을 하지 않기 위해 노력하거나 어떤 일이 발생하지 않도록 막다. 피하다: *Exercise will help you avoid heart disease.* 운동은 심장병을 막는 데 도움이 될 것이다. / *Avoid drinking alcohol while taking this medicine.* 이 약을 복용하는 동안에는 술을 마시지 마라. ✗DON'T SAY "avoid to do something"✗ "avoid to do something"과 같이 to부정사는 쓰지 않는다. **2** to deliberately stay away from someone or something ‖ 사람이나 사물에서 일부러 떨어져 있다: *I was told to avoid stress.* 나는 스트레스를 피하라는 말을 들었다. – **avoidable** *adj* – **avoidance** *n* [U]

a·vow /əˈvaʊ/ *v* [T] FORMAL to say or admit something publicly ‖ 어떤 것을 공개적으로 말하거나 인정하다. 공언[인정]하다 – **avowal** *n* [C, U]

a·vowed /əˈvaʊd/ *adj* said or admitted

publicly ‖ 공공연히 말하거나 인정한. 공언한: *an avowed atheist* 스스로 인정한 무신론자 – **avowedly** /əˈvaʊɪdli/ *adv*

a·wait /əˈweɪt/ *v* [T] FORMAL **1** to wait for something ‖ 무엇을 기다리다: *Briggs is awaiting trial for murder.* 브리그스는 살인죄로 재판을 기다리고 있다. **2** to be about to happen to someone ‖ 누군가에게 일어나려고 하다: *A terrible surprise awaited them.* 그들에게는 대단히 놀라운 일이 기다리고 있었다.

a·wake¹ /əˈweɪk/ *adj* **1** not sleeping ‖ 잠자지 않는. 깨어 있는: *I was wide awake* (=completely awake) *before dawn.* 나는 새벽까지 완전히 깨어 있었다. **2 be awake to sth** FORMAL to understand a situation and its possible effects ‖ 상황과 그 가능한 결과를 이해하다. …을 알아채다. …에 세심한 주의를 하다

awake² *v* **awoke, awoken** [I, T] LITERARY **1** to stop sleeping ‖ 잠자기를 멈추다. (잠에서)깨다[깨우다]: *The noise awoke me.* 나는 시끄러운 소리에 잠이 깼다. **2** to suddenly begin to feel an emotion, or to make someone do this ‖ 갑자기 감정을 느끼기 시작하거나 느끼게 하다. 갑자기 알아채다[깨닫게 하다]

a·wak·en /əˈweɪkən/ *v* ⇨ AWAKE²

awaken sb/sth to *phr v* [T] FORMAL to begin to understand a situation and its possible effects, or to make someone do this ‖ 상황과 그 가능한 결과를 이해하기 시작하거나 이해하게 하다. 깨닫다. 깨닫게 하다: *Churches are awakening to the needs of their older members.* 교회는 나이든 교인들의 요구를 깨닫기 시작하고 있다.

a·wak·en·ing /əˈweɪkənɪŋ/ *n* a situation when you suddenly realize that you understand or feel something ‖ 어떤 것을 이해하거나 느끼는 것을 갑자기 깨닫는 상황. 자각. 인식: *Anyone who thinks that this job is easy will have a rude awakening.* (=a time when s/he suddenly realizes that it is not easy) 이 일이 쉽다고 생각하는 사람은 어느 순간 쉽지 않다는 것을 깨닫게 될 것이다.

a·ward¹ /əˈwɔːrd/ *v* [T] to officially give someone an award ‖ 상을 남에게 공식적으로 주다. 수여하다: *He was awarded the Nobel Prize.* 그는 노벨상을 받았다. / *A large sum of money was awarded to the survivors.* 거액의 돈이 생존자들에게 주어졌다.

award² *n* a prize or money given to someone for a special reason ‖ 특별한 이유로 사람에게 주어지는 상이나 상금: *the award for best actor* 최우수 배우상 / *an* *award of $10,000 to each victim* 희생자 각자에게 주어지는 만 달러의 보상금

a·ware /əˈwɛr/ *adj* realizing that something is true, exists, or is happening ‖ 어떤 것의 사실[존재, 발생]을 깨닫는. 알아 차린. 인식하고 있는: *Are you aware of the dangers of smoking?* 흡연의 위험성을 알고 있습니까? / *Were you aware (that) your son has been taking drugs?* 아드님이 마약을 복용해 왔다는 것을 알고 있었습니까? / *Sheila is very politically/environmentally aware.* (=she knows a lot about what is happening in politics etc.) 쉴라는 정치[환경] 문제에 매우 밝다. / *"Are there any more problems?" "Not that I'm aware of."* "더 이상의 문제가 있습니까?" "제가 알고 있는 바로는 없어요." —opposite UNAWARE

a·ware·ness /əˈwɛrnɪs/ *n* [U] knowledge or understanding of a particular subject or situation ‖ 특정한 주제나 상황에 대한 지식이나 이해. 인식. 자각: *The TV ads are meant to raise the public's awareness of environmental issues.* 그 TV 광고는 환경 문제에 대한 국민의 각성을 불러일으키기 위한 것이다.

a·wash /əˈwɑʃ, əˈwɔʃ/ *adj* **1 awash with/in** too full of something ‖ 어떤 것으로 가득찬. 넘치는: *TV is awash with talk shows.* TV는 토크쇼로 넘쳐난다. **2** covered with water or another liquid ‖ 물이나 다른 액체로 덮힌. 물로 덮힌. 침수된

a·way¹ /əˈweɪ/ *adv* **1** to or at a different place from someone or something ‖ 사람이나 사물과는 다른 곳으로[에]. 저리로. 저쪽으로: *Go away!* 저리 가! / *Diane drove away quickly.* 다이안은 재빨리 운전해서 가버렸다. / *Move away from the fire!* 불에서 멀리 떨어져라. **2 3 miles/40 feet etc. away** at a particular distance from a place ‖ 한 장소에서 특정한 거리를 떨어져. 3마일/40피트 떨어져: *a town about 50 miles away from Chicago* 시카고에서 약 50마일 떨어진 읍내 **3** into a safe or enclosed place ‖ 안전하거나 둘러싸인 곳으로: *Put all your toys away now, please.* 장난감은 모두 지금 치우거라. **4 2 days/3 weeks etc. away** at a particular time in the future ‖ 미래의 특정한 시간에. 이틀/3주 앞두고 있는: *Christmas is only a month away.* 크리스마스는 단지 한 달 남아 있다. **5** not at home or in your usual place of work ‖ 집이나 평소 일하는 곳에 없는. 부재중인: *I'm sorry, Ms. Parker is*

away this week. 죄송합니다. 파커 씨는 이번 주 부재중입니다. **6** completely gone or used up ‖ 완전히 사라지거나 다 써 버린: *All the water had boiled away.* 물이 모두 끓어서 증발해 버렸다. / *The music died away.* 음악 소리가 완전히 사라졌다. **7** all the time, or continuously ‖ 항상 또는 계속해서. 쉬지 않고: *He's been working away on the patio all day.* 그는 하루 종일 안뜰에서 일하고 있다.

away² *adj* playing on your opponent's sports field rather than your own ‖ 홈 경기장이 아닌 상대방 경기장에서 경기하는. 원정(경기)의: *The away team is ahead by four runs.* 원정팀이 4점을 앞서고 있다. —opposite HOME²2

awe /ɔ/ *n* [U] **1** a feeling of great respect and admiration, and sometimes a slight fear ‖ 대단한 존경과 감탄의 감정 및 때로는 약간의 두려움. 경외(敬畏): *The beauty of the chapel filled them with awe.* 그 교회당의 아름다움에 그들은 경외심으로 가득찼다. **2 be/stand in awe of sb** to respect someone and be slightly afraid of him/her ‖ 남을 존경하며 약간 두려워하다. 경외하다 – **awed** *adj*: *an awed silence* 경외심으로 인한 침묵

awe·in·spir·ing /ˈ. ,.../ *adj* making you feel awe ‖ 경외심을 느끼게 하는: *an awe-inspiring achievement* 경외심을 불러 일으키는 업적

awe·some /ˈɔsəm/ *adj* **1** so impressive, serious, or difficult that it makes you feel awe ‖ 경외심을 느끼게 할 정도로 매우 인상적인[심각한, 어려운]. 무시무시한. 어마어마한: *an awesome responsibility* 두려움을 느끼게 할 정도의 [어마어마한] 책임 **2** SLANG extremely good ‖ 극도로 좋은. 최고의: *That concert was awesome!* 그 콘서트는 끝내줬어!

awe·struck /ˈɔstrʌk/ *adj* feeling great awe ‖ 대단한 경외심을 느끼는. 위엄에 눌린: *We gazed awestruck at the pyramids.* 우리는 경외심을 가지고 피라미드를 쳐다보았다.

aw·ful¹ /ˈɔfəl/ *adj* **1** very bad or unpleasant ‖ 매우 나쁘거나 불쾌한. 형편없는: *an awful movie* 졸작의 영화 / *This soup tastes awful!* 이 수프는 맛이 형편없어! **2** SPOKEN used in order to emphasize how much of something there is, or how good, bad etc. something is ‖ 어떤 것이 얼마나 많이 있는지 또는 얼마나 좋거나 나쁜지 등을 강조하는 데에 쓰여. 대단한. 굉장한: *I have an awful lot* (=a very large amount) *of work to do.* 내가 해야 할 일이 산더미처럼 있다. **3 look/feel awful** to look or feel sick ‖ 아프게 보이거

나 느끼다.

awful² *adv* SPOKEN NONSTANDARD very ‖ 매우: *She's awful cute.* 그녀는 아주 귀엽다.

aw·ful·ly /'ɔfli/ *adv* SPOKEN very ‖ 매우. 대단히: *Helen looks awfully tired.* 헬렌은 몹시 피곤해 보인다.

a·while /ə'waɪl/ *adv* for a period of time, when you cannot say exactly how long ‖ 정확히 얼마나 긴지 말할 수 없는 일정한 기간 동안. 얼마[잠시] 동안: *Gil stood at the window awhile, watching for Sarah.* 길은 창가에 서서 한동안 사라를 지켜보았다.

awk·ward /'ɔkwəd/ *adj* **1** making you feel so embarrassed that you are not sure what to do or say ‖ 무엇을 하거나 말해야 할지 모를 정도로 심한 당혹감을 느끼게 하는. 난처한. 어색한: *There was an awkward pause in the conversation.* 대화 중에 어색한 침묵이 흘렀다. **2** causing a problem or making things difficult ‖ 문제를 일으키거나 일을 어렵게 하는. 골치 아픈. 곤란한: *This is kind of an awkward time for me, could I call you back?* 지금은 곤란한데 제가 다시 전화해도 될까요? / *You're just being awkward!* (=causing problems intentionally) 당신 일부러 문제를 일으키는군! **3** difficult to use or handle ‖ 사용하거나 다루기 어려운: *an awkward-sized box* 다루기 어려운 크기의 상자 **4** moving or behaving in a way that does not seem relaxed or comfortable ‖ 편하거나 안정되지 않는 태도로 움직이거나 행동하는. 어색한. 미숙한: *an awkward teenager* 미숙한 십대 **– awkwardly** *adv* **– awkwardness** *n* [U]

awn·ing /'ɔnɪŋ/ *n* a sheet of material outside a store, tent etc. used for protection from the sun or the rain ‖ 햇빛이나 비를 막기 위해 사용하는 가게·텐트 바깥 부분의 천. 차양. 비막이

a·woke /ə'woʊk/ *v* the past tense of AWAKE ‖ awake의 과거형

a·wok·en /ə'woʊkən/ *v* the PAST PARTICIPLE of AWAKE ‖ awake의 과거 분사형

AWOL /'eɪˌwɔl/ *adj* Absent Without Leave; absent from your military group without permission ‖ Absent Without Leave(무단 이탈)의 약어; 군대에서 무단 이탈한: *Private Ames has gone AWOL.* 아메스 병사는 탈영했다.

a·wry /ə'raɪ/ *adj* LITERARY **go awry** to not happen in the way that was planned ‖ 계획된 대로 일어나지 않다. 실패하다

axe¹, ax /æks/ *n* **1** a tool with a heavy metal blade on a long handle, used for cutting wood ‖ 나무를 벨 때 사용하는 것으로 긴 손잡이에 무거운 금속 날이 있는 도구. 도끼 **2 give sb/sth the axe** INFORMAL to dismiss someone from his/her job, or get rid of something ‖ 사람을 해고하거나 사물을 제거하다: *The TV station gave Brown the axe.* TV 방송국은 브라운을 해고했다. **3 have an axe to grind** to do or say something again and again because you want people to accept your ideas or beliefs ‖ 자신의 사상이나 믿음을 사람들이 받아들이기를 원해서 어떤 것을 거듭하거나 말하다. 다른 속셈이 있다: *I have no political axe to grind.* 나는 정치적인 속셈을 가지고 있지 않다.

axe², ax *v* [T] INFORMAL to suddenly dismiss someone from his/her job, or get rid of something ‖ 사람을 갑자기 해고하거나 사물을 제거하다: *Did you hear they're axing 500 jobs?* 그들이 500개의 일자리를 없애려 한다는 얘기 들었니?

ax·i·om /'æksiəm/ *n* a rule or principle that is considered by most people to be true ‖ 대부분의 사람들이 진실이라고 여기는 법칙이나 원칙. 자명한 이치. 격언

ax·i·o·mat·ic /ˌæksiə'mætɪk/ *adj* a principle that is axiomatic does not need to be proved because people can see that it is true ‖ 원리가 진실임을 사람들이 알 수 있기 때문에 증명할 필요가 없는. 공리(公理)의 **– axiomatically** *adv*

ax·is /'æksɪs/ *n,* **plural axes 1** the imaginary line around which something turns, for example the Earth ‖ 지구와 같은 회전체가 도는 가상적인 선. 축(선) **2** a line at the side or bottom of a GRAPH that you measure the positions of points on ‖ 점의 위치를 측정하는 그래프의 옆이나 밑의 선. 수평축(선)·수직축(선)

axis

ax·le /'æksəl/ *n* the BAR that connects two wheels on a vehicle ‖ 차량의 두 바퀴를 연결하는 가로장. 차축

aye /aɪ/ *adv* SPOKEN FORMAL used in order to say yes, especially when voting ‖ 특히 표결할 때 예라고 말하는 데에 쓰여. 찬성! 예!

AZ the written abbreviation of Arizona ‖ Arizona(애리조나 주)의 약어

Bb

B, b /biː/ the second letter of the English alphabet ‖ 영어 알파벳의 둘째 자.

B /biː/ *n* **1** the second highest grade you can get on a test or piece of school work ‖ 시험이나 학교 과제물에서 얻을 수 있는 두 번째로 높은 점수. 비(B) **2** [C, U] the seventh note in the musical SCALE of C, or the musical KEY based on this note ‖ C 음계의 일곱째 음이나 이 음을 기조로 한 조(調). 나 음. 나 조

b the written abbreviation of born ‖ born 의 약어: *A. Lincoln, b. 1809* 링컨 1809년 탄생

B.A. *n* Bachelor of Arts; a university degree in a subject such as history or literature ‖ Bachelor of Arts(문학사)의 약어; 역사나 문학 등의 과목의 대학 학위 —compare B.S.

baa /bɑ, bæ/ *v* [I] to make the sound a sheep makes ‖ 양이 내는 소리를 내다

bab·ble /ˈbæbəl/ *v* [I, T] to talk a lot in a way that does not make sense ‖ 뜻이 안 통하는 말을 많이 하다. 중얼중얼 말하다: *a baby just beginning to babble* 옹알 옹알 말하기를 갓 시작한 아기 —**babble** *n* [C, U]

babe /beɪb/ *n* **1** SPOKEN an attractive young man or woman ‖ 매력적인 젊은 남자나 여자. 매력덩어리: *Brad's a total babe.* 브래드는 정말 매력적인 사람이다. **2** SPOKEN a way of speaking to someone you like and know well ‖ 좋아하며 잘 아는 사람에 대한 호칭. 자기: *Hey, babe, how are you?* 어, 자기, 좀 어때? **3** SPOKEN a way of speaking to a woman, often considered offensive ‖ 여성에 대한 종종 모욕적인 호칭. 아가씨 **4** LITERARY a baby ‖ 아기

ba·boon /bæˈbun/ *n* a large African or south Asian monkey with a small tail ‖ 아프리카나 남아시아산의 몸집이 크고 꼬리가 짧은 원숭이. 비비

ba·by /ˈbeɪbi/ *n* **1** a very young child who has not yet learned to talk ‖ 말을 채 배우지 못한 어린아이. 아기. 젖먹이: *Joyce had a baby* (=gave birth to a baby) *in September.* 조이스는 9월에 아기를 낳았다. / *Pam is expecting a baby.* (=will have a baby) 팸은 임신 중이다. / *a crying baby* 우는 아기 **2** a very young animal or plant ‖ 아주 어린 동물이나 식물: *baby birds* 새끼 새 **3** SPOKEN **a)** a way of speaking to someone you love ‖

사랑하는 사람에 대한 호칭. 자기: *Bye, baby. I'll be back by six.* 자기, 안녕. 6시까지 돌아올게. **b)** a way of speaking to a woman, often considered offensive ‖ 여성에 대한 종종 모욕적인 호칭. 아가씨 **4** SPOKEN a word meaning someone who behaves in a stupid or silly way, used especially by children ‖ 특히 아이들이 사용하는 말로 어리석거나 바보스럽게 행동하는 사람을 의미하는 말. 바보 **5** **baby boom** a time when a lot of babies are born in a particular country ‖ 특정한 나라에서 아기들이 많이 출생하는 시기. 베이비 붐

baby boom·er /ˈ.. ˌ../ *n* INFORMAL someone born between 1946 and 1965, when a lot of babies were born ‖ 많은 아기들이 출생된 1946년에서 1965년 사이에 태어난 사람. 베이비 붐 세대

baby car·riage /ˈ.. ˌ../, **baby bug·gy** /ˈbeɪbi ˌbʌgi/ *n* a small bed with wheels, used for pushing a baby around outdoors ‖ 옥외에서 아기를 미는 데 사용하는 바퀴 달린 작은 침대. 유모차

ba·by·ish /ˈbeɪbiɪʃ/ *adj* DISAPPROVING like a baby or suitable for a baby ‖ 아기 같거나 아기에게 어울리는. 유치한: *babyish games* 유치한 게임

ba·by·sit /ˈbeɪbiˌsɪt/ *v* **babysat, babysat, babysitting** [I, T] to take care of someone's children while the parents are not at home ‖ 부모가 부재 중에 남의 아이를 돌보다. 애를 봐 주다 —**babysitter** *n* —**babysitting** *n* [U]

ba·by·talk /ˈbeɪbiˌtɔk/ *n* [U] words or sounds that you make when talking to a baby ‖ 아기에게 이야기할 때 내는 말이나 소리. 아기말(투)

bach·e·lor /ˈbætʃələ, ˈbætʃlə/ *n* a man who is not married ‖ 결혼하지 않은 남자. 미혼남. 총각

bachelor par·ty /ˈ... ˌ../ *n* a party given for a man the night before his wedding ‖ 결혼 전날 밤에 신랑을 위하여 열어 주는 파티. 총각 파티

bach·e·lor's de·gree /ˈ... ˌ../ *n* ⇨ B.A.

back¹ /bæk/ *n*

1 ▶BODY 신체◀ **a)** the part of a person's or animal's body that goes from the neck to the BUTTOCKS or the tail ‖ 목에서 엉덩이나 꼬리에 이르는 사람이나 동물의 신체 부위. 등: *My back was*

back²

really aching. 등이 정말 아팠다. / *The cat arched its back and hissed.* 그 고양이는 등을 잔뜩 구부리고 가르릉 소리를 내었다. **b)** the bone that goes from your neck to your BUTTOCKs ‖ 목에서 엉덩이까지 뻗은 뼈. 등뼈: *He broke his back in a motorcycle accident.* 그는 오토바이 사고로 등뼈가 부러졌다.

2 ▶PART OF STH …의 부분◀ [singular, U] the part of something that is furthest from the way that it moves or faces ‖ 움직이거나 마주하고 있는 쪽에서 가장 멀리 떨어진 부분. 뒤(쪽): *a grocery list on the back of an envelope* 봉투 뒷면에 있는 식료품 목록 / *The index is at the back of the book.* 색인은 책의 뒤쪽에 있다. / *The pool's in back of the house.* 수영장은 집의 뒤곁에 있다. / *Kids should always wear seat belts, even in back.* (=in the seats behind the driver in a car) 아이들은 뒷좌석에 있어도 항상 안전벨트를 매야 한다. / *Tom's working on the car out back.* (=behind a house or other building) 톰은 건물 뒤곁의 차에서 일하고 있다. —opposite FRONT¹

3 ▶SEAT 좌석◀ the part of a seat that you lean against when you are sitting ‖ 앉을 때 기댈 수 있는 의자의 부분. 등받이

4 behind sb's back without the person who is concerned knowing about what is being said or done ‖ 관련된 사람이 거론되거나 진행되는 일에 대해서 알지 못하는. …이 없는 데서. 은밀히: *I can't believe she said that about me behind my back!* 내가 없는 곳에서 그녀가 나에 대해 그렇게 얘기했다니 믿을 수 없어!

5 at/in the back of your mind a thought or feeling at the back of your mind is affecting you, although you are not thinking about it directly ‖ 생각이나 감정이 직접적으로 생각하고 있지는 않지만 영향을 미치는. 마음 속에. 내심으로: *There was always a slight fear in the back of his mind.* 그의 마음 속에는 항상 약간의 두려움이 있었다.

6 get off my back! SPOKEN said when you want someone to stop telling you to do something ‖ 남이 자기에게 어떤 것을 하라고 말하는 것을 그치기를 원할 때 쓰여. 그만 좀 해라!: *I'll do it in a minute. Just get off my back!* 잠시 후에 할 테니까 제발 이제 그만 좀 해!

7 be on sb's back SPOKEN to keep telling someone to do something, in a way that annoys him/her ‖ 귀찮아 할 정도로 어떤 것을 하라고 남에게 계속 말하다. 잔소리하다: *The boss has been on my back about being late.* 사장은 내가 늦는

다고 계속 잔소리를 해댄다.

8 have your back to the wall INFORMAL to be in a very difficult situation ‖ 매우 어려운 상황에 처하다. 궁지에 몰리다: *A lot of small businesses have their backs to the wall in this slow economy.* 많은 영세 기업이 이러한 불경기로 몹시 어려운 상황에 처해 있다. —see also **turn your back (on)** (TURN¹)

back² adv 1 where someone or something was before ‖ 사람이나 사물이 전에 있던 곳에. 원위치에: *Put the milk back in the refrigerator.* 우유를 냉장고에 도로 갖다 놓아라. / *Roger said he'd be back in an hour.* 로저는 한 시간 안에 돌아오겠다고 말했다. **2** in or into the condition that someone or something was in before ‖ 사람이나 사물이 전에 있던 상태로. 다시. 도로: *I woke up at 5 a.m. and couldn't get back to sleep.* 나는 새벽 5시에 깬 뒤에 다시 잠을 이루지 못했다. **3** in the direction that is behind you ‖ 뒷방향으로. 뒤에: *George glanced back to see if he was still being followed.* 조지는 아직도 미행을 당하고 있는지 보려고 힐끗 뒤 돌아보았다. **4** as a reply or reaction to what someone has done ‖ 남이 한 것에 대한 대답이나 반응으로. 답례로: *Can you call me back later?* 나중에 다시 전화해 주시겠어요? / *Sarah smiled, and the boy grinned back.* 사라가 미소짓자 소년도 따라 씩 웃었다. **5** away from the front of something or away from a person or thing ‖ 사물의 앞 또는 사람이나 사물에게서 떨어져. 뒤로: *Her hair was pulled back in a ponytail.* 그녀는 머리를 말꼬리처럼 뒤로 묶었다. / *Stand back from the fire!* 불에서 물러서라! **6** in or toward an earlier time ‖ 이전에. 이전으로: *This all happened about three years back.* 이 모든 것이 약 3년 전에 일어났다. **7 back and forth** in one direction and then in the opposite direction ‖ 한 쪽으로 그러고 나서 반대 쪽으로. 왔다갔다. 이리저리(로): *He walked back and forth across the floor.* 그는 마루를 가로질러 왔다갔다 했다.

back³ v 1 [I, T] to move in the direction that is behind you, or to make someone or something move in this way ‖ 뒤쪽으로 움직이거나 움직이게 하다. 후진하다[시키다]: *Teresa backed the car down the narrow driveway.* 테레사는 좁은 진입로로 차를 후진시켰다. / *We slowly backed away from the snake.* 우리는 뱀을 보고 슬슬 뒤로 물러섰다. **2** [T] to support someone or something, especially by using your money or power ‖ 사람이나 사물을 특히 돈이나 권력을 이용해 지지하다. 뒷받침하다: *The bill is backed by several environmental groups.* 몇몇 환경 단체들은 그 법안을 지지한다. **3** [T] to risk money on the team, person, horse etc. that you think will win something ‖ 승산이 있으리라고 생각되는 팀·사람·말 등에 돈을 걸다. 베팅하다: *Which team did you back in the Superbowl?* 슈퍼볼 경기에서 어느 팀에 돈을 걸었니?

back down *phr v* [I] to accept defeat or admit that you are wrong in an argument or fight ‖ 논쟁이나 싸움에서 패배를 받아들이거나 틀렸음을 인정하다: *Rosen backed down when he saw how big the other guy was.* 로젠은 상대방이 얼마나 덩치가 큰지 보고서는 졌다고 인정했다.

back off *phr v* [I] **1** to move in the direction that is behind you, away from something ‖ 어떤 것과 떨어져 뒤로 움직이다. 물러서다: *Back off a little, you're too close.* 좀 뒤로 떨어져, 너무 가깝잖아. **2** to stop trying to make someone do or think something ‖ 어떤 사람에게 어떤 것을 하거나 생각하게 하려는 것을 멈추다. 그만두다: *Back off! I don't need your advice.* 그만둬! 네 충고는 필요 없어.

back onto sth *phr v* [T] to have something very near to the back ‖ 사물이 뒤쪽으로 매우 가까이 있다. …과 등을 맞대고 있다: *These houses back onto a busy road.* 이 집들은 번잡한 도로를 등지고 있다.

back out *phr v* [I] to decide not to do something you promised to do ‖ 하기로 약속한 것을 하지 않기로 결정하다. 약속을 취소하다: *They backed out of the deal at the last minute.* 그들은 막판에 가서 거래를 취소했다.

back up *phr v* **1** [T **back sb/sth ↔ up**] to support what someone is doing or saying, or show that it is true ‖ 남이 하거나 말하는 것을 지지하거나 그것이 사실임을 보이다. 뒷받침하다: *He had evidence on video to back up his claim.* 그는 주장을 뒷받침할 비디오로 된 증거물을 가지고 있었다. **2** [I, T **back sth ↔ up**] to make a car go backward ‖ 차를 뒤쪽으로 가게 하다. 차를 후진하다[시키다] **3** [I] to move in the direction that is behind you ‖ 뒤쪽으로 움직이다. 물러서다: *Back up a little so they can get by.* 그들이 지나갈 수 있게 좀 뒤로 물러서라. **4** [I, T **back sth ↔ up**] to make a copy of information on a computer ‖ 컴퓨터상의

정보를 복사하다. 백업하다 **5 be backed up** traffic that is backed up is moving very slowly ‖ 교통이 아주 천천히 움직이다. 정체되다

back⁴ *adj* **1** in the back or behind something ‖ 사물의 뒤쪽에 있는: *the back door* 뒷문 **2 back street/road** a street or road that is away from the main streets of a town or area ‖ 어떤 도시나 지역의 중심가에서 떨어진 길이나 도로. 뒷길. 변두리길 **3 back rent/taxes/pay** money that someone owes for rent, tax etc. from an earlier date ‖ 집세·세금 등의 지불 기한이 넘은 돈. 밀린 집세/세금/임금: *We owe $350 in back taxes!* 우리 350달러의 세금이 연체되었어!

back·ache /ˈbækeɪk/ *n* [C, U] a dull pain or general pain in your back ‖ 허리가 뻐근하거나 아픈 증세. 요통

back·bit·ing /ˈbæk,baɪtɪŋ/ *n* [U] criticism of someone who is not present ‖ 없는 사람에 대한 비판. 험담. 중상: *The coach made sure there was never any backbiting in the locker room.* 그 코치는 탈의실에서 어떠한 험담도 없었음을 확신했다.

back·bone /ˈbækboʊn/ *n* **1** ⇨ SPINE **2 the backbone of** the most important part of an activity, group, or set of ideas, on which other parts depend ‖ 다른 부분들이 의존하는, 활동[집단, 일련의 생각]의 가장 중요한 부분. 중추. 핵심: *The cocoa industry is the backbone of Ghana's economy.* 코코아 산업은 가나 경제의 중추이다. **3** [U] courage and determination ‖ 용기와 결단. 기개: *Fight for what you believe – show some backbone!* 너의 신념을 위해 싸워서 용기를 보여 봐!

back·break·ing /ˈbæk,breɪkɪŋ/ *adj* backbreaking work is very difficult and tiring ‖ 일이 대단히 어렵고 고된.

back·date /ˌbækˈdeɪt/ *v* [T] to write an earlier date on a document or check than the date when it was really written ‖ 문서나 수표에 그것이 실제로 작성된 날짜보다 이전의 날짜를 쓰다. 소급시키다: *a pay increase backdated to January* 1월까지 소급한 봉급 인상분

back·drop /ˈbækdrɑp/ *n* **1** the conditions in which something happens, and which help to explain it ‖ 어떤 일의 발생하여 그것을 설명하는 데 도움을 주는 상황. 배경: *The company's growth must be seen against the backdrop of the city's economic expansion.* 그 회사의 성장은 그 도시의 경제 팽창을 배경으로 이

루어졌다고 봐야 한다. **2** a painted cloth behind a stage, or the scenery behind something you are looking at ‖ 무대 뒤의 색칠한 천, 또는 바라보는 것 뒤의 경관. 배경(막)

back·er /'bækɚ/ *n* someone who supports a plan, organization, country etc., especially by providing money ‖ 특히 자금을 제공하여 계획·조직·국가 등을 지원하는 사람. 지원[후원]자: *financial backers of the new gun club* (=people who give money to the club) 새 사격 클럽의 재정적 후원자들

back·fire /'bækfaɪɚ/ *v* [I] **1** if a plan or action backfires, it has an effect that is the opposite of what you intended ‖ 계획이나 행동이 의도했던 것과 반대의 결과를 낳다. 예상을 뒤엎다[빗나가다] **2** if a car backfires, it makes a sudden loud noise because the engine is not working correctly ‖ 차가 엔진이 제대로 작동하지 않아서 갑자기 큰 소음을 내다. 역화(逆火)를 일으키다

back·gam·mon /'bæk,gæmən/ *n* [U] a game for two players, using flat round pieces and DICE on a special board ‖ 특수 판 위에서 주사위와 동글납작한 말을 써서 하는 2인용 게임. 서양 주사위 놀이

back·ground /'bækgraʊnd/ *n* **1** the type of education, experiences, and family that someone has ‖ 사람이 보유한 교육·경험·가족의 유형. 경력. 배경: *The kids here have very different religious backgrounds* 여기 있는 아이들은 매우 다양한 종교적 배경을 가지고 있다. **2** the sounds, things, movements etc. that are in or happening in a place or picture but that are not the main thing you see or hear ‖ 듣거나 보는 것의 주요소는 아니지만 공간이나 그림 속에 존재하거나 일어나는 소리·물건·동작 등. 배경: *I could hear cars honking in the background.* 나는 뒷배경에서 울리는 자동차의 경적 소리를 들을 수 있었다. **3** [singular, U] ⇨ BACKDROP

backhanded /'bæk,hændɪd/ *adj* **backhanded compliment** a statement that seems to express praise or admiration, but is actually insulting ‖ 칭찬이나 찬사를 하는 듯하지만 실제로는 모욕하는 말. 비꼬는 듯한 칭찬

back·ing /'bækɪŋ/ *n* **1** [U] support or help, especially with money ‖ 특히 자금의 지원이나 후원: *The agency has provided financial backing for the project.* 그 기구는 그 프로젝트에 재정적 후원을 제공해 왔다. **2** material that is used to make the back of an object ‖ 물건의 뒤를 받치는 데에 쓰이는 재료. 등판. 안감

back·lash /'bæklæʃ/ *n* [singular] a strong reaction against a particular event, decision, or social development ‖ 특정 사건[결정, 사회 발전] 등에 대항하는 격렬한 반응. 반발. 반동: *a political backlash against immigrants* 이민자들에 대한 정치적 반발

back·log /'bæklɔg, -lɑg/ *n* work that still needs to be done and should have been done earlier ‖ 여전히 해야 될 필요가 있고 이미 했어야 하는 일. 잔무. 잔업: *a huge backlog of orders from customers* 고객들로부터의 막대한 주문 잔고

back·pack[1] /'bækpæk/ *n* a bag you carry on your back when you are walking or camping ‖ 걷거나 캠핑할 때 등에 메는 가방. 배낭

back·pack[2] *v* [I] to go walking and camping carrying a BACKPACK ‖ 배낭을 지고 걷거나 캠핑하러 가다. **– backpacker** *n* **– backpacking** *n* [U]

back seat /,. './ *n* **1** the seat behind where the driver sits in a car ‖ 운전석 뒤쪽의 좌석. 뒷좌석 **2 back seat driver** someone who gives unwanted advice to the driver of a car ‖ 운전자에게 달갑지 않은 충고를 하는 사람. 운전할 때 참견하는 사람 **3 take a back seat** to accept or be put in a less important position ‖ 덜 중요한 지위를 수락하거나 그러한 상태에 놓이다. 뒤로 물러나다. 나서지 않다: *His career has taken a back seat while he helps raise his two children.* 그가 두 아이들의 뒷바라지를 하는 동안 일은 뒷전으로 미루어졌다.

back·side /'bæksaɪd/ *n* INFORMAL the part of your body on which you sit ‖ 앉는 신체 부위. 엉덩이

back·space /'bækspeɪs/ *v* [I] to move backward toward the beginning of the line that you are typing (TYPE) on a computer or TYPEWRITER ‖ 컴퓨터나 타자기로 타자를 치고 있는 행의 앞쪽으로 역행하다. 한 스페이스 물리다

back·stage /,bæk'steɪdʒ/ *adv* in or toward the area behind the stage in a theater ‖ 극장의 무대 뒤편에서[으로]

back-to-back /,. . '. ./ *adj, adv* **1** happening one after the other ‖ 연이어 발생하는. 잇따른. 잇따르는: *We played two concerts back-to-back.* 우리는 연이어 두 번의 콘서트를 했다. / *back-to-back baseball games* 더블헤더 야구 경기 **2** with someone's or something's back against another person's or thing's back ‖ 사람이나 물건이 다른 사람이나 물건의

bad¹

등을 마주한. 맞댄. 맞대고: *The chairs were placed back-to-back.* 의자들은 등을 맞대어 놓여 있었다.

back·track /'bæktræk/ *v* [I] **1** to go back the way you have just come ‖ 방금 온 길로 되돌아가다. 되밟다: *We had to backtrack about a mile.* 우리는 1마일이나 왔던 길을 되돌아가야 했다. **2** to do or say something again in a different way ‖ 어떤 것을 다른 방식으로 다시 하거나 말하다: *The witness backtracked, adding some new facts to his story.* 증인은 말을 바꿔 자신의 이야기에 새로운 사실들을 덧붙였다.

back·up /'bækʌp/ *n* **1** a copy of something that you can use if the original thing is lost or does not work ‖ 원본이 분실되거나 제 기능을 하지 못할 경우 사용할 수 있는 복사본. 백업(판): *Make a backup of any work you do on the computer.* 컴퓨터상에서 하는 어느 작업이나 복사본을 만들어라. **2** [C, U] someone or something that provides help or support when it is needed ‖ 필요할 때 도움이나 원조를 제공하는 사람이나 사물. 후원(자[품]): *Several police cars provided backup for the officers.* 몇 대의 경찰차가 관리들을 호위했다.

back·ward¹ /'bækwɚd/, **backwards** *adv* **1** in the direction that is behind you ‖ 뒤쪽으로: *She took a step backwards, startled.* 그녀는 놀라서 한 걸음 뒤로 물러섰다. —opposite FORWARD¹ **2** toward the beginning or the past ‖ 시초나 과거로. 거슬러서: *Can you say the alphabet backward?* 알파벳을 거꾸로 말할 수 있습니까? —opposite FORWARD¹ **3** with the back part in front ‖ 뒷부분이 앞으로. 거꾸로: *Your t-shirt is on backwards.* 네 티셔츠는 앞뒤를 바꿔 입었다.

back·ward² *adj* **1** made toward the direction that is behind you ‖ 뒤쪽을 향한: *She left without a backward glance.* 그녀는 뒤도 돌아보지 않고 떠났다. **2** developing slowly and less successfully than others ‖ 남보다 더디고 처지게 발전하는. 부진한: *a backward child* 지진아

back·wa·ter /'bæk,wɔtɚ, -,wɑ-/ *n* a town or place far away from cities, where not much happens ‖ 도시에서 멀리 떨어져 일이 별로 일어나지 않는 읍이나 장소. 벽촌. 벽지

back·woods /,bæk'wʊdz/ *n* [plural] an area in the forest that is far from any towns ‖ 어느 도시에서든 멀리 떨어진 산간 지역. 오지 –**backwoods** *adj* : *a backwoods town* 오지의 마을

back·yard, back yard /,bæk'yɑrd/ *n* the area of land behind a house ‖ 집 뒤의 터. 뒤뜰

bacon /'beɪkən/ *n* [U] long thin pieces of SALT*ed* or SMOKED meat from the back or sides of a pig ‖ 돼지의 등이나 옆구리 살을 소금에 절이거나 훈제한 길고 가는 조각. 베이컨

bac·te·ri·a /bæk'tɪriə/ *n* [plural] very small living things, some of which can cause disease ‖ 일부는 질병을 유발할 수도 하는, 매우 작은 생명체. 박테리아

bad¹ /bæd/ *adj* **worse, worst** **1** not good and unpleasant ‖ 좋지 않고 불쾌한. 나쁜: *I'm afraid I have some bad news for you.* 당신에게 좀 나쁜 소식이 있는 것 같아요. / *a really bad smell* 정말 고약한 냄새 **2** low in quality or below an acceptable standard ‖ 질이 낮거나 수용 기준 이하인. 기준 미달의. 불충분한: *She was the worst teacher I ever had.* 그녀는 내가 만났던 선생님들 중 최악이었다. / *Brian is really bad at sports.* 브라이언은 스포츠는 정말 못한다. **3** damaging or harmful ‖ 손상을 입히는, 해로운: *Smoking is bad for your health.* 흡연은 건강에 해롭다. / *Pollution in the lake is having a bad effect on fish stocks.* 호수의 오염이 물고기떼에게 악영향을 주고 있다. **4** serious or severe ‖ 심각한, 지독한: *a bad cold* 지독한[심한] 감기 / *The traffic near the airport was even worse today than it was yesterday.* 오늘 공항 주변의 교통이 어제보다 훨씬 나빴다. **5 too bad** SPOKEN said when you are sorry that something unpleasant has happened to someone ‖ 남에게 불쾌한 일이 일어난 것이 유감스러울 때 쓰여. 정말 안된! *It's too bad she had to give up teaching when she got sick.* 그녀가 아파서 교직을 그만두어야 했다니 참 안됐다. **6** not fit to eat ‖ 먹기에 적절치 않은. 상한: *The milk has gone bad.* 우유가 상했다. **7 feel bad** to feel ashamed or sorry about something ‖ 어떤 것에 대해 부끄러움이나 미안함을 느끼다: *I felt really bad about missing your birthday.* 네 생일을 잊은 것에 대하여 정말 미안했다. **8** permanently injured or not working correctly ‖ 영구적으로 손상을 입거나 제대로 움직이지 않는. 불량한. 결함이 있는: *The fever left him with a bad heart.* 그는 열 때문에 심장이 나빠졌다. **9 not bad** SPOKEN used when you think something is acceptable ‖ 사물이 받아들일 만하다고 여겨질 때 쓰여. 나쁘지 않은. 그저 그런: *"How are you?" "Oh, not bad."* "어떻게 지내?" "어, 그저 그래."

10 comparative **badder,** superlative **baddest** SLANG extremely good ‖ 굉장히 좋은. 훌륭한: *That's a bad song!* 정말 끝내주는 곡이네! **11 bad language/ words** swearing or rude words ‖ 욕하거나 무례한 말. 욕설 **12 bad off** NONSTANDARD ⇨ **badly off** (BADLY)

bad² *adv* SPOKEN NONSTANDARD ⇨ BADLY

badge /bædʒ/ *n* a small piece of metal that you wear or carry to show people that you work for a particular organization ‖ 특정 조직에서 일하는 것을 표시하기 위하여 착용하거나 지니는 작은 금속 조각. 배지: *a police officer's badge* 경찰관 배지

badg·er /ˈbædʒɚ/ *n* an animal with black and white fur that lives in holes in the ground ‖ 땅속의 굴에서 사는 흑·백의 털을 지닌 동물. 오소리

bad·lands /ˈbædlændz/ *n* [plural] an area of rocks and hills where no crops can be grown ‖ 작물이 자랄 수 없는, 암석과 구릉으로 된 지역. 불모지

bad·ly /ˈbædli/ *adv* **worse, worst 1** in an unsatisfactory or unsuccessful way ‖ 만족스럽거나 성공적이지 못한 방식으로. 형편없이: *a badly written book* 졸렬하게[형편없이] 쓰여진 책 / *I sing very badly.* 나는 노래를 형편없이 부른다[잘 부르지 못한다]. ✗DON'T SAY "I sing very bad."✗ (이 뜻으로) "I sing very bad."라고는 하지 않는다. —opposite WELL¹ **2** very much or seriously ‖ 아주 몹시 또는 심하게. 대단히: *The refugees badly need food and clean water.* 난민들은 음식과 깨끗한 물을 몹시 필요로 한다. **3 badly off** not having things or money that you need ‖ 필요한 물건이나 돈이 없는. 궁한. 쪼들리는: *The tax changes left many middle-class Americans worse off.* 조세 변화로 중산층의 많은 미국인들이 더 가난해졌다.

bad·min·ton /ˈbædˌmɪnt³n/ *n* [U] a game in which players hit a small object with feathers across a net and try not to let it touch the ground ‖ 선수들이 깃털 달린 작은 물체를 네트를 가로질러 쳐 가며 지면에 떨어지지 않도록 하는 경기. 배드민턴

bad·mouth /ˈbædmaʊθ/ *v* [T] INFORMAL to talk about someone in a way that criticizes him/her ‖ 남에 대하여 비판하는 투로 말하다. 헐뜯다. 중상하다: *Ken's in trouble for badmouthing one of his employees.* 켄은 직원 한 명을 헐뜯어 곤경에 처해 있다.

baf·fle /ˈbæfəl/ *v* [T] if something baffles you, you cannot understand it at all ‖ 사물이 전혀 이해할 수 없게 만들다. 어리둥절[당황]하게 하다 —**baffling** *adj*

baf·fled /ˈbæfəld/ *adj* unable to understand something at all ‖ 어떤 것을 전혀 이해할 수 없는. 어리둥절한: *Scientists are completely baffled by the results.* 과학자들은 그 결과에 완전히 당황했다.

bag¹ /bæg/ *n* **1** a container made of paper, plastic, cloth etc. that opens at the top ‖ 종이·플라스틱·천 등으로 된, 윗부분이 열리는 용기. 봉지. 가방. 자루: *a shopping bag* 쇼핑백 / *packing a bag for the weekend* 주말용 가방 싸기 **2** the amount a bag can hold ‖ 자루 하나에 담을 수 있는 양: *two bags of rice per family* 가족당 두 자루의 쌀 **3 in the bag** certain to be won or to be a success ‖ 승리나 성공이 확실한: *We thought we had the game in the bag, but they beat us.* 우리는 그 경기의 승리가 따 놓은 당상이라고 여겼지만 그들이 우리를 이겼다. **4 bags** dark circles or loose skin around your eyes ‖ 눈가의 둥그스름한 검은 부분이나 늘어진 피부

bag² *v* **-gged, -gging** [T] **1** to put things in a bag ‖ 가방에 물건을 집어넣다: *He got a job bagging groceries at the supermarket.* 그는 슈퍼마켓에서 봉지에 식료품을 담는 일을 구했다. **2** SPOKEN to decide not to do something ‖ 어떤 것을 하지 않기로 결심하다: *I'm tired of waiting. Bag this-I'm leaving.* 기다리는 데 지쳤어. 집어치워. 나 간다.

ba·gel /ˈbeɪgəl/ *n* a type of bread that is shaped like a ring ‖ 반지처럼 생긴 빵의 일종. 베이글 —see picture at BREAD

bag·ful /ˈbægfʊl/ *n* the amount a bag can hold ‖ 자루 하나에 담을 수 있는 양. 한 자루분의 양

bag·gage /ˈbægɪdʒ/ *n* [U] **1** all the bags, boxes etc. that someone carries when s/he is traveling ‖ 여행시 들고 다니는 모든 가방·상자 등. 여행용 수화물 **2** beliefs, opinions, and experiences from the past that influence the way a person or society behaves or thinks ‖ 사람이나 사회의 행동이나 사고 방식에 영향을 끼치는 과거로부터의 신념·의견·경험. 관습: *cultural baggage* 문화적 관습

Bag·gies /ˈbægiz/ *n* [plural] TRADEMARK small plastic bags used for keeping food in ‖ 음식을 보관하는 데 쓰는 작은 비닐백 —**baggie** *n*

bag·gy /ˈbægi/ *adj* hanging in loose folds ‖ 느슨하게 주름져 늘어진. 헐렁한. 늘어진: *a baggy t-shirt* 헐렁한 티셔츠

bag la·dy /ˈ. ͵. ./ *n* INFORMAL an

impolite word for a woman who lives on the street and carries all her possessions with her ‖ 소지품을 모두 갖고 다니며 거리에서 생활하는 여성을 무례하게 이르는 말. 여자 부랑자

bag·pipes /'bægpaɪps/ n [plural] a Scottish musical instrument which is played by forcing air out of a bag through pipes ‖ 파이프를 통해 공기를 자루 밖으로 밀어내어 연주하는 스코틀랜드 악기. 백파이프

bail¹ /beɪl/ n [U] money left with a court of law so that someone can be let out of prison while waiting for his/her TRIAL ‖ 재판을 기다리는 동안 사람이 교도소에서 석방될 수 있도록 법원에 맡긴 돈. 보석금: *The prisoner was let out on bail.* ‖ 수감자는 보석으로 석방됐다. / *Marshall's father stood/posted bail for him.* (=paid the bail) 마셜의 아버지는 그를 위해 보석금을 지불했다.

bail² v [I, T] to remove water from the bottom of a boat ‖ 배의 바닥에서 물을 제거하다. (물을) 퍼내다

bail out phr v **1** [T **bail** sb/sth **out**] to do something to help someone out of trouble, especially financial problems ‖ 남을 곤경, 특히 재정적 문제에서 벗어나도록 돕는 일을 하다. 구제하다: *bailing out a company* 회사를 회생시키기 **2** [T **bail** sb ↔ **out**] to give money to a court of law so that someone can leave prison until his/her TRIAL ‖ 재판에 회부될 때까지 사람이 교도소에서 풀려날 수 있게 법원에 돈을 맡기다. 보석금을 지불하다 **3** [I] INFORMAL to escape from a situation that you no longer want to be involved in ‖ 더 이상 연루되고 싶지 않은 상황에서 빠져나오다. 벗어나다. 손을 떼다: *After ten years in the business, McArthur is bailing out.* 맥아더는 10년간 하던 사업을 정리하고 있다. **4** [T **bail** sth ↔ **out**] to remove water from the bottom of a boat ‖ 배의 바닥에서 물을 제거하다. 물을 퍼내다 **5** [I] to escape from a plane, using a PARACHUTE ‖ 낙하산을 이용해 비행기에서 탈출하다

bail·out /'beɪlaʊt/ n a situation in which someone provides money to help someone else who has financial problems ‖ 재정적 곤경에 빠진 누군가를 돕기 위해 자금을 제공하는 상황. (자금 지원에 의한) 긴급 구제 조치: *the government bailout of the savings and loan organizations* 저축·대출 기관에 대한 정부의 자금 지원

bait¹ /beɪt/ n [singular, U] **1** food used for attracting fish, animals, or birds so that you can catch them ‖ 물고기[동물, 새]를 잡을 수 있도록 유인하는 데에 쓰는 먹이. 미끼 **2** something you use in order to try to make someone do something or buy something ‖ 남에게 어떤 것을 하거나 구매하게 하려고 사용하는 것. 미끼. 유혹물: *He made the CD player sound so good, I took the bait and bought it.* 그가 CD플레이어 소리를 너무나 듣기 좋게 해 놓아 나는 그것에 혹해 그것을 사버렸다.

bait² v [T] **1** to put food on a hook to catch fish, or in a trap to catch animals ‖ 물고기나 동물을 잡기 위해 갈고리나 덫에 음식을 놓다. 미끼를 달다 **2** to laugh at or TEASE someone in an unkind way ‖ 사람을 가혹하게 비웃거나 놀리다. 못살게 굴다

bake /beɪk/ v [I, T] to cook food in an OVEN, using dry heat ‖ 오븐의 음식물을 건조열을 이용해 요리하다. 굽다: *I'm baking a cake for Laurie.* 나는 로리에게 줄 케이크를 굽고 있다.

bak·er /'beɪkə/ n someone whose job is to BAKE bread, cakes, cookies etc. ‖ 빵·케이크·과자 등을 굽는 직업인. 제빵사. 빵 제조업자

bak·er·y /'beɪkəri/ n a place where bread, cakes, cookies etc. are made or sold ‖ 빵·케이크·과자 등을 만들거나 파는 곳. 제과점

bake sale /'. ./ n an occasion when the members of a school group, church organization etc. make sweet foods and sell them in order to make money for the organization ‖ 학교 단체·교회 기관 등의 회원들이 기금 마련을 위해 맛있는 음식을 만들어 파는 행사

bal·ance¹ /'bæləns/ n **1** [singular, U] a state in which your weight is evenly spread so that you are steady and not likely to fall ‖ 무게가 골고루 퍼져 안정되고 넘어지지 않는 상태. 균형: *Billy was walking on top of the fence and lost his balance.* 빌리는 울타리 위를 걷다가 균형을 잃었다. (=was unable to stay steady) / *Tricia could not keep her balance* (=could not stay steady), *and fell on the ice.* 트리시아는 균형을 잡지 못하고 빙판 위에 넘어졌다. / *I was still off balance* (=unable to stay steady) *when he hit me again.* 그가 나를 다시 쳤을 때 나는 여전히 균형을 잡지 못하고 있었다. **2** [singular] a state in which opposite qualities or influences have or are given equal importance ‖ 상반된 성질이나 세력이 동등한 중요성을 띠거나 부여받는 상태. 조화: *The car's designers wanted to strike a balance between safety and* *style.* (=make sure that two things have equal importance) 그 자동차 설계자들은 안전성과 스타일 사이의 조화를 꾀하고 싶었다. **3** the amount of something that remains after some has been used or spent ‖ 어떤 것의 일부를 사용하거나 소비한 후 남은 양. 잔여. 나머지: *a bank balance* (=the money you have left in the bank) 은행 잔고 **4 be/hang in the balance** to be in a situation where the result of something could be good or bad ‖ 어떤 것의 결과가 좋거나 나쁠 수 있는 상태에 놓여 있다. 불안정[미결정] 상태에 있다: *With the war still going, thousands of peoples' lives hang in the balance.* 전쟁이 아직 계속되고 있어 수천 명의 생명이 불안정한 상태에 있다.

balance² *v* **1** [I, T] to get into a steady position, without falling to one side or the other, or to put something in this position ‖ 한쪽으로 쏠리지 않고 안정된 위치에 놓이거나 두다. 균형을 유지하다 [유지시키다]: *The man balanced a spinning plate on a tall stick.* 그 남자는 긴 막대 위에서 돌아가는 접시의 균형을 유지시켰다. **2** [I, T] to have equal amounts of money being paid and spent, or to make two amounts of money equal ‖ 번 금액과 소비한 금액이 일치하거나 두 금액을 똑같이 만들다. 수지가[를] 맞다 [맞추다]: *Congress is attempting to balance the budget.* 의회는 예산 수지를 맞추려고 하고 있다. **3** [T] to give equal importance to two or more things ‖ 두 개 이상의 것에 동등한 중요성을 부여하다. 균형을 유지시키다: *A working mother has to balance her home life with a career.* 일하는 엄마는 가정 생활과 직업 활동의 균형을 맞추어야 한다. **4** [T] to consider one thing in relation to something else ‖ 어떤 것을 다른 것과 관련지어 생각하다. 비교하여 검토하다: *The need for a new road must be balanced against the damage to the environment.* 새로운 도로의 필요성은 환경에 미칠 악영향을 비교하여 검토되어야 한다.

bal·anced /ˈbælənst/ *adj* **1** giving equal attention to all sides or opinions; fair ‖ 모든 측면이나 견해에 동등한 주의를 기울이는. 균형 감각을 갖춘; 공정한: *balanced reporting of the election campaign* 선거 운동에 관한 공정한 보도 **2** including the right amount of different kinds of things or people ‖ 적정량의 다른 종류의 사물이나 사람을 포함하는. 균형잡힌: *a balanced diet* 균형잡힌 식단

balance sheet /ˈ.. ./ *n* a written statement of the money and property a business has, and how much money it has paid for goods and services ‖ 한 사업체가 소유한 돈이나 자산 및 재화와 용역에 지출한 금액을 기재한 명세서. 대차대조표

bal·co·ny /ˈbælkəni/ *n* **1** a structure built onto the outside of a high window, so that you can stand or sit outside ‖ 높이 달린 창문 외부에 서거나 앉아 있을 수 있도록 만든 구조물. 발코니 —see picture on page 945 **2** the seats upstairs in a theater ‖ 극장의 위층 좌석

bald /bɔld/ *adj* **1** having little or no hair on your head ‖ 머리카락이 거의 없거나 전혀 없는. 머리가 벗어진. 대머리의 **2** not having enough of the substance that normally covers something ‖ 보통 어떤 것을 덮고 있는 물질이 충분하지 않은. 닳아 버린: *bald tires* 닳은 타이어

bald ea·gle /ˈ. ,./ *n* a large North American wild bird that represents the US on money, official signs etc. ‖ 화폐·국장(國章) 등에서 미국을 상징하는 북미 지역의 큰 야생 조류. 흰머리수리

bald·ing /ˈbɔldɪŋ/ *adj* becoming BALD ‖ 대머리가 되어가는

bale /beɪl/ *n* a large amount of something such as paper or HAY that is tied tightly together ‖ 종이나 건초 등의 상당량을 함께 단단히 묶은 것. 꾸러미

bale·ful /ˈbeɪlfəl/ *adj* expressing a desire to harm someone ‖ 남에게 해악을 끼치려는 욕구를 나타내는. 악의가 있는: *a baleful look* 악의에 찬 얼굴

balk /bɔk/ *v* [I] to refuse to do something unpleasant or difficult ‖ 불쾌하거나 어려운 일을 하는 것을 거부하다: *Several managers balked at enforcing the decision.* 몇몇 부장들은 그 결정 사항의 시행을 거부했다. **– balky** *adj*

ball /bɔl/ *n* **1** a round object that is thrown, hit, kicked etc. in a game, or any object shaped like this ‖ 경기에서 던지고 치고 (발로) 차는 둥근 물체나 이와 비슷한 물체. 공: *yellow tennis balls* 노란색 테니스 공 / *a ball of yarn* 털실 뭉치 **2 on the ball** INFORMAL able to think or act quickly ‖ 재빠르게 생각하거나 행동할 수 있는: *If we had been on the ball, this might not have happened.* 우리가 기민했다면 이런 일은 일어나지 않았을 텐데. **3 have a ball** INFORMAL to have a very good time ‖ 즐거운 시간을 보내다. 즐기다: *We had a ball last night!* 우리는 어젯밤에 정말 즐거운 시간을 보냈어! **4 set/start the ball rolling** to begin an activity or event ‖ 활동이나 행사를 시작

하다: *You set the ball rolling, and we'll help you out when you need us.* 네가 시작해라. 그러면 필요할 때 우리가 도울게. **5** a ball that is thrown toward the hitter outside the correct area in baseball ‖ 야구에서 정확한 구역을 벗어난, 타자 쪽으로 투구한 공. 볼 **6** a large formal occasion where people dance ‖ 사람들이 춤추는, 대규모의 격식을 갖춘 행사. 무도회 **7 the ball of the foot/hand/thumb** the rounded part at the base of your largest toe or at the base or top of your thumb ‖ 엄지발가락 기부의 둥근 부분, 또는 엄지손가락 기부나 위쪽의 둥근 부분 —see also BALLS **play ball** (PLAY¹)

bal·lad /'bæləd/ *n* **1** a simple song, especially about love ‖ 특히 사랑에 관한 간결한 노래. 발라드 **2** a short story in the form of a poem ‖ 시의 형식을 갖춘 짤막한 이야기. 발라드

bal·le·ri·na /ˌbælə'rinə/ *n* a female BALLET dancer ‖ 여성 발레 무용수. 발레리나

bal·let /bæ'leɪ, 'bæleɪ/ *n* **1** a performance in which a story is told using dance and music, without any speaking ‖ 대사 없이 춤과 음악으로 이야기를 전하는 공연. 발레: *the ballet "Swan Lake"* 발레 "백조의 호수" **2** [U] this type of dancing as an art form ‖ 예술 형태로서의 이러한 종류의 춤. 발레 **3** a group of ballet dancers who work together ‖ 함께 공연을 하는 일단의 무용수. 발레단: *the Bolshoi ballet* 볼쇼이 발레단

ball game /'. ./ *n* **1** a game of baseball, basketball, or football ‖ 야구[농구, 축구] 경기. 구기(球技) **2 a whole new ball game/a different ball game** a situation that is very different from the one you were in before ‖ 이전의 상황과는 상당히 다른 상황. 아주 새로운/다른 사태: *I've used word processors, but this is a whole new ball game.* 나는 워드 프로세서를 써 왔지만 이것은 전혀 새로운 것이다.

bal·lis·tic /bə'lɪstɪk/ *adj* **go ballistic** SPOKEN to suddenly become very angry ‖ 갑자기 화가 치밀다. 격노하다

bal·lis·tics /bə'lɪstɪks/ *n* [U] the study of how objects move through the air when they are thrown or shot from a gun ‖ 물체가 던져지거나 발사될 때 공중을 이동하는 방법에 대한 학문. 탄도학

bal·loon¹ /bə'lun/ *n* **1** a small brightly colored rubber bag that can be filled with air ‖ 공기를 채울 수 있는 작고 밝은 색깔의 고무 주머니. 풍선 **2** ⇨ HOT AIR

BALLOON

balloon² *v* [I] to become larger in size or amount ‖ 크기나 양이 커지다. 늘어나다. 불어나다: *Paul's weight has ballooned to 300 pounds since he left college.* 폴의 몸무게는 대학 졸업 이후 300파운드로 불었다.

bal·lot /'bælət/ *n* **1** a piece of paper that you use to vote ‖ 투표에 쓰는 종이조각. 투표 용지 **2** [C, U] a system of voting in secret, or an occasion when you vote in this way ‖ 비밀리에 투표하는 방식이나 경우. 비밀 투표: *We're holding a ballot to decide the chairmanship.* 회장직을 결정짓기 위해 우리는 비밀 투표를 하고 있다.

ballot box /'.. ../ *n* **1 the ballot box** the process of voting, or the time when voting happens ‖ 투표의 과정이나 투표가 이뤄지는 때. 투표(시기): *The voters will give their opinion of the Governor at the ballot box.* 유권자들은 투표로 주지사에 대한 의견을 표출할 것이다. **2** a box that BALLOT papers are put in during the vote ‖ 투표시 투표 용지를 집어 넣는 상자. 투표함

ball park /'. ../ *n* **1** a field for playing baseball, with seats for people to watch the game ‖ 경기를 관람할 수 있는 좌석을 갖춘 야구 경기용 구장. 야구 경기장 **2 a ball park figure/estimate** a number or amount that is almost but not exactly correct ‖ 거의 비슷하나 정확하게 맞지 않는 수나 양. 어림셈한 수[견적]: *Can you give us a ball park figure?* 대략적인 수치를 알려 주겠니? **3 in the (right) ball park** INFORMAL close to the amount, price etc. that is correct ‖ 정확한 양·값 등에 가까운. 근사치의: *"Does $3000 sound too high?" "No, that's in the right ball park."* "3000달러가 너무 비싸게 들리니?" "아니, 그 정도면 적당해."

ball·point pen /ˌbɔlpɔɪnt 'pɛn/ *n* a pen with a small ball at the end that rolls ink onto the paper ‖ 종이 위에 잉크를 흘리는 작은 볼이 끝에 달린 펜. 볼펜

ball·room /'bɔlrum/ *n* a large room where formal dances take place ‖ 격식을 갖춘 춤을 추는 큰 실내. 무도장

balls /bɔlz/ *n* [plural] SLANG courage and determination ‖ 용기와 결단. 배짱. 담력: *It took balls to be that tough with Mr. Dozier.* 도지에 씨에게 그렇게 강경하게 나가기 위해서는 배짱이 필요했다.

balm /bam/ *n* [U] an oily liquid that you rub onto your skin to reduce pain ‖ 통증을 경감시키기 위해 피부에 바르는 유성 수지. 발삼

balm·y /'bɑmi/ *adj* balmy weather or air is warm and pleasant ‖ 날씨나 공기가 따뜻하고 쾌적한

ba·lo·ney /bə'louni/ *n* [U] **1** INFORMAL something that is silly or not true ‖ 어이없거나 사실이 아닌 것. 허튼소리: *His explanation sounded like a bunch of baloney to me.* 그의 설명은 허튼소리투성이로 들렸다. **2** NONSTANDARD ⇨ BOLOGNA

bam·boo /,bæm'bu·/ *n* [C, U] a tall plant with hard hollow stems, often used for making furniture ‖ 종종 가구를 만드는 데에 쓰는, 줄기가 딱딱하고 속이 빈 키 큰 나무. 대나무

bam·boo·zle /bæm'buzəl/ *v* [T] INFORMAL to trick or confuse someone ‖ 남을 속이거나 혼란스럽게 하다. 기만하다

ban¹ /bæn/ *n* an official order that does not allow something to be used or done ‖ 어떤 것의 사용이나 실행을 허락하지 않는 공식 명령. 금지령: *a global ban on nuclear testing* 핵실험에 대한 전 세계적인 금지령

ban² *v* **-nned, -nning** [T] to say that something must not be done, used etc. ‖ 어떤 것이 실행·사용되어서는 안 된다는 것을 밝히다. 금지하다: *The city council banned smoking in public areas in 1995.* 시의회는 1995년에 공공장소에서의 흡연을 금지했다.

ba·nal /bə'næl, bə'nɑl, 'beɪnl/ *adj* ordinary and not interesting ‖ 평범하고 흥미롭지 않은. 진부한: *a banal love song* 진부한 연가 **– banality** /bə'næləti/ *n* [C, U]

ba·nan·a /bə'nænə/ *n* **1** a long curved yellow fruit ‖ 길게 휜 노란색 과일. 바나나 —see picture on page 944 **2 go bananas** to get very excited, upset, or angry ‖ 몹시 흥분하다[심란해지다, 화나다]: *The kids went bananas and tore open the boxes.* 아이들은 매우 흥분해 하여 상자를 뜯었다.

banc·as·sur·ance /'bæŋkə,ʃʊrəns/ *n* [U] the combining of banking and insurance activities in one organization ‖ 은행 업무와 보험 업무를 한 조직 내로 병합한 것. 방카쉬랑스

band¹ /bænd/ *n* **1** a group of musicians, especially a group that plays popular music ‖ 특히 대중 음악을 연주하는 음악가들의 집단. 악단. 밴드 —compare ORCHESTRA **2** a group of people who work together to achieve the same aims ‖ 공동의 목적을 달성하기 위해 함께 일하는 일단의 사람들. 일행. 무리: *a small band of terrorists* 소규모의 테러범 일당 **3** a narrow piece of material with one end joined to the other to form a circle ‖ 한쪽 끝과 다른 쪽 끝을 연결하여 원을 이루는 좁다란 물건. 띠. 밴드: *Her hair was pulled back with a rubber band.* 그녀의 머리는 고무 밴드로 뒤로 묶여 있었다. **4** a line of a different color; STRIPE ‖ 다른 색으로 된 선; ⓟ stripe: *a fish with a black band along its back* ‖ 등을 따라 검은 줄무늬가 나 있는 물고기 **5** one of the parts or groups that something is divided into ‖ 나뉜 부분이나 집단 중의 하나. 층. 부류: *My new job puts us in a higher tax band.* 나의 새 직업으로 인하여 우리는 고액 납세자층에 속하게 된다.

band² *v*

band together *phr v* [I] to join with other people in order to work toward achieving an aim ‖ 목표 달성을 추진하기 위해 다른 사람들과 뭉치다. 단합[단결]하다. 연대[동맹]하다: *150 families have banded together to try to keep drug dealers out of the neighborhood.* 150여 가정이 마약상들을 동네에서 추방하기 위해 뭉쳤다.

band·age¹ /'bændɪdʒ/ *n* a piece of cloth that you wrap around an injured part of someone's body ‖ 사람 몸에 난 상처 부위를 감싸는 천조각. 붕대

bandage² *v* [T] to put a BANDAGE on a part of someone's body that is injured ‖ 상처입은 신체 부위에 붕대를 감다

Band-Aid /'bænd eɪd/ *n* TRADEMARK a small piece of material that sticks to your skin to cover small wounds ‖ 작은 상처를 덮으려고 피부에 붙이는 작은 물건. 반창고. 밴드

ban·dan·na /bæn'dænə/ *n* a square piece of colored cloth that you can wear over your head or around your neck ‖ 머리에 쓰거나 목에 두르는 사각형의 색깔 있는 천조각. 손수건. 스카프

ban·dit /'bændɪt/ *n* OLD-FASHIONED someone who robs people ‖ 사람들을 약탈하는 사람. 강도. 산적

band·stand /'bændstænd/ *n* a small building in a park that has a roof but no walls, used for musical performances ‖ 지붕만 있고 벽이 없는, 음악 공연에 쓰이는 공원 내의 작은 건물. 연주(무)대

band·wag·on /'bænd,wægən/ *n* **jump/climb on the bandwagon** to start doing something because a lot of other people are doing it ‖ 다른 많은 사람들이 하고 있어서 어떤 일을 하기 시작하다. 시류[대세]에 편승하다: *Like many companies, PELCO has jumped on the environmental bandwagon.* (=started to give attention to the environment) 많은 기업들처럼 펠코사도 환경 문제라는 시류에 편승했다.

ban·dy /'bændi/ *v*

bandy sth **about/around** *phr v* [T] to mention people or facts, especially to seem important or interesting ‖ 특히 중요하거나 재미있어 보이도록 사람이나 사실을 언급하다. 소문을 내다. 입방아에 올리다: *Her name was bandied about in connection with the recent scandal.* 그녀의 이름이 최근의 스캔들과 관련해서 사람들의 입방아에 올랐다.

bane /beɪn/ *n* **bane of sb's existence** HUMOROUS someone or something that causes you problems ‖ 문제를 일으키는 사람이나 사물. 화근. 골칫거리: *Physics was the bane of my existence in high school.* 물리학은 내 고등학교 시절 골칫거리였다.

bang¹ /bæŋ/ *v* **1** [I, T] to make a loud noise, especially by hitting something against something hard ‖ 특히 사물을 단단한 다른 사물에 부딪혀서 큰 소리를 내다. 쿵[쾅] 소리나게 부딪치다 : *Larren was banging on the wall with his fist.* 라렌은 주먹으로 벽을 쾅쾅 두드리고 있었다. / *The screen door banged shut behind him.* 방충문이 그의 뒤에서 쾅 하고 닫혔다. **2** [T] to hit a part of your body against something hard and hurt it ‖ 단단한 것에 신체의 일부를 부딪혀 다치다. 쾅 부딪치다: *I banged my knee on the corner of the bed.* 나는 침대 모서리에 무릎을 부딪쳤다.

bang

bang² *n* **1** a sudden loud noise, usually made by something hard hitting something else or by something exploding ‖ 보통 단단한 것을 다른 것에 부딪히게 하거나 어떤 것을 폭발시켜 나는 갑작스런 큰 소리. 쿵[쾅] 소리. 꿍음: *The door slammed shut with a bang.* 문이 쾅 소리를 내며 닫혔다. **2 get a bang out of** sth SPOKEN to enjoy something very much ‖ 어떤 것을 대단히 즐기다. …으로 크게 재미보다: *I really got a bang out of seeing those guys last night!* 나는 어젯밤 그 친구들을 만나서 재미가 좋았다. **3 with a bang** in a way that is very exciting or noticeable ‖ 꽤 흥미롭거나 눈에 띄게. 요란하게. 대대적으로: *He began his presidential campaign with a bang.* 그는 대대적으로 대통령 선거 유세

를 시작했다. —see also BANGS

bang³ *adv* INFORMAL directly or exactly ‖ 똑바로 또는 정확히. 딱. 꼭: *They've built a parking lot bang in the middle of town.* 그들은 읍의 한 중앙에 주차장을 만들었다.

bang⁴ *interjection* said in order to make the sound of a gun or bomb ‖ 총이나 폭탄 소리를 내는 데에 쓰여. 팡. 탕. 빵: *"Bang! Bang! You're dead!"* Tommy shouted. "탕! 탕! 너는 죽었다!"라고 토미는 소리쳤다.

banged-up /ˌ. '../ *adj* INFORMAL damaged or injured ‖ 손상되거나 다친. 부서진: *a banged-up old car* 파손된 낡은 차

bangs /bæŋz/ *n* [plural] hair that is cut straight across your FOREHEAD ‖ 이마를 가로질러 반듯이 자른 머리. 가지런한 앞머리

ban·ish /'bænɪʃ/ *v* [T] to punish someone by making him/her leave a place and stay out of it for a long time ‖ 사람에게 어떤 장소에서 떠나 오랫동안 돌아오지 못하게 하는 벌을 주다. 추방하다: *The king banished Roderigo from the court.* 왕은 로드리고를 궁정에서 추방했다.

ban·is·ter /'bænəstɚ/ *n* a row of upright pieces of wood or metal with a BAR along the top that you hold onto when using a set of stairs ‖ 계단을 이용할 때 붙잡는 봉이 상단에 부착되어 있는, 똑바로 세운 나무나 금속의 열. 난간동자

ban·jo /'bændʒoʊ/ *n* a musical instrument with four or more strings, a circular body, and a long neck ‖ 네 개 이상의 현·둥근 몸통부·긴 목으로 이루어진 악기. 밴조

bank¹ /bæŋk/ *n* **1** a business that keeps and lends money, or the office or building belonging to this business ‖ 돈을 보관·대출해 주는 사업, 또는 이 사업에 속하는 사무실이나 건물. 은행(업): *I went to the bank at noon to deposit my check.* 나는 정오에 수표를 예치하러 은행에 갔다. **2** land along the side of a river or lake ‖ 강이나 호수의 측면을 따라 있는 땅. 제방. 둑: *trees lining the river bank* 강둑을 따라 줄지어 있는 나무들 —see usage note at SHORE **3 blood/sperm/ organ etc. bank** a place where human blood etc. is stored until someone needs it ‖ 사람의 피 등이 필요할 때까지 저장되는 곳. 혈액/정자/장기 은행[보관소] **4** a large number of machines etc. arranged close together in a row ‖ 열을 지어 서로 가깝게 배열해 놓은 많은 수의

B

기계 등: *a bank of television screens along the wall* 벽을 따라 늘어선 텔레비전 화면들 **5** a large pile of snow, sand etc. ‖ 눈·모래 등의 큰 무더기. 더미 **6 cloud/fog etc. bank** a lot of clouds, thick mist etc. that you can see the edge of ‖ 가장자리를 볼 수 있는 잔뜩 낀 구름·자욱한 안개 등. 구름/안개층

bank² *v* **1** [I] to make a plane, car etc. slope to one side when it is turning ‖ 비행기·차 등이 방향을 틀 때 한쪽으로 기울게 하다. 기체[차체]를 기울이다[틀다]. 기우뚱하다: *The lead plane banked and turned toward Honolulu.* 선두 비행기가 한쪽으로 기울더니 호놀룰루 쪽으로 방향을 틀었다. **2** [I, T] to put or keep money in a bank ‖ 돈을 은행에 넣거나 보관하다. 예금[예치]하다: *Do you bank at First National?* 당신은 퍼스트 내셔널 은행에 예금합니까? **3** [I] to have steep sides like a hill ‖ 언덕처럼 가파른 면을 이루다. 경사지다. 급경사로 비탈지다: *The race track banks steeply in the third turn.* 그 경주 트랙은 세 번째 회전(구간)에서 급경사져 있다. **4** [T] also **bank up** to put a lot of wood, coal etc. on a fire to keep it burning for a long time ‖ 불이 장시간 계속 타도록 많은 나무·석탄 등을 불 속에 넣다. 쌓아 올리다

bank on *sb/sth phr v* [T] to depend on something happening or someone doing something ‖ 어떤 일이 일어나거나 어떤 사람이 어떤 일을 할 것에 의지하다. 기대하다. …에 희망을 걸다: *We were banking on Jesse being here to help.* 우리는 제시가 여기 와서 도와줄 것으로 기대하고 있다.

bank·er /'bæŋkɚ/ *n* someone who works in a bank in an important position ‖ 은행의 중요 직위에서 일하는 사람. 은행가

bank·ing /'bæŋkɪŋ/ *n* [U] the business of a bank ‖ 은행 업무

bank·rupt¹ /'bæŋkrʌpt/ *adj* unable to pay your debts ‖ 빚을 갚을 수 없는. 파산 [도산]한: *Many small businesses went bankrupt during the recession.* 많은 영세 기업들이 불황 중에 도산했다.

bankrupt² *v* [T] to make someone become bankrupt ‖ 남을 파산시키다.

bank·rupt·cy /'bæŋk,rʌptsi/ *n* [C, U] a situation in which you officially say that you are unable to pay your debts ‖ 빚을 갚을 수 없다고 공식 선언한 상태. 파산 (상태). 파산 선언: *The company lost so much money it was forced to declare bankruptcy.* 그 회사는 많은 돈을 손해 봐서 파산을 선언해야 했다.

bank tell·er /'. ,../ *n* ⇨ TELLER

ban·ner¹ /'bænɚ/ *n* **1** a long piece of cloth on which something is written, often carried between two poles ‖ 무엇인가를 적어 종종 두 개의 장대에 매단 긴 천조각. 현수막: *voters waving election banners* 선거 현수막을 흔들고 있는 유권자들 **2** LITERARY a flag ‖ 기. 깃발 **3** a belief or principle ‖ 신념이나 원칙. 구호: *Civil rights groups have achieved a lot under the banner of fair and equal treatment.* 시민 운동 단체들은 공정하고 동등한 대우라는 기치 아래 많은 것을 성취했다.

banner² *adj* excellent ‖ 최고의. 일류[일급]의: *a banner year for American soccer* 미국 축구 최고의 해

ban·quet /'bæŋkwɪt/ *n* a formal meal for many people ‖ 많은 사람들을 위한 공식 식사. 연회

ban·ter /'bæntɚ/ *n* [U] conversation that has a lot of jokes in it ‖ 장난기 섞인 말이 많이 들어 있는 대화. 농담. 놀림 – **banter** *v* [I]

bap·tism /'bæptɪzəm/ *n* [C, U] a Christian ceremony in which someone is touched or covered with water to welcome him/her into the Christian faith ‖ 크리스트교를 믿게 됨을 환영하여 물을 묻히거나 적시는 크리스트교 의식. 세례. 침례. 영세 – **baptismal** /bæp'tɪzməl/ *adj*

Bap·tist /'bæptɪst/ *adj* relating to the Protestant church whose members believe that BAPTISM is only for people old enough to understand its meaning ‖ 침례는 신도들이 그 의미를 이해할 정도의 나이든 사람만을 위한 것이라고 믿는 개신교 교회에 관한. 침례파의

bap·tize /'bæptaɪz, bæp'taɪz/ *v* [T] to perform a BAPTISM ‖ 침례[세례]를 행하다

bar¹ /bɑr/ *n* **1** a place that serves alcoholic drinks, where you go to meet other people ‖ 술이 제공되며 다른 사람들을 만나러 가는 곳. 술집. 바: *We went to that bar called the Owl last night.* 우리는 어젯밤 아울이라는 술집에 갔다. **2** the long table inside a bar where alcoholic drinks are sold and served ‖ 술을 팔거나 손님에게 제공하는 술집 내의 긴 테이블: *O'Keefe stood at the bar, drinking and watching the girls.* 오키프는 바에 서서 술을 마시며 여자들을 쳐다보고 있었다. **3** a small block of solid material that is longer than it is wide ‖ 폭보다 길이가 더 긴 단단한 작은 물질. 막대 모양의 것: *a bar of soap* 비누 한 개 / *a candy bar* 막대 사탕 **4 behind bars** in prison ‖ 감옥

에 있는. 수감 중인 **5 the bar** the profession of being a lawyer, or lawyers considered as a group ‖ 변호사로서의 직업, 또는 집단으로서의 변호사들. 변호사업. 변호사단. 법조(계) —see also SALAD BAR, SNACK BAR

bar² v **-rred, -rring** [T] **1** to put a piece of wood or metal across a door or window to prevent people from going in or out ‖ 사람들이 드나드는 것을 막기 위해 문이나 창문에 나무나 금속 조각을 가로질러대다. 빗장을 지르다 **2** to officially prevent something from happening or someone from doing something ‖ 어떤 일이 일어나거나 사람이 어떤 일을 하는 것을 공식적으로 막다. 금하다. 저지하다: *Photographers are barred from taking pictures inside the courtroom.* 사진 기자들은 법정 안에서 사진을 찍는 것이 금지되어 있다.

bar·bar·i·an /bɑrˈbɛriən/ n someone who is considered to be bad because s/he is violent, does not respect people's ideas or property etc. ‖ 폭력적이고 다른 사람의 생각이나 재산 등을 존중하지 않기 때문에 악랄하다고 간주되는 사람. 야만인: *You're behaving like a barbarian!* 너는 마치 야만인처럼 행동하고 있어! – **barbarous** /ˈbɑrbərəs/ adj

bar·bar·ic /bɑrˈbærɪk, -ˈbɛrɪk/ adj violent and cruel ‖ 폭력적이고 잔인한. 야만적인: *a barbaric act of terrorism* 야만적인 테러 행위

bar·be·cue¹ /ˈbɑrbɪˌkyu/ n **1** a party at which food is cooked and eaten outdoors ‖ 야외에서 음식을 요리해서 먹는 파티. 야외[바비큐] 파티: *We're having a barbecue on Saturday.* 우리는 토요일에 야외 (바비큐) 파티를 연다. **2** a metal frame for cooking food on outdoors ‖ 야외에서 음식을 올려 놓고 굽는 금속제 틀. 석쇠. 불고기판

barbecue² v [T] to cook food outdoors on a BARBECUE ‖ 야외에서 불판 위에 음식을 굽다.

barbed wire /ˌbɑrbd ˈwaɪɚ/ n [U] wire with short sharp points on it, usually used for making fences ‖ 짧고 날카로운 가시가 달려 있고 보통 울타리를 만드는 데 쓰는 철사줄. 가시철사줄

bar·bell /ˈbɑrbɛl/ n a long piece of metal with heavy round pieces at each end, that you lift to become stronger ‖ 양 끝에 무겁고 둥근 판이 달려 있으며 힘을 기르기 위해 들어올리는 금속제의 긴 봉. 역기. 바벨

bar·ber /ˈbɑrbɚ/ n a man whose job is to cut men's hair ‖ 남성의 머리를 깎는 직업인. 이발사

bar·bi·tu·rate /bɑrˈbɪtʃərɪt/ n [C, U] a drug that makes people calm or makes them sleep ‖ 사람을 안정시키거나 잠들게 하는 약. 바르비투르산염. 신경 안정제

bar code /ˈ. ˌ./ n a group of thin and thick lines on a product that a computer in a store reads to find the price and other information ‖ 가게 내의 컴퓨터로 가격과 다른 정보를 찾아 읽을 수 있는 제품 표면의 가늘고 두꺼운 줄의 조합. 바코드

bare¹ /bɛr/ adj **1** not covered by clothes ‖ 옷으로 가려지지 않은. 벌거벗은: *bare legs/feet/shoulders* 벗은[맨] 다리[발, 어깨] —compare NAKED **2** empty, or not covered by anything ‖ 텅비거나 아무것도 덮히지 않은. 헐벗은. 횅댕그렁한: *bare and treeless hills* 헐벗고 나무 하나 없는 언덕 **3** having or including only the least amount of something that you need ‖ 필요한 것 중 단지 최소한의 양만 가지고 있거나 포함하고 있는. 가까스로의. 겨우 …뿐인. 극소량의: *The refugees took only the bare necessities/essentials.* (=the most necessary things they owned) 난민들은 겨우 최소한의 생필품[기본적인 것]만을 챙겼을 뿐이다. / *a report giving just the bare facts* 단지 최소한의 사실만을 제공하는 보도

bare² v [T] to let something that is not usually seen be seen by uncovering it ‖ 보통 보이지 않는 것을 벗겨서 보이게 하다. …을 드러내다[나타내다]: *The dog bared its teeth and growled.* 그 개가 이빨을 드러내고 으르렁거렸다.

bare·back /ˈbɛrbæk/ adj, adv on a horse without a SADDLE ‖ 안장 없는 말등의[에]: *riding bareback* 안장 없이 말타기

bare-bones /ˈ. ˌ./ adj INFORMAL having only the most basic things, information, qualities etc. that are needed ‖ 필요한 가장 기초적인 것·정보·특성 등만을 갖고 있는. 최소한의. 가장 기본적인: *a bare-bones style of drawing* 기본 골격만 그리는 소묘법 / *a bare-bones existence* 근근이 생활함

bare·foot /ˈbɛrfʊt/ adj, adv not wearing any shoes or socks ‖ 신발이나 양말을 전혀 신고 있지 않는. 맨발의: *We walked barefoot in the sand.* 우리는 맨발로 모래 밭을 걸었다. / *barefoot children* 맨발의 아이들

bare·ly /ˈbɛrli/ adv **1** hardly existing, happening, true etc.; just ‖ 거의 존재하지 않거나 일어나지 않거나 사실이 아닌; 겨우: *She was barely 18 when she had her first child.* 그녀는 첫 아이를 낳았을

B

때 겨우 18살이었다. / *I could barely stay awake.* 나는 간신히 잠들지 않고 깨어 있었다. **2** used in order to emphasize that something happens immediately after a previous action ‖ 이전의 행동 직후에 어떤 일이 일어남을 강조하는 데에 쓰여. …하자마자: *He'd barely sat down when she started asking questions.* 그가 앉자마자 그녀는 질문을 던지기 시작했다. —compare RARELY

barf /barf/ *v* [I] SPOKEN ⇨ VOMIT¹ – **barf** *n* [U]

bar·gain¹ /'bargən/ *n* **1** something bought for less than its usual price ‖ 일반 가격보다 싸게 산 것. 할인품. 특가[특매]품: *At $8500, this car is a real bargain.* 8,500달러라면 이 차는 정말 특가품이다[좋은 가격에 사는 것이다]. **2** an agreement to do something in return for something else ‖ 다른 것에 대한 대가로 어떤 것을 하기로 하는 협정. 흥정. 협상. 타협: *Let's make/strike a bargain – you'll shop and I'll cook.* 자 타협[협상]을 하자. 네가 장봐 오면 나는 요리할게. / *The company drove a hard bargain in the negotiations.* (=they made sure the agreement was favorable to them) 그 회사는 그 협상을 한치의 양보도 없이 몰아갔다. — **bargainer** *n*

bargain² *v* [I] **1** to discuss the conditions of a sale, agreement etc. ‖ 판매·협정 등의 조건을 의논하다. 협상[흥정]하다: *The players were bargaining with the owners for higher pay.* 선수들은 높은 보수를 놓고 구단주와 협상 중에 있었다. **2 more than sb bargained for** INFORMAL more difficult than you expected ‖ 예상보다 더 어려운. …이 …하기로 한 것보다 훨씬 더한: *I got more than I bargained for in this job.* 나는 이 일로 예상보다 훨씬 더한 어려움을 겪었다.

bargain on sth *phr v* [T] to expect that something will happen and make it part of your plans ‖ 어떤 일이 생겨서 계획의 일부가 될 것으로 예상하다. 고려하다. 참작하다: *I hadn't really bargained on things being so expensive there.* 나는 그곳의 물가가 그렇게 비싸리라고는 전혀 예상치 못했다.

bar·gain·ing chip /'... ,./ *n* something that one person or group in a business deal or political agreement has, that can be used in order to gain an advantage in the deal ‖ 사업상 흥정이나 정치적 협상에서 사람이나 집단이 보유하여 이득을 얻는 데 사용될 수 있는 것. 승부수: *The country's oil supply will be used as a bargaining chip in the talks.* 그 나라의 석유 공급은 협상에서 비장의 카드로 이용될 것이다.

barge¹ /bardʒ/ *n* a boat with a flat bottom, used for carrying goods ‖ 바닥이 평평하고, 물자를 운반하는 데 쓰이는 보트. 짐배. 바지선

barge² *v* [I] INFORMAL to walk somewhere quickly, often pushing against people or things ‖ 종종 사람이나 물건을 밀치면서 빨리 걷다: *Dana barged past the guards at the door.* 다나는 문에 있는 경비원들을 밀어제치고 들어갔다.

barge in/into *phr v* [I] to interrupt someone or go into a place when you were not invited ‖ 어떤 사람을 방해하거나 초청받지 않은 곳에 들어가다. 끼어들다. 난입하다: *Matt's mom barged in on them while they were in bed.* 매트의 엄마는 그들이 침대에 누워 있는 중에 불쑥 들어왔다.

bar·i·tone /'bærə,toun/ *n* a man who sings in a low voice ‖ 저음으로 노래하는 남성. 바리톤 —compare BASS¹ (2)

bark¹ /bark/ *v* **1** [I] to make the sound that a dog makes ‖ 개가 내는 소리를 내다. 짖다 **2** [T] also **bark out** to say something quickly in a loud voice ‖ 큰 소리로 어떤 것을 빨리 말하다. 소리를 질러대며 말하다: *"What's your name?" barked the officer.* "이름이 뭐야?"라고 경찰관이 소리질렀다. **3 be barking up the wrong tree** INFORMAL to have a wrong idea or be making a mistake about something ‖ 잘못 알고 있거나 어떤 것에서 오류를 범하다. 헛다리 짚다: *I realize now that I was barking up the wrong tree.* 내가 지금까지 헛다리 짚고 있었다는 것을 이제야 알겠다.

bark² *n* **1** the sound a dog makes ‖ 개 짖는 소리 **2** [U] the outer cover on the TRUNK and branches of a tree ‖ 나무 몸통·가지의 외피. 수피. 나무 껍질 **3 sb's bark is worse than his/her bite** SPOKEN used in order to say that someone talks more angrily than s/he behaves ‖ 사람이 행동보다 말로 더 화를 낸다는 것을 말하는 데에 쓰여. 입심만큼 고약하지 않다

bar·ley /'barli/ *n* [C, U] a plant that produces a grain used in making food and alcohol ‖ 음식·술을 만드는 데 쓰이는 곡식을 생산해 내는 식물. 보리

barn /barn/ *n* a large building on a farm for storing crops or keeping animals in ‖ 곡식을 저장하거나 가축을 가두기 위한 농장의 큰 건물. 곳간. 축사

bar·na·cle /'barnəkəl/ *n* a small sea

animal with a hard shell that sticks firmly to rocks, boats etc. ‖ 바위·보트 등에 단단히 들러붙는 딱딱한 껍질을 가진 작은 바다 동물. 따개비. 삿갓조개

barn·yard /'bɑrnyɑrd/ *n* the area on a farm around a BARN ‖ 농가의 곳간 주변 지역. 헛간 마당

ba·rom·e·ter /bə'rɑmətə/ *n* an instrument for measuring changes in the air pressure and weather, or for calculating height above sea level ‖ 기압·날씨의 변화를 측정하거나 해발 고도를 산정하는 기구. 기압계. 고도계 – **barometric** /,bærə'mɛtrɪk/ *adj*

ba·roque /bə'roʊk/ *adj* relating to the very decorated style of art, music, buildings etc. that was common in Europe in the 17th century ‖ 17세기 유럽에서 유행한 미술·음악·건축물 등의 매우 화려한 양식에 관한. 바로크 양식의

bar·racks /'bæriks/ *n* [plural] a group of buildings in which soldiers live ‖ 군인들이 거주하는 일단의 건물. 막사. 병영

bar·rage /bə'rɑʒ/ *n* **1** a lot of actions, sounds, questions etc. that happen very quickly after each other ‖ 연달아서 매우 빠르게 일어나는 많은 동작·소리·질문 등. 연발. 연속: *a barrage of insults/abuse* 빗발치는 모욕[학대] ‖ 연속 사격 **2** the continuous shooting of guns ‖ 연속 사격

bar·rel¹ /'bærəl/ *n* **1** a large container with curved sides and a flat top and bottom ‖ 옆면이 곡선을 이루고 위아래가 평평한 큰 용기. (중배 부른) 통. 맥주통: *a barrel for collecting rain water* 빗물받이용 통 **2** a unit used for measuring liquids, especially oil, equal to about 42 gallons or 159 liters ‖ 약 42갤런이나 159리터에 상당하는 액체, 특히 기름의 계량 단위. 배럴 **3** the part of a gun that the bullets are shot through ‖ 발사된 총알이 통과하는 부분. 총신. 총열 **4 not be a barrel of laughs** SPOKEN HUMOROUS to not be enjoyable ‖ 즐겁지 않은. 재미 없는: *The meeting wasn't exactly a barrel of laughs.* 그 모임은 그렇게 재미있지는 않았다. **5 have sb over a barrel** INFORMAL to put someone in a situation where s/he is forced to do something ‖ 남을 어쩔 수 없이 어떤 것을 하게 하는 상황에 몰아 넣다. 남을 궁지에 몰아 넣다 : *I didn't really want to work overtime, but my boss had me over a barrel.* 나는 정말로 초과 근무를 하고 싶지 않았지만 사장이 억지로 시켰다.

barrel² *v* [I] to move very fast in a vehicle ‖ 자동차를 타고 고속으로 달리다. 쏜살같이 질주하다: *We were barreling down the road at 90 miles an hour.* 우리는 시속 90마일로 쏜살같이 내달리고 있었다.

bar·ren /'bærən/ *adj* land that is barren cannot grow plants ‖ 땅이 식물이 자랄 수 없는. 불모의. 메마른

bar·rette /bə'rɛt/ *n* a small plastic or metal object for holding your hair in a particular position ‖ 머리카락을 특정 위치에 고정시키는 작은 플라스틱이나 금속제 물체. 머리핀[클립]

bar·ri·cade¹ /'bærə,keɪd/ *n* something that is put across a road, door etc. for a short time to prevent people from going past ‖ 사람이 지나가는 것을 막기 위해 잠시 동안 도로·문 등에 가로질러 설치하는 것. 바리케이드. 도로 봉쇄용 장애물

barricade² *v* [T] to build a BARRICADE ‖ 바리케이드를 치다. 장애물로 가로막다: *Winters barricaded the door with the bookcase.* 윈터스는 책장으로 문을 가로막았다.

bar·ri·er /'bæriə/ *n* **1** something such as a rule, situation, or problem that prevents or limits what people can do ‖ 사람이 할 수 있는 일을 막거나 제한하는 규칙[상황, 문제] 등의 것. 장벽. 장애: *an attempt to reduce trade barriers* 무역 장벽을 줄이려는 노력 **2** a type of fence that prevents people from passing through a place ‖ 사람들이 통과하는 것을 막는 일종의 울타리. 방벽. 방책: *The police put up barriers to hold back the crowds.* 경찰은 군중을 저지하기 위해 방벽을 설치했다. **3** a physical object that separates two areas, groups of people etc. ‖ 두 지역·사람들의 집단 등을 가르는 물체. 경계: *The Alps form a natural barrier across Europe.* 알프스 산맥은 유럽을 가르는 자연적 경계를 이룬다.

bar·ring /'bɑrɪŋ/ *prep* unless there are ‖ 무엇이 없는 한. …이 없다면. …을 제외하고는: *Barring any last minute problems, we should finish Friday.* 최종적인 문제를 제외하고는 우리는 금요일까지 끝내야 한다.

bar·ri·o /'bæri,oʊ/ *n* a part of an American city where many poor, Spanish-speaking people live ‖ 스페인어를 구사하는 가난한 사람들이 많이 사는 미국 도시의 구역. 스패니시 타운

bar·room /'bɑr,rum/ *adj* INFORMAL happening in a BAR ‖ 주점에서 일어나는: *a barroom conversation* 주점에서 나누는 대화

bar·tend·er /'bɑr,tɛndə/ *n* someone whose job is to make and serve drinks in a BAR ‖ 주점에서 술을 만들어 제공하는

B

직업인. 바텐더

bar·ter /'bɑrtɚ/ *v* [I, T] to exchange goods, work, or services for other goods or services instead of money ‖ 상품[노동, 용역]을 돈 대신에 다른 상품이나 용역으로 교환하다. 물물 교환하다

base¹ /beɪs/ *v* [T] to use a city, town etc. as your main place of business or activities ‖ 대도시·소도시 등을 사업이나 활동의 주요 거점으로 삼다. 기지[기반]로 하다: *a law firm based in Denver* 덴버 시를 거점으로 한 법률 회사

base sth **on/upon** sth *phr v* [T] to do something or develop something using a particular piece of information as the reason or starting point ‖ 특정 정보를 근거나 출발점으로 삼아 어떤 것을 하거나 개발하다. …을 기초[근거]로 하다: *Discrimination based on race or sex is forbidden by law.* 인종·성별에 근거한 차별은 법률로 금지된다. / *The movie was based on Amelia Earhart's life.* 그 영화는 아멜리아 에어하트의 삶에 기반을 두었다.

base² *n*

1 ▶LOWEST PART 최하부◀ the lowest part or surface of something, especially the part on which it stands or where it is attached to something else ‖ 사물의 최하부나 표면, 특히 사물이 놓여 있거나 다른 것에 붙는 부분. 기초. 기저: *a black vase with a round base* 바닥이 둥근 검은 꽃병 / *Waves crashed against the base of the cliff.* 파도가 절벽의 아래 부분에 부딪혔다. / *the base of the skull* 두개골의 기초(구조)

2 ▶MAIN PART 주요부◀ all the people, companies, money etc. that form the main part of something ‖ 어떤 것의 주요 부분을 이루는 모든 사람·회사·돈 등. 기반. 중추: *Roosevelt had a broad base of political support.* 루즈벨트는 광범위한 정치 기반[지지 세력]을 가지고 있었다. / *an attempt to improve the economic base* (=things that produce jobs and money) *of inner-city areas* 도심 빈민 지역의(일자리와 돈을 창출하는) 경제적 토대를 개선하려는 노력 / *The country's manufacturing base* (=companies that make things) *shrank by 15% during the recession.* 그 나라의 생산 기반은 불황 중에 15%가 줄어들었다.

3 ▶COMPANY 회사◀ the main place where the work of a company or organization is done ‖ 회사나 조직의 업무가 수행되는 중심지. 본사. 본부: *Microsoft's base is in Redmond.* 마이크로 소프트사의 본사는 레드몬드에 있다.

4 ▶MILITARY 군사◀ a permanent place where people in the army, navy etc. live and work ‖ 육군·해군 등에서 군인들이 항구적으로 거주하고 일하는 곳. 기지

5 ▶IDEAS 사상◀ something from which new things or ideas develop or are made ‖ 새로운 사물이나 생각이 발전하거나 만들어지는 것. 기원. 원천: *Both French and Spanish come from a Latin base.* 프랑스어와 스페인어는 둘 다 라틴어에서 기원하고 있다.

6 off base INFORMAL completely wrong ‖ 완전히 잘못된. 크게 틀린[벗어난]: *The estimate he gave for painting the house seems way off base.* 집에 페인트칠을 하려고 그가 낸 견적은 크게 틀린 것 같다.

7 touch/cover all the bases to do or think about something thoroughly, so that all possible problems are dealt with ‖ 어떤 것에 대해 철저히 하거나 생각해서 모든 가능한 문제를 처리하다. 만반의 준비를 하다. 만사에 빈틈없게[철저히] 하다: *OK, I think we've covered all the bases – we should be ready for whatever happens.* 좋아, 우리는 만반의 준비를 해왔어. 어떤 일이 일어나도 대비할 수 있을 거야.

8 ▶SUBSTANCE/MIXTURE 물질/혼합◀ the main part of something, to which other things can be added ‖ 다른 것들이 첨가될 수 있는 어떤 것의 주요 부분. 주성분. 기제(基劑): *paints with a water base* 물을 주성분으로 하는[수성] 페인트

9 ▶BASEBALL 야구◀ one of the four places that a player must touch in order to get a point ‖ 선수가 점수를 획득하기 위해 반드시 접촉해야 하는 4곳 중 하나. 루(壘). 베이스

base·ball /'beɪsbɔl/ *n* **1** [U] an outdoor game in which two teams of nine players try to get points by hitting a ball and running around four bases ‖ 9명의 선수로 된 2개의 팀이 공을 치고 4개의 베이스 주위를 달려 득점을 시도하는 야외 운동 경기. 야구 —see picture on page 946 **2** the ball used in this game ‖ 이 경기에 사용되는 공. 야구공

base·ment /'beɪsmənt/ *n* a room or rooms in a building that are under the level of the ground ‖ 건물 내 지표(地表)보다 낮은 방이나 방들. 지하실. 지하층 —see picture on page 945

bas·es /'beɪsiz/ the plural of BASIS ‖ basis의 복수형

bash¹ /bæʃ/ *v* [I, T] **1** to hit someone or something hard, causing pain or damage ‖ 사람이나 물건을 세게 쳐서 고통이나 손상을 일으키다. 후려치다. 세게

때리다: *He bashed his toe on the coffee table.* 그는 커피 테이블에 발가락을 부딪쳤다. **2** to criticize someone or something a lot ‖ 사람이나 어떤 것을 심하게 비판하다: *The local newspaper has recently been bashing the city's court system.* 지역 신문은 최근에 시의 사법 제도에 대해 맹비난을 해오고 있다.

bash² *n* INFORMAL a large party ‖ 큰 파티. 대연회: *They're having a big bash over at the club tonight.* 그들은 오늘 밤 클럽에서 대대적인 파티를 벌이고 있다.

bash·ful /ˈbæʃfəl/ *adj* easily embarrassed; shy ‖ 쉽게 당황하는. 숫기 없는; 부끄러워하는

bash·ing /ˈbæʃɪŋ/ *n* [U] **gay-bashing/liberal-bashing etc.** the act of criticizing or physically attacking a particular person or group of people ‖ 특정인이나 사람들의 집단을 비난하거나 물리적으로 공격하는 행위. 동성애자/자유주의자 공격: *The police say they think the attack was an incident of gay-bashing.* 경찰은 그 폭행을 동성애자에 대한 공격 사건인 것 같다고 말한다.

ba·sic /ˈbeɪsɪk/ *adj* **1** forming the main or most necessary part of something ‖ 어떤 것의 중심이나 가장 필수적인 부분을 이루는. 기본적인. 근본적인: *the basic principles of mathematics* 수학의 근본원리 / *There are two basic problems here.* 여기에는 2가지 근본적인 문제가 있다. **2** simple or not fully developed ‖ 단순하거나 완전히 발전되지 않은. 기초적인. 초보적인: *basic health care for children* 아동에 대한 기초적 건강 관리 —see also BASICS

ba·si·cally /ˈbeɪsɪkli/ *adv* **1** SPOKEN used when giving the most important reason or fact about something, or a simple explanation of something ‖ 사물에 대한 가장 중요한 이유나 사실을 밝힐 때, 또는 간략한 설명을 제시할 때 쓰여. 기본[근본]적으로. 원래는. 본래부터: *Well, basically the teacher said he'll need extra help with math.* 그런데 본래부터 선생님은 그에게 수학 과외 지도가 필요할 것이라고 말했다. **2** in the main or most important ways ‖ 중심적이거나 가장 중요한 점에서. 요컨대. 골자를 따지면: *Norwegian and Danish are basically the same.* 노르웨이인과 덴마크인은 근본적으로 동일하다.

ba·sics /ˈbeɪsɪks/ *n* [plural] **1 the basics** the most important part of something, from which other things, ideas etc. can develop ‖ 다른 것·생각 등이 발전될 수 있는 가장 중요한 부분. 근본. 기초: *a class in the basics of first aid* 응급 처치의 기초반 **2 get/go back to basics** to return to teaching or doing the most important or the simplest part of something ‖ 어떤 것의 가장 중요하거나 기본적인 부분을 가르치거나 하는 것으로 돌아가다. 기본에 충실하다: *If you really want to learn this, we'll have to go back to basics.* 네가 정말로 이것을 배우고 싶으면 우리는 기본으로 돌아가야 할 것이다.

ba·sin /ˈbeɪsən/ *n* **1** a large area of land that is lower in the center than at the edges ‖ 가장자리 쪽보다 중심부가 더 낮은 대지. 분지: *the Amazon basin* 아마존 분지 **2** a large bowl, especially one for water ‖ 특히 물을 담는 큰 대접. 대야

ba·sis /ˈbeɪsɪs/ *n, plural* **bases** /ˈbeɪsiz/ **1 on the basis of** because of a particular fact or reason ‖ 특정 사실이나 이유 때문에. …을 기준[근거]로: *Employers may not discriminate on the basis of race or sex.* 고용주들은 인종이나 성별을 근거로 차별해선 안 된다. **2 on a weekly/informal/freelance etc. basis** happening at a particular time or in a particular way ‖ 특정한 시간에 또는 특정한 방식으로 일어나는. 매주/비공식/자유계약의 조건으로: *Meetings are held on a monthly basis.* 회의는 매달 열린다. **3** the information or ideas from which something develops ‖ 어떤 것이 전개되는 정보나 사상. 기저(基底). 기조(基調). 토대: *The fear of Communism formed the basis of American foreign policy at that time.* 공산주의에 대한 두려움이 당시 미국 외교 정책의 기저를 이루었다.

bask /bæsk/ *v* [I] **1** to enjoy sitting or lying somewhere warm ‖ 따뜻한 곳에서 앉거나 누워 있기를 즐기다. 열·햇볕을 쬐다. 일광욕을 하다: *a snake basking in the sun* 햇볕을 쬐고 있는 뱀 **2** to enjoy the attention or approval of someone ‖ 누군가의 주목이나 인정을 누리다. 향유하다. …을 듬뿍 받다: *She basked in her mother's praise.* 그녀는 어머니의 칭찬을 흠뻑 받았다.

bas·ket /ˈbæskɪt/ *n* **1** a container made of thin pieces of dried plants, wire etc. woven together, used for carrying or holding things ‖ 건조시킨 식물의 가는 줄기·철사 등을 서로 엮어서 물건을 운반하거나 담아 두는 데 쓰는 용기. 바구니. 광주리: *a basket full of fruit* 과일로 가득찬 바구니 **2** a net with a hole at the bottom, through which you throw the ball in basketball ‖ 밑부분에 구멍이 뚫려 있어 농구 경기에서 공을 던져 넣는 그물

망. 농구골의 그물

bas·ket·ball /ˈbæskɪt,bɔl/ *n* **1** [U] a game in which two teams of five players try to get points by throwing a ball through a net ‖ 5명의 선수로 구성된 두 팀이 망 속으로 공을 던져 점수를 획득하려 하는 운동 경기. 농구 —see picture on page 946 **2** the ball used in this game ‖ 이 경기에서 사용되는 공. 농구공

basket case /ˈ.. ,./ *n* INFORMAL someone who is so nervous and worried that s/he cannot deal with a situation ‖ 불안·걱정이 지나쳐 상황에 대처할 수 없는 사람. 노이로제에 걸린 사람: *Mom was a complete basket case at our wedding.* 엄마는 우리 결혼식에서 너무 긴장한 나머지 어찌할 바를 몰랐다.

bass¹ /beɪs/ *n* **1** a type of electric GUITAR with four strings that plays low notes ‖ 4개의 현으로 저음부 곡조를 연주하는 전자 기타의 일종. 베이스(기타) **2** a man who sings the lowest range of musical notes ‖ 악보의 최저음 영역을 노래하는 사람. 베이스. 저음 성악가 **3** [U] the lower half of the whole range of musical notes ‖ 악보상의 전체 음역 중 중간 이하의 저음부 **4** ⇨ DOUBLE BASS — **bass** *adj* : *a bass guitar/drum* 베이스 기타[드럼]

bass² /bæs/ *n* [C, U] a fish that lives both in the sea and in rivers, or the meat from this fish ‖ 바다와 강에서 서식하는 물고기, 또는 이 생선의 살. 배스. (유럽산) 농어

bas·si·net /,bæsɪˈnɛt/ *n* a small bed that looks like a basket, used for a very young baby ‖ 영아·유아용으로 쓰이는 바구니 모양의 작은 침대. 요람

bas·soon /bəˈsun, bæ-/ *n* a long wooden musical instrument with a low sound, played by blowing into a thin curved metal pipe and pressing buttons ‖ 가늘고 굽은 금속 파이프에 바람을 불어넣고 버튼을 눌러 연주하는 낮은 소리를 내는 긴 목관 악기. 바순. 파곳

bas·tard /ˈbæstəd/ *n* **1** SPOKEN a rude word for a man you do not like or are angry with ‖ 좋아하지 않거나 화를 돋우는 남자를 무례하게 이르는 말. 녀석. 새끼: *You stupid bastard!* 이 멍청한 자식아! **2** OLD-FASHIONED someone whose parents were not married when s/he was born ‖ 결혼하지 않은 부모에게서 태어난 사람. 사생아. 서출

bat¹ /bæt/ *n* **1** a long wooden stick used for hitting the ball in baseball ‖ 야구 경기에서 공을 치는 데 쓰는 긴 나무 방망이. 배트 **2** a small animal like a mouse with wings, that flies at night ‖ 밤에 날아다니는 날개 달린 쥐와 비슷한 작은 동물. 박쥐 **3 right off the bat** SPOKEN done immediately ‖ 곧바로 행해진. 즉시. 주저하지 않고 바로: *She said yes right off the bat!* 그녀는 즉시 '예'라고 했어! **4 like a bat out of hell** SPOKEN very fast ‖ 매우 빠르게. 맹[전]속력으로: *He came running out of the house like a bat out of hell.* 그는 맹속력으로 그 집에서 달려 나오고 있었다. **5 be at bat** to be the person who is trying to hit the ball in baseball ‖ 야구 경기에서 공을 칠 사람이 되다. 타석에 들어서다

bat² *v* **-tted, -tting 1** [I] to hit a ball with a bat ‖ 방망이로 공을 치다: *Brent is up to bat next.* (=he will try to hit the ball next) 브렌트가 다음 타석에 오른다. **2 bat your eyes/eyelashes** to open and close your eyes quickly, especially to try to look sexually attractive ‖ 특히 성적으로 매력적으로 보이도록 눈을 빠르게 깜박이다. 윙크하다: *She's always batting her eyelashes at Tom.* 그녀는 항상 톰에게 추파를 던진다. **3** [I, T] to hit something lightly with your hand ‖ 손으로 어떤 것을 가볍게 때리다: *kittens batting at balls of paper* 종이뭉치를 살짝 치고 있는 새끼고양이들 **4 without batting an eye** INFORMAL without showing any emotion or guilty feelings ‖ 어떠한 감정이나 죄의식을 조금도 보이지 않고. 눈 하나 깜작하지 않고: *He used to tell the worst lies without batting an eye.* 그는 눈 하나 깜작하지 않고 가장 나쁜 거짓말을 해대곤 했다. **5 go to bat for sb** INFORMAL to help someone and give him/her support ‖ 남을 돕고 지지해 주다. 남을 변호해 주다[감싸주다]: *Andy really went to bat for me with my manager.* 앤디는 정말로 내 상관으로부터 나를 감싸주었다. **6 bat a thousand** INFORMAL to be very successful ‖ 매우 성공적이다. 대성공을 거두다

batch /bætʃ/ *n* **1** a group of things or people that you deal with at the same time ‖ 동시에 처리하는 사물이나 사람의 집단. 묶음. 무리. 일단: *the latest batch of reports* 가장 최신판 기사 묶음 **2** a number of things made at the same time ‖ 동시에 만들어진 많은 수의 물건. 한 회[차례]분: *a batch of cookies* 한 판에 구워진 과자

bat·ed /ˈbeɪtɪd/ *adj* **with bated breath** in a very excited and anxious way ‖ 매우 흥분되고 걱정하여. 숨을 죽이고: *I waited for her answer with bated breath.* 나는 숨죽이며 그녀의 대답을 기다렸다.

bath /bæθ/ *n, plural* **baths** /bæðz, bæθs/ **1** an act of washing your body in a bathtub ‖ 욕조에서 몸을 씻는 행위. 목욕: *You need to take a bath before you go to bed.* 잠자리에 들기 전에 목욕해야 한다. / *Dan, will you give the kids a bath tonight?* (=wash them) 댄, 오늘 밤 아이들 목욕을 시켜 주겠어요? **2** water that you sit or lie in to wash yourself ‖ 몸을 씻기 위해 들어앉아 있거나 누워 있는 곳의 물. 목욕물: *I love to sit and soak in a hot bath.* 나는 뜨거운 목욕물에 들어 앉아 푹 담그기를 좋아한다. / *Lisa ran a bath* (=put water in a bathtub) *for herself.* 리사는 욕조에 자신이 쓸 물을 받았다.

bathe /beɪð/ *v* **1** [I] to wash your whole body ‖ 몸 전체를 씻다. 목욕하다: *Water was scarce, and we only bathed once a week.* 물이 너무 부족해서 우리는 일주일에 한 번만 목욕했다. **2** [T] to wash someone else, usually in a bathtub ‖ 보통 욕조에서 다른 사람을 씻기다. 목욕시키다 **3** [T] to wash an injury with a liquid medicine ‖ 약물로 상처를 씻어 내다. 소독하다 **4 be bathed in** to be lit in a particular type of light ‖ 특정한 종류의 (불)빛으로 빛나다: *The beach sparkled, bathed in the clear light of morning.* 해변은 맑은 아침 햇살에 반짝이며 빛났다.

bathing suit /'beɪðɪŋ ,sut/ *n* a piece of clothing you wear for swimming ‖ 수영용으로 입는 옷 (한 벌). 수영복

bath·robe /'bæθroʊb/ *n* a long loose piece of clothing made of thick cloth, worn especially before or after you take a SHOWER or bath ‖ 특히 샤워나 목욕 전·후에 입는, 두꺼운 천으로 만든 길고 헐렁한 의복. 목욕 가운. 욕의(浴衣)

bath·room /'bæθrum/ *n* **1** the room in a house where there is a toilet and usually a bathtub or a SHOWER and SINK ‖ 집안에서 변기와 보통 욕조나 샤워기·세면대가 있는 방. 욕실 **2 go to the bathroom** to use the toilet ‖ 화장실을 사용하다. 화장실에 가다: *Mommy, I have to go to the bathroom!* 엄마 나 화장실에 가야 해요! —compare RESTROOM, —see usage note at TOILET

bath·tub /'bæθtʌb/ *n* a large container you fill with water to sit in and wash yourself in ‖ 물을 채우고 들어앉아 몸을 씻는 큰 통. 욕조. 목욕통

ba·tik /bə'tik, bæ-/ *n* [C, U] a method of using WAX to put colored patterns on cloth, or cloth that has been colored in this way ‖ 천에 색무늬를 넣기 위해 밀납을 사용하는 방법, 또는 이 방법으로 염색된 천. 납결(臘纈) 염색(법)[(천)]

ba·ton /bə'tan/ *n* **1** a short stick, used by the leader of a group of musicians to direct the music ‖ 음악(연주)를 지휘하기 위해 악단의 지휘자가 사용하는 짧은 막대. 지휘봉 **2** a metal stick that you spin and throw into the air ‖ 빙빙 돌리며 공중으로 집어던지는 금속봉. 배턴

bat·tal·ion /bə'tælyən/ *n* a large group of soldiers that is formed from several smaller groups ‖ 몇 개의 작은 집단으로 이루어진 대규모의 병사들의 집단. (군 편제상의) 대대

bat·ter¹ /'bætɚ/ *n* **1** [C, U] a mixture of flour, eggs, milk etc. used for making cakes, some types of bread etc. ‖ 케이크·특정 종류의 빵 등을 만드는 데 쓰는 밀가루·달걀·우유 등의 혼합물. 반죽 **2** the person who is trying to hit the ball in baseball ‖ 야구 경기에서 공을 치려는 사람. 타자 —see picture on page 946

bat·ter² *v* [I, T] to hit someone or something hard, usually in a way that injures or damages him, her, or it ‖ 보통 상처가 나거나 손상을 입힐 정도로 사람이나 물건을 세게 때리다. 강타[구타]하다: *Waves were battering against the rocks.* 파도가 바위를 강타하고 있었다. – **battering** *n* [C, U]

bat·tered /'bætɚd/ *adj* **1** old and slightly damaged ‖ 낡고 약간 파손된. 너덜너덜한: *a battered old paperback book* 너덜너덜하고 낡은 종이 표지를 한 책 **2 battered woman/child etc.** a woman etc. who has been violently hurt by someone that s/he lives with ‖ 함께 사는 사람에게 심하게 상처를 입은 여자 등. 매맞는[학대받는] 여자/어린이

bat·ter·y /'bætəri/ *n* **1** an object that provides electricity for something such as a radio or car ‖ 라디오나 자동차 등의 물건에 전기를 공급하는 물체. 전지. 배터리 **2** [U] the crime of beating someone ‖ 남을 구타하는 범죄. 폭행[폭력]죄 **3** a set of many things of the same type ‖ 같은 종류의 많은 것으로 이루어진 한 세트. 일련: *a battery of medical tests* 일련의 의학적 검사 **4** several large guns used together ‖ 함께 사용되는 여러 개의 대포. 함포. 포대

bat·tle¹ /'bætl/ *n* **1** [C, U] a fight between two armies, especially during a longer war ‖ 특히 긴 전쟁 중의 두 군대 간의 싸움. 전투: *the battle of Bunker Hill* 벙커 힐 전투 / *Thousands of soldiers were killed in battle.* (=during a war or battle) 수천 명의 군인들이 전투에서 전사했다. **2** a situation in which two people or groups compete or argue with each other ‖ 두 사람이나 집단이 서로 경쟁하거나 다투는 상태. 분쟁: *a long and costly legal battle* 장기간의 비용이 많이 드는 법정 분쟁 **3** an attempt to solve a difficult problem ‖ 어려운 문제를 해결하려는 노력. 투쟁: *the battle against racial discrimination* 인종 차별에 반대하는 투쟁

battle² *v* [I, T] to try very hard to achieve something when this is very difficult ‖ 아주 힘들 때에 어떤 것을 이루기 위해 몹시 애를 쓰다. 분투하다: *My mother battled bravely against breast cancer for years.* 내 어머니는 수년 동안 유방암에 맞서 꿋꿋하게 싸웠다.

bat·tle·ground /'bætl̩ˌɡraʊnd/, **bat·tle·field** /'bætl̩ˌfild/ *n* **1** a subject that people argue about ‖ 사람들이 논쟁하는 주제. 쟁점. 논점: *Prayer in schools has become a political battleground.* 학교에서의 예배는 정치적 쟁점이 되어 왔다. **2** a place where a battle has been fought ‖ 전투가 벌어진 장소. 전장터

bat·tle·ship /'bætl̩ˌʃɪp/ *n* a very large ship used in wars ‖ 전투에 쓰이는 매우 큰 배. 전함

baud rate /'bɔd ˌreɪt/ *n* TECHNICAL a measurement of how fast information is sent to or from a computer ‖ 정보가 컴퓨터로 또는 컴퓨터에서 전송되는 속도. 보드 속도. 보드율

bawd·y /'bɔdi/ *adj* bawdy songs, jokes etc. are about sex ‖ 노래·농담 등이 성에 관한. 외설적인. 야한. 상스러운

bawl /bɔl/ *v* [I] INFORMAL to cry in a noisy way ‖ 시끄럽게 울다. 엉엉 소리내어 울다: *By the end of the movie I was bawling.* 영화가 끝나갈 때 나는 엉엉 울고 있었다.

bawl sb ↔ **out** *phr v* [T] INFORMAL to speak angrily to someone because s/he has done something wrong ‖ 남이 잘못을 저질러서 화를 내며 말하다. 야단치다. 꾸짖다: *Mom bawled me out for not cleaning my room.* 엄마가 방청소를 안 한다고 나를 크게 야단쳤다.

bay /beɪ/ *n* **1** a part of the ocean that is enclosed by a curve in the land ‖ 육지의 굴곡에 의해 둘러싸인 바다의 일부. 만 (灣) **2 keep/hold sth at bay** to prevent something dangerous or unpleasant from happening or coming too close ‖ 위험하거나 불쾌한 일이 발생하거나 임박해 오는 것을 막다. 저지하다. 떼어 놓다: *The dogs kept the intruder at bay.* 그 개들이 침입자를 못 들어오게 저

지했다. **3** an area used for a special purpose that is partly separated from the area surrounding it ‖ 주위를 둘러싼 구역에서 부분적으로 분리되어 특별한 목적으로 쓰이는 구역. 격실. … 칸: *the plane's cargo bay* 비행기의 화물칸

bay·o·net /'beɪənɪt, -ˌnɛt, ˌbeɪəˈnɛt/ *n* a long knife attached to the end of a RIFLE (=type of gun) ‖ 소총의 끝에 부착된 긴 칼. 총검

bay·ou /'baɪu, 'baɪoʊ/ *n* a large area of slow moving water in the Gulf states of the US with plants growing out of it ‖ 유속이 느리며 물 밖으로 식물이 자라는 미국의 멕시코 만 연안 주의 넓은 지역. (호수의) 후미. 소택성 호수 —compare SWAMP¹

ba·zaar /bəˈzɑr/ *n* **1** an occasion when a lot of people sell various things to collect money for a good purpose ‖ 좋은 목적에 쓸 돈을 모으기 위해 많은 사람들이 여러 가지 물건을 파는 행사. 바자(회): *the annual church bazaar* 교회의 연례 바자 **2** a place, usually outdoors, where a lot of different things are sold, especially in the Middle East ‖ 특히 중동 지역에서 수많은 이색적인 물건이 판매되는 보통 옥외 장소. 야외 장터. 시장(가)

BB gun /'bibi ˌɡʌn/ *n* a gun that uses air pressure to shoot small metal balls ‖ 압축 공기로 작은 금속 탄환을 쏘는 총. BB총

BBQ /'bɑrbɪˌkyu/ a written abbreviation for BARBECUE ‖ barbecue의 약어

B.C. *adv* Before Christ; used in order to show that a date is a particular number of years before the birth of Christ ‖ Before Christ(기원전)의 약어; 연대가 그리스도 탄생 전의 특정한 연도임을 나타내는 데 쓰여: *The Great Pyramid dates from around 2600 B.C.* 그 대(大)피라미드는 기원전 약 2600년부터 비롯된다. —compare A.D.

be¹ /bi/ *auxiliary verb*

PRESENT TENSE (현재 시제)

singular (단수)	*plural* (복수)
I **am**, I'**m**	we **are**, we'**re**
you **are**, you'**re**	you **are**, you'**re**
he/she/it **is**	
he'**s**/she'**s**/it'**s**	they **are**, they'**re**

PAST TENSE (과거 시제)

singular (단수)	*plural* (복수)
I **was**	we **were**
you **were**	you **were**

he/she/it **was**   they **were**

PAST PARTICIPLE (과거 분사) **been**

PRESENT PARTICIPLE (현재 분사) **being**

NEGATIVE *short forms* (부정 단축형)
aren't, isn't, wasn't, weren't

1 used with a PRESENT PARTICIPLE to form the continuous tenses of verbs ‖ 현재 분사와 함께 동사의 진행형을 만드는 데에 쓰여: *Jane was reading by the fire.* 제인은 난롯가에서 독서를 하고 있었다. / *Don't talk to me while I'm* (=I am) *working.* 내가 일하는 동안은 나에게 말을 걸지 마라. **2** used with a PAST PARTICIPLE to form the PASSIVE ‖ 과거 분사와 함께 수동태를 만드는 데에 쓰여: *Smoking is not permitted on this flight.* 이 비행기에서는 흡연이 허용되지 않습니다. **3** used in order to show what might happen in the future, in CONDITIONAL sentences ‖ 조건문에서 앞으로 일어날 일을 나타내는 데에 쓰여: *If I were rich, I'd buy myself a Rolls Royce.* 내가 부자라면 롤스 로이스 차를 살 텐데. **4** used in order to show what you expect will happen in the future ‖ 앞으로 일어나리라고 예상되는 일을 나타내는 데에 쓰여: *I'll be* (=I will be) *leaving tomorrow.* 나는 내일 출발할 겁니다. **5 is to/are to/were to etc.** FORMAL used in order to say what must happen or what has been arranged ‖ 반드시 일어날 일이나 예정된 일을 말하는 데에 쓰여: *The children are to go to bed by 8:00.* 그 아이들은 8시까지는 잠자리에 들어야 한다. —see also BEEN

be² *v* **1** [I, linking verb] used in order to give the name, date, or position of something or someone, or to describe it in some way ‖ 명칭이나 날짜 또는 사물이나 사람의 위치를 말하거나 어떤 식으로든 그것을 묘사하는 데에 쓰여: *January is the first month of the year.* 1월은 일년의 첫 번째 달이다. / *The concert was last night.* 그 콘서트는 어젯밤에 있었다. / *Julie wants to be a doctor.* 줄리는 의사가 되고 싶어한다. / *Where is Tom?* 톰은 어디 있습니까? / *It's* (=it is) *going to be hot today.* 오늘은 날씨가 덥겠다. / *I'm* (=I am) *hungry.* 배가 고프다. **2 there is/are/were etc.** used in order to show that something or someone exists ‖ 사물이나 사람이 있다는 것을 나타내는 데에 쓰여: *Last night there were only eight people at choir practice.* 어젯밤 합창 연습에 단지 여덟 사람만 있었다. /

There's (=there is) *a hole in the knee of your jeans.* 네 청바지 무릎에 구멍이 났다. —see also **let sb/sth be** (LET) —compare BECOME

beach /biʧ/ *n* an area of sand or small stones at the edge of an ocean or a lake ‖ 바다나 호수의 가장자리에 있는 모래나 자갈이 있는 지역. 해변. 바닷가. 호숫가

beach ball /'. ,./ *n* a large plastic ball that you fill with air and play with at the beach ‖ 공기를 채워서 해변에서 가지고 노는 큰 비닐 공. 비치볼

bea·con /'bikən/ *n* a flashing light, used as a signal to warn or guide boats, planes etc. ‖ 배·비행기 등에 경고하거나 안내하기 위한 신호로 쓰이는 번쩍이는 불빛. 신호 등·불

bead /bid/ *n* **1** a small ball of plastic, wood, glass etc., usually used for making jewelry ‖ 보통 장신구를 만드는 데 사용하는 플라스틱·나무·유리 등으로 만든 작은 알. 구슬 **2** a small drop of liquid ‖ 작은 액체 방울: *beads of sweat* 땀방울

bead·y /'bidi/ *adj* beady eyes are small and shiny ‖ 눈이 작고 반짝이는

bea·gle /'bigəl/ *n* a dog that has smooth fur, large ears, and short legs, sometimes used in hunting ‖ 때때로 사냥에 쓰이며 부드러운 털·커다란 귀·짧은 다리를 가진 개

beak /bik/ *n* the hard pointed mouth of a bird ‖ 새의 단단하고 뾰족한 입. 부리 —see picture at BILL¹

beak·er /'bikɚ/ *n* a glass cup with straight sides used in a LABORATORY (=place where people do scientific tests) ‖ 실험실에서 사용하는 측면이 곧게 뻗은 유리컵. 비커

beam¹ /bim/ *n* **1** a line of light shining from something such as the sun, a lamp etc. ‖ 태양·램프 등에서 비치는 한 줄기 빛. 광선: *The beam of the flashlight flickered and went out.* 손전등 불빛이 깜박이더니 꺼졌다. / *a laser beam* 레이저 광선 **2** a long heavy piece of wood or metal used in building houses, bridges etc. ‖ 집·다리 등의 건축에 쓰이는 길고 육중한 목재나 금속재. 들보. 도리 **3** a line of energy or light that you cannot see ‖ 볼 수 없는 한 줄기의 에너지나 빛

beam² *v* **1** [I] to smile or look at someone in a very happy way ‖ 남에게 행복하게 미소짓거나 바라보다: *Uncle Willie beamed at us proudly.* 윌리 삼촌은 우리를 보고 자랑스럽게 미소지었다. **2** [I, T] to send out energy, light, radio, or television signals etc. ‖ 에너지[빛, 라

디오나 텔레비전 전파] 등을 보내다: *the first broadcast beamed across the Atlantic* 대서양을 가로지른 첫 방송

bean /biːn/ *n* **1 a)** the seed of one of many types of PEA plants, that is cooked as a food ‖ 각종 콩과 식물 중의 하나로, 음식으로 조리되는 열매. 콩 **b)** a POD (=seed case) from one of these plants that is eaten as a vegetable when it is young ‖ 연할 때 야채로 먹는 콩과 식물의 깍지 **2** a plant that produces these beans ‖ 콩이 열리는 식물. 콩과 식물 **3 a** seed used in making some types of food or drinks ‖ 여러 형태의 음식이나 음료를 만드는 데에 쓰이는 열매: *coffee beans* 커피 콩 **4 not know/care beans (about sth)** to not know anything or care about someone or something ‖ 사람이나 사물에 대하여 아무것도 모르거나 상관하지 않다. (…에 대하여) 전혀 모르다[개의치 않다]: *He doesn't care beans about his family.* 그는 가족에게 전혀 신경을 쓰지 않는다.

bear¹ /beːr/ *v* **bore, borne, bearing** [T]

1 ▶BE RESPONSIBLE 책임지다◀ FORMAL to be responsible for or accept something ‖ 어떤 것을 책임지거나 받아들이다: *In this case, you must bear some of the blame yourself.* 이번 사건에 너 자신이 어느 정도 비난을 감수해야 한다.

2 ▶DEAL WITH STH …에 대처하다◀ to bravely accept or deal with a painful or unpleasant situation ‖ 고통스럽거나 불쾌한 상황을 용감하게 받아들이거나 대처하다. 참다. 견디다: *The pain was almost more than she could bear.* 그 고통은 그녀가 거의 참을 수 없는 지경이었다.

3 bear a resemblance/relation etc. to sth to be similar to something, or to be related to someone or something in some way ‖ 사물과 비슷하거나 사람 또는 사물과 어떤 면으로 관련되어 있다. …과 유사성/관련성이 있다: *The final script bore no resemblance to the one he'd originally written.* 마지막 대본은 그가 원래 쓴 대본과 유사성이 없었다.

4 bear (sth) in mind to consider a fact when you are deciding or judging something ‖ 일을 결정하거나 판단할 때 어떤 사실을 고려하다. 명심[유념]하다: *Bear in mind that this method does not always work.* 이 방법이 항상 효과가 있는 것은 아니라는 것을 명심해라.

5 bear fruit a) if a plan or decision bears fruit, it is successful ‖ 계획이나 결정이 성공하다. 결실을 맺다 **b)** if a tree bears fruit, it produces fruit ‖ 나무가 열

매를 맺다

6 ▶MARK/NAME 표시/이름◀ FORMAL to have or show a particular mark, name, piece of information etc. ‖ 특정한 표시·이름·정보 등을 지니거나 나타내다: *He bore the scars for the rest of his life.* 그는 여생 동안 그 상처를 지녔다.

7 can't bear to dislike something a lot, and get upset or annoyed about it ‖ 어떤 것을 몹시 싫어하여 화나 짜증을 내다. 참지 못하다: *She was the kind of person who couldn't bear to throw anything away.* 그녀는 뭐든지 버리는 것을 참을 수 없어 하는 부류의 사람이었다.

8 ▶WEIGHT 무게◀ to support the weight of something ‖ 어떤 것의 무게를 지탱하다. 버티다: *The ice wasn't thick enough to bear his weight.* 그 얼음은 그의 체중을 지탱할 만큼 두껍지 않았다.

9 bear with me SPOKEN used in order to politely ask someone to be patient while you do something ‖ 무엇을 할 동안 남에게 정중하게 참고 있으라고 요구하는 데 쓰여: *Bear with me for a minute while I check the files.* 파일을 검색하는 동안 잠시 기다려.

10 bear right/left to turn right or left ‖ 오른쪽이나 왼쪽으로 돌다: *Bear left where the road divides.* 길이 갈라지는 곳에서 왼쪽으로 돌아라.

11 ▶BABY 아기◀ FORMAL to give birth to a baby ‖ 아기를 낳다. 출산하다

12 ▶CARRY 운반하다◀ FORMAL to carry something ‖ 무엇을 운반하다. 나르다: *The seeds are borne long distances by the wind.* 그 씨들은 바람에 의해 멀리까지 날아간다. —see also **bring sth to bear (on)** (BRING)

bear down on sb/sth *phr v* [T] to move quickly toward someone or something, especially in a threatening way ‖ 특히 위협적으로 어떤 사람이나 물건쪽으로 신속히 움직이다. 돌진하다. 덮치다: *We ran as the truck bore down on us.* 그 트럭이 우리를 향해 돌진하자 우리는 내달렸다.

bear sb/sth **out** *phr v* [T] to show that something is true ‖ 어떤 것이 사실임을 보여 주다. …을 실증하다: *Research bears out the claim that boys receive more attention in the classroom.* 연구는 소년들이 교실에서 보다 많은 보살핌을 받고 있다는 주장을 실증한다.

USAGE NOTE bear, stand, tolerate, put up with

Use these words to talk about accepting or dealing with a bad situation. **Bear** is more formal, and means that someone is being brave: *The pain was almost too much to bear.* **Stand** is usually used in the phrase "can't stand": *I can't stand this noise!* **Tolerate** and **put up with** mean the same thing, but **tolerate** is more formal: *Why do you put up with being treated so badly? / I'm surprised she tolerates his behavior.* ✗DON'T SAY "support" instead of any of these words.✗ 이 단어들은 나쁜 상황의 수용이나 대처를 언급하는 데 쓰인다. **bear**는 더 격식적이고 사람이 용감함을 의미한다: 고통이 너무 심해서 거의 참을 수 없었다. **stand**는 보통 "can't stand"의 구로 사용된다: 이 소음 못 참겠네! **tolerate**와 **put up with**는 같은 뜻이나 **tolerate**가 더 격식적이다: 너는 그렇게 부당하게 취급받는데 왜 참니? / 나는 그녀가 그의 행동을 참는 것에 놀랐다. 이들 단어 대신에 "support"를 쓰지는 않는다.

bear² *n* **1** a large strong heavy animal with thick fur that eats fruit, insects, and some flesh ‖ 과일·곤충과 약간의 고기를 먹으며 두꺼운 털가죽을 지닌 체구가 크고 강하며 육중한 동물. 곰 **2** INFORMAL something very difficult to do or deal with ‖ 하거나 다루기에 매우 어려운 것: *That last test was a real bear!* 그 마지막 시험은 정말 어려웠어!

bear·a·ble /ˈbɛrəbəl/ *adj* a situation that is bearable is difficult or unpleasant but can be accepted or dealt with ‖ 상황이 어렵거나 불쾌하지만 수용하거나 대처할 수 있는. 견딜 수 있는: *His letters made her loneliness bearable.* 그의 편지가 그녀의 외로움을 견딜 수 있게 해 주었다. —opposite UNBEARABLE

beard /bɪrd/ *n* the hair that grows over a man's chin ‖ 남성의 턱에 나는 털. 턱수염 – **bearded** *adj* —see picture at HAIRSTYLE

bear·er /ˈbɛrɚ/ *n* **1** FORMAL someone who owns a legal document such as a PASSPORT ‖ 여권 등의 법률 서류를 소지한 사람. 소지[지참]인 **2** LITERARY someone who brings you something such as a message, letter etc ‖ 전하는 말·편지 등을 가져오는 사람. 전달자. 사자: *the bearer of bad news* 나쁜 소식의 전달자 **3** someone who carries something ‖ 어떤 것을 운반하는 사람: *a flag bearer* 기수 —see also PALLBEARER

bear hug /ˈ. ./ *n* the action of putting your arms around someone and holding him/her very tightly, especially to show

loving feelings ‖ 특히 애정의 표시로 남을 팔로 감아 꼭 껴안는 행위. 침찬 포옹

bear·ing /ˈbɛrɪŋ/ *n* **1 have a bearing on sth** to have some influence on or to be related to something ‖ 어떤 것에 어떤 영향을 주거나 관련되다: *The new information has no bearing on the case.* 새 정보는 그 사건에 아무런 영향도 미치지 못했다. **2 get/lose your bearings** to find out exactly where you are, or to not know exactly where you are ‖ 현재의 위치를 정확히 알거나 모르다. 방향을 알다/잃다: *Apparently the boat lost its bearings in the fog.* 분명히 그 배는 안개 속에서 방향을 잃었다. **3** [singular, U] the way someone moves or stands ‖ 사람이 움직이거나 서 있는 방식. 태도. 몸가짐: *an elderly man with a military bearing* 군인다운 태도를 지닌 노인

bear·ish /ˈbɛrɪʃ/ *adj* relating to a decrease in prices in the STOCK MARKET ‖ 주식 시장에서 가격의 감소와 관련된. 하락세의. 약세의: *The market has been bearish this week.* 주식 시장은 금주에 하락세였다. —compare BULLISH

bear mar·ket /ˌ. ˈ../ *n* a situation in which the value of SHAREs in business decreases ‖ 주식의 가치가 하락하는 상황. 약세 시장 —compare BULL MARKET

beast /bist/ *n* LITERARY an animal, especially a wild or dangerous one ‖ 특히 거칠고 위험한 동물. 짐승

beat¹ /bit/ *v* **beat, beat, beaten**
1 ▶DEFEAT 패배시키다◀ [T] to defeat someone in a game, competition etc., or to do better than someone or something ‖ 게임·시합 등에서 남을 이기거나, 남이나 어떤 것을 능가하다: *Stein beat me at chess in 44 moves.* 스타인은 체스에서 44수(手)만에 나를 이겼다. / *Hank Aaron finally beat the record for home runs set by Babe Ruth.* 행크 아론은 마침내 베이브 루스가 세운 홈런 기록을 깼다.
2 ▶HIT SB 남을 때리다◀ [T] to hit someone many times with your hand, a stick etc. ‖ 손·막대기 등으로 남을 여러 번 때리다: *He used to come home drunk and beat us.* 그는 술 취해 집에 와서는 우리를 때리곤 했다.
3 ▶HIT STH …을 치다◀ [I, T] to hit something regularly or continuously ‖ 어떤 것을 규칙적으로 또는 계속적으로 치다: *waves beating on/against the shore* 해안에 철썩이는 파도
4 ▶FOOD 음식◀ [I, T] to mix foods together quickly using a fork or a special kitchen tool ‖ 포크나 특별한 주방 용구를 사용하여 음식을 빨리 섞다. 휘젓

B

다: *Beat the eggs and add them to the sugar mixture.* 계란을 휘저어 설탕 혼합물에 넣어라.

5 ▶SOUND 소리◀ [I, T] to make a regular sound or movement, or to make something do this ‖ 규칙적으로 소리를 내거나 움직이다, 또는 규칙적으로 소리를 내게 하거나 움직이게 하다. 고동치다. 고동치게 하다: *My heart seemed to be beating much too fast.* 내 심장은 너무 빠르게 고동치는 것 같았다. / *beating time on the drum* (=making regular sounds for other musicians to follow) 드럼으로 박자를 맞추기

6 beat around the bush to avoid talking about the main point of a subject, often because it is unpleasant or embarrassing ‖ 화제의 요점이 종종 불쾌하거나 거북스러워서 그에 대한 언급을 회피하다. 에둘러 말하다: *Stop beating around the bush, and say it!* 빙 둘러 이야기하지 말고 요점을 말해!

7 beat the rush INFORMAL to do something early in order to avoid problems because later everyone will be doing it ‖ 나중에 모두가 그 일을 할 것이므로 문제를 피하기 위해 서둘러서 어떤 것을 하다: *Shop early and beat the Christmas rush!* 성탄절에는 혼잡하니 서둘러 쇼핑하십시오!

SPOKEN PHRASES

8 [T] to be better or more enjoyable than something else 다른 일보다 더 낫거나 즐겁다: *It's not the greatest job, but it beats waitressing for the rest of my life.* 그것이 아주 대단한 일은 아니지만 내 여생을 웨이트리스로 일하는 것보다는 좋다. / *You can't beat* (=nothing is better than) *San Diego for good weather.* 날씨가 좋기로는 샌디에이고가 제일이다.

9 (it) beats me used in order to say that you cannot understand or do not know something ‖ 어떤 것을 이해할 수 없거나 모른다고 말하는 데에 쓰여. 글쎄: *"What kind of books does she write?" "Beats me. She makes good money, though."* "그녀는 어떤 책을 쓰고 있니?" "모르지만 돈은 많이 벌어."

10 beat it! an impolite way to tell someone to leave ‖ 남에게 떠나라고 하는 무례한 어법. 꺼져!

—see also **off the beaten track/path** (BEATEN) —see usage note at HIT¹

beat down *phr v* **[I] 1** if the sun beats down, it shines brightly and makes things hot ‖ 햇빛이 밝고 따갑게 비치다. 햇빛이 내리쬐다 **2** if the rain beats down, it rains very hard ‖ 비가 억수로 오다

beat sb/sth ↔ **off** *phr v* **[T]** to hit someone who is attacking you until s/he goes away ‖ 공격하는 사람이 사라질 때까지 때리다. 쫓아 버리다. 격퇴하다

beat sb ↔ **out** *phr v* **[T]** INFORMAL to defeat someone in a competition ‖ 시합에서 남을 이기다: *By winning the game, Notre Dame beat out Georgia Tech for the number one position in the country.* 그 경기에 승리하여 노트르 데임 팀은 조지아 테크 팀을 제치고 1위로 올라섰다.

beat sb **to** sth *phr v* **[T]** to get or do something before someone else is able to ‖ 남보다 앞서서 어떤 것을 얻거나 하다. 남의 선수를 치다: *I called to ask about buying the car, but someone had beaten me to it.* 나는 그 자동차 구입에 대한 문의를 하려고 전화했으나 누군가가 선수를 쳤다.

beat sb ↔ **up** *phr v* **[T] 1** to hit someone until they are badly hurt ‖ 남을 심하게 상처 입을 정도로 때리다: *My boyfriend went crazy and beat me up.* 내 남자 친구는 이성을 잃고 나를 심하게 때렸다. **2 beat yourself up** to blame yourself too much for something bad that has happened ‖ 일어난 나쁜 일에 대하여 지나치게 자책하다: *Don't beat yourself up over this!* 이 일에 대해 너무 자책하지 마라!

beat up on sb *phr v* **[T]** to hit someone younger or weaker than you until s/he is badly hurt ‖ 어리거나 약한 사람을 심한 상처를 입을 때까지 때리다. 늘씬 때려눕히다

beat² *n* **1** one of a series of regular movements, sounds, or hitting actions ‖ 연속되는 규칙적인 동작[소리, 때리는 행위]의 하나하나: *a strong heart beat* 강한 심장 박동 / *the beat of the drum* 북소리 **2 a) [singular]** the main pattern of strong musical notes that are repeated in a piece of music ‖ 곡에서 반복되는 강한 음조의 주요 패턴. 박자: *The song has a beat you can dance to.* 그 노래는 네가 춤출 수 있는 박자를 가지고 있다. **b)** one of the notes in this pattern ‖ 이 패턴의 음표의 하나. 비트. 강렬한 리듬 **3 [singular]** a subject or an area of a city that someone is responsible for as his/her job ‖ 사람이 업무로 맡고 있는 분야나 도시의 구역. 활동 분야[구역]: *journalists covering the political beat* 정치 부문을 담당하는 기자들 / *a police* *officer on the beat* (=working in his/her area) 담당 구역을 순찰 중인 경찰관

beat³ *adj* INFORMAL very tired ‖ 매우 피곤한: *You look beat!* 너 피곤해 보이는데!

beat·en /'bitn/ *adj* **off the beaten track/path** far away from places that people usually visit ‖ 사람이 흔히 가는 장소에서 멀리 떨어진. 잘 알려지지 않은: *a little hotel off the beaten track* 잘 알려지지 않은 작은 호텔

beat·er /'bitə/ *n* **1** a kitchen tool that is used for mixing foods together ‖ 음식을 섞는 데 사용되는 주방 용구. 교반기 **2 wife/child beater** someone who hits his wife or his/her child ‖ 아내나 아이를 구타하는 사람. 아내/자녀 폭행[학대]자

beat·ing /'bitɪŋ/ *n* **take a beating** to be defeated or criticized very badly ‖ 크게 패배하거나 비난받다: *The soccer team took a beating in the semifinals.* 그 축구 팀은 준결승전에서 참패했다.

beat-up /ˌ. '../ *adj* old and slightly damaged ‖ 오래되어 다소 망가진: *a beat-up old car* 못쓰게 된 낡은 차

beaut /byut/ *n* [singular] SPOKEN something that is very good ‖ 아주 좋은 것: *That last catch was a beaut.* 그 마지막으로 잡은 것은 끝내주는 것이었다.

beau·ti·cian /byu'tɪʃən/ *n* OLD-FASHIONED ⇨HAIRDRESSER

beau·ti·ful /'byutⁿəfəl/ *adj* **1** a woman, girl, or child who is beautiful is very attractive to look at ‖ 여성[소녀, 어린이]이 몹시 매력있게 보이는. 아름다운: *the most beautiful woman in the world* 세상에서 가장 아름다운 여자 / *What a beautiful baby!* 참 예쁜 아기구나! **2** very attractive to look at or good to listen to ‖ 매우 매력적으로 보이거나 좋게 들리는: *a beautiful gray wool dress* 아름다운 회색 모직 드레스 / *beautiful music* 아름다운 음악 / *The views from the mountaintop were beautiful.* 산꼭대기에서 본 경치는 아름다웠다.

USAGE NOTE beautiful, pretty, handsome, good-looking, cute

Use these words to say that someone is attractive. **Beautiful** is a very strong word meaning "extremely attractive": *a beautiful movie star.* **Pretty, handsome, good-looking,** and **cute** are all less strong ways of describing attractive people, and are used more often than **beautiful**. Use **pretty** only for describing younger women and girls. Use **handsome** for describing men, although we

---

sometimes use it for describing attractive older women. Use **good-looking** for both men and women. Use **cute** for babies, children, and young men and women.
이 단어들은 사람이 매력적이라는 것을 말하는 데 쓰인다. **beautiful**은 "아주 매력적인"이라는 뜻의 강도가 강한 단어이다: 아름다운 영화 배우. **pretty·handsome·good-looking**과 **cute**는 매력적인 사람을 묘사하는 강도가 다소 떨어지는 어휘로 **beautiful**보다 더 자주 쓰인다. **pretty**는 오로지 젊은 여성과 소녀의 묘사에만 쓰인다. **handsome**은 매력적인 나이든 여성을 묘사하는 데에 간혹 쓰이기는 하지만 일반적으로 남성의 묘사에 쓰인다. **good-looking**은 남성·여성 가리지 않고 쓰이며, **cute**는 아기·어린이·젊은 남녀에게 두루 쓰인다.

beau·ty /'byuti/ *n* **1** [U] a quality that things, places, or people have that makes them very attractive to look at ‖ 사물[장소, 사람]이 외관상 매우 매력적으로 보이게 하는 성질. 아름다움. 미(美): *a woman of great beauty* 대단히 아름다운 여성 / *the beauty of America's national parks* 미국 국립 공원의 아름다움 **2** [U] a quality that something such as a poem, piece of music etc. has that gives you a feeling of pleasure ‖ 즐거움을 주는 시·음악 등이 지니고 있는 성질: *the beauty of Keats' poetry* 키츠 시의 아름다움 **3** INFORMAL something that is very good ‖ 아주 멋있는 것: *His new car's a beauty.* 그의 새 자동차는 끝내준다. **4 the beauty of** a good quality that makes something especially suitable or useful ‖ 어떤 것을 적합하게 하거나 유용하게 하는 속성. 장점. 이점: *The beauty of this type of exercise is that you can do it anywhere.* 이런 운동의 장점은 어디서나 할 수 있다는 점이다. **5** OLD-FASHIONED a woman who is very beautiful ‖ 아주 아름다운 여성. 미녀

beauty sa·lon /'.. ..,./, **beauty parlor** /'.. ,../ *n* ⇨ SALON

bea·ver /'bivə/ *n* an animal with thick fur, a flat tail, and sharp teeth that it uses to cut down trees for building DAMs ‖ 두툼한 털가죽에 납작한 꼬리가 있으며, 날카로운 이빨로 나무를 베어 넘어뜨려 둑을 만드는 동물. 비버

be·bop /'bibɑp/ *n* a style of JAZZ music ‖ 재즈 음악의 한 형태. 비밥

be·came /bɪ'keɪm/ *v* the past tense of BECOME ‖ become의 과거형

be·cause /bɪˈkɔz, -ˈkʌz/ *conjunction* **1** for the reason that ‖ 어떤 이유 때문에: *You can't go, because you're too young.* 너는 너무 어려서 갈 수 없다. **2 because of** as a result of a particular thing or of someone's actions ‖ 특정한 일이나 남의 행동의 결과로: *We weren't able to have the picnic because of the rain.* 우리는 비가 와서 소풍갈 수 없었다. —see also **just because** (JUST)

beck·on /ˈbɛkən/ *v* [I, T] to move your hand or arm to show that you want someone to move toward you ‖ 남을 자기 쪽으로 오라고 표시하기 위하여 손이나 팔을 움직이다. 손짓하다: *He beckoned her to join him.* 그는 그녀에게 자기와 함께 하자고 손짓했다. / *He beckoned to her.* 그는 그녀에게 손짓했다.

be·come /bɪˈkʌm/ *v* **became, become, becoming 1** [linking verb] to begin to be something, or to develop in a particular way ‖ 어떤 것이 되기 시작하거나 특정하게 전개되다: *The weather had become warmer.* 날씨는 더 따뜻해졌다. / *In 1960 Kennedy became the first Catholic president.* 1960년에 케네디는 첫 번째 가톨릭 신자 대통령이 되었다. / *It is becoming harder to find good housing for low-income families.* 저소득 가정이 알맞은 집을 찾기는 더 어려워지고 있다. / *She started to become anxious about her son* 그녀는 아들이 걱정되기 시작했다. ✗DON'T SAY "She started to be anxious about her son."✗ "She started to be anxious about her son."이라고는 하지 않는다. **2 what/whatever became of...?** used in order to ask what happened to a person or thing ‖ 사람이나 사물에 일어난 일을 묻는 데에 쓰여. …은 어떻게 되었지?: *Whatever became of Grandma's dishes?* 할머니의 접시가 어떻게 됐냐? **3** [T] FORMAL to be suitable for someone ‖ 사람에게 어울리다: *I don't think that dress becomes you, dear.* 여보, 그 옷은 당신에게 어울리지 않는다고 생각해.

> **USAGE NOTE become, get, and go**
>
> Use these words to talk about situations or states that develop. **Become** is more formal: *He's becoming very successful. / Prague has become popular with tourists.* **Get** is more informal: *It's getting dark outside. / I'm getting hungry.* Use **go** in some fixed expressions: *Have you gone crazy?*

이 단어들은 상황이나 상태의 전개에 대한 언급에 쓰인다. **become**은 보다 격식적이다: 그는 상당히 성공하고 있다. / 프라하는 관광객들에게 인기가 있는 곳이 되었다. **get**은 보다 비격식적이다: 밖은 어두워지고 있다. / 배가 고파진다. 몇몇 관용 표현에서는 **go**가 쓰인다: 당신 미쳤어?

be·com·ing /bɪˈkʌmɪŋ/ *adj* OLD-FASHIONED becoming clothes or styles look attractive on you ‖ 옷이나 스타일이 매력적으로 보이는. 어울리는

bed[1] /bɛd/ *n* **1** [C, U] a piece of furniture for sleeping on ‖ 그 위에서 잠을 자는 데에 쓰이는 가구. 침대: *an old brass bed* 낡은 놋쇠 침대 / *I was lying in bed reading.* 나는 침대에 누워서 독서를 하고 있었다. / *She looked like she had just gotten out of bed.* 그녀는 방금 잠자리에서 일어난 것 같았다. / *What time do you usually put the kids to bed?* 너는 보통 몇 시에 아이들을 재우냐? / *Jamie usually goes to bed around seven o'clock.* 제이미는 보통 7시 경에 잠자리에 든다. / *Sara, have you made your bed yet?* 사라야 이미 잠자리는 봐 놓았지? (=pulled the sheets etc. into place) / *Come on, it's time for bed.* (=time to go to sleep) 자, 잠잘 시간이다. **2 go to bed with sb** INFORMAL to have sex with someone ‖ 남과 성교하다 **3** the ground at the bottom of the ocean, a river, or a lake ‖ 바다[강, 호수]의 바닥 **4** a special area of ground that has been prepared for plants to grow in ‖ 식물을 재배하기 위해 마련된 특별한 지역의 땅. 못자리. 화단: *rose beds* 장미 화단 **5** a layer of something that forms a base on which other things are put ‖ 다른 물건을 놓는 기반이 되는 물건의 층: *potato salad on a bed of lettuce* 상추 위에 얹은 감자 샐러드 **6 sb got up on the wrong side of the bed** SPOKEN said when someone is slightly angry or annoyed for no particular reason ‖ 특별한 이유없이, 좀 화가 나거나 짜증이 날 때 쓰여. 기분이 나쁘다

bed[2] *v* **-dded, -dding**
bed down *phr v* [I] to make yourself comfortable and sleep in a place where you do not usually sleep ‖ 보통은 잠을 자지 않는 곳에서 편안히 자다: *I'll just bed down on the sofa.* 소파에서 좀 잘게.

bed and break·fast /ˌ. . ˈ../, **B&B** *n* a small comfortable hotel like a house where you are served breakfast ‖ 아침 식사가 제공되는 집처럼 작고 편안한 호텔

bed·clothes /'bɛdkloʊz, -kloʊðz/ *n* [plural] ⇨ BEDDING

bed·ding /'bɛdɪŋ/ *n* [U] **1** the sheets, BLANKETs etc. that you put on a bed ‖ 침대에 까는 시트·담요 등. 침구류 **2** material that an animal sleeps on ‖ 동물이 깔고 자는 재료. 깔집

bed·lam /'bɛdləm/ *n* [singular, U] a lot of wild noisy activity in a place ‖ 어떤 곳의 시끌벅적함. 아수라장: *The classroom was bedlam.* 그 교실은 난장판이었다.

bed·pan /'bɛdpæn/ *n* a container used as a toilet by someone who has to stay in bed ‖ 누워서 지내야만 하는 사람이 변기로 쓰는 용기. (환자용) 요강

be·drag·gled /bɪ'drægəld/ *adj* looking dirty, wet, and messy ‖ 더럽고 축축하고 엉망으로 보이는. 지저분한: *bedraggled hair* 지저분한 머리

bed·rid·den /'bɛd,rɪdn/ *adj* unable to get out of bed because you are old or very sick ‖ 늙거나 몹시 아파서 일어날 수 없는. 누워서만 지내는

bed·room /'bɛdrum/ *n* a room with a bed in it, where you sleep ‖ 침대가 있는 잠을 자는 방. 침실

bed·side /'bɛdsaɪd/ *n* the area around a bed ‖ 침대 주변. 침대 곁. 머리맡: *His family has been at his bedside all night.* 그의 가족은 밤새도록 그의 침대 곁에 있었다. / *a bedside table/lamp* 침대가의 테이블[램프]

bed·spread /'bɛdsprɛd/ *n* a large piece of cloth that covers the top of a bed, including the PILLOWs ‖ 베개를 포함하여 침대를 덮는 대형 천. 침대 덮개

bed·stead /'bɛdstɛd/ *n* the frame of a bed ‖ 침대틀

bed·time /'bɛdtaɪm/ *n* [C, U] the time when you usually go to bed ‖ 보통 잠자리에 드는 시간. 취침 시간: *It's way past your bedtime!* 잘 시간이 한참 지났어!

bee

bee　　wasp　　hornet

bee /bi/ *n* a yellow and black insect that flies, makes HONEY, and can sting you ‖ 날아다니며, 꿀을 만들고, 침을 쏘는 노랗고 검은 곤충. 벌 —see also SPELLING BEE

beech /bitʃ/ *n* [C, U] a tree with smooth gray branches and dark green leaves, or the hard wood of this tree ‖ 미끈한 회색 가지와 암녹색 잎을 가진 나무나 그 단단한 목재. 너도밤나무(목재)

beef¹ /bif/ *n* **1** [U] meat from a cow ‖ 쇠고기 **2** INFORMAL a complaint ‖ 불평. 불만: *The guy had a beef with the manager and yelled at him for about 15 minutes.* 그 사람은 매니저에게 불만이 있어서 약 15분 동안 그에게 고함을 쳤다. —see usage note at MEAT

beef² *v* [I] INFORMAL to complain ‖ 불평하다: *The kids are beefing about their homework assignment.* 어린이들은 숙제에 대해 불평을 하고 있다.

beef sth ↔ **up** *phr v* [T] INFORMAL to improve something, especially to make it stronger or more interesting ‖ 더 강하거나 흥미있게 하려고 무엇을 개선하다. 강화[증강]하다: *Security around the White House has been beefed up since the attack.* 백악관 주변의 경계가 그 공격 이후 강화되었다.

beef·y /'bifi/ *adj* a beefy man is big, strong, and usually fat ‖ 남자가 덩치가 크고 튼튼하며 일반적으로 뚱뚱한. 건장한

bee·hive /'bihaɪv/ *n* ⇨ HIVE

bee·line /'bilaɪn/ *n* **make a beeline for** sth INFORMAL to go quickly and directly toward someone or something ‖ 사람이나 사물을 향하여 신속히 곧장 가다. …으로 직행하다: *The bear made a beeline for the woods.* 그 곰은 숲으로 곧장 갔다.

been /bɪn/ *v* **1** the PAST PARTICIPLE of BE ‖ be의 과거 분사형 **2 have/has been** used in order to say that someone has gone to a place and come back ‖ 사람이 어떤 장소에 갔다가 되돌아온 것을 말하는 데에 쓰여: *Sandy has just been to Japan.* 샌디는 일본에 막 다녀오는 길이다. / *Have you been to see Katrina's new house?* 당신은 카트리나의 새 집에 가 본 적이 있습니까? —see usage note at GO¹ —see picture at GO¹

beep /bip/ *v* **1** [I] if a machine beeps, it makes a short high sound ‖ 기계가 짧고 높은 소리를 내다. 삑 소리를 내다: *The computer beeps when you push the wrong key.* 키를 잘못 누르면 컴퓨터는 삑 소리를 낸다. **2** [I, T] if a horn beeps or you beep it, it makes a loud sound ‖ 경적이 큰 소리를 내다. 경적이[경적을] 울리다 **3** [T] to telephone someone who has a BEEPER ‖ 무선 호출기 소지인에게 전화하다 –**beep** *n*

beep·er /'bipɚ/ *n* a small machine that you carry with you that makes a sound to tell you to telephone someone; PAGER

‖ 전화를 해달라고 알리는 소리를 내는 작은 휴대 기계. 무선 호출기; 圈 pager

beer /bɪr/ *n* [C, U] an alcoholic drink made from grain, or a glass, can, or bottle of this drink ‖ 곡물로 만든 알코올 음료, 또는 이 음료가 든 잔[캔, 병]. 맥주 (가 든 잔[캔, 병]) —see also ROOT BEER

bees·wax /ˈbizwæks/ *n* [U] **1** a substance produced by BEEs, used in making CANDLES and furniture polish ‖ 양초나 가구 광택제 제조에 쓰이는 벌이 만들어 내는 물질. 밀랍 **2 none of your beeswax** SPOKEN a way of telling someone that something is private and s/he does not have the right to know about it ‖ 남에게 사적(私的)인 것이라 그 것에 대하여 알 권리가 없다고 말하는 어법. 당신이 알 바 아니야

beet /bit/ *n* a dark red round root that is cooked and eaten as a vegetable ‖ 요리하여 채소로 먹는 검붉고 둥근 뿌리. 비트

bee·tle /ˈbitl/ *n* an insect with a hard round back that covers its wings ‖ 날개를 덮는 딱딱하고 둥근 등을 가진 곤충. 딱정벌레

be·fit /bɪˈfɪt/ *v* **-tted, -tting** [T] FORMAL to be suitable or seem right for someone ‖ 어떤 사람에게 적합하거나 알맞아 보이다. 어울리다: *a funeral befitting a national hero* 국민적 영웅에 어울리는 장례식 **– befitting** *adj*

be·fore¹ /bɪˈfɔr/ *prep* **1** earlier than something ‖ 어떤 것보다 일찍. (이)전에: *I usually shower before having breakfast.* 나는 아침 식사 전에 보통 샤워를 한다. / *Denise got there before me.* 데니스는 나보다 일찍 그곳에 도착했다. / *He arrived the day before yesterday.* (=two days ago) 그는 그저께 도착했다. **2** ahead or in front of someone or something ‖ 어떤 사람이나 사물보다 먼저 또는 앞에: *There were ten people before us in line.* 우리 앞에 열 사람이 줄 서 있었다. / *The priest knelt before the altar.* 그 사제는 제단 앞에 무릎을 꿇었다. **3** in a more important position than someone or something ‖ 어떤 사람이나 사물보다 더 중요한 위치에: *His wife and children come before* (=are more important than) *his job.* 그는 아내와 아이들을 직업보다 더 중요시한다. **4** at a particular distance in front of a place as you travel toward it ‖ 앞으로 가다가 어떤 장소 앞의 특정한 지점에서: *Turn right just before the stop light.* 신호등 바로 앞에서 우회전해라. **5** in a situation where something is being considered by

someone so that a decision can be made ‖ 남이 결정을 내릴 수 있도록 어떤 것이 검토되고 있는 상황에. (재판을 받기 위하여) …의 앞에: *The case is now before the Supreme Court.* 그 사건은 지금 대법원에서 심리 중이다.

before² *adv* at an earlier time ‖ 이전에: *They'd met before, at one of Sandra's parties.* 그들은 전에 산드라가 연 한 파티에서 만났다.

before³ *conjunction* **1** earlier than the time when something happens ‖ 어떤 일이 일어나기 전에. …보다 전에[앞서서]: *It will be several days before we know the results.* 며칠이 지나야 우리는 그 결과를 알게 된다. / *John wants to talk to you before you go.* 존은 네가 가기 전에 너와 이야기하고 싶어한다. **2** so that something bad does not happen ‖ 나쁜 일이 일어나지 않도록: *You'd better lock your bike before it gets stolen.* 자전거를 도난당하지 않게 자물쇠를 채우는 것이 좋다. **3 before you know it** SPOKEN used in order to say that something will happen very soon ‖ 어떤 일이 금방 일어날 거라고 말하는 데에 쓰여. 눈 깜짝할 사이에. 곧: *We'd better get going – it'll be dark before you know it.* 서두르는 게 좋겠다. 곧 어두워질 테니.

be·fore·hand /bɪˈfɔrˌhænd/ *adv* before something else happens or is done ‖ 다른 일이 일어나거나 끝나기 전에. 사전에. 미리: *You should never eat a piece of fruit without washing it beforehand.* 과일을 씻기 전에는 결코 먹어서는 안 된다.

be·friend /bɪˈfrɛnd/ *v* [T] FORMAL to become someone's friend, especially someone who needs your help ‖ 특히 도움을 필요로 하는 사람의 친구가 되다. 을 돌봐주다

be·fud·dled /bɪˈfʌdld/ *adj* completely confused ‖ 몹시 혼란스러운. 당혹스러운: *Annie looked a little befuddled.* 애니는 좀 당황한 것 같았다.

beg /bɛg/ *v* **-gged, -gging 1** [I, T] to ask for something in an urgent or anxious way ‖ 어떤 것을 절박하거나 초조하게 청하다. 간청하다: *I begged him to stay, but he wouldn't.* 나는 그에게 머물러 줄 것을 간청했으나 그는 들어 주지 않았다. / *He sank to his knees and begged for forgiveness.* 그는 풀썩 무릎을 꿇고 용서를 빌었다. **2** [I, T] to ask someone for food, money etc. because you are very poor ‖ 매우 가난해서 남에게 음식·돈 등을 청하다. 구걸하다: *homeless families begging for food* 음식을 구걸하는 집 없는 가족들 **3** [I] if an animal such as a dog begs, it asks for food ‖ 개 등의 동물이 음식을 달라고 조르다 **4 I beg your pardon** SPOKEN **a)** used in order to ask someone politely to repeat something ‖ 남에게 어떤 것을 반복해 달라고 정중히 부탁하는 데에 쓰여. 다시 한 번 말씀해 주십시오: *"It's 7:00." "I beg your pardon?" "It's 7:00."* "7시다." "다시 한 번 말씀해 주시겠어요?" "7시라고." **b)** used in order to say you are sorry ‖ 미안하다고 말하는 데에 쓰여. 미안합니다: *Oh, I beg your pardon, did I hurt you?* "오, 미안합니다. 다치지 않았어요?" **c)** FORMAL used in order to show that you strongly disagree with or disapprove of something someone has said ‖ 남이 한 말에 대한 강한 반대나 불만을 나타내는 데에 쓰여. 실례[죄송]합니다만: *"You never had to work hard in your life!" "I beg your pardon – I believe that I have!"* "너는 살면서 한 번도 일을 열심히 한 적이 없어!" "죄송합니다만 저는 열심히 일했다고 생각해요."

beg·gar /ˈbɛɡɚ/ *n* **1** someone who lives by asking people for food and money ‖ 사람들에게 음식과 돈을 구걸하여 살아가는 사람. 거지. 걸인 **2 beggars can't be choosers** SPOKEN used in order to say that if you need something, you have to accept what you are given, even if it is not what you would like ‖ 무엇인가가 필요하면 마음에 들지 않더라도 주어지는 것을 받을 수 밖에 없다는 것을 말하는 데에 쓰여. 빌어먹는 놈이 콩밥을 마다할까

be·gin /bɪˈɡɪn/ *v* **began, begun, beginning 1** [I, T] to start doing or feeling something, or to start to happen or exist ‖ 무엇을 하거나 느끼기 시작하다, 또는 일어나거나 존재하기 시작하다: *The meeting will begin at 10:00.* 집회는 10시에 시작될 예정입니다. / *He began his career 30 years ago.* 그는 30년 전에 그의 직업에 발을 디뎠다. / *Let's begin with exercise 5.* 연습 문제 5부터 시작합시다. / *I began to realize that he was lying.* 나는 그가 거짓말을 하고 있는 것을 깨닫기 시작했다. ✗DON'T SAY "I became to realize."✗ "I became to realize."라고는 하지 않는다. **2 to begin with a)** used in order to introduce the first or most important point ‖ 첫 번째 또는 가장 중요한 사항을 도입하는 데에 쓰여. 우선. 무엇보다도 먼저: *To begin with, photography is not really an art form at all.* 무엇보다도 먼저 사진 촬영술은 전혀 참다운 예술 형태가 아니다. **b)** used in order to say what something was like at the start ‖ 애초에 사물이 어떤 모양이었

는지 말하는 데에 쓰여. 처음에는: *The children helped me to begin with, but they soon got bored.* 아이들이 처음에는 나를 도왔지만 곧 싫증을 냈다. —see usage note at START¹

be·gin·ner /bɪˈɡɪnɚ/ *n* someone who has just started to do or learn something ‖ 어떤 것을 막 하거나 배우기 시작한 사람. 초보자. 초심자

be·gin·ning /bɪˈɡɪnɪŋ/ *n* [C usually singular] the start or first part of something ‖ 어떤 것의 시작이나 첫 부분: *the beginning of the book* 책의 첫 부분 / *Placement tests are given at the beginning of the year.* 반 배치 고사는 학년 초에 치른다. / *The whole trip was a disaster from beginning to end.* 그 여행 전체가 처음부터 끝까지 재난이었다.

be·gin·nings /bɪˈɡɪnɪŋz/ *n* [plural] the early part or early signs of something that later develops and becomes bigger or more important ‖ 나중에 발달되어 더 커지거나 중요해지는 어떤 것의 초기 부분이나 모습: *From its beginnings as a small rural shop, the store grew to be the US's second largest chain.* 그 상점은 초창기의 조그만 시골 상점에서 성장하여 미국의 두 번째로 큰 체인점이 되었다.

be·grudge /bɪˈɡrʌdʒ/ *v* [T] to feel upset or JEALOUS because of something that you think is unfair ‖ 불공정하다고 여겨지는 일로 인하여 기분을 상하거나 질투하다. 시기하다: *Honestly, I don't begrudge him his success.* 솔직히 나는 그의 성공을 시기하지 않는다.

be·guile /bɪˈɡaɪl/ *v* [T] to persuade or trick someone into doing something, especially by saying nice things to him/her ‖ 특히 기분 좋은 말을 하여 남이 어떤 것을 하도록 설득하거나 속이다. 기만하다

be·gun /bɪˈɡʌn/ *v* the PAST PARTICIPLE of BEGIN ‖ begin의 과거 분사형

be·half /bɪˈhæf/ *n* **on behalf of sb/on sb's behalf** if you do something on behalf of someone, you do it for him/her or instead of him/her ‖ 어떤 사람을 위하여 또는 대신하여: *He agreed to speak on her behalf.* 그는 그녀 대신에 연설하기로 동의했다.

be·have /bɪˈheɪv/ *v* **1** [I] to do or say things in a particular way ‖ 특정한 방식으로 행동하거나 말하다: *Lions in a zoo do not behave like lions in the wild.* 동물원의 사자들은 야생의 사자처럼 행동하지 않는다. / *You behaved bravely in a very difficult situation.* 매우 어려운 상황에서 너는 용감하게 행동했다. **2** [I, T] to do or

B

say things in a way that people think is good or correct ‖ 사람들이 착하거나 옳다고 여기는 방식으로 일을 하거나 말하다: *Tom was quieter than his brother and knew how to behave.* 톰은 자기 동생보다 말수가 적고 처세법을 알았다. / *If you behave yourself, you can stay up late.* 얌전히 굴면 늦게까지 자지 않고 있어도 좋다.

be·hav·ior /bɪˈheɪvyɚ/ *n* [U] **1** the way that a person or animal does or says things, or a particular example of this ‖ 사람이나 동물이 일을 하거나 말하는 방식 또는 그 특정한 본보기. 행동. 행위: *Can TV shows affect children's behavior?* 텔레비전 쇼가 아이들의 행동에 영향을 미칠까요? / *Your behavior is not acceptable in my classroom!* 너의 행동은 내 교실에서는 용납할 수 없어! **2** the things that an object, substance etc. normally does ‖ 물체·물질 등이 정상적으로 움직이는 일. 작동. 작용: *the behavior of cancer cells* 암세포의 작용

be·head /bɪˈhɛd/ *v* [T] to cut someone's head off ‖ 남의 목을 베다. 참수하다

be·hind¹ /bɪˈhaɪnd/ *prep* **1** at or toward the back of something ‖ 어떤 것의 뒤쪽에[으로]: *I was driving behind a truck on the freeway.* 나는 고속도로에서 트럭 뒤에서 차를 몰고 있었다. / *The liquor store is right behind* (=just behind) *the supermarket.* 그 주류 판매점은 슈퍼마켓 바로 뒤에 있다. **2** not as successful or advanced as someone or something else ‖ 남이나 다른 것만큼 성공하거나 진보하지 못한. …보다 뒤져서: *The Lakers were four points behind the Celtics at half time.* 레이커스 팀은 전반전 종료시 셀틱스 팀보다 4점 뒤져 있었다. / *Work on the new building is three months behind schedule.* 새 건물에 대한 작업이 계획보다 3개월 늦어졌다. **3** supporting a person, idea etc. ‖ 사람·사상 등을 지지하여: *Congress is behind the President on this issue.* 의회는 이 문제에 관해 대통령을 지지하고 있다. **4** responsible for something, or causing something to happen ‖ 어떤 것에 책임이 있거나 일어나는 일의 원인이 되어. …의 이면[배후]에: *The police believe a local gang is behind the killings.* 경찰은 지역 조직폭력단이 그 살인의 배후라고 생각하고 있다.

behind² *adv* **1** at or toward the back of something ‖ 어떤 것의 뒤쪽에[으로]: *Several other runners followed close behind.* 몇 명의 다른 주자가 바로 뒤에 따라왔다. **2** in the place where someone

or something was before ‖ 사람이나 사물이 전에 있던 곳에. 뒤에: *I got there and realized I'd left the tickets behind.* 나는 그곳에 도착해서야 표를 놔두고 왔다는 것을 알았다. / *Barb stayed behind to wait for Tina.* 바브는 티나를 기다리려고 뒤에 남았다. **3 be/get behind** to be late or slow in doing something ‖ 어떤 것을 하는 데에 늦거나 더디다: *I'm a little behind; I think I'll stay late and finish this.* 일이 좀 더디니 늦게까지 남아서 이 일을 마쳐야겠다.

behind³ *n* INFORMAL the part of your body that you sit on ‖ 앉을 때 닿는 신체 부분. 엉덩이.

be·hold /bɪˈhoʊld/ *v* [T] LITERARY to see something ‖ 어떤 것을 보다. 목격하다 – **beholder** *n*

beige /beɪʒ/ *n* [U] a pale yellow-gray color ‖ 연하고 노르스름한 회색빛이 감도는 색. 베이지 – **beige** *adj*

be·ing /ˈbiɪŋ/ *n* **1** a living thing, such as a person ‖ 인간처럼 살아 있는 것. 생명체. 생물: *strange beings from outer space* 외계에서 온 이상한 생명체 **2 come into being** to begin to exist ‖ 존재하기 시작하다. 출현하다. 생기다: *Their political system came into being in the early 1900s.* 그들의 정치 제도는 1900년대 초반에 생겨났다.

be·lat·ed /bɪˈleɪtɪd/ *adj* happening or arriving late ‖ 늦게 발생하거나 도착한. 뒤늦은: *a belated birthday card* 뒤늦은 생일 (축하) 카드

belch /bɛltʃ/ *v* **1** [I] to let air from your stomach come out in a noisy way through your mouth ‖ 요란한 소리를 내며 위 속의 공기를 입 밖으로 나오게 하다. 트림하다 **2** [T] to produce a lot of smoke, fire etc. from a particular area ‖ 특정 장소에서 많은 연기·불 등을 만들어 내다. 내뿜다: *factories belching blue smoke* 푸른 연기를 뿜어대는 공장들

be·lie /bɪˈlaɪ/ *v* [T] FORMAL to make someone have a false idea about something ‖ 남에게 어떤 것에 대한 잘못된 생각을 갖게 하다. …을 속이다. …을 거짓으로[잘못] 전하다: *Her strong voice belied the horror of her story.* 그녀의 힘찬 목소리 때문에 그 이야기의 공포스러움이 잘못 전달되었다.

be·lief /bəˈlif/ *n* **1** [singular, U] the feeling that something is definitely true or definitely exists ‖ 어떤 것이 확실히 사실이거나 분명히 존재한다는 느낌. 믿음. 확신: *the medieval belief that the sun went around the earth* 태양이 지구 둘레를 돈다는 중세의 믿음 / *a child's belief* *in Santa Claus* 산타클로스의 존재에 대한 아이들의 믿음 **2** [singular] the feeling that someone or something is good and can be trusted ‖ 사람이나 사물이 좋거나 믿을 만하다는 느낌. 믿음. 신뢰. 신임. 신용: *a strong belief in the importance of education* 교육의 중요성에 대한 강한 신뢰 / *Contrary to popular belief* (=unlike what most people believe), *eating carrots does not improve your eyesight.* 흔히 사람들이 믿고 있는 것과 달리 당근을 먹는 것이 시력을 향상시키지는 않는다. **3** [C usually plural] an idea that you think is true ‖ 자신이 생각하는 것이 옳다는 신념. 믿음. 확신. 소신: *religious beliefs* 종교적 신념

be·liev·a·ble /bəˈlivəbəl/ *adj* able to be believed ‖ 믿을 수 있는. 신뢰할 만한: *a believable love story* 믿을 만한 사랑 이야기 —opposite UNBELIEVABLE

be·lieve /bəˈliv/ *v* **1** [T] to be sure that something is true or that someone is telling the truth ‖ 어떤 것이 옳거나 어떤 사람이 사실을 말하고 있음을 확신하다. 믿다: *Young children often believe (that) animals can understand them.* 어린아이들은 종종 동물이 자신들의 말을 알아들을 수 있다고 믿는다. / *Believe me, I've been there, and it's not nice.* 절 믿으세요. 거기에 가본 적이 있는데 별로 좋지 않아요. / *He said Chris started the fight, but no one believed him.* 그는 크리스가 먼저 싸움을 걸었다고 말했지만, 아무도 그의 말을 믿지 않았다. ✗DON'T SAY "... no one believed in him."✗ "... no one believed in him."이라고는 하지 않는다. **2** [T] to think that something is true, although you are not completely sure ‖ 완전히 확신하지는 않아도 어떤 것을 사실로 생각하다. …이라 믿다: *I believe (that) she'll be back on Monday.* 난 그녀가 월요일날 돌아올 것이라 믿는다. / *The jury believed him to be guilty.* 배심원들은 그가 유죄라고 판단했다. **3** [I] to have religious faith ‖ 종교적 믿음을 갖다

SPOKEN PHRASES

4 can't/don't believe sth said when you are very surprised or shocked ‖ 매우 놀라거나 충격을 받을 때 쓰여. …을 믿을 수 없다/믿지 않는다: *I can't believe you lied to me!* 네가 나에게 거짓말을 했다니 믿을 수가 없어! **5 would you believe it** said when you are surprised or slightly angry about something ‖ 놀라거나 약간 화가 날 때 쓰여. 믿을 수 있겠니[았습니까]: *Would you believe it, he even remembered my birthday!* 대체 믿을 수 있겠니, 그는 내 생일조차 잊어 버렸어! **6 believe it or not** said when you are going to say something that is true but surprising ‖ 놀라운 사실을 말할 때 쓰여. 믿거나 말거나: *Believe it or not, I kissed him.* 믿거나 말거나, 나는 그에게 키스했다.

believe in *phr v* [T] **1** to be sure that something or someone definitely exists ‖ 사물이나 사람이 분명히 존재한다고 확신하다. (…의 존재를) 믿다: *Do you believe in ghosts?* 유령의 존재를 믿습니까? **2** to think that someone or something is good, or to trust him, her, or it ‖ 사람이나 사물을 좋다고 생각하거나 믿다. 신뢰하다: *He believes in the democratic system.* 그는 민주주의 체제를 신뢰한다. / *If you believe in yourself, you can do anything.* 자신감이 있으면 당신은 무엇이든 할 수 있다.

be·liev·er /bəˈlivər/ *n* **1** someone who believes that a particular idea or thing is very good ‖ 특정 생각이나 일이 매우 좋다고 믿는 사람. 신봉자: *I'm a firm/great believer in healthy eating.* 나는 건강한 식사의 확고한[열렬한] 신봉자다. **2** someone who believes in a particular religion ‖ 특정 종교를 믿는 사람. 신자

be·lit·tle /bɪˈlɪtl/ *v* [T] FORMAL to say or do things that make someone or something seem less important ‖ 사람이나 사물의 중요성이 덜해 보이게 만드는 말이나 행동을 하다. 과소평가하다. 경시하다: *I don't want to belittle her efforts, but it's not enough.* 그녀의 노력을 경시하고 싶지는 않지만, 이건 불충분하다.

bell /bɛl/ *n* **1** a hollow metal object shaped like a cup that makes a sound when it is hit by a piece of metal that hangs down inside it ‖ 안쪽에 달린 금속 조각이 부딪쳐 소리를 내는 컵처럼 생긴 속이 빈 금속 물체. 종: *church bells* 교회 종 / *The bell rang for school to start.* 종소리가 수업의 시작을 알렸다. **2** an electronic piece of equipment that makes a noise as a signal or warning ‖ 신호나 경고로 소리를 내는 전자 장치. 벨: *We ran out of the classroom as soon as the bell rang.* 벨이 울리자마자 우리는 교실에서 뛰쳐나왔다. **3 alarm/warning bells** something that makes you realize that there may be a problem with something you are doing ‖ 진행 중인 일에 문제의 가능성을 알리는 것. 경보/경고

벨 —see also **ring a bell** (RING²)

bell bot·toms /ˈ. ˌ../ n [plural] a pair of pants with legs that are wide at the bottom ‖ 다리 끝자락의 통이 넓은 바지. 나팔바지. 판탈롱

bel·lig·er·ent /bəˈlɪdʒərənt/ adj ready to fight or argue ‖ 싸우거나 논쟁할 태세가 된. 호전[전투]적인 – **belligerence** n [U]

bel·low /ˈbɛloʊ/ v [I, T] to shout something in a very loud low voice ‖ 매우 크고 낮은 음성으로 소리지르다. 고함치다. 포효하다

bell pep·per /ˌ. ˈ../ n ⇨ PEPPER¹

bel·ly /ˈbɛli/ n INFORMAL 1 your stomach, or the part of your body between your chest and the top of your legs ‖ 위(부분), 또는 가슴과 다리 상부 사이의 신체 부분. 배. 복부 2 **go belly up** to fail ‖ 실패하다. 도산하다: *The store went belly up in 1969.* 그 가게는 1969년에 도산했다.

belly but·ton /ˈ.. ˌ../ n INFORMAL the small hollow or raised place in the middle of your stomach ‖ 배 중앙의 작은 구멍이나 불룩 튀어나온 부분. 배꼽 —see picture at BODY

be·long /bɪˈlɔŋ/ v [I] 1 to be in the right place or situation ‖ 마땅한 장소나 상황에 있다. 속하다. 어울리다: *Please put the chair back where it belongs.* 의자를 원래 있던 곳에 가져다 놓으세요. / *Books like that don't belong in the classroom.* 그런 책들은 교실에 있어서는 안 된다. 2 to feel happy and comfortable in a place, or with a group of people ‖ 어떤 곳에 있거나 일단의 사람들과 함께 있을 때 행복해 하다. 편안함을 느끼다: *I'm going back to Colorado where I belong.* 내집 같은 곳, 콜로라도로 돌아갈 것이다.

belong to phr v [T] 1 [**belong to** sth] to be a member of a group or organization ‖ 단체나 기관의 구성원이다. …에 속하다: *Mary and her husband belong to the yacht club.* 메리와 그녀 남편은 요트 클럽 소속이다. 2 [**belong to** sb] to be the property of someone ‖ 어떤 사람의 소유물이다: *Who does this umbrella belong to?* 이 우산은 누구의 것입니까?

be·long·ings /bɪˈlɔŋɪŋz/ n [plural] the things that you own, especially things that you are carrying with you ‖ 소유하는 물건, 특히 지니고 있는 물건. 소지품

be·loved /bɪˈlʌvd, bɪˈlʌvɪd/ adj LITERARY loved very much ‖ 아주 많이 사랑받는 – **beloved** n [singular]

be·low¹ /bɪˈloʊ/ prep 1 in a lower place or position than something, or on a lower level than something ‖ 어떤 것보다 낮은 곳이나 위치에, 또는 어떤 것보다 낮은 수준에. …의 아래에: *Can you read the writing below the picture?* 사진 아래 글을 읽어 주시겠어요? / *A corporal is below a captain in rank.* 계급상 상병은 대위보다 아래이다. 2 less than a particular number, amount etc. ‖ 특정한 수나 양보다 더 적은. …의 이하의: *It was 20° below zero outside.* 바깥은 영하 20도였다. / *Sales for this year are well below last year's.* 올해 판매량은 작년보다 훨씬 못하다. —compare UNDER¹

be·low² adv 1 in a lower place or position, or on a lower level ‖ 더 낮은 곳[위치, 수준]에. 아래(쪽)에: *Jake lives in the apartment below.* 제이크는 아래층 아파트에 산다. 2 less than a particular number ‖ 특정한 수보다 적게. 이하로: *It was 10° below outside.* (=10° below zero in temperature) 바깥은 영하 10도였다. 3 on a later page, or lower on the same page ‖ 페이지 후반이나 같은 페이지의 아래쪽에: *For more information, see below.* 더 많은 정보를 알려면 아래를 참조하세요.

belt¹ /bɛlt/ n 1 a band of leather, cloth etc. that you wear around your waist ‖ 허리에 두르는 가죽·천 등으로 만든 띠. 혁대. 벨트 2 a circular band of material such as rubber that moves parts of a machine ‖ 기계 부품을 움직이는, 고무 등으로 된 회전띠. 벨트: *The car's fan belt is loose.* 자동차의 팬 벨트가 느슨하다. 3 a large area of land that has particular qualities ‖ 특정한 속성을 지닌 넓은 지역. 지대. 벨트: *the farm belt states* (=states with lots of farms) 농장 지대(로 이루어진) 주(州)들 —see also SEAT BELT

belt² v [T] INFORMAL 1 to hit someone or something hard ‖ 사람이나 사물을 세게 치다 2 also **belt** sth ↔ **out** to sing a song loudly ‖ 큰 소리로 노래부르다

belt·way /ˈbɛltˌweɪ/ n **the Beltway a)** a road that goes around a city in order to keep traffic away from the center ‖ 중심부의 교통을 분산시키기 위해 도시를 우회하는 도로. 순환 도로 **b)** a group of people in large US cities, who are involved in government ‖ 미국 대도시에서 정부와 관련된 일을 하는 일단의 사람들: *a discussion inside/outside the Beltway* 정부 내부[외부] 관계자의 토론

be·mused /bɪˈmyuzd/ adj slightly confused ‖ 약간 혼란스러운. 멍한

bench¹ /bɛntʃ/ n 1 a long seat for two

or more people, for sitting on outdoors ‖ 두 명 이상의 사람들이 야외에서 앉을 수 있는 긴 의자. 벤치 **2 the bench a)** the job of a judge in a court ‖ 법원 판사직: *He was appointed to the bench in 1974.* 그는 1974년에 판사직에 임명되었다. **b)** the place where a judge sits in a court ‖ 법정에서 판사가 앉는 자리. 법관석. 판사석

bench² *v* [T] to make a sports player stay out of a game for a period of time ‖ 일정 시간 동안 운동 선수를 시합에서 빼다. 후보 선수로 벤치에서 대기하다

bench·mark /'bɛntʃmɑrk/ *n* something used as a standard to measure another number, rate, level etc. against ‖ 다른 수·비율·수준 등을 계측하는 데 대한 기준이 되는 것. 기준: *7.5% is the current benchmark set by banks for loan rates.* 은행이 정한 현행 대출이율 기준은 7.5%이다.

bend¹ /bɛnd/ *v* **bent, bent, bending** [I, T] **1** to move a part of your body so that it is no longer straight or so that you are no longer standing upright ‖ 더 이상 곧거나 바로 선 자세가 되지 않도록 신체 일부를 움직이다. 굽다. 굽히다: *He bent down/over to tie his shoelace.* 그는 신발끈을 묶으려고 구부렸다. / *Bend your knees slightly.* 무릎을 약간 구부려 보세요. **2** to make something straight have a curved shape, or to become curved in shape ‖ 곧은 사물을 굽은 모양이 되게 하거나 굽은 모양이 되다. 휘게 하다. 휘어지다: *Heavy rains had bent the wheat to the ground.* 폭우 때문에 밀이 땅에 쓰러졌다. **3 bend over backwards** to try very hard to help ‖ 돕기 위해 매우 애쓰다: *The neighbors bent over backwards to help when we moved into the house.* 우리가 그 집으로 이사할 때 이웃 사람들이 도와 주려고 많이 애썼다. **4 bend the rules** to allow someone to do something that is not normally allowed ‖ 보통 금지된 일을 누군가에게 하도록 허락하다. 규칙을 왜곡하다

bend² *n* a curve in something, especially a road or river ‖ 특히 길이나 강 등의 휘어진 부분. 굽은 곳. 굽이: *The creek goes around a bend by the farm.* 시내가 농장을 끼고 굽이쳐 흐른다.

be·neath¹ /bɪ'niθ/ *prep* FORMAL **1** under or below something ‖ 어떤 것의 밑이나 아래에 있는: *the warm sand beneath her feet* 그녀 발 밑의 따뜻한 모래 **2** not good enough for someone ‖ 누군가에게 충분히 좋지 않은. …에 미치지 않는: *She seemed to think that talking to us was beneath her.* 그녀는 우리와의 대화를 수준 이하로 생각하는 것처럼 보였다.

beneath² *adv* under or below something ‖ 어떤 것의 밑이나 아래에: *He stood on the bridge, looking at the water beneath.* 그는 밑에 흐르는 물을 바라보며 다리 위에 서 있었다.

ben·e·dic·tion /ˌbɛnə'dɪkʃən/ *n* a prayer that asks God to protect and help someone ‖ 신에게 누구를 보호하고 도와 달라고 비는 기도. 축복의 기도. 축도

ben·e·fac·tor /'bɛnəˌfæktɚ/ *n* FORMAL someone who gives money to someone else or helps him/her ‖ 남에게 돈을 기부하거나 돕는 사람. 후원자. 은인

ben·e·fi·cial /ˌbɛnə'fɪʃəl/ *adj* good or useful ‖ 좋거나 득이 되는. 유용한. 유익한: *The agreement will be beneficial to both groups.* 그 합의는 두 단체 모두에게 유익할 것이다.

ben·e·fi·ci·ar·y /ˌbɛnə'fɪʃi,ɛri, -'fɪʃəri/ *n* FORMAL **1** someone who gets an advantage because of something ‖ 어떤 것 때문에 이득을 얻는 사람. 수혜자: *Inner city residents will be the chief beneficiaries (=will get the most advantages) of this policy.* 이 정책으로 도심 거주자들이 가장 큰 혜택을 받을 것이다. **2** someone who gets money when someone dies ‖ 어떤 사람이 죽었을 때 돈을 받는 사람. (유산의) 수령인

ben·e·fit¹ /'bɛnəfɪt/ *n* **1** money or help that you get from something such as insurance or the government, or as part of your job ‖ 보험 회사나 정부, 또는 직장에서 받는 돈이나 도움. 혜택. 수당: *The company provides medical benefits.* 그 회사는 의료 수당을 지급한다. / *social security benefits* 사회 복지 수당 **2** [C, U] something that gives you an advantage, that helps you, or that has a good effect ‖ 득 또는 도움이 되거나 좋은 효과가 있는 것. 이득. 이점: *The aid program has brought lasting benefits to the area.* 원조 프로그램은 그 지역에 지속적인 이득을 가져왔다. / *Liu Han translated what he had said for my benefit.* (=in order to help me) 리우 한은 나를 위해서 자기가 한 말을 통역해 주었다. **3** a performance, concert etc. that is done in order to make money for a CHARITY (=organization that helps people) ‖ 자선 단체의 모금을 위한 공연·콘서트 등 **4 give sb the benefit of the doubt** to believe someone even though it is possible that s/he is lying ‖ 거짓말일지라도 어떤 사람을 믿다. 의심스러운 점을 선의로 해석하다

benefit² *v* **-fited, -fiting,** *also* **-fitted, -fitting 1** [T] to help someone, or to be useful to him/her ‖ 남을 돕거나 남에게 득이 되다: *These policy changes mainly benefit cities in the South.* 이러한 정책 변화는 주로 남부 도시에 이득이 된다. **2** [I] to get an advantage or help from something ‖ 어떤 것에서 (이)득을 보거나 도움을 얻다: *The whole nation benefits by/from having skilled and educated workers.* 국가 전체가 숙련되고 교육받은 근로자들을 보유하여 득을 보고 있다.

be·nev·o·lent /bə'nɛvələnt/ *adj* FORMAL kind, generous, and helpful ‖ 친절하고 관대하며 도움이 되는. 자비심[인정] 많은

be·nign /bɪ'naɪn/ *adj* **1** TECHNICAL not likely to hurt you or cause CANCER ‖ 해를 끼치거나 암을 유발할 가능성이 없는. 양성의: *a benign tumor* 양성 종양 **2** FORMAL kind and unlikely to harm anyone ‖ 친절하며 누구에게도 해를 끼칠 것 같지 않은. 인자한. 자상한 —compare MALIGNANT

bent¹ /bɛnt/ the past tense and PAST PARTICIPLE of BEND ‖ bend의 과거·과거 분사형

bent² *adj* **1 be bent on** to be determined to do something or have something ‖ 어떤 것을 하거나 갖기로 결심하다: *Mendez was bent on getting a better job.* 멘데즈는 더 나은 직업을 구하기로 결심했다. **2** curved and no longer flat or straight ‖ 휘어져서 더 이상 평평하거나 곧지 않은. 굽은: *The grass was bent where he'd been lying on it.* 그가 누워 있었던 잔디가 짓눌려져 있었다. **3 bent out of shape** SPOKEN angry or annoyed ‖ 화나거나 성가신. 짜증나는: *Hey, don't get all bent out of shape!* 이봐! 그렇게 화내지 마!

bent

bent³ *n* [singular] a natural skill or ability ‖ 천성적인 재주나 능력. 소질: *Rebecca has an artistic bent.* 레베카는 예술적 소질이 있다.

be·queath /bɪ'kwiθ, bɪ'kwið/ *v* [T] FORMAL to arrange for someone to get something that belongs to you after your death ‖ 남에게 사후에 자신의 소유물을 갖도록 조치하다. …에게 유증하다

be·quest /bɪ'kwɛst/ *n* FORMAL money or property that you BEQUEATH to someone ‖ 어떤 사람에게 유증(遺贈)하는 돈이나 재산. 유산

be·rate /bə'reɪt/ *v* [T] FORMAL to speak angrily to someone because s/he has done something wrong ‖ 어떤 사람에게 일을 잘못하여 화를 내며 말하다. …을 호되게 꾸짖다

be·reaved¹ /bə'rivd/ *adj* FORMAL having had someone you love die ‖ 사랑하는 사람이 죽은. 사별한. 여읜 — **bereavement** *n* [C, U]

bereaved² *n* **the bereaved** the person or people whose friend or relative has died ‖ 친구나 친지와 사별(死別)한 사람(들). 유가족

be·reft /bə'rɛft/ *adj* FORMAL completely without something ‖ 어떤 것이 전혀 없는. (…을) 잃은[빼앗긴]: *bereft of all hope* 모든 희망이 사라진

be·ret /bə'reɪ/ *n* a soft round hat that is almost flat ‖ 부드럽고 밋밋한 둥근 모자. 베레모

ber·ry /'bɛri/ *n* one of several types of small soft fruits with very small seeds ‖ 매우 작은 씨가 있는 작고 물렁한 여러 종류의 과일 중 하나. 베리

ber·serk /bə'sɔk, -'zɔk/ *adj* **go berserk** INFORMAL to become very angry and violent in a crazy way ‖ 제정신이 아닌 상태로 매우 화가 나고 폭력적이 되다. 광포해지다: *The guy went berserk and started hitting Paul.* 그 남자는 광포해지더니 폴을 때리기 시작했다.

berth /bəθ/ *n* **1** a place to sleep on a train or boat ‖ 열차나 배의 잠자는 곳. 침대. 침상 **2** a place near land where a ship can be kept ‖ 배를 세워 두는 육지 근처의 장소. 정박지

be·set /bɪ'sɛt/ *v* **beset, beset, besetting** [T] FORMAL to make someone have a lot of trouble or problems ‖ 남에게 많은 골칫거리나 문제 등을 갖게 하다. …을 괴롭히다[시달리다 하다]: *The family was beset by financial difficulties.* 그 가족은 돈에 쪼들렸다.

be·side /bɪ'saɪd/ *prep* **1** next to or very close to someone or something ‖ 사람이나 사물의 옆이나 아주 가까이에: *Gary sat down beside me.* 게리는 내 옆에 앉았다. / *a cabin beside the lake* 호숫가의 오두막 **2** used in order to compare two people or things ‖ 두 명 또는 두 가지를 비교하는 데 쓰여. …과 비교하면: *Pat looked big and clumsy beside her sister.* 패트는 언니에 비하여 크고 볼품없어 보였다. **3 be beside the point** to not be important compared to something else ‖ 다른 것과 비교하여 중요하지 않다: *"I'm not hungry." "That's beside the point, you need to eat!"* "난 배고프지 않

아." "그건 중요한 게 아니야, 넌 먹어야
해!" **4 be beside yourself (with)** to feel
a particular emotion very strongly ‖ 특정
한 감정을 격하게 느끼다. 제정신이 아니
다: *The boy was beside himself with
fear.* 그 소년은 심한 공포를 느꼈다.

be·sides¹ /bɪˈsaɪdz/ *adv* **1** SPOKEN said
when giving another reason ‖ 다른 이유
를 들 때에 쓰여. 그리고 또: *I wanted to
help her out. Besides, I needed the
money.* 난 그녀를 돕고 싶었어. 그리고 돈
도 필요했고. **2** in addition to ‖ 그 이외에.
게다가: *Besides going to college, she
works 15 hours a week.* 대학에 다니는
것말고도 그녀는 주당 15시간 일한다.

besides² *prep* in addition to something
or someone ‖ 어떤 것이나 어떤 사람 이외
에도. …에 더하여: *Who's going to be
there besides David and me?* 데이비드와
나 이외에 누가 거기에 갑니까?

USAGE NOTE besides and except

Use **besides** to mean "in addition to
someone or something": *Is there
anything to drink besides coffee? /
Who is coming besides your parents?*
Except means that someone or
something is not included: *I
remembered to pack everything
except my toothbrush.*
besides는 "어떤 것에 더하여, 누구 이
외에도"를 의미한다: 커피 이외에 마실
것이 있나요? / 부모님 이외에 누가 오
십니까? **except**는 어떤 사람이나 사물
이 포함되지 않음을 의미한다: 나는 칫
솔을 제외하고는 잊지 않고 짐을 모두
쌌다.

---

be·siege /bɪˈsiːdʒ/ *v* [T] FORMAL **1
besieged by** surrounded by a lot of
people ‖ 많은 사람들에게 둘러싸인. 포위
된: *a rock star besieged by fans* 팬들에
둘러싸인 록스타 **2** to send a lot of
letters, ask a lot of questions, or annoy
someone often ‖ 많은 편지를 보내거나 수
많은 질문을 하거나, 또는 종종 남을 성가
시게 하다. …을 퍼붓다[괴롭히다]: *The
radio station was besieged by letters of
complaint.* 그 라디오 방송국에 불만 사항
을 적은 편지들이 쇄도했다. **3** to
surround a place with an army ‖ 군대가
장소를 둘러싸다. 포위하다

best¹ /bɛst/ *adj* [the superlative of
"good"] "good"의 최상급] better in
quality, skill etc. than anyone or
anything else ‖ 자질이나 기술 등에서 다
른 어떤 사람이나 사물보다 더 나은. 최상
의. 최고의: *the best player on the team*

팀의 최우수 선수 / *What's the best way
to get to El Paso?* 엘 파소로 가는 가장 좋
은 방법이 무엇입니까? / *It's one of the
best books I've ever read.* 그것은 내가
이제껏 읽은 최고의 책 중의 하나다. / *my
best friend* (=the one I know and like
the most) 내 가장 친한 친구

best² *adv* [the superlative of "well"]
"well"의 최상급] **1** to the greatest
degree ‖ 최상의 정도로. 가장 잘[훌륭하
게]: *Helene knows him best.* 헬렌이 그를
가장 잘 안다. / *Which song do you like
best?* 어떤 노래를 가장 좋아하니? **2** in a
way that is better than any other ‖ 다른
어떤 것보다 낫게. 최고로. 가장 잘: *It
works best if you oil it thoroughly first.*
먼저 그것에 속속들이 기름칠을 하면 작동
이 가장 잘 된다.

best³ *n* [singular] **1** someone or
something that is better than any others
‖ 다른 어느 것보다 더 좋은 사람이나 사
물. 가장 좋은[우수한, 훌륭한] 사람[사
물]: *Which stereo is the best?* 어떤 스테
레오가 가장 좋은 것입니까? **2** a situation
or result that is better than any other
you could achieve ‖ 달성할 수 있는 다른
어느 것보다 나은 상황이나 결과. 최고(의
상태): *All parents want the best for
their children.* 모든 부모들은 자기 자식
이 최고가 되기를 바란다. **3 do your
best** to try very hard to achieve
something ‖ 어떤 것을 이루려고 매우 열
심히 노력하다. 최선을 다하다: *I did my
best, but I still didn't pass.* 나는 최선을
다했지만, 아직 통과하지 못했다. **4 at
best** used in order to emphasize that
something is not very good, even when
you consider it in the best possible way
‖ 어떤 것에 대해 가능한 한 가장 좋게 생
각해 봐도 그다지 좋지 않음을 강조하는
데에 쓰여. 기껏해야. 고작: *At best, sales
have been good but not great.* 판매량은
기껏해야 괜찮은 수준이지, 대단한 것은
아니다. **5 at your/its best** performing
as well or as effectively as you are able
to ‖ 할 수 있는 만큼 가장 잘, 또는 효과적
으로 해내는. 최고의 상태인. 진가를 가장
잘 발휘하는: *The movie shows
Hollywood at its best.* 그 영화는 헐리우
드를 가장 잘 보여 준다. **6 make the
best of sth** to accept a bad situation
and do what you can to make it better ‖
안 좋은 상황을 받아들여 이를 개선하기
위해 할 수 있는 일을 하다. …을 가장 잘
이용하다: *It's not going to be fun, but
we'll have to make the best of it.* 재미있
지는 않겠지만 어떻게든 해 봐야 될 거야.
7 be for the best to be the best thing

to do or happen, although you do not like it ‖ 비록 마음에 들지는 않지만 하거나 발생하기에 가장 나은 것이 되다. 잘 된 일이다: *She's upset that they broke up, but it's probably for the best.* 그들이 헤어진 것에 그녀는 매우 화가 났지만, 아마 (따지고 보면) 잘 된 일일 것이다. — see study note on page 931

best⁴ *v* [T] LITERARY to defeat someone ‖ 어떤 사람을 이기다

bes·tial /'bɛstʃəl, 'bis-/ *adj* behaving like an animal, especially in a cruel way ‖ 특히 잔인하게 동물처럼 행동하는. 짐승[야수] 같은 – **bestiality** /ˌbɛstʃi'æləti, ˌbis-/ *n* [U]

best man /ˌ. './ *n* [singular] the man at a wedding who stands beside and helps the man who is getting married ‖ 결혼식에서 신랑 곁에 서서 도와주는 남자. 신랑 들러리

be·stow /bɪ'stoʊ/ *v* [T] FORMAL to give someone something, especially something important ‖ 누군가에게 특히 중요한 것을 주다. 수여하다

best·sell·er /ˌbɛst'sɛlɚ/ *n* a new book that a lot of people have bought ‖ 많은 사람들이 구입한 신간 서적. 베스트셀러 – **best-selling** *adj*

bet¹ /bɛt/ *v* **bet, bet, betting** [I, T] to risk money on the result of a race, game etc. ‖ 경주·경기 등의 결과에 돈을 걸다. 내기하다: *Brad bet 50 bucks on the Bears to win.* 브래드는 베어스 팀이 승리한다는 데에 50달러를 걸었다. / *Dad bet Mom ten dollars that I wouldn't pass my driver's test.* 아빠는 내가 운전 면허 시험에서 떨어질 것이라는 데에 엄마와 10달러 내기를 했다.

SPOKEN PHRASES

1 I/I'll bet a) said when you think something is true or likely to happen 어떤 것이 사실이거나 일어날 것 같다고 생각할 때에 쓰여. 틀림없이 (…이다): *I'll bet that made her mad!* 틀림없이 그녀는 그 일 때문에 화났을 거야! / *I bet it will rain tomorrow.* 내일은 틀림없이 비가 올 것이다. **b)** said in order to show that you agree with someone or understand how s/he feels ‖ 남에게 동의하거나 남의 감정을 이해한다는 것을 표현하는 데에 쓰여. 그러겠지: *"I was furious." "I bet you were!"* "난 몹시 화가 났어." "아무렴, 그랬겠지!" **c)** said in order to show you do not believe someone ‖ 남을 믿지 않는다는 것을 나타내는 데에 쓰여. 설마 그럴라고: *"I was really worried about you."*

"Yeah, I'll bet." "난 정말 네 걱정 많이 했어." "설마, 그랬겠어." **2 you bet (your life)!** said in order to agree with someone, or to say that you are definitely going to do something ‖ 누군가에게 동의하거나 반드시 어떤 것을 할 것이라고 말하는 데에 쓰여. 물론, 틀림없이 (…이다): *"Are you coming along?" "You bet!"* "너 함께 갈 거니?" "물론이지!"

bet² *n* **1** an agreement to risk money on the result of a race, game etc. ‖ 경주·경기 등에 돈을 건다는 약속. 내기: *Higgins had a bet on the World Series.* 히긴스는 월드 시리즈에 돈을 걸었다[내기했다]. **2** the money that you risk ‖ 건 돈. 내기돈: *a $10 bet* 10달러의 내기돈 **3 your best bet** SPOKEN said in order to give someone advice about the best thing to do ‖ 어떤 사람에게 가장 하기 좋은 것에 대해 조언하는 데에 쓰여. (네가 할 수 있는) 최선의 방법[길]: *Your best bet would be to take Highway 9.* 9번 고속도로를 타는 것이 가장 좋을 것이다. **4 a good bet** something that is likely to be useful or successful ‖ 유용하거나 성공적으로 보이는 것. 성공적인(괜찮은) 것: *The earrings seemed like a good bet for a birthday present.* 생일 선물로 귀걸이가 괜찮아 보였다. **5 a safe bet** something that seems almost certain ‖ 거의 확실해 보이는 것: *It's a pretty safe bet that the Arnolds will be at that party.* 아놀드네가 그 파티에 오리라는 것은 거의 확실하다.

bet·cha /'bɛtʃə/ SPOKEN NONSTANDARD a short form of "bet you" ‖ "bet you"의 단축형: *I betcha I can run faster than you.* 내가 너보다 더 빨리 뛸 수 있다는 것을 장담한다.

be·tray /bɪ'treɪ/ *v* [T] **1** to be disloyal to a friend, your country etc., for example by telling a secret ‖ 예를 들어 비밀을 누설함으로써 친구·조국 등에 불충하다. 배신[배반]하다: *Kaplan went to jail rather than betray his friends.* 카플란은 친구들을 배신하기보다 감옥에 갔다. **2** to show an emotion you were trying to keep hidden ‖ 숨기려 애써 온 감정을 나타내다. 무심코 드러내다: *Keith's voice betrayed his nervousness.* 키스의 목소리에 초조함이 드러났다.

be·tray·al /bɪ'treɪəl/ *n* [C, U] the act of betraying your country, a friend etc. ‖ 조국·친구 등에 대한 배신 행위. 배반

bet·ter¹ /'bɛtɚ/ *adj* **1** [the comparative of "good" "good"의 비교급] higher in quality, or more useful, suitable, interesting etc. than something or someone else || 다른 사물이나 사람보다 더 고급의[더 유용한, 더 적합한, 더 흥미 있는]. …보다 좋은[나은]: *He's applying for a better job.* 그는 더 나은 직장을 구하고 있다. / *The weather is a lot better than it was last week.* 날씨는 지난 주보다 훨씬 더 좋다. / *The Mexican place across the street has much better food.* 길 건너에 있는 멕시코 식당에는 훨씬 더 고급 음식이 있다. / *I'll feel better if I can talk to someone about this.* 이것에 대해서 누군가에게 얘기할 수 있다면 기분이 더 나아질 텐데. **2** [the comparative of "well" "well"의 비교급] **a)** less sick or painful than before || 이전보다 덜 아프거나 덜 고통스러운. 차도가 있는: *He had the flu, but he's much better now.* 그는 감기에 걸렸었지만 지금은 훨씬 괜찮아졌다. / *I hope your sore throat gets better.* 너의 인후염이 낫길 바래. / *Dana's feeling a little better since he started taking the penicillin.* 페니실린을 쓰기 시작한 이후로 다나는 약간 더 나아진 것을 느끼고 있다. **b)** completely well again after being sick || 앓고 난 후 완전히 다시 나은. 회복한: *I don't think you should go swimming until you're better.* 나는 네가 완전히 회복할 때까지 수영하러 가서는 안 된다고 생각한다. **3 get better** to improve || 향상되다. 좋아지다: *Her tennis game is getting a lot better.* 그녀의 테니스 실력은 훨씬 더 향상되고 있다. **4 have seen better days** INFORMAL to be in a bad condition || 나쁜 상태가 되다. 좋은 시절[전성기]이 지나다: *The sofa had definitely seen better days.* 그 소파는 확실히 낡았다.

better² *adv* [the comparative of "well" "well"의 비교급] **1** to a higher degree; more || 더 높은 수준으로; (더욱) 많이: *Which one do you like better?* 어느 것이 더 좋니? / *Marilyn knows New York a lot better than I do.* 마릴린은 뉴욕에 대해서 나보다 훨씬 더 많이 안다. **2** in a better way || 더 좋게. 더 낫게: *Tina speaks French better than her sister.* 티나는 그녀의 동생보다 프랑스어를 더 잘한다. **3 better late than never** used in order to say that it is better for something to happen late rather than not happen at all || 어떤 일이 전혀 일어나지 않으니 늦더라도 일어나는 편이 낫다고 말하는 데에 쓰여. 늦더라도 하는 게 나은 **4 the sooner/bigger etc., the better** used in order to emphasize that something should happen as soon as possible, that it should be as big as possible etc. || 어떤 것이 가능한 한 빨리 일어나거나 가능한 한 커야 한다고 강조하는 데에 쓰여. 빠를수록/클수록 더 좋다: *She liked hot baths – the hotter the better.* 그녀는 온수욕을 좋아했는데, 물이 뜨거울수록 더 좋아했다. —see picture on page 931

SPOKEN PHRASES

5 had better (do sth) a) used in order to say that you or someone else should do something || 자신이나 다른 사람이 어떤 것을 해야 한다고 말하는 데 쓰여. …하는 편이 낫다: *It's getting late, you had better get changed.* 늦어지고 있으니 갈아 타는 것이 좋겠다. **b)** said when threatening someone || 남을 협박할 때에 쓰여. …하는 것이 좋을 것이다: *You'd better not tell Dad about this.* 아빠에게 이것을 말하지 않는 게 좋을 거야. **6 be better (to do sth)** said when giving advice about what someone should do || 남에게 해야 할 일에 대해 충고해 줄 때 쓰여. …하는 편이 낫다: *It's better if she doesn't stand for too long.* 그녀는 너무 오랫동안 서 있지 않는 것이 좋다.

—see also BETTER OFF

better³ *n* **1 get the better of sb a)** if a feeling gets the better of you, you do not control it when you should || 감정을 통제하지 못하다. 감정을 억누르지 못하다: *Finally, his curiosity got the better of him and he read Dee's letter.* 결국 그는 호기심을 억누르지 못하고 디의 편지를 읽었다. **b)** to defeat someone || 남을 패배시키다: *Jack usually manages to get the better of his opponents.* 잭은 대개 상대를 어떻게든 패배시킨다. **2 for the better** in a way that improves the situation || 상황을 개선시키는 방법으로. 더 나은 쪽으로: *Smaller classes are definitely a change for the better.* 학급의 규모가 더 작아지는 것은 확실히 더 나은 쪽으로의 변화이다.

better⁴ *v* [T] FORMAL to achieve something that is higher in quality, amount etc. than something else || 다른 것보다 질적·양적으로 더 나은 것을 성취하다. …을 개선하다[향상시키다] – **betterment** *n* [U]

better off /ˌ.. '.../ *adj* **1** more successful, richer, or having more advantages than you did before || 이전보다 더 성공한[부유해진, 많은 이점을 가진]. 더 좋은 상태인. 더 잘 사는: *The* *more prepared you are, the better off you'll be.* 더 많이 준비할수록 더 성공할 것이다. / *Most businesses in the area are better off than they were 10 years ago.* 그 지역의 대개의 사업체들은 10년 전보다 더 나아졌다. **2 be better off doing sth** SPOKEN said when giving advice about what someone should do ‖ 남에게 반드시 해야 할 것에 대해 충고할 때에 쓰여. …해야 한다: *You're better off leaving early.* (=should leave early) 너는 일찍 떠나야 한다.

bet·ween¹ /bɪ'twin/ *prep* **1** in or into the space or time that separates two things, people, events etc. ‖ 두 개의 사물·사람·사건 등을 가르는 공간이나 시간 속에 또는 속으로. …의 사이에: *Jay was sitting between Kate and Lisa.* 제이는 케이트와 리사 사이에 앉아 있었다. / *You know I don't want you to eat between meals.* 네가 간식 먹는 것을 내가 싫어하는 거 알잖아. —see also IN-BETWEEN **2** used in order to show a range of amounts, distances, times etc. ‖ 양·거리·시간의 범위를 나타내는 데에 쓰여. …사이에: *Why don't you come over between seven and eight?* 7시에서 8시 사이에 오는 게 어때? / *The project will cost between 10 and 12 million dollars.* 그 프로젝트는 천만 달러에서 천 이백만 달러의 비용이 들 것이다. ✗DON'T SAY "*between 10 to 12 million dollars.*"✗ "*between 10 to 12 million dollars*"라고 는 하지 않는다. **3** used in order to show that something is divided or shared by two people, places, or things ‖ 어떤 것이 두 사람[장소, 물건]에 의해 분할되거나 공유되는 것을 나타내는 데에 쓰여. …사이에. 모두 합하여: *We had about two loads of laundry between us.* 우리에게는 세탁물이 거의 두 짐이나 있었다. / *Linda and Dave split a milkshake between them.* 린다와 데이브는 밀크셰이크를 나누어 먹었다. **4** used in order to show a relationship between two people, things, events etc. ‖ 두 사람·사물·사건 사이의 관계를 나타내는 데에 쓰여. …의 사이에: *What's the difference between the two computers?* 두 컴퓨터 사이의 차이가 뭐냐? / *Trade relations between the countries have improved.* 두 나라간의 무역 관계는 개선되었다. **5** used in order to show how two places are connected ‖ 두 장소가 어떻게 연결되는지를 나타내는 데에 쓰여. …간의: *the highway between Fresno and Visalia* 프레스노와 비살리아 간[사이를 잇는] 고속도로 **6 between you and me** SPOKEN

said before you tell someone a secret or a private opinion ‖ 남에게 비밀이나 개인적인 생각을 말할 때에 쓰여. 우리끼리 이야기인데: *Between you and me, I thought she looked ugly.* 우리끼리 이야기인데, 난 그녀가 못생겼다고 생각했어.

USAGE NOTE between and among

Use **between** to talk about being in the middle of two people, things, times etc.: *They arrived between 2:30 and 3:00.* Use **among** to talk about being in the middle of three or more people, things etc.: *I found this old photo among her letters.* 두 사람·사물·시간 사이의 일에 대해 언급할 때 **between**을 쓴다: 그들은 두 시 반에서 세 시 사이에 도착했다. 셋 이상의 사람·사물 사이의 일에 대해 언급할 때 **among**을 쓴다: 그녀의 편지 속에서 이 오래 된 사진을 발견했다.

---

between² *adv* in or into the space that separates two things, people etc., or in or into the time that separates two events ‖ 두 사물·사람을 떼어 놓는 공간 속에(서), 두 사건을 구분짓는 시간 속에 (서). 사이에(서): *two yards with a fence between* 사이에 울타리가 쳐진 두 개의 마당 —see also IN-BETWEEN

bev·eled /'bɛvəld/ *adj* beveled glass or wood has edges that slope slightly ‖ 유리나 나무의 가장자리가 약간 경사진. 비스듬한. 사면으로 된

bev·er·age /'bɛvrɪdʒ, 'bɛvərɪdʒ/ *n* FORMAL a drink ‖ 음료: *alcoholic beverages* 알코올성 음료

bev·y /'bɛvi/ *n* **a bevy of** a large group, especially of people ‖ 특히 사람의 큰 집단. 무리. 떼: *a bevy of artists* 한 무리의 예술가들

be·ware /bɪ'wɛr/ *v* [I, T] used in order to warn someone to be careful ‖ 남에게 조심하라고 경고하는 데에 쓰여. 조심[경계]하다: *Beware of the dog!* 개조심!

be·wil·dered /bɪ'wɪldərd/ *adj* very confused and not sure what to do or think ‖ 매우 혼란스러워서 무엇을 하거나 생각해야 할지 확신하지 못하는. 당혹한. 당황한 —**bewilderment** *n* [U]

be·wil·der·ing /bɪ'wɪldərɪŋ/ *adj* making you feel very confused ‖ 몹시 혼란스럽게 하는. 당혹케 하는: *a bewildering number of choices* 갈피를 잡을 수 없게 하는 많은 대안들

be·witched /bɪ'wɪtʃt/ *adj* so interested in or attracted by someone or something that you cannot think clearly

‖ 사람이나 사물에 대단히 흥미를 느끼거나 매료되어 명확하게 생각할 수 없는. 넋을 잃은. 홀린 – **bewitching** *adj*

be·yond¹ /bɪˈyɑnd/ *prep* **1** on or to the farther side of something ‖ 어떤 것의 저편에[으로]. …의 너머에[로]: *The ocean was beyond the dunes.* 바다는 모래 언덕 너머에 있었다. **2** not within someone's ability or skill ‖ 사람의 능력이나 기술의 범위 안에 있지 않는. (…이)미치지 않는: *an apple just beyond my reach* 내 손이 닿을락 말락 하는 곳에 있는 사과 / *Chemistry was beyond my understanding.* 화학은 내가 이해하기에는 벅찼다. **3** used when something is not possible ‖ 어떤 것이 가능하지 않을 때에 쓰여. …할 수 없을 정도의: *In just six years, the town had changed beyond all recognition.* (=it could not be recognized) 불과 6년 만에 그 도시는 알아볼 수 없을 정도로 변했다. / *I think that this time the car is beyond repair.* (=it cannot be repaired) 이번에는 그 차는 수리할 수 없을 것 같다. **4** more than a particular amount, level, or limit ‖ 특정한 양[수준, 한계] 이상의. …보다 더 많이: *The population has grown beyond estimated levels.* 인구가 추정한 수준 이상으로 늘어났다. **5** later than a particular time, date etc. ‖ 특정한 시간·날짜보다 더 나중에. …을 지나서: *The ban has been extended beyond 1998.* 그 금지령은 1998년 이후에까지 연장되었다. **6 it's beyond me why/what etc.** SPOKEN said when you do not understand something ‖ 어떤 것을 이해하지 못할 때에 쓰여. 나로서는 알 수 없다: *It's beyond me why they ever got married at all.* 나는 그들이 도대체 왜 결혼을 했는지 모르겠다. **7** besides ‖ 그것 이외에(는): *Santa Fe doesn't have much industry beyond tourism.* 산타페는 관광 부분 이외의 산업은 많이 발달하지 않았다.

beyond² *adv* **1** on or to the farther side of something ‖ 어떤 것의 저편에 또는 저편으로: *a view from the mountains with the plains beyond* 산에서 본 그 너머 평원의 경치 **2** later than a particular time, date etc. ‖ 특정한 시간·날짜 등보다 나중에. 그 이후로: *planning for the year 2000 and beyond* 2000년과 그 이후를 위한 계획 수립

bias /ˈbaɪəs/ *n, plural* **biases** /ˈbaɪəsiz/ [C, U] an opinion about whether something is good or bad that influences how you deal with it ‖ 어떤 것을 다루는 데 영향을 주는 그것의 좋고 나

쁨에 대한 견해. 편견. 선입관: *We believe the court's decision reveals a bias against Hispanics.* 우리는 법원의 판결이 라틴 아메리카계 사람들에 대한 편견을 드러낸다고 생각한다. – **bias** *v* [T]

bi·ased /ˈbaɪəst/ *adj* **1** unfairly influenced by someone's opinion ‖ 남의 의견에 불공정하게 영향을 받은. 편견을 가진. 치우친: *a biased report* 편파적인 보도 **2** unfairly preferring one person or group over another ‖ 다른 쪽보다 한 사람이나 집단을 불공정하게 선호하는. 편애하는: *My mother liked mine best, but of course she's biased!* 어머니는 내가 하는 일은 뭐든지 제일 마음에 들어하셨는데 그것은 물론 편애였다! —opposite UNBIASED

bib /bɪb/ *n* a piece of cloth that you tie under a baby's chin to protect his/her clothes while s/he eats ‖ 아기들이 음식을 먹을 때 옷을 버리지 않도록 턱 밑에 묶어 주는 천 조각. 턱받이

bi·ble /ˈbaɪbəl/ *n* **1 the Bible** the holy book of the Christian religion ‖ 기독교의 성서. 성경(책) **2** a copy of this book ‖ 한 권의 성서 **3** a useful and important book on a particular subject ‖ 특정 분야의 유용하고 중요한 책. 권위 있는 서적: *This textbook is the medical student's bible.* 이 교재는 의대생들의 필독서이다.

bib·li·og·ra·phy /ˌbɪbliˈɑɡrəfi/ *n* a list of all the books and articles used in the preparation of another book, or a list of books and articles on a particular subject ‖ 다른 책의 준비에 쓰인 모든 책·논문 목록, 또는 특정 주제에 대한 책·논문 목록. 문헌[도서] 목록

bi·cen·ten·ni·al /ˌbaɪsɛnˈtɛniəl/ *n* the day or year exactly 200 years after an important event ‖ 어떤 중요한 사건이 있은 후 정확히 200년이 되는 날이나 해. 200주년 기념일: *The US had its bicentennial in 1976.* 1976년에 미국은 건국 200주년을 맞았다.

bi·ceps /ˈbaɪsɛps/ *n, plural* **biceps** the large muscle on the front of your upper arm ‖ 위팔의 앞쪽의 큰 근육. 이두박근

bick·er /ˈbɪkɚ/ *v* [I] to argue about something that is not very important ‖ 그다지 중요하지 않은 일로 논쟁하다. 말다툼하다: *The kids were bickering about/over who would sleep in the top bunk.* 그 아이들은 누가 침대의 꼭대기 층에서 잘 것인지를 놓고 말다툼을 하고 있었다.

bi·cy·cle¹ /ˈbaɪsɪkəl/ *n* a vehicle with two wheels that you ride by pushing the PEDALs with your feet ‖ 발로 페달을 밟으면서 타는 바퀴가 두 개 달린 탈것. 자전거

bicycle² *v* [I] ⇨ BIKE²

bid¹ /bɪd/ *n* **1** an offer to do some work for someone at a particular price ‖ 남에게 특정 가격에 어떤 일을 해준다는 제안. 입찰: *The company accepted the lowest bid for the project.* 그 회사는 그 프로젝트를 가장 낮은 입찰가에 낙찰시켰다. **2** an attempt to achieve or gain something ‖ 어떤 것을 성취하거나 얻으려는 시도. 노력: *Clinton's successful bid for the presidency in 1992* 1992년의 클린턴의 성공적인 대통령 선거 입후보 **3** an offer to pay a particular price for something ‖ 어떤 것에 대해 특정 값을 매긴다는 제안. 입찰(금). 매긴 값: *a bid of $50 for the plate* 그 접시를 50달러로 입찰함

bid² *v* **bid, bid, bidding** **1** [I, T] to offer to pay a particular price for something ‖ 어떤 것에 특정 값을 지불하기로 제안하다. (값을) 매기다: *Foreman bid $150,000 for an antique table.* 경매 중개인은 고(古) 탁자에 150,000달러를 매겼다. **2** [I] to offer to do some work for someone at a particular price ‖ 특정한 값으로 어떤 사람에게 어떤 일을 해준다고 제안하다. …에 입찰하다: *Four aerospace companies were invited to bid for the contract.* 네 개의 항공 우주 회사가 계약에 대한 입찰을 요청받았다.

bid³ *v* **bade** *or* **bid, bid** *or* **bidden, bidding** [T] LITERARY **1 bid sb good morning/goodbye etc.** to say good morning etc. to someone ‖ 남에게 인사 등을 말하다. …에게 안녕하세요[잘 가세요]라고 말하다 **2** to tell someone to do something ‖ 남에게 무엇을 하라고 말하다. 명령하다

bid·ding /ˈbɪdɪŋ/ *n* [U] **1** the activity of offering to pay a particular price for something, or offering to do some work ‖ 어떤 것에 대해 특정 값을 지불하거나 어떤 일을 해준다고 제안하는 행위. 입찰 **2 do sb's bidding** LITERARY to do what someone tells you to do ‖ 남이 시키는 대로 하다

bide /baɪd/ *v* **bide your time** to wait until the right time to do something ‖ 어떤 것을 할 호기가 올 때까지 기다리다. 때를 기다리다

bi·en·ni·al /baɪˈɛniəl/ *adj* happening once every two years ‖ 2년마다 한 번 발생하는. 격년의. 2년마다의

bi·fo·cals /ˈbaɪˌfoukəlz, baɪˈfoukəlz/ *n* [plural] a pair of special glasses made so that you can look through the upper part to see things that are far away and through the lower part to see things that are close ‖ (렌즈의) 윗부분은 멀리 있는 것을, 아랫부분은 가까이 있는 것을 볼 수 있도록 만들어진 특수 안경. 원시·근시 양용 안경

big /bɪg/ *adj* **-gger, -ggest** **1** of more than average size, amount etc.; large ‖ 평균적인 크기·양 이상의; 큰: *big baggy t-shirts* 크고 헐렁한 티셔츠 / *There's a big age difference between them.* 그들은 나이 차가 크게 난다. / *That boy gets bigger every time I see him.* 저 소년은 내가 볼 때마다 자란다. **2** important or serious ‖ 중요한, 중대한: *The big game is on Friday.* 금요일에 중요한 경기가 있다. / *The company lost a big contract this year.* 그 회사는 올해 중요한 계약 한 건을 놓쳤다. **3** INFORMAL older ‖ 나이가 더 많은. 손위의: *This is my big sister.* 이쪽은 저의 누나[언니]입니다. **4** doing something to a large degree ‖ 어떤 것을 극심하게 하는. 굉장한. 지독한: *I've never been a big baseball fan.* 나는 결코 광적인 야구팬은 아니었다. / *Both the girls are big eaters.* (=they eat a lot) 그 두 소녀는 모두 대식가이다. **5** successful or popular ‖ 성공한, 인기 있는: *The song was a big hit.* 그 노래는 크게 히트했다. / *Microsoft is big in the software market.* 마이크로소프트사는 소프트웨어 시장에서 성공한 기업이다. / *I knew I'd never make it big as a professional golfer.* 나는 결코 프로 골프 선수로서 출세할 수 없다는 것을 알았다. **6 be big on** SPOKEN to like doing something very much or to be very interested in it ‖ 어떤 것을 하는 것을 매우 좋아하거나 어떤 것에 매우 관심을 가지다: *Jenny's big on health food these days.* 제니는 요즘 건강 식품에 매우 관심을 가진다.

USAGE NOTE big and large

Use **big** and **large** with countable nouns to describe size. **Big** is more informal than **large**: *She was wearing a really big hat.* / *a large company.* Use **large** to describe amounts: *a large amount of information* ✗"DON'T SAY" *a big amount.*"✗ Use **big** to describe how important something is: *a big problem/issue / I have big news!* ✗DON'T SAY *"a large problem."*✗ 크기를 나타낼 때 가산 명사에는 **big**과 **large**를 쓴다. **big**은 **large**보다 더 비격식적으로 쓰인다: 그녀는 정말 큰 모자를 쓰고 있었다. / 대기업. 양을 나타낼 때는 **large**를 쓴다: 막대한 양의 정보. "a big amount"라고는 하지 않는다.

어떤 일의 중요한 정도를 나타낼 때에는 **big**을 쓴다: 큰 문제[쟁점] / 중대 뉴스가 있어! "a large problem"이라고는 하지 않는다.

big·a·my /ˈbɪɡəmi/ *n* [U] the crime of being married to two people at the same time ‖ 두 사람과 동시에 결혼하는 죄. 중혼죄 - **bigamist** *n* - **bigamous** *adj*

Big Ap·ple /ˌ. ˈ../ *n* INFORMAL New York City ‖ 뉴욕 시

big broth·er /ˌ. ˈ../ *n* any person, organization, or system that seems to control people's lives and restrict their freedom ‖ 사람의 생활을 통제하거나 자유를 제한하는 사람[조직, 체제]. 독재자. 독재 조직[체제]

big busi·ness /ˌ. ˈ../ *n* [U] very large companies that are considered as a group that influences the politics, the industry etc. of a country ‖ 한 나라의 정치·산업 등에 영향을 미치는 조직으로 간주되는 거대 기업. 대기업. 재벌

big deal /ˌ. ˈ./ *n* SPOKEN **1** an important event or situation ‖ 중요한 사건이나 상황. 대단한 것. 중대사: *Marian hates cooking, so getting invited for dinner is a big deal!* 요리를 싫어하는 마리안이 저녁 식사에 초대하는 것은 굉장한 일이야! **2** said when you do not think something is as important as someone else thinks it is ‖ 무엇을 타인이 생각하는 만큼 중요시 하지 않을 때에 쓰여. 별거 아니야: *His idea of a pay raise is giving me 50¢ more an hour – big deal!* 그가 급료를 인상한다는 것은 시간당 50센트를 더 준다는 거야, 대수롭지 않은 거지! **3 no big deal** said in order to show that you are not upset or angry about something that has just happened ‖ 방금 일어난 일에 대해 기분 나쁘거나 화나지 않았음을 나타내는 데에 쓰여. 별일 아니야: *"I'm really sorry about all this!" "No big deal."* "이 모든 일에 정말 미안해!" "별일 아닌데 뭘."

Big Dip·per /ˌ. ˈ../ *n* a group of seven bright stars seen in the northern sky in the shape of a bowl with a long handle ‖ 긴 손잡이가 달린 사발 모양을 한 북쪽 하늘에서 볼 수 있는 일곱 개의 밝은 별 무리. 북두칠성

big·gie /ˈbɪɡi/ *n* **no biggie** SPOKEN ⇨ **no big deal** (BIG DEAL)

big gov·ern·ment /ˌ. ˈ../ *n* [U] government, when people think it is controlling their lives too much ‖ 국민들의 생활을 지나치게 통제한다고 여겨지는 정부. 거대 정부

big·head·ed /ˈbɪɡhɛdɪd/ *adj* someone who is bigheaded thinks s/he is better than other people ‖ 자신을 타인들보다 더 잘났다고 생각하는. 자부심이 강한

big-league /ˈ. ˌ./ *adj* INFORMAL ⇨ MAJOR-LEAGUE

big mouth /ˈ. ˌ./ *n* INFORMAL someone who tells people things that should be secret ‖ 비밀로 해야 할 것들을 사람들에게 말해버리는 사람. 떠버리

big name /ˌ. ˈ./ *n* a famous person, especially an actor, musician etc. ‖ 특히 배우·음악가 등의 유명인: *a club where all the big names from Hollywood go* 할리우드의 유명인들이 모두 가는 클럽 – **big name** *adj* : *big name Broadway entertainers* 브로드웨이의 유명 연예인들

big·ot /ˈbɪɡət/ *n* someone who is BIGOTED ‖ 편협한 사람. 고집쟁이

big·ot·ed /ˈbɪɡətɪd/ *adj* having such strong opinions about race, religion, or politics that you are unwilling to listen to other people's opinions ‖ 인종·종교·정치에 대해 다른 사람들의 의견을 들으려고 하지 않는 강한 의견을 가진. 편협한 (의견을 가진). 고집불통의

big·ot·ry /ˈbɪɡətri/ *n* [U] BIGOTED behavior or beliefs ‖ 편협한 행동이나 신념

big shot /ˈ. ˌ./ *n* INFORMAL someone who is very important or powerful in business or politics ‖ 사업이나 정치에서 중요하거나 세력 있는 사람. 거물. 유력자: *They could have hired one of the big shots, but they chose Miller because he works hard.* 그들은 거물 중의 한 사람을 고용할 수 있었지만 밀러가 일을 열심히 하기 때문에 그를 뽑았다.

big-tick·et /ˌ. ˈ../ *adj* very expensive ‖ 매우 비싼: *Customers aren't buying big ticket items like CD players.* 고객들은 CD 플레이어와 같이 매우 비싼 품목들은 구매하려 하지 않는다.

big time¹ /ˈ. ˌ./ *adv* SPOKEN said in order to emphasize something that has just been said ‖ 방금 한 말을 강조하는 데에 쓰여: *"So, I'm in trouble, huh?" "Yeah, big time!"* "그러니까, 나 곤란한 상황이지, 그렇지?" "그래, 아주 곤란한 상황이야!"

big time² *n* **the big time** INFORMAL the position of being very famous or important, for example in politics or sports ‖ 예를 들어 정치나 스포츠에서의 매우 유명하거나 중요한 위치. 일류. 최고 수준: *The coaches don't think he's ready for the big time yet.* 코치들은 그가 아직 일류급의 수준은 아니라고 생각한다. –

big-time *adj* : *big-time drug dealers* 거물급 마약상들

big·wig /ˈ. ˌ./ *n* INFORMAL an important person ‖ 중요 인물. 거물: *one of the bigwigs in the movie business* 영화계의 거물 중의 한 사람

bike¹ /baɪk/ *n* INFORMAL **1** a bicycle ‖ 자전거: *kids riding their bikes in the street* 길에서 자전거를 타고 있는 아이들 / *We went for a bike ride around the lake today.* 오늘 우리는 호숫가로 자전거를 타러 갔다. **2** a MOTORCYCLE ‖ 오토바이

bike² *v* [I] to travel on a bicycle ‖ 자전거로 여행하다

bik·er /ˈbaɪkə/ *n* someone who rides a MOTORCYCLE, especially as part of a group ‖ 특히 집단의 일원으로서 오토바이를 타는 사람

bi·ki·ni /bɪˈkini/ *n* a piece of clothing in two parts that women wear for swimming ‖ 투피스로 된 여성용 수영복. 비키니

bi·lat·er·al /baɪˈlæt̬ərəl/ *adj* **bilateral agreement/treaty etc.** an agreement etc. between two groups or countries ‖ 양 집단이나 국가 사이의 협정 등. 상호 조약: *bilateral Mideast peace talks* 양국 간 중동 평화 회담 — **bilaterally** *adv*

bile /baɪl/ *n* [U] **1** a liquid produced by the LIVER to help the body DIGEST food ‖ 체내의 소화를 돕기 위해 간에서 생성되는 액체. 담즙 **2** LITERARY strong anger and hate ‖ 강렬한 노여움과 증오. 울화. 역정

bi·lin·gual /baɪˈlɪŋgwəl/ *adj* **1** able to speak two languages ‖ 두 가지 언어를 구사할 수 있는 **2** containing or expressed in two languages ‖ 두 언어를 포함하거나 두 언어로 표현된: *a bilingual dictionary* 대역 사전

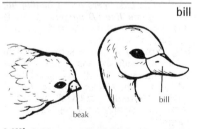

bill

beak

bill¹ /bɪl/ *n* **1** a list of things you have bought or services you have used and the amount you have to pay for them ‖ 구매품이나 이용한 서비스·지불해야 할 금액의 목록. 계산서. 청구서: *I have to remember to pay the phone bill this week.* 나는 이번 주에 전화 요금을 잊지 않고 내야 한다. **2** a piece of paper money ‖ 지폐: *a ten-dollar bill* 10달러짜리 지폐 **3** a plan for a law, written down for a government to decide on ‖ 정부가 결정하기 바라는 바를 적은 법률案. 법안: *a Senate tax bill* 상원의 세금 법안 **4** a wide or long beak on a bird such as a duck ‖ 오리 등의 새의 납작하고 긴 부리 —see also **foot the bill** (FOOT²)

bill² *v* [T] **1** to send a bill to someone ‖ 남에게 청구서를 보내다. (계산서로) 청구하다: *They've billed me for things I didn't buy.* 그들은 내가 구매하지도 않은 물건에 대한 청구서를 보냈다. **2 bill sth as** to advertise something in a particular way ‖ 특정한 방식으로 어떤 것을 광고하다: *The boxing match was billed as "the fight of the century."* 그 권투 경기는 "세기의 대결"로 광고되었다.

bill·board /ˈbɪlbɔrd/ *n* a very large sign used for advertising, especially next to a road ‖ 특히 길 옆에 있는 광고용 대형 간판. 게시판. 광고판

bill·fold /ˈbɪlfoʊld/ *n* ⇨ WALLET

bil·liards /ˈbɪlyədz/ *n* [plural] a game like POOL in which the balls go into the holes in a special order ‖ 특정한 규정에 따라 구멍에 공을 넣는 풀과 유사한 게임. 당구

bil·lion /ˈbɪlyən/ *number, plural* **billion** *or* **billions** 1,000,000,000 ‖ 10억: *$7 billion* 70억 달러 / *Billions of dollars have been invested.* 수십억 달러가 투자되었다. – **billionth** *number*

bill of rights /ˌ. . ˈ./ *n* **1** an official written list of the most important rights of the citizens of a country ‖ 한 국가의 국민이 가져야 할 가장 중요한 권리를 공식적으로 기록한 목록. 권리 선언. 기본권에 관한 선언 **2 the Bill of Rights** this document in the US ‖ 미국의 권리 장전

bil·low /ˈbɪloʊ/ *v* [I] to swell like a sail because of the wind ‖ 바람에 의해 돛처럼 부풀다. 펄럭이다. 부풀어 오르다: *clouds billowing overhead* 머리 위에서 뭉게뭉게 피어오르는 구름

billy goat /ˈbɪli ˌgoʊt/ *n* INFORMAL a word meaning a male goat, used especially when speaking to children ‖ 특히 아이들에게 말할 때 쓰여 숫염소를 뜻하는 단어

bim·bo /ˈbɪmboʊ/ *n* SLANG an insulting word meaning an attractive but stupid woman ‖ 매력적이지만 멍청한 여자를 뜻하는 모욕적인 단어. 경박한 여자

bi·month·ly /baɪˈmʌnθli/ *adj, adv* happening or being done every two months, or twice each month ‖ 두 달마다 또는 한 달에 두 번 발생하거나 행해지

는. 격월의. 한 달에 두 번의: *a bimonthly magazine* 격월로 간행되는 잡지 / *The magazine is published bimonthly.* 그 잡지는 격월로 간행된다.

bin /bɪn/ *n* a large container for storing things ‖ 대형 저장 용기. 저장소

bi·na·ry /ˈbaɪˌnɛri, ˈbaɪnəri/ *adj* TECHNICAL **1 the binary system** a system of counting, used in computers, in which only the numbers 0 and 1 are used ‖ 컴퓨터에서 숫자 0과 1만 사용하는 계산 체계. 이진법 **2** consisting of two things or parts ‖ 두 개나 두 부분으로 이루어진

bind¹ /baɪnd/ **bound, bound, binding** *v* [T] **1 a)** to tie someone so that s/he cannot move ‖ 남을 움직일 수 없게 묶다. 매다: *His legs were bound with rope.* 그의 다리는 밧줄로 묶였다. **b)** to tie things firmly together or wrap something tightly with cloth, rope etc. ‖ 물건을 함께 단단히 묶거나 천·밧줄 등으로 꽉 싸매다. 감다. 매다: *sticks bound together with twine* 끈 실로 같이 동여맨 막대기 **2** also **bind together** to form a strong relationship between two people, countries etc. ‖ 두 사람이나 두 국가 사이의 강한 결속을 형성하다. 결합[단결]시키다: *Religious belief binds the community together.* 종교적 신념은 지역 사회를 단결시킨다. **3** to make someone obey something such as a law or promise ‖ 남을 법이나 약속 등에 따르게 하다. 구속[속박]하다: *The countries are bound by the treaty to reduce the number of nuclear weapons.* 그 나라들은 조약에 의해 핵무기를 축소하기로 되어 있다. **4** to fasten the pages of a book together and put them in a cover ‖ 책의 페이지를 하나로 묶어 한 표지에 넣다. 제책[장정]하다. 합본하다

bind² *n* an annoying or difficult situation ‖ 골치 아프거나 난처한 상황. 곤경: *I'm so mad at him for putting me in this bind!* 나를 이런 곤경에 빠뜨린 그에게 너무 화가 나!

bind·er /ˈbaɪndɚ/ *n* a cover for holding loose sheets of paper, magazines etc. together ‖ 서류·잡지 등의 철하지 않은 낱장을 함께 보관하는 덮개. 바인더

bind·ing¹ /ˈbaɪndɪŋ/ *adj* a contract, agreement etc. that is binding must be obeyed ‖ 계약·협약 등이 지켜져야 하는. 구속력이 있는. 의무적인: *The contract isn't binding until you sign it.* 그 계약은 서명하기 전까지는 구속력이 없다.

binding² *n* **1** the cover of a book ‖ 책표지 **2** [U] material sewn along the edge of a piece of cloth for strength or decoration ‖ 견고함이나 장식을 목적으로 천의 가장자리를 따라 꿰맨 것. 바인딩. 가장자리 장식

binge¹ /bɪndʒ/ *n* INFORMAL a short period of time when you do too much of something ‖ 어떤 것을 지나치게 많이 하는 짧은 한 때. 실컷[진탕] 즐기기: *He went on a drinking binge last week.* (=drank too much alcohol) 그는 지난주에 술을 진탕 마셨다.

binge² *v* [I] to eat a lot of food in a very short time, especially as a result of an EATING DISORDER ‖ 특히 섭식 장애의 결과로 매우 짧은 시간 동안 많은 음식을 먹다. 과식하다

bin·go /ˈbɪŋgoʊ/ *n* [U] a game in which you win if a set of numbers chosen by chance are the same as a line of numbers on your card ‖ 임의로 선택한 일련의 숫자들이 자신의 카드에 있는 숫자 열과 같을 때 이기는 게임. 빙고

bin·oc·u·lars /bɪˈnɑkyəlɚz, baɪ-/ *n* [plural] a pair of glasses like short TELESCOPEs used for looking at distant objects ‖ 멀리 있는 물체를 보는 데에 쓰이는 짧은 망원경 같은 쌍안경

bi·o·chem·is·try /ˌbaɪoʊˈkɛmɪstri/ *n* [U] the scientific study of the chemistry of living things ‖ 생명체의 화학 작용에 대한 과학적인 연구. 생화학 **– biochemist** *n* **– biochemical** /ˌbaɪoʊˈkɛmɪkəl/ *adj*

bi·o·de·grad·a·ble /ˌbaɪoʊdɪˈgreɪdəbəl/ *adj* a material, product etc. that is biodegradable is able to change or decay naturally so that it does not harm the environment ‖ 물질·생산품 등이 환경에 유해하지 않게 자연적으로 변하거나 부패할 수 있는. 생물 분해성이 있는: *Most plastic is not biodegradable.* 대부분의 플라스틱은 생물 분해성이 없다.

bi·og·ra·pher /baɪˈɑgrəfɚ/ *n* someone who writes a BIOGRAPHY ‖ 전기 작가

bi·og·ra·phy /baɪˈɑgrəfi/ *n* [C,U] a book about a particular person's life, or all books like this considered as a group ‖ 특정 인물의 일생에 관한 책이나 집합적으로 본 이러한 종류의 모든 책. 일대기. 전기. 전기물

bi·o·log·i·cal /ˌbaɪəˈlɑdʒɪkəl/ *adj* relating to BIOLOGY ‖ 생물학에 관한. 생물학의: *a biological process* 생물학적 진보

biological war·fare /ˌ..ˌ... ˈ../ *n* [U] methods of fighting a war in which living things such as BACTERIA are used in order to harm the enemy ‖ 적을 해치는 데에 박테리아 등의 생물을 이용하는 전쟁 방법. 생물전. 세균전

bi·ol·o·gy /baɪˈɑlədʒi/ *n* [U] the scientific study of living things ‖ 생물체에 대한 과학적인 연구. 생물학 – **biologist** *n*

bi·o·pic /ˈbaɪoʊˌpɪk/ *n* a movie that tells the story of someone's life ‖ 사람의 일생에 대한 줄거리를 전해 주는 영화. 전기물

bi·op·sy /ˈbaɪˌɑpsi/ *n* the act of taking cells, skin etc. from someone who is sick, in order to learn more about his/her disease ‖ 병에 대해 좀더 많은 것을 알기 위해 환자의 세포·피부 등을 떼내는 행위. 생체 검사

bi·o·tech·nol·o·gy /ˌbaɪoʊtɛkˈnɑlədʒi/ *n* [U] the use of living things such as cells and BACTERIA in science and industry to make drugs, chemicals etc. ‖ 과학과 산업에서 약·화학 제품 등을 만들기 위한 세포와 박테리아 등의 생물의 이용. 생물[인간] 공학

bi·par·ti·san /baɪˈpɑrtəzən/ *adj* consisting of or representing two political parties ‖ 두 개의 정당으로 구성되거나 두 정당을 대표하는. 양당 연립의: *a bipartisan committee in the Senate* 상원의 양당 연립 위원회

bi·ped /ˈbaɪpɛd/ *n* TECHNICAL any animal with two legs, including humans ‖ 인간을 포함한 두 발 짐승

bi·plane /ˈbaɪpleɪn/ *n* an old-fashioned type of plane with two sets of wings ‖ 날개가 네 개[두 쌍] 달린, 비행기의 옛날 형태. 복엽(비행)기

birch /bɚtʃ/ *n* [C,U] a tree with BARK like paper that comes off easily, or the wood of this tree ‖ 나무 껍질이 종이처럼 쉽게 벗겨지는 나무나 이 나무의 재목. 자작나무(재목)

bird /bɚd/ *n* **1** an animal with wings and feathers that lays eggs and can usually fly ‖ 날개와 깃털이 있고 알을 낳으며, 보통 날 수 있는 동물. 새 **2 give/flip sb the bird** SLANG to put your middle finger up to make a very offensive sign at someone ‖ 남에게 매우 모욕적인 표시를 하기 위해 가운뎃손가락을 세우다. **3 sth is for the birds** SPOKEN said when you think something is useless or stupid ‖ 어떤 것이 쓸모없고 어리석다고 생각될 때에 쓰여. …이 형편없다: *Working in this heat is for the birds!* 이런 더위 속에서 일하는 것은 어리석은 일이야! —see also **early bird** (EARLY¹), **kill two birds with one stone** (KILL¹)

bird-brained /ˈ. ˌ./ *adj* INFORMAL silly or stupid ‖ 어리석거나 멍청한

bird·ie /ˈbɚdi/ *n* INFORMAL ⇨

SHUTTLECOCK

bird of prey /ˌ. . ˈ./ *n* any bird that kills other birds and small animals for food ‖ 먹이로 다른 새·작은 동물을 죽이는 새. 맹금류

bird·seed /ˈbɚdsid/ *n* [U] a mixture of seeds for feeding birds ‖ 새 먹이용인 씨앗의 혼합물. 새 모이

bird's eye view /ˌ. . ˈ./ *n* a view from a very high place ‖ 매우 높은 곳에서 본 광경. 전경. 조감도: *From our hotel room, we had a bird's eye view over the city.* 우리는 호텔 방에서 그 도시의 전경을 만끽했다.

birth /bɚθ/ *n* **1 give birth (to)** if a woman gives birth, she produces a baby from her body ‖ 여성이 아이를 낳다. 출산하다: *Jo gave birth to a baby girl at 6:20 a.m.* 조는 오전 6시 20분에 여자 아기를 출산했다. **2** [C,U] the time when a baby comes out of its mother's body ‖ 산모의 몸에서 아기가 나온 시간. 출산[탄생] (시간): *He died soon after the birth of their child.* 그는 아기가 태어난 직후 죽었다. / *The baby weighed 7 pounds at birth.* 태어났을 때 그 아기의 몸무게는 7파운드였다. **3** [U] someone's family origin ‖ 가족의 기원. 가계. 혈통: *Her grandfather was French by birth.* 그녀의 할아버지는 프랑스계 혈통이셨다. **4 the birth of sth** the time when something begins to exist ‖ 어떤 것이 존재하기 시작한 시기. 사물의 기원[발생]: *the birth of the new democracy* 새로운 민주주의의 발생

birth cer·tif·i·cate /ˈ. .ˌ.../ *n* an official document that has information about your birth printed on it ‖ 사람의 출생 정보를 기록한 공식 문서. 출생 증명서

birth con·trol /ˈ. .ˌ./ *n* [U] various methods of controlling the number of children you have ‖ 산아[임신]를 조절하는 다양한 방법. 산아 제한 방법

birth·day /ˈbɚθdeɪ/ *n* the date on which someone was born, usually celebrated each year ‖ 보통 매년 기념하는 탄생일. 생일: *a birthday present/card* 생일 선물[카드] / *When is your birthday?* 생일이 언제니? / *Happy Birthday!* (=said to someone on his/her birthday) 생일 축하해!

birth·mark /ˈbɚθmɑrk/ *n* an unusual mark on someone's body at birth ‖ 태어났을 때 몸에 있는 독특한 표시. 모반

birth·rate /ˈbɚθreɪt/ *n* the number of births for every 100 or 1000 people during a particular time ‖ 특정기간 동안

100명 또는 1000명당 출생수. 출생률
bis·cuit /'bɪskɪt/ *n* a type of bread that is baked in small round shapes || 작고 둥근 모양으로 구운 빵의 일종. 비스킷
bi·sect /'baɪsɛkt, baɪ'sɛkt/ *v* [T] TECHNICAL to divide something into two equal parts || 어떤 것을 두 개로 똑같이 나누다. …을 이등분하다 – **bisection** /'baɪ,sɛkʃən, baɪ'sɛkʃən/ *n* [U]
bi·sex·u·al¹ /baɪ'sɛkʃuəl/ *adj* **1** sexually attracted to both men and women || 성적으로 남성·여성 모두에게 끌리는. 양성애의 **2** having qualities or features of both sexes || 양성의 성질이나 모습을 가진. (자웅)양성의
bisexual² *n* someone who is sexually attracted to both men and women || 성적으로 남성·여성 모두에게 끌리는 사람. 양성애자
bish·op /'bɪʃəp/ *n* a priest with a high rank who is in charge of the churches and priests in a large area || 광범위한 지역 내에 있는 교회나 성직자들을 책임지고 있는 고위직의 사제. 주교
bi·son /'baɪsən/ *n* TECHNICAL ⇨ BUFFALO
bit¹ /bɪt/ *n*
1 a (little) bit slightly, but not very || 약간. 조금: *I'm a little bit tired.* 나는 약간 피곤하다.
2 quite a bit a fairly large amount || 양이 상당히 많은: *He's willing to pay us quite a bit of money.* 그는 우리에게 많은 돈을 기꺼이 내려고 한다.
3 ▶SMALL PIECE 작은 조각◀ a small amount or piece of something || 어떤 것의 적은 양이나 조각: *The floor was covered in tiny bits of glass.* 바닥이 작은 유리 조각들로 덮여 있다.
4 ▶COMPUTER 컴퓨터◀ a unit for measuring the amount of information a computer can use || 컴퓨터가 다룰 수 있는 정보의 양을 측정하는 데에 쓰는 단위. 비트
5 to bits into small pieces || 작은 조각으로: *I tore the letter to bits and burned it.* 나는 그 편지를 갈기갈기 찢어서 태워 버렸다.
6 ▶TIME 시간◀ a short amount of time || 짧은 시간: *We'll talk about the Civil War in just a bit.* 우리는 잠시 남북 전쟁에 대해 이야기할 것이다. / *I could see that she was learning, bit by bit.* (=gradually) 나는 그녀가 점차 터득하고 있다는 것을 알 수 있었다.
7 every bit as just as || 마찬가지로. 똑같이: *Ray was every bit as good-looking as his brother.* 레이는 그의 형과 마찬가지로 미남이었다.

8 ▶TOOL 도구◀ a part of a tool for cutting or making holes || 자르거나 구멍을 내는 연장의 일부
9 ▶HORSE 말◀ a piece of metal that is put in the mouth of a horse to control its movements || 말의 입에 넣어 말의 동작을 제어하는 금속 조각. 재갈
bit² *v* the past tense of BITE || bite의 과거형
bitch¹ /bɪtʃ/ *n* **1** SPOKEN a rude word for a woman who you dislike || 싫어하는 여성에게 쓰는 모욕적인 단어. 나쁜년. 화냥년: *You bitch!* 나쁜 년! **2 be a bitch** SLANG to cause problems or be difficult || 문제를 야기하거나 곤란해지다: *I love this sweater but it's a bitch to wash.* 이 스웨터는 마음에는 들지만 세탁하는 데 어려움이 있다. **3** a female dog || 암캐
bitch² *v* [I] IMPOLITE to complain or say unkind things about someone or something || 사람이나 사물에 대해 불평하거나 나쁘게 말하다. 투덜거리다: *He's been bitching about the fact that Jimmy owes him money all day.* 지미가 그에게 빚졌다는 사실에 대해 그는 하루 종일 투덜거리고 있다.
bitch·y /'bɪtʃi/ *adj* SLANG tending to complain or say unkind things about people || 남에 대해 불평하거나 나쁘게 말하는 경향이 있는. 남을 헐뜯는
bite¹ /baɪt/ *v* **bit, bitten, biting 1** [I, T] to cut or crush something with your teeth || 이로 어떤 것을 자르거나 으깨다. 깨물다. 물어 뜯다: *He bit a huge piece out of the cookie.* 그는 쿠키를 크게 한 조각 깨물었다. / *I had just bitten into the apple.* 나는 방금 사과를 베어 물었다. / *Be careful of the dog; he bites.* 개한테 물리지 않도록 조심해라. / *She bites her fingernails.* 그녀는 손톱을 (습관적으로) 깨문다. / *Marta got bitten by a snake.* 마르타는 뱀에게 물렸다. **2 bite sb's head off** SPOKEN to speak to someone very angrily, especially when there is no good reason to do this || 특히 남에게 그럴 만한 이유가 없을 때 화내며 말하다. …에게 퉁명스럽게 말하다: *I asked if she wanted help, and she bit my head off!* 내가 그녀에게 도움이 필요하냐고 물었더니만 그녀는 그럴 필요 없다며 퉁명스럽게 말했어! **3 bite the dust** INFORMAL to die, fail, be defeated, or stop working || 죽다 [실패하다, 패배하다, 고장나다]: *My*

bite

Chevy finally bit the dust last week. 내 쉐비 자동차가 결국 지난 주에 완전히 고장나 버렸다. **4 bite the bullet** to do something even though it is unpleasant ‖ 비록 꺼려지는 일이지만 어떤 것을 하기로 결정하다. 울며 겨자먹기로 하다: *We had to bite the bullet and buy a car we couldn't really afford.* 우리는 결코 차를 살 여유가 없었지만 그렇게 해야만 했다. **5 bite off more than you can chew** to try to do more than you are able to do ‖ 능력 이상의 일을 하려고 시도하다. 힘에 부치는 일을 하려고 하다 **6** [I] to have the effect that was intended, especially a bad effect ‖ 의도했던 특히 나쁜 효과를 가져오다: *The new tobacco taxes have begun to bite.* 새로운 담뱃세는 악영향을 가져오기 시작했다. **7** if a fish bites, it takes food from a hook ‖ 물고기가 낚싯바늘의 미끼를 물다

bite² *n* **1** the act of cutting or crushing something with your teeth, or the piece of food that is cut ‖ 이빨로 어떤 것을 자르거나 으깨는 행위나 깨문 음식의 한 조각. 한 입(분량): *Can I have a bite of your steak?* 네 스테이크 한 입만 먹을 수 있을까? / *He took a bite of the cheese.* 그는 치즈를 한 입 먹었다. **2** a wound made when an animal or insect bites you ‖ 동물이나 벌레 등이 물었을 때 생기는 상처. 문[물린] 상처: *I'm covered in mosquito bites!* 나는 모기에 물린 자국투성이야! **3 a bite (to eat)** INFORMAL a quick meal ‖ 가벼운 식사: *We can grab a bite at the airport before we go.* 우리는 가기 전에 공항에서 가벼운 식사를 할 수 있다. **4** an occasion when a fish takes the food from a hook ‖ 물고기가 낚싯바늘의 미끼를 물기

bite-size /'. ,./, **bite-sized** *adj* the right size to fit in your mouth easily ‖ 딱한 입에 들어갈 만한 크기의. 한 입 크기의: *bite-size pieces of chicken* 한 입 크기의 치킨 조각

bit·ing /'baɪtɪŋ/ *adj* **1** a biting wind is cold and unpleasant ‖ 바람이 차고 불쾌한. 매서운. 살을 에는 듯한 **2** biting criticisms or remarks are very unkind ‖ 비평이나 말이 매우 냉정한. 신랄한

bit·ten /'bɪtˈn/ *v* the PAST PARTICIPLE of BITE ‖ bite의 과거 분사형

bit·ter /'bɪtɚ/ *adj* **1** very angry because you feel something bad or unfair has happened to you ‖ 자신에게 나쁘거나 부당한 일이 일어났다고 느껴 매우 화가 난. 성난. 분개하는: *Kyle's bitter voice showed how upset he was.* 카일의 성난 목소리는 그가 얼마나 화가 났는지를 보여

주었다. **2** having a strong taste, like coffee without sugar ‖ 설탕을 넣지 않은 커피처럼 강한 맛을 내는. 맛이 쓴 **3** air that is bitter is cold and unpleasant ‖ 공기가 차고 불쾌한. 매서운. 살을 에는 듯한: *a bitter wind* 살을 에는 듯한 바람 — see usage note at TEMPERATURE **4 to/until the bitter end** until the end, even though unpleasant things happen ‖ 비록 불쾌한 일이 생기더라도 끝까지. 막판[최후]까지: *The UN stayed in the war zone until the bitter end.* 유엔은 어려움을 무릅쓰고 끝까지 그 전쟁 지역에 머물렀다. — **bitterly** *adv* — **bitterness** *n* [U]

bit·ter·sweet /,bɪtɚ'swit/ *adj* pleasant, but sad too ‖ 즐겁지만 슬픈. 시원섭섭한. 달콤쌉쌀한: *a bittersweet goodbye* 시원섭섭한 이별

bi·week·ly /baɪ'wikli/ *adj, adv* **1** happening or being done every two weeks ‖ 격주로 일어나거나 행해지는. 격주의 **2** twice each week ‖ 일주일에 두 번: *a biweekly meeting* 일주일에 두 번 하는 회의 / *We now meet biweekly.* 우리는 이제 일주일에 두 번 만난다.

bi·zarre /bɪ'zar/ *adj* very unusual and strange ‖ 매우 희한하고 이상한. 기묘한. 별난: *We had some very bizarre discussions last night.* 우리는 지난 밤에 몇 가지 매우 별난 토론을 했다. / *a bizarre coincidence* 기묘한 일치

blab /blæb/ *v* **-bbed, -bbing** [I] SPOKEN to talk too much, especially when you say things you are not supposed to ‖ 특히 해서는 안 되는 것을 너무 많이 얘기하다. 비밀을 무심코 누설하다. 지각 없이 지껄이다: *Marty will blab on and on if you let him.* 마티는 그냥 두면 분별 없이 계속 지껄여댈 것이다.

blab·ber·mouth /'blæbɚ,maʊθ/ *n* SPOKEN a word meaning someone who BLABs, used especially by children ‖ 특히 아이들이 쓰는 말로, 비밀까지 말해 버리는 사람을 뜻하는 단어. 입이 싼 사람

black¹ /blæk/ *adj* **1** having a color that is darker than every other color, like the sky at night ‖ 밤하늘처럼 다른 모든 색깔보다 더 어두운 색을 가진. 검은. 흑색의: *a black dress* 검은 옷 / *The mountains looked black against the sky.* 그 산은 하늘에 대비되어 검게 보였다. / *It was pitch black* (=completely dark), *and I fell over the chair.* 칠흑같이 어두워 의자 위로 넘어지고 말았다. **2 Black** someone who is black has very dark skin, and is from a family that was originally from Africa ‖ 조상이 아프리카

인인 피부가 매우 검은 사람. 흑인: *Over half the students here are Black.* 여기 학생들의 절반 이상이 흑인이다. **3 black coffee** does not have milk in it ‖ 커피가 프림을 넣지 않은. 블랙의: *Do you take your coffee black?* 커피 블랙으로 마실 거니? **4 black sheep** someone who is different from the rest of a group or family, especially in a way that is considered to be bad ‖ 특히 좋지 않다고 생각되게, 집단이나 가족의 나머지 구성원과 다른 사람. 말썽꾸러기. 두통거리 – **blackness** *n* [U]

black² *n* **1** [U] a black color ‖ 검은 색 **2** also **Black** someone who has very dark skin, and whose family originally came from Africa ‖ 조상이 아프리카인인 피부가 매우 검은 사람. 흑인 **3 in black and white a)** in writing ‖ 서면으로: *The rules are there in black and white for everybody to see.* 그 규칙들은 모든 사람이 볼 수 있게 서면으로 되어 있다. **b)** in a very simple way, as if there are clear differences between good and bad ‖ 좋고 나쁨의 확실한 구별이 있듯이 매우 단순하게. 양단적[이분법적인] 사고 방식으로: *Dad sees things in black and white, so for him, what we're doing is wrong.* 아버지는 모든 것을 양단적 사고 방식으로 보기에 우리가 하는 일은 아버지 측면에서 틀린 것이다. **4 be in the black** to have more money than you owe ‖ 지불해야 될 돈보다 더 많은 돈을 가지고 있다. 흑자이다: *We're in the black for the first time in 3 years.* 우리는 3년 만에 처음으로 흑자를 내고 있다. —opposite **be in the red** (RED²)

USAGE NOTE black

Using **black** as a noun when talking about someone's race is usually offensive. However, it is acceptable in some situations, for example when you are comparing racial groups: *Relations between blacks and whites in the area are good.* Using **Black** as an adjective is less offensive: *a Black man.* However, **African** is usually the best choice of adjective: *an African-American woman.*
사람의 인종을 말할 때 명사로 **black**을 사용하는 것은 일반적으로 모욕적인 언사이다. 그러나 인종적 집단을 비교할 때와 같은 상황에서는 무방하다: 이 지역에서 흑인과 백인의 관계는 좋다. 형용사로 **Black**을 사용하는 것은 덜 모욕적인 언사이다: 흑인 남자. 그러나,

African이 형용사로선 일반적으로 최상의 선택이다: 아프리카계 미국 여성.

black³ *v*
black out *phr v* [I] to become unconscious ‖ 의식이 없게 되다. 기절하다: *Sharon blacked out while she was swimming.* 샤론은 수영을 하던 중에 의식을 잃었다.

black and blue /ˌ. . ˈ./ *adj* skin that is black and blue has dark marks on it because it has been injured ‖ 피부에 상처를 입어 거무스레한 자국이 있는. 멍든

black belt /ˈ. ˌ./ *n* **1** a high rank in some types of Asian fighting sports, especially JUDO and KARATE ‖ 특히 유도·가라데 등의 아시아 격투기에서의 상위 등급. 검정띠 **2** someone who has this rank ‖ 검정띠 등급을 가진 사람. 유단자

black·ber·ry /ˈblæk,bɛri/ *n* a very sweet black or dark purple BERRY ‖ 매우 달며 진한 또는 검은 자줏빛이 나는 딸기. 검은딸기

black·bird /ˈblækbɚd/ *n* a common American and European bird, the male of which is completely black ‖ 수컷은 완전히 검은색인 미국·유럽산의 흔한 새. 찌르레기과[지빠귓과]의 새

black·board /ˈblækbɔrd/ *n* a dark smooth surface on the wall, usually in a school, which you write on with CHALK ‖ 보통 학교의 벽에 걸린, 분필로 글을 쓰는 표면이 검고 매끄러운 것. 칠판. 흑판

black·en /ˈblækən/ *v* [I, T] to become black, or to make something do this ‖ 검게 되다, 또는 검게 만들다: *Smoke had blackened the kitchen walls.* 연기로 부엌 벽이 검게 그을렸다.

black eye /ˌ. ˈ./ *n* skin around someone's eye that becomes dark because it has been hit ‖ 맞아서 거무스레해진 눈 언저리 피부. 멍든 눈

black·head /ˈblækhɛd/ *n* a small spot on someone's skin that has a black center ‖ 사람 피부에 있는 중앙이 검은 작은 여드름. (위가 검은) 여드름

black hole /ˌ. ˈ./ *n* TECHNICAL an area in outer space into which everything near it is pulled, including light ‖ 빛을 포함한 주위의 모든 것을 빨아들이는 우주의 한 구역. 블랙 홀

black hu·mor /ˌ. ˈ../ *n* [U] jokes, funny stories etc. that deal with the unpleasant parts of human life ‖ 인간 생활의 불쾌한 부분을 다루는 농담·웃기는 이야기 등. 블랙 유머

black·jack /ˈblækdʒæk/ *n* a card game, usually played for money, in which you try to get as close to 21 points as possible || 가능한 한 21점에 근접한 점수를 얻으려는 보통 돈을 걸고 하는 카드 게임. 블랙잭

black·list /'blæk,lɪst/ v to make a list of people, countries, products etc. that are not approved of, and should therefore be avoided || 인정받지 않아서 기피되는 사람·나라·제품 등의 리스트를 만들다. 블랙리스트에 올리다: *Ritter is blacklisted in most of the nightclubs in Phoenix.* 리터는 피닉스에 있는 대부분의 나이트 클럽에 블랙리스트로 올라가 있다. – **blacklist** n

black mag·ic /, '../ n [U] magic that is believed to use the power of the Devil for evil purposes || 사악한 목적으로 악마의 힘을 사용한다고 믿는 마술. 검은 마술

black·mail /'blækmeɪl/ n the practice of making someone do what you want by threatening to tell secrets about him/her || 남에게 비밀을 밝히겠다고 위협을 해서 원하는 것을 하게 만드는 행위. 공갈. 협박 – **blackmail** v [T] – **blackmailer** n

black mar·ket /, '../ n the system by which people illegally buy and sell goods, foreign money etc. that are difficult to obtain || 사람들이 구하기 힘든 물건이나 외국환을 불법적으로 사고 파는 체제. 암거래. 암시장: *The drug might be available on the black market.* 그 약은 암시장에서 구할 수 있을 것이다.

black·out /'blækaʊt/ n 1 a period of time when the lights do not work, because the electricity supply has failed || 전력 공급의 중단으로 전등이 켜지지 않는 시기. 정전: *The cause of the blackout in New York is not known yet.* 뉴욕에서의 정전 원인이 아직 밝혀지지 않았다. 2 an occasion when you suddenly become unconscious || 갑작스럽게 의식을 잃는 경우. 기절. 실신. 기억 상실: *He's suffered from blackouts since he came back from the war.* 그는 전쟁에서 되돌아온 후 기억 상실로 고통받고 있다. —see also **news blackout** (NEWS)

black·smith /'blæksmɪθ/ n someone who makes and repairs things made of iron, especially HORSESHOEs || 특히 편자 등의 철제품을 만들고 수리하는 사람. 대장장이

black-tie /'. ,./ adj a party or social event that is black-tie is one at which you have to wear formal clothes || 파티나 사교 모임이 정장을 해야 하는. 정장 차림의

black·top /'blæktɑp/ n [C, U] the thick

black substance used for covering roads || 도로 포장에 쓰이는 걸쭉하고 검은 물질. 아스팔트

blad·der /'blædɚ/ n the organ in the body that stores waste liquid until it is ready to leave the body || 소변이 몸을 빠져 나오기 전에 저장되는 신체 기관. 방광

blade /bleɪd/ n 1 the flat cutting part of a knife, tool, or weapon || 칼[도구, 무기]의 납작하게 생긴 자르는 부분. (칼)날: *The blade needs to be kept sharp.* 그 날은 날카롭게 유지되어야 한다. / *razor blades* 면도날 2 a leaf of grass or a similar plant || 풀이나 그와 유사한 식물의 잎. 잎사귀 3 the flat wide part of an OAR, PROPELLER etc. || 노·프로펠러 등의 판판하고 넓은 부분. 노깃. 날개

blah¹ /blɑ/ adj SPOKEN 1 not having an interesting taste, appearance, character etc. || 구미가 당기는 맛·외형·성격 등을 지니지 않은. 싱거운. 시시한: *The color of the walls is kind of blah.* 벽색깔이 별로다. 2 slightly sick or unhappy || 약간 아프거나 행복하지 않은: *I feel really blah today.* 오늘 정말 기분이 별로야.

blah² n [U] **blah, blah, blah** SPOKEN said when you do not want to say or repeat something because it is boring || 지루하기 때문에 어떤 것을 말하거나 반복하는 것을 원하지 않을 때에 쓰여. 어쩌고 저쩌고: *Oh, you know Michelle; it's blah, blah, blah about her kids all the time.* 아, 너 미쉘 알지. 내내 자기 애들 얘기만 재잘재잘 하더군.

blame¹ /bleɪm/ v [T] 1 to say or think that someone is responsible for something bad || 어떤 잘못에 대해 누군가에게 책임이 있다고 말하거나 생각하다. 책임을 지우다: *It's not fair to blame Charlie – he didn't know anything.* 찰리에게 책임을 묻는 것은 부당해. 그는 아무 것도 몰랐어. / *Mom blamed herself for Keith's problems.* 엄마는 키스의 문제를 자신의 탓으로 돌렸다. / *Don't try to blame this on me!* 이것에 대해 나에게 책임을 전가하려고 하지 마! 2 **I don't blame you/them etc.** SPOKEN said when you think it was right or reasonable for someone to do what s/he did || 누군가가 한 일이 옳거나 합당했다고 생각할 때에 쓰여. 당신이/그들이 그렇게 할 만도 합니다: *I don't blame her for not letting her kids see that movie!* 그녀가 자기 아이들에게 그 영화를 못 보게 할 만도 하지!

blame² n [U] responsibility for a mistake or for something bad || 실수나

잘못에 대한 책임. 책망. 비난: *Because she's the older child, she usually gets the blame*. 그 여자애가 좀더 나이가 많기 때문에 대개 꾸중을 듣는다. / *You shouldn't have to take the blame* (=say it was your fault) *if Rader did it.* 레이더가 그것을 했다면 너는 자책할 필요없다.

blame·less /'bleɪmlɪs/ *adj* not guilty of anything bad ‖ 아무 잘못도 없는. 비난할여지 없는. 나무랄 데 없는: *blameless behavior* 나무랄 데 없는 행동

blanch /blæntʃ/ *v* **1** [I] to become pale because you are afraid or shocked ‖ 두렵거나 놀라서 창백해지다: *Nick blanched at the sight of blood.* 닉은 유혈 광경에 창백해졌다. **2** [T] to put vegetables, fruit, or nuts into boiling water for a short time ‖ 야채[과일, 견과류]를 잠깐동안 끓는 물에 넣다. 살짝 데치다

bland /blænd/ *adj* **1** without any excitement, strong opinions, or special character ‖ 자극[강한 주장, 특별한 특징]이 없는. 무덤덤한: *bland TV shows* 재미없는 TV 쇼 **2** bland food has very little taste ‖ 음식의 맛이 거의 없는. 맛이 부드러운. 순한: *bland cheese* 맛이 순한 치즈

blank¹ /blæŋk/ *adj* **1** without any writing, print, or recorded sound ‖ 어떤 글도 써 있지 않은[인쇄되지 않은, 음이 녹음되지 않은]. 백지의. 공백의: *a blank sheet of paper* 백지장 **2 go blank a)** to be suddenly unable to remember something ‖ 갑자기 기억할 수 없게 되다. 정신이 희미해지다: *My mind went blank as I stood up to speak.* 말하려고 일어섰을 때 정신이 희미해졌다. **b)** to stop showing any images, writing etc. ‖ 영상·글 등을 보여 주기를 멈추다. 깜깜해지다. 어두워지다: *The screen suddenly went blank.* 그 스크린이 갑자기 나가 버렸다. **3** showing no expression, understanding, or interest ‖ 표정[이해, 흥미] 없어 보이는. 멍한. 무표정한: *a blank look* 멍한 표정

blank² *n* **1** an empty space on a piece of paper, where you are supposed to write a word or letter ‖ 글이나 편지를 쓰고자 하는 종이의 여백. 빈칸. 공간: *Fill in the blanks on the application form.* 신청서 양식의 빈칸을 채우세요. **2** a CARTRIDGE (=container for a bullet in a gun) that has an explosive but no bullet ‖ 화약만 들어있고 탄알이 없는 탄약통. 공포탄: *The police were only firing blanks.* 그 경찰들은 공포탄만 쏘고 있었다. – **blankness** *n* [U]

blank check /ˌ. './ *n* [singular] **1** a check that has been signed but has not had the amount written on it ‖ 금액은 쓰여 있지 않지만 서명이 되어 있는 수표. 백지 수표 **2** INFORMAL the authority to do whatever you want, without any limits ‖ 어떤 제한도 없이 원하는 무엇이든 할수 있는 권한. 자유 재량권[행동권]

blan·ket¹ /'blæŋkɪt/ *n* **1** a heavy cover that keeps you warm in bed ‖ 침대에서 몸을 따뜻하게 해 주는 두꺼운 덮개. 담요. 모포 **2** LITERARY a thick covering of something ‖ 어떤 것을 덮는 두꺼운 것. 덮개: *a blanket of snow on the mountains* 온 산을 뒤덮은 눈

blanket² *adj* **blanket statement** a statement that affects everyone or includes all possible cases ‖ 모든 사람에게 영향을 미치거나 모든 가능한 경우를 포함하는 말. 일괄적인 진술: *You shouldn't make blanket statements about all single parents.* 당신은 모든 편부모에 대해서 일괄적인 진술을 하지 말아야 한다.

blank·ly /'blæŋkli/ *adv* in a way that shows no expression, understanding, or interest ‖ 아무런 표정[이해, 흥미] 없이. 무표정하게. 멍하니. 멍청하게: *When I walked in, he was staring blankly at the wall.* 내가 걸어 들어갔을 때 그는 멍하니 벽을 응시하고 있었다.

blank verse /ˌ. './ *n* [U] poetry that does not RHYME ‖ 운을 달지 않은 시. 무운시(無韻詩)

blare /blɛr/ *v* [I, T] to make a very loud unpleasant noise ‖ 매우 크고 불쾌한 소리를 내다. 요란하게 울리다: *blaring horns* 시끄러운 경적 소리 / *a radio blaring out music* 음악 소리를 쿵쿵 울려 대는 라디오 – **blare** *n* [singular]

bla·sé /blɑˈzeɪ/ *adj* not worried or excited about things that most people think are important, impressive etc. ‖ 대부분의 사람들이 중요하고 인상적이라 생각하는 것에 대해 걱정하지도 흥분하지도 않는. 무관심[무감동]한: *The fans are more blasé about the playoffs this year than they were last year.* 그 팬들은 작년보다 올해의 플레이오프전에 대해 더 무관심하다.

blas·phe·mous /'blæsfəməs/ *adj* showing disrespect for God or people's religious beliefs ‖ 신이나 사람들의 종교적 믿음에 불경함을 나타내는. 신성 모독의. 불경스러운: *a blasphemous book* 불경스러운 책

blas·phe·my /'blæsfəmi/ *n* [C, U] something you say or do that is insulting to God or to people's religious beliefs ‖

신이나 종교적인 믿음을 모욕하는 말이나 행동. 모독(적인 언행) – **blaspheme** /blæsˈfim, ˈblæsfim/ *v* [I, T]

blast¹ /blæst/ *n* **1** an explosion, or the very strong movement of air that it causes‖폭발 또는 폭발로 인한 공기의 매우 강한 움직임. 폭풍: *The blast knocked him forward.* 폭풍 때문에 그는 앞쪽으로 넘어졌다. **2** [singular] SPOKEN an enjoyable and exciting experience‖즐겁고 흥분시키는 경험. 기쁨. 황홀 상태: *We had a blast at Mitch's party.* 우리는 미치의 파티에서 즐거운 한 때를 보냈다. **3** **full blast** as strongly, loudly, or fast as possible‖가능한 한 강하게[크게, 빠르게]: *When I got home, she had the TV on full blast.* 내가 집에 왔을 때 그녀는 텔레비전 소리를 한껏 올려 놓았다. **4** a sudden strong movement of wind or air‖바람이나 공기의 갑작스러운 강한 움직임. 돌풍: *a blast of icy air* 찬 공기의 돌풍 **5** a sudden very loud noise‖갑작스런 매우 큰 소리: *a trumpet blast* 트럼펫의 요란한 소리

blast² *v* **1** [I, T] to break a large amount of rock into pieces using explosives‖폭발물을 사용해서 거대한 암석을 조각내어 부수다. 폭파하다[시키다]: *Workers had to blast through the side of the mountain to build the road.* 일꾼들은 도로를 내기 위해 산의 한 쪽 면을 폭파시켜야 했다. **2** [I, T] also **blast out** to produce a lot of loud noise, especially music‖특히 음악 같은 큰 소리를 내다: *How can you hear anything with the radio blasting?* 라디오 소리가 이렇게 큰데 어떻게 무슨 소리를 들을 수 있니? **3** [T] to attack a place or person with bombs or large guns‖지역이나 사람을 폭탄이나 장총으로 공격하다: *Two gunmen blasted their way into the building.* 두 명의 총잡이들이 빌딩 안으로 들어가며 총알 세례를 퍼부었다. **4** [T] to criticize something very strongly‖어떤 것을 심하게 비난하다. …을 혹평하다: *The President's remarks were quickly blasted by Democratic leaders.* 대통령의 발언은 민주당의 지도자들에게 바로 비난받았다.

blast off *phr v* [I] if a SPACECRAFT blasts off, it leaves the ground‖우주선이 지상을 떠나다. 발사되다

blast·ed /ˈblæstɪd/ *adj* SPOKEN said in order to show you are annoyed‖짜증났음을 나타내는 데에 쓰여. 신경질나는. 빌어먹을: *Next year there'll be two of these blasted forms to fill out.* 내년에는 기입해야 할 빌어먹을 양식이 두 개나 될

것이다.

blast-off /ˈ. ./ *n* [U] the moment when a SPACECRAFT leaves the ground‖우주선이 지상에서 벗어나는 순간. 우주선의 발사: *10 seconds till blast-off!* 발사 10초 전!

bla·tant /ˈbleɪʔnt/ *adj* very noticeable and offensive‖몹시 눈에 띄며 무례한. 빤한. 뻔뻔스러운: *blatant discrimination* 명백한 차별 대우 – **blatantly** *adv*

blaze¹ /bleɪz/ *v* [I] to burn or shine very brightly and strongly‖매우 밝고 강렬하게 불타거나 빛나다. 활활 타다. 번쩍이다: *a fire blazing in the fireplace* 벽난로에서 활활 타고 있는 불꽃 / *a Christmas tree blazing with lights* 불빛으로 밝게 빛나는 크리스마스 트리

blaze² *n* [singular] **1** a very bright light or color‖매우 밝은 빛이나 색. 섬광. (타는 듯한)광채: *a blaze of sunshine* 눈부신 햇빛 **2** the strong bright flames of a fire‖강하고 밝은 화염. 불꽃. 불. 화재: *Fire officials continued searching for the cause of the blaze.* 소방 관계자들은 계속해서 그 화재의 원인을 찾았다. / *a cheerful blaze in the fireplace* 벽난로에서 활활 타오르는 불꽃 **3 in a blaze of glory/publicity** receiving a lot of praise or public attention‖많은 칭찬이나 대중의 주목을 받는. 대대적인 영광/인기를 얻으며: *In 1987, in a blaze of publicity, Maxwell launched a new newspaper.* 1987년에 맥스웰은 폭발적인 주목을 받으며 새 신문을 발행했다.

blaz·er /ˈbleɪzɚ/ *n* a suit JACKET (=piece of clothing like a short coat) without matching pants‖하의와는 별개의 재킷: *a wool blazer* 울 재킷

blaz·ing /ˈbleɪzɪŋ/ *adj* **1** extremely hot‖극도로 뜨거운. 타는 듯한: *a blazing summer day* 타는 듯한 여름날 **2** very bright because of strong emotions‖격정으로 인해 매우 밝은. 강렬한: *blazing eyes* 이글거리는 눈(빛)

bleach¹ /blitʃ/ *n* [U] a chemical used in order to make things white or to kill GERMs‖물체를 희게 하거나 세균을 죽이는 데에 쓰이는 화학 물질. 표백제

bleach² *v* [T] to make something white by using chemicals or the light of the sun‖어떤 것을 화학 물질이나 햇빛으로 이용하여 희게 하다. 표백[바래게] 하다: *bleached hair* 탈색된 머리

bleach·ers /ˈblitʃɚz/ *n* [plural] a structure in a GYM or a park, that has several rows of seats where people sit to watch sports games‖운동 경기를 관람하기 위해 사람들이 앉는 좌석을 여러 열

갖춘 운동장이나 공원의 구조물. 관람석
—compare GRANDSTAND

bleak /blik/ *adj* **1** without anything to
make you feel cheerful or hopeful ‖ 기운
이 나거나 희망을 느끼게 하는 것이 없는.
어두운. 흐린: *Without a job, Carlo's
future seemed bleak.* 직업이 없이는 칼로
의 미래가 어두워 보였다. **2** cold and
without any pleasant or comfortable
features ‖ 싸늘하며 어떠한 유쾌함이나 안
락함도 없는. 음산한: *a bleak November
day* 음산한 11월의 하루 – **bleakness**
n [U]

blear·y /'blɪri/ *adj* unable to see clearly
because you are tired ‖ 피곤하여 명확히
볼 수 없는. 흐린. 녹초가 된: *Sam
jumped up, looking bleary-eyed.* 샘은 침
침한 시야로 뛰어올랐다. – **blearily** *adv*

bleat /blit/ *v* [I] to make the sound that
a sheep, goat, or young cow makes ‖ 양
[염소, 송아지]이 우는 소리를 내다. 매애
[음매] 하고 울다 – **bleat** *n*

bleed /blid/ *v* **bled** /bled/, **bled**,
bleeding 1 [I] to lose blood, especially
from an injury ‖ 특히 상처가 나서 피를
흘리다. 출혈하다: *The cut on his
forehead was bleeding again.* 그의 이마
에 난 상처에서 또 다시 피가 흘러 내리고
있었다. **2** [T] to make someone pay a lot
of money for something, especially
when s/he does not have much money ‖
특히 많은 돈을 가지지 않은 사람에게 어
떤 것에 대한 많은 돈을 지불하게 하다. 돈
을 뜯기다: *Many poor countries are
being bled dry by debt.* (=they have to
pay all their money to repay debts) 많은
가난한 나라들은 부채 상환으로 돈이 고갈
되고 있다.

blem·ish /'blɛmɪʃ/ *n* a small mark that
spoils the appearance of something or
someone ‖ 사물이나 사람의 외관을 망치
는 작은 자국. 흠. 얼룩: *a small blemish
on her cheek* 그녀의 뺨에 난 작은 기미
– **blemished** *adj*

blend¹ /blɛnd/ *v* [I, T] **1** to thoroughly
mix two or more foods together to form
a single substance ‖ 하나의 물질을 만들
기 위해 두 가지 이상의 음식물을 완전히
섞다. 섞다. 섞이다: *Blend the eggs with
the sugar.* 달걀에 설탕을 섞어라. **2** to
combine two different qualities, things
etc. so that you cannot see the
difference between them ‖ 두 물질 간의
차이를 알 수 없도록 두 개의 다른 물질·
물건 등을 결합하다: *a story that blends
fact and fiction* 사실과 허구를 결합한 이
야기 / *These immigrants did not blend
easily into American society.* 이들 이민

자들은 미국 사회에 쉽게 융합하지 못했다.

blend in *phr v* [I] to be similar to other
things or people ‖ 다른 사물이나 사람들
과 유사하다. 비슷하다. 어울리다: *Jessie
never blended in with the other
children at school.* 제시는 학교에서 다른
아이들과 결코 잘 어울리지 못했다.

blend² *n* a combination ‖ 결합: *the right
blend of sunshine and soil for growing
grapes* 포도를 재배하기 위한 햇빛과 토양
의 적절한 조화

blended fam·i·ly /ˌ.. '../ *n* a family in
which one or both parents have
children from previous marriages living
with the family ‖ 한쪽 또는 양쪽 부모가
이전 결혼에서 데려온 아이들과 같이 사는
가정. 혼합 가족

blend·er /'blɛndɚ/ *n* a small electric
machine that you use to mix liquids
together, or to make soft foods more
liquid ‖ 액체를 섞거나 부드러운 음식을
보다 유동성 있게 만드는 데에 쓰는 소형
전기 기구. 혼합기. 믹서

bless /blɛs/ *v* [T] **1 bless you** SPOKEN
said when someone SNEEZES ‖ 상대가 재
채기할 때에 쓰여. 이런. 조심해요 **2** to
protect, help, and make good things
happen to someone ‖ 보호하고 도와주어
누군가에게 좋은 일이 일어나게 하다. 축
복하다: *Thank you, and God bless you.*
고마워요, 신의 축복이 있기를. **3** to ask
God to make something holy ‖ 어떤 것을
신성하게 하기 위해 신에게 빌다. 축성하
다: *The priest blessed the bread and
wine.* 목사님은 빵과 포도주를 축성했다.
4 bless him/her etc. SPOKEN said in
order to show that you like someone or
are pleased by something s/he has done
‖ 누군가를 좋아하거나 그 사람이 한 일로
기쁘다는 것을 나타내는 데에 쓰여. 참 고
맙다: *"Donna cleaned up." "Oh, bless
her heart."* "도나가 청소를 싹 했어요."
"어머, 정말 기특하구나." **5 be blessed
with** to be lucky enough to have
something, especially a good quality ‖ 특
히 양질의 것을 가질 만큼 운이 좋다. …의
복[행운]을 운 좋게 받다: *I'm blessed
with good eyesight.* 나는 운 좋게도 시력
이 좋다.

bless·ed /'blɛsɪd/ *adj* holy, or loved by
God ‖ 신성한, 또는 신의 은총을 입은. 축
복 받은

bless·ing /'blɛsɪŋ/ *n* **1** something that
is good or helps you ‖ 좋거나 도움이 되
는 것. 축복: *The rain was a real blessing
after all that heat.* 그 비는 혹서 뒤의 정
말 반가운 비였다. **2** [U] someone's
approval or encouragement for a plan,

activity etc. ‖ 계획·활동 등에 대한 누군가의 승인이나 격려: *We want to get married, Dad, but we want your blessing first.* 아빠, 우린 서로 결혼하길 원하지만 먼저 아빠의 결혼 승낙을 위해요. **3 a mixed blessing** something that is both good and bad ‖ 동시에 좋기도 하고 나쁘기도 한 것: *The color printer is a mixed blessing – it looks good but takes too long to print.* 컬러 인쇄기는 좋기도 하고 나쁘기도 하다. 좋아 보이지만 인쇄하는 데 너무 오래 걸리기 때문이다. **4 a blessing in disguise** something that seems to be bad but that you later realize is good ‖ 나쁜 것처럼 보이지만 나중에 좋게 인식되는 것. 전화위복: *He had a small heart attack which was a blessing in disguise because we hadn't known he had a heart problem.* 그는 가벼운 심장 마비를 일으켰으나 전화위복이 되었다. 왜냐하면 우리는 그가 심장 질환이 있었다는 것을 몰랐었기 때문이다. **5** [singular, U] protection and help from God, or the prayer in which you ask for this ‖ 신의 보호와 도움, 또는 이것을 비는 기도

blew /blu/ *v* the past tense of BLOW ‖ blow의 과거형

blight /blaɪt/ *n* [singular, U] something that damages or spoils something else, or the condition of being damaged or spoiled ‖ 다른 것을 손상시키거나 망치는 것, 또는 손상되거나 망친 상태: *an area suffering from urban blight* (=severe problems that only a city has) 도시 환경의 황폐함으로 고통 받는 지역 **– blight** *v* [T]

blight·ed /ˈblaɪtɪd/ *adj* damaged or spoiled ‖ 손상되거나 망친: *the blighted downtown area* 황폐한 도심 지역

blimp /blɪmp/ *n* an aircraft without wings that looks like a very large BALLOON with an engine ‖ 매우 큰 풍선같이 생긴, 엔진이 달린 날개 없는 비행선

blind¹ /blaɪnd/ *adj* **1** unable to see ‖ 볼 수 없는. 눈먼. 장님의: *She was born blind.* 그녀는 장님으로 태어났다. / *People with the disease often go blind.* (=become blind) 사람들은 종종 질병 때문에 장님이 된다. **2 the blind** people who cannot see ‖ 볼 수 없는 사람들. 장님들. 눈 먼 사람들 **3** showing that you are not thinking carefully about something ‖ 어떤 것에 관해 주의깊게 생각하지 않고 있음을 나타내는. 맹목적인. 분별 없는: *They have blind faith in the government.* (=they approve of it even when it is not good) 그들은 정부에 대한 맹목적인 믿음을 가지고 있다. **4** not noticing or realizing something ‖ 어떤 것을 깨닫거나 인식하지 못하는: *The White House seems blind to the struggles of the middle class.* 백악관은 중산층의 어려움을 인식하지 못하는 것 같다. **5 blind corner/bend/curve** a corner etc. that you cannot see around when you are driving ‖ 운전할 때에 볼 수 없는 구석 등. 사각(死角) 지대 **6 the blind leading the blind** a situation in which someone who does not know much about a subject is helping someone else who knows nothing about it ‖ 한 주제에 대해 많이 알지도 못하는 사람이 전혀 알지 못하는 사람을 돕는 상황. 장님이 장님을 인도하는 상황 **7 blind as a bat** HUMOROUS not able to see well ‖ 잘 볼 수 없는. 앞을 내다보지 못하는 **– blindly** *adv* **– blindness** *n* [U] —see also **turn a deaf ear/turn a blind eye** (TURN¹)

blind² *v* [T] **1** to make someone unable to see, either permanently or for a short time ‖ 영원히 또는 잠시 동안 볼 수 없게 하다. 눈을 멀게 하다: *The deer was blinded by our headlights.* 그 사슴은 우리 차의 전조등 때문에 잠시 눈이 보이지 않게 되었다. **2** to make someone unable to recognize the truth about something ‖ 누군가를 어떤 것에 대한 진실을 인식할 수 없게 하다. 깨닫지 못하게 하다: *Being in love blinded me to his faults.* 사랑에 빠진 나는 그의 결점을 깨닫지 못했다.

blind³ *n* a piece of cloth or other material that you pull down to cover a window ‖ 창문을 가리기 위해 끌어 당겨 내리는 천이나 다른 재료. 블라인드 —see also VENETIAN BLIND

blind date /ˌ. './ *n* an occasion when someone arranges for two people who have not met before to go on a DATE ‖ 전에 만난 적이 없는 두 사람을 데이트시켜 주기 위해 제삼자가 주선한 상황. 주선에 의한 모르는 사람 사이의 데이트. 미팅

blind·fold /ˈblaɪndfoʊld/ *n* a piece of cloth that you use to cover someone's eyes so that s/he cannot see ‖ 볼 수 없도록 눈을 가리는 데에 쓰는 천조각. 눈가리개 **– blindfold** *v* [T]

blind·side /ˈblaɪndsaɪd/ *v* [T] to hit the side of a car with your car in an accident ‖ (자동차)사고에서 자기 차로 다른 차의 측면을 치다. 블라인드 사이드에서 공격하다

blind spot /ˈ. ,./ *n* **1 have a blind spot** to be unwilling to think about something, or pretend you cannot understand it ‖ 어떤 것에 대해 생각하려

들지 않거나 이해하지 못하는 척하다: *He has a blind spot when it comes to his daughter's problems.* 그는 자기 딸의 문제점에 관해서는 모르는 척 한다. **2** the part of the road that you cannot see when you are driving a car ‖ 차를 운전할 때 볼 수 없는 도로의 일부. 사각(死角) 지대: *The other car was right in my blind spot.* 상대편의 차가 내 차의 오른쪽 사각 지대에 있었다.

blink /blɪŋk/ *v* **1** [I, T] to open and close your eyes quickly ‖ 재빨리 눈을 떴다가 감다. 깜박이다: *He blinked as he stepped out into the sunlight.* 햇빛이 내리쬐는 곳으로 걸어 나왔을 때 그는 눈을 깜박거렸다. **2** if a light blinks, it goes on and off quickly and repeatedly ‖ 불빛이 빠르게 되풀이 하며 켜졌다 꺼졌다 하다. 깜박거리다: *The answering machine light was blinking.* 자동 응답기 불빛이 깜박거리고 있었다.

blink·ers /'blɪŋkəz/ *n* [plural] the small lights on a car that flash to show which direction you are turning ‖ 자동차가 어떤 방향으로 향할 것인지 보여 주기 위해 깜박거리는 자동차의 작은 불빛. 방향 지시등

blip /blɪp/ *n* **1** a flashing light on a RADAR screen ‖ 레이더 스크린상에 비치는 번쩍이는 불빛. 블립 **2** INFORMAL a sudden and temporary change from the way something typically happens ‖ 어떤 것이 일어나는 전형적인 방식에서 벗어난 갑작스럽고 일시적인 변화. 단발적인 변동: *I think the loss of this game is just a blip – the team will continue to win.* 이번 게임에 진 것은 일시적인 현상일 뿐이다. 그 팀은 앞으로는 계속 이길 것이다.

bliss /blɪs/ *n* [U] perfect happiness ‖ 완벽한 행복. 지극한 기쁨 **– blissful** *adj* **– blissfully** *adv*

blis·ter¹ /'blɪstə/ *n* **1** a painful swollen area on the skin containing a clear liquid, caused by a burn or by being rubbed too much ‖ 화상이나 심하게 문질러서 피부에 생기는, 맑은 액체를 함유한 부풀어올라 아픈 부위. 물집 **2** a slightly raised area on the surface of a metal, painted wood etc. ‖ 금속·페인트 칠한 나무 등의 표면상의 약간 올라간 부위. 불룩한 부분. 기포

blister² *v* [I, T] to develop blisters or to make blisters form ‖ 물집이 생기거나 물집을 만들다 **– blistered** *adj*

blis·ter·ing /'blɪstərɪŋ/ *adj* criticizing someone very strongly ‖ 사람을 매우 신랄하게 비판하는. 통렬한: *Berkowski sent a blistering memo to his staff.* 버코스키는 자기 직원에게 따끔한 메모를 보냈다.

blithe /blaɪð, blaɪθ/ *adj* LITERARY happy and not worried ‖ 행복하고 걱정이 없는. 쾌활한. 명랑한 **– blithely** *adv* : *"I don't care!" she said blithely.* "난 상관 없어!" 하고 그녀는 명랑하게 말했다.

blitz /blɪts/ *n* **1** a situation in football when a lot of football players attack the QUARTERBACK ‖ 미식 축구에서 모든 선수들이 일제히 쿼터백을 공격하는 상황 **2** a situation when you use a lot of effort to achieve something, often in a short time ‖ 어떤 것을 달성하기 위해 종종 단시간 내에 모든 노력을 다하는 상황. 전격적인 맹공격[공세]: *an advertising blitz* 전격적인 광고 활동 **3** a sudden military attack, especially from the air ‖ 특히 공중에서의 갑작스런 군사 공격. 공습(空襲) **– blitz** *v* [T]

bliz·zard /'blɪzəd/ *n* a long heavy storm with a lot of wind and snow ‖ 많은 바람과 눈을 동반한 장기간의 심한 눈보라. 블리자드 **—see usage note at** WEATHER¹

bloat·ed /'bloʊtɪd/ *adj* looking or feeling larger than usual because of being too full of water, food, gas etc ‖ 물·음식·가스 등이 너무 꽉 차서 평소보다 더 커 보이거나 더 크게 느껴지는. 부은: *Sonny felt bloated with all the holiday food.* 소니는 연휴에 먹은 온갖 음식 때문에 몸이 부은 느낌이 들었다.

blob /blɑb/ *n* a small drop of a thick liquid ‖ 걸쭉한 액체의 작은 방울: *blobs of paint* 페인트 방울

bloc /blɑk/ *n* a large group of people or countries with the same political aims, working together ‖ 동일한 정치적 목표를 갖고 함께 일하는 대규모 집단의 사람이나 국가들. 연합. 블록: *the liberal bloc in Congress* 의회 내의 자유주의 연합

block¹ /blɑk/ *n*

1 ▶SOLID MATERIAL 고체 물질◀ a piece of a solid material with straight sides ‖ 평평한 면으로 된 고체 덩어리. 토막: *a block of concrete* 콘크리트 한 덩어리 / *children playing with wooden blocks* 나무 토막[블록]을 가지고 노는 아이들

2 ▶IN A CITY 도시에서◀ **a)** the distance along a city street from where one street crosses it to the next ‖ 시내 도로의 교차점에서 다음 교차 지점까지 나 있는 거리. 블록: *We're just two blocks from the bus stop.* 우리는 버스 정류장에서 딱 두 블록 떨어져 있다. / *the sixteen hundred block of Glenwood Drive* (=where the buildings are numbered from 1600 to 1699) (건물에 1600부터 1699까지 번호가 매겨진) 글렌우드 드라이브(도로)의 1,600블록 **b)** a square area of houses or buildings formed by four streets ‖ 사방에 도로가 나 있는 집이나 건물들의 사각형 구역: *Let's walk around the block.* 이 블록을 걸어다닙시다. / *We were the first family on our block to get a swimming pool.* 우리가 사는 블록에서 수영장이 있는 집은 우리집이 최초였다.

3 ▶RELATED GROUP 관련 집단◀ a group of things of the same kind, that are related in some way ‖ 어떤 면에서 관련있는, 동일한 종류로 이루어진 일단의 사물. 연속된 한 벌. 한 조: *Jason says he can get a block of seats* (=set of seats next to each other) *for the play.* 제이슨은 그 연극을 볼 연이은 한 조의 좌석을 확보할 수 있다고 한다.

4 ▶AMOUNT 양◀ a continuous amount of something ‖ 어떤 것의 연속된 양: *To delete a block of text, highlight it, then press Del.* 텍스트의 한 블록을 삭제하려면, 하이라이트를 주고 나서[블록을 선정하여] Del 키를 누르면 된다. / *a block of time to do homework* 숙제할 시간

5 ▶UNABLE TO THINK 생각 할 수 없는◀ [singular] a condition in which you are not able to think, learn, write etc. as you normally can ‖ 평소와는 다르게, 생각하고 배우고 쓰는 등의 일을 할 수 없는 상태: *After her first novel, she had writer's block for a year.* 그녀는 첫 번째 소설을 탈고한 후 1년간 아무 것도 쓰지 못했다.

6 ▶STOPPING MOVEMENT 동작 저지◀ something that stops things moving through or along something else ‖ 어떤 것이 다른 것을 통과하거나 따라가지 못하게 막는 것. 장애물. 방해물: *Police put up a road block after the accident.* 사고 후에 경찰은 도로 차단물을 세웠다.

7 ▶SPORTS 스포츠◀ a movement in sports that stops an opponent going forward ‖ 스포츠에서 상대편이 앞으로 나아가지 못하도록 하는 동작. 방해. 블록

8 ▶COMPUTER 컴퓨터◀ a physical unit of stored information on a computer DISK ‖ 컴퓨터 디스크에 저장된 정보의 물리적 단위

block² *v* [T] **1** also **block up** to prevent anything from moving through a narrow space by filling it ‖ 좁은 공간을 메워 아무 것도 통과할 수 없게 막다. 차단하다: *My nose is blocked up.* 코가 꽉 막혔어. / *It looks like the sink is blocked.* 싱크대가 막힌 것 같다. **2** to prevent

anyone or anything from moving past a place ‖ 어떤 사람이나 어떤 것이 어떤 곳을 지나가지 못하게 막다. 봉쇄하다: *Whose car is blocking the driveway?* 차도를 막고 있는 차가 누구의 것입니까? **3** to stop something happening, developing, or succeeding ‖ 어떤 것이 발생[발전, 성공]하는 것을 막다: *The county council blocked the idea for a new shopping mall.* 주의회는 새 쇼핑몰에 대한 안(案)의 통과를 저지했다. **4** to prevent someone from seeing a view, getting light etc. ‖ 누군가가 광경을 보는 것·빛을 쏘이는 것 등을 못하게 막다. 시야를 가리다: *Could you move a little? You're blocking my view.* 약간 움직일 수 있겠니? 네가 내 시야를 막고 있어.

block sth ↔ **off** *phr v* [T] to completely close a road or path ‖ 도로나 길을 완전히 막다. 차단하다: *The freeway exit's blocked off.* 고속도로 출구가 완전히 차단되었다.

block out *phr v* **1** [T **block** sth ↔ **out**] to stop light passing through something ‖ 빛이 어떤 것을 통과하지 못하게 하다. (빛의 통과를)막다. 차단하다: *Witnesses said the black smoke blocked out the sun.* 목격자들은 검은 연기가 햇빛을 차단했다고 말했다. **2** [I,T **block** sth ↔ **out**] to try to ignore something or stop yourself remembering a bad experience ‖ 어떤 것을 애써 무시하다 또는 나쁜 경험을 기억하지 않으려고 하다: *She had managed to block her childhood out completely.* 그녀는 용케도 어린 시절의 기억을 완전히 잊었다. **3** [T **block** sth ↔ **out**] to decide that you will use a particular time only for a particular purpose ‖ 특정 목적을 위해 일정 시간을 사용하기로 결정하다. 할애하다: *I try to block out four hours a week for research.* 나는 일주일에 네 시간은 연구하는 데 할애하려 한다.

block·ade /blɑˈkeɪd/ *n* the action of surrounding an area with soldiers or ships to stop people or supplies leaving or entering a place ‖ 사람이나 물자가 어떤 장소의 출입을 하지 못하도록 그 지역을 군인이나 선박들로 둘러싸는 행위. 봉쇄. 폐쇄: *a naval blockade* 해군을 이용한 봉쇄 — **blockade** *v* [T]

block·age /ˈblɑkɪdʒ/ *n* **1** something that is stopping movement in a narrow place ‖ 좁은 곳에서 움직임을 막는 것. 장애물[봉쇄]물: *a blockage in the drain* 하수구에 막혀 있는 것 **2** [U] the state of being blocked or prevented from doing something ‖ 막히거나 어떤 것을 못하도록

차단된 상태. 봉쇄 상태. 저해: *the blockage of army movements* 군대 이동의 봉쇄

block·bust·er /'blɑk,bʌstər/ *n* INFORMAL a book or movie that is very successful ‖ 매우 성공적인 책이나 영화. 블록버스터: *Spielberg's new blockbuster* 스필버그의 새 블록버스터 영화

block·head /'blɑkhɛd/ *n* INFORMAL a very stupid person ‖ 매우 멍청한 사람. 바보. 얼간이. 멍청이

block par·ty /'. ,../ *n* a party that is held in the street for all the people living in the area ‖ 한 지역에 사는 모든 사람들을 위해 거리에서 열리는 파티

blog /blɑg/ *n* a web page that is made up of information about a particular subject, in which the newest information is always at the top of the page ‖ 최신 정보가 항상 페이지 맨 위에 오는 특정 주제에 대한 정보로 이루어진 웹페이지. 블로그

blond¹, blonde /blɑnd/ *adj* **1** blond hair is pale or yellow ‖ 머리카락이 밝거나 노란색인. 밝은색 머리카락의. 금발의 **2** someone who is blond has blond hair ‖ 사람이 금발 머리를 가진

blond², blonde *n* INFORMAL someone with BLOND hair ‖ 금발 머리의 사람: *a good-looking blonde* 잘생긴 금발 머리의 사람

blood /blʌd/ *n* **1** [U] the red liquid that your heart pumps through your body ‖ 심장에서 밀어내 온몸으로 퍼지는 붉은 액체. 피. 혈액: *Put pressure on the wound to stop the blood flow.* 피가 흐르는 것을 막으려면 상처부위를 지압하세요. / *The Red Cross asks people to give/donate blood.* 적십자에서는 사람들에게 헌혈을 부탁한다. / *The doctor said she'd do a blood count/test.* (=see if anything is wrong with the blood) 의사는 그녀에게 혈구 수 [혈액]검사를 받아 보라고 했다. **2 in cold blood** in a deliberate way without any emotion ‖ 감정 없이 신중하게. 냉혹하게: *a murder in cold blood* 냉혹한 살인자 **3** [U] the family or race to which you belong ‖ 자신이 속한 가문이나 인종. 혈통: *You look like you've got some Irish blood.* 당신은 약간 아일랜드 혈통을 지닌 것처럼 보입니다. / *a blood relative* (=related by birth, not by marriage) 혈족 **4 new blood** new members in a group or organization who bring new ideas and energy ‖ 참신한 생각과 활기를 가져다 주는 단체나 조직의 신입 회원들. 신참들: *We need some new blood in the department.* 그 부서에 신참들이 몇 명

필요하다. **5 bad blood** angry feelings between people about something bad that happened in the past ‖ 과거에 일어난 좋지 않은 일에 대한 사람들간의 악감정: *There was some bad blood between Jose and Arriola over a woman.* 한 여인을 사이에 두고 호세와 아리올라 사이에 좋지 않은 감정이 있었다. **6 -blooded** having a particular type of blood ‖ 특정 유형의 피를 가진. (…한)피[기질]를 가진: *Fish are cold-blooded.* 어류는 냉혈 동물이다.

blood-and-guts /,. . './ *adj* INFORMAL full of action and violence ‖ 액션과 폭력으로 가득찬: *a blood-and-guts movie* 폭력이 난무하는 영화

blood bank /'. ,./ *n* a supply of blood that people have given, to be used in hospitals for treating sick people ‖ 병원에서 환자 치료에 쓰기 위해 사람들이 수혈한 피의 저장고. 혈액 은행

blood·bath /'blʌdbæθ/ *n* [singular] the violent killing of many people at the same time ‖ 동시에 많은 사람들에게 저지르는 폭력적인 살해. 대학살

blood·cur·dling /'blʌd,kədl-ɪŋ/ *adj* extremely frightening ‖ 극도로 무서운. 등골이 오싹한. 소름끼치는: *a blood-curdling scream* 소름끼치는 비명

blood·hound /'blʌdhaʊnd/ *n* a large dog with a very good sense of smell ‖ 후각이 매우 예민한 큰 개. 블러드하운드

blood·less /'blʌdlɪs/ *adj* **1** without killing or violence ‖ 살인이나 폭력이 없는. 무혈의: *a bloodless revolution* 무혈혁명 **2** extremely pale ‖ 극도로 창백한. 핏기없는: *bloodless cheeks* 창백한 볼

blood pres·sure /'. . ,../ *n* [U] the force with which blood travels through your body, that can be measured by a doctor ‖ 의사가 측정할 수 있는, 혈액이 신체를 순환하는 힘. 혈압: *a special diet for people with high/low blood pressure* 고혈압[저혈압] 환자를 위한 특별 식단

blood·shed /'blʌdʃɛd/ *n* [U] the killing of people, usually in fighting or a war ‖ 보통 전투나 전쟁에서의 살인. 살상. 살육

blood·shot /'blʌdʃɑt/ *adj* bloodshot eyes look slightly red ‖ 눈이 약간 붉은. 충혈된

blood·stain /'blʌdsteɪn/ *n* a mark or spot of blood ‖ 핏자국이나 피의 얼룩. 혈흔 **– bloodstained** *adj*

blood·stream /'blʌdstrim/ *n* [singular] blood as it flows around the body ‖ 신체를 순환하는 피. 혈류: *Drugs were found in her bloodstream.* 그녀의 혈류에서 마약이 검출되었다.

blood·thirst·y /'blʌd,θɜːsti/ adj showing that someone enjoys doing violent things or watching violence ‖ 사람이 폭력적인 행동을 하거나 보는 것을 즐기는 경향을 보이는. 피에 굶주린. 잔인한: *bloodthirsty attacks* 잔인한 공격

blood type /'. ./ n one of the groups into which human blood is divided, including A, B, AB, and O ‖ 인간의 혈액을 A, B, AB, O로 분류한 그룹 중 하나. 혈액형

blood ves·sel /'. ,../ n one of the tubes through which blood flows in your body ‖ 체내에서 피가 흐르는 관의 하나. 혈관

blood·y /'blʌdi/ adj 1 covered in blood, or losing blood ‖ 피로 뒤덮인, 또는 피를 잃어가는: *a bloody nose* 피를 흘리고 있는 2 with a lot of injuries or killing ‖ 부상이나 죽음이 난무하는: *a bloody fight* 유혈 전투

bloom[1] /blum/ n [C, U] a flower or flowers ‖ 꽃 한 송이 또는 꽃들: *lovely yellow blooms* 예쁜 노란 꽃들 / *roses in bloom* (=with flowers completely open) 만개(滿開)한 장미

bloom[2] v [I] 1 to open as flowers ‖ 꽃이 피다. 개화하다: *lilacs blooming in the spring* 봄에 피는 라일락 2 to look happy and healthy or successful ‖ 행복하고 건강하거나 성공적으로 보이다: *Sheila bloomed like a woman in love.* 쉴라는 사랑에 빠진 여인처럼 행복해보였다.

bloom·er /'blumɚ/ n **late bloomer** INFORMAL someone who grows or becomes successful at a later age than most people ‖ 대부분의 사람들에 비해 늦은 나이에 성장하거나 성공한 사람

bloop·er /'blupɚ/ n INFORMAL an embarrassing mistake made in front of other people ‖ 다른 사람들 앞에서 저지른 부끄러운 실수

blos·som[1] /'blɑsəm/ n [C, U] a small flower, or all the flowers on trees or bushes ‖ 작은 꽃, 또는 나무나 관목숲에 핀 모든 꽃: *peach blossoms* 복숭아꽃

blossom[2] v [I] 1 if trees blossom, they produce flowers ‖ 나무가 꽃을 피우다: *a blossoming plum tree* 꽃이 핀 자두나무 2 to become happier, more beautiful, or successful ‖ 더 행복해지다[더 아름다워지다, 더 성공하다]. 발전하여 (…이)되다: *By the end of the year she had blossomed into an excellent teacher.* 연말에는 그녀는 더욱 훌륭한 선생님이 되었다.

blot[1] /blɑt/ v **-tted, -tting** [T] to press soft paper or cloth on to a wet spot or surface in order to dry it ‖ 젖은 부분을 말리기 위해 부드러운 종이나 헝겊으로 누르다. 물기를 없애다. 닦아내다: *Blot wet hair with a towel, but don't rub it.* 젖은 머리를 수건으로 문지르지 말고 눌러서 말려라.

blot sth ↔ out phr v [T] to hide or remove something completely ‖ 어떤 것을 완전히 숨기거나 제거하다: *He tried to blot out his memory of Marcia.* 그는 마르시아에 대한 기억을 완전히 지우려 했다. / *clouds blotting out the sun* 태양을 완전히 가린 구름

blot[2] n 1 a mark or spot that spoils something or makes it dirty ‖ 어떤 것을 망치거나 더럽히는 자국이나 흠. 얼룩: *ink blots* 잉크 자국 2 a building, structure etc. that is ugly and spoils the appearance of a place ‖ 이상하게 생겨 경관을 망치는 건물·구조물 등: *a blot on the landscape* 경관을 해치는 것

blotch /blɑtʃ/ n a colored or dirty mark on something ‖ 어떤 것 위에 채색되거나 때묻은 자국. 얼룩. – **blotched** adj

blotch·y /'blɑtʃi/ adj blotchy skin is covered with pink or red marks ‖ 피부가 분홍이나 붉은 자국으로 덮인. (피부에)붉은 반점이 있는. 홍반성의

blot·ter /'blɑtɚ/ n a large piece of BLOTTING PAPER kept on the top of a desk ‖ 책상 위에 놓는 대형 압지

blotting pa·per /'.. ,../ n [U] soft thick paper used for drying wet ink on a page after writing ‖ 글을 쓴 후 종이 위의 젖은 잉크를 말리는 데에 쓰는 부드럽고 두꺼운 종이. 압지

blouse /blaʊs/ n a shirt for women ‖ 여성용 셔츠. 블라우스: *a summer blouse* 여름철 블라우스 —see picture at CLOTHES

blow[1] /bloʊ/ v blew, blown, blowing
1 ▶WIND MOVING 바람의 움직임◀ [I] if the wind or a current of air blows, it moves ‖ 바람이나 공기의 흐름이 움직이다. 바람이 불다: *A cold wind was blowing from the east.* 동쪽에서 차가운 바람이 불어오고 있었다.
2 ▶WIND MOVING STH 바람이 어떤 것을 움직임◀ [I, T] to move something, or to be moved, by the force of the wind or a current of air ‖ 바람이나 공기 흐름의 힘으로 어떤 것을 움직이거나 어떤 것이 움직여지다. (바람에)날리다, (바람에)불어 …을 날리다: *The wind must have blown the door shut/open.* 바람 때문에 문이 닫힌[열린] 것이 틀림없다. / *curtains blowing in the breeze* 미풍에 나부끼는 커튼
3 ▶USING YOUR MOUTH 입의 사용◀

a) [I, T] to send air out through your mouth ‖ 입을 통해 공기를 내보내다. 입김을 불다: *Renee blew on her soup to cool it a little.* 르네는 수프를 식히려고 후후 불었다. **b)** [T] to make or shape something by sending air out of your mouth and into a substance ‖ 공기를 입에서 어떤 물질 안으로 불어 넣어 어떤 것을 만들거나 형성하다. …을 불어대다: *The kids are on the back porch blowing bubbles.* 아이들이 뒷현관에서 비눗방울을 불고 있다. / *ornaments made of blown glass* 유리를 불어 만든 공예품

4 blow your nose to clean your nose by forcing air through it into a cloth or TISSUE(=piece of soft paper) ‖ 헝겊이나 티슈에 공기를 강제로 내뿜어 콧속을 깨끗이 하다. 코를 풀다

5 ▶MAKE A SOUND 소리를 내다◀ [I, T] to make a sound by sending air through a musical instrument or a horn ‖ 악기나 나팔에 공기를 불어 소리를 내다. (…을) 울리다: *Listen – can you hear the train whistle blowing?* 들어봐. 기차가 경적을 울리는 소리가 들리니?

6 ▶STOP WORKING 고장◀ [I, T] also **blow out** if a piece of equipment blows or if something blows it, it suddenly stops working completely ‖ 기기 등이 갑자기 작동을 완전히 멈추다. 고장나다. 고장내다: *You're lucky you didn't blow the whole engine.* 엔진 전체를 고장낸 것은 아니니 다행이군요.

7 blow sth to bits/pieces INFORMAL **a)** to destroy an idea, plan etc. by showing that it cannot work or be true ‖ 효과가 없거나 사실이 아님을 보임으로써 생각·계획 등을 엉망으로 만들다. 무효화하다: *The new data's blown their theory to pieces.* 새로운 데이터로 인해 그들의 이론이 수포로 돌아갔다. **b)** to completely destroy a building or structure with an explosion ‖ 폭발물로 건물이나 구조물을 완전히 파괴하다. 무너뜨리다

8 blow the whistle (on sb) INFORMAL to tell the public or someone in authority about something wrong that someone has done ‖ 누군가의 잘못을 대중이나 담당자에게 말하다. 고자질하다

SPOKEN PHRASES

9 ▶RUIN STH 어떤 것을 망치다◀ [T] to ruin something, or lose a good opportunity, by making a mistake or being careless ‖ 실수나 부주의로 인해 일을 망치다, 또는 좋은 기회를 놓치다: *I blew it by talking too much in the interview.* 나는 면접에서 말을 너무 많이 해서 망쳤다.

10 ▶LEAVE 떠나다◀ [T] to leave a place quickly ‖ 어떤 장소를 빨리 떠나다: *Let's blow this joint.* (=*leave this place*) 빨리 여기를 떠나자.

11 ▶SPEND MONEY 돈을 쓰다◀ [T] to spend a lot of money at one time in a careless way ‖ 돈을 한번에 흥청망청 많이 쓰다. 한꺼번에 날리다: *He got a big insurance payment, but he blew it all on a new stereo.* 그는 보험금을 많이 받았지만 새 스테레오를 사는데 다 날려 버렸다.

12 blow your top/stack to suddenly become extremely angry ‖ 갑자기 극도로 화가 나다. 울화통을 터트리다: *If you tell Dad about the car, he'll blow his top.* 네가 아빠에게 차 이야기를 꺼낸다면 버럭 화내실 거다.

13 blow sb's mind to make someone feel very surprised by something ‖ 사람을 무엇인가에 매우 놀라게 하다: *That's what really blew my mind about Michael.* 그 점이 내가 정말 마이클에게 놀랐던 점이다.

blow away *phr v* [T] **1** [**blow** sb **away**] SPOKEN to completely surprise someone; AMAZE ‖ 남을 정말 놀라게 하다; 慇 amaze: *It just blows me away to think how fast Graham has grown.* 그레이엄이 얼마나 빠르게 성장했는지를 생각하면 정말 놀라울 뿐이다. **2** [**blow** sb/sth ↔ **away**] INFORMAL to completely destroy something or kill someone with a weapon ‖ 무엇을 완전히 파괴하거나 무기로 사람을 죽이다: *Stop or I'll blow you away.* 거기 멈춰! 안 그러면 쏘아 죽여버리겠다. **3** [**blow** sb ↔ **away**] INFORMAL to defeat someone completely, especially in a sports game ‖ 특히 스포츠 경기에서 상대편을 완전히 패배시키다. 이기다: *The Giants blew away the Rams 31-0.* 자이언츠는 램스를 31대 0으로 대파(大破)했다.

blow down *phr v* [I, T **blow** sth ↔ **down**] if the wind blows something down, or if it blows down, the wind makes it fall ‖ 바람이 불어 무엇이 넘어지거나 어떤 것을 넘어뜨리다: *A big tree had blown down and was blocking the road.* 큰 나무가 바람에 쓰러져 길을 막고 있었다.

blow into sth *phr v* [T] INFORMAL to arrive without warning ‖ 예고도 없이 나타나다. 홀연히 나타나다: *Look who just blew into town!* 마을에 홀연히 나타난 저

사람 좀 봐!

blow off *phr v* [T] **1** [**blow** sth ↔ **off**] to damage someone or something, or explode in a way that makes part of that person or thing come off ‖ 사람이나 사물을 손상시키다, 또는 사람이나 사물의 일부가 떨어져나가게 폭파시키다: *a soldier whose leg was **blown off** by a land mine* 지뢰에 다리가 잘려나간 군인 **2** [**blow** sb/sth ↔ **off**] SPOKEN to treat someone or something as unimportant, for example by not doing what you were expected to do ‖ 남이 기대하는 일을 하지 않는 등의 방식으로, 사람이나 사물을 중요하지 않게 대하다. 무시하다: *I blew off my 8 a.m. class again.* 오전 8시 수업을 또 듣지 않았다.

blow out *phr v* [I, T **blow** sth ↔ **out**] to make a fire suddenly stop burning, or to stop burning ‖ 갑자기 불을 끄다, 또는 불이 꺼지다: *Bobbi shut her eyes and blew out her birthday candles.* 보비는 눈을 감고 생일 촛불을 껐다.

blow over *phr v* **1** [I, T **blow** sth ↔ **over**] if the wind blows something over, or if it blows over, the wind makes it fall ‖ 바람이 불어서 어떤 것이 넘어지거나 어떤 것을 넘어뜨리다: *Our fence blew over during the storm.* 폭풍으로 우리집 울타리가 쓰러졌다. **2** [I] to end, or no longer be important ‖ 끝나다, 또는 더 이상 중요하지 않다: *Matt was hoping the whole problem with Tim would blow over.* 매트는 팀과의 모든 문제가 해결되기를 바라고 있었다.

blow up *phr v* **1** [I, T **blow** sth ↔ **up**] to destroy something, or to be destroyed, by an explosion ‖ 폭발로 어떤 것을 파괴하거나 파괴되다: *A car was blown up near the embassy.* 대사관 근처에서 차량이 폭파되었다. / *The Tatleys' gas boiler blew up last night.* 태틀리 집의 가스 보일러가 지난 밤 폭발했다. **2** [T **blow** sth ↔ **up**] to fill something with air or gas ‖ 공기나 가스로 어떤 것을 채우다: *Come and help me blow up the balloons.* 이리 와서 풍선에 바람넣는 것 좀 도와줘. **3** [I] SPOKEN to shout angrily at someone ‖ 남에게 화를 내며 소리치다: *I'm sorry I blew up at you earlier, Julie.* 전에 네게 화내고 소리질러서 미안해, 줄리. **4** [T **blow** sth ↔ **up**] to make a photograph larger ‖ 사진을 확대하다: *I'd like to have this picture blown up.* 이 사진을 확대하고 싶어요.

blow² *n* **1** a hard hit with a hand, tool, or weapon ‖ 손, 도구 또는 무기로 세게 때림. 구타. 일격: *a blow to/in the stomach* 배에 맞은 일격 **2** an event that makes you very unhappy or shocks you ‖ 언짢게 하거나 충격을 주는 사건. 정신적 타격: *Not getting the job was a blow to Kate's confidence.* 직장을 구하지 못해 케이트는 자신감에 타격을 입었다. / *The death of their father was a terrible blow.* 그들 아버지의 죽음은 청천벽력이었다. **3** the act of blowing ‖ 부는 행위: *Give the candles a good blow.* 촛불을 잘 불어 봐라. **4 come to blows** if two people come to blows, they get so angry that they start hitting each other ‖ 두 사람이 너무 화가 나 서로 때리기 시작하다. 치고 받고 싸우다

blow-by-blow /ˌ. . '. ./ *adj* a blow-by-blow description, account etc. gives the details of an event as it happens ‖ 묘사·설명 등이 어떤 사건이 일어난 그대로 세부 사항을 알려주는. 매우 상세한

blow dry /'. ./ *v* [T] to dry hair using an electric machine that you hold in your hand ‖ 손에 쥐는 전기 기구로 머리를 말리다. 헤어 드라이어로 말리다: *blow dried hair* 헤어 드라이어로 말린 머리

blown /bloʊn/ *v* the PAST PARTICIPLE of BLOW ‖ blow의 과거 분사형

blow-out /'bloʊaʊt/ *n* INFORMAL **1** the sudden bursting of a TIRE ‖ 타이어의 갑작스런 파열. 펑크 **2** a big expensive meal or a large party ‖ 매우 비싼 식사나 큰 파티 **3** an easy victory in a sports game ‖ 스포츠 경기에서의 수월한 승리

blow-torch /'bloʊ.tɔrtʃ/ *n* a piece of equipment that is held in the hand and produces a small, very hot flame, used for welding (WELD) metal ‖ 작고 매우 뜨거운 화염을 내는, 손에 잡히는 금속 용접용 기기. 용접용 화염 발사 장치

blow-up /'. ./ *n* **1** a photograph, or part of a photograph, that has been made larger ‖ 확대된 사진이나 사진의 일부분. 확대(사진) **2** INFORMAL a sudden loud argument ‖ 갑작스런 격렬한 논쟁. 격론

blubber¹ /'blʌbɚ/ *n* [U] the fat of sea animals, especially WHALEs ‖ 바다 동물 특히 고래의 지방

blubber² *v* [I] INFORMAL to cry in a noisy way ‖ 시끄럽게 울다. 엉엉 소리내어 울다: *Anna tried to talk but could only blubber.* 안나는 말을 하려 했지만 엉엉 울 수 밖에 없었다.

blud·geon /'blʌdʒən/ *v* [T] to hit someone many times with something heavy ‖ 무거운 물체로 남을 수차례 때리다.

blue¹ /blu/ *adj* **1** having the same color

as a clear sky during the day ‖ 낮시간 동안의 청명한 하늘 색과 같은. 푸른. 파란: *the blue lake water* 푸르른 호수의 물 / *a dark/light blue dress* 짙은[엷은] 청색 드레스 **2** INFORMAL sad and without hope ‖ 슬프고 희망이 없는. 우울한: *I've been feeling kind of blue lately.* 최근에 계속 기분이 울적하다. **3 do sth till you're blue in the face** INFORMAL to do something a lot but without achieving what you want ‖ 어떤 것을 열심히 하나 원하는 바를 얻지 못하다. 얼굴이 파랗게 질릴 때까지 …을 하다: *You can argue till you're blue in the face, but I won't change my mind.* 네가 질리도록 주장해 봤자 나는 결코 마음을 바꾸지 않을 것이다. —see also **once in a blue moon** (ONCE¹)

blue² *n* [U] **1** a blue color ‖ 푸른색. 청색: *We're painting the bedroom blue.* 우리는 침실을 청색으로 칠할 것이다. **2 out of the blue** INFORMAL when you are not expecting something to happen ‖ 어떤 것이 일어나리라고 예상치 않을 때에 쓰여. 느닷없이. 뜻밖에: *The call from Judge Richey came out of the blue.* 뜻밖에 져지 리치에게서 전화가 왔다. —see also BLUES

blue·bell /'blubɛl/ *n* a small plant with blue flowers that grows in the forest ‖ 숲에서 자라는 푸른 꽃이 피는 작은 식물

blue·ber·ry /'blu,bɛri/ *n* a small dark blue round BERRY ‖ 짙은 청색의 작고 둥근 베리. 블루베리: *blueberry muffins* 블루베리 머핀

blue·bird /'blubɚd/ *n* a small North American wild bird that sings and has a blue back and wings ‖ 푸른 등과 날개가 있고 노래하는, 자그마한 북미산 야생 조류. 블루버드

blue-blood·ed /,. '../ *adj* belonging to a royal or NOBLE family ‖ 왕가 또는 귀족 가문에 속하는. 왕가[귀족] 태생의 – **blue-blood** /'. ./ *n* [U]

blue book /'. ./ *n* **1** a book with a blue cover that is used in colleges for writing answers to test questions ‖ 대학에서 시험 문제의 답안 작성에 쓰는 표지가 청색인 책. 대학의 시험 답안지 **2** a book with a list of prices that you should expect to pay for any used car ‖ 중고차에 지불할 것이 예상되는 가격 목록을 적은 책

blue cheese /,. './ *n* [C, U] a strong-tasting pale cheese with blue spots in it ‖ 푸른 점이 박힌 강한 맛의 흰색 치즈. 블루 치즈

blue chip /'. ,./ *adj* considered to be important, profitable, and unlikely to disappoint you ‖ 중요하고 이익이 되리라 여겨지며 실망시키지 않을 것 같은. 우량의: *a blue-chip investment* 전망 있는 투자 – **blue chip** *n*

blue col·lar /,. '../ *adj* blue collar workers do jobs such as repairing machines and working in factories ‖ 노동자가 기계를 수리하며 공장에서 일하는 직종의. 블루 칼라의. 육체 노동을 하는 —see usage note at CLASS¹

blue·grass /'blugræs/ *n* [U] a type of COUNTRY AND WESTERN music from the southern and western US, using string instruments such as the VIOLIN ‖ 바이올린 등의 현악기로 연주하는 미국 남서부의 일종의 컨트리·웨스턴 음악. 블루그래스

blue·jay /'bludʒeɪ/ *n* a common North American wild bird that has blue, black, and white feathers ‖ 파란색, 검정색, 흰색의 깃털이 있는 북미산의 흔한 야생 조류. 아메리카어치

blue jeans /'. ./ *n* [plural] ⇨ JEANS

blue law /'. ./ *n* INFORMAL a law that limits the time when people can drink alcohol, work on Sundays etc. ‖ 일요일 등에 음주·노동하는 시간을 제한하는 법. 청교도적 금법(禁法)

blue mov·ie /,. '../ *n* a movie showing sexual activity ‖ 성행위를 보여 주는 영화. 도색[포르노] 영화

blue·print /'blu,prɪnt/ *n* **1** a plan for achieving something ‖ 어떤 것을 달성하기 위한 계획. 청사진: *a blueprint for health care reform* 의료 개혁의 청사진 **2** a print of a plan for a building, machine etc. ‖ 건물·기계 등을 위한 설계도. 청사진

blue rib·bon /,. '../ *n* a small piece of blue material given to someone who wins a competition ‖ 경쟁의 승자에게 주는 푸른 소재의 작은 조각. 청색 리본

blues /bluz/ *n* [plural] **1** a slow sad style of music that came from the Afro-American culture ‖ 미 흑인 문화에서 기원한 느리고 슬픈 스타일의 음악. 블루스: *a blues singer* 블루스 가수 **2 have/get the blues** INFORMAL to be or become sad ‖ 슬프거나 슬퍼지다. 우울하다[해지다]

bluff¹ /blʌf/ *v* [I, T] to pretend to be more confident that you are, or to pretend to know something that you do not know ‖ 실제보다 더 자신감 있는 척하거나 모르는 것을 아는 체하다. 허세를 부려서 (남을) 속이다. 허풍떨다: *I could tell Sunderland was bluffing because he kept looking away.* 선더랜드가 계속 눈길을 피하고 있었기 때문에 나는 그가 속이고 있다는 것을 알 수 있었다.

bluff² *n* [C, U] **1** the action of bluffing ‖ 허세부리는 행위: *Grolsky's threat to resign is no more than a bluff.* 그롤스키의 사임하겠다는 협박은 단지 허풍에 지나지 않았다. **2 call sb's bluff** to tell someone to do what s/he threatens because you believe s/he has no intention of doing it ‖ 그럴 의도가 없다고 믿고 위협하는 일을 해 보라고 말하다. 허세에 도전[응답]하다: *If the general calls our bluff, we'd better have enough men in there to fight.* 그 장군이 우리의 허세에 도전한다면, 우리는 거기서 싸울 충분한 병사들이 있는 것이 좋겠다. **3** a very steep cliff or slope ‖ 매우 가파른 절벽이나 경사: *Pine Bluff, Arkansas.* 아칸소 주에 있는 파인 절벽

blunder¹ /'blʌndɚ/ *n* a careless or stupid mistake ‖ 부주의하거나 어리석은 실수. 큰 실수[실책]: *a terrible political blunder* 대단한 정치적 실수

blunder² *v* [I] **1** to make a careless or stupid mistake ‖ 부주의하거나 어리석은 실수를 하다 **2** to move in an unsteady way as if you cannot see well ‖ 잘 보이지 않는 듯이 불안정하게 움직이다. 비틀거리다. 머뭇거리다

blunt¹ /blʌnt/ *adj* **1** not sharp or pointed ‖ 날카롭거나 뾰족하지 않은. 무딘: *blunt scissors* 무딘 가위 / *a blunt table knife* 무딘 식탁용 나이프 — compare DULL¹ —see picture at SHARP¹ **2** speaking in an honest way even if it upsets people ‖ 남을 화나게 하더라도 솔직하게 말하는: *Did you have to be so blunt?* 너 그렇게 무례할 정도로 솔직해야 했니? – **bluntness** *n* [U]

blunt² *v* [T] to make something less sharp or less strong ‖ 어떤 것을 날카로움이나 강함이 덜하게 하다. ⋯을 무디게 만들다: *a blunted axe* 무딘 도끼 / *The whiskey had blunted his senses.* 위스키가 그의 감각을 둔화시켰다.

blunt·ly /'blʌnt⁽ˡ⁾li/ *adv* speaking in a direct, honest way that sometimes upsets people ‖ 사람을 화나게 할 정도로 직설적이고 솔직하게 말하는. 무뚝뚝하게. 쌀쌀맞게: *To put it bluntly, you're failing the class.* 솔직히 말하면 넌 반에서 낙제야.

blur¹ /blɚ/ *n* [singular] **1** something that you cannot see clearly ‖ 선명하게 볼 수 없는 것. 희미한 상태. 흐릿함: *a blur of horses running past* 말들이 뛰어 지나가는 희미한 모습 **2** something that is difficult to remember ‖ 기억하기 어려운 것. 희미함: *The next day was all a blur.* 다음날의 기억은 온통 희미했다.

blur² *v* **-rred, -rring** [I, T] **1** to become difficult to see, or to make something difficult to see, because the edges are not clear, or to make something do this ‖ 가장자리가 명확하지 않아서 보기 어렵게 되다, 또는 보기 어렵게 만들다, 또는 어떤 것을 흐리게 만들다. 흐릿해지다. 흐리게 하다: *Tears blurred my vision.* 눈물 때문에 시야가 흐려졌다. **2** to make the difference between two things less clear ‖ 두 사물의 차이의 명확함을 덜하게 하다. 둔화시키다: *Differences in social classes have been blurred.* 사회 계층 간의 차이가 둔화되었다.

blurb /blɚb/ *n* a short description giving information about a book, new product etc. ‖ 책·새 제품 등에 대해 정보를 제공하는 짧은 말. 추천문. 선전문

blurred /blɚd/ *adj* **1** also **blur·ry** /'blɚi/ not clear in shape, or making it difficult to see shapes ‖ 형체가 명확하지 않은, 또는 형체를 보기 어렵게 만드는. 희미한. 흐릿한: *blurred vision* 몽롱한 시야 / *blurry photos* 흐릿한 사진 **2** difficult to understand or remember clearly ‖ 명확히 이해하거나 기억하기 어려운. 애매한. 희미한: *blurred memories* 희미한 기억

blurt /blɚt/ *v* [T] also **blurt out** to say something suddenly and without thinking, usually because you are nervous or excited ‖ 대개 긴장하거나 흥분하여 갑작스레 생각 없이 어떤 것을 말하다. 불쑥 말하다. 무심코 말하다: *"But I love you!" Ted blurted.* "하지만 난 널 사랑해!"라고 테드가 불쑥 말했다.

blush¹ /blʌʃ/ *v* [I] to become red in the face, usually because you are embarrassed ‖ 대개 부끄러워 얼굴이 빨개지다. 얼굴을 붉히다: *She's so shy, she blushes when she talks.* 그녀는 수줍음을 잘 타서 이야기할 때 얼굴이 빨개진다.

blush² *n* **1** the red color on your face that appears when you are embarrassed, confused, or ashamed ‖ 당황[혼란, 수치]스러울 때 얼굴에 나타나는 붉은 색조. 홍조 **2** [U] cream or powder used for making your cheeks slightly red or pink ‖ 뺨을 약간 붉거나 분홍색으로 만들기 위해 사용하는 크림이나 파우더

blus·ter¹ /'blʌstɚ/ *v* [I] **1** to talk loudly and behave as if what you are doing is extremely important ‖ 자신이 하고 있는 일이 상당히 중요한 것처럼 소리높여 말하고 행동하다. 허세부리다 **2** if the wind blusters, it blows violently ‖ 바람이 세차게 불다. 거세게 몰아치다

bluster² *n* [U] noisy, proud talk ‖ 소란스럽고 자만에 찬 말. 허세

blus·ter·y /'blʌstəri/ *adj* blustery weather is very windy ‖ 날씨가 바람이 많이 부는: *a blustery winter day* 바람이 많이 부는 겨울날

Blvd. the written abbreviation of boulevard ‖ boulevard의 약어

BO, B.O. *n* [U] SLANG body odor; an unpleasant smell from someone's body ‖ body odor(체취)의 약어; 몸에서 나는 불쾌한 냄새

boa con·strict·or /ˌboʊə kənˈstrɪktər/ *n* a large tropical snake that kills animals for food by crushing them ‖ 동물을 압사시켜 잡아먹는 거대한 열대산 뱀. 보아뱀

boar /bɔr/ *n* **1** a male pig kept on a farm for breeding ‖ 교배용으로 농장에서 기르는 수퇘지 **2** a wild pig ‖ 야생 돼지

board¹ /bɔrd/ *n*

1 ▶FOR DOING THINGS ON 사물을 올려 놓는 것◀ a flat piece of wood, plastic etc. that you use for a particular purpose ‖ 특정 목적을 위해 사용하는 나무·플라스틱 등의 평평한 조각. (···)판 [대]: *a cutting board* 재단대 / *Where's the chess board?* 체스판 어디 있니?

2 ▶GROUP OF PEOPLE 사람들의 집단◀ a group of people in an organization who make the rules and important decisions ‖ 조직에서 규칙이나 중요한 사항들을 결정하는 일단의 사람들. ···위원회: *the local school board* 지역 학교 위원회 / *a board of directors* 이사회

3 ▶FOR INFORMATION 정보용◀ a flat wide piece of wood, plastic etc. where information is written or shown ‖ 정보를 쓰거나 보여주는 나무·플라스틱 등으로 만든 평평하고 넓은 조각. 칠판. 게시판: *Your vocabulary words for this week are on the board.* 이번 주에 배울 단어는 칠판에 있습니다. —see also BLACKBOARD, BULLETIN BOARD

4 ▶FOR BUILDING 건축용◀ a long thin flat piece of wood used for making floors, walls, fences etc. ‖ 바닥·벽·울타리 등을 만드는 데에 쓰는 길고 얇으며 평평한 조각. 널빤지. 판자

5 on board on a plane, ship etc. ‖ 비행기·배 등에 타고. 탑승[승선]하여: *No one on board was hurt.* 탑승객 중 아무도 다치지 않았다.

6 take sth on board to accept a suggestion, idea etc. and do something about it ‖ 제안·생각 등을 받아들여 그것에 대한 뭔가를 하다. ···을 참작하다: *We'll try to take some of your points on board.* 당신이 말하는 바를 참작해 보도록 하겠습니다.

7 across the board if something happens across the board, it affects everyone in a particular group ‖ 특정 집단의 모든 이들에게 영향을 끼쳐. 일률적으로. 모든 구성원을 포함하여: *increases in pay across the board* 일률적인 봉급 인상

8 ▶MEALS 식사◀ [U] the meals that are provided for you when you pay to stay somewhere ‖ 어느 곳에 머무르기 위해 돈을 지불하면 제공받는 식사: *Room and board is $3000 per semester.* 한 학기당 숙식비는 3,000달러입니다.

board² *v* [I, T] **1** to get on a plane, ship, train etc. in order to travel somewhere ‖ 어디로 가기 위해 비행기·배·기차 등에 타다. (···에) 탑승[승선]하다: *We invite our first class passengers to board the plane now.* 1등석 승객분들은 지금 탑승해 주십시오. **2** [I] to allow passengers onto a plane, ship, train etc. ‖ 승객들을 비행기·배·기차 등에 타게 하다: *Flight 503 for Toronto is now boarding.* 토론토행 503편은 현재 탑승 중입니다.

board sth ↔ **up** *phr v* [T] to cover a window or door with wooden boards ‖ 창문이나 문을 나무 판자로 가리다: *The house next door has been boarded up for months.* 옆집은 몇 개월 동안 문에 판자가 대져 있었다.

board·er /'bɔrdə/ *n* someone who pays to live in another person's house with some or all of his/her meals provided ‖ 다른 사람의 집에 거주하기 위해 돈을 지불하고 식사를 제공받는 사람. 하숙인

board game /'. ./ *n* an indoor game played with wooden or plastic pieces that you move on a specially designed board made of wood or thick CARDBOARD ‖ 나무 판자나 두꺼운 보드지로 만든, 특별히 고안된 판 위에서 나무나 플라스틱 말을 움직여 하는 실내 게임. 보드 게임

board·ing·house /'bɔrdɪŋˌhaʊs/ *n* a private house where you pay to sleep and eat ‖ 돈을 내고 숙식을 하는 가정집. 하숙집

boarding school /'.. ./ *n* a school where students live as well as study ‖ 학생들이 공부뿐만 아니라 거주도 하는 학교. 기숙 학교

board·room /'bɔrdrum/ *n* a room where the DIRECTORs of a company have meetings ‖ 회사의 이사진들이 회의하는 방. 이사[중역] 회의실

board·walk /'bɔrdwɔk/ *n* a raised path made of wood, usually built next to the ocean ‖ 보통 해변가 옆에 지어 놓은, 나무

boast¹

(판자)를 올려 만든 길. 널빤지를 깐 해안 산책길

boast¹ /boʊst/ v 1 [I, T] to talk too proudly about your abilities, achievements etc. in order to make people admire you; BRAG ‖ 사람들에게 인정받기 위해 자신의 능력·성취한 일 등을 지나치게 자랑하여 말하다. 뽐내다. 자랑하다; 㕮 brag: *I don't want to sound like I'm boasting, but I'm sure I can do the job.* 자랑하는 것처럼 보이기는 싫지만, 전 그 일을 확실히 할 수 있습니다. 2 [T] to have a good feature ‖ 좋은 특성을 지니다. …을 갖추다[가지고 있다]: *The new athletic center boasts an Olympic-sized swimming pool.* 새 체육 센터는 올림픽용 규모의 수영장을 갖추고 있다. – **boastful** adj

boast² n something you like telling people because you are very proud of it ‖ 자랑스럽게 생각하기 때문에 사람들에게 말하고 싶은 것. 자랑(거리)

boat /boʊt/ n 1 a vehicle that travels across water ‖ 물을 건너갈 수 있는 운송 수단. 배: *fishing boats* 고기잡이배[어선] / *You can only get to the island by boat.* 배를 타야만 그 섬에 갈 수 있다. — compare SHIP¹ 2 **be in the same boat (as)** to be in the same unpleasant situation as someone else ‖ 다른 누군가와 똑같이 불쾌한 상황에 놓여 있다. (바람직하지 않은) 같은 입장[운명]에 있다: *We're all in the same boat, so stop complaining.* 우리는 모두 같은 처지야. 그러니 불평하지 마. —see also **miss the boat** (MISS¹), **rock the boat** (ROCK²)

boat peo·ple /'. ,../ n [plural] people who escape from bad conditions in their country in small boats ‖ 작은 배를 타고 자국의 악조건에서 탈출하는 사람들. (이주) 난민. 보트 피플

bob¹ /bɑb/ v **-bbed, -bbing 1** [I] to move up and down ‖ 위아래로 움직이다: *a boat bobbing up and down on the water* 물 위에서 상하로 움직이는 배 **2** [T] to cut someone's hair so that it is the same length all the way around his/her head ‖ 머리 둘레와 머리카락 길이가 같도록 머리를 자르다. 보브 스타일로[단발로] 자르다

bob² n a way of cutting hair so that it is the same length all the way around your head ‖ 머리 둘레와 머리카락의 길이를 완전히 같게 자르는 방법. (짧은) 단발 머리

bob·bin /'bɑbɪn/ n a small round object that you wind thread onto ‖ 실을 감는 작고 둥근 물건. 실패

bob·cat /'bɑbkæt/ n a North American wild cat that has no tail ‖ 꼬리가 없는 북미산 야생 고양이. 스라소니. 살쾡이류

bob·sled /'bɑbslɛd/, **bob·sleigh** /'bɑbsleɪ/ n a small vehicle with two long thin metal blades that is used for racing down a special ice track ‖ 특수 얼음 트랙을 타고 경주하는 데 쓰이는, 두 개의 길고 얇은 금속 날이 달린 작은 탈것. 봅슬레이 – **bobsled** v [I]

bode /boʊd/ v **bode well/ill** LITERARY to be a good or bad sign for the future ‖ 미래에 관한 좋거나 나쁜 징조가 되다. 밝은/불길한 전조가 되다

bod·ice /'bɑdɪs/ n the part of a woman's dress above her waist ‖ 여성용 드레스의 허리 위쪽 부분. 보디스. 여성복의 몸통 부분

bod·i·ly¹ /'bɑdl-i/ adj relating to the human body ‖ 인간의 신체와 관계된. 신체의: *bodily functions* 신체 기능

bodily² adv by moving all of your body or someone else's body ‖ 자신이나 타인의 전신을 움직여. 송두리째: *She had to be carried bodily to bed.* 그녀의 전신을 들어 침대로 옮겨야 했다.

bod·y /'bɑdi/ n **1 ▶PHYSICAL BODY 신체◀ a)** the physical structure of a person or animal ‖ 사람이나 동물의 신체 구조: *a strong healthy body* 강하고 건강한 신체 **b)** the central part of a person or animal's body, not including the head, arms, legs or wings ‖ 머리[팔, 다리, 날개]를 제외한 사람이나 동물의 몸통: *a short body and long legs* 짧은 몸통과 긴 다리 **c)** the body of a dead person ‖ 죽은 사람의 신체. 시체. 시신: *They flew his body home to his parents.* 그들은 그의 시신을 항공편으로 부모님이 계신 그의 고향으로 보냈다. ✗DON'T SAY "his dead body."✗ "his dead body"라고는 하지 않는다. —see picture at HEAD and EYE **2 ▶GROUP OF PEOPLE 사람의 무리◀** a group of people who work together for a particular purpose ‖ 특정한 목적을 위해 함께 일하는 사람들의 집단. 단체. 회: *the governing body of a university* 대학의 이사회 / *the president of the student body* (=all the students in a school or college) 총학생회장 **3 a/the body of sth a)** a large amount or collection of something ‖ 어떤 것의 많은 양이나 전체. 대부분: *a body of literature* 대부분의 문학 **b)** the main, central, or most important part of something ‖ 어떤 것의 주된[중심된, 가장 중요한] 부분: *the body of the report* 기사

body

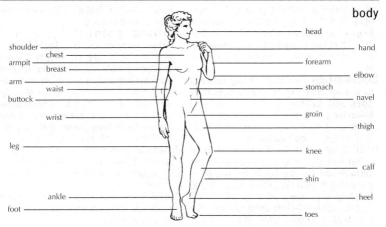

shoulder
chest
armpit
breast
arm
waist
buttock
wrist

leg

ankle

foot

head
hand
forearm
elbow
stomach
navel
groin
thigh

knee
calf
shin
heel

toes

의 본문

4 -bodied   a) having a particular type of body ‖ 특정한 형태의 몸을 가진. …형[타입]의: *thick-bodied men* 몸집이 큰 남자들 **b)** having a particular amount of taste ‖ 특정한 만큼의 맛이 나는: *full-bodied red wine* 풍부한 맛을 가진 적포도주

5 ▶VEHICLE 차량◀ the main structure of a vehicle, not including the engine, wheels etc. ‖ 엔진·바퀴 등을 포함하지 않은 탈것의 주요 구조. 동체. 차체: *The body of the airplane was broken in two.* 그 비행기의 동체는 두 동강 났다.

6 body and soul with all your effort and attention ‖ 모든 노력과 주의를 기울여. 혼신의 힘으로: *devoting yourself body and soul to a cause* 대의명분에 몸과 마음을 다함

7 keep body and soul together to manage to continue to live, although you may not have much money ‖ 많은 돈을 가지고 있지는 않지만 근근이 살아가다. 연명하다

body build·ing /ˈ.. ˌ../ *n* [U] an activity in which you do hard physical exercise in order to develop big muscles ‖ 근육을 잘 발달시키려고 힘든 육체 운동을 하는 활동. 보디 빌딩 **– body builder** *n*

bod·y·guard /ˈbɑdiˌgɑrd/ *n* a person or group of people whose job is to protect an important person ‖ 주요 인물을 보호하는 직업인이나 그 무리. 보디가드. 경호원(단)

body lan·guage /ˈ.. ˌ../ *n* [U] changes in your body position and movements that show what you are feeling or thinking ‖ 감정이나 생각을 드러내는 몸의 자세와 움직임의 변화. 바디 랭귀지. 신체 언어

body o·dor /ˈ.. ˌ../ *n* ⇨ BO

bod·y·work /ˈbɑdiˌwɜrk/ *n* [U] work done to repair the frame of a vehicle, not including the engine, wheels etc. ‖ 엔진·바퀴 등을 제외한 차체 구조를 수리하는 작업: *I know a garage that does good bodywork.* 나는 차체 수리를 잘 하는 자동차 정비소를 안다.

bog¹ /bɑg, bɔg/ *n* [C, U] an area of wet muddy ground that you can sink into ‖ 속으로 빠질 수 있는 축축한 진흙 땅의 지역. 늪. 소택지

bog² *v* **-gged, -gging be/get bogged down** to be or become too involved in dealing with something so that you cannot finish an activity that is more important ‖ 더욱 중요한 활동을 끝낼 수 없을 정도로 어떤 일을 처리하는 데 너무 몰두하게 되다. 난항에 빠지다: *The negotiations are getting bogged down in details.* 그 협상은 세부 사항에서 난항에 빠져 있다.

bo·gey·man /ˈbʊgiˌmæn/ *n* ⇨ BOOGIE MAN

bog·gle /ˈbɑgəl/ *v* **the mind boggles/sth boggles the mind** INFORMAL used in order to say that something is difficult to believe or very confusing ‖ 어떤 일이 믿기 어렵거나 매우 혼란스럽다고 말하는 데에 쓰여. 질려서 위축되다. 상상할 수 없다: *The paperwork you have to fill out just boggles the mind.* 기입 해야 하는 문서 작업은 상상조차 할 수 없다.

bo·gus /ˈboʊgəs/ *adj* **1** INFORMAL not true or real, although someone tries to make you think it is; FAKE ‖ 누군가가 비

록 사실이라고 생각하게끔 유도해도 진실이나 실제가 아닌. 거짓의; 🔞 **fake:** *a bogus insurance claim* 허위 보험금 청구 **2** SLANG completely worthless ‖ 전혀 가치 없는: *a bogus movie* 형편없는 영화

bo·he·mi·an /boʊˈhimiən/ *adj* relating to a way of living in which someone does not accept society's rules of behavior ‖ 사회의 행동 규범을 받아들이지 않는 생활 방식과 관련된. 방랑적인. 자유 분방한 – **bohemian** *n*

boil¹ /bɔɪl/ *v* **1** [I, T] if a liquid boils, it is hot enough for BUBBLEs to rise to the surface and for the liquid to change to gas ‖ 액체가 기화(氣化)하며 액체 표면에 보글보글 끓는 방울이 생길 정도로 충분히 뜨겁다. 끓다. 끓이다: *Drop the noodles into boiling salted water.* 끓는 소금물에 면을 넣어라. / *Turn off the heat – the water has boiled.* 불을 꺼라. 물이 끓잖아. **2** [I, T] if something containing liquid boils, the liquid inside it is boiling ‖ 무엇에 들어 있는 액체가 끓다: *Ben, the kettle's boiling.* 벤, 주전자가 끓고 있어. **3** also **boil up** [I, T] to cook food in boiling water ‖ 끓는 물에 음식을 요리하다. 삶다. 삶아지다: *Boil the vegetables for 10 minutes.* 10분 동안 그 야채를 끓는 물에 데쳐라.

boil down to sth *phr v* [T] **it (all) boils down to** used in order to say what the main cause or point of something is ‖ 주요한 원인이나 요소가 무엇인지 말하는 데에 쓰여. 요약하면 …이다. 문제는 …으로 귀결된다: *It all boils down to how much money you have.* 모든 것을 요약하자면 당신이 얼마나 많은 돈을 가지고 있느냐의 문제이다.

boil over *phr v* [I] if a liquid boils over, it flows over the side of a container because it is boiling ‖ 액체가 끓어서 용기 밖으로 흐르다. 끓어 넘치다

boil² *n* **1** [singular] the act or state of boiling ‖ 끓이는 행위나 끓는 상태: *Bring the soup to a boil and cook for 5 minutes.* 수프를 5분 동안 끓여서 요리해라. **2** a painful infected swelling under the skin ‖ 피부 밑에서 부풀어오른 아픈 감염 부위. 부스럼. 종기

boil·er /ˈbɔɪlɚ/ *n* a container for boiling water that is part of a steam engine, or that is used for providing heat in a house ‖ 증기 엔진의 한 부분인 또는 가정에 열을 공급하기 위해 사용하는, 물을 끓이는 용기. 보일러

boil·ing /ˈbɔɪlɪŋ/, **boiling hot** *adj* too hot ‖ 너무 뜨거운: *It's boiling hot in here!* 이곳은 지독하게 덥군! —see usage note at TEMPERATURE

boiling point /ˈ.. ˌ./ *n* **1** the temperature at which a liquid boils ‖ 액체가 끓는 온도. 끓는점. 비등점 **2** a point at which people can no longer deal with a problem calmly ‖ 문제를 더 이상 조용히 처리할 수 없는 지점. 흥분·분노 등이 폭발하는 순간. 최고조: *Frustrations with the military government finally reached a boiling point.* 군사 정부에 대한 실망이 마침내 최고조에 도달했다.

bois·ter·ous /ˈbɔɪstərəs/ *adj* noisy and cheerful ‖ 떠들썩하고 흥겨운. 야단법석인: *boisterous children* 야단법석을 떠는 아이들

bold /boʊld/ *adj* **1** showing that you are confident and willing to take risks ‖ 자신감이 있고 위험을 기꺼이 감수하겠다는 것을 나타내는. 대담한. 용감한: *Yamamoto's plan was bold and original.* 야마모토의 계획은 대담하고 독창적이었다. **2** writing, shapes, or colors that are bold are very clear and strong or bright ‖ 글씨[모양, 색깔]가 매우 명확한[강한, 밝은]. 뚜렷한. 눈에 띄는: *wallpaper with bold stripes* 밝은 줄무늬가 들어간 벽지 – **boldly** *adv* – **boldness** *n* [U]

bo·lo·gna /bəˈloʊni/ *n* a type of cooked meat often eaten in SANDWICHes ‖ 종종 샌드위치에 끼워 먹는 요리된 고기의 일종. 볼로냐 소시지

bol·ster¹ /ˈboʊlstɚ/ *v* [T] also **bolster up 1** to improve someone's opinion about himself/herself ‖ 자기 자신에 대한 생각을 향상시키다.…을 고무하다: *Roy's promotion seems to have bolstered his confidence.* 로이의 승진은 그의 자신감을 더욱 북돋우어 주는 것 같다. **2** to improve something by supporting it ‖ 어떤 것을 지지하여 향상시키다.…을 강화하다: *New reports have bolstered the committee's research.* 새로운 보고서는 그 위원회의 연구를 지지했다.

bolster² *n* a long firm PILLOW ‖ 길고 단단한 베개. (베개 밑에 까는) 덧베개

bolt¹ /boʊlt/ *n* **1** a piece of metal that you slide across a door or window to close or lock it ‖ 문이나 창문을 닫거나 잠그기 위해 지르는 금속 조각. 빗장 **2** a screw with a flat head and no point, for fastening two pieces of metal together ‖ 두 개의 금속 조각을 함께 조이기 위한, 뾰족한 끝이 없고 납작한 머리를 가진 나사. 볼트 **3 bolt of lightning** LIGHTNING that appears as a white line in the sky ‖ 하늘에 흰 줄처럼 보이는 번갯불. 한 줄기의 번개 —see also THUNDERBOLT **4** a large long roll of cloth ‖ 크고 긴 천 한 두루마리. 한 통[필]

bolt² *v* **1** [I] to suddenly start to run very fast because you are frightened ‖ 무서워서 갑자기 아주 빨리 뛰기 시작하다: *When the horse bolted, I fell off.* 말이 놀라 갑자기 달려 나가면서 나는 떨어지고 말았다. **2** [I, T] to close or lock a door or window with a bolt ‖ 빗장으로 문이나 창문을 닫거나 잠그다. 빗장이 채워지다. 빗장을 걸다 **3** [T] also **bolt down** to eat very quickly ‖ 매우 빨리 먹다: *Kevin bolted his lunch and ran out the door.* 케빈은 허겁지겁 점심을 먹고나서 밖으로 내달렸다. **4** [I, T] to fasten two things together using a BOLT ‖ 볼트를 이용해서 두 개의 물체를 고정시키다. 볼트로 죄다 [고정되다]

bolt³ *adv* **sit/stand bolt upright** to sit or stand with your back very straight, because something has frightened you ‖ 어떤 것이 무서워서 등을 매우 곧추세워 앉거나 서다. 똑바로 앉다[서다]: *Suddenly Dennis sat bolt upright in bed.* 데니스는 갑자기 침대에 똑바로 앉았다.

bomb¹ /bɑm/ *n* **1** a weapon made of material that will explode ‖ 폭발하는 물질로 만든 무기. 폭탄: *bombs dropping on the city* 도시에 떨어지는 폭탄 **2** the bomb⇨ NUCLEAR WEAPON **3** a container in which insect poison, paint etc. is kept under pressure ‖ 살충제·페인트 등을 담는 압력 용기. 고압 분무식 용기: *a flea bomb* (=used for killing FLEAS) 벼룩 퇴치 분무기

bomb² *v* **1** [T] to attack a place by exploding a bomb there, or by dropping a bomb by plane ‖ 어떤 지역에 폭탄을 터뜨리거나 비행기로 폭탄을 투하하여 공격하다: *Terrorists threatened to bomb the building.* 테러범들은 그 빌딩을 폭파시키겠다고 위협했다. **2** [I, T] SPOKEN to fail a test very badly ‖ 시험을 완전히 망치다: *I bombed my history test.* 나는 역사 시험을 망쳤다. **3** [I] if a play, movie, or joke bombs, it is not successful ‖ 연극·영화·농담 등이 성공적이지 못하다. 실패하다

bom·bard /bɑmˈbɑrd/ *v* [T] **1** to attack a place by firing a lot of guns at it, or dropping bombs on it ‖ 총알 세례를 퍼붓거나 폭탄을 떨어뜨려 공격하다. …을 폭격[포격]하다: *The town was bombarded from all sides.* 그 도시는 사방에서 공격을 받았다. **2** to continue to ask someone too many questions or give him/her too much information ‖ 누군가에게 너무 많은 질문을 계속해서 물어보다, 또는 너무

많은 정보를 주다. 질문 공세를 펴다: *Teachers are continually bombarded with new materials.* 교사들은 끊임없는 새로운 자료의 홍수 속에 산다. –
bombardment *n*

bombed /bɑmd/ *adj* SLANG drunk ‖ 술에 취한

bomb·er /ˈbɑmɚ/ *n* **1** a plane that carries and drops bombs ‖ 폭탄을 적재하여 투하하는 비행기. 폭격기 **2** someone who puts a bomb somewhere ‖ 어딘가에 폭탄을 설치하는 사람.

bomb·shell /ˈbɑmʃɛl/ *n* INFORMAL a shocking piece of news ‖ 깜짝 놀랄 만한 소식. 폭탄 선언: *Last night she dropped the bombshell and told him she wouldn't marry him.* 어젯밤에 그녀는 그와 결혼하지 않겠다고 그에게 폭탄 선언을 했다.

bo·na fide /ˈboʊnə ˌfaɪd, ˈbɑnə-/ *adj* real, true, and not pretending to be something else ‖ 실제이며 사실이어서 다른 것인체 하지 않는. 진짜의. 진심의: *We need a bona fide expert on the subject.* 우리는 그 주제에 대한 진짜 전문가가 필요하다.

bo·nan·za /bəˈnænzə, boʊ-/ *n* a lucky or successful situation in which people can make a lot of money ‖ 많은 돈을 벌 수 있는 운이 좋거나 성공적인 상황. 횡재: *a financial bonanza for the movie industry* 영화계의 재정적 횡재

bond¹ /bɑnd/ *n* **1** a feeling or interest that unites two or more people or groups ‖ 둘 이상의 사람이나 집단을 결속시키는 감정이나 관심. 유대. 결속: *a strong bond of affection between the two women* 두 여자 사이의 강한 애정의 결속 **2** an official document promising that a government or company will pay back money that it has borrowed, often with INTEREST ‖ 정부나 회사가 보통 이자와 함께 빌린 돈을 상환하겠다고 약속하는 공식 문서. 공채. 국채. 사채. 채권: *US savings* BONDS 미합중국 저축성 채권 — see also BONDS

bond² *v* [I] **1** to develop a special relationship with someone ‖ 누군가와 특별한 관계를 발전시키다. 유대를 형성하다: *The two older children never really bonded.* 그 나이든 두 아이들은 결코 친밀한 관계를 맺지 못했다. **2** if two things bond to each other, they become firmly stuck together ‖ 서로 딱 달라붙다. 밀착[접합]하다

bond·age /ˈbɑndɪdʒ/ *n* [U] the state of having your freedom limited or being prevented from doing what you want ‖

원하는 것을 금지당하거나 자유가 제한된 상태. 속박. 굴종

bond·ing /'bɑndɪŋ/ *n* [U] OFTEN HUMOROUS a process in which a special relationship develops between two or more people ‖ 두 명 이상의 사람 사이에 특별한 관계를 발전시키는 과정. 긴밀한 유대[결속]: *The guys went away for the weekend to do some male bonding.* (=bonding between men) 그 사내들은 남자들간의 우정을 결속시키기 위해 주말에 여행을 갔다.

bonds /bɑndz/ *n* [plural] LITERARY something that limits your freedom ‖ 자유를 제한하는 것. 속박. 구속

bone¹ /boʊn/ *n* **1** one of the hard parts that form the frame of a human or animal body ‖ 사람이나 동물의 골격을 형성하는 단단한 부분의 하나. 뼈대. 뼈: *a broken bone in his arm* 그의 부러진 팔뼈 / *the thigh bone* 넓적다리뼈 **2 make no bones about (doing) sth** to not feel nervous or ashamed about doing or saying something ‖ 어떤 것을 하거나 말하는 것에 대해 긴장하거나 수줍어하지 않다. 개의치 않다. 감추지 않다: *She makes no bones about her religious beliefs.* 그녀는 자기의 종교적 믿음을 숨기려 하지 않는다. **3 be chilled/frozen to the bone** to be extremely cold ‖ 몹시 춥다 **4 a bone of contention** something that causes arguments between people ‖ 사람들 사이에 논쟁을 야기시키는 것. 분쟁의 근원: *His smoking has been a bone of contention between us.* 그의 흡연이 우리 사이의 다툼의 원인이었다.

bone² *v* [T] to remove the bones from fish or meat ‖ 생선이나 고기에서 뼈를 제거하다. (뼈를) 바르다

bone up on sth *phr v* [T] INFORMAL to study something a lot for an examination ‖ 시험을 위하여 어떤 것을 열심히 공부하다: *I should bone up on my grammar before the test.* 나는 시험 치기 전에 문법 공부를 열심히 해야 한다.

bone dry /ˌ. './ *adj* completely dry ‖ 바짝 마른

bon·fire /'bɑnˌfaɪɚ/ *n* a large outdoor fire either for burning waste, or for a celebration ‖ 쓰레기를 태우거나 축하하기 위한 야외의 큰 불. 모닥불. 큰 화톳불

bon·gos /'bɑŋgoʊz/, **bongo drums** /'bɑŋgoʊ ˌdrʌmz/ *n* a pair of small drums that you play with your hands ‖ 손으로 연주하는 작은 한 쌍의 드럼. 봉고

bon·net /'bɑnɪt/ *n* a warm hat for a baby that ties under his/her chin ‖ 턱 아래에서 끈을 매는 아기용의 따뜻한 모자.

보닛

bo·nus /'boʊnəs/ *n* **1** money added to someone's pay, especially as a reward for good work ‖ 특히 일을 잘 한 것에 대한 보상으로 봉급에 추가되는 돈. 보너스: *a Christmas bonus* 크리스마스 보너스 **2** something good that you did not expect in a situation ‖ 어떤 상황에서 기대하지 않았던 뜻밖의 좋은 일. 뜻밖의 선물: *The fact that our house is so close to the school is a bonus.* 우리집이 학교와 아주 가깝게 있다는 사실은 뜻밖의 즐거움이다.

bon·y /'boʊni/ *adj* **1** very thin ‖ 매우 야윈. 앙상한: *a bony hand* 앙상한 손 **2** full of bones ‖ 뼈가 많은: *bony fish* 가시가 많은 생선

boo¹ /bu/ *v* [I, T] to shout BOO to show that you do not like a person, performance etc. ‖ 사람·공연 등을 좋아하지 않는다는 것을 보이기 위해 "우" 하고 소리치다. 비난[야유]하다

boo² *n, interjection* **1** a noise made by people who do not like a person, performance etc. ‖ 어떤 사람이나 공연 등을 좋아하지 않는 사람들이 내는 소리. 우 **2** a word you shout suddenly to someone to try to frighten him/her as a joke ‖ 장난으로 사람을 놀라게 하기 위해 갑자기 소리치는 말. 꽥

boob /bub/ *n* SLANG a woman's breast ‖ 여자의 가슴. 유방

boo-boo /'bubu/ *n* a word meaning a silly mistake or a small injury, used when speaking to children ‖ 아이들에게 사용하는 말로 어리석은 실수나 가벼운 상처를 의미하는 말. 바보[멍청한]짓

boob tube /'. ./ *n* SPOKEN ⇨ TV

boo·by prize /'bubi ˌpraɪz/ *n* a prize given as a joke to the person who is last in a competition ‖ 시합에서 꼴찌한 사람에게 재미로 주는 상. 최하위상. 꼴찌상

booby trap /'.. ˌ./ *n* a hidden bomb that explodes when you touch something else that is connected to it ‖ 연결된 다른 부분을 건드리면 폭발하는 위장 폭탄. 부비 트랩 – **booby-trapped** *adj*

boo·gie man /'bugi ˌmæn/ *n* an imaginary man who frightens children ‖ 아이들을 겁먹게 하는 상상의 남자. 악귀. 귀신

book¹ /bʊk/ *n* **1** a set of printed pages held together in a cover so that you can read them ‖ 읽을 수 있도록 표지로 함께 엮은 일련의 인쇄물. 책. 서적: *a book about/on photography* 사진첩 / *Have you read this book?* 이 책 읽어 봤니? **2** a set of sheets of paper held together in

boom²

a cover so that you can write on them ‖ 필기할 수 있도록 표지로 함께 엮은 종이 묶음. 공책. 연습장. 기록부: *an address book* 주소록 —compare NOTEBOOK **3** a set of things such as stamps, tickets etc. held together inside a paper cover ‖ 종이 표지 안으로 함께 묶은 우표나 회수권 등의 묶음. 철(綴). 다발. 세트: *a book of matches* 성냥 한 갑 **4 by the book** exactly according to rules or instructions ‖ 정확히 규칙이나 지시대로: *Around here, we do everything by the book, understand?* 이곳에서는 만사를 규칙대로 한다. 알아? —see also BOOKS, **throw the book at sb** (THROW)

book² *v* **1** [T] to arrange for someone such as a speaker or singer to perform on a particular date ‖ 강연자나 가수 등이 강연이나 공연할 특정한 날짜를 미리 정하다. …을 계약[예약]하다: *They have a speaker booked for next Tuesday.* 그들은 연설자가 다음 주 화요일에 연설할 수 있게 예정해 놓았다. **2** [I, T] to arrange with a hotel to stay there at a particular time in the future ‖ 앞으로 특정한 시간에 머물겠다고 호텔에 예약하다: *I've booked a room for us at the Hilton.* 힐튼 호텔에 우리가 지낼 방 하나를 예약해 두었다. **3** [T] to put someone's name officially in police records, with the charge made against him/her ‖ 경찰 기록부에 공식적으로 혐의가 있는 어떤 사람의 이름을 올리다. 입건하다: *Ramey was booked on suspicion of murder.* 라미는 살인 혐의로 입건됐다.

book·case /ˈbʊk-keɪs/ *n* a piece of furniture with shelves to hold books ‖ 책을 보관하는 선반이 달린 가구. 책장

book·end /ˈbʊkɛnd/ *n* one of a pair of objects that you put at each end of a row of books to prevent them from falling ‖ 책이 쓰러지지 않게 책의 열 양끝에 놓는 한 쌍의 물체 중 하나. 북엔드

bookie /ˈbʊki/ *n* INFORMAL someone whose job is to collect money that people BET on a race, sport etc. and who pays them if they win ‖ 사람들이 경주·경기 등에 건 돈을 모아 이긴 사람들에게 돈을 지불하는 직업인. 물주. 마권업자

book·ing /ˈbʊkɪŋ/ *n* an arrangement in which a hotel, theater etc. agrees to let you have a particular room, seat etc. at a future time ‖ 호텔의 특정 방·극장의 특정 좌석 등을 장차 사용할 수 있게 정해 둠. 예약: *Cheaper prices are available on early bookings.* 일찍 예약하면 보다 더 싼 가격으로 이용할 수 있다.

book·keep·ing /ˈbʊkˌkipɪŋ/ *n* [U] the job or activity of recording the financial accounts of an organization ‖ 조직체의 재무 계정을 기록하는 일이나 활동. 부기(簿記) – **bookkeeper** *n*

book·let /ˈbʊklɪt/ *n* a very short book that contains information ‖ 정보를 담은 매우 짧은 분량의 책. 소책자. 팸플릿: *a booklet on AIDS* 에이즈에 대한 팸플릿

book·mak·er /ˈbʊkˌmeɪkɚ/ *n* ⇨ BOOKIE

book·mark /ˈbʊkmɑrk/ *n* **1** a piece of paper that you put in a book to show you the last page you have read ‖ 읽은 책의 마지막 페이지를 나타내기 위해 책갈피에 꽂아 두는 종이 조각. 서표. 갈피표 **2** a way of saving the address of a page on the Internet, so that you can find it again easily ‖ 인터넷 상의 웹페이지 주소를 저장해서 쉽게 다시 찾을 수 있게 하는 방식. 즐겨찾기. 북마크

books /bʊks/ *n* [plural] written records of the financial accounts of a business ‖ 기업의 재무 계정의 기록. 회계 장부

book·shelf /ˈbʊkʃɛlf/ *n*, *plural* **bookshelves** /-ʃɛlvz/ a shelf on a wall or a piece of furniture with shelves, used for holding books ‖ 책을 보관하는 데 사용하는 선반이 달린 가구나 벽에 붙은 선반. 서가(書架). 책장

book·store /ˈbʊkstɔr/ *n* a store that sells books ‖ 책을 파는 가게. 서점. 책방

book·worm /ˈbʊkwɚm/ *n* INFORMAL someone who likes to read very much ‖ 읽는 것을 매우 좋아하는 사람. 독서광. 책벌레

boom¹ /bum/ *n* **1** a rapid increase of activity or interest in something ‖ 어떤 것에 대한 활동과 관심의 급속한 증가. 급격한 발전. 붐: *a boom in sales* 매출의 급신장 / *the building boom in the 1980s* 1980년대의 건축붐 / *The fitness boom started in the 70s.* 건강에 대한 급격한 관심이 70년대에 생기기 시작하였다. **2** a loud deep sound that you can hear for several seconds after it begins ‖ 소리가 난 뒤로 수초 간 들리는 크고 낮은 소리. 울림소리. 여음: *the boom of guns in the distance* 멀리서 쿵 하고 울리는 포성

boom² *v* **1** [I] to make a loud deep sound ‖ 크고 낮은 소리를 내다. 울려 퍼지다: *Chris's voice boomed above the others.* 크리스의 목소리는 다른 사람들 목소리 속에서 크고 묵직하게 울렸다. **2** to grow rapidly especially in value ‖ 특히 가치면에서 급속히 증대하다 – **booming** *adj* —see also **baby boom** (BABY)

boom box /ˈ. ˌ./ *n* INFORMAL ⇨ GHETTO BLASTER

boo·mer·ang /ˈbuːmə,ræŋ/ *n* a curved stick that comes back to you when you throw it ‖ 던지면 자신에게 되돌아오는 구부러진 막대기. 부메랑

boom town /ˈ. ˌ./ *n* INFORMAL a city that suddenly becomes very successful because of new industry ‖ 새로운 산업 때문에 급속히 번창한 도시. 신흥 도시

boon /buːn/ *n* LITERARY something that is very useful and makes your life a lot easier ‖ 매우 유용하고 삶을 훨씬 용이하게 만드는 것. 혜택. 은혜. 이익

boon·docks /ˈbundɑks/, **boo·nies** /ˈbuːniz/ *n* [plural] INFORMAL **the boondocks/boonies** a place that is a long way from any town ‖ 도시에서 멀리 떨어진 곳. 오지. 벽지. 시골 구석: *Ken's family live way out in the boondocks.* 켄의 가족은 아주 오지에 산다.

boor /bʊr/ *n* someone who behaves in an unacceptable way in social situations ‖ 사회적으로 받아들여질 수 없는 방식으로 행동하는 사람. 버릇없는[야비한] 사람 **– boorish** *adj*

boost¹ /buːst/ *n* **1** [singular] something that helps someone be more successful and confident, or that helps something increase or improve ‖ 어떤 사람을 더욱 성공하고 자신감 있게 도와주거나 어떤 것이 증가하거나 향상하게 도와주는 것. 후원. 격려. 응원: *Some women may need an extra boost from vitamins.* 어떤 여자들은 비타민으로 특별히 기분을 돋우는 것이 필요할 수 있다. / *a real boost to the American fashion industry* 미국 패션업계에 대한 실질적 후원 **2 give sb a boost** to lift or push someone so s/he can get over or onto something high or tall ‖ 들어올리거나 밀어서 높은 곳을 넘기나 닿을 수 있도록 남을 돕다. …을 들어[밀어]올리다: *Give your brother a boost.* 네 동생을 들어올려 주어라.

boost² *v* [T] **1** to increase something such as production, sales etc. because they are not as high as you want them to be ‖ 자신이 원하는 만큼 높지 않기에 생산·매출 등을 증가시키다: *The new facility will help boost oil production.* 그 새로운 설비는 석유 생산을 증가시키는 데 도움을 줄 것이다. **2 boost sb's confidence/ego etc.** to make someone feel more confident and less worried ‖ 남을 더욱 자신감을 갖고 걱정을 덜하게 만들다. …에게 자신감/자아를 북돋다: *I think Kathy's new job has boosted her ego.* 캐시의 새 직업이 그녀에게 더욱 자신감을 갖게 한 거라고 생각한다. **3** to help someone get over or onto something high or tall by lifting or pushing him/her up ‖ 들어올리거나 밀어서 높은 곳을 넘거나 닿을 수 있도록 남을 돕다. 들어[밀어]올리다

boost·er /ˈbuːstə/ *n* **1** a small quantity of a drug that increases the effect of one that was given before ‖ 전에 주어진 것의 효과를 증진시키는 소량의 약. 효능 촉진제. 보조약: *a measles booster* 홍역의 보조약 **2 confidence/morale/ego etc. booster** something that BOOSTs someone's confidence etc. ‖ 자신감을 증진시키는 것. 자신감/사기/자아를 고무시키는 것: *The letters from people at home are a great morale booster for the soldiers.* 고향의 가족들에게서 온 편지는 군인들의 사기를 크게 진작시켜 준다. **3** someone who gives a lot of support to a person, organization, or idea ‖ 사람[조직, 생각]을 전폭적으로 지원하는 사람: *The Williamstown High School Booster Club* 윌리엄스타운 고등학교 후원회 **4** a ROCKET that provides more power for a SPACECRAFT ‖ 우주선에 더 많은 동력을 제공해 주는 로켓. 보조 추진 장치. 부스터

boot¹ /buːt/ *n* **1** a type of shoe that covers your whole foot and the lower part of your leg ‖ 발 전체와 무릎 아랫부분을 덮는 신발의 일종. 부츠. 장화: *hiking boots* 하이킹용 장화 **2 to boot** SPOKEN used at the end of a list of remarks to emphasize the last one ‖ 마지막 말을 강조하기 위해 열거하는 말의 끝에 쓰여. 게다가. 또한: *Jack's tall, handsome, and rich to boot.* 잭은 키가 크고 잘 생겼으며 게다가 부자이다.

boot² *v* [I, T] also **boot up** to make a computer ready to be used by putting in its instructions ‖ 컴퓨터에 명령어를 입력해서 사용할 수 있도록 준비를 하다. 컴퓨터를 구동[부팅]하다[시키다] **2** [T] INFORMAL to kick someone or something hard ‖ 사람이나 사물을 세게 걷어차다: *Joe booted the ball across the field.* 조는 공을 운동장 저편으로 찼다.

boot camp /ˈ. ./ *n* a training camp for people who have joined the Army, Navy, or Marines ‖ 육군[해군, 해병대]에 입대한 사람들을 위한 훈련소. 신병 훈련소

boot·ee /ˈbuːti/ *n* a sock that a baby wears instead of a shoe ‖ 신발 대신에 신는 유아용 양말. 털실로 짠 아기 신발

booth /buːθ/ *n* **1** a small, partly enclosed place where one person can do something privately ‖ 한 사람이 사적으로

어떤 것을 할 수 있는 작고 부분적으로 막힌 장소. 칸막이 방. 부스: *a phone booth* 전화 박스 / *a voting booth* 기표소 **2** a partly enclosed place in a restaurant with a table between two long seats ‖ 두 개의 긴 좌석 사이에 탁자가 있는 음식점의 칸막이 자리 **3** a place at a market or FAIR where you can buy things, play games, or find information ‖ 물건을 사거나 게임을 하거나 정보를 얻을 수 있는 시장이나 견본시의 한 코너. 매점. 부스

boot·leg /'but'leg/ *adj* bootleg products are made and sold illegally ‖ 물건을 불법적으로 만들어 파는. 밀조[밀수, 밀매]의 – **bootlegging** *n* [U] – **bootlegger** *n*

boot·straps /'butstræps/ *n* **pull yourself up by your bootstraps** to get out of a difficult situation by your own effort ‖ 스스로의 노력으로 어려운 상황을 헤쳐 나가다

boo·ty /'buţi/ *n* LITERARY valuable things taken or won by the winners in a war, competition etc. ‖ 전쟁·경쟁 등에서 승자가 노획하거나 받은 가치있는 물건. 전리품. 상

booze¹ /buz/ *n* [U] INFORMAL alcoholic drinks ‖ 알코올 음료. 술

booze² *v* [I] INFORMAL to drink a lot of alcohol ‖ 술을 많이 마시다. – **boozer** *n*

bop¹ /bɑp/ *v* -**pped**, -**pping** [I] to hit someone gently ‖ 사람을 부드럽게 치다.

bop² *n* **1** a gentle hit ‖ 살짝 때림 **2** ⇨ BEBOP

bor·der¹ /'bɔrdɚ/ *n* **1** the official line that separates two countries ‖ 두 나라를 나누는 공식적인 선. 국경선: *the border between the US and Mexico* 미국과 멕시코 사이의 국경선 **2** a band along the edge of something such as a picture or piece of material ‖ 그림이나 물체와 같은 것의 가장자리를 두른 띠. 테두리: *a skirt with a red border* 가장자리가 붉은 치마

border² *v* [T] **1** to share a border with another country ‖ 다른 나라와 경계를 나누다. 접하다: *Spain borders Portugal.* 스페인은 포르투갈과 접해 있다 **2** to form a line around the edge of something ‖ 어떤 것의 가장자리 주위로 줄을 서다. 줄지어 서다: *willow trees bordering the river* 강 주위에 죽 늘어선 버드나무

border on sth *phr v* [T] to be very close to reaching an extreme feeling or quality ‖ 거의 극도의 감정이나 특성에 달해 있다. …과 비슷하다: *Jane's math skills border on genius.* 제인의 수학 실력은 천재에 가깝다.

bor·der·line¹ /'bɔrdɚˌlaɪn/ *adj* very close to being unacceptable ‖ 받아들일

수 없는 상태에 매우 가까운. 아슬아슬한. 어중간한: *His grades are borderline; unless he works hard, he won't graduate.* 그의 성적은 어중간하여 열심히 공부하지 않으면 졸업하지 못할 것이다.

borderline² *n* **1** [singular] the point at which one quality, condition etc. ends and another begins ‖ 하나의 특성·상태 등이 끝나고 다른 것이 시작되는 지점. 경계: *the borderline between admiration and love* 숭배와 사랑의 경계 **2** a border between two countries ‖ 두 나라간의 경계(선). 국경선

bore¹ /bɔr/ *v* **1** [T] to make someone feel bored, especially by talking too much ‖ 특히 말을 너무 많이 해서 사람을 지루하게 느끼게 하다. …을 지루하게 하다: *I'm sorry to bore you with all the details.* 너무 세세하게 말해서 당신을 지루하게 만들어 미안해요. **2** [I, T] to make a deep round hole in a hard surface ‖ 딱딱한 표면에 깊고 둥근 구멍을 파다. (…에) 구멍을 뚫다 **3** the past tense of BEAR ‖ bear의 과거형

bore into sb *phr. v* [T] if someone's eyes bore into you, they look at you in a way that makes you feel uncomfortable ‖ 남의 눈이 불쾌한 기분이 들 정도로 바라보다. …을 뚫어지게 쳐다보다

bore² *n* **1** someone who makes other people feel bored, especially because they talk too much about something ‖ 특히 어떤 것에 대해 지나치게 말이 많아 사람들을 지루하게 하는 사람. 지겨운 사람: *Ralph is such a bore!* 랄프는 정말 지겨운 사람이야! **2** [singular] something you have to do but do not like ‖ 좋아하지 않지만 해야 하는 것. 따분한 것: *Ironing is a real bore.* 다리미질은 정말 따분해.

bored /bɔrd/ *adj* tired and impatient because you do not think something is interesting or because you have nothing to do ‖ 흥미가 없거나 할 일이 없어서 지루하며 참을 수 없는. 지겨운: *George got bored with his job, so he quit.* 조지는 그가 하는 일이 진저리나서 회사를 그만두었다. / *Can't we do something else? I'm bored stiff/bored to tears.* (=extremely bored) 우리 다른 거 하면 안 되니? 정말 지겨워 죽겠어. / *I'm so bored!* 정말 지겨워! ✗DON'T SAY "I'm so boring."✗ "I'm so boring"이라고는 하지 않는다.

bore·dom /'bɔrdəm/ *n* [U] the feeling you have when you are bored ‖ 지루할 때 느끼는 감정. 권태

bor·ing /'bɔrɪŋ/ *adj* not interesting in any way ‖ 흥미 없는. 지루한: *I thought the book was boring.* 그 책은 지루하다고

생각했다.

born /bɔrn/ *adj* **1 be born** when a person or animal is born, it comes out of its mother's body or out of an egg ‖ 사람이나 동물이 모체 또는 알에서 나오다. 태어나다. 부화하다: *I was born in the South.* 나는 남부에서 태어났다. / *Lincoln was born on February 12.* 링컨은 2월 12일에 태어났다. / *She was born into a wealthy family.* 그녀는 부유한 가정에서 태어났다. **2 be born to do/be sth** to be very good at doing a particular job, activity etc. ‖ 특정한 일·활동 등을 매우 잘 하다. 타고나다: *Mantle was born to play baseball.* 맨틀은 야구하는 감각을 타고났었다. **3 born leader/teacher etc.** someone who has a natural ability to lead, teach etc. ‖ 어떤 것을 이끌거나 가르치는 데 타고난 능력을 가진 사람. 타고난 지도자/교사 **4** something that is born starts to exist ‖ 어떤 것이 존재하기 시작하다. …이 출현하다: *Unions were born out of* (=started because of) *a need for better working conditions.* 노동 조합은 보다 나은 근로 조건을 위한 필요성에서 생겨났다.

born-a·gain /ˈ. .ˌ./ *adj* **born-again Christian** someone who has become an EVANGELICAL Christian after having an important religious experience ‖ 중요한 종교적 체험을 한 후 열성적인 크리스천이 된 사람. 거듭난 크리스천

borne /bɔrn/ *v* the PAST PARTICIPLE of BEAR ‖ bear의 과거 분사형

bor·ough /ˈbɚou, ˈbʌrou/ *n* a town or part of a large city that is responsible for managing its own schools, hospitals, roads etc. ‖ 자체의 학교·병원·도로 등을 관리하는 책임이 있는 소도시 또는 대도시의 구. 자치시[구, 군]

borrow

Jerry borrowed a CD from Sue.
Sue lent Jerry a CD.

Jerry gave it back later.

bor·row /ˈbɑrou, ˈbɔrou/ *v* [I, T] **1** to use something that belongs to someone else and give it back to him/her later ‖ 다른 사람 소유의 물건을 사용하고 후에 돌려 주다. (…을)빌리다. 차용하다: *Could I borrow your bike tomorrow?* 내일 네 자전거 좀 빌릴 수 있을까? / *We'll have to borrow money from the bank for the house.* 우리는 집 때문에 은행에서 돈을 빌려야 할 것이다. —opposite LEND **2** to take or copy ideas or words ‖ 생각이나 말을 취하거나 베끼다. 모방하다. 차용하다: *English has borrowed many words from French.* 영어는 프랑스어에서 많은 단어를 차용했다. – **borrower** *n* —see usage note at LEND

bor·row·ings /ˈbɑrouɪŋz/ *n* [plural] the total amount of money that a person, company, or organization has borrowed, usually from a bank ‖ 개인 [회사, 조직]이 보통 은행에서 빌린 전체 금액. 차용[대출]금

bos·om /ˈbuzəm/ *n* **1 bosom buddy** INFORMAL a very close friend ‖ 매우 가까운 친구 **2** OLD-FASHIONED a woman's chest ‖ 여성의 가슴. 유방

boss¹ /bɔs/ *n* **1** the person who employs you or who is in charge of your work ‖ 고용한 사람이나 일을 감독하는 사람. 사장. 상사: *Our boss let us leave early today.* 사장은 오늘 우리를 일찍 퇴근하게 했다. **2** [singular, U] the person who is the strongest in a relationship, who controls a situation etc. ‖ 어떤 관계에서 가장 강한 힘을 가지고 어떤 상황을 통제하는 사람. 보스. 우두머리. 장. 두목: *You have to let them know who's boss.* (=make sure you are in control) 당신이 실권을 가지고 있다는 것을 그들에게 보여 줘야 한다.

boss² *v* [T] also **boss around** to tell people to do things, give them orders etc., especially when you have no authority to do it ‖ 특히 그렇게 할 만한 권한이 없을 때 사람들에게 지시나 명령 등을 하다. 이것저것 명령[지시]하다: *Stop bossing me around!* 나에게 이래라저래라 명령하지 마라!

boss·y /ˈbɔsi/ *adj* always telling other people what to do, in a way that is annoying ‖ 항상 짜증내는 투로 남에게 무엇을 하라고 말하는. 거들먹거리는: *Ruth's okay, but she can be bossy.* 루스라면 괜찮기는 한데 그녀는 거만하게 굴 가능성도 있다.

bot·a·ny /ˈbɑt⌐n-i/ *n* [U] the scientific study of plants ‖ 식물의 과학적 연구. 식물학 – **botanical** /bəˈtænɪkəl/ *adj* :

botanical gardens 식물원 − **botanist**
/'bɑt‿nɪst/ *n*

botch /bɑtʃ/ *v* [T] INFORMAL also **botch up** to do something badly because you were careless or did not have the skill to do it well ‖ 부주의하거나 잘할 기술이 없어서 일을 엉망으로 하다. …을 망쳐 놓다: *She really botched my haircut this time.* 그녀는 이번에 나의 이발을 완전히 망쳐 버렸다.

both /bouθ/ *quantifier, pronoun* **1** used in order to talk about two people or things together ‖ 두 사람이나 사물을 함께 말하는 데에 쓰여. 양자[쪽]. 쌍방. 둘 다: *They both have good jobs.* 그들은 둘 다 좋은 직업을 가지고 있다. / *Hold it in both hands.* 그것을 양 손으로 잡아라. / *Both women are famous writers.* 두 여자 모두 유명한 작가들이다. / *Both of my grandfathers are farmers.* 나의 할아버지와 외할아버지 두 분 모두 농부이다. **2 both… and…** used in order to emphasize that something is true of two people, things, situations etc. ‖ 두 사람·사물·상황이 사실이라는 것을 강조하는 데에 쓰여. …뿐만 아니라 …도: *Dan plays both football and basketball.* 댄은 축구뿐만 아니라 농구도 한다. —see usage note at EACH[1]

both·er[1] /'bɑðɚ/ *v* **1** [I, T] to make someone feel slightly annoyed or upset, especially by interrupting what s/he is doing ‖ 특히 하고 있는 일을 방해함으로써 남을 약간 짜증나게 하거나 화나게 하다. (…을) 괴롭히다. 귀찮게 하다: *"Why didn't you ask me for help?" "I didn't want to bother you."* "왜 도와 달라고 요청하지 않았느냐?" "당신을 귀찮게 하고 싶지 않았습니다." **2** [I, T] to make the effort to do something ‖ 어떤 것을 하기 위해 노력하다. …에 신경쓰다. 마음 졸이다: *I'll never get the job, so why bother applying?* 나는 그 일자리를 얻지 못할 텐데 왜 애써 지원하느라 사서 고생해? **3 sorry to bother you** SPOKEN said in order to politely interrupt what someone is doing ‖ 남이 하고 있는 일을 정중하게 방해하는 데 쓰여. 폐를 끼치게 되어[귀찮게 해서] 죄송합니다: *Sorry to bother you, but I have a few questions.* 귀찮게 해서 죄송합니다만 몇 가지 질문이 있습니다. **4** [T] to upset or frighten someone by trying to hurt him/her, touch him/her sexually etc. ‖ 남을 성적으로 해를 끼치거나 만지려고 함으로써 화나게 하거나 접먹게 하다. 성적으로 모욕[추행]하다: *If that man's bothering you, tell the police.* 만일 저 남자가 너에게 추근대면 경찰에 신고해라.

bother[2] *n* someone or something that slightly annoys or upsets you ‖ 조금 귀찮게 하거나 심란하게 하는 사람이나 사물. 골칫거리: *"Thanks for your help." "That's okay; it's no bother at all."* (=it is not difficult to help) "도와줘서 고마워." "괜찮아. 별 일 아닌데 뭘." − **bothersome** *adj*

Bo·tox /'boutɑks/ *n* [U] TRADEMARK a substance that makes muscles relax, which can be INJECTED into the skin around some one's eyes to make the lines disappear and the skin look younger and more attractive ‖ 주름살을 제거하고 피부가 더 젊고 매력적으로 보이도록 눈 주위 피부에 주입할 수 있는, 근육을 이완시키는 물질. 보톡스 (주사액)

bot·tle[1] /'bɑtl/ *n* **1** a container with a narrow top for keeping liquids in, usually made of glass or plastic ‖ 보통 유리나 플라스틱으로 만들어서, 액체를 담아 두는 위쪽이 좁은 용기. 병: *a wine bottle* 포도주병 / *a baby's bottle* 젖병 — see picture at CONTAINER **2** the amount of liquid that a bottle contains ‖ 한 병에 담는 액체의 양. 한 병의 양: *We drank the entire bottle.* 우리는 한 병을 다 마셨다. **3 hit the bottle** to start drinking a lot of alcohol regularly ‖ 규칙적으로 많은 술을 마시기 시작하다

bottle[2] *v* [T] to put a liquid into a bottle after you have made it ‖ 액체를 만들어서 병에 담다: *wine bottled in California* 캘리포니아산 포도주

bottle sth ↔ **up** *phr v* [T] to not allow yourself to show strong feelings or emotions ‖ 격렬한 느낌이나 감정을 보여 주려 하지 않다. …을 억지로 참다: *You shouldn't bottle up your anger like that.* 그렇게 화를 억지로 참아서는 안 된다.

bottled /'bɑtld/ *adj* **bottled water/beer etc.** water, beer etc. that is sold in a bottle ‖ 병에 넣어 파는 물·맥주 등. 병에 든 물/병맥주

bot·tle·neck /'bɑtl‚nɛk/ *n* **1** a place in a road where the traffic cannot pass easily, so that cars are delayed ‖ 차가 막혀서 교통이 원활히 소통될 수 없는 도로의 지점. 좁은 통로. 병목 지점 **2** a delay in part of a process that makes the whole process take longer ‖ 전체 과정을 지연시키는 과정의 지체 부분. 장애 요인: *a bottleneck in factory production* 공장 생산에서의 장애 요인

bot·tom[1] /'bɑtəm/ *n* **1** the lowest part of something ‖ 어떤 것의 최저부. 아랫부

분: *The fruit at the bottom of the basket was spoiled.* 바구니의 제일 밑바닥에 있는 과일은 상했다. **2** the flat surface on the lowest side of an object ‖ 물체의 최저면의 평평한 표면. 밑바닥: *What's on the bottom of your shoe?* 당신 신발은 밑창이 무엇으로 되어 있느냐? **3** the lowest position in an organization or company, or on a list etc. ‖ 조직이나 회사 또는 명단 등에서 가장 낮은 위치. 말단: *He started at the bottom, and now he manages the store.* 그는 밑바닥부터 시작해서 지금은 가게를 경영한다. **4** INFORMAL a word meaning the part of your body that you sit on, used especially when talking to children ‖ 보통 아이들에게 말할 때 사용하는 말로 앉을 때 닿는 신체 부위를 뜻하는 말. 궁둥이 **5** the ground under an ocean, river etc., or the flat land in a valley ‖ 바다·강의 밑바닥 땅이나 계곡의 평평한 땅. 바닥: *The bottom of the river is rocky.* 강바닥은 암석투성이다. **6** the part of a set of clothes that you wear on the lower part of your body ‖ 몸의 아랫도리에 입는 옷 한 벌의 일부. 하의: *pajama bottoms* 파자마의 바지 **7 get to the bottom of sth** INFORMAL to find the cause of a problem or situation ‖ 문제나 상황의 원인을 밝히다. 진상을 규명하다: *We've got to get to the bottom of this!* 우리는 이것의 진상을 규명해야 해! —compare TOP¹ —see also ROCK BOTTOM

bottom² *adj* in the lowest place or position ‖ 장소나 위치가 가장 아래의. 바닥의. 최하부의: *The papers are in the bottom drawer.* 그 서류는 맨 밑 서랍에 있다.

bottom³ *v*

bottom out *phr v* [I] if a situation, price etc. bottoms out, it stops getting worse or lower, usually before it starts improving again ‖ 상황·가격 등이 일반적으로 다시 향상되기 시작하기 전에 더 악화되거나 떨어지는 것을 멈추다. 바닥을 치다: *The decrease in car sales has finally bottomed out.* 자동차 매출의 감소는 마침내 바닥을 쳤다.

bot·tom·less /'bɑtəmlɪs/ *adj* **1** extremely deep ‖ 매우 깊은 **2** seeming to have no end ‖ 끝이 없는 것 같은. 무한한: *a bottomless supply of money* 끝없는 자금의 공급

bottom line /... './ *n* **the bottom line a)** the main fact about a situation that you must accept, even though you may not like it ‖ 좋아하지 않더라도 받아들여야만 하는 상황에 대한 주요한 사실. 최종

결과. 요점: *The bottom line is that we have to win this game.* 요점은 이 경기에서 이겨야만 한다는 것이다. **b)** the profit or the amount of money that a business makes or loses ‖ 기업이 벌거나 잃는 수익이나 액수. 순이익[손실]

bough /baʊ/ *n* LITERARY a main branch on a tree ‖ 나무의 주된 가지. 큰 가지

bought /bɔt/ *v* the past tense and PAST PARTICIPLE of BUY ‖ buy의 과거·과거 분사형

boul·der /'boʊldɚ/ *n* a large stone or piece of rock ‖ 큰 돌이나 바위덩이

bou·le·vard /'bʊləvɑrd, 'bu-/ *n* a wide road in a town or city ‖ 읍이나 도시의 넓은 도로. 대로. 넓은 가로수길

bounce¹ /baʊns/ *v* **1** [I, T] if a ball or other object bounces, it hits a surface and then immediately moves away from it, or you make it move in this way ‖ 공이나 다른 물체가 표면을 친 후 바로 그 표면에서

bounce

멀어지다, 또는 이와 같이 움직이게 하다. 공 등이[을] 튀다[튀기다]: *The ball bounced off the wall and hit Marie on the nose.* 그 공은 벽에 되튀어 마리의 코를 때렸다. **2** [I] to move up and down, especially because you are walking or jumping on a surface that is made of rubber, has springs etc. ‖ 특히 고무로 되어 있거나 스프링이 있는 표면을 걷거나 뛰는 까닭에 위아래로 움직이다. 뛰어오르다. 뛰듯이 걷다: *Don't bounce on the bed.* 침대 위에서 뛰지 마라. **3** [I, T] if a check bounces or a bank bounces a check, the bank will not pay any money because there is not enough money in the account of the person who wrote it ‖ 수표에 이서한 사람의 계좌에 돈이 부족해서 은행이 돈을 지불하지 않다. 수표가 부도가 나다 **4** [I] to walk quickly and with a lot of energy ‖ 재빠르고 힘차게 걷다: *The kids came bouncing down the stairs.* 그 아이들은 계단을 요란하게 걸어 내려갔다. **5 bounce ideas off sb** to ask someone for his/her opinion about an idea, plan etc. before you decide something ‖ 어떤 것을 결정하기 전에 아이디어·계획 등에 관해 사람에게 의견을 물어보다: *Could I bounce a few ideas off you?* 당신에게 몇 가지 의견을 물어봐도 될까요?

bounce back *phr v* [I] to feel better quickly, or to become successful again after having a lot of problems ‖ 많은 문제를 겪은 후 속히 호전되거나 다시 성공하게 되다. 곧 회복하다: *Experts expect the economy to bounce back.* 전문가들은 경제가 곧 회복될 거라 예상한다.

bounce² *n* **1** [C, U] the quality that makes things able to BOUNCE, or an act of bouncing ‖ 물건을 튈 수 있게 하는 성질, 또는 튀는 행위. 탄성. 튀어오르기. 도약: *Catch the ball on the first bounce.* 공을 원바운드로 잡아라. **2** [U] the ability to BOUNCE ‖ 튀는 능력. 탄력. 반발력

bounc·er /'baʊnsə/ *n* someone whose job is to keep people who behave badly out of a club, BAR etc. ‖ 클럽·술집 등에서 좋지 않은 행동을 하는 사람을 제지하는 직업인. 경비원

bounc·ing /'baʊnsɪŋ/ *adj* a word meaning healthy and active, used especially about babies ‖ 특히 아기에게 쓰여, 건강하고 활기있는. 힘찬. 활발한: *a bouncing baby boy* 건강하고 활기찬 사내아기

bounc·y /'baʊnsi/ *adj* **1** able to BOUNCE or be bounced easily ‖ 튈 수 있거나 쉽게 튀어지는. 탄력 있는. 잘 튀는: *a bouncy ball* 잘 튀는 볼 / *a bouncy bed* 탄력 있는 침대 **2** happy and full of energy ‖ 즐겁고 활기가 가득한. 활기찬. 생동하는

bound¹ /baʊnd/ *v* the past tense and PAST PARTICIPLE of BIND ‖ bind의 과거·과거 분사형

bound² *adj* **1 be bound to** to be certain to do something ‖ 틀림없이 어떤 것을 하다. …할 운명이다: *She's such a nice girl that she's bound to make friends.* 그녀는 정말 멋진 소녀여서 반드시 친구가 따르게 되어 있다. **2** tied up and unable to move ‖ 꽁꽁 묶여 움직일 수 없는. 얽매인. 동여 매어진: *Their bodies were discovered bound and gagged.* 그들의 시신은 입이 틀어막히고 꽁꽁 묶인 채 발견되었다. **3** having a legal or moral duty to do something ‖ 법적 또는 도덕적으로 어떤 것을 할 의무가 있는. …해야 하는: *The company is bound by law to provide us with safety equipment.* 그 회사는 법적으로 우리에게 안전 보호 장비를 제공할 의무가 있다. **4 -bound** controlled or limited by something, so that you cannot do what you want ‖ 무엇에 의해 통제 또는 제한되어 원하는 것을 할 수 없는. …에 묶인[매인]: *a fog-bound airport* 안개에 묶인 공항 **5 bound and determined** determined to do or achieve something, even if it is difficult ‖ 어려움에도 불구하고 어떤 것을 하거나 이루기로 결심한. …하기로 굳게 결심한[결의에 찬]: *He's bound and determined to become one of baseball's premier players.* 그는 최고의 야구 선수가 되기 위해 결의에 차 있다. **6** intending to go in a particular direction or to a particular place ‖ 특정 방향이나 특정 장소로 가려고 하는. …에 가기로 된. …행의: *a plane bound for Peru* 페루행 항공기

bound³ *v* **1 be bounded by** if a place is bounded by another place or thing, its edges are marked by that place or thing ‖ 한 장소의 외곽이 다른 장소나 사물에 의해 구분되다. 범위[경계]가 정해지다: *The neighborhood is bounded by Decoto Road, Fremont Boulevard, and Interstate 880.* 그 동네는 디카토 로드, 프레몽 불리바드, 그리고 인터스테이트(고속 도로) 880 번과 경계를 접하고 있다. **2** [I] to move quickly and with a lot of energy ‖ 빠르고 힘차게 움직이다. 내닫다. 내달리다: *George came bounding down the stairs.* 조지는 내달려서 계단을 내려왔다.

bound⁴ *n* a long or high jump made with a lot of energy ‖ 많은 힘을 들여서 멀게 또는 높게 뛰기. 도약: *With one bound he had left his seat and was half way to the door.* 그는 자리에서 벌떡 일어나더니 어느새 문 쪽을 향하고 있었다. —see also BOUNDS

bound·a·ry /'baʊndəri, -dri/ *n* **1** the line that marks the edge of a surface, space, or area of land inside a country ‖ 한 나라 안의 지표면[공간, 구역]의 가장자리를 표시하는 선. 경계선: *The Mississippi forms a natural boundary between Tennessee and Arkansas.* 미시시피 강은 테네시 주와 아칸소 주 사이의 자연적 경계선을 이루고 있다. —compare BORDER¹ **2** the highest or most extreme limit that something can reach ‖ 어떤 것이 도달할 수 있는 가장 높거나 극단적인 한계: *the boundaries of human knowledge* 인간 지식의 한계

bound·less /'baʊndlɪs/ *adj* without any limits or end ‖ 제한이나 끝이 없는: *boundless optimism* 끝없는 낙관주의

bounds /baʊndz/ *n* [plural] legal or social limits or rules ‖ 법적 또는 사회적 제한이나 규율. 한도. 한정: *His imagination knows no bounds.* (=has no limits) 그의 상상력은 끝이 없다 —see also OUT-OF-BOUNDS

boun·ti·ful /'baʊntɪfəl/ *adj* LITERARY large or generous ‖ 크거나 많은. 풍성한. 넉넉한: *a bountiful harvest* 풍성한 수확

boun·ty /'baʊnti/ n 1 [U] LITERARY a generous amount of something, especially food || 사물 특히 음식이 넉넉함. 후함. 풍부함 2 money that is given as a reward for catching a criminal || 범인 체포의 대가로 주는 돈. 현상금 − **bountiful** adj : a bountiful harvest 풍성한 수확

bou·quet /boʊ'keɪ, bu-/ n 1 a group of flowers given to someone as a present or carried at a formal occasion || 선물로서 다른 사람에게 주거나 공식 행사에 들고 다니는 꽃다발. 부케 2 [C, U] the smell of a wine || 포도주의 향: a rich bouquet 물씬 풍기는 포도주 향

bour·bon /'bɚbən/ n [U] a type of American WHISKEY made from corn || 옥수수로 만든 미국산 위스키 종류. 버본 위스키

bour·geois /bʊr'ʒwɑ, 'bʊrʒwɑ/ adj DISAPPROVING too interested in having a lot of possessions and a high position in society || 상당한 재산의 소유와 높은 사회적 지위에 지나친 관심을 갖는. 부르주아근성의. 속된. 속물적인

bour·geoi·sie /ˌbʊrʒwɑ'zi/ n the bourgeoisie⇨ MIDDLE CLASS

'bout /baʊt/ SPOKEN NONSTANDARD ⇨ ABOUT

bout /baʊt/ n 1 a short period of time during which you do something a lot or suffer from a particular illness || 일을 많이 하거나 특정 질병으로 고생하는 짧은 기간. 한 차례. 한 바탕: a bout of drinking 한 차례의 주연 / a bout of the flu 한 바탕 치러낸 감기 2 a BOXING or WRESTLING competition || 권투나 레슬링 경기. 대전. 시합

bou·tique /bu'tik/ n a small store that sells very fashionable clothes or decorations || 아주 유행하는 의상이나 장신구를 파는 작은 가게. 부티끄

bo·vine /'boʊvaɪn/ adj TECHNICAL relating to cows, or like a cow || 소에 관한, 또는 소 같은. 소의

bow¹ /baʊ/ v [I, T] to bend your head or the top part of your body forward, as a sign of respect or as a way of thanking an AUDIENCE after you perform || 존경의 표시로, 또는 공연 후 청중에 대해 감사하여 머리나 신체의 윗부분을 앞으로 숙이다. 절하다. 인사하다

bow down phr v [I] to bend forward from your waist, especially when you are already kneeling, in order to pray || 특히 기도하기 위해 이미 무릎을 꿇고 있을 때 허리를 앞으로 굽히다. 무릎을 꿇고 바닥에 엎드리다

bow out phr v [I] to decide not to take part in something any longer || 어떤 것에 더 이상 참여하지 않기로 결정하다. …에서 빠지다. …에서 물러나다[그만두다]: Two more Republicans have bowed out of the presidential race. 또 다른 공화당원 2명도 대통령 경선에서 사퇴했다.

bow to sb/sth phr v [T] to finally agree to do something that other people want you to do, even though you do not want to || 본인은 하고 싶지 않지만 다른 사람들이 해 주기를 원하는 것을 하기로 마침내 동의하다. …에 따르다. 순종[굴복]하다: Congress may bow to public pressure and reduce the gas tax. 의회는 종내에는 여론의 압력에 굴복하여 유류세를 줄일 것이다.

bow² /boʊ/ n 1 a knot of cloth or string with a curved part on each side || 양 끝이 구부러진 천이나 줄의 매듭. 나비 매듭. 리본: a girl with a red bow in her hair 머리에 붉은 리본을 단 소녀 2 a tool used for shooting ARROWs, made of a piece of wood held in a curve by a tight string || 팽팽한 줄로 나무를 휘어 잡아 맨, 화살을 쏘는 데 쓰이는 도구. 활 3 a long thin piece of wood with hair stretched tightly from one end to the other, used for playing STRING instruments || 줄을 한쪽 끝에서 다른 쪽 끝까지 팽팽하게 잡아당겨 현악기의 연주에 쓰이는 가늘고 긴 나무. 현악기의 활

bow³ /baʊ/ n 1 the act of bowing (BOW) || 인사하는 행위. 절. 경례 2 take a bow to BOW at the end of a performance to receive APPLAUSE || 공연의 끝에 관중의 갈채를 받아들여 인사하다. 갈채의 답례로 인사하다 3 the front part of a ship || 배의 앞부분. 선수(船首). 이물

bow⁴ /boʊ/ v [I] to bend or curve || 굽거나 구부러지다. 휘다

bow·el /'baʊəl/ n [C usually plural] the part of the body below the stomach where food is made into solid waste material || 음식물이 고체 찌꺼기로 만들어지는 위(胃) 밑에 있는 신체 부분. 창자. 장(腸)

bowl¹ /boʊl/ n 1 a wide round container that is open at the top, used for holding liquids, food etc. || 윗부분이 터져 있어 액체·음식 등을 담는 데 쓰이는 넓고 둥근 그릇. 대접. 주발. 단지: Mix the eggs and butter in a large bowl. 큰 대접에다 계란과 버터를 섞어라. / a soup bowl 수프 그릇 2 also **bowlful** the amount that a bowl will hold || 그릇에 담을 수 있는 양. 한 그릇 분: a bowl of rice 쌀 한 그릇 분량 3 the part of an object that is shaped like a bowl ‖ 모양이 사발처럼 생긴 물체의 부분. 통. …기(器): *a toilet bowl* 변기 **4** also **Bowl** a special game played by two of the best football teams after the normal playing season ‖ 정규 시합 기간이 끝난 후 두 최고 미식 축구 팀이 치르는 특별 경기. 미식 축구 선수권전: *the Rose Bowl* 로즈 볼, 전미 대학 미식 축구 선수권전

bowl[2] *v* [I, T] to play the game of BOWLING ‖ 볼링을 하다

bowl sb ↔ **over** *phr v* [T] to surprise, please, or excite someone very much ‖ 남을 매우 놀라게[즐겁게, 흥분되게] 하다: *When Tony met Angela, he was completely bowled over.* 토니는 안젤라를 만났을 때 매우 놀랐다.

bow·legged /ˈboʊˌlɛgɪd, -ˌlɛgd/ *adj* having legs that curve out at the knee ‖ 무릎 부근이 밖으로 휘어진 다리를 가진. 안짱다리의

bowl·ing /ˈboʊlɪŋ/ *n* [U] an indoor game in which you roll a heavy ball to try to knock down a group of objects shaped like bottles ‖ 무거운 볼을 굴려 병 모양의 목표물을 쓰러뜨리려는 실내 게임. 볼링: *Let's go bowling!* 볼링 하러 가자!

bowl·ing al·ley /ˈ.. ˌ../ *n* a building where you can go BOWLING ‖ 볼링을 할 수 있는 건물. 볼링장

bow tie /ˈboʊ taɪ/ *n* a short piece of cloth tied in the shape of a BOW, which men wear around their necks ‖ 활 모양으로 매듭이 나 있어 남자들이 목에 매는 짧은 천조각. 나비 넥타이

box[1] /baks/ *n* **1** a container for putting things in, especially one with four stiff straight sides ‖ 물건을 넣는, 특히 4면이 직각으로 반듯한 용기. 상자. 박스: *a cardboard box* 골판지 박스 —see picture at CONTAINER **2** the amount that a box can hold ‖ 상자에 담을 수 있는 양. (박스) 한 상자분: *a box of candy* 사탕 한 상자 **3** a small area in a larger space such as a theater or court ‖ 극장이나 법정 등의 넓은 공간 중의 작은 구역. …석(席). (소형의) 칸막이 실: *the jury box* 배심원석 **4** a small square on an official form for people to write information in ‖ 사람들이 정보를 기입할 수 있는 공문서 양식상의 작은 사각 칸. 빈칸. 공란: *Write your name and address in the box at the top.* 성명과 주소를 상단의 공란에 기입해 넣으시오. **5** ➪P.O. BOX

box[2] *v* **1** [I, T] to fight someone with your hands as a sport while wearing big leather GLOVES ‖ 손에 큰 가죽 글로브를 끼고 시합으로서 남과 싸우다. 권투 시합

을 하다. 복싱 경기를 하다 **2** [T] to put things in a box or in boxes ‖ 상자 하나 또는 여러 개의 상자에 물건을 담다. 상자에 넣다[담다]. 박스로 포장하다 **3** [T] to draw a box around something on a page ‖ 페이지 상의 어떤 것에 네모 표시를 하다. 박스 괄호로 싸다

box sb/sth ↔ **in** *phr v* [T] **1** to enclose someone or something in a small space where it is not possible to move freely ‖ 사람이나 사물을 자유롭게 움직일 수 없는 작은 공간에 가두다. 꼼짝 못하게 둘러싸다: *The Honda in the driveway has boxed my car in.* 혼다가 내 차를 꼼짝 못하게 집 진입로를 막아 버렸다. **2 feel boxed in** to feel that you are limited in what you can do in a difficult situation ‖ 어려운 상황에서 할 수 있는 일의 제한을 받는다고 느끼다. 속박되다. 몰아세워지다

box·car /ˈbakskar/ *n* a railroad car with high sides and a roof that is used for carrying goods ‖ 높은 측면과 지붕이 있는, 물건을 운반하는 데에 쓰이는 철도 차량. 유개 화차

box·er /ˈbaksɚ/ *n* **1** someone who boxes, especially as a job ‖ 특히 직업으로 권투를 하는 사람. 권투 선수. 복서: *a heavyweight boxer* 헤비급 권투 선수 **2** a dog with short light brown hair and a flat nose ‖ 짧고 밝은 갈색의 털과 납작코를 가진 개. 복서

boxer shorts /ˈ.. ˌ./ *n* [plural] loose underwear for men ‖ 남성용의 헐렁한 속옷. 사각팬티

box·ing /ˈbaksɪŋ/ *n* [U] the sport of fighting with your hands while wearing big leather GLOVES ‖ 손에 큰 가죽 글로브를 낀 채로 싸우는 운동 경기. 권투 시합. 복싱

box of·fice /ˈ. ˌ../ *n* a place in a theater, concert hall etc. where tickets are sold ‖ 극장·공연장 등에서 표를 파는 곳. 매표소

box spring /ˈ. ˌ./ *n* a base containing metal springs that you put under a MATTRESS to make a bed ‖ 매트리스 밑에 넣어 침대를 만드는 금속제 스프링이 들어 있는 기부(基部). 침대용 스프링

boy[1] /bɔɪ/ *n* **1** a male child or young man ‖ 남자 아이 또는 어린 남자. 소년: *a school for boys* 남학교 **2** someone's son, especially a young one ‖ 특히 남의 어린 아들: *How old is your boy?* 댁의 아들은 몇 살입니까? **3 paper/delivery etc. boy** a young man who does a particular job ‖ 특정한 일을 하는 소년. 신문 배달 소년/배달 소년 **4 city/local etc. boy** INFORMAL a man of any age from a particular place or social group ‖ 나이를 불문한 특정 지역이나 사회 계층 출신의 남자. 도시/지방 출신남자: *I'm just a country boy.* 나는 촌놈에 지나지 않아. **5 the boys** INFORMAL a group of men who are friends and often go out together ‖ 친구 사이로서 종종 같이 어울려 노는 한 무리의 남자. 패거리. 동료들: *playing cards with the boys* 친구들과 카드 놀이 하기 **6** SPOKEN used when speaking to a male animal, such as a horse or a dog ‖ 말이나 개 등의 수컷 동물에게 말할 때에 쓰여: *Good boy, Patches!* 잘했어, 패치스!

boy², oh boy *interjection* said in order to emphasize a statement ‖ 진술을 강조 하는 데에 쓰여. 아이구, 저런. 어머나: *Boy, is he mad!* 저런, 그 사람 정말 미쳤 구나!

boy·cott /ˈbɔɪkɑt/ *v* [T] to refuse to buy something, use something, or take part in something as a way of protesting ‖ 항의 방법으로 어떤 것을 사거나 쓰거나 참 여하는 것을 거부하다. 불매 동맹을 맺다. 보이콧하다: *We boycott all products tested on animals.* 우리는 동물에게 실험 한 모든 제품들을 보이콧한다. **– boycott** *n*

boy·friend /ˈbɔɪfrɛnd/ *n* a boy or man with whom you have a romantic relationship ‖ 애정 관계를 맺고 있는 소 년이나 남자. 남자 친구

boy·hood /ˈbɔɪhʊd/ *n* [U] LITERARY the time in a man's life when he is very young ‖ 한 남자의 일생 중 매우 어린 시 기. 소년기[시절]

boy·ish /ˈbɔɪ-ɪʃ/ *adj* looking or behaving like a boy ‖ 소년처럼 보이거나 행동하는. 소년다운: *his boyish laughter* 그의 소년 같은 웃음

Boy Scouts /ˈ. ./ *n* an organization for boys that teaches them practical skills and helps develop their character ‖ 소년들에게 실용적 기술을 가르치고 인 격 발달을 돕는 청소년 단체. 보이 스카우 트 **—compare** GIRL SCOUTS

bo·zo /ˈboʊzoʊ/ *n* INFORMAL someone who you think is stupid or silly ‖ 멍청하 거나 바보 같다고 생각되는 사람. 놈. 녀 석

bps, BPS /ˌbi pi ˈes/ *n* [U] TECHNICAL bits per second; a measurement of how fast a computer or MODEM can send or receive information ‖ bits per second(초 당 비트수)의 약어; 컴퓨터나 모뎀이 정보 를 주고 받는 속도 측정 단위

bra /brɑ/ *n* a piece of underwear that a woman wears to support her breasts ‖ 여성들이 젖가슴을 지지하기 위해 입는 속 옷. 브래지어

brace¹ /breɪs/ *v* [T] **1** to prepare for something unpleasant that is going to happen ‖ 앞으로 벌어질 불쾌한 일에 대비 하다. 마음의 준비를 하다. 마음을 다잡 다: *Brace yourself for some bad news!* 나쁜 소식에 대비해 마음 준비 단단히 해 라! **2** to prevent something from falling or moving by supporting it ‖ 어떤 것을 받쳐서 떨어지거나 움직이는 것을 막다. 떠받치다. 보강하다. 강화하다

brace² *n* something used or worn in order to support something ‖ 어떤 것을 지지하기 위해 사용하거나 착용하는 것. 보조[보호]대: *Jill had to wear a neck brace for six weeks.* 질은 6주 동안 목 보 호대를 차야 했다. **—see also** BRACES

brace·let /ˈbreɪslɪt/ *n* a band or chain that you wear around your wrist or arm as a decoration ‖ 장신구로서 손목이나 팔 둘레에 끼는 띠나 사슬. 팔찌 **—see picture at** JEWELRY

brac·es /ˈbreɪsɪz/ *n* [plural] a connected set of wires that people, especially children, have to put on their teeth to make them straight ‖ 사람 특히 아이들이 이를 교정하기 위해 착용해야 하 는, 철사를 연결하여 만든 장치. 치열 교정 기

brac·ing /ˈbreɪsɪŋ/ *adj* bracing air or weather is cold and makes you feel very awake and healthy ‖ 공기나 날씨가 차가 워서 정신을 깨우고 건강한 느낌이 들게 하는. 상쾌한. 기운을 돋우는

brack·et¹ /ˈbrækɪt/ *n* **1 income/ tax/age etc. bracket** an income etc. that is inside a particular range ‖ 소득 등이 특정 범위 안에 드는 구분. 소 득층/납세자층/연령층: *Your new job puts you in the highest tax bracket.* 새로 운 직업으로 당신은 고위 납세자층에 들게 됩니다. **2** one of the pair of marks [ ] put around words to show that the rest of the writing can be read and understood without these words ‖ 이 단 어가 없어도 나머지를 읽고 이해할 수 있 음을 표시하기 위해 단어에 두르는 한 쌍 의 기호 [ ] 중의 하나. 각[대]괄호: *All grammar information is given in brackets.* 모든 문법 정보는 각 괄호 안에 주어진다. **3** a piece of metal, wood, or plastic put in or on a wall to support something such as a shelf ‖ 선반 등을 받 치기 위해 벽 속 또는 벽 위에 박는 금속 [나무, 플라스틱]제. 까치발. 받침대. 보 강재

bracket² *v* [T] to put BRACKETs around a written word, piece of information etc. ‖ 쓰여진 단어·정보 등에 괄호를 치다. 괄호 안에 넣다. 괄호로 묶다

brack·ish /'brækɪʃ/ *adj* brackish water is not pure because it is slightly salty ‖ 물이 약간 짜서 순수하지 않은. 짭짤한

brag /bræg/ *v* **-gged, -gging** [I, T] to talk too proudly about what you have done, what you own etc. ‖ 자신이 해 온 일, 소유한 것 등에 대해 너무나 자랑스럽게 말하다. 허풍을 떨다. 과장하다: *Todd's always bragging about how smart he is.* 토드는 항상 자신의 머리가 좋다고 자랑을 해댄다.

brag·gart /'brægət/ *n* someone who BRAGs ‖ 허풍을 떠는 사람. 허풍쟁이

braid¹ /breɪd/ *n* [C, U] a length of hair or a narrow band of material that has been separated into three parts and then woven together ‖ 세 가닥으로 나누어 서로 꼰 긴 머리나 좁고 긴 띠. 땋은 머리[밴드]: *a girl with her hair in braids* 머리를 땋은 소녀 / *a red jacket with gold braid* 금색 띠가 쳐진 빨간 재킷 – **braided** *adj* —see picture at HAIRSTYLE

braid² *v* [T] to make a BRAID ‖ 땋은 머리를 하다. 머리카락을[끈을] 땋다

braille /breɪl/ *n* [U] a form of printing with raised round marks that blind people can read by touching ‖ 맹인들이 만져서 읽도록 돌기한 둥근 점 표시로 된 인쇄 형태. 점자 (인쇄)

brain¹ /breɪn/ *n* **1** [C, U] the organ inside your head that controls how you think, feel, and move ‖ 사람의 생각·느낌·동작을 제어하는 머리 속 기관. 뇌. 두뇌: *Jorge suffered brain damage in the accident.* 호르헤는 사고로 뇌손상을 입었다. **2** the ability to think clearly and learn quickly ‖ 명확히 사고하고 빠르게 학습하는 능력. 지능. 지력: *She's nice, but she doesn't have much of a brain.* 그녀는 착하지만 머리는 그다지 좋지 않다. **3** INFORMAL someone who is very intelligent ‖ 매우 지적인 사람. 영리하고 똑똑한 사람. 수재: *Some of the best brains in the country are here tonight.* 국내의 몇몇 최고의 수재들이 오늘 밤 여기에 있다. **4 have sth on the brain** INFORMAL to be always thinking about something ‖ 항상 어떤 것에 대해 생각하다. …에 늘 정신이 팔려 있다: *I have that song on the brain today.* 나는 오늘 그 노래만 내내 생각하고 있다. —see also NO-BRAINER

brain² *v* [T] OLD-FASHIONED to hit someone on the head very hard ‖ 누군가의 머리를 세게 때리다. 정수리[머리]를

내려치다: *I'll brain you if you don't be quiet!* 조용히 하지 않으면 네 머리를 쥐어박을 거야!

brain·child /'breɪntʃaɪld/ *n* [singular] INFORMAL an idea, organization etc. that someone has thought of without any help from anyone else ‖ 다른 사람의 도움 없이 생각해 낸 생각·조직 등. 발명[고안](품): *The personal computer was the brainchild of a man named Steve Jobs.* 개인용 컴퓨터는 스티브 조브스라는 사람이 고안해 낸 것이다.

brain·less /'breɪnlɪs/ *adj* INFORMAL silly and stupid ‖ 바보 같고 멍청한. 어리석은. 머리가 나쁜: *You brainless idiot!* 이 멍청이 바보야!

brains /breɪnz/ *n* [plural] **1** the ability to think clearly and learn quickly ‖ 명확히 사고하고 빨리 학습하는 능력. 지능. 머리. 지력. 사고력: *If he had any brains he'd figure it out for himself.* 그가 조금만 머리를 썼더라면, 그 혼자서 알아냈을 것이다. / *Use your brains, veronica.* 머리를 써라, 베로니카. **2 be the brains behind sth** to be the person who thought of and developed a particular plan, system, organization etc. ‖ 특별한 계획·체제·조직 등을 생각해 내고 개발한 사람이 되다. …의 핵심 두뇌[브레인]가 되다: *Bill Gates is the brains behind Microsoft* 빌 게이츠는 마이크로 소프트사의 핵심 두뇌이다. —see also **pick sb's brain(s)** (PICK¹), **rack your brain(s)** (RACK²)

brain·storm /'breɪnstɔrm/ *n* [singular] INFORMAL a sudden intelligent idea ‖ 갑작스러운 비상한 생각. 착상. 묘안. 문득 떠오르는[창의적인] 생각: *I've just had a brainstorm!* 방금 좋은 수가 생각났어!

brain·storm·ing /'breɪn,stɔrmɪŋ/ *n* [U] the act of meeting with a group of people in order to try to develop ideas and think of ways to solve problems ‖ 아이디어를 개발하고 문제에 대한 해결책을 생각해 내기 위해 일단의 사람들과 회의하는 활동. 브레인 스토밍. 자유롭게 착상을 내놓는 회의: *a brainstorming session* 브레인 스토밍 회의

brain·wash /'breɪnwɑʃ, -wɔʃ/ *v* [T] to make someone believe something that is not true by using force, confusing him/her, or continuously repeating it over a long period of time ‖ 남에게 강제로[혼란시켜서, 장기간 계속 반복해서] 사실이 아닌 것을 믿게 만들다. …에게 …을 믿게 세뇌시키다 – **brainwashing** *n* [U]

brain·y /'breɪni/ *adj* INFORMAL able to think clearly and learn quickly ‖ 명확히

사고하고 빨리 학습할 수 있는. 머리가 좋은. 총명한. 현명한: *Out of all of us, Richard was always the brainy one.* 우리 모두 중에서 리차드가 언제나 총명했다.

braise /breɪz/ *v* [T] to cook meat or vegetables slowly in a small amount of liquid in a closed container ‖ 뚜껑이 닫힌 용기에 소량의 물을 넣고 고기나 채소를 천천히 요리하다. 조리다. 소량의 물로 뭉근하게 끓이다

brake¹ /breɪk/ *n* **1** a piece of equipment that makes a vehicle go more slowly or stop ‖ 차량을 좀 더 천천히 가게 하거나 멈추게 만드는 장치. 브레이크. 제동 장치: *My car needs new brakes.* 내 차는 브레이크를 새로 갈아야 한다. **2 put the brakes on sth** to stop something that is happening ‖ 어떤 것이 발생하는 것을 막다. …하지 못하게 저지하다. 제동을 걸다: *efforts to put the brakes on rising prices* 물가 상승에 제동을 걸려는 노력들

brake² *v* [I] to make a vehicle go more slowly or stop by using its BRAKE ‖ 브레이크를 써서 차량이 좀 더 천천히 가거나 멈추게 하다. 브레이크로 제동을 걸다. 브레이크를 밟다: *She had to brake suddenly to avoid a dog in the road.* 그녀는 도로에 있는 개를 피하기 위해 급제동을 걸어야 했다.

bran /bræn/ *n* [U] the crushed outer skin of wheat or a similar grain ‖ 밀이나 유사한 곡식의 분쇄한 껍질. 겨

branch¹ /bræntʃ/ *n* **1** part of a tree that grows out from the TRUNK (=main stem) and has leaves, fruit, or smaller branches growing from it ‖ 나무의 몸통에서 자라나고, 잎[열매, 작은 가지]이 그 위에 자라는 나무의 부분. 가지. 나뭇가지 **2** one part of something larger such as an organization, a subject of study, or a family ‖ 조직[학문 분야, 가문] 등의 더 큰 것의 한 부분. 부문. 분과. 분야. 지점: *The company has branches in Dallas and Toronto.* 그 회사는 댈러스와 토론토에 지사가 있다. / *a branch of medicine* 약학 부문 **3** a smaller, less important part of something that leads away from the larger, more important part of it ‖ 더 크고 중요한 부분에서 떨어져 나온 사물의 더 작고 덜 중요한 부분. 지선(支線). 지류(支流). 지엽(枝葉): *a branch of the Missouri River* 미주리 강의 지류

branch² *v* [I] also **branch off** to divide into two or more smaller, narrower, or less important parts ‖ 둘 이상의 더 작은[더 좁은, 덜 중요한] 부분으로 나누다. 갈라지다. 분기(分岐)하다: *Turn off where the road branches to the right.* 도로가 오른쪽으로 갈라지는 곳에서 우회전하시오.

branch out *phr v* [I] to do something new in addition to what you usually do ‖ 일상적으로 하는 것에 추가로 새로운 것을 하다. 활동 영역을 늘리다[확장하다]: *The bookstore has decided to branch out into renting movies.* 그 서점은 비디오를 대여하여 사업 영역을 확장하기로 결정했다.

brand¹ /brænd/ *n* **1** a type of product made by a particular company ‖ 특정 회사에 의해 생산된 제품의 종류. 상표. 브랜드: *different brands of soap* 서로 다른 상표의 비누 **2 brand of humor/politics/religion etc.** a particular type of humor, politics etc. ‖ 특정 유형의 유머·정치·종교: *You know what I think of Jerry's brand of humor.* 제리 특유의 유머를 내가 어떻게 생각하는지 너는 알지. **3** a mark burned into an animal's skin that shows whom it belongs to ‖ 누구 소유인가를 나타내도록 동물의 가죽에 불로 지진 자국. 소인(燒印). 낙인

brand² *v* [T] **1** to make a mark on something such as an animal, in order to show whom it belongs to ‖ 소유주를 나타내도록 동물 등에 표시를 하다. …에 소인[낙인]을 찍다 **2** to consider someone as a very bad type of person, often unfairly ‖ 다른 사람을 매우 나쁜 유형의 사람으로, 종종 부당하게 간주하다. …이라는 낙인을 찍다: *Pete got branded as a troublemaker when he was a kid.* 피트는 어렸을 때 문제아로 낙인 찍혔다.

bran·dish /ˈbrændɪʃ/ *v* [T] to wave something around in a dangerous and threatening way ‖ 어떤 것을 위험하게, 또 위협적으로 휘두르다. …을 휘두르다[내두르다]: *He burst into the store brandishing a knife.* 그는 칼을 휘두르며 가게에 난입했다.

brand name /ˈ. ./ *n* the name a company gives to the goods it has produced ‖ 회사가 생산한 제품에 붙인 이름. 상표(명). 제품명: *brand names such as Jell-O and Coca-Cola* 젤오·코카콜라 등의 상표(명)

brand-new /ˌbrænˈnu/ *adj* new and not used ‖ 새롭고 사용되지 않은. 신(제)품인. 신형의: *a brand-new car* 신형 차

bran·dy /ˈbrændi/ *n* [C, U] a strong alcoholic drink made from wine, or a glass of this drink ‖ 포도주로 만든 독한 술, 또는 이 술 한 잔. 브랜디(한 잔)

brash /bræʃ/ *adj* behaving too confidently and speaking too loudly ‖ 지

bread

나치게 자신있게 행동하고 지나치게 크게 말하는. 버릇 없는. 무례한: *a brash young man* 무례한 젊은이

brass /bræs/ *n* **1** [U] a very hard bright yellow metal that is a mixture of COPPER and ZINC ‖ 구리와 아연의 합금으로 매우 단단하고 밝은 노랑색을 띠는 금속. 황동. 놋쇠 **2 the brass (section)** the people in an ORCHESTRA or band who play musical instruments such as the TRUMPET or horn ‖ 오케스트라나 밴드에서 트럼펫이나 호른 등의 악기를 연주하는 연주자들. 금관 악기부 **3 get down to brass tacks** INFORMAL to start talking about the most important details or facts ‖ 가장 중요한 세부 내용이나 사실들에 대해 이야기를 시작하다. (문제의)핵심 [요점]을 찌르다. 본론으로 들어가다

bras·siere /brə'zɪr/ *n* ⇨ BRA

brass knuck·les /ˌ. '../ *n* [plural] a set of metal rings worn over your KNUCKLES, used as a weapon ‖ 주먹에 끼어 무기로 쓰는 한 쌍의 금속제 고리

brass·y /'bræsi/ *adj* **1** like BRASS in color ‖ 황동색이 나는 **2** sounding loud and unpleasant ‖ 크고 불쾌하게 소리나는. 시끄러운 금속성이 나는 **3** someone who is brassy talks loudly and behaves in a way that is too confident ‖ 사람이 큰 소리로 떠들고 지나치게 자신만만한 태도로 행동하는. 뻔뻔스러운. 철면피의

brat /bræt/ *n* INFORMAL a badly behaved child ‖ 불량하게 행동하는 아이. 악동. 녀석: *Stop acting like a spoiled brat.* 버릇 없는 악동 같은 짓 좀 그만둬.

bra·va·do /brə'vɑdoʊ/ *n* [U] behavior that is intended to show how brave you are, but is often unnecessary ‖ 종종 쓸데없이 자신이 용감하다는 것을 보여주려는 의도로 하는 행위. 허세. 허장성세

brave¹ /breɪv/ *adj* dealing with danger, pain, or difficult situations with courage ‖ 위험[고통, 어려운 상황]을 용기있게 처리하는. 용감한. 씩씩한. 두려움을 모르는. 불굴의: *brave soldiers* 용감한 군인들 / *her brave fight against cancer* 그녀의 암과의 불굴의 투쟁 – **bravely** *adv* – **bravery** *n* [U]

brave² *v* [T] to deal with a difficult, dangerous, or unpleasant situation ‖ 어려운[위험한, 불쾌한] 상황에 대처하다. 용감하게 …에 맞서다. …을 무릅쓰다: *15,000 people braved the hot sun to see Mandela.* 1만5천명의 사람들이 만델라를 보기 위해 뜨거운 햇볕도 불사했다.

brave³ *n* a young fighting man from a Native American tribe ‖ 미국 원주민 부족의 젊은 전사

bra·vo /'brɑvoʊ, brɑ'voʊ/ *interjection* said in order to show your approval when someone, especially a performer, has done well ‖ 사람, 특히 연주자가 잘했을 때에 호감을 나타내는 데에 쓰여. 브라보. 잘한다

brawl¹ /brɔl/ *n* a noisy fight, especially in a public place ‖ 특히 공공 장소에서의 떠들썩한 싸움질. 소동

brawl² *v* [I] to fight in a noisy way, especially in a public place ‖ 특히 공공 장소에서 떠들썩하게 싸우다: *brawling in the street* 길거리에서의 소동

brawn /brɔn/ *n* [U] physical strength ‖ 육체적인 힘. 체력. 완력: *You have the brains, I have the brawn.* 너는 머리가 좋고, 나는 체력이 좋다. – **brawny** *adj*: *brawny arms* 억센 팔

bray /breɪ/ *v* [I] if a DONKEY brays, it makes a loud sound ‖ 당나귀가 시끄럽게 울다

bra·zen¹ /'breɪzən/ *adj* showing that you do not feel ashamed about your behavior ‖ 자신의 행동에 부끄러워하지 않음을 보여주는. 뻔뻔스러운. 철면피의: *a brazen lie* 뻔뻔스런 거짓말 – **brazenly** *adv*

brazen² *v*

brazen sth ↔ **out** *phr v* [T] to deal with a difficult or embarrassing situation by appearing to be confident rather than ashamed ‖ 부끄러워하기보다 확신에 찬 모습을 보여 어렵거나 곤혹스러운 상황에 대처하다. 뻔뻔스럽게 맞서다[밀고 나아가다]

bra·zier /'breɪʒɚ/ *n* a metal pan that holds a fire ‖ 불을 담아 두는 금속제의 화로

breach /britʃ/ *n* **1** [C, U] an act of breaking a law, rule, agreement etc. ‖ 법률·규칙·협정 등을 깨는 행위. 불이행. 위반: *You are in breach of your contract.* 너는 계약을 위반하고 있다. **2** a hole or broken place in a wall or a similar structure, especially one made during a military attack ‖ 특히 군사 공격 중 만들어진 성벽이나 그 유사 구조물의 구멍이나 부서진 부위. 갈라진 틈. 터진 곳 – **breach** *v* [T]

bread /brɛd/ *n* [U] **1** a common food made from flour, water, and YEAST ‖ 밀가루·물·효모로 만든 흔한 식품. 빵: *We need a loaf of bread.* (=large piece of bread that can be cut into pieces) 우리는 빵 한 덩어리가 필요하다. / *bread and butter* 버터를 바른 빵 **2** SLANG money ‖ 돈 **3 sb's bread and butter** INFORMAL where the owner of a business gets

bread

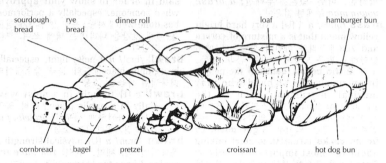

sourdough bread | rye bread | dinner roll | loaf | hamburger bun

cornbread | bagel | pretzel | croissant | hot dog bun

most of his/her income from ‖ 한 사업체의 주인이 주요 수입을 벌어 들이는 곳. 생계. 생활 수단: *Tourists are our bread and butter.* 관광객은 우리의 생계 수단이다. **4 daily bread** the money that you need in order to live ‖ 사는 데 필요한 돈. 생계비. 양식 **5 know which side your bread is buttered on** INFORMAL to know who to be nice to in order to get advantages for yourself ‖ 자기의 이득을 얻기 위해 누구에게 친절해야 하는지를 알다. 자기의 이해 관계[타산]에 밝다

bread·bas·ket /'brɛd,bæskɪt/ *n* **1** [singular] INFORMAL the part of a country or other large area that provides most of the food ‖ 대부분의 식량을 생산하는 한 나라의 일부 지역이나 다른 대규모 지역. 곡창 지대: *The midwest is the breadbasket of America.* 중서부는 미국의 곡창 지대이다. **2 a** basket for holding or serving bread ‖ 빵을 담거나 내놓는 바구니. 빵 바구니

bread·crumbs /'brɛdkrʌmz/ *n* [plural] very small pieces of bread used in cooking ‖ 요리할 때에 쓰는 빵 부스러기. 빵가루

bread·ed /'brɛdɪd/ *adj* covered in BREADCRUMBS, then cooked ‖ 빵가루를 입혀 요리한. 빵가루를 뿌린: *breaded veal* 빵가루를 뿌린 송아지 고기

breadth /brɛdθ, brɛtθ/ *n* [U] **1** the distance from one side of something to the other, especially something very wide; width ‖ 특히 매우 넓은 사물의 한 쪽에서 다른 쪽까지의 거리. 폭; width **2 a** wide range or variety ‖ 넓은 범위나 변화: *No one can match Dr. Brennan's breadth of knowledge.* 브레넌 박사의 폭 넓은 지식은 아무도 필적할 수 없다.

bread·win·ner /'brɛd,wɪnɚ/ *n* the member of a family who earns the

money to support the others ‖ 가족을 부양하기 위해 돈을 버는 가족의 구성원. 가족 부양자

break¹ /breɪk/ *v* **broke, broken, breaking**
1 ▶IN PIECES 조각조각으로◀ [T] if something breaks or someone breaks it, it separates into two or more pieces, especially because it has been hit or dropped ‖ 특히 부딪치거나 떨어뜨려서 둘 또는 그 이상의 조각으로 나눠지다. 깨뜨리다. 부수다: *Careful, those glasses break easily.* 조심해라. 그 유리는 깨지기 쉽다. / *I broke off a piece of the candy bar for Kathy.* 캐시에게 줄 막대 사탕을 부러뜨렸다. / *They had to break the window to get into the house.* 그들은 집으로 들어가기 위해 창문을 부숴야 했다.
2 ▶BODY PART 신체 부위◀ [T] if you break a part of your body, the bone splits into two or more pieces ‖ 뼈가 둘 또는 그 이상의 조각으로 나눠지다. 부러뜨리다. 골절시키다: *Sharon broke her leg skiing.* 샤론은 스키를 타다가 다리가 부러졌다.
3 ▶END STH …을 끝내다◀ [I, T] to not continue, or to end something ‖ 어떤 것을 계속하지 않거나 끝내다: *Dee's laugh broke the silence.* 디의 웃음은 침묵을 깨뜨렸다. / *I don't smoke anymore, but it was hard to break the habit.* 나는 더 이상 담배를 피우지 않지만 습관을 고치기가 어려웠다.
4 ▶NOT WORK 작동되지 않다◀ [I, T] to damage something such as a machine so that it does not work, or to become damaged in this way ‖ 기계 등을 작동되지 못할 정도로 손상시키다. 또는 작동되지 않을 만큼 망가지다. 고장나다. 고장내다: *You've broken the TV?* 네가 그 TV 고장냈지? / *It just broke. I didn't even*

touch it! 그냥 고장 난 거야. 나는 건드리지도 않았어!

5 ▶SURFACE/SKIN 표면/피부◀ [T] to damage the surface of something so that it splits or has a hole in it ‖ 찢어지거나 구멍이 생기게 물건의 표면을 손상시키다. 찢다. 터지게 하다: *Do not use this product if the seal has been broken.* 밀봉된 부분이 터져 있으면 이 제품을 사용하지 마시오.

6 break loose/free to suddenly become free or able to move without any restrictions ‖ 갑자기 자유로워지거나 아무 제약 없이 움직일 수 있게 되다. 벗어나다. 해방되다: *I broke free from him and ran.* 나는 그에게서 탈출하여 달아났다.

7 break a law/rule to disobey a law or rule ‖ 법률이나 규칙을 어기다: *What's wrong? We're not breaking any rules.* 무슨 일이야? 우리는 전혀 규칙을 어기고 있지 않아.

8 break a promise/an agreement/your word to not do what you promised to do ‖ 하기로 약속한 것을 하지 않다. 약속/협정/말을 어기다: *politicians who break their election promises* 선거 공약을 어기는 정치인들

9 break your neck INFORMAL to hurt yourself very badly ‖ 심하게 다치다: *Get the ice off the sidewalk; we don't want people breaking their necks.* 보도 위의 얼음을 치워라. 우리는 사람들이 크게 다치는 것을 원치 않아.

10 break for lunch/coffee etc. to stop working in order to eat or drink something ‖ 어떤 것을 먹거나 마시기 위해 일을 중단하다. 점심/커피를 마시려고 일손을 놓다: *We broke for lunch at about 12:30.* 우리는 일을 멈추고 12시 30분경에 점심을 먹었다.

11 break a record to do something faster or better than it has ever been done before ‖ 전보다 어떤 것을 더 빠르게 하거나 더 잘하다. 기록을 갱신하다: *He decided he would retire if he broke the world record.* (=beat the best one in the world) 그는 세계 기록을 갱신하면 은퇴하기로 결심했다.

12 break the news to sb to tell someone about something bad that has happened ‖ 일어난 나쁜 일을 남에게 말하다: *Freddy didn't want to break the news to Mom.* 프레디는 엄마에게 그 소식을 전하고 싶지 않았다.

13 ▶NEWS/EVENT 뉴스/사건◀ if news about an important event breaks, it becomes known by everyone after having been secret ‖ 뉴스·사건이 비밀스런 상태였다가 모든 이들에게 알려지다. 소식이 전해[알려]지다: *The next morning, the news broke that Monroe was dead.* 다음 날 아침에 몬로가 죽었다는 소식이 전해졌다.

14 break even to neither make a profit nor lose money ‖ 수익이나 손실이 없게 되다. 득실 없이 끝나다: *We broke even in our first year of business.* 우리는 사업 첫 해에 손익이 없었다.

15 ▶DAY 날◀ if day breaks, light begins to show in the sky as the sun rises ‖ 해가 뜨며 하늘에 빛이 보이기 시작하다. 날이 새다[밝다]

16 ▶WAVE 파도◀ if a wave breaks, it begins to look white on top because it is coming close to the shore ‖ 파도가 해변 가까이 다가와서 윗부분이 하얗게 보이기 시작하다. 부서지다 —see also **break the ice** (ICE¹)

break away *phr v* [I] **1** to escape ‖ 도망치다. 달아나다: *Nelson broke away from the policemen.* 넬슨은 경찰관으로부터 도망쳤다. **2** to change what you have been doing because it limits your freedom, is boring etc. ‖ 하고 있는 일이 자유를 제한하며 지루해서 바꾸다. 벗어나다: *teenagers trying to break away from their parents* 부모에게서 벗어나고자 하는 십대들

break down *phr v* **1** [I] if a large machine breaks down, it stops working ‖ 큰 기계가 작동을 멈추다. 고장나다: *A truck had broken down in the middle of the intersection.* 트럭 한 대가 교차로 한 가운데서 고장났다. **2** [I] if a discussion, system, opinion etc. breaks down, it fails or stops existing ‖ 토론·시스템·의견 등이 실패하거나 존재하지 않게 되다. 좌절되다. 중단되다: *The talks broke down completely in June 1982.* 그 회담은 1982년 6월에 완전히 중단됐다. / *breaking down the divisions between racial groups* 인종간의 분열 타파 **3** [T **break** sth ↔ **down**] to hit something, such as a door, so hard that it falls down ‖ 문 등을 세게 쳐서 넘어뜨리다. …을 부수다 **4 break down and do sth** to finally do something that you did not want to do, because someone has persuaded or forced you ‖ 남이 설득하거나 강요해서 결국은 원하지 않은 일을 하다. 굴복하다: *He finally broke down and admitted he'd stolen it.* 그는 마침내 굴복하고 그것을 훔쳤다고 시인했다. **5** [I, T] if a substance breaks down or is broken down, it is reduced or changed, usually as a result of a chemical process

‖ 대개 화학 작용의 결과로 어떤 물질이 감소 또는 변화되다. 분해하다[시키다]: *Wastes in the water are **broken down** using bacteria.* 물 속의 찌꺼기는 박테리아를 이용하여 분해된다. **6** [I] to be unable to stop yourself from crying ‖ 울음을 멈출 수 없다. 울음을 터뜨리다: *She **broke down** several times during the funeral.* 그녀는 장례식 때 여러 번 울음을 터뜨렸다. **7** [T **break** sth ↔ **down**] to make something such as a job, report, plan etc. simpler by dividing it into parts ‖ 일·보고서·계획 등을 더 단순하게 세분화하다. 분류[분석]하다: *You can **break** the exam question **down** into three parts to make it easier.* 너는 시험 문제를 더 쉽게 하기 위해서 세 부분으로 분류할 수 있다.

break in *phr v* **1** [I] to enter a building using force, in order to steal something ‖ 물건을 훔치기 위해 건물에 무단으로 들어가다. 침입하다: *They **broke in** through that window.* 그들은 그 창문을 통해 침입했다. **2** [T **break** sb/sth ↔ **in**] to make a person or animal become used to the work she, he, or it has to do ‖ 사람이나 동물을 해야 할 일에 익숙해지게 하다. …을 훈련시키다[길들이다]: *a training camp for **breaking in** new soldiers* 신병을 훈련시키는 훈련소 **3** [I] to interrupt someone when s/he is speaking ‖ 다른 사람이 이야기할 때 방해하다. 대화에 끼어들다. 참견하다: *The operator **broke in** saying, "You need another 75¢ to continue the call."* 전화 교환원이 중간에 끼어들며 이야기했다. "통화를 계속하시려면 75센트가 더 필요합니다." **4** [I,T **break** sth ↔ **in**] if you break shoes or boots in, or they break in, they become more comfortable because you have been wearing them ‖ 신발이나 부츠 등을 신어서 더 편해지다. 신어서 길들이다[길이 들다]

break into sth *phr v* [T] **1** to enter a building using force in order to steal something ‖ 물건을 훔치기 위해 무단으로 건물에 들어가다. 침입하다: *We think she **broke into** the room through the back window.* 그가 뒤 창문을 통해 그 방에 침입했으리라 생각된다. **2 break into a run** to suddenly begin running ‖ 갑자기 뛰기 시작하다 **3** to become involved in a new activity, especially a business activity ‖ 특히 기업 활동 등의 새로운 활동에 참여하다. 진출하다: *companies trying to **break into** the Eastern European markets* 동유럽 시장에 진출하려는 기업들

break off *phr v* **1** [T] to end a relationship, especially a political or romantic one ‖ 특히 정치적 또는 연애 관계를 끝내다. 청산하다. 헤어지다: *They've **broken off** their engagement.* 그들은 파혼했다. **2** [I, T] to suddenly stop doing something, especially talking to someone ‖ 특히 남에게 이야기하는 것을 갑자기 멈추다. (…을) 중단하다: *She **broke off**, forgetting what she wanted to say.* 그녀는 하고자 하는 말을 잊어버리자 이야기를 중단했다.

break out *phr v* [I] **1** if something bad such as a disease, fire, or war breaks out, it begins to happen ‖ 질병[화재, 전쟁] 등의 안 좋은 일이 발생하기 시작하다. 일어나다. 발발하다: *Last night fire **broke out** in the 12th Street warehouse.* 어젯밤에 12번가 창고에서 불이 났다. **2** to change the way you live or behave, especially because you are bored ‖ 특히 지루해서 생활 방식이나 행동 방식을 바꾸다. …에서 벗어나다: *You've got to **break out of** this rut!* (=stop doing the same things all the time) 너는 판에 박힌 생활을 벗어나야 해! **3** to suddenly begin to have red spots on your skin, especially on your face ‖ 피부, 특히 얼굴에 붉은 반점이 갑자기 생기다: *Chocolate makes me **break out**.* 나는 초콜릿을 먹으면 붉은 반점이 생긴다. **4 break out in a sweat** to start sweating (SWEAT) ‖ 땀이 나기 시작하다 **5** to escape from prison ‖ 교도소에서 탈출하다. 탈옥하다

break through *phr v* **1** [T **break through** sth] to change or end a way of thinking ‖ 사고 방식을 바꾸거나 없애다. …을 타파하다: *It's difficult to **break through** cultural differences and meet people in a new country.* 새로운 나라에서 문화적 차이를 극복하고 사람들을 만나는 일은 어렵다. **2** [I, T] if the sun breaks through, you can see it through the clouds ‖ 해가 구름 사이로 보이다. 해가 나타나다[비치다]

break up *phr v* **1** [T **break** sth ↔ **up**] to separate something into smaller parts because it is too big, too long, or too boring ‖ 사물이 너무 커서[길어, 지루해서] 여러 작은 부분으로 나누다. 해체하다: *Large companies were being **broken up** to encourage competition.* 경쟁을 북돋우기 위해 대기업들이 해체되고 있었다. **2** [I] to end a marriage or romantic relationship, or to stop being together as a group ‖ 결혼이나 연애 관계를 끝내다, 또는 한 집단으로서 더 이상 함께 하지 않다. 헤어지다. 정리하다: *Troy and I* *broke up last month.* 트로이와 나는 지난 달에 헤어졌다. / *When did the Beatles break up?* 비틀즈가 언제 해체됐지? **3** [I, T] if a fight breaks up or someone breaks it up, the people stop fighting or are made to do this ‖ 싸움을 멈추거나 중단시키다. **4** [I] if a crowd or meeting breaks up, people start to leave ‖ 군중이나 모임의 사람들이 떠나기 시작하다. 흩어지다. 해산하다 **5** [I,T **break** sth ↔ **up**] to break, or break something into small pieces ‖ 깨지거나 무엇을 작은 조각으로 깨뜨리다. 부서지다. 부수다: *The ship broke up on the rocks.* 배가 바위에 부딪쳐 산산조각났다. / *We used shovels to break up the soil.* 우리는 삽으로 흙을 파헤쳤다.

break with sb/sth *phr v* [T] to leave a group or organization because you have had a disagreement with them ‖ 의견이 일치하지 않아서 단체나 조직을 떠나다. 관계를 끊다: *The Socialists needed money after they broke with the Communists.* 사회주의자들은 공산주의자들과 관계를 끊은 후 돈이 필요했다.

**break² ** *n*

1 ▶A REST 휴식◀ a period of time when you stop working in order to rest, eat, or travel ‖ 휴식[식사, 여행]하기 위해 일을 중단하는 기간. 휴식(기): *Matthews spoke for three hours without taking a break.* 매튜즈는 쉬지 않고 세 시간 동안 연설했다. / *lunch/coffee break* (=when you stop to eat lunch or drink coffee) 점심[커피] 시간: *We needed a break, so we went up to the mountains for a few days.* 우리는 휴식이 필요해서 며칠 동안 등산을 했다. / *Spring Break* (=spring vacation from college) *is at the end of March.* 봄방학은 3월 말이다. —see usage note at VACATION

2 ▶STH STOPS …이 중단되다◀ a period of time when something stops for a while and then starts again ‖ 어떤 일이 잠시 동안 중단했다가 다시 시작하는 기간. 중단. 중지: *There was a break of two years between his last book and this one.* 그의 마지막 책과 이 책 사이에는 2년간의 공백이 있었다. / *a break in the conversation* 대화의 중단

3 give sb a break SPOKEN to stop annoying, criticizing, or being unkind to someone ‖ 남을 괴롭히거나, 비난하거나 또는 불친절하게 대하지 않다. 한 번 봐주다: *Give me a break, you guys! I can't get the money until Friday.* 좀 봐줘! 금요일까지는 그 돈을 구할 수가 없어.

4 ▶A CHANCE 기회◀ a chance to do

something that improves your job ‖ 일을 향상시키는 것을 할 기회. 운. 호기: *The band's big break came when they sang on a local TV show.* 그 악단이 지방 TV 쇼에서 노래를 불렀을 때에 큰 기회가 찾아왔다.

5 ▶END/CHANGE 끝/변화◀ [singular] a situation when a relationship or something traditional ends suddenly or changes completely ‖ 관계나 전통적인 것이 갑자기 끝나거나 완전히 변화할 때의 상황. 절교. 단절: *In a break with tradition, the city council decided not to have a parade.* 전통과 단절하는 의미에서 시의회는 퍼레이드를 하지 않기로 결정했다.

6 ▶A SPACE 공간◀ a space between two things or in a group of things ‖ 두 사물이나 한 무리의 사물들 사이의 공간. 틈. 빈 공간: *a break in the clouds* 구름 사이의 빈 공간

7 ▶BONE 뼈◀ a place where a bone in someone's body has broken ‖ 신체 내의 뼈가 부러진 곳. 골절 부위(部位)

break·a·ble /'breɪkəbəl/ *adj* made of material that breaks easily ‖ 쉽게 깨지는 재료로 만들어진. 깨지기 쉬운

break·age /'breɪkɪdʒ/ *n* FORMAL something that has been broken ‖ 파손물: *All breakages must be paid for.* 모든 파손물은 변상해야 한다.

break·away /'breɪkə‚weɪ/ *adj* **breakaway group/party/movement etc.** a group etc. that has been formed by people who left another group because of a disagreement ‖ 불일치로 인해 다른 집단을 형성한 집단. 분리 집단/분당/분리 운동

break·down /'breɪkdaʊn/ *n* **1** [C, U] the failure of a system or relationship ‖ 시스템이나 관계의 실패. 단절. 결렬: *a breakdown in the peace talks* 평화 회담의 결렬 **2** an occasion when a car or a piece of machinery stops working ‖ 차나 기계의 작동이 중단되는 경우. 고장. 파손 **3** ⇨ NERVOUS BREAKDOWN **4** a statement explaining the details of something such as a bill ‖ 계산서 등의 상세한 설명서. 명세. 내역: *I'd like a breakdown of these figures, please.* 저는 이 수치의 세부 내역을 알고 싶습니다.

break·fast /'brɛkfəst/ *n* [C, U] the meal you have in the morning ‖ 아침 식사. 조반: *I had bacon and eggs for breakfast.* 아침 식사로 베이컨과 계란을 먹었다. / *Did you have time to eat breakfast?* 아침 식사 했니? —see usage note at MEAL TIMES

break-in /'. ./ *n* an act of entering a building illegally using force ‖ 건물에 불법적·강제적으로 들어가는 행위. 무단 침입

break·ing point /'.. ,./ *n* [U] the point at which someone or something is no longer able to work well or deal with problems ‖ 사람이나 사물이 더 이상 일을 잘할 수 없거나 문제를 처리할 수 없는 시점. 한계점: *He was at breaking point. I thought he was going to kill me.* 그가 한계에 다다랐기 때문에 나를 죽일 거라 생각했다.

break·neck /'breɪknɛk/ *adj* extremely and often dangerously fast ‖ 아주, 그리고 종종 위험스러울 정도로 빠른. 맹렬한 속도의: *She was driving at breakneck speed.* 그녀는 무시무시한 속도로 차를 몰고 있었다.

break·through /'breɪkθru/ *n* an important new discovery in something you have been studying ‖ 연구해 온 것에 있어 중요하고 새로운 발견. 획기적 발전. 비약적 전진: *Scientists have made an important breakthrough in the treatment of heart disease.* 과학자들은 심장 질환의 치료에 획기적 발전을 해 왔다.

break·up /'breɪkʌp/ *n* [C, U] **1** the act of ending a marriage or other relationship ‖ 결혼 생활이나 다른 관계를 끝내는 행위. 이별. 헤어짐 **2** the separation of an organization, country etc. into smaller parts ‖ 조직·나라 등이 작은 부분으로 분리됨. 분열. 분할: *the breakup of Yugoslavia* 유고슬라비아의 분열

break·wa·ter /'breɪk,wɔtɚ, -,wɑtɚ/ *n* a strong wall built out into the sea to protect the shore from the force of the waves ‖ 파도의 힘으로부터 해안을 보호하기 위해 바다에 세워 놓은 튼튼한 벽. 방파제

breast /brɛst/ *n* **1** one of the two round raised parts on a woman's chest ‖ 여성의 가슴에 있는 두 개의 둥글고 봉긋한 부분의 하나. 유방 —see picture at BODY **2** [C, U] the part of the body, especially a bird's body, between the neck and the stomach, or the meat from this ‖ 목과 배 사이에 있는, 특히 새의 몸통 부분 또는 이 부위의 고기. 가슴살: *turkey breast* 칠면조 가슴살

breast-feed /'. ,./ *v* [I, T] if a woman breast feeds, she feeds a baby with milk from her breasts ‖ 젖먹이에게 모유를 먹이다. …을 모유로 키우다

breast·stroke /'brɛst̬stroʊk/ *n* [U] a way of swimming in which you push your arms out from your chest and then bring them back to your side ‖ 팔을 가슴에서 쭉 내뻗었다가 옆구리로 가져가는 수영법. 평영(平泳)

breath /brɛθ/ *n* **1** [U] the air that comes out of your lungs when you breathe ‖ 숨을 쉴 때 폐에서 나오는 공기. 호흡. 숨: *I can smell alcohol on your breath.* 네 입에서 술 냄새가 난다. / *The cat has bad breath.* (=it smells bad) 그 고양이는 입 냄새가 심하다. **2** [C, U] the act of breathing air into your lungs, or the amount of air you breathe ‖ 숨쉴 때 공기가 폐 속으로 들어감, 또는 들이마시는 공기의 양. 숨쉬기. 폐활량: *Take a big/deep breath* (=breathe in a lot of air once) *and try to calm down.* 심호흡을 하고 진정해라. **3 be out of breath** to have difficulty breathing because you have just been running or exercising ‖ 방금 달리거나 운동을 해서 숨을 쉬기가 곤란한. 숨이 차다. 숨을 헐떡이다: *Lily was out of breath when she answered the phone.* 릴리는 전화를 받았을 때 숨을 헐떡였다. **4 hold your breath a)** to breathe in and close your mouth to keep the air in your lungs ‖ 숨을 들이마시고 폐에 공기를 유지하기 위해 입을 다물다. 숨을 참다: *I couldn't hold my breath anymore.* 나는 더 이상 숨을 참을 수 없었다. **b)** to wait anxiously to see what is going to happen ‖ 무슨 일이 일어나는가를 보기 위해 초조하게 기다리다. 숨을 죽이고 기다리다: *We were all holding our breath, waiting for the winner to be announced.* 우승자가 발표되기를 기다리며 우리 모두는 숨 죽이고 기다렸다. **5 save your breath/don't waste your breath** SPOKEN used in order to tell someone that it is not worth saying anything ‖ 남에게 아무 말할 가치도 없다고 이야기할 때에 쓰여. 잠자코 있다. 말을 삼가다: *Save your breath - he won't listen anyway.* 잠자코 있어라. 어차피 그는 들으려 하지 않을 테니까. **6 catch your breath** to begin breathing normally again after you have been running or exercising ‖ 뛰거나 운동한 후에 다시 평상시처럼 숨쉬기 시작하다. 한숨 돌리다: *I had to sit down to catch my breath.* 나는 앉아서 한숨 돌려야 했다. **7 a breath of fresh air** something that is different, exciting, and enjoyable ‖ 다르고 재미있으며 즐거운 것. 기운을 북돋아 주는 것: *Your happy face is like a breath of fresh air around here.* 너의 행복한 얼굴이 이곳 분위기를 즐겁게 해주는

것 같구나. **8 take your breath away** to be extremely beautiful or exciting ‖ 대단히 아름답거나 흥미롭다: *a view that will take your breath away* 숨이 막힐 정도로 아름다운 경치 **9 under your breath** in a quiet voice ‖ 조용한 목소리로. 속삭이며: *"I hate you," he muttered under his breath.* "네가 미워."라고 그는 작은 소리로 중얼거렸다.

breath·a·ble /'briðəbəl/ *adj* **1** clothing that is breathable allows air to pass through it easily ‖ 옷이 공기를 잘 통과시키는. 통기성(通氣性)이 있는 **2** able to be breathed ‖ 호흡할 수 있는. 호흡하기에 알맞은: *breathable air* 호흡하기 좋은 공기

Breath·a·lyz·er /'brɛθə,laɪzə/ *n* TRADEMARK a piece of equipment used by the police to see if a car driver has drunk too much alcohol ‖ 운전자가 지나치게 많은 술을 마셨는지 확인하기 위해 경찰관이 쓰는 기구. 음주 측정기 – **breathalyze** *v* [T]

breathe /brið/ *v* **1** [I, T] to take air into your lungs and send it out again ‖ 폐로 공기를 들이마시고 다시 내뿜다. 숨쉬다. 호흡하다: *Relax and breathe deeply.* (=take in a lot of air) 긴장을 풀고 심호흡을 해라. **2** [I, T] to blow air, smoke, or smells out of your mouth ‖ 입에서 공기[연기, 냄새]를 불어 내다. 내뿜다. 풍기다: *Stop breathing garlic all over me.* 나한테 마늘 냄새 좀 풍기지 마라. **3 breathe a sigh of relief** to stop being worried about something ‖ 어떤 일에 대해 걱정을 멈추다. 안도의 한숨을 쉬다: *We all breathed a sigh of relief as he climbed off the roof.* 그가 지붕에서 내려왔을 때 우리 모두는 안도의 한숨을 내쉬었다. **4 breathe down sb's neck** INFORMAL to watch what someone is doing so carefully that it makes him/her feel nervous or annoyed ‖ 긴장시키거나 기분 나쁘게 할 정도로 남이 하고 있는 일을 주의깊게 지켜보다. 감시하다: *I can't work with you breathing down my neck.* 나를 감시하는 당신과 같이 일을 할 수 없다. **5 not breathe a word** to not tell anyone about a secret ‖ 비밀에 대해 누구에게도 말하지 않다. 비밀을 지키다: *Promise not to breathe a word to anyone.* 비밀을 지킨다고 약속해라. **6 breathe life into sth** to change a situation so that people feel more excited or interested ‖ 더욱 흥분하거나 호기심을 불러일으키도록 상황을 바꾸다. …에 생기를 불어넣다: *Some new teachers might breathe a little life into*

this school. 몇몇 새로 오신 선생님들이 이 학교에 생기를 약간 불어넣을 수 있을 것이다.

breathe in *phr v* [I, T **breathe** sth ↔ **in**] to take air, smoke, a particular type of smell etc. into your lungs ‖ 공기·연기·특정한 냄새 등을 폐로 들이쉬다. 숨을 들이 쉬다: *breathing in the fresh sea air* 신선한 바다 공기를 마심

breathe out *phr v* [I, T **breathe** sth ↔ **out**] [I] to send air, smoke, a particular type of smell etc. from your lungs ‖ 폐에서 공기·연기·특정한 냄새 등을 내쉬다. 숨을 내쉬다: *OK, now breathe out slowly.* 좋아, 이제 천천히 내쉬어라.

breath·er /'briðə/ *n* INFORMAL a short period of rest from an activity ‖ 활동 후 잠시의 휴식. 잠깐 쉼: *OK, everybody, let's take a 20 minute breather.* 자, 여러분 20분 동안 휴식합시다.

breath·less /'brɛθlɪs/ *adj* having difficulty breathing in a normal way ‖ 정상적으로 숨쉬는 데에 어려움이 있는. 숨쉬기가 곤란한 – **breathlessly** *adv*

breath·tak·ing /'brɛθ,teɪkɪŋ/ *adj* extremely impressive, exciting, or surprising ‖ 몹시 인상적인[흥미진진한, 깜짝 놀랄 만한]. 가슴을 뛰게 하는. 굉장한: *breathtaking scenery* 정말 멋있는 풍경

breath·y /'brɛθi/ *adj* if someone's voice is breathy, you can hear his/her breath when s/he speaks ‖ 말할 때에 음성에서 숨소리를 들을 수 있는. 음성이 기식음(氣息音)이 섞인

breed¹ /brid/ *v* **bred** /brɛd/, **bred**, **breeding 1** [I] if animals breed, they have babies ‖ 동물이 새끼를 낳다: *Rats can breed every six weeks.* 쥐는 6주마다 새끼를 낳는다. **2** [T] to keep animals or plants in order to produce babies, or to develop new animals or plants ‖ 새끼를 낳거나 새로운 동·식물을 개발하기 위해 동물이나 식물을 기르다. 사육하다. 품종 개량하다: *He breeds horses.* 그는 말을 사육한다. **3** [T] to cause a particular feeling or condition ‖ 특정한 감정이나 상태를 야기하다. …을 일으키다. …의 원인이 되다: *The crowded living conditions bred disease and crime.* 밀집한 생활 환경이 질병과 범죄의 원인이 됐다.

breed² *n* **1** a type of animal, especially one that people have kept to breed ‖ 특히 번식시키기 위한 동물의 일종. 품종: *What breed is your dog?* 당신 개는 어떤 품종입니까? **2** a particular type of person or type of thing ‖ 특정 유형의 사람이나 사물. 종족. 종류: *the first in a* *new breed of home computers* 신기종 가 정용 컴퓨터들 중 최고품

breed·er /'bridɚ/ *n* someone who breeds animals or plants ‖ 동물이나 식물을 기르는 사람. 사육자. 육종가

breed·ing /'bridɪŋ/ *n* [U] **1** the act or process of animals producing babies ‖ 동물이 새끼를 생산하는 행위나 과정. 번식. 생식 **2** the activity of keeping animals or plants in order to produce babies, or to develop new types ‖ 새끼를 낳거나 새로운 종류를 개발하기 위해 동물이나 식물을 기르는 행위. 사육. 품종 개량 **3** OLD-FASHIONED polite social behavior ‖ 예의 바른 사회적 행동. 교양. 예의 범절

breeding ground /'.. ,./ *n* a place or situation where something grows or develops ‖ 어떤 것이 자라거나 발달하는 장소나 상황. 사육장. 온상: *Universities were a breeding ground for protests against the war.* 대학은 반전 데모의 온상이었다.

breeze[1] /briz/ *n* **1** a light gentle wind ‖ 가볍고 온화한 바람. 산들바람. 미풍 — see usage note at WEATHER[1] **2 be a breeze** SPOKEN to be very easy to do ‖ 어떤 것을 하는 것이 매우 쉽다: *Learning to drive was a breeze.* 운전을 배우는 일은 매우 쉬웠다. —see also **shoot the breeze** (SHOOT[1])

breeze[2] *v* [I] INFORMAL to walk somewhere in a quick confident way ‖ 빠르고 확신에 찬 태도로 어딘가로 걸어가다. 거침없이 나아가다: *She breezed into my office and sat down.* 그녀는 내 사무실에 거침없이 들어와 앉았다.

breeze through sth *phr v* [T] INFORMAL to finish a piece of work or pass a test very easily ‖ 아주 쉽게 일을 끝마치거나 시험에 합격하다. 거침없이 해내다: *Sherry breezed through her final exams.* 셰리는 기말 시험을 쉽게 치렀다.

breez·y /'brizi/ *adj* **1** cheerful, confident, and relaxed ‖ 쾌활하고 자신있으며 긴장하지 않은. 기운찬: *his breezy manner* 그의 쾌활한 태도 **2** breezy weather is when the wind blows in a fairly strong way ‖ 바람이 상당히 강하게 부는. 산들바람이 부는

breth·ren /'brɛðrən/ *n* [plural] OLD-FASHIONED male members of an organization, especially a religious group ‖ 특히 종교 집단과 같은 조직의 남성 회원들. 형제들. 남성 신도

brev·i·ty /'brɛvəti/ *n* [U] FORMAL **1** the quality of expressing something in very few words ‖ 어떤 것을 몇 마디로 표현하는 특성. 간결함: *We appreciated the speaker's brevity.* 우리는 그 연사의 간결한 연설에 감사했다. **2** shortness of time ‖ 시간의 짧음: *the brevity of the meeting* 짧은 모임

brew[1] /bru/ *v* **1** [I, T] if tea or coffee brews or you brew it, boiling water is poured over it to make it ready to drink ‖ 차나 커피가[를] 끓는 물을 부어 마시게 되다[하다]. 끓다. 끓이다 **2** [I] if something unpleasant is brewing, it will happen soon ‖ 불쾌한 일이 곧 일어나다. 일어나려고 하다: *There's a storm brewing.* 폭풍우가 몰려오고 있다. **3** [T] to make beer ‖ 맥주를 양조하다

brew[2] *n* a drink that is brewed, such as tea, coffee, or beer ‖ 차[커피, 맥주] 등의 끓인[양조한] 음료

brew·er /'bruɚ/ *n* a person or company that makes beer ‖ 맥주를 만드는 사람이나 회사. 맥주 양조업자

brew·er·y /'bruəri/ *n* a place where beer is made, or a company that makes beer ‖ 맥주를 제조하는 곳이나 회사. 맥주 양조장[회사]

bribe[1] /braɪb/ *n* money or gifts that you use to persuade someone to do something, usually something dishonest ‖ 보통 부정한 일을 하도록 남을 설득하는 데에 사용하는 돈이나 선물. 뇌물: *politicians accused of taking bribes* 뇌물을 받은 혐의로 고발된 정치인들

bribe[2] *v* [T] to give someone a BRIBE ‖ 남에게 뇌물을 주다: *They say he bribed the policeman to let him go.* 그들은 그가 그 경찰관에게 풀어 달라고 뇌물을 주었다고 말한다.

brib·er·y /'braɪbəri/ *n* [U] the act of giving or taking BRIBEs ‖ 뇌물을 주거나 받는 행위. 뇌물 수수

bric-a-brac /'brɪk ə ,bræk/ *n* [U] small inexpensive objects, used for decoration in a house ‖ 집안의 장식품으로 쓰이는 작고 값싼 물건

brick[1] /brɪk/ *n* [C, U] a hard block of baked clay used for building walls, houses etc. ‖ 벽·집 등을 짓는 데에 쓰이는 단단하게 구운 진흙 덩어리. 벽돌

brick[2] *v*

brick sth ↔ **up** *phr v* [T] to fill or close a space by building a wall of bricks in it ‖ 벽돌로 벽을 만들어 공간을 메우거나 막다. 벽돌로 막다[메우다]: *bricked up windows* 벽돌로 막은 창문

brick·lay·er /'brɪk,leɪɚ/ *n* someone whose job is to build things with bricks ‖ 벽돌로 건축하는 직업인. 벽돌공 — **bricklaying** *n* [U]

bri·dal /ˈbraɪdl/ *adj* relating to a BRIDE or a wedding ‖ 신부나 결혼식과 관련된. 신부의. 결혼식의: *a bridal gown* 신부 드레스

bride /braɪd/ *n* a woman at the time she gets married or just after she is married ‖ 결혼식 때의 또는 결혼 직후의 여성. 신부. 새색시

bride·groom /ˈbraɪdɡrum/ *n* ⇨ GROOM²

brides·maid /ˈbraɪdzmeɪd/ *n* a woman who helps the BRIDE and stands beside her during her wedding ‖ 결혼식 때 신부를 도와 주고 그 옆에 서 있는 여성. 신부 들러리

bridge¹ /brɪdʒ/ *n* **1** a structure built over a river, road etc., that allows people or vehicles to cross from one side to the other ‖ 사람이나 차량이 한쪽에서 다른 쪽으로 건널 수 있게 하는 강·도로 등 위에 건설된 건축물. 다리. 교량: *the Brooklyn Bridge* 브루클린 다리 **2** something that provides a connection between two ideas or subjects ‖ 두 사상이나 주제 사이에 연관성을 제공하는 것. 다리. 가교: *His new book acts as a bridge between art and science.* 그의 새 책은 예술과 과학 사이의 가교 역할을 한다. **3 the bridge** the raised part of a ship from which it can be controlled ‖ 배를 통제할 수 있는 배의 높은 부분. 선교(船橋). 브리지. 참교 **4** [U] a card game for four players who play in pairs ‖ 네 사람이 짝을 지어 하는 카드 게임. 브리지 **5 the bridge of your nose** the upper part of your nose between your eyes ‖ 눈 사이의 코의 윗부분. 콧마루 **6** a piece of metal for keeping a false tooth in place ‖ 가짜 이빨을 제자리에 박혀 있게 하기 위한 금속 조각. 가공 의치(架工義齒)

bridge² *v* [T] **1 bridge the gap (between)** to reduce the difference between two things ‖ 두 사물 사이의 차이를 줄이다: *attempting to bridge the gap between rich and poor* 빈부의 격차를 줄이려는 시도 **2** to build or form a bridge over something ‖ 어떤 것 위에 다리를 건설하다: *a log bridging the stream* 시냇물 위에 놓인 통나무 다리

bridle¹ /ˈbraɪdl/ *n* a set of leather bands put on a horse's head to control its movements ‖ 말의 동작을 조종하기 위해 말 머리에 씌운 한 세트의 가죽 끈. 굴레

bridle² *v* **1** [T] to put a BRIDLE on a horse ‖ 말에 굴레를 씌우다. **2** [I, T] to show anger, especially by making a proud upward movement of your chin ‖ 특히 거만하게 턱을 치켜들면서 분노를 표현하다. (…에)화내다. 분개하다: *Amy bridled at the insult.* 에이미는 그 모욕적인 말을 듣고 분개했다.

brief¹ /brif/ *adj* **1** continuing for a short time ‖ 짧은 시간 동안 계속되는. 잠시의. 단시간의: *a brief look at the newspaper* 신문을 잠시 훑어봄 **2** using only a few words and not describing things in detail ‖ 사물을 상세히 설명하지 않고 단지 몇 마디만 쓰는. 간결한. 간략한: *I'll try to be brief.* 간략하게 말하겠다. / *a brief letter* 짧은 편지 / *Here is the news in brief.* 여기 짤막한 소식이 있다. – **briefly** *adv*

brief² *n* **1** a set of instructions about someone's duties or jobs ‖ 의무나 일에 관한 일련의 지시(사항): *My brief is to increase sales.* 나의 임무는 판매를 증대시키는 것이다. **2** a short statement giving facts about a law case ‖ 소송 사건에 관한 사실을 제공하는 짧은 진술(서). 소송 사건 적요서

brief³ *v* [T] to give someone all the information about a situation that s/he will need ‖ 누군가에게 필요로 하는 상황에 관한 모든 정보를 제공하다. (…에게) 개요를 알리다. 요약하다: *Before we go in, let me brief you on what to expect.* 들어가기 전에 예상되는 일에 대해 간략히 요약하고자 합니다. – **briefing** *n* [C, U]

brief·case /ˈbrifkeɪs/ *n* a case used for carrying papers or documents ‖ 보고서나 서류를 담는 가방. 서류 가방

briefs /brifs/ *n* [plural] men's or women's underwear worn on the lower part of the body ‖ 하체에 입는 남녀 속옷. 팬티

bri·gade /brɪˈɡeɪd/ *n* **1** a large group of soldiers forming part of an army ‖ 군대를 이루는 대규모 집단의 병사들. 여단 **2** USUALLY HUMOROUS a group of people who have similar qualities or beliefs ‖ 유사한 특성이나 신념을 가진 사람들의 집단. 단체: *the diaper brigade* (=a group of babies) 아기 집단

brig·a·dier gen·er·al /ˌbrɪɡədɪr ˈdʒɛnərəl/, **Brigadier General** *n* an officer who has a high rank in the Army, Air Force, or Marines ‖ 육군[공군, 해병대]의 고위급 장교. 준장

bright /braɪt/ *adj* **1** shining strongly or with plenty of light ‖ 강하게 빛나거나 빛으로 가득한. 밝은. 눈부신: *a bright sunny day* 화창한 날 / *bright lights* 밝은 불빛 **2** intelligent ‖ 똑똑한. 영리한: *Vicky is a very bright child.* 비키는 매우 영리한 아이다. / *a bright idea* 명안(名案) **3** bright colors are strong and easy to see

‖ 색이 강렬해서 쉽게 눈에 띄는. 선명한: *Her pants were bright red.* 그녀의 바지는 선명한 빨간색이었다. **4 cheerful** ‖ 쾌활한: *a bright smile* 쾌활한 미소 **5 likely to be successful** ‖ 성공할 듯한. 장래가 촉망되는. 유망한: *You have a bright future ahead of you!* 너는 장래가 촉망되는구나! **6 bright and early** SPOKEN very early in the morning ‖ 아침 일찍: *I'll be here bright and early to pick you up.* 너를 태우러 아침 일찍 이곳으로 오겠다. **7 look on the bright side** to see the good things about something that is bad in other ways ‖ 다른 측면으로 보면 나쁜 것에 대해 좋은 면을 보다. 낙관하다. 긍정적으로 생각하다: *Look on the bright side – at least you didn't lose your job.* 긍정적으로 생각해라. 적어도 너는 직장을 잃지는 않았잖아. **– brightly** *adv* **– brightness** *n* [U] —see also BRIGHTS

bright·en /'braɪtn/, **brighten up** *v* [I, T] **1** to become brighter or more pleasant, or to make something do this ‖ 더 밝아지거나 즐거워지다, 또는 어떤 것을 더 밝거나 즐겁게 하다: *Flowers would brighten up this room.* 꽃은 이 방의 분위기를 환하게 해줄 것이다. / *The weather should brighten in the afternoon.* 날씨는 오후에 개인다. **2** to become more cheerful, or to make someone else feel like this ‖ 더 쾌활해지거나 누군가를 쾌활하게 느끼게 하다: *She brightened up when she saw us coming.* 그녀는 우리가 오는 걸 보자 명랑해졌다.

brights /braɪts/ *n* [plural] car HEADLIGHTs when they are on as brightly as possible ‖ 가능한 한 밝게 켜져 있을 때의 자동차의 전조등.

bril·liant /'brɪlyənt/ *adj* **1** brilliant light or color is very bright and strong ‖ 빛이나 색깔이 매우 밝고 강렬한. 빛나는. **2** extremely intelligent ‖ 매우 똑똑한. 영특한: *a brilliant scientist* 명민한 과학자 **– brilliance** *n* [U] **– brilliantly** *adv*

brim[1] /brɪm/ *n* **1** the part of a hat that sticks out to protect you from sun and rain ‖ 모자의 햇빛·비를 막도록 튀어나온 부분. 테두리. 챙 **2 the brim** the top of a container, such as a glass ‖ 유리잔 등의 그릇의 윗부분. 가장자리. 언저리: *The glass was full to the brim.* 유리잔은 넘칠 만큼 가득 찼다.

brim[2] *v* **-mmed, -mming** [I] to be very full of something ‖ 어떤 것으로 가득 차다. 넘칠 정도로 차다: *His eyes brimmed with tears.* 그의 눈은 눈물이 글썽했다.

brim over *phr v* [I] to be full of an emotion or have a lot of ideas ‖ 어떤 감

brine /braɪn/ *n* [U] water that contains a lot of salt ‖ 많은 소금이 함유된 물. 소금물 **– briny** *adj*

bring /brɪŋ/ *v* **brought, brought, bringing** [T] **1** to take someone or something to the place you are now, to the place you are going to, or to the person you are speaking to or about ‖ 사람이나 사물을 지금 있는 장소로[가려고 하는 곳으로, 말하고 있는 사람에게로] 데려가다. …을 가져오다. …을 데려가다[오다]: *I brought these pictures to show you.* 당신에게 보여 주기 위해 이 그림을 가져왔습니다. / *Can I bring a friend with me to the party?* 파티에 친구를 데려가도 되겠니? / *Rob brought her a glass of water.* 로브는 그녀에게 물 한 잔을 갖다 주었다. **2** to cause a particular type of result or reaction ‖ 특정한 결과나 반응을 일으키다. …을 생기게 하다[야기시키다]: *The article in the newspaper brought angry letters from readers.* 그 신문 기사는 독자들의 항의 편지를 야기시켰다. / *The fishing industry brings lots of money into the area.* 그 지역은 어업으로 인해 많은 돈을 벌어 들인다. **3** to make someone come to a place ‖ 남을 어떤 장소로 오게 하다: *"What brings you here?" "I need to discuss something with Mike."* "여기 무슨 일로 왔어요?" "마이크와 뭔가 상의하려고요." **4 not bring yourself to do sth** to not be able to do something, especially because you know it will upset or harm someone ‖ 특히 누군가를 화나게 하거나 해를 끼친다는 것을 알기 때문에 어떤 것을 할 수 없다: *Brenda couldn't bring herself to tell him that Helen was dead.* 브렌다는 헬렌이 죽었다는 소식을 그에게 전할 수 없었다. **5 bring sth to an end** to do something that shows that an event or situation is at an end ‖ 사건이나 상황이 끝이라는 것을 나타내 보이는 일을 하다. …을 끝내다: *The President's speech brought the Democratic Conference to an end.* 대통령의 연설로 민주당 전당 대회가 끝났다. **6 bring sth to sb's attention** a phrase used especially in formal writing that means to tell someone something ‖ 남에게 무엇을 말한다는 것을 뜻하는, 특히 격식적인 글에서 쓰는 어구: *Thank you for bringing the problem to our attention.* 그 문제에 대해 언급해 주셔서 감사합니다. **7 bring sth to bear (on)** to use something in order to get the result you want ‖ 원하는 결과를 얻기 위해 어떤 것을 사용하다: *Pressure had been brought* *to bear on the governor from state Democrats.* 주 민주당원들이 주지사에게 압력을 가해 왔다.

bring sth ↔ **about** *phr v* [T] to make something happen ‖ 어떤 것을 생기게 하다. 일으키다: *"They say the bank is closing." "What brought that about?"* 그 은행이 문 닫는다고 하더라." "무엇 때문에 그런 일이 생겼을까?"

bring sb/sth **around** *phr v* **1 bring the conversation around to** to change the subject of a conversation gradually to something new ‖ 대화의 주제를 점진적으로 새로운 것으로 바꾸다: *Ginny tried to bring the conversation around to the subject of marriage.* 지니는 대화 주제를 결혼으로 바꾸려 했다. **2** [T **bring** sb **around**] to make someone conscious again after s/he has been unconscious ‖ 의식 불명의 사람을 다시 의식이 들게 하다. 의식을 회복시키다. 제정신이 들게 하다

bring back *phr v* **1** [T **bring** sth ↔ **back**] to start using something again that had been used in the past ‖ 과거에 쓰던 것을 다시 쓰기 시작하다. (…을) 부활시키다: *Many states have voted to bring back the death penalty.* 상당수의 주들이 사형 제도를 부활시키기로 가결했다. **2** [T **bring back** sth] to make you remember something ‖ 어떤 것을 생각나게 하다. 기억[상기]시키다: *The smell of suntan lotion brought back memories of the summer.* 선탠 로션 냄새가 그 여름의 기억을 상기시켰다.

bring sb/sth **down** *phr v* [T] **1** to make something fall or come down ‖ 어떤 것을 떨어뜨리거나 내리다. …을 내리다[감소시키다]: *We are taking action to bring inflation down.* 우리는 인플레이션을 떨어뜨리기 위해 조치를 취하고 있다. **2 bring down a government/president etc.** to force a government etc. to stop being in control of a country ‖ 강제로 정부가 나라를 통치하지 못하게 하다. 정부를 전복시키다/대통령을 하야시키다

bring sth ↔ **forth** *phr v* [T] FORMAL to make something happen, appear, or become available ‖ 어떤 것을 발생하게[나타나게, 유용하게] 하다. 제안[제시]하다: *No evidence has been brought forth against Mr. Keele.* 킬레 씨에게 불리한 어떤 한 증거도 제시되지 않았다.

bring sth ↔ **forward** *phr v* [T] **1** to change the date or time of something so that it happens sooner than it was originally planned to ‖ 원래 계획된 것보다 더 빨리 일어나도록 일의 날짜나 시간

을 변경하다. …의 일정을 앞당기다: *They had to bring the wedding forward because Lynn got a new job.* 그들은 린이 새 직장을 잡아서 결혼 날짜를 앞당겨야 했다. **2** to introduce or suggest a new plan or idea ‖ 새로운 계획이나 아이디어를 소개하거나 제안하다. …을 제시하다: *Many arguments were brought forward supporting the changes.* 그 개혁을 지지하는 주장이 많이 나왔다.

bring sb/sth ↔ **in** *phr v* **1** [T **bring** sb ↔ **in**] to ask or persuade someone to become involved in a discussion, help with a problem etc. ‖ 남에게 토론에 참여해서 문제 등을 해결하는 데 돕도록 요청하거나 설득하다. …을 참여[관련, 개입]시키다: *The police had to bring the FBI in to help with their search.* 경찰은 그들을 수색하는 데 도움을 얻기 위해 미국 연방 수사국을 개입시켜야 했다. **2** [T **bring** sth ↔ **in**] to earn or produce a particular amount of money ‖ 특정한 액수의 돈을 벌거나 생기게 하다: *The painting should bring in at least a million dollars.* 그 그림은 적어도 백만 달러를 벌어들일 것이다. **3 bring in a verdict** if a court or JURY brings in a verdict, it says whether someone is guilty or not ‖ 법원이나 배심원이 남의 유죄 여부를 공표하다. 평결을 내리다

bring sth ↔ **off** *phr v* [T] to succeed in doing something that is very difficult ‖ 어려운 일을 성공적으로 해내다: *She'll get a promotion if she brings off the deal.* 그녀가 그 거래를 성사시키면 승진할 것이다.

bring sth ↔ **on** *phr v* [T] to make something bad or unpleasant happen or begin ‖ 나쁘거나 불쾌한 일이 생기게 하다. …을 가져오다: *Her illness was brought on by working too much.* 과도한 업무로 그녀는 병이 났다.

bring sth ↔ **out** *phr v* [T] **1** to make something become easier to notice, see, taste etc. ‖ 어떤 것을 더 쉽게 알아채거나 보거나 또는 맛보게 하다. 뚜렷이 나타내다: *The red paint brings out the red in the curtains.* 빨간 페인트가 커튼의 빨간색을 뚜렷이 나타낸다. **2 bring out the best/worst in sb** to emphasize someone's best or worst qualities ‖ 사람의 가장 좋은 점이나 나쁜 점을 강조하다. 남의 좋은/나쁜 점을 끌어내다: *Becoming a father has brought out the best in Dan.* 아버지가 되자 댄의 가장 좋은 점이 두드러지게 나타났다. **3** to produce and begin to sell a new product, book, record etc. ‖ 새 제품·책·

음반 등을 생산하여 판매하기 시작하다. (상품 등을) 내놓다. 출시하다: *I heard that they're **bringing out** a new kind of home computer.* 그들이 신기종의 가정용 PC를 출시할 거라고 들었어.

bring sb ↔ **together** *phr v* [T] if an event brings a group of people together, it makes them care about each other more ‖ 사람들을 서로 더욱 배려하게 만들다: *Stuart's death really brought the family together.* 스튜어트의 죽음으로 그 가족 관계가 더욱 끈끈해졌다.

bring sb/sth ↔ **up** *phr v* [T] **1** to start to talk about a particular subject or person ‖ 특정한 주제나 사람에 대하여 말하기 시작하다. …을 (화제로) 내놓다: *Why do you always **bring up** your old girlfriends?* 너는 왜 항상 옛날 여자 친구들 얘기를 꺼내냐? **2** to educate and care for a child until s/he is old enough to be independent ‖ 독립할 만큼 충분히 성장할 때까지 아이를 교육시키고 돌보다. 양육하다: *She brought up three children by herself.* 그녀 혼자서 세 아이를 길렀다. / *I was brought up a Catholic/Muslim etc.* (=taught to believe a particular religion) 나는 가톨릭[회교]을 믿으며 자랐다. **3 bring** sb **up on charges** if the police bring someone up on charges, they say officially that they think s/he is guilty of a crime ‖ 경찰이 누군가를 어떤 범죄에 대해 유죄로 생각한다고 공식적으로 말하다. …에게 범죄 혐의를 두다

brink /brɪŋk/ *n* **be on the brink of** to be about to begin a new or different situation ‖ 새롭거나 다른 상황이 막 시작되려 하다. …직전이다: *Scientists say they're on the brink of a major discovery.* 과학자들은 대발견 직전에 있다고 말한다.

brisk /brɪsk/ *adj* **1** quick and full of energy ‖ 민첩하며 기운이 충만한. 활기찬. 팔팔한. 기운찬: *a brisk walk* 활기찬 걸음걸이 **2** trade or business that is brisk is very busy ‖ 장사나 사업이 매우 바쁜. 장사가 잘되는. 활황인 **3** weather that is brisk is cold and clear ‖ 날씨가 차고 청명한. 날씨가 쾌적한 – **briskly** *adv*

bris·tle[1] /ˈbrɪsəl/ *n* [C, U] short stiff hair, wire etc. ‖ 짧고 뻣뻣한 털·철사 등. 센털. 강모: *a brush with short bristles* 짧은 강모로 된 솔

bristle[2] *v* [I] **1** to behave in a way that shows you are very angry or annoyed ‖ 매우 화나거나 짜증나 있음을 보여 주는 태도로 행동하다. 노기를 띠다. 화를 내다: *He bristled at my suggestion.* 그는 내 제안에 화를 냈다. **2** if an animal's hair bristles, it stands up stiffly because the animal is afraid or angry ‖ 두렵거나 화가 나서 동물의 털이 빳빳이 일어서다

bris·tly /ˈbrɪsəli, -sli/ *adj* **1** bristly hair is short and stiff ‖ 머리털이 짧고 뻣뻣한 **2** a bristly part of your body has short stiff hairs on it ‖ 신체에 난 털이 짧고 뻣뻣한. 억센 털의: *a bristly face* 억센 털이 난 얼굴

britch·es /ˈbrɪtʃɪz/ *n* INFORMAL **1 too big for your britches** too confident in a way that annoys other people ‖ 다른 사람들을 짜증나게 할 정도로 너무 자신만만한. 거만한 **2** HUMOROUS pants ‖ 바지

Brit·ish[1] /ˈbrɪtɪʃ/ *adj* relating to or coming from Great Britain ‖ 대영 제국과 관련되거나 대영 제국산의. 영국(산)의

British[2] *n* **the British** the people of Great Britain ‖ 영국민. 영국인

Brit·on /ˈbrɪtˈn/ *n* someone from Great Britain ‖ 그레이트 브리튼 사람. 영국인

brit·tle /ˈbrɪtl/ *adj* **1** hard but easily broken ‖ 단단하지만 깨지기 쉬운: *brittle glass* 깨지기 쉬운 유리 **2** a system, relationship etc. that is brittle is easily damaged or destroyed ‖ 시스템·관계 등이 쉽게 손상되거나 파괴되는. 불안정한: *a brittle friendship* 믿을 수 없는 우정 **3** showing no kind feelings ‖ 온화한 감정이 없음을 나타내는. 성마른. 냉담한: *his brittle nature* 화를 잘 내는 그의 성질

bro /broʊ/ *n* SLANG ⇨ BROTHER[1]

broach /broʊtʃ/ *v* **broach the subject/question etc.** to introduce something as a subject of conversation ‖ 어떤 것을 화제로 도입하다. 주제/문제를 화제로 삼다: *It's often difficult to broach the subject of sex.* 섹스를 화제로 삼는 것은 종종 곤란하다.

broad /brɔd/ *adj* **1** very wide ‖ 매우 넓은: *broad shoulders* 딱 벌어진 어깨 **2** including many different kinds of things or people ‖ 많은 다른 종류의 사물이나 사람을 포함하는: *a movie that appeals to a broad range of people* 광범위한 영역의 사람들에게 호소하는 영화 **3** concerning only the main ideas or parts of something ‖ 어떤 것의 주된 생각이나 부분에만 관련된. 일반적인. 개괄적인: *Could you give me a broad idea of your plans?* 당신 계획의 개괄적인 개념을 말해 주시겠습니까? **4 in broad daylight** during the day when it is light ‖ 밝은 낮 동안에. 대낮에: *He got stabbed in the street in broad daylight.* 그는 대낮에 거리에서 칼에 찔렸다.

broad·cast[1] /ˈbrɔdkæst/ *n* a program on the radio or television ‖ 라디오나 텔

레비전상의 프로그램. (1회의) 방송 (프로
그램): *a news broadcast* 뉴스 방송

broadcast² *v* **broadcast** *or*
broadcasted, broadcast *or*
broadcasted, broadcasting 1 [I, T]
to send out a radio or television
program ‖ 라디오나 텔레비전 프로그램을
내보내다. …을 방송하다: *Channel 5 will
broadcast the game at 6 o'clock.* 5번 채
널에서 6시에 그 게임을 방송할 것이다. **2**
[T] to tell something to a lot of people ‖
어떤 것을 많은 사람들에게 말하다. …을
퍼뜨리다. 선전하다. 떠벌리다: *If I tell
you, don't go broadcasting it all over
the office.* 너한테 말하면 회사 전체에 떠
벌리고 다니지 마라.

broad·cast·er /ˈbrɔdˌkæstɚ/ *n*
someone who speaks on radio and
television programs ‖ 라디오·텔레비전
프로그램에서 말하는 사람. 방송자. 아나
운서 —compare NEWSCASTER

broad·cast·ing /ˈbrɔdˌkæstɪŋ/ *n* [U]
the business of making radio and
television programs ‖ 라디오·텔레비전
프로그램을 제작하는 사업. 방송(업)

broad·en /ˈbrɔdn/ *v* **1** [T] also
broaden out to increase something
such as your knowledge, experience, or
number of activities ‖ 지식[경험, 활동]
등을 증가시키다. …을 넓히다: *Broaden
your knowledge with reading.* 독서로 당
신의 지식을 넓히시오. **2** [I, T] also
broaden out to make something
wider, or to become wider ‖ 어떤 것을
[이] 더 넓히거나 넓어지다: *The river
broadens out here.* 그 강은 이곳에서 넓
어진다. **3 broaden your mind** if
something broadens your mind, it
makes it easier for you to accept other
people's beliefs, ways of doing things
etc. ‖ 다른 사람들의 믿음·행동 방식 등을
받아들이기 더 쉽게 하다. 마음을 넓게 하
다: *Maybe traveling will broaden his
mind.* 아마 여행이 그의 마음을 너그럽게
만들 것이다.

broad·ly /ˈbrɔdli/ *adv* **1** in a general
way ‖ 일반적으로. 대체로. 개괄적으로: *I
know broadly what to expect.* 나는 대략
무슨 일이 일어날 것인지 안다. **2**
smile/grin broadly to have a big smile
on your face ‖ 얼굴에 큰 미소를 띠다. 활
짝/이를 드러내고 웃다

broad·mind·ed /ˌbrɔdˈmaɪndɪd/ *adj*
willing to respect opinions or behavior
that are very different from your own ‖
자신과 매우 다른 의견이나 행동을 기꺼이
존중해 주는. 너그러운. 관대한

broadside¹ /ˌbrɔdˈsaɪd/ *adv* with the

longest side facing you ‖ 마주하고 있는
가장 긴 측면으로. 옆으로: *He hit the car
broadside.* 그는 그 차의 측면을 받았다.

broadside² *v* [T] to crash into the side
of another vehicle ‖ 다른 차량의 측면에
부딪히다.

Broad·way /ˈbrɔdweɪ/ *n* a street in
New York that is known as the center of
American theater ‖ 미국 연극의 중심지로
알려진 뉴욕의 거리. 브로드웨이

bro·cade /broʊˈkeɪd/ *n* [U] thick heavy
cloth that has a pattern of gold and
silver threads ‖ 금·은실로 무늬를 넣은
두껍고 무거운 천. 비단. 양단

broc·co·li /ˈbrɑkəli/ *n* [U] a green
vegetable with thick groups of small
dark green flower-like parts ‖ 진녹색의
작은 꽃처럼 생긴 것들이 뭉쳐 있는 녹색
야채. 브로콜리 —see picture on page
944

bro·chure /broʊˈʃʊr/ *n* a thin book that
gives information or advertises
something ‖ 정보를 제공하거나 어떤 것을
광고하는 얇은 책자. 소책자

brogue /broʊɡ/ *n* **1** a strong leather
shoe, especially one with a pattern in
the leather ‖ 특히 가죽에 무늬가 있는 튼
튼한 가죽 신발. 구두 **2** an ACCENT,
especially an Irish or Scottish one ‖ 특히
아일랜드나 스코틀랜드 사투리

broil /brɔɪl/ *v* [I, T] if you broil
something, or if something broils, you
cook it under or over direct heat ‖ 어떤
것을[이] 불 바로 아래나 위에서 요리하다
[되다]. 굽다[구워지다]: *broiled chicken*
석쇠로 구운 닭고기

broil·er /ˈbrɔɪlɚ/ *n* a special area of a
STOVE used for cooking food under
direct heat ‖ 요리용 스토브의, 불이 바로
닿는 특정한 부분. 그릴. 굽는 기구

broke¹ /broʊk/ *adj* **1** INFORMAL
completely without money ‖ 돈이 한푼도
없는. 빈털터리의: *I'm flat broke.* 나는 완
전히 빈털터리이다. **2 go broke** INFORMAL
if a company or business goes broke, it
can no longer operate because it has no
money ‖ 회사나 사업이 자금이 없어서 더
이상 운영될 수 없다. 파산하다: *The
record store went broke last year.* 그 음
반 가게는 작년에 망했다. **3 go for
broke** INFORMAL to take big risks trying
to achieve something ‖ 어떤 것을 성취하
기 위해 대단한 위험을 무릅쓰다. 전력을
다하다. 죽을 각오로 버티다: *Let's go for
broke and enter the race!* 죽을 각오로 경
주에 임하자!

broke² *v* the past tense of BREAK ‖ break
의 과거형

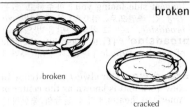

broken

broken

cracked

bro·ken¹ /'broʊkən/ *adj* **1** not working correctly ‖ 제대로 작동하지 않는. 고장난: *a broken clock* 고장난 시계 / *How did the lawn mower get broken?* 잔디 깎는 기계가 어떻게 고장났나요? **2** cracked or in pieces because of being hit, dropped etc. ‖ 부딪치거나 떨어져서 깨지거나 조각난. 고장난. 부서진: *a broken leg* 부러진 다리 / *a broken plate* 깨진 접시 **3** not continuous ‖ 계속되지 않는. 중단된: *a broken white line* 끊어진 흰 선 **4** a broken relationship is one that has been destroyed by the separation of a husband and wife ‖ 부부의 결별로 인해 관계가 깨진. 파탄한: *a broken marriage* 깨진 결혼생활 / *Jenny comes from a broken home.* (=her parents separated) 제니는 결손 가정의 자녀이다. **5** extremely mentally or physically weak after suffering a lot ‖ 많은 고통을 겪은 후에 정신적으로나 육체적으로 극도로 약한. 쇠(약)한: *a broken man* 폐인 **6 broken agreement/promise etc.** a situation in which someone did not do what s/he promised to ‖ 남이 하기로 약속한 것을 하지 않은 상황. 파기된 협정/약속 **7 broken English/French etc.** English, French etc. that is spoken very slowly, with a lot of mistakes ‖ 아주 천천히 실수투성이로 말하는 영어·프랑스어 등. 엉터리 영어/프랑스어

broken² *v* the PAST PARTICIPLE of BREAK ‖ break의 과거 분사형

broken-down /ˌ.. '.-/ *adj* broken, old, and needing a lot of repair ‖ 깨지고 낡아 많은 수선이 필요한. 고장난. 무너진: *a broken-down trailer* 고장난 트레일러

broken-heart·ed /ˌ.. '.--/ *adj* very sad, especially because someone you love has died or left you ‖ 특히 사랑하는 사람이 죽거나 떠나서 매우 슬픈. 비탄[절망]에 빠진

bro·ker¹ /'broʊkɚ/ *n* someone whose job is to buy and sell property, insurance, etc. for someone else ‖ 남에게 부동산·보험 등을 사고 파는 직업인. 브로커. 중개업자: *a real estate broker* 부동산 중개인 —see also STOCKBROKER

broker² *v* [T] to arrange the details of a deal, plan etc. so that everyone can agree to it ‖ 모든 사람이 동의할 수 있도록 거래·계획 등의 세부 사항을 조정하다. …을 중개하다: *an agreement brokered by the UN* UN이 중개한 협정

bro·ker·age /'broʊkərɪdʒ/ *n* [U] the business of being a BROKER ‖ 중개업

bron·chi·tis /brɑŋˈkaɪtɪs/ *n* [U] an illness that affects your breathing and makes you cough ‖ 호흡에 영향을 주고 기침을 유발하는 병. 기관지염 — **bronchitic** /brɑŋˈkɪtɪk/ *adj*

bron·co /'brɑŋkoʊ/ *n* a wild horse ‖ 야생마

bron·to·sau·rus /ˌbrɑntəˈsɔrəs/ *n* a large DINOSAUR with a very long neck and body ‖ 목과 몸이 매우 긴 거대한 공룡. 브론토사우루스

bronze¹ /brɑnz/ *n* **1** [U] a hard metal that is a mixture of COPPER and TIN ‖ 구리와 주석을 혼합한 경금속. 청동 **2** [U] a dull red-brown color ‖ 흐릿한 적갈색. 청동색 **3** a work of art made of bronze ‖ 청동으로 만든 예술 작품: *a bronze by Henry Moore* 헨리 무어의 청동 작품

bronze² *adj* **1** made of BRONZE ‖ 청동으로 만든 **2** having the red-brown color of bronze ‖ 청동의 적갈색인. 청동색의

bronze med·al /ˌ. '../ *n* a prize that is given to the person who finishes third in a race, competition etc., usually made of BRONZE ‖ 경주·경기 등에서 3위를 한 사람에게 수여되는 보통 청동으로 만든 상. 동메달

brooch /broʊtʃ, brutʃ/ *n* a piece of jewelry that you fasten to your clothes ‖ 옷에 고정시키는 보석 조각. 브로치

brood¹ /brud/ *v* [I] to think about something that you are worried, angry, or sad about for a long time ‖ 오랫동안 걱정하는[화가 나는, 슬픈] 것에 대해 생각하다. 곰곰이 생각하다. 숙고하다: *Don't just sit there brooding about your problems.* 거기에 그냥 앉아서 네 문제를 곰곰이 생각만 하고 있지 마라.

brood² *n* a family of young birds ‖ 한배의 새끼 새

brook /brʊk/ *n* a small stream ‖ 작은 내. 시내. 개울

broom /brum, brʊm/ *n* a large brush with a long handle, used for sweeping floors ‖ 바닥을 쓰는 데에 사용하는 긴 손잡이가 달린 큰 솔. 비

broom·stick /'brum,stɪk, 'brʊm-/ *n* the long thin handle of a BROOM ‖ 비의 길고 가는 손잡이. 빗자루

broth /brɔθ/ *n* [U] a soup made by

cooking meat or vegetables in water and then removing them ‖ 고기나 야채를 물에 넣어 삶은 후 건져내어 만든 수프. 국: *beef broth* 소고기 수프

broth·el /'brɑθəl, 'brɔ-, -ðəl/ *n* a house where men pay to have sex with PROSTITUTEs ‖ 남자들이 돈을 내고 매춘부와 성관계를 가지는 곳. 매춘굴

broth·er¹ /'brʌðɚ/ *n* **1** a male who has the same parents as you ‖ 자신과 부모가 같은 남자. 형[오빠]. 아우[남동생]: *Isn't that your big/little* (=older or younger) *brother?* 저 사람은 너의 형[아우] 아니니? —see picture at FAMILY **2** SPOKEN a word meaning a male friend, used especially by African Americans ‖ 특히 아프리카계 미국인들이 쓰는 남자 친구를 의미하는 말 **3** a man who belongs to the same race, religion, organization etc. as you ‖ 자신과 같은 인종·종교·조직 등에 속해 있는 남자. 형제 **4** ⇨ MONK: *Brother Francis* 프란시스 수도사 – **brotherly** *adv* —compare SISTER

brother² *interjection* **Oh brother!** said when you are annoyed or surprised ‖ 화가 나거나 놀랐을 때에 쓰여. 이런 원!

broth·er·hood /'brʌðɚˌhʊd/ *n* **1** [U] OLD-FASHIONED a feeling of friendship between people ‖ 사람들간의 우정. 형제애: *peace and brotherhood* 평화와 형제애 **2** OLD-FASHIONED a men's organization formed for a particular purpose ‖ 특정한 목적을 위해 형성된 남자들의 조직. 동업 조합

brother-in-law /'.. .. ,./ *n* **1** the brother of your husband or wife ‖ 남편이나 아내의 형제. 처남. 시동생. 아주버니 **2** the husband of your sister ‖ 자매[누이]의 남편. 형부. 제부. 매형. 매제 —see picture at FAMILY

broth·er·ly /'brʌðɚli/ *adj* showing helpfulness, love, loyalty etc., like a brother would ‖ 형제처럼 도움·사랑·충성을 보여 주는. 형제의. 형제 같은[다운]: *brotherly love* 형제애

brought /brɔt/ *v* the past tense and PAST PARTICIPLE of BRING ‖ bring의 과거·과거 분사형

brou·ha·ha /'bruhɑhɑ/ *n* [U] INFORMAL unnecessary noise and activity; COMMOTION ‖ 쓸데없는 소음과 행동. 소란. 야단법석; ㊅ commotion: *a big brouhaha going on in the street* 거리에서 계속되는 소동

brow /braʊ/ *n* **1** ⇨ FOREHEAD **2** ⇨ EYEBROW

brow·beat /'braʊbit/ *v* [T] to force someone to do something by

continuously asking him/her to do it, especially in a threatening way ‖ 특히 위협적으로 남에게 어떤 것을 하도록 계속해서 강요하다: *Don't let them browbeat you into doing anything.* 그들이 너에게 어떤 일을 하라고 협박하게 내버려 두지 마라.

brown¹ /braʊn/ *adj* having the same color as earth, wood, or coffee ‖ 흙[나무, 커피]과 같은 색을 띤. 갈색의: *brown shoes* 갈색 신발 – **brown** *n* [C, U]

brown² *v* [I, T] to become brown, or to make food do this ‖ 갈색이 되거나 음식을 갈색이 되게 하다. 노릇노릇 타다[타게 하다]: *brown the meat in hot oil* 뜨거운 기름에 고기를 노릇노릇하게 굽다

brown-bag /,. './ *v* [I] INFORMAL to bring your lunch to work in a small brown paper bag ‖ 작은 갈색 종이 가방에 점심을 넣어 일하는 곳에 가지고 가다. 도시락을 지참하다: *"I'm brown-bagging this week."* "난 이번 주는 도시락을 싸서 다닐 거야.

brown·ie /'braʊni/ *n* **1** a thick flat piece of chocolate cake ‖ 두툼하고 납작한 초콜릿 케이크 조각 **2** **get/earn brownie points** INFORMAL if you do something to get brownie points, you do it to get praise ‖ 칭찬 받기 위해 어떤 것을 하다. 아첨으로 점수를 따다

Brown·ies /'braʊniz/ *n* the part of the GIRL SCOUTS that is for younger girls ‖ 걸스카우트의 유년단원

brown·stone /'braʊnstoʊn/ *n* **1** [U] a type of red-brown stone, often used for building in the eastern US ‖ 종종 미국 동부에서 건축 재료로 쓰이는 적갈색 유형의 돌. 갈색 사암 **2** a house with a front made of this stone ‖ 정면이 이 적갈색 돌로 만들어진 집

browse /braʊz/ *v* [I] **1** to look at the goods in a store without wanting to buy anything ‖ 상점에서 상품을 살 생각 없이 구경하다. 훑어보다: *"Can I help you?" "No thanks. I'm just browsing."* "도와 드릴까요?" "아닙니다. 그냥 구경하는 거에요." **2** to read only the most interesting parts of a book, magazine etc. ‖ 책·잡지 등의 가장 흥미로운 부분만 읽다. 띄엄띄엄 읽다. 훑어보다: *I was browsing through the catalog, and I found this.* 카탈로그를 여기저기 훑어보다가 이것을 찾았다.

brows·er /'braʊzɚ/ *n* a computer program that lets you find and use information on the INTERNET ‖ 인터넷상에서 정보를 검색해 이용하게 하는 컴퓨터 프로그램. 브라우저

bruise¹ /bruz/ *n* a mark on the skin of a person or piece of fruit where it has been damaged by a hit or a fall ‖ 부딪치거나 떨어져서 손상된 사람의 피부나 과일 표면에 생긴 자국. 멍. 상처. 흠: *That's a nasty bruise you've got.* 너 멍이 심하게 들었구나.

bruise² *v* [I, T] to become bruised, or to bruise a person or piece of fruit ‖ 멍들거나 사람이나 과일을 멍들게 하다: *He fell and bruised his knee.* 그는 넘어져서 무릎에 멍이 들었다. / *a bruised apple* 상한 사과 – **bruising** *n* [U]

brunch /brʌntʃ/ *n* [C, U] a meal eaten in the late morning, as a combination of breakfast and LUNCH ‖ breakfast와 lunch의 합성어로 늦은 아침에 먹는 식사. 브런치 —see usage note at MEAL TIMES

bru·nette /bruˈnɛt/ *n* a woman with dark brown hair ‖ 짙은 갈색 머리카락을 가진 여자

brunt /brʌnt/ *n* **bear/take the brunt of sth** to have to deal with the worst part of something bad ‖ 좋지 않은 일의 최악의 부분에 대처해야 하다. …에 정면으로 맞서다: *Women usually bear the brunt of caring for the ill.* 여자들은 보통 환자를 간호하는 어려움을 견뎌야 한다.

brush¹ /brʌʃ/ *n* **1** an object that you use for cleaning, painting etc., made with BRISTLES, or thin pieces of plastic attached to a handle ‖ 손잡이에 가는 플라스틱 조각이 부착된, 뻣뻣한 털로 만든 청소·페인트칠 등에 쓰이는 물건. 브러시. 솔 —see also HAIRBRUSH, PAINTBRUSH, TOOTHBRUSH **2** [singular] the movement of brushing something ‖ 어떤 것을 쓰는 동작. 솔질: *I'll just give my hair a quick brush.* 빨리 머리 빗질만 할게. **3** [U] small bushes and trees covering an open area of land ‖ 광활한 땅을 덮고 있는 관목(숲). 관목[삼림] 지대: *a brush fire* 덤불 숲의 화재 **4 a brush with death/the law** an occasion when you just manage to avoid death or prison ‖ 죽음이나 투옥을 가까스로 모면한 상황

brush² *v* **1** [T] to use a brush to clean something or to make it look smooth and neat ‖ 어떤 것을 깨끗하게 하거나 매끄럽고 단정하게 하려고 솔을 이용하다. …을 솔질하다: *Go brush your teeth.* 가서 이를 닦아

brush

라. / *He didn't brush his hair.* 그는 머리를 빗지 않았다. **2** [T] to remove something with a brush or your hand ‖ 어떤 것을 솔이나 손으로 제거하다. …을 솔로 털다: *She brushed the crumbs off her lap.* 그녀는 무릎 위의 부스러기를 털어냈다. **3** [I, T] to touch someone or something lightly by chance as you pass ‖ 지나가면서 모르고 사람이나 사물을 살짝 건드리다. …을 스치다: *Her hair brushed against my arm.* 그녀의 머리카락이 내 팔에 살짝 닿았다.

brush sb/sth ↔ **aside** *phr v* [T] to refuse to listen to someone or consider someone's opinion ‖ 남에게 귀를 기울이거나 남의 의견을 고려하는 것을 거부하다. …을 무시하[일축, 묵살]하다: *He brushed her objections aside.* 그는 그녀의 반대를 일축했다.

brush sth ↔ **off** *phr v* [T] to refuse to talk about something ‖ 어떤 것에 대해서 이야기하기를 거부하다. 무시하다: *The President calmly brushed off their questions about his health.* 대통령은 자신의 건강에 대한 그들의 질문을 태연하게 무시했다.

brush up (on) sth *phr v* [I] to quickly practice and improve your skills or knowledge of a subject ‖ 한 주제에 대한 기술이나 지식을 서둘러 익히거나 향상시키다: *I have to brush up on my French before I go to Paris.* 나는 파리에 가기 전에 프랑스어를 빨리 익혀야 한다.

brush-off /'. ./ *n* [singular] INFORMAL a clear refusal to accept someone's friendship, invitations etc. ‖ 남의 우정·초대 등에 응하지 않겠다는 분명한 거절: *I thought she really liked me, but she gave me the brush-off.* 나는 그녀가 나를 정말로 좋아한다고 생각했는데, 나를 매정하게 거절했다.

brusque /brʌsk/ *adj* using very few words in a way that seems impolite ‖ 예의 없어 보일 정도로 거의 말이 없는. 무뚝뚝한. 퉁명스러운: *a brusque manner* 무뚝뚝한

brus·sels sprout /'brʌsəl ˌspraʊt/ *n* a small round green vegetable that has a slightly bitter taste ‖ 약간 쓴맛이 나는 작고 둥근 녹색 채소. 싹양배추

bru·tal /'brutl/ *adj* **1** very cruel and violent ‖ 매우 잔인하고 폭력적인. 야만적인: *a brutal attack* 잔인한 공격 **2** not sensitive to people's feelings ‖ 사람의 감정에 민감하지 않은. 냉엄한. 혹독한: *the brutal truth* 냉엄한 진실 – **brutally** *adv* – **brutality** /bruˈtæləti/ *n* [C, U]

bru·tal·ize /'brutlˌaɪz/ *v* [T] to treat

someone in a cruel and violent way ‖ 남을 잔인하고 폭력적으로 다루다. 잔인한 [야비한] 짓을 하다

brute¹ /bruːt/ *n* **1** someone who is rough, cruel, and not sensitive ‖ 거칠고 잔인하며 이해심이 없는 사람. 짐승(같은 사람). 망나니: *Her husband is a real brute.* 그녀의 남편은 정말 짐승 같은 사람이다. **2** an animal, especially a large one ‖ 특히 덩치 큰 동물

brute² *adj* **brute force/strength** physical strength that is used rather than thought or intelligence ‖ 생각이나 지능 대신 사용되는 물리적인 힘. 폭력. 완력

brut·ish /'bruːtɪʃ/ *adj* very cruel ‖ 매우 잔인한. 야만적인: *brutish behavior* 잔인한 행동

B.S. *n* Bachelor of Science; a university degree in a subject such as chemistry or mathematics ‖ Bachelor of Science(이학사)의 약어; 화학이나 수학 등의 과목의 대학 학위 —compare B.A.

BS, bs *n* SPOKEN ⇨ BULLSHIT¹

bub /bʌb/ *n* SPOKEN used in order to speak to a man or boy ‖ 남자나 소년에게 말하는 데에 쓰여. 젊은이. 자네: *Hey bub, what are you up to?* 이봐 자네, 커서 뭐 하려고 그래?

bub·ble¹ /'bʌbəl/ *n* **1** a ball of air in a liquid or solid substance ‖ 액체나 고체 물질의 공기 방울. 거품: *soap bubbles* 비눗방울 **2 burst sb's bubble** INFORMAL to destroy someone's beliefs or hopes about something ‖ 어떤 것에 대한 남의 신념이나 희망을 무너뜨리다: *I don't want to burst your bubble, but I don't think this will work.* 너를 실망시키고 싶지는 않지만 이 일은 잘 될 것 같지 않다.

bub·ble² *v* [I] **1** to produce bubbles ‖ 거품이 생기다: *Heat the sauce until it starts to bubble.* 소스에 거품이 생길 때까지 가열해라. **2** also **bubble over** to be full of a particular emotion ‖ 특정한 감정으로 가득 차다. …으로 달아오르다 [흥분하다]: *The kids were bubbling over with excitement.* 아이들은 흥분으로 잔뜩 들떠 있었다.

bubble

bubble gum /'.. ,./ *n* [U] a type of CHEWING GUM that you can blow into a round shape ‖ 둥근 모양으로 불 수 있는 껌의 일종. 풍선껌

bub·bly¹ /'bʌbli/ *adj* **1** full of BUBBLEs ‖ 거품으로 가득 찬. 거품투성이의 **2** cheerful and friendly ‖ 명랑하고 상냥한: *a bubbly personality* 명랑한 성격

bubbly² *n* [U] INFORMAL ⇨ CHAMPAGNE

buck¹ /bʌk/ *n* **1** SPOKEN a dollar ‖ 달러: *Could you lend me 20 bucks?* 내게 20달러를 빌려줄 수 있니? **2 pass the buck** to try to make someone else responsible for something that you should deal with ‖ 자신이 처리해야 하는 일을 남이 책임지게 하다. 남에게 책임을 넘기다: *You can't keep passing the buck!* 계속해서 네 책임을 남에게 떠넘기면 안 돼! **3 buck naked** SPOKEN wearing no clothes ‖ 옷을 입지 않은. 나체의: *He was standing outside buck naked.* 그는 옷을 입지 않은 채로 밖에 서 있었다. **4** the male of some animals, such as DEER, rabbits etc. ‖ 사슴·토끼 등의 수컷 동물

buck² *v* **1** [I] if a horse bucks, it kicks its back feet up in the air ‖ 말이 허공에 대고 뒷발질하다 **2** [T] to throw a rider off by jumping in this way ‖ 말이 뒷발질하며 뛰어서 등에 탄 사람을 떨어뜨리다 **3** [T] INFORMAL to oppose something ‖ 어떤 것에 반대하다. …에 저항하다: *He's finally realized he can't buck the system.* (=avoid the usual rules) 그는 결국 자신이 그 제도에 저항할 수 없다는 것을 깨달았다.

buck·et /'bʌkɪt/ *n* **1** an open container with a handle, used for carrying and holding things, especially liquids ‖ 특히 액체를 나르거나 담아두는 데에 쓰는, 손잡이가 있고 뚜껑이 없는 용기. 양동이 **2** the amount that a bucket will hold ‖ 한 양동이에 들어가는 양: *a bucket of water* 양동이 한 통의 물 —see also **a drop in the ocean/bucket** (DROP²), **kick the bucket** (KICK¹)

buck·le¹ /'bʌkəl/ *v* **1** [I, T] to fasten a buckle, or be fastened with a buckle ‖ 버클을 죄거나 버클로 조여지다: *The strap buckles at the side.* 그 가죽끈은 옆쪽에서 채운다. / *Tim buckled up his belt.* 팀은 벨트를 채웠다. **2** [I] if your knees buckle, they become weak and bend ‖ 무릎이 약해져서 구부러지다 **3** [I, T] to bend because of heat or pressure, or to make something do this ‖ 열이나 압력으로 인해 휘거나 무엇을 휘게 하다

buckle down *phr v* [I] INFORMAL to start working seriously ‖ 진지하게 일하기 시작하다. 일에 착수하다: *You'd better buckle down or you'll never get your degree.* 너는 전력을 다해 공부해야 해. 그렇지 않으면 결코 학위를 따낼 수 없을 거

야.

buckle up *phr v* [I] to fasten your SEAT BELT in a car, aircraft etc. ‖ 자동차·항공기 등에서 안전벨트를 매다

buckle² *n* a metal fastener used for attaching the two ends of a belt or STRAP, for fastening a shoe, bag etc., or for decoration ‖ 벨트나 가죽끈의 양끝을 잇는[신발이나 가방 등을 채우는, 장식하는] 데에 쓰이는 금속 죔쇠. 버클

buck teeth /ˌ. ˈ./ *n* [plural] teeth that stick forward out of your mouth ‖ 입에서 앞쪽으로 튀어나온 이빨. 뻐드렁니 – **buck-toothed** /ˈbʌktuθt/ *adj*

bud¹ /bʌd/ *n* **1** SPOKEN ➪ BUDDY **2** a young flower or leaf that is still tightly rolled up ‖ 아직 단단히 말려 있는 어린 꽃이나 잎. 싹. 눈 —see also **nip sth in the bud** (NIP¹)

bud² *v* **-dded, -dding** [I] to produce buds ‖ 싹트다

Bud·dhis·m /ˈbudɪzəm, ˈbu-/ *n* [U] the belief and religion based on the teachings of Siddhartha Gautama Buddha ‖ 부처의 가르침을 기초로 한 신앙과 종교. 불교 – **Buddhist** *n* – **Buddhist** *adj*

bud·ding /ˈbʌdɪŋ/ *adj* beginning to develop ‖ 발전하기 시작하는. 신진의: *a budding poet* 떠오르는 시인 / *a budding relationship* 발전하기 시작하는 관계

bud·dy /ˈbʌdi/ *n* **1** SPOKEN used in order to speak to a man or boy ‖ 남자나 소년을 부르는 데에 쓰여. 이봐, 녀석: *Hey, buddy! Leave her alone!* 어이, 이봐! 그녀를 혼자 있게 둬! / *Thanks, buddy!* 이봐, 고마워! **2** INFORMAL a friend ‖ 친구: *We're good buddies.* 우리는 좋은 친구야.

budge /bʌdʒ/ *v* [I, T] **1** to move, or to move someone or something from one place to another ‖ 움직이거나 사람이나 사물을 한 장소에서 다른 장소로 움직이게 하다: *It's useless. The car won't budge.* 소용없어. 그 차는 꼼짝도 않을 거야. / *Mark hasn't budged from his room all day.* 마크는 하루 종일 자기 방에서 꼼짝도 하지 않았다. **2** to make someone change his/her opinion ‖ 사람에게 의견을 바꾸게 하다: *The workers refused to budge from their demands.* 노동자들은 그들의 요구 사항을 바꾸려 하지 않았다.

budg·et¹ /ˈbʌdʒɪt/ *n* a plan of how to spend the money that is available in a particular period in time, or the money itself ‖ 특정 기간 내에 쓸 수 있는 돈의 소비 방법에 대한 계획, 또는 그 돈 자체. 예산(안). 경비 비용: *a budget of $2 million for the project* 그 계획에 대한 2

백만 달러의 예산 / *We have to try to cut/trim the budget.* (=find ways to spend less) 우리는 경비를 줄일 방법을 찾아야 한다. / *balance the budget* (=make the money that goes out of the budget equal to the money that comes in) 수지 균형을 맞추다 – **budgetary** /ˈbʌdʒəˌtɛri/ *adj* : *budgetary limits* 예산 한도

budget² *v* [I] to carefully plan and control how much you will spend ‖ 얼마의 돈을 쓸 것인지에 대해 신중하게 계획하고 조절하다. 예산을 짜다[세우다]: *I'm budgeting for a new computer.* (=planning to save enough money for one) 나는 새 컴퓨터를 사기 위한 예산을 세우고 있다.

budget³ *adj* very low in price ‖ 값이 매우 싼: *a budget flight* (값)싼 항공편

buff¹ /bʌf/ *n* **1** movie/jazz/computer etc. buff someone who is interested in and knows a lot about movies, JAZZ etc. ‖ 영화·재즈 등에 대해서 관심이 있고 많이 아는 사람. 영화/재즈/컴퓨터광 **2** in the buff INFORMAL wearing no clothes ‖ 옷을 입지 않은. 알몸의

buff² *v* [T] to make a surface shine by polishing it with something soft ‖ 부드러운 것으로 표면을 문질러 광이 나게 하다. …을 연마하다[닦다]

buf·fa·lo /ˈbʌfəˌlou/ *n, plural* **buffalos, buffaloes,** *or* **buffalo** **1** a large animal like a cow with a very large head and thick hair on its neck and shoulders; BISON ‖ 머리가 매우 크고 목과 어깨에 무성한 털이 나 있는 소처럼 큰 동물. 버팔로; ㉮ bison **2** an animal like a large black cow with long curved horns that lives in Africa and Asia ‖ 아프리카와 아시아에서 서식하는 길고 굽은 뿔을 가진 크고 검은 소와 같은 동물. 물소

buff·er /ˈbʌfɚ/ *n* **1** something that protects one thing from being affected by another thing ‖ 다른 것에 영향을 받지 않도록 막아 주는 존재. 방패가 되는 것. 완충기[역]: *The walls are a buffer against noise from the airport.* 그 벽은 공항의 소음을 막는 완충재 역할을 한다. / *Support from friends can provide a buffer against stress.* 친구들의 지지는 스트레스를 막는 완충 역할을 제공할 수 있다. **2** buffer zone a safe or quiet area where fighting or dangerous activity is not allowed to happen ‖ 전투나 위험한 행동이 일어나는 것을 허용하지 않는 안전하거나 조용한 지역. 완충 지대. 비무장 중립 지대: *The armies have agreed to a 20 mile buffer zone in the north.* 그 군대

들은 북쪽에 20마일의 비무장 중립지대를 세우는 데에 합의했다. **3 a place in a computer's memory for storing information for a short time** ‖ 일시적으로 정보를 저장하는 컴퓨터의 기억 장소. 버퍼

buf·fet¹ /bə'feɪ, bʊ-/ n a meal in which people serve themselves at a table and then move away to eat ‖ 사람들이 직접 자신의 테이블로 음식을 가져와서 먹는 식사. 뷔페(식 식사)

buf·fet² /'bʌfɪt/ v [T] to make someone or something move by hitting him, her, or it again and again ‖ 사람이나 사물을 거듭하여 쳐서 움직이게 하다. …을 치다 [때려눕히다]: *boats buffeted by the wind and the rain* 바람과 비로 인해 밀려간 배들

buf·foon /bə'fun/ n someone who does silly things that make you laugh ‖ 남을 웃게 하는 어리석은 짓을 하는 사람. 어릿광대 **– buffoonery** n [U]

bug¹ /bʌg/ n **1** INFORMAL any small insect, especially one you think is unpleasant ‖ 특히 불쾌하게 여기는 모든 작은 곤충. 벌레: *a tiny little green bug* 아주 작은 녹색 벌레 **2** INFORMAL a GERM (=very small creature) that causes an illness that is not very serious ‖ 아주 심각하지는 않은 질병을 유발하는 매우 작은 생물체. 병원균. 세균: *a flu bug* 독감 바이러스 **3 the travel/skiing/writing etc. bug** INFORMAL a sudden strong interest in doing something that usually only continues for a short time ‖ 보통 단기간 동안만 지속되는, 어떤 것을 하는 것에 대한 갑작스러운 대단한 관심. 여행/스키/집필 광: *After going to India, I got the travel bug.* 인도에 간 이후로 나는 여행에 사로잡혔다. **4** a small mistake in a computer program that stops it from working correctly ‖ 정상적으로 작동하는 것을 저지하는 컴퓨터 프로그램의 작은 오류. 버그 **5** a small piece of electronic equipment for listening secretly to other people's conversations ‖ 남의 대화를 몰래 듣기 위한 작은 전자 장비. 도청기

bug² v **-gged, -gging** [T] **1** SPOKEN to annoy someone ‖ 남을 화나게 하다: *Stop bugging me!* 나를 짜증나게 하지 마! **2** to use a BUG in order to listen secretly to other people's conversations ‖ 남의 대화를 몰래 듣는 데에 도청기를 사용하다. 도청 장치를 설치하다. 도청하다: *Are you sure this room isn't bugged?* 너는 이 방에 도청 장치가 없다고 확신하니?

bu·gle /'byugəl/ n a musical instrument like a TRUMPET, which is used in the army to call soldiers ‖ 병사들을 소집하기 위해 군대에서 쓰는 트럼펫 같은 악기. 군대 나팔

build¹ /bɪld/ v **built, built, building 1** [I, T] to make a structure such as a house, factory, ship etc. ‖ 집·공장·배 등의 구조물을 만들다. 짓다, 건설하다: *building a new bridge* 새로운 다리의 건설 / *More homes are being built near the lake.* 호수 근처에 더 많은 집들이 지어지고 있다. **2** [T] to make something develop or form ‖ 어떤 것을 발달시키거나 형성시키다: *working to build a more peaceful world* 보다 더 평화로운 세계를 만들기 위한 작업 **3 confidence-building/muscle-building/character-building etc** making someone's confidence, muscles etc. grow or develop ‖ 사람의 자신감·근육 등을 키우거나 발달시키기. 자신감 향상/근육 발달/인격 발달

build sth ↔ **into** *phr v* [T] **1** to make something a permanent part of a system, agreement etc. ‖ 어떤 것을 체제·협정 등의 영구한 일부분으로 만들다. 조항 등을 부가하다: *A completion date was built into the contract.* 완료일은 계약서에 부가되어 있었다. **2** to make something so that it is a permanent part of a structure, machine etc. ‖ 어떤 것을 구조물·기계 등의 영구적인 일부분으로 만들다. …의 일부로 짜 넣다: *The alarm was small enough to be built into a watch.* 그 경보 장치는 시계에 장착될 정도로 작았다.

build on *phr v* [T **build on** sth] to use your achievements in order to develop ‖ 발전시키기 위해 자신의 성취물을 이용하다. …을 발판으로 삼다: *We hope to build on the success of our products.* 우리는 제품의 성공을 발판으로 삼길 기대한다.

build up *phr v* **1** [I,T **build** sth ↔ **up**] if something builds up or you build it up, it gradually increases or grows ‖ 어떤 것이 점점 늘거나 커지다, 또는 무엇을 늘리거나 키우다: *You need to build up your strength.* 너는 체력을 키울 필요가 있다. / *They've built up a reputation as a reliable car dealer.* 그들은 믿을 만한 자동차 거래자로 신망을 쌓았다. **2 build up sb's hopes** to make someone think that s/he will get something that s/he wants, often in a way that is unfair ‖ 남에게 종종 부당한 방법으로 원하는 것을 얻을 것이라고 생각하게 하다. …의 희망을 부추기다: *Don't build up the kids' hopes – they'll just be disappointed.* 아이들에게

희망을 가지도록 부추기지 마, 그들은 실망만 하게 될 거야.

build up to sth *phr v* [T] to gradually prepare for a particular moment or event || 특정한 순간이나 사건을 위해 점진적으로 준비하다: *All the activity was building up to something, but I didn't know what.* 모든 활동이 무언가를 위해 준비되고 있었지만 나는 그것이 어떤 것인지 몰랐다.

build² *n* [singular, U] the shape and size of someone's body || 사람 몸의 형태와 크기. 체격: *She has black hair and a slim build.* 그녀는 검은 머리에 날씬한 체격이다.

build·ing /ˈbɪldɪŋ/ *n* 1 a structure such as a house, church, or factory, that has a roof and walls || 지붕과 벽이 있는 집[교회, 공장] 등의 구조물. 건물: *I was surrounded by tall buildings.* 나는 높은 건물들에 둘러싸였다. ✗DON'T SAY "high buildings."✗ "high buildings"라고는 하지 않는다. 2 [U] the process or business of building things || 건축 과정이나 건축업

building block /ˈ.. ˌ./ *n* 1 a block of wood or plastic for young children to build things with || 아이들의 쌓기 놀이용 나무나 플라스틱 블록 2 [plural] the pieces or parts that make it possible for something big or important to exist || 크거나 중요한 것이 존재할 수 있게 하는 조각이나 부분. (중요한) 구성 요소: *Reading and writing are the building blocks of our education.* 읽기와 쓰기는 우리 교육의 중요한 구성 요소이다.

build·up /ˈbɪldʌp/ *n* 1 [singular, U] a gradual increase || 점진적인 증가. 증강: *The buildup of traffic on the roads is causing problems in the city.* 도로 교통량의 증가는 도시의 여러 문제를 유발하고 있다. 2 a description of someone or something that says that he, she, or it is very special or important || 아주 특별하거나 중요하다고 말하는 사람이나 사물에 대한 묘사. 선전. 광고: *The magazine had a great buildup, but I don't like it much.* 그 잡지는 많은 광고를 했지만 그다지 마음에 들지는 않는다. 3 the length of time spent preparing for an event || 행사를 준비하는 데 보낸 기간. 사전 준비: *the long buildup to the opening of the new mall* 새로운 상점의 개업을 위한 오랜 준비 (기간)

built¹ /bɪlt/ the past tense and PAST PARTICIPLE of BUILD || build의 과거·과거분사형

built² *adj* SLANG a word used by men to describe a woman with large breasts,

considered OFFENSIVE by many women || 많은 여성들이 모욕적이라고 여기는 말로, 가슴이 큰 여성을 가리키는 남성들이 쓰는 말. 여성의 가슴이 빵빵한

built-in /ˌ. ˈ./ *adj* forming a part of something that cannot be separated from it || 분리될 수 없는 사물의 일부를 이루고 있는. 붙박이의. 고유한: *built-in cupboards* 붙박이 찬장 / *Children have a built-in sense of survival.* 어린이들은 생존 본능을 타고 난다.

bulb /bʌlb/ *n* 1 the glass part of an electric light, that the light shines from || 빛을 내는 전등의 유리 부분. 전구: *a 40 watt bulb* 40와트 전구 2 a root shaped like a ball that grows into a plant || 식물로 자라는 공 모양의 뿌리. 구근: *tulip bulbs* 튤립 구근

bul·bous /ˈbʌlbəs/ *adj* fat and round || 뚱뚱하고 둥근. 통통한. 볼록한: *a bulbous nose* 주먹코

bulge¹ /bʌldʒ/ *n* a curved place on the surface of something, caused by something under or inside it || 밑이나 내부에 있는 것 때문에 표면이 굽은 부분. 불룩한 부분. 돌출: *Trent could see the bulge of a gun under the man's jacket.* 트렌트는 그 남자의 재킷 아래로 불룩 튀어나온 권총을 볼 수 있었다.

bulge², bulge out *v* [I] to stick out in a rounded shape || 둥근 모양으로 튀어나오다. 부풀어 오르다: *His stomach bulged out.* 그의 배는 불룩했다.

bu·li·mi·a /bəˈlimiə, bu-/ *n* [U] a mental illness that makes someone eat too much and then VOMIT because s/he is afraid of gaining weight || 지나치게 많이 먹고 나서 살찌는 것을 염려해 구토를 하게 하는 정신병. 병적 과식증. 식욕 이상 항진 – **bulimic** /bəˈlimɪk/ *adj*

bulk /bʌlk/ *n* 1 **the bulk of** sth the main or largest part of something || 어떤 것의 주요 부분, 또는 가장 큰 부분. 대부분: *The bulk of the work has already been done.* 일의 대부분은 이미 끝냈다. 2 [C, U] the large size of something or someone || 사람이나 사물의 거대함. 거대한 사람[것]: *Greg squeezed his bulk into the car.* 그레그는 자신의 거대한 몸을 차 안으로 밀어넣었다. 3 **in bulk** in large quantities || 많은 양으로. 대량으로: *We buy our paper in bulk.* 우리는 대량으로 종이를 구매한다.

bulk·y /ˈbʌlki/ *adj* big and heavy || 크고 무거운. 부피가 큰: *a bulky package* 부피가 큰 소포

bull /bʊl/ *n* 1 a male cow, or the male of some other large animals, such as an

ELEPHANT or WHALE ‖ 황소, 또는 코끼리나 고래 등의 큰 동물의 수컷 **2** [U] INFORMAL ⇨ BULLSHIT¹ **3 take the bull by the horns** INFORMAL to bravely or confidently deal with a difficult, dangerous, or unpleasant problem ‖ 어렵거나 위험하거나 불쾌한 문제를 용감하거나 자신있게 다루다. 과감히 문제에 맞서다: *I just took the bull by the horns, hoping Sam wouldn't get mad.* 나는 샘이 화내지 않기를 바라며 그냥 과감히 맞섰다.

bull·dog /'bʊldɔg/ *n* a dog with a large head, a flat nose, a short neck, and short thick legs ‖ 큰 머리·납작한 코·짧은 목·짧고 굵은 다리의 개. 불도그

bull·doze /'bʊldoʊz/ *v* [T] to move dirt and rocks, destroy buildings etc. with a BULLDOZER ‖ 불도저로 쓰레기·바위를 제거하거나 빌딩 등을 부수다. 불도저로 제거하다[고르다]

bull·doz·er /'bʊl,doʊzɚ/ *n* a powerful vehicle with a broad metal blade, used for moving dirt and rocks, destroying buildings etc. ‖ 쓰레기·바위를 제거하거나 빌딩 등을 부수는 데에 쓰는 넓적한 쇳날이 달린 강력한 차. 불도저

bul·let /'bʊlɪt/ *n* a small round piece of metal that is fired from a gun ‖ 권총에서 발사되는 작고 둥근 금속 조각. 총알. 총탄

bul·le·tin /'bʊlət'n, 'bʊlətɪn/ *n* **1** a short official news report or announcement that is made to tell people about something important ‖ 중요 사항에 대해 사람들에게 알리는 짤막한 공식 뉴스 보도나 발표. 공보. 속보: *a news bulletin* 뉴스 속보 **2** a letter or printed statement that a group or organization produces to tell people its news ‖ 단체나 조직의 소식을 알리기 위해 만드는 편지나 인쇄된 성명서. 회보

bulletin board /'... ,./ *n* **1** a board on a wall that you put information or pictures on ‖ 정보나 그림을 붙이는 벽 면의 판자. 게시판. 공고판 **2** a place in a system of computers where you can read messages or leave messages for anyone to read ‖ 메시지를 읽거나 다른 사람이 읽도록 메시지를 남기는 컴퓨터 시스템의 부분. 전자 게시판

bull·fight /'bʊlfaɪt/ *n* a type of entertainment in some countries, in which a man fights and kills a BULL ‖ 몇몇 나라에서 하는 남자가 황소와 싸워서 죽이는 오락의 일종. 투우 **– bullfighter** *n* **– bullfighting** n [U]

bull·horn /'bʊlhɔrn/ *n* a piece of equipment that you hold up to your mouth when you talk, to make your voice louder ‖ 말할 때 목소리를 더 크게 내기 위해 입에 대는 장비. 확성기

bul·lion /'bʊlyən/ *n* [U] blocks of gold or silver ‖ 금이나 은 덩어리. 금[은]괴

bull·ish /'bʊlɪʃ/ *adj* relating to an increase in prices in the STOCK MARKET ‖ 주식 시장에서의 주가 상승에 관한. 상승세의 **—compare** BEARISH

bull mar·ket /,. '../ *n* a situation in which the value of SHAREs in business increases ‖ 주식 시장에서 주가가 상승하는 상황. 강세 시장 **—compare** BEAR MARKET

bull·pen /'bʊlpɛn/ *n* the area in a baseball field in which PITCHERs practice throwing ‖ 야구장에서 투수가 공 던지기 연습을 하는 지역. 불펜

bull's-eye /'. ./ *n* the center of a TARGET that you try to hit when shooting ‖ 총을 쏠 때 맞추려고 하는 과녁의 중심

bull·shit¹ /'bʊlʃɪt/ *interjection, n* SPOKEN a very impolite word meaning something that is stupid and completely untrue ‖ 어떤 것이 어리석고 완전히 거짓이라는 의미의 매우 무례한 말. 허튼소리. 개소리

bullshit² *v* [I, T] INFORMAL a very impolite word meaning to say something that is BULLSHIT ‖ 거짓말하다라는 의미의 매우 무례한 말. 허튼소리를 하다 **– bullshitter** *n*

bul·ly /'bʊli/ *v* [T] to threaten to hurt someone or frighten him/her, especially someone weaker or smaller than you ‖ 특히 자신보다 더 약하거나 작은 사람을 다치게 하거나 겁주겠다고 위협하다. 골리다. 못살게 굴다 **– bully** *n*

bum¹ /bʌm/ *n* INFORMAL **1** DISAPPROVING someone who has no home or job, and who usually asks people on the street for money ‖ 집이나 직업이 없어 보통 거리에서 돈을 구걸하는 사람. 부랑자 **2** INFORMAL someone who is very lazy ‖ 매우 게으른 사람. 게으름뱅이: *Get out of bed, you bum!* 어서 일어나, 이 게으름뱅이야! **3 beach/ski etc. bum** someone who spends all of his/her time on the beach, skiing (ski) etc. ‖ 해변에서, 또는 스키를 타는 데 온종일 시간을 보내는 사람. 해변/스키 광

bum² *v* **-mmed, -mming** [T] SLANG to ask someone if you can borrow or have something ‖ 어떤 것을 빌리거나 가져도 되는지 남에게 묻다. …을 빌리다[얻다]: *Can I bum a cigarette?* 담배 한 대 빌릴 수 있을까요?

bum around *phr v* SLANG **1** [I, T] to spend time doing nothing, or in a very lazy way ‖ 아무것도 하지 않거나 빈둥거리며 시간을 보내다: *We were just bumming around at home yesterday.* 우리는 어제 집에서 그냥 빈둥거리면서 지냈다. **2** [T **bum around** sth] to travel around living very cheaply and having few plans ‖ 매우 저렴하게 지내며 거의 계획 없이 여행하다. 방랑[떠돌이] 여행하다: *bumming around Africa* 아프리카에서의 떠돌이 여행

bum³ *adj* INFORMAL bad and useless ‖ 나쁘고 쓸모없는. 시시한. 보잘것없는: *Andy gave me some bum advice about buying a car.* 앤디는 나에게 차 구매에 대한 몇 가지 시시한 조언을 해 주었다.

bum·ble·bee /'bʌmbəlˌbi/ *n* a large hairy BEE ‖ 털이 많은 큰 벌. 호박벌

bum·bling /'bʌmblɪŋ/ *adj* behaving in a careless way and making a lot of mistakes ‖ 부주의하게 행동하고 실수를 많이 하는. 무능력한. 신통하지 못한

bummed /bʌmd/, **bummed out** *adj* SPOKEN feeling disappointed ‖ 실망한: *I'm really bummed that we can't go!* 우리가 갈 수 없어서 정말 실망이야!

bum·mer /'bʌmɚ/ *n* [singular] SPOKEN a situation that is disappointing ‖ 실망스러운 상황. 실패. 실망: *You can't go? What a bummer.* 너는 갈 수 없다고? 이거 실망인 걸.

bump¹ /bʌmp/ *v* **1** [I, T] to hit or knock against something, especially by accident ‖ 특히 우연히 어떤 것과 부딪치거나 충돌하다: *It was so dark I bumped into a tree.* 너무 깜깜해서 나무에 쾅 부딪쳤다. / *Don't bump your head!* 머리 부딪치지 않게 조심해! **2** [I] to move up and down as you move forward, in a vehicle ‖ 차 안에서 앞으로 갈 때 위아래로 움직이다. 덜컹덜컹 흔들리며 가다: *We bumped along the dirt road.* 우리는 비포장 도로를 따라 덜컹거리며 지나갔다.

bump into sb *phr v* [T] INFORMAL to meet someone when you were not expecting to ‖ 예상하지 않게 누군가를 만나다. 우연히 만나다: *Guess who I bumped into this morning?* 나 오늘 아침에 누구를 만났는지 아니?

bump sb ↔ **off** *phr v* [T] INFORMAL to kill someone ‖ 남을 죽이다

bump² *n* **1** an area of skin that is swollen because you have hit it on something ‖ 어떤 것에 부딪쳐서 부은 피부의 부위. 타박상. 혹: *a bump on his head* 그의 머리에 생긴 혹 **2** a small raised area on a surface ‖ 표면 위로 약

간 올라온 부분. 융기부: *a bump in the road* 도로의 융기부 **3** a movement in which one thing hits against another thing, or the sound that this makes ‖ 어떤 것이 다른 것에 부딪치는 동작이나 부딪칠 때 나는 소리. 쿵[쾅](하는 소리): *The elevator stopped with a bump.* 엘리베이터가 쿵 하고 멈췄다.

bump·er /'bʌmpɚ/ *n* the part at the front and back of a car that protects it if it hits anything ‖ 자동차가 무언가에 부딪칠 때 보호하는 자동차의 앞뒤쪽의 부분. 완충 장치. 범퍼 —see also picture on page 943

bumper

bumper

bumper² *adj* very large ‖ 매우 큰. 아주 풍부한: *a bumper crop* 대풍작

bumper stick·er /'.. ˌ../ *n* a small sign with a message on it on the BUMPER of a car ‖ 자동차의 범퍼에 붙이는 문자가 적힌 작은 표시판

bumper-to-bumper /ˌ.. . '../ *adj, adv* with a lot of cars that are very close together ‖ 많은 자동차들이 아주 가까이 붙어 있는. 꼬리에 꼬리를 문[물고]: *bumper-to-bumper traffic* 교통 체증 / *driving bumper-to-bumper* (자동차들의) 꼬리에 꼬리를 문 운전

bump·y /'bʌmpi/ *adj* **1** a bumpy surface has a lot of raised parts on it ‖ 표면에 융기된 부분이 많은. 울퉁불퉁한: *a bumpy road* 울퉁불퉁한 길 **2** a bumpy trip by car or plane is uncomfortable because of bad road or weather conditions ‖ 자동차나 비행기로 하는 여행이 나쁜 도로나 날씨 때문에 불편한. 어려움이 있는

bun /bʌn/ *n* **1** a type of bread that is small and round ‖ 일종의 작고 둥근 빵. 소형 롤빵: *a hamburger bun* 햄버거용 둥근 빵 **2** a HAIRSTYLE in which a woman fastens her hair in a small round shape at the back of her head ‖ 머리 뒤쪽에 작고 둥근 모양으로 머리카락을 고정시킨 여성의 헤어스타일. 쪽진 머리. 트레머리 —see also BUNS

bunch¹ /bʌntʃ/ *n* [singular] a group or number of similar people or things, or a large amount of something ‖ 비슷한 사람이나 물건들의 집합이나 수, 또는 어떤 것의 많은 양. 송이. 다발. 무리: *The doctor asked me a bunch of questions.* 그 의사는 내게 많은 질문을 했다. / *a bunch of grapes* 한 송이의 포도 / *There are a* *whole bunch of little restaurants by the beach.* 해변가에는 매우 작은 레스토랑들이 옹기종기 모여 있다.

bunch² *v* [I, T] **1** also **bunch together** to stay close together in a group, or to form a group ‖ 함께 모여 있거나 그룹을 형성하다. 무리를 짓다: *The kids stood bunched together behind their mother.* 아이들은 자신들의 엄마 뒤에 무리를 지어서 있었다. **2** also **bunch up** to pull material together tightly in folds ‖ 무엇을 접어서 촘촘하게 당기다. 주름을 잡다: *My skirt's all bunched up.* 내 스커트는 완전히 주름이 잡혀 있다.

bun·dle¹ /'bʌndl/ *n* **1** a group of things such as papers, clothes, or sticks that are fastened or tied together ‖ 하나로 고정되어 있거나 묶여 있는 일단의 종이[옷, 막대기] 등의 것. 다발. 뭉치. 묶음: *a bundle of newspapers* 신문 한 뭉치 **2** SOFTWARE that is included with the computer you buy ‖ 구매한 컴퓨터에 포함되어 있는 소프트웨어. 번들 제품[소프트웨어] **3** [singular] INFORMAL a lot of money ‖ 많은 돈: *That car must have cost a bundle.* 그 차는 매우 비쌀 것이다. **4 be a bundle of nerves/laughs etc.** INFORMAL to be very nervous, a lot of fun etc. ‖ 몹시 신경질적이다. 매우 재미있다

bundle² *v* [I, T] **1** also **bundle up** to make a bundle ‖ 다발 짓다. 포장하다. 싸다: *Bundle up those old clothes.* 저 낡은 옷가지들을 꾸려라. **2** also **bundle up** to dress warmly because it is cold ‖ 추워서 따뜻하게 옷을 입다 **3** to move quickly in a particular direction or into a particular place, or to make someone or something do this ‖ 특정한 방향이나 장소로 재빨리 움직이거나 사람이나 사물을 특정한 방향이나 장소로 재빨리 움직이게 하다: *The police bundled him into a car.* 경찰은 그를 차 안에 재빨리 태웠다.

bun·ga·low /'bʌŋgə,lou/ *n* a small house that has only one level ‖ 단층의 작은 집. 방갈로(식 주택)

bun·gle /'bʌŋgəl/ *v* [T] to do something badly ‖ 무엇을 서투르게 하다. 실책[실수]하다: *They bungled the job completely.* 그들은 그 일을 완전히 망쳐 놨다. **– bungler** *n* **– bungling** *adj*

bun·ion /'bʌnyən/ *n* a painful sore on your big toe ‖ 엄지발가락의 통증. 건막류(腱膜瘤)

bunk /bʌŋk/ *n* **1** a narrow bed that is attached to the wall, for example on a train or a ship ‖ 기차나 배의 벽에 붙어 있는 좁은 침대. 침상 **2** INFORMAL something that is not true or that does

not mean anything ‖ 사실이 아니거나 아무 의미없는 것. 허튼소리

bunk beds /'. ./ *n* [plural] two beds that are attached together, one on top of the other ‖ 한 침대가 다른 하나의 침대 위로 붙어 있는 두 개의 침대. 이단 침대

bun·ker /'bʌŋkɚ/ *n* a strongly built shelter for soldiers, usually under the ground ‖ 보통 지하에 견고하게 만든 군인용 은신처. 벙커. 엄폐호

bun·ny /'bʌni/, **bunny rabbit** *n* a word meaning a rabbit, used especially by or to children ‖ 특히 어린아이가 또는 어린아이에게 쓰는 토끼를 뜻하는 말

buns /bʌnz/ *n* [plural] SLANG your BUTTOCKs ‖ 궁둥이

buoy¹ /'bui, bɔɪ/ *n* an object that floats on the water, used for showing boats which parts of the water are safe or dangerous ‖ 선박을 위해 물의 어느 부분이 안전하거나 위험한지를 표시하는 데에 쓰여, 물에 띄우는 물체. 부이. 부표

buoy², **buoy up** *v* [T] **1** to make someone feel happier, more confident etc. ‖ 남을 보다 행복해 하거나 자신감이 들게 하다. 기운을 북돋우다. 고무하다: *Success buoyed his confidence.* 성공은 그를 자신에 차게 했다. **2** to keep profits, prices etc. at a high level ‖ 이익·가격 등을 높은 수준으로 유지하다

buoy·ant /'bɔɪənt/ *adj* **1** cheerful and confident ‖ 쾌활하고 자신만만한. 명랑한. 기운찬: *a buoyant mood* 활기찬 분위기 **2** buoyant prices etc. tend not to fall ‖ 가격 등이 떨어지지 않는. 상승 경향에 있는 **3** able to float ‖ 뜰 수 있는. 부양성 있는 **– buoyancy** *n* [U] **– buoyantly** *adv*

bur·den¹ /'bɚdn/ *n* FORMAL **1** something that is difficult, or that worries you because you are responsible for it ‖ 어려운 것이나 책임져야 할 걱정거리. 부담: *I don't want to be a burden on my children when I'm old.* 나는 늙어서 자식들에게 짐이 되고 싶지 않다. **2 the burden of proof** the duty to prove something ‖ 어떤 것을 증명할 의무. 입증 책임 **3** LITERARY something heavy that you have to carry ‖ 나르기에 무거운 것. 짐

burden² *v* [T] **1** to make someone worry or cause trouble for him/her ‖ 남을 걱정시키거나 문제를 일으키다. …에게 무거운 짐[부담]을 지우다. 괴롭히다: *I won't burden you with my problems.* 내 문제로 너에게 부담을 주고 싶지 않다. **2** to make someone carry something heavy ‖ 남에게 무거운 것을 나르게 하다.

bu·reau /'byʊroʊ/ *n* **1** a government

department or part of a government department ‖ 정부 국이나 정부 국의 한 부서. (관청의) 국[부]: *the Federal Bureau of Investigation* 연방 수사국 **2** an office or organization that collects or provides information ‖ 정보를 수집하거나 제공하는 사무소나 조직. 사무국[소]. 안내소: *an employment bureau* 직업 안내소 **3** ⇨ CHEST OF DRAWERS

bu·reauc·ra·cy /byʊˈrɑkrəsi/ *n* **1** [U] an official system that is annoying or confusing because it has too many rules, long processes etc. ‖ 너무 많은 규칙과 긴 절차 등으로 짜증나게 하거나 혼돈을 일으키는 공무원 제도. 관료제 **2** [C, U] the officials in a government or business who are employed rather than elected ‖ 선출되지 않고 고용된 정부나 기업의 관료

bu·reau·crat /ˈbyʊrəˌkræt/ *n* someone who works in a BUREAUCRACY and follows official rules very carefully ‖ 관료 사회에서 일하고 공적 규칙을 매우 잘 따르는 사람. 관료. 관리

bu·reau·crat·ic /ˌbyʊrəˈkrætɪk/ *adj* involving a lot of complicated official rules and processes ‖ 복잡한 공적 규칙과 절차를 많이 포함함. 관료적인

bur·geon·ing /ˈbədʒənɪŋ/ *adj* growing, increasing, or developing very quickly ‖ 매우 빨리 자라는[증가하는, 발달하는]: *the city's burgeoning population* 급속히 증가하는 도시의 인구

burg·er /ˈbəgə/ *n* INFORMAL ⇨ HAMBURGER

bur·glar /ˈbəglə/ *n* someone who goes into buildings, cars etc. in order to steal things ‖ 물건을 훔치기 위해 건물이나 차 등으로 들어가는 사람. 강도 —see usage note at THIEF

bur·glar·ize /ˈbəgləˌraɪz/ *v* [T] to go into a building, car etc. and steal things from it ‖ 건물이나 차 안으로 들어가서 물건을 훔치다. 도둑질하다

bur·gla·ry /ˈbəgləri/ *n* [C, U] the crime of going into a building, car etc. to steal things ‖ 물건을 훔치기 위해 건물이나 차 등으로 들어가는 범죄. 강도죄. 가택 침입죄

bur·i·al /ˈbɛriəl/ *n* [C, U] the act or ceremony of putting a dead body into a grave ‖ 무덤에 시체를 묻는 행위나 의식. 매장. 장례식

bur·lap /ˈbələp/ *n* [U] a type of thick rough cloth ‖ 두껍고 거친 천의 일종. 올이 굵은 천. 누런 삼베

bur·ly /ˈbəli/ *adj* a burly man is big and strong ‖ 사람이 우람하고 튼튼한. 건장한

burn¹ /bən/ *v* **burned, burned** or

burnt, burning 1 [I, T] to damage something or hurt someone with fire or heat, or to be hurt or damaged in this way ‖ 불이나 열로 사물을 손상시키거나 사람을 다치게 하거나, 또는 불이나 열로 다치거나 손상되다. 불에 데다[타다]: *Ricky burned his hand on the stove.* 리키는 난로에 손을 데었다. / *My toast is burning!* 토스트가 타고 있어! / *I've burned the turkey to a crisp!* (=cooked it until it is black) 나는 칠면조를 새까맣게 태웠어! **2** [I] to produce heat and flames ‖ 열기와 불꽃을 만들다: *Is the fire still burning?* 아직 불꽃이 남아 있니? **3 get burned** SPOKEN **a)** to be emotionally hurt by someone or something ‖ 사람이나 사물에 의해 감정적으로 상처받다: *Sally's really afraid of getting burned in a relationship again.* 샐리는 관계가 다시 어긋나 상처받는 것을 정말 염려한다. **b)** to lose a lot of money, especially in a business deal ‖ 특히 사업 거래에서 많은 돈을 잃다 **4** [I, T] if you burn a FUEL, or if it burns, it is used for producing power, heat, light etc. ‖ 연료를[가] 전력·열·빛의 발생을 위해 쓰다[쓰이다]. 연소하다[연소시키다]. 타다[태우다]: *Cars burn gasoline.* 자동차는 가솔린을 연소시킨다. **5** [I] also **burn up** to feel hot in an unpleasant way ‖ 불쾌하게 뜨겁게 느끼다. 확 타오르다: *My face is burning up.* 얼굴이 화끈거린다. **6** [I] LITERARY if a light or lamp burns, it shines or produces light ‖ 등이나 램프가 빛을 발하다 **– burned** *adj* **– burnt** *adj*

burn sth **↔ down** *phr v* [I, T] if a building burns down or is burned down, it is destroyed by fire ‖ 건물이 불에 의해 파괴되다. 다 타다. 전부 태워 버리다

burn sth **↔ off** *phr v* [T] **burn off energy/fat/calories** to use energy etc. by doing physical exercise ‖ 운동을 해서 에너지 등을 소비하다. 에너지/지방/칼로리를 소진하다

burn out *phr v* **1** [I,T **burn** sth **↔ out**] if a fire burns out or burns itself out, it stops burning because there is no coal, wood etc. left ‖ 남은 석탄·나무 등이 없어 불타지 않다. 연료를 다 써 버리다 **2** [I,T **burn** sth **↔ out**] if an engine or electric wire burns out or is burned out, it stops working because it has become too hot ‖ 엔진이나 전선이 과열되어 작동하지 않다. …을 태워서 못쓰게 만들다. 타서 끊어지다 **3 be burned out a)** to feel very tired ‖ 매우 피곤해 하다. 지치다: *I was completely burned out after my finals.* 나는 기말 시험 이후에 완전히 지쳐 버렸

다. **b)** if a building, car etc is burned out, the inside of it is destroyed by fire ‖ 불에 의해 건물·차 등의 내부가 다 타서 없어지다

burn up *phr v* **1** [I,T **burn sth ↔ up**] if something burns up or is burned up, it is completely destroyed by fire or great heat ‖ 불이나 엄청난 열에 의해 완전히 파괴되다. 재로 만들다. 몽땅 타버리다 **2** [T **burn** sb **up**] INFORMAL to make someone angry ‖ 남을 화나게 하다: *The way she treats him really burns me up.* 그를 대하는 그녀의 태도는 나를 정말 화나게 해.

burn² *n* an injury or mark caused by fire or heat ‖ 불이나 열에 의해 생긴 상처나 자국. 화상: *a burn on her arm* 그녀 팔의 화상

burn·er /'bɚnɚ/ *n* **1** the part of a STOVE that produces heat or a flame ‖ 난로의 열이나 불꽃을 일으키는 부분. 버너 **2 put sth on the back burner** INFORMAL to delay dealing with something until a later time ‖ 어떤 것을 나중에 처리하기로 연기하다. 나중으로 미루다

burn·ing /'bɚnɪŋ/ *adj* **1** on fire ‖ 불타는: *a burning house* 불타고 있는 집 **2** feeling very hot ‖ 매우 뜨겁게 느끼는. 화끈거리는: *a burning fever* 화끈대는 열 **3 burning ambition/need etc.** a very strong need etc. ‖ 매우 강한 욕구 등. 강렬한 포부/욕구 **4 burning question/issue** a very important question that must be answered quickly ‖ 빨리 응답해야 할 아주 중요한 문제. 화급한 현안/문제

bur·nish /'bɚnɪʃ/ *v* [T] to polish metal until it shines ‖ 반짝일 때까지 금속을 닦다. 갈다. 광을 내다 – **burnished** *adj*

burnt¹ /bɚnt/ *v* a past tense and PAST PARTICIPLE of BURN¹ ‖ burn¹의 과거·과거분사형

burnt² *adj* having been burned ‖ 탄. 연소된: *burnt sugar* 탄 설탕

burp /bɚp/ *v* INFORMAL **1** [I] if you burp, gas comes up from your stomach and makes a noise ‖ 위에서 가스가 나와서 소리가 나다. 트림하다 **2** [T] to help a baby get rid of stomach gas, especially by rubbing his/her back ‖ 아기의 등을 쓰다듬어 위의 가스를 제거하는 것을 돕다. 트림시키다 – **burp** *n*

bur·ri·to /bəˈritoʊ/ *n* a Mexican food made from a TORTILLA folded around meat or beans with cheese ‖ 고기나 콩을 치즈와 함께, 구운 옥수수빵으로 싼 멕시코 음식. 부리토

bur·row¹ /'bɚoʊ, 'bʌroʊ/ *v* [T] to make a hole or passage in the ground ‖ 지하에

굴이나 통로를 만들다. 굴[땅굴]을 파다: *Gophers had burrowed under the wall.* 땅다람쥐들이 담 밑에 땅굴을 팠었다.

bur·row² *n* a passage in the ground made by an animal such as a rabbit or a FOX ‖ 토끼나 여우 등 동물이 만든 지하 통로. 굴

bur·sar /'bɚsɚ, -sɑr/ *n* someone at a college who is responsible for the money that is paid by students ‖ 학생들이 낸 돈을 책임지고 있는 대학의 직원. 회계원. 출납원

burst¹ /bɚst/ *v* **burst, burst, bursting 1** [I, T] to break open or apart suddenly and violently, or to make something do this ‖ 갑자기 심하게 부서지거나 쪼개지다, 또는 무엇을 부수거나 쪼개다. 파열[폭발]하다[시키다]: *a game in which kids sit on balloons to try to burst them* 아이들이 풍선 위에 앉아 터뜨리려고 하는 게임 **2 be bursting** to be very full of something ‖ 어떤 것으로 가득 차다: *This town is bursting with tourists.* 이 도시는 관광객들로 가득 차 있다. / *School classrooms are bursting at the seams.* (=are too full of students) 교실은 학생들로 대만원이다. **3** [I] to move suddenly, quickly, and often violently ‖ 돌연히 빠르고 격렬하게 움직이다. 갑자기 …하다: *She burst through the door of my room.* 그녀는 내 방문을 벌컥 열고 들어왔다. **4 be bursting with pride/confidence/energy etc.** to be very proud, confident etc. ‖ 상당한 자긍심이나 자신 등이 있다. 자존심/자신/활력이 넘치다 —see also **burst** sb's **bubble** (BUBBLE¹)

burst in on sb/sth *phr v* [T] to interrupt something suddenly and noisily ‖ 갑자기 요란하게 어떤 것을 방해하다. …에 난입하다: *John's secretary burst in on the meeting with the news.* 존의 비서는 갑자기 회의에 끼어들어 뉴스를 알렸다.

burst into sth *phr v* [T] to suddenly start to do something ‖ 갑자기 어떤 것을 하기 시작하다: *Ellen burst into tears.* (=began crying) 엘렌은 갑자기 울음을 터뜨렸다. / *The car hit a tree and burst into flames.* (=began burning) 그 차는 나무를 받고 갑자기 화염에 휩싸였다.

burst out *phr v* **1 burst out laughing/crying** to suddenly start to laugh or cry ‖ 갑자기 웃거나 울기 시작하다. 갑자기 웃음/울음을 터뜨리다 **2** [T] to suddenly say something forcefully ‖ 갑자기 무엇인가를 강력히 말하다. 별안간 강력히 말하다: *"I don't believe it!" she* *burst out angrily.* "난 안 믿어!" 그녀는 화를 내며 불쑥 말했다.

burst² *n* **1 a burst of sth** a short sudden period of increased activity, loud noise, or strong feeling ‖ 활동[큰 소음, 격한 감정]이 갑작스럽게 증가되는 순간. 돌발. 분출: *A sudden burst of energy made her decide to clean the house.* 갑작스레 활력이 넘쳐 그녀는 집안 청소를 했다. **2** the action of something bursting, or the place where it has burst ‖ 파열 행위, 또는 파열된 곳: *a burst in the water pipes* 수도관의 파열된 부분

bur·y /'bɛri/ *v* [T] **1** to put a dead body into a grave ‖ 무덤에 시체를 넣다. 매장하다: *Aunt Betty was buried in Woodlawn Cemetery.* 베티 숙모는 우드론 공동묘지에 묻혔다. **2** to cover something with something else so that it cannot be seen ‖ 어떤 것을 보이지 않게 다른 것으로 덮다. 감추다. 덮어 가리다: *The dog buried a bone.* 개는 뼈다귀를 감추어 두었다. / *His glasses were buried under a pile of newspapers.* 그의 안경은 신문 뭉치 밑에 덮혀 있었다. **3** to ignore a feeling or memory and pretend that it does not exist ‖ 감정이나 기억을 묵살하여 없는 척하다. 묻어두다. 잊다

bus¹ /bʌs/ *n, plural* **buses** a large vehicle that people pay to travel on ‖ 사람들이 요금을 지불하고 여행을 하는 큰 차. 버스: *Are you going to drive or go by bus?* 직접 운전할 거니 아니면 버스를 타고 갈 거니? / *Five people got on the bus.* 다섯 명이 버스를 탔다. ✗DON'T SAY "... get in the bus."✗ "... get in the bus" 라고는 하지 않는다.

bus² *v* **-sed, -sing** [T] **1** to take a group of people somewhere in a bus ‖ 버스로 일단의 사람들을 어딘가로 태워다 주다: *Many children are being bused to schools in other areas.* 많은 아이들이 다른 지역의 학교로 버스 통학을 하고 있다. **2** to take away dirty dishes from the tables in a restaurant ‖ 식당에서 테이블에 있는 더러운 접시들을 치우다: *Frank has a job busing tables.* 프랭크는 식당에서 먹고 난 식기를 치우는 일을 하고 있다.

bus·boy /'bʌsbɔɪ/ *n* a man whose job is to take away dirty dishes from the tables in a restaurant ‖ 식당에서 테이블의 더러운 접시들을 치우는 직업인. 버스보이

bush /bʊʃ/ *n* **1** a short plant like a small tree with a lot of branches ‖ 가지가 많은 작은 나무처럼 생긴 작은 식물. 관목 **2**

the bush wild country that has not been cleared in Australia or Africa ‖ 오스트레일리아나 아프리카의 개간이 안 된 야생 지역. 오지(奧地) —see also **beat around the bush** (BEAT¹)

bushed /bʊʃt/ *adj* INFORMAL very tired ‖ 매우 지친. 기진맥진한: *I'm bushed.* 나는 기진맥진했다.

bush·el /'bʊʃəl/ *n* a unit for measuring dry food, equal to 8 gallons or 36.4 liters ‖ 8 갤런이나 36.4 리터에 해당하는 건조 식품의 계량 단위. 부셸

bush·y /'bʊʃi/ *adj* bushy hair or fur grows thickly ‖ 머리털이나 부드러운 털이 빽빽하게 자란. 무성한: *a bushy tail* 털이 무성한 꼬리

bus·i·ly /'bɪzəli/ *adv* in a busy way ‖ 바쁘게. 부지런히

busi·ness /'bɪznɪs/ *n*
1 ▶WORK DONE BY COMPANIES◀ 기업의 업무◀ [U] the activity of buying or selling goods or services ‖ 물건이나 서비스를 사고파는 행위. 장사. 매매. 거래: *We do a lot of business with people in Texas.* 우리는 텍사스 사람들과 거래를 많이 한다.
2 ▶YOUR JOB◀ 직업◀ [U] the work that you do as your job to earn money ‖ 돈을 버는 직업으로서 하는 일: *Al's gone to Japan on business.* (=because of his job) 앨은 업무차 일본에 갔다.
3 be in business to be operating as a company ‖ 사업에 종사하다: *He's in business for himself.* (=he owns a small company) 그는 자영업에 종사하고 있다.
4 go into business/go out of business to begin or stop operating as a company ‖ 회사 운영을 시작하거나 중단하다. 회사를 시작하다/폐업하다
5 ▶AMOUNT OF WORK◀ 업무량◀ [U] the amount of work a company is doing, or the amount of money the company is making ‖ 회사가 처리하는 업무량 또는 벌어들이는 돈의 액수: *Our business is good/bad/slow during the winter.* 우리 회사는 겨울 동안의 거래가 호황[불황, 부진]이다.
6 ▶A COMPANY◀ 회사◀ an organization that produces or sells goods or services ‖ 상품이나 서비스를 생산하거나 판매하는 조직. 회사. 기업. 상점: *He runs a printing business in Chicago.* 그는 시카고에서 인쇄소를 경영하고 있다.
7 ▶PERSONAL LIFE◀ 사생활◀ [U] something about your life that you do not think other people have the right to know ‖ 타인들은 알 권리가 없다고 생

각하는 사생활에 관한 것: *It's none of your business how much I earn.* 내가 얼마를 버는지는 네가 알 바가 아니다. / *Why don't you just mind your own business!* (=used in order to tell someone rudely that you do not want his/her advice, help etc.) (원하지 않는 조언·도움 등을 주는 사람에게 무례하게 쓰여) 네 일이나 잘 하지 그래!
8 ▶SUBJECT/ACTIVITY 주제/활동◀ [singular] a subject, event, or activity that you have a particular opinion of ‖ 특정한 의견을 가지고 있는 주제[사건, 활동]: *Rock climbing can be a risky business.* 암벽 등반은 위험한 일이 될 수 있다.
9 get down to business to start dealing with an important subject ‖ 중요한 과제를 처리하기 시작하다. 일에 착수하다
10 mean business INFORMAL to be determined to do something ‖ 무엇을 하기로 결정하다. 진정[진심]이다: *I could tell from the look on his face that he meant business.* 나는 그의 얼굴 표정에서 진심이라는 것을 알 수 있었다.
11 have no business doing sth if someone has no business doing something, he or she should not do it ‖ 누군가가 어떤 일을 해서는 안 되다: *He was drunk and had no business driving.* 그는 술을 마셔서 운전을 하면 안 되었다.
—see also BIG BUSINESS
business card /'.. ,./ *n* a card that shows your name, the name of your company, the company's address etc. ‖ 성명·회사명·회사 주소 등을 보여주는 카드. 업무용 명함
busi·ness·like /'bɪznɪs,laɪk/ *adj* effective and practical in the way you do things ‖ 일을 하는 방식이 능률적이고 실용적인. 사무적인: *a businesslike attitude* 사무적인 태도
busi·ness·man /'bɪznɪs,mæn/, **busi·nesswom·an** /'bɪznɪs-,wʊmən/ *n* someone who works at a fairly high level in a company or has his/her own business ‖ 회사에서 상당히 고위직에서 일하는 사람이나 자신의 사업을 하는 사람. 실업가. 경영자. 사업가
bus·ing /'bʌsɪŋ/ *n* [U] a system in which students ride buses to schools that are far from where they live, so that a school has students of different races ‖ 학교가 다른 인종의 학생을 받을 수 있도록 학생이 거주 지역에서 멀리 떨어져 있는 학교로 버스를 타고 통학하는 제도. 버스 통학 (제도)

bus lane /'. ./ *n* a part of a wide street that only buses can use ‖ 버스만 다닐 수 있는 대로의 부분. 버스 전용 차선
bus sta·tion /'. ,../ *n* a place where buses start and finish their trips ‖ 버스가 이동을 시작하거나 마치는 장소. 버스 종점[터미널]
bus stop /'. ./ *n* a place at the side of a road, marked with a sign, where buses stop for passengers ‖ 승객을 위해 버스가 정차하는 도로변의 간판이 있는 곳. 버스 정류장
bust¹ /bʌst/ *v* [T] **1** NONSTANDARD to break something ‖ 어떤 것을 깨뜨리다: *I busted my watch.* 나는 시계를 깨뜨렸다. **2 bust sb (for sth)** INFORMAL if the police bust someone, they catch someone who has done something illegal ‖ 경찰이 불법행위를 한 사람을 붙잡다. 체포하다 **3 bust your butt/ass** SLANG an impolite phrase meaning to try very hard to do something ‖ 어떤 일을 하는 데에 대단히 노력하는 것을 뜻하는 무례한 어구. 뼈 빠지게 노력하다: *Tim's been busting his ass to finish on time.* 팀은 제시간에 끝마치기 위해 뼈 빠지게 애써오고 있다.
bust² *n* **1** a woman's breasts, or the measurement around a woman's breasts and back ‖ 여자의 가슴, 또는 가슴과 등 둘레의 치수. 버스트: *a 34 inch bust* 가슴 둘레 34인치 **2** INFORMAL a situation in which the police go into a place in order to catch people doing something illegal ‖ 경찰이 불법 행위를 하는 사람을 잡으려고 어떤 장소에 침투하는 상황. 급습: *a drug bust* 마약 단속 **3** a model of someone's head, shoulders, and upper chest ‖ 사람의 머리·어깨·가슴 윗부분의 모형. 흉상(胸像): *a bust of Beethoven* 베토벤 흉상
bust³ *adj* **go bust** a business that goes bust stops operating because it does not have enough money ‖ 기업이 충분한 돈이 없어서 운영을 중단하다. 도산하다
bust·er /'bʌstɚ/ *n* **1** INFORMAL something that ends a situation, or that stops a particular activity ‖ 상황을 끝내거나 특정한 활동을 정지시키는 것. 파괴하는 것: *The storm should be a drought-buster.* 폭풍으로 틀림없이 가뭄이 해소될 것이다. **2** SPOKEN used when speaking to a man who is annoying you, or who you do not respect ‖ 자신을 괴롭히거나 존경하지 않는 사람에게 말을 걸 때 쓰여. 이봐: *Keep your hands off me, buster!* 이봐, 나한테 손대지 마!
bus·tle¹ /'bʌsəl/ *n* [singular] busy and

usually noisy activity ‖ 분주하고 종종 시끄러운 활동. 활기. 번잡: *the bustle of the big city* 활기에 찬 대도시 – **bustling** *adj*

bustle² *v* [I] to move around quickly, looking very busy ‖ 아주 바쁜 듯이 분주히 돌아다니다: *Linda bustled around the kitchen.* 린다는 부엌을 분주히 왔다갔다 했다.

busy¹ /'bɪzi/ *adj* **1** spending time working or doing something, so that you do not have time to do other things ‖ 무엇을 하느라 시간을 보내서 다른 일을 할 시간이 없는. 바쁜. 분주한: *I'm busy with a customer right now – can I call you back?* 나는 지금 고객이 있어서 바쁘거든. 내가 네게 다시 전화해도 되지? / *He's busy studying for his finals.* 그는 지금 기말 시험 공부하느라 바쁘다. / *a busy mother* 분주한 어머니 **2** a busy place is full of people or vehicles, or has a lot happening in it ‖ 장소가 사람이나 자동차로 가득하거나 많은 일이 일어나는: *a busy airport* 바삐 돌아가는 공항 **3** a telephone that is busy is being used ‖ 전화가 사용 중인. 통화 중인 **4** a pattern or design that is busy is full of too many details ‖ 무늬나 디자인이 너무 많은 요소로 가득한. 야한. 요란하게 장식한 – **busily** *adv*

busy² *v* **busy yourself with** to do something in order to make time seem to go faster ‖ 어떤 일을 해서 시간이 빨리 가는 것처럼 느끼다. …으로 바쁘다: *He busied himself with cleaning.* 그는 청소하느라 바빴다.

bus·y·bod·y /'bɪzi,badi, -,bʌdi/ *n* someone who is too interested in other people's private activities ‖ 남의 사생활에 지나친 관심을 갖는 사람. 참견하기 좋아하는 사람

but¹ /bət; *strong* bʌt/ *conjunction* **1** used before you say something that is different or the opposite from what you have just said ‖ 방금 말한 것과 다르거나 반대의 것을 말하기 전에 쓰여. 그러나: *Mom didn't like the movie, but Dad loved it.* 엄마는 그 영화를 좋아하지 않았지만 아빠는 좋아했다. / *Learning Chinese was difficult, but I got this job because of it.* 중국어를 배우는 것은 어려웠지만 그 덕분으로 이 일자리를 얻었다. **2** used before you give the reason why something did not happen or is not true ‖ 일이 발생하지 않거나 진실이 아닌 이유를 제시하기 전에 쓰여. 그렇지만: *Carla was supposed to come tonight, but her husband took the car.* 칼라는 오늘 밤 오

기로 되어 있었지만 그녀의 남편이 차를 가지고 나갔다. **3** used in order to show surprise at what has just been said ‖ 방금 말한 것에 대한 놀라움을 나타내는 데에 쓰여. 이런. 그것 참: *"I have to leave tomorrow." "But you only got here this morning!"* "나는 내일 떠나야 한다." "이런, 여기에 겨우 오늘 아침에야 왔잖아!"

SPOKEN PHRASES

4 used in order to introduce a new subject ‖ 새 주제를 도입하는 데에 쓰여. 그런데: *That's why I've been so busy this week. But, how are you anyway?* 그래서 나는 이번 주에 바빴어. 그런데 어쨌든 너는 어떻게 지내니? **5 but then (again)**... used in order to show that what you have just said is not as surprising as it seems ‖ 보는 바와 같이 방금 말한 것이 놀라운 것이 아니라는 것을 나타내는 데에 쓰여. 그렇지만 (한편). 그런데 어쨌든: *He doesn't have a strong French accent, but then he has lived in this country for 35 years.* 그에게 강한 프랑스어 억양은 없지만 그래도 그는 이 나라에서 35년을 살았다. **6** used after phrases such as "excuse me" and "I'm sorry" ‖ "excuse me"와 "I'm sorry"등의 구 (句) 뒤에 쓰여. …합니다만: *I'm sorry, but you're not allowed to go in there.* 미안합니다만 거기 들어가서는 안 됩니다. / *Excuse me, but didn't you go to Laney High School?* 실례지만 래니 고등학교에 다니지 않니?

but² *prep* except for ‖ …을 제외하고는. …밖에는. 이외에는: *Joe can come any day but Monday.* 조는 월요일 이외에는 어느 날이나 올 수 있다. / *There's nobody here but me.* 나밖에는 여기 아무도 없다.

USAGE NOTE but and except

Use **but** and **except** to talk about someone or something that is not included in a particular group: *I'll eat anything except liver. / Everyone's here but Mary.* In formal and written English, only **but** can be used after words like "none," "all," "nobody," "anywhere," "everything," or after question words like "who," "where," and "what": *We looked everywhere but in the shed. / Who but John would do that?*
but과 **except**는 특정 집단에 포함되지 않은 사람이나 사물에 대하여 말할 때

쓰인다: 나는 간 이외에는 무엇이든 먹겠다. / 메리를 제외하고는 모두 여기에 있다. 격식체·문어체 영어에서 **but** 은 "none," "all," "nobody," "anywhere," "everything" 같은 단어 다음이나 "who," "where," "what" 같은 의문사 다음에만 쓸 수 있다: 우리는 헛간을 제외하고는 모든 곳을 살펴보았다. / 존 이외에 누가 그것을 하겠느냐?

butch /bʊtʃ/ *adj* SLANG a woman who is butch looks, behaves, or dresses like a man ‖ 여성이 남자처럼 보이는[행동하는, 옷을 입는]. 여성이 사내 같은

butch·er¹ /'bʊtʃɚ/ *n* someone who owns or works in a store that sells meat ‖ 육류 판매점의 소유자나 일꾼. 푸줏간 주인[종업원]

butcher² *v* [T] **1** to kill animals and prepare them to be used as meat ‖ 동물을 죽여 고기로 쓸 수 있도록 준비하다. 도살하다 **2** to kill people in a cruel way ‖ 잔인하게 사람들을 죽이다. 학살하다 – **butchery** *n* [U]

but·ler /'bʌtlɚ/ *n* the main male servant of a house ‖ 집의 우두머리 남자 하인. 집사

butt¹ /bʌt/ *n* **1** INFORMAL the part of your body that you sit on; BUTTOCKS ‖ 자리에 앉는 신체의 부위. 궁둥이; buttocks: *Jody bruised her butt falling off the slide.* 조디는 비탈길에서 나가떨어져 궁둥이에 멍이 들었다. **2 get your butt in/out/over etc.** SPOKEN used in order to rudely tell someone to go somewhere or do something ‖ 어떤 곳에 가거나 어떤 것을 하라고 남에게 무례하게 말할 때 쓰여: *Get your butt out of that bed!* 그 침대에서 나오기나 해! **3 be the butt of** to be the person or thing that other people often make jokes about ‖ 종종 타인들의 조롱거리인 사람이나 사물이 되다. 비웃음거리가 되다: *Poor John is always the butt of everyone's jokes.* 모든 사람들이 가엾은 존을 항상 비웃음의 대상으로 삼는다. **4** the end of a cigarette after most of it has been smoked ‖ 거의 다 피우고 남은 담배의 끝부분. 담배꽁초 **5** the end of the handle of a gun ‖ 총의 손잡이의 끝부분. 개머리판 —see also **bust your butt/ass** (BUST¹), **a pain in the ass/butt** (PAIN¹)

butt² *v* [I, T] if a person or animal butts something or someone, it hits or pushes him, her, or it with its head ‖ 사람이나 동물이 머리나 뿔로 받거나 밀다

butt in *phr v* [I] INFORMAL to become involved in someone else's private situation or conversation ‖ 다른 사람의 사적인 상황이나 대화에 끼어들다. 참견하다. 간섭하다

butt out *phr v* [I] INFORMAL used in order to tell someone to stop being involved in something private ‖ 사적인 일에 끼어들지 말라고 남에게 말하는 데 쓰여. 참견[간섭]하지 않다: *This has nothing to do with you, so just butt out!* 이것은 너하고 아무 상관 없으니까 간섭하지 마!

butte /byut/ *n* a large hill with steep sides and a flat top ‖ 경사면이 가파르고 정상이 평평한 큰 언덕. 평원의 고립된 언덕[산]

but·ter¹ /'bʌtɚ/ *n* [U] a yellow food made from milk or cream that you spread on bread or use in cooking ‖ 빵에 바르거나 요리할 때 쓰는 우유나 크림으로 만든 노란색 식품. 버터 – **buttery** *adj*

butter² *v* [T] to spread butter on something ‖ 어떤 것에 버터를 바르다

butter sb ↔ **up** *phr v* [T] INFORMAL to say nice things to someone so that s/he will do what you want ‖ 원하는 것을 해주도록 남에게 상냥히 말하다. 알랑거리다

but·ter·cup /'bʌtɚˌkʌp/ *n* a small shiny yellow wild flower ‖ 작고 빛나는 노란색의 야생화. 미나리아재비

but·ter·fin·gers /'bʌtɚˌfɪŋgɚz/ *n* [singular] INFORMAL someone who often drops things ‖ 물건을 자주 떨어뜨리는 사람. 부주의한 [서투른] 사람

but·ter·fly /'bʌtɚˌflaɪ/ *n* **1** an insect with large and usually colored wings ‖ 보통 색깔 있는 큰 날개를 가진 곤충. 나비 **2 have butterflies (in your stomach)** INFORMAL to feel very nervous ‖ 매우 초조해 하다. 안절부절 못하다. 조마조마하다

but·ter·milk /'bʌtɚˌmɪlk/ *n* [U] the liquid that remains after butter has been made, used for drinking or cooking ‖ 마시거나 요리에 쓰이는 버터를 만들고 난 뒤에 남는 액체. 버터밀크. 탈지유

but·ter·scotch /'bʌtɚˌskatʃ/ *n* [C, U] a type of candy made from butter and sugar boiled together ‖ 버터와 설탕을 함께 끓여서 만든 사탕의 일종. 버터스카치

but·tock /'bʌtək/ *n* [C usually plural] FORMAL one of the soft parts of your body that you sit on ‖ 자리에 앉는 신체의 말랑한 부위의 한 쪽. 한 쪽 궁둥이. 볼기 —see picture at BODY

but·ton¹ /'bʌtn/ *n* **1** a small round flat object on your shirt, coat etc. that you pass through a hole to fasten it ‖ 셔츠·코

트 등에 달려 있어 구멍에 넣어 잠그는 작고 둥글며 납작한 것. 단추 **2** a small round object on a machine that you press to make it work ‖ 기계를 작동하기 위해 누르는 기계에 달린 작고 둥근 물건. 누름단추: *Push this button to make the machine stop.* 기계를 정지시키려면 이 버튼을 눌러라. **3** a small metal or plastic pin with a message or picture on it ‖ 그 위에 메시지나 그림이 있는 작은 금속이나 플라스틱 핀. 기장(記章). 배지

button², button up *v* [I, T] to fasten something with buttons, or to be fastened with buttons ‖ 어떤 것을[이] 단추로 잠그다[잠기다]: *Button up your coat.* 네 코트의 단추를 채워라.

but·ton·hole /'bʌtˌn,houl/ *n* a hole for a button to be put through to fasten a shirt, coat etc. ‖ 셔츠·코트 등을 채우기 위해 단추를 집어 넣는 구멍. 단춧구멍

but·tress¹ /'bʌtrɪs/ *v* [T] FORMAL to do something to support a system, idea etc. ‖ 체제·사상 등을 지지하기 위하여 어떤 것을 하다: *the government's policy of buttressing democracy all over the world* 전 세계의 민주주의를 지지하는 정부의 정책

buttress² *n* a structure built to support a wall ‖ 벽을 지지하기 위해 세워진 구조물. 부벽(扶壁). 버트레스

bux·om /'bʌksəm/ *adj* a woman who is buxom has large breasts ‖ 여성이 가슴이 큰. 가슴이 풍만한

buy¹ /baɪ/ *v* **bought, bought, buying 1** [I, T] to get something by paying money for it ‖ 돈을 내고 무엇을 입수하다. 사다. 구매하다: *Did you buy Cheryl that book?* 너는 셰릴에게 그 책을 사 주었니? / *I bought my car from our neighbors.* 나는 이웃 사람한테서 차를 샀다. / *He bought his house for $100,000.* 그는 10만 달러에 집을 샀다. **2** [T] INFORMAL to believe an explanation or reason for something ‖ 사물에 대한 설명이나 이유를 믿다. 받아들이다: *If we tell the police it was an accident, do you think they'll buy it?* 만일 우리가 그것이 사고였다고 경찰에 말한다면 그들이 믿으리라고 생각하니? **3 buy time** INFORMAL to do something in order to get more time to finish something ‖ 일을 끝낼 더 많은 시간을 얻으려고 어떤 것을 하다. 시간을 벌다 **4** [T] also **buy off** INFORMAL to pay money to someone in order to persuade him/her to do something dishonest ‖ 남을 꼬드겨 부정한 일을 하게 하려고 돈을 지불하다. 매수하다: *They say the judge was bought.* 그

들은 판사가 매수되었다고 말한다.

buy into sth *phr v* [T] **1** to buy part of a business or organization ‖ 기업이나 조직의 일부를 사다. 주주가 되다: *I used the money to buy into a computer company.* 나는 컴퓨터 회사의 주식을 사들이는 데 돈을 썼다. **2** to believe in an idea ‖ 어떤 사상을 믿다: *women who buy into the idea of having a "perfect body"* "완벽한 신체"의 소유에 대한 생각을 믿는 여자들

buy sb/sth ↔ **out** *phr v* [T] to gain control of a business by buying all the SHAREs in it that you do not already own ‖ 전에 소유하지 않았던 주식을 모두 사들여 기업을 장악하다. 독점하다

buy up sth ↔ *phr v* [T] to quickly buy as much as you can of something ‖ 가능한 한 많은 물건을 신속히 사다. 매점하다: *He bought up all the copies of the magazine in the store.* 그는 가게에서 그 잡지를 몽땅 사들였다.

buy² *n* **be a good/bad buy** to be worth or not worth the price you paid ‖ 지불한 가격의 가치가 있거나 없다. 싸게 잘 사다/잘못 사다: *These shoes were a good buy; they've really lasted well.* 이 구두들은 싸게 잘 샀다. 정말 오래 잘 신고 있다.

buy·er /'baɪɚ/ *n* **1** someone who is buying or has bought something ‖ 어떤 것을 사거나 산 사람. 구매자. 구입자: *We've found a buyer for our boat.* 우리는 우리 배의 구매자를 찾았다. **2** someone whose job is to choose and buy the goods that a store or company will sell ‖ 상점이나 회사가 팔 물건을 선정하여 구입하는 직업인. 구매 담당원

buy·out /'baɪaʊt/ *n* a situation in which someone gains control of a company by buying all of its SHAREs ‖ 사람이 회사의 주식을 모두 사서 회사를 장악하는 상황. 매점(買占): *a management buyout* 경영권 매점

buzz¹ /bʌz/ *v* **1** [I] to make a continuous noise like the sound of a BEE ‖ 벌이 내는 것과 같은 소음을 계속 내다. 윙윙소리를 내다: *What's making that buzzing noise?* 뭐가 저 윙윙거리는 소리를 내느냐? **2** [I] if a group of people or a place is buzzing, people are making a lot of noise because they are excited ‖ 일단의 사람이나 장소가 흥분으로 인해 많은 소음을 내다. 웅성거리다. 떠들썩하다: *The room buzzed with excitement.* 그 방은 흥분으로 시끌벅적했다. **3** [I, T] to call someone by pressing a buzzer ‖ 버저를 눌러 남을 부르다. 호출하다: *Tina buzzed* *for her secretary.* 티나는 버저를 눌러서 비서를 불렀다.

buzz off *phr v* [I] INFORMAL used in order to tell someone to go away in an impolite way ‖ 남에게 무례하게 나가라고 말하는 데에 쓰여. 꺼져

buzz² *n* 1 a continuous noise like the sound of a BEE ‖ 벌이 내는 것과 같은 계속적인 소음. 윙윙소리 2 [singular] INFORMAL a strong feeling of excitement, pleasure, or success, especially one you get from alcohol or drugs ‖ 특히 술이나 마약에서 얻는 흥분이나 즐거움 또는 성취에 대한 강렬한 감정. 얼근히 취함. 열광: *A couple of glasses of that punch will give you a real buzz.* 저 펀치 2잔이면 너는 정말 얼근히 취할 것이다.

buz·zard /ˈbʌzəd/ *n* a large wild bird that eats dead animals ‖ 죽은 동물을 먹는 커다란 야생 조류. 말똥가리

buzz·er /ˈbʌzə/ *n* a small thing like a button that makes a buzzing sound when you push it, for example on a door ‖ 출입문 등에 붙어 있어서 누르면 윙윙소리를 내는 단추 모양의 작은 물체. 버저. 경적

buzz·word /ˈbʌzwəd/ *n* a word or phrase relating to a particular subject, which is only popular for a limited time ‖ 한정된 시간에만 유행하는 특정한 주제에 관한 말이나 구(句). 전문적인 어감의 유행어. 전문 용어

by¹ /baɪ/ *prep* 1 used with PASSIVE forms of verbs to show who did something or what caused something ‖ 누가 어떤 일을 했는지, 무엇이 어떤 일을 일어나게 했는지를 나타내기 위해 동사의 수동형과 함께 쓰여. …에 의하여: *a play (written) by Shakespeare* 셰익스피어가 쓴 희곡 / *a film made by Steven Spielberg* 스티븐 스필버그가 만든 영화 / *Her money is controlled by her family.* 그녀의 돈은 가족이 관리한다. 2 near ‖ 가까이에. 옆에: *He was standing by the window.* 그는 창가에 서 있었다. 3 past ‖ 지나서. 경유하여: *Two dogs ran by me.* 개 두 마리가 나를 急 스쳐 달렸다. 4 using or doing a particular thing ‖ 특정한 것을 사용하거나 행하여. …으로. …에 의하여: *Send the letter by airmail.* 편지를 항공우편으로 보내라. / *Carolyn earns extra money by babysitting.* 캐롤린은 아기 돌보기로 부수입을 얻고 있다. / *We went from New York to Philadelphia by car/plane/train/bus.* 우리는 뉴욕에서 필라델피아까지 자동차[비행기, 열차, 버스]로 갔다. —see usage note at TRANSPORTATION 5 no later than a particular time ‖ 특정한 시간보다

늦지 않은. …까지(는). …즘(에는): *This report has to be done by 5:00.* 이 보고서는 5시까지 마쳐야 한다. 6 **by mistake/accident** without intending to do something ‖ 어떤 일을 할 의도가 없이. 실수로/우연히: *She locked the door by mistake.* 그녀는 실수로 문을 잠갔다. 7 according to a particular way of doing things ‖ 일을 하는 특정한 방식에 따라. …에 따라서. …에 의거하여: *By law, cars cannot pass a school bus that has stopped.* 법에 따라 자동차는 정지해 있는 학교 버스를 추월할 수 없다. 8 used in order to show which part of something that someone holds ‖ 사람이 잡고 있는 물건의 부분을 나타내는 데에 쓰여: *I picked up the pot by the handle.* 나는 손잡이로 주전자를 집어 들었다. / *She grabbed him by the arm.* 그 여자는 그 남자의 팔을 잡았다. 9 used in order to show a distance, amount, or rate ‖ 거리[수량, 비율]를 나타내는 데에 쓰여: *The room is 24 feet by 36 feet.* 그 방은 폭 24피트 길이 36피트이다. / *Are you paid by the hour?* 너는 시급으로 받느냐? 10 **by the way** SPOKEN used in order to begin talking about a subject that is not related to the one you were talking about ‖ 지금까지 말하고 있던 것과 관련 없는 주제에 대해 말을 시작하기 위해 쓰여. 그런데. 어쨌든. 한편: *Oh, by the way, Vicky called while you were out.* 아, 그런데 말이지 네가 외출했을 때 비키가 전화했어. 11 **(all) by yourself** completely alone ‖ 혼자서. 홀로: *They left the boy by himself for two days!* 그들은 이틀 동안 그 소년을 혼자 내버려 두었어! 12 **day by day/little by little etc.** used in order to show that something happens gradually ‖ 어떤 일이 점진적으로 일어나는 것을 나타내는 데에 쓰여. 나날이/조금씩: *Little by little he began to understand the language.* 조금씩 그는 그 언어를 이해하기 시작했다.

by² *adv* 1 past ‖ …을 지나서: *One or two cars went by, but nobody stopped.* 한두 대의 차가 지나갔으나 멈춰서는 사람이 아무도 없었다. / *Three hours went by before we heard any news.* 세 시간이 지나서야 비로소 우리는 어떤 뉴스를 들었다. 2 **come/stop/go by** to visit or go to a place for a short time when you intend to go somewhere else afterward ‖ 나중에 다른 장소에 가려고 할 때 잠시 방문하거나 어떤 장소에 가다. 들르다: *Come by (=come to my house, office etc.) any time tomorrow.* 내일 아무 때나 들러라. / *I had to stop by the supermarket on the* *way home.* 집에 가는 길에 슈퍼마켓에 잠깐 들러야 했다. **3 by and large** used when talking generally about something ‖ 사물에 관하여 일반적으로 말할 때 쓰여. 대체로. 전반적으로: *By and large, the more questions you ask now, the easier it will be.* 대체로 지금 네가 질문을 더 많이 할수록 그 일은 더 쉽게 풀리게 된다.

bye /baɪ/, **bye-bye** /ˌ. ˈ., ˈ. ./ *interjection* SPOKEN goodbye ‖ 안녕. 잘 있어: *Bye, Sandy! See you later.* 안녕, 샌디! 나중에 봐.

by·gone /ˈbaɪgɔn, -gɑn/ *adj* **bygone days/age/era etc.** an expression meaning a period in the past ‖ 과거의 기간을 의미하는 표현. 지나간 날/시기/시대

by·gones /ˈbaɪgɔnz, -gɑnz/ *n* **let bygones be bygones** INFORMAL to forgive someone for something bad that s/he has done to you ‖ 남이 저지른 좋지 않은 일에 대하여 남을 용서하다. 지난 일을 잊어버리다. 지난 일은 지난 일일 뿐이다

by·law /ˈbaɪlɔ/ *n* a rule made by an organization ‖ 조직에 의해 만들어진 규정. 내규. 준칙

by·line /ˈbaɪlaɪn/ *n* a line at the beginning of a newspaper or magazine article that gives the writer's name ‖ 필자의 성명을 써넣는, 신문이나 잡지 기사가 시작되는 행(行). 타이틀 밑의 필자명을 쓰는 행(行)

BYOB *adj* Bring Your Own Bottle; used in order to describe a party or event that you bring your own alcoholic drinks to ‖ Bring Your Own Bottle(술은 각자 지참)의 약어; 자신이 마실 술을 본인이 갖고 가는 파티나 행사를 말하는 데에 쓰여

by·pass[1] /ˈbaɪpæs/ *n* **1** a road that goes around a town or other busy place rather than through it ‖ 도시나 다른 번잡한 장소를 통과하지 않고 돌아가는 길. 우회로(迂廻路) **2** a medical operation that repairs the system of arteries (ARTERY) around the heart ‖ 심장 근처의 관상동맥 조직을 치료하는 의료 수술. 관상동맥 바이패스 수술

bypass[2] *v* [T] to avoid a place by going around it ‖ 돌아가서 어떤 장소를 피하다. 우회하다: *If we bypass the town, we'll save time.* 시내를 우회하면 시간이 절약될 것이다.

by-prod·uct /ˈ. ˌ../ *n* **1** a substance that is produced during the process of making something else ‖ 다른 것을 만드는 과정에서 생산되는 물질. 부산물: *Whey is a by-product of milk.* 유장(乳漿)은 우유의 부산물이다. **2** an unexpected result of an event or of something you do ‖ 사건이나 하는 일에 대한 예상치 않은 결과. 부작용: *The patient's ideas about men are a by-product of her relationship with her father.* 남성에 대한 그 환자의 생각은 그녀의 아버지와의 관계에서 나온 부작용이다.

by·stand·er /ˈbaɪˌstændɚ/ *n* someone who watches what is happening without taking part ‖ 무슨 일이 일어나는지를 보고만 있고 참여하지는 않는 사람. 구경꾼. 방관자: *Several innocent bystanders were killed by the gunman.* 몇몇 무고한 구경꾼들이 무장 범인에게 살해당했다.

byte /baɪt/ *n* a unit for measuring the amount of information a computer can use, equal to 8BITS ‖ 8비트에 해당하는 컴퓨터가 사용할 수 있는 정보량의 측정 단위. 바이트

by·way /ˈbaɪˌweɪ/ *n* a small road or path that is not used very much ‖ 그다지 이용되지 않는 작은 도로나 오솔길. 골목길. 옆길. 뒷길

by·word /ˈbaɪwɚd/ *n* the name of someone or something that has become so well known for a particular quality, that it represents that quality ‖ 어떤 특성을 대표할 정도의 특정한 속성으로 잘 알려진 사람이나 사물의 이름. 별명. 대명사: *His name has become a byword for honesty in the community.* 그의 이름은 지역 사회에서 정직의 대명사가 되었다.

C c

C, c /si/ **1** the third letter of the English alphabet ‖ 영어 알파벳의 셋째 자 **2** the ROMAN NUMERAL (=number) for 100 ‖ 100을 나타내는 로마 숫자

C¹ /si/ *n* **1** a grade given to a student's work to show that it is of average quality ‖ 평균 수준을 나타내는 학업 성적. 시(C): *I got a C in biology.* 나 생물학 과목에서 C를 받았어. **2** [C, U] the first note in the musical SCALE of C MAJOR, or the musical KEY based on this note ‖ 다 장조의 첫째 음이나 이 음을 기조로 한 음조. 다 음. 다 조

C² the written abbreviation of CELSIUS or CENTIGRADE ‖ celsius 또는 centigrade의 약어

c. **1** the written abbreviation of CENT ‖ cent의 약어 **2** the written abbreviation of CIRCA ‖ circa의 약어

C&W *n* [U] ▷ COUNTRY AND WESTERN

CA the written abbreviation of California ‖ California(캘리포니아 주)의 약어

cab /kæb/ *n* **1** ▷ TAXI **2** the part of a truck or train where the driver sits ‖ 트럭이나 기차의 운전석 —see picture on page 943

cab·a·ret /ˌkæbəˈreɪ/ *n* [C, U] entertainment such as music and dancing performed in a restaurant while customers eat and drink ‖ 손님들이 음식점에서 식사·음주를 하는 동안 공연되는 음악·춤 등의 쇼. 카바레

cab·bage /ˈkæbɪdʒ/ *n* [C, U] a large round vegetable with thick green or purple leaves that can be cooked or eaten raw ‖ 익히거나 날로 먹을 수 있는, 두꺼운 녹색이나 자주색 잎이 달린 크고 둥근 채소. 양배추 —see picture on page 944

cab·bie, cabby /ˈkæbi/ *n* INFORMAL someone who drives a CAB ‖ 택시 운전사

cab·in /ˈkæbɪn/ *n* **1** a small house made of wood, usually in a forest or the mountains ‖ 보통 숲이나 산속에 있는 나무로 만든 작은 집. 오두막집: *a log cabin* 통나무 오두막집 **2** a small room in which you sleep on a ship ‖ 선상의 작은 침실. (여객선의) 객실 **3** the area inside a plane where the passengers sit ‖ 비행기 내의 승객들이 앉는 구역. 캐빈. 객실

cab·i·net /ˈkæbənɪt/ *n* **1** a piece of furniture with doors and shelves or drawers, used for storing or showing things ‖ 물건을 저장하거나 전시하는 데 쓰이는 문과 선반, 또는 서랍이 달린 가구. 장식장. 진열장: *a filing cabinet* 서류 캐비닛 / *the kitchen cabinets* 찬장 —see picture at KITCHEN **2** an important group of politicians who make decisions or advise the leader of a government ‖ 사안들을 결정하거나 정부 수반에게 고문 역할을 하는 정치인들의 중요 집단. 대통령 고문단. 각료들

ca·ble¹ /ˈkeɪbəl/ *n* **1** [C, U] a plastic or rubber tube containing wires that carry electronic signals, telephone messages etc. ‖ 전기 신호·전화 전언 등을 전달하는 전선을 싸고 있는 플라스틱 또는 고무로 된 관. 케이블. 전선: *an underground telephone cable* 지하 전화 케이블 **2** [U] a system of broadcasting television by cable that is paid for by the person watching it ‖ 시청자가 수신료를 내는, 케이블을 통한 텔레비전 방송 시스템. 케이블 방송: *I'll wait for the movie to come out on cable.* 나는 케이블 방송에서 그 영화가 방영되기를 기다릴 것이다. **3** [C, U] a thick strong metal rope used on ships, to support bridges etc. ‖ 선박의 선교 등을 지탱하기 위해 배에서 사용하는 굵은 금속제 밧줄 **4** ▷ TELEGRAM

ca·ble² *v* [I, T] to send a TELEGRAM ‖ 전보를 보내다.

cable car /ˈ.. ˌ./ *n* **1** a vehicle that is pulled by a CABLE along the road, used like a bus by people in a city ‖ 도시에서 사람들이 버스처럼 이용하는, 도로를 따라 케이블에 의해 움직이는 차량. 전차 **2** a vehicle that hangs from a CABLE and carries people up mountains ‖ 케이블에 달려 사람을 산 위로 수송하는 차량. 케이블 카

cable tel·e·vi·sion /ˌ.. ˈ..../, **cable TV** *n* [U] ▷ CABLE¹

ca·boose /kəˈbus/ *n* a small railroad car at the end of a train ‖ 열차 맨 뒤에 있는 작은 차량. 차장차

cache /kæʃ/ *n* a group of things that are hidden, or the place where they are hidden ‖ 숨겨진 일단의 물건들이나 물건이 숨겨진 장소. 감춘 물건. 은닉처: *Police found a cache of weapons in the house.* 경찰은 그 집에서 무기 은닉처를 찾아냈다.

ca·chet /kæˈʃeɪ/ *n* [U] a quality that is good or desirable ‖ 좋거나 바람직한 특

성, 명성: *It's a great college, but it doesn't have the same cachet as Harvard.* 그 대학은 훌륭하지만 하버드 대학만큼의 명성은 없다.

cack·le /'kækəl/ *v* [I] **1** to make the loud unpleasant noise a chicken makes ‖ 닭이 크고 불쾌한 소리를 내다. 꼬꼬댁거리며 울다 **2** to laugh or talk in a loud rough voice ‖ 시끄럽고 거친 목소리로 크게 웃거나 이야기하다. – **cackle** *n*

cac·tus /'kæktəs/ *n*, *plural* **cacti** /'kæktaɪ/ or **cactuses** a desert plant with thick smooth stems and needles instead of leaves ‖ 두껍고 부드러운 줄기와 잎 대신 가시가 있는 사막 식물. 선인장

ca·dav·er /kə'dævə/ *n* a dead human body ‖ 죽은 사람의 몸. 시체

cad·dy /'kædi/ *n* someone who carries the equipment for someone who is playing GOLF ‖ 골프 치는 사람의 장비를 운반하는 사람. 골프 캐디

ca·dence /'keɪdns/ *n* a word meaning a regular pattern of sound, used especially to describe the way someone's voice gets louder or softer ‖ 특히 사람의 목소리가 더 커지거나 부드러워지는 양상을 묘사하는 데 쓰이는 소리의 일정한 패턴을 의미하는 단어. 가락, 리듬, 억양

ca·det /kə'dɛt/ *n* someone who is studying to become an officer in the military or the police ‖ 군대나 경찰에서 장교가 되려고 공부하는 사람. 사관 생도

ca·dre /'kædri, 'kɑ-, -dreɪ/ *n* FORMAL a small group of specially trained people in a profession, political party, or military force ‖ 전문 직업[정당, 군대]에서 특별히 훈련된 소규모의 사람들. 간부진, 중견 요원: *a cadre of highly trained scientists* 고도로 훈련된 과학자 집단

cae·sar·e·an /sɪ'zɛriən/ *n* ⇨ CESAREAN

ca·fe, café /kæ'feɪ, kə-/ *n* **1** a small restaurant ‖ 간이 식당. 카페 **2** a part of a WEBSITE which has general information about the website, discussion groups, a place to read or leave messages for other users etc ‖ 웹사이트·토론 그룹과 다른 사용자를 위한 메시지를 남기거나 읽을 수 있는 곳 등에 대한 일반적인 정보가 담겨 있는 웹사이트의 한 부분. 웹 카페

caf·e·te·ri·a /,kæfə'tɪriə/ *n* a restaurant where people get their own food and take it to a table to eat it ‖ 손수 식탁으로 음식을 날라다가 먹는 음식점. 카페테리아: *the school cafeteria* 교내 카페테리아

caf·feine /kæ'fin, 'kæfin/ *n* [U] a chemical substance in coffee, tea, and

some other drinks that makes people feel more active ‖ 커피, 차 및 다른 음료에 들어 있어 사람들이 보다 활력적인 기분이 들게 하는 화학 물질. 카페인: *a caffeine-free cola* (=one without caffeine) 카페인이 없는 콜라

cage[1] /keɪdʒ/ *n* a structure made of wires or BARs in which birds or animals can be kept ‖ 새나 동물을 가둬 두는 철망이나 빗장으로 만든 구조물. 우리

cage[2] *v* **1** [T] to put an animal or bird in a CAGE ‖ 동물이나 새를 우리에 가두다. **2 feel caged in** to feel uncomfortable and annoyed because you cannot go outside ‖ 밖으로 나갈 수 없어 불편하고 화가 나다

cag·ey /'keɪdʒi/ *adj* INFORMAL not willing to talk about your plans or intentions ‖ 계획이나 의도에 대해 말하려 하지 않는. 정체를 드러내지 않는: *The White House is being very cagey about the contents of the report.* 백악관은 그 보고서의 내용을 공개하려 하지 않고 있다.

ca·hoots /kə'huts/ *n* INFORMAL **be in cahoots (with)** to be working secretly with others, usually to do something that is not honest ‖ 보통 정직하지 못한 일을 하기 위해 남들과 비밀스럽게 일하다. 공모[결탁]하다: *Was Roger really in cahoots with the drug smugglers?* 로저가 정말 마약 밀매업자들과 한패였단 말입니까?

ca·jole /kə'dʒoʊl/ *v* [T] to persuade someone to do something by praising him/her or making promises to him/her ‖ 칭찬하거나 약속함으로써 사람이 어떤 일을 하도록 설득하다. 감언으로 꾀다[부추기다]: *Mom and Dad would try to cajole us into eating our vegetables.* 엄마와 아빠는 우리가 야채를 먹도록 부추겼다.

Ca·jun /'keɪdʒən/ *n* a member of a group of people in southern Louisiana whose family originally came from the French-speaking part of Canada ‖ 본래 캐나다의 프랑스어 사용 지방 출신의 가족으로 루이지애나 주 남부에 살고 있는 사람들 – **Cajun** *adj*

cake[1] /keɪk/ *n* **1** [C, U] a sweet food made by baking a mixture of flour, fat, sugar, and eggs ‖ 밀가루·지방·설탕·계란을 섞은 것을 구워 만든 단 음식. 케이크: *a birthday cake* 생일 케이크 / *Do you want a piece of cake?* 케이크 한 조각 드실래요? **2** a small piece of something, made into a flat shape ‖ 편평한 모양으로 만들어진 어떤 것의 작은 조각: *a cake of* *soap* 비누 한 개 **3 be a piece of cake** INFORMAL to be very easy ‖ 매우 쉽다. 식은 죽 먹기이다: *Go on, jump off the high dive, Ben. It's a piece of cake!* 어서, 벤, 다이빙대에서 뛰어내려. 정말 식은 죽 먹기야! **4 have your cake and eat it too** INFORMAL to have all the advantages of something without any of the disadvantages ‖ 아무런 손해없이 어떤 것의 모든 이익을 취하다. (돈 등을) 저축하고도 싶고 쓰고도 싶다

cake² *v* **be caked in/with** to be covered with a thick layer of something ‖ 어떤 것의 두꺼운 층으로 뒤덮이다: *Irene's boots were caked with mud.* 아이린의 부츠는 진흙 범벅이었다.

ca·lam·i·ty /kə'læməti/ *n* a very bad, unexpected event that causes a lot of damage or suffering ‖ 많은 손해나 고통을 유발하는 예상치 못한 매우 나쁜 사건. 재난. 참사: *Sudan suffered a number of calamities in the 1980s.* 수단은 1980년대에 수많은 재난으로 고통받았다. – **calamitous** *adj*

cal·ci·um /'kælsiəm/ *n* [U] a silver-white metal that is an ELEMENT and that helps form teeth, bones, and CHALK ‖ 치아·뼈·석회암의 형성을 돕는 은백색의 금속 원소. 칼슘

cal·cu·late /'kælkyə,leɪt/ *v* [I, T] **1** to find out something or measure something using numbers ‖ 어떤 것을 알아내거나 숫자를 이용해 측정하다. 계산하다: *These instruments calculate distances precisely.* 이 기기는 거리를 정확하게 측정한다. **2 be calculated to do sth** to be intended to have a particular effect ‖ 특정 효과를 갖도록 의도되다. …하도록 고안되다: *The ads are calculated to attract Hispanic buyers.* 그 광고들은 라틴 아메리카계의 구매자들을 겨냥한 것이다.

cal·cu·lat·ed /'kælkyə,leɪtɪd/ *adj* **1 calculated risk/gamble** something you do after thinking carefully, although you know it may have bad results ‖ 나쁜 결과를 초래할 수 있다는 것을 알면서도 심사 숙고한 뒤에 하는 일. 계획된 위험/모험 **2** deliberately and carefully planned to have a particular effect ‖ 특정 효과를 내기 위해 치밀하고 섬세하게 계획된. 면밀히 계산[계획]된: *It was a calculated attempt to make the governor look silly.* 그것은 주지사를 멍청하게 보이게 하기 위해 면밀히 계획된 시도였다.

cal·cu·lat·ing /'kælkyə,leɪtɪŋ/ *adj* DISAPPROVING tending to make careful plans to get what you want, without caring about how it affects other people ‖ 원하는 바를 얻기 위해 다른 사람에게 어떤 영향을 미칠지는 고려하지 않고 면밀한 계획을 세우는 경향이 있는. 계산[타산]적인: *He's just another calculating politician.* 그는 단지 또 한 명의 타산적인 정치인일 뿐이다.

cal·cu·la·tion /,kælkyə'leɪʃən/ *n* [C usually plural, U] the act of adding, multiplying, or dividing numbers to find out an amount, price etc. ‖ 양·값 등을 알아내기 위해 수를 더하는[곱하는, 나누는] 행위. 계산: *By their calculations, the debt will be paid off in four years.* 그들이 계산한 바에 따르면, 4년 내에 빚이 청산될 것이다.

cal·cu·la·tor /'kælkyə,leɪtə/ *n* a small machine that can add, multiply, divide etc. numbers ‖ 덧셈·곱셈·나눗셈 등을 할 수 있는 작은 기계. 계산기

cal·cu·lus /'kælkyələs/ *n* [U] the part of mathematics that studies changing quantities, such as the speed of a falling stone or the slope of a curved line ‖ 떨어지는 돌의 속도나 곡선의 기울기 등의 변하는 수치를 연구하는 수학의 한 부분. 계산법

cal·en·dar /'kæləndə/ *n* **1** a thing with pages that show the days and months of a year, that you usually hang on the wall ‖ 보통 벽에 걸어 놓는, 1년의 날짜·월(月)을 나타내는 페이지들로 구성된 것. 달력 **2** all the things that you plan to do in the next days, months etc. ‖ 다음 날·다음 달 등에 하기로 계획한 모든 일들. 일정: *My calendar is full this week.* 이번 주는 일정이 꽉 차 있다. **3** a system that divides and measures time in a particular way ‖ 특정 방법으로 시간을 나누고 측정하는 체계. 역법(曆法): *the Jewish calendar* 유대력 **4 calendar year/month** a period of time that continues from the first day of the month or year until the last day of the month or year ‖ 달이나 해의 첫날부터 마지막 날까지 연속되는 기간. 역년(曆年)/역월(曆月)

calf /kæf/ *n, plural* **calves** /kævz/ **1** the part at the back of your leg between your knee and foot ‖ 무릎과 발 사이의 다리 뒷부분. 장딴지 —see picture at BODY **2** the baby of a cow, or of some other large animals such as the ELEPHANT ‖ 소나 코끼리 등의 큰 동물의 새끼

cal·i·ber /'kæləbə/ *n* **1** the level of quality or ability that someone or something has achieved ‖ 사람이나 사물이 이뤄낸 품질이나 능력의 수준. 역량:

musicians of the highest caliber 최고의
역량을 지닌 음악가들 **2** the width of a
bullet or the inside part of a gun ‖ 총알
의 직경이나 총의 구경

cal·i·brate /ˈkælə,breɪt/ *v* [T]
TECHNICAL to mark an instrument or tool
so you can use it for measuring ‖ 측정하
는 데에 쓸 수 있도록 계기나 도구에 표시
하다. 눈금을 매기다 **– calibration**
/,kæləˈbreɪʃən/ *n* [C, U]

cal·i·co /ˈkæli,koʊ/ *n* [U] a light cotton
cloth with a small pattern on it ‖ 작은 무
늬가 있는 가벼운 면으로 된 천. 캘리코

call¹ /kɔl/ *v*

1 ▶TELEPHONE 전화하다◀ [I, T] to
telephone someone ‖ 누구에게 전화하다:
*I called about six o'clock but no one was
home.* 여섯시쯤 전화했지만 아무도 집에
없었습니다. / *He said he'd call me
tomorrow.* 그가 내일 내게 전화한다고 했
다. —see usage note at TELEPHONE

2 ▶DESCRIBE 묘사하다◀ [T] to describe
someone or something in a particular
way, or to say that s/he has a particular
quality ‖ 사람이나 사물을 특정한 방식으
로 묘사하거나 사람이 특정한 성질이 있다
고 말하다: *News reports have called it
the worst disaster of this century.* 뉴스
보도는 그것을 금세기 최악의 참사라 했다.

3 ▶ASK/ORDER 요청하다/명령하다◀ [T]
to ask or order someone to come to you
‖ 누구에게 와 달라고 부탁하거나 명령하
다: *Will somebody please call an
ambulance?* 누구 구급차 좀 불러 줄래요?
/ *I can hear Mom calling me; I'd better
go.* 엄마가 날 부르는 소리가 들려. 가는
것이 좋겠어.

4 ▶ARRANGE 준비하다◀ [T] to arrange
for something to happen at a particular
time ‖ 어떤 일이 특정 시간에 일어나도록
준비하다. 소집하다. 열다: *A meeting
was called for 3 p.m. Wednesday.* 회의
가 수요일 오후 세 시에 소집되었다.

5 ▶SAY/SHOUT 말하다/소리치다◀ [I, T]
to say or shout something because you
want someone to hear you ‖ 남에게 잘
들리도록 말하거나 소리치다: *"I'm
coming!" Paula called down the stairs.*
"갑니다!"라고 파울라는 계단을 내려가며
소리쳤다.

6 be called to have a particular name ‖
특정한 이름을 갖다. …이라 불리다: *What
was that movie called again?* 그 영화 제
목이 뭐라고 그랬죠?

7 ▶NAME 이름◀ [T] to give a person or
pet a name ‖ 사람이나 애완 동물에게 이
름을 붙이다: *They finally decided to call
the dog "Torka."* 그들은 결국 그 개를

"토르카"라고 부르기로 했다.

8 call the shots INFORMAL to be the
person who decides what to do in a
situation ‖ 어떤 상황에서 무엇을 할지 결
정하는 사람이 되다: *I
think it would be okay, but I'm not the
one calling the shots around here.* 괜찮
을 것 같기는 한데 나는 이곳의 결정권자
가 아니다.

9 call it a day SPOKEN said when you
want to stop working, either because
you are tired or because you have done
enough ‖ 피곤하거나 충분히 했기 때문에
일을 끝내고 싶을 때에 쓰여. 그만 끝내다
[마치다]: *Come on, guys, let's call it a
day.* 자, 여러분, 오늘은 이만 끝냅시다.

call back *phr v* [I, T **call** sb **back**] to
telephone someone again, or to
telephone someone who tried to
telephone you earlier ‖ 남에게 다시 전화
걸거나 앞서 자신에게 전화를 걸었던 사람
에게 전화를 걸다: *Okay, I'll call back
around three.* 알겠습니다, 세 시쯤 다시
전화드리죠. / *Ms. Brinston is on another
line; can she call you back later?* 브린
스톤 씨는 통화 중이신데 나중에 그녀가
전화를 드려도 될까요?

call for sb/sth *phr v* [T] **1** to demand or
need something in a particular situation
‖ 특정 상황에서 무엇을 요구하거나 필요
로 하다: *Representatives are calling for
an investigation into the scandal.* 국회
의원들은 그 추문에 대한 조사를 요구하고
있다 / *a situation that calls for
immediate action* 즉각적인 조치를 요하
는 상황 **2** to say that a particular type of
weather is likely to happen ‖ 특정 형태
의 날씨가 될 것이라 말하다. 예보하다:
The forecast calls for more rain. 일기 예
보에서는 더 많은 비가 내릴 것이라 한다.

call in *phr v* **1** [T **call** sb ↔ **in**] to ask or
order someone to come and help you
with a difficult situation ‖ 남에게 와서 어
려운 상황에 처해 있는 자신을 도와 달라
고 요청하거나 명령하다. 원조를 구하다:
*The governor called in the National
Guard to deal with the riots.* 주지사는 주
방위군에게 폭도들을 진압하라고 명령했
다. **2** [I] to telephone the place where
you work, especially to report
something ‖ 특히 어떤 일을 보고하기 위
해 직장에 전화하다: *Jan called in sick
this morning.* (=telephoned to say that
she was too sick to come to work) 잔은
오늘 아침 직장에 전화를 걸어 아파서 출
근하지 못한다고 말했다. **3** to telephone
a radio or television show to give your
opinion or ask a question ‖ 의견을 제안

하거나 질문하기 위해 라디오나 텔레비전 방송에 전화를 걸다.

call sb/sth ↔ **off** *phr v* [T] **1** to decide that a planned event will not happen ‖ 계획된 일이 일어나지 않도록 결정하다. 취소하다: *The game had to be called off due to bad weather.* 악천후 때문에 그 경기를 취소해야 했다. **2** to order a dog or person to stop attacking someone ‖ 개나 사람에게 어떤 사람에 대한 공격을 중단하라고 명령하다: *Call off your dog!* 네 개를 (사람을 공격하지 못하도록) 불러들여!

call on sb/sth *phr v* [T] **1** to formally ask someone to do something ‖ 남에게 어떤 일을 하라고 공식적으로 요청하다: *The UN has called on both sides to start peace talks.* 유엔은 양측 모두에게 평화 회담에 착수할 것을 요청했다. **2** to visit someone for a short time ‖ 누구를 짧은 기간 동안 방문하다: *a salesman calling on customers* 고객을 방문하는 세일즈맨

call out *phr v* **1** [I, T **call** sth ↔ **out**] to say something loudly ‖ 어떤 것을 크게 말하다. 소리치다: *"Hey!" she called out to him as he got into his car.* "이봐요!"라고 그가 차에 탔을 때, 그녀가 소리쳤다. **2** [T **call** sb/sth ↔ **out**] to ask or order someone to come and help you with a difficult situation ‖ 남에게 와서 어려운 상황에 처해 있는 자신을 도와 달라고 요청하거나 명령하다. 도움을 구하다: *"Where's Dr. Cook?" "She's been called out."* "쿡, 의사 선생님 어디 계신가요?" "왕진 나가셨어요."

call up *phr v* **1** [I, T **call** sb ↔ **up**] to telephone someone ‖ 남에게 전화하다. 전화를 걸다: *Why don't you call Susie up and see if she wants to come?* 수지에게 전화해서 오고 싶은지 알아 보는 게 어때? **2** [T **call** sth ↔ **up**] to make information appear on a computer screen ‖ 정보를 컴퓨터 화면에 뜨게 하다.

call² *n* **1** an attempt to talk to someone by telephone ‖ 전화로 누구와 얘기하려는 시도. 전화. 통화: *She's expecting a call from the office soon.* 그녀는 사무실에서 곧 걸려올 전화를 기다리고 있다. / *I got a call yesterday from Teresa; she's fine.* 어제 테레사한테 전화 왔어. 그녀는 괜찮데. / *Just give me a call from the airport when you arrive.* 공항에 도착하면 바로 내게 전화해 줘. / *I have to make a telephone call.* 전화 걸어야 해. / *Ask him to return my call* (=telephone me back) *when he comes home.* 그가 집에 돌아오면 나한테 전화해 달라고 말해 줘. / *Can I make a local call?* (=a call made within the city or area where you

are) 시내 전화 좀 써도 될까요? —see usage note at TELEPHONE **2 be on call** ready to go to work if you are needed ‖ 자신을 필요로 한다면 일하러 갈 준비가 되어 있는: *Heart surgeons are on call 24 hours a day.* 심장 외과의들은 24시간 내내 대기 상태이다. **3** a shout or cry ‖ 외침이나 울부짖는 소리: *a call for help* 도움을 구하는 외침 **4 no call for sth/no call to do sth** SPOKEN used in order to tell someone that his/her behavior is wrong or that something is unnecessary ‖ 남에게 행동이 잘못되었거나 무엇이 불필요하다는 것을 말하는 데에 쓰여: *She had no call to talk to you like that.* 그녀가 네게 그렇게[그런 식으로] 말할 필요는 없었다. **5 a)** a decision made by someone in a sports game ‖ 스포츠 경기에서 누군가가 내리는 결정. 판정: *All the calls went against us.* 모든 (심판의)판정이 우리에게 불리했다. **b)** a decision ‖ 결정. 판단: *"Where should we eat tonight?" "I don't know, it's your call."* "우리 오늘 저녁 어디서 먹지?" "모르겠어, 네가 결정해." **6** a short visit for a particular reason ‖ 특정한 이유로 인한 짧은 방문: *We should pay Jerry and his wife a call since we're driving through Ohio.* 우리가 오하이오 주를 통과해 가고 있으니 제리와 그의 아내를 방문해야 돼. **7** a request or demand for someone to do something ‖ 남에게 어떤 일을 하라는 요청이나 요구: *Phillip said he'd received a call from God to preach.* 필립은 자기가 하나님으로부터 전도하라는 부름을 받았다고 했다.

call·er /'kɔlɚ/ *n* someone who is making a telephone call ‖ 전화 거는 사람. 발신자: *Didn't the caller say who she was?* 전화 건 사람이 자신이 누구라고 말 안 하던가요?

call girl /'. ./ *n* ➪ PROSTITUTE¹

cal·lig·ra·phy /kə'lɪgrəfi/ *n* [U] the art of writing using special pens or brushes, or the beautiful writing produced in this way ‖ 특별한 펜이나 붓을 사용하여 쓰는 기술이나 이런 기술로 쓰여진 아름다운 글씨. 서법. 필적

call-in /'. ./ *n* a radio or television program in which people telephone to give their opinions or ask questions ‖ 사람들이 전화해서 자신의 의견을 내거나 질문하는 라디오나 텔레비전 프로그램. 시청자[청취자] 전화 참가 프로그램

call·ing /'kɔlɪŋ/ *n* a strong desire or feeling of duty to do a particular type of work, especially work that helps other people ‖ 특히 타인을 돕는 일과 같이 특정

형태의 일을 하고자 하는 강한 욕구나 의
무감. 소명. 사명: *He felt a calling to
become a teacher.* 그는 교사가 되어야 한
다는 소명을 느꼈다.

cal·lous /'kæləs/ *adj* unkind and not
caring that other people are suffering ||
불친절하고 다른 사람들이 고통받는 것에
신경쓰지 않는. 냉담한 **– callousness** *n*
[U] **– callously** *adv*

cal·lus /'kæləs/ *n* an area of hard
rough skin || 딱딱하고 거친 피부 부위. 굳
은살: *Ron has calluses on his feet from
walking so much.* 론은 너무 많이 걸어서
발에 굳은살이 있다. **– callused** *adj*

calm¹ /kɑm/, **calm down** *v* [I, T] to
become quiet after you have been
angry, excited, or upset, or to make
someone become quiet || 화난[흥분된, 당
황한] 후에 가라앉거나 또는 남을 가라앉
히다. 진정하다[시키다]: *Calm down and
tell me what happened.* 진정하고 무슨
일이 일어났는지 말해 봐. / *It took a
while to calm the kids down.* 아이들을
달래는 데 시간이 걸렸다. / *Matt was
trying to calm the baby by singing to it.*
매트는 노래를 불러 아이를 달래려 했다.

calm² *adj* **1** relaxed and not angry or
upset || 긴장이 풀려 화나거나 흥분하지 않
은. 차분한: *The nurse was speaking in a
calm and patient voice.* 간호사는 침착하
고 참을성 있는 목소리로 말하고 있었다.
/ *Please, everyone, try to keep/stay
calm!* 여러분, 제발 진정하세요! **2**
completely still, or not moving very
much || 완전히 정지해 있거나 움직임이
거의 없는. 잔잔한: *the calm water of the
lake* 잔잔한 호수의 물 **3** not windy || 바람
이 불지 않는: *a calm clear beautiful day*
바람 한 점 없이 청명하고 아름다운 날 **–
calmly** *adv*

calm³ *n* **1** [singular, U] a time that is
quiet and peaceful || 조용하고 평화로운
시간. 고요. 평온 **2 the calm before the
storm** a peaceful situation just before a
big problem or argument || 큰 문제나 논
쟁 직전의 평온한 상황. 폭풍 전의 고요

cal·o·rie /'kæləri/ *n* **1** a unit for
measuring the amount of ENERGY a
particular food can produce || 특정 음식
이 낼 수 있는 에너지의 양을 측정하는 단
위. 칼로리: *An average potato has about
90 calories.* 감자 하나에는 평균 90칼로
리가 함유되어 있다. **2 count calories** to
try to control your weight by calculating
the number of calories you eat || 섭취하
는 칼로리 수를 계산하여 체중을 조절하려
고 하다. 칼로리를 계산하다 **3** TECHNICAL
a unit for measuring heat || 열량을 측정

하는 단위. 칼로리

calves /kævz/ *n* the plural of CALF ||
calf의 복수형

ca·ma·ra·der·ie /ˌkæmˈrɑdəri, kɑm-/ *n*
[U] a feeling of friendship that the
people in a group have, especially when
they work together || 특히 함께 일하는
집단 내의 사람들이 느끼는 친밀감. 동료
의식: *the camaraderie of firefighters* 소
방관들의 동료 의식

cam·cord·er /'kæmˌkɔrdə/ *n* a small
piece of equipment like a camera that
you can hold in one hand to record
pictures and sound on a VIDEO || 한 손에
들고 비디오 테이프에 사진·소리를 기록하
는 카메라와 비슷한 작은 기기. 캠코더

came /keɪm/ *v* the past tense of COME ||
come의 과거형

cam·el /'kæməl/ *n* a large animal with
a long neck and one or two HUMPs
(=large raised parts) on its back, that
lives in the desert and carries goods or
people || 목이 길고 등에 한 개 또는 두 개
의 혹이 달린, 사막에 살고 물건이나 사람
을 실어 나르는 큰 동물. 낙타

ca·mel·lia /kəˈmilyə/ *n* a large sweet-
smelling red, pink, or white flower || 크
고 달콤한 향기가 나는 빨간[분홍, 흰]색
의 꽃. 동백꽃

cam·e·o /'kæmiou/ *n* **1** a small part in
a movie or play acted by a famous actor
|| 유명 배우가 출연한 영화나 연극에서의
사소한 역. 까메오: *Whoopi Goldberg
makes a cameo appearance in the
movie.* 우피 골드버그가 그 영화에 까메오
로 출연한다. **2** a piece of jewelry with a
raised shape, usually of a person's face,
on a dark background || 어두운 배경에
대개 사람 얼굴을 도드라진 형상으로 조각
한 보석. 양각 조각한 보석. 카메오: *a
cameo brooch* 양각[카메오] 브로치

cam·er·a /'kæmrə, -ərə/ *n* a piece of
equipment used for taking photographs,
making films, or producing television
pictures || 사진이나 영화, 또는 텔레비전
프로그램을 찍는 데 쓰이는 장비. 카메라

cam·er·a·man /'kæmrəˌmæn, -mən/,
cam·er·a·wom·an /'kæmrəˌwumən/
n someone who operates a camera for a
television or film company || 방송사나 영
화사에서 카메라를 작동하는 사람. 카메라
맨

ca·mi·sole /'kæmɪˌsoul/ *n* a light piece
of clothing that women wear on the top
half of their bodies under other clothes
|| 여성이 상반신의 다른 옷 속에 입는 가
벼운 옷. 속옷. 캐미솔

cam·o·mile /'kæməˌmil/ *n* [C, U] a

plant with small white and yellow flowers, often used for making tea ‖ 종종 차를 만드는 데 쓰는 하얗고 노란 작은 꽃이 달린 식물. 카밀레

cam·ou·flage¹ /ˈkæməˌflɑʒ, -ˌflɑdʒ/ *n* [C, U] the act of hiding something by making it look the same as the things around it, or the things you use to do this ‖ 주위 배경과 똑같아 보이게 만들어 어떤

camouflage

것을 숨기는 행위, 또는 이렇게 하기 위해 사용하는 것. 위장. 변장. 카무플라주: *a soldier in camouflage* 위장한 군인 / *The Arctic fox's white fur is an excellent winter camouflage.* 북극 여우의 흰 털은 훌륭한 겨울용 위장술이다.

cam·ou·flage² /ˈkæməflɑʒ, -flɑdʒ/ *v* [T] to hide something by making it look like the things around it ‖ 어떤 것을 주위 배경과 비슷하게 보이게 만듦으로써 어떤 것을 숨기다. 위장[은폐]하다: *Hunters camouflage the traps with leaves and branches.* 사냥꾼들은 나뭇잎과 가지로 덫을 은폐한다.

camp¹ /kæmp/ *n* [C, U] **1** a place where people stay in tents in the mountains, forest etc. for a short time ‖ 사람들이 짧은 기간 동안 산·숲 등에서 텐트를 치고 머무는 장소. 텐트촌. 캠프: *After hiking all morning, we returned to camp.* 아침 내내 하이킹을 하고 우리는 캠프로 돌아왔다. **2** a place where children go to stay for a short time and do special activities ‖ 아이들이 짧은 기간 가서 머물며 특별 활동을 하는 장소. 캠프: *summer/scout/basketball camp* 여름[스카우트, 농구] 캠프 **3** a place where people are kept for a particular reason, when they do not want to be there ‖ 사람들이 원치 않아도 특정한 이유로 그들을 가두어 두는 곳: *a refugee/prison/labor camp* 난민 [수감, 노동] 캠프 —see also DAY CAMP

camp² *v* [I] to set up a tent or shelter in a place and stay there for a short time ‖ 어떤 장소에 텐트나 천막을 치고 짧게 머무르다. 야영(캠핑)하다: *Where should we camp tonight?* 우리 오늘 밤 어디서 야영하지? **– camping** *n* [U]: *We're going to go camping in Yellowstone Park this summer.* 우리는 이번 여름에 옐로우스톤 공원으로 야영하러 갈 것이다.

camp out *phr v* [I] to sleep outdoors, usually in a tent ‖ 대개 텐트를 치고 야외

에서 자다. 야영하다: *The kids like to camp out in the backyard.* 아이들은 뒤뜰에서 야영하는 것을 좋아한다.

cam·paign¹ /kæmˈpeɪn/ *n* a series of actions that are intended to achieve a particular result, especially in business or politics ‖ 특히 사업이나 정치에서 특정한 결과를 달성할 의도로 하는 일련의 행동. 캠페인. 조직적 활동: *Nixon's 1968 presidential campaign* 1968년 닉슨의 대통령 선거 운동 / *a campaign for/ against equal rights for homosexuals* 동성애자의 동등한 권리에 대한 찬성[반대] 운동[캠페인]

campaign² *v* [I] to do things publicly to try to achieve a particular result, especially in business or politics ‖ 특히 사업이나 정치에서 특정 결과를 달성하기 위해 어떤 일을 공개적으로 하다. 캠페인을 벌이다: *We're campaigning for/against the right to smoke in public places.* 우리는 공공 장소에서의 흡연권 찬성[반대] 캠페인을 벌이고 있다.

camp·er /ˈkæmpə/ *n* **1** someone who is staying in a tent or shelter for a short time ‖ 짧은 기간 텐트나 천막에 머무르는 사람. 캠프하는 사람 **2** a vehicle that has beds and cooking equipment so that you can stay in it while you are on vacation ‖ 침대와 요리 시설을 갖추고 있어 휴가 중 머물 수 있는 차량. 캠핑용 자동차 **3 happy camper** SPOKEN HUMOROUS someone who seems to be happy with his/her situation ‖ 자신의 상황에 행복해 하는 듯 보이는 사람

Camp·fire /ˈkæmpfaɪə/ *n* an organization for girls and boys that teaches them practical skills and helps develop their character ‖ 실용적인 기술을 가르치고 인성 계발을 도와주는 소년·소녀를 위한 단체. 캠프파이어

camp·ground /ˈkæmpɡraʊnd/ *n* a place where people who are on vacation can stay in tents, CAMPERs etc. ‖ 휴가차 온 사람들이 텐트나 캠핑용 자동차 등에 머무를 수 있는 장소. 캠핑장. 야영장

camp·site /ˈkæmpsaɪt/ *n* a place where you can camp ‖ 야영할 수 있는 장소. 야영지: *We found a good campsite under a tree.* 우리는 나무 밑에 있는 훌륭한 야영지를 찾아냈다.

cam·pus /ˈkæmpəs/ *n* the land or buildings of a college ‖ 대학의 부지나 건물. 캠퍼스: *Many students live on campus.* 많은 학생들이 캠퍼스에서 생활한다.

can¹ /kən; *strong* kæn/ *modal verb* **1** to be able to do something or know how to

C

do something ‖ 어떤 일을 할 수 있거나 어떤 일을 하는 방법을 알다: *I can't* (=cannot) *swim!* 난 수영할 줄 몰라! / *Jean can speak French fluently.* 진은 프랑스어를 유창하게 구사할 수 있다. / *We can't afford a vacation this year.* 우리는 올해 휴가갈 여유가 없다. **2** to be allowed to do something ‖ 어떤 일을 하도록 허락받다: *You can go out when you've finished your homework.* 숙제를 다 끝내면 나가도 좋다. / *In soccer, you can't touch the ball with your hands.* (=it is against the rules) 축구에서는 손으로 공을 건드릴 수 없다. **3** SPOKEN used in order to ask someone to do something or give you something ‖ 남에게 어떤 것을 하거나 달라고 부탁하는 데에 쓰여: *Can I have a cookie?* 쿠키 좀 먹어도 될까요? / *Can you help me take the clothes off the line?* 줄에서 빨래 걷는 것을 좀 도와 주시겠어요? **4** used in order to show what is possible or likely ‖ 가능하거나 가망성 있는 것을 나타내는 데에 쓰여: *It can't be Steve; he's in New York right now.* 스티브일 리가 없다. 그는 지금 뉴욕에 있는걸. / *I still think the problem can be solved.* 나는 여전히 그 문제를 풀수 있다고 생각한다. **5** used with the verbs "see," "hear," "feel," "smell," and "taste," and with verbs relating to thinking, to show that an action is happening ‖ "see","hear", "feel", "smell", "taste"의 동사 및 생각과 관련된 동사와 함께 사용하여, 어떤 행위가 일어나고 있음을 나타내는 데에 쓰여: *Nancy can't understand why I'm so upset.* 낸시는 내가 왜 이렇게 흥분했는지 모른다. / *I can see Ralph coming now.* 지금 랄프가 오는 게 보인다. **6** used in order to show what often happens or how someone often behaves ‖ 종종 어떤 일이 일어나는지, 또는 누가 어떻게 행동하는지를 나타내는 데에 쓰여: *It can get pretty cold here at night.* 여기서는 밤에 꽤 추워질수 있다. —see also COULD —see study note on page 932

USAGE NOTE can

Can is used instead of the PRESENT CONTINUOUS with many verbs relating to physical or mental ability: *I can smell something burning.* / *Can you believe that?* ✗DON'T SAY "I am smelling something burning" or "Are you believing that?"✗
can은 신체적이거나 정신적인 능력에 관계된 많은 동사들과 함께 현재 진행형을 대신해 쓰인다: 뭔가 타는 냄새가 난다. / 저것을 믿을 수 있겠니? "I am smelling something burning" 또는 "Are you believing that?"과 같이 진행형을 쓰지 않는다.

can² /kæn/ *n* **1** a metal container in which food or liquid is kept without air ‖ 음식이나 액체를 진공 상태로 보관하는 금속 용기. 깡통. 캔: *Soft drink cans may be recycled.* 음료수 깡통은 재활용할수 있다. / *a can of tuna fish* 참치 캔 한통 / *a large can of paint* 큰 페인트 한통 —see picture at CONTAINER **2 a (whole) can of worms** a complicated situation that causes a lot of problems when you start to deal with it ‖ 대처하려 할 때 많은 문제를 일으키는 복잡한 상황 **3** SLANG a toilet ‖ 변기 **4** OLD-FASHIONED SLANG BUTTOCK**s** ‖ 엉덩이 **5** OLD-FASHIONED SLANG prison ‖ 감옥

can³ /kæn/ *v* **1** to preserve food by putting it in a closed container without air ‖ 음식을 진공의 밀폐된 용기에 담아 보관하다. 음식을 통조림하다: *My mother likes to can vegetables from the garden.* 우리 엄마는 뜰에서 기른 채소를 통조림하는 것을 좋아한다. **2** SPOKEN to dismiss someone from their job ‖ 직장을 그만두게 하다. …을 해고시키다 **3 can it!** SPOKEN used in order to tell someone impolitely to stop talking or making a noise ‖ 남에게 말이나 소리내는 것을 중지하라고 무례하게 말하는 데에 쓰여

Ca·na·di·an¹ /kəˈneɪdiən/ *adj* relating to or coming from Canada ‖ 캐나다와 관계되거나 캐나다 출신의. 캐나다(산)의

Canadian² *n* someone from Canada ‖ 캐나다 출신의 사람. 캐나다인

ca·nal /kəˈnæl/ *n* a long narrow stream of water for ships or boats to travel along or to bring water from somewhere ‖ 선박이나 배가 다니는, 또는 어딘가로부터 물을 끌어오는 길고 좁은 수로. 운하: *the Panama Canal* 파나마 운하

ca·nar·y /kəˈnɛri/ *n* a small yellow bird that sings and is often kept as a pet ‖ 종종 애완용으로 기르는, 노래하는 작고 노란 새. 카나리아

can·cel /ˈkænsəl/ *v* [T] **1** to say or decide that something you have planned will not happen ‖ 계획한 것이 일어나지 않으리라고 말하거나 결정하다. 취소하다: *I had to cancel my trip.* 나는 여행을 취소해야 했다. **2** to tell someone that you no longer want something ‖ 더 이상 어떤 것을 원하지 않는다고 남에게 말하다: *We're canceling our subscription to the* *magazine*. 우리는 잡지 구독을 취소하려 한다.

cancel out *phr v* [T] to have an equal but opposite effect on something, so that a situation does not change ‖ 어떤 것에 동등하지만 정반대의 효과를 미쳐서 결과적으로 상황이 변하지 않다. 상쇄하다: *The big meal I ate canceled out the exercise I had done*. 내가 먹은 엄청난 양의 식사로 살빼기 운동이 허사가 되었다.

can·cel·la·tion /ˌkænsə'leɪʃən/ *n* [C, U] a decision or statement that a planned activity or event will not happen ‖ 계획했던 활동이나 사건이 일어나지 않을 것이라는 결정이나 진술. 취소: *The plane is full right now, but sometimes there are cancellations*. 지금 당장은 비행기 좌석이 꽉 차 있지만, 가끔 취소하는 경우도 있습니다.

Can·cer /'kænsə/ *n* **1** [singular] the fourth sign of the ZODIAC, represented by a CRAB ‖ 게로 상징되는 황도 12궁의 넷째 별자리. 게자리 **2** someone born between June 21 and July 22 ‖ 6월 21일에서 7월 22일 사이에 태어난 사람. 게좌 태생자

cancer *n* [C, U] a serious disease in which the body's cells increase too fast, producing a growth that may lead to death ‖ 사망에 이를 수도 있는 종양을 생성해 내는, 체세포가 급속히 증가하는 심각한 질병. 암: *breast/lung/bowel cancer* 유방/폐/대장암 / *He died of cancer at the age of 63*. 그는 63세의 나이에 암으로 사망했다. **– cancerous** *adj*

can·did /'kændɪd/ *adj* directly truthful, even when the truth may be unpleasant or embarrassing ‖ 사실이 불쾌하거나 부끄러운 경우라도 매우 솔직한. 정직한. 숨김 없는: *a candid article on birth control for teenagers* 10대 청소년들의 피임에 관한 사실적인 기사 **– candidly** *adv*

can·di·da·cy /'kændədəsi/ *n* [C, U] the fact of being a CANDIDATE, usually for a political position ‖ 보통 어떤 정치적 지위의 후보자가 되는 것. 입후보: *She announced her candidacy at the convention*. 그녀는 그 대회에서 입후보를 표명했다.

can·di·date /'kændədə,deɪt, -dɪt/ *n* someone who applies for a job or is trying to be elected to a political position ‖ 어떤 직업에 지원하거나 정치적 지위에 선출되기 위해 노력하는 사람. 지원자. 후보자: *Which candidate are you voting for?* 어떤 후보자에게 투표할 거니? / *Sara seems to be a likely candidate*

for the job. 사라는 그 일에 안성맞춤인 후보자로 보인다.

can·died /'kændid/ *adj* cooked in or covered with sugar ‖ 설탕으로 조리하거나 설탕으로 덮인. 설탕 절임의: *candied fruit* 설탕 절임 과일

can·dle /'kændl/ *n* a round stick of WAX with a piece of string through the middle that you burn to produce light ‖ 태워서 불을 만들어 내는 줄이 중앙을 관통하는, 왁스로 만든 둥근 모양의 막대. 양초

can·dle·stick /'kændl,stɪk/ *n* a specially shaped metal or wooden object used for holding CANDLEs ‖ 초를 고정시키는 데에 쓰이는 특별한 형태의 금속이나 목제 제품. 촛대

can·dor /'kændə/ *n* [U] the quality of being honest and truthful ‖ 정직하고 진실한 성품. 성실(성)

can·dy /'kændi/ *n* **1** [C, U] a sweet food made of sugar or chocolate, or a piece of this ‖ 설탕이나 초콜릿으로 만든 달콤한 음식 또는 이것의 조각. 과자. 사탕 **2 mind/brain/eye etc. candy** INFORMAL something that is entertaining or pleasant to look at, but that does not make you think ‖ 보기에는 재미있고 즐겁지만 생각하지 못하게 하는 것. 정신/두뇌/눈을 혹하게 하는 것: *A lot of TV shows are just mind candy*. 많은 TV 쇼 프로그램은 정신을 멍하게 만들 뿐이다.

candy bar /'.. ./ *n* a long narrow BAR of candy, usually covered with chocolate ‖ 보통 초콜릿으로 덮인 길고 좁은 막대 사탕

candy cane /'.. ./ *n* a stick of hard sugar with a curved shape, colored red and white ‖ 색이 빨갛고 하얀, 구부러진 모양의 단단한 설탕 막대. 지팡이 모양 사탕 과자

cane¹ /keɪn/ *n* a long thin stick, usually with a curved handle, used for helping you walk ‖ 보통 구부러진 손잡이가 있고 걷기 보조용으로 쓰이는 길고 가는 막대. 지팡이

cane² *v* [T] to punish someone by hitting him/her with a cane ‖ 남을 막대기로 때려 벌 주다. 매로 때리다.

ca·nine /'keɪnaɪn/ *adj* relating to dogs ‖ 개에 관련된. 개의

can·is·ter /'kænəstə/ *n* a metal container with a lid used for storing dry food or a gas ‖ 건조 식품이나 가스의 저장에 쓰이는 뚜껑이 달린 금속 용기. 깡통: *a flour/sugar/salt canister* 밀가루[설탕, 소금] 통

can·ker /'kæŋkə/, **canker sore**

/'.. ,./ n [U] a sore area on the flesh of people or animals or on the wood of trees, caused by illness or a disease ‖ 사람이나 동물의 살 위나 나무의 목질 위에 질병으로 생긴 문드러진 부위. 헌데. 궤양

can·na·bis /'kænəbɪs/ n [U] TECHNICAL ⇨ MARIJUANA

canned /kænd/ adj **1** preserved without air in a container ‖ 용기 안에 공기 없이 보존된. 통조림으로 된: *canned tomatoes* 토마토 통조림 **2 canned music/laughter/applause** music etc. that has been recorded and is used on television or radio programs ‖ 녹음되어 텔레비전이나 라디오 프로그램에 쓰이는 음악 등. 녹음된 음악/웃음/박수 소리

can·ner·y /'kænəri/ n a factory where food is put into cans ‖ 식품을 깡통 속에 넣는 공장. 통조림 공장

can·ni·bal /'kænəbəl/ n someone who eats human flesh ‖ 사람 고기를 먹는 사람. 식인종 **– cannibalism** n [U] **– cannibalistic** /ˌkænəbə'lɪstɪk/ adj

can·non /'kænən/ n a large gun, fixed to the ground or on wheels, used in past times ‖ 땅이나 바퀴 위에 고정되어 과거에 쓰였던 큰 포. 대포

can·not /'kænɑt, kə'nɑt, kæ-/ modal verb the negative form of CAN ‖ can의 부정형: *I cannot accept your offer.* 당신의 제안을 받아들일 수 없습니다.

can·ny /'kæni/ adj smart, careful, and showing that you understand a situation very well ‖ 영리하고 주의깊고 상황을 매우 잘 이해하고 있음을 보여주는. 눈치빠른. 재치있는

ca·noe /kə'nu/ n a long light narrow boat that is pointed at both ends, which you move using a PADDLE ‖ 양 끝이 뾰족하고 노를 사용해 움직이는 길고 가볍고 좁은 배. 카누 **– canoe** v [I]

can·on /'kænən/ n **1** FORMAL a generally accepted rule or standard for behaving or thinking ‖ 일반적으로 인정된 행동이나 사고의 규칙이나 기준. 규범 **2** an established law of the Christian church ‖ 크리스트교 교회의 정립된 법령. 교회법

can o·pen·er /'. ,../ n a tool used for opening cans of food ‖ 통조림 식품을 여는 데에 쓰이는 도구. 통조림[깡통] 따개

can·o·py /'kænəpi/ n a cover attached above a bed or seat, used as a decoration or as a shelter ‖ 침대나 의자 위에 부착되어 장식으로나 가리개로 쓰이는 덮개. 차양. 캐노피 **– canopied** adj

can't /kænt/ modal verb the short form of "cannot" ‖ "cannot"의 단축형: *I can't*

go with you today. 오늘 너와 같이 갈 수 없다.

can·ta·loupe /'kæntəlˌoʊp/ n [C, U] a type of MELON with a hard green skin and sweet orange flesh ‖ 단단한 녹색 껍질과 달콤한 오렌지색 과육으로 채워진 일종의 멜론. 칸탈루프 **—see picture on page 944**

can·tan·ker·ous /kæn'tæŋkərəs/ adj bad-tempered and complaining ‖ 성미가 고약하고 불평을 늘어놓는. 까탈스러운. 심술궂은: *a cantankerous old man* 심술궂은 노인

can·teen /kæn'tin/ n **1** a small container for carrying water or other drinks ‖ 물이나 다른 음료를 담아 나르는 작은 용기. 물통. 수통 **2** a store or place where people in the military can buy things or go to be entertained ‖ 군인들이 물건을 사거나 즐기러 가는 매점이나 장소. 피엑스(PX). 접대소

can·ter /'kæntɚ/ v [I, T] when a horse canters, it runs fast, but not as fast as possible ‖ 말이 최대한은 아니지만 빨리 달리다. 구보로 달리다 **– canter** n

Can·to·nese /ˌkæntən'iz/ n [U] a language used in Hong Kong and parts of southern China ‖ 홍콩과 중국 남부 지방에서 쓰이는 언어. 광둥어

can·vas /'kænvəs/ n **1** [U] a type of strong cloth that is used for making tents, sails, bags etc. ‖ 텐트·돛·가방 등을 만드는 데에 쓰이는 일종의 질긴 천. 즈크 천 **2** a piece of canvas on which a picture is painted ‖ 그 위에 그림을 그리는 캔버스 천 조각

can·vass /'kænvəs/ v [I, T] to try to get information or support for a political party by going from place to place within an area and talking to people ‖ 구역 내 여기저기를 돌아다니며 연설하여 정당을 위한 정보나 지지를 얻으려 하다. 선거 운동[유세]을 하다: *Someone was here canvassing for the Democrats.* 누군가가 민주당을 위해 이곳에서 선거운동을 하고 있었다.

can·yon /'kænyən/ n a deep valley with very steep sides ‖ 매우 가파른 경사면이 있는 깊은 계곡. 협곡: *the Grand Canyon* 그랜드 캐니언(협곡)

cap¹ /kæp/ n **1** a soft flat hat with a curved part sticking out at the front ‖ 앞면에 구부러진 부분이 튀어나와 있는 부드럽고 납작한 모자. 챙이 달린 모자: *a baseball cap* 야구 모자 **2** something that covers and protects the end or top of something ‖ 물체의 끝이나 상단을 덮어 보호하는 것. 덮개. 뚜껑: *a bottle cap* 병

뚜껑 / *Put the cap back on that pen!* 그 펜의 뚜껑을 도로 닫아라! **3** a limit on the amount of money that someone can earn or spend ‖ 어떤 사람이 벌거나 소비할 수 있는 금액의 한도. 상한: *There's a cap on the amount of money you can earn and still receive Social Security.* 돈을 벌면서 여전히 사회 보장 수당을 탈 수 있는 소득에는 상한이 있다

cap² *v* [T] **1** to be the last and usually best thing that happens in a game, situation etc. ‖ 게임·상황 등에서 보통 최상의 마무리가 되다. 최상[최선]으로 마무리하다: *Wilkes capped a perfect season by winning the 100 meter sprint.* 윌크스는 100미터 경주에서 우승하여 시즌을 완벽하게 마무리했다. **2** to cover the top of something ‖ 어떤 것의 위를 덮다. 덮개[뚜껑]를 씌우다: *All her front teeth are capped.* 그녀는 앞니 전부를 씌웠다. / *the snow-capped peaks of the Rocky Mountains* 록키 산맥의 눈 덮인 봉우리들 **3** to limit the amount of something, especially money, that can be used or spent ‖ 사물의 양, 특히 쓰거나 소비될 수 있는 금액을 제한하다. 상한[한도]을 정하다: *The law caps the amount of interest that credit card companies can charge.* 법은 신용 카드 회사가 부과할 수 있는 이자의 상한을 정하고 있다.

ca·pa·bil·i·ty /ˌkeɪpəˈbɪləti/ *n* the ability of a machine, person, or organization to do something, especially something difficult ‖ 특히 어려운 일을 할 수 있는 기계[사람, 조직]의 능력. 역량: *The country has the capability to produce nuclear weapons.* 그 나라는 핵무기를 생산할 수 있는 역량이 있다. / *What you can do depends on your computer's graphics capability.* 당신이 무엇을 할 수 있는가는 당신 컴퓨터의 그래픽 구현 능력에 달려 있습니다.

ca·pa·ble /ˈkeɪpəbəl/ *adj* [C, U] **1** having the power, skill, or other qualities that are needed to do something ‖ 어떤 일을 하는 데에 필요한 역량[기술, 여타 특성]을 가지고 있는. … 할 능력[힘]이 있는: *Do you think he is capable of murder?* 그가 살인을 저지를 수 있다고 생각하십니까? —opposite INCAPABLE **2** skillful and effective ‖ 능숙하고 효과적인. 유능한: *Mary Beth is a capable lawyer.* 메리 베스는 유능한 변호사이다.

ca·pac·i·ty /kəˈpæsəti/ *n* **1** [singular, U] the amount that something can hold, produce, or carry ‖ 사물이 수용[생산, 운반]할 수 있는 양. 용량. 용적. 수용력:

My computer has a capacity of 400 megabytes. 내 컴퓨터의 용량은 400 메가바이트이다. / *The theater was filled to capacity.* (=completely full) 그 극장은 수용 한도까지 찼다. **2** [singular, U] the ability to do or produce something ‖ 어떤 일을 하거나 생산할 수 있는 능력. 수행[생산] 능력: *Jan has a real capacity for hard work.* 잰은 힘든 일을 해낼 만한 충분한 역량이 있다. / *The factory is not yet working at full capacity.* 그 공장은 아직 생산 능력을 완전 가동하지 않고 있다. **3** [singular] someone's job, position, or duty ‖ 사람의 업무[입장, 임무]: *She has traveled a lot in her capacity as a photojournalist.* 그녀는 사진 기자로서 직업상 여행을 많이 하고 있다.

cape /keɪp/ *n* **1** a long loose piece of clothing without SLEEVEs, that fastens around your neck and hangs from your shoulders ‖ 목 둘레에 매어 어깨에서 늘어뜨린, 소매없는 길고 헐렁한 천. 케이프. 망토: *Batman's black cape* 배트맨의 검은 망토 **2** a large piece of land surrounded on three sides by water ‖ 삼면이 바다로 싸인 큰 땅덩어리. 곶. 갑: *Cape Cod* 케이프 코드

ca·per¹ /ˈkeɪpə/ *n* **1** a small dark green part of a flower used in cooking to give a sour taste to food ‖ 음식에 신 맛을 내기 위해 요리할 때 쓰는 진녹색의 작은 꽃 부분. 케이퍼 **2** a planned activity, especially an illegal or dangerous one ‖ 특히 불법적이거나 위험한, 계획된 행동. 불법 행위. 계획 범죄

ca·per² *v* [I] to jump around and play in a happy excited way ‖ 뛰어다니며 기분좋게 흥분해서 놀다. 흥분해서 깡충깡충 뛰어다니다. 까불거리며 장난치다

cap·il·lar·y /ˈkæpəˌlɛri/ *n* a very small narrow tube that carries blood around your body —compare ARTERY, VEIN ‖ 피를 온 몸 곳곳에 운반하는 매우 작고 좁은 관. 모세 혈관

cap·i·tal¹ /ˈkæpətl/ *n* **1** the city where a country or state's central government is ‖ 나라나 주(州)의 중앙 정부가 있는 도시. 수도. 주도: *The New York state capital is Albany.* 뉴욕 주의 주도는 올버니이다. —compare CAPITOL **2** ⇨ **capital letter** (CAPITAL²) **3** [singular, U] money or property you use to start a business or to make more money ‖ 사업을 시작하거나 더 많은 돈을 벌기 위해 쓰는 돈 또는 재산. 자본(금). (사업) 밑천[자산] **4** a place that is important for a particular activity ‖ 특정 활동에 중요한 장소. 중심지. 활동 무대[중심]: *Hollywood is the* *capital of the movie industry.* 할리우드는 영화 산업의 중심지이다. —see picture on page 930

capital² *adj* **1** relating to money, machines, products, or property that can be used to create more wealth ‖ 더 많은 부를 창출하는 데 쓰일 수 있는 돈[기계, 상품, 재산]에 관한. 자산[자본]의: *We need a bigger capital investment to improve our schools.* 우리 학교를 발전시키기 위해서도 더 많은 자본 투자가 필요하다. **2 capital letter** a letter of the alphabet that is printed in its large form, used at the beginning of a word or sentence ‖ 단어나 문장의 첫머리에 쓰이는, 큰 글자체로 인쇄된 글자. 대문자 **3 capital offense/crime** a crime that is bad enough to be punished by death ‖ 사형 처벌을 받을 만큼 나쁜 범죄. 사형에 처해지는 중범죄

cap·i·tal·ism /ˈkæpət̬lˌɪzəm/ *n* [U] an economic and political system in which businesses belong mostly to private owners, not to the government ‖ 기업들이 국가가 아니라 주로 개인 소유주에게 속하는 경제·정치 체제. 자본주의(체제) —compare COMMUNISM, SOCIALISM

cap·i·tal·ist /ˈkæpət̬l-ɪst/ *n* someone who supports or takes part in CAPITALISM ‖ 자본주의를 지지하거나 자본주의 체제에 참여하는 사람. 자본주의자 – **capitalist** *adj*

cap·i·tal·i·za·tion /ˌkæpət̬l-əˈzeɪʃən/ *n* [U] the total value of a company, based on the value of its SHAREs ‖ 주식의 가치에 기반을 둔 회사의 총가치. 증권 자본

cap·i·tal·ize /ˈkæpət̬lˌaɪz/ *v* [T] **1** to write a letter of the alphabet using a CAPITAL letter ‖ 대문자로 알파벳을 쓰다. 알파벳 대문자를 쓰다 **2** to supply a business with money so that it can operate ‖ 운영할 수 있도록 기업에 자금을 공급하다. 자본을 투자[출자]하다

capitalize on sth *phr v* [T] to use something in order to gain an advantage ‖ 이익을 얻기 위해 어떤 것을 이용하다. …을 기화로 삼다: *The President should capitalize on his popularity and get that law passed.* 대통령은 자신의 인기를 이용해서 그 법률을 통과시켜야 한다.

capital pun·ish·ment /ˌ... ˈ.../ *n* [U] the punishment of legally killing someone for a crime s/he has done ‖ 범죄를 저지른 사람을 합법적으로 죽이는 처벌. 사형 —see also DEATH PENALTY

Cap·i·tol /ˈkæpət̬l/ *n* **the Capitol** the building in which the people who make laws for the US or one of its 50 states meet ‖ 미합중국의 법을 제정하는 사람들이나 50개 주의 의원들이 모여 회의하는 건물. 미국 국회 의사당 —compare CAPITAL¹

Capitol Hill /ˌ... ˈ./ *n* [singular] the US Congress ‖ 미국 연방 의회: *The debate about gun control is continuing on Capitol Hill.* 총포 규제에 대한 논의가 의회에서 계속되고 있다.

ca·pit·u·late /kəˈpɪtʃəˌleɪt/ *v* [I] to stop fighting someone and accept his/her conditions or demands ‖ 누군가와 싸움을 멈추고 조건이나 요구를 받아들이다. 조건[요구]에 굴복하다 – **capitulation** /kəˌpɪtʃəˈleɪʃən/ *n* [C, U]

cap·puc·ci·no /ˌkæpəˈtʃinoʊ, ˌkɑ-/ *n* [C, U] a type of Italian coffee made with hot milk ‖ 뜨거운 우유로 만든 이탈리아 커피의 일종. 카푸치노

ca·price /kəˈpris/ *n* [C, U] a sudden and unreasonable change in someone's opinion or behavior ‖ 남의 견해나 행동상의 갑작스럽고 불합리한 변화. 변덕. 충동적 변화

ca·pri·cious /kəˈprɪʃəs/ *adj* likely to suddenly change decisions, emotions, conditions etc. without warning ‖ 예고 없이 결정·감정·조건 등을 갑자기 잘 바꾸는. 자주 변하는. 변덕스러운: *Helen's just as capricious as her mother was.* 헬렌은 꼭 그녀 어머니만큼이나 변덕스럽다. / *capricious spring weather* 변덕스러운 봄철 날씨 – **capriciously** *adv*

Cap·ri·corn /ˈkæprɪˌkɔrn/ *n* **1** [singular] the tenth sign of the ZODIAC, represented by a GOAT ‖ 염소로 상징되는 황도 12궁의 열째 별자리. 염소자리 **2** someone born between December 22 and January 19 ‖ 12월 22일부터 1월 19일 사이에 태어난 사람. 염소좌 태생자

cap·size /ˈkæpsaɪz, kæpˈsaɪz/ *v* [I, T] if a boat capsizes or you capsize it, it turns over in the water ‖ 보트가 물 속에서 뒤집혀지거나 보트를 뒤집다. 보트가 [를] 뒤집히다. 전복되다. 전복시키다

cap·sule /ˈkæpsəl/ *n* **1** a very small object with medicine inside that you swallow whole ‖ 안에 약이 들어 있어 통째로 삼키는 매우 작은 물체. 알약. 캡슐 —see picture at MEDICINE **2** the part of a space vehicle in which people live and work ‖ 사람들이 거주하고 일하는 우주선의 일부분. 우주 캡슐

cap·tain¹ /ˈkæptən/ *n* **1** also **Captain** someone who commands a ship or aircraft ‖ 선박이나 항공기를 지휘하는 사람. 선장[함장]. 기장 **2** also **Captain** an officer who has a middle rank in the Army, Navy, Air Force, or Marines ‖ 육군[해군, 공군, 해병대]의 중간 계급을 가진 지휘관. 대위 **3** someone who leads a team or group ‖ 팀이나 단체를 이끄는 사람. 지도자. 장. 대장(隊長): *the football team captain* 축구팀 주장

captain² *v* [T] to lead a team or group of people as their CAPTAIN ‖ 사람들의 대장으로서 팀이나 일단의 사람들을 이끌다. 지휘하다

cap·tion /'kæpʃən/ *n* words written above or below a picture that explain the picture ‖ 그림의 위나 아래에 쓰여 그것을 설명하는 말. 설명(문). 캡션

cap·ti·vate /'kæptə,veɪt/ *v* [T] to attract and interest someone very much ‖ 남을 매우 끌리게 하거나 흥미를 갖게 하다. 마음을 사로잡다. 매혹시키다: *Alex was captivated by her beauty.* 알렉스는 그녀의 아름다움에 매혹되었다. – **captivating** *adj*

cap·tive¹ /'kæptɪv/ *adj* **1** kept as a prisoner or in a small space ‖ 죄수로서 또는 좁은 공간에 갇힌. 수감[투옥]된. 감금된: *captive animals* 갇혀 있는 동물들 **2 captive audience** a group of people who listen to or watch someone or something because they have to, not because they want to ‖ 하고 싶어서가 아니라 해야 하기 때문에 사람이나 사물을 듣거나 바라보는 일단의 사람들. (정신없이) 사로잡힌 청중 **3 take/hold sb captive** to make someone become a prisoner, or to keep someone as a prisoner ‖ 어떤 사람을 죄수가 되게 하거나 죄수로 가두다. …을 포로로 잡다. …을 죄수로 구금하다

captive² *n* someone who is kept as a prisoner, especially in a war ‖ 특히 전쟁에서 죄수로 잡혀 있는 사람. 전쟁 포로

cap·tiv·i·ty /kæp'tɪvəti/ *n* [U] the state of being kept as a prisoner or in a small space ‖ 죄수로서, 또는 좁은 공간에 갇혀 있는 상태. 감금. 속박: *Many animals won't breed in captivity.* 많은 동물들이 갇힌 상태에서는 번식을 하지 않는다.

cap·tor /'kæptɚ/ *n* FORMAL someone who keeps a person or animal as a prisoner or in a small space ‖ 사람이나 동물을 죄수로 또는 좁은 공간에 가두는 사람. 포획자. 체포자

cap·ture¹ /'kæptʃɚ/ *v* [T] **1** to catch someone in order to keep him/her as a prisoner ‖ 사람을 죄수로 감금하기 위해 붙잡다. 체포하다. 포획하다: *Lester was captured at the airport.* 레스터는 공항에서 체포되었다. **2** to take control of

something, often by using force ‖ 종종 무력을 써서 어떤 것을 지배하다. 공략하다. 함락시키다: *They've captured a large share of the market.* 그들은 시장의 많은 부분을 장악했다. / *a town captured by an enemy* 적에게 함락된 도시 **3** to catch an animal without killing it ‖ 죽이지 않고 동물을 포획하다. 사로잡다. 생포하다 **4** to succeed in showing or describing something by using pictures or words ‖ 그림이나 문구를 써서 무엇을 보여주거나 묘사하는 데에 성공하다. …을 성공적으로 표현하다[설명하다]: *His new book really captures what the 1920s were like.* 그의 새 책은 1920년대를 잘 나타내고 있다. **5 capture sb's imagination/attention** to make someone feel very interested in what you are saying or showing ‖ 자신이 말하거나 보여주는 것에 대해 남이 깊은 흥미를 느끼게 하다. 마음을 혹하게 하다. 남의 상상력/주의력을 사로잡다 **6** TECHNICAL to put something in a form that a computer can use ‖ 무엇을 컴퓨터에서 쓸 수 있는 형태로 입력하다. …으로 (전환)입력하다: *The data is captured by an optical scanner.* 그 데이터는 광학 스캐너로 입력된다.

capture² *n* [U] **1** the act of catching someone in order to keep him/her as a prisoner, or of catching an animal ‖ 사람을 죄수로 가두기 위해 붙잡거나 동물을 잡는 행위. 체포. 구속. 생포: *Higgins avoided capture by hiding in the woods.* 히긴스는 숲 속에 숨어서 체포되는 것을 면했다. **2** the act of taking control of something, often by using force ‖ 종종 무력을 써서 어떤 것을 지배하는 행위. 획득. 공략. 함락

car /kɑr/ *n* **1** a vehicle with four wheels and an engine, used for traveling from one place to another ‖ 한 곳에서 다른 곳으로 여행하는 데 쓰이는, 네 개의 바퀴와 엔진이 달린 차량. 자동차: *That's Lynn's new car.* 그것은 린의 새 차다. / *Joe got in the car and buckled his seatbelt.* 조는 차에 타서 안전벨트를 맸다. / *Wait for me here; don't get out of the car.* 여기서 나를 기다려, 차 밖으로 나오지 말고. **2** one of the connected parts of a train ‖ 열차의 연결된 차량 중의 하나. 한 칸[량]: *I'll meet you in the dining/sleeping car.* 식당칸[침대칸]에서 만나자.

ca·rafe /kə'ræf/ *n* a glass bottle with a wide top, used for serving wine or water at meals ‖ 식사 때 포도주나 물을 따라 주는 데에 쓰는 상단이 넓은 유리병

car·a·mel /'kærəməl, -,mɛl, 'kɑrməl/ *n*

[C, U] candy made of cooked sugar, butter, and milk ‖ 설탕·버터·우유를 가열해 만든 사탕. 캐러멜

car·at /'kærət/ *n* a unit for measuring the weight of jewels, equal to 200 MILLIGRAMs ‖ 2백 밀리그램에 상당하는, 보석의 무게를 재는 단위. 캐럿 —see also KARAT

car·a·van /'kærə,væn/ *n* a group of people with animals or vehicles, who travel together ‖ 동물이나 차량으로 함께 여행하는 일단의 사람들. 캐러밴

car·bo·hy·drate /,kɑrbou'haɪdreɪt, -drɪt, -bə-/ *n* [C, U] a substance in some foods that provides your body with heat and energy ‖ 인체에 열량과 에너지를 제공하는 음식에 함유된 물질. 탄수화물

car·bon /'kɑrbən/ *n* [U] a chemical that is an ELEMENT and that forms into DIAMONDs, and is in GASOLINE, coal etc. ‖ 원소로서 다이아몬드를 만들고, 석유·석탄 등에 들어 있는 화학물질. 탄소

car·bon·at·ed /'kɑrbə,neɪtɪd/ *adj* carbonated drinks have a lot of BUBBLEs in them ‖ 음료수가 그 안에 거품이 많은. 탄산가스를 함유하는

carbon cop·y /,.. '../ *n* **1** someone or something that is very similar to another person or thing ‖ 다른 사람이나 사물과 매우 닮은 사람이나 사물. 판박이. 복사판: *The robbery is a carbon copy of one that took place last year.* 그 강도 사건은 지난해 일어났던 건의 복사판이다. **2** a copy of something made using CARBON PAPER ‖ (복사용) 먹지를 써서 만든 어떤 것의 복사본. 부본(副本)

carbon di·ox·ide /,kɑrbən daɪ-'ɑksaɪd/ *n* [U] the gas produced when animals breathe out, when CARBON is burned in air, or when animals and plants decay ‖ 동물이 숨을 내쉴 때[탄소가 공기 중에서 연소될 때, 동·식물이 부패할 때] 생기는 가스. 이산화 탄소

carbon mon·ox·ide /,kɑrbən mə'nɑksaɪd/ *n* [U] a poisonous gas produced when engines burn gasoline ‖ 엔진이 휘발유를 연소할 때 생기는 유독 가스. 일산화 탄소

carbon pap·er /'.. ,../ *n* [C, U] thin paper with a blue or black substance on one side, that you put between two sheets of paper to make a copy of what you write on the top sheet ‖ 맨 윗장에 쓰는 것을 복사하기 위해 두 장의 종이 사이에 끼우는, 한 면이 청색이나 흑색 물질로 된 얇은 종이. 먹지

car·bu·re·tor /'kɑrbə,reɪtɚ/ *n* the part of an engine that mixes the air and GASOLINE so they can burn in the engine to provide power ‖ 동력을 공급하도록 공기와 가솔린을 섞어 엔진에서 연소할 수 있게 해주는 엔진의 일부분. 기화기

car·cass /'kɑrkəs/ *n* the body of a dead animal ‖ 죽은 동물의 시체

car·cin·o·gen /kɑr'sɪnədʒən/ *n* TECHNICAL a substance that can cause CANCER ‖ 암을 유발하는 물질. 발암 물질 – **carcinogenic** /,kɑrsɪnə'dʒɛnɪk/ *adj*

card

credit card

birthday card

playing cards

postcards

card¹ /kɑrd/ *n* **1** a small piece of plastic or stiff paper that shows information about someone or something ‖ 사람이나 사물에 대한 정보를 나타내는 플라스틱 또는 빳빳한 작은 종이 조각. 카드. 명함: *a credit/library/business card* 신용 카드 [도서관 카드, 명함] **2** a piece of folded stiff paper, usually with a picture on the front and a message inside, that you send to people on special occasions ‖ 보통 겉면에 그림이 있고 안에 메시지를 적어 특별한 때에 사람들에게 보내는, 빳빳하게 접힌 종이. 인사장. 축하 카드. 연하장: *a birthday card* 생일축하 카드 **3** one of a set of 52 small pieces of stiff paper with pictures or numbers on them, that are used for playing games —see also CARDS ‖ 그림이나 글자가 위에 적혀 있는, 게임에 쓰이는 52장의 빳빳한 종이 세트 중의 한 장. (카드 놀이)패. 카드 —see also CARDS **4** ⇨ POSTCARD **5** **play your cards right** INFORMAL to do the things that make you succeed in getting what you want ‖ 원하는 것을 성공적으로 얻게 해주는 일을 하다. 정확하게 목표에 따른 일을 하다. 일을 능숙하게 처리하다 **6** **put/lay your cards on the table** INFORMAL to be completely honest about what your plans and intentions are ‖ 계획하고 의도하는 바에

대해 완전히 솔직해지다. 계획[비밀]을 털어 놓다. 속셈을 공개하다 **7 the flat piece of plastic inside a computer that has small electrical things attached to it, that allows the computer to do specific jobs** ‖ 작은 전자 부품들이 부착되어 컴퓨터가 특정 작업을 수행하게 하는 컴퓨터 내부의 납작한 플라스틱 조각. 기판. 카드

card² v [T] **to ask someone to show a card proving that s/he is old enough to be in a particular place or to buy alcohol or cigarettes** ‖ 누군가에게 특정 장소에 들어가거나 술이나 담배를 살 수 있는 적정 연령임을 증명하는 카드 제시를 요구하다. 신분증을 보여 달라고 하다

card·board /'kardbɔrd/ n [U] **a thick material like stiff paper, used especially for making boxes** ‖ 특히 박스를 만드는 데 쓰이는 빳빳한 종이 같은 두꺼운 소재. 골판지

card cat·a·log /ˌ. '.../ n **a set of cards that contain information about something, especially books in a library, and are arranged in a particular order** ‖ 특정 순서로 정렬된, 특히 도서관의 책에 대한 정보를 담고 있는 일련의 카드. 색인 카드. 분류 카드

car·di·ac /'kardi,æk/ adj TECHNICAL **relating to the heart or to heart disease** ‖ 심장이나 심장병에 관련된. 심장(병)의

cardiac ar·rest /ˌ... .'./ n TECHNICAL ⇨ HEART ATTACK

car·di·gan /'kardəgən/ n **a SWEATER that is fastened at the front with buttons** ‖ 앞쪽에서 단추를 채우는 스웨터. 카디건

car·di·nal¹ /'kardn-əl, -nəl/ adj **very important or basic** ‖ 매우 중요하거나 기본적인. 주된. 주요한: a cardinal rule 주요 규칙

cardinal² n **1 a common North American wild bird that is a bright red color** ‖ 북미 대륙에 흔한 밝은 빨간색의 야생 조류. 붉은 홍관조 **2 a priest of high rank in the Roman Catholic Church** ‖ 로마 가톨릭 교회의 고위 사제. 추기경

cardinal num·ber /ˌ... .'../ n **any of the numbers 1, 2, 3 etc. that show the quantity of something** ‖ 사물의 수량을 표시하는 1,2,3 등의 숫자. 기수(基數) — compare ORDINAL NUMBER

car·di·ol·o·gy /ˌkardi'alədʒi/ n [U] **the study or science of medical treatment of the heart** ‖ 심장의 의학적 치료에 대한 연구나 과학. 심장(병)학

cards /kardz/ n [plural] **1 a set of 52 small pieces of stiff paper with pictures or numbers on them, used for playing games** ‖ 빳빳한 종이 위에 그림이나 숫자

가 있는, 게임에 쓰이는 52장의 작은 종이 세트. 카드: a deck of cards (=set of cards) 카드 한 벌 **2 games played with such a set** ‖ 카드 한 벌로 하는 게임. 카드놀이[게임]: I'm going over to Herb's to play cards. 나는 카드놀이 하러 허브네 집에 간다.

card ta·ble /'. ˌ../ n **a small light table that you can fold, on which you can play cards** ‖ 카드 놀이를 할 수 있으며 접을 수 있는 작고 가벼운 테이블. 접이형 테이블

care¹ /kɛr/ v [I, T] **to be concerned about or interested in someone or something** ‖ 사람이나 사물에 대해 걱정하거나 관심을 가지다. (…에)마음 쓰다.(…을)염려하다: He doesn't care about anybody but himself. 그는 자신 이외엔 아무도 신경쓰지 않는다. / I don't care what you do. 네가 무엇을 하든 관심없어.

SPOKEN PHRASES

1 who cares? used in order to say in an impolite way that you do not care about something because you do not think it is important ‖ 어떤 일을 중요하게 생각지 않아서 상관하지 않겠다고 무례하게 말하는 데 쓰여. 누가 신경쓰나?[아무도 신경 쓰지 않는다] **2 I/he/they etc. couldn't care less** used in order to say in an impolite way that someone does not care at all about something ‖ 어떤 것에 대해 전혀 개의치 않음을 무례하게 말하는 데 쓰여. 나/그/그들은 전혀 관심 없다[신경 쓰지 않는다] **3 what do I/you/they etc. care?** used in order to say in an impolite way that someone does not care at all about something ‖ 남이 어떤 것에 대해 전혀 개의치 않는다고 무례하게 말하는 데 쓰여. 나/너/그들이 왜 상관해?: What does he care? He'll get his money whatever happens. 그가 왜 신경 써? 어쨌든 그는 자신의 돈을 받을 거잖아. **4** FORMAL **to like or want something** ‖ 어떤 것을 좋아하거나 원하다. 바라다: Would you care to meet us after the show? 쇼가 끝난 다음에 우리와 만나 주시겠습니까? / I don't really care for peanuts. 나는 땅콩을 정말 좋아하지 않는다.

---

care for sb/sth phr v [T] **1 to help someone when s/he is sick or not able to do things for himself/herself** ‖ 남이 아프거나 스스로 어떤 일을 할 수 없을 때 도와 주다. …을 돌보다[간호하다]: Angie cared for her mother after her stroke. 앤지는 뇌졸중으로 쓰러진 어머니를 돌보

고 있다. **2 to do things to keep
something in good condition or working
correctly** ‖ 사물을 좋은 상태로 유지하거
나 올바르게 작동하게 어떤 일들을 하다.
유지 관리하다. 손질하다: *instructions on
caring for your new sofa* 새 소파 관리
[손질] 지침

care² n

**1 ▶HELP 도움◀ [U] the process of
helping someone who is sick or not able
to do things for himself/herself** ‖ 아프거
나 스스로 어떤 일을 할 수 없는 사람을
돕는 과정. 돌보기. 간호: *Your father will
need constant medical care.* 당신의 아버
지는 지속적인 치료가 필요합니다. / *the
care of young children* 어린 아이들 돌보
기

**2 ▶LOOKING AFTER STH …의 관리◀
[U] the process of doing things to
something so that it stays in good
condition and works correctly** ‖ 사물이
좋은 상태로 유지되어 올바르게 작동하도
록 어떤 일들을 하는 과정. 관리: *With
proper care, your washing machine
should last years.* 잘만 관리하면 세탁기
는 수년간 쓸 수 있습니다.

**3 take care of a) to watch and help
someone** ‖ 남을 보살피고 돕다. 돌보다:
Who's taking care of the baby? 누가 애
들을 돌보고 있습니까? **b) to do things to
keep something in good condition or
working correctly** ‖ 사물을 좋은 상태로
유지하거나 올바르게 작동하게 어떤 일들
을 하다. 관리[손질]하다: *Karl will take
care of the house while we're on
vacation.* 우리의 휴가 기간 동안 카알이
집을 관리할 것이다. **c) to do the work or
make the arrangements that are
necessary for something to happen** ‖ 어
떤 일이 일어나는 데 필요한 작업이나 준
비를 하다. 책임지고 …을 처리하다: *I'll
take care of making the reservations.* 내
가 예약을 책임질게. **d) to pay for
something** ‖ 어떤 일에 대해 지불하다. 계
산을 치르다: *Don't worry about the bill,
it's taken care of.* 계산 걱정은 마라, 이미
지불돼 있다.

**4 ▶CAREFULNESS 주의◀ [U]
carefulness to avoid damage, mistakes
etc.** ‖ 손상·실수 등을 피하는 조심성. 주
의: *Handle the package with care.* 포장
물 취급 주의 / *You'd better put more
care into your work!* 당신은 일에 좀 더
주의를 기울이는 게 좋겠어요!

**5 ▶WORRY 걱정◀ [C, U] feelings of
worry, concern, or unhappiness** ‖ 걱정
[근심, 불행]의 감정. 한탄. 고뇌: *Eddie
doesn't have a care in the world.*

(=doesn't have any problems or
worries) 에디는 세상 걱정할 게 없다

6 take care a)SPOKEN **used when
saying goodbye to family or friends** ‖ 가
족이나 친구들에게 작별 인사를 할 때에 쓰
여. 건강 조심해. 잘 지내 **b) to be
careful** ‖ 조심하다. 주의하다: *It's very
icy, so take care driving home.* (길이)매
우 미끄러우니까, 집까지 운전 조심해요.

**7 care of used when sending letters to
someone at someone else's address** ‖ 다
른 사람 주소지에 있는 어떤 사람에게 편
지를 보낼 때 쓰여. 전교(轉交). 댁내(宅
內): *Just send the package to me care of
my cousin.* 소포를 내 사촌집 주소를 써서
내게 보내 주시오.

ca·reen /kə'rin/ *v* [I] **to move quickly
forward in an uncontrolled way,
making sudden sideways movements** ‖
갑자기 옆으로 쏠리며 걷잡을 수 없이 빠
르게 앞으로 움직이다. 옆으로 휙 미끄러
지다: *Morillo's truck careened down
the embankment and burst into flames.*
모릴로의 차는 제방을 굴러 내려가 불이
붙었다.

ca·reer¹ /kə'rır/ *n* **1 a job or profession
that you have been trained for and
intend to do for a long time** ‖ 이제까지
훈련 받아왔고 오랫동안 할 마음이 있는
일이나 전문 분야. 직업: *a career in law*
법률직[변호사직] **2 the period of time in
your life that you spend working** ‖ 일생
중 일하면서 보낸 기간. 이력. 경력: *Will
spent most of his career as a teacher.* 윌
은 그의 경력의 대부분을 교사로 보냈다.
—see usage note at JOB

career² *adj* **intending to make a
particular job your career** ‖ 특정 직업으
로 경력을 쌓으려 하는. 직업적인: *a
career soldier* 직업군인

care·free /'kɛrfri/ *adj* **without any
problems or worries** ‖ 어떤 문제나 걱정
이 없는. 근심[걱정] 없는. 평안한: *a
carefree summer vacation* 평안한 여름
휴가

care·ful /'kɛrfəl/ *adj* **1 (be) careful!**
SPOKEN **used in order to tell someone to
think about what s/he is doing so that
something bad does not happen** ‖ 하고
있는 일에 나쁜 일이 생기지 않도록 잘 생
각해서 하라고 말하는 데에 쓰여. 조심해
라 **2 trying very hard to avoid doing
anything wrong or damaging something**
‖ 잘못을 범하거나 사물에 손상을 주지 않
도록 지극히 노력하는. 조심[주의]하는: *a
careful driver* 조심스런 운전자 / *Anna
was careful not to upset Steven.* 애나는
스티븐의 화를 돋구지 않도록 조심했다. /

Be careful with that ladder! 그 사다리 조심해! **3** paying a lot of attention to detail ‖ 세심한 데까지 많은 주의를 기울이는. 꼼꼼한. 면밀한. 신중한: *Dr. Eng did a careful examination.* 엥박사는 꼼꼼하게 검사했다. – **carefully** *adv* – **carefulness** *n* [U]

care·giv·er /ˈkɛrˌɡɪvɚ/ *n* someone who takes care of a child or of someone who is old or sick ‖ 어린이[노인, 환자]를 돌보는 사람. 유모. 보모. 간병인

care·less /ˈkɛrlɪs/ *adj* **1** not paying enough attention to what you are doing ‖ 하고 있는 일에 충분한 주의를 기울이지 않는. 부주의한. 태만한. 소홀한: *It was very careless of you to leave your keys in the car.* 차 안에 열쇠를 남겨 두다니 매우 부주의했다. **2** done without much effort or attention to detail ‖ 세심한 데까지 많은 노력이나 주의를 기울이지 않고 수행된. 정성[공]을 들이지 않은. 성의없이 대충 한: *This is very careless work – do it again!* 이 일은 너무 성의가 없군. 다시 하도록 해! – **carelessly** *adv* – **carelessness** *n* [U]

care pack·age /ˈ. ˌ../ *n* a package of food, candy etc. that is sent to someone living away from home, especially a student at college ‖ 가족을 떠나서 생활하는 사람, 특히 대학생에게 보내는 음식·과자 등의 꾸러미. 위문품. 소포

carer /ˈkɛrɚ/ *n* ⇨ CAREGIVER

ca·ress /kəˈrɛs/ *v* [T] to gently touch or kiss someone in a way that shows you love him/her ‖ 사랑의 표현으로 부드럽게 만지거나 키스하다. …을 애무하다. 어루만지다 – **caress** *n*

care·tak·er /ˈkɛrˌteɪkɚ/ *n* **1** someone whose job is to take care of a building or someone's land ‖ 건물이나 다른 사람의 땅을 관리해 주는 직업인. (건물·재산)관리인 **2** someone such as a nurse who takes care of other people ‖ 다른 사람들을 돌보는 간호사 등의 사람. 간병인 **3 caretaker government/administration** a government that has power only for a short time between the end of one government and the start of another ‖ 전임 정부의 만료와 차기 정부의 출범 사이에 단기간만 권한을 갖는 정부. 과도[임시] 정부

car·go /ˈkɑrɡoʊ/ *n, plural* **cargoes** [C, U] the goods being carried in a ship, plane, TRUCK etc. ‖ 배·비행기·트럭 등으로 운반되어지는 물자. 화물: *a cargo of oil* 석유 화물

Car·ib·be·an¹ /ˌkærɪˈbi·ən, kəˈrɪbi·ən/ *n* **the Caribbean** the Caribbean Sea (=sea east of Mexico), and the islands in it ‖ (멕시코 동쪽 바다)카리브 해와 그 지역 내의 군도

Caribbean² *adj* relating to or coming from the Caribbean ‖ 카리브에 관한 또는 카리브산(産)의. 카리브(산)의.

cari·bou /ˈkærəbu/ *n* a North American REINDEER ‖ 북미산 순록. 카리부

car·i·ca·ture¹ /ˈkærəkətʃɚ, -ˌtʃʊr/ *n* [C, U] a funny picture or description of someone that makes him/her look or seem more silly or amusing than s/he really is ‖ 사람을 실제보다 바보 같거나 재미있게 만드는 익살스런 그림 또는 묘사. 풍자화. 캐리커처

caricature² *v* [T] to draw or describe someone in a way that makes him/her seem silly or amusing ‖ 어떤 사람을 바보 같거나 재미있어 보이게 그리거나 묘사하다. …을 풍자적으로 그리다. 캐리커처로 표현하다 – **caricaturist** *n*

car·ing /ˈkɛrɪŋ/ *adj* providing care and support for others ‖ 다른 사람에 대한 관심과 지원을 제공하는. 남을 배려하는. 돌봐 주는: *a warm and caring person* 따뜻하고 배려 깊은 사람

car·jack·ing /ˈkɑrˌdʒækɪŋ/ *n* [C, U] the crime of using a weapon to force the driver of a car to drive you somewhere or give you his/her car ‖ 무기를 써서 운전자에게 강제로 다른 곳으로 가게 하거나 차를 강탈하는 범죄. 카재킹 – **carjacker** *n* – **carjack** *v* [T]

car·nage /ˈkɑrnɪdʒ/ *n* [U] FORMAL the killing and wounding of lots of people or animals, especially in a war ‖ 특히 전쟁에서 많은 사람이나 동물의 살상(殺傷). 대학살. 살육

car·nal /ˈkɑrnl/ *adj* FORMAL relating to the body or to sex ‖ 육체나 성에 관련된. 육욕의. 성욕의: *carnal desires* 육욕[성욕] – **carnally** *adv*

car·na·tion /kɑrˈneɪʃən/ *n* a sweet-smelling white, pink, or red flower ‖ 흰[분홍·붉은] 색의 향기나는 꽃. 카네이션

car·ni·val /ˈkɑrnəvəl/ *n* **1** [C, U] a public celebration with dancing, drinking, and entertainment, or the period when this takes place ‖ 춤·음주·놀이를 즐기는 대중 축제, 또는 이 행사가 열리는 기간. 사육제[카니발](기간): *carnival time in Rio* 리오의 축제 기간 **2** a noisy outdoor event where you can ride on special machines and play games for prizes ‖ 특별한 놀이 기구를 타거나 경품 게임을 할 수 있는 시끌벅적한 야외 행사

car·ni·vore /ˈkɑrnəˌvɔr/ *n* an animal

that eats meat ‖ 고기를 먹는 동물. 육식 동물 – **carnivorous** /kɑrˈnɪvərəs/ *adj*

car·ol¹ /ˈkærəl/ *n* ⇨ CHRISTMAS CAROL

carol² *v* [I] to sing CHRISTMAS CAROLs ‖ 크리스마스 캐럴을 부르다.

ca·rouse /kəˈraʊz/ *v* [I] to drink a lot of alcohol, be noisy, and have fun ‖ 많은 술을 마시며 소란스럽게 즐기다. 술마시며 흥청거리다. 떠들썩하게 술마시며 놀다

car·ou·sel /ˌkærəˈsɛl/ *n* **1** the circular moving belt that you collect your bags and SUITCASEs from at an airport ‖ 공항에서 손가방·여행 가방을 찾는 회전식 벨트. 소화물 환수대 **2** ⇨ MERRY-GO-ROUND **3** a circular piece of equipment that you put photographic SLIDEs into for showing on a SLIDE PROJECTOR ‖ 슬라이드 영사기에 투사용 사진 슬라이드 필름을 넣는 회전식 장비. 슬라이드트레이

carp¹ /kɑrp/ *n* [C, U] a large fish that lives in lakes or rivers, or the meat from this fish ‖ 호수나 강에서 사는 큰 물고기, 또는 이 물고기의 살. 잉어(고기)

carp² *v* [I] to complain about something or criticize someone all the time ‖ 항상 사물에 대해 불평하거나 다른 사람을 비판하다. 트집 잡다. 잔소리 하다

car·pen·ter /ˈkɑrpəntɚ/ *n* someone whose job is making and repairing wooden objects ‖ 나무 제품을 만들거나 수리하는 직업인. 목수. 대목

car·pen·try /ˈkɑrpəntri/ *n* [U] the art or work of a carpenter ‖ 목공 기술이나 목공예(품)

car·pet¹ /ˈkɑrpɪt/ *n* **1** [C, U] a heavy woven material for covering all of a floor and stairs, or a piece of this material ‖ 마루와 계단 전체를 덮는 두껍게 짠 직물, 또는 이 직물의 조각. 양탄자. 융단. 카펫 —compare RUG **2 a carpet of leaves/flowers etc.** LITERARY a thick layer of leaves etc. ‖ 나뭇잎 등의 두꺼운 층. 나뭇잎/꽃잎 등이 융단같이 깔린 층

carpet² *v* [T] to cover something with a carpet ‖ 카펫으로 사물을 덮다. 카펫을 깔다

car·pet·ing /ˈkɑrpətɪŋ/ *n* [U] ⇨ CARPET¹

car pool /ˈ. ./ *n* **1** a group of car owners who agree to drive everyone in the group to work, school etc. on different days, so that only one car is used at a time ‖ 각기 다른 요일에 한 번에 한 대를 이용해, 직장·학교까지 차를 태워 주기로 합의한 차량 소유주들의 집단. 카풀제[모임] **2** a group of cars owned by a company or other

organization so its members can use them ‖ 회사나 여타 조직에 의해 소유되어 그 조직원들이 사용할 수 있는 차량군(群). 공용차(제도)

car·port /ˈkɑrpɔrt/ *n* a shelter for a car that has a roof and is often built against the side of a house ‖ 지붕이 있고 종종 집 벽면에 잇대 지은 차량용 창고. 간이 차고 —compare GARAGE

car·riage /ˈkærɪdʒ/ *n* **1** a vehicle with wheels that is pulled by a horse ‖ 말이 끄는 바퀴 달린 차량. 마차 **2** the movable part of a machine that supports another part ‖ 다른 부분을 지원하는 기계의 움직이는 부분. 구동부: *a typewriter carriage* 타자기의(용지) 구동부 **3** [U] FORMAL the way someone walks and moves his/her head and body ‖ 사람이 걸으면서 머리와 신체를 움직이는 방식. 행동거지. 몸가짐. 자세. 태도 **4** ⇨ BABY CARRIAGE

car·ri·er /ˈkæriɚ/ *n* **1** a person or thing that moves goods or passengers from one place to another ‖ 물자나 승객을 한 곳에서 다른 곳으로 옮기는 사람이나 사물. 운반인[대]. 운송인[기] **2** someone who passes a disease to other people without having it himself/herself ‖ 자신은 질병에 걸리지 않고 다른 사람에게 옮기는 사람. 병균 매개자. 보균자

car·rot /ˈkærət/ *n* a long thick orange root with a pointed end, eaten raw or cooked as a vegetable ‖ 생으로 먹거나 야채로 요리해 먹는, 끝이 뾰족한 길고 두꺼운 오렌지색 뿌리. 당근 —see picture on page 944

car·rou·sel /ˌkærəˈsɛl/ *n* another spelling of CAROUSEL ‖ carousel의 다른 철자형

car·ry /ˈkæri/ *v*

1 ▶TAKE SOMEWHERE 다른 곳으로 나르다◀ [T] to take something somewhere by holding it, supporting it etc. ‖ 어떤 것을 들고, 받쳐서 다른 곳으로 가지고 가다. 운반[운송]하다. 나르다: *Can you carry that suitcase for me?* 저 가방 좀 날라 줄래? / *The bus was carrying 25 passengers.* 버스는 25명의 승객을 태우고 있었다. / *These pipes will carry oil across the desert.* 이 파이프는 사막을 가로질러 석유를 운반할 것이다. —see picture on page 947

2 ▶INFORMATION/NEWS ETC. 정보/뉴스 등◀ [T] to contain a particular piece of information, story, advertisement etc. ‖ 특정 정보·기사·광고 등을 게재하다. 보도하다. 싣다: *All the newspapers carried articles about the plane crash.* 모든 신문들이 비행기 추락 기사를 보도했다.

3 ▶HAVE WITH YOU 소지하다◀ [T] to have something with you in your pocket, on your belt, in your bag etc. ‖ 사물을 주머니 속에[벨트에 차고, 가방 속에 넣어서]소지하다. 가지고 다니다. 지참[휴대]하다: *Larry always carries a gun.* 래리는 항상 총을 소지하고 다닌다.

4 ▶DISEASE 질병◀ [T] to have a disease and pass it to others ‖ 질병을 보유하고 다른 사람에게 옮기다. 전(파)하다. 퍼뜨리다: *The disease was carried by rats.* 그 병은 쥐 때문에 옮겨졌다.

5 ▶AVAILABLE TO USE/BUY 사용/구매할 수 있는◀ [T] to have something that is available for people to use or buy ‖ 사람들이 사용 또는 구매할 수 있도록 어떤 것을 보유하다. (재고로) 가지고 있다[갖추고 있다]: *All our products carry a 1 year guarantee.* 우리의 모든 제품은 1년간 품질이 보증된다. / *I'm sorry, we don't carry that brand anymore.* 미안합니다. 그 제품은 더 이상 취급하지 않습니다.

6 be/get carried away to be or become so excited that you are no longer in control of what you do or say ‖ 너무 흥분되어서 더 이상 행동·발언을 조절하지 못하다. 흥분해서 정신을 뺏기다. 열광하다: *I got carried away and bought three suits!* 나는 그 양복이 너무 맘에 들어서 세 벌이나 샀어!

7 ▶MOVE 움직임◀ to hold your body in a particular way as you move ‖ 움직일 때 특정하게 자세를 취하다. 처신하다. 특정 행동거지로 움직이다: *It was obvious by the way they carried themselves that they were soldiers.* 그들이 군인이라는 것은 행동거지로 보아 분명했다.

8 carry weight to have some influence over someone ‖ 다른 사람에 대해 영향력을 갖다. 무게[비중]이 크다: *Lee's opinions carry a lot of weight with the boss.* 리의 의견은 사장에게 큰 영향력을 발휘한다.

9 ▶RESULT 결과를 낳다◀ [T] to have something as a usual or necessary result ‖ 보통 또는 당연한 결과로 어떤 것을 갖다. …한 결과로 나타나다: *Murder carries a life sentence in this state.* 살인은 이 주에서 종신형[무기 징역]을 받게 된다. / *The job carries certain risks.* 그 일은 상당한 위험이 따른다.

10 carry sth too far to do or say too much about something ‖ 어떤 것에 대해 너무 많은 일을 하거나 지나치게 많은 말을 하다. 도를 지나치다[넘다]: *It was funny at first, but you've carried the joke too far.* 처음에는 재미있었지만 너의 농담은 도를 넘어섰다.

11 ▶SUPPORT 지탱하다◀ [T] to support the weight of something else ‖ 여타 다른 것의 무게를 지탱하다. 지지하다. 떠받치다: *Those columns carry the whole roof.* 그 기둥은 전체 지붕을 떠받치고 있다.

12 ▶TRAVEL/GO 여행하다/가다◀ [I] to be able to go as far as a particular place or a particular distance ‖ 특정 장소나 거리만큼 멀리 갈 수 있다. …까지 이르다, 미치다]. 도달하다: *The boom carried as far as the lake.* 쾅 하는 소리가 호수까지 도달했다. / *These bullets carry for two miles.* 이 총알은 2마일이나 날아간다.

13 ▶ELECTION 선거에 이기다◀ [T] to win an election in a state or particular area ‖ 어떤 주·특정 구역의 선거에서 승리하다. 지지를 획득하다[얻어내다]: *Reagan carried California in 1980.* 레이건은 1980년 캘리포니아주 선거에서 승리했다.

14 ▶BEHAVE 행동하다◀ [T] to behave in a particular way or have a particular quality ‖ 특정하게 행동하거나 어떤 특성을 갖다. 행동거지를 …하게 보이다[나타내다]. …한 행동 특징이 있다: *Kevin always carries himself well.* (=stands and walks straight) 케빈은 항상 자세를 똑바로 하고 걷는다. / *Matthew's voice did not carry much conviction* (=he did not sound certain). 매튜의 목소리는 확신 있게 들리지 않았다.

15 be carried to be approved by a vote ‖ 투표에 의해 승인되다. 통과되다. 가결되다: *The motion has been carried.* 그 동의안은 가결되었다.

16 carry a tune to sing correctly ‖ 정확하게 노래하다. 곡조에 맞춰 노래부르다

17 ▶MATHEMATICS 산술◀ [T] also **carry over** to move a total to the next row of figures for adding to other numbers ‖ 다른 숫자에 더하기 위해 합계치를 다음 열의 수치로 옮기다. 이월해서 합산하다

carry sth ↔ **forward** *phr v* [T] ➪ **carry over**

carry sth ↔ **off** *phr v* [T] **1** to do something successfully ‖ 어떤 일을 성공적으로 하다. 완수하다. 잘 해내다: *I really don't know how I managed to carry that presentation off!* 내가 그 발표를 어떻게 잘 해 낼 수 있었는지 정말 모르겠어! **2** to win a prize ‖ 상을 획득하다. 수상하다: *Fred carried off all the top awards at the banquet.* 프레드는 시상식장에서 모든 최고상을 수상했다.

carry on *phr v* **1** [I,T **carry on** sth] to

continue doing something ‖ 어떤 일을 계속해서 하다. 계속해서 …하다. 속행하다: *You'll get sick if you carry on working like that.* 너는 계속해서 그렇게 일하다간 병에 걸릴 것이다. **2** [I] SPOKEN to behave in a silly or excited way ‖ 바보같이 또는 흥분해서 행동하다. 속없이[야단스럽게] 행동하다. 소란을 피우다: *We won't get anything done if you two don't stop carrying on!* 너희 둘이 계속 소란 피우면 우리는 아무것도 끝내지 못할 거야! **3** [I] OLD-FASHIONED to have a sexual relationship with someone when you should not ‖ 남과 해서는 안 될 성관계를 맺다. 정을 통하다. 바람피다

carry sth ↔ **out** *phr v* [T] **1** to do something that needs to be organized and planned ‖ 조직적·계획적이어야 할 어떤 일을 실행하다. 수행해 내다. 성취[달성]하다: *Teenagers carried out a survey on attitudes to drugs.* 십대 청소년들이 마약에 대한 태도에 관한 설문 조사를 수행해 냈다. **2 carry out an order/threat etc.** to do something that you have said you will do or that someone has told you to do ‖ 하겠다고 한 일 또는 누군가가 하라고 한 일을 수행하다. 명령/협박을 이행하다: *I'm supposed to carry out her instructions and report back.* 나는 그녀의 지시를 이행하고 결과를 보고하기로 되어 있다.

carry sth ↔ **over** *phr v* [T] to make an amount of something available to be used at a later time ‖ 현재 쓸 수 있는 일정 분량을 나중에 이용할 수 있게 만들다. 이용을 다음으로 넘기다. 이월해서 쓸 수 있게 하다: *Can I carry over my vacation time to next year?* 내 휴가 기간을 내년으로 넘겨서 쓸 수 있을까요?

carry through *phr v* [T] **1** [**carry** sth ↔ **through**] to complete or finish something successfully ‖ 어떤 일을 성공적으로 완료하거나 끝내다. 끝까지 실행하다. 완수[달성]하다: *Once he starts a project, he always carries it through.* 그는 일단 하나의 사업 계획을 시작하면 언제나 끝까지 해낸다. **2** [**carry** sb **through** (sth)] to help someone to manage during an illness or a difficult period ‖ 와병중이나 어려운 시기를 견디어 내도록 돕다. …이 …을 뚫고 나가게 [이겨내게] 지원하다: *Joe's courage carried him through Amanda's death.* 조의 용기가 그에게 아만다의 죽음을 견디어 내게 했다.

car·ry·all /ˈkæriˌɔl/ *n* a large soft bag, usually made of cloth ‖ 보통 천으로 된 크고 유연한 가방. 여행용 큰 가방

carry-on /ˈ.. ˌ./ *adj, n* a bag that you can take on a plane with you ‖ 소지하고 비행기에 탈 수 있는 가방. 기내 휴대 수하물

car·ry·out /ˈkæriˌaʊt/ *n* ⇨ TAKEOUT

car seat /ˈ. ./ *n* a special seat for babies or young children that you attach to the seat of a car ‖ 유아나 아동을 위해 자동차의 좌석에 부착하는 특수 의자. 유아용 보조 의자

car·sick /ˈ. ./ *adj* feeling sick because of the movement of traveling in a car ‖ 차 속에서 주행의 흔들림에 의해 구역질이 나는. 차멀미의 **– carsickness** *n* [U]

cart¹ /kɑrt/ *n* **1** a large wire basket on wheels used in a SUPERMARKET ‖ 슈퍼마켓에서 사용되는 바퀴 달린 큰 철망 바구니. 수레형 장바구니 **2** a vehicle with two or four wheels ‖ 두 개 또는 네 개의 바퀴가 달린 수레. 카트: *a golf cart* 골프카트 / *a wooden cart drawn* (=pulled) *by a horse* 말이 끄는 목제 수레 **3** a small table on wheels, used for moving and serving food ‖ 이동하면서 음식을 제공하는 데 쓰이는, 바퀴 달린 작은 테이블. 푸드카트 **4 put the cart before the horse** to do things in the wrong order ‖ 잘못된 순서로 일을 하다. 순서를 뒤바꾸다. 본말을 전도하다

cart² *v* [I, T] to carry or take something or someone somewhere ‖ 사물이나 사람을 어떤 곳으로 실어 나르거나 데려가다. 운반하다: *Workers carted away several tons of trash.* 일꾼들이 수 톤의 쓰레기를 실어 냈다. / *The sheriff carted him off to jail.* 보안관이 그를 유치장으로 호송했다.

car·tel /kɑrˈtɛl/ *n* [U] a group of companies that work together to control prices on a particular product ‖ 특정 제품에 대한 가격을 함께 통제하는 일군의 기업들. 담합. 카르텔

car·ti·lage /ˈkɑrtl-ɪdʒ/ *n* [C, U] a strong substance that stretches and that is around the joints in your body ‖ 신체의 관절 부위를 싸고 있고 늘어나는 강한 조직. 연골(낭)

car·tog·ra·phy /kɑrˈtɑɡrəfi/ *n* [U] the skill or practice of making maps ‖ 지도를 제작하는 기술이나 업무. 지도 제작(법) **– cartographer** *n*

car·ton /ˈkɑrt'n/ *n* a box made from stiff paper or plastic, used for holding food or drinks ‖ 빳빳한 종이나 플라스틱으로 만들어져 음식물이나 음료수를 담는 데 쓰는 박스. 카턴: *a milk carton* 우유 박스 —see picture at CONTAINER

car·toon /kɑrˈtun/ *n* **1** a funny short

movie made using characters that are drawn and not real ‖ 실재 인물이 아닌 그림으로 그려진 등장 인물로 만든 재미있는 짧은 영화. 만화 영화. 카툰: *a Bugs Bunny cartoon* 벅스 버니(토끼) 만화 영화 **2** a funny drawing, usually in a newspaper, that tells a joke or something humorous about the news ‖ 보통 신문에 실려 뉴스에 대한 농담이나 우스개 소리를 하는 재미있는 그림. 시사 만화. 풍자화 – **cartoonist** *n*

car·tridge /ˈkɑrtrɪdʒ/ *n* **1** a small piece of equipment that you put inside something to make it work ‖ 어떤 것이 작동하도록 끼워 넣는 작은 부품. 카트리지: *computer case cartridges* 컴퓨터 게임 카트리지 **2** a tube containing explosive material and a bullet for a gun ‖ 폭발물·총알이 들어 있는 통. 탄창. 탄약통

cart·wheel /ˈkɑrt˺-wil/ *n* a movement in which you turn completely over by throwing yourself sideways onto your hands with your arms straight and bringing your legs straight over your head ‖ 팔을 쭉 펴서 손을 짚고 다리를 똑바로 머리 위로 올리며 몸을 옆으로 던져 완전히 몸을 뒤짚는 동작. 옆으로 재주넘기 – **cartwheel** *v* [I]

cartwheel

carve /kɑrv/ *v* **1** [T] to cut something, especially wood or stone, into a particular shape ‖ 특히 나무나 돌을 특정한 형상으로 깎다. 조각하다. 새기다: *Their totem poles are carved from a single tree.* 그들의 토템폴[수호 장승]은 통나무로 조각되어 있다. **2** [I, T] to cut cooked meat into smaller pieces with a large knife ‖ 큰 칼로 조리된 고기를 작은 조각으로 잘라내다. 썰어내다. 베어내다: *Dad always carves the turkey.* 언제나 아빠가 칠면조 고기를 자른다. **3** [T] also **carve out** to become successful by working hard, especially in business ‖ 특히 사업에서 열심히 일해서 성공하게 되다. 사업을 일구어 내다[개척하다]: *She has carved a niche/place/career for herself in the competitive world of advertising.* 그녀는 경쟁이 치열한 광고업계에서 혼자 힘으로 틈새[영역, 경력]을 개척해 왔다.

carve sth ↔ **up** *phr v* [T] DISAPPROVING to divide something into different parts ‖ 사물을 각각 다른 부분으로 나누다. 분

할하다. 가르다: *The Assembly is carving up the area into new electoral districts.* 의회는 그 지역을 새로운 선거구로 분할하고 있다.

carv·ing /ˈkɑrvɪŋ/ *n* **1** an object made by cutting wood, stone etc. ‖ 나무·돌 등을 깎아서 만든 물체. 조각물[품] **2** [U] the activity or skill of cutting wood, stone etc. ‖ 나무·돌 등을 조각하는 행위나 기술. 조각(술)

car wash /ˈ. ./ *n* a place where you can take your car to be washed with special equipment ‖ 특수 장비로 차를 세차할 수 있는 곳. 세차장

cas·cade¹ /kæˈskeɪd/ *n* **1** a stream of water that falls over rocks ‖ 바위 위에서 떨어지는 물의 흐름. 폭포 **2** something that seems to flow or hang down ‖ 흘러 내리거나 매달려 있는 모양의 것. 물결 모양으로 드리워진 상태: *Her hair fell in a cascade of soft curls.* 그녀의 부드러운 곱슬머리가 물결처럼 흘러 내렸다.

cas·cade² *v* [I, T] to flow in large amounts ‖ 대량으로 흐르다. 폭포처럼 떨어지다[뜨리다]

case¹ /keɪs/ *n*

1 ▶SITUATION/EXAMPLE 경우/예◀ [C usually singular] a particular situation that exists, or an example of that situation ‖ 존재하는 특정한 상황, 또는 그 상황의 예(例): *The action was a clear case of sexual harassment.* 그 행위는 명백한 성희롱을 한 경우였다. / *People working together can make a difference, and this certainly seems to be the case in Maria's neighborhood.* 사람들은 함께 일해서 변화를 이룰 수 있고 마리아의 이웃은 분명하게 이 실례가 된 것으로 보인다. / *Some flowers can't survive the cold – impatiens are a case in point.* (=a clear example) 몇몇 꽃들은 추위에 견디지 못한다. 봉선화가 대표적인 예이다. / *No one should be here after hours, but in your case I'll make an exception.* 아무도 업무 시간 후에는 여기에 있을 수가 없습니다만 당신의 경우에는 예외로 하겠습니다.

2 ▶COURT 법정◀ a question that must be decided in a court of law ‖ 법정에서 결정되어져야 하는 문제. 소송(사건): *a court case dealing with cruelty to animals* 동물 학대를 다루는 소송 사건

3 ▶POLICE 경찰◀ an event or set of events that the police deal with ‖ 경찰이 다루는 한 사건이나 일련의 사고들: *Sturgis is investigating a murder case.* 스터기스는 살인 사건을 수사중이다.

4 ▶ARGUMENT 논쟁◀ all the facts or

reasons that support one side of an argument ‖ 논쟁하고 있는 한 쪽을 지지하는 모든 사실과 이유. 논거. 논증: *The prosecution's case against him is very strong.* 그를 반박할 검찰측의 논거는 매우 강하다. / *There is a good case for changing the rule.* 그 규칙을 변경시키는 데에는 충분한 논거가 있다.
5 (just) in case a) used in order to say that someone should do something because something else might happen or be true ‖ 다른 어떤 일이 일어나거나 사실일 수 있기 때문에 남에게 어떤 것을 해야 한다고 말하는 데 쓰여. …인 경우에는. …에 대비하여: *Take your umbrella in case it rains.* 비올 것에 대비하여 우산을 가지고 가거라. **b)** used like "if" ‖ "만일"의 의미로 쓰여: *In case you missed the program, here's a summary of the story.* 그 프로그램을 못보고 놓쳤다면, 여기 그 내용의 요약본이 있다.
6 ▶CONTAINER 용기◀ a container for storing something ‖ 물건을 담는 용기. 그릇. 상자: *a jewelry case* 보석 상자 / *a case of wine* 포도주 한 상자
7 in case of if or when something happens ‖ 어떤 일이 발생하면, 또는 발생할 때. 만약 …인 경우에는: *In case of your death, your family will receive $50,000.* 당신이 사망한다면 당신 가족은 5만 달러를 받게 됩니다.
8 ▶DISEASE/ILLNESS 병/질환◀ an example of a disease or illness, or the person suffering this disease or illness ‖ 병이나 질환의 증례(症例), 또는 이 병이나 질환에 걸려 있는 환자. 병상[증상]. 환자: *There have been ten cases of malaria in the village recently.* 최근에 말라리아 환자가 10명 발생했다. / *a bad case of sunburn* 심하게 볕에 탄 증세
9 in that case SPOKEN used in order to describe what you will do or what will happen as a result of something ‖ 어떤 것의 결과로 무엇이 일어날 것이라든지 또는 자신이 무엇을 할 것이라고 설명하는 데에 쓰여. 그럴 경우에는: *"I'll be home late tonight." "Well, in that case, I won't cook dinner."* "오늘 저녁 늦게 집에 올 거야." "알았어, 그러면 저녁 식사 준비 하지 않을게."
10 in any case used in order to say that a fact or situation remains the same even if other things change ‖ 비록 다른 것들이 변한다 해도 사실이나 상황이 같은 상태를 유지할 것이라고 말하는 데 쓰여. 어떠한 경우에도: *Sure we'll take you home – we're going that way in any case.* 우리가 반드시 너를 집에 데려다 주

겠다. 무슨 일이 있어도 그렇게 할게.
11 be on sb's case/get off sb's case SPOKEN to be criticizing someone a lot, or to stop criticizing him/her ‖ 남을 심하게 비난하다, 또는 비난하는 것을 멈추다.
12 ▶GRAMMAR 문법◀ [C, U] TECHNICAL the form of a word, usually a noun, that shows its relationship to other words in a sentence ‖ 문장에서 다른 단어와의 관계를 보여 주는, 일반적으로 명사의 단어 형태. 격(格) —see also LOWER CASE, UPPER CASE
case² v 1 be cased in to be surrounded by a substance ‖ 물질로 둘러싸이다: *The building girders are cased in cement.* 그 건물의 대들보는 시멘트로 발라져 있다.
2 case the joint/place SLANG to look around a place so that something can be stolen from it later ‖ 나중에 어떤 것을 도둑질할 수 있게 장소를 살피다. 미리 답사하다. 사전 조사를 하다
case·load /'keɪsloʊd/ *n* the number of people a doctor, lawyer etc. has to deal with ‖ 의사·변호사 등이 담당하는 사람의 수. 담당[취급] 건수
case stud·y /ˌ. ˈ../ *n* a detailed study of a particular person, group, or situation over a long period of time ‖ 장기간에 걸쳐서 하는 특정한 사람[단체, 상황]에 관한 상세한 연구. 사례 연구
case·work /'keɪswɚk/ *n* [U] work done to help particular people or families with their social problems ‖ 사회적 문제를 가진 특정의 사람이나 가족을 돕기 위해 행하는 일. 사회 복지 사업 – **caseworker** *n*
cash¹ /kæʃ/ *n* [U] **1** money in the form of coins and bills ‖ 동전·지폐 형태의 돈. 현금: *"Are you paying by credit card?" "No, I'll pay cash."* "신용 카드로 지불할 거예요?" "아뇨, 현금으로 지불하겠습니다." / *He had about $200 in cash in his wallet.* 그는 지갑에 약 200달러의 현금을 가지고 있었다. **2** INFORMAL money in the bank ‖ 은행에 있는 돈. 은행 잔고: *I'm kind of short of cash at the moment.* 나는 현재 잔고가 부족하다.
cash² v [T] to exchange a check for money ‖ 수표를 현금으로 교환하다. 환전하다: *Can I get this check cashed here?* 이 수표를 여기에서 현금으로 바꿀 수 있습니까? – **cashable** *adj*
cash in *phr v* **1** [I] to gain advantages from a situation ‖ 어떤 상태에서 이득을 얻다: *Brooks is cashing in on his new-found popularity.* 최근에 유명해진 덕을 보고 있다. **2** [T **cash** sth ↔ **in**] to exchange something for its value in

money ‖ 어떤 것의 가치만큼 돈으로 바꾸다.: *We decided to cash in our insurance policy early.* 우리는 초기에 보험 증서를 현금으로 바꾸기로 결정했다.

cash cow /ˌ. './ *n* INFORMAL a business or product you can always depend on to make a profit ‖ 이윤을 창출하기 위해 항상 의존할 수 있는 사업이나 제품. 돈벌이가 되는 상품[사업]

cash crop /ˌ. './ *n* a crop that is grown to be sold rather than to be used by the people growing it ‖ 재배해서 사용하기보다는 판매 목적으로 재배되는 작물. 환금(換金) 작물

cash·ew /ˈkæʃu, kæˈʃu/ *n* a small curved nut that you can eat, or the tropical American tree on which these nuts grow ‖ 식용의 작고 구부러진 견과, 또는 이런 견과가 자라는 열대 아메리카산 나무. 캐슈

cash flow /ˈ. ./ *n* [singular, U] the movement of money into and out of a company ‖ 기업으로 들어오고 나가는 돈의 움직임. 현금의 흐름[유입과 유출]

cash·ier /kæˈʃɪɚ/ *n* someone whose job is to receive and pay out money in a store ‖ 가게에서 돈을 받고 잔돈을 거슬러 주는 직업인. 현금 출납원

cash·mere /ˈkæʒmɪr, ˈkæʃ-/ *n* [U] a type of fine soft wool ‖ 가늘고 부드러운 양털. 캐시미어: *an expensive cashmere sweater* 값비싼 캐시미어 스웨터

cash on de·liv·er·y /ˌ. . .ˈ.../ *n* [singular] ⇨ C.O.D.

cash reg·is·ter /ˈ. ˌ.../ *n* a machine used in stores to keep money in and to show how much customers have to pay ‖ 손님이 얼마나 지불해야 하는지 보여 주고 돈을 보관하기 위해 가게에서 사용하는 기계. 금전 등록기

cash-strapped /ˈ. ./ *adj* not having enough money ‖ 돈을 충분히 가지고 있지 않은: *a cash-strapped company* 자금 사정이 좋지 않은 회사

cas·ing /ˈkeɪsɪŋ/ *n* an outer layer of rubber, metal etc. that covers and protects something inside of it ‖ 안에 있는 물건을 덮어 보호하는 고무·금속 등의 바깥층. 포장(재료)

ca·si·no /kəˈsinoʊ/ *n* a place where people try to win money by playing games ‖ 사람들이 게임을 해서 돈을 따려고 하는 장소. 카지노

cask /kæsk/ *n* a round wooden container used for holding wine, or the amount contained in this ‖ 포도주를 보관하는 데 사용하는 둥근 나무로 된 통, 또는 그 통에 담긴 양. 통. 한 통의 양

cas·ket /ˈkæskɪt/ *n* ⇨ COFFIN

cas·se·role /ˈkæsəˌroʊl/ *n* [C, U] a mixture of meat and vegetables that are cooked together slowly, or the large dish that this food is served in ‖ 서서히 함께 요리되는 고기와 야채의 혼합물이나 이 요리를 담는 큰 식기. 찜냄비(요리)

cas·sette /kəˈsɛt/ *n* a small flat plastic case used for playing or recording sound or pictures; TAPE ‖ 소리나 화상을 재생하거나 기록하는 데 사용되는 작고 납작한 플라스틱 상자. 카세트; ㈜ tape

cast¹ /kæst/ *v* cast, cast, casting [T]
1 ▶MOVIE/TV 영화/텔레비전◀ to give an actor a part in a movie, play etc. ‖ 영화·연극 등에서 배우에게 배역을 주다. 역을 맡기다
2 cast light on/onto a) to explain or give new information about something ‖ 어떤 것에 대한 새로운 정보를 설명하거나 제시하다: *Can you cast any light on the meaning of these figures?* 이들 수치들의 의미에 대해 설명해 주실 수 있습니까? **b)** LITERARY to send light onto a surface ‖ 표면에 빛을 내다. 비추다
3 cast a shadow LITERARY to make a shadow appear on something ‖ 그림자를 어떤 것 위에 나타나게 하다. 그림자를 드리우다: *trees casting a shadow across the lawn* 잔디밭을 가로질러 그림자를 드리우는 나무
4 cast a spell on/over a) to make someone feel very strongly attracted to something and keep his/her attention completely ‖ 사람을 어떤 것에 강하게 매료시키고 관심을 사로잡다. …을 매혹시키다 **b)** to say magic words to make something happen ‖ 어떤 것이 일어나게 주문을 읊다. …에 대한 주문을 걸다
5 cast doubt on to make someone feel less certain about something ‖ 어떤 것에 대한 확신을 덜 느끼게 하다. 의심하게 하다: *I didn't mean to cast doubt on Arthur's version of the story.* 나는 아서가 전하는 그 이야기를 의심하려는 것은 아니었다.
6 cast a vote to vote in an election ‖ 선거에서 투표하다.
7 ▶ART 예술◀ to make something by pouring metal or plastic into a specially shaped container ‖ 특수 형틀에 금속물이나 플라스틱을 부어 어떤 것을 만들다. 주조하다: *a statue of Lincoln cast in bronze* 청동으로 주조한 링컨의 동상
8 ▶THROW 던지다◀ to throw something somewhere ‖ 어떤 것을 어디에 던지다: *fishermen casting their nets into the sea* 바다에 그물을 던지는 어부들

cast sb/sth ↔ **aside** *phr v* [T] to get rid of something or someone in a careless way ‖ 사물이나 사람을 경솔하게 없애다. 제거하다. 버리다: *The new policy casts aside decades of work.* 그 새 정책으로 수십년간 해온 일은 없어지게 된다.

cast off *phr v* **1** [I, T **cast off** sth] to untie the rope that keeps a boat on shore so that it can sail away ‖ 출항할 수 있게 해안가에 배를 매어 둔 밧줄을 풀다. **2** [T **cast** sb/sth ↔ **off**] LITERARY to get rid of something or someone ‖ 사물이나 사람을 제거하다. 버리다: *a country that has cast off Communist rule* 공산주의 지배에서 벗어난 나라

cast sb/sth ↔ **out** *phr v* [T] LITERARY to make someone or something go away using force ‖ 사람이나 사물을 무력을 사용해서 쫓아 버리다. 내쫓다

cast² *n* **1** all of the actors in a movie ‖ 영화의 출연자 전원. 캐스트. 배역: *an all-star cast* 스타 총출연 **2** a hard cover for a part of your body that supports a broken bone while it gets better ‖ 부러진 뼈가 낫는 동안에 지지하도록 신체의 일부에 씌우는 딱딱한 덮개. 깁스: *a leg cast* 다리에 한 깁스 **3** a container with a special shape into which you can pour metal or plastic to make a particular object ‖ 특정한 물체를 만들기 위해 금속이나 플라스틱 용액을 부을 수 있게 한 특별한 모양의 틀. 거푸집. 주형(鑄型) **4** an act of throwing a fishing line ‖ 낚싯줄을 던지는 행위. 던지기

cast·a·way /ˈkæstəˌweɪ/ *n* someone who is alone on an island after his/her ship has sunk ‖ 배가 가라앉은 후 무인도에 홀로 남은 사람. 표류자

caste /kæst/ *n* [C, U] one of the social classes in India into which people are born, that cannot be changed ‖ 사람이 태어나면서 갖게 되고 바꿀 수 없는 인도의 사회 계층의 하나. 인도의 세습적 계급 제도. 카스트

cast·er /ˈkæstə/ *n* a small wheel fixed to the bottom of a piece of furniture so it can be moved ‖ 움직일 수 있게 하기 위해 가구 밑에 부착해 놓은 작은 바퀴. 이동용 바퀴

cas·ti·gate /ˈkæstəˌgeɪt/ *v* [T] FORMAL to criticize or punish someone in a severe way ‖ 사람을 가혹하게 비판하거나 벌주다. (…을)혹평하다. 징계[응징]하다 – **castigation** /ˌkæstəˈgeɪʃən/ *n* [U]

cast·ing /ˈkæstɪŋ/ *n* [U] the act of choosing actors for a movie, play etc. ‖ 영화·연극 등에서 배우를 선정하는 행위. 캐스팅: *a casting director* 배역 감독

cast i·ron /ˌ ˈ../ *n* [U] a type of iron that is very hard but breaks easily ‖ 매우 단단하나 쉽게 깨지는 철의 종류. 주철(鑄鐵)

cast-i·ron /ˌ ˈ../ *adj* **1** made of CAST IRON ‖ 주철로 만든: *a cast-iron skillet* 주철로 만든 후라이팬 **2** INFORMAL very hard or strong ‖ 매우 단단하거나 강한: *a cast-iron stomach* (=one that does not get upset) 튼튼한 위장

cas·tle /ˈkæsəl/ *n* a very large strong building built in past times to protect the people inside from attack ‖ 안에 있는 사람들을 공격으로부터 보호하기 위해 예전에 지은 매우 크고 튼튼한 건물. 성 (城)

cast·off /ˈkæstɔf/ *n* INFORMAL something you no longer want, that you give to someone else who can use it ‖ 어떤 것을 더 이상 원하지 않아서 사용할 수 있는 다른 사람에게 준 것. 버림받은 것 – **cast-off** *adj*

cas·trate /ˈkæstreɪt/ *v* [T] to remove the sexual organs of a male animal or a man ‖ 수컷 동물이나 남성의 성 기관을 제거하다. 거세하다 – **castration** /kæˈstreɪʃən/ *n* [C, U]

cas·u·al /ˈkæʒuəl, -ʒəl/ *adj* **1** not formal, or not for a formal situation ‖ 격식을 차리지 않은, 또는 격식적인 상황을 위한 것이 아닌. 격의 없는. 평상시의: *casual clothes* 격식을 차리지 않은 옷[평상복] / *a casual meal* 격식 차리지 않은 간단한 음식 **2** relaxed and not worried about things ‖ 일에 관해 긴장을 풀고 걱정하지 않는. 대수롭지 않게 여기는: *His casual attitude toward work really irritates me.* 일에 대한 그의 태평한 태도는 정말 나를 짜증나게 한다. **3** without any clear aim or serious interest ‖ 뚜렷한 목표나 진지한 관심 없이. 건성의: *a casual glance at the newspapers* 신문을 건성으로 대충 훑어봄 / *She wanted something more than a casual relationship.* 그녀는 가벼운 관계 이상의 특별함을 원했다. **4** happening by chance without being planned ‖ 미리 계획하지 않고 우연히 일어나는. 우발적인. 즉석의: *a casual remark* 무심코 한 말 **5** temporary, or used for only a short time ‖ 일시적인, 또는 단지 잠시 동안 사용되는. 임시의: *casual workers* 임시 노동자들 – **casually** *adv* – **casualness** *n* [U]

cas·u·al·ty /ˈkæʒəlti, -ʒuəlti/ *n* **1** someone who is hurt in an accident or a battle ‖ 사고나 전쟁에서 다친 사람. 사상 [부상]자: *The army suffered heavy casualties.* (=a lot of people were hurt or killed) 그 군대는 막대한 사상자를 내는 피해를 입었다. **2 be a casualty of** to suffer because of a particular action || 특정한 조치로 어려움을 겪다. …의 희생자가 되다: *The city library is the latest casualty of the cutbacks.* 그 시립 도서관이 가장 최근에 예산 삭감조치에 희생되었다.

cat /kæt/ *n* **1** a small animal with four legs that is often kept as a pet or used for catching mice (MOUSE) || 종종 애완용으로 기르거나 쥐를 잡는 데 이용하는 네 발 달린 작은 동물. 고양이 **2** a large animal that is related to this animal, such as a lion || 사자 등 이 동물과 동족관계에 있는 큰 동물. 고양잇과 동물 **3 let the cat out of the bag** INFORMAL to tell a secret without intending to || 뜻하지 않게 비밀을 말하다. 무심코 비밀을 누설하다

cat·a·clysm /'kætə,klɪzəm/ *n* LITERARY a sudden violent event or change, such as a big flood or EARTHQUAKE || 큰 홍수나 지진 등의 갑작스럽고 격렬한 사건이나 변화. 격변 **– cataclysmic** /,kætə'klɪzmɪk/ *adj*

cat·a·log¹, catalogue /'kætl,ɔg, -,ag/ *n* **1** a book with pictures and information about goods or services that you can buy || 구매할 수 있는 상품이나 서비스에 대한 그림과 정보가 실린 책. 카탈로그: *the Sears catalog* 시어스 백화점 카탈로그 **2** a list of the objects, paintings, books etc. in a place || 한 장소에 있는 물건·그림·서적 등의 목록. 카탈로그. 일람표. 안내서: *a museum catalog* 박물관 안내서

catalog² *v* [T] to put a list of things into a particular order and write it into a CATALOG || 물건의 목록을 특정 순서대로 카탈로그에 써 넣다. …을 목록에 싣다. …의 목록을 만들다

cat·a·lyst /'kætl-ɪst/ *n* **1** someone or something that makes an important event or change happen || 중요한 사건이나 변화를 일으키는 사람이나 사물. 계기. 자극. 촉매. 요인: *The women's movement became a catalyst for change in the workplace.* 여성 운동은 일터에서 변화를 일으키는 계기가 되었다. **2** a substance that makes a chemical reaction happen more quickly, without being changed itself || 그 자체는 변화하지 않고 화학적 반응을 보다 촉진시키는 물질. 촉매

cat·a·ma·ran /,kætəmə'ræn/ *n* a SAILBOAT with two separate HULLs (=the part that goes in the water) || 두 개의 분리된 선체를 가진 범선. 쌍동선

cat·a·pult¹ /'kætə,pʌlt, -,pʊlt/ *v* [T] **1** to become famous or successful extremely suddenly || 느닷없이 유명해지거나 성공하다: *The character of "Rocky" catapulted Stallone to stardom.* Rocky의 주연은 스탤론을 스타의 지위로 급부상시켰다. **2** to shoot something from a CATAPULT, or to throw something with the movement of a catapult || 투석기에서 어떤 것을 쏘다, 또는 투석기의 움직임으로 어떤 것을 던지다. …을 발사하다

cat·a·pult² *n* a machine for throwing heavy stones or balls || 무거운 돌이나 공을 던지는 기계. 투석기. 캐터펄트

cat·a·ract /'kætə,rækt/ *n* a change in the LENS of someone's eye that makes him/her slowly lose his/her sight || 시력을 서서히 잃게 하는 눈의 수정체의 변화. 백내장(白內障)

ca·tas·tro·phe /kə'tæstrəfi/ *n* [C, U] a terrible event that causes a lot of destruction or suffering || 많은 파괴나 고통을 초래하는 끔찍한 사건. 큰 재난. 대참사: *catastrophes such as the Chernobyl explosion* 체르노빌 폭발과 같은 대참사 **– catastrophic** /,kætə's-trafɪk/ *adj*

catch¹ /kætʃ/ *v* **caught, caught, catching**

catch

1 ▶HOLD 잡다◀ [I, T] to get hold of and stop something that is moving through the air || 공중에서 움직이는 것을 잡아서 멈추게 하다. 붙잡다: *Denise caught the bride's bouquet.* 드니스는 신부의 부케를 잡았다. / *Here's your red ball, Sammy. Catch!* 새미, 여기 너의 붉은 색 공이 있다. 잡아 봐!

2 ▶STOP/TRAP 중단시키다/잡다◀ [T] to stop and hold someone or something after you have been chasing or hunting him, her, or it || 사람이나 사물을 추적하거나 사냥몰이한 후 붙잡다: *Look at all the fish we caught, Wes.* 웨스, 우리가 잡은 모든 물고기들을 봐.

3 ▶SEE/SMELL 보다/냄새 맡다◀ [T] to see or smell something for a moment || 잠깐 동안 어떤 것을 보거나 냄새 맡다: *I suddenly caught sight of Luisa in the crowd.* 순간 나는 군중 속에서 루이사의 모습을 보았다. / *Yuck – did you catch a whiff of his aftershave?* (=did you smell it?) 왝. 그가 면도후 바른 스킨로션의 냄

새를 맡아 보았니?

4 catch sb's eye to make someone notice someone or something ‖ 어떤 사람이 다른 사람이나 사물을 알아채게 하다. …의 주의[주목]를 끌다: *A photograph on his desk caught my eye.* 책상 위의 사진이 내 시선을 끌었다.

5 ▶GET SICK 아프다◀ [T] to get an illness ‖ 병에 걸리다: *Put your coat on! You don't want to catch (a) cold!* 외투를 입어라! 감기에 걸리고 싶지 않잖아!

6 catch (on) fire to start burning, especially accidentally ‖ 특히 사고로 불이 타기 시작하다. 불이 붙다

7 catch your breath to begin breathing normally again after you have been running or exercising ‖ 달리거나 운동을 하고 난 후 다시 평소대로 숨을 쉬기 시작하다. 숨을 돌리다

8 ▶NOT BE TOO LATE 너무 늦지 않다◀ [T] to not be too late to do something, talk to someone etc. ‖ 무엇을 하기에·누구에게 말하기에 너무 늦지는 않다: *I'm catching the 7:30 bus.* 나는 7시 30분 버스를 늦지 않게 탈 것이다. / *If you hurry you might catch her before she leaves.* 서두른다면 그녀가 떠나기 전에 만날 수도 있다.

9 ▶FIND SB DOING STH 사람이 …을 하는 것을 발견하다◀ [T] to find someone doing something wrong or illegal ‖ 사람이 그릇되거나 불법적인 일을 하는 것을 발견하다. 포착하다: *I caught him sleeping with another woman.* 나는 그가 다른 여자와 자고 있는 것을 발견했다. / *A store detective caught him red-handed.* (=saw him stealing) 매장 감시원은 물건을 슬쩍하고 있는 그를 목격했다.

10 ▶ATTACHED 달라붙다◀ [I, T] to become attached to or stuck on something, or to make something do this ‖ 어떤 것에 들러붙거나 끼이게 되다, 또는 어떤 것이 이렇게 되게 하다. …이 걸리다[걸리게 하다]: *His shirt caught on the fence and tore.* 그의 셔츠는 울타리에 걸려 찢어졌다.

11 catch sb's interest/imagination to make someone feel interested in something ‖ 남에게 어떤 것에 흥미를 느끼게 하다. …에게 관심/상상력을 일으키다: *a story that will catch children's imaginations* 아이들의 상상력을 자극할 만한 이야기

12 catch sb by surprise/catch sb off guard to do something or happen in an unexpected way, so that someone is not ready to deal with it ‖ 다른 사람이 대처할 준비가 되지 않도록 예기치 않게 어떤

일을 하거나 일어나다. 허(점)를 찌르다/무방비 상태에서 벌어지다

13 ▶STOP PROBLEM/DISEASE 문제점/병을 막다◀ [T] to discover a problem, especially a disease, and stop it from developing ‖ 문제점, 특히 질병을 발견하고 그것이 더 진행되는 것을 막다: *It's a type of cancer that can be cured, if it is caught early.* 그것은 조기에 발견하여 막으면 치유될 수 있는 종류의 암이다.

SPOKEN PHRASES

14 not catch sth to not hear or understand something clearly ‖ 어떤 것을 확실히 듣거나 이해하지 못하다: *I'm sorry, I didn't catch your name.* 미안합니다만 당신의 이름을 제대로 듣지 못했습니다.

15 sb wouldn't be caught dead doing sth said in order to emphasize that you would never do something ‖ 어떤 것을 결코 하지 않겠다는 것을 강조하는 데에 쓰여. 절대 …하지 않을거야: *I wouldn't be caught dead wearing a dress like that!* 절대로 저 따위 옷은 입지 않을거야!

16 you won't catch me doing sth used in order to say you would never do something ‖ 어떤 것을 결코 하지 않겠다고 말하는 데에 쓰여. 절대 …하지 않을거야: *You won't catch me ironing his shirts!* 절대 그의 셔츠를 다림질하지 않을 거야!

17 Catch you later! used in order to say goodbye ‖ 작별 인사로 말하는 데 쓰여. 안녕!, 나중에 봐!

---

catch on *phr v* [I] **1** to begin to understand something ‖ 어떤 것을 이해하기 시작하다: *Usually a couple of the children will catch on quickly and help the others.* 대개 몇몇 아이들이 빨리 이해하기 시작하여 다른 아이들을 도울 것이다. **2** to become popular ‖ 유명해지다. 인기를 얻다: *Rollerblades have sure caught on -* you see them everywhere now. 롤러블레이드는 확실히 히트쳤어. 지금은 어디에서든 그걸 볼 수 있잖아.

catch up *phr v* [I] **1** to come up from behind someone or something and reach the same point ‖ 어떤 사람이나 사물의 뒤에서 따라가서 같은 지점에 도달하다. 뒤따라 잡다: *I had to run to catch up with her.* 그녀를 따라잡기 위해 달려야 했다. **2** to reach the same standard or level as someone or something else ‖ 다른 사람이나 사물과 같은 기준이나 수준에 도달하다: *The US spent a lot of money* *trying to catch up with/to the Soviet Union in space exploration.* 미국은 우주 탐사에서 소비에트 연방을 따라잡기 위해 많은 돈을 들였다.

catch up on sth *phr v* [T] to do something that needs to be done that you have not had time to do in the past ‖ 과거에 시간이 없어 못했던 해야 할 일을 하다. 뒤처진 일을 따라잡다: *I need to catch up on some work.* 미처 못한 일을 만회해야 한다.

catch² *n* **1** the act of catching something that has been thrown or hit ‖ 던지거나 친 것을 잡는 행위. 잡기. 포구: *That was a great catch!* 정말 멋지게 잡아냈어! **2** [U] a game in which two or more people throw a ball to each other ‖ 두 명 이상의 사람이 서로에게 공을 던지는 게임. 캐치볼: *Let's play catch.* 캐치볼하자. **3** INFORMAL a hidden problem or difficulty ‖ 숨겨진 문제나 어려움. 함정: *The rent is so low there must be a catch.* 임대료가 너무 싸. 틀림없이 무슨 문제가 있을 거야. **4** a quantity of something that has been caught, usually fish ‖ 보통 물고기의 잡힌 양. 어획량: *a large catch of tuna fish* 다량의 참치 어획량 **5** a hook for fastening something and holding it shut ‖ 어떤 것에 채워서 잠가 두는 걸쇠. 잠금쇠: *the catch on my necklace* 내 목걸이의 잠금쇠

Catch-22 /ˌkætʃ twɛnti 'tu/ *n* [singular, U] a situation that you cannot escape from because of something that is part of the situation itself ‖ 어떤 것이 상황 자체의 일부분이어서 피할 수 없는 상황. 딜레마: *You can't get a job without experience, and you can't get experience without a job. It's a Catch-22.* 경험 없이는 직업을 구할 수 없고 직업 없이는 경험을 쌓을 수 없다. 그건 딜레마이다.

catch·er /'kætʃə/ *n* the baseball player who SQUATs behind the place where the BATTER stands, in order to catch missed balls ‖ 타자가 놓친 공을 잡기 위해 타석 뒷쪽에 쭈그리고 앉아 있는 야구 선수. 포수 —see picture on page 946

catch·ing /'kætʃɪŋ/ *adj* INFORMAL a disease or illness that is catching is infectious ‖ 질병이나 질환이 전염성인. 옮기 쉬운

catch phrase /'. ./ *n* a word or phrase that is easy to remember and is repeated by a political party, newspaper etc. ‖ 정당·신문 등에서 반복하는, 기억하기 쉬운 말이나 구절. 캐치프레이즈. 이목을 끄는 문구

catch·y /'kætʃi/ *adj* pleasant and easy to remember ‖ 재미있고 기억하기 쉬운. 사람의 마음을 끄는: *a catchy song* 재미있고 외기 쉬운 노래

cat·e·chism /'kætə,kɪzəm/ *n* a set of questions and answers about the Christian religion that people learn before becoming members of the church ‖ 교회의 신도가 되기 전에 배우는 기독교에 관한 문답서. 교리 문답서

cat·e·gor·i·cal /ˌkætə'gɔrɪkəl, -'gɑr-/ *adj* clearly stating that something is true ‖ 어떤 것이 사실이라고 명확히 말하는. 단언적인. 절대적인: *Foxe gave a categorical denial of his guilt.* 폭스는 자신의 범죄사실에 대해 단호히 부인했다. **– categorically** *adv*

cat·e·go·rize /'kætəgə,raɪz/ *v* [T] to put people or things into groups according to what type they are; CLASSIFY ‖ 사람이나 사물이 어떤 유형이냐에 따라서 그룹으로 나누다. …을 범주로 나누다. 분류하다; 🔁 classify: *We've categorized the wines by region.* 우리는 포도주를 지역별로 분류했다.

cat·e·go·ry /'kætə,gɔri/ *n* a group of people or things that have the same qualities ‖ 같은 성질을 가진 사람이나 사물의 집단. 범주: *Voters fall into* (=belong to) *one of three categories.* 투표자들은 세 가지 범주 중 하나에 속한다.

ca·ter /'keɪtə/ *v* [I, T] to provide and serve food and drinks at a party ‖ 파티에서 음식과 마실 것을 공급하거나 제공하다. 주문에 따라 음식을 조달하다: *Who's catering your daughter's wedding?* 어느 업체가 따님의 결혼식 음식을 조달합니까? **– caterer** *n*

cater to sb *phr v* [T] to provide a particular group of people with something that they need or want ‖ 특정 그룹 사람들에게 필요하거나 원하는 것을 제공하다. 조건을 충족시키다. 요구를 채워 주다: *newspapers that cater to business people* 사업가들의 요구를 충족시키는 신문

cat·er·pil·lar /'kætə,pɪlə, 'kætə-/ *n* a small creature with a long rounded body and many legs, that eats leaves ‖ 길고 둥그런 몸에 많은 다리를 가지고 나뭇잎을 먹는 작은 생물. 애벌레

cat·fish /'kæt'fɪʃ/ *n* [C, U] a common fish with long hairs around its mouth that lives mainly in rivers and lakes, or the meat from this fish ‖ 주로 강·호수에서 살며 입 주위에 긴 수염을 가진 흔한 물고기, 또는 이 물고기의 살코기. 메기

ca·thar·tic /kə'θɑrtɪk/ *adj* helping you

to deal with difficult emotions and get rid of them || 심란한 감정에 대처하여 그 것을 없애는 데 도움이 되는. 카타르시스 의: *Talking to a counselor can be a cathartic experience.* 상담자와 상담하는 것은 카타르시스적 경험이 될 수 있다. – **catharsis** /kəˈθɑrsɪs/ *n*

ca·the·dral /kəˈθidrəl/ *n* the main church in a particular area, that a BISHOP is responsible for || 주교가 관리하 는 특정 지역에서의 주교좌 성당. 대성당

cath·e·ter /ˈkæθəṭɚ/ *n* a thin tube that is put into someone's body to take away liquids || 체액을 배출시키기 위해 체내에 삽입하는 가는 관. 도뇨관(導尿管)

Cath·o·lic /ˈkæθlɪk, -θəlɪk/ *adj* relating to the Roman Catholic Church || 로마 가 톨릭 교회와 관련된. 로마 가톨릭 교회의 – **Catholic** *n* – **Catholicism** /kəˈθɑləˌsɪzəm/ *n* [U]

catholic *adj* FORMAL not limited to only a few things || 단지 몇몇의 것들에 한정되 지 않은. 한쪽으로 치우치지 않은. 폭넓 은: *Susan has catholic tastes in music.* 수잔은 음악에 관한 폭넓은 취향을 가 지고 있다.

cat·nap /ˈkætˌnæp/ *n* INFORMAL a short sleep during the day || 낮 동안의 짧은 잠. 낮잠. 선잠

cat·nip /ˈkætˌnɪp/ *n* [U] a type of grass with a pleasant smell that cats are attracted to || 고양이들이 좋아하는 상쾌 한 향이 나는 풀의 일종. 개박하

cat·sup /ˈkɛtʃəp, ˈkæ-/ *n* [U] ⇨ KETCHUP

cat·tail /ˈkæt-teɪl/ *n* a plant that grows near water and has groups of brown flowers and seeds that look like the tail of a cat || 물 근처에서 자라며, 고양이 꼬 리처럼 생긴 갈색 꽃 무리와 씨앗을 가진 식물. 부들

cat·tle /ˈkæṭl/ *n* [plural] cows and BULLs kept on a farm || 목장에서 기르는 암소 및 황소. 소(떼)

cat·ty /ˈkæṭi/ *adj* INFORMAL deliberately unkind in what you say about someone || 누군가에 대해 일부러 통명스럽게 말하 는. 악의에 찬. 심술궂은 – **cattiness** *n* [U] – **cattily** *adv*

cat·ty-cor·nered /ˈ.. ˌ../ *adv* ⇨ KITTY-CORNER

cat·walk /ˈkætˌwɔk/ *n* **1** a long raised path that MODELs walk on in a fashion show || 패션쇼에서 모델들이 걷는 단을 쌓 아 올린 긴 통로. 객석으로 뻗은 무대 **2** a narrow structure built along something such as a bridge or above a stage, that is being built or repaired || 건설 또는 보

수되고 있는 다리나 무대 위 등을 따라 지 어진 좁은 구조물. 다리·무대의 천장 가 까이 있는 횡단교의 좁은 보행 통로

Cau·ca·sian /kɔˈkeɪʒən/ *adj* someone who is Caucasian belongs to the race that has pale skin || 흰색 피부를 가진 인 종에 속한. 백인의 – **Caucasian** *n*

cau·cus /ˈkɔkəs/ *n* a group of people in a political party, who meet to discuss and decide on political plans || 정치 계획 을 토론·결정하려고 모이는 정당내의 사람 들의 그룹. 정당의 지방 위원회[대회]

caught /kɔt/ *v* the past tense and PAST PARTICIPLE of CATCH || catch의 과거·과거 분사형

cau·li·flow·er /ˈkɔlɪˌflaʊɚ, ˈkɑ-/ *n* [C, U] a white vegetable with short firm stems and thick groups of small round flower-like parts || 짧고 단단한 줄기와 여 러 겹의 작고 둥근 꽃 모양의 부분을 가진 흰 야채. 꽃양배추 —see picture on page 944

'cause /kəz/ *conj* SPOKEN because || …때 문에

cause¹ /kɔz/ *n* **1** a person, event, or thing that makes something happen || 어 떤 일을 일으키는 사람[사건, 사물]. 이유. 원인: *What was the cause of the accident?* 그 사고의 원인은 무엇이었니? **2** [U] good reasons for feeling or behaving in a particular way || 특정한 방 식으로 느끼거나 행동하는 타당한 이유. 근거. 동기: *She had no cause for complaint.* 그녀는 불평할 만한 타당한 이 유가 없었다. **3** a principle or aim that a group of people support or fight for || 일 단의 사람들이 지지하거나 투쟁하는 원칙 이나 목표. 명분. 주의. 주장. 신조: *I don't mind giving money if it's for a good cause.* 대의를 위해서라면 돈을 주 는 것은 신경쓰지 않는다.

cause² *v* [T] to make something happen || 어떤 것을 일으키다. 야기하다. 원인이 되다: *Heavy traffic is causing long delays on the freeway.* 교통 폭주로 고속 도로에 장시간 정체가 일어나고 있다. / *We still don't know what caused the computer to crash.* 우리는 무엇 때문에 컴퓨터가 고장났는지 아직 모른다.

caus·tic /ˈkɔstɪk/ *adj* **1 caustic remark/comment etc.** something you say that is extremely unkind or full of criticism || 아주 냉정하거나 비판이 가득 한 말. 신랄한 말/논평 **2** a caustic substance can burn through things by chemical action || 물질이 화학적 작용에 의해 물건을 태울 수 있는. 가성(苛性)의: *caustic soda* 가성 소다

cau·tion[1] /'kɔʃən/ *n* [U] **1** the quality of doing something carefully, not taking risks, and avoiding danger ‖ 모험을 하지 않고 위험성을 피하여 어떤 것을 주의깊게 하는 성질. 주의. 경계: *Mulder moved with caution through the dark house.* 멀더는 조심스럽게 어두운 집 안에서 몸을 움직였다. / *You should use caution when driving at night.* 밤에 운전할 때에는 주의해야 한다. **2** word/note of caution a warning to be careful ‖ 조심하라는 경고. 경고의 말/표시: *One note of caution: never try this trick at home.* 한 마디의 경고: 절대 집에서 이 묘기를 하지 말 것

caution[2] *v* [T] FORMAL to warn someone that something might be dangerous or difficult ‖ 어떤 것이 위험하거나 어려울 수 있다고 누구에게 경고하다. 주의하다: *The children were cautioned against talking to strangers.* 그 아이들은 낯선 사람과 말하지 말라는 주의를 들었다.

cau·tion·ar·y /'kɔʃə,nɛri/ *adj* giving advice or warning ‖ 충고나 경고를 하는: *a cautionary tale* 교훈적인 이야기

cau·tious /'kɔʃəs/ *adj* careful to avoid danger ‖ 위험을 피하기 위해 주의하는. 신중한. 주의를 기울이는: *a cautious driver* 신중한 운전자

cav·a·lier /,kævə'lɪr/ *adj* not caring or thinking about other people ‖ 다른 사람에 대해 신경쓰거나 생각하지 않는. 제멋대로의. 거만한: *The foreman had a cavalier attitude towards workers' safety.* 그 감독은 노동자의 안전에는 무관심한 태도였다.

cav·al·ry /'kævəlri/ *n* soldiers who fight while riding on horses ‖ 말을 타고 싸우는 군인. 기병대

cave[1] /keɪv/ *n* a large natural hole in the side of a cliff or under the ground ‖ 절벽의 측면이나 지하에 나 있는 큰 자연적인 구멍. 동굴

cave[2] *v*

cave in *phr v* [I] **1** to fall down or inwards ‖ 아래로 또는 안쪽으로 꺼지다. 움푹 패다. 함몰하다: *The roof of the old house had caved in.* 그 낡은 집의 지붕이 푹 꺼져 버렸다. **2** to stop opposing something because you have been persuaded or threatened ‖ 설득당하거나 위협을 받아서 어떤 것에 반대하는 것을 멈추다. 항복하다. 약화되다: *Now is not the time to cave in to their demands.* 지금은 그들의 요구에 굴복할 때가 아니다. **– cave-in** *n*

cave·man /'keɪvmæn/ *n* someone who

lived in a CAVE many thousands of years ago ‖ 수천 년 전에 동굴에서 살았던 사람. 혈거인(穴居人)

cav·ern /'kævən/ *n* a large deep CAVE ‖ 크고 깊은 동굴 **– cavernous** *adj*

cav·i·ar /'kævi,ɑr/ *n* [U] the salted eggs of various types of large fish, eaten as a special expensive food ‖ 특별히 값비싼 음식물로서 식용하는, 각종 큰 생선의 소금에 절인 알. 캐비어

cav·i·ty /'kævəti/ *n* **1** a hole in a tooth made by decay ‖ 썩어서 치아에 생긴 구멍. 충치 **2** a hole or space inside something solid ‖ 딱딱한 물체 속의 구멍이나 공간. 움푹 들어간 곳. 공동(空洞)

ca·vort /kə'vɔrt/ *v* [I] to jump or dance in a noisy, playful, or sexual way ‖ 시끄럽게[신이 나서, 선정적으로] 뛰거나 춤추다. 뛰어다니다. 흥청거리다

CB *n* [C, U] Citizens Band; a radio on which people can speak to each other over short distances ‖ Citizens Band(민간 주파수대 무선)의 약어; 근거리에 있는 사람들이 서로 말할 수 있는 무선 통신

CBS *n* Columbia Broadcasting System; one of the national companies that broadcasts television and radio programs in the US ‖ Columbia Broadcasting System(콜롬비아 방송사)의 약어; 미국 전국으로 텔레비전과 라디오 프로그램을 방송하는 회사 중 하나

CBT *n* [U] **1** computer-based testing; a way of taking standard tests such as the GRE on a computer ‖ computer-based testing (컴퓨터 이용 시험)의 약어; GRE 등 평가 시험을 컴퓨터로 보는 방식 **2** computer-based training; the use of computers to teach people to do something ‖ computer-based training(컴퓨터 이용 교육 훈련)의 약어; 컴퓨터를 이용해서 사람들에게 어떤 것을 하도록 가르치기

cc **1** the abbreviation of "cubic centimeter" ‖ cubic centimeter의 약어: *a 2000 cc engine* 2000cc짜리 엔진 **2** the abbreviation of CARBON COPY; used at the end of a business letter to show that you are sending a copy to someone else ‖ carbon copy의 약어; 상업 서신의 말미에, 발신인이 누구에게 복사본을 보내고 있다는 것을 알릴 때 사용하여

CD *n* **1** Compact Disc; a small circular piece of hard plastic on which recorded sound or information can be stored ‖ Compact Disc(콤팩트 디스크)의 약어; 녹음된 소리나 정보를 저장할 수 있는 딱딱한 플라스틱으로 된 작은 원형 조각 **2** ⇨ CERTIFICATE OF DEPOSIT

CD burn·er /.' . .,./, **burner** *n* compact disc burner; a piece of computer equipment that records music, images, or other information onto a CD ‖ compact disc burner(CD 기록기)의 약어; 음악[영상, 다른 정보]를 CD에 기록하는 컴퓨터 장비

CD play·er /,. '. .,./ *n* a piece of equipment used for playing music CDs ‖ 음악 시디를 재생하는 데 사용하는 기기. 시디 플레이어

CD-ROM /,si di 'rɑm/ *n* [C, U] Compact Disc Read-Only Memory; a CD on which large quantities of information can be stored to be used by a computer ‖ Compact Disc Read-Only Memory(판독 전용 기억 공간)의 약어; 컴퓨터에 의해 사용되는 대량의 정보를 저장할 수 있는 시디. 시디롬

cease /sis/ *v* [I, T] FORMAL to stop doing something or to make an activity stop happening ‖ 무엇을 하는 것을 그만두거나 어떤 행위가 일어나지 못하도록 조치를 취하다. 중지하다[시키다]: *By noon the rain had ceased.* 정오에 비가 그쳤다. / *He never ceases to amaze me.* (=I am always surprised by what he does) 나는 그가 하는 일에 언제나 놀란다.

cease·fire /,sis'faɪɚ, 'sisfaɪɚ/ *n* an agreement for both sides in a war to stop fighting for a period of time ‖ 전쟁에서 양측이 일정 기간 동안 전투를 중지하려는 합의. 정전

cease·less /'sislɪs/ *adj* FORMAL continuing for a long time without stopping ‖ 오랜 시간 동안 멈추지 않고 계속되는. 끊임없는. 중단없는: *She was tired of her parents' ceaseless arguing.* 그녀는 부모님의 끊임없는 언쟁에 질렸다. **– ceaselessly** *adv*

ce·dar /'sidɚ/ *n* [C, U] a tall tree with leaves shaped like needles that do not fall off in winter, or the red sweet-smelling wood of this tree ‖ 겨울에도 떨어지지 않는 바늘처럼 생긴 잎이 달린 키 큰 나무, 또는 붉고 달콤한 향이 나는 이 나무의 목재. 개잎갈나무 (목재)

cede /sid/ *v* [T] FORMAL to give something, usually land, to another country or person, often after losing a war ‖ 종종 전쟁에서 패한 후 다른 나라나 사람에게 보통 영토 등을 주다. 할양하다

ceil·ing /'silɪŋ/ *n* **1** the inside surface of the top part of a room ‖ 방 제일 윗부분의 안쪽 면. 방의 천장 **2** an official upper limit on things such as wages or rents ‖ 임금이나 임대료 등의 공식적인 최고 한도. 상한

cel·e·brate /'sɛlə,breɪt/ *v* **1** [I, T] to do something special because of a particular event or special occasion ‖ 특정 행사나 특별한 경우라서 특별한 것을 하다. 축하[경축, 기념]하다: *We should celebrate Dad's birthday at a restaurant.* 우리는 음식점에서 아빠의 생신을 축하해야 한다. **2** [T] FORMAL to praise someone or something in speech or writing ‖ 연설이나 글로서 사람이나 사물을 칭송하다. 찬양하다

cel·e·brat·ed /'sɛlə,breɪtɪd/ *adj* famous or talked about a lot ‖ 유명한 또는 회자(膾炙)되는. …으로 이름난: *Chicago is celebrated for its architecture.* 시카고는 건축으로 유명하다.

cel·e·bra·tion /,sɛlə'breɪʃən/ *n* **1** an occasion or party when you celebrate something ‖ 어떤 것을 축하하는 행사나 파티: *New Year's celebrations* 새해 축하 행사 **2** the act of celebrating ‖ 축하하는 행위: *There'll be a party in celebration of his promotion.* 그의 승진을 축하하는 파티가 있을 예정이다.

ce·leb·ri·ty /sə'lɛbrəti/ *n* a famous person, especially someone in the entertainment business ‖ 특히 연예계에서 유명한 사람. 저명[유명] 인사

cel·er·y /'sɛlɚi/ *n* [U] a vegetable with long firm pale green stems, often eaten raw ‖ 보통 날로 먹는 길고 단단한 열은 초록색의 줄기가 있는 채소. 셀러리 —see picture on page 944

ce·les·tial /sə'lɛstʃəl/ *adj* LITERARY relating to the sky or heaven ‖ 하늘이나 천상과 관련된. 천체의

cel·i·bate /'sɛləbɪt/ *adj* not having sex, especially for religious reasons ‖ 특히 종교적 이유로 인해 성관계를 갖지 않는. 금욕주의의 **– celibacy** /'sɛləbəsi/ *n* [U]

cell /sɛl/ *n* **1** a small room in a police station or prison where prisoners are kept ‖ 죄수가 수감되는 경찰서의 작은 방이나 감옥. 유치장. 감방 **2** the smallest part of an animal or plant that can exist on its own ‖ 단독으로 존재할 수 있는, 동물이나 식물을 구성하는 가장 부분. 세포: *red blood cells* 적혈구 세포

cel·lar /'sɛlɚ/ *n* a room under a house or restaurant ‖ 집이나 음식점 지하에 있는 방. 지하 저장실: *a wine cellar* 포도주 지하 저장실

cel·list /'tʃɛlɪst/ *n* someone who plays the CELLO ‖ 첼로 연주자. 첼리스트

cel·lo /'tʃɛloʊ/ *n* a large wooden musical instrument, shaped like a VIOLIN, that you hold between your knees and play by pulling a BOW (=special stick) across wire strings ‖ 무릎 사이에 끼고 활로 금속 현을 켜서 연주하는, 바이올린처럼 생긴 큰 목제 악기. 첼로

cel·lo·phane /'sɛlə,feɪn/ *n* TRADEMARK a thin transparent material used for wrapping food ‖ 음식을 포장하는 데 사용하는 얇고 투명한 물질. 셀로판

cel·lu·lar /'sɛlyələ/ *adj* relating to the cells in a plant or animal ‖ 식물이나 동물의 세포와 관계된. 세포의. 세포상의

cellular phone /,... './ *n* a telephone that you can carry with you, that works by using a network of radio stations to pass on signals ‖ 신호를 보내는 무선 기지국망을 이용해 작동하는 휴대할 수 있는 전화. 핸드폰. 휴대 전화

cel·lu·lite /'sɛlyə,laɪt/ *n* [U] fat that is just below someone's skin and that makes it look uneven and unattractive ‖ 피부를 울퉁불퉁하고 보기 흉하게 만드는, 피부 바로 밑의 지방. 셀룰라이트

cel·lu·loid /'sɛlyə,lɔɪd/ *n* TRADEMARK a substance like plastic, used in past times to make film ‖ 과거에 필름을 만드는 데 쓰였던 플라스틱 같은 물질. 셀룰로이드

cel·lu·lose /'sɛlyə,loʊs/ *n* [U] the material that the cell walls of plants are made of and that is used for making plastics, paper etc. ‖ 식물 세포벽의 주요 성분이며, 플라스틱·종이 등을 만드는 데 쓰는 물질. 셀룰로오스. 섬유소

Cel·si·us /'sɛlsiəs, -ʃəs/ *n* [U] a temperature scale in which water freezes at 0° and boils at 100° ‖ 물이 0도에서 얼고 100도에서 끓는 온도 측정 기준. 섭씨

ce·ment¹ /sɪ'mɛnt/ *n* [U] **1** a gray powder used in building, that becomes hard when mixed with water and allowed to dry ‖ 물과 혼합해서 건조시키면 딱딱해지는, 건축에 쓰이는 회색 가루. 시멘트 **2** a substance used to fill holes or as a glue ‖ 구멍을 막거나 접착제로 사용하는 물질. 접합제

cement² *v* [T] **1** to cover something with CEMENT ‖ 시멘트로 어떤 것을 덮다 **2** to make a relationship stronger ‖ 관계를 더 강하게 하다. 굳게 하다. 다지다: *China has cemented its trade connections with the US.* 중국은 미국과의 무역 관계를 공고히 해 왔다.

cem·e·tery /'sɛmə,tɛri/ *n* an area of land where dead people are buried ‖ 죽은 사람들이 묻히는 부지. 매장지. 공동묘지

cen·sor /'sɛnsə/ *v* [T] to examine books, movies etc. in order to remove anything that is OFFENSIVE, politically dangerous etc. ‖ 불쾌감을 주며 정치적으로 위험한 것을 삭제할 목적으로 책·영화 등을 조사하다. 검열하다 – **censor** *n*

cen·sor·ship /'sɛnsə,ʃɪp/ *n* [U] the practice or system of CENSORing something ‖ 어떤 것을 검열하는 일이나 제도

cen·sure /'sɛnʃə/ *v* [T] FORMAL to officially criticize someone for something s/he has done wrong ‖ 남이 잘못한 일에 대해서 공식적으로 비판하다. 책망하다 – **censure** *n*

cen·sus /'sɛnsəs/ *n* an official count of all the people in a country, including information about their ages, jobs etc. ‖ 연령·직업 등의 정보를 포함하는 한 나라의 공식적인 전체 인구수. 인구[국세] 조사

cent /sɛnt/ *n* **1** a unit of money that is worth 1/100 of a dollar. Its sign is ¢. ‖ 1달러의 100분의 1의 가치를 지니는 화폐 단위. 센트. 기호는 ¢ **2 put in your two cents' worth** INFORMAL to give your opinion about something ‖ 어떤 것에 대한 의견을 밝히다.

cen·ten·ni·al /sɛn'tɛniəl/, **cen·tenary** /sɛn'tɛnəri/ *n* the day or year exactly 100 years after an important event ‖ 중요한 사건 이후로 정확히 100년이 되는 날이나 연도. 100주년 (기념일)

cen·ter¹ /'sɛntə/ *n* **1** the middle part or point of something ‖ 어떤 것의 중간 부분이나 지점. 중앙. 한가운데: *I work in the center of the city.* 나는 도심에서 일한다. / *the center of the table* 테이블 한가운데 **2** a place or building used for a particular purpose ‖ 특정 목적을 위해 사용되는 장소나 건물. 센터: *a shopping center* 쇼핑 센터 / *the Kennedy Space Center* 케네디 우주 센터 **3** a place where most of the important things happen that relate to a business or activity ‖ 사업 또는 활동에 관계되는 대부분의 중요한 일이 일어나는 장소. 주요 지점. 중심지: *the center of the country's music industry* 그 나라 음악 산업의 중심지 / *a major banking center* 주요 금융 지점 **4 be the center of attention** to be the person to whom people are giving the most attention ‖ 사람들에게 가장 주목받는 사람이 되다. **5 the center** a position in politics that is not extreme ‖ 정치에서 극단적이지 않은 위치. 중도 **6** in basketball, the player who usually plays in the middle of the action ‖ 농구에서, 보통 중앙의 역할을 담당하는 선수. 센터 —see picture on page 946 **7** in football, the player who starts the ball moving in each PLAY ‖ 미식 축구에서, 매 플레이마다 공을 먼저 다루기 시작하는 선수. 센터 —see usage note at MIDDLE¹

center² v [T] to move something to a position at the center of something else ‖ 어떤 것을 다른 것의 중앙 위치로 옮기다. 중심에 놓다: *Stand back and tell me if the painting is centered.* 뒤로 물러서서 그림이 중앙에 있는지 말해 줘.

center around sth *phr v* [I, T] if your thoughts, activities etc. center around something, it is the main thing you think is important ‖ 사고·행동 등이 자신이 중요하게 생각하는 주된 것이 되다. …에 집중하다. …을 우선 순서로 (중앙에) 두다: *Their whole life centers around that kid of theirs!* 그들 인생의 전부는 그들의 저 아이에게 집중되어 있다.

center on sth *phr v* [T] to pay more attention to one thing or person than anything or anyone else ‖ 다른 사물이나 사람보다 하나의 사물이나 사람에 더 많은 주의를 기울이다. 집중하다: *The discussion centered on gun control.* 그 토론은 총기 규제 문제에 집중되었다.

center field /ˌ.. ˈ./ n [singular] the area in baseball in the center of the OUTFIELD ‖ 야구에서 외야의 중심부. 센터 (필드)

cen·ter·fold /ˈsentɚˌfoʊld/ n a picture of a woman with no clothes on that covers the two pages in the middle of a magazine ‖ 잡지 중앙의 두 페이지에 걸친, 옷을 입지 않은 여자 사진. (누드 사진의) 삽입 페이지

center of grav·i·ty /ˌ.. . ˈ.../ n the point on an object at which it will balance ‖ 물체가 평형을 이루는 지점. 무게 중심. 중심

cen·ter·piece /ˈsentɚˌpis/ n 1 a decoration in the middle of a table, usually made of flowers ‖ 테이블 중앙의, 보통 꽃으로 만들어 놓은 장식품 2 the centerpiece of the most important part of something ‖ 어떤 것의 가장 중요한 부분. 주요 특징: *the centerpiece of Canada's foreign policy* 캐나다 대외 정책의 주요 부분

Cen·ti·grade /ˈsentɚˌɡreɪd/ n ⇨ CELSIUS

cen·ti·me·ter /ˈsentɚˌmitɚ/, *written abbreviation* **cm** n a unit for measuring length, equal to 1/100 of a meter or 0.39 inches ‖ 1미터의 100분의 1, 또는 0.39 인치에 해당하는 길이 측정 단위. 센티미터

cen·ti·pede /ˈsentɚˌpid/ n a very small creature with a long thin body and many legs ‖ 몸이 길고 가늘며, 다리가 많

이 달린 아주 작은 생명체. 지네(류)

cen·tral /ˈsentrəl/ adj 1 in the middle of an object or area ‖ 물체나 지역의 중앙에 있는. 중앙[중심]의: *Central Asia* 중앙 아시아 / *the central part of the house* 집의 중심부 2 controlling or used by everyone or everything in a whole country or a large organization ‖ 국가 전체나 대규모 조직의 모든 사람이나 사물에 의해 통제되거나 사용되는. 중앙의. 주요한: *The computers are linked to a central database.* 컴퓨터는 중앙 데이터 베이스에 연결되어 있다. 3 the most important ‖ 가장 중요한. 핵심인: *These questions have played a central role in the history of the US.* (=they have been very important) 이 문제들은 미국 역사에서 핵심적인 역할을 해 왔다. 4 convenient because of being near the center ‖ 중심지 근처에 있어서 편리한: *I want a hotel that's central.* 나는 중심지 근처에 있는 편리한 호텔을 원한다. – **centrally** adv

Central Eu·rope n ⇨ EASTERN EUROPE

Central In·tel·li·gence A·gen·cy /ˌ.. ˌ.... ˌ../ n [singular] ⇨ CIA

cen·tral·ize /ˈsentrəˌlaɪz/ v [T] to change a government or organization so that it is controlled in one place, by one main group of people ‖ 정부나 조직을 변화시켜, 한 곳에서 하나의 주된 집단의 사람들이 통제하도록 하다. 중앙 집권화하다

cen·tu·ry /ˈsentʃəri/ n 1 one of the 100-year periods counted forward or backward from the year of Christ's birth ‖ 예수 탄생 연도를 전후로 하여 산정되는 100년 단위의 기간 중 하나. 세기: *technology for the twenty-first century* 21세기의 기술 / *My grandparents moved west at the turn of the century.* (=in or around the year 1900) 나의 조부모님은 (1900년을 전후로 한) 세기의 전환기에 서부로 이주하셨다. 2 a period of time equal to 100 years ‖ 100년에 해당하는 기간

CEO n Chief Executive Officer; the person with the most authority in a large company ‖ Chief Executive Officer(최고 경영자)의 약어; 대기업에서 최고 권한을 가진 사람

ce·ram·ics /səˈræmɪks/ n [plural, U] objects produced by shaping pieces of clay and baking them until they are hard, or the art of making them ‖ 점토로 모양을 만들어 단단해질 때까지 구워서 만든 물건, 또는 그것을 만드는 기예. 도자기 공예. 요업 (제품) – **ceramic** adj

ce·re·al /ˈsɪriəl/ n 1 [C, U] breakfast food that is made from grain and usually eaten with milk ‖ 보통 우유를 곁들여 먹는, 곡물로 만든 아침 식사 음식. 시리얼 **2** a plant grown to produce grain for foods, such as wheat, rice etc. ‖ 밀, 쌀 등의 식용 곡식을 만들기 위해 키우는 식물. 곡물(류)

ce·re·bral /sə'ribrəl, 'sɛrə-/ *adj* TECHNICAL relating to or affecting the brain ‖ 뇌와 관계된 또는 뇌에 영향을 미치는. 뇌의

cer·e·mo·ni·al /ˌsɛrə'mouniəl/ *adj* used in a ceremony ‖ 의식에 쓰이는. 의식의. 의식용의: *Native American ceremonial pipes* 아메리카 원주민의 의식용 파이프 – **ceremonially** *adv*

cer·e·mo·ny /'sɛrəˌmouni/ *n* **1** a formal or traditional set of actions used at an important social or religious event ‖ 중요한 사회적 또는 종교적 행사에서 사용되는 공식적이거나 전통적인 일련의 행위. 의식. 제전: *The treaty was signed during a ceremony at the White House.* 그 조약은 백악관에서 거행한 의식에서 체결되었다. / *Pastor Hetland conducted/performed the marriage ceremony.* 헤틀랜드 목사가 그 결혼식을 주재했다. **2** [U] formal words and actions used on special occasions ‖ 특별한 행사에서 사용되는, 격식적인 말·행동: *With great ceremony, the Mayor opened the new concert hall.* 그 시장은 거창한 개관식과 함께 새 콘서트홀을 개관했다.

cer·tain¹ /'sɚt̚n/ *determiner, pron* **1** a certain thing, person, idea etc. is a particular thing, person etc. that you are not naming or describing exactly ‖ 사물·사람·생각 등이 정확히 명명하거나 묘사할 수 없는. 어떤: *The plant grows on a certain island in the South China Sea.* 그 식물은 남지나해의 어떤 섬에서 자란다. / *There are certain things I just can't talk about with her.* 그녀에게 말할 수 없는 어떤 것들이 있다. **2** some, but not a lot ‖ 약간 있지만 많지 않은. 다소의: *In certain ways he can be good to work for.* 어떤 면에서 그는 그 일에 적합할 수 있다. / *I had to spend a certain amount of time practicing, but it wasn't hard.* 나는 연습하는 데 다소의 시간을 보내야 했지만 힘들지는 않았다. **3 to a certain extent** partly, but not completely ‖ 부분적으로, 전적으로는 아닌. 어느 정도는: *I agree with you to a certain extent, but I think there are other problems too.* 어느 정도는 당신 의견에 동의하지만, 다른 문제들도 있다고 생각합니다.

certain² *adj* **1** completely sure and without any doubts ‖ 전적으로 확신하며 아무런 의심이 없는. 확실한: *I'm not certain (that) he's telling me the truth.* 나는 그가 내게 진실을 말하고 있다고 확신하지 않는다. / *No one was certain what to expect.* 아무도 무슨 일이 일어날지 확신할 수 없었다. / *Are you certain about that?* 그것에 대해 확신합니까? **2 know/say for certain** to know something without any doubt ‖ 의심의 여지없이 어떤 것을 알다. …을 확실히 알다/말하다: *I can't say for certain when her plane will arrive.* 그녀가 탄 비행기가 언제 도착할지 확실히 말할 수 없다. **3** something that is certain will definitely happen or is definitely true ‖ 어떤 것이 반드시 일어나거나 틀림없이 사실인. 확실히 …한: *It's almost certain that the enemy will attack from the north.* 적이 북쪽에서 공격할 것이라는 점은 거의 확실하다. / *He's certain to be offered the job.* 그가 그 일을 제안받으리라는 것은 확실하다. **4 make certain (that)** to do something in order to be sure about a fact, about what to do etc. ‖ 어떤 사실·할 일 등에 대해 확실히 하기 위해 어떤 것을 하다. …을 확인하다. 틀림없이 (…하도록) 하다: *Employers are required to make certain that all employees are treated fairly.* 고용주들은 반드시 모든 직원들이 공정하게 대우받도록 해야 한다. —compare UNCERTAIN —see usage note at SURE¹

cer·tain·ly /'sɚt̚nli/ *adv* without any doubt ‖ 아무 의심없이. 틀림없이. 확실히. 물론: *Diana certainly spends a lot of money on clothes.* 다이애나는 확실히 옷 사는 데 많은 돈을 쓴다. / *"Can I borrow your notes?" "Certainly!"* (=yes, of course) "노트 좀 빌릴 수 있을까요?" "그럼요, 물론이죠!" —see usage note at SURE¹

cer·tain·ty /'sɚt̚nti/ *n* **1** [U] the state of being completely sure about something ‖ 어떤 것에 대해 전적으로 확신하는 상태. …에 대한 확신: *We cannot say with complete certainty whether your wife will be all right.* 당신의 아내가 괜찮을지 확실하게 장담할 수 없습니다. **2** something that is definitely true or will definitely happen ‖ 틀림없이 사실인 또는 앞으로 틀림없이 일어날 일. 확실한 것. 불가피한 일: *Ginny had to face the certainty that she was pregnant.* 지니는 자신이 임신한 사실을 직시해야 했다.

cer·ti·fi·a·ble /ˌsɚt̚ə'faɪəbəl/ *adj* INFORMAL crazy ‖ 미친. 정신 이상인: *If you ask me, that guy is certifiable.* 내 생

각에는, 그 남자는 제 정신이 아니다.

cer·tif·i·cate /sə'tɪfəkɪt/ n an official document that states the facts about something or someone ‖ 사물이나 사람에 대한 사실을 진술하는 공식 문서. 증명서. 증서: a birth/marriage/death certificate (=giving details of someone's birth etc.) 출생[결혼, 사망] 증명서 —see also GIFT CERTIFICATE

certificate of de·pos·it /.,... ...'../ n TECHNICAL a bank account that you must leave a particular amount of money in for a particular amount of time in order to get INTEREST ‖ 이자를 얻기 위해, 일정 기간 동안 일정 금액의 돈을 예치해 두어야 하는 은행 계좌. 정기 예금 증서

cer·ti·fied /'sətəfaɪd/ adj having successfully completed the training for a profession ‖ 어떤 전문 직업을 위한 훈련 과정을 성공적으로 끝마친. 보증된. 공인의: a certified nurse 유자격 간호사 – **certification** /,sətəfə'keɪʃən/ n [U]

certified check /,... './ n a check that you get from a bank for a particular amount of money ‖ 은행에서 발행하는 일정 금액의 수표. 보증 수표

certified mail /,... './ n [U] a method of sending mail in which the person it is sent to must sign his/her name to prove s/he has received it ‖ 우편 수취를 증명하기 위해 수취인이 서명해야 하는 우편 발송 방식. 배달 증명 우편

certified pub·lic ac·count·ant /,... ,... .'../ n ⇨ CPA

cer·ti·fy /'sətə,faɪ/ v [T] 1 to officially state that something is true or that a document is correct ‖ 어떤 것이 사실이거나 서류가 정확하다는 것을 공식적으로 언급하다. 보증[증명]하다: Two doctors certified that the patient was dead. 두 명의 의사가 그 환자가 사망했음을 증명했다. 2 to give someone an official paper that states that s/he has completed a course of training ‖ 남에게 훈련 과정의 수료를 명시한 공식 문서를 주다. 수료[수수]증을 수여하다: He has been certified as a mechanic. 그는 기계공 수료증을 받았다.

cer·vix /'səvɪks/ n TECHNICAL the narrow opening into a woman's UTERUS ‖ 여성의 자궁으로 나 있는 좁은 입구. 자궁 경관 – **cervical** /'səvɪkəl/ adj

ce·sar·e·an /sɪ'zɛriən/, **cesarean section** /.,... '../ n an operation in which a woman's body is cut open to take a baby out ‖ 아기를 꺼내려고 여성의 몸을 절개하는 수술. 제왕 절개 수술

ces·sa·tion /sɛ'seɪʃən/ n FORMAL the act of stopping something ‖ 어떤 것을 중단시키는 행위. 정지. 중단: the cessation of nuclear tests 핵 실험의 중단

cess·pool /'sɛspul/ n a container under the ground where waste water from a house is collected, especially SEWAGE ‖ 특히 하수 등 집안의 오수가 모아지는 땅 밑의 통. 지하의 하수통

CFC n CHLOROFLUOROCARBON; one of the gases that are used in AEROSOLs, REFRIGERATORs etc., and in making some plastics ‖ chlorofluorocarbon(염화불화탄소)의 약어; 분무기·냉장고 등에, 또한 몇몇의 플라스틱 제작에 쓰이는 가스 중의 하나

chafe /tʃeɪf/ v [I, T] 1 if a part of your body chafes or if something chafes it, it becomes sore because of something rubbing against it ‖ 어떤 것에 피부가 쓸려서 헐다. 따끔거리다. 따끔거리게 하다 2 also **chafe at** to be or become impatient or annoyed ‖ 참을 수 없거나 없게 되다, 또는 짜증나다. 신경질[화]나다

cha·grin /ʃə'grɪn/ n [U] FORMAL a feeling of being disappointed and annoyed because something has not happened the way you hoped ‖ 어떤 일이 바라던 대로 일어나지 않아 실망하고 화난 감정. 원통함. 분함

chagrin v **be chagrined** FORMAL to be annoyed and disappointed ‖ 화나고 실망하다. 원통하다

chain¹ /tʃeɪn/ n 1 [C, U] a series of metal rings connected together in a line, used as jewelry or for fastening things, supporting weights etc. ‖ 보석으로 또는 사물을 고정시키거나 무게를 지탱하는 데 사용

chain

link

하는 일렬로 연결된 일련의 금속 고리. 쇠사슬. 체인: a delicate gold chain 정교한 금 목걸이 / The snow is so bad, you'll probably need chains on the tires. 눈이 너무 심하네요, 타이어에 체인을 감는 게 좋겠어요. 2 **chain of events** a connected series of events that lead to a particular result ‖ 특정 결과로 이어지는 일련의 연관된 사건: the chain of events that caused World War I 제1차 세계 대전을 일으킨 일련의 사건 3 a group of stores, hotels etc. that are owned by the same person or company ‖ 동일한 사람이나 회사가 소유한 일단의 상점·호텔 등. 체인점 4 mountains, lakes, or islands that are close together in a line ‖ 일렬로 서로 가까이 붙어있는 산[호수, 섬] **5 in chains** prisoners in chains have heavy chains fastened around their legs or arms, to prevent them from escaping ‖ 죄수들이 도망가지 못하도록 다리나 팔에 무거운 쇠사슬 채운. 족쇄를 채워. 구속되어

chain² *v* [T] to use a chain to fasten one thing or person to another ‖ 어떤 사물이나 사람을 다른 것에 묶기 위해 체인을 사용하다. …을 …에 쇠사슬로 매다: *a bicycle chained to a fence* 울타리에 체인으로 묶여 있는 자전거

chain let·ter /ˌ. '../ *n* a letter that is sent to several people who send copies to more people ‖ 몇 사람에게 보내면 그 수취인들이 더 많은 사람들에게 사본을 보내는 편지. 행운의 편지

chain of com·mand /ˌ. . . ./ *n* a system in an organization by which decisions are made and passed from people at the top of the organization to people lower down ‖ 조직에서 결정이 내려지면 그 조직의 상층부터 말단까지 전해지는 체계. 상명 하달식 체계

chain re·ac·tion /ˌ. '.., '. .,./ *n* a series of events or chemical changes, each of which causes the next one ‖ 어떤 하나가 다음 것을 유발시키는 일련의 사건이나 화학 변화. 연쇄 작용. 학학적 연쇄 반응

chain·saw /'tʃɛmsɔ/ *n* [U] a tool used for cutting wood, consisting of a circular chain with sharp edges that is moved by a motor ‖ 모터로 작동되며 날카로운 날을 가진 회전식 쇠사슬로 이루어진, 나무를 자르는 연장. 동력 쇠사슬 톱

chain-smoke /'. ., . . './ *v* [I, T] to smoke cigarettes one after the other ‖ 담배를 연속해서 피우다. 줄담배 피우다 – **chain-smoker** *n*

chair¹ /tʃɛr/ *n* **1** a piece of furniture for one person to sit on, that has a back, a seat, and four legs, and that can be moved ‖ 등받이·좌석·네 개의 다리로 이루어져 있고 옮길 수 있으며, 한 사람이 앉을 수 있는 가구. 의자 **2** someone who is in charge of a meeting, a committee, or a university department ‖ 어떤 모임[위원회, 대학 학부]을 책임지고 있는 사람. 의장. 위원장. 학과장 **3** [singular] INFORMAL ⇨ ELECTRIC CHAIR

chair² *v* [T] to be the CHAIRPERSON of a meeting or committee ‖ 회의나 위원회의 의장이 되다

chair·per·son /'tʃɜr,pɚsən/, **chair·man** /'tʃɛrmən/, **chair-**

woman /'tʃɛr,wʊmən/ *n* **1** someone who is in charge of a meeting or committee ‖ 회의나 위원회의 책임자. 의장. 위원장 **2** someone who is in charge of a large organization ‖ 거대 조직의 책임자

USAGE NOTE chairman

Chairman can be used for both men and women, but many people prefer to use **chairperson**, especially if the sex of the person is not known.
chairman은 남·녀 모두에 사용할 수 있지만 특히 성별을 모를 경우 **chairperson**을 쓰는 것을 선호한다.

---

cha·let /ʃæˈleɪ, ˈʃæleɪ/ *n* a small wooden house with a steeply sloping roof ‖ 가파른 경사의 지붕이 있는 작은 나무 집. 샬레

chalk¹ /tʃɔk/ *n* **1** [U] soft white rock ‖ 부드럽고 하얀 암석. 백악 **2** [C, U] small sticks of this substance used for writing or drawing ‖ 글을 쓰거나 그리는 데 쓰는, 백악으로 만들어진 작은 막대. 분필. 초크 – **chalky** *adj*

chalk² *v* [I, T] to write or draw with CHALK ‖ 분필로 쓰거나 그리다

chalk sth ↔ **up** *phr v* [T] INFORMAL to succeed in winning or getting something ‖ 어떤 것을 이기거나 얻는 데 성공하다: *Boston chalked up another win over Detroit last night.* 어젯밤 보스턴은 디트로이트를 상대로 다시 한 번 승리를 거두었다.

chalk·board /'tʃɔkbɔrd/ *n* ⇨ BLACKBOARD

chalk·y /'tʃɔki/ *adj* similar to CHALK, or containing CHALK ‖ 백악과 비슷하거나 백악을 함유한. 백악의. 백악질의

chal·lenge¹ /'tʃæləndʒ/ *n* [C, U] **1** something new, exciting, or difficult that needs a lot of skill and effort to do ‖ 하려면 많은 기술과 노력을 요하는 새로운[흥미진진한, 어려운] 일. 도전: *the challenge of a new job* 새로운 일에 대한 도전 / *Can American businesses meet the Japanese challenge?* (=can they do just as well?) 미국의 사업이 일본의 도전에 대처할 수 있을까? / *The President faces a serious challenge to his leadership.* (=he must be ready to deal with it) 대통령은 자신의 지도력에 대한 심각한 도전에 직면하고 있다. **2** the act of questioning whether something is right, fair, or legal ‖ 어떤 것이 옳은지[공정한지, 적법한지] 의문을 갖는 일. 도전. 의의. 항의: *If I make any decisions myself, my boss thinks it's a direct* *challenge to her authority.* 나 혼자 어떤 결정을 내리면, 내 상사는 그것이 자신의 권위에 대한 직접적인 도전이라고 간주한다. **3** an invitation from someone to compete or fight ‖ 경쟁하거나 격투하려는 사람으로부터의 제안. 도전. 결투 신청

challenge² *v* [T] **1** to question whether something is right, fair, or legal ‖ 어떤 것이 옳은지[정당한지, 적법한지]에 대해 의문을 갖다. 문제 삼다: *At meetings, she would often challenge the director's views.* 회의에서 그녀는 종종 감독의 견해를 문제 삼았다. **2** to invite someone to compete or fight against you ‖ 남에게 자신과 경쟁하거나 결투하자고 제안하다. 도전하다: *We were challenged to a game of tennis.* 우리는 테니스 시합을 제안받았다. **3** to test someone's skills and ability, or to encourage him/her to do this ‖ 남의 기술·능력을 시험하다, 또는 남을 독려하여 기술·능력을 발휘하게 하다: *Nothing about school seems to challenge Brenda any more.* 학교에 관한 한 어느 것도 더 이상 브렌다의 능력을 시험하지 못하는 것 같다. – **challenger** *n*

chal·lenged /ˈtʃæləndʒd/ *adj* **visually/mentally/physically challenged** a phrase meaning that someone has difficulty with seeing, thinking, or doing things, used in order to be polite ‖ 보는 [생각하는, 일을 하는] 데 어려움이 있는 사람을 정중하게 이르는 말. 시각/정신적/육체적 장애가 있는

chal·leng·ing /ˈtʃæləndʒɪŋ/ *adj* difficult in an interesting way ‖ 흥미롭지만 어려운. 흥미를 일게 하는. 해 볼 만한: *a challenging new job* 해 볼 만한 새로운 일

cham·ber /ˈtʃeɪmbɚ/ *n* **1** a room used for a special purpose ‖ 특정 목적에 쓰이는 방. …실: *a gas/torture chamber* (=used for killing people by gas or for hurting them) 가스[고문]실 / *the council's chamber in the Town Hall* 관청 내의 회의실 **2** an enclosed space inside something, such as your body or a machine ‖ 몸이나 기계 등의 안쪽의 막힌 공간. 실(室). 약실: *a gun with six chambers* 6연발 권총 **3** a group of people who make laws for a country, state etc. ‖ 국가·주 등에서 법률을 제정하는 사람들의 집단. 의회: *The Senate is the upper chamber of Congress.* 상원은 국회의 상부 의회이다.

chamber mu·sic /ˈ.. ˌ../ *n* [U] CLASSICAL MUSIC written for a small group of performers ‖ 소규모 집단의 연주자용으로 작곡된 클래식 음악. 실내악

Chamber of Com·merce /ˌ.. '../ *n*

an organization of business people in a town or city whose aim is to encourage business ‖ 사업을 장려하려는 읍이나 시에 있는 사업가들의 조직. 상공 회의소

chambers /ˈtʃeɪmbɚz/ *n* the offices used by judges ‖ 판사가 쓰는 사무실. 판사실

cha·me·leon /kəˈmilyən, kəˈmiliən/ *n* **1** a small LIZARD (=type of animal) whose skin changes and becomes the same color as the things around it ‖ 피부색이 변하여 주변과 같은 색이 되는 작은 도마뱀. 카멜레온 **2** someone who changes his/her ideas, behavior etc. to fit different situations ‖ 다른 상황에 맞추기 위해 자신의 생각·행동 등을 바꾸는 사람. 지조 없는 사람

cham·o·mile /ˈkæməˌmil/ *n* [U] ⇨ CAMOMILE

champ /tʃæmp/ *n* INFORMAL ⇨ CHAMPION¹

cham·pagne /ʃæmˈpeɪn/ *n* [U] a French white wine that has a lot of BUBBLEs and is often drunk on special occasions ‖ 거품이 많고 종종 특별한 경우에 마시는 프랑스산 백포도주. 샴페인

cham·pi·on¹ /ˈtʃæmpiən/ *n* **1** a person, team etc. that has won a competition, especially in sports ‖ 특히 스포츠 시합에서 이긴 사람·팀 등. 챔피언: *the reigning national soccer champions* (=the champions right now) 현 국내 축구 챔피언 팀 **2** **champion of** someone who publicly fights for and defends an aim, idea, group etc. ‖ 목적·사상·단체 등을 위해 공개적으로 싸우며 옹호하는 사람. 옹호[대변]자: *a champion of the homeless* 집 없는 사람들의 대변자

champion² *v* [T] to publicly fight for an aim, idea, group etc ‖ 목적·사상·단체 등을 위해 공개적으로 싸우다. 대변[옹호]하다: *people championing gay rights* 동성애자 인권을 옹호하는 사람들

cham·pi·on·ship /ˈtʃæmpiənˌʃɪp/ *n* **1** a competition or series of competitions to find the best player or team in a particular sport ‖ 특정 스포츠에서 최우수 선수나 팀을 가려내기 위한 시합 또는 일련의 시합. 선수권 대회: *the US basketball championships* 미국 농구 선수권 대회 **2** the position or period of being a champion ‖ 챔피언의 지위 또는 챔피언 자리에 머무르는 기간: *Can she win the championship again?* 그녀가 다시 챔피언 자리를 지킬 수 있을까?

chance¹ /tʃæns/ *n* **1** a time or situation that you can use to do something that you want to do; opportunity ‖ 하고 싶은

것을 하기 위해 쓸 수 있는 시간이나 상황. 기회: *Now I'll have/get a chance to find out what her husband looks like.* 이제야 나는 그녀 남편이 어떻게 생겼는지 볼 기회가 생기겠군. / *If you'll just give me a chance, I'll tell you what happened.* 내게 기회를 준다면 무슨 일이 일어났는지 말해 주겠다. / *You should take the chance* (=use the opportunity) *to travel while you're young.* 젊을 때 여행할 기회를 가져야 합니다. / *Mr. Yates has given us a second chance to pass the test.* (=another chance after you have failed the first time) 예이츠 씨는 우리에게 그 테스트에 통과할 두 번째 기회를 주었다. **2** [C, U] how possible or likely it is that something is true or that someone will succeed ‖ 어떤 것이 사실이거나 어떤 사람이 성공할 가능성이나 개연성의 정도. 승산. 가망: *What are Deirdre's chances of getting the job?* 디어드레가 그 일자리를 잡을 가망성이 얼마나 될까? / *There's a chance she left her keys in the office.* 그녀가 사무실에 열쇠를 놓아 두었을 가능성이 있다. / *Chances are* (=it is likely) *they're stuck in traffic.* 그들이 교통 체증 때문에 오도 가도 못하는 것 같다. **3 by any chance** SPOKEN used in order to ask politely whether something is true ‖ 어떤 것이 사실인지 정중하게 물을 때 쓰여. 혹시. 행여나: *Are you Ms. Hughes' daughter, by any chance?* 혹시, 휴스 여사의 따님이십니까? **4 fat chance!/not a chance!** SPOKEN said when you are sure that something could never happen ‖ 어떤 것이 결코 일어날 수 없을 것이라 확신할 때에 쓰여. 그럴 가능성은 없어!: *"Maybe you'll win the lottery." "Sure, fat chance!"* "어쩌면 네가 복권에 당첨될지 몰라." "물론, 그럴 리 없지!" **5 take a chance** to do something that involves risk ‖ 위험 부담이 있는 어떤 것을 하다. 위험을 무릅쓰고 해 보다: *You take a chance investing money in stocks, but the gains can be huge.* 위험 부담을 안고 주식 투자를 하면 큰 이득을 볼 수 있다. **6** [U] the way things happen without being planned or caused ‖ 계획이나 원인 없이 일이 일어나는 방식. 우연: *We met by chance at a friend's party.* 우리는 한 친구네 집 파티에서 우연히 만났다. —see also **stand a chance (of doing sth)** (STAND¹)

USAGE NOTE chance and opportunity

Use these words to talk about

---

something you are able to do because of luck: *I had the opportunity to visit Boston. / I had no chance to see him.* **Chance** can also mean a possibility: *There is a chance that I will see him.* ✗DON'T SAY "There is an opportunity that I will see him."✗ 운좋게 어떤 것을 할 수 있다고 언급하는 데 이 단어들을 사용한다: 나는 보스턴에 방문할 기회가 있었다. / 나는 그를 볼 기회가 없었다. **chance**는 또한 가능성을 의미하기도 한다: 내가 그를 만나게 될 가능성이 있다. "There is an opportunity that I will see him."이라고는 하지 않는다.

chance² *v* [T] INFORMAL to do something that involves a risk ‖ 위험 부담이 있는 어떤 것을 하다. …에 부딪쳐 보다: *You could always ride the subway, if you're willing to chance it.* 당신이 기꺼이 위험 부담을 안고 해보고 싶다면 언제든지 지하철을 타면 됩니다.

chance on/upon sth *phr v* [T] LITERARY to meet someone or find something when you are not expecting to ‖ 기대하지 않았는데 사람을 만나거나 사물을 찾다. 뜻밖에 …하다

chance³ *adj* not planned; accidental ‖ 계획되지 않은; 우연의: *a chance encounter* (=when you meet someone by accident) 우연한 마주침[만남]

chan·cel·lor /'tʃænsələ/ *n* **1** the head of some universities ‖ 일부 대학의 수장 (首長). 학장: *the Chancellor of UCLA* UCLA 학장 **2** the head of the government in some countries ‖ 일부 국가에서의 정부 수반. (독일 등의) 수상

chanc·y /'tʃænsi/ *adj* INFORMAL uncertain or involving risks ‖ 불확실하거나 위험 부담이 있는. 믿을 것이 못 되는: *The weather there can be chancy in the spring.* 그곳의 봄 날씨는 불확실하다.

chan·de·lier /ˌʃændə'lɪr/ *n* a large decoration that holds lights or CANDLEs, hangs from the ceiling, and is covered with small pieces of glass ‖ 천장에 매달려 전등이나 촛불이 들어 있는, 작은 유리 조각으로 덮인 커다란 장식물. 샹들리에

change¹ /tʃeɪndʒ/ *v* **1** [I, T] to become different, or to make someone or something become different ‖ 달라지다, 변(화)하다. …을 바꾸다[고치다]: *In the fall, its leaves change from green to gold.* 가을에 그 나뭇잎들은 녹색에서 황금색으로 변한다. / *Ed changed after Ricky died.* 리키가 죽은 후 에드는 변했

다. / *There are plans to change the voting system.* 투표 방식을 변경시킬 계획이 있다. / *Let me know if you change your mind.* (=change your decision, plan, or opinion) 마음이 바뀌면 제게 알려주세요. **2** [I, T] to stop having or doing one thing and start something else instead ‖ 한 가지를 갖거나 하는 것을 중단하고 대신 다른 것을 (갖거나 하기) 시작하다: *You'll have to change in Denver.* (=get on a different plane) 덴버에서 다른 비행기를 갈아타야 할 겁니다. / *Would you mind changing places* (=exchanging positions) *with me?* 저와 자리를 바꿔 주실 수 있겠습니까? **3** [I, T] to take off your clothes and put on different ones ‖ 옷을 벗고 다른 옷으로 갈아 입다. 복장을 바꾸다: *Go upstairs and change into your play clothes.* 위층으로 올라가서 연극 의상으로 갈아 입어라. / *Eric went to get changed.* 에릭은 옷 갈아 입으러 갔다. / *change the baby* (=put a clean DIAPER on the baby) 아기 기저귀를 갈아 채우다. **4** [T] **a)** to exchange a unit of money for smaller units that add up to the same value ‖ 한 단위의 돈을 총액이 같은 가치의 보다 작은 단위의 돈으로 교환하다. 잔돈으로 바꾸다: *Can you change a $10 bill?* 10달러짜리 지폐를 잔돈으로 바꾸어 주실 수 있습니까? **b)** to exchange money from one country for money from another ‖ 한 나라의 돈을 다른 나라의 돈으로 바꾸다. 환전하다: *I want to change my dollars into pesos.* 달러화를 페소화로 환전하고 싶습니다. **5 change the sheets** to put clean SHEETs on a bed ‖ 침대에 깨끗한 시트를 깔다. 침대 시트를 갈다 **6 change hands** to become someone else's property ‖ 다른 사람의 재산이 되다. 주인이 바뀌다: *The house has changed hands twice in the last ten years.* 그 집은 지난 10년간 주인이 두 번 바뀌었다.

change sth ↔ **around** *phr v* [T] to move things into different positions ‖ 물건을 다른 위치로 옮기다. 위치를 바꾸다: *The room looks bigger since we changed the furniture around.* 가구 위치를 바꾼 후로 방이 더 넓어 보인다.

change over *phr v* [I] to stop doing or using one thing and start doing or using something different ‖ 하거나 사용하던 것을 멈추고 다른 것을 하거나 사용하기 시작하다. 변경하다. 교체하다: *Will the US ever change over to the metric system?* 미국이 언젠가는 미터법 체계로 교체할까?

change² *n* **1** [C, U] the process or result when something or someone becomes different ‖ 사물이나 사람이 달라지는 과정 또는 결과. 변화: *a change in the weather* 날씨의 변화 / *a change of leadership* 지도력의 변화 / *Grandpa's health has taken a change for the worse.* (=become worse) 할아버지의 건강이 악화되었다. **2** a new or different thing or person used instead of something or someone else ‖ 다른 사물이나 사람 대신 사용되는 새롭거나 다른 사물이나 사람. 교환(되는 것). 교체(되는 사람): *Take a change of clothes with you.* 갈아 입을 옷을 챙겨라. / *The car needs an oil change.* 그 차는 오일 교환이 필요하다. **3** [C usually singular] something that is interesting or enjoyable because it is different from what is usual ‖ 평상시와 다르기 때문에 흥미롭거나 즐거운 것. 기분 전환: *Why don't we go out for a change?* 기분 전환하러 외출하는 게 어때? **4** [U] the money that you get back when you pay for something with more money than it costs ‖ 가격보다 더 많은 돈을 낼 때 되돌려 받는 돈. 거스름돈: *That's 32¢ change, ma'am.* 32센트 거스름돈입니다, 아주머니. **5** [U] money in the form of coins ‖ 동전의 형태로 된 돈. 잔돈: *I have about a dollar in change.* 나에게 잔돈으로 1달러쯤 있다. **6** [U] coins or small bills that you give in exchange for the same amount of money in a larger unit ‖ 큰 단위의 돈과 같은 액수로 교환해 주는 동전 또는 소액 지폐. 잔돈: *Do you have change for a dollar?* 1달러 바꿔 줄 잔돈 있습니까?

change·a·ble /ˈtʃeɪndʒəbəl/ *adj* likely to change, or changing often ‖ 변할 것 같은, 또는 자주 변하는. 변하기 쉬운. 변덕스러운: *changeable weather* 변화 무쌍한 날씨

change·o·ver /ˈtʃeɪnˌdʒoʊvɚ/ *n* a change from one activity or system to another ‖ 하나의 활동이나 체계에서 다른 것으로의 전환. 변환. 변경

chan·nel¹ /ˈtʃænl/ *n* **1** a particular television station ‖ 특정 텔레비전 방송국. 채널: *What's on channel 2?* 2번 채널에서 무슨 프로그램을 하고 있습니까? **2** a long passage dug into the earth that water or other liquids can flow along ‖ 물이나 다른 액체가 따라 흐를 수 있도록 땅에 파 놓은 긴 통로. 도랑 **3** water that connects two seas ‖ 큰 두 바다를 연결하는 바다. 해협: *the English Channel* 영국 해협 **4** the deepest part of a river, sea etc. that ships can sail through ‖ 배가 항해할 수 있는, 강·바다 등의 가장 깊은 부

분. 물길. 수로 **5 channel hop/surf**
INFORMAL to change from one television
channel to another again and again ‖ 텔
레비전 채널을 계속해서 다른 채널로 바꾸
다. 채널을 돌리다

channel² *v* [T] **1** to use something such
as money or energy for a particular
purpose ‖ 특정 목적을 위해 자금이나 에
너지 등을 쓰다. 돌리다. 쏟다: *Wayne
needs to channel his creativity into
something useful.* 웨인은 자신의 창조성
을 뭔가 유용한 것에 쓸 필요가 있다. **2** to
cut a deep line or space into something
‖ 어떤 것에 깊은 선이나 공간을 내다. …
에 수로[도랑]을 파다

channels /ˈtʃænlz/ *n* [plural] ways of
sending or obtaining information about
a particular subject ‖ 특정 주제에 관한
정보를 보내거나 얻는 과정. 전달 경로[수
단]: *You'll have to go through official
channels for help.* 도움을 얻으려면 공식
경로를 통해야 할 것이다.

chant¹ /tʃænt/ *v* [I, T] **1** to repeat a
word or phrase again and again ‖ 단어
나 어구를 되풀이해서 말하다. 구호를 외
치다: *Crowds of chanting supporters
filled the streets.* 구호를 외치는 지지자들
의 무리가 거리를 가득 메웠다. **2** to sing
or say a religious song or prayer using
only one note or TONE ‖ 한 음이나 톤을
사용해서 종교적인 노래나 기도문을 부르
거나 말하다. 찬송하다

chant² *n* **1** words or phrases that are
repeated again and again ‖ 계속 반복되
는 단어나 어구. 반복하는 말. 구호: *The
crowd responded with chants of
"Resign! Resign!"* 군중들은 "사퇴하라! 사
퇴하라!"는 구호로 응답했다. **2** a
religious song with a regularly repeated
tune ‖ 규칙적으로 반복되는 선율의 종교
적인 노래. 성가

Cha·nu·kah /ˈhɑnəkə/ *n* [U] ⇨
HANUKKAH

cha·os /ˈkeɪɑs/ *n* [U] a state of
complete disorder and confusion ‖ 완전
한 무질서와 혼돈 상태: *After the
earthquake, the city was in chaos.* 지진
이 일어난 후 그 도시는 지독한 혼란 상태
에 빠졌다.

cha·ot·ic /keɪˈɑtɪk/ *adj* a situation that
is chaotic is very disorganized and
confusing ‖ 상황 등이 매우 비조직적이며
혼란스러운. 대혼란[무질서]의. 혼돈된:
*The lunchroom was chaotic, with kids
shouting and throwing things.* 아이들이
소리치며 물건을 던지는 바람에 학교 식당
이 아주 혼란스러웠다.

chap·el /ˈtʃæpəl/ *n* a small church or a
room where Christians have religious
services ‖ 크리스트교인들이 예배를 드리
는 작은 교회나 방. 예배당[실]

chap·e·rone¹ /ˈʃæpəˌroʊn/ *n* an older
person who is responsible for young
people on social occasions ‖ 사교계의 행
사에서 젊은 사람을 돌봐 주는 나이 많은
사람. 샤프롱: *My parents are going to be
chaperones at the dance on Friday.* 금요
일 무도회에서 부모님이 보호자가 되어 주
실 거다.

chaperone² *v* [T] to go somewhere
with someone as his/her CHAPERONE ‖ 어
떤 사람을 돌봐 주는 역할로서 함께 어떤
곳에 가다. 따라다니며 돌봐 주다

chap·lain /ˈtʃæplɪn/ *n* a minister who is
responsible for the religious needs of
people in a part of the army, a hospital,
a prison etc. ‖ 군대·병원·감옥 등에 있는
사람들의 종교적인 요구를 담당하는 성직
자. 지도 신부. 군목(軍牧)

chapped /tʃæpt/ *adj* skin that is
chapped is sore and cracked as a result
of cold weather or wind ‖ 추운 날씨나 바
람 때문에 피부가 쓰라리고 갈라진. 튼.
거칠어진: *chapped lips* 갈라진 입술 –
chap *v* [T]

chaps /tʃæps/ *n* [plural] leather covers
that protect your legs when you ride a
horse ‖ 말을 탈 때 다리를 보호하는 가죽
덮개. 가죽 바지

chap·ter /ˈtʃæptɚ/ *n* **1** one of the parts
into which a book is divided ‖ 책이 나뉘
어진 부분 중 하나. 장(章) **2** a particular
period or event in someone's life or in
history ‖ 사람의 삶이나 역사에서 특정한
시기 또는 사건. (중요한) 한 구획[시기]:
a sad chapter in our country's history
우리 나라 역사의 슬픈 시기 **3** the local
members of a large organization or club
‖ 거대한 조직이나 클럽의 지방 회원들.
지부. 분회: *the Boise chapter of the
Sierra Club* 시에라 클럽의 보이스 분회

char·ac·ter /ˈkærɪktɚ/ *n* **1** [C, U] all of
the qualities that make one person,
place, or thing different from another ‖
하나의 사람[장소, 사물]을 다른 것과 구
별짓게 하는 모든 성질. 특성: *There's a
very serious side to her character.* 그녀
의 성격에는 매우 심각한[진지한] 면이 있
다. / *All these new buildings have really
changed the character of this town.* 이
모든 새 건물들이 이 도시의 특성을 정말
로 변화시켰다. **2** [U] the good qualities
that make someone or something
special, interesting, valuable etc. ‖ 사람
이나 사물을 특별하게 [흥미롭게, 가치있
게] 만드는 좋은 특성. 명성. 평판: *an old*

house with a lot of character 유서 깊은 오래된 집 **3 a person in a book, play, movie etc.** ‖ 책·연극·영화 등에 나오는 사람. 등장 인물: *I don't like the main character in the book.* 나는 그 책의 주인공이 마음에 들지 않는다. **4 a person of a particular kind** ‖ 특정 부류의 사람. ···한 [성격의] 인물: *Dan's a strange character.* 댄은 이상한 성격의 인물이다. **5 an unusual and humorous person** ‖ 유별나고 익살맞은 사람. 괴짜: *Charlie's such a character!* 찰리는 정말 괴짜야! **6 a letter, mark, or sign used in writing, printing,or computing** (COMPUTE) ‖ 기록[인쇄, 계산]에 사용되는 문자[부호, 기호]. 자체. 서체: *Chinese characters* 한자

char·ac·ter·is·tic¹ /ˌkærɪktəˈrɪstɪk/ *n* a special quality or feature that someone or something has ‖ 사람이나 사물이 지니는 특별한 성질 또는 특징. 특색. 특질: *the characteristics of a good manager* 훌륭한 경영인의 특징 / *Each wine has particular characteristics.* 각각의 포도주는 독특한 특성을 지니고 있다.

characteristic² *adj* typical of a particular thing or person ‖ 특정 사물이나 사람에게 전형적인. 특유한: *Mark, with characteristic kindness, offered to help.* 특유의 친절함을 지닌 마크가 도움을 주었다. **– characteristically** *adv*

char·ac·ter·ize /ˈkærɪktəˌraɪz/ *v* [T] **1** to be typical of someone or something ‖ 사람이나 사물의 특징이다. ···의 특징[특색]을 나타내다: *Alzheimer's disease is characterized by memory loss.* 알츠하이머 병은 기억력 상실로 특징지워진다. **2** to describe the character of someone or something in a particular way ‖ 사람이나 사물의 특성을 특정하게 기술하다. ···으로 묘사하다: *His book characterizes Eisenhower as a natural leader.* 그의 책은 아이젠하워를 타고난 지도자로 묘사하고 있다. **– characterization** /ˌkærɪktərəˈzeɪʃən/ *n* [C, U]

cha·rade /ʃəˈreɪd/ *n* a situation that seems to be true or serious, but that everyone knows is not ‖ 사실로 또는 진정한 것으로 보이나 모든 사람들이 그렇지 않다는 것을 아는 상황. 속이 들여다 보이는 상황. 뻔히 알 수 있는 구실: *Their happy marriage is just a charade.* 그들의 행복한 결혼이란 것은 그저 속이 뻔히 들여다보이는 거짓에 불과하다.

cha·rades /ʃəˈreɪdz/ *n* [U] a game in which one person uses only actions to show the meaning of a word or phrase, and other people have to guess what it is ‖ 한 사람이 몸짓만을 사용하여 단어나 어구의 의미를 나타내면 다른 사람들이 무엇인지 추측하는 게임. 제스처 게임

char·coal /ˈtʃɑrkoʊl/ *n* [U] a black substance made of burned wood, used for burning or drawing ‖ 불탄 나무로 만든, 불을 지피거나 그림 그릴 때 쓰는 검은 물질. 숯. 목탄

charge¹ /tʃɑrdʒ/ *n*
1 ▶MONEY 돈◀ [C, U] the amount of money you have to pay for a particular thing ‖ 특정한 것에 대해 지불해야 하는 금액. 경비. 요금: *There's a $70 charge for every extra piece of luggage.* 추가되는 수하물마다 70달러의 요금이 붙는다. / *We deliver free of charge.* (=at no cost) 무료로 배달해 드립니다.
2 be in charge (of) to be the person who controls or is responsible for someone or something ‖ 사람이나 사물을 지휘하거나 책임지는 사람이다: *Who is in charge of the department?* 누가 그 부서의 책임자입니까?
3 take charge (of) to take control of someone or something ‖ 사람이나 사물의 관리를 떠맡다. 책임지다: *Diane took charge of the business when her husband died.* 남편이 사망했을 때 다이앤이 그 사업을 떠맡았다.
4 ▶CRIME 범죄◀ an official statement saying that someone is guilty of a crime ‖ 누군가가 죄가 있다고 말하는 공식 진술. 혐의. 고소. 고발: *He's in court on charges of murder.* 그는 살인 혐의로 재판 중이다. / *The charge against her was shoplifting.* 그녀에 대한 고소 내용은 상점에서 물건을 훔친 것이다. / *They decided not to bring/press charges.* (=make official charges) 그들은 공식적인 고발을 하지 않기로 했다. / *Somebody else confessed, so the police had to drop the charges against him.* (=decide to stop making charges) 다른 누군가가 자백해서 경찰은 그를 무혐의 처리를 해야만 했다.
5 ▶ELECTRICITY 전기◀ [U] electricity that is put into a piece of electrical equipment ‖ 전기 기기에 투입되는 전기. 충전: *The charge didn't last very long in the batteries.* 배터리의 충전이 그리 오래 가지 않았다.
6 get a charge out of sth to enjoy something very much ‖ 어떤 것을 매우 즐기다: *I got a real charge out of seeing Jane win that prize.* 나는 제인이 그 상을 수상하는 것을 보고 정말 즐거웠다.
7 ▶ATTACK 공격◀ an attack in which people, animals etc. move forward quickly ‖ 사람·동물 등이 앞으로 재빠르게

움직이며 하는 공격. 급습. 돌격

8 ▶EXPLOSIVE 폭발물◀ an explosive material put into a gun or weapon ‖ 총이나 무기에 투입하는 폭발 물질. 총포에 재는 장전(물)

charge² *v* **1** [I, T] to ask for a particular amount of money for something you are selling ‖ 판매하는 것에 대해 특정 금액을 요구하다. 요금을 청구하다 [매기다]: *How much do you charge for your eggs?* 계란이 얼마입니까? **2** [T] to record the cost of something in someone's account, so that s/he can pay for it later ‖ 나중에 남이 계산할 수 있도록 하기 위해 사물의 가격을 남의 계정에 기록하다. 남 앞으로 달아 놓다: *Charge the room to my account.* 방 값을 제 앞으로 달아 놓으세요. / *"Would you like to pay cash?" "No, I'll charge it."* (=pay with a CREDIT CARD) "현금으로 계산하시겠습니까?" "아니요, 신용 카드로 하겠습니다." **3** [T] to state officially that someone is guilty of a crime ‖ 사람이 유죄라는 것을 공식적으로 진술하다. 고소[고발]하다: *Ron's been charged with assault.* 론은 폭행 혐의로 고소당했다. **4** [I, T] to put electricity into a piece of electrical equipment such as a BATTERY ‖ 배터리 등의 전기 기기에 전기를 축적하다. 충전하다: *Leave the phone on its base to charge overnight.* 밤새 충전될 수 있도록 전화기를 전화기 받침대 위에 놓아 두시오. **5** [I, T] to run very fast, often in order to attack someone or something ‖ 종종 다른 사람이나 사물을 공격하기 위해 매우 빨리 달리다. 돌격[돌진]하다

charge ac·count /'. .,./ *n* an account you have with a store that allows you to take goods away with you immediately and pay for them later ‖ 물건을 즉시 가져가고 지불을 나중에 할 수 있게 하는 자신이 상점에 갖고 있는 계정. 외상 (계정)

charge card /'. ./ *n* ⇨ CREDIT CARD

char·i·ot /'tʃæriət/ *n* a vehicle with two wheels pulled by a horse, used in ancient times in battles and races ‖ 고대에 전투와 경주에서 쓰였던, 말이 끄는 바퀴가 두 개 달린 탈것. 이륜 마차 – **charioteer** /ˌtʃæriə'tɪr/ *n*

cha·ris·ma /kə'rɪzmə/ *n* [U] the natural ability to attract other people and make them admire you ‖ 다른 사람들을 매혹시켜 숭배하게 만들 수 있는 타고난 능력. 카리스마 – **charismatic** /ˌkærɪz'mætɪk/ *adj*

char·i·ta·ble /'tʃærətəbəl/ *adj* **1** relating to money or gifts given to people who need help, or organizations that give this type of help ‖ 도움을 필요로 하는 사람들에게 제공하는 돈이나 선물, 또는 이런 종류의 도움을 주는 단체들과 관련된. 자선의[을 위한]: *The money went to a charitable group.* 그 돈은 자선 단체로 들어갔다. **2** kind and generous ‖ 친절하고 관대한. 자비로운 – **charitably** *adv*

char·i·ty /'tʃærəti/ *n* **1** an organization that gives money or help to people who need it ‖ 도움이 필요한 사람들에게 돈이나 원조를 제공하는 단체. 자선 단체: *Several charities sent aid to the flood victims.* 몇몇 자선 단체들이 수재민들에게 원조를 보냈다. **2** [U] charity organizations in general ‖ 일반적인 자선 단체: *It's strange that poorer people donate more money to charity.* 이상하게도 더 가난한 사람들이 자선 단체에 더 많은 돈을 기부한다. **3** [U] money or gifts given to people who need help ‖ 도움이 필요한 사람들에게 제공하는 돈이나 선물. 구호[품]: *She's too proud to accept charity.* 그녀는 구호 물자를 받기에는 너무 자존심이 강하다.

char·la·tan /'ʃɑrlətən/ *n* someone who pretends to have special skills or knowledge that s/he does not really have ‖ 사실은 없으면서 특수 기술이나 지식이 있는 체하는 사람. 허풍선이. 사기꾼

charm¹ /tʃɑrm/ *n* **1** [C, U] the special quality someone or something has that makes people like him, her, or it ‖ 사람들이 좋아하게 만드는 사람이나 사물의 특별한 특성. 매력: *This town has a charm you couldn't find in a big city.* 이 도시는 대도시에서 찾을 수 없는 매력이 있다. **2** an object, phrase, or action believed to have special magic powers ‖ 특별한 마법의 힘이 있다고 여겨지는 대상물[어구, 행위]. 부적. 주문: *a lucky charm* 행운의 부적 **3 work like a charm** to happen exactly as you had hoped, or have the result you wanted ‖ 바라던 그대로 (일·사건이) 일어나거나 바라던 결과를 얻다. 기이하게도 잘 되어 가다

charm² *v* [T] to please someone or make him/her like you ‖ 남을 기쁘게 하거나 그 사람이 자기를 좋아하게 하다. …을 황홀하게 하다[매혹시키다]: *a story that has charmed youngsters for generations* 수세대에 걸쳐 젊은이들을 사로잡았던 이야기 – **charmer** *n*

charmed /tʃɑrmd/ *adj* lucky in a way that seems magical ‖ 마술처럼 보일 정도로 운이 좋은: *Until she was 18, Liz seemed to live a charmed life.* (=a life in

which many good things happened) 열여
덟 살 때까지 리즈는 이상하게도 좋은 일
만 일어나는 삶을 산 듯했다.

charm·ing /'tʃɑrmɪŋ/ *adj* very pleasing
or attractive ‖ 매우 기쁘게 하거나 매력을
끄 는. 매력적인. 유쾌한: *What a
charming house!* 정말 매력적인 집이군!
– **charmingly** *adv*

charred /tʃɑrd/ *adj* something that is
charred is so burnt that it has become
black ‖ 너무 타서 새까맣게 된. 까맣게 탄
– **char** *v* [I, T]

chart¹ /tʃɑrt/ *n* **1** information that is
shown in the form of a picture, GRAPH
etc. ‖ 그림, 그래프 등의 형태로 보여지는
정보. 표. 도표: *a weather chart* 기상도
2 the charts a list of the most popular
records ‖ 가장 인기 있는 음반 목록. 인기
곡 순위표: *That song was top of the
charts for over 6 weeks.* 그 노래는 6주
가 넘게 순위에서 1위 곡이었다. **3** a
detailed map of the sea or stars ‖ 바다나
별의 세부적인 지도. 해도. 별자리표

chart² *v* [T] **1** to record information
about a situation or set of events over a
period of time ‖ 일정 기간에 걸쳐 상황이
나 일련의 사건들에 관한 정보를 기록하
다. …을 기록하다: *a report charting the
progress of the housing program* 주택 계
획의 경과를 기록한 보고서 **2** to make a
map of an area, or to draw lines on a
map to show where you have traveled ‖
어떤 지역의 지도를 만들거나 여행한 곳을
나타내려고 지도 위에 선을 그리다. …을
지도로 만들다. …을 지도에 그리다

char·ter¹ /'tʃɑrtɚ/ *n* **1** a statement of
the principles, duties, and purposes of
an organization ‖ 단체의 신조·의무·목적
등에 관한 성명서. 헌장: *the UN charter*
유엔 헌장 **2** [C, U] the practice of
paying money to a company to use their
boats, aircraft etc., or the plane, boat
etc. that is used in this way ‖ 배·항공기
등을 사용하기 위해 회사에 돈을 지불하는
일, 또는 돈을 지불하고 사용하는 비행기
·배 등. (배·비행기 등의) 전세 계약. 전
세 비행기[배]: *The airline is now
primarily a charter service.* 그 항공 회사
는 현재 주로 비행기를 전세 운영하고 있
다.

charter² *v* [T] **1** to pay a company for
the use of their boat, plane etc. ‖ 선박·
비행기 등의 사용의 대가로 회사에 돈을
지불하다. (선박·비행기 등을) 전세 계
약으로 임대하다: *We'll have to charter a
bus.* 우리는 전세 버스를 임대해야 한다.
2 to say officially that a town,
organization, or university exists and

has special rights ‖ 읍[단체, 대학]이 존
재하며 특권을 갖는다는 것을 공식적으로
밝히다. …의 설립을 인가하다

charter flight /'.. ˌ./ *n* a plane trip
that is arranged especially for a
particular group or for a particular
purpose ‖ 특정 집단이나 특정 목적을 위
해 특별히 마련된 비행기 여행. 전세기
(편)

charter mem·ber /ˌ.. '../ *n* an
original member of a club or
organization ‖ 클럽이나 단체의 창립 회원

char·treuse /ʃɑr'truz, -'trus/ *n* [U] a
bright yellow-green color ‖ 밝은 황록색
– **chartreuse** *adj*

chase¹ /tʃeɪs/ *v* **1** [I, T] to quickly
follow someone or something in order to
catch him, her, or it ‖ 사람이나 사물을
잡기 위해 빠르게 뒤쫓다. …을 쫓다. …
을 추격[추적]하다: *a cat chasing after
a mouse* 쥐를 쫓는 고양이 / *Cops chased
the mugger down the street.* 경찰들은 거
리에서 강도를 추격했다. **2** [T] to make
someone or something leave ‖ 사람이나
사물을 떠나게 하다. …을 쫓아내다[내쫓
다]: *There was a racoon in the yard, but
the dog chased it away.* 뜰에 너구리가
있었는데, 개가 내쫓았다. **3** [I] to rush or
hurry somewhere ‖ 어딘가에 급히 가거
나 서두르다: *Those kids are always
chasing in and out!* 저 아이들은 항상 들
락날락한단 말이야! **4** [T] to try very
hard to make someone like you in a
romantic way ‖ 남이 자기를 사랑하게 하
려고 매우 애쓰다. …을 끈질기게 쫓아다
니다: *Sherry's been chasing me for
months.* 셰리는 몇 개월째 내가 좋다고 쫓
아다니고 있다.

chase² *n* **1** the act of following
someone or something quickly in order
to catch him, her, or it ‖ 사람이나 사물
을 잡기 위해 재빨리 쫓아가는 행위. 추
적. 추격: *The movie ended with a long
car chase.* 그 영화는 긴 차 추격 장면으로
끝났다. **2 give chase** LITERARY to chase
someone or something ‖ 사람이나 사물을
쫓아가다. 추격하다 **3 cut to
the chase** INFORMAL to immediately
begin to do or discuss the most
important part of something ‖ 어떤 것의
가장 중요한 부분을 즉시 하거나 논의하기
시작하다. 본론으로 들어가다

chasm /'kæzəm/ *n* **1** [singular] a big
difference between ideas or groups of
people ‖ 사람들의 생각이나 집단 사이의
큰 차이. 틈. 간격. 간극: *the chasm
between rich and poor people* 부자와 가
난한 자들 사이의 간극 **2** a very deep

hole between two areas of rock or ice ‖ 바위나 얼음의 두 지대 사이의 매우 깊은 구멍. 깊게 갈라진 틈

chas·sis /'tʃæsi, 'ʃæ-/ *n, plural* **chassis** the frame on which the body, engine etc. of a vehicle is built ‖ 탈것의 몸체·엔진 등이 건조되는 틀. (자동차의) 섀시[차대]. (비행기의) 각부(脚部)

chaste /tʃeɪst/ *adj* OLD-FASHIONED not having sex with anyone, or not with anyone except the person you are married to ‖ 누구와도 성관계를 갖지 않는, 또는 자기 배우자 이외에는 누구와도 성관계를 갖지 않는. 정절을 지키는

chas·ten /'tʃeɪsən/ *v* [T] FORMAL to make someone realize that his/her behavior is wrong, and that it must change ‖ 어떤 사람에게 그 자신의 행동이 잘못되어 꼭 고쳐야 한다는 것을 깨닫게 하다. 벌하여 바로잡다

chas·tise /tʃæs'taɪz, 'tʃæstaɪz/ *v* [T] FORMAL to criticize or punish someone severely ‖ 누군가를 가혹하게 비난하거나 벌주다. 질책하다. (매질하여) 벌하다 – **chastisement** *n* [C, U]

chas·ti·ty /'tʃæstəti/ *n* [U] the state of not having sex with anyone, or not with anyone except the person you are married to ‖ 누구와도, 또는 배우자를 제외한 누구와도 성관계를 갖지 않는 상태. 순결. 정절

chat¹ /tʃæt/ *v* **-tted, -tting** [I] **1** to talk in a friendly and informal way ‖ 친근하고 격의없이 이야기하다. 잡담하다 **2** to communicate with several people in a chat room on the Internet ‖ 인터넷 상의 대화방에서 몇몇 사람들과 대화하다. 채팅하다

chat² *n* [C, U] a friendly informal conversation ‖ 친근하고 격의없는 대화. 잡담

cha·teau /ʃæ'tou/ *n, plural* **chateaux** /-'touz/ *or* **chateaus** a castle or large country house in France ‖ 프랑스의 성이나 대저택

chat room /'../ *n* a place on the Internet where you can write messages to other people and receive messages back from them immediately, so that you can have a conversation while you are ONLINE ‖ 다른 사람들에게 메시지를 써 보내고 즉시 답신을 받을 수 있어서 접속 중인 동안 대화를 나눌 수 있는 인터넷 상의 장소. 채팅 룸. 대화방

chat·ter¹ /'tʃætɚ/ *v* [I] **1** to talk a lot about things that are not important ‖ 대수롭지 않은 일에 대해서 많이 이야기하다. 시시한 내용을 재잘재잘 지껄이다 **2**

to make short high sounds ‖ 짧고 높은 소리를 내다. 요란한 소리를 내다: *monkeys chattering in the trees* 나무에서 요란한 소리를 내는 원숭이들 **3** if your teeth chatter, they knock together because you are cold ‖ 추워서 이가 딱딱 맞부딪치다. (이가) 덜덜 떨리다

chatter² *n* [U] **1** a conversation about something that is not important ‖ 중요하지 않은 일에 관한 대화. 잡담 **2** a series of short high sounds or hard quick sounds ‖ 연속된 짧고 높은 소리나 무겁고 짧게 끊어지는 소리. 딱딱[덜컹덜컹, 탕탕] 하는 소리: *the continuous chatter of machinery* 계속되는 기계의 덜컹거리는 소리

chat·ter·box /'tʃætɚˌbɑks/ *n* OLD-FASHIONED someone who talks too much ‖ 이야기를 너무 많이 하는 사람. 수다쟁이

chat·ty /'tʃæti/ *adj* INFORMAL **1** liking to talk a lot ‖ 이야기를 많이 하기 좋아하는. 수다스러운 **2** having a friendly informal style ‖ 친근하고 격의없는 말씨를 가진. 기탄없는. 허물없는: *a chatty letter* 정답게 이야기하는 투의 편지

chauf·feur¹ /'ʃoufɚ, ʃou'fɚ/ *n* someone whose job is to drive a car for someone else ‖ 다른 사람의 차를 운전해 주는 직업인. 고용 운전사

chauffeur² *v* [T] to drive a car for someone else, especially when it is your job or duty ‖ 특히 직업이나 의무로서 다른 사람을 위해 차를 운전하다: *I spent all day chauffeuring my kids everywhere.* 나는 내 아이들을 차에 태우고 사방으로 다니며 하루 종일 지냈다.

chau·vin·ism /'ʃouvəˌnɪzəm/ *n* [U] a strong belief that your sex or country is better than the other sex or other countries ‖ 자신의 성(性)이나 국가가 다른 성(性)이나 국가보다 우월하다는 강한 믿음. 극단적인 성차별주의. 광신적[맹목적] 애국주의. 쇼비니즘: *fears that ethnic chauvinism will lead to civil war* 맹목적인 인종 차별주의로 인해 내전이 일어날 것이라는 두려움

chau·vin·ist /'ʃouvənɪst/ *n* someone who believes that his/her sex, country etc. is better than the other sex, other countries etc. ‖ 자신의 성·국가 등이 다른 성·국가보다 우월하다고 믿는 사람. 극단적 성차별주의자. 맹목적 애국주의자 – **chauvinist** *adj* : *Ernie's just a male chauvinist pig.* 어니는 아무도 못 말리는 맹목적인 남성 우월주의자이다. – **chauvinistic** /ˌʃouvə'nɪstɪk/ *adj*

cheap¹ /tʃip/ *adj* **1** not expensive, or

lower in price than you expected ‖ 비싸지 않은, 또는 예상보다 가격이 낮은. 값이 싼: *Their fruit is really cheap.* 그 집 과일은 정말 싸다. / *Those jeans are dirt cheap!* (=very low in price) 그 청바지는 아주 싸구나! **2** of bad quality ‖ 질이 안 좋은. 후진: *Judy's shoes looked cheap to me.* 주디 신발은 질이 안 좋아 보였다. **3** not liking to spend money ‖ 돈 쓰기를 좋아하지 않는. 인색한: *He's so cheap we didn't even go out on my birthday.* 그는 너무나 구두쇠여서 내 생일 조차도 외식을 안 했다. **4** behaving in a way that is unkind or not respectful to other people, just because it is easy to do ‖ 단지 하기 쉬워서 남에게 불친절하거나 존중하지 않는 방식으로 행동하는. 말보는: *He made some cheap shot* (=an unkind criticism) *about her looks.* 그는 그녀의 외모에 대해 가혹한 비난을 했다. **5** behaving in a way that shows you do not respect or care about yourself, so that other people do not respect you ‖ 스스로를 존중하거나 배려하지 않는 것을 보여 남들이 자신을 존중하지 않게 행동하는. 하찮은. 보잘것없는: *He made me feel cheap.* 그 때문에 나 스스로가 하찮게 여겨졌다. **6 cheap thrill** excitement that does not take much effort to get ‖ 큰 노력을 들이지 않고 얻는 재미 – **cheaply** *adv* – **cheapness** *n* [U]

cheap² *adv* **1** at a low price ‖ 낮은 가격으로. 싸게. 저가(低價)에: *I was lucky to get it so cheap.* 나는 운좋게 그것을 아주 싸게 샀다. / *Cars like that don't come cheap.* (=are expensive) 그런 차는 비싸다. / *Flights to Rio are going cheap.* (=selling for a lower price than usual) 리오행 비행기표를 평소보다 싸게 팔고 있다. **2** INFORMAL in a way that makes someone difficult to respect ‖ 사람을 존경하기 어렵게 만드는 방식으로. 저속하게: *I wish she wouldn't act so cheap.* 나는 그녀가 그렇게 저속하게 행동하지 않기를 바란다.

cheap·en /ˈtʃipən/ *v* **1** [T] to make someone or something seem to have less worth ‖ 사람이나 물건이 가치가 덜한 것으로 보이게 하다. 품위[가치]를 떨어뜨리다: *As an actress, I'd be cheapening myself by doing TV commercials.* 여배우로서 나는 TV 상업 광고에 출연하여 품위를 떨어뜨리게 될 거다. **2** [I, T] to become lower in price or value, or to make something do this ‖ 가격이나 가치가 낮아지다, 또는 어떤 것을 이렇게 하게 하다. 값이 싸지다. 가치를 내리다: *The dollar's rise in value has cheapened*

imports. 달러 가치의 상승은 수입품의 가격을 떨어뜨렸다.

cheap·skate /ˈtʃipskeɪt/ *n* INFORMAL someone who does not like spending money or giving gifts ‖ 돈을 쓰거나 선물을 주는 것을 싫어하는 사람. 구두쇠

cheat

Mike was cheating in the Spanish test.

cheat¹ /tʃit/ *v* **1** [I] to behave in a dishonest way in order to win or gain something ‖ 어떤 것을 이기거나 얻기 위해서 부정하게 행동하다. 속임수를 쓰다: *He always cheats when we play cards.* 우리가 카드놀이를 할 때 그는 항상 속임수를 쓴다. **2** [T] to trick or deceive someone ‖ 사람에게 속임수를 쓰거나 속이다. 기만하다. 사기치다: *The salesman cheated me out of $100.* 그 영업 사원은 나를 속여 100달러를 사취했다. **3 feel cheated** to feel that you have been treated wrongly or unfairly ‖ 부정하게 또는 부당하게 취급당해 왔다고 느끼다 – **cheating** *n* [U]

cheat on sb *phr v* [T] to be unfaithful to your husband, wife, or sexual partner by secretly having sex with someone else ‖ 다른 사람과 몰래 성관계를 가져서 남편·부인·섹스 파트너에게 불성실하다. 외도하다. 바람을 피우다: *I think Dan's cheating on Debbie again.* 나는 댄이 데비 몰래 다시 바람을 피우고 있다고 생각한다.

cheat² *n* someone who is dishonest and CHEATS ‖ 부정직하고 속임수를 쓰는 사람. 사기[첩잡]꾼: *You're a liar and a cheat!* 너는 거짓말쟁이에 협잡꾼이야!

check¹ /tʃek/ *v* **1** [I, T] to do something or look at something to find out if it is done, correct, in good condition etc. ‖ 어떤 것의 실행·정확성·양호한 상태 등을 알아보기 위해 어떤 것을 하거나 살펴보다. 검사[확인]하다: *"Did Barry lock the back door?" "I don't know – I'll check."* "배리가 뒷문을 잠갔지요?" "모르겠네요. 제가 점검해 보겠습니다." / *I need to check the mailbox; I'm expecting a letter.* 나는 우편함을 확인해 봐야 해. 편지를 기다리고 있거든. / *Make sure you double check* (=check them twice) *the* *spellings of these names.* 이 이름들의 철자를 두 번 확인하여 틀림없도록 해라. **2** [I] to ask permission to do something or to ask whether something is correct or true ‖ 어떤 것을 할 수 있도록 허가를 요청하거나 어떤 것이 정확하거나 사실인지를 물어보다: *Check with Jim to see if you can leave early.* 네가 일찍 출발할 수 있는지 짐에게 문의해 봐라. / *Can you check whether we're still having a meeting?* 여전히 회의 계획이 있는지 확인할 수 있니? **3** [T] to put someone's bags, coat etc. in a special place where they can be kept safe ‖ 안전하게 보관할 수 있는 특별한 장소에 가방·외투 등을 두다. 소지품을 임시로 맡기다[보관하다]: *Can I check that for you, sir?* 그것을 보관해 드릴까요, 손님? **4** [T] to try hard to stop yourself from doing something ‖ 자신의 행동을 자제하려고 애쓰다. 억제하다. 참다: *I had to check the urge to laugh out loud.* 나는 웃음이 크게 터져 나오려는 것을 참아야 했다. **5** [T] to stop something bad from getting worse ‖ 나쁜 것이 더 악화되는 것을 막다. 저지[방해]하다: *The treatment checks the spread of the cancer.* 그 치료는 암의 확산을 막는다.

check in *phr v* [I, T] to go to the desk at a hotel, airport etc. and say that you have arrived ‖ 호텔·공항 등의 프런트에 가서 도착했음을 말하다. 체크인하다. 탑승 절차를 밟다: *Please check in at gate number 5.* 5번 탑승구로 탑승해 주세요.

check sth ↔ **off** *phr v* [T] to make a mark (√) next to an answer, something on a list etc. to show that it is correct, finished, or that you have noticed it ‖ 어떤 것의 정확함[완성됨, 인되었음]을 나타내기 위해 해답이나 목록에 있는 사항 옆에 표시하다. …에 점검표(√)를 하다: *Check their names off the list as they arrive.* 그들이 도착하면 성명에 점검 표시를 해라.

check on sb/sth *phr v* [T] to make sure that someone or something is doing what he, she, or it is supposed to be doing ‖ 사람이나 사물이 하도록 되어 있는 일을 하고 있는지 확인하다. 조사 확인하다: *I have to go check on the roast.* 나는 가서 불고기를 확인해 봐야 돼.

check out *phr v* **1** [T **check** sth ↔ **out**] INFORMAL to make sure that something is actually true, correct, or acceptable ‖ 어떤 것이 정말 맞는지[정확한지, 받아들일 수 있는 것인지]를 확인하다: *The police checked out his story with the other suspects.* 경찰은 다른 용의자들에게서 그

의 말이 사실인지를 확인 조사했다. / *We thought we'd check out this new restaurant Jim says is so good.* 우리는 짐이 말한 이 새 식당이 그렇게 훌륭한지 확인해 봐야겠다고 생각했다. **2** [T **check** sb/sth ↔ **out**] SPOKEN to look at someone or something because he, she, or it is interesting or attractive ‖ 사람이나 사물이 흥미롭고 매력이 있어서 쳐다보다: *Check it out, man! This place is great!* 이봐, 이것 좀 봐! 이곳은 대단해! **3** [I] if something checks out, it is proven to be true, correct, or acceptable ‖ 어떤 것이 진실한[정확한, 받아들일 수 있는] 것으로 입증되다: *If your references check out, you can start the job on Monday.* 자네의 신원 조회가 끝나면 월요일부터 일을 시작할 수 있네. **4** [I] to pay the bill and leave a hotel ‖ 계산을 하고 호텔을 나오다. 체크아웃하다: *You must check out before 12 o'clock.* 12시 전에 체크아웃하셔야 합니다. **5** [T **check** sth ↔ **out**] to borrow books from a library ‖ 도서관에서 책을 빌리다. 대출하다: *You can only check out 5 books at a time.* 한 번에 5권만 대출할 수 있습니다.

check sth ↔ **over** *phr v* [T] to look carefully at someone or something to make sure that he, she, or it is in an acceptable condition ‖ 받아들일 수 있는 상황인지 확인하기 위해 사람이나 사물을 주의깊게 살펴보다. 조사하다. 점검[검토]하다: *Can you check over my paper for spelling mistakes?* 철자에 잘못이 있는지 내 논문을 봐 주실래요? / *The doctor checked her over and couldn't find anything wrong.* 의사가 그녀를 검진했으나 어떤 이상도 발견할 수 없었다.

check up on sb/sth *phr v* [T] to try to find out if someone is doing what s/he is supposed to be doing, or that something is correct ‖ 남이 해야 할 일을 하고 있는지, 또는 어떤 것이 정확한지 확인하려고 애쓰다. 철저히 조사하다: *Are you trying to check up on me, or what?* 나를 조사하라도 하겠다는 거야 뭐야?

check² *n*

1 ▶ **EXAMINATION** 조사 ◀ an examination to find out if something is correct, true, or safe ‖ 어떤 것이 정확[진실, 안전]한지를 확인하려는 조사. 검사. 조사: *a security check* 안전 검사 / *I want a check on the quality of all goods leaving the factory.* 나는 공장에서 출하되는 모든 상품의 품질 검사를 원한다. / *They're doing spot checks for drugs.* (=quick checks of one thing in a group of things, done without warning) 그들은

마약 색출을 위해 무작위로 아무거나 조사하고 있다. / *I want you to do/run a check on this blood sample.* (=find out information about it) 네가 이 혈액 샘플을 분석하기를 바란다.

2 ▶MONEY 돈◀ one of a set of printed pieces of paper that you can sign and use to pay for things ‖ 서명하고 나서 물건 가격을 지불하는 데 사용하는 종이 인쇄물의 하나. 수표: *a check for $50* 50달러짜리 수표 / *Can I pay by check?* 수표로 지불해도 괜찮습니까?

3 ▶CONTROL 통제◀ [singular] something that controls something else ‖ 다른 것을 통제하는 것. 억제. 저지: *The policy should act as a check on inflation.* 그 정책은 인플레이션을 억제하는 작용[역할]을 할 것이다. / *We've kept the disease in check for over a year now.* 우리는 현재 그 질병을 1년 이상 억제시켜 왔다.

4 ▶BILL 청구서◀ a list that you are given at a restaurant that shows what you have eaten and how much you must pay ‖ 무엇을 먹고 얼마를 지불해야 하는지를 나타내는 식당에서 주는 명세서. 계산서: *Can I have the check, please?* 계산서를 주시겠습니까?

5 ▶MARK 표시◀ a mark (√) that you put next to an answer, something on a list etc. to show that it is correct, finished, or that you have noticed it ‖ 어떤 것의 정확함[완성됨, 확인됨]을 나타내려고 해답이나 목록에 있는 사항 옆에 써넣는 표시. 점검표[√]

6 hat/coat check **a)** a place in a restaurant, theater etc. where you can leave your coat, bag etc. ‖ 식당·극장 등에서 외투·가방 등을 맡길 수 있는 장소. 물품 보관소 **b)** a ticket that you are given so you can claim your things from this place ‖ 보관소에서 물건을 찾을 수 있도록 교부된 물표. 보관증

7 ▶SQUARES 정방형◀ a pattern of squares on something ‖ 사물에 새겨진 사각형 무늬. 바둑판[체크] 무늬: *a tablecloth with red and white checks* 빨강과 흰 바둑판[체크] 무늬가 있는 식탁보

check·book /ˈtʃɛkbʊk/ *n* a small book of checks that your bank gives you ‖ 은행에서 주는 작은 수표책. 수표장

check card /ˈ. ./ *n* a special plastic card, similar to a CREDIT CARD, that you can use to pay for things directly from your CHECKING ACCOUNT ‖ 자신의 은행 당좌 예금 계좌에서 곧바로 대금을 지불하는 데 쓸 수 있는, 신용카드와 비슷한 특수 신용 카드. 체크 카드

checked /tʃɛkt/ *adj* having a regular pattern of different colored squares ‖ 다른 색으로 된 정방형의 규칙적인 무늬가 있는. 바둑판[체크] 무늬의: *a checked skirt* 체크 무늬 치마 —see picture at PATTERN

check·ered /ˈtʃɛkəd/ *adj* marked with squares of two different colors ‖ 상이한 두 가지 색깔로 된 사각형들로 표시된. 체크 무늬의: *a checkered flag* 체크 무늬 깃발

check·ers /ˈtʃɛkəz/ *n* [U] a game for two players, using a set of 12 flat round pieces each and a special board with 64 squares ‖ 각각 12개의 납작하면서 둥근 말과 64개 정방형 눈의 특수한 판을 사용해서 두 사람이 하는 놀이. 서양 장기

check-in /ˈ. ./ *n* [U] the process of going to the desk at an airport, hotel etc. and saying that you have arrived ‖ 호텔·공항 등의 프런트에 가서 도착했음을 알리는 절차. 탑승 수속. 투숙 절차. 체크인: *Be at the check-in counter* (=place where you go to say that you have arrived) *an hour before your plane leaves.* 비행기 출발 1시간 전에 탑승 수속을 밟으셔야 합니다. —see also **check in** (CHECK[1])

checking ac·count /ˈ.. .ˌ./ *n* a bank account that you can take money out of at any time ‖ 언제든지 돈을 찾을 수 있는 은행 계좌. 당좌 예금

check·list /ˈtʃɛk.lɪst/ *n* a list of things you have to do for a particular job or activity ‖ 특정한 업무나 활동을 위해 해야 할 일의 목록. 확인표

check·out coun·ter /ˈtʃɛk-aʊt ˌkaʊntə/ *n* the place in a SUPERMARKET where you pay for things ‖ 슈퍼마켓 등에서 물건 값을 지불하는 곳. 계산대

check·point /ˈtʃɛkpɔɪnt/ *n* a place where someone official, such as a police officer, stops people and cars to examine them ‖ 경찰관 등의 공무원이 검문을 위해 사람·차를 정지시키는 곳. 검문소

check-up /ˈtʃɛk-ʌp/ *n* an occasion when a doctor or DENTIST examines you to see if you are healthy ‖ 건강 상태를 알아보려고 의사나 치과 의사가 검사하는 경우. 건강 진단: *Dentists recommend regular check-ups to help prevent tooth decay.* 치과 의사는 충치 예방 차원에서 정기 진단을 권고한다.

ched·dar /ˈtʃɛdə/ *n* [U] a firm smooth yellow or orange cheese ‖ 단단하면서 매끄러운 노랗거나 오렌지 색깔의 치즈. 체더 치즈

cheek /tʃik/ n **1** the soft round part of your face below your eyes ‖ 눈 아래 부드럽고 둥근 얼굴 부위. 뺨. 볼: *He kissed her lightly on the cheek.* 그는 그녀의 뺨에 가볍게 키스했다. —see picture at HEAD¹ **2** SLANG ⇨ BUTTOCK

cheek·bone /ˈtʃikboʊn/ n the bone just below your eye ‖ 눈 바로 아래에 있는 뼈. 광대뼈

cheep /tʃip/ v [I] to make a high noise like a young bird ‖ 새끼 새처럼 고음의 시끄러운 소리를 내다. 삐악삐악[찍찍] 울다 – **cheep** n

cheer¹ /tʃɪr/ v [I, T] to shout approval, encouragement etc ‖ 소리쳐 찬성하거나 격려하다. 성원하다. 환호하다: *The audience cheered as the band began to play.* 밴드의 연주가 시작되자 관객은 갈채를 보냈다.

cheer sb **on** phr v [T] to encourage someone by cheering for him/her ‖ 누군가를 환호하여 격려하다. …을 응원하다: *Hansen's family was there cheering him on.* 한센의 가족들은 거기서 그를 응원하고 있었다.

cheer up phr v **1** [T **cheer** sb ↔ **up**] to make someone feel happier ‖ 남의 기분을 더 신나게 하다. (…을)격려하다. 기운나게 하다: *I tried to cheer her up by taking her out to dinner.* 나는 저녁 외식으로 그녀의 기운을 북돋으려고 했다. **2** [I] to become happier ‖ 더 기분이 좋아지다. 기운내다. 유쾌해지다: *Cheer up, Connie!* 기운내라, 코니!

cheer² n **1** a shout of approval and happiness ‖ 찬성과 기쁨의 외침. 환호. 갈채: *The crowd gives a cheer as Griffey hits a home run!* 관중들은 그리피가 홈런을 치자 환호했다! **2 three cheers for** sb SPOKEN used in order to tell people to shout in order to praise someone ‖ 누군가를 칭찬하기 위해 사람들에게 소리치라고 말하는 데에 쓰어. …을 위해 만세 삼창

cheer·ful /ˈtʃɪrfəl/ adj **1** happy and feeling good ‖ 행복하고 기분 좋은. 쾌활한. 명랑한: *Nancy gave me a cheerful grin.* 낸시는 나를 보고 쾌활하게 씩 웃었다. **2** pleasant and making you feel happy ‖ 즐거우며 행복을 느끼게 하는. 유쾌한. 상쾌한: *a cheerful kitchen* 쾌적한 부엌 – **cheerfully** adv – **cheerfulness** n [U]

cheer·lead·er /ˈtʃɪrˌlidɚ/ n someone who encourages a crowd to CHEER at a sports event ‖ 운동 경기에서 환호하도록 관중을 격려하는 사람. 치어리더

cheer·y /ˈtʃɪri/ adj smiling and cheerful ‖ 미소지으며 명랑한. 기분 좋은. 유쾌한: *a little boy with a cheery smile* 유쾌한 미소를 띤 작은 소년

cheese /tʃiz/ n [C, U] **1** a solid food made from milk, that is usually white or yellow ‖ 우유로 만든 대개 희거나 노란색의 굳은 식품. 치즈 **2 say cheese** SPOKEN said when you want people to smile as you take a photograph of them ‖ 사진 촬영을 하면서 사람들에게 미소지으라고 말할 때에 쓰어. '김치' 하세요. 웃으세요

cheese·burg·er /ˈtʃizˌbɚgɚ/ n a HAMBURGER with cheese on it ‖ 치즈를 곁들인 햄버거. 치즈버거

cheese·cake /ˈtʃizkeɪk/ n [C, U] a sweet cake made with soft white cheese ‖ 부드러운 흰 치즈로 만든 달콤한 케이크. 치즈케이크 —see picture at DESSERT

cheese·cloth /ˈtʃizklɔθ/ n [U] a type of very thin cotton cloth, used in cooking ‖ 요리에 쓰이는 가는 면직물의 일종. 무명천

chees·y /ˈtʃizi/ adj INFORMAL cheap and not of good quality, or not sincere ‖ 값싸고 질이 좋지 않거나 진지하지 않은. 싸구려의. 하찮은: *a really cheesy movie* 정말 볼품없는 영화 / *a cheesy grin* 천박하게 씩 웃는 웃음

chee·tah /ˈtʃitə/ n an African wild cat that has black spots, long legs, and is able to run very fast ‖ 검은 반점과 긴 다리를 가진, 매우 빨리 달릴 수 있는 아프리카산 야생 고양잇과. 치타

chef /ʃɛf/ n the chief cook in a restaurant ‖ 음식점의 일급 요리사. 주방장

chem·i·cal¹ /ˈkɛmɪkəl/ adj relating to substances used in chemistry, or involving the changes that happen when two substances combine ‖ 화학에서 쓰이는 물질과 관련된, 또는 두 물질이 결합했을 때 일어나는 변화를 포함하는. 화학 작용의: *a chemical reaction* 화학 반응 – **chemically** adv

chemical² n a substance that is used in or produced by a chemical process ‖ 화학 작용으로 사용되거나 생성된 물질. 화학 제품: *chemicals used in agriculture* 농업에 사용된 화학 제품

chem·ist /ˈkɛmɪst/ n a scientist who has a special knowledge of chemistry ‖ 화학에 대한 전문 지식을 가진 과학자. 화학자: *a research chemist for a drug company* 제약 회사의 화학 연구원

chem·is·try /ˈkɛməstri/ n [U] **1** the science of studying substances and what happens to them when they change or combine with each other ‖ 물질을 연구하

고 물질이 변화하거나 서로 결합할 때 발생하는 것을 연구하는 학문. 화학 **2** the way substances combine in a particular process, thing, person etc. ‖ 특별한 과정·사물·사람 등에서 물질이 결합하는 방식. 화학 반응[작용]. 화학적 성질. 마음이 통함: *This drug causes changes to the body's chemistry.* 이 약은 신체의 화학 반응에 변화를 일으킨다.

che·mo·ther·a·py /ˌkimoʊ'θɛrəpi/ *n* [U] the treatment of CANCER using special drugs ‖ 특별한 약품을 사용하는 암치료. 화학 요법

cher·ish /'tʃɛrɪʃ/ *v* [T] to love and take good care of someone or something ‖ 사람이나 사물을 사랑하며 잘 돌보다. …을 소중히 여기다: *He has been forced to sell cherished possessions to pay his debts.* 그는 애장품을 팔아서 빚을 갚으라고 강요받고 있다.

cher·ry /'tʃɛri/ *n* **1** a small round soft red fruit with a large seed ‖ 큰 씨가 있고 작고 둥글며 연한 붉은색 과실. 버찌 — see picture on page 944 **2** [C, U] a tree that produces cherries, or the wood of this tree ‖ 버찌가 열리는 나무, 또는 버찌나무의 목재. 벚나무(재목)

cher·ub /'tʃɛrəb/ *n* an ANGEL shown in paintings as a small child with wings ‖ 그림에서 날개 달린 작은 아이로 표현되는 천사. 케루빔(천사). 아기 천사

chess /tʃɛs/ *n* [U] a game for two players, using a set of 16 pieces each and a special board with 64 squares ‖ 각 16개의 말과 64개의 정방형 눈을 가진 특수한 판을 이용한 2인용 놀이. 서양 장기

chest /tʃɛst/ *n* **1** the front part of your body between your neck and stomach ‖ 목과 배 사이에 있는 신체의 앞 부위. 가슴. 흉곽: *a man with a hairy chest* 가슴에 털이 많이 난 남자 **2** a large strong box with a lid, used for storing things ‖ 물건을 보관하는 데에 쓰는 뚜껑이 있는 크고 단단한 상자. 궤: *We keep our blankets in a cedar chest.* 우리는 담요를 시더 재목으로 만든 상자에 보관한다. **3** get sth off your chest to tell someone about something that you are worried about ‖ 걱정하고 있는 일에 대해 누군가에게 말하다. 속을 털어놓아 짐을 덜다

chest·nut /'tʃɛsnʌt/ *n* **1** a smooth red-brown nut you can eat ‖ 먹을 수 있는 매끄러운 적갈색의 견과. 밤 **2** [C, U] the tree on which these nuts grow, or the wood of this tree ‖ 이러한 견과가 자라는 나무, 또는 이 나무의 목재. 밤나무. 밤나무 목재 **3** [U] a dark red-brown color ‖ 진한 적갈색 – **chestnut** *adj*

chest of drawers /ˌ. . './ *n* a piece of furniture with drawers that clothes can be kept in ‖ 옷을 보관하는 서랍이 달린 가구. 서랍장

chew /tʃu/ *v* [I, T] to crush food with your teeth before swallowing it ‖ 삼키기 전에 음식물을 이로 으깨다. 씹다: *We gave the dog a bone to chew on.* 우리는 개에게 물어뜯으라고 뼈다귀를 주었다. / *Come on, baby, chew it up,* (=chew it completely) *there's a good girl.* 자 아가야, 잘 씹어 먹어, 착하지.

chew sb **out** *phr v* [T] INFORMAL to talk angrily to someone who has done something you do not like ‖ 마음에 들지 않는 일을 저지른 사람에게 화를 내면서 말하다. …을 호되게 꾸짖다: *Mom chewed me out for getting home late.* 엄마는 내가 늦게 귀가했다고 몹시 꾸짖었다.

chewing gum /'.. ,./ *n* [U] ⇨ GUM¹

chew·y /'tʃui/ *adj* needing to be chewed ‖ 씹어야 하는. 잘 씹히지 않는: *moist chewy brownies* 눅눅하고 잘 씹히지 않는 아몬드 초콜릿 케이크

chic /ʃik/ *adj* fashionable and showing good judgment about style ‖ 유행을 따르며 세련된 감각을 보여주는. 멋진. 맵시 있는: *a chic clothes store* 유행을 따르는 [세련된] 옷가게

Chi·ca·no /tʃɪ'kɑnoʊ/ *n* a US citizen whose family came from Mexico ‖ 가족이 멕시코 출신인 미국 시민. 멕시코계 미국 시민

chick /tʃɪk/ *n* **1** a baby bird, especially a baby chicken ‖ 새끼새, 병아리 **2** INFORMAL a word meaning a young woman, that some people consider offensive ‖ 젊은 여성을 뜻하는, 일부의 사람들이 모욕적으로 여기는 말. 계집애

chick·a·dee /'tʃɪkə,di/ *n* a small North American wild bird with a black head ‖ 검은 머리를 가진 작은 북미산 야생 조류. 미국 박새

chick·en¹ /'tʃɪkən/ *n* **1** a common farm bird that is kept for its meat and eggs ‖ 고기와 달걀을 얻기 위해 사육하는 농장의 일반 조류. 닭 **2** [U] the meat from this bird ‖ 이 새의 고기. 닭고기: *fried chicken* 튀긴 닭고기 **3** INFORMAL someone who lacks courage ‖ 용기가 부족한 사람. 겁쟁이: *"You won't jump? What a chicken!"* "안 뛰어 내려? 이런 겁쟁이!"

chick·en² *adj* INFORMAL having no courage ‖ 용기 없는. 겁많은. 소심한: *He was too chicken to dive off the high board.* 그는 너무 겁이 많아 높은 다이빙대에서 뛰어내리지 못했다.

chick·en³ *v*

chicken out *phr v* [I] INFORMAL to decide not to do something because you are afraid || 겁이 나서 어떤 것을 하지 않기로 결정하다. 뒷걸음치다. 꽁무니를 빼다: *They chickened out at the last minute.* 그들은 마지막 순간에 꽁무니를 뺐다.

chick·en·feed /'tʃɪkən,fid/ *n* [U] INFORMAL a small unimportant amount of money || 작고 하찮은 금액. 푼돈. 잔돈: *To a millionaire, $1000 is chickenfeed.* 백만장자에게 1000달러는 푼돈이다.

chicken pox, chickenpox /'tʃɪkən,pɑks/ *n* [U] a disease that children often get that causes ITCHY spots on the skin and a fever || 피부에 가려운 반점과 열을 야기하는 종종 어린이들이 걸리는 질병. 수두

chide /tʃaɪd/ *v* [I, T] LITERARY to speak in an angry way to someone who has done something wrong || 잘못된 일을 저지른 사람에게 화를 내면서 말하다. 꾸짖다. 질책하다

chief¹ /tʃif/ *n* the leader of a group or organization || 단체나 조직의 지도자. 장. 우두머리: *the chief of police* 경찰서장

chief² *adj* **1** most important || 가장 중요한. 주된. 주요한: *The customers' chief complaint was the poor service.* 고객들의 주된 불만은 형편없는 서비스였다. **2** highest in rank || 최고위직의. 우두머리의: *the chief political reporter for the Washington Post* 워싱턴 포스트 신문의 정치 보도부장

Chief Executive /ˌ. .ˈ.../ *n* the President of the United States || 미국 대통령

chief ex·ec·u·tive of·fi·cer /ˌ. .ˌ... ˈ../ *n* ⇨ CEO

chief jus·tice /ˌ. ˈ../ *n* the most important judge in a court of law, especially in the US Supreme Court || 특히 미국 대법원에서 가장 중요한 판사. 대법원장

chief·ly /'tʃifli/ *adv* mainly || 주로. 대개: *They had borrowed a lot of money, chiefly from Dan's parents.* 그들은 주로 댄의 부모한테서 많은 돈을 빌렸다.

chief·tain /'tʃiftən/ *n* the leader of a tribe || 부족의 지도자. 족장. 추장

chif·fon /ʃɪ'fɑn/ *n* [U] a soft thin material used for make women's clothing, scarves (SCARF) etc. || 여자 옷·스카프 등을 만드는 데에 사용되는 부드럽고 얇은 직물. 시퐁

chi·hua·hua /tʃɪ'wawə/ *n* a very small dog from Mexico with smooth short hair || 털이 부드럽고 짧은 멕시코산의 매우 작은 개. 치와와

child /tʃaɪld/ *n, plural* **children** /'tʃɪldrən/ **1** a young person who is not yet fully grown || 아직 완전히 성장하지 않은 어린 사람. 아이. 아동. 어린이: *The children may start ballet lessons at the age of six.* 아이들은 6세에 발레 교습을 시작해도 괜찮다. **2** a son or daughter || 아들이나 딸. 자녀. 자식: *Dan has a child from a previous marriage.* 댄은 전처 소생의 자식이 하나 있다. / *Are you planning to have children?* (=give birth to children) 출산 계획이 있니? **3 child's play** something that is very easy to do || 하기에 아주 쉬운 일. 누워서 떡먹기: *Stealing the money was child's play to him.* 그에게 돈을 훔치는 일은 식은 죽 먹기였다.

child·bear·ing /'tʃaɪld,bɛrɪŋ/ *n* **1** [U] the process of being PREGNANT and then giving birth || 임신하고 아이를 낳는 과정. 출산. 분만 **2 childbearing age** the period of time during which a woman is old enough to give birth to a baby || 여자가 출산을 하기에 나이가 충분한 기간. 출산 적령기

child·birth /'tʃaɪldbɔθ/ *n* [U] the act of giving birth || 아이를 낳는 행위. 출산

child·care /'tʃaɪldkɛr/ *n* [U] an arrangement in which someone takes care of children while their parents are at work || 아이의 부모가 근무하는 동안 아이를 돌봐주기로 한 약속. 보육. 육아

child·hood /'tʃaɪldhʊd/ *n* [C, U] the time when you are a child || 어린 시절. 유년기: *happy childhood memories* 행복한 유년 시절의 추억

child·ish /'tʃaɪldɪʃ/ *adj* **1** typical of a child || 어린 아이 특유의. 어린애 같은: *a childish game* 어린이다운 놀이 **2** DISAPPROVING behaving in a way that makes you seem younger than you really are || 실제보다 더 어려 보이게 행동하는. 어린애 같은. 유치한: *Stop being so childish.* 너무 어린애처럼 굴지 마라. – **childishly** *adv*

child·less /'tʃaɪldlɪs/ *adj* having no children || 자식이 없는: *childless couples* 아이가 없는 부부 – **childlessness** *n* [U]

child·like /'tʃaɪldlaɪk/ *adj* APPROVING having the character, qualities etc. of a child || 어린이의 품성과 특성을 가진. 천진한. 어린애 같은. 순진한: *childlike innocence* 어린애 같은 천진무구함

child·proof /'tʃaɪldpruf/ *adj* designed to prevent a child from hurting something or being hurt || 어린아이가 사물을 건드리지 못하도록, 또는 다치지 않

도록 고안된. 어린이에게 안전한. 어린이는 다룰 수 없는: *a childproof cap on a pill bottle* 어린애는 열 수 없는 알약병 뚜껑

child·ren /'tʃɪldrən/ the plural of CHILD ‖ child의 복수형 —see picture at FAMILY

USAGE NOTE children

Baby and **infant** both mean "a very young child," but **infant** is more formal. A child who can walk and is under the age of 3 is a **toddler**. Children aged 13 to 19 are **teenagers**. Use the informal word **kids** to talk about all young people and children.

baby와 **infant**는 모두 "매우 어린 아이"를 의미하지만 **infant**는 더 격식차린 말이다. 걸을 수 있는 3세 이하 아이는 **toddler**(아장거리는 아이)라고 한다. 13세에서 19세까지의 아이들은 **teenagers**(10대)라고 한다. 모든 젊은 사람들과 아이들에 관하여 말할 때에는 **kids**라는 비격식어를 쓴다.

---

child sup·port /'. .,./ *n* [U] money that someone pays regularly to his/her former husband or wife in order to help support his/her children ‖ 자녀 양육을 돕기 위하여 전 남편이나 처에게 정기적으로 지급하는 돈. 자녀 양육비

chil·i /'tʃɪli/ *n, plural* **chilies 1** [U] a dish made with beans and usually meat cooked with chilies ‖ 콩과 대개 칠레고추로 요리한 고기로 만든 음식. 칠리 **2** [C, U] a small thin type of red pepper with a very hot taste, often used in cooking ‖ 아주 매운 맛을 지니며 요리에서 자주 사용되는 작고 가는 형태의 붉은 고추. 칠레고추 —see picture on page 944

chill¹ /tʃɪl/ *v* **1** [I, T] to make something or someone very cold ‖ 사물이나 사람을 아주 차게 하다. 식히다. 냉장하다. 차갑게[춥게] 하다: *This wine should be chilled before serving.* 이 포도주는 차게 해서 드십시오. **2** [I] also **chill out** to relax instead of feeling angry or nervous ‖ 노여움이나 초조함 대신 마음을 누그러뜨리다. 냉정해지다: *Chill out, Dave, it doesn't matter.* 진정해라, 데이브. 그건 중요하지 않아. **3** [T] to make someone feel very cold ‖ 사람을 매우 춥게 느끼게 하다. 춥게 하다: *The wind chilled me to the bone.* 바람 때문에 추위가 뼛속까지 스며들었다.

chill² *n* **1** [singular] a feeling of coldness ‖ 차가운 느낌. 냉기: *a chill in the early morning air* 이른 아침 공기의 서늘함 **2** a slight feeling of fear ‖ 약간 무

서운 느낌. 오싹함: *a horror movie that sends chills through the audience* (=makes them feel afraid) 관객의 간담을 서늘하게 하는 공포 영화 **3** a slight sickness with a fever ‖ 열이 나는 가벼운 질병. 한기. 오한: *I must have caught a chill from walking in the snow.* 나는 눈길을 걸어서 오한이 난 것이 틀림없다.

chill³ *adj* extremely cold ‖ 아주 추운. 냉랭한: *a chill wind* 차가운 바람

chil·ling /'tʃɪlɪŋ/ *adj* making you feel frightened because something is cruel, violent, or dangerous ‖ 어떤 것이 잔인해서[폭력적이어서, 위험해서] 무섭게 느끼게 하는. 오싹한. 소름끼치는: *a chilling report on child abuse* 아동 학대에 관한 소름끼치는 보고서

chill·y /'tʃɪli/ *adj* **1** cold enough to make you feel uncomfortable ‖ 불쾌감을 느끼게 할 만큼 추운. 싸늘한. 으스스한: *a chilly room* 싸늘한 방 —see usage note at TEMPERATURE **2** unfriendly ‖ 비우호적인. 쌀쌀한. 적개심이 있는: *Relations between the two countries have been chilly since the incident.* 두 나라 사이의 관계는 그 사건 이후 냉담해졌다.

chime¹ /tʃaɪm/ *n* the ringing (RING) sound of a bell or clock ‖ 종이나 시계의 울리는 소리: *the chime of the doorbell* 현관의 초인종 소리

chime² *v* [I, T] to make a ringing (RING) sound, especially in order to show what time it is ‖ 특히 몇 시인지를 알리기 위해 울리는 소리를 내다. (시간을) 소리를 내 알리다: *The clock chimed six.* 시계가 6시를 알렸다.

chime in *phr v* [I] to agree with what someone has just said, often by repeating it or adding to it slightly ‖ 남이 방금 말한 내용을 종종 반복하거나 거기에 약간 추가해서 동의하다. 맞장구치다: *"Yes, the kids could go too," Maria chimed in.* "네, 아이들도 갈 수 있을 거예요."라고 마리아는 맞장구를 쳤다.

chim·ney /'tʃɪmni/ *n* a pipe inside a building for smoke from a fire to go out through the roof ‖ 불에서 생긴 연기가 지붕을 통해 내보내는 건물 내부에 있는 연통. 굴뚝 —see picture on page 945

chim·pan·zee /,tʃɪmpæn'zi/, **chimp** /tʃɪmp/ *n* a very intelligent small African APE (=animal like a monkey) ‖ 매우 영리하고 몸집이 작은 아프리카산 유인원. 침팬지

chin /tʃɪn/ *n* the front part of your face below your mouth ‖ 입 아래에 있는 얼굴의 앞면. 턱 —see picture at HEAD¹

chi·na /'tʃaɪnə/ *n* [U] **1** a hard white

substance made by baking a particular type of clay ‖ 특정한 종류의 찰흙을 구워서 만든 단단하고 하얀 물질. 경질(硬質) 도기 **2** plates, cups, and dishes made from this clay ‖ 이 찰흙으로 된 접시·잔·식기. 도자기 제품: *We were given a lot of china as wedding presents.* 우리는 결혼 선물로 도자기 제품을 많이 받았다.

Chi·na·town /ˈtʃaɪnəˌtaʊn/ *n* [C, U] an area in a city where there are Chinese restaurants and stores, and where a lot of Chinese people live ‖ 중국 식당과 상점들이 있고 중국인들이 많이 거주하는 도시의 일정 지역. 중국인 거리. 차이나 타운

Chi·nese¹ /ˈtʃaɪˈniz/ *adj* **1** relating to or coming from China ‖ 중국과 관련되거나 중국 출신의. 중국(산)의 **2** relating to a Chinese language ‖ 중국어와 관련된. 중국어의

Chi·nese² /ˈtʃaɪˈniz/ *n* **1** [U] any of the languages that come from China, such as Mandarin or Cantonese ‖ 만다린(표준 중국어)이나 광둥어 등의 중국에서 나온 언어. 중국어 **2 the Chinese** the people of China ‖ 중국인

chink /tʃɪŋk/ *n* **1** a narrow crack or hole in something that lets light or air through ‖ 빛이나 공기를 통과시키는 사물의 가는 틈새나 구멍. 갈라진 틈: *a chink in the wall* 벽에 있는 좁은 틈새 **2** a short ringing sound made by metal or glass objects hitting each other ‖ 금속이나 유리 제품이 서로 부딪칠 때 나는 짧은 울림 소리. 짤랑짤랑. 땡그랑: *the chink of glassware* 유리 그릇의 땡그랑 소리

chi·nos /ˈtʃinoʊz/ *n* [plural] loose pants made from heavy cotton ‖ 두툼한 무명으로 만든 헐렁한 바지. 치노

chintz /tʃɪnts/ *n* [U] smooth cotton cloth with brightly colored patterns on it ‖ 화사한 색깔의 무늬가 있는 부드러운 면직물. 사라사 무명: *chintz covers on the chairs* 사라사 무명 의자 덮개

chin-up /ˈ. ./ *n* an exercise in which you hang on a BAR and pull yourself up until your chin is above the bar ‖ 철봉에 매달려서 아래턱이 철봉 위로 올 때까지 몸을 끌어 올리는 운동. 턱걸이

chip¹ /tʃɪp/ *n*

1 ▶COMPUTER 컴퓨터◀ a small piece of SILICON that has a set of electronic parts and their connections attached to it, used in computers ‖ 일련의 전자 부품들이 서로 연결돼 부착된 컴퓨터용 작은 실리콘 조각. 칩

2 ▶FOOD 음식◀ a thin dry piece of FRIED potato or of a TORTILLA ‖ 튀긴 감자나 납작하게 구운 옥수수빵의 얇고 마른 조각: *chips and salsa* 칠레소스를 곁들인 얇게 썬 감자 튀김 / *barbecue flavor potato chips* 바비큐 맛이 나는 감자 튀김

3 ▶CRACK/MARK 금/자국◀ a crack or mark left when a small piece is broken off something ‖ 작은 조각이 떨어져 나가 생긴 금이나 흔적. 이빠진 자국. 흠: *This plate has a chip in it.* 이 접시에는 이빠진 흠이 있다.

4 ▶SMALL PIECE 작은 조각◀ a small piece of wood, stone etc. that has broken off something ‖ 어떤 것에서 떨어져 나간 나무·돌 등의 작은 조각[부스러기]: *Chips of wood can be used around plants to control weeds.* 대팻밥은 잡초를 억제하기 위해 풀 주변에 사용될 수 있다.

5 bargaining chip something that you can use or exchange in order to get something else you want ‖ 원하는 다른 것을 얻기 위해 사용하거나 교환할 수 있는 사물. 거래·교섭을 유리하게 이끄는 재료. 비장[최후]의 수단: *The terrorists were using the hostages as bargaining chips to gain the release of the prisoners.* 테러분자들은 죄수들의 석방을 위해 비장의 최후 수단으로 인질들을 이용하고 있었다.

6 ▶GAME 게임◀ a small flat colored piece of plastic used in games to represent money ‖ 게임에서 돈을 대신하는 데에 사용되는 플라스틱으로 만든 작고 납작한 색깔 있는 조각. 칩: *a gambling chip* 도박 칩

7 have a chip on your shoulder INFORMAL to become angry easily about something because you think you have been treated unfairly in the past ‖ 과거에 부당하게 대우 받아왔다고 생각하여 어떤 것에 쉽게 화내다. 부당한 대접으로 기분 나빠서 걸핏하면 싸우려고 들다. 시비조이다: *He's always had a chip on his shoulder about not going to college.* 그는 대학을 다니지 않은 것에 대해 항상 시비조로 나온다.

8 be a chip off the old block INFORMAL to be like one of your parents in the way you look or behave ‖ 모습이나 행동 방식에서 부모의 한쪽을 닮다 —see also BLUE

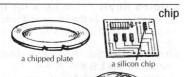

a chipped plate　　　　a silicon chip

potato chips

CHIP

chip² *v* [I, T] to break a small piece off something accidentally, or to become broken in this way‖ 우연히 어떤 것에서 작은 조각을 떼어내거나 이렇게 떼어지다. 빠지다. 벗겨내다 – **chipped** *adj* : *chipped fingernail polish* 벗겨진 손톱 매니큐어

chip sth ↔ **away** *phr v* ‖ 어떤 것에서 작은 조각을 떼어내다: *Sandy chipped away the plaster covering the tiles.* 샌디는 타일을 덮고 있는 석고를 벗겨냈다.

chip away at sth *phr v* [T] to break small pieces off something to make it less effective or destroy it‖ 능률을 떨어뜨리거나 파괴시키기 위해 사물에서 조각을 내다. …을 조금씩 깎아[벗겨] 내다. 조금씩 깎다: *All this new paperwork is chipping away at the time teachers can spend preparing for classes.* 이 모든 새로운 문서 업무는 교사가 수업을 준비할 시간을 조금씩 잡아먹고 있다.

chip in *phr v* [I, T] to give help, money, advice etc. to add to what other people are giving‖ 다른 사람이 주는 것에 덧붙여 도움·돈·충고 등을 제공하다. 제각기 돕다[갹출하다, 조언하다]: *Tanya's classmates have chipped in more than $100 to help her buy the special wheelchair.* 타냐의 반 친구들은 그녀가 특수 휠체어를 사는 데 도움을 주기 위해 100달러 이상을 내놓았다.

chip·munk /'tʃɪpmʌŋk/ *n* a small brown North American animal similar to a SQUIRREL, that has black and white lines on its fur‖ 다람쥐와 비슷하고 털에 흑백의 선이 있는 작은 갈색의 북미산 동물. 얼룩다람쥐

chip·per /'tʃɪpɚ/ *adj* happy and healthy‖ 행복하고 건강한. 기운찬. 쾌활한: *Grandma's feeling pretty chipper again now that her back is better.* 할머니는 지금 허리가 호전되어 다시 기분이 훨씬 좋아진 상태이다.

chi·ro·prac·tor /'kaɪrə,præktɚ/ *n* a doctor who treats sickness by pressing on and moving the bones in your back‖ 등뼈를 압박하고 움직여서 질병을 치료하는 의사. 척추 지압(요법)사

chirp /tʃɚp/ *n* the short high sound made by birds and some insects‖ 새들과 곤충들이 내는 짧고 날카로운 소리. 짹짹[찍찍]거리는 소리: *the chirp of crickets* 귀뚜라미의 찍찍거리는 소리 – **chirp** *v* [I]

chis·el¹ /'tʃɪzəl/ *n* a metal tool with a sharp edge, used for cutting wood or stone‖ 나무나 돌을 절단하는 데에 사용하는 끝이 날카로운 금속 연장. 조각칼. 끌

chisel² *v* [T] to cut or shape something with a CHISEL‖ 끌로 어떤 것을 자르거나 형상을 만들다. 끌로 깎다. 조각하다: *Small figures of deer, buffalo, and men have been chiseled into the sandstone.* 사슴·물소·사람의 작은 형상이 사암(砂岩)에 조각되어 있다.

chit /tʃɪt/ *n* a short note that shows how much money someone owes or has paid‖ 갚아야하거나 지불한 금액을 나타내는 짧은 쪽지. 청구서. 영수증

chit-chat /'tʃɪt-tʃæt/ *n* [U] INFORMAL informal conversation about unimportant things‖ 중요하지 않은 일에 관한 격식 없는 대화. 잡담. 수다

chiv·al·rous /'ʃɪvəlrəs/ *adj* FORMAL showing polite and kind behavior toward women‖ 여자에게 예절 바르고 친절한 행동을 보이는. 정중한. 예의 바른 – **chivalry** /'ʃɪvəlri/ *n* [U]

chives /tʃaɪvz/ *n* [plural] a plant with long thin leaves that taste like onion, used in cooking‖ 요리할 때 사용하는, 양파 같은 맛을 내며 길고 가는 잎을 가진 식물. 골파

chlo·ri·nate /'klɔrə,neɪt/ *v* [T] to make water clean by putting CHLORINE in it to kill BACTERIA‖ 세균을 죽이기 위해 물에 염소를 넣어 물을 깨끗하게 하다. 물을 염소로 살균하다: *Public swimming pools have to be chlorinated.* 대중 수영장은 염소로 살균하여야 한다.

chlo·rine /'klɔrin, klɔ'rin/ *n* [U] a yellow-green gas that is an ELEMENT and is often used for keeping swimming pools clean‖ 종종 수영장의 물을 깨끗하게 유지하는 데 사용하는 황록색 기체 원소. 염소

chlo·ro·fluo·ro·car·bon /,klɔrəˌfluroʊ'karbən/ *n* TECHNICAL ⇨ CFC

chlo·ro·form /'klɔrə,fɔrm/ *n* [U] a colorless liquid with a strong smell that was used in medicine as an ANESTHETIC in past times‖ 과거에 의학용 마취제로 사용되었던 무색의 강한 냄새가 나는 용액. 클로로포름

chlo·ro·phyll /'klɔrə,fɪl/ *n* [U] the green substance in the stems and leaves of plants‖ 식물의 줄기와 잎에 있는 녹색 물질. 엽록소

chock-full /,tʃak 'ful·/ *adj* INFORMAL completely full‖ 완전히 가득차 있는. 꽉 들어찬: *a bus chock-full of people* 사람들로 초만원인 버스

choc·o·hol·ic, chocaholic /,tʃakə'-hɔlɪk/ *n* HUMOROUS someone who likes chocolate very much and eats a lot of it ‖ 초콜릿을 몹시 좋아해서 많이 먹는 사람. 초콜릿 중독자

choco·late /'tʃaklɪt/ *n* **1** [U] a sweet hard brown food eaten for pleasure, or used for giving foods a special taste ‖ 즐거움을 위해서 먹거나 음식에 특별한 맛을 내기 위해 사용하는 달고 굳은 갈색의 식품. 초콜릿: *a chocolate bar* 초콜릿 바 / *chocolate ice cream* 초콜릿 아이스크림 **2** a candy covered with chocolate ‖ 초콜릿을 입힌 사탕: *a box of chocolates* 한 상자의 초콜릿 사탕

chocolate chip /ˌ.. './ *n* [C usually plural] a small piece of chocolate put in foods such as cookies and cakes ‖ 쿠키와 케이크 등의 식품에 넣은 작은 초콜릿 조각. 초콜릿 알갱이

choice¹ /tʃɔɪs/ *n* **1** [singular, U] the right to choose or the chance to choose between two or more things ‖ 둘 또는 그 이상의 사물 가운데에서 선택할 권리나 기회: *a choice between 31 flavors of ice cream* 31가지 아이스크림 맛 중 한 가지의 선택 / *The bookstore has a wide choice of magazines.* 그 서점에는 다양한 종류의 많은 잡지들이 있다. / *If you had a choice* (=were able to choose), *where would you want to live?* 네게 선택권이 있다면 어디에서 살기를 원하니? / *He **had no choice** * (=it was the only thing he could do) *but to move back into his parents' house.* 그는 부모님 집으로 다시 들어가는 것 외에는 다른 방도가 없었다. / *We were **given a choice** * (=allowed to choose) *between doing volleyball or basketball first in P.E.* 우리는 체육 시간에 먼저 배구나 농구 둘 중에 하나를 선택할 기회가 주어졌다. **2** the act of choosing something ‖ 어떤 것을 고르는 행위. 고르기. 선택: *The price of the car influenced our choice.* 자동차 가격은 우리의 선택에 영향을 미쳤다. / *He left the choice of hotels to his wife.* 그는 호텔을 선택할 기회를 아내에게 맡겼다. / *Shea has had to **make some hard choices** about budgeting.* 시아는 예산 편성에 관해 몇 가지 어려운 선택을 해야만 했다. **3** one of several things that you can choose, or the range of things you can chose from ‖ 선택할 수 있는 여러 가지 것 중의 하나, 또는 선택할 수 있는 일의 범위. 선택의 범위[종류]: *The menu had several choices of soup.* 메뉴에는 여러 가지 종류의 수프가 있었다. / *You will have a **choice of five questions** on the test.* 너는 시험에서 5개의 문제 가운데 한 개를 선택하게 될 것이다. **4** [C

usually singular] the person or thing that someone has chosen ‖ 선택한 사람이나 사물. 고른 사람[것]: *Going to Hawaii was our first choice, but we couldn't really afford it.* 하와이에 가는 것이 우리의 첫 번째 선택이었지만 우리는 실제로 그렇게 할 여유가 없었다. **5 the drug/treatment/magazine etc. of choice** the thing that a particular group of people prefer ‖ 특정한 집단의 사람들이 선호하는 것. 가장 좋은[최적의] 약/치료/잡지: *It is the treatment of choice for this particular disease.* 이것은 이 특이한 질병에 가장 좋은 치료법이다. **6 by choice** done because you want to ‖ 자신이 원해서 한. 스스로 선택하여. 좋아서: *Can anyone really believe that homeless people are homeless by choice?* 노숙자들이 자신들이 원해서 노숙자 생활을 한다고 누가 정말로 믿을 수 있겠나?

choice² *adj* having a high quality or standard ‖ 품질이나 수준이 높은. 뛰어난. 상품인: *choice fruit/vegetables/meat* 최상품 과일[채소, 고기]

choir /kwaɪə/ *n* a group of people who sing together, especially in a church or school ‖ 특히 교회나 학교에서 같이 노래하는 사람들의 집단. 합창단. 성가대: *The school choir is putting on a concert Friday.* 학교 합창단은 금요일에 연주회를 연다.

choke¹ /tʃoʊk/ *v* **1** [I, T] to prevent someone from breathing, or to be prevented from breathing because something is blocking your throat or because there is not enough air ‖ 어떤 것이 목구멍을 막거나, 공기가 충분하지 않아서 숨을 쉬지 못하게 하다, 또는 숨을 쉬지 못하다. 질식시키다. 숨이 막히다: *Don't give her that fish – she'll choke on the bones.* 그녀에게 그 생선을 주지 마라, 가시에 질식하게 될 거야. / *The fumes were choking me.* 나는 매연으로 숨이 막혔다. **2** [T] to fill a space or passage with something that is harmful or not wanted ‖ 해롭거나 원치 않는 것으로 공간이나 통로를 메우다. 막다. 채우다: *The pipe was **choked with** leaves.* 그 관은 나뭇잎으로 꽉 차서 막혔다. / *highways choked by pollution* 공해로 가득 찬 고속도로 **3** [I, T] if your voice is choked or choking with an emotion, it sounds strange and not very loud because the emotion is so strong ‖ 감정이 아주 격해서 목소리가 이상하고 아주 크지 않게 들리다. 목이 메다[메이게 하다]: *Cranston read his statement in a voice choked with emotion.* 크랜스턴은 감정이 북받쳐

목이 메이는 목소리로 성명서를 낭독했다.
4 [I] SPOKEN to fail at doing something, especially a sport ‖ 특히 스포츠에서 어떤 것을 하는 데 실패하다: *They were great all season, but choked in the playoffs.* 그들에게는 최고의 시즌이었지만 플레이오프전에서 낭패를 봤다.

choke sth ↔ **back** *phr v* [T] to control a strong feeling so that you do not show it ‖ 격앙된 감정을 나타내지 않으려고 자제하다: *Annelise choked back tears as she tried to explain.* 애너리즈는 설명하려고 할 때 눈물이 나오려는 것을 참았다.

choke sth ↔ **down** *phr v* [T] to eat something with difficulty, especially because you are ill or upset ‖ 특히 아프거나 화가 나서 어떤 것을 힘들게 먹다. 음식을 겨우 삼키다: *He managed to choke down a sandwich.* 그는 샌드위치를 간신히 씹어 삼켰다.

choke off *phr v* [T] to prevent something from going where it was meant to go ‖ 사물이 예정했던 목적지에 가는 것을 막다. 그만두게 하다. 중단시키다: *A blockade has choked off their main food supply.* 봉쇄로 인해 그들의 주요 식품 공급이 중단되었다.

choke up *phr v* [I] **be choked up** to feel such strong emotions about something that you are almost crying ‖ 어떤 것에 대하여 울음을 터뜨릴 것 같은 격한 감정을 느끼다. 감정이 격하여 말문이 막히다: *He was so choked up about his award that he could hardly speak.* 그는 자신이 상을 타게 된 것에 감격하여 거의 말을 할 수가 없었다.

choke² *n* **1** the act or sound of choking (CHOKE) ‖ 숨이 막히는 것이나 그 소리. 질식 **2** a piece of equipment that controls the amount of air going into a car engine ‖ 자동차 엔진에 들어가는 공기의 양을 조절하는 장치. 내연 기관의 공기 조절 장치

choke chain /'. ./ *n* a chain that is fastened around the neck of a dog to control it ‖ 개를 통제하기 위해 개의 목 둘레에 채우는 사슬. 개목걸이

chok·er /'tʃoukə/ *n* a piece of jewelry or narrow cloth that fits closely around your neck ‖ 사람의 목 둘레에 꼭 끼는 보석이나 가는 천 조각. 목걸이. 넥타이. 스카프

chol·er·a /'kɑlərə/ *n* [U] a serious infectious disease that attacks the stomach and BOWELs ‖ 위와 창자를 공격하는 심각한 전염병. 콜레라

cho·les·ter·ol /kə'lɛstə,rɔl, -,roul/ *n* [U] a substance in fat, blood, and other cells in your body, that can sometimes cause heart disease ‖ 때때로 심장병을 일으킬 수 있는 신체의 지방·혈액·기타 세포 내에 있는 물질. 콜레스테롤

choose /tʃuz/ *v* **chose, chosen, choosing** [I, T] **1** to decide which one of a number of things, possibilities, people etc. that you want ‖ 수많은 사물·가능성·사람 중에 원하는 하나를 결정하다. 고르다. 선택하다: *Everything looks so good, I don't know what to choose.* 모두 아주 좋아 보여서 나는 무엇을 선택해야 할지 모르겠다. / *They chose Roy to be the team captain.* 그들은 로이를 주장으로 선정했다. / *You'll have to choose between taking French or Spanish.* 너는 불어나 스페인어 가운데에서 하나를 선택해 수강해야만 할 것이다. / *a large selection of drinks to choose from* 선택할 수 있는 종류가 아주 많은 주류[음료수] **2** to decide or prefer to do something ‖ 어떤 것을 하기를 결정하거나 선호하다: *Donna chose to quit her job after she had the baby.* 도나는 아기를 가진 후 직장을 그만두기로 결정했다. **3 there is little/nothing to choose between** used in order to say that two or more things are very much alike ‖ 둘 또는 그 이상의 사물이 아주 많이 비슷하다고 말하는 데에 쓰여. …사이에 우열은 별로 [조금도] 없다: *There's so little to choose between those two, I just don't know who to vote for.* 저 두 사람은 아주 유사해서 나는 누구에게 투표를 해야 할지 정말 모르겠다.

choos·y /'tʃuzi/ *adj* difficult to please ‖ 만족시키기 어려운. 가리는. 까다로운: *Jean's very choosy about what she eats.* 진은 먹는 것을 몹시 가린다.

chop¹ /tʃɑp/ *v* **-pped, -pping 1** [T] also **chop up** to cut something, especially food, into small uneven pieces ‖ 특히 음식물을 울퉁불퉁한 작은 조각으로 자르다. …을 잘게 썰다: *Chop up some onions.* 양파 몇 개를 잘게 썰어라. / *Chop the tomatoes into fairly large pieces.* 토마토를 좀 큰 조각으로 잘라라. **2** [I, T] to cut something by hitting it many times with a heavy sharp tool such as an AXE ‖ 도끼 등의 무겁고 날카로운 연장으로 여러 차례 쳐서 물건을 자르다. 찍어[잘라]내다: *Greta was out chopping wood for the fire.* 그레타는 밖에서 장작을 패고 있었다.

chop sth ↔ **down** *phr v* [T] to make a tree fall down by cutting it with a heavy sharp tool such as an AXE ‖ 도끼 등의 무겁고 날카로운 연장으로 나무를 잘라서 쓰

러뜨리다. 찍어[잘라]내다

chop sth ↔ **off** *phr v* [T] to remove something by cutting it with a heavy sharp tool so that it is no longer connected to something else ‖ 무겁고 날 카로운 연장으로 어떤 것을 잘라 다른 것에 더 이상 연결되지 않게 제거하다. 베어[잘라] 내다: *Mitch's foot was chopped off in a horrible accident.* 미치의 발은 끔찍한 사고로 절단되었다.

chop² *n* **1** a small flat piece of meat on a bone ‖ 뼈에 붙어 있는 작고 얇은 고깃점: *a pork chop* 돼지고기 토막 **2** a quick hard hit with the side of your hand or with a heavy sharp tool ‖ 손의 옆부분이나 무겁고 날카로운 도구로 하는 빠르고 격렬한 타격. 짧은 일격: *a karate chop* 당수 타격

chop·per /'tʃɑpɚ/ *n* **1** INFORMAL ⇨ HELICOPTER **2** a type of MOTORCYCLE on which the front wheel is far in front of the BARs you use to control the vehicle ‖ 앞바퀴가 오토바이를 운전하는 데 사용하는 핸들 앞쪽에 멀리 떨어져 있는 오토바이의 일종. 개조 오토바이 **3 choppers** SLANG teeth ‖ 이. 치아

chop·py /'tʃɑpi/ *adj* choppy water has many small waves ‖ 많은 작은 물결이 있는. 파도가 이는. 물결이 치는 – **choppiness** *n* [U]

chop·sticks /'tʃɑpstɪks/ *n* [plural] a pair of thin sticks used for eating food, especially by people in Asia ‖ 특히 아시아인들이 음식을 먹을 때 사용하는 가느다란 막대기 한 벌. 젓가락

chop suey /'tʃɑp 'sui/ a Chinese dish made of bean sprouts, other types of vegetables and meat, which is served with rice ‖ 콩나물과 다른 종류의 야채·고기로 만들어져 밥과 함께 제공되는 중국요리. 찹수이. 잡채

cho·ral /'kɔrəl/ *adj* intended to be sung by a CHOIR (=group of people that sing), or involving this type of singing ‖ 합창단이 부르기로 되어 있거나 이런 종류의 노래를 포함하는. 합창단[곡]의: *choral music* 합창 음악

chord /kɔrd/ *n* **1** a combination of two or more musical notes played at the same time ‖ 동시에 연주되는 둘 또는 그 이상의 음표의 결합. 화음 **2 strike a chord** to say or do something that people react well to because they feel it is familiar or true ‖ 사람들에게 친숙하거나 진실하게 느껴져 공감이 가는 것을 말하거나 행하다. 심금을 울리다: *I think our campaign has struck a chord with the public.* 우리 캠페인이 대중들의 심금

을 울렸다고 나는 생각한다.

chore /tʃɔr/ *n* **1** a job that you have to do regularly, especially work that you do in a house or on a farm ‖ 특히 집이나 농장에서 하는 일로 규칙적으로 해야 하는 일. 허드렛일. 잡일: *Do your chores before you go to school!* 학교 가기 전에 네 몫의 자질구레한 일을 하거라! **2** something you have to do that is boring and unpleasant ‖ 해야 하는 지루하고 언짢은 일. 지루한 일. 싫은 일: *Grocery shopping is such a chore.* 식품 구입은 정말 귀찮은 일이다.

cho·re·og·ra·phy /ˌkɔriˈɑgrəfi/ *n* [U] the art of arranging how dancers should move during a performance ‖ 공연하는 동안 무용수들이 어떻게 움직여야 하는지를 미리 정하는 기술. 안무 – **choreographer** *n*

chor·tle /'tʃɔrtl/ *v* [I] to laugh because something is funny or pleases you ‖ 어떤 것이 재미있거나 즐겁게 만들어 웃다. 기쁜 듯이 웃다 – **chortle** *n*

cho·rus /'kɔrəs/ *n* **1** the part of a song that is repeated after each VERSE (=main part of a song) ‖ 각 절 뒤에 반복되는 노래 부분. 후렴 **2** a group of people who sing together ‖ 같이 노래 부르는 일단의 사람들. 합창단 **3** a piece of music written to be sung by a large group of people ‖ 대규모 집단의 사람들이 노래를 부르도록 쓰여진 곡. 합창곡: *the Hallelujah Chorus* 할렐루야 합창곡 **4** a group of singers and dancers in a show ‖ 쇼에 출연하는 가수·무용수들의 집단 **5** something said or expressed by a lot of people at the same time ‖ 동시에 많은 사람들이 말하거나 표현하는 것. 일제히 내는 소리: *a chorus of howls and whistles* 여러 사람이 일제히 내는 외침과 휘파람 소리

chose /tʃouz/ *v* the past tense of CHOOSE ‖ choose의 과거형

chosen /'tʃouzən/ *v* the PAST PARTICIPLE of CHOOSE ‖ choose의 과거 분사형

chow¹ /tʃau/ *n* [U] SLANG food ‖ 음식. 식사: *It's chow time!* (=time to eat) 식사 시간이다

chow² *v*

chow down *phr v* [I] SPOKEN to eat a lot of food ‖ 많은 음식을 먹다: *We really chowed down at Larry's house last night.* 우리는 어젯밤 래리의 집에서 음식을 진짜 많이 먹었다.

chow·der /'tʃaudɚ/ *n* [U] a thick soup made with milk, vegetables, and usually fish ‖ 우유·야채·흔히 생선으로 만든 진한 수프. 차우더: *clam chowder* 대합 차우더

Christ /kraɪst/ *n* ⇨ JESUS

chris·ten /'krɪsən/ v [T] **1 be christened** to be given your name and be made a member of a Christian church at a religious ceremony soon after you are born ‖ 태어난 직후 종교적인 의식을 통해 세례명을 받고 크리스트교 교회의 신자가 되다: *She was christened Elizabeth Ann.* 그녀는 엘리자베스 앤이라는 세례명을 받았다. **2** to name a ship, airplane etc. at a special ceremony ‖ 특별한 의식에서 선박·비행기 등에 이름을 붙이다. 명명하다

chris·ten·ing /'krɪsənɪŋ/ n [C, U] a religious ceremony at which you are CHRISTENed ‖ 세례를 받는 종교적 의식. 세례식

Chris·tian /'krɪstʃən, 'krɪʃtʃən/ adj based on Christianity, or believing in it ‖ 기독교 신앙에 기초를 두거나 기독교를 믿는. 크리스트교의: *Christian ministers* 기독교 성직자 / *Christian values* 기독교의 가치 – **Christian** n

Chris·ti·an·i·ty /ˌkrɪstʃi'ænəti/ n [U] the religion based on the life and teachings of Jesus Christ ‖ 예수 그리스도의 생애와 가르침에 기초를 둔 종교. 크리스트교

Christian Sci·ence /ˌ.. '../ n [U] a church whose members believe that they can cure their own illnesses using their minds rather than with medical help ‖ 신자들이 자신들의 질병을 의학적 도움보다는 자신의 마음을 이용해서 치유할 수 있다고 믿는 교회. 크리스천 사이언스 – **Christian Scientist** n

Christ·mas /'krɪsməs/ n [C, U] **1** a Christian holiday on December 25 that celebrates the birth of Christ, when people give and receive gifts ‖ 12월 25일에 사람들이 선물을 주고받으며 예수의 탄생을 축하하는 기독교 축일. 크리스마스 **2** the period of time just before and after this day ‖ 크리스마스 직전 및 직후의 기간: *What did you do over Christmas?* 크리스마스 기간에 너는 무얼 했니?

Christmas car·ol /'.. ˌ../ n a Christian song sung at Christmas ‖ 크리스마스에 부르는 기독교 노래. 크리스마스 캐럴

Christmas Day /ˌ.. './ n [C, U] December 25 ‖ 12월 25일. 성탄절

Christmas Eve /ˌ.. './ n [C, U] December 24, the day before Christmas ‖ 크리스마스 전날인 12월 24일. 크리스마스 이브

Christmas tree /'.. ˌ./ n a real or artificial tree that you put inside your house and decorate for Christmas ‖ 집안에 놓고 크리스마스 장식을 하는 실제 또는 인조 나무. 크리스마스 트리

chrome /kroʊm/ **chro·mi·um** /'kroʊmiəm/ n [U] a hard metal substance used for covering objects with a shiny protective surface ‖ 윤이 나는 보호 표면으로 물체를 도금하는 데에 쓰는 단단한 금속 물질. 크롬 (도금): *chrome fenders on a car* 크롬 도금을 한 자동차의 펜더

chro·mo·some /'kroʊməˌsoʊm, -ˌzoʊm/ n TECHNICAL a part of every living cell that controls the character, shape etc. that a plant or animal has ‖ 식물이나 동물이 가지는 특성·모양 등을 관장하는 모든 생물 세포의 일부분. 염색체

chron·ic /'krɑnɪk/ adj **1** a chronic disease or illness is one that cannot be cured ‖ 질병이나 병이 치료될 수 없는. 만성인: *chronic arthritis* 만성 관절염 **2** a chronic problem, difficulty, or type of behavior is one that you cannot get rid of or that keeps happening again ‖ 문제 [어려움, 행동 유형]가 제거할 수 없거나 계속해서 다시 생기는. 상습적인. 고질적인: *chronic unemployment* 고질적인 실업 – **chronically** adv

chron·i·cle /'krɑnɪkəl/ n a written record of historical events, arranged in the order in which they happened ‖ 일어난 순서대로 배열된, 역사적 사건의 문서 기록. 연대기 – **chronicle** v [T]

chron·o·log·i·cal /ˌkrɑnl'ɑdʒɪkəl/ adj arranged according to when something happened ‖ 어떤 일이 일어난 순서대로 배열된. 연대순의: *a list of World Series champions in chronological order* 연대순에 따른 월드 시리즈 챔피언의 목록 – **chronologically** adv

chro·nol·o·gy /krə'nɑlədʒi/ n a list of events arranged according to when they happened ‖ 일어난 때에 따라 배열된 사건의 목록. 연표: *a chronology of the 20th century* 20세기의 연표

chrys·a·lis /'krɪsəlɪs/ n a MOTH or BUTTERFLY at the stage of development when it has a hard outer shell, before becoming a LARVA and then an adult ‖ 유충이 되고 나서 성충이 되기 전 발달 단계인 딱딱한 외피를 하고 있을 때의 나방이나 나비. 번데기 —compare COCOON

chrys·an·the·mum /krɪ'sænθəməm/ n a garden plant with large brightly colored flowers ‖ 크고 밝은 색의 꽃이 피는 원예 식물. 국화

chub·by /'tʃʌbi/ adj a word meaning

slightly fat, used especially about children ‖ 특히 어린아이에게 쓰여 약간 뚱뚱한을 뜻하는 단어. 토실토실한. 오동통한 **– chubbiness** *n* [U] —see usage note at FAT[1]

chuck /tʃʌk/ *v* [T] INFORMAL to throw something in a careless or relaxed way ‖ 어떤 것을 무심코 아무렇게나 던지다. 팽개치다: *Chuck that magazine over here, would you?* 그 잡지 좀 여기로 던져 주시겠습니까?

chuck sth ↔ **away/out** *phr v* [T] INFORMAL to throw something away ‖ 어떤 것을 내버리다: *We had to chuck out a lot of stuff when we moved.* 우리는 이사할 때 많은 잡동사니들을 버려야 했다.

chuck sb ↔ **out** *phr v* [T] INFORMAL to force someone to leave a place ‖ 어떤 장소를 떠나라고 남에게 강요하다. 쫓아내다: *There was a fight, and some guys got chucked out of the bar.* 술집에서 싸움이 나서 남자들 몇 명이 쫓겨났다.

chuck·le /'tʃʌkəl/ *v* [I] to laugh quietly ‖ 조용하게 웃다. 낄낄거리다: *Terry chuckled to himself as he read his book.* 테리는 책을 읽으면서 혼자 낄낄거렸다. **– chuckle** *n*

chug /tʃʌg/ *v* **-gged, -gging 1** [I] if a car, boat, or train chugs, it makes a repeated low sound while moving ‖ 자동차[배, 기차] 등이 움직이는 동안 반복되는 낮은 소리를 내다. 통통[직칙] 소리를 내다 **2** [T] INFORMAL to drink all of something without stopping ‖ 어떤 것을 멈추지 않고 다 마시다. 단숨에 들이켜다. 꿀꺽꿀꺽 마시다: *Chug that beer and let's go.* 저 맥주를 다 마시고 가자. **– chug** *n* [C usually singular]

chum /tʃʌm/ *n* OLD-FASHIONED a good friend ‖ 좋은 친구. 단짝

chump /tʃʌmp/ *n* INFORMAL someone who is silly or stupid, and who can be easily deceived ‖ 어리석거나 우둔해서 쉽게 속일 수 있는 사람. 얼간이. 등신

chunk /tʃʌŋk/ *n* **1** a large piece of something ‖ 어떤 것의 큰 조각. 덩어리: *a chunk of cheese* 치즈 한 덩어리 **2** a large part or amount of something ‖ 어떤 것의 상당한 부분이나 양: *Having to get a new car took a big chunk out of her savings.* 새 차를 구입하느라 그녀는 저축의 상당 부분을 축냈다.

chunk·y /'tʃʌŋki/ *adj* **1** thick and heavy ‖ 두껍고 무거운. 묵직한: *chunky jewelry* 묵직한 장신구 **2** someone who is chunky has a broad heavy body ‖ 사람이 몸이 펑 퍼짐하고 무거운. 땅딸막한. 육중한

church /tʃɝtʃ/ *n* **1** a building where Christians go to have religious services ‖ 기독교인이 예배를 보러 가는 건물. 교회 **2** [U] the religious services in a church ‖ 교회에서의 예배(식): *Come over after church.* 예배 끝나고 와라. **3** also **Church** one of the separate groups within the Christian religion ‖ 크리스트교 내의 분리된 파의 하나. 교파. …교: *the Catholic Church* 가톨릭교

churl·ish /'tʃɝlɪʃ/ *adj* not polite or friendly ‖ 예의바르거나 우호적이지 못한. 무례한. 무뚝뚝한

churn[1] /tʃɝn/ *n* a container in which milk is shaken until it forms butter ‖ 버터가 만들어질 때까지 우유를 휘젓는 용기. 교반기

churn[2] *v* **1 make sb's stomach churn** to make someone feel sick because s/he is nervous or frightened ‖ 긴장되거나 놀라서 울렁거리게 하다 **2** [T] to make butter using a CHURN ‖ 교반기를 사용하여 버터를 만들다 **3** [I, T] also **churn up** if water churns or if it is churned, it moves around violently ‖ 물이 세차게 움직이거나 세게 휘젓다: *Buck tried to shout above the roar of the churning water.* 벅은 세차게 흐르는 물의 굉음보다 더 크게 소리치려고 했다.

churn sth ↔ **out** *phr v* [T] INFORMAL to produce large quantities of something ‖ 어떤 것을 대량 생산하다: *She churns out about three new books every year.* 그녀는 매년 신간 서적을 3권이나 낸다.

churn sth ↔ **up** *phr v* [T] if something churns up the ground, water, dust etc., it makes the ground etc. turn over or move a lot ‖ 땅·물·먼지 등을 뒤엎거나 많이 흔들다: *Tractors had churned up the muddy fields.* 트랙터들이 진흙 밭을 갈아엎었다.

chute /ʃut/ *n* **1** a long narrow structure that slopes down, so that things or people can slide down it from one place to another ‖ 물건이나 사람이 한 장소에서 다른 장소로 미끄러져 내려가도록 아래로 경사진 길고 좁은 구조물. 슈트. 활송(滑送): *a mail chute* 우편물 활송 장치 **2** INFORMAL ⇨ PARACHUTE[1]

chutzpah /'hʊtspə/ *n* [U] INFORMAL too much confidence, which is often considered to be rude ‖ 흔히 무례하게 여겨지는 과도한 자신감. 뻔뻔스러움. 철면피함: *Only Klinkman would have the chutzpah to say what he did.* 클링크만이 뻔뻔스럽게 자신이 한 일을 말하려고 했다.

CIA *n* Central Intelligence Agency ‖ Central Intelligence Agency(미국 중앙 정

보국)의 약어; the department of the US government that collects secret information about other countries ‖ 다른 나라들에 대한 비밀 정보를 모으는 미국 정부의 기관

ci·der /ˈsaɪdɚ/ n [C, U] a drink made from apples ‖ 사과로 만든 음료. 사과즙. 사과 주스

ci·gar /sɪˈgɑr/ n a thing that people smoke, that is made from tobacco leaves that have been rolled into a thick tube shape ‖ 담배잎을 굵은 관 모양으로 말아 피우는 것. 시가. 엽궐련

cig·a·rette /ˌsɪgəˈrɛt, ˈsɪgəˌrɛt/ n a thing that people smoke, that is made from finely cut tobacco leaves that have been rolled inside a thin tube of paper ‖ 잘게 썬 담배잎을 가는 종이 관 속에 말아서 사람들이 피우는 것. 궐련. 담배

cinch¹ /sɪntʃ/ n **be a cinch** INFORMAL **a)** to be almost certain to happen ‖ 거의 확실히 일어나다: The Cubs are a cinch to win the National League East. 커브스 팀이 동부 내셔널 리그에서 우승할 것이 확실하다. **b)** to be very easy to do ‖ 하는 것이 아주 쉽다: The written test was a cinch, but the oral one – well, I don't know. 그 필기 시험은 아주 쉬웠지만 구술 시험은, 글쎄 잘 모르겠네.

cinch² v [T] to pull a belt, STRAP etc. tightly around something ‖ 어떤 것의 둘레를 벨트·끈 등으로 바짝 당기다. 단단히 매다[죄다]

cin·der /ˈsɪndɚ/ n a very small piece of burned wood, coal etc. ‖ 불에 탄 나무·석탄 등의 아주 작은 조각. 타다 남은 덩어리. 뜬숯

cin·e·ma /ˈsɪnəmə/ n [singular U] **1** the art or business of making movies ‖ 영화를 제작하는 예술이나 산업. 영화 예술[산업]: an important director in German cinema 독일 영화의 중요한 감독 **2** OLD-FASHIONED ⇨ MOVIE THEATER

cin·e·ma·to·gra·phy /ˌsɪnəməˈtɑgrəfi/ n [U] TECHNICAL the skill or study of making movies ‖ 영화를 제작하는 기술이나 학문. 영화 촬영술 **– cinematographer** n

cin·na·mon /ˈsɪnəmən/ n [U] a sweet-smelling brown SPICE used especially in baking cakes and cookies ‖ 특히 케이크와 쿠키를 굽는 데 쓰는 달콤한 냄새가 나는 갈색의 향신료. 계피(桂皮). 육계

ci·pher /ˈsaɪfɚ/ n a secret system of writing; CODE ‖ 비밀스런 글쓰기의 방식. 암호: 위 CODE

cir·ca /ˈsɚkə/, written abbreviation **c.** prep FORMAL used with dates to show that something happened on nearly, but not exactly, that date ‖ 정확하지 않지만 거의 그 날짜에 일어났다는 것을 나타내는 데에 날짜와 함께 쓰여. …즘. 경: He was born circa 1100. 그는 1100년경에 태어났다.

cir·cle¹ /ˈsɚkəl/ n a completely round shape ‖ 완전히 둥근 모양. 원(형) **—see** picture at SHAPE¹ **1** a group of people or things forming the shape of a circle ‖ 원형을 이룬 사람이나 사물들의 집단: a circle of chairs 원형으로 놓인 의자들 **2** a group of people who know each other or have a common interest ‖ 서로 알고 공통의 관심을 가진 사람들의 집단. 그룹. 사회. – 계: a large circle of friends 광범위한 친구 관계 / Myers' new book has caused an uproar in literary circles. 마이어스의 새 책은 문학계에 큰 소동을 일으켰다. **3 come full circle** to end in the same situation in which you began, even though there have been changes during the time in between ‖ 중간에 변화도 있었지만 시작했던 것과 동일한 상황으로 끝나다. 원점으로 되돌아오다: After the experiments of the 1960s, education has come full circle in its methods of teaching reading. 1960년대의 실험 단계가 지나고 교육은 읽기 교수법으로 되돌아왔다. **4 go around in circles** to think or argue about something a lot without deciding anything or making any progress ‖ 어떠한 결정도 하지 않거나 진전도 하지 못하고 어떤 것에 대해 많이 생각하거나 논의하다. 제자리 걸음을 하다. 공전(空轉)하다

circle² v **1** [T] to draw a circle around something ‖ 어떤 것 둘레에 원을 그리다: Circle the correct answer. 정답에 동그라미를 치시오. **2** [I, T] to move in a circle around something ‖ 어떤 것 주위를 원형으로 움직이다. 선회하다: a plane circling an airport before landing 착륙하기 전에 공항을 선회하는 비행기

cir·cuit /ˈsɚkɪt/ n **1** [singular] all the places that are usually visited by someone who is doing a particular activity ‖ 특정한 활동을 하는 사람이 항상 방문하는 모든 장소. 순회 구역. 일주: Hayes will get rich out of the lecture/talk show/cabaret circuit. 헤이즈는 순회 강연[토크쇼, 카바레 연주]으로 부자가 될 것이다. **2** the complete circle that an electric current travels ‖ 전류가 완전히 한 바퀴 도는 회로. 전기의 회로(回路). 회선

circuit board /ˈ.. ./ n a set of connections between points on a piece of electrical equipment that uses a thin line of metal to CONDUCT (=carry) the electricity ‖ 전기를 전도하기 위해 얇은 금속선을 사용하는, 전자 장치 위의 부분들을 한 세트로 연결해 놓은 것. 회로기판

circuit break·er /ˈ.. ˌ../ *n* a piece of equipment that stops an electric current if it becomes dangerous ‖ 전류가 위험해지면 전류를 차단시키는 장비. 차단기

circuit court /ˌ.. ˈ./ *n* a court of law in a US state that meets in different places within the area it is responsible for ‖ 담당하는 지역 내의 곳곳에서 열리는 미국 주의 재판소. 순회 재판소

cir·cu·i·tous /sərˈkyuətəs/ *adj* FORMAL going from one place to another in a way that is longer than the most direct way ‖ 한 장소에서 다른 장소로 최직선 거리보다 먼 길로 가는. 빙 돌아가는. 우회의: *the river's circuitous course* 강의 우회 수로

cir·cuit·ry /ˈsərkətri/ *n* [U] a system of electric CIRCUITs ‖ 전기 회로 시스템. 전기 회로도[망]

cir·cu·lar¹ /ˈsərkyələ/ *adj* **1** shaped like a circle ‖ 원처럼 생긴. 원형의 **2** moving around in a circle ‖ 원형으로 움직이는. 순환하는: *a circular journey* 순회 여행 **3 circular argument/discussion/ logic etc.** an argument etc. in which you always return to the same statements or ideas that were expressed at the beginning ‖ 처음에 표현되었던 동일한 말이나 생각으로 항상 돌아가는 논쟁 등. 원점을 맴도는 토론/토의/논리 – **circularity** /ˌsərkyəˈlærəti/ *n* [U]

circular² *n* a printed advertisement or notice that is sent to a lot of people at the same time ‖ 많은 사람에게 동시에 보내지는 인쇄된 광고나 통지서. 안내장. 광고 전단: *Did you see that circular from the new supermarket?* 새 슈퍼마켓에서 보낸 그 전단을 봤소?

cir·cu·late /ˈsərkyəˌleɪt/ *v* **1** [I, T] to move around within a system, or to make something do this ‖ 시스템 내에서 돌거나 무엇을 돌게 하다. 순환하다[시키다]: *blood circulating around the body* 인체를 순환하는 피 **2** [I] if information, facts, or ideas circulate, they become known by many people ‖ 정보[사실, 사상]가 모든 사람들에게 알려지다. 퍼지다. 유포되다: *There's a rumor circulating about Midori and Mr. Trenton.* 미도리와 트렌턴 씨에 대한 소문이 나돌고 있다. **3** [T] to send or give information, facts, goods etc. to a group of people ‖ 일단의 사람에게 정보·사실·물건 등을 보내거나

주다. 배포하다. 제공하다: *I'll circulate the report at the meeting.* 모임에서 그 보고서를 배포할 것이다. **4** [I] to talk to a lot of different people in a group, especially at a party ‖ 특히 파티에서 한 그룹의 다른 많은 사람들에게 이야기하다. 유포하다 – **circulatory** /ˈsərkyələˌtɔri/ *adj*

cir·cu·la·tion /ˌsərkyəˈleɪʃən/ *n* **1** [C, U] the movement of blood around your body ‖ 신체를 도는 혈액의 움직임. 혈액 순환: *Dick has bad circulation.* 딕은 혈액 순환이 나쁘다. **2 in/out of circulation a)** used by a group or society and passing from one person to another, or no longer doing this ‖ 한 집단이나 사회에서 사용되며 한 사람에게서 다른 사람으로 전해지는, 또는 더 이상 이렇게 되지 않는. 유통[통용]되는/되지 않는: *The government has reduced the number of $100 bills in circulation.* 정부는 유통 중인 100달러 지폐의 수를 줄였다. **b)** INFORMAL having or not having an active social life ‖ 활동적인 사회 생활을 하거나 하지 않는: *Archie's out of circulation until after his operation.* 아치는 수술이 끝날 때까지 사회 활동을 하지 않는다. **3** [singular] the average number of copies of a newspaper, magazine, or book that are usually sold over a particular period of time ‖ 특정 기간에 걸쳐 판매되는 신문[잡지, 책]의 평균 권수. 판매[발행] 부수: *a magazine with a circulation of 400,000* 발행 부수가 40만부인 잡지

cir·cum·cise /ˈsərkəmˌsaɪz/ *v* [T] **1** to cut off the skin at the end of the PENIS (=male sex organ) ‖ 남자 성기 끝의 포피(包皮)를 잘라내다. 포경 수술을 하다 **2** to cut off a woman's CLITORIS (=part of her sex organs) ‖ 여자 성기의 음핵(陰核)을 잘라내다. 음핵 제거 수술을 하다 – **circumcision** /ˌsərkəmˈsɪʒən/ *n* [C, U]

cir·cum·fer·ence /sərˈkʌmfrəns/ *n* [C, U] the distance around the outside of a circle or a round object ‖ 원이나 둥근 물체의 외부 둘레. 원둘레. 외주(外周): *The earth's circumference is nearly 25,000 miles.* 지구 둘레는 약 25,000마일이다. —see picture at DIAMETER

cir·cum·spect /ˈsərkəmˌspɛkt/ *adj* FORMAL thinking carefully about things before doing them; CAUTIOUS ‖ 일을 하기 전에 깊이 생각하는. 용의주도한. 신중한; 🔲 cautious: *In politics you have to be more circumspect about what you say in public.* 정치 활동에서 당신은 대중들 앞에서 하는 말에 더 신중해야 한다.

cir·cum·stance /ˈsərkəmˌstæns/ *n* [U]

the combination of facts, events, and luck that influences your life, that you cannot control ‖ 자신이 통제할 수 없는, 삶에 영향을 끼치는 사실·사건·운의 결합. 상황. 환경: *Circumstance played a large part in her getting the job.* 주변 환경이 그녀가 그 일자리를 잡는 데 큰 역할을 했다.

cir·cum·stan·ces /'sɚkəm,stænsɪz/ *n* [plural] **1** the facts or conditions that affect a situation, action, event etc. ‖ 상황·행동·사건 등에 영향을 미치는 사실이나 조건. 사정. 형편: *You shouldn't judge him until you know the circumstances.* 사정을 알 때까지 그에 대해 함부로 판단을 내려서는 안 된다. **2 under/in the circumstances** used in order to say that a particular situation makes an action, decision etc. necessary or acceptable ‖ 특정한 상황이 어떤 행동·결정 등을 필요하게 하거나, 수용하게 만든 다고 말하는 데 쓰여. 형편상. 상황에 맞 춰: *Under the circumstances, I think we did the best we could.* 현 상황에서 우리는 할 수 있는 최선을 다했다고 생각한다. **3 under/in no circumstances** used in order to emphasize that something must not happen ‖ 어떤 일이 절대 발생해서는 안 된다는 것을 강조하는 데 쓰여. 결코 [어떠한 상황에서도] …하지 않는: *Under no circumstances are you to leave this house!* 어떤 일이 있어도 너는 이 집을 떠 날 수 없어!

cir·cum·stan·tial /ˌsɚkəm'stænʃəl/ *adj* making you believe that something is true, because of the events or facts relating to it, but not able to be proved ‖ 증명할 수는 없지만 관련된 사건이나 사실 때문에 어떤 것이 사실이라고 믿게 하는. 정황적인: *The circumstantial evidence strongly suggested that he was guilty.* 그 정황 증거는 그가 유죄임을 강력히 시사했다.

cir·cum·vent /ˌsɚkəm'vɛnt, 'sɚ-kəm,vɛnt/ *v* [T] FORMAL to avoid something, especially a rule or law that restricts you ‖ 특히 자신을 제한하는 규칙이나 법을 회피하다. 모면하다: *The company has opened an office abroad in order to circumvent the tax laws.* 그 회사는 세법(稅法)을 피하기 위해 해외에 사무실을 냈다. – **circumvention** /ˌsɚkəm'vɛnʃən/ *n* [U]

cir·cus /'sɚkəs/ *n* **1** a group of people and animals that travel to different places performing skillful tricks as entertainment, or a performance by these people and animals ‖ 흥행으로 능

숙한 묘기를 공연하며 여러 지역을 여행하는 일단의 사람·동물, 또는 이 사람·동물들의 연기. 유랑 극단. 서커스 **2** [singular] INFORMAL a meeting, group of people etc. that is very noisy and uncontrolled ‖ 매우 시끄럽고 무절제한 모임·일단의 사람. 야단법석. 떠들썩한 사람들: *Our office turns into a circus on Friday afternoons.* 우리 사무실은 금요일 오후에는 떠들썩해진다.

cir·rho·sis /sɪ'roʊsɪs/ *n* [U] a serious disease of the LIVER, often caused by drinking too much alcohol ‖ 흔히 지나친 음주로 인해 걸리는 심각한 간 질환. 간경변(肝硬變)

cis·tern /'sɪstɚn/ *n* a container in which water is stored inside a building ‖ 건물 내부의 물을 저장하는 통. 물탱크

ci·ta·tion /saɪ'teɪʃən/ *n* **1** an official order for someone to appear in court or pay a FINE for doing something illegal ‖ 법원에 출두하라는 또는 불법적인 일에 대해 벌금을 지불하라는 공식적인 명령. 소환: *a traffic citation* 교통 위반 딱지 **2** a FORMAL statement publicly praising someone's actions or achievements ‖ 남의 행동이나 업적을 공공연하게 찬양하는 공식 발표. 표창: *a citation for bravery* 용감한 행동에 대한 표창 **3** [C, U] a line taken from a book, speech etc., or the act of using this line ‖ 책·연설 등에서 발췌한 문장, 또는 이 문장을 사용하는 행위. 인용(문)

cite /saɪt/ *v* [T] **1** to mention something as an example or proof of something else ‖ 어떤 것의 예나 증거로서 어떤 것을 언급하다. 인용하다: *The mayor cited the latest crime figures as proof of the need for more police.* 그 시장은 경찰이 더 필요하다는 증거로 최근의 범죄 수치를 인용했다. **2** LAW to order someone to appear before a court of law because s/he has done something wrong ‖ 잘못한 사람에게 법원에 출두하라고 명령하다. 법정에 소환하다. …에게 출두 명령을 내리다: *He was cited for speeding.* 속도 위반으로 그는 법정에 소환되었다. **3** to publicly praise someone ‖ 어떤 사람을 공개적으로 칭찬하다. 치하[표창]하다: *Officer Johnson was cited for bravery.* 존슨 경찰관은 용감한 행위로 표창받았다.

cit·i·zen /'sɪtəzən/ *n* **1** someone who lives in a particular town, state, or country ‖ 특정한 시(주, 나라)에 사는 사람. 시민. 주민. 거주자: *the citizens of Poland* 폴란드 거주자 **2** someone who legally belongs to a particular country, whether s/he lives there or not ‖ 거주 여

부와 상관없이 특정한 나라에 법률적으로 속한 사람. 공민. 국민 **3 second class citizen** someone who feels unimportant because of the way other people treat him/her ‖ 다른 사람들이 그를 대하는 태도로 인해 스스로를 중요하지 않다고 여기는 사람. 이등 시민

citizens band /'... ,./ n [U] ⇨ CB

cit·i·zen·ship /'sɪtəzən,ʃɪp/ n [U] the legal right of belonging to a particular country ‖ 특정한 나라에 속하는 법적 권리. 시민권

cit·rus /'sɪtrəs/ adj **1** a citrus fruit, such as an orange, has a thick skin, juicy flesh, and grows on a tree ‖ 껍질이 두껍고 과육에 즙이 많으며 나무에서 자라는 오렌지 등의 과일의. 감귤류의 **2** a citrus tree grows this fruit ‖ 이 과일이 자라는 나무의. 감귤류 나무의

cit·y /'sɪti/ n **1** a large important town ‖ 크고 중요한 도회지. 시. 도시: New York City 뉴욕 시 **2** the people who live in a city ‖ 도시에 거주하는 사람들. 도시의 주민[시민]: The city has been living in fear since last week's bombing. 전 시민이 지난주의 폭격 이후로 두려워하며 살고 있다.

city coun·cil /,.. '../ n the group of elected officials who are responsible for making a city's laws ‖ 시의 법률 제정을 담당하는 선출된 관료 집단. 시의회

city hall /,.. './ n [C, U] the local government of a city, or the building it uses as its offices ‖ 도시의 지방 자치체, 또는 지방 자치체가 사무실로 사용하는 건물. 시당국. 시청

civ·ic /'sɪvɪk/ adj relating to a city or its citizens ‖ 도시나 도시의 시민과 관련된. 도시의. 시민의: It's your civic duty to vote. 투표하는 것은 시민의 의무이다.

civ·ics /'sɪvɪks/ n [U] a school subject dealing with the rights and duties of citizens and the way government works ‖ 시민의 권리와 의무, 정부가 활동하는 방법을 다루는 학과목. 시민론. 시정학

civ·il /'sɪvəl/ adj **1** relating to the people or things in a country that are not part of military or religious organizations ‖ 군사적이나 종교적인 조직의 일부가 아닌 한 나라의 사람이나 사물과 관련된. 일반 시민의. 민간인의: We were married in a civil ceremony, not in church. 우리는 교회가 아닌 일반 예식으로 결혼했다. **2** relating to the laws concerning the private affairs of citizens, such as laws about business or property, rather than with crime ‖ 범죄에 관한 것이 아니라 사업이나 재산에 관

련된 법률 등의 시민의 사적인 일과 관련된 법률에 관한. 민법의. 민사의: a civil lawsuit 민사 소송 **3** relating to the people who live in a country ‖ 한 나라에 사는 사람들과 관련된. 시민의: The leaders must take care not to start new civil unrest. 지도자들은 시민의 불안을 새로이 야기시키지 않도록 조심해야 한다. **4** polite but not really very friendly ‖ 아주 다정하지는 않지만 예의 바른. 정중한: At least try to be civil to him, even if you don't like him. 그를 좋아하지 않더라도 적어도 정중하게 대하도록 해라. – **civilly** adv

civil dis·o·be·di·ence /,.. ..'..'.../ n [U] actions done by a large group of people in order to protest against the government, but without being violent ‖ 격렬하지 않으나 정부에 대해 항의하기 위해 대규모 집단의 사람들이 취하는 행동. 시민 불복종

civil en·gi·neer·ing /,.. ..'../ n [U] the planning, building, and repair of roads, bridges, large buildings etc. ‖ 도로·교량·큰 건물 등을 설계·건설·보수하는 일. 토목 공학

civilian /sə'vɪlyən/ n anyone who is not a member of the military or police ‖ 군인이나 경찰이 아닌 모든 사람. 민간인: Many innocent civilians were killed in the attack. 습격을 받아 많은 무고한 민간인이 살해되었다. – **civilian** adj

civ·i·li·za·tion /,sɪvələ'zeɪʃən/ n **1** [C, U] a society that is well organized and developed ‖ 조직화되고 발달된 사회. 문명: modern American civilization 현대 미국 문명 / the ancient civilizations of Greece and Rome 그리스와 로마의 고대 문명 **2** [U] all the societies in the world considered as a whole ‖ 전체로서 바라본 세계의 모든 사회. 문명 세계: The book looks at the relationship between religion and civilization. 그 책은 종교와 문명 사이의 관계를 고찰하고 있다.

civ·i·lize /'sɪvə,laɪz/ v [T] to improve a society so that it is more organized and developed ‖ 보다 조직화되고 발달되도록 사회를 개선하다. 문명화하다. 개화하다: The Romans hoped to civilize all the tribes of Europe. 로마인들은 유럽의 모든 종족들을 개화시키고 싶어했다.

civ·i·lized /'sɪvə,laɪzd/ adj **1** well organized and developed socially ‖ 조직화되고 사회적으로 발달된. 문명화된: Care for the disabled is essential in a civilized society. 신체 장애자들에 대한 배려는 문명화된 사회에서 필수적이다. **2** behaving in a polite and sensible way ‖

예의 바르고 분별 있게 행동하는. 교양 있
는. 세련된: *That's not the civilized way
to deal with things.* 그것은 일을 처리하
는 세련된 방법이 아니다. —opposite
UNCIVILIZED

civil rights /ˌ.. './ *n* [plural] the legal
rights that every person in a particular
country has. In the US, these include
the right to have the same treatment
whatever your race or religion is ‖ 특정
국가의 모든 사람이 가지는 법적 권리. 미
국에서는 인종이나 종교가 무엇이든 동등
한 대우를 받을 권리가 여기에 포함된다.
시민권. 공민권

civil serv·ant /ˌ.. '../ *n* someone who
works in the civil service ‖ 관청에서 일하
는 사람. 공무원

civil serv·ice /ˌ.. '../ *n* **the civil
service** the government departments
that deal with all the work of the
government except the military ‖ 군대를
제외한 정부의 모든 일을 처리하는 정부
부처. 행정 기관. (정부) 관청

civil war /ˌ.. './ *n* [C, U] a war in
which opposing groups of people from
the same country fight each other ‖ 같은
나라의 반대 집단의 사람들이 서로 싸우는
전쟁. 내란. 내전

clack /klæk/ *v* [I, T] if you clack
something or if it clacks, it makes a
continuous short hard sound ‖ 계속해서
짧고 딱딱한 소리를 내다. 딱딱[딸깍]하는
소리를 내다: *We could hear Grandma's
knitting needles clacking together.* 우리
는 할머니의 뜨개바늘들이 서로 딸깍거리
는 소리를 들을 수 있었다. – **clack** *n*
[singular]

clad /klæd/ *adj* LITERARY wearing or
covered in a particular thing ‖ 특정한 것
을 입거나 덮은: *a lady clad in silk and
lace* 비단옷과 레이스를 차려입은 숙녀 /
an armor-clad ship 군함

claim¹ /kleɪm/ *v* **1** [T] to state that
something is true, even if it has not
been proved ‖ 증명되지 않았지만 어떤 것
이 사실이라고 진술하다. 주장[단언]하다:
*Scientists now claim that a cure can be
found.* 현재 과학자들은 치유가 가능하다
고 주장한다. / *Ask Louie, he claims to
be an expert.* 자칭 전문가라고 주장하는
루이에게 물어봐라. / *She claims to have
written the book herself.* 그녀는 그 책을
본인이 썼다고 주장한다. **2** [I, T] to
officially ask for money that you have a
right to receive ‖ 받을 권리가 있는 돈을
공식적으로 요청하다: *The damage is too
slight to claim on insurance.* 그 피해는
너무 경미해서 보험금을 요구할 수 없다.

/ *Congress intends to make welfare
harder to claim.* ✗DON'T SAY "harder to
demand"✗ 의회는 생활보호대상 청구를
더 어렵게 하려고 한다. "harder to
demand"라고는 하지 않는다. **3** [T] to
state that you have a right to something,
or to take something that belongs to you
‖ 무엇에 대한 권리가 있다고 진술하다,
또는 자신의 물건을 가져가다: *Will
whoever lost an earring please come to
the front office to claim it.* 귀걸이를 잃으
신 분은 안내실로 오셔서 찾아가세요. **4** if
something claims lives, people die
because of it ‖ 어떤 것 때문에 사람들이
죽다. (인명을) 빼앗다: *That year, plane
crashes claimed 216 lives.* 그 해에 비행
기 추락으로 216명의 생명을 앗아갔다.

claim² *n* **1** [C, U] an act of officially
saying that you have a right to receive
or own something, or the state of
having this right ‖ 무엇을 받거나 소유할
권리가 있다고 공식적으로 말함, 또는 이
러한 권리를 가진 상태. 요구[청구](할 권
리)): *The contract proves he has no
claim on the house.* 그 계약서는 그가 그
집에 대한 권리가 없다는 것을 증명한다.
/ *insurance claims* 보험금 지급 청구 **2** a
statement that something is true, even
if it has not been proved ‖ 증명되지 않았
지만 무엇이 사실이라는 진술. 주장:
*Cardoza denied claims that he was
involved in drug smuggling.* 카도자는 그
가 마약 밀수에 연루되었다는 주장을 부인
했다. **3 claim to fame** a reason that
someone or something ought to be
famous ‖ 사람이나 사물이 유명해진 이유:
*Her chief/main claim to fame is the men
she married.* 그녀가 유명해진 주된 이유
는 그녀가 결혼했던 남자들 때문이다.

clair·voy·ant /klɛrˈvɔɪənt/ *n* someone
who says s/he can see what will happen
in the future ‖ 미래에 무슨 일이 일어날지
알 수 있는 사람. 통찰력이 있는 사람. 천
리안 – **clairvoyance** *n* [U] – **clair·
voyant** *adj*

clam¹ /klæm/ *n* **1** [C, U] a small sea
animal that has a shell and lives in sand
and mud, or the meat from this animal
‖ 껍데기가 있고 모래와 진흙에 사는 작은
바다 동물, 또는 이 동물의 살. 대합 조개
2 as happy as a clam INFORMAL very
happy ‖ 매우 행복한

clam² *v* **-mmed, -mming**

clam up *phr v* [I] INFORMAL to suddenly
stop talking, especially when you are
nervous or shy ‖ 특히 긴장하거나 수줍을
때 갑자기 이야기를 중단하다. 침묵을 지
키다. 입을 다물다: *Lou always clams up*

if you ask him too many questions about his past. 루는 자기의 과거에 대해 너무 많은 질문을 하면 항상 입을 다문다.

clam·ber /ˈklæmbɚ, ˈklæmɚ/ v [I] to climb something that is difficult to climb, using your hands and feet ‖ 손과 발을 써서 오르기 힘든 것에 오르다. 기어 오르다: *Jenny and I clambered up the side of the hill.* 제니와 나는 그 언덕의 경사면을 힘들게 기어올라갔다.

clam·my /ˈklæmi/ adj wet, cold, and sticky in a way that is unpleasant ‖ 불쾌하게 습하고 차가우며 끈적끈적한: *clammy hands* 축축한 손

clam·or¹ /ˈklæmɚ/ n [singular, U] 1 a very loud continuous noise ‖ 매우 시끄럽고 끊임없는 소음. 떠들썩함: *a clamor of voices in the next room* 옆방의 떠들썩한 소리 2 a complaint or a demand for something ‖ 어떤 것에 대한 불평이나 요구. (요구·항의·불만의) 함성. 외침. 아우성. 원성 – **clamorous** adj

clamor² v [I, T] to complain about or demand something loudly ‖ 어떤 것에 대해 불평하거나 큰 소리로 요구하다. (…을) 외치다. 부르짖다: *All the kids were clamoring for attention at once.* 모든 아이들이 당장 관심을 가져 달라고 시끄럽게 소리치고 있었다.

clamp¹ /klæmp/ v [T] 1 to hold something tightly so that it does not move ‖ 움직일 수 없도록 어떤 것을 꽉 잡다. …을 꽉 죄다: *He clamped his hand over her mouth.* 그는 손으로 그녀의 입을 꽉 막았다. 2 to fasten or hold two things together with a CLAMP ‖ 죔쇠로 두 물건을 한데 묶거나 고정하다: *Clamp the boards together until the glue dries.* 아교가 마를 때까지 그 판자를 고정시켜라.

clamp down phr v [I] to stop or limit an activity, especially a criminal activity ‖ 어떤 행동, 특히 범죄 행위를 막거나 제한하다. 단속[탄압]하다: *The police are clamping down on drunk drivers.* 경찰은 음주 운전자들을 단속하고 있다.

clamp² n a tool used for fastening or holding things together tightly ‖ 물건을 꽉 묶거나 고정하는 데에 사용하는 도구. 클램프. 죔쇠

clamp·down /ˈklæmpdaʊn/ n a sudden action by the government, police etc. to stop a particular activity ‖ 특정한 활동을 막기 위해 정부·경찰 등이 벌이는 갑작스러운 활동. 일제 단속: *a clampdown on illegal immigration* 불법 이민에 대한 일제 단속

clan /klæn/ n INFORMAL a large family, especially one that is all together at once ‖ 특히 동시에 함께 있는 대가족. 한 집안: *The whole clan will be coming over for Thanksgiving.* 온 집안이 추수 감사절을 지내러 올 것이다.

clan·des·tine /klænˈdɛstɪn/ adj secret and often illegal ‖ 비밀스럽고 종종 불법적인. 남몰래 행해지는: *a clandestine meeting* 비밀 모임

clang /klæŋ/ v [I, T] to make a loud sound like metal being hit ‖ 금속이 부딪치는 것과 같은 큰 소리를 내다. 쨍[땡그랑] 하고 울리다: *a bell clanging in the distance* 멀리서 땡그랑 하고 울리는 종소리 – **clang** n

clank /klæŋk/ v [I, T] to make a short loud sound like metal objects hitting each other ‖ 금속 물체가 서로 부딪치는 것과 같은 짧고 큰 소리를 내다. 철꺽 소리나다[나게 하다]: *clanking chains* 철꺽거리는 쇠사슬 – **clank** n

clap¹ /klæp/ v 1 [I, T] **a)** to hit your hands together loudly and continuously to show that you approve of something ‖ 어떤 것을 찬성한다는 것을 나타내기 위해 큰 소리로 계속해서 손뼉을 치다. 박수 갈채를 보내다: *The audience was clapping wildly as she sang the last words of the song.* 청중은 그녀가 그 노래의 마지막 가사를 부를 때 열렬하게 박수 갈채를 보내고 있었다. **b)** to hit your hands together one or two times to get someone's attention ‖ 남의 주의를 끌기 위해 한두 번의 손뼉을 치다: *The coach clapped his hands and yelled, "OK, listen up!"* 그 코치는 손뼉을 치고 "좋아, 잘 들어!"라고 고함쳤다. 2 **clap sb on the back/shoulder** to hit someone on the back or shoulder with your hand in a friendly way ‖ 남의 등이나 어깨를 손으로 친근하게 치다. …의 등/어깨를 가볍게 두드리다 – **clapping** n [U]

clap² n 1 **clap of thunder** a very loud sound made by THUNDER ‖ 천둥이 내는 매우 큰 소리 2 the sound that you make when you hit your hands together ‖ 손뼉칠 때 나는 소리 3 **the clap** SLANG ⇨ GONORRHEA

clap·board /ˈklæbɚd, ˈklæpbɔrd/ n [C, U] a cover for the sides of a house made of many long thin boards, or one of these boards ‖ 여러 개의 길고 가는 판자로 만든 가옥 측면의 덮개, 또는 이들 판자 중의 하나. 널빤지 지붕. 물막이 판자

clap·per /ˈklæpɚ/ n a piece of metal hung inside a bell that hits the bell to make it ring ‖ 쳐서 종소리를 내는 종의 안쪽에 매달린 금속 조각. 추

clar·i·fy /'klærə,faɪ/ v [I, T] to make something easier to understand by explaining it in more detail ‖ 어떤 것을 더 자세히 설명하여 보다 이해하기 쉽게 하다. 분명하게 하다. 명백히 하다: *His explanation did not clarify the matter for me.* 그 문제에 대한 그의 설명은 나에게는 명확하지 못했다. **– clari·fi·cation** /,klærəfə'keɪʃən/ n [C, U]

clar·i·net /,klærə'nɛt/ n a wooden musical instrument shaped like a long black tube, that you play by blowing into it ‖ 불어서 연주하는 길고 검은 관 모양의 목관 악기. 클라리넷 **– clarinetist** n

clar·i·ty /'klærəti/ n [U] **1** the quality of speaking, writing, or thinking in a clear way ‖ 명확하게 말하는[쓰는, 생각하는] 특성. 뚜렷함. 명쾌함: *the clarity of Irving's writing style* 어빙의 명료한 문체 / *I was amazed at his clarity of mind* (=how clearly he could think) *even at age 95.* 나는 그가 95세인데도 정신이 초롱초롱한 데에 놀랐다. **2** the ability to be seen or heard clearly ‖ 명확하게 보이거나 들리는 능력. 투명. 맑음: *the clarity of the TV picture* 선명한 텔레비전 화상

clash¹ /klæʃ/ v **1** [I] to fight or argue with someone ‖ 남과 싸우거나 논쟁하다. 격돌하다: *Soldiers clashed with rebels near the border.* 군인들은 국경 근처에서 반군과 격돌했다. **2** [I] if two colors or patterns clash, they look very bad together ‖ 두 색깔이나 무늬가 어울리지 않다: *That red tie clashes with your jacket.* 그 빨간 넥타이는 너의 재킷과 어울리지 않는다. **3** [I] if two events clash, they happen at the same time in a way that causes problems ‖ 두 행사가 동시에 일어나 문제를 야기하다. (···과)겹치다: *Unfortunately, the concert clashes with my evening class, so I can't go.* 불행히도 그 연주회가 내 저녁 수업과 겹쳐서 갈 수가 없다. **4** [I, T] to make a loud sound by hitting two metal objects together ‖ 두 금속 물체가 부딪쳐서 큰 소리를 내다. 쩽그렁 울리다

clash² n **1** a fight or argument between two people, armies etc. ‖ 두 사람·군대 사이의 싸움이나 논쟁. 충돌. 격돌: *a clash between Democrats and Republicans in the Senate* 상원에서 민주당원과 공화당원간의 논쟁 **2** a loud sound made by two metal objects hitting together ‖ 두 금속 물체가 부딪치는 커다란 소리. 쩽그렁 소리: *the clash of the cymbals* 심벌즈의 쩽그렁 소리

clasp¹ /klæsp/ n **1** a small metal object used for fastening a bag, belt, piece of jewelry etc. ‖ 손가방·벨트·장신구 등을 잠그는 데에 쓰는 작은 금속물. 걸쇠. 죔쇠 **2** [singular] a tight firm hold; GRIP ‖ 꽉 쥠. 거머쥐기; 圏 grip

clasp² v [T] **1** to hold someone or something tightly in your hands or arms ‖ 사람이나 사물을 손이나 팔로 꽉 잡다. ···을 꽉 쥐다: *The President and the Prime Minister clasped hands.* (=shook each other's hands) 대통령과 총리는 악수했다. **2** to fasten something with a CLASP ‖ 걸쇠로 물건을 잠그다

class¹ /klæs/ n

1 ▶GROUP OF STUDENTS 학생 집단◀ **a)** a group of students who are taught together ‖ 함께 배우는 학생 집단. 학급. 반: *a small class of ten people* 10명으로 된 소규모 학급 **b)** a group of students who will finish college or HIGH SCHOOL in the same year ‖ 같은 해에 대학이나 고등학교를 졸업하는 학생 집단. 동기생. 동창생: *Our class had its 30th reunion this year.* 우리 동기생은 올해 30주년 동창회를 가졌다. / *I was class of '96/'74/'88.* (=I finished in 1996, 1974 etc.) 나는 1996[1974, 1988]년도 졸업생이다.

2 ▶TEACHING PERIOD 수업 시간◀ [C, U] a period of time during which students are taught ‖ 학생들이 배우는 시간. 수업 시간: *When's your next class?* 다음 수업 시간은 언제니? / *Bob wasn't in class today.* 보브는 오늘 수업 시간에 없었다.

3 ▶SUBJECT 과목◀ a set of lessons in which you study a particular subject ‖ 특정한 주제를 공부하는 일련의 강의. ···수업: *a class in computer design* 컴퓨터 디자인 수업 / *a Spanish/math/science class* 스페인어[수학, 과학] 수업

4 ▶IN SOCIETY 사회에서◀ **a)** a group of people in a society that earn a similar amount of money, have similar types of job etc. ‖ 사회 내에서 비슷한 금액의 돈을 벌고 유사한 종류의 직업 등을 가진 사람들의 집단. 계층: *The Republicans are promising tax cuts for the middle class.* 공화당원들은 중산층에 대한 감세를 약속하고 있다. **b)** [U] the system in which people are divided into such groups ‖ 사람들이 그러한 집단으로 나뉘어진 제도. 계급[계층]제. 신분 제도: *the class system in Britain* 영국의 신분 제도

5 ▶QUALITY 질◀ a group into which people or things are divided according to how good they are ‖ 사람이나 사물을 좋은 정도에 따라 나눈 집단. 등급: *We can't afford to travel first class* (=the

most expensive way) *on the plane.* 우리
는 비행기 1등석으로 여행할 여유가 없다.
/ *As a tennis player, he's not in the
same class as Sampras.* (=not as good
as Sampras) 테니스 선수로서 그는 샘프
라스만큼 잘하지 못한다.
6 ▶STYLE/SKILL 스타일/기술◀ a
particular style, skill, or way of doing
something that makes people admire
you ‖ 사람들을 감탄하게 만드는, 무엇을
하는 특정한 스타일[기술, 방식]. 기품.
품위: *I think she's one of the only
actresses in Hollywood with class.* 나는
그녀가 할리우드의 비길 데 없이 기품 있
는 여배우들 중 한 사람이라고 생각한다.
7 ▶PLANTS/ANIMALS 식물/동물◀ a
group of plants, animals, words etc.
that can be studied together because
they are similar ‖ 유사해서 함께 연구되
는 식물·동물·단어 등의 집단. 부류. 강
(綱): *There are four main word classes* :
nouns, verbs, adjectives, and adverbs.
명사, 동사, 형용사, 부사의 네 가지 주요
어군(語群)이 있다.

CULTURE NOTE social classes

There are several phrases that are
used when talking about the type of
job that someone does and the money
s/he earns. **Blue collar workers** do
physical work that may or may not
need a lot of skill, but that does not
need a high level of education.
Plumbers and electricians, and
people who work in factories,
restaurants, and stores are blue
collar workers. **White collar
workers** work in offices, banks,
schools etc., and do work that
involves information and needs a
higher level of education. Managers,
teachers, lawyers, and doctors are
white collar workers. **Lower class**
describes people's income rather than
the kind of job they do. Both white
collar and blue collar workers who do
not earn a lot of money, are not
managers, or who do not own their
own business or their own home,
would consider themselves to be
lower class. **Middle class** describes
people who earn enough money to
have a fairly comfortable life. They
often own a small business or are
managers or teachers. People in this
class usually own their own home and
have a high level of education. **Upper**

class describes people who are not
quite rich, but are very comfortable.
They are usually managers with a
high position, people who own very
successful businesses, or are doctors
or lawyers.
사람들이 일해서 돈을 버는 직종에 대해
말할 때에 사용하는 몇 가지 어구가 있
다. **blue collar workers**(블루 칼라
층)는 많은 기술이 필요하거나 불필요한
육체적인 노동을 하되 높은 교육 수준을
요하지 않는다. 배관공·전기 기술자와
공장·식당·상점에서 일하는 사람들은
블루 칼라층이다. **white collar
workers**(화이트 칼라층)는 사무실·은
행·학교 등에서 정보와 관련된 일을 하
며 높은 교육 수준을 요한다. 매니저·교
사·변호사·의사들은 화이트 칼라층이
다. **lower class**(하류층)는 사람들의
직종보다 사람들의 수입을 표현한다. 많
은 돈을 벌지 못하거나 매니저가 아니거
나 또는 자신의 기업이나 집을 소유하지
않은 화이트 칼라층과 블루 칼라층도 자
기 자신을 하류층이라고 생각한다.
middle class(중류층)은 꽤 안락한 생
활을 할 만큼의 충분한 돈을 버는 사람
들을 일컫는다. 그들은 때로 영세 기업
을 소유하거나 매니저 혹은 교사들이다.
이 계층의 사람은 대개 자기 소유의 집
을 가지고 있으며 교육수준이 높다.
upper class(상류층)은 아주 부유하지
는 않지만 매우 안락한 생활을 하는 사
람들을 일컫는다. 그들은 대개 높은 지
위를 가진 매니저이거나, 매우 성공한
기업을 소유한 사람이거나 의사 혹은 변
호사들이다.

---

class² *v* [T] to decide that someone or
something belongs in a particular group
‖ 사람이나 사물을 특정한 집단에 속하는
것으로 결정하다. …을 분류하다: *Heroin
and cocaine are classed as hard drugs.*
헤로인과 코카인은 습관성 약물로 분류된
다.

class·ac·tion /ˌ. ˈ../ *adj* a class-action
LAWSUIT is one that a group of people
bring to a law court for themselves and
all other people with the same problem
‖ 일단의 사람들이 자신과 다른 사람들 모
두를 위해 동일한 문제로 법정에 소송을
제기하는. 집단 소송의 – **class action**
n [C, U]

clas·sic¹ /ˈklæsɪk/ *adj* **1** a classic book,
movie etc. is important and has been
popular for a long time ‖ 책·영화 등이
중요하고 오랫동안 인기가 있는. 고전의.
빼어난: *the classic rock music of the
sixties* 1960년대의 고전 록 음악 **2 a**

classic example/case etc. a typical or very good example etc. ‖ 대표적인 또는 아주 좋은 예 등. 전형적인 예/사례: *Forgetting to release the emergency brake is a classic mistake that many new drivers make.* 사이드 브레이크를 풀어 놓는 것을 잊어버리는 일은 많은 초보 운전자들이 범하는 전형적인 실수다. **3** a classic style of dressing, art etc. is attractive in a simple or traditional way ‖ 의복·예술 등의 스타일이 간소하거나 전통적인 방식으로 매력을 끄는. 고전적인. 유행에 좌우되지 않는: *a classic blue suit* 고전적인 청색 양복

classic² *n* **1** a book, movie etc. that is important and has been popular for a long time ‖ 중요하고 오랫동안 인기가 있는 책·영화 등. 고전: *"Gone With The Wind" is a classic movie about the Civil War.* "바람과 함께 사라지다"는 남북 전쟁에 관한 고전 영화다. **2** something that is very good and one of the best examples of its kind ‖ 매우 훌륭하여 그 종류 중에 최상의 표본 중 하나. 명품: *The '65 Ford Mustang is a classic!* 1965년형 포드 무스탕은 명품이야!

clas·si·cal /ˈklæsɪkəl/ *adj* **1** based on a traditional set of ideas, especially in art or science ‖ 특히 예술이나 과학에서 전통적인 사상 체계에 바탕을 둔. 고전의. 전통적인: *classical Indian dance* 전통적인 인디언 춤 **2** belonging to the CULTURE of ancient Greece and Rome ‖ 고대 그리스와 로마 문화에 속하는. 고대 그리스·로마의. 고전(시대, 양식)의: *classical architecture* 고전 양식의 건축

classical mu·sic /ˌ... ˈ../ *n* [U] music that was written especially in Europe in past times by COMPOSERs such as Bach, Mozart, Beethoven etc. ‖ 특히 과거에 유럽에서 바흐·모차르트·베토벤 등의 작곡가가 쓴 음악. 클래식 음악

clas·sics /ˈklæsɪks/ *n* [U] the study of the languages, literature, and history of ancient Greece and Rome ‖ 고대 그리스·로마의 언어·문학·역사에 관한 연구

clas·si·fi·ca·tion /ˌklæsəfəˈkeɪʃən/ *n* **1** [U] the act of putting people or things into a group ‖ 사람이나 사물을 한 집단에 놓기. 분류. 구별: *the classification of wines according to their region* 지역에 따른 포도주의 분류 **2** a group or class into which something is put ‖ 사물이 분류된 집단이나 부류. 유형. 범주. 등급: *Each college is given a classification according to its size.* 각 대학은 규모에 따라 등급이 매겨진다.

clas·si·fied /ˈklæsəˌfaɪd/ *adj* classified information, documents etc. are kept secret by the government or an organization ‖ 정보·문서 등이 정부나 기관에 의해 비밀로 유지되는. 기밀로 취급되는. 비밀의

classified ad /ˌ... ˈ./ *n* a small advertisement you put in a newspaper if you want to buy or sell something ‖ 물건을 사거나 팔고 싶을 때 신문에 내는 작은 광고. 항목별 광고. 안내 광고

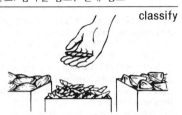

classify

The shells are classified according to shape.

clas·si·fy /ˈklæsəˌfaɪ/ *v* [T] **1** to put animals, plants, books etc. into groups ‖ 동물·식물·책 등을 그룹별로 두다. 분류하다. 등급별로 나누다: *Whales are classified as mammals rather than fish.* 고래는 어류라기보다는 포유 동물로 분류된다. **2** to make information or documents secret ‖ 정보 문서를 비밀로 하다. 기밀 취급하다: *The military has classified the results of the weapons tests.* 군 당국은 무기 시험의 결과를 기밀로 취급했다.

class·mate /ˈklæsmeɪt/ *n* someone who is in the same class as you at school or college ‖ 학교나 대학에서 같은 학급에 속한 사람. 급우. 반 친구: *An old classmate of mine from high school is visiting.* 나의 옛 고등학교 급우가 방문할 예정이다.

class·room /ˈklæsrum, -rʊm/ *n* **1** a room in a school where students are taught ‖ 학교에서 학생들이 배우는 방. 교실 **2 in the classroom** in schools or classes in general ‖ 일반적으로 학교나 학급에서: *Religion is rarely even discussed in the classroom.* 종교는 교실에서 좀처럼 논의되지 않는다.

class·work /ˈklæswɚk/ *n* [U] school work that you do during class rather than at home ‖ 가정에서보다 수업 중에 하는 학교 공부. 수업 —compare HOMEWORK

class·y /ˈklæsi/ *adj* INFORMAL stylish and fashionable ‖ 현대적이며 유행하는. 고급의. 세련된: *a classy place to shop* 고급 쇼핑 장소

clat·ter /ˈklætɚ/ *v* **1** [I, T] to make a

loud unpleasant noise by hitting hard objects together ‖ 단단한 물체가 부딪쳐서 크고 불유쾌한 소리를 내다. 덜거덕[쩽그렁] 소리를 내다: *The pots clattered to the floor.* 항아리가 바닥에 부딪쳐 쩽그렁 소리를 냈다. **2** [I] to move quickly and with a lot of noise ‖ 많은 소음을 내며 빨리 움직이다. 소리를 내며 나아가다: *a horse clattering down the street* 거리를 덜거덕 소리를 내며 나아가는 말 – **clatter** *n* [singular, U]

clause /klɔz/ *n* **1** a part of a written law or legal document ‖ 성문법(成文法) 또는 법률 문서의 일부. 조목. 조항: *A clause in the contract states when payment must be made.* 계약서의 한 조항에는 지급해야 하는 시기가 명시되어 있다. **2** TECHNICAL in grammar, a group of words that contains a subject and a verb, but which is usually only part of a sentence. In the sentence "Jim is the only one who knows the answer," "who knows the answer" is a clause ‖ 문법에서 주어와 술어를 포함하고 있으나 대개 문장의 일부만을 이루는 어구. 절. "Jim is the only one who knows the answer (짐은 그 정답을 아는 유일한 사람이다)."라는 문장에서 "who knows the answer"는 하나의 절이다.

claus·tro·pho·bi·a /ˌklɔstrəˈfoʊbiə/ *n* [U] a feeling of fear or anxiety about being in a small enclosed place or in a crowd of people ‖ 작은 폐쇄 공간 또는 군중 속에 있는 상태에 대해 느끼는 공포나 불안. 폐쇄[밀실]공포증 – **claus·trophobic** /ˌklɔstrəˈfoʊbɪk/ *adj*

claw¹ /klɔ/ *n* **1** a sharp curved hard part on the toe of an animal or bird ‖ 짐승이나 새의 날카롭게 구부러진 단단한 발가락 부위. (갈고리) 발톱 **2** a curved part of the body on some insects and sea animals such as CRABs that is used for attacking and holding things ‖ 일부 곤충·게 등의 바다 동물이 목표물을 공격하거나 잡는 데 사용하는 몸의 구부러진 부위. 집게발

claw² *v* [I, T] to tear or pull at something using CLAWs ‖ 발톱으로 어떤 것을 찢거나 당기다. …을 할퀴다[쥐어뜯다]: *Ow! Your kitten just clawed me!* 아야! 네 새끼고양이가 방금 나를 할퀴었어!

clay /kleɪ/ *n* [U] heavy soil that is soft and sticky when wet, but hard when dry or baked ‖ 축축할 때는 부드럽고 끈적끈적하지만 마르거나 구울 때는 딱딱한 무거운 흙. 점토. 찰흙: *a clay pot* 점토 항아리

clean¹ /klin/ *adj*

1 ▶NOT DIRTY 더럽지 않은◀ **a)** not dirty or messy ‖ 더럽지 않거나 어지르지 않은. 깨끗한: *Are your hands clean?* 네 손 깨끗하니? / *The kitchen looks cleaner than it did before.* 부엌이 전보다 더 깨끗해 보인다. **b)** not containing anything harmful or dirty ‖ 해롭거나 더러운 것이 포함되지 않은. 순수한: *clean water/air* 깨끗한 물[공기]

2 ▶NO SEX/CRIME ETC. 섹스/범죄 등이 없음◀ not involving sex, drugs, or anything illegal ‖ 섹스[마약, 불법적인 일]와 관련 없는: *kids having good clean fun* 건전한 오락을 하는 어린이들 / *Billy's been clean* (=hasn't done anything illegal, especially take drugs) *for over a year now.* 빌리는 현재 1년 넘게 (마약 등의 불법을 저지르지 않고) 건전하게 지내 왔다.

3 ▶HONEST 정직한◀ honest, fair, and not breaking any rules ‖ 정직하고 공정하며 규칙을 어기지 않는. 정정당당한: *a clean fight* 깨끗한 시합

4 come clean INFORMAL to tell the truth or admit that you have done something wrong ‖ 사실을 말하거나 잘못했음을 시인하다. 자백[실토]하다: *Josh finally came clean about denting the car.* 조시는 차를 찌그러뜨린 일을 결국 실토했다.

5 make a clean break to leave a place or stop a relationship completely, so that you do not have any more connections with that place or person ‖ 어떤 장소나 사람과 더 이상 연관을 맺지 않도록 장소를 떠나거나 관계를 완전히 끊다. (관계를) 깨끗이 정리하다. 청산하다: *She wanted to make a clean break with the past.* 그녀는 과거를 깨끗이 정리하길 원했다.

6 ▶NOT USED 사용하지 않은◀ not yet used ‖ 아직 사용하지 않은: *a clean sheet of paper* 백지 한 장

7 ▶SMOOTH 매끈한◀ having a smooth edge ‖ 가장자리가 매끈한. 반듯한: *a clean cut on his leg* 그의 다리에 난 매끈하게 베인 상처

8 ▶DESIGN 디자인◀ having a simple and attractive style or design ‖ 단순하고 매력적인 스타일이나 디자인을 가진: *the car's clean lines* 잘 빠진 차 모양

9 a clean bill of health something that says that a person, building etc. is healthy or safe ‖ 사람·건물 등이 건강하거나 안전하다는 것을 나타내는 것. 건강 증명서: *Three months after the operation, Jim was given a clean bill of health.* 수술한 지 3개월 후에 짐은 건강 증명서를 받았다. – **cleanness** *n* [U]

clean² *v* **1** [I, T] to remove dirt from something ‖ 어떤 것에서 먼지를 제거하다. 깨끗해지다[하게 하다]. 청소하다: *I need to clean the bathtub.* 나는 욕조를 청소해야 한다. / *He's been cleaning for hours!* 그는 몇 시간 동안 청소하고 있구나! **2** [T] to take out the inside parts of a fish, bird etc. so it can be cooked ‖ 요리하기 위해 생선·새 등의 내장을 빼다.

clean out *phr v* [T] **1** [**clean** sth ↔ **out**] to make the inside of a car, room, house etc. clean, especially by removing things from it ‖ 특히 물건을 제거함으로써 차·방·집 등의 내부를 깨끗이 하다. 청소[정돈]하다: *We cleaned out the garage Sunday.* 우리는 일요일에 차고를 청소했다. **2** [**clean** sb/sth ↔ **out**] INFORMAL to steal everything from a place or from someone ‖ 어떤 장소나 사람에게서 모든 것을 훔치다: *Two armed men cleaned out the computer store.* 무장한 두 남자가 컴퓨터 가게를 몽땅 털었다. **3** [**clean** sb ↔ **out**] to spend all of your money on something so that you have none left ‖ 남은 돈이 없을 정도로 어떤 것에 모두 소비하다. 다 써버리다: *The new refrigerator really cleaned me out.* 그 새 냉장고를 사느라 완전 무일푼이 되었다.

clean up *phr v* [I,T **clean** sb/sth ↔ **up**] **1** to make something or someone clean and neat ‖ 사물이나 사람을 청소하거나 말쑥하게 하다: *Clean up your room – it's a mess!* 네 방 청소를 해라. 방이 엉망이잖니! **2** to remove dirt from something, especially your own body ‖ 어떤 것에서, 특히 자신의 몸에서 더러움을 제거하다. 몸단장하다: *Go upstairs, get cleaned up, and then we can go.* 위층에 올라가서, 옷차림을 말쑥하게 하면 갈 수 있다. **3 clean up your act** INFORMAL to begin to behave in a better way ‖ 더 좋은 태도로 행동하기 시작하다. 품행을 단정하게 하다: *You'll have to clean up your act if you want to impress Diane's parents.* 다 이젠 부모님께 잘 보이려면 너는 점잖게 행동해야 될 거다. —see also CLEANUP

clean³ *adv* completely ‖ 완전히. 모조리: *I'm sorry, I clean forgot about your birthday.* 미안한데, 네 생일을 까맣게 잊어 버렸어.

clean-cut /ˌ. '../ *adj* a man who is clean-cut dresses neatly in CONSERVATIVE clothes and has a short haircut ‖ 사람이 수수한 옷차림으로 말끔하게 차려입고 짧은 머리 스타일을 한. 단정한. 품위 있고 건실한

clean·er /ˈklinɚ/ *n* **1** someone whose job is to clean something ‖ 어떤 것을 청소하는 직업인. 청소부 **2** a machine or substance used for cleaning something ‖ 물건을 청소하는 데에 쓰는 기계나 물질. 세탁기. 청소기. 세제: *a vacuum cleaner* 진공 청소기 **3 take sb to the cleaners** INFORMAL to get all of someone's money, especially in a way that is not honest ‖ 특히 정직하지 못한 방법으로 남의 돈을 모두 취득하다. …을 빈털터리로 만들다. 남의 돈[재산]을 털어먹다: *The insurance company will take you to the cleaners if you're not careful.* 그 보험 회사는 조심하지 않으면 너를 빈털터리로 만들 것이다. —see also DRY CLEANERS

clean·ing /ˈklinɪŋ/ *n* [U] the process of making something clean and neat ‖ 물건을 깨끗하고 말쑥하게 만드는 과정. 청소. 세탁: *A woman comes twice a week to do the cleaning.* 여자 한 명이 일주일에 두 번 청소하러 온다.

clean·li·ness /ˈklɛnlinɪs/ *n* [U] the practice or state of being clean ‖ 깨끗이 하기, 또는 깨끗한 상태. 청결

clean·ly /ˈklinli/ *adv* quickly and smoothly in a neat way ‖ 산뜻한 형태로 신속하고 원활하게. 깔끔하게: *The branch snapped cleanly in two.* 그 가지는 탁 하고 단번에 두 동강이 났다.

cleanse /klɛnz/ *v* [T] to make something completely clean ‖ 어떤 것을 철저히 깨끗이 하다. 세척하다: *Cleanse the wound with alcohol.* 알코올로 상처를 깨끗이 씻어내다.

cleans·er /ˈklɛnzɚ/ *n* [C, U] a substance used for cleaning your skin or things like SINKs ‖ 피부나 개수대 같은 것을 닦는 데에 사용하는 물질. 세제

clean-shav·en /ˌ. '../ *adj* a man who is clean-shaven has cut off all the hair on his face ‖ 얼굴의 수염을 모두 깨끗하게 깎은. 깨끗이 면도한

clean-up /ˈklinʌp/ *n* a process in which you clean something thoroughly ‖ 물건을 철저하게 닦아내는 과정. 청소. 소제: *The cleanup of the oil spill took months.* 누출된 기름을 완전히 제거하는 데에 몇 개월이 걸렸다. – **cleanup** *adj*

clear¹ /klɪr/ *adj*

1 ▶SIMPLE/EASY 간단한/쉬운◀ easy to understand, hear, read, or see ‖ 이해하기[듣기, 읽기, 보기] 쉬운. 명쾌한: *Are the instructions clear?* 지시 사항이 이해가 됩니까? / *Most of the photographs were sharp and clear.* 대부분의 사진이 또렷하고 선명하다.

2 ▶CERTAIN 확실한◀ certain, and

impossible to doubt, question or make a mistake about || 확실하여 그에 대해 의심이나 의문을 품거나 실수가 불가능한. 확실한: *The newest tests make it clear that the drug is safe.* 가장 최근의 테스트는 그 약이 안전하다는 것을 확실히 보여 준다.

3 ▶SEE THROUGH 관통해서 보다◀ easy to see through rather than colored or dirty || 채색되거나 더럽지 않아 꿰뚫어 보기 쉬운. 투명한. 비치는: *Clear glass bottles go in this box.* 투명 유리병은 이 상자에 넣는다. / *a clear mountain lake* 산의 투명한 호수

4 ▶NOT BLOCKED 막히지 않은◀ not blocked or covered || 막히거나 덮이지 않은. 뻥 뚫린: *a clear view of the harbor* 항구의 뻥 뚫린 시야

5 ▶NO MARKS 자국이 없는◀ not having marks, spots etc. || 자국·흠 등이 없는: *smooth clear skin* 매끈하고 깨끗한 피부 / *a clear sky* (=with no clouds) 구름 한 점 없는 하늘

6 a clear head the ability to think quickly and well || 신속하게 잘 생각할 수 있는 능력. 명석함. 명철함: *Dee always has a clear head when things are stressful.* 디는 스트레스를 받을 때 명석함을 발휘한다.

7 (as) clear as mud HUMOROUS used in order to say that something is difficult to understand || 어떤 것이 이해하기 어렵다고 말하는 데에 쓰여: *As usual, the directions for putting the bed together were as clear as mud!* 늘 그렇듯이 그 침대 조립법은 이해하기 어려워!

clear² *v*

1 ▶MAKE NEAT 단정하게 만들다◀ [T] to make a place neat by removing things from it || 물건을 치움으로써 어떤 장소를 깨끗이 하다. 치우다: *If you clear the table* (=take away the dishes, forks etc.), *I'll make the coffee.* 네가 식탁을 치우면 내가 커피를 끓일게.

2 ▶REMOVE 제거하다◀ [T] to remove something or someone from a place || 어떤 장소에서 사물이나 사람을 제거하다: *Trucks have just finished clearing the wreck from the road.* 트럭이 도로의 잔해 제거 작업을 막 끝냈다. / *The area was cleared of workers as a safety precaution.* 안전 예방 조치로서 일꾼들을 그 지역에서 대피시켰다.

3 ▶LEGAL CHARGE 법적 혐의◀ [T] to prove that someone is not guilty of something || 사람이 어떤 것에 대해 무죄라는 것을 입증하다. 결백을 밝히다: *The jury cleared Johnson of the murder*

charge. 배심원은 살인 혐의를 받고 있는 존슨의 무죄를 선언했다.

4 ▶WEATHER 날씨◀ [I] if the weather, sky etc. clears, it becomes better or there is more sun || 날씨·하늘 등이 개이거나 더 화창해지다

5 ▶PERMISSION 허가◀ [T] to give or get official permission to do something || 무엇을 할 수 있는 공식 허가를 주거나 받다: *Has the plane been cleared for landing?* 비행기의 착륙 허가가 떨어졌습니까?

6 ▶CHECK 수표◀ [I, T] if a check clears, the bank allows the money to be paid into the account of the person who received the check || 수표의 금액이 수취인의 계좌로 입금될 수 있도록 은행에서 허가하다. 교환[결제]되다

7 clear your throat to cough so you can speak clearly or in order to get someone's attention || 또렷하게 말하거나 주의를 끌기 위해 기침을 하다. 목을 가다듬다. 헛기침을 하다

8 clear the air to do something in order to end an argument or bad situation || 논쟁이나 나쁜 상황을 종식시킬 무언가를 하다. 의혹[걱정]을 일소하다: *The White House hopes that the investigation will clear the air.* 백악관에서는 조사를 통해 의혹을 해소하기를 바란다.

9 ▶GO OVER 넘어가다◀ [T] to go over something without touching it || 어떤 것에 닿지 않고 그 위로 가다: *The plane barely cleared the fence as it came down.* 비행기가 불시착하면서 간신히 울타리 위로 빠져나갔다.

10 ▶DEBT 빚◀ [T] to get rid of a debt by paying all the money you owe || 빚진 돈을 모두 갚아서 빚을 없애다

clear sth ↔ **away** *phr v* [T] to make a place look neat by removing things or putting them where they belong || 물건을 치우거나 원래 있던 자리에 놓음으로써 어떤 장소를 깔끔하게 보이게 하다: *Clear all these toys away before you go to bed.* 자기 전에 이 장난감을 모두 치워라.

clear out *phr v* **1** [I,T **clear** sth ↔ **out**] to make a place neat by removing things from it || 물건을 치워 어떤 장소를 깨끗이 하다. 치우다: *I need to clear out that closet.* 저 옷장을 치울 필요가 있다. **2** [I] INFORMAL used in order to angrily tell someone to leave a place || 남에게 어떤 곳을 떠나라고 화내어 말하는 데에 쓰여: *The campers were told to clear out by 9:00.* 야영자들은 9시까지 떠나라는 말을 들었다.

clear up *phr v* **1** [T **clear** sth ↔ **up**] to

explain something or make it easier to understand ‖ 어떤 것을 설명하거나 이해하기 쉽게 하다. 문제·수수께끼·의심 등을 풀다: *We have some facts that will clear up the mystery.* 우리는 그 미스터리를 풀어 줄 몇 가지 사실을 안다. **2** [I] if the weather clears up, it gets better ‖ 날씨가 좋아지다. 화창해지다: *I hope it clears up by the weekend.* 주말까지는 날씨가 좋아지길 바란다. **3** [T **clear** sth ↔ **up**] to make a place look neat by putting things where they belong ‖ 물건을 원래 있던 곳에 놓음으로써 어떤 곳을 깔끔하게 보이게 하다. 치우다: *We should clear up the basement before your parents visit.* 네 부모님이 오시기 전에 우리는 지하실을 치워야 한다. **4** [I] if an infection clears up, it gets better ‖ 전염병이 나아지다. 병을 고치다

clear³ *adv* **1** away from something, or out of the way ‖ 어떤 것으로부터 떨어져서, 또는 길에서 벗어나서. 방해되지 않게 비켜서: *Firemen pulled the driver clear of the wreckage.* 소방관들은 그 운전자를 파괴된 차에서 끌어냈다. **2 steer/stay clear of** to avoid someone or something because of possible danger or trouble ‖ 위험이나 문제 발생의 소지가 있어서 사람이나 사물을 피하다: *Drivers should stay clear of Malta Bridge because of the ice.* 운전자들은 빙판 때문에 말타 브리지를 피해야 합니다. **3 clear to** sth all the way to a place or time that is distant ‖ 멀리 있는 장소나 시간까지 내내. 줄곧: *You can see clear to the Rockies today.* 오늘은 멀리 록키 산맥까지 볼 수 있다.

clear⁴ *n* **in the clear** not guilty of something or not having difficulties because of something ‖ 어떤 것에 대해 유죄가 아닌, 또는 어떤 것 때문에 어려움을 겪지 않는. 혐의가 풀린. 책임[근심]이 없는: *The debt is being paid off, but we're not in the clear yet.* 빚은 다 갚았지만 우리는 아직 안심할 처지는 아니다.

clear·ance /'klırəns/ *n* [C, U] **1** the process of getting official permission or approval to do something ‖ 어떤 것을 하기 위한 공식 허가나 승인을 얻는 과정. 절차. 승인: *shipping and customs clearance* 선적 및 통관 **2** the distance that is needed between one object and another one that is under or next to it, so that they do not touch each other ‖ 하나의 물체와 그 옆이나 아래에 있는 다른 물체가 서로 닿지 않도록 필요한 거리. 간격. 틈. 여유: *the clearance between the bridge and the tops of trucks* 다리와 트럭 꼭대기 사이의 간격

clearance sale /'.. ,./ *n* a sale in which goods are sold very cheaply to get rid of them ‖ 상품들을 다 없애려고 헐값에 판매함. 떨이. 재고 정리 판매

clear-cut /'klırkʌt/ *n* an area of forest in which all the trees have been cut down ‖ 나무를 모두 베어 낸 숲의 한 지역. 개벌지(皆伐地) – **clearcut** *v* [T]

clear-cut /. '../ *adj* impossible to be uncertain about; definite ‖ 불확실하기가 불가능한. 명확한; 정확한: *clear-cut goals* 명확한 목표

clear-headed /, '../ *adj* able to think in a clear and sensible way ‖ 명확하고 지각있게 사고할 수 있는. 명석한 – **clear-headedness** *n* [U]

clear·ing /'klırıŋ/ *n* a small area in a forest where there are no trees ‖ 나무가 전혀 없는 숲의 작은 지역. 개간지

clear·ly /'klırli/ *adv* **1** without any doubt ‖ 어떠한 의심도 없이. 명확히. 분명하게: *Clearly, he felt he was to blame.* 틀림없이 그는 자신이 비난받을 것이라고 생각하였다. **2** in a way that is easy to see, understand, hear etc ‖ 보고 이해하며 듣기 쉬운 방법으로. 알기 쉽게. 분명히: *I clearly remember that time in my life.* 난 내 삶에서 그 시기를 확실히 기억한다.

clear-sight·ed /, '../ *adj* showing that someone is able to understand things easily and make good judgments ‖ 사람이 일을 쉽게 이해하고 훌륭한 판단을 내린다는 것을 보여 주는. 명석한: *a clear-sighted analysis of the problem* 문제에 대한 명석한 분석

cleat /klit/ *n* one of a set of pieces of metal or hard rubber attached to the bottom of a sports shoe to stop it from slipping on the ground ‖ 땅 위에서 미끄러지지 않게 스포츠화 바닥에 부착한 금속 조각이나 딱딱한 고무. 미끄럼막이

cleats /klits/ *n* [plural] a pair of shoes with cleats attached to them ‖ 미끄럼막이가 부착된 신발 한 켤레

cleav·age /'klivıdʒ/ *n* [C, U] the space between a woman's breasts ‖ 여성의 가슴 사이의 공간. 유방 사이의 오목한 곳

clea·ver /'klivɚ/ *n* a large square knife used for cutting up large pieces of meat ‖ 큰 고깃덩어리를 자르는 데에 쓰는 큰 사각형 식칼. (푸주의) 큰 식칼

clef /klɛf/ *n* a sign at the beginning of a line of written music to show the PITCH of the notes ‖ 음높이를 보여 주기 위해 악보의 첫머리에 표시하는 기호. 음자리표

cleft¹ /klɛft/ *n* a narrow crack in the ground or in rocks ‖ 땅이나 바위의 좁게

갈라진 틈

cleft² *adj* partly split or divided ‖ 부분적으로 쪼개지거나 나뉜. 갈라진: *a cleft chin* 움푹 들어간 곳이 있는 턱

clem·en·cy /ˈklɛmənsi/ *n* [U] FORMAL **grant/give sb clemency** to forgive someone for a crime and make his/her punishment less severe ‖ 누군가의 죄를 용서하고 너무 가혹하지 않게 처벌하다. 죄인에게 인정을 베풀다

clench /klɛntʃ/ *v* [T] to close your hands or your mouth tightly, in order to hold something or because you feel angry or determined ‖ 어떤 것을 잡기 위해서 또는 화가 나거나 결심이 굳기 때문에 손이나 입을 꽉 쥐거나 다물다. 거머쥐다. 악물다: *He had a cigar clenched between his teeth.* 그는 이 사이에 시가를 단단히 물었다. / *Raising clenched fists, the demonstrators sang the national anthem.* 시위자들은 불끈 쥔 주먹을 올리며 국가를 불렀다. – **clench** *n*

cler·gy /ˈklɚdʒi/ *n* [plural] the official leaders of religious activities in organized religions, such as priests, RABBIs, and MULLAHs ‖ 목사·율법학자·물라 등의 조직화된 종교에서 종교 활동의 공식 지도자. 성직자. 승려

cler·gy·man /ˈklɚdʒimən/, **cler·gywoman** /ˈklɚdʒiˌwʊmən/ *n* a male or female member of the CLERGY ‖ 남성이나 여성 성직자

cler·ic /ˈklɛrɪk/ *n* an official leader in an organized religion ‖ 조직화된 종교의 공식 지도자. 성직자. 목사

cler·i·cal /ˈklɛrɪkəl/ *adj* **1** relating to office work ‖ 사무에 관계한. 사무(직)의: *a clerical worker* 사무직 근로자 **2** relating to the CLERGY ‖ 성직에 관한. 성직자의: *a clerical collar* 성직복의 깃

clerk /klɚk/ *n* **1** someone who deals with people arriving at a hotel ‖ 호텔에 도착하는 사람들을 대하는 사람. 객실 담당원: *Please return your keys to the desk clerk.* 객실 담당원에게 열쇠를 반납하십시오. **2** someone whose job is to keep records, accounts etc. in an office ‖ 사무실에서 기록·회계 등의 일을 하는 직업인. 사무원 —see also SALES CLERK

clev·er /ˈklɛvɚ/ *adj* **1** able to use your intelligence to do something, especially in a slightly dishonest way ‖ 무엇을 하는 데에 특히 약간 정직하지 못한 방법으로 지력(知力)을 사용할 수 있는. 영리한. 교활한: *a lawyer's clever tricks* 변호사의 영리한 속임수 **2** able to learn things quickly ‖ 무엇을 빨리 배울 수 있는. 머리가 잘 도는. 똑똑한 **3** showing ability or skill, especially in making things ‖ 특히 물건을 만드는 데에 능력이나 기술을 나타내는. 솜씨[재주]가 좋은: *Bill's very clever with his hands.* (=good at making things) 빌은 손재주가 좋다. – **cleverly** *adv* – **cleverness** *n* [U]

cli·ché /kliˈʃeɪ/ *n* DISAPPROVING an idea or phrase that has been used so much that it is no longer effective or does not have any meaning ‖ 너무 많이 쓰여서 더 이상 효과적이지 않거나 어떤 의미도 갖지 않는 단어나 어구. 진부한 상투어. 케케묵은 말: *The cliché "better late than never" is true in this case.* "하지 않는 것보다는 늦더라도 하는 것이 낫다"라는 진부한 말이 이 경우에는 들어맞는다.

click¹ /klɪk/ *v* **1** [I, T] to make a short hard sound, or to make something produce this sound ‖ 짧고 딱딱한 소리를 내다, 또는 어떤 것이 이러한 소리를 내게 하다. 찰깍 소리가 나다[소리를 내다]: *The dog's toenails clicked on the wooden floor.* 그 개의 발톱이 나무 바닥 위에서 딸깍딸깍 소리를 냈다. / *clicking your heels together* 철컥하고 구두 뒤축을 부딪치기 **2** INFORMAL to suddenly understand something ‖ 어떤 것을 갑자기 이해하다. 퍼뜩 떠오르다[알게 되다]: *I was having a lot of trouble with algebra until one day it just clicked.* 어느 날 대수학이 갑자기 이해될 때까지 나는 대수학 때문에 고생을 많이 했다. **3** [I] INFORMAL to like someone and share his/her ideas, opinions etc. ‖ 남을 좋아하여 그 사람의 생각·의견 등을 공유하다. 남녀가 눈이 맞다. 좋아하게 되다: *We clicked the first time we met.* 우리는 처음 만났을 때 눈이 맞았다.

click on sth *phr v* [T] to press a button on a computer MOUSE in order to choose something from the screen that you want the computer to do ‖ 컴퓨터 실행 작업을 화면에서 선택하기 위해 컴퓨터 마우스 버튼을 누르다. 클릭하다

click² *n* a short hard sound ‖ 짧고 딱딱한 소리: *the click of a key in the lock* 자물쇠에서 열쇠가 딸깍거리는 소리

cli·ent /ˈklaɪənt/ *n* someone who pays for services or advice from a person or organization ‖ 사람이나 단체로부터 받은 서비스나 자문에 대해 돈을 지불하는 사람. 고객: *a lawyer with several important clients* 몇몇 중요한 고객이 있는 변호사

cli·en·tele /ˌklaɪənˈtɛl, ˌkliɑn-/ *n* [singular] the people who regularly go to a store, restaurant etc ‖ 상점·음식점 등에 정기적으로 가는 사람들. 단골: *a* *young clientele* 젊은 단골

cliff /klɪf/ *n* a high rock or piece of land with a steep side ‖ 가파른 경사가 있는 높은 바위나 땅의 부분. 절벽

cliff·hang·er /'klɪf,hæŋɚ/ *n* INFORMAL a story or competition that is exciting because you do not know the result until the very end ‖ 마지막 순간까지 결과를 모르기 때문에 흥미진진한 이야기나 시합. 손에 땀을 쥐게 하는 사건[경쟁]: *The show's writers have produced a real cliffhanger ending.* 그 쇼의 작가들은 손에 땀을 쥐게 하는 결말을 만들어 냈다.

cli·mac·tic /klaɪ'mæktɪk/ *adj* forming a very exciting or important part of a story or event, especially near the end of it ‖ 특히 결말에 가까워져서 이야기나 사건의 가장 흥미진진하거나 중요한 부분을 이루는. 최고조의. 절정의. 클라이맥스의: *the final climactic scene of the play* 그 연극의 마지막 클라이맥스 장면

cli·mate /'klaɪmɪt/ *n* 1 the typical weather conditions in a particular area ‖ 특정 지역의 전형적인 기상 여건. 기후: *a hot and humid climate* 덥고 습한 기후 2 the general feeling or situation in a place at a particular time ‖ 특정 시기에 어떤 지역의 일반적 감정이나 상황. 풍토. 추세. 경향: *the present economic climate* 현 시점의 경제 여건

cli·max[1] /'klaɪmæks/ *n* 1 the most important or exciting part of a book, movie, situation etc, that usually happens at the end ‖ 대개 끝 부분에서 일어나는, 책·영화·상황 등의 가장 중요하거나 흥미로운 부분. 최고조. 절정. 클라이맥스: *Winning the gold medal was the climax of his sports career.* 금메달 수상은 그의 스포츠 경력의 절정이었다. 2 ⇨ ORGASM

cli·max[2] *v* [I, T] to reach the most important or exciting part of something ‖ 가장 중요하거나 흥미진진한 부분에 도달하다. 최고조[절정, 클라이맥스]에 이르다: *The strike climaxed two weeks of protests.* 파업은 2주간의 시위에서 절정을 이루었다.

climb[1] /klaɪm/ *v* [I, T] 1 to move up, down, or across something using your hands and feet, especially when this is difficult to do ‖ 특히 하기가 어려울 때 손·발을 사용하여 어떤 것을 기어오르거나 내려오다, 또는 건너다:

climb

climber

Kids like to climb trees. 아이들은 나무 타는 것을 좋아한다. / *Climbing down the ladder was harder than climbing up.* 사다리를 내려오는 것은 올라가기보다 더 어려웠다. / *He tried to climb over the fence.* 그는 울타리를 타고 넘으려 애썼다. 2 [I] to move gradually to a higher position ‖ 점차 높은 위치로 움직이다. 오르다. 상승하다. 출세[승진]하다: *We watched as the plane climbed into the sky.* 우리는 비행기가 하늘로 상승하는 것을 지켜보았다. 3 [I] to increase in number, amount, or level ‖ 수나 양이 증가하다, 수준이 오르다: *The temperature was climbing steadily.* 온도가 꾸준히 상승하고 있었다. 4 **climb the ladder** to move to a better position in your social or professional life ‖ 사회나 직업 생활에서 더 나은 지위로 나아가다. 평판·지위 등이 높아지다. 승진하다: *women trying to climb the economic ladder* 경제적 지위를 높이기 위해 노력하는 여성들 5 **climbing the walls** SPOKEN to be very worried or impatient ‖ 매우 걱정하거나 초조해하는: *When he hadn't gotten back by midnight, I was climbing the walls.* 그가 자정까지 돌아오지 않자 나는 매우 마음을 졸였다.

climb[2] *n* 1 a process in which you move up toward a place while using a lot of effort ‖ 많은 노력을 들여 어떤 곳을 향해 오르는 과정. 오르기: *a tough climb to the top of the mountain* 산 정상까지의 험난한[고된] 등반 2 an increase in value or amount ‖ 가치나 양에서의 증가. 상승: *a steady climb in house prices* 집값의 꾸준한 상승 3 the process of improving your professional or social position ‖ 직업적 또는 사회적 지위가 높아지는 과정. 출세. 승진: *a politician's climb to power* 한 정치인의 권력 쟁취

climb·er /'klaɪmɚ/ *n* someone who climbs rocks, mountains etc. as a sport ‖ 스포츠로 바위·산 등을 오르는 사람. 등반[등산]객 —see picture at CLIMB[1] —see also SOCIAL CLIMBER

climb·ing /'klaɪmɪŋ/ *n* [U] the sport of climbing mountains or rocks ‖ 산이나 바위를 오르는 스포츠. 등산. 등반: *Let's go climbing this weekend.* 이번 주말에 등산하러 가자.

clinch /klɪntʃ/ *v* [T] INFORMAL to finally agree on something or get something after trying very hard ‖ 마침내 어떤 것에 동의하거나 매우 힘들게 노력한 후 어떤 것을 얻다. 매듭짓다: *A last-minute touchdown clinched the game for the Saints.* 세인트 팀이 막판 터치다운으로

승리를 언어냈다. / *I think I know how we can clinch this deal.* 나는 우리가 이 거래를 성사시킬 수 있는 방법을 알 것 같다. – **clinch** *n*

clinch·er /ˈklɪntʃɚ/ *n* INFORMAL a fact or action that finally persuades someone to do something, or that ends an argument or competition ‖ 마침내 누군가가 어떤 것을 하도록 설득시키거나 논쟁이나 경쟁을 끝내는 사실이나 행위. 결정적 요인[수단, 방법, 말]. 결정타: *The real clincher was her threat to sue the city.* 진짜 결정타는 도시를 상대로 고소하겠다는 그녀의 협박이었다.

cling /klɪŋ/ *v* **clung, clung, clinging** [I] **1** to hold someone or something tightly, especially because you do not feel safe ‖ 특히 안전하다고 느끼지 않기 때문에 사람이나 사물을 꽉 잡다. 매달리다: *a climber clinging onto a rock* 바위를 꼭 붙잡고 있는 등반객 / *They clung to each other and cried.* 그들은 서로 꽉 잡고 울었다. **2** to stick to something ‖ 어떤 것에 착 들러붙다: *The wet shirt clung to his body.* 젖은 셔츠가 그의 몸에 들러붙었다.

cling to sth *phr v* [T] to continue to believe or do something, even though it may no longer be true or useful ‖ 더 이상 사실이거나 유용하지 않더라도 어떤 것을 계속 믿거나 행하다. 고수하다. …에 집착하다: *The villagers still clung to their traditions.* 그 마을 사람들은 여전히 자신들의 전통을 고수했다.

cling·ing /ˈklɪŋɪŋ/ *adj* DISAPPROVING too dependent on another person ‖ 타인에게 너무 의존하는. 기대는. 의존적인: *a clinging child* 남에게 기대는 아이

cling·y /ˈklɪŋi/ *adj* **1** fitting or sticking tightly to your body ‖ 몸에 꼭 맞거나 착 달라붙는: *a clingy dress* 몸에 착 붙는 드레스 **2** ⇨ CLINGING

clin·ic /ˈklɪnɪk/ *n* **1** a place where medical treatment is given to people who do not need to stay in a hospital ‖ 병원에 입원할 필요가 없는 사람들이 진료를 받는 곳. 외래 환자 진찰실. 진료소. 클리닉: *a dental clinic* 치과 진료소 **2** a small hospital in an area far away from large cities ‖ 대도시에서 멀리 떨어진 지역의 작은 병원: *a rural health clinic* 시골 보건소 **3** a meeting during which a professional person gives advice or help to people ‖ 전문가가 사람에게 조언이나 도움을 주는 모임. 상담소: *a marriage clinic* 결혼 상담소

clin·i·cal /ˈklɪnɪkəl/ *adj* **1** relating to treating or testing people who are sick ‖ 아픈 사람을 치료하거나 검사하는 것과 관계된. 임상의: *The drug has undergone a number of clinical trials.* 그 약은 수 차례의 임상 실험을 거쳤다. **2** considering only the facts and not influenced by emotions ‖ 사실만을 고려하며 감정의 영향을 받지 않는. 분석적인. 냉정한: *a cold clinical attitude toward the homeless* 노숙자들에 대한 차갑고 분석적인 태도 – **clinically** *adv*

clin·i·cian /klɪˈnɪʃən/ *n* a doctor who studies diseases by examining people ‖ 사람들을 진찰함으로써 질병을 연구하는 의사. 임상 의사[의학자]

clink /klɪŋk/ *v* [I, T] if pieces of glass or metal clink or you clink them, they make a short ringing sound because they have been hit together ‖ 유리나 금속이 서로 부딪쳐서 짧게 울리는 소리를 내다. 쨍[땡] 울리다[울리게 하다] – **clink** *n* [singular]

clip¹ /klɪp/ *n* **1** a small metal or plastic object for holding things together ‖ 물건을 함께 묶어 놓는 데에 쓰는 작은 금속이나 플라스틱 물체. 클립: *a paper clip* 서류 클립 **2** a short part of a movie or television program that is shown by itself, especially as an advertisement ‖ 특히 광고로서 단독으로 보여 주는 영화나 텔레비전 프로그램의 짧은 부분. 비디오 클립: *clips from Fox's new movie* 폭스사 신작 영화의 비디오 클립 **3** a container for bullets in a gun ‖ 총에서 총알이 담긴 용기. 탄창 **4 at a good/rapid/fast clip** quickly ‖ 신속히. 재빠르게: *Julie turned and headed down the beach at a fast clip.* 줄리는 방향을 바꿔 재빠르게 해변으로 향했다.

clip² *v* **-pped, -pping 1** [I, T] to put a CLIP on things to hold them together ‖ 물건들을 한데 묶어 두기 위해 클립을 끼우다. 클립으로 고정시키다: *She'd clipped her business card to the letter.* 그녀는 자기 명함을 편지에 클립으로 끼워 놓았다. **2** [T] to cut something out of a newspaper, magazine etc. in order to use it or save it ‖ 사용하거나 모아 놓을 목적으로 신문·잡지 등에서 어떤 것을 자르다. 오려내다: *Tara showed him an ad she'd clipped out of the Sunday paper.* 태러는 선데이 신문에서 오려낸 광고를 그에게 보여 주었다. **3** [T] to cut small amounts from something in order to make it look neater ‖ 더 단정하게 보이게 하려고 어떤 것에서 적은 양을 잘라내다. 깎다: *clipping a hedge* 산울타리 깎기

clip·board /ˈklɪpbɔrd/ *n* a small flat board with a CLIP on the top that holds paper so that you can write on it ‖ 위쪽에 종이를 고정시키는 클립이 있어서 필기 가능한 작고 평평한 판. 클립보드

clip-on /ˈ. ./ *adj* able to attach to something using a CLIP ‖ 클립을 사용하여 어떤 것에 부착할 수 있는. 핀이 달린. 클립으로 채우는: *clip-on earrings* 클립으로 고정되는 귀걸이

clip·pers /ˈklɪpərz/ *n* [plural] a tool for cutting something ‖ 물건을 자르는 데에 쓰는 도구. 깎는 기구: *nail clippers* 손톱깎이

clip·ping /ˈklɪpɪŋ/ *n* **1** an article or picture that you cut out of a newspaper or magazine ‖ 신문이나 잡지에서 오린 기사나 사진 **2** [C usually plural] a small piece cut from something bigger ‖ 큰 것에서 잘라낸 작은 부분. 잘린[깎인] 것: *a pile of grass clippings* 깎아 놓은 잔디 더미

clique /klik, klɪk/ *n* DISAPPROVING a small group of people that do not want others to join their group ‖ 남들이 자신들의 집단에 가입하는 것을 원하지 않는 소집단의 사람들. 배타적인 소집단. 파벌. 도당

clit·o·ris /ˈklɪtərɪs/ *n* a small part of a woman's outer sex organs, where she can feel sexual pleasure ‖ 여성의 외음부에 있는, 성적 쾌락을 느낄 수 있는 작은 부분. 음핵. 클리토리스

cloak[1] /kloʊk/ *n* a warm piece of clothing like a coat that hangs from your shoulders and does not have SLEEVES ‖ 어깨에서부터 늘어지며 소매가 없는, 외투 같은 따뜻한 옷. 망토

cloak[2] *v* [T] LITERARY to cover or hide something ‖ 어떤 것을 덮거나 숨기다. 은폐하다: *The early stages of the negotiations were cloaked in secrecy.* 교섭 초기 단계는 비밀에 부쳐졌다.

cloak-and-dag·ger /ˌ. . ˈ../ *adj* very secret and mysterious ‖ 매우 은밀하고 신비스러운. 음모의. 첩보 활동의: *cloak-and-dagger methods of obtaining information* 정보를 획득하는 은밀한 방법

cloak·room /ˈkloʊk-rum/ *n* a room in a school, MUSEUM etc. where you can leave your coat, bags etc. for a short time ‖ 학교·박물관 등에서 잠시 동안 외투·가방 등을 맡겨 놓을 수 있는 방. 휴대품 보관소

clob·ber /ˈklɑbər/ *v* [T] INFORMAL **1** to hit someone hard ‖ 사람을 세게 치다. 호되게 때리다: *Do it now or I'll clobber you!* 그것을 당장 해라. 안 그러면 너를 때릴 거야! **2** to defeat someone easily ‖ 남을 쉽게 이기다: *Our football team got*

clobbered again last Friday. 우리 미식축구팀은 지난 금요일 또다시 패배했다.

clock[1] /klɑk/ *n* **1** an instrument in a room or building that shows the time ‖ 시간을 나타내는 방이나 건물 안의 기구. 시계: *a big clock on the schoolroom wall* 교실 벽에 걸린 큰 시계 / *We left as the clock struck three.* (=made three loud noises to show the time) 시계가 3시를 알렸을 때 우리는 떠났다. / *The kitchen clock is five minutes slow/fast.* (=shows a time that is five minutes less or more than the right time) 부엌 시계는 5분 느리다[빠르다]. / *Don't forget to set your clocks back/ahead tonight.* (=change the time the clocks show to one hour earlier or later) 오늘 밤 시계를 한 시간 뒤로[앞으로] 맞추어 놓는 것을 잊지 마라 **2 turn/put/set the clock back** to go back to the ways things were done before, rather than trying new ideas or methods ‖ 새로운 생각이나 방법을 시도하기보다 과거에 했던 방식으로 돌아가다. 과거로 돌아가다: *Women's groups warned that the law would turn the clock back fifty years.* 여성 단체는 그 법안이 50년 전 과거로 돌아가는 것이라고 경고했다. **3 around the clock** all day and all night without stopping ‖ 멈추지 않고 밤낮을 계속하여. 밤낮 없이: *We've been working around the clock to get done on time.* 우리는 제시간에 일을 끝마치기 위해 밤낮 없이 일해 오고 있다. **4 race/work against the clock** to work quickly in order to finish something before a particular time ‖ 특정한 시간 전에 어떤 것을 끝내기 위해 신속하게 일하다. 시간[촌각]을 다투다: *Doctors are racing against the clock to find a cure for AIDS.* 의사들은 에이즈의 치료법을 발견하기 위해 촌각을 다투고 있다. **5 watch the clock** to keep looking to see what time it is because you are bored or do not want to work ‖ 지루하거나 일하기 싫어서 계속 몇 시인지 지켜보다. 퇴근 시간만을 기다리다 —see also **punch a clock** (PUNCH[1])

clock[2] *v* [T] to measure how long it takes to travel a particular distance ‖ 특정 거리를 이동하는 데에 시간이 얼마나 걸리는지 측정하다. 시간을 재다: *She clocked her best time in the 200-meter sprint.* 그녀는 200미터 경주에서 자신의 최고 기록을 냈다.

clock in/out *phr v* [I] to record on a special card the time when you begin or stop working ‖ 일을 시작하거나 마친 시간을 특별한 카드에 기록하다. 출·퇴근

시간을 기록하다: *I clocked in at 8:00 this morning.* 나는 오늘 아침 8시에 출근 시간을 기록했다.

clock up sth *phr v* [T] to reach a particular number or amount ‖ 특정 수 나 양에 이르다: *We clocked up 125,000 miles on our old car.* 우리의 낡은 차는 125,000마일을 주행했다.

clock ra·di·o /ˌ. '.../ *n* a clock that you can set so that it turns on a radio to wake you up ‖ 잠을 깨기 위해 정해진 시 간에 라디오가 켜지도록 맞출 수 있는 시 계. 시계가 있는 라디오

clock·wise /'klɑk-waɪz/ *adv* moving in the same direction as the HANDs (=parts that point to the time) of a clock ‖ 시계 바늘과 같은 방향으로 움직이는. 시계 방 향으로 도는: *Turn the dial clockwise.* 다 이얼을 시계 방향으로 돌려라. – **clock·wise** *adj* —opposite COUNTERCLOCKWISE

clock·work /'klɑk-wɔrk/ *n* [U] **1 like clockwork a)** INFORMAL easily and without problems ‖ 문제 없이 쉽게: *Fortunately, production has been going like clockwork.* 다행스럽게도 생산은 순 탄하게 진행되어 오고 있다. **b)** at the same time every day, week, or month ‖ 매일[매주, 매달] 같은 시간에. 정확히. 규칙적으로: *At 6:30 every evening, like clockwork, Ari would milk the cows.* 아 리는 매일 저녁 6시에 정확히 소젖을 짠 다. **2** machinery that you make work by turning a key around several times ‖ 태 엽을 여러 번 돌려 작동시키는 기계. 태엽 장치: *clockwork toy soldiers* 태엽 장치가 되어 있는 장난감 군인

clod /klɑd/ *n* **1** a solid piece of clay or earth ‖ 흙이나 토양의 덩어리 **2** INFORMAL someone who is not graceful and behaves in a stupid way ‖ 세련되지 않고 멍청하게 행동하는 사람. 바보. 얼간이

clog /klɑg/, **clog up** *v* **-gged, -gging** [I, T] to block something or become blocked ‖ 어떤 것을 막다, 또는 막히다: *potato peelings clogging up the drain* 하 수구를 막히게 한 감자 껍질 /*freeways clogged with heavy traffic* 교통 체증으 로 꽉 막힌 고속도로

clogs /klɑgz/ *n* shoes made of wood or with a wooden bottom ‖ 나무로 만들어졌 거나 나무 바닥으로 된 신발. 나막신

clone¹ /kloʊn/ *n* TECHNICAL **1** an exact copy of a plant or animal that is made in an artificial way ‖ 인공적인 방법으로 만 들어진 식물이나 동물의 정확한 복사. 복 제 **2** a computer that can use SOFTWARE that was written for a different computer ‖ 다른 컴퓨터용으로 만들어진

소프트웨어를 사용할 수 있는 컴퓨터. 호 환 가능한 컴퓨터: *an IBM clone* IBM 컴 퓨터와 호환 가능한 컴퓨터

clone² *v* [T] to produce a plant or an animal that is a CLONE ‖ 복제 식물이나 동물을 만들어 내다. …을 복제하다

close¹ /kloʊz/ *v* [I, T] **1** to shut something or to become shut ‖ 어떤 것을 닫다, 또는 닫히다: *Rita walked over and closed the curtains.* 리타는 걸어가서 커 튼을 쳤다. / *The hinges creaked slightly as the door closed.* 문을 닫을 때 경첩이 살짝 삐걱거렸다. / *Close your eyes and go to sleep.* 눈을 감고 자거라. **2** to stop allowing the public to use a store, road, school etc. for a limited time ‖ 제한된 시 간 동안 일반 사람들이 상점·도로·학교 등 을 이용하지 못하게 하다. 일시적으로 문 을 닫다[폐쇄하다]: *What time does the mall close tonight?* 오늘 밤 그 쇼핑센터 는 몇 시에 문을 닫습니까? / *Prentice Street has been closed to traffic.* 프렌티 스가의 교통이 일시적으로 폐쇄되었다. **3** to end something, or to end ‖ 어떤 것을 끝내다, 또는 끝나다: *the closing (=final) days of the Christmas shopping season* 크리스마스 쇼핑 시즌의 막바지 기간 / *Professor Schmidt closed his speech with a quote from Tolstoy.* 슈미트 교수는 톨스토이의 인용문으로 연설을 마쳤다. **4** also **close down** to stop all work at a business or factory ‖ 사업체나 공장에서 의 모든 일을 중단하다. 휴업[폐업]하다: *Hundreds of timber mills have closed since World War II.* 제2차 세계 대전 이 후 수백 개의 제재소가 폐업했다. / *closing down local newspapers* 지방 신 문의 폐간 —see usage note at OPEN²

close in *phr v* [I] to move closer in order to catch someone or something ‖ 사람이나 사물을 잡기 위해 가까이 가다. 다가가다: *a tiger closing in for the kill* 먹잇감을 잡기 위해 다가가는 호랑이

close² /kloʊs/ *adj* **closer, closest** **1** ▶NEAR 가까운◀ **a)** near in space; not far ‖ 공간적으로 가까운; 멀지 않은: *We live close to the school.* 우리는 학교 근처에[가까이에] 산다. / *The victim was shot at close range.* (=from very near) 그 피살자는 매우 가까운 거리에서 총에 맞았다. **b)** near in time ‖ 시간적으로 가 까운: *By the time we left it was close to midnight.* 우리가 떠날 때는 자정에 가까 운 시간이었다.

2 ▶ALMOST 거의◀ almost at a particular level, in a particular state, like a particular thing, etc. ‖ 거의 특정 수준이나 상태에 달한. 특정물과 비슷한:

They haven't reached an agreement yet, but they're close. 그들은 아직은 아니지만 거의 합의에 도달했다. / *Inflation is now close to 6%.* 지금 물가 상승률이 거의 6%에 달한다. / *Do you have any shoes that are closer in color to this scarf?* 이 스카프와 색이 비슷한 신발이 있나요?

3 ▶**CAREFUL** 주의깊은◀ giving careful attention to details ‖ 세부 사항에 대해 세심한 주의를 기울이는. 엄밀한: *Take a closer look at the facts.* 그 사실들을 좀 더 세밀하게 고찰해 봐라. / *Scientists are keeping a close watch on the volcano.* 과학자들은 그 화산을 세심히 관찰하고 있다. / *The jury paid very close attention to the evidence.* 배심원들은 그 증거에 세심한 주의를 기울였다.

4 ▶**LIKING SB** 사람을 좋아하는◀ liking or loving someone very much ‖ 사람을 매우 좋아하거나 사랑하는. 친한: *Are you very close to your sister?* 당신은 당신 누이와 사이가 아주 좋습니까? / *We were pretty close friends in high school.* 우리는 고등학교에서 아주 친한 친구 사이였다.

5 ▶**AT WORK** 직장에서◀ working and talking together often ‖ 자주 함께 일하고 이야기하는: *Our job required close contact with the general manager.* 우리 일은 총지배인과 긴밀한 협의를 필요로 했다.

6 ▶**IN SPORTS** 스포츠에서◀ if a competition is close, the teams are not very far apart in points ‖ 시합에서 팀의 점수 차가 많이 벌어지지 않은. 막상막하인. 접전인: *Right now it's too close to call.* (=no one can say who the winner will be) 지금 당장은 누가 이길지 아무도 모른다.

7 ▶**ALMOST BAD** 거의 나쁜◀ INFORMAL used when you just manage to avoid something bad, such as an accident ‖ 사고 등의 나쁜 일을 가까스로 피했을 때 쓰여. 위기일발의. 구사일생의: *I had a couple of close calls, but they weren't my fault.* 나에게 위기일발의 순간이 몇 번 있었지만 내 잘못은 아니었다.

8 close relation/relative a member of your family, such as a parent, brother, or sister ‖ 부모, 형제, 또는 자매 등의 가족 구성원. 인척. 친척

9 ▶**WEATHER** 날씨◀ too warm, and without any fresh air ‖ 너무 덥고 신선한 공기가 없는. 후텁지근한: *Further inland, the trees became denser and the air more close.* 더 깊은 오지에서는 나무가 더 빽빽해지고 공기도 더 후텁지근해졌다.
– **closely** *adv* – **closeness** *n* [U]

close³ /klous/ *adv* **1** very near ‖ 매우 가까이에. 근처에: *The woman held her baby close.* 그 여인은 아기를 꼭 안고 있었다. / *The grocery store is close by.* 식료품점은 근처에 있다. / *You're planting your tomatoes too close together.* 넌 토마토를 너무 배게 심고 있다. **2 come close to (doing) sth** to almost do something ‖ 거의 어떤 것을 하다. 하마터면 …할 뻔하다: *I was so angry I came close to hitting him.* 난 너무 화가 나서 하마터면 그를 칠 뻔했다. —see usage note at NEAR¹

close⁴ /klouz/ *n* [singular] the end of an activity or period of time ‖ 활동이나 일정 기간의 끝. 마감: *His retirement brought to a close a wonderful career.* 그의 은퇴로 훌륭한 경력에 종지부를 찍었다. / *Summer days finally drew to a close.* 마침내 여름날이 막바지에 가까워졌다.

closed /klouzd/ *adj* **1** shut, especially for a particular period of time ‖ 특히 특정 기간 동안 닫힌: *Sorry, the store's closed on Sundays.* 죄송합니다, 일요일에는 휴점합니다. **2** restricted to a particular group of people ‖ 특정 집단의 사람들에게 제한된. 배타적인. 비공개의: *a closed meeting between the mayor and community leaders* 시장과 지역 사회 유지들간의 비공개 회의 **3** not willing to accept new ideas or influences ‖ 새로운 생각이나 영향을 받아들이려고 하지 않는. 폐쇄적인. 배타적인: *a closed society* 폐쇄적인 사회

closed cir·cuit tel·e·vi·sion /ˌ. ˌ.. '.../ *n* [C, U] a system in which many cameras send pictures to a set of televisions that someone watches to see if any crimes are happening in a building or area ‖ 어떤 건물이나 지역에서 범죄가 일어나는지 지켜볼 수 있도록 많은 카메라가 일련의 텔레비전 수상기로 영상을 전송하는 체계. 폐회로 텔레비전. 시시티브이(CCTV)

closed shop /ˌ. '../ *n* a factory, store etc. where all the workers must belong to a particular UNION ‖ 모든 노동자가 반드시 특정 노조에 속해야 하는 공장·상점 등. 노동 조합원만을 고용하는 사업장

close-knit /ˌklous 'nɪt/ *adj* a close-knit group of people such as a family have good relationships with each other and care about each other ‖ 가족 등의 집단 구성원들이 서로 좋은 관계를 가지며 돌봐 주는. 굳게 뭉친. 긴밀한

close-set /ˌklous 'sɛt/ *adj* close-set eyes are very near to each other ‖ 눈이 서로 매우 가까이 붙어 있는. 서로 한데

clothes

jacket

dress   skirt   pants   sweats

coat

sweater   sweatshirt   shirt   blouse

몰린

clos·et¹ /'klɑzɪt/ *n* **1** a tall cupboard that you keep your clothes in, built into the wall of a room ‖ 옷을 보관해 놓는, 방 벽에 붙박이로 설치된 큰 벽장. 옷장. 붙박이장 **2 come out of the closet** INFORMAL to tell people that you are HOMOSEXUAL ‖ 남들에게 동성애자라는 사실을 밝히다. 커밍아웃하다. 동성애자임을 공공연히 드러내다

closet² *adj* **closet liberal/homosexual etc.** someone who does not admit in public what s/he thinks or does in private ‖ 사적으로 인정하거나 하는 일을 공개 석상에서 인정하지 않는 사람. 숨은 자유주의자/동성애자

close-up /'klous ʌp/ *n* a photograph that someone takes from very near ‖ 사람이 매우 가까이에서 찍는 사진. 근접 촬영. 클로즈업: *a close-up of the children* 아이들을 근접 촬영한 사진

clo·sure /'klouʒɚ/ *n* [C, U] the act of permanently closing a building, factory, school etc ‖ 건물, 공장, 학교 등을 영구적으로 닫는 행위. 폐쇄. 폐업. 폐점: *We were surprised at the closure of the hospital.* 우리는 그 병원의 폐업 사실에 놀랐다.

clot¹ /klɑt/ *n* a place where blood or another liquid has become thick and almost solid ‖ 피나 다른 액체가 엉겨서 거의 고체가 된 곳. 끈끈한 덩어리. 응혈: *a blood clot in his leg* 그의 다리에 생긴 응혈

clot² *v* **-tted, -tting** [I, T] to become thicker and more solid, or to make a liquid do this ‖ 더 걸쭉해져서 굳어지다, 또는 액체를 이런 상태로 만들다. 엉기(게 하)다. 응고하다[시키다]: *a disease in which the blood does not clot* 혈액이 응고되지 않는 병 / *clotted cream* 고형 크림

cloth /klɔθ/ *n* **1** [singular, U] material that is made from cotton, wool etc. and used for making things such as clothes ‖ 옷 등의 물건을 만드는 데에 쓰는, 면·모 등으로 된 직물. 천. 옷감: *pants made from a hard-wearing cloth* 질긴 천으로 만든 바지. **2** a piece of material that is used for a particular purpose ‖ 특정 용도의 천 조각: *Put the dough in a bowl, and cover it with a damp cloth.* 반죽된 것을 사발에 넣은 다음 축축한 천으로 덮어라.

USAGE NOTE cloth, fabric, and material

Use **cloth** as an uncountable noun to talk about the cotton, wool etc. that is used for making clothes: *red silk cloth.* **Fabric** can be countable or uncountable, and can be used about things other than clothes: *What kind of fabric are your pants made of? / fine Italian fabrics.* When **material** is an uncountable noun, it means the same as **fabric**: *There isn't enough material to make curtains.*

옷을 만드는 데 쓰는 면·모 등을 언급할 때는 불가산 명사인 **cloth**를 사용한다: 붉은색 비단 천. **fabric**은 가산 명사나 불가산 명사 모두 될 수 있으며 옷 이외의 것에 관해서도 사용할 수 있다: 당신 바지는 어떤 종류의 천으로 만든 것입니까? / 질 좋은 이탈리아제 직물. **material**이 불가산 명사로 쓰이면 **fabric**과 같은 의미를 가진다: 커튼을 만들 충분한 천이 없다.

clothe /klouð/ v [T] **1** to provide clothes for someone ‖ 남에게 옷을 제공하다: *They could barely keep the family fed and clothed.* 그들은 간신히 가족들의 의식을 해결할 수 있었다. **2** [I, T] to dress someone or be dressed in a particular way ‖ 특정 방식으로 남에게 옷을 입히거나 입고 있다: *The kids were fast asleep, still fully clothed.* 아이들은 옷을 그대로 입은 채로 곯아떨어졌다.

clothes /klouz, klouðz/ n [plural] the things that people wear to cover their bodies or keep warm ‖ 사람들이 몸을 덮거나 따뜻하게 하기 위해 입는 것. 옷. 의복: *She likes casual clothes.* 그녀는 캐주얼한 의상을 좋아한다.

clothes·line /'klouzlaɪn/ n a rope on which you hang clothes outside to dry ‖ 옷을 말리려고 바깥에 거는 줄. 빨랫줄

clothes·pin /'klouzpɪn/ n a small wooden or plastic object that you use for fastening clothes to a CLOTHESLINE ‖ 옷을 빨랫줄에 고정시키기 위해 사용하는, 작은 나무나 플라스틱의 물건. 빨래집게 —see picture at PIN¹

cloth·ing /'klouðɪŋ/ n [U] clothes that people wear ‖ 사람들이 입는 옷. 의류: *The refugees needed food and clothing.* 난민들은 음식과 의류가 필요했다.

cloud¹ /klaud/ n **1** [C, U] a white or gray MASS floating in the sky that consists of very small drops of water ‖ 매우 작은 물방울로 이루어져 하늘에 떠다니는 회거나 회색인 덩어리. 구름: *Storm clouds moved closer overhead.* 먹구름이 머리 위로 몰려왔다. **2** a large amount of smoke or dust, or a large number of other things moving together ‖ 많은 양의 연기나 먼지, 또는 함께 움직이는 많은 수의 다른 것들. 자욱한 연기[먼지]. …떼: *They left a cloud of dust behind them.* 그들이 떠나고 난 뒤 먼지가 자욱했다. / *clouds of flies* 파리떼 **3** something that makes you feel unhappy or afraid ‖ 불행함이나 두려움을 느끼게 하는 일. 어두운 그림자. 암운: *Ryder resigned under a cloud of suspicion.* 라이더는 의심을 받는 수모를 당하고 사임했다. **4 be on cloud nine** INFORMAL to be very happy ‖ 아주 행복하다: *When Caitlin was born, Adam was on cloud nine.* 케이틀린이 태어났을 때 아담은 너무 행복했다.

cloud² v **1** [I, T] also **cloud up** to make something difficult to see through ‖ 어떤 것을 뚫고 보기 어렵게 하다. 흐리게 하다: *Steam clouded up the windows.* 유리창에 김이 서렸다. **2** [T] to make something less easy to understand or

think about ‖ 어떤 것을 이해하거나 생각하기 어렵게 하다. 문제 등을 애매하게 하다: *These unnecessary details are only clouding the issue.* 이런 불필요한 세부사항들은 쟁점을 애매하게 만들 뿐이다.

cloud over phr v [I] if the sky clouds over, it becomes dark and full of clouds ‖ 하늘이 어두워지고 구름으로 뒤덮이다. 온통 흐려지다

cloud·burst /'klaudbɚst/ n a sudden storm of rain ‖ 갑작스런 호우

cloud·y /'klaudi/ adj **1** dark and full of clouds ‖ 어둡고 구름이 가득한. 흐린: *a cloudy day* 흐린 날 **2** cloudy liquids are not clear or transparent ‖ 액체 등이 맑거나 투명하지 않은. 뿌연. 흐린

clout /klaut/ n [U] INFORMAL power or influence ‖ 권력이나 영향력: *Several Christian groups have been gaining political clout in Washington.* 몇몇 기독교 단체들이 워싱턴에서 정치적 영향력을 획득해 왔다.

clove /klouv/ n one of the separate pieces that a GARLIC plant (=plant like a small onion) is made up of ‖ 마늘류 식물을 구성하는 각각의 비늘줄기. 쪽

clo·ver /'klouvɚ/ n a small plant with three round leaves on each stem ‖ 각각의 줄기에 세 개의 둥근 잎이 달린 작은 식물. 클로버. 토끼풀

clown¹ /klaun/ n a performer who wears funny clothes and tries to make people laugh, especially in a CIRCUS ‖ 특히 서커스에서 우스꽝스러운 옷을 입고 사람들을 웃기는 배우. 어릿광대

clown² v [I] to behave in a way that makes other people laugh ‖ 다른 사람들을 웃기는 방식으로 행동하다. 어릿광대 노릇을 하다: *A couple of boys were clowning around, trying to impress the girls.* 몇몇 소년들은 여자 아이들의 눈에 띄기 위해 어릿광대 노릇을 하고 있었다.

club¹ /klʌb/ n **1** a group of people who meet together to do something they are interested in ‖ 자신들이 흥미를 갖는 일을 하기 위해 함께 모인 사람들의 집단. 클럽. 동호회: *the drama club* 드라마 동호회 **2** ⇨ NIGHTCLUB **3** an organization for people who share a particular interest or enjoy similar activities, or the building where they meet ‖ 특정 관심사를 공유하거나 비슷한 활동을 즐기는 사람들을 위한 단체, 또는 그러한 사람들이 모이는 건물. 동호회. 클럽 (회관): *It costs $600 a year to join the health club.* 헬스 클럽 가입비가 1년에 600불이다. **4** a specially shaped stick for hitting a ball in some sports ‖ 일부 스포츠에서 공을 치

는 데에 쓰는 특별한 모양의 막대. 타구봉. 클럽: *a golf club* 골프 클럽[타구봉] **5** a playing card with one or more figures with three leaves on it ‖ 카드놀이에서 세 개의 잎이 달린 무늬가 하나나 그 이상 들어 있는 카드. 클로버 패: *the five of clubs* 클로버 패 5 **6** a heavy stick that is used as a weapon ‖ 무기로 사용하는 묵직한 막대기. 곤봉

club² *v* **-bbed, -bbing** [T] to beat or hit someone with a club ‖ 사람을 곤봉으로 때리거나 치다.

club·house /'klʌbhaʊs/ *n* a building used by a club ‖ 동호회에서 사용되는 건물. 클럽 회관

club sand·wich /ˌ. '../ *n* three pieces of bread with meat and cheese between them ‖ 세 장의 빵 사이에 고기와 치즈를 넣어 만든 것. 클럽 샌드위치

club so·da /ˌ. '../ *n* [C, U] water filled with BUBBLEs that is often mixed with other drinks ‖ 종종 다른 음료와 섞는, 거품이 가득 찬 물. 탄산수

cluck /klʌk/ *v* [I] to make a noise like a HEN ‖ 암탉처럼 소리를 내다. 꼬꼬 울다 – **cluck** *n*

clue¹ /klu/ *n* **1** an object, piece of information, reason etc. that helps you find an answer to a problem or solve a crime ‖ 문제에 대한 해답을 찾거나 범죄 해결을 돕는 물건·정보·추리력 등. 실마리. 단서: *The police are searching for clues to the identity of the murderer.* 경찰은 살인자의 신원에 대한 실마리를 찾고 있다. **2 not have a clue** INFORMAL to not have any idea about the answer to a question, how to do something, what a situation is etc. ‖ 문제의 답·무언가를 하는 방법·현재 상황 등에 대한 생각이 전혀 없는. 짐작도 못 하는: *Brian doesn't have a clue about how she feels.* 브라이언은 그녀의 기분이 어떤지 짐작도 못 한다. / *"Where's Jamie?" "I don't have a clue."* "제이미 어디니?" "전혀 모르겠는 걸."

clue²

clue sb ↔ **in** *phr v* [T] INFORMAL to give someone information about something ‖ 남에게 사물에 대한 정보를 주다: *He clued me in on how the washing machine works.* 그는 내게 세탁기 작동법을 알려 주었다.

clump¹ /klʌmp/ *n* a group of trees, bushes etc. growing close together ‖ 한데 모여 자라는 나무·덤불 등의 무리. 숲. 덤불

clump² *v* [I] to walk with slow noisy steps ‖ 느리게 시끄러운 걸음으로 걷다. 쿵쿵거리며 걷다: *I could hear Grandpa*

clumping around in the basement. 나는 할아버지가 지하실에서 쿵쿵거리며 걷는 소리를 들을 수 있었다.

clum·sy /'klʌmzi/ *adj* **1** moving in an awkward way and tending to break things ‖ 서투르게 움직이며 물건을 망가뜨리는 경향이 있는. 서투른. 솜씨 없는: *At 13, she was clumsy and shy.* 열세 살 때 그녀는 서투르고 수줍음이 많았다. / *a clumsy attempt to catch the ball* 공을 잡으려는 어설픈 시도 **2** a clumsy object is difficult to use and is often large and heavy ‖ 물건이 사용하기 어려우며 종종 크고 무거운. 쓰기 불편한 **3** done carelessly or badly, without enough thought ‖ 충분히 생각하지 않고 부주의하거나 형편없이 한: *The clumsy solution pleased almost nobody.* 형편없는 해결책은 거의 아무도 만족시키지 못했다. – **clumsily** *adv* – **clumsiness** *n* [U]

clung /klʌŋ/ *v* the past tense and PAST PARTICIPLE of CLING ‖ cling의 과거·과거분사형

clunk /klʌŋk/ *v* [I, T] to make the loud sound of two heavy objects hitting each other ‖ 두 개의 무거운 물체가 서로 부딪쳐 큰 소리를 내다. 쿵하고 둔탁한 소리를 내다 – **clunk** *n*

clunk·er /'klʌŋkɚ/ *n* INFORMAL an old car or other machine that does not work very well ‖ 잘 작동하지 않는 오래된 차나 다른 기계. 고물 자동차[기계]

clunk·y /'klʌŋki/ *adj* heavy and awkward to wear or use ‖ 입거나 사용하기에 무겁고 어색한. 맵시가 안 나는. 볼품없는: *clunky old boots* 볼품없는 낡은 부츠

clus·ter¹ /'klʌstɚ/ *n* a group of things of the same kind that are very close together ‖ 매우 가깝게 붙어 있는 같은 종류의 물건의 집단. 무리. (열매의) 송이: *a cluster of grapes* 포도 한 송이

cluster² *v* [I, T] to come together or be together in a group, or to be put together in a group ‖ 한 무리로 한데 모이다, 또는 한 무리로 모아지다. (··· 둘레에) 몰리다. 한 무리로 만들다: *The tulips were clustered around the fence.* 튤립이 울타리 둘레에 군생했다.

clutch¹ /klʌtʃ/ *v* [T] to hold something tightly ‖ 물건을 꽉 잡다. 움켜잡다: *Jamie stood there, clutching her purse.* 제이미는 지갑을 움켜쥔 채 그곳에 서 있었다.

clutch² *n* **1** the PEDAL in a car that you press with your foot when you change GEARs ‖ 자동차에서 기어를 바꿀 때 발로 누르는 페달. 클러치 —see picture on page 943 **2** an important but difficult situation, in which what you do can make the difference between success or failure ‖ 무엇을 하느냐에 따라 성패의 차이를 낼 수 있는, 중요하지만 어려운 상황. 중대한 국면: *Henderson came through in the clutch,* (=succeeded in the situation) *hitting a home run in the ninth inning.* 헨더슨은 9회에서 홈런을 쳐 경기 최대의 고비를 넘겼다. **3 sb's clutches** OFTEN HUMOROUS the control that someone has over you ‖ 남에게 군림하려는 지배력. …의 수중[손아귀]

clut·ter¹ /ˈklʌtə-/ *v* [T] to make something messy by filling it with things ‖ 어떤 것을 물건들로 가득 채워 엉망으로 만들다. 어지럽히다[어질러 놓다]: *His desk is always cluttered with paper.* 그의 책상은 언제나 종이로 어질러져 있다.

clutter² *n* [U] a lot of things scattered in a messy way ‖ 엉망으로 흩어져 있는 많은 물건. 잡동사니. 혼란 (상태): *I can't stand all this clutter!* 난 이런 어질러진 상태를 참을 수 없어!

cm *n* the written abbreviation of CENTIMETER ‖ centimeter의 약어

CNN *n* Cable News Network; an organization that broadcasts television news programs all over the world ‖ Cable News Network (케이블 뉴스 네트워크)의 약어; 텔레비전 뉴스를 전 세계에 방송하는 기구

CO the written abbreviation of Colorado ‖ Colorado(콜로라도 주)의 약어

Co. /koʊ/ the abbreviation of COMPANY, which is usually written rather than spoken ‖ 보통 구어에서보다는 문어에서 쓰는 company의 약어.

c/o /ˌsi ˈoʊ/ the written abbreviation of "in care of"; used when you are sending a letter for someone to another person who will keep it for him/her ‖ "in care of(…전교(轉交))"의 약어; 누군가에게 보낼 편지를 대신 맡아 줄 타인에게 보낼 때 쓰여: *Send the letter to me c/o Anne Miller, 8 Brown St., Peoria, IL* 일리노이 주 피오리아 시 브라운 8번가의 앤 밀러 씨 전교로 편지를 보내라.

coach¹ /koʊtʃ/ *n* **1** someone who trains a person or team in a sport ‖ 스포츠에서 사람이나 팀을 훈련시키는 사람. 코치: *a basketball coach* 농구 코치 **2** a less expensive type of seat on a plane or train ‖ 비행기 또는 기차의 덜 비싼 좌석. 이등석. 이코노미 클래스: *Many business people have begun flying coach to save money.* 많은 사업가들이 돈을 절약하기 위해 이등석을 타기 시작했다. **3** someone who gives private lessons in singing,

acting etc. ‖ 노래·연기 등을 개인 교습해 주는 사람. 성악[연기] 지도자

coach² *v* [I, T] **1** to train a person or team in a sport ‖ 스포츠에서 사람이나 팀을 훈련시키다. 코치하다: *He coaches our tennis team.* 그는 우리 테니스팀을 코치한다. **2** to give someone private lessons in singing, acting etc. ‖ 노래·연기 등의 개인 교습을 하다. (…을) 지도하다

co·ag·u·late /koʊˈægyə.leɪt/ *v* [I, T] to change from a liquid into a thicker substance or a solid ‖ 액체에서 걸쭉한 물질이나 고체로 변하다. 응고[응결]하다: *Egg white coagulates when it is cooked.* 계란 흰자는 가열되면 응고한다. **– coagulation** /koʊˌægyəˈleɪʃən/ *n* [U]

coal /koʊl/ *n* [U] a black mineral that is dug from the earth and is burned for heat ‖ 땅에서 채굴하여 열을 내기 위해 태우는 검은색 광물. 석탄: *a coal fire* 석탄 불 / *coal miners* 광부 —see also CHARCOAL, COALS

co·a·lesce /ˌkoʊəˈlɛs/ *v* [I] FORMAL to grow together or combine so as to form one group ‖ 함께 자라다, 또는 한 집단을 형성하기 위해 결합하다. 하나로 합체하다. 연합하다

co·a·li·tion /ˌkoʊəˈlɪʃən/ *n* a union of separate political parties or people for a special purpose, usually for a short time ‖ 특별한 목적을 위한 보통 일시적인, 각 정당이나 사람들간의 결합. 연합. 연립: *Italy's coalition government* 이탈리아의 연립 정부

coals /koʊlz/ *n* [plural] burning pieces of coal ‖ 불타는 석탄 —see also **rake sb over the coals** (RAKE)

coarse /kɔrs/ *adj* **1** rough and thick, not smooth or fine ‖ 부드럽거나 섬세하지 않고 거칠고 두꺼운: *A coarse cloth was made from local wool.* 거친 천은 지방 양모로 만들어졌다. **2** rude and offensive ‖ 무례하고 공격적인. 거친. 난폭한: *The guys were making coarse jokes about the women at the bar.* 그 놈들은 바에 있는 여성들에 대한 상스러운 농담을 하고 있었다. **– coarsely** *adv* **– coarseness** *n* [U]

coars·en /ˈkɔrsən/ *v* [I, T] to make something COARSE or to become coarse ‖ 무엇을 거칠게 만들거나 거칠어지다. 조잡하게 만들다[되다]: *Washing dishes can coarsen your hands.* 설거지하는 일은 네 손을 거칠게 만들 수 있다.

coast¹ /koʊst/ *n* **1** the land next to the ocean ‖ 바다 옆에 있는 육지. 해안. 연안. 해변: *the Pacific coast* 태평양 연안 —see usage note at SHORE **2 from coast to**

coast across all of the US ‖ 미국 전역을 가로질러. 대서양 연안에서 태평양 연안까지. 전국에 걸쳐: *Their market now stretches from coast to coast.* 그들의 시장은 현재 전국적으로 뻗어 있다. **3 the coast is clear** INFORMAL used in order to say that there is no one who might see you or catch you ‖ 자신을 보거나 잡을 사람이 없다는 것을 말하는 데에 쓰여. 모든 위험이 사라지다. 눈에 띄는 위험[장애물]이 없다: *Let's leave now while the coast is clear!* 위험이 사라진 지금 떠나자! – **coastal** *adj*

coast² *v* [I] **1** to do something without using any effort ‖ 어떠한 노력도 하지 않고 어떤 것을 하다. 힘들이지 않고[고생하지 않고] 하다[되다, 살다]: *Wilson coasted to victory in the election.* 윌슨은 힘들이지 않고 선거에서 승리했다. **2** to keep moving in a vehicle without using more power ‖ 더 이상의 동력을 쓰지 않고 차량이 계속 움직이다. 관성[타성]에 의해 달리다[전진하다]: *Andretti's car coasted to a stop.* 안드레티의 차는 관성으로 전진하다가 멈춰 섰다.

coast·er /ˈkoustɚ/ *n* a small round MAT you put under a glass or bottle to protect a table ‖ 식탁을 보호하기 위해 유리잔이나 병 밑에 받치는 작고 둥근 매트. 받침 접시

coast guard /ˈ. ./ *n* **the Coast Guard** the military organization whose job is to watch for ships in danger and prevent illegal activity at sea ‖ 배가 위험에 처해 있는지 감시하고 바다에서의 불법 행위를 방지하는 일이 임무인 군사 조직. 해안 경비대

coast·line /ˈkoustlaɪn/ *n* the edge of the coast ‖ 해안의 가장자리. 해안선: *a rocky coastline* 바위가 많은 해안선

coat¹ /kout/ *n* **1** a piece of clothing with long SLEEVEs that you wear over your other clothes to protect them or to keep you warm ‖ 몸을 보호하거나 따뜻하게 하기 위해 다른 옷 위에 입는 긴 소매가 달린 옷. 외투. 코트: *her heavy winter coat* 그녀의 두꺼운 겨울 코트 / *a lap coat* 무릎까지 오는 코트 —see picture at CLOTHES **2** a layer of something that covers a surface ‖ 표면을 덮는 어떤 것의 층. 칠. 도금: *a coat of paint* 페인트 칠 **3** an animal's fur, wool, or hair ‖ 동물의 털[양모, 머리카락]. 모피: *a dog with a black and brown coat* 검정색과 갈색 털이 난 개

coat² *v* [T] to cover a surface with a layer of something ‖ 표면을 어떤 것의 층으로 덮다: *The books were thickly coated with dust.* 그 책들은 먼지가 수북이 쌓여 있었다.

coax /kouks/ *v* [T] to persuade someone to do something by talking gently and kindly ‖ 온화하고 친절하게 누군가에게 무언가를 하도록 설득하다. 달래어 …하게 하다: *The boy's mother coaxed him into eating a little.* 그 소년의 어머니는 그를 달래어 음식을 조금 먹게 했다.

cob /kab/ *n* the long hard middle part of an EAR of corn ‖ 옥수수 열매의 길고 딱딱한 중간 부분. 옥수수 속대: *corn on the cob* 속채로 찌거나 구워 버터를 바른 옥수수

cob·bled /ˈkabəld/ *adj* covered with round flat stones ‖ 둥글고 평평한 돌들로 덮인. 자갈로 포장한. 자갈을 깐: *a cobbled street* 자갈 포장 도로

cob·bler /ˈkablɚ/ *n* **1** [C, U] cooked fruit covered with a mixture like sweet bread ‖ 달콤한 빵 같은 혼합물로 씌운 조리된 과일. 코블러: *peach cobbler* 복숭아 코블러 **2** OLD-FASHIONED someone who makes shoes ‖ 신발을 만드는 사람. 제화공

co·bra /ˈkoubrə/ *n* an African or Asian poisonous snake ‖ 아프리카나 아시아산의 독사. 코브라

cob·web /ˈkabwɛb/ *n* a very fine network of sticky threads made by a SPIDER in order to catch insects ‖ 거미가 곤충들을 잡기 위해 친 끈끈한 줄로 된 매우 섬세한 망. 거미줄

Co·ca-Co·la /ˌkoukə ˈkoulə/, **Coke** *n* [C, U] TRADEMARK a sweet brown SOFT DRINK ‖ 달며 갈색의 청량 음료. 코카콜라

co·caine /kouˈkeɪn, ˈkoukeɪn/ *n* [U] a drug used for preventing pain, or taken illegally for pleasure ‖ 고통을 막기 위해 쓰는, 또는 환락을 위해 불법적으로 복용하는 약물. 코카인

cock¹ /kak/ *n* ⇨ ROOSTER

cock² *v* [T] **1** to raise or move part of your head or face ‖ 머리나 얼굴 부분을 들거나 움직이다. 치켜올리다: *Jeremy cocked his head to one side and smiled.* 제레미는 한쪽으로 머리를 치켜들며 웃었다. **2** to pull back the part of a gun that hits the back of a bullet, so that you are ready to shoot ‖ 총의 총알의 후미를 치는 부분을 뒤로 당겨서 발사할 준비를 하다. 총의 공이치기를 당기다 **3** to put your hat on at an angle ‖ 모자를 비스듬히 쓰다.

cock-a-doo·dle-doo /ˌkak ə ˌdudl ˈdu/ *n* the loud sound make by a ROOSTER ‖ 수탉이 내는 큰 소리. 수탉의 울음소리. 꼬끼오

cock·a·ma·mie /'kɑkə,meɪmi/ *adj*
INFORMAL silly and hard to believe ‖ 이치
에 맞지 않아서 믿기 힘든. 어처구니없는:
a cockamamie excuse 어처구니없는 변명

cock·eyed /'kɑkaɪd/ *adj* INFORMAL **1**
not sensible or practical ‖ 분별없거나 실
질적이지 못한. 잘못된. 혼란된: *a
cockeyed idea* 잘못된 생각 **2** not
straight or level ‖ 똑바르지 못하거나 수
평이 아닌. 삐뚤어진: *His hat was on
cockeyed.* 그의 모자가 삐딱하게 씌어졌
다.

cock·pit /'kɑk,pɪt/ *n* the part of a plane
or racing car in which the pilot or driver
sits ‖ 조종사나 운전자가 앉는 비행기나
경주용 자동차의 부분. 조종실. 운전석 —
see picture at AIRPLANE

cock·roach /'kɑk-roʊtʃ/ *n* a large
black or brown insect that often lives
where food is kept ‖ 종종 음식을 보관하
는 곳에 사는 크고 검은색 또는 갈색의 벌
레. 바퀴벌레

cock·sure /ˌkɑk'ʃʊr/ *adj* INFORMAL too
confident about what you know or what
you can do ‖ 알고 있는 것 또는 할 수 있
는 것에 대해 너무 자신만만한. 확신하는.
자부심이 강한: *a cocksure professional
skydiver* 자신만만한 프로 스카이다이버

cock·tail /'kɑkteɪl/ *n* **1** an alcoholic
drink made from a mixture of different
drinks ‖ 서로 다른 음료를 혼합시켜 만든
알코올성 음료. 혼합주(混合酒). 칵테일
2 a small dish of specially prepared food
eaten at the start of a meal ‖ 식사 처음
에 먹는 특별히 준비된 간단한 음료. 전채
(前菜): *a shrimp cocktail* 새우 전채

cocktail lounge /'.. ,./ *n* a public
room in a hotel or restaurant where
people can buy alcoholic drinks ‖ 술을
살 수 있는 호텔이나 레스토랑의 대중적인
장소. 바. 휴게실

cocktail par·ty /'.. ,./ *n* a formal
party where alcoholic drinks are served
‖ 술이 나오는 공식 파티. 칵테일 파티

cock·y /'kɑki/ *adj* INFORMAL too
confident about yourself and what you
can do ‖ 자신과 자신이 할 수 있는 것에
대해 너무 자신 있어하는. 자만심이 강한.
뽐내는: *Howitt was young and cocky.* 호
위트는 젊고 자부심이 강했다. –
cockiness *n* [U]

co·coa /'koʊkoʊ/ *n* **1** [U] a dark brown
chocolate powder used in cooking to
make cakes, cookies etc. ‖ 케이크·쿠키
등을 만들기 위한 요리에 쓰이는 어두운
갈색 초콜릿 가루. 코코아 **2** [C, U] a hot
drink made from this powder, sugar,
and milk or water ‖ 코코아 가루·설탕·우

유나 물로 만든 뜨거운 음료. 코코아 음료:
a cup of cocoa 코코아 한 잔

co·co·nut /'koʊkə,nʌt/ *n* [C, U] a white
fruit that has a hard brown shell and
produces a liquid that looks like milk ‖
껍질은 딱딱한 갈색이며 우유처럼 생긴 액
체가 나오는 하얀 과일. 코코넛 —see
picture on page 944

co·coon /kə'kun/ *n* **1** a bag of silky
threads that some young insects make
to cover and protect themselves while
they are growing ‖ 새끼 벌레가 자라는
동안 감싸서 보호하기 위해 견실로 만들어
진 자루. 고치 **2** a place where you feel
comfortable and safe ‖ 안락하고 안전하
다고 느끼는 곳: *He needs to come out of
his cocoon and have some sort of social
life.* 그는 자신의 안식처에서 벗어나 여러
가지 사회 생활을 경험할 필요가 있다. –
cocoon *v* [T]

C.O.D. *adv* the abbreviation of "cash on
delivery"; a system in which you pay for
something when it is delivered ‖ "cash
on delivery(대금 상환 인도)"의 약어; 물
건이 배달될 때 지불하는 방식: *Send the
equipment C.O.D.* 그 장비를 대금 상환 인
도 방식으로 보내라.

cod /kɑd/ *n* [C, U] a large sea fish that
lives in the North Atlantic, or the meat
from this fish ‖ 북대서양산 큰 바다 생선,
또는 이 생선의 살. 대구. 대구살

code¹ /koʊd/ *n* **1** a set of rules or laws
that tell people how to behave in their
lives or in particular situations ‖ 사람들
의 삶이나 특정한 상황에서의 행동 방식을
알려 주는 일련의 규칙이나 법규. 규준.
관례. 규정: *a strong moral code* 엄격한
도덕률 / *The restaurant was fined for
Health and Safety Code violations.* 그 식
당은 건강 안전 법규 위반으로 벌금이 부
과되었다. / *The school has a dress code.*
(=set of rules about what kind of clothes
people can wear) 그 학교는 복장 규정이
있다. **2** [C, U] a system of words,
letters, or signs that are used instead of
ordinary writing in order to send secret
messages ‖ 비밀 전언을 보내기 위해 일반
적인 글 대신 쓰이는 단어[문자, 기호]의
체계. 암호. 약호: *Important reports
were sent in code.* 중요한 보고는 암호로
보내졌다. **3** a set of numbers, letters, or
other marks that show what something
is ‖ 어떤 것이 무엇인지를 나타내는 일련
의 숫자[문자, 기타 표시]. 코드: *All
products are marked with a bar code.*
(=set of thick and thin black lines) ‖ 모든
상품은 바 코드로 표시되어 있다. —see
also AREA CODE, ZIP CODE

code² *v* [T] to put a message into CODE ‖ 메시지를 암호로 넣다. 암호[신호]로 하다. 코드화하다 – **coded** *adj*

co·ed /ˈkoʊɛd/ *adj* where students of both sexes study or live together ‖ 남녀 학생들이 함께 공부하거나 생활하는 곳의. 남녀 공학의: *co-ed dormitories* 남녀 공학 기숙사

co·erce /koʊˈɚs/ *v* [T] FORMAL to force someone to do something by threatening him/her ‖ 위협하여 남에게 어떤 것을 하도록 강요하다. 억지로 …시키다: *The women were coerced into hiding the drugs.* 그 여자들은 마약을 숨길 것을 강요받았다.

co·er·cion /koʊˈɚʃən, -ʒən/ *n* [U] the use of threats or authority to make someone do something s/he does not want to do ‖ 남이 원하지 않는 일을 시키기 위한 위협 또는 권위의 사용. 강제. 강요: *Their confessions may have resulted from police coercion.* 그들의 자백은 경찰의 강요에 의한 것일지도 모른다. – **coercive** /koʊˈɚsɪv/ *adj*

co·ex·ist /ˌkoʊɪɡˈzɪst/ *v* [I] to exist together in spite of having different opinions, needs, or political systems ‖ 다른 의견(수요, 정치 체제)에도 불구하고 함께 존재하다. 공존하다: *Can the two countries coexist after the war?* 그 두 나라는 전후에 공존할 수 있을까? – **coexistence** *n* [U]

cof·fee /ˈkɔfi, ˈkɑ-/ *n* [C, U] **1** a brown powder that is made by crushing the beans of the coffee tree ‖ 커피나무의 콩을 갈아서 만든 갈색 분말. 커피 **2** a hot brown drink made from this powder ‖ 이 분말로 만든 뜨거운 갈색 음료. 커피: *Do you want a cup of coffee?* 커피 한 잔 하시겠어요?

coffee cake /ˈ.. ./ *n* [C, U] a sweet heavy cake, usually eaten along with coffee ‖ 보통 커피와 함께 먹는, 단맛이 강한 케이크. 커피 케이크

coffee house /ˈ.. ./ *n* a small restaurant where people go to talk and drink coffee ‖ 사람들이 이야기하고 커피를 마시러 가는 작은 음식점. 커피점

coffee ma·chine /ˈ.. ./ *n* a machine that gives you a hot drink when you put money into it ‖ 돈을 넣으면 뜨거운 음료가 나오는 기계. 커피 자판기

cof·fee·mak·er /ˈ.. ./ *n* an electric machine that makes a pot of coffee ‖ 커피를 만드는 전기 기구. 커피메이커 —see picture at KITCHEN

coffee shop /ˈ.. ./ *n* a small restaurant that serves cheap meals ‖ 싼

식사를 제공하는 작은 식당. 커피숍

coffee ta·ble /ˈ.. ./ *n* a small low table in a LIVING ROOM for putting drinks and magazines on ‖ 음료와 잡지를 놓는 데 쓰는 거실의 작고 낮은 탁자

cof·fin /ˈkɔfɪn/ *n* the box in which a dead person is buried ‖ 시신을 묻는 상자. 관(棺)

cog /kɑg/ *n* **1** a tooth around the edge of a wheel that makes it move or be moved by another wheel in a machine ‖ 기계에서 바퀴를 움직이거나 다른 바퀴로 인해 움직여지는 바퀴 가장자리 둘레의 이. (톱니바퀴의) 이 **2 a cog in the machine/wheel** an unimportant worker in a large organization ‖ 큰 조직 속의 중요하지 않은 근로자. 조직 내의 일원

co·gent /ˈkoʊdʒənt/ *adj* a cogent reason or argument is clear, reasonable, and easy to believe ‖ 이유나 논의가 분명하고 합당하여 믿기 쉬운. 설득력 있는 – **cogently** *adv* – **cogency** *n* [U]

co·gnac /ˈkɑnyæk, ˈkɔn-, ˈkoʊn-/ *n* [C, U] a strong alcoholic drink made from wine ‖ 포도주로 만든 독한 알코올 음료. 코냑

co·hab·it /ˌkoʊˈhæbɪt/ *v* [I] if two unmarried people cohabit, they live together as if they are married ‖ 결혼하지 않은 사람들이 마치 결혼한 것처럼 같이 살다. 동거하다 – **cohabitation** /koʊˌhæbəˈteɪʃən/ *n* [U]

co·her·ent /koʊˈhɪrənt/ *adj* clear and easy to understand ‖ 명백하여 쉽게 이해되는. 논리 정연한. 일관성 있는: *a coherent answer* 일관성 있는 대답 – **coherently** *adv* – **coherence** *n* [U]

co·he·sion /koʊˈhiʒən/ *n* [U] the ability to fit together or stay together well ‖ 함께 잘 어울리거나 잘 지내는 능력. 접착. 결합. 유대: *Religious beliefs can provide cohesion among diverse groups of people.* 종교적 믿음은 다양한 집단의 사람들 간에 유대감을 제공해 줄 수 있다.

coil¹ /kɔɪl/, **coil up** *v* [I, T] to wind or twist into a round shape, or to wind or twist something in this way ‖ 둥근 모양으로 감기거나 꼬이다, 또는 이렇게 어떤 것을 감거나 꼬다: *Dad coiled up the hose.* 아빠는 그 호스를 둘둘 감았다.

coil² *n* **1** a length of wire, rope etc. that has been wound into a round shape ‖ 둥근 모양으로 감긴 한 사리의 철사·밧줄 등. 똘똘 감은 것 **2** TECHNICAL a piece of wire that is wound into a continuous shape in order to carry an electrical current ‖ 전류를 전달하도록 계속 말아 놓은 감긴 철사. 코일

coin¹ /kɔɪn/ *n* **1** a piece of money made of metal ‖ 금속으로 만든 돈. 동전. 경화 (硬貨): *Uncle Henry collects foreign coins.* 헨리 아저씨는 외국 동전을 모은다. **2 toss/flip a coin** to choose or decide something by throwing a coin into the air and guessing which side will show when it falls ‖ 동전을 공중에 던져 떨어질 때 어느 쪽이 나타날지 알아맞힘으로써 어떤 것을 선택하거나 결정하다. 동전을 던져서 결정하다

coin² *v* [T] **1** to invent a new word or phrase that many people start to use ‖ 많은 사람들이 쓰기 시작하는 새로운 단어나 어구를 고안하다. 신조어를 만들다: *I wonder who coined the word "cyberpunk"?* "사이버펑크"라는 단어는 누가 만들어 냈을까? **2** to make coins from metal ‖ 금속으로 동전을 만들다. 주조하다

co·in·cide /ˌkoʊɪnˈsaɪd/ *v* [I] to happen at the same time ‖ 동시에 발생하다. 일치 [부합]하다: *Their wedding anniversary coincides with Thanksgiving.* 그들의 결혼 기념일은 추수 감사절과 겹친다.

co·in·ci·dence /koʊˈɪnsədəns/ *n* [C, U] a situation in which two things happen together by chance, in a surprising way ‖ 놀랍게도 두 가지 일이 우연하게 같이 일어나는 상황. 동시 발생. (우연의) 일치: *By coincidence, my husband and my father have the same first name.* 우연히도 내 남편과 아버지는 이름이 같다. / *It's no coincidence that veterans are more likely to smoke than other people.* 참전 용사들이 다른 사람들보다 담배를 더 많이 피우는 것은 당연하다. – **coincidental** /koʊˌɪnsəˈdɛntl/ *adj* – **coincidentally** *adv*

coke /koʊk/ *n* **1 Coke** [C, U] TRADEMARK ⇨ COCA-COLA **2** [U] INFORMAL ⇨ COCAINE

COLA /ˈkoʊlə/ *n* [singular] Cost of Living Adjustment; an increase in wages or SOCIAL SECURITY payments that is equal to the amount that prices, rents etc. have increased ‖ Cost of Living Adjustment(생계비 조정)의 약어; 물가·집세 등의 인상분에 상응하는 임금이나 사회 보장 지급비의 인상

co·la /ˈkoʊlə/ *n* [C, U] a sweet brown SOFT DRINK, or a glass of this drink ‖ 달콤한 갈색 청량 음료, 또는 이 음료 한 잔. 콜라 (한 잔)

col·an·der /ˈkɑləndə, ˈkʌ-/ *n* a metal or plastic bowl with a lot of small holes in the bottom and sides, used for separating liquid from food ‖ 음식에서 액체를 거르는 데 쓰는, 밑바닥과 옆면에 작은 구멍이 많이 나 있는 금속이나 플라스틱 그릇. 여과기

cold¹ /koʊld/ *adj*

1 ▶TEMPERATURE 온도◀ having a low temperature ‖ 낮은 온도를 가진. 저온의. 추운. 찬: *a cold clear day in March* 3월의 춥고 맑게 갠 날 / *It was cold in the car.* 차 안은 추웠다. / *Let's go inside; I'm cold.* 안으로 들어가자. 나는 추워. / *Your coffee's getting cold.* 네 커피가 식고 있다. (=becoming cold) —see usage note at TEMPERATURE

2 ▶FOOD 음식◀ cold food has been cooked, but is not eaten while it is warm ‖ 요리된 음식을 따뜻할 때 먹지 않은. 식은: *cold chicken* 식어버린 닭고기

3 ▶UNFRIENDLY 친절하지 않은◀ without friendly feelings ‖ 우호적인 느낌이 없는. 냉담한. 쌀쌀한. 불친절한: *a polite but cold greeting* 예의는 바르나 쌀쌀 맞은 인사

4 leave sb cold to not interest someone at all ‖ 남에게 아무런 흥미를 주지 않다: *Shakespeare leaves me cold.* 셰익스피어는 나에게 아무런 흥미도 주지 못한다.

5 get/have cold feet INFORMAL to suddenly feel that you are not brave enough to do something ‖ 어떤 것을 할 만큼 용감하지 않다고 갑자기 느끼다. …하는 것에 겁을 먹다. 두려워하다: *She was getting cold feet about getting married.* 그녀는 결혼하는 것에 겁을 먹고 있었다.

6 cold snap a sudden short period of very cold weather ‖ 갑작스러운 짧은 기간의 매우 추운 날씨. 갑자기 엄습하는 한파

7 cold spell a period of several days or weeks of very cold weather ‖ 매우 추운 날씨가 며칠이나 몇 주 지속되는 기간

8 give sb/sth the cold shoulder to deliberately ignore a person or idea ‖ 어떤 사람이나 생각을 고의적으로 무시하다. 냉대하다 – **coldness** *n* [U]

cold² *n* **1** a common illness that makes it difficult to breathe through your nose and makes your throat hurt ‖ 코로 숨쉬는 것을 어렵게 만들고 목구멍을 아프게 하는 흔한 질병. 감기: *You sound like you have a cold.* 너 감기 걸린 것 같다. / *Did you catch a cold?* (=get a cold) 감기 걸렸니? **2 the cold** a low temperature or cold weather ‖ 저온이나 추운 날씨. 추위: *She's not really dressed for the cold.* 그녀는 추위에 맞게 옷을 차려 입지 않았다.

3 out in the cold not included ‖ 포함되지 않은. 무시[묵살]되어. 냉대받은: *The policy seems to leave many gay students out in the cold.* 정책은 다수의 동성애자 학생들을 무시하는 것 같다.

cold³ *adv* **1** suddenly and completely ‖ 갑자기·완전히: *In the middle of his speech, he stopped cold.* 그는 연설 도중에 갑자기 멈췄다. **2 out cold** INFORMAL unconscious, especially because of being hit on the head ‖ 특히 머리를 부딪혀 의식을 잃은. 기절한

cold-blood·ed /ˌ. '../ *adj* **1** not seeming to have any feelings ‖ 어떠한 감정도 지니지 않은 듯한. 냉혹한. 피도 눈물도 없는: *a cold-blooded killer* 잔인한 살인자 **2** cold-blooded animals have a body temperature that changes with the air or ground temperature ‖ 동물의 신체 온도가 공기나 지면의 온도에 따라 변하는. 냉혈[변온]의

cold cuts /ˈ. ./ *n* [plural] thin pieces of different kinds of cold cooked meat ‖ 얇게 저민 각종 냉육(冷肉)

cold-heart·ed /ˌ. '../ *adj* without sympathy or pity ‖ 동정심이나 연민이 없는. 인정머리 없는. 매정한: *a cold-hearted man* 매정한 사람

cold·ly /ˈkoʊldli/ *adv* without friendly feelings ‖ 우호적인 느낌이 없이. 차갑게. 냉담하게. 쌀쌀맞게: *"I'm busy," said Sarah coldly.* "저 바빠요."라고 사라는 쌀쌀맞게 말했다.

cold sore /ˈ. ./ *n* a painful spot on the inside or outside of your mouth that you sometimes get when you are sick ‖ 아플 때 가끔 입 안팎에 생기는 아픈 부위. 입가의 발진

cold tur·key /ˌ. '../ *n* [U] **go cold turkey** to suddenly stop a bad habit, such as taking drugs or smoking, without using any other drugs to help you do this ‖ 도움이 되는 다른 어떤 약도 쓰지 않고 마약이나 흡연 등의 나쁜 습관을 갑자기 중단하다. 단번에 끊다

cold war /ˌ. '../ *n* **1** an unfriendly political relationship between two countries that do not actually fight with each other ‖ 실제로 서로 싸우진 않는 두 나라 사이의 비우호적인 정치적 관계. 냉전 **2 the Cold War** this type of relationship between the US and the Soviet Union, after World War II ‖ 2차 세계 대전 후 미국과 소비에트 연방 간의 냉전 관계. 미·소 간의 냉전

cole slaw /ˈkoʊl slɔ/ *n* [U] a SALAD made with thinly cut raw CABBAGE ‖ 잘게 썬 날양배추로 만든 샐러드. 콜슬로

col·ic /ˈkɑlɪk/ *n* [U] severe pain in the stomach and BOWELs of babies ‖ 아기들의 위·장의 심한 통증. 복통. 배앓이

col·lab·o·rate /kəˈlæbəˌreɪt/ *v* [I] **1** to work together for a special purpose ‖ 특별한 목적을 위해 함께 일하다. 공동으로 일하다. 합작하다: *The two authors collaborated on translating the novel.* 그 두 저자는 공동으로 그 소설을 번역했다. **2** to help a country that your country is at war with ‖ 자국과 전쟁 중인 나라를 돕다. 적국에 협력하다: *He was accused of collaborating with the Nazis.* 그는 나치에 부역한 죄로 기소되었다. **– collaborator** *n*

col·lab·o·ra·tion /kəˌlæbəˈreɪʃən/ *n* [U] **1** the act of working together to make or produce something ‖ 어떤 것을 만들거나 생산하기 위해 함께 일하는 행위. 협력. 합작: *Our departments worked in close collaboration on the project.* 우리 부서는 그 계획에 긴밀히 협력하면서 작업했다. **2** the act of helping an enemy during a war ‖ 전시(戰時) 중 적을 돕는 행위. 적국에의 협력[부역]

col·lage /kəˈlɑʒ, koʊ-/ *n* **1** a picture made by sticking various materials onto a surface ‖ 표면에 여러 가지 재료를 붙여서 제작하는 그림. 콜라주 **2** [U] the art of making pictures in this way ‖ 여러 가지 재료를 붙여서 그림을 제작하는 기술. 콜라주 기법

col·lapse¹ /kəˈlæps/ *v* [I] **1** to fall down or inward suddenly ‖ 갑자기 아래로 또는 안으로 무너지다. 붕괴하다: *Many buildings collapsed during the earthquake.* 지진이 나면서 많은 건물이 붕괴됐다. **2** to fall down and perhaps become unconscious ‖ 쓰러져서 그대로 의식을 잃다. 졸도하다. 실신하다: *She collapsed on hearing the news.* 그 소식을 듣자 그녀는 졸도했다. **3** to fail suddenly and completely ‖ 갑자기·완전히 실패하다. 망하다: *a business venture that collapsed* 망한 벤처 사업

col·lapse² *n* [singular] **1** a sudden failure in the way something works ‖ 일의 작동 방식에서의 갑작스러운 실패. 좌절. 붕괴: *the collapse of communism in Eastern Europe* 동유럽에서의 공산주의의 붕괴 **2** the act of falling down or inward ‖ 아래로나 안으로 무너져 내림. 함몰. 붕괴: *Floods caused the collapse of the bridge.* 홍수로 다리가 함몰되었다.

col·laps·i·ble /kəˈlæpsəbəl/ *adj* able to be folded up into a smaller size ‖ 작은 크기로 접을 수 있는. 조립식인: *collapsible chairs* 접는 의자

col·lar¹ /'kɑlə/ *n* **1** the part of a shirt, coat, dress etc. that fits around your neck ‖ 셔츠·코트·드레스 등의 목 둘레에 해당하는 부분. 칼라. 깃 **2** a band put around an animal's neck ‖ 동물의 목에 거는 끈. 동물의 목걸이

collar² *v* [T] INFORMAL to catch and hold someone ‖ 어떤 사람을 붙잡다. 체포하다. 붙들다: *Two policemen collared the suspect near the scene.* 두 경찰관은 현장 근처에서 용의자를 체포했다.

col·lar·bone /'kɑlə,boʊn/ *n* one of a pair of bones that go from the base of your neck to your shoulders ‖ 목 밑부분에서 어깨까지 이어지는 한 쌍의 뼈 중의 하나. 쇄골

col·late /kə'leɪt, kɑ-, 'koʊleɪt, 'kɑ-/ *v* [T] to arrange things such as papers in the right order ‖ 종이 등을 올바른 순서대로 배열하다. (페이지를) 맞추다. 정돈하다

col·lat·er·al /kə'lætərəl/ *n* [singular U] TECHNICAL property or money that you promise to give to someone if you cannot pay back a debt ‖ 빚을 갚을 수 없을 때 남에게 주기로 약속한 재산이나 돈. 담보물

col·league /'kɑlig/ *n* someone you work with, especially in a profession ‖ 특히 직업상 함께 일하는 사람. 동료: *His colleagues described him as a man of great patience.* 그의 동료들은 그를 인내심이 많은 사람이라고 말했다.

col·lect¹ /kə'lɛkt/ *v* **1** [T] to take things and put them together ‖ 사물을 가져다 한데 두다. 모으다: *I'm still collecting data for my research paper.* 내 연구 논문을 위해 아직 자료를 수집하는 중이다. **2** [T] to get and keep things of a particular kind that interest you ‖ 흥미를 갖는 특정한 종류의 물건을 취득해 보관하다. 수집하다: *A lot of boys collect baseball cards.* 많은 소년들이 야구 카드를 수집한다. **3** [I, T] to get money from people ‖ 사람들에게서 돈을 얻다. 모금[수금]하다: *kids collecting for charity* 자선 기금을 모금하는 어린이들 / *Does this ruling apply to taxes that have already been collected?* 이 판결이 이미 징수된 세금에도 적용됩니까? **4** [I] to come or gather together ‖ 한데 오거나 모이다. 쌓이다: *Dust had collected in the corners of the room.* 먼지가 방 구석에 쌓였다. **5** [T] to obtain something, especially because you have achieved something to get it ‖ 특히 그것을 획득한 무엇인가를 이뤄냈기 때문에 어떤 것을 획득하다: *"Beauty and the Beast"*

collected four Oscar nominations. "미녀와 야수"는 4개 부문 오스카상 후보에 올랐다.

collect² *adv* **1 call/phone someone collect** if you call someone collect, the person who gets the call pays for it ‖ 전화를 받는 사람이 요금을 지불하다. 수신자 부담으로 전화를 걸다 **2 collect call** a telephone call that is paid for by the person who receives it ‖ 전화 받는 사람이 요금을 지불하는 전화. 수신자 부담 전화 (통화)

col·lect·ed /kə'lɛktɪd/ *adj* **1** put together in one book or as a COLLECTION ‖ 한 권의 책이나 모음집으로 한데 모은. 수집한: *the collected works of Emily Dickinson* 에밀리 디킨슨 전집 **2** in control of yourself and your thoughts, feelings etc ‖ 자신과 자신의 생각·감정 등을 통제하는. 침착한. 냉정한: *Jason seemed calm and collected.* 제이슨은 차분하고 침착해 보였다.

col·lect·i·ble /kə'lɛktəbəl/ *n* an object that you keep as part of a group of similar things ‖ 일단의 유사한 사물의 일부로서 보관하는 물건. 수집할 가치가 있는 것. 수집품: *a store that sells antiques and collectibles* 골동품과 수집품을 판매하는 상점

col·lec·tion /kə'lɛkʃən/ *n* **1** a set of similar things that you keep or put together ‖ 보관하거나 모으는 일련의 유사한 물건들. 수집(물). 컬렉션: *a stamp collection* 우표 수집 / *a collection of toy soldiers* 장난감 병정 수집 **2** [U] the act of bringing together things of the same type from different places ‖ 다른 출처에서 동일한 유형의 사물을 한데 가져오는 행위. 수집: *the collection of reliable information* 믿을 만한 정보의 수집 **3** several stories, poems, pieces of music etc. that are put together ‖ 한데 모은 여러 이야기·시·음악 작품 등. 모음집: *a collection of Jimi Hendrix songs* 지미 헨드릭스 노래 모음집 **4** [C, U] the act of taking something away from a place ‖ 한 장소에서 어떤 것을 가져가는 행위. 수거: *Garbage collection is on Fridays.* 쓰레기 수거는 금요일에 한다. **5** [C, U] the act of asking for money from people for a particular purpose ‖ 특정한 목적을 위해 사람들에게 돈을 요구하는 행위. 모금. 징수: *We're planning to have a collection for UNICEF.* 유니세프를 위한 모금을 할 예정이다. / *tax collection* 세금 징수

col·lec·tive /kə'lɛktɪv/ *adj* shared or done by all the members of a group together ‖ 한 집단의 모든 구성원이 공유

하거나 행하는. 집단의. 공동의: *We had made a collective decision.* 우리는 집단적인 결정을 내렸다. / *collective farms* 집단 농장 – **collectively** *adv*

collective bar·gain·ing /ˌ.,.. ˈ...ˌ/ *n* [U] talks between employers and unions about wages, working conditions etc. ‖ 임금·근로 조건 등에 관한 사용자와 노조 간의 협의. 노사간의 단체 교섭

col·lec·tor /kəˈlɛktə/ *n* **1** someone whose job is to collect things ‖ 어떤 것을 징수하는 직업인. 수금원: *a tax collector* 징세원 **2** someone who collects things for pleasure ‖ 재미삼아 물건을 수집하는 사람. 수집가: *a rock collector* 돌 수집가

col·lege /ˈkɑlɪdʒ/ *n* **1** [C, A] a large school where you can study after high school ‖ 고등학교를 졸업한 후에 공부할 수 있는 규모가 큰 학교. 대학: *My oldest son is in college.* (=is a student at a college) 나의 큰아들은 대학에 재학 중이다. **2** the part of a university that teaches a particular subject ‖ 특정한 과목을 가르치는 종합 대학의 일부. 단과 대학: *the college of fine arts* 미술 (단과) 대학

col·lide /kəˈlaɪd/ *v* [I] **1** to crash violently into something ‖ 어떤 것에 격렬하게 부딪히다. 충돌하다: *His car collided with a bus.* 그의 차는 버스와 충돌했다. **2** to strongly oppose someone ‖ 누군가를 심하게 반대하다. 상충하다. 충돌하다: *The President collided with Congress over the proposed bill.* 대통령은 제출된 법안을 놓고 의회와 충돌했다.

col·lie /ˈkɑli/ *n* a middle-sized dog with long hair, kept as a pet or trained to look after sheep ‖ 애완 동물로 기르거나 양을 돌보도록 훈련받은 긴 털을 가진 중형견. 콜리

col·li·sion /kəˈlɪʒən/ *n* [C, U] **1** a violent crash in which one vehicle hits another ‖ 한 차량이 다른 차량에 부딪히는 격렬한 충돌: *a head-on collision* (=between cars going in opposite directions) 정면 충돌 **2** a strong disagreement or fight ‖ 강한 불일치나 싸움. 충돌. 격돌: *a collision between police and demonstrators* 경찰과 데모대 간의 충돌 **3 be on a collision course** to be likely to have trouble because your aims are very different from someone else's ‖ 자신의 목표가 다른 사람의 목표와 많이 달라서 문제가 발생하기 쉽다. 충돌 노선[상태]에 있다: *Religion and politics are on a collision course over the issue.* 종교계와 정계는 그 문제를 놓고 의견이 상충되고 있다.

col·lo·qui·al /kəˈloʊkwiəl/ *adj* used informal conversations ‖ 비격식적인 대화에 쓰이는. 구어(체)의. 구어적인: *colloquial expressions* 구어체 표현 – **colloquially** *adv* – **colloquialism** *n*

col·lu·sion /kəˈluʒən/ *n* [U] FORMAL the act of agreeing secretly with someone else to do something dishonest or illegal ‖ 부정직하거나 불법적인 일을 하기 위해 다른 사람과 은밀하게 결탁하는 행위. 공모. 결탁

co·lon /ˈkoʊlən/ *n* **1** the mark (:) used in writing to introduce a list, examples etc. ‖ 나열·예시 등을 도입하기 위한 글에 쓰이는 부호. 콜론 **2** part of the large tube that takes waste matter down from your stomach ‖ 위(胃)에서 노폐물을 내려 보내는 큰 관의 일부. 결장

colo·nel, Colonel /ˈkənl/ *n* an officer who has a middle rank in the Army, Air Force, or Marines ‖ 육군·공군·해병대의 중간 계급인 장교. 대령

co·lo·ni·al /kəˈloʊniəl/ *adj* **1** relating to the control of countries by a more powerful distant country ‖ 원거리에 있는 보다 강력한 국가가 다른 여러 나라를 지배하는 것과 관련된. 식민지의: *the end of colonial rule in India* 인도에서의 식민 통치의 종식 **2** also **Colonial** relating to the time when the US was a COLONY of England ‖ 미국이 영국의 식민지였던 시기와 관련된. 영국 식민지(시대)의: *a Colonial-style brick house* 영국 식민지 시대풍의 벽돌집 – **colonialism** *n* [U] – **colonialist** *adj, n*

col·o·nize /ˈkɑləˌnaɪz/ *v* [I, T] to control a country or area and send your own people to live there ‖ 나라나 지역을 지배하여 자국민을 그곳에 살게 하다. 식민지를 만들다: *Australia was colonized in the 18th century.* 호주는 18세기에 식민지화되었다. – **colonization** /ˌkɑlənəˈzeɪʃən/ *n* [U]

col·o·ny /ˈkɑləni/ *n* **1** a country or area that is ruled by another country ‖ 다른 나라의 지배를 받는 나라나 지역. 식민지. 식민국 **2** a group of people from the same country or with the same interests, who live together ‖ 함께 사는, 같은 나라 출신이거나 같은 흥미를 가진 일단의 사람. 동종의 사람들의 그룹[거주지]: *an artists' colony* 예술인 촌 **3** a group of the same type of animals or plants living or growing together ‖ 함께 살거나 자라는 같은 종류의 동물 또는 식물 집단. 떼. 군(群): *an ant colony* 개미 떼

col·or¹ /ˈkʌlə/ *n* **1** red, blue, yellow,

etc. || 빨강·파랑·노랑 등. 색. 빛깔: *the colors of the rainbow* 무지개 빛깔 / *houses painted bright colors* 밝은 색으로 페인트칠한 집들 / *"What color is your new car?" "Blue."* "당신의 새 차는 무슨 색이에요?" "파란색입니다." ✗DON'T SAY *"What color does your new car have?"*✗ "What color does your new car have?" 라고 하지 않는다 **2** [U] the quality of having colors || 색깔을 띰. 컬러. 색상: *These pages need more color.* 이 페이지들에는 더 많은 색깔이 있어야 한다. / *color television* 컬러 텔레비전 **3** [C, U] a paint, pencil, DYE etc. that has a color || 색깔이 있는 페인트·연필·물감 등: *a big box of crayons, with 64 colors* 64색의 크레용이 들어 있는 큰 상자 / *The color is washing out of my shirt.* 내 셔츠에서 물이 빠지고 있다. **4** [C, U] how dark or light someone's skin is || 사람의 피부가 어둡거나 밝은 정도. 피부색. 탄 피부: *You've got some color – have you been out in the sun?* 너는 좀 탔구나. 밖에서 선탠했니? **5 people of color** people whose skin is brown, black etc. || 피부가 갈색·검은색 등인 사람들. 유색 인종: *a conference of writers of color* 유색 인종 작가 회의 **6** [U] the appearance of someone's skin, that shows how healthy s/he is || 얼마나 건강한지를 보여주는 피부의 겉모습. 혈색. 안색: *Katie has a healthy color in her cheeks.* 케이티의 뺨은 건강한 혈색을 띤다. —see also COLORS

color² *v* **1** [T] to give color to something || 어떤 것에 색깔을 부여하다. 채색하다. 염색하다: *Do you color your hair?* 네 머리 물들였니? **2** [I, T] to put color onto a drawing or picture, or to draw a picture using colored pencils or pens || 그림 또는 사진에 색칠하거나 색연필 또는 색펜을 사용하여 그림을 그리다: *Give Grandma the picture you colored, Jenny.* 제니야, 네가 색칠한 그림을 할머니에게 드려라. **3** [T] to influence your opinion about something || 어떤 것에 대한 의견에 영향을 끼치다: *Personal feelings color his judgment.* 사적인 감정은 그의 판단을 영향을 미친다.

color bar /ˈ.. ˌ./ *n* ⇨ COLOR LINE

col·or·blind /ˈ.. ˌ./ *adj* **1** not able to see the difference between particular colors || 특정한 색깔들 간의 차이를 구별할 수 없는. 색맹의 **2** treating all races of people fairly || 모든 인종을 공평하게 대하는. 인종 차별을 하지 않는: *Equal rights laws are supposed to be colorblind.* 평등권 법률은 인종 차별을 하지 않기로 되어 있다.

color·co·or·di·nat·ed /ˌ.. .ˈ..../ *adj* clothes or decorations that are color-coordinated have colors that look good together || 옷이나 장식이 한데 어울리는. 색상을 띤. 색상을 맞춘. 배색의

col·ored¹ /ˈkʌləd/ *adj* **1** having a color rather than being black or white || 검정색이나 흰색 이외의 색깔을 가진: *brightly colored tropical birds* 밝은 색깔의 열대 새 **2** OFFENSIVE having dark skin || 검은 피부를 가진. 흑인의

colored² *n* OFFENSIVE someone who has dark skin || 검은 피부를 가진 사람. 흑인

color·fast /ˈkʌləˌfæst/ *adj* colorfast clothing has a color that will not become lighter when you wash or wear it || 옷을 세탁하거나 입을 때, 옷의 색상이 더 연해지지 않는. 변색되지 않는. 색이 바래지 않는

col·or·ful /ˈkʌləfəl/ *adj* **1** having a lot of bright colors || 매우 밝은 색을 띤. 화려한: *a colorful stained-glass window* 화려한 스테인드글라스 창문 **2** interesting and full of variety || 흥미있고 변화가 많은. 다채로운: *a colorful career* 다양한 경력 – **colorfully** *adv*

col·or·ing /ˈkʌlərɪŋ/ *n* **1** [U] the color of something, especially someone's hair, skin, eyes, etc. || 특히 사람의 머리털·피부·눈 등의 색깔. 피부색. 안색. 혈색: *Mandy had her mother's dark coloring.* 만디는 어머니와 같은 검은 피부색을 가졌다. **2** [C, U] a substance used for giving a particular color to something, especially food || 특히 음식 등에 특정한 색을 채색하는 데 쓰이는 물질. 착색제. 색소

coloring book /ˈ... ˌ./ *n* a book full of pictures that are drawn without color so that a child can color them in || 어린이가 색칠할 수 있도록 채색 없이 윤곽만 그려진 그림이 많은 책. 색칠하기 그림책

col·or·less /ˈkʌləlɪs/ *adj* **1** not having any color || 색이 전혀 없는. 무색의: *a colorless gas* 무색 가스 (기체) **2** not interesting or exciting; boring || 재미나 흥미가 없는; 지루한

color line /ˈ.. ˌ./ *n* a set of US laws in the past that did not let black people do the same things as white people || 과거에 흑인들이 백인들과 똑같은 일을 하지 못하게 했던 일련의 미국법. 백인과 유색 인종 간의 차별(법)

col·ors /ˈkʌləz/ *n* [plural] the colors that are used as a sign to represent a team, school, club etc. || 팀·학교·클럽 등을 대표하는 표시로 쓰이는 색깔: *UCLA's colors are blue and gold.* UCLA

의 색깔은 청색과 황금색이다.

co·los·sal /kə'lasəl/ *adj* very large ‖ 매우 큰. 거대한. 어마어마한: *a colossal building* 거대한 빌딩 / *They've run up colossal debts.* 그들은 막대한 빚을 지고 있다.

co·los·sus /kə'lasəs/ *n* someone or something that is very large or very important ‖ 매우 크거나 매우 중요한 사람 또는 사물. 거장. 위대한 사람

colt /koʊlt/ *n* a young male horse ‖ 어린 수말. 수망아지

col·umn /'kaləm/ *n* **1** a tall thin round structure used as a support for part of a building or as a decoration ‖ 건물의 지주나 장식으로 쓰이는 높고 가늘면서 둥근 구조물. 기둥 **2** an article by a particular writer that appears regularly in a newspaper or magazine ‖ 신문이나 잡지에 규칙적으로 등장하는 특정한 필자의 기사. 칼럼. 기고란: *an advice column* 신문·잡지의 신상(身上) 상담란 **3** something with a long narrow shape ‖ 길고 폭이 좁은 모양의 것. 기둥 모양의 것: *a column of smoke* 연기 기둥 **4** one of the long narrow sets of printed lines that go down the page of a newspaper or book ‖ 신문이나 책의 페이지를 따라 내려가는 길고 좁게 인쇄된 여러 줄들의 하나. 단(段) **5** a long moving line of people, vehicles etc. ‖ 움직이는 사람·차량 등의 긴 줄. 행렬: *A column of tanks rolled through the streets.* 탱크의 행렬이 거리를 천천히 통과하여 달렸다.

col·um·nist /'kaləmnɪst, 'kaləmɪst/ *n* someone who regularly writes an article for a newspaper or magazine ‖ 신문·잡지에 정기적으로 기사를 쓰는 사람. 칼럼니스트. 특설란 집필자

co·ma /'koʊmə/ *n* a state in which someone is not conscious for a long time, usually after an accident or illness ‖ 사람이 대개 사고나 병이 난 후 오랫동안 의식이 없는 상태. 혼수 상태: *Ben was in a coma for six days.* 벤은 엿새 동안 혼수 상태였다.

co·ma·tose /'koʊmə,toʊs, 'ka-/ *adj* **1** TECHNICAL in a COMA ‖ 혼수 상태인. 인사불성인 **2** INFORMAL very tired or in a deep sleep ‖ 몹시 피곤하거나 깊은 잠에 빠진: *Denny's usually comatose after he works nights.* 데니는 밤에 일한 후엔 곯아떨어진다.

comb¹ /koʊm/ *n* a flat piece of plastic or metal with a row of thin parts like teeth on one side, that you use to make your hair neat ‖ 머리카락을 가지런히 하는 데에 쓰는 한쪽 면에 가는 조각들이 치아처

럼 일렬로 나열되어 있는 플라스틱이나 금속의 납작한 조각. 빗

comb² *v* [T] **1** to make your hair neat with a comb ‖ 빗으로 머리칼을 가지런히 하다. 머리를 빗다: *Go comb your hair.* 가서 머리 빗어라. **2** to search a place thoroughly ‖ 어떤 장소를 철저히 조사하다. 구석구석 뒤지다. 샅샅이 수색하다: *Police combed the woods for the missing boy.* 경찰은 실종된 소년을 찾기 위해 숲을 샅샅이 수색했다.

comb sth ↔ **out** *phr v* [T] to make messy hair neat and smooth ‖ 헝클어진 머리를 가지런히·부드럽게 하다. (흐트러진 머리를)빗질하다: *Let me comb out the tangles.* 내가 헝클어진 머리를 빗질해 줄게.

com·bat¹ /'kambæt/ *n* [U] fighting during a war ‖ 전시의 싸움. 전투: *Her husband was killed in combat.* 그녀의 남편은 전투 중에 사망했다. –**combat** *adj*

com·bat² /kəm'bæt, 'kambæt/ *v* [T] **1** to try to stop something bad from happening or getting worse ‖ 나쁜 일이 일어나거나 악화되는 것을 막으려고 노력하다. 싸우다. 맞서다: *new measures to combat inflation* 인플레이션을 막기 위한 새로운 조치 / *drugs to combat depression* 우울증을 억제하기 위한 약물 **2** to fight against someone, especially in a war ‖ 특히 전쟁에서 남과 싸우다. 전투하다

com·bat·ant /kəm'bæt'nt/ *n* someone who fights in a war ‖ 전쟁에서 싸우는 사람. 전투원

com·ba·tive /kəm'bæt̬ɪv/ *adj* showing eagerness to fight or argue ‖ 싸우거나 언쟁하기를 좋아하는 듯한. 전투적인. 호전적인: *Paul was in a combative mood.* 폴은 곧 싸울 기세였다.

com·bi·na·tion /,kambə'neɪʃən/ *n* **1** two or more different things, substances etc. that are used or put together ‖ 둘 이상의 다른 사물·물질 등이 사용 또는 결합된 것. 배합. 결합: *A combination of factors led to the decision.* 그 결정에는 여러 가지 요인들이 작용했다. / *Vitamin C should be taken in combination with other vitamins for the best results.* 비타민 C 는 최상의 효과를 위해서 다른 비타민과 같이 섭취해야 한다. **2** a particular arrangement or way of putting two or more things together ‖ 둘 이상의 사물을 결합하는 특정한 배열이나 방식. 배합: *She was dressed in an unusual combination of colors.* 그녀는 독특하게 색깔을 맞추어 옷

을 입었다. **3** a series of numbers or letters you need to open a COMBINATION LOCK ‖ 조합 자물쇠를 여는 데 필요한 일련의 숫자나 문자. 자물쇠의 숫자[문자] 조합 **4** [U] used in order to show that something has more than one job or can do more than one thing ‖ 사물이 한 가지 이상의 기능을 갖거나 할 수 있음을 나타내는 데에 쓰여. 복합 기능을 가진 것. 겸용: *a combination washer-dryer* 세탁 건조기 겸용

combination lock /ˌ.... ˈ./ *n* a lock that is opened by using a special series of numbers or letters ‖ 특별한 일련의 숫자나 문자를 사용하여 여는 자물쇠. 숫자[문자] 조합 자물쇠

com·bine¹ /kəmˈbaɪn/ *v* **1** [I, T] if you combine two or more things, ideas, or qualities, or if they combine, they begin to work or exist together ‖ 둘 이상의 사물[생각, 성질]이 함께 작용하거나 존재하기 시작하다. 결합하다[시키다]: *The two car makers combined to form a new company.* 두 자동차 회사가 합병하여 새로운 회사가 되었다. / *It was the heat combined with the jet lag that made her feel so tired.* 그녀를 그토록 지치게 한 것은 시차증과 더불어 작용한 더위 때문이었다. / *The Dodge Viper combines speed with power.* 다지 바이퍼는 속도와 힘을 결합시킨다. **2** [I, T] if two or more substances combine or if you combine them, they mix together to produce a new substance ‖ 둘 이상의 물질이 한데 섞여 새로운 물질을 만들어 내다. 혼합하다[시키다]: *Next, combine the flour with the milk and eggs.* 다음으로 밀가루에 우유와 계란을 혼합해라. **3** [T] to do two different activities at the same time ‖ 동시에 두 가지 다른 활동을 하다. 겸(비)하다. 양립시키다: *It's hard to combine family life with a career.* 가정 생활과 사회적 성공을 양립시키기는 어렵다.

com·bine² /ˈkɑmbaɪn/ *n* **1** also **combine harvester** a large machine used on a farm to cut a crop and separate the grain at the same time ‖ 수확물을 베면서 동시에 알곡을 분리시키기 위해 농장에서 쓰는 큰 기계. 콤바인 **2** a group of people, businesses etc. that work together ‖ 함께 일하는 일단의 사람·기업 등. 연합체. 기업 합동

combo /ˈkɑmboʊ/ *n* INFORMAL **1** a small group of musicians who play dance music ‖ 댄스 음악을 연주하는 소규모 그룹의 음악가들. 소규모의 댄스 악단. 캄보 **2** a combination of things, especially

food at a restaurant ‖ 물질, 특히 식당 음식들의 결합. 세트 음식: *I'll have the fish combo and a beer.* 생선 세트와 맥주를 먹을게.

com·bus·ti·ble /kəmˈbʌstəbəl/ *adj* able to catch fire and burn easily ‖ 쉽게 불이 붙어서 탈 수 있는. 가연성인. 불붙기 쉬운: *Gasoline is highly combustible.* 가솔린은 가연성이 높다. – **combustible** *n*

com·bus·tion /kəmˈbʌstʃən/ *n* [U] the process of burning ‖ 불타는 작용. 연소. 발화

come /kʌm/ *v* **came, come, coming** [I]

1 ▶MOVE TO …으로 이동하다◀ to move to or toward the person who is speaking or the place that s/he is talking about ‖ 말하고 있는 사람이나 언급되고 있는 장소로 이동하다. 오다. 가다: *She asked me to come and look at the report.* 그녀는 그 보고서를 와서 보라고 나에게 말했다. / *Come here, right now!* 지금 당장 이리로 와라! / *The car came slowly up the driveway.* 그 차는 서서히 집앞 진입로로 들어왔다.

2 ▶ARRIVE 도착하다◀ to arrive somewhere ‖ 어딘가에 도착하다: *When Bert came home from work, he looked tired.* 버트는 직장에서 귀가했을 때 피곤해 보였다. / *The boxes will come later in the truck.* 그 상자들은 트럭으로 나중에 도착할 것이다.

3 ▶VISIT 방문하다◀ to visit somewhere ‖ 어딘가를 방문하다: *She comes here every summer.* 그녀는 여름마다 이곳을 방문한다.

4 ▶HAPPEN 일어나다◀ to begin to happen ‖ 일어나기 시작하다. 도래하다: *Spring came early that year.* 그 해에 봄은 일찍 왔다.

5 ▶LIST/COMPETITION ETC. 목록/시합 등◀ to have a particular position in the order of something ‖ 사물의 순서에서 특정한 위치에 있다: *Jason came first/last in the 10K race.* 제이슨은 10킬로미터 경주에서 일등[꼴찌]으로 들어왔다.

6 ▶LIGHT 빛◀ if light comes in or through something, you can see it in a particular place ‖ 빛이 특정한 장소에서 보이다. 빛이 나타나다: *The morning sun came through the doorway.* 아침해가 대문간을 비추었다.

7 ▶TRAVEL 이동하다◀ to travel in a particular way or for a particular distance or time to get somewhere ‖ 어딘가에 도착하기 위해 특정한 방식으로 또는 특정한 거리나 시간 동안 이동하다: *He* *had to come over the Bay Bridge, because of the traffic on the Golden Gate.* 그는 골든 게이트의 교통 때문에 베이브리지를 건너야 했다.

8 come open/loose/undone etc. to become open, loose etc. ‖ 열리다, 느슨해지다, 풀리다: *Your shoe's come untied.* 네 신발 풀어졌다.

9 come in to exist or be available ‖ 존재하거나 입수 할 수 있다: *People come in all shapes and sizes.* 사람들의 모습과 몸집은 각양각색이다. / *This shoe doesn't come in size 11.* 이 신발은 11사이즈가 없습니다.

10 come as a surprise to sb to make someone feel surprised ‖ 누구를 놀라게 하다: *It didn't come as a surprise to learn she was pregnant.* 그녀가 임신했다는 것을 알고 놀라지 않았다.

11 sb/sth has come a long way used in order to say that someone or something has achieved or developed a lot ‖ 사람이나 사물이 크게 성취하거나 발전했음을 말하는 데에 쓰여. 장족의 발전을 이루다: *Jackie has come a long way since she first started teaching.* 잭키는 교직 일을 처음 시작한 이래 장족의 발전을 이루었다.

12 ▶LENGTH/HEIGHT 길이/높이◀ to reach a particular height or length ‖ 특정한 높이나 길이에 도달하다: *The grass came up to our knees* 그 풀은 우리 무릎까지 닿았다.

13 come naturally/easily to sb to be easy for someone to do ‖ 어떤 사람에게는 …하는 것이 수월하다: *Acting came naturally to Rae.* 연기하는 것이 레이에게는 쉬웠다.

14 in the years/days to come in the future ‖ 미래에. 장래에

SPOKEN PHRASES
---

15 how come? used in order to ask someone why something happened or is true ‖ 일이 왜 일어났는지 또는 그것이 사실인지 묻는 데에 쓰여. 어찌하여. 왜: *"She's moving to Alaska." "How come?"* "그녀는 알래스카로 이사갈 거야." "왜?" / *So, how come we haven't met your boyfriend yet?* 그러니까, 어째서 우리가 아직까지 네 남자 친구를 만나지 않았지?

16 here comes sb said when someone is about to arrive at the place where you are ‖ 자신이 있는 장소에 누군가가 막 도착할 때에 쓰여: *Here comes Karen now.* 카렌이 이제 오네.

17 come to think of it said when you have just realized or remembered something ‖ 무엇을 막 깨닫거나 기억했을 때에 쓰여. 생각해 보니. 그러고 보니: *Come to think of it, Cooper did mention it to me.* 생각해 보니, 쿠퍼가 나에게 그 말을 했어.

come about *phr v* [I] to happen or develop ‖ 일어나거나 발전하다: *The rules have come about slowly, as a result of the way we work.* 우리가 작업하는 방식의 결과로 그 규칙은 서서히 생겨났다.

come across *phr v* **1** [T **come across sb/sth**] to meet someone or discover something, usually by chance ‖ 보통 우연히 사람을 만나거나 사물을 발견하다. 우연히 만나다[찾아내다]: *I had come across the article in a magazine.* 나는 우연히 잡지에서 그 기사를 발견했다. **2** [I] to have a particular effect on people ‖ 사람들에게 특정한 영향을 미치다. 인상을 주다: *Brody comes across as being mean, but actually he's nice.* 브로디는 비열한 인상을 주지만 실제로는 멋진 사람이다. / *I thought his speech came across well/badly.* 나는 그의 연설이 좋은[나쁜] 인상을 주었다고 생각했다.

come along *phr v* [I] **1** to happen, especially at a time that you do not expect ‖ 특히 생각지도 않은 시간에 일어나다. 나타나다. 등장하다: *Jobs like this don't come along very often!* 이런 일자리는 자주 나타나지 않아! **2** to develop or improve ‖ 발달하거나 향상하다. 진보하다. 잘 자라다: *The corn crop is coming along fine this year.* 옥수수 작물이 올해는 잘 자라고 있다.

come around *phr v* [I] **1** to visit someone ‖ 누구를 방문하다: *Why don't you come around at 10:00?* 10시에 방문하는 게 어때요? **2** if someone comes around, s/he decides to agree with you after disagreeing with you ‖ 의견이 일치하지 않다가 동의하기로 결정하다. 의견[태도]을 바꾸다. …에 동조하다: *Alyssa finally came around and decided to help.* 앨리사는 마침내 생각을 바꾸어 돕기로 결정했다. **3** if a regular event comes around, it happens as usual ‖ 규칙적인 행사가 평소처럼 일어나다. 돌아오다: *I can't believe his birthday is coming around already.* 벌써 그의 생일이 돌아오다니 믿을 수 없군.

come at sb *phr v* [T] to move toward someone in a threatening way ‖ 위협적으로 남에게 접근하다. …에게 덤벼들다

come back *phr v* [I] **1** to return from a

place ‖ 어떤 곳에서 돌아오다: *When is
your sister coming back from Europe?*
네 여동생은 유럽에서 언제 돌아오니? **2
come back to sb** to be remembered,
especially suddenly ‖ 특히 갑자기 생각나
다. … 에게 문득 떠오르다: *Then,
everything Williams had said came
back to me.* 그때 윌리엄스가 했던 말이
모두 떠올랐다. —see also COMEBACK
come between sb *phr v* [T] to cause
trouble between two or more people ‖
둘이나 그 이상의 사람들 사이에서 문제를
야기하다. … 사이를 갈라놓다. 끼어들다.
방해하다: *Don't let money come
between you and David.* 돈이 당신과 데
이비드 사이를 벌어지게 하지 마라.
come by sth *phr v* **1** [T] to visit
someone for a short time before going
somewhere else ‖ 다른 곳을 가기 전에 잠
시 동안 남을 방문하다. 잠깐 들르다: *I'll
come by about 6:00 to pick up the
clothes.* 옷을 가지러 6시경에 들를게요. **2
be hard to come by** to be difficult to
get ‖ 구하기 어렵다: *Good jobs are hard
to come by right now.* 좋은 직업을 지금
당장 구하기는 어렵다.
come down *phr v* [I] **1** to become lower
in price, level etc. ‖ 가격·수준 등이 더
낮아지다: *Wait until the price
comes down to buy the computer.* 컴퓨
터를 사려면 가격이 떨어질 때까지 기다려
라. **2** if something tall comes down, it
falls or is pulled down ‖ 키가 큰 것이 넘
어지거나 쓰러지다.
come down on sth *phr v* [T] **1** to
punish someone severely ‖ 누구를 심하
게 벌주다: *The school came down hard
on the students who were caught
drinking.* 그 학교는 음주하다 잡힌 학생
들에게 호되게 벌주었다. **2 come down
on the side of sth** to decide to support
something ‖ 어떤 것을 지지하기로 결정하
다. … 의 편을 들다. … 에 찬성하다: *The
court came down on the side of the
boy's father.* 법원은 그 소년의 아버지 손
을 들어 주었다.
come down to *phr v* [T] if a difficult or
confusing situation comes down to one
thing, that thing is the basic problem or
the most important thing you have to do
to solve it ‖ 어렵거나 당혹스러운 상황의
풀어야 될 근본적인 문제 또는 가장 중요
한 것이 되다. … 으로 요약[귀결]되다: *It
comes down to this: How much time do
we have left?* 지금 중요한 것은 우리에게
남은 시간이 얼마나 있느냐 하는 것이다.
come down with sth *phr v* [T] to
become infected with a particular

illness ‖ 특정한 병에 감염되다. … 에 걸리
다. … 으로 몸져 눕다: *I think I'm
coming down with the flu.* 독감에 걸렸
나봐요.
come forward *phr v* [I] to offer to help
someone in an official position with a
crime or problem ‖ 범죄나 문제에 대해
담당자에게 돕겠다고 제의하다. 나서다.
자원하다: *Several people came forward
with information about the robbery.* 여러
사람들이 강도 사건에 대한 정보를 주겠다
고 나섰다.
come from *phr v* [T] **1** to have been
born in a particular place ‖ 특정 장소에
서 태어나다. … 의 출신이다. 태생이다:
"Where do you come from?" "Texas."
"어디 출신이니?" "텍사스." **2** to have
first existed, been made, or produced in
a particular place, thing, or time ‖ 특정
한 장소[사물, 시간]에 처음으로 존재하다
[만들어지다, 생산되다]. … 에서 기원[유
래]하다. (… 의)산물이다: *Milk comes
from cows.* 우유는 젖소에서 만들어진다.
*/ The lines she read come from a
Dickens novel.* 그녀가 읽은 구절은 디킨
스 소설에서 따온 것이다. **3** if a sound
comes from a place, it begins there ‖ 소
리가 어떤 장소에서 시작하다. … 에서 나
다: *I heard a weird sound coming from
the closet.* 나는 벽장에서 나는 이상 야릇
한 소리를 들었다.
come in *phr v* **1** [I] to arrive or be
received ‖ 도착하거나 받다: *Reports
were coming in from Mexico about a
huge earthquake.* 큰 지진에 대한 보도가
멕시코에서 들어오고 있었다. **2** to enter a
room or house ‖ 방이나 집에 들어가다: *I
recognized him when he came in.* 그가
들어왔을 때 나는 그를 알아봤다. */ Please
come in and take a seat.* 들어와서 앉으
세요. **3 come in first/second etc.** to
finish first, second etc. in a race or
competition ‖ 경주나 시합에서 첫 번째나
두 번째로 끝마치다. 1등/2등으로 들어오
다: *Trey came in second in the sack
race.* 트레이는 자루 경주에서 2등으로 골
인했다. **4** to become fashionable or
popular ‖ 유행하거나 인기를 얻다:
Platform shoes came back in (=were
popular again) *in the 1990s.* 통굽구두가
1990년대에 다시 유행했다. —opposite
go out (GO¹) **5** when the TIDE comes in,
it rises ‖ 조수가 높아지다. 밀물이 되다 —
opposite **go out** (GO¹)
come into sth *phr v* [T] **1** to begin to be
in a particular state or position ‖ 특정한
상태나 위치에 있기 시작하다. … 이 되다.
… 에 이르다: *As we turned the corner,*

the town came into view. 우리가 모퉁이를 돌았을 때 그 읍내가 눈에 들어왔다. / *The new law comes into effect tomorrow.* 그 새 법은 내일 발효한다. **2 come into money** to receive money because someone has died and given it to you ‖ 누군가가 죽어서 자신에게 주어지는 돈을 받다. …을 상속하다

come of sth *phr v* [T] **1** to result from ‖ (결과로서)생기다. …에 기인하다: *What good can come of getting so angry?* 그렇게 화내는 것이 무슨 도움이 되겠는가? **2 come of age** to become a particular age, usually 18 or 21, when you are considered legally old enough to be responsible for your actions ‖ 행동에 책임을 질 수 있는 법적인 나이로 여겨지는 보통 18세나 21세의 특정한 나이가 되다. 성년이 되다

come off *phr v* **1** [I, T **come off** sth] to no longer be on something, connected to it, or fastened to it ‖ 더 이상 어떤 것에 있지[연결되지, 묶여 있지] 않다. 떨어지다. 빠지다. 벗겨지다: *A button came off my coat yesterday.* 단추 하나가 어제 내 외투에서 떨어졌다. / *Ink had come off onto her hands.* 그녀 손에 묻은 잉크가 빠졌다. **2** [I] to happen in a particular way ‖ 특정한 방식으로 일어나다. 행해지다: *The wedding came off as planned.* 결혼식은 계획했던 대로 치러졌다. **3 Come off it!** SPOKEN said when you think someone is being stupid or unreasonable ‖ 사람이 어리석거나 이치에 맞지 않는다고 생각할 때에 쓰여. 바보 같은 소리 마라!: *Oh, come off it! You're acting like a child.* 바보 같은 소리 마라! 왜 어린 아이처럼 구는 거야.

come on *phr v* [I] **1** if a light or machine comes on, it starts working ‖ 전등이나 기계가 작동하기 시작하다. 켜지다: *The lights suddenly came on in the theater.* 극장에 전등이 갑자기 켜졌다. **2** if a television or radio program comes on, it starts ‖ 텔레비전이나 라디오 프로그램이 시작되다. 방송이 시작되다: *What time does the show come on?* 그 쇼는 몇 시에 시작하니? **3** if an illness comes on, you start to have it ‖ 병들기 시작하다

SPOKEN PHRASES

come on! **a)** used in order to tell someone to hurry, or to come with you ‖ 남에게 서두르라고 하거나 자신을 따르라고 말하는 데에 쓰여. 서둘러. 빨리. 이리와: *Come on, Sam! We have to go now.* 빨리 해, 샘! 우리는 지금 가야 해. / *Come on. I'll show you where*

it is. 이리 와, 그것이 어디에 있는지 가르쳐 줄게. **b)** said in order to encourage someone to do something ‖ 남에게 무엇을 하라고 격려하는 데에 쓰여. 어서. 기운을 내: *Come on, it's not that hard.* 어서 해봐, 그것은 그다지 어렵지 않아. **c)** used in order to say that you do not believe what someone has just said ‖ 남이 방금 한 말을 믿을 수 없을 때에 쓰여. 제발. 어이없군: *Oh, come on, don't lie to me!* 오, 제발 나에게 거짓말하지 마라!

come on to sb *phr v* [T] INFORMAL to do or say something that makes it clear that you are sexually interested in someone ‖ 누구에게 성적으로 관심 있다는 것을 명백하게 하는 행동이나 말을 하다. …에게 추파를 던지다[추근대다]

come out *phr v* [I]
1 ▶BECOME KNOWN 알려지다◀ to become known, after being hidden ‖ 숨겨져 있던 이후에 알려지다. 퍼지다: *The news came out that the Mayor was very sick.* 시장이 매우 아프다는 뉴스가 흘러 나왔다.

2 ▶TV/RADIO 텔레비전/라디오◀ if something you say comes out in a particular way, you say it in that way or it is understood by someone in that way ‖ 무엇을 특정한 방식으로 말하다, 또는 특정한 방식으로 남에게 이해되다. …으로 드러나다[이해되다]: *When I try to explain, it comes out wrong, and she gets mad.* 내가 설명하려 하자 그것이 잘못 이해되어 그녀는 화를 냈다.

3 ▶SAY PUBLICLY 공개적으로 말하다◀ to say something publicly or directly ‖ 무엇을 공개적으로, 또는 직접적으로 말하다. 생각[태도]을 밝히다: *Senator Peters has come out against abortion.* 피터스 상원의원은 낙태에 반대 의사를 밝혔다. / *Why don't you just come out and say what you think?* 당신이 생각하는 바를 밝혀서 말하는 것이 어떻습니까?

4 ▶SELL 팔다◀ to begin to be sold ‖ 팔리기 시작하다. 출시되다. 출판되다: *When does his new book come out?* 그의 신간 서적이 언제 나옵니까?

5 ▶DIRT 때◀ if dirt or a mark comes out of cloth, it can be washed out ‖ 때나 얼룩이 씻겨 나가다. 지워지다

6 come out well/badly/ahead etc. to finish an action or process in a particular way ‖ 행동이나 과정을 특정한 방식으로 끝마치다. 잘/나쁘게/미리 나오다: *I can never get cakes to come out right.* 제대로 된 케이크를 나는 단 한 번

도 만들지 못 한다.

7 ▶ PHOTOGRAPH 사 진 ◀ if a photograph comes out, it looks the way it is supposed to ‖ 사진이 예상했던 대로 나오다. 사진이 …하게 나오다

8 ▶SUN/MOON 태양/달◀ when the sun, moon, or stars come out, they appear in the sky ‖ 태양[달, 별]이 하늘 에 모습을 드러내다. 나오다. 뜨다

come out with sth *phr v* [T] to say something, especially in a way that is not expected ‖ 특히 예기치 않게 말하다. (느닷없이)말하다: *Tanya came out with a really stupid remark.* 타냐는 불쑥 정말 로 어리석은 말을 했다.

come over *v* **1** [I] to visit someone ‖ 남을 방문하다: *Can I come over and see the kitten tonight?* 오늘 밤에 방문해 서 새끼 고양이를 볼 수 있을까요? **2** [T **come over** sb] if an emotion or feeling comes over someone, s/he begins to feel it ‖ 사람이 감정이나 느낌을 느끼기 시작 하다. 감정이 엄습하다: *A wave of sleepiness came over her.* 밀려오는 졸음 이 그녀를 엄습했다.

come through sth *phr v* [T] to continue to live, exist, be strong, or succeed after a difficult or dangerous time ‖ 어렵거나 위험한 시기 후에 계속해 서 살다[존재하다, 강해지다, 성공하다]. 이겨내다. 극복하다: *Their house came through the storm without much damage.* 그들의 집은 큰 피해 없이 폭풍 우를 이겨냈다.

come to *phr v* **1 come to do** sth to begin to think or feel a particular way after knowing someone or doing something a long time ‖ 누군가를 알고 난 후 또는 오랫동안 무엇을 실행한 후 특 정한 방식을 생각하거나 느끼기 시작하다. …하게 되다. …하기 시작하다: *Gabby was coming to hate all the rules at camp.* 개비는 캠프장의 모든 규칙을 싫어 하게 되었다. **2 come to** sb if an idea or memory comes to you, you suddenly realize or remember it ‖ 생각이나 기억이 갑자기 떠오르거나 기억나다: *Later that afternoon, the answer came to him.* 그 날 오후 늦게, 그 대답이 그에게 떠올랐다. **3 come to $20/$3** etc. to add up to a total of $20, $3 etc. ‖ 다 합해서 총액이 $20, $3 등이 되다: *That comes to $24.67, ma'am.* 사모님, 총액은 24달러 67센트입니다. **4 when it comes to** sth relating to a particular subject ‖ 특정한 주제와 관련해서. …에 대해서[관해서]라 면: *When it comes to fixing computers I know nothing.* 컴퓨터 수리에 관한 것이

라면 나는 아무것도 모른다. **5** [I] to become conscious again after having been unconscious ‖ 의식을 잃었다가 다시 의식이 있게 되다. 의식을 되찾다. 정신이 들다

come under sth *phr v* [T] **1 come under attack/fire/pressure** etc. to experience something unpleasant such as an attack, criticism etc. ‖ 공격·비판 등의 불쾌한 일을 경험하다. 공격/비난/ 압박 받다: *The future of the orchestra has come under threat.* 그 오케스트라의 앞날은 위협받아 왔다. **2** to be controlled or influenced by something such as a set of rules ‖ 일련의 규칙 등에 지배받거나 영 향받다: *All doctors come under the same rules of professional conduct.* 모든 의사는 동일한 직업 윤리 강령에 구속 받 는다.

come up *phr v* [I] **1** to be mentioned or suggested ‖ 언급되거나 제시되다. 화제에 오르다. 상정되다: *The subject didn't come up at the meeting.* 그 주제는 그 모 임에서 언급되지 않았다. **2 be coming up** to be happening soon ‖ 곧 일어날 것 이다. 다가오다: *Isn't your anniversary coming up?* 네 기념일이 곧 다가오니? **3** when the sun or moon comes up, it rises ‖ 태양이나 달이 떠오르다 **4** if a problem comes up, it suddenly happens ‖ 문제가 갑자기 발생하다: *Something's come up, so I won't be able to go with you Thursday.* 갑자기 일이 생겨서 목요 일에 너와 함께 갈 수 없을 거야

come up against sb/sth *phr v* [T] to have to deal with difficult problems or people ‖ 어려운 문제나 사람을 해결하거 나 다루어야 하다. 맞서다. 대항하다: *The novel's about a man who comes up against racism in a Midwest town.* 그 소설은 한 미국 중서부 도시의 인종 차별 주의에 맞선 한 남자에 관한 이야기이다.

come upon sb/sth *phr v* [T] LITERARY to find or discover something by chance ‖ 우연히 무엇을 찾거나 발견하다

come up with sth *phr v* [T] **1** to think of an idea, plan, reply etc ‖ 생각·계획 ·대답 등을 생각해 내다: *I couldn't come up with a good excuse for being late.* 나 는 지각한 것에 대한 좋은 핑계를 생각해 내지 못했다. **2** to be able to produce a particular amount of money ‖ 특정한 액 수의 돈을 만들 수 있다. 돈을 마련하다: *I'll never be able to come up with $2000!* 나는 절대로 2,000달러를 마련할 수 없을 거야!

come·back /ˈkʌmbæk/ *n* **1 make/stage a comeback** a) to become powerful, popular, or famous again after being unknown for a long time ‖ 오랫동안 무명으로 지낸 후에 다시 세력을 얻다[인기를 얻다, 유명해지다]. 복귀하다. 재기하다. 인기를 만회하다: *No one knew then that Tina Turner would make such a big comeback.* 티나 터너가 그렇게 크게 재기하리라고는 그 당시 어느 누구도 몰랐다. **b)** to play better in a sports competition after playing badly ‖ 스포츠 시합에서 경기를 잘 못하다가 다시 나아지다. 경기를 만회하다: *The Knicks made a remarkable comeback in the fourth quarter.* 닉스 팀은 4쿼터에서 상당한 만회를 했다. **2** a quick reply that is smart or funny ‖ 영특하거나 재미있는 재빠른 대답. 응답. 응수: *I can never think of a good comeback when I need one.* 나는 필요한 순간에 적당한 응답을 생각하지 못 한다.

co·me·di·an /kəˈmidiən/, **come-dienne** /kəˌmidiˈɛn/ *n* **1** a man or woman whose job is to tell jokes and make people laugh ‖ 농담을 해서 사람들을 웃기는 남자 또는 여자 직업인. 코미디언 **2** INFORMAL someone who is amusing ‖ 남을 즐겁게 하는 사람. 익살꾼: *Dan was always trying to be the class comedian.* 댄은 항상 반 아이들을 웃기려고 애썼다.

come·down /ˈkʌmdaʊn/ *n* INFORMAL a situation that is not as good as one that you were in before ‖ 전에 있었던 상황만큼 좋지 않은 상황. 몰락. 전락: *From boxing champion to prison cook – what a comedown!* 권투 챔피언이 교도소 요리사가 되다니, 엄청난 전락이군!

com·e·dy /ˈkɑmədi/ *n* **1** [C, U] a funny movie, play etc. that makes people laugh ‖ 사람을 웃기는 재미있는 영화·연극 등. 코미디. 희극: *a new Jim Carey comedy* 짐 캐리의 새로운 코미디 영화. **2** [U] the funny quality of something that makes you laugh ‖ 남을 웃기는 것의 재미있는 특성. 희극적인 요소

come-on /ˈkʌmɑn/ *n* INFORMAL **1** something that someone does to try to make someone else sexually interested in him/her ‖ 다른 사람에게 성적으로 관심을 갖게 하려는 것. 유혹하는 것. 섹스 어필: *I know a come-on when I see one.* 나는 사람을 보면 성적 매력을 잘 간파한다. **2** an attempt to get people to buy something using an advertisement ‖ 광고를 이용해 물건을 사게 하려는 시도: *We'll give you 20% off everything, and that's not a come-on!* 모든 품목을 20% 할인해 드립니다. 실망하지 않을 겁니다!

com·et /ˈkɑmɪt/ *n* an object in the sky like a very bright ball with a tail, that moves around the sun ‖ 태양 주위를 움직이는, 꼬리 달린 아주 밝은 공 모양의 하늘에 있는 물체. 혜성

come·up·pance /kʌmˈʌpəns/ *n* **get your comeuppance** INFORMAL to be punished or have something bad happen to you because you have done something bad ‖ 나쁜 일을 해서 처벌받거나 자신에게 나쁜 일이 일어나다. 당연한 응보를 받다: *I know he's treated you badly, but he'll get his comeuppance!* 그가 네게 심하게 굴었다는 거 알아, 하지만 그는 응분의 대가를 받게 될 거야.

com·fort¹ /ˈkʌmfət/ *n* **1** [U] a feeling of being physically relaxed and satisfied ‖ 육체적으로 편안하거나 만족한 느낌. 안락: *These chairs are designed for comfort.* 이들 의자는 안락하게 디자인되었다. **2** [U] a way of living in which you have everything you need to be happy ‖ 행복에 필요한 모든 것을 가진 생활 방식. 안락한 생활: *He envied the people living in comfort in those big houses.* 그는 저런 대저택에서 안락하게 사는 사람들을 부러워했다. **3** [U] a feeling of being calm or hopeful after having been worried or sad ‖ 걱정이나 슬픔 뒤의 차분하거나 희망에 찬 느낌. 위안: *He can take comfort from the fact that his family will be with him.* 그는 가족과 함께 있게 된다는 사실로 위안을 삼을 수 있다. **4 (be) a comfort to sb** to help someone feel calm or less worried ‖ 누군가가 진정하거나 덜 걱정하게 돕다. …에게 위안이 되다: *She was a great comfort to me while I was in the hospital.* 내가 병원에 입원해 있는 동안 그녀는 나에게 큰 위안이 되었다. **5 be too close for comfort** something bad that is too close for comfort, worries or upsets you because it is too close in distance or time ‖ 나쁜 일이 거리 또는 시간상으로 너무 근접하여 걱정되거나 당혹스럽다. 아슬아슬하다: *The lion in the safari park got a little too close for my comfort.* 사파리 공원의 그 사자는 나와 너무 가까이 있어 아슬아슬했다. —opposite DISCOMFORT

comfort² *v* [T] to make someone feel less worried by being kind to him/her ‖ 남에게 친절하게 대해서 덜 걱정하게 하다. …을 위로[위안]하다 – **comforting** *adj* – **comfortingly** *adv*

com·fort·a·ble /ˈkʌmftəbəl, ˈkʌmfətəbəl/ *adj* **1** feeling physically relaxed and satisfied ‖ 육체적으로 편안하고 만족감을 느끼는. 안락한. 쾌적한:

Come in and make yourself comfortable. 들어와서 편히 쉬세요. **2** making you feel physically relaxed and satisfied ‖ 육체적으로 편안함·만족감을 느끼게 하는. 안락함[쾌적함]을 주는: *a comfortable sofa* 안락한 소파 **3** not worried about what someone will do or about what will happen ‖ 남이 무엇을 할 것인지 또는 무슨 일이 일어날지에 대해 걱정하지 않는. 마음 편한: *I feel very comfortable with him.* 나는 그와 함께 있으면 아주 마음이 편하다. **4** having enough money to live on without worrying ‖ 걱정 없이 살아갈만큼 충분한 돈이 있는. 풍족한: *We're not rich, but we are comfortable.* 우리는 부자는 아니지만 풍족하다. – **comfortably** *adv* — opposite UNCOMFORTABLE

com·fort·er /ˈkʌmfətəʳ/ *n* a thick cover for a bed ‖ 침대용 두꺼운 덮개

com·fy /ˈkʌmfi/ *adj* SPOKEN ➪ COMFORTABLE

com·ic¹ /ˈkɑmɪk/ *adj* funny or amusing ‖ 우습거나 재미있는: *a comic moment* (=short funny situation) 웃기는 순간 / *At least Marlene was there to give us comic relief.* (=make us laugh in a serious situation) 그래도 그곳에 말린이 있어서 우리는 웃으며 긴장을 풀었다.

comic² *n* **1** ➪ COMEDIAN **2** ➪ COMIC BOOK —see also COMICS

com·i·cal /ˈkɑmɪkəl/ *adj* funny, especially in a strange or unexpected way ‖ 특히 이상하거나 예기치 않은 방법으로 웃기는. 익살맞은. 우스운: *men wearing comical hats* 우스꽝스러운 모자를 쓰고 있는 남자들 – **comically** *adv*

comic book /ˈ.. ./ *n* a magazine that tells a story using pictures that are drawn like COMIC STRIPs ‖ 연재 만화처럼 그려진 그림을 사용해 이야기를 전하는 잡지. 만화 잡지[책]

com·ics /ˈkɑmɪks/ *n* [plural] the part of a newspaper that has COMIC STRIPs ‖ 신문의 연재 만화가 있는 부분. 연재 만화 (란)

comic strip /ˈ.. ./ *n* a series of pictures that are drawn that tell a short funny story ‖ 짧고 재미있는 이야기를 전하는, 일련의 그려진 그림. 연재 만화

com·ing¹ /ˈkʌmɪŋ/ *n* **1 the coming of** the time when someone or something arrives or begins ‖ 사람이나 사물이 도착하거나 시작하는 때. 도착. 도래: *With the coming of the railroad, the population in the west grew quickly.* 철도의 출현으로 서부의 인구가 급격히 증가했다. **2 comings and goings** the things that

people do during a particular time or in a particular place ‖ 특정한 시간 동안 또는 장소에서 사람들이 하는 일. 행동. 동정: *The camera records the comings and goings of the bank's customers.* 그 카메라는 은행 고객들의 동정을 녹화한다.

coming² *adj* happening soon ‖ 곧 일어나는. 다가오는: *preparing for the coming winter* 다가올 겨울을 대비하는 —see also UP-AND-COMING

com·ma /ˈkɑmə/ *n* the mark (,) used in writing to show a short pause ‖ 짧은 휴지(休止)를 나타내기 위해 글에 쓰는 기호. 콤마. 쉼표

com·mand¹ /kəˈmænd/ *n* **1** an order that must be obeyed ‖ 복종해야 하는 명령. 지령. 지시: *The driver did not respond to a command to stop.* 그 운전자는 정지하라는 지시를 따르지 않았다. **2** [U] the total control of a group of people or a situation ‖ 일단의 사람이나 상황에 대한 완전한 통제. 지휘. 통솔: *How many officers are under your command?* 몇 명의 장교가 당신의 지휘 하에 있습니까? / *Who is in command here?* 누가 여기를 지휘하고 있나요? **3 have a command of sth** to have knowledge of something, especially a language, or the ability to use something ‖ 특히 언어에 대한 지식, 또는 어떤 것을 사용할 능력을 가지다. …을 자유 자재로 사용하다: *Fukiko has a good command of English.* 후키코는 영어가 유창하다. **4** an instruction to a computer to do something ‖ 컴퓨터에 무엇을 하라는 지시. 명령(어) **5 be in command of yourself** to be able to control your emotions and thoughts ‖ 감정·생각을 통제할 수 있다. 자신을 통제하다

command² *v* **1** [I, T] to tell someone to do something, especially if you are a king, military leader etc. ‖ 특히 왕·군 지휘관 등이 남에게 무엇을 하라고 말하다. 명령하다. 지시하다: *General Patton commanded the tank crews to attack.* 패튼 장군은 전차대원들에게 공격하라고 명령했다. —see usage note at ORDER² **2** [T] to get attention, respect etc. because you are important or popular ‖ 중요하거나 인기가 있어서 관심을 끌거나 존경을 받다: *He commands one of the highest fees in Hollywood.* 그는 할리우드에서 가장 높은 보수를 받는 사람 중의 한 명으로 이름이 높다.

com·man·dant /ˈkɑmənˌdɑnt/ *n* the chief officer in charge of a military organization ‖ 군 조직을 책임지는 최고 장교. 사령관. 지휘관

com·man·deer /ˌkamən'dɪr/ v [T] to take someone else's property for your own use ‖ 자신이 사용하려고 남의 재산을 가져가다. 탈취하다. 강제로 빼앗다: *The hotel was commandeered for use as a war hospital.* 그 호텔은 징발되어 군 병원으로 사용되었다.

com·mand·er, Commander /kə'mændɚ/ n an officer who has a middle rank in the Navy ‖ 해군에서 중간 계급을 가진 장교. 해군 중령

com·mand·ing /kə'mændɪŋ/ adj 1 having the authority or confidence to give orders ‖ 명령하는 권위나 확신을 가진. 지휘하는. 위엄 있는: *a commanding officer* 부대 지휘관 / *a commanding voice* 위압적인 목소리 2 from much higher or much farther ahead than is usual ‖ 보통보다 훨씬 더 높은 곳이나 훨씬 멀리 앞선 곳에서. 전망이 좋은. 압도적인: *a commanding view* 전망이 좋은 경치 / *a commanding lead in the polls* 여론 조사에서의 압도적인 우세

com·mand·ment /kə'mændmənt/ n **the Ten Commandments** a set of rules in the Bible that tell people how they should behave ‖ 사람이 어떻게 행동해야 하는지 가르쳐 주는 성경의 일련의 계율. 십계명

com·man·do /kə'mændoʊ/ n a soldier who is specially trained to make quick attacks into enemy areas ‖ 적진에 기습 공격하도록 특수 훈련된 병사. 특공대원

com·mem·o·rate /kə'mɛmə,reɪt/ v [T] to remember someone or something by a special action, ceremony, object etc. ‖ 특별한 행동·의식·물건 등으로 사람이나 사물을 기억하다. 기념하다: *a plaque commemorating those who died during the war* 전쟁 때 죽은 사람을 기념하는 작고 납작한 패(牌) – **commemoration** /kə,mɛmə'reɪʃən/ n [U] – **commemorative** /kə'mɛmərətɪv/ adj

com·mence /kə'mɛns/ v [I, T] FORMAL to begin or start something ‖ 무엇을 시작하거나 개시하다: *Work should commence on the new building immediately.* 곧 새 건물에서 일이 시작된다.

com·mence·ment /kə'mɛnsmənt/ n 1 FORMAL [C, U] the beginning of something ‖ 어떤 것의 시작. 개시: *the commencement of the trial* 재판의 개시 2 a ceremony at which students who have finished HIGH SCHOOL are given their DIPLOMAs ‖ 고등학교를 졸업한 학생들이 졸업장을 받는 의식. 졸업식

com·mend /kə'mɛnd/ v [T] FORMAL 1

to praise someone or something, especially in public ‖ 특히 대중 앞에서 사람이나 사물을 칭찬하다. 칭송하다: *The three firefighters were commended for their bravery.* 그 세 명의 소방관들은 용감한 행동으로 칭송 받았다. 2 to tell someone that something is good; RECOMMEND ‖ 남에게 어떤 것이 좋다고 말하다. 추천하다; 㳠 recommend

com·mend·a·ble /kə'mɛndəbəl/ adj FORMAL deserving praise ‖ 칭찬할 만한 – **commendably** adv

com·men·da·tion /ˌkamən'deɪʃən/ n FORMAL an honor or prize given to someone for being brave or successful ‖ 용감하거나 성공한 것에 대해 남에게 주어지는 훈장이나 상

com·men·su·rate /kə'mɛnsərɪt, -ʃərɪt/ adj FORMAL matching something else in size, quality, or length of time ‖ 크기[질·시간의 길이]에서 다른 것에 필적하는. (…과) 같은[동등한]. 상응하는: *a salary commensurate with your experience* 당신의 경험에 상응하는 봉급

com·ment[1] /'kamɛnt/ n [C, U] 1 an opinion that you give about someone or something ‖ 사람이나 사물에 대해 내놓는 의견. 논평. 비평: *Do you want to make any comments about the proposal?* 그 제안에 대해 논평할 말이 있습니까? 2 **no comment** SPOKEN said when you do not want to answer a question, especially in public ‖ 특히 대중들 앞에서 질문에 대답하기를 원하지 않을 때에 쓰여. 할 말 없습니다

comment[2] v [I, T] to give an opinion about someone or something ‖ 사람이나 사물에 대한 의견을 내놓다. 논평[비평]하다: *The police have refused to comment on the investigation until it is completed.* 경찰은 수사가 끝날 때까지 논평을 거부했다.

com·men·tar·y /'kamən,tɛri/ n 1 a description of an event that is broadcast on the television or radio, or written in a newspaper ‖ 텔레비전이나 라디오에 방송되거나 신문에 실린 행사에 대한 설명. 실황 방송. 시사 해설: *an exciting commentary on the game* 시합의 흥미진진한 실황 방송 2 [C, U] a book or article that explains or discusses something, or the explanation itself ‖ 어떤 것을 설명하거나 논한 책이나 기사, 또는 그 설명 자체. 주석서. 해설: *The article was an interesting commentary on life in a Chinese village.* 그 기사는 중국인 마을의 생활에 관한 흥미 있는 해설이었다. 3 **be a sad/tragic etc. commentary** to be a sign or example of how bad something is ‖ 어떤 것이 얼마나 나쁜지에 대한 징조나 본보기가 되다. 슬픈/비극적인 징후[예]이다: *It's a sad commentary on our culture that we need constant entertainment.* 우리가 끊임없이 오락을 필요로 한다는 것은 우리 문화의 슬픈 징후이다.

com·men·tate /'kɑmən,teɪt/ v [I] to describe an event as it is being broadcast on television or radio ‖ 텔레비전이나 라디오로 방송되고 있는 행사를 설명하다. 실황 방송[해설]을 하다

com·men·ta·tor /'kɑmən,teɪtɚ/ n someone whose job is to COMMENTATE ‖ 방송에서 논평하는 직업인. 실황 방송 아나운서. 해설자

com·merce /'kɑmɚs/ n [U] the buying and selling of goods and services ‖ 재화와 용역을 사고 팔기. 상업. 무역: *interstate commerce* (=among US states) 주간(州間) 무역

com·mer·cial¹ /kə'mɚʃəl/ adj 1 relating to business and the buying and selling of things ‖ 사업과 물건의 매매와 관련된. 상업(상)의: *commercial activity* 상업 활동 2 relating to making money or a profit ‖ 돈을 벌거나 이익을 내는 것과 관련된. 영리(본위)의. 돈벌이 위주의: *a movie that was a huge commercial success* 상업적으로 대단히 성공한 영화 – **commercially** adv

commercial² n an advertisement on television or radio ‖ 텔레비전이나 라디오상의 광고. 상업 광고: *There are too many commercials on TV these days.* 요즈음은 텔레비전에 광고가 너무 많다.

commercial bank /,.. '. / n TECHNICAL the type of bank that most people use, that provides services to both customers and businesses ‖ 고객과 기업 양쪽 모두에게 서비스를 제공하는, 대다수 사람들이 이용하는 은행. 상업[시중] 은행

com·mer·cia·li·sm /kə'mɚʃə,lɪzəm/ n [U] the practice of being more concerned with making money than with the quality of what you sell ‖ 판매하는 물건의 질보다 돈을 버는 데 더 관심이 있는 행위. 영리[상업]주의

com·mer·cial·ize /kə'mɚʃə,laɪz/ v [T] to make money or profits, often in a way that people disapprove of ‖ 종종 사람들이 인정하지 않는 방법으로 돈을 벌거나 이익을 내다. 상업화[영리화]하다: *Christmas is getting so commercialized!* 크리스마스가 너무 상업화되고 있어! – **commercialization** /kə,mɚʃələ'zeɪʃən/

n [U]

com·mie /'kɑmi/ n INFORMAL ⇨ COMMUNIST

com·mis·e·rate /kə'mɪzə,reɪt/ v [I] FORMAL to express your sympathy for someone who is unhappy about something ‖ 어떤 일로 불행한 사람에게 동정을 표하다. 애처로워하다 – **commiseration** /kə,mɪzə'reɪʃən/ n [C, U]

com·mis·sion¹ /kə'mɪʃən/ n 1 [C, U] an amount of money paid to someone for selling something ‖ 어떤 것을 판매한 사람에게 주는 금액. 커미션. 수수료: *Salespeople earn a 30% commission on/for each new car.* 판매원은 새 차 한 대당 30%의 수수료를 번다. 2 a group of people who have been given the official job of finding out about something or controlling something ‖ 공식적으로 어떤 것을 알아내거나 조정하는 업무를 부여받은 사람들의 집합체. 위원회: *A commission is being set up to look at the welfare system.* 복지 제도를 검토하기 위한 위원회가 설립되고 있는 중이다. 3 a piece of work that someone, especially an artist or a musician, is asked to do ‖ 특히 미술가나 음악가가 해달라고 부탁한 작품. 의뢰[주문](품): *a commission for a new sculpture* 새 조각상 주문 4 **out of commission** a) not working correctly, or not able to be used ‖ 제대로 작동하지 않거나 사용할 수 없는. 고장나서. 사용 불능의: *I'm afraid the toilet's out of commission until the plumber gets here.* 배관공이 이곳에 올 때까지 화장실을 사용할 수 없을 것 같아요. b) INFORMAL ill or injured ‖ 아프거나 다친 5 the official authority to be an officer in the military ‖ 군대에서 장교가 되는 공식적인 승인. 장교 임관 6 **the commission of a crime/felony etc.** FORMAL the act of doing something illegal ‖ 불법적인 일을 하는 행위. 범죄/중죄 등을 범함

commission² v [T] to ask someone, especially an artist or musician, to do a piece of work for you ‖ 어떤 사람, 특히 미술가나 음악가에게 작품을 해달라고 부탁하다. …을 의뢰[주문]하다: *John Williams has been commissioned to write another movie score.* 존 윌리엄스는 또 다른 영화 음악을 작곡해 달라는 의뢰를 받았다.

com·mis·sion·er /kə'mɪʃənɚ/ n someone who is officially in charge of a police department, sports organization etc. ‖ 경찰서·스포츠 기구 등을 공식적으로 책임지고 있는 사람. 경찰서장[청장]

커미셔너. 최고 책임자

com·mit /kə'mɪt/ v **-tted, -tting** [T] **1** to use all of the time and energy that you can in order to achieve something ‖ 무언가를 성취하기 위해 가능한 시간·정력을 모두 쓰다. 전념[헌신]하다: *I don't think she's ready to commit herself to marriage.* 나는 그녀가 결혼 생활을 할 준비가 되어 있다고 생각하지 않아. / *His father's whole life was committed to education.* 그의 아버지는 평생을 교육에 헌신하셨다. **2** to promise to use money, time, people etc. for a particular purpose ‖ 돈·시간·사람 등을 특정한 목적에 사용할 것을 약속하다: *They are unwilling to commit that many soldiers to the UN.* 그들은 그렇게 많은 병사들을 유엔에 보내는 것을 내켜 하지 않는다. / *The city has committed itself to cleaning up the environment.* 그 도시는 환경을 정화하겠다고 약속했다. **3** to do something wrong or illegal ‖ 옳지 않거나 불법적인 일을 저지르다: *Stolen cars are used by criminals to commit other crimes.* 다른 범죄를 저지르기 위해 범죄자들은 도난차량을 사용한다.

com·mit·ment /kə'mɪtmənt/ n **1** [C, U] a promise to do something or behave in a particular way ‖ 어떤 것을 하거나 특정한 방식으로 행동하겠다는 약속. 서약. 공약: *Volunteers must be able to make a commitment of four hours a week.* 자원 봉사자는 일주일에 4시간을 제공하겠다고 약속할 수 있어야 한다. / *a store's commitment to providing quality service* 양질의 서비스를 제공하겠다는 상점의 약속 **2** [U] the hard work and loyalty that someone gives to an organization, activity, or person ‖ 누군가가 조직[활동, 사람]에게 바치는 많은 수고와 충성. 헌신: *I'm impressed with Glen's deep commitment to coaching the kids.* 아이들을 헌신적으로 가르치는 글렌에게 나는 감명을 받았다. **3** [C, U] the use of money, time, people etc. for a particular purpose ‖ 특정한 목적을 위한 돈·시간·사람 등의 이용: *a large commitment of resources to research and development* 자원의 연구·개발에의 대규모 이용

com·mit·ted /kə'mɪtɪd/ adj willing to work very hard at something ‖ 무언가에 매우 열심히 일하고자 하는. 헌신적인: *a committed teacher* 헌신적인 교사

com·mit·tee /kə'mɪti/ n a group of people chosen to do a particular job, make decisions etc. ‖ 특정한 일을 하거나 결정 등을 하기 위해 뽑힌 일단의 사람들.

위원회: *I'm on the finance committee.* 나는 재무 위원회 소속이다.

com·mod·i·ty /kə'mɑdəti/ n TECHNICAL a product that is bought and sold ‖ 사거나 파는 제품. 상품: *agricultural commodities* 농산품

com·mo·dore, Commodore /'kɑmə,dɔr/ n an officer who has a high rank in the Navy ‖ 해군에서 높은 계급의 장교. 해군 준장

com·mon¹ /'kɑmən/ adj **1** existing in large numbers ‖ 많은 수효로 존재하는. 흔한: *Foxes are very common around here.* 이 주변에는 여우가 아주 흔하다. **2** happening often and to many people, or in many places ‖ 다수의 사람들에게 또는 여러 장소에서 자주 일어나는. 흔히 있는: *Heart disease is common among smokers.* 심장병은 흡연자들 사이에 빈번하다. / *It's common for new fathers to feel jealous of their babies.* 초보 아빠가 자기 아이에게 질투를 느끼는 일은 흔히 있는 일이다. ✗DON'T SAY "It is common that."✗ "It is common that."이라고는 하지 않는다. **3** belonging to, or shared by two or more people or things ‖ 둘 이상의 사람이나 사물에 속하거나 공유된. 공통의: *a common goal* 공통 목표 / *problems that are common to all big cities* 모든 대도시의 공통된 문제 / *It's common knowledge* (=something everyone knows) *that Sam's an alcoholic.* 샘이 알코올 중독자라는 것은 모든 사람이 다 아는 사실이다. **4 the common good** what is best for everyone in a society ‖ 사회의 모든 사람에게 최선의 것. 공익: *They truly believed they were acting for the common good.* 그들은 공익을 위해 활동하고 있다고 진짜로 믿었다. **5 common ground** facts, opinions, and beliefs that a group of people can agree on, in a situation in which they are arguing about something ‖ 어떤 것에 대해 논쟁하는 상황에서 한 집단의 사람들이 동의한 사실·의견·신념. 공통점. 공통 기반: *Let's see if we can establish some common ground.* 우리가 어떤 공통의 기반을 마련할 수 있는지 알아보자. **6** ordinary and not special in any way ‖ 평범하여 어떤 면에서도 특별하지 않은. 평범한. 보통의: *They can put a man on the moon, but they can't cure the common cold.* 우리는 달에 인간을 보낼 수 있으면서도 그 흔한 감기는 치유하지 못한다.

common² n **1 have sth in common (with sb)** to have the same qualities and interests as another person or group ‖ 다른 사람이나 집단과 같은 특성

과 흥미를 갖다. …과 공통점이 있다: *Terry and I have a lot in common.* 테리와 나는 공통점이 많이 있다. **2 a word meaning a public park, used mostly in names** ‖ 대개 이름으로 사용되는, 공원을 뜻하는 단어: *walking on Boston Common* 보스톤 공원을 걷기

com·mon-law /ˈ.. ˌ./ *adj* **common-law marriage/husband/wife a relationship that is considered in law to be a marriage because the man and woman have lived together a long time** ‖ 남녀가 오랫동안 함께 살아서 법적으로 부부로 간주되는 관계. 내연[사실혼] 관계/내연의 남편/내연의 아내

com·mon·ly /ˈkɑmənli/ *adv* **usually, or by most people** ‖ 보통, 또는 대부분의 사람들에 의해. 흔히. 일반적으로: *a bird commonly found in Malaysia* 말레이시아에서 흔히 발견되는 새 / *the most commonly used computer* 가장 흔히 사용되는 컴퓨터

com·mon·place /ˈkɑmənˌpleɪs/ *adj* **very common or ordinary** ‖ 매우 흔하거나 일상적인. 흔해 빠진. 보통인: *Expensive foreign cars are commonplace in this Chicago suburb.* 이곳 시카고 교외에서는 비싼 외제차가 매우 흔하다.

common sense /ˌ.. ˈ./ *n* [U] **the ability to behave in a sensible way and make practical decisions** ‖ 분별 있게 행동하고 실용적인 결정을 내리는 능력. 상식. 양식: *Use your common sense for once!* 한 번이라도 상식적으로 생각해라!

com·mon·wealth /ˈkɑmənˌwɛlθ/ *n* FORMAL **a group of countries that are related politically or economically, for example the group of countries that have a strong relationship with Great Britain** ‖ 정치적으로나 경제적으로 관련된 나라의 집단으로 예를 들면 영국과 긴밀한 관계가 있는 나라의 집단. 연방

com·mo·tion /kəˈmoʊʃən/ *n* [singular, U] **sudden noisy activity or arguing** ‖ 갑작스런 시끄러운 행동이나 논쟁. 소동. 소란: *Hicks caused a commotion by going next door and demanding to use the phone.* 힉스는 옆집에 가서 전화를 이용하자면서 소란을 피웠다.

com·mu·nal /kəˈmyunl/ *adj* **shared by a group of people** ‖ 일단의 사람들이 공유하는. 공동의: *a communal bathroom* 공동 화장실

com·mune¹ /ˈkɑmyun/ *n* **a group of people who live and work together and share their possessions** ‖ 함께 거주하고 일하며 소유물을 공유하는 일단의 사람들.

생활 공동체: *Kyle belonged to a commune in the 1960s.* 카일은 1960년대에 공동체 생활을 했다.

com·mune² /kəˈmyun/ *v* [I] **to try to communicate without using words** ‖ 말을 사용하지 않고 의사 소통하려 하다. 마음이 통하다. 교감하다: *I often walk on the beach to commune with nature.* 나는 종종 자연과 교감하기 위해 바닷가를 거닌다.

com·mu·ni·ca·ble /kəˈmyunɪkəbəl/ *adj* **a communicable disease is infectious** ‖ 병이 전염성인

com·mu·ni·cate /kəˈmyunəˌkeɪt/ *v* **1** [I] **to express your thoughts and feelings so other people understand them** ‖ 다른 사람들이 이해하도록 생각과 감정을 표현하다. 의사 소통하다: *Jack and I just can't communicate any more.* 잭과 나는 더 이상 의사 소통이 안 된다. **2** [I, T] **to exchange information or conversation with other people using words, signs, letters, telephones etc.** ‖ 말·신호·편지·전화 등을 사용하여 다른 사람들과 정보나 대화를 교환하거나 대화를 나누다. 정보를 전달하다. 연락하다: *We've communicated our offer to their director.* 우리는 그들의 이사에게 우리의 제의를 전달했다. / *They managed to communicate with each other by using sign language.* 그들은 서로 수화를 이용해 간신히 의사를 교환했다.

com·mu·ni·ca·tion /kəˌmyunəˈkeɪʃən/ *n* **1** [U] **the process of speaking, writing etc., by which people exchange information** ‖ 사람들이 정보를 교환하는 말하기·쓰기 등의 절차. 의사 소통. 연락. 통신: *The pilot was in constant communication with the control tower.* 그 조종사는 관제탑과 끊임없이 연락을 취하고 있었다. / *Radio and television are important means of communication.* (=ways of sending information somewhere) 라디오와 텔레비전은 중요한 통신 수단이다. **2** [U] **the way people express their thoughts and feelings or share information** ‖ 사람들이 생각과 감정을 표현하거나 정보를 공유하는 방법. 의사 소통: *We have a real communication problem in this family!* (=we do not express our feelings well) 우리 가족은 정말로 (감정을 잘 표현하지 못하는) 의사 소통에 문제가 있다! **3** FORMAL **a letter, message, or telephone call** ‖ 편지, 전언, 전화

com·mu·ni·ca·tions /kəˌmyunəˈkeɪʃənz/ *n* [plural] **1 the various ways of sending and receiving information,**

such as radio, telephone, television etc. ‖ 라디오·전화·텔레비전 등의 정보를 보내고 받는 다양한 방법. 통신 기관[시설]: *global communications satellites/ networks* 세계적인 통신 위성/망 / *The power failure disrupted communications at the airport.* 정전으로 공항의 통신 시설이 두절되었다. **2** the study of using radio, TV, and film to communicate ‖ 의사 소통을 위해 라디오·텔레비전·영화를 이용하는 것에 대한 연구. 통신학. 정보 전달학: *a degree in communications* 정보 전달학 학위

com·mu·ni·ca·tive /kə'myunɪkətɪv, -,keɪtɪv/ *adj* willing or able to talk or give information ‖ 말하려 하거나 할 수 있는 또는 정보를 주고자 하거나 줄 수 있는. 이야기하기 좋아하는. 터놓고 이야기하는: *Customers complained that the sales clerks were not very communicative.* 고객들은 판매원들이 말을 잘 하지 않는다고 불평했다. —opposite UNCOMMUNICATIVE

com·mun·ion /kə'myunyən/ *n* [U] **1** FORMAL a special relationship with someone or something in which you feel that you understand him, her, or it very well ‖ 특정한 사람이나 사물을 아주 잘 이해한다고 느끼는 특별한 관계. 교류. 교감: *Prayer is a form of communion between people and God.* 기도는 사람과 신 사이의 교감의 한 형태이다. **2 Communion** the Christian ceremony in which people eat bread and drink wine as signs of Christ's body and blood ‖ 그리스도의 몸과 피의 상징으로 사람이 빵을 먹고 포도주를 마시는 기독교 의식. 성찬식

com·mu·ni·qué /kə'myunə,keɪ, -,myunə'keɪ/ *n* an official report or announcement ‖ 공식 보도나 발표. 성명서. 코뮈니케

com·mu·nism /'kɑmyə,nɪzəm/ *n* [U] a political system in which the government controls all the production of food and goods and there is no privately owned property ‖ 정부가 식량과 상품의 모든 생산을 통제하며 사유 재산이 없는 정치 제도. 공산주의

com·mu·nist /'kɑmyənɪst/ *n* someone who supports or takes part in COMMUNISM ‖ 공산주의를 지지하거나 참여하는 사람. 공산주의자 – **communist** *adj*

com·mu·ni·ty /kə'myunəti/ *n* **1** the people who live in the same area, town etc., or who have the same interests, religion, race etc. ‖ 같은 지역·도시 등에 사는 사람이나 같은 이해 관계·종교·인종 등을 가진 사람들. 지역 공동체. 지역 사회. …계: *They've done a lot for our*

local communities. 그들은 우리 지역 사회를 위해 많은 일을 했다. / *the Asian community* 아시아 공동체 **2 the community** society and the people in it ‖ 사회와 그 사회 사람들. 대중. 일반 사회: *a plan to get young police officers out into the community* 젊은 경찰관들을 일반 사회로 나가게 하려는 계획

community col·lege /.,… '../ *n* a college that people can go to for two years to learn a skill or prepare for a university ‖ 사람들이 기술을 배우거나 4년제 대학을 준비하기 위해 2년간 다닐 수 있는 단과 대학. 지역 사회 대학

community prop·er·ty /.,… '../ *n* [U] LAW property that is considered to be owned equally by both a husband and wife ‖ 남편과 부인 두 사람이 동등하게 소유하는 것으로 간주되는 재산. 부부 공동 재산

community serv·ice /.,… '../ *n* [U] work that someone does to help other people without being paid, especially as punishment for a crime ‖ 특히 범죄에 대한 처벌로서 대가 없이 다른 사람들을 돕기 위해 하는 일. 사회 봉사 활동

com·mute¹ /kə'myut/ *v* **1** [I] to travel regularly in order to get to work ‖ 직장에 출근하기 위해 규칙적으로 이동하다. 통근하다: *Jerry commutes from Scarsdale to New York every day.* 제리는 스카스데일에서 뉴욕까지 매일 통근한다. / *I commute all the way to St. Louis from here.* 나는 여기에서 멀리 세인트 루이스까지 통근한다. **2** [T] FORMAL to change the punishment given to a criminal to one that is less severe ‖ 범죄자에게 부여한 처벌을 덜 중한 것으로 바꾸다. 감형하다: *Her sentence was commuted from death to life imprisonment.* 그녀에 대한 선고는 사형에서 무기 징역으로 감형되었다.

commute² *n* [C usually singular] the trip made in commuting (COMMUTE) ‖ 통근시의 이동. 통근(거리): *It's a long commute from Monroe to downtown.* 먼로에서 시내까지는 통근 거리가 멀다.

com·mut·er /kə'myutə'/ *n* someone who regularly travels in order to get to work ‖ 직장에 출근하기 위해 규칙적으로 이동하는 사람. 통근자

com·pact¹ /'kɑmpækt, kəm'pækt/ *adj* **1** small, but designed well so that everything fits neatly into the available space ‖ 작지만 잘 설계되어서 모든 것이 필요한 공간 속으로 잘 들어가는. 소형(小型)의: *a compact computer* 소형 컴퓨터 / *a new compact pickup truck* 새로운 소

형 픽업 트럭 **2** fitting closely into a
small space ‖ 작은 공간에 꽉 들어찬. 빽
빽한. 촘촘한: *Look for plants with
healthy leaves and a compact shape.* 건
강한 잎과 촘촘한 모양을 가진 식물을 찾
아라.

com·pact² /ˈkɑmpækt/ *n* **1** a small flat
container with a mirror, containing
powder for a woman's face ‖ 여성의 얼
굴용 분이 담겨 있으며 거울이 달린 작고
납작한 용기. 휴대용 분갑. 콤팩트 **2** a
small car ‖ 소형 자동차 **3** FORMAL an
agreement between two or more people,
countries etc. ‖ 둘 이상의 사람·나라 등
사이의 동의. 협약. 협정

com·pact³ /kəmˈpækt/ *v* [T] to press
something together so that it becomes
smaller or more solid ‖ 물건을 더 작아지
거나 단단해지도록 함께 누르다. 압축하다
– **compacted** *adj*

compact disc /ˌkɑmpækt ˈdɪsk/ *n* ⇨
CD

com·pan·ion /kəmˈpænyən/ *n* **1**
someone whom you spend a lot of time
with, especially someone who is a
friend ‖ 많은 시간을 함께 보내는 사람, 특
히 친구. 벗. 동반자: *He was my only
companion during the war.* 그는 전쟁 기
간 동안 나의 유일한 벗이었다. **2** one of a
pair of things that go together or can be
used together ‖ 함께 붙어 다니거나 사용
하는 한 쌍의 물건 중 하나. 짝[쌍]의 한
쪽: *There used to be a companion to
that ornament, but I broke it.* 그 장신구
의 한 짝이 있었지만, 내가 그것을 깨뜨렸
다. **3** used in the title of books that
explain something about a particular
subject ‖ 특정한 주제에 대한 것을 설명
하는 책 제목에 쓰여. 지침서. 안내서:
The Fisherman's Companion 낚시꾼 안내
서

com·pan·ion·a·ble /kəmˈpænyənəbəl/
adj pleasantly friendly ‖ 기분 좋게 친근
한. 붙임성이 있는. 서글서글한: *They sat
in a companionable silence.* 그들은 정감
어린 침묵 속에 앉아 있었다.

com·pan·ion·ship /kəmˈpænyənˌʃɪp/
n [U] a friendly relationship ‖ 친근한 관
계. 친교. 사림. 교제: *When Stan died, I
missed his companionship the most.* 스
탠이 죽자 나는 그와의 교우를 가장 그리
워했다.

com·pa·ny /ˈkʌmpəni/ *n* **1** an
organization that makes or sells goods
or services ‖ 상품이나 용역을 만들거나
파는 조직. 회사. 상사: *a bus company* 버
스 회사 / *What company do you work
for?* 너는 어느 회사에 근무하니? **2** [U]

the act of being with someone so that
s/he does not feel lonely ‖ 남이 외로움을
느끼지 않게 함께 있음. 동석. 동행: *I
wasn't much company for Aunt
Margaret.* 나는 마가렛 이모[고모]와 많
은 시간을 함께 보내지 못했다. / *Why
don't you come with me? I could use the
company.* 저와 함께 가는 게 어때요? 일
행이 있으면 해서요. / *At least Carol had
the dog to keep her company.* (=to stay
with her) 적어도 캐롤에게는 그녀 곁을
지켜줄 개가 있었다. **3** [U] one or more
guests, or someone who is coming to
see you ‖ 한 사람 이상의 손님이나 자신을
만나러 오는 사람: *We're having
company tonight, so be back home by
five.* 오늘 밤 손님이 오니까 다섯 시까지
집으로 돌아와라. **4** [singular, U] the
group of people that you are friends
with or spend time with ‖ 함께 하는 친구
나 함께 시간을 보내는 일단의 사람들. 친
구. 벗. 일행: *I don't like the company
she keeps.* 나는 그녀가 사귀는 그 친구가
싫다. **5 part company** to no longer
work together or agree with each other
‖ 더 이상 함께 일하지 않거나 서로 부합
하지 않다. 헤어지다. 교제[친교]를 끊다:
*The show's writer and director have
now parted company.* 그 쇼의 작가와 연
출가는 현재 작업을 같이 하지 않는다. **6**
a group of about 120 soldiers who are
usually part of a larger group ‖ 보통 큰
집단의 일부인 약 120명 정도의 군인 집
단. 중대

com·pa·ra·ble /ˈkɑmpərəbəl/ *adj*
FORMAL similar to something else in size,
number, quality etc. ‖ 크기·수·질 등이
다른 것과 비슷한. 유사한. 동등한: *Is the
pay rate comparable to that of other
companies?* 봉급 수준이 다른 회사의 봉
급 수준과 비슷합니까?

comparative¹ /kəmˈpærətɪv/ *adj* **1**
showing what is different and similar
between things of the same kind ‖ 같은
종류의 물건 사이의 차이점·유사점을 보여
주는. 비교의. 비교에 의한: *a comparative study of European languages* 유럽
언어의 비교 연구 **2** measured or judged
when compared with something of the
same kind ‖ 같은 종류의 물건과 비교하여
측정되거나 판단되는. 상대적인. 상당한:
the comparative wealth of Kuwait (=its
wealth compared with the rest of the
world) (세계의 다른 나라와 비교한) 쿠웨
이트의 상대적인 부

comparative² *n* **the comparative**
TECHNICAL in grammar, the form of an
adjective or adverb that shows an

increase in quality, quantity, degree etc. For example, "better" is the comparative of "good" ‖ 문법에서 질·양·정도 등의 증가를 나타내는 형용사나 부사의 형태. 비교급. 예를 들어 "better"는 "good"의 비교급이다. —see study note on page 931

com·par·a·tive·ly /kəmˈpærətɪvli/ *adv* as compared to something else or to a previous state ‖ 다른 것이나 이전의 상태와 비교하여. 비교적. 어느 정도: *The children were comparatively well-behaved today.* 그 아이들은 오늘 비교적 얌전했다.

com·pare[1] /kəmˈpɛr/ *v* [T] **1** to examine or judge two or more things in order to show how they are similar to or different from each other ‖ 얼마나 서로 유사하거나 다른지 보여 주려고 두 가지 이상의 물건을 검사하거나 판단하다. 비교 [대조]하다. 견주다: *I'm healthy compared to most people.* 대부분의 사람들과 비교해서 나는 건강하다. / *Compared with our old house, this one's a lot bigger.* 우리 옛집과 비교하면 이 집은 아주 크다. / *Compare these wines and tell us what you think.* 이들 포도주를 비교하여 당신의 생각을 말해라. **2** to say that something or someone is like someone or something else, or that it is equally good, large etc. ‖ 사물이나 사람이 다른 사람이나 사물과 비슷한 점, 또는 마찬가지로 좋거나 중요한 점 등을 말하다. 비유하다. 비기다: *Tammy has often been compared to Janet Jackson.* 태미는 종종 재닛 잭슨에 비유된다. / *The oranges out here don't compare with* (=are not as good as) *the Florida ones.* 타지의 오렌지는 플로리다산 오렌지와 비교가 안 된다. **3 compare notes (with sb)** INFORMAL to talk with someone in order to find out if his/her experience is the same as yours ‖ 남의 경험이 자신의 것과 같은지 알아보려고 이야기하다. 의견 [인상, 정보]을 교환하다: *She and I both have allergies, and we are always comparing notes.* 그녀와 나는 둘 다 알레르기가 있어서 우리는 항상 의견을 나눈다.

compare[2] *n* **beyond/without compare** LITERARY a quality that is beyond compare is the best of its kind ‖ (품)질면에서 같은 종류 중에 최상의. 비교가 안될 정도로. 비할 데 없이: *a beauty beyond compare* 비할 데 없는 미인

com·par·i·son /kəmˈpærəsən/ *n* **1** [U] the process of comparing two people or things ‖ 두 사람이나 사물을 비교하는 과정. 비교. 견줌: *In comparison with his older brother, he's a much better student.* 그의 형과 비교하면 그는 훨씬 나은 학생이다. / *My last job was so boring that this one seems great by comparison.* 내 지난번 일은 너무 지루했었는데 이번 일은 비교적 괜찮아 보인다. **2** a statement or examination of how similar two things, people etc. are ‖ 두 사물·사람 등이 얼마나 비슷한지에 대한 진술이나 조사. 비교. 대조: *a comparison of crime figures in Chicago and Detroit* 시카고와 디트로이트의 범죄 수치 비교 / *You can't make a comparison between American and Japanese schools – they're too different.* 미국 학교와 일본 학교를 비교할 수는 없는데, 너무나 다르기 때문이다. / *Many writers have tried to draw comparisons* (=show similarities) *between the two presidents.* 많은 작가들이 두 대통령 사이의 유사점을 끌어내려고 했다. **3 there's no comparison** used when you think that someone or something is much better than someone or something else ‖ 사람이나 사물이 다른 사람이나 사물보다 훨씬 더 좋다고 생각할 때 쓰여. 비교할 바 못 되다: *There's just no comparison between canned vegetables and fresh ones.* 통조림한 야채와 신선한 야채는 비교가 되지 않는다.

com·part·ment /kəmˈpɑrtmənt/ *n* a smaller enclosed space inside something larger ‖ 큰 물체 내부에 있는 더 작은 밀폐된 공간. 칸막이. 분실. 작은 방. 간: *a car's glove compartment* 물건을 넣어 두는 자동차의 작은 서랍[칸] / *the luggage compartment on a plane* 비행기의 수화물 칸

com·part·men·tal·ize /kəm.pɑrtˈmɛntəl.aɪz/ *v* [T] to divide things into separate groups; CATEGORIZE ‖ 사물을 분리된 집단으로 나누다. 분류 [구분]하다; 伊 categorize

com·pass /ˈkʌmpəs/ *n* **1** an instrument that shows directions ‖ 방향을 나타내는 도구. 컴퍼스. 나침반: *All I had was a map and a compass.* 내가 가진 것은 지도와 나침반이 전부였다. **2** an instrument with a sharp point, used for drawing circles or measuring distances on maps ‖ 원을 그리거나 지도에서 거리를 측정하는 데 사용되는 끝이 날카로운 도구. 제도용 컴퍼스

compass

com·pas·sion /kəmˈpæʃən/ n [U] a strong feeling of sympathy for someone who is suffering ‖ 고통받고 있는 사람에 대한 강한 연민의 감정. 동정. 측은히 여기는 마음: *She's really upset - can't you show a little compassion?* 그녀는 정말 기분이 엉망이야. 연민의 감정을 조금이라도 보여 줄 수 없니? / *compassion for the poor* 가난한 사람에 대한 연민

com·pas·sion·ate /kəmˈpæʃənɪt/ adj feeling sympathy for people who are suffering ‖ 고통받고 있는 사람에 대해 동정심을 느끼는. 인정 많은. 가엾게 여기는: *a caring compassionate man* 배려 깊고 인정 많은 남자

com·pat·i·ble[1] /kəmˈpætəbəl/ adj **1** able to exist or be used together without causing problems ‖ 문제를 일으키지 않고 함께 존재하거나 사용할 수 있는. 겸용식의. 호환성이 있는: *PC-compatible software* (=able to be used with personal computers) 개인용 컴퓨터와 호환성이 있는 소프트 웨어 / *We wanted a trail that would be compatible with the rest of the park.* 우리는 공원의 다른 지역과 잘 어울리는 오솔길을 원했다. **2** two people who are compatible are able to have a good relationship, because they share interests, ideas etc. ‖ 두 사람이 흥미·생각 등을 공유하기 때문에 좋은 관계를 가질 수 있는. 양립[공존]할 수 있는. 화합[협력]할 수 있는 – **compatibility** /kəmˌpætəˈbɪləti/ n [U] —opposite INCOMPATIBLE

compatible[2] n a computer that can operate the same programs as a more famous type of computer ‖ 더 유명한 컴퓨터 기종과 같은 프로그램을 작동시킬 수 있는 컴퓨터. 호환성이 있는 장치[기종]: *programs for IBM PCs and compatibles* IBM 개인용 컴퓨터와 이것과 호환성이 있는 컴퓨터용 프로그램

com·pa·tri·ot /kəmˈpeɪtriət/ n someone who was born in or is a citizen of the same country as someone else ‖ 다른 사람과 같은 나라에 태어나거나 같은 나라의 시민인 사람. 동포. 겨레

com·pel /kəmˈpɛl/ v **-lled, -lling** [T] to force someone to do something ‖ 남에게 어떤 일을 하도록 강제하다. 억지로 … 시키다: *On Monday, Ozawa said he felt compelled to resign.* 월요일에 오자와는 자신이 권고 사직당할 것 같다고 말했다. —see also COMPULSION

com·pel·ling /kəmˈpɛlɪŋ/ adj so interesting or exciting that you have to pay attention ‖ 너무 재미있거나 흥미있어서 주의를 끌 수 밖에 없는. 주목하지 않을 수 없는: *It's a compelling story about one man's courage.* 그것은 한 남자의 용기를 다룬 흥미진진한 이야기이다.

com·pen·di·um /kəmˈpɛndiəm/ n FORMAL a book that contains a complete collection of facts, drawings etc. on a particular subject ‖ 특정한 주제에 관한 사실·그림 등의 철저히 모아 놓은 책. 개론. 해설서: *a baseball compendium* 야구 해설서

com·pen·sate /ˈkɑmpənˌseɪt/ v **1** [I] to reduce or balance the bad effect of something ‖ 어떤 것의 나쁜 영향을 줄이거나 균형을 맞추다. 상쇄하다. 보충하다: *Her intelligence more than compensates for her lack of experience.* 그녀의 지성은 경험 부족을 메우고도 남는다. / *A wet June doesn't compensate for a dry winter.* 비 오는 6월이 가문 겨울을 상쇄하지는 못한다. **2** [I, T] to pay someone money because s/he has suffered injury, loss, or damage ‖ 어떤 사람이 부상[손실, 손해]을 입어 돈을 지불하다. 보상하다. 배상하다: *Survivors were given $20,000 each to help compensate for their losses.* 생존자들은 그들이 입은 손실에 대한 보상으로 각자 2만 달러씩 지급 받았다. – **compensatory** /kəmˈpɛnsəˌtɔri/ adj

com·pen·sa·tion /ˌkɑmpənˈseɪʃən/ n **1** [U] money paid to someone because s/he has suffered injury, loss, or damage ‖ 부상[손실, 손해]을 입은 사람에게 지급된 돈. 보상금. 배상금: *Ralph still hasn't been paid compensation for his back injury.* 랄프는 허리 부상에 대한 보상금을 아직 받지 못했다. / *They were each given $500 as/in compensation.* 그들은 보상금으로 각각 500달러를 지급 받았다. **2** [C, U] something that makes a bad situation seem better ‖ 나쁜 상황을 더 좋아 보이게 하는 것. 보상. 벌충: *One of the few compensations of losing my job was seeing more of my family.* 실직에 대한 약간의 이점 중의 하나는 내 가족을 더 많이 마주하는 것이었다.

com·pete /kəmˈpit/ v [I] to try to win or gain something, or try to be better or more successful than someone else ‖ 이기거나 얻으려 하다, 또는 남보다 더 좋아지거나 성공하려고 노력하다. 경쟁하다. 겨루다: *Kids start competing for college places as early as 10th grade.* 아이들은 고1 때부터 대학에 들어가기 위해 경쟁하기 시작한다. / *We just can't compete with/against big companies like theirs.* 우리는 그들과 같은 대기업과[대기업을 상대로] 경쟁할 수는 없다. / *How many*

305   **complain**

runners will be competing in the race? 몇 명의 주자가 그 경주에 출전하니?

com·pe·tent /ˈkɑmpətənt/ *adj* **1** having enough skill or knowledge to do something to a satisfactory standard ‖ 만족스러운 수준으로 무엇을 할 만큼 충분한 기술이나 지식이 있는. 유능한: *Olive's a very competent teacher.* 올리브는 매우 유능한 교사이다. **2** satisfactory, but not especially good ‖ 특별히 좋지는 않지만 만족스러운. 알맞은. 적당한: *They did a competent job fixing the roof.* 그들은 만족스럽게 지붕을 수리했다. – **competence** *n* [U] – **competently** *adv* —opposite INCOMPETENT

com·pe·ti·tion /ˌkɑmpəˈtɪʃən/ *n* **1** [U] a situation in which people or organizations COMPETE with each other ‖ 사람이나 조직이 서로 경쟁하는 상황. 경쟁: *The competition between the two sisters is obvious.* 두 자매는 서로 경쟁하는 것이 분명하다. / *There's a lot of competition for the promotion.* 승진 경쟁이 심하다. / *Prices have gone down due to competition among the airlines.* 항공사 간의 경쟁으로 인해 가격이 인하되었다. / *Judy is in competition with* (=competing with) *four others for the role.* 주디는 그 배역을 놓고 다른 네 명과 경쟁하고 있다. **2** [singular, U] the people or groups that are competing against you, especially in business ‖ 특히 사업에서 자신과 경쟁하는 사람들이나 집단. 경쟁자: *trying to sell more than the competition* 경쟁자보다 더 많이 판매하려는 노력 **3** an organized event in which people or teams COMPETE against each other ‖ 사람이나 팀이 서로 대항하여 경쟁하는 조직화된 행사. 경기. 대회. 경연: *a dancing competition* 무용 대회 / *Teams from 10 different schools entered the competition.* 10개의 각기 다른 학교팀이 시합에 참가했다.

com·pet·i·tive /kəmˈpɛtətɪv/ *adj* **1** determined to be more successful than other people or companies ‖ 다른 사람이나 회사보다 더 성공하고자 결심하는. 경쟁적인: *Steve's very competitive.* 스티브는 매우 경쟁적이다. / *What can we do to maintain our competitive edge?* (=ability to be more successful) 강한 경쟁력을 유지하기 위해 우리는 무엇을 할 수 있나? **2** relating to competition ‖ 경쟁과 관련된. 경쟁의: *competitive sports* 경기 / *a competitive market* 경쟁 시장 **3** competitive prices or wages are similar to the prices that are charged or the wages that are paid by other stores or companies ‖ 가격이나 임금이 다른 가게나 회사가 매기거나 지불하는 것과 유사한. 경쟁에 의해 정해지는. 자유 경쟁에 의한 – **competitiveness** *n* [U]

com·pet·i·tor /kəmˈpɛtətə/ *n* a person, team, company etc. that is competing with another one ‖ 다른 사람과 경쟁하는 사람[팀, 회사]등. 경쟁자[팀]. 경쟁 상대: *Last year we sold twice as many computers as our competitors.* 작년에 우리는 경쟁사보다 컴퓨터를 두 배나 많이 판매했다.

com·pi·la·tion /ˌkɑmpəˈleɪʃən/ *n* a book, list, record etc. that puts together many different pieces of information, music etc. ‖ 많은 다른 정보·음악 등을 한데 모은 책·목록·기록 등. 편집[편찬]된 것: *a compilation of love songs* 연가 모음집

com·pile /kəmˈpaɪl/ *v* [T] to make a book, list, record etc. using different pieces of information, music etc. ‖ 다른 정보·음악 등을 사용하여 책·목록·기록 등을 만들다. 편집하다: *The report is compiled from a survey of 5,000 households.* 그 보고서는 5,000가구를 설문 조사하여 작성되었다.

com·pla·cent /kəmˈpleɪsənt/ *adj* pleased with what you have achieved so that you stop trying to improve or change things ‖ 어떤 것을 개선하거나 변화하려는 노력을 중단할 만큼 성취한 것에 기뻐하는. 자기 만족의: *Yes, we've been winning, but we're not going to get complacent.* 예, 우리는 승리하고 있지만 자만하지는 않을 겁니다. – **complacency** *n* [U]

com·plain /kəmˈpleɪn/ *v* [I, T] **1** to say that you are annoyed, not satisfied, or unhappy about something or someone ‖ 사물이나 사람에 대한 짜증[불만족, 불쾌감]을 토로하다. 불평하다. 투덜대다: *Fred's always complaining about something.* 프레드는 항상 무언가에 대해 불평하고 있다. / *Dee complained that she couldn't find a job anywhere.* 디는 어디에서도 직업을 구할 수 없었다고 불평했다. / *I'm going to complain to the manager!* 나는 그 매니저에게 불만을 얘기할 거야! **2 I can't complain** SPOKEN said when you think a situation is satisfactory even though there may be a few problems ‖ 약간의 문제가 있다 하더라도 상황이 만족스럽다고 생각할 때 쓰여: *I still don't feel too great, but I can't complain.* 아직도 기분이 그리 좋지는 않지만 별 불만은 없다.

complain of sth *phr v* [T] to say that

you feel sick or have a pain in a part of your body ‖ 아프거나 몸의 부위에 통증이 있다고 말하다. 고통을 호소하다: *Tom's been complaining of pain in his chest.* 톰은 가슴의 통증을 호소해 왔다.

com·plaint /kəmˈpleɪnt/ *n* **1** [C, U] a statement in which someone complains about something ‖ 누가 무엇에 대해 불평하는 말. 불평. 불만. 푸념. 고소: *a complaint against five police officers* 다섯 명의 경찰에 대한 고소 / *I want to make a complaint!* (=complain formally to someone) 나는 고소하고 싶어! / *I've had a lot of complaints about your work.* 나는 네 일에 불만이 많았다. ✗DON'T SAY "a complaint for something."✗ "a complaint for something"이라고는 하지 않는다 **2** something that you complain about ‖ 불평하는 것. 불평[불만]의 대상[원인]: *My only complaint is the high prices they charge.* 나의 유일한 불만은 그들이 청구한 가격이 높다는 점이다. **3** an illness that affects a particular part of your body ‖ 신체의 특정 부위에 영향을 미치는 병. …병[질환]: *a serious liver complaint* 심각한 간 질환

com·ple·ment¹ /ˈkɑmpləmənt/ *n* **1** someone or something that emphasizes the good qualities of another person or thing ‖ 다른 사람이나 사물의 좋은 성질을 강조하는 사람이나 사물. 보충[보완]물. 보충하여 완전하게 하는 것: *A fine wine is a complement to a good meal.* 훌륭한 식사에는 고급 포도주가 있어야 제격이다. **2** the number or quantity needed to make a group complete ‖ 집단을 이루는 데 필요한 수나 양. 정원. 정수. 정량: *The English department already has its full complement of teachers.* 영어과는 이미 영어 교사 정원을 확보하고 있다. **3** TECHNICAL in grammar, a word or phrase that follows a verb and describes the subject of the verb. In the sentence "You look angry," "angry" is a complement ‖ 문법에서 동사의 뒤에 오고 동사의 주제를 기술하는 단어나 어구. 보어. "You look angry,"라는 문장에서 "angry"는 보어이다. —compare COMPLIMENT¹

com·ple·ment² /ˈkɑmplə,mɛnt/ *v* [T] to emphasize the good qualities of another person or thing, especially by adding something that was needed ‖ 특히 필요한 것을 덧붙임으로써 다른 사람이나 사물의 좋은 성질을 강조하다. 보충[보완]하다: *Terry and Jim really complement each other.* 테리와 짐은 서로를 잘 보완한다. — **complementary**

/ˌkɑmpləˈmɛntri, -mɛntəri/ *adj* : *complementary colors* 보색

com·plete¹ /kəmˈplit/ *adj* **1** having all the parts, details, facts etc. that are necessary or usual ‖ 필수적이거나 통상적인 부분·세부·사실 등을 모두 가지고 있는. 전부 갖추어져 있는. 완전한: *You'll find complete cooking instructions on the cans.* 깡통 위에서 충분한 요리 설명을 볼 수 있을 것이다. / *the complete works of Shakespeare* 셰익스피어 전집 / *a complete sentence* 완전한 문장 / *Christmas just didn't seem complete without Dad there.* 아빠가 크리스마스 때 안 계셔서 뭔가 빠진 듯했다. —opposite INCOMPLETE **2** INFORMAL a word meaning in every way, used in order to emphasize what you are saying; total ‖ 말하고자 하는 바를 강조하는 데에 쓰여, 모든 점에서를 뜻하는 단어. 온전한. 철저한. 전적인; 완전한: *Bart's a complete idiot!* 바트는 정말 멍청이다! / *Their wedding announcement came as a complete surprise.* 그들의 결혼 발표는 정말 뜻밖이었다. **3** finished ‖ 완성된. 끝난. 완결된: *Our research is nearly complete.* 우리의 연구는 거의 완성 단계에 있다. **4 complete with** including or containing something additional ‖ 추가물이 포함된. …이 완비된. …을 갖춘: *The house comes complete with a swimming pool.* 그 집은 수영장을 갖추고 있다. — **completeness** *n* [U]

complete² *v* [T] **1** to finish doing or making something ‖ 무엇을 하거나 만드는 것을 끝내다. 마무리짓다. 완결하다: *The book took five years to complete.* 그 책을 완성하는 데 5년이 걸렸다. **2** to make something whole or perfect by adding what is missing ‖ 빠진 것을 더함으로써 무엇을 완전하게 하다. 모두 갖추다: *I need one more stamp to complete my collection.* 우표 한 장만 더 있으면 내 수집품은 완성된다.

com·plete·ly /kəmˈplitˈli/ *adv* in every way; totally ‖ 모든 점에서. 완전히; 전적으로: *I completely forgot about your birthday.* 나는 너의 생일을 까맣게 잊어버리고 있었어.

com·ple·tion /kəmˈpliʃən/ *n* [U] the state of being finished, or the act of finishing something ‖ 끝마친 상태, 또는 무엇을 끝마치는 행위. 완성. 완료: *Repair work is scheduled for completion in April.* 보수 공사는 4월에 완공될 예정이다. / *the completion of the $80 million project* 8,000만 달러 짜리 프로젝트의 완성

com·plex¹ /kəmˈplɛks, kɑm-, ˈkɑmplɛks/ *adj* **1** consisting of many closely connected parts or processes ‖ 밀접하게 관련된 많은 부분이나 과정으로 이루어진. 복합의. 통합의: *There's a complex network of roads connecting the two cities.* 두 도시를 연결하는 통합된 도로망이 있다. **2** full of small details, and therefore difficult to understand or explain ‖ 작은 세부 사항들로 가득차서 이해하거나 설명하기 어려운. 까다로운. 복잡한: *"This is a very complex issue,"* Morrison said. "이것은 아주 복잡한 문제야."라고 모리슨은 말했다.

com·plex² /ˈkɑmplɛks/ *n* **1** a group of buildings or one large building used for a particular purpose ‖ 특정한 목적에 쓰는 일단의 건물이나 대형 건물. 단지. 복합체: *They're building a new shopping complex downtown.* 그들은 시내에 새 쇼핑 센터를 짓고 있다. **2** an emotional problem in which someone is too anxious about something or thinks too much about it ‖ 무엇에 대해 너무 걱정하거나 너무 많이 생각하는 감정적인 문제. 콤플렉스: *Linda has a real complex about her appearance.* 린다는 자신의 외모에 대해 정말로 콤플렉스를 가지고 있다.

com·plex·ion /kəmˈplɛkʃən/ *n* the natural color and appearance of the skin on your face ‖ 얼굴 피부의 자연적인 색깔이나 모습. 안색: *a pale/dark complexion* 창백한[거무스름한] 안색

com·plex·i·ty /kəmˈplɛksəti/ *n* [U] the state or quality of being complicated and detailed ‖ 복잡하고 상세한 상태나 특성. 복잡(함). 복잡성: *the complexity of the book's plot* 책의 복잡한 줄거리

com·pli·ance /kəmˈplaɪəns/ *n* [U] FORMAL the act of obeying a rule or law ‖ 규칙이나 법을 따르는 행위. 복종. 준수: *Compliance with the law is expected of everyone.* 모든 사람에게 법을 준수하는 것이 요구된다.

com·pli·ant /kəmˈplaɪənt/ *adj* willing to obey or agree to other people's wishes and demands ‖ 타인의 소망과 요구에 기꺼이 복종하거나 동의하는. 고분고분한. 순종하는: *a compliant little girl* 유순한 작은 소녀 – **compliantly** *adv*

com·pli·cate /ˈkɑmpləˌkeɪt/ *v* [T] to make something difficult to understand or deal with ‖ 무엇을 이해하거나 다루기 어렵게 하다. 복잡하게[뒤얽히게] 하다: *It's a serious problem, complicated by the fact that we have no experience in this area.* 그것은 우리가 이 분야에 경험이 없다는 사실로 인해 복잡해진 심각한 문제이다.

com·pli·cat·ed /ˈkɑmpləˌkeɪt̬ɪd/ *adj* difficult to understand or deal with ‖ 이해하거나 다루기 어려운. 까다로운. 복잡한: *Don't ask me such complicated questions.* 그렇게 까다로운 문제를 내게 물어 보지 마라. / *It's a complicated situation.* 그것은 복잡한 상황이다. — opposite SIMPLE

com·pli·ca·tion /ˌkɑmpləˈkeɪʃən/ *n* **1** [C usually plural] a medical problem or illness that happens while someone is already ill ‖ 이미 병들어 있는 동안에 일어나는 의료상의 문제나 병. 합병증: *Mrs. Potter died Thursday of complications following surgery.* 포터 부인은 수술 후의 합병증으로 목요일에 죽었다. **2** [C, U] a problem or situation that makes something more difficult to understand or deal with ‖ 무엇을 이해하거나 다루기 더 어렵게 하는 문제나 상황. 골칫거리. 까다로운 문제: *The drop in student numbers added further complications.* 학생 수의 감소로 어려움이 더 가중되었다.

com·plic·i·ty /kəmˈplɪsəti/ *n* [U] FORMAL the act of being involved in a crime with other people ‖ 다른 사람들과 함께 범죄에 관여하는 행위. 공범. 공모. 연루

com·pli·ment¹ /ˈkɑmpləmənt/ *n* something you say or do in order to praise someone or show that you admire or respect him/her ‖ 남을 칭찬하기 위해 또는 감탄이나 존경한다는 것을 나타내기 위해 하는 말이나 행동. 찬사. 칭찬: *"You look great." "Thanks for the compliment."* "멋있어 보이네요." "칭찬 감사합니다." / *I took it as a compliment that Rickey even knew my name.* 리키가 내 이름도 안다는 것이 내게는 찬사로 여겨졌다. / *This is the highest compliment anyone has ever paid me.* 이것은 이제껏 내가 받았던 최고의 찬사이다. —compare COMPLEMENT¹ —see also COMPLIMENTS

com·pli·ment² /ˈkɑmpləˌmɛnt/ *v* [T] to say something to someone that expresses praise, admiration, or respect ‖ 칭찬[감탄, 존경]을 표현하는 말을 남에게 하다. 칭찬[찬양]하다: *That's the first time Bob has complimented me on my hair.* 보브가 내 머리 스타일을 칭찬한 것은 처음이다.

com·pli·men·ta·ry /ˌkɑmpləˈmɛntri, -ˈmɛntəri/ *adj* **1** expressing praise, admiration, or respect ‖ 찬양[감탄, 존

경]을 표현하는. 칭찬하는. 찬사의. 경의를 표하는: *Your teacher made some very complimentary remarks about your work.* 네 선생님이 네 성적에 대해 상당히 칭찬을 하시더구나. —opposite UNCOMPLIMENTARY **2** given free to people ‖ 사람에게 무료로 주어지는: *complimentary tickets* 무료 입장권

com·pli·ments /'kɑmpləmənts/ *n* [plural] **1** praise, admiration, or good wishes ‖ 칭찬[감탄, 안부]: *Please give my compliments to the chef.* 요리사에게 찬사 좀 전해 주세요. **2 with the compliments of/with sb's compliments** FORMAL used by a person or company when he, she, or it sends or gives something to you ‖ 사람이나 회사가 무엇을 남에게 보내거나 줄 때 쓰여. …근정(謹呈): *Please accept these tickets with our compliments.* 저희가 삼가 드리는 이 표를 받아주세요.

com·ply /kəm'plaɪ/ *v* [I] FORMAL to do what you have to do or are asked to do ‖ 해야 할 일이나 부탁받은 일을 하다. 따르다. 응하다: *Those who fail to comply with the law will be fined.* 그 법을 따르지 않는 사람은 벌금을 물게 된다.

com·po·nent /kəm'poʊnənt/ *n* one of several parts that make up a whole machine or system ‖ 기계 전체나 시스템 전체를 구성하는 여러 부분 중의 하나. 구성 요소. 부품: *stereo components* 스테레오 부품

com·pose /kəm'poʊz/ *v* **1 be composed of** to be formed from a group of substances or parts ‖ 일단의 물질이나 부분들로 형성되다. …로 구성되다: *Water is composed of hydrogen and oxygen.* 물은 수소와 산소로 구성되어 있다. —compare COMPRISE **2** [T] to combine together with other things or people to form something ‖ 어떤 것을 형성하기 위해 다른 사물이나 사람을 결합하다. 구성하다. 조립하다: *the letters that compose a word* 단어를 구성하는 문자들 **3** [I, T] to put sounds, words, colors or images together to form a piece of art ‖ 하나의 예술 작품을 만들기 위해 소리[말, 색깔, 영상]를 한데 모으다. 작곡[작화]하다. 구도하다: *Schumann was better at composing music than playing it.* 슈만은 음악을 연주하는 것보다는 작곡하는 데에 더 능숙했다. —see usage note at COMPRISE

com·posed /kəm'poʊzd/ *adj* calm, rather than upset or angry ‖ 당황하거나 화를 내기보다는 침착한. 조용한. 차분한

com·pos·er /kəm'poʊzɚ/ *n* someone who writes music ‖ 곡을 쓰는 사람. 작곡가

com·pos·ite /kəm'pɑzɪt/ *adj* made up of different parts or materials ‖ 다른 부분이나 물질로 이루어진. 합성의: *a composite drawing* 합성화(畵) – **composite** *n*

com·po·si·tion /ˌkɑmpə'zɪʃən/ *n* **1** [U] the way in which something is made up of different parts, members etc. ‖ 무엇이 다른 부분이나 구성원 등으로 만들어지는 방식. 합성. 구성: *the chemical composition of plants* 식물의 화학적 구성 **2** [C, U] a piece of music or a poem, or the art of writing one ‖ 음악 작품이나 시, 또는 그 작법. 작곡[창작, 작문](법) **3** [C, U] a short piece of writing about a particular subject that is done at school; ESSAY ‖ 학교에서 하는 특정한 주제에 대한 짧은 글. 작문; ㊀ essay **4** [U] the way in which the different parts of a painting or photograph are arranged ‖ 그림이나 사진의 다른 부분들이 배열되는 방식. 구도

com·post /'kɑmpoʊst/ *n* [U] a mixture of decayed leaves, plants etc. used for improving the quality of soil ‖ 토양을 기름지게 하는 데에 쓰이는 썩은 나뭇잎·식물 등의 혼합물. 두엄. 퇴비

com·po·sure /kəm'poʊʒɚ/ *n* [singular, U] a calm feeling that you have when you feel confident about dealing with a situation ‖ 상황을 다루는 데 자신감을 느낄 때 가지는 차분한 감정. 침착. 평정

com·pound¹ /'kɑmpaʊnd/ *n* **1** something that consists of a combination of two or more parts ‖ 둘 또는 둘 이상의 부분의 결합으로 이루어지는 것. 혼합물. 합성물: *a chemical compound* 화합물 **2** an area that contains a group of buildings and is surrounded by a fence or wall ‖ 일단의 건물을 포함하여 울타리나 벽으로 둘러싸여 있는 지역. 구역. 지구: *a prison compound* 포로 수용소 **3** TECHNICAL in grammar, a noun or adjective consisting of two or more words. The noun "ice cream" is a compound ‖ 문법에서 두 단어나 두 단어 이상의 단어로 구성되어 있는 명사나 형용사. 복합어. 합성어. "ice cream"이라는 명사는 복합어이다.

com·pound² /kəm'paʊnd/ *v* [T] **1** to make a difficult situation worse by adding more problems ‖ 문제를 더 추가시킴으로써 어려운 상황을 악화시키다. 가중시키다: *Our difficulties were compounded by other people's* *mistakes.* 다른 사람들의 실수로 우리들은 더욱 곤경에 처하게 되었다. **2** TECHNICAL to pay INTEREST that is calculated on both the sum of money and the INTEREST it is making ‖ 돈의 합계와 그 돈의 이자, 이 둘을 근거로 계산된 이자를 지불하다. 이자를 복리로 지불하다

com·pre·hend /ˌkɑmprɪˈhɛnd/ *v* [I, T] FORMAL to understand something ‖ 무엇을 이해하다: *The judge said it was difficult to fully comprehend* (=understand completely) *the actions of the police in this matter.* 그 판사는 이 사건에서 경찰관의 행동을 완전히 이해하기가 힘들다고 말했다.

com·pre·hen·si·ble /ˌkɑmprɪˈhɛnsəbəl/ *adj* able to be understood ‖ 이해할 수 있는: *A book like that is not comprehensible to the average student.* 그와 같은 책은 보통의 학생은 이해할 수 없다. —opposite INCOMPREHENSIBLE

com·pre·hen·sion /ˌkɑmprɪˈhɛnʃən/ *n* [U] the ability to understand something, or knowledge about something ‖ 무엇을 이해하는 능력, 또는 무엇에 대한 지식. 이해(력): *Some politicians seem to have no real comprehension of what it's like to be poor.* 몇몇 정치인은 가난이 무엇인지 실제로 이해하지 못하는 것 같다. / *a test of reading/listening comprehension* (=a student's ability to understand written or spoken language) 읽기[듣기] 능력 시험

com·pre·hen·sive /ˌkɑmprɪˈhɛnsɪv/ *adj* including everything that is necessary ‖ 필요한 모든 것을 포함하는. 포괄적인. 광범위한: *comprehensive health insurance* 종합 건강 보험

com·press /kəmˈprɛs/ *v* [I, T] to press something or make it smaller so that it takes up less space ‖ 공간을 덜 차지하도록 물건을 누르거나 작게 하다. …을 꽉 누르다. 압축[압착]하다: *The garlic is dried and compressed into a pill.* 마늘을 말려서 압착하여 환약을 만들었다. / *electronically compressing data* 전자 공학적으로 압축한 자료 —**compressed** *adj* —**compression** /kəmˈprɛʃən/ *n* [U]

com·prise /kəmˈpraɪz/ *v* FORMAL **1** [linking verb] to consist of particular parts, groups etc. ‖ 특정한 부분·집단 등으로 구성되다. …으로 이루어지다. …을 포함하다: *New York City comprises Manhattan, Queens, Brooklyn, The Bronx, and Staten Island.* 뉴욕 시는 맨해튼·퀸스·브루클린·브롱크스·스태튼 아일랜드로 이루어진다. ✗DON'T SAY "is comprised of" "is comprised of"라고는 하지 않는다.✗ **2** [T] to form part of a larger group ‖ 큰 집단의 일부를 구성하다: *Women comprise over 75% of our staff.* 여성이 우리 직원의 75% 이상을 차지한다.

USAGE NOTE comprise, be composed of, consist of

Use these phrases to talk about the parts that things are made of, or the things that something contains. Each of the following sentences means the same thing, but the patterns are different: *The United States comprises 50 states. / The United States is composed of 50 states. / The United States consists of 50 states.* ✗DON'T SAY "is comprised of" or "is consisted of."✗ 사물을 구성하는 부분, 또는 사물을 포함하는 것에 대해 말할 때 이 어구를 쓴다. 다음 각각의 문장은 같은 의미이나 문형은 다르다: 미국은 50개 주로 구성된다. "is comprised of" 또는 "is consisted of"라고는 하지 않는다.

com·pro·mise¹ /ˈkɑmprəˌmaɪz/ *n* [C, U] an agreement that is achieved after everyone involved accepts less than what s/he wanted at first ‖ 모든 관련자들이 처음에 원했던 것보다 못한 것을 수용한 후에 이루어지는 합의. 타협: *There is still hope that the warring sides will reach a compromise.* 싸우는 양측이 타협에 이를 것이라는 희망은 아직 있다. / *No one at the meeting was prepared to make compromises.* 그 모임에서 아무도 타협할 준비가 되어 있지 않았다.

compromise² *v* **1** [I] to end an argument by making an agreement in which everyone involved accepts less than what s/he wanted at first ‖ 모든 관련자들이 처음에 원했던 것보다도 못한 것을 받아들이는 데에 합의함으로써 논쟁을 끝내다. 타협하여 해결하다: *We managed to compromise on a price for the car.* 우리는 그럭저럭 차의 가격에 타협했다. / *Look, I'll compromise with you and pay half of the cost.* 저기요, 저는 당신과 흥정해서 절반 가격만 지불할게요. **2** [T] to do something in a way that does not match a legal or moral standard, for example in order to spend less money or get more power ‖ 예를 들면 돈을 적게 쓰거나 힘을 더 얻기 위해 법적이나 도덕적 기준에 맞지 않게 일을 하다. (명예·신용 등을)위태롭게 하다: *Safety has clearly been compromised in the building's* *construction.* 그 건물을 지으면서 분명 안전이 소중히 다루어졌다.

com·pro·mis·ing /'kɑmprə,maɪzɪŋ/ *adj* proving that you have done something morally wrong, or making it seem like you have done so ‖ 도덕적으로 나쁜 일을 한 것을 증명하는, 또는 그렇게 일을 한 것처럼 보이게 하는. 명예[체면]를 손상시키는. 더럽히는: *a compromising photograph* 명예를 손상시키는 사진

comp time /'kɑmp ,taɪm/ *n* [U] vacation time that you are given instead of money because you have worked more hours than you should have ‖ 일해야 하는 시간 이상을 일해서 돈 대신에 받는 휴가 기간. 보상 휴가. 대휴(代休)

com·pul·sion /kəm'pʌlʃən/ *n* 1 a strong unreasonable desire to do something ‖ 어떤 것을 하려는 강한 비이성적인 욕구. 충동: *Drinking is a compulsion with her.* 그녀에게 있어 음주는 끊기 어려운 충동이다. 2 [singular, U] a force or influence that makes someone do something ‖ 사람에게 어떤 것을 하게 하는 힘이나 영향. 강제. 강요. 강박: *Remember that you are under no compulsion to sign the agreement.* 너에게 그 협정에 서명하도록 강요하지 않는다는 것을 기억해라. —see also COMPEL

com·pul·sive /kəm'pʌlsɪv/ *adj* very difficult to stop or control ‖ 멈추거나 제어하기 매우 어려운. 강박적인: *compulsive eating* 폭식[과식] – **compulsively** *adv*

com·pul·so·ry /kəm'pʌlsəri/ *adj* having to be done because it is a rule or law ‖ 규칙이나 법률이어서 행해져야 하는. 강제적인. 의무적인: *Attendance is compulsory in all classes.* 모든 수업시간에는 반드시 출석해야 한다.

com·punc·tion /kəm'pʌŋkʃən/ *n* [U] **have/feel no compunction about** FORMAL to not feel guilty or sorry about something although other people may think that it is wrong ‖ 다른 사람들이 그 일이 그르다고 생각하더라도 그것에 대해 죄책감이나 미안함을 느끼지 않다. 뉘우치지 않다: *I have no compunction about saying what I think.* 생각한 것을 말하는 것에 대하여 나는 아무런 거리낌이 없다.

com·pute /kəm'pyut/ *v* [I, T] FORMAL to calculate an answer, total, result etc. ‖ 해답·합계·결과 등을 계산하다. 산출[산정]하다 – **computation** /,kɑmpyə'teɪʃən/ *n* [C, U]

com·put·er /kəm'pyutər/ *n* an electronic machine that stores information and uses sets of instructions called PROGRAMs to help you find, organize, or change the information ‖ 정보를 저장하고, 프로그램이라 불리는 일련의 명령을 사용하여 정보를 찾는[조직화하는, 변환하는] 전자 기계. 컴퓨터: *a personal computer* 개인용 컴퓨터 / *We do all our work on computer.* 우리는 컴퓨터로 모든 일을 한다.

com·put·er·ize /kəm'pyutə,raɪz/ *v* [T] to use a computer to control the way something is done, to store information etc. ‖ 일 처리 방식을 제어하거나 정보 등을 저장하기 위해 컴퓨터를 사용하다. 컴퓨터화하다. 컴퓨터로 처리하다 – **computerization** /kəm,pyutərə'zeɪʃən/ *n* [U]

computer lit·er·ate /,.. '.../ *adj* able to use a computer ‖ 컴퓨터를 사용할 수 있는

com·put·ing /kəm'pyutɪŋ/ *n* [U] the use of computers as a job, in a business etc. ‖ 사업 등에서 업무로서의 컴퓨터의 사용

com·rade /'kɑmræd/ *n* FORMAL a friend, especially someone who shares difficult work or the same aims as you ‖ 특히 어려운 일이나 같은 목표를 공유하는 친구. 동료. 동지 – **comradeship** *n* [U]

con¹ /kɑn/ *v* [T] INFORMAL to trick someone, either to take his/her money or to get him/her to do something ‖ 돈을 취하거나 일을 시키려고 남을 속이다. 사기치다: *That guy tried to con me out of $20.* 그 녀석이 내 돈 20달러를 사취하려고 했다.

con² *n* 1 INFORMAL a trick to get someone's money or make someone do something ‖ 남의 돈을 취하거나 남에게 어떤 일을 시키기 위한 속임수. 사기: *The ads you see in the paper are just a con.* 당신이 신문에서 보는 광고는 사기에 불과하다. 2 SLANG ⇨ CONVICT²

con art·ist /'. ,../ *n* INFORMAL someone who tricks people in order to get money from them ‖ 금전을 우려내려고 사람들을 속이는 사람. 사기꾼. 협잡꾼

con·cave /,kɑn'keɪv/ *adj* TECHNICAL curved inward like a bowl ‖ 사발처럼 안으로 굽은. 오목한. 요면(凹面)형의: *a concave lens* 오목 렌즈 —opposite CONVEX

con·ceal /kən'sil/ *v* [T] FORMAL to hide something carefully ‖ 조심스럽게 물건을 숨기다. 감추다. 보이지 않게 하다: *She tried to conceal her emotions from Ted.* 그녀는 테드에게 자신의 감정을 숨기려 했다. – **concealment** *n* [U]

con·cede /kən'sid/ *v* 1 [T] to admit

that something is true although you wish that it were not true ‖ 어떤 것이 사실이 아니길 바라지만 사실임을 용인하다. 인정하다: *Even the critics conceded that the movie was a success.* 비평가들조차 그 영화가 성공작이라고 인정했다. **2** [I, T] to admit that you are not going to win a game, argument, battle etc. ‖ 경기·토론·싸움 등에서 승리할 수 없다고 시인하다. (패배 등을) 인정하다: *Hawkins conceded defeat in the leadership election.* 호킨스는 지도자 선거에서 패배를 인정했다. **3** [T] to let someone have something although you do not want to ‖ 원하지 않지만 남에게 어떤 것을 갖게 하다. 주다. 허용하다: *The Lakers conceded 12 points in a row to the Suns.* 레이커스 팀은 선즈 팀에게 연속하여 12점을 허용했다.

con·ceit /kənˈsit/ *n* [U] an attitude that shows that you have too much pride in your abilities, appearance etc. ‖ 자신의 능력·외모 등에 대단한 자부심을 가지고 있음을 나타내는 태도. 자만

con·ceit·ed /kənˈsitɪd/ *adj* behaving in a way that shows too much pride in your abilities, appearance etc. ‖ 자신의 능력·외모 등에 너무 많은 자부심을 주는 식으로 행동하는. 자만하는. 우쭐대는: *I don't want to seem conceited, but I know I'll win.* 자만하는 것으로 보이고 싶지는 않지만 내가 이길 거라는 걸 안다.

con·ceiv·a·ble /kənˈsivəbəl/ *adj* able to be believed or imagined ‖ 믿거나 상상할 수 있는: *It is conceivable that the experts are wrong.* 그 전문가들이 잘못이라고 생각할 수도 있다. **–conceivably** *adv* —opposite INCONCEIVABLE

con·ceive /kənˈsiv/ *v* **1** [T] to imagine a situation or what something is like ‖ 상황이나 사물이 어떤 모습인지를 상상하다. …을 마음 속에 그리다: *It is impossible to conceive of the size of the universe.* 우주의 크기를 상상하는 것은 불가능하다. **2** [T] to think of a new idea or plan ‖ 새로운 아이디어나 계획에 대해 생각하다. 고안하다. 착상하다: *It was Dr. Salk who conceived the idea of a polio vaccine.* 소아 마비 백신에 대한 아이디어를 생각해 낸 사람은 소크 박사였다. **3** [I, T] to become PREGNANT ‖ 임신하다.

con·cen·trate¹ /ˈkɑnsənˌtreɪt/ *v* **1** [I] to think very carefully about something you are doing ‖ 하고 있는 일을 매우 주의 깊게 생각하다. 집중하다. 골몰하다: *With all this noise, it's hard to concentrate.* 이 소음 때문에 집중하기 힘들다. **2** to be present in large numbers or amounts in

a particular place ‖ 특정한 장소에 다수 또는 다량으로 존재하다. 집중하다: *Most of New Zealand's population is concentrated in the north island.* 대부분의 뉴질랜드 인구는 북쪽 섬에 집중되어 있다. **3** [T] to make a liquid stronger by removing most of the water from it ‖ 물질에서 대부분의 물을 제거함으로써 액체를 더 진하게 만들다. 농축하다

concentrate on sth *phr v* [T] to give most of your attention to one thing ‖ 한 가지 일에 모든 주의를 기울이다. …에 집중하다: *I want to concentrate on my career for a while before I have kids.* 아이를 갖기 전 한동안은 내 일에 전념하고 싶다.

con·cen·trate² *n* [C, U] a substance or liquid that has been made stronger by removing most of the water from it ‖ 수분의 대부분을 제거함으로써 더 진해진 물질이나 액체. 응축[농축]물. 농축 음료: *orange juice concentrate* 농축 오렌지 주스

con·cen·trat·ed /ˈkɑnsənˌtreɪtɪd/ *adj* **1** showing a lot of determination or effort ‖ 큰 결심이나 노력을 보이는. 집중된: *He made a concentrated effort to raise his grades.* 그는 자신의 성적을 올리기 위해 노력을 집중했다. **2** a substance that is concentrated has had some of the liquid removed from it ‖ 어떤 물질이 액체의 일부를 제거한. 액체가 농축된. 진한

con·cen·tra·tion /ˌkɑnsənˈtreɪʃən/ *n* **1** [U] the ability to think very carefully about something for a long time ‖ 어떤 일에 대해 오랫동안 매우 주의깊게 생각하는 능력. 집중. 전념: *Mendez has amazing powers of concentration.* 멘데즈는 놀랄 만한 집중력이 있다. **2** [C, U] a large amount of something in a particular place ‖ 특정한 곳에 있는 물질의 많은 양. 농축. 응축. 농도: *Tests show high concentrations of chemicals in the water.* 실험 결과는 그 물 속에 화학 약품의 농도가 높다는 것을 나타낸다.

concentration camp /ˌ...ˈ. ./ *n* a prison for enemy soldiers or for people who are considered dangerous during a war ‖ 전쟁 중에 적군이나 위험인물들을 수용하는 교도소. 강제 수용소

con·cen·tric /kənˈsɛntrɪk/ *adj* TECHNICAL having the same center ‖ 동일한 중심을 가진. 동심(同心)의: *concentric circles* 동심원

con·cept /ˈkɑnsɛpt/ *n* an idea of how something is, or how something should be done ‖ 사물이 어떠한지, 또는 그것이

어떻게 이루어져야 하는지에 대한 생각. 개념. 관념. 구상: *Jerry has no concept of how difficult being a parent is.* 제리는 부모가 되는 것이 얼마나 어려운지에 대한 관념이 없다.

con·cep·tion /kənˈsɛpʃən/ *n* **1** an idea about something, or a basic understanding of something ‖ 어떤 사물에 대한 생각, 또는 그것의 기본적인 이해. 관념. 개념: *One common conception of democracy is that it means "government by the people."* 민주주의에 대한 하나의 일반적인 개념은 "국민에 의한 정부"를 의미한다는 것이다. **2** [U] the process by which a woman or female animal becomes PREGNANT, or the time when this happens ‖ 여성이나 동물의 암컷이 수태하는 과정, 또는 이런 일이 일어나는 시기. 수정(受精). 수태. 임신

con·cep·tu·al /kənˈsɛptʃuəl/ *adj* FORMAL dealing with CONCEPTs, or based on them ‖ 개념을 다루는, 또는 개념에 입각한. 개념의[에 관한]. 개념상의: *plans that are in the conceptual stage* 개념상의 단계에 있는 계획 – **conceptually** *adv*

con·cern¹ /kənˈsɚn/ *n* **1** [C, U] a feeling of worry about something important, or the thing that worries you ‖ 중요한 일에 대해 걱정하는 감정, 또는 걱정시키는 일. 걱정. 염려. 근심: *There is growing concern about the rise in drug-related crimes.* 마약 관련 범죄의 증가에 대한 우려가 늘고 있다. / *Your father's health is giving the doctors cause for concern.* 네 아버지의 건강이 의사들의 걱정거리가 되고 있다. **2** [C, U] something important that worries you or involves you ‖ 걱정되거나 관련된 중요한 일. 관심사. 중대사: *The destruction of the rainforest is of concern to us all.* 열대 우림의 파괴는 우리 모두의 관심사다. / *Our main concern is for the children's safety.* 우리의 주된 관심사는 아이들의 안전이다. **3** [singular, U] a feeling of wanting someone to be happy and safe ‖ 남이 행복하고 안전하길 바라는 감정. 관심. 배려: *Anne's concern for her elderly mother* 노모에 대한 앤의 배려 **4 to whom it may concern** used at the beginning of a formal letter when you do not know the person you are writing to ‖ 편지의 수취인을 알지 못할 때 격식 차린 편지의 첫머리에 쓰여. 관계자 제위[각위]

concern² *v* [T] **1** to affect someone or involve him/her ‖ 남에게 영향을 주거나 누구에 관계하다: *What we're planning* *doesn't concern you.* 우리가 계획하는 것은 당신과는 관계없다. **2** to make someone feel worried or upset ‖ 남을 걱정시키거나 기분 나쁘게 하다. 염려하다. 속을 태우다: *My daughter's problems at school concern me greatly.* 학교에 다니는 내 딸의 문제로 나는 걱정을 많이 한다. **3** to be about something or someone ‖ 사물이나 사람에 관련되다. …에 관계[관여]하다: *Many of Woody Allen's movies concern life in New York.* 우디 알렌이 나온 많은 영화들은 뉴욕 생활에 대한 것이다. **4 concern yourself** to become involved in something that interests or worries you ‖ 흥미를 주거나 걱정시키는 일에 관여되다. 관여하다: *You don't need to concern yourself with this, Jan.* 잰아, 너는 이 일에 신경쓸 필요 없어.

con·cerned /kənˈsɚnd/ *adj* **1** involved in something or affected by it ‖ 어떤 일에 관여하고 있는, 또는 그것의 영향을 받는: *It was a shock for all concerned.* (=everyone involved) 그것은 모든 관련자들에게 충격이 있었다. / *Everyone concerned with the car industry will be interested.* 자동차 산업에 관련된 사람은 누구나 흥미를 가질 것이다. **2** worried about something important ‖ 중요한 어떤 일에 대해 걱정하는: *We're concerned about the results of the test.* 우리는 그 시험의 결과가 걱정스럽다. **3** believing that something is important ‖ 어떤 일이 중요하다고 믿는: *Some people are more concerned with just making money.* 몇몇 사람은 돈벌이에만 더 관심이 있다. **4 as far as sth is concerned** used in order to show which subject or thing you are talking about ‖ 이야기하고 있는 어떤 주제나 사물을 나타내는 데에 쓰여. …에 관한 한: *As far as money is concerned, the club is doing fairly well.* 돈에 관한 한 그 클럽은 아주 잘 운영되고 있다. **5 as far as sb is concerned** used in order to show what someone's opinion on a subject is ‖ 어떤 주제에 대한 사람의 의견이 무엇인지를 보여 주기 위해 쓰여. …에 관한 한. …로서는: *As far as I'm concerned, the whole idea is crazy.* 나로서는 그 모든 생각이 터무니없다. —see usage note at NERVOUS

con·cern·ing /kənˈsɚnɪŋ/ *prep* FORMAL about, or relating to ‖ …에 대한, 또는 …에 관련한: *We have questions concerning the report.* 우리는 그 보도에 관해 의문이 있다.

con·cert /ˈkɑnsɚt/ *n* **1** a performance given by musicians or singers ‖ 음악가나

가수가 개최하는 공연. 음악회. 연주회.
콘서트: *a rock/jazz/orchestra concert* 록/
재즈/오케스트라 콘서트 **2 in concert**
(with) a) playing or singing at a
concert ‖ 콘서트에서 연주하거나 노래하
는 : *Live, tonight, in concert, it's*
Madonna! 오늘 밤에 라이브 콘서트하는
사람은 마돈나다! **b)** FORMAL done
together with someone else ‖ 다른 사람
과 함께 하는. (…과) 협력[공조]하는:
police working in concert with local
authorities 지방 당국과 협력하는 경찰
con·cert·ed /kən'sɚtɪd/ *adj* **a**
concerted effort/attempt etc.
something that is done by people
working together in a determined way ‖
결연한 자세로 함께 일하는 사람들에 의해
행해지는 일. 협력에 의한 노력/시도:
Courtland County officials have made a
concerted effort to raise the standards
of education. 코틀랜드 군 관리들은 교육
수준을 높이기 위해 일치 단결하여 노력했
다.
con·cer·to /kən'tʃɛrtoʊ/ *n* a piece of
CLASSICAL MUSIC, usually for one
instrument and an ORCHESTRA ‖ 보통 독
주 악기와 오케스트라용의 클래식 음악 작
품. 협주곡. 콘체르토
con·ces·sion /kən'sɛʃən/ *n* **1**
something that you let someone have in
order to end an argument ‖ 논쟁을 끝내
기 위해 남에게 허용하는 것. 양보. 승인:
Neither side is willing to make
concessions on/about the issue of pay.
임금 문제에 관해 양측 모두 양보하려들지
않는다. **2** a special right given to
someone by the government, an
employer etc. ‖ 정부·사용자 등이 어떤 사
람에게 주는 특별한 권리. 면허. 특혜. 이
권. 특권: *tax concessions for married*
people 기혼자들에 대한 세제 혜택. **3** the
right to have a business in a particular
place, especially in a place owned by
someone else ‖ 특정 장소, 특히 다른 사
람이 소유한 장소에서 영업하는 권리. 영
업 허가
concession stand /.'.. ,./ *n* a small
business that sells food, drinks, and
other things at sports events, theaters
etc. ‖ 스포츠 경기·극장 등에서 음식·음료
등을 파는 조그만 상점. 매점
con·ci·erge /kɔn'syɛrʒ/ *n* someone in
a hotel whose job is to help guests with
problems, give advice about local places
to go etc. ‖ 손님들의 문제를 도와 주고 지
역의 방문할 장소 등을 조언해 주는 호텔
의 직업인. 접객 담당자. 안내인
con·cil·i·a·tion /kən,sɪli'eɪʃən/ *n* [U]

FORMAL the process of trying to end an
argument between people ‖ 사람들 사이
의 논쟁을 종식시키려는 과정. 달래기. 회
유 . 조정 . 화해 **– conciliate**
/kən'sɪli,eɪt/ *v* [T]
con·cil·i·a·to·ry /kən'sɪliə,tɔri/ *adj*
FORMAL intended to make someone stop
being angry with you or with someone
else ‖ 어떤 사람이 자신 또는 다른 사람에
게 화내는 것을 막으려 하는. 달래는. 회
유하는: *a conciliatory remark* 회유성 발
언
con·cise /kən'saɪs/ *adj* short and
clear, without using too many words ‖
말을 너무 많이 하지 않고 짧고 분명한. 간
명한. 간결한: *a concise answer* 간결한
답변 **– concisely** *adv* **– concise-**
ness *n* [U]
con·clude /kən'klud/ *v* **1** [T] to decide
something after considering all the
information you have ‖ 가지고 있는 모든
정보를 참작한 후 어떤 결을 결정하다. 결
론을 내리다[짓다]: *Doctors have*
concluded that sunburn can lead to
skin cancer. 의사들은 햇볕에 피부를 태
우는 것이 피부암을 일으킬 수 있다는 결
론을 내렸다. **2** [T] to complete
something that you have been doing ‖ 계
속해 오던 일을 완결하다. 종결[완료]하
다: *The study was concluded last*
month. 연구는 지난달에 종결됐다. **3** [I,
T] to end a meeting, speech, piece of
writing etc. by doing or saying one final
thing ‖ 마지막 하나를 하거나 말함으로써
회의·연설·작문 등을 끝내다. 끝맺음하다.
…을 끝으로 종료하다: *The carnival*
concluded with a fireworks display.
불꽃 놀이로 축제를 마쳤다. **4** [T] to
successfully finish something or agree
on something ‖ 일을 성공적으로 끝내거나
일에 대해 합의하다. …을 맺다. 체결하
다: *This lecture concludes the course.* 이
강의를 끝으로 과정은 끝이 난다. **–**
concluding *adj* : *concluding remarks*
맺음 말[결어(結語)]
con·clu·sion /kən'kluʒən/ *n* **1**
something that you decide after
considering all the information you have
‖ 가진 모든 정보를 고려한 후 결정하는
것. 결론. 결정. 판정: *I've come to the*
conclusion that she's lying. 나는 그녀가
거짓말 하고 있다는 결론에 도달했다. /
It's hard to draw any conclusions
without more data. 추가 자료 없이 어떤
결론을 내리기는 힘들다. / *Megan, you're*
jumping to conclusions. (=deciding
something is true without knowing all
the facts) 메건, 너는 성급하게 결론을 내

리고 있다. **2 the end or final part of something** ‖ 어떤 일의 끝이나 최종 부분. 끝맺음. 결말. 종결: *Your essay's fine, but the conclusion needs more work.* 너의 에세이는 훌륭하지만 결론 부분에 손질이 필요하다. **3 in conclusion** FORMAL used in speech or a piece of writing to show that you are about to finish ‖ 연설이나 작문을 끝내려는 것을 나타내는 데 쓰여. 끝으로. 결론적으로 —see also FOREGONE CONCLUSION

con·clu·sive /kən'klusɪv/ *adj* showing without any doubt that something is true ‖ 추호도 의심을 하지 않고 어떤 것이 사실임을 나타내는. 결정적인: *There is no conclusive evidence connecting him with the crime.* 그를 그 범죄와 연관시킬 결정적인 증거는 아무것도 없다. – **conclusively** *adv*

con·coct /kən'kakt/ *v* [T] **1** to invent a story, plan, or excuse, especially in order to deceive someone ‖ 특히 다른 사람을 속이기 위해 이야기[계획, 변명]를 꾸며내다. 거짓말을 지어내다: *She concocted a story about her mother being sick.* 그녀는 어머니가 아프다는 거짓말을 꾸며냈다. **2** to make something unusual by mixing different things together ‖ 상이한 것들을 함께 섞어서 특별한 것을 만들어 내다. 조합[혼합]해서 …을 만들다: *Lou concocts wonderful things in the kitchen.* 루는 부엌에서 (이것 저것 섞어서)굉장한 것을 만든다. – **concoction** *n*

con·course /'kankɔrs/ *n* a large hall or open place in an airport, train station etc. ‖ 공항·기차역 등의 넓은 홀이나 탁 트인 공간. 중앙 홀. 광장

con·crete¹ /kan'krit, 'kankrit/ *adj* **1** made of CONCRETE ‖ 콘크리트로 만들어진. 콘크리트의: *a concrete floor* 콘크리트 바닥 **2** clearly based on facts, not on beliefs or guesses ‖ 믿음이나 추측이 아닌 사실에 명백히 근거한. 구체적인. 실재적인: *We need concrete evidence to prove that he did it.* 그가 했다는 것을 증명하기 위해서 우리는 구체적인 증거가 필요하다. – **concretely** *adv*

con·crete² /'kankrit/ *n* a substance used for building that is made by mixing sand, water, small stones, and CEMENT ‖ 모래·물·자갈·시멘트를 섞어서 만드는 건축 용도의 재료. 콘크리트

con·cur /kən'kɚ/ *v* **-rred, -rring** [I] FORMAL to agree with someone or have the same opinion ‖ 남에게 동의하거나 같은 의견을 갖다. 의견 일치를 보다: *Dr. Hastings concurs with the decision of the medical board.* 헤이스팅스 박사는 병원 이사회의 결정에 동의했다. – **concurrence** *n* [U]

con·cur·rent /kən'kɚənt, -'kʌrənt/ *adj* FORMAL **1** existing or happening at the same time ‖ 동시에 존재하거나 발생하는. 공존하는. 동시 발생의: *In 1992, di Gesu's work was displayed in three concurrent art exhibitions.* 1992년 디 게수의 작품은 동시에 3개의 미술 전시회에서 전시되었다. **2** FORMAL in agreement ‖ 일치한. 같은 의견인: *concurrent opinions* 일치된 견해[의견 일치] – **concurrently** *adv*

con·cus·sion /kən'kʌʃən/ *n* [C, U] a small amount of damage to the brain that makes you become unconscious or feel sick, caused by hitting your head ‖ 머리를 부딪쳐서 생긴, 의식 불명 또는 구토증이 나게 하는 가벼운 뇌 손상. 뇌진탕

con·demn /kən'dɛm/ *v* [T] **1** to say very strongly that you do not approve of someone or something ‖ 사람이나 사물을 용인하지 않는다는 것을 강력히 말하다. 비난하다. 힐난하다: *Plans to dump nuclear waste here have been condemned by local residents.* 핵 폐기물을 이곳에 버리는 계획은 지역 주민들에게 비난받아 왔다. **2** to give a severe punishment to someone who is guilty of a crime ‖ 죄를 범한 사람을 엄중히 처벌을 하다. 형을 선고하다: *a murderer who was condemned to death* 사형이 선고된 살인범 **3** to force someone to live in an unpleasant way or to suffer ‖ 사람을 불행하게 살게 하거나 고통받게 하다. 운명지우다. 비참한 삶을 살게 하다: *The orphans were condemned to a life of poverty.* 고아들은 빈곤하게 살 수 밖에 없었다. **4** to say officially that a building is not safe enough to be lived in or used ‖ 건물이 거주하거나 사용하기에 안전하지 않다고 공식 발표하다. 사용 금지[용도 폐지] 처분하다

con·dem·na·tion /,kandəm'neɪʃən/ *n* [C, U] an expression of very strong disapproval ‖ 매우 강한 반대의 표현. 비난. 책망: *Condemnation of the plans came from across the community.* 그 계획에 대한 비난의 목소리가 사회 전반으로부터 터져 나왔다.

con·den·sa·tion /,kandən'seɪʃən/ *n* [U] small drops of water that appear when steam or hot air touches something that is cool, such as a window ‖ 증기나 뜨거운 공기가 유리창 등의 차가운 물체에 닿을 때 나타나는 작은 물방울. 응축. 결정체

con·dense /kənˈdɛns/ v **1** [T] to make a speech or piece of writing shorter by using fewer words to say the same thing ‖ 말이나 글을 더 적은 단어를 사용해 짧게 해서 동일한 의미를 표현하다. 간략화하다. 요점[단축]하다 **2** [I, T] if gas or hot air condenses, it becomes a liquid as it becomes cooler ‖ 가스나 뜨거운 공기가 더 차가워지면서 액체가 되다. 응결하다. 액화하다 **3** [T] to make a liquid thicker by removing some of the water from it ‖ 액체에서 어느 정도의 수분을 제거하여 더 진하게 만들다. 농축시키다: *condensed soup* 진한 수프

con·de·scend /ˌkɑndɪˈsɛnd/ v [I] **1** OFTEN HUMOROUS to agree to do something even though you think that you should not have to do it ‖ 반드시 해야 할 필요가 없다고 생각하면서도 어떤 일을 하는 데에 동의하다. 체면치레로[선심쓰듯이] …하기로 하다. 생색내며 …하다: *Do you think you can condescend to helping your sister?* 너는 생색을 내며 누이를 도울 수 있다고 생각하느냐? **2 condescend to sb** to behave as if you are better or more important than someone else ‖ 자신이 다른 사람보다 뛰어나거나 더 중요한 것처럼 행동하다. 뻐기다. 으스대다 **– condescension** /ˌkɑndəˈsɛnʃən/ n [U]

con·de·scend·ing /ˌkɑndɪˈsɛndɪŋ/ adj showing that you think you are better or more important than other people ‖ 자신이 다른 사람들보다 더 훌륭하거나 더 중요하다고 생각하고 있음을 보여주는. 우월감을 보이는. 으스대는: *I can't stand his condescending attitude!* 나는 그의 으스대는 태도를 참을 수가 없어!

con·di·ment /ˈkɑndəmənt/ n FORMAL something that you add to food when you are eating it to make it taste better ‖ 음식을 먹을 때 맛을 더 좋게 하기 위해 음식에 추가하는 것. 양념. 향신료

con·di·tion¹ /kənˈdɪʃən/ n [C, U] **1** the particular state that someone or something is in ‖ 사람이나 사물이 처해 있는 특정한 상황. 형편. 현황: *I'm not buying the car until I see what condition it's in.* 내가 그 차의 상태를 점검해 볼 때까지 그 차를 사지 않겠다. / *The VCR is still in pretty good condition.* VCR은 아직 상태가 아주 좋다. **2** something that must happen or be done before something else can happen or be done ‖ 다른 것이 일어나거나 수행되려면 먼저 반드시 일어나거나 수행되어야 하는 것. 조건. 요건: *a set of conditions for getting into college* 대학

에 입학하기 위한 일련의 요건들 / *Grandma sent some money for Steve on condition that* (=if) *he save it.* 할머니는 절약한다는 조건으로 스티브에게 돈을 조금 보내주었다. **3** the state of health of a person or animal ‖ 사람이나 동물의 건강 상태. …할 건강 조건: *Molly is in no condition to return to work.* (=too sick or upset to work) 몰리는 일에 복귀할 건강 상태가 아니다. / *a bad heart condition* (=that has affected you for a long time) 오래된 심장 질환 —see also CONDITIONS

con·di·tion² v [T] **1** to make a person or animal behave in a particular way by training him, her, or it over a period of time ‖ 사람이나 동물을 일정 기간에 걸쳐 훈련시켜 특정하게 행동하게 하다. 길들여서 …하게 하다: *Pavlov conditioned the dogs to expect food at the sound of a bell.* 파블로프는 개가 종소리를 듣고 먹이를 기대하도록 훈련시켰다. **2** to make your hair easy to comb by putting a special liquid on it ‖ 특수 액체를 머리에 발라서 빗질하기 쉽게 해 주다. 컨디셔액으로 머리를 보호하다

con·di·tion·al /kənˈdɪʃənəl/ adj **1** if an offer, agreement etc. is conditional, it will only be done if something else happens ‖ 다른 어떤 일이 발생할 경우에만 제안·협정 등이 성사되는. 조건에 따라 정해지는. 조건부의: *Our buying the house is conditional on our loan approval.* 대출이 승인돼야 우리는 그 집을 산다. **2** TECHNICAL a conditional sentence is one that usually begins with "if" or "unless," and states something that must be true or must happen before something else can be true or happen ‖ 문장이 보통 "if"나 "unless"로 시작하며 사전에 다른 것이 실현되거나 발생해야 어떤 것이 실현되거나 발생한다고 말하는. 조건을 나타내는. 조건문(條件文)의

con·di·tion·er /kənˈdɪʃənɚ/ n a special liquid that you put on your hair after washing it to make it easier to comb ‖ 머리를 감고 나서 빗으로 빗기 쉽도록 머리에 바르는 특수 액체. 헤어 컨디셔너

con·di·tion·ing /kənˈdɪʃənɪŋ/ n [U] the process by which people or animals learn to behave in a particular way ‖ 사람이나 동물이 특정하게 행동하도록 학습하는 과정. 조건 학습. 적응[순응] 과정. …화하기: *social conditioning* 사회적 적응[사회화 과정]

con·di·tions /kənˈdɪʃənz/ [plural] **1** the situation in which people live or work, especially the physical things that affect them ‖ 사람들이 생활하거나 일하는 상황, 특히 사람들에게 영향을 끼치는 물리적인 것들. 상태. 형편: *Poor living/working conditions are part of their daily lives.* 가난한 주거 환경[열악한 근로 조건들]이 그들의 일상 생활을 이루고 있다. **2** the weather at a particular time ‖ 특정 시간의 날씨. 기상 조건: *Icy conditions on the roads are making driving dangerous.* 도로 결빙으로 운전이 위험해지고 있다.

con·do /'kɑndoʊ/ *n* INFORMAL ⇨ CONDOMINIUM

con·do·lence /kən'doʊləns/ *n* [C usually plural, U] sympathy for someone when something very bad has happened ‖ 사람에게 매우 나쁜 일이 일어났을 때 느끼는 동정심. 조의. 애도: *My condolences on your mother's death.* 자당의 별세에 대하여 조의를 표합니다.

con·dom /'kɑndəm/ *n* a thin piece of rubber that a man wears over his PENIS during sex to stop a woman becoming PREGNANT, or to protect against disease ‖ 여성이 임신되는 것을 막거나 질병에서 보호하기 위해 남성이 성교시에 성기에 씌우는 얇은 고무. 콘돔

con·do·min·i·um /,kɑndə'mɪniəm/ *n* a building that consists of separate apartments, each of which is owned by the people living in it, or one of these apartments ‖ 분할된 아파트들로 이루어져 각각의 아파트를 그곳에 사는 사람들이 소유하는 건물, 또는 이 아파트들 중의 하나. 콘도(미니엄)

con·done /kən'doʊn/ *v* [T] to approve of behavior that most people think is wrong ‖ 대부분의 사람들이 나쁘다고 생각하는 행위를 승인하다. 묵과하다. 비행을 용서하다: *I cannot condone the use of violence.* 나는 폭력의 사용을 묵인할 수 없다.

con·du·cive /kən'dusɪv/ *adj* FORMAL **be conducive to** to provide conditions that make it easier to do something ‖ 어떤 일을 더 쉽게 할 수 있는 조건을 제공하다. 도움이 되다. 공헌하다: *The sunny climate is conducive to outdoor activities.* 햇볕이 쨍한 날씨는 야외 활동에 좋다.

con·duct¹ /kən'dʌkt/ *v* **1** [T] to do something in order to find out or prove something ‖ 어떤 것을 발견하거나 증명하기 위해 어떤 일을 하다. 수행[처리, 실시]: *Dr. Hamilton is conducting an experiment for the class.* 해밀턴 박사는 수업을 위해서 실험을 하고 있다. **2** [I, T]

to stand in front of a group of musicians or singers and direct their playing or singing ‖ 일단의 음악가나 성악가 앞에 서서 그들이 연주하거나 노래하는 것을 지시하다. 지휘하다: *the Boston Pops Orchestra, conducted by John Williams.* 보스턴 팝 오케스트라, 지휘자 존 윌리엄스 **3** [T] if something conducts electricity or heat, it allows the electricity or heat to travel along or through it ‖ 전기나 열이 지나가거나 통과하게 하다. 전기·열을 전도하다 **4 conduct yourself** FORMAL to behave in a particular way ‖ 특정한 방식으로 행동하다. …에 맞게 처신하다. 처신을 잘하다: *He conducted himself well in the job interview.* 그는 구직 면접을 잘 치렀다. **5** [T] to show someone a place as part of an official TOUR ‖ 공식 관람의 한 부분으로서 남에게 어떤 장소를 보여 주다. 안내하다. 수행하여 둘러보게 하다: *A guide will conduct us through the museum.* 안내자가 우리에게 박물관을 안내하여 줄 것이다.

con·duct² /'kɑndʌkt, -dəkt/ *n* [U] FORMAL **1** the way someone behaves ‖ 사람이 행동하는 방식. 처신. 태도. 품행 **2** the way a business or activity is organized and done ‖ 사업이나 활동이 조직되어 수행되는 방식. 운영. 경영. 수행: *The mayor was not satisfied with the conduct of the meeting.* 시장은 그 회의의 진행 방식이 맘에 들지 않았다.

con·duc·tor /kən'dʌktɚ/ *n* **1** someone who CONDUCTS a group of musicians or singers ‖ 연주단이나 합창단을 지휘하는 사람. 지휘자 **2** someone who is in charge of a train or the workers on it ‖ 열차나 열차 승무원을 관리하는 사람. 열차 차장

cone

traffic cone   ice cream cone   pine cone

cone /koʊn/ *n* **1** a hollow or solid object with a round base and a point at the top ‖ 둥근 밑변과 뾰족한 상단을 가진, 속이 비거나 단단한 물체. 원추. 원뿔: *an orange traffic cone* 오렌지색 (원뿔형) 교통 표지판 **2** ⇨ ICE CREAM CONE **3** the hard brown woody fruit of a PINE or FIR

tree ‖ 소나무나 전나무의 단단한 갈색의
나무 열매. 솔방울

con·fed·er·a·cy /kən'fɛdərəsi/ *n* **1 the
Confederacy** the southern states that
fought against northern states in the
American Civil War ‖ 미국 남북 전쟁에서
북부 주들에 대항해 싸운 남부 주들. 남부
연맹[연합] **2** ⇨ CONFEDERATION –
confederate /kən'fɛdərɪt/ *adj*

con·fed·er·ate /kən'fɛdərɪt/ *n* a
soldier in the Confederacy ‖ 남부 연맹의
군인. 남군(南軍)

con·fed·e·ra·tion /kən,fɛdə'reɪʃən/ *n* a
group of people, political parties, or
organizations that have united in order
to achieve an aim ‖ 목적을 달성하기 위해
결합한 사람[정당, 단체]의 집단. …의 연
합[연맹, 동맹](체): *a confederation of
47 insurance agencies* 47개 보험 대리점
들의 연합체 – **confederate** /kən-
'fɛdə,reɪt/ *v* [I, T]

con·fer /kən'fɚ/ *v* **-rred, -rring 1** [I]
to discuss something with other people
so everyone can give his/her opinion ‖ 모
든 사람이 자신의 의견을 낼 수 있도록 다
른 사람들과 어떤 것을 의논하다. 협의[상
의]하다: *The lawyers are conferring on
this matter.* 변호사들이 이 문제에 대해
의논 중이다. **2 confer a degree/honor
etc. on sb** to give someone a degree
etc. in order to reward him/her ‖ 어떤
사람에게 포상하기 위해 학위 등을 주다.
…에게 학위/명예를 수여하다

con·fer·ence /'kɑnfrəns/ *n* [C, U] **1** a
large formal meeting in which people
exchange ideas about business, politics
etc., especially for several days ‖ 사람들
이 특히 수일 동안 사업·정치 등에 대해
의견을 교환하는 대규모의 공식 모임. 회
의. 회합. 협의회: *a sales conference* 판
매 회의 / *a conference room/center* 회의
실[대회의장] **2** a private meeting in
which a few people discuss something ‖
몇 사람이 어떤 일을 의논하는 사적인 회
의: *Ms. Chen is in conference at the
moment.* 첸 여사는 지금 회의 중입니다.

conference call /'.. ,./ *n* a telephone
conversation in which several people in
different places can all talk to each
other ‖ 서로 다른 곳에 있는 수명의 사람
들이 서로에게 모두 이야기할 수 있는 전
화 대화. 여럿이 하는 전화 회의

con·fess /kən'fɛs/ *v* [I, T] **1** to admit
that you have done something wrong or
illegal ‖ 나쁜 일이나 불법적인 일을 했음
을 시인하다. 자인[자백]하다. 고백하다:
It didn't take long for her to confess. 그
녀가 자백하기까지는 오래 걸리지 않았다.

/ *Jared wouldn't confess to the
beating.* 제러드는 구타에도 불구하고 자
백하지 않을 것이다. **2** to admit
something that you feel embarrassed
about ‖ 어떤 일에 대해 난처하게 느꼈음
을 인정하다. 토로[실토]하다. …을 털어
놓다: *Lyn confessed that she had fallen
asleep in class.* 린은 수업 중에 졸았다고
털어놓았다. **3** to tell a priest or God
about the wrong things you have done ‖
자신이 저지른 잘못을 사제나 신에게 말하
다. 고백[고해]하다. 고해 성사를 하다 –
confessed *adj*

con·fes·sion /kən'fɛʃən/ *n* **1** a
statement that you have done something
wrong or illegal ‖ 잘못이나 불법을 저질
렀다는 진술. 고백. 자백. 자인: *He made
a full confession at the police station.*
그는 경찰서에서 모두 자백했다. **2** [C, U]
the act of CONFESS*ing* to a priest ‖ 사제에
게 고백하는 행위. 고백(성사)

con·fet·ti /kən'fɛti/ *n* [U] small pieces
of colored paper thrown into the air at a
wedding, party etc. ‖ 결혼식·파티 등에서
공중에 뿌리는 작은 색종이 조각

con·fi·dant, confidante /'kɑn-
fə,dɑnt/ *n* someone to whom you tell
secrets or personal information ‖ 비밀
이나 사적인 정보를 말할 수 있는 사람.
믿을 만한 사람. 절친한 친구

con·fide /kən'faɪd/ *v* [T] to tell a secret
to someone you trust ‖ 신뢰하는 사람에
게 비밀을 말하다. …을 털어놓다[고 이야
기하다]: *Joel confided to her that he
didn't want to study medicine.* 조엘은
의학을 공부하고 싶지 않다고 그녀에게 털
어 놓았다.

confide in sb *phr v* [T] to tell someone
you trust about something that is very
private ‖ 매우 사적인 것에 대하여 자신이
신뢰하는 사람에게 말하다. 속내를 털어놓
다: *I don't trust her enough to confide
in her.* 그녀에게 속내를 털어놓을 만큼 그
녀를 믿지는 못한다.

con·fi·dence /'kɑnfədəns/ *n* **1** [U]
belief in your own or someone else's
ability to do things well ‖ 일을 잘 할 수
있다는, 자신 또는 다른 사람의 능력에 대
한 믿음. 신용. 신임. 자신(감): *She has
no confidence in my driving ability.* 그
녀는 내 운전 실력을 믿지 않고 있다. /
*Living in another country gave me more
confidence.* 다른 나라에서 생활한 경험이
내게 더 큰 자신감을 주었다. **2** [U] the
feeling that something is true, or that it
will produce good results ‖ 어떤 일이 사
실이거나 좋은 결과를 낳으리라는 느낌.
확신. 신념: *Young people today have no*

confidence in the future. 오늘날의 젊은 이들은 미래에 대한 신념이 없다. / *I have confidence (that) it will work.* 나는 그 것이 잘 될 것이라고 확신하고 있다. **3** [U] a feeling of trust that someone will not tell your secrets to other people ‖ 어떤 사람이 자신의 비밀을 다른 사람들에게 말 하지 않을 것이라고 믿는 감정. 신뢰(감): *It took a long time to gain his confidence.* (=make him feel he could trust me) 그의 신뢰를 얻기까지 시간이 오래 걸렸다. **4** a secret or a piece of information that is personal ‖ 사적인 비 밀이나 정보. 개인 비밀. 속내

con·fi·dent /'kɑnfədənt/ *adj* **1** sure that you can do something well ‖ 어떤 일 을 잘 할 수 있다고 확신하는. 굳게 믿는. 자신 만만한: *We won't continue until you feel confident about using the equipment.* 우리는 네가 장비 사용에 대 해 자신감을 가질 때까지는 계속하지 않겠 다. / *She seems very confident of winning.* 그녀는 승리에 대해 확신하는 것 같다. ✗DON'T SAY "She seems very confident of herself."✗ "She seems very confident of herself"라고는 하지 않는다. —compare SELF-CONFIDENT **2** very sure that something is going to happen ‖ 어떤 일이 일어날 것이라고 확신하는. …할 것 임을 의심하지 않는: *I'm confident (that) he'll help us out.* 나는 그가 우리들을 도 와줄 것이라고 확신한다. –**confidently** *adv*

con·fi·den·tial /ˌkɑnfə'dɛnʃəl/ *adj* intended to be kept secret ‖ 비밀로 유지 하려는 의도의. 기밀[비밀]의. 은밀한: *a confidential report* 비밀 보고(서) – **confidentially** *adv*

con·fig·u·ra·tion /kənˌfɪgjə'reɪʃən/ *n* the way that the things in a place or the parts of something are arranged ‖ 한 장 소의 물건들이나 어떤 것의 각 요소들이 배열된 방식. 배치. 형태. 구성: *a table arranged in a U-shaped configuration* U 자 형태로 배열된 탁자

con·fine /kən'faɪn/ *v* [T] **1** to happen in only one place or time, or affect only one group of people ‖ 오직 한 장소나 한 때에 일어나다, 또는 한 집단의 사람들에 게만 영향을 미치다. …에 한(정)하다. 국 한하다: *The fire was confined to one building.* 불은 건물 한 곳에만 났다. / *This problem is not confined to the western world.* 이 문제는 서방 세계에만 국한된 것이 아니다. **2** to have to stay in a place, especially because you are ill ‖ 특히 아파서 한 곳에 머물려야 하다. 꼼짝 못하고 …에 (남아) 있다: *Rachel is*

confined to her bed. 레이첼은 (아파서) 침대에 꼼짝 않고 누워 있어야 한다. **3** to keep someone or something within the limits of a particular subject or activity ‖ 사람이나 사물을 특정한 주제나 활동 범 위 안에 잡아 두다. 분야나 활동을 …으로 제한하다: *Try to confine yourself to spending $120 a week.* 일주일에 120달 러만 지출하도록 절제해 봐라. **4** to make someone stay in a place s/he cannot leave, such as a prison ‖ 남을 나갈 수 없 는 교도소 등에 머무르게 하다. 가두다. 감금하다

con·fined /kən'faɪnd/ *adj* a confined space or area is very small ‖ 공간이나 구 역이 매우 작은. 한정된

con·fine·ment /kən'faɪnmənt/ *n* [U] the act of making someone stay in a room or area, or the state of being there ‖ 누군가를 방이나 구역에 머물게 하 는 행위, 또는 거기에 있는 상태. 가둠. 갇 힘. 감금. 유폐: *Ellie hated the confinement of living in an apartment.* 엘리는 아파트에 갇혀 살기를 싫어했다. —see also SOLITARY CONFINEMENT

con·fines /'kɑnfaɪnz/ *n* [plural] the walls, limits or borders of something ‖ 벽 또는 사물의 한계나 경계. 범위. 변경: *His son has only seen him within the confines of the prison.* 그의 아들은 오직 교도소 안에서만 그를 봤을 뿐이다.

con·firm /kən'fɚm/ *v* [T] **1** to say or prove that something is definitely true ‖ 무엇이 분명히 사실이라고 말하거나 입증 하다. 확언[확증]하다: *Dr. Martin confirmed the diagnosis of cancer.* 마틴 박사는 암진단을 확언했다. / *Can you confirm that she really was there?* 당신 은 그녀가 정말 거기에 있었다고 확언할 수 있습니까? **2** to tell someone that a possible plan, arrangement etc. is now definite ‖ 남에게 가능성 있는 계획·준비 등이 이제 확실하게 정해졌다고 말하다. 확 정하다. 굳히다: *Please confirm your reservations 72 hours in advance.* 당신 의 예약을 72시간 전에 확인해 주세요.

con·fir·ma·tion /ˌkɑnfɚ'meɪʃən/ *n* [C, U] a statement or letter that says that something is definitely true, or the act of saying this ‖ 무엇이 분명히 사실이라고 말하는 진술이나 서한, 또는 그렇게 말하 는 행위. 확정(서). 확언. 확인: *We're waiting for confirmation of the report.* 우리는 그 보고의 사실 확인을 기다리고 있다.

con·firmed /kən'fɚmd/ *adj* **a confirmed bachelor/alcoholic etc.** someone who seems completely happy with his/her way of life ‖ 자신의 생활 방식에 완전히 만족하고 있는 듯한 사람. 굳어진 독신주의자/알코올 중독자: *Charlie was a confirmed bachelor, until he met Helen.* 찰리는 헬렌을 만날 때까지는 독신에 만족하는 사람이었다.

con·fis·cate /ˈkɑnfəˌskeɪt/ v [T] to officially take someone's property away from him/her, usually as a punishment ‖ 보통 벌로서 남의 재산을 공식적으로 빼앗다. 압수[몰수, 압류]하다: *The police confiscated his gun when they arrested him.* 경찰은 그를 체포했을 때 그의 총을 압수했다. – **confiscation** /ˌkɑnfəˈskeɪʃən/ n [C, U]

con·flict¹ /ˈkɑnˌflɪkt/ n [C, U] **1** disagreement between people, groups, countries etc. ‖ 사람·집단·국가 등 사이의 불일치. 반목. 대립. 갈등: *The two groups have been in conflict with each other for years.* 두 단체는 수년 동안 서로 반목해 왔다. / *a conflict between father and son* 아버지와 아들의 갈등 / *conflicts over who owns the land* 토지의 소유권을 둘러싼 대립 **2** a situation in which you have to choose between opposing things ‖ 서로 반대되는 것들 사이에서 선택해야 하는 상황. 모순[상충] 상황. 갈등 국면: *In a conflict between work and family, I would always choose my family.* 일과 가정이 상충되는 상황이라면 나는 언제나 가정을 선택하겠다. **3** a war or fight in which weapons are used ‖ 무기가 사용되는 전쟁이나 전투

con·flict² /kənˈflɪkt/ v [I] if two ideas, beliefs, opinions etc. conflict, they cannot both be true ‖ 두 개의 사상·믿음·의견 등이 양쪽 모두가 사실일 수 없다. 모순[상반]되다. 대립[충돌]하다: *What she just said conflicts with what she said before.* 그녀가 방금 말한 것은 전에 말한 것과 상충된다. / *We have heard many conflicting opinions on the subject.* 우리는 그 주제에 대한 많은 상반되는 의견을 들었다.

conflict of in·ter·est /ˌ.. ˈ../ n a situation in which you cannot legally be involved in one business activity, because you have connections with another business that would gain an unfair advantage from your involvement ‖ 다른 사업에 참여한 상태에서 어떤 사업 활동에 개입시 부당 이득을 볼 수 있기 때문에 법적으로 그 사업에 관계할 수 없게 된 상황. 이해 상충

con·form /kənˈfɔrm/ v [I] **1** to behave in the way that most people do ‖ 대부분의 사람들이 하는 대로 행동하다. 순응[순종]하다. 말을 잘 듣다: *There's always pressure on kids to conform.* 아이들에게는 항상 말을 잘 들으라는 압력이 가해진다. **2** to obey or follow an established rule, pattern, etc. ‖ 제정되어 있는 규칙·양식 등을 준수하거나 따르다. 규정을 지키다[엄수하다]: *Seatbelts must conform to safety standards.* 안전 벨트는 안전 기준에 맞아야 한다. – **conformity** n [U]

con·form·ist /kənˈfɔrmɪst/ n someone who behaves or thinks too much like everyone else ‖ 다른 모든 사람들과 너무 똑같이 행동하거나 생각하는 사람. 순응자. 신봉자 —opposite NONCONFORMIST

con·found /kənˈfaʊnd/ v [T] to be impossible to explain, often in a way that worries or surprises you ‖ 종종 사람을 걱정시키거나 놀라게 하는 식으로 설명하기가 불가능하다. 당혹[어리둥절]하게 하다. 어안이 벙벙해지다: *Her illness confounded the doctors.* 그녀의 병은 의사들을 어리둥절하게 했다.

con·front /kənˈfrʌnt/ v [T] **1** to try to make someone admit s/he has done something wrong ‖ 누군가에게 잘못했음을 시인하게 하려 하다. 따지다. 들이대고 맞서다. 대립하다: *I'm afraid to confront her about her drinking.* 나는 그녀의 음주 문제를 그녀에게 따지기가 두렵다. **2** to have to deal with something difficult or unpleasant, usually in a brave way ‖ 어렵거나 불쾌한 일을 보통 용감하게 대처해야 하다. 대결[대항]하다. 직면하다: *Sooner or later you'll have to confront your problems.* 조만간에 당신은 당신의 문제에 직면해야 할 것입니다. **3** to behave in a threatening way toward someone ‖ 남에게 위협적으로 행동하다. 가로막고 대치하다: *Security guards confronted us at the door.* 경비원들이 문에서 우리를 가로막았다.

con·fron·ta·tion /ˌkɑnfrənˈteɪʃən/ n [C, U] a situation in which there is a lot of angry disagreement ‖ 매우 화가 나서 다투고 있는 상태. 대결. 대립. 대치. 충돌: *Stan doesn't like confrontations.* 스탠은 충돌이 일어나는 것을 좋아하지 않는다.

con·fuse /kənˈfyuz/ v [T] **1** to make someone feel unable to think clearly or understand something ‖ 어떤 사람에게 사물을 명확히 생각하거나 이해할 수 없다는 느낌이 들게 하다. 혼란시키다. 당황하게 하다: *His directions really confused me.* 그의 지시는 정말로 나를 혼란스럽게 했다. **2** to think wrongly that one person, thing or idea is really someone or something else ‖ 어떤 사람[사물, 생

각]을 실제로 다른 사람이나 사물로 잘못 생각하다. 혼동하다. 착각하다: *It's easy to confuse Sue with her sister. They look so much alike.* 수는 그녀의 동생과 혼동하기 쉽다. 그들은 정말 똑같다.

con·fused /kənˈfyuzd/ *adj* **1** unable to understand something clearly ‖ 사물을 분명히 이해할 수 없는. 혼란[혼미]해진. 당황한: *I'm totally confused.* 나는 완전히 혼란스러웠다. / *If you're confused about anything, call me.* 무엇이든지 혼동되는 점이 있다면 제게 전화하세요. **2** not clear or not easy to understand ‖ 분명하지 않거나 쉽게 이해되지 않는. 불명확[애매]한. 구별[식별]되지 않는: *a confused answer* 애매한 답변 / *confused instructions* 불명확한 지시

con·fus·ing /kənˈfyuzɪŋ/ *adj* difficult to understand because there is no clear order or pattern ‖ 명백한 질서나 양식이 없어서 이해하기 어려운. 혼란스러운. 어리둥절한: *The diagram is really confusing.* 그 도표는 정말 혼란스럽다.

con·fu·sion /kənˈfyuʒən/ *n* **1** [C, U] a state of not understanding what is happening or what something means ‖ 일어나고 있는 일이나 어떤 것이 의미하는 바를 이해하지 못하는 상태. 혼미. 혼동: *There's a lot of confusion about/over the new rules.* 새 규칙에 대해[을 두고] 많은 혼란이 있다. **2** [U] a situation in which there is a lot of activity that is difficult to understand or control ‖ 이해하거나 제어하기 어려운 활동이 많은 상태. 혼란 (상태). 뒤죽박죽(된) 상태: *After the explosion the airport was a scene of total confusion.* 폭발 후 공항은 완전히 아수라장이 되었다.

con·geal /kənˈdʒil/ *v* [I] if a liquid such as blood congeals, it becomes thick or solid ‖ 피 등의 액체가 진해지거나 고형화되다. 엉기다. 응고[응결]하다

con·gen·i·al /kənˈdʒinyəl/ *adj* FORMAL pleasant in a comfortable and relaxed way ‖ 편안하고 느긋하게 기분 좋은. 마음에 드는. 마음[기분]이 맞는: *a congenial host* 마음에 드는 주인

con·gen·i·tal /kənˈdʒɛnətl/ *adj* TECHNICAL affecting someone from the time s/he is born ‖ 태어날 때부터 사람에게 영향을 끼치는. 타고난. 선천적인: *a congenital heart problem* 선천적인 심장 질환

con·gest·ed /kənˈdʒɛstɪd/ *adj* **1** too full or blocked because of too many vehicles or people ‖ 탈것이나 사람이 너무 많아 꽉 차거나 막힌. 혼잡[밀집]한. 교통 체증 상태의: *the problem of*

congested freeways 혼잡한 고속도로 문제 **2** a congested nose, chest etc. is filled with thick liquid that does not flow easily ‖ 코·가슴 등이 잘 흐르지 않는 진한 액체로 가득찬. 꽉 막힌 울혈[충혈]이 된 – **congestion** /kənˈdʒɛstʃən/ *n* [U]

con·glom·er·ate /kənˈglɑmərɪt/ *n* **1** a large company made up of many different smaller companies ‖ 다수의 상이한 작은 회사로 이루어진 큰 회사. 복합 [거대] 기업 **2** a substance, such as rock, made up of many small pieces held together ‖ 많은 작은 조각들이 함께 뭉쳐져 이루어진 바위 등의 사물. 집합 (체). 집괴(集塊). 역암(礫岩)

con·glom·er·a·tion /kənˌglɑməˈreɪʃən/ *n* a group of many different things gathered together ‖ 함께 모아진 다수의 상이한 사물들의 집단. 복합(체)

con·grats /kənˈgræts/ *interjection* ⇨ CONGRATULATIONS

con·grat·u·late /kənˈgrætʃəˌleɪt/ *v* [T] to tell someone that you are happy because s/he has achieved something, or because something good has happened to him/her ‖ 누군가가 어떤 일을 성취해서, 또는 좋은 일이 누군가에게 일어나서 즐겁다고 말하다. …에게 …을 축하[경하]하다. 축하의 말을 하다: *I want to congratulate you on a fine achievement.* 당신의 훌륭한 업적에 대해 축하드리고 싶습니다. – **congratulatory** /kənˈgrætʃələˌtɔri/ *adj*

con·grat·u·la·tions /kənˌgrætʃəˈleɪʃəns/ *n* [plural] ESPECIALLY SPOKEN used in order to CONGRATULATE someone ‖ 남을 축하하기 위해 쓰여. 축하. 경하. 경축: *You won? Congratulations!* 이겼다고? 축하해! / *Congratulations on your engagement!* 약혼을 축하합니다!

con·gre·gate /ˈkɑŋgrəˌgeɪt/ *v* [I] to come together in a group ‖ 한 집단으로 모이다. 집합[집결]하다: *Ducks congregate here in the fall.* 가을에는 야생오리들이 이곳에 모인다.

con·gre·ga·tion /ˌkɑŋgrəˈgeɪʃən/ *n* a group of people gathered in a church for a religious service, or the people who usually go to a particular church ‖ 예배를 위해 교회에 모인 사람들의 집단, 또는 보통 특정 교회에 다니는 사람들. (교회의) 회중. 신도들. 교인들

Con·gre·ga·tion·al /ˌkɑŋgrəˈgeɪʃənl/ *adj* relating to a Protestant church in which each CONGREGATION makes its own decisions ‖ 각 교단이 독자적으로 결정하는 프로테스탄트 교회의. 조합 교회의 – **Congregationalist** *n, adj*

con·gress /ˈkɑŋgrɪs/ n **1 Congress** the group of people elected to make laws for the US, consisting of the Senate and the House of Representatives ‖ 상원과 하원으로 구성되어 미국의 법을 제정하도록 선출된 일단의 사람들. 국회: *The bill has been approved by both houses of Congress.* 법안이 상하원 모두에 의해 승인되었다. / *an act of Congress* 의회 활동 **2** a meeting of representatives of different groups, countries, etc. to exchange information and make decisions ‖ 서로 다른 집단·나라 등의 대표자들이 정보를 교환하고 결의를 하는 회의. 대회. 학회. 대표 회의 – **congressional** /kənˈgrɛʃənəl/ adj

con·gress·man /ˈkɑŋgrɪsmən/, **con·gress·wom·an** /ˈkɑŋgrɪsˌwʊmən/ n someone who is elected to be in CONGRESS ‖ 의회에 출석하도록 선출된 사람. 미연방 의회 의원

con·i·cal /ˈkɑnɪkəl/, **conic** /ˈkɑnɪk/ adj shaped like a CONE, or relating to cones ‖ 원뿔 모양의, 또는 원뿔에 관한. 원뿔(형)의

con·i·fer /ˈkɑnəfɚ/ n any tree that makes CONEs (=hard woody brown fruit) ‖ 솔방울을 맺는 나무의 총칭. 침엽수. 구과(毬果) 식물 – **coniferous** /kəˈnɪfərəs, koʊ-/ adj

con·jec·ture /kənˈdʒɛktʃɚ/ n [C, U] FORMAL the act of guessing about things when you do not have enough information ‖ 사물들에 대한 충분한 정보가 없을 때 그 것들을 추측하기. 억측. 짐작: *The report is based purely on conjecture.* 그 보고는 순전히 추측에 근거를 두고 있다. – **conjecture** v [I, T]

con·ju·gal /ˈkɑndʒəgəl/ adj FORMAL relating to marriage or married people ‖ 결혼이나 결혼한 사람들과 관련된. 결혼[혼인]의. 부부(간)의

con·ju·gate /ˈkɑndʒəˌgeɪt/ v [T] TECHNICAL to give all the parts of a verb in a fixed order ‖ 동사의 모든 부분을 정해진 방식으로 제시하다. 동사를 활용 변화시키다. 동사를 활용하다: *Try conjugating these irregular verbs.* 이 불규칙 동사들을 활용 변화시켜 봐라. – **conjugation** /ˌkɑndʒəˈgeɪʃən/ n [C, U]

con·junc·tion /kənˈdʒʌŋkʃən/ n **1 in conjunction with** working, happening, or being used with someone or something else ‖ 어떤 사람이나 사물과 협력해서[같이 일어나서, 같이 쓰여서]. …과 연대[연계]하여. …과 함께[공동으로]: *There are worksheets for use in conjunction with the training video.* 훈련용 비디오와 함께 쓰이는 연습 문제지가 있다. **2** TECHNICAL in grammar, a word such as "but," "and," or "while," that connects parts of sentences, phrases, or CLAUSEs ‖ 문법에서 문장[구, 절]의 부분들을 연결하는 "but", "and", "while" 등의 단어. 접속사

con·jure /ˈkɑndʒɚ/ v [I, T] to make something appear using magic ‖ 마술을 부려서 물건이 나타나게 하다. 마술로 출현시키다. 불러내다 – **conjurer**, **conjuror** n

conjure sth ↔ **up** phr v [T] **1** make an image, idea, memory etc. very clear and strong in someone's mind ‖ 이미지·생각·기억 등을 사람의 마음속에 매우 분명하고 강렬하게 하다. 상기시키다. 상상하게 하다: *Maria conjured up the whole Mediterranean for us in her talk.* 마리아가 하는 말에서 우리는 지중해의 전체 이미지를 떠올렸다. **2** to make something appear as if by magic ‖ 마술을 부리듯이 사물을 나타나게 하다. 출현시키다. 불러내다: *Pete can conjure up a meal out of whatever is in the fridge.* 피트는 냉장고에 있는 아무것으로나 식사를 뚝딱 만들어 낼 수 있다.

con·man /ˈkɑnˌmæn/ n INFORMAL someone who gets money or valuable things from people by tricking them ‖ 사람들을 속여서 돈이나 귀중품을 취하는 사람. 사기꾼

con·nect /kəˈnɛkt/ v **1** [I, T] to attach two or more things together ‖ 2개 이상의 사물을 한데 붙이다. 접속하다. 연결하다: *Next, you have to connect this bolt to the base.* 다음에는 이 나사를 바닥에 결합시키세요. / *I can't see how these hoses connect.* 나는 이들 호스를 어떻게 연결하는지 알 수가 없다. —opposite DISCONNECT **2** to realize that two facts, events, or people have a relationship ‖ 두 가지 사실[사건, 사람들]이 연관되어 있음을 알게 되다. 관련시켜[연관지어, 결부시켜] 생각하다: *I never connected her with Sam.* 나는 결코 그녀를 샘과 연관시켜 생각하지 못했다. **3** [T] to attach something to a supply of electricity, gas, etc. ‖ 물체를 전기·가스 등의 공급원에 연결하다. 잇다: *Is the TV connected yet?* 텔레비전이 이미 연결되어 있습니까? —opposite DISCONNECT **4** [I] to be planned so that passengers can continue their trip on a different plane, train, bus, etc. ‖ 승객들이 다른 비행기·열차·버스 등으로 여행을 계속할 수 있도록 마련되다. 갈아탈 수 있게 준비되다. 연계[환승]편이 마련되다: *a connecting* *flight to Omaha* 오마하행 환승 항공편 **5** [T] to attach telephone lines so that people can speak ‖ 사람들이 통화할 수 있도록 전화선을 연결하다. 접속시키다 — opposite DISCONNECT **6** [I] if people connect, they feel that they like and understand each other ‖ 사람들이 서로 좋아하고 이해함을 느끼다. 마음이 통하다. 유대감이 형성되다: *I really felt I connected with Jim's parents.* 나는 정말로 짐의 부모와 마음이 통한다고 느꼈다.

con·nect·ed /kə'nɛktɪd/ *adj* **1** joined to or relating to something else ‖ 다른 것에 연결되거나 관련된. 연관[결합]된: *Kai's problems are partly connected with drug abuse.* 카이의 문제는 부분적으로 마약 중독과 관련되어 있다. — opposite UNCONNECTED **2 well-connected** having important or powerful friends or relatives ‖ 중요하거나 힘이 있는 친구나 친척이 있는. 든든한 배경을 가진. 연고[연줄]가 좋은: *a wealthy and well-connected lawyer* 부유하고 배경이 든든한 변호사

con·nec·tion /kə'nɛkʃən/ *n* **1** [C, U] a relationship between things, people, ideas etc. ‖ 사물·사람·생각 등 간의 관계. 관련[연관](성): *What's the connection between the two events?* 두 사건 사이에 어떤 관계가 있니? / *This has no connection with our conversation.* 이것은 우리의 대화와 전혀 관련이 없습니다. **2** [U] the joining together of two or more things, especially by electricity, telephone, computer etc. ‖ 특히 전기·전화·컴퓨터 등의 2가지 이상의 것들을 결합하는 것. 연결. 접속. 이음: *There must be a loose connection – I'm not getting any power.* 단락된 곳이 있는게 틀림없다. 전기가 전혀 안 들어오거든. **3** a plane, bus, or train that leaves at a time that allows passengers from an earlier plane, bus, or train to use it to continue their trip ‖ 이전 비행기[버스, 열차]의 승객들이 여행을 계속할 수 있도록 일정 시간에 맞춰 출발하는 비행기[버스, 열차]. 환승[연계] 교통편: *I barely made/missed the connection* (=did or did not get the flight, train etc.) *to Boston.* 나는 간신히 [아슬아슬하게] 보스톤행 환승편을 탔다[놓쳤다]. **4 in connection with** concerning something ‖ 어떤 것에 관련된. … 과 연관시켜: *Police are questioning a man in connection with the crime.* 경찰은 범죄와 관련해서 한 남자를 심문하고 있다.

con·nec·tions /kə'nɛkʃənz/ *n* [plural] people who can help you because they have power ‖ 권력을 가지고 있어서 도움을 줄 수 있는 사람. 든든한 배경[연줄, 연고]: *Ramsey has connections* (=knows powerful people); *maybe he can help you.* 램지는 든든한 배경을 가지고 있어서 아마 너를 도울 수 있을 것이다.

con·nive /kə'naɪv/ *v* [I] to secretly work to achieve something wrong or illegal, or to allow something illegal to happen ‖ 그릇되거나 불법적인 일을 이루기 위해, 또는 불법적인 일이 일어나도록 비밀리에 일을 꾸미다. 음모를 꾸미다. …과 공모하다: *She's conniving with Tony to get Grandma's money.* 그녀는 할머니의 돈을 우려먹기 위해 토니와 공모 중이다. **– connivance** *n* [C, U]

con·nois·seur /ˌkɑnə'sɚ, -'sʊɚ/ *n* someone who knows a lot about something such as art, good food, music etc. ‖ 예술·좋은 음식·음악 등에 대해 많이 아는 사람. 감정인. 감식가. 전문가: *a true connoisseur of fine wines* 좋은 포도주의 진정한 감식가

con·no·ta·tion /ˌkɑnə'teɪʃən/ *n* an idea or a feeling that a word makes you think of, rather than the actual meaning of the word ‖ 단어의 실제 의미보다 단어로 인해 떠오르는 관념이나 느낌. 언외의[함축적] 의미: *a negative/positive connotation* 부정적[긍정적] 함축 **– connote** /kə'noʊt/ *v* [T]

con·quer /'kɑŋkɚ/ *v* **1** [I, T] to win control of a land or country by attacking an enemy or fighting in a war ‖ 적을 공격하거나 전쟁에서 싸워 땅이나 나라에 대한 지배권을 획득하다. 무력으로 획득하다. 정복하다: *Egypt was conquered by the Ottoman Empire in 1517.* 이집트는 1517년 오스만 제국에 의해 정복당했다. **2** [T] to gain control over a feeling or a problem that you have ‖ 갖고 있는 감정이나 문제에 대해 제어할 수 있게 되다. 조절하다. 극복하다: *I didn't think I'd ever conquer my fear of heights.* 나는 고소 공포증을 극복했던 적이 없다고 생각했다. **– conqueror** *n*

con·quest /'kɑŋkwɛst/ *n* **1** [singular, U] the act of defeating or controlling a group of people ‖ 사람들의 집단을 패배시키거나 지배하는 행위. 정복. 점령: *the Spanish conquest of the Incas and the Aztecs* 잉카족과 아즈텍족에 대한 스페인의 정복 **2** HUMOROUS someone who is persuaded to love or have sex with someone ‖ 설득당해서 누군가와 사랑하거나 성교를 하게 된 사람. 이성의 꾀임에 넘어간 사람: *Jane was just another of* *his many conquests.* 제인은 그가 꾀어낸 많은 여자들 중 또 한 명일 뿐이었다.

con·science /ˈkɑnʃəns/ *n* [U] **1** the set of feelings that tell you whether what you are doing is morally right or wrong ‖ 자신이 하고 있는 일이 도덕적으로 옳은 지 그른지에 대해 판단하는 일련의 감정 들. 선악의 판단력. 양심: *Pete acts like he has a guilty conscience.* (=as if he has done something wrong) 피트는 마치 죄나 지은 것처럼 행동한다 / *At least my conscience is clear.* (=I know I have done nothing wrong) 최소한 나는 양심에 꺼리끼는 것이 없다. **2 on sb's conscience** making someone feel guilty all the time for doing or not doing something ‖ 어떤 일을 하거나 하지 않아 서 항상 죄의식을 느끼게 하는. 양심에 걸 리는. 가책을 느끼는: *Tim's suicide is always going to be on his mother's conscience.* 팀의 자살로 그의 어머니는 항상 죄책감을 갖게 될 것이다.

con·sci·en·tious /ˌkɑnʃiˈɛnʃəs/ *adj* showing a lot of care and attention ‖ 많 은 조심성과 주의력을 보이는. 조심스러 운. 신중한: *a conscientious worker* 신중 한 노동자

con·scious /ˈkɑnʃəs/ *adj* **1** noticing or realizing something; AWARE ‖ 무엇을 알 아 차리거나 인식하고 있는; 윤 aware: *Jodie was very conscious of the fact that he was watching her.* 조디는 그가 자신을 주시하고 있다는 사실을 매우 잘 알고 있었다. **2** awake and able to understand what is happening around you ‖ 깨어 있어서 주변에서 일어나는 일 을 알 수 있는. 각성하고 있는. 의식이 있 는: *Owen was still conscious when they arrived at the hospital.* 그들이 병원에 도 착했을 때 오웬은 아직 의식이 있었다. **3** intended or planned ‖ 의도되거나 계획 된. 의도적인. 고의의. 의식적인: *Jenny made a conscious effort/decision to smoke less.* 제니는 담배를 줄이려고 의식 적으로 노력했다[결심했다]. — **consciously** *adv* —opposite UNCONSCIOUS¹

con·scious·ness /ˈkɑnʃəsnɪs/ *n* [U] **1** the condition of being awake and understanding what is happening around you ‖ 깨어 있어서 주변에서 일어 나는 일을 아는 상태. 의식[지각, 자각, 각성](상태): *Charlie fell down the stairs and lost consciousness.* 찰리는 계단에 서 떨어져 의식을 잃었다. **2** the understanding that you or a group of people have about a situation ‖ 자신이나 일단의 사람들이 상황에 대해 가지고 있는

이해. 공통의 의식[생각]. 일반적인 견해: *a consciousness raising effort* (=effort to make people understand and care about a problem) (사람들에게 문제를 이 해하고 관심을 갖게 하려는) 의식 고양을 위한 노력

cons·cript /kənˈskrɪpt/ *v* [T] FORMAL ⇨ DRAFT² – **conscription** /kənˈskrɪpʃən/ *n* [U]

con·se·crate /ˈkɑnsəˌkreɪt/ *v* [T] to have a special ceremony that makes a particular place or building holy ‖ 특정 장소나 건물을 성스럽게 하는 특별 의식을 거행하다. …을 신성하게 하다. …을 봉 헌(奉獻)[성별(聖別)]하다: *consecrating a church* 교회의 봉헌

con·sec·u·tive /kənˈsɛkyətɪv/ *adj* consecutive numbers or periods of time happen one after the other ‖ 숫자나 시기 가 연달아서 일어나는. 연속되는. 계속 이 어지는: *It rained for three consecutive days.* 3일간 연속해서 비가 왔다. – **consecutively** *adv*

con·sen·sus /kənˈsɛnsəs/ *n* [singular, U] an agreement that everyone in a group reaches ‖ 한 집단 내의 모든 사람 들이 도달한 합의. 대다수의 의견. 총의 (總意): *The consensus of opinion is that the military is not to blame.* 대다수의 의 견은 군대가 비난받아서는 안 된다는 것이 다.

con·sent¹ /kənˈsɛnt/ *n* [U] permission to do something ‖ 어떤 것을 하기 위한 허 가. 동의. 승낙. 허락: *We need your parents' written consent before you can join.* 너는 가입하기 전에 부모의 동의서가 필요하다.

consent² *v* [I] formal to give your permission for something to happen ‖ 어 떤 것이 일어나도록 허가하다. 동의하다. 승낙하다: *Father will never consent to Jenny's marrying Tom.* 아버지는 제니가 톰과 결혼하는 것을 결코 허락하지 않을 것이다.

con·se·quence /ˈkɑnsəˌkwɛns, -kwəns/ *n* **1** something that happens as a result of a particular action ‖ 특정 행 동의 결과로 벌어지는 것. 결말. 귀결. 결 과: *Think about the consequences if you drop out of college.* 대학을 중퇴한다면 그 결과에 대해 생각해 봐라. / *Much has happened as a consequence of my meeting with the board.* 나와 그 위원회 의 만남의 결과로서 많은 일들이 일어났 다. **2** FORMAL importance ‖ 중요성. 중대 함: *a matter of little/no consequence* 거 의[전혀] 중요하지 않은 문제

con·se·quent·ly /ˈkɑnsəˌkwɛntli,

-kwənt-/ *adv* as a result ‖ 결과로서. 따라서: *Reports aren't trusted; consequently, managers are refusing to believe the budget reports.* 보고서는 신뢰성이 없다. 그래서 이사들은 예산 보고서를 믿지 않으려 하고 있다.

con·ser·va·tion /ˌkɑnsəˈveɪʃən/ *n* [U] 1 the protection of natural things such as wild animals, forests, or beaches from being harmed or destroyed ‖ 야생 동물[숲, 해변] 등 자연물들에 대한 손상이나 파괴로부터의 보호. 보존 2 the controlled use of a limited amount of water, gas, electricity etc. to prevent the supply from being wasted ‖ 제한된 양의 물·가스·전기 등의 공급이 낭비되는 것을 막기 위한 사용의 통제. 보존[보호] 관리 –**conservationist** *n*

con·serv·a·tism /kənˈsɚvəˌtɪzəm/ *n* [U] the belief that any changes to the way things are done must happen slowly and have very good reasons ‖ 일을 하는 방식에 대한 모든 변화는 반드시 천천히 일어나야 하고 아주 충분한 이유가 있어야 한다고 믿는 신념. 보수성. 보수주의: *political conservatism* 정치적 보수주의

con·serv·a·tive /kənˈsɚvəṭɪv/ *adj* 1 preferring to continue doing things the way they are being done or have been proven to work, rather than risking changes ‖ 변화의 위험을 겪기보다 현재하고 있는 방식이나 효과가 있다고 입증된 방식으로 일을 계속 하기를 선호하는. 급격한 변화를 싫어하는. 보수적인: *a very conservative attitude to education* 교육에 대한 매우 보수적인 태도 / *a politically conservative family* 정치적으로 보수적인 가족 2 not very modern in style, taste etc.; traditional ‖ 스타일·기호 등에서 그다지 현대적이지 않은; 전통적인. 보수적인. 수수한: *a conservative business suit* 전통 스타일의 양복 3 a **conservative estimate** a guess that is deliberately lower than the possible amount ‖ 가능치보다 의도적으로 낮게 잡은 추정치. 조심스런 [신중한] 평가치[견적] –**conservatively** *adv* –**conservative** *n*

con·serv·a·tor /kənˈsɚvəṭɚ/ *n* LAW someone who is legally responsible for the property of a person who cannot take care of it himself/herself ‖ 스스로 관리할 수 없는 사람의 재산을 법적으로 책임지는 사람. 보호 관리인. 후견인

con·serv·a·to·ry /kənˈsɚvəˌtɔri/ *n* 1 a school where students are trained in music or acting ‖ 학생들이 음악이나 연기

(演技) 교육을 받는 학교. 예술 학교 2 ⇨ GREENHOUSE

con·serve /kənˈsɚv/ *v* [T] to prevent something from being wasted, damaged, or destroyed ‖ 사물이 낭비[손상, 파괴]되는 것을 막다. 유지[보존]하다: *Conserve water: fix any leaking pipes and faucets.* 물을 보존합시다. 물이 새는 모든 파이프와 수도꼭지는 고칩시다.

con·sid·er /kənˈsɪdɚ/ *v* [I, T] to think about something very carefully ‖ 사물에 대해 매우 신중히 생각하다. 숙고하다. 고려[고찰]하다: *Has John ever considered applying for a loan?* 존은 대출 신청을 생각해 보았습니까? ✗DON'T SAY "considered to apply"✗ "considered to apply"라고는 하지 않는다. 1 [T] to remember particular facts or details when making a judgment or decision about something ‖ 사물에 대해 판단이나 결정을 할 때 특정 사실이나 세부 사항을 기억하다. …한 점을 참작[감안]하다. …을 고려하다: *If you consider how hard she studied, she really should have gotten higher grades.* 그녀가 얼마나 열심히 공부했는가를 감안한다면 그녀는 정말 높은 점수를 받았어야 한다. 2 [T] to think of someone or something in a particular way ‖ 사람이나 사물을 특정하게 생각하다. …이라고 여기다[생각하다]. 간주하다: *Mrs. Greenwood was considered to be an excellent teacher.* 그린우드 부인은 훌륭한 선생으로 간주되었다. / *We consider it important to get the Director's advice on this.* 우리는 이것에 대한 감독의 충고를 받아들이는 것이 중요하다고 생각한다. / *Greg should consider himself lucky* (=be glad) *he wasn't badly hurt.* 그레그는 심하게 다치지 않은 것을 다행으로 여겨야 한다. 3 [T] to think about someone or his/her feelings, and try to avoid upsetting him/her ‖ 남이나 남의 감정에 대해 생각하여 성나게 하지 않기 위해 노력하다. 주의[관심]를 기울이다. 배려하다: *It's all right for you, but have you considered the children?* 너는 괜찮지만 아이들은 고려해 봤느냐?

con·sid·er·a·ble /kənˈsɪdərəbəl/ *adj* large enough to be noticeable or to have noticeable effects ‖ 관심을 끌 수 있거나 눈에 띄는 효과를 낼 만큼 충분히 큰. 상당한. 적지[작지] 않은: *A considerable amount of time and money was spent on the project.* 그 계획에 상당한 시간과 돈이 소모됐다. –**considerably** *adv* : *It's considerably colder tonight.* 오늘 밤은 상당히 더 춥다.

con·sid·er·ate /kən'sɪdərɪt/ *adj* always thinking and caring about other people's feelings, wants, or needs etc. ‖ 다른 사람들의 감정[욕구, 필요] 등을 항상 생각하고 마음 쓰는. 동정심[인정·이해심] 많은. 사려 깊은: *You really should be more considerate of your neighbors.* 정말로 이웃에 대해 더 관심을 가져야 한다. – **considerately** *adj* – opposite INCONSIDERATE

con·sid·er·a·tion /kən,sɪdə'reɪʃən/ *n* **1** a particular fact or detail that you need to think about, especially when making a decision ‖ 특히 결정을 내릴 때 고려할 필요가 있는 특정 사실이나 세부 사항. 고려 사항[대상]: *There are financial considerations to remember.* 기억해야 될 금전적 고려 사항들이 있다. **2** [U] the quality of thinking and caring about other people's feelings, wants, or needs etc. ‖ 다른 사람들의 감정[욕구, 필요] 등을 생각하고 마음을 쓰는 특성. 배려. 사려: *Show a little consideration for the lady's feelings!* 여성들의 감정에 대해 조금이라도 배려해 봐라! **3** [U] FORMAL careful thought and attention ‖ 주의 깊은 생각과 관심. 고찰. 숙고: *After further consideration, we decided not to sue.* 좀 더 숙고해 본 다음에 우리는 제소하지 않기로 결정했다. **4 take sth into consideration** to remember a particular fact or detail when making a decision or judgment ‖ 결정이나 판단을 할 때 특정 사실이나 세부 내용을 상기하다. …을 고려에 넣다. 참작[감안]하다: *Of course, we'll take into consideration the fact that you were sick.* 물론 우리는 네가 아팠다는 사실을 참작할 것이다.

con·sid·ered /kən'sɪdəd/ *adj* **1 considered opinion/judgment** an opinion based on careful thought ‖ 주의 깊은 생각에 기초한 의견. 신중한 견해/판단 **2 all things considered** after thinking about all the facts ‖ 모든 사실들에 대해 생각한 후에. 모든 사항들을 고려해서: *All things considered, I think the meeting went pretty well.* 모든 사항을 고려해 볼 때 그 회의는 아주 성공적이었다고 생각한다.

con·sid·er·ing /kən'sɪdərɪŋ/ *prep, conjunction* used before stating a fact that you know has had an effect on a particular situation ‖ 알고 있는 사실이 특정 상황에 영향을 끼친 점을 말하기 전에 쓰여. …을 고려하면[참작하면]: *Considering we missed the bus, we're actually not too late.* 우리가 버스를 놓쳤다는 점을 고려하면 실제로 우리는 그다지

늦지 않았다.

con·sign /kən'saɪn/ *v* [T] FORMAL

consign sb/sth ↔ **to** sth *phr v* [T] to decide that someone or something is no longer important enough to pay attention to ‖ 사람이나 사물이 주의를 기울일 만큼 더 이상 중요하지 않다고 결정하다. 중요치 않은 것으로 치부되다[내몰리다]: *I'm not ready to be consigned to an old folks' home yet!* 나는 아직 양로원으로 내몰릴 지경까지는 아니다.

con·sign·ment /kən'saɪnmənt/ *n* **1** a quantity of goods that is sent to someone in order to be sold ‖ 판매를 위해 누군가에게 보내진 상당량의 상품들. 위탁판매품. 위탁 화물 **2 on consignment** goods that are on consignment are being sold by a store owner for someone else, for a share of the profit ‖ 이익을 공유하기 위해 가게 주인이 다른 사람을 대신하여 상품을 판매하여. 위탁 판매로

con·sist /kən'sɪst/ *v*

consist of sth *phr v* [T] to be made of or contain a number of different things ‖ 수많은 서로 다른 것들로 만들어지거나 포함하다. 이루어지다. 구성되다: *The show at the Mexican Museum consists of over 30 paintings.* 멕시코 미술관의 전시회는 30점 이상의 미술품으로 구성되어 있다. / *a sauce consisting of cream, onions, and herbs* 크림·양파·허브로 만들어진 소스 —see usage note at COMPRISE

con·sist·en·cy /kən'sɪstənsi/ *n* **1** the quality of always being the same, or of always behaving in an expected way ‖ 항상 동일하게 되는 특성, 또는 항상 예상한 대로 행동하는 특성. 일관성. 일치: *There's no consistency in the way they apply the rules.* 그들이 규칙을 적용하는 방식에는 일관성이 없다. —opposite INCONSISTENCY **2** [C, U] how thick or firm a substance is ‖ 물질의 진하거나 견고한 정도. 물질의 농도[밀도]. 굳기: *a dessert with a nice creamy consistency* 맛있는 크림 상태의 후식

con·sist·ent /kən'sɪstənt/ *adj* **1** always happening in the same way or having the same attitudes, quality etc. ‖ 항상 동일하게 발생하거나 같은 태도·특성 등을 갖는. 일관[일치]하는. 변함 없는: *I've tried to be consistent in applying the rules.* 나는 규칙 적용에 있어서 일관성을 유지하도록 애써 왔다. **2 be consistent with** to say the same thing or follow the same principles as something else ‖ 같은 것을 말하거나 다

른 것과 같은 원칙을 따르다. 양립[조화, 일치]하다. 모순되지 않다: *His story is not consistent with the facts.* 그의 이야기는 사실과 일치하지 않는다. - **consistently** *adv* : *consistently high sales* 지속적인 높은 판매(율) —opposite INCONSISTENT

con·so·la·tion /ˌkansəˈleɪʃən/ *n* [C, U] someone or something that makes you feel better when you are sad or disappointed || 슬프거나 실망할 때 기분이 좋아지게 하는 사람이나 사물. 위안(물). 위로(하는 사람[것]): *They were still together, and at least that was one consolation.* 그들은 아직 함께 있었고 최소한 그것은 하나의 위안이 되었다.

con·sole /kənˈsoʊl/ *v* [T] to help someone who is sad or disappointed to feel better || 슬프거나 실망한 사람의 기분이 좋아지도록 돕다. 위로[위안]하다: *No one could console her when her first child died.* 그녀의 첫째 아이가 죽었을 때 아무도 그녀를 위로할 수 없었다. / *Danny consoled himself with the thought that Matt couldn't go either.* 대니는 매트 역시 갈 수 없다는 생각을 하며 스스로를 달랬다.

con·sol·i·date /kənˈsaləˌdeɪt/ *v* [I, T] **1** to combine two or more things such as organizations, duties, jobs, or large amounts of money to form a single thing that is more effective || 보다 효율적인 단일체를 만들기 위해 두 가지 이상의 조직[의무, 업무, 거액의 돈] 등을 결합하다. 합병하다. 통합 정리하다: *By consolidating their resources they could afford to buy new businesses.* 자산을 통합 정리하여 그들은 새 기업체를 인수할 수 있었다. **2** to make your power or level of success stronger so that it will continue || 힘 또는 성공의 수준을 계속 유지할 수 있도록 더욱 강화하다. 굳건하게 하다: *Advertising helped them consolidate their leading position in Europe.* 광고는 그들이 유럽에서 선두적인 위치를 공고히 하는 데 기여했다. - **consolidation** /kənˌsaləˈdeɪʃən/ *n* [C, U]

con·som·mé /ˌkansəˈmeɪ/ *n* [U] a thin clear meat soup || 묽고 맑은 고기 수프. 콩소메

con·so·nant /ˈkansənənt/ *n* TECHNICAL any letter of the English alphabet except a, e, i, o, and u || 영어 알파벳에서 a·e·i·o·u를 제외한 모든 글자. 자음(자) —compare VOWEL

con·sort /kənˈsɔrt/ *v* FORMAL
consort with sb *phr v* [T] to spend time with a person or group that is

morally bad || 도덕적으로 나쁜 사람이나 집단과 시간을 보내다. (나쁜 대상과) 사귀다[교제하다, 어울리다]

con·sor·ti·um /kənˈsɔrʃiəm, -tiəm/ *n* a combination of several companies, organizations etc. working together || 함께 일하는 여러 회사·조직체 등의 결합. 합작 기업: *a consortium of banks* 합작 은행

con·spic·u·ous /kənˈspɪkyuəs/ *adj* very easy to notice because of being different || 차이가 나기 때문에 매우 알아보기 쉬운. 눈에 잘 띄는. 뚜렷한: *There's still a very conspicuous burn mark on the seat.* 좌석에는 여전히 눈에 매우 잘 띄는 불에 탄 자국이 있다. - **conspicuously** *adv* —opposite INCONSPICUOUS

con·spir·a·cy /kənˈspɪrəsi/ *n* [C, U] a secret plan made by two or more people to do something harmful or illegal || 해치거나 불법적인 일을 하기 위해 두 사람 이상이 꾸미는 은밀한 계획. 음모. 공모

con·spir·a·tor /kənˈspɪrətər/ *n* someone who is part of a group that secretly plans something harmful or illegal || 위험하거나 불법적인 일을 은밀히 꾸미는 집단의 일원. 공모자. 음모자 - **conspiratorial** /kənˌspɪrəˈtɔriəl/ *adj*

con·spire /kənˈspaɪɚ/ *v* [I] **1** to secretly plan with other people to do something harmful or illegal || 위험하거나 불법적인 일을 하기 위해 다른 사람들과 은밀히 계획하다. 공모하다. 음모를 꾸미다: *a company conspiring with local stores to fix prices* 가격을 정하기 위해 지역 상점들과 담합한 회사 **2** FORMAL to happen at the same time and cause a bad result || 동시에 일어나 나쁜 결과를 초래하다. 겹치다: *Events conspired to ensure he lost the election.* 그가 선거에서 떨어졌다는 것을 확신시키는 사건이 겹쳐서 일어났다.

con·stant /ˈkanstənt/ *adj* **1** happening regularly or all the time || 규칙적으로 또는 항상 일어나는. 끊임없는. 연속적인: *The children must be kept under constant supervision.* 그 아이들은 계속 주의깊게 살펴야 한다. **2** staying the same for a period of time || 일정 기간 동안 같은 상태를 지속하는. 불변의. 일정한: *driving at a constant speed* 일정한 속도로 운전하기 - **constancy** *n* [singular, U]

con·stant·ly /ˈkanstəntli/ *adv* always or regularly || 항상 또는 규칙적으로. 언제나. 끊임없이: *Marla is constantly on the phone!* 말라는 언제나 전화통에 매달려 있

구나!

con·stel·la·tion /ˌkɑnstəˈleɪʃən/ n a group of stars that forms a particular pattern and has a name ‖ 특정한 형태를 형성하고 하나의 이름을 가진 별 무리. 별자리

con·ster·na·tion /ˌkɑnstəˈneɪʃən/ n [U] a feeling of shock or worry that makes it difficult for you to decide what to do ‖ 무엇을 해야 할지 결정하기 어렵게 하는 충격이나 우려의 느낌. 깜짝 놀람. 대경실색

con·sti·pa·tion /ˌkɑnstəˈpeɪʃən/ n [U] the condition of someone being unable to empty his/her BOWELs ‖ 사람이 대변을 볼 수 없는 상태. 변비 – **constipated** /ˈkɑnstəˌpeɪtɪd/ adj

con·stit·u·en·cy /kənˈstɪtʃuənsi/ n an area of the country that has one or more elected officials, or all the people who live and vote there ‖ 한 명 이상의 선임된 공직자가 가는 한 나라의 지역, 또는 그 지역에서 살면서 투표하는 모든 사람들. 선거구. 유권자

con·stit·u·ent /kənˈstɪtʃuənt/ n 1 someone who lives and votes in a particular area represented by one or more elected officials ‖ 한 사람 이상의 선임된 공직자가 대표하는 특정 지역에 살면서 투표하는 사람. 선거인. 유권자 2 one of the parts that forms something ‖ 사물을 형성하는 부분들 중 하나. 구성 요소. 성분: *The FBI has found the constituents of a bomb inside the warehouse.* FBI는 창고 안에 있는 폭탄의 성분을 알아냈다. – **constituent** adj

con·sti·tute /ˈkɑnstəˌtut/ v [linking verb] FORMAL 1 if several parts constitute something, they form it together ‖ 여러 부분들이 함께 어떤 것을 형성하다. 구성하다: *Students constituted the majority of the people in the bar.* 술집에 있는 대다수가 학생들이었다. 2 to be considered to be something ‖ 어떤 것으로 생각되다. 간주되다: *According to Marx, money "constitutes true power."* 마르크스에 의하면 돈은 "진정한 권력으로 간주된다".

con·sti·tu·tion /ˌkɑnstəˈtuʃən/ n 1 also **Constitution** a set of laws and principles that describes the power and the purpose of a particular government, organization etc. ‖ 특정 정부·조직 등의 권력과 목적을 기술한 일련의 법률과 원칙. 헌법: *the Constitution of the United States* 미합중국 헌법 2 [singular] the ability of your body to fight disease and illness ‖ 병·질환과 싸우는 신체의 능력.

체질: *a boy with a strong/weak constitution* 튼튼한[약한] 체질의 소년

con·sti·tu·tion·al /ˌkɑnstəˈtuʃənəl/ adj 1 officially allowed or restricted by the set of rules that a government or organization has ‖ 정부나 조직이 가지고 있는 일련의 규칙에 의해 공식적으로 허용되거나 규제되는. 헌법(상)의. 합법적인: *a constitutional right to privacy* 사적 자유에 대한 헌법상의 권리 —opposite UNCONSTITUTIONAL 2 relating to a CONSTITUTION ‖ 헌법과 관련된: *a constitutional amendment* (=change to the original set of laws) 헌법 수정 3 relating to someone's health ‖ 건강에 관련된. 체질[기질]의: *a constitutional weakness* 체질적인 허약

con·strain /kənˈstreɪn/ v [T] to limit what someone or something can do or become, by laws, rules, or by force ‖ 사람이나 사물이 할 수 있는 것이나 될 수 있는 것을 법[규칙, 힘]으로 제한하다. 제약하다: *They're constrained to work within very strict rules.* 그들은 매우 엄격한 규칙 안에서 일하도록 제약을 받았다.

con·strained /kənˈstreɪnd/ adj 1 prevented from developing, improving, or doing what you really want ‖ 발전이나 개선, 또는 정말 하고 싶어 하는 것을 방해 받은. 제약을 받은: *Victor felt more and more constrained by his father's firm.* 빅터는 자기 아버지 회사에 의해 더욱더 구속당하는 느낌을 받았다. 2 a constrained smile or manner seems too controlled and is not natural ‖ 웃음 또는 태도가 지나치게 억제되고 자연스럽지 못한. 부자연스러운. 어색한 —opposite UNCONSTRAINED

con·straint /kənˈstreɪnt/ n something that restricts what you are doing ‖ 하고 있는 것을 제한하는 것. 억제. 속박: *working under time/budget constraints* 제한된 시간[예산]하에서의 작업

con·strict /kənˈstrɪkt/ v [T] to make something smaller, tighter, or narrower ‖ 사물을 더욱 작게[빡빡하게, 좁게] 만들다. 압축[억제]하다: *Anna felt the tears coming, her throat constricting.* 애너는 눈물이 흐르고 목이 메는 것을 느꼈다. – **constriction** /kənˈstrɪkʃən/ n [C, U]: *constriction of the arteries* 동맥의 수축

con·struct /kənˈstrʌkt/ v [T] 1 to build something large such as a building, bridge etc. ‖ 빌딩·다리 등과 같은 큰 구조물을 짓다. 건설[건조]하다: *Right now they're constructing another runway.* 바로 지금 그들은 또 다른 활주

로를 건설 중이다. **2** to join words, ideas etc. **together** to make a sentence, argument, or system || 문장[주장, 체계] 을 만들기 위해 말·생각 등을 한데 결합시 키다. 구성하다. 구축하다: *Boyce has constructed a new theory of management.* 보이스는 새로운 경영 이론 을 구축해 왔다.

con·struc·tion /kənˈstrʌkʃən/ *n* [U] the process or method of building something large such as a house, road etc. || 집·도로 등의 큰 구조물을 짓는 과 정이나 방법. 건축. 건설: *Several new offices are under construction.* (=being built) 여러 개의 새 사무실이 건축 중에 있다. / *a construction worker* 건설 노동 자 —compare DESTRUCTION

construction pa·per /.ˈ.. ,../ *n* [U] a thick colored paper that is used especially by children at school || 특히 학 교에서 아이들이 사용하는 두꺼운 색종이. 공작용 색판지

con·struc·tive /kənˈstrʌktɪv/ *adj* intended to be helpful, or likely to produce good results || 유익하게 하려는, 또는 좋은 결과를 가져올 가능성이 있는. 건설적인: *I'm always glad to hear constructive criticism.* 나는 건설적인 비 평을 듣는 것을 항상 기뻐한다.

con·strue /kənˈstru/ *v* [T] to understand something in a particular way || 무엇을 특정한 방식으로 이해하다. (…의) 뜻으로 해석[간주]하다: *What you think is friendly behavior might be construed as flirting.* 당신이 친절한 행 동이라 여기는 것이 집적거리는 것으로 간 주될 수 있다. —opposite MISCONSTRUE

con·sul /ˈkɑnsəl/ *n* an official who lives in a foreign city and whose job is to help citizens of his/her own country who also live or work there || 외국 도시에 거주하 며, 그곳에 거주하거나 일하는 자국민을 돕는 일을 하는 공무원. 영사 – **consular** *adj*

con·sul·ate /ˈkɑnsəlɪt/ *n* the official building where a CONSUL lives and works || 영사가 거주하며 일하는 공식적인 건물. 영사관

con·sult /kənˈsʌlt/ *v* [T] to ask or look for advice, information, etc. from someone or something that should have the answers || 해답을 갖고 있는 사람이나 사물에서 조언·정보 등을 구하거나 찾다. 의견을 묻다. 상담하다: *Consult your physician if your symptoms persist.* 증상 이 계속된다면 의사와 상담해라.

consult with sb *phr v* [T] to ask for someone's permission or advice before

making a decision || 결정하기 전에 남의 허락이나 조언을 구하다. 상의[상담]하다: *You may want to consult with your lawyer first.* 당신은 먼저 당신 변호사와 상담하고 싶을지도 모른다.

con·sul·tan·cy /kənˈsʌltənsi/ *n* a company that gives advice and training in a particular area of business to people in other companies || 다른 회사의 사람들에게 특정 사업 분야에 대한 조언과 교육을 하는 회사. 컨설턴트 회사

con·sult·ant /kənˈsʌltənt/ *n* someone with a lot of experience in a particular area of business whose job is to give advice about it || 특정한 사업 분야에 경험 이 많고 그 분야에 대해 조언해 주는 직업 인. 컨설턴트. 상담역: *a marketing consultant* 마케팅 컨설턴트

con·sul·ta·tion /ˌkɑnsəlˈteɪʃən/ *n* [C, U] **1** a discussion in which people who are affected by a decision can say what they think should be done || 어떤 결정에 영향을 받게 되는 사람들이 그렇게 되어야 한다는 자기들의 생각을 말할 수 있는 토 론. 협의: *The changes were made completely without consultation.* 그 변화 는 전적으로 협의없이 이루어졌다. **2** a meeting in which you get advice from a professional, or the advice s/he gives || 전문가에게 조언을 구하는 모임, 또는 전 문가가 제공하는 조언. (전문가의) 회의. 자문. 상담: *The school counselor is always available for consultation.* 그 학 교의 상담자는 항상 상담이 가능하다.

con·sume /kənˈsum/ *v* [T] **1** to completely use time, energy, goods etc. || 시간·에너지·물건 등을 완전히 사용하 다. 소모하다. 다 써버리다: *His work seems to consume all his time these days.* 요즘 그는 모든 시간을 일하는 데 쓰는 것 같다. **2** to eat or drink something || 무엇을 먹거나 마시다: *Americans in general consume a lot of beef.* 미국인들은 일반적으로 쇠고기를 많이 먹는다. **3 be consumed with passion/guilt/rage etc.** to have a very strong feeling that you cannot ignore || 묵살할 수 없는 매우 격한 감정을 가지다. 열중하게 하다. 사로잡다. 열정/죄의식/ 분노에 사로잡히다 **4** if a fire consumes something, it completely destroys it || 불 이 어떤 것을 완전히 파괴하다. 태워 버리 다. 소멸시키다

con·sum·er /kənˈsumɚ/ *n* **1** someone who buys or uses goods and services || 재화나 용역을 사거나 이용하는 사람. 소 비자: *We received many calls from consumers saying they liked the old* *smell better.* 우리는 소비자들로부터 옛날 향기가 더 좋다는 전화를 여러 통 받았다. **2** [singular] all the people who buy goods and services, considered as a group ‖ 집단으로 간주되는 재화·용역을 사는 모든 사람. 소비자: *Our job is to make sure food is safe before it reaches the consumer.* 우리 직업은 음식이 소비자에게 도착하기까지 안전한가를 확인하는 것이다. / *consumer products* 소비재 — compare CUSTOMER, PRODUCER

con·sum·er·is·m /kənˈsuːmə,rɪzəm/ *n* [U] the idea or belief that buying and selling things is the most important activity a person or society can do ‖ 물건을 사고 파는 것이 인간이나 사회가 할 수 있는 가장 중요한 활동이라는 생각이나 믿음. 소비주의

con·sum·mate¹ /ˈkɑnsəmɪt/ *adj* very skillful, or without any faults or weaknesses ‖ 매우 솜씨 좋은, 또는 어떤 결점이나 약점이 없는. 완벽한. 최고의. 유능한: *a consummate politician* 더할 나위 없이 유능한 정치인

con·sum·mate² /ˈkɑnsə,meɪt/ *v* [T] FORMAL **1** to make a marriage or a relationship complete by having sex ‖ 성관계를 가짐으로써 결혼이나 관계를 완전하게 하다. (결혼을) 완성시키다 **2** to make something such as an agreement complete ‖ 계약 등을 완전하게 하다. 완성[완료]하다 – **consummation** /,kɑnsəˈmeɪʃən/ *n* [U]

con·sump·tion /kənˈsʌmpʃən/ *n* [U] **1** the amount of electricity, gas etc. that is used ‖ 사용한 전기·가스 등의 양. 소비량: *We intend to reduce water consumption by up to 30% a year.* 우리는 물 소비량을 1년에 30퍼센트까지 감소시키려 한다. **2** FORMAL the act of eating or drinking ‖ 먹거나 마시는 행위: *The consumption of alcohol is not permitted on these premises.* 이 구내에서는 음주가 허용되지 않습니다.

con·tact¹ /ˈkɑntækt/ *n* **1** [U] communication with a person, organization, country etc. ‖ 사람·조직·나라 등과의 의사 소통. 연락: *Have you kept/stayed in contact with any of your school friends?* 네 학교 친구들 중 누구와 연락하고 지내니? / *We don't have much contact with other departments.* 우리는 다른 부서들과 접촉이 그리 많지 않다. **2** [U] the state of touching or being close to someone or something ‖ 사람이나 사물과 접촉하거나 가까워지는 상태. 접촉. 교제: *Kids come in contact with all kinds of germs at*

school. 아이들은 학교에서 모든 종류의 병원균과 접촉하고 있다. **3** someone you know who may be able to help you or give you advice ‖ 도움이나 조언을 줄 가능성이 있는 아는 사람. 연고. 연줄: *I've got a few contacts in the movie industry.* 나는 영화계에 약간의 연줄을 가지고 있다. **4** ⇨ CONTACT LENS **5** an electrical part that completes a CIRCUIT when it touches another part ‖ 또 다른 부분과 접촉하는 경우 회로가 완성되는 전기 부분. 접촉점. 접속 장치

contact² *v* [T] to telephone or write to someone ‖ 남에게 전화를 걸거나 편지를 쓰다. …에게 연락하다: *I've been trying to contact you for the past three days!* 난 지난 3일간 너에게 연락하려고 애써오고 있다. ✗DON'T SAY "I've been trying to contact with you."✗ "I've been trying to contact with you."라고는 하지 않는다.

contact lens /ˈ.. ,.. ,.. ˈ./ *n* a small round piece of plastic you put on your eye to help you see clearly ‖ 선명하게 볼 수 있게 도와 주는 눈에 착용하는 작고 둥근 플라스틱 조각. 콘택트 렌즈 —see picture at LENS

con·ta·gious /kənˈteɪdʒəs/ *adj* **1** a disease that is contagious can be passed from person to person by touch or through the air ‖ 병이 접촉이나 공기를 통해서 한 사람에게서 다른 사람으로 옮겨질 수 있는. 전염하는. 전염성의 **2** having a disease like this ‖ 이와 같은 병을 가진. 전염병에 걸린 **3** a feeling, attitude, action etc. that is contagious is quickly felt or done by other people ‖ 감정·태도·행동 등이 다른 사람들이 금방 감지하거나 행하게 되는. 옮겨지기 쉬운. 잘 퍼지는: *Jeannie's laughter was contagious.* 지니의 웃음은 전파성이 있었다.

con·tain /kənˈteɪn/ *v* [T] **1** to have something inside, or have something as a part ‖ 안에 무엇이 들어 있거나 무엇을 부분으로서 가지고 있다. 포함하다. 함유하다: *We also found a wallet containing $43.72.* 우리는 또한 43달러 72센트가 들어 있는 지갑을 발견했다. / *a report that contained some shocking information* 깜짝 놀랄 만한 정보가 들어 있는 보고서 **2** to control the emotions you feel ‖ 느끼는 감정을 조절하다. 감정을 누르다[억제하다]: *Greg was so excited he could hardly contain himself.* 그레그는 너무 흥분해서 거의 감정을 조절할 수 없었다.

con·tain·er /kənˈteɪnə/ *n* something such as a box, a bowl, a bottle etc. that can be filled with something ‖ 물건을 채워 넣을 수 있는 상자·그릇·병 등의 것. 용

pack of cigarettes

packet of seeds

box of chocolates

carton of milk

tube of toothpaste

jar   bottle

can of soup   gas can

crate

pot

pitcher   jug

기: *an eight-gallon container* 8갤런짜리 용기

con·tain·ment /kən'teɪnmənt/ n [U] the act of keeping something controlled, such as the cost of a plan or the power of an unfriendly country ‖ 기획 비용이나 비우호 국가의 권력 등을 통제하는 행위. 억제. 봉쇄

con·tam·i·nate /kən'tæmə,neɪt/ v [T] **1** to spoil something by adding a dangerous or poisonous substance to it ‖ 위험하거나 독성이 있는 물질을 추가해서 어떤 것을 망쳐놓다. 더럽히다. 불결하게 하다. 오염시키다: *Lead in plumbing can contaminate drinking water* 수도 배관에 있는 납성분은 식수를 오염시킬 수 있다. **2** to influence someone or something in a way that has a bad effect ‖ 나쁜 결과를 일으키는 쪽으로 사람이나 사물에 영향을 미치다. 타락시키다. 악영향을 미치다: *Lack of trust will contaminate your whole relationship.* 믿음이 부족한 것은 당신의 전반적인 인간 관계를 악화시킬 것이다. **–contamination** /kən,tæmə'neɪʃən/ n [U]

contd the written abbreviation of "continued" ‖ "continued"의 약어

con·tem·plate /'kɑntəm,pleɪt/ v [T] to think quietly and seriously for a long time about something you intend to do, or in order to understand something ‖ 하려는 것에 대해, 또는 사물을 이해하려고 오랫동안 조용하고 진지하게 생각하다. …을 심사숙고하다: *I can't even contemplate taking a vacation right now.* (=it is not possible, so it is not worth thinking about) 지금 당장은 휴가를 얻는 것에 대해 생각조차 할 수 없다.

–contemplation /,kɑntəm'pleɪʃən/ n [U]

con·tem·pla·tive /kən'tɛmplətɪv/ adj spending a lot of time thinking seriously and quietly ‖ 많은 시간을 진지하고 조용하게 생각하는 데 보내는. 묵상하는

contemporary¹ /kən'tɛmpə,rɛri/ adj **1** belonging to the present time; modern ‖ 현재에 속한. 당대의; 현대의: *a museum of contemporary art* 현대 미술 박물관 **2** happening or existing in the same period of time ‖ 같은 시대에 일어나거나 존재하는. 동시대의

contemporary² n someone who lives in the same period of time as a particular person or event ‖ 특정한 사람이나 사건과 같은 시대를 사는 사람. 동시대인: *Mozart was greatly admired by his contemporaries.* 모차르트는 그와 동시대의 사람들에게 크게 칭송받았다.

con·tempt /kən'tɛmpt/ n [U] **1** a feeling that someone or something does not deserve any respect ‖ 사람이나 사물이 존경을 받을 만한 가치가 없다는 느낌. 업신여김. 경멸: *Stephen's contempt for foreigners was well known.* 스티븐이 외국인을 경멸한다는 것은 유명하다. **2 contempt of court** not doing what a judge or court of law has told you to ‖ 재판관이나 법정이 지시한 것을 행하지 않음. 법정 모독죄: *Cooper was fined $100 for contempt of court.* 쿠퍼는 법정 모독죄로 100달러의 벌금을 물었다.

con·tempt·i·ble /kən'tɛmptəbəl/ adj not deserving any respect ‖ 존경할 만하지 않은. 경멸할 만한: *contemptible behavior* 경멸할 만한 행동 **–contemptibly** adv

con·temp·tu·ous /kənˈtɛmptʃuəs/ *adj* showing that you believe someone or something does not deserve any respect ∥ 사람이나 사물이 존경할 만한 가치가 없다고 믿는 것을 보여주는. 경멸적인. 업신여기는: *I hate her contemptuous attitude toward my mother.* 나는 우리 엄마를 대하는 그녀의 경멸적인 태도가 밉다.

con·tend /kənˈtɛnd/ *v* [I] **1** to argue or claim that something is true ∥ 무엇이 사실이라고 논쟁하거나 주장하다. 싸우다. 다투다: *Some critics contend that the changes will create even more problems.* 어떤 비평가들은 그 변화가 심지어 더 많은 문제점을 야기시킬 것이라고 주장한다. **2** to compete for something ∥ 어떤 것을 위해 다투다. 경쟁하다: *Twelve teams are contending for the title.* 12팀이 선수권을 위해 경쟁하고 있다.

contend with sth *phr v* [T] to deal with a problem or difficult situation ∥ 문제나 어려운 상황을 다루다. 해결하다: *I have enough to contend with, without you yelling!* 네가 소리치지만 않으면 나는 충분히 해결할 수 있어!

con·tend·er /kənˈtɛndɚ/ *n* someone who is involved in a competition ∥ 경쟁에 참가하는 사람. 경쟁자

content¹ /ˈkɑntɛnt/ *n* [singular] **1** the amount of a substance that something contains ∥ 어떤 것에 들어 있는 물질의 양. 함유량: *Peanut butter has a high fat content.* 땅콩 버터는 지방 함유량이 높다. **2** the ideas, information, or opinions that are expressed in a speech, book etc. ∥ 연설·책 등에서 표현되는 생각[정보, 의견]. 내용: *I like the content of the story but I don't think it's very well written.* 그 이야기의 내용은 마음에 들지만 그리 잘 쓰여졌다고는 생각하지 않는다. **3** the information contained in a WEBSITE, considered separately from the software that makes the website work ∥ 웹사이트에 포함되어 있으나 사이트를 가동시키는 소프트웨어와는 별개로 생각되는 정보. 컨텐트 —see also CONTENTS

content² /kənˈtɛnt/ *adj* happy or satisfied because you have what you want or need ∥ 원하거나 필요한 것을 가지고 있어서 기쁘거나 만족스러운: *Gary's content to sit at home in front of the TV all day.* 게리는 하루 종일 텔레비전 앞에서 편하게 앉아 있는 것에 만족한다. / *I'd say she's pretty content with her job.* 나는 그녀가 일에 매우 만족하고 있다고 말하고 싶군요. – **contentment** *n* [U]

content³ *v* [T] **content yourself with** sth to do or have something that is not what you really want, but is still satisfactory ∥ 진정으로 원하는 것은 아니나 아직은 만족할 만한 것을 하거나 가지다. …에 만족하다: *Jack's driving, so he'll have to content himself with a soft drink.* 잭은 운전하고 있어서 청량음료를 마시는 것으로 만족해야 할 것이다.

content⁴ *n* [U] **do sth to your heart's content** to do something as much as you want ∥ 원하는 만큼 무엇을 하다. 충분히[마음껏] …을 하다: *For $8 you can eat to your heart's content at Big Al's Diner.* 8달러면 Big Al's Diner 음식점에서 마음껏 먹을 수 있다.

con·tent·ed /kənˈtɛntɪd/ *adj* satisfied or happy ∥ 만족하거나 행복한: *a contented cat curled up by the fire* 불 옆에서 몸을 웅크리고 만족해 하는 고양이 —opposite DISCONTENTED

con·ten·tion /kənˈtɛnʃən/ *n* **1** a belief or opinion that someone expresses ∥ 사람이 표현하는 신념이나 의견. 주장. 논점. 의도: *It is my contention that bicycle helmets should be required.* 나의 주장은 자전거 헬멧을 착용해야 한다는 것이다. **2** [U] a situation in which people or groups are competing ∥ 사람들이나 단체들이 서로 경쟁하는 상황. 다툼. 경쟁: *Twenty teams are in contention for the NFL playoffs.* NFL 플레이오프전에 20팀이 경쟁하고 있다. **3** [U] arguments and disagreement between people ∥ 사람들간의 논쟁과 불일치. 말다툼: *City planning has been a bone of contention* (=subject that people argue about) *for a long time.* 도시 계획은 오랫동안 쟁점이 되어 왔다.

con·ten·tious /kənˈtɛnʃəs/ *adj* likely to cause a lot of argument ∥ 많은 논쟁을 야기하는 경향이 있는. 논쟁을 불러일으키는: *one of the most contentious issues in biotechnology* 생물 공학에서 가장 많은 논쟁을 불러일으키는 문제 중의 하나 – **contentiously** *adv*

con·tents /ˈkɑntɛnts/ *n* [plural] **1** the things that are in a box, bag, room etc. ∥ 상자·가방·방 안에 있는 물건들. 안에 든 것. 내용물: *Customs officers searched through the contents of his luggage.* 세관원들은 그의 수화물의 내용물을 철저히 조사했다. **2** the words or ideas that are written in a book, letter etc. ∥ 책·편지 등에 기록된 말이나 생각. 내용: *The contents of the document are still unknown.* 그 서류의 내용은 아직 알려져 있지 않다. / *the table of contents* (=a list at the beginning of a book that tells you what is in it) (안에 들어 있는 것

을 알려 주는, 책 앞부분의) 목차
con·test¹ /'kɑntɛst/ *n* **1** a competition, usually a small one ‖ 보통 작은 경기. 시합. 대회: *a contest to see who can run the fastest* 누가 가장 빨리 달릴 수 있는지 보기 위한 시합. / *a pie-eating contest* 파이먹기 대회 **2** a struggle to win control or power ‖ 지배력이나 권력을 획득하려는 싸움. 투쟁: *the excitement of a political contest* 흥분을 자아내는 정치적 다툼 **3 no contest** INFORMAL used in order to say that a choice or a victory is not at all difficult ‖ 선택이나 승리가 전혀 어렵지 않다고 말하는 데 쓰여. 식은 죽 먹기: *In the end, it was no contest, with the Dolphins beating the Bengals 37-13.* 결국 돌핀 팀은 벵골 팀을 37대 13으로 쉽게 승리했다.
con·test² /kən'tɛst/ *v* [T] **1** to say formally that you do not think something is right or fair ‖ 무엇이 옳거나 공정하다고 생각하지 않음을 격식을 갖춰 말하다. 이의[이론]를 제기[주장]하다. 논쟁하다: *We intend to contest the judge's decision.* 우리는 그 판사의 결정에 대해 이의를 제기할 작정이다. **2** to compete for something ‖ 어떤 것을 놓고 다투다. 겨루다: *contesting a seat on the city council* 시의회의 자리를 놓고 벌이는 경쟁
con·test·ant /kən'tɛstənt/ *n* someone who competes in a CONTEST ‖ 시합에서 경쟁하는 사람. 경쟁자
con·text /'kɑntɛkst/ *n* **1** the situation, events, or information that relate to something, and help you understand it better ‖ 어떤 것과 관련되어 보다 잘 이해하도록 도움을 주는 상황[사건, 정보]. 배경: *The events have to be considered in their historical context.* 그 사건은 역사적 배경이 고려되어야 한다. **2** the words and sentences that come before and after a word and that help you understand its meaning ‖ 단어 앞뒤에 놓여 의미를 이해하는 데 도움을 주는 말이나 문장. 전후 관계. 문맥: *"Smart" can mean "intelligent" or "sarcastic," depending on the context.* "smart"는 문맥에 따라서 "영리한" 또는 "빈정대는"의 뜻이 될 수 있다. **3 take sth out of context** to repeat a sentence or phrase without describing the situation in which it was said, so that its meaning is not clear ‖ 언급된 상황을 묘사하지 않고 문장이나 구를 반복해서 그 의미가 명확하지 않다. 전후 관계를 무시하고 어떤 것을 인용하다: *Journalists had taken his comments completely out of context.* 기

자들은 전후 관계를 무시하고 그의 논평을 철저히 인용했다.
con·tig·u·ous /kən'tɪgyuəs/ *adj* FORMAL next to something, or sharing the same border ‖ 사물 옆의, 또는 같은 경계선을 공유하는. 인접한. 근접한: *the 48 contiguous States* 미국의 인접한 48개 주
con·ti·nent /'kɑntənənt, 'kɑnt¬n-ənt/ *n* one of the main areas of land on the earth ‖ 지구상에 있는 육지의 주요 지역의 하나. 대륙: *the continent of Africa* 아프리카 대륙
con·ti·nen·tal /ˌkɑntən'ɛntl/ *adj* relating to a large area of land ‖ 육지의 넓은 지역과 관련된. 대륙의. 대륙에 관한: *flights across the continental US* 아메리카 대륙을 횡단하는 비행
continental break·fast /ˌ.... '../ *n* a breakfast consisting of coffee, juice, and a sweet ROLL (=type of bread) ‖ 커피·주스·스위트 롤로 구성된 아침 식사
con·tin·gen·cy /kən'tɪndʒənsi/ *n* an event or situation that might happen and could cause problems ‖ 발생하여 문제를 야기시킬 수 있는 사건이나 상황. 우연한 사건. 부수적인 일: *Of course there are contingency plans to cope with any computer failures.* 물론 컴퓨터 고장에 대처할 부수적인 계획들이 있다.
con·tin·gent¹ /kən'tɪndʒənt/ *adj* FORMAL dependent on something that may or may not happen in the future ‖ 장차 일어날지 일어나지 않을지 모를 일에 달려 있는. …에 의존적인. (…을) 조건으로 하는: *The purchase of the house is contingent on/upon a satisfactory inspection.* 그 집의 매입 여부는 충분한 조사에 달려 있다.
contingent² *n* a group of people who have the same aims or are from the same area, and who are part of a larger group ‖ 목표나 출신지가 같은 사람들의 집단이면서 보다 큰 집단의 부분인 일단의 사람들. 파견단. 분견대: *By late summer, a contingent of scientists had arrived.* 늦여름에 과학자들의 파견단이 도착했다.
con·tin·u·al /kən'tɪnyuəl/ *adj* repeated often over a long period of time ‖ 종종 오랜 기간에 걸쳐 반복되는. 끊임없는. 연속적인: *Their continual arguing really upset me.* 그들의 끊임없는 다툼은 정말로 내 기분을 엉망진창으로 만들었다. – **continually** *adv*

USAGE NOTE continual and continuous

Use these words to talk about the way something happens and how long it continues. Use **continual** when something is repeated often over a long time: *The telephone has been ringing continually.* Use **continuous** when something continues without stopping: *The Salsa Club offers continuous music and entertainment from 5 pm to midnight.* 이 단어들은 일이 일어나는 방식과 얼마나 오랫동안 계속되느냐를 언급하는 데에 사용한다. **continual**은 어떤 일이 종종 장기간에 걸쳐 반복될 때 사용한다: 전화기가 줄곧 울려대고 있다. **continuous**는 일이 멈추지 않고 계속될 때 사용한다: 살사 클럽에서는 오후 5시부터 자정까지 계속해서 음악과 쇼를 한다.

con·tin·u·a·tion /kən,tɪnyu'eɪʃən/ n **1** something that follows after or is joined to something else and seems a part of it ‖ 후속하거나 다른 것에 연결되어 그것의 한 부분처럼 보이는 것. 연장 (부분). 지속: *the continuation of our economic success* 우리 경제의 지속적인 성공 **2** [U] the act or state of continuing for a long time without stopping ‖ 멈추지 않고 오랫동안 계속되는 행동이나 상태. 계속함. 존속: *the continuation of family traditions* 가풍의 존속

con·tin·ue /kən'tɪnyu/ v **1** [I, T] to keep happening, existing, or doing something without stopping ‖ 멈추지 않고 계속 일어나다[존재하다, 일을 하다]. 계속되다. 계속하다: *The city's population will continue to grow.* 도시의 인구는 계속 증가할 것이다. / *Do you plan on continuing with your education?* 교육을 계속할 계획이십니까? **2** [I, T] to start doing something again after a pause ‖ 잠깐 중단된 후 다시 무엇을 하기 시작하다. (…을) 계속하다: *To be continued...* (=used at the end of a program to say that the story will be finished later) (나중에 이야기가 마무리되리라는 것을 말하려고 프로그램 끝에 쓰여) 다음 편에 계속 **3** [I] to go further in the same direction ‖ 같은 방향으로 좀 더 가다. 이어지다. 뻗어 있다: *Route 66 continues on to Texas from here.* 66번 노선은 여기서부터 텍사스까지 이어진다.

continuing ed·u·ca·tion /..,... ../ n [U] classes for adults, often on subjects that relate to their jobs ‖ 성인을 대상으로 하는, 종종 직업에 관련된 주제에 대한 강의. 성인 교육

con·ti·nu·i·ty /,kɑntə'nuəti/ n [U] the state of continuing over a long period of time without being interrupted or changing ‖ 방해받거나 변화하지 않고 오랜 기간에 걸쳐 계속되는 상태. 연속 (상태). 계속성: *Changing doctors can affect the continuity of your treatment.* 의사를 바꾸는 것은 당신이 치료를 계속하는 데 영향을 미칠 수 있다.

con·tin·u·ous¹ /kən'tɪnyuəs/ adj **1** continuing to happen or exist without stopping or pausing ‖ 중단하거나 쉬지 않고 계속 일어나거나 존재하는. 계속적인. 끊임없는: *These plants need a continuous supply of fresh water.* 이들 식물은 끊임없는 신선한 물 공급이 필요하다. **2** without any spaces or holes in it ‖ 안에 공간이나 구멍이 없는. 빈틈없는. 이어진. 연속된: *a continuous line of cars* 끊임없이 이어진 자동차의 행렬 − **continuously** adv —see usage note at CONTINUAL

continuous² n **the continuous** TECHNICAL in grammar, the form of a verb that shows that an action or activity is continuing to happen, and is formed with "be" and the PRESENT PARTICIPLE. In the sentence "She is watching TV," "is watching" is in the continuous form ‖ 문법에서 행동이나 활동이 계속해서 일어나는 것을 보여주는 동사의 한 형태로 be 동사와 현재 분사로 이루어진다. 진행형. "She is watching TV." 문장에서 "is watching"은 진행형이다.

con·tort /kən'tɔrt/ v [I, T] to twist your face or body so that it does not have its normal shape ‖ 정상적인 모양을 지니지 않도록 얼굴이나 몸을 비틀다. 일그러지다[일그러뜨리다]. 찌푸리다 − **contortion** /kən'tɔrʃən/ n [C, U]

con·tour /'kɑntʊr/ n the shape of the outer edges of something such as an area of land or someone's body ‖ 땅이나 신체의 한 부분 등의 외곽선의 형태. 윤곽

con·tra·band /'kɑntrə,bænd/ n [U] goods that are brought into or taken out of a country illegally ‖ 불법적으로 한 나라로 들여오거나 한 나라에서 가지고 나가는 물품. 밀수품 − **contraband** adj

con·tra·cep·tion /,kɑntrə'sɛpʃən/ n [U] the practice or methods of making it possible for a woman to have sex without becoming PREGNANT; BIRTH CONTROL ‖ 여성이 임신되지 않고 성관계를 가능하게 하는 수단이나 방법. 피임(법); ㉤ birth control

con·tra·cep·tive /,kɑntrə'sɛptɪv/ n [U] a drug, object, or method used so that a woman can have sex without becoming

PREGNANT ‖ 여성이 임신되지 않고 성관계를 가능하게 하기 위해 사용하는 약[물체, 방법]. 피임약[기구, 법] **– con·traceptive** adj

con·tract¹ /'kɑntrækt/ n 1 a legal written agreement between two people, companies etc. that says what each side must do for the other ‖ 두 사람·회사 사이의 각 측이 상대 측에게 해야 하는 사항을 언급한 법적인 서면 약정. 계약(서): *Stacy signed a three year contract with a small record company.* 스테이시는 작은 레코드 회사와 3년간의 계약에 서명했다. **2** INFORMAL an agreement to kill someone for money ‖ 돈을 위해 사람을 죽이는 계약. 살인 청부

con·tract² /kən'trækt/ v 1 [T] to get a CONTAGIOUS illness ‖ 전염병에 걸리다: *Just after high school, he contracted polio.* 그는 고등학교를 졸업하자마자 척수성 소아마비에 걸렸다. **2** [I] to become smaller or tighter ‖ 더 작아지거나 더 좁아지다. 수축하다: *Scientists say the universe will begin to contract.* 과학자들은 우주가 더욱 좁아지기 시작할 것이라고 말한다. **—opposite** EXPAND

contract³ /'kɑntrækt/ v [T] to sign a contract to do something ‖ 무엇을 하는 계약에 서명하다. …을 계약하다

contract sth ↔ **out** phr v [T] to arrange to have a job done by a person or company outside your own organization ‖ 자신의 조직 외부 사람이나 회사가 일을 하도록 배정하다. 외부에 하청을 주다[시키다]

con·trac·tion /kən'trækʃən/ n 1 TECHNICAL a very strong movement of a muscle in which it suddenly becomes tight, used especially about the muscles that become tight when a woman is going to give birth ‖ 특히 여성이 출산하려고 할 때 근육이 경직되는 것에 대해서 쓰여, 갑자기 근육이 매우 강하게 수축되는 움직임. (근육의) 수축. 진통 **2** [U] the process of becoming smaller or shorter ‖ 보다 작아지거나 짧아지는 과정. 축소. 단축 **3** TECHNICAL a short form of a word or words, such as "don't" for "do not" ‖ "do not"을 "don't"로 축약하는 것 등의 단어나 말의 축약형

con·trac·tor /'kɑn,træktɚ, kən'træk-/ n a person or company that does work or supplies material for other companies ‖ 다른 회사를 위해 일하거나 물품을 공급해 주는 사람이나 회사. 청부업자

con·trac·tu·al /kən'træktʃuəl/ adj agreed in a contract ‖ 계약에서 동의된. 계약(상)의. 계약으로 보증된: *contractual obligations* 계약상의 의무

con·tra·dict /,kɑntrə'dɪkt/ v 1 [T] if a statement, story, fact etc. contradicts another one, it is very different from or the opposite of the other one ‖ 진술·이야기·사실 등이 나머지 것과 매우 다르거나 반대되다. …에 상반되다. 모순되다: *The witnesses' reports contradicted each other.* 증인들의 진술은 서로 상반되었다. **2** [I, T] to say that what someone else has just said is wrong or not true ‖ 남이 방금 말한 것이 그르거나 사실이 아니라고 말하다. 반박하다. 부정하다: *You shouldn't contradict me in front of the kids.* 당신은 아이들 앞에서 나를 반박하지 말아야 한다. **3 contradict yourself** to say something that is the opposite of what you have said before ‖ 이전에 말한 것과 반대되는 것을 말하다. 모순된 말을 하다 **– contradictory** /,kɑntrə'dɪktəri/ adj

con·tra·dic·tion /,kɑntrə'dɪkʃən/ n 1 a difference between two stories, facts etc. that means they cannot both be true ‖ 양쪽 모두가 사실일 수 없음을 의미하는 두 이야기·사실 등 간의 차이. 모순: *There's a contradiction between what they say and what they do.* 그들이 말하는 것과 행동하는 것과는 차이가 있다. **2** [U] the act of saying that what someone has just said is wrong or not true ‖ 누군가가 방금 말한 것이 그르거나 사실이 아님을 말하는 행위. 반박. 부정

con·trap·tion /kən'træpʃən/ n INFORMAL a piece of equipment that looks strange ‖ 이상하게 보이는 장치. 진기한 장치[고안물]

con·tra·ry¹ /'kɑn,trɛri/ n FORMAL 1 **on the contrary** used in order to show that the opposite of what has just been said is actually true ‖ 방금 말한 것이 실제로는 사실과 반대되는 것임을 나타내는 데 쓰여. 이와 반대로. 오히려: *We didn't start the fire. On the contrary, we helped put it out.* 우리는 불을 내지 않았다. 오히려 불을 끄는 것을 도왔다. **2 to the contrary** showing that the opposite is true ‖ 반대되는 것이 사실이라는 것을 보여 주는. 그것과는 반대로[의]: *In spite of rumors to the contrary, their marriage is fine.* 소문과는 반대로[달리] 그들의 결혼 생활은 괜찮다.

contrary² adj 1 completely different or opposite ‖ 완전히 다르거나 반대되는: *Lying to her would be contrary to everything I believe in.* 그녀에게 거짓말하는 것은 내가 믿는 모든 것과 완전히 반

대뇌는 일이다. **2 contrary to popular belief** used in order to show that something is true even though people may think the opposite ‖ 사람들이 반대로 생각할지언정 어떤 것이 사실이라는 것을 보여 주기 위해 쓰여: *Contrary to popular belief, gorillas are shy and gentle.* 사람들이 반대로 생각할지 모르지만 고릴라는 수줍음 많고 온순한 동물이다.

contrary³ /ˈkɑntrɛri/ *adj* deliberately doing or saying the opposite of what someone else wants ‖ 일부러 다른 사람이 원하는 것과 반대로 하거나 말하는. 고집센: *Angela was an extremely contrary child.* 안젤라는 정말 고집센 아이였다.

con·trast¹ /ˈkɑntræst/ *n* **1** [C, U] a large difference between two people, situations, ideas etc. that are compared ‖ 비교되는 두 사람·상황·생각 등 간의 큰 차이. 대조. 대비. 현저한 차이: *the contrast between the rich and poor in America* 미국에서의 부자와 가난한 사람 사이의 뚜렷한 차이 **2 in contrast (to)** used when comparing objects or situations that are completely different from each other ‖ 서로 완전히 다른 사물이나 상황을 비교할 때 쓰여. …과 대조하여: *Claire is tall and dark, in sharp/marked contrast to her mother, who is short and fair.* 클레어는 키가 작고 피부가 흰 자기 엄마와는 현격하게[두드러지게] 대조를 이루어 키가 크고 피부가 까무잡잡하다. **3** [U] the differences in color or in light and darkness on photographs, a television picture etc. ‖ 사진·텔레비전 화상 등의 색깔의 차이나 밝고 어두움의 차이. 콘트라스트. 대조 (법)

con·trast² /kənˈtræst/ *v* **1** [T] to compare two people, ideas, objects etc. to show how they are different from each other ‖ 서로 얼마나 차이가 나는지 보여 주기 위해 두 사람·생각·물체 등을 비교하다. 대비하다: *The lecture contrasted Chinese characters with the western alphabet.* 그 강의는 한자와 서양 알파벳을 대비했다. **2** [I] if two things contrast, they are very different from each other ‖ 두 사물이 서로 매우 다르다. 현저히 차이가 나다: *His views on religion contrast sharply with my own.* 종교에 관한 그의 견해는 나와는 상당히 다르다. **- contrasting** *adj*

con·tra·vene /ˌkɑntrəˈvin/ *v* [T] FORMAL to do something that is not allowed by a law or a rule ‖ 법이나 규칙에서 허용되지 않는 것을 하다. 위반하다 **- contravention** /ˌkɑntrəˈvɛnʃən/ *n* [C, U]

con·trib·ute /kənˈtrɪbyut, -yət/ *v* **1** [I, T] to give money, help, or ideas to something that other people are also giving to ‖ 다른 사람들도 내고 있는 것에 돈[도움, 생각]을 제공하다. 기부하다. 주다: *We all contributed $5 toward his present.* 우리 모두는 그의 선물 값으로 5달러씩 냈다. **2 contribute to sth** to help make something happen ‖ 어떤 것이 일어나게 도와 주다. …에 도움이 되다. 공헌하다. 기여하다: *An electrical problem may have contributed to the crash.* 전기 이상으로 그 사고가 일어났는지 모른다. **3** to write something for a newspaper or magazine ‖ 신문이나 잡지에 어떤 것을 쓰다. 기고하다 **- contributor** *n* **- contributory** *adj*

con·tri·bu·tion /ˌkɑntrəˈbyuʃən/ *n* **1** something that is given or done to help something else be a success ‖ 다른 것이 성공하는 것을 돕기 위해 제공하거나 행한 것. 기여(한 것): *The Mayo Clinic has made important contributions to cancer research.* 메이요 클리닉은 암 연구에 중요한 기여를 했다. **2** an amount of money that is given to help pay for something ‖ 어떤 것에 지불하는 데 돕기 위해 제공된 돈의 액수. 기부금: *Would you like to make a contribution to the Red Cross?* 적십자에 기부하시겠습니까? **3** a piece of writing that is printed in a newspaper or magazine ‖ 신문이나 잡지에 인쇄된 글. 기고 작품

con·trite /kənˈtraɪt/ *adj* feeling guilty and sorry for something bad that you have done ‖ 자기가 한 좋지 않은 것에 대해 죄책감과 미안함을 느끼는. 뉘우치는. 회개하는 **- contrition** /kənˈtrɪʃən/ *n* [U]

con·trive /kənˈtraɪv/ *v* [T] to manage to do something difficult or to invent something by being very smart or dishonest ‖ 어려운 일을 가까스로 해내거나 매우 약삭빠르고 정직하지 못한 방법으로 어떤 것을 발명하다. 어떻게 해서든지 …하다. …을 고안하다: *Somehow she contrived to get herself invited to the governor's ball.* 어쨌든 그녀는 주지사가 개최하는 무도회에 가까스로 초대되었다.

con·trived /kənˈtraɪvd/ *adj* seeming false and not natural ‖ 잘못되고 자연스럽지 않아 보이는. 부자연스러운: *Alice spoke with a contrived southern accent.* 앨리스는 부자연스러운 남쪽 지방의 어투로 말했다.

con·trol¹ /kənˈtroʊl/ *n* **1** [U] the power or ability to make someone or something do what you want ‖ 사람이나 사물이 원하는 것을 하게 만드는 힘이나 능력. 통제(력). 지배(력): *They don't have any control over their son.* 그들은 자기들의 아들을 어찌할 수가 없다. / *The car went out of control* (=could not be controlled) *and hit a tree.* 그 차는 제어할 수 없게 되어 나무를 들이받았다. / *A military spokesman said the situation was now under control.* (=being controlled) 당시 상황은 통제하에 있었다고 군대 대변인은 말했다. / *These events are beyond our control.* (=not possible for us to control) 이 사건들은 우리가 통제할 수 없다. **2** [U] the power to rule or govern a place, organization, or company ‖ 장소[조직, 회사]를 지배하는 힘. 장악. 관리. 지휘(권): *Rioters took control of the prison.* 폭도들은 감옥을 점거했다. / *The airport is now under the control of UN troops.* 그 공항은 지금 유엔 부대의 통제하에 있다. / *The government is no longer in control of the country.* 정부는 더 이상 그 나라를 통제하지 못한다. **3** [C, U] the action or method of limiting the amount or growth of something ‖ 무엇의 양이나 성장을 제한하는 행동이나 방법. 통제: *After four hours firefighters brought the fire under control.* (=stopped it from getting worse) 네 시간 후 소방관들은 불길을 잡았다. **4** [U] the ability to remain calm even when you are angry or excited ‖ 화가 나거나 흥분했을 때조차 차분함을 유지하는 능력. 억제[제어]. 냉정: *I just lost control* (=became unable to control my behavior) *and punched him!* 나는 냉정을 잃고 그에게 한방 먹여 버렸어! **5** something that you use to make a television, machine, vehicle etc. work ‖ 텔레비전·기계·탈것 등을 작동시키기 위해 사용하는 것. 조종[제어] 장치 – **controlled** *adj*

control² *v* **-lled, -lling** [T] **1** to make someone or something do what you want or work in a particular way ‖ 원하는 것을 사람이나 사물에게 하게 하다, 또는 특정한 방식으로 일하게 하다. …을 통제하다: *If you can't control your dog you should put it on a leash.* 당신 개를 당신 뜻대로 제어할 수 없으면 개에게 개줄을 달아놔야 한다. **2** to limit the amount or growth of something ‖ 어떤 것의 양이나 성장을 제한하다. 억제하다. 방지하다: *It was impossible to control the flooding on the Ogallala River.* 오갈라라 강의 범람을 막는 것은 불가능했다. **3** to rule or govern a place, organization, or

company, or to have more power than someone else ‖ 장소[조직, 회사]를 관리하거나 지배하다, 또는 다른 사람보다 더 많은 힘을 가지다. 단속하다. 지휘하다: *Rebels control all the roads into the capital.* 반란군들이 수도로 진입하는 모든 도로를 통제한다. **4** to make yourself behave calmly, even if you feel angry, excited, or upset ‖ 화가 나도[흥분해도, 기분이 엉망일 때에도] 차분하게 행동하다. 감정을 억제하다. 자제하다: *I was furious, but I managed to control myself.* 나는 격분했지만 간신히 참았다.

control freak /ˈ. ./ *n* INFORMAL someone who is too concerned about controlling all the details in every situation s/he is involved in ‖ 자기를 둘러싸고 있는 모든 상황의 온갖 세부 사항을 통제하는 데 열중하는 사람. 자기 뜻대로 하고 싶어하는 사람

con·trol·ler /kənˈtroʊlə/ *n* TECHNICAL someone whose job is to collect and pay money for a government or company department ‖ 정부나 회사의 부서에 돈을 징수하고 지불하는 직업인. 회계 감사관: *the state controller* 주 회계 감사관

control tow·er /ˈ. ,../ *n* a building at an airport from which planes are watched and guided as they come down and go up ‖ 비행기가 착륙·이륙할 때 살펴보고 안내해 주는 공항에 있는 빌딩. 관제탑

con·tro·ver·sial /ˌkɑntrəˈvəʃəl/ *adj* something that is controversial causes a lot of disagreement, because many people have strong opinions about it ‖ 많은 사람들이 무엇에 강한 이견을 가지고 있어서 많은 불화를 일으키는. 논쟁의 대상이 되는. 논쟁의 여지가 있는: *the controversial subject of abortion* 낙태에 관한 논쟁거리 – **controversially** *adv*

con·tro·ver·sy /ˈkɑntrəˌvəsi/ *n* [C, U] a serious disagreement among many people over a plan, decision etc., over a long period of time ‖ 장기간에 걸친 계획·의사 결정 등에 관한 다수의 사람들 간의 심각한 불일치. 논쟁: *There is a lot of controversy over the use of this drug.* 이 약의 사용에 관한 많은 논쟁이 있다.

con·va·lesce /ˌkɑnvəˈlɛs/ *v* [I] to spend time getting well after a serious illness ‖ 중병을 겪고 난 후 회복하는 데 시간을 보내다. 건강을 회복하다 – **convalescence** *n* [singular] – **convalescent** *n*

con·va·les·cent /ˌkɑnvəˈlɛsənt/ *adj* **convalescent home/hospital etc.** a place where people stay when they need care from doctors and nurses but are not sick enough to be in a hospital ‖ 입원할 만큼 아프지는 않지만 의사나 간호사의 치료를 받아야 될 때 머무르는 곳. 회복기 환자 집/요양소

con·vene /kən'vin/ *v* [I, T] FORMAL if a group of people convenes, or if someone convenes them, they come together for a formal meeting ‖ 공식적인 모임에 일단의 사람들이 함께 모이다. 소집되다. 소집하다

con·ven·ience /kən'vinyəns/ *n* 1 [U] the quality of being suitable or useful for a particular purpose, especially because it makes something easier ‖ 특히 어떤 것은 더 용이하게 하기 때문에, 특정한 목적을 위해 적당하거나 유용한 성질. 편리함. 편의: *I like the convenience of living near my work.* 나는 직장 근처에 살아 편해서 좋다. 2 [U] what is easiest and best for someone ‖ 누군가에게 가장 용이하고 좋은 것. 편리한 사정. 형편이 좋은 때: *The package can be delivered at your convenience.* (=at a time that is best for you) 그 짐은 당신이 편리한 때에 배달될 수 있다. 3 a service, piece of equipment etc. that is useful because it saves you time or work ‖ 시간과 노동을 줄이기 때문에 유용한 서비스·장비 등. 유용품. 편리한[편의] 시설: *modern conveniences* 현대적인 편의 시설 — opposite INCONVENIENCE[1]

convenience store /.'.. ,./ *n* a store where you can buy food, newspapers etc. and that is often open 24 hours each day ‖ 대개 매일 24시간 문을 열어 놓는 식료품·신문 등을 살 수 있는 가게. 편의점

con·ven·ient /kən'vinyənt/ *adj* 1 useful to you because it makes something easier or saves you time ‖ 무엇을 보다 용이하게 하거나 시간을 절약해 주기 때문에 유용한. 편리한: *It's more convenient for me to pay by credit card.* 신용 카드로 지불하는 것이 나에겐 더욱 편리하다. 2 near and easy to get to ‖ 가깝고 도달하기에 쉬운. 가기 쉬운: *a convenient place to shop* 가게와 가까운 장소 — **conveniently** *adv* —opposite INCONVENIENT

con·vent /'kɑnvɛnt, -vənt/ *n* a place where NUNs (=religious women) live and work ‖ 수녀들이 살고 일하는 곳. 여자 수도[수녀]회

con·ven·tion /kən'vɛnʃən/ *n* 1 a large formal meeting of people who belong to the same profession, organization etc. ‖ 같은 직업·조직 등에 속한 사람들의 대규모 공식적인 모임. 대회. 집회: *an astronomy convention* 천문학 대회 2 [C, U] behavior and attitudes that most people in society think are normal and right ‖ 사회 대부분의 사람들이 정상적이고 옳다고 생각하는 행동·태도. 관습. 관례: *We broke with convention* (=did something unusual) *and had our wedding at the beach.* 우리는 관례를 깨고 해변에서 결혼식을 올렸다. 3 a formal agreement between countries ‖ 국가들 간의 공식적인 합의. 협약. 협정: *the Geneva convention on human rights* 인권에 관한 제네바 협정

con·ven·tion·al /kən'vɛnʃənəl/ *adj* 1 always following the behavior and attitudes that most people in society think are normal and right, so that you seem boring ‖ 항상 사회 대부분의 사람들이 정상적이고 옳다고 생각하는 행동이나 태도를 따라서 지루해 보이는. 사회적 관습에 따른. 진부한. 틀에 박힌: *My parents have very conventional attitudes about sex.* 내 부모님들은 성에 관해서 매우 진부한 태도를 가지고 계신다. 2 a conventional method, product, practice etc. is one that has been used for a long time ‖ 방법·제품·실행 등이 오랫동안 사용되어 온. 재래[종래]의. 관습[관례]의 : *Acupuncture is one alternative to conventional medicine.* 침술은 종래의 의학에 대한 하나의 대체 의학이다. 3 conventional weapons and wars do not use NUCLEAR explosives ‖ 무기·전쟁이 핵폭탄을 쓰지 않는. 재래식의 – **conventionally** *adv*

con·verge /kən'vərdʒ/ *v* [I] to move or come together from different directions to meet at the same point ‖ 같은 지점에 모이기 위해서 다른 방향으로부터 함께 움직이거나 오다.(한 점에) 모이다. 집결하다: *Thousands of fans converged on the stadium to watch the game.* 수천 명의 팬들이 그 경기를 관람하기 위해 경기장에 모였다. – **convergence** *n* [C, U]

con·ver·sant /kən'vərsənt/ *adj* FORMAL having knowledge or experience of something ‖ 어떤 것에 대한 지식이나 경험을 가진. 정통한. 밝은: *Are you conversant with word processors?* 워드 프로세서를 잘 다루니?

con·ver·sa·tion /,kɑnvə'seɪʃən/ *n* [C, U] 1 a talk between two or more people in which people ask questions, exchange news etc. ‖ 질문하거나 소식을 교환하는 등의 두 사람 또는 그 이상의 사람들간의 대화: *Don't interrupt while your mother and I are having a* *conversation.* 네 어머니와 내가 대화를 나누고 있는 중에는 방해하지 마라. / *The two women were deep in conversation.* (=they were concentrating on their conversation) 두 여성이 서로의 대화에 푹 빠져 있었다. / *He struck up a conversation with* (=began to talk to) *a man at the bus stop.* 그는 버스 정류장에서 한 남자와 애기하기 시작했다. **2 make conversation** to talk to someone to be polite, not because you really want to ‖ 진정으로 대화하고 싶지 않아서 남에게 예의바르게 말하다. 의례적인 말을 하다 – **conversational** *adj* – **conversationally** *adv*

con·verse¹ /kən'vɝs/ *v* [I] FORMAL to have a conversation with someone ‖ 남과 대화를 하다. 담화하다. 의견을 나누다

con·verse² /'kɑnvɝs/ *n* [singular] **the converse** FORMAL the opposite of something ‖ 어떤 것의 반대. 역(逆): *The converse can also be true in some cases.* 그 반대가 어떤 경우에는 또한 진실일 수 있다. – **converse** /kən'vɝs, 'kɑnvɝs/ *adj* – **conversely** *adv*

con·ver·sion /kən'vɝʒən, -ʃən/ *n* [C, U] **1** the act or process of changing something from one form, system, or purpose to another ‖ 한 형태[체제, 목적]에서 다른 것으로 바꾸는 행위 또는 과정. 전환. 변환: *Canada's conversion to the metric system* 캐나다의 미터법 전환 **2** a change in which someone accepts a completely new religion, belief etc. ‖ 사람이 새로운 종교·신념 등을 완전히 받아들이는 변화. 개종. 전향: *Tyson's conversion to Islam surprised the media.* 타이슨의 이슬람교로의 개종은 대중 매체를 놀라게 했다.

con·vert¹ /kən'vɝt/ *v* [I, T] **1** to change or make something change from one form, system, or purpose to another ‖ 하나의 형태[체제, 목적]를 다른 것으로 바꾸거나 어떤 것을 변화시키다. 전환[변경]하다[시키다]: *We're going to convert the garage into a workshop* 우리는 차고를 작업장으로 변경시키려고 한다. **2** to accept or make someone accept a completely new religion, belief etc. ‖ 새로운 종교·신념 등을 완전히 받아들이거나 받아들이게 하다. 개종[전향]하다[시키다]: *My wife has converted me to aerobics.* (=persuaded me to do it so that I enjoy it now) 내 아내는 내가 에어로빅을 하도록 설득했다.

con·vert² /'kɑnvɝt/ *n* someone who has accepted a completely new religion, belief etc. ‖ 새로운 종교·신념 등을 완전

히 수용한 사람. 개종자. 전향자

con·vert·i·ble¹ /kən'vɝtəbəl/ *adj* **1** something convertible is able to change or be arranged so it becomes or can be used for something else ‖ 사물이 변화할 수 있거나 조정될 수 있어서 다른 것이 되거나 다른 것으로 사용될 수 있는. 변화[전환]할 수 있는: *a convertible couch* (=one that unfolds to become a bed) 컨버터블형의[펼치면 침대가 되는] 의자 **2** TECHNICAL money that is convertible can be exchanged for another type of money ‖ 돈이 다른 형태의 돈으로 교환될 수 있는. 태환성이 있는

convertible² *n* a car with a roof that you can fold back or remove ‖ 지붕을 뒤로 젖히거나 없앨 수 있는 자동차. 무개차. 오픈카 —see picture on page 943

con·vex /ˌkɑn'vɛks·, kən-/ *adj* TECHNICAL curved outwards, like the outside edge of a circle ‖ 원의 바깥 가장자리와 같이 바깥으로 굽은. 볼록한: *a convex lens* 볼록 렌즈 —opposite CONCAVE

con·vey /kən'veɪ/ *v* [T] FORMAL to communicate a message or information, with or without using words ‖ 말을 사용하거나 사용하지 않고 전언이나 정보를 전달하다. 알리다. 표현하다: *Please convey my thanks to her.* 그녀에게 감사하다고 전해 주세요.

con·vey·or belt /.'.. ,./ *n* a long continuous moving band of rubber or metal, used in a place such as a factory or airport to move things from one place to another ‖ 공장이나 공항 등의 장소에서 물건을 한 곳에서 다른 곳으로 이동시키는 데 사용하는 길게 이어져 움직이는 고무나 금속 밴드. 컨베이어 벨트

con·vict¹ /kən'vɪkt/ *v* [T] to prove or announce that someone is guilty of a crime after a TRIAL in a court of law ‖ 법정에서 재판 후 남이 유죄임을 입증하거나 알리다. 선고하다. 판결하다: *Both men were convicted of fraud.* 두 사람은 사기죄의 판결을 받았다. —opposite ACQUIT

con·vict² /'kɑnvɪkt/ *n* someone who has been proved to be guilty of a crime and sent to prison ‖ 유죄임이 판명되어 교도소로 보내진 사람. 죄수. 기결수

con·vic·tion /kən'vɪkʃən/ *n* [C, U] **1** a very strong belief or opinion ‖ 매우 강력한 믿음이나 의견. 확신. 신념: *his firm religious convictions* 그의 확고한 종교적 신념 **2** an official announcement in a court of law that someone is guilty of a crime ‖ 법정에서 남이 유죄임을 공표함. 유죄 판결[선고]: *Bradley's conviction* *for theft was no surprise.* 브래들리의 절도죄에 대한 유죄 판결은 놀라운 것이 아니었다. —opposite ACQUITTAL

con·vince /kən'vɪns/ *v* [T] to make someone feel certain that something is true ‖ 남에게 무엇이 사실이라는 것을 확신시키다. 설득[납득]시키다: *The defense lawyers failed to convince the jury that Booth was innocent.* 피고측 변호사들은 부스가 무죄라는 것을 배심원들에게 납득시키는 데 실패했다. —compare PERSUADE

con·vinced /kən'vɪnst/ *adj* be convinced to feel certain that something is true ‖ 어떤 것이 사실이라는 것을 확실히 느끼다. 확신하다: *Her folks were convinced she was doing drugs.* 그녀의 식구들은 그녀가 약물을 복용하고 있다는 것을 확신했다.

con·vinc·ing /kən'vɪnsɪŋ/ *adj* making you believe that something is true or right ‖ 어떤 것이 사실이거나 옳다는 것을 믿게 만드는. 납득시키는. 설득력이 있는: *a convincing argument* 설득력 있는 논쟁 – **convincingly** *adv*

con·viv·i·al /kən'vɪviəl/ *adj* FORMAL friendly and pleasantly cheerful ‖ 우호적이며 기분 좋게 유쾌한. 들뜬. 명랑한: *a convivial atmosphere* 우호적인 분위기 – **conviviality** /kən,vɪvi'æləti/ *n* [U]

con·vo·lut·ed /'kɑnvə,lutɪd/ *adj* FORMAL complicated and difficult to understand ‖ 이해하기 복잡하고 어려운: *convoluted legal language* 복잡한 법률 용어

con·voy /'kɑnvɔɪ/ *n* [C, U] a group of vehicles or ships traveling together ‖ 함께 이동하는 차량이나 선박의 무리. 호송[호위]대: *a convoy of army trucks* 육군 트럭의 호송대

con·vulse /kən'vʌls/ *v* be convulsed with laughter to be laughing a lot ‖ 심하게 웃다. 포복절도하다

con·vul·sion /kən'vʌlʃən/ *n* an occasion when someone cannot control the violent movements of his/her body, because s/he is sick ‖ 사람이 아파서 격렬한 신체의 움직임을 통제할 수 없는 경우. 경련. 발작: *An overdose of the drug can cause convulsions.* 과량의 약물 복용은 발작을 유발할 수 있다.

coo /ku/ *v* **1** [I] to make a sound like the low cry of a DOVE or a PIGEON ‖ 비둘기의 낮은 울음 같은 소리를 내다. 구구 울다 **2** [I, T] to make soft loving noises ‖ 부드러운 사랑의 소리를 내다. 정답게 속삭이다: *a mother cooing to her baby* 아기에게 사랑을 속삭이는 어머니

cook¹ /kʊk/ *v* **1** [I, T] to prepare food for eating by using heat ‖ 열을 이용하여 먹을 음식을 마련하다. 요리하다: *Whose turn is it to cook supper tonight?* 오늘 저녁 요리 당번이 누구지? / *Grandma's cooking for the whole family on Thanksgiving.* 추수 감사절 날 할머니는 가족 전체를 위해 요리 중이시다. **2** [I] to be prepared for eating by using heat ‖ 가열하여 먹을 준비가 되다. 익다: *How long will it take the stew to cook?* 스튜가 요리되는 데 얼마나 걸릴까? **3** be cooking with gas SPOKEN to be doing something in the correct or best way, so that it is successful ‖ 성공하도록 올바른 또는 최선의 방법으로 무엇을 하고 있다.

cook sth ↔ **up** *phr v* [T] **1** INFORMAL to invent an excuse, reason, plan etc. that is slightly dishonest or will not work ‖ 약간 부정직하거나 효과가 없을 변명·이유·계획 등을 만들어 내다. 날조하다. 꾸며대다: *She refused to be part of a scheme that Lawrence had cooked up.* 그녀는 로렌스가 꾸며낸 계획에 동참하기를 거부했다. **2** to prepare food, especially quickly ‖ 특히 신속히 음식을 조리하다: *The oatmeal cooks up quickly in the microwave.* 오트밀은 전자렌지에서 빨리 조리된다.

cook² *n* someone who cooks and prepares food ‖ 음식을 요리하고 마련하는 사람. 요리사: *Kevin works as a cook in an Italian restaurant.* 케빈은 이탈리아 레스토랑에서 요리사로 근무한다. / *My cousin's a great cook.* 내 사촌은 대단한 요리사이다.

cook·book /'kʊkbʊk/ *n* a book that tells you how to prepare and cook food ‖ 음식을 마련하고 조리하는 방법을 알려 주는 책. 요리책

cooked /kʊkt/ *adj* ready for eating and not raw ‖ 날것이 아니라 먹도록 마련된. 조리된. 익힌: *cooked vegetables* 익힌 야채

cook·ie /'kʊki/ *n* **1** a small flat sweet cake ‖ 작고 납작하며 달콤한 케이크. 쿠키. 과자: *chocolate chip cookies* 초콜릿 칩 과자 **2** TECHNICAL information which a computer PROGRAM on the Internet leaves in your computer so that the program will recognize you when you use it again ‖ 인터넷 상의 컴퓨터 프로그램이 다시 접속한 이용자를 인식할 수 있도록 이용자의 컴퓨

cookie

터에 남겨 두는 정보. 쿠키

cook·ing¹ /ˈkʊkɪŋ/ *n* [U] **1** the act of making food and cooking it ‖ 음식을 만들고 조리하는 행위. 요리: *I hate cooking.* 나는 요리하는 것이 싫어. **2** food made in a particular way or by a particular person ‖ 특정한 방법이나 특정인에 의해 만들어진 음식. …식 요리: *Italian cooking* 이탈리아(식) 요리

cooking² *adj* **1** suitable for cooking or used in cooking ‖ 요리하는 데 적합하거나 요리에 쓰이는. 요리용의: *cooking oil* 요리용 기름 **2** SLANG doing something very well ‖ 무엇을 매우 잘 하고 있는: *The band is really cooking tonight.* 그 밴드는 오늘 밤 무척 잘 하고 있다.

cool¹ /kul/ *adj* **1** SPOKEN said in order to show that you agree with something or that it does not annoy you ‖ 어떤 것에 동의하거나 귀찮지 않음을 나타내는 데 쓰여: *"Do you mind if I bring my sister?" "No, that's cool."* "내 여동생을 데려가도 되겠니?" "그럼, 좋아." **2** SPOKEN said in order to show approval, especially of someone or something that is fashionable, attractive, or relaxed ‖ 특히 유행에 맞는[매력적인, 편안한] 사람이나 물건에 대해 인정하는 것을 보이는 데 쓰여. 멋있는. 끝내주는: *He's a really cool guy.* 그는 정말 멋진 녀석이다. **3** low in temperature but not cold ‖ 기온이 낮지만 춥지 않은. 서늘한. 시원한: *a cool summer evening* 서늘한 여름 저녁 —see usage note at TEMPERATURE **4** calm and not nervous or excited ‖ 침착하고 긴장되거나 흥분되지 않은. 냉정한. 냉철한: *a cool calculating politician* 냉철하고 용의주도한 정치인 **5** unfriendly ‖ 우호적이지 않은. 냉담한. 열의 없는: *a cool welcome* 냉대 —**coolness** *n* [U] —**coolly** /ˈkul-li/ *adv*

cool² *v* **1** [I, T] also **cool down** to make something slightly colder or to become slightly colder ‖ 어떤 것을 약간 더 차갑게 만들거나 차가워지다. 식다. …을 식히다: *Allow the cake to cool before cutting it.* 케이크를 자르기 전에 식혀라. **2** [I] feelings or relationships that cool become less strong ‖ 감정이나 관계가 덜 강렬해지다. 식다. 소원해지다: *Their feelings for each other seem to be cooling.* 서로에 대한 그들의 감정은 식어가는 듯하다. **3 cool it** SPOKEN used to tell someone to stop being angry ‖ 남에게 화내지 말라고 말하는 데 쓰여. 진정해: *Will you stop shouting and just cool it!* 고함 좀 치지 말고 진정해라!

cool down *phr v* [I] **1** to become calm

after being angry ‖ 화낸 후 차분해지다. 진정하다: *The long walk home helped me cool down.* 집까지 오래 걸었더니 마음을 진정시키는 데 도움이 되었다. **2** to do gentle physical exercises after doing more difficult exercises, so that you do not get injuries ‖ 부상당하지 않도록 더 힘든 운동을 한 뒤에 부드러운 육체 운동을 하다. 완화하는 마무리 운동을 하다

cool off *phr v* [I] **1** to return to a normal temperature after being hot ‖ 뜨거워진 후에 평상시의 온도로 되돌아가다. 식다. 차가워지다: *The kids cooled off by going for a swim.* 아이들은 수영하러 감으로써 더위를 식혔다. **2** to become calm after being angry ‖ 화낸 후 차분해지다. 진정하다. 냉정을 찾다: *You need to cool off before trying to talk to her again.* 그녀에게 다시 이야기하려고 하기 전에 너는 냉정해져야겠다.

cool³ *n* [U] **1 the cool** a temperature that is cool ‖ 차가운 기온. 냉기. 서늘함: *the cool of a spring morning* 봄날 아침의 서늘 **2 keep your cool** to stay calm in a difficult situation ‖ 곤란한 상황 속에서 냉정을 지키다. 침착함을 유지하다: *He was starting to annoy her, but she kept her cool.* 그가 그녀를 괴롭히기 시작했지만 그녀는 냉정을 지켰다. **3 lose your cool** to stop being calm in a difficult situation ‖ 곤란한 상황에서 냉정함을 잃다: *Nick lost his cool when Ryan yelled at him.* 라이언이 그에게 소리쳤을 때 닉은 냉정함을 잃었다.

cool·er /ˈkulɚ/ *n* a container in which you can keep food or drinks cool ‖ 음식이나 음료를 시원하게 유지시킬 수 있는 용기. 냉각용 용기

coop¹ /kup/ *n* a cage for hens ‖ 닭장

coop² *v*

coop sb ↔ **up** *phr v* [T] to make someone stay indoors, or in a small space ‖ 사람을 건물 안이나 비좁은 공간에 머무르게 하다. 가두다. 감금하다: *After being cooped up all morning, we were happy to go outside.* 아침 내내 갇혀 있다가 밖에 나오니 우리는 행복했다.

co·op·er·ate /kouˈɑpəˌreɪt/ *v* [I] **1** to work with someone else to achieve something that you both want ‖ 공동으로 원하는 것을 얻기 위해 남과 함께 작업하다. 협력[협동]하다: *The local police are cooperating with the FBI in the search for the killers.* 지방 경찰은 살인자들의 수색 작업에 FBI와 공조하고 있다. **2** to do what someone asks you to do ‖ 남이 요청하는 것을 하다. 협조하다: *We can deal with this problem, if you're willing to* *cooperate.* 당신이 기꺼이 협조한다면 우리는 이 문제를 해결할 수 있다.

co·op·er·a·tion /koʊˌɑpəˈreɪʃən/ *n* [U] **1** the act of working with someone else to achieve what you both want || 공동으로 원하는 것을 얻기 위해 남과 함께 작업하는 행위. 협력. 협동: *The sales team will be working in cooperation with other departments.* 영업팀은 다른 부서와 협력하여 일하게 될 것이다. **2** willingness to work with other people, or to do what they ask you to do || 다른 사람과 기꺼이 함께 작업하거나 남이 요청하는 것을 행함. 협조. 원조: *I'd like to thank you for your cooperation.* 당신의 협조에 감사를 표하고 싶습니다.

co·op·era·tive¹ /koʊˈɑprətɪv/ *adj* **1** willing to help || 기꺼이 도와 주는. 협조적인: *I've always found her very cooperative.* 그녀가 매우 협조적이라는 것을 나는 언제나 알고 있다. **2** made, done, or owned by people working together || 함께 일하는 사람들이 만든[행하는, 소유한]. 협동하는. 협력적인: *a cooperative farm venture* 협동 농장 기업 – **cooperatively** *adv*

cooperative² *n* a company, farm etc. that is owned and operated by people working together || 함께 일하는 사람들이 소유하고 운영하는 회사·농장 등. 협동 조합[농장]: *They turned their business into a cooperative.* 그들은 사업을 협동 조합으로 전환했다.

co-opt /koʊˈɑpt/ *v* [T] DISAPPROVING to use something that was not originally yours to help you do something, or to persuade someone to help you || 자신의 일을 도모하기 위해 원래 자기 것이 아닌 무엇을 사용하거나, 또는 자신을 돕도록 사람을 설득하다. (남의 것을) 마음대로 쓰다. (반대자를) 흡수하다: *Conservative Christians have been accused of co-opting the Republican party.* 보수적인 기독교인들이 공화당을 흡수했다는 비난을 받았다.

co·or·di·nate /koʊˈɔrdnˌeɪt/ *v* [T] **1** to organize people or things so that they work together well || 효과적으로 함께 작업할 수 있도록 사람 또는 물건을 조직화하다. 협력[조정]하다: *Liza is coordinating our sales effort.* 리자는 우리의 영업 노력에 협조하고 있다. **2** to make the parts of your body work together well || 신체의 부위들이 함께 작용하게 하다. 조화시키다: *Her movements were perfectly coordinated.* 그녀의 동작은 완벽하게 조화되었다.

co·or·di·na·tion /koʊˌɔrdnˈeɪʃən/ *n* [U] **1** the organization of people or things so that they work together well || 효과적으로 함께 일하기 위한 사람이나 사물의 조직. 협력. 조정: *the coordination of research teams* 연구팀의 협조 **2** the way that the parts of your body work together to do something || 신체 부위들이 무엇을 하기 위해 함께 작용하는 방식. 조화: *Skating in pairs takes good coordination.* 짝을 지어 스케이트를 타는 데에는 조화가 잘 되어야 한다.

co·or·di·na·tor /koʊˈɔrdnˌeɪtər/ *n* someone who organizes the way people work together || 사람들이 함께 일하는 방식을 조직화시키는 사람. 코오디네이터. 제작 진행 책임자

coo·ties /ˈkutiz/ *n* [plural] a word meaning lice (LOUSE), used by children as an insult when they do not want to play with or sit with another child || 이를 뜻하는 단어로, 아이들이 다른 아이와 같이 놀거나 앉고 싶지 않을 때 모욕적인 언사로 쓰여: *Jenny has cooties.* 제니는 이가 있대요.

cop /kɑp/ *n* INFORMAL a police officer || 경찰관, 순경

cope /koʊp/ *v* [I] to deal successfully with something || 어떤 일을 성공적으로 다루다. 대처하다: *How do you cope with all this work?* 이 모든 일에 어떻게 대처합니까?

cop·i·er /ˈkɑpiər/ *n* a machine that quickly copies documents onto paper by photographing them || 문서를 그대로 사진 찍어 종이에 신속하게 복사하는 기계. 복사기

co·pi·lot /ˈkoʊ ˌpaɪlət/ *n* a pilot who helps the main pilot fly an airplane || 주조종사가 비행하는 것을 도와 주는 조종사. 부조정사

co·pi·ous /ˈkoʊpiəs/ *adj* produced in large amounts || 다량으로 생산되는. 풍부한: *He always takes copious notes.* 그는 언제나 필기를 잔뜩 한다. – **copiously** *adv*

cop-out /ˈ. ./ *n* INFORMAL something you do or say in order to avoid doing something || 어떤 일 하는 것을 피하기 위해 행동하거나 말하는 것. 구실. 도피: *Blaming failing grades on TV is a cop-out.* 나쁜 성적을 텔레비전 탓으로 돌리는 것은 변명에 불과하다. – **cop out** *v*

cop·per /ˈkɑpər/ *n* [U] an orange-brown metal that is an ELEMENT and is often used to make wire || 종종 전선을 만드는 데에 쓰는 황갈색의 금속 원소. 구리. 동 – **copper** *adj*

cop·ter /ˈkɑptər/ *n* INFORMAL ⇨

HELICOPTER

cop·u·late /'kɑpyə,leɪt/ v [I] FORMAL to
have sex ‖ 성관계를 갖다 – **copulation**
/,kɑpyə'leɪʃən/ n [U]

cop·y¹ /'kɑpi/ n **1** something that is
made to look exactly like something else
‖ 다른 것과 정확히 똑같아 보이도록 만들
어진 것. 사본. 모방: *Please make me a
copy of the report.* 저에게 그 보고서를
복사해 주세요. / *a very good copy of Van
Gogh's famous painting* 반 고흐의 유명
한 미술 작품 중의 뛰어난 모사품 **2** one
of many books, magazines etc. that are
exactly the same ‖ 완전히 똑같은 다수의
책. 잡지 등 중의 하나. 1부. 1권: *a copy of
Irving's new novel* 어빙의 신간 소설본 **3**
[U] TECHNICAL something written to be
printed, especially for an advertisement
‖ 특히 광고용으로 인쇄하기 위해 작성된
것. 광고문: *We need someone who can
write good copy.* 우리는 훌륭한 광고문을
작성할 수 있는 사람이 필요하다.

copy² v **1** [T] to make a thing that is
exactly like something else ‖ 다른 것과
완전히 같은 것을 만들다. 복사하다. …을
베끼다: *Could you copy this tape for me?*
이 테이프를 복사해 주실 수 있겠어요? **2**
[T] to do something that someone else
has done, or behave like someone else
‖ 다른 사람이 했던 것을 하거나 다른 사
람처럼 행동하다. 모방하다. 본뜨다: *The
system has been copied by other
organizations, and has worked well.* 그
체제를 다른 조직들이 모방하여 잘 운영하
고 있다. **3** [I, T] to write exactly what
someone else has written ‖ 다른 사람이
작성한 것을 똑같이 쓰다. 베끼다. 커닝하
다: *He copied his friend's answers
during the test.* 그는 시험보는 동안 친구
의 답안을 커닝했다.

cop·y·cat /'kɑpi,kæt/ n INFORMAL **1** a
word used by children to criticize
someone who copies other people's
clothes, behavior etc. ‖ 남의 옷·행동 등
을 따라하는 사람을 비난하기 위해 아이들
이 쓰는 말. 흉내쟁이 **2 copycat
crime/murder etc.** a crime, murder
etc. that someone has copied from
another person ‖ 다른 사람을 모방해서
하는 범죄·살인 등. 모방 범죄/살인

cop·y·right /'kɑpi,raɪt/ n [C, U] the
legal right to produce and sell a book,
play, movie, or record ‖ 책[연극, 영화,
음반]을 제작하고 판매하는 법적 권리. 저
작권. 판권

cor·al /'kɔrəl, 'kɑrəl/ n [U] a hard
colored substance that grows in warm
sea water ‖ 따뜻한 바닷물 속에서 자라는
단단하고 색이 있는 물질. 산호

cord /kɔrd/ n [C, U] **1** a piece of wire
covered with plastic for connecting
electrical equipment to the supply of
electricity ‖ 전기를 공급하기 위해 전기
기구에 연결하는 플라스틱으로 싸여 있는
전선. 코드: *an extension cord for the TV*
TV용 확장 코드 **2** a piece of thick string
or thin rope ‖ 두꺼운 줄 또는 가는 밧줄.
끈. 실

cor·dial /'kɔrdʒəl/ adj friendly and
polite but formal ‖ 우호적이고 예의바르
면서도 격식 있는. 진심에서 우러난. 친절
한: *a cordial greeting* 진심어린 인사 –
cordiality /,kɔrdʒi'æləti/ n [U] –
cordially /'kɔrdʒəli/ adv

cord·less /'kɔrdlɪs/ adj a cordless
piece of equipment uses a BATTERY
instead of a CORD ‖ 코드 대신 배터리를
쓰는 무선 장비의. 코드 없는. 무선의: *a
cordless telephone* 무선 전화기

cor·don¹ /'kɔrdn/ n a line of police,
soldiers, or vehicles that are put around
an area to protect or enclose it ‖ 어떤 것
을 보호하고 둘러싸기 위해 그 주변에 배
치하는 경찰[군인, 차량]의 행렬. 비상선.
저지선: *Several protesters tried to push
through the police cordon.* 여러 명의 항
의자들이 경찰 저지선을 밀어붙치려고 시
도했다.

cordon² v

cordon sth ↔ **off** phr v [T] to surround
and protect an area with police officers,
soldiers, or vehicles ‖ 경찰관[군인, 차량]
으로 지역을 둘러싸고 보호하다. 비상선을
치다. 차단하다: *Police have cordoned
off the building where the bomb was
found.* 경찰은 폭발물이 발견된 빌딩을 차
단했다.

cords /kɔrdz/ n [plural] INFORMAL
CORDUROY pants ‖ 코르덴 바지

cor·du·roy /'kɔrdə,rɔɪ/ n [U] thick
strong cotton cloth with raised lines on
one side ‖ 한 쪽 면에 돋아진 선들이 있는
두껍고 질긴 면직물. 코르덴 천: *a
corduroy jacket* 코르덴 재킷

core¹ /kɔr/ n **1** the central or most
important part of something ‖ 어떤 것의
중심 또는 가장 중요한 부분. 핵심: *The
city is the core of a large industrial
area.* 그 도시는 대단위 산업 지역의 중심
지이다. **2** the hard central part of an
apple or PEAR ‖ 사과나 배의 딱딱한 중심
부. 속. 심 **3** the central part of the
earth or any other PLANET ‖ 지구나 다른
행성의 중심부. 중심 핵 **4** a group of
people who do important work in an
organization ‖ 조직 내에서 중요한 일을

하는 일단의 사람들. 핵심. 중요 집단:
*The department has a small core of
experienced staff.* 그 부서에는 경력자들
로 구성된 소수의 핵심 집단이 있다. **5**
the central part of a NUCLEAR REACTOR ‖
원자로의 핵심부. 노심 —see also
HARDCORE

core² *v* [T] to remove the hard center of
a piece of fruit ‖ 과일의 딱딱한 중심부를
제거하다. 심을 빼내다

cork¹ /kɔrk/ *n* **1** [U] the light outer part
of a particular type of tree that is used
for making things ‖ 물건을 만드는 데 쓰
는 특정한 나무의 가벼운 바깥 부분. 코르
크 나무 외피: *cork mats* 코르크 돗자리 **2**
a round piece of this material that is put
into the top of a bottle to keep liquid
inside ‖ 병 속의 액체를 보존하기 위해 병
입구에 끼우는 코르크의 둥근 조각. 코르
크 마개

cork² *v* [T] to close a bottle tightly by
putting a CORK in it ‖ 코르크 마개를 끼워
넣어 병을 단단히 막다. 코르크 마개를 하
다

cork·screw /'kɔrkskru/ *n* a tool used
for pulling CORKs out of bottles ‖ 병에서
코르크 마개를 빼는 데 쓰는 도구. 코르크
따개

corn /kɔrn/ *n* [U] **1** a tall plant with
yellow seeds that are cooked and eaten
as a vegetable ‖ 야채로 요리해서 먹는 노
란 씨가 있는 키 큰 식물. 옥수수: *an ear
of corn* (=the top part of a corn plant on
which these yellow seeds grow) 옥수수
열매 / *steak and corn on the cob* (=an
ear of corn that is boiled and eaten as a
vegetable) 스테이크와 속대에 붙은 옥수
수 —see picture on page 944 **2** a thick,
hard, and painful area of skin on your
foot ‖ 발에 생기는 두껍고 딱딱하여 아픈
피부 부위. 티눈

corn·bread /'kɔrnbrɛd/ *n* [U] bread
that is made from CORNMEAL ‖ 옥수수 가
루로 만든 빵. 옥수수빵 —see picture at
BREAD

cor·ne·a /'kɔrniə/ *n* the strong
transparent covering on the outer
surface of your eye ‖ 안구의 외부 표면을
감싸는 단단하고 투명한 덮개. 각막 –
corneal *adj*

corned beef /ˌkɔrn'bif-/ *n* [U] BEEF
that has been preserved in salt water
and SPICEs ‖ 소금물과 양념에 절인 쇠고
기. 콘비프

cor·ner¹ /'kɔrnɚ/ *n* **1** the point at
which two lines, surfaces, or edges
meet ‖ 두 개의 선[면, 모서리]이 만나는
점. 모서리. 가장자리: *a table in the*

corner of the room 방 구석에 놓인 탁자.
/ *a calendar on the corner* of her desk
그녀의 책상 모서리에 놓인 달력 —see
picture at EDGE¹ **2** the place where two
roads, streets, or paths meet ‖ 두 갈래의
도로[길, 통로]가 만나는 지점. 길모퉁이:
*Meet me on the corner of 72nd and
Central Park.* 72번가 센트럴 파크의 모퉁
이에서 만나자. / *We went to a place
around the corner for coffee.* 우리는 커
피를 마시러 길모퉁이 쪽으로 갔다. /
When you turn the corner (=go around
the corner) *you'll see a video store.* 길모
퉁이를 돌면 비디오 가게를 찾을 수 있을
거야. **3** a distant part of the world ‖ 세상
에서 동떨어진 곳. 외딴 곳. 후미진 곳:
*You can hear Voice of America in almost
every corner of the world.* 당신은 세계
도처에서 Voice of America 방송을 청취
할 수 있습니다. **4 see sth out of the
corner of your eye** to notice something
without turning your head ‖ 머리를 돌리
지 않고 어떤 것을 인지하다. 곁눈질로 어
떤 것을 보다 —see also **cut corners**
(CUT¹)

corner² *v* [T] **1** to move closer to a
person or an animal so that he, she, or
it cannot escape ‖ 사람 또는 동물이 도망
칠 수 없도록 더 가까이 다가가다. 궁지에
몰아넣다. 꼼짝 못하게 하다: *Gibbs
cornered Cassetti after the meeting and
asked for his decision.* 기브스는 회의가
끝나고 카세티를 궁지에 몰며 그의 결단을
요구했다. **2 corner the market** to sell
or produce all of a particular type of
goods ‖ 특정한 모든 종류의 상품을 팔거
나 만들다. 시장을 독점하다. 매점하다

cor·ner·stone /'kɔrnɚˌstoun/ *n* **1** a
stone set at one of the bottom corners of
a building, often as part of a special
ceremony ‖ 종종 특별한 의식의 일부로
건물의 바닥 한쪽 귀퉁이에 세운 돌. 귀돌
2 something that is very important
because everything else depends on it ‖
다른 모든 것의 바탕이 되는 매우 중요한
것. 기초: *Free speech is the cornerstone
of democracy.* 자유로운 연설은 민주주의
의 기본이다.

cor·net /kɔr'nɛt/ *n* a small musical
instrument like a TRUMPET ‖ 트럼펫과 같
은 작은 악기. 코넷

corn·flakes /'kɔrnfleɪks/ *n* [plural] a
type of breakfast food made from corn
‖ 옥수수로 만든 아침 식사의 한 종류. 콘
플레이크

corn·meal /'kɔrnmil/ *n* [U] a rough
type of flour made from crushed dried
corn ‖ 건조시킨 옥수수를 갈아 만든 곱지

않은 가루. 옥수수 가루

corn·starch /ˈkɔrnstɑrtʃ/ *n* [U] a fine white flour made from corn, used in cooking to make liquids thicker ‖ 요리할 때 액체를 걸쭉하게 만드는 데 쓰는, 옥수수를 곱게 빻아 만든 흰 가루. 콘스타치. 녹말

corn·y /ˈkɔrni/ *adj* INFORMAL old, silly, and too familiar to be interesting ‖ 오래되고 시시하며 흥미를 주기엔 너무 익숙한. 진부한: *a corny song from the '40s* 40년대의 진부한 노래

cor·o·na·ry¹ /ˈkɔrəˌnɛri/ *adj* concerning or relating to the heart ‖ 심장에 관한, 또는 심장에 관련된. 심장의: *coronary disease* 심장 질환

coronary² *n* ⇨ HEART ATTACK

cor·o·na·tion /ˌkɔrəˈneɪʃən/ *n* a ceremony in which someone officially becomes a king or queen ‖ 공식적으로 왕이나 왕비가 되는 의식. 대관(식)

cor·o·ner /ˈkɔrənə/ *n* an official whose job is to discover the cause of someone's death, if it is sudden or unexpected, especially by examining his/her body ‖ 특히 사체를 검사함으로써 갑작스럽거나 예기치 않은 사인(死因)을 밝히는 직업인. 검시관

cor·po·ral, Corporal /ˈkɔrpərəl/ *n* the lowest noncommissioned officer in the Army or Marines, or someone who has this rank ‖ 육군 또는 해군에서 최하위의 분대장급의 직급이나 이 계급의 사람. 병장

cor·po·ral pun·ish·ment /ˌ... ˈ.../ *n* [U] the punishment of someone by hitting him/her ‖ 사람을 때리는 처벌. 태형. 체벌

cor·po·rate /ˈkɔrpərɪt/ *adj* belonging to or relating to a CORPORATION ‖ 법인에 속하거나 관련된. 법인의: *They're building new corporate headquarters.* 그들은 새로운 법인 본부를 설립하고 있다. **– corporately** *adv*

cor·po·ra·tion /ˌkɔrpəˈreɪʃən/ *n* a large business organization that is owned by SHAREHOLDERS ‖ 주주들이 소유하고 있는 대규모 사업 조직. 법인. 조합: *an executive position in a large corporation* 대단위 법인 내의 실무직

corps /kɔr/ *n* [singular] TECHNICAL **1** a trained group of people with special duties in the military ‖ 군대에서 특수 임무를 띤 일단의 훈련된 사람들. 병과. 군단: *the Naval Air Corps* 해군 항공단 **2** a group of people who do a particular job ‖ 특정한 일을 하는 사람들의 집단. …단 [대]: *the press corps* 기자단

corpse /kɔrps/ *n* a dead body ‖ 사체. 송장. 유해

cor·pu·lent /ˈkɔrpyələnt/ *adj* FORMAL very fat ‖ 매우 뚱뚱한. 비만한

cor·pus·cle /ˈkɔrˌpʌsəl/ *n* a red or white blood cell in your body ‖ 신체의 붉거나 흰 혈액 세포. 적[백]혈구

cor·ral¹ /kəˈræl/ *n* an enclosed area where cattle, horses etc. are kept ‖ 소·말 등을 가두어 둘러싼 장소. 울타리. 우리

corral² *v* [T] to put animals into a CORRAL ‖ 울타리 속에 동물을 넣다. 우리에 가두다

cor·rect¹ /kəˈrɛkt/ *adj* **1** right or without any mistakes ‖ 올바른 또는 어떠한 실수도 없는. 옳은. 정확한: *the correct answers* 정답 / *"Your name is Ives?" "Yes, that's correct."* "당신 이름이 아이브즈입니까?" "예, 맞습니다." **2** suitable for a particular occasion or use ‖ 특정한 경우나 용도에 적합한. 적절한. 타당한: *the correct procedure for making an application* 정식 지원 절차 **– correctly** *adv* **– correctness** *n* [U] —opposite INCORRECT

correct² *v* [T] to make something right or better ‖ 어떤 것을 올바르게 만들거나 개선하다. 수정[교정]하다: *Your eyesight can be corrected with better glasses.* 더 좋은 안경으로 당신의 시력을 교정할 수 있습니다. / *Teachers spend hours correcting papers.* 교사들은 숙제를 교정하는 데 많은 시간을 쏟아 일한다.

cor·rec·tion /kəˈrɛkʃən/ *n* a change in something that makes it right or better ‖ 올바르거나 더 좋게 만드는 변화. 수정. 개선: *Johnson made a few corrections to the article before allowing it to be printed.* 그 기사를 싣기 전에 존슨은 몇 가지를 수정했다.

cor·rec·tive /kəˈrɛktɪv/ *adj* FORMAL intended to make something right or better, after being wrong or not working correctly ‖ 잘못되거나 제대로 작동하지 않아 올바르게 만들거나 개선하려는. 수정하는. 올바르게 하는: *corrective lenses for the eyes* 시력 교정 렌즈

cor·re·la·tion /ˌkɔrəˈleɪʃən, ˌkɑr-/ *n* [C, U] a relationship in which two things happen together and may have an effect on each other ‖ 두 가지 사건이 함께 일어나 서로에게 영향을 끼칠 수 있는 관계. 상호 [상관] 관계: *There's a high correlation between hot weather and this type of illness.* 더운 날씨와 이러한 종류의 질병은 높은 상관 관계가 있다. **– correlate** /ˈkɔrəˌleɪt/ *v* [I, T]

cor·re·spond /ˌkɔrəˈspɑnd, ˌkɑr-/ v [I] **1** if two things correspond, they are like each other or relate to each other ‖ 두 가지 사건이 서로 같거나 관련되다. 일치 [부합]하다: *The name on the envelope doesn't correspond with the one on the letter.* 봉투에 적힌 이름과 편지에 적힌 이름이 일치하지 않는다. / *His salary doesn't correspond to his responsibilities.* 그의 봉급은 그가 맡은 일과는 맞지 않는다. **2** if two people correspond, they write letters to each other ‖ 두 사람이 서로에게 편지를 쓰다. 편지 왕래하다. 통신하다: *They've been corresponding for years.* 그들은 오랫동 안 서신 교환을 해오고 있다.

cor·re·spond·ence /ˌkɔrəˈspɑndəns, ˌkɑr-/ n [U] **1** letters that people write ‖ 사람들이 쓰는 편지. 서한: *I try to type all my correspondence.* 나는 내 편지를 모두 타이핑하려 한다. **2** the activity of writing letters ‖ 편지를 쓰는 행위. 서신 왕래 : *His correspondence with Hemingway continued until his death.* 그와 헤밍웨이와의 서신 왕래는 그가 죽을 때까지 계속되었다.

correspondence course /..'.. ˌ./ n a course of lessons that you receive by mail and do at home ‖ 우편으로 받거나 집에서 하는 수강 과정. 통신 교육 과정

cor·re·spond·ent /ˌkɔrəˈspɑndənt, ˌkɑr-/ n **1** someone whose job is to report news from a distant area or about a particular subject to a newspaper or television ‖ 멀리 떨어진 지역의 뉴스나 특정 주제를 신문이나 텔레비전에 보도하는 직업인. 통신원. 특파원: *the White House correspondent* 백악관 통신원 / *the London correspondent for the Los Angeles Times* LA 타임즈의 런던 통신원 **2** someone who writes to another person regularly ‖ 다른 사람에게 정기적으로 편지를 쓰는 사람: *I like getting her letters; she's a good correspondent.* 나는 그녀가 보내는 편지를 좋아한다. 그녀는 편지를 잘 쓰기 때문이다.

cor·re·spond·ing /ˌkɔrəˈspɑndɪŋ, ˌkɑr-/ adj similar or matching ‖ 유사하거나 어울리는. 대응[상응]하는: *a promotion and a corresponding increase in salary* 승진과 그에 상응하는 봉급 인상 – **correspondingly** adv

cor·ri·dor /ˈkɔrədə, -ˌdɔr, ˈkɑr-/ n **1** a passage between two rows of rooms ‖ 두 줄로 늘어서 있는 방들 사이의 통로. 복도: *The elevator's at the end of the corridor.* 엘리베이터는 복도 끝에 있다. **2** a narrow area of land within a large area, especially one used for traveling from one place to another ‖ 특히 한 곳에서 다른 곳으로 여행하는 데 쓰이는 넓은 지역 내의 좁은 지역. 회랑 지대: *the New York – Washington DC corridor* 뉴욕과 워싱턴 DC간 회랑 지대

cor·rob·o·rate /kəˈrɑbəˌreɪt/ v [T] FORMAL to support an opinion or claim with new information or proof ‖ 새로운 정보나 증거로 견해나 주장을 뒷받침하다. 확인[확증]하다: *Can you corroborate his story?* 그의 이야기를 뒷받침할 수 있어? – **corroboration** /kəˌrɑbəˈreɪʃən/ n [U] – **corroborative** /kəˈrɑbərətɪv/ adj : *corroborative evidence* 뒷받침할 수 있는 증거

cor·rode /kəˈroʊd/ v [I, T] to destroy something slowly or be destroyed slowly, especially by chemicals ‖ 특히 화학 약품에 의해 서서히 파괴하거나 파괴되다. 부식하다[되다]: *metal doors corroded by rust* 녹슬어 부식된 금속 문

cor·ro·sion /kəˈroʊʒən/ n [U] **1** the process of becoming slowly destroyed by chemicals ‖ 화학 약품에 의해 서서히 파괴되는 과정. 부식 **2** a substance such as RUST (=weak red metal) that is produced by this process ‖ 부식 작용에 의해 발생하는 녹 등의 물질 – **corrosive** /kəˈroʊsɪv/ adj

cor·ru·gat·ed /ˈkɔrəˌgeɪtɪd, ˈkɑr-/ adj formed in rows of folds that look like waves ‖ 물결처럼 생긴 주름이 연속적으로 이루어진. 골이 진. 주름 잡힌: *corrugated cardboard* 골판지

cor·rupt¹ /kəˈrʌpt/ adj **1** dishonest and ready to accept money to do something illegal ‖ 부정직하여 불법적인 일을 하기 위해 기꺼이 돈을 받는. 부정한. 뇌물이 통하는: *a corrupt judge who took a bribe* 뇌물을 받은 부정한 판사 **2** very bad morally ‖ 도덕적으로 매우 나쁜. 부도덕한. 타락한: *a corrupt society* 부패한 사회 – **corruptly** adv

corrupt² v [T] **1** to make someone dishonest or immoral ‖ 누군가를 부정직하고 부도덕하게 만들다. 타락[부패] 시키다: *Bakker's Christian ministry was corrupted by greed.* 배커스 크리스천 교단의 목사들은 탐욕으로 부패했다. **2** to change or spoil something so that it is not as good ‖ 어떤 것을 좋지 않게 변화시키거나 망치다. 오염시키다: *a traditional culture corrupted by outside influences* 외부의 영향으로 오염된 전통 문화 **3** to change the information in a computer so that it does not work correctly ‖ 제대

로 작동되지 않도록 컴퓨터 안의 정보를
바꾸다. – **corruptible** *adj*

cor·rup·tion /kə'rʌpʃən/ *n* [U] **1**
dishonest or immoral behavior ‖ 부정직
하거나 부도덕한 행실. 타락. 부패: *We
must fight against corruption in city
politics.* 우리는 시정(市政)의 부패에 맞서
싸워야 한다. **2** the act or process of
making someone dishonest or immoral
‖ 부정직하거나 부도덕하게 만드는 행위
나 과정. 부정. 타락: *the corruption of
today's youth by drugs* 오늘날 젊은이들
의 마약으로 인한 타락

cor·sage /kɔr'saʒ/ *n* a small group of
flowers that a woman wears on her
dress for special occasions ‖ 여성이 특별
한 경우에 드레스에 다는 작은 꽃다발. 코
르사주. 꽃장식

cor·set /'kɔrsɪt/ *n* a type of underwear
that fits very tightly, that women in past
times wore in order to look thinner ‖ 과
거에 여성들이 더 날씬하게 보이기 위해
입었던 아주 꼭 끼는 속옷의 한 종류. 코르
셋

cor·tege /kɔr'tɛʒ/ *n* FORMAL a line of
people, cars etc. that move slowly in a
funeral ‖ 장례식에서 천천히 이동하는 사
람·차량 등의 행렬. 장례 행렬

cos·met·ic /kaz'mɛtɪk/ *adj* **1** intended
to make your skin or body more
beautiful ‖ 피부나 신체를 더 아름답게 만
들기 위한. 화장용의. 성형의: *cosmetic
surgery* 성형 외과 **2** dealing only with
the appearance of something ‖ 어떤 것의
외형만을 다루는. 표면적인. 가식적인:
cosmetic changes to the policy 정책의 표
면적인 변화 – **cosmetically** *adv*

cos·me·ti·cian /ˌkazmə'tɪʃən/ *n*
someone who is trained to put
COSMETICS on other people ‖ 다른 사람에
게 화장을 해주는 교육을 받은 사람. 메이
크업아티스트

cos·met·ics /kaz'mɛtɪks/ *n* [plural]
substances such as creams or powders
that are used in order to make your face
and skin more attractive ‖ 얼굴·피부를
더 매력적으로 만들기 위해 쓰는 크림이나
분가루 등의 물질. 화장품

cos·mic /'kazmɪk/ *adj* **1** relating to the
whole universe, or happening in, or
coming from space ‖ 우주 전체와 관련된
[우주에서 발생한, 우주에서 온]. 우주의.
우주에 관한: *cosmic radiation* 우주 복사
에너지 **2** INFORMAL relating to the
meaning of the universe ‖ 우주라는 의미
와 관계된. 우주와 관련된: *philosophers
asking cosmic questions* 우주에 관한 문
제를 제기하는 철학자들 – **cosmically**
adv

cos·mo·naut /'kazmɛˌnɔt/ *n* an
ASTRONAUT from Russia or the former
Soviet Union ‖ 러시아나 구 소련의 우주
비행사

cos·mo·pol·i·tan /ˌkazmə'palətn, -
lət'n/ *adj* **1** consisting of people from
many different parts of the world ‖ 다양
한 세계 각국의 사람들로 이루어진. 전세
계에 속하는. 범세계적인: *a
cosmopolitan city like New York* 뉴욕과
같은 국제 도시 **2** showing wide
experience of different people and
places ‖ 상이한 사람들과 지역들에 대한
광범위한 경험을 나타내는. 세계주의적인.
보편적인: *a cosmopolitan outlook* 세계주
의적인 시각

cos·mos /'kazmous, -məs/ *n* **the
cosmos** the universe considered as a
whole system ‖ 통일된 체계로 본 우주

cost[1] /kɔst/ *n* **1** [C, U] the amount of
money you must pay in order to buy,
do, or produce something ‖ 어떤 것을 구
매[실행, 생산]하는 데 지불해야 하는 액
수. 값. 비용: *Will $100 cover the cost
of books?* (=be enough to pay for them)
이 책 전부에 100달러면 되겠습니까? /
the high/low cost of educating children
높은[낮은] 자녀 교육비 —compare
PRICE[1] **2** [singular] something that you
must give or lose in order to get
something else ‖ 어떤 것을 얻기 위해 주
거나 잃어야만 하는 것. 희생. 대가: *War
is never worth its cost in human life.* 전
쟁은 결코 인간의 생명까지 희생할 만한
가치가 있는 것이 아니다. / *He saved his
family, at the cost of his own life.* 그는
자신의 생명을 바쳐서 가족을 구했다. **3
at all costs/at any cost** whatever
happens, or whatever effort is needed ‖
무슨 일이 있더라도 또는 어떠한 노력이
수반되더라도. 무슨 수를 써서라도: *We
need to get that contract, at any cost.* 무
슨 일이 있어도 우리는 그 계약을 성사시
켜야 한다. **4 at cost** for the same price
that you paid ‖ 지불했던 것과 같은 가격
으로. 원가로. 구입 가격으로: *We had to
sell the van at cost.* 우리는 원가로 트럭
을 팔아야 했다. —see also COSTS

USAGE NOTE cost

Use **cost** to talk about how much you
have to pay for something: *How much
does this CD cost? / the cost of having
the TV repaired.* Use **price** only to
talk about the amount of money you
have to pay to buy something in a

store, restaurant etc.: *Their prices seem pretty high.* Use **charge** to talk about the amount of money someone makes you pay: *They charged me $35 to deliver the couch.* Use **value** to talk about how much something such as jewelry or furniture is worth: *He sold the house for less than its real value.* Use **expense** to talk about a very large amount of money: *the expense of health care.*

cost는 물건 값으로 얼마를 지불해야 되는가에 대해 이야기할 때 쓴다: 이 CD는 얼마입니까? / TV수리비 **price**는 상점·식당 등에서 물건을 구매하는 데 지불해야 되는 액수를 말할 때 쓴다: 물건 값이 꽤 비싼 것 같군요. **charge**는 누군가가 자신에게 지불해야 되는 액수에 대해 말할 때 쓴다: 그들은 나에게 소파 배달비로 35달러를 청구했다: **value**는 보석이나 가구 등의 값비싼 물건 값을 말할 때 쓴다: 그는 실제 가격 이하로 그 집을 팔았다. **expense**는 매우 큰 금액에 대해 이야기할 때 쓴다: 의료 비용

cost² *v* [T] **1** to have a particular price ‖ 특정한 가격을 갖다. 비용이 들다: *This dress cost $75.* 이 드레스는 75달러이다. / *It'll cost you less to drive than to take the train.* 기차 타는 것보다 자가운전이 비용이 덜 들 것이다. **2** to make someone lose something ‖ 누군가가 어떤 것을 잃게 하다. 희생을 치르게 하다: *Your mistake cost us the deal.* 네 실수로 인해 우리는 그 거래를 놓쳤다. **3 cost an arm and a leg** INFORMAL to be extremely expensive ‖ 극도로 비싸다. 상당한 비용이 나가다: *I love these boots, but they cost an arm and a leg.* 저는 이 부츠가 정말 마음에 들지만 너무 비싸네요.

cost³ *v* **costed, costed, costing** to calculate the price to be charged for a job, someone's time etc ‖ 일·근무 시간 등에 대해 매겨지는 값을 산정하다. 비용을 계산하다: *The electrician costed the job at $400.* 전기 기술자는 그 일에 400달러의 비용을 산정했다.

co·star¹ /'kou star/ *n* one of two or more famous actors who work together in a movie or play ‖ 영화나 연극에서 공동으로 작업하는 두 명 이상의 유명한 배우들 중 한 명. 공연자. 조연자

co·star² *v* [I] to be working in a movie or play with other famous actors ‖ 영화나 연극에서 다른 유명 배우들과 함께 작업하다. 공연하다. 출연하다

cost ef·fec·tive /'. .,../ *adj* producing the best profits or advantages at the lowest cost ‖ 최저 비용으로 최대의 수익이나 이점을 낳는. 비용 효과가 큰: *It's more cost-effective to take public transportation.* 대중 교통을 이용하는 것이 비용 효과가 더 크다.

cost·ly /'kɔstli/ *adj* **1** costing a lot of money ‖ 많은 비용이 드는. 값비싼. 사치스러운: *a costly vacation* 사치스러운 휴가 **2** causing a lot of problems or making you lose something important ‖ 많은 문제를 야기시키거나 중요한 것을 잃게 만드는. 손해가 많은. 큰 희생이 따르는: *The Vietnam War was costly in terms of both human life and American pride.* 베트남 전쟁은 인간의 생명과 미국의 자존심 양 측면에서 큰 희생이 따랐다.

cost of liv·ing /,. . '../ *n* [singular] the average amount that people spend to buy food, pay bills, own a home etc. in a particular area ‖ 특정 지역에서 식품을 사고 청구서 대금을 치르며 집을 소유하는 데 드는 평균값. 생활비. 생계비: *The cost of living is much higher in California than in Iowa.* 아이오와보다 캘리포니아의 생계비가 훨씬 높다.

costs /kɔsts/ *n* [plural] **1** the money that you must regularly spend in a business, or on your home, car etc ‖ 사업체[주택, 자동차] 등에 정기적으로 지출해야 하는 돈. 비용. 지출: *We're trying to cut costs* (=spend less money) *by driving a smaller car.* 우리는 소형차를 운행하여 비용을 절감하려 하고 있다. **2** the money that you must pay to lawyers if you are involved in a legal case ‖ 법정 소송을 할 때 변호사에게 지불해야 되는 돈. 비용. 경비: *Burdell lost the case and was ordered to pay the defense's costs.* 버델은 소송에 져서 피고측 비용을 부담하라는 명령을 받았다.

cos·tume /'kɑstum/ *n* [C, U] **1** clothes worn to make you look like someone in a particular job or something such as an animal, GHOST etc. ‖ 특정한 직업인이나 동물·유령처럼 보이도록 입는 옷. 복장. 의상: *a prize for the best Halloween costume* 할로윈 최고 복장상 **2** the clothes that were typical of a particular period of time, a country, an activity etc. ‖ 특정한 시대·국가·활동 등을 대표했던 복장. 옷차림

costume jew·el·ry /'.. ,..., ,.. '../ *n* [U] cheap jewelry that looks expensive ‖ 비싸게 보이는 싼 보석. 모조 장신구

cot /kɑt/ *n* a light narrow bed that folds up ‖ 포개지는 가볍고 좁은 침대. (휴대용) 간이 침대

cot·tage /ˈkɑtɪdʒ/ *n* a small house, especially in the country ‖ 특히 시골에 있는 작은 집. 소주택. 작은 별장

cottage cheese /ˌ.. ˈ./ *n* [U] a type of soft wet white cheese ‖ 부드럽고 촉촉한 흰 치즈의 일종. 코티지 치즈

cot·ton /ˈkɑtˀn/ *n* [C, U] **1** cloth made from the cotton plant ‖ 목화 식물로 만든 천. 무명. 면직물: *a cotton shirt* 면 셔츠 **2** a plant that produces seeds covered in soft white hair that is used for making thread and cloth ‖ 실과 천을 만드는 데 쓰며 부드러운 흰 털로 덮인 씨앗을 생산하는 식물. 목화. 면화

cotton ball /ˈ.. ˌ./ *n* a small soft ball made from cotton, used for cleaning skin ‖ 피부를 닦는 데 쓰는 작고 부드러운 면 뭉치. 정제솜. 탈지면

cotton can·dy /ˌ.. ˈ../ *n* [U] a type of sticky pink candy that looks like cotton ‖ 목화처럼 생긴 끈적끈적한 분홍색 사탕의 일종. 솜사탕

cot·ton·wood /ˈkɑtˀn,wʊd/ *n* a North American tree with seeds that look like cotton ‖ 목화처럼 생긴 씨가 있는 북미산 나무. 미루나무

couch¹ /kaʊtʃ/ *n* a comfortable piece of furniture, usually with a back and arms, on which more than one person can sit ‖ 보통 등받이와 팔걸이가 있고 한 사람 이상이 앉을 수 있는 안락한 가구. 소파

couch² *v* **be couched in sth** FORMAL to be expressed in a particular way in order to be polite or not offend someone ‖ 공손하게 또는 다른 사람을 불쾌하게 하지 않기 위해 특정하게 표현되다. 나타내다. 말하다: *His refusal was couched in polite terms.* 그는 공손한 말로 거절했다.

couch po·ta·to /ˈ. .,./ *n* INFORMAL someone who spends a lot of time sitting and watching television ‖ 앉아서 텔레비전을 보는 데 많은 시간을 보내는 사람. TV 중독자

couch potato

cou·gar /ˈkugɚ/ *n* a large pale brown wild cat from the mountains of western North and South America ‖ 북미와 남미 서부 산악 지대의 연갈색의 큰 야생 고양이. 쿠거

cough¹ /kɔf/ *v* [I] to push air out of your throat with a sudden rough sound, especially because you are sick ‖ 특히 병에 걸려서 갑작스런 거친 소리를 내며 목에서 공기를 뿜어내다. 기침하다: *He's been coughing and sneezing all day.* 그는 하루 종일 기침과 재채기를 해대고 있다.

cough up *phr v* **1** [I, T **cough** sth ↔ **up**] INFORMAL to unwillingly give someone money, information etc ‖ 다른 사람에게 마지못해 돈·정보 등을 주다. 마지못해 내놓다[실토하다]. 토해내다: *I'm trying to get my Dad to cough up some money for a motorcycle.* 나는 아빠에게서 오토바이 살 돈을 어느 정도 받아내려 한다. **2** [T **cough up** sth] to get something out of your throat or lungs by coughing ‖ 기침으로 목이나 폐에서 어떤 것을 나오게 하다. 기침하여 토해내다: *We got worried when she started coughing up blood.* 그녀가 피를 토해내기 시작하자 우리는 걱정이 되었다.

cough² *n* **1** the sound made when you cough ‖ 기침할 때 내는 소리. 콜록콜록 소리: *She gave a nervous cough before speaking.* 그녀는 말하기 전에 성마른 기침을 했다. **2** **have a cough** to have an illness in which you cough a lot ‖ 기침을 많이 하는 병에 걸리다. 감기에 걸리다: *I have a terrible cough and a headache.* 나는 기침이 심하고 두통이 있다.

cough drop /ˈ. ./ *n* a type of medicine like a piece of candy that you suck when you have a cough ‖ 기침할 때 빨아 먹는 알사탕 같은 약 종류. 기침을 멎게 하는 드롭스. 진해정

cough syr·up /ˈ. ,./ *n* [U] a thick liquid medicine that you take when you have a cough ‖ 기침할 때 먹는 진한 액체. 진해(鎮咳) 시럽. 기침약

could /kəd; *strong* kʊd/ *modal verb* **1** used in order to talk about what you were able to do ‖ 할 수 있었던 것을 말하는 데 쓰여. …할 수 있었다: *Could you hear that all right?* 그것이 잘 들립니까? / *I looked everywhere, but I couldn't* (=could not) *find it.* 나는 사방을 둘러 봤지만 그것을 찾을 수 없었다. **2** used in order to show that something might be possible or might happen ‖ 어떤 일이 가능하거나 발생할 수 있음을 나타내는 데 쓰여: *Most accidents in the home could easily be prevented.* 가정에서 일어나는 대부분의 사고들은 쉽게 예방될 수 있다. / *It could be weeks before they're finished.* 그들이 끝마치기까지는 수 주일이 걸릴지 모른다. **3** used instead of "can" when reporting what someone said ‖ 다른 사람이 말했던 것을 전할 때 "can" 대신에 쓰여: *He said we could smoke if we wanted.* 그는 우리가 원하면 담배를 피워도 괜찮다고 말했다. **4** used in order to politely ask if someone is allowed to do something || 어떤 일을 하는 것이 허용되는지를 정중하게 묻는 데에 쓰여: *Could I ask you a couple of questions?* 몇 가지 질문을 여쭤볼 수 있을까요? **5** used in order to politely ask someone to do something || 누군가에게 어떤 것을 해줄 것을 정중하게 요청하기 위해 쓰여: *Could you deposit this check at the bank for me?* 이 수표를 내 대신에 은행에 예금해 주실 수 있습니까? **6 I couldn't believe sth** used when you are very surprised about something || 어떤 일에 대해 상당히 놀랐을 때 쓰여. 나는 믿을 수가 없었다. 믿어지지 않았다: *I couldn't believe how easy it was.* 나는 그것이 얼마나 쉬운지 믿을 수가 없었다. —see also CAN¹ —see study note on page 932

SPOKEN PHRASES

7 said when you are annoyed because you think someone should have done something 어떤 사람이 그 일을 했어야 한다고 생각하기 때문에 짜증이 났을 때 쓰여: *You could have told me you were going to be late!* 늦을 거라고 나한테 말할 수도 있었잖니! **8 I could have strangled/hit/killed etc. sb** used in order to emphasize that you were very angry with someone || 어떤 사람에게 매우 화가 났음을 강조하는 데에 쓰여. 나는 …을 목 조를/때릴/죽일 수도 있었다: *I could have murdered Kerry for telling Jason that!* 케리가 제이슨에게 그 말을 했다면 나는 그녀를 죽이고도 남았을 거야! **9 I couldn't care less** used when you are not at all interested in something || 어떤 일에 전혀 관심이 없을 때 쓰여. 전혀 신경쓰지 않다: *I couldn't care less what he says – I'm not going!* 나는 그가 한 말에 눈꼼만큼도 개의치 않아. 난 안 갈거야! **10** used in order to suggest doing something || 어떤 일을 할 것을 제안하는 데에 쓰여: *We could always stop and ask directions.* 우리는 언제든 멈춰서 길을 물어볼 수 있다.

---

could·n't /'kʊdnt/ *modal verb* the short form of "could not" || "could not"의 단축형: *We just couldn't stop laughing.* 우리는 그저 계속 웃을 수밖에 없었다.

coun·cil /'kaʊnsəl/ *n* **1** a group of people who are elected as part of a town or city government || 구 또는 시 행정 부분에 선출된 일단의 사람들. 심의[평

의]회(위원). 지방 의회(의원) **2** a group of people who make decisions for a church, organization etc., or who give advice || 교회·단체 등을 위한 결정을 내리거나 조언을 하는 일단의 사람들. (자문) 위원회. 이사회: *the UN Security Council* 유엔 안전 보장 이사회

coun·cil·man /'kaʊnsəlmən/, **coun·cil·wom·an** /'kaʊnsəl,-wʊmən/ *n* a COUNCILOR

coun·cil·or /'kaʊnsələʳ/ *n* a member of a COUNCIL || 위원회의 구성원. (지방 의회) 의원

coun·sel¹ /'kaʊnsəl/ *n* [U] **1** LAW a lawyer or group of lawyers who speak for someone in a court of law || 법정에서 다른 사람을 대변하는 변호인이나 변호인단. 법률 고문: *The counsel for the defense gave her opening statement.* 피고의 변호사는 그녀를 대신해 모두(冒頭) 진술을 했다. **2 keep your own counsel** to not talk about your private thoughts and opinions || 사적인 생각·의견을 말하지 않다. 잠자코 있다 **3** FORMAL advice || 충고

counsel² *v* [T] FORMAL to listen to and advise someone || 어떤 사람 말을 듣고서 조언해 주다. 상담해 주다: *Tyrone got a job counseling teenagers about drugs.* 타이론은 마약에 대해 청소년들에게 상담해 주는 일자리를 얻었다.

coun·sel·ing /'kaʊnsəlɪŋ/ *n* [U] advice given to people about their personal problems or difficult decisions || 사적인 문제나 어려운 결정에 대해 사람들에게 해주는 조언. 상담. 지도: *She's been getting career counseling.* 그녀는 직업 상담을 받아오고 있다.

coun·sel·or /'kaʊnsələʳ/ *n* **1** someone whose job is to help people with their personal problems or with difficult decisions || 사적인 문제나 어려운 결정을 해야 하는 사람들을 돕는 직업인. 조언자. 상담역. 고문: *a marriage counselor* 결혼 상담가 **2** also **Counselor** a name used when speaking to a lawyer in court || 법정에서 변호사에게 말할 때 쓰는 명칭. 변호인 **3** someone who takes care of a group of children at a CAMP || 야영장에서 일단의 아동을 돌봐주는 사람. 지도원. 지도 교사

count¹ /kaʊnt/ *v* **1** [T] also **count up** to calculate the total number of things in a group || 한 집단 내의 사물의 총숫자를 계산하다. 셈하다. 총계를 내다. 합산하다: *The nurses counted the bottles of medicine as they put them away.* 간호사들은 약병을 치우면서 총숫자를 세었다. **2**

[I, T] also **count up** to say numbers in order, one by one or in groups || 차례로 [하나씩, 집단별로] 수를 세다. 세어 나가다: *My daughter is learning to count in French.* 내 딸은 프랑스어로 숫자 세는 것을 배우고 있다. / *He's only three, but he can count to ten.* 그는 겨우 3살이지만 10까지 셀 수 있다. **3** [I] to be officially allowed or accepted || 공식적으로 허용되거나 받아들여지다 || …을 인정[승인]하다: *"I won!" "You cheated, so it doesn't count."* "내가 이겼다!" "너는 속임수를 썼으니까 인정 할 수 없어." **4** [T] to include someone or something in a total || 사람이나 사물을 총계에 넣다. 셈에 넣다. …을 넣어 생각[계산]하다: *There are five in our family, counting me.* 우리 가족은 나를 포함해서 5명이다. **5** [T] to consider something or someone in a particular way || 사물이나 사람을 특정하게 생각하다. …으로 여기다: *I count her as one of my best friends.* 나는 그녀를 가장 친한 친구들 중 하나로 생각한다. / *You should count yourself lucky that you weren't badly hurt.* 너는 심하게 다치지 않은 것을 천만다행으로 여겨야 한다. **6** [I] to be important or valuable || 중요하거나 가치 있게 되다. 영향력이 있게 되다: *I felt my opinion didn't count for much.* 나는 내 의견이 그다지 중요시되지 않는다고 느꼈다. **7 be able to count sth on one hand** SPOKEN used in order to emphasize how small the number of something is || 어떤 것의 수가 얼마나 적은지 강조하는 데에 쓰여. …을 한 손으로 꼽을 수 있다. 한 손으로 셀 정도로 적다: *I can count on one hand the number of times he's come to visit me.* 그가 나를 방문한 횟수는 한 손으로 꼽을 수 있다.

count down *phr v* [I,T **count** sth ↔ **down**] to count the number of days, minutes etc. left until a particular moment or event || 특정한 순간이나 사건까지 남아 있는 날짜·분 등의 숫자를 세다. 수를 큰 것부터 거꾸로 세다. 카운트다운하다: *Okay, get ready to count down to midnight.* (=on New Year's Eve) 그럼 자정까지 카운트다운할 준비합시다.

count sb **in** *phr v* [T] INFORMAL to include someone or something in an activity || 사람이나 사물을 활동에 포함시키다. …에 껴주다. 축[한 패]에 넣다: *If you're going dancing, count me in.* 춤추러 가려면 나도 끼워 줘.

count on sb/sth *phr v* [T] **1** to depend on someone or something || 다른 사람이나 사물에 의지하다. 기대하다: *You can always count on him to help.* 너는 언제나 그가 도와줄 것이라 기대해도 좋다. **2** to expect someone to do something, or something to happen || 누군가가 어떤 일을 하리라고, 또는 어떤 일이 일어나리라고 기대하다. 예상하다: *We didn't count on this many people coming.* 우리는 이렇게 많은 사람이 올 것이라 예상하지 못했다.

count out *phr v* [T] **1** [**count** sb **out**] INFORMAL to not include someone or something in an activity || 사람이나 사물을 활동에 포함하지 않다. 제외하다. …을 셈에서 빼다: *If you're looking for a fight, count me out.* 싸우고 싶다면, 나는 좀 빼줘. **2** [**count out** sth] to lay things down one by one as you count them || 어떤 것들을 세면서 하나씩 내려놓다. …을 세어 나가다. 숫자를 하나하나 세다: *Jamie counted out the number of spoons needed.* 제이미는 필요한 숟가락의 숫자를 하나씩 세어 나갔다.

count² *n* **1** [C usually singular] the process of counting, or the total that you get when you count things || 숫자를 세는 과정, 또는 어떤 것들을 셀 때 얻는 총수. 셈하기. 계산. 총계. 합계: *The final count showed that Gary had won by 110 votes to 86.* 최종 집계는 게리가 110표 대 86표로 이긴 것으로 나타났다. / *At the last/latest count* (=the last time you counted), *46 students were interested in the trip.* 최종[최근] 집계에서 46명의 학생이 그 여행에 관심이 있는 것으로 나타났다. **2** [C usually singular] a measurement that shows the total number of things in a particular group || 특정 집단 내의 어떤 것의 총수를 나타내는 측정치. …수치. …기준[수준](량): *The pollen count is high today.* (=the amount of plant material in the air is high) 오늘 꽃가루 수치가 높습니다. **3 keep count** to know the total of something || 어떤 것의 총계를 알다. 정확한 수를 알다. 총계를 파악하다: *Are you keeping count of the people you've invited?* 당신은 초청한 사람들의 총수를 파악하고 있습니까? **4 lose count** to forget the total number of something || 어떤 것의 총수를 잊다. 정확한 수를 모르다. (수셈을 놓쳐서) 총계 파악을 못하다: *I've lost count of how many times she's been married.* 나는 그녀가 몇 번이나 결혼했는지 까먹었다. **5** LAW one of the crimes that the police say someone has done || 경찰이 주장하는, 어떤 사람이 저지른 범죄 중의 하나. 죄목. 기소 사항: *He's guilty on two counts of robbery.* 그

는 두 건의 강도 행위 죄목이 있다.

count·a·ble /ˈkaʊntəbəl/ adj
countable noun a noun such as "book",
that has a singular and a plural form ‖
단수형과 복수형을 갖는 "book" 등의 명
사. 가산(可算) 명사 —opposite
UNCOUNTABLE —see study note on page
940

count·down /ˈkaʊntˌdaʊn/ n the act of
counting backward to zero before
something happens, especially before a
space vehicle is sent into the sky ‖ 어떤
일이 발생하기 전, 특히 우주선이 하늘로
발사되기 전에 0까지 거꾸로 세는 행위.
초읽기. 카운트다운: The countdown has
begun at Cape Canaveral. 케이프 커네버
럴 기지에서 카운트다운이 시작됐다.

coun·te·nance¹ /ˈkaʊntənəns/ n
LITERARY your face or your expression ‖
얼굴이나 표정. 안색. 용모

countenance² v [T] FORMAL to support
or approve of something ‖ 어떤 일을 지
지하거나 승인하다. 격려하다. 찬동하다:
We cannot countenance violent
behavior. 우리는 폭력 행위는 묵인할 수
없다.

coun·ter¹ /ˈkaʊntər/ n 1 a flat surface
in the kitchen where you work, prepare
food etc. ‖ 음식 등을 조리하거나 준비하
는 부엌의 평평한 평면. 조리대 2 a
narrow table or flat surface in a store or
bank where you go to be served ‖ 가게나
은행에 가서 일을 보는 좁은 테이블이나
평평한 평면. 계산대. 판매대. 창구: the
checkout counter in a supermarket 슈퍼
마켓의 계산대 3 **over the counter** over
the counter medicines can be bought
without a PRESCRIPTION from your doctor
‖ 약을 의사의 처방전 없이 살 수 있는 4
under the counter secretly and not
legally ‖ 비밀리에 불법적으로. 몰래. 암기
래로. 비합법 거래로: They pay her
under the counter for her dishwashing
job. 그녀의 접시닦이 일에 대해 그들은 불
법적으로[세금 보고 없이] 월급을 주고 있
다.

counter² v [I, T] to react to an action,
criticism, argument etc. by doing or
saying something that will have an
opposite effect ‖ 반대 효과를 갖는 어떤
일을 하거나 말해서 행동·비판·주장 등에
대응하다. 반박[논박]하다. 되받아치다.
역습[반격]하다: Bradshaw countered the
protests by saying that the plan had
been approved by school officials. 브래
드쇼는 그 계획이 학교 당국에 의해 승인
되었던 것이라고 말하며 항의에 대해 반박
했다.

counter³ adv in a way that is opposite
to someone else's opinion, ideas etc. ‖
다른 사람의 견해·생각 등에 반대되게. 역
으로. 거꾸로. 반대로: His ideas always
run counter to my own. 그의 생각은 항
상 내 생각과 어긋난다. – **counter** adj

coun·ter·act /ˌkaʊntərˈækt/ v [T] to
reduce or prevent the bad effect of
something by doing something that has
the opposite effect ‖ 반대 효과를 갖는 일
을 해서 어떤 일의 나쁜 영향을 줄이거나
막다. …의 효과를 반감시키다[중화시키
다, 반대로 작용하게 하다]

coun·ter·at·tack /ˈkaʊntərəˌtæk/ n an
attack on an enemy that has attacked
you ‖ 자신을 공격한 적에 대한 공격. 반격
– **counterattack** /ˌ...ˈ./ v [I, T]

coun·ter·bal·ance /ˈkaʊntərˌbæləns/ v
[T] to have an effect that is the opposite
of the effect of something else ‖ 다른 것
의 효과에 반대되는 효과를 갖다. 균형잡
히게 하다. 평형을 유지하다: Good sales
in Europe have counterbalanced the
weak sales in the US. 유럽에서의 판매
호조가 미국에서의 판매 약세를 균형 잡히
게 했다. – **counterbalance** n

coun·ter·clock·wise /ˌkaʊntərˈklɑk-
waɪz/ adj, adv moving in the opposite
direction to the HANDs (=parts that point
to the time) on a clock ‖ 시계 바늘 반대
방향으로 움직이는. 시계 반대 방향의[으
로] —opposite CLOCKWISE

coun·ter·feit¹ /ˈkaʊntərfɪt/ adj made to
look exactly like something else in order
to deceive people ‖ 사람들을 속이기 위해
다른 것과 꼭 닮게 만든. 가짜의. 모조의.
위조의: counterfeit money 위조 화폐

counterfeit² v [T] to copy something
exactly in order to deceive people ‖ 사람
들을 속이기 위해 어떤 것을 똑같이 복제
하다. …을 위조하다. 위조품[모조품]을
만들다 – **counterfeiter** n

coun·ter·part /ˈkaʊntərˌpart/ n a
person or thing that has the same job or
purpose as someone or something else
in a different place ‖ 다른 곳의 다른 사람
이나 사물과 똑같은 일이나 목적을 갖고
있는 사람이나 사물. 걸맞는 역의 한쪽[상
대역]. 대응물: a meeting between the
US president and his French
counterpart 미·불 정상 회담

coun·ter·pro·duc·tive /ˌkaʊntər-
prəˈdʌktɪv/ adj achieving the opposite
result to the one you want ‖ 원하는 것과
반대되는 결과를 낳는. 역효과의[를 초래
하는]. 비생산적인: Punishing children
too harshly can be counterproductive.
어린이들에게 너무 심하게 벌을 주면 역효

과를 초래할 수 있다.

coun·ter·sign /ˈkaʊntəˌsaɪn/ v [T] to sign something that someone else has already signed ‖ 다른 사람이 이미 서명한 어떤 것에 서명하다. 부서하다. 확인 도장을 찍다: *My boss will countersign the check.* 사장이 그 수표에 확인 서명을 할 것이다.

count·less /ˈkaʊntlɪs/ adj too many to be counted ‖ 너무 많아서 셀 수 없는. 헤아릴 수 없이 많은. 무수한: *She spent countless hours making that clock.* 그녀는 그 시계를 만드는 데에 수많은 시간을 보냈다.

coun·try[1] /ˈkʌntri/ n 1 a nation or state with its land and people ‖ 영토와 국민이 있는 국가나 나라: *Bahrain became an independent country in 1971.* 바레인은 1971년에 독립 국가가 되었다. 2 the people of a nation or state ‖ 국가나 주(州)의 사람들. 국민. 대중. 민중: *a peace-loving country* 평화를 사랑하는 국민 3 **the country** the land that is outside cities or towns, especially land that is used for farming ‖ 도시나 읍 외곽의, 특히 경작에 쓰이는 땅. 시골. (농)촌

country[2] adj in the area outside cities, or relating to this area ‖ 도시 외곽 지역의, 또는 이 지역에 관한. 시골[전원]의. 농촌의[지방의]: *clean country air* 맑은 시골 공기

country and west·ern /ˌ.. . ˈ../, **country** n [U] a type of popular music from the southern and western US ‖ 미국 남부·서부에서 기원한 대중 음악의 일종. 컨트리 뮤직

country club /ˈ.. ˌ./ n a sports and social club, especially for rich people ‖ 특히 부유층을 위한 스포츠·사교 클럽

coun·try·man /ˈkʌntrimən/ n OLD-FASHIONED someone from your own country ‖ 본국 출신의 사람. 같은 나라 사람. 동향 사람. 동포

coun·try·side /ˈkʌntriˌsaɪd/ n [U] a word meaning the area outside cities and towns, used especially when you are talking about its beauty ‖ 도시나 읍 외곽 지역을 의미하며 특히 그 경관을 이야기할 때 쓰이는 단어. 지방. 시골. 농촌[전원] 지역: *the peaceful countryside* 평화로운 시골 —compare COUNTRY

coun·ty /ˈkaʊnti/ n a large area of land within a state or country that has its own government to deal with local matters ‖ 지역 문제를 해결하기 위한 자체 정부를 가지고 있는 나라나 국가 내의 지역. 카운티. 군(郡) 단위

county fair /ˌ.. ˈ./ n an event that happens each year in a particular COUNTY, with games, competitions for the best farm animals, for the best cooking etc. ‖ 특정 카운티에서 각종 게임이나 최고의 가축·최고 요리 등의 경연이 열리는 연례 행사. 카운티[군(郡)] 품평회 [축제]

coup /ku/ n 1 also **coup d'état** /ˌku deɪˈtɑ/ an act in which citizens or the army suddenly take control of the government by force ‖ 시민들이나 군대가 갑자기 무력으로 정부의 통치권을 빼앗는 행위. 쿠데타. 혁명. 정권 탈취: *President Aristide fled from a military coup in Haiti.* 아리스타이드 대통령은 아이티의 군사 쿠데타를 피해 도망쳤다. 2 something you do that is successful ‖ 성공적으로 한 일. 통쾌한 성과. 대성공: *Getting that job was quite a coup.* 그 일자리를 얻은 것은 대단한 성과였다.

cou·ple[1] /ˈkʌpəl/ n 1 **a couple of** INFORMAL **a)** a small number of things ‖ 사물의 적은 수. 몇몇: *We leave in a couple of days.* 우리는 며칠 내로 떠난다. / *I need to make a couple (of) phone calls.* 나는 전화를 몇 통 걸어야 한다. **b)** two things or people of the same kind ‖ 같은 종류의 2가지 사물이나 사람들. 2개[명]. 쌍. 짝: *I think they have a couple (of) kids now.* 나는 지금 그들이 아이를 두 명 두었다고 생각한다. 2 two people who are married or who have a romantic relationship ‖ 결혼했거나 애정 관계의 두 사람. 커플. 부부. 한 쌍의 남녀: *the young couple next door* 이웃집의 젊은 부부

USAGE NOTE couple

Use **couple** to talk about any two things of the same kind: *There are a couple of cars parked outside.* Use **pair** to talk about something that has two main parts of a similar shape that are joined together: *a pair of pants / a pair of scissors.* **Pair** is also used to talk about two things that are used together as a set: *a pair of shoes.*
couple은 종류가 같은 두 가지 사물을 말하는 데에 쓰인다: 밖에 주차된 차가 두 대 있다. **pair**는 유사한 모양의 두 주요 부분이 하나로 연결되어 있는 것을 말하는 데에 쓰인다: 바지 한 벌/가위 한 개. **pair**는 하나의 세트로서 함께 쓰이는 두 개의 사물에 대해 말할 경우 쓰인다: 신발 한 켤레

---

couple[2] v FORMAL [T] to join two things together, especially two vehicles ‖ 두 개

의 사물, 특히 두 대의 차량을 함께 연결하다. 서로 잇다. 결합하다
coupled with *phr v* [T] to happen, exist, or be used together ∥ 함께 일어나다[존재하다, 사용되다]. 연결[관련]되어 …하다. 동시에 …하다. 짝을 이루다: *Technology coupled with better health care means people live longer.* 더 나은 의료와 결부된 기술은 사람들이 더 오래 산다는 것을 의미한다.
cou·pon /'kupɑn, 'kyu-/ *n* **1** a small piece of paper that you can use to pay less money for something or get it free ∥ 어떤 것에 대해 돈을 적게 지불하거나 무료로 얻는 데 쓸 수 있는 작은 종잇조각. 쿠폰. 할인권. 우대권: *a coupon for fifty cents off a jar of coffee* 커피 한 통당 50센트 할인 쿠폰 **2** a printed form used when you order something, enter a competition etc. ∥ 물건을 주문하거나 경기장 등에 들어갈 때 쓰는 인쇄된 양식. 상품 교환권. 경기 입장권
cour·age /'kɚɪdʒ, 'kʌr-/ *n* [U] the ability to be brave when you are in danger, a difficult situation etc. ∥ 위험·어려운 상황 등에 처했을 때 용감해질 수 있는 능력. 용기. 담력. 대담성: *It must have taken a lot of courage for him to drive again after the accident.* 그가 사고 후에 다시 운전하기까지는 분명 대단한 용기가 필요했을 것이다.
cou·ra·geous /kə'reɪdʒəs/ *adj* brave and not afraid ∥ 용감하며 두려워하지 않는. 담력 있는. 대담한: *a courageous hero* 용감한 영웅 — **courageously** *adv*
cou·ri·er /'kʊriɚ, 'kɚ-/ *n* someone who delivers messages ∥ 전갈을 전달하는 사람. 사자(使者). 급사(急使)
course¹ /kɔrs/ *n*
1 of course **a)** used when what you or someone else has just said is not surprising ∥ 자신이나 다른 사람이 방금 한 말이 놀라운 것이 아닐 때 쓰여. 당연히. 마땅히: *The insurance has to be renewed every year, of course.* 당연히 그 보험은 매년 갱신되어야 한다. **b)** SPOKEN used in order to agree with someone or to give permission to someone ∥ 누군가에게 동의하거나 허가해 주는 데에 쓰여. 물론: *"Can I borrow your notes?" "Of course you can."* "네 노트 좀 빌릴 수 있어?" "물론, 그렇게 해." **c)** SPOKEN said in order to emphasize that what you are saying is true or correct ∥ 언급하고 있는 것이 사실이거나 올바르다는 것을 강조하는 데에 쓰여. 맞아: *"You'll tell her?" "Of course!"* "그녀에게 말할 거니?" "물론이지!"

2 of course not SPOKEN said in order to emphasize that you are saying no to something, or that something is not true or correct ∥ 어떤 일에 안 된다고 말하는 것, 또는 어떤 일이 사실이 아니거나 올바르지 않다는 것을 강조하는 데에 쓰여: *"Do you mind if I come a little late?" "Of course not."* "조금 늦게 와도 괜찮을까요?" "물론 괜찮습니다."
3 course of action an action you can take in a particular situation ∥ 특정 상황에서 취할 수 있는 행동. 행동 방침. 방책: *The best course of action is to speak to her alone.* 최선의 방책은 그녀 혼자에게 말하는 것이다.
4 ▶SPORTS 운동경기◀ an area of land or water on which a race is held or a particular type of sport is played ∥ 경주가 열리거나 특정 종류의 운동 경기가 펼쳐지는 육상이나 수중 지역. 경기장. 경기 코스: *a race course* 경주 코스 / *a golf course* 골프 코스
5 ▶DIRECTION 방향◀ the direction of movement that someone or something takes ∥ 사람이나 사물이 취하는 움직임의 방향. 진로. 노정(路程): *During the flight we had to change course.* 비행중에 우리는 항로를 바꿔야 했다.
6 ▶SCHOOL 학교◀ a class in a particular subject ∥ 특정 교과 강의. 교과[교육](과정). 과목: *I'm taking an evening course in math.* 나는 수학 야간 강의를 듣고 있다.
7 in/during the course of FORMAL during a process or period ∥ 과정이나 기간 중에. …하는 도중[중간]에: *During the course of our conversation, I found out that he had worked in France.* 우리가 대화를 나누던 중에 나는 그가 프랑스에서 일했었다는 것을 알았다.
8 ▶WAY STH DEVELOPS 사물의 발전과정◀ the usual or natural way that something happens, develops etc ∥ 사물이 발생하고 발전하는 등의 통상적이거나 자연적인 과정. 생장[성장](과정). 진행 과정: *a major event that changed the course of history* 역사의 흐름을 바꾼 주요한 사건
9 ▶MEAL 식사◀ the parts of a meal ∥ 식사의 일부분. …요리(차례). 식사의 순서: *Fish is often our main course.* 생선이 가끔 우리의 주요리가 된다.
course² *v* [I] LITERARY if a liquid courses somewhere, it flows rapidly ∥ 액체가 어딘가로 빠르게 흐르다
court¹ /kɔrt/ *n* **1** [C, U] a room or building in which a judge, lawyers, and other people officially decide whether

someone is guilty of a crime and what the punishment should be ‖ 어떤 사람이 유죄인지 아닌지, 어떤 벌을 받아야 하는지를 판사·변호사 그리고 기타 사람들이 공식적으로 결정하는 실내나 건물. 법원. 법정. 재판소: *He had to appear in court as a witness.* 그는 법정에 증인으로 출두해야 했다. / *We decided to take them to court* (=make them be judged in a court) *to get our money back.* 우리는 돈을 되돌려 받기 위해 그들을 법정에 세우기로 결정했다. / *The case should go to court* (=start being judged in a court) *in August.* 그 사건은 8월에 법정에서 재판을 받을 것이다. / *The insurance company settled out of court.* (=they made an agreement without going to a court) 보험 회사는 법정 밖에서 해결했다. **2 the court** the judge, lawyers, and other people who officially decide whether someone is guilty of a crime and what the punishment should be ‖ 어떤 사람이 범죄에 대해 유죄인지 무슨 벌을 받아야 하는지를 공식적으로 결정하는 판사·변호사·기타 사람들. 재판정: *The court decided he wasn't guilty.* 재판정은 그가 무죄라는 판결을 내렸다. **3** [C, U] an area that has been made specially for playing some types of sports ‖ 어떤 종류의 운동 경기를 치르기 위해 특별히 만들어진 구역. 구기 경기장. 코트: *a tennis court* 테니스 코트 **4** the official place where a king or queen lives and works ‖ 왕이나 여왕이 거주하고 집무하는 공식 장소. 궁정. 왕궁. 조정

court² *v* **1** [T] to pay attention to someone important so that s/he will like or help you in some way ‖ 중요한 사람에게 관심을 기울여서 자신을 어떤 면으로 마음에 들게 하거나 돕게 하다. …에게 알랑거리다. 비위를 맞추다. 아첨을 떨다: *Politicans are courting voters before the elections.* 정치인들은 선거를 앞두고 유권자들에게 잘 보이려 하고 있다. **2 court disaster/danger etc.** to do something that makes a problem or failure more likely ‖ 문제를 일으키거나 실패할 것 같은 일을 하다. 재앙을 불러들이다. 재난/위험을 자초하다: *The Hamiltons are courting disaster if they invite both Jim and Lynne to the party.* 해밀턴가가 짐과 린 둘을 파티에 초청한다면 재앙을 자초하고 있는 것이다. **3** [I, T] OLD-FASHIONED to have a romantic relationship with someone, especially someone you are likely to marry ‖ 특히 결혼하게 될 사람과 애정 관계를 맺다. 구애[구혼]하다. 결혼을 전제로 교제하다

cour·te·ous /'kɔtiəs/ *adj* FORMAL polite and respectful ‖ 정중하고 존경을 표하는. 공손한. 예의바른: *a courteous reply* 공손한 대답 – **courteously** *adv*

cour·te·sy /'kɔtəsi/ *n* **1** [U] polite and respectful behavior to other people ‖ 다른 사람에 대한 정중하고 존중하는 태도. 공손함. 예의바름: *She didn't have the courtesy to apologize.* 그녀는 사과할 정도의 예의도 없었다. **2** a polite action or remark ‖ 정중한 행동이나 발언. 예의: *As a courtesy to your hosts, you should reply quickly to invitations.* 주최측에 대한 예의로 초청에 대해 빨리 참석여부를 답해줘야 한다.

court·house /'kɔrthaʊs/ *n* a building containing courts of law and government offices ‖ 법정이나 정부 사무소가 있는 건물. 법원 청사. 관청

court-mar·tial /'. ,../ *n, plural* **courts-martial** *or* **court-martials 1** a military court that deals with people who break military law ‖ 군법을 어기는 사람을 다루는 군사 법정. 군법 회의 **2** an occasion when someone is judged by a military court ‖ 군사 법정에서 심판받는 경우. 군법 회의 회부. 군사 법정에 의한 재판: *He'll face a court-martial on drug charges.* 그는 마약 혐의로 군법 회의에 회부될 것이다. – **court-martial** *v* [T]

court·room /'kɔrtrum/ *n* the room where a CASE is judged by a court of law ‖ 소송 사건을 재판하는 법원의 실내. 재판정. 법정

court·ship /'kɔrtʃɪp/ *n* [C, U] OLD-FASHIONED the time when a man and a woman have a romantic relationship before getting married ‖ 남자와 여자가 결혼하기 전에 애정 관계를 갖는 시기. 구혼[구애](기간)

court·yard /'kɔrtyɑrd/ *n* an open space that is surrounded by walls or buildings ‖ 담장이나 건물에 의해 둘러싸인 열린 공간. 뜰. 안마당

cous·in /'kʌzən/ *n* the child of your AUNT or UNCLE ‖ 숙모[고모, 이모]나 숙부[고모부, 이모부]의 자녀. 사촌 —see picture at FAMILY

cove /koʊv/ *n* a small area on the coast that is partly surrounded by land and is protected from the wind ‖ 육지가 부분적으로 에워싸서 바람을 막는 해안의 작은 구역. 작은 만(灣). 후미

cov·e·nant /'kʌvənənt/ *n* a formal agreement between two or more people or groups ‖ 둘 이상의 사람이나 단체간의 공식적인 협정. 계약. 서약

cov·er¹ /'kʌvɚ/ *v* [T]

1 ▶PUT STH OVER STH◀ 어떤 것 위에 무엇을 씌우다◀ also **cover up** to put something over the top of something else in order to hide or protect it ‖ 숨기거나 보호하기 위해 어떤 것을 다른 것 위에 올려 놓다. …을 덮다[싸다, 가리다]: *Cover the pan and simmer the beans for two hours.* 냄비 뚜껑을 덮고 2시간 동안 콩을 삶으시오.

2 ▶BE OVER STH◀ 어떤 것 위에 있다◀ to be on top of something or spread over something ‖ 사물 위에 놓여 있거나 펼쳐져 있다. …위에 펴다[퍼지다]. …의 표면에 놓(이)다: *His bedroom walls are covered with posters.* 그의 침실 벽은 포스터로 도배되어 있다.

3 ▶INCLUDE◀ 포함하다◀ to include or deal with something ‖ 어떤 것을 포함하거나 다루다. 망라하다. 범위가 …에 이르다. …으로 구성되다: *The class covers twentieth century American poetry.* 그 수업은 20세기 미국시를 다룬다.

4 ▶NEWS◀ 뉴스◀ to report the details of an event for a newspaper or a television or radio program ‖ 신문[TV, 라디오 프로그램]을 위해 사건의 세부 내용을 보도하다. 취재하여 보도[방송]하다: *Scully will be covering the World Series this year.* 스컬리가 올해 월드 시리즈 경기를 취재 보도할 것이다.

5 ▶PAY FOR STH◀ 어떤 것의 값을 지불하다◀ to be enough money to pay for something ‖ 어떤 것의 값을 지불할 충분한 돈이 있다. 돈이 …하기에 충분하다: *That should be enough to cover the tip too.* 그 정도면 팁을 지불하기에도 충분하다.

6 ▶INSURANCE◀ 보험◀ to protect someone from loss, especially through insurance ‖ 특히 보험을 통해 사람의 손실을 보호하다. 손실을 막아 주다[메우다]. 보험으로 보상하다: *a policy that covers medical expenses* 의료비를 보상해 주는 보험 증서

7 ▶DISTANCE◀ 거리◀ to travel a particular distance ‖ 특정 거리를 이동하다. 나아가다. 답파하다: *We should cover another 50 miles before lunch.* 우리는 점심 전에 50마일을 더 가야 한다.

8 a) cover for sb to do the work that someone else usually does, but that s/he cannot do because s/he is sick or not present ‖ 보통은 다른 사람이 하는 일이지만 그 사람이 아프거나 자리에 없어서 할 수 없게 된 일을 하다. 대신[대리]하다. 대행하다: *Will you cover for Ruth again today?* 오늘도 또 루스 대신에 일할 겁니까? **b)** to prevent someone from getting into trouble by lying about where s/he is ‖ 다른 사람의 소재에 대해 거짓말을 해서 그 사람이 곤란해지는 것을 막다. 소재를 숨겨 주다[덮어 주다]: *Can you cover for me? Just say I had an appointment.* 내 소재 좀 둘러대 줄래? 그저 약속이 있었다고 말해줘.

9 ▶GUN◀ 총◀ to aim a gun at a person or a place in order to protect someone from being attacked or to prevent someone from escaping ‖ 누군가가 공격당하는 것을 막기 위해 또는 도주를 막기 위해 사람이나 장소에 총을 겨냥하다. 사정 안에 두다[지키다]. 엄호 사격하다: *We'll cover you while you run for it.* 네가 그쪽으로 뛰는 동안 우리가 엄호할 것이다. / *The police covered the back entrance.* 경찰이 뒷문을 지키고 있었다.

10 cover (all) the bases INFORMAL to make sure that you can deal with any situation or problem ‖ 어떤 상황이나 문제든지 다룰 수 있게 확실히 하다. 모든 준비를 다하다. 만전을 기해 준비하다

cover sth ↔ **up** *phr v* [T] to prevent mistakes or unpleasant facts from being known ‖ 잘못이나 불쾌한 사실이 알려지는 것을 막다. …을 알아채지 못하게 하다 [숨기다]. 은폐하다: *A lot of people tried to cover up the Watergate affair.* 많은 사람들이 워터게이트 사건을 은폐하려 했었다.

cover up for sb *phr v* [T] to protect someone by hiding unpleasant facts about him/her ‖ 누군가에 대한 불쾌한 사실들을 숨겨서 그 사람을 보호하다. 은폐해[감추어] 주다: *The mayor's friends tried to cover up for him.* 시장의 친구들은 그의 잘못을 감추어 주려 했다.

cover² *n* **1** something that protects something else by covering it ‖ 다른 것을 덮어서 보호해 주는 것. 덮개. 뚜껑. 가리개: *a plastic cover over the bowl* 대접 위의 플라스틱 뚜껑 **2** the outside of a book, magazine etc. ‖ 책·잡지 등의 바깥면. 커버. 표지: *Rolling Stone magazine always has interesting covers.* 롤링 스톤지의 표지는 항상 흥미롭다. **3** [U] shelter or protection from bad weather or attack ‖ 나쁜 날씨나 공격으로부터의 피난처나 보호물. 은폐[엄폐, 엄호](물). 은신처: *The soldiers ran for cover when the shooting started.* 병사들은 총격이 시작되자 엄폐물을 찾아 뛰었다. / *We took cover from the rain under a tree.* 우리는 나무 아래서 비를 피했다. **4** something that hides something or keeps it secret ‖ 어떤 것을 숨겨 주거나 비밀로 지켜 주는 것. 은폐[은닉]하는 것. 숨기기 위한

핑계[구실, 위장](물): *The company is just a cover for the Mafia.* 회사는 단지 마피아 조직을 위한 위장물일 뿐이다. **5** [U] insurance against loss, injury, or damage ∥ 손실[상해, 손해]에 대한 보험: *We'll need cover for theft.* 우리는 도난에 대비한 보험이 필요할 것이다. **6 under cover** pretending to be someone else in order to do something without being noticed ∥ 눈에 띄지 않고 어떤 일을 하기 위해 다른 사람인 체하는. 위장[변장]한. 숨어서[몰래] 하는: *Policemen working under cover arrested several drug dealers.* 위장 근무 경찰이 여러 명의 마약 거래상을 체포했다. **7 cover your tracks** to be careful not to leave any signs that could let people know where you have been or what you have done ∥ 자신이 어디에 있었는지 또는 무슨 일을 했는지 사람들이 알 수 없게 어떤 흔적도 남기지 않도록 주의하다. 자취[발자국]를 지우다. 종적을 감추다 —see also COVERS

cov·er·age /ˈkʌvrɪdʒ/ *n* [U] **1** the amount of time and space given on television or by a newspaper to report something ∥ 어떤 일을 보도하기 위해 텔레비전이나 신문에 주어진 시간·공간의 크기. 보도 시간[범위]: *excellent news coverage of the elections* 선거에 관한 훌륭한 뉴스 보도 **2** things that are included in insurance ∥ 보험에 포함돼 있는 것들. 보험 담보(사항). 보상[적용] 범위: *Make sure your policy will give you accident coverage.* 사고 보상이 되는지 당신 보험 약관을 확인하세요.

cov·er·alls /ˈkʌvɚˌɔlz/ *n* [plural] a piece of clothing that covers your upper and lower body, usually worn over your clothes to keep them clean while you work ∥ 보통 일할 때 옷을 깨끗하게 유지하기 위해 그 위에 입는 상하체를 덮는 옷. 상하가 붙은 작업복. 커버올 —see picture at OVERALLS

cover charge /ˈ.. ˌ./ *n* money that you have to pay in a restaurant in addition to the cost of food and drinks ∥ 음식점에서 음식과 음료 대금에 추가로 지불해야 하는 돈. 봉사료

cov·er·ing /ˈkʌvrɪŋ, -ərɪŋ/ *n* something that covers or hides something else ∥ 다른 것을 덮거나 감춰 주는 것. 뚜껑. 덮개. 씌우개. 가리개. 외피. 피복: *a light covering of snow* 살짝 쌓인 눈

cover let·ter /ˈ.. ˌ./ *n* a letter that you send with another letter or a package to explain what it is or give more information ∥ 내용물이 무엇인지 설명하

거나 더 자세한 정보를 주기 위해 편지나 소포와 함께 보내는 글. 첨부서[설명서]: *Always include a typed cover letter with your résumé.* 항상 이력서에 타자로 친 첨부서를 포함시켜라.

cov·ers /ˈkʌvɚz/ *n* [plural] BLANKETs, SHEETs (=large pieces of cloth) etc. that cover you in bed ∥ 침대에서 덮는 담요·시트 등. 이불. 침구

co·vert /ˈkoʊvɚt, ˈkʌ-, koʊˈvɚt/ *adj* secret or hidden ∥ 비밀이거나 감춰진. 암암리의. 비공개의. 드러나지 않은: *the covert actions of spies* 간첩들의 비밀 공작들 **– covertly** *adv*

cover-up /ˈ.. ˌ./ *n* an attempt to prevent people knowing about something shameful or illegal ∥ 수치스럽거나 불법적인 일에 대해 다른 사람들이 알지 못하게 막는 시도. 은폐. 은닉. 무마: *CIA officials denied there had been a cover-up.* CIA 관리들은 은폐 공작이 있었다는 것을 부인했다.

cov·et /ˈkʌvɪt/ *v* [T] LITERARY to have a strong desire to possess something that someone else has ∥ 다른 사람이 가진 사물을 소유하려는 강한 욕망을 갖다. 몹시 탐내다[갈망하다]. …을 욕심내다 **– covetous** *adj*

cow¹ /kaʊ/ *n* **1** an adult female farm animal that is kept for its milk and meat ∥ 우유와 고기를 얻기 위해 사육되는 가축의 다 자란 암컷. 암소. 젖소 —compare BULL, STEER² **2 have a cow** SPOKEN to be very angry or surprised about something ∥ 어떤 것에 대해 매우 화가 나거나 놀라다. 갑자기 흥분[동요]하다: *It was just an accident. Don't have a cow!* 그것은 그저 사고였어. 너무 흥분하지 마! **3** the female of some large land and sea animals, such as the ELEPHANT or the WHALE ∥ 코끼리·고래 등의 바다나 육지에서 사는 몸집이 큰 동물의 암컷

cow² *v* [T] to make someone afraid or control him/her by using violence or threats ∥ 폭력을 쓰거나 협박을 하여 다른 사람을 두려워하게 하거나 통제하다. 폭력·위협으로 억누르다[으르다]. 겁을 주어 …하게 하다. …하도록 강요하다: *The children were cowed into obedience.* 아이들은 복종하도록 위협을 받았다.

cow·ard /ˈkaʊɚd/ *n* DISAPPROVING someone who is not brave in dangerous situations ∥ 위험한 상황에서 용감하지 않은 사람. 겁쟁이. 비겁자 **– cowardly** *adj*

cow·ard·ice /ˈkaʊɚdɪs/ *n* [U] a lack of courage ∥ 용기의 부족. 비겁. 소심

cow·boy /ˈkaʊbɔɪ/ *n* a man whose job

is to take care of cattle ‖ 소를 돌보는 남자 직업인. 목동. 카우보이

cow·er /ˈkauɚ/ v [I] to bend low and move back because you are afraid ‖ 겁이 나서 낮게 구부리거나 뒤로 물러나다. 움츠리다. 웅크리다. 위축하다: *The hostages were cowering in a corner.* 인질들은 구석에 웅크리고 있었다.

cow·girl /ˈkaugɚl/ n a woman whose job is to take care of cattle ‖ 소를 돌보는 여자 직업인.

co-work·er /ˈkou,wɚkɚ/ n someone who works with you ‖ 함께 일하는 사람. 동료. 협력자

coy /kɔɪ/ adj a person or action that is coy seems quiet or shy but is really trying to attract attention ‖ 사람 또는 행동이 조용하고 수줍어하는 것처럼 보이지만 실제로는 관심을 끌려고 하는. 수줍은 체하는. 얌전 빼는: *a coy smile* 수줍은 듯한 미소 **- coyly** adv

coy·ote /kaɪˈouti, ˈkaɪ-out/ n a wild animal like a dog that lives in western North America and Mexico ‖ 북미 서부와 멕시코에 사는 개과의 야생 동물. 코요테

co·zy /ˈkouzi/ adj small, comfortable, and warm ‖ 작고 편안하며 따뜻한. 아늑한. 안락한: *a cozy cabin in the woods* 숲속의 아늑한 오두막집 **- cozily** adv **- coziness** n [U]

CPA n Certified Public Accountant; an ACCOUNTANT who has passed all of his/her examinations ‖ Certified Public Accountant(공인 회계사)의 약어; 모든 시험에 합격한 회계사

CPR n cardiopulmonary resuscitation; a set of actions that you do to help someone who has stopped breathing or whose heart has stopped beating ‖ cardiopulmonary resuscitation(심폐 소생술)의 약어; 호흡이 끊어졌거나 심장 박동이 중지된 사람을 돕기 위해 하는 일련의 조치들.

CPU n Central Processing Unit; the part of a computer that controls and organizes what the computer does ‖ Central Processing Unit(중앙 처리 장치)의 약어; 컴퓨터가 하는 일을 제어하고 조직화하는 부분.

crab /kræb/ n [C, U] a sea animal with a round flat shell and its two large CLAWs on front legs, or the meat from this animal ‖ 둥글고 넓적한 껍데기와 앞다리에 2개의 큰 집게를 가진 바다 동물, 또는 이 동물의 살. 게(살)

crab·by /ˈkræbi/ adj easily annoyed or upset ‖ 쉽게 짜증내거나 화를 내는. 심술궂은. 성미가 까다로운[고약한]: *Mom*

gets really crabby right before dinner. 엄마는 저녁 식사 직전에 신경이 매우 날카로워 진다.

crack¹ /kræk/ v

1 ▶BREAK 깨지다◀ [I, T] to break something so that lines appear on its surface, or to break in this way ‖ 사물의 표면에 금이 생기도록 어떤 것을 깨다, 또는 이런 식으로 깨어지다. 갈라지(게 하)다. 조개(지)다: *Two of my best plates cracked in the dishwasher.* 가장 좋은 접시 2개가 식기 세척기 안에서 깨졌다.

2 ▶NOISE OF BREAKING 파열음◀ [I, T] to make a loud sudden noise that sounds like something breaking, or to make something do this ‖ 물건이 부서지는 것 같은 크고 갑작스러운 소리를 내다, 또는 어떤 것을 그런 소리가 나게 하다. 파열음을 내다[나게 하다]. 부러지는 소리를 내다[나게 하다]: *A stick cracked under his foot.* 막대가 그의 발 밑에서 딱 소리를 내며 부러졌다.

3 ▶HIT STH 어떤 것을 세게 때리다◀ [I, T] to accidentally hit something very hard ‖ 사고로 어떤 것을 매우 세게 치다. 갑자기[쾅소리가 나게] 부딪치다. (딱 소리나게)일격을 가하다: *Carly tripped and cracked her head on the sidewalk.* 칼리는 발이 걸려서 보도에 머리를 쾅 찧었다.

4 ▶LOSE CONTROL 통제력을 잃다◀ [I] to lose control of your emotions or tell a secret because someone or something is making you feel extremely anxious ‖ 어떤 사람이나 사물 때문에 매우 불안해져 자신의 감정을 제어하지 못하거나 비밀을 누설하다. 자제력을 상실하다. 녹초가 되어[기운이 꺾여] 무너지다: *a spy who never cracked under questioning* 심문에 결코 굴복하지 않는 스파이

5 ▶EGG/NUT 알/견과◀ [T] to break the shell of an egg, nut etc. in order to get the food inside it ‖ 알·견과 등의 속에 들어 있는 먹을 것을 꺼내기 위해 껍데기를 깨뜨리다.

6 ▶VOICE 음성◀ [I] if your voice cracks, it suddenly get softer or louder because you feel a strong emotion ‖ 강렬한 감정을 느껴서 음성이 갑자기 낮아지거나 커지다. 목소리가 쉬다[갈라지다]

7 ▶SOLVE 풀다◀ [T] to solve a problem or a CODE ‖ 문제나 암호를 풀다. 해독하다. 해석[해결]하다

8 crack a joke INFORMAL to tell a joke ‖ 농담을 말하다. 우스개 소리를 하다: *John keeps cracking jokes about my hair.* 존은 내 머리 스타일에 대해 계속 농담을 해댄다.

9 not be all sth is cracked up to be

INFORMAL not as good as people say it is ‖ 사람들이 말하는 만큼 좋지는 않은. 소문보다 못한: *Life as a model isn't all it's cracked up to be.* 모델로서의 삶은 겉보기만큼 좋지는 않다.

crack down *phr v* [I] to become more strict when dealing with someone's bad behavior or an illegal activity ‖ 사람들의 악행이나 불법 행위를 다룰 때 더 엄격해지다. 단속을 강화하다. 일제 단속하다: *Police are cracking down on drunk drivers.* 경찰은 음주 운전자들에 대한 단속을 강화하고 있다. – **crackdown** *n*

crack up *phr v* INFORMAL **1** [I, T] to laugh a lot at something, or to make someone laugh a lot ‖ 어떤 것 때문에 크게 웃거나 남을 크게 웃게 만들다: *Sue just cracks me up!* 수가 나를 배꼽잡고 웃게 만드네! **2** [I] to become unable to think clearly or behave normally because you are tired, worried, too busy etc. ‖ 피곤하고 걱정되며 너무 바빠서 올바로 생각하거나 정상적으로 행동할 수 없게 되다. 넋이 나가다[빠지다]. 어쩔 줄 모르다

crack² *n* **1** a very narrow space between two things ‖ 2개의 사물 사이의 매우 좁은 틈. 갈라진 골. 깨어진 틈: *Can you open the window a crack?* 창문을 조금 열어 주시겠어요? **2** a thin line on the surface of something that is damaged ‖ 파손된 사물 표면의 가는 금. 균열: *These cracks on the wall are from last year's earthquake.* 벽에 난 이 금들은 작년 지진 때 생긴 것이다. **3** INFORMAL a cruel joke or remark ‖ 심한 농담이나 발언. 비꼬는 말. 조롱: *Stop making cracks about my sister!* 내 누이를 놀리지 마! **4 a crack at** INFORMAL an attempt to do or use something ‖ 어떤 것을 하거나 이용하려는 시도. 기회. 찬스: *Okay, Dave, let's take/have a crack at fixing this bike.* 좋아, 데이브, 이 자전거를 고쳐 보자. **5** a sudden loud noise that sounds like a stick breaking ‖ 막대가 부러지는 것 같은 갑작스런 큰 소리. 딱[탁] 하는 소리: *the cracks of the fireworks* 폭죽이 탁탁 터지는 소리. **6** a pure form of the drug COCAINE that some people take illegally for pleasure ‖ 일부 사람들이 쾌락을 위해 불법적으로 복용하는 코카인의 순수 결정체. **7 the crack of dawn** the very early time in the morning when the sun appears ‖ 해가 뜨는 아침의 매우 이른 시간. 동틀 무렵. 첫새벽

crack³ *adj* having a lot of skill ‖ 상당한 기술이 있는. 솜씨가 좋은[탁월한]. 능수한: *a crack shot* (=someone who is very

good at shooting) 기막힌 사격 선수

crack·down /'. ./ *n* [C usually singular] an effort to stop bad or illegal behavior by being strict and determined ‖ 나쁘거나 불법적인 행위를 엄격하고 단호하게 막는 노력. 단속 강화. 일제 단속: *a national crackdown on illegal immigrants* 불법 이민자들에 대한 전국적인 일제 단속

cracked /krækt/ *adj* something that is cracked has thin lines on its surface because it is damaged ‖ 사물이 파손되어 표면에 가는 금들이 있는. 금이 간. 갈라진. 균열이 생긴. 깨진. 부서진 —see picture at BROKEN¹

crack·er /'krækə/ *n* **1** a type of hard dry bread that is thin and flat ‖ 얇고 납작한, 딱딱하고 마른 빵의 일종. 크래커. 비스킷: *cheese and crackers* 치즈와 크래커 **2** someone who illegally breaks into a computer system in order to steal information or stop the system from working properly ‖ 정보를 훔치거나 시스템의 정상 작동을 막기 위해 불법적으로 컴퓨터 시스템에 침투하는 사람. 크래커. 악덕 해커

crack·le /'krækəl/ *v* [I] to make a lot of short noises that sound like something burning in a fire ‖ 사물이 불 속에서 타는 소리 같은 짧은 소음을 많이 내다. 탁탁[바지직] 소리가 나다: *a log fire crackling in the fireplace* 벽난로 속에서 탁탁 소리내며 타는 장작 불꽃 / *a radio program crackling with static* 전파 방해로 찌지직 소리를 내는 라디오 프로그램 – **crackle** *n*

crack·pot /'krækpɑt/ *adj* slightly crazy or strange ‖ 약간 미치거나 이상한. 엉뚱한. 기괴한: *a crackpot idea* 엉뚱한 생각 – **crackpot** *n*

cra·dle¹ /'kreɪdl/ *n* **1** a small bed for a baby, that can swing gently from side to side ‖ 좌우로 부드럽게 흔들 수 있는 유아용 작은 침대. 요람 **2 the cradle of** the place where something important began ‖ 중요한 일이 시작됐던 장소. 발상[발생]지. 기원. 근원: *Some say Athens was the cradle of democracy.* 어떤 사람들은 아테네가 민주주의의 발상지였다고 말한다.

cradle² *v* [T] to gently hold someone or something ‖ 사람이나 사물을 부드럽게 잡다. 양손으로 안 듯이 잡다[받치다]: *Tony cradled his baby daughter in his arms.* 토니는 자기 딸아이를 조심스럽게 두팔에 안았다.

craft /kræft/ *n* **1** a job or activity that you need to have a lot of skill to do, especially one in which you make things ‖ 특히 물건을 만들 때 숙련된 솜씨가 필요한 일이나 행위. 공예. 수공예: *a craft such as knitting* 뜨개질 등의 공예 **2** *plural* **craft** a boat, ship, or plane ‖ 보트[선박, 비행기]

crafts·man /'kræftsmən/ *n* someone who has a lot of skill in a particular craft ‖ 특정 공예에 숙련된 기술을 가진 사람. 숙련공. 장인: *furniture made by the finest craftsmen* 최고의 장인이 만든 가구 – **craftsmanship** *n* [U]

craft·y /'kræfti/ *adj* good at deceiving people in order to get what you want ‖ 원하는 것을 얻기 위해 사람을 속이는 데 뛰어난. 교활한. 약삭빠른. 간교한 – **craftily** *adv*

crag·gy /'krægi/ *adj* a craggy mountain or cliff is very steep and is covered with large sharp rocks ‖ 산이나 절벽이 매우 가파르며 크고 날카로운 바위들로 덮인. 깎아지른 듯한. 바위가 많은. 바위가 험하게 돌출한

cram /kræm/ *v* **-mmed, -mming 1** [T] to force something into a small space ‖ 사물을 좁은 공간으로 억지로 집어 넣다. 밀어 넣다. 쑤셔 넣다: *You should see how many clothes we crammed into that suitcase!* 우리가 얼마나 많은 옷을 그 가방 속에 쑤셔 담았는지 네가 봐야 하는데! **2** [T] to fill an area with too many people ‖ 어떤 곳이 사람들로 넘치다. …을 사람들이 가득 채우다[메우다]. (움직이지 못할 정도로) 꽉 차다: *The mall was totally crammed with Christmas shoppers.* 상가는 크리스마스 쇼핑객들로 미어터졌다. **3** [I] to prepare yourself for a test by studying a lot of information very quickly ‖ 매우 짧은 시간에 많은 내용을 공부하여 시험에 대비하다. 벼락치기 공부를 하다: *Julia stayed up all night cramming for her math final.* 줄리아는 벼락치기로 수학 기말 시험 공부를 하느라 밤을 꼬박 새웠다. – **crammed** *adj*

cramp /kræmp/ *n* a severe pain that you get when a muscle becomes very tight ‖ 근육이 경직될 때 생기는 심한 통증. 경련. 쥐: *I have a cramp in my wrist from writing all day.* 하루 종일 글을 썼더니 손목에 쥐가 난다. – **cramping** *n* [U]

cramped /kræmpt/ *adj* uncomfortable because there is not enough space ‖ 공간이 충분하지 않아 불편한. 비좁고 갑갑한: *I can never sleep on planes because I always feel so cramped.* 나는 비행기안에서는 늘 비좁고 답답해서 전혀 잠을 잘 수 없다.

cramps /kræmps/ *n* [plural] pain that women get during MENSTRUATION ‖ 여성이 생리 기간에 겪는 통증. 생리통

cran·ber·ry /'kræn,bɛri/ *n* a small sour red BERRY ‖ 작고 새콤한 붉은 딸기류의 과실. 덩굴월귤. 크랜베리: *cranberry sauce* 크랜베리 소스

crane[1] /kreɪn/ *n* **1** a large machine with a thick strong wire that builders use to lift heavy things ‖ 건축업자가 무거운 물건을 들어올리는 데 쓰는 굵고 튼튼한 쇠줄이 달린 큰 기계. 기중기 **2** a tall water bird with very long legs ‖ 매우 긴 다리를 가진 키가 큰 물새. 두루미. 학

crane[2] *v* [I, T] to look around or over something by stretching or leaning ‖ 몸을 늘이거나 뻗어서 사물을 둘러보거나 넘겨보다. 목을 길게 빼다: *All the kids craned their necks to see who Mrs. Miller was talking to.* 밀러 여사와 말하고 있는 사람이 누구인지를 보려고 아이들은 모두 목을 길게 뺐다.

cra·ni·um /'kreɪniəm/ *n* TECHNICAL the bones in an animal's or person's head that cover the brain ‖ 동물이나 사람의 뇌를 싸고 있는 머리 뼈. 두개골

crank[1] /kræŋk/ *n* **1** **crank call** INFORMAL a telephone call intended as a joke or made in order to frighten, annoy, or upset someone ‖ 장난할 의도로, 또는 사람을 놀라게[귀찮게, 기분 나쁘게] 하려고 거는 전화. 장난 전화 **2** INFORMAL someone who easily becomes angry or annoyed ‖ 쉽게 화를 내거나 짜증을 내는 사람. 변덕쟁이. 까다로운 사람 **3** a handle on a piece of equipment that you turn in order to move something ‖ 무엇을 작동시키기 위해 돌리는 장비에 부착된 손잡이. ㄴ자 꼴의 손잡이

crank[2] *v* INFORMAL

crank sth **out** *phr v* [T] to produce a lot of something very quickly ‖ 무엇을 매우 급하게 많이 생산하다. (별 노력 없이) 기계적으로 만들어 내다: *He cranks out novels at the rate of one a year.* 그는 소설을 1년에 한 권 꼴로 기계적으로 써낸다.

crank sth ↔ **up** *phr v* [T] to make the sound from a radio etc. a lot louder ‖ 라디오 등의 소리를 더 크게 하다: *Hey, Vince, crank up the stereo!* 어이, 빈스, 스테레오 소리 좀 키워!

crank·y /'kræŋki/ *adj* very easily annoyed or made angry, especially because you are tired ‖ 특히 피곤해서 아주 쉽게 짜증을 내거나 화를 내는. 심술궂은: *Steve woke up cranky this morning.* 스티브는 오늘 아침에 짜증을 내며 일어

났다.

crap /kræp/ *n* [U] INFORMAL **1** an impolite word for something that you think is very bad, wrong, or untrue ‖ 아주 나쁘거나 잘못되었거나 사실이 아니라고 생각하는 것을 무례하게 이르는 말. 허풍. 허튼 말. 과장: *That movie was crap.* 그 영화는 순 엉터리였다. **2** an impolite word for things that you do not need or want ‖ 필요하지 않거나 원하지 않는 사물을 경멸하여 이르는 말. 쓰레기. 잡동사니: *What's all this crap doing on my desk?* 내 책상 위의 이 모든 잡동사니들은 도대체 뭐야? – **crappy** *adj*

craps /kræps/ *n* [U] a game played for money in which you throw two DICE ‖ 돈을 걸고 두 개의 주사위를 던져 승부를 가리는 게임. 주사위 도박

crash¹ /kræʃ/ *v* **1** [I, T] to have an accident in which a car, plane etc. hits something and is badly damaged ‖ 차·비행기 등이 물체와 부딪쳐 심하게 파손되는 사고가 나다. 충돌하다. 추락하다: *We crashed straight into the car ahead of us.* 우리는 앞에 있는 차를 곧장 들이받았다. **2** [I, T] if a computer crashes or you crash it, it suddenly stops working ‖ 컴퓨터가 갑자기 작동을 멈추거나 컴퓨터를 갑자기 작동을 멈추게 하다 **3** [I] SPOKEN **a)** also **crash out** to go to sleep very quickly because you are very tired ‖ 매우 피곤해서 아주 빨리 잠자리에 들다: *I crashed out on the sofa watching TV.* 나는 소파에서 TV를 보다가 그만 잠이 들고 말았다. **b)** to stay at someone's house for the night ‖ 하룻밤 남의 집에 머물다: *You can crash at our place if you can't get a ride home.* 집에 돌아갈 차가 없으면 우리 집에서 자도 돼. **4** [I, T] to make a sudden loud noise, especially by hitting or breaking something ‖ 특히 무엇을 치거나 부수어 갑자기 큰 소리를 내다. …이 꽝하고 박살나다. …을 (와르르) 무너뜨리다: *A baseball crashed into/through our living room window.* 야구공이 우리 집 거실 유리창을 요란하게 깨뜨리고 들어왔다. **5** [I] if the STOCK MARKET crashes, STOCKs suddenly become worth less money than before ‖ 주가가 이전보다 갑자기 떨어지다. 폭락하다 **6** [T] if you crash a party or event, you go to it although you have not been invited ‖ 파티나 행사에 초청되지 않았는데도 가다. 밀고(몰래) 들어가다

crash² *n* **1** a very bad accident involving cars, planes etc. that have hit something ‖ 자동차·비행기 등이 어떤 것에 부딪쳐 일어난 아주 큰 사고. 충돌: *Both the passenger and the driver were killed in the crash.* 그 충돌 사고로 승객과 운전자가 모두 죽었다. **2** an occasion when a computer suddenly stops working ‖ 컴퓨터가 갑자기 작동하지 않는 경우. 컴퓨터 프로그램상의 고장 **3** a sudden loud noise that sounds like something breaking or hitting something else ‖ 물체가 깨지거나 다른 물체에 부딪치는 소리 같은 갑작스런 큰 소음. 요란한 소리: *a crash of plates falling on the floor* 마루바닥에 접시가 떨어지는 요란한 소리 **4** an occasion when a business or a financial system suddenly fails and STOCKs become worth much less money than before ‖ 사업이나 재무 시스템이 갑자기 무너지고 주식의 가치가 이전보다 크게 떨어지는 상황. 도산. 파멸: *the crash of the New York Stock Exchange* 뉴욕 증권 거래소의 붕괴

crash course /ˌ. ˈ./ *n* a course in which you try to learn a particular subject very quickly ‖ 특정 과목을 매우 빠른 시일에 배우는 과정. 집중 강좌. 특강

crash di·et /ˌ. ˈ../ *n* an attempt to make yourself thinner quickly by strictly limiting how much you eat ‖ 식사량을 엄격히 제한하여 빨리 날씬해지려는 시도. 과격한 다이어트

crash hel·met /ˈ. ˌ../ *n* a very strong hat that covers and protects someone's whole head, worn by people who drive race cars, MOTORCYCLEs, etc. ‖ 경주용 자동차나·모터 사이클 등을 운전하는 사람이 머리를 감싸서 보호하기 위해 쓰는 아주 튼튼한 모자. 사고 방지용 헬멧

crash land·ing /ˌ. ˈ../ *n* **make a crash landing** to try to fly a damaged plane to the ground in a way that will not damage it more ‖ 파손된 비행기를 더 이상 파손되지 않도록 착륙시키려고 하다. 불시착시키다. 동체 착륙시키다

crass /kræs/ *adj* offensive or rude ‖ 모욕적인, 무례한: *Dick made a crass remark about her weight.* 딕은 그녀의 몸무게에 대한 모욕적인 말을 했다.

crate /kreɪt/ *n* a large wooden or plastic box used for sending things a long distance ‖ 먼곳으로 물건을 발송하는 데 쓰는 큰 나무 또는 플라스틱 상자. (수송·포장용의) 나무 상자[틀]: *a crate of wine* 와인 한 상자

cra·ter /ˈkreɪtər/ *n* **1** a round hole in the ground made by something that has fallen on it or exploded on it ‖ 물체가 땅에 떨어지거나 폭발이 일어나서 생긴 지상의 둥근 구멍. 폭탄 등의 파열로 땅에 생

긴 구덩이. 폭탄 자국: *a bomb crater* 폭 탄으로 생긴 구멍 / *craters on the moon's surface* 달 표면의 분화구 **2** the round open top of a VOLCANO ‖ 화산 꼭대기의 둥글게 파인 곳. 분화구

crave /kreɪv/ v [T] to have a very strong desire for something ‖ 어떤 것에 대해 매우 강렬한 욕망을 가지다. …을 열망하다: *Most little kids crave attention.* 대부분의 어린아이들은 자기에게 관심을 가져 주기를 몹시 바란다.

crav·ing /ˈkreɪvɪŋ/ n a very strong desire for something ‖ 어떤 것에 대한 매우 강렬한 바람. 갈망: *I have a major craving for chocolate chip cookies.* 나는 초콜릿 칩 과자를 굉장히 먹고 싶다.

craw·dad /ˈkrɔdæd/, **craw·fish** /ˈkrɔˌfɪʃ/ n ⇨ CRAYFISH

crawl¹ /krɔl/ v [I] **1** to move on your hands and knees or with your body close to the ground ‖ 손·무릎으로 또는 땅바닥에 가까이 몸을 숙이고 움직이다. 기어가다: *When did your baby start crawling?* 네 아기는 언제부터 기어다니기 시작했니? / *There's a bee crawling on your arm!* 네 팔에 벌이 기어가고 있어! **2** to move very slowly ‖ 매우 천천히 움직이다. 서행하다: *We got stuck behind a truck crawling along at 25 mph.* 우리 차는 시속 25마일로 서행하는 트럭 뒤에서 꼼짝하지 못하고 따라갔다. **3 be crawling with** to be completely covered with insects, people etc. ‖ 곤충·사람 등으로 온통 뒤덮이다. 우글[득실]거리다: *Oh gross! Nibby's dog dish is crawling with ants!* 윽 징그러워! 니비의 개밥 그릇에 개미들이 우글거리고 있어!

crawl² n **1** a very slow speed ‖ 매우 느린 속도. 서행: *Traffic has slowed to a crawl.* 차량들이 기어가듯이 서행했다. **2** a fast way of swimming in which you lie on your stomach and move one arm and then the other over your head ‖ 배를 깔고 엎드려서 머리 위로 한 팔을 젓고 그 다음 다른 팔을 저어 빠르게 수영하는 방식. 크롤(수영법)

crawl

cray·fish /ˈkreɪˌfɪʃ/ n [C, U] a small animal that is similar to a LOBSTER and lives in rivers and streams, or the meat from this animal ‖ 강이나 냇물에 사는, 왕새우와 비슷한 작은 동물, 또는 이 동물의 살. 가재. 가재살

cray·on /ˈkreɪɑn, -ən/ n a stick of colored WAX that children use to draw pictures ‖ 어린이들이 그림을 그리기 위해 쓰는 색깔 있는 왁스 막대. 크레용

craze /kreɪz/ n a fashion, game, type of music etc. that becomes very popular for a short amount of time ‖ 단기간에 매우 널리 알려진 유행·게임·음악 형태 등. (일시적인) 열광적 대유행. 대인기: *the latest teenage craze* 십대들 사이에서의 최신의 대유행

crazed /kreɪzd/ adj wild, strange, or crazy ‖ 사나운[이상한, 미친]. 발광한. 정신 이상의: *a crazed evil laugh* 광기어린 사악한 웃음 소리

cra·zy /ˈkreɪzi/ adj INFORMAL **1** very strange or not very sensible ‖ 아주 이상하거나 너무 지각이 없는. 미친(듯한). 머리가 돈: *You must be crazy to drive in that snow!* 저 눈 속에서 차를 몰다니 너 정말 미쳤구나! / *Whose crazy idea was it to go hiking in November?* 11월에 하이킹을 간다는 미친 생각을 누가 했느냐? **2 be crazy about sb/sth** to like someone or something very much ‖ 사람이나 사물을 매우 좋아하다. 열중하다. 홀딱 빠지다: *Lee and John are crazy about skiing.* 리와 존은 스키타는 것에 홀딱 빠져 있다. **3** angry or annoyed ‖ 화내는, 짜증내는: *Shut up! You're driving me crazy!* 닥쳐! 정말 짜증나게 하네! / *Dad's going to go crazy* (=be very angry) *when he hears that I flunked math.* 아빠는 내가 수학에 낙제했다는 말을 들으면 무섭게 화내실 거다. **4 like crazy** very much or very quickly ‖ 매우 많이, 매우 빨리. 몹시. 맹렬히. 무서운 기세로: *These mosquito bites on my leg are itching like crazy.* 내 다리의 이 부위들이 모기에 물려 가려워 미치겠다. / *We ran like crazy to the bus stop.* 우리는 버스 정류장까지 미친듯이 달렸다. **5** mentally ill ‖ 정신적으로 병든: *I feel so alone, sometimes I wonder if I'm going crazy.* 나는 너무 외로워져서 때때로 내가 미치는 것이 아닌가 하는 의구심이 든다. **– crazily** adv **– craziness** n [U]

creak /krik/ v [I] if something such as a door, wooden floor, or old bed creaks, it makes a long high noise when you push it, step on it, or sit on it ‖ 문을 열거나, 마룻바닥을 디디거나, 낡은 침대에 앉을 때 길고 날카로운 소음이 나다. 삐걱거리다. 끽끽 소리나다 **– creak** n **– creaky** adj

cream¹ /krim/ n **1** [U] a thick yellow-white liquid that can be separated from milk ‖ 우유에서 분리되는 걸쭉한 황백색의 액체. 유지: *Do you take cream and* *sugar in your coffee?* 너는 커피에 크림과 설탕을 타니? **2** [U] a pale yellow-white color ‖ 엷은 황백색. 크림색 **3** [C, U] a food containing cream or something similar to it ‖ 크림이나 크림 비슷한 것이 든 음식. 크림을 넣은 요리: *banana cream pie* 바나나 크림 파이 / *cream of mushroom soup* 크림을 넣은 버섯 수프 **4** [C, U] a thick smooth substance that you put on your skin to make it feel soft, treat a medical condition etc. ‖ 피부를 부드럽게 하거나 피부병을 치료하기 위해 바르는 걸쭉하고 부드러운 물질. 화장용·약용 크림: *The doctor recommended a cream to put on my sunburn.* 의사는 나의 화상에 바를 크림을 추천해 주었다. **5 the cream of the crop** the best of a particular group ‖ 특정 집단 속의 최고의 것이나 사람. 가장 정선된 것. 가장 좋은 것: *"We're unable to get the cream of the crop,"* admitted the athletic director. "우리는 최고의 선수를 확보할 수가 없다."고 감독은 시인했다. **– creamy, cream** adj

cream² *v* [T] **1** to mix foods together until they become a thick smooth mixture ‖ 걸쭉하고 부드러운 혼합물이 될 때까지 음식물을 함께 섞다. 휘저어 크림 상태로 하다: *Next, cream the butter and sugar.* 다음에는 버터나 설탕을 섞어 크림 상태로 만들어라. **2 cream sb** INFORMAL to hit someone very hard or easily defeat someone in a game, competition etc. ‖ 남을 매우 세게 때리다, 또는 게임·시합 등에서 남을 쉽게 이기다: *We got creamed 25 runs to 2.* 우리는 25대 2로 쉽게 물러섰다.

cream cheese /ˌ. './ *n* [U] a type of soft white smooth cheese ‖ 하얗고 매끈거리는 연한 치즈의 일종. 크림 치즈

creamer /ˈkrimɚ/ *n* [U] a substance you can use instead of milk or cream in coffee or tea ‖ 커피나 차에 우유나 크림 대신에 사용할 수 있는 물질. 크리머

crease¹ /kris/ *n* **1** a line on a piece of cloth, paper etc. where it has been folded or IRONed ‖ 접거나 다림질해서 옷·종이 등에 생긴 선. 접은 자국. (바지에) 세운 주름: *pants with creases down the front* 아랫단 앞쪽에 주름을 잡은 바지 **2** a fold in someone's skin; WRINKLE ‖ 사람의 피부의 주름; ⇨ wrinkle

crease² *v* [T] to make a line appear on a piece of cloth, paper etc. by folding or crushing it ‖ 옷이나 종이 등을 접거나 눌러서 줄이 생기게 하다. 접은 자국을 내다. 주름지게 하다 **– creased** adj

cre·ate /kriˈeɪt/ *v* [T] **1** to make something exist ‖ 어떤 것을 존재하게 하다. 창조하다. 생성하다: *Scientists believe the universe was created by a big explosion.* 과학자들은 우주가 대폭발로 생성되었다고 믿는다. / *Why do you want to create problems for everyone?* 너는 왜 모든 사람들에게 말썽을 일으키려고 하느냐? **2** to invent something new ‖ 새로운 것을 발명하다. 창작하다: *Janet created a wonderful chocolate dessert for the party.* 자넷은 파티에 쓸 훌륭한 초콜릿 디저트를 만들었다.

cre·a·tion /kriˈeɪʃən/ *n* **1** [U] the act of creating (CREATE) something ‖ 사물을 만들어내는 행위. 창조. 창작: *the creation of 300 new jobs* 300개의 새로운 직업의 창출 **2** [U] the whole universe and all living things ‖ 온 우주와 모든 생물들. 피창조물. 만물 **3** something that has been created ‖ 창조되어진 것. 창작물. 산물. 예술 작품: *this year's fashion creations* 올해에 새롭게 유행하는 것 **4 the Creation** the act by God of making the universe and everything in it, according to the Bible ‖ 성경에서 우주와 우주의 만물을 창조한 하나님의 행위. 천지 창조

cre·a·tive /kriˈeɪtɪv/ *adj* **1** producing or using new and effective ideas ‖ 새롭고 효과적인 아이디어를 안출하거나 사용하는. 창조적인. 독창적인: *a creative solution to our problems* 우리의 문제에 대한 독창적인 해결책 **2** good at using your imagination and skills ‖ 상상력과 기술을 잘 사용하는. 창조[창작, 독창]력이 있는: *a creative young author* 창의성이 있는 젊은 작가 **– creatively** adv

cre·a·tiv·i·ty /ˌkrieɪˈtɪvɪti/ *n* [U] the ability to use your imagination to produce or use new ideas, make things etc. ‖ 새로운 아이디어를 안출하거나 사용하기 위해, 또는 사물을 만들기 위해 상상력을 사용하는 능력. 창조성[력, 작용]. 독창력

cre·a·tor /kriˈeɪtɚ/ *n* **1** someone who CREATEs something ‖ 무엇을 창조하는 사람. 창조[창작]자: *Walt Disney, the creator of Mickey Mouse* 미키 마우스를 만들어낸 월트디즈니사 **2 the Creator** God ‖ 조물주. 하나님

crea·ture /ˈkritʃɚ/ *n* **1** any living thing such as an animal, fish, or insect, except plants ‖ 식물을 제외한 동물·물고기·곤충 등의 모든 생물. 피창조물. 생명이 있는 것: *Native Americans believe that all living creatures should be respected.* 아메리칸 인디언들은 모든 생명체들은 존중되어야 한다고 믿는다. **2** an imaginary animal or person, or one that is very strange ‖ 상상의 또는 아주 기이한 동물이나 사람: *creatures from outer space* 외계에서 온 생명체 **3 a creature of sth** someone who is a creature of something is influenced by it a lot or has a quality produced by it ‖ 무엇에 의해 많은 영향을 받는 사람, 또는 무엇에 의해 형성된 성질을 가지는 사람. 예속자. 노예. …의 예속물[노예]: *Today's kids are creatures of television.* 오늘날의 아이들은 텔레비전의 노예이다. **4 creature comforts** things that people need to feel comfortable, such as warmth, good food, comfortable furniture etc. ‖ 따뜻함·좋은 음식·편안한 가구 등 안락함을 느끼는 데 필요한 것들. 육체적 위안이 되는 것. 의식주 **5 creature of habit** someone who always does things in the same way or at the same time ‖ 항상 동일한 방식으로 또는 일정한 시간에 일을 하는 사람. 습관의 포로

cre·dence /ˈkridns/ *n* [U] FORMAL the acceptance of something as true ‖ 어떤 것을 사실로 받아들임. 신임. 신뢰: *His ideas quickly gained credence* (=started to be believed) *among economists.* 그의 사상은 경제학자들 사이에서 급속히 신뢰를 얻었다.

cre·den·tials /krəˈdenʃəlz/ *n* [plural] someone's education, achievements, experience etc., that prove that s/he has the ability to do something ‖ 어떤 것을 할 능력이 있다는 것을 증명하는, 사람의 교육·성취 업적·경험 등. 자격. 경력

cred·i·bil·i·ty /ˌkredəˈbiləti/ *n* [U] the quality of being CREDIBLE ‖ 믿을 수 있는 특성. 신뢰성. 진실성: *The scandal has ruined his credibility as a leader.* 그 스캔들은 지도자로서의 그의 신뢰성을 깨뜨려 버리고 말았다.

cred·i·ble /ˈkrɛdəbəl/ *adj* deserving to be believed, or able to be trusted ‖ 믿을 만한 가치가 있는, 신뢰할 수 있는. 신용할 수 있는. 확실한: *a credible witness* 믿을 만한 증인 **– credibly** *adv*

cred·it¹ /ˈkrɛdɪt/ *n* **1** [U] an arrangement with a bank, store etc. that allows you to buy something and pay for it later ‖ 고객이 물건을 사고 나중에 지불해도 좋다는 은행·가게 등의 승인. 신용 대출. 외상: *We bought a new stove on credit.* 우리는 외상으로 새 난로를 샀다. / *six months of interest-free credit* (=credit with no additional charge) 6개월 무이자 외상 **2** [U] approval or praise for doing something good ‖ 좋은 일을 한 것에 대한 인정 또는 칭찬. 명성: *They never give Jess any credit for all the*

extra work he does. 그들은 제스가 한 모든 잔업에 대해 어떤 칭찬도 하는 법이 없다. / *I can't take all the credit; Nicky helped a lot too!* 모든 것을 내 공으로만 돌릴 수는 없어요. 니키도 정말 많이 도와주었거든요. / *Much to Todd's credit, the dance was a great success.* (=Todd deserves praise for organizing it) 토드의 많은 기여 덕분으로 댄스 공연은 대성공이었다. **3 be in credit** to have money in your bank account ‖ 은행 계좌에 돈이 있다 **4 be a credit to sb/sth** to be so successful or good that everyone who is connected with you can be proud of you ‖ 아주 성공적이거나 훌륭해서 관련 있는 모든 사람들이 자랑스럽게 여길 수 있다. …의 영예이다. 명예가 되다: *Jo's a credit to her family.* 조는 가족의 자랑거리이다. **5** a unit that shows you have completed part of a college course ‖ 대학의 교과 과정 일부를 끝마쳤음을 나타내는 단위. 학점. 이수 단위: *a 5-credit class* 5학점짜리 강의 **6 have sth to your credit** to have achieved something ‖ 무엇을 성취하다: *She already has two best-selling novels to her credit.* 그녀는 이미 자기 이름으로 출간된 2개의 베스트셀러 소설이 있다. **7** [U] the belief that something is true or correct ‖ 어떤 것이 사실이거나 정확하다는 믿음. 신용. 신뢰. 신빙성: *The witness's story is gaining credit with the jury.* 그 증인의 증언은 배심원의 신뢰를 얻고 있다. **—see also** CREDITS

credit² *v* [T] **1** to add money to a bank account ‖ 은행 계좌에 추가로 돈을 넣다. 입금하다: *For some reason the bank has credited my account with an extra $237.* 어떤 이유로 그 은행은 나의 계좌에 추가로 237달러를 입금했다. **—opposite** DEBIT² **2 credit sb/sth with sth** to believe or admit that someone or something has a particular quality ‖ 사람이나 사물이 특정한 성질을 가지고 있음을 믿거나 인정하다: *I wouldn't have credited him with that much intelligence.* 나는 그가 그렇게 똑똑하다고는 생각하지 못했다.

cred·it·a·ble /ˈkrɛdɪtəbəl/ *adj* deserving praise or approval ‖ 칭찬하거나 인정할 만한. 존경할 만한. 훌륭한: *a creditable piece of scientific research* 훌륭한 과학적인 연구 **– creditably** *adv*

credit card /ˈ.. ˌ./ *n* a small plastic card that you use to buy goods or services and pay for them later ‖ 물건을 구입하거나 서비스를 받고 비용을 나중에 지불하는 데 쓰는 작은 플라스틱 카드. 크

레디트 카드. 신용 카드 —see picture at
CARD¹

credit lim·it /ˈ.. ˌ../ *n* the amount of
money that you are allowed to borrow
or spend using your CREDIT CARD ‖ 크레
디트 카드를 사용해서 돈을 빌리거나 지불
할 수 있게 허용된 금액. 대출 여신 한도.
신용 한도

cred·i·tor /ˈkrɛdət̬ə/ *n* a person, bank,
or company that you owe money to ‖ 돈
을 되돌려받아야 할 개인[은행, 회사]. 채
권자. 빚쟁이 —compare DEBTOR

credit rat·ing /ˈ.. ˌ../ *n* a judgment
made by a bank or other company
about how likely a person or a business
is to pay debts ‖ 개인이나 회사가 채무를
상환할 가능성에 대해 은행이나 다른 회사
가 하는 판단. 신용 등급

cred·its /ˈkrɛdɪts/ *n* **the credits** a list
of all the people involved in making a
television program or movie ‖ 텔레비전
프로나 영화를 제작하는 데 관련된 모든
사람들의 명단. 크레디트

cre·do /ˈkridoʊ/ *n* a short statement
that expresses a belief or rule that a
particular person or group has ‖ 특정인
또는 집단이 가지고 있는 믿음이나 규칙을
표현하는 짧은 문구. 신조: *Dad's credo
has always been, "Never give up!"* 아버
지의 신조는 언제나 "절대 포기하지 마
라!"이다.

creed /krid/ *n* a set of beliefs or
principles, especially religious ones ‖ 특
히 일련의 종교적인 믿음이나 원칙. 교리.
신조. 주의. 강령

creek /krik, krɪk/ *n* **1** a small narrow
stream or river ‖ 작고 좁은 개울 또는 강.
시내 **2 be up the creek** SPOKEN to be in
a difficult situation ‖ 어려운 상황에 처하
다. 곤경에 빠지다: *I'll really be up the
creek if I don't pay my bills by Friday.*
내가 금요일까지 청구서를 지불하지 않으
면 정말 난처해질 것이다.

creep¹ /krip/ *v* **crept, crept,
creeping** [I] **1** to move very carefully
and quietly so that no one will notice
you ‖ 아무도 알지 못하게 아주 조심스럽
고 조용하게 움직이다. 살금살금 걷다:
*She crept down the hall, trying not to
wake up her mom.* 그녀는 엄마를 깨우지
않으려고 홀 아래로 애써 살금살금 걸어
내려갔다. **2** to move very slowly ‖ 매우
천천히 움직이다. 서행하다: *a tractor
creeping along the road at 15 mph* 도로
를 따라 시속 15마일로 기어가고 있는 트
랙터 **3** to gradually begin to appear ‖ 점
차 나타나기 시작하다: *Bitterness crept
into his voice.* 그의 목소리에 점차 괴로

움이 나타나기 시작했다.

creep² *n* **1** someone you dislike a lot,
especially because s/he annoys you or
frightens you a little ‖ 특히 귀찮게 하거
나 다소 놀라게 해서 매우 싫어하는 사람.
꼴보기 싫은 녀석: *Get lost, you little
creep!* 꺼져, 징그러운 꼬마 녀석! **2 give
sb the creeps** a person or place that
gives you the creeps makes you feel
nervous and slightly frightened ‖ 사람이
나 장소가 불안하게 하고 약간 놀라게 하
다. 섬뜩하게 하다. 소름끼치게[전율하게]
하다: *That house gives me the creeps.*
그 집은 나를 섬뜩하게 한다. **– creepy**
adj

cre·mate /ˈkrimeɪt, krɪˈmeɪt/ *v* [T] to
burn the body of a dead person ‖ 사체
(死體)를 태우다. 화장하다 **– cremation**
/krɪˈmeɪʃən/ *n* [U]

cre·ma·to·ri·um /ˌkriməˈtɔriəm/ *n*,
plural **crematoriums, crematoria** a
building in which the bodies of dead
people are CREMATEd ‖ 사체를 화장하는
건물. 화장터

cre·ole /ˈkrioʊl/ *n* **1** [C, U] a language
that is a combination of a European
language and one or more others ‖ 유럽
언어와 하나 이상의 다른 언어가 결합된
언어. 크리올어 **2 Creole a)** someone
whose family was originally from both
Europe and Africa ‖ 가족의 태생이 유럽
과 아프리카 양쪽인 사람 **b)** someone
whose family were originally French
SETTLERs in the southern US ‖ 가족의 태
생이 미국 남부의 프랑스 정착민인 사람
– creole *adj*

crepe, crêpe /kreɪp/ *n* **1** [U] thin light
cloth with very small folded lines on its
surface, made from cotton, silk, wool
etc. ‖ 면·비단·모 등으로 만든, 표면에 아
주 작은 주름들이 있는 얇고 가벼운 옷감.
크레이프 **2** a very thin PANCAKE ‖ 매우 얇
은 팬케이크

crepe pa·per /ˈ. ˌ../ *n* [U] thin
brightly colored paper with small folded
lines on its surface, used as a
decoration at parties ‖ 파티 장식으로 쓰
는, 표면에 작은 주름들이 있는 얇고 밝은
색종이. (장식용)주름 종이

crept /krɛpt/ the past tense and PAST
PARTICIPLE of CREEP ‖ creep의 과거·과거
분사형

cre·scen·do /krəˈʃɛndoʊ/ *n* a sound or
a part of a piece of music that becomes
gradually louder ‖ 소리나 악곡의 한 부분
의 세기가 점점 커지는 것. 크레셴도

cres·cent /ˈkrɛsənt/ *n* a curved shape
that is wider in the middle and pointed

on the ends ‖ 중간은 넓고 양 끝은 뾰족한 휘어진 형상. 초승달 모양(의 것): *a crescent moon* 초승달

crest /krɛst/ *n* **1** [C usually singular] the top of something such as a mountain, hill, or wave ‖ 산·언덕·파도 등의 꼭대기. 정상. 정점 **2** a pointed group of feathers on top of a bird's head ‖ 새 머리의 꼭대기에 있는 일단의 뾰족한 깃털. 볏. 관모. 도가머리

crest·fall·en /'krɛst,fɔlən/ *adj* disappointed and sad ‖ 실망하고 슬픈. 의기 소침한. 풀이 죽은

cre·vasse /krə'væs/ *n* a deep wide crack, especially in thick ice ‖ 특히 두꺼운 빙하의 깊고 넓게 깨진 틈

crev·ice /'krɛvɪs/ *n* a narrow crack, especially in rock ‖ 특히 바위의 좁게 갈라진 틈

crew /kru/ *n* **1** all the people that work together on a ship, plane etc. ‖ 선박·항공기 등에서 함께 근무하는 모든 사람들. 선원. 승무원 **2** a group of people with special skills who work together on something ‖ 함께 어떤 일을 하는 특별한 기술을 가진 일단의 사람들. 조. 반: *the movie's cast and crew* 영화의 배역 및 제작진

crew cut /'. ./ *n* a very short hair style for men ‖ 매우 짧은 남자의 머리 스타일. 크루커트

crib /krɪb/ *n* **1** a baby's bed with BARs around the sides ‖ 가장 자리에 난간이 있는 아기 침대 **2** SLANG the place where someone lives ‖ 사람이 사는 장소. (조그만) 집[방]

crib death /'. ./ *n* the unexpected death of a healthy baby while s/he is asleep ‖ 잠자는 도중에 건강한 아기의 돌연한 사망. 유아의 사망

crib sheet /'. ./ *n* INFORMAL something on which answers to questions are written, usually used in order to cheat on a test ‖ 보통 시험칠 때 커닝하는 데 쓰이는 것으로 질문에 대한 해답이 적힌 것. 커닝 페이퍼

crick /krɪk/ *n* a sudden stiff feeling in a muscle in your neck or back ‖ 목이나 등의 근육이 갑자기 뻣뻣해지는 느낌. 근육 경련

crick·et /'krɪkɪt/ *n* **1** a small brown insect that makes a short loud noise by rubbing its wings together ‖ 날개를 서로 비벼서 짧고 큰 소리를 내는 작은 갈색의 곤충. 귀뚜라미 **2** [U] a game in which two teams try to get points by hitting a ball and running between two sets of special sticks ‖ 두 팀이 공을 치고 특별한

2개의 막대기 사이를 달려서 득점을 하려고 하는 경기. 크리켓

crime /kraɪm/ *n* **1** [U] illegal activity in general ‖ 일반적으로 불법적인 행위. 범죄 (행위): *There's some petty crime* (=crime that is not serious) *in our neighborhood, but not much serious crime.* (=crime that is more violent) 우리 동네에는 약간의 경범죄는 있지만 중범죄는 많지 않다. / *methods of crime prevention* (=ways to stop crime) 범죄 방지 수단 **2** an illegal action that can be punished by law ‖ 법에 의해 처벌되는 불법적인 행위. (범)죄: *crimes against the elderly* 노인에 대한 범죄 / *She committed a number of crimes in the area.* 그녀는 그 지역에서 여러 번 범죄를 저질렀다. ✗DON'T SAY "do a crime"✗ "do a crime"이라고는 하지 않는다. **3 it's a crime** SPOKEN said when you think something is wrong ‖ 어떤 것이 잘못이라고 생각될 때에 쓰여. 나쁜 짓이다: *It's a crime to throw away all that food.* 저 음식을 모두 내버리는 것은 죄악이다.

crim·i·nal¹ /'krɪmənəl/ *adj* **1** relating to crime ‖ 범죄에 관련된. 범죄의: *a criminal record* (=an official record of crimes someone has done) 전과 기록 **2** INFORMAL wrong but not illegal ‖ 잘못이지만 불법은 아닌. 부당한. 어리석은: *It's criminal to charge so much for popcorn at the movies!* 영화관에서 팝콘을 그렇게 비싸게 파는 것은 말도 안돼! – **criminally** *adv*

criminal² *n* someone who is proved guilty of a crime ‖ 범죄에 대해 유죄로 증명된 사람. 범인. 죄인

crimp¹ /krɪmp/ *n* **put a crimp in/on** to reduce or restrict something, so that it is difficult to do something else ‖ 어떤 것을 줄이거나 제한해서 다른 것을 하기가 어려워지다. (계획 등을) 방해하다: *Falling wheat prices have put a crimp on farm incomes.* 밀의 가격 하락은 농가 소득을 감소시켰다.

crimp² *v* [T] to restrict the development, use, or growth of something ‖ 사물의 발전[사용, 성장]을 제한하다. 방해하다. 저지하다: *The lack of effective advertising has crimped sales.* 효과적인 광고의 부족으로 판매가 부진했다.

crim·son /'krɪmzən/ *n* [U] a dark slightly purple red color ‖ 어둡고 약간 자줏빛이 도는 붉은 색. 심홍색 – **crimson** *adj*

cringe /krɪndʒ/ *v* [I] **1** to move back or away from someone or something because you are afraid ‖ 두려워서 사람이나 물체로부터 뒷걸음치거나 떨어지다. (겁이 나서) 움츠리다: *a dog cringing in the corner* 구석에 움츠리고 있는 개 **2** to feel embarrassed by something ‖ 어떤 것에 의해 당혹감을 느끼다: *Paul cringed at the thought of having to speak in public.* 대중 앞에서 연설해야 한다는 생각에 폴은 난감해졌다. – **cringe** *n*

crin·kle /ˈkrɪŋkəl/, **crinkle up** *v* [I, T] to become covered with very small folds, or to make something do this ‖ 아주 작은 주름들로 덮이다 또는 어떤 것을 덮이게 하다. 주름지다[잡다]: *Mandy crinkled up her nose in disgust.* 맨디는 진저리나서 콧 잔등을 잔뜩 찌푸렸다. – **crinkled** *adj* – **crinkly** *adv*

crip·ple¹ /ˈkrɪpəl/ *n* **1** OFFENSIVE someone who cannot walk ‖ 걸을 수 없는 사람. 절뚝발이. 불구자 **2 emotional cripple** DISAPPROVING someone who is not able to deal with his/her own or other people's feelings ‖ 자기 자신이나 타인의 감정을 다룰 수 없는 사람. 정서 장애자

cripple² *v* [T] **1** to injure someone so s/he cannot walk or use his/her arms ‖ 걸을 수 없거나 팔을 쓸 수 없게 사람을 다치게 하다. 불구가 되게 하다 **2** to make something very weak or damage it ‖ 어떤 것을 매우 약하게 만들거나 손상을 가하다. 약화시키다. 무능하게 만들다: *The country's economy has been crippled by drought.* 그 나라의 경제는 가뭄으로 큰 타격을 받았다. – **crippled** *adj* – **crippling** *adj*

cri·sis /ˈkraɪsɪs/ *n, plural* **crises** /ˈkraɪsiz/ [C, U] **1** a very bad or dangerous situation that might get worse, especially in politics or ECONOMICS ‖ 특히 정치나 경제에서 더욱 악화될 가능성이 있는 아주 나쁜 또는 위험한 상황. 위기. 공황: *the worst budget crisis in a decade* 10년 동안의 최악의 예산 위기 / *the hostage crisis* 인질 위기 **2** a time when an emotional problem or illness is at its worst ‖ 정서적 문제 또는 질병이 최악의 상태에 있는 시기. 고비: *I had reached a crisis in my personal life.* 내 개인적인 삶에서 고비에 봉착했다.

crisp /krɪsp/ *adj* **1** APPROVING dry and hard enough to be broken easily ‖ 쉽게 부서질 만큼 물기가 없고 단단한. 파삭파삭한: *nice crisp pastry* 맛있고 파삭파삭한 페이스트리 **2** fruit and vegetables that are crisp are firm and fresh ‖ 과일·야채 등이 단단하고 신선한 **3** paper or clothes that are crisp are fresh, clean,

and stiff ‖ 종이나 옷 등이 새로우면서 깨끗하고 빳빳한. 파삭파삭 소리나는: *a crisp $20 bill* 빳빳한 20달러짜리 지폐 **4** weather that is crisp is cold and dry ‖ 기후 등이 차갑고 건조한. 서늘한. 상쾌한: *a crisp winter morning* 쌀쌀한 겨울 아침 – **crisply** *adv*

crisp·y /ˈkrɪspi/ *adj* CRISP and good to eat ‖ 먹기에 신선하고 좋은: *crispy bacon* 신선하고 먹기 좋은 베이컨

criss·cross /ˈkrɪskrɔs/ *v* [I, T] **1** to travel many times from one side of an area to the other ‖ 한 지역의 한 쪽으로부터 다른 쪽으로 여러 차례 돌아다니다. 종횡으로 움직이다: *crisscrossing the country by plane* 그 나라를 비행기로 종횡무진하기 **2** to make a pattern of straight lines that cross over each other ‖ 서로 교차하는 직선 형태를 만들다. 교차하다 – **crisscross** *n*

cri·te·ri·a /kraɪˈtɪriə/ *n singular* **criterion** /-ˈtɪriən/ [plural] facts or standards used in order to help you judge or decide something ‖ 무엇을 판단하거나 결정하는 것을 돕는 데에 사용되는 사실이나 기준. 규범. 표준: *What are the main criteria for awarding the prize?* 상을 수여하는 주요 기준이 무엇입니까?

crit·ic /ˈkrɪtɪk/ *n* **1** someone whose job is to judge whether a movie, book etc. is good or bad ‖ 영화·책 등이 좋은지 나쁜지를 판단하는 직업인. 비평가. 평론가: *a literary critic for The Times* 타임즈지의 문학 비평가 **2** someone who judges a person, idea etc. ‖ 사람·생각 등을 신랄하게 비판하는 사람. 혹평가: *a critic of the plans for developing Yosemite* 요세미테 개발 계획에 대한 혹평가

crit·i·cal /ˈkrɪtɪkəl/ *adj* **1** severely judging people or things, sometimes in an unfair way ‖ 때로는 부당하게 사람이나 사물을 가혹하게 평가하는. 혹평하는. 비판적인: *Darren was critical of the plan to reorganize the company.* 회사의 구조 조정 계획에 대해 대렌은 비판적이었다. **2** very important, because what happens in the future depends on it ‖ 장래의 일을 좌우하는 아주 중요한. 결정적인: *This next phase is critical to the project's success.* 이 다음 단계는 프로젝트의 성공에 결정적인 것이다. **3** very serious or dangerous, because a situation could get better or worse ‖ 상황이 더 좋아지거나 나빠질 수 있기 때문에 매우 심각하거나 위험한. 위기의: *Seth is at a critical stage in his recovery from his operation.* 세스는 수술 회복기의

가장 중요한 단계에 있다. **4 making judgments about whether someone or something is good or bad** ‖ 사람이나 사물이 좋은지 나쁜지를 판단하는. 비평적인: *a critical analysis of the play* 그 연극에 대한 비평적인 분석 – **critically** *adv*

criti·cism /ˈkrɪtəˌsɪzəm/ *n* [C, U] **1** the act of judging whether someone or something is good or bad ‖ 사람이나 사물이 좋은지 나쁜지를 판단하는 행위. 비평 : *I'm always willing to hear constructive criticism.* (=helpful advice) 나는 건설적인 비판은 항상 기꺼이 들으려고 한다. **2** written or spoken remarks that show that you do not approve of someone or something ‖ 사람이나 사물을 인정하지 않음을 나타내는 글이나 말. 비난: *There is growing criticism of the President's decision.* 대통령의 결정에 대한 비난이 커지고 있다.

crit·i·cize /ˈkrɪtəˌsaɪz/ *v* **1** [I, T] to judge someone or something severely ‖ 사람이나 사물을 호되게 평가하다. 비난하다: *Journalists criticized the White House for cutting the Social Security budget.* 언론인들은 사회 보장 예산의 삭감에 대해 백악관을 비난했다. **2** [T] ⇨ CRITIQUE[2]

cri·tique[1] /krɪˈtik/ *n* [C, U] an article, book etc. that makes judgments about the good and bad qualities of someone or something ‖ 사람이나 사물의 좋고 나쁜 점에 대해 판단을 하는 기사·책 등. 비평. 평론. 서평

critique[2] *v* [T] to judge whether someone or something is good or bad ‖ 사람이나 사물이 좋은지 나쁜지를 판단하다. 비평하다: *a group of artists meeting to critique each others' work* 상호 작품을 비평하기 위한 일단의 예술가들의 모임

crit·ter /ˈkrɪtɚ/ *n* INFORMAL an animal, fish, or insect; creature ‖ 동물[물고기, 곤충]; 생물

croak[1] /kroʊk/ *v* **1** [I] to make a deep low sound like the sound a FROG makes ‖ 개구리가 내는 소리처럼 깊고 낮은 소리를 내다. 개굴개굴 울다 **2** [I, T] to speak in a low deep voice as if you have a sore throat ‖ 목이 쉰 것처럼 낮고 깊은 목소리로 말하다. 쉰[침울한] 소리로 말하다 **3** [I] SLANG to die ‖ 죽다. 뻗다

croak[2] *n* a low deep sound made in the throat, like the sound a FROG makes ‖ 개구리가 내는 소리와 같은 낮고 굵은 목소리. 쉰 목소리

cro·chet /kroʊˈʃeɪ/ *v* [I, T] to make clothes, hats etc. from YARN, using a special needle with a hook at one end ‖ 한 쪽 끝에 고리가 있는 특수한 바늘을 사용해서 실로 옷·모자 등을 만들다. …을 코바늘로 뜨다. 코바늘 뜨기로 하다 – **crochet** *n* [U]

crock /krɑk/ *n* **sth is a crock** SPOKEN an impolite expression used in order to say that something is not true or that you do not believe someone ‖ 어떤 것이 사실이 아니거나 어떤 사람을 믿지 않는다는 것을 말하는 데에 쓰는 무례한 표현. …은 허풍[허황된 이야기]이다

crock·er·y /ˈkrɑkəri/ *n* [U] dishes made from clay ‖ 찰흙으로 만든 그릇. 도자기. 도기

croc·o·dile /ˈkrɑkəˌdaɪl/ *n* a large REPTILE (=type of animal) that has a long body and a long mouth with sharp teeth, and lives in hot wet areas ‖ 몸통과 입이 길고 이빨이 날카로운, 열대 습지대에서 사는 커다란 파충류. 악어

cro·cus /ˈkroʊkəs/ *n* a small purple, yellow, or white flower that appears in early spring ‖ 초봄에 피는 작은 자줏빛의 [노란, 하얀] 꽃. 크로커스

crois·sant /krwɑˈsɑnt/ *n* a soft bread ROLL shaped in a curve ‖ 둥글게 휜 형태의 부드러운 빵. 크루아상. 초승달형 빵 —see picture at BREAD

cro·ny /ˈkroʊni/ *n* INFORMAL someone that you spend a lot of time with, especially someone you help unfairly by using your power or authority ‖ 많은 시간을 함께 보내는 사람, 특히 권력이나 권위를 이용해서 불공정하게 도와주는 사람. 한패

crook[1] /krʊk/ *n* **1** INFORMAL someone who is not honest ‖ 정직하지 않은 사람. 사기꾼. 도둑: *Politicians are just a bunch of crooks.* 정치인들이야말로 사기꾼 무리이다. **2 the crook of your arm** the inside part of your arm where it bends at the elbow ‖ 팔이 굽혀지는 팔꿈치의 안쪽 부분. 팔의 굴곡 부위

crook[2] *v* [I, T] to bend something, especially your finger or arm ‖ 어떤 것, 특히 손가락이나 팔을 굽히다. 구부리다 [구부러지다]

crook·ed /ˈkrʊkɪd/ *adj* **1** twisted or not straight ‖ 꼬이거나 똑바르지 않은. 구부러진. 비뚤어진: *crooked country roads* 구부러진 시골 도로 **2** INFORMAL not honest ‖ 정직하지 않은. 부정한: *a crooked cop* 부정한 경찰 – **crookedly** *adv*

croon /krun/ *v* [I, T] to sing or speak in a soft gentle voice ‖ 부드럽고 조용한 목소리로 노래하거나 말하다. 낮은 목소리로 감상적으로 노래하다. 낮게 중얼거리는

듯한 소리를 내다: *crooning love songs* 잔잔한 목소리로 연가를 노래하기 - **crooner** *n*

crop¹ /krɑp/ *n* **1** a plant such as corn, wheat etc. that is grown by a farmer and used as food ‖ 농부가 재배하여 식용으로 쓰는 옥수수·밀 등의 식물. 농작물 **2** the amount of corn, wheat etc. that is produced in a single season ‖ 한 계절에 생산된 옥수수·밀 등의 양. 수확고. 작황: *a bumper crop* (=a very large amount) *of barley* 보리 풍작 **3 a crop of** INFORMAL a group of people, problems etc. that arrive at the same time ‖ 동시에 다다른 일단의 사람·문제 등: *this year's crop of college freshmen* 한 무리의 금년도 대학 신입생

crop² *v* **-pped, -pping** [T] **1** to make something smaller or shorter by cutting it ‖ 사물을 잘라서 더 작거나 짧게 만들다. 끝[가장자리(등)]을 자르다: *cropped hair* 짧게 자른 머리 **2** if an animal crops grass, it makes it shorter by eating the top part ‖ 동물이 풀의 윗부분을 뜯어 먹어서 짧아지게 하다. (풀 등을) 뜯어먹다

crop up *phr v* [I] to happen or appear suddenly in an unexpected way ‖ 예기치 않게 갑자기 발생하거나 나타나다: *Several problems cropped up soon after we bought the car.* 우리가 차를 산지 얼마 안되어 뜻밖에 여러 문제들이 발생했다.

cro·quet /kroʊ'keɪ/ *n* [U] an outdoor game in which you hit heavy balls under curved wires using a wooden hammer ‖ 나무 망치로 무거운 공을 쳐서 휜 철사 밑을 통과시키는 옥외 게임. 크로케

cross¹ /krɔs/ *v* **1** [I, T] to go from one side of a road, river, place etc. to the other side ‖ 도로·강·장소 등의 한 쪽에서 다른 쪽으로 가다. 건너다. 횡단하다: *Look both ways before crossing the street!* 길을 건너기 전에 좌우를 살펴봐라! **2** [T] if two or more roads, lines etc. cross, they go across each other ‖ 2개 이상의 도로·선 등이 서로 엇갈려 지나다. 교차하다. 가로지르다: *There's a post office where Main Street crosses Elm.* 메인스트리트와 엘름이 교차하는 곳에 우체국이 있다. **3** [T] if you cross your arms or legs, you put one on top of the other ‖ 한 팔이나 다리를 다른 쪽 팔이나 다리 위에 얹다. 팔짱을 끼다. 가부좌하다: *a big man standing at the door with his arms crossed* 팔짱을 낀 채 문에 서 있는 몸집이 큰 남자 **4 cross your mind** if something crosses your mind, you think about it ‖ 어떤 것에 대하여 생각하다. 생각이 마음에 떠오르다: *It never crossed my mind that she might be sick.* 나는 그녀가 아플지도 모른다는 것은 생각도 못했다. **5** [T] to mix two or more breeds of animal or plant to form a new breed ‖ 새로운 품종을 만들기 위해 둘 이상의 동물이나 식물의 품종을 섞다. 교배하다. 접붙이다: *crossing a horse with a donkey to get a mule* 노새를 얻기 위해 말과 당나귀를 교배하기 **6 cross my heart (and hope to die)** SPOKEN a phrase used especially by children to promise that what you have said is true ‖ 자기가 한 말이 사실이라는 것을 맹세하기 위해 특히 아이들이 쓰는 어구. 가슴에 십자가를 긋고 맹세하다 **7 cross yourself** to move your hand across your chest in the shape of a cross, as a sign of Christian faith ‖ 크리스트교인이 믿음의 표시로 손으로 가슴을 가로질러 십자를 그리다. 성호를 긋다

cross sth ↔ **off** *phr v* [I, T] to draw a line through something on a list to show that it is not needed or that it has been done ‖ 필요하지 않거나 이미 완성되었다는 것을 나타내기 위해 목록에 있는 것에 사선을 긋다. 선을 그어 지우다: *Cross off their names as they arrive.* 그들이 도착하면 이름에 선을 그어 지워라.

cross sth ↔ **out** *phr v* [T] to draw a line through something that you have written or drawn, especially to show that it is wrong ‖ 쓰거나 그린 것에, 특히 잘못 되었다는 표시로, 선을 긋다. 줄을 그어 지우다: *a handwritten letter with a few words crossed out* 몇몇 단어들에 줄을 그어 지운 손으로 쓴 편지

cross² *n* **1** a wooden post with another post crossing it near the top, that people were NAILed to as a punishment in ancient times ‖ 고대에 형벌로 사람을 못박았던, 꼭대기 근처에 다른 기둥을 교차시킨 나무 기둥. 십자가 **2** an object in the shape of a cross that is used as a decoration or as a sign of the Christian faith ‖ 장식 또는 크리스트 교인의 믿음의 표시로 쓰이는 십자 모양의 물체: *She wore a tiny gold cross around her neck.* 그녀는 작은 금 십자상 목걸이를 걸었다. **3** a mixture of two or more things, breeds, qualities etc. ‖ 둘 이상의 물건·품종·성질 등의 혼합물. 잡종. 혼혈. 절충. 중간물: *His dog is a cross between a retriever and a collie.* 그의 개는 리트리버와 콜리의 교잡종이다.

cross³ *adj* OLD-FASHIONED annoyed and angry ‖ 화난. 성을 잘 내는

cross·bow /'krɔsboʊ/ *n* a weapon used

in past times to shoot ARROWs with a lot of force ‖ 큰 힘을 들여 화살을 쏘는 데 쓰였던 과거의 무기. 쇠뇌

cross·check /ˌkrɔsˈtʃɛk, ˈkrɔstʃɛk/ v [T] to make sure that something is correct by using a different method to calculate it again ‖ 어떤 것을 다른 방법으로 다시 계산하여 그것이 정확하다는 것을 확인하다. 대조하여 정확성을 조사하다. 크로스 체크하다

cross·coun·try /ˌ. ˈ../ adj 1 across fields and not along roads ‖ 도로를 따라 가지 않고 들판을 횡단하는: cross-country running 크로스 컨트리 경주 2 from one side of a country to the other side ‖ 나라의 한 쪽에서 다른 쪽까지. 나라를 횡단하는: a cross-country flight 전국 횡단 비행

cross·cul·tur·al /ˌ. ˈ../ adj belonging to or involving two or more societies, countries, or CULTUREs ‖ 둘 이상의 사회·국가·문화에 속하거나 관련된. 서로 다른 문화 상호간의. 비교 문화적(인)

cross·dress /ˈ. ./ v [I] to wear the clothes of the opposite sex, especially for sexual pleasure ‖ 특히 성적 쾌감을 위해 이성(異性)의 옷을 입다 **– cross-dressing** n [U]

cross·ex·am·ine /ˌ. .ˈ../ v [I, T] to ask someone questions about something s/he has just said to see if s/he is telling the truth, especially in a court of law ‖ 특히 법정에서 상대방이 방금 한 말이 사실인가를 확인하기 위해 질문을 하다. …에게 반대 신문을 하다 **– cross-examination** /ˌ. ...ˈ../ n [C, U]

cross·eyed /ˈ. ./ adj having eyes that look inward toward the nose ‖ 코 쪽을 향해 안쪽을 쳐다보는 눈을 가진. 사팔뜨기의

cross·fire /ˈkrɔsfaɪæ/ n [U] 1 **be caught in the crossfire** to be involved in a situation in which other people are arguing ‖ 다른 사람들이 논쟁하는 상황에 말려들다. (질문 등의) 일제 공격을 받다 2 bullets from two or more different directions that pass through the same area ‖ 동일 지역을 통과하는 둘 이상의 다른 방향에서 날아오는 탄환. 십자포화

cross·ing /ˈkrɔsɪŋ/ n 1 a marked place where you can safely cross a road, railroad, river etc. ‖ 안전하게 건널 수 있다고 표시된 도로·철로·강 등 장소. 횡단로. 건널목. 도하 지점 2 a place where two roads, lines etc. cross ‖ 두 개의 도로·선 등이 교차하는 장소. 교차점 3 a trip across the ocean ‖ 대양을 횡단하는 여행. 항해. 도항

cross-legged

Tony is sitting cross-legged.

Kara is sitting with her legs crossed.

cross·leg·ged /ˈkrɔs ˌlɛgɪd, -lɛgd/ adv in a sitting position with your knees wide apart and your feet crossed ‖ 무릎을 넓게 벌리고 발을 교차시킨 자세로 앉아. 가부좌[책상다리]를 하고: children sitting cross-legged on the floor 마루에 가부좌하고 앉아 있는 아이들 **– cross-legged** adj

cross·o·ver /ˈkrɔsˌoʊvæ/ adj moving or changing from one type of group, style, period etc. to another ‖ 한 유형의 집단·양식·시기 등에서 또 다른 것으로 이동하거나 변화하는. 교차[전향]하는. 크로스오버의: the band's crossover move from jazz into pop music 그 밴드의 재즈에서 팝 음악으로의 전향 움직임

cross·pur·pos·es /ˌ. ˈ../ n [plural] **be at cross-purposes** if two people are at cross-purposes, they do not understand each other because they do not know that they want, or are talking about different things ‖ 두 사람이 원하는 것을 몰라서 서로 이해하지 못하거나 다른 것에 대해 이야기하다. 서로의 의도를 오해하다. 서로 빗나간 말을 하다

cross·ref·er·ence /ˈ. ,...,ˌ. ˈ../ n a note in a book that directs you to look in a different place in the same book for more information ‖ 더 많은 정보를 얻기 위해 같은 책의 다른 부분을 보라고 안내하는 책의 표시. (같은 책 속의) 상호 참조

cross·roads /ˈkrɔsroudz/ n, plural crossroads 1 a place where two roads meet and cross each other ‖ 두 길이 서로 만나서 교차하는 곳. 교차로 2 a time in your life when you have to make an important decision that will affect your future ‖ 장래에 영향을 미칠 중대한 결정을 해야 하는 인생의 한 시기. 기로. 중대한 갈림길: Neale's career was at a crossroads. 닐의 생애는 기로에 서 있었다.

cross sec·tion, cross-section /ˈ. ,../ n 1 something that has been cut in half so that you can look at the inside, or a drawing of this ‖ 내부를 볼 수 있게 하기 위해서 반으로 자른 것, 또는 이러한 그림. 횡단면. 단면도: *a cross section of the brain* 뇌의 단면도 **2** a group of people or things that is typical of a larger group ‖ 보다 큰 그룹을 대표하는 사람이나 사물의 집단. 대표적인 단면[실례]: *a cross-section of the American public* 대표적인 미국 사람들

cross street /ˈ. ./ n a street that crosses another street ‖ 다른 길과 교차하는 길. 교차로: *The nearest cross streets are Victory and Reseda Blvd.* 가장 가까운 교차로는 빅토리와 레세다 대로이다.

cross·walk /ˈkrɔswɔk/ n a specially marked place for people to walk across a street ‖ 도로를 건너는 사람들을 위해 특별하게 표시가 되어있는 지역. 횡단보도

crossword puz·zle /ˈkrɔswəd ˌpʌzəl/, **crossword** n a game in which you write the words that are the answers to questions in a special pattern of squares with numbers in their corners ‖ 구석에 숫자가 적힌 특별한 형태의 사각형 칸들 안에 질문의 해답을 써넣는 게임. 십자말풀이

crotch /krɑtʃ/ n the part of your body between the tops of your legs, or the part of a piece of clothing that covers this ‖ 다리의 맨 윗부분 사이의 신체 부위, 또는 이것을 감싸고 있는 옷의 부분. 가랑이

crotch·et·y /ˈkrɑtʃəti/ adj INFORMAL easily annoyed or made angry ‖ 쉽게 짜증내거나 화내는. 괴팍한: *a crotchety old man* 괴팍한 노인

crouch /krautʃ/, **crouch down** v [I] to lower your body close to the ground by bending your knees and back ‖ 무릎과 등을 굽혀 지면 가까이로 몸을 낮추다. 웅크리다: *We crouched down behind your wall to hide.* 우리는 숨기 위해서 당신의 벽 뒤에 웅크렸다. —see picture on page 947

crow¹ /krou/ n **1** a large shiny black bird that makes a loud sound ‖ 큰 소리로 우는 광택있는 검은색의 큰 새. 까마귀 **2** [singular] the loud sound that a ROOSTER makes ‖ 수탉이 내는 큰 소리. 수탉의 울음 소리 **3 as the crow flies** measured in a straight line ‖ 일직선으로 측정된. 일직선으로. 가장 가까운 길로: *My house is ten miles from here as the crow flies.* 우리 집은 여기에서 직선 거리로 10마일이다.

crow² v [I] to make the loud sound of a ROOSTER ‖ 수탉이 큰 소리를 내다. (수탉

이) 울다

crow·bar /ˈkroubɑr/ n a strong iron BAR used for lifting or opening things ‖ 물건을 들어올리거나 열기 위해 사용하는 강철 막대. 쇠지레

crowd¹ /kraud/ n **1** a large group of people in a particular place ‖ 특정한 장소에 떼지어 있는 사람들의 무리. 군중. 관중: *A crowd gathered to watch the parade.* 군중들이 시가 행진을 보기 위해 모였다. **2** a group of people who are friends, work together etc ‖ 친구·함께 일하는 사람 등의 무리. 그룹. 동료: *I guess the usual crowd will be at the party.* 나는 평소의 친구들이 파티에 참석하리라 생각한다.

crowd² v **1** [I, T] if people crowd somewhere or around something, they gather together in large numbers, filling a particular place ‖ 많은 사람들이 특정한 장소를 가득 채우다. 모여들다. 붐비다. 떼를 짓다: *People crowded around the scene of the accident.* 사람들이 사고 현장 주변에 운집했다. **2** [T] to make someone angry by moving too close to him/her or by asking him/her to do too much for you ‖ 너무 가까이 다가가거나 지나친 요구를 하여 남을 화나게 만들다. 졸라대다. 다그치다: *Stop crowding me!* 나를 졸라대지마!

crowd sb/sth ↔ **out** phr v [T] to force someone or something out of a place or situation ‖ 사람이나 사물을 어떤 장소나 상황에서 강제로 밀어내다. 구축(驅逐)하다: *The big supermarkets have been crowding out small grocery stores for years.* 대형 슈퍼마켓은 수년 동안 작은 식료품 가게들을 몰아내 왔다.

crowd·ed /ˈkraudɪd/ adj too full of people or things ‖ 사람들이나 물건들로 가득찬. 대만원인: *a crowded room* 사람들로 가득찬 방

crown¹ /kraun/ n **1** a circle made of gold that a king or queen wears on his/her head ‖ 왕이나 여왕이 머리에 쓰는 금으로 만든 원형 물건. 왕관 **2** the top part of a hat, head, or hill ‖ 모자[머리, 언덕]의 상단 부분. 꼭대기. 정수리: *a hat with a high crown* 춤이 높은 모자 **3** an artificial top for a damaged tooth ‖ 손상된 치아를 위한 인공적인 덮개. 인공치관(齒冠) **4** the position you have if you have won a sports competition ‖ 스포츠 경기에서 이긴 경우 차지하게 되는 지위. 왕좌. 타이틀: *He lost the heavyweight boxing crown in 1972.* 그는 1972년에 헤비급 권투 챔피언 자리를 잃었다. **5 the crown** the position of being king or queen ‖ 왕이나 여왕의 지위

crown² *v* [T] **1** to put a CROWN on someone's head, so that s/he officially becomes king or queen ‖ 머리에 왕관을 씌워 공식적으로 왕이나 왕비의 자리에 앉게 하다. 왕위에 앉히다: *He was crowned at the age of six.* 그는 여섯 살 때 왕위에 올랐다. **2** to do something or get something that is the best and usually last thing in a series of things you have done or gotten ‖ 행하거나 가졌던 일련의 것들 중에서 최고이자 최후의 것을 하거나 가지다. …의 최후를 장식하다. 유종의 미를 거두다: *His successful career was crowned by the best actor award.* 그의 성공적인 이력은 최우수 배우상으로 유종의 미를 거두었다. **3** to put a protective top on a damaged tooth ‖ 손상된 치아에 보호막을 씌우다. 인공치관을 씌우다

crown·ing /ˈkraʊnɪŋ/ *adj* being the best and usually last of a series of things ‖ 일련의 것들 중 대개 최고이자 최후의. 정상의. 더없는: *Winning a fourth championship was her crowning achievement.* 네 번째 우승으로 그녀는 최고의 금자탑을 쌓았다.

crown prince /ˌ. ˈ./, **crown princess** /ˌ. ˈ../ *n* the child of a king or queen, who will be the next king or queen ‖ 차기 왕이나 여왕이 될 왕이나 여왕의 아이. 황태자(비). 왕세자(빈)

cru·cial /ˈkruʃəl/ *adj* extremely important ‖ 극히 중요한. 결정적인: *crucial decisions involving millions of dollars* 수백만 달러가 걸린 지극히 중요한 결정 **– crucially** *adv*

cru·ci·fix /ˈkrusəˌfɪks/ *n* a CROSS with a figure of Christ on it ‖ 예수의 형상이 달려 있는 십자가. 십자가상

cru·ci·fix·ion /ˌkrusəˈfɪkʃən/ *n* **1** [C, U] the act of killing someone by fastening him/her to a CROSS and leaving him/her to die ‖ 사람을 십자가에 매달아 죽게하는 살해 행위. 십자가에 못 박힘. 십자가형 **2 the Crucifixion** the death of Christ in this way, or a picture or object that represents it ‖ 예수의 십자가에서의 죽음, 또는 이것을 표현하는 그림이나 물체

cru·ci·fy /ˈkrusəˌfaɪ/ *v* [T] **1** to kill someone by fastening him/her to a CROSS and leaving him/her to die ‖ 사람을 십자가에 매달아 죽이다 **2** to criticize someone severely and cruelly, especially in public ‖ 특히 공개적으로 사람을 가혹하고 잔인하게 비평하다: *Gardner was crucified by the press for his offensive comments.* 가드너는 모욕적인 발언 때문에 언론의 맹비난을 받았다.

crud /krʌd/ *n* [U] INFORMAL something that is very unpleasant to look at, taste, smell etc. ‖ 모양·맛·냄새 등이 매우 불쾌한 것: *I can't get this crud off my shoe.* 내 신발에서 이 지저분한 것을 없앨 수가 없다. **– cruddy** *adj*

crude /krud/ *adj* **1** offensive or rude, especially in a sexual way ‖ 특히 성적으로 불쾌감을 주거나 무례한. 노골적인: *One of the young men yelled something crude at her.* 젊은 남자들 중 한 명이 그녀에게 외설적인 말들을 외쳐댔다. **2** in a natural or raw condition ‖ 천연의, 또는 날것의. 미가공의. 정제하지 않은: *crude oil* 원유 **3** not developed to a high standard, or made with little skill ‖ 높은 수준으로 발전되지 않은, 또는 미숙한 기술로 만들어진. 허술한. 세련되지 못한: *a crude shelter in the forest* 숲속의 허술한 대피소 **– crudely** *adv*

cru·el /ˈkruəl/ *adj* **1** deliberately hurting people or animals or making them feel unhappy ‖ 일부러 사람이나 동물을 다치게 하거나 기분을 상하게 하는. 잔인한. 무자비한. 모진: *Children can be very cruel to each other.* 아이들은 서로에게 매우 잔인해질 수 있다. / *Keeping animals in cages seems cruel.* 우리에 동물을 가두어 놓는 것은 잔혹해 보인다. **2** making someone feel very unhappy ‖ 남에게 매우 불행한 느낌을 주는. 심한 고통을 주는. 끔찍한: *Her father's death was a cruel blow.* (=a sudden event that seems unfair and makes you unhappy) 그녀에게 아버지의 죽음은 끔찍한 충격이었다. **– cruelly** *adv*

cru·el·ty /ˈkruəlti/ *n* **1** [U] behavior that is cruel ‖ 잔인한 태도. 잔혹[잔인]함. 냉혹함: *cruelty to animals* 동물 학대 **2** a cruel action ‖ 잔인한 행동

cruise¹ /kruz/ *v* **1** [I] to sail along slowly ‖ 천천히 항해하다. 순항하다: *boats cruising on Lake Michigan* 미시건 호수를 순항하는 배 **2** [I] to move at a steady speed in a car, plane etc. ‖ 자동차·비행기 등을 타고 일정한 속도로 움직이다: *We cruised along at 65 miles per hour.* 우리는 시속 65마일의 일정한 속도로 달렸다. **3** INFORMAL [I, T] to drive a car without going to any particular place ‖ 일정한 목적지가 없이 차를 몰다: *Terry and I were out cruising Friday night.* 테리와 나는 금요일 밤에 정처없이 차를 몰고 다니고 있었다. **4** [I, T] SLANG to look for a sexual partner in a public place ‖ 공공 장소에서 성적인 파트너를 찾다. 쏘다니다

cruise² *n* a vacation in which you travel

on a large boat ‖ 큰 배로 여행하면서 보
내는 휴가. 유람[순양] 항해: *a Caribbean
cruise* 카리브해 유람 항해

cruiser /'kruzə/ *n* a large fast WARSHIP
‖ 크고 빠른 전투함. 순양함: *a battle
cruiser* 순양 전함

cruise ship /. ./ *n* a large ship with
restaurants, BARs, etc. that people
travel on for a vacation ‖ 사람들이 휴가
여행하는 식당·술집 등을 갖춘 대형 선
박. 유람선

crumb /krʌm/ *n* **1** a very small piece of
dry food, especially bread or cake ‖ 특히
빵이나 케이크 같은 마른 음식의 매우 작
은 조각. 부스러기 **2** a very small amount
of something ‖ 사물의 아주 작은 양. 소
량: *a few crumbs of information* 정보의
단편들

crum·ble /'krʌmbəl/ *v* **1** [I, T] to break
apart into small pieces, or make
something do this ‖ 작은 조각으로 부스러
지다, 또는 물건을 부스러지게 하다. 부스
러지다[뜨리다]: *an old stone wall,
crumbling with age* 세월과 더불어 허물
어지고 있는 오래된 돌담 **2** [I] to lose
power, become weak, or fail ‖ 힘을 잃
다[약해지다, 실패하게 되다]: *the
crumbling Roman empire* 쇠망해 가는 로
마 제국.

crum·my /'krʌmi/ *adj* SPOKEN bad or
unpleasant ‖ 나쁘거나 불쾌한. 볼품없는.
값싼: *What a crummy movie!* 싸구려 영
화 같으니라구!

crum·ple /'krʌmpəl/ *v* [I, T] to crush
something so that it becomes smaller
and bent, or to be crushed in this way ‖
어떤 것을 보다 작게 구부러지도록 찌부러
뜨리거나 이렇게 찌부러지다. 구겨지다.
구기다: *The front of the car crumpled
from the impact.* 차가 충돌하여 앞부분이
찌그러졌다.

crunch¹ /krʌntʃ/ *v* **1** [I] to make a
sound like something being crushed ‖ 부
서지는 것 같은 소리를 내다. 바삭바삭 소
리내다. 자박자박 밟고 가다: *Our feet
crunched on the frozen snow.* 우리는 얼
어붙은 눈 위를 뽀드득뽀드득 소리를 내며
걸었다. **2** [I, T] to eat hard food in a
way that makes a noise ‖ 딱딱한 음식을
소리내며 먹다. 오도독[와삭와삭] 씹다:
The dog was crunching on a bone. 그
개는 뼈를 오도독오도독 깨물어 먹고 있었
다. **- crunchy** *adj*

crunch² *n* **1** [singular] a noise like the
sound of something being crushed ‖ 깨
어지는 것 같은 소리. 깨무는 소리. 저벅
저벅 밟는 소리: *I could hear the crunch
of their footsteps on the gravel.* 나는 자

갈 위를 자박자박 걷는 그들의 발소리를
들을 수 있었다. **2 the crunch** INFORMAL
a) a difficult situation caused by a lack
of something, especially money or time
‖ 특히 돈이나 시간이 부족해서 야기된 어
려운 상황. 위기: *We're all feeling the
crunch these days.* 요즘 우리 모두는 위
기감을 느끼고 있다. **b)** also **crunch
time** a period when you have to make
the most effort to make sure you
achieve something ‖ 어떤 것을 확실히 이
루기 위해서 최선의 노력을 해야 하는 시
기. 결정적 시기

cru·sade¹ /kru'seɪd/ *n* a determined
attempt to change something because
you think you are right ‖ 옳다고 생각하
기 때문에 어떤 것을 변화시키려는 결연한
시도. (옹호, 개혁, 박멸) 운동: *a
crusade for better schools* 더 좋은 학교
를 만들기 위한 개혁 운동

crusade² *v* [I] to take part in a CRUSADE
‖ (옹호, 개혁, 박멸) 운동에 참가하다:
*students crusading against nuclear
weapons* 핵무기 반대 운동에 참가하고 있
는 학생들 **- crusader** *n*

crush¹ /krʌʃ/ *v* [T] **1** to press
something so hard that it breaks or is
damaged, or to injure someone
seriously this way ‖ 깨지거나 손상이 되
도록 물체를 세게 누르다, 또는 남에게 이
런 식으로 심한 상처를 입히다. 눌러 찌부
러뜨리다. 으깨다. 뭉개다: *crushing
grapes to make wine* 포도주를 만들기 위
한 포도 으깨기 / *people crushed beneath
a collapsing building* 붕괴된 건물 아래에
깔린 사람들 **2** to completely defeat
someone or something ‖ 사람이나 일을
완전히 패배시키거나 타파하다: *The
uprising was crushed by the military.* 그
반란은 군대에 의해 진압되었다. **3** to
make someone feel extremely upset,
shocked, sad etc. ‖ 남을 아주 당황스럽게
[충격을 받게, 슬프게] 만들다: *Pete was
crushed by his wife's sudden death.* 피
트는 아내의 갑작스러운 죽음에 큰 충격을
받았다.

crush² *n* **1** INFORMAL a feeling of
romantic love for someone, especially
someone older than you are ‖ 특히 자신
보다 나이 많은 사람에 대한 낭만적인 사
랑의 감정. 짝사랑: *Ben has a crush on
his teacher.* 벤은 선생님을 짝사랑한다. **2**
[singular] a crowd of people pressed so
close together that it is difficult for them
to move ‖ 움직이기 어려울 정도로 빽빽하
게 모여 있는 많은 사람들의 무리. 대군중

crust /krʌst/ *n* [C, U] **1** the hard brown
outer surface of bread ‖ 빵의 딱딱한 갈

색 표면. 빵 껍질 **2** the baked outer part of foods such as PIEs ‖ 파이 같은 음식의 구운 바깥 부분. 파이 껍질 **3** a thin hard covering on the surface of something ‖ 어떤 것의 표면에 있는 얇고 딱딱한 껍질: *the earth's crust* 지각(地殼)

crus·ta·cean /krʌˈsteɪʃən/ *n* TECHNICAL one of a group of animals such as a CRAB that have a hard outer shell and several pairs of legs, and that usually live in water ‖ 단단한 껍데기와 여러 개의 발을 가진, 주로 물 속에 사는 게 등의 동물의 한 무리. 갑각류 – **crustacean** *adj*

crust·y /ˈkrʌsti/ *adj* **1** having a hard CRUST ‖ 딱딱한 껍질을 가진. 외피가 딱딱한: *crusty bread* 껍질이 딱딱한 빵 **2** INFORMAL easily annoyed and not patient ‖ 쉽게 화내고 참지 못하는. 화를 잘 내는. 심술궂은: *a crusty old man* 심술궂은 노인

crutch /krʌtʃ/ *n* **1** [C usually plural] a special stick that you put under your arm to help you walk when you have hurt your leg ‖ 다리를 다쳤을 때 걷는 데 도움을 주기 위해 팔 밑에 끼는 특수한 막대기. 목발 **2** DISAPPROVING something that gives you support or help ‖ 지원해 주거나 도와 주는 것. 의지물[처]: *Tom uses those pills as a crutch.* 톰은 그 약들에 의존하고 있다.

crux /krʌks/ *n* **the crux** the most important part of a problem, question, argument etc. ‖ 문제점·질문·논쟁 등의 가장 중요한 부분. 핵심. 급소: *The crux of the matter is whether she intended to commit murder.* 그 사건의 핵심은 그녀가 살인을 저지를 의도가 있었느냐 없었느냐이다.

cry¹ /kraɪ/ *v* **cried, cried, crying 1** [I] to produce tears from your eyes, usually because you are unhappy or hurt ‖ 보통 불행하거나 다쳤기 때문에 눈에서 눈물을 흘리다. 울다: *The baby was crying upstairs.* 아기가 위층에서 울고 있었다. / *I always cry at sad movies.* 나는 슬픈 영화를 보면 항상 운다. **2** [T] to shout something loudly ‖ 무엇이라고 크게 소리치다: *"Stop!" she cried.* "멈춰"라고 그녀는 소리쳤다. **3 for crying out loud** SPOKEN said when you feel annoyed with someone ‖ 누군가에게 짜증이 날 때에 쓰여. 제발: *For crying out loud, will you shut up!* 제발 조용히 좀 해줄래! **4 cry over spilled milk** INFORMAL to waste time worrying about something that cannot be changed ‖ 돌이킬 수 없는 것에 대해 걱정하며 시간을 낭비하다. 지나간 일을 후회하다 **5** [I] if animals and birds

cry, they make a loud sound ‖ 동물과 새가 큰 소리를 내다. 울다. 짖다: *Listen to the gulls crying.* 갈매기들이 우는 소리를 들어 봐. **6 cry wolf** to often ask for help when you do not need it, so that people do not believe you when you really need help ‖ 종종 필요하지 않을 때 도움을 요청해서 실제로 도움이 필요할 때는 사람들이 믿지 못하다. 허보를 전하다. 거짓경보를 울리다

cry out *phr v* **1** [I, T] to make a loud sound or shout something loudly ‖ 큰 소리를 내거나 무엇을 크게 소리치다: *He cried out in pain.* 그는 고통으로 소리쳤다. **2 be crying out for sth** to need something urgently ‖ 긴급하게 어떤 것을 필요로 하다: *The health care system is crying out for reform.* 보건 제도는 개혁이 절실히 필요하다.

cry² *n, plural* **cries 1** a loud sound showing fear, pain, shock etc. ‖ 공포·고통·충격 등을 나타내는 큰 소리. 외침: *a baby's cry* 아기의 울음 소리 **2** a loud shout ‖ 큰 고함(소리): *Miller heard a cry of "Stop, thief!"* 밀러는 "거기 서, 도둑놈아!"라는 고함 소리를 들었다. **3** a sound made by a particular animal or bird ‖ 특정한 동물이나 새가 내는 소리. 울음 소리: *the cry of the eagle* 독수리의 울음 소리 **4** [singular] a period of time during which you cry ‖ 울음(을 우는 때): *You'll feel better after you've had a good cry.* 실컷 울고 나면 기분이 한결 좋아질 거야. **5** a phrase used in order to unite people in support of a particular action or idea ‖ 특정한 행동이나 사상을 지지하며 사람들을 결속시키는 데에 쓰이는 문구. 슬로건. 표어: *a war/battle cry* 전쟁[전투] 슬로건

cry·ba·by /ˈkraɪˌbeɪbi/ *n* INFORMAL someone who cries or complains too much ‖ 너무 심하게 울거나 불평하는 사람. 울보. 불평꾼

cry·ing /ˈkraɪ-ɪŋ/ *adj* **1 a crying need for sth** a serious need for something ‖ 어떤 것에 대한 심각한 필요. 급선무: *There's a crying need for better housing.* 더 좋은 집이 절실히 필요하다. **2 it's a crying shame** SPOKEN used in order to say that you are angry and upset about something ‖ 어떤 것에 대해 화나고 기분이 상해 있음을 말하는 데에 쓰여: *It's a crying shame the way she treats that child.* 그녀가 그 아이를 대하는 태도는 정말 분노가 치밀게 한다.

crypt /krɪpt/ *n* a room under a church, used in past times for burying people ‖ 예전에 사람을 매장하는 데에 쓰인 교회

밑의 방. 성당 지하실

cryptic /'krɪptɪk/ *adj* having a hidden meaning that is not easy to understand ‖ 이해하기 쉽지 않은 숨은 의미를 가진. 수수께끼 같은. 애매한: *a cryptic message* 수수께끼 같은 메시지 — **cryptically** *adv*

crys·tal /'krɪstəl/ *n* **1** [C, U] rock that is clear like ice, or a piece of this ‖ 얼음처럼 투명한 돌, 또는 이것의 조각. 수정. 투명한 광석 **2** [U] clear glass that is of very high quality ‖ 질이 아주 좋은 투명한 유리. 크리스털 유리: *crystal wine glasses* 크리스털 포도주[와인]잔 **3** a small piece of a substance with a particular shape, formed naturally when this substance becomes solid ‖ 어떤 물질이 굳을 때 자연스레 생기는 특정 형태를 가진 물체의 작은 조각. 결정(체): *sugar and salt crystals* 설탕과 소금의 결정체 **4** the clear plastic or glass cover on a clock or watch ‖ 손목시계나 탁상시계의 투명한 플라스틱 또는 유리 덮개

crystal ball /ˌ.. './ *n* a magic glass ball that you look into in order to see the future ‖ 미래를 보기 위해 안을 들여다보는 마술 유리 공

crystal clear /ˌ.. './ *adj* **1** very clearly stated and easy to understand ‖ 아주 분명히 언급되어 이해하기 쉬운. 아주 명료한: *I made it crystal clear that you weren't allowed to go!* 너는 못간다고 내가 분명히 말했지! **2** completely clean and clear ‖ 완전히 깨끗하고 투명한: *The lake was crystal clear.* 그 호수는 수정같이 맑았다.

crys·tal·lize /'krɪstəˌlaɪz/ *v* [I, T] **1** to make a substance form CRYSTALs ‖ 물질을 결정체로 만들다. 결정시키다. 결정체가 되다: *At what temperature does sugar crystallize?* 설탕은 몇 도에서 결정체가 되느냐? **2** to make an idea, plan etc. become clear in your mind ‖ 생각·계획 등을 마음속에 명백해지게 하다. 구체화되다. 구체화시키다: *The team had several ideas that gradually crystallized into a plan.* 그 팀은 점차 하나의 계획으로 구체화된 여러 가지 아이디어를 가지고 있었다. — **crystallization** /ˌkrɪstələˈzeɪʃən/ *n* [U]

c-sec·tion /'si ˌsɛkʃən/ *n* ⇨ CESAREAN

CT the written abbreviation of Connecticut ‖ Connecticut(코네티컷 주)의 약어

cub /kʌb/ *n* the baby of a wild animal such as a lion or bear ‖ 사자나 곰 등의 야생 동물의 새끼

cub·byhole /'kʌbi ˌhoʊl/ *n* a small

space or a small room for working or storing things in ‖ 일하거나 물건을 저장하기 위한 작은 공간이나 방. 작은 반침 [벽장]

cube¹ /kyub/ *n* **1** a solid object with six equal square sides ‖ 동일한 사각형 면이 여섯 개인 단단한 물체. 정육면체. 입방체: *a sugar cube* 각설탕 **2 the cube of sth** the number you get when you multiply a number by itself twice ‖ 어떤 숫자에 그 수를 두 번 제곱했을 때 구해지는 수. 세제곱: *The cube of 3 is 27.* 3의 세제곱은 27이다.

cube² *v* [T] **1** to multiply a number by itself twice ‖ 한 숫자에 그 수를 두 번 제곱하다. 세제곱하다: *3 cubed is 27.* 3을 세제곱하면 27이 된다. **2** to cut something into CUBEs ‖ 어떤 것을 정육면체로 자르다.

cu·bic /'kyubɪk/ *adj* **cubic inch/centimeter/yard etc.** a measurement of space in which the length, width, and height are all equal ‖ 길이·너비·높이가 모두 같은 공간의 측정치. 세제곱 인치/센티미터/야드

cu·bi·cle /'kyubɪkəl/ *n* a small enclosed part of a room ‖ 방의 한쪽을 막아놓은 작은 공간. 칸막이한 장소. 작은 열람실: *cubicles in the library for studying in* 공부하기 위한 도서관의 열람석

Cub Scouts /'. ./ *n* the part of the BOY SCOUTS that is for younger boys ‖ 어린 소년들을 대상으로 하는 보이 스카우트의 일부. 보이 스카우트의 유년단원

cuck·oo¹ /'kuku/ *adj* INFORMAL crazy or silly ‖ 미친, 어리석은

cuckoo² *n* a gray European bird that puts its eggs in other birds' NESTs and that has a call that sounds like its name ‖ 자기의 알을 다른 새의 둥지에 넣고 자기 이름과 같은 울음소리를 내는 회색의 유럽산 새. 뻐꾸기

cu·cum·ber /'kyu ˌkʌmbɚ/ *n* a long thin rounded vegetable with a dark green skin, usually eaten raw ‖ 일반적으로 날로 먹는, 껍질이 진초록색이며 길고 가는 둥근 야채. 오이 —see picture on page 944

cud·dle¹ /'kʌdl/ *v* [I, T] to hold someone or something very close to you with your arms around him, her, or it ‖ 사람이나 물체에 두 팔을 둘러 매우 가깝게 안다. …을 꼭 껴안다. 포옹하다: *Chris cuddled her new puppy.* 크리스는 자신의 새 강아지를 껴안았다.

cuddle up *phr v* [I] to lie or sit very close to someone or something ‖ 사람이나 물체에 매우 가까이 눕거나 앉다. 바싹

달라붙다. 달라붙어 자다: *The children cuddled up to each other in the dark.* 아이들은 어둠 속에서 서로 바싹 달라붙어 있었다.

cuddle² *n* [singular] an act of cuddling (CUDDLE) ‖ 껴안는 행동. 포옹. 껴안기: *Give me a cuddle.* 날 껴안아 주세요.

cud·dly /'kʌdli/ *adj* someone or something that is cuddly makes you want to CUDDLE him, her, or it ‖ 사람이나 물체가 껴안고 싶게 만드는. 귀여운: *a cuddly baby* 귀여운 아기

cue /kyu/ *n* **1** a word or action that is a signal for someone to speak or act in a play, movie etc. ‖ 연극·영화 등에서 사람이 대사나 연기를 하는 데 신호가 되는 단어나 행동. 큐. 신호: *Tony stood by the stage, waiting for his cue.* 토니는 그의 신호를 기다리며 무대 옆에 서 있었다. **2** an action or event that is a signal for something else to happen ‖ 다른 어떤 일이 일어날 신호가 되는 행동이나 사건. 단서. 힌트. 조짐: *a cue for prices to rise again* 가격이 다시 오를 조짐 **3 (right) on cue** happening or done at exactly the right moment ‖ 정확한 순간에 정확히 일어나거나 행해지는. 예정대로. 때맞춰: *I was just asking where you were when you walked in, right on cue.* 네가 어디 있는지 묻고 있었는데 때맞추어 네가 걸어들어 왔다. **4 take your cue from sb** to do something similar to what someone else does, especially in order to behave in the right way ‖ 특히 적절하게 행동하기 위해 다른 사람이 하는 것과 비슷한 행동을 하다. 남에게서 힌트를 얻다: *Wayne took his cue about which fork to use from the guy sitting next to him.* 웨인은 옆에 앉아 있는 사람이 하는 대로 따라서 포크를 사용했다. **5** a long straight wooden stick used for hitting the ball in games such as POOL ‖ 포켓 당구와 같은 게임에서 볼을 치기 위해 사용되는 길게 쭉 뻗은 나무 막대기. 큐. 당구채

cuff¹ /kʌf/ *n* **1** the end part of a SLEEVE (=the arm of a shirt, dress etc.) ‖ 소매의 끝부분. 소맷부리 **2** a narrow band of cloth turned up at the bottom of your pants ‖ 바지의 밑단에 위로 접힌 천의 가는 띠. 바지끝의 접단. 커프스 **3 off-the-cuff** without previous thought or preparation ‖ 사전에 생각이나 준비 없이. 즉석에서. 즉흥적으로: *an off-the-cuff remark* 즉흥적인 발언 —see also CUFFS

cuff² *v* [T] to put HANDCUFFS on someone ‖ 남에게 수갑을 채우다: *Cuff him and take him to the station.* 그를 수갑 채워 경찰서로 데려가.

cuff link /'. ./ *n* a small piece of jewelry that a man uses instead of a button to hold the CUFF on his shirt together ‖ 남성이 셔츠의 커프스를 채우기 위해 단추 대신에 사용하는 작은 보석 조각. 커프스 링크

cuffs /kʌfs/ *n* [plural] INFORMAL ⇨ HANDCUFFS

Cui·sin·art /'kwizɪn,ɑrt/ *n* TRADEMARK ⇨ FOOD PROCESSOR

cui·sine /kwi'zɪn/ *n* [U] a particular style of cooking ‖ 독특한 형태의 요리: *French cuisine* 프랑스 요리

cul-de-sac /,kʌl də 'sæk, ,kʊl-/ *n* a street that is closed at one end ‖ 한 쪽 끝이 막혀 있는 길. 막힌 길. 막다른 골목

cul·i·nar·y /'kʌlə,nɛri, 'kyu-/ *adj* FORMAL relating to cooking ‖ 요리와 관련된. 요리(용)의

cull /kʌl/ *v* FORMAL **1** [T] to find or choose information from many different places ‖ 여러 다른 곳에서 정보를 찾거나 선택하다. 고르다. 추려내다. 발췌하다: *data culled from various sources* 여러 가지 자료에서 빼낸 데이터 **2** [I, T] to kill the weakest animals in a group ‖ 무리에서 가장 약한 동물을 죽이다. 도태되다[하다] **– cull** *n*

cul·mi·nate /'kʌlmə,neɪt/ *v* [T] FORMAL **culminate in sth** to result in something ‖ 어떤 것의 결과를 얻다. 어떤 것으로 끝나다: *a series of arguments that culminated in a divorce* 이혼으로 귀결된 일련의 다툼

cul·mi·na·tion /,kʌlmə'neɪʃən/ *n* [singular, U] the final or highest point of something, especially after a long period of effort or development ‖ 특히 장기간의 노력과 발전을 한 후의 어떤 것의 최종적인 또는 가장 높은 지점. 정상. 최고조. 절정: *That discovery was the culmination of his life's work.* 그 발견은 그의 일생의 업적 중 최고의 것이었다.

cu·lottes /ku'lɑts, 'kulɑts/ *n* [plural] women's pants that stop at the knee and are shaped to look like a skirt ‖ 무릎까지 오고 치마처럼 생긴 여성용 바지. 퀼로트. 치마바지

cul·pa·ble /'kʌlpəbəl/ *adj* FORMAL deserving blame; guilty ‖ 비난할 만한; 유죄의 **– culpability** /,kʌlpə'bɪləti/ *n* [U]

cul·prit /'kʌlprɪt/ *n* **1** someone who is guilty of a crime or of doing something wrong ‖ 범죄에 대해 유죄이거나 잘못을 저지른 사람. 범인. 죄인 **2** INFORMAL the reason for a particular problem or difficulty ‖ 특정한 문제나 어려움의 원인:

High labor costs are the main culprit for the rise in prices. 높은 인건비는 가격 상승의 주요 원인이다.

cult /kʌlt/ *n* **1** an extreme religious group that is not part of an established religion || 기존의 종교 분파가 아닌 극단적인 종교 단체. 사이비 종교. 광신적 교단 **2** a particular fashion, style, movie, group etc. that has become very popular among a small number of people || 소수의 사람들 사이에서 매우 인기 있는 특정한 패션·양식·영화·단체 등: *a cult movie* 컬트 영화

cul·ti·vate /'kʌltə,veɪt/ *v* [T] **1** to prepare and use land for growing crops || 곡식을 재배하기 위해 땅을 일구어 이용하다. 경작하다 **2** to develop a particular skill or quality in yourself || 내재되어 있는 특정한 기술이나 특성을 발전시키다. …을 양성하다[기르다]. …을 계발하다: *cultivating a knowledge of art* 예술에 대한 소양을 함양하기 **3** to develop a friendship with someone, especially someone who can help you || 특히 도움을 줄 수 있는 사람과 우정을 발전시키다. …을 기르다. 관계를 깊이 하다: *Although the president has carefully cultivated relations with his country's powerful military, his future as leader is not entirely secure.* 대통령이 자국의 강력한 군부와 관계를 돈독히 하려고 신중히 노력해 왔음에도 불구하고 지도자로서 그의 미래는 완전히 안정적이지는 않다.

cul·ti·vat·ed /'kʌltə,veɪtɪd/ *adj* **1** intelligent and extremely polite in social situations || 사교적 상황에서 지적이고 아주 예의바른. 교양 있는. 세련된: *a cultivated gentleman* 교양 있는 신사 **2** used for growing crops || 곡물을 재배하는 데 사용되는. 경작[재배]의: *cultivated fields* 경작지

cul·ti·va·tion /ˌkʌltə'veɪʃən/ *n* [U] **1** the preparation and use of land for growing crops || 곡물을 재배하기 위한 땅의 준비와 사용. 경작. 재배: *These fields have been under cultivation (=used for growing crops) for over 50 years.* 이 밭은 50년 넘게 경작되어 왔다. **2** the deliberate development of a particular skill or quality || 특정 기술이나 특성을 공들여 개발시킴. 수련. 수양

cul·tur·al /'kʌltʃərəl/ *adj* **1** relating to a particular society and its way of life || 특정 사회와 그 사회의 생활 방식과 관련된. 문화의. 문화적인: *England has a rich cultural heritage.* 영국은 풍부한 문화 유산을 가지고 있다. **2** relating to art, literature, music etc. || 미술·문학·음악 등과 관련된. 교양의. 문화적인: *The city is trying to promote cultural activities.* 그 도시는 문화 활동을 증진시키기 위해 노력하고 있다. **– culturally** *adv*

cul·ture /'kʌltʃɚ/ *n* **1** [C, U] the art, beliefs, behavior, ideas etc. of a particular society or group of people || 특정 사회나 일단의 사람들이 갖고 있는 예술·믿음·행동·생각 등. 문화: *the culture of ancient Greece* 고대 그리스의 문화 / *youth culture* 청년 문화 / *students learning about American culture* 미국 문화에 대해 배우고 있는 학생들 **✗**DON'T SAY "the American culture"**✗** "the American culture"라고는 하지 않는다 **2** [U] activities relating to art, literature, music etc. || 미술·문학·음악 등과 관련된 활동. 예술. 문화(활동): *Boston is a good place for anyone who is interested in culture.* 보스턴은 예술 활동에 흥미를 가진 사람에게는 좋은 곳이다. **3 culture shock** the strange feelings that someone has when s/he visits a foreign country or a new place for the first time || 사람이 처음으로 외국이나 새로운 곳을 방문할 때 가지게 되는 낯선 감정. 문화적 충격 **4** [C, U] the process of growing BACTERIA for scientific use, or the bacteria produced by this || 과학적 용도로 세균을 성장시키는 과정, 또는 이렇게 배양된 세균. 세균의 배양. 배양균

cul·tured /'kʌltʃɚd/ *adj* intelligent, polite, and interested in art and music || 지적이고 예의바르며 미술이나 음악에 흥미를 가진. 교양 있는. 세련된: *a handsome cultured man* 잘생기고 세련된 남자

cum·ber·some /'kʌmbɚsəm/ *adj* **1** slow and difficult || 느리고 어려운. 번거로운. 성가신: *Getting a passport can be a cumbersome process.* 여권 발급은 번거로운 과정이 될 수 있다. **2** heavy and difficult to move or use || 움직이거나 사용하기에 무겁고 어려운. 거추장스러운: *cumbersome equipment* 거추장스러운 장비

cu·mu·la·tive /'kyumyələtɪv, -,leɪ-/ *adj* increasing gradually as more of something is added or happens || 어떤 것이 더 추가되거나 일어남으로써 점점 더 증가하는. 누적되는. 점증적인: *the cumulative effect of air pollution* 대기 오염의 누적 효과 **– cumulatively** *adv*

cun·ning /'kʌnɪŋ/ *adj* good at deceiving people || 사람을 속이는 데 능숙한. 교활한. 간사한. 약삭빠른: *a cunning criminal* 교활한 범죄자 **– cunning** *n* [U] **– cunningly** *adv*

cup¹ /kʌp/ *n* **1** a small round container with a handle, used for drinking from, or the liquid it contains ‖ 마실 때 사용하는 손잡이가 달린 작고 둥근 용기나 이 용기가 담고 있는 액체. 잔. 한 잔(의 양): *a cup and saucer* 잔과 잔 받침 / *a cup of coffee* 커피 한 잔 **2** a unit for measuring liquids or dry foods, equal to half a PINT ‖ 반 파인트(분량)에 해당하는, 액체나 건조 식품을 측정하는 단위. 계량컵 한 컵: *Stir in a cup of flour.* 밀가루 한 컵을 넣어서 섞어라. **3** a specially shaped container that is given as a prize in a competition ‖ 시합에서 상으로 주어지는 특별한 모양의 용기. 우승컵 **4** something round and hollow that is shaped like a cup ‖ 컵 같은 모양의 둥글고 속이 빈 물건. 잔 모양의 것: *the cup of a flower* 꽃 받침

cup² *v* **-pped, -pping** [T] to form your hands into the shape of a cup ‖ 손을 컵 모양으로 만들다. 잔 모양으로 오므리다: *Greta cupped her hands around the mug.* 그레타는 머그잔을 양손으로 감쌌다.

cup·board /'kʌbəd/ *n* a piece of furniture for storing clothes, plates, food etc., that is usually attached to a wall and has shelves and a door ‖ 보통 벽에 붙어 있고 선반과 문이 달린, 옷·접시·음식 등을 보관하는 데에 쓰는 가구. 붙박이장. 벽장. 찬장

cup·cake /'kʌpkeɪk/ *n* a small round cake ‖ 작고 둥근 케이크. 컵케이크

cur·a·ble /'kyʊrəbəl/ *adj* able to be cured ‖ 치료될 수 있는. 치료 가능한: *a curable disease* 치료할 수 있는 병 — opposite INCURABLE

cu·ra·tor /'kyʊ,reɪtə, -ətə, kyʊ'reɪtə/ *n* someone who is in charge of a MUSEUM ‖ 박물관[미술관]의 책임을 맡고 있는 사람. 전시 책임자. 큐레이터

curb¹ /kəb/ *n* the edge of a street between where cars can drive and where people can walk ‖ 차가 주행할 수 있는 곳과 사람들이 걸어다닐 수 있는 곳 사이의 길 가장자리. (보도의)연석 (緣石): *Larry tripped on the curb.* 래리는 연석에 걸려 넘어졌다.

curb
curb
drain

curb² *v* [T] to control or limit something ‖ 어떤 것을 통제하거나 제한하다. 어떤 것을 구속하다. 억제하다: *Doctors are trying to curb the spread of the disease.* 의사들은 병의 확산을 억제하기 위해 노력하고 있다.

curd /kəd/ *n* [C usually plural] the thick substance that forms in milk when it becomes sour ‖ 우유가 상할 때 그 안에 형성되는 걸쭉한 물질. 응유(凝乳)

cur·dle /'kədl/ *v* [I, T] to become thicker or form CURDS, or to make a liquid do this ‖ 더 걸쭉해지거나 응유가 되다, 또는 액체를 이런 식으로 굳게 만들다. 응고하다[시키다]: *The milk got too warm and curdled.* 그 우유는 너무 데워져서 응고되었다.

cure¹ /kyʊə/ *v* [T] **1** to make an injury or illness better, so that the person who was sick is well ‖ 부상이나 병을 호전시켜 아팠던 사람이 좋아지다. …을 치료하다. 병을 고치다. 건강을 회복하다: *Penicillin will cure most infections.* 페니실린은 대부분의 전염병을 치료해 줄 것이다. — compare HEAL **2** to solve a problem or improve a bad situation ‖ 문제를 해결하거나 나쁜 상황을 개선하다: *No one can completely cure unemployment.* 누구도 실업 문제를 완전하게 해결할 수는 없다. **3** to preserve food, leather etc. by drying it, hanging it in smoke, or covering it with salt ‖ 식품·가죽 등을 건조시키되[연기 속에 매달아, 소금에 절여서] 보존하다

cure² *n* **1** a medicine or medical treatment that can cure an illness or disease ‖ 병을 치료할 수 있는 약제나 의학적 치료. 치료(법): *a cure for cancer* 암 치료 **2** something that solves a problem or improves a bad situation ‖ 문제를 풀거나 나쁜 상황을 개선시키는 것. 해결책: *There's no easy cure for poverty.* 가난을 해결하는 쉬운 방법은 없다.

cur·few /'kəfyu/ *n* a time during which everyone must stay indoors ‖ 모든 사람들이 집안에 머물러 있어야 하는 시간(대). 통행 금지(시간): *The government imposed a curfew from sunset to sunrise.* 정부는 일몰 때부터 일출 때까지 통행 금지령을 내렸다.

cu·ri·o /'kyʊri,oʊ/ *n* a small object that is valuable because it is old, beautiful, or rare ‖ 오래되거나 아름답거나 희귀해서 가치가 있는 작은 물체. 골동품. 진귀한 물건

cu·ri·os·i·ty /,kyʊri'ɑsəti/ *n* [singular, U] the desire to know something or to learn about something ‖ 어떤 것을 알고자 하거나 배우고자 하는 욕구. 호기심: *Children have a natural curiosity about the world around them.* 아이들은 그들 주변의 세계에 대한 타고난 호기심이 있

다. / *Just out of curiosity, how old are you?* 그저 호기심에서 묻는데, 나이가 어떻게 돼요? / *I just had to satisfy my curiosity, so I opened the box.* 나는 호기심을 이기지 못하고 그 상자를 열어 보았다.

cu·ri·ous /ˈkyʊriəs/ *adj* **1** wanting to know or learn about something ‖ 어떤 것에 대해 알거나 배우고 싶은. 호기심이 있는: *We were curious about what was going on next door.* 우리는 옆집에서 무슨 일이 일어나고 있는지 궁금했다. / *I was curious to see how it worked.* 나는 그것이 어떻게 작동되는지 알고 싶었다. **2** strange or unusual in a way that makes you interested ‖ 흥미가 일도록 이상하거나 진귀한. 호기심을 끄는. 진기한. 기묘한: *a curious noise* 이상한 소리 / *Joe's remark had a curious effect on Peter.* 조의 말은 피터의 호기심을 끌었다. – **curiously** *adv*

curl¹ /kɚl/ *n* **1** a piece of hair that hangs down in a curved shape ‖ 구부러진 모양으로 늘어지는 머리카락. 곱슬곱슬한 머리칼: *a little girl with blonde curls* 금발의 곱슬머리인 작은 소녀 **2** something that forms a curved shape ‖ 구부러진 모양을 이루는 것. 똘똘 만 것: *chocolate curls* 똘똘 말린 초콜릿 – **curly** *adj*

curl² *v* [I, T] **1** to form a curved shape, or to make something do this ‖ 구부러진 모양이 되거나 어떤 것을 구부러진 모양으로 되게 하다. 곱슬곱슬해지다. …을 곱슬곱슬하게 하다: *I don't know if I should curl my hair or leave it straight.* 머리를 말아야 할지 생머리로 놔둬야 할지 모르겠다. **2** to move while forming a curved shape, or to make something do this ‖ 구부러진 모양을 이루면서 움직이거나 움직이게 하다. 비틀(리)다. 소용돌이치(게 하)다: *Thick smoke curled from the chimney.* 진한 연기가 굴뚝에서 소용돌이치며 올라갔다.

curl up *phr v* [I] **1** to lie or sit with your arms and legs bent close to your body ‖ 팔과 다리를 몸에 가깝게 구부린 채 눕거나 앉다. 몸을 웅크리다[움츠리다]: *Pepe curled up on the couch to watch some TV.* 페페는 소파 위에서 몸을 웅크린 채 TV를 봤다. **2** if paper, leaves etc. curl up, their edges become curved and point up ‖ 종이·잎 등의 가장자리가 구부러지며 위를 향하게 되다. 끝(부분)이 오그라들다: *The old photos had begun to curl up and turn yellow.* 낡은 사진들의 끝이 오그라들고 색이 누렇게 변하기 시작했다.

curl·er /ˈkɚlɚ/ *n* [C usually plural] a small metal or plastic tube that hair is wound around in order to curl it ‖ 머리를 곱슬거리게 하려고 마는 금속이나 플라스틱 관. 컬 핀[클립]

curl·ing i·ron /ˈkɚlɪŋ ˌaɪɚn/ *n* a piece of electrical equipment that you heat and use to curl your hair ‖ 머리를 곱슬거리게 하기 위해 열을 가하여 사용하는 전기 기구. 고대기

cur·rant /ˈkɚənt, ˈkʌr-/ *n* a small round red or black BERRY, usually dried ‖ 주로 말린 상태의 작고 둥글며 붉거나 검은 장과(漿果). 건포도

cur·ren·cy /ˈkɚənsi, ˈkʌr-/ *n* **1** [C, U] the particular type of money that a country uses ‖ 한 국가에서 사용하는 특정 유형의 돈. 통화: *Polish currency* 폴란드 화폐 **2** [U] the state of being generally accepted or used ‖ 널리 수용되거나 쓰이는 상태. 통용. 유통: *Some of the songs had been in currency for a hundred years.* 어떤 노래들은 백년 동안이나 불리어 왔다.

cur·rent¹ /ˈkɚənt, ˈkʌr-/ *adj* happening or being used right now, but not likely to last a long time ‖ 바로 지금 일어나거나 사용되지만 오래 지속될 것 같진 않은. 지금의. 현재의. 통용하고 있는: *Sales for the current year* (=this year) *are low.* 금년은 판매가 저조하다. / *Denise's current boyfriend* 데니스의 현재 남자 친구 —see usage note at NEW

current² *n* **1** a continuous movement of water or air in a particular direction ‖ 물이나 공기의 특정 방향으로의 끊임없는 움직임. 흐름. 유동: *There's a strong current in the river.* 강의 물살이 세다. **2** a flow of electricity through a wire ‖ 전선을 통한 전기의 흐름. 전류: *Turn off the electric current before changing that fuse.* 그 퓨즈를 교체하기 전에 전원을 차단해라.

cur·rent·ly /ˈkɚəntli/ *adv* at the present time ‖ 현재. 지금은: *She's currently studying in Japan.* 그녀는 현재 일본에서 공부하고 있다.

cur·ric·u·lum /kəˈrɪkyələm/ *n, plural* **curricula** /-kyələ/ *or* **curriculums** all of the subjects that are taught at a school, college etc. ‖ 학교·대학 등에서 배우는 모든 과목. 커리큘럼. 교과 과정

cur·ry /ˈkɚi, ˈkʌri/ *n* [C, U] a mixture of SPICEs that is used for giving food a hot taste ‖ 음식에 매운 맛을 가미하는 데에 쓰는 향신료의 혼합물. 카레

curse¹ /kɚs/ *v* **1** [I] to swear because you are very angry ‖ 매우 화나서 욕하다:

We heard him cursing at the lawn mower because it wouldn't start. 우리는 그가 작동하지 않는 잔디 깎는 기계에 대고 욕하는 소리를 들었다. **2** [T] to say or think bad things about someone or something ‖ 사람이나 사물에 대해 나쁘게 말하거나 생각하다. 모독하다. 악담하다: *I cursed myself for not buying the car insurance sooner.* 나는 자동차 보험에 빨리 가입하지 않은 스스로를 책망했다. **3** to ask God or a magical power to do something bad to someone ‖ 남에게 나쁜 일이 일어나게 해 달라고 신이나 마술적인 힘에 요청하다. 저주하다

curse² *n* **1** a swear word, or words, that you say because you are very angry ‖ 매우 화가 나서 말한 욕(설) **2** a word or sentence that asks God or a magical power to do something bad to someone ‖ 남에게 나쁜 일을 내려 달라고 신이나 마술적 힘에 요청하는 말이나 문장. 저주 (의 말). 주문: *It feels like someone has put a curse on my career.* 누군가 내 인생을 저주한 것 같다.

cursed /kɜːst/ *adj* **be cursed with** to suffer because of a problem that you have and cannot get rid of ‖ 벗어날 수 없는 문제를 지니고 있기 때문에 고통받다. 나쁜 습관 등을 갖고 있다. …으로 시달리다: *Randy's cursed with a bad back.* 랜디는 허리가 좋지 않아 시달리고 있다.

cur·sor /ˈkɜːsɚ/ *n* a mark that you can move on a computer screen that shows you where you are writing ‖ 컴퓨터 스크린상에서 글을 쓰고 있는 위치를 나타내는 움직일 수 있는 표시. 커서

cur·so·ry /ˈkɜːsəri/ *adj* done quickly without much attention to detail ‖ 세심한 부분까지 많은 주의를 기울이지 않고 신속하게 이루어진. 황급한. 겉핥기의: *After a cursory glance/look at the menu, Grant ordered coffee.* 메뉴를 대충 본 다음 그랜트는 커피를 주문했다.

curt /kɜːt/ *adj* using very few words when you speak to someone, in a way that seems rude ‖ 남에게 말할 때, 무례해 보일 만큼 거의 말을 하지 않는. 무뚝뚝한. 퉁명스러운 – **curtly** *adv*

cur·tail /kɚˈteɪl/ *v* [T] FORMAL to reduce or limit something ‖ 어떤 것을 줄이거나 제한하다. …을 단축[축소]하다: *new laws to curtail immigration* 이민을 제한하는 새로운 법률 – **curtailment** *n* [U]

cur·tain /ˈkɜːtn/ *n* a large piece of hanging cloth that can be pulled across a window, stage, or SHOWER ‖ 창문[무대, 샤워룸]에 걸려 있어 한쪽에서 다른 쪽으로 잡아 당길 수 있게 되어 있는 커다란 천. 커튼: *Can you pull/draw the curtains for me?* (=close the curtains) 커튼 좀 쳐 줄래?

curt·sy, curtsey /ˈkɜːtsi/ *v* [I] if a woman curtsies to someone, she bends her knees and puts one foot forward as a sign of respect ‖ 여성이 존경의 표시로 무릎을 꿇고 한 발을 내밀다. …에게 무릎을 굽혀 인사[절]하다 – **curtsy** *n*

curve¹ /kɜːv/ *n* **1** a line that bends like part of circle ‖ 원의 일부처럼 구부러진 선. 곡선: *a sharp curve in the road* 도로의 급커브 **2** a method of giving grades based on how a student's work compares with other students' work ‖ 한 학생의 (학업)성취도를 다른 학생들의 성취도와 비교를 통해 점수를 주는 방식. 상대 평가

curve² *v* [I, T] to bend or move in the shape of a curve, or to make something do this ‖ 곡선 형태로 구부러지거나 움직이다, 또는 어떤 것을 이렇게 만들다. …을 [이] 굽히다[휘다]: *a golf ball curving through the air* 공중에서 휘면서 날아가는 골프 공 – **curved** *adj* – **curvy** *adj*

cush·ion¹ /ˈkʊʃən/ *n* **1** a soft, usually square PILLOW that you put on a chair, floor etc. so you can sit or lie on it to make yourself more comfortable ‖ 의자·바닥 등에 놓고 그 위에 보다 더 편히 앉거나 누울 수 있는, 푹신하고 보통 사각형인 베개. 쿠션. 방석 **2** something, especially money, that prevents you from being affected by a situation immediately ‖ 어떤 상황에 의해 즉각 영향 받는 것을 막아 주는 것, 특히 돈. …을 완화시키는 것. 저축. 비상금: *If I lose my job, my savings will provide a cushion for a while.* 내가 직장을 잃는 다 해도 저축해 놓은 돈으로 얼마 동안은 버틸 것이다.

cushion² *v* [T] to reduce the effects of something unpleasant ‖ 불쾌한 일의 영향을 줄이다. …의 영향을 약화시키다: *This time, James wasn't there to cushion the blow.* (=help make a bad situation less bad) 이번에는 바람막이가 해줄 제임스가 그 자리에 없었다.

cuss /kʌs/ *v* [I] INFORMAL to use offensive language; swear ‖ 모욕적인 말을 하다. 악담[저주]하다; 욕하다

cuss sb out *phr v* [T] INFORMAL to swear and shout at someone because you are very angry ‖ 매우 화가 나서 남에게 욕하고 소리치다

cus·tard /ˈkʌstɚd/ *n* a soft baked mixture of milk, eggs, and sugar ‖ 우유·

달걀·설탕의 혼합물을 구워 낸 부드러운
것. 커스터드

cus·to·di·an /kəˈstoʊdiən/ *n* someone
who takes care of a public building ‖ 공
공 건물을 관리하는 사람. 관리인[자]

cus·to·dy /ˈkʌstədi/ *n* [U] **1** the right to
take care of a child, given by a court
when the child''s parents are legally
separated ‖ 아이의 부모가 법적으로 헤어
질 때, 법원이 부여한 아이를 돌볼 권리.
양육권: *My ex-wife has custody of the
kids*. 나의 전처가 아이들의 양육권을 갖고
있다. / *The judge awarded us joint
custody*. (=both parents will take care
of the child) 판사는 우리에게 공동 양육
권을 부여했다. **2 in custody** being kept
in prison by the police until going to
court ‖ 기소되기 전까지 경찰에 의해 구금
된: *Two robbery suspects are being held
in custody*. 두 명의 강도 용의자들이 현
재 구금되어 있다. **– custodial**
/kəˈstoʊdiəl/ *adj*

cus·tom /ˈkʌstəm/ *n* [C, U] something
that is done by people in a particular
society because it is traditional ‖ 특정 사
회에서 전통이기 때문에 사람들이 하는
일. 관습. 풍속. 관례: *the custom of
throwing rice at weddings* 결혼식에서 쌀
을 던지는 풍습 / *Chinese customs and
culture* 중국의 관습과 문화 —see also
CUSTOMS —compare HABIT —see usage
note at HABIT

cus·tom·ar·y /ˈkʌstəˌmɛri/ *adj*
something that is customary is normal
because it is the way it is usually done ‖
으레 행해지는 방식이기 때문에 정상적인.
관습에 따른. 통례의: *It is customary
for a local band to lead the parade*. 현
지 악단이 퍼레이드를 이끄는 것이 관례이
다. **– customarily** /ˌkʌstəˈmɛrəli/ *adv*

custom-built /ˌ.. ˈ./ *adj* a custom-
built car, machine etc. is built specially
for the person buying it ‖ 차·기계 등이
해당 구매자를 위해서 특별히 제작된. 주
문 생산한. 맞춤인

cus·tom·er /ˈkʌstəmɚ/ *n* someone who
buys goods or services from a store,
company etc. ‖ 가게·회사 등에서 상품이
나 용역을 사는 사람. 손님. 고객: *Dow is
one of our biggest customers*. 다우는 우
리의 최대 고객 중 한 명이다.

USAGE NOTE customer

When you go out to buy things, you
are a **shopper**; but when you buy
goods from a particular store, you are
that store's **customer**: *The mall is*

---

full of shoppers. / *We don't get many
customers in the evenings*. If you are
paying someone such as a lawyer for
professional services, you are a
client, but if you are seeing a doctor
you are a **patient**. If you are staying
in a hotel, you are a **guest**.
물건을 사러 나가는 사람은 **shopper**
이다; 그러나 특정 가게에서 상품을 구
입할 때는 그 가게의 **customer**가 된
다 : 그 쇼핑몰은 쇼핑객으로 가득 차
있다./저녁에는 손님들이 많이 없습니다.
전문적인 서비스에 대한 대가로 변호사
등에게 돈을 지불할 때, 그 사람은
client이지만 의사에게 진찰하러 간다
면, 그 때는 **patient**이며 호텔에 머무
를 때는 **guest**이다.

cus·tom·ize /ˈkʌstəˌmaɪz/ *v* [T] to
change something to make it more
useful for you, or to make it look special
or unusual ‖ 고객에게 더 유용하게 하기
위해, 또는 특별하거나 독특해 보이게 하
려고 물건을 변화시키다. 맞춤으로 만들
다: *a customized software package* 제품
에 맞춰 끼워 파는[주는] 소프트웨어

custom-made /ˌ..ˈ./ *adj* a custom-
made shirt, pair of shoes, etc. is made
specially for the person buying it ‖ 셔츠·
신발 등이 해당 구매자를 위해 특별히 제
작된. 주문하여 만든. 맞춤인

cus·toms /ˈkʌstəmz/ *n* [plural] the
place where your bags are checked for
illegal goods when you go into a country
‖ 입국시 불법 소지물을 검사하는 곳. 세
관: *It shouldn't take too long to clear
customs*. (=be allowed into a country
after being checked) 세관을 통과하는 데
에는 그리 오랜 시간이 걸리진 않을 거야.

cut¹ /kʌt/ *v* **cut, cut, cutting**
1 ▸USE KNIFE/SCISSORS◂ 칼/가위를 사용
하다◂ [I, T] to use a knife, scissors etc.
to divide something into pieces, remove
a piece from something, open
something etc. ‖ 물건을 여러 조각으로 나
누며 조각을 잘라내고 개봉하기 위해 칼·
가위 등을 사용하다. 자르다: *Abby, go cut
Grandpa a piece of pie*. 애비, 가서 할아
버지께 파이 한 조각 잘라 드려라. / *Cut
some cheese into cubes and add them
to the salad*. 치즈를 네모지게 잘라 샐러
드에 넣어라. / *Uncle Bert used a saw to
cut a hole in the ice*. 버트 삼촌은 톱으로
얼음에 구멍을 냈다.
2 ▸REDUCE◂ 줄이다◂ [T] to reduce the
amount of something, especially
something such as time or money ‖ 특히
시간이나 금액 등을 줄이다: *The company*

had to close several factories to cut costs. 그 회사는 비용을 절감하기 위해 몇 몇 공장을 폐쇄해야 했다. / *The number of soldiers had to be cut in half.* 군인들은 절반으로 수를 줄여야 했다.

3 ▶MAKE SHORTER 짧게 만들다◀ [T] to make something shorter using a knife, scissors etc. ‖ 칼·가위 등을 사용하여 물건을 짧게 하다. …을 잘라내다: *A neighbor boy cuts our grass once a week.* 우리 잔디는 일주일에 한 번씩 이웃집 소년이 깎아 준다. / *Where did you get your hair cut?* 너 머리 어디서 잘랐니?

4 ▶INJURE 상처를 입히다◀ [T] to injure yourself or someone else using a sharp object such as a knife, so that you start bleeding ‖ 칼 등의 날카로운 물체로 자신이나 남을 다치게 하여 피가 나기 시작하다. …을 베다: *He cut his finger on a piece of broken glass.* 그는 깨진 유리 조각에 손가락을 베었다. / *Sarah says her head got cut open when she fell.* 새라는 떨어져서 자기 머리가 깨졌다고 말한다.

5 cut sb free/loose to cut something such as a rope or metal in order to let someone escape ‖ 남이 탈출할 수 있도록 밧줄이나 금속 등을 끊다. (밧줄·금속 등을 끊어) …을 자유롭게 해주다: *Firemen were carefully cutting the driver free from the wreckage.* 소방관들은 조심스럽게 파괴된 차에서 운전사를 빼내고 있었다.

6 cut class/school to not go to a class or to school when you ought to ‖ 출석해야 할 때 수업을 듣지 않거나 학교에 가지 않다. 수업을/학교를 빠지다[빼먹다]

7 cut corners to do something in a way that is not as good as it should be, in order to save time, effort, or money ‖ 시간[노력, 돈]을 아끼려고 규정보다 좋지 않게 무엇을 하다. 일을 날림으로 하다: *Parents are worried that the city is cutting corners in education.* 부모들은 시의 교육이 제대로 이루어지지 않는 것에 대해 걱정한다.

8 cut sth short to end something earlier than you had planned to end it ‖ 계획했던 것보다 어떤 것을 빨리 마치다. …을 급히 끝나게 하다. 조기 중단시키다: *His career was cut short by a back injury.* 그는 허리 부상으로 예상보다 일찍 활동을 중단했다.

9 cut a record/CD/album to record music to be sold to the public ‖ 대중에게 팔기 위한 음악을 녹음하다. 음반을 취입하다

SPOKEN PHRASES

10 cut it/that out! used in order to tell someone to stop doing something that is annoying you ‖ 남에게 귀찮게 굴지 말라고 말하는 데에 쓰여. 그만해. 닥쳐: *Cut that out, you two, or you'll go to your rooms.* 너희들 그만 좀 해, 안 그러면 각자 방으로 보내 버릴 거야.

11 cut sb some slack to allow someone to do something without criticizing him/her or making it more difficult ‖ 비난하거나 더 어렵게 만들지 않고 남이 하는 일을 허용하다. …에게 여유[기회]를 주다: *He's only been here two weeks! Cut him some slack – he'll learn.* 그는 여기에 온지 고작 2주 됐어! 그에게 시간을 좀 주면 곧 배우게 될 거야.

12 cut the crap an impolite way of telling someone to talk only about what is important, instead of wasting time on other things ‖ 다른 것들에 시간 낭비하지 말고 오직 중요한 것만 얘기하라고 남에게 무례하게 말하는 방식. 헛소리 집어 치워: *Cut the crap and tell me what you really mean, Nicholas.* 헛소리 그만하고 정말 하고 싶은 말을 해 봐, 니콜라스.

13 not cut it to not be good enough ‖ 충분히 좋지는 않다: *Barry's just not cutting it as a journalist.* 배리는 언론인으로서 아직 좀 부족하다.

14 cut it close to leave yourself only just enough time or money to do something ‖ 자신에게 어떤 것을 간신히 할 시간이나 돈만 남기다. 아슬아슬하게 하다: *He cut it pretty close but he made it to the airport all right.* 꽤 아슬아슬했지만 그는 제때 공항에 도착했다.

cut across sth *phr v* [T] **1** to go across an area rather than around it ‖ 어떤 지역을 에둘러 가기보다는 가로질러 가다. …을 가로지르다: *Sherman cut across three lanes of traffic to the exit.* 셔먼은 출구까지 세 차선을 단숨에 가로질렀다. **2** if a problem or feeling cuts across different groups of people, they are all affected by it ‖ 어떤 문제나 정서가 다양한 집단의 사람들에게 두루 영향을 미치다

cut back *phr v* [I, T **cut** sth ↔ **back**] to reduce the amount, size, cost etc. of something ‖ 어떤 것의 양·크기·비용 등을 줄이다. 절감[삭감]하다: *The company is attempting to cut back on expenses.* 그

회사는 비용을 절감하려 하고 있다.

cut down *phr v* **1** [I, T **cut** sth ↔ **down**] to reduce the amount of something, especially something you do, eat, buy etc. ∥ 특히 행하거나 먹거나 사는 것 등의 양을 줄이다: *I'm trying to cut down on my drinking.* 나는 음주를 줄이려고 애쓰고 있다. **2** [T **cut** sth ↔ **down**] to cut the main stem of a tree so that it falls to the ground ∥ 나무의 줄기를 베어 땅에 쓰러뜨리다: *Beautiful old oaks had been cut down to build houses.* 집을 지으려고 오래된 아름다운 떡갈나무들을 베었다.

cut in *phr v* [I] **cut in front/cut in line** to unfairly go in front of other people who are waiting to do something ∥ 어떤 것을 하려고 기다리는 다른 사람들 앞으로 부당하게 끼어들다. 새치기하다. 추월하다: *Some idiot cut in front of me on the freeway and almost caused an accident.* 어떤 멍청한 놈이 고속도로에서 날 추월해서 하마터면 사고날 뻔했어.

cut off *phr v* [T] **1** [**cut** sth ↔ **off**] to remove a piece from something using a sharp tool such as a knife ∥ 칼 등의 날카로운 도구를 사용하여 물체의 일부분을 제거하다. …을 잘라내다: *Cut the top off a large ripe pineapple.* 잘 익은 큰 파인애플의 윗부분을 잘라내라. **2** [**cut** sth ↔ **off**] to stop the supply of something ∥ 어떤 것의 공급을 중단하다: *They're going to cut off our electricity if you don't pay that bill.* 네가 그 요금을 내지 않으면 전기 공급이 중단될 거야. **3** **be/get cut off** to be unable to finish talking to someone because something is wrong with the telephone connection ∥ 전화 연결에 문제가 있어서 대화를 끝까지 못하다. 통화 중에 전화가 끊기다 **4** [**cut** sb/sth ↔ **off**] to separate someone or something from other people or things, or to prevent them from going somewhere ∥ 사람이나 사물을 다른 사람들이나 사물로로부터 떼어 놓거나 어딘가로 가지 못하게 막다. …을 (…으로부터) 따돌리다. 고립시키다: *A heavy snowfall cut us off from the town.* 폭설로 인해 우리는 읍내로부터 고립되었다. **5** [**cut** sb **off**] to interrupt someone ∥ 남의 말을 끊다: *He cut her off in mid-sentence.* 그는 그녀가 말하는 도중에 끼어들었다.

cut out *phr v* **1** [T **cut** sth ↔ **out**] to remove a piece from something using a sharp tool such as a knife or scissors ∥ 칼이나 가위 등의 날카로운 도구를 사용하여 물체의 일부분을 제거하다. …을 잘라내다: *The children can cut star shapes out of colored paper.* 아이들은 색종이를 별 모양으로 자를 수 있다. **2** [I] if a motor cuts out, it stops working suddenly ∥ 모터가 갑자기 작동을 멈추다 **3** **not be cut out for/not be cut out to be** to not have the qualities that would make you suitable for a particular job or activity ∥ 특정한 일이나 활동에 적합한 자질을 갖추지 못하다: *I decided I wasn't really cut out to be a teacher.* 나는 교사가 될 자질이 정말 없다고 결론 내렸다.

cut sth ↔ **up** *phr v* [T] to cut something into smaller pieces ∥ 사물을 보다 작은 조각들로 자르다: *Cut up two carrots and three potatoes.* 당근 두 개와 감자 세 개를 썰어라.

cut² *n* **1** a wound that you get if a sharp object cuts your skin ∥ 날카로운 물체가 피부를 베어 생긴 상처. 베인 상처: *Luckily, I only got a few cuts and bruises.* 다행스럽게도 나는 몇 군데 베인 상처와 타박상만 입었다. **2** a reduction in the size, number, or amount of something ∥ 어떤 것의 크기[수, 양]의 줄어듦: *Workers were forced to take a cut in pay.* 노동자들은 강제로 임금을 삭감당했다. / *the promise of new tax cuts* 새로운 세금 인하 약속 **3** INFORMAL ⇨ HAIRCUT **4** INFORMAL someone's share of something, especially money ∥ 특히 돈에 대한 몫: *Everyone's taking a cut of the profits.* 모든 사람들이 배당된 이익을 챙기고 있다. **5** a piece of meat that is cut so you can cook it ∥ 요리할 수 있도록 자른 고깃덩어리: *tender cuts of beef* 소고기의 부드러운 부위 **6** the shape or style of your clothes ∥ 옷의 모양이나 스타일: *a well-cut suit* 잘 빠진 양복 **7** **be a cut above (the rest)** to be better than someone or something else ∥ 다른 사람이나 사물보다 더 낫다. 한 수 위다: *The movie is a cut above most made-for-TV films.* 그 영화는 대부분의 텔레비전용 영화보다 더 낫다.

cut and dried /ˌ. . ./ *adj* a situation that is cut and dried is certain to happen because it has already been planned or decided, and nothing can be done to change it ∥ 상황이 이미 계획되거나 결정되었기 때문에 일어날 것이 확실하며 이를 변화시키기 위해 할 수 있는 일이 아무 것도 없는. (말·행위 등이) 미리 준비[결정]되어 있는: *The outcome of the election is already cut and dried.* 선거 결과는 이미 결정적이다.

cut·back /ˈkʌtbæk/ *n* a reduction that is made in something such as the number of people in an organization or the amount of money spent by the government ‖ 조직의 인원수나 정부가 지출하는 금액 등의 축소: *a number of cutbacks in funding for public libraries* 수 차례에 걸친 공공 도서관 기금의 삭감

cute /kyut/ *adj* **1** cute people are attractive in the way they look or behave ‖ 생김새나 행동하는 방식이 매력적인. 귀여운. 깜직한: *What a cute little baby!* 정말 귀여운 어린애네! / *Tim is so cute.* 팀은 너무 귀여워 **2** cute things are attractive and pretty ‖ 사물이 매력적이고 예쁜. 멋진. 근사한: *That's a cute skirt.* 저 치마 멋지다. **3** smart in a way that can be rude ‖ 무례할 정도로 건방진: *Don't pay any attention to him; he's just trying to be cute.* 그에게 전혀 신경쓸 것 없어. 단지 뽐내려고 저러는 거야. ─ **cutely** *adv* ─ **cuteness** *n* [U] ─see usage note at BEAUTIFUL

cute·sy, cutesie /'kyutsi/ *adj* INFORMAL too pretty or smart in a way that is annoying ‖ 밉살스러울 정도로 너무 예쁘거나 영리한. 귀엽게[똑똑하게] 보이는: *a cutesy dress with a lot of frills* 주름 장식을 많이 달아 귀엽게 보이는 드레스

cu·ti·cle /'kyutɪkəl/ *n* the hard thin skin at the bottom of your FINGERNAILs ‖ 손톱 뿌리 쪽의 딱딱하고 얇은 피부

cut·ler·y /'kʌtˡləri/ *n* [U] knives, forks, and spoons ‖ 나이프와 포크 및 스푼

cut·let /'kʌtˡlɪt/ *n* a small piece of meat ‖ 작은 고기 조각. 얇게 저민 고기

cut·off /'kʌtɔf/ *n* a limit or level at which you must stop doing something ‖ 하던 일을 중단해야 하는 제한선이나 수준. 마감 시한. 통과 최저선: *The cutoff date for applying was June 3rd.* 응모 마감일은 6월 3일이었다.

cut·offs /'kʌtɔfs/ *n* [plural] a pair of SHORTS that you make by cutting off the legs of an old pair of pants ‖ 낡은 바지의 다리 부분을 잘라 만든 반바지

cut-rate /ˌ. '../, **cut-price** *adj* cheaper than the normal price ‖ 정상 가격보다 싼. 할인한. 할인 가격의: *cut-rate insurance* 할인된 보험료

cut·ter /'kʌtɚ/ *n* a tool that cuts things ‖ 물건을 자르는 도구. 절단기: *wire cutters* 전선 [철사]절단기 / *a cookie cutter* 쿠키 모양을 찍는 틀

cut-throat /'kʌtˈθroʊt/ *adj* willing to do anything to succeed ‖ 성공하기 위해 기꺼이 어떤 일이라도 하는. 필사적인. 격렬한: *the cutthroat competition of software companies* 소프트웨어 회사들 간의 죽기

살기식 경쟁

cut·ting /'kʌtɪŋ/ *adj* unkind and intended to upset someone ‖ 불친절하고 남을 화나게 하려는 의도의. 빈정거리는. 신랄한: *a cutting remark* 빈정거리는 말

cutting edge /ˌ.. '../ *n* **be at/on the cutting edge** to be working on the most advanced stage or development of something ‖ 어떤 것의 가장 진보한 단계나 발달한 상태에서 일하다. 최첨단의: *Her designs are at the cutting edge of fashion.* 그녀의 디자인은 패션의 최첨단에 서있다.

cy·a·nide /'saɪəˌnaɪd/ *n* [U] a very strong poison ‖ 매우 강한 독. 청산가리

cy·ber·ca·fé, cyber cafe /'saɪbɚˌkæfeɪ/ *n* a CAFE that has computers which are connected to the Internet for customers to use ‖ 인터넷을 연결한 컴퓨터를 갖춰 고객들이 이용할 수 있게 한 카페. 사이버[인터넷] 카페

cy·ber·crime, cyber crime /'saɪbɚˌkraɪm/ *n* [C,U] criminal activity that involves the use of computers or the Internet ‖ 컴퓨터나 인터넷 사용과 관련된 범죄 행위. 사이버[인터넷] 범죄

cy·ber·punk /'saɪbɚˌpʌŋk/ *n* [U] a character in stories about life in a future society in which computers are very important ‖ 컴퓨터가 매우 중요한 역할을 하는 미래 사회의 생활에 관한 이야기 속에 등장하는 인물

cy·ber·space /'saɪbɚˌspeɪs/ *n* [U] all the connections between computers in different places, considered as a real place where information, messages, pictures etc. exist ‖ 정보·메시지·사진 등이 있는 실제 장소로 여겨지는, 각기 다른 장소에 있는 컴퓨터들 간의 모든 연결망. 사이버 공간

cy·ber·stalk·ing /'saɪbɚˌstɔkɪŋ/ *n* [U] the illegal use of the Internet, E-MAIL, or other electronic communication systems to follow someone or threaten them ‖ 다른 사람 뒤를 쫓거나 위협하기 위해 인터넷[이 메일, 다른 전자 통신 시스템]을 불법 사용하기. 사이버 스토킹

cy·ber·ter·ror·ist /'saɪbɚˌtɛrərɪst/ *n* someone who uses the Internet to damage computer systems, especially for political purposes ‖ 특히 정치적 목적을 위해 인터넷을 이용하여 컴퓨터 시스템을 손상시키는 사람. 사이버 테러리스트

cy·cle /'saɪkəl/ *n* a number of related events that happen again and again in the same order ‖ 동일한 순서로 거듭 반복해서 일어나는 많은 연관된 사건들. 주기: *the life cycle of flowering plants* 개화

식물의 생명 주기
cy·clic /'saɪklɪk, 'sɪ-/, **cyclical**
/'saɪklɪkəl, 'sɪ-/ *adj* happening again
and again in a regular pattern ‖ 일정한
형태로 거듭하여 일어나는. 주기적인 –
cyclically *adv*
cy·clone /'saɪkloʊn/ *n* a strong wind
that moves in a circle ‖ 원을 그리며 움직
이는 강풍. 사이클론. 열대성 저기압 —
see usage note at WEATHER
cyl·in·der /'sɪləndɚ/ *n* **1** a shape,
object, or container with circular ends
and straight sides, such as a can ‖ 깡통
과 같이 끝부분이 둥글고 옆면이 일직선인
모양[물체, 용기]. (원)기둥. 원통 **2** the
hollow part of a car engine in which the
PISTON moves up and down ‖ 자동차 엔진
내에서 피스톤이 상하로 움직이는 비어 있
는 부분. (펌프·엔진의)실린더. 기통: *a
six-cylinder engine* 6기통 엔진
cy·lin·dri·cal /sə'lɪndrɪkəl/ *adj* in the
shape of a CYLINDER ‖ (원)기둥 모양의. 원
통형의
cym·bal /'sɪmbəl/ *n* a musical
instrument made of a round metal
plate, played by hitting it with a stick or
hitting two of them together ‖ 둥근 금속
판으로 만들어져 막대로 치거나 두 개를
서로 맞부딪쳐 연주하는 악기. 심벌즈
cyn·ic /'sɪnɪk/ *n* someone who believes

that people do things only to help
themselves and not to help other people
‖ 사람이란 자기 자신만을 돕기 위해 무엇
인가를 하며 타인을 돕지 않는 존재라 믿
는 사람. 냉소적인 사람: *Working in
politics has made Sheila a cynic.* 쉴라는
정치계에서 일하더니 냉소적인 사람이 되
었다. – **cynicism** /'sɪnə,sɪzəm/ *n* [U]
cyn·i·cal /'sɪnɪkəl/ *adj* unwilling to
believe that someone has good or
honest reasons for doing something ‖ 남
이 어떤 것을 하는 데 좋거나 정직한 이유
가 있다는 것을 믿으려 하지 않는. 냉소적
인: *Since her divorce she's become very
cynical about men.* 그녀는 이혼한 이후
로 남자에 대해 아주 냉소적이 되었다. –
cynically *adv*
cyst /sɪst/ *n* a small LUMP in someone's
body that grows and fills with liquid ‖ 액
체가 들어 차며 커지는 인체 내의 작은 혹.
낭포
czar /zɑr/ *n* **1** INFORMAL a government
official who is responsible for important
decisions in a particular area ‖ 특정 영
역에서 중대한 결정을 내릴 책임이 있는
정부 관료: *the President's drugs czar* 대
통령 직속 마약 단속 책임자 **2** a male
ruler of Russia before 1917 ‖ 1917년(러
시아 혁명) 이전에 러시아의 남성 통치자.
(제정 시대의) 러시아 황제. 차르

Dd

D, d /di/ **1** the fourth letter of the English alphabet ‖ 영어 알파벳의 넷째 자 **2** the number 500 in the system of ROMAN NUMERALS ‖ 로마 숫자 체계에서, 500

D /di/ *n* **1** a low grade on a test or piece of school work ‖ 시험이나 학업에서의 낮은 점수. 디(D): *a D in chemistry* 화학 과목의 D학점 **2** [C, U] the second note in the musical SCALE of C, or the musical KEY based on this note ‖ 다 장조에서의 두 번째 음이나 이 음을 기조로 한 조(調). 라 음. 라 조

d. the abbreviation of died ‖ died의 약어: *d.1937* 1937년 사망

d /d/ **1** the short form of WOULD ‖ would 의 단축형: *Ask her if she'd* (=she would) *like to go with us.* 그녀가 우리와 같이 가고 싶어 하는지 물어 봐라. **2** the short form of HAD ‖ had의 단축형: *If I'd* (=I had) *only known you were there!* 네가 거기 있었다는 것만 알았어도!

D.A. *n* the abbreviation of DISTRICT ATTORNEY ‖ district attorney의 약어

dab¹ /dæb/ *n* a small amount of a substance ‖ 어떤 물질의 소량. 조금. 약간: *a dab of butter* 버터 약간

dab² *v* **-bbed, -bbing** [I, T] **1** to quickly and lightly touch something several times in order to dry it ‖ 건조시키기 위해 어떤 것을 빠르고 가볍게 몇 번 치다. …을 가볍게[토닥토닥] 두드리다: *Emily dabbed at her eyes with a handkerchief.* 에밀리는 손수건으로 눈물을 가볍게 찍어냈다. **2** [T] to quickly put a small amount of a substance onto something ‖ 소량의 물질을 어떤 것 위에 빨리 바르다. 살짝 칠하다: *She dabbed some suntan lotion onto her cheeks.* 그녀는 약간의 선탠로션을 뺨에 살짝 발랐다.

dab

dab·ble /'dæbəl/ *v* [I] to do something or be involved in something in a way that is not serious ‖ 깊이 빠지지 않고서 어떤 일을 하거나 어떤 일에 관계하다. 취미삼아 …을 조금 해보다. …에 손대 보다: *My husband dabbles in art.* 내 남편은 취미삼아 미술을 한다.

dachs·hund /'dɑkshʊnt, -hʊnd/ *n* a small dog with short legs and a long body ‖ 다리가 짧고 몸이 긴 작은 개. 닥스훈트

dad /dæd/, **daddy** /'dædi/ *n* INFORMAL father ‖ 아빠

daf·fo·dil /'dæfə,dɪl/ *n* a tall yellow flower that appears in early spring ‖ 초봄에 피는 키가 큰 노란색의 꽃. 나팔수선화

dag·ger /'dægɚ/ *n* a short pointed knife used as a weapon ‖ 짧고 끝이 뾰족한 무기용 칼. 단검[도]. 비수

dai·ly /'deɪli/ *adj* **1** happening, done, or produced every day ‖ 날마다 일어나는[행해지는, 생산되는]. 매일의. 일간의: *daily flights to Miami* 매일 취항하는 마이애미행 항공편 / *a daily newspaper* 일간 신문 **2** relating to a single day ‖ 하루에 관계된: *a daily rate of pay* 일당(日當) **3** daily life the things you do every day ‖ 매일 하는 일. 일과. 일상: *the weather and its effect on daily life* 날씨 및 일상생활에 날씨가 미치는 영향 **–daily** *adv*

dain·ty /'deɪnti/ *adj* small, pretty, and delicate ‖ 작고 예쁘며 섬세한. 날씬하고 가냘픈: *a dainty china doll* 날씬하고 가냘픈 중국 인형 **–daintily** *adv*

dair·y /'dɛri/ *n* **1** a place on a farm where milk is kept and butter and cheese are made ‖ 농장의 우유를 저장하고 버터와 치즈를 만드는 장소. 우유 가공소. 낙농장 **2** a company that buys and sells milk, butter etc. ‖ 우유와 버터 등을 사고 파는 회사. 유제품 판매소[회사] **3** **dairy products** milk and foods made from milk, such as butter, cheese, or YOGURT ‖ 버터[치즈, 요구르트]등의 우유로 만드는 유제품. 낙농제품

dai·sy /'deɪzi/ *n* a white flower with a bright yellow center ‖ 중심부가 연한 노란색인 흰 꽃. 데이지

dally /'dæli/ *v* [I] OLD-FASHIONED to move slowly or waste time ‖ 천천히 움직이거나 시간을 낭비하다. 빈둥거리다. 꾸물거리다: *children dallying on their way to school* 꾸물거리며 학교에 가는 중인 아이들

dal·ma·tian /dæl'meɪʃən/ *n* a dog with white fur and small black spots ‖ 흰 털에 작고 검은 점이 있는 개. 달마시안

dam¹ /dæm/ *n* a wall built across a river

in order to make a lake behind it or to produce electricity ‖ 뒷편에 호수를 만들거나 전력을 생산하기 위해 강을 가로질러 세운 벽. 댐. 둑

dam² v **-mmed, -mming** [T] to build a dam across a river ‖ 강을 가로질러 댐을 건설하다.

dam sth ↔ **up** *phr v* [T] to stop the flow of a stream, river etc. ‖ 시내·강 등의 흐름을 막다. 댐으로 …의 흐름을 막다: *Falling rocks have dammed up the creek.* 낙석(落石)이 지류[시내]를 막아 버렸다.

dam·age¹ /'dæmɪdʒ/ *n* [U] **1** physical harm done to something, so that it is broken or injured ‖ 깨지거나 부상을 입도록 어떤 것에 가해지는 물리적 위해. 손상. 손해: *The tests show some brain/liver damage.* 검사 결과 약간의 뇌[간] 손상이 있다. / *Was there any damage to your car?* 당신 차에 어떤 피해[손상]가 있습니까? / *The earthquake caused serious/severe damage to the freeway system.* 지진 때문에 고속도로 체계가 심하게 망가졌다[훼손되었다]. / *Don't worry, the kids can't do any damage.* 걱정하지 마, 아이들은 아무 것도 망가뜨릴 수 없어. **2** a bad effect on someone or something ‖ 사람이나 사물에 대한 나쁜 영향. 손상. 훼손: *the damage to Symon's reputation* 사이먼에 대한 명예 훼손 —see also DAMAGES

damage² v [T] **1** to physically harm someone or something ‖ 사람이나 사물에 물리적으로 해를 입히다. 손상하다. 해치다: *The storm damaged the tobacco crop.* 폭풍으로 인해 담배 수확이 피해를 입었다. **2** to have a bad effect on someone or something ‖ 사람이나 사물에 대해 나쁜 영향을 끼치다. 손상시키다. 훼손하다: *The scandal has badly damaged his ability to control Congress.* 그 스캔들로[추문으로] 인해 그의 의회 장악력이 심하게 손상되었다. **– damaging** *adj*

dam·ag·es /'dæmɪdʒɪz/ *n* [plural] LAW money that someone must pay to someone else for harming that person or his/her property ‖ 사람이나 재산에 입힌 피해에 대해 상대방에게 지불해야 하는 돈. 손해 배상금: *The court ordered her to pay $2000 in damages.* 법원은 그녀에게 2,000달러의 손해 배상금을 지급하라고 명령했다.

dame /deɪm/ *n* OLD-FASHIONED a woman ‖ 여성

dam·mit /'dæmɪt/ *interjection* NONSTANDARD said when you are annoyed or angry ‖ 성가시거나 화날 때에 쓰여. 제기랄. 젠장. 빌어먹을: *Hurry up, dammit!* 서둘러라, 젠장!

damn¹ /dæm/ *adj* SPOKEN OFFENSIVE said when you are angry or annoyed about something ‖ 어떤 것에 대해 화나거나 성가실 때에 쓰여: *Turn off that damn TV!* 그 빌어먹을 텔레비전 좀 꺼!

damn² *adv* SPOKEN OFFENSIVE **1** used in order to emphasize something ‖ 어떤 일을 강조할 때에 쓰여: *We're damn lucky we got here ahead of the storm.* 폭풍이 몰아치기 전에 이곳에 도착하다니 우린 정말 운이 좋다. **2 damn well** used in order to emphasize how determined or sure you are about something ‖ 어떤 일에 대한 단호함이나 확신의 정도를 강조하는 데에 쓰여: *He knows damn well he shouldn't drive my car.* 그는 내 차를 운전해서는 안 된다는 것을 확실히 알고 있다.

damn³ *interjection* SPOKEN OFFENSIVE said when you are annoyed or disappointed ‖ 성가시거나 실망했을 때에 쓰여. 제기랄. 젠장. 빌어먹을: *Damn! I forgot my wallet!* 젠장, 지갑을 깜빡했네!

damn⁴ *n* SPOKEN OFFENSIVE **not give a damn** said in order to emphasize that you do not care at all about something ‖ 어떤 것에 대해 전혀 신경 쓰지 않는다는 것을 강조하는 데 쓰여: *I don't give a damn if he's sorry!* 그가 미안하든 말든 신경 안 써!

damn⁵ v [T] **damn it/you/sb etc.** SPOKEN OFFENSIVE said when you are very angry ‖ 매우 화가 났을 때에 쓰여. 제기랄. 젠장. 빌어먹을: *Damn it! This is the third time those kids have broken the window.* 빌어먹을! 그 애들이 유리창 깨뜨린 게 이번이 세 번째야.

damned¹ /dæmd/ *adj* SPOKEN OFFENSIVE **1** ⇨ DAMN² **2 I'll be damned** said when you are surprised ‖ 놀랐을 때에 쓰여. 정말 놀라워[놀랐어]: *Well, I'll be damned! When did you get here, Tom?* 이런, 정말 놀랐어. 너 언제 이곳에 왔니, 톰? **3 damned if** used in order to emphasize that you do not want something to happen, or that you do not know something ‖ 어떤 일이 일어나기를 바라지 않거나 어떤 일을 모른다는 것을 강조하는 데에 쓰여. …이면 손에 장을 지진다. 어떤 일이 있어도 …않다: *I'll be damned if I'll sleep on the floor!* 내가 바닥에서 자면 손에 장을 지진다! / *Damned if I know!* (=I don't know) (절대로)나는 모른다[내가 알면 손에 장을 지진다]. **4 damned if you do, damned if you**

don't used in a situation where the result will be bad whether or not you do something ‖ 어떤 일을 하든 안 하든 나쁜 결과가 발생할 상황에서 쓰여. **5 be damned** to be punished by God after your death by being sent to HELL ‖ 사후에 지옥에 감으로써 신에게 벌을 받다.

damned² *adv* SPOKEN ⇨ DAMN²

damn·est, damndest /'dæmdɪst/ *adj* SPOKEN **1** said when you think something is very surprising or strange ‖ 어떤 일이 매우 놀랍거나 이상하다고 생각할 때에 쓰여. 아주 별다른[놀라운]: *It was the damnedest thing I ever saw!* 그것은 내가 이제껏 본 것 중 가장 기이했어! **2 do your damnedest** to try as hard as you can to achieve something ‖ 어떤 것을 달성하기 위해 할 수 있는 최대한의 노력을 하다.

damn·ing /'dæmɪŋ/ *adj* proving or showing that something is very bad or wrong ‖ 어떤 일이 매우 나쁘거나 잘못된 것이라고 증명하거나 보여 주는. 죄를 모면할 수 없는. 증거 등이 꼼짝 못할 만한: *a damning article about pollution* 오염에 대한 꼼짝달싹할 수 없는 기사

damp /dæmp/ *adj* slightly wet, usually in a cold and unpleasant way ‖ 보통 차갑고 불쾌하게 약간 젖은. 축축한: *My swimsuit is still damp.* 내 수영복은 여전히 축축하다. – **dampness** *n* [U]

damp·en /'dæmpən/ *v* [T] **1** to make something slightly wet ‖ 어떤 것을 약간 젖게 하다. 축축하게 하다. 축이다: *Dampen the clothes before ironing them.* 옷을 다리기 전에 축축하게 만들어라. **2 dampen sb's enthusiasm/spirits** to make someone feel less excited or interested about something ‖ 어떤 것에 대해 흥미나 관심을 덜 갖게 하다. …의 열정/기운을 꺾다

damp·er /'dæmpə/ *n* **put a damper on sth** to stop something from being enjoyable ‖ 어떤 것을 유쾌하지 않게 하다. 흥을 깨다. …의 트집을 잡다

dam·sel /'dæmzəl/ *n* **damsel in distress** HUMOROUS a young woman who needs help ‖ 도움을 필요로 하는 젊은 여성

dance¹ /dæns/ *v* **1** [I] to move your feet, body, and arms to match the style and speed of music ‖ 음악의 형식과 속도에 맞춰 발·몸·팔을 움직이다. 춤추다: *Juan and Roberta danced to the radio.* 후안과 로베타는 라디오(음악)에 맞춰 춤을 추었다. **2 dance the waltz/tango etc.** to do a particular type of dance ‖ 특정한 형태의 춤을 추다. 왈츠/탱고를 추

다 – **dancing** *n* [U]: *We used to go dancing pretty regularly.* 우리는 꽤 정기적으로 춤추러 가곤 했다.

dance² *n* **1** a party for dancing ‖ 춤추는 파티. 댄스파티: *a school dance* 학교 댄스파티 **2** an act of dancing ‖ 춤추는 행위. 춤. 무용: *May I have this dance?* (=will you dance with me?) 저와 함께 춤을 추실래요? **3** a particular set of movements that you perform with music ‖ 음악에 맞춰 움직이는 일련의 특정한 동작. 춤: *The only dance I know is the foxtrot.* 내가 아는 유일한 춤은 폭스트롯[4박자의 사교춤]이다. **4** [U] the art or activity of dancing ‖ 춤추는 기술이나 행위. 무용: *dance lessons* 무용 교습

danc·er /'dænsə/ *n* someone who dances, especially as a job ‖ 특히 직업으로써 춤추는 사람. 댄서. 무희

dan·de·li·on /'dændə,laɪən/ *n* a small bright yellow wild flower that becomes a white ball of seeds when it dies ‖ 선명한 노란색의 꽃이 지면 흰색 공 모양의 씨가 되는 작은 야생화. 민들레

dan·druff /'dændrəf/ *n* [U] small white pieces of dead skin from your head that show in your hair or on your clothes ‖ 머릿속이나 옷 위에서 볼 수 있는 작고 하얀, 머리의 죽은 피부 조각. 비듬

dan·dy /'dændi/ *adj* HUMOROUS very good ‖ 아주 좋은. 최고급의: *This gadget makes a dandy present for a cook.* 이 기계는 요리사에게는 최고의 선물이다.

dang /dæŋ/ *interjection* SPOKEN a word meaning DAMN that people consider less offensive ‖ damn과 같은 의미이나 사람들이 보다 덜 기분 상해 하는 단어

dan·ger /'deɪndʒə/ *n* **1** [U] the possibility that someone or something will be harmed ‖ 사람이나 사물이 해를 입을 가능성. 위험(성): *Is there any danger of infection?* 감염의 위험이 있습니까? / *The UN wants to move civilians who are in danger.* (=in a dangerous situation) UN은 위험에 처한 민간인들을 이동시키고 싶어 한다. **2** something or someone that may harm you ‖ 해를 끼칠 수도 있는 사물이나 사람. 위험(요인): *What are the dangers of scuba diving?* 스쿠버 다이빙의 위험한 점은 무엇입니까? **3** [C, U] the possibility that something unpleasant will happen ‖ 불쾌한 일이 일어날 가능성. 위기. 위험. 위험한 것: *Margie is in danger of losing her job.* 마지는 직장을 잃게 될 위험에 처해 있다.

dan·ger·ous /'deɪndʒərəs/ *adj* **1** able or likely to harm you ‖ 해를 입을 수 있거나 해를 입힐 가능성이 있는. 위험한: *a*

dangerous criminal 위험한 범죄자 / *It's dangerous for women to walk alone at night.* 여자가 밤에 혼자 걸어다니는 것은 위험하다. **2** likely to cause problems or involving a lot of risk ‖ 문제를 일으킬 것 같거나 대단한 위험을 수반하는. 위험한. 위태로운: *The company is in a dangerous financial position.* 그 회사는 재정상황이 위태롭다. – **dangerously** *adv*

dan·gle /'dæŋgəl/ *v* [I, T] to hang or swing loosely, or to make something do this ‖ 느슨하게 매달려 있거나 흔들리다, 또는 사물을 이렇게 하게 만들다. …에 매달려 늘어지다(게 하다). 대롱거리(게 하)다: *keys dangling from a chain* 체인에 대롱대롱 달려 있는 열쇠

da·nish /'deɪnɪʃ/, **Danish pas·try** /ˌ.. '../ *n* a round slightly flat sweet bread, usually with fruit in the middle ‖ 보통 가운데에 과일이 들어 있는, 둥글고 약간 납작하며 달콤한 빵. 데이니시 페이스트리

dank /dæŋk/ *adj* a dank place is wet and cold in an unpleasant way ‖ 장소 등이 불쾌하게 습기가 있고 추운. 눅눅한. 축축한

dap·per /'dæpɚ/ *adj* a dapper man is neatly dressed ‖ 남자가 깔끔하게 차려입은. 단정한. 맵시 있는

dare¹ /dɛr/ *v* **1** [T] to try to persuade someone to do something dangerous ‖ 남에게 위험한 일을 하도록 설득하려고 애쓰다. 남에게 …해 보라고 꼬드기다: *I dare you to jump!* 뛰어내릴 수 있으면 뛰어내려 봐! **2** [I] to be brave enough to do something, used especially in negative sentences ‖ 특히 부정문에 쓰여 어떤 일을 할 만큼 충분히 용감하다. 감히 …할 용기가 있다: *Robbins wouldn't dare tell the boss he's wrong.* 로빈은 상사에게 그가 잘못이라고 감히 말할 용기가 없다. **3 don't you dare** SPOKEN said in order to warn someone against doing something ‖ 남에게 어떤 일을 하지 말라고 경고하는 데에 쓰여: *Don't you dare tell!* 너 입도 뻥긋하지 마라! **4 how dare you/he etc.** SPOKEN said when you are very upset about what someone has said or done ‖ 남이 한 말이나 행동에 매우 화가 났을 때 쓰여. 어떻게 감히 네가/그가: *How dare you say that!* 어떻게 네가 감히 그런 말을 할 수 있지!

dare² *n* a suggestion that someone should do something dangerous to prove that s/he is not afraid ‖ 두려워하지 않는다는 것을 입증하기위해 위험한 일을 해야 한다는 제안. 감히 함. 도전

dare·dev·il /'dɛrˌdɛvəl/ *n* someone who likes doing dangerous things ‖ 위험한 일을 하기 좋아하는 사람. 덤비는[저돌적인] 사람 – **daredevil** *adj*

dar·ing¹ /'dɛrɪŋ/ *adj* **1** willing to do things that might be dangerous, or involving danger ‖ 위험할 수 있거나 위험을 수반하는 일을 기꺼이 하는. 대담한: *a daring adventure* 대담한 모험 **2** new or unusual in a way that is sometimes shocking ‖ 가끔 충격을 줄 정도로 새롭거나 유별난. 비범한. 참신한: *a daring movie* 참신한 영화

daring² *n* [U] courage to do dangerous things ‖ 위험한 일을 하는 용기. 대담(성). 용감(성)

dark¹ /dɑrk/ *adj* **1** with very little or no light ‖ 빛이 거의 없거나 전혀 없는. 어두운: *Turn on the light; it's dark in here.* 불을 켜라, 이곳은 어둡다. **2** closer to black than to white in color ‖ 색상에서 흰색보다는 검은색에 더 가까운. 짙은. 진한: *a dark blue tie* 짙은 푸른색 타이 / *Lewis has dark hair.* 루이스의 머리색은 검다. —compare LIGHT² **3 get dark** to become night ‖ 밤이 되다. 어두워지다: *We'd better go home, it's getting dark.* 집에 가는 것이 좋겠어. 날이 어두워지고 있으니. **4** a dark person has brown skin, hair, or eyes ‖ 사람의 피부[머리카락, 눈동자]가 갈색인. 다갈색의. 거무스름한: *a small dark woman* 작고 까무잡잡한 여인 **5** threatening, mysterious, or frightening ‖ 위협적인[신비로운, 소름끼치게 하는]. 험악한. 미지의: *a dark side to his character* 그 남자 성격의 사악한 면 **6** LITERARY unhappy or without hope ‖ 즐겁지 않거나 희망이 없는. 암울한: *the dark days of the war* 암울한 전쟁의 나날

dark² *n* **1 the dark** a situation in which there is no light ‖ 빛이 전혀 없는 상황. 어둠. 암흑: *My son is afraid of the dark.* 내 아들은 어둠을 두려워한다. **2 after dark** at night ‖ 밤에: *Don't go out after dark.* 밤에는 밖에 나가지 말아라. **3 before dark** before night has begun ‖ 밤이 시작되기 전에. 어둡기 전에: *Mom wants us home before dark.* 엄마는 우리들이 어둡기 전에 집에 들어오기를 바라신다. **4 in the dark** INFORMAL knowing nothing about something important because no one has told you about it ‖ 아무도 말을 해주지 않아서 중요한 무엇인가에 대해 전혀 모르고 있는. 알지 못하고 [모르고] 있는. 깜깜한: *Employees were kept in the dark* (=not told) *about the possible layoffs.* 종업원들은 해고가 있으

리라는 것을 전혀 모르고 있었다.

dark·en /ˈdɑrkən/ v [I, T] to make something dark, or to become dark ‖ 어떤 것을 어둡게 하다, 또는 어떤 것이 어두워지다: *The sky darkened before the storm.* 폭풍 전에 하늘이 어두워졌다.

dark horse /ˌ. ˈ./ n someone who is not well known and who surprises people by winning a competition ‖ 잘 알려지지 않았으나 시합에서 승리하여 사람들을 깜짝 놀라게 하는 사람. 다크호스. 의외의 역량을 가진 신예

dark·ly /ˈdɑrkli/ adv in an unpleasant or threatening way ‖ 불쾌하거나 위협적인 방법으로. 암울하게. 험악하게: *scientists speaking darkly about the future* 미래에 대해 암울하게 말하는 과학자들.

dark·ness /ˈdɑrknɪs/ n [U] a place or time when there is no light, or the lack of light ‖ 빛이 전혀 없는 장소나 시간, 또는 빛의 부족. 어둠. 암흑: *the darkness of a winter morning* 겨울날 아침의 어두컴컴함 / *The whole room was in darkness.* 방 전체가 어두웠다.

dark·room /ˈdɑrkrum/ n a special room with a red light or no light, where film is taken out of a camera and made into a photograph ‖ 카메라에서 필름을 꺼내 사진으로 인화하는, 붉은 불빛이 있거나 빛이 없는 특별한 방. 암실

dar·ling¹ /ˈdɑrlɪŋ/ n SPOKEN used when speaking to someone you love ‖ 사랑하는 사람에게 말할 때에 쓰여. 여보. 내 사랑. 자기: *Come here, darling.* 이리 와, 자기

darling² adj much loved ‖ 매우 사랑하는 [받는]: *my darling child* 나의 사랑하는 아이

darn¹ /dɑrn/ v [T] **1 darn it!** SPOKEN said when you are annoyed about something ‖ 어떤 것에 대해 성가실 때 쓰여. 젠장[빌어먹을, 제기랄]: *Darn it! I broke my shoelace.* 젠장, 구두끈이 끊어졌잖아. —see also DAMMIT **2 I'll be darned** SPOKEN said when you are surprised about something ‖ 어떤 일에 대해 놀랐을 때 쓰여. **3** to repair a hole in clothes by sewing thread through it many times ‖ 실로 여러 번 꿰매서 옷에 난 구멍을 수선하다. 꿰매다. 짜깁다: *darning socks* 양말 꿰매기

darn² also **darned** adv SPOKEN said in order to emphasize how bad or good someone or something is ‖ 사람이나 사물의 나쁘거나 좋은 정도를 강조하는 데에 쓰여. 터무니없이. 지독히: *a darned good movie* 정말 좋은 영화

darn³ also **darned** adj SPOKEN said in order to emphasize how bad, stupid etc. someone or something is, especially when you are annoyed ‖ 특히 화가 나서, 사람이나 사물의 못되고 어리석은 정도를 강조하는 데에 쓰여: *The darn fool got lost.* 그 바보 머저리가 잃어버렸다. —see also DAMN¹

dart¹ /dɑrt/ n **1** a small object with a sharp point that you can throw or shoot as a weapon or in games ‖ 무기나 놀이용으로 던지거나 쏠 수 있는 끝이 뾰족한 작은 물체. 다트. 작은 화살: *a poisoned dart* 독화살 **2** a small fold stitched into a piece of clothing to make it fit better ‖ 더 잘 맞도록 옷의 일부를 작게 접어 꿰맨 부분. —see also DARTS

dart² v [I] to move suddenly and quickly in a particular direction ‖ 특정 방향으로 갑작스럽고 재빨리 움직이다. 날쌔게 움직이다. 돌진하다: *The dog darted into the street.* 개가 거리로 날쌔게 뛰어들었다.

darts /dɑrts/ n [U] a game in which you throw DARTS at a circular board ‖ 원형 판에 다트를 던지는 게임. 화살 던지기 게임

dash¹ /dæʃ/ v **1** [I] to run somewhere very quickly ‖ 어딘가로 매우 빨리 달려가다. 돌진하다. 급히 가다: *She dashed into the room just before the boss arrived.* 그녀는 사장이 도착하기 직전에 급하게 방으로 달려 들어갔다. **2 dash sb's hopes** to ruin someone's hopes completely ‖ 남의 희망을 완전히 망치다. 희망을 무참히 짓밟다: *Her hopes of running in the Olympics were dashed after the accident.* 올림픽 게임에 출전한다는 그녀의 희망은 사고 이후에 산산조각났다. **3** [T] to make something hit violently against something else, usually so that it breaks ‖ 어떤 사물을 다른 것에 격렬하게 부딪쳐서 보통 깨지게 하다. …을 박살내다: *The ship was dashed against the rocks.* 그 배는 바위에 부딪쳐 박살났다.

dash off phr v [I] to leave somewhere very quickly ‖ 어딘가에서 매우 신속히 떠나다: *Tim dashed off after class.* 팀은 수업이 끝난 후 급히 떠났다.

dash² n **1 make a dash for** to run a short distance very quickly ‖ 짧은 거리를 매우 빨리 달리다. 돌진하다. 전속력으로 달리다: *I made a dash for the house to get my umbrella.* 우산을 가져가려고 집까지 전속력으로 달려갔다. **2** a small amount of something ‖ 사물의 소량: *a dash of lemon* 소량의 레몬(즙) **3** a mark (-) used in writing to separate thoughts in a sentence ‖ 문장에서 생각을 구분하기

위해 쓰는 표시 (-). 대시 기호 **4** ⇨
DASHBOARD

dash·board /'dæʃbɔrd/ *n* the board at
the front of a car that has the controls
on it ‖ 제어 장치들이 있는 차 앞쪽의 판.
계기판 —see picture on page 943

DAT *n* [U] digital audio tape; a type of
TAPE used in order to record music,
sound, or information in DIGITAL form ‖
digital audio tape(디지털 오디오 테이프)
의 약어; 음악[소리, 정보 등]을 디지털 형
태로 저장하는 데 쓰이는 테이프의 일종

da·ta /'deɪtə, 'dætə/ *n* [U, plural]
information or facts ‖ 정보나 사실. 쟈료.
데이타: *He's collecting data for his
report.* 그는 보고서를 위한 자료를 수집하
고 있다.

D

da·ta·base /'deɪtə,beɪs/ *n* a large
amount of DATA stored in a computer
system so that you can find and use it
easily ‖ 쉽게 찾아 쓸 수 있도록 컴퓨터 시
스템에 저장된 방대한 양의 자료. 데이터
베이스

da·ta pro·cess·ing /'.. ,../ *n* [U] the
use of computers to store and organize
information, especially in business ‖ 특
히 업무에서, 정보를 저장하고 체계화하기
위해 컴퓨터를 사용하는 일. (컴퓨터에 의
한)데이터 처리

date¹ /deɪt/ *n* **1** a particular day of the
month or of the year, shown by a
number ‖ 숫자로 표시되는 월이나 년 중
의 특정한 날. 날짜. 일: *"What's today's
date?" "It's August 11th."* "오늘이 며칠
이지?" "8월 11일." / *Have you set a
date* (=chosen a day) *for the wedding?*
결혼 날짜 잡았니? **2** an arrangement to
meet someone you like in a romantic
way ‖ 좋아하는 사람과 연애 기분으로 만
나는 약속. 데이트. (미리 정한) 이성과의
만날 약속: *Mike's going (out) on a date
on Friday.* 마이크는 금요일 날 데이트하
러 간다. **3** an arrangement to meet at a
particular time or place ‖ 특정 시간이나
장소에서 만날 약속: *Let's make a date
to see that new movie.* 그 신작 영화를 볼
날짜를 잡자. **4** someone you have a date
with ‖ 데이트 상대: *My date's taking me
out to dinner.* 데이트 상대가 저녁 식사에
나를 데리고 갈 거야. **5 to date** up to
now ‖ 현재까지. 이제[오늘(날)]까지:
*This is the best research on the subject
to date.* 이것은 그 주제에 관한 현재까지
의 최고의 연구이다. **6 at a later date**
at some time in the future ‖ 미래의 언
젠가. 나중에. 앞으로: *This will be
discussed at a later date.* 이점에 대해서
는 훗날 논의할 것이다. **7** a small sweet

sticky brown fruit with a single long
seed ‖ 긴 씨가 하나 들어 있는 작고 달콤
하며 전득전득한 갈색 과일. 대추야자 —
see also OUT-OF-DATE, UP-TO-DATE

date² *v* **1** [I, T] to have a romantic
relationship with someone ‖ 다른 사람과
연애 관계를 갖다. …와 사귀다[데이트하
다]: *How long have you been dating
Mona?* 모나와 사귄 지 얼마나 되었지? **2**
[T] to write the date on something ‖ 어
떤 것에 날짜를 적다: *a letter dated May
1, 1998* 1998년 5월 1일자 편지 **3** [T] to
find out when something old was made
or how long it has existed ‖ 오래된 사물
등이 언제 만들어졌는지 또는 얼마나 오랫
동안 존재해 왔는지 알아내다. …의 시기
[시점, 연대]를 산정[추정]하다:
*Geologists date these rocks to 30
million years ago.* 지질학자들은 이 암석
들이 3천만 년 전 것이라고 추정한다.

date from/date back to *phr v* [I] to
have existed or been made at a
particular time ‖ 특정 시기에 존재했거나
만들어졌다. …부터 시작되다[기산되다].
…으로 거슬러 올라가다: *Independence
Hall dates from the 17th century.* 독립
기념관은 17세기에 건립되었다.

dat·ed /'deɪtɪd/ *adj* no longer
fashionable ‖ 더 이상 유행하지 않는. 시
대에 뒤떨어진. 낡은: *These shoes are
really dated.* 이 구두는 정말 구식이다.

date rape /'. ./ *n* [C, U] a RAPE that
happens on a date ‖ 데이트 중에 일어나
는 강간. 데이트 상대에 의한 성폭행

daub /dɔb/ *v* [T] to paint something in a
careless way ‖ 어떤 것을 아무렇게나 칠
하다. (…을) 서툴게 그리다

daugh·ter /'dɔtə/ *n* your female child
‖ 자신의 여자 아이. 딸 —see picture at
FAMILY

daugh·ter-in-law /'.. . ,./ *n, plural*
daughters-in-law the wife of your son
‖ 아들의 아내. 며느리 —see picture at
FAMILY

daunt /dɔnt, dɑnt/ *v* [T] to make
someone afraid or less confident ‖ 남을
겁나게 하거나 자신감이 줄어들게 하다.
위압하다. 기죽게 하다. 기를 꺾다:
*Cooper is feeling daunted by his new
responsibilities.* 쿠퍼는 자신의 새 책임
때문에 위축되어 있다.

daunt·ing /'dɔntɪŋ/ *adj* frightening in a
way that makes you feel less confident ‖
자신감을 떨어뜨릴 정도로 겁나게 하는.
위압적인. 기를 꺾는: *a daunting task* 기
죽게 하는[벅찬] 일

da·ven·port /'dævən,pɔrt/ *n* a large
SOFA ‖ 대형 소파

daw·dle /'dɔdl/ v [I] INFORMAL to waste time by doing things too slowly ‖ 일을 너무 느리게 해서 시간을 낭비하다. 꾸물대다: *Stop dawdling; we'll be late.* 꾸물대지 마. 우리 늦겠어.

dawn[1] /dɔn/ n [C, U] **1** the time of day when light first appears ‖ 하루 중 처음 (태양)빛이 나올 때의 시간. 새벽. 동틀녘: *We talked until dawn.* 우리는 새벽까지 이야기 했다. / *The boat left at the crack of dawn.* (=very early in the morning) 그 배는 동틀 무렵에 떠났다. **2** **the dawn of** the time when something is just beginning to develop ‖ 어떤 일이 막 발달하기 시작하고 있는 때. 시작. 시초. 발단: *the dawn of civilization* 문명의 태동기

dawn[2] v [I] if a day or morning dawns, it begins ‖ 날이나 아침이 시작되다. 날이 새다. 동이 트다: *The morning dawned cool and clear.* 상쾌하고 맑은 아침이 밝았다.

dawn on sb *phr v* [T] to realize something ‖ 무엇을 깨닫다: *It suddenly dawned on me that he was right.* 갑자기 그가 옳았다는 생각이 들었다.

day /deɪ/ n

1 ▶**24 HOURS** 24시간◀ a period of time equal to 24 hours ‖ 24시간에 해당하는 기간. 하루: *I'll be back in ten days.* 열흘 후에 돌아올게. / *We're leaving for Arizona the day after tomorrow.* 우리는 모레 애리조나로 출발한다. / *I saw Margo downtown the day before yesterday.* 나는 그저께 시내에서 마고를 보았다. ✗DON'T SAY "We're leaving for Arizona after tomorrow" or "I saw Margo before yesterday."✗ "We're leaving for Arizona after tomorrow." 또는 "I saw Margo before yesterday."라고는 하지 않는다.

2 ▶**MORNING UNTIL NIGHT** 아침부터 밤까지◀ [C, U] the period of time between when it becomes light in the morning and when it becomes dark in the evening, when most people are awake ‖ 아침 밝을 때부터 저녁 어두워질 때까지 사이의 대부분의 사람들이 깨어 있는 시간. 낮(동안). 주간: *The days begin to get longer in the spring.* 봄에는 낮이 길어지기 시작한다. / *a beautiful summer day* 아름다운 여름 낮

3 ▶**WORK** 일◀ a period of work within a 24 hour period ‖ 24시간 중에서 일하는 시간. 근로 시간: *Jean works an eight-hour day.* 진은 하루 8시간 일한다. / *I need a day off* (=a day when you do not have to work). 나는 하루 휴무가 필요하다.

다. / *It's been a long day* (=a day when you had to get up early and were busy all day). 정말 긴 하루였다. / *Jan's been studying all day.* (=for the whole day) 잰은 하루 종일 공부하고 있다. / *Jim had a really bad/good day at work.* 짐은 직장에서 정말 일진이 나빴다[좋았다]. / *I have Spanish class every day.* 나는 매일 스페인어 수업이 있다.

4 ▶**POINT IN TIME** 시점◀ a period or point in time ‖ 시기나 시점: *back in the days before the war* 전쟁 이전 시점으로 거슬러가다 / *It's not safe to walk the streets these days.* (=now, as opposed to the past) 요즈음 거리를 걸어다니는 것은 안전하지 않다. / *Things were different in my day.* (=when I was young) 어린 시절에는 상황이 달랐다. / *We'll buy our dream home one/some day.* (=at some time in the future) 우리는 언젠가 꿈꿔온 집을 살 것이다. / *To this day* (=until now) *we haven't heard the whole story.* 지금까지 우리는 전체 이야기를 듣지 못했다. / *Grandpa was telling stories about the good old days.* (=a time in the past that was better than the present) 할아버지는 좋았던 옛 시절에 관한 이야기를 들려 주셨다.

5 **the other day** INFORMAL within the last few days ‖ 지난 며칠 이내에. 며칠 전에: *I saw Randy the other day.* 나는 요전에 랜디를 보았다.

6 **make someone's day** INFORMAL to make someone very pleased or happy ‖ 남을 매우 기쁘거나 즐겁게 하다: *That card made my day.* 그 카드가 나를 아주 즐겁게 했다.

7 **(has) had its day** no longer popular or successful ‖ 더 이상 인기 없거나 더 이상 성공적이지 못한: *The old steam trains were something to see, but they've had their day.* 오래된 증기 기차는 보기엔 특별하지만 한물갔다.

8 **those were the days** SPOKEN used in order to say that a time in the past was better than the present time ‖ 과거 시절이 현재보다 나았다고 말하는 데에 쓰여. 그때가 좋았지

9 **day after day/day in day out** continuously ‖ 계속해서. 끊임없이. 매일매일. 날마다: *I drive the same route to work day in day out.* 나는 출근하기 위해 날마다 똑같은 길을 운전한다.

10 **from day to day/day by day** from each day to the next ‖ 하루에서 그 다음 날까지. 나날이. 하루하루: *You change your mind from day to day.* 너는 하루하루 마음이 바뀌는구나. —see also DAYS[2],

DAILY, **call it a day** (CALL[1])

day·break /'deɪbreɪk/ n [U] the time of day when light first appears ‖ 하루 중 (태양)빛이 처음으로 나타나는 시간. 새벽. 동틀 녘: *We broke camp at daybreak.* 우리는 동틀 녘에 야영천막을 걷었다.

day camp /'. ./ n a CAMP where children do activities, sports etc. during the day, but go home at night ‖ 아이들이 낮 시간 동안에는 (과외)활동, 스포츠 등을 하지만, 밤에는 집에 돌아가는 캠프. 주간 캠프

day·care /'deɪkɛr/ n [U] the care of children while their parents are at work ‖ 부모가 직장에서 일하는 동안 어린이들을 보살피는 것. 주간 탁아[보육]: *a daycare center* 보육원[탁아소] / *My youngest is in daycare.* 내 막내 아이는 탁아소에 맡기고 있다.

day·dream[1] /'deɪdrɪm/ v [I] to think about pleasant things so that you forget what you should be doing ‖ 해야 할 일을 잊어 버릴 정도로 즐거운 일에 대해 생각하다. 몽상하다. 공상에 잠기다: *Joan sat at her desk, daydreaming about Tom.* 조안은 책상에 앉아 톰에 대한 공상에 잠겼다. **– daydreamer** n

daydream[2] n the pleasant thoughts you have when you DAYDREAM ‖ 공상에 잠겨 있을 때 가지는 즐거운 생각. 몽상. 백일몽

Day·Glo /'deɪgloʊ/ adj TRADEMARK having a very bright orange, green, yellow, or pink color ‖ 아주 밝은 주황색[녹색, 노란색, 핑크색]을 지닌. 형광색의. 화려한

day·light /'deɪlaɪt/ n [U] the light produced by the sun during the day ‖ 낮 시간 동안 태양이 만들어 내는 빛. 햇빛. 일광: *There's more daylight in summer.* 여름에는 일광시간이 길어진다. / *She was attacked in broad daylight.* (=during the day when everyone could see) 그녀는 백주에 강간당했다.

day·lights /'deɪlaɪts/ n [plural] INFORMAL **1 scare/frighten the living daylights out of sb** to frighten someone a lot ‖ 사람을 크게 위협하다. 사람을 몹시 두려워하게[놀라게] 하다. … 을 기절시키다[시킬 정도이다] **2 beat the living daylights out of sb** to hit someone many times and hurt him/her ‖ 사람을 여러 번 때려 다치게 하다.

daylight sav·ing time /,.. '.. ,./, **daylight savings** n [U] the time in the spring when clocks are set one hour ahead of standard time ‖ 봄에 시계를 표준 시간보다 한 시간 앞당겨 맞춰 놓는 시기. 일광 절약 시간. 섬머 타임

days[1] /deɪz/ n LITERARY life ‖ 삶. 생(애): *He began his days in a small town.* 그는 작은 마을에서 생애를 시작했다.

days[2] adv during each day ‖ 낮 동안 (에). 주간에: *This week I work days; next week it's nights.* 이번 주에 나는 주간 근무고, 다음 주는 야간 근무다.

day·time /'deɪtaɪm/ n the time between when it gets light in the morning and when it gets dark in the evening ‖ 아침에 빛이 나서 저녁에 어두워질 때까지의 시간. 낮. 주간: *I've never been here in/during the daytime.* 나는 낮 시간에 [동안] 이곳에 와 본 적이 없다.

day-to-day /,. . '. ./ adj happening every day as a regular part of life ‖ 삶의 규칙적인 부분으로서 매일 발생하는. 나날의. 매일매일의: *our day-to-day routine at work* 직장에서 보내는 매일매일의 일과

day trad·ing /'. ,./ n [U] the activity of using a computer to buy and sell SHARES on the Internet, often buying and selling very quickly to make a profit out of small price changes ‖ 컴퓨터를 이용해서 인터넷상에서 주식을 사고 파는, 종종 소폭의 가격 변동에서 이익을 얻기 위해 재빠르게 사고 파는 활동. 당일치기 거래[단타 매매] **– day trader** n [C]

daze /deɪz/ n **in a daze** unable to think clearly ‖ 명료하게 생각할 수 없는. 멍해진. 아찔해진

dazed /deɪzd/ adj unable to think clearly, usually because you are shocked, have been hurt etc. ‖ 보통 충격이나 상처 등을 입어서 명료하게 생각할 수 없는. 멍해진. 아찔해진. 어리둥절해진: *dazed victims of the bombing* 폭격으로 정신이 멍해진 희생자들

daz·zle /'dæzəl/ v [T] **1** to make someone unable to see by shining a strong light in his/her eyes ‖ 사람의 눈에 강한 빛을 쐬어 볼 수 없게 만들다. 눈을 부시게 하다: *deer dazzled by our headlights* 우리의 헤드라이트에 눈이 부신 사슴 **2** to make someone admire someone or something a lot ‖ 남으로 하여금 어떤 사람이나 사물을 매우 존경하도록 하다. 현혹시키다. 감탄하게 하다: *We were all dazzled by her talent and charm.* 우리는 모두 그녀의 재능과 매력에 매료되었다.

daz·zling /'dæzlɪŋ/ adj very impressive, exciting, or interesting ‖ 매우 인상적인[흥분시키는, 흥미로운]. 현혹적인. 눈부신: *a dazzling performance* 현혹적인 공연

D.C. District of Columbia; the area containing the city of Washington, the CAPITAL of the US ‖ District of Columbia(콜럼비아 특별 구역)의 약어; 미국의 수도인 워싱턴을 포함하는 지역

DC *n* [U] direct current; the type of electric current that comes from batteries (BATTERY) ‖ direct current(직류)의 약어; 배터리에서 나오는 전류의 종류 —compare AC

DDT *n* [U] a chemical used in order to kill insects, that is now illegal ‖ 곤충 살충용의, 현재는 불법인 화학 약품. 디디티

DE the written abbreviation of Delaware ‖ Delaware(델라웨어 주)의 약어

dea·con /'dikən/, **dea·con·ess** /'dikə,nɛs/ *n* an official in some Christian churches ‖ 일부 교회에서의 관리. 집사

dead¹ /dɛd/ *adj*

1 ▶NOT ALIVE 살아 있지 않은◀ no longer alive ‖ 더 이상 살아 있지 않은. 죽은: *Her mom's been dead for two years.* 그녀의 어머니가 돌아가신 지 2년이 되었다. / *Two boys found a dead body* (=a dead person) *by the train tracks.* 두 소년이 기차 선로 옆에서 시체를 발견했다.

2 ▶NOT WORKING 작동하지 않는◀ not working, especially because there is no power ‖ 특히 전력이 없어서 작동하지 않는. 꺼진. 끊어진: *Is the battery dead?* 건전지가 다 되었습니까? / *The phones went dead during the storm.* 폭풍 중에 전화가 불통됐다.

3 ▶PLACE 장소◀ a place that is dead does not have anything interesting happening in it ‖ 장소 등에서 흥미 있는 일이 일어나지 않는. 활기 없는: *The bar is usually dead until around 10:00.* 술집은 대체로 10시 경까지는 활기가 없다.

4 ▶NOT USED 사용하지 않는◀ no longer used or no longer able to be used ‖ 더 이상 사용하지 않거나 사용할 수 없는: *a dead language* 사어(死語)

5 ▶TIRED 피곤한◀ INFORMAL very tired ‖ 매우 피곤한: *I think I'll go to bed early, I'm absolutely dead.* 일찍 자야 할 것 같아, 완전히 녹초가 되었거든.

6 ▶PART OF BODY 몸의 일부◀ a part of your body that is dead has no feeling in it for a short time ‖ 몸의 일부분이 일시적으로 감각이 없는. 마비된. 저린: *I'd been sitting so long my legs went dead.* 너무 오래 앉아 있어서 다리가 저렸다.

7 over my dead body SPOKEN used when you are determined not to allow something to happen ‖ 단호하게 어떤 일이 일어나는 것을 허락하지 않겠다고 할

때 쓰여. 내가 죽고 나서야. 내 눈에 흙이 들어가기 전에는: *You'll marry him over my dead body!* 내 눈에 흙이 들어가기 전에는 그 남자랑 결혼할 생각 마라!

8 SPOKEN also **dead meat** *in serious trouble* ‖ 심각한 곤경에 처한. 큰일 난: *If anything happens to the car, you're dead!* 만약 그 차에 무슨 일이라도 생기면 죽을 줄 알아! —see also **sb wouldn't be caught dead doing sth** (CATCH¹)

USAGE NOTE dead and died

Use **dead** as an adjective to talk about things or people that are no longer alive: *I think this plant is dead.* **Died** is the past tense and past participle of "die": *She died of a heart attack.*
이미 살아 있지 않은 사물이나 사람에 대해 말할 때 형용사 **dead**를 쓴다: 이 식물은 죽은 것 같다. **died**는 die의 과거·과거 분사형이다: 그녀는 심장 마비로 사망했다.

---

dead² *adv* **1** INFORMAL completely or extremely ‖ 완전히, 극도로. 전적으로: *Paula stopped dead when she saw us.* 폴라는 우리를 보자 완전히 멈춰 섰다. / *The baby was up all night; I'm dead tired.* 아이가 밤새 잠을 안 자서 난 몹시 지쳐 있다. **2** INFORMAL directly or exactly ‖ 바로, 정확히. 정통으로: *You can't miss it; it's dead ahead.* 너는 찾을 수 있을 거야. 바로 앞쪽에 있거든.

dead³ *n* **1 in the dead of winter/night** in the middle of winter or the night when everything is quiet ‖ 모든 것이 고요한 한겨울이나 한밤중에 **2 the dead** people who have died ‖ 죽은 사람. 고인 (故人)

dead·en /'dɛdn/ *v* [T] to make a feeling or sound less strong ‖ 감각이나 소리를 덜 강하게 하다. 무디게 하다. 둔화시키다: *a drug to deaden the pain* 고통을 완화시키는 약

dead end /ˌ. './ *n* **1** a street with no way out at one end ‖ 한 쪽 끝에서 밖으로 나가는 길이 없는 거리. 막다른 거리 **2** a job or situation from which no more progress is possible ‖ 더 이상의 진전이 불가능한 일이나 상황

dead·line /'dɛdlaɪn/ *n* a time by which you must finish something ‖ 어떤 일을 마쳐야 하는 시간. 최종 기한. 마감 시간: *Can you meet the 5:00 deadline?* 5시 마감 시한에 맞출 수 있나요?

dead·lock /'dɛdlɑk/ *n* [C, U] a situation in which a disagreement cannot be settled ‖ 불일치가 해결되지 않는 상황. 교착 상태. 정체: *the UN's attempt to break the deadlock* (=end it) *in the region.* 그 지역의 교착 상태를 타개하려는 UN의 시도

dead·ly /'dɛdli/ *adj* **1** very dangerous and likely to cause death ‖ 매우 위험하고 죽게 할 수 있는. 치명적인: *a deadly virus* 치명적인 바이러스 **2** complete or total, often in an unpleasant or frightening way ‖ 보통 불쾌하거나 위협적일 정도로 완전하거나 전적인. 지극히 정확한: *Brian hit the target with deadly accuracy.* 브라이언은 극히 정확하게 목표물을 명중시켰다.

dead·pan /'dɛdpæn/ *adj* sounding and looking like you are completely serious when you are not ‖ 심각하지 않은데도 매우 진지하게 들리고 진지해 보이는. 심각[진지]한 체하는: *a deadpan expression* 심각한 체하는 표현

deaf /dɛf/ *adj* **1** unable to hear ‖ 들을 수 없는. 귀가 먼. 청각 장애의: *I'm deaf in my right ear.* 나는 오른쪽 귀가 안 들린다. **2 the deaf** people who are deaf ‖ 귀가 먼 사람들. 청각 장애인들 **3 deaf to sth** unwilling to listen to something ‖ 어떤 것을 들으려 하지 않는. …에 귀를 기울이지 않는: *The guards were deaf to the prisoners' complaints.* 교도관들은 수감자들의 불만에 귀를 기울이지 않았다. **4 fall on deaf ears** to not be listened to ‖ 듣지 않다. 귀기울이지 않다. 무시하다: *My warning fell on deaf ears.* 내 경고에 (아무도) 귀기울이지 않았다. – **deafness** *n* [U]

deaf·en /'dɛfən/ *v* [T] to make it difficult for you to hear anything ‖ 어떤 것도 듣기 어렵게 만들다. 귀를 먹게 하다. 못 듣게 하다 – **deafening** *adj* : *deafening music* 귀를 먹먹하게 하는 음악

deal¹ /dil/ *n* **1** an agreement or arrangement, especially in business or politics ‖ 특히 사업이나 정치에서의 협정이나 계약. 거래: *They've just signed a new deal with their record company.* 그들은 자신들의 음반 회사와 새 계약을 막 체결했다. / *You can get some good deals at the new travel agency.* (=buy something at a good price) 당신은 새 여행사에서 싼 가격에 좋은 여행 상품들을 살 수 있습니다. **2 it's a deal** SPOKEN used in order to say that you agree to something, especially when you get something in return ‖ 특히 대가로 어떤 것을 받을 때, 그것에 동의한다고 말하는 데 쓰여. 좋아: *"I'll give you $100." "It's*

a deal." "네게 100달러를 줄게." "좋아." **3 a great/good deal** a large quantity of something ‖ 어떤 것의 다량. 많음. 상당한 양: *He knows a great deal more* (=a lot more) *than I do about computers.* 그는 컴퓨터에 대해 나보다 훨씬 더 많이 안다. **4** the way someone is treated in a particular situation ‖ 특정 상황에서 사람이 취급받는 방식. 대우. 대접: *Women often get a raw deal* (=unfair treatment) *from their employers.* 여성들은 종종 고용주에게 부당한 대우를 받는다. **5 what's the deal?** SPOKEN used when you want to know what is happening ‖ 무슨 일이 일어나고 있는지 알고 싶을 때에 쓰여. 무슨 일이야?: *So what's the deal? Why is he so mad?* 무슨 일이야? 그가 왜 그렇게 화난 거야? **6** someone's turn to give out playing cards in a game ‖ 게임에서 어떤 사람이 카드를 도를 차례: *It's your deal.* 네가 카드를 도를 차례야. —see also BIG DEAL

deal² *v* dealt, dealt /dɛlt/, dealing **1** [I, T] also **deal out** to give out playing cards to players in a game ‖ 카드 게임에서 카드를 도르다: *Whose turn is it to deal?* 누가 패를 도를 차례야? **2** [I, T] to buy and sell illegal drugs ‖ 불법 마약을 사고 팔다: *He was arrested for dealing cocaine.* 그는 코카인을 거래한 혐의로 체포되었다.

deal with sb/sth *phr v* [T] **1** to take the correct action for a problem, piece of work etc. ‖ 문제·일 등에 대해 올바른 조치를 취하다. 처리[대처]하다: *Who's dealing with the new account?* 누가 신규 예금을 담당하고 있습니까? **2** to not lose confidence or to not become too upset in a difficult situation ‖ 어려운 상황에서 자신감을 잃지 않거나 지나치게 흥분하지 않다. 대처하다. 참다: *I can't deal with any more crying children today.* 난 오늘 우는 아이들을 더 이상 어쩔 수 없다. **3** to do business with someone or have a business connection with someone ‖ 남과 거래하거나 사업적 관계를 갖다. 거래[관계]하다. 장사하다: *We've been dealing with their company for ten years.* 우리는 10년간 그들의 회사와 거래해 오고 있다. **4** to be about a particular subject ‖ 특정 주제에 관계[관련]하다. 취급하다. 논하다: *a book dealing with 20th century art* 20세기 예술을 다루고 있는 책

deal in sth *phr v* [T] to buy and sell a particular type of product ‖ 특정 유형의 생산품을 사고 팔다. 거래[취급]하다: *a business dealing in medical equipment*

의료 장비 거래 사업

deal·er /'dilɚ/ n 1 someone who buys and sells a particular product ‖ 특정 상품을 사고 파는 사람. 상인. 무역업자: *a car dealer* 자동차상 2 someone who gives out the playing cards in a game ‖ 카드 게임에서 패를 도르는 사람. 딜러

deal·er·ship /'dilɚˌʃɪp/ n a business that sells the products of a particular company, especially cars ‖ 특정 회사의 제품, 특히 자동차를 판매하는 사업: *a Ford dealership* 포드 자동차 판매업

deal·ing /'dilɪŋ/ n [U] the buying and selling of things ‖ 물건을 사고 팖. 매매. 거래: *problems with drug dealing in the school* 학교 내의 마약 거래 문제

deal·ings /'dilɪŋz/ n [plural] personal or business relations with someone ‖ 남과의 개인적 또는 업무상의 관계. 거래: *Have you had any dealings with IBM?* IBM사와 거래합니까?

dean /din/ n an official with a high rank in some universities ‖ 일부 대학에서의 고위 관리. 학장. 학과장: *Dean of Arts* 인문대 학장

dear¹ /dɪr/ interjection said when you are surprised, annoyed, or upset ‖ 놀라거나 성가시거나 화날 때에 쓰여. 어머나. 맙소사: *Oh dear! I forgot to phone Jill.* 오, 맙소사! 질에게 전화하는 걸 깜빡 했군.

dear² n SPOKEN used when speaking to someone you like or love ‖ 좋아하거나 사랑하는 사람에게 말할 때에 쓰여. 사랑스런 사람[아기, 여보, 애인 등]: *How was your day, dear?* 하루가 어땠어, 여보?

dear³ adj 1 used before a name or title at the beginning of a letter ‖ 편지의 서두에서 이름이나 직함 앞에 쓰여. 친애하는. 존경하는: *Dear Sue, …* 사랑하는 수에게… / *Dear Dr. Ward, …* 친애하는 워드 박사 님 께 … 2 much loved and very important to you ‖ 대단히 사랑스럽고 소중한: *She's a dear friend.* 그녀는 소중한 친구다.

dear·ly /'dɪrli/ adv very much ‖ 아주 많이. 매우. 몹시: *I'd dearly love to go to Hawaii.* 난 하와이에 너무나 가고 싶다.

dearth /dɚθ/ n FORMAL a lack of something ‖ 어떤 것의 부족

death /dɛθ/ n 1 [C, U] the end of a person or animal's life ‖ 사람이나 동물의 종말. 죽음: *Maretti lived in Miami until his death.* 마레티는 죽을 때까지 마이애미에 살았다. / *The number of deaths from AIDS is increasing.* 에이즈로 인한 사망자 수가 증가하고 있다. / *He choked to death* (=choked until he died) *on a*

fish bone. 그는 생선 가시에 걸려 질식사했다. 2 **bored/scared to death** INFORMAL very bored or afraid ‖ 아주 지루하거나/두려운 3 the end of something ‖ 어떤 것의 끝. 종말. 종결: *the death of Communism* 공산주의의 붕괴 —see also **be sick (and tired) of, be sick to death of** (SICK¹)

death·bed /'dɛθbɛd/ n sb's deathbed the point in time when someone is dying and will be dead very soon ‖ 사람이 죽음에 임박한 시점. 임종. 죽음의 자리: *Marquez flew home to be with his mother, who was on her deathbed.* 마르께즈는 고향집으로 가 어머니의 임종하는 것을 지켰다.

death pen·al·ty /'. ,.../ n the legal punishment of being killed for a serious crime ‖ 중범죄자를 죽이는 법적 형벌. 사형: *Gilmore was given the death penalty for murder.* 길모어는 살인죄로 사형을 선고받았다. —see also CAPITAL PUNISHMENT

death row /ˌ './ n [U] the part of a prison where prisoners are kept while they wait to be punished by being killed ‖ 죄수가 사형을 기다리는 동안 머무는 감옥의 구역. 사형수 감방: *He's been on death row for three years.* 그는 3년간 사형수 감방에 수감되어 있다.

death trap /'. ./ n INFORMAL a vehicle or building that is in such bad condition that it is dangerous ‖ 위험할 만큼 열악한 상태에 놓인 차량이나 건물. 위험 건축물 [교통 수단]

de·base /dɪ'beɪs/ v [T] to reduce the quality or value of something ‖ 어떤 것의 질이나 가치를 떨어뜨리다. 낮추다. 저하시키다 – **debasement** n [C, U]

de·bat·a·ble /dɪ'beɪt̬əbəl/ adj an idea or problem that is debatable is one for which two or more different opinions or answers could be true or right ‖ 어떤 생각이나 문제에서, 두 가지 이상의 다른 의견이나 답이 사실이거나 옳을 수 있는. 논쟁의 여지가 있는

de·bate¹ /dɪ'beɪt/ n 1 a discussion or argument on a subject that people express different opinions about ‖ 사람들이 다른 의견을 발표하는 어떤 주제에 대한 토론이나 논쟁: *a debate on/about equal pay* 균등 임금에 관한 논쟁 2 [U] the process of discussing a subject or question ‖ 어떤 주제나 질문에 관해 토론하는 과정. 논의: *After much debate, the committee decided to raise the fees.* 많은 논의를 거친 후, 그 위원회는 요금을 인상하기로 결정했다.

de·bate² v 1 [I, T] to discuss a subject formally with someone so that you can make a decision or solve a problem ‖ 어떤 주제에 관해 결정을 내리거나 문제를 해결할 수 있도록 공식적으로 남과 토론하다. 논의하다: *The Senate is debating the future of health care.* 상원에서는 의료 보장제도의 미래에 관해 토론하고 있다. / *We were debating which person to hire.* 우리는 누구를 고용할지에 대해 논의하고 있었다. 2 [T] to seriously consider something ‖ 어떤 것에 대해 진지하게 고려하다. 숙고하다: *I was debating whether to go to work.* 나는 일하러 갈 것인지 따져보고 있었다.

de·bauched /dɪ'bɔʃt/ adj someone who is debauched drinks too much alcohol, takes drugs, or has an immoral attitude about sex ‖ 지나치게 술을 마시는[마약을 하는, 성에 대해 부도덕한 태도를 가진]. 방탕한. 문란한. 타락한 **– debauchery** n [U]

de·bil·i·tate /dɪ'bɪlə.teɪt/ v [T] to make someone weak, especially from sickness, heat, or lack of food ‖ 특히 질병[더위, 음식 부족]으로 사람을 쇠약하게 하다: *debilitated by disease* 질병으로 쇠약해진 **– debilitating** adj **– debility** n

deb·it¹ /'dɛbɪt/ n a record of the money that you have taken out of your bank account ‖ 은행 계좌에서 출금한 돈의 기록. 차변 기입

debit² v [T] to take money out of a bank account ‖ 은행 계좌에서 돈을 찾다. 출금하다: *The sum of $50 has been debited from your account.* 네 계좌에서 총 50달러를 출금했다. **—opposite** CREDIT²

deb·o·nair /,dɛbə'nɛr/ adj a man who is debonair is fashionable and behaves in a confident way ‖ 남자가 유행 감각이 있고 자신감 있게 행동하는. 서글서글한. 사근사근한. 유쾌한

de·brief /di'brif/ v [T] to ask someone such as a soldier to give a report of a job that s/he has done ‖ 군인 등의 사람에게 수행한 일에 대해 보고할 것을 요청하다. 임무의 결과를 물어보다. 보고를 듣다 **– debriefing** n

de·bris /dɪ'bri/ n [U] the pieces of something that are left after it has been destroyed ‖ 파괴된 후 남은 사물의 조각. 잔해. 파편: *The street was full of debris after the explosion.* 폭발 후 거리는 잔해로 가득했다.

debt /dɛt/ n 1 money that you owe to someone ‖ 남에게 빚진 돈. 빚: *Gordon can finally pay off his debts.* 고든은 마침내 그의 빚을 갚을 수 있다. 2 [U] the state of owing money to someone ‖ 남에게 빚진 상태. 부채. 채무: *a company heavily in debt* (=owing a lot of money) 막대한 부채를 진 회사 3 **be in sb's debt** to be very grateful to someone for what s/he has done for you ‖ 자신에게 해 준 일에 대해 남에게 매우 고마워하다. …의 신세[은혜]를 지고 있다

debt·or /'dɛtɚ/ n a person, group, or organization that owes money ‖ 돈을 빚진 사람[집단, 조직]. 채무자

de·bug /di'bʌg/ v [T] to take the mistakes out of a computer PROGRAM ‖ 컴퓨터 프로그램에서 오류를 없애다. 결함을 고치다

de·bunk /di'bʌŋk/ v [T] to show that an idea or belief is false ‖ 어떤 생각이나 믿음이 잘못된 것임을 보여주다. 정체를 폭로하다. 가면을 벗기다: *She set out to debunk the myth that French cooking is difficult.* 그녀는 프랑스 요리가 어렵다는 잘못된 믿음을 깨기 위해 (프랑스) 음식을 차려냈다.

de·but /deɪ'byu, 'deɪbyu/ n the first time that a performer or sports player performs in public, or the first time something is available to the public ‖ 연주자나 운동 선수가 사람들 앞에서 처음으로 공연이나 경기하는 때, 또는 어떤 것이 처음으로 대중에게 공개되는 때. 데뷔. 초연. 첫 공개: *the band's debut album* 그 밴드의 데뷔 앨범 / *Foster made her debut in movies at a young age.* 포스터는 어린 나이에 영화계에 데뷔했다.

deb·u·tante /'dɛbyu,tɑnt/ n a girl who has just formally begun going to parties etc. in rich people's society ‖ 부유층의 사교계 파티 등에 정식으로 갓 나가기 시작한 소녀. 사교계에 처음 나온 소녀

dec·ade /'dɛkeɪd/ n a period of time equal to 10 years ‖ 10년에 해당하는 기간. 10년간

dec·a·dent /'dɛkədənt/ adj more interested in pleasure than anything else ‖ 다른 어떤 것보다 쾌락에 더 흥미 있는. 퇴폐적인. 타락으로 향하는: *decadent behavior* 퇴폐적인 행위 **– decadence** n [U]

de·caf /'dikæf/ n [U] DECAFFEINATED coffee ‖ 카페인을 제거한 커피

de·caf·fein·at·ed /di'kæfə,neɪtɪd/ adj coffee, tea, or COLA that is decaffeinated has had the CAFFEINE removed ‖ 커피[차, 콜라]에서 카페인을 제거한. 카페인 없는

de·cal /'dikæl/ n a piece of paper with a picture on it that you stick onto a surface ‖ 표면 위에 붙이는 그림이 새겨진 종이. 판박이 그림. 스티커

de·cant·er /dɪˈkæntɚ/ n a glass container for alcoholic drinks ‖ 주류용 유리 용기. 디캔터

dec·ath·lon /dɪˈkæθlɑn, -lən/ n [singular] a competition with ten running, jumping, and throwing events ‖ 10가지의 달리기·뛰기·던지기 종목으로 이루어진 경기. 10종 경기

de·cay¹ /dɪˈkeɪ/ n [U] the process, state, or result of decaying ‖ 썩는 과정[상태, 결과]. 부패. 쇠퇴. 붕괴: *The building has fallen into decay over the last few years.* 그 건물은 지난 몇 년에 걸쳐 붕괴되어 오고 있다. / *the decay of the country's morals* 국가 도덕성의 붕괴

decay² v 1 [I, T] to be slowly destroyed by natural chemical processes, or to destroy something in this way ‖ 자연적 화학 작용으로 서서히 썩다, 또는 이렇게 사물을 썩게 하다. 부패하다[시키다]: *The dead animal had started to decay.* 죽은 동물이 부패하기 시작했다. / *Sugar decays teeth.* 설탕은 이빨을 썩게 한다. 2 [I] to become weaker or less important, or to no longer be in good condition, because of not being taken care of ‖ 돌보지 않아서 더 약해지거나 덜 중요해지다, 또는 더 이상 좋은 상태에 있지 않다. 쇠퇴하다. 시들다: *the decaying downtown area* 쇠퇴하는 번화가 구역

de·ceased /dɪˈsist/ n FORMAL **the deceased** someone who has died ‖ 죽은 사람. 고인(故人) – **deceased** adj

de·ceit /dɪˈsit/ n [U] behavior that is intended to make someone believe something that is not true ‖ 남에게 사실이 아닌 것을 믿게 하려는 의도의 행위. 속임. 사기. 책략. 기만: *the government's history of deceit and prejudice in its dealings with Native Americans* 미국 인디언들과의 관계에서 기만과 편견으로 일관한 정부의 역사.

de·ceit·ful /dɪˈsitfəl/ adj intending to make someone believe something that is not true ‖ 의도적으로 남에게 사실이 아닌 것을 믿게 하려고 하는. 남을 속이는[속일 작정인]. 협잡의

de·ceive /dɪˈsiv/ v [T] 1 to make someone believe something that is not true ‖ 남에게 사실이 아닌 것을 믿게 하다. 속이다. 사기를 치다: *Cusack tried to deceive the police.* 쿠삭은 경찰을 속이려 애썼다. 2 **deceive yourself** to pretend to yourself that something is not true, though you know that it is true ‖ 어떤 것이 사실임을 알면서도 스스로에게는 사실

이 아닌 척 가장하다. 자신을 속이다. 현실 도피적으로 생각하다: *Stop deceiving yourself! She's never coming back!* 정신 차려! 그녀는 절대 돌아오지 않아!

De·cem·ber /dɪˈsɛmbɚ/, written abbreviation **Dec.** n the twelfth month of the year ‖ 한 해의 열두 번째 달. 12월. —see usage note at JANUARY

de·cen·cy /ˈdisənsi/ n [U] the quality of being honest and, and respecting other people ‖ 정직하고 예의 바르며 다른 사람을 존중하는 성질. 고상함. 예의 바름: *You could at least have the decency to call if you know you're late.* 늦는다고 생각되면 적어도 전화해 주는 예의는 있어야지요.

de·cent /ˈdisənt/ adj 1 acceptable and good enough ‖ 충분히 수용할 만하고 좋은. 제대로 된. 알맞은: *Don't you have a decent pair of shoes?* 좀 괜찮은 신발 없습니까? 2 honest and good ‖ 정직하고 좋은. 고상한. 점잖은: *Dr. Green was a decent man.* 그린 박사는 예의 바른 사람이었다. 3 wearing enough clothes to not show too much of your body ‖ 신체를 지나치게 드러내지 않기 위해 충분한 옷을 입은. (남 앞에 나설 수 있는) 단정한 옷차림의: *Don't come in, I'm not decent.* 들어오지 마. 옷을 제대로 안 입었어. – **decently** adv

de·cen·tral·ize /diˈsɛntrəˌlaɪz/ v [T] to move parts of a government, organization etc. from one central place to several smaller ones ‖ 정부·기구 등의 부서를 하나의 중심부에서 여러 개의 작은 곳으로 옮기다. 탈중앙화하다. 분산시키다. 지방 분권화하다 – **decentralization** /diˌsɛntrələˈzeɪʃən, ˌdisɛn-/ n [U]

de·cep·tion /dɪˈsɛpʃən/ n [C, U] the act of deliberately making someone believe something that is not true ‖ 고의로 남에게 사실이 아닌 것을 믿게 하는 행위. 속임. 사기. 기만: *People were outraged when they learned of the deception.* 사람들은 자신들이 속았다는 걸 알았을 때 분노했다.

de·cep·tive /dɪˈsɛptɪv/ adj able to make someone believe something that is not true ‖ 남에게 사실이 아닌 것을 믿게 할 수 있는. 남을 속이는. 기만적인: *deceptive advertising* 기만적인 광고 – **deceptively** adj

dec·i·bel /ˈdɛsəˌbɛl, -bəl/ n TECHNICAL a unit for measuring how loud a sound is ‖ 소리의 크기를 측정하는데 쓰는 단위. 데시벨

de·cide /dɪˈsaɪd/ v 1 [I, T] to make a

choice or judgment about something ‖
어떤 것에 대해 선택하거나 판단하다. 결
정하다. 결심하다: *I've decided to stay
at home.* 난 집에 머물기로 결정했어. /
*Jane decided against going to
Washington on vacation.* 제인은 휴가 때
워싱턴에 가지 않기로 결정했다. / *Ted
decided (that) the car would cost too
much.* 테드는 그 차가 너무 비싸다고 판단
했다. / *I can't decide whether/if I want
fish or chicken.* 저는 생선을 먹을지 닭을
먹을지 결정을 못 내리겠습니다. **2
deciding factor** a very strong reason
that forces you to make a particular
decision ‖ 특정 결정을 내릴 수 밖에 없게
하는 매우 강력한 이유. 결정적 요인 **3** [T]
to influence the result of a game,
competition etc. ‖ 게임·시합 등의 결과에
영향을 미치다. 승패를 가르다. 승부를 정
하다: *One punch decided the fight.* 한 방
의 펀치가 그 싸움의 승부를 판가름했다.

decide on sth *phr v* [T] to choose one
thing from many possible choices ‖ 여러
가능한 선택들 중 하나를 고르다. 정하다:
*Have you decided on a name for the
baby?* 아기 이름을 정했니?

de·cid·ed /dɪˈsaɪdɪd/ *adj* definite and
easy to notice ‖ 명확하며 알아차리기 쉬
운. 분명한. 뚜렷한: *a decided change for
the worse* 더 악화된 쪽으로의 분명한 변
화 **– decidedly** *adv*

de·cid·u·ous /dɪˈsɪdʒuəs/ *adj*
deciduous trees have leaves that fall off
in autumn ‖ 나무가 가을에 잎이 떨어지
는. 낙엽성인 **–compare** EVERGREEN

dec·i·mal¹ /ˈdɛsəməl/ *adj* based on the
number ten ‖ 숫자 10에 기반한. 10진법
의: *a decimal system* 10진법

decimal² *n* TECHNICAL a number less
than one that is shown by a mark (.)
followed by the number of TENTHs, then
the number of HUNDREDTHs etc. ‖ 소수점
첫째 자릿수, 다음으로 소수점 둘째 자릿
수 등이 뒤따르며 (.)부호로 표시되는 1보
다 작은 수. 소수: *The decimal .37 is
equal to the fraction ³⁷/₁₀₀.* 소수 0.37은
분수 100분의 37과 동일하다.

decimal point /ˈ... ˌ./ *n* the mark (.)
in a DECIMAL, used in order to separate
whole numbers from TENTHs,
HUNDREDTHs etc. ‖ 정수를 소수점 첫째 자
릿수, 소수점 둘째 자릿수 등과 구분을 하
기 위하여 소수에서 사용하는 점 표시(.).
소수점

dec·i·mate /ˈdɛsəˌmeɪt/ *v* [T] to
destroy a large part of something ‖ 사물
의 많은 부분을 파괴하다. 대량 살해하다.
제거하다: *Disease decimated the*

population. 질병으로 많은 사람들이 목숨
을 잃었다.

de·ci·pher /dɪˈsaɪfɚ/ *v* [T] to find the
meaning of something that is difficult to
read or understand ‖ 읽거나 이해하기 어
려운 것의 의미를 찾아내다. 파악[판독,
해독]하다: *deciphering a code* 암호 해독
/ *I can't decipher his handwriting.* 나는
그의 필적을 판독할 수가 없다.

de·ci·sion /dɪˈsɪʒən/ *n* **1** a choice or
judgment that you make ‖ 사람이 내리는
선택이나 판단. 결정: *We'll make a
decision by Friday.* 우리는 금요일까지
결정을 내릴 것이다. / *Gina's decision to
go to college* 대학에 가겠다는 지나의 결
정 / *Do you expect to reach a decision
soon?* 곧 결정할 수 있을 거라 예상하십니
까? / *a decision about where to go on
vacation* 휴가 때 어디에 갈 것인지에 대
한 결정 **2** [U] the ability to make choices
or judgments quickly ‖ 선택이나 판단을
신속히 내릴 수 있는 능력. 결단력

decision-mak·ing /ˈ... ˌ.../ *n* [U] the
action of deciding on something, or the
ability to decide something ‖ 어떤 것에
대해 결정하는 행위, 또는 어떤 것을 결정
하는 능력. 의사 결정: *Most of the
decision-making is done by elected
officials.* 대부분의 의사 결정은 선출된 관
리들이 한다.

de·ci·sive /dɪˈsaɪsɪv/ *adj* **1** having a
great effect on the result of something ‖
어떤 것의 결과에 지대한 영향을 미치는.
결정적인: *a decisive moment in his
career* 그의 경력에 있어서 결정적인 순간
2 good at making decisions quickly ‖ 결
정을 신속히 내리는 데 능한. 단호한. 결
단력이 있는: *We need a strong decisive
leader.* 우리는 강하고 결단력이 있는 지
도자가 필요하다. **3** definite and not able
to be doubted ‖ 분명하고 의심할 수 없는.
명확한: *a decisive advantage* 분명한 이
익 **– decisively** *adv*

deck¹ /dɛk/ *n* **1** a
wooden floor outside
the back of a house,
used for relaxing on ‖
집의 뒤쪽 옥외에 휴식
용으로 만들어진 나무
바닥. 나무로 된 베란
다 **2** a set of playing
cards ‖ 게임용 카드의
한 벌: *Take one from
the top of the deck.* 한
벌의 카드에서 맨 윗장을 하나 뽑아라. **3**
the outside top level of a ship that you
can walk on, or any of the levels on a
ship, plane, or bus ‖ 걸어다닐 수 있는 배

deck

바깥의 평평한 상단, 또는 배[비행기, 버스]의 모든 평면. 갑판. 바닥층: *Let's go up on deck.* 갑판으로 올라가자.

deck² *v* [T] **1** also **deck** sb/sth ↔ **out** to make someone or something more attractive, especially for a special occasion ‖ 특히 특별한 경우에 사람이나 사물을 더 매력적으로 만들다. …을 꾸미다[장식하다]: *The street was decked out with flags for the big parade.* 그 거리는 대형 퍼레이드를 위해 깃발로 장식되었다. **2** SLANG to hit someone so hard that s/he falls over ‖ 남을 아주 세게 쳐서 쓰러뜨리다. …을 때려눕히다

dec·la·ra·tion /ˌdɛkləˈreɪʃən/ *n* [C, U] **1** a statement saying that something has officially begun or happened ‖ 어떤 것이 공식적으로 시작됐거나 발생했음을 알리는 진술. 공표. 선언: *a declaration of war* 선전(宣戰) 포고 **2** an official statement that gives information ‖ 정보를 제공하는 공식 진술. 고지. 고시

de·clare /dɪˈklɛr/ *v* [T] **1** to state officially and publicly that something is happening or that something is true ‖ 어떤 것이 일어나고 있거나 사실이라는 것을 공식적이고 공개적으로 말하다. 공표하다. 선언하다. 단언하다: *The US declared war on England in 1812.* 미국은 1812년에 영국에 선전포고했다. / *The doctor declared that she was dead.* 의사는 그녀가 죽었다고 공식 선언했다. / *The bridge has been declared unsafe.* 그 다리는 안전하지 않다고 공표되었다. / *Jones was declared the winner.* 존스가 승자로 선언됐다. **2** to say clearly and publicly what you think or feel ‖ 생각하거나 느끼는 바를 분명하고 공개적으로 말하다. 표명하다: *Parson declared (that) he would never go back there.* 파슨은 그곳에 절대로 돌아가지 않겠다는 입장을 표명했다. **3** to make an official statement saying how much money you have earned, what property you own etc. ‖ 돈을 얼마나 벌었고 소유한 재산이 무엇인지 등에 관해 공식 진술하다. 신고하다: *You must declare your full income.* 당신의 모든 수입을 신고해야 합니다.

de·cline¹ /dɪˈklaɪn/ *v* **1** [I] to decrease in quality, quantity, importance etc. ‖ 질·양·중요성 등이 감소하다. 쇠퇴[감퇴]하다. 기울다. 내려가다: *As his health has declined, so has his influence.* 그의 건강이 약해짐에 따라 영향력도 쇠퇴해 갔다. **2** [I, T] to refuse something, usually politely ‖ 어떤 것을 보통 정중히 거절하다. 거부하다: *We asked them to come, but they declined.* 우리는 그들에게 오라고 했지만 그들은 정중히 거절했다. / *The senator declined to make a statement.* 그 상원 의원은 성명 발표를 정중히 거절했다. —see usage note at REFUSE¹

decline² *n* [singular, U] a gradual decrease in the quality, quantity, or importance of something ‖ 사물의 질[양, 중요성]의 점진적 감소. 약화. 쇠퇴: *New car sales are on the decline.* 신차의 판매량이 감소하고 있다. / *a decline in profits* 이익의 점진적 감소

de·code /diˈkoʊd/ *v* [T] to discover the meaning of a secret or complicated message ‖ 비밀이나 복잡한 전언의 의미를 알아내다. 암호 등을 해독[번역]하다

de·com·pose /ˌdikəmˈpoʊz/ *v* [I, T] to decay or to make something do this ‖ 썩다, 또는 사물을 썩게 하다. 부패하다[시키다] –**decomposition** /ˌdikɑmpəˈzɪʃən/ *n* [U]

de·cor /ˈdeɪkɔr, deɪˈkɔr/ *n* [C, U] the furniture and decoration of a place ‖ 어떤 장소의 가구와 장식(물). 실내 장식

dec·o·rate /ˈdɛkəˌreɪt/ *v* [T] **1** to make something look more attractive by adding pretty things to it ‖ 예쁜 것을 덧붙여서 어떤 것을 더 매력적으로 보이게 만들다. 장식하다. 꾸미다: *This year we're decorating the Christmas tree with big red bows.* 올해 우리는 대형 붉은색 나비매듭 리본으로 크리스마스트리를 장식하려 한다. **2** to give someone an official sign of honor, such as a MEDAL ‖ 남에게 메달 등을 공식적인 명예의 표시로 주다. …에게 훈장을 수여하다: *He was decorated for bravery in the war.* 그는 무공(武功)으로 훈장을 받았다.

dec·o·ra·tion /ˌdɛkəˈreɪʃən/ *n* **1** something pretty that you add in order to make something look more attractive ‖ 물건을 더 매력적으로 보이도록 덧붙이는 예쁜 물체. 장식품: *Christmas decorations* 크리스마스 장식품 **2** [U] the way in which something is decorated ‖ 어떤 것이 장식되는 방식. 꾸밈. 장식: *the tasteful decoration of their living room* 그들의 고상한 거실 장식 **3** an official sign of honor, such as a MEDAL, that is given to someone ‖ 남에게 주어지는 메달 등의 공식적인 명예의 표시. 훈장

dec·o·ra·tive /ˈdɛkərətɪv/ *adj* pretty or attractive ‖ 예쁘거나 매력적인. 장식(용)의: *a decorative pot* 장식용 화분

dec·o·ra·tor /ˈdɛkəˌreɪtɚ/ *n* someone who chooses furniture, paint, curtains etc. for houses, offices etc. as his/her job ‖ 집·사무실 등에 쓸 가구·페인트·커튼 등을 고르는 직업인. 장식가

de·cor·um /dɪˈkɔrəm/ *n* [U] behavior that is respectful and correct for a particular occasion ‖ 특정한 경우에 맞는 정중하고 적절한 행동. 예의바름 – **decorous** /ˈdɛkərəs/ *adj*

de·coy /ˈdikɔɪ/ *n* something that is used in order to lead a person or a bird into a trap ‖ 사람이나 새를 덫으로 이끄는 데 사용하는 것. 미끼. 유인책 – **decoy** *v* [T]

de·crease¹ /dɪˈkris, ˈdikris/ *v* [I, T] to become less in size, number, or amount, or to make something do this ‖ 크기[수, 양]이 줄어들다, 또는 어떤 것을 줄어들게 하다. 감소하다[시키다]: *The company's profits decreased in 1992.* 1992년에 회사 이윤이 감소했다. — opposite INCREASE¹

de·crease² /ˈdikris, dɪˈkris/ *n* [C, U] the process of reducing something, or the amount by which it is reduced ‖ 어떤 것을 줄이는 과정, 또는 줄어든 양. 감소(량). 감퇴(량): *a decrease in sales* 판매의 감소

de·cree¹ /dɪˈkri/ *n* an official command or decision ‖ 공식 명령이나 결정. 법령. 포고

decree² *v* [T] to make a DECREE ‖ 공식 명령을 내리다. 포고하다. 판결하다

de·crep·it /dɪˈkrɛpɪt/ *adj* old and in bad condition ‖ 오래되고 불량한 상태인. 낡은. 약해진. 노쇠한. 늙어빠진

de·crim·i·nal·ize /diˈkrɪmənəˌlaɪz/ *v* [T] to state officially that something is no longer illegal ‖ 어떤 것이 더 이상 불법적이지 않다고 공식 선언하다. …을 해금하다. 기소[처벌] 대상에서 제외하다 – **decriminalization** /diˌkrɪmɪnələˈzeɪʃən/ *n* [U]

de·cry /dɪˈkraɪ/ *v* [T] FORMAL to state publicly that you do not approve of something ‖ 어떤 것을 찬성하지 않는다고 공개적으로 말하다. …을 헐뜯다[깎아내리다]. …을 공공연히 비난하다

ded·i·cate /ˈdɛdəˌkeɪt/ *v* [T] **1** to say that something such as a book, movie, song etc. has been written, made, or sung in honor of someone ‖ 책·영화·노래 등이 남에게 경의를 표하여 쓰여졌다고[만들어졌다고, 불려졌다고] 말하다. (…에게 …을) 바치다[헌정하다]: *The book is dedicated to his mother.* 그 책은 자기 어머니에게 바쳐졌다[헌정되었다]. **2** **dedicate yourself/your life to sth** to use all your energy, time, effort etc. for one particular thing ‖ 특정한 한 가지 일을 위해 모든 에너지·시간·노력 등을 사용하다. …에 전념[헌신]하다/일생을 바치다: *I've dedicated my life to my work.*

나는 내 일생을 그 일에 전념해 왔다. **3** to state in an official ceremony that something such as a building or bridge will be given someone's name ‖ 공식 기념식에서, 건물이나 다리등의 물체에 사람의 이름이 붙여질 것임을 언명하다. (신축 건물 등을) 개소[개관]하다: *a chapel dedicated to Saint Paul* 성 바울이라 이름이 붙여진 예배당

ded·i·cat·ed /ˈdɛdəˌkeɪtɪd/ *adj* working very hard for a particular purpose ‖ 특정 목적을 위해 매우 열심히 일하는. 헌신[전념]하는: *She's very dedicated to her job.* 그녀는 자기 일에 매우 열심이다.

ded·i·ca·tion /ˌdɛdɪˈkeɪʃən/ *n* **1** [U] the hard work or effort that someone puts into a particular activity ‖ 사람이 특정 활동에 쏟아 붓는 고된 일이나 노력. 헌신: *He shows great dedication to his work.* 그는 자기 일에 대단한 노력을 보인다. **2** the act or ceremony of dedicating (DEDICATE) something to someone ‖ 어떤 것을 남에게 바치는 행위나 의식. 헌납(식). 헌당(식) **3** the words used in dedicating a book ‖ 책을 헌정하는 데 쓰이는 말. 헌정사

de·duce /dɪˈdus/ *v* [T] FORMAL to make a judgment based on the information that you have ‖ 가지고 있는 정보에 근거하여 판단을 내리다. 추론하다. 연역하다

de·duct /dɪˈdʌkt/ *v* [T] to take away an amount or a part from a total ‖ 총액에서 일정량이나 일부를 빼다. 공제하다: *Taxes are deducted from your pay.* 봉급에서 세금이 공제된다. – **deductible** *adj*

de·duct·i·ble /dɪˈdʌktəbəl/ *n* the part of a bill you must pay before the insurance company will pay the rest ‖ 보험 청구 금액 중 보험 회사가 나머지를 지불하기 전에 본인이 내야 하는 일부 금액. 본인 부담금. 공제금액

de·duc·tion /dɪˈdʌkʃən/ *n* [C, U] **1** the process of taking away an amount from a total, or the amount that is taken away ‖ 총액에서 일정액을 빼는 과정, 또는 공제된 액수. 공제(액). 차감(액): *You can receive a tax deduction for giving money to charity.* (=you can pay less tax if you give money to charity) 자선 단체에 돈을 기부하면 세금 공제를 받을 수 있다. **2** the process of making a judgment about something, based on the information that you have ‖ 가지고 있는 정보에 근거하여, 어떤 것에 대한 판단을 내리는 과정. 추론. 연역: *a game that teaches logic and deduction* 논리와 추론을 가르쳐 주는 게임

deed /did/ *n* **1** LITERARY an action ‖ 행

동: *good deeds* 훌륭한 행동 **2** LAW an official paper that is a record of an agreement, especially one that says who owns property ‖ 특히 재산 소유자를 밝히는 계약을 기록한 공식 문서. 증서

deem /dim/ *v* [T] FORMAL to consider something in a particular way ‖ 어떤 것을 특정한 방식으로 고려하다. 여기다. 생각하다: *The judge deemed several of the questions inappropriate.* 그 판사는 몇 가지 질문이 부적절하다고 여겼다.

deep¹ /dip/ *adj*

1 ▶GO FAR IN/DOWN 안쪽[아래쪽]으로 멀리 가다◀ going far down or far in from the top, the front, or the surface of something ‖ 위쪽[앞쪽, 사물의 표면]으로부터 아래쪽이나 안쪽으로 멀리 간. 깊은: *The water's not very deep here.* 여기는 물이 그다지 깊지 않다. / *Terry had a deep cut in his forehead.* 테리는 이마에 깊은 상처를 입었다. / *a shelf 3 feet long and 8 inches deep* 길이가 3피트이고 폭이 8인치인 선반

2 ▶FEELING/BELIEF 느낌/믿음◀ a deep feeling or belief is very strong and sincere ‖ 감정이나 믿음이 매우 강렬하고 진지한: *deep feelings of hatred* 강한 증오

3 ▶SOUND 소리◀ a deep sound is very low ‖ 소리가 매우 낮은. 굵은. 저음의: *a deep voice* 굵은 목소리

4 ▶COLOR 색깔◀ a deep color is dark and strong ‖ 색깔이 진하고 강렬한. 짙은: *a deep blue sky* 짙은 파란 하늘

5 ▶SERIOUS 진지한◀ serious and often difficult to understand ‖ 진지하면서 종종 이해하기 어려운. 난해한: *a deep conversation about the meaning of life* 인생의 의미에 관한 심오한 대화

6 deep sleep a sleep that is difficult to wake up from ‖ 깨어나기 어려운 잠. 숙면

7 take a deep breath to breathe in a lot of air at once, especially in order to do something difficult or frightening ‖ 특히 어렵거나 무서운 일을 하기 위해 한 번에 많은 공기를 들이마시다. 심호흡하다: *I took a deep breath and plunged into the water.* 나는 심호흡하고 나서 물속으로 뛰어들었다.

8 be in deep trouble/water INFORMAL to be in serious trouble or in an extremely difficult situation ‖ 심각한 문제나 지극히 어려운 상황에 처해 있다. 곤경에 빠지다: *If mom sees you doing that,*

you'll be in deep trouble! 네가 그것을 하는 것을 엄마가 알면 너는 곤경에 빠질 것이다.

9 deep in debt owing a lot of money ‖ 많은 돈을 빚지고 있는. 빚에 쪼들리는

10 deep in thought/conversation thinking so hard or talking so much that you do not notice anything else ‖ 너무 깊이 생각하거나 너무 많이 말하여 다른 것을 알아차지 못하는. 깊은 생각에 잠겨/대화에 심취하는: *Martin sat at his desk, deep in thought.* 마틴은 책상에 앉아 깊은 생각에 잠겼다.

11 go off the deep end INFORMAL to suddenly become angry or violent ‖ 갑자기 화를 내거나 사나워지다. 자제심을 잃다. 욱하다 —see also DEPTH

deep² *adv* **1** far into something ‖ 사물 속 깊이. …의 깊숙한 곳까지. 깊은 곳에: *He stepped deep into the mud.* 그는 진흙탕 속으로 깊이 걸어 들어갔다. **2 deep down** **a)** if you feel or know something deep down, then you are sure about it even though you may not admit it ‖ 어떤 것을 인정하지는 않을지라도 마음으로는 확신하는. 내심(으로): *Deep down, I knew she was gone forever.* 나는 내심으로 그녀가 영영 가 버렸다는 것을 알았다. **b)** if someone is good, evil etc. deep down, that is what s/he is really like even though s/he hides it ‖ 사람이 비록 선함·악함 등을 숨기고 있지만 그 사람의 내심에 있는 실제 모습의. 본심은: *He seems mean, but deep down he's really very nice.* 그는 비열하게 보이지만 실제로 본심은 아주 괜찮다. **3 two/three etc. deep** in two, three etc. rows or layers ‖ 둘·셋 등의 줄이나 겹으로. 두/세 겹 — see also **run deep** (RUN)

deep·en /'dipən/ *v* [I, T] to make something deeper or to become deeper ‖ 어떤 것을[이] 더 깊게 하거나 깊어지다. 짙어지다. 짙게 하다

deep freeze /ˌ. '. / *n* ⇨ FREEZER

deep fried /ˌ. '. ./ *adj* cooked in a lot of hot oil ‖ 많은 뜨거운 기름 속에서 요리된. 많은 기름으로 튀긴 —**deep fry** *v* [T]

deep·ly /'dipli/ *adv* extremely or very much ‖ 지극히 또는 매우 많이. 깊이. 깊게: *The Americans did not want to get deeply involved in a European war.* 미국인들은 유럽 전쟁에 깊이 개입하고 싶지 않았다.

deep-seat·ed /ˌ. '../, **deep-rooted** *adj* a deep-seated feeling or idea is strong and very difficult to change ‖ 감정이나 생각이 강하고 바꾸기가 매우 어려운. 뿌리 깊은. 심층의

deer /dɪr/ *n, plural* **deer** a large wild animal that lives in forests, the male of which has long horns that look like tree branches || 수컷은 나뭇가지 같은 긴 뿔을 가진, 숲 속에 서식하는 몸집이 큰 야생 동물. 사슴

de·face /dɪ'feɪs/ *v* [T] to spoil the appearance of something, especially by writing or making marks on it || 특히 어떤 것의 표면에 낙서나 표시를 해서 외관을 손상하다. 흉하게 하다: *walls defaced by graffiti* 낙서로 손상된 벽

de·fame /dɪ'feɪm/ *v* [T] FORMAL to write or say something that makes people have a bad opinion of someone || 어떤 사람에 대하여 나쁜 견해를 가지도록 someone가 를 쓰거나 말하다. 중상하다. 비방하다 – **defamation** /ˌdɛfə'meɪʃən/ *n* [U] – **defamatory** /dɪ'fæməˌtɔri/ *adj*

de·fault¹ /dɪ'fɔlt/ *v* [I] to not do something that you are legally supposed to || 법적으로 하기로 되어 있는 일을 하지 않다. 이행하지 않다: *He defaulted on his loan payments.* 그는 대출금 변제를 이행하지 않았다.

default² *n* **1** [U] failure to do something that you are supposed to do || 하기로 되어 있는 일을 하지 않음. 불이행. 태만: *a default on his mortgage payments* 그의 주택 융자금 변제 불이행 / *The other team never arrived, so we won by default.* (=because they failed to arrive) 상대 팀이 도착하지 않아서 우리는 부전승으로 이겼다. **2** [C usually singular] the way in which things will be arranged on a computer screen unless you change them || 변경하지 않는 한 컴퓨터 화면에 배열되도록 예정된 방식. 디폴트. 하드[소프트]웨어의 초기 설정

de·feat¹ /dɪ'fit/ *v* [T] **1** to win a victory over someone || 남을 누르고 승리를 얻다. …을 패배시키다. 물리치다: *Michigan defeated USC in Saturday's game.* 미시간 팀은 토요일 경기에서 USC 팀을 패배시켰다. **2** to make something fail || 어떤 것을 실패하게 하다. …을 좌절시키다. 꺾다: *The plan was defeated by a lack of money.* 그 계획은 자금 부족으로 좌절되었다.

defeat² *n* **1** [C, U] failure to win or succeed || 이기거나 성공하지 못함. 패배. 패전: *He'll never admit defeat.* (=admit that he has failed) 그는 결코 패배를 인정하지 않을 것이다. / *The vote resulted in a serious defeat for the governor.* 투표의 결과는 주지사의 참패였다. **2** [singular] victory over someone or something || 사람이나 사물에 대한 승리. 타파. 정복: *The defeat of racism is our main goal.* 인종 차별을 타파하는 것이 우리의 주요한 목표다.

de·feat·ist /dɪ'fitɪst/ *n* someone who expects to fail || 실패하리라 예상하는 사람. 패배주의자

def·e·cate /'dɛfəˌkeɪt/ *v* [I] FORMAL to get rid of waste matter from your BOWELS || 창자에서 노폐물을 배출하다. 배변하다 – **defecation** /ˌdɛfə'keɪʃən/ *n* [U]

de·fect¹ /'difɛkt, dɪ'fɛkt/ *n* a fault or a lack of something that makes something not perfect || 사물을 완전하지 못하게 하는 결함이나 부족. 결점. 약점. 단점: *The cars are tested for any defects before being sold.* 자동차는 판매되기 전에 결함 여부에 대한 검사를 받는다. / *a birth defect* (=something that makes a baby not normal) 선천적 결함

de·fect² /dɪ'fɛkt/ *v* [I] to leave your own country or a group and join or go to an opposing one || 자신의 조국이나 집단을 떠나 반대편에 합류하거나 가다. 이탈[배반]하다. 망명하다 – **defection** /dɪ'fɛkʃən/ *n* [C, U] – **defector** /dɪ'fɛktər/ *n*

de·fec·tive /dɪ'fɛktɪv/ *adj* not made correctly or not working correctly || 제대로 제작되지 않은, 또는 제대로 작동하지 않는. 결함이 있는. 불충분한: *defective machinery* 결함이 있는 기계

de·fend /dɪ'fɛnd/ *v* **1** [T] to protect someone or something from being attacked or taken away || 사람이나 사물이 공격이나 제거당하지 않도록 보호하다. 방어하다. 지키다: *You should learn to defend yourself.* 너는 네 자신을 지키는 법을 배워야 한다. / *Soldiers defended the fort from attack.* 군인들은 공격으로부터 요새를 방어했다. **2** [T] to use arguments to protect something or someone from criticism || 비판으로부터 사물이나 사람을 보호하기 위하여 논쟁을 하다. 변호[변론]하다. 변명하다: *How can you defend the use of animals for cosmetics testing?* 동물을 화장품 시험에 이용하는 것을 너는 어떻게 변론할 수 있느냐? / *He had to defend himself against their charges.* 그는 그들의 비난에 대항해 스스로를 변호해야 했다. **3** [I, T] to protect your GOAL in a game, and prevent your opponents from getting points || 경기에서 자신의 골을 지키며 상대방의 득점을 막다. **4** [T] to be a lawyer for someone who is said to be guilty of a crime || 범죄 혐의를 받는 사람을 위해 변

호사가 되다. 변호하다 **– defender** *n* **–**
defensible /dɪˈfɛnsəbəl/ *adj*
de·fend·ant /dɪˈfɛndənt/ *n* LAW the
person in a court of law who has been
charged with doing something illegal ‖
불법 행위로 기소돼 법정에 선 사람. 피고
(인) **—compare** PLAINTIFF
de·fense¹ /dɪˈfɛns/ *n* **1** [U] the act of
protecting someone or something from
attack or criticism ‖ 공격이나 비난으로부
터 사람이나 사물을 보호하는 행위. 변호.
옹호. 변명. 항변: *Senator Stevens*
spoke today in defense of the bill to
make handguns illegal. 스티븐스 상원
의원은 오늘 권총을 불법화하는 법안에 대
한 옹호 발언을 했다. **2** [U] the weapons
and people that a country uses to
protect itself from attack ‖ 국가가 공격으
로부터 자국을 보호하기 위해 사용하는 무
기와 사람. 방어. 수비. 방위: *the*
country's military defense 국가의 군사
방위 / *Defense spending* (=spending
money on weapons etc.) *has increased.*
방위비가 증가했다. **3** something that is
used for protection against something
else ‖ 다른 것에 대항하여 보호하는 데에
쓰이는 것. 방어물[시설, 수단]: *Vitamin*
C is my defense against colds. 비타민 C
는 내 감기 예방책이다. **4** the things that
are said in a court of law to prove that
someone is not guilty of a crime ‖ 범죄에
대해 무죄임을 증명하기 위해 법정에서 진
술하는 것. 변론: *Our defense is pretty*
weak. 우리의 변론은 너무 미약하다. **5**
the defense the people in a court of
law who are trying to show that
someone is not guilty of a crime ‖ 법정에
서 어떤 사람이 무죄라는 것을 증명하기
위해 노력하는 사람들. 피고측(변호인단):
Is the defense ready to call their first
witness? 변호인은 첫 증인을 소환할 준비
가 되어 있습니까?
de·fense² /ˈdifɛns/ *n* [U] the players in
a game such as football whose main job
is to try to prevent the other team from
getting points ‖ 미식축구 등의 경기에서
상대 팀이 득점하는 것을 막으려는 것이
주요 임무인 선수. 수비수 **—see picture**
on page 946
de·fense·less /dɪˈfɛnslɪs/ *adj* unable
to protect yourself from being hurt or
criticized ‖ 해를 입거나 비판 받는 것으로
부터 자신을 보호할 수 없는. 무방비의
defense mech·a·nism /ˈ. .ˌ…/ *n* **1**
a process in your brain that makes you
forget things that are too unpleasant or
painful to think about ‖ 생각하기에 너무
불쾌하고 고통스러운 일을 잊게 하는 뇌의

작용. 방어 기제 **2** a natural reaction in
your body that protects you from illness
or danger ‖ 질병이나 위험으로부터 자신
을 보호하는 신체의 자연 반응. 방어 반응
de·fen·sive¹ /dɪˈfɛnsɪv/ *adj* **1** used or
intended for protection against attack ‖
공격에 대해 방어하기 위해 쓰이거나 방어
목적의. 방어(용)의: *defensive weapons*
방어 무기 **2** behaving in a way that
shows you think someone is criticizing
or attacking you ‖ 어떤 사람이 자신을 비
판하거나 공격한다는 생각을 나타내는 방
식으로 행동하는. 수세의. 방어적인: *She*
got really defensive when I asked her
why she hadn't finished. 내가 그녀에게
끝마치지 못한 이유를 물었을 때 그녀는
바로 방어적이 되었다. **3** relating to the
DEFENSE in sports such as football ‖ 미식
축구 등의 스포츠에서 수비와 관련된. 수
비의: *a defensive play* 수비 플레이 **–**
defensively *adv* **– defensiveness** *n*
[U]
defensive² *n* **on the defensive** having
to react to criticism or an attack ‖ 비판
이나 공격에 반응을 보이는. 수세에 있는.
수세를 취하는: *Danton was on the*
defensive after Roberts disagreed with
him. 댄턴은 로버츠가 의견을 달리 한 후
수세를 취하고 있었다.
de·fer /dɪˈfɚ/ *v* **-rred, -rring** [T] to
delay something until a later date ‖ 더
나중으로 어떤 것을 연기하다. 늦추다. 미
루다: *His military service was deferred*
until he finished college. 그는 대학을 졸
업할 때까지 병역을 연기했다.
defer to sb/sth *phr v* [T] FORMAL to
accept someone's opinion or decision
because you have respect for that
person ‖ 누군가에 대한 존경심이 있어서
그의 의견이나 결정을 받아들이다. 따르
다. 맡기다: *She had more experience, so*
I deferred to her suggestions. 그녀는 더
많은 경험을 했으므로 나는 그녀의 제안에
따랐다.
def·er·ence /ˈdɛfərəns/ *n* [U] FORMAL
behavior that shows you respect
someone and are willing to accept
his/her opinions or judgment ‖ 누군가를
존경해서 기꺼이 그의 의견이나 판단을 받
아들이는 것을 나타내는 행동. 복종. 경의
– deferential /ˌdɛfəˈrɛnʃəl/ *adj*
de·fi·ant /dɪˈfaɪənt/ *adj* refusing to do
what someone tells you to do because
you do not respect him/her ‖ 그 사람을
존경하지 않아서 하라는 것을 하지 않는.
시비조의. 도전적인. 반항적인 **–**
defiance *n* [U] **– defiantly** *adv*
de·fi·cien·cy /dɪˈfɪʃənsi/ *n* [C, U] **1** a

lack of something that is needed ‖ 필요로 하는 사물의 부족. 결핍: *a vitamin deficiency* 비타민 결핍 **2** 충분히 좋지 않은 상태. 결함: *the deficiencies of the public transportation system* 대중 교통 체계의 문제점

de·fi·cient /dɪ'fɪʃənt/ *adj* **1** not having or containing enough of something ‖ 어떤 것을 충분히 가지거나 포함하지 않은. 부족한. 결핍된: *food deficient in iron* 철분이 부족한 음식 **2** not good enough ‖ 충분히 좋지 않은. 결함 있는. 불완전한

def·i·cit /'dɛfəsɪt/ *n* the difference between the amount of money that a company or country has and the higher amount that it needs ‖ 회사나 국가가 보유하고 있는 금액과 필요한 더 많은 금액 사이의 차액. 적자: *Our records show a deficit of $2.5 million.* 우리의 기록에 의하면 250만 달러의 적자가 있다.

de·file /dɪ'faɪl/ *v* [T] FORMAL to make something less pure, good, or holy ‖ 어떤 것을 덜 순수하게[좋게, 신성하게] 만들다. 더럽히다. 손상시키다. 모독하다: *graves defiled by Nazi symbols* 나치의 상징물로 인해 손상된 무덤들

de·fine /dɪ'faɪn/ *v* [T] **1** to show or describe what something is or means ‖ 사물이 무엇인지 또는 무엇을 의미하는지를 나타내거나 묘사하다. 정의(定義)를 내리다: *Some words are hard to define.* 몇몇 단어들은 정의하기가 어렵다. **2** to clearly show the limits or shape of something ‖ 사물의 경계나 형상을 뚜렷이 나타내다. 한정하다. 분명히 하다: *The footprints were sharply defined in the snow.* 발자국이 눈 속에 선명하게 나타나 있었다. – **definable** *adj*

def·i·nite /'dɛfənɪt/ *adj* clearly known, seen, or stated, and completely certain ‖ 분명히 알려지거나 보여지거나 진술되어 아주 확실한. 뚜렷한. 명확한: *They want to leave Monday; John was very definite about it.* 그들은 월요일에 떠나기를 원한다. 존은 그 점에 관해 아주 분명했다 ./ *We don't have a definite arrangement yet.* 우리는 아직 확실한 계획이 없다. —opposite INDEFINITE

definite ar·ti·cle /,... '.../ *n* ⇨ ARTICLE

def·i·nite·ly /'dɛfənɪtli/ *adv* certainly and without any doubt ‖ 확실하여 의심할 여지 없이. 분명하게. 틀림없이: *That was definitely the best movie I've seen all year.* 그 영화는 분명 내가 1년간 봤던 영화 중 최고였다. / *It's definitely not the right time to tell her.* 그녀에게 말할 적절한 시기는 분명 아니다.

def·i·ni·tion /,dɛfə'nɪʃən/ *n* **1** a phrase or sentence that says exactly what a word, phrase, or idea means ‖ 단어[구, 생각]가 뜻하는 것을 정확히 전달하는 구나 문장. 설명. 정의 **2** [U] the clearness of something such as a picture or sound ‖ 사진이나 소리 등의 선명함. 선명도. 해상력(解像力): *The photograph lacks definition.* 그 사진은 선명도가 떨어진다.

de·fin·i·tive /dɪ'fɪnətɪv/ *adj* **1** a definitive book, description etc. is considered to be the best and cannot be improved ‖ 책·서술 등이 최고라서 더 이상 개선될 수 없다고 생각되는. 가장 신뢰할 만한. 가장 확실한: *Wasserman's definitive book on wine* 포도주에 관한 바서만의 믿을만한 저서 **2** a definitive statement, answer etc. cannot be doubted or changed ‖ 진술이나 답변 등이 의심스럽거나 변경될 수 없는. 최종적인. 결정적인. 분명한: *The group has taken a definitive stand against pornography.* 그 단체는 음란물에 반대하는 분명한 입장을 취했다. – **definitively** *adv*

de·flate /dɪ'fleɪt, di-/ *v* **1** [I, T] if something deflates or if you deflate it, it becomes smaller because the air or gas inside it comes out —opposite INFLATE ‖ 안에 있던 공기나 가스가 빠져나가서 더 작아지다. 공기를 빼다. 오므라들게 하다 **2** [T] to make someone feel less important or confident ‖ 남에게 중요성이나 자신감을 덜 느끼게 하다. 풀 죽게 하다. 기를 꺾다: *I'd love to deflate that ego of his!* 그의 자존심을 꺾어 버리고 싶어! **3** [T] TECHNICAL to change the economic rules or conditions in a country so that prices become lower or stop rising ‖ 가격이 더 떨어지게 하거나 상승하지 못하도록 국가의 경제 법규나 조건을 바꾸다. (통화를) 수축시키다 – **deflation** /dɪ'fleɪʃən/ *n* [U]

de·flect /dɪ'flɛkt/ *v* **1** [I, T] to turn something in a different direction by hitting it, or to be turned in this way ‖ 어떤 것을 쳐서 다른 방향으로 돌리거나 이렇게 돌려지다. 빗나가다. 빗나가게 하다: *The ball was deflected into the crowd.* 그 공은 빗맞아 관중에게로 날아갔다. **2 deflect attention/criticism/ anger etc.** to stop people paying attention to something, criticizing it etc. ‖ 사람들이 사물에 주의를 기울이거나 비판하는 일 등을 하지 못하게 하다. 관심/비판/분노를 피하다 – **deflection** /dɪ'flɛkʃən/ *n* [C, U]

de·form /dɪ'fɔrm/ *v* [T] to change the

usual shape of something so that its usefulness or appearance is spoiled ‖ 사물의 유용성이나 외관이 손상되도록 정상적인 형상을 바꾸다. …을 변형시키다. 흉하게 하다. 일그러뜨리다: *The disease had deformed his left hand.* 질병으로 그의 왼손이 흉해졌다. – **deformed** *adj* – **deformation** /ˌdifɔrˈmeɪʃən/ *n* [C, U]

de·form·i·ty /dɪˈfɔrməti/ *n* [C, U] a condition in which part of someone's body is not the normal shape ‖ 신체의 일부가 정상적인 형태가 아닌 상태. 불구. 기형

de·fraud /dɪˈfrɔd/ *v* [T] to deceive a person or organization in order to get money from him, her, or it ‖ 돈을 얻으려고 사람이나 조직을 속이다. 속여서 빼앗다. 사취하다

de·frost /dɪˈfrɔst/ *v* **1** [I, T] if frozen food defrosts, or if you defrost it, it gets warmer until it is not frozen ‖ 냉동 식품 등을 얼지 않은 상태가 되게 하다. 해동(解凍)시키다 **2** [I, T] if a FREEZER or REFRIGERATOR defrosts, or if you defrost it, it is turned off so that the ice inside it melts ‖ 냉동기·냉장고의 전원을 꺼서 얼음이[을] 녹다[녹이다]. **3** [T] to remove ice or steam from the windows of a car by blowing warm air onto them ‖ 자동차 유리창의 얼음이나 김을 따뜻한 공기를 불어서 제거하다. 성에를 없애다

deft /dɛft/ *adj* quick and skillful ‖ 신속하고 솜씨 좋은. 능숙한: *a deft catch* 호수비(好守備) – **deftly** *adv*

de·funct /dɪˈfʌŋkt/ *adj* FORMAL no longer existing or useful ‖ 더 이상 존재하지 않거나 쓸모가 없는. 죽은. 소멸한. 쇠퇴한

de·fuse /diˈfyuz/ *v* [T] **1** to stop a bomb from exploding ‖ 폭탄의 폭발을 막다. 신관을 제거하다 **2** to improve a difficult situation ‖ 어려운 상황을 개선하다. 누그러뜨리다. 완화시키다: *Tim tried to defuse the tension.* 팀은 긴장을 완화시키려고 했다.

de·fy /dɪˈfaɪ/ *v* [T] **1** to refuse to obey someone or something ‖ 사람이나 어떤 것에 복종하기를 거부하다. 무시[거역, 반항]하다: *He defied his father's wishes and joined the army.* 그는 아버지의 바람을 거스르고 군에 입대했다. **2 defy description/analysis/imagination etc.** to be almost impossible to describe or understand ‖ 묘사하거나 이해하는 것이 거의 불가능하다. 형언[분석/상상]할 수 없다: *The place just defies description.* 그 장소는 뭐라고 형언할 수가 없다.

de·gen·er·ate[1] /dɪˈdʒɛnəˌreɪt/ *v* [I] to

become worse ‖ 악화되다. 저하[쇠퇴, 퇴보]하다. 타락하다: *The party soon degenerated into a drunken brawl.* 파티는 곧바로 주정꾼들의 소란으로 엉망이 되어 버렸다. – **degeneration** /dɪˌdʒɛnəˈreɪʃən/ *n* [U]

de·gen·e·rate[2] /dɪˈdʒɛnərɪt/ *adj* **1** worse than before in quality ‖ 이전보다 품질이 나빠진. 저하된. 악화된 **2** having very low moral standards ‖ 매우 낮은 도덕 수준을 가진. 퇴폐한. 타락한 – **degenerate** *n*

de·grade /dɪˈgreɪd, di/ *v* [T] **1** to treat someone without respect, or to make people lose their respect for someone ‖ 누군가를 존경심 없이 대하거나 사람들이 존경심을 잃게 하다. 체면을 손상하다. 품위를 떨어뜨리다: *Don't degrade yourself by arguing with him.* 그 사람과 다퉈서 너의 품위를 떨어뜨리지 마라. / *Pornography degrades women.* 음란물은 여성들의 품위를 떨어뜨린다. **2** FORMAL to make a situation or condition worse ‖ 상황이나 상태를 악화시키다: *The proposed law could degrade safety standards.* 입법안은 안전 기준을 저하시킬 수 있다. – **degradation** /ˌdɛgrəˈdeɪʃən/ *n* [U]

de·grad·ing /dɪˈgreɪdɪŋ/ *adj* making people lose their respect for someone, or making you feel that other people have lost respect for you ‖ 사람에 대한 존경심을 잃게 하는, 또는 남들이 자신에 대한 존경심을 잃어 버렸다고 느끼게 하는. 품위를 떨어뜨리는. 체면[자존심]을 손상하는: *She treats her children in a degrading way.* 그녀는 자녀들을 모욕적으로 대한다.

de·gree /dɪˈgri/ *n* **1** a unit for measuring temperature or the size of an angle ‖ 온도나 각도의 크기를 측정하는 단위. 도 **2** [C, U] the level or amount of something, especially of ability or progress ‖ 특히 능력이나 발달의 수준이나 양. 정도. 범위: *students with different degrees of ability* 각기 다른 수준의 능력을 가진 학생들 / *To what degree can he be trusted?* 그를 어느 정도까지 신뢰할 수 있을까? **3** a course of study at a university, or the QUALIFICATION given to someone who has successfully completed this ‖ 대학에서의 공부 과정, 또는 이 과정을 성공적으로 끝마친 자에게 수여되는 자격. 학사. 학위: *a law degree* 법학사 / *a degree in history* 역사학 학위

de·hy·drate /diˈhaɪdreɪt/ *v* **1** [T] to remove all the water from something ‖ 어떤 것에서 모든 수분을 제거하다. 탈수

하다 **2** [I] to lose too much water from your body ‖ 신체의 수분이 너무 많이 빠져 나가다. 탈수하다. 탈수 상태가 되다 – **dehydrated** *adj* – **dehydration** /ˌdihaɪˈdreɪʃən/ *n* [U]

deign /deɪn/ *v* **deign to do sth** HUMOROUS to agree to do something that you think you are too important to do ‖ 하기에는 자존심이 허락하지 않는 일을 하는 것에 동의하다. 황송하게도[송구스럽게도] …해 주시다: *She finally deigned to join us for lunch.* 그녀는 마침내 황송하게도 우리와 점심을 같이 하기로 하셨다.

de·i·ty /ˈdiəti, ˈdeɪ-/ *n* a god or GODDESS ‖ 신이나 여신

dé·jà· vu /ˌdeɪʒɑ ˈvu/ *n* [U] the feeling that what is happening now has happened before in exactly the same way ‖ 현재 발생하는 일이 과거에 아주 똑같이 발생했던 것으로 느끼는 감정. 기시감(旣視感)

de·ject·ed /dɪˈdʒɛktɪd/ *adj* sad and disappointed ‖ 슬프고 낙심한. 기가 죽은. 풀 죽은. 의기소침한: *a dejected look* 풀 죽은 표정 – **dejectedly** *adv* – **dejection** /dɪˈdʒɛkʃən/ *n* [U]

de·lay¹ /dɪˈleɪ/ *v* **1** [I, T] to wait until a later time to do something ‖ 무엇을 하는 것을 나중까지 기다리다. 연기하다. 지체하다: *We've decided to delay the trip until next month.* 우리는 다음 달까지 여행을 연기하기로 결정했다. / *Don't delay, call us today!* 지체하지 말고 오늘 우리한테 전화해! **2** [T] to make someone or something late ‖ 사람이나 사물을 늦게 하다. 지연시키다: *Our flight was delayed by bad weather.* 우리 비행편이 악천후로 지연되었다. – **delayed** *adj*

delay² *n* [C, U] a situation in which someone or something is made to wait, or the length of the waiting time ‖ 사람이나 사물을 기다리게 하는 상황, 또는 대기 시간. 지체. 지연 (시간): *There are severe delays on Route 95 because of an accident.* 사고로 인해 95번 도로는 심하게 지체되고 있다. / *Delays of two hours or more are common.* 두 시간 이상의 지체는 흔한 일이다. / *Do it without delay!* 그 일을 지체없이 하도록 해!

de·lec·ta·ble /dɪˈlɛktəbəl/ *adj* FORMAL very pleasant to taste, smell etc. ‖ 맛이나 냄새 등이 아주 기분 좋은

del·e·gate¹ /ˈdɛləgɪt/ *n* someone who is chosen to speak, vote, and make decisions for a group ‖ 집단을 대표해 연설·투표·결정을 하도록 뽑힌 사람. 대리자. 대표자: *Delegates from 50 colleges met to discuss the issue.* 50개 대학의 대

표들이 그 문제를 논의하기 위해 만났다.

del·e·gate² /ˈdɛləˌgeɪt/ *v* [I, T] to give part of your work or the things you are responsible for to someone in a lower position than you ‖ 보다 하위직에 있는 사람에게 자신이 책임 맡고 있는 일이나 업무의 일부를 주다. 위임하다: *Smaller jobs should be delegated to your assistant.* 사소한 업무는 조수에게 넘겨주어야 한다.

del·e·ga·tion /ˌdɛləˈgeɪʃən/ *n* **1** a small group of people who are chosen to speak, vote, and make decisions for a larger group or organization ‖ 더 큰 집단이나 조직을 위해 연설·투표·결정하도록 뽑힌 사람들의 작은 집단. 대표단. 파견단: *A UN delegation was sent to the peace talks.* 유엔 대표단은 평화 회담을 위해 파견되었다. **2** [U] the process of delegating (DELEGATE) work ‖ 업무를 위임하는 과정. 위임: *the delegation of authority* 권한의 위임

de·lete /dɪˈlit/ *v* [T] **1** to remove a letter, word etc. from a piece of writing ‖ 문장에서 글자·단어 등을 제거하다. 지우다 **2** to remove a piece of information from a computer's MEMORY ‖ 컴퓨터 메모리에서 일부 자료를 제거하다. 삭제하다 – **deletion** /dɪˈliʃən/ *n*

del·i /ˈdɛli/ *n* INFORMAL a small store that sells cheese, cooked meat, SALADs, breads etc. ‖ 치즈·조리된 고기·샐러드·빵 등을 파는 작은 가게

de·lib·er·ate¹ /dɪˈlɪbrɪt, -bərɪt/ *adj* **1** intended or planned ‖ 의도된 또는 계획된. 고의의. 계획적인: *I'm sure her story was a deliberate attempt to confuse us.* 나는 그녀가 우리를 혼란스럽게 하기 위해 그 이야기를 했다고 확신한다. **2** deliberate speech, thought, or movement is slow and careful ‖ 연설[생각, 움직임]이 느리고 주의 깊은. 깊이 생각한. 사려 깊은. 신중한

de·lib·er·ate² /dɪˈlɪbəˌreɪt/ *v* [I, T] to think about something very carefully, especially a TRIAL ‖ 어떤 것, 특히 재판을 매우 주의 깊게 생각하다. 심사숙고하다: *The jury deliberated for 3 days before finding him guilty.* 배심원단은 3일간의 심사숙고 끝에 그의 유죄를 결정했다.

de·lib·er·ate·ly /dɪˈlɪbrɪtli/ *adv* not happening by accident; planned ‖ 우연히 발생하지 않은. 고의로. 일부러; 계획된: *She deliberately spilled coffee on my dress!* 그녀가 일부러 내 옷에 커피를 쏟았어!

de·lib·er·a·tion /dɪˌlɪbəˈreɪʃən/ *n* [C, U] careful thought or discussion about a

problem ‖ 어떤 문제에 대한 주의 깊은 생각이나 의논. 숙고. 심사. 심의: *The committee will finish its deliberations today.* 위원회는 오늘 심의를 마칠 것이다.

del·i·ca·cy /'dɛlɪkəsi/ *n* **1** [U] the quality of being delicate ‖ 정밀한 성질. 민감함. 정교함: *the delicacy of the clock's machinery* 시계의 기계 장치의 정교함 / *The delicacy of the situation means we have to be very careful about what we say.* 우리가 하는 말에 매우 주의를 기울여야 한다는 것은 사태가 미묘함을 뜻한다. **2** a particular food that tastes very good or that is expensive and rare ‖ 맛이 아주 좋거나 값이 비싸며 흔하지 않은 특별한 음식. 진미. 별미: *In France, snails are considered a delicacy.* 프랑스에서는 달팽이 요리를 별미로 여긴다.

del·i·cate /'dɛlɪkɪt/ *adj* **1** made in a way that is not solid or is weak and therefore easily damaged ‖ 견고하지 않거나 약하게 만들어져서 손상되기 쉬운. 깨지기 쉬운. 상하기 쉬운. 연약한: *a delicate piece of lace* 손상되기 쉬운 레이스 **2** needing to be done very carefully in order to avoid causing problems ‖ 문제 발생을 피하기 위해 매우 주의 깊게 할 필요가 있는. 세심한 주의를 요하는. 다루기 어려운. 요령이 필요한: *doctors performing a delicate operation on her eye* 그녀의 눈에 세심한 주의를 요하는 수술을 하는 의사들 **3** a part of the body that is delicate is attractive and graceful ‖ 신체의 일부가 매력적이고 우아한. 고상한: *long delicate fingers* 길고 우아한 손가락 – **delicately** *adv*

del·i·ca·tes·sen /ˌdɛlɪkə'tɛsən/ *n* ⇨ DELI

de·li·cious /dɪ'lɪʃəs/ *adj* having a very enjoyable taste or smell ‖ 매우 기분 좋은 맛이나 향이 나는. (매우) 맛있는. 향긋한: *That chocolate cake was delicious!* 그 초콜릿 케이크는 맛있었어!

de·light¹ /dɪ'laɪt/ *n* **1** [U] a feeling of great pleasure or satisfaction ‖ 대단한 즐거움이나 만족의 감정. 큰 기쁨. 환희: *Krystal laughed with delight.* 크리스탈은 유쾌하게 웃었다. **2** something that makes you feel very happy or satisfied ‖ 상당한 행복감이나 만족감을 느끼게 하는 것. 즐거움(을 주는 것). 기쁜 일: *the delights of owning your own home* 자신의 집을 갖는 즐거움

delight² *v* [T] to give someone a feeling of satisfaction and enjoyment ‖ 사람에게 만족·즐거움의 감정을 주다. …을 기쁘게 [즐겁게] 하다: *This movie classic will delight the whole family.* 이 고전 영화는 온 가족이 즐겁게 볼 수 있다.

delight in sth *phr v* [T] to enjoy something very much, especially something unpleasant ‖ 특히 유쾌하지 않은 것을 매우 많이 즐기다: *twins who delight in confusing people* 사람들이 혼동하는 것을 즐거워 하는 쌍둥이

de·light·ed /dɪ'laɪtɪd/ *adj* very happy or satisfied ‖ 매우 행복하거나 만족스러운. 즐거워하고 있는: *We were delighted to hear their good news.* 그들의 좋은 소식을 듣고 우리는 즐거웠다.

de·light·ful /dɪ'laɪtfəl/ *adj* very nice or enjoyable ‖ 매우 좋거나 즐거운. 유쾌한. 기분 좋은: *a delightful book for children* 어린이들이 즐길 수 있는 책

de·lin·e·ate /dɪ'lɪni,eɪt/ *v* [T] to describe something carefully so that it is easy to understand ‖ 이해하기 쉽도록 사물을 주의 깊게 묘사하다. …을 정확히 서술하다

de·lin·quen·cy /dɪ'lɪŋkwənsi/ *n* [U] behavior that is illegal or socially unacceptable ‖ 불법적이거나 사회적으로 용납되지 않는 행위. 과실. 범죄: *the problem of juvenile delinquency* (=crime done by young people) 청소년 비행 문제

de·lin·quent /dɪ'lɪŋkwənt/ *adj* **1** late in paying the money you owe ‖ 빚진 돈의 상환이 늦은. 연체[체납]되어 있는: *delinquent loans* 연체된 대출금 **2** young people who are delinquent do illegal things ‖ 젊은이들이 불법적인 일을 하는. 비행의. 사회 규범을 어기는 – **delinquent** *n*

de·lir·i·ous /dɪ'lɪriəs/ *adj* **1** confused, anxious, and excited because you are very sick ‖ 너무 아파서 혼란스럽고 불안하며 흥분되는. 의식이 혼탁한[혼미한]. 헛소리하는 **2** extremely happy and excited ‖ 극도로 행복하고 흥분된. 광란의: *people delirious with joy* 미칠 듯이 기뻐하는 사람들 – **delirium** /də'lɪriəm/ *n* [C, U]

de·liv·er /dɪ'lɪvɚ/ *v* **1** [I, T] to take a letter, package, goods etc. to a particular place ‖ 편지·소포·상품 등을 특정한 장소에 가져가다. 전하다. 배달하다: *I used to deliver newspapers when I was a kid.* 나는 어렸을 때 신문 배달을 하곤 했다. / *I'm having some flowers delivered for her birthday.* 나는 그녀의 생일에 꽃을 좀 배달시키려 한다. **2** [T] to make a speech to a lot of people ‖ 많은 사람들에게 연설하다. 말하다. 강의하다: *Rev. Whitman delivered a powerful* *sermon about love and forgiveness.* 휘트만 목사는 사랑과 용서에 대하여 설득력 있는 설교를 했다. **3** [I, T] to do the things that you have promised ‖ 약속했던 일을 하다. 약속을 이행하다: *Voters are angry that politicians haven't delivered on their promises yet.* 정치인들이 아직 공약을 지키지 않아 유권자들은 분개하고 있다. **4 deliver a baby** to help a woman with the birth of her baby ‖ 여성이 아기를 출산하는 것을 돕다 **5** [T] to get votes or support from a particular group of people ‖ 일단의 특정한 사람들로부터 표나 지지를 얻다. 모으다: *We're expecting Rigby to deliver the blue collar vote.* 우리는 리그비가 노동계층의 표를 모으기를 기대하고 있다.

de·liv·er·y /dɪˈlɪvəri/ *n* **1** [C, U] the act of taking something to someone's house, work etc. ‖ 물건을 누군가의 집·직장 등으로 갖다 주는 행위. 배달. 송달. 인도: *Pizza Mondo offers free delivery for any pizza over $10.* 몬도 피자 가게는 10달러가 넘는 피자는 무료로 배달을 해준다. **2** the process of a baby being born ‖ 아기를 낳는 과정. 분만: *Mrs. Haims was rushed into the delivery room* (=hospital room where a baby is born) *at 7:42 p.m.* 하임즈 여사는 오후 7시 42분에 분만실로 급히 들어갔다. **3** [singular] the way that someone speaks or performs in public ‖ 사람들 앞에서 말하거나 행동하는 방식. 말투. 전달 방식: *Your speech is good, but you'll have to improve your delivery.* 네 연설 내용은 훌륭했지만 말투는 개선해야 할 것이다.

del·ta /ˈdɛltə/ *n* a low area of land where a river separates into many smaller rivers flowing toward an ocean ‖ 바다로 흘러 들어가는, 많은 작은 강들로 갈라지는 낮은 지역. 삼각주: *the Mississippi Delta* 미시시피 강의 삼각주

de·lude /dɪˈlud/ *v* [T] to make someone believe something that is not true; deceive ‖ 사실이 아닌 것을 사람들에게 믿게 하다. 속이다. 현혹시키다. 착각하게 하다; 기만하다: *Don't delude yourself—Jerry won't change his mind.* 착각하지 마라. 제리는 그의 마음을 바꾸지 않을 거야. **– deluded** *adj*

del·uge¹ /ˈdɛlyudʒ/ *n* **1** a large flood, or a period of time when it rains continuously ‖ 대홍수, 또는 비가 계속 오는 시기 **2** a large amount of something such as letters, questions etc. that someone gets at the same time ‖ 동시에 받는 다량의 편지·질문 등의 것. 쇄도

deluge² *v* [T] **1** to send a lot of letters, questions etc. to someone at the same time ‖ 누군가에게 많은 편지·질문 등을 동시에 보내다. (…에) 쇄도하다. 쏟아지다: *The radio station was deluged with complaints.* 그 라디오 방송국에는 불만 사항이 쇄도했다. **2** LITERARY to completely cover something with water ‖ 물로 무엇을 완전히 덮다. …을 넘치게 하다. 범람시키다

de·lu·sion /dɪˈluʒən/ *n* [C, U] a false belief about something that you wish were true ‖ 사실이기를 바랐던 것에 대한 잘못된 믿음. 현혹. 착각: *Walter's still under the delusion that his wife loves him.* 월터는 아직도 부인이 자기를 사랑하고 있다고 착각하고 있다.

de·luxe /dɪˈlʌks/ *adj* having a better quality and more expensive price than other similar things ‖ 다른 유사 제품보다 품질이 더 좋고 가격이 더 비싼. 호화로운. 사치스러운: *a deluxe queen-sized bed* 호화로운 퀸사이즈 침대

delve /dɛlv/ *v*

delve into *phr v* [T] to search for more information about someone or something ‖ 사람이나 사물에 대한 더 많은 자료를 찾다. 탐구하다. 깊이 파고들다: *Reporters are always delving into actors' personal lives.* 기자들은 항상 배우들의 사생활을 깊이 파고들고 있다.

dem·a·gogue /ˈdɛməˌɡɑɡ/ *n* DISAPPROVING a political leader who tries to make people feel strong emotions in order to influence their opinions ‖ 사람들의 견해에 영향을 미치기 위해 사람들에게 격한 감정을 느끼게 하려는 정치적 지도자. 선동자. 선동 정치가 **– demagogic** /ˌdɛməˈɡɑɡɪk, -ˈɡɑdʒɪk/ *adj*

de·mand¹ /dɪˈmænd/ *n* **1** [singular, U] the need or desire that people have for particular goods or services ‖ 특정한 상품이나 용역에 대하여 사람들이 갖는 필요나 욕구. 수요: *There isn't any demand for leaded gas anymore.* 더 이상 가연(可鉛) 휘발유에 대한 수요는 없다. **2** a strong request that shows you believe you have the right to get what you ask for ‖ 요구하는 것을 얻을 권리가 있다는 믿음을 나타내는 강한 요청. 청구. 요구: *Union members will strike until the company agrees to their demands.* 노동조합원들은 회사가 그들의 요구를 들어줄 때 까지 파업을 할 것이다. **3 be in demand** to be wanted by a lot of people ‖ 많은 사람들이 원하고 있다. 수요가 있다: *She's been in great demand ever since her book was published.* 그녀의 책이 출간된 이후 많은 사람들이 그녀를 찾

게 됐다. —see also DEMANDS

demand² *v* **1** [T] to ask strongly for something, especially because you think you have a right to do this ‖ 특히 그럴 권리가 있다고 여겨 어떤 것을 강력히 요청하다. 요구하다. 청구하다: *The President demanded the release of all the hostages.* 대통령은 모든 인질들의 석방을 요구했다. / *Horrocks was demanding that he give the checks to her.* 호록스는 그가 그녀에게 수표를 줄 것을 요구하고 있었다. **2** [I, T] to order someone to tell you something ‖ 어떤 것을 말하라고 사람에게 명령하다. 캐묻다. 심문하다: *"What are you doing here?" she demanded.* "여기서 무엇을 하고 있습니까?"라고 그녀는 캐물었다. **3** [T] something that demands your time, skill, attention etc. makes you use a lot of your time, skill etc. ‖ 어떤 것이 시간·기술·주의 등을 많이 쓰게 하다. … 을 필요로 하다: *The baby demands most of her time.* 그녀는 대부분의 시간을 아기에게 쓴다. —see usage notes at ASK, RECOMMEND

de·mand·ing /dɪˈmændɪŋ/ *adj* making you use a lot of your time, skill, attention etc. ‖ 많은 시간·기술·주의 등을 쓰게 하는. 지나치게 요구하는. 빡빡한: *a very demanding job* 매우 빡빡한 업무

de·mands /dɪˈmændz/ *n* [plural] the difficult or annoying things that a job, situation etc. forces you to do ‖ 직무·상황 등이 억지로 하게 하는 어렵거나 귀찮은 일. 요구 사항: *women dealing with the demands of family and career* 가족과 직장을 모두 충족시켜야 하는 여성들 / *The school makes heavy demands on its teachers.* 교사들은 학교에서 과중한 업무에 시달린다.

de·mean /dɪˈmin/ *v* [T] to treat someone without respect, or to make people lose respect for someone ‖ 존경심 없이 사람을 대하다, 또는 사람들에게 어떤 사람에 대한 존경심을 잃게 하다. 버릇없이 굴다. … 의 품위를 떨어뜨리다

de·mean·ing /dɪˈminɪŋ/ *adj* making someone feel very embarrassed or ashamed ‖ 사람을 매우 당황스럽거나 부끄럽게 느끼게 하는. 품위를 떨어뜨리는: *a demeaning job* 품위를 떨어뜨리는 일

de·mean·or /dɪˈminɚ/ *n* [singular, U] FORMAL the way someone behaves, dresses, speaks etc., that shows what his or her character is like ‖ 사람의 품성을 나타내는, 행동하고 옷을 입고 말하는 방식. 태도. 거동. 처신

de·ment·ed /dɪˈmɛntɪd/ *adj* behaving in a way that is crazy or very strange ‖ 미친 듯이 또는 매우 이상하게 행동하는. 머리가 돈. 실성한. 발광한

de·mer·it /dɪˈmɛrɪt/ *n* a mark that is given to a student to warn him/her not to cause any more trouble at school ‖ 학교에서 더 이상 문제를 일으키지 않도록 경고하기 위해서 학생에게 부여하는 점수. 벌점

de·mise /dɪˈmaɪz/ *n* [U] **1** the failure of someone or something that used to be successful ‖ 과거에 성공적이었던 사람이나 사물의 실패. 소멸. 종료: *the demise of the steel industry* 철강 산업의 쇠퇴 **2** FORMAL the death of a person ‖ 사람의 죽음. 사망

dem·o /ˈdɛmoʊ/ *n* INFORMAL an example of a piece of recorded music, SOFTWARE etc. that you play or show to someone who you hope will buy more ‖ 더 많이 사기를 바라는 사람에게 작동시키거나 보여주는 음악·소프트웨어 등의 미리 만들어진 견본. 시청용 음반[테이프]. 선전용 견본: *a demo tape* 데모 테이프

de·moc·ra·cy /dɪˈmɑkrəsi/ *n* **1** [U] a system of government in which everyone in a country can vote to elect its leaders ‖ 지도자를 선출하기 위해 국내의 모든 사람들이 투표할 수 있는 정치 제도. 민주주의. 민주 정치(체제) **2** a country that allows its people to elect its government officials ‖ 국민들에게 공무원을 선출하도록 하는 국가. 직접 민주주의 국가 **3** [U] a situation or society in which everyone is socially equal and has the same right to vote, speak etc. ‖ 모두가 사회적으로 평등하고, 동등한 투표권과 발언권 등을 지닌 상황이나 사회. 평등(사회)

dem·o·crat /ˈdɛməˌkræt/ *n* **1 Democrat** someone who supports or is a member of the DEMOCRATIC PARTY in the US ‖ 미국에서 민주당을 지지하거나 그 구성원인 사람. 민주당원 **2** someone who believes in or works to achieve DEMOCRACY —compare REPUBLICAN² ‖ 민주주의를 신봉하거나 이룩하려고 활동하는 사람. 민주주의(옹호)자

dem·o·crat·ic /ˌdɛməˈkrætɪk/ *adj* **1** organized by a system in which everyone has the same right to vote, speak etc. ‖ 모두가 동등한 투표권과 발언권 등을 지닌 체제로 조직된. 민주주의의: *a democratic way of making decisions* 민주주의적인 의사 결정 방식 **2** controlled by leaders who are elected by the people of a country ‖ 국민이 선출한 지도자가 통치하는. 민주 정치의: *a democratic government* 민주주의 정부

Democratic Par·ty /ˌ...ˌ.. '../ n
[singular] one of the two main political
parties of the US ‖ 미국의 2대 주요 정당
의 하나. 민주당 —see culture note at
PARTY

dem·o·graph·ics /ˌdɛmə'græfɪks/ n
[plural] the changes in the number of
people or types of people that live in an
area ‖ 일정 지역에 거주하는 사람들의 수
나 형태의 변화. 인구 실태[통계]

de·mol·ish /dɪ'mɑlɪʃ/ v [T] **1** to
completely destroy a building ‖ 건물을
완전히 파괴하다. 부수다. 무너뜨리다. 철
거 하 다 : *Several old houses were
demolished to make space for a new
park.* 여러 채의 낡은 집들이 신설 공원의
부지를 마련하기 위해 철거되었다. **2** to
prove that an idea or opinion is
completely wrong ‖ 생각이나 견해가 완
전히 틀렸다는 것을 증명하다. 뒤엎다. 뒤
집다: *Every one of his arguments was
demolished by the defense lawyer.* 그의
주장은 피고측 변호사에 의해 모조리 뒤집
혔다.

dem·o·li·tion /ˌdɛmə'lɪʃən/ n [C, U] the
act or process of completely destroying
a building ‖ 건물을 완전히 파괴하는 행위
나 과정. 파괴. 분쇄

de·mon /'dimən/ n an evil spirit ‖ 악령.
악마 – **demonic** /dɪ'mɑnɪk/ adj

dem·on·strate /'dɛmən,streɪt/ v [T] **1**
to prove something clearly ‖ 어떤 것을
분명히 증명하다. 논증하다: *Our studies
demonstrate that fewer college
graduates are finding jobs.* 우리 연구에
따르면 극히 소수의 대학 졸업자들이 구직
활동을 하고 있다. **2** to show or describe
how to use or do something ‖ 어떤 것을
사용하거나 수행하는 법을 보여 주거나 기
술하다. 시범을 보이다. 설명하다: *Our
aerobics instructor always demon-
strates each new movement first.*
우리 에어로빅 강사는 항상 각각의 새 동
작을 먼저 시범을 보여 준다. **3** to show
that you have a particular skill, quality,
or ability ‖ 보유한 특정한 기술[소질, 능
력]을 보이다. 표출하다: *The contest gave
her a chance to demonstrate her ability.*
그 경연은 그녀에게 자신의 능력을 보여
줄 기회를 제공했다. **4** to meet with
other people in order to protest or
support something in public ‖ 공개적으
로 어떤 것을 항의하거나 지지하기 위해
다른 사람들과 회합하다. 시위 운동을 하
다. 데모하다

dem·on·stra·tion /ˌdɛmən'streɪʃən/ n
1 an event at which a lot of people meet
to protest or support something in

public ‖ 공개적으로 어떤 것에 대해 항의
나 지지를 하기 위해 많은 사람들이 모이
는 행사. 시위 운동. 데모: *Students
staged/held a demonstration against
the war.* 학생들은 전쟁에 반대하는 시위
를 했다. **2** [C, U] the act of showing and
explaining how to do something ‖ 어떤
것을 하는 방법을 보여 주면서 설명하는
행위. 실물 설명. 실연(實演): *She gave a
demonstration on how to use the
electronic dictionary.* 그녀는 전자 사전을
어떻게 사용하는지를 실제로 보여 주면서
설명했다. **3** proof that someone or
something has a particular quality,
ability, emotion etc. ‖ 사람이나 사물이
특정한 성질·능력·감정 등을 지니고 있다
는 증명. 입증: *People gathered around
the school in a demonstration of support
for the missing children.* 사람들이 미아
들에 대한 후원의 표시로 학교 주변에 모
였다.

de·mon·stra·tive /dɪ'mɑnstrətɪv/ adj
willing to show how much you care
about someone ‖ 누군가에 대하여 얼마나
많은 관심을 갖고 있는가를 나타내려는.
감정을 노골적으로 나타내는. 심정을 토
로하는: *He loves me, but he's not very
demonstrative.* 그는 나를 사랑하지만, 너
무 감정을 표현하지 않는다.

dem·on·stra·tor /'dɛmən,streɪtɚ/ n
someone who meets with other people
in order to protest or support something
in public ‖ 공개적으로 어떤 것을 항의하
거나 지지하기 위해 다른 사람들과 회합을
하는 사람. 데모[시위] 참가자

de·mor·al·ize /dɪ'mɔrə,laɪz, dɪ-, -
'mɑr-/ v [T] to make someone lose his
or her confidence or courage ‖ 누군가의
자신감이나 용기를 잃게 하다. 의기소침하
게 하다. 사기를 꺾다: *The soldiers were
demoralized by the defeat.* 병사들은 패
배로 인해 사기가 꺾였다. – **demoral-
izing** adj

de·mote /dɪ'moʊt, di-/ v [T] to make
someone have a lower rank or less
important position ‖ 누군가를 낮은 직위
나 비중이 덜한 직책을 갖게 하다. 강등시
키다. 지위를 낮추다 – **demotion**
/dɪ'moʊʃən/ n [C,U] —opposite PROMOTE

de·mure /dɪ'myʊr/ adj a girl or woman
who is demure is shy, quiet, and always
behaves well ‖ 소녀나 여성이 수줍어하고
조용하며 항상 바르게 행동하는. 얌전한.
새치름한

den /dɛn/ n **1** a room in a house where
people relax, read, watch television etc.
‖ 사람들이 휴식·독서·텔레비전 시청 등
을 하는 방. 아담한 사실. 서재 **2** the

home of some types of animals such as lions and foxes (FOX) ‖ 사자·여우 등의 일부 동물의 집. (동)굴

de·ni·al /dɪˈnaɪəl/ *n* **1** [C, U] a statement saying that something is not true ‖ 어떤 것이 사실이 아니라고 말하는 진술. 부정: *Diaz made a public denial of the rumor.* 디아즈는 소문에 대해 공개적으로 부정했다. **2** [U] a condition in which you refuse to admit or believe that something bad exists or has happened ‖ 좋지 않은 일이 있거나 발생했다는 것을 인정하거나 믿기를 거부하는 상태. 부인: *She went through a phase of denial after her child's death.* 그녀는 아이가 죽은 것을 부인하는 과정을 겪었다. **3** FORMAL the act of refusing to allow someone to have or do something ‖ 누군가가 어떤 것을 갖거나 하는 것의 허용을 거부하는 행위. 거절(하는 행위): *the denial of basic human rights* 기본적 인권의 불인정 —see also DENY

den·i·grate /ˈdɛnɪˌɡreɪt/ *v* [T] to do or say things in order to make someone or something seem less important or good ‖ 사람이나 사물의 중요성이나 양호함이 덜해 보이게 하기 위해 어떤 것을 하거나 말하다. 중상하다. 헐뜯다

den·im /ˈdɛnəm/ *n* [U] a type of strong cotton cloth used for making JEANS ‖ 진을 만드는 데 쓰이는 일종의 질긴 면직물. 데님

de·nom·i·na·tion /dɪˌnɑməˈneɪʃən/ *n* **1** a religious group that is part of a larger religious organization ‖ 대규모 종교 조직의 분파인 종교 집단. 종파. 교파 **2** the value of coins, BILLs, BONDs etc. ‖ 경화·지폐·채권 등의 가치. 화폐 (단위) 금액. 액면가: *bills in denominations of $1 and $5* 1달러와 5달러 단위의 지폐들

de·note /dɪˈnoʊt/ *v* [T] to represent or mean something ‖ 사물을 표현하거나 의미하다. 표시하다. 지시하다: *Each X on the map denotes 500 people.* 지도상의 X 표는 각기 500인을 나타낸다.

de·nounce /dɪˈnaʊns/ *v* [T] to publicly express disapproval of someone or something ‖ 사람이나 사물에 대해 공개적으로 불만을 표현한다. 공공연히 비난하다: *The bishop denounced the film as being immoral.* 주교는 그 영화가 부도덕하다고 공공연히 비난했다.

dense /dɛns/ *adj* **1** made of or containing a lot of things or people that are very close together ‖ 서로 매우 밀착된 많은 사물이나 사람들로 구성되거나 포함하는. 밀집한. 빽빽한. 촘촘한: *the city's dense population* 그 도시의 밀집한

인구 / *dense forests of pine trees* 무성한 소나무 숲 **2** difficult to see through or breathe in ‖ 관통해서 보거나 숨을 들이쉬기가 곤란한. 짙은. 농후한: *dense clouds of smoke* 구름처럼 자욱한 연기 **3** INFORMAL stupid ‖ 우둔한 **– densely** *adv*

den·si·ty /ˈdɛnsəti/ *n* [U] **1** how crowded something is ‖ 사물이 밀집한 정도. 밀도: *a high density neighborhood* (=very crowded neighborhood) 인구 과밀 지역 **2** TECHNICAL the relationship between an object's weight and the amount of space it fills ‖ 물체의 무게와 그것이 차지하는 공간과의 관계. 밀도

dent[1] /dɛnt/ *n* **1** a mark made when you hit or press something so that its surface is bent ‖ 어떤 것을 때리거나 눌러서 표면이 구부러져 생긴 흔적. 움푹 들어간 곳: *a big dent in the car* 자동차의 크게 팬 자국

dent

2 make a dent in sth INFORMAL to reduce the amount of something ‖ 사물의 양을 줄이다. 감소시키다: *I haven't made a dent in the money I have to pay back on my loan.* 갚아야 할 대출 금액을 줄이지 못했다.

dent[2] *v* [T] to hit or press something so that its surface is bent and marked ‖ 표면이 구부러지거나 자국이 나도록 어떤 것을 때리거나 누르다. …에 두드린 자국을 내다. 움푹 들어가게 하다: *Some idiot dented my car door last night.* 어떤 얼간이들이 지난밤에 내 차 문을 움푹 들어가게 했다. **– dented** *adj*

den·tal /ˈdɛntl/ *adj* relating to your teeth ‖ 치아에 관련된. 이의. 치과용의: *dental care* 치과 치료

dental floss /ˈ.., ./ *n* [U] a thin string that you use to clean between your teeth ‖ 치아 사이를 깨끗이 하는 데 쓰는 가는 실. 치실

den·tist /ˈdɛntɪst/ *n* someone whose job is to treat people's teeth ‖ 사람의 치아를 치료하는 직업인. 치과 의사 —see usage note at DOCTOR[1]

den·tures /ˈdɛntʃɚz/ *n* [plural] artificial teeth worn to replace the natural ones that someone has lost; FALSE TEETH ‖ 상실한 자연 치아를 대체하기 위해 끼는 인공 치아. 틀니. 의치; (동) false teeth

de·nun·ci·a·tion /dɪˌnʌnsiˈeɪʃən/ *n* a public statement in which you criticize someone or something ‖ 사람이나 사물을 비판하는 공개적인 진술. 공공연한 비난

de·ny /dɪˈnaɪ/ v [T] 1 to say that something is not true ‖ 어떤 것이 사실이 아니라고 말하다. 부인하다. 부정하다: *Simmons denied that he had murdered his wife.* 시몬스는 자신이 부인을 살해했다는 것을 부인했다. 2 to refuse to allow someone to have or do something ‖ 누가 무엇을 갖거나 하는 것을 허용하지 않다. 응하지 않다. 거절하다: *They denied him entry into the country.* 그들은 그의 입국을 허용하지 않았다. —see also DENIAL

de·o·dor·ant /diˈoʊdərənt/ n [C, U] a substance that you put on the skin under your arms to stop you from smelling bad ‖ 겨드랑이에서 악취가 나는 것을 막기 위해 바르는 물질. 방취제

de·o·dor·ize /diˈoʊdəˌraɪz/ v [T] to remove an unpleasant smell or to make it less noticeable ‖ 불쾌한 냄새를 제거하거나 불쾌한 냄새를 덜 나게 하다. 악취를 없애다

de·part /dɪˈpɑrt/ v [I] to leave ‖ 떠나다. 출발하다: *All passengers departing for New York on flight UA179 should go to Gate 7.* 뉴욕으로 출발하는 UA179 항공편의 모든 승객들은 7번 출구로 가주십시오. / *The train will depart from platform 7.* 열차는 7번 플랫폼에서 출발합니다.

depart from sth *phr v* [T] FORMAL to start to use new ideas or do something in an unusual or unexpected way ‖ 유별나거나 예상외로 새로운 아이디어를 이용하거나 어떤 것을 하기 시작하다. 벗어나다. 어긋나다: *a treatment for cancer that departs from the usual methods* 일반적인 방법을 벗어난 암 치료법

de·part·ment /dɪˈpɑrtˈmənt/ n 1 any of the groups of people that form a part of a large organization such as a college, government, or business ‖ 대학 [정부, 기업] 등의 대조직의 일부를 구성하는 사람들의 집단. 부. 과: *the design department in a large advertising company* 큰 광고 회사의 디자인 부서 / *the English department* 영어과 2 a specific area in a large store where a particular type of product is sold ‖ 특정 종류의 상품을 판매하는 큰 상점의 특정 구역. 상품별 매장. 코너: *the men's department* (=sells clothes for men) 남성복 코너

department store /.ˈ. ˌ./ n a large store that sells many different products such as clothes, kitchen equipment etc. ‖ 의류·주방 용품 등의 여러 다양한 상품

을 판매하는 대형 상점. 백화점

de·par·ture /dɪˈpɑrtʃɚ/ n 1 [C, U] the action of leaving a place, especially to travel in a plane, car, etc. ‖ 특히 비행기·자동차 등으로 여행하려고 특정 장소를 떠나는 행위. 출발: *Check in at the airport an hour before departure.* 출발 한 시간 전에 공항에서 탑승 수속을 밟으세요. 2 FORMAL a change from what is usual or expected ‖ 통상적이거나 예상된 것으로부터의 변경. 이탈

de·pend /dɪˈpɛnd/ v **it/that depends** SPOKEN used in order to say that because you do not know what will happen yet, you cannot decide ‖ 아직 무엇이 일어날지 몰라서 결정할 수 없다고 말하는 데에 쓰여. 그것은 형편에 달렸다. 사정 나름이다: *"Are you coming to my house later?" "It depends. I might have to work."* "나중에 우리 집에 올래?" "상황 봐서. 난 아마 일해야 할 거야."

depend on/upon *phr v* [T] 1 to need the help, support, or existence of someone or something else ‖ 어떤 사람이나 사물의 원조[지원, 존재]를 필요로 하다. 의지하다. 의존하다: *Children depend on their parents for almost everything.* 어린이들은 거의 모든 것을 부모에게 의지한다. 2 to change because of other things that happen or change ‖ 다른 것이 발생하거나 변하기 때문에 변하다. …에 달려 있다. …나름이다: *The amount you spend depends on how/where you live.* 네가 소비하는 양은 네가 어떻게[어디에] 사느냐에 달려 있다. 3 to trust someone or something ‖ 사람이나 사물을 신뢰하다. 믿다: *Sometimes I think you're the only person I can depend on.* 때때로 나는 내가 믿을 수 있는 사람은 너뿐이라고 생각한다.

de·pend·a·ble /dɪˈpɛndəbəl/ adj able to be trusted ‖ 믿을 수 있는: *a dependable employee* 믿음직한 종업원

de·pend·ent¹ /dɪˈpɛndənt/ adj 1 needing someone or something else in order to exist, be successful etc. ‖ 존재하거나 성공하기 위해 어떤 사람이나 사물을 필요로 하는. 의지하는. 의존적인: *dependent children* 의존적인 아이들 2 **be dependent on/upon** FORMAL to change because of other things that happen or change ‖ 다른 일이 발생하거나 변경되어서 변하다. …에 의해 결정[좌우]되는. …나름인: *Your success is dependent on how hard you work.* 너의 성공은 네가 얼마나 열심히 일하느냐에 달려 있다. —opposite INDEPENDENT

dependent² n someone, especially a

child, who needs someone else to provide him/her with food, money, clothing etc. ‖ 특히 아이처럼 음식·돈·옷 등을 제공해 줄 사람이 필요한 사람. 남에게 의지해서 생활하는 사람

de·pict /dɪˈpɪkt/ v [T] to clearly describe a character, situation, or event in a story or by using pictures ‖ 이야기로 또는 그림을 사용하여 성격[상황, 사건]을 명확히 서술하다. 그리다. 묘사하다: *The painting depicts the Fall of Rome.* 그 그림은 로마의 멸망을 묘사한 것이다.

de·plete /dɪˈplit/ v [T] to reduce the amount of something ‖ 사물의 양을 줄이다. 격감시키다. 고갈시키다: *Many of our forests have been depleted by the paper industry.* 제지 산업으로 인해 우리의 많은 산림이 고갈되어 왔다.

de·plor·a·ble /dɪˈplɔrəbəl/ adj FORMAL deserving strong disapproval ‖ 몹시 못마땅하게 여길 만한. 한탄할 만한: *the deplorable act of illegally polluting our rivers* 불법적으로 우리 강을 오염시키는 통탄할 만한 행위

de·plore /dɪˈplɔr/ v [T] FORMAL to severely criticize something that you disapprove of ‖ 못마땅한 일을 혹독하게 비판하다. 맹렬히 비난하다: *a statement deploring the use of chemical weapons* 화학 무기 사용을 통렬히 비난하는 성명

de·ploy /dɪˈplɔɪ/ v [T] to organize the soldiers, military equipment etc. that may be used in an attack ‖ 공격에 이용할 수 있는 군인·군 장비 등을 구성하다. 배치[편성]하다: *Nuclear missiles were being deployed in Europe.* 핵미사일이 유럽에 배치되고 있었다.

de·port /dɪˈpɔrt/ v [T] to force a foreigner to return to the country s/he came from ‖ 강제로 외국인을 자신이 온 나라로 돌아가게 하다. 추방하다 – **deportation** /ˌdipɔrˈteɪʃən/ n [C, U]

de·pos·it¹ /dɪˈpɑzɪt/ n **1** part of the price of a house, car etc. that you pay first so that it will not be sold or given to anyone else ‖ 타인에게 팔리거나 넘어가지 않도록 우선 지불하는 집·자동차 등의 값의 일부. 계약금. 보증금. 예약금: *We put down a deposit on the house yesterday.* 우리는 어제 그 집에 대한 계약금을 지불했다. **2** an amount of money that is added to someone's bank account ‖ 누군가의 은행 계좌에 추가되는 금액. 예금: *I'd like to make a deposit please.* 예금을 하려고 합니다. **3** an amount or layer of a substance in a particular place ‖ 특정 장소에 있는 물질의 양이나 층: *rich deposits of gold in the*

hills 그 산의 풍부한 금 매장량

deposit² v [T] **1** to put money into a bank account ‖ 은행 계좌에 돈을 입금하다. 예금하다 **2** LITERARY to put something down, especially in a particular place ‖ 특히 특정한 장소에 어떤 것을 내려놓다

de·pot /ˈdipoʊ/ n **1** a small train or bus station ‖ 열차나 버스의 간이 정류장. 철도역. 정거장 **2** a place where goods are stored ‖ 물건을 저장하는 곳. 창고

de·praved /dɪˈpreɪvd/ adj morally unacceptable and evil ‖ 도덕적으로 받아들일 수 없고 사악한. 부패한. 타락한: *a depraved murderer* 사악한 살인자 – **depravity** /dɪˈprævəti/ n [U]

de·pre·ci·ate /dɪˈpriʃiˌeɪt/ v [I] to become less valuable ‖ 가치가 덜하게 되다. 가치가 떨어지다: *A new car depreciates as soon as it is driven.* 새 차는 타기 시작하자마자 가치가 떨어진다.

de·press /dɪˈprɛs/ v [T] **1** to make someone feel very sad ‖ 누군가를 매우 슬프게 하다: *The news depressed my father.* 그 소식은 내 아버지를 우울하게 만들었다. **2** to reduce the amount or value of something ‖ 사물의 분량이나 가치를 떨어뜨리다. 약화[하락]시키다: *The value of the peso fell, depressing the nation's economy.* 국가 경제가 침체됨으로써 페소화의 가치는 떨어졌다.

de·pressed /dɪˈprɛst/ adj **1** very sad ‖ 매우 슬픈. 의기소침한. 우울한: *I got really depressed just thinking about her.* 나는 그녀에 대한 생각만 해도 정말 슬퍼졌다. **2** not having enough jobs or business activity to make an area, industry etc. successful ‖ 지역·산업 등을 성공시키기 위한 충분한 일이나 사업 활동이 없는. 불황의: *a depressed economy* 불경기

de·press·ing /dɪˈprɛsɪŋ/ adj making you feel sad ‖ 슬퍼지게 하는. 우울한: *It's so depressing – we should have won.* 너무 슬프다. 우리가 이겼어야 했는데.

de·pres·sion /dɪˈprɛʃən/ n **1** [C, U] a feeling of sadness and a loss of hope ‖ 슬프고 희망을 잃어버린 감정. 의기소침. 침울. 우울(증): *The patient is suffering from depression.* 그 환자는 우울증에 시달리고 있다. **2** [C, U] a long period when businesses are not very active and many people do not have jobs ‖ 사업이 그다지 활발하지 않고 많은 사람들이 직업을 가지지 못하는 오랜 기간. 불황. 불경기: *the Great Depression of the 1930s* 1930년대의 대공황 **3** an area of a surface that is lower than the other

parts ‖ 다른 부분보다 더 낮은 표면 지역.
침하한 곳. 함몰된 곳

de·prive /dɪˈpraɪv/ v

deprive sb **of** sth *phr v* [T] to take
something that someone needs away
from him/her ‖ 남에게서 그 사람이 필요
한 것을 빼앗다: *The troops had been
deprived of food, water, and electricity.*
그 군대는 식량과 물, 그리고 전기를 탈취
당했다.

de·prived /dɪˈpraɪvd/ adj not having or
giving someone the things that are
considered to be necessary for a
comfortable or happy life ‖ 안락하고 행
복한 삶을 위해 필요하다고 생각되는 것을
가지지 못하거나 누군가에게 주지 못한.
혜택 받지 못한. 빈곤한. 불우한: *a
deprived childhood* 불우한 어린 시절

dept. the written abbreviation of
DEPARTMENT ‖ department의 약어

depth /dɛpθ/ n 1 [C usually singular]
a) the distance from the top of
something to the bottom of it ‖ 사물의 꼭
대기에서 밑바닥까지의 거리. 깊이: *a lake
with a depth of 30 feet* 30피트 깊이의 호
수 **b)** the distance from the front of an
object to the back of it ‖ 물체의 앞면에서
뒷면까지의 거리. 안길이: *the depth of the
shelves* 선반의 안길이 2 [U] how serious
and important someone's feelings,
conversations etc. are ‖ 감정·대화 등의
심각하고 중요한 정도. 감정 등의 깊이[강
도]: *the depth of their friendship* 깊은 그
들의 우정 3 **in depth** including all the
details ‖ 모든 세부 사항을 포함한. 상세
한. 철저한. 깊이 있는: *He gave us an in
depth report on the problem.* 그는 그 문
제에 관해 상세한 보고를 했다.

dep·u·ty /ˈdɛpyəti/ n 1 someone who
has the second most powerful position
in an organization ‖ 조직 내에서 두 번째
로 강력한 지위를 가진 사람. 대리(인).
부관: *the deputy vice president of the
Foundation* 재단의 부총재 2 someone
whose job is to help a SHERIFF ‖ 보안관을
돕는 직업인. 보안관 대리

de·rail /dɪˈreɪl, di-/ v [I, T] to make a
train come off a railroad track ‖ 열차를
철도 궤도에서 벗어나게 하다. 탈선하다
[시키다]

de·ranged /dɪˈreɪndʒd/ adj behaving in
a crazy or dangerous way ‖ 미친듯 또는
위험하게 행동하는. 광적인: *a deranged
criminal* 제 정신이 아닌 범죄자

der·by /ˈdɚbi/ n 1 a type of horse race
‖ 경마의 일종. 더비: *the Kentucky
Derby* 켄터키 더비[대경마] 2 a stiff
round hat for men worn in past times ‖

과거에 남성들이 썼던 뻣뻣한 둥근 모자.
중산모

der·e·lict[1] /ˈdɛrəˌlɪkt/ adj a building,
boat etc. that is derelict is in bad
condition because no one uses it ‖ 건물·
배 등이 아무도 사용하지 않아 상태가 나
쁜. 헐어빠진. 버려진. 유기된

derelict[2] n OFFENSIVE someone who has
no home or money ‖ 집이나 돈이 없는 사
람. 부랑자

de·ride /dɪˈraɪd/ v [T] FORMAL to say
something that shows you think
something is silly or has no value ‖ 어떤
것이 어리석고 가치가 없다는 생각을 나타
내는 말을 하다. …을 비웃다. 조소하다
 – derision /dɪˈrɪʒən/ n [U] **– derisory**
/dɪˈraɪsəri/ adj

de·riv·a·tion /ˌdɛrəˈveɪʃən/ n 1 [C, U]
the origin of something, especially a
word or phrase ‖ 특히 단어나 구의 기원.
어원 2 a word that comes from another
word or language ‖ 다른 단어나 언어에서
생긴 낱말. 파생어

de·riv·a·tive /dɪˈrɪvətɪv/ adj developing
or coming from something else, and
often not as good ‖ 다른 것에서 발전하거
나 생긴 것으로 종종 좋지 않은. 유도된.
이끌어 낸. 파생적인 **– derivative** n

de·rive /dɪˈraɪv/ v 1 [T] to get
something such as happiness, strength,
or satisfaction from someone or
something ‖ 사람이나 사물로부터 행복
[힘, 만족감] 등을 얻다. 이끌어 내다: *He
derives a lot of pleasure from meeting
people.* 그는 사람들을 만남으로써 많은
기쁨을 얻는다 2 [I] to develop or come
from something else ‖ 다른 것으로부터
발전하거나 생기다. 유래하다: *This word
is derived from Latin.* 이 단어는 라틴어
에서 유래한다.

der·ma·ti·tis /ˌdɚməˈtaɪtɪs/ n [U] a
disease of the skin that makes it swell,
become red, and be painful ‖ 붓고 붉어
지며 통증을 유발하는 피부 질환. 피부염

de·rog·a·to·ry /dɪˈrɑgəˌtɔri/ adj
insulting or criticizing someone or
something ‖ 사람이나 사물을 모욕하거나
비난하는. 경멸적인: *"Bitch" is a
derogatory term for a woman.* "Bitch"라
는 말은 여성에 대한 경멸어이다.

der·rick /ˈdɛrɪk/ n the tall tower over
an oil well that holds the DRILL ‖ 굴착 장
비가 설치된 유정(油井) 위에 있는 높은
탑. 유정탑

de·scend /dɪˈsɛnd/ v [I, T] FORMAL to
go down or move from a higher level to
a lower one ‖ 높은 수준에서 낮은 수준으
로 내려가거나 움직이다. 하강하다: *a*

plane descending to the airport 공항에 착륙하고 있는 비행기 —opposite ASCEND

descend from sb *phr v* [T] **be descended from** sb to be related to someone who lived a long time ago ‖ 오래 전에 살았던 사람과 혈연 관계가 있다. …의 자손이다: *My father's family is descended from the Pilgrims.* 내 아버지 가족은 미국 최초 이주자들의 자손이다.

descend on/upon sb *phr v* [T] INFORMAL if a lot of people descend on a place or on you, they arrive at a place or at your house ‖ 많은 사람들이 어떤 장소나 어떤 사람의 집에 도착하다. …에 방문하다[몰려들다]: *Thousands of tourists descend on Athens each year.* 수천 명의 관광객들이 매년 아테네에 몰려든다.

de·scend·ant /dɪˈsɛndənt/ *n* someone who is related to a person who lived a long time ago ‖ 오래 전에 살았던 사람과 혈연 관계가 있는 사람. 자손. 후손: *a descendant of African slaves* 아프리카 노예의 자손 —compare ANCESTOR

de·scent /dɪˈsɛnt/ *n* **1** [C, U] a movement down, or the process of going down ‖ 아래로 움직이거나 내려가는 과정. 강하: *a plane beginning its descent* 하강하기 시작하는 비행기 — opposite ASCENT **2** [U] your family origins, especially the country that you came from ‖ 가족의 기원, 특히 출신국. 가계. …계: *We're Irish by descent.* 우리는 아일랜드계 사람들이다.

de·scribe /dɪˈskraɪb/ *v* [T] to say what someone or something is like by giving details ‖ 사람이나 사물의 모습을 자세히 말하다. 묘사하다. 서술[기술]하다: *Can you describe the man?* 그 남자를 묘사할 수 있겠니? / *It's hard to describe how I feel.* 내 기분이 어떤지 설명하기가 어렵다. / *Would you describe Jim as a good worker?* 짐이 좋은 일꾼이라고 보십니까?

de·scrip·tion /dɪˈskrɪpʃən/ *n* [C, U] a piece of writing or a speech that gives details about what someone or something is like ‖ 사람이나 사물이 어떻게 생겼는지에 대한 자세한 설명을 하는 글이나 말. 설명(서). 묘사. 기술: *Police have a detailed description of the missing child.* 경찰은 미아에 대한 상세한 인상 착의를 가지고 있다. / *You fit the description of* (=look like) *a man seen running from the scene.* 당신은 그 현장에서 도망치다 목격된 남자와 생김새가 일치한다.

de·scrip·tive /dɪˈskrɪptɪv/ *adj* giving a description of something using words or pictures ‖ 말이나 사진을 사용하여 사물의

대한 묘사를 하는. 묘사[서술, 기술]적인. 설명적인

des·e·crate /ˈdɛsəˌkreɪt/ *v* [T] to damage something holy ‖ 어떤 것의 신성함을 손상시키다. …의 신성을 더럽히다. 모독하다 – **desecration** /ˌdɛsəˈkreɪʃən/ *n* [U]

de·seg·re·gate /diˈsɛgrəˌgeɪt/ *v* [T] to end a system in which people of different races are kept separate ‖ 다른 인종의 사람들을 따로 분리하는 제도를 없애다. 인종 차별을 폐지하다: *an attempt to desegregate the schools* 학교에서의 인종 차별을 철폐하려는 시도 – **desegregation** /ˌdisɛgrəˈgeɪʃən/ *n* [U] – **desegregated** /diˈsɛgrəˌgeɪtɪd/ *adj*

des·ert¹ /ˈdɛzət/ *n* [C, U] a very large area of land where it is very hot and dry ‖ 매우 덥고 건조한 매우 광활한 땅. 사막: *the Sahara desert* 사하라 사막

de·sert² /dɪˈzət/ *v* **1** [T] to leave someone alone and not help him/her any more ‖ 남을 홀로 남겨 두고 더 이상 돕지 않다. …을 버리다: *My boyfriend deserted me when I got pregnant.* 내 애인은 내가 임신했을 때 나를 버렸다. **2** [T] to leave a place so that it is empty ‖ 어떤 장소를 떠나 그곳이 텅 비다. …을 비우다: *Everyone deserted the village and fled to the hills.* 모든 이들이 마을을 빠져나와 언덕으로 도피했다. **3** [I] to leave the army without permission ‖ 허락 없이 군대를 떠나다. 탈영하다 – **desertion** /dɪˈzəʃən/ *n* [C, U]

de·sert·ed /dɪˈzətɪd/ *adj* empty and quiet, especially because the people who are usually there have left ‖ 특히 사람들이 보통 있던 곳에서 떠나서 텅 비어 조용한. 인기척 없는: *At night the streets are deserted.* 밤에 거리들은 텅 빈다.

de·sert·er /dɪˈzətə/ *n* a soldier who leaves the army without permission ‖ 허락 없이 군대를 떠난 군인. 탈영병

de·serve /dɪˈzəv/ *v* [T] if someone deserves something, s/he should get it because of the way s/he has behaved ‖ 누군가가 자신의 행동 방식 때문에 어떤 것을 얻어야 마땅하다. 받을 만하다. …을 받을 가치가 있다: *After all that work you deserve a rest!* 그 모든 일을 했으니 당신은 쉴 만해! / *Migrant workers deserve to make more than $3 an hour.* 이주 노동자들은 시간당 3달러 이상을 받을 만하다. / *The drug dealer got what he deserved.* (=received the right punishment) 그 마약 거래상은 응분의 벌을 받았다. – **deserved** *adj*

de·sign¹ /dɪˈzaɪn/ *n* **1** [U] the way that

something has been planned or made ‖ 어떤 것이 계획되고 만들어진 방식. 설계. 기획: *We're working to improve the design of the computer.* 우리는 컴퓨터의 설계를 개선하는 일을 하고 있다. **2** a pattern used for decorating something ‖ 무엇인가를 장식하기 위해 쓰이는 무늬. 도안. 디자인: *curtains with a floral design* 꽃 무늬 커튼 **3** a drawing or plan that shows how something will be made or what it will look like ‖ 사물을 만들려는 방법이나 모습을 나타내는 그림이나 계획. 기획[설계](도). 도안: *Have you seen the designs for the new store?* 새 가게의 설계도를 본 적 있니? **4** [U] the art or process of making drawings or plans for something ‖ 사물에 대한 그림을 그리거나 계획을 세우는 기술이나 과정. 도안법. 설계법[술]: *Vicky studied graphic design at college.* 비키는 대학에서 그래픽 디자인을 배웠다. **5 have designs on sth** to want something and be planning a way to get it ‖ 어떤 것을 원해서 그것을 얻기 위한 방법을 계획하다. …을 노리다

design² *v* **1** [I, T] to make a drawing or plan of something that will be made or built ‖ 제작이나 건설될 것의 그림을 그리거나 계획을 세우다. …을 디자인[설계, 기획]하다. 도안을 그리다: *Armani is designing some exciting new suits for the fall.* 아르마니는 멋진 가을용 새 정장 몇 벌을 디자인 중이다 **2** [T] to plan or develop something for a particular purpose ‖ 특정 목적을 위해 어떤 것을 계획하거나 발전시키다. 기획[설계, 고안]하다: *an engine designed to give more power* 더 큰 동력을 내도록 고안된 엔진 / *a video game designed for children* 어린이용으로 기획된 비디오 게임

des·ig·nate /'dɛzɪɡˌneɪt/ *v* [T] to choose someone or something for a particular job or purpose ‖ 특정한 일이나 목적을 위하여 사람이나 사물을 선택하다. 지명[임명]하다. 선정하다: *a check-out line designated for shoppers who will pay cash* 현금으로 지불할 구매자들을 위해 지정된 계산대

des·ig·nat·ed driv·er /ˌ.... '../ *n* someone who drives his/her friends to a party, BAR etc. and agrees not to drink alcohol ‖ 술을 마시지 않겠다고 약속하고 파티나 술집 등에 친구들을 운전해 데려다 주는 사람. 지명 운전자

des·ig·na·tion /ˌdɛzɪɡ'neɪʃən/ *n* [C, U] **1** the act or state of designating (DESIGNATE) something ‖ 어떤 것을 지정하는 행위나 상태. 지정. 지명: *the designation of 100 acres around the lake as a protected area for wildlife* 호수 주위의 100에이커에 대한 야생 동물 보호 구역 지정 **2** the description or title that someone or something is given ‖ 사람이나 사물에게 주어진 묘사나 칭호. 명칭. 호칭: *Any beef with the designation "extra lean" must only have 5% of its weight in fat.* "extra lean(초저지방육)"이라는 호칭이 붙은 쇠고기는 총무게 중 지방이 5퍼센트만 있어야 한다.

de·sign·er /dɪ'zaɪnə/ *n* someone whose job is to make plans or patterns for clothes, jewelry etc. ‖ 옷·보석 등에 대해 기획하거나 무늬를 만드는 직업인. 디자이너

de·sir·a·ble /dɪ'zaɪrəbəl/ *adj* FORMAL **1** worth having or doing because it is useful or popular ‖ 유용하고 인기가 있기 때문에 가지거나 할 가치가 있는. 바람직한: *a desirable job with a big law firm* 큰 법률 회사에 근무하는 멋진 일 **2** someone who is desirable is sexually attractive ‖ 사람이 성적으로 매력 있는 **-desir·ability** /dɪˌzaɪrə'bɪləti/ *n* [U]

de·sire¹ /dɪ'zaɪə/ *n* **1** a strong hope or wish ‖ 강한 소망이나 바람. 욕구. 욕망: *students with strong desire for knowledge* 지식에 대한 강한 욕구를 가진 학생들 / *I have no desire to meet her.* 나는 그녀를 만나고 싶지 않다. **2** FORMAL a strong wish to have sex with someone ‖ 누군가와 성교를 몹시 하고 싶어함. 성욕

desire² *v* [T] **1 leave a lot to be desired** said when something is not as good as it should be ‖ 사물이 예상만큼 좋지 않을 때 쓰여. 유감스러운 점이 많다: *This coffee leaves a lot to be desired!* 이 커피는 개선의 여지가 아주 많다! **2** FORMAL to want or hope for something very much ‖ 어떤 것을 몹시 원하거나 소망하다. 바라다. 갈망하다: *All those desiring to vote must come to the meeting.* 투표하고자 하는 모든 사람들은 그 회의에 참석해야만 한다. **3** FORMAL to want to have sex with someone ‖ 누군가와 성교하기를 원하다. 성욕을 느끼다

USAGE NOTE desire, want, and wish

Use **want** to talk about things you would like to do or have: *He wants to talk to you.* Use **desire** and **wish** only in very formal writing or in literature: *He wishes to speak with you. / She has everything her heart desires.*
want는 하고 싶은 것이나 가지고 싶은 것에 대해 이야기할 때 쓴다: 그는 당신

에게 말하고 싶어한다. **desire**와 **wish**
는 매우 격식 차린 글이나 문학에서만
사용한다: 그는 당신과 이야기하기를 소
망합니다. / 그녀는 마음으로 바라는 모
든 것을 가지고 있다.

de·sir·ous /dɪˈzaɪrəs/ *adj* FORMAL
wanting someone or something very
much ‖ 사람이나 사물을 몹시 원하는. 간
절히 바라는. 갈망하는

de·sist /dɪˈzɪst, dɪˈsɪst/ *v* [I] FORMAL to
stop doing something ‖ 어떤 것을 하는
것을 그만두다. …을 그치다

desk /dɛsk/ *n* **1** a piece of furniture
like a table that you sit at to write and
work ‖ 앉아서 글을 쓰고 업무를 보는 탁
자 같은 가구. 책상 **2** a place where you
can get information at a hotel, airport
etc. ‖ 호텔·공항 등에서 정보를 얻을 수
있는 곳. 프런트. 접수처: *You should
check in at the hotel desk first.* 먼저 호
텔 프런트에서 체크인을 해야 합니다.

desk·top com·put·er /ˌdɛsktɑp
kəmˈpyutɚ/ *n* a computer that is small
enough to be used on a desk ‖ 책상 위에
서 쓸 수 있을 정도로 작은 컴퓨터. 데스크
톱[탁상용] 컴퓨터 —compare LAPTOP

desk·top pub·lish·ing /ˌ.. ˈ.../, **DTP**
n [U] the work of producing magazines,
books etc. using a DESKTOP COMPUTER ‖
데스크톱 컴퓨터를 써서 잡지·책 등을 제
작하는 작업. 데스크톱 출판

des·o·late /ˈdɛsəlɪt/ *adj* **1** empty and
not attractive ‖ 텅 비어 마음을 끌지 않
는. 황량한. 황폐한: *the desolate terrain
of the Moon* 달의 황량한 지형 **2** feeling
very sad and lonely ‖ 매우 슬프고 외로움
을 느끼는. 고독한. 쓸쓸한: *He was
desolate when his wife died.* 그는 아내가
죽자 쓸쓸했다. – **desolation**
/ˌdɛsəˈleɪʃən/ *n* [U]

de·spair¹ /dɪˈspɛr/ *n* [U] a feeling of
being very unhappy and having no hope
at all ‖ 매우 불행하며 전혀 희망이 없는
느낌. 절망. 낙담: *Nancy's suicide left
him in deep despair.* 낸시의 자살은 그
를 깊은 절망의 나락으로 빠뜨렸다.

despair² *v* [I] to feel that there is no
hope at all ‖ 전혀 희망이 없다고 느끼다.
절망하다: *The trapped miners despaired
of ever being found alive.* 매몰된 광부들
은 과연 살아서 발견될지에 대해 절망적이
었다.

des·per·ate /ˈdɛsprɪt, -pərɪt/ *adj* **1**
willing to do anything to change a very
bad situation, and not caring about
danger ‖ 매우 나쁜 상황을 변화시키려고
위험도 감수한 채 무엇이든 하려 하는. 필

사적인. 모든 것을 건: *prisoners making
a desperate attempt to escape* 필사적인
탈출을 시도하는 죄수들 **2** needing or
wanting something very much ‖ 어떤 것
을 아주 많이 필요로 하거나 원하는. …을
몹시 갖고[하고] 싶어하는: *By then I was
so broke I was desperate for a job.* 빈털
터리가 되었을 때에야 비로소 일자리가 절
실했다. **3** a desperate situation is very
bad, serious, or dangerous ‖ 상황이 매
우 나쁜[심각한, 위험한]. 절망적인. 지독
한: *There is a desperate shortage of food
in the city.* 그 도시는 심각한 식량 부족을
겪고 있다. – **desperately** *adv*

de·sper·a·tion /ˌdɛspəˈreɪʃən/ *n* [U] a
strong feeling that you will do anything
to change a very bad situation ‖ 아주 나
쁜 상황을 바꾸기 위해 어떤 것이든 하고
자 하는 강렬한 감정. 필사적임: *The
drowning man grabbed at the life raft in
desperation.* 물에 빠진 남자는 필사적으
로 구명보트를 꽉 잡았다.

de·spic·a·ble /dɪˈspɪkəbəl/ *adj*
extremely unpleasant or cruel ‖ 대단히
불쾌하거나 잔인한. 비열한. 야비한

de·spise /dɪˈspaɪz/ *v* [T] to dislike
someone or something very much ‖ 사람
이나 사물을 몹시 싫어하다. 경멸하다. 얕
보다: *He despised her from the moment
they met.* 그들이 만났던 순간부터 그는
그녀를 몹시 싫어했다.

de·spite /dɪˈspaɪt/ *prep* in spite of
something ‖ 어떤 것에도 불구하고:
*Despite the doctors' efforts, the patient
died.* 의사들의 노력에도 불구하고 그 환
자는 사망했다.

de·spond·ent /dɪˈspɑndənt/ *adj*
unhappy and without hope ‖ 즐겁지 않으
며 희망이 없는. 낙심한. 풀이 죽은. 비관
하는 – **despondency** *n* [U] –
despondently *adv*

des·pot /ˈdɛspət, -pɑt/ *n* someone,
especially the ruler of a country, who
uses power in a cruel and unfair way ‖
잔인하고 부당하게 권력을 행사하는 사람.
특히 한 나라의 지배자. 독재자. 폭군 –
despotic /dɛˈspɑtɪk/ *adj*

dessert

cake   pie   cheesecake

sundae   Jell-o

des·sert /dɪˈzət/ *n* [C, U] sweet food served after the main part of a meal ‖ 주요리 후에 제공되는 달콤한 음식. 후식. 디저트

des·ti·na·tion /ˌdɛstəˈneɪʃən/ *n* the place that someone or something is going to ‖ 사람이나 사물이 가기로 예정된 곳. 목적지. 도착지: *The Alamo is a popular tourist destination in Texas.* 알라모는 텍사스의 인기 있는 관광지이다.

des·tined /ˈdɛstnd/ *adj* seeming certain to happen at some time in the future, because of FATE ‖ 운명 때문에 미래의 어느 때에 반드시 일어날 것 같은. (…할) 운명인: *She seemed destined for an acting career.* 그녀는 연기자가 될 운명처럼 보였다.

des·ti·ny /ˈdɛstəni/ *n* [C, U] the things that will happen to someone in the future, or the power that controls this; FATE ‖ 미래에 사람에게 일어날 일이나 이것을 통제하는 힘. 운명. 숙명; 随 fate: *a nation fighting to control its destiny* 나라의 운명을 결정하기 위해 싸우고 있는 나라

des·ti·tute /ˈdɛstəˌtut/ *adj* having no money, no place to live, no food etc. ‖ 돈·살 곳·먹을 것 등이 없는. 가난한. 곤한: *The floods left thousands of people destitute.* 그 홍수로 수천 명의 수재민이 생겼다. – **destitution** /ˌdɛstəˈtuʃən/ *n* [U]

de·stroy /dɪˈstrɔɪ/ *v* [T] to damage something very badly, so that it cannot be used or no longer exists ‖ 사물을 아주 심하게 손상시켜서 사용할 수 없거나 더 이상 존재하지 않다. 파괴하다: *a building completely destroyed by fire* 화재로 완전히 파괴된 건물

de·struc·tion /dɪˈstrʌkʃən/ *n* [U] the act or process of destroying something ‖ 어떤 것을 파괴하는 행위나 과정. 파괴: *Scientists are trying to stop the destruction of the ozone layer.* 과학자들은 오존층의 파괴를 막으려고 노력하고 있다. – **destructive** /dɪˈstrʌktɪv/ *adj*

de·tach /dɪˈtætʃ/ *v* [T] to remove part of something that is designed to be removed ‖ 제거하도록 고안된 사물의 부분을 없애다. 떼어내다. 분리하다: *Unsnap the buttons to detach the hood from the jacket.* 재킷에서 모자를 떼어내기 위해 단추를 풀어라. – **detachable** *adj*

de·tached /dɪˈtætʃt/ *adj* not reacting to something in an emotional way ‖ 감정적으로 어떤 것에 반응하지 않는. 초연한: *Rescue workers must remain detached*

to do their jobs well. 구조대원들은 일을 잘 하기 위해 냉정함을 유지해야 한다. – **detachment** *n* [U]

de·tail /ˈditeɪl, dɪˈteɪl/ *n* [C, U] a single fact or piece of information about something ‖ 어떤 것에 관한 하나의 사실이나 정보. 세부 (내용). 항목: *Dad planned our vacation down to the smallest detail.* 아빠는 우리의 휴가를 가장 작은 세부 사항까지 계획했다. / *Dr. Blount described the process in detail.* (=using lots of details) 블론트 박사는 그 과정을 상세하게 기술했다. / *There's no need to go into detail* (=give a lot of details) *about the contract at this early stage.* 지금 초기 단계에서 계약에 관해 상세히 기술할 필요는 없다.

de·tailed /dɪˈteɪld, ˈditeɪld/ *adj* containing or using a lot of information or facts ‖ 많은 정보나 사실들을 포함하거나 사용한. 상세한. 세부적인: *a detailed examination of the body* 신체 정밀 검사

de·tain /dɪˈteɪn/ *v* [T] to officially stop someone from leaving a place ‖ 사람이 한 장소에서 떠나는 것을 공식적으로 막다. …을 구금하다: *The police detained two suspects for questioning.* 경찰은 심문하기 위해 두 용의자를 구금했다.

de·tect /dɪˈtɛkt/ *v* [T] to notice or discover something, especially something that is not easy to see, hear etc. ‖ 특히 보거나 듣기에 쉽지 않은 것을 알아차리거나 발견하다. …을 찾아내다[발견하다]. 감지[간파]하다: *I detected the faint smell of perfume in the air.* 나는 공기 중에서 희미한 향수 냄새를 감지했다. – **detectable** *adj* – **detection** /dɪˈtɛkʃən/ *n* [U]

de·tec·tive /dɪˈtɛktɪv/ *n* a police officer whose job is to discover information about crimes and to catch criminals ‖ 범죄에 대한 정보를 찾고 범죄자를 잡는 경찰관. 형사

de·tec·tor /dɪˈtɛktə/ *n* a machine or piece of equipment that finds or measures something ‖ 어떤 것을 발견하거나 측정하는 기계나 장비. 탐지기: *the metal detectors at the airport* 공항의 금속 탐지기

dé·tente /deɪˈtɑnt/ *n* [C, U] FORMAL a state in which two countries that are not friendly toward each other agree to behave in a more friendly way ‖ 서로에게 우호적이지 않은 두 나라가 좀 더 우호적으로 행동하자고 동의한 상태. 긴장 완화. 데탕트

de·ten·tion /dɪˈtɛnʃən/ *n* **1** [U] the state of being kept in prison ‖ 감옥에 가

뒤 놓은 상태. 구금. 감금: *a political prisoner who was released after five years of detention* 5년간의 구금 후에 풀려난 정치범 **2** [C, U] a punishment in which students who have behaved badly must stay at school for a short time after other students have left ‖ 나쁜 행동을 한 학생들이 다른 학생들이 하교한 후 잠시 동안 학교에 남아야 하는 벌. 방과 후 학교에 남는 벌

de·ter /dɪˈtɚ/ *v* **-rred, -rring** [T] to make someone not want to do something by making it difficult, or by threatening him/her with a punishment ‖ 남이 어떤 것을 하기 어렵게 만들거나 벌로 위협해서 하고 싶어하지 않게 만들다. …을 그만두게[단념하게] 하다: *a new program to deter crime in the inner cities* 도심 빈민가의 범죄를 방지하려는 새 프로그램

de·ter·gent /dɪˈtɚdʒənt/ *n* [C, U] a liquid or powder containing soap, used for washing clothes, dishes etc. ‖ 옷·접시 등을 씻는 데에 사용하는 비누를 포함한 액체나 가루. 세제

de·te·ri·o·rate /dɪˈtɪriəˌreɪt/ *v* [I] to become worse ‖ 더 나빠지다. 악화되다. 저하하다: *My grandmother's health is deteriorating quickly.* 우리 할머니의 건강이 급격히 악화되고 있다. – **deterioration** /dɪˌtɪriəˈreɪʃən/ *n* [U]

de·ter·mi·na·tion /dɪˌtɚməˈneɪʃən/ *n* [U] the quality of continuing to try to do something even when it is difficult ‖ 일을 하기 어려울 때에도 계속하려고 노력하는 성질. 결심. 결단: *Marco has shown great determination to learn English.* 마르코는 영어를 배우는 데 대단한 결의를 보였다.

de·ter·mine /dɪˈtɚmɪn/ *v* [T] **1** FORMAL to find out the facts about something ‖ 어떤 것에 대한 사실을 알아내다. 측정하다: *Using sonar, they determined exactly where the ship had sunk.* 그들은 수중 음파 탐지기를 이용하여 배가 가라앉은 곳을 정확히 알아냈다. **2** to decide something, or to influence a decision about something ‖ 어떤 것을 결정하거나 어떤 것에 대한 결정에 영향을 미치다: *The number of incoming students will determine the size of the classes.* 신입생의 수에 따라서 학급 규모가 결정될 것이다.

de·ter·mined /dɪˈtɚmɪnd/ *adj* having a strong desire to continue to do something even when it is difficult ‖ 일을 하기 어려운 상황에서도 계속하고자 하는 강한 욕구를 가진. 굳게 결심한. 결연한:

She's a very determined woman. 그녀는 매우 단호한 여자다.

de·ter·min·er /dɪˈtɚmənɚ/ *n* TECHNICAL in grammar, a word that is used before an adjective or a noun in order to show which thing you mean. In the phrases "the car" and "some cars," "the" and "some" are determiners ‖ 문법에서, 의미하는 것을 나타내기 위해 형용사나 명사 앞에 쓰는 단어. 한정사. "the car"와 "some cars"의 구에서 "the"와 "some"은 한정사이다

de·ter·rent /dɪˈtɚənt/ *n* something that makes someone not want to do something ‖ 남으로 하여금 뭔가를 하고 싶지 않게 만드는 것. 억지[제지]물: *Car alarms can be an effective deterrent to burglars.* 자동차 도난 경보기는 효과적인 도난 방지물이 될 수 있다. – **deterrence** *n* [U]

de·test /dɪˈtɛst/ *v* [T] to hate someone or something very much ‖ 사람이나 사물을 몹시 싫어하다: *I detest drivers who follow too closely!* 나는 너무 가깝게 따라 붙는 운전자들은 질색이야!

det·o·nate /ˈdɛtˌneɪt, -təˌneɪt/ *v* [I, T] to explode, or to make something do this ‖ 폭발하거나 어떤 것을 폭발시키다: *Nuclear bombs were detonated in tests in the desert.* 핵폭탄을 시험 삼아 사막에서 터뜨렸다. – **detonation** /ˌdɛtˈnˈeɪʃən/ *n* [C, U]

det·o·na·tor /ˈdɛtˌnˌeɪtɚ, -təˌneɪtɚ/ *n* a small object used in order to make a bomb explode ‖ 폭탄을 터뜨리기 위해 사용되는 작은 물체. 기폭 장치

de·tour¹ /ˈditʊr/ *n* a way of going from one place to another that is longer than the usual way, because you want to avoid traffic, go somewhere special etc. ‖ 교통 정체를 피하거나 특정한 장소로 가고 싶어서 한 곳에서 다른 곳으로 이동하는 데 평소보다 더 멀리 가는 길. 우회로: *We made a detour to avoid the street repairs.* 우리는 도로 보수 공사를 피하기 위하여 우회했다.

detour² *v* [I, T] to make a DETOUR ‖ 우회하다[시키다]

de·tox /ˈditɑks/ *n* [U] INFORMAL a special treatment to help people stop drinking alcohol or taking drugs ‖ 사람들이 술을 마시거나 마약을 복용하는 것을 끊는 데에 도움을 주는 특별한 치료. 중독 치료

de·tract /dɪˈtrækt/ *v*

detract from sth *phr v* [T] to make something seem less good than it really is ‖ 어떤 것을 실제보다 덜 좋은 것처럼 보

이게 하다. (가치·명성 등을) 떨어뜨리다 [줄이다]. 손상시키다: *The billboards lining the streets detract from the city's beauty.* 길거리에 늘어서 있는 옥외 광고물은 도시의 미관을 해친다.

det·ri·ment /'dɛtrəmənt/ *n* [U] FORMAL harm or damage that is done to something ‖ 어떤 것에 가해진 손해나 손상: *He works long hours, to the detriment of his marriage.* 그는 결혼 생활을 희생해 가면서까지 장시간 일한다. – **detrimental** /,dɛtrə'mɛntl/ *adj*

de·val·ue /di'vælyu/ *v* **1** [I, T] TECHNICAL to reduce the value of a country's money, especially in relation to the value of another country's money ‖ 특히 다른 나라의 화폐 가치와 비교해서 한 나라의 화폐 가치를 떨어뜨리다. 평가가[를] 절하되다[시키다] **2** [T] to make someone or something seem less important or valuable ‖ 사람이나 사물을 중요성이나 가치가 덜해 보이게 만들다. – **devaluation** /di,vælyu'eɪʃən/ *n* [C, U]

dev·as·tate /'dɛvə,steɪt/ *v* [T] **1** to make someone feel extremely sad or shocked ‖ 사람을 극도로 슬프거나 놀라게 만들다. …을 압도하다. 망연자실하게 하다: *Hannah was devastated by the sudden death of her mother.* 한나는 어머니의 갑작스러운 죽음으로 망연자실해 있었다. **2** to damage something, or to destroy something completely ‖ 어떤 것을 손상시키거나 완전히 파괴시키다. …을 황폐시키다. 유린하다: *Bombing raids devastated the city of Dresden.* 폭격으로 드레스덴 도시가 완전히 파괴되었다. – **devastation** /,dɛvə'steɪʃən/ *n* [U]

dev·as·tat·ing /'dɛvə,steɪtɪŋ/ *adj* **1** badly damaging or destroying something ‖ 어떤 것을 심하게 손상시키거나 파괴하는. 황폐시키는. 파괴적인: *The drought has had a devastating effect on crops.* 농작물은 가뭄으로 심각한 피해를 입었다. **2** making someone feel extremely sad or shocked ‖ 사람을 극도로 슬프게 하거나 깜짝 놀라게 하는. 굉장한. 압도하는 듯한. 충격적인: *the devastating news of her sister's death* 그녀의 언니가 죽었다는 충격적인 소식

de·vel·op /dɪ'vɛləp/ *v* **1** [I, T] to grow or change into something bigger or more advanced, or to make someone or something do this ‖ 더 커지거나 더 진전된 것으로 성장하거나 변화하다, 또는 이렇게 성장시키거나 변화시키다. 발전[발달, 발육]하다[시키다]: *It's hard to believe that a tree can develop from a small seed.*

작은 씨앗이 나무로 성장할 수 있다는 것은 믿기 어렵다. / *plans to develop the local economy* 지역 경제를 발전시키기 위한 계획 **2** [T] to make a new idea or product successful by working on it for a long time ‖ 오랫동안 계속 연구함으로써 새로운 생각이나 제품을 성공적으로 만들다. 개발[전개]하다: *scientists developing new drugs to fight AIDS* 에이즈를 퇴치하기 위한 신약을 개발 중인 과학자들 **3** [T] to begin to have a quality or illness ‖ 특성이나 병을 가지기 시작하다. 나타내다. 발현하다[시키다]: *Her baby developed a fever during the night.* 그녀의 아기는 밤 동안에 열이 나기 시작했다. **4** [I] to begin to happen, exist, or be noticed ‖ 발생하기[존재하기, 알게 되기] 시작하다: *Clouds are developing over the mountains.* 구름이 산 위로 (뭉게뭉게) 피어나고 있다. **5** [T] to use land to build things that people need ‖ 사람들이 필요한 것을 짓기 위해 땅을 사용하다. 땅을 개발[조성]하다: *This area will be developed over the next five years.* 이 지역은 향후 5년간에 걸쳐 개발될 것이다 **6** [T] to make pictures out of film from a camera ‖ 카메라 필름으로 사진을 만들다. 현상하다: *I have three rolls of film to develop.* 나는 필름 3통을 현상해야 한다.

de·vel·oped /dɪ'vɛləpt/ *adj* **1** larger, more advanced, or stronger ‖ 보다 커진 [향상된, 강해진]. 발달한: *a child with fully developed social skills* 사회성이 완전히 발달한 아이 / *well developed muscles* 잘 발달된 근육 **2 developed countries/nations** rich countries that have many industries, comfortable living for most people, and usually elected governments ‖ 많은 산업을 가지고 있고 대다수의 사람들이 안락한 삶을 누리며 대개 선출된 정부가 있는 부유 국가. 선진국

de·vel·op·er /dɪ'vɛləpə/ *n* someone who makes money by buying land and then building houses, factories etc. on it ‖ 땅을 사서 그 땅에 집·공장 등을 지어서 돈을 버는 사람. 택지 개발업자

de·vel·op·ing /dɪ'vɛləpɪŋ/ *adj* **1** growing or changing ‖ 성장하거나 변화하고 있는: *a developing child* 성장하고 있는[자라나는] 아이 **2 developing countries/nations** countries without much money or industry, but that are working to improve life for their people ‖ 돈이나 산업은 많지 않지만 국민들의 생활을 향상시키기 위해 노력하고 있는 나라. 개발도상국

de·vel·op·ment /dɪ'vɛləpmənt/ *n* **1** [U]

the process of becoming bigger, stronger, or more advanced‖더욱 커지는[강해지는, 진전되는] 과정. 발달. 성장: *the development of skin cancer* 피부암의 진행 / *economic/industrial development* 경제[산업] 성장 **2** a new event that changes a situation‖상황을 변화시키는 새로운 사건. 새로운 뉴스. 새 정세: *Our reporter in Denver has the latest developments.* 덴버에 주재한 기자가 최신 뉴스를 전해 드리겠습니다. **3** a change that makes a product, plan, idea etc. better‖제품·계획·생각 등을 보다 좋게 만드는 변화. 개발: *new developments in computer technology* 컴퓨터 기술의 새로운 개발 **4** [U] the process of planning and building new streets, buildings etc. on land‖땅 위에 새로운 도로·빌딩 등을 계획하고 짓는 과정. 토지의 개발: *100 acres ready for development* 개발을 위해 준비된 100 에이커의 땅 **5** land that has buildings on it that were all planned together‖일괄적 계획으로 지은 건물이 있는 땅. 개발지. 주택 단지: *a housing development* 주택 단지

de·vi·ant /'diviənt/, **de·vi·ate** /ˌdiviɪt/ *adj* FORMAL different, in a bad way, from what is normal‖정상적인 것과는 나쁜 쪽으로 다른. 규범에서 벗어난. 비정상적인: *deviant behavior* 일탈 행위 – **deviant** *n*

de·vi·ate /'diviˌeɪt/ *v* [I] FORMAL to be or become different from what is normal or acceptable‖정상적이거나 수용할 수 있는 것과 다르거나 다르게 되다. 벗어나다. 빗나가다. 일탈하다: *The results of this study deviate from the earlier study.* 이 연구의 결과는 이전의 연구와 차이가 있다. – **deviate** /'diviɪt/ *n*

de·vi·a·tion /ˌdivi'eɪʃən/ *n* [C, U] FORMAL a noticeable difference from what is expected or normal, especially in behavior‖특히 행동에서 예상되거나 정상적인 것과의 확연한 차이. 벗어남. 탈선. 일탈: *The school does not allow deviation from the rules.* 그 학교는 학칙에서 벗어나는 것을 허용하지 않는다.

de·vice /dɪ'vaɪs/ *n* **1** a machine or tool that is usually small and usually electronic, that does a special job‖특정한 일을 하는 대개 작은 전자식 기계나 도구. 장치. 기기: *a device for separating metal from garbage* 쓰레기에서 금속을 분리하는 장치 **2** a way of achieving a particular purpose‖특정한 목적을 이루는 방법. 방책: *a language learning device* 언어 습득 방법 —see usage note

at MACHINE¹

dev·il /'dɛvəl/ *n* **1 the Devil** the most powerful evil spirit; Satan‖가장 강력한 악령. 악마; 사탄 **2** any evil spirit‖악령. 악귀

dev·il·ish /'dɛvəlɪʃ/ *adj* OLD-FASHIONED very bad, difficult, or unpleasant‖매우 나쁜[어려운, 불쾌한]. 악마 같은. 심한 – **devilishly** *adv*

dev·il's ad·vo·cate /ˌ.. '.../ *n* someone who pretends to disagree with you in order to have a good discussion about something‖어떤 것에 대한 만족스러운 토론을 하려고 의견을 달리하는 체하는 사람. 고의로 반대 입장을 취하는 사람: *Let me play devil's advocate and say that you should take the job even though the pay is less.* 비록 봉급은 적지만 나는 네가 그 일을 해야 한다고 반대 입장에 서서 말하겠다.

de·vi·ous /'diviəs/ *adj* using tricks or lies to get what you want‖원하는 것을 얻기 위해 술수나 거짓말을 사용하는. 솔직하지 않은. 속임수의. 교활한: *a devious way of not paying taxes* 세금을 내지 않는 부정직한 방법

de·vise /dɪ'vaɪz/ *v* [T] to plan or invent a way of doing something‖어떤 것을 하는 방법을 계획하거나 고안하다: *A teacher devised the game as a way of making math fun.* 선생님은 수학을 재미있게 하는 방법으로 그 게임을 고안해 냈다.

de·void /dɪ'vɔɪd/ *adj* **devoid of sth** not having a particular quality at all‖전혀 특정한 성질을 가지고 있지 않은. …이 결여된[없는]. …이 빠진: *The food is completely devoid of taste.* 그 음식은 맛이 전혀 없다.

de·vote /dɪ'voʊt/ *v* [T] **1 devote time/money/attention to sth** to give your time, money etc. to something‖어떤 것에 시간·돈 등을 제공하다. …에 시간을 바치다/돈을 들이다/전념하다: *She devotes her time on the weekends to her family.* 그녀는 주말에는 가족들과 시간을 보낸다. **2 devote yourself to sth** to do everything that you can to achieve something or help someone‖어떤 것을 성취하거나 남을 돕기 위해 할 수 있는 모든 것을 하다. 전념[몰두]하다: *He has devoted himself to finding out who killed his son.* 그는 자기 아들을 죽인 사람을 찾는 데 몰두했다.

de·vot·ed /dɪ'voʊtɪd/ *adj* giving someone or something a lot of love, concern, and attention‖사람이나 사물에 많은 사랑·관심·주의를 기울이는. 헌신

적인: *a devoted wife/father* 헌신적인 아
내[아버지] – **devotedly** *adv*

dev·o·tee /ˌdɛvəˈtiː, -ˈteɪ, -vou-/ *n*
someone who enjoys or admires
someone or something very much ‖ 사람
이나 사물을 아주 몹시 즐기거나 칭송하는
사람. 심취자. 열성가. 애호가. 팬(fan)
…광(狂): *a video game devotee* 비디오
게임광

de·vo·tion /dɪˈvouʃən/ *n* [U] 1 a strong
feeling of love that you show by paying
a lot of attention to someone or
something ‖ 사람이나 사물에 많은 주의를
기울여 보여주는 격한 사랑의 감정. 헌
신(적인 사랑). 전념: *He should be
admired for his devotion to duty.* 의무
를 다하는 그의 모습은 존경받아야 한다.
2 strong religious feeling ‖ 열렬한 종교적
감정. 신앙(심)

de·vour /dɪˈvauɚ/ *v* [T] 1 to eat
something quickly because you are very
hungry ‖ 몹시 배가 고프기 때문에 뭔가를
급하게 먹다. …을 게걸스럽게 먹다 2 if
you devour information, books etc. you
read a lot very quickly ‖ 많은 정보·책 등
을 매우 빨리 읽다. 탐독하다

de·vout /dɪˈvaut/ *adj* having very
strong religious beliefs ‖ 매우 열렬한 종
교적 믿음을 가진. 독실한: *a devout
Jew/Muslim* 독실한 유대교도[회교도] –
devoutly *adv*

dew /duː/ *n* [U] small drops of water
that form on outdoor surfaces during
the night ‖ 밤 사이에 옥외의 표면에 생기
는 작은 물방울. 이슬

dex·ter·i·ty /dɛkˈstɛrəti/ *n* [U] skill in
using your hands to do things ‖ 무엇인가
를 하기 위해 손을 쓰는 기술. 솜씨 좋
음. 손재주 – **dexterous, dextrous**
/ˈdɛkstrəs/ *adj*

di·a·be·tes /ˌdaɪəˈbitiz, -ˈbitɪs/ *n* [U] a
disease in which there is too much
sugar in the blood ‖ 혈액에 당이 너무 많
은 병. 당뇨병

di·a·bet·ic /ˌdaɪəˈbɛtɪk/ *n* someone who
has DIABETES ‖ 당뇨병 환자 – **diabetic**
adj

di·a·bol·i·cal /ˌdaɪəˈbɑlɪkəl/ *adj* very
bad, evil, or cruel ‖ 매우 나쁜[사악한, 잔
인한]. 극악무도한: *a diabolical killer* 잔
인한 살인자

di·ag·nose /ˌdaɪəgˈnous, ˈdaɪəgˌnous/ *v*
[T] to find out what illness a person has
or what is wrong with something ‖ 사람
에게 무슨 병이 있는지 또는 사물에 무엇
이 잘못되었는지를 찾아내다. …을 진단하
다: *Her doctor diagnosed cancer.* 그녀의
의사는 암 진단을 내렸다. / *He was*

diagnosed as having hepatitis. 그는 간
염에 걸렸다는 진단을 받았다.

di·ag·no·sis /ˌdaɪəgˈnousɪs/ *n, plural*
diagnoses [C, U] the result of
diagnosing (DIAGNOSE) someone or
something ‖ 사람이나 사물을 진찰한 결
과. 진단. 판정: *The doctor gave/made a
diagnosis of pneumonia.* 의사는 폐렴이
라고 진단을 내렸다. – **diagnostic**
/ˌdaɪəgˈnɑstɪk/ *adj*

di·ag·o·nal /daɪˈægənəl/ *adj* 1 a
diagonal line is straight and sloping ‖ 선
이 직선이며 비스듬한. 대각선의: *a
diagonal line across the field* 경기장을
가로지르는 대각선 / *diagonal parking
spaces* 대각으로 비스듬한 주차 공간 2
going from one corner of a square
shape to the opposite corner ‖ 정사각형
모양의 한 모서리에서 맞은편 모서리까지
가 는. 사선의 – **diagonal** *n* –
diagonally *adv* —see picture at
VERTICAL

di·a·gram /ˈdaɪəˌgræm/ *n* a drawing
that shows how something works,
where something is, what something
looks like etc. ‖ 어떤 것의 작동 방법·위
치·생김새 등을 보여주는 그림. 도해. 도
식. 설계도: *a diagram of a car engine* 자
동차 엔진의 설계도

di·al¹ /ˈdaɪəl/ *v* [I, T] to turn the wheel
with numbers on a telephone, or to
press the buttons on a telephone ‖ 전화
기의 숫자 다이얼을 돌리거나 전화기 버튼
을 누르다. (다이얼을 돌려, 버튼을 눌러)
전화를 걸다: *Dial 911–there's been an
accident.* 911에 전화해. 사고가 났어. /
Put the money in before you dial. 전화를
걸기 전에 돈을 넣으시오. —see usage
note at TELEPHONE

di·al² *n* 1 the round part of a clock,
watch, machine etc. that has numbers
that show you the time or a
measurement ‖ 시간이나 측정치를 나타
내는 숫자가 있는 벽시계·손목시계·기계
등의 둥근 부분. 문자반. 눈금판 2 the
part of a radio or television that you
turn to find different stations, or that
shows which station you are listening to
‖ 다른 방송국을 찾기 위해 돌리거나 청취
하고 있는 방송국이 어디인지를 보여 주는
라디오나 텔레비전의 부분. 다이얼 3 the
wheel with holes for fingers on some
telephones ‖ 일부 전화기에 손가락을 넣
는 구멍이 있는 원반. 전화기의 숫자반.
다이얼

di·a·lect /ˈdaɪəˌlɛkt/ *n* [C, U] a form of
a language that is spoken in one area in
a different way than it is spoken in

other areas ‖ 다른 지역에서 말하는 것과 다른 방식으로 한 지역에서 말하는 언어 형식. (지방) 사투리. 방언: *a dialect of Arabic* 아라비아 방언 / *The children speak only in the local dialect.* 그 아이들은 오직 지방 사투리로만 말한다.

di·a·logue, dialog /ˈdaɪəˌlɔg, -ˌlɑg/ *n* [C, U] **1** a conversation in a book, play, or film ‖ 책[연극, 영화]에서의 대화: *The dialogue in the movie didn't seem natural.* 그 영화에서의 대화는 자연스러워 보이지 못했다 **2** a formal discussion between countries or groups in order to solve problems ‖ 문제를 해결하기 위한 나라나 집단들간의 공식적인 토론. 회담. 대담. 토의: *an opportunity for dialogue between the fighting countries* 전쟁을 하고 있는 나라간의 회담 기회

dialogue box, dialog box /ˈ... ˌ/ *n* a box that appears on your computer screen when the PROGRAM you are using needs to ask you a question before it can continue to do something ‖ 사용중인 프로그램이 어떤 작업을 계속 수행하기에 앞서서 사용자에게 질문할 필요가 있을 경우 컴퓨터 화면에 뜨는 상자. 대화상자

dial tone /ˈ.. ./ *n* the sound that you hear when you pick up a telephone ‖ 전화기를 들었을 때 들리는 소리. 발신음

di·am·e·ter /daɪˈæmət̬ə/ *n* a line or measurement from one side of a circle to the other that passes through the center ‖ 원의 중앙을 통과하는 원의 한 쪽 면에서 다른 쪽 면까지의 선이나 길이. 직경. 지름: *a wheel two feet in diameter* 직경이 2피트인 바퀴

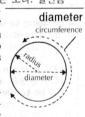

diameter
circumference
radius
diameter

di·a·met·ri·cal·ly /ˌdaɪəˈmɛtrɪkli/ *adv* **diametrically opposed** completely different or opposite ‖ 완전히 다르거나 정반대의: *The women hold diametrically opposed views on abortion.* 그 여자들은 낙태에 관해 정반대의 견해를 가지고 있다.

di·a·mond /ˈdaɪmənd, ˈdaɪə-/ *n* [C, U] **1** a clear, very hard, valuable stone, used in jewelry and in industry ‖ 보석·공업용으로 사용되는 투명하고 매우 단단하며 값비싼 보석. 다이아몬드: *a diamond ring* 다이아몬드 반지 **2** a shape with four straight points that stands on one of its points ‖ 하나의 지점을 기초로 하여 네 개의 일직선의 지점으로 이루어진

모양. 마름모꼴 —see picture at SHAPE¹ **3** a playing card with red diamond shapes on it ‖ 붉은색 다이아몬드 모양을 가진 게임용 카드. 다이아몬드 패

di·a·per /ˈdaɪpə, -ˈdaɪə-/ *n* a piece of material that is put between a baby's legs and fastened around its waist ‖ 아기의 다리 사이에 넣어 허리에 묶는 물건. 기저귀: *I think we need to change the baby's diaper.* (=put on a new one) 나는 아기의 기저귀를 갈아 주어야 한다는 생각이 든다.

di·a·phragm /ˈdaɪəˌfræm/ *n* **1** the muscle between your lungs and your stomach that controls your breathing ‖ 폐와 위 사이에서 호흡을 조정하는 근육. 격막. 횡격막 **2** a small round rubber object that a woman can put inside her body to stop her from getting PREGNANT ‖ 여성이 임신되는 것을 막기 위해 몸속에 집어넣는 작고 둥근 고무 제품. (피임용) 페서리

di·ar·rhe·a /ˌdaɪəˈriə/ *n* [U] an illness in which waste from the BOWELS is watery and comes out often ‖ 장에서 묽은 배설물이 자주 나오는 질병. 설사

di·a·ry /ˈdaɪəri/ *n* a book in which you write down important or interesting things that happen in your life ‖ 생활에서 일어난 중요하거나 흥미있는 일들을 기록한 책. 일기(장). 일지: *I'm going to keep a diary* (=write in it regularly) *this summer.* 나는 이번 여름에 일기를 쓸 거야.

dice¹ /daɪs/ *n, plural* **dice 1** a small block of wood or plastic with a different number of spots on each side, used in games ‖ 각 면에 각기 다른 숫자의 점이 있어 게임에 사용되는 나무나 플라스틱 재질의 작은 토막. 주사위: *Jeanie rolled the dice.* 지니는 주사위를 던졌다. **2 no dice** SPOKEN said when you refuse to do something ‖ 어떤 것 하기를 거절할 때에 쓰여. 반대. 거부. 안 됨: *I asked if I could borrow the car but she said no dice.* 내게 차를 빌려줄 수 있는지 물어보았지만 그녀는 절대 안 된다고 말했다.

dice² *v* [T] to cut food into small square pieces ‖ 음식물을 네모지게 작은 조각으로 자르다. 주사위 꼴로 자르다: *Dice the carrots.* 당근을 주사위 꼴로 잘라라.

dic·ey /ˈdaɪsi/ *adj* INFORMAL risky and possibly dangerous ‖ 아슬아슬하고 위험스런. 위기의: *a dicey situation* 위험한 상황

di·chot·o·my /daɪˈkɑt̬əmi/ *n* FORMAL the difference between two things or ideas that are not like each other ‖ 서

로 같지 않은 두 가지 사물이나 생각 사이의 차이(점). 양분(됨). 이분. 괴리: *a dichotomy between what he says and what he does* 그가 말하는 것과 행하는 것 사이의 괴리

dic·tate /'dɪkteɪt, dɪk'teɪt/ *v* **1** [I, T] to say words for someone else to write down ‖ 다른 사람이 받아쓰도록 단어를 말하다. 받아쓰게 하다. 구술하다: *She dictated a letter to her secretary.* 그녀는 비서에게 편지를 받아쓰게 했다. **2** [I, T] to tell someone exactly what s/he must do ‖ 어떤 사람에게 해야 할 일을 정확하게 말하다. 명령하다. 지시하다: *You can't dictate how I should live my life!* 네가 나에게 인생을 어떻게 살라고 지시할 수는 없지!: *Federal funds have to be used as dictated by Washington* 연방 기금은 워싱턴 정부의 지시대로 사용되어야 한다 **3** [T] to influence or control something ‖ 어떤 것에 영향을 미치거나 통제하다. …에 영향을 주다. …을 좌우하다: *The weather will dictate whether we can go or not.* 우리가 갈 수 있는지 없는지는 날씨가 좌우할 것이다.

dic·ta·tion /dɪk'teɪʃən/ *n* **1** [U] the act of saying words for someone to write down ‖ 어떤 사람이 받아쓰게 단어를 불러주는 행위. 받아쓰기. 구술 **2** sentences that a teacher reads out to test your ability to understand and write a language correctly ‖ 언어를 정확히 이해하고 쓸 수 있는 능력을 시험하기 위해 교사가 읽어 주는 문장. 받아쓰기[구술](시험): *Dictations are the hardest part of learning French.* 받아쓰기가 프랑스어 학습 중 가장 어려운 부분이다.

dic·ta·tor /'dɪkteɪtə/ *n* a leader of a country who controls everything, and who people usually do not like and are afraid of ‖ 사람들이 보통 좋아하지 않고 두려워하며 모든 것을 통제하는 국가의 지도자. 독재자 **– dictatorial** /,dɪktə'tɔriəl/ *adj*

dic·ta·tor·ship /dɪk'teɪtəˌʃɪp, 'dɪkteɪtə-/ *n* **1** [U] government that is by a DICTATOR ‖ 독재자에 의한 정부. 독재 정권 **2** a country under the control of a DICTATOR ‖ 독재자의 지배 하에 있는 국가. 독재 국가

dic·tion /'dɪkʃən/ *n* [U] the way in which someone pronounces words ‖ 사람이 단어를 발음하는 방식. 말투. 어법. 발성법

dic·tion·ar·y /'dɪkʃəˌnɛri/ *n* a book that gives a list of words in ALPHABETICAL order, with their meanings in the same or another language ‖ 알파벳 순서의 단어 목록에 같거나 다른 언어로 그 단어의 의미를 제공하는 책. 사전. 사서

did /dɪd, d; *weak* dəd/ *v* the past tense of DO ‖ do의 과거형

di·dac·tic /daɪ'dæktɪk/ *adj* FORMAL speech or writing that is didactic is intended to teach people a lesson ‖ 연설이나 글이 사람들에게 교훈을 가르쳐 줄 의도로 된. 교훈적인. 설교적인

did·n't /'dɪdnt/ *v* the short form of "did not" ‖ "did not"의 단축형: *He didn't say anything to me.* 그는 나에게 아무 말도 하지 않았다.

die /daɪ/ *v* **died, died, dying** [I] **1** to stop living ‖ 죽다. 사망하다: *Hector's upset because his dog died.* 헥터는 자기 개가 죽어서 상심해 있다. / *Mrs. Chen died of/from* (=because of) *heart disease.* 첸 부인은 심장병으로 사망했다. **2** to disappear or stop existing ‖ 사라지거나 존재하지 않게 되다. 소멸하다. 없어지다: *Her hope of returning home never died.* 집으로 돌아가려는 그녀의 희망은 결코 사라지지 않았다 **3** INFORMAL if a machine or motor dies, it stops working ‖ 기계나 모터가 작동을 멈추다. 시동이 꺼지다. 움직이지 않게 되다: *My car died when I was stopped at a red light.* 빨간 신호등에서 차를 멈추자 차의 시동이 꺼졌다.

SPOKEN PHRASES

4 be dying to do something to want to do something very much ‖ 어떤 것을 매우 하고 싶어하다. 간절히[애타게] …하고 싶어하다. …하고 싶어 못 견디다: *I'm dying to meet her brother.* 나는 그녀의 동생을 만나고 싶어 못 견디겠다. **5 be to die for** something that is to die for is extremely good ‖ 어떤 것이 상당히 좋다. 훌륭하고 멋지다. 끝장나다: *Max's chocolate cake is to die for!* 맥스가 만든 초콜릿 케이크는 둘이 먹다 한 사람이 죽어도 모를 정도야! **6 die laughing** to laugh a lot ‖ 많이 웃다. 포복절도하다: *I nearly died laughing when Jerry fell in the swimming pool.* 제리가 수영장에서 넘어졌을 때 나는 정말 우스워 죽을 뻔했다. **7 I could have died** said when you are very surprised or embarrassed ‖ 매우 놀라거나 당황했을 때 쓰여. 까무러치게 놀라다[당황하다]: *I could've died when I realized there was a hole in the back of my skirt.* 내 치마 뒤에 구멍이 났다는 것을 알고서 나는 까무러칠 뻔했다.

—see usage note at DEAD¹

die away phr v [T] if a sound dies away it becomes weaker and then stops ‖ 소리가 점차 약해지다가 그치다. 희미해져 사라지다: *The sound of her footsteps gradually died away.* 그녀의 발자국 소리가 점차 희미하게 사라졌다.

die down phr v [I] to become less strong or violent ‖ 덜 강해지거나 난폭해지다. 차츰 가라앉다. 누그러지다: *The wind finally died down this morning.* 바람은 오늘 아침 마침내 잠잠해졌다.

die off phr v [I] to die one at a time until none is left ‖ 하나도 남지 않을 때까지 한 번에 하나씩 죽어가다. 하나씩[차례차례] 죽다: *All the elm trees are dying off.* 모든 느릅나무들이 하나씩 차례차례 죽어가고 있다.

die out phr v [I] to disappear completely so that no one or no part is left ‖ 완전히 사라져서 아무도, 또는 어떤 부분도 남지 않다. 사멸[전멸]하다. 자취를 감추다: *The last bears in this area died out 100 years ago.* 이 지역의 마지막 곰들은 백 년 전에 자취를 감췄다.

die·hard /ˈdaɪhɑrd/ adj INFORMAL unwilling to stop doing something or stop supporting someone even though other people have ‖ 비록 다른 사람들은 중단했지만, 하던 일이나 사람에 대한 지원을 중단하려 하지 않는. 끝까지 저항하는. 완고한. 군센: *a diehard group of Grateful Dead fans* 그레이트풀 데드 그룹의 열렬한 팬클럽

die·sel en·gine /ˌdizəl ˈɛndʒɪn, -səl-/, **diesel** n an engine used in buses, TRUCKs, and some cars that uses DIESEL FUEL ‖ 버스·트럭·경유를 사용하는 차량에 쓰이는 엔진. 디젤 엔진

diesel fu·el /ˌ.. ˈ.., ˌ.. ˌ../, **diesel** n [U] a type of fuel that only burns under extreme pressure, and is cheaper than GASOLINE ‖ 극도의 압력 하에서만 연소하고 휘발유보다 가격이 싼 연료의 한 종류. 디젤 연료. 경유

di·et¹ /ˈdaɪət/ n 1 [C, U] the type of food that you eat each day ‖ 매일 먹는 음식의 종류. 일상 음식. 주식: *A healthy diet and exercise are important for good health.* 건강식과 운동은 건강 유지에 중요하다. 2 a plan to eat only particular kinds or amounts of food ‖ 특정 종류나 분량의 음식만을 먹는 계획. 규정식[식이요법] 식단: *a low-fat diet* 저지방 식단 / *No dessert for me – I'm on a diet.* (=trying to become thinner) 후식은 사양합니다. 다이어트 중이거든요.

diet² v [I] to eat less or eat only particular foods in order to lose weight ‖ 체중을 줄이기 위해 덜 먹거나 특정 음식만 먹다. 규정식을 취하다. 식이 요법을 하다: *Jill's always dieting.* 질은 항상 다이어트 중이다.

dif·fer /ˈdɪfɚ/ v [I] 1 to be different ‖ 다르다. 차이가 나다[있다]: *The students differ in their ability to understand English.* 학생들은 영어를 이해하는 능력에서 차이가 난다. / *His views differ from mine.* 그의 견해는 나와 다르다. 2 FORMAL to have different opinions ‖ 다른 의견을 갖다. 생각[의견]이 다르다[맞지 않다]: *The two groups differ on/about/over where to have the meeting.* 두 집단은 회의를 개최할 장소를 놓고 의견을 달리 한다.

dif·fer·ence /ˈdɪfrəns/ n 1 a way in which two or more things are not like each other ‖ 두 개나 그 이상의 것들이 서로 같지 않음. 다름. 상이: *There are many differences between public and private schools.* 공립학교와 사립학교간에는 다른 점이 많다. 2 [singular, U] the fact of not being the same as something else, or an amount by which one thing is not the same as another ‖ 다른 것과 같지 않은 점, 또는 하나가 다른 것과 똑같지 않은 정도. 차이(점). 격차: *What's the difference in price?* 가격차가 얼마나 납니까? / *There's an age difference of 4 years between the two children.* 두 아이들간에 네 살 터울이 난다. / *Can you tell the difference between the twins?* (=recognize that they are different) 쌍둥이들 사이의 차이점을 알아 볼 수 있습니까? 3 **make a difference/make all the difference** to have a good effect on a situation or person ‖ 상황이나 사람에 대해 좋은 영향을 주다. 좋아지게 하다. 변화/많은 차이를 가져오다: *Swimming twice a week can make a big difference in the way you feel.* 일주일에 두 번 수영을 하면 확연히 달라진 자신을 느낄 수 있다. 4 **make no difference** to have no effect on a situation or person ‖ 상황이나 사람에게 영향이 없다. 전혀 차이가 없다. 아무 문제가 안 된다: *It makes no difference to me what you do.* 네가 무엇을 하든 내게는 문제가 되지 않는다. 5 **have your differences** to have disagreements with or different opinions from someone ‖ 어떤 사람과 일치하지 않거나 다른 의견을 갖다. 각자 다른 점을 가지다. 의견이 서로 다르다: *We've had our differences, but we're still friends.* 우리는 서로 다르지만 여전히 친구다. 6 **difference of opinion** a disagreement ‖ 불일치. 의견 차이:

Perkins left his job because of a difference of opinion with his boss. 퍼킨스는 상사와의 의견 차이로 직장을 떠났다.

dif·fer·ent /'dɪfrənt/ *adj* **1** not like something or someone else, or not the same as before ‖ 다른 사물이나 사람과 같지 않은, 또는 전과 같지 않은. 다른. 달라진: *Have you had a haircut? You look different.* 너 머리 깎았니? 달라 보인다. / *New York and Chicago are very different from each other.* 뉴욕과 시카고는 서로 매우 다르다. / *My new job's different than anything I've done before.* 나의 새로운 일은 이전에 했던 그 어떤 일과도 다르다. **2** separate ‖ 분리된, 별개의. 서로 다른. 여러 가지의: *The bookstore has a lot of different books about Kennedy.* 그 서점은 케네디에 대한 여러 가지 책들을 많이 비치하고 있다. **3** SPOKEN unusual, often in a way that you do not like ‖ 종종 좋아하지 않게 특이한. 색다른. 별난: *"How do you like my shirt?" "Well, it's different."* "내 셔츠 어때?" "글쎄, 특이한데." – **differently** *adv*

USAGE NOTE different

We use both **different from** and **different than** to talk about two things that are not the same: *My new school is different from/than my old one.* However, most teachers prefer **different from**.

different from과 **different than**은 둘 다 같지 않은 두 가지 것에 대해 이야기할 때 쓴다: 내 새 학교는 옛 학교와 다르다. 그러나, 대부분의 교사들은 **different from**을 선호한다.

---

dif·fer·en·ti·ate /ˌdɪfə'rɛnʃiˌeɪt/ *v* **1** [I, T] to recognize or express the difference between things or people ‖ 사물이나 사람들 사이의 차이를 인식하거나 나타내다. 식별[분간]하다. 구별하다: *Most people couldn't differentiate between the two types of soft drink.* 대부분의 사람들이 그 두 가지의 청량음료를 서로 구분하지 못했다 **2** [T] to make one thing different from another ‖ 한 가지를 다른 것과 다르게 만들다. 차이 나게 하다. 차별화하다: *Our company tries to differentiate its products from the competitors.* 우리 회사는 제품을 경쟁사와 차별화하려고 한다. – **differentiation** /ˌdɪfəˌrɛnʃi'eɪʃən/ *n* [U]

dif·fi·cult /'dɪfəˌkʌlt/ *adj* **1** not easy to do or understand ‖ 하거나 이해하기가 쉽지 않은. 어려운. 곤란한. 힘든: *She sometimes finds math difficult.* 그녀는 때때로 수학을 어렵게 느낀다. **2** involving a lot of problems and causing trouble ‖ 많은 문제를 포함하여 말썽을 일으키는. 괴로운. 고통스러운: *His home life is difficult right now.* 그의 가정 생활은 지금 순탄하지 못하다. / *The bus strike is making life difficult for commuters.* 버스 파업으로 통근자들이 생활에 불편을 겪고 있다. **3** someone who is difficult is never satisfied, friendly, or pleased ‖ 사람이 결코 만족하지[다정하지, 기뻐하지] 않는. 다루기 힘든. 완고한. 까탈스러운. 무뚝뚝한.

dif·fi·cul·ty /'dɪfɪˌkʌlti/ *n* **1** [U] the state of being hard to do ‖ 하기가 힘든 상태. 어려움. 곤란: *David's having difficulty (in) finding a job.* 데이비드는 직업을 찾는 데 어려움을 겪고 있다. / *She spoke with difficulty.* 그녀는 어렵게 말했다. / *Their business is in financial difficulty.* 그들의 사업은 재정적으로 어려움에 처해 있다. **2** [usually plural] a problem or something that causes trouble ‖ 문제나 말썽을 일으키는 것. 곤경. 난제. 장애: *a country with economic difficulties* 경제적 곤경에 처한 나라 / *We ran into difficulties* (=had trouble) *buying the house.* 우리는 그 집을 사는 데 어려움에 부딪쳤다. **3** [U] how hard something is to understand ‖ 사물이 이해되기 어려운 정도. 난이도: *The books vary in level of difficulty.* 서적들은 난이도별로 다양하다.

dif·fuse¹ /dɪ'fyus/ *adj* FORMAL **1** spread over a large area or in many places ‖ 넓은 지역이나 많은 장소에 퍼져 있는. 널리 퍼진. 사방에 뿌려진. 방대한. 확산된: *a large and diffuse organization* 크고 방대한 조직 **2** using too many words and not expressing ideas clearly ‖ 너무 많은 말을 사용하며 생각을 분명히 표현하지 못하는. 산만한. 장황한: *a diffuse and complicated book* 장황하고 복잡한 책

dif·fuse² /dɪ'fyuz/ *v* [I, T] FORMAL **1** to make ideas, information etc. available to many people ‖ 생각·정보 등을 많은 사람들에게 이용할 수 있게 하다. 퍼뜨리다. 유포시키다. 전파[보급, 확산]하다: *a policy diffused throughout the company* 회사 전체로 확산된 정책 **2** to make a bad feeling less strong ‖ 나쁜 감정을 덜 격하게 하다. 마음을 풀다. 가라앉히다. 누그러뜨리다: *Mara tried telling jokes to diffuse the tension.* 마라는 긴장을 완화하기 위해 농담을 해보았다. **3** to make heat, a gas, light etc. spread over a larger area ‖ 열·가스·빛 등을 넓은 지역으로 퍼져 나가게 하다. 방산[산란]시키다. 발산하다

dig¹ /dɪg/ v **dug, dug, digging** 1 [I, T] to break up and move earth with a tool, your hands, or a machine ‖ 연장[손, 기계]으로 흙을 부수어서 옮기다. (땅을) 파다 [파헤치다]: *The kids enjoyed digging in the sand.* 아이들은 모래를 파며 즐겁게 놀았다. / *Dig a large hole.* 큰 구덩이를 파라. 2 [I, T] to get something by digging ‖ 파서 어떤 것을 얻다. 캐다. 발굴[채굴]하다: *dig coal* 석탄을 채굴하다 / *dig for gold* 금을 찾아 땅을 파다 3 **dig your own grave** INFORMAL to do something that will make you have problems later ‖ 나중에 문제를 일으키게 될 일을 하다. 제 무덤을 파다 4 [T] SPOKEN to like something or someone ‖ 사물이나 사람을 좋아하다. 즐기다: *You really dig her, don't you?* 너 정말로 그녀를 좋아하는구나, 그렇지?

shovel

dig in *phr v* [I] SPOKEN to start eating food that is in front of you ‖ 앞에 있는 음식을 먹기 시작하다. 맛있게 먹다: *Come on everyone – dig in!* 모두 어서 와. 먹자!

dig into *phr v* [I, T **dig** sth **into** sth] to push hard into something, or to make something do this ‖ 어떤 것 속으로 강하게 밀어 넣거나 어떤 것을 이렇게 되게 하다. …을[으로] 찔러 넣다[찌르다]: *She dug her fingernails into my arm.* 그녀는 손톱으로 내 팔을 쿡 찔렀다.

dig sth ↔ **up** *phr v* [T] 1 to remove something from under the earth with a tool or your hands ‖ 연장이나 손으로 땅 속에서 어떤 것을 제거하다. 파내다. 파서 없애다: *Beth was digging up weeds.* 베스는 잡초를 제거하고 있었다. 2 INFORMAL to find hidden or forgotten information by careful searching ‖ 주의깊은 탐색으로 숨겨지거나 잊혀졌던 정보를 찾아내다. 배경[과거, 정보]을 캐내다: *See what you can dig up on the guy.* 네가 그 남자에 대해 캐낼 수 있는 정보를 알아봐라.

dig sth ↔ **out** *phr v* [T] 1 to get something out of a place using a tool or your hands ‖ 연장이나 손으로 한 장소에서 어떤 것을 꺼내다. 파내다. 발굴하다: *We had to dig our car out of the snow.* 우리는 눈 속에 빠진 우리 차를 꺼내야 했다. 2 to find something that you have not seen for a long time, or that is not easy to find ‖ 오랫동안 보지 못했거나 찾기에 쉽지 않은 것을 찾아내다. 발견하다. 들추어내다: *Mom dug her wedding dress out of the closet.* 엄마는 옷장에서 자신의 웨딩 드레스를 발견했다.

dig² n 1 an unkind thing you say to annoy someone ‖ 남을 짜증나게 하는 불친절한 말. 빈정대기. 비꼬기: *Sally keeps making digs about my work.* 샐리는 내 작업에 대해 계속해서 빈정대고 있다. 2 a small quick push that you give someone with your finger or elbow ‖ 손가락이나 팔꿈치로 짧게 재빨리 사람을 밀기. 쿡 찌르기: *a dig in the ribs* 갈비뼈[옆구리] 찌르기 3 the process of digging in a place in order to find ancient objects to study ‖ 연구 목적으로 고대의 유물을 찾기 위해 한 장소를 파헤치는 과정. 발굴

di·gest¹ /daɪˈdʒɛst, dɪ-/ v [T] 1 to change food in the stomach into a form your body can use ‖ 위 속의 음식물을 인체가 이용 가능한 형태로 변화시키다. 소화시키다[하다]: *Some babies can't digest cow's milk.* 어떤 아기들은 우유를 소화하지 못한다. 2 to understand something after thinking about it carefully ‖ 어떤 것에 대해 주의 깊게 생각한 후에 이해하다. 터득하다: *It took a while to digest the theory.* 그 이론을 이해하는 데 한참 걸렸다.

di·gest² /ˈdaɪdʒɛst/ n a short piece of writing that gives the most important facts from a book, report etc. ‖ 책·보고서 등으로부터 가장 중요한 사실만 알려 주는 짤막한 글. 요약. 적요. 개요

di·ges·tion /daɪˈdʒɛstʃən, dɪ-/ n [C, U] the process or ability to DIGEST food ‖ 음식물을 소화시키는 과정이나 능력. 소화 (작용·기능). 소화력: *I've always had good digestion.* 나는 항상 소화가 잘 된다. **– digestive** *adj*

dig·it /ˈdɪdʒɪt/ n 1 any of the numbers from 0 to 9 ‖ 0에서 9까지의 숫자. 아라비아 숫자: *a seven-digit phone number* 일곱 자릿수의 전화 번호 2 TECHNICAL a finger or toe ‖ 손가락. 발가락

dig·i·tal /ˈdɪdʒɪtl/ *adj* 1 giving information in the form of numbers ‖ 정보를 숫자 형태로 주는. 디지털의: *a digital clock* 디지털 시계 2 using a system in which information is represented in the form of changing electrical signals ‖ 정보가 전기 신호를 변환시키는 형태로 표시되는 체제를 사용하는. 디지털(방식)의: *It's a digital recording of the concert.* 이것은 콘서트를 디지털 방식으로 녹음한 것이다.

dig·ni·fied /ˈdɪgnəˌfaɪd/ *adj* calm,

serious, proud, and making people feel respect ‖ 조용하고 진지하고 자신에 차 있으며 사람들로 하여금 존경심을 느끼게 하는. 위엄[품위] 있는. 당당한. 고귀한: *a dignified leader* 위엄 있는 지도자 — opposite UNDIGNIFIED

dig·ni·tar·y /'dɪgnə,tɛri/ *n* someone who has an important official position ‖ 중요한 공직에 있는 사람. 고관. 고위 인사: *foreign dignitaries* 외국 고위 인사

dig·ni·ty /'dɪgnəti/ *n* [U] **1** calm serious behavior, even in difficult situations, that makes people respect you ‖ 어려운 상황에서조차 사람들로 하여금 존경하게 하는 차분하고 진지한 행동. 위엄. 품위. 위풍. 기품: *a woman of compassion and dignity* 동정심과 기품을 가진 여성 **2** the quality of being serious and formal ‖ 진지하고 격식 있게 행동하는 특성. 존엄성. 신성함. 고귀함. 권위: *Lawyers must respect the dignity of the court.* 변호사는 반드시 법정의 권위를 존중해야 한다.

di·gress /daɪ'grɛs, dɪ-/ *v* [I] FORMAL to begin talking about something that is not related to the subject you were talking about ‖ 말하고 있던 주제와 관련 없는 것에 대해 말하기 시작하다. (주제에서) 벗어나다[빗나가다]. 여담을 하다 – **digression** /daɪ'grɛʃən/ *n* [C, U]

di·lap·i·dat·ed /də'læpə,deɪtɪd/ *adj* old, broken, and in very bad condition ‖ 낡고 부서지고 상태가 아주 나쁜. 허물어진. 낡아빠진. 황폐한: *a dilapidated old house* 쓰러져 가는 낡은 집 – **dilapidation** /dɪ,læpə'deɪʃən/ *n* [U]

di·late /daɪ'leɪt, 'daɪleɪt/ *v* [I, T] to become wider or more open ‖ 더 넓어지거나 열리게 되다. 확장되다[하다]. 팽창하다[시키다]: *Her eyes were dilated.* 그녀는 눈을 크게 떴다. – **dilation** /daɪ'leɪʃən/ *n* [U]

di·lem·ma /də'lɛmə/ *n* a situation in which you have to make a difficult choice between two actions ‖ 두 가지 행동 사이에서 어려운 선택을 해야 하는 상황. 진퇴양난. 딜레마. 궁지. 기로: *We're in a dilemma about whether to move or not.* 우리는 이동해야 할 것인지 말 것인지 기로에 놓여 있다.

dil·i·gent /'dɪlədʒənt/ *adj* someone who is diligent always works hard and carefully ‖ 사람이 항상 열심히 그리고, 주의 깊게 일하는. 근면한. 부지런한. 부단히 노력하는: *a diligent student* 근면한 학생 – **diligently** *adv* – **diligence** *n* [U]

dill /dɪl/ *n* [U] a plant whose seeds and leaves are used in cooking ‖ 씨와 잎이 요리에 쓰이는 식물. 미나릿과의 풀. 딜

dill pick·le /,. '../ *n* a CUCUMBER that is preserved in VINEGAR (=a sour-tasting liquid) ‖ 식초에 절인 오이. 딜로 양념한 오이 피클

di·lute /dɪ'lut, daɪ-/ *v* [T] to make a liquid weaker or thinner by mixing another liquid with it ‖ 한 액체에 다른 액체를 혼합하여 더 약하거나 묽게 하다. 희석하다: *diluted fruit juice* 묽게 한 과일 주스 / *Dilute the paint with oil.* 페인트에 기름을 섞어 묽게 만들어라. – **dilute** *adj* – **dilution** /daɪ'luʃən, dɪ-/ *n* [C, U]

dim¹ /dɪm/ *adj* **1** not bright or easy to see well ‖ 밝지 않거나 제대로 보기가 쉽지 않은. 어둠침침[어슴푸레]한. 흐릿한: *a dim room with a tiny window* 작은 창이 달린 어둠침침한 방 / *the dim outline of a building* 건물의 흐릿한 윤곽 **2** **dim recollection/awareness etc.** something that is difficult for someone to remember, understand etc. ‖ 사람이 기억하고 이해하기 어려운 것. 희미한 기억/인식: *a dim memory of her old house* 그녀의 옛날 집에 대한 희미한 기억 **3** **take a dim view of** to disapprove of something ‖ 어떤 것을 인정하지 않다. …을 의심[회의]하다. 비관적으로 보다 – **dimly** *adv*

dim² *v* **-mmed, -mming** [I, T] **1** to become less bright, or to make something do this ‖ 덜 밝아지거나 어떤 것을 덜 밝아지게 하다. 어둠침침하다[하게 하다]. 희미해지다[하게 하다]: *Can you dim the lights?* 조명을 낮출 수 있습니까? **2** if a feeling or quality dims, it grows weaker ‖ 감정이나 특성이 약해지다. 희박해지다. 어렴풋[어슴푸레]해지다: *The painful memory began to dim.* 고통스런 기억이 희미하게 사라지기 시작했다.

dime /daɪm/ *n* **1** a coin worth 10 cents (=10/100 of a dollar), used in the US and Canada ‖ 미국과 캐나다에서 사용되는 10센트 가치의 동전. 10센트 (주화). 다임 **2** **a dime a dozen** INFORMAL very common and not valuable ‖ 매우 평범하고 가치 없는. 흔해 빠진. 싸구려의: *Jobs like his are a dime a dozen.* 그가 하는 일은 흔해 빠진 것이다. **3** **on a dime** within a small area ‖ 좁은 지역 내에. 좁은 곳에서: *He can park on a dime.* 그는 좁은 곳에 주차시킬 수 있다.

di·men·sion /dɪ'mɛnʃən, daɪ-/ *n* **1** a part of a situation that affects the way you think about it ‖ 어떤 것을 생각하는 방식에 영향을 미치는 상황의 일부. 차원. 국면. 양상: *The baby added a new dimension to our life at home.* 아기로 인해 우리 가정생활은 새로운 모습을 띠게

되었다. **2** a measurement of space in a particular direction, such as length, height, or width ‖ 길이[높이, 폭] 등 특정한 간격을 측정한 값. 길이[높이, 폭]의 값[치수]

di·men·sions /dɪˈmɛnʃənz/ *n* [plural] **1** the measurement or size of something ‖ 사물의 치수나 크기. 부피. 면적. 용적: *What are the dimensions of the room?* 방의 크기가 어떻게 됩니까? **2** the seriousness of a problem ‖ 문제의 심각성 : *They didn't realize the true dimensions of the crisis.* 그들은 위기에 대한 실제적 심각성을 인식하지 못했다.

dime store /ˈ. ./ *n* a store that sells different types of inexpensive things ‖ 상이한 종류의 값싼 물건들을 파는 가게. 싸구려 잡화점

di·min·ish /dɪˈmɪnɪʃ/ *v* [I, T] to become smaller or less important, or to make something do this ‖ 더 작아지거나 덜 중요해지다, 또는 사물을 이렇게 하게 하다. 줄(이)다. 축소[감소]되다[시키다]: *the country's diminishing political influence* 점점 축소되는 그 나라의 정치적 영향력

di·min·u·tive /dɪˈmɪnyətɪv/ *adj* FORMAL very small ‖ 아주 작은. 소형의. 자그마한: *a diminutive man* 자그마한 사람

dim·ple /ˈdɪmpəl/ *n* a small hollow place on your cheek or chin, especially one that forms when you smile ‖ 뺨이나 턱에, 특히 웃을 때 생기는 움푹 들어간 작은 자국. 보조개 – **dimpled** *adj* —see picture at HEAD¹

din /dɪn/ *n* a loud, continuous, and unpleasant noise ‖ 크고 계속적이며 불쾌한 소음. 쿵쾅 울리는 소리[소음]

dine /daɪn/ *v* [I] FORMAL to eat dinner ‖ 정찬을 먹다. 식사하다

dine on *phr v* [T] FORMAL to eat a particular type of food for dinner, especially expensive food ‖ 정찬으로 특정 종류, 특히 비싼 음식을 먹다. …요리를 대접받다. …을 식사로 먹다: *We dined on lobster.* 우리는 바닷가재 요리를 식사로 먹었다.

dine out *phr v* [I] FORMAL to eat in a restaurant ‖ 식당에서 식사하다. 외식하다

din·er /ˈdaɪnɚ/ *n* **1** a small restaurant that serves inexpensive meals ‖ 값싼 식사를 제공하는 작은 식당. 작은[간이] 식당 **2** someone who is eating in a restaurant ‖ 식당에서 식사하는 사람. 식사 손님

ding-dong /ˈdɪŋ dɔŋ, -dɑŋ/ *n* [U] the noise made by a bell ‖ 종이 울리는 소리. 땡땡[딩동](소리)

din·ghy /ˈdɪŋi/ *n* a small open boat usually used for taking people between a ship and the shore ‖ 큰 배와 해변 사이에서 보통 사람을 나르는 데 쓰이는 작고 지붕이 없는 배. 거룻배

din·gy /ˈdɪndʒi/ *adj* dirty and in bad condition ‖ 더럽고 상태가 불량한. 지저분한. 초라한: *a dingy room* 지저분한 방

dining room /ˈ.. ˌ./ *n* a room where you eat meals in a house or hotel ‖ 집이나 호텔에서 식사하는 방. 식당

din·ner /ˈdɪnɚ/ *n* **1** [C, U] the main meal of the day, usually eaten in the evening ‖ 보통 저녁에 먹는 하루의 주요 식사. 저녁 식사. 정찬: *We had fish for dinner.* 우리는 저녁으로 생선을 먹었다 / *Grandma had everyone over for Thanksgiving dinner.* 할머니는 우리 모두를 추수 감사절 식사에 초대했다. **2** a formal occasion when an evening meal is eaten, often to celebrate something ‖ 종종 어떤 일을 축하하기 위해 저녁 식사를 하는 공식 행사. 만찬. 향연. 축하연: *There was a dinner in honor of his retirement.* 그의 은퇴를 기념하는 축하연이 열렸다. —see usage note at MEAL TIMES

din·ner·time /ˈdɪnɚˌtaɪm/ *n* [U] the time in the early evening when people eat dinner, usually between 5 and 7 o'clock ‖ 보통 5시와 7시 사이의 사람들이 저녁을 먹는 이른 저녁 시간(대). 저녁 식사 시간(대)

di·no·saur /ˈdaɪnəˌsɔr/ *n* one of many types of animal that lived in ancient times and no longer exist ‖ 고대에 살았던 이제는 존재하지 않는 많은 종류의 동물 중의 하나. 공룡

dip¹ /dɪp/ **-pped, -pping** *v* **1** [T] to put something into a liquid and quickly lift it out again ‖ 사물을 액체 속에 넣었다 다시 재빨리 꺼내다. 잠깐 담그다[적시다]: *Janet dipped her feet into the water.* 재닛은 물 속에 발을 잠깐 담갔다. **2** INFORMAL to go down or become lower ‖ 밑으로 내려가거나 낮아지다. 침하하다. 떨어지다. 감소하다: *Nighttime temperatures dipped below freezing.* 밤 기온이 영하로 떨어졌다.

dip into sth *phr v* [T] to use some of an amount of money that you have ‖ 가지고 있는 돈 중의 일부를 사용하다. (저금 등을) 헐다: *Medical bills forced her to dip into her savings.* 치료비 때문에 그녀는 저금에 손을 대야 했다.

dip² *n* **1** [C, U] a thick mixture that you can dip food into before you eat it ‖ 음식을 먹기 전에 담갔다 먹을 수 있는 진한 혼합물. 찍어 먹는 소스: *a sour cream* *dip for the potato chips* 감자 칩을 찍어 먹는 신 크림 소스 **2** an occasion when the level or amount of something becomes lower ‖ 어떤 것의 정도나 양이 더 낮아지는 경우. 하강. 하락. 급강하. 급락: *a dip in prices* 가격의 급락 **3** a place where the surface of something is lower than the rest of the area ‖ 어떤 곳의 지표가 나머지 지역보다 더 낮은 곳. 움푹 팬 곳: *a dip in the road* 도로의 움푹 팬 곳 **4** INFORMAL a quick swim ‖ 잠깐의 수영. 한 번 헤엄치기: *Is there time for a dip before lunch?* 점심 식사 전에 잠깐 수영할 짬이 있을까요?

diph·the·ri·a /dɪf'θɪriə, dɪp-/ *n* [U] a serious infectious disease of the throat that makes breathing difficult ‖ 호흡을 곤란하게 하는 심한 목 전염병. 디프테리아

di·plo·ma /dɪ'ploʊmə/ *n* an official paper showing that someone has successfully finished a course of study ‖ 사람이 성공적으로 공부 과정을 마쳤음을 나타내는 공식 문서. 졸업장[증서]. 학위(증서): *a high school diploma* 고등학교 졸업장

di·plo·ma·cy /dɪ'ploʊməsi/ *n* [U] **1** the management of political relations between countries ‖ 국가들간 정치 관계의 관리. 외교(술): *an expert at international diplomacy* 국제 외교 전문가 **2** skill in dealing with people and difficult situations successfully ‖ 사람과 어려운 상황을 성공적으로 다루는 기술. 수완. 교제[처세]술: *Bill handles personnel problems with diplomacy.* 빌은 인사 문제를 수완 좋게 다룬다.

dip·lo·mat /'dɪplə,mæt/ *n* someone who officially represents his/her country in a foreign country ‖ 외국에서 공식적으로 자국을 대표하는 사람. 외교관. 외교 사절

dip·lo·mat·ic /,dɪplə'mætɪk/ *adj* **1** relating to the management of political relations between countries ‖ 국가들간 정치 관계의 관리에 관한. 외교(상)의. 외교에 관한: *Feingold plans to join the diplomatic service.* 페인골드는 외교 업무에 참여할 계획이다. **2** good at dealing with people in a way that causes no bad feelings ‖ 나쁜 감정이 들지 않게 사람을 잘 다루는. 대인 관계에 능숙한[능수능란한]. 수사학이 뛰어난: *Try to be diplomatic when you criticize his work.* 그의 작업을 비판할 때는 될 수 있으면 말을 가려가면서 해라. —**diplomatically** *adv*

dip·stick /'dɪpstɪk/ *n* a stick used for measuring the amount of liquid in a container, such as oil in a car's engine ‖ 자동차 엔진의 기름 등 용기 안에 든 액체의 양을 측정하는 데 쓰는 막대. 게이지 막대[봉(棒)]

dire /daɪə/ *adj* **1** extremely serious or terrible ‖ 아주 심각하거나 지독한. 무시무시한. 끔찍한. 비참한: *Max is in dire trouble with the tax office.* 맥스는 세무서와 세금 문제로 심각한 상황에 처해 있다. / *a family in dire poverty/need* 지독한 가난[빈곤]에 처한 가족 **2 be in dire straits** to be in an extremely difficult or serious situation ‖ 매우 힘들거나 심각한 상황에 처하다. 심한 곤궁에 빠지다. 절박한[긴박한·극단적인] 사태에 직면하다

di·rect¹ /də'rɛkt, daɪ-/ *adj* **1** saying exactly what you mean in an honest way ‖ 의미하는 바를 진솔하게 정확히 말하는. 솔직한. 탁 터놓는. 단도직입적인: *It's better to be direct when talking with the management.* 경영진과 대화할 때는 솔직하게 말하는 것이 좋다. **2** done without involving any people, actions, processes etc. that are not necessary ‖ 불필요한 어떤 사람·행위·과정 등을 개입시키지 않고 이루어진. 직접적인: *direct government help for the unemployed* 실업자에 대한 직접적인 정부의 지원 **3** going straight from one place to another without stopping or changing direction ‖ 멈추거나 방향 전환 없이 한 장소에서 다른 곳으로 곧장 가는. 직행의. 일직선의: *We got a direct flight to Cairo.* 우리는 카이로 직행 항공편을 탔다. **4** likely to change something immediately ‖ 어떤 것을 즉시 변화시킬 것 같은. 즉효의. 직접의: *new laws that have a direct impact on health care* 건강 서비스에 직접적인 영향을 주는 새 법안 **5** exact or total ‖ 정확하거나 총체적인. 순전한. 글자 그대로의: *a direct translation from French* 프랑스어의 축자 번역[직역] —**directness** *n* [U] —opposite INDIRECT

direct

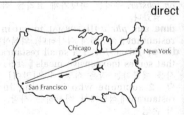

I'm flying direct from New York to San Francisco, but coming back via Chicago.

direct² *v* [T] **1** to give attention, money,

information etc. to a particular person, group etc. ‖ 특정 사람·집단 등에게 관심·돈·정보 등을 주다. …을 …으로 돌리다[나아가게 하다]. 향하게[집중하게] 하다: *My remark was directed at Tom, not at you.* 내 말은 네가 아니라 톰에게 한 것이다 / *money directed towards community projects* 공동체 사업 계획에 투입된 자금 **2** to aim something in a particular direction ‖ 특정 방향으로 사물을 겨누다. 조준[겨냥]하다. …으로 돌리다[지향하다]: *He directed the light towards the house.* 그는 불빛을 집 쪽으로 비추었다. **3** to be in charge of something ‖ 사물의 책임을 맡다. …을 관리하다. 지도하다: *Hanley was asked to direct the investigation.* 핸리는 조사를 책임지도록 요청받았다 **4** to give actors in a play, movie etc. instructions about what to do ‖ 연극·영화 등에서 배우에게 무엇을 할 것인가에 대한 지시를 내리다. 감독하다. 연출하다. 지휘하다: *Who's directing the school play this year?* 올해 학교 연극을 누가 연출합니까? **5** FORMAL to tell someone the way to a place ‖ 남에게 어떤 장소에 가는 길을 알려 주다. 길을 가르쳐 주다. 안내하다: *He directed me to the airport.* 그는 나에게 공항으로 가는 길을 가르쳐 주었다. —see usage note at LEAD¹

direct³ *adv* **1** without stopping or changing direction ‖ 멈추거나 방향 전환 없이. 곧바로. 곧장. 직행으로: *You can fly direct from London to Nashville.* 너는 런던에서 내슈빌로 곧장 비행할 수 있다. **2** without dealing with anyone else first ‖ 다른 사람을 먼저 대하지 않고. 직접[우선](적으로). 직통으로: *You'll have to contact the manager direct.* 네가 직접 지배인을 만나야 할 것이다.

di·rec·tion /də'rɛkʃən, daɪ-/ *n* **1** the way that someone or something is moving, facing, or aimed ‖ 사람이나 사물이 움직이는[마주보는, 향해진] 쪽. 방향. 방위. 코스: *We took a walk in the opposite direction from the hotel.* 우리는 호텔의 반대쪽으로 산책했다. / *Brian drove off in the direction of the party.* (=toward the party) 브라이언은 파티가 는 길로 차를 몰고 가 버렸다. **2** the general way in which someone or something changes or develops ‖ 사람이나 사물이 변화하거나 발전해 가는 일반적인 과정. 진행 방향[과정]: *Suddenly the conversation changed direction.* 갑자기 대화의 화제가 바뀌었다. **3** [U] control, guidance, or advice ‖ 통제. 지도. 충고. 명령. 지시. 감독. 관리: *The company's*

been successful *under Martini's direction.* 회사는 마티니의 관리하에 성공해 왔다. **4** [U] a general purpose or aim ‖ 일반적 목적 또는 목표: *Sometimes I feel that my life lacks direction.* 나는 때때로 내 인생에 목표가 결여되어 있음을 느낀다. **5 sense of direction** the ability to know which way to go in a place you do not know well ‖ 잘 모르는 장소에서 갈 길을 아는 능력. 방향 감각: *Matt's always getting lost; he has no sense of direction.* 매트는 항상 길을 잃는다. 그는 방향 감각이 없다. **6** [U] the instructions given to actors and other people in a play, movie etc. ‖ 연극·영화 등에서 배우와 다른 사람들에게 하는 지시. 감독. 연출

di·rec·tions /də'rɛkʃənz, daɪ-/ *n* [plural] instructions about how to go from one place to another, or about how to do something ‖ 한 장소에서 다른 장소로 가는 방법, 또는 어떤 일을 하는 방법에 대한 지침. 설명. 안내: *Could you give me directions to the theater?* 극장으로 가는 길을 가르쳐 줄 수 있습니까? / *Read the directions at the top of the page.* 페이지 상단의 지시 사항을 읽으세요.

di·rec·tive /də'rɛktɪv/ *n* an official order or instruction to do something ‖ 어떤 일을 하라는 공식적 명령이나 지시. 지령. 훈령

di·rect·ly /də'rɛktli, daɪ-/ *adv* **1** only involving people or actions that are necessary ‖ 꼭 필요한 사람이나 행동만 관계하여. 직접적으로. 곧장: *programs aimed directly at people on welfare* 생활 보호 대상자들을 직접 겨냥한 프로그램 **2** exactly ‖ 정확히. 똑바로. 바로: *Lucas sat directly behind us.* 루카스는 바로 우리 뒤에 앉았다.

direct ob·ject /.. '../ *n* ⇨ OBJECT¹

di·rec·tor /də'rɛktə, daɪ-/ *n* **1** someone who controls or manages a company, organization, or activity ‖ 회사[조직, 활동]를 지휘하거나 관리하는 사람. 지휘자. 관리자. 중역. 이사: *Her new job is marketing director of Sun Life.* 그녀의 새 직업은 선 라이프사의 마케팅 이사이다. **2** someone who gives instructions to actors and other people in a movie or play ‖ 영화나 연극에서 배우와 다른 사람들에게 지시를 내리는 사람. 감독. 연출가

di·rec·to·ry /də'rɛktəri, daɪ-/ *n* a book or list of names, facts, events etc., arranged in ALPHABETICAL order ‖ 알파벳 순으로 배열된 이름·사실·사건 등의 책이

나 목록

dirt /dət/ *n* **1** earth or soil ‖ 땅이나 흙. 토양. 토사: *a dirt road* 비포장도로 **2** any substance, such as dust or mud, that makes things not clean ‖ 먼지나 진흙 등의, 물체를 지저분하게 하는 모든 물질. 오물. 쓰레기: *The floor was covered with dirt!* 바닥은 먼지로 덮여 있었어! **3** INFORMAL information about someone's private life or activities that might give people a bad opinion about him/her ‖ 사람들에게 나쁜 인상을 줄 수 있는 어떤 사람의 사적인 생활이나 행위에 대한 정보. 추문. 부도덕한 비밀

dirt cheap /ˌ. './ *adj, adv* INFORMAL extremely cheap ‖ 지극히 싼[싸게]. 지독한 헐값의[으로]. 거저나 다름없는[이]: *We got this chair dirt cheap at a sale.* 우리는 이 의자를 세일 행사에서 거저나 다름없이 샀다.

dirt·y[1] /'dəti/ *adj* **1** not clean ‖ 깨끗하지 않은. 더러운. 불결한: *dirty dishes in the sink* 개수대 속의 지저분한 접시들 **2** concerned with sex in a way that is considered immoral ‖ 부도덕하게 여겨지게 성과 관련된. 추잡한. 상스러운. 음란한. 외설적인: *dirty jokes* 상스러운 농담들 **3** unfair or dishonest ‖ 정당하지 못한. 부정직한. 비열한. 교활한: *a dirty fighter* 비열한 권투 선수 **4 do sb's dirty work** to do an unpleasant or dishonest job for someone ‖ 어떤 사람을 위해 불쾌하거나 부정한 일을 대신하다. (다른 사람의) 뒤치다꺼리를 해 주다. 하수인 노릇을 하다: *I told them to do their own dirty work.* 나는 그들에게 자신들의 뒤치다꺼리나 잘 하라고 말했다.

dirt·y[2] *v* [T] to make something not clean ‖ 어떤 것을 깨끗하지 않게 하다. …을 더럽히다. 불결하게 하다

dis /dɪs/ *v* [T] SLANG to make unfair and unkind remarks about someone ‖ 남에 대해 부당하고 무례한 발언을 하다. 무시하며 말하다. 무례하게 말대꾸하다

dis·a·bil·i·ty /ˌdɪsə'bɪləti/ *n* **1** a physical or mental condition that makes it difficult for someone to do the things most people are able to do ‖ 대부분의 사람들이 할 수 있는 일들을 하기 힘들게 만드는 육체적 또는 정신적 조건. 무능[무력, 무자격] 상태. 장애: *Her disability doesn't keep her from working.* 그녀의 장애 상태가 그녀가 일하는 것을 막지는 못한다. **2** [U] the state of having a disability ‖ 장애를 가진 상태. 불구 상태: *learning to live with disability* 장애를 안고 살아가는 법을 배우기

dis·a·bled /dɪs'eɪbəld/ *adj* **1** someone who is disabled cannot use a part of his/her body properly ‖ 사람이 신체의 일부를 적절하게 사용할 수 없는. 불구의. 신체 장애가 있는: *a disabled worker* 장애 노동자 **2 the disabled** people who are disabled ‖ 신체 장애가 있는 사람들. 신체 장애자들: *The bank has an entrance for the disabled.* 그 은행에는 장애인들을 위한 출입구가 있다. – **disablement** *n* [U]

dis·ad·van·tage /ˌdɪsəd'væntɪdʒ/ *n* **1** something that may make someone less successful than other people ‖ 어떤 사람을 다른 사람들보다 덜 성공적으로 만들 수 있는 것. 열세. 불리한 위치[상태, 입장]: *Your main disadvantage is lack of experience.* 너의 가장 불리한 점은 경험 부족이다. / *I was at a disadvantage because I didn't speak Spanish.* 나는 스페인어를 말하지 않았기 때문에 불리한 입장에 처했다. **2** something that is not good or causes problems ‖ 좋지 않거나 문제를 일으킬 수 있는 것. 약점. 취약점. 불리한 점: *The only disadvantage of the job is the traveling.* 이 직업의 유일한 단점은 돌아다닌다는 것이다. – **disadvantageous** /ˌdɪsædvən'teɪdʒəs, -væn-/ *adj*

dis·ad·van·taged /ˌdɪsəd'væntɪdʒd/ *adj* having social DISADVANTAGEs such as a lack of money or education, that make it difficult for someone to succeed ‖ 사람을 성공하기 어렵게 하는 돈이나 교육의 부족 등 사회적으로 불리한 점을 가진. 사회[경제]적으로 혜택받지 못한. 가난한: *disadvantaged members of society* 사회의 혜택을 받지 못한 구성원들

dis·af·fect·ed /ˌdɪsə'fɛktɪd/ *adj* no longer loyal because you are not satisfied with your leader, ruler etc. ‖ 지도자·지배자 등에게 만족하지 않아서 더 이상 충성하지 않는. 마음이 떠난[이반(離反)된]. 불평불만을 품은: *Candidates are trying to attract disaffected voters.* 후보자들은 등을 돌린 유권자들의 관심을 끌려고 애쓰고 있다. – **disaffection** /ˌdɪsə'fɛkʃən/ *n* [U]

dis·a·gree /ˌdɪsə'griː/ *v* [I] **1** to have or express a different opinion from someone else ‖ 다른 사람과 다른 의견을 가지거나 표현하다. 이견(異見)을 보이다. 동의하지 않다: *Roth doesn't like anybody who disagrees with him.* 로스는 자기와 의견이 다른 사람은 아무도 좋아하지 않는다. / *We disagree about the best way to solve the problem.* 우리는 그 문제를 푸는 가장 좋은 방법에 대해 다른 의견을 갖고 있다. **2** if statements or reports about the same thing disagree, they are different from each other ‖ 같은 일에 대한 진술이나 보고가 서로 다르다. 상이하다. 일치하지 않다. 차이가 나다 **disagree with** *phr v* [T] to make you feel sick ‖ 구역질나게 하다. 체질[입맛]에 맞지 않다: *Crab meat disagrees with me.* 게살은 내 입맛에 맞지 않는다.

dis·a·gree·a·ble /ˌdɪsəˈgriəbəl/ *adj* **1** not enjoyable or pleasant ‖ 즐겁지 않거나 불쾌한. 마음에 들지 않는. 싫은: *a disagreeable experience* 불쾌한 경험 **2** unfriendly and having a bad temper ‖ 불친절하고 고약한 성미를 가진. 까다로운. 무뚝뚝한: *a disagreeable person* 까다로운 사람

dis·a·gree·ment /ˌdɪsəˈgrimənt/ *n* **1** [C, U] the state of having a different opinion from someone ‖ 어떤 사람과 의견이 다른 상태. 상이. 의견 차이: *She had a disagreement with the store's manager.* 그녀는 상점의 지배인과 의견이 달랐다. / *There was a slight disagreement over who should pay the bill.* 누가 비용을 지불할 것인가를 놓고 약간의 의견 차이가 있었다. **2** [U] differences between two statements, reports etc. that should be similar ‖ 유사해야 될 두 개의 진술·보고 등 간의 차이(점). 불일치(점). 상이점: *There was major disagreement between the witnesses' statements.* 목격자들의 진술 사이에 중요한 차이점이 있었다.

dis·al·low /ˌdɪsəˈlaʊ/ *v* [T] FORMAL to officially refuse to allow something because a rule has been broken ‖ 규칙이 지켜지지 않았기 때문에 어떤 일의 승인을 공식적으로 거부하다. 허가[인가]하지 않다. 각하하다. 심판은 골을 인정하지 않았다. *The referee disallowed the goal.* 심판은 골을 인정하지 않았다.

dis·ap·pear /ˌdɪsəˈpɪr/ *v* [I] **1** to become impossible to see or find ‖ 보거나 찾기가 불가능해지다. 사라지다. 보이지 않게 되다: *The cat had disappeared under the couch.* 고양이가 소파 밑으로 사라졌다. / *a plane disappearing behind the clouds* 구름 뒤로 사라진 비행기 **2** to stop existing ‖ 존재하지 않게 되다. 소멸하다. 멸종되다: *Many species of plants and animals disappear every year.* 많은 종류의 동식물들이 매년 사라져 가고 있다. **3** to **disappear into thin air** to suddenly become impossible to find with no explanation ‖ 갑자기 아무 설명 없이 찾기가 불가능해지다. 증발하다. 허공으로 사라지다 – **disappearance** *n* [C, U] —see usage note at LOSE

dis·ap·point /ˌdɪsəˈpɔɪnt/ *v* [T] to make someone unhappy because something s/he hoped for does not happen or is not as good as s/he expected ‖ 바라던 어떤 일이 일어나지 않거나 기대했던 만큼 좋지 않아서 사람을 즐겁지 않게 하다. 실망[낙담]시키다. 기대에 어긋나다: *I'm sorry to disappoint you, but the trip is canceled.* 실망시켜서 미안합니다만 여행이 취소되었습니다.

dis·ap·point·ed /ˌdɪsəˈpɔɪntɪd/ *adj* unhappy because something did not happen, or because something or someone is not as good as you hoped it would be ‖ 어떤 일이 일어나지 않았거나, 또는 사물이나 사람이 기대한 만큼 좋지 않아서 즐겁지 않은. 실망한. 낙담한. 기대에 어긋난: *Are you disappointed (that) you didn't get an invitation?* 초청을 받지 못해서 실망스럽니? / *We were disappointed with the election results.* 우리는 선거 결과에 낙담했다. / *I've been disappointed in his work.* 나는 그가 하는 일에 실망했다.

dis·ap·point·ing /ˌdɪsəˈpɔɪntɪŋ/ *adj* not as good as you expected or hoped something would be ‖ 어떤 일의 결과가 기대했거나 희망했던 만큼 좋지 않은. 기대에 어긋나는. 실망[낙담]시키는: *disappointing test scores* 실망스런 시험 점수 – **disappointingly** *adv*

dis·ap·point·ment /ˌdɪsəˈpɔɪntˈmənt/ *n* **1** [U] a feeling of sadness because something is not as good as you expected or has not happened ‖ 어떤 일이 기대했던 것만큼 좋지 않거나 실현되지 않았기 때문에 생긴 슬픈 감정. 실망. 낙담. 기대에 어긋남: *his disappointment at not being chosen for the job* 그 업무에 임명되지 못한 데에 대한 그의 실망감 **2** someone or something that is not as good as you hoped or expected ‖ 희망했거나 기대했던 만큼 좋지 못한 사람이나 사물. 기대에 어긋나는 사람[것]. 실망시키는 것[원인]: *What a disappointment that movie was!* 그 영화 정말 실망스럽구나! / *Kate feels like she's a disappointment to her family.* 케이트는 자신이 가족들에게 실망스런 존재인 양 느끼고 있다.

dis·ap·prov·al /ˌdɪsəˈpruvəl/ *n* [U] a feeling or opinion that someone else is behaving badly ‖ 다른 사람이 잘못 행동하는 것에 대한 감정이나 의견. 불찬성. 불승인. 불만: *public disapproval of the war* 전쟁에 대한 대중의 반대 / *People were looking with disapproval at our clothes.* 사람들은 우리 옷을 불만스럽게 바라보고 있었다. / *Marion shook her*

head in disapproval. 매리언은 찬성하지
않는다고 머리를 저었다.
dis·ap·prove /ˌdɪsəˈpruːv/ v [I] to
think that something is bad, wrong etc.
‖ 어떤 것을 나쁘고 잘못된 것 등으로 생
각하다. 좋지 않은 의견을 가지다. 승인
[인가, 찬성]하지 않다. 불만을 품다:
Her parents disapprove of her lifestyle.
그녀의 부모님은 그녀의 생활 방식을 찬성
하지 않는다.
dis·arm /dɪsˈɑrm/ v 1 [I] to reduce the
size of the army, navy etc. and the
number of weapons ‖ 육군·해군 등의 규
모와 무기의 숫자를 줄이다. 군비를 축소
하다[제한하다]: *Both sides must disarm
before the peace talks.* 양측은 평화 회담
전에 군비를 축소해야 한다. 2 [T] to take
away someone's weapons ‖ 남의 무기를
빼앗다. 무장 해제시키다: *Police
disarmed the two men.* 경찰은 두 남자에
게서 무기를 빼앗았다. 3 [T] to make
someone less angry and more friendly ‖
남을 덜 화나게 하고 더 친밀하게 하다. 화
를 풀게 하다. 마음을 누그러지게 하다:
Susie's reply disarmed him. 수지의 대답
은 그의 마음을 누그러뜨렸다.
dis·ar·ma·ment /dɪsˈɑrməmənt/ n [U]
the reduction in numbers or size of a
country's weapons, army, navy etc. ‖ 한
나라의 무기·육군·해군 등의 숫자나 규모
의 감축. 군비 축소: *plans for nuclear
disarmament* 핵무기 감축 계획
dis·arm·ing /dɪsˈɑrmɪŋ/ adj making
you feel less angry and more friendly or
trusting ‖ 화를 누그러뜨려 더욱 친밀하게
느끼게 하거나 신뢰감을 느끼게 하는. 적
개심[의혹, 서먹함]을 없애는. 마음을 부
드럽게 하는: *a disarming smile* 마음을
풀게 하는 미소
dis·ar·ray /ˌdɪsəˈreɪ/ n [U] FORMAL the
state of being messy or not organized ‖
어지럽혀지거나 정돈되지 않은 상태. 무질
서. 혼란: *papers in disarray on the
desk* 책상 위에 어지럽게 널린 종이들
dis·as·ter /dɪˈzæstɚ/ n [C, U] 1 a
sudden event such as an accident, flood,
or storm that causes great harm or
damage ‖ 큰 손해나 손상을 입히는 사고
[홍수, 폭풍] 등 갑작스런 사건. 재난. 재
해. 참사: *an air disaster in which 329
people died* 329명이 사망한 항공기 참사
2 **natural disaster** a disaster caused by
nature ‖ 자연에 의해 초래된 재난. 자연
재해: *The 1994 flood of the Mississippi
was a terrible natural disaster.* 1994년
미시시피 강의 홍수는 지독한 자연 재해였
다. 3 a complete failure ‖ 완전한 실패
(작). 구제 불능(인 것)[사람]): *What a*

disaster that party was! 그 파티는 완전
한 실패작이었어!
dis·as·trous /dɪˈzæstrəs/ adj very bad
or ending in failure ‖ 매우 나쁘거나 실패
로 끝나는. 비참[불행]한. 재해[재난]를
일으키는: *The whole evening was
disastrous.* 그 날 밤은 온통 비참한 일투
성이였다. – **disastrously** adv
dis·a·vow /ˌdɪsəˈvaʊ/ v [T] FORMAL to
state that you are not responsible for
something, or that you do not know
about it ‖ 어떤 일에 대해 책임이 없거나
알지 못한다고 말하다. …의 책임을 부정
하다. …과의 관계를 부인하다: *The
President has disavowed any knowledge
of the affair.* 대통령은 그 사건에 대해 아
는 바가 전혀 없다고 부인했다. –
disavowal n [C, U]
dis·band /dɪsˈbænd/ v [I, T] FORMAL to
stop existing as an organization ‖ 조직으
로서 존재하지 않게 되다. 해체[해산]하다
[되다]
dis·be·lief /ˌdɪsbəˈlif/ n [U] a feeling
that something is not true or does not
exist ‖ 어떤 것이 사실이 아니거나 존재하
지 않는다는 느낌. 불신. 의혹: *I looked at
him in disbelief.* 나는 못미더워 하면서
그를 바라보았다. – **disbelieve**
/ˌdɪsbəˈliv/ v [T] – **disbelieving** adj
disc /dɪsk/ n ⇨ DISK
dis·card /dɪˈskɑrd/ v [T] to get rid of
something ‖ 어떤 것을 없애다. 버리다.
폐기하다: *discarding old clothes* 헌 옷들
의 폐기 – **discard** /ˈdɪskɑrd/ n
dis·cern /dɪˈsɚn, dɪˈzɚn/ v [T] FORMAL
to see, notice, or understand something
by looking at it or thinking about it
carefully ‖ 사물을 주의 깊게 지켜보거나
생각함으로써 알아내다[인식하다, 이해하
다]. 식별[판별, 분간]하다: *Walters
couldn't discern any difference between
the two plants.* 월터스는 두 식물간의 차
이를 조금도 알아낼 수 없었다. –
discernible adj – **discernibly** adv
dis·cern·ing /dɪˈsɚnɪŋ, -ˈzɚ-/ adj able
to make good judgments about people,
styles, and things ‖ 사람·양식·사물에 대
해 판단을 잘 할 수 있는. 안목 있는. 분
별력[통찰력] 있는: *the discerning
traveler's guide to the Southeast* 미국 남
동부에 대한 훌륭한 여행 안내서
dis·charge¹ /dɪsˈtʃɑrdʒ/ v 1 [T] to
allow someone to go or to send him/her
away from a place ‖ 남을 가게 하거나 한
장소에서 떠나게 하다. 내보내다: *Blanton
was discharged from the hospital last
night.* 블랜튼은 어젯밤 병원에서 퇴원했
다. 2 [I, T] to send, pour, or let out

something from something else, especially a liquid or gas ‖ 특히 액체나 가스 등의 것을 다른 것으로부터 배출하다 [쏟아내다, 방출하다]. 뿜어내다: *Sewage was discharged into the ocean.* 하수가 바다로 배출되었다. / *The gun accidentally discharged.* (=it shot a bullet) 총이 사고로 발사됐다. **3** [T] FORMAL to perform a duty or promise ‖ 의무나 약속을 이행하다. 행하다. 역할을 다하다

dis·charge² /'dɪstʃɑrdʒ/ *n* **1** [U] the action of sending someone or something away ‖ 사람이나 사물을 내보내는 행위. 방출. 유출. 발사. 제대. 퇴원. 해고: *After his discharge from the army, he got married.* 군대에서 제대한 후, 그는 결혼했다 **2** [C, U] a substance that comes out of something, especially a wound or part of your body ‖ 특히 상처나 신체 부위에서 나오는 물질. 분비물. 고름. 진물: *infected discharge from the cut on her leg* 그녀 다리의 베인 상처에서 나오는 감염된 진물[고름]

dis·ci·ple /dɪ'saɪpəl/ *n* **1** a follower of a religious teacher, especially one of the 12 original followers of Christ ‖ 종교적 스승의 추종자, 특히 예수의 12제자 중 한 명. 사도 **2** a follower of any great leader or teacher ‖ 어떤 위대한 지도자나 스승의 추종자

dis·ci·pli·nar·i·an /ˌdɪsəplə'nɛriən/ *n* someone who believes that people should obey rules and who makes them do this ‖ 사람들이 반드시 규칙에 복종해야 한다고 믿으며 복종하게 하는 사람. 가르침이 엄한[규율을 강요하는] 사람. 엄격한 교사: *Sam's father is a strict disciplinarian.* 샘의 아버지는 엄격하게 규율을 지키는 사람이다.

dis·ci·pline¹ /'dɪsəplɪn/ *n* **1** [C, U] a way of training your mind and body so that you control your actions and obey rules ‖ 행동을 절제하고 규율에 복종하도록 마음과 몸을 훈련하는 방법. 단련. 수양. 수련: *It takes a lot of self discipline to study so hard.* 아주 열심히 공부하는 데는 많은 자기 수양이 필요하다. / *military discipline* 군기(軍紀) 훈련 **2** [U] the result of such training ‖ 그러한 훈련의 결과. 규율. 기강: *maintaining discipline in the classroom* 교실 내에서 규율 잡기 **3** [U] punishment for not obeying rules ‖ 규율에 복종하지 않는 데 대한 벌. 훈계. 징계: *That child needs discipline.* 그 아이는 훈계가 필요하다. **4** FORMAL an area of knowledge or teaching ‖ 지식이나 가르침의 영역. 학과.

학문 (분야)

discipline² *v* [T] **1** to train someone to behave or act in a particular way ‖ 사람을 특정하게 처신하거나 행동하도록 훈련시키다. 단련[수양]시키다: *sergeants disciplining the soldiers* 병사들을 훈련시키는 하사 **2** to punish someone ‖ 남을 벌주다. 처벌[징계]하다: *The staff members were disciplined for their carelessness.* 보좌진은 그들의 부주의함 때문에 징계를 받았다.

dis·claim /dɪs'kleɪm/ *v* [T] FORMAL to say that you are not responsible for or do not know anything about something ‖ 어떤 일에 대해 책임이 없거나 아무것도 모른다고 말하다. 부인[거부]하다: *The group has disclaimed any involvement in the attack.* 그 단체는 습격 사건에 대한 어떠한 개입도 부인했다.

dis·claim·er /dɪs'kleɪmər/ *n* FORMAL a statement that you are not responsible for or do not know about something, often used in advertising ‖ 종종 광고에서 쓰이는, 어떤 일에 책임이 없거나 모른다고 하는 말. 부인[거부, 기권] 발표(문)

dis·close /dɪs'kloʊz/ *v* [T] to make something known publicly ‖ 어떤 일을 공개적으로 알리다. 실토하다. 폭로하다. (드러냄으로써) 나타내다[밝히다]: *GM did not disclose details of the agreement.* GM은 협정의 세부 내용을 밝히지 않았다.

dis·clo·sure /dɪs'kloʊʒər/ *n* [C, U] a secret that someone tells people, or the act of telling this secret ‖ 사람들에게 말한 비밀, 또는 이 비밀을 말하는 행위. 탄로. 발각. 적발. 폭로. 발표: *the disclosure of corruption in the mayor's office* 그 시장 직무의 부패에 대한 폭로

dis·co /'dɪskoʊ/ *n* **1** [U] a type of dance music with a strong repeating beat that was first popular in the 1970s ‖ 1970년대에 최초로 대중화된, 강하게 반복되는 박자를 가진 댄스곡의 일종. 디스코 음악 **2** a place where people dance to recorded popular music ‖ 녹음된 대중음악에 맞춰 사람들이 춤을 추는 장소. 디스코장[클럽]

dis·col·or /dɪs'kʌlər/ *v* [I, T] to change color, or to make something change color, so that it looks unattractive ‖ 어떤 것의 색을 바꾸거나 변화시켜서 매력이 없어 보이다. 변색시키다. 퇴색하다: *His teeth were discolored from smoking.* 그의 치아는 담배를 피워서 변색됐다. – **discoloration** /dɪsˌkʌlə'reɪʃən/ *n* [C, U]

dis·com·fort /dɪs'kʌmfət/ *n* **1** [U] slight pain or an unpleasant feeling ‖ 가

벼운 고통이나 불쾌한 느낌. 불편. 불안: *Your injury isn't serious, but it may cause some discomfort.* 당신의 부상은 심하지는 않지만 약간 불편할 수 있습니다. **2** something that makes you uncomfortable ‖ 불편하게 만드는 것. 곤란한[힘든] 상황[조건]. 고생: *the discomforts of long distance travel* 장거리 여행의 고생스러움

dis·con·cert·ing /ˌdɪskənˈsɜtɪŋ/ *adj* making someone feel slightly embarrassed, confused, or worried ‖ 사람을 약간 당황스럽게[혼란스럽게, 걱정스럽게] 느끼게 하는. 당황하게 하는. 불안하게 하는: *It was disconcerting to be watched while I worked.* 일하는 동안 감시당하는 것은 불안하게 하는 일이었다. – **disconcert** *v* [T] – **disconcerted** *adj*

dis·con·nect /ˌdɪskəˈnɛkt/ *v* [T] **1** to take out the wire, pipe etc. that connects a machine or piece of equipment to something ‖ 기계나 장비를 어떤 것에 연결시키는 선·관 등을 떼어내다. …을 분리하다[잘라내다]. 연결을 해제하다: *Disconnect the cables before you move the computer.* 컴퓨터를 옮기기 전에 모든 연결선을 분리하시오. **2** to remove the supply of power to something such as a telephone line or a building ‖ 전화선이나 건물 등의 동력 공급원을 제거하다. 접속[연결]을 차단하다: *I tried to call, but the phone had been disconnected.* 나는 전화를 걸려고 했지만 전화는 불통이었다. – **disconnection** /ˌdɪskəˈnɛkʃən/ *n* [C, U]

dis·con·tent /ˌdɪskənˈtɛnt/ *n* [U] a feeling of not being happy or satisfied ‖ 행복하지 않거나 만족하지 못한 감정. 불만(족). 불평. 부족감

dis·con·tent·ed /ˌdɪskənˈtɛntɪd/ *adj* unhappy or not satisfied ‖ 행복하지 않거나 만족하지 않은. 불만스러운. 만족스럽지 못한. 불만[불평]을 품은: *After two years, I began to get discontented with my job.* 2년이 지나자 나는 내 직업에 대해 불만이 생기기 시작했다.

dis·con·tin·ue /ˌdɪskənˈtɪnyu/ *v* [T] to stop doing or providing something ‖ 어떤 것을 하거나 제공하는 것을 중단하다. 정지[중지]하다: *Five bus routes will be discontinued.* 5개의 버스 노선이 폐지될 것이다. – **discontinuation** /ˌdɪskənˌtɪnyuˈeɪʃən/ *n* [U]

dis·cord /ˈdɪskɔrd/ *n* **1** [U] FORMAL disagreement between people ‖ 사람들 사이의 불일치. 불화. 알력. 부조화: *fears that the law will increase racial discord*

그 법이 인종간 불화를 키울 것이라는 우려 **2** [C, U] an unpleasant sound produced by musical notes that do not go together well ‖ 서로 잘 화합하지 않는 음조에 의해 생성된 불쾌한 소리. 불협화음 – **discordant** *adj*

dis·count[1] /ˈdɪskaʊnt/ *n* a reduction in the usual price of something ‖ 사물의 통상 가격의 인하. 할인. 에누리: *I got this jacket at a huge discount.* 나는 이 재킷을 대폭 할인해서 샀다.

dis·count[2] /dɪsˈkaʊnt/ *v* [T] **1** to reduce the price of something ‖ 어떤 것의 가격을 내리다. 할인하다: *a good wine, discounted to $3.99* 고급 포도주, 3.99달러로 할인 **2** to regard something as unlikely to be true or important ‖ 어떤 것을 사실이 아니거나 중요하지 않은 것으로 여기다. …에 주의를 기울이지 않다. 무시하다. 신용[신뢰]하지 않다: *Scientists discounted his method of predicting earthquakes.* 과학자들은 지진을 예측하는 그의 방법을 무시했다.

dis·cour·age /dɪˈskɜrɪdʒ, -ˈskʌr-/ *v* [T] **1** to persuade someone not to do something, especially by making it seem difficult or unpleasant ‖ 특히 어렵거나 불쾌하게 보이게 해서 어떤 사람이 어떤 것을 하지 못하도록 설득하다. …하기를 그만두게[못하게] 하다. 단념시키다: *Keith's mother tried to discourage him from joining the navy.* 키스의 어머니는 그가 해군에 입대하는 것을 단념시키려고 노력했다. **2** to make someone less confident or less willing to do something ‖ 어떤 일을 하는 데 자신을 잃거나 하고 싶어하지 않게 만들다. 용기를 잃게 하다. …을 낙담[좌절, 실망]시키다: *Her failure on the first two attempts had discouraged her.* 처음 두 번의 시도가 실패로 끝나서 그녀는 용기를 잃었다. **3** to make something become less likely to happen ‖ 어떤 일이 일어날 가능성을 낮게 만들다. 방해[훼방]하다. 제지[억제]하다: *Put the plant in a cold room to discourage growth.* 성장을 억제하도록 그 식물을 추운 방에 두시오. —opposite ENCOURAGE

dis·cour·aged /dɪˈskɜrɪdʒd, -ˈskʌr-/ *adj* no longer having the confidence you need to continue doing something ‖ 어떤 일을 계속하는 데 필요한 자신감이 더 이상 없는. 용기를 잃은. 낙담한. 낙심한: *Children may get discouraged if they are criticized too often.* 아이들은 너무 자주 야단맞으면 자신감을 잃게 될지도 모른다.

dis·cour·age·ment /dɪˈskɜrɪdʒmənt,

-'skʌr-/ *n* **1** [C, U] a feeling of being DISCOURAGED ‖ 자신감을 잃어버린 느낌. 낙심. 낙담. 좌절. 실망 **2** [U] the act of trying to DISCOURAGE someone from doing something ‖ 어떤 사람이 어떤 일을 하지 못하게 노력하는 행위. 낙담[좌절]시키기. 만류[제지, 방해](행위)

dis·cour·ag·ing /dɪˈskɔɪdʒɪŋ, -skʌr-/ *adj* making you lose the confidence you need to continue doing something ‖ 어떤 일을 계속하는 데 필요한 자신감을 잃게 하는. 낙담[좌절]시키는. 기를 꺾는. 신명이 나지 않게 만드는: *It was very discouraging to see my sister do it so easily.* 내 누이가 그것을 그렇게 쉽게 해내는 것을 보고 나는 기가 꺾였다.

dis·course /ˈdɪskɔrs/ *n* **1** a serious speech or piece of writing on a particular subject ‖ 특정 주제에 대한 진지한 연설이나 글. 강연[설교](문). 논문. 논평: *a discourse on the history of Indian society* 인디언 사회의 역사에 대한 논문 **2** [U] serious conversation between people ‖ 사람들 사이의 진지한 대화. 담화. 담론. 토론. 토의: *a chance for meaningful discourse between the two leaders* 두 지도자 사이에 의미 있는 담론을 가질 기회

dis·cour·te·ous /dɪsˈkɔtiəs/ *adj* FORMAL not polite ‖ 정중하지 않은. 무례한. 버릇없는 **- discourtesy** *n* [C, U]

dis·cov·er /dɪˈskʌvɚ/ *v* **1** [T] to find something that was hidden or that people did not know about before ‖ 감춰졌거나 사람들이 전에는 알지 못했던 것을 찾아내다. 발견하다. 발굴하다: *Benjamin Franklin discovered electricity.* 벤자민 프랭클린은 전기를 발견했다. **2** [I, T] to find out something that is a fact, or the answer to a question ‖ 사실 또는 문제에 대한 해답이 되는 것을 알아내다. 깨닫다. 찾아내다: *Did you ever discover who sent you the flowers?* 누가 당신에게 꽃을 보냈는지 알아냈습니까? **- discoverer** *n*

dis·cov·er·y /dɪˈskʌvri, -vəri/ *n* **1** a fact, thing, or answer to a question that someone discovers ‖ 사람이 발견해 낸 사실[사물, 해답]. 발견된 것. 발견(물): *Einstein made an important scientific discovery.* 아인슈타인은 중요한 과학적 발견을 했다. **2** [U] the act of finding something that was hidden or not known before ‖ 숨겨져 있었거나 전에는 알려지지 않았던 어떤 것을 찾아내는 행위. 발굴. 발견(하기): *the discovery of oil in Texas* 텍사스 유전의 발견

dis·cred·it /dɪsˈkrɛdɪt/ *v* [T] to make people stop trusting or having respect for someone or something ‖ 사람들이 어떤 사람이나 사물을 믿거나 존경하지 않게 하다. …을 신뢰[존경]하지 않게 하다. 불신하다. 신용[신뢰]을 잃게 하다: *the newspaper's attempt to discredit the senator* 그 상원 의원의 평판을 손상시키려는 신문사의 노력 **- discredit** *n* [U]

dis·creet /dɪˈskrit/ *adj* careful about what you say or do so that you do not upset or embarrass people ‖ 사람들을 화나게 하거나 당황하게 하지 않도록 말하거나 행동하는 것에 주의하는. 신중한. 조심스러운. 지각[분별] 있는: *a discreet romance between co-workers* 직장 동료 간의 조심스러운 연애 **- discreetly** *adv*

dis·crep·an·cy /dɪˈskrɛpənsi/ *n* [C, U] a difference between two amounts, details etc. that should be the same ‖ 똑같아야 할 두 가지 양·내용 등 사이의 차이(점). 격차. 불일치[어긋남](의 정도): *How do you explain the discrepancies in these totals?* 이 총계들 사이의 차이를 어떻게 설명하시겠습니까?

dis·cre·tion /dɪˈskrɛʃən/ *n* [U] **1** the ability to be careful about what you say or do in a particular situation, so that you do not upset or embarrass people ‖ 특정 상황에서 말하거나 행하는 것에 조심해서 사람들을 화나거나 당황하지 않게 하는 능력. 분별[지각](력). 신중(함): *This situation must be handled with discretion.* 이 상황은 신중하게 처리되어야 한다. **2** the ability to decide what is the right thing to do in a situation ‖ 어떤 상황에서 해야 할 바른 일을 결정하는 능력. 결정[판단, 선택] 능력. 자유재량: *Pay raises are left to the manager's discretion.* 봉급 인상은 관리자의 자유재량에 맡겨져 있다. **- discretionary** *adj*

dis·crim·i·nate /dɪˈskrɪmə,neɪt/ *v* **1** [I] to treat a person or group differently from another in an unfair way ‖ 사람이나 집단을 다른 사람이나 집단과 달리 불공정하게 대하다. 차별 대우하다. 차별하다: *a law that discriminates against immigrants* 이민자를 차별하는 법 **2** [I, T] to recognize a difference between things ‖ 사물들간의 차이를 인식하다. 구별[판별, 식별]하다. 분간하다: *You must learn to discriminate between facts and opinions.* 당신은 사실과 의견 사이의 차이를 구별하는 법을 배워야 합니다.

dis·crim·i·nat·ing /dɪˈskrɪmə,neɪtɪŋ/ *adj* able to judge what is of good quality and what is not ‖ 질이 좋은 것과 질이 좋지 않은 것을 판단할 수 있는. 식별력[식견]이 있는: *fine food for those with discriminating taste* 맛을 아는 분들을 위

한 고급 음식
dis·crim·i·na·tion /dɪˌskrɪmə'neɪʃən/ n
[U] **1** the practice of treating one group
of people differently from another in an
unfair way ‖ 한 집단의 사람들을 다른 집
단의 사람들과 달리 불공평하게 대우하는
일. 차별(대우): *sex discrimination* 성차
별 / *working to stop discrimination
against the disabled* 장애인에 대한 차별
을 막기 위해 일하기 **2** the ability to
judge what is of good quality and what
is not ‖ 질이 좋은 것과 좋지 않은 것을 판
단하는 능력. 선별력. 판단력

dis·cus /'dɪskəs/ n [singular] a sport in
which you throw a heavy plate-shaped
object as far as you can ‖ 접시 모양의 무
거운 물체를 최대한 멀리 던지는 운동 경
기. 원반던지기 경기

dis·cuss /dɪ'skʌs/ v [T] to talk about
something with someone in order to
exchange ideas or decide something ‖ 생
각을 교환하거나 무엇을 결정하기 위해 누
군가와 어떤 것에 대해 이야기하다. …을
의논[논의]하다. 토론[토의]하다: *I
wanted to discuss my plans with my
father.* 나는 내 계획들을 아버지와 의논하
고 싶었다.

dis·cus·sion /dɪ'skʌʃən/ n [C, U] the
act of discussing something, or a
conversation in which people discuss
something ‖ 어떤 것을 의논하는 행위, 또
는 사람들이 어떤 것을 의논하는 대화. 의
논. 토론. 평의. 심의: *I want to have a
discussion about your behavior in
class.* 나는 네 수업 태도에 대해 이야기해
보고 싶다. / *The subject now under
discussion* (=being discussed) *is the
Vietnam War.* 지금 토론 중인 주제는 베
트남 전쟁이다.

dis·dain¹ /dɪs'deɪn/ n [U] FORMAL a lack
of respect for someone or something,
because you think he, she, or it is not
important or not good enough ‖ 사람이
나 사물이 중요하지 않거나 충분히 좋지
않다고 생각해서 그것에 대한 존경심이 결
여됨. 경멸. 모멸. 멸시: *Mason's
disdain for people without education* 교
양 없는 사람들에 대한 메이슨의 경멸 –
disdainful *adj*

disdain² *v* [T] FORMAL to feel DISDAIN
for someone ‖ 어떤 사람에 대해 경멸을
느끼다. 경멸[모멸, 멸시]하다

disease /dɪ'ziz/ n [C, U] an illness or
unhealthy condition that can be named
‖ 병명으로 불릴 수 있는 병이나 건강하지
못한 상태. 질병. 질환: *My uncle has
heart disease.* 내 삼촌은 심장병을 가지고
있다. / *Tina suffers from a rare brain*

disease. 티나는 희귀한 뇌 질환을 앓고 있
다. / *Lack of clean water can cause
disease.* 깨끗한 물의 부족은 질병을 초래
할 수 있다. – **diseased** *adj*

> **USAGE NOTE disease, illness,** and
> **sickness**
>
> Although we often use **disease** and
> **illness** to mean the same thing, it is
> a **disease** that actually makes you
> sick: *He suffers from heart disease.*
> **Illness** is the state of being sick:
> *Janey missed a lot of school because
> of illness.* **Sickness** is a particular
> type of illness: *radiation sickness /
> motion sickness.*
> 간혹 **disease**와 **illness**는 동일한 의
> 미에 쓰이지만, 실제로 사람을 아프게
> 하는 것은 **disease**이다: 그는 심장병
> [질환]을 앓고 있다. **illness**는 아프고
> 있는 상태이다: 제이니는 아파서 학교를
> 많이 빼먹었다. **sickness**는 특정 형태
> 의 병을 나타낸다: 방사선병 / (탈것으로
> 인한) 멀미

dis·em·bark /ˌdɪsɪm'bɑrk/ v [I, T] to
get off or be taken off a ship or plane ‖
배나 비행기에서 내리거나 내려지다. 상륙
하다[시키다]. 양륙하다[시키다] –
disembarkation /ˌdɪsɛmbɑr'keɪʃən/ n
[U]

dis·em·bod·ied /ˌdɪsɪm'bɑdid/ adj **1** a
disembodied sound or voice comes from
someone who cannot be seen ‖ 소리나
음성이 볼 수 없는 사람에게서 나오는. 실
체가 없는. 현실에 존재하지 않는 **2**
without a body ‖ 육체가 없는:
disembodied spirits 육신을 떠난 영혼

dis·en·chant·ed /ˌdɪsɪn'tʃæntɪd/ adj
no longer liking or believing in the value
of someone or something ‖ 사람이나 사
물의 가치를 더 이상 좋아하지 않거나 믿
지 않는. 믿음을 잃은. 환멸을 느낀: *She
was becoming disenchanted with her
marriage.* 그녀는 결혼 생활에 대해 환멸
을 느껴가고 있었다. – **disenchant-
ment** *n* [U]

dis·en·fran·chised /ˌdɪsɪn'fræntʃaɪzd/
adj not having any rights, especially the
right to vote, and not feeling part of
society ‖ 특히 투표할 권리 등 어떤 권리
도 가지지 않아서 사회의 한 구성원으로
느끼지 않는. 공민권을 빼앗긴[박탈당한].
구성원의 특권[권리]을 박탈당한 –
disenfranchise *v* [T]

dis·en·gage /ˌdɪsɪn'geɪdʒ/ v [I, T] to
separate something from something else
that was holding it or connected to it ‖

붙어 있거나 연결되어 있는 다른 것으로부터 어떤 것을 분리하다. 풀어[떼어, 빼어]놓다. 떨어지게 하다: *Disengage the gears when you park the car.* 차를 주차할 때 기어를 풀어 놓으시오. –

disengagement *n* [U]

dis·en·tan·gle /ˌdɪsɪnˈtæŋɡəl/ *v* [T] to separate different ideas or pieces of information that have become confused together ‖ 서로 뒤섞여 있는 상이한 생각이나 정보의 단편들을 분리하다. 얽힘[매듭]을 풀다[풀어내다]. 풀어내 해결하다: *Investigators had to disentangle Maxwell's complicated financial affairs.* 조사관들은 맥스웰의 뒤얽힌 금융 사고를 해결해야 했다.

dis·fa·vor /dɪsˈfeɪvɚ/ *n* [U] FORMAL a feeling of dislike or disapproval ‖ 싫어하거나 불찬성하는 감정. 혐오. 멸시. 불쾌. 냉대

dis·fig·ure /dɪsˈfɪɡyɚ/ *v* [T] to spoil the appearance of someone or something ‖ 사람이나 사물의 외관을 손상시키다. 아름다움을 훼손시키다. 추하게 하다: *His face was badly disfigured in the accident.* 그의 얼굴은 사고로 심하게 손상되었다. – **disfigurement** *n* [C, U]

dis·grace¹ /dɪsˈɡreɪs, dɪˈskreɪs/ *n* [singular, U] **1** something that makes people feel DISAPPROVING or ashamed ‖ 사람들이 싫어하게 만들거나 부끄럽게 여기게 하는 것. 수치[불명예](가 되는 것). 오점. 망신거리: *That old suit of yours is a disgrace.* 너의 그 낡은 양복은 창피스럽다. / *Doctors like you are a disgrace to our hospital.* 당신들 같은 의사들은 우리 병원의 수치입니다. **2 be in disgrace** to be regarded with disapproval because of something you have done ‖ 이미 한 어떤 것 때문에 불만스럽게 여겨지다. 수치스럽게 되다. 면목을 잃게 되다: *Harry left the school in disgrace.* 해리는 수치스럽게 학교를 떠났다.

disgrace² *v* [T] to do something so bad that people lose respect for you ‖ 아주 나쁜 짓을 해서 사람들의 존경(심)을 잃게 되다. …에 수치[불명예]가 되다. 명예[이름]를 더럽히다: *Peter disgraced himself last night by getting drunk and starting a fight.* 피터는 지난 밤 술에 취해 싸움을 벌여서 망신을 당했다.

dis·grace·ful /dɪsˈɡreɪsfəl/ *adj* completely unacceptable ‖ 전혀 용인할 수 없는. 수치스러운. 불명예의. 꼴불견의: *Your manners are disgraceful!* 너의 태도는 꼴불견이야!

dis·grun·tled /dɪsˈɡrʌntəld/ *adj* annoyed, disappointed, and not satisfied ‖ 짜증나며 실망스럽고 만족스럽지 못한. 언짢은. 불만인. 기분이 상한: *disgruntled employees* 불만에 찬 근로자들

dis·guise¹ /dɪsˈɡaɪz, dɪˈskaɪz/ *v* [T] **1** to change the usual appearance, sound etc. of someone or something ‖ 사람이나 사물의 평소의 모습·음성 등을 바꾸다. 변장[변성]하다. 위장[가장]하다: *She disguised herself as a man.* 그녀는 남자로 변장했다. **2** to hide something so that people will not notice it ‖ 사람들이 못 알아보도록 어떤 것을 숨기다. 감추다. 덮어서 모르게 하다: *We can't disguise the fact that the business is losing money.* 우리는 사업이 손해보고 있다는 사실을 숨길 수 없다.

disguise² *n* [C, U] something that you wear to change your appearance and hide who you really are, or the act of wearing this ‖ 모습을 바꾸거나 진짜 정체를 숨기기 위해 입는 것, 또는 이러한 것을 입는 행위. 변장. 위장. 가장. 분장: *He traveled to Russia in disguise.* 그는 위장을 하고 러시아로 여행을 떠났다.

dis·gust¹ /dɪsˈɡʌst, dɪˈskʌst/ *n* [U] a strong feeling of dislike and disapproval ‖ 싫어하고 용인하지 않는 강한 감정. 혐오. 반감. 진저리: *Joe was filthy, and everyone was looking at him with disgust.* 조는 지저분했고 그래서 모두들 그를 혐오스럽게 보고 있었다. / *We waited an hour before leaving in disgust.* 우리는 한 시간을 기다리다가 진저리를 내고 떠났다.

disgust² *v* [T] to make someone feel strong dislike and disapproval ‖ 사람이 심하게 싫어하고 반대하게 만들다. …에 혐오감을 일으키다. 진저리나게[메스껍게] 하다: *The dirt and smells of the city disgusted him.* 그 도시의 더러움과 악취가 그를 메스껍게 했다.

dis·gust·ed /dɪsˈɡʌstɪd/ *adj* feeling or showing DISGUST ‖ 혐오감을 느끼거나 보이는. 정떨어진. 진저리나는. 싫증난: *I felt sorry for Al, but Mike just looked disgusted and told him to get a job.* 나는 앨이 안됐다고 느꼈지만, 마이크는 완전히 정나미가 떨어진 듯 그에게 일자리를 구하라고 말했다.

dis·gust·ing /dɪsˈɡʌstɪŋ/ *adj* very unpleasant or unacceptable ‖ 아주 불쾌하거나 용납할 수 없는. 구역질나는. 메스꺼운. 진절머리 나는. 정나미가 떨어지는: *The smell in there is disgusting!* 거기서 나는 냄새는 구역질이 나! / *Fifteen dollars for a salad is disgusting!* 샐러드 하나에 15달러라니 정나미가 뚝 떨어지는

군! – **disgustingly** *adv*

dish¹ /dɪʃ/ *n* **1** a round container with low sides, used for holding food ‖ 음식을 담는 데 쓰는, 납작한 둥근 그릇. 접시: *a serving dish* (음식을 공용으로 담는 큰) 서빙 접시 **2** food cooked or prepared in a particular way ‖ 특정하게 조리되거나 준비된 음식. … 요리(한 가지): *a wonderful pasta dish* 맛있는 파스타 요리 —see also DISHES

dish² *v*

dish sth ↔ **out** *phr v* [T] INFORMAL **1** to give something to people ‖ 무엇을 사람들에게 주다. 나누어 주다. 제공하다: *He's always dishing out unwanted advice.* 그는 언제나 원치 않는 조언을 해주고 있다. **2** to serve food to people ‖ 음식을 사람들에게 주다. 담아 주다. 음식을 내놓다: *Dad dished out the barbecued steaks.* 아빠는 구운 스테이크를 접시에 담아 내놓았다. **3 sb can dish it out but s/he can't take it** INFORMAL used in order to say that someone criticizes others but does not like to be criticized ‖ 사람이 다른 사람들을 비판하지만 비판받기는 싫어한다는 것을 말하는 데 쓰여. …가 비판할 줄만 알지 비판을 받는 것은 못하다

dish sth ↔ **up** *phr v* [I, T] to put the food for a meal onto plates ‖ 식사를 위해 음식을 접시에 담다. 음식상을 차리다. 요리를 접시에 담아 내놓다: *Will you help me dish up dinner?* 저녁 식사 차리는 것을 도와주시겠어요?

dis·heart·ened /dɪsˈhɑrtˈnd/ *adj* feeling disappointed and without hope and confidence ‖ 실망해서 희망과 자신이 없어짐을 느끼는. 희망[용기]을 잃은. 낙담[좌절]한 – **dishearten** *v* [T]

dis·heart·en·ing /dɪsˈhɑrtˈn-ɪŋ/ *adj* making you lose hope and confidence ‖ 희망과 자신을 잃게 만드는. 낙담[좌절]시키는. 실망한: *It was disheartening to see that the changes we made didn't help.* 우리가 이뤄낸 변화가 도움이 되지 않는다는 것을 알고 실망스러웠다. – **dishearteningly** *adv*

dish·es /ˈdɪʃɪz/ *n* [plural] all the plates, cups, bowls etc. that are used during a meal ‖ 식사 중에 이용되는 모든 접시·컵·대접 등. 그릇. 식기: *The dishes go in the cupboard near the stove.* 식기들은 난로 옆의 찬장에 넣는다. / *It's your turn to do the dishes.* (=wash the dishes) 네가 설거지할 차례다.

di·shev·eled /dɪˈʃɛvəld/ *adj* very messy ‖ 매우 지저분한. 단정치 못한. 난잡한: *She looked tired and disheveled.*

그녀는 피곤하고 부스스해 보였다.

dis·hon·est /dɪsˈɑnɪst/ *adj* not honest ‖ 정직하지 않은. 부정직[불성실]한. 속임수[사기]의: *a dishonest politician* 부정직한 정치인 – **dishonestly** *adv*

dis·hon·est·y /dɪsˈɑnɪsti/ *n* [U] dishonest behavior ‖ 부정직한 행위. 부정(행위). 사기. 기만

dis·hon·or¹ /dɪsˈɑnɚ/ *n* [U] FORMAL a state in which people no longer respect you or approve of you ‖ 다른 사람들이 더 이상 존경하지 않거나 인정하지 않는 상태. 불명예. 망신. 치욕. 체면 손상: *His behavior brought dishonor on the family.* 그의 행위는 가족에게 불명예가 되었다.

dishonor² *v* [T] FORMAL to do something bad that makes people stop respecting you ‖ 다른 사람들의 존경을 받을 수 없게 하는 나쁜 일을 하다. 부정행위를 해서 명예·체면을 잃게 하다

dis·hon·or·a·ble /dɪsˈɑnərəbəl/ *adj* not morally correct or acceptable ‖ 도덕적으로 옳지 않거나 용납되지 않는. 불명예[수치]스러운. 비열한. 천한: *a dishonorable man* 비열한 남자 – **dishonorably** *adv*

dish rack /ˈ. ./ *n* a thing in which you put dishes to dry ‖ 말리려고 식기를 놓는 물건. 식기 건조대 —see picture at KITCHEN

dish·tow·el /ˈdɪʃtaʊəl/ *n* a cloth used for drying dishes ‖ 그릇의 물기를 닦는 데 사용하는 천. 마른 행주

dish·wash·er /ˈdɪʃˌwɑʃɚ/ *n* a machine that washes dishes ‖ 그릇을 씻는 기계. 식기 세척기 —see picture at KITCHEN

dis·il·lu·sion /ˌdɪsəˈluʒən/ *v* [T] to make someone realize that something s/he thought was true or good is not really true or good ‖ 남이 사실이거나 좋다고 여기는 것이 실은 그렇지 않다는 것을 깨닫게 하다. 환상을 버리게 하다. 미몽을 깨우치다: *I hate to disillusion you, but she won't pay you.* 환상을 깨고 싶진 않지만, 그녀는 네게 돈을 지불하지 않을 거야. – **disillusionment** *n* [U]

dis·il·lu·sioned /ˌdɪsəˈluʒənd/ *adj* disappointed because you have lost your belief that someone or something is good or right ‖ 사람이나 사물이 좋거나 옳다는 믿음을 잃었기 때문에 실망한. …에 환멸을 느낀[느끼는]

dis·in·fect /ˌdɪsɪnˈfɛkt/ *v* [T] to clean something with a chemical that destroys bacteria ‖ 박테리아를 파괴하는 화학 약품으로 어떤 것을 깨끗이 하다. 소독[살균]하다

dis·in·fect·ant /ˌdɪsɪnˈfɛktənt/ *n* [C, U]

a chemical that destroys BACTERIA ‖ 박테리아를 파괴하는 화학 약품. 소독약. 멸균제

dis·in·her·it /,dɪsɪn'hɛrɪt/ v [T] to prevent someone from receiving any of your money or property after your death ‖ 자신이 죽은 후에 누군가를 자신의 돈이나 재산을 받지 못하게 하다. …에게서 상속권을 빼앗다: *Crowley disinherited his son.* 크룰리는 아들의 상속권을 박탈했다.

dis·in·te·grate /dɪs'ɪntə,greɪt/ v [I] **1** to break up into small pieces ‖ 작은 조각들로 깨뜨리다. 분해하다: *The heat had made the foam rubber disintegrate.* 열기가 발포 고무를 분해시켰다. **2** to become weaker and be gradually destroyed ‖ (쇠)약해지고 점차로 파괴되다. 붕괴하다: *The whole project just disintegrated through lack of interest.* 모든 계획은 관심 부족으로 무산되었다. – **disintegration** /dɪs,ɪntə'greɪʃən/ n [U]

dis·in·ter·est·ed /dɪs'ɪntrɪstɪd, -'ɪntə,rɛstɪd/ adj **1** able to judge a situation fairly because you will not gain an advantage from it ‖ 어떤 것으로부터 얻을 이익이 없기 때문에 상황을 공정하게 판단할 수 있는. 공평무사한. 사심 없는: *a disinterested observer of the voting process* 투표 진행 과정에 대한 공평무사한 감시자 **2** NONSTANDARD not interested ‖ 흥미 없는. 관심 없는 – **disinterest** n [U]

USAGE NOTE disinterested

We often use **disinterested** to mean "not interested." However, many teachers think this is incorrect. If you want to say that someone is "not interested," use **uninterested**: *She seemed uninterested in the details.* "무관심한[흥미 없는]"의 뜻으로 종종 **disinterested**를 사용한다. 하지만 많은 교사들은 이것이 틀린 표현이라고 생각한다. 누가 "무관심하다[흥미 없다]"고 말하고 싶을 때는, **uninterested**를 쓴다: 그녀는 자세한 사항에는 무관심해 보였다.

---

dis·joint·ed /dɪs'dʒɔɪntɪd/ adj disjointed speaking or writing is not easy to understand because the words or ideas are not arranged in a reasonable order ‖ 단어나 생각이 합리적인 순서로 배열되지 않아서 말이나 글이 이해하기 쉽지 않은. (말·글 등이) 종잡을 수 없는. 지리멸렬한

disk /dɪsk/ n **1** a small flat piece of plastic or metal used for storing information in a computer ‖ 컴퓨터에 정보를 저장하는 데 쓰이는 작고 납작한 플라스틱 또는 금속 조각. 디스크 —see also HARD DISK **2** ⇨ DISKETTE **3** a flat object in the shape of a circle ‖ 원 모양의 납작한 물체. 디스크: *a metal disk* 금속 디스크 **4** a flat piece of CARTILAGE (=a strong substance that stretches) between the bones of your back ‖ 등뼈 사이에 있는 연골부의 납작한 부분. 추간판

disk drive /'. ./ n a piece of equipment in a computer that is used in order to get information from a DISK or to store information on one ‖ 디스크에서 정보를 얻거나[불러오거나] 정보를 저장하는 데 쓰이는 컴퓨터 내의 장치. 디스크 드라이브

disk·ette /dɪ'skɛt/ n a small square plastic object that you put into a computer, that is used for storing information ‖ 컴퓨터에 집어넣어 정보를 저장하는 데 쓰이는 작은 사각형 플라스틱 물체. 디스켓

disk jock·ey /'. ,../ n ⇨ DJ

dis·like¹ /dɪs'laɪk/ v [T] to not like someone or something ‖ 사람이나 사물을 좋아하지 않다. …을 싫어하다: *Why do you dislike her so much?* 왜 너는 그녀를 그렇게 싫어하니?

dislike² n [C, U] a feeling of not liking someone or something ‖ 사람이나 사물을 좋아하지 않는 감정. 싫음. 혐오. 반감: *She shared her mother's dislike of housework.* 그녀는 자기 엄마처럼 가사 일을 싫어했다.

dis·lo·cate /dɪs'loʊkeɪt, 'dɪsloʊ,keɪt/ v [T] to put a bone out of its normal place ‖ 뼈를 정상 위치에서 빠지게 하다. 관절을 삐게 하다. 뼈를 탈구시키다: *I dislocated my shoulder playing football.* 나는 축구하다가 어깨뼈가 탈구됐다. – **dislocation** /,dɪsloʊ'keɪʃən/ n [C, U]

dis·lodge /dɪs'lɑdʒ/ v [T] to force or knock something out of its position ‖ 무엇을 어떤 위치에서 몰아내거나 비우다. 제거하다. 쫓아내다: *Lee dislodged a stone as he climbed over the old wall.* 리는 오래된 벽을 오르면서 돌을 치웠다.

dis·loy·al /dɪs'lɔɪəl/ adj not loyal ‖ 충성스럽지 않은. 불성실한. 배신의: *He was accused of being disloyal to his country.* 그는 조국을 배신한 혐의로 기소되었다. – **disloyalty** /dɪs'lɔɪəlti/ n [C, U]

dis·mal /'dɪzməl/ adj very bad, and making you feel unhappy and without hope ‖ 아주 나쁘고, 불행하며 희망이 없

게 느끼도록 하는. 우울한. 비참한. 형편
없는: *dismal weather* 음울한 날씨 / *the team's dismal record in the past month* 지난 달 그 팀의 형편없는 기록[성적] –
dismally *adv*

dis·man·tle /dɪsˈmæntəl/ *v* [I, T] **1** to take something apart so that it is in separate pieces ‖ 어떤 것을 여러 부분이 되도록 나누다. 분해[해체]하다: *I'll have to dismantle the engine.* 나는 엔진을 분해해 봐야겠다. **2** to gradually get rid of a system or organization ‖ 체계나 조직을 점진적으로 제거하다. 허물다. 폐지하다: *plans to dismantle the existing tax laws* 기존의 세법을 점진적으로 폐지하려는 계획

dis·may¹ /dɪsˈmeɪ/ *n* [U] a strong feeling of being disappointed and unhappy ‖ 실망한·불행한 강한 느낌. 낙담. 환멸. 경악: *Jan read the news of the disaster with dismay.* 잰은 그 참사 기사를 읽고 대경실색했다.

dismay² *v* [T] to make someone feel worried, disappointed, and upset ‖ 어떤 사람을 걱정하고 실망하고 화나게 하다. 놀라게[당황하게] 하다. 환멸을 느끼게 하다: *I was dismayed to hear that you were moving.* 난 네가 이사할 거라는 소식을 듣고 매우 실망했어.

dis·mem·ber /dɪsˈmɛmbər/ *v* [T] FORMAL to cut or tear a body into pieces ‖ 신체를 여러 부분으로 자르거나 째다. 신체 부위를 잘라 내다

dis·miss /dɪsˈmɪs/ *v* [T] **1** to refuse to consider someone's idea, opinion etc. ‖ 남의 생각·의견 등에 대해 고려하기를 거절하다. 무시하다. 퇴짜 놓다. 거들떠보지 않다: *He dismissed the idea as impossible.* 그는 그 생각이 불가능하다며 거들떠보지 않았다 **2** FORMAL to remove someone from his/her job ‖ 어떤 사람을 직장에서 나가게 하다. 해고[해임]하다: *If you're late again you'll be dismissed!* 다시 한 번 늦으면 당신은 해고야! **3** to send someone away or allow him/her to go ‖ 어떤 사람을 멀리 보내다, 또는 가도록 허락하다. 해산시키다. 떠나게 하다: *Class is dismissed.* 수업은 이만 끝. – **dismissal** *n* [C, U]

dis·mis·sive /dɪsˈmɪsɪv/ *adj* refusing to consider someone or something seriously ‖ 사람이나 사물에 대해 진지하게 고려하지 않는. 멸시하는. 오만한: *Freud was much too dismissive of religion.* 프로이드는 종교를 지나치게 경멸했다.

dis·mount /dɪsˈmaʊnt/ *v* [I] to get off a horse, bicycle, or MOTORCYCLE ‖ 말[자전

거, 오토바이]에서 내리다

dis·o·be·di·ent /ˌdɪsəˈbidiənt/ *adj* deliberately not doing what you are told to do ‖ 하라고 시키는 일을 의도적으로 하지 않는. 복종하지 않는. 반항적인: *a disobedient child* 반항적인 아이 – **disobedience** *n* [U]

dis·o·bey /ˌdɪsəˈbeɪ/ *v* [I, T] to refuse to do what you are told to do, or to refuse to obey a rule or law ‖ 시키는 일을 하기를 거부하거나 규칙이나 법을 준수하기를 거부하다. 불복종하다. 거역하다. 순종하지 않다: *Drivers who disobey the speed limit will be fined.* 제한 속도를 지키지 않는 운전자는 벌금을 물게 된다.

dis·or·der /dɪsˈɔrdər/ *n* **1** [U] a situation in which things or people are very messy or not organized ‖ 사물이나 사람들이 매우 엉망이거나 조직화되지 않은 상황. 무질서. 혼란: *The house was in a state of complete disorder.* 그 집은 완전히 엉망이 된 상태였다 **2** civil/public disorder a situation in which many people disobey the law and are difficult to control ‖ 많은 사람들이 법을 준수하지 않아서 통제하기 어려운 상황. 시민/대중의 소요 **3** a disease or illness that prevents part of your body from working correctly ‖ 신체 일부가 제대로 기능하지 못하게 하는 질병. 장애. 이상. (질)병: *a rare liver disorder* 희귀한 간 질환

dis·or·der·ly /dɪsˈɔrdərli/ *adj* **1** messy ‖ 엉망인. 난잡한: *clothes left in a disorderly heap* 너저분한 더미로 놓여진 옷가지들 **2** noisy or violent in public ‖ 공연하게 소란스럽거나 폭력적인. 무도한. 난폭한. 치안을 해치는: *Jerry was charged with being drunk and disorderly.* 제리는 술에 취해 난동을 부렸다는 혐의를 받았다.

dis·or·ga·nized /dɪsˈɔrgəˌnaɪzd/ *adj* not arranged or planned in a clear order, or not planned at all ‖ 분명한 순서에 따라 배열 또는 계획되지 않거나 전혀 계획되지 않은. 무질서한. 혼란한: *The meeting was disorganized and too long.* 그 회의는 무질서했으며 너무 길었다 – **disorganization** /dɪsˌɔrgənəˈzeɪʃən/ *n* [U]

dis·o·ri·ent·ed /dɪsˈɔriəntɪd/ *adj* confused and not really able to understand what is happening ‖ 혼란스럽고 무슨 일이 일어나고 있는지 정말 이해할 수 없는. 어리둥절한. 방향 감각을 잃은. 정신적 혼란에 빠진: *You'll feel disoriented for a while after the operation.* 수술 후에는 잠시 혼미함을 느

낄 겁니다. – **disorientation** /dɪs-ˌɔːriənˈteɪʃən/ *n* [U]

dis·own /dɪsˈoʊn/ *v* [T] to say that you no longer want to have any connection with someone or something ‖ 더 이상 남이나 다른 것과의 어떠한 관계도 원치 않는다고 말하다. …와 인연을 끊다[의절하다]: *Her family disowned her for marrying him.* 그녀가 그 남자와 결혼했다는 이유로 가족들은 그녀와의 인연을 끊었다.

dis·par·age /dɪˈspærɪdʒ/ *v* [T] FORMAL to criticize someone or something in a way that shows you do not think he, she, or it is very good or important ‖ 사람이나 사물이 아주 좋거나 중요하다고 생각하지 않음을 나타내어 사람이나 사물을 비난하다. 비하하다. 경시하다. 깔보다. …의 평판[신용]을 떨어뜨리다: *Clay's humor tends to disparage women and gays.* 클레이의 유머는 여성과 동성애자들을 비하하는 경향이 있다.

dis·par·a·ging /dɪˈspærədʒɪŋ/ *adj* showing that you think someone or something is not very good or important ‖ 사람이나 사물을 그다지 좋거나 중요하지 않게 생각한다는 것을 보여 주는. 비하[경시]하는: *disparaging remarks/comments* 비하하는 말/논평

dis·par·ate /ˈdɪspərɪt/ *adj* FORMAL very different and not related to each other ‖ 매우 다르고 서로 관련이 없는. 본질적으로 다른[상이한]: *The project brought together several disparate groups to work on a common problem.* 서로 다른 몇몇 단체들이 공통의 문제를 해결하려고 그 프로젝트에 참여했다. – **disparately** *adv*

dis·par·i·ty /dɪˈspærət̬i/ *n* [C, U] FORMAL a difference between things, especially an unfair difference ‖ 사물들 간의 특히 불공정한 차이. 불일치. 불균형: *a huge disparity between our salaries* 우리 월급간의 심각한 불균형

dis·pas·sion·ate /dɪsˈpæʃənɪt/ *adj* not easily influenced by personal feelings ‖ 개인 감정에 의해 쉽게 영향 받지 않는. 감정에 좌우되지 않는. 냉정한: *a dispassionate opinion* 냉정한 의견 – **dispassionately** *adv*

dis·patch[1] /dɪˈspætʃ/ *v* [T] to send someone or something away ‖ 사람이나 사물을 멀리 보내다. …을 파견하다. …을 발송하다: *The packages were dispatched yesterday.* 그 소포들은 어제 발송했다.

dispatch[2] *n* a message sent between government or military officials, or sent to a newspaper by one of its writers ‖ 정부나 군 관계자 간에, 또는 신문 기자가 신문사에 보내는 전언. (군사·외교 등에 관해서 보내어지는) 공문. (신문 기자의) 특전

dis·pel /dɪˈspɛl/ *v* **-lled, -lling** [T] FORMAL to stop someone believing or feeling something ‖ 남이 어떤 것을 믿거나 느끼지 못하게 하다. (걱정·공포·의심 등을) 떨쳐버리다: *Mark's calm words dispelled our fears.* 마크의 침착한 말이 우리의 공포를 떨쳐냈다.

dis·pen·sa·ry /dɪˈspɛnsəri/ *n* a place where medicines are prepared and given out in a hospital ‖ 병원에서 약을 조제해 나누어 주는 곳. 조제실

dis·pen·sa·tion /ˌdɪspənˈseɪʃən, -pɛn-/ *n* [C, U] special permission to do something that is not usually allowed ‖ 보통 허가되지 않는 일을 할 수 있게 하는 특별한 허락. 특별 허가[면제]

dis·pense /dɪˈspɛns/ *v* [T] FORMAL **1** to give something to people, especially a particular amount of something ‖ 사람들에게 특히 물건의 특정 양을 주다. 분배하다: *The soldiers helped to dispense supplies.* 군인들이 물자 배분을 도왔다 **2** to give or provide people with advice, information etc. ‖ 사람들에게 충고·정보 등을 주거나 제공하다. 베풀다: *a clinic dispensing advice on family planning* 가족계획에 관한 조언을 제공하는 진료소

dispense with sth *phr v* [T] FORMAL to not use or do something that you usually use or do, because it is no longer necessary ‖ 보통 사용하거나 행하던 것을 더 이상 필요하지 않기 때문에 사용하거나 행하지 않다. …없이 지내다

dis·pens·er /dɪˈspɛnsɚ/ *n* a machine that gives you things such as drinks or money when you press a button ‖ 버튼을 누르면 음료수나 돈 등을 제공하는 기계. 자동 판매기. 현금 지급기

dis·perse /dɪˈspɚs/ *v* [I, T] to scatter in different directions, or to make something do this ‖ 사방으로 흩어지다, 또는 흩어지게 하다. 해산하다[시키다]: *The police used tear gas to disperse the crowd.* 군중을 해산시키기 위해 경찰이 최루가스를 사용했다. – **dispersal** *n* [U]

dis·pir·it·ed /dɪˈspɪrɪt̬ɪd/ *adj* LITERARY sad and without hope ‖ 슬프며 희망이 없는. 기운 없는. 의기소침한

dis·place /dɪsˈpleɪs/ *v* [T] **1** to take the place of someone or something by becoming more important or useful ‖ 더 중요하거나 유용해져서 다른 사람이나 사물의 자리를 차지하다. …을 대신하다: *Coal is being displaced by natural gas* *as a major source of energy.* 천연가스가 주요 에너지원으로서 석탄을 대신하고 있다. **2** to make a group of people or animals leave the place where they normally live ‖ 일단의 사람들이나 동물들을 평소 살던 곳에서 떠나게 하다. …을 강제 추방하다 – **displacement** n [U]

dis·play¹ /dɪˈspleɪ/ n **1** [C, U] an arrangement of things for people to look at ‖ 사람들이 보도록 사물을 배열함. 전시. 진열: *a display of African masks* 아프리카의 가면 전시 **2** a show or performance intended to entertain people ‖ 사람들을 즐겁게 할 목적의 쇼나 공연: *a fireworks display* 불꽃놀이(쇼) **3 be on display** something that is on display is in a public place where people can look at it ‖ 물건 등이 사람들이 볼 수 있는 공공장소에 있다. 전시[진열]되어 있다 **4** the act of clearly showing a feeling, attitude, or quality ‖ 감정[태도, 성질]을 분명히 드러내는 행위. (감정의) 노출. 표현: *Displays of affection* (=showing loving feelings for someone) *are disapproved of in many cultures.* 많은 문화권에서 스스럼없는 애정 표현은 허용하지 않는다.

display² v [T] **1** to put things where people can see them easily ‖ 사람들이 쉽게 볼 수 있는 곳에 사물을 놓다. 진열하다: *tables displaying pottery and other crafts* 도자기와 다른 공예품들을 진열한 테이블 **2** to clearly show a feeling, attitude, or quality ‖ 감정[태도, 성질]을 분명히 나타내다. 표출하다: *He displayed no emotion at Helen's funeral.* 그는 헬렌의 장례식에서 어떤 감정도 표출하지 않았다.

dis·pleased /dɪsˈplizd/ adj FORMAL annoyed and not satisfied ‖ 언짢고 불만족스러운. 못마땅한. 불만인: *Many employees were displeased with the decision.* 많은 직원들이 그 결정을 못마땅해했다. – **displease** v [T]

dis·pleas·ure /dɪsˈplɛʒɚ/ n [U] FORMAL the state of being DISPLEASED ‖ 불만족스러운 상태. 불만. 언짢음: *The audience showed their displeasure by leaving as the orchestra played.* 청중들은 오케스트라가 연주하는 동안 자리를 뜨는 것으로 불만을 표시했다.

dis·pos·a·ble /dɪˈspoʊzəbəl/ adj intended to be used once or for a short time and then thrown away ‖ 한 번, 또는 잠깐 쓰고서 버릴 수 있도록 만들어진. 1회용의: *disposable razors* 1회용 면도기

disposable in·come /.,… '../ n the amount of money you have after paying

all your bills, taxes etc., that you can spend on things you want ‖ 모든 청구액, 세금 등을 지불한 후, 원하는 것에 쓸 수 있는 나머지 금액. 가처분[실질] 소득

dis·pos·al /dɪˈspoʊzəl/ n **1** [U] the act of getting rid of something ‖ 어떤 것을 제거하는 행위. 처분. 처리: *the safe disposal of radioactive waste* 핵폐기물의 안전한 처리 **2 at sb's disposal** available for someone to use ‖ 어떤 사람이 쓸 수 있는. …이 임의 처분할 수 있는: *My car and driver are at your disposal.* 내 차와 기사는 당신 마음대로 쓰실 수 있습니다. **3** ⇨ GARBAGE DISPOSAL

dis·pose /dɪˈspoʊz/ v
dispose of sth *phr* v [T] **1** to get rid of something ‖ 어떤 것을 없애다. 처리[처분]하다: *How did the killer dispose of his victims' bodies?* 그 살인자는 피해자들의 사체를 어떻게 처리했나요? **2** to deal with something such as a problem or question successfully ‖ 문제나 질문 등에 성공적으로 훌륭히 대처하다. 문제를 (최종적으로) 처리하다. 결정짓다: *The court quickly disposed of the case.* 법원은 신속히 그 사건을 처리했다.

dis·posed /dɪˈspoʊzd/ adj FORMAL **1 be disposed to do sth** to feel willing to do something or behave in a particular way ‖ 어떤 것을 기꺼이 하거나 특정한 방식으로 행동하고 싶은 마음이 들다. …하고픈 마음이 나다[생기다]: *I don't feel disposed to interfere.* 난 방해하고 싶은 마음 없어. **2 well/favorably disposed (to)** liking or approving of something ‖ 무엇을 좋아하거나 승인하는. …에 대해 호감을 갖는: *The countries seem favorably disposed to a conference.* (=they want one) 그 나라들은 회담에 대해 호감을 갖고 있는 것 같다.

dis·po·si·tion /ˌdɪspəˈzɪʃən/ n FORMAL the way someone tends to behave ‖ 사람이 행동을 하는 방식. 기질. 성질. 성미: *a nervous disposition* 신경질적인 기질

dis·pos·sess /ˌdɪspəˈzɛs/ v [T] FORMAL to take property or land away from someone ‖ 남에게서 재산이나 토지를 빼앗다. 몰수하다 – **dispossession** /ˌdɪspəˈzɛʃən/ n [U]

dis·pro·por·tion·ate /ˌdɪsprəˈpɔrʃənɪt/ adj too much or too little in relation to something else ‖ 다른 것에 비해 너무 많거나 적은. …과 불균형인: *the disproportionate amount of money being spent on defense projects* 방위 사업에 소요되는 과다한 비용 – **disproportionately** adv

dis·prove /dɪsˈpruv/ v [T] to prove that

something is false ‖ 어떤 일이 잘못된 것이라는 점을 증명하다. …의 오류를 입증하다. 논박[반증]하다: *evidence that disproves Lane's claim* 레인의 주장을 논박하는 증거

dis·pute¹ /dɪ'spyut/ *n* [C, U] **1** a serious argument or disagreement ‖ 심각한 논쟁이나 의견 차이. 언쟁. 분쟁. 쟁의: *a pay dispute* 임금 쟁의 / *The land's ownership is in dispute.* (=being argued about) 그 토지의 소유권은 분쟁 중에 있다. / *The bus drivers are still in dispute with* (=having an argument with) *their employers over pay.* 버스 기사들은 임금을 둘러싸고 사용자 측과 여전히 논쟁 중이다. **2 be beyond dispute** to clearly be true, so that no one can question it or argue about it ‖ 명백하게 사실이어서 누구도 그것에 의문을 제기하거나 논쟁할 수 없다. 논의할 여지가 없다. 명백하다: *The facts are beyond dispute.* 그 사실은 명백하다. **3 be open to dispute** to not be completely certain, so that people can question it or argue about it ‖ 전적으로 확실하지 않아서 사람들이 의문을 제기하거나 논쟁할 수 있다. 논쟁의 여지가 있다: *The results of this research are still open to dispute.* 이 연구 결과는 여전히 논쟁의 소지가 있다.

dispute² *v* [I, T] to argue or disagree with someone, especially about whether something is true ‖ 특히 무엇이 사실인지 아닌지에 대해서 누구와 논쟁하거나 의견을 달리 하다. 논쟁[언쟁]하다: *The question was hotly disputed* (=argued about with strong feelings) *in the Senate.* 그 문제에 대해 상원에서 격론이 벌어졌다.

dis·qual·i·fy /dɪs'kwɑlə,faɪ/ *v* [T] to stop someone from taking part in an activity or competition, usually because s/he has done something wrong ‖ 어떤 사람이 옳지 않은 일을 해서 활동이나 시합에 참여하지 못하게 하다. 자격을 박탈하다: *Dennis was disqualified from the competition for cheating.* 데니스는 부정 행위를 했다는 이유로 시합에 참가하는 자격을 박탈당했다. **– disqualification** /dɪs,kwɑləfə'keɪʃən/ *n* [C, U]

dis·re·gard¹ /,dɪsrɪ'gɑrd/ *v* [T] to ignore something ‖ 어떤 것을 무시하다. …에 주의하지 않다: *The judge ordered us to disregard the lawyer's last statement.* 판사는 우리에게 변호사의 최후 진술을 무시하라고 명령했다.

disregard² *n* [U] the act of ignoring something, especially something important ‖ 특히 중요한 것을 무시하는 행위. 무시. 경시. 등한시: *Thomas' actions show a total disregard for the law.* 토마스의 행동은 그가 법을 완전히 무시하고 있다는 것을 보여 준다.

dis·re·pair /,dɪsrɪ'pɛr/ *n* [U] the state of being in a bad condition and needing to be repaired ‖ 나쁜 상태에 있으며 수리를 요하는 상태. 파손 (상태). 황폐: *The old house has been allowed to fall into disrepair.* 그 낡은 집은 방치되어 황폐해졌다.

dis·rep·u·ta·ble /dɪs'rɛpyəṭəbəl/ *adj* not respected and thought to be involved in dishonest activities ‖ 존경받지 못하며 부정직한 활동에 연루되어 있다고 여겨지는. 평판이 좋지 않은: *your disreputable friends* 평판이 나쁜 당신 친구들

dis·re·pute /,dɪsrə'pyut/ *n* [U] FORMAL **bring sb/sth into disrepute** to make people stop trusting or having respect for someone or something ‖ 사람들로 하여금 어떤 사람이나 사물에 대해 신뢰하거나 존중하지 못하게 하다. …의 평판을 떨어뜨리다: *Your behavior has brought the whole school into disrepute.* 너의 행동이 학교 전체의 명예를 실추시켰어.

dis·re·spect /,dɪsrɪ'spɛkt/ *n* [U] lack of respect or politeness ‖ 존경심이나 예의바름의 모자람. 실례. 무례. 불경 **– disrespectful** *adj* **– disrespectfully** *adv*

dis·rupt /dɪs'rʌpt/ *v* [T] to stop a situation, event etc. from continuing in its usual way ‖ 상황·사건 등이 평소대로 진행되지 못하게 하다. …을 혼란[중단, 두절, 불통]시키다: *A crowd of protesters tried to disrupt the meeting.* 시위 군중은 그 회의를 무산시키려고 했다. **– disruption** /dɪs'rʌpʃən/ *n* [C, U] **– disruptive** /dɪs'rʌptɪv/ *adj*

dis·sat·is·fac·tion /dɪ,sæṭɪs'fækʃən, dɪs,sæ-/ *n* [U] a feeling of not being satisfied ‖ 만족스럽지 않은 느낌. 불만(족). 불평: *The poll shows voters' dissatisfaction with politicians.* 그 여론조사는 정치인들에 대한 유권자들의 불만을 보여 준다.

dis·sat·is·fied /dɪ'sæṭɪs,faɪd/ *adj* not satisfied because something is not as good as you had expected ‖ 기대했던 것만큼 좋지 않기 때문에 불만족스러운. 불만인. 만족 못한: *If you are dissatisfied with this product, please return it for a full refund.* 만약 이 제품이 만족스럽지 않으시다면 전액 환불해 드립니다.

dis·sect /dɪ'sɛkt, daɪ-/ *v* [T] **1** to cut up the body of a plant or animal in order to study it ‖ 연구할 목적으로 식물이나 동물의 몸체를 잘라내다. 해부[절개]하다 **2** to examine something in great detail ‖ 어떤 것을 매우 자세하게 조사하다. 분석하다: *The book dissects historical data to show how Napoleon ran his army.* 그 책은 나폴레옹이 어떻게 자신의 군대를 움직였는지 보여 주는 역사적 자료를 분석하고 있다. **– dissection** /dɪ'sɛkʃən/ *n* [C, U]

dis·sem·i·nate /dɪ'sɛmə,neɪt/ *v* [T] FORMAL to spread information, ideas etc. to as many people as possible ‖ 가능한 한 많은 사람들에게 정보나 생각 등을 퍼뜨리다. 보급[유포]하다: *a Web site that disseminates health information* 건강 정보를 보급하는 웹 사이트 **– dissemination** /dɪ,sɛmə'neɪʃən/ *n* [U]

dis·sen·sion /dɪ'sɛnʃən/ *n* [C, U] disagreement that often leads to argument ‖ 종종 언쟁으로 이어지는 의견 차이. 불화. 의견 충돌

dis·sent¹ /dɪ'sɛnt/ *n* [U] refusal to accept an opinion that most people accept ‖ 대부분의 사람들이 받아들이는 의견에 대해 인정하기를 거부함. 이의. 불찬성: *political dissent* 정치적 이견

dissent² *v* [I] to say that you refuse to accept an opinion that most people accept ‖ 대부분의 사람들이 받아들이는 의견을 인정하지 않는다고 말하다. 이의를 제기하다. 의견을 달리하다: *Two of the court's nine judges dissented from the opinion.* 아홉 명 중 두 명의 판사가 그 의견에 이의를 제기했다. **– dissenter** *n* **–** opposite ASSENT

dis·ser·ta·tion /,dɪsɚ'teɪʃən/ *n* a long piece of writing about a subject, especially one that you write at a university to get a PH.D. ‖ 특히 대학에서 박사 학위를 받기 위해 쓰는, 한 주제에 관한 긴 글. 박사 (학위) 논문

dis·serv·ice /dɪ'sɚvɪs, dɪs'sɚ-/ *n* [singular, U] something that harms someone or something ‖ 사람이나 사물에 해를 끼치는 것. 폐. 해: *The players' actions have done a great disservice to the game.* 그 선수들의 행동은 경기에 큰 지장을 주었다.

dis·si·dent /'dɪsədənt/ *n* someone who publicly criticizes an opinion, group, government etc. ‖ 어떤 의견·집단·정부 등을 공공연하게 비판하는 사람. 반대자. 반체제 인사 **– dissidence** *n* [U] **– dissident** *adj*

dis·sim·i·lar /dɪ'sɪmələ, dɪs'sɪ-/ *adj* not the same ‖ 같지 않은. 다른: *countries with dissimilar legal systems*

상이한 법 제도를 가진 나라들 **– dissimilarity** /dɪ,sɪmə'lærəti/ *n* [C, U]

dis·si·pate /'dɪsə,peɪt/ *v* FORMAL [I, T] to gradually disappear, or to make something do this ‖ 점점 사라지다, 또는 사라지게 하다. 없어지다. 분산시키다. 일소하다: *The smoke gradually dissipated.* 연기가 점점 사라졌다.

dis·so·ci·ate /dɪ'soʊʃi,eɪt, -si,eɪt/ *v* [T] FORMAL to believe or claim that one thing or person has no relation to another ‖ 어떤 일이나 사람이 다른 것과 관계가 없다고 믿거나 주장하다. …과의 관계를 부인하다. 분리해서 생각하다: *We have disassociated ourselves from any kind of terrorist activity.* 우리는 어떤 종류의 테러 활동과도 관계를 끊었다. **– dissociation** /dɪ,soʊsi'eɪʃən, -,soʊʃi-/ *n* [U]

dis·so·lute /'dɪsə,lut/ *adj* FORMAL having bad or immoral habits ‖ 나쁘거나 부도덕한 습관을 지닌. 방종[방탕]한. 무절제한: *a dissolute life* 방탕한 생활

dis·so·lu·tion /,dɪsə'luʃən/ *n* [U] FORMAL the act of ending a marriage, business arrangement etc. ‖ 결혼·사업 계약 등을 끝내는 행위. 이혼. 해지. 해약

dis·solve /dɪ'zɑlv/ *v* **1** [I, T] to mix with a liquid and become part of it, or to make something do this ‖ 액체와 섞여 그것의 일부분이 되다, 또는 일부분이 되게 하다. 용해되다[시키다]. 녹(이)다: *Dissolve the tablets in warm water.* 따뜻한 물에 알약을 녹여라 / *The aspirin dissolves quickly.* 그 아스피린은 빨리 녹는다. **2** [T] to end a marriage, business arrangement etc. ‖ 결혼·사업 계약 등을 종결하다. 이혼하다. 취소하다 **3** [I] to become weaker and disappear ‖ (세)약해지다. 사라지다. 소멸하다. 수그러들다: *Our fears gradually dissolved.* 우리의 공포는 점점 사라졌다.

dis·suade /dɪ'sweɪd/ *v* [T] FORMAL to persuade someone not to do something ‖ 어떤 것을 하지 말라고 남을 설득하다. 설득하여 …을 단념시키다: *a program to dissuade teenagers from drinking* 10대들의 음주를 단념시키는 프로그램

dis·tance¹ /'dɪstəns/ *n* **1** [C, U] the amount of space between two places or things ‖ 두 개의 장소나 사물 사이의 공간적 차이. 거리. 간격: *What's the distance from Louisville to Memphis?* 루이빌에서 멤피스까지 거리가 얼마나 되지? / *The church is still some distance* (=a fairly long distance) *away.* 교회는 아직도 꽤 멀리 떨어져 있다. **2** [singular] a point or place that is far away, but close enough to be seen or heard ‖ 약간 떨어져 있으나 보거나 들을 수는 있을 만한 지점이나 장소: *The ruins look very impressive from a distance.* 멀리 떨어져서 보면 그 폐허는 매우 인상적으로 보인다. / *That's Long Island in the distance over there.* 저쪽에 멀리 있는 곳이 롱아일랜드이다. / *The Empire State Building is visible at a distance of several miles.* 엠파이어 스테이트 빌딩은 몇 마일 떨어져서도 보인다. **3 within walking/driving distance** near enough to walk or drive to ‖ 걸어가거나 차 타고 갈 만큼 충분히 가까운: *The lake is within driving distance of my house.* 그 호수는 우리 집에서 차 타고 갈 수 있는 거리에 있다. **4 keep your distance** to stay far away from someone or something ‖ 사람이나 사물에서 멀리 떨어져 있다. 일정한 거리를 두다: *Mark could see that the guy was drunk, so he kept his distance.* 마크는 그 남자가 술에 취해 있는 것을 보고 떨어져 있었다. **5 keep sb at a distance** to avoid telling someone your private thoughts or feelings ‖ 사적인 생각이나 감정을 남에게 말하기를 꺼리다. 남과 가까이 하지 않다: *We've known each other for years, but I've always felt she keeps me at a distance.* 우리는 서로 알고 지낸 지 수년이 되었지만 난 언제나 그녀가 나를 멀리 한다는 느낌을 받아 왔다. **6 [U]** an amount of time between two events ‖ 두 사건 사이의 시간(간격). 사이

distance² *v* **distance yourself** to say that you are not involved with someone or something, or to try to become less involved with someone or something ‖ 어떤 사람이나 일에 개입되지 않았다고 말하거나 개입을 덜 하기 위해 애쓰다. …에 가까이 가지 않다. …과 거리를 두다: *Tony tried to distance himself from the company's position.* 토니는 회사의 입장과 거리를 두려고 노력했다.

dis·tant /'dɪstənt/ *adj* **1** far away from where you are now, or at a much different time than now ‖ 현재 있는 곳에서 멀리 떨어진, 또는 현재와는 시간적으로 아주 다른 때에. 먼. 오랜: *the distant hills* 먼 언덕 / *the distant past* 오래된 과거 **2** unfriendly and showing no emotion ‖ 우호적이지 않으며 감정을 표현하지 않는. 냉담한. 쌀쌀한: *Jeff's been kind of distant lately.* 제프는 최근 들어 좀 서먹서먹했다. **3** not very closely related ‖ 관계가 그리 가깝지 않은. 관계가 먼: *a distant cousin* (촌수가) 먼 사촌

dis·taste /dɪs'teɪst/ *n* [singular, U] a feeling of dislike for someone or something ‖ 사람이나 사물을 싫어하는 감정. 싫음. 혐오(감): *a distaste for office work* 사무직에 대한 거부감

dis·taste·ful /dɪs'teɪstfəl/ *adj* very unpleasant or offensive ‖ 매우 불쾌하거나 기분 상하게 하는. 싫은. 기분 나쁜: *I just want to forget the whole distasteful affair.* 나는 그저 그 모든 불쾌한 일을 잊고 싶을 뿐이다. **– distastefully** *adv*

dis·tend /dɪ'stɛnd/ *v* [I, T] FORMAL to swell because of pressure from inside, or to make something do this ‖ 내부의 압력으로 부풀다, 또는 어떤 것을 이렇게 부풀게 하다. 팽창하다[시키다]: *His stomach was distended from lack of food.* 못 먹어서 그의 위는 부어 있었다. **– distension** /dɪ'stɛnʃən/ *n* [U]

dis·till /dɪ'stɪl/ *v* [T] to heat a liquid so that it becomes a gas and then let it cool so that it becomes liquid again, in order to make it more pure or in order to make a strong alcoholic drink ‖ 더 순수하게 만들거나 독한 술을 만들기 위해 액체를 가열하여 기체로 만들었다가 냉각시켜 다시 액체로 만들다. 증류하다: *distilled water* 증류수 **– distillation** /ˌdɪstə'leɪʃən/ *n* [C, U]

dis·till·er·y /dɪ'stɪləri/ *n* a factory where alcoholic drinks are produced by DISTILLING ‖ 증류 기법으로 술을 생산하는 공장. 증류소. 증류주 양조장

dis·tinct /dɪ'stɪŋkt/ *adj* **1** clearly different or separate ‖ 분명히 다르거나 분리된. 별개의: *The two types of monkeys are quite distinct from each other.* 그 두 종류의 원숭이는 서로 확연히 구별된다. **2** clearly seen, heard, understood etc. ‖ 분명히 보이거나 들리거나 이해되는 등. 뚜렷한. 명백한. 분명한: *There's a distinct possibility that we'll all lose our jobs.* 우리 모두가 직장을 잃을 가능성이 분명히 있다. **– distinctly** *adv*

dis·tinc·tion /dɪ'stɪŋkʃən/ *n* **1** a clear difference between things ‖ 어떤 것간의 확연한 차이. 구별. 차별: *The school makes no distinction between male and female students.* (=the school does not treat male and female students differently) 그 학교는 남학생과 여학생 사이에 어떠한 차별도 두지 않는다. **2 a** special honor given to someone ‖ 사람이 얻는 특별한 명예. 영예. 훈장: *Neil Armstrong had the distinction of being the first man on the moon.* 닐 암스트롱은 최초로 달에 착륙한 사람이라는 영예를 얻었다. **3 [U]** the quality of being unusually good ‖ 특별하게 좋은 성질. 탁월(성). 우수(성). 비범(성): *a poet of distinction* 비범한 시인

dis·tinc·tive /dɪ'stɪŋktɪv/ *adj* clearly marking a person or thing as different from others ‖ 사람이나 사물을 다른 사람이나 사물과 확연히 구별짓는. 특이[독특]한. 뚜렷이 구별되는: *Chris has a very distinctive laugh.* 크리스는 매우 독특한 웃음을 지녔다. **- distinctively** *adv* **- distinctiveness** *n* [U]

dis·tin·guish /dɪ'stɪŋgwɪʃ/ *v* 1 [I, T] to recognize or understand the difference between two similar things, people etc. ‖ 두 가지 비슷한 사물·사람 등의 차이를 인식하거나 이해하다. …을 분간하다. 식별[판단]하다: *Young children often can't distinguish between TV programs and commercials.* 어린 아이들은 흔히 텔레비전 프로그램과 광고를 분간하지 못한다. 2 [T] to be able to see, hear, or taste something, even if it is difficult ‖ 어렵더라도 어떤 것을 보거나 듣거나 맛볼 수 있다. …을 (시각·청각·미각 등에 의해서) 분명히 알(아차리)다: *It was so noisy it was difficult to distinguish what he was saying.* 너무 시끄러워서 그가 무슨 말을 하는지 알아듣기가 어려웠다. 3 [T] to be the thing that makes someone or something different from other people or things ‖ 사람이나 사물을 다른 사람이나 사물과 다르게 만드는 것이 되다. …을 특징지우다. …과 구별이 되다: *The bright feathers distinguish the male peacock from the female.* 수컷 공작새의 눈부신 깃털은 암컷과 구별된다. 4 **distinguish yourself** to do something so well that people notice you, praise you, or remember you ‖ 어떤 것을 너무나 잘해서 사람들이 주목[칭찬, 기억]하다. 이름을 떨치다: *Eastwood distinguished himself as an actor before becoming a director.* 이스트우드는 영화 감독이 되기 전에 배우로서 이름을 떨쳤다. **- distinguishable** *adj*

dis·tin·guished /dɪ'stɪŋgwɪʃt/ *adj* 1 very successful and therefore admired or respected ‖ 매우 성공하여 칭찬받거나 존경을 받는. 뛰어난. 발군의: *a distinguished medical career* 뛰어난 의료 활동 2 looking important and successful ‖ 중요하고 성공적으로 보이는. 고귀한. 위엄있는: *a distinguished looking man* 위엄있어 보이는 남자 — opposite UNDISTINGUISHED

dis·tort /dɪ'stɔrt/ *v* [T] 1 to explain a fact, statement etc. so that it seems to mean something different from what it

really means ‖ 실제 의미하는 것과는 다른 것을 의미하는 것처럼 보이게 사실·진술 등을 설명하다. …을 왜곡하다: *a reporter accused of distorting the facts* 사실 왜곡의 비난을 받고 있는 기자 2 to change the shape or sound of something so it is strange or unclear ‖ 이상하거나 분명치 않게 사물의 형상이나 소리를 변화시키다. …을 찌그러뜨리다. 비틀다: *Bruno's face was distorted with rage.* 브루노의 얼굴이 분노로 일그러졌다. **- distorted** *adj* **- distortion** /dɪ'stɔrʃən/ *n* [C, U]

dis·tract /dɪ'strækt/ *v* [T] to make someone look at or listen to something when s/he should be giving attention to something else ‖ 다른 것에 주의를 기울여야 되는 사람에게 어떤 것을 보거나 듣게 하다. 산만하게 하다: *Don't distract me while I'm driving!* 내가 운전할 때는 정신 사납게 하지 마라.

dis·tract·ed /dɪ'stræktɪd/ *adj* anxious and not able to think clearly ‖ 걱정이 되어 명확하게 생각할 수 없는. 마음이 산란해진. 혼란스러운: *Laura seems distracted - she must be worried about her finals.* 로라는 왠지 심란해 보인다. 틀림없이 기말 시험 걱정 때문에 그럴 것이다.

dis·trac·tion /dɪ'strækʃən/ *n* [C, U] something that takes your attention away from what you are doing ‖ 하고 있는 일에서 주의를 빼앗는 것. 주의를 산만하게 하는 것: *I study in the library; there are too many distractions at home.* 집에는 주의를 산만하게 하는 것들이 많아서 나는 도서관에서 공부한다.

dis·traught /dɪ'strɔt/ *adj* extremely anxious or upset ‖ 몹시 걱정하거나 상심한. 몹시 동요된. 미칠 듯한: *A policewoman was trying to calm the boy's distraught mother.* 여자 경찰이 몹시 흥분해 있는 그 소년의 엄마를 진정시키려 애쓰고 있었다.

dis·tress¹ /dɪ'strɛs/ *n* [U] 1 a feeling of extreme worry and sadness ‖ 극도의 근심과 슬픔. 고뇌. 번민. 비탄. 비통: *Children suffer emotional distress when their parents divorce.* 아이들은 부모가 이혼할 때 정신적 고통을 겪는다. 2 a situation in which someone suffers because s/he does not have any money, food etc. ‖ 돈·음식 등이 없어서 고통받는 상황. 빈곤. 곤궁. 궁지: *money to help families in distress* 빈곤 가정을 돕는 돈 3 **be in distress** if a ship, plane etc. is in distress, it is in danger of sinking or crashing ‖ 배·비행기 등이 가라앉거나 추

락할 위험에 처하다 - **distressed** *adj*

distress² *v* [T] to make someone feel very worried or upset ‖ 사람을 매우 걱정시키거나 상심하게 하다. …을 (심한 정신적 고통으로) 괴롭히다: *We were shocked and distressed to learn of Thomas's death.* 우리는 토마스의 사망 소식을 듣고 충격과 비탄에 잠겼다.

dis·tress·ing /dɪ'strɛsɪŋ/ *adj* making someone feel very worried or upset ‖ 사람을 매우 걱정시키거나 상심하게 하는. 괴로운. 고민스러운

dis·trib·ute /dɪ'strɪbyət/ *v* [T] **1** to give something such as food or medicine to each person in a large group ‖ 음식이나 약 등의 것을 큰 집단 내의 각자에게 나누어 주다. …을 분배하다[할당하다]: *The Red Cross is distributing food and clothing to the refugees.* 적십자는 난민들에게 음식과 의복을 분배하고 있다. **2** to supply goods to stores, companies etc. in a particular area ‖ 특정 지역의 가게·회사 등에 물건을 공급하다. 유통시키다. 배포[배달]하다: *Most of the steel is distributed by rail.* 철강의 대부분은 철도로 유통된다.

dis·tri·bu·tion /ˌdɪstrə'byuʃən/ *n* [U] the act of giving something to each person in a large group, or supplying goods to stores, companies etc. ‖ 물건을 큰 집단 내의 각자에게 나누어 주는 일, 또는 가게·회사 등에 물건을 공급하는 일. 분배. 유통: *the distribution of tickets for the concert* 콘서트 입장권의 분배

dis·tri·bu·tor /dɪ'strɪbyətɚ/ *n* **1** a company or person that supplies goods to stores or other companies ‖ 가게나 여타 회사에 물건을 공급하는 회사나 개인. 배급업자. 유통 회사 **2** a part of a car's engine that sends an electric current to the SPARK PLUGs ‖ 점화 플러그에 전류를 보내는 자동차 엔진의 부품. 배전기

dis·trict /'dɪstrɪkt/ *n* a particular area of a city, country etc., especially an area officially divided from others ‖ 도시·국가 등에서 특히 다른 곳과 공식적으로 분리된 특정 지역. 지구. 구역. 관할구: *the manufacturing district* 공장 지대

district at·tor·ney /ˌ.. '../, **D.A.** *n* a lawyer who works for the government in a particular DISTRICT and brings criminals to court ‖ 특정 지역에서 정부에 소속되어 범죄자들을 재판받게 하는 법률가. 지방 검사

district court /ˌ.. './ *n* a court where people are judged in cases involving national rather than state law ‖ 주(州)법보다는 연방법에 관련된 사건에 대하여 사람들을 재판하는 법정. 연방 지방 법원

dis·trust¹ /dɪs'trʌst/ *n* [U] a feeling that you cannot trust someone ‖ 남을 신뢰할 수 없는 감정. 불신. 의혹. 의심: *Many people regard politicians with distrust.* 많은 사람들이 정치인들을 불신을 갖고 바라본다. - **distrustful** *adj* - **distrustfully** *adv*

distrust² *v* [T] to not trust someone or something ‖ 사람이나 사물을 신뢰하지 않다. 불신하다. 의심하다: *Do you have any reason to distrust Arnold?* 아놀드를 신뢰하지 않는 이유라도 있습니까?

dis·turb /dɪ'stɚb/ *v* [T] **1** to interrupt what someone is doing by making a noise, asking a question etc. ‖ 소리를 내거나 질문을 하거나 하여 남이 하는 일을 방해하다. 훼방놓다: *Try not to disturb other users of the library.* 도서관의 다른 이용자들을 방해하지 않도록 해라. **2** to make someone feel worried or upset ‖ 남을 걱정하게 하거나 상심하게 하다. 불안하게[당황스럽게] 하다: *I was disturbed to hear that Don and Betty were getting divorced.* 나는 돈과 베티가 이혼한다는 소식에 당황스러웠다.

dis·turb·ance /dɪ'stɚbəns/ *n* **1** [C, U] something that interrupts you so that you cannot continue what you are doing ‖ 하고 있던 일을 계속할 수 없도록 방해하는 것. 방해(물). 장애. 폐해: *People are complaining about the disturbance caused by the work on the roads.* 사람들은 도로 공사로 길이 막힌다고 불평하고 있다. **2** a situation in which people fight or behave violently in public ‖ 사람들이 사람들 앞에서 싸우거나 폭력적으로 행동하는 상황. 소동. 소란. 소요: *The police arrested three men for creating a disturbance at the bar.* 경찰은 술집에서 소동을 일으킨 죄로 세 남자를 체포했다.

dis·turbed /dɪ'stɚbd/ *adj* not behaving in a normal way because of mental or emotional problems ‖ 정신적 또는 감정적 문제로 인해 정상적으로 행동하지 않는. 정신 이상의. 신경증의

ditch¹ /dɪtʃ/ *n* a long narrow hole in the ground for water to flow through, usually at the side of a field, road etc. ‖ 보통 밭·도로 등의 옆에 물이 흐르도록 땅에 낸 길고 좁은 구덩이. 도랑. 수로. 배수구

ditch² *v* [T] INFORMAL to get rid of something because you do not need it ‖ 필요하지 않기 때문에 어떤 것을 없애다. 내버리다. 팽개쳐 버리다: *The bank robbers ditched the stolen car as soon as they could.* 은행 강도들은 훔친 차를

가능한 한 빨리 내버렸다.

dith·er /'dɪðɚ/ *v* [I] to be unable to make a decision ‖ 결정을 내릴 수 없다. 갈피를 못 잡다. 우유부단하다: *He's been dithering about what to do.* 그는 무엇을 해야 할지 갈피를 못 잡고 있다.

dit·to¹ /'dɪtou/ *interjection* INFORMAL said when you agree with someone about something, or when something is the same as something else ‖ 어떤 것에 관해 남에게 동의할 때, 또는 어떤 것이 다른 것과 같을 때 쓰여. 동감이야. (나도) 마찬가지야: *"I love pepperoni pizza!" "Ditto!"* "나는 페퍼로니 피자를 너무 좋아해!" "나도!"

dit·to² *n* a mark (") that you write beneath a word in a list so that you do not have to write the same word again ‖ 같은 단어를 다시 쓸 필요가 없도록 목록의 단어 밑에 쓰는 기호("). 상동 부호

dit·ty /'dɪti/ *n* HUMOROUS a short simple song or poem ‖ 짧고 간단한 노래나 시

dive¹ /daɪv/ *v* **dived or dove, dived, diving** [I] **1** to jump into the water with your head and arms going in first ‖ 머리와 팔이 먼저 들어가도록 물에 뛰어들다. 다이빙하다: *Harry dived into the swimming pool.* 해리는 수영장으로 뛰어들었다. **2** to swim under water using special equipment to help you breathe ‖ 호흡을 도와주는 특수 장비를 사용하여 물밑에서 수영하다. 잠수하다: *treasure hunters diving to look at the old shipwreck* 옛 난파선을 찾기 위해 잠수하여 보물을 찾는 사람들 **3** to go down through the air or water very quickly and suddenly ‖ 매우 빠르고 갑작스럽게 공기 중이나 물 속으로 뛰어내리다. (급)강하하다: *birds swooping and diving in the air* 공중에서 급강하하는 새들 **4** to jump forward or sideways quickly to catch something or to avoid something ‖ 뭔가를 잡거나 피하기 위해 앞쪽이나 옆쪽으로 재빨리 점프하다. 다이빙하다: *Ripken dived to his left and caught the ball.* 립켄은 왼쪽으로 몸을 날려 공을 잡았다.

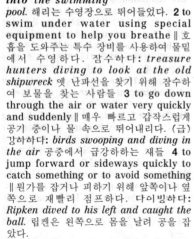

dive

dive² *n* **1** a jump into the water with your head and arms going in first ‖ 머리와 팔이 먼저 들어가도록 물 속으로 뛰어듦. 다이빙 **2** INFORMAL a place such as a bar or a hotel that is cheap and dirty ‖ 싸고 지저분한 술집이나 호텔 등의 장소. 음침한 술집. 싸구려 호텔: *We ate at a dive out by the airport.* 우리는 공항 근처 싸구려 식당에서 식사했다.

div·er /'daɪvɚ/ *n* **1** someone who swims under water using special equipment to help him/her breathe ‖ 호흡을 돕는 특수 장비를 사용하여 물 속에서 수영하는 사람. 잠수부: *a scuba diver* 스쿠버 다이빙하는 사람 **2** someone who DIVEs into the water ‖ 물 속으로 잠수하는 사람

di·verge /də'vɚdʒ, daɪ-/ *v* [I] to become separate or different, or to go in two different directions ‖ 갈라지거나 달라지다, 또는 서로 다른 두 방향으로 가다. 분기하다. 빗나가다: *The new plan diverges considerably from the original one.* 새로운 계획은 애초의 것과는 상당히 다르다. **–divergence** *n* [C, U] **–divergent** *adj* —opposite CONVERGE

di·verse /də'vɚs, daɪ-/ *adj* very different from each other ‖ 서로 매우 다른. 다양한. 가지가지의: *New York is one of the most culturally diverse cities in the world.* 뉴욕은 전 세계에서 문화적으로 가장 다양한 도시 중 하나이다.

di·ver·si·fy /də'vɚsə,faɪ, daɪ-/ *v* [I, T] if a company diversifies, it begins to make new products or to become involved in new types of business in addition to what it already does ‖ 회사가 새로운 제품을 생산하기 시작하거나 이미 하던 사업에 더하여 새로운 형태의 사업에 관계하기 시작하다. (사업을) 다각화하다. …을 다양화하다: *They started as a computer company and then diversified into software.* 그들은 컴퓨터 회사로 시작해서 소프트웨어 쪽으로 사업을 다각화했다. **–diversification** /də,vɚsə-fə'keɪʃən/ *n* [U]

di·ver·sion /də'vɚʒən, daɪ-/ *n* **1** [C, U] a change in the direction or purpose of something ‖ 어떤 것의 방향이나 목적의 변경. 전환. (자금 등의) 유용[전용]: *the illegal diversion of money from the project* 그 프로젝트에 쓰이는 자금의 불법 유용 **2** something that takes your attention away from what someone else is trying to do ‖ 다른 사람이 하려고 하는 일에서 자신의 주의를 다른 데로 돌리게 하는 것. 주의를 빼앗는 것: *The prisoners created a diversion to allow the others time to escape.* 수감자들은 다른 이들이 탈옥할 시간을 주려고 주의를 다른 데로 돌렸다. **3** FORMAL an activity that you do for pleasure or amusement ‖ 즐거움이나 놀이를 위해 하는 활동. 기분 전환. 오락(물): *Fishing is a pleasant diversion.* 낚시는 기분 전환에 아주 좋다.

di·ver·si·ty /də'vɚsɪti, daɪ-/ *n* [C, U] a range of different people or things; variety ‖ 폭넓은 다양한 사람들이나 사물들. 다양(성): *the religious diversity of the US* 미국의 종교적 다양성

di·vert /də'vɚt, daɪ-/ *v* [T] **1** to change the direction or purpose of something ‖ 어떤 것의 방향이나 목적을 변경하다. 방향을 전환시키다. (자금 등을) 유용[전용]하다: *Traffic is being diverted to avoid the accident.* 사고 때문에 차량을 우회시키고 있다. **2 divert (sb's) attention from sth** to stop someone from paying attention to something ‖ 남이 어떤 것에 주의를 기울이지 못하도록 하다. (주의를) 딴 데로 돌리다: *The tragedy has diverted attention from the country's political problems.* 그 비극(적 사건)으로 그 나라의 정치 문제는 사람들의 관심에서 벗어났다. **3** FORMAL to amuse or entertain someone ‖ 사람을 재미있거나 즐겁게 하다. 기분을 전환시키다: *a game to divert the children* 어린이를 즐겁게 해주는 게임

di·vest /dɪ'vɛst, daɪ-/ *v*
divest sb **of** sth *phr v* [T] FORMAL to take something away from someone ‖ 사람에게서 어떤 것을 빼앗다. 박탈하다

di·vide /də'vaɪd/ *v* **1** [I, T] to separate something, or to become separated, into two or more parts ‖ 어떤 것을 2개 이상의 부분으로 분리하다, 또는 분리되다. 가르다[갈라지다]. 나누다[나뉘다]: *The class divided into groups.* 학급이 몇 개의 그룹으로 나누어졌다. / *Brenda's trying to divide her time between work and school.* 브렌다는 시간을 쪼개서 직장과 학교를 다니느라 애쓰고 있다. **2** [T] to keep two areas separate from each other ‖ 두 지역을 서로 갈라놓다. 분리하다: *the long border dividing America from Canada* 미국과 캐나다의 경계를 이루고 있는 긴 국경선. **3** [T] also **divide up** to separate something into two or more parts and share it among two or more people ‖ 어떤 것을 둘 이상으로 쪼개서 그것을 둘 이상의 사람들이 나누어 갖다. 배분하다. 쪼개다: *The money will be divided equally among his children.* 그 돈은 아이들에게 똑같이 분배될 것이다. **4** [I, T] to calculate how many times one number is contained in a larger number ‖ 큰 수(數)에 어떤 수(數)가 몇 배 포함되는지를 계산하다. 나누다. 나눗셈하다: *15 divided by 3 is 5.* 15 나누기 3은 5이다. **5** [T] to make people disagree and form groups with different opinions ‖ 사람들에게 동의하지 않게 하

여 다른 의견을 가진 그룹을 형성하게 하다. …의 사이를 갈라놓다. 이간하다. 분열시키다: *Congress is divided over whether to raise taxes or cut spending.* 의회는 조세를 인상할 것인지 지출을 축소할 것인지를 두고 분열되어 있다.

div·i·dend /'dɪvə,dɛnd, -dənd/ *n* **1** a part of a company's profit that is paid to people who have SHARES in the company ‖ 회사의 주식을 가진 사람들에게 지급되는 회사 이익의 일부. 배당금 **2 pay dividends** to get an advantage at a later time from something that you are doing now ‖ 현재 하고 있는 일로부터 나중에 이익을 얻다. 장래에 유용하다: *Studying hard at school will pay dividends when you apply for college.* 학교에서 열심히 공부하는 것이 대학에 지원할 때 도움이 될 것이다.

di·vid·er /də'vaɪdɚ/ *n* **1** something that divides something else into two or more parts ‖ 다른 것을 두 부분 이상으로 나누는 것. 분할물: *the center divider on a road* 도로의 중앙 분리대 **2** a stiff piece of paper used in order to keep other papers separate ‖ 다른 종이들을 분리시키는 데 쓰이는 빳빳한 종이. 가름쪽

di·vine /də'vaɪn/ *adj* having the qualities of God, or coming from God ‖ 신의 특성을 지니거나 신으로부터 온. 신의. 신에 의한

div·ing /'daɪvɪŋ/ *n* [U] the activity of jumping into water with your head and arms first ‖ 머리와 팔을 앞으로 하고 물속으로 뛰어드는 행위. 다이빙

diving board /'.. ,./ *n* a board above a SWIMMING POOL from which you can jump into the water ‖ 물 속으로 뛰어들 수 있는 수영장 위에 있는 대(臺). 다이빙 도약대

di·vin·i·ty /də'vɪnəti/ *n* **1** [U] the study of God and religious beliefs; THEOLOGY ‖ 신과 종교적 믿음에 관한 학문. 신학; 윤 theology **2** [U] the quality of being like God ‖ 신과 같은 성질. 신성(神性) **3** a male or female god ‖ 남성이나 여성 신

di·vis·i·ble /də'vɪzəbəl/ *adj* able to be divided, especially by another number ‖ 특히 다른 수(數)에 의해 나누어질 수 있는. 나눌 수 있는. 나누어 떨어지는: *15 is divisible by 3 and 5.* 15는 3과 5로 나누어 떨어진다.

di·vi·sion /də'vɪʒən/ *n* **1** [C, U] the act of dividing something into two or more parts or groups, or the way that it is divided ‖ 어떤 것을 둘 이상의 부분이나 집단으로 나누는 행위, 또는 나누어지는 방식. 분할. 분배: *the division of the* *students into groups for discussion* 토론을 위한 학생들의 그룹별 분할 / *the division of the money between the government departments* 정부 부처 간의 예산의 분배 **2** [C, U] a disagreement among members of a group ‖ 집단 구성원 사이의 불일치. 의견의 불일치. 분열: *strong divisions in the Republican party* 공화당 내의 격렬한 분열 양상 **3** [U] the process of calculating how many times a small number will go into a larger number ‖ 작은 수(數)가 큰 수(數)에 몇 배가 들어갈 것인지를 계산하는 과정. 나눗셈 —compare MULTIPLICATION **4** a group within a large company, army, organization etc. ‖ 큰 회사·군대·조직 등의 내부의 한 집단. 부(部). 국(局). 사단(師團): *the finance division of the company* 회사의 경리부

di·vi·sive /dəˈvaɪsɪv, -ˈvɪs-/ *adj* causing a lot of disagreement among people ‖ 사람들 사이에 많은 불화를 일으키는. 알력을 만드는: *Abortion is one of the most divisive issues in America.* 낙태는 미국에서 가장 많이 논란이 되는 문제 중의 하나이다.

di·vorce¹ /dəˈvɔrs/ *n* [C, U] the legal ending of a marriage ‖ 결혼의 법적인 종료. 이혼: *She finally got a divorce after six years of unhappiness.* 그녀는 6년간의 불행한 결혼 생활 끝에 마침내 이혼을 했다. – **divorced** *adj*

divorce² *v* **1** [I, T] to legally end a marriage ‖ 합법적으로 결혼을 끝내다. 이혼하다: *My parents got divorced when I was ten.* 내가 열 살 때 부모님이 이혼했다. **2** to separate two ideas, values, organizations etc. ‖ 두 개의 생각·가치·조직 등을 분리하다: *Some of his ideas are completely divorced from reality.* (=not based on real experience or sensible thinking) 그의 생각 중 몇 가지는 완전히 현실과 동떨어져 있다.

di·vor·cée /dəˌvɔrˈseɪ, -ˈsi/ *n* a woman who has legally ended her marriage ‖ 결혼을 법적으로 끝낸 여자. 이혼녀

di·vulge /dəˈvʌldʒ, daɪ-/ *v* [T] to give someone information, especially about something that was secret ‖ 특히 비밀이었던 일에 대한 정보를 남에게 주다. 누설하다: *Wolf refused to divulge the names of those who helped.* 울프는 도움을 주었던 사람들의 이름을 밝히기를 거부했다.

Dix·ie /ˈdɪksi/ *n* INFORMAL the southern states of the US ‖ 미국 남부의 여러 주

diz·zy /ˈdɪzi/ *adj* **1** having a feeling of not being able to balance yourself, especially after spinning around or

because you feel sick ‖ 특히 빙빙 돈 후에 또는 몸이 아파서 균형을 잡지 못하는 느낌을 갖는. 현기증 나는. 어질어질한 **2** HUMOROUS someone who is dizzy is silly or stupid ‖ 우스운, 어리석은 – **dizziness** *n* [U]

DJ /ˈdi dʒeɪ/ *n* DISK JOCKEY; someone whose job is to play the music on a radio show or in a club where you can dance ‖ Disk Jockey(디스크 자키)의 약어; 라디오 쇼 프로나 춤출 수 있는 클럽에서 음악을 틀어주는 직업인

DNA *n* [U] TECHNICAL deoxyribonucleic acid; an acid that carries GENETIC information in a cell ‖ deoxyribonucleic acid(디옥시리보 핵산)의 약어; 세포에서 유전인자 정보를 전달하는 산

do¹ /də; *strong* du/ *auxiliary verb*

PRESENT TENSE (현재 시제)

singular (단수)	*plural* (복수)
I **do**	we **do**
you **do**	you **do**
he/she/it **does**	thery **do**

PAST TENSE (과거 시제)

singular (단수)	*plural* (복수)
I **did**	we **did**
you **did**	you **did**
he/she/it **did**	they **did**

PAST PARTICIPLE (과거 분사) **done**

PRESENT PARTICIPLE (현재 분사) **doing**

NEGATIVE *short forms* (부정 단축형) **don't, doesn't, didn't**

1 used with another verb to form questions or negatives ‖ 의문형이나 부정형을 만들기 위해 다른 동사와 함께 쓰여: *Do you have a VCR?* VCR을 가지고 있습니까? / *What time does Linda usually go to bed?* 린다는 보통 몇 시에 잠자리에 드니? / *Mark doesn't think he's going to get that job he applied for.* 마크는 자신이 지원했던 직장을 얻지 못하리라 생각한다. **2** SPOKEN used at the end of a sentence to make a question or to ask someone to agree with it ‖ 의문형을 만들거나 사람에게 동의를 구하기 위해 문장의 끝에 쓰여: *That dress looks really nice on her, doesn't it?* 그 옷은 그녀에게 정말 잘 어울린다, 안 그래? **3** used in order to emphasize the main verb ‖ 본동사를 강조하는 데에 쓰여: *He hasn't been here in* *a while, but he does come to visit us most weekends.* 그는 얼마 동안 여기 오지 않았지만 거의 주말이면 우리를 찾아온다. **4** used in order to avoid repeating another verb ‖ 다른 동사의 반복을 피하는 데에 쓰여: *"Go clean up your room." "I already did!"* "가서 방 청소 해라." "이미 했어요!" / *"Craig really likes Thai food." "So do I."* "크레이그는 태국 음식을 정말 좋아해." "나도 그래." / *"I didn't like the movie." "Neither did I."* "나는 그 영화를 좋아하지 않았어." "나도 안 좋아했어." / *Emilio speaks much better English than he did a year ago.* 에밀리오는 1년 전보다 영어를 훨씬 더 잘 한다.

do² /du/ *v* **1** [T] to perform an action or job ‖ 행동을 하거나 업무를 수행하다: *Have you done your homework yet?* 벌써 숙제를 다 했니? / *It's Jim's turn to do the dishes.* 짐이 접시를 닦을 차례다. / *"What are you doing?" "Making cookies."* "뭐 하고 있니?" "과자 만들고 있어." **2** [I] to make progress or be successful ‖ 발전하거나 성공하다: *How is Jayne doing in her new job?* 제인은 새 일을 잘 하고 있니? / *Neil has done well this year in his chemistry class.* 닐은 금년에 화학 과목에서 점수를 잘 받았다. **3** [T] to have a particular effect on something or someone ‖ 사물이나 사람에 특별한 영향을 미치다: *The new car factory has done a lot for* (=had a good effect on) *the local economy.* 이 새 자동차 공장은 지역 경제에 좋은 영향을 미쳤다. / *Let's go to the beach. Come on, it will do you good.* (=make you feel better or happier) 해변으로 가자. 자, 어서. 기분이 아주 좋아질 거야. **4 do your hair/nails/makeup etc.** to spend time making your hair, nails etc. look good ‖ 머리·손톱 등을 보기 좋게 하는 데 시간을 보내다. 머리를 하다/손톱 손질을 하다/화장을 하다 **5** [T] to travel at a particular speed or to travel a particular distance ‖ 특정한 속도로 이동하거나 특정 거리를 이동하다. 나아가다. …속도로 나아가다: *This car will do 0 to 60 miles per hour in six seconds.* 이 차는 6초에 시속 60마일까지 낸다. **6** [I, T] to be suitable ‖ 적합하다. 알맞다[알맞게 하다]: *The recipe calls for butter, but margarine will do.* 그 요리법에는 버터가 필요하지만 마가린도 괜찮다. / *I wanted to get a new dress for the wedding, but my blue one will have to do.* (=be good enough, even though you would like something better) 나는 결혼식에 새 드레스를 입고 싶지만 내 푸른색 드레스로도

괜찮을 것이다. **7 what do you do (for a living)?** SPOKEN used in order to ask someone what his/her job is ‖ 남의 직업이 무엇인지를 묻는 데 쓰여. 무슨 일을 합니까? 직업이 뭐예요? —see also **How are you (doing)?/How's it going?** (HOW), **how do you do?** (HOW) —see usage note at MAKE¹

do away with *phr v* [T] INFORMAL **1** [do away with sth] to get rid of something ‖ 어떤 것을 제거하다. 버리다. 폐지하다: *Some senators would like to do away with affirmative action laws.* 몇몇 상원의원들은 차별 철폐법을 폐기하고 싶어한다. **2** [do away with sb] to kill someone ‖ 사람을 죽이다

do sb in *phr v* [T] INFORMAL **1** to make someone feel very tired ‖ 사람을 매우 피곤하게 느끼게 하다. 지치게 하다: *That long walk did me in.* 장시간 걸어서 나는 지쳤다. **2** to kill someone ‖ 사람을 죽이다

do sth over *phr v* [T] to do something again, especially because you did it wrong the first time ‖ 특히 처음에 일을 잘못해서 다시 하다. 되풀이하다. 한 번 더 하다: *If there are mistakes, the teacher makes you do it over.* 잘못된 것들이 있으면 선생님이 너희에게 한 번 더 시키신다.

do with sth *phr v* [T] **1 have/be to do with** to be about something, related to something, or involved in something ‖ 어떤 것에 대한 것이다[어떤 것에 관련되다, 어떤 것에 포함되다]. …과 관련이 있다: *The book has to do with new theories in physics.* 그 책은 물리학의 새 이론에 관한 것이다. / *Diane wanted nothing to do with the party for Sara.* (=she did not want to be involved at all) 다이앤은 사라를 위한 파티는 전혀 상관하고 싶지 않았다 / *Jack's job is something to do with marketing.* (=related to marketing, but you are not sure exactly how) 잭의 일은 마케팅과 다소 관계가 있다.

SPOKEN PHRASES

1 what has sb done with sth? used in order to ask where someone has put something ‖ 어떤 사람에게 물건을 둔 곳을 묻는 데에 쓰여: *What have you done with the scissors?* 가위 어디에 두었니? **2 what sb does with himself/herself** the activities that someone does as a regular part of his/her life ‖ 누군가가 생활의 일부로서 규칙적으로 하는 활동: *What is your* *dad doing with himself since he retired?* 너의 아빠는 퇴임 후에 무얼 하고 지내시니? **3 what is sb doing with sth?** used in order to ask why someone has something ‖ 남에게 왜 물건을 가지고 있는지를 묻는 데에 쓰여: *What are you doing with my wallet?* 네가 왜 내 지갑을 가지고 있니?

—see also **make do** (MAKE¹)
do without *phr v* **1** [I, T **do without** sth] to manage to continue living or doing something ‖ 특정한 것 없이 계속 생활을 꾸려 나가거나 어떤 것을 하다. …없이 견디다: *It's almost impossible to do without a car in Los Angeles.* LA에서 자동차 없이 지낸다는 것은 거의 불가능하다. **2 can do without** SPOKEN used in order to say that something is annoying you or making it difficult for you ‖ 어떤 것이 귀찮게 하거나 곤란하게 한다고 말하는 데에 쓰여: *I could do without all this hassle at work.* 나는 직장에서 이 모든 말다툼이 없었으면 한다.

USAGE NOTE do

If someone asks what you have **done to** something, you have probably changed it in some way: *What did you do to your hair?* However, if someone asks what you have **done with** something, s/he wants to know where it is: *What did you do with my book?* If someone asks what you **do**, s/he wants to know what kind of work you do: *"What do you do, Sally?" "I'm a doctor."* However, if s/he asks what you **are doing**, s/he wants to know what activity you are doing at that particular moment: *"What are you doing, Sally? "I'm making lunch."*
done to를 사용한 의문문은 사물을 어떤 방식으로 변경한 것인지를 물을 때 쓰인다: "네 머리를 어떻게 한 거야?" 그러나 **done with**는 물건의 소재를 물을 때 쓰인다: "내 책을 어디 두었니?" **do**는 직업이 무엇인지를 물을 때 쓰인다: "샐리야, 네 직업은 뭐니?" "나는 의사야." 그러나 **are doing**은 어느 특정 순간에 무슨 일을 하고 있는지를 물을 때 쓰인다: "샐리야, 지금 뭐 하고 있니?" "점심 식사 준비하고 있어."

---

do³ *n* **dos and don'ts** things that you should or should not do in a particular situation ‖ 특정한 상황에서 사람이 해야 할 일이나 해서는 안 될 일. 주의 사항: *I'm still learning all the dos and don'ts of the job.* 나는 아직도 그 일의 모든 주의 사항을 익히고 있다.

d.o.b. the written abbreviation for date of birth (=the day you were born) ‖ date of birth(생일)의 약어

do·ber·man pin·scher /ˌdoʊbərmən ˈpɪntʃər/, **doberman** *n* a large black and brown dog with very short hair, often used in order to guard property ‖ 경비견으로 쓰이는 털이 매우 짧고 몸집이 큰 검은 갈색의 개. 도베르만 (핀셔)

doc /dɑk/ *n* SPOKEN ⇨ DOCTOR¹

doc·ile /ˈdɑsəl/ *adj* quiet and easy to control ‖ 조용하고 통제하기 쉬운. 순한. 고분고분한: *a docile animal* 순한 동물

dock¹ /dɑk/ *n* a place where goods are put onto or taken off of ships or trucks ‖ 선박이나 트럭에 물건을 싣거나 내리는 장소. 부두. 선창

dock² *v* **1** if a ship docks or you dock it, you sail it into a DOCK ‖ 배를 선거(船渠)에 넣다 **2 dock sb's pay** to reduce the amount of money that you pay someone ‖ 남에게 지불하는 금액을 줄이다. 삭감하다. 빼다: *If you come in late one more time, we'll have to dock your pay.* 한 번만 더 지각하면 감봉 처분될 겁니다.

dock·et /ˈdɑkɪt/ *n* **1** LAW a list of legal cases that will take place in a particular court ‖ 특정 법원에서 처리할 소송 사건 목록. 소송 사건 일람표 **2** TECHNICAL a short document that shows what is in a package or describes goods that are being delivered ‖ 소포 내용을 나타내거나 인도 물품을 기재한 간단한 문서. 꼬리표

doc·tor¹ /ˈdɑktər/ *n* **1** someone whose job is to treat people who are sick ‖ 아픈 사람을 치료하는 직업인. 의사: *You really should see a doctor about that cough.* 그 감기는 정말 병원에 가야 해. **2** someone who has the highest level of degree given by a university ‖ 대학교에서 수여하는 최고의 학위를 가진 사람. 박사: *a Doctor of Philosophy* 철학 박사

USAGE NOTE doctor

Use **Doctor** for both doctors and DENTISTs. **Physician** is a formal word for a medical doctor, while a **surgeon** is a medical doctor who can operate on you.
의사와 치과 의사 모두에게 **doctor**를 쓴다. **physician**은 내과 의사에 대한 격식어이며 **surgeon**은 수술을 할 수 있는 외과 의사를 말한다.

doctor² *v* [T] to change something, especially in a way that is not honest ‖ 특히 정직하지 않은 방법으로 어떤 것을 변경하다. 변조하다: *The police may have doctored the evidence.* 경찰이 증거를 변조했을지도 모른다.

doc·trine /'dɑktrɪn/ *n* a belief or set of beliefs, especially religious or political beliefs ‖ 특히 종교적 또는 정치적 신념이나 신념 체계. 교리. 신조: *the Christian doctrine of the Holy Trinity* 성 삼위 일체의 기독교 교리 – **doctrinal** *adj*

doc·u·dra·ma /'dɑkyə,drɑmə/ *n* a movie, usually for television, that is based on a true story ‖ 실화에 기초한, 일반적으로 텔레비전용 영화. 다큐멘터리 드라마

doc·u·ment¹ /'dɑkyəmənt/ *n* **1** a piece of paper that has official information written on it ‖ 공식적인 정보가 기재된 서류. (공)문서: *You'll need to sign a few legal documents.* 몇 가지 법률 문서에서 명하셔야 하겠습니다. **2** a piece of work that you write on a computer ‖ 컴퓨터에서 글을 쓰는 일 – **documentary** /,dɑkyə'mɛntəri, -'mɛntri/ *adj*

doc·u·ment² /'dɑkyə,mɛnt/ *v* [T] to write about something, photograph it etc. in order to have information that you can keep ‖ 정보를 보관하려고 어떤 것에 대해 기재하고 촬영하다. 기록하다: *a TV program documenting the daily life of a teenage mother* 10대 어머니의 일상 생활을 기록한 TV 프로

doc·u·men·ta·ry /,dɑkyə'mɛntri, -'mɛntəri/ *n* a movie or television program that gives facts and information on something ‖ 어떤 것에 대한 사실과 정보를 제공하는 영화나 텔레비전 프로그램. 기록물. 다큐멘터리: *a documentary about alcoholism* 알코올 중독에 관한 다큐멘터리

doc·u·men·ta·tion /,dɑkyəmən'teɪʃən/ *n* [U] official documents that are used in order to prove that something is true or correct ‖ 어떤 것이 사실이거나 정확하다는 것을 증명하는 데 쓰이는 공식 문서. 증거 서류

dodge¹ /dɑdʒ/ *v* **1** [I, T] to move quickly in order to avoid someone or something ‖ 사람이나 사물을 피하려고 급히 움직이다. 재빨리 몸을 비키다: *dogs dodging in and out of city traffic* 도시의 차량들 사이를 허둥지둥 피해다니는 개들 **2** [T] to avoid talking about something or doing something that you do not want to do ‖ 어떤 것에 대한 언급을 회피하거나 하기 싫은 일을 피하다. 둘러대다.

교묘하게 벗어나다: *Senator O'Brian skillfully dodged the reporter's question.* 오브라이언 상원의원은 기자들의 질문을 교묘하게 따돌렸다.

dodge² *n* something dishonest you do in order to avoid a responsibility or law ‖ 책임이나 법을 회피하려고 행하는 부정직한 일. 속임수: *a tax dodge* 탈세

doe /doʊ/ *n* a female DEER ‖ 암사슴

does /dəz, z, s; strong dʌz/ *v* the third person singular of the present tense of DO ‖ do의 3인칭 단수 현재형

does·n't /'dʌzənt/ *v* the short form of "does not" ‖ "does not"의 단축형: *The plant doesn't look healthy.* 그 식물은 상태가 좋아 보이지 않는다.

dog¹ /dɔg/ *n* **1** a very common animal with four legs that is often kept as a pet or used for guarding buildings ‖ 흔히 애완용으로 기르거나 건물을 지키는 데에 쓰이는 네 발 달린 매우 흔한 동물. 개 **2** OFFENSIVE an ugly woman ‖ 못생긴 여자. 추녀 **3** something that is not of good quality ‖ 품질이 좋지 않은 것. 실패작. 보잘것없는 것: *It was a dog of a movie.* 그것은 형편없는 영화였다. **4 dog eat dog** used when describing a situation in which people do anything they can to get what they want ‖ 원하는 것을 얻기 위해서라면 뭐든지 할 수 있는 상황을 설명하는 데에 쓰여. 인정 사정 없는[가차없는] 행동: *Advertising is a dog-eat-dog business.* 광고업이란 것은 (먹느냐 먹히느냐의) 치열한 경쟁 사업이다. —see also **top dog** (TOP²)

dog² *v* **-gged, -gging** [T] if a problem or bad luck dogs you, it causes trouble for a long time ‖ 문제점이나 불운 등이 오랫동안 곤란을 야기하다. 재난[불행] 등이 따라다니다: *Bad luck has dogged the team for the whole season.* 시즌 내내 불운이 그 팀을 따라다녔다.

dog-eared /'. ./ *adj* dog-eared books have the corners of their pages folded or torn ‖ 책 페이지 구석이 접히거나 찢어진. 책장의 귀가 접힌

dog·ged /'dɔgɪd/ *adj* determined to do something even though it is difficult ‖ 곤란하더라도 어떤 것을 하기로 결심한. 끈질긴. 불굴의: *Barry's dogged efforts to learn Greek.* 그리스어를 배우려는 배리의 끈질긴 노력 – **doggedly** *adv*

doggone /,dɔ'gɔn./, **doggone it** *interjection* OLD-FASHIONED said when you are annoyed ‖ 짜증날 때 쓰여. 제기랄. 빌어먹을: *Doggone it, I said leave that alone!* 젠장, 내가 내버려 두라고 했잖아! – **doggone** *adj*

dog·gy, doggie /'dɔgi/ *n* a word meaning dog, used by or when speaking to young children ‖ 어린 아이들이 사용하는 또는 어린 아이에게 말할 때 쓰는 개를 의미하는 말. 강아지. 멍멍이

doggy bag /'.. ../ *n* a small bag for taking home the food you did not eat from a meal at a restaurant ‖ 식당에서 식사 중 먹지 않은 (남은) 음식을 집에 가져오는 데에 쓰는 작은 봉지

doggy paddle /'.. ../ *n* ⇨ DOG PADDLE

dog·house /'dɔghaʊs/ *n* **1 be in the doghouse** INFORMAL to be in a situation in which someone is angry or annoyed with you ‖ 어떤 사람이 상대에게 화가 나거나 짜증나 있는 상황에 처해 있다. 면목이 없다. 미움을 사다: *If Andy finds out I spent that money, I'll be in the doghouse.* 만일 내가 그 돈을 써버린 것을 앤디가 안다면 그는 화를 낼 거야. **2** a little building for a dog to sleep in ‖ 개가 잠자는 작은 집. 개집

dog·ma /'dɔgmə, 'dɑgmə/ *n* [C, U] an important belief or set of beliefs that people are supposed to accept without doubting them ‖ 사람들이 의심 없이 수용하게 되는 중요한 믿음이나 믿음 체계. 교리. 신조: *church dogma* 교회 교리 / *political dogmas* 정치적 신조

dog·mat·ic /dɔg'mætɪk, dɑg-/ *adj* having beliefs or ideas that you will not change and that you think other people should accept ‖ 자신의 믿음이나 생각을 바꾸려 하지 않고 다른 사람들이 받아들여야 한다고 생각하는. 독선적인. 독단적인 **– dogmatically** *adv*

do-good·er /'du ,gʊdɚ/ *n* INFORMAL someone who does things to help people who have less than s/he does, but who sometimes gets involved when s/he is not wanted ‖ 자신보다 가난한 사람들을 돕는 일을 하지만 때로는 남이 원치 않는 데도 개입하는 사람. 독선적인 자선가

dog pad·dle /'. ,../ *n* [singular] INFORMAL a simple way of swimming that you do by moving your arms and legs like a swimming dog ‖ 개가 헤엄치듯이 팔과 다리를 움직여서 하는 간단한 수영 방식. 개헤엄

dog tag /'. ./ *n* small piece of metal a soldier wears on a chain around his/her neck, with his/her name, blood type, and official number written on it ‖ 군인이 군번줄에 매어 목에 거는 것으로 성명·혈액형·군번을 기재한 작은 금속 조각. 군번표

dog·wood /'dɔgwʊd/ *n* an eastern North American tree or bush with flat white or pink flowers ‖ 흰색이나 분홍색의 납작한 꽃이 피는 미국의 동북부의 나무나 관목. 층층나무

do·ing /'duɪŋ/ *n* **1 be sb's (own) doing** to be someone's fault ‖ 누군가의 잘못이다. 자업자득이다: *His bad luck was all his own doing.* 그의 불운은 모두 그 자신의 자업자득이다. **2 take some doing** to be hard work ‖ 어려운 일이다. 매우 힘들다. 대단히 어렵다: *Getting this old car to run is going to take some doing.* 이 낡은 차를 굴러가게 하는 것은 대단히 힘들 것이다.

dol·drums /'doʊldrəmz, 'dɑl-/ *n* [plural] INFORMAL **1** a state in which something is not improving or developing ‖ 어떤 것이 개선되거나 발전하지 않는 상태. 침체(기). 불경기: *The building industry is temporarily in the doldrums.* 건축산업은 일시적으로 침체에 빠져 있다. **2** [plural] a state in which you feel sad; DEPRESSION ‖ 사람이 슬프게 느끼는 상태. 우울. 침울; ㉠ depression: *Beat the post-Christmas doldrums – visit the Children's Museum.* 크리스마스가 끝났다고 우울해하지 말고 어린이 박물관에 가 봐라.

dole /doʊl/ *v*

dole sth ↔ **out** *phr v* [T] to give something such as money, food, advice etc. in small amounts to a lot of people ‖ 돈·음식·충고 등을 많은 사람에게 조금씩 주다. …을 베풀다: *people doling out candy on Halloween* 할로윈 날에 사탕을 조금씩 나누어 주는 사람들

dole·ful /'doʊlfəl/ *adj* very sad ‖ 매우 슬픈. 침울한. 우울한. 슬픔[비탄, 수심]에 잠긴: *She had such a doleful expression on her face.* 그녀는 아주 우울한 표정을 하고 있었다.

doll /dɑl/ *n* a child's toy that looks like a small person ‖ 작은 사람처럼 생긴 어린이 장난감. 인형

dol·lar /'dɑlɚ/ *n* **1** the standard unit of money used in the US, Canada, Australia, New Zealand etc. Its sign is $ and it is worth 100 cents ‖ 미국·캐나다·호주·뉴질랜드 등에서 사용되는 표준 화폐 단위로 기호는 $, 100센트와 가치가 동일함: *The company has a $7 million debt.* 그 회사는 7백만 달러의 부채가 있다. **2** a piece of paper money or a coin of this value ‖ 지폐 한 장이나 지폐 한 장 가치의 동전. 1달러 지폐[동전]

USAGE NOTE dollar

Say "a two billion dollar debt" or "a

fifty dollar loan," but write "a $2 billion debt" or "a $50 loan."
말할 때는 "a two billion dollar debt" 또는 "a fifty dollar loan"이라고 하지만 쓸 때는 "a $2 billion debt" 또는 "a $50 loan"이라고 한다.

dol·lop /ˈdɑləp/ *n* a small amount of soft food, usually dropped from a spoon ‖ 보통 한 스푼에서 덜어낸 적은 양의 부드러운 음식 덩어리. 소량: *a dollop of whipped cream* 거품을 낸 약간의 크림

dol·ly /ˈdɑli/ *n* **1** SPOKEN a word meaning a DOLL, used when speaking to children ‖ 어린이에게 말할 때 쓰는, 인형을 뜻하는 단어 **2** a flat frame on wheels, used for moving heavy objects ‖ 무거운 물건을 움직이는 데에 쓰는 바퀴 달린 넙적한 틀. 작은 바퀴가 달린 수레

dol·phin /ˈdɑlfɪn, ˈdɔl-/ *n* a sea animal like a large gray fish with a long pointed nose ‖ 코가 길고 뾰족하며 큰 회색 물고기처럼 생긴 바다 동물. 돌고래

do·main /douˈmeɪn, də-/ *n* **1** the range of things that are included in a particular subject, type of art, or activity ‖ 특정한 주제[예술의 형태, 활동]에 포함되어 있는 사물의 범위. 분야. 영역: *the domain of science fiction* 공상 과학 소설 분야 **2** a particular place or activity that is controlled by one person or government ‖ 한 사람이나 정부에 의해 지배되는 특정한 지역이나 활동. 영역. 판도: *In the past, politics has been mainly a male domain.* 과거에 정치는 주로 남성들의 전유물이었다.

domain name /.ˈ.,./ *n* a company's or organization's address on the Internet. A domain name is followed by an abbreviation which shows its type, for example .com for company, or its country of origin, for example .uk for the United Kingdom. ‖ 회사를 나타내는 com, 영국을 나타내는 .uk 등 유형이나 철처를 보여 주는 약어를 수반하는, 회사나 조직의 인터넷 상의 주소. 도메인 네임

dome /doum/ *n* a round curved roof on a building or room ‖ 건물이나 실내 위쪽이 둥글게 굽은 지붕. 돔. 둥근 지붕[천장] –
domed *adj*

dome

do·mes·tic /dəˈmɛstɪk/ *adj* **1** happening within one country and not involving any other countries ‖ 한 나라 안에서 발생하고 다른 나라와는 관련되지 않은. 국내의. 자국의: *Canada's domestic affairs* 캐나다의 국내 문제 **2** relating to family relationships and life at home ‖ 가족 관계와 가정 생활에 관련된. 가정의. 가사의: *a victim of domestic violence* (=violence between members of the same family) 가정 폭력의 희생자 **3** someone who is domestic enjoys spending time at home and is good at cooking, cleaning etc. ‖ 가정에서 시간을 보내는 것을 즐기며 음식·청소 등을 잘하는. 가정적인. 살림꾼의

do·mes·ti·cat·ed /dəˈmɛstɪˌkeɪtɪd/ *adj* domesticated animals live with people as pets or work for them on a farm ‖ 동물이 애완용으로 사람들과 같이 살거나 농장에서 사람들을 위해 일하는. 동물이 길들여진 – **domesticate** *v* [T] – **domestication** /dəˌmɛstəˈkeɪʃən/ *n* [U] —compare TAME¹

do·mes·tic·i·ty /ˌdoumɛˈstɪsəti/ *n* [U] life at home with your family, or the state of enjoying this life ‖ 가족과 같이 하는 가정 생활이나 가정 생활을 즐기는 상태. 가정적임

dom·i·cile /ˈdɑmə,saɪl, ˈdou-/ *n* LAW the place where someone officially lives ‖ 사람이 공식적으로 거주하는 장소. 주소. 거주지

dom·i·nance /ˈdɑmənəns/ *n* [U] great power, control, or importance ‖ 큰 힘[지배력, 중요성]. 우세. 지배: *the Soviet Union's past dominance over/in Eastern Europe* 과거 동유럽에 대한 소련의 지배

dom·i·nant /ˈdɑmənənt/ *adj* **1** strongest, most important, or most noticeable ‖ 가장 강한[가장 중요한, 아주 현저한]. 지배적인. 우세한: *TV news is the dominant source of information in our society.* TV 뉴스는 우리 사회에서 주요한 정보의 출처이다. **2** controlling other people or things, or showing this quality ‖ 다른 사람이나 사물을 지배하거나 이런 성질을 나타내는. 지배적인. 우위를 차지하는: *her husband's dominant behavior* 그녀 남편의 독불장군적 행동

dom·i·nate /ˈdɑmə,neɪt/ *v* **1** [I, T] to have power and control over someone or something ‖ 사람이나 사물에 대한 힘과 통제력을 갖다. 지배하다. 복종시키다: *For sixty years France had dominated Europe.* 60년간 프랑스는 유럽을 지배했었다. **2** [I, T] to be the most important feature of something ‖ 어떤 것의 가장 중요한 특징이 되다. …의 우위를 차지하다. 우세하다: *The murder trial has been dominating the news this week.* 살인 재

판이 이번 주 뉴스를 석권하고 있다. **3** [T] to be larger or more noticeable than anything else in a place or situation ‖ 장소나 상황에서 다른 어떤 일보다 더 크게 또는 더 현저하게 되다. 두드러지다. …을 특색 있게 하다: *A large wooden desk dominates the room.* 커다란 나무 책상이 그 방을 딱 차지하고 있다. / *Nursing used to be a profession dominated by women.* 간호 일은 예전에는 여성들이 압도적으로 많은 직업이었다. – **domination** /ˌdɑməˈneɪʃən/ *n* [U]

dom·i·neer·ing /ˌdɑməˈnɪrɪŋ/ *adj* trying to control other people without considering how they feel or what they want ‖ 다른 사람들의 감정이나 원하는 것은 고려하지 않고 그들을 지배하려 하는. 폭군적인. 횡포를 부리는: *his domineering father* 폭군적인 그의 아버지

do·min·ion /dəˈmɪnyən/ *n* [U] the power or right to rule people ‖ 사람들을 지배하는 힘이나 권리. 지배권[력]. 통치력[권]

dom·i·no /ˈdɑməˌnoʊ/ *n, plural* **dominoes 1** a small piece of wood, plastic etc. with a different number of spots on each half of its top side, used in playing a game ‖ 윗면 중간에 각기 다른 숫자의 점이 새겨진 작은 나무·플라스틱 등의 게임용 조각. 도미노 **2 the domino effect** a situation in which one event or action causes several other things to happen, one after the other ‖ 하나의 사건이나 행위가 여러 다른 일을 연쇄적으로 발생하게 하는 상황. 도미노 효과

dom·i·noes /ˈdɑməˌnoʊz/ *n* [U] the game played using dominoes (DOMINO) ‖ 도미노를 사용하여 하는 게임. 도미노 놀이

do·nate /ˈdoʊneɪt, doʊˈneɪt/ *v* [I, T] **1** to give something useful to a person or organization that needs help ‖ 도움이 필요한 사람이나 조직에게 유용한 것을 주다. 기부하다: *Our school donated $500 to the Red Cross.* 우리 학교는 적십자사에 500달러를 기부했다. **2 donate blood/organs etc.** to allow some of your blood or a part of your body to be used for medical purposes ‖ 혈액이나 신체의 일부를 의료 목적으로 쓰이도록 허용하다. 헌혈하다/장기 기증하다

do·na·tion /doʊˈneɪʃən/ *n* [C, U] something, especially money, that you give to help a person or organization ‖ 사람이나 조직을 돕기 위해 주는 것으로 특히 돈. 기부금: *Please make a donation to UNICEF.* 유니세프에 기부해 주세요.

done¹ /dʌn/ *v* the PAST PARTICIPLE of DO ‖ do의 과거 분사형 —see usage note at DO¹

done² *adj* **1** finished or completed ‖ 끝나거나 완성된: *The job's almost done.* 그 일은 거의 다 끝났다. **2** cooked enough to be eaten ‖ 먹을 수 있게 충분히 요리된. 잘 익은: *I think the hamburgers are done.* 햄버거가 다 익은 것 같아. **3 done!** SPOKEN said in order to accept a deal that someone offers you ‖ 어떤 사람이 제시한 거래를 수락하는 데에 쓰여. 좋아! 알았어!: *"I'll give you $50 for it and that's my final offer." "Done!"* "그 값으로 50달러 주겠네. 이것이 마지막 제안이야." "좋아!" **4 be done for** INFORMAL to be in serious trouble or likely to fail ‖ 심각한 문제에 처하거나 실패할 것 같다. 결딴나다. 다 틀리다: *If we get caught, we're done for.* 잡히면 우린 끝장이다.

don·key /ˈdɑŋki, ˈdʌŋ-, ˈdɔŋ-/ *n* a gray or brown animal like a horse, but smaller and with longer ears ‖ 말과 비슷하지만 더 긴 귀를 가지고 몸집은 더 작은 회색이나 갈색 동물. 당나귀

do·nor /ˈdoʊnɚ/ *n* **1** a person, group etc. that gives something, especially money, in order to help an organization ‖ 조직을 돕기 위해 특히 돈 등을 내는 개인이나 집단 등. 기증자. 기부자: *The Museum received $10,000 from an anonymous donor.* 그 박물관은 익명의 기증자로부터 1만 달러를 받았다. **2** someone who allows some of his/her blood or part of his/her body to be used for medical purposes ‖ 자신의 혈액이나 신체의 일부를 의료 목적으로 쓰이도록 허락하는 사람. 헌혈자. 장기 제공자

don't /doʊnt/ *v* the short form of "do not" ‖ "do not"의 단축형: *I don't know how to ski.* 나는 스키를 탈 줄 모른다.

do·nut /ˈdoʊnʌt/ *n* ⇨ DOUGHNUT

doo·dad /ˈdudæd/, **doo·hick·ey** /ˈduˌhɪki/ *n* INFORMAL a small object whose name you have forgotten or do not know ‖ 그 이름을 잊어버렸거나 알지 못하는 작은 물건: *What's this doodad for?* 이 물건이 무엇에 쓰는 것이지?

doo·dle /ˈdudl/ *v* [I, T] to draw lines, shapes etc. without really thinking about what you are doing ‖ 실제로 무슨 일을 하고 있는지 생각하지 않고 선·모양 등을 그리다. 무의미한 낙서를 끄적거리다: *Stein was doodling on a napkin.* 스타인은 냅킨에 아무 생각없이 낙서를 하고 있었다. – **doodle** *n*

doom¹ /dum/ *n* [U] **1** destruction,

death, or failure that you are unable to avoid ‖ 피할 수 없는 파괴[죽음, 실패]. 운명. 비운. 파멸: *a terrible sense of doom* 파멸할 것 같은 끔찍한 느낌 **2 doom and gloom** HUMOROUS a state or attitude in which there is no hope for the future ‖ 미래에 대한 희망이 없는 상태나 태도. 어두운 전망: *Chloe's always full of doom and gloom.* 클로는 항상 절망 속에 빠져 있다.

doom² *v* [T] to make someone or something certain to fail, be destroyed, or die ‖ 사람이나 사물을 확실히 실패하게 [파괴되게, 죽게] 하다. …할 운명[비운]에 처하게 하다: *He was doomed to repeat the same mistakes his parents made.* 그는 그의 부모가 한 똑같은 실수를 되풀이할 비운에 놓여 있었다. – **doomed** *adj*

dooms·day /'dumzdeɪ/ *n* ▷ JUDGMENT DAY

door /dɔr/ *n* **1** a large tall flat piece of wood, glass etc. that you push or pull in order to go into a building, room, car etc., or to open a piece of furniture ‖ 건물·실내·자동차 등에 들어가거나 가구를 열기 위하여 밀거나 당기는 나무·유리 등으로 만든 크고 높으며 넓적한 부분. 문. 문짝: *Could someone please open/close/shut the door for me?* 누가 문 좀 열어 [닫아] 주시겠어요? / *Don't forget to lock the front/back/side door.* 앞[뒷, 옆]문을 잠그는 것을 잊지 마라. / *How many times do I have to tell you not to slam the door?* (=shut it very hard) 문을 (쾅하고) 세게 닫지 말라고 내가 몇 번이나 말해야 하겠니? / *Did you hear someone knock on/at the door?* 누군가 문을 두드리는 소리를 들었어요? **2** the space made by an open door ‖ 문을 열어서 생기는 공간: *You just go out/through this door and turn right.* 너는 바로 이 문을 나가서 [통해서] 오른쪽으로 돌아라. **3 next door** in the room, house etc. next to where you are ‖ 자신이 있는 곳 옆에 있는 방·집 등에. 옆방에, 옆집에: *the people who live next door* 옆집에 사는 사람들 **4 at the door** if someone is at the door, s/he is waiting for you to open it ‖ 문을 열어 주기를 기다리고 있는. 문앞[현관]에 있는 **5 answer/get the door** to open the door to see who is there ‖ (현관)문에 누가 있는지 확인하려고 문을 열다. 응대하러 나가다/(현관)문을 열어 주다: *Mary, would you get the door?* 메리, 문 좀 열어 주겠어요? **6 two/three etc. doors down** a particular number of rooms, houses etc. away from where

you are ‖ 자신이 있는 곳에서 특정한 수의 방·집 등이 떨어져 있는. 두/세 집[방]째에[건너]: *Her office is just two doors down.* 그녀의 사무실은 바로 두 방 건너에 있다. **7 show/see sb to the door** to walk with someone to the main door of a building ‖ 건물의 대문까지 남과 같이 걷다. …을 문간까지 배웅하다 **8 (from) door to door a)** between one place and another ‖ 한 장소에서 다른 장소의 사이에. 여기에서 거기까지: *If you drive it should only take you 20 minutes door to door.* 자동차로 가면 여기에서 거기까지 20분밖에 안 걸린다. **b)** going to each house on a street to sell something, collect money etc. ‖ 물건을 팔거나 돈 등을 걷으려고 거리의 집집마다 다니는: *We went door to door asking people to sponsor us in the race.* 우리는 사람들에게 그 경주의 스폰서가 되어 달라고 요청하면서 가가호호 방문했다.

door·bell /'dɔrbɛl/ *n* a button by the door of a house that you press to make a sound so that the people inside know you are there ‖ 집안에 있는 사람이 현관에 사람이 있음을 알 수 있도록 벨 소리를 내기 위해 누르는 집의 현관 옆에 있는 버튼. 현관의 초인종

door·knob /'dɔrnɑb/ *n* a round handle that you turn to open a door ‖ 돌려서 문을 여는 둥근 손잡이. 문의 손잡이

door·man /'dɔrmæn, -mən/ *n* a man who works in a hotel or apartment building watching the door, helping people find taxis etc. ‖ 문을 지키거나 택시를 잡아 주는 등 호텔이나 아파트에서 근무하는 사람. 문지기. 수위

door·mat /'dɔrmæt/ *n* **1** a thick piece of material just outside a door for you to clean your shoes on ‖ (출입자의) 신발을 닦기 위해 현관 바로 밖에 두는 두툼한 것. 신발 흙털개 **2** INFORMAL someone who lets other people treat him/her badly and never complains ‖ 다른 사람들이 자신을 심하게 대하도록 내버려두며 불평을 전혀 안 하는 사람. 동네북(과 같은 사람)

door prize /'. ./ *n* a prize given to someone who has the winning number on his/her ticket for a show, dance etc. ‖ 공연·댄스 등의 입장권의 당첨 번호 소지자에게 주는 상. 당첨자 상품

door·step /'dɔrstɛp/ *n* **1** a step just outside a door to a building ‖ 건물의 문 바로 바깥의 계단. 현관의 계단 **2 on your doorstep** very near to where you live or are staying ‖ 자신이 살거나 머물고 있는 곳에서 아주 가까이에. 바로 눈앞에: *Wow! You have the beach right on* *your doorstep!* 와! 바로 문앞에 해변이 있구나!

door·stop /'dɔrstɑp/ *n* something you put under or against a door to keep it open ‖ 문이 열려 있도록 문 아래에 괴거나 문에 받쳐놓는 것. 문 버팀쇠[멈추개]

door·way /'dɔrweɪ/ *n* the space where the door opens into a room or building ‖ 문이 실내나 건물 쪽으로 열리는 공간. 문간. 출입구

dope¹ /doʊp/ *n* INFORMAL **1** [U] a drug that is taken illegally for pleasure ‖ 쾌락을 위해서 불법적으로 먹는 약. 마약 **2** a stupid person ‖ 어리석은 사람. 멍청이

dope², **dope up** *v* [I, T] INFORMAL to give a drug to a person or animal to make him, her, or it sleep, feel better, or work better ‖ 사람이나 동물에게 잠들게[더 기분 좋아지게, 더 일을 잘하게] 하려고 약을 주다. 수면제[마약, 흥분제]를 주다: *athletes doping up to improve their performance* 경기 성적을 높이기 위해 약물을 복용하는 운동선수들 – **doping** *n* [U]

dork /dɔrk/ *n* INFORMAL someone who you think is silly or stupid because s/he behaves strangely or wears strange clothes ‖ 이상하게 행동하거나 이상한 옷을 입어서 어수룩해 보이는 사람. 촌뜨기. 얼간이: *I look like such a dork in that picture.* 나는 그 사진에서 정말 얼뜨기처럼 보인다. – **dorky** *adj*

dorm /dɔrm/ *n* INFORMAL a large building at a school or college where students live ‖ 학생들이 거주하는 학교나 대학의 큰 건물. 기숙사

dor·mant /'dɔrmənt/ *adj* not active or not producing any effects at the present time ‖ 현재 활동을 하지 않거나 어떤 작용도 일으키지 않는. 활발하지 못한. 활동을 중지하고 있는: *a dormant volcano* 휴화산 – **dormancy** /'dɔrmənsi/ *n* [U]

dor·mi·to·ry /'dɔrmə,tɔri/ *n* **1** a large room in a HOSTEL, CONVENT etc. with many beds in it ‖ 많은 침대를 갖고 있는 유스호스텔·수도원 등의 큰 방. 공동 침실 **2** ⇨ DORM

dorsal /'dɔrsəl/ *adj* TECHNICAL on or relating to the back of a fish or animal ‖ 물고기나 동물의 등 위의 또는 그와 관련된. 등(쪽)의: *a whale's dorsal fin* 고래의 등지느러미

DOS /dɑs, dɔs/ *n* [U] TRADEMARK Disk Operating System; SOFTWARE used in a computer system to make all the different parts work together ‖ Disk Operating System(디스크 운영 체계)의 약어; 컴퓨터 시스템에서 모든 부분들이 함께 작동하도록 사용하는 소프트웨어

dose /doʊs/ *n* **1** also **do·sage** /'doʊsɪdʒ/ a measured amount of medicine ‖ 정해진 약의 양(量). 복용량: *The average adult dose is 300 mg daily.* 평균적인 성인 복용량은 하루 300mg 이다. **2** the amount of something that you experience at one time ‖ 한 번에 경험하는 어떤 것의 양. 어떤 분량: *I can only handle Jason in small doses.* (=for short amounts of time) 나는 아주 잠시만 제이슨을 봐줄 수 있다.

dos·si·er /'dɑsi,eɪ, 'dɔ-/ *n* a set of papers that include detailed information about someone or something ‖ 사람이나 사물에 관한 상세한 자료가 포함된 서류 한 벌. 어떤 문제에 관한 서류 일체: *The police keep dossiers on all their prisoners.* 경찰은 모든 죄수들에 관한 신상명세서를 보관하고 있다.

dot¹ /dɑt/ *n* **1** a small round mark or spot ‖ 작은 둥근 표시나 점. 반점: *The stars look like small dots of light in the sky.* 별들이 하늘에 점점이 뿌려진 작은 불빛처럼 보인다. **2 on the dot** exactly at a particular time ‖ 특정한 시간에 정확히. 제시간에. 정각에: *Parry arrived at nine o'clock on the dot.* 패리는 9시 정각에 도착했다.

dot² *v* **-tted, -tting** [T] **1** to mark something by putting a DOT on it or above it ‖ 물건에 또는 물건 위에 점을 찍어 표시를 하다. 점을 찍다: *She never dots her "i's."* 그녀는 철자 "i"에서 점을 찍는 법이 없다. **2** to spread things over a wide area and fairly far apart ‖ 꽤 멀리까지 넓은 지역 위에 어떤 것을 흩어지게 하다. 점재해 있다. 산재시키다: *We have over 20 stores dotted around the state.* 우리는 주(州)의 요소요소에 20개 이상의 점포를 개점하고 있다.

dot-com, **dot.com**, **dot com** /,dɑt'kɑm/ *adj* INFORMAL relating to a person or company whose business is done using the Internet or involves the Internet. ‖ 인터넷을 이용하거나 연관해서 사업을 하는 개인이나 회사와 관련된. 닷컴(사업자[기업])의: *a dot-com company* 닷컴 기업 / *dot-com millionaires* ‖ 닷컴 백만장자 – **dot-com** *n* [C]

dote /doʊt/ *v*

dote on sb/sth *phr v* [T] to love and care about someone more than other people think you should ‖ 다른 사람들이 당연하게 생각하는 것 이상으로 남을 사랑하고 보살피다. 맹목적으로 사랑하다: *Steve just dotes on his little grandson.* 스티브는 그의 어린 손자를 지나치게 사랑

한다. **– doting** *adj*

dot·ted line /ˌ.. './ *n* a printed or drawn line made of a lot of DOTS ‖ 많은 점들로 인쇄되거나 그려진 선. 점선: *Please sign on the dotted line.* 점선 위에 서명하세요.

dou·ble¹ /'dʌbəl/ *adj* **1** twice the usual amount or size ‖ 보통 양이나 크기의 두 배인. 갑절의: *I'll have a double whiskey.* 나는 위스키 두 잔을 마시겠다. **2** having two parts that are exactly the same ‖ 정확히 똑같은 두 개의 부분을 가진. 두 겹의. 쌍으로 된. 이중의: *a double line* 이중선 / *double doors* 이중으로 된 문들 **3** intended to be used by two people ‖ 두 사람이 사용하게 된. 2인용의: *a double room/bed* 2인용 방/침대 — compare SINGLE¹ **4 double meaning/ nature etc.** two very different or opposite meanings, qualities, etc. that one thing has at the same time ‖ 한 가지의 것이 두 개의 매우 다르거나 반대되는 의미·성질을 동시에 가지는. 이중적인. 이중적 의미/성질: *For years Jack had led a double life.* (=one part of his life was very different from the other) 잭은 수년간 이중생활을 했다.

dou·ble² *v* **1** [I] to become twice as large or twice as much ‖ 크기나 양이 두 배가 되다. 배가 되다: *Our house has doubled in value since we bought it.* 우리 집은 구입한 이후 그 가치가 두 배가 되었다. **2** [T] to make something be twice as large or twice as much ‖ 사물의 크기나 양을 두 배로 만들다: *The new job will double my salary.* 새로 얻은 직장에서 내 봉급은 지금의 두 배가 될 것이다.

double as *sb/sth phr v* [T] to have a second use, job, or purpose ‖ 제2의 용도[업무·목적]를 가지다. …의 역(役)을 하다. 겸무하다: *The sofa doubles as a bed.* 그 소파는 침대 역할도 한다.

double back *phr v* [I] to turn around and go back in the direction you just came from ‖ 방금 왔던 방향에서 뒤돌아서 되돌아가다. 정반대의 방향으로 나아가다: *I doubled back and headed south to Houston.* 나는 오던 길을 되돌아 휴스턴을 향해 남쪽으로 갔다.

double up, double over *phr v* [I] to suddenly bend at the waist because you are laughing too much or are in pain ‖ 너무 많이 웃거나 고통으로 갑자기 허리를 굽히다. (폭소·고통 등으로 사람·몸을) 구부리다: *Greene doubled over from a kick to his stomach.* 그린은 그의 배를 차여서 몸을 웅크렸다.

dou·ble³ *n* **1** [C, U] something that is twice the size, quantity, value, or strength of something else ‖ 다른 사물의 크기[양, 가치, 힘]의 두 배의 것: *I'll have a whiskey please – make it a double.* 위스키 더블로 주세요 **2 sb's double** someone who looks very similar to someone else ‖ 다른 사람과 아주 닮아 보이는 사람. 꼭 닮은 사람 **3 on the double** INFORMAL very soon or immediately ‖ 매우 빨리 또는 즉시. 당장에: *I want that report here on the double!* 여기에 당장 그 보고서를 가져와! —see also DOUBLES

double⁴ *adv* **see double** to have a problem with your eyes so that you see two things instead of one ‖ 눈에 이상이 있어 사물이 하나가 아닌 둘로 보이다. 상이 겹쳐 보이다

double⁵ *determiner* twice as much or twice as many ‖ 수·양이 두 배만큼 많은: *The car is worth double the amount we paid for it.* 그 차는 우리가 지불한 액수의 두 배의 가치가 있다.

double bass /ˌdʌbəl 'beɪs/ *n* a very large wooden musical instrument, shaped like a VIOLIN, that you play while standing up by pulling a special stick across wire strings ‖ 특수 막대로 철사 줄을 가로질러 당기며 서서 연주하는. 바이올린 모양의 아주 큰 목제 악기. 콘트라베이스

double boil·er /ˌ.. '../ *n* a pot for cooking food, made of one pot resting on top of another pot that has hot water in it ‖ 뜨거운 물이 담겨 있는 다른 냄비 위에 하나의 냄비가 놓여 있는 요리용 냄비. 중탕 냄비

double-breast·ed /ˌ.. '../ *adj* a double-breasted JACKET (=coat that has two rows of buttons on the front) ‖ 상의가 앞면에 두 줄의 단추가 달린. 더블의

double-check /ˌ..'./ *v* [T] to check something again to find out if it is safe, ready, correct etc. ‖ 사물의 안전성·준비성·정확성 등을 알아보기 위해 다시 검사하다. 두 번 확인하다. 재대조하다: *I think I turned off the oven, but let me go double check.* 오븐의 스위치를 끈 것 같지만 가서 다시 한 번 확인해 볼게.

double chin /ˌ.. './ *n* an additional fold of skin under someone's chin that looks like a second chin ‖ 사람의 턱 아래에 제2의 턱처럼 보이는 접힌 피부. 이중턱

double-cross /ˌ.. './ *v* [T] to cheat someone whom you have encouraged to trust you ‖ 어떤 사람에게 자기를 믿으라고 해 놓고 속이다. …을 배반하다: *He* *was killed for double-crossing his Mob bosses.* 그는 자신의 마피아 조직 두목을 배신했다고 살해당했다. – **double cross** *n*

double date /ˌ.. './ *n* an occasion in which two COUPLEs meet to go to a movie, restaurant etc. together ‖ 두 쌍이 만나서 함께 극장·식당 등에 가는 것. 더블 데이트. – **double-date** *v* [I, T]

double du·ty /ˌ.. './ *n* **do double duty** to do more than one job or be used for more than one purpose at the same time ‖ 동시에 한 개 이상의 업무를 하거나 한 가지 이상의 목적으로 쓰여지다. 두 가지 직무를 겸하고 있다: *The lids on the pots do double duty as plates when we're camping.* 냄비 뚜껑은 우리가 캠핑할 때 접시 역할도 겸한다.

double fea·ture /ˌ.. '../ *n* two movies that you watch for the price of a single ticket ‖ 표 한 장의 가격으로 관람하는 영화 두 편. 2편 동시 상영

double-head·er /ˌ.. './ *n* two baseball games that are played one after the other ‖ 연달아 두 번 경기하는 야구 게임. 더블헤더

double-joint·ed /ˌ.. '../ *adj* able to move the joints in your arms, fingers etc. backward as well as forward ‖ 팔·손가락 등의 관절을 앞뒤로 움직일 수 있는. 이중 관절이 있는. 잘 휘는

double-park /ˌ.. './ *v* [I, T] to leave a car on the road beside another car that is already parked there ‖ 이미 주차되어 있는 다른 차의 옆 도로로 차를 세우다. 이중[병렬] 주차하다: *I got a ticket for double-parking.* 나는 이중 주차로 교통 위반 딱지를 받았다. – **double-parking** *n* [U]

dou·bles /'dʌbəlz/ *n* [U] a tennis game played by two pairs of players ‖ 두 쌍의 선수들이 하는 테니스 게임. (테니스 등의) 복식 시합

double-spaced /ˌ.. './ *adj* a piece of writing that is double-spaced has a line of space between every line of writing ‖ 글쓰기에서 각 행 사이에 한 줄씩 여백이 있는. 한 줄씩 띄우고 타자한

double stand·ard /ˌ.. '../ *n* a rule or principle that is unfair because it treats one group or type of people more severely than another in the same situation ‖ 동일한 상황에서 한 집단이나 한 유형의 사람들을 다른 집단이나 유형보다 더 가혹하게 대하는, 불공정한 규칙이나 원칙. 이중 기준[잣대]. 차별: *There is a double standard that says men can want sex but women aren't supposed to.* 남자는 섹스를 원할 수 있지만 여자들은 그렇지 않다는 말은 이중 잣대이다.

double take /ˈ.. ˌ./ *n* **do a double take** to suddenly look at someone or something again because you are surprised by what you originally saw or heard ‖ 당초에 보거나 들은 것에 의해 놀라서 갑자기 사람이나 사물을 다시 보다. 갑자기 한 번 더 보다. 뒤돌아보다

double talk /ˈ.. ˌ./ *n* [U] INFORMAL speech that seems to be serious and sincere, but actually has another meaning or no meaning ‖ 심각하고 진지한 듯이 보이지만 실제로는 또 다른 의미가 있거나 전연 무의미한 말. 그럴 듯한 [앞뒤가 안 맞는] 말: *Don't be fooled by the double talk you'll get from the salesmen.* 세일즈맨한테서 들을 수 있는 그럴 듯한 말에 속지 마라.

double vi·sion /ˌ.. '../ *n* [U] a medical condition in which you see two of everything ‖ 모든 사물이 두 개로 보이는 의학적인 증세. 복시(複視). 이중시

double wham·my /ˌdʌbəl 'wæmi/ *n* INFORMAL two bad things that happen at the same time or one after the other ‖ 동시에 또는 연달아 일어나는 두 가지 나쁜 일. 이중의 재난. 이중고

dou·bly /'dʌbli/ *adv* **1** twice as much ‖ 두 배로. 배가하여: *doubly painful* 2배나 아픈 **2** in two ways ‖ 두 가지 방법으로. 이중으로. 두 가지로: *Rita was doubly distrusted, as a woman and as a foreigner.* 리타는 여자로서 또 외국인으로서 이중으로 불신을 당했다.

doubt¹ /daʊt/ *n* **1** the feeling of being unable to trust or believe in someone or something ‖ 어떤 사람이나 사물을 신뢰하거나 믿을 수 없는 상태의 감정. 의심. 회의: *Dad's always had serious doubts about Meg's boyfriend.* 아빠는 항상 메그의 남자 친구에 대해 깊은 의심을 했다. / *He was in doubt about what he should do.* 그는 자신이 무엇을 해야 하는지에 대해 회의에 빠져 있었다. / *I have no doubt that* (=I believe that) *Marshall was speaking the truth.* 마셜이 사실을 말하고 있었다는 것을 전혀 의심하지 않는다. **2 no doubt** used when emphasizing that you think something is probably true ‖ 어떤 것이 틀림없이 사실로 생각된다고 강조할 때 쓰여. 의심할 바 없이. 확실히: *No doubt he's married and has three kids by now.* 그는 결혼해서 현재 아이가 셋인 것은 확실하다. **3 without/beyond doubt** used in order to emphasize what you think is true ‖ 생각하는 것이 사실임을 강조하는 데에 쓰여. 의심할 여지없이:

Your mom is without a doubt the best cook this side of Texas! 네 엄마는 여기 텍사스 쪽에서는 의심할 여지없이 최고의 요리사야!

doubt² *v* [T] **1** to think that something may not be true or that it is unlikely ‖ 어떤 것이 사실이 아닐지도 모르거나 그럴 것 같지 않다고 생각하다. 의심하다. 미심쩍게 여기다: *I doubt (that) anyone was really paying attention.* 어느 누가 정말로 관심을 쏟고 있었을까 의심스럽다. **2** to not trust or believe in someone or something ‖ 사람이나 사물을 신뢰하지 않거나 믿지 않다: *We doubted her willingness to help the group.* 우리는 그녀가 자진해서 그 단체를 돕겠다는 것을 믿지 않았다.

doubt·ful /ˈdaʊtʰfəl/ *adj* **1** probably not true or not likely to happen ‖ 필시 사실이 아니거나 일어날 것 같지 않은. 의심스러운. 불확실한: *It's doubtful that we'll get to take a vacation this summer.* 우리가 이번 여름에 휴가를 가질 수 있을지는 잘 모른다. **2** unable to be trusted or believed ‖ 신뢰하거나 믿을 수 없는. 의심을 품게 하는: *his doubtful character* 그의 신뢰할 수 없는 성격 **3** feeling doubt ‖ 의심스럽게 느끼는. 의심하고 있는: *Corrine believed him, but Henry was doubtful.* 코린은 그를 믿었지만 헨리는 믿지 않았다. – **doubtfully** *adv*

doubt·less /ˈdaʊtʰlɪs/ *adv* very likely ‖ 매우 있을 법한. 의심할 바 없이. 확실히: *Jim doubtless knew that he was going to be fired.* 짐은 자기가 해고당할 거라는 것을 확실히 알고 있었다.

dough /doʊ/ *n* [U] **1** a soft mixture of flour and water etc. that you bake to make bread or cookies ‖ 빵이나 과자를 만들기 위해 굽는, 밀가루와 물 등의 부드러운 혼합물. 밀가루 반죽 **2** INFORMAL money ‖ 돈

dough·nut /ˈdoʊnʌt/ *n* a small round cake that is usually shaped like a ring ‖ 대개 고리 모양처럼 생긴 작고 둥근 빵. 도넛

dour /ˈdaʊɚ, dʊr/ *adj* very severe and not smiling ‖ 매우 엄하고 웃지 않는. 뚱한. 부루퉁한: *a dour expression* 언짢은 표정

douse /daʊs/ *v* [T] to stop something burning by throwing water on it ‖ 어떤 것에 물을 끼얹어 불타는 것을 막다. 불을 끄다: *20 firefighters quickly doused the blaze.* 20명의 소방관들이 황급히 불길을 잡았다.

dove¹ /dʌv/ *n* a type of small white PIGEON (=bird) often used as a sign of peace ‖ 종종 평화의 상징으로 사용되는 작고 흰 비둘기 종류

dove² /doʊv/ *v* a past tense of DIVE ‖ dive의 과거형

dow·dy /ˈdaʊdi/ *adj* a dowdy woman wears clothes that are old-fashioned or that are not attractive ‖ 여성이 구식이거나 맵시 없는 옷을 입는. 촌스러운. 모양 없는

down¹ /daʊn/ *adv* **1** from above a place or position toward a lower place or position ‖ 위쪽의 장소나 위치에서 아래쪽의 장소나 위치를 향하여. 낮은 곳으로. 아래쪽으로: *She looked down at the street from her window.* 그녀는 자기 방의 창문에서 거리를 내려다보았다. / *The sun goes down about 5:00 in the winter.* 해는 겨울에 5시경에 진다. **2** from a position in which someone or something is standing up to a position in which he, she, or it is lying flat or sitting ‖ 사람이나 사물이 서 있는 자세에서 납작 엎드리거나 앉아 있는 자세로: *Come in and sit down.* 들어와서 앉아라. / *trees blown down by the big storm* 심한 폭풍에 쓰러진 나무들 **3** toward or in the south ‖ 남쪽으로. 남쪽에: *Gail drove down to North Carolina to see her brother.* 게일은 그녀의 오빠[동생]를 만나려고 노스캐롤라이나로 차를 몰고 내려갔다. **4** in a direction away from the person speaking ‖ 화자(話者)로부터 떨어진 쪽에. 저쪽: *Could you go down to the store* *and get some bread?* 저쪽 가게에 가서 빵 좀 사다 줄 수 있습니까? **5** SPOKEN used in order to emphasize where something is when it is in a different place from the person who is speaking ‖ 어떤 것이 말하고 있는 사람과 다른 장소에 있을 때 그것이 있는 위치를 강조하는 데에 쓰여: *I saw her earlier today down on Main Street.* 나는 오늘 일찍 그녀를 거기 메인가(街)에서 보았다. **6** to a lower level of noise, strength, activity etc ‖ 소음·강도·활동 등의 보다 낮은 수준으로. 약하게. 낮게: *Can you turn the TV down? I'm on the phone.* 텔레비전 볼륨 좀 낮춰 줄래? 전화 통화 중이야. / *Slow down! You're going too fast.* 속도 좀 늦춰! 너무 빨리 가잖아. **7** to a level, state, or condition that is lower or worse than before ‖ 전보다 낮거나 나쁜 수준[상태, 조건]으로. 떨어져. 내려가: *Exports are down this year by 10%.* 올해 수출은 10 퍼센트 떨어졌다. / *Everything in the store has been marked down.* (=given a lower price) 그 가게의 모든 물품의 가격이 내렸다. **8** on paper, or in writing ‖ 종이 위에, 또는 글로 써서: *When you know the answer, write it down in the blank.* 답을 알면 빈칸에 써 넣으시오. / *I have his number down somewhere.* 그의 전화번호를 어딘가에 써 놓았는데. **9** in a low place ‖ 낮은 곳에. 아래에: *The cows are down in the valley.* 소들이 아래쪽 계곡에 있다. —see also **come down with** (COME¹)

down² *adj* **1** sad ‖ 슬픈. 우울한: *I've never seen Bret looking so down.* 지금껏 브레트가 그렇게 우울해 하는 모습을 본 적이 없다. **2** behind in a game by a particular number of points ‖ 특정한 점수로 게임에서 뒤진: *We were down by 6 points at half-time.* 우리는 전반전에 6점 차이로 뒤졌다. **3** not working or operating ‖ 작동하지 않는, 가동하지 않는: *The computers were down this afternoon.* 그 컴퓨터들은 오늘 오후에 작동되지 않았다. **4** SPOKEN used in order to say that a particular number of things in a list are finished ‖ 목록에 있는 특정 수의 것들이 끝났다고 말하는 데에 쓰여. …까지 끝낸: *That's two down. Only two more to do.* 두 개는 끝냈어. 두 개만 더 하면 돼. **5 be down on** SPOKEN to have a bad opinion of someone or something ‖ 사람이나 사물에 대해 나쁜 견해를 가지다. 편견을 갖다. 싫어하다: *Why is Jerome so down on work?* 제롬은 일하는 것을 왜 그렇게 싫어하니?

down³ *prep* **1** toward the ground or a lower point, or in a lower position ‖ 땅쪽으로[더 낮은 지점으로, 더 낮은 위치에]. …의 밑에[으로]: *The bathroom is down those stairs.* 욕실은 저 계단 밑에 있다. **2** along or toward the far end of something ‖ 사물의 먼 끝을 따라서 또는 먼 끝으로: *We walked down the beach as the sun rose.* 우리는 해가 떠오를 때 해변 끝을 따라 걸었다. / *They live down the road from us.* 그들은 우리 집에서 떨어진 길 끝에 산다. **3 down the road/line** SPOKEN at some time in the future ‖ 미래의 어느 때에: *We'd like to have children sometime down the line.* 우리는 먼 훗날 언젠가 아이들을 가지고 싶다.

down⁴ *v* [T] to drink something very quickly ‖ 사물을 매우 빨리 마시다: *Matt downed his coffee and left for work.* 매트는 커피를 재빨리 마시고 일하러 떠났다.

down⁵ *n* [U] thin soft feathers or hair ‖ 가늘고 부드러운 깃털이나 머리털. 솜털

down-and-out /ˌ. . ˈ./ *adj* having no luck or money ‖ 운이나 돈이 없는. 몰락한. 무일푼의

down·cast /ˈdaʊnkæst/ *adj* sad or upset because something bad has happened ‖ 나쁜 일이 발생해서 슬프거나 기분이 나쁜. 의기소침한. 풀이 죽은: *Jason looked downcast as his mother left.* 제이슨은 자기 어머니가 떠나자 풀이 죽어 보였다.

down·er /ˈdaʊnɚ/ *n* **1** [singular] SPOKEN an experience that makes you feel unhappy ‖ 불행함을 느끼게 하는 경험. 불쾌한 경험: *Failing my last exam was a real downer.* 지난번 시험에서 낙제한 것은 정말 불쾌한 경험이었다. **2** INFORMAL a drug that makes you feel very relaxed or sleepy ‖ 아주 편안하게 하거나 졸리게 하는 약. 진정제. 신경 안정제

down·fall /ˈdaʊnfɔl/ *n* a sudden loss of money, power, social position etc., or something that leads to this ‖ 돈·힘·사회적 지위 등의 갑작스러운 상실, 또는 이러한 상실에 이르게 되는 것. 파멸·몰락(의 원인): *Greed will be his downfall.* 탐욕으로 그는 파멸에 이를 것이다.

down·grade /ˈdaʊngreɪd/ *v* [T] to give someone a less important job, or to make something seem less important ‖ 남에게 덜 중요한 일을 주다, 또는 사물을 덜 중요해 보이게 하다. …을 경시하다[강등시키다]: *He may be downgraded to assistant manager.* 그는 부지배인으로 강등될지 모른다.

down·heart·ed /ˌdaʊnˈhɑrt̮ɪd/ *adj* **be downhearted** to feel sad about something ‖ 어떤 것에 대해 슬픔을 느끼다. 낙담하다. 기가 죽다

down·hill¹ /ˌdaʊnˈhɪl/ *adv* **1** toward the bottom of a hill or toward lower land ‖ 언덕 밑으로 또는 보다 낮은 땅으로. 내리받이에. 언덕을 내려가서: *The truck's brakes failed, and it rolled downhill.* 트럭의 브레이크가 고장 나서 언덕 아래로 굴러 떨어졌다. **2 go downhill** to become worse ‖ 더 나빠지다. 악화되다: *After he lost his job, things went downhill.* 그가 실직하고 난 후에 상황은 더 나빠졌다.

downhill² *adj* **1** on a slope that goes down to a lower point ‖ 더 낮은 지점으로 내려가는 경사에 있는. 내리막의: *downhill skiing* 활강 스키 **2 be (all) downhill** to get worse ‖ 더 나빠지다. 악화되다: *We got three runs in the first inning, but it was all downhill from there.* 우리는 1회에 3점을 냈지만 그 뒤로 상황은 악화되었다.

down·load /ˈdaʊnloʊd/ *v* [T] to move information from one part of a computer system to another, or from one computer to another using a MODEM ‖ 컴퓨터 시스템의 한 부분에서 다른 부분으로 정보를 옮기다, 또는 모뎀을 이용하여 한 컴퓨터에서 다른 컴퓨터로 정보를 옮기다. …을 다운로드하다

down pay·ment /ˌ. ˈ../ *n* the first payment you make on something expensive that you will pay for over a longer period ‖ 장기에 걸쳐 지불할 비싼 사물에 대한 첫 지불. 할부의 첫 납입금: *a down payment on a car* 자동차의 할부금 중 첫 납입금

down·play /ˈdaʊnpleɪ/ *v* [T] to make something seem less important than it really is ‖ 사물을 실제보다 덜 중요한 것처럼 만들다. …을 경시하다. 얕보다: *Fred downplayed the seriousness of his illness.* 프레드는 자기 병의 심각성을 가볍게 여겼다.

down·pour /ˈdaʊnpɔr/ *n* a lot of rain that falls in a short time ‖ 짧은 시간에 내리는 많은 비. 억수. 호우

down·right /ˈdaʊnraɪt/ *adv* INFORMAL thoroughly and completely ‖ 철저하게, 완전하게. 매우: *You're just downright lazy.* 당신은 정말로 게으르군.

down·riv·er /ˌdaʊnˈrɪvɚ/ *adv* ⇨ DOWNSTREAM

down·side /ˈdaʊnsaɪd/ *n* **the downside** the negative side of something ‖ 사물의 부정적인 측면. 불리한 면: *The downside of the plan is the cost.* 그 계획의 부정적인 측면은 비용 문제이다.

down·size /ˈdaʊnsaɪz/ *v* [I, T] to make a company smaller by reducing the number of people who work there ‖ 회사에서 일하는 사람의 수를 줄임으로써 회사를 더 작게 만들다. 인력·규모를 줄이다. 감량하다 – **downsizing** *n* [U]

down·spout /ˈdaʊnspaʊt/ *n* a pipe that carries rain water away from the roof of a building ‖ 빌딩의 지붕에서 빗물을 옮기는 파이프. 빗물받이 홈통 —see picture on page 945

Down's Syn·drome /ˈ. ˌ../ *n* [U] a condition that someone is born with that stops him/her from developing normally both mentally and physically ‖ 정신적·육체적 양쪽으로 정상적 발달이 멈추도록 태어난 사람의 증세. 다운 증후군

down·stairs /ˌdaʊnˈstɛrz/ *adv* **1** on or going toward a lower floor of a building, especially a house ‖ 특히 집 등의 건물 아래층에 또는 아래층으로 내려 가는: *Run downstairs and answer the door.* 아래층으로 뛰어내려가 누군가 봐라. **2 the downstairs** the rooms on the ground floor of a house ‖ 집의 바닥 층에 있는 방. 아래층 방. 1층: *Let's paint the downstairs blue.* 아래층 방들을 푸른색으로 페인트칠하자. – **downstairs** /ˈdaʊnstɛrz/ *adj* : *the downstairs rooms* 아래층의 방들 —opposite UPSTAIRS¹

down·state /ˌdaʊnˈsteɪt/ *adj, adv* in or toward the southern part of a state ‖ 주의 남부에, 또는 남부로. 주 남부의[에서]: *He lives downstate, near the city.* 그는 도시 근처의 남부에 산다.

down·stream /ˌdaʊnˈstrim/ *adv* in the direction the water in a river or stream flows ‖ 강이나 시내의 물이 흘러가는 방향에. 흐름에 따라. 하류로 —opposite UPSTREAM

down·time /ˈdaʊntaɪm/ *n* [U] **1** the time when a computer is not working ‖ 컴퓨터가 작동되지 않는 때. 컴퓨터의 중지 시간 **2** INFORMAL time spent relaxing ‖ 휴식하며 보내는 시간. 휴식 시간

down-to-earth /ˌ. . ˈ./ *adj* practical and honest ‖ 실제적이고 정직한. 현실적인. 세상 물정에 밝은: *He liked her down-to-earth way of talking.* 그는 그녀가 현실적이고 정직하게 말하는 것을 좋아했다.

down·town¹ /ˌdaʊnˈtaʊn/ *n* [U] the business center of a city or town ‖ 대도시나 소도시의 상업 지구. 상업 중심 지구. 도심: *The university is 20 minutes* *from downtown.* 그 대학은 도심에서 20 분 거리에 있다. / *downtown Phoenix* 피 닉스 상업 중심 지구 **-downtown** /'daʊntaʊn/ *adj* : *a downtown hotel* 번화 가에 있는 호텔

downtown² *adv* to or in the business center of a city or town ‖ 대도시나 소도 시의 상업 지구로[에]. 번화가에: *Do you work downtown?* 도심 중심가에서 일하 니? / *We went downtown to eat and see a movie.* 우리는 음식을 먹고 영화를 보기 위해 도심의 번화가에 갔다.

down·trod·den /'daʊn,trɑdn/ *adj* LITERARY treated badly or without respect by people in positions of power ‖ 권력자들로부터 부당하거나 하찮게 대 우받는. 압박[탄압]받는. 짓밟힌

down·turn /'daʊntɜn/ *n* a time during which business activity is reduced and conditions become worse ‖ 상거래 활동 이 감소되고 상황이 악화되는 시기. 경기 의 하강 [침체] (기): *an economic downturn* 경제 침체 / *a downturn in the number of product orders* 상품 주문 수량의 감소 —opposite UPTURN

down·ward¹ /'daʊnwɚd/, **down-wards** *adv* from a higher place or position to a lower one ‖ 보다 높은 장소 나 위치에서 보다 낮은 장소나 위치로. 아 래쪽으로. 아래를 향하여: *Tim pointed downward at his shoes.* 팀은 아래쪽 자 기 신발을 가리켰다. —opposite UPWARD²

downward² *adj* going or moving down to a lower level or place ‖ 더 낮은 수준이 나 장소로 내려가는, 또는 밑으로 움직이 는. 하향의. 하락하는: *a quick downward movement* 재빨리 아래로 향하는 움직임

down·wind /,daʊn'wɪnd/ *adj, adv* in the same direction that the wind is moving ‖ 바람이 불고 있는 방향과 같은 방향의[으로]. 순풍으로

down·y /'daʊni/ *adj* having thin soft feathers or hair ‖ 가늘고 부드러운 깃털 이나 머리털을 가진. 솜털 같은. 솜털이 난. 폭신한: *the baby's downy head* 아기 의 솜털이 난 머리

dow·ry /'daʊri/ *n* money or property that women in some societies bring to their new husband from their families ‖ 일부 사회에서 여성들이 그들의 가족에게 서 받아 그들의 남편에게 가져가는 돈이나 재산. 지참금. 재산. 재물

doze /doʊz/ *v* [I] to sleep for a short time ‖ 짧은 시간 동안 자다. 선잠자다. 졸 다: *He dozed for an hour.* 그는 1시간 동 안 선잠을 잤다.

doze off *phr v* [I] to fall asleep when you do not intend to do so ‖ 잠 잘 생각이

없을 때 잠이 들다. 꾸벅꾸벅[깜박] 졸다: *I usually doze off watching TV.* 텔레비전 을 보면서 나는 보통 꾸벅꾸벅 존다.

doz·en /'dʌzən/ *n* [determiner, n] **1** a group of 12 things ‖ 12개의 1조. 1다스: *a dozen eggs* 계란 1판 **2 dozens (of)** INFORMAL a lot of something ‖ 많은 것. 수 십. 다수: *We looked at dozens of houses before we found this one.* 우리는 이 집을 찾아내기 전에 수십 채의 집들을 둘러보았 다.

Dr. /'dɑktɚ/ the written abbreviation of Doctor ‖ doctor의 약어

drab /dræb/ *adj* not bright in color, or not interesting ‖ 색깔이 밝지 않은, 또는 흥미 없는. 칙칙한. 단조로운: *a drab coat* 색깔이 칙칙한 코트

dra·co·ni·an /dræ'koʊniən/ *adj* FORMAL very strict and severe ‖ 매우 엄격하고 혹 독한. 가혹한: *draconian laws* 엄격한 법 률

draft¹ /dræft/ *n* **1** a piece of writing, drawing etc. that is not yet in its finished form ‖ 아직 완성된 형태를 갖추 지 못한 일련의 글·그림 등. 밑그림. 초고: *Make a draft of your paper first.* 우선 리포트의 초고를 작성해라. / *This is only a first draft.* 이것은 단지 초안에 불과하 다. **2 the draft** a system in which people must fight for their country when it is in a war ‖ 국민이 전쟁 상황시 국가를 위해 싸워야 하는 제도. 징병[징모] **3** a current of air ‖ 공기의 흐름. 통풍. 외풍: *a draft coming through a crack in the walls* 벽의 갈라진 틈으로 새어 들어오는 바람 **4** a system in American sports in which PROFESSIONAL teams choose players from colleges for their teams ‖ 프로팀이 자기 팀을 위하여 대학에서 선수 들을 뽑는 미국 스포츠 제도. 드래프트제: *He was chosen in the third round of the NFL draft this year.* 그는 올해 NFL 드래 프트의 3라운드에서 뽑혔다. **5** a written order for money to be paid by a bank ‖ 은행이 돈을 지불하라는 명령서. 지급 명 령서. 어음

draft² *v* [T] **1** to write a plan, letter, report etc. that you will need to change before it is finished ‖ 완성되기 전에 변경 이 필요할 수 있는 계획·편지·보고서 등을 쓰다. …을 기초하다. 초고를 쓰다: *The House plans to draft a bill on education.* 백악관은 교육에 대한 법안을 입안할 계획 이다. **2** to order someone to fight for his/her country during a war ‖ 어떤 사람 에게 전쟁 중에 조국을 위해 싸우라고 명 령하다: *Jim was drafted into the army.* 짐은 군대에 징집되었다.

draft³ *adj* **1** not finished ‖ 끝나지[완성하지] 않은: *the draft treaty* 미체결 조약 **2** used for pulling loads ‖ 짐수레를 끄는 데에 쓰는. 하역용의: *a draft horse* 짐수레를 끄는 말

draft beer /,. './ beer that is fresh because it has not been kept in cans or bottles ‖ 깡통이나 병에 넣어 저장하지 않아서 신선한 맥주. 생맥주

draft dodg·er /'. ,../ *n* someone who illegally avoids joining the military service ‖ 군대에 가는 것을 불법적으로 기피하는 사람. 징병 기피자

drafts·man /'dræftsmən/, **drafts-wom·an** /'dræfts,wumən/ *n* someone whose job is to make detailed drawings of a building, machine etc. ‖ 건물·기계 등의 상세한 제도(製圖)를 하는 직업인. 제도공

draft·y /'dræfti/ *adj* with currents of air flowing through ‖ 통풍되는 공기의 흐름이 있는. 통풍이 잘 되는. 외풍이 있는: *a drafty room* 외풍이 있는 방

drag¹ /dræg/ *v* - **gged, -gging**

drag

1 ▶PULL 끌다◀ [T] to pull someone or something heavy along the ground or away from somewhere ‖ 무거운 사람 또는 사물을 지면을 따라서 끌거나 어딘가에서 끌어내다. …을 질질 끌다. 끌어당기다: *Ben dragged his sled through the snow.* 벤은 눈을 헤치고 자기의 썰매를 질질 끌었다. / *protestors dragged away by police* 경찰에 의해 끌려가는 항의자들

2 ▶GO SOMEWHERE 어디로 가다◀ [T] to make someone go somewhere that s/he does not want to go ‖ 사람을 가고 싶어하지 않는 어떤 곳으로 가게 하다. 끌고 가다: *Mom dragged us to a concert last night.* 엄마는 어제 저녁 우리를 콘서트에 끌고 갔다.

3 drag yourself away (from) to stop doing something, although you do not want to ‖ 원하지는 않지만 어떤 일을 그만두다: *Drag yourself away from the TV and come for a swim.* 텔레비전 그만 보고 수영하러 가자.

4 ▶BORING 지겨운◀ [I] if time or an event drags, it is boring and seems to go very slowly ‖ 시간이나 사건이 따분하거나 매우 늦게 가는 듯하다. 일이 지겹다: *Friday afternoons really drag.* 금요일 오후는 정말 시간이 가지 않는 것 같다.

5 ▶COMPUTER 컴퓨터◀ [T] to move something on a computer screen by pulling it along with the MOUSE ‖ 마우스로 끌어서 컴퓨터 화면 위의 어떤 것을 움직이다. 드래그하다

6 ▶TOUCHING GROUND 지면에 닿은◀ [I] if something is dragging along the ground, part of it is touching the ground as you move ‖ 움직일 때 사물의 일부분이 땅에 닿다. 지면에 질질 끌다

7 drag your feet INFORMAL to take too much time to do something because you do not want to do it ‖ 어떤 일을 하기 싫어서 시간을 지나치게 많이 끌다. 일부러 꾸물거리다: *The police are being accused of dragging their feet on this case.* 경찰은 이 사건에 대해 일부러 꾸물거리고 있다고 비난받고 있다.

8 drag yourself up/over/along etc. to move somewhere when it is difficult ‖ 힘든 상황에서 어디엔가로 움직이다. …위로/건너서/따라 간신히 움직이다: *I dragged myself out of bed to call the doctor.* 나는 의사를 부르기 위해 간신히 침대 밖으로 나왔다.

drag sb/sth ↔ into *phr v* [T] to make someone get involved in a situation even though s/he does not want to ‖ 어떤 사람이 원하지 않는데도 어떤 상황에 관련시키다. …을 …에 끌어들이다: *I'm sorry to drag you into this mess.* 이 혼란 속으로 당신을 끌어들여 미안합니다.

drag on *phr v* [I] to continue for too long ‖ 너무 오랫동안 계속하다. 지루하게 끌다: *The meeting dragged on all afternoon.* 그 회의는 오후 내내 지루하게 계속되었다.

drag sth ↔ out *phr v* [T] to make a situation or event last longer than necessary ‖ 상황이나 사건을 필요 이상으로 지속시키다. 질질 끌다: *How long are you going to drag this discussion out?* 이 토론을 얼마나 질질 끌 거냐?

drag² *n* **1 a drag** INFORMAL something or someone that is boring or uninteresting ‖ 지루하거나 흥미 없는 사람이나 사물. 따분한[싫증나는] 사람[것, 장소]: *"I have to stay home tonight." "What a drag."* "오늘 밤 집에 있어야만 해." "정말 따분하겠군." **2 a drag on sth** someone or something that prevents someone from making progress ‖ 남이 진행하는 것을 방해하는 사람이나 사물. …의 방해물. 장애물: *Marriage would be a drag on my career.* 결혼은 나의 경력에 장애물이 될 것이다. **3** the act of breathing in smoke from your cigarette ‖ 담배 연기를 들이마시는 행위. 한 모금: *Al took a drag on his cigarette.* 앨은 담

배 한 모금을 들이마셨다 **4 in drag** INFORMAL a man who is in drag is wearing women's clothes ‖ 남성이 여성의 옷을 입은. 여장을 한

drag·on /'drægən/ *n* a large imaginary animal that has wings, a long tail, and can breathe out fire ‖ 날개와 긴 꼬리를 가지고 있고 불을 뿜어낼 수 있다는 큰 상상의 동물. 용

drag·on·fly /'drægən,flaɪ/ *n* a flying insect with a long brightly colored body ‖ 밝은 색깔의 긴 몸통을 가진 날아다니는 곤충. 잠자리

drag race /'. ./ *n* a car race over a short distance ‖ 단거리 자동차 경주

drain¹ /dreɪn/ *v* **1 a)** [T] also **drain off** to make a liquid flow away from something ‖ 어떤 것에서 액체를 흘려보내다. 배출시키다. (물기를) 없애다[빼내다]: *They drained the water out of the lake.* 그들은 호수의 물을 빼내었다. / *Drain off the fat from the meat.* 고기에서 지방을 빼내어라. **b)** [I] if something drains, the liquid in it or on it flows away ‖ 어떤 사물의 안 또는 위에 있는 액체가 흘러나가다. (물기가) 빠져나가다: *Let the pasta drain well.* 파스타에서 물기를 잘 빼내라. **2** [T] to make someone feel very tired ‖ 사람을 매우 피곤하게 하다. …을 소모시키다. 기진맥진하게 하다: *The argument drained me completely.* 그 논쟁으로 나는 완전히 지쳐버렸다. **3** [I] if the color drains from your face, you suddenly become pale ‖ 얼굴이 갑자기 창백해지다 **4** [T] to drink all the liquid in a glass, cup etc. ‖ 유리잔·컵 등에 있는 액체를 모두 마시다. 잔을 비우다. …을 죽 들이키다: *Lori quickly drained her cup.* 로리는 잔을 재빨리 쭉 들이켜 버렸다.

drain² *n* **1** a pipe or hole that dirty water or other waste liquids DRAIN into ‖ 더러운 물이나 다른 폐수를 흘려보내는 관이나 구멍. 배수구. 하수관: *The drain in the sink is blocked.* 싱크대의 배수구가 막혔다. —see picture at CURB **2 be a drain on sth** to use too much time, money etc. ‖ 너무 많은 시간·돈 등을 사용하다. 소모하다: *Doing a graduate degree has been a drain on Fran's savings.* 프랜의 저금은 석사학위를 따느라 바닥났다. **3 down the drain** INFORMAL wasted or having no result ‖ 낭비된 또는 결과물이 없는. 헛수고가 된: *There's another $50 down the drain.* 추가로 50달러를 날렸다.

drain·age /'dreɪnɪdʒ/ *n* [U] **1** a system of pipes or passages in the ground for carrying water or waste liquids ‖ 물이나 폐수를 나르기 위한 땅 속의 관이나 수로 장치. 배수(설비). 배수구: *drainage ditches* 배수구(排水溝) **2** the process by which water or waste liquids flow through this system ‖ 배수 장치를 통해 물이나 폐수를 흘려보내는 과정. 배수. 방수

drained /dreɪnd/ *adj* very tired ‖ 매우 지친: *I felt so drained after my parents left.* 나는 부모님이 떠난 후 몹시 피곤함을 느꼈다.

drain·er /'dreɪnɚ/, **drain·board** /'dreɪnbɔrd/ *n* a flat area next to a 'SINK where you put dishes to dry ‖ 식기를 건조시키기 위해 놓아 두는 싱크대 옆에 있는 평평한 곳. 식기 건조대

dra·ma /'drɑmə, 'dræmə/ *n* **1** a play for the theater, television, radio etc. ‖ 극장·텔레비전·라디오 등을 위한 극. 드라마. 희곡 **2** [U] the study of drama ‖ 드라마에 대한 학문. 극문학: *drama classes* 극문학 수업[반] **3** [C, U] an exciting and unusual situation or event ‖ 자극적이고 평범하지 않은 상황이나 사건. 극적인 사건[상황]: *the drama of a sea rescue* 극적인 해난 구조 상황

dra·mat·ic /drə'mætɪk/ *adj* **1** sudden and noticeable ‖ 갑작스럽고 주목할 만한. 급격한: *a dramatic change in temperature* 온도의 급격한 변화 **2** exciting and impressive ‖ 자극적이고 감동을 주는. 극적인. 인상적인: *a dramatic speech about the dangers of drugs* 마약의 위험성에 관한 인상적인 연설 **3** related to the theater or plays ‖ 극장이나 연극과 관련된. 연극[희곡]의. 극 형식의: *Miller's dramatic works* 밀러의 극작품 **4** showing feelings in a way that makes other people notice you ‖ 다른 사람들을 주목하게 만드는 투로 감정을 표현하는. 연극조의. 박진감 넘치는: *Don't be so dramatic.* 그렇게 호들갑떨지 마. – **dramatically** *adv*

dra·mat·ics /drə'mætɪks/ *n* **1** [plural] behavior that shows a lot of feeling but is not sincere ‖ 많은 감정을 드러내지만 심각하지 않은 행동. 연극조의 행동. 연기: *I'm really tired of your dramatics.* 당신의 연기가 정말 지겹다. **2** [U] the study or practice of skills used in DRAMA, such as acting ‖ 연기 등의 드라마에서 사용되는 기술에 대한 학문이나 교습. 연기술. 연출법

dram·a·tist /'dræmətɪst, 'drɑ-/ *n* someone who writes plays, especially serious ones ‖ 특히 진지한 연극을 쓰는 사람. 극작가

dram·a·tize /'dræmə,taɪz, 'drɑ-/ v **1** to make a book or event into a play ‖ 책이나 사건을 극화시키다. 각색하다: *a dramatized children's story* 각색된 동화 **2** to make an event seem more exciting than it really is ‖ 사건을 실제보다 더욱 흥미로워 보이게 만들다. …을 과장하다: *The incident was dramatized by the newspaper.* 그 사고는 신문에 의해 더욱 과장되었 다. – **dramatization** /,dræmətə'zeɪʃən/ n

drank /dræŋk/ v the past tense of DRINK ‖ drink의 과거형

drape /dreɪp/ v [T] to let something, especially cloth, hang or lie somewhere loosely ‖ 특히 옷을 아무렇게나 어딘가에 걸거나 놓다. …을 축 늘어뜨리다. 되는 대로 놓다: *a scarf draped over her shoulders* 그녀의 어깨에 늘어뜨린 스카프 —see also DRAPES

drap·er·y /'dreɪpəri/ n [C, U] cloth or clothing that is arranged in folds over something ‖ 어떤 것 위로 접어 정리한 천이나 옷. 주름잡힌 천[옷]

drapes /dreɪps/ n [plural] heavy curtains ‖ 무거운 커튼: *We need new drapes for the living room.* 거실에 새 커튼이 필요하다.

dras·tic /'dræstɪk/ adj extreme, sudden, and often violent or severe ‖ 극심한, 갑작스러운, 종종 격렬하거나 가혹한. 철저한. 과감한. 급격한: *The President promised drastic changes in health care.* 대통령은 의료 서비스에 있어서 과감한 변혁을 약속했다. – **drastically** adv

draw¹ /drɔ/ v **drew, drawn, drawing** **1** ▶PICTURE 그림◀ [I, T] to make a picture of something with a pencil or a pen ‖ 연필이나 펜으로 어떤 것을 그리다: *Could you draw me a map?* 나에게 지도를 그려줄 수 있습니까? / *He drew an elephant on the paper.* 그는 종이에 코끼리를 그렸다.

2 draw (sb's) attention to make someone notice something ‖ 남을 어떤 것에 주목하게 만들다. (…의) 주의[이목]을 끌다. …을 환기시키다: *Because she's tall, Roz draws attention in a crowd.* 로즈는 키가 크기 때문에 대중들 속에서 눈에 확 띈다. / *I'd like to draw your attention to the six exit doors in the plane.* 나는 당신에게 비행기에 6개의 비상구가 있다는 것을 환기시켜 주고 싶다.

3 draw a conclusion to decide that something is true after thinking carefully about it ‖ 어떤 일에 대하여 신중하게 생각한 뒤에 그것이 진실하다고 결

정하다: *It's difficult to draw conclusions from so little data.* 아주 적은 자료로 결론을 도출한다는 것은 어렵다.

4 draw a distinction/comparison to make someone understand that two things are different from or similar to each other ‖ 남에게 두 개의 물건이 서로 다르거나 비슷하다는 것을 이해시키다. 구별시키다. 구분 짓다: *We have to draw a distinction between what is right and wrong for our children.* 우리는 아이들에게 무엇이 옳고 그른지 구별시켜야 한다.

5 ▶PULL SB/STH 사람/사물을 끌어당기다◀ [T] to make someone or something move by pulling him/her or it gently ‖ 사람이나 사물을 부드럽게 끌어 움직이게 하다. …을 끌어당기다. 잡아끌다: *Grant drew me aside to tell me the news.* 그랜트는 나에게 그 소식을 얘기하려고 나를 옆으로 끌어당겼다.

6 draw the curtains to open or close the curtains ‖ 커튼을 열다 또는 치다

7 ▶ATTRACT/INTEREST 매혹됨/흥미를 끔◀ [T] to attract or interest people ‖ 사람을 매혹시키거나 흥미를 끌다: *"Batman Forever" drew large crowds on the first day.* 영화 "Batman Forever"는 개봉 첫날 많은 관객을 끌었다. / *What could have drawn Alex to drugs?* 왜 알렉스가 마약에 빠졌느냐?

8 ▶TAKE CARD ETC. 카드 등을 뽑다◀ [T] to take a playing card, piece of paper, number etc. from a group of other cards or papers ‖ 기타 카드나 종이 뭉치에서 게임 카드·종이 조각·숫자 등을 뽑다. 제비를 뽑다: *Lotto numbers are drawn on Saturdays.* 로또 숫자는 토요일에 추첨한다.

9 draw a blank INFORMAL to be unable to think or remember something ‖ 어떤 것을 생각하거나 기억할 수 없다. 실패하다. 어떠한 응답도 얻지 못하다. 아무것도 건지지 못하다: *I drew a blank when I tried to remember the number.* 내가 그 숫자를 기억해내려고 노력했을 때 아무것도 얻지 못했다.

10 draw the line (at) to refuse to do something because you do not approve of it ‖ 어떤 것을 인정하지 않기 때문에 그것을 하는 것을 거절하다. …에 선을 긋다. 한계를 짓다: *I don't mind helping you, but I draw the line at telling lies.* 나는 너를 도와주고 싶지만 거짓말하는 것은 거절한다.

11 ▶TAKE OUT 꺼내다◀ to remove something from its place or container ‖ 장소나 용기에서 어떤 것을 제거하다. …을 꺼내다. 빼내다: *Suddenly Ed drew a*

gun/knife. 갑자기 에드는 총[칼]을 뽑았
다. / *She drew $50 out of the bank*. 그녀
는 은행에서 50달러를 인출했다.

12 draw fire/criticism to be criticized
‖ 비난받다: *The company drew criticism
for putting chemicals into the river*. 그
회사는 강에 화학물질을 버렸다고 비난받
았다.

13 ▶RECEIVE MONEY 돈을 받다◀ [T] to
receive an amount of money regularly
from the government ‖ 정부로부터 정기
적으로 일정 액수의 돈을 받다: *people
drawing unemployment benefits* 실업 수
당을 받고 있는 사람들

14 draw up/along/beside etc. if a
vehicle draws up etc., it moves near you
‖ 탈것이 자신의 근처로 움직이다. …에
바짝 따라붙다[다가서다]: *A police car
drew up behind me*. 경찰차가 내 뒤에 바
짝 다가왔다.

15 draw a check (on sth) to write a
check for taking money out of a bank ‖
은행에서 돈을 찾기 위해 수표에 서명하
다. 어음[수표]을 발행하다: *a check
drawn on a British bank* 브리티시 은행
에서 발행한 수표

16 ▶LIQUID 액체◀ [T] to take liquid
from the place where it is contained,
especially water, beer, or blood ‖ 특히
물[맥주, 피] 등이 들어 있는 곳에서 액체
를 빼내다

17 draw near/close LITERARY to move
closer in time or space ‖ 시간 또는 공간
적으로 더 가까이 움직이다. 다가오다. 접
근하다: *Summer vacation is drawing
near*. 여름 방학이 가까이 다가오고 있다.

18 ▶PULL VEHICLE 탈것을 끌다◀ [T]
to pull a vehicle using an animal ‖ 동물
을 이용해서 탈것을 끌다: *a carriage
drawn by six horses* 여섯 마리의 말이 끄
는 마차

draw back *phr v* [I] to move back from
something ‖ 어떤 것으로부터 뒤로 움직이
다. 뒷걸음치다. (뒤로) 물러서다: *The
crowd drew back to let the police by*. 군
중들은 경찰이 지나가도록 뒤로 물러섰다.

draw sb ↔ **into** *phr v* [T] to make
someone become involved in something
‖ 사람을 어떤 일에 연관시키다. …을 …
에 끌어들이다: *I let myself be drawn
into the argument*. 나는 그 논쟁에 말려
들었다. / *Keith refused to be drawn in
during the argument*. 케이스는 그 논쟁
중에 말려드는 것을 거부했다.

draw on *phr v* to use your money,
experiences etc. to help you do
something ‖ 어떤 일을 하는 데 도움을 주
는 돈·경험 등을 사용하다: *A good writer

draws on his or her own experience*. 좋
은 작가는 자기 자신의 경험을 이용한다.

draw up *phr v* [T] to prepare a written
document ‖ 문서를 작성하다: *We drew
up some guidelines for the new
committee*. 우리는 새 위원회의 몇 개의
지침을 문서로 작성했다.

draw² *n* **1** the act of taking a playing
card, number etc. ‖ 게임 카드·숫자 등을
뽑는 행동. 제비뽑기. 추첨: *Come on,
Doug, it's your draw*. 자, 도그, 자네 차례
야 / *the lottery draw* 복권 추첨 **2**
something or someone that a lot of
people are willing to pay to see ‖ 많은 사
람들이 가까이 보려고 하는 것이나 사람.
인기 있는 것[사람]: *The Lakers are
always a big draw*. 레이커스팀은 항상 사
람들에게 큰 인기가 있다. **3** ⇨ TIE²

draw·back /'drɔbæk/ *n* something that
can cause trouble ‖ 곤란함을 야기시킬
수 있는 것. 장애. 방해. 결점: *The big
drawback to the plan is that it takes a
long time*. 그 계획의 큰 결점은 시간이 오
래 걸린다는 것이다.

draw·bridge /'drɔbrɪdʒ/ *n* a bridge
that can be pulled up to let ships go
under it ‖ 밑으로 배가 지나갈 수 있도록
들어올릴 수 있는 다리. 도개교(跳開橋)

drawer /drɔr/ *n* a part of a piece of
furniture that slides in and out and is
used for keeping things in ‖ 밀어 넣었다
뺐다 하는, 안에 물건을 보관하는 데 사용
되는 가구류의 일부. 서랍: *The pens are
in the top drawer of my desk*. 펜은 내 책
상 맨 위 서랍에 있다.

draw·ing /'drɔ-ɪŋ/ *n* **1** a picture you
make with a pen, pencil etc. ‖ 펜·연필
등으로 그린 그림. 스케치. 데생: *She
showed us a drawing of the house*. 그녀
는 우리에게 그 집의 그림을 보여 주었다.
2 [U] the art or skill of making pictures
with a pen, pencil etc. ‖ 펜·연필 등으로
그림을 그리는 예술 또는 기술. 스케치 기
법[기술]: *I've never been good at
drawing*. 나는 그림을 잘 그려본 적이 전
혀 없다[그림 솜씨가 형편없다].

drawing board /'.. ,./ *n* **back to the
drawing board** to start working on a
plan or idea again after an idea you
have tried has failed ‖ 시도했던 생각이
실패한 후에 다시 계획이나 생각을 실행하
기 시작하다. 처음부터 다시 시작하다. 백
지로 돌리다: *They rejected our proposal,
so it's back to the drawing board*. 그들이
우리 제안을 거절해서, 처음부터 다시 시
작했다.

drawl /drɔl/ *n* [U] a way of speaking
with vowels that are longer ‖ 모음을 보

다 길게 말하는 방법. 느린 말투: *a Southern drawl* 남부 지방의 느린 말투 – **drawl** *v* [I, T]

drawn¹ /drɔn/ *v* the PAST PARTICIPLE OF DRAW ‖ draw의 과거 분사형

drawn² *adj* someone who is drawn has a thin pale face because s/he is sick or worried ‖ 아프거나 걱정을 하고 있어서 사람의 얼굴이 야위고 창백해진. 찡그린

drawn-out /ˌ. '.·/ *adj* seeming to pass very slowly ‖ 매우 천천히 지나가는 듯한. 장시간 연장된. 지루한: *a long drawn-out speech* 지루하게 질질 끄는 연설

draw·string /'drɔstrɪŋ/ *n* a string through the top of a bag, piece of clothing etc. that you can pull tight or make loose ‖ 단단히 조여 당기거나 느슨하게 풀 수 있는 가방의 꼭대기(부분)·옷 등을 두르는 줄. 가방·옷 등을 졸라매는 끈

dread¹ /drɛd/ *v* [T] to feel very worried about something ‖ 어떤 일에 대해 매우 걱정하다. 두려워하다: *Jill's really dreading her interview.* 질은 면접 보는 것을 정말 걱정하고 있다. / *I dread going to the dentist tomorrow.* 나는 내일 치과에 갈 일이 걱정이다.

dread² *n* [U] a strong fear of something that may or will happen ‖ 일어날 가능성이 있는 일에 대한 강한 공포심. 공포. 걱정

dread·ful /'drɛdfəl/ *adj* very bad ‖ 매우 나쁜. 지루한. 몹시 불쾌한[저속한]: *a dreadful movie* 저속한 영화 – **dreadfully** *adv*

dread·locks /'drɛdlɑks/ *n* [plural] a way of arranging your hair in which it hangs in lots of thick pieces that look like rope ‖ 밧줄처럼 생긴 두꺼운 머리칼을 많이 매달아 머리를 다듬는 방법. 드레드헤어

dream¹ /drim/ *n* 1 a series of thoughts, pictures, and feelings you have when you are asleep ‖ 잠잘 때 가지게 되는 일련의 생각·장면·감정. 꿈: *I had a funny dream last night.* 나는 어젯밤에 재미있는 꿈을 꾸었다. 2 **beyond your wildest dreams** better than anything you imagined or hoped for ‖ 상상한 또는 기대한 것보다 더 나은. 꿈에도 생각지 않은. 믿을 수 없을 정도로 3 **a dream come true** something that you have wanted to happen for a long time ‖ 오랫동안 일어나기를 원했던 것. 오랜 소망. 포부. 이상: *Owning this boat is a dream come true.* 이 배를 소유한 것은 나의 오랜 소망이 이루어진 것이다.

dream² *v* **dreamed** *or* **dreamt**

/drɛmt/, **dreamed** *or* **dreamt**, **dreaming** 1 [I, T] to think about something that you would like to happen ‖ 일어나기 원하는 것에 대해 생각하다. 꿈꾸다. 상상하다: *She dreamed about/of becoming a pilot.* 그녀는 비행기 조종사가 되는 꿈을 가졌다. 2 [I, T] to have a dream while you are asleep ‖ 자는 동안에 꿈을 꾸다: *I often dream that I'm falling.* 나는 자주 떨어지는 꿈을 꾼다. 3 **dream on** SPOKEN said when you think that what someone is hoping for will not happen ‖ 남이 바라고 있는 것이 일어나지 않을 거라고 생각할 때 쓰여: *You really believe we'll win? Dream on!* 너는 정말 우리가 이길 거라고 믿고 있니? 꿈 같은 이야기야!

dream sth ↔ **up** *phr v* [T] to think of a plan or idea, especially an unusual one ‖ 특히 평범하지 않은 계획 또는 구상에 대해 생각하다. 생각해 내다. 착상하다: *Who dreams up these TV commercials?* 이 텔레비전 광고들은 누가 착상을 하지?

dream³ *adj* the best you can imagine ‖ 상상할 수 있는 가장 좋은. 꿈 같은. 이상적인. 환상적인: *A Porsche is my dream car.* 포르셰는 내가 꿈꿔 온 차야.

dream·er /'drimɚ/ *n* someone who has plans that are not practical ‖ 실제적이지 않은 계획을 가진 사람. 공상[몽상]가

dream·y /'drimi/ *adj* 1 someone who is dreamy likes to imagine things ‖ 어떤 일을 상상하기 좋아하는. 꿈꾸는 2 like something in a dream, or like you are imagining something ‖ 꿈속의 일 같은, 또는 어떤 것을 상상하고 있는 것 같은. 꿈 같은. 환상[공상]적인: *a dreamy look* 꿈꾸는 듯한 표정 3 pleasant, peaceful, and relaxing ‖ 즐겁고 평온하며 느긋한: *dreamy music* 차분한 음악 – **dreamily** *adv*

drear·y /'drɪri/ *adj* dull and uninteresting ‖ 지루하고 흥미가 없는. 따분한: *a dreary afternoon of rain* 비 오는 따분한 오후 – **drearily** *adv* – **dreariness** *n* [U]

dredge /drɛdʒ/ *v* [I, T] to remove mud or sand from the bottom of a river ‖ 강바닥에서 진흙이나 모래를 제거하다. 강바닥을 긁어내다

dredge sth ↔ **up** *phr v* [T] INFORMAL 1 to start talking about something that happened a long time ago ‖ 오래 전에 일어난 것에 대해 말하기 시작하다. 캐내다. 새삼스레 생각해 내다: *Why do the papers have to dredge up that old story?* 왜 신문들은 저 옛날 이야기를 새삼스럽게 캐내야 하는 거니? 2 to pull something up from the bottom of a river ‖ 강 밑바닥에서 어떤 것을 퍼올리다

dredg·er /ˈdrɛdʒər/, **dredge** *n* a machine or ship used for removing mud or sand from the bottom of a river, lake etc. ‖ 강·호수 등의 밑바닥에서 진흙이나 모래를 제거하기 위해 사용되는 기계나 배. 준설기[선]

dregs /drɛgz/ *n* [plural] **1** small solid pieces in a liquid, that sink to the bottom ‖ 밑바닥에 가라앉는 액체 속의 작은 고체 조각. 찌꺼기: *coffee dregs* 커피 찌꺼기 **2 the dregs of society** OFFENSIVE people that you think are the least important or useful ‖ 중요성이나 유용성이 가장 적다고 생각되는 사람. 쓰레기 같은 사람. 보잘것없는 사람

drench /drɛntʃ/ *v* [T] to make something completely wet ‖ 어떤 것을 완전히 젖게 하다. …을 흠뻑 적시다: *I forgot my umbrella and got drenched.* 나는 우산을 두고 와서 비를 흠뻑 맞았다.

dress[1] /drɛs/ *v* **1** [I, T] to put clothes on someone or yourself ‖ 남에게 옷을 입히다, 또는 자신이 옷을 입다: *Hurry up and get dressed!* 서둘러서 옷 입어! / *Can you dress the kids while I make breakfast?* 내가 아침 식사 준비하는 동안 애들 옷 좀 입혀줄래요? **2** [I] to wear a particular type of clothes ‖ 특별한 종류의 옷을 입다: *Dress warmly; it's cold out.* 따뜻하게 입어라. 바깥이 춥다. / *teenagers dressed in black* 검은 옷을 입고 있는 십대들 **3 dress a wound/cut etc.** to clean and cover a wound to protect it ‖ 상처를 보호하기 위해 세척을 하고 싸다. 상처[벤곳]에 붕대를 감다

Sarah's going trick or treating dressed up as a witch.

dress down *phr v* [I] to wear clothes that are more informal than you usually wear ‖ 평상시 입는 것보다 더욱 격식 차리지 않은 옷을 입다. 약식 복장[간편한 옷]을 입다

dress up *phr v* **1** [I] to wear clothes that are more formal than you usually wear ‖ 평소에 입는 것보다 더욱 격식 차린 옷을 입다. 성장(盛裝)하다. 잘 차려입다: *Should we dress up to go to the club?* 클럽에 가려면 정장을 해야 하니? **2** [I, T **dress** sb ↔ **up**] to wear special clothes, shoes etc. for fun ‖ 재미로 특별한 옷·신발 등을 입거나 신다. 가장[분장]

하다: *She dressed up as a witch for Halloween.* 그녀는 할로윈 축제를 위해 마녀로 분장을 했다. / *old clothes for the kids to dress up in* 아이들이 분장하기 위한 낡은 옷들

USAGE NOTE dress, put on, and wear

Use **dress** to mean "put on clothes" or "wear a particular type of clothes": *David dressed quickly. / She always dresses fashionably.* If you **put on** a piece of clothing, you dress yourself in that thing: *You'd better put on your sweater before going out.* Use **wear** to mean that you have something on your body: *Is that a new shirt you're wearing?* **dress**는 "옷을 입다" 또는 "특정한 종류의 옷을 입다"의 뜻으로 쓴다: 데이비드는 빨리 옷을 입었다. / 그녀는 항상 유행에 맞게 옷을 입는다. **put on**은 옷 한 점 한 점을 입다의 뜻으로 쓴다: 외출하기 전에 스웨터를 입는 게 좋겠어. **wear**는 몸에 어떤 것을 입다[걸치다]의 뜻으로 쓴다: 네가 입고 있는 것은 새 셔츠니?

---

dress[2] *n* **1** a piece of clothing worn by a woman or girl, that covers the top of her body and some or all of her legs ‖ 상체와 다리의 일부 또는 전체를 가리는 여성이나 소녀들이 입는 옷. 여성복. 드레스: *Do you like my new dress?* 내 새 드레스 마음에 드니? —see picture at CLOTHES **2 casual/informal dress** clothes that are not formal in style ‖ 격식 차리지 않은 스타일의 옷. 평상복: *It's casual dress for dinner tonight.* 오늘 밤 저녁 식사는 평상복 차림이다. **3 evening/national etc. dress** special clothes that you wear for a particular occasion ‖ 특정한 경우를 위해 입는 특별한 옷. 이브닝드레스/민족 전통 의상

dress[3] *adj* used for formal occasions ‖ 격식 차린 경우에 사용되는. 정장[예복]의: *a dress shirt* 정장용 셔츠

dress code /ˈ. ./ *n* a standard of what you should wear for a particular situation ‖ 특정한 상황에 무엇을 입어야 하는지에 대한 기준. 복장 규정: *The company has a strict dress code.* 그 회사는 엄격한 복장 규정을 가지고 있다.

dress·er /ˈdrɛsər/ *n* ⇨ CHEST OF DRAWERS

dress·ing /ˈdrɛsɪŋ/ *n* **1** [C, U] a mixture of liquids that you can pour over food ‖ 음식에 부을 수 있는 유동 혼합물. 드레싱: *salad dressing* 샐러드 드레

싱 **2** [C, U] ⇨ STUFFING **3** a special piece of material used for covering and protecting a wound ‖ 상처를 덮거나 보호하는 데 사용되는 특별한 재료. 상처 처치 용품: *a clean dressing for the cut* 베인 데를 소독하는 처치 용품

dressing room /'.. ,./ *n* a room where an actor gets ready to act on stage, on TV etc. ‖ 배우가 무대·텔레비전 등에서 연기할 준비를 하는 방. 분장실

dress·mak·er /'drɛs,meɪkɚ/ *n* ⇨ SEAMSTRESS

dress re·hear·sal /'. .,../ *n* the last time actors practice a play, using all the clothes, objects etc. that will be used in the real performance ‖ 배우들이 실제 공연에서 사용될 모든 의상·소품 등을 사용해서 연극을 연습하는 마지막 시간. 총[본] 연습

dress sense /'. ./ *n* [U] the ability to choose clothes that make you look attractive ‖ 매력적으로 보이기 위해 옷을 고르는 능력. 멋을 부리는 센스. 복장의 감각

dress·y /'drɛsi/ *adj* suitable for formal occasions ‖ 공식 행사에 적합한. 정장을 입어야 하는. 정장용의: *a dressy skirt* 정장용의 스커트

drew /dru/ *v* the past tense of DRAW ‖ draw의 과거형

drib·ble /'drɪbəl/ *v* **1** [I] if liquid dribbles, it comes out of something in a thin irregular stream ‖ 액체가 가늘고 불규칙적으로 흘러 나오다. 액체가 똑똑 떨어지다. 줄줄 흐르다: *Ice cream dribbled from his mouth.* 아이스크림이 그의 입에서 줄줄 흘러내렸다. **2** [T] to move a ball forward by bouncing (BOUNCE) or kicking it again and again ‖ 공을 반복해서 (손으로) 되튀기거나 (발로) 차서 앞으로 움직이다. 드리블하다 **- dribble** *n*

dribs and drabs /,drɪbz ən 'dræbs/ *n* [plural] **in dribs and drabs** in small irregular amounts over a period of time ‖ 일정 기간 동안 작고 불규칙적인 양으로. 아주 소량으로. 조금씩: *News is coming in dribs and drabs.* 뉴스가 조금씩 흘러나오고 있다.

dried¹ /draɪd/ *v* the past tense and PAST PARTICIPLE of DRY ‖ dry의 과거·과거 분사형

dried² *adj* dried food or flowers have had all the water removed from them ‖ 음식이나 꽃에서 모든 물기를 제거시킨. 건조시킨

drift¹ /drɪft/ *v* [I] **1** to move very slowly through the air or on the surface of water ‖ 공기를 통해 매우 천천히 움직이

다, 또는 물의 표면에서 매우 천천히 움직이다다. 바람이나 물의 흐름에 밀려가다. 떠돌다. 표류하다: *We watched their boat drift along the shore.* 우리는 해변을 따라 표류하는 그들의 배를 지켜보았다. **2** to move or go somewhere without any plan or purpose ‖ 계획이나 목적 없이 어디엔가로 움직이거나 가다. 정처 없이 헤매다[나아가다]: *Julie stood up and drifted towards the window.* 줄리는 일어나 무작정 창문 쪽으로 향해 갔다. **3** to gradually change from being in one condition, situation etc. into another ‖ 한 조건·상황 등에서 또 다른 조건·상황으로 점점 변하다: *During the ambulance ride he drifted in and out of consciousness.* 앰뷸런스가 달리고 있는 동안 그는 의식이 들었다 나갔다 했다. **4** snow or sand that drifts is moved into a large pile by the wind ‖ 눈이나 모래가 바람에 날려 큰 더미로 쌓이다. 날려서 쌓이다

drift apart *phr v* [I] if people drift apart, they gradually stop having a relationship ‖ 사람들이 점점 교제를 끊다. 소원해지다. 멀어지다: *Over the years my college friends and I have drifted apart.* 수년 동안 내 대학 친구와 나는 점점 소원해졌다.

drift² *n* **1** a large pile of snow, sand etc. that has been blown by the wind ‖ 바람에 날려 많이 쌓인 눈·모래 등. 퇴적물: *All the roads in Lake Tahoe were blocked with snow drifts.* 타호 호수의 모든 도로는 눈이 날려 쌓여서 봉쇄되었다. **2 catch/get sb's drift** to understand the general meaning of what someone says ‖ 어떤 사람이 하는 말의 일반적인 의미를 이해하다: *I don't speak Spanish very well but I think I got her drift.* 나는 스페인어를 잘은 못하지만 그녀가 하는 말은 알아들은 것 같다. **3** a gradual change or development in a situation, people's opinion etc. ‖ 상황·여론 등의 점차적인 변화 또는 진보. 동향: *a long downward drift in the birth rate* 출산율의 장기적인 하향 추세 **4** a very slow movement ‖ 매우 느린 이동. 표류: *the drift of the continents away from each other* 서로간에 멀어져 가며 표류하는 대륙들

drift·er /'drɪftɚ/ *n* someone who is always moving to a different place or doing different jobs ‖ 항상 다른 장소로 이동하거나 다른 일을 하는 사람. 표류자. 떠돌이. 직장을 전전하는 사람

drift·wood /'drɪftwʊd/ *n* [U] wood floating in the ocean or left on the shore ‖ 대양에 떠다니거나 해안가에 버려진 목

재. 유목(流木)

drill' /drɪl/ *n* **1** a tool or machine used for making holes in something hard ‖ 딱딱한 물건에 구멍을 내는 데에 쓰이는 도구나 기계. 드릴: *an electric drill* 전기 드릴 / *a dentist's drill* 치과 의사용 드릴 **2** [C, U] a method of teaching something by making students or soldiers repeat the same lesson, exercise etc. many times ‖ 학생 또는 군인들에게 여러 차례 같은 교과·훈련 등을 반복시켜 어떤 것을 가르치는 방법. 연습. 훈련: *a spelling drill* 철자 연습 **3 fire/emergency etc. drill** an occasion when you practice what you should do during a dangerous situation ‖ 위험한 상황 동안에 하여야 할 것을 훈련하는 일. 소방/비상 훈련: *We had a tornado drill at school yesterday.* 우리는 어제 학교에서 토네이도 대비 훈련을 했다.

drill² *v* **1** [I, T] to make a hole with a drill ‖ 드릴로 구멍을 뚫다: *We'll have to drill some holes in the wall to put up the shelves.* 우리가 벽에 선반을 달기 위해서는 몇 개의 구멍을 뚫어야 할게다. / *drilling for oil in Texas* 텍사스의 석유 굴착 공사 **2** [T] to teach soldiers or students something by repeating the same exercise, lesson etc. many times ‖ 군인이나 학생들에게 동일한 훈련·학과 등을 여러 차례 반복시켜서 어떤 것을 가르치다. 훈련[연습]시키다

drill sth **into** sb *phr v* [T] to continue telling something to someone until s/he knows it very well ‖ 어떤 일을 남이 잘 알 때까지 계속 이야기하다: *Momma drilled into my head that I should never talk to strangers.* 엄마는 낯선 사람에게 절대로 말을 해서는 안 된다고 나에게 반복하여 가르쳤다.

drily /'draɪli/ *adv* ⇨ DRYLY

drink' /drɪŋk/ *n* **1** [C, U] liquid that you can drink, or an amount of liquid that you drink ‖ 마실 수 있는 액체(의 양). 음료(량): *Could I have a drink of water please?* 물 한 잔 주시겠습니까? / *food and drink* 음식과 음료 **2** an alcoholic drink ‖ 알코올 음료. 술: *Let's go find a quiet bar and have a drink.* 조용한 술집에 가서 한 잔 하자.

drink² *v* **drank, drunk, drunking 1** [I, T] to pour a liquid into your mouth and swallow it ‖ 입에 액체를 부어서 삼키다. 마시다: *What would you like to drink?* 무엇을 마시고 싶으세요? / *Charlie drinks way too much coffee.* 찰리는 커피를 끔찍스레 너무 많이 마신다. **2** [I] to drink alcohol, especially too much or too often

‖ 특히 너무 많이 또는 너무 자주 술을 마시다: *"Whiskey?" "No, thanks, I don't drink."* "위스키 어때?" "괜찮아, 난 안 마셔."

drink sth ↔ **in** *phr v* [T] to listen, look at, feel, or smell something in order to enjoy it ‖ 사물을 즐기려고 듣다[보다, 느끼다, 냄새 맡다]. …에 도취하다: *We spent the day drinking in the sights and sounds of Paris.* 우리는 파리를 보고 듣는 데에 도취하여 하루를 보냈다.

drink to sth *phr v* [T] to wish someone success, good health etc. before having an alcoholic drink ‖ 술을 마시기 전에 어떤 사람의 성공·건강 등을 기원하다. 건배하다. 축배를 들다: *Let's all drink to their happiness as a married couple!* 결혼한 한 쌍의 행복을 위해 우리 모두 건배합시다.

drink·er /'drɪŋkɚ/ *n* someone who often drinks alcohol ‖ 술을 자주 마시는 사람. 술꾼: *Greg's always been a heavy drinker.* (=has always drunk a lot) 그레그는 항상 술고래였다.

drink·ing foun·tain /'.. ˌ../ *n* a piece of equipment in a public place that produces a stream of water for you to drink from ‖ 사람이 마시게 물줄기를 뿜어내는 공공장소에 있는 장치. 음용 분수

drinking prob·lem /'.. ˌ../ *n* [singular] someone who has a drinking problem drinks too much alcohol ‖ 술을 너무 많이 마셔서 생기는 문제. 음주 문제

drip' /drɪp/ *v* **-pped, -pping 1** [I] to produce small drops of liquid ‖ 액체의 작은 방울들을 만들다. 방울져 떨어지다: *Did you turn off the faucet? It sounds like it's still dripping.* 수도꼭지를 잠갔니? 아직 물방울이 떨어지는 것 같은 소리가 난다. / *a brush dripping with paint* 페인트가 뚝뚝 떨어지는 솔 **2** [I, T] to fall in the shape of a small drop, or have something falling in small drops ‖ 작은 방울 형태로 뚝뚝 떨어지다, 또는 어떤 것을 작은 방울 형태로 뚝뚝 떨어지게 하다: *Sweat was dripping off his arms.* 땀이 그의 팔에서 방울져 떨어지고 있었다. / *Her finger was dripping blood.* 그의 손가락에서 피가 뚝뚝 떨어지고 있었다.

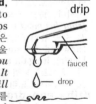
drip

faucet

drop

The faucet is dripping.

drip² *n* **1** one of the small drops of liquid that falls from something ‖ 어떤 것에서 떨어지는 작은 한 방울 **2** [singular,

U] the action or sound of a liquid falling in small drops ‖ 작게 방울져 떨어지는 액체의 움직임이나 소리: *the drip of rain from the roof* 지붕에서 나는 빗방울 떨어지는 소리 **3** INFORMAL someone who is boring and annoying ‖ 지루하고 귀찮은 사람. 따분한 사람

drip-dry /ˌ. ˈ./ *adj* clothes that are drip-dry do not need to be IRONed ‖ 옷이 다림질할 필요가 없는

drive¹ /draɪv/ *v* **drove, driven, driving 1** [I, T] to make a car, bus etc. move and control where it goes ‖ 자동차·버스 등을 움직여 가는 곳을 조정하다. 운전하다: *I can't drive.* 나는 운전을 못 한다. / *Farrah drives a red Porsche.* 파라는 빨간색 포르셰를 몰고 다닌다. **2** [I, T] to travel in a car or take someone somewhere by car ‖ 차로 여행하다, 또는 자동차로 사람을 어딘가에 데려다 주다. 차로 가다. 차로 데려가다: *We're driving up/down to Washington this weekend.* 우리는 이번 주말에 자동차로 워싱턴으로 올라[내려]간다. / *Would you mind driving me to the airport?* 공항까지 저를 태워다 주시겠습니까? **3** [T] to make people, animals, or an activity move somewhere ‖ 사람[동물, 활동]을 어딘가로 움직이게 하다. 몰(아내)다: *Our party was driven indoors by the heavy rain.* 폭우로 인해 우리 파티는 집안으로 옮겨졌다. / *The gang activity drove business away from the town.* 갱단의 활동으로 사업은 그 시로부터 쫓겨났다. **4** [T] to strongly influence someone to do something ‖ 어떤 일을 하도록 남에게 강력한 영향을 주다: *Driven by jealousy, Mel decided to read his girlfriend's diary.* 질투한 나머지 멜은 여자 친구의 일기를 읽어 보기로 작정했다. **5 drive sb crazy/nuts/insane etc.** to make someone feel very annoyed and angry ‖ 남을 매우 성가시고 화나게 하다. 미치게[성나게] 하다: *The kids are driving me crazy!* 아이들이 나를 미치게 해! **6 drive sb up the wall** SPOKEN to make someone extremely annoyed ‖ 사람을 극도로 귀찮게 하다: *All the barking is driving me up the wall!* 하도 짖어대어서 내 신경을 곤두서게 하는군! **7** [T] to hit something very hard ‖ 사물을 매우 세게 때리다. 박다: *driving a nail into the wall* 못을 벽에 두드려 박기

drive sb ↔ **away** *phr v* [T] to behave in a way that makes someone want to leave you ‖ 남이 자기를 떠나고 싶게 만들게 행동하다. 쫓아버리다: *If you keep on drinking I guarantee you'll drive her away.* 네가 계속 술을 먹으면 단언하건대 너는 그녀를 쫓아버리게 될 것이다.

drive off *phr v* **1** [I] if a driver or a car drives off then he, she, or it leaves ‖ 운전사 또는 차가 떠나다 **2** [I,T **drive** sb ↔ **off**] to force someone or something to go away from you ‖ 사람이나 사물에게 떠나도록 강요하다. 쫓아버리다: *The army used tear gas to drive off the rioting crowds.* 군대는 폭도들을 해산시키려고 최루 가스를 사용했다.

drive sth ↔ **up** *phr v* [T] to make prices, costs etc. increase ‖ 가격·비용 등을 인상시키다: *The price of gasoline was driven up by at least 5% during the Gulf War.* 휘발유 가격은 걸프전 동안에 최소한 5% 인상되었다.

drive² *n* **1** a trip in a car ‖ 자동차 여행: *Let's go for a drive.* 드라이브 가자. / *Our house is just a twenty minute drive from the city.* 우리 집은 자동차로 시내에서 꼭 20분 걸린다. **2** a strong natural need, such as hunger, that people or animals must satisfy ‖ 사람이나 동물이 충족해야 하는 배고픔 등의 강렬한 본능적 욕구. 충동: *the male sex drive* 남성의 성적 충동 **3** a planned effort by an organization to achieve a particular result ‖ 특정한 결과를 달성하려는 조직의 계획된 노력. 운동: *an economy/efficiency drive* 절약[능률] 운동 **4** [U] a determination to succeed ‖ 성공하려는 결의. 과단성. 투지: *I've never met anyone who has as much drive as he has.* 그 사람만큼 투지가 넘치는 사람은 만나본 적이 없다 **5** the power from an engine that makes the wheels of a car, bus etc. turn ‖ 차·버스 등의 바퀴를 회전시키는 엔진의 힘. 구동. 전동(傳動): *a four-wheel drive pickup* 4륜 구동 픽업 [소형 트럭]

drive-by /ˈ. ./ *adj* **drive-by shooting/killing** the act of shooting someone from a moving car ‖ 주행 중인 차에서 사람을 쏘는 행위. 주행 중인 차에서의 총격

drive-in¹ /ˈ. ./ *n* a place where you can watch movies outdoors while sitting in your car ‖ 자동차에 앉은 채로 야외에서 영화를 관람할 수 있는 장소. 드라이브인

drive-in² *adj* **drive-in restaurant/ bank/movie** a restaurant etc. where you stay in your car to be served ‖ 차 안에 타고 있는 채로 서비스를 받을 수 있는 식당 등. 드라이브인 식당/은행/ 영화관

driv·el /ˈdrɪvəl/ *n* [U] something written or said that is silly or does not mean anything ‖ 어리석거나 아무 뜻도 없이 쓰거나 말한 것. 쓸데없는 말. 허튼 소리: *Walter was talking complete drivel.* 월터는 전연 실없는 소리를 지껄이고 있었다.

driv·en /'drɪvən/ the PAST PARTICIPLE of DRIVE ‖ drive의 과거 분사형

driv·er /'draɪvɚ/ *n* someone who drives ‖ 운전하는 사람. 운전자

driver's li·cense /'.. ,../ *n* a official card with your name, picture etc. on it that says you are legally allowed to drive ‖ 법적으로 운전을 허가한다고 기록된 성명·사진 등이 있는 공식 카드. 운전면허증

drive-through /'. ./ *adj* a drive-through restaurant, bank etc. can be used without getting out of your car ‖ 식당·은행 등이 차에서 내리지 않고 이용할 수 있는: *We ordered food at the drive-through window.* 우리는 (차에 탄 채 서비스를 받는) 드라이브 스루 창구에서 음식을 주문했다.

drive·way /'draɪvweɪ/ *n* the road or area for cars between a house and the street ‖ 집과 거리 사이에 있는 차량용 도로나 구역. 사유(私有) 차도 —see picture on page 945

driz·zle¹ /'drɪzəl/ *n* [singular, U] weather that is a combination of mist and light rain ‖ 안개와 가랑비가 결합된 날씨. 이슬비 —see usage note at WEATHER

drizzle² *v* **it drizzles** if it drizzles, mist and light rain come out of the sky ‖ 하늘에서 안개와 가랑비가 내리다. 이슬비가 내리다: *It started to drizzle.* 이슬비가 내리기 시작했다.

droll /droʊl/ *adj* OLD-FASHIONED unusual and slightly funny ‖ 이상하고 약간 재미있는. 우스꽝스러운

drone¹ /droʊn/ *v* [I] to make a continuous low noise ‖ 계속적인 낮은 소음을 내다. 윙윙거리다: *An airplane droned overhead.* 비행기가 머리 위에서 윙윙거렸다.

drone on *phr v* [I] to talk in a boring way for a long time ‖ 장시간 지겹게 말하다. 단조롭게 이야기하다: *The Principal droned on about his plans for our school.* 교장은 우리 학교를 위한 그의 계획에 대해 단조롭게 계속 말했다.

drone² *n* a low continuous noise ‖ 계속되는 낮은 소음. 윙윙 소리: *the drone of the lawnmower* 잔디 깎는 기계의 윙윙 소리

drool /drul/ *v* [I] **1** to have SALIVA (=the liquid in your mouth) flow from your mouth ‖ 입에서 침을 흘리다. 군침을 흘리다: *At the sight of food the dog began to drool.* 음식물을 보고 개는 군침을 흘리기 시작했다. **2** to show in a silly way that you like someone or something a lot ‖ 분별없이 사람이나 사물을 몹시 좋아하는 태도를 드러내다. 열광하다: *Sarah was drooling over the lead singer through the whole concert!* 사라는 콘서트 내내 리드 싱어에게 그저 열광하고 있었어!

droop /drup/ *v* [I] to hang or bend down ‖ 아래로 축 늘어지거나 구부러지다. 수그러지다. 시들다: *Can you water the plants – they're starting to droop.* 나무에 물 좀 줄래. 시들기 시작하고 있어.

drop¹ /drɑp/ *v* **-pped, -pping**
1 ▶LET GO 놓다◀ [T] to suddenly or accidentally let go of something you are holding or carrying, so that it falls ‖ 갖고 있거나 운반하는 것을 갑자기 또는 우연히 놓아 떨어뜨리다: *One of the waiters tripped and dropped a tray full of food.* 웨이터 중 한 명이 발을 헛디뎌서 음식이 가득 담긴 쟁반을 떨어뜨렸다.
2 ▶FALL 떨어지다◀ [I] to fall ‖ 떨어지다: *The bottle rolled off the table and dropped onto the floor.* 병이 테이블에서 굴러 마루 위에 떨어졌다. / *He dropped into his chair with a sigh.* 그는 한숨을 쉬면서 의자에 털썩 앉았다.
3 ▶TAKE IN A CAR 차에 태우다◀ [T] also **drop off** to take someone or something to a place in a car, when you are going on to somewhere else ‖ 다른 곳에 가면서 사람이나 사물을 차로 어떤 장소에 데려다 주다. 내려주다: *I'll drop you at the corner, okay?* 모퉁이에서 너를 내려줄게. 괜찮지? / *She drops the kids off at school on her way to work.* 그녀는 직장에 가는 길에 학교 앞에 아이들을 내려준다.
4 drop by/in to visit someone when you have not arranged to come at a particular time ‖ 특정한 시간에 가기로 정하지 않고 남을 방문하다. 잠깐 들르다: *Doris and Ed dropped by on Saturday.* 도리스와 에드가 토요일에 불쑥 방문했다.
5 ▶DECREASE 줄다◀ [I] to decrease to a lower level or amount ‖ 낮은 수준이나 양으로 줄다. 내리다. 떨어지다: *The price of wheat dropped steadily during the late 1920s.* 밀의 가격이 1920년대 후반에 꾸준히 하락했다.
6 ▶STOP DOING STH 일하는 것을 멈추다◀ [T] to stop doing something or stop planning to do something ‖ 무엇을 하거나 하려는 계획을 중단하다. 중지하다: *We've dropped the idea of going by*

plane. 우리는 비행기로 가는 생각을 접었다. / *At the sound of the alarm, the men dropped everything* (=stopped everything they were doing) *and ran for safety.* 경보 소리에 사람들은 하던 일을 모두 멈추고 안전을 위해 도망쳤다. / *I wasn't doing very well, so I decided to drop French.* (=stop studying French) 나는 그다지 잘 하지를 못해서 불어 공부를 중단하기로 했다.

7 ▶STOP INCLUDING 포함시키지 않다◀ [T] to decide not to include someone or something ‖ 사람이나 사물을 포함하지 않기로 결정하다. 빼다. 제명하다: *Morris has been dropped from the team.* 모리스는 그 팀에서 제명되었다.

8 ▶STOP TALKING 말을 그만두다◀ [T] to stop talking about something, especially because it is upsetting someone ‖ 특히 남의 기분을 상하게 하므로 무엇에 대해 말하는 것을 중지하다: *She didn't understand, so I let it drop.* 그녀가 이해하지 못해서 나는 그만두었다. / *Drop it, man, it's just a rumor.* 그만 둬, 이 사람아. 그것은 소문일 뿐이야.

9 ▶STOP RELATIONSHIP 관계를 끊다◀ [T] to stop having a relationship with someone, especially suddenly ‖ 특히 갑자기 남과의 관계를 끊다. 절교하다. 헤어지다: *Marian has dropped all her old friends since she started college.* 마리안은 대학 생활을 시작한 이래 오랜 친구들과 절교했다.

10 drop dead a) to die suddenly and unexpectedly ‖ 갑자기·뜻밖에 죽다. 급사하다 **b)** SPOKEN used in order to tell someone to be quiet, stop annoying you etc., in an angry way ‖ 남에게 화가 나서 조용히 하고 귀찮게 하지 말라는 등의 말을 하는 데에 쓰여. 입 닥쳐

11 work/run etc. until you drop INFORMAL to do something until you are extremely tired ‖ 지칠 때까지 일을 하다

12 drop sb a line INFORMAL to write to someone ‖ 남에게 편지를 간단히 쓰다: *Drop us a line sometime.* 나중에 우리에게 간단한 편지를 보내라.

13 drop a hint to say something in a way that is not direct ‖ 직접적이 아닌 방식으로 어떤 것을 말하다. 넌지시 힌트를 주다: *I've dropped a few hints about what I want for my birthday.* 내 생일에 내가 무엇을 원하는지에 관해 몇 가지 힌트를 주었다.

14 be dropping like flies INFORMAL used in order to say that a lot of people are getting sick with the same illness ‖ 같은 질병으로 많은 사람들이 아픈 것을 말하는

데에 쓰여 —see also **drop/lower your eyes** (EYE¹)

drop off *phr v* [I] **1** to begin to sleep ‖ 잠들기 시작하다. 잠들다: *The baby dropped off to sleep in the car.* 아기는 꾸벅꾸벅 졸다가 차 안에서 잠들었다. **2** to become less in level or amount ‖ 수준이나 양이 줄어들다. 쇠퇴하다: *The demand for leaded fuel dropped off in the late 1970s.* 유연 휘발유에 대한 수요는 1970년대 후반에 들어 줄어들었다

drop out *phr v* [I] to stop going to school or stop an activity before you have finished it ‖ 끝내기 전에 학교에 다니는 것을 중지하거나 활동을 중지하다. 중퇴하다. 낙오하다: *teenagers dropping out of high school* 고등학교를 중퇴하는 10대들 / *The injury forced him to drop out of the race.* 그 상처로 인해서 그는 경주에서 낙오했다.

drop² n 1 a very small amount of liquid that falls in a round shape ‖ 둥근 형태로 떨어지는 소량의 액체. 한 방울: *Big drops of rain splashed on the sidewalk.* 큰 빗방울이 인도 위에서 튀겼다. / *a tear drop* 눈물 한 방울 —see picture at DRIP¹ **2** a small amount of a liquid ‖ 액체의 소량: *Add a couple drops of lemon juice.* 레몬 주스 두세 방울을 넣어라. **3** [singular] a distance from something down to the ground ‖ 사물에서 지상까지의 거리. 낙하 거리. 낙차: *It's a twenty-five foot drop from this cliff.* 이 절벽에서 낙하 거리는 25피트이다. **4** [singular] a decrease in the amount, level, or number of something ‖ 사물의 양[수준, 숫자]의 감소. 저하: *a drop from 72% to 34%* 72%에서 34%로의 감소 **5 a drop in the ocean/bucket** an amount of something that is too small to have any effect ‖ 어떤 영향력을 가지기에는 너무나 적은 사물의 양. 극소량 —see also DROPS

drop·out /'drɑp-aʊt/ *n* someone who leaves school or college without finishing it ‖ 학교나 대학을 끝마치지 않고 떠난 사람. 탈락자. 중퇴자

drop·per /'drɑpɚ/ *n* a short glass tube with a hollow rubber part at one end, used for measuring liquid in drops ‖ 속이 빈 고무 부분이 한 쪽 끝에 달려, 방울로 액체를 측정하는 데에 쓰는 짧은 유리관. 스포이트

drop·pings /'drɑpɪŋz/ *n* [plural] solid waste from animals or birds ‖ 동물이나 새의 고형 배설물. 동물의 똥

drops /drɑps/ *n* [plural] **eye/ear/nose drops** medicine that you put in your eye etc. in drops ‖ 눈 등에 방울로 투입하는

약. 점안약/점이약/점비약

drought /draʊt/ n a long period of dry weather when there is not enough water ‖ 충분한 물이 없는, 장기간에 걸친 건조한 날씨. 가뭄: *In the sixth year of drought more than half the corn crop was lost.* 6년째 가뭄으로 옥수수 수확량의 반 이상을 잃었다. —see usage note at WEATHER

drove[1] /droʊv/ the past tense of DRIVE ‖ drive의 과거형

drove[2] n a large group of animals or people that move or are moved together ‖ 함께 움직이(게 하)는 동물이나 사람의 큰 집단. 가축 떼. 군중: *Tourists come in droves to see the White House.* 백악관을 보기 위해 관광객들이 무리 지어 들어온다. / *a drove of cattle* 소 떼

drown /draʊn/ v 1 [I, T] to die by being under water too long, or to kill someone in this way ‖ 물속에 너무 오래 있어서 죽거나 죽게 하다. 익사하다[시키다]: *Two surfers drowned near Santa Cruz yesterday.* 두 명의 서핑하던 사람들이 어제 산타크루스 근처에서 익사했다. / *Five people were drowned in the flood.* 홍수 때문에 다섯 명이 익사했다. 2 [T] also **drown out** to prevent a sound from being heard by making a louder noise ‖ 더 큰 소리를 내서 (다른)소리를 들리지 않게 하다. 소리를 잠재우다: *We put on some music to drown out their yelling.* 우리는 그들의 고함 소리를 듣지 않으려고 약간의 음악을 틀었다. 3 [T] to completely cover something with liquid ‖ 어떤 것을 액체로 완전히 덮다: *Dad always drowns his pancakes in/with maple syrup.* 아빠는 항상 팬케이크를 메이플 시럽[단풍 당밀]으로 완전히 뒤덮는다. 4 **drown your sorrows** to drink a lot of alcohol in order to forget your problems ‖ 문제를 잊기 위해 많은 술을 마시다. 술로 슬픔을 달래다

drown·ing /ˈdraʊnɪŋ/ n [C, U] death caused by staying under water too long ‖ 물속에 너무 오래 있음으로 해서 유발되는 죽음. 익사: *a fear of drowning* 익사에 대한 공포 / *accidental drowning* 불의의 익사

drows·y /ˈdraʊzi/ adj tired and almost asleep ‖ 피곤하여 거의 졸린. 졸리는. 꾸벅꾸벅 조는: *The doctor said the pills might make me feel drowsy.* 의사는 그 약이 졸음을 유발할 수 있다고 했다. – **drowsiness** n [U]

drudge /drʌdʒ/ n someone who does difficult boring work ‖ 어렵고 지루한 일을 하는 사람. 기계적으로 일하는 사람 –

drudge v [I]

drudg·er·y /ˈdrʌdʒəri/ n [U] difficult boring work ‖ 어렵고 지루한 일. 고역

drug[1] /drʌg/ n 1 an illegal substance that people smoke, INJECT etc. for pleasure ‖ 사람들이 쾌락을 위해 피우고, 주사하는 등의 불법 물질. 마약: *Bill was accused of taking/using drugs.* 빌은 마약 복용 혐의로 기소되었다. / *My mom thinks I'm on drugs.* (=using drugs regularly) 우리 엄마는 내가 마약을 상용한다고 생각한다. / *Dave's been doing drugs* (=using drugs regularly) *since he was thirteen.* 데이브는 열세 살 때부터 마약을 사용해 왔다. / *the problem of drug abuse* (=the use of illegal drugs) 마약 남용의 문제 / *drug dealing* (=selling illegal drugs) *in the neighborhood* 인근에서의 마약 거래 / *He was sent to prison for selling hard drugs.* (=dangerous illegal drugs such as HEROIN and COCAINE) 그는 중독성이 강한 마약 판매 혐의로 수감되었다. 2 a medicine or a substance for making medicines ‖ 약이나 약을 만드는 물질: *She's on some kind of drug for her depression.* 그녀는 우울증 때문에 약물 치료를 받고 있다.

drug[2] v -gged, -gging [T] to put drugs into someone's body, usually to prevent him/her from moving or from feeling pain ‖ 보통 움직이거나 고통을 느끼지 못하게 하기 위해 남의 몸에 약물을 주입하다. …을 마약으로 마비시키다: *A man has been arrested for drugging and strangling 14 victims.* 14명의 피해자들에게 마약을 주입하여 교살한 혐의로 한 남자가 체포되었다.

drug·store /ˈdrʌgstɔr/ n a store where you can buy medicines, beauty products etc.; PHARMACY ‖ 약·화장품 등을 살 수 있는 가게. 드러그스토어; 유 pharmacy

drum[1] /drʌm/ n 1 a musical instrument made of skin stretched over a circular frame, which you play by hitting it with your hand or a stick ‖ 원형의 틀 위로 가죽을 팽팽히 펴 만든, 손이나 막대로 쳐서 연주하는 악기. 북. 드럼: *Fred plays guitar and I play the drums.* (=a set of drums) 프레드는 기타를, 나는 드럼을 연주한다. 2 something that looks like a drum, especially part of a machine ‖ 북처럼 생긴, 특히 기계의 한 부분. (기계의) 몸통. 드럼 3 a large round container for storing liquids such as oil, chemicals etc. ‖ 석유·화학 약품 등의 액체를 저장하는 데에 쓰는 크고 둥근 용기. 드럼통

drum[2] v -mmed, -mming [I, T] to hit the surface of something again and again in a way that sounds like drums ‖ 북소리처럼 들리도록 어떤 표면을 반복해서 치다. …을 북을 치듯 둥둥[쿵쿵] 울리다. …을 율동적으로 치다: *He drummed his fingers on the table.* 그는 손가락으로 테이블을 탁탁 쳤다. / *rain drumming on the roof* 지붕 위에 툭툭 떨어지는 빗물

drum sth **into** sb *phr v* [T] to say something to someone so often that s/he cannot forget it ‖ 남에게 무엇을 잊을 수 없도록 자주 말하다. 귀가 따갑도록 말하다. 거의 세뇌시키다: *Patriotism was drummed into us at school.* 학교에서 애국심에 대해 귀에 못이 박히도록 들었다.

drum sb **out** of sth *phr v* [T] to force someone to leave an organization ‖ 남을 강제로 조직에서 떠나도록 하다. …을 …에서 내쫓다[추방하다]: *soldiers drummed out of the military* 군대에서 축출당한 군인들

drum sth ↔ **up** *phr v* [T] to obtain help, money etc. by asking a lot of people ‖ 많은 사람들에게 부탁하여 도움·돈 등을 얻다. 모으다. 획득하다: *a group drumming up support for the "Save the Whales" campaign* "고래를 살리자"라는 캠페인에 대한 지지를 호소하는 단체

drum·mer /ˈdrʌmɚ/ *n* someone who plays the drums ‖ 북을 치는 사람. 드러머

drum·stick /ˈdrʌmˌstɪk/ *n* **1** the leg of a chicken, TURKEY etc., cooked as food ‖ 음식으로 요리한 닭·칠면조 등의 다리 **2** a stick that you use to hit a drum ‖ 북을 치는 데에 쓰는 막대. 북채

drunk¹ /drʌŋk/ *adj* unable to control your behavior, speech etc. because you have drunk too much alcohol ‖ 술을 너무 많이 마셔서 행동·말 등을 통제할 수 없는. 술 취한: *We got totally drunk at Sue's party.* 우리는 수의 파티에서 완전히 취했다.

drunk² the PAST PARTICIPLE of DRINK ‖ drink의 과거 분사형

drunk³, drunk·ard /ˈdrʌŋkɚd/ *n* DISAPPROVING someone who is drunk or often gets drunk ‖ 술 취해 있거나 자주 술에 취하는 사람. 술고래

drunk·en /ˈdrʌŋkən/ *adj* **1** drunk ‖ 술(에) 취한: *a drunken crowd* 술 취한 군중 **2** resulting from or related to drinking too much alcohol ‖ 지나친 음주에 기인되거나 그와 관련된. 취중의. 술에 취한: *drunken shouting* 술김에 고래고래 소리 지르는 것 **– drunkenness** *n* [U] **– drunkenly** *adv*

dry¹ /draɪ/ *adj* **1** having no water or other liquid inside or on the surface; not wet ‖ 안 또는 표면에 물이나 다른 액체가 없는; 젖지 않은. 마른. 건조한: *Can you check and see if the laundry's dry yet?* 세탁물이 벌써 말랐는지 봐 주겠니? / *dry dusty ground* 건조하고 먼지투성이인 땅[바닥] **2** dry weather does not have much rain or MOISTURE ‖ 날씨가 비가 많이 오지 않거나 습기가 적은. 건조한: *The weather tomorrow will be cold, dry, and sunny.* 내일 날씨는 춥고 건조하며 맑을 예정입니다. / *March was a really dry month.* 3월은 정말 건조했다. **3** if your mouth, throat, or skin is dry, it does not have enough of the natural liquid that is usually in it ‖ 입[목구멍, 피부]이 평소만큼의 자연적인 물기가 없는. 마른. 건조한: *Do you have any lotion? My skin's really dry.* 로션 있니? 내 피부가 정말 건조하네. **4 dry wine/champagne etc.** wine etc. that is not sweet ‖ 포도주 등이 달지 않은. 담백한. 달지 않은 포도주/샴페인: *a glass of dry white wine* 담백한 백포도주 한 잔 **5** humor or a voice that is dry says funny things in a serious way ‖ 유머나 목소리 등이 재미있는 이야기를 심각하게 하는. 시치미 떼고[천연덕스럽게] 하는

dry² *v* **dried, dried, drying** [I, T] to become dry, or to make something do this ‖ 마르거나 무엇을 마르게 하다. 건조하다[시키다]: *It'll only take me a few minutes to dry my hair.* 머리 말리는 데에 몇 분밖에 안 걸릴 거야.

dry off *phr v* [I, T] to become dry, or to make the surface of something dry ‖ 건조해지거나 무엇의 표면을 건조시키다: *The kids played in the ocean and then dried off in the sun.* 아이들은 바다에서 놀다가 햇볕에 몸을 말렸다.

dry out *phr v* [I,T **dry** sth ↔ **out**] to dry completely, or to dry something completely ‖ 완전히 마르거나 무엇을 완전히 마르게 하다: *Keep the dough covered so that it doesn't dry out.* 밀가루 반죽이 마르지 않도록 덮어 놓아라.

dry up *phr v* **1** [I, T] a river, lake, or area of land that dries up has no more water in it ‖ 강[호수, 토지]에 더 이상 물이 없다. 바싹 마르다: *During the drought all the reservoirs dried up.* 가뭄 동안 모든 저수지가 바싹 말라 버렸다. **2** [I] if a supply of something dries up, there is no more of it ‖ 사물의 공급이 더 이상 없다. 바닥나다: *Our research project was canceled when the money dried up.* 자금이 바닥나자 우리의 연구 프로젝트가 취소되었다.

dry clean /ˈ. ./ *v* [T] to clean clothes with chemicals instead of water ‖ 물 대

신 화학 제품으로 옷을 세탁하다. 드라이 클리닝하다

dry clean·ers /ˌ '..ˌ '. ˌ../ *n* a place where you take clothes to be DRY CLEANed ‖ 옷을 드라이클리닝하러 가져가는 곳. 드라이클리닝점

dry·er /'draɪə/ *n* a machine that dries things, especially clothes or hair ‖ 특히 옷이나 머리털을 말리는 기계. 건조기. 드라이어

dry goods /'../ *n* [plural] things that are made from cloth, such as clothes, sheets, and curtains ‖ 옷·시트·커튼 등의 천으로 만든 물건. 직물류

dry ice /ˌ '.ˌ / *n* [U] CARBON DIOXIDE in a solid state, often used for keeping food and other things cold ‖ 종종 음식 및 다른 것들을 차게 유지하는 데에 쓰는 고체 상태의 이산화탄소. 드라이 아이스

dry·ly /'draɪli/ *adv* speaking in a serious way, although you are actually joking ‖ 실제로 농담을 하고 있지만 진지하게 말하여. 무미건조하게

dry run /ˌ '.ˌ / *n* an occasion when you practice for an important event ‖ 중요한 행사를 위해 연습하는 경우. 예행 연습

DSL *n* digital subscriber line; a telephone line that has special equipment which allows it to receive information from the Internet, or send information at very high speeds ‖ digital subscriber line(디지털 인터넷 가입자 회선)의 약어; 정보를 최고속으로 인터넷으로부터 받거나 보낼 수 있게 하는 특수 장비가 부착된 전화선.

du·al /'duəl/ *adj* having two of something, or two parts ‖ 두 가지나 두 부분을 가진. 이중의: *My wife has dual nationality; her parents are Brazilian but she was born in the States.* 내 아내는 이중 국적을 가지고 있다. 그녀의 부모님은 브라질 사람이지만 그녀는 미국에서 태어났다.

dub /dʌb/ *v* **-bbed, -bbing** [T] **1** to replace the original sound recording of a film, television show etc. with another sound recording ‖ 영화·텔레비전 쇼 등에 원래 녹음되어 있는 소리를 다른 소리로 녹음하여 대체하다. 더빙하다. 음향 효과를 넣다[입히다]: *They're showing an Italian movie that's been dubbed into English.* 그들은 영어로 더빙된 이탈리아 영화를 보여주고 있다. **2** to give someone or something a humorous name that describes his, her, or its character ‖ 사람이나 사물의 특성을 묘사하는 재미있는 이름을 붙이다. …에게 …이라는 별명을 붙이다: *We dubbed our star quarterback*

"The King." 우리는 유명한 쿼터백에게 "왕"이라는 별명을 붙였다.

du·bi·ous /'dubiəs/ *adj* **1 be dubious** to have doubts about whether something is good, true etc. ‖ 사물이 좋은지·사실인지 등에 대해 의심하다. 의심스럽다. 미덥지 않다: *Your father and I are a little dubious about your getting married so young.* 네 아버지와 나는 네가 너무 어린 나이에 결혼하는 것에 대해 좀 불안하다. **2** not seeming honest, safe, valuable etc. ‖ 정직하고, 안전하고, 가치가 있는 것 같지 않은. 수상한: *a dubious partnership* 수상한 협력 관계

duch·ess /'dʌtʃɪs/ *n* a woman with the highest social rank below a PRINCESS, or the wife of a DUKE ‖ 공주 바로 아래의 최고의 사회적 지위를 지닌 여성이나 공작의 아내. 옹주. 공작 부인

duck¹ /dʌk/ *n* **1** a common water bird with short legs and a wide beak that is used for its meat, eggs, and soft feathers ‖ 고기·알·부드러운 깃털을 사용하기 위해 기르는 다리가 짧고 부리가 넓은 흔한 물새. 오리 **2** [U] the meat from this bird ‖ 오리 고기: *roast duck* 구운 오리 고기

duck² *v* **1** [I, T] to lower your body or head very quickly, especially to avoid being hit or seen ‖ 특히 구타나 보이는 것을 피하기 위해 재빨리 몸이나 머리를 낮추다. 머리·몸 등을 휙 숙이다: *She had to duck her head to get through the doorway.* 출입구를 통과하기 위해 그녀는 머리를 재빨리 숙여야 했다. **2** [T] INFORMAL to avoid something that is difficult or unpleasant ‖ 어렵거나 불쾌한 것을 피하다: *His campaign speech ducked all the major issues.* 그의 선거 운동 연설은 모든 주요한 주제들을 피해갔다. **3** [T] to push someone or something under water ‖ 사람이나 물건을 물속으로 밀어 넣다. …을 물속으로 처박다: *Doug ducked his head in the stream to cool off.* 더그는 머리를 식히기 위해 개울 물속에 처박았다.

duck·ling /'dʌklɪŋ/ *n* a young duck ‖ 새끼 오리

duct /dʌkt/ *n* **1** a pipe or tube in a building that liquid, air, electric cables etc. go through ‖ 액체·기체·전력선 등이 통과하는 건물 내의 파이프나 관. (물·가스 등의) 도관. 덕트 **2** a thin narrow tube inside your body, a plant etc. that liquid, air etc. goes through ‖ 액체·기체 등이 통과하는 신체·식물 등 내부의 얇고 긴 관. 도관: *a tear duct* 눈물관

dud /dʌd/ *adj* INFORMAL not working or

useless ‖ 작동하지 않거나 쓸모없는. 가짜의. 가치 없는: *a couple of dud batteries* 몇 개의 쓸모없는 배터리 – **dud** *n* —see also DUDS

dude /dud/ *n* SLANG used when talking to a man or a group of people, male or female ‖ 한 사람[일단의 사람들, 남성, 여성]에게 말을 걸 때 쓰여. 이봐. 친구: *Hey, dudes, how's it going?* 이봐, 요즘 어떻게 지내?

dude ranch /'. ./ *n* a vacation place where you can ride horses and live like a COWBOY ‖ 카우보이처럼 말을 타고 생활할 수 있는 휴가지. 관광용 목장

duds /dʌdz/ *n* [plural] HUMOROUS clothes ‖ 옷

due¹ /du/ *adj* **1 be due** to be expected to happen or arrive at a particular time ‖ 특정 시간에 발생하거나 도착하리라고 예상되다. …할 예정이다. …하기로 되어 있다: *The flight from Chicago is due at 7:48 p.m.* 시카고발 비행기가 오후 7시 48분에 도착할 예정이다 / *My library books are due back tomorrow.* 도서관 책은 내일 반납하기로 되어 있다. / *The movie isn't due to start until 10:30.* 영화는 10시 30분이 되기까지는 시작하지 않을 것이다. **2 due to** because of ‖ …때문에: *Our bus was late due to heavy traffic.* 교통 체증 때문에 우리 버스가 늦었다. / *His success is due to hard work.* 그의 성공은 열심히 일한 덕택이다. **3** needing to be paid ‖ 지불될 필요가 있는. 마땅히 지불되어야 할: *The first installment of $250 is now due.* 250달러 중 첫 번째 할부금을 지금 내야 한다. **4** deserved by someone or owed to someone ‖ 누군가가 받을 만한 또는 누군가에게 빚진. 마땅히 치러져야 할. 주어져야 할: *He never got the recognition he was due for his help.* 그는 도와준 것에 대해 마땅히 받아야 할 인정을 받지 못했다. / *Much of the credit is due to our backup team.* 우리를 후원한 팀에게 많은 공적이 돌아가야 한다. **5 in due course/time** at a more suitable time in the future ‖ 미래의 보다 적당한 시기에. 머지않아. 때가 되면: *The committee will answer your complaints in due course.* 그 위원회는 당신의 불만 사항에 대해 머지않아 회신할 것입니다.

due² *adv* **due north/south/east/west** directly or exactly north etc. ‖ 똑바로 또는 정확히 북쪽 등. 정북/정남/정동/정서

due³ *n* **give sb his/her due** to admit that someone has good qualities even though you are criticizing him/her ‖ 남을 비판할지라도 그 사람이 가진 좋은 특성을

인정하다. 남을 공정하게 대하다[다루다]: *Mr. Johnston was a bad teacher, but to give him his due, he did try hard.* 존스턴 씨는 나쁜 교사였지만, 공정하게 대하자면, 그는 열심히 노력했다. —see also DUES

du·el /'duəl/ *n* a fight in past times between two people with guns or swords ‖ 옛날에 두 사람 간에 총이나 칼로 한 싸움. 결투 – **duel** *v* [I]

due proc·ess /ˌ. '../, **due process of law** /ˌ. ˌ.... './ *n* [U] LAW a set of laws that must be obeyed to protect someone's legal rights when s/he goes to court ‖ 사람이 재판을 받을 때 법적 권리를 보호받기 위해 준수해야 하는 일련의 법률. 정당한 법의 절차

dues /duz/ *n* [plural] the money that you pay to be a member of an organization ‖ 어떤 단체의 회원이 되기 위해 내는 돈. 회비

du·et /du'ɛt/ *n* a piece of music written for two performers ‖ 두 명의 연주자를 위해 쓰여진 곡. 2중창[주]곡

duf·fel bag /'dʌfəl ˌbæg/ *n* a cloth bag with a round bottom and a string around the top to tie it closed ‖ 바닥이 둥글고 꼭대기 부분에 달린 끈으로 묶어서 닫는 천 가방. 스크제 (원통형인) 잡낭

duffel coat /'...ˌ./ *n* a coat made of rough heavy cloth, usually with a HOOD and TOGGLES (=buttons shaped like tubes) ‖ 보통 두건과 토글 단추가 달린, 거칠고 무거운 천으로 만든 코트. 더플 코트

dug /dʌg/ *v* the past tense and PAST PARTICIPLE OF DIG ‖ dig의 과거·과거 분사형

dug·out /'dʌgaʊt/ *n* a low shelter at the side of a sports field, where players and team officials sit ‖ 경기장 옆에 선수와 팀 관계자들이 앉는 낮은 대기소. 더그아웃

duke /duk/ *n* a man with the highest social rank below a PRINCE ‖ 왕자 아래의 최고의 사회적 계급을 가진 남자. 공작

dull¹ /dʌl/ *adj* **1** not interesting or exciting ‖ 흥미롭거나 자극적이지 않은. 단조로운. 재미없는. 지루한: *What a dull party!* 정말 지루한 파티군! **2** not bright or shiny ‖ 밝거나 빛나지 않는. 흐릿한: *a dull gray sky* 흐릿한 회색 하늘 **3** a dull sound is not clear or loud ‖ 소리가 분명하지 않거나 크지 않은. 둔탁한: *I heard a dull thud from upstairs.* 나는 위층에서 나는 둔탁한 소리를 들었다. **4** a dull pain is not severe ‖ 아픔이 심각하지 않은. 둔한: *a dull ache in my shoulder* 어깨의 둔한 통증 **5** not sharp; BLUNT ‖ 날카롭지 않

은. 무딘; 圏 blunt: *a dull knife* 무딘 칼 **6** not able to think quickly or understand things easily ‖ 사물을 빨리 생각하거나 쉽게 이해할 수 없는. 머리가 둔한[나쁜]: *a dull student* 우둔한 학생 – **dully** *adv* – **dullness** *n* [U]

dull² *v* [T] to make something become less sharp, less clear etc. ‖ 사물의 예리함·명확성 등을 덜하게 하다. 무디게[둔하게] 하다: *a drug to dull the pain* 진통제

du·ly /'duli/ *adv* FORMAL at the correct time or in the correct way ‖ 정확한 시간에, 또는 정확하게. 제시간에. 지체없이: *Your suggestion has been duly noted.* 당신의 제안은 지체없이 적어두었습니다.

dumb /dʌm/ *adj* **1** INFORMAL stupid ‖ 어리석은. 멍청한. 아둔한: *What a dumb idea!* 정말 멍청한 생각이군! **2** OLD-FASHIONED unable to speak; MUTE ‖ 말할 수 없는. 벙어리의; 圏 mute.

dumb·bell /'dʌmbɛl/ *n* **1** two weights connected by a short piece of metal that you lift for exercise ‖ 들어올려서 운동을 하는 것으로 짧은 금속 부분으로 연결된 두 개의 무거운 물건. 아령 **2** INFORMAL someone who is stupid ‖ 멍청한 사람. 바보. 멍청이

dumb·found·ed /ˌdʌmˈfaʊndɪd/ *adj* so surprised that you cannot speak ‖ 너무 놀라서 말을 잇지 못하는. 말문이 막힌: *He stared at me, dumbfounded.* 그는 말문이 막힌 채 나를 빤히 쳐다봤다.

dum·my¹ /'dʌmi/ *n* **1** INFORMAL someone who is stupid ‖ 멍청한 사람. 바보. 멍청이 **2** a figure made to look like a person ‖ 사람처럼 보이게 만든 형상. 마네킹. 인형

dummy² *adj* a dummy tool, weapon etc. looks like a real one but does not work ‖ 도구·무기 등이 실제의 것처럼 보이지만 작동하지 않는. 모형[모조]의: *a dummy rifle* 모형 소총

dump¹ /dʌmp/ *v* [T] **1** to drop or put something somewhere in a careless way, sometimes in order to get rid of it ‖ 때때로 물건을 처분하기 위해, 어딘가에 아무렇게나 떨어뜨리거나 놓다. …을 아무렇게나 내던지다: *illegal chemicals dumped in the river* 강에 아무렇게나 버려진 불법 화학 제품 / *They dumped their bags on the floor and left.* 그들은 가방을 바닥에 내동댕이치고 떠나 버렸다. **2** to suddenly end a relationship ‖ 갑자기 관계를 끝내다. 남을 버리다: *Tammy dumped her boyfriend.* 태미는 자기 남자 친구를 차버렸다.

dump² *n* **1** a place where unwanted waste is taken and left ‖ 불필요한 쓰레기들을 가져와 내버리는 곳. 쓰레기 하치장: *I'm going to take those boxes down to the dump.* 저 상자들을 쓰레기장에 가지고 내려갈 거야. **2** INFORMAL a place that is unpleasant because it is dirty, ugly, or boring ‖ 더럽거나 추하거나 지루해서 불쾌한 장소. 누추한[지저분한] 장소: *This town's a real dump.* 이 읍은 정말 지저분하구나. **3 be down in the dumps** INFORMAL to feel very sad ‖ 매우 슬프다. 의기소침하다

dump·ster /'dʌmpstə/ *n* TRADEMARK a large metal container used for holding waste ‖ 쓰레기를 담는 데에 쓰는 대형 금속 용기. 금속제 대형 쓰레기통

dump truck /'. ./ *n* a vehicle with a large open container at the back that can pour sand, soil etc. onto the ground ‖ 모래·흙 등을 땅에 쏟아 부을 수 있도록 뒤쪽에 대형의 덮개가 없는 적재함이 달린 차량. 덤프 트럭

dump·y /'dʌmpi/ *adj* INFORMAL short and fat ‖ 키가 작고 뚱뚱한. 땅딸막한: *a dumpy little man* 땅딸막한 남자

dunce /dʌns/ *n* INFORMAL OFFENSIVE someone who is slow at learning things ‖ 일을 배우는 데에 느린 사람. 바보. 열등생

dune /dun/ *n* a hill made of sand near the ocean or in the desert ‖ 바닷가나 사막의 모래로 된 언덕

dung /dʌŋ/ *n* [U] solid waste from animals, especially large ones ‖ 동물의 고형 배설물, 특히 큰 것. 똥

dun·geon /'dʌndʒən/ *n* a prison under the ground, used in past times ‖ 옛날에 사용되었던 지하 감옥

dunk /dʌŋk/ *v* [T] **1** to quickly put something that you are eating into coffee, milk etc., and take it out again ‖ 먹고 있던 것을 재빨리 커피·우유 등에 담갔다가 다시 꺼내다. …을 커피, 우유 등에 잠그다 **2** to push someone under water for a short time as a joke ‖ 장난삼아 잠시 동안 남을 물속에 밀어 넣다 **3** to jump up toward the basket in a game of basketball and throw the ball down into it ‖ 농구 경기에서, 골 그물로 점프하여 그 안으로 공을 집어넣다. 덩크 슛하다 —see picture on page 946 – **dunk** *n*

dun·no /də'noʊ/ SPOKEN NONSTANDARD I **dunno** a short form of "I do not know" ‖ "I do not know"의 단축형

du·o /'duoʊ/ *n* two people who do something together, especially play music or sing ‖ 특히 음악을 연주하거나 노래를 부르는 등, 무언가를 함께 하는 두 사람. 2인조

dupe /dup/ v [T] to trick or deceive someone ‖ 남을 속이거나 기만하다: *Many older people were duped into buying worthless insurance.* 많은 노인들이 속아 넘어가서 쓸모없는 보험에 가입했다. – **dupe** n

du·plex /'dupleks/ n a type of house that is divided so that it has two separate homes in it ‖ 집이 나뉘어 두 개의 분리된 가정이 있는 주택의 형태. 2세대용 주택

du·pli·cate[1] /'dupləkɪt/ n an exact copy of something that you can use in the same way ‖ 똑같은 방식으로 사용할 수 있는 어떤 사물의 정확한 복사본. 사본. 부본. 복제: *We'd better make a duplicate of that key.* 그 열쇠의 복사품을 만들어 놓는 것이 좋겠어.

du·pli·cate[2] /'duplə,keɪt/ v [T] to copy something exactly ‖ 물건을 똑같이 복사하다. 재현하다. 되풀이하다: *a machine that duplicates the movements of the human hand* 인간의 손 동작을 똑같이 재현하는 기계 – **duplication** /,duplə'keɪʃən/ n [U]

du·plic·i·ty /du'plɪsəti/ n [U] FORMAL dishonest behavior that is intended to deceive someone ‖ 남을 속일 의도로 하는 부정직한 행위. 기만. 허위

dur·a·ble /'durəbəl/ adj 1 staying in good condition for a long time ‖ 오랫동안 좋은 상태를 유지하는. 내구력이 있는. 튼튼한: *durable clothing* 내구성이 있는 옷 2 FORMAL continuing for a long time ‖ 오랫동안 계속되는: *a durable peace* 항구적인 평화 – **durability** /,durə'bɪləti/ n [U]

du·ra·tion /du'reɪʃən/ n [U] FORMAL the length of time that something continues ‖ 사물이 지속되는 시간의 길이. 계속[지속, 존속] 기간: *Food was rationed for the duration of the war* 전쟁이 지속되는 동안에는 식량이 배급되었다.

du·ress /du'rɛs/ n [U] FORMAL under duress as a result of using illegal or unfair threats ‖ 불법적이거나 부당한 위협을 사용한 결과로서. 강요되어. 협박당하여: *Her confession was made under duress.* 그녀의 자백은 강요를 당한 것이었다.

dur·ing /'durɪŋ/ prep 1 all through a particular period of time ‖ 특정 기간 내내. 죽: *I try to swim every day during the summer.* 나는 여름 내내 매일 수영하려고 한다. 2 at some point in a period of time ‖ 특정 기간 중의 어떤 시점에. …동안[사이]에: *Henry died during the night.* 헨리는 밤 사이에 죽었다.

dusk /dʌsk/ n [U] the time before it gets dark when the sky is becoming darker ‖ 어두워지기 전, 하늘이 어둑어둑해지는 시간. 해질녘. 황혼(녘)

dust[1] /dʌst/ n [U] extremely small pieces of dirt, sand etc. that are like a dry powder ‖ 마른 분가루같이 아주 작은 흙·모래 등. 먼지. 티끌: *The truck drove off in a cloud of dust.* 그 트럭은 뭉게뭉게 피어오르는 먼지 속을 달려갔다. / *a thick layer of dust on the table* 테이블 위에 두껍게 쌓인 먼지

dust[2] v 1 [I, T] to clean the dust from something ‖ 어떤 것에서 먼지를 치우다. …의 먼지를 털다: *I just dusted the living room.* 나는 방금 거실의 먼지를 청소했다. 2 [T] to cover something with a fine powder ‖ 어떤 것을 미세한 가루로 덮다. …에 미세한 가루를 뿌리다: *Lightly dust the cakes with sugar.* 케이크에 설탕을 살짝 뿌려라.

dust sth ↔ **off** phr v [T] to clean something using a dry cloth or your hand ‖ 마른 천이나 손을 사용해 어떤 것을 청소하다: *She dusted the snow off Billy's coat.* 그녀는 빌리의 외투에서 눈을 털었다.

dust jack·et /'. ../ n a thick folded piece of paper that fits over the cover of a book ‖ 책의 표지에 꼭 맞게 접힌 두꺼운 종이. 책 커버[덮개]

dust·pan /'dʌstpæn/ n a flat container with a handle that you use with a brush to remove dust and waste from the floor ‖ 바닥의 먼지와 쓰레기를 치우기 위해 솔과 함께 사용하는, 손잡이가 달린 납작한 용기. 쓰레받기

dust·y /'dʌsti/ adj covered or filled with dust ‖ 먼지로 뒤덮이거나 먼지로 가득 찬. 먼지투성이의: *a dusty room* 먼지투성이 방

Dutch[1] /dʌtʃ/ adj 1 relating to or coming from the Netherlands ‖ 네덜란드와 관련된, 또는 네덜란드에서 온. 네덜란

드(인)의 **2** relating to the Dutch language ‖ 네덜란드어와 관계된. 네덜란드어의

Dutch² *n* **1** [U] the language used in the Netherlands ‖ 네덜란드에서 사용하는 언어. 네덜란드어 **2 the Dutch** the people of the Netherlands ‖ 네덜란드 국민. 네덜란드인

dutch *adj* **go dutch (with sb)** to share the cost of something such as a meal in a restaurant ‖ 식당에서 식사 등의 비용을 함께 나누다. (…와) 비용을 각자 부담하다

du·ti·ful /ˈdutɪfəl/ *adj* always obeying other people, doing what you are supposed to do, and behaving in a loyal way ‖ 항상 다른 사람들에게 복종하며 해야 할 일을 하고 충성스럽게 행동하는. 본분을 지키는[다하는]. 순종하는[충실한] **– dutifully** *adv*

du·ty /ˈduti/ *n* **1** [C, U] something that you have to do because you think it is right ‖ 옳다고 여기기 때문에 해야 하는 일. 의무: *I feel it's my duty to help you.* 당신을 돕는 건 제 의무라는 생각이 들어요. / *The government has a duty to provide education.* 정부는 교육 서비스를 제공할 의무가 있다. / *jury duty* 배심원으로서의 의무 **2** [C, U] something that you have to do because it is part of your job ‖ 직무의 일부이기 때문에 해야 하는 일. 맡은 일. 임무: *The soldiers were expected to do their duty.* 그 군인들은 자신들의 임무를 수행할 것으로 기대됐다. / *Please report for duty tomorrow morning.* 내일 아침에 출근해 주십시오. / *his duties at the airport* 공항에서의 그의 직무 **3 be on/off duty** to be working or not working at a particular time ‖ 특정 시간에 근무하거나 하지 않다. 근무 시간 중이다[당번이다]/근무 시간이 아니다[비번이다]: *Is she the nurse who was on duty last night?* 그녀가 어젯밤에 근무했던 간호사인가요? **4** a tax you pay on something, especially on goods you bought in another country ‖ 특히 다른 나라에서 산 물건에 대해 지불하는 세금. 관세

duty-free /ˌ.. ˈ./ *adj* duty-free goods can be brought into a country without paying tax on them ‖ 세금을 내지 않고 어떤 나라에 물건을 수입할 수 있는. 면세의 **– duty-free** *adv*

DVD *n* digital versatile disc; special kind of CD that can store large amounts of music, VIDEOs, and computer information ‖ digital versatile disc(디지털 방식의 다기능 디스크)의 약어; 대용량의 음악·비디오·컴퓨터 정보를 저장할 수 있는 특수한 종류의 콤팩트 디스크

dwarf¹ /dwɔrf/ *n* **1** an imaginary creature that looks like a small man ‖ 작은 사람처럼 생긴 상상의 피조물. 난쟁이. 소인: *Snow White and the Seven Dwarfs* 백설 공주와 일곱 난쟁이 **2** a person, animal, or plant that does not grow to the normal height ‖ 정상적인 키까지 자라지 않은 사람[동물, 식물]. 난쟁이. 소형 동식물

dwarf² *v* [T] to be so big that other things seem very small ‖ 너무 커서 다른 것들이 매우 작아 보이다. …을 대조적으로 작아 보이게 하다: *The church is dwarfed by the surrounding office buildings.* 주변의 회사 빌딩들 때문에 교회가 매우 작아 보였다.

dweeb /dwib/ *n* SLANG a weak, slightly strange person who is not popular or fashionable ‖ 인기 있거나 세련되지 않은, 약하고 약간 이상한 사람. 얼간이

dwell /dwɛl/ *v* **dwelt** *or* **dwelled, dwelt** *or* **dwelled, dwelling** [I] LITERARY to live in a particular place ‖ 특정 장소에 살다. 거주하다: *They dwelt on an island.* 그들은 어떤 섬에 살았다.

dwell on/upon sth *phr v* [T] to think or talk for too long about something, especially something unpleasant ‖ 특히 불쾌한 일에 대해 너무 오래 생각하거나 이야기하다. …을 곰곰이 생각하다. …을 장황하게 말하다: *There's no point in dwelling on the past.* 과거의 일을 장황하게 말하는 데에 요점이 없다.

dwell·er /ˈdwɛlə/ *n* **city/town/cave dweller etc.** a person or animal that lives in a city, town etc. ‖ 도시·읍 등에 사는 사람이나 동물. 도시/읍/동굴 거주자

dwell·ing /ˈdwɛlɪŋ/ *n* FORMAL a house, apartment etc. where people live ‖ 사람들이 거주하는 집·아파트 등. 주거. 주택

dwelt /dwɛlt/ *v* the past tense and PAST PARTICIPLE OF DWELL ‖ dwell의 과거·과거분사형

dwin·dle /ˈdwɪndl/ *v* [I] to gradually become fewer or smaller ‖ 점차 적어지거나 작아지다. 줄어들다: *Their supplies have dwindled away to almost nothing.* 그들의 물자는 점점 줄어들어서 거의 아무것도 남아 있지 않았다. **– dwindling** *adj*

dye¹ /daɪ/ *n* [C, U] a substance you use to change the color of your hair, clothes etc. ‖ 머리털·옷 등의 색깔을 바꾸는 데에 쓰는 물질. 물감. 염료

dye² *v* [T] to give something a different color using a DYE ‖ 염료를 사용하여 어떤

것에 다른 색을 입히다. 염색하다: *Brian dyed his hair green.* 브라이언은 머리를 초록색으로 염색했다.

dyed-in-the-wool /ˌ. . . ˈ.·/ *adj* having strong beliefs or opinions that will never change ‖ 결코 변하지 않을 강한 신념이나 의견을 가진. 철저한. 골수의: *a dyed-in-the-wool Republican* 골수 공화당원

dy·ing /ˈdaɪ-ɪŋ/ *v* the PRESENT PARTICIPLE of DIE ‖ die의 현재 분사형

dy·nam·ic /daɪˈnæmɪk/ *adj* **1** interesting, exciting, and full of energy ‖ 흥미롭고 신나며 활력으로 가득 찬. 힘찬. 활동적인. 정력적인: *a dynamic young man* 활동적인 젊은 남자 **2** continuously moving or changing ‖ 끊임없이 움직이거나 변화하는. (역)동적인: *a dynamic society* 역동적인 사회 **3** TECHNICAL relating to a force or power that causes movement ‖ 움직임을 유발하는 힘이나 능력에 관계된. 역학적인. 동역학의: *dynamic energy* 역학 에너지

dy·nam·ics /daɪˈnæmɪks/ *n* [U] **1** the way in which systems or people behave, react, and affect each other ‖ 체제나 사람들이 행동하고 반응하며 서로 영향을 미치는 방식. 역학 (관계). 성장[변화, 발달]의 역사: *family dynamics* 가족 역학 / *the dynamics of power in large businesses* 대기업 내 권력의 역학 관계 **2** the science concerned with the movement of objects and with the forces related to movement ‖ 물체의 움직임 및 움직임과 관계된 힘에 관한 과학(적 학문). 동역학

dy·na·mism /ˈdaɪnəˌmɪzəm/ *n* [U] the quality of being DYNAMIC ‖ 역동적인 성질. 활력. 패기

dy·na·mite¹ /ˈdaɪnəˌmaɪt/ *n* [U] a powerful explosive ‖ 강력한 폭발물. 다이너마이트

dynamite² *v* [T] to damage or destroy something with DYNAMITE ‖ 다이너마이트로 어떤 것에 손상을 끼치거나 파괴하다. …을 다이너마이트로 폭파하다

dy·na·mo /ˈdaɪnəˌmoʊ/ *n* **1** INFORMAL someone who has a lot of energy and is very excited about what s/he does ‖ 에너지가 충만하고 자신이 하고 있는 일에 아주 흥미를 느끼는 사람. 정력가 **2** a machine that changes some other form of power into electricity ‖ 다른 형태의 힘을 전기로 바꾸는 기계. 발전기

dy·nas·ty /ˈdaɪnəsti/ *n* a family of kings or other rulers who have ruled a country for a long time, or the period of time during which this family rules ‖ 한 나라를 오랫동안 지배해 왔던 왕이나 기타 통치자의 가족, 또는 이 가족이 통치한 기간. 명문. 지배자층. 왕조 (지배): *the Ming dynasty* 명(왕)조 **– dynastic** /daɪˈnæstɪk/ *adj*

dys·en·ter·y /ˈdɪsənˌtɛri/ *n* [U] a serious disease of the BOWELs that makes someone pass much more waste than usual ‖ 사람이 평소보다 많은 양의 배설물을 배출하는 장의 중병. 설사. 이질

dys·func·tion·al /dɪsˈfʌŋkʃənl/ *adj* not working normally or not showing normal social behavior ‖ 정상적으로 작용하지 않거나 정상적인 사회적 행위를 보이지 않는. 기능 장애의. 비정상의: *dysfunctional relationships within the family* 가족 내의 비정상적 관계

dys·lex·i·a /dɪsˈlɛksiə/ *n* [U] a condition that makes it difficult for someone to read ‖ 읽는 데 어려움을 일으키는 상태. 난독증. 독서 장애 **– dyslexic** /dɪsˈlɛksɪk/ *adj*

Ee

E, e /i/ the fifth letter of the English alphabet ‖ 영어 알파벳의 다섯째 자

E¹ /i/ *n* [C, U] the third note in the musical SCALE of C, or the musical KEY based on this note ‖ 다음계의 셋째 음이나 이음을 기초로 한 조(調). 마 음. 마 조

E² 1 the written abbreviation of EAST or EASTERN ‖ east, 또는 eastern의 약어 2 SLANG the abbreviation of ECSTASY, an illegal drug ‖ 불법 마약인 ecstasy의 약어

each¹ /itʃ/ *determiner, pron* every single one of two or more things, considered separately ‖ 두 개 이상의 것들 중 독립된 것으로 간주되는 개개의 것. 각자. 각각. 제각각: *Each student will be given a book.* 각 학생들은 책을 한 권씩 받을 것이다. / *I gave a piece of candy to each of the children.* 나는 아이들 각각에게 사탕 하나씩을 주었다.

USAGE NOTE each, every, all, and **both**

Use **each** with a singular countable noun to mean "every person or thing in a group, considered separately": *Each child at the party will get a balloon.* Use **every** with a singular countable noun to mean "every person or thing in a group, considered together": *Every child in the class passed the test.* Use **all** with a plural countable noun to mean "every one of a group of things or people": *All of the children enjoyed the trip.* Use **both** with a plural countable noun to mean "two people or things in a group, considered together": *Both of our children are in college.*

each는 "독립된 것으로 간주되는 그룹 내의 모든 사람이나 사물"을 뜻하는 단수의 가산 명사와 함께 쓰인다: 그 파티에 있는 각각의 아이는 풍선 하나씩을 받을 것이다. **every**는 "전체로서 간주되는 그룹 내의 모든 사람이나 사물"을 뜻하는 단수의 가산 명사와 함께 쓰인다: 그 반의 모든 아이들이 시험에 합격했다. **all**은 "일단의 사물이나 사람 모두"를 뜻하는 복수의 가산 명사와 함께 쓰인다: 모든 아이들이 여행을 즐겼다. **both**는 "일괄적으로 간주되는 한 그룹 내의 두 사람이나 사물"을 뜻하는 복수의 가산 명사와 함께 쓰인다: 우리 아이들은 두 명 모두 대학에 다닌다.

---

each² *adv* for or to every one ‖ 모든 것을 위해, 또는 모든 것에게. 각각(에 대하여). 제각기: *The tickets are $5 each.* 표들은 각각 5달러씩이다. / *You kids can have two cookies each.* 너희 아이들은 각각 과자 두 개씩을 먹을 수 있다.

each oth·er /ˌ. '../ *pron* used in order to show that each of two people does something to the other person, or that each of several people does something to each of the others ‖ 두 명이 각각 또는 몇몇 사람들이 각각 상대방에게 어떤 것을 하는 것을 나타내는 데에 쓰여. 서로. 상호간: *Susan and Robert kissed each other.* 수잔과 로버트는 서로 키스했다. / *The two kids played with each other all morning.* 그 두 아이들은 오전 내내 서로 장난쳤다. / *It's normal for people to ignore each other in an elevator.* 엘리베이터 안에서 사람들이 서로 못 본 체하는 것은 정상이다.

USAGE NOTE each other and **one another**

Some teachers prefer to use **each other** when talking about two people or things, and **one another** when talking about many people or things: *The two leaders shook hands with each other. / All the leaders shook hands with one another.* **One another** is also more formal than **each other**.

어떤 교사들은 두 명 또는 두 개의 사물에 대해 말할 때는 **each other**를, 여러 사람 또는 여러 개의 사물에 대해 말할 때는 **one another**를 사용한다: 그 두 지도자는 서로 악수했다. / 모든 지도자들이 서로 악수했다. 또한 **one another**는 **each other**보다 더 격식 차린 말이다.

---

ea·ger /ˈigər/ *adj* 1 having a strong desire to do something or a strong interest in something ‖ 어떤 것을 하고자 하는 강렬한 열망이 있는, 또는 어떤 것에 강한 흥미가 있는. …을 갈망[열망]하는: *I've been eager to meet you.* 저는 당신을 몹시 만나고 싶었습니다. / *a young woman eager for success* 성공을 갈망하는 젊은 여성 2 **eager to please** willing to do anything that people want ‖ 사람들이 원하는 어떤 것이라도 기꺼이 하는 —

eagerly *adv* – **eagerness** *n* [U]

ea·gle /ˈigəl/ *n* a large wild bird with a beak like a hook, that eats small animals, birds etc. ‖ 갈고리처럼 생긴 부리가 있고 작은 동물·새 등을 잡아먹는 큰 야생 조류. 독수리

eagle-eyed /ˌ.. ˌ./ *adj* very good at seeing or noticing things ‖ 사물을 보거나 알아차리는 데 매우 능한. 관찰력[시력]이 날카로운[좋은]: *an eagle-eyed teacher* 관찰력이 예리한 교사

ear /ɪr/ *n* **1** the part of your body that you hear with ‖ 듣는 신체 부위. 귀: *Stop shouting in my ear!* 내 귀에 대고 소리치지 마! —see picture at HEAD¹ **2** [U] the ability to hear, recognize, or copy sounds, especially in music and languages ‖ 특히 음악과 언어에 있어서 소리를 듣는[인식하는, 흉내내는] 능력. 청력. 음을 분간하는 힘: *Joel has a good ear for music.* 조엘은 음악을 잘 안다. **3** the top part of plants that produce grain ‖ 곡물이 나는 식물의 윗부분. 이삭: *an ear of corn* 옥수수 이삭 **4 be up to your ears in sth** INFORMAL to be very busy with something ‖ 어떤 일로 몹시 바쁜: *I'm up to my ears in work.* 일하느라 너무 바쁘다. **5 go in one ear and out the other** INFORMAL to be heard and then forgotten immediately ‖ 듣고 즉시 잊어버리다 **6 be all ears** INFORMAL to be very interested in listening to someone ‖ 남의 말에 매우 관심을 기울이고 듣다. 경청하다: *Go ahead, I'm all ears.* 어서 말해, 열심히 듣고 있어. **7 be out on your ear** INFORMAL to be forced to leave a place because of something you have done wrong ‖ 잘못한 일 때문에 어떤 곳에서 강제로 쫓겨나다: *If you come to work that late again, you'll be out on your ear!* 당신 또 한번 지각하면, 해고될 줄 알아! —see also **play it by ear** (PLAY¹), **wet behind the ears** (WET¹)

ear·drum /ˈɪrdrʌm/ *n* a tight thin MEMBRANE (=layer like skin) over the inside of your ear that allows you to hear sound ‖ 소리를 들을 수 있도록 귀 안쪽에 걸쳐 있는 팽팽하고 얇은 막. 고막

ear·lobe /ˈɪrloʊb/ *n* the soft piece of flesh at the bottom of your ear ‖ 귀 밑의 부드러운 살. 귓불

ear·ly¹ /ˈərli/ *adj* **1** near to the beginning of a day, year, someone's life etc. ‖ 하루·일년·인생 등의 시작 무렵의. 초기의. 이른: *She woke in the early morning.* 그녀는 이른 아침에 일어났다. / *a man in his early twenties* 20대 초반의 남자 **2** before the usual or expected

time ‖ 평상시나 예정된 시간 전의. 여느 때보다 이른. 조금 이른: *The train was ten minutes early.* 열차가 평상시보다 10분 빨랐다. **3** existing before other people, events, machines etc. of the same kind ‖ 동종의 다른 사람·사건·기계 등보다 먼저 존재했던. 예전의: *early settlers in New England* 뉴잉글랜드의 초기 정착민들 **4 at the earliest** used in order to say that a particular time is the soonest that something can happen ‖ 어떤 일이 발생할 수 있는 가장 빠른 특정한 시간을 말하는 데에 쓰여. 빨라도: *He'll arrive on Monday at the earliest.* 그는 빨라도 월요일은 되어야 도착할 것이다. **5 the early hours** the time between MIDNIGHT and morning ‖ 자정과 아침 사이의 시간. 이른 아침. 새벽 **6 the early days** the time when something had just started to be done or to exist ‖ 어떤 일이 막 시작되었거나 막 생기기 시작한 시기. 초창기: *the early days of television* TV가 등장한 초창기 **7 early bird** someone who gets up early or arrives early ‖ 일찍 일어나거나 도착하는 사람 —opposite LATE¹

early² *adv* **1** before the usual, arranged, or expected time ‖ 평소[정해진, 예정된] 시간 전에. (여느 때보다) 일찍: *You should arrive early if you want a good seat.* 좋은 자리를 원한다면 일찍 도착해야 한다. **2** near the beginning of a particular period of time ‖ 특정 시기의 시작 무렵에. 초기에. 일찍이: *These flowers were planted early in the spring.* 이 꽃들은 이른 봄에 심었다. / *I'll have to leave early tomorrow morning.* 나는 내일 아침에 일찍 떠나야 한다. **3** near the beginning of an event, story, process etc. ‖ 사건·이야기·과정 등의 시작 무렵에. 초(창)기에: *I realized early on that this relationship wasn't going to work.* 나는 이 관계가 잘 되지 않을 거라는 것을 초기에 깨달았다. —opposite LATE²

ear·mark /ˈɪrmɑrk/ *v* [T] to save something to be used for a particular purpose ‖ 특정 목적에 쓰기 위해 사물을 확보해 두다: *We've earmarked funds for the new bridge.* 우리는 새 다리 건설을 위한 기금을 확보해 두었다.

ear·muffs /ˈɪrmʌfs/ *n* [plural] two pieces of material attached to the ends of a band, that you wear to keep your ears warm ‖ 귀를 따뜻하게 하기 위해 착용하는, 띠의 양 쪽 끝에 달린 두 개의 물체. 방한용 귀싸개

earn /ərn/ *v* [T] **1** to get money by working ‖ 일을 해서 돈을 얻다. 돈을 벌

다: *Alan earns $30,000 a year.* 앨런은 1
년에 3만 달러를 번다. **2** to make a profit
from business, or from putting money in
a bank, lending it etc. ‖ 사업[은행 예금,
대금(貸金)]으로 이익을 보다. 수익[이자]
을 올리다: *I earned $5000 from my
investments last year.* 나는 지난해 5천
달러의 투자 수익을 올렸다. **3** to get
something that you deserve ‖ 받을 만한
자격이 있는 어떤 것을 받다: *She earned
her place on the team by practicing
hard.* 그녀는 열심히 연습해서 그 팀에서
자기 위치를 확보했다. **4 earn a living** to
work to get enough money to pay for
the things you need ‖ 필요한 것들에 지불
하기에 충분한 돈을 벌기 위해 일하다. 생
계를 이어가다: *He earned his living as a
writer.* 그는 작가로서 생계를 이어갔다.
—see usage note at GAIN¹

ear·nest¹ /'ɚnɪst/ *adj* serious and
sincere ‖ 진지하고 진실한. 성실한: *an
earnest young man* 성실한 젊은이 –
earnestly *adv* – **earnestness** *n* [U]

earnest² *n* **1 in earnest** happening
more seriously or with greater effort
than before ‖ 전보다 더 진지하게, 또는
더 많은 노력을 기울여 일어나는. 진정으
로. 진지하게. 본격적으로: *Soon they
were talking in earnest about business
plans.* 그들은 곧 사업 계획에 대해 본격
적으로 이야기하고 있었다. **2 be in
earnest** to be serious about what you
are saying ‖ 자신이 말하고 있는 것에 대
해 진지하다: *I'm sure he was in earnest
when he said he was going to quit.* 나는
그가 그만둘 것이라고 말할 때 진심이었다
고 믿는다.

earn·ings /'ɚnɪŋz/ *n* [plural] **1** the
money that you earn by working ‖ 일해
서 버는 돈. 수입. 소득 **2** the profit that
a company makes ‖ 회사가 올리는 이익.
수익

ear·phones /'ɪrfoʊnz/ *n* [plural]
electrical equipment that you put over
or into your ears to listen to a radio,
TAPE DECK etc. ‖ 라디오, 테이프 덱 등을
듣기 위해 귀 위에 얹거나 안 쪽에 넣는
전기 기구. 이어폰

ear·plug /'ɪrplʌg/ *n* [C usually plural] a
small piece of rubber that you put into
your ear to keep out noise or water ‖ 소
음이나 물을 막기 위해 귀 안에 넣는 고무
조각. 귀마개

ear·ring /'ɪrɪŋ/ *n* [C usually plural] a
piece of jewelry that you fasten to your
ear ‖ 귀에 고정시키는 보석. 귀걸이 —see
picture at JEWELRY

ear·shot /'ɪrʃat/ *n* **within earshot/out**

of earshot near enough or not near
enough to hear what someone is saying
‖ 남이 말하는 것을 듣기에 충분히 가깝거
나 가깝지 않은. 소리가 들리는/들리지 않
는 곳에

ear-split·ting /'. ˌ../ *adj* very loud ‖ 소
리가 매우 큰. 귀청이 찢어질 듯한: *an
ear-splitting scream* 귀청이 찢어질 듯한
비명

earth /ɚθ/ *n* **1** [singular] also **Earth**
the world that we live in, especially
considered as a PLANET ‖ 특히 하나의 행
성으로 간주되는, 우리가 사는 세계. 지구:
The Earth moves around the sun. 지구는
태양 둘레를 공전한다. / *The space
shuttle is returning to the earth.* 우주
왕복선은 지구로 복귀하고 있다. / *the
most beautiful woman on earth* 지구상
에서 가장 아름다운 여인 —compare
WORLD —see picture at ORBIT¹ and
GREENHOUSE EFFECT **2** [U] the substance
that plants, trees etc. grow in; dirt ‖ 식
물·나무 등이 자라는 물질; 흙: *footprints
in the wet earth* 젖은 흙 속에 새겨진 발
자국 **3 what/why/how etc. on
earth...?** SPOKEN said when you are
asking a question about something that
you are very surprised or annoyed
about ‖ 매우 놀랍거나 짜증스러운 것에
대해 물어볼 때에 쓰여. 도대체: *What on
earth did you do to your hair?* 도대체 네
머리에 무슨 짓을 한 거냐? —see also
DOWN-TO-EARTH

USAGE NOTE earth, world, and land

The **earth** is the planet we live on:
*The earth moves around the sun
every 365 days.* The **world** is a place
with people, countries etc.: *It's one of
the largest countries in the world.*
You can also use **earth** to mean "the
world": *It's the highest mountain on
earth.* ✗DON'T SAY "in earth" or "on
the world."✗ When you compare the
earth's surface to the ocean, use
land: *After weeks at sea, the sailors
saw land.* When you compare it to the
sky, use **earth**: *The spacecraft
returned to earth safely.*
earth는 우리가 사는 행성을 말한다:
지구는 365일마다 태양 둘레를 공전한
다. **world**는 사람·국가 등이 있는 장소
를 뜻한다: 그 나라는 세계에서 가장 큰
나라 중의 하나이다. "세계"라는 의미로
earth를 쓸 수 있다: 그것은 세계에서
가장 높은 산이다. "in earth"나 "on the
world"라고는 하지 않는다. 지구 지표면

을 바다와 비교할 때는 **land**를 쓴다: 몇 주간을 바다에서 보낸 후 선원들은 육지를 보았다. 하늘과 비교할 때는 **earth**를 쓴다: 우주선은 무사히 지구로 귀환했다.

earth·ly /'ɔ˞θli/ *adj* **1 no earthly reason/use/chance etc.** no reason, use etc. at all ‖ 어떤 이유·쓰임 등이 전혀 없는. 아무런 이유/소용/가망 없는: *There's no earthly reason for me to go.* 내가 가야 할 아무런 이유가 없다. **2** LITERARY relating to life on Earth rather than in heaven ‖ 천상이 아닌 지상에서의 삶과 관계된. 현세의: *all my earthly possessions* 속세의 나의 온갖 소유물

earth·quake /'ɔ˞θkweɪk/ *n* a sudden shaking of the earth's surface that often causes a lot of damage ‖ 종종 큰 피해를 일으키는 지구 표면의 갑작스런 진동. 지진

earth·shat·ter·ing /'. ,.../, **earth-shaking** /'. ,./ *adj* surprising or shocking and very important ‖ 놀랍거나 충격적이고 매우 중요한. 세계를 떠들썩하게 하는: *It's interesting, but not earth-shattering.* 그것은 흥미롭지만, 세상을 떠들썩하게 할 것은 아니야.

earth·worm /'ɔ˞θwɔ˞m/ *n* ⇨ WORM¹

earth·y /'ɔ˞θi/ *adj* **1** talking about sex and the human body in a direct and impolite way ‖ 직접적이며 무례하게 성(性)과 몸에 대해 이야기하는. 저속한: *Jimmy has an earthy sense of humor.* 지미는 저속한 유머 감각이 있다. **2** tasting, smelling, or looking like earth or soil ‖ 토양이나 흙 맛이 나는[냄새가 나는, 처럼 보이는]. 흙 맛의. 흙내의. 흙 모양의: *mushrooms with an earthy flavor* 흙냄새가 나는 버섯 – **earthiness** *n* [U]

ease¹ /iz/ *n* [U] **1 with ease** if you do something with ease, it is very easy for you to do it ‖ 어떤 것을 하기에 매우 쉽게. 쉽게: *Randy climbed the ladder with ease.* 랜디는 쉽게 사다리를 올랐다. **2 at ease a)** feeling comfortable and confident ‖ 편안하고 자신 있는: *She tried to make the new students feel at ease.* 그녀는 신입생들이 편안하게 느낄 수 있도록 노력했다. / *You always look ill at ease* (=not relaxed) *in a suit.* 너는 정장만 입으면 항상 편해 보이지 않는다. **b)** SPOKEN used in order to tell soldiers to stand in a relaxed way with their feet apart ‖ 군인들에게 발을 벌린 채 편안한 자세로 서 있으라고 말할 때에 쓰여. 쉬어! **3** the ability to feel or behave in a natural or relaxed way ‖ 자연스럽게 또

는 편하게 느끼거나 행동하는 능력. 소탈함. 자연스러움: *He had a natural ease which made him very popular.* 그는 천성적인 소탈함 때문에 매우 인기를 끌었다. **4 a life of ease** a comfortable life, without problems or worries ‖ 문제나 걱정거리가 없는 안락한 삶

ease² *v* **1** [I, T] to make something less severe or difficult, or to become less severe or difficult ‖ 어떤 일을 덜 심각하거나 덜 어렵게 만들다, 또는 덜 심각하거나 덜 어렵게 되다. 느슨하게 하다[느슨해지다]. 누그러뜨리다[누그러지다]: *He was given drugs to ease the pain.* 그는 고통을 완화시키는 약을 받았다. / *Tensions in the region have eased slightly.* 그 지역의 긴장이 약간 완화되었다. **2** [T] to move something slowly and carefully into another place ‖ 어떤 것을 다른 곳으로 천천히 조심스럽게 옮기다: *Ease the patient onto the bed.* 환자를 침대 위로 조심스럽게 옮겨라.

ease up *phr v* [I] **1** also **ease off** if something, especially something that annoys you, eases off or eases up, it becomes less or gets better ‖ 특히 괴롭게 하던 것이 덜해지거나 나아지다. 누그러지다. 완화되다: *The rain is starting to ease up.* 비가 잦아들기 시작한다. **2** to stop being unpleasant to someone ‖ 남에게 불쾌하게 구는 것을 그만두다: *Ease up on Roger, will you; he's doing all right.* 로저 좀 괴롭히지 마, 알겠어? 잘 하고 있잖아. **3** to do something more slowly or less often than before ‖ 어떤 것을 예전보다 더 천천히, 또는 덜 자주 하다. …을 줄이다: *I think it's time you eased up on the cigarettes.* 내 생각엔 네가 담배를 줄일 때가 된 것 같다.

ea·sel /'izəl/ *n* a frame that you put a painting on while you paint it ‖ 그림을 그리는 동안 올려놓는 틀. 이젤. 화가(畫架)

eas·i·ly /'izəli/ *adv* **1** without difficulty ‖ 어려움 없이. 쉽게: *I can easily finish it today.* 나는 그것을 오늘 쉽게 끝낼 수 있다. **2** without doubt; definitely ‖ 의심 없이; 확실히: *She is easily the most intelligent girl in the class.* 그녀는 확실히 반에서 가장 똑똑한 소녀다.

east¹, East /ist/ *n* **1** [singular, U] the direction from which the sun rises ‖ 태양이 뜨는 방향. 동(東)(쪽): *Which way is east?* 어느 쪽이 동쪽입니까? **2 the east** the eastern part of a country, state etc. ‖ 국가·주 등의 동부(東部): *Rain will spread to the east later today.* 오늘 늦게 비가 동부까지 내릴 것이다. **3 the**

E

East a) the countries in Asia, especially China, Japan, and Korea ‖ 아시아 국가들, 특히 중국·일본·한국. 동양 **b)** the countries in the eastern part of Europe, especially the ones that had Communist governments ‖ 유럽 동부의 국가들, 특히 공산주의 정부 치하였던 국가들. 동유럽권 **c)** the part of the US east of the Mississippi River, especially the states north of Washington, D.C. ‖ 미국의 미시시피 강 동쪽 지방, 특히 워싱턴 D.C. 북쪽의 주들. 미국의 동부 지방 **4 back East** in the East, or to the East of the US ‖ 미국 동부에 또는 동부로: *My son goes to college back East.* 내 아들은 동부에 있는 대학에 다닌다. —see usage note at NORTH³

east² *adj* **1** in, to, or facing east ‖ 동쪽에 있는, 동쪽으로의, 또는 동쪽을 향하는: *12 miles east of Portland* 포틀랜드 동쪽으로 12마일 / *the east coast of the island* 그 섬의 동해안 **2 east wind** a wind coming from the east ‖ 동쪽에서 불어오는 바람. 동풍

east³ *adv* toward the east ‖ 동쪽으로: *Go east on I-80 to Omaha.* 80번 고속도로를 타고 동쪽으로 오마하까지 가라. / *The window faces east.* 창문이 동쪽으로 나 있다.

east·bound /ˈistbaʊnd/ *adj* traveling or leading toward the east ‖ 동쪽으로 여행하거나 동쪽으로 이끄는: *eastbound traffic* 동쪽으로 가는 교통편 / *the eastbound lanes of the freeway* 동쪽으로 가는 고속도로 차선

Eas·ter /ˈistɚ/ *n* [C, U] **1** a Christian holiday on a Sunday in March or April to celebrate Christ's return to life after his death ‖ 예수의 죽음 후 부활을 축하하는, 3월이나 4월의 일요일에 거행되는 크리스도교의 축일. 부활절 날 **2** the period of time just before and after this day ‖ 부활절 날 전후의 기간. 부활절: *We went skiing in Vermont at Easter.* 우리는 부활절에 버몬트에 스키 타러 갔다.

Easter Bun·ny /ˌ.. ˈ../ *n* [singular] an imaginary rabbit that children believe brings colored eggs and chocolate at Easter ‖ 부활절에 채색한 달걀과 초콜릿을 가져다준다고 아이들이 믿는 상상 속의 토끼

Easter egg /ˈ.. ˌ./ *n* an egg that has been colored and decorated ‖ 채색하고 장식한 달걀. 부활절 장식용 달걀

east·er·ly /ˈistɚli/ *adj* **1** in or toward the east ‖ 동쪽에 있는 또는 동쪽으로 향하는: *sailing in an easterly direction* 동쪽으로의 항해 **2** easterly winds come

from the east ‖ 바람이 동쪽에서 불어오는

east·ern /ˈistɚn/ *adj* **1** in or from the east part of an area, country, state etc. ‖ 어떤 지역·나라·주 등의 동부에 있는 또는 동부로부터의: *eastern Oregon* 오리건 주 동부 **2 Eastern** in or from the countries in Asia, especially China, Japan, and Korea ‖ 아시아 국가, 특히 중국·일본·한국의 또는 중국·일본·한국으로부터의. 동양의: *Eastern religions* 동양의 종교들 **3** in or from the countries in the eastern part of Europe, especially the ones that used to have Communist governments ‖ 동부 유럽 국가들, 특히 공산주의 체제였던 나라들의 또는 그 나라들로부터의. 동유럽권의 —see usage note at NORTH³

east·ern·er, Easterner /ˈistɚnɚ/ *n* someone who comes from the EASTERN part of a country or the eastern HEMISPHERE ‖ 한 나라의 동쪽 지역, 또는 동반구에서 온 사람. 동부인

Eastern Eu·rope /ˌ.. ˈ../ *n* the eastern part of Europe, including places such as Poland and part of Russia ‖ 폴란드와 러시아의 일부 등을 포함하는 동부 유럽. 동유럽 –**Eastern European** *adj*

east·ern·most /ˈistɚnmoʊst/ *adj* farthest east ‖ 가장 동쪽의. 극동의: *the easternmost part of the island* 그 섬의 극동 지역

east·ward /ˈistwɚd/ *adj, adv* toward the east ‖ 동쪽을 향하는[여]

eas·y¹ /ˈizi/ *adj* **1** not difficult ‖ 어렵지 않은. 쉬운: *Making brownies is easy.* 초콜릿 케이크를 만드는 것은 쉽다. / *I want a book that's easy to read.* 난 읽기 쉬운 책을 원해. / *Having a computer will definitely make things a lot easier.* 컴퓨터가 있으면 분명 일이 훨씬 더 쉬워질 것이다. **2** comfortable and not feeling worried or anxious ‖ 편안하고 걱정이나 근심이 없는: *I imagine Paul has a very easy life.* 폴은 매우 편안한 삶을 사는 것 같아. **3 I'm easy** SPOKEN used in order to show that you do not mind what choice is made ‖ 무엇을 선택하든 개의치 않는다는 것을 나타내는 데에 쓰여. 아무래도 상관 없어: *"Do you want to go to the movies or out to eat?" "Oh, I'm easy."* "영화 보고 싶니, 아니면 외식하고 싶니?" "오, 난 아무래도 상관없어." **4 easy money** INFORMAL money that you do not have to work hard to get ‖ 열심히 일하지 않아도 버는 돈. 쉽게 버는 돈 **5** INFORMAL DISAPPROVING someone who is easy has a lot of sexual partners ‖ 사람이 성관계 파트너가 많이 있는 **6 eggs**

over easy eggs cooked on a hot surface and turned over quickly before serving, so that the YOLKs (=YELLOW PART) are not completely cooked ‖ 뜨거운 표면에서 익힌 다음 내놓기 전에 재빨리 뒤집어 노른자위가 충분히 익지 않은 계란

easy² *adv* **1 take it easy a)** to relax and not do very much ‖ 긴장을 풀고 너무 많이 하지 않다. 서두르지 않다. 느긋하게 쉬다: *I'm going to take it easy this weekend.* 이번 주말에는 느긋이 쉴래. **b)** SPOKEN used in order to tell someone to become less upset or angry ‖ 남에게 흥분이나 화를 가라앉히라고 말하는 데에 쓰여. 진정해! **2 go easy on/with sth** INFORMAL to not use too much of something ‖ 어떤 것을 너무 많이 쓰지 않다. 주의해서 쓰다: *My doctor said that I should go easy on the salt.* 의사는 내가 소금을 과용하지 말아야 한다고 말했다. **3 go easy on sb** INFORMAL to be more gentle and less strict or angry with someone ‖ 남에게 보다 부드러우며 덜 엄격하게 하거나 화를 잘 내지 않다. 너그럽게 대하다: *Go easy on Peter – he's having a hard time at school.* 피터를 너그럽게 봐줘. 요즘 학교에서 힘들어 하고 있어. **4 rest/sleep easy** to be able to relax because you are not worried or anxious ‖ 걱정이나 근심이 없기 때문에 긴장을 풀 수 있다. 편히 쉬다/자다: *I won't rest easy until I know she's safe.* 그녀가 안전하다는 것을 알 때까지 난 편히 쉴 수 없을 거야. **5 easy does it** SPOKEN used in order to tell someone to be careful, especially when s/he is moving something ‖ 특히 남이 물건을 옮기고 있을 때 조심하라고 말하는 데에 쓰여. 조심하다 **6 easier said than done** SPOKEN used when it would be difficult to actually do what someone has suggested ‖ 남이 제안한 일을 실제로 실행에 옮기기가 어려울 때에 쓰여. 말하기는 쉽지만 행하기는 어렵다: *I should just tell her to go away, but that's easier said than done.* 난 그녀에게 그저 떠나라고 말해야 하는데 그게 말이 쉽지 잘 안 된다.

easy chair /ˈ.. ˌ./ *n* a large comfortable chair ‖ 대형 안락의자

eas·y·go·ing /ˌiziˈgoʊɪŋ/ *adj* not easily worried or annoyed ‖ 쉽게 걱정하거나 화내지 않는. 느긋한. 마음 편한: *Phil's a pretty easygoing person.* 필은 상당히 느긋한 사람이다.

easy lis·ten·ing /ˌ.. ˈ../ *n* [U] music that is relaxing to listen to ‖ 듣기 편한 음악

eat /it/ *v* **ate, eaten** /ˈiˀtn/, **eating 1** [I, T] to put food in your mouth and swallow it ‖ 음식을 입 속에 넣고 삼키다. 먹다: *Eat your dinner!* 저녁 먹어라! / *eat like a horse/bird* (=eat a lot or eat very little) 많이 [조금] 먹다 / *eat right* (=eat food that keeps you healthy) 몸에 좋은 음식을 섭취하다 **2** [I] to have a meal ‖ 식사하다: *What time do we eat?* 우리 몇 시에 식사하지? **3 eat sb alive/eat sb for breakfast** INFORMAL to be very angry with someone ‖ 남에게 매우 화내다 **4 eat your heart out** INFORMAL used in order to say that someone should be sad or JEALOUS ‖ 남이 틀림없이 슬프거나 질투할 것이라고 말하는 데에 쓰여: *Yeah, I just bought a new convertible. Eat your heart out, Jay.* 이 봐, 나 방금 컨버터블형으로 새 차 뽑았어. 샘나지, 제이 **5 what's eating him/her/you?** SPOKEN said in order to ask why someone seems annoyed or upset ‖ 남이 화나 있거나 심란해 보이는 까닭을 묻는 데에 쓰여. 무슨 일이냐? **6 eat your words** INFORMAL to admit that what you said was wrong ‖ 자신이 했던 말이 잘못이라고 인정하다: *I had to eat my words when he turned up on time after all.* 그가 결국 제 시간에 나타났을 때 난 내가 한 말이 틀렸음을 인정해야 했다. **7 eat crow/eat humble pie** INFORMAL to be forced to admit that you were wrong and say that you are sorry ‖ 마지못해 자신의 잘못을 인정하고 미안하다고 하다 **8** [T] also **eat up** SPOKEN to use all of something until it is gone ‖ 사물이 없어질 때까지 다 쓰다. …을 써서 없애다: *That car of mine just eats money.* 나의 저 차는 돈 먹는 기계일 뿐이야.

eat sth ↔ **away, eat away at** sth *phr v* [T] to gradually remove or reduce the amount of something ‖ 어떤 것의 양을 점차 없애거나 감소시키다: *Rust had eaten away at the metal frame.* 녹이 슬어 그 철골이 부식되었다.

eat into sth *phr v* [T] **1** to gradually reduce the amount of time, money etc. that is available ‖ 이용 가능한 시간·돈 등의 양을 서서히 감소시키다: *All these car expenses are really eating into our savings.* 이 차들에 들어가는 모든 비용 때문에 저축한 돈이 점점 줄어들고 있다. **2** to damage or destroy something ‖ 어떤 것을 손상시키거나 파괴하다: *This acid will eat into the surface of the metal.* 이 산은 금속 표면을 손상시킬 것이다.

eat out *phr v* [I] to eat in a restaurant ‖ 음식점에서 먹다. 외식하다: *I don't feel* *like cooking. Let's eat out tonight.* 나 요리하기 싫은데, 오늘 밤 외식하자.

eat sth ↔ **up** *phr v* [I, T] SPOKEN to eat all of something ‖ 전부를 먹다. 다 먹어치우다: *Come on, Kaylee, eat up!* 자, 케일리, 다 먹어치워!

eat·er /'itə/ *n* **big/light/fussy etc. eater** someone who eats a lot, not much, only particular things etc. ‖ 많이·많지 않게·특정 음식만 먹는 사람. 대식가/소식가/식성이 까다로운 사람

eat·ing dis·or·der /'.. .,../ *n a* medical condition in which you do not eat normal amounts of food or do not eat regularly ‖ 정상적인 양의 음식을 먹지 않거나 규칙적으로 먹지 않는 의학적 증세. 섭식 장애 —see also ANOREXIA, BULIMIA

eaves /ivz/ *n* [plural] the edges of a roof that stick out beyond the walls ‖ 담 너머로 돌출된 지붕의 가장자리. 처마: *birds nesting under the eaves* 처마 밑에 둥지를 튼 새들

eaves·drop /'ivzdrɑp/ *v* **-pped, -pping** [I] to listen secretly to other people's conversations ‖ 다른 사람들의 대화를 몰래 엿듣다. 도청하다 – **eavesdrop·per** *n* —compare OVERHEAR

eavesdrop

ebb¹ /ɛb/ *n* **1 ebb and flow** a situation or state in which something increases and decreases in a type of pattern ‖ 어떤 것이 한 형태로 증가하고 감소하는 상황 또는 상태. 성쇠. 증감: *the ebb and flow of consumer demand* 소비자 수요의 증감 **2 be at a low ebb** to be in a bad state or condition ‖ 나쁜 상태나 형편에 처해 있다: *By March 1933, the economy was at its lowest ebb.* 1933년 3월까지 경제 상황은 최악이었다. **3** [singular, U] the flow of the sea away from the shore, when the TIDE goes out ‖ 조수가 빠져나갈 때 해안으로부터 멀어지는 바닷물의 흐름. 썰물. 간조

ebb² *v* [I] **1** LITERARY to gradually decrease ‖ 서서히 감소하다: *His courage slowly ebbed away.* 그는 점점 용기를 잃었다. **2** if the TIDE ebbs, it flows away from the shore ‖ 조수가 해안으로부터 멀어지다. 간조가 되다

eb·o·ny /'ɛbəni/ *n* **1** [C, U] a tree with dark hard wood, or the wood itself ‖ 검고 단단한 목재, 또는 그 나무. 흑단 (나무) **2** [U] LITERARY a black color ‖ 검은색 – **ebony** *adj*

e-book /'. ./ *n* also **electronic book** a book that you read on a computer screen or on a special small computer that you can hold in your hands, and that is not printed on paper ‖ 컴퓨터 화면이나 손에 쥘 수 있는 특수 소형 컴퓨터로 볼 수 있으며, 종이로 인쇄되지 않는 책. 전자책

e·bul·lient /ɪ'bʌlyənt, ɪ'bʊl-/ *adj* FORMAL very happy and excited ‖ 매우 즐겁고 흥분된. 열광적인: *an ebullient mood* 열광적인 분위기 – **ebullience** *n* [U]

e-busi·ness /'. ,../ *n* [C] electronic business; the activity of buying and selling goods and services and doing other business activities using a computer and the Internet ‖ electronic business(전자 사업)의 약어; 컴퓨터와 인터넷을 이용해 재화와 용역을 사고 팔며 기타 사업 활동을 하는 행위

e-cash /'. ./ *n* [U] money that can be used to buy things on the Internet, but that does not exist in a physical form or belong to any particular country ‖ 인터넷 상에서 물건을 사는 데에 쓸 수 있지만, 물리적 형태로 존재하거나 어떤 특정 국가에 속하지 않는 돈. 전자 화폐

ec·cen·tric¹ /ɪk'sɛntrɪk/ *adj* behaving in a way that is unusual and strange ‖ 유별나고 이상하게 행동하는. 엉뚱한. 별난: *That old lady has some eccentric habits.* 저 나이든 여인은 별난 습관들이 좀 있다. – **eccentricity** /,ɛksɛn'trɪsəti/ *n* [C, U]

eccentric² *n* an unusual and strange person ‖ 유별나고 이상한 사람. 괴짜

ec·cle·si·as·ti·cal /ɪ,klizi'æstɪkəl/ *adj* relating to the Christian church ‖ 크리스트 교회에 관한: *ecclesiastical history* 크리스트 교회의 역사

ech·o¹ /'ɛkoʊ/ *n, plural* **echoes** a sound that you hear again because it was made near something such as a wall or a hill ‖ 벽이나 언덕 등의 가까이에서 소리를 냈기 때문에 다시 들을 수 있는 소리. 메아리. 반향음

echo² *v* **echoed, echoed, echoing 1** [I] if a sound echoes, it is heard again because it was made near something such as a wall or a hill ‖ 소리가 벽이나 언덕 등의 가까이에서 났기 때문에 다시 들리다. 소리가 울리다[반향하다]: *voices echoing around the cave* 동굴 주위에 울려 퍼지는 목소리 **2 echo with** to be full of a sound ‖ 어떤 소리로 가득 차다: *The* *theater echoed with laughter and applause.* 그 극장에는 웃음소리와 박수갈채가 울려 퍼졌다. **3** [T] to repeat what someone else has said ‖ 남이 말했던 것을 되풀이하다. 남의 말을 되풀이하다: *This report simply echoes what I said two weeks ago.* 이 보고서는 내가 2주 전에 말한 내용을 반복하고 있을 뿐이다.

é·clair /eɪˈklɛr, ɪ-/ *n* a long cake covered with chocolate and filled with cream ‖ 크림을 넣어 초콜릿을 씌운 긴 케이크. 에클레어

e·clipse¹ /ɪˈklɪps/ *n* a short time when you cannot see the sun because the moon is in front of it, or when you cannot see the moon because it is covered by the earth's shadow ‖ 달이 해의 정면에 있어 해를 볼 수 없거나, 또는 달이 지구의 그림자에 가려져 달을 볼 수 없는 짧은 시간. 일식. 월식

eclipse² *v* [T] **1** to become more powerful, famous, important etc. than someone or something else ‖ 다른 사람이나 사물보다 더 힘 있고 유명하고 중요하게 되다. 다른 것을 능가하다: *a 100-meter record that was eclipsed only ten days after it was set* ‖ 수립된 지 열흘만에 갱신된 100미터 기록 **2** to make the sun or moon disappear in an ECLIPSE ‖ 일식 또는 월식으로 해나 달을 보이지 않게 하다

e·co·log·i·cal /ˌikəˈlɑdʒɪkəl, ˌɛ-/ *adj* **1** relating to the way that plants, animals, and people are related to each other and to their environment ‖ 식물·동물·인간이 상호 간에 그리고 각각의 환경과 관계 맺는 방식에 관련된. 생태의: *ecological problems caused by the huge oil spill* 대규모 기름 유출로 야기된 생태 문제 **2** concerned with making or keeping the environment healthy ‖ 환경을 건강하게 만들거나 보존하는 데에 관한. 환경의: *an ecological study* 환경 연구 **– ecologically** *adv*

e·col·o·gy /ɪˈkɑlədʒi/ *n* [singular, U] the way in which plants, animals, and people are related to each other and to their environment, or the study of this ‖ 식물·동물·인간이 상호 간에 그리고 각각의 환경과 관계 맺는 방식, 또는 이를 연구하는 학문. 생태(학) **– ecologist** *n*

ec·o·nom·ic /ˌɛkəˈnɑmɪk, ˌi-/ *adj* relating to business, industry, and managing money ‖ 사업·산업·자금 관리에 관계된. 경제의: *economic development* 경제 발전 **– economically** *adv*

ec·o·nom·i·cal /ˌɛkəˈnɑmɪkəl, ˌi-/ *adj* using time, money, products, etc.

without wasting any ‖ 어떤 것도 낭비하지 않고 시간·돈·제품 등을 쓰는. 절약하는. 검소한. 알뜰한: *an economical way to produce energy* 경제적인 에너지 생산 방법 **– economically** *adv*

ec·o·nom·ics /ˌɛkəˈnɑmɪks, ˌi-/ *n* [U] the study of the way in which money, goods, and services are produced and used ‖ 돈·재화·용역이 생산되고 사용되는 방식에 대한 연구. 경제학

e·con·o·mist /ɪˈkɑnəmɪst/ *n* someone who studies ECONOMICS ‖ 경제학을 연구하는 사람. 경제학자

e·con·o·mize /ɪˈkɑnəˌmaɪz/ *v* [I] to save something such as money, time, effort, etc. by using it carefully and not wasting it ‖ 신중하게 쓰고 낭비하지 않음으로써 돈·시간·노력 등을 절약하다: *We're trying to economize on food costs.* 우리는 식품비를 절약하려고 애쓰고 있다.

e·con·o·my¹ /ɪˈkɑnəmi/ *n* **1** the way that money, businesses, and products are organized in a particular country, area etc. ‖ 특정 국가·지역 등에서 돈·사업·제품이 조직되는 방식. 경제: *A new factory would help the local economy.* (=in a particular town or city) 새 공장은 지역 경제에 도움을 줄 것이다. / *the growing economies of southeast Asia* 동남 아시아의 성장하는 경제 **2** [U] the careful use of money, time, products etc. so that nothing is wasted ‖ 아무것도 낭비하지 않도록 돈·시간·물건 등의 신중한 사용. 절약. 검약

economy² *adj* **economy size/ package etc.** the biggest container that a product is sold in ‖ 제품을 넣어 파는 가장 큰 용기. 절약형 사이즈/포장

economy class /ˈ.ˌ.. ./, ˌ.ˈ./ *n* [U] the cheapest way to travel on a plane ‖ 비행기로 여행하는 가장 값싼 수단. 비행기의 보통석[이코노미 클래스]

e·co·sys·tem /ˈikoʊˌsɪstəm/ *n* all the animals and plants in a particular area, and the way in which they are related to each other and to their environment ‖ 특정 지역의 모든 동·식물과 그것들이 상호 간에, 그리고 환경과 관계를 맺는 방식. 생태계

ec·sta·sy /ˈɛkstəsi/ *n* **1** [C, U] a feeling of extreme happiness ‖ 매우 행복한 느낌. 황홀경: *Fans sang along, in ecstasy at hearing their old favorites.* 팬들은 그들의 과거의 애창곡을 듣는 황홀경에 빠져 함께 따라 불렀다. **2 Ecstasy** [U] an illegal drug used especially by young people to give a feeling of happiness and

E

energy ‖ 특히 젊은이들이 쓰는, 도취감과 활력을 주는 불법 마약. 엑스터시

ec·stat·ic /ɪkˈstætɪk, ɛk-/ adj feeling extremely happy and excited ‖ 매우 기쁘고 흥분한. 무아지경에 빠진. 황홀한: *Luke is ecstatic about being accepted at Harvard.* 루크는 하버드 입학 허가를 받고 기뻐 날뛰고 있다.

ec·u·men·i·cal /ˌɛkyəˈmɛnɪkəl/ adj bringing together different Christian churches, or supporting this ‖ 다른 크리스트 교회들을 한데 불러 모으는, 또는 이를 지지하는. 전(全) 크리스트 교회의

ec·ze·ma /ˈɛksəmə, ˈɛgzəmə, ɪgˈzimə/ n [U] a condition in which skin becomes dry and red, and begins to ITCH ‖ 피부가 건조하고 벌개져서 가렵게 되는 상태. 습진

ed. n [singular, U] INFORMAL the abbreviation of EDUCATION ‖ education의 약어: *the adult ed. department* 성인 교육 분과

E

ed·dy /ˈɛdi/ n a circular movement of water, wind, dust etc. ‖ 물·바람·먼지 등의 소용돌이 **- eddy** v [I]

edge¹ /ɛdʒ/ n **1** the part of something that is farthest from the center ‖ 사물의 중심에서 가장 먼 부분. 가장자리: *She had sewn ribbon on the edge of the cloth.* 그녀는 천의 가장자리에 리본을 꿰맸다. / *a lake with houses around the edge* 집들로 둘러싸인 호수 **2** the thin sharp part of a tool used for cutting ‖ 절단하는 데에 쓰는 연장의 얇고 날카로운 부분. 날 **3** an advantage in a competition, game, or fight ‖ 경쟁[게임, 싸움]에서의 우세: *This new software should give our company an edge in the market.* 이 새 소프트웨어로 우리 회사가 시장에서 우위를 점하게 될 것이다. **4 be on edge** to feel nervous because you are expecting something bad to happen ‖ 나쁜 일이 일어날 것이라 예상하기 때문에 조마조마하다. 몹시 초조하다. 신경이 곤두서다: *Rudy was on edge all night.* 루디는 밤새 몹시 초조했다.

edge² v **1** [I, T] to move slowly and gradually, or to make something do this ‖ 천천히·점진적으로 움직이거나 이렇게 움직이게 하다: *Ramon edged the gun toward my hand.* 라몬은 내 손을 향해 총을 움직였다. / *Witnesses edged away from the scene.* 목격자들은 현장에서 슬금슬금 떠났다. **2** [T] to put something on the edge or border of something else ‖ 사물을 다른 사물의 가장자리나 경계에 놓다: *sleeves edged with gold thread* 금실로 테두리를 두른 소매 **3** [I, T] to develop or increase slowly and gradually, or to make something do this ‖ 서서히 점진적으로 발전하거나 증가하다, 또는 어떤 것을 이렇게 하도록 하다: *The price of gasoline is edging up.* 휘발유 가격이 서서히 상승하고 있다

edge·wise /ˈɛdʒwaɪz/ adv **1 not get a word in edgewise** to not be able to say something in a conversation because someone else is talking too much ‖ 대화에서 남이 너무 말을 많이 해서 어떤 것을 말할 수 없다. 말할 기회를 얻지 못하다: *When Ann's mother is here I can't get a word in edgewise.* 앤의 엄마가 여기 있으면 내가 말할 기회가 없다. **2** with the edge or thinnest part forward ‖ 가장자리나 가장 가는 부분을 앞으로 향하고: *Slide the table in edgewise.* 탁자 모서리를 앞으로 해서 밀어라.

edg·y /ˈɛdʒi/ adj nervous and easy to upset ‖ 초조하고 화나기 쉬운. 신경이 곤두선: *Bill was edgy after a hard day at work.* 빌은 직장에서 힘든 시간을 보낸 후 신경이 곤두섰다.

ed·i·ble /ˈɛdəbəl/ adj something that is edible is safe or acceptable to eat ‖ 어떤 것이 먹기에 안전한, 또는 먹을 수 있는. 식용의 **—opposite** INEDIBLE

e·dict /ˈidɪkt/ n FORMAL an official public order made by someone in a position of power ‖ 권력의 지위에 있는 사람이 내린 공식 명령. 칙령. 포고

ed·i·fice /ˈɛdəfɪs/ n FORMAL a large building ‖ 큰 건물

ed·i·fy /ˈɛdəˌfaɪ/ v [T] FORMAL to improve someone's mind or character by teaching him/her something ‖ 누군가에게 무엇을 가르쳐서 마음이나 품성을 개선시키다. 덕성을 함양하다. 계발하다 **– edification** /ˌɛdəfəˈkeɪʃən/ n [U]

ed·it /ˈɛdɪt/ v [T] to prepare a book, movie, article etc. for people to read or see by arranging the parts, correcting mistakes, and deciding which parts to keep ‖ 부분별로 배열하고 잘못을 고치고 어떤 부분을 유지시켜야 하는지를 결정해서 책·영화·기사 등을 사람들이 읽거나 보도록 준비하다. 편집하다

e·di·tion /ɪˈdɪʃən/ n the form that a book is printed in, or the total numbers of a particular book produced at one time ‖ 책이 인쇄된 양식이나 한 번에 제작된 특정한 책의 전체 부수. 간행물의 판

edge

corner edge

edge

(版). 같은 판의 발행 부수: *the newest edition of a dictionary* 최신판 사전

ed·i·tor /ˈɛdətəʳ/ *n* **1** the person who decides what should be included in a newspaper, magazine etc. ‖ 신문·잡지 등에서 실어야 할 내용을 결정하는 사람. 주필. 편집장 **2** someone who prepares a book, movie etc. for printing or broadcasting by deciding what to include and checking for any mistakes ‖ 포함시킬 내용을 결정하고 오류에 대한 점검을 하여 인쇄나 방송을 하려고 책·영화 등을 준비하는 사람. 편집자 – **editorial** /ˌɛdəˈtɔriəl/ *adj*

ed·i·to·ri·al /ˌɛdəˈtɔriəl/ *n* a piece of writing in a newspaper that gives the opinion of the writer rather than reporting facts ‖ 사실 보도보다는 필자의 견해를 제공하는 신문의 일련의 글. 사설: *an editorial on* (=about) *gun control laws* 총포 규제법에 관한 사설

ed·u·cate /ˈɛdʒə.keɪt/ *v* [T] to teach someone, especially in a school or college ‖ 특히 학교나 대학에서 사람을 가르치다. 교육하다: *Most Americans are educated in public schools.* 대다수의 미국인들은 공립학교에서 교육을 받는다. / *We need to educate ourselves about environmental issues.* 우리는 환경 문제에 대해 스스로를 교육할 필요가 있다. – **educator** *n*

ed·u·cat·ed /ˈɛdʒə.keɪtɪd/ *adj* **1** having knowledge as a result of studying or being taught ‖ 학습이나 배움의 결과로 지식을 지닌. 교육을 받은. 교양 있는: *Frank comes from a well-educated family.* 프랭크는 교양 있는 가문 출신이다. **2 educated guess** a guess that is likely to be correct because you know something about the subject ‖ 주제에 대해서 무언가를 알기 때문에 정확할 것이라는 추측. 경험에 의한 추측

ed·u·ca·tion /ˌɛdʒəˈkeɪʃən/ *n* [singular, U] **1** the process of learning in a school or other program of study ‖ 학교나 다른 학습 프로그램상의 배우는 과정. 교육: *parents saving for their kids' college education* 자녀의 대학 교육을 위해 저축하고 있는 부모를 **2** the work of teaching in schools and colleges ‖ 학교·대학교에서 가르치는 일. 교직: *jobs in higher education* (=colleges) 대학에서 가르치는 일

ed·u·ca·tion·al /ˌɛdʒəˈkeɪʃənəl/ *adj* **1** relating to teaching and learning ‖ 가르치고 배우는 것과 관련된. 교육의: *educational opportunities for high school graduates* 고교 졸업생을 위한 교육의 기회 **2** teaching you something that you did not know ‖ 알지 못했던 것을 가르치는. 교육적인: *It was really educational, one of the best jobs I've had.* 그것은 정말 배운 바가 많은, 내가 가진 최고의 직업 중 하나였다. – **educationally** *adv*

ed·u·tain·ment /ˌɛdʒuˈteɪnmənt/ *n* [U] movies, television programs, or computer SOFTWARE that both educate and entertain children ‖ 아이들을 교육하면서 즐거움도 주는 영화[텔레비전 프로그램, 컴퓨터 소프트웨어). 에듀테인먼트. 오락성을 겸비한 시청각 교육

eel /il/ *n* a long thin fish that looks like a snake ‖ 뱀처럼 생긴 길고 가는 물고기. 장어

ee·rie /ˈɪri/ *adj* strange and frightening ‖ 이상하고 무서운. 으스스한. 기분 나쁜. 무시무시한: *an eerie light* 으스스한 불빛 – **eerily** *adv*

ef·fect¹ /ɪˈfɛkt/ *n* **1** [C, U] a result, or a reaction to something or someone ‖ 결과, 또는 사물이나 사람에 대한 반응. 영향. 효과: *the effects of a long illness* 오랜 질병의 영향 / *Seeing him so upset really had an effect on Mom.* 그가 그렇게 심란해 하는 것을 보고 엄마는 정말로 영향을 받았다. / *Red has the effect of making the room seem warmer.* 빨간색은 방을 더욱 따뜻하게 보이게 하는 효과가 있다. **2 put sth into effect** to make a plan or idea happen ‖ 계획이나 생각을 발현시키다. …을 실행[시행]하다: *Nothing had been done to put the changes into effect.* 변화를 일으키려는 어떤 조치도 취해지지 않았다. **3 come/go into effect** to start officially ‖ 공식적으로 시작하다. 발효하다: *The new tax laws come into effect January 1st.* 그 새 조세법은 1월 1일자로 발효된다. **4 take effect** to start to have results, or to start being used ‖ 효과가 생기기 시작하다, 또는 사용되기 시작하다. 듣다. 효험이 있다: *The drug should take effect in about ten minutes.* 그 약은 약 10분 이내에 약효가 나타난다. **5 in effect** used when you are describing what the real situation is, instead of what it seems to be ‖ 어떻게 보이는가보다는 실제 상황이 어떤지를 기술할 때 쓰여. 사실상. 본질적으로는: *Ellie is his secretary, but in effect she's the manager.* 엘리는 그의 비서이지만 사실상 그녀는 지배인이다. — compare AFFECT, EFFECTS

effect² *v* [T] FORMAL to make something happen ‖ 무엇을 발생하게 하다. 초래하다. 달성하다

ef·fec·tive /ɪˈfɛktɪv/ *adj* **1** producing the result that was wanted or intended ‖ 원하거나 의도된 결과를 일으키는. 효과적인. 효험이 있는: *a very effective medicine for headaches* 두통에 아주 효과적인 약 —opposite INEFFECTIVE **2** done with skill, or having a skillful way of doing things ‖ 기술적으로 이룬, 또는 어떤 일을 솜씨있게 하는. 역량 있는: *an effective politician/speech* 역량 있는 정치인[감동적인 연설] —opposite INEFFECTIVE **3 be/become effective** to be in use, or to start to be in use officially ‖ 사용되다, 또는 공식적으로 사용되기 시작하다. 실시 중이다. 유효하다: *These prices are effective from April 1.* 이 가격들은 4월 1일부터 유효하다. – **effectiveness** *n* [U]

ef·fec·tive·ly /ɪˈfɛktɪvli/ *adv* **1** in a way that produces the result you wanted ‖ 자신이 원하는 결과를 가져오는 방식으로. 효과적으로. 유효하게: *He didn't deal with the problem very effectively.* 그는 그 문제를 매우 효과적으로 처리하지 못했다. **2** actually; really ‖ 실제적으로; 사실상: *By parking here you effectively prevented everyone from leaving.* 네가 여기에 주차해서 모든 사람이 사실상 차를 빼지 못했다.

ef·fects /ɪˈfɛkts/ *n* [plural] FORMAL the things that someone owns; BELONGINGS ‖ 사람이 소유하는 것들. 소유물. 소지품; 兪 belongings —see also SPECIAL EFFECTS

ef·fem·i·nate /ɪˈfɛmənɪt/ *adj* a man or boy who is effeminate behaves like a woman or girl ‖ 남자나 소년이 여자나 소녀처럼 행동하는. 사내답지 못한. 여자같이 나약한

ef·fer·ves·cent /ˌɛfərˈvɛsənt/ *adj* **1** TECHNICAL a liquid that is effervescent has BUBBLES of gas rising in it ‖ 액체가 기포가 일어나는. 부글부글 끓는 **2** someone who is effervescent is very active and cheerful ‖ 사람이 매우 활동적이고 쾌활한. 활기찬. 기운이 넘치는 – **effervescence** *n* [U]

ef·fi·cient /ɪˈfɪʃənt/ *adj* working well, quickly, and without wasting time, energy, or effort ‖ 일을 빨리 잘 하고 시간[에너지, 노력]을 낭비하지 않는. 유능한. 실력 있는. 능률적인: *a very efficient secretary/organization* 아주 유능한 비서[능률적인 조직] – **efficiency** *n* [U] – **efficiently** *adv* —opposite INEFFICIENT

ef·fi·gy /ˈɛfədʒi/ *n* a figure of a particular person that is usually burned in order to show that the person is not liked ‖ 특정한 사람을 좋아하지 않음을 나타내기 위해 보통 태워 버리는 특정인의 형상. 인형. 우상

ef·flu·ent /ˈɛfluənt/ *n* [C, U] FORMAL liquid waste that flows out of a place ‖ 어떤 장소에서 흘러나오는 액체 폐기물. 폐수. 오수

ef·fort /ˈɛfərt/ *n* **1** [U] the physical or mental energy needed to do something ‖ 어떤 일을 하는 데 필요한 육체적 또는 정신적 에너지. 노력: *Kenny's teacher wants him to put more effort into his work.* 케니의 선생님은 그가 공부에 더 많은 노력을 기울이기를 원한다. / *I'm so tired, I can't do anything that takes any effort.* 나는 너무 피곤해서 힘이 드는 일은 어떤 일도 할 수 없다. / *Is it really worth the effort to move these boxes?* 이 상자들을 과연 애써서 옮겨야 하는 걸까? **2** [C, U] an attempt to do something that may be difficult ‖ 어려울 것 같은 일을 하려는 시도. 분투: *Sheila's very nice when you make the effort to know her better.* 실러를 좀 더 알려고 들면 그녀는 상당히 괜찮은 편이다. / *This is an effort to help the homeless.* 이것은 집 없는 사람들을 도우려는 활동이다. / *Tom will do anything in his efforts to* (=in order to) *please his wife.* 톰은 아내를 즐겁게 하려고 무슨 일이든지 할 것이다.

ef·fort·less /ˈɛfərtlɪs/ *adj* done skillfully in a way that seems easy ‖ 쉬워 보이는 방식으로 능숙하게 하는. 노력이 필요 없는. 쉬운: *Brad's seemingly effortless skiing* 겉보기에 힘들이지 않고 타는 브래드의 스키 타는 솜씨. – **effortlessly** *adv*

ef·fu·sive /ɪˈfyusɪv/ *adj* showing strong, excited feelings ‖ 격하며 흥분된 감정을 보이는. 지나치게 감정적인. 과장된. 심정을 토로한: *effusive greetings* 지나치게 감정적인 인사말 – **effusively** *adv*

EFL English as a Foreign Language; the methods used for teaching English to people whose first language is not English, and who do not live in an English-speaking country ‖ English as a Foreign Language (외국어로서의 영어)의 약어; 모국어가 영어가 아니고 영어 사용 국가에서 거주하지 않는 사람에게 영어를 가르치는 데 사용되는 방법

e.g. /ˌi ˈdʒi/ a written abbreviation that means "for example" ‖ "for example"을 의미하는 약어. 예를 들면: *the Gulf States, e.g. Texas, Louisiana, and Mississippi* 멕시코 만 연안의 여러 주(州), 예를 들면 텍사스 주, 루이지애나 주, 미시시피 주

e·gal·i·tar·i·an /ɪˌgælə'tɛriən/ *adj* believing that everyone should have the same rights and opportunities ‖ 모든 사람이 동일한 권리와 기회를 지녀야 한다고 믿는. 평등주의의 – **egalitarianism** *n* [U]

egg¹ /ɛg/ *n* **1** a slightly round object with a hard surface that contains a baby bird, insect, snake etc. ‖ 새끼 새·곤충·뱀 등이 들어 있는 표면이 딱딱하고 약간 둥근 물질. 알: *We saw two eggs in the bluebird's nest.* 우리는 지빠귀의 둥지에서 알 2개를 보았다. **2** an egg from a chicken, used as food ‖ 음식으로 사용되는 닭의 알. 달걀 **3** a cell produced inside a female that can develop into a new animal or person when it joins with a SPERM ‖ 정자와 결합해서 새로운 동물이나 사람으로 성장하게 될 여성의 체내에서 생산되는 세포. 난자. 난세포

egg² *v*

egg sb ↔ **on** *phr v* [T] to encourage someone to do something that is not wise for him/her to do ‖ 현명하지 못한 일을 하도록 남을 고무시키다. 부추기다. 꼬드기다. 충동질하다: *He wouldn't have dived off the bridge if people hadn't egged him on.* 사람들이 그에게 충동질하지만 않았다면 그는 다리에서 뛰어내리지 않았을 것이다.

egg·head /'ɛghɛd/ *n* INFORMAL someone who is very educated but not very practical ‖ 상당한 교육을 받은 사람이지만 아주 현실적이지 못한 사람. 지식인

egg·plant /'ɛgplænt/ *n* [C, U] a large shiny dark purple fruit that is cooked and eaten as a vegetable ‖ 야채로 요리해서 먹는 크고 윤기 나는 짙은 자줏빛 과일. 가지 —see picture on page 944

egg·shell /'ɛgʃɛl/ *n* [C, U] the hard outside part of a bird's egg ‖ 새 알의 딱딱한 바깥 부분. 알껍질

e·go /'igoʊ/ *n* **1** the opinion that you have about yourself ‖ 자기 자신에 대해 가지고 있는 의견. 자기. 자아: *Her boyfriend has a big ego.* (=thinks he is very interesting or important) 그녀의 남자 친구는 자존심이 무척 강하다. **2 ego trip** INFORMAL something that someone does for himself/herself because it makes him/her feel good or important ‖ 자신을 훌륭하거나 중요하다고 느끼게 하기 때문에 사람이 스스로 하는 것. 자만. 자기 도취

e·go·tism /'igəˌtɪzəm/, **e·go·ism** /'igoʊɪzəm/ *n* the belief that you are more interesting or important than other people, or behavior that shows

this ‖ 다른 사람들보다 자신이 더 재미있거나 중요하다는 믿음, 또는 이것을 나타내는 행동. 자기 중심(주의) 성향. 이기. 자기 본위 – **egotistical** /ˌigə'tɪstɪkəl/ *adj* – **egotist** /'igətɪst/ *n*

e·gre·gious /ɪ'gridʒəs/ *adj* FORMAL an egregious ERROR (=mistake), failure etc. is extremely bad and noticeable ‖ 잘못·실패 등이 현저하게 나쁘고 눈에 띄는. 지독한 – **egregiously** *adv*

eight /eɪt/ *number* **1** 8 ‖ 8 **2** eight o'clock ‖ 8시: *Dinner will be at eight.* 저녁 식사는 8시에 있습니다.

eight·een /ˌeɪ'tin/ *number* 18 ‖ 18 – **eighteenth** *number*

eighth /eɪtθ/ *number* **1** 8th ‖ 여덟 번째 **2** 1/8 ‖ 8분의 1

eight·y /'eɪti/ *number* **1** 80 ‖ 80 **2 the eighties a)** the years between 1980 and 1989 ‖ 1980년과 1989년 사이의 해. 80년대 **b)** the numbers between 80 and 89, especially when used in measuring temperature ‖ 특히 온도를 측정하는 데 쓰여 80과 89 사이의 숫자. 80도대 – **eightieth** /'eɪtiɪθ/ *number*

ei·ther¹ /'iðə, 'aɪ-/ *conj* used in order to begin a list of possibilities separated by "or" ‖ "or"에 의해 분리되는 가능성 있는 사항을 시작하는 데 쓰여. …이든 (아니면) …이든 어느 한 쪽: *There's either coffee or tea to drink.* 마실 것으로는 커피나 차가 있습니다. / *Either say you're sorry, or get out!* 미안하다고 말하든가 아니면 나가라!

> **USAGE NOTE** either… or and neither… nor
>
> When you use these phrases in formal speech or writing, use a singular verb if the second noun is singular: *If either Doris or Meg calls, please take a message.* / *Neither Theo nor Garth is very tall.* If the second noun is plural, use a plural verb: *If either my sister or my parents come, please let them in.* In informal speech, the verb is usually plural.
> 격식 차린 말이나 글에서 이 구(句)를 사용하는 경우에 두 번째 명사가 단수이면 단수 동사를 쓴다: 도리스나 메그가 전화를 하면 메모 부탁드려요. / 테오도 가스도 모두 키가 아주 크지 않다. 두 번째 명사가 복수이면 복수 동사를 쓴다: 내 여동생이나 부모님이 오시면 들여 보내 주세요. 비격식적인 말에서 동사는 보통 복수형이다.

either² *determiner, pron* **1** one or the

other of two ‖ 둘 중의 하나 또는 다른 하나. 어느 하나의. 어느 쪽의: *I've lived in New York and Chicago, but I don't like either city very much.* 나는 뉴욕과 시카고에 살았지만 나는 두 도시 모두 그렇게 많이 좋아하지 않는다. / *Do you want to meet, or just talk on the phone?" "Either way is fine."* "너 만나고 싶니, 전화로 얘기하고 싶니?" "어느 쪽이든 괜찮아." **2** one and the other of two things; each ‖ 두 가지 중에 하나와 다른 하나; 양쪽의: *He was standing there with a policeman on either side of him.* 그는 양쪽에 경찰관을 대동하고 그곳에 서 있었다. —compare BOTH

USAGE NOTE either, neither, none, and any

In formal speech and writing, use these pronouns with a singular verb : *None/neither of us has seen the exhibit.* / *Is any of the paintings for sale?* In informal speech, you can use a plural verb: *Have either of you ever been to Dallas?*
격식을 차린 말과 글에서 이들 대명사는 단수 동사와 같이 사용된다: 우리들 가운데 아무도[어느 누구도] 전시회를 보지 않았다. / 그림 가운데 어느 것이 판매용입니까? 비격식적으로 말할 때에는 복수 동사를 사용해도 된다: 너희들 모두 댈러스에 가본 적이 있니?

---

either³ *adv* **1** used in negative sentences to mean also ‖ 부정문에서 또한을 의미하는 데 쓰여: *"I haven't seen 'Batman' yet." "I haven't either."* "아직 '배트맨'을 보지 못했어." "나도 보지 못했어." **2 me either** SPOKEN NONSTANDARD used in order to say that something is also true about you ‖ 무언가가 자신에게도 사실임을 말하는 데에 쓰여. 나도 그래: *"I don't like broccoli." "Me either."* "나는 브로콜리를 좋아하지 않아." "나도 그래."

e·jac·u·late /ɪ'dʒækyə,leɪt/ *v* [I, T] when a male ejaculates, SPERM comes out of his PENIS ‖ 남성의 성기에서 정액이 나오다. 사정하다 – **ejaculation** /ɪ,dʒækyə'leɪʃən/ *n* [C, U]

e·ject /ɪ'dʒɛkt/ *v* **1** [T] to push or throw out with force ‖ 힘으로 밀거나 쫓아내다. 빼내다. 내뿜다: *The plane had to eject most of its fuel as it went down.* 그 비행기는 추락하면서 연료를 거의 배출해야 했다. **2** [I] to jump out of a plane that is going to crash ‖ 추락하게 될 비행기에서 뛰쳐나오다. 탈출하다 **3** [T] to make

something come out of a machine by pressing a button ‖ 버튼을 눌러서 물건을 기계에서 나오게 하다. 꺼내다: *Rewind and eject the tape.* 테이프를 되감아서 빼내라. – **ejection** /ɪ'dʒɛkʃən/ *n* [C, U]

eke /ik/ *v*

eke sth ↔ **out** *phr v* [T] LITERARY **1** to make something such as food or money last a long time by using small amounts of it, or by adding something else ‖ 음식물이나 돈 등을 조금씩 사용하거나 다른 것을 추가해서 오랫동안 남아 있게 하다. **2 eke out a living/existence** to get just enough food or money to live on ‖ 겨우 생활해 나갈 만큼의 음식물이나 돈을 얻다. 그럭저럭 생계를 꾸려나가다

e·lab·o·rate¹ /ɪ'læbrɪt/ *adj* having a lot of small details or parts that are connected together in a complicated way ‖ 복잡하게 서로 연결된 다수의 사소한 세부 사항이나 부분들을 가진. 정교한. 꼼꼼한: *The Nelsons are planning an elaborate Thanksgiving dinner.* 넬슨 가족은 추수 감사절 만찬을 꼼꼼히 준비하고 있다. / *wallpaper with an elaborate design* 정교한 디자인으로 된 벽지 – **elaborately** *adv*

e·lab·o·rate² /ɪ'læbə,reɪt/ *v* [I, T] to give more details about something you have said or written ‖ 말한 것이나 글로 쓴 것에 대한 더욱 상세한 내용을 제공하다. 상세하게 말하다[설명하다]: *Would you please elaborate on your earlier statement?* 전번에 말씀하신 것을 좀 더 상세히 말씀해 주시겠습니까? – **elaboration** /ɪ,læbə'reɪʃən/ *n* [U]

an elaborate pattern

a simple pattern

elaborate

e·lapse /ɪ'læps/ *v* [I] FORMAL if a period of time elapses, it passes ‖ 일정 시간이 경과하다. 지나다

e·las·tic /ɪ'læstɪk/ *adj* able to stretch and then go back to its usual shape or size ‖ 늘어났다가 그것의 원래 모양이나 크기로 돌아갈 수 있는. 신축성[탄력]이 있는. 유연한: *an elastic waistband* 신축성 있는 허리띠 – **elasticity** /ɪ,læs'tɪsəti/ *n* [U] – **elastic** /ɪ'læstɪk/ *n*

e·lat·ed /ɪ'leɪtɪd/ *adj* extremely happy and excited ‖ 매우 기쁘고 흥분한. 우쭐한. 의기양양한: *I was elated when Mary told me she was pregnant.* 메리가 임신했다고 말했을 때 나는 매우 기뻤다. – **elation** /ɪ'leɪʃən/ *n* [U]

el·bow¹ /ˈɛlboʊ/ *n* **1** the joint where your arm bends ‖ 팔이 구부러지는 곳에 있는 관절. 팔꿈치 —see picture at BODY **2 elbow room** INFORMAL enough space, so that you can move easily ‖ 쉽게 움직일 수 있을 만한 충분한 공간. 자유로운 행동 범위. 충분한 여유: *Let's sit in a booth. There's more elbow room.* 부스에 앉자. 여유 공간이 더 있네. **3 elbow grease** INFORMAL hard physical effort ‖ 힘든 육체적인 일. 팔을 쓰는 일. 육체 노동: *All it needs is a little elbow grease to get the cabin cleaned up.* 객실 청소에는 약간의 육체 노동만이 필요할 뿐이다.

elbow² *v* [T] to push someone with your elbows, especially in order to move past him/her ‖ 특히 지나쳐 움직이기 위해 팔꿈치로 남을 밀치다. 밀어제치고 나아가다: *She elbowed her way through the crowd.* 그녀는 팔꿈치로 군중을 헤치고 나아갔다.

el·der¹ /ˈɛldɚ/ *adj* **elder brother/sister** an older brother or sister in a family ‖ 가족 중의 나이가 더 많은 남자 또는 여자 형제. 손위의 형/누나: *My elder sister is a nurse.* 내 누나는 간호사이다.

USAGE NOTE elder and older

Use **elder** to talk about the members of a family: *Nick is my elder brother.* Use **older** to compare the age of people or things: *My sister is two years older than I am.* ✗DON'T SAY "elder than."✗
가족 구성원에 대해 말할 때는 **elder**를 쓴다: 닉은 나의 형이다. 사람이나 사물의 나이를 비교하는 데에는 **older**를 쓴다: 내 누이는 나보다 2살 더 많다. "elder than"이라고는 하지 않는다.

---

elder² *n* **1** [C usually plural] someone who is older than you are ‖ 자신보다 나이가 많은 사람. 연장자: *Young people should have respect for their elders.* 젊은이들은 어른들을 공경해야 한다. **2** an older person who is important and respected ‖ 중요하고 존경받는 나이든 사람. 노인. 어른: *the town elders* 읍의 노인들

el·der·ly /ˈɛldɚli/ *adj* **1** a word meaning old, used in order to be polite ‖ 정중하게 쓰이는 노인을 의미하는 말. 초로의. 나이가 지긋한: *an elderly woman with white hair* 머리가 희끗한 나이 지긋한 여자 **2 the elderly** people who are old ‖ 나이든 사람들. 노인층: *a home that provides care for the elderly*

노인들을 보살펴 주는 집 —compare OLD, ANCIENT —see usage note at OLD

el·dest /ˈɛldɪst/ *adj* **eldest son/daughter/brother/sister** the oldest son etc. in a family ‖ 가족 중 제일 나이 많은 아들 등. 장남/장녀/맏형/큰 누나

e·lect¹ /ɪˈlɛkt/ *v* [T] **1** to choose someone for an official position by voting ‖ 투표로 공직자를 뽑다. 선출하다: *Clinton was elected President in 1992.* 클린턴은 1992년에 대통령에 당선되었다. **2 elect to do sth** FORMAL to choose to do something ‖ 어떤 것을 하기로 선택하다. 결정[채택]하다: *Hanley elected to take early retirement.* 핸리는 조기 퇴직하기로 결정했다.

elect² *adj* **president-elect/senator-elect etc.** the person who has been elected but has not officially started his/her job ‖ 당선은 되었지만 직무를 공식적으로 시작하지 않은 사람. 대통령/상원 의원 당선자

e·lec·tion /ɪˈlɛkʃən/ *n* an occasion when you vote in order to choose someone for an official position ‖ 공직자를 선출하기 위해 투표하는 행사. 선거. 표결: *The election results are still coming in.* 선거 결과가 아직 들어오고 있다. – **electoral** /ɪˈlɛktərəl/ *adj*

CULTURE NOTE elections

In the US, there are elections to choose a President and Vice-President every four years. Every two years, all of the members of the House of Representatives and one-third of the Senators are elected. The period of office for a Senator is six years; for a President it is four years; and for a Representative it is two years. A President can only serve for eight years.
미국에서는 4년마다 대통령과 부통령을 뽑는 선거를 한다. 2년마다 모든 하원 의원과 상원 의원 3분의 1을 선출한다. 상원 의원의 재임 기간은 6년이며 대통령은 4년, 하원 의원은 2년이다. 대통령은 8년 동안만 재임할 수 있다.

---

e·lec·tive¹ /ɪˈlɛktɪv/ *n* a subject that a student chooses to study, but that s/he does not have to study in order to GRADUATE ‖ 학생이 공부하기 위해 선택을 하지만 졸업을 목적으로 반드시 공부할 필요는 없는 과목. 선택 과목

elective² *adj* an elective office, position etc. is one for which there is an election ‖ 공직·지위 등이 선거를 통한 것인. 선거

로 임용되는

e·lec·to·ral col·lege /.,... '../ *n*
[singular] a group of people chosen by
the votes of the people in each US state,
who come together to elect the
president ‖ 대통령을 선출하기 위해 함께
모인, 미국 각 주의 주민들이 투표로 선출
한 일단의 사람들. (대통령) 선거인단

e·lec·tor·ate /ɪˈlɛktərɪt/ *n* [singular] all
the people who are allowed to vote in an
election ‖ 선거에서 투표를 하도록 허용된
모든 사람들. 선거인. 유권자

e·lec·tric /ɪˈlɛktrɪk/ *adj* **1** needing
electricity in order to work ‖ 작동하는 데
전기가 필요한. 전기의. 전기로 움직이는:
an electric oven 전기 오븐 / *an electric
guitar* 전기 기타 **2** making people feel
very excited ‖ 사람을 매우 흥분시키는.
충격적인. 감동을 주는: *The atmosphere
at the concert was electric.* 콘서트 분위
기는 감동적이었다.

USAGE NOTE electric and electrical

Use **electric** as an adjective before
the names of things that need
electricity in order to work: *an
electric clock / electric lights.* Use
electrical as a more general word to
talk about people and their work, or
about things that use or produce
electricity: *an electrical engineer / My
dad's company imports electrical
goods.*
작동하는 데 전기가 필요한 사물의 이름
앞에 형용사로 **electric**을 쓴다: 전기
시계/전깃불. 전기를 사용하거나 생산하
는 사람들과 그들의 업무, 또는 사물에
대해 말할 때 더욱 일반적인 단어로서
electrical을 쓴다: 전기 기사 / 우리 아
빠 회사는 전기 제품을 수입한다.

---

e·lec·tri·cal /ɪˈlɛktrɪkəl/ *adj* relating to
or using electricity ‖ 전기에 관련되거나
전기를 사용하는. 전기의: *an electrical
fault* 전기 고장 / *electrical goods* 전기 제
품 —see usage note at ELECTRIC

electric chair /.'.. ,./ *n* **the electric
chair** a chair in which criminals are
killed using electricity ‖ 전기를 사용하여
범죄자들을 죽이는 의자. 사형용 전기의자

e·lec·tri·cian /ɪˌlɛkˈtrɪʃən, i-/ *n*
someone whose job is to fit and repair
electrical equipment ‖ 전기 장치를 설치
하고 수리하는 직업인. 전기 기술자

e·lec·tric·i·ty /ɪˌlɛkˈtrɪsəti, i-/ *n* [U] **1**
the power that is carried by wires and
used in order to provide heat or light, to
make machines work etc. ‖ 전선에 의해

이송되며 열이나 빛을 제공하고 기계를 작
동시키는 데 쓰이는 힘. 전기. 전력: *The
electricity went out* (=stopped working)
during the storm. 폭풍이 부는 동안 전기
가 나갔다. **2** a feeling of excitement ‖ 흥
분된 감정. 격한 감정. 충격: *You could
feel the electricity in the air!* 너는 흥분된
분위기를 느낄 수 있을 거야!

e·lec·tri·fy /ɪˈlɛktrəˌfaɪ/ *v* [T] **1** to
make people feel very excited or
interested ‖ 사람들을 매우 흥분시키거나
흥미를 느끼게 하다. 감동[흥분]시키다:
Guns 'n' Roses electrified the crowd. 건
즈 앤 로즈즈는 군중을 흥분의 도가니로
몰아넣었다. **2** to make electricity
available in a particular area ‖ 특정한
지역에서 전기를 사용할 수 있게 하다. 전
력을 공급하다 – **electrified** *adj* –
electrifying *adj*

e·lec·tro·cute /ɪˈlɛktrəˌkyut/ *v* [T] to
kill someone by passing electricity
through his/her body ‖ 사람의 몸에 전기
를 통하게 하여 죽이다. 감전시켜 죽이다.
전 기 처 형 하 다 – **electrocution**
/ɪˌlɛktrəˈkyuʃən/ *n* [U]

e·lec·trode /ɪˈlɛktroʊd/ *n* the point at
which electricity enters or leaves
something such as a BATTERY ‖ 배터리
등에 전기가 들어가거나 나오는 지점. 전
극

e·lec·trol·y·sis /ɪˌlɛkˈtrɑlɪsɪs/ *n* [U] the
process of using electricity to remove
hair from your face, legs etc. ‖ 얼굴·다
리 등의 털을 제거하려고 전기를 이용하는
과정. 전기 분해 요법

e·lec·tron /ɪˈlɛktrɑn/ *n* a very small
piece of matter that moves around the
nucleus (=central part) of an atom ‖ 원
자핵 주위를 움직이는 매우 작은 물질. 전
자 —compare NEUTRON, PROTON

e·lec·tron·ic /ɪˌlɛkˈtrɑnɪk/ *adj* **1**
electronic equipment, such as
computers or televisions, that uses
electricity in special ways ‖ 컴퓨터나 텔
레비전 등의 장비가 특수한 방식으로 전기
를 이용하는. 전자 활동에 의한 **2** using
electronic equipment ‖ 전자 장비를 사용
하는. 전자의 – **electronically** *adv*

electronic bank·ing /,....'../ *n* [U] a
service provided by banks that allows
people to pay money from one account
to another, pay bills etc. using the
Internet ‖ 인터넷을 이용해서 사람들이 한
계좌에서 다른 계좌로의 이체·청구액의 결
제 등을 하도록 은행이 제공하는 서비스.
전자식 은행 업무

e·lec·tron·ics /ɪˌlɛkˈtrɑnɪks/ *n* [U] the
study of making equipment, such as

computers or televisions, that uses electricity in special ways ‖ 특별한 방식으로 전기를 이용하는 컴퓨터나 텔레비전 등의 장비를 만드는 학문. 전자 공학

el·e·gant /ˈɛləgənt/ adj very beautiful and graceful ‖ 매우 아름답고 고상한. 우아한. 기품이 있는: *a tall elegant woman* 키가 크고 우아한 여인 **– elegance** *n* [U] **– elegantly** *adv*

el·e·gy /ˈɛlədʒi/ *n* a poem or song that shows that you are sad for someone who has died, or sad about something in the past ‖ 죽은 사람이나 과거의 어떤 일에 대해 슬픔을 나타내는 시나 노래. 애가. 만가

el·e·ment /ˈɛləmənt/ *n* **1** a simple chemical substance such as oxygen or gold, that is made of only one type of atom ‖ 오직 한 가지 종류의 원자로 이루어진 산소나 금 등의 단순한 화학 물질. 원소. (구성) 분자[요소, 성분] —compare COMPOUND **2 an element of danger/ truth/risk etc.** a small amount of danger, truth, risk etc. ‖ 약간의 위험·진실·모험 등: *There's an element of truth in what he says.* 그가 말한 내용에는 약간의 진실이 있다. **3** one part of a plan, system, piece of writing etc. ‖ 계획·체제·글 등의 한 부분. 요소: *a movie with all the elements of a great love story* 위대한 사랑 이야기의 모든 요소를 갖춘 영화 **4 be in your element** to be in a situation that you enjoy, because you are good at it ‖ 어떤 것에 능숙하기 때문에 즐기는 입장에 있다. 자기의 진가를 발휘할 수 있는 처지에 있다: *When talking about wine, Glenn is really in his element.* 와인에 관한 얘기가 나오면 글렌은 정말로 자기의 진가를 발휘하게 된다. —see also ELEMENTS

el·e·men·tal /ˌɛləˈmɛntəl/ adj an elemental feeling is simple, basic, and strong ‖ 감정이 단순하며 근본적이고 강렬한

el·e·men·ta·ry /ˌɛləˈmɛntri, -ˈmɛntəri/ adj **1** relating to the first and easiest part of a subject ‖ 특정 과목의 처음이며 가장 쉬운 부분과 관련된. 초보의. 초급의: *a book of elementary math exercises* 기초 수학 수련장 **2** simple or basic ‖ 단순한, 기본의. 기본적인: *the elementary human need for food* 기본적인 인간의 식욕 **3** relating to an ELEMENTARY SCHOOL ‖ 초등학교에 관련된. 초등학교의

elementary school /.. ˈ.. ˌ./ *n* a school in the US for the first six or eight years of a child's education; GRADE SCHOOL ‖ 어린이 교육의 최초 6년 또는 8년을 위한 미국의 학교. 초등학교; 吊 grade school

el·e·ments /ˈɛləmənts/ *n* [plural] weather, especially bad weather ‖ 특히 나쁜 기후. 악천후: *A tent provided shelter from the elements.* 텐트는 악천후로부터 피난처 구실을 했다.

el·e·phant /ˈɛləfənt/ *n* a very large gray animal with two TUSKS (=long curved teeth), big ears, and a trunk (=a long nose) that it can use to pick things up ‖ 두 개의 엄니·큰 귀·물건을 집어올리는 데 쓸 수 있는 긴 코를 가진 매우 큰 회색의 동물. 코끼리

el·e·vate /ˈɛləˌveɪt/ *v* [T] FORMAL **1** to make someone more important, or to make something better ‖ 사람을 더욱 중요하게 하거나 어떤 것을 더욱 좋아지게 하다. 승진시키다. 향상시키다: *Sloane was elevated to the rank of captain.* 슬로엔은 대위 계급으로 진급되었다. **2** to raise someone or something to a higher position or level ‖ 사람이나 사물을 보다 높은 위치나 수준으로 올리다. 높이다: *This drug tends to elevate body temperature.* 이 약은 체온을 상승시키는 경향이 있다.

el·e·va·tion /ˌɛləˈveɪʃən/ *n* **1** a height above the level of the sea ‖ 바다의 기준 수위로부터의 높이. 해발: *We camped at an elevation of 10,000 feet.* 우리는 해발 1만 피트 높이에 캠프를 설치했다. **2** [U] FORMAL the act of making someone more important ‖ 사람을 더욱 중요하게 하는 행위. 승진. 등용: *the judge's elevation to the Supreme Court* 그 판사의 대법원으로의 등용 **3** [C, U] FORMAL an increase in the quantity or level of something ‖ 사물의 양이나 수준의 증가. 상승. 향상. 증진: *Elevation of blood pressure can cause headaches.* 혈압의 상승이 두통을 유발할 수 있다.

el·e·va·tor /ˈɛləˌveɪtə/ *n* a machine in a building that takes people from one level to another ‖ 사람을 한 층에서 다른 층으로 실어다 주는 건물 내의 기계. 엘리베이터

e·lev·en /ɪˈlɛvən/ *number* **1** 11 ‖ 11 **2** eleven o'clock ‖ 11시: *an appointment at eleven* 11시의 약속

e·lev·enth /ɪˈlɛvənθ/ *number* **1** 11th ‖ 11번째 **2** 1/11 ‖ 11분의 1 **3 eleventh hour** the latest possible time ‖ 최후의 가능한 시간. 최후의 기회. 막판: *the eleventh hour cancellation of her wedding* 그녀의 마지막 순간의 결혼 취소

elf /ɛlf/ n, plural **elves** a small imaginary person with pointed ears ‖ 뾰족한 귀를 가진 상상의 작은 인간. 작은 요정(妖精) – **elfin** /ˈɛlfɪn/ adj

e·lic·it /ɪˈlɪsɪt/ v [T] FORMAL to get information, a reaction etc. from someone, when this is difficult ‖ 정보·반응 등을 얻기 어려울 때 남으로부터 정보·반응 등을 얻다. 알아내다. 끌어내다: *Short questions are more likely to elicit a response.* 짧은 질문이 응답을 더 잘 이끌어낼 것 같다.

el·i·gi·ble /ˈɛlədʒəbəl/ adj **1** able or allowed to do something ‖ 어떤 일을 할 수 있거나 할 수 있게 허용되는. …할 자격이 있는. 선출되는 데 알맞은: *In the US you're eligible to vote at the age of 18.* 미국에서는 18세에 투표할 자격이 있다. **2** an eligible man or woman would be good to marry because s/he is rich, attractive etc. ‖ 남성이나 여성이 부유하고 매력적이어서 결혼하기에 좋은. 결혼 상대로서 알맞은[바람직한] – **eligibility** /ˌɛlədʒəˈbɪləti/ n [U]

e·lim·i·nate /ɪˈlɪmɪˌneɪt/ v [T] **1** to get rid of something completely ‖ 무엇을 완전히 제거하다. 삭제하다: *a plan to eliminate all nuclear weapons* 모든 핵무기를 폐기하기 위한 계획 **2 be eliminated** to be defeated in a sports competition, so that you can no longer take part in it ‖ 스포츠 경기에서 패배하여 더 이상 참가할 수 없다. 실격되다. 탈락되다

e·lim·i·na·tion /ɪˌlɪməˈneɪʃən/ n [U] **1** the removal or destruction of something ‖ 사물의 제거 또는 파괴. 배출. 배제: *The elimination of unemployment is still our goal.* 실업 문제를 없애는 것이 여전히 우리의 목표이다. **2 process of elimination** a way of finding out the answer to something by getting rid of other answers that are not correct until only one is left ‖ 해답이 한 개만 남을 때까지 정확하지 않은 다른 대답을 삭제하여 어떤 것에 대한 해답을 찾는 방법. 소거(消去) 과정

e·lite /eɪˈlit, ɪ-/ n a small group of people who are powerful or important because they have money, knowledge, special skills etc. ‖ 돈·지식·특별한 기술 등이 있어서 권력이 있거나 중요한 작은 집단의 사람들. 엘리트. 정예

e·lit·ist /eɪˈlitɪst, ɪ-/ adj DISAPPROVING an elitist system, government etc. is one in which a small group of people have much more power than other people ‖ 체제·정부 등에서 작은 집단의 사람들이 다른 사람들보다 더 많은 권력을 가지는. 엘리트에 의한 지배의. 정예주의의 –

elitism n [U]

elk /ɛlk/ n a large DEER with a lot of hair around its neck ‖ 목 근처에 털이 많은 몸집이 큰 사슴. 엘크. 큰사슴

el·lip·ti·cal /ɪˈlɪptɪkəl/, **el·lip·tic** /ɪˈlɪptɪk/ adj shaped like a circle but with slightly flat sides; OVAL ‖ 원형이지만 옆이 약간 납작한. 타원형의; 冏 oval: *the elliptical orbit of the planets* 행성의 타원형 궤도

elm /ɛlm/ n [C, U] a large tall tree with broad leaves, or the wood of this tree ‖ 넙적한 잎사귀를 가진 크고 높은 나무, 또는 이 나무의 재목. 느릅나무(재목)

e·lon·gat·ed /ɪˈlɔŋɡeɪtɪd/ adj long and thin ‖ 길고 가는: *elongated shadows* 가늘고 긴 그림자 – **elongate** v [I, T]

e·lope /ɪˈloʊp/ v [I] to go away secretly with someone to get married ‖ 결혼할 사람과 몰래 달아나다. 애인과 가출하다 – **elopement** n [C, U]

el·o·quent /ˈɛləkwənt/ adj able to express your ideas, opinions, or feelings clearly, in a way that influences other people ‖ 다른 사람에게 영향을 미치도록 자신의 생각[의견, 감정]을 분명히 표현할 수 있는. …을 잘 나타내는. 유창한. 감명을 주는: *He gave an eloquent speech after dinner.* 그는 만찬 뒤에 감명을 주는 연설을 했다. – **eloquently** adv – **eloquence** n [U]

else /ɛls/ adv **1** a word meaning "in addition," used after words beginning with "any-," "no-," "some-," and after question words ‖ "any-"·"no-"·"some-"으로 시작하는 단어 뒤와 의문사 뒤에 쓰이는 "추가로"를 의미하는 말. 그밖의. 다른: *Clayton needs someone else to help him.* 클레이턴은 다른 사람의 도움이 필요하다. / *There's nothing else to do.* 다른 할 일은 아무것도 없다. / *What else can I get you?* 다른 무엇을 갖다 드릴까요? **2** a word meaning "different," used after words beginning with "any-," "no-," "some-," and after question words ‖ "any-"·"no-"·"some-"으로 시작하는 단어 뒤와 의문사 뒤에 쓰이는 "다른"을 뜻하는 말: *Is there anything else to eat?* 다른 먹을 것이 있느냐? / *She was wearing someone else's coat.* (=not her own coat) 그녀는 다른 사람의 코트를 입고 있었다. / *Well, what else can I do?* 그럼, 내가 무슨 다른 일을 할 수 있을까? **3 or else** used when saying what the result of not doing something will be ‖ 어떤 일을 하지 않은 결과가 어떠할 것이라고 말

할 때에 쓰여. 그렇지 않으면: *They said she'd have to pay, or else she'd go to jail.* 그들은 그녀가 값을 치러야 하고 그렇지 않으면 그녀는 교도소에 가게 될 거라고 말했다. **4 if nothing else** used when a situation gives you one opportunity, or has one good result, even though there are no others ‖ 상황이 한 차례 기회를 주거나 다른 일이 없더라도 한 가지 좋은 결과가 있을 때에 쓰여. 적어도. 최소한: *It's boring, but if nothing else, I can get my homework done.* 지루해, 하지만 최소한 숙제를 끝마칠 수는 있겠다.

else·where /'ɛlswɛr/ *adv* in or to another place ‖ 다른 장소에서[로]: *Most of the city's residents were born elsewhere.* 대다수의 그 도시 거주자들은 다른 곳에서 태어났다.

e·lu·ci·date /ɪ'lusəˌdeɪt/ *v* [I, T] FORMAL to explain very clearly something that is difficult to understand ‖ 이해하기 어려운 것을 아주 분명하게 설명하다. 해명하다. 밝히다

e·lude /ɪ'lud/ *v* [T] **1** to avoid being found or caught by someone, especially by tricking him/her ‖ 특히 사람을 속여서 누군가에게 발견되거나 잡히는 것을 피하다. 잘 피하다. 교묘하게 벗어나다: *Jones eluded the police for six weeks.* 존스는 6주 동안 경찰을 따돌렸다. **2** if something that you want eludes you, you do not find it or achieve it ‖ 자신이 원하는 것을 발견하거나 달성하지 못하다. (바라는 것이) 손에 들어오지 않다: *Success has eluded him so far.* 성공이 그에게서 아주 멀리 날아가 버렸다. **3** if a fact, someone's name etc. eludes you, you cannot remember it ‖ 사실·남의 이름 등을 기억하지 못하다. 생각나지 않다: *Her name eludes me at the moment.* 나는 지금 그녀의 이름이 생각나지 않는다.

e·lu·sive /ɪ'lusɪv/ *adj* difficult to find, or difficult to remember ‖ 발견하기 어렵거나 기억하기 어려운. 눈에 띄지 않는. 교묘히 피하는: *The fox is a sly elusive animal.* 여우는 교활하고 잘 잡히지 않는 동물이다.

elves /ɛlvz/ *n* the plural of ELF ‖ elf의 복수형

'em /əm/ *pron* SPOKEN NONSTANDARD them ‖ 그들을: *Tell the kids I'll pick 'em up after school.* 방과 후에 내가 태우러 간다고 아이들에게 말해라.

e·ma·ci·at·ed /ɪ'meɪʃiˌeɪtɪd/ *adj* extremely thin because of illness or lack of food ‖ 질병이나 식량 부족으로 몹시 마른. 수척한. 초췌한 —see usage note at THIN¹

e-mail, email /'i meɪl/ *n* [U] electronic mail; a system in which you can quickly send letters, information, reports etc. from your computer to someone else who is using a computer ‖ electronic mail (전자 우편)의 약어; 편지·정보(자료)·보고서 등을 자신의 컴퓨터에서 다른 컴퓨터 사용자에게 신속하게 보낼 수 있는 시스템 – **e-mail, email** *v* [T] —see culture note at INTERNET

em·a·nate /'ɛməˌneɪt/ *v*
emanate from sth *phr v* [T] to come from or out of something ‖ 어떤 것으로부터 나오다. 발산하다. 퍼지다: *Wonderful smells were emanating from the kitchen.* 굉장히 좋은 냄새가 부엌에서 나고 있었다.

e·man·ci·pate /ɪ'mænsəˌpeɪt/ *v* [T] FORMAL to make someone free from social, political, or legal rules that limit what s/he can do ‖ 할 수 있는 것을 제한하는 사회적[정치적, 법적] 규제로부터 사람을 자유롭게 하다. 해방하다 – **emancipated** *adj* – **emancipation** /ɪˌmænsə'peɪʃən/ *n* [U]

em·balm /ɪm'bɑm/ *v* [T] to use chemicals to prevent a dead body from decaying ‖ 사체의 부패를 방지하기 위해 화학제품을 사용하다. 방부 처리하다

em·bank·ment /ɪm'bæŋkmənt/ *n* a wide wall of earth or stones built to stop water from flooding an area, or to support a road or railroad ‖ 한 지역의 홍수가 나지 않도록 물을 차단하거나 도로나 철로를 지탱하기 위해 구축한 흙이나 돌로 만든 넓은 벽. 둑. 제방

em·bar·go¹ /ɪm'bɑrgoʊ/ *n* **embargoes** an official order to stop trade with another country ‖ 다른 나라와 무역을 중지하라는 공식적인 명령. 무역 금지령. 수출입 금지: *The UN imposed an arms embargo on the country.* UN은 그 국가에 대해 무기 수출 금지 조치를 내렸다.

embargo² *v* **embargoed, embargoed, embargoing** [T] to officially stop particular goods from being traded with another country ‖ 특정 품목에 대해 타국과 무역하는 것을 공식적으로 금지하다. 통상을 정지시키다

em·bark /ɪm'bɑrk/ *v* [I] to go onto a ship or plane ‖ 선박이나 비행기에 오르다. 승선하다. 탑승하다 —opposite DISEMBARK

embark on/upon sth *phr v* [T] to start something new, difficult, or exciting ‖ 새로운[어려운, 흥미 있는] 일을 시작하다. 진출하다. 착수하다: *Hal is embarking on a new career.* 핼은 새로

운 일을 시작하고 있다.

em·bar·rass /ɪmˈbærəs/ v [T] to make someone feel EMBARRASSED ‖ 남을 당황하게 하다. 난처하게 만들다: *I hope I didn't embarrass you in front of your friends.* 네 친구들 앞에서 너를 난처하게 하지 않았기를 바란다.

em·bar·rassed /ɪmˈbærəst/ adj ashamed, anxious, or nervous, especially in front of other people ‖ 특히 다른 사람들 앞에서 부끄러운[불안한, 긴장하는]. 당황한. 절쩔매는: *I felt embarrassed about how dirty my house was.* 나는 내 집이 얼마나 지저분한지 당황했다. —see usage note at GUILTY

em·bar·ras·sing /ɪmˈbærəsɪŋ/ adj making you feel EMBARRASSED ‖ 난처하게 하는. 성가신. 귀찮은: *He asked a lot of embarrassing questions.* 그는 난처한 질문을 많이 했다.

em·bar·rass·ment /ɪmˈbærəsmənt/ n [U] the feeling that you have when you are EMBARRASSED ‖ 난처한 경우에 가지는 감정. 당황. 낭패: *Billy looked down and tried to hide his embarrassment.* 빌리는 눈을 내리뜨고 자신의 당혹감을 감추려고 했다.

em·bas·sy /ˈɛmbəsi/ n a group of officials who represent their country in a foreign country, or the building they work in ‖ 외국에서 자기 나라를 대표하는 일단의 공무원들이나 그들이 근무하는 건물. 대사관 (직원)

em·bat·tled /ɪmˈbæt̪ld/ adj FORMAL **1** surrounded by enemies, especially in a war ‖ 특히 전쟁에서 적에게 둘러싸인. 포위된: *the embattled city* 적에게 포위된 도시 **2** an embattled person, company etc. has many problems or difficulties ‖ 사람·회사 등이 많은 문제나 어려움을 가진

em·bed /ɪmˈbɛd/ v **-dded, -dding** [T] **1** to put something firmly and deeply into something else ‖ 사물을 다른 사물 속으로 단단하게 깊숙이 넣다. 박아 넣다: *A piece of glass was embedded in his hand.* 유리 조각이 그의 손에 박혔다. **2** if your ideas, feelings, or attitudes are embedded, you believe them very strongly ‖ 생각[감정, 태도] 등을 매우 강렬하게 믿다. 깊이 새겨 두다: *The idea of freedom is deeply embedded in America's values.* 자유 사상은 미국의 가치에 깊이 새겨져 있다.

em·bel·lish /ɪmˈbɛlɪʃ/ v [T] **1** to make something more beautiful by adding decorations to it ‖ 사물에 장식물을 추가하여 더욱 아름답게 하다. 아름답게 꾸미다. 장식하다: *a crown embellished with gold stars* 금으로 만든 별들로 장식한 왕관 **2** to make a story or statement more interesting by adding details to it that are not true ‖ 사실이 아닌 세부 사항을 추가하여 이야기나 말을 더욱 재미있게 하다. 재미있게 꾸미다. 윤색[수식]하다: *Larry couldn't help embellishing the story.* 래리는 그 이야기를 재미있게 꾸미지 않을 수 없었다. **– embellishment** n [C, U]

em·ber /ˈɛmbɚ/ n a piece of wood or coal that stays red and very hot after a fire has stopped burning ‖ 불이 꺼진 뒤에 붉고 매우 뜨거운 상태를 유지하는 나무나 석탄의 조각. (꺼져가는 불 속의) 붉은 장작[석탄]

em·bez·zle /ɪmˈbɛzəl/ v [I, T] to steal money from the place where you work ‖ 일하는 곳에서 돈을 훔치다. 횡령하다. 착복하다 **– embezzlement** n [U] **– embezzler** n

em·bit·tered /ɪmˈbɪt̪ɚd/ adj feeling anger, sadness, or hatred because of unpleasant or unfair things that have happened to you ‖ 불쾌하거나 불공정한 일이 발생하여 분노[슬픔, 증오]를 느끼는 **– embitter** v [T]

em·bla·zon /ɪmˈbleɪzən/ v [T] to put a name, design etc. on something such as a piece of clothing so that it can be seen clearly ‖ 분명히 보이도록 옷 등에 이름·무늬 등을 넣다. 문장(紋章)으로 꾸미다[장식하다]

em·blem /ˈɛmbləm/ n a picture, shape, or object that represents a country, company, idea etc. ‖ 국가·회사·생각 등을 대표하는 그림[형상, 물건]. 문장(紋章). 상징: *The bald eagle is the national emblem of the US.* 흰머리수리는 미국의 상징이다.

em·bod·y /ɪmˈbadi/ v [T] to be the best example of an idea or quality ‖ 생각이나 성질에 관한 가장 좋은 예이다. 구현하다. 나타내다: *Mrs. Miller embodies everything I admire in a teacher.* 밀러 여사는 내가 교사로서 훌륭하다고 생각하는 모든 점을 보여 준다. **– embodiment** n [U]

em·boss /ɪmˈbɔs, ɪmˈbɑs/ v [T] to decorate the surface of metal, leather, paper etc. with a raised pattern ‖ 금속·가죽·종이 등의 표면을 돋은 무늬로 장식하다. 도드라진 무늬를 내다. 돋을새김으로 하다 **– embossed** adj : *embossed stationery* 돋을새김이 된 편지지

em·brace /ɪmˈbreɪs/ v [T] **1** to put your arms around someone and hold him/her in a caring way ‖ 사람에게 손을 둘러 사랑스럽게 안다. 껴안다. 포옹하다: *Rob reached out to embrace her.* 로브는 그녀를 안기 위해 손을 뻗었다. **2** FORMAL to eagerly accept ideas, opinions, religions etc. ‖ 생각·의견·종교 등을 적극적으로 받아들이다. 기꺼이 받아들이다. 쾌히 승낙하다: *young men who are embracing Islam* 이슬람을 기꺼이 받아들이는 청년들 – **embrace** *n* : *a tender embrace* 부드러운 포옹

em·broi·der /ɪmˈbrɔɪdɚ/ *v* **1** [I, T] to decorate cloth by sewing a picture or pattern on it with colored threads ‖ 색실로 옷 위에 그림이나 무늬를 수놓아서 옷을 장식하다 **2** [T] to add untrue details to a story to make it more interesting or exciting ‖ 이야기를 더 재미있거나 흥미롭게 하기 위해 사실이 아닌 사항을 추가하다. (이야기 등을) …으로 꾸미다. 윤색하다 – **embroidery** *n* [U]

em·broil /ɪmˈbrɔɪl/ *v* [T] **be embroiled in** to be involved in a difficult situation ‖ 어려운 상황에 연루되다. …에 휘말리다: *Soon the whole group was embroiled in a fierce argument.* 곧 전체 그룹이 극심한 다툼에 휘말렸다.

em·bry·o /ˈɛmbriˌoʊ/ *n* an animal or human that has not yet been born and has just begun to develop ‖ 아직 태어나지 않고 이제 막 발육하기 시작한 동물이나 사람. 태아 —compare FETUS

em·bry·on·ic /ˌɛmbriˈɑnɪk/ *adj* not fully developed ‖ 충분히 발달하지 않은. 미발달의: *the country's embryonic nuclear weapons program* 국가의 초기 단계의 핵무기 계획

em·cee /ˌɛmˈsi/ *n* master of ceremonies; someone who introduces the performers on a television program or at a social event ‖ 사회자; 텔레비전 프로그램이나 사회적인 행사에서 출연자를 소개하는 사람 – **emcee** *v* [I, T]

em·er·ald /ˈɛmərəld/ *n* a valuable bright green jewel ‖ 값비싼 밝은 녹색의 보석. 에메랄드

e·merge /ɪˈmɚdʒ/ *v* [I] **1** to appear after being hidden ‖ 숨었다가 나타나다: *The sun emerged from behind the clouds.* 구름 뒤편에서 태양이 떠올랐다. / *New evidence has emerged during the trial.* 새 증거가 재판 과정에서 드러났다. **2** to have a particular quality or position after experiencing a difficult situation ‖ 어려운 상황을 겪은 뒤에 특정한 성질이나 지위를 가지다. 벗어나다. 빠져 나오다. 일어서다: *She emerged from the divorce a stronger person.* 그녀는 이혼에서 헤어

나 더 강한 사람이 되었다. – **emergence** *n* [U]

e·mer·gen·cy /ɪˈmɚdʒənsi/ *n* an unexpected and dangerous situation that you must deal with immediately ‖ 즉시 처리해야 하는 예기치 않은 위험한 상황. 비상 사태: *Call an ambulance! This is an emergency!* 구급차를 불러! 비상 사태다! – **emergency** *adj* : *an emergency exit* 비상구

emergency room /.ˈ… ˌ./ *n* the part of a hospital that immediately treats people who have been hurt in a serious accident ‖ 심각한 사고로 다친 사람을 즉시 치료하는 병원의 일부. 응급 치료실

e·mer·gent /ɪˈmɚdʒənt/ *adj* beginning to develop and be noticeable ‖ 발전하여 눈에 띄기 시작하는. 나타나는. 신생의. 신흥의: *the emergent nations of Eastern Europe and Africa* 동부 유럽과 아프리카의 신흥 국가들

e·mer·i·tus /ɪˈmɛrətəs/ *adj* a PROFESSOR emeritus is no longer working but still has an official title ‖ 교수 등이 더 이상 근무하지는 않지만 아직 공식 직명은 가지고 있는. 명예 퇴직의. 전직 예우의

em·ery board /ˈɛmri ˌbɔrd/ *n* a NAIL FILE made from thick card covered with a mineral powder ‖ 광석 가루를 씌운 두꺼운 카드로 만든 손톱 미는 줄

em·i·grant /ˈɛməgrənt/ *n* someone who leaves his/her own country to live in another ‖ 다른 나라에서 살기 위해 자기 나라를 떠나는 사람. (다른 나라로의) 이민. 이주민: *an emigrant to the United States* 미국으로의 이민[이주민] —compare IMMIGRANT

em·i·grate /ˈɛməˌgreɪt/ *v* [I] to leave your own country in order to live in another ‖ 다른 나라에서 살기 위해 자신의 나라를 떠나다. (다른 나라로) 이주하다. 이민 가다: *Maria emigrated from Canada three years ago.* 마리아는 3년 전에 캐나다에서 이민 갔다. – **emigration** /ˌɛməˈgreɪʃən/ *n* [C, U] —compare IMMIGRATION

USAGE NOTE emigrate, immigrate, and migrate

Use **emigrate** to talk about people who have left their country in order to live in another one: *My grandparents emigrated from Italy.* Use **immigrate** to talk about people who are entering a country in order to live there: *Yuko immigrated to the US last year.* Use **migrate** to talk about birds that go to another part of the world in the fall and the spring. 다른 나라에서 살기 위해 자기 나라를 떠나는 사람들에 대해 말할 때는 **emigrate**를 쓴다: 나의 할아버지는 이 탈리아에서 이민 갔다. 이민 갈 나라에 입국하는 사람들에 대해 말할 때는 **immigrate**를 쓴다: 유코는 작년에 미국으로 이민 왔다. 가을과 봄에 세계의 다른 장소로 이동하는 새에 관해서 말할 때는 **migrate**를 쓴다

em·i·nent /ˈɛmənənt/ adj famous and admired by many people ‖ 유명하고 많은 사람들에 의해 칭찬받는. 저명한. 탁월한: *an eminent professor of medicine* 유명한 의대 교수

eminent do·main /ˌ... .ˈ./ n LAW the right of the US government to pay for and take someone's private land so it can be used for a public purpose ‖ 개인의 사유지에 대해 보상하고 사유지를 취득하여 공공 목적을 위해 사용할 수 있는 미국 정부의 권리. 토지 수용권

em·i·nent·ly /ˈɛmənəntˈli/ adv FORMAL completely, and without any doubt ‖ 완전하고 어떠한 의심도 없이. 뛰어나게. 현저하게. 두드러지게: *He's eminently qualified to do the job.* 그는 그 직무를 수행할 뛰어난 자격을 갖추고 있다.

e·mir /ɛˈmɪɚ, i-/ n a Muslim ruler, especially in Asia and parts of Africa ‖ 특히 아시아와 아프리카 지역에서의 회교도 지도자. (아랍의) 수장[왕족]. 아랍 토후

e·mir·ate /ˈɛmərɪt/ n the country ruled by an EMIR ‖ 아랍 토후가 지배하는 국가. 아랍 토후국

em·is·sar·y /ˈɛmə‚sɛri/ n someone who is sent with an official message, or who must do other official work ‖ 공식적인 전언을 갖고 파견되거나, 또는 다른 공적 업무를 해야 하는 사람. 사절. 밀사: *an emissary from the Italian government* 이탈리아 정부의 사절

e·mis·sion /ɪˈmɪʃən/ n [C, U] the sending out of gas, heat, light, sound etc., or the gas etc. that is sent out ‖ 가스·열·빛·소리 등의 방출, 또는 방출된 가스. 배출[방사](물질): *an emissions test* (=a test to make sure the gases your car sends out are at the right level) 배기 물질 테스트

e·mit /ɪˈmɪt/ v **-tted, -tting** [T] FORMAL to send out gas, heat, light, sound etc. ‖ 가스·열·빛·소리 등을 내뿜다. 방출하다: *The kettle emitted a shrill whistle.* 주전자가 날카로운 휘파람 소리를 내뱉었다.

Em·my /ˈɛmi/ n a prize given every year to the best program, actor etc. on US television ‖ 미국 텔레비전의 최우수 프로그램·배우 등에게 매년 수여하는 상. 에미상

e·mo·ti·con /ɪˈmoʊtɪkən/ n one of a set of special signs that is used to show an emotion in E-MAIL and on the Internet, often by making a picture. This word comes from a combination of the words 'emotion' and 'ICON' ‖ 종종 그림으로 만들어서 이메일이나 인터넷 상에서 감정을 나타내는 데에 쓰이는 일련의 특수 부호들 중의 하나로 'emotion'과 'icon'의 합성어. 이모티콘

e·mo·tion /ɪˈmoʊʃən/ n [C, U] a strong human feeling such as love or hate ‖ 사랑이나 증오 등의 인간의 강렬한 느낌. 감정: *David doesn't usually show his true emotions.* 데이비드는 보통 자기의 진실한 감정을 나타내지 않는다. / *Her voice was full of emotion.* 그녀의 목소리에는 감정이 풍부했다.

e·mo·tion·al /ɪˈmoʊʃənəl/ adj **1** making people have strong feelings ‖ 강렬한 감정을 갖게 하는. 감동[감격]적인: *The end of the movie was really emotional.* 영화의 마지막은 너무나 감동적이었다. **2** showing your emotions to other people, especially by crying ‖ 특히 울어서 다른 사람들에게 감정을 나타내는. 감정에 호소하는. 감상적인: *Please don't get all emotional.* 감상에 젖지 마세요. **3** relating to your feelings or how they are controlled ‖ 자신의 감정 또는 그것을 어떻게 다스리는지와 관련된. 감정[정서]의. 심리상의: *the emotional development of children* 아이의 정서 발달 **4** influenced by what you feel rather than what you know ‖ 무엇을 아는가보다는 무엇을 느끼는가에 의해 영향을 받는. 감정적[주정적]인: *an emotional response to the problem* 그 문제에 대하여 감정에 기인한 반응 **– emotionally** adv

e·mo·tive /ɪˈmoʊtɪv/ adj making people have strong feelings ‖ 사람들에게 강렬한 감정을 갖게 하는. 감정[정서]의. 감동을 불러일으키는. 감격시키는: *an emotive speech about the effects of war* 전쟁의 영향에 대한 감동을 불러일으키는 연설

em·pa·thy /ˈɛmpəθi/ n [U] the ability to understand someone else's feelings and problems ‖ 다른 사람의 감정과 문제를 이해하는 능력. 감정 이입. 남과의 공감 **– empathize** v [I] —compare SYMPATHY

em·per·or /ˈɛmpərɚ/ n the ruler of an EMPIRE ‖ 제국의 통치자. 황제. 제왕

em·pha·sis /ˈɛmfəsɪs/ n, *plural* **emphases** /ˈɛmfəsiz/ [C, U] special importance ‖ 특별히 중요함. 강조: *Jamieson's report puts/places an emphasis on the need for working conditions.* 재미슨의 보고서는 근로 조건 개선의 필요성을 강조하고 있다.

em·pha·size /'ɛmfə,saɪz/ *v* [T] to show that an opinion, idea, quality etc. is important ‖ 의견·생각·성질 등이 중요하다는 것을 나타내다. …을 강조하다. 중요시하다: *My teacher emphasized the importance of grammar.* 우리 선생님은 문법의 중요성을 강조하셨다. ✗DON'T SAY "…emphasize on."✗ "…emphasize on"이라고는 하지 않는다.

em·phat·ic /ɪm'fætɪk/ *adj* done or said in a way that shows something is important or should be believed ‖ 어떤 것이 중요하거나 믿어져야 함을 나타내는 식으로 행하거나 말하는. 강경한. 단호한: *Dale's answer was an emphatic "No!"* 데일의 대답은 단호하게 "아니요"였다. – **emphatically** *adv*

em·phy·se·ma /,ɛmfə'zimə, -'si-/ *n* [U] a serious disease that affects the lungs, making it difficult to breathe ‖ 폐에 영향을 끼쳐 호흡하기 곤란하게 하는 심각한 질병. 기종(氣腫). 폐기종

em·pire /'ɛmpaɪɚ/ *n* **1** a group of countries that are all controlled by one ruler or government ‖ 한 지배자나 정부가 모두 지배하는 일단의 나라들. 제국 **2** a group of organizations that are all controlled by one person or company ‖ 한 사람이나 회사가 모두 지배하는 일단의 조직체: *a media empire* 미디어 왕국

em·pir·i·cal /ɪm'pɪrɪkəl, ɛm-/ *adj* based on practical experience rather than on ideas ‖ 생각보다 실제적인 경험에 기반을 둔. 경험[실험]상의: *an empirical approach to studying sociology* 사회학 연구에 대한 경험적 접근법

em·ploy /ɪm'plɔɪ/ *v* [T] **1** to pay someone to work for you ‖ 돈을 주고 자신을 위해 일하다. 고용하다: *The factory employs over 2000 people.* 그 공장은 2,000명 이상의 사람을 고용한다. **2** to use a particular object, method, or skill in order to achieve something ‖ 어떤 일을 달성하기 위해 특정한 물건[방법, 기술]을 쓰다. 사용[적용]하다: *research methods employed by scientists* 과학자들이 사용하는 연구 방법

em·ploy·ee /ɪm'plɔɪ-i, ,ɪmplɔɪ'i, ,ɛm-/ *n* someone who is paid to work for a person, organization, or company ‖ 남[조직체, 회사]을 위해 돈을 받고 일하는 사람. 종업원. 고용인: *a government employee* 국가[정부] 고용인

em·ploy·er /ɪm'plɔɪɚ/ *n* a person, company, or organization that employs people ‖ 사람을 고용하는 사람[회사, 조직체]. 사용자. 고용주: *The shoe factory is the largest employer in this area.* 그 신발 회사는 이 지역 최대의 사용자이다.

em·ploy·ment /ɪm'plɔɪmənt/ *n* [U] **1** work that you do to earn money ‖ 돈을 벌기 위해 하는 일. 일자리. 직업: *Steve's still looking for employment.* 스티브는 아직 일자리를 찾고 있는 중이다. **2** the use of an object, method, skill etc. to achieve something ‖ 어떤 일을 달성하기 위해 물건·방법·기술 등을 사용함: *the employment of weapons to gain control of the area* 그 지역을 지배하기 위한 무기의 사용 —compare UNEMPLOYMENT

em·po·ri·um /ɪm'pɔriəm/ *n* a word meaning a large store, used in the names of stores ‖ 점포의 이름에 쓰이는 큰 상점을 뜻하는 단어. 백화점. 대규모 슈퍼마켓

em·pow·er /ɪm'paʊɚ/ *v* [T] to give someone the confidence, power, or right to do something ‖ 어떤 일을 하기 위한 신임[권력, 권리]을 남에게 주다. 권리[권한]를 주다: *Our aim is to empower women to defend themselves.* 우리의 목표는 여성에게 자위권을 주는 것이다.

em·press /'ɛmprɪs/ *n* the female ruler of an EMPIRE, or the wife of an EMPEROR ‖ 제국의 여성 통치자, 또는 황제의 부인. 여왕. 왕비. 황후(皇后)

emp·ty¹ /'ɛmpti/ *adj*
1 having nothing inside ‖ 안에 아무것도 없는. 빈. 든 것이 없는: *Your glass is empty – would you like some more wine?* 당신 잔이 비었네요. 포도주를 좀 더 드시겠어요? / *an empty box* 빈 상자 **2** not filled with people, or not being used by anyone ‖ 사람들로 가득 차지 않은, 또는 누군가가 사용하지 않은. 비어 있는: *Is this seat empty?* 이 자리가 비어 있습니까? / *an empty restaurant* 사람이 없는 레스토랑 **3** unhappy because nothing seems interesting, important, or worth doing ‖ 아무것도 흥미롭고[중요하게], 할 만하게] 보이지 않아서 불행한. 공허한. 무의미한: *After the divorce, my life felt empty.* 이혼 후 나의 삶은 공허했다. **4 empty words/promises/gestures**

empty

empty

full

etc. words etc. that are not sincere and therefore have no meaning ‖ 진지하지 않아서 의미가 없는[말 등. 실속 없는[말 뿐인] 말/약속/몸짓 **5 on an empty stomach** without having eaten anything first ‖ 처음에 아무것도 먹지 않아. 공복으로. 빈속으로: *You shouldn't go to school on an empty stomach.* 너는 공복으로 학교에 가서는 안 된다. **6 empty nest (syndrome)** a situation in which parents become sad because their children have grown up and left home ‖ 아이들이 자라 집을 떠나서 부모들이 슬픈 상황. 공소(空巢)[빈 집](증후군)

empty² *v* **1** [T] also **empty out** to remove everything that is inside of something else ‖ 다른 물건의 속에 있는 모든 것을 없애다. …을 내쏟다[비우다]. 꺼내다: *I found your umbrella when I was emptying out the closet.* 벽장을 비우고 있을 때 나는 네 우산을 발견했다. / *Troy, please empty the dishwasher.* 트로이야, 자동 식기 세척기 안의 식기를 꺼내 봐라. **2** [T] to pour the things that are in a container into or onto something else ‖ 용기에 있는 것들을 다른 것에 쏟다. 옮기다. 옮겨 담다: *Empty the contents of one pudding package into a large bowl.* 한 푸딩 용기 안에 있는 내용물을 큰 사발에 쏟아라. **3** [I, T] to leave a place, vehicle etc., or to make someone do this ‖ 장소나 탈것 등을 떠나다, 또는 남에게 이렇게 하게 하다: *Judge Sinclair ordered the courtroom to be emptied.* 싱클레어 판사는 법정을 비우라고 명령했다. **4** [I] to flow into a large area of water ‖ 넓은 수역(水域)으로 흘러들다: *the place where Waddell Creek empties into the ocean* 와델 샛강이 바다로 흘러 들어 가는 곳

empty-hand·ed /ˌ.. ˈ../ *adj* without gaining or getting anything ‖ 어떤 것도 얻거나 가지지 않은. 빈손의. 손에 든 것이 없는: *The thieves fled the building empty-handed.* 그 도둑들은 빈손으로 그 건물에서 달아났다.

em·u·late /ˈɛmyəˌleɪt/ *v* [T] FORMAL to try to do something or behave in the same way as someone; copy ‖ 남과 똑같은 방식으로 어떤 것을 하거나 행동하려고 하다. 흉내내다; 복사하다: *Children emulate their parents' behavior.* 아이들은 부모의 행동을 흉내낸다.

en·a·ble /ɪˈneɪbəl/ *v* [T] to make someone or something able to do something ‖ 사람이나 사물이 어떤 것을 할 수 있게 하다. …을 가능하게 하다: *The new plastic enables us to make our*

products more cheaply. 그 새 플라스틱으로 우리는 제품을 더 싸게 만들 수 있다.

en·act /ɪˈnækt/ *v* [T] to make something a law ‖ 어떤 것을 법률로 만들다. 법률을 제정하다. 법규화하다: *The measure was enacted to prevent tax abuses.* 그 조치는 세금 남용을 막기 위해 제정되었다.

en·am·el /ɪˈnæməl/ *n* [U] **1** a substance like glass that is put on metal, clay etc. for decoration or for protection ‖ 장식용이나 보호용으로 금속이나 점토 등에 입힌 유리 같은 물질. 에나멜 **2** the hard smooth outer surface of your teeth ‖ 치아의 딱딱하며 부드러운 외피. 법랑질. 에나멜질

en·am·ored /ɪˈnæmɚd/ *adj* FORMAL **be enamored of** to like and admire someone or something very much ‖ 사람이나 사물을 아주 많이 좋아하고 감탄하다. …에 반하다. 빠지다: *Not everyone in town is quite so enamored of the new building.* 도시의 누구나가 새 건물을 대단히 좋아하는 것은 아니다.

en·case /ɪnˈkeɪs/ *v* [T] to cover or surround something completely ‖ 어떤 것을 완전히 덮거나 둘러싸다. (케이스, 상자 등에) 집어 넣다: *art objects encased in a glass box* 유리 상자 안에 넣은 예술품

en·chant·ed /ɪnˈtʃæntɪd/ *adj* something that is enchanted has been changed by magic so that it has special powers ‖ 어떤 것이 특별한 힘을 지니도록 마법에 의해 변화된. 마법에 걸린: *an enchanted forest* 마법의 숲

en·chant·ing /ɪnˈtʃæntɪŋ/ *adj* very pleasant in a way that makes you feel very interested, happy, or excited ‖ 상당한 흥미로움[행복감, 흥분]을 느끼게 하여 매우 즐거운. 매혹적인. 황홀하게 하는: *an enchanting movie about young love* 젊은이의 사랑에 관한 매혹적인 영화

en·chi·la·da /ˌɛntʃəˈlɑdə/ *n* a Mexican food made from a corn TORTILLA rolled around meat or beans and covered with a hot-tasting liquid ‖ 고기나 콩 주위를 둘둘 말아 매운 맛이 나는 소스를 칠한 토르티야로 만든 멕시코 음식. 엔칠라다

en·clave /ˈɛnkleɪv, ˈɑŋ-/ *n* a place or group of people that is surrounded by areas or groups of people that are different from it ‖ 상이한 지역 또는 사람들의 집단으로 둘러싸인 장소나 사람들 집단. 소수 민족 거주지. 고립된 지역[소집단]: *the Italian-American enclave in New York* 뉴욕의 이탈리아계 미국인 거주지

en·close /ɪnˈkloʊz/ v [T] **1** to put something inside an envelope with a letter ‖ 편지와 함께 어떤 것을 봉투 안에 넣다. 동봉하다: *A copy of the article is enclosed.* 한 장의 기사가 동봉되어 있다. **2** to surround an area, especially with a fence or wall ‖ 특히 울타리나 벽으로 지역을 둘러싸다. 에워싸다: *A high wall enclosed the yard.* 높은 벽이 뜰을 둘러쌌다. – **enclosed** adj

en·clo·sure /ɪnˈkloʊʒɚ/ n **1** an area that is surrounded by something such as a wall or fence ‖ 벽이나 울타리 같은 것으로 둘러싸인 지역. 울타리. 구내: *The animals are kept in a large enclosure.* 그 동물들은 넓은 울타리 안에서 사육된다. **2** things such as documents, photographs, money etc. that you send with a letter ‖ 편지와 함께 보내진 문서·사진·돈 등의 물건. 동봉물

en·com·pass /ɪnˈkʌmpəs/ v [T] **1** to include a range of ideas, subjects etc. ‖ 일련의 생각·주제 등을 포함하다. 망라하다: *Crosby's career encompassed radio, records, TV, and movies.* 크로스비의 경력은 라디오·레코드·텔레비전·영화를 망라했다. **2** to completely cover or surround an area ‖ 지역을 완전히 덮거나 둘러싸다. 에워싸다: *a national park encompassing 400 square miles* 400평방 마일을 둘러싸고 있는 국립공원

en·core /ˈɑŋkɔr/ n an additional performance that is performed because the people listening want to hear more ‖ 청중이 더 듣고 싶어 해서 연주하는 추가 공연. 앙코르 연주

en·coun·ter¹ /ɪnˈkaʊntɚ/ v [T] **1** to experience something bad that you have to deal with ‖ 해결해야 할 나쁜 일을 경험하다. 직면하다: *She encountered a lot of difficulties trying to get her article published.* 그녀는 자신의 논문을 출판하려는 데 많은 어려움을 겪었다. **2** FORMAL to see someone or something that you were not expecting to see ‖ 볼 것이라 기대하지 않은 사람이나 사물을 보다. 우연히 만나다

encounter² n **1** a dangerous or unpleasant meeting between two people or groups ‖ 두 사람이나 집단 사이에 위험하거나 불쾌한 만남: *one of the bloodiest encounters of the Civil War* 남북 전쟁에서 피비린내 나는 교전 중의 하나 **2** an occasion when you meet someone without planning to ‖ 만날 계획 없이 남과 만나는 경우. 우연히 만남: *I had an encounter with my ex-boyfriend the other day.* 요전 날 예전의 남자 친구와 우연히 만났다.

en·cour·age /ɪnˈkɚɪdʒ, -ˈkʌr-/ v [T] **1** to help someone become confident or brave enough to do something ‖ 어떤 일을 할 만큼 자신감을 갖거나 용감해지도록 누군가를 돕다. 격려하다. 용기[기운]를 북돋우다: *My drama teacher encouraged me to try out for the school play.* 우리 연극 선생님은 학교 연극을 시험 삼아 해보라고 나를 격려했다. **2** to make something become more likely to happen ‖ 어떤 일이 더 잘 일어나게 하다. 촉진하다: *a plant food that encourages growth* 성장을 촉진하는 식물 음식 – **encouragement** n [C, U] —opposite DISCOURAGE

en·cour·ag·ing /ɪnˈkɚɪdʒɪŋ/ adj giving you hope and confidence ‖ 희망과 자신감을 주는. 격려가 되는. 용기를 북돋아 주는: *This time, the news is more encouraging.* 이번에, 그 소식은 기운을 더욱 북돋아 주고 있다. – **encouragingly** adv

en·croach /ɪnˈkroʊtʃ/ v [T] **1** to cover more and more land in a way that affects or changes that land ‖ 땅에 영향을 주거나 변화시켜 점점 더 땅을 덮다. 침식하다. 잠식[침범]하다: *The forest fire is now encroaching on the town of Bridgeway.* 그 삼림 화재가 현재 브리지웨이 읍으로 침범하고 있다. **2** to take away more and more of someone's time, rights etc. ‖ 남의 시간·권리 등을 점점 더 빼앗다. 침해하다: *Recent court decisions have allowed the government to encroach on people's lives.* 최근의 법원 결정은 정부가 사람들의 삶을 침해하도록 허용했다.

en·crust·ed /ɪnˈkrʌstɪd/ adj covered with something hard and sharp, such as jewels, ice, or dried mud ‖ 보석이나 얼음, 또는 마른 진흙 같은 딱딱하고 날카로운 것으로 덮인

en·cum·ber /ɪnˈkʌmbɚ/ v [T] FORMAL to make someone have difficulty moving or doing something ‖ 누군가가 움직이거나 어떤 일을 하는 데 어려움을 갖게 하다. 방해하다. 지장을 주다 – **encumbrance** /ɪnˈkʌmbrəns/ n

en·cy·clo·pe·di·a /ɪnˌsaɪkləˈpidiə/ n a book, set of books, or CD that contains facts about many subjects or about one particular subject ‖ 많은 주제나 하나의 특정한 주제에 관한 사실을 포함하는 책[책 세트, CD]. 백과사전

end¹ /ɛnd/ n
1 ▶LAST PART 마지막 부분◀ the last part of something such as a period of

time, activity, book, or movie ‖ 일정 시간[활동, 책, 영화] 등의 마지막 부분. 결말. 말미: *Of course, the hero died at the end of the story.* 물론 그 영웅은 소설의 마지막 부분에서 죽었다. / *Rob's moving to Maine at the end of September.* 로브는 9월 말에 메인으로 이사가려고 한다.

2 ▶FARTHEST POINT 가장 먼 곳◀ the farthest point of a place or thing ‖ 장소나 물건의 가장 먼 곳. 끝. 선단. 말단: *Mr. Williams sent us to the end of the line.* 윌리엄스 씨는 우리를 그 줄의 끝으로 보냈다. / *the deep/shallow end of the pool* 물웅덩이의 가장 깊은[얕은] 곳 / *the north/south end of the lake* 호수의 북[남]단

3 ▶OF A SITUATION 상황의 ◀ a situation in which something is finished or no longer exists ‖ 어떤 일이 끝나거나 더 이상 존재하지 않는 상황: *Their relationship had come to an end.* (=had finished) 그들의 관계는 끝났다. / *the UN's latest plan to put an end to* (=stop) *the war* 전쟁을 종식시키기[끝내기] 위한 유엔의 최근 계획

4 in the end after a lot of thinking or discussion; finally ‖ 많이 생각하거나 토론한 후; 마침내. 결국: *In the end, we decided to go to Florida.* 마침내 우리는 플로리다로 가기로 결정했다.

5 make ends meet to have just enough money to buy what you need ‖ 단지 필요한 것을 살 만큼만 돈을 가지다. 수입 내에서 살다. 수지를 맞추다: *It's been hard to make ends meet since Ray got laid off.* 레이가 일시 해고당한 이래 수지를 맞추기가 어려웠다.

6 it's not the end of the world SPOKEN used in order to say that a problem is not too serious or bad ‖ 문제가 너무 심각하거나 나쁘지 않다고 말하는 데에 쓰여. 그것이 세상의 마지막[끝]은 아니다: *If you don't get the job, it's not the end of the world.* 당신이 직업이 없다고 해서 그것이 세상의 종말은 아니다.

7 ▶RESULT 결과◀ FORMAL the result that you hope to achieve ‖ 달성하고 싶은 결과: *Stalin wanted a weak China, and worked to that end.* (=to achieve that result) 스탈린은 약한 중국을 원했고 그 결과를 달성하기 위해 노력했다.

8 at the end of your rope extremely annoyed, upset, and impatient because you cannot control, change, or achieve something ‖ 어떤 일을 제어[변화, 달성]할 수 없어서 매우 괴롭고 화나며 참을 수 없는. 한계에 다다른

9 end to end with the end of something

next to the end of something else ‖ 어떤 것의 끝을 다른 것의 끝에 붙여. 끝과 끝을 이어: *cars parked end to end* 끝과 끝을 이어 주차하는 차들

10 ▶IN SPORTS 스포츠에서◀ in football, one of two players who play on the outside of the TACKLEs and try to catch the ball ‖ 미식축구에서 태클 바깥 구역에서 경기를 하며 공을 잡으려고 하는 두 선수 중의 한 명. 엔드. 공격[수비]의 최전선의 양쪽 끝 선수 —see also **go off the deep end** (DEEP¹)

end² v [I, T] to finish or stop, or to make something do this ‖ 끝나거나 중단하다, 또는 끝나게[중단시키게] 하다: *World War II ended in 1945.* 2차 세계대전은 1945년에 끝났다. / *Janet's party didn't end until 4 o'clock in the morning.* 재닛의 파티는 새벽 4시까지 끝나지 않았다. / *Lucy decided to end her relationship with Jeff.* 루시는 제프와 관계를 끝내기로 결심했다.

end in sth *phr v* [T] to have a particular result or to finish in a particular way ‖ 특별한 결과가 있거나 특별하게 끝나다. …으로 끝나다. 결국 …이 되다: *The meeting ended in a huge argument.* 그 모임은 큰 논쟁으로 끝났다.

end up *phr v* [I] to come to be in a place, situation, or condition that you did not expect or intend ‖ 기대하거나 의도하지 않았던 장소[상황, 조건]에 있게 되다. 결국[마침내, 끝내] …이 되다: *Whenever we go out to dinner I always end up paying the bill.* 식사하러 갈 때마다 내가 항상 돈을 지불하게 된다.

en·dan·ger /ɪnˈdeɪndʒɚ/ *v* [T] to put someone or something in a dangerous or harmful situation ‖ 사람이나 사물을 위험하거나 해로운 상황에 처하게 하다. …을 위험에 빠뜨리다. 위태롭게 하다: *Smoking seriously endangers your health.* 흡연은 심각하게 당신의 건강을 위태롭게 한다.

en·dan·gered spe·cies /.,.. '../ *n* a type of animal or plant that soon might not exist ‖ 곧 존재하지 않을지도 모르는 동물이나 식물의 종류. 멸종 위기의 생물[종]

en·dear /ɪnˈdɪr/ *v*

endear sb to sb *phr v* [T] to make someone be liked by other people ‖ 사람을 다른 사람들이 좋아하게 만들다. 따르게[사랑받게] 하다: *His speech did not endear him to the voters.* 그의 연설은 유권자에게 호감을 사지 못했다.

en·dear·ing /ɪnˈdɪrɪŋ/ *adj* making

someone like or love you ‖ 좋아하거나 사랑하게 만드는. 사랑을 받는. 남이 따르는: *an endearing smile* 귀여운 미소

en·dear·ment /ɪnˈdɪrmənt/ *n* something you say that shows your love for someone ‖ 남에 대한 자신의 사랑을 나타내는 말. 애정(의 표시)

en·deav·or[1] /ɪnˈdɛvɚ/ *n* [C, U] an attempt or effort to do something new or different ‖ 새롭거나 다른 일을 하기 위한 시도나 노력: *The artist fails in his endeavor to create a new style.* 그 예술가는 새로운 스타일을 창조하려는 노력에 실패한다.

endeavor[2] *v* [I] FORMAL to try very hard ‖ 아주 열심히 노력하다. …하려고 애쓰다: *One must always endeavor to do one's best.* 사람은 항상 최선의 노력을 다해야 한다.

en·dem·ic /ɛnˈdɛmɪk, ɪn-/ *adj* regularly happening in a particular place or among a particular group of people ‖ 특정한 장소나 특정한 집단의 사람들 사이에서 규칙적으로 일어나는. 어떤 지방 특유[고유]의. 풍토성의: *Violent crime is now endemic in parts of the city.* 폭력 범죄는 현재 그 도시 지역의 특이한 면이다.

end·ing /ˈɛndɪŋ/ *n* the end of a story, movie, play etc. ‖ 소설·영화·연극 등의 끝부분. 종결. 결말: *a happy ending* 행복한 결말

en·dive /ˈɛndaɪv/ *n* [C, U] a vegetable with bitter-tasting leaves that are eaten raw in SALADs ‖ 샐러드에서 날로 먹는 쓴 맛이 나는 잎을 가진 야채. 꽃상추

end·less /ˈɛndlɪs/ *adj* continuing for a very long time, especially in a way that is annoying ‖ 특히 괴롭히듯이 매우 오랫동안 계속되는. 끝없는. 영원한: *his endless complaining* 그의 끝없는 불평

en·dorse /ɪnˈdɔrs/ *v* [T] **1** to officially say that you support or approve of someone or something ‖ 사람이나 사물을 지지하거나 찬성한다고 공식적으로 말하다. 보증[승인]하다: *The company endorses a policy of equal pay for women.* 그 회사는 여성들에 대해 동등한 급여 정책을 승인한다. **2** to sign your name on the back of a check ‖ 수표 뒷면에 자신의 이름을 서명하다. 배서하다 – **endorsement** *n* [C,U]

en·dow /ɪnˈdaʊ/ *v* [T] **1** to give an ENDOWMENT to a college, hospital etc. ‖ 대학·병원 등에 기부금을 내다. 기부하다 **2 be endowed with talent/resources/rights etc.** FORMAL to have or be given a good quality, feature, or ability ‖ 좋은 성질이나 용모, 또는 능력을 가지거나 주어지다. 재능/재원/능력을 가지다

en·dow·ment /ɪnˈdaʊmənt/ *n* [C, U] a large amount of money or property that is given to a college, hospital etc. so that it has an income ‖ 대학·병원 등에 제공되어 수입이 되는 큰 액수의 돈이나 재산. 기부금

en·dur·ance /ɪnˈdʊrəns/ *n* [U] the ability to remain strong and patient even though you feel pain or have problems ‖ 고통을 느끼거나 문제가 있을지라도 강하고 참을성 있게 유지하는 능력. 인내(력). 참을성: *Jogging will help increase your endurance.* 조깅은 너의 인내력을 증진시키는 데 도움이 될 것이다.

en·dure /ɪnˈdʊr/ *v* [T] to suffer pain or deal with a very difficult situation for a long time ‖ 오랫동안 고통을 겪거나 매우 어려운 상황에 대처하다. 견디다. 참다: *People in the war-torn country have endured months of fighting.* 전쟁으로 파괴된 나라의 국민은 수개월의 전투를 견뎌냈다.

en·dur·ing /ɪnˈdʊrɪŋ/ *adj* continuing to exist in spite of difficulties ‖ 어려움에도 불구하고 계속 존재하는. 오래 지속되는. 영속적인: *an enduring relationship* 영속적인 관계

end zone /ˈ. ./ *n* the end of a football field to which you carry or catch a ball to win points ‖ 점수를 얻기 위해 공을 가지고 가거나 잡는 미식축구장의 끝. 엔드 존 —see picture on page 946

en·e·my /ˈɛnəmi/ *n* **1** someone who hates you and wants to harm you or prevent you from being successful ‖ 자신을 미워하고 해치고 싶어하거나 자신이 성공하는 것을 저지하는 사람. 적. 원수: *Judge Lonza has made a lot of enemies during her career.* 론자 판사는 자신의 판사 생활 동안 많은 적을 만들어 왔다. **2** the person or group of people that you are fighting in a war ‖ 전쟁에서 싸우고 있는 사람이나 사람들 집단. 적군: *a surprise attack on the enemy* 적군에 대한 기습 공격

en·er·get·ic /ˌɛnɚˈdʒɛtɪk/ *adj* very active ‖ 매우 활동적인. 정력적인. 힘이 넘치는: *Sam's kids are really energetic.* 샘의 아이들은 정말 활동적이다. – **energetically** *adv*

en·er·gy /ˈɛnɚdʒi/ *n* [C, U] **1** the ability to be active and do a lot of work or activities without being tired ‖ 활동적이고 지치지 않고 많은 일이나 활동을 하는 능력. 정력. 활력: *I'm finally getting my energy back after my surgery.* 나는 수술

E

후에 마침내 활력을 되찾았다. **2** power from burning heat, coal etc. that produces heat and makes machines work ‖ 열을 내고 기계를 작동시키는 석유·석탄 등을 연소시켜서 얻는 힘. 에너지: *atomic energy* 원자 에너지[원자력] / *the world's energy resources* 세계의 에너지 자원

en·force /ɪnˈfɔrs/ v [T] to make people obey a rule or law ‖ 사람들에게 규칙이나 법을 지키게 하다. 준수하게 하다. 시행하다: *They're strict here about enforcing the speed limit.* 그들은 이 곳에서 제한 속도를 엄격히 지키게 한다. – **enforcement** n [U] – **enforceable** adj

en·fran·chise /ɪnˈfrænˌtʃaɪz/ v [T] FORMAL to give a group of people rights, especially the right to vote ‖ 한 집단의 사람에게 특히 투표권을 주다. …에게 공민[참정]권을 부여하다 —opposite DISENFRANCHISE

en·gage /ɪnˈgeɪdʒ/ v [T] FORMAL **1** to make someone remain interested in something ‖ 사람으로 하여금 어떤 일에 흥미를 가지게 하다. 끌다. 사로잡다: *a storyteller able to engage the children's imaginations* 어린이의 상상력을 끌 수 있는 이야기꾼 **2** to employ someone ‖ 사람을 고용하다: *I suggest that you engage a good accountant.* 좋은 회계사를 채용할 것을 제안합니다.

engage in phr v [T] **1** involve yourself in an activity ‖ 어떤 활동에 관여하다. 종사[참여]하다: *They're engaging in a price war with three other companies* 그들은 세 개의 다른 회사와 가격 전쟁에 참여하고 있다. **2** FORMAL **engage sb in (a) conversation** to begin talking to someone ‖ 남에게 말하기 시작하다. 대화에 끼다[참여하다]

en·gaged /ɪnˈgeɪdʒd/ adj two people who are engaged have agreed to marry each other ‖ 두 사람이 결혼하기로 서로 동의한. 약혼한: *Viv and Tyrell got engaged last month.* 비브와 티렐은 지난 달에 약혼했다. / *Sheri's engaged to a guy in the Army.* 셰리는 군대에서 어떤 사람과 약혼했다. ✗DON'T SAY "engaged with someone."✗ "engaged with someone"이라고는 하지 않는다.

en·gage·ment /ɪnˈgeɪdʒmənt/ n **1** an agreement to marry someone ‖ 남과 결혼하기로 한 합의. 약혼: *Charlene and I have broken off our engagement.* (=decided to end it) 샬렌과 나는 파혼했다 **2** FORMAL an arrangement to do something or meet someone ‖ 어떤 일을

하거나 남을 만나기로 한 약속: *an engagement calendar* 예정표

en·gag·ing /ɪnˈgeɪdʒɪŋ/ adj attracting people's attention and interest ‖ 사람들의 관심이나 흥미를 끄는. 매력적인: *an engaging personality* 매력적인 성격

en·gen·der /ɪnˈdʒɛndər/ v [T] FORMAL to be the cause of something such as a situation, action, or emotion ‖ 상황[행동, 감정] 등의 원인이 되다. …을 일으키다

en·gine /ˈɛndʒɪn/ n **1** a piece of machinery that produces power from oil, steam, electricity etc. and uses it to make something move ‖ 석유·증기·전기 등으로 힘을 내고 사물을 움직이는 데 사용하는 기계. 엔진. 발동기: *the engine of a car* 자동차 엔진 / *a jet engine* 제트기 엔진 **2** the part of a train that pulls the other CARs along a railroad ‖ 철도를 따라서 다른 차를 끄는 기차의 일부. 기관차

en·gi·neer¹ /ˌɛndʒəˈnɪr/ n **1** someone who designs the way roads, bridges, machines etc. are built ‖ 도로·교량·기계 등의 건설 방법을 설계하는 사람. 엔지니어. 기사. 기술자: *a software engineer* 소프트웨어 기사 **2** someone who controls the engines on a ship, plane, or train ‖ 배[비행기, 기차]의 엔진을 조종하는 사람. 기관사

engineer² v [T] to secretly and effectively arrange something ‖ 어떤 일을 은밀하고 효과적으로 미리 계획하다. 비밀 계획을 짜다[꾀하다]. 공작하다: *He had powerful enemies who engineered his downfall.* 그에게는 자신의 파멸을 획책하는 막강한 적이 있었다.

en·gi·neer·ing /ˌɛndʒəˈnɪrɪŋ/ n [U] the profession or activity of designing the way roads, bridges, machines etc. are built ‖ 도로·교량·기계 등의 건설 방법을 설계하는 직업이나 활동. 엔지니어링. 공학

En·glish¹ /ˈɪŋglɪʃ/ n **1** [U] the language used in places such as the US, Canada, and Great Britain ‖ 미국·캐나다·영국 등에서 쓰는 언어. 영어 **2 the English** [plural] the people of England ‖ 영국 국민. 영국인

English² adj **1** relating to the English language ‖ 영어와 관련된. 영어의. 영어로 쓰인 **2** relating to or coming from England ‖ 영국과 관련되거나 영국 출신의. 영국의

en·grave /ɪnˈgreɪv/ v [T] to cut words or pictures onto the surface of metal, wood, glass etc. ‖ 문자나 그림을 금속·나무·유리 등의 표면에 새기다. 조각하다:

an engraved trophy 문자가 새겨진 트로피

en·grav·ing /ɪnˈɡreɪvɪŋ/ *n* [T] a picture printed from an ENGRAVEd piece of metal or wood ‖ 새겨진 금속이나 나무 조각으로 인쇄한 그림. 제판. 판화

en·grossed /ɪnˈɡroʊst/ *adj* so interested in something that you do not notice anything else ‖ 다른 것을 알아차리지 못할 만큼 어떤 것에 열중한. 몰두한: *Kit was in a corner, completely engrossed in a book.* 키트는 구석에서 완전히 책에 몰두했다.

en·gross·ing /ɪnˈɡroʊsɪŋ/ *adj* so interesting that you do not notice anything else ‖ 다른 것을 알아차리지 못하게 할 만큼 매우 흥미 있는. 마음을 빼앗는: *an engrossing story* 빠져들게 하는 소설

en·gulf /ɪnˈɡʌlf/ *v* [T] **1** to suddenly affect someone so strongly that s/he feels nothing else ‖ 아무것도 느낄 수 없을 만큼 아주 강력하게 남에게 갑작스레 영향을 미치다. 덮치다. 빠지다: *Fear engulfed him as he approached the stage.* 그가 무대에 다가갔을 때 공포가 그를 덮쳤다. **2** to completely surround or cover something ‖ 사물을 완전히 둘러싸거나 덮다. …을 삼키다. 휩쓸리게 하다: *a home engulfed in flames* 불길에 휩싸인 집

en·hance /ɪnˈhæns/ *v* [T] to make something such as a taste, feeling, or ability better ‖ 맛[감정, 능력] 등을 더 좋게 하다. 높이다. 늘리다: *Adding lemon juice will enhance the flavor.* 레몬 주스를 더 넣으면 맛이 더 나을 것이다. – **enhancement** *n* [C, U]

e·nig·ma /ɪˈnɪɡmə/ *n* a person, thing, or event that is strange, mysterious, and difficult to understand ‖ 이상하고 신비하며 이해하기 어려운 사람[사물, 사건]. 수수께끼 같은 인물[것]: *That man will always be an enigma to me.* 그 사람은 항상 나에게는 수수께끼 같은 인물이 될 것이다. – **enigmatic** /ˌɛnɪɡˈmætɪk/ *adj*

en·joy /ɪnˈdʒɔɪ/ *v* [T] **1** if you enjoy something, it gives you pleasure ‖ 어떤 것이 즐거움을 주다. 즐기다: *Did you enjoy the movie?* 영화 좋았니? / *I really enjoy walking the dog.* 나는 개와 산책하는 것을 정말 즐긴다. ✗DON'T SAY "I enjoy to walk the dog."✗ "I enjoy to walk the dog."이라고 하지 않는다. **2 enjoy yourself** to be happy and have fun in a particular situation ‖ 특별한 상황에 기뻐하고 즐거워하다. 유쾌하게 지내다. 즐기

다: *She was determined to enjoy herself at the prom even though she was by herself.* 그녀는 비록 혼자이지만 학교 댄스 파티에서 즐기기로 작정했다. **3** to have a particular ability, advantage, or success ‖ 특정한 능력[장점, 성공]을 가지다. 향유하다. 누리다: *The team has enjoyed some success this season.* 그 팀은 이번 시즌에 약간의 성공을 거두었다. – **enjoyment** *n* [U]

en·joy·a·ble /ɪnˈdʒɔɪəbəl/ *adj* giving you pleasure ‖ 즐거움을 주는. 즐거운. 재미있는: *an enjoyable afternoon/concert/ book* 즐거운 오후[즐거운 콘서트, 재미있는 책]

en·large /ɪnˈlɑrdʒ/ *v* [T] to become bigger, or to make something become bigger ‖ 더 커지다, 또는 어떤 것을 더 커지게 하다. 확대[확장]하다: *I'm going to get some of these pictures enlarged.* 이 사진들 중 몇 개를 확대시키고자 합니다.

en·large·ment /ɪnˈlɑrdʒmənt/ *n* a photograph that has been printed again in a larger size ‖ 큰 사이즈로 다시 인화한 사진. 확대 사진

en·light·en /ɪnˈlaɪtˈn/ *v* [T] FORMAL to explain something to someone so that s/he finally understands it ‖ 마침내 어떤 것을 이해하도록 남에게 설명해주다. 계발[계몽]하다. 깨우쳐 주다 – **enlightening** *adj*: *an enlightening experience* 깨우침을 주는 경험

en·light·ened /ɪnˈlaɪtˈnd/ *adj* wise, fair, and sensible because you know what is true and what is false ‖ 무엇이 사실이고 거짓인지를 알기 때문에 현명하며 공정하고 분별이 있는. 이치를 아는. 개화된. 정통한: *an enlightened progressive company that treats its employees well* 종업원에 대한 처우가 좋은 깨이고 진보적인 회사

en·list /ɪnˈlɪst/ *v* **1** [T] to persuade someone to help you, do a job for you etc. ‖ 자신을 돕거나 자신을 위한 일 등을 하도록 어떤 사람을 설득하다. (남의 협력·지지를) 얻어 내다. 협력을 요청하다: *Moore enlisted the help of four friends to move the piano.* 무어는 피아노를 옮기기 위해 친구 네 명의 도움을 얻었다. **2** [I] to join the army, navy etc. ‖ 육군·해군 등에 합류하다. 입대하다. 병적에 들어가다: *My grandfather enlisted when he was 18.* 우리 할아버지는 18살에 입대하셨다. – **enlistment** *n* [C, U]

en·liv·en /ɪnˈlaɪvən/ *v* [T] to make something more interesting or exciting ‖ 어떤 것을 더 재미있거나 흥미롭게 하다. 활기 띠게 하다. 북돋우다

E

en masse /ɑn ˈmæs, -ˈmɑs, ɛn-/ *adv*
together as one group ‖ 한 무리로서 함
께. 집단으로: *City councilors threatened
to resign en masse.* 시 의원들은 총사되
를 하겠다고 위협했다.

en·mi·ty /ˈɛnməti/ *n* [U] feelings of
hatred and anger; ANIMOSITY ‖ 미움과 분
노의 감정. 원한. 악의. 적대감; 倂
animosity

e·nor·mi·ty /ɪˈnɔrməti/ *n* [singular, U]
the fact of being very large or serious ‖
매우 크거나 심각한 사실. (문제·일 등
의) 막대함[곤란함, 무모함]: *He could
not understand the enormity of his
crime.* 그는 자신이 저지른 범죄의 심각성
을 이해할 수 없었다.

e·nor·mous /ɪˈnɔrməs/ *adj* extremely
large in size or amount ‖ 크기나 양이 지
극히 큰. 거대한: *You should see their
house – it's enormous!* 네가 그들의 집을
봐야 하는데. 어마어마하더라! / *an
enormous amount of work to finish* 끝내
야 할 엄청난 양의 일

e·nor·mous·ly /ɪˈnɔrməsli/ *adv*
extremely or very much ‖ 지극히 또는 아
주 많이. 매우. 엄청나게. 막대하게: *an
enormously popular writer* 대단히 인기
있는 작가

e·nough¹ /ɪˈnʌf/ *adv*
1 as big, as well, as
far, as much etc. as
necessary ‖ 필요한 만
큼 큰·잘·멀리·많이
등. 충분히: *This bag
isn't big enough to
hold all my stuff.* 이
가방은 내 물건을 다
담을 만큼 크지 않다. /
*I couldn't see well enough to read the
sign.* 나는 잘 안 보여서 그 기호를 읽을
수 없었다. 2 not very, but in an
acceptable way ‖ 대단하지는 않지만 받아
들일 정도로. 그럭저럭. 어지간히: *She's
nice enough, but I don't think she likes
me.* 그녀는 그런 대로 멋있지만 나를 좋아
하는 것 같지는 않다. 3 **sth is bad
enough...** SPOKEN said when one thing is
bad, but another thing is worse ‖ 한 가
지 일도 나쁘지만 다른 하나가 더 나쁠 때
쓰여: *It's bad enough that I have to work
late – then you make jokes about it!* 내가
야근을 해야 하는 것도 안 좋은데 너는 그
걸 가지고 농담까지 해! 4 **strangely/
oddly/funnily enough** SPOKEN said
when what you have just said or are
about to say is strange ‖ 자신이 방금 말
했거나 말하려는 내용이 이상할 때 쓰여.
정말 이상하게/묘하게/기묘하게도:

enough
Her bag isn't big enough.

*Funnily enough, I met him today after
not having seen him for months.* 참으로
이상하게도 몇 달 동안 그를 못 보다가 오
늘 그를 만났다. —see also **sure enough**
(SURE²) —see usage note at TOO

USAGE NOTE using **enough** in
sentences

Enough is used after adjectives or
adverbs, but it is usually used before
a noun: *They're rich enough to have
three cars.* / *I can't walk fast enough
to keep up with you.* / *Do we have
enough money for the tickets?* In
sentences with "there" as the subject,
enough can also be used after a
noun: *There's room enough for
everyone.*
enough는 형용사나 부사 뒤에 쓰이나
대개 명사 앞에 쓰인다: 그들은 차를 세
대나 가질 만큼 부자다. / 나는 당신을
따라갈 만큼 빨리 걸을 수 없다. / 우리
가 표를 살 만한 돈이 있니? 주어로서
"there"가 있는 문장에서 **enough**는
명사 뒤에도 쓰일 수 있다: 모든 사람이
들어갈 공간이 충분하다.

enough² *determiner, pron* 1 as much
or as many as necessary ‖ 필요한 만큼
수량이 많은. 족한: *Do we have enough
food for everybody?* 모든 사람에게 충분
한 음식이 있니? / *I think we've done
enough for one day.* 하루 양은 충분히 한
것 같다. / *He doesn't earn enough to
pay the rent.* 그는 임대료를 낼 만큼 많이
벌지 못한다. 2 **have had enough (of)** to
be very annoyed with someone or
something ‖ 사람이나 사물에 매우 화가
나다. 더 이상 참을 수 없다: *I'd had
enough of the neighbors' noise, so I
called the police.* 이웃의 소음에 더 이상
참을 수 없어서 경찰에 신고했다.

en·rage /ɪnˈreɪdʒ/ *v* [T] to make
someone very angry ‖ 남을 몹시 화나게
하다. 격노하게 하다: *Ed was enraged
at/by what Dee said to me.* 에드는 디가
나에게 한 말에 분노했다. – **enraged**
adj

en·rich /ɪnˈrɪtʃ/ *v* [T] to improve the
quality of something ‖ 어떤 것의 질을 향
상시키다. 높이다. …을 풍부하게 하다:
*activities to enrich your language
ability* 당신의 언어 능력을 향상시키기 위
한 활동 / *vitamin-enriched flour* 비타민
이 강화된 밀가루 – **enrichment** *n* [U]

en·roll, enrol /ɪnˈrol/ *v* [I, T] to make
yourself or another person officially a
member of a course, school etc. ‖ 자신이

나 다른 사람을 공식적으로 특정 과정·학교 등의 회원이 되게 하다. 등록하다[시키다]. 입회[입학]하다[시키다]: *More students are enrolling in special education classes.* 더 많은 학생들이 특수 교육반에 등록하고 있다.

en·roll·ment /ɪnˈrəlmənt/ n [C, U] the number of students who are ENROLLed in a course or class, or the process of enrolling them ‖ 특정 과정이나 수업에 등록하는 학생 수, 또는 학생들을 등록시키는 과정. 등록[입학]자 수. 등록. 입학. 입회: *Enrollment was high this year.* 올해는 입학자 수가 많았다.

en route /ɑn ˈruːt, ɛn-/ adv on the way ‖ 도중에. 도상에: *Dinner will be served en route to Dallas.* 댈러스로 가는 도중에 저녁 식사가 제공됩니다.

en·sconce /ɪnˈskɑns/ v [T] FORMAL OR HUMOROUS to put someone in a safe and comfortable place ‖ 사람을 안전하고 안락한 장소에 두다. …에 자리잡다. 편히 앉다: *Martha ensconced herself in the biggest chair.* 마사는 가장 큰 의자에 편히 앉았다.

en·sem·ble /ɑnˈsɑmbəl/ n a small group of musicians who play together regularly ‖ 정기적으로 함께 연주하는 소규모 집단의 음악가들. 합주[합창]단

en·shrine /ɪnˈʃraɪn/ v [T] FORMAL to put something in a special place so that people can see it and remember it ‖ 사람이 보고 기억할 수 있게 어떤 것을 특별한 장소에 놓다. 모시다. 안치하다: *civil rights enshrined in the Constitution* 헌법에 명시된 시민권

en·sign /ˈɛnsən/ n 1 also **Ensign** an officer who has a low rank in the Navy or Coast Guard ‖ 해군이나 해안 경비대의 낮은 계급의 장교. 해군 소위 2 a flag on a ship that shows what country the ship belongs to ‖ 선박의 소속 국가를 나타내기 위해 선박에 다는 기. 국기

en·slave /ɪnˈsleɪv/ v [T] FORMAL 1 to put someone into a situation that is difficult to escape from ‖ 사람을 탈출하기 어려운 상황에 두다. …을 포로로 하다 2 to make someone a SLAVE ‖ 사람을 노예로 만들다. 예속시키다

en·sue /ɪnˈsuː/ v [I] FORMAL to happen after something, often as a result of it ‖ 종종 어떤 것의 결과로서 그 이후에 일어나다. 계속되다. 잇따라 일어나다: *They received the report, and a long discussion ensued.* 그들은 그 보고를 받고서 긴 토론에 들어갔다. – **ensuing** adj : *The ensuing battle was fierce.* 그 다음 전투는 치열했다.

en·sure /ɪnˈʃʊr/ v [T] to do something to be certain of a particular result ‖ 특정한 결과를 보장하는 어떤 것을 하다. …를 확실하게 하다. 보증[보장]하다: *We must ensure that standards are maintained.* 우리는 기준이 유지되도록 확실히 해야 한다.

en·tail /ɪnˈteɪl/ v [T] to make something necessary, or have something as a necessary part ‖ 어떤 것을 필요하게 만들거나 필요한 부분으로 가지다. (…을) 수반하다. 필요로 하다: *Does your new job entail much traveling?* 네 새 직업은 외근을 많이 하니?

en·tan·gle /ɪnˈtæŋɡəl/ v [T] 1 be **entangled in/with** to make someone be involved with someone or something bad ‖ 남을 나쁜 사람이나 일에 관련시키다. 말려들게[얽히게] 하다. 관계를 맺게 하다 : *He became entangled with dishonest business partners.* 그는 부정한 사업 동업자와 관계를 맺게 되었다. 2 to make something be twisted or caught in something else ‖ 어떤 것을 다른 것에 꼬이거나 잡히게 하다. 걸리게하다: *a fish entangled in the net* 그물에 걸린 물고기 – **entanglement** n [C, U]

en·ter /ˈɛntɚ/ v 1 [I, T] to go or come into a place ‖ 어떤 장소에 들어가거나 들어오다: *When the President entered, we stood up.* 대통령이 들어왔을 때 우리는 일어섰다. / *Army tanks entered the capital.* 육군 탱크가 수도에 진입했다. 2 [T] to go inside something ‖ 어떤 것의 안으로 들어가다. 파고들다: *The infection hasn't entered her bloodstream.* 그 전염 물질은 그녀의 혈류에는 침투하지 않았다. 3 [T] to start working in a particular profession, or studying at a particular university, school etc. ‖ 특정한 직업으로 일하기 시작하다, 또는 특정한 대학·학교 등에서 공부하기 시작하다. …의 길에 접어들다. …에 입학하다: *Julia's planning to enter the Navy.* 줄리아는 해군에 입대할 예정이다. / *Many older students are now entering university.* 나이 든 학생들이 현재 대학에 많이 입학하고 있다. 4 [T] to start to take part in an activity ‖ 활동에 참가하기 시작하다. 참가[가담]하다: *There was a great feeling of national pride after we entered the war.* 우리나라가 그 전쟁에 참전한 후 커다란 국민적 자긍심이 생기게 되었다. 5 [I, T] to take part in something such as a competition or to arrange for someone else to do this ‖ 시합 등에 참가하거나 다른 사람이 시합 등에 참가하도록 준비하다. 출전하다[시키다]. 참가를 신청하다: *She entered* *the competition and won.* 그녀는 시합에 참가하여 이겼다. / *Mary entered her son in the race.* 메리는 그 경주에 자신의 아들을 출전시켰다. **6** [T] to put information into a computer by pressing the keys, or to write information on a form, document etc. ‖ 키를 눌러서 컴퓨터에 정보를 입력하다, 또는 용지·문서 등에 정보를 쓰다. 기입[기록]하다: *Enter your name on the form.* 용지에 본인의 이름을 기입하세요. **7** [T] to begin a period of time ‖ 일정한 기간이 시작되다. 돌입하다. 들어가다: *The economy is entering a period of growth.* 경제가 성장기에 들어가고 있다.

enter into sth *phr v* [T] **1** to start doing something, discussing something etc. ‖ 어떤 것을 하거나 토론하기 시작하다 : *Both sides must enter into negotiations.* 양측은 협상을 시작해야 한다. **2** to be considered as a reason for something ‖ 어떤 것에 대한 이유로 고려되다. …에 구성요소[요인, 일부분]로 들어[계산되어]있다: *Money didn't enter into my decision to leave.* 떠나기로 한 내 결정에 돈이 고려되지는 않았다. **3 enter into an agreement/contract etc.** FORMAL to officially make an agreement ‖ 공식적으로 계약을 맺다. 협상/계약 등을 맺다

en·ter·prise /ˈɛntəˌpraɪz/ *n* **1** a company, organization, or business, especially a new one ‖ 특히 새로운 회사[조직체, 사업]. 기업: *The store is a family enterprise.* (=owned by one family) 그 상점은 가족 기업이다. **2** a large and complicated plan or process that you work on with other people ‖ 다른 사람과 함께 작업하는 크고 복잡한 계획이나 과정. 어렵고 대담한 계획. 사업 계획: *The show is a huge enterprise that takes a year to plan.* 그 쇼는 계획을 세우는 데 일년이 걸리는 큰 사업이다. **3** [U] the ability to work hard and think of new ideas, especially in business ‖ 특히 사업상 열심히 일하고 새로운 아이디어를 생각해내는 능력. 진취적 기상. 모험심: *We have a great product due to the enterprise and energy of this team.* 이 팀의 진취성과 활기 덕택에 우리는 큰 성과가 있다. **4** [U] the activity of starting and running businesses ‖ 사업을 시작하고 경영하는 활동. 기업[사업] 경영: *private enterprise* 사기업 —see also FREE ENTERPRISE

en·ter·pris·ing /ˈɛntəˌpraɪzɪŋ/ *adj* able and willing to do things that are new or difficult ‖ 새롭거나 어려운 일을

할 수 있고 기꺼이 하고자 하는. 진취적인. 적극[모험]적인: *an enterprising law student* 진취적인 법학도

en·ter·tain /ˌɛntəˈteɪn/ *v* **1** [T] to do something that interests and amuses people ‖ 사람의 관심을 끌고 재미있게 하는 일을 하다. 즐겁게[재미있게] 하다: *He spent the next hour entertaining us with jokes.* 그는 농담으로 우리를 즐겁게 해주면서 그 다음 시간을 보냈다. **2** [I, T] to treat someone as a guest by providing food and drink for him/her ‖ 음식과 음료를 제공함으로써 누군가를 손님으로 대접하다. 환대하다. 향응을 베풀다: *Mike's entertaining clients at JoJo's restaurant.* 마이크는 조조 레스토랑에서 고객을 접대하고 있다. **3** [T] FORMAL to consider or think about an idea, doubt, suggestion etc. ‖ 생각·의심·제안 등을 고려하거나 생각하다. 마음에 품다

en·ter·tain·er /ˌɛntəˈteɪnə/ *n* someone whose job is to amuse people and make them laugh ‖ 사람을 즐겁게 하고 웃게 하는 직업인. 연예인: *a circus entertainer* 곡예사

en·ter·tain·ing /ˌɛntəˈteɪnɪŋ/ *adj* amusing and interesting ‖ 즐거우며 재미있는. 유쾌한: *an entertaining movie/book* 재미있는 영화[책] / *an entertaining evening* 유쾌한 저녁

en·ter·tain·ment /ˌɛntəˈteɪnmənt/ *n* [U] things such as television, movies etc. that amuse or interest people ‖ 사람을 즐겁게 하거나 흥미를 끄는 텔레비전·영화 등의 것. 오락. 연예: *the entertainment industry* 연예 산업 / *What do people do for entertainment in this town?* 이 도시에서는 사람들이 오락으로 무엇을 합니까?

en·thrall /ɪnˈθrɔl/ *v* [T] to completely hold someone's attention and interest ‖ 남의 관심과 흥미를 완전히 사로잡다. 매혹하다. 열중하게 하다: *We were enthralled by the new play.* 우리는 새 연극에 매혹되었다. **– enthralling** *adj*

en·thuse /ɪnˈθuz/ *v* [I] to talk about something with excitement and admiration ‖ 흥분과 감탄으로 어떤 것에 대해 이야기하다. …에 열중[열광, 감격]하다: *Jeff showed us pictures and enthused about his trip to Africa.* 제프는 우리에게 그림을 보여주며 자신의 아프리카 여행 이야기를 신나게 했다.

en·thu·si·as·m /ɪnˈθuziˌæzəm/ *n* [U] a strong feeling of interest, excitement, or admiration about something ‖ 어떤 것에 대한 흥미[흥분, 감탄]의 강렬한 느낌. 열광. 열중. 열정. 열의: *He sang with* *enthusiasm.* 그는 열정적으로 노래했다. / *A few of the kids showed enthusiasm for art.* 몇몇 어린이들은 예술에 대한 열정을 보였다. – **enthusiast** /ɪnˈθuziəst/ *n*

en·thu·si·as·tic /ɪnˌθuziˈæstɪk/ *adj* showing a lot of interest and excitement about something ‖ 어떤 것에 대한 많은 흥미와 흥분을 보이는. 열심[열광적]인: *I was really enthusiastic about going to the party.* 나는 파티에 가는 데에 정말 열성적이었다. – **enthusiastically** *adv*

en·tice /ɪnˈtaɪs/ *v* [T] to persuade someone to do something by offering him/her something nice ‖ 남에게 멋진 것을 제안함으로써 어떤 일을 하도록 설득하다. 유혹[유인]하다. 꼬드기다. 부추기다: *another ad trying to entice people into buying a new car* 사람들을 유혹해서 새 차를 사게 하려는 또다른 광고 – **enticing** *adj* : *enticing smells from the kitchen* 부엌에서 나는 식욕을 자극하는 냄새 – **enticement** *n* [C, U]

en·tire /ɪnˈtaɪə/ *adj* a word meaning whole or complete, used in order to emphasize what you are saying ‖ 말하고자 하는 것을 강조하는 데 쓰이는 전부나 완전함을 뜻하는 단어. 전체의. 온전한: *I've spent my entire day cooking.* 나는 하루종일 요리하면서 보냈다. / *The entire wheat crop was lost to bad weather.* 밀 수확 전체가 악천후로 유실됐다.

en·tire·ly /ɪnˈtaɪəli/ *adv* completely ‖ 완전히. 온전히. 전부: *Things are entirely different now.* 지금은 사정이 완전히 다르다. / *The decision is entirely yours.* 결정은 전적으로 너의 몫이다.

en·tire·ty /ɪnˈtaɪəti, -ˈtaɪrəti/ *n* [U] **in sth's entirety** using or affecting all of something ‖ 사물의 전체를 이용하거나 전체에 영향을 미치는. 전부. 온전히. 완전한 형태로. 전체적으로: *The speech is published in its entirety.* 그 연설은 원고 그대로 출간된다.

en·ti·tle /ɪnˈtaɪtl/ *v* [T] **1** to give someone the right to have or do something ‖ 다른 사람에게 어떤 것을 하거나 가질 수 있는 권리를 주다. 자격을 부여하다[주다]: *This coupon entitles you to 50¢* off a box of cornflakes. 이 쿠폰으로 콘플레이크 한 상자를 50센트 싸게 살 수 있다. **2** to give a title to a book, play etc., or to have a particular title ‖ 책·희곡 등에 명칭을 주거나 특정 명칭을 갖다. …으로 부르다. 표제[제목, 이름, 칭호]를 붙이다: *a book entitled "The Stone Diaries"* "더 스톤 다이어리즈"라는 제목의 책

en·ti·tle·ment /ɪnˈtaɪtlmənt/ *n* [C, U] the official right to have or receive something, or the amount you receive ‖ 어떤 것을 갖거나 받을 수 있는 공식적 권리, 또는 받은 것의 크기. 권리[자격](부여): *an employee's entitlement to free medical care* 무료 치료를 받을 종업원들의 권리

en·ti·ty /ˈɛntəti/ *n* FORMAL something that exists as a single and complete unit ‖ 단일하고 완전한 단위로 존재하는 것. 단일체. 독립체. 단독의[독립된] 존재(물): *The treaty made East and West Germany a single economic entity.* 그 조약으로 동서독은 하나의 경제 단일체가 되었다.

en·to·mol·o·gy /ˌɛntəˈmɑlədʒi/ *n* [U] the scientific study of insects ‖ 곤충에 관한 과학적 연구. 곤충학 – **entomologist** *n*

en·tou·rage /ˌɑntʊˈrɑʒ/ *n* a group of people who travel with an important person ‖ 중요 인사와 함께 여행하는 사람들의 집단. 수행원. 측근[추종자]들: *the President's entourage* 대통령의 수행원들

en·trails /ˈɛntreɪlz/ *n* [plural] the inside parts of a person or animal, especially the BOWELS ‖ 사람이나 동물의 내부 장기로서 특히 창자. 장

en·trance /ˈɛntrəns/ *n* **1** a door, gate, or other opening that you go through to enter a place ‖ 어떤 장소에 들어가기 위해 지나가는 문[대문, 기타 열린 곳]. 입구. 출입문. 현관: *Meet us at the main entrance to the school.* 학교 정문에서 만나자. **2** [U] the right or opportunity to enter a place, become a member of a profession, university etc. ‖ 어떤 장소에 들어가거나 전문직·대학 등의 일원이 될 권리나 기회. 들어가기. 입장. 입회. 입학. 입사: *Entrance will be denied to those without tickets.* 표가 없는 사람들은 입장할 수 없다. / *There will be an entrance fee of $30.* 입장료는 30달러 입니다. **3 make an entrance** to come into a place in a way that makes people notice you ‖ 다른 사람들이 알아볼 수 있게 어떤 장소로 들어오다. 입장하다. 등장하다: *She loves to make an entrance at a party.* 그녀는 파티에 참석하기를 좋아한다. —compare ENTRY

en·tranced /ɪnˈtrænst/ *adj* very interested in and pleased with something ‖ 어떤 것에 매우 흥미 있어 하며 즐거워하는. …에 황홀해진[매혹된]. 기뻐 어쩔 줄 모르는: *The children were entranced by the performance.* 아이들은 공연에 매혹되었다. – **entrance** *v* [T]

en·trant /ˈɛntrənt/ *n* FORMAL someone who enters a competition ‖ 시합에 참가하는 사람. 경기 참가자

en·trap /ɪnˈtræp/ *v* **-pped, -pping** [T] FORMAL to deceive someone so that s/he is caught doing something illegal ‖ 다른 사람을 속여 불법 행위 중에 잡다. 덫에 걸리게 하다. 덫을 놓아 잡다. 함정에 빠뜨려 잡다 **– entrapment** *n* [U]

en·treat /ɪnˈtrit/ *v* [T] FORMAL to ask someone, with a lot of emotion, to do something ‖ 남에게 어떤 것을 해달라고 간절하게 요청하다. 간청[탄원]하다 **– entreaty** *n* [C, U]

en·trée /ˈɑntreɪ/ *n* the main dish of a meal ‖ 식사의 주요리. 앙트레

en·trenched /ɪnˈtrɛntʃt/ *adj* strongly established and not likely to change ‖ 굳건히 확립되어서 변할 것 같지 않은. 확립된. 확고한: *entrenched values and attitudes* 확고한 가치관과 태도

en·tre·pre·neur /ˌɑntrəprəˈnɜ, -ˈnʊr/ *n* someone who starts a company, arranges business deals, and takes risks in order to make a profit ‖ 회사를 창업해서 사업상 거래를 계획하고 이익을 내기 위해 위험을 감수하는 사람. 사업[기업]가 **– entrepreneurial** /ˌɑntrəprəˈnʊriəl/ *adj*

en·trust /ɪnˈtrʌst/ *v* [T] to give someone something to be responsible for ‖ 남에게 책임져야 할 임무를 주다. …을 맡기다[위탁]하다. …하는 책임을 부여하다: *Bergen was entrusted with delivering the documents.* 버겐은 서류를 전달하는 책임을 맡았다.

en·try /ˈɛntri/ *n* **1** the act of coming or going into a place ‖ 어떤 장소에 들어오거나 들어가는 행위. 입장. 입국: *What was your point of entry into the United States?* 미국에 입국한 목적이 무엇이었습니까? **2** [U] the right or opportunity to enter a place or become a member of a group ‖ 어떤 장소에 들어가거나 한 집단의 구성원이 될 권리나 기회. 진입. 입회. 입사. 입학: *the entry of new firms into the market* 새 기업들의 시장으로의 진입 **3** also **entryway** a door, gate, or passage that you go through to go into a place ‖ 어떤 장소에 들어가기 위해 통과하는 문[대문, 통로]. 현관. 입구. 출입구 **4** something written or printed in a book, list etc. ‖ 책자·목록 등에 쓰이거나 인쇄된 것. 기재[기입](사항). 표제(어): *a dictionary entry* 사전의 표제어 **5** [U] the act of recording information on paper or in a computer ‖ 정보를 종이나 컴퓨터에 기록하는 행위. 기장. 기록. 입력:

data entry 데이터 입력 **6** a person or thing in a competition, race etc. ‖ 경기·경주 등에 참가한 사람이나 사물. 경기 참가자. 출품작: *the winning entry* 우승작[자] **7** the act of entering a competition, race etc. ‖ 경기·경주 등에 참가하는 행위. 참가. 출장: *Entry is open to anyone over 18.* 18세 이상 누구나 참가 할 수 있다.

en·twine /ɪnˈtwaɪn/ *v* [T] **1** be **entwined to** be closely connected with each other in a complicated way ‖ 복잡하게 서로 긴밀히 연결되다. 얽히다. 엉키다: *The two sisters' lives were deeply entwined.* 그 두 자매의 삶은 서로 깊이 얽혀져 있었다. **2** to twist something around something else ‖ 사물을 다른 것 주위에 감다. 엮다. 휘감다: *flowers entwined in her hair* 그녀의 머리에 휘감아진 꽃

e·nu·mer·ate /ɪˈnuməˌreɪt/ *v* [T] FORMAL to name a list of things, one by one ‖ 사물의 목록을 하나하나 거론하다. 일일이 들다. 열거하다

e·nun·ci·ate /ɪˈnʌnsiˌeɪt/ *v* FORMAL **1** [I, T] to pronounce words or sounds clearly ‖ 낱말이나 소리를 똑똑히 발음하다. 분명하게 발음하다 **2** [T] to express ideas or principles clearly and firmly ‖ 생각이나 원칙을 분명하고 확고하게 표현하다. 명확하게 말하다. 공표[선언]하다 **– enunciation** /ɪˌnʌnsiˈeɪʃən/ *n* [C, U]

en·vel·op /ɪnˈvɛləp/ *v* [T] to cover something completely ‖ 사물을 완전히 덮다. 감싸다: *a building enveloped in flames* 화염 속에 휩싸인 건물 **– enveloping** *adj*

en·ve·lope /ˈɛn-və,loʊp, ˈɑn-/ *n* the paper cover in which you put a letter ‖ 편지를 넣는 종이 표지. 편지 봉투

envelope

en·vi·a·ble /ˈɛnviəbəl/ *adj* making you wish you had something or could do something ‖ 어떤 것을 가지거나 할 수 있으면 하고 바라는. 부러운. 샘나는. 선망의 대상이 되는: *an enviable position in the company* 회사 내의 탐나는 직책 **– enviably** *adv*

en·vi·ous /ˈɛnviəs/ *adj* wishing that you had someone else's qualities or things ‖ 다른 사람의 자질이나 물건을 가졌으면 하고 바라는. 부러워하는. 시샘[시기, 질투]하는: *Jackie was envious of Sylvia's success.* 재키는 실비아의 성공을 시기했다. **– enviously** *adv* —see usage note at JEALOUS

en·vi·ron·ment /ɪnˈvaɪ(ə)nmənt/ n **1 the environment** the land, water, and air in which people, animals, and plants live ‖ 사람·동물·식물들이 사는 땅·물·공중. 자연 환경: *laws to protect the environment* 환경보호법 **2** [C, U] the situations, people etc. that influence the way in which people live and work ‖ 사람들이 생활하고 일하는 방식에 영향을 주는 상황·사람들 등. 주위 (상황). 여건: *a pleasant work environment* 쾌적한 근무 환경

en·vi·ron·men·tal /ɪnˌvaɪ(ə)nˈmɛntl/ adj relating to or affecting the air, land, or water on Earth ‖ 지구의 대기[땅, 물]에 관련되거나 영향을 미치는. 환경의[상의]: *environmental damage caused by oil spills* 기름 유출에 의한 환경 파괴 – **environmentally** adv

en·vi·ron·men·tal·ist /ɪnˌvaɪ(ə)n-ˈmɛntl-ɪst/ n someone who is concerned about protecting the environment ‖ 환경 보호에 관심을 갖는 사람. 환경 보호주의자

en·vi·rons /ɪnˈvaɪrənz, ɛn-/ n [plural] FORMAL the area surrounding a place ‖ 한 장소를 둘러싼 지역. 주변. 근교

en·vi·sion /ɪnˈvɪʒən/, **en·vis·age** /ɪnˈvɪzɪdʒ/ v [T] to imagine something as a future possibility ‖ 어떤 것을 장래 가능성으로서 상상하다. 마음에 그리다. 상상하다. 계획하다: *Eve had envisioned a career as a diplomat.* 이브는 직업으로 외교관을 꿈꿨었다.

en·voy /ˈɛnvɔɪ, ˈɑn-/ n someone who is sent to another country as an official representative ‖ 공식 대표로서 다른 나라에 보내진 사람. 사절. 특사. 전권 공사

en·vy¹ /ˈɛnvi/ n [U] **1** the feeling of wanting to have the qualities or things that someone else has ‖ 다른 사람이 가진 자질이나 물건을 가지고 싶어하는 감정. 부러움. 선망. 시기. 시샘: *She was looking with envy at Pat's new shoes.* 그녀는 팻의 새 구두를 부러운 눈으로 바라보고 있었다. **2 be the envy of** to be something that other people admire and want ‖ 다른 사람들이 감탄하고 바라는 것이다. 선망의 대상[부러워하는 것]이다: *Our social programs are the envy of other cities.* 우리의 사회 보장 시책은 다른 도시들의 선망의 대상이다.

envy² v [T] to wish you had the qualities or things that someone else has ‖ 다른 사람이 가진 자질이나 사물을 가졌으면 하다. …을 부러워하다. 시기[시샘]하다: *I envy Nina – she gets to travel all over*

the world in her job! 나는 직업상 전세계를 여행하는 니나가 부럽다! / *I envy you your house.* 나는 너의 집이 부럽다. ✗DON'T SAY "I envy your house."✗ "I envy your house"라고는 하지 않는다.

en·zyme /ˈɛnzaɪm/ n TECHNICAL a chemical substance produced by living cells in plants and animals, that causes changes in other chemical substances ‖ 식물과 동물의 살아있는 세포로 만들어져 다른 화학 물질의 변화를 일으키는 화학 물질. 효소

ep·au·let /ˌɛpəˈlɛt, ˈɛpəˌlɛt/ n a shoulder decoration on a military uniform ‖ 군복의 어깨 장식. 견장

ephem·er·al /ɪˈfɛmərəl/ adj existing only for a short time ‖ 짧은 시간 동안만 존재하는. 단명한. 순식간의. 덧없는

ep·ic¹ /ˈɛpɪk/ adj **1** full of brave action and excitement ‖ 용맹한 행동과 재미로 가득 찬. 서사시의. 서사시적인. 영웅적인: *an epic journey* 서사시적 여정 **2** very big, long, or impressive ‖ 매우 큰[긴, 감동적인]. 웅장한: *an epic movie* 장편 영화

epic² n **1** a book or movie that tells a long story ‖ 긴 이야기를 해 주는 책이나 영화. 장편. 서사시적 작품: *"Gone with the Wind," an epic about the Civil War* 남북 전쟁을 그린 서사시적 작품인, "바람과 함께 사라지다" **2** a long poem about what gods or important people did in past times ‖ 신이나 중요 인물들이 과거에 했던 일에 대한 장시(長詩). 서사시. 사시(史詩): *Homer's epic "The Odyssey"* 호머의 서사시 "오디세이"

ep·i·cen·ter /ˈɛpəˌsɛntɚ/ n TECHNICAL the place on the Earth's surface above the point where an EARTHQUAKE begins ‖ 지진이 시작되는 지점 위의 지표면상의 위치. 진앙. 진원지

ep·i·dem·ic /ˌɛpəˈdɛmɪk/ n **1** the rapid spread of an infectious disease among many people in the same area ‖ 같은 지역 내 많은 사람들 사이에서 전염병의 급속한 확산. 유행(성). 만연. 창궐: *a typhoid epidemic* 장티푸스의 창궐 **2** something bad that develops and spreads quickly ‖ 급속하게 발전되어 퍼지는 악성적인 것. 만연: *an epidemic of crime* 범죄의 만연 – **epidemic** adj

ep·i·gram /ˈɛpəˌgræm/ n a short amusing poem or saying that expresses a wise idea ‖ (마음을) 즐겁게 해 주는 짧은 시나 현명한 생각을 표현한 명언. 경구. 금언

ep·i·lep·sy /ˈɛpəˌlɛpsi/ n [U] a disease of the brain that causes someone to become unconscious, and often move his/her body in a violent uncontrolled way‖ 사람의 의식을 잃게 하고 종종 통제할 수 없이 격렬하게 몸을 움직이게 하는 뇌질환. 간질병

ep·i·lep·tic /ˌɛpəˈlɛptɪk/ n someone who has EPILEPSY‖ 간질병이 있는 사람. 간질 환자 – **epileptic** adj

ep·i·logue /ˈɛpəˌlɔg, -ˌlɑg/ n a speech or piece of writing added to the end of a book, movie, or play‖ 책[영화·연극]의 말미에 추가된 연설이나 문장. 끝맺음 말. 에필로그

E·pis·co·pal /ɪˈpɪskəpəl/ adj relating to the Protestant church in America that developed from the Church of England‖ 영국 국교회에서 발전된 미국 내 개신교에 관련된. 성공회의 – **Episcopalian** /ɪˌpɪskəˈpeɪliən/ adj

ep·i·sode /ˈɛpəˌsoʊd/ n 1 a television or radio program that is one of a series of programs that tell a story‖ TV나 라디오 프로그램 중 하나의 이야기를 풀어내는 연속물 중의 한 회분. 1편. 1회분: The final episode will be broadcast next week. 마지막 회가 다음 주에 방송될 것이다. 2 an event, or a short time that is different from the time around it‖ 하나의 사건, 또는 나머지 시간과는 다른 짧은 시간. 삽화적인 사건. 기간: She's had several episodes of depression lately. 그녀는 최근에 수 차례의 우울증 증세를 보였다. – **episodic** /ˌɛpəˈsɑdɪk/ adj

e·pis·tle /ɪˈpɪsəl/ n FORMAL OR HUMOROUS a long and important letter‖ 장문의 중요한 편지. 서간. 서한

ep·i·taph /ˈɛpəˌtæf/ n a statement about a dead person, on the stone over his/her grave‖ 무덤 묘비에 쓰인 죽은 사람에 대한 글. 비문(碑文). 묘비명

ep·i·thet /ˈɛpəˌθɛt/ n an adjective or short phrase used for describing someone‖ 사람을 묘사하기 위해 쓰인 형용사나 짧은 문구. 형용어구. 별명

e·pit·o·me /ɪˈpɪtəmi/ n **the epitome of** the perfect example of something‖ 어떤 것의 완벽한 실례. 본보기. 전형: He was the epitome of a good doctor – caring and knowledgeable. 그는 친절하고 전문 지식을 갖춘 훌륭한 의사의 전형이었다.

e·pit·o·mize /ɪˈpɪtəˌmaɪz/ v [T] to be the perfect or most typical example of something‖ 어떤 것의 완벽하거나 가장 전형적인 실례가 되다. …의 전형[본보기]이 되다: Chicago's busy liveliness seemed to epitomize the US. 활기에 찬 시카고는 미국의 전형인 듯했다.

ep·och /ˈɛpək/ n a period in history during which important events or

developments happened‖ 중요한 사건이나 발전이 이루어진 역사상의 시기. 신기원. 획기적인 시대[시기]

e·qual¹ /ˈikwəl/ adj **1** the same in size, value, amount etc.‖ 크기·가치·양 등에서 같은. 동일한. 균일한. 똑같은. 동등한. 등가[동격]의: Divide the dough into three equal parts. 반죽을 똑같이 세 등분해라. / The country's population growth is equal to 2% a year. 그 국가의 인구 성장률은 연 2%에 달한다. **2** having the same rights, chances etc. as everyone else, or giving everyone the same rights, chances etc.‖ 다른 사람과 똑같은 권리·기회 등을 가진, 또는 모든 사람에게 똑같은 권리·기회를 주는. 평등한: The Constitution says that all people are created equal. 헌법에 모든 사람은 평등하게 태어났다고 쓰여 있다. / We are equal partners in the business. 우리는 사업상 대등한 동업자이다. **3 on equal footing/terms** with neither side having any advantages over the other‖ 어느 쪽도 다른 쪽보다 유리한 점을 갖지 않는. 대등한 입장/조건으로: The contest was fair, with the two sides starting on equal footing. 경연 대회는 양측이 대등한 입장으로 시작해서 공평했다.

equal² v **1** [linking verb] to be the same as something else in size, number, amount etc.‖ 크기·수·양 등에서 다른 것과 똑같다. 동등하다. 비등하다: Four plus four equals eight. 4 더하기 4는 8이다. **2** [T] to be as good as something or someone else‖ 다른 사물이나 사람만큼 좋다. …에 미치다. 필적하다. 맞먹다: He has equalled the Olympic record! 그가 올림픽 기록에 맞먹는 성적을 냈어!

equal³ n someone who is as important, intelligent etc. as you are, or who has the same rights and opportunities as you do‖ 자신만큼 중요한·지적인 등의 사람, 또는 자신만큼 권리와 기회를 가진 사람. 동등한[대등한] 사람. 맞먹는[필적하는] 사람: My boss treats her employees as equals. 우리 사장은 그녀의 직원들을 대등한 사람으로 대한다. / Rembrandt was an artist without equal. (=no one was as good as he) 렘브란트와 필적할 예술가는 없었다.

e·qual·i·ty /ɪˈkwɑləti/ n [U] the state of having the same conditions, opportunities, and rights as everyone else‖ 다른 모든 사람과 똑같은 조건·기회·권리를 가진 상태. 균등. 평등. 대등. 등가: Women haven't achieved equality in the work force. 여성들은 노동력 부분에서 평등성을 달성하지 못했다. —

opposite INEQUALITY

e·qual·ize /ˈikwəˌlaɪz/ v [T] to make two or more things equal in size, value etc. ‖ 두 개 이상의 사물을 크기·가치 등에서 같게 하다. 평등[대등]하게 하다. 균일하게[고르게] 하다: *equalizing pay rates in the steel industry* 철강 업계의 임금을 균등하게 하기

e·qual·ly /ˈikwəli/ adv **1** to the same degree or limit ‖ 똑같은 정도나 한도로. 균등[동등, 평등]하게: *The candidates are equally qualified for the job.* 지원자[후보]들은 똑같이 그 직무에 맞는 자격을 갖추고 있다. **2** in parts that are the same size ‖ 같은 크기의 부분들로. 균일[동일]하게. 똑같이: *We'll divide the work equally.* 우리는 일을 똑같이 나눌 것이다.

equal sign /ˈ.. ˌ./ n the sign (=), used in mathematics to show that two amounts or numbers are the same ‖ 수학에서 두 개의 양이나 숫자가 같다는 것을 나타내는 데에 쓰는 기호(=). 등호

e·qua·nim·i·ty /ˌikwəˈnɪməti, ˌɛk-/ n [U] FORMAL calmness in a difficult situation ‖ 어려운 상황 속에서의 침착함. 평정. 냉정

e·quate /ɪˈkweɪt/ v [T] FORMAL to consider that one thing is the same as something else ‖ 한 가지 것을 다른 것과 동일하다고 간주하다. 동등[대등]하게 생각하다[다루다]. 동일시하다: *Don't equate criticism with blame.* 비판을 비난과 동일시하지 마라.

e·qua·tion /ɪˈkweɪʒən/ n a statement in mathematics showing that two quantities are equal, for example 2*x*+4=10 ‖ 예를 들어 2*x*+4=10처럼 2개의 수량이 같다는 것을 나타내는 수학의 표현 방식. 방정식. 등식

e·qua·tor /ɪˈkweɪt̬ɚ/ n [singular, U] **the equator** an imaginary circle around the Earth, that divides it equally into its northern and southern halves ‖ 지구를 남반구와 북반구로 똑같이 절반으로 나누는 가상의 원. 적도 – **equatorial** /ˌɛkwəˈtɔriəl/ adj

e·ques·tri·an /ɪˈkwɛstriən/ adj relating to horse riding ‖ 승마와 관련된. 기수의. 기마의. 마상(馬上)의

e·qui·lat·er·al /ˌikwəˈlæt̬ərəl/ adj having all sides equal ‖ 모든 변이 동일한. 등변의: *an equilateral triangle* 정삼각형

e·qui·lib·ri·um /ˌikwəˈlɪbriəm/ n [U] **1** a balance between opposing forces, influences etc. ‖ 상반되는 힘·영향(력) 간의 균형. 평형: *The supply and the demand for money must be kept in equilibrium.* 화폐에 대한 수요와 공급은 균형을 유지해야 한다. **2** a calm emotional state ‖ 차분한 정서적 상태. 마음의 평정. 침착

e·quine /ˈikwaɪn, ˈɛ-/ adj relating to horses, or looking like a horse ‖ 말과 관련되거나 말처럼 생긴. 말의[같은]. 말과(科)의

e·qui·nox /ˈikwəˌnɑks, ˈɛ-/ n one of the two times each year when day and night are equal in length everywhere ‖ 밤낮의 길이가 어디에서나 같은 매년 두 번의 시기 중 하나. 주야 평분시[점]

e·quip /ɪˈkwɪp/ v **-pped, -pping** [T] **1** to provide a person, group, building etc. with the things that are needed for a particular purpose ‖ 사람·집단·건물 등에 특정 목적을 위해 필요한 것들을 제공하다. 마련하다. 장비하다. 설비를 갖추다: *The new school will be equipped with computers.* 새 학교에는 컴퓨터가 설치될 것이다. **2** to prepare someone for a particular purpose ‖ 사람을 특정 목적을 위해 준비시키다. 치장[단장]시키다. 익혀서 … 할 수 있게 하다: *Your education should equip you for a good job.* 여러분의 교육은 좋은 직업을 얻도록 자신을 준비시키는 것입니다. – **equipped** adj

e·quip·ment /ɪˈkwɪpmənt/ n [U] the tools, machines etc. that you need for a particular activity ‖ 특정 활동에 필요한 연장·기계 등. 비품. 설비. 장비: *camera equipment* 카메라 장비 / *We bought several new pieces of equipment for the chemistry lab.* 우리는 화학 실험실에 놓을 새 장비를 여러 점 구입했다.

eq·ui·ta·ble /ˈɛkwət̬əbəl/ adj FORMAL fair and equal to everyone involved ‖ 관련자 모두에게 공정하고 평등한. 공평한: *We'll find an equitable solution to the problem.* 우리는 그 문제에 대한 공정한 해결책을 찾을 것이다.

eq·ui·ty /ˈɛkwəti/ n [U] **1** FORMAL a situation in which everyone is fairly treated ‖ 모든 사람들이 공평하게 대우받는 상황. 공평. 공정. 공명정대 **2** TECHNICAL the value of something you own, such as a house or SHAREs, after you have taken away the amount of money you still owe on it ‖ 아직 빚지고 있는 액수를 차감한 후의 주택이나 주식 등 소유하고 있는 것의 가치. 순자산. 재산·물건의 순가

e·quiv·a·lent¹ /ɪˈkwɪvələnt/ adj equal in value, purpose, rank etc. to something or someone else ‖ 가치·목적·

지위 등에서 다른 것이나 다른 사람과 동등한. 대등한. 등가의. (…에) 상당하는: *The atomic bomb has power equivalent to 10,000 tons of dynamite.* 원자 폭탄은 다이너마이트 1만 톤에 상당하는 위력을 가진다.

equivalent² *n* something that has the same value, size, etc. as something else ‖ 다른 것과 같은 가치·크기 등을 가진 것. 동등한 것. 상당[등가]물: *Some French words have no equivalents in English.* 어떤 프랑스어 낱말들은 그에 상응하는 영어 낱말이 없다.

e·quiv·o·cal /ɪˈkwɪvəkəl/ *adj* **1** deliberately not clear or definite in meaning ‖ 의도적으로 의미상 분명치 않거나 명확하지 않은. 애매한. 결정적이지 않는: *an equivocal answer* 애매한 대답 **2** difficult to understand or explain ‖ 이해하거나 설명하기가 어려운. 해석하기 힘든. 모호한. 난해한: *The results of the test were equivocal.* 시험 결과는 납득하기 힘들었다. —opposite UNEQUIVOCAL

ER *n* ⇨ EMERGENCY ROOM

e·ra /ˈɪrə, ˈɛrə/ *n* a long period of time that begins with a particular date or event ‖ 특정 날짜나 사건으로 시작되는 장기간의 시간. 연대. 시기. 시대: *the Reagan era* 레이건 시대

e·rad·i·cate /ɪˈrædəˌkeɪt/ *v* [T] to completely destroy something ‖ 어떤 것을 철저히 파괴하다. 박멸하다. 근절[전멸]시키다: *Smallpox has been eradicated.* 천연두는 완전 근절되었다. – **eradication** /ɪˌrædəˈkeɪʃən/ *n* [U]

e·rase /ɪˈreɪs/ *v* [T] to completely remove written or recorded information so that it cannot be seen or heard ‖ 기록되거나 녹음된 정보를 깨끗이 제거해서 보거나 들을 수 없다. 지우다. 말소[삭제]하다: *Erase any incorrect answers.* 틀린 답은 모두 지우시오. / *Ben erased one of my favorite tapes.* 벤이 내가 가장 좋아하는 테이프 중 하나를 지워 버렸다.

e·ras·er /ɪˈreɪsɚ/ *n* **1** a piece of rubber used for erasing (ERASE) pencil marks from paper ‖ 종이에 쓰인 연필 자국을 지우는 데에 쓰는 고무 조각. (고무) 지우개 —see picture at ERASE **2** an object used for cleaning marks from a BLACKBOARD ‖ 칠판에 쓴 것을 지우는 데에 쓰는 물건. 칠판 지우개

e·rect¹ /ɪˈrɛkt/ *adj* in a straight upright position ‖ 똑바로 선 자세의. 수직의. 곧추 선: *standing erect* 똑바로 서 있기

erect² *v* [T] **1** FORMAL to build something ‖ 어떤 것을 짓다. 세우다. 건립[건설]하다: *a statue erected in honor of Lincoln* 링컨 대통령을 기념해서 세워진 동상 **2** to put something in an upright position ‖ 사물을 똑바로 서게 놓다. 똑바로 세우다. 곧추[곧두]세우다: *The tents for the fair were erected overnight.* 밤새 박람회용 천막이 세워졌다.

e·rec·tion /ɪˈrɛkʃən/ *n* **1** the swelling of a man's PENIS during sexual excitement ‖ 성적 흥분 중의 남성 성기의 부풀어 오름. 발기 **2** [U] the act of ERECT*ing* something ‖ 물체를 세우는 행위. 건립. 건설: *the erection of a new church* 새 교회의 건립

e·rode /ɪˈroʊd/ *v* **1** [I, T] to destroy something gradually by the action of wind, rain, or acid, or to be destroyed in this way ‖ 사물을 바람[비, 산성]의 작용으로 점차 파괴하다. 부식[침식]하다[시키다]. 마멸되다[시키다]: *The cliffs had been eroded by the sea.* 절벽이 바다에 의해 침식되었다. **2** [I,T] to gradually destroy someone's power, authority etc., or be destroyed ‖ 다른 사람의 힘·권위 등을 점차 파괴하다. 또는 파괴되다. 잠식하다[시키다]. 침해하다: *Congress reversed a series of Supreme Court decisions that had eroded civil rights.* 의회는 시민권을 잠식해 왔던 대법원의 일련의 결정을 뒤집었다.

e·ro·sion /ɪˈroʊʒən/ *n* [U] the process of eroding (ERODE) something ‖ 사물을 부식하는 과정. 침식. 파괴: *soil erosion* 토양 침식 / *the erosion of society's values* 사회 가치(기준)의 파괴

e·rot·ic /ɪˈrɑtɪk/ *adj* relating to sexual love and desire ‖ 성적인 사랑과 욕구에 관한. 성애의. 성욕의: *erotic pictures* 춘화[외설적 그림이나 사진] – **erotically** *adv* – **eroticism** /ɪˈrɑtəsɪzəm/ *n* [U]

err /ɛr, ɚ/ *v* [I] **1 err on the side of caution/mercy etc.** to be too careful, too kind etc. rather than risk making mistakes ‖ 실수할 우려가 아니라 오히려 너무 조심하거나 너무 친절하다. 지나치게 조심/관대하다: *Doctors would prefer to err on the side of caution, by keeping newborns in the hospital longer.* 의사들은 신생아들을 병원에 더 오래 두면서 지나칠 정도로 주의를 기울이려 한다. **2** FORMAL to make a mistake ‖ 실수하다

er·rand /ˈɛrənd/ *n* a short trip that you make to take a message or buy something ‖ 전언을 받아 오거나 물건을

사기 위해 잠깐 다녀오는 것. 심부름. 볼일: *I have errands to do downtown.* 나는 시내에서 볼일이 있다. / *Could you run an errand for Grandma?* 할머니 심부름 좀 다녀오겠니?

er·rant /'ɛrənt/ *adj* **1** FORMAL going in the wrong direction ‖ 잘못된 방향으로 가는. 길을 잘못 든. 길을 잃은: *Rainer caught the errant pass.* 레이너는 길을 잘못 접어들었다. **2** HUMOROUS behaving in a bad or irresponsible way ‖ 나쁘거나 무책임하게 행동하는. 정도에서 벗어난. 불륜을 저지르는: *an errant husband* 불륜을 저지르는 남편

er·rat·ic /ɪ'rætɪk/ *adj* changing often or moving in an irregular way, without any reason ‖ 아무 이유 없이 자주 바뀌거나 불규칙하게 움직이는. 변덕스런. 일정치 못한. 잘 변하는: *erratic eating habits* 불규칙한 식습관[식생활] – **erratically** *adv*

er·ro·ne·ous /ɪ'rouniəs/ *adj* FORMAL incorrect ‖ 맞지 않은. 잘못된. 틀린: *erroneous statements* 잘못된 진술 – **erroneously** *adv*

er·ror /'ɛrɚ/ *n* [C, U] a mistake that causes problems ‖ 문제를 일으키는 잘못. 오류. 실수. 과오. 착오: *an accident caused by human error* (=by a person rather than a machine) 사람의 실수로 일어난 사고 / *The company admitted it was in error.* (=made a mistake) 그 회사는 자신들이 실수했다고 인정했다. / *Kovitz apologized yesterday for his error in/of judgment.* (=a decision that was a mistake) 코비츠는 그의 판단 착오에 대해 어제 사과했다.

USAGE NOTE error and mistake

A **mistake** is something that you do by accident, or that is the result of a bad judgment: *I'm sorry; I took your pen by mistake.* / *We made a mistake in buying this car.* An **error** is a mistake that you do not realize that you are making, that can cause problems: *You've made a serious error in calculating your taxes.*

mistake는 우연히 또는 잘못된 판단의 결과로 범하는 것이다: 미안합니다. 실수로 당신 펜을 가져갔습니다. / 우리는 이 차를 사면서 실수를 저질렀다. **error**는 잘못을 저지르고 있으며 문제를 초래할 수도 있다는 것을 인식하지 못하는 잘못이다: 당신은 세금을 계산하면서 중대한 오류를 범했습니다.

---

er·u·dite /'ɛryə,daɪt, 'ɛrə-/ *adj* FORMAL showing a lot of knowledge ‖ 지식이 많음을 보이는. 유식[박식]한. 학구적인: *an erudite speech* 박식한 연설 – **erudition** /,ɛryə'dɪʃən/ *n* [U]

e·rupt /ɪ'rʌpt/ *v* [I] **1** to happen suddenly ‖ 갑자기 발생하다. 발발하다. 복받쳐[쏟아져, 터져] 나오다: *Violence erupted after the demonstrations.* 시위 후에 갑자기 폭력 사태가 벌어졌다. **2** if a VOLCANO erupts, it sends out smoke, fire, and rock into the sky ‖ 화산이 연기·불·암석을 공중으로 뿜어내다. 분화[분출, 폭발]하다 **3** to appear suddenly on the skin ‖ 피부에 갑자기 나타나다. 발진하다. 돋아나다: *A rash erupted on his arms.* 뾰루지가 그의 팔에 돋아났다.

es·ca·late /'ɛskə,leɪt/ *v* **1** [I, T] if violence or a war escalates or is escalated, it becomes more serious ‖ 폭력이나 전쟁이 더 심각해지다. 단계적으로 확대[증대, 악화]되다[시키다]: *Fighting has escalated in several areas.* 몇몇 지역에서 전투가 격렬해졌다. **2** [I] to become higher or increase ‖ 더 높아지거나 증가하다. 오르다. 올라가다. 상승[증가]하다: *Housing prices escalated recently.* 주택 가격이 최근에 상승했다. – **escalation** /,ɛskə'leɪʃən/ *n* [C, U]

es·ca·la·tor /'ɛskə,leɪtɚ/ *n* a set of stairs that move and carry people from one level of a building to another ‖ 건물의 한 층에서 다른 층으로 움직이며 사람을 실어 나르는 일련의 계단. 에스컬레이터

es·ca·pade /'ɛskə,peɪd/ *n* an exciting adventure or series of events that may be dangerous ‖ 위험할지 모르는 흥미진진한 모험이나 일련의 사건들. 분별없이 벌이는 일. 엉뚱한 짓

es·cape¹ /ɪ'skeɪp/ *v* **1** [I, T] to leave a dangerous place, especially when someone is trying to catch you or stop you from leaving ‖ 특히 어떤 사람이 잡으려 하거나 떠나지 못하게 막으려 할 때 위험한 곳을 벗어나다. 피해서 도망치다[빠져 나오다]. 탈출[도피]하다: *Many people were killed trying to escape (from) the war zone.* 많은 사람들이 전쟁 지역을 벗어나려다 사망했다. / *Most passengers escaped the fire.* 대부분의 승객들이 화재를 피해 빠져 나왔다. **2** [I, T] to stop thinking about an unpleasant situation ‖ 불쾌한 상황에 대해 생각하는 것을 중단하다. …에서 도

escape

The dog escaped through a gap in the fence.

피하다. 회피하다: *Children use TV to escape (from) reality.* 아이들은 현실에서 도피하기 위해 TV를 이용한다. **3** [T] to not be noticed by someone ‖ 다른 사람에게 주목받지 않게 되다. 눈에서 벗어나다. 눈에 띄지 않게 숨다: *Nothing escapes Bill's attention.* 빌의 주목을 받지 않는 것은 아무 것도 없다. – **escaped** *adj*

escape² *n* **1** [C, U] the act of escaping ‖ 도피하는 행위. 도망. 빠져 나감. 탈출: *There's no chance of escape.* 도주할 가망은 없다. / *He made a daring escape from jail.* 그는 대담하게 탈옥했다. **2** [U] a way to forget about an unpleasant situation ‖ 불쾌한 상황을 잊기 위한 방법. (현실) 도피(수단). 일상 탈출: *Books are a good form of escape.* 책은 현실을 잊기 위한 좋은 수단이다.

es·cap·ism /ɪ'skeɪp,ɪzəm/ *n* [U] a way of forgetting about an unpleasant situation and think of pleasant things ‖ 불쾌한 상황을 잊고 즐거운 것들을 생각하는 방식. 현실 도피(주의·생활): *The world looks to Hollywood for escapism.* 사람들은 현실 도피를 위해 할리우드로 눈을 돌린다. – **escapist** *adj*

es·chew /ɛs'tʃu/ *v* [T] FORMAL to deliberately avoid doing, using, or having something ‖ 고의로 어떤 것을 하기[사용하기, 갖기]를 회피하다. 피하다. 삼가다. 멀리하다: *a man who eschews violence* 폭력을 멀리하는 남자

es·cort¹ /ɪ'skɔrt, 'ɛskɔrt/ *v* [T] **1** to go somewhere with someone, especially in order to protect him/her ‖ 특히 어떤 사람을 보호하기 위해 함께 어딘가에 가다. (경호하기 위해) 수행하다. 호위해 가다. 호송하다: *Armed guards escorted the prisoners into the courthouse.* 무장한 교도관들이 죄수들을 법정으로 호송해 갔다. **2** to go with someone of the opposite sex to a social event ‖ 사교 행사에 이성과 함께 가다. 동반하다. 바래다주다. 에스코트하다: *The princess was escorted by her cousin.* 공주는 그녀의 사촌이 에스코트했다.

es·cort² /'ɛskɔrt/ *n* the person or people who ESCORT someone ‖ 다른 사람을 에스코트하는 사람. 보호자. 호송자. 호위대: *The Governor travels with a police escort.* 주지사는 경찰 경호를 받으며 이동한다. / *prisoners transported under escort* (=with an escort) 호위를 받으며 이송된 죄수들

Es·ki·mo /'ɛskə,moʊ/ *n* a word meaning a member of one of the Native American tribes in Alaska or northern Canada, that some people consider OFFENSIVE ‖ 일부 사람들이 기분 상해하는, 알래스카나 북부 캐나다에 사는 북미 원주민 종족들 중의 한 종족의 일원을 의미하는 말. 에스키모인 —compare INUIT

ESL *n* English as a Second Language; the methods used for teaching English to people whose first language is not English, who are living in an English-speaking country ‖ English as a Second Language (제2언어로서의 영어)의 약어; 제1언어[모국어]가 영어가 아니면서 영어 상용국에서 사는 사람들에게 영어를 가르치기 위해 쓰는 교습법

e·soph·a·gus /ɪ'sɑfəgəs/ *n* the tube that goes from the mouth to the stomach ‖ 입에서 위로 이어진 관. 식도

es·o·ter·ic /,ɛsə'tɛrɪk/ *adj* known and understood only by a few people ‖ 소수의 사람들에게만 알려지고 이해되는. 심원한. 난해한. 비법의. 비전(祕傳)의: *esoteric teachings* 비법의 가르침

ESP *n* extrasensory perception; knowledge of other people's thoughts, of ghosts etc. that is gained not by seeing or hearing things, but in a way that cannot be explained ‖ extrasensory perception (초감각적 지각·초능력)의 약어; 보거나 들어서가 아니라 설명할 수 없는 방식으로 다른 사람의 생각·귀신 등을 아는 것

es·pe·cial·ly /ɪ'spɛʃəli/ *adv* **1** used in order to emphasize that something is more important, or happens more with one thing than with others ‖ 어떤 것이 더 중요하거나, 다른 것들보다 어떤 것이 더 자주 발생한다는 것을 강조하는 데에 쓰여. 특히. 특별히: *Everyone's excited about the trip, especially Doug.* 모두들 여행 때문에 흥분되어 있는데 특별히 더그는 더하다. / *Drive carefully, especially at night.* 특히 밤에는 조심해서 운전해라. **2** to a particularly high degree, or more than usual ‖ 특별히 정도가 심하게 또는 통상적인 것 이상으로. 특별하게. 각별하게. 비상하게: *I'm especially looking forward to seeing the new baby.* 나는 그 갓난아기를 특히나 빨리 보고 싶다. **3** for a particular purpose, reason etc. ‖ 특정 목적·이유 등으로. 특정하게. 특별히: *These flowers are especially for you.* 이 꽃들은 특별히 너를 위한 것이다. —compare SPECIALLY

es·pi·o·nage /'ɛspiə,nɑʒ/ *n* [U] the activity of finding out secret information and giving it to a country's enemies or a company's competitors ‖ 비밀 정보를 찾아내서 적국이나 경쟁 회사에게 주는 행

위. 간첩[첩보] 활동. 스파이 행위

ESPN *n* a CABLE TELEVISION company that broadcasts sports programs in the US ‖ 미국 내에서 스포츠 경기 프로그램을 방영하는 케이블 텔레비전 회사

es·pouse /ɛ'spaʊz, ɪ-/ *v* [T] FORMAL to believe in and support an idea, especially a political one ‖ 특히 정치적인 사상을 믿고 지원하다. 신봉[지지, 옹호]하다: *anti-drug policies espoused by the government* 정부의 지원을 받는 마약 퇴치 정책

es·pres·so /ɛ'sprɛsoʊ/ *n* [C, U] very strong coffee that you drink in small cups ‖ 작은 컵으로 마시는 매우 진한 커피. 에스프레소 커피

es·say /'ɛseɪ/ *n* a short piece of writing about a particular subject, especially as part of a course of study ‖ 특히 학업 과정의 부분으로서, 특정 주제에 대한 짧은 글. 에세이. 수필. 소론(小論)

es·sence /'ɛsəns/ *n* **1** [singular] the most basic and important quality of something ‖ 사물의 가장 기초적이고 중요한 성질. 특성. 본질. 진수: *The essence of his argument is that we shouldn't use cars when we can walk.* 그의 주장의 핵심은 우리가 걸을 수 있을 때는 차를 이용하지 말아야 한다는 것이다. / *In essence,* (=the most basic thing, said in a shortened form) *he said we should send more food aid.* 기본적으로, 그는 우리가 더 많은 식량 구호품을 보내야 한다고 말했다. **2** [U] a liquid that has a strong smell or taste and is obtained from a plant, flower etc. ‖ 강한 향이나 맛이 나며 식물·꽃 등에서 추출한 액체. 원액. 추출물. 정유. 향수: *vanilla essence* 바닐라 원액

es·sen·tial¹ /ɪ'sɛnʃəl/ *adj* **1** important and necessary ‖ 중요하고 필수적인. 절대 필요한. (필수)불가결한: *Good food is essential for your health.* 좋은 음식은 건강에 필수 불가결하다. **2** the essential parts, qualities, or features of something are the ones that are most important, typical, or easily noticed ‖ 사물의 가장 중요한[전형적인, 쉽게 눈에 띄는] 요소[성질, 특성]의. 본질[근원]적인: *What is the essential difference between these two books?* 이 두 책 사이의 가장 근본적인 차이는 무엇입니까?

essential² *n* [C usually plural] something that is important and necessary ‖ 중요하고 필수적인 것. 필수품. 필수 사항: *We provide people with the bare essentials* (=the most necessary things) *such as food and clothing.* 우리는 사람들에게 음식과 의복 같은 최소한의 필수품을 제공합니다.

es·sen·tial·ly /ɪ'sɛnʃəli/ *adv* relating to the most important or basic qualities of something ‖ 사물의 가장 중요하거나 기본적인 특질에 관련해서. 본래. 본질적으로. 기본적으로: *Your argument is essentially correct.* 너의 주장은 본질적으로 옳다.

es·tab·lish /ɪ'stæblɪʃ/ *v* [T] **1** to start something such as a company, system, situation etc., especially one that will exist for a long time ‖ 회사·체계·상황 등 특히 오랫동안 지속될 것을 시작하다. 설립[창설]하다. 확립[제정]하다: *The school was established in 1922.* 그 학교는 1922년에 설립되었다. **2** to begin a relationship, conversation etc. with someone ‖ 다른 사람과 관계·대화 등을 시작하다. 관계를 맺다[설정하다]. 대화를 나누다: *The group has established contacts with other groups overseas.* 그 단체는 해외의 다른 단체들과 접촉했다. **3** to get yourself a position or to be respected because of something you have done or a quality you have ‖ 한 일이나 가지고 있는 자질 때문에 지위를 얻거나 존경받다. 명성을 얻다. 출세하다. 기반을 잡다: *He's established himself as the most powerful man in the state.* 그는 주(州) 내에서 가장 영향력 있는 유지로 명성을 쌓았다. **4** to find out facts that will prove that something is true ‖ 어떤 것이 사실임을 입증할 사실을 찾아내다. 확증[입증, 증명]하다. …임을 분명히 하다: *His lawyer established that Shea did not know the victim.* 그의 변호사는 쉬어가 그 피해자를 모른다는 것을 입증했다.

es·tab·lish·ment /ɪ'stæblɪʃmənt/ *n* **1** FORMAL an institution, especially a business, store, hotel etc. ‖ 특히 사업체·매장·호텔 등의 시설: *an educational establishment* 교육 기관 **2 the Establishment** the organizations and people in a society who have a lot of power and who often are opposed to change or new ideas ‖ 많은 권력을 가지고 있고 종종 변화나 새로운 사상에 반대하는 사회 내 조직과 사람들. 기성 권력 기구[체제]. 특권 계급. 지배층. 기득권층 **3** [U] the act of starting something such as a company, organization, system etc. ‖ 회사·조직·체제 등의 것을 시작하는 행위. 설립. 창설. 수립. 확립: *the establishment of new laws protecting children* 어린이를 보호하는 새 법의 제정

es·tate /ɪ'steɪt/ *n* **1** a large area of land in the country, usually with one large house on it ‖ 보통 하나의 대저택이 들어선 시골의 넓은 대지. 부지. 사유지. 대저택의 토지[택지] **2** [singular] LAW all of someone's property and money, especially everything that is left after s/he dies ‖ 특히 죽은 후에 남긴 모든 재산과 돈. 전 재산. 유산: *She left her entire estate to my mother.* 그녀는 전 재산을 내 어머니에게 남겼다.

es·teem[1] /ɪ'stim/ *n* [U] FORMAL a feeling of respect and admiration for someone ‖ 다른 사람에 대한 존경과 칭송의 감정. 존중. 호의적인 의견[평판]: *She was held in high esteem by everyone on the team.* 그녀는 팀 내 모든 사람들에게 대단히 존경 받았다. —see also SELF-ESTEEM

esteem[2] *v* [T] FORMAL to respect and admire someone ‖ 다른 사람을 존경하고 칭송하다. 존중하다. 높이 평가하다: *a highly esteemed (=greatly respected) artist* 높이 평가되는 예술가

es·thet·ic /ɛs'θɛtɪk/ *adj* relating to beauty and the study of beauty ‖ 아름다움과 미의 연구에 관련된. 미의. 미학의. 심미안이 있는: *an esthetic point of view* 미학적 관점[견지] – **esthetically** *adv*

es·thet·ics /ɛs'θɛtɪks/ *n* [U] the study of beauty, especially beauty in art ‖ 특히 예술에서의 미에 대한 연구. 미학

es·ti·ma·ble /'ɛstəməbəl/ *adj* FORMAL deserving respect and admiration ‖ 존경과 칭송할 가치가 있는. 존중할 만한

es·ti·mate[1] /'ɛstə,meɪt/ *v* [T] to judge the value, size etc. of something ‖ 사물의 가치·크기 등을 평가하다. 산정하다. 어림잡다: *It is estimated that 75% of our customers are adult men.* 우리 고객의 75%가 성인 남자인 것으로 추정된다. – **estimated** *adj*

es·ti·mate[2] /'ɛstəmɪt/ *n* **1** a calculation or judgment of the value, size etc. of something ‖ 사물의 가치·크기 등의 계산이나 평가. 어림(잡음). 추정: *I'd say it's about 200 miles to the mountains, but that's just a rough estimate.* (=a calculation that is not very exact) 나는 산까지 약 2백 마일이라고 보지만 그것은 어디까지나 개략적인 추정치다. **2** a statement of how much it will probably cost to build or repair something ‖ 어떤 것을 짓거나 수리하는 데에 소요될 추정액의 계산서. 견적서: *I got three estimates so I could pick the cheapest.* 나는 세 가지 견적서를 받아서 가장 싼 쪽을 선택할 수 있었다.

es·ti·ma·tion /,ɛstə'meɪʃən/ *n* [U] your judgment or opinion of the value of someone or something ‖ 사람이나 사물의 가치에 대한 자신의 판단이나 의견. 평가. 견해: *In my estimation, McEnery has been a great mayor.* 내가 보기에 맥에너리는 훌륭한 시장이었다.

es·tranged /ɪ'streɪndʒd/ *adj* **1** no longer living with your husband or wife ‖ 더 이상 남편이나 부인과 같이 살지 않는. 별거 중인. 따로 사는 **2** no longer having any relationship with a relative or friend ‖ 더 이상 친척이나 친구와 아무 관계를 갖지 않는. 관계가 멀어진[소원해진]. 내왕이 끊어진: *Molly is estranged from her son.* 몰리는 그녀의 아들과 내왕을 끊고 있다. – **estrangement** *n* [C, U] FORMAL

es·tro·gen /'ɛstrədʒən/ *n* [U] TECHNICAL a HORMONE (=chemical substance) that is produced by a woman's body ‖ 여성의 신체에서 생산되는 호르몬. 난포 호르몬. 에스트로겐

es·tu·ar·y /'ɛstʃu,ɛri/ *n* the wide part of a river where it goes into the ocean ‖ 바다로 흘러드는 강의 넓은 부분. 하구. 강어귀

et al. /,ɛt 'ɑl, -'æl/ *adv* FORMAL used after a list of names to mean that other people, who are not named, are also involved in something ‖ 거명되지 않은 다른 사람들도 역시 어떤 일에 관련되어 있음을 나타내기 위해 명단 뒤에 쓰여. … 외. 그리고 다른 사람들: *"The Human Embryo" by Brodsky, Rosenblum et al.* "인간 배아", 브로드스키, 로젠블럼 외 공저

etc. /ɛt 'sɛtrə, -'tərə/ *adv* the written abbreviation of "et cetera"; used after a list to show that there are many other similar things or people that could be added ‖ "et cetera"의 약어; 다른 유사한 사물이나 사람들이 많이 추가될 수 있음을 보이기 위해 목록 뒤에 쓰여. 기타. … 등등. … 따위: *cars, ships, planes etc.* 자동차, 선박, 항공기 등등

etch /ɛtʃ/ *v* [I, T] to cut lines on a metal plate, piece of glass, stone etc. to form a picture ‖ 그림이 형성되도록 금속판·유리·돌 등의 표면에 선을 새기다. 식각(蝕刻)하다. 에칭하다

e·ter·nal /ɪ'tənl/ *adj* continuing for ever ‖ 영원히 계속되는. 영구한. 무한한: *eternal life* 영생 – **eternally** *adv*

e·ter·ni·ty /ɪ'tənəti/ *n* **1 an eternity** a period of time that seems long because you are annoyed, anxious etc. ‖ 짜증나거나 걱정돼서 길게 여겨지는 시간. 무한

한[아주 오랜] 시간. 영원: *We waited for what seemed like an eternity.* 우리는 한 없이 오랫동안 기다렸다. **2** [U] time without any end, especially the time after death that some people believe continues for ever ‖ 어떤 끝도 없는 시간, 특히 일부 사람들이 영원히 계속되리라 믿는 사후의 시간. 영원(성). 영겁

e·ther /'iθɚ/ *n* [U] a clear liquid, used in past times to make people sleep during a medical operation ‖ 수술 중 사람을 잠들게 하려고 예전에 사용했던 맑은 액체. 에테르

e·the·re·al /ɪ'θɪriəl/ *adj* very delicate and light, in a way that does not seem real ‖ 실재하는 것으로 보이지 않게 매우 섬세하고 가벼운. 이 세상 것이 아닌. 절묘[영묘]한

eth·ic /'εθɪk/ *n* an idea or belief that influences people's behavior and attitudes ‖ 사람들의 행위와 태도에 영향을 주는 사상이나 믿음. 가치 (체계). 윤리. 도덕: *the Christian ethic* 기독교 윤리 —see also ETHICS

eth·i·cal /'εθɪkəl/ *adj* **1** relating to principles of what is right and wrong ‖ 옳고 그름의 원리에 관한. 윤리[도덕]상의: *The use of animals in scientific tests raises some difficult ethical questions.* 과학적 실험에 동물을 이용하는 것은 몇 가지의 곤란한 윤리적 문제를 일으킨다. **2** morally good and correct ‖ 도덕적으로 좋고 올바른. 윤리[도덕]적인: *Is it ethical to use drugs to control unacceptable behavior?* 용납할 수 없는 행위를 통제하기 위해 마약을 사용하는 것이 윤리적인가? **– ethically** *adv*

eth·ics /'εθɪks/ *n* **1** [plural] moral rules or principles of behavior for deciding what is right and wrong ‖ 옳고 그름을 결정하기 위한 도덕 규칙이나 행동 원칙들. 도덕. 윤리(규범) **2** [U] the study of moral rules and behavior ‖ 도덕적 규칙과 행동에 관한 연구. 윤리학

eth·nic /'εθnɪk/ *adj* relating to a particular race, nation, tribe etc. ‖ 특정 인종·국가·종족 등에 관한. 민족의: *ethnic food* 민족 음식

e·thos /'iθɑs/ *n* [singular] the set of ideas and moral attitudes belonging to a person or group ‖ 사람이나 집단이 갖고 있는 사상과 도덕적 태도의 경향. 특질. 기질. 정신. 기풍. 풍조: *the competitive spirit in the American ethos* 미국인 특질인 경쟁심

et·i·quette /'εtɪkɪt/ *n* [U] the formal rules for polite behavior in society or in a particular group ‖ 사회나 특정 집단 내의 예절 바른 행위에 대한 공식 규칙. 예의. 예법. 에티켓

et·y·mol·o·gy /ˌεtə'mɑlədʒi/ *n* [U] the study of the origins, history, and meanings of words ‖ 단어의 기원·역사·의미에 관한 연구. 어원학 **– etymological** /ˌεtəmə'lɑdʒɪkəl/ *adj*

EU *n* the written abbreviation of the European Union ‖ European Union(유럽 연합)의 약어

Eu·cha·rist /'yukərɪst/ *n* **the Eucharist** the bread and wine that represent Christ's body and blood and are used during a Christian ceremony, or the ceremony itself ‖ 예수의 몸과 피를 상징하며 기독교 의식 중에 사용되는 빵과 포도주, 또는 그 의식 자체. 성찬(식)

eu·lo·gize /'yulə,dʒaɪz/ *v* [T] FORMAL to praise someone or something very much ‖ 사람이나 사물을 매우 칭찬하다. 찬양하다

eu·lo·gy /'yulədʒi/ *n* [C, U] FORMAL a speech or piece of writing that praises someone or something very much, especially at a funeral ‖ 특히 장례식에서 사람이나 사물을 대단히 칭찬하는 연설이나 문장. 추도문[사]

eu·nuch /'yunɪk/ *n* a man who has had his TESTICLEs removed ‖ 고환이 제거된 남자. 거세된 남자. 고자. 내시. 환관

eu·phe·mism /'yufə,mɪzəm/ *n* a polite word or expression that you use instead of a more direct one to avoid shocking or upsetting someone ‖ 누군가에게 충격이나 혼란을 주는 것을 피하기 위해 직접적인 것 대신에 쓰는 정중한 말이나 표현. 완곡어법[어구] **– euphemistic** /ˌyufə'mɪstɪk/ *adj* **– euphemistically** *adv*

eu·pho·ri·a /yu'fɔriə/ *n* [U] a feeling of extreme happiness and excitement ‖ 극도로 행복하고 흥분된 느낌. 행복감. 도취감 **– euphoric** /yu'fɔrɪk/ *adj*

eu·ro /'yuərou/ *n* a unit of money that can be used in most countries of the EU ‖ 유럽 연합 대부분의 국가에서 사용 가능한 화폐 단위. 유로

Eu·rope /'yurəp/ *n* one of the seven CONTINENTs, that includes land north of the Mediterranean Sea and west of the Ural mountains ‖ 지중해의 북쪽과 우랄산맥의 서쪽 땅을 포함하는, 7개 대륙 중의 하나. 유럽

Eu·ro·pe·an¹ /ˌyurə'piən/ *adj* relating to or coming from Europe ‖ 유럽과 관련되거나 유럽 출신의. 유럽(산)의

European² *n* someone from Europe ‖ 유럽 출신의 사람. 유럽인

eu·tha·na·sia /ˌyuθə'neɪʒə/ *n* [U] the painless killing of people who are very ill or very old in order to stop them suffering ‖ 매우 아프거나 나이가 많은 사람들이 고통 받지 않도록 통증 없이 죽이는 일. 안락사

e·vac·u·ate /ɪ'vækyu,eɪt/ *v* [T] to move people from a dangerous place to a safer place ‖ 위험한 장소에서 더 안전한 장소로 사람을 이동시키다. 피난[대피] 시키다: *During the flood, we were all evacuated to higher ground.* 홍수 중에 우리는 모두 고지대로 대피했다. – **evacuation** /ɪ,vækyu'eɪʃən/ *n* [C, U]

e·vac·u·ee /ɪ,vækyu'i/ *n* someone who has been EVACUATEd ‖ 피난한 사람. 피난자. 대피자

e·vade /ɪ'veɪd/ *v* [T] **1** to avoid doing something you should do, or avoid talking about something ‖ 해야 할 일을 하지 않고 회피하거나 어떤 일에 대해 말하기를 피하다. 기피하다. 빠져나가다: *If you try to evade paying taxes you risk going to prison.* 당신이 세금 납부를 기피하려는 것은 교도소에 갈 위험을 무릅쓰는 것입니다. / *Briggs was evading the issue.* 브리그스는 쟁점을 회피하고 있었다. **2** to avoid being caught by someone who is trying to catch you ‖ 붙잡으려고 하는 사람에게 잡히는 것을 피하다. (모) 면하다. 벗어나다: *He evaded capture by hiding in a cave.* 그는 동굴에 숨어서 잡히는 것을 모면했다.

e·val·u·ate /ɪ'vælyu,eɪt/ *v* [T] FORMAL to carefully consider something or someone in order to judge him, her, or it ‖ 사물이나 사람을 판단하기 위해 주의 깊게 생각하다. 평가하다: *Our work is evaluated regularly.* 우리 업무는 정기적으로 평가된다.

e·val·u·a·tion /ɪ,vælyu'eɪʃən/ *n* [C, U] the act of considering and judging something or someone, or a document in which this is done ‖ 사물이나 사람을 검토하고 판단하는 행위, 또는 이렇게 처리된 서류. 평가(서): *an evaluation of new surgical techniques* 새로운 외과 수술 기법에 대한 평가

e·van·gel·i·cal /ˌivæn'dʒɛlɪkəl, ˌɛvən-/ *adj* believing that religious ceremonies are not as important as Christian faith and studying the Bible, and trying to persuade other people to accept these beliefs ‖ 종교 의식은 기독교 신앙만큼 중요하지 않다고 믿고, 성경을 공부하며 다른 사람들도 이 믿음을 받아들이도록 설득하는. 복음주의의

e·van·ge·list /ɪ'vændʒəlɪst/ *n* someone who travels from place to place in order to try to persuade people to become Christians ‖ 사람들을 기독교인이 되도록 설득하려고 도처로 다니는 사람. 복음 전도자. 선교사 – **evangelism** *n* [U] – **evangelistic** /ɪ,vændʒə'lɪstɪk/ *adj*

e·vap·o·rate /ɪ'væpə,reɪt/ *v* **1** [I, T] if a liquid evaporates or if something evaporates, it changes into steam ‖ 액체가 증기로 변하거나 액체를 증기로 변하게 하다. 증발하다[시키다]. 기화하다[시키다] **2** [I] to slowly disappear ‖ 천천히 사라지다. 소멸하다: *Support for the idea has evaporated.* 그 생각에 대한 지지는 온 데 간 데 없다. – **evaporation** /ɪ,væpə'reɪʃən/ *n* [U]

e·va·sion /ɪ'veɪʒən/ *n* [C, U] **1** the act of avoiding doing something you should do ‖ 당연히 해야 할 일을 하지 않고 피하는 행위. 회피. 발뺌: *tax evasion* 탈세 **2** the act of deliberately avoiding talking about something or dealing with something ‖ 어떤 일에 대해 언급하거나 취급하는 것을 고의적으로 회피하는 행위. 변명. 구실: *a speech full of lies and evasions* 거짓과 변명으로 가득 찬 연설

e·va·sive /ɪ'veɪsɪv/ *adj* **1** not willing to answer questions directly ‖ 직접적으로 질문에 대답하려고 하지 않는. 도피[회피] 적인. 모면하려는: *an evasive answer* 모면하려는 대답 **2 evasive action** an action someone does to avoid being injured or harmed ‖ 누군가가 다치거나 해 입는 것을 피하기 위해 하는 행동. 회피 [탈출] 행위

eve /iv/ *n* **1** [C usually singular] the night or day before a religious day or a holiday ‖ 종교적 행사일이나 휴일의 전날 밤이나 전날. 전날(밤). 전야. 이브: *a party on New Year's Eve* 신년 전야 파티 **2 the eve of** the time just before an important event ‖ 중요한 행사의 바로 전 시간. 직전: *on the eve of the election* 선거 직전에

e·ven¹ /'ivən/ *adv* **1** used in order to emphasize that something is surprising or unexpected ‖ 어떤 일이 놀랍거나 예상치 않은 것임을 강조하는 데에 쓰여. 심지어 …조차(도): *Even Arnie was bored by the game, and he loves baseball.* 심지어 야구를 좋아하는 아니 조차도 그 경기는 지루해 했다. / *Carrie doesn't even like cookies!* 캐리는 과자를 좋아하지도 않아! **2** used in order to make a comparison stronger ‖ 비교를 더 강하게 하는 데에 쓰여. 더욱[한층] (더): *I know even less about calculus than my son does.* 나는 내 아들보다 미적분에 대해 훨씬 더 모른

다. **3 even if** used in order to show that what you have just said will not change for any reason ‖ 방금 말한 것이 어떤 이유에서든 변하지 않을 것임을 보이는 데에 쓰여. 비록 …일지라도. …라 하더라도: *I wouldn't go into that place, even if you paid me!* 네가 돈을 내준다 해도 나는 그 곳에 들어가지 않을래! **4 even though** used in order to emphasize that although one thing happens or is true, something else also happens or is true ‖ 한 가지 일이 일어나거나 사실이더라도 다른 일 역시 일어나거나 사실임을 강조하는 데에 쓰여. …임에도 불구하고. 비록 …일지라도: *She wouldn't go onto the ski slope, even though Tom offered to help her.* 그녀는 톰이 도와주겠다고 말했음에도 불구하고 스키 활강 코스는 타려고 하지 않았다. **5 even so** although that is true ‖ 그것이 사실이지만. 그렇기는 하나. 그렇다 하더라도: *They made lots of money that year, but even so the business failed.* 그들은 그 해에 많은 돈을 벌었지만 그래도 사업은 실패했다.

even² *adj* **1** flat, level, or smooth ‖ 평평한. 고른. 매끈한. 평탄한: *The floor has to be even before we put the boards down.* 마루판을 놓기 전에 바닥을 평탄하게 해야 한다. **2** an even rate, temperature etc. does not change much ‖ 비율·온도 등이 많이 변하지 않는. 균등한. 고른. 들쭉날쭉하지 않는: *Store the chemicals at an even temperature.* 화학 약품을 일정 온도에서 보관하시오. **3** separated by equal spaces ‖ 고른 간격으로 분리된. 균일한. 등분의. 규칙적인: *his even white teeth* 그의 고른 하얀 치아 **4 be even** INFORMAL to no longer owe someone money ‖ 더 이상 남에게 빚지고 있지 않다. (빚이) 없다. 대차가 없다: *If you give me $5, we'll be even.* 네가 나에게 5달러를 주면 우리는 주고받을 게 없게 된다. **5** an even number can be divided by 2 ‖ 2로 나누어지는 숫자의. 짝수[우수]의: *2, 4, 6, 8 etc. are even numbers.* 2, 4, 6, 8 등은 짝수이다. —opposite ODD **6 get even** INFORMAL to harm someone just as much as s/he has harmed you ‖ 누군가가 해를 끼친 만큼 꼭 그대로 해를 입히다. …에게 되갚음하다. 복수하다: *No matter how long it takes, I'll get even with him one day.* 아무리 오래 걸릴지라도, 나는 언젠가 그에게 복수할 것이다. **– evenness** *n* [U] —see also **break even** (BREAK¹) — opposite UNEVEN

even³ *v*

even out *phr v* [I,T **even** sth ↔ **out**] to become equal or level, or to make

something do this ‖ 동일하거나 균등해지다, 또는 사물을 이렇게 만들다. 대등[균등]하다[하게 하다]: *Some students are being bused in order to even out enrollment at the two schools.* 두 학교의 학생수를 균등하게 맞추기 위해 일부 학생들을 버스로 통학시키고 있다.

even up *phr v* [I,T **even** sth ↔ **up**] to become equal or the same, or to make something do this ‖ 동등하거나 똑같아지다, 또는 사물을 이렇게 만들다. 동등[동일]하다[하게 하다]. 막상막하가 되다[되게 하다]: *O'Malley hit a home run to even up the score.* 오맬리는 동점 홈런을 쳤다.

even-handed /ˌ.. ˈ.../ *adj* giving fair and equal treatment to everyone ‖ 모든 사람을 공평하고 동등하게 대우해 주는. 공정한. 공평한: *Justice must be even-handed.* 정의는 공명정대해야 한다.

eve·ning /ˈivnɪŋ/ *n* **1** [C, U] the end of the day and the early part of the night ‖ 낮의 끝이자 밤의 이른 시간. 저녁(때): *I have a class on Thursday evenings.* 나는 매주 목요일 저녁에 수업이 있다. **2 (Good) Evening** SPOKEN said in order to greet someone when you meet him/her in the evening ‖ 저녁 시간에 사람을 만났을 때 인사하는 데에 쓰여. 안녕하세요: *Evening, Rick.* 안녕, 릭.

evening gown /ˈ.. ./, **evening dress** *n* a dress worn by women for formal occasions in the evening ‖ 저녁의 공식 행사를 위해 여성이 입는 옷. 야회복. 이브닝 드레스

evening wear /ˈ.. ./ *n* [U] special clothes worn for formal occasions in the evening ‖ 저녁의 공식 행사를 위해 입는 특별한 옷. 야회복

evening wear

e·ven·ly /ˈivənli/ *adv* **1** with equal amounts or numbers of something spread all through an area or divided among a group of people ‖ 어떤 것이 동일한 양이나 수로 한 지역에 두루 퍼져 있거나 한 무리의 사람들 사이에 분배되어. 균등하게: *We divided the money evenly.* 우리는 돈을 똑같이 나누었다. / *He spread the butter evenly on his toast.* 그는 토스트에 버터를 고루 펴 발랐다. **2** in a steady or regular way ‖ 일정하게. 규칙적으로: *I could hear the baby breathing evenly in her crib.* 나는 침대에서 자고 있는 아기의 규칙적인 숨소리를 들을 수 있었다. / *evenly spaced rows of* *young trees* 일정한 간격으로 열을 이룬 묘목 **3 if two teams are evenly matched, they have an equal chance of winning** ‖ 두 팀의 이길 승산이 똑같아. 대등하게

e·vent /ɪ'vɛnt/ *n* **1 something that happens, especially something important, interesting, or unusual** ‖ 특히 중요하거나 흥미있거나 평범하지 않은 일이 일어나는 것. 사건: *the most important events of the 1990s* 1990년대의 가장 중요한 사건들 **2 a performance, sports competition, party etc. that has been arranged for a particular date and time** ‖ 특정한 날짜와 시간에 준비된 공연·스포츠 경기·파티 등. 행사. 종목: *"Which event are you entered in?" "The long jump."* "너는 무슨 종목에 참가하니?" "멀리뛰기야." **3 in any event** **whatever happens or whatever situation** ‖ 어떤 일이 일어나든, 또는 상황이 어떻든. 아무튼. 좌우간. 여하튼: *My career, after this trial, is probably over in any event.* 이 재판 후에는 어쨌든 내 경력도 아마 끝장날 것이다. **4 in the event of rain/fire/an accident etc.** **used in order to tell people what they should do or what will happen if something else happens** ‖ 어떤 일이 일어난다면 무엇을 해야 하는지, 또는 어떤 사태가 되는지를 사람들에게 말하는 데에 쓰여. 비가 올/불이 날/사고가 날 경우에는: *Britain agreed to support the US in the event of war.* 영국은 전쟁이 날 경우 미국을 지원하기로 합의했다.

e·vent·ful /ɪ'vɛntˀfəl/ *adj* **full of interesting or important events** ‖ 흥미있거나 중요한 사건들로 가득한. 다사다난한: *an eventful meeting* 흥미있고 중요한 행사들로 가득한 모임

e·ven·tu·al /ɪ'vɛntʃuəl/ *adj* **happening at the end of a process** ‖ 과정의 마지막에 일어나는. 최종적인. 결과의. 궁극의: *China's eventual control of Hong Kong* 중국의 홍콩에 대한 궁극적인 지배

e·ven·tu·al·i·ty /ɪ,vɛntʃu'æləti/ *n* FORMAL **a possible event or result, especially an unpleasant one** ‖ 일어날지 모르는, 특히 불쾌한, 사건이나 결과

e·ven·tual·ly /ɪ'vɛntʃəli, -tʃuəli/ *adv* **after a long time** ‖ 오랜 시간 후에. 마침내. 결국: *He worked so hard that eventually he made himself sick.* 그는 너무 열심히 일한 나머지 결국에는 병에 걸렸다.

ev·er /'ɛvɚ/ *adv* **1 a word meaning at any time, used mostly in questions, negatives, comparisons, or sentences with "if"** ‖ 주로 의문문이나 부정문이나 비교문, 또는 "if"가 든 문장에 쓰여 언제라도를 뜻하는 단어: *Nothing ever makes Paula angry.* 폴라는 그 어떤 것에도 화를 내지 않는다. / *Have you ever eaten snails?* 달팽이를 먹어 보았냐? / *If you're ever in Wilmington, give us a call.* 언제라도 당신이 윌밍턴에 오면 우리에게 전화해 주세요. / *That was one of the best meals I've ever had.* 그건 내가 먹어본 음식 중 최고중의 하나였다. / *Jim's parents hardly ever* (=almost never) *watch TV.* 짐의 부모님은 거의 텔레비전을 보지 않는다. **2 ever since** **continuously since** ‖ 그 후 계속하여. 줄곧: *He started teaching here when he was 20, and he's been here ever since.* 그는 20살 때 여기에서 가르치기 시작해서 줄곧 여기서 가르치고 있다. **3 ever-growing/ever-increasing etc.** **continuously becoming longer etc.** ‖ 끊임없이 계속되는. 계속 자라는/증가하는: *the ever-growing population problem* 계속 증가하는 인구 문제

ev·er·green /'ɛvɚ,grin/ *adj* **evergreen trees have leaves that do not fall off in winter** ‖ 나무가 겨울에 떨어지지 않는 잎을 가진. 상록의 (잎을 가진) – **evergreen** *n* —compare DECIDUOUS

ev·er·last·ing /,ɛvɚ'læstɪŋ·/ *adj* **continuing for ever** ‖ 영원히 계속되는: *everlasting peace* 영구히 계속되는 평화

ev·er·more /,ɛvɚ'mɔr/ *adv* LITERARY **always; FOREVER** ‖ 항상; ⓟ forever

ev·ery /'ɛvri/ *determiner* **1 each one of a group of people or things** ‖ 한 무리의 사람이나 물건의 개개의 하나. 모든: *Every student will take the test.* 모든 학생들이 그 시험을 볼 것이다. / *He told Jan every single thing* (=all the things) *I said.* 그는 내가 한 말을 전부 잰에게 말했다. **2 used in order to show how often something happens** ‖ 무엇이 얼마나 자주 일어나는지 나타내는 데에 쓰여. 매(每)…. …마다: *We get the newspaper every day.* 우리는 매일 그 신문을 받아본다. / *Change the oil in the car every 5000 miles.* 그 차의 엔진 오일을 주행거리 5,000마일마다 교환해라. / *He came to see us every other day.* (=every two days) 그는 이틀에 한 번씩 우리를 만나러 왔다. / *I still see her every now and then/every so often.* (=sometimes but not often) 나는 여전히 이따금 그녀를 만난다. **3 one in every 100/3 in every 5 etc.** **used in order to show how often something affects a particular group of people or things** ‖ 사물이 일단의 특정한 사람들이나 사물들에 얼마나 자주 영향을 미치는지 나타내는 데에 쓰여. 100에 하나

/다섯 중에 셋: *One in every three couples live together without being married.* 세 커플 중 한 커플은 결혼하지 않고 동거한다. **4 every which way** INFORMAL in every direction ‖ 모든 방향으로. 사방팔방으로: *People were running every which way.* 사람들은 사방팔방으로 도망가고 있었다. —see usage note at EACH¹

ev·ery·bod·y /'ɛvri,bɑdi, -,bʌdi/ *pron* ⇨ EVERYONE

ev·ery·day /'ɛvri,deɪ/ *adj* ordinary, usual, or happening every day ‖ 흔한, 평범한, 매일 일어나는: *Stress is just part of everyday life.* 스트레스는 일상적인 생활의 일부라고 볼 수 있다.

ev·ery·one /'ɛvri,wʌn/, **everybody** *pron* **1** every person involved in a particular activity or in a particular place ‖ 특정한 활동이나 특정한 장소에 관련된 모든 사람. 모두: *Is everyone ready to go?* 모두 갈 준비가 되어 있느냐? / *They gave a small prize to everyone who ran in the race.* 그들은 그 경주에서 뛴 모든 이에게 조그만 상을 주었다. / *Where is everybody?* (=where are the people that are usually here) 모두 어디 갔냐? / *I was still awake but everybody else* (=all the other people) *had gone to bed.* 나는 아직 깨어 있었지만 다른 모든 사람들은 자고 있었다. / *Everyone but* (=all the people except) *Lisa went home.* 리자를 제외하고는 모두 집에 갔다. **2** all people in general ‖ 일반적인 모든 사람. 만인: *Everyone has bad days.* 누구에게나 좋지 않은 시절은 있다. —see usage notes at EVERY, PRONOUN

ev·ery·place /'ɛvri,pleɪs/ *adv* SPOKEN ⇨ EVERYWHERE

ev·ery·thing /'ɛvri,θɪŋ/ *pron* **1** each thing or all things ‖ 개개의 것이나 모든 것: *I think everything is ready for the party.* 파티 준비는 모두 끝난 것 같다. /

I've forgotten everything I learned about math in school. 나는 학교에서 수학에 대해 배운 것을 몽땅 잊어버렸다. / *There's only bread left. They've eaten everything else.* (=all other things) 오로지 빵만 남겨놓고 그 밖의 다른 것은 그들이 모두 먹어 버렸다. **2** used when you are talking in general about your life or about a situation ‖ 자신의 삶이나 상황에 관해 일반적으로 얘기할 때 쓰여: *"How's everything at work these days?" "It's been really busy!"* "요즘 일하고 있는 것이 어때?" "정말 바빠 죽겠어!" **3** be/mean everything to be the thing that matters most ‖ 가장 중요한 것이다: *Money isn't everything.* 돈이 전부가 아니다. **4 and everything** SPOKEN a phrase meaning all the things related to what you have just said ‖ 방금 말한 것과 관련된 모든 것을 의미하는 구. 기타 등등. 그밖에 여러 가지: *She's at the hospital having tests and everything, but they don't know what's wrong.* 그녀는 병원에서 이것저것 여러 가지 검사를 받고 있지만 의사들은 뭐가 잘못되었는지 알지 못한다. —compare NOTHING¹

ev·ery·where /'ɛvri,wɛr/ *adv* in or to every place ‖ 모든 곳에[으로]. 어디든지. 어디나: *The dog follows me everywhere.* 그 개는 어디든지 나를 따라온다. / *I've looked everywhere for my keys.* 나는 열쇠를 찾기 위해 구석구석 뒤졌다. —compare NOWHERE

e·vict /ɪ'vɪkt/ *v* [T] to legally force someone to leave the house s/he is renting from you ‖ 세 들어 사는 사람을 법적으로 강제로 떠나게 하다. 법적으로 퇴거시키다. 쫓아내다: *Carl was evicted when he didn't pay his rent.* 칼은 집세를 내지 않아서 강제 퇴거당했다. – **eviction** /ɪ'vɪkʃən/ *n* [C, U]

ev·i·dence /'ɛvədəns/ *n* **1** [U] facts, objects, or signs that make you believe that something exists or is true ‖ 어떤 것이 존재하거나 사실이라고 믿게 만드는 사실[물체, 표시]. 증거. 근거: *The police have evidence that the killer was a woman.* 경찰은 살인자가 여자였다는 증거를 가지고 있다. / *scientists looking for evidence of life on other planets* 다른 행성에 생명체가 살고 있다는 증거를 찾고 있는 과학자들 / *I had to give evidence* (=tell the facts) *in my brother's trial.* 나는 내 형의 재판에서 증언을 해야 했다. **2 be in evidence** FORMAL to be easily seen or noticed ‖ 쉽게 보이거나 눈에 띄다: *The police were very much in evidence at the march.* 경찰들은 그 행진에서 눈에

아주 쉽게 떠었다.

ev·i·dent /ˈɛvədənt/ adj easily noticed or understood ‖ 쉽게 알아차리거나 이해하는. 명백한. 분명한: *It's evident that you've been drinking again.* 네가 다시 음주를 해오고 있는 것은 분명하다. – **evidently** adv

e·vil¹ /ˈivəl/ adj deliberately cruel or harmful ‖ 일부러 잔인하거나 해롭게 하는. 나쁜. 사악한: *an evil dictator responsible for the death of millions of people* 수백만 명의 죽음에 책임을 져야 할 사악한 독재자

evil² n FORMAL **1** [U] actions and behavior that are morally wrong and cruel ‖ 도덕적으로 그릇되고 잔인한 행동과 행위. 악행. 악: *the battle between good and evil* 선과 악의 싸움 **2** something that has a very cruel, harmful, or unpleasant effect ‖ 매우 잔인하거나 해롭거나 불쾌한 결과를 가져오는 것. 폐해. 해악: *the evils of alcohol* 술의 해악

e·voc·a·tive /ɪˈvɑkətɪv/ adj making people remember something by reminding them of a feeling or memory ‖ 사람들에게 감정이나 기억을 일깨워 줌으로써 무엇을 생각나게 하는. 환기시키는. 불러일으키는: *The scent of bread baking is evocative of my childhood.* 빵을 굽는 냄새를 맡으니 나의 어린 시절이 떠오른다.

e·voke /ɪˈvoʊk/ v [T] to produce a strong feeling or memory in someone ‖ 사람의 강한 감정이나 기억을 자아내다. 환기시키다. 불러일으키다: *Hitchcock's movies can evoke a sense of terror.* 히치콕의 영화는 공포감을 불러일으킬 수 있다. – **evocation** /ˌɛvəˈkeɪʃən, ˌivoʊ-/ n [C, U]

ev·o·lu·tion /ˌɛvəˈluʃən/ n [U] **1** the scientific idea that plants and animals develop gradually from simpler to more complicated forms ‖ 식물과 동물이 단순한 형태에서 보다 복잡한 형태로 점차로 발전한다는 과학적인 사고. 진화 **2** the gradual change and development of an idea, situation, or object ‖ 생각[상황, 물체]의 점진적 변화와 발전. 진전: *the evolution of the home computer* 가정용 컴퓨터의 발전 – **evolutionary** adj

e·volve /ɪˈvɑlv/ v [I, T] to develop by gradually changing or to make something do this ‖ 점진적으로 변화하여 발전하다, 또는 발전시키다. 진화하다[시키다]: *Did man evolve from apes?* 사람은 유인원에서 진화했느냐?

ewe /yu/ n a female sheep ‖ 양의 암컷.

양양

ex /ɛks/ n [C usually singular] INFORMAL someone's former wife, husband, GIRLFRIEND, or BOYFRIEND ‖ 누군가의 전(前)부인[남편, 여자 친구, 남자 친구]

ex·ac·er·bate /ɪɡˈzæsɚˌbeɪt/ v [T] FORMAL to make a bad situation worse ‖ 나쁜 상황을 더 나빠지게 만들다. 악화시키다: *The drugs they gave her only exacerbated the pain.* 그들이 그녀에게 준 약은 고통을 악화시키기만 했다. – **exacerbation** /ɪɡˌzæsɚˈbeɪʃən/ n [U]

ex·act¹ /ɪɡˈzækt/ adj correct and including all the necessary details ‖ 정확하고 필요한 세목을 모두 포함한. 정확한. 엄밀한: *The exact time is 2:47.* 정확한 시간은 2시 47분이다. / *It has been nine months, to be exact.* 정확히 말하면 9개월이었다.

exact² v [T] FORMAL to demand and get something from someone by using threats, force etc. ‖ 위협과 완력 등으로 남에게 어떤 것을 요구하여 얻어내다. 강요하다: *the penalty exacted for breaking the rules* 규칙 위반에 강제로 가해지는 벌칙.

ex·act·ing /ɪɡˈzæktɪŋ/ adj demanding a lot of care, effort, and attention ‖ 많은 관심·노력·주의를 요구하는. 매우 힘든: *an exacting piece of work* 매우 힘든 일

ex·act·ly /ɪɡˈzæktli/ adv **1** used in order to emphasize that a particular number, amount, or piece of information is completely correct ‖ 특정한 수나 양, 또는 정보가 완전히 옳다는 것을 강조하는 데에 쓰여. 틀림없이. 정확히. 꼭: *We got home at exactly six o'clock.* 우리는 정확히 6시에 집에 도착했다 / *I don't know exactly where she lives.* 나는 그녀가 살고 있는 곳을 정확히 알지 못한다. **2** SPOKEN said in order to emphasize a statement or question ‖ 진술이나 질문을 강조하는 데에 쓰여: *That's exactly what I've been trying to tell you!* 그게 바로 당신에게 말하고자 했던 것이야! **3** SPOKEN said when you agree with what someone is saying ‖ 남이 말하는 것에 동의할 때에 쓰여. 바로 그렇습니다: *"So we should spend more on education?" "Exactly!"* "그러니까 우리는 교육에 더 많은 돈을 들여야 합니까?" "예, 바로 그렇습니다."

ex·ag·ger·ate /ɪɡˈzædʒəˌreɪt/ v [I, T] to make something seem better, larger, worse etc. than it really is ‖ 사물을 실제보다 더 좋게·더 크게·더 나쁘게 보이게 하다. 과장하다. 과대시하다: *Charlie says that everyone in New York has a gun,* *but I'm sure he's exaggerating.* 찰리는 뉴욕에 있는 모든 사람들이 총을 가지고 있다고 말하지만 나는 그가 과장하고 있다고 확신한다. **– exaggerated** *adv* – **exaggeration** /ɪɡˌzædʒəˈreɪʃən/ *n* [C, U]

ex·alt /ɪɡˈzɔlt/ *v* [T] FORMAL to praise someone ‖ 남을 칭찬하다

ex·al·ta·tion /ˌɛɡzɔlˈteɪʃən, ˌɛksɔl-/ *n* [C, U] FORMAL a very strong feeling of happiness ‖ 매우 강렬한 행복한 감정. 의기양양. 기고만장

ex·alt·ed /ɪɡˈzɔltɪd/ *adj* FORMAL **1** having a very high rank and highly respected ‖ 상당히 높은 지위와 존경을 함께 받고 있는. 고귀한. 고상한 **2** filled with a feeling of great happiness ‖ 매우 행복한 감정으로 충만한. 의기양양한

ex·am /ɪɡˈzæm/ *n* **1** an official test of knowledge or ability in a particular subject ‖ 특정 주제의 지식이나 능력에 대한 공식적인 검사. 시험: *a chemistry exam* 화학 시험 / *When do you take/have your final exams?* 마지막 시험은 언제 봅니까? **2** a set of medical tests ‖ 일련의 의학적 검사: *an eye exam* 시력 검사

ex·am·i·na·tion /ɪɡˌzæməˈneɪʃən/ *n* **1** the process of looking at something carefully in order to see what it is like or find out something ‖ 상태를 알아보거나 무엇인가를 발견하기 위해 주의 깊게 사물을 살펴보는 과정. 조사: *a detailed examination of the photographs* 그 사진의 세밀한 조사 **2** FORMAL ⇨ EXAM

ex·am·ine /ɪɡˈzæmɪn/ *v* [T] **1** to look at something carefully in order to make a decision, find out something etc. ‖ 무엇을 결정하고 발견하기 위해서 어떤 것을 주의 깊게 살펴보다. 조사하다. 검토하다. 검사하다: *The doctor examined me thoroughly.* 의사는 나를 철저히 검진했다. / *The police examined the room for fingerprints.* 경찰은 지문을 찾기 위해 그 방을 조사하였다. **2** FORMAL to ask someone questions to get information or to test his/her knowledge about something ‖ 정보를 얻거나 사물에 대한 지식을 시험하려고 남에게 질문을 하다. 시험하다: *On Friday, you will be examined on American history.* 여러분 금요일에 미국사 시험이 있습니다. – **examiner** *n*

ex·am·ple /ɪɡˈzæmpəl/ *n* **1** someone or something that you mention to show what you mean, show that something is true, or show what something is like ‖ 뜻하는 것[사물의 진실, 사물의 모습]을 보여 주려고 언급한 사람이나 사물. 예.

보기: *This church is a good example of Gothic architecture.* 이 교회는 고딕 건축물의 좋은 예이다. / *Can anyone give me an example of a transitive verb?* 누가 나에게 타동사의 예를 들어 줄 수 있습니까? / *Everything costs too much. The price of meat, for example,* (=as an example) *has doubled since April.* 모든 것이 너무 비싸다. 예를 들어 고기 가격은 4월 이후로 두 배가 되었다. **2** someone whose behavior is very good and should be copied by other people ‖ 행동이 매우 훌륭하여 다른 사람들이 본받아야 하는 사람. 모범. 본보기: *Parents should set an example for their children.* (=parents should behave in a good way so their children will behave in a good way) 부모는 자녀들에게 좋은 본보기가 되어야 한다. **3 make an example of sb** to punish someone for doing something so that other people will be afraid to do the same thing ‖ 다른 사람들이 똑같은 행동을 하기가 두렵도록 어떤 사람이 한 행위에 대해 벌을 주다. …을 본보기로 벌주다

ex·as·per·ate /ɪɡˈzæspəˌreɪt/ *v* [T] to make someone feel very annoyed by continuing to do something that upsets him/her ‖ 기분 상하게 하는 짓을 계속하여 남을 매우 화나게 하다: *His refusal to agree has exasperated his lawyers.* 그는 동의하는 것을 거절하여 담당 변호사들을 화나게 하였다. – **exasperating** *adj* – **exasperation** /ɪɡˌzæspəˈreɪʃən/ *n* [U]

ex·as·per·at·ed /ɪɡˈzæspəˌreɪtɪd/ *adj* feeling annoyed because someone is continuing to do something that upsets you ‖ 남이 기분 상하게 하는 짓을 계속해서 화가 난. 분노한

ex·ca·vate /ˈɛkskəˌveɪt/ *v* [I, T] **1** to dig a hole in the ground ‖ 땅에 구멍을 파다 **2** to dig up the ground in order to find something that was buried there in an earlier time ‖ 이전에 묻혀 있던 것을 발견하기 위해서 땅을 파내다. 발굴하다: *archeologists excavating an ancient city* 고대 도시를 발굴하고 있는 고고학자들 – **excavation** /ˌɛkskəˈveɪʃən/ *n* [C, U]

ex·ceed /ɪkˈsid/ *v* [T] FORMAL **1** to be more than a particular number or amount ‖ 특정한 수나 양보다 더 많다. 웃돌다: *The cost must not exceed $150.* 비용은 150달러를 상회해서는 안 된다. **2** to go beyond an official or legal limit ‖ 공식적인 또는 법적인 제한을 넘는다. 초과하다: *a fine for exceeding the speed limit* 제한 속도 초과에 대한 벌금

ex·ceed·ing·ly /ɪkˈsidɪŋli/ *adv* FORMAL extremely ‖ 대단히. 매우: *The show has* *done exceedingly well.* 그 쇼는 대단히 훌륭했다.

ex·cel /ɪk'sɛl/ *v* **-lled, -lling** [I] FORMAL to do something very well, or much better than most people ‖ 무엇을 매우 잘 하거나 대부분의 사람보다 훨씬 더 잘하다. 탁월하다. 남보다 뛰어나다: *I've never excelled at math.* 나는 수학을 잘 했던 적이 전혀 없었다. / *That was a great meal! You've really excelled yourself* (=done even better than usual) *this time.* 정말 맛있는 식사였어요! 당신 이번에는 정말 평소보다 훨씬 잘 만들었어요.

ex·cel·lence /'ɛksələns/ *n* [U] the quality of being excellent ‖ 뛰어난 성질. 탁월. 우수. 우월: *an honor given for academic excellence* 학문적 우수성에 대해 주어진 영예

ex·cel·lent /'ɛksələnt/ *adj* **1** extremely good or of very high quality ‖ 대단히 좋거나 매우 질이 좋은. 우수한: *Jim's in excellent health.* 짐은 대단히 건강이 좋다. / *That was an excellent meal.* 그것은 훌륭한 식사였다. **2** SPOKEN said when you approve of something ‖ 무엇을 인정할 때 쓰임. 매우 좋아: *"There's a party at Becky's house tonight." "Excellent!"* "오늘 저녁 베키의 집에서 파티가 있어." "그거 좋지!" – **excellently** *adv*

ex·cept[1] /ɪk'sɛpt/ *prep* **except (for)** used in order to show the things or people who are not included in a statement ‖ 언급하는 것에 포함되지 않는 물건이나 사람을 나타내는 데에 쓰임. …이 없으면. …을 제외하고는. … 이외에는: *Everyone went to the show, except for Scott and Danny.* 스코트와 대니를 제외하고는 모두 다 그 쇼를 보러 갔다. / *We're open every day except Monday.* 월요일을 제외하고는 매일 영업을 합니다. / *I don't know anything about it, except what I've read in the newspaper.* 신문에서 읽은 것을 제외하고는 나는 그것에 관해 아무것도 알지 못한다. —see usage note at BESIDES[2]

except[2] *conjunction* **except (that)** used in order to show that the statement you have just made is not true or not completely true ‖ 방금 한 말이 (전혀) 사실이 아니라는 것을 나타내는 데 쓰임. …을 제외하고: *It is like all the other houses, except that it's painted bright blue.* 밝은 청색으로 칠이 되어 있는 것을 제외하고는 그 집은 다른 모든 집들과 마찬가지다. / *I have earrings just like those, except they're silver.* 나도 은 제품이란 점을 빼고는 그것들과 꼭 같은

귀걸이가 있다. / *I'd go, except it's too far.* 너무 멀지만 않다면 가겠다. —see usage note at BUT[1]

except[3] *v* [T] FORMAL to not include something ‖ 무엇을 포함하지 않다. …을 제외하다

ex·cept·ed /ɪk'sɛptɪd/ *adj* not included ‖ 포함하지 않은. 제외한: *He's not interested in anything, politics excepted.* 그는 정치를 제외한 어떤 것에도 흥미를 느끼지 못한다.

ex·cept·ing /ɪk'sɛptɪŋ/ *prep* FORMAL not including ‖ 포함하지 않고. 제외하고

ex·cep·tion /ɪk'sɛpʃən/ *n* [C, U] **1** someone or something that is not included in something ‖ 어떤 것에 포함되지 않는 사람이나 사물. 제외. 예외: *It's been very cold, but today's an exception.* 날씨가 요즘 매우 추웠지만 오늘은 예외이다. / *We don't usually take credit cards, but for you we'll make an exception.* (=not include you in this rule) 우리는 보통 신용 카드를 받지 않지만 당신은 예외로 하겠다. / *Everyone has improved, with the possible exception of Simon.* (=everyone has improved except Simon) 사이먼을 제외한 모든 사람의 성적이 올랐다. **2 be no exception** used in order to say that something is not different than before or than the other things mentioned ‖ 사물이 전과, 또는 언급한 다른 사물과 다르지 않다고 말하는 데에 쓰임. 예외가 아니다: *March weather is usually changeable and this year was no exception.* 3월의 날씨는 보통 변덕이 심한데 올해도 예외는 아니다. **3 without exception** FORMAL used in order to say that something is true of all the people or things in a group ‖ 어떤 것이 집단 내의 모든 사람이나 사물에 들어맞는다는 것을 말하는 데에 쓰임. 예외 없이. 모조리: *Almost without exception, teachers said that students do not work hard enough.* 거의 예외 없이 선생님들은 학생들이 아주 열심히 공부하지 않는다고 말했다.

ex·cep·tion·al /ɪk'sɛpʃənəl/ *adj* **1** unusually good ‖ 매우 좋은. 아주 우수한: *an exceptional student* 아주 뛰어난 학생 **2** unusual and not likely to happen often ‖ 유별나서 자주 일어날 것 같지 않은. 각별한. 예외적인: *The teachers were doing their best under exceptional circumstances.* 선생님들은 이례적인 상황하에서 최선을 다하고 있었다. – **exceptionally** *adv*

ex·cerpt /'ɛksɚpt/ *n* a short piece of writing or music taken from a longer book, poem etc. ‖ 장편의 저서·시구(詩句) 등에서 인용한 짧은 글이나 곡. 인용(구). 발췌(곡)

ex·cess¹ /'ɛksɛs, ɪk'sɛs/ n 1 [singular, U] a larger amount of something than is needed, usual, or allowed ‖ 필요한[보통의, 허용된] 것보다 더 많은 양. 초과. 과잉. 과다: *There is an excess of alcohol in his blood.* 그는 혈중 알코올 농도가 높다. 2 **in excess of** more than a particular amount ‖ 특정한 양보다 많은. …을 초과하여: *Our profits were in excess of $5 million.* 우리의 수익은 5백만 달러를 넘었다. 3 **do sth to excess** to do something too much or too often ‖ 무엇을 너무 많이 또는 너무 자주 하다. 지나치게 …하다: *He drinks to excess.* 그는 과도하게 술을 마신다. —see also EXCESSES

excess² adj additional and more than is needed or allowed ‖ 추가되어 필요하거나 허용된 것 이상인. 초과한. 여분의: *a charge of $75 for excess baggage* 초과 수하물에 대한 75달러의 요금

ex·cess·es /ɪk'sɛsɪz, 'ɛksɛsɪz/ n [plural] actions that are socially or morally unacceptable ‖ 사회적 또는 도덕적으로 받아들일 수 없는 행동. 못된 짓. 난폭: *the army's excesses during the last war* 지난 전쟁시의 군대의 만행

ex·ces·sive /ɪk'sɛsɪv/ adj much more than is reasonable or necessary ‖ 알맞거나 필요한 것보다 많은. 과도한. 과다한. 터무니없는: *Don's wife left him because of his excessive gambling.* 돈의 심한 노름 때문에 그의 아내는 그를 떠났다. – **excessively** adv

ex·change¹ /ɪks'tʃeɪndʒ/ n 1 [C, U] the act of exchanging one thing for another, or the act of doing something to someone at the same time as s/he does it to you ‖ 한 가지 사물을 다른 것으로 바꾸는 행위, 또는 남이 자신에게 하는 대로 동시에 남에게 어떤 행동을 하는 행위. 교환. 주고받기: *an exchange of political prisoners* 정치범의 교환 / *I gave Larry my bike in exchange for some video games.* (=I gave him my bike, and he gave me some video games) 나는 래리의 비디오 게임과 내 자전거를 맞바꾸었다. 2 an angry argument between two people or groups ‖ 두 사람 또는 그룹 간의 격렬한 논쟁 3 an arrangement in which a student, teacher etc., visits another country to work or study ‖ 학생·교사 등이 근무·연구차 타국을 방문하는 경우에 맺는 협정 4 ⇨ STOCK EXCHANGE

exchange² v [T] to give something to someone who gives you something else ‖ 자신에게 다른 것을 주는 사람에게 대신 어떤 것을 주다. …을 교환하다: *This shirt is too big. Can I exchange it for a smaller one?* 이 셔츠는 너무 큽니다. 작은 것으로 교환할 수 있을까요? – **exchangeable** adj

exchange rate /.'. ,./ n the value of the money of one country compared to the money of another country ‖ 다른 나라의 돈과 비교한 한 나라의 돈의 가치. 환율. 외환 시세

ex·cise¹ /'ɛksaɪz, -saɪs/ n [C, U] the government tax on particular goods produced and used inside a country ‖ 국내에서 생산되고 사용되는 특정한 물품에 대한 정부의 세금. 물품세. 소비세

ex·cise² /ɪk'saɪz/ v [T] FORMAL to remove something completely by cutting it out ‖ 무엇을 잘라 완전히 제거하다. 잘라내다: *Doctors excised the tumor.* 의사들은 종양을 잘라냈다. – **excision** /ɪk'sɪʒən/ n [C, U]

ex·cit·a·ble /ɪk'saɪtəbəl/ adj easily excited ‖ 쉽게 흥분하는. 격하기 쉬운

ex·cite /ɪk'saɪt/ v [T] 1 to make someone feel happy, eager, or nervous ‖ 남을 행복한[의욕적인, 신경질적인] 느낌이 들게 만들다. 자극하다. 흥분시키다: *That movie was good, but it didn't really excite me very much.* 그 영화는 좋았지만 나를 대단히 흥분시킬 정도는 아니었다. 2 to make someone have strong feelings ‖ 남에게 강력한 느낌을 주다: *The murder trial has excited a lot of public interest.* 그 살인 사건의 재판은 일반인의 큰 관심을 불러일으켰다.

ex·cit·ed /ɪk'saɪtɪd/ adj happy, interested, or hopeful because something good has happened or will happen ‖ 좋은 일이 일어났거나 일어날 이기 때문에 행복한[흥미 있는, 희망적인]. 흥분한. 들뜬: *The kids are really excited about our trip to California.* 그 아이들은 캘리포니아 여행을 하게 되어 매우 들떠 있다. – **excitedly** adv

ex·cite·ment /ɪk'saɪtmənt/ n [U] the feeling of being excited ‖ 흥분된 감정. 격앙: *Ann couldn't hide her excitement at the possibility of meeting the Senator.* 앤은 그 상원 의원을 만날 수 있게 되어 흥분을 감출 수가 없었다.

ex·cit·ing /ɪk'saɪtɪŋ/ adj making you feel happy or interested in something ‖ 어떤 것에 즐거움이나 흥미를 느끼게 하는. 흥분시키는. 흥미로운: *an exciting story* 흥미 있는 이야기

ex·claim /ɪk'skleɪm/ v [I, T] to say something suddenly because you are surprised, excited, or angry ‖ 깜짝 놀라서[흥분하여, 화나서] 무엇이라고 갑자기 말하다. 외치다. 소리치다: *"Wow!" exclaimed Bobby, "Look at that car!"* 와! 저 자동차 좀 봐!"라고 보비는 소리쳤다. – **exclamation** /ˌɛksklə'meɪʃən/ n

ex·cla·ma·tion point /..'.. ../, **exclamation mark** n the mark (!) used in writing after a sentence or word that expresses surprise, excitement, or anger ‖ 놀람[흥분, 노여움]을 나타내는 문장이나 단어 뒤의 글에 쓰이는 부호. 감탄 부호(!)

ex·clude /ɪk'sklud/ v [T] **1** to not allow someone to enter a place, or to do something ‖ 남에게 어떤 곳에 들어오거나 어떤 일을 하는 것을 허락하지 않다. 못 들어오게[못 하게] 하다: *In the Army, women usually are excluded from fighting.* 군대에서 여성은 일반적으로 전투에서 제외된다. **2** to deliberately not include something ‖ 일부러 무엇을 포함시키지 않다. 제외하다: *Some of the data was excluded from the report.* 어떤 자료들은 보고서에서 제외되었다.

ex·clud·ing /ɪk'skludɪŋ/ prep not including ‖ 포함하지 않고. …을 제외하고: *The trip costs $1300, excluding airfare.* 그 여행 경비는 항공 요금을 제외하고 1,300달러가 든다.

ex·clu·sion /ɪk'skluʒən/ n [U] **1** a situation in which someone is not allowed to do something or something is not used ‖ 사람이 무엇을 하도록 허용받지 못한 상황, 또는 어떤 것이 사용되지 않은 상황. 제외. 배제: *the former exclusion of professional athletes from the Olympics* 올림픽에서의 프로 선수의 사전 제외 **2 do sth to the exclusion of** to do something so much that you do not do, consider, or have time for something else ‖ 그 밖의 것은 하지 않을[고려하지 않을, 할 시간이 없을] 정도로 무엇을 많이 하다. …을 제쳐두고 …하다: *He works constantly, to the exclusion of everything else.* 그는 다른 모든 것을 제쳐두고 계속 일만 한다.

ex·clu·sive¹ /ɪk'sklusɪv, -zɪv/ adj **1** exclusive places, organizations etc. are for people who have a lot of money, or who belong to a high social class ‖ 장소·조직 등이 돈이 많거나 높은 사회적 계층에 속한 사람들을 위한. 고급의. 특권층에 한정된: *an exclusive Manhattan hotel* 고급 맨해튼 호텔 **2** used by only one person or group, and not shared ‖ 공유되지 않고 오직 한 사람이나 한 집단에 의해 사용되는. 독점적인: *a car for the*

exclusive use of the Pope 교황 전용차 **3** **exclusive of** not including ‖ 포함하지 않고. …을 제외하고: *The trip cost $450, exclusive of meals.* 그 여행은 식사비를 제외하고 450달러 들었다.

exclusive² n an important news story that is in only one newspaper, magazine, television news program etc. ‖ 오직 한 신문·잡지·텔레비전 뉴스 프로 등에만 있는 중요한 뉴스 기사. 특종

ex·clu·sive·ly /ɪk'sklusɪvli, -zɪv-/ adv only ‖ 단지. 오로지: *This offer is available exclusively to those who call now.* 이 신청은 지금 전화하는 사람들에게만 유효하다.

ex·com·mu·ni·cate /ˌɛkskə'myunə,keɪt/ v [T] to punish someone by not allowing him/her to continue to be a member of a church ‖ 어떤 사람에게 교인의 자격을 중지시킴으로써 벌을 주다. 추방[파문]하다 – **excommunication** /ˌɛkskə,myunə'keɪʃən/ n [C, U]

ex·cre·ment /'ɛkskrəmənt/ n [U] FORMAL the solid waste from a person's or animal's body ‖ 사람이나 동물의 몸에서 나온 고형의 노폐물. 대변

ex·crete /ɪk'skrit/ v [I, T] FORMAL to get rid of waste from the body through the BOWELS, or to get rid of waste liquid through the skin ‖ 창자를 통해 몸속의 노폐물을 내보내거나 피부를 통해 몸 속의 쓸모없는 액체를 내보내다. …을 배설하다. 분비하다

ex·cru·ci·at·ing /ɪk'skruʃi,eɪtɪŋ/ adj extremely painful ‖ 매우 고통스러운: *The pain in my knee was excruciating.* 나는 무릎의 통증으로 몹시 괴로웠다. – **excruciatingly** adv

ex·cur·sion /ɪk'skɚʒən/ n a short trip, usually made by a group of people ‖ 일반적으로 단체로 하는 단기 여행. 유람: *an excursion to Sea World* 시 월드 관광 여행

ex·cus·a·ble /ɪk'skyuzəbəl/ adj behavior or words that are excusable are easy to forgive ‖ 행동이나 말이 용서될 수 있는. 변명이 되는 —opposite INEXCUSABLE

ex·cuse¹ /ɪk'skyuz/ v [T] **1 excuse me** SPOKEN **a)** said when you want to politely get someone's attention in order to ask a question ‖ 질문을 하기 위해 정중히 남의 이목을 끌고 싶을 때 쓰여. 실례합니다만: *Excuse me, is this the right bus for the airport?* 실례합니다만, 이것이 공항행 버스 맞습니까? **b)** used in order to say you are sorry when you have done something that is embarrassing or rude ‖ 당혹케 하거나 무례한 짓을 했을 때 미안하다고 말하는 데에 쓰여. 죄송합니다: *Oh, excuse me, I didn't mean to step on your foot.* 아, 죄송합니다. 실수하여 당신 발을 밟았습니다. **c)** used in order to politely tell someone that you are leaving a place ‖ 어떤 장소에서 떠나려는 것을 남에게 정중히 알리려는 데에 쓰여: *Excuse me, I'll be right back.* 실례합니다만 금방 돌아올게요. **d)** used in order to ask someone to repeat what s/he has just said ‖ 남에게 방금 한 말을 되풀이해 달라고 부탁하는 데에 쓰여. 다시 한 번 말씀해 주십시오: *"What time is it?" "Excuse me?" "I asked what time it is."* "몇 시죠?" "뭐라고 하셨죠?" "몇 시냐고 물었습니다." **e)** used in order to ask someone to move so you can go past him/her ‖ 남에게 지나갈 수 있도록 비켜 달라고 요청하는 데에 쓰여: *Excuse me, I need to get through.* 실례합니다만, 좀 지나가겠습니다. **2** to forgive someone, usually for something not very serious ‖ 일반적으로 아주 중요하지 않은 일에 대해 남을 용서하다: *Please excuse my bad handwriting.* 악필인 점을 양해해 줘요. **3** to not make someone do something that s/he is supposed to do ‖ 남이 하기로 한 일을 하지 못하게 하다. 면(제)하다: *You are excused from doing the dishes tonight.* 오늘 밤 설거지하는 것 면제해 줄게[안 해도 돼]. —see usage note at APOLOGIZING

excuse² /ɪk'skyus/ *n* **1** a reason that you give to explain why you did something wrong ‖ 잘못한 까닭을 설명하려고 제시하는 이유. 변명. 해명: *His excuse for being late wasn't very good.* 지각에 대한 그의 변명은 그다지 합당치는 않았다. **2** a false reason that you give to explain why you are or are not doing something ‖ 무엇을 하려는 또는 하지 않으려는 까닭을 설명하기 위해 제시하는 거짓 이유. 핑계: *I'll make an excuse and get away from the party early.* 나는 핑계를 대고 그 파티에서 일찍 나오겠다.

USAGE NOTE excuse and reason

An **excuse** is the explanation that you give when you have not done something that you should have done, or when you have done something wrong: *What's your excuse for not doing your homework?* A **reason** is a fact that explains why something happens, exists, or is true: *The reason I'm tired is that the neighbors had a noisy party.*

excuse는 해야 할 것을 하지 못했을 때 또는 잘못을 저질렀을 때 하는 설명이다: 숙제를 하지 못한 데에 대해 너는 뭐라 말할 거니? **reason**은 무엇이 일어나는[존재하는, 진실인] 까닭을 설명하는 사실이다: 내가 피곤한 이유는 이웃들이 소란스러운 파티를 했기 때문이다.

---

ex·ec /ɪg'zɛk/ *n* INFORMAL a business EXECUTIVE ‖ 기업의 간부. 임원

ex·e·cute /'ɛksɪˌkyut/ *v* [T] **1** to kill someone, especially as a legal punishment for a crime ‖ 특히 범죄에 대한 법적 처벌로서 남을 사형시키다 **2** FORMAL to do something that you have planned ‖ 계획한 것을 하다. 실행하다: *These ideas require money and materials to execute.* 이 아이디어들을 실행하는 데에는 돈과 재료가 필요하다.

ex·e·cu·tion /ˌɛksɪ'kyuʃən/ *n* **1** [C, U] the act of killing someone, especially as a legal punishment for a crime ‖ 범죄에 대한 법적 처벌로서 남을 사형시키는 행위. 사형 집행: *An hour before the execution, a crowd gathered outside the jail.* 사형 집행 1시간 전에 군중들이 교도소 밖에 모였다. **2** [U] FORMAL a process in which you do something that you have planned to do ‖ 하려고 계획했던 것을 하는 과정. 실행: *the planning and execution of urban policy* 도시 정책의 계획과 시행

ex·e·cu·tion·er /ˌɛksɪ'kyuʃənə/ *n* someone whose job is to kill someone else as a legal punishment for a crime ‖ 범죄에 대한 법적 처벌로서 남을 사형시키는 직업인. 사형 집행인

ex·ec·u·tive¹ /ɪg'zɛkyətɪv/ *n* someone whose job is to decide what a company or business will do ‖ 회사나 기업이 할 것을 결정하는 직업인. 경영 간부. 중역. 임원

executive² *adj* **1** relating to making decisions, especially in a company or business ‖ 회사나 기업에서 의사 결정을 하는 것과 관련된. 중역의. 이사의: *an executive committee* 이사회. 집행 위원회 **2 executive branch** the part of a government that approves decisions and laws and organizes how they will work ‖ 결정 사항·법률을 승인하고 그것들을 효율적으로 작용시킬 방법을 체계화하는 정치의 한 부문. 행정부 —compare JUDICIARY, LEGISLATURE

ex·ec·u·tor /ɪg'zɛkyətə/ *n* LAW someone

who deals with the instructions in a WILL ‖ 유언으로 지시한 것을 처리하는 사람. 유언 집행자

ex·em·pla·ry /ɪɡ'zɛmpləri/ *adj* FORMAL **1** excellent and extremely good, and used as an example ‖ 우수하고 매우 좋아 표본으로 쓰이는. 본보기의. 모범적인: *the students' exemplary behavior* 학생들의 모범적인 행동 **2** severe and used as a warning ‖ 엄격하며 경고로 쓰이는. 경고 [본보기]가 되는: *an exemplary punishment* 본보기로서의 처벌

ex·em·pli·fy /ɪɡ'zɛmplə,faɪ/ *v* [T] FORMAL to be a very typical example of something, or to give an example like this ‖ 어떤 것의 매우 전형적인 예이다, 또는 이와 같은 예를 들다. …의 좋은 예가 되다. 예증하다: *Stuart exemplifies the kind of student we like at our school.* 스튜어트는 학교에서 우리가 좋아하는 학생의 전형적인 예이다.

ex·empt¹ /ɪɡ'zɛmpt/ *adj* having special permission not to do a duty, pay for something etc., that you would usually have to do ‖ 보통은 이행해야 하는 의무·지불 등을 하지 않아도 되는 특별한 허가를 받은. 면제된: *The money is exempt from state taxes.* 그 돈은 주세(州稅)가 면제되어 있다.

exempt² *v* [T] to give someone special permission not to do something, pay for something etc., that s/he would usually have to do ‖ 남에게 무엇을 행하고 지불하는 등의 일반적으로 해야만 하는 것을 하지 말라고 특별히 허락하다. 면제하다: *Children are exempted from this rule.* 아이들은 이 규칙에서 제외된다.

ex·emp·tion /ɪɡ'zɛmpʃən/ *n* **1** an amount of money that you do not have to pay tax on in a particular year ‖ 특정한 해에 내는 것이 면제된 세금 액수. 세금 공제액: *a tax exemption for gifts to charity* 자선품에 대한 세금 공제액 **2** [C, U] permission not to do something, pay for something etc., that you would usually have to do ‖ 무엇을 행하고 지불하는 등의 일반적으로 해야만 하는 것을 하지 말라는 허락. 면제. 해제: *an exemption from military service* 병역 면제

ex·er·cise¹ /'ɛksɚ,saɪz/ *n* **1** [C, U] physical activity that you do regularly in order to stay strong and healthy ‖ 튼튼함과 건강을 유지하기 위해 정기적으로 하는 육체적인 운동: *stretching exercises for the back* 등을 위한 스트레칭 운동 / *Have you done your stomach exercises today?* 오늘 복부 운동을 했니? **2** a set of

written questions that test your skill or knowledge ‖ 기술이나 지식을 시험해 보는 일련의 질문들. 연습 문제: *For homework, do exercises 1 and 2.* 숙제로 1번과 2번 연습 문제를 해라. **3** a set of military actions that are not part of a war, but that allow soldiers to practice their skills ‖ 전쟁의 일부분은 아니지만 군인들에게 기술을 연마시키는 일련의 군사적 행동. 군대의 연습[훈련] **4** FORMAL the use of power, a right etc. in order to make something happen ‖ 무엇을 일으키기 위한 힘·권리 등의 사용. 행사: *laws that protect the exercise of our freedom of speech* 언론 자유의 행사를 보장해 주는 법률들

exercise² *v* [I, T] **1** to do physical activities regularly so that you stay strong and healthy ‖ 튼튼함과 건강을 유지하기 위해 정기적으로 육체적 활동을 하다. 운동하다[시키다]: *Hilary exercises by walking to work.* 힐러리는 직장까지 걷는 운동을 한다. **2** FORMAL to use power, a right etc. to make something happen ‖ 무엇이 일어나도록 힘과 권리 등을 사용하다. 행사하다: *She exercised her influence to get Rigby the position.* 그녀는 리그비에게 그 자리를 주기 위해 자기의 영향력을 행사했다.

exercise bike /'... ,./ *n* a bicycle that does not move and is used indoors for exercise ‖ 굴러가지 않고 실내에서 운동용으로 사용하는 자전거

ex·ert /ɪɡ'zɚt/ *v* [T] **1 exert authority/pressure etc.** to use your authority etc. to make something happen ‖ 무엇이 일어나도록 권한 등을 사용하다. 권한을 행사하다/압력을 가하다: *The UN is exerting pressure on the countries to stop the war.* 유엔은 전쟁을 중단시키려고 그 나라들에 압력을 가하고 있다. **2 exert yourself** to make a strong physical or mental effort ‖ 세찬 육체적 또는 정신적 노력을 하다. 분투하다

ex·er·tion /ɪɡ'zɚʃən/ *n* [C, U] strong physical or mental effort ‖ 세찬 육체적 또는 정신적 노력. 분투: *Paul's face was red with exertion.* 폴은 힘든 일을 하여 얼굴이 새빨개졌다.

ex·hale /ɛks'heɪl, ɛk'seɪl/ *v* [I, T] to breathe air, smoke etc. out of your mouth ‖ 입에서 공기나 담배 연기를 내뿜다. 숨을 내쉬다: *Take a deep breath, then exhale slowly.* 숨을 깊이 들이마시고 나서 천천히 내쉬어라. —opposite INHALE

ex·haust¹ /ɪɡ'zɔst/ *v* [T] **1** to make someone very tired ‖ 사람을 매우 지치게

하다. 기진맥진하게 하다: *The trip totally exhausted us.* 우리는 그 여행으로 완전히 기진맥진해 버렸다. **2** to use all of something ‖ 어떤 것을 전부 사용하다. 다 써버리다. 고갈시키다: *We are in danger of exhausting the world's oil supply.* 우리는 전 세계적 원유 고갈의 위험에 처해 있다.

ex·haust² n **1** [U] the gas that is produced when a machine is working ‖ 기계가 작동할 때 생기는 가스. 배기 가스: *Car exhaust is the main reason for pollution in the city.* 자동차 배기 가스는 도시 오염의 요인이다. **2** also **exhaust pipe** a pipe on a car or machine that exhaust comes out of ‖ 배기 가스를 배출하는 자동차나 기계의 관. 배기관

ex·haust·ed /ɪgˈzɔstɪd/ adj extremely tired ‖ 매우 지친. 기진맥진한: *Ron was exhausted from lack of sleep.* 론은 수면 부족으로 녹초가 되어 있었다.

ex·haust·ing /ɪgˈzɔstɪŋ/ adj making you feel extremely tired ‖ 매우 지치게 하는: *an exhausting trip* 몹시 고단한 여행

ex·haus·tion /ɪgˈzɔstʃən/ n [U] the state of being extremely tired ‖ 매우 지친 상태. 극도의 피로. 기진맥진: *Neil is suffering from mental exhaustion.* 닐은 극도의 정신적 피로를 겪고 있다.

ex·haus·tive /ɪgˈzɔstɪv/ adj extremely thorough ‖ 아주 철저한: *The rescue team made an exhaustive search of the area.* 구조팀은 그 지역을 아주 철저히 조사했다. **– exhaustively** adv

ex·hib·it¹ /ɪgˈzɪbɪt/ v **1** [I, T] to put something in a public place so people can see it ‖ 사람들이 볼 수 있게 공공 장소에 어떤 것을 놓다. 진열하다. 전시하다: *The art gallery will exhibit some of Dali's paintings.* 그 화랑은 달리의 그림 몇 점을 전시할 것이다. **2** [T] FORMAL to show a quality, sign, emotion etc. in a way that people easily notice ‖ 사람들이 쉽게 알 수 있도록 특질·신호·감정 등을 나타내 보이다: *The patient exhibited symptoms of heart disease.* 그 환자는 심장병의 징후를 나타냈다.

exhibit² n **1** something that is put in a public place so people can see it ‖ 사람들이 볼 수 있게 공공 장소에 놓은 것. 전시품. 진열품: *a new sculpture exhibit at the museum* 미술관에 새로 전시된 조각품 **2** something that is shown in a court of law to prove that someone is guilty or not guilty ‖ 사람이 죄가 있는지 없는지를 입증하기 위해 법정에 제시되는 것. 증거물

ex·hi·bi·tion /ˌɛksəˈbɪʃən/ n [C, U] a public show where you put something so people can see it ‖ 사물을 사람들이 볼 수 있게 놓아 두는 공개 전시(회). 전람[전시]회: *A collection of rare books is on exhibition at the city library.* 수집된 희귀본들은 시립 도서관에 전시 중이다. / *an exhibition of historical photographs* 역사적인 사진의 전시

ex·hi·bi·tion·ism /ˌɛksəˈbɪʃəˌnɪzəm/ n [U] **1** behavior that makes people notice you, but that most people think is not acceptable ‖ 대부분의 사람들이 마음에 들어 하지 않는다고 여기면서도 사람들이 자신을 알아보게 만드는 행동. 과시벽. 현시벽 **2** a mental problem in which someone likes to show his/her sexual organs to other people in public places ‖ 사람이 공공 장소에서 다른 사람들에게 자신의 성기를 보여 주고 싶어하는 정신적인 문제. 노출증 **– exhibitionist** n

ex·hil·a·rat·ed /ɪgˈzɪləˌreɪtɪd/ adj feeling extremely happy and excited ‖ 매우 행복하고 격앙된 느낌의. 들뜬: *Rita was exhilarated when she first saw the ocean.* 리타는 처음 바다를 보자 몹시 들떴다.

ex·hil·a·ra·ting /ɪgˈzɪləˌreɪtɪŋ/ adj making you feel extremely happy and excited ‖ 매우 행복하고 격앙된 기분을 느끼게 하는. 들뜨게 하는: *The balloon ride was exhilarating.* 그 기구에 타는 것은 기분을 들뜨게 했다.

ex·hil·a·ra·tion /ɪgˌzɪləˈreɪʃən/ n [U] a feeling of being extremely happy and excited ‖ 매우 행복하고 격앙된 느낌. 명랑. 들뜬 기분 **– exhilarate** /ɪgˈzɪləˌreɪt/ v [T]

ex·hort /ɪgˈzɔrt/ v [T] FORMAL to try to persuade someone to do something ‖ 남에게 무엇을 하도록 설득하려고 애쓰다. 강력히 권고하다 **– exhortation** /ˌɛksɔrˈteɪʃən, ˌɛgzɔr-/ n [C, U]

ex·hume /ɪgˈzum, ɛksˈhyum/ v [T] FORMAL to remove a dead body from the ground after it has been buried ‖ 묻혀 있던 시체를 지하에서 들어 내다. 시체를 발굴하다 **– exhumation** /ˌɛksyuˈmeɪʃən/ n [C, U]

ex·ile¹ /ˈɛgzaɪl, ˈɛksaɪl/ v [T] to force someone to leave his/her country and live in another country, usually for political reasons ‖ 일반적으로 정치적인 이유로 어떤 사람을 강제로 자기 나라를 떠나 다른 나라에서 살게 하다. …을 국외 추방하다. 망명시키다 **– exiled** adj

ex·ile² n **1** [U] a situation in which someone is EXILED ‖ 사람이 국외 추방된 상태. 망명. 추방: *a writer who lives in* *exile in Britain* 영국에서 망명 생활을 하고 있는 작가 **2** someone who has been EXILEd ‖ 국외 추방된 사람. 망명자

ex·ist /ɪgˈzɪst/ *v* [I] **1** to be real or alive ‖ 실제하거나 살아 있다. 존재[현존]하다: *Do ghosts really exist?* 유령이 정말 존재할까? ✗DON'T SAY "It is existing/they are existing."✗ "It is existing/they are existing"과 같이 진행형을 쓰지 않는다. **2** to stay alive, especially in difficult conditions ‖ 특히 어려운 조건에서 살아 있다. 존속하다. 생존하다: *Poor families in our city are barely able to exist in the winter.* 우리 도시에 사는 가난한 가정은 겨울을 나기가 힘들다.

ex·ist·ence /ɪgˈzɪstəns/ *n* **1** [U] the state of existing ‖ 존재하는 상태. 존재. 현존: *Do you believe in the existence of God?* 당신은 신의 존재를 믿습니까? / *laws that are already in existence* 이미 존재하는 법률 **2** the type of life that someone has, especially when it is difficult ‖ 특히 어려울 때의 생활 방식. 생활상: *a terrible existence* 끔찍한 생활상

ex·ist·ing /ɪgˈzɪstɪŋ/ *adj* present now and available to be used ‖ 현재 존재하며 사용 가능한. 기존의. 현존하는: *We need new computers to replace the existing ones.* 우리는 기존의 컴퓨터를 대체할 새 컴퓨터가 필요하다.

ex·it¹ /ˈɛgzɪt, ˈɛksɪt/ *n* **1** a door through which you can leave a room, building etc. ‖ 방, 건물 등을 빠져나갈 수 있는 문. 출구: *There are two exits at the back of the plane.* 비행기 뒤쪽에 두 개의 출구가 있다. **2** the act of leaving a room, theater stage etc. ‖ 방, 극장 무대 등을 떠나는 행위. 나감. 퇴거. 퇴장: *The President made a quick exit after his speech.* 대통령은 연설 후 재빠르게 퇴장했다. **3** a small road that you can drive on to leave a larger road ‖ 더 큰 도로에서 나가기 위해 타는 작은 도로. 고속도로 등의 출구: *Take exit 23 into the city.* 그 도시로 진입하는 23번 출구로 나가라.

exit² *v* **1** [I] to leave a place ‖ 어떤 장소를 떠나다: *The band exited through a door behind the stage.* 그 밴드는 무대 뒤편의 문으로 빠져나갔다. **2** [I, T] to stop using a computer or computer program ‖ 컴퓨터나 컴퓨터 프로그램 사용을 중단하다

ex·o·dus /ˈɛksədəs/ *n* [singular] a situation in which a lot of people leave a particular place at the same time ‖ 많은 사람들이 특정 장소를 동시에 떠나는 상황. 집단 이주: *the exodus of Russian scientists to America* 러시아 과학자들의

미국으로의 집단 이주

ex·on·er·ate /ɪgˈzɑnəˌreɪt/ *v* [T] FORMAL to officially say that someone who has been blamed for something is not guilty ‖ 어떤 혐의를 받은 사람이 무죄라고 공적으로 언급하다. 혐의를 면제하다: *Ross was exonerated from all charges of child abuse.* 로스는 아동 학대에 관한 모든 혐의를 벗었다. **–exoneration** /ɪgˌzɑnəˈreɪʃən/ *n* [U]

ex·or·bi·tant /ɪgˈzɔrbətənt/ *adj* an exorbitant price, demand etc. is much higher or greater than it should be ‖ 가격·요구 등이 적정 수준보다 훨씬 높거나 큰. 터무니없이 많은[높은, 큰]. 과도한: *It's a nice hotel but the prices are exorbitant!* 호텔은 훌륭하지만 요금이 터무니없이 비싸!

ex·or·cize /ˈɛksɔrˌsaɪz, -sə-/ *v* [T] to force evil spirits to leave a place or someone's body by using special words and ceremonies ‖ 특별한 주문과 의식으로 어떤 장소나 사람의 몸에서 악령을 쫓아내다. 몰아내다 **–exorcism** /ˈɛksɔrˌsɪzəm, -sə-/ *n* [C, U] **–exorcist** /ˈɛksɔrsɪst/ *n*

ex·ot·ic /ɪgˈzɑtɪk/ *adj* unusual and exciting because of a connection with a foreign country ‖ 외국과 연관되어 특이하고 흥미로운. 이국적인. 색다른. 진귀한: *an exotic flower from Africa* 아프리카산의 이국적인 꽃 **–exotically** *adv*

ex·pand /ɪkˈspænd/ *v* [I, T] to become larger in size, area, activity, or number, or to make something become larger ‖ 크기[지역, 활동, 수]가 더 커지다, 또는 더 크게 만들다. …이[을] 늘[리]다. 팽창하다[시키다]: *The population of Texas expanded rapidly in the '60s.* 60년대에 텍사스 주 인구가 급격히 증가했다. / *McDonalds is beginning to expand (=open new stores) in Asia.* 맥도널드가 아시아에서 늘기 시작하고 있다. **–expandable** *adj* —compare CONTRACT²

expand on/upon sth *phr v* [T] FORMAL to add more details or information to something that you have already said ‖ 자신이 이미 말한 것에 더 자세한 사항이나 정보를 첨가하다. …에 부연하다

ex·panse /ɪkˈspæns/ *n* a very large area of water, sky, land etc. ‖ 물·하늘·땅 등의 매우 넓은 지역. 광활한 공간[장소]: *the vast expanse of the Pacific Ocean* 광활한 태평양

ex·pan·sion /ɪkˈspænʃən/ *n* [U] the process of increasing in size, number, or amount ‖ 크기[수, 양]가 커지는 과정. 확대. 확장. 팽창: *a period of economic* *expansion* 경제 팽창기 — **expansionist** *adj*

ex·pan·sive /ɪkˈspænsɪv/ *adj* **1** very friendly and willing to talk a lot ‖ 매우 친근하고 말을 많이 하고자 하는. 활달한: *After dinner, Mr. Woods relaxed and became more expansive.* 저녁 식사 후 우즈 씨는 긴장을 풀고 더 활달해졌다. **2** very large and wide in area ‖ 지역이 매우 크고 넓은. 광활한. 광범위의: *a window with an expansive view of the beach* 넓찍한 해변 경관이 보이는 창문

ex·pa·tri·ate /ɛksˈpeɪtriɪt/ *n* someone who lives in a foreign country ‖ 외국에 사는 사람. 국외 거주자 — **expatriate** *adj*

ex·pect /ɪkˈspɛkt/ *v* [T] **1** to think that something will happen ‖ 어떤 일이 일어날 것이라 생각하다. 예상하다. 기대하다: *The hotel bill was more than we expected it to be.* 호텔 요금이 우리 예상보다 더 많이 나왔다. / *We expect her to arrive any day.* 우리는 그녀가 언제든 도착할 것을 기대한다. / *I expect (that) Beth will do well on the test.* 나는 베스가 그 시험을 잘 치러낼 것이라고 기대한다. **2** to demand that someone do something because it is his/her duty ‖ 어떤 사람에게 의무가 있어서 그 일을 하라고 요구하다: *You are expected to return all books by Monday.* 월요일까지 모든 책을 반납하도록 하세요. / *Wanda's parents expect too much of her.* (=think she can do more than she really can) 완다의 부모님은 그녀에게 너무 큰 기대를 하신다. **3 be expecting** if a woman is expecting, she is going to have a baby soon ‖ 여성이 곧 아이를 낳을 예정이다. 임신 중이다. 출산 예정이다 —see usage note at WAIT¹

ex·pect·an·cy /ɪkˈspɛktənsi/ *n* [U] the feeling that something exciting or interesting is about to happen ‖ 재미있거나 흥미로운 일이 곧 일어날 것이라는 느낌. 기대: *a look of expectancy in her eyes* 기대에 찬 그녀의 눈빛 —see also LIFE EXPECTANCY

ex·pect·ant /ɪkˈspɛktənt/ *adj* **1** hopeful that something good or exciting will happen ‖ 좋거나 신나는 일이 일어나기를 희망하는. 기대를 가진: *An expectant crowd gathered at the movie premiere.* 기대에 찬 군중들이 영화 시사회장에 모였다. **2 expectant mother/father** someone whose baby will be born soon ‖ 곧 아이를 낳게 될 사람. 예비 엄마/아빠 — **expectantly** *adv*

ex·pec·ta·tion /ˌɛkspɛkˈteɪʃən/ *n* **1** [C, U] the belief or hope that something will happen ‖ 어떤 일이 일어날 것이라는 믿음이나 희망. 예상. 기대: *Sales of the car have exceeded expectations.* (=have been better than expected) 자동차 판매액이 예상을 뛰어넘었다. / *expectations that the dollar will drop in value* 달러 가치가 하락할 것이라는 예상 **2** [C usually plural] a feeling or belief about the way something should be or how someone should behave ‖ 사물이 어떠해야 한다는 방식 또는 사람이 행동해야 하는 방식에 대한 느낌이나 믿음. 기대치: *The movie did not live up to our expectations.* (=was not as good as we thought it would be) 그 영화는 우리 기대에 미치지 못했다. / *My parents have high expectations* (=believe I should succeed) *about my future.* 우리 부모님은 내 미래에 대한 큰 기대감을 갖고 계신다.

ex·pe·di·en·cy /ɪkˈspidiənsi/ also **expedience** /ɪkˈspidiəns/ *n* [C, U] what is useful, easy, or necessary to do in a particular situation, even if it is morally wrong ‖ 도덕적으로 잘못 되었을지라도 특정 상황에서 하기에는 쓸모 있는[쉬운, 필요한] 것. 편의. 방편: *The governor vetoed the bill as an act of political expediency.* 그 주지사는 정략적 방편으로서 그 법안에 거부권을 행사했다.

ex·pe·di·ent /ɪkˈspidiənt/ *adj* helpful or useful, sometimes in a way that is morally wrong ‖ 가끔 도덕적으로 나쁘게 도움이 되거나 쓸모있는. 편리한. 유리한. 방편의. 편의주의의. 정략적인: *We thought it would be expedient to consult a lawyer.* 우리는 변호사와 상의하는 것이 상책이라고 생각했다. — **expedient** *n*

ex·pe·dite /ˈɛkspəˌdaɪt/ *v* [T] to make a process, action etc. happen more quickly ‖ 과정·행동 등을 더 신속히 일어나게 하다. 일을 촉진시키다. 신속히 처리하다: *More money would, of course, expedite things.* 물론 돈이 더 있으면 일을 빨리 처리할 수 있겠지.

ex·pe·di·tion /ˌɛkspəˈdɪʃən/ *n* **1** a long and carefully organized trip, especially to a dangerous place ‖ 오랫동안 신중히 계획된, 특히 위험한 장소로의 여행. 원정. 탐험: *an expedition to the North Pole* 북극 탐험 **2** a short trip, usually made for a particular purpose ‖ 대개 특정 목적을 위해 이루어진 짧은 여행. 나들이. 외출: *a shopping expedition* 쇼핑 나들이

ex·pel /ɪkˈspɛl/ *v* **-lled, -lling** [T] **1** to officially make someone leave a school, organization, or country ‖ 사람을 학교[단체, 나라]에서 공식적으로 떠나게 하다. …을 …에서 추방하다[쫓아내다]:

Larry was expelled from school for smoking. 래리는 담배를 피워서 퇴학당했다. **2** to force air, water, or gas out of something ‖ 공기[물, 가스]를 어떤 것에서 내보내다. …을 배출[방출]하다

ex·pend /ık'spɛnd/ *v* [T] FORMAL to use money, time, energy etc. to do something ‖ 어떤 것을 하기 위해 돈·시간·에너지 등을 쓰다. 소비[소모]하다: *A lot of effort has been expended on this research project.* 이 연구 사업계획에 많은 공을 들였다.

ex·pend·a·ble /ık'spɛndəbəl/ *adj* not needed enough to be kept or saved ‖ 보관하거나 절약하지 않아도 되는. 소모해도 되는. 소모적인: *Health clinics for the poor are not expendable.* 빈민들을 위한 보건소는 없어서는 안 된다.

ex·pend·i·ture /ık'spɛndətʃɚ/ *n* FORMAL **1** [C, U] the total amount of money that a person or organization spends ‖ 사람이나 단체가 쓰는 총금액. 경비. 비용. 지출. 소비: *US expenditure on welfare programs went down by 5%.* 미국 정부의 복지비 지출이 5%까지 감소되었다 **2** [U] the action of spending or using time, money, effort etc. ‖ 시간·돈·노력 등을 쓰거나 사용하는 일. 소비. 소모

ex·pense /ık'spɛns/ *n* [C, U] **1** the amount of money you spend on something ‖ 사물에 소비하는 금액. 비용: *Sally's parents spared no expense* (=spent all the money necessary to buy the best things) for her wedding. 샐리의 부모님은 샐리의 결혼 비용을 몽땅 부담했다. **2 at the expense of** achieved by harming someone or something else ‖ 다른 사람이나 사물에 해를 끼쳐서 달성된. …을 희생시켜. …의 희생을 치르고: *The cars were produced quickly, at the expense of safety.* 자동차들은 안전성은 고려되지 않고 빠른 속도로 생산되었다. **3 at sb's expense** achieved by someone else paying for something, being harmed by something etc. ‖ 어떤 일에 대하여, 또는 어떤 일로 손상된 것에 대하여 다른 사람이 대가를 치러 이루어진. …의 돈[비용]으로. 남에게 폐를 끼치고: *Education is provided at the public's expense.* 교육은 공공의 비용으로 제공된다. —see also EXPENSES

expense ac·count /.'..,./ *n* money that is available to someone who works for a company so that s/he can pay for hotels, meals etc. when traveling for work ‖ 회사 직원이 업무상 출장시 호텔·식사 등의 비용을 지불하는 데에 쓸 수 있는 돈. 필요 경비

ex·pens·es /ık'spɛnsız/ *n* [plural] **1** money that you spend on travel, hotels, meals etc. when you are working, and that your employer gives back to you later ‖ 업무상의 여행·호텔·식사 등에 돈을 지출하고 추후에 고용주로부터 돌려받는 돈. 경비 **2 all expenses paid** having all of your costs for hotels, travel, meals etc. paid for by someone else ‖ 호텔·여행·식사 등에 소요되는 모든 비용을 다른 사람이 지불하는. 모든 비용을 상대방이 부담하여: *The prize is an all expenses paid trip to Hawaii.* 상금은 하와이 여행 총비용이다.

ex·pen·sive /ık'spɛnsıv/ *adj* costing a lot of money ‖ 돈이 많이 드는. 비싼. 고가의: *an expensive piece of jewelry* 고가의 보석 —opposite INEXPENSIVE

ex·pe·ri·ence¹ /ık'spıriəns/ *n* **1** [U] knowledge or skill that you gain from doing a job or activity ‖ 직업이나 활동을 통해 얻은 지식이나 기술. 경험. 체험: *Do you have any experience in the publishing business?* 출판업계 경험이 있습니까? **2** [U] knowledge that you gain about life and the world by being in different situations and meeting different people ‖ 다른 상황에 놓여 다른 사람들을 만남으로 해서 얻어지는 삶과 세계에 대한 지식. 경험으로 얻은 지식[지혜]: *In my experience, a credit card is always useful.* 내 경험상, 신용 카드는 언제나 유용하다. **3** something that happens to you and has an effect on how you feel or what you think ‖ 발생하여 느낌이나 생각에 영향을 미치는 것. 경험한 일: *Visiting Paris was a wonderful experience.* 파리 방문은 대단한 경험이었다. / *People often say they have had similar experiences.* 종종 사람들은 자신들이 비슷한 경험이 있다고 말한다.

experience² *v* [T] to be influenced or affected by something that happens to you or by emotions, pain etc. ‖ 사람에게 일어난 일이나 감정·고통 등에 의해 영향을 받다. …을 경험하다[겪다]: *The company is experiencing problems with its computer system.* 그 회사는 컴퓨터 시스템의 문제를 겪고 있다. / *The patient is experiencing a lot of pain.* 그 환자는 엄청난 고통을 겪고 있다.

ex·pe·ri·enced /ık'spıriənst/ *adj* having particular skills or knowledge because you have done something often or for a long time ‖ 어떤 것을 자주, 또는 오랫동안 해왔기 때문에 특정한 기술이나 지식을 가지고 있는. 경험 있는. …에 숙달한[노련한]: *an experienced pilot* 노련

한 조종사 —opposite INEXPERIENCED

ex·per·i·ment¹ /ɪk'spɛrəmənt/ n **1** a scientific test done to show how something will react in a particular situation, or to prove that an idea is true ‖ 어떤 것이 특정 상황에서 어떻게 반응하는지를 보여 주거나 어떤 생각이 사실이라는 것을 입증하기 위해 시행되는 과학적 시험. 실험: *They performed/did experiments on rats to test the drug.* 그들은 그 약을 시험하기 위해 쥐를 대상으로 실험했다. **2** a process in which you try a new idea, method etc. in order to find out if it is effective ‖ 새로운 생각·방법 등이 효과적인지 찾아내기 위해 이를 시험해 보는 과정. 시험. 시도: *St. Mary's School is an experiment in bilingual education.* 세인트 메리 학교는 2개어 병용 교육을 시도하고 있다.

ex·per·i·ment² /ɪk'spɛrə,mɛnt/ v [I] **1** to try using various ideas, methods, materials etc. in order to find out how effective or good they are ‖ 다양한 생각·방법·재료 등이 얼마나 효과적인지 또는 얼마나 좋은지를 알아내기 위해 그것들을 써보다. 시험[시도]하다: *Many teenagers experiment with drugs.* 많은 10대들이 시험 삼아 마약을 해보고 있다. **2** to do a scientific test in order to find out if a particular idea is true or to obtain more information ‖ 특정 생각이 맞는지 알아내기 위해 또는 더 많은 정보를 얻기 위해 과학적인 시험을 하다. 실험하다: *Scientists often experiment on animals when testing new products.* 과학자들은 신제품을 시험할 때 종종 동물을 대상으로 실험한다. **– experimentation** /ɪk,spɛrəmən'teɪʃən/ n [U]

ex·per·i·men·tal /ɪk,spɛrə'mɛntəl/ adj **1** used for or related to EXPERIMENTs ‖ 실험에 쓰이거나 관련된. 실험의: *experimental research* 실험 연구 **2** using or testing new ideas ‖ 새로운 생각을 써보거나 시험하는. 실험적인: *an experimental theater group* 실험 극단 **– experimentally** adv

ex·pert /'ɛkspɔt/ n someone with special skills or knowledge of a subject, gained as a result of training or experience ‖ 훈련이나 경험의 결과로 얻어진 특정 주제에 관한 특수한 기술이나 지식을 갖춘 사람. 전문가: *an expert on/in ancient Egyptian art* 고대 이집트 예술의 전문가 **– expert** adj **– expertly** adv

ex·per·tise /,ɛkspɔ'tiz/ n [U] a special skill or knowledge that you learn by experience or training ‖ 경험이나 훈련을 통해 배우는 특수한 기술이나 지식. 전문적 기술[지식, 의견]: *We should use his medical expertise to our advantage.* 우리는 그의 전문적 의학 지식을 우리에게 유리하게 사용해야 한다.

ex·pi·ra·tion /,ɛkspə'reɪʃən/ n [U] the end of a period of time during which an official document or agreement is allowed to be used ‖ 공식 문서 또는 협약의 사용이 허용되는 기간의 종결. (기한의) 만료[만기]: *the expiration of the treaty* 그 조약의 만료

expiration date /..'.. ,./ n the date when something stops being safe to eat or to use ‖ 먹거나 쓰는데에 안전하지 못하게 되는 날짜. 유통 기한: *The milk is past its expiration date.* 그 우유는 유통 기한이 지났다.

ex·pire /ɪk'spaɪɚ/ v [I] **1** if a document expires, you cannot legally continue to use it beyond a particular date ‖ 서류 등을 특정 날짜가 지난 후 법적으로 계속 사용할 수 없다. 기한이 다 되다[끝나다]. 만료하다. 만기가 되다: *My driver's license expires in September.* 내 운전 면허증은 9월에 만료된다. **2** LITERARY to die ‖ 죽다. 숨을 거두다

ex·plain /ɪk'spleɪn/ v [I, T] **1** to say or write something so that it is easy to understand ‖ 어떤 것을 이해하기 쉽도록 말하거나 쓰다. 설명하다: *Could you explain the rules to me?* 제게 규칙을 설명해 주시겠어요? ✗DON'T SAY "explain me the rules."✗ "explain me the rules." 라고는 하지 않는다. / *Can someone explain how this thing works?* 이것의 작동 방법을 누가 설명해 줄 수 있습니까? ✗DON'T SAY "explain me how it works."✗ "explain me how it works." 라고는 하지 않는다. **2** to give or be the reason for something ‖ 어떤 것에 대한 이유를 제시하거나 이유가 되다. …을 해명[변명]하다: *Brad never explained why he was late.* 브래드는 지각한 이유를 전혀 말하지 않았다.

explain sth ↔ **away** phr v [T] to make something seem to be less important or not your fault ‖ 어떤 일을 덜 중요하거나 자신의 잘못이 아닌 것처럼 보이게 하다. …을 둘러대다. 발뺌하다: *Claire tried to explain away the bruises on her arm.* 클레어는 팔의 타박상에 대해 둘러대려고 했다.

ex·pla·na·tion /,ɛksplə'neɪʃən/ n **1** what you say or write to make something easier to understand ‖ 어떤 것을 더 이해하기 쉽도록 말하거나 쓰는 것. 설명: *a detailed explanation of how* *to write a proposal* 제안서 작성 방법에 대한 상세한 설명 **2** [C, U] the reason something happened or why you did something ‖ 어떤 것이 발생한 이유 또는 어떤 일을 한 이유. 원인. 해명. 변명: *Smith could not give an explanation for the blood on his jacket.* 스미스는 자신의 재킷에 묻은 피에 대해 해명할 수 없었다.

ex·plan·a·to·ry /ɪkˈsplænəˌtɔri/ *adj* giving information about something or describing how something works ‖ 어떤 것에 대한 정보를 주는 또는 작동 방법을 설명하는. 설명[주석]적인. 설명을 위한: *an explanatory booklet* 설명서 —see also SELF EXPLANATORY

ex·ple·tive /ˈɛksplətɪv/ *n* FORMAL a rude word that you use when you are angry or in pain ‖ 화가 나거나 고통스러울 때 쓰는 무례한 말. 욕설

ex·pli·ca·ble /ɪkˈsplɪkəbəl, ˈɛksplɪ-/ *adj* able to be easily understood or explained —opposite INEXPLICABLE ‖ 쉽게 이해되거나 설명될 수 있는. 해명할 수 있는

ex·plic·it /ɪkˈsplɪsɪt/ *adj* **1** expressed in a way that is very clear ‖ 매우 분명하게 표현되는. (설명 등이)명쾌한. 명백[명확]한: *The workers were given explicit instructions.* 노동자들은 분명한 지시를 받았다. **2** language or pictures that are explicit describe or show a lot of sex or violence ‖ 말이나 사진 등에 성(性)과 폭력이 많이 묘사되거나 나타나는. 적나라한. 노골적인 – **explicitly** *adv*

ex·plode /ɪkˈsploʊd/ *v* **1** [I, T] to burst into small pieces, making a loud noise and causing damage, or to make something do this ‖ 큰 소음을 내고 피해를 입히면서 산산조각이 나며 터지다, 또는 이렇게 만들다. 폭발하다[시키다]: *The car bomb exploded at 6:16.* 자동차에 설치된 폭탄은 6시 16분에 폭발했다. / *In 1949 the USSR exploded its first atomic bomb.* 1949년에 구소련은 자국의 첫 핵폭탄을 터뜨렸다. **2** [I] to suddenly become very angry ‖ 갑자기 매우 화가 나다. (감정 등이) 폭발하다: *Susie exploded when I told her I'd wrecked her car.* 수지는 내가 그녀의 차를 파손시켰다고 말하자 갑자기 버럭 화를 냈다. **3** [I] if the population explodes, it suddenly increases ‖ 인구 등이 갑자기 증가하다. 폭발적으로 증가하다

ex·ploit¹ /ɪkˈsplɔɪt/ *v* [T] **1** to treat someone unfairly in order to gain what you want ‖ 원하는 것을 얻기 위해 남을 부당하게 대우하다. …을 착취하다:

Children were exploited in factories in the 19th century. 19세기에 아이들은 공장에서 착취당했다. **2** to use something effectively and completely ‖ 어떤 것을 효과적으로 완벽하게 쓰다. 개발[개척]하다: *The country must exploit its resources more effectively.* 국가는 자원을 보다 효율적으로 개발해야 한다. – **exploitation** /ˌɛksplɔɪˈteɪʃən/ *n* [U]

ex·ploit² /ˈɛksplɔɪt/ *n* [C usually plural] a brave, exciting, and interesting action ‖ 용감하고 감동적이며 흥미로운 행위. 영웅적 행위. 위업: *a book about Annie Oakley's exploits* 애니 오클리의 위업에 관한 책

ex·plo·ra·tion /ˌɛkspləˈreɪʃən/ *n* [C, U] **1** a trip to a place you have not been, or a place where you are looking for something ‖ 가보지 않았거나 무언가를 찾고 있는 장소로의 여행. 탐험. 탐사: *exploration for oil* 석유 탐사 / *space exploration* 우주 탐험 **2** an examination or discussion about something to find out more about it ‖ 어떤 것에 대해 더 많이 알아내기 위한 조사나 토론. 조사. 연구. 탐구: *an exploration of spiritual issues* 영적인 문제에 관한 연구

ex·plo·ra·to·ry /ɪkˈsplɔrəˌtɔri/ *adj* done in order to find out more about something ‖ 어떤 것에 관해 더 많이 알아내기 위해 행해지는. 탐구를 위한. 탐험의. 예비적인: *exploratory surgery on his knee* 그의 무릎에 대한 예비적인 수술

ex·plore /ɪkˈsplɔr/ *v* **1** [I, T] to travel through an unfamiliar area in order to find out what it is like ‖ 낯선 지역이 어떤 곳인지 알아보기 위해 여행하다. (미지의 지역·세계를) 탐험하다: *We spent a week exploring the Oregon coastline.* 우리는 오리건 해안선을 탐험하며 1주일을 보냈다. **2** [I] to discuss, examine, or think about something carefully ‖ 어떤 것에 대해 신중히 토론[조사, 생각]하다. …을 연구[탐색, 조사]하다: *We're exploring new solutions to the problem.* 우리는 그 문제에 관한 새로운 해결책을 연구 중이다.

ex·plor·er /ɪkˈsplɔrə/ *n* someone who travels to places that have not been visited before ‖ 전인미답(前人未踏)의 장소를 여행하는 사람. 탐험가

ex·plo·sion /ɪkˈsploʊʒən/ *n* **1** [C, U] the action of something exploding, or a loud noise that sounds like something exploding ‖ 폭발하는 것, 또는 폭발하는 것 같은 큰 소리. 폭발[파열](음): *a nuclear explosion* 핵폭발 / *an explosion of thunder* 천둥의 굉음 **2** a sudden or

quick increase in number or amount ‖
수나 양의 갑작스럽거나 빠른 증가. 급증:
the population explosion 인구 급증[폭
발]

ex·plo·sive[1] /ɪkˈsploʊsɪv/ *n* a
substance that can cause an explosion ‖
폭발을 일으킬 수 있는 물질. 폭발물

explosive[2] *adj* **1** able or likely to
explode ‖ 폭발할 수 있는 또는 폭발할 것
같은. 폭발성의: *Dynamite is highly
explosive.* 다이너마이트는 폭발성이 매우
높다. **2** likely to suddenly become
violent and angry ‖ 갑자기 난폭하고 화를
내는 경향이 있는. (사람의 기질 등이) 격
정적인: *the teenager's explosive
behavior* 10대들의 격정적인 행동 **3** able
to make people argue and become
angry ‖ 사람들을 논쟁하게 하여 화나게
할 수 있는. 감정을 격하게 할 수 있는.
격정적인: *the explosive issue of abortion*
격론을 불러일으키는 낙태 문제

ex·po /ˈɛkspoʊ/ *n* ⇨ EXPOSITION

ex·po·nent /ɪkˈspoʊnənt, ˈɛkspoʊ-/ *n*
someone who supports a particular
idea, belief etc. and tries to persuade
others to accept it ‖ 특정 생각·신념 등을
지지하며 남들이 이를 받아들이도록 설득
하려는 사람. (주의의) 주창자[옹호자]:
an exponent of socialism 사회주의의 주
창자[옹호자]

ex·port[1] /ˈɛkspɔrt/ *n* [C, U] the business
of selling and sending products to
another country, or the products that
are sold ‖ 제품을 다른 나라에 판매하고
보내는 일, 또는 판매되는 제품. 수출. 수
출품: *The Government has banned the
export of lumber.* 정부는 목재의 수출을
금지했다. / *Wheat is one of our country's
chief exports.* 밀은 우리나라의 주요 수출
품 중 하나이다. —compare IMPORT[1]

ex·port[2] /ɪkˈspɔrt/ *v* [I, T] to send and
sell goods to another country ‖ 재화를 다
른 나라로 보내서 판매하다. 수출하다 –
exporter *n* – **exportation** /ˌɛks-
pɔrˈteɪʃən/ *n* [U] —compare IMPORT[2]

ex·pose /ɪkˈspoʊz/ *v* [T] **1** to show
something that is usually covered or not
able to be seen ‖ 대개 덮여 있거나 보이
지 않는 것을 보여 주다. 노출하다: *Her
skin has never been exposed to the sun.*
그녀의 피부는 햇빛에 노출된 적이 없다.
2 to put someone in a situation, place
etc. that could be harmful or dangerous
‖ 사람을 해롭거나 위험할 수 있는 상황·
장소 등에 두다. (위해·위험 등에) 노출
시키다. 빠뜨리다: *Smoking exposes
people to the risk of lung cancer.* 흡연은
사람들을 폐암의 위험에 노출시킨다. **3** to

help someone experience new ideas,
TRADITIONs etc. ‖ 사람이 새로운 생각·전
통 등을 경험하도록 돕다. 접촉시키다. 접
하게[닿게] 하다: *The Shinsekis exposed
me to Japanese art.* 신세키 부부는 내가
일본 예술을 접할 수 있도록 도움을 주었
다. **4** to tell people the truth about a
dishonest person, event, or situation ‖
사람들에게 부정한 사람[사건, 상황]에 대
한 사실을 이야기하다. …을 폭로하다[드
러내다]. 신고하다: *We threatened to
expose him to the police.* 우리는 그를 경
찰에 신고하겠다고 위협했다 **5** to allow
light onto a piece of film in a camera in
order to produce a photograph ‖ 사진을
만들어 내기 위해 빛이 카메라 내부의 필
름 위에 쏘이게 하다. 필름을 노출하다.
감광시키다

ex·po·sé /ˌɛkspoʊˈzeɪ/ *n* a television or
newspaper story that tells people about
a dishonest person, event, or situation
‖ 사람들에게 부정한 사람[사건, 상황]에
대해 밝히는, 텔레비전이나 신문상의 이야
기. 폭로 기사

ex·posed /ɪkˈspoʊzd/ *adj* not protected
or covered ‖ 보호되거나 감추어지지 않은.
노출된. 드러나 있는: *tiny plants
growing out of the exposed rocks* (비바
람에) 노출된 바위에서 자라는 작은 식물

ex·po·si·tion /ˌɛkspəˈzɪʃən/ *n* **1** [C, U]
a detailed explanation that is easy to
understand ‖ 이해하기 쉬운 자세한 설명.
상세한 해설 **2** a large public event at
which you show and sell a particular
type of product ‖ 특정 종류의 제품을 전
시하고 판매하는 대형 공개 행사. 박람회.
전시회

ex·po·sure /ɪkˈspoʊʒər/ *n* **1** [C, U] the
state of being put into a harmful
situation without any protection ‖ 어떤
보호도 없이 위험한 상황에 놓여진 상태.
노출: *Skin cancer is often caused by too
much exposure to the sun.* 피부암은 흔
히 너무 많은 햇빛에 노출되어 발생한다.
2 [U] an opportunity to experience new
ideas, events, methods etc. ‖ 새로운 생
각·사건·방법 등을 경험할 기회: *My first
exposure to classical music was at
college.* 내가 처음으로 클래식 음악을 접
한 것은 대학에서였다. **3** get/receive
exposure to be written or talked about
in newspapers or on television ‖ 신문이
나 텔레비전에서 쓰여지거나 이야기되다.
(언론에서) 다루다. 방영되다: *The issue
has received a lot of exposure in the
press.* 그 문제는 언론에서 많이 다루어져
왔다. **4** [C, U] the action of telling
people about a dishonest person, event,

or situation ‖ 부정한 사람[사건, 상황]에 대해 사람들에게 이야기하는 행위. 폭로: *We threatened him with public exposure.* 우리는 공개적으로 폭로하겠다고 그를 협박했다. **5** [U] the harmful effects of staying outside for a long time when the weather is extremely cold ‖ 날씨가 극도로 추울 때에 밖에 장시간 머물러 있어서 발생하는 결과. 노출에 의한 악영향: *Three climbers died of exposure in the Himalayas.* 세 명의 등산가가 히말라야의 악천후의 영향으로 사망했다. **6** the part of a film in a camera that is used for producing a photograph ‖ 사진을 만들어내는 데에 쓰이는 카메라 내의 필름의 일부. (필름의) 한 토막[화면]: *This roll has 36 exposures.* 이 필름 한 통은 36장으로 되어 있다.

ex·press¹ /ɪkˈsprɛs/ *v* [T] **1** to use words or actions in order to let people know what you are thinking or feeling ‖ 자신이 생각하거나 느끼는 바를 사람들에게 알리기 위해 말이나 행동을 하다. 표현하다. 나타내다: *A number of people expressed the fear that they would never get another job.* 많은 사람들이 다른 직업을 구하지 못할 것이라는 것에 두려움을 나타냈다. / *It's hard sometimes for children to express themselves.* 때때로 아이들이 자신을 표현하는 것은 어려운 일이다. **2 express an interest in sth** to say that you are interested in something ‖ 어떤 것에 관심 있다고 말하다. …에 관심을 표현하다: *She expressed an interest in seeing the old map.* 그녀는 오래된 지도를 살펴보는 것에 대해 관심을 나타냈다.

express² *adj* **1** specific, deliberate, or exact ‖ 특정한, 숙고한, 정확한. 명시된. 명백한: *It was her express wish that you inherit her house.* 당신이 그녀의 집을 상속받는 것은 그녀의 분명한 바람이었습니다. **2 express train/bus** a train or bus that travels quickly and does not stop in many places ‖ 많은 장소에 정차하지 않고 빠르게 운행되는 열차나 버스. 고속 열차/버스

ex·pres·sion /ɪkˈsprɛʃən/ *n* **1** a word or phrase that has a particular meaning ‖ 특정한 의미를 지니는 단어나 구. 표현: *You use the expression "break a leg" to wish an actor good luck.* 배우에게 행운을 빈다고 할 때 "break a leg"라는 표현을 쓴다. **2** a look on someone's face that shows what s/he is thinking or feeling ‖ 생각이나 느낌을 나타내는 얼굴 표정: *a cheerful expression* 활기찬 표정 **3** [C, U] something that you say, do, or write

that shows what you think or feel ‖ 생각이나 느낌을 나타내기 위해 말하는[행하는, 쓰는] 것. 표시: *I'm sending these flowers as an expression of my thanks.* 감사의 표시로 이 꽃을 보냅니다.

ex·pres·sion·less /ɪkˈsprɛʃənlɪs/ *adj* an expressionless face or voice does not show what someone feels or thinks ‖ 얼굴이나 목소리에서 감정이나 생각이 나타나지 않는. 감정 표현이 없는

ex·pres·sive /ɪkˈsprɛsɪv/ *adj* showing what someone thinks or feels ‖ 생각하거나 느끼는 것을 나타내는. 표현하는. 의미심장한: *He has really expressive eyes.* 그는 정말 표정이 풍부한 눈을 가지고 있다.

ex·press·ly /ɪkˈsprɛsli/ *adv* FORMAL in a detailed or exact way ‖ 자세하거나 정확하게. 정확히. 명백히: *Mr. Samson expressly asked you to leave.* 삼손 씨는 분명히 너에게 떠나 달라고 요구했다.

ex·press·way /ɪkˈsprɛsˌweɪ/ *n* a very wide road in a city on which cars can travel at a fast speed ‖ 차들이 빠른 속도로 달릴 수 있는 도시 내의 아주 넓은 도로. 고속도로

ex·pro·pri·ate /ɛksˈproʊpriˌeɪt/ *v* [T] FORMAL to take away someone's private property for public use ‖ 남의 사유 재산을 공공의 용도로 빼앗다. 수용(收用)하다 – **expropriation** /ɛksˌproʊpriˈeɪʃən/ *n* [C, U]

ex·pul·sion /ɪkˈspʌlʃən/ *n* [C, U] the official act of making someone leave a country, school, or organization ‖ 사람을 국가[학교, 단체]에서 떠나게 하는 공식적 행위. 추방. 제적. 제명: *the expulsion of Communists from the government* 정부에서의 공산주의자들에 대한 축출

ex·quis·ite /ɪkˈskwɪzɪt, ˈɛkskwɪ-/ *adj* extremely beautiful and delicate, and seeming to be perfect ‖ 극도로 아름답고 섬세하며 완벽해 보이는. 매우 아름다운. 훌륭한. 절묘한. 정교한: *an exquisite piece of jewelry* 정교한 보석 한 점 – **exquisitely** *adv*

ex·tem·po·ra·ne·ous /ɪkˌstɛmpəˈreɪniəs, ɛk-/ *adj* spoken or done without any preparation or practice ‖ 어떤 준비나 연습 없이 말하거나 행해진. 즉석의. 즉흥적인: *an extemporaneous speech* 즉석 연설

ex·tend /ɪkˈstɛnd/ *v* **1** [I] to continue, reach, or stretch ‖ 지속하다, 도달하다, 뻗치다. 확장하다. 뻗다: *The river extends for more than 200 miles through the Grand Canyon.* 그 강은 그

랜드 캐년을 통과해 200마일 이상 뻗어 있다. / *The 90° weather extended into late September.* 90도에 육박하는 날씨가 9월 말까지 계속되었다. **2** [T] to increase something in size or amount of time ‖ 시간의 크기나 양에 있어서 어떤 것을 증가시키다. 연장하다: *Immigration is extending her visa by another six months.* 출입국관리소는 그녀의 비자를 6개월 더 연장해 주고 있다. **3** [I, T] to be able to be used in more than one way or by more than one person or group ‖ 하나 이상의 방법으로, 또는 한 명이나 하나의 단체 이상이 쓸 수 있게 되다. …의 범위를 넓히다[확대하다]: *My insurance policy can be extended to cover my family too.* 내 보험 증권은 가족에게도 확대 적용될 수 있다. **4** [T] FORMAL to offer someone help, thanks, sympathy etc. ‖ 남에게 도움·감사·동정 등을 주다. 베풀다: *We'd like to extend a welcome/greeting to all our new members.* 우리 신입 회원들 모두에게 따뜻한 환영/인사의 말을 전하고 싶습니다. **5** [T] to stretch out a part of your body ‖ 신체 일부를 바깥쪽으로 뻗다. 내밀다

ex·tend·ed fam·i·ly /.ˌ.. ˈ../ *n* a family that includes parents, children, grandparents, AUNTs etc. ‖ 부모·아이들·조부모·고모 등을 포함하는 가족. 확대 가족 —compare NUCLEAR FAMILY

ex·ten·sion /ɪkˈstɛnʃən/ *n* **1 a)** the set of additional numbers for a particular telephone line in a large building ‖ 대형 빌딩 내의 특정 전화선에 대한 일련의 부가 번호. 내선(번호). 구내 전화(번호): *Hello, I'd like extension 1334, please.* 안녕하세요. 내선 1334번 부탁합니다. **b)** one of the telephones in a house, that all have the same number ‖ 번호가 모두 같은 집안의 전화기들 중 하나 **2** [C usually singular] an additional period of time that someone is given to finish a job, pay money that s/he owes etc. ‖ 일을 끝내거나 빚진 돈을 갚는 데에 주어진 추가 기간. 연장. 연기. 유예: *The professor gave me a two-week extension on my paper.* 교수님은 내 논문 기한을 2주 연장해 주셨다. **3** [C, U] the process of making something bigger or longer, or the part that is added in this process ‖ 어떤 것을 더 크거나 길게 하는 과정, 또는 이 과정에서 추가된 부분. 확장. 확대. 연장. 확장[연장] 부분: *The city is building an extension to the subway line.* 시에서는 지하철의 연장선을 건설 중이다. **4** [singular, U] the process of increasing something that is already

there ‖ 이미 그곳에 있는 것을 늘리는 과정. 확대: *the extension of Soviet power in Eastern Europe* 동유럽 내 소련 영향력의 확대

extension cord /.ˈ.. ˌ./ *n* an additional piece of electric wire that you attach to another wire in order to make it longer ‖ 전기선을 더 길게 만들기 위해 다른 전기선에 덧붙이는 추가 전선. (전기 기기의) 연장[이음] 코드

ex·ten·sive /ɪkˈstɛnsɪv/ *adj* **1** containing a lot of information, details, work etc. ‖ 많은 정보·세부 사항·작업 등을 포함하는. 광범위한: *Doctors have done extensive research into the effects of stress.* 의사들은 스트레스의 영향에 대한 폭넓은 연구를 해 왔다. **2** very large in the size, amount, or degree of something ‖ 사물의 크기[양, 정도]가 매우 큰. 막대한: *Forests were destroyed due to extensive logging.* 막대한 양의 벌목으로 인해 삼림이 파괴되었다.

ex·tent /ɪkˈstɛnt/ *n* **1** [U] the limit, size, or degree of something ‖ 어떤 일의 한도[크기, 정도]: *What's the extent of the damage?* 피해 정도는 얼마나 됩니까? **2 to some extent/to a certain extent/to a large extent** used when saying that something is partly but not completely true ‖ 전체가 사실인 것은 아니지만 부분적으로는 사실이라는 것을 말할 때 쓰여. 어느 정도는[다소]/대부분은 [크게]: *To some extent, you're right.* 어느 정도는 네가 옳다. **3 to such an extent that/to the extent that/to the extent of** used when saying that something is affected or influenced so much that something else happens ‖ 어떤 일이 다른 일로부터 많은 영향을 받아 발생하는 것을 말할 때에 쓰여. …할 정도까지: *The building was damaged to such an extent that it had to be knocked down.* 그 건물은 철거해야 할 정도까지 훼손됐었다.

ex·te·ri·or¹ /ɪkˈstɪriɚ/ *n* the appearance or outside surface of something ‖ 사물의 모습이나 바깥 표면. 외관. 외형. 외모: *the exterior of the house* 집의 외관 / *Her calm exterior hid her intense anger.* 그녀의 차분한 겉모습은 강렬한 분노를 감춘 것이었다. —opposite INTERIOR¹

exterior² *adj* on the outside or outside surface of something ‖ 바깥쪽에 있는, 또는 외면에 있는. …의 외부의. 외면적인. 외관상의: *the exterior walls of the church* 교회의 외벽 —opposite INTERIOR²

ex·ter·mi·nate /ɪkˈstɚməˌneɪt/ *v* [T] to kill most or all members of a particular group of people, animals, or insects ‖ 특정 무리의 사람들[동물, 곤충]의 대부분, 또는 전부를 죽이다. 박멸하다. 멸종[전멸]시키다 **– exterminator** n **– extermination** /ɪkˌstɜːmə'neɪʃən/ n [C, U]

ex·ter·nal /ɪk'stɜːnl/ adj **1** coming from outside something ‖ 사물의 바깥쪽에서 오는. 외부에서 오는. 외인적인: *The plant must live in constantly changing external conditions.* 식물은 끊임없이 변화하는 외부 조건 속에서 살아야 한다. **2** relating to the outside of something ‖ 사물의 바깥쪽과 관련된. 외부의. 외부에 쓰는: *This medicine is for external use only.* 이 약은 외용(外用)으로만 쓴다. **—** opposite INTERNAL

ex·tinct /ɪk'stɪŋkt/ adj an extinct plant, animal, or language no longer exists ‖ 식물[동물, 언어] 등이 더 이상 존재하지 않는. 사멸한. 멸종한

ex·tinc·tion /ɪk'stɪŋkʃən/ n [U] the state of being EXTINCT ‖ 멸종 상태. 멸종. 단절. 소멸: *Greenpeace believes that whales are in danger of extinction.* 그린피스는 고래가 멸종 위기에 처해 있다고 믿고 있다.

ex·tin·guish /ɪk'stɪŋgwɪʃ/ v [T] **1** to make a fire or light stop burning or shining ‖ 불이나 빛이 타거나 빛나는 것을 멈추게 하다. 끄다. 소화[소등]하다: *Please extinguish all cigarettes.* 담뱃불을 모두 꺼주세요. **2** LITERARY to destroy an idea or feeling ‖ 생각이나 감정을 파괴하다. 잃게 하다: *The news extinguished all hope of his return.* 그 뉴스로 인해 그가 돌아오리라는 모든 희망이 사라졌다.

ex·tin·guish·er /ɪk'stɪŋgwɪʃər/ n ⇨ FIRE EXTINGUISHER

ex·tol /ɪk'stoʊl/ v **-lled, -lling** [T] to praise something very much ‖ 어떤 일을 아주 많이 칭찬하다. 격찬[칭송, 찬양]하다: *Jaime was extolling the virtues of being vegetarian.* 제이미는 채식주의자의 장점을 격찬하고 있었다.

ex·tort /ɪk'stɔːrt/ v [T] to force someone to give you money by threatening him/her ‖ 남을 위협하여 강제로 돈을 받다. 강요로 돈을 빼앗다[강탈하다]: *The policemen were actually extorting money from drug dealers.* 경찰이 사실상 마약 밀매업자들로부터 돈을 강취(強取)하고 있었다. **– extortion** /ɪk'stɔːrʃən/ n [U]

ex·tor·tion·ate /ɪk'stɔːrʃənɪt/ adj too expensive or unfair ‖ 너무 비싸거나 부당한. 폭리의. 터무니없는. 엄청난: *an extortionate price for a hotel room* 터무

니없이 요금이 비싼 호텔 방

ex·tra¹ /'ɛkstrə/ adj more than the usual or standard amount of something ‖ 어떤 것의 평소 또는 기준량 이상인. 여분의: *a large mushroom pizza with extra cheese* 보통보다 더 많은 치즈가 들어 있는 대형 버섯 피자

extra² adv **1** being more money than the usual amount ‖ 평소보다 더 많은 금액으로. 할증의. 별도[추가]의: *You have to pay extra if you want to travel first class.* 1등석으로 여행하려면 추가 요금을 내야 합니다. **2** used when emphasizing an adjective or adverb ‖ 형용사나 부사를 강조할 때에 쓰여. 특별[각별]히. 남달리: *If you're extra good I'll buy you an ice cream.* 네가 특별히 잘 하면 아이스크림을 사줄게.

extra³ n **1** something that is added to a product or service and that usually costs more ‖ 상품이나 용역에 추가되어 대개 값이 더 나가는 것. 가외의 것: *a car with extras such as a sun roof and CD player* 선루프와 시디플레이어 등의 별도 추가 사양이 장착된 차 **2** an actor who is not a main character in a movie but pretends to be part of a crowd ‖ 영화의 주인공이 아닌 군중의 일부를 연기하는 배우. 엑스트라. 단역 배우

ex·tract¹ /ɪk'strækt/ v [T] **1** to remove an object or substance from the place where it belongs or comes from ‖ 어떤 물체나 물질을 그것이 있는 곳이나 생겨난 곳에서 떼어내다. …에서부터 뽑다[빼내다]. 추출하다: *I'm having my wisdom teeth extracted.* 나는 사랑니를 뽑으려고 한다. / *Olive oil is extracted from green olives.* 올리브기름은 초록색 올리브에서 추출된다. **2** to make someone give you information, money etc. that s/he does not want to give ‖ 정보·돈 등을 제공하고 싶어하지 않는 사람에게 그것들을 제공하게 만들다. …을 얻다. 끌어내다. 끄집어내다: *The police couldn't extract any information from him.* 경찰은 그에게서 어떤 정보도 캐내지 못했다.

ex·tract² /'ɛkstrækt/ n **1** a small part of a story, poem, song etc. ‖ 이야기, 시, 노래 등의 일부. 발췌: *an extract from "A Midsummer Night's Dream"* "한 여름밤의 꿈"에서의 발췌 **2** [C, U] a substance that is removed from a root, flower etc. by a special process ‖ 특수한 과정에 의해 뿌리·꽃 등에서 추출된 물질: *vanilla extract* 바닐라 추출물

ex·trac·tion /ɪk'strækʃən/ n **1** [C, U] the process of removing an object or substance from something else ‖ 다른 사

물에서 물체나 물질을 빼내는 과정. 적출. 추출: *the extraction of coal and other natural resources* 석탄 및 다른 천연 자원의 추출 **2 of French/Irish etc. extraction** having family members who come from France etc. even though you were born in another country ‖ 다른 나라에서 태어났다 하더라도 가족들이 프랑스 등의 출신인. 프랑스/아일랜드계의

ex·tra·cur·ric·u·lar /ˌɛkstrəkəˈrɪkyələ/ *adj* extracurricular activities are sports, classes etc. that you do for fun and are not part of the usual work you do for school ‖ 학교 수업의 일부로서가 아니라 재미로 스포츠·수업 등 교과목 외의 활동을 하는. 정식 과목 이외의. 과외의

ex·tra·dite /ˈɛkstrəˌdaɪt/ *v* [T] to send someone who may be guilty of a crime back to the country where the crime happened ‖ 어떤 범죄에 대한 혐의를 받고 있는 사람을 그 범죄가 발생한 나라로 넘겨주다. 도주 범인 등을 당국에 인도하다 **– extradition** /ˌɛkstrəˈdɪʃən/ *n* [C, U]

ex·tra·ne·ous /ɪkˈstreɪniəs/ *adj* FORMAL not directly related to a particular subject or problem ‖ 특정 주제나 문제에 직접적으로 연관되지 않은. 본질과 관계없는. …과 관계없는. 본질에서 벗어난. 이질적인: *His report contains too many extraneous details.* 그의 보고서에는 직접 관련이 없는 세부 사항들이 지나치게 많이 포함되어 있다.

ex·traor·di·nar·y /ɪkˈstrɔrdnˌɛri/ *adj* very unusual, special, or surprising ‖ 매우 특이한[특별한, 놀랄 만한]. 비범한. 별난: *Ellington had an extraordinary musical talent.* 엘링턴은 비범한 음악적 재능을 갖고 있다.

ex·trap·o·late /ɪkˈstræpəˌleɪt/ *v* [I, T] FORMAL to use the information you already know in order to guess what will happen ‖ 일어날 일을 추측하기 위해 이미 알고 있는 정보를 이용하다. 추론[추정]하다

ex·tra·ter·res·tri·al /ˌɛkstrətəˈrɛstriəl/ *n* a living creature that people think may live on another PLANET ‖ 다른 행성에 살지도 모른다고 생각되는 생명체. 지구 밖의 생물. 우주인 **– extraterrestrial** *adj*

ex·trav·a·gant /ɪkˈstrævəgənt/ *adj* **1** spending a lot of money on things that are not necessary, or costing a lot of money ‖ 필요하지 않거나 값이 많이 나가는 것에 많은 돈을 쓰는. 사치스러운: *the extravagant lifestyles of movie stars* 영화 배우들의 사치스러운 생활 /

extravagant parties 사치스러운 파티 **2** unusual and exciting, but not practical or reasonable ‖ 특이하고 흥미롭지만 실용적이거나 합리적이지 않은. 터무니없는. 도를 지나친: *extravagant claims that the drug cures AIDS* 마약이 에이즈를 치료한다는 터무니없는 주장 **– extravagantly** *adv* **– extravagance** *n* [C, U]

ex·treme¹ /ɪkˈstrim/ *adj* **1** very great ‖ 매우 심한. 극도의. 극심한. 지나친: *Mountain climbers face extreme danger.* 등산가들은 극심한 위험에 직면한다. **2** extreme opinions, actions, conditions etc. are not acceptable because they are very unusual or unreasonable ‖ 견해·행동·상태 등이 너무 특이하거나 합리적이지 않아서 받아들일 수 없는. 극단적인: *Mr. Wong uses extreme methods to discipline his students.* 웡 씨는 학생들을 훈련시키기 위해 극단적인 방법들을 사용한다. **3 extreme example/case** the strangest, most unusual, or most unlikely possibility ‖ 가장 이상한[특이한, 가능성이 없는]. 희박한[희귀한] 예/경우: *In an extreme case, pregnant women who use this drug may harm the baby.* 가능성은 희박하지만 이 약을 임산부가 복용한다면 태아에게 해로울 수 있습니다.

extreme² *n* **1** one of the limits to a range of things, such as temperatures, actions, or emotions ‖ 온도[행동, 감정] 등의 범위의 한계. 극단. 극도: *Seals can survive extremes of hot summers and very cold winters.* 바다표범은 극심한 여름 더위와 매서운 겨울 날씨에서 살아남을 수 있다. / *between the extremes of joy and depression* 기쁨과 슬픔의 극단 사이에 **2 in the extreme** to a very great degree or amount ‖ 매우 심한 정도나 양까지. 극단적으로. 극도로. 극히

ex·treme·ly /ɪkˈstrimli/ *adv* to a very great degree ‖ 매우 심한 정도까지. 극단적으로. 극도로. 대단히: *Wilma's little girl is extremely pretty.* 윌마의 작은딸은 아주 예쁘다.

ex·trem·ist /ɪkˈstrimɪst/ *n* someone who has extreme political aims, and who is willing to do unusual or illegal things to achieve them ‖ 극단적인 정치적 목표를 갖고 있으면서 그것을 달성하기 위해 통상적이 아니거나 불법적인 일들을 하려고 하는 사람. 극단론자. 과격주의자 **– extremist** *adj* **– extremism** *n* [U]

ex·trem·i·ties /ɪkˈstrɛmətiz/ *n* [plural] your hands, feet, legs, or arms ‖ 손, 발, 다리, 팔. 수족

ex·trem·i·ty /ɪkˈstrɛməti/ *n* the area

farthest from something ‖ 어떤 것으로부터 가장 먼 지역. 맨 끝. 선단. 말단: *the city's northern extremity* 도시의 최북단

ex·tri·cate /'ɛkstrəˌkeɪt/ *v* [T] to get someone out of a place or a difficult situation ‖ 사람을 어떤 장소나 어려운 상황에서 빼내다. 구출하다: *They couldn't extricate themselves from the huge crowd of people.* 그들은 거대한 인파 속에서 빠져나올 수 없었다.

ex·tro·vert·ed /'ɛkstrəˌvɜˈtɪd/ *n* confident and enjoying being with other people ‖ 남들과 같이 있는 것에 자신있어 하고 즐거워하는. 사교적인. 외향적인 – **extrovert** *n* —compare INTROVERTED

ex·u·ber·ant /ɪg'zubərənt/ *adj* very happy, excited, and full of energy ‖ 매우 행복한·흥분된·활기로 가득한. 원기 왕성한. 활기찬: *the exuberant bride* 활기찬 신부 – **exuberance** *n* [U]

ex·ude /ɪg'zud, ɪk'sud/ *v* **1** [T] to show that you have a lot of a particular feeling ‖ 특정한 느낌을 많이 가지고 있음을 보이다. 발산하다. 드러내다: *new students exuding excitement* 흥분을 감추지 못하는 신입생들 **2** [I, T] to flow out slowly and steadily, or to make liquid do this ‖ 액체가 서서히 꾸준하게 흘러나오다. 또는 이렇게 흘러 나오게 하다

ex·ult /ɪg'zʌlt/ *v* [I] to be very happy and proud because you have achieved something ‖ 어떤 일을 달성했기 때문에 매우 행복하고 자랑스러워하다. (…으로) 기뻐 날뛰다. 미칠 듯이 기뻐하다: *The people exulted over the defeat of their enemy.* 사람들은 적을 물리친 것에 대해 뛸 듯이 기뻐했다. – **exultant** *adj* – **exultation** /ˌɛgzʌl'teɪʃən, ˌɛksʌl-/ *n* [U]

eye

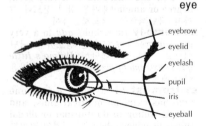

- eyebrow
- eyelid
- eyelash
- pupil
- iris
- eyeball

eye¹ /aɪ/ *n*

1 ▶SEE 보다◀ one of the two parts of your body that you see with ‖ 사물을 볼 수 있는 2개의 신체 부위중 하나. 눈: *Gina has blue eyes.* 지나는 푸른 눈을 가지고 있다. / *My eyes are going bad; I think I need glasses.* 나는 시력이 나빠지고 있어서 안경을 써야 할 것 같아.

2 keep an eye on sb/sth INFORMAL to watch what someone or something does in order to prevent something bad from happening ‖ 나쁜 일이 일어나지 못하도록 사람이 행하는 일이나 사물이 어떻게 되어 가는 것을 주시하다. …을 감시하다. …에서 눈을 떼지 않다: *Can you keep an eye on the baby while I go to the store?* 내가 가게 가는 동안 아이 좀 봐줄래?

3 lay/set eyes on sb/sth SPOKEN a phrase meaning to see someone or something ‖ '사람이나 사물을 보다'라는 의미의 어구: *The first time I laid eyes on him I knew I liked him.* 그를 처음 보았을 때 내가 그를 좋아한다는 것을 알았다.

4 cannot take your eyes off sb/sth to be unable to stop looking at someone or something because s/he or it is so attractive or interesting ‖ 사람이나 사물이 아주 매력적이거나 흥미로워서 계속 바라보다. …에서 눈을 뗄 수 없다: *You looked so pretty I just couldn't take my eyes off you.* 네가 너무 예뻐 보여서 난 그저 눈을 뗄 수 없었어.

5 make eye contact to look directly at someone while s/he is looking at you ‖ 자신을 바라보고 있는 사람을 똑바로 쳐다보다. 눈을 맞추다: *We made eye contact on the bus.* 우리는 버스에서 눈을 맞췄다.

6 keep an eye out for sb/sth to look around in order to find someone or something, even though you are doing other things at the same time ‖ 다른 일을 하고 있더라도 사람이나 사물을 찾기 위해 동시에 주변을 둘러보다. …을 살피다[경계하다]. 빈틈없이 감시하다: *Keep an eye out for Rick's car.* 릭의 차를 잘 지켜봐라.

7 in the eyes of the law/world/police etc. in the opinion or the judgment of the law, world, etc. ‖ 법·세계 등의 의견이나 판단에 있어서. 법/세계/경찰의 관점[견해]에서: *Divorce is a sin in the eyes of the Catholic Church.* 가톨릭 교회의 관점에서 보면 이혼은 죄악이다.

8 have your eye on sb to notice someone that you think is so attractive or interesting that you want to meet him/her ‖ 자신이 생각하기에 만나보고 싶을 정도로 아주 매력적이고 관심이 가는 사람을 주목하다. …에 눈독을 들이고 있다. …을 탐내고 있다: *Mark really has his eye on Yvonne.* 정말로 마크는 이본에게 눈독을 들이고 있다.

9 have your eye on sth to have noticed something that you want to buy or have ‖ 사거나 갖고 싶은 것에 주목하다: *Harris has his eye on a two-story*

house in Woodside. 해리스는 우드사이드
에 있는 2층 집에 눈독을 들이고 있다.

10 drop/lower your eyes to look down,
especially because you are shy,
embarrassed, or ashamed ‖ 특히 수줍어
서[당황해서, 창피해서] 내려다보다. 눈을
떨구다[내리깔다]: *She looked up, saw
him staring at her, and lowered her
eyes again.* 그녀는 위를 올려다보고 그가
자신을 빤히 쳐다보는 것을 알고는, 다시
눈을 떨구었다.

**11 blue-eyed/one-eyed/bright-eyed
etc.** having blue eyes, one eye, bright
eyes etc. ‖ 푸른 눈의, 애꾸눈의, 눈매가 시
원한

12 ▶NEEDLE 바늘◀ the hole in a needle
that you put thread through ‖ 실을 꿰어
넣는 바늘의 구멍. 바늘 구멍

13 ▶STORM 폭풍◀ the calm center of a
storm such as a CYCLONE or HURRICANE ‖
싸이클론이나 허리케인 등 폭풍의 고요한
중심. 태풍의 눈 —see also **catch sb's
eye** (CATCH¹), **look sb in the eye** (LOOK¹)

eye² *v* **eyed, eyed, eyeing or eying**
[T] to look at someone in a way that
shows you think s/he is sexually
attractive ‖ 상대방에게 성적 매력이 있다
고 생각한다는 것을 나타내는 투로 상대를
쳐다보다. 유혹의 눈길로 바라보다:
*Sarah kept eyeing my boyfriend all
night.* 사라는 밤새 내 남자 친구를 유혹의
눈길로 바라보았다.

eye·ball /ˈaɪbɔl/ *n* the whole of your
eye, including the part that is inside
your head ‖ 머리 속에 있는 부분을 포함
하는 눈 전체. 눈알, 안구 —see picture
at EYE¹

eye·brow /ˈaɪbraʊ/ *n* the line of short
hairs above your eye ‖ 눈 위에 있는 짧은
털로 이루어진 선. 눈썹 —see picture at
EYE¹ and HEAD¹

eye-catch·ing /ˈ. ͵../ *adj* something
that is eye-catching is so unusual or
attractive that you notice it ‖ 사물이 아

주 독특하거나 매력적이어서 주목하게 되
는. 남의 눈길을 끄는: *an eye-catching
dress* 눈길을 끄는 드레스

eye·lash /ˈaɪlæʃ/ *n* one of the small
hairs that grow on the edge of your
EYELID ‖ 눈꺼풀 가장자리에서 자라는 짧은
털들 중의 하나. 속눈썹 —see picture at
EYE¹

eye·lid /ˈaɪˌlɪd/ *n* the piece of skin that
covers your eye when it is closed ‖ 눈을
감을 때 눈을 덮는 피부 부위. 눈꺼풀 —
see picture at EYE¹

eye-o·pen·er /ˈ. ͵.../ *n* [singular] an
event, situation etc. that makes you
learn something surprising ‖ 어떤 놀라
운 것을 알게 하는 사건·상황 등. 놀라운
경험. 눈이 휘둥그레지는 사실: *The
documentary about runaway children
was a real eye-opener for me.* 가출한 아
이들에 관한 다큐멘터리는 나에게 정말 놀
라운 사건이었다.

eye·shad·ow /ˈaɪ͵ʃædoʊ/ *n* [U] a
colored powder women put over their
eyes to make them look attractive ‖ 매력
적으로 보이려고 여성들이 눈에 바르는 색
깔 있는 파우더. 아이섀도우

eye·sight /ˈaɪsaɪt/ *n* [U] the ability to
see ‖ 볼 수 있는 능력. 시력: *Grandma is
slowly losing her eyesight.* 할머니는 서
서히 시력을 잃어가고 있다.

eye·sore /ˈaɪsɔr/ *n* something ugly in a
place that makes an area look less nice
‖ 어떤 지역을 덜 좋아 보이게 하는 추한
것. 눈에 거슬리는 것. 눈의 가시: *The
old mall has become an eyesore.* 낡은 쇼
핑센터는 눈에 거슬리는 존재가 되어 버렸
다.

eye·wit·ness /͵aɪˈwɪtˈnɪs, ˈaɪ͵wɪtˈnɪs/
n someone who has seen a crime,
important event etc. ‖ 범죄·중대한 사건
등을 본 사람. 목격자. 증인: *According to
an eyewitness, the bomb exploded at
exactly 3:00 p.m.* 목격자에 따르면 폭탄
은 정확히 오후 세 시에 터졌다.

Ff

F, f /ɛf/ the sixth letter of the English alphabet ‖ 영어 알파벳의 여섯째 자

F¹ /ɛf/ n **1** a failing grade on a test or piece of school work ‖ 시험 또는 학업에서의 낙제 점수. 에프 **2** [C, U] the fourth note in the musical SCALE of C, or the musical KEY based on this note ‖ 다음계의 넷째 음이나 이 음을 기초로 한 조(調). 바 음. 바 조

F² **1** the written abbreviation of FAHRENHEIT ‖ Fahrenheit의 약어: *Water boils at 212° F.* 물은 화씨 212도에서 끓는다. **2** the written abbreviation of FEMALE ‖ female의 약어 **3** the written abbreviation of FALSE ‖ false의 약어

fa·ble /'feɪbəl/ n a short story, often about animals, that teaches a moral lesson ‖ 도덕적 교훈을 주는, 종종 동물에 관한 짧은 이야기. 우화

fab·ric /'fæbrɪk/ n **1** [C, U] cloth used for making clothes, curtains etc. ‖ 옷·커튼 등을 만드는 데 쓰는 천. 직물 **2** the basic structure of something such as a society, system etc. ‖ 사회·체제 등의 기본 구조. 조직. 구성 —see usage note at CLOTH

fab·ri·cate /'fæbrə,keɪt/ v [T] to make up a story, piece of information etc. in order to deceive someone; lie ‖ 사람을 속이기 위해 이야기·정보 등을 꾸미다. 조작하다. 위조하다; 거짓말하다 — **fabrication** /,fæbrə'keɪʃən/ n [C, U]

fab·u·lous /'fæbyələs/ adj **1** extremely good or impressive ‖ 매우 좋거나 인상적인. 훌륭한. 놀라운. 굉장한. 아주 멋진: *You look fabulous!* 너 대단히 멋져 보이는데! **2** unusually large in amount or size ‖ 양이나 크기에서 유별나게 큰. 엄청난: *a fabulous sum of money* 엄청난 금액 — **fabulously** adv

fa·cade, façade /fə'sɑd/ n **1** a way of behaving that hides your real feelings or character ‖ 실제의 감정이나 성격을 숨기는 행동 방식. (특히 허위의) 겉치레: *Behind that cheerful facade she's really a lonely person.* 그녀는 겉으로 보기에는 쾌활해 보이지만 실제로는 고독한 사람이다. **2** the front of a building ‖ 건물의 앞면. 정면

face¹ /feɪs/ n

1 ▶FRONT OF YOUR HEAD 앞이마◀ the front part of your head, where your eyes, nose, and mouth are ‖ 눈·코·입이 있는 머리의 앞면. 얼굴: *Jodi has such a pretty face.* 조디의 얼굴은 정말 예쁘다. / *He had a surprised look on his face.* 그의 얼굴은 놀란 표정이었다. —see picture at HEAD¹

2 ▶EXPRESSION 표정◀ an expression on someone's face ‖ 사람 얼굴의 표정: *Carl was making faces at Lisa all morning.* (=using his face to try to make her laugh, or to annoy her) 칼은 아침 내내 리사에게 (웃기거나 화나게 하는 등의) 이런 저런 표정을 짓고 있었다. / *I just couldn't keep a straight face.* (=avoid laughing) 나는 웃지 않고는 배길 수 없었다.

3 in the face of when dealing with difficult situations or danger ‖ 어려운 상황이나 위험을 처리하는 경우. …을 아랑곳하지 않고. …에도 불구하고: *cities that did well, even in the face of budget cuts* 예산의 삭감에도 불구하고 (사업을) 잘 수행한 시(市)들

4 face to face if you are face to face with someone, you are looking directly at him/her ‖ 어떤 사람을 직접적으로 쳐다보고 있는. 얼굴을 직접 맞대고: *I've never met her face to face. We've only talked on the phone.* 나는 그녀를 직접 대면한 적은 없다. 우리는 단지 전화상으로만 이야기했다.

5 ▶SURFACE 표면◀ an outside surface of an object, usually on its front ‖ 대개 사물의 앞쪽에 있는 외부 표면. 정면: *a clock face* 시계의 문자반(盤) / *the north face of Mount Rainier* 레이니어 산의 북쪽 면

6 come/be face to face with sth to have to deal with something unpleasant ‖ 불쾌한 일을 처리해야 하다. 직면하다: *It was the first time he'd ever come face to face with death.* 그가 죽음에 맞닥뜨린 것은 그것이 처음이었다.

7 on the face of it when you first consider something, before you know the details ‖ 상세한 내용을 알기 이전에, 그것에 대해 처음 고려할 때. 보기에는. 얼핏 보아서는. 표면상: *On the face of it, the data is not very helpful.* 표면상으로 그 자료는 그다지 도움이 되지 않는다.

8 lose/save face to lose or avoid losing the respect of other people ‖ 다른 사람의 존경을 잃거나 잃는 것을 피하다. 체면을 잃다/체면을 세우다: *If I win, Mosad will*

lose face and hate me even more. 만일 내가 이기면 모사드는 체면을 잃어 나를 더욱 미워할 것이다.

9 say sth to sb's face to say something to someone directly ‖ 남에게 무엇을 직접 말하다. 남의 면전에서[노골적으로] …을 말하다: *I'd never say it to his face, but his breath stinks.* 나는 그의 면전에 대고 이야기하지 않았는데도, 그의 입 냄새가 코를 찌른다.

10 what's-his-face/what's-her-face SPOKEN used instead of someone's name when you cannot remember it ‖ 남의 이름을 기억할 수 없을 때 그 대신에 쓰여. 아무개(라는 사람): *There's a letter from what's-his-face for Troy.* 트로이에게 와 무개한테서 온 편지 한 통이 있다.

11 in your face INFORMAL behavior, remarks etc. that are in your face are very direct and make people feel uncomfortable ‖ 행동·발언 등이 매우 직접적이어서 불편함을 느끼게 하는. 면전에서. 공공연히

12 get out of my face SPOKEN used in order to tell someone rudely to go away because s/he is annoying you ‖ 자신을 귀찮게 하기 때문에 남에게 가 버리라고 무례하게 말하는 데에 쓰여. 꺼져

face² *v* [T] **1** also **face up to** to accept that a difficult situation or problem exists, and to be willing to deal with it ‖ 곤란한 상황이나 문제가 존재한다는 것을 받아들이고 그것을 기꺼이 처리하려고 하다. …을 인정하다[용감히 맞서다]. …을 직시하다[직접 부딪치다]: *I hope that's the worst problem we'll have to face.* 나는 저것이 우리가 직시해야 할 최악의 문제이기를 바란다. / *Randy refuses to face the fact that he needs help.* 랜디는 자신이 도움이 필요하다는 사실을 인정하고 싶어하지 않는다. **2** to be turned or pointed in a particular direction or toward someone or something ‖ 특정 방향을 향해 또는 사람이나 사물 쪽으로 돌리거나 가리키다. …쪽을 향하다. …에 면해 있다: *Dean turned to face me.* 딘은 내 쪽을 향해 몸을 돌렸다. / *a north-facing window* 북향(北向)으로 나있는 창 / *apartments that face the ocean* 바다를 마주한 아파트 **3 be faced with sth** to be in a situation where you have to deal with something difficult ‖ 어려운 일을 처리해야 할 상황에 있다. …의 처지[상황]에 직면하다: *She's faced with some very tough choices.* 그녀는 몇 가지 아주 어려운 선택을 해야 할 처지에 직면했다. **4** to deal with someone, or talk to someone, when this is difficult ‖ 사람을 대하거나

사람에게 말하기 어려운 경우에 사람과 대면하거나 사람에게 말하다. (문제 등을 남과) 정면으로 상의하다: *You're going to have to face him sooner or later.* 너는 조만간 그와 직접 상의해야 할 것이다. **5** to play against an opponent or team in a game or competition ‖ 게임이나 경기에서 상대방 또는 상대 팀과 경기를 하다. 승부를 겨루다: *The Jets face the Dolphins in two weeks.* 제츠 팀은 2주 안에 돌핀스 팀과 시합을 한다.

face sb ↔ **down** *phr v* [T] to deal in a strong and confident way with someone who opposes you ‖ 반대하는 사람에게 강력하고 소신 있게 대처하다. 굴복시키다: *Yeltsin faced down a coup.* 옐친은 쿠데타를 진압했다.

face off *phr v* [I] to get in a position in which you are ready to fight, argue, or COMPETE with someone ‖ 어떤 사람과 싸움[논쟁, 경기]을 할 준비가 된 상태에 있다. 대결하다: *The two candidates will face off in the election in November.* 두 후보는 11월 선거에서 대결하게 된다.

face·less /ˈfeɪslɪs/ *adj* a faceless person, organization etc. is boring or is not easily noticed ‖ 사람·조직 등이 고리타분하거나 쉽게 눈에 띄지 않는. 특징이 없는. 정체불명의

face·lift /ˈfeɪslɪft/ *n* **1** a medical operation in which doctors remove loose skin on someone's face in order to make him/her look younger ‖ 사람을 더 젊어 보이게 하려고 의사가 얼굴의 늘어진 피부를 제거하는 의료 수술. 미용[안면] 성형술. 주름살 제거 수술 **2 give sth a facelift** to make something look newer or better by working on it or repairing it ‖ 사물에 작업을 하거나 수선을 해서 더 새롭게 또는 더 좋게 만들다. 개장(改裝)하다

fac·et /ˈfæsɪt/ *n* **1** one of several parts of someone's character, a situation etc. ‖ 사람의 성격·상황 등의 여러 부분 중의 하나. 한 면. 양상. 국면: *You've only seen one facet of his personality.* 너는 그의 성격 중 한 단면만을 본 것이다. **2** one of the flat sides of a cut jewel ‖ 절단한 보석의 평면 중의 하나. 깎은 면

fa·ce·tious /fəˈsiʃəs/ *adj* intended to be funny, but annoying or not suitable instead ‖ 재미있게 하려고 하지만 오히려 사람을 귀찮게 하거나 적절하지 않은. 까부는. 경박한 **– facetiously** *adv*

face val·ue /ˈ. ˌ../ *n* [U] **1** the value that is written on something such as a coin, STOCK etc., but that may not actually be what the coin etc. is worth ‖

실제 가치와 다를 수 있는 화폐·주식 등의 것에 쓰여진 가치. 액면가치: *A Treasury note with a face value of $10,000 was sold for $9998.* 액면가 1만 달러의 미국 재무부 채권이 9998 달러에 매각되었다. **2 take sth at face value** to accept something without thinking that it might not be as good or true as it seems ‖ 보이는 것 만큼 좋지 않거나 사실이 아닐지도 모른다는 생각없이 어떤 것을 받아들이다. …을 액면 그대로 믿다: *Don't take anything Burgess tells you at face value.* 버제스가 너에게 한 말을 액면 그대로 믿지 마라.

fa·cial¹ /ˈfeɪʃəl/ *adj* on the face, or relating to the face ‖ 얼굴에 있는, 또는 얼굴과 관련된. 얼굴의. 안면의: *facial hair* 얼굴에 난 털

facial² *n* a process in which your face is specially cleaned ‖ 얼굴을 특별히 깨끗하게 하는 과정. 미안술. 안면 마사지

fac·ile /ˈfæsəl/ *adj* too simple and showing a lack of careful thought or understanding ‖ 너무 단순하고 주의 깊은 생각이나 이해가 부족한 것을 나타내는. 경박한. 피상적인: *a facile argument against abortion* 낙태에 반대하는 피상적인 주장

fa·cil·i·tate /fəˈsɪləˌteɪt/ *v* [T] FORMAL to make it easier for something to happen ‖ 어떤 일이 일어나는 것을 더 수월하게 하다. 촉진하다. 조성하다: *We've hired more people to facilitate the enrollment of new students.* 우리는 신입생 등록을 용이하게 하기 위해 인원을 더 채용했다.

fa·cil·i·ties /fəˈsɪlətiz/ *n* [plural] rooms, equipment, or services that are provided for a particular purpose ‖ 특정 목적을 위해 마련된 방[설비, 용역]. 편의. 편익. 설비. 시설: *The college has excellent research facilities.* 그 대학은 우수한 연구 시설을 갖추고 있다.

fa·cil·i·ty /fəˈsɪləti/ *n* **1** a place or building used for a particular purpose ‖ 특정한 목적에 쓰이는 장소나 건물. 시설. 설비: *a sports facility* 스포츠 시설 **2** [singular] an ability to do or learn something easily ‖ 어떤 것을 쉽게 하거나 배우는 능력. 재능. 솜씨. 재주: *a facility for languages* 언어에 대한 재능

fac·sim·i·le /fækˈsɪməli/ *n* **1** an exact copy of a picture, piece of writing etc. ‖ 그림·글 등의 정확한 복사. 복제. 모사 **2** ⇨ FAX

fact /fækt/ *n* **1** something that is known to be true, or that has definitely happened ‖ 사실로 알려져 있는 것, 또는 틀림없이 발생한 일. 사실. 진실. 진상: *What are the facts of/in this case?* 이 사건의 진상은 무엇이냐? / *interesting facts about plants* 식물에 관한 흥미있는 사실 / *I appreciate the fact that you're willing to help.* 네가 기꺼이 돕겠다는 사실에 대해 나는 고맙게 생각한다. **2 in fact/as a matter of fact a)** used in order to add information ‖ 정보를 추가하는 데에 쓰여. 사실상. 실제로는: *I know her really well, in fact I had dinner with her last week.* 나는 그녀를 아주 잘 안다. 사실 지난주에 그녀와 저녁 식사를 했다. **b)** used in order to emphasize that something is true, especially when it is surprising ‖ 특히 놀랄 만한 경우에 어떤 것이 사실이라는 것을 강조하는 데 쓰여: *It's cheaper to fly, as a matter of fact.* 실제로는 비행기로 가는 편이 더 비용이 적게 든다. **3 sth is a fact of life** used in order to say that a situation exists and must be accepted ‖ 특정 상황이 존재하며 (그것을) 받아들여야 한다는 것을 말하는 데 쓰여. …이 현실이다: *Violent crime seems to have become a fact of life.* 강력 범죄가 현실이 되어 버린 것 같다. **4 the facts of life a)** the details about sex and how babies are born ‖ 성(性) 및 아기가 어떻게 태어나는지에 대한 상세한 설명. 성[출산]에 관한 상세 이야기: *Most parents have difficulty talking to their children about the facts of life.* 대다수의 부모들은 아기가 어떻게 태어나는 지에 관한 상세한 내용을 자녀에게 이야기해 주는 데에 어려움을 느낀다. **b)** the way life really is, with all its problems and difficulties ‖ 문제·어려움으로 가득 찬 실제의 인생살이. 힘든 인생의 현실

fac·tion /ˈfækʃən/ *n* a small group of people within a larger group, who have different ideas from the other members ‖ 다른 구성원들과 다른 생각을 가진 보다 큰 집단 내에 있는 소규모의 사람들. 당파. 파벌 **– factional** *adj*

fac·tor /ˈfæktɚ/ *n* **1** one of several things that influence or cause a situation ‖ 어떤 상황에 영향을 미치거나 원인이 되는 여러 것 중의 하나. 요소. 요인: *The weather could be an important factor in tomorrow's game.* 내일 경기에서는 날씨가 중요한 요인이다. **2** TECHNICAL a number that divides into another number exactly ‖ 다른 숫자를 (나머지없이) 정확하게 나누는 숫자. 인수(因數): *3 is a factor of 15.* 3은 15의 인수이다.

fac·to·ry /ˈfæktəri/ *n* a building or

F

group of buildings where goods are produced in large quantities ‖ 제품이 대량으로 생산되는 건물이나 그 건물들의 집합. 공장: *a shoe factory* 구두 공장

fac·tu·al /ˈfæktʃuəl/ *adj* based on facts ‖ 사실에 기초한. 사실의. 실제의 – **factually** *adv*

fac·ul·ty /ˈfækəlti/ *n* **1 the faculty a)** all the teachers in a particular school or college ‖ 특정한 학교나 대학의 모든 교사: *a faculty meeting* 교수 회의 **b)** the teachers in a particular department of a school or college ‖ 학교나 대학교의 특정 학부의 교수단: *the history faculty* 역사 학부 교수단 **2** FORMAL a natural ability, such as the ability to see or think ‖ 보거나 생각하는 능력 등의 타고난 능력. 재능. 수완: *the faculty of hearing* 청각

fad /fæd/ *n* something that someone likes or does for a short time, or that is fashionable for a short time ‖ 사람들이 잠시 좋아하거나 행하는 것, 또는 잠깐동안 유행하는 것. 일시적 유행: *a fad for big baggy t-shirts* 큰 자루 같은 티셔츠의 일시적 유행

fade /feɪd/ *v* **1** [I] also **fade away** to gradually disappear or become weaker ‖ 점차 사라지거나 약해지다. 희미해지다. 바래다: *Hopes of a peace settlement are beginning to fade.* 평화 정착에 대한 희망이 사라지기 시작하고 있다. **2** [I, T] to lose color or brightness, or to make something do this ‖ 색깔이나 선명도를 잃다, 또는 잃게 하다. 바래다[바래게 하다]. 희미해지다[흐릿해지다]: *faded jeans* 색이 바랜 진 바지

fade out *phr v* [I, T **fade** sth ↔ **out**] to disappear slowly or become quieter, or to make a picture or sound do this ‖ 천천히 사라지거나 더 조용해지다, 또는 상(象)이나 소리를 점점 사라지거나 조용해지게 만들다. 서서히 사라지[게 하]다. 작아지[게 하]다

Fahr·en·heit /ˈfærənˌhaɪt/ *n* [U] a scale of temperature in which water freezes at 32° and boils at 212° ‖ 물이 32도에서 얼고 212도에서 끓는 온도를 측정하는 눈금. 화씨

fail¹ /feɪl/ *v* **1** [I, T] to be unsuccessful in doing something ‖ 어떤 일을 하는 데 성공하지 못하다. 실패하다. 낙제하다: *Doctors failed to save the girl's life.* 의사들은 소녀의 생명을 구하지 못했다. / *I failed my math test.* 나는 수학 시험에서 낙제를 했다. **2** [I] to not do what is expected or needed ‖ 예상하거나 필요한 일을 하지 않다. …을 못하다: *Larry failed to present his proposal on time.*

래리는 자신의 제안을 때맞춰 제시하지 못했다. / *The wheat crop failed* (=did not grow) *due to drought.* 밀농사가 가뭄으로 인해 흉작이었다. **3 I fail to see/understand** used in order to show that you are annoyed by something that you do not accept or understand ‖ 받아들이거나 이해할 수 없는 일로 인해 화가 난다는 것을 보이는 데에 쓰여: *I fail to see the humor in this situation.* 나는 이런 상황에서 그러한 유머를 이해하지 못하겠다. **4** [I] if a bank, company etc. fails, it has to stop operating because of a lack of money ‖ 자금 부족으로 은행·회사 등이 운영을 중지하다. 파산하다. 도산하다 **5** [I] to stop working correctly or at all ‖ 제대로 또는 전혀 작동하지 못하다. 고장나다. 끊어지다: *The engine failed just after the plane took off.* 비행기가 이륙 직후 엔진이 고장 났다. **6 your courage/nerve fails** if your courage fails, you do not have it when you need it ‖ 필요할 때 용기가 없다 **7 failing sight/health** sight or health that is becoming worse ‖ 악화되고 있는 시력이나 건강

fail² *n* **without fail** FORMAL **a)** if you do something without fail, you always do it ‖ 무엇을 언제나 하는. 꼭. 반드시: *Barry comes over every Friday without fail.* 배리는 금요일마다 꼭 온다. **b)** used when telling someone that s/he must do something ‖ 어떤 일을 해야 한다고 남에게 말할 때에 쓰여. 틀림없이. 어김없이: *I want that work finished by tomorrow, without fail!* 그 작업을 내일까지 틀림없이 끝내줘야 해!

fail·ing¹ /ˈfeɪlɪŋ/ *n* a fault or weakness ‖ 결점이나 약점. 단점: *He loved her in spite of her failings.* 그는 그녀의 단점에도 불구하고 그녀를 사랑했다.

failing² *prep* used in order to say that if one thing is not possible or available, there is another one you could try ‖ 어떤 한 가지가 불가능하거나 이용할 수 없을 경우 시도해 볼 수 있는 다른 하나가 있음을 말하는 데에 쓰여. …이 없는 경우. …이 아니면: *We will probably have the conference at the Hyatt, or failing that at the Fairmont.* 우리는 아마도 하야트(호텔), 아니면 페어몬트에서 회담을 할 것이다.

fail-safe /ˈ. ˌ./ *adj* **1** a fail-safe machine, piece of equipment etc. will stop working if one part of it breaks or stops working correctly ‖ 기계·장비의 일부분이 고장나거나 제대로 작동하지 않으면 작동을 멈추는. (고장에 대비한) 안전

장치의. 2중 안전 장치를 장비한 **2 a fail-safe plan is certain to succeed** ‖ 계획이 성공이 확실한

fail·ure /'feɪlyɚ/ *n* **1** [C, U] a lack of success in achieving or doing something ‖ 어떤 것의 달성이나 수행에 성공하지 못함. 실패. 파산. 낙제: *The recession has caused the failure of many small businesses.* 경기 침체로 많은 소규모 기업들이 도산했다. / *Are teachers to blame for students' failure to learn?* 학생들의 학업 부진에 대해 교사들을 비난할 수 있을까요? / *The whole project ended in failure.* 전체 사업 계획은 실패로 끝났다. **2** someone or something that is not successful ‖ 성공하지 못한 사람이나 사물. 실패자. 낙오자. 실패작: *I feel like such a failure.* 나는 그런 실패자를 좋아하고 싶은 마음이 든다. **3** an occasion when a machine or part of your body stops working in the correct way ‖ 기계나 신체의 일부가 제대로 작동하지 않는 경우. 고장. 기능의 정지[부전(不全)]: *He died of heart failure.* 그는 심장 마비로 죽었다. / *the failure of the computer system* 컴퓨터 시스템의 고장 **4** the act of not doing something you should do or are expected to do ‖ 해야 할 일 또는 하리라고 예상한 일을 하지 않는 행위. 태만. 불이행: *We were worried about his failure to contact us.* 우리는 그와 연락이 안 되어 걱정했다.

faint¹ /feɪnt/ *adj* **1** difficult to see, hear, smell etc. ‖ 보고, 듣고, 냄새 맡는 것 등이 어려운. 약한. 희미한: *a faint sound* 희미한 소리 **2 a faint possibility/chance etc.** a very small or slight possibility etc. ‖ 매우 적거나 약간의 가능성 등. 희박한[실낱 같은] 가능성/기회: *There's still a faint hope that they might be alive.* 그들이 생존해 있을 수도 있다는 실낱 같은 희망이 여전히 존재한다. **3** feeling weak and as if you are about to become unconscious ‖ 기운이 없이 곧 의식 불명이 될 것 같은. 현기증이 나는: *He was faint with hunger.* 그는 배가 고파서 어지러웠다. **4 not have the faintest idea** to not know anything at all about something ‖ 어떤 것에 대해 전혀 아무것도 알지 못하다: *I don't have the faintest idea what you are talking about.* 네가 무슨 말을 하는지 전혀 모르겠어. – **faintly** *adv*

faint² *v* [I] to become unconscious for a short time ‖ 잠시 의식 불명이 되다. 기절하다. 까무러치다 – **faint** *n*

fair¹ /fɛr/ *adj* **1 ▶REASONABLE** 정당한◀ reasonable

and acceptable according to what people normally accept as being right ‖ 사람들이 보통 옳다고 받아들이는 것에 비추어 이치에 맞고 수용할 만한. 정당한. 올바른: *That's not fair! You went last time—I want to go.* 그것은 공평하지 않아! 너는 지난번에 갔잖아. (이번엔) 내가 가고 싶어. / *What do you think is the fairest solution?* 너는 가장 정당한 해결 방법이 무엇이라고 생각하니?

2 ▶EQUAL 동등한◀ treating everyone in an equal way ‖ 모든 사람을 동등하게 대우하는. 동등한. 공평한: *That law isn't fair to women.* 그 법률은 여성에게는 공정하지 않다.

3 ▶AVERAGE 평균◀ neither particularly good nor particularly bad ‖ 특별히 좋지도 특별히 나쁘지도 않은. 어지간한. 보통[평균] 정도의: *Her written work is excellent but her practical work is only fair.* 그녀의 서면상의 업무는 우수하지만 그녀의 실제 업무는 보통 정도일 뿐이다.

4 ▶ACCORDING TO RULES 규칙에 따른◀ played or done according to the rules ‖ 규칙에 따라 경기하거나 행해진. 규칙에 맞는. 정정당당한: *free and fair elections* 자유롭고 정정당당한 선거

5 fair share a reasonable and acceptable amount of something ‖ 이치에 맞고 받아들일 수 있는 사물의 양. 공평한[정당한] 몫: *Tim's had more than his fair share of bad luck this year.* 팀은 금년에 그가 받을 만한 몫 이상의 악운을 겪었다.

6 ▶HAIR/SKIN 머리털/피부◀ light in color ‖ 색깔이 밝은

7 ▶WEATHER 날씨◀ sunny ‖ 갠. 맑은

8 fair game someone or something that you can criticize or try to get ‖ 비판할 수 있거나 얻고자 시도할 수 있는 사람이나 사물. (공격·조소 등의) 좋은 목표[대상]: *Reporters seem to think movie stars are fair game just because they are public figures.* 기자들은 영화 배우들이 공인(公人)이기 때문에 그들을 비판의 좋은 대상으로 생각하는 것 같다.

9 give/get a fair shake to treat someone, or to be treated, fairly, so that everyone has the same chance ‖ 모든 사람들이 동일한 기회를 갖도록 사람을 공정하게 대우하거나 대우받다. 공평한 취급[대우]를 하다/받다: *Women don't always get a fair shake in business.* 여성들은 업계에서 항상 공정한 대우를 받지 못한다.

10 ▶BEAUTY 아름다움◀ LITERARY beautiful ‖ 아름다운 – **fairness** *n* [U]

fair² *adv* **1 fair and square** in a fair and honest way ‖ 공평하고 정직하게. 올바르게. 정당하게: *They won fair and square.* 그들은 정정당당하게 승리했다. **2** play fair to play or behave in a fair and honest way ‖ 공평하고 정직하게 경기를 하거나 행동하다

fair³ *n* **1** an outdoor event, at which there are large machines to ride on, games to play, and sometimes farm animals being judged and sold ‖ 올라타는 대형 기구 및 놀이와 때로는 감정을 받고 매매되는 가축들이 있는 야외 행사. 품평회 **2** a regular event where companies show and advertise their products ‖ 회사가 자사 제품을 전시하고 광고하는 정기적인 행사. 박람회. 견본 시장: *a trade fair* 무역 박람회

fair·ground /ˈfɛrgraʊnd/ *n* an open space on which a fair takes place ‖ 박람회가 개최되는 공개된 공간. 개최장. 전람회장

fair·ly /ˈfɛrli/ *adv* **1** more than a little, but much less than very ‖ a little(약간의)보다는 많지만 very(매우·아주)보다는 아주 적은. 상당히. 패: *She speaks English fairly well.* 그녀는 영어를 상당히 잘 구사한다. **2** in a way that is honest or reasonable ‖ 정직하거나 정당하게. 정정당당하게. 합법적으로: *I felt that I hadn't been treated fairly.* 나는 정당하게 대우를 받지 못했다고 느꼈다.

fair·y /ˈfɛri/ *n* a very small imaginary creature with magic powers, that looks like a person with wings ‖ 날개 달린 사람처럼 생긴 마력을 지닌 아주 작은 상상의 피창조물. 요정

fairy tale /ˈ.. ˌ./ *n* a story for children in which magical things happen ‖ 마술적인 일이 일어나는 어린이들을 위한 이야기. 동화

fait ac·com·pli /ˌfeɪt əkɑmˈpli, ˌfɛt ækɔmˈpli/ *n* [singular] something that has already happened and cannot be changed ‖ 이미 발생하여 변경할 수 없는 일. 기정 사실

faith /feɪθ/ *n* **1** [U] a strong belief that someone or something can be trusted to be right or to do the right thing ‖ 사람이나 사물이 옳거나 옳은 일을 한다고 믿을 수 있는 강한 신념. 자신. 확신: *I have great faith in her ability to succeed.* 나는 그녀가 성공할 만한 능력을 가졌다고 확신한다. **2** [U] belief and trust in God ‖ 신에 대한 믿음과 신뢰. 신앙: *a strong faith in God's power to heal* 병을 치료하는 신의 권능에 대한 강한 믿음 **3 in good faith** with honest and sincere intentions

‖ 정직하고 진지한 의도로. 성실하게: *The guy who sold me the car claimed he had acted in good faith.* 나에게 자동차를 판 매한 녀석이 자기가 성실하게 굴었다고 주장했다. **4** a religion ‖ 종교: *the Jewish faith* 유대교

faith·ful /ˈfeɪθfəl/ *adj* **1** showing loyalty and giving continuous support to someone or something ‖ 사람이나 사물에 충성을 보이며 지속적인 지원을 하는. 충실한. 성실한: *a faithful friend* 신의가 두터운 친구 **2** describing an event or copying an image exactly ‖ 사건을 정확히 설명하거나 상(像)을 정확히 복사하는. (원본 등에) 충실한. 정확한: *a faithful reproduction of the original picture* 원본 그림의 정확한 복원 **3** loyal to your wife, BOYFRIEND etc. by not having a sexual relationship with anyone else ‖ 다른 사람과 성관계를 갖지 않고 처·애인 등에게 충실한. 정숙한. 독실한 – **faithfulness** *n* [U]

faith·ful·ly /ˈfeɪθfəli/ *adv* in a faithful way ‖ 충실히. 성실하게. 틀림없이: *He visited his aunt faithfully.* 그는 꾸준히 숙모를 방문했다.

faith·less /ˈfeɪθlɪs/ *adj* FORMAL not able to be trusted ‖ 신뢰할 수 없는: *a faithless friend* 신뢰할 수 없는 친구

fake¹ /feɪk/ *n* **1** a copy of a valuable object, painting etc. that is intended to deceive people ‖ 사람을 속이고자 가치 있는 물건·회화 등을 복사한 것. 모조품. 위조품: *We thought it was a Picasso, but it was a fake.* 우리는 피카소 작품이었다고 생각했으나 그것은 모조품이었다. **2** someone who does not really have the knowledge, skills etc. that s/he claims to have ‖ 자신이 소유하고 있다고 주장하는 지식·기술 등을 실제로 소유하지 않은 사람. 사기꾼. 협잡꾼: *It turned out her doctor was a fake.* 그녀의 의사는 가짜로 판명되었다.

fake² *adj* made to look like a real material or object in order to deceive people ‖ 사람을 속이기 위해 물질 또는 물건을 실물처럼 보이게 만든. 위조[모조]의. 가짜의. 겉치레의: *fake fur* 인조 모피

fake³ *v* **1** [T] to make an exact copy of something, or to make up figures or results, in order to deceive people ‖ 사람을 속이기 위해 사물을 똑같이 복사하거나, 또는 숫자나 결과를 똑같이 꾸미다. …을 날조[조작]하다. 위조[모조]하다: *He faked his uncle's signature on the check.* 그는 수표에 자기 삼촌의 서명을 날조했다. **2** [I, T] to pretend to be sick, or to be interested, pleased etc. when you are not || 실제 그렇지 않을 때 아프거나 흥미가 있거나 즐거운 척하다. …인 체하다. 가장하다: *I thought he was really hurt but he was just faking it.* 나는 그가 실제로 다쳤다고 생각했지만 다친 척하고 있을 뿐이었다. **3** to pretend to move in one direction, but then move in another, especially when playing a sport || 특히 운동 경기 시에 한쪽 방향으로 움직이는 척하지만 사실은 다른 방향으로 움직이다. 페인트(feint)를 쓰다. …하는 체하다: *Everett faked a pass and ran with the ball.* 에버렛은 패스하는 척하면서 공을 몰았다.

fake sb **out** *phr v* [T] to deceive someone by making him/her think you are planning to do one thing when you are really planning something else || 실제로는 다른 일을 계획하면서 다른 사람에게는 특정한 일을 계획하고 있다고 생각하게 만들어 사람을 속이다

fal·con /ˈfælkən, ˈfɔl-/ *n* a large bird that is often trained to hunt small animals || 종종 작은 동물들을 사냥하도록 훈련된 큰 새. 매

fall¹ /fɔl/ *v* **fell, fallen, falling** [I]

fall

1 ▶THINGS FALLING 사물이 떨어짐◀ to move or drop down toward the ground || 지상으로 이동하거나 떨어지다. 낙하[추락]하다. 내리다: *as the rain/snow began to fall* 비[눈]가 내리기 시작할 무렵 / *Some of the big trees fell over in the storm.* 큰 나무 몇 그루가 폭풍에 쓰러졌다. / *apples that had fallen from the trees* 나무에서 떨어진 사과들

2 ▶PERSON FALLING 사람이 넘어짐◀ to accidentally fall onto the ground when you are standing, walking, running etc. || 사람이 서 있거나 걷거나 달리는 등의 경우에 땅바닥에 우연히 넘어지다. 쓰러지다: *Don't worry, I'll catch you if you fall.* 걱정 마라. 네가 넘어지면 내가 붙잡아 줄게. / *I slipped and fell down the stairs.* 나는 미끄러져 계단에서 굴러 떨어졌다.

3 ▶LOWER LEVEL/AMOUNT 보다 낮은 수준/양◀ to become lower in level, degree, quantity, or quality || 수준[정도, 양, 질]이 낮아지다. 감소하다. 내리다. 약해지다: *Temperatures should fall below zero tonight.* 오늘 밤 기온은 영하로 내려간다. / *The number of traffic deaths fell by 10% last year.* 교통 사고 사망자 수는 작년에 10%까지 감소했다.

4 fall asleep/ill etc. to start to sleep, be sick etc. || 잠자거나 아프기 시작하다. 잠들다/병들다: *I fell asleep at 8:30.* 나는 8시 30분에 잠들었다. / *Everyone fell silent as Beth walked in.* 베스가 걸어 들어오자 모두들 조용해졌다.

5 fall in love to begin to love someone || 누군가를 사랑하기 시작하다. 사랑에 빠지다: *Your father and I fell in love during the war.* 너의 아버지와 나는 전쟁 중에 사랑에 빠졌다.

6 ▶GROUP/PATTERN 집단/형태◀ to be part of a particular group, pattern, or range || 특정 그룹[형태, 범위]의 일부가 되다. …의 분야에 들다. 범위에 들어가다: *These substances fall into two categories.* 이들 물질은 2개의 범주에 들어간다.

7 fall into place to become organized or easy to understand || 조직화되거나 쉽게 이해되다. (논의·이야기 등이) 앞뒤가 맞다: *If you have a good outline for your paper, the rest just falls into place.* 네 논문의 개요만 잘 되어 있다면 나머지는 앞뒤가 딱 맞는다.

8 ▶HAPPEN 발생하다◀ to happen, especially at a particular time || 특히 특정한 시간에 발생하다: *Christmas falls on a Monday this year.* 금년에 크리스마스는 월요일이다.

9 ▶LIGHT/DARKNESS 밝음/어두움◀ if light or darkness falls, it makes something brighter or darker || 무엇이 더 밝아지거나 어두워지다: *A shadow fell across his face, hiding his expression.* 그림자가 그의 얼굴에 드리워져 그의 표정은 숨겨졌다. / *The lights came on as darkness/night fell on the city.* 도시에 어둠[밤]이 깔리자[되자] 불이 켜졌다.

10 ▶HANG DOWN 매달리다◀ to hang loosely || 축 늘어지다: *Maria's hair fell over her shoulders.* 마리아의 머리카락은 그녀의 어깨 위로 길게 늘어져 있었다.

11 fall short (of) to fail to achieve the result or standard you wanted || 원하는 결과나 기준을 달성하는 데 실패하다. 못미치다. 미달하다. 불충분하다. 부족하다: *Her newest book fell short of my expectations.* 그녀의 신간 서적은 나의 기대에 미치지 못했다.

12 ▶FACE 표정◀ if your face falls, you suddenly look sad or disappointed || 갑자기 슬퍼 보이거나 실망한 것처럼 보이다: *Carla's face fell as she read the dreadful news.* 칼라의 표정은 끔찍한 뉴스를 읽으면서 침울해 보였다.

13 fall flat to fail to produce the effect you wanted || 바라던 효과를 낳는 데 실패

하다. (농담 등이) 효과[반응]가 없다:
Your joke about the nuns really fell flat,
didn't it? 수녀들에 대한 네 농담은 정말
로 반응이 없었지. 안 그래?

14 fall into poverty/despair etc. to
start being poor, sad etc. ‖ 가난해지고
슬퍼지기 시작하다. 가난/절망에 빠지다:
an old house allowed to fall into
disrepair 황폐하게 방치된 낡은 집

15 ▶ DIE 죽다 ◀ to be killed or
destroyed in a war ‖ 전쟁에서 죽거나 파
괴되다: *The first man to fall in battle*
was only 18. 전투에서 첫 전사자는 18세
밖에 되지 않았다.

16 ▶ LOSE POWER 힘을 잃다◀ to fail or
lose power ‖ 권력이 쇠퇴하거나 또는 권
력을 상실하다. 몰락하다: *After World*
War II, the British Empire fell. 세계 2차
대전 후 대영제국은 몰락했다.

fall apart *phr v* [I] **1** to separate into
small pieces ‖ 작은 조각들로 갈라지다.
산산이 부서지다: *The old book fell apart*
in my hands. 그 낡은 책은 내 손안에서
조각나 버렸다. **2** to stop working
effectively ‖ 효과적으로 작동을 못하다.
무너지다. 붕괴되다: *The country's*
economy was falling apart. 국가 경제가
붕괴되고 있었다. **3** to start having
problems dealing with life or your
emotions ‖ 생활 또는 감정을 처리하는 데
문제를 갖기 시작하다: *When Pam left, I*
thought I was going to fall apart. 팸이
떠났을 때 나는 마음이 찢어질 것 같았다.

fall back on sth *phr v* [T] to use
something that is familiar or easy after
something new or difficult has failed to
work ‖ 새롭거나 어려운 것을 하는 데 실
패한 후에 익숙하거나 쉬운 것을 이용하
다. …에 의지하다. …에 의거하다:
Theaters are falling back on old
favorites rather than risking money on
new plays. 극장들은 새 연극에 위험을 무
릅쓰고 돈을 투자하기보다는 오래된 인기
작품에 의존하고 있다.

fall behind *phr v* [I, T] to not finish
something by the time you are supposed
to ‖ 예정된 시간까지 어떤 일을 완성하지
못하다. 늦어지다. 뒤지다: *The*
manufacturers have fallen behind
schedule. 제작자들은 일정보다 뒤쳐졌다.

fall for *phr v* [T] **1** [**fall for** sth] to be
tricked into believing something that is
not true ‖ 사실이 아닌 것을 믿도록 기만
당하다. …에 속다: *We told him we were*
Italian and he fell for it! 우리가 이탈리
아인이라고 그에게 말했고 그는 그것을 곧
이들었어! **2** [**fall for** sb] to suddenly feel
romantic love for someone ‖ 누구에게 갑

자기 연정을 품다. 미치다. 홀딱 반하다:
Samantha fell for a man half her age.
사만다는 자기 나이의 반밖에 안 되는 남
자에게 홀딱 반했다.

fall off *phr v* [I] to become less in
quality, amount etc. ‖ 질·양 등에서 적어
지다. 저하하다. 쇠퇴하다. 줄어들다:
Demand for records has fallen off
recently. 음반에 대한 수요가 최근 감소했
다.

fall out *phr v* [I] if a tooth or your hair
falls out, it drops out of the place where
it grows ‖ 치아나 머리카락이 자라는 자리
에서 빠지다

fall through *phr v* [I] to fail to happen
or be completed ‖ 발생하거나 완성되지
못하다. 수포로 돌아가다. 실현되지 않다:
The deal fell through at the last
minute. 그 거래는 마지막 순간에 수포로
돌아갔다.

fall² *n* **1** the season between summer
and winter, when the weather becomes
cooler; AUTUMN ‖ 여름과 겨울 사이의 기
후가 서늘해지는 계절. 가을; ㋐ autumn:
Brad's going to Georgia Tech in the fall.
브래드는 가을에 조지아 공과 대학에 갈
거다. / *Dad's going to retire this fall.* 아
빠는 이번 가을에 은퇴하실 거다. /
last/next fall (=the fall before or after
this one) 작년[내년] 가을 **2** a decrease
in the level, quantity, price etc. of
something ‖ 사물의 수준·양·가격 등의 하
락. 저하: *a sudden fall in temperature*
기온의 갑작스런 저하 —opposite RISE² **3**
the act of falling ‖ 떨어지는 행위. 추락:
He had a bad fall from a ladder. 그는 사
다리에서 떨어져 심하게 다쳤다. **4**
[singular] a situation when someone or
something is defeated or loses power ‖
사람이나 사물이 패배하거나 권력을 상실
한 상황. 몰락. 붕괴. 멸망: *the fall of*
Rome 로마의 멸망 —see also FALLS

fal·la·cious /fəˈleɪʃəs/ *adj* FORMAL
containing or based on false ideas ‖ 잘못
된 생각을 포함하거나 또는 그에 기초한.
허위의. 잘못된. 불합리한: *a fallacious*
argument 불합리한 논쟁 – **fallaciously**
adv

fal·la·cy /ˈfæləsi/ *n* a false idea or
belief ‖ 그릇된 생각이나 믿음. 착오. 오
신: *the fallacy that money brings*
happiness 돈이 행복을 가져온다는 잘못
된 생각

fall·en /ˈfɔlən/ the past participle of fall
‖ fall의 과거 분사형

fall guy /ˈ. ./ *n* INFORMAL someone who
is punished for someone else's crime or
mistake ‖ 다른 사람의 범죄 또는 잘못으

F

로 처벌되는 사람. 죄를 대신 뒤집어쓰는 사람

fal·li·ble /'fæləbəl/ *adj* able to make a mistake ‖ 잘못을 할 수 있는. 잘못하기 쉬운 - **fallibility** /,fælə'bɪləti/ *n* [U] — opposite INFALLIBLE

fall·out /'fɔːlaʊt/ *n* [U] **1** the dangerous RADIOACTIVE dust that is left in the air after a NUCLEAR explosion ‖ 핵폭발 후에 대기 중에 남아 있는 유해 방사성 먼지. 방사성 낙진 **2** the bad results or effects of an event ‖ 사건의 나쁜 결과나 효과. 부산물: *The fallout from the scandal cost him his job.* 스캔들의 여파로 그는 직장을 잃었다

falls /fɔːlz/ *n* [plural] ⇨ WATERFALL

false /fɔːls/ *adj* **1** not true or correct ‖ 사실이 아니거나 정확하지 않은. 그릇된. 옳지 않은: *He gave the police false information.* 그는 경찰에 허위 정보를 제공했다. **2** not real, but intended to seem real ‖ 진짜가 아니지만 진짜처럼 보이려는. 가짜의. 위조[인조]의: *false eyelashes* 가짜 속눈썹 **3** not sincere or honest ‖ 진지하거나 정직하지 않은. 허위의. 거짓된: *Her smile and welcome seemed false.* 그녀의 미소와 환대는 거짓되어 보였다. **4 false alarm** a warning of something bad that does not happen ‖ 일어나지 않는 나쁜 일에 대한 경고. 허위 정보: *We thought there was a fire, but it was a false alarm.* 우리는 화재가 발생했다고 생각했으나 그것은 허위 경보였다. **5 false start** an unsuccessful attempt to begin a process or event ‖ 과정이나 행사를 시작하기 위한 성공적이지 못한 시도. 잘못된 출발. 부정한 스타트: *After several false starts, the show finally began.* 여러 차례 잘못된 시도 끝에 드디어 쇼가 시작되었다. **6 under false pretenses** if you get something under false pretenses, you get it by deceiving people ‖ 사람을 속여서 무엇을 얻다. 사취(詐取)하다 - **falsely** *adv* - **falsity** *n* [U]

false·hood /'fɔːlshʊd/ *n* FORMAL a statement that is not true ‖ 사실이 아닌 말. 거짓말. 기만

false teeth /, . './ *n* [plural] ⇨ DENTURES

fal·set·to /fɔːl'sɛtoʊ/ *n* a very high male voice ‖ 남자의 매우 높은 목소리. 남성의 가성(假聲) - **falsetto** *adj, adv*

fal·si·fy /'fɔːlsə,faɪ/ *v* [T] to change information and make it untrue ‖ 정보를 바꿔서 허위로 만들다. 왜곡하다. 위조[변조]하다: *He was accused of falsifying the company's records.* 그는 회사 기록을

위조한 혐의로 기소되었다. - **falsification** /,fɔːlsəfə'keɪʃən/ *n* [C, U]

fal·ter /'fɔːltər/ *v* [I] **1** to become weaker, less determined etc. ‖ 더욱 약해지다. 결심 등이 흔들리다. 쇠퇴하다: *The economy is faltering.* 그 경제는 휘청거리고 있다. **2** to speak or move in a way that seems weak or uncertain ‖ 약하거나 불확실하게 말하거나 움직이다. 더듬더듬 말하다. 비틀거리다: *She faltered for a moment.* 그녀는 잠시 비틀거렸다.

fame /feɪm/ *n* [U] the state of being known about by a lot of people because of your achievements ‖ 업적으로 인하여 많은 사람들에게 알려진 상태. 명성. 명망: *Elizabeth Taylor's rise to fame came in the movie "National Velvet."* 엘리자베스 테일러는 영화 "녹원의 천사"로 유명해졌다. —see also **claim to fame** (CLAIM²)

famed /feɪmd/ *adj* known about by a lot of people ‖ 많은 사람들에게 알려진. 유명한. 이름난: *mountains famed for their beauty* 아름답기로 유명한 산들

fa·mil·iar /fə'mɪlyər/ *adj* **1** someone or something that is familiar is easy to recognize because you have seen or heard him, her, or it before ‖ 사람이나 사물이 전에 보거나 들었기 때문에 알아보기 쉬운. 친숙한. 익은: *Your face looks familiar to me.* 너의 얼굴은 나에게 낯익어 보인다. / *the familiar sounds of the classroom* 교실의 익숙한 소리 **2 be familiar with** to have a good knowledge of something ‖ 무엇을 훤히 알고 있다. 정통하다: *Are you familiar with his books?* 당신은 그의 책을 훤히 알고 있습니까? **3** friendly and INFORMAL in speech, writing etc. ‖ 연설·문장 등이 친근하고 격식을 차리지 않은: *Vic has an easy familiar style of writing.* 빅의 문체는 쉽고 딱딱하지 않다.

fa·mil·iar·i·ty /fə,mɪl'yærəti, -,mɪli'ær-/ *n* [U] **1** a good knowledge of something ‖ 어떤 것을 잘 알고 있음. 정통함: *a familiarity with Russian poetry* 러시아 시에 정통함 **2** relaxed and friendly behavior ‖ 느긋하고 친근한 행동. 친밀함

fa·mil·iar·ize /fə'mɪlyə,raɪz/ *v* **1 familiarize yourself with sth** to learn about something so that you understand it ‖ 무엇을 이해 하기 위해 배우다. …에 익숙해지다: *I spent the first few weeks familiarizing myself with the new job.* 나는 새 직업에 익숙해지는 데 처음 몇 주를 보냈다. **2** [T] to teach someone about something so that s/he understands it ‖ 남이 이해할 수 있게 무엇을 가르치다. 널

family

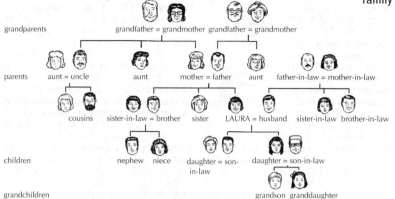

grandparents   grandfather = grandmother   grandfather = grandmother

parents   aunt = uncle   aunt   mother = father   aunt   father-in-law = mother-in-law

cousins   sister-in-law = brother   sister   LAURA = husband   sister-in-law   brother-in-law

children   nephew   niece   daughter = son-in-law   daughter = son-in-law

grandchildren   grandson   granddaughter

리 알리다: *We'd like to familiarize you with the new regulations.* 우리는 여러분께 새 규정을 널리 알리고 싶습니다. – **familiarization** /fə,mɪlyərə'zeɪʃən/ *n* [U]

fa·mil·iar·ly /fə'mɪlyɚli/ *adv* in an informal or friendly way ‖ 격식 차리지 않고, 친밀하게

fam·i·ly /'fæmli, -məli/ *n* **1** [C, U] any group of people who are related to each other, especially a mother, father, and their children ‖ 일단의 서로 관련된 사람들, 특히 어머니와 아버지 및 그 자녀. 가족: *Do you know the family next door?* 당신은 옆집 가족을 압니까? / *a car that will comfortably seat a family of five* (=a family with five people in it) 다섯 식구가 안락하게 탈 수 있는 차 / *Heart disease runs in our family.* (=is common in our family) 심장병은 우리 집안 내력이다. / *Terry wants to work in the family business.* (=a small business owned by one family) 테리는 가족이 운영하는 작은 업체에서 일하기를 원한다. **2** children ‖ 아이들, 자녀들: *Steve and Linda want to start a family* (=have children) *next year.* 스티브와 린다는 내년에 첫 아이를 가지기를 원한다. / *the problems of raising a family* (=educating and caring for your children) 아이 양육 문제 **3** a group of related animals, plants, languages etc. ‖ 관련된 동물·식물·언어 등의 집단. 과 (科). 족. 군: *tigers and other members of the cat family* 고양잇과의 호랑이와 다른 동물들

family plan·ning /,.. '../ *n* [U] the practice of controlling the number of children that are born by using

CONTRACEPTIVEs ‖ 피임 기구를 사용하여 태어나는 아이들의 수를 조절하는 행위. 산아 제한. 가족 계획

family room /'.. ,./ *n* a room in a house where the family can play games, watch television etc. ‖ 가족이 놀이·텔레비전 시청 등을 할 수 있는 방. 가정 내 오락실. 거실

family tree /,.. './ *n* a drawing that gives the names of all the members of a family and shows how they are related to each other ‖ 가족 전원의 이름을 보여주고 서로 어떤 관계인지를 나타내는 그림. 가계도

fam·ine /'fæmɪn/ *n* [C, U] a situation in which a large number of people have little or no food for a long time ‖ 수많은 사람이 오랫동안 음식을 거의 또는 전혀 먹지 못하는 상황. 기근. 굶주림

fam·ished /'fæmɪʃt/ *adj* INFORMAL very hungry ‖ 몹시 배고픈. 굶주린: *What's for dinner? I'm famished.* 저녁은 뭐야? 배고파 죽겠어.

fa·mous /'feɪməs/ *adj* known about or recognized by a lot of people ‖ 많은 사람에게 알려지거나 인정된. 유명한. 이름난: *a famous actor* 유명한 배우 / *France is famous for its food and wine.* 프랑스는 음식과 포도주로 유명하다. / *Da Vinci's world-famous* (=recognized by everyone) *portrait of the Mona Lisa* 다빈치의 세계적으로 유명한 모나리자의 초상화 – **famously** *adv*

fan¹ /fæn/ *n* **1** someone who likes a particular sport, type of music etc. very much, or who admires a famous person ‖ 특정 스포츠·특정 종류의 음악 등을 매우 좋아하거나 유명한 사람을 존경하는 사람. 열렬한 애호가[지지자]. 팬: *He was a* *big fan of Elvis Presley.* 그는 엘비스 프레슬리의 열광적인 팬이었다. **2** a machine, or a thing that you wave with your hand, that makes the air move so that you become cooler ‖ 시원해지도록 공기를 움직이게 하는 기계나 손으로 흔드는 물건. 선풍기. 부채: *a ceiling fan* 천장 선풍기

fan

fan² *v* **-nned, -nning** [T] to make air move around near something by waving a FAN, piece of paper etc. ‖ 부채나 한 장의 종이 등을 부쳐서 공기를 어떤 것 가까이로 움직이게 하다. 부채질하다: *She fanned her face with a newspaper.* 그녀는 신문으로 얼굴에 부채질했다.

fan out *phr v* [I, T **fan** sth ↔ **out**] to spread out from a central point, or to make something do this ‖ 중심에서 퍼져 나가다, 또는 퍼져 나가게 하다. 부채꼴로 퍼지다[펴다]: *The soldiers fanned out and walked into the jungle.* 병사들은 부채꼴로 흩어져서 정글 속으로 걸어 들어갔다.

fa·nat·ic /fə'nætɪk/ *n* someone whose beliefs and behavior are extreme, especially concerning religion or politics ‖ 특히 종교나 정치에 관하여 믿음과 행동이 극단적인 사람. 광신자 **– fanatic** *adj* **– fanaticism** /fə'nætə͵sɪzəm/ *n* [U]

fan·ci·ful /'fænsɪfəl/ *adj* imagined rather than based on facts ‖ 사실에 입각하기보다는 오히려 상상적인. 공상적인: *fanciful ideas* 공상적인 생각

fan club /'. ./ *n* an organization for FANs of a particular team, famous person etc. ‖ 특정한 팀·유명한 사람 등의 팬을 위한 조직체. 팬클럽. 후원회

fan·cy¹ /'fænsi/ *adj* **1** expensive and not simple or ordinary ‖ 비싸며 단순하거나 평범하지 않은. 고급의. 일류의: *a fancy hotel* 고급 호텔 **2** having a lot of decorations ‖ 장식이 많은: *I'd just like plain brown shoes, nothing fancy.* 나는 장식이 없이 그저 수수한 갈색 구두를 좋아한다. **3** needing technical skill ‖ 기교를 요하는. 곡예의. 묘기의: *fancy skiing* 곡예 스키 타기 **4** high quality ‖ 높은 품질의. 최상품의. 특선의: *fancy eggs* 최상품 달걀 **– fancily** *adv*

fan·cy² *n* [singular] OLD-FASHIONED a feeling that you like something or someone ‖ 사물이나 사람을 좋아하는 감정. 기호. 애호: *Grant's taken a fancy to you!* 그랜트는 당신을 좋아해!

fan·cy³ *v* [T] **1** to consider that something is true ‖ 무엇을 사실로 간주하다. …이라고 생각하다: *Hiram fancies himself a good writer.* 하이람은 자기를 훌륭한 작가라고 자처한다. **2** OLD-FASHIONED to like or want something ‖ 무엇을 좋아하거나 원하다

fan·fare /'fænfɛr/ *n* a short piece of music played on a TRUMPET to introduce an important person or event ‖ 중요 인물이나 행사를 소개하기 위해 트럼펫으로 연주하는 짧은 악곡. 팡파르

fang /fæŋ/ *n* a long sharp tooth of an animal such as a snake or dog ‖ 뱀이나 개 등의 동물의 길고 날카로운 이빨. 독아 (毒牙). 송곳니. 엄니

fan mail /'. ./ *n* [U] letters sent to famous people by their FANs ‖ 팬들이 유명인들에게 보내는 편지. 팬레터

fan·ny /'fæni/ *n* INFORMAL the part of your body that you sit on; BOTTOM ‖ 앉는 신체 부위. 엉덩이; ㊋ bottom

fan·ta·size /'fæntə͵saɪz/ *v* [I, T] to imagine something strange or pleasant happening to you ‖ 이상하거나 유쾌한 것이 일어나고 있다고 상상하다. 공상을 펼치다. …을 공상하다: *I used to fantasize that I was a famous dancer.* 나는 내가 유명한 무용가라는 공상을 하곤 했다.

fan·tas·tic /fæn'tæstɪk/ *adj* **1** extremely good, attractive, enjoyable etc. ‖ 매우 좋고 매력적이며 즐거운. 굉장한. 멋진: *You look fantastic!* 너 굉장히 멋져 보인다! / *We had a fantastic trip to New Orleans.* 우리는 뉴올리언스로 즐거운 여행을 했다. **2** SPOKEN used when someone has just told you something good ‖ 남이 방금 좋은 말을 했을 때 쓰여: *"Hey Mom, I passed my math test!" "Fantastic!"* "엄마, 나 수학 시험 합격했어!" "장하구나!" **3** very large ‖ 엄청나게 큰: *She spends fantastic amounts of money on clothes.* 그녀는 옷에 엄청난 돈을 쓴다. **4** strange or unreal ‖ 이상한, 비현실적인: *a fantastic dream* 이상한 꿈 **– fantastically** *adv*

fan·ta·sy /'fæntəsi, -zi/ *n* [C, U] imagined situations that are not related to the real world ‖ 현실 세계와는 관련이 없는 상상의 상황. 몽상. 공상: *When I was young, I had fantasies about becoming a race car driver.* 어린 시절에 나는 경주차 운전자가 되는 꿈을 꿨다[공상을 했다].

FAQ, faq /fæk, ͵ɛf eɪ 'kyu/ *n* [C usually plural] frequently asked question(s); on WEBSITEs, a list of questions that users often ask about the website, and answers to them. ‖ frequently asked question(s)(자주 하는 질문)의 약어; 웹사이트 상의 사용자들이 자주 묻는 질문과 그에 대한 답변들의 목록

far¹ /fɑr/ *adv* **farther, farthest** *or* **further, furthest**

1 ▶DISTANCE 거리◀ moving over a long distance ‖ 장거리를 이동하여. 멀리: *I don't want to drive very far.* 나는 아주 멀리까지 운전하고 싶지 않아. / *The boat had moved farther away from the dock.* 그 배는 부두에서 아득히 멀어져 갔다. / *Let's see who can swim the farthest.* 누가 가장 멀리 헤엄치는가 보자. ✗DON'T SAY "I walked far." SAY "I walked a long way."✗ "I walked far."라고는 하지 않고 "I walked a long way."라고 한다.

2 ▶AMOUNT/DEGREE 양/정도◀ very much or to a great degree ‖ 몹시, 훨씬: *Our new car is far better than the old one.* 우리의 새 차는 낡은 차보다 훨씬 낫다. / *a plane flying far above the clouds* 구름보다 훨씬 높이 날고 있는 비행기

3 **so far** until a particular time, point, degree etc. ‖ 특정한 시간·시점·정도 등까지. 지금[여태]까지는: *We haven't had any problems so far.* 지금까지는 우리에게 어떠한 문제도 없었다.

4 **how far have you gotten (with sth)?** used when asking how much of something someone has done or achieved ‖ 남에게 일을 얼마나 했는지 또는 달성했는지 물을 때 쓰여: *How far have you gotten with painting the kitchen?* 부엌 페인트칠하는 일은 얼마나 했느냐?

5 **sb will/should go far** used in order to say that you think someone will be successful ‖ 어떤 사람이 성공하리라고 생각한다고 말하는 데에 쓰여: *She's a good dancer and should go far.* 그녀는 훌륭한 무용수여서 분명히 성공할 거야.

6 **as far as possible** as much as possible ‖ 가능한 한: *We try to buy from local stores as far as possible.* 우리는 가능한 한 지역 상점에서 사려고 한다.

7 **go so far as to do sth** to behave in a way that seems surprising or extreme ‖ 깜짝 놀라거나 지나쳐 보일 정도로 행동하다. 심지어 …하기까지 하다: *He even went so far as to call her a liar.* 그는 심지어 그녀를 거짓말쟁이라고 부르기까지 했다.

8 **go too far** to do something too much or in an extreme way so that people are angry ‖ 사람들이 화를 낼 정도로 지나치

거나 극단적으로 어떤 것을 하다. 도를 지나치다: *He's always been a little rude, but this time he went too far.* 그는 항상 좀 무례하지만 이번에는 도를 지나쳤다.

9 **not go far** if something does not go far, there is not enough of it to do what you need ‖ 필요한 것을 하기에 충분하지 못한: *A dollar doesn't go far anymore.* (=it does not buy enough) 1달러로는 이제 살 만한 게 별로 없다.

SPOKEN PHRASES

10 **as far as I know/as far as I can remember** said when you think that something is true, although you do not know or cannot remember all the facts ‖ 모든 사실을 알거나 기억하지는 못하지만 어떤 것이 사실로 여겨질 때 쓰여. 내가 아는/기억하는 한에서는: *Cole wasn't even there, as far as I can remember.* 콜은 내가 기억하는 한 거기에도 없었어.

11 **so far so good** said when things have been happening successfully until now ‖ 일이 지금까지는 성공적으로 진행되어 오고 있을 때 쓰여. 지금까지는 순조롭다: *"How's your new job?" "So far so good."* "너의 새 직업은 어떠니?" "지금까지는 그런 대로 괜찮아."

—see also **as far as sb's concerned** (CONCERNED)

far² *adj* **farther, farthest,** *or* **further, furthest**

1 if something is far, it is a long distance from something else ‖ 사물이 다른 것에서 먼 거리에 있는. 먼, 멀리 떨어진: *We can walk if it's not far.* 멀지 않으면 우리는 걸을 수 있다. / *Denver's farther away than I thought.* 덴버는 내가 생각했던 것보다 더 멀리 떨어져 있다. / *Aim at the target that's farthest from you.* 너에게서 가장 멀리 떨어져 있는 과녁을 겨누어라.

2 most distant from where you are ‖ 있는 곳에서 가장 멀리 떨어진: *The parking lot is on the far side of the building.* 주차장은 그 건물의 가장 먼 쪽에 있다.

3 **how far** used when asking the distance between two places or the distance someone has traveled ‖ 두 지점 사이의 거리나 사람이 움직인 거리를 물을 때 쓰여: *How far is Boston from here?* 여기서부터 보스턴까지의 거리는 얼마니?

4 **the far left/right** people who have political opinions that are much more extreme than those of most people ‖ 대부분의 사람들보다 훨씬 극단적인 정치적

F

견해를 가진 사람들. 극좌파/극우파

5 be a far cry from to be very different from something else ‖ 다른 것과 전혀 다르다: *Europe was a far cry from what Tom had expected.* 유럽은 톰이 기대한 것과 전혀 달랐다.

far·a·way /ˈfɑrəˌweɪ/ *adj* **1** LITERARY distant ‖ 먼: *faraway cities* 먼 도시 **2 faraway look** an expression on your face that shows that you are not thinking about what is around you ‖ 주위에 있는 것을 생각하고 있지 않다는 것을 나타내는 얼굴 표정. 멍한 표정

farce /fɑrs/ *n* **1** [singular] an event or situation that is badly organized and does not happen in the way it should ‖ 구성이 졸렬하고 마땅히 일어나야 하는 식으로 일어나지 않는 사건이나 상황. 웃음거리: *I'm telling you, the trial was a total farce.* 정말이야, 그 재판은 완전히 웃음거리였어. **2** a humorous play in which a lot of silly things happen ‖ 많은 우스운 사건들이 일어나는 익살스런 연극. 소극(笑劇) – **farcical** *adj*

fare¹ /fɛr/ *n* **1** the price you pay to travel by train, plane, bus etc. ‖ 열차·비행기·버스 등으로 여행하려고 지불하는 값. 요금. 운임: *Air fares are going up again.* 비행기 요금이 다시 오를 기미다. **2** a passenger in a taxi ‖ 택시 승객

fare² *v* [I] FORMAL to succeed in a particular situation ‖ 특정한 상황에서 성공하다. 해나가다. 살아 나가다: *Women are now faring better in politics.* 이제는 정치에서 여성이 더 잘 해내고 있다.

Far East /ˌ. ˈ./ *n* **the Far East** the part of Asia that is the farthest east, including areas such as Hong Kong and Japan ‖ 홍콩·일본 등의 지역을 포함하는 동쪽 끝에 있는 아시아 지역. 극동

fare·well /ˌfɛrˈwɛl/ *n, interjection* **1** FORMAL goodbye ‖ 안녕, 잘 가거라: *It is time to bid farewell to our friends.* (=say goodbye to them) 우리 친구들에게 작별을 고할 때다. **2 farewell party/drink** a party or drink that you have with someone who is leaving ‖ 떠나는 사람과 가지는 파티나 마시는 술. 송별회/송별주

far-fetched /ˌ. ˈ../ *adj* unlikely to be true ‖ 사실일 것 같지 않은. 무리한. 당치 않은: *I thought her story was pretty far-fetched.* 나는 그녀의 이야기가 상당히 억지스럽다고 생각했다.

far-flung /ˌ. ˈ./ *adj* very far away or spread over a wide area ‖ 멀리 떨어진, 널리 퍼진: *the far-flung cities of the world* 세계 도처에 있는 도시들

far gone /ˌ. ˈ./ *adj* INFORMAL very ill, drunk, crazy etc. ‖ 병이 심한, 곤드레 만드레가 된, 미친: *She's too far gone to understand what's happening.* 그녀는 너무 취해서 무슨 일이 일어나는지 몰랐다.

farm¹ /fɑrm/ *n* an area of land used for raising animals or growing food ‖ 동물을 사육하거나 식량을 재배하는 데에 사용되는 지역. 농장. 농원

farm² *v* [I, T] to use land for growing crops, raising animals etc. ‖ 농작물 재배·동물 사육 등을 위해 땅을 이용하다. 농사를 짓다. 경작[사육]하다: *Our family has farmed here for years.* 우리 가족은 오랫동안 이곳에서 농사를 지었다.

farm sth ↔ out *phr v* [T] to send work to other people instead of doing it yourself ‖ 손수 하지 않고 다른 사람들에게 일을 맡기다. 위탁하다. 하청 주다: *Most of the editing is farmed out.* 대부분의 편집 일은 하청을 준다.

farm·er /ˈfɑrmə/ *n* someone who owns or manages a farm ‖ 농장을 소유하거나 관리하는 사람. 농장주. 농장 관리자. 농부

farm·hand /ˈfɑrmhænd/ *n* someone who is employed to work on a farm ‖ 농장에서 일하도록 고용된 사람. 농장 노동자. 일꾼

farm·ing /ˈfɑrmɪŋ/ *n* [U] the practice or business of raising animals or growing crops on a farm ‖ 농장에서 동물을 사육하거나 농작물을 재배하는 일. 농사. 농업. 농장 경영. 사육업

farm·yard /ˈfɑrmyɑrd/ *n* the area next to or around farm buildings ‖ 농장 건물의 옆이나 주변 지역. 농장 부지

far-off /ˌ. ˈ./ *adj* LITERARY distant in time or space ‖ 시간적으로나 공간적으로 먼. 멀리 떨어진: *a far-off land* 먼 지역

far-out /ˌ. ˈ./ *adj* INFORMAL unusual or strange ‖ 유별나거나 이상한. 기발한: *far-out clothes* 이상한 옷

far-reach·ing /ˌ. ˈ../ *adj* having a big influence or effect ‖ 영향이나 효과가 광범위한: *This will be the most far-reaching tax reform in our history.* 이것은 우리 역사상 가장 광범위한 조세 개혁일 것이다.

far·sight·ed /ˈfɑrˌsaɪtɪd/ *adj* **1** able to see distant things more clearly than close ones ‖ 가까이 있는 것보다 멀리 있는 것을 더 잘 볼 수 있는. 원시의 **2** APPROVING considering what will happen in the future ‖ 앞으로 일어날 일을 생각하는. 선견지명이 있는. 앞을 내다보는: *a farsighted economic plan* 앞을 내다보는 경제 정책

fart /fɑrt/ *v* [I] INFORMAL an impolite

word meaning to make air come out of your BOWELS ‖ 장에서 가스를 나오게 하다 의 뜻인 정중하지 못한 단어. 방귀를 뀌다 – **fart** *n*

fart around *phr v* [I] INFORMAL an impolite phrase meaning to waste time not doing very much ‖ 열심히 일하지 않고 시간을 낭비하다의 뜻인 정중하지 못한 어구. 빈둥빈둥 놀다: *Stop farting around and help me out.* 빈둥빈둥 놀지 말고 나를 도와 줘.

far·ther /ˈfɑrðɚ/ *adj, adv* the COMPARATIVE of FAR ‖ far의 비교급 — compare FURTHER¹

> **USAGE NOTE farther and further**
>
> Use **farther** to talk about distance: *The bar's just a little farther down the street.* Use **further** to talk about time, quantities, or degrees: *House prices will probably drop further next year. / I don't want to discuss this any further.* We also use **further** to talk about distance, but many teachers think this is incorrect.
> **farther**는 거리를 말하는 데에 쓰인다: 그 술집은 거리 아래쪽으로 조금 떨어져 있다. **further**는 시간이나 양, 또는 정도를 말하는 데에 쓰인다: 주택 가격은 아마도 내년에 더 떨어질 것이다. / 나는 더 이상 이 문제를 논의하고 싶지 않다. 또한 거리를 말하는 데에 **further**를 쓰기도 하지만 많은 교사들이 이것을 옳지 않은 것으로 여긴다.

far·thest /ˈfɑrðɪst/ *adj, adv* the SUPERLATIVE of FAR ‖ far의 최상급

fas·ci·nate /ˈfæsəˌneɪt/ *v* [T] to attract or interest someone very much ‖ 남을 매혹하거나 흥미를 끌다: *Mechanical things fascinate me.* 기계에 관한 일은 나를 매료시킨다.

fas·ci·nat·ing /ˈfæsəˌneɪtɪŋ/ *adj* extremely interesting, especially because you are learning something new ‖ 특히 새로운 일을 배우고 있기 때문에 매우 흥미로운. 매혹적인. 흥미진진한: *a fascinating subject/film/woman* 매혹적인 주제[영화, 여성]

fas·ci·na·tion /ˌfæsəˈneɪʃən/ *n* [singular, U] the state of being very interested in something ‖ 어떤 것에 매우 흥미 있는 상태. 매혹. 매료: *Jan had a fascination with/for movie stars.* 잰은 영화 배우들에게 매료되어 있었다.

fas·cism /ˈfæʃɪzəm/ *n* [U] an extreme political system in which people's lives are completely controlled by the state ‖ 국민의 삶이 완전히 국가의 통제를 받는 극단적인 정치 제도. 파시즘

fas·cist /ˈfæʃɪst/ *n* **1** someone who supports FASCISM ‖ 파시즘을 지지하는 사람. 파시즘 신봉자 **2** someone who is cruel and unfair ‖ 잔인하고 불공정한 사람 – **fascist** *adj*

fash·ion¹ /ˈfæʃən/ *n* **1** [C, U] the popular style of clothes, hair, behavior etc. at a particular time ‖ 특정 시기에 인기 있는 스타일의 옷·머리·행동 등. 패션. 유행: *Hats are now in fashion again.* 모자가 지금 다시 유행하고 있다. / *Shoes like that went out of fashion years ago.* 그런 신발은 몇 년 전에 유행이 지났다. / *She always buys the latest fashions.* 그녀는 항상 최근에 유행하는 물건을 산다. **2** [U] the business or study of making or selling clothes ‖ 옷의 제조나 판매에 대한 일이나 연구: *the assistant fashion editor at Vogue* 보그지의 패션 부(副)편집장 **3 in a** ... **fashion** FORMAL in a particular way ‖ 특정한 방법으로: *Albert smiled in a tired fashion.* 앨버트는 피곤한 듯이 웃었다.

fashion² *v* [T] FORMAL **1** to shape or make something with your hands or a few tools ‖ 손이나 몇 개의 도구로 물건을 모양내거나 만들다: *fashioning a dress out of old curtains* 낡은 커튼으로 옷을 만들기 **2** to influence and form someone's ideas and opinions ‖ 남의 생각과 견해에 영향을 끼쳐 형성하다: *Our attitudes to politics are often fashioned by the media.* 정치에 대한 우리의 태도는 종종 언론에 의해 형성된다.

fash·ion·a·ble /ˈfæʃənəbəl/ *adj* popular, especially for a short time ‖ 특히 잠깐 동안 인기 있는. 유행하는: *Long skirts are fashionable now.* 긴 치마가 지금 유행하고 있다. / *a fashionable restaurant* 인기가 많은 음식점 — opposite UNFASHIONABLE

fashion show /ˈ.. ˌ./ *n* an event at which new styles of clothes are shown to the public ‖ 새 스타일의 옷을 대중에게 보여 주는 행사. 패션 쇼. 의상 발표회

fast¹ /fæst/ *adj*

1 ▶MOVING QUICKLY 빨리 움직이는◀ moving, or able to move quickly ‖ 빨리 움직이거나 움직일 수 있는: *a fast runner* 빠른 주자 / *a fast car* 빠른 차

2 ▶DONE QUICKLY 신속히 이뤄진◀ doing something or happening in a short time ‖ 단시간에 하거나 일어나는. 신속한: *The subway is the fastest way to get downtown.* 지하철은 시내로 나가는 가장 빠른 방법이다. / *a fast reader* 글을

빨리 읽는 사람

3 ►CLOCK/WATCH 괘종시계/손목시계◄
showing time that is later than the true
time ‖ 실제 시간보다 더 나중의 시간을 나
타내는. 빠른: *Is it really 5:00, or is my
watch fast?* 정말 다섯 시야? 아니면 내
시계가 빠른 건가?

4 pull a fast one INFORMAL to trick
someone ‖ 남을 속이다: *Don't try and
pull a fast one on me.* 나를 애써 속이려
하지 마라.

5 fast track a way of achieving
something more quickly than it is
normally done ‖ 정상적으로 하는 것보다
일을 더 빨리 성취하는 방법. 출세 가도.
고속 승진 코스: *young professionals on
the fast track for promotion* 승진 가도
를 달리는 젊은 전문가들

6 the fast lane an exciting way of
living that involves dangerous or
expensive activities ‖ 위험하고 사치스러
운 활동을 포함하는 재미있는 생활 방식:
living life in the fast lane 위험하고 자극
적인 삶을 살기

7 make sth fast to tie something such
as a boat or tent firmly to something
else ‖ 다른 것에 배나 텐트 등을 단단히
묶다

8 COLOR ⇨ COLORFAST

fast² *adv* **1** moving quickly ‖ 빠르게 움직
여. 빨리. 날쌔게: *He likes driving fast.*
그는 차를 빨리 모는 것을 좋아한다. **2** in
a short time ‖ 짧은 시간에. 신속하게:
You're learning fast. 너는 빨리 배우고
있어. **3 fast asleep** sleeping very
deeply ‖ 깊이 잠들어 있는: *The baby's
fast asleep.* 그 아이는 깊이 잠들어 있다.
4 firmly or tightly ‖ 단단히, 굳게, 꽉: *The
boat's stuck fast in the mud.* 그 배는 진
창에 푹 빠져 있다. / *Walter began to
fall, but the rope held him fast.* 월터는
떨어지기 시작했지만 밧줄로 꽉 매져 있었
다. **5 hold fast to** to continue to believe
in or support an idea, principle etc. ‖ 사
상이나 원칙 등을 계속 믿거나 지지하다:
*In spite of everything, her father held
fast to his religion.* 만사를 제쳐 놓고 그
녀의 아버지는 종교에 매달렸다. **6 not so
fast** SPOKEN said when telling someone
to do something more slowly or
carefully ‖ 남에게 일을 보다 천천히 또는
조심스럽게 하라고 말할 때에 쓰여. 서두
르지 마라: *Not so fast! You'll scrape the
paint.* 서두르지 마! 칠 벗겨질라.

fast³ *n* a period of time during which
someone eats very little or nothing,
usually for religious reasons ‖ 보통 종교
적인 이유로 사람이 음식을 거의 또는 전

혀 먹지 않는 기간. 단식 기간 – **fast** *v* [I]

fas·ten /'fæsən/ *v* **1** [I, T] to join
together the two sides of something so
that it is closed, or to become joined in
this way ‖ 닫히도록 물건의 양쪽을 결합시
키거나 이렇게 결합되다. 잠그다. 잠기다:
Fasten your seat belts. 안전띠를 매시오.
/ *I'm too fat. My skirt won't fasten.* 나는
너무 뚱뚱해. 치마가 채워지지가 않아. **2**
[T] to firmly close a window, gate etc.
so it will not open ‖ 열리지 않도록 창문·
문 등을 단단히 잠그다 **3** [T] to attach
something firmly to another object ‖ 무
엇을 다른 물체에 단단히 부착하다: *Jill
fastened a flower onto her dress.* 질은
자신의 드레스에 꽃을 달았다.

fas·ten·ing /'fæsənɪŋ/ *n* something you
use to hold another thing shut or in the
right position ‖ 다른 물건을 잠그거나 올
바른 위치에 고정시키는 데에 쓰이는 물
건. 죄는[잠그는, 채우는] 제구(諸具)

fast food /ˌ. './ *n* [U] inexpensive food,
for example, HAMBURGERs, that is
prepared and served quickly in a
restaurant ‖ 음식점에서 신속하게 준비되
어 제공되는, 예를 들면 햄버거 같이 비싸
지 않은 음식. 패스트푸드. 즉석 식품

fast for·ward /ˌ. '../ *n* [singular] the
button that you push on a machine to
make a TAPE wind more quickly ‖ 테이프
를 보다 신속히 감기 위해 누르는 기계상
의 버튼. 고속 감기 버튼

fas·tid·i·ous /fæ'stɪdiəs, fə-/ *adj* very
careful about small details in your
appearance, work etc. ‖ 용모나 일 등의
세심한 부분에 매우 주의하는. 꼼꼼한 –
fastidiously *adv*

fat¹ /fæt/ *adj* **1** weighing too much ‖ 무
게가 너무 많이 나가는. 살찐. 뚱뚱한:
Chris is worried about getting fat. 크리
스는 살찌는 것을 걱정한다. **2** thick or
wide ‖ 두툼한, 불룩한: *a big fat letter
from Grandma* 할머니에게서 온 두툼한
편지 **3** INFORMAL containing or worth a
lot of money ‖ 고액의, 돈이 많은: *I
should get a nice fat check at the end of
the month.* 나는 이달 말에 상당한 고액
수표를 받게 됐다. **4 fat chance** SPOKEN
said when something is very unlikely to
happen ‖ 일이 거의 일어날 것 같지 않을
때 쓰여. 희박한 가망성: *What, Max get a
job? Fat chance!* 뭐, 맥스가 직업을 잡는
다고? 거의 불가능한 일이야!

USAGE NOTE fat

Fat means that someone weighs too
much, but this word is not very polite.

Use **plump** in order to be polite: *Grandma was always fairly plump.* Use **chubby** to describe babies or young children. **Overweight** means that someone weighs too much, and is often used by doctors or people who are worried about their weight. **Obese** means that someone is extremely fat in a way that is dangerous to his/her health.

fat은 사람이 체중이 너무 많이 나가는 것을 의미하는데 이 단어는 그다지 정중하지 못하다. 정중한 표현에는 **plump**가 쓰인다: 할머니는 늘 상당히 풍만했다. 아기나 어린이들에게는 **chubby**를 쓴다. **overweight**는 체중이 너무 많이 나가는 것을 뜻하는데 종종 의사나 자신의 체중을 염려하는 사람들이 사용한다. **obese**는 사람이 건강에 위험할 정도로 몹시 뚱뚱한 것을 뜻한다.

fat² *n* **1** [U] a substance that is under the skin of people and animals, that helps keep them warm ‖ 사람과 동물의 피하(皮下)에 있으며 보온을 도와주는 물질. 지방. 비계: *Take two chicken breasts, and cut off all the fat.* 닭고기 두 마리 가슴살을 가져와서 지방을 모두 잘라내라. **2** [C, U] an oily substance in some foods ‖ 일부 음식에 있는 기름. 지방: *food that is low/high in fat* 지방이 적은/많은 음식 **3** [C, U] a thick oily substance taken from animals or plants and used in cooking ‖ 동물이나 식물에서 추출해 요리할 때 사용하는 진한 지방질. 유지(油脂): *Fry the potatoes in oil or melted fat.* 감자를 기름이나 녹인 유지에 튀기시오.

fa·tal /'feɪtl/ *adj* **1** resulting in someone's death ‖ 누군가의 죽음을 초래하는. 치명적인: *a fatal accident/injury* 치명적인 사고[부상] / *a disease that proved fatal* (=killed someone) 사망자를 낸 병 **2** having a very bad effect ‖ 매우 나쁜 영향을 끼치는. 파멸적인. 치명적인: *Her fatal mistake was to marry too young.* 그녀의 치명적인 실수는 너무 일찍 결혼했다는 점이었다. / *There's a fatal flaw* (=serious weakness) *in his argument.* 그의 주장에는 치명적인 약점이 있다. **– fatally** *adv*

fa·tal·ism /'feɪtl,ɪzəm/ *n* [U] the belief that there is nothing you can do to prevent events from happening ‖ 일이 일어나는 것을 막기 위해 할 수 있는 일이 아무것도 없다는 신념. 운명[숙명]론 **– fatalistic** /,feɪtl'ɪstɪk/ *adj*

fa·tal·i·ty /feɪ'tæləti, fə-/ *n* a death in an accident or violent attack ‖ 사고나 격렬한 공격에 의한 죽음. 불의의 죽음: *This year there have been fewer traffic fatalities.* 금년에는 교통 사망자가 거의 없었다.

fate /feɪt/ *n* **1** the things that happen to someone ‖ 사람에게 일어나는 일: *No one knows what the fate of the refugees will be.* 아무도 그 피난민의 앞날이 어떻게 될지 모른다. / *Their fate is sealed.* (=something unpleasant is certain to happen) 그들의 앞날에 어두운 그림자가 드리워져 있다. **2** [U] a power that is believed to control what happens in people's lives ‖ 사람의 삶에 일어나는 일을 지배하고 있다고 여겨지는 힘. 운명: *Fate brought us together.* 운명이 우리를 맺어 주었다. / *By a lucky twist of fate, we were on the same plane.* 거짓말처럼 운 좋게 우리는 같은 비행기에 탔다. **3 a fate worse than death** HUMOROUS an experience that seems like the worst thing that could happen to you ‖ 발생 가능한 것 중 가장 최악의 것으로 보이는 경험. 쓰라린 경험

fat·ed /'feɪtɪd/ *adj* **be fated to** certain to happen or to do something because a mysterious force is controlling events ‖ 신비한 힘이 사건을 지배하기 때문에 어떤 것이 일어나거나 어떤 것을 하는 것이 확실한. 운명지어진. 숙명적인: *We were fated to meet.* 우리는 숙명적으로 만났다.

fate·ful /'feɪtfəl/ *adj* having an important, usually bad effect on future events ‖ 중대하며 일반적으로 장차 나쁜 영향을 끼치는. 운명을 결정하는: *a fateful decision* 운명을 결정짓는 결단

fat farm /'. ./ *n* INFORMAL a place where people who are fat can go to lose weight and improve their health ‖ 살찐 사람이 살을 빼고 건강을 증진시키기 위해 가는 곳. 체중 감량 도장. 단식원

fat-free /,. '. / *adj* food that is fat-free does not have any fat in it ‖ 음식이 지방분이 없는. 무지방의: *fat-free yogurt* 무지방 요구르트

fa·ther¹ /'faðɚ/ *n* **1** your male parent ‖ 부친. 아버지 **2 Father** a priest, especially in the Roman Catholic Church ‖ 특히 로마 가톨릭 교회의 성직자. 신부: *Do you know Father Vernon?* 버논 신부님을 아십니까? **3 the father of sth** the man who was responsible for starting something ‖ 어떤 것의 출발의 기원이 된 사람. 창시자: *George Washington is the father of our country.* 조지 워싱턴은 미국의 국부(國父)이다.

father² *v* [T] to become a male parent ‖

아버지가 되다: *his desire to father a child* 한 아이의 아버지가 되려는 그의 욕구

fa·ther·hood /'faðəˌhʊd/ *n* [U] the state of being a father ‖ 아버지임, 부권

father-in-law /'.. ˌ./ *n* the father of your husband or wife ‖ 남편이나 아내의 아버지. 시아버지, 장인 —see picture at FAMILY

fa·ther·ly /'faðəli/ *adj* typical of a kind or concerned father ‖ 다정하거나 자상한 아버지의 전형인. 아버지다운: *talking in a fatherly way* 자애로운 아버지처럼 말함

Father's Day /'.. ˌ./ *n* a holiday in the US and Canada on the third Sunday of June in honor of fathers ‖ 미국과 캐나다에서 아버지들을 기리는 날로 6월 셋째 주 일요일. 아버지날

fath·om¹ /'fæðəm/ *v* [T] to understand what something means after thinking about it carefully ‖ 주의깊게 생각한 후에 어떤 것의 의미를 파악하다

fathom² *n* a unit for measuring how deep water is, equal to 6 feet or 1.83 meters ‖ 6피트나 1.83미터에 해당하는 수심 측정 단위

F fa·tigue /fə'tig/ *n* [U] **1** extreme tiredness ‖ 심한 피로: *They were cold, and weak with fatigue, but not hurt.* 그들은 춥고 피로로 약해졌으나 다치지는 않았다. **2** TECHNICAL weakness in a substance such as metal, that may cause it to break ‖ 부러지게 만들 수도 있는 금속 등의 물질의 약함. 피로. 약화 – **fatigue** *v* [T]

fa·tigues /fə'tigz/ *n* [plural] army clothes that fit loosely ‖ 헐렁하게 입는 군복. 작업복. 전투복

fat·ten /'fæt'n/ *v* [I, T] to make an animal become fatter so that it is ready to eat, or to become fat and ready to eat ‖ 먹을 수 있도록 동물을 살찌게 하거나 먹기 좋게 살이 찌다. 살찌우다. 살찌다: *fattened pigs* 살찐 돼지

fatten sb/sth **up** *phr v* [T] OFTEN HUMOROUS to make a thin person or animal fatter ‖ 마른 사람이나 동물을 살찌우다: *Grandma always thinks she needs to fatten me up.* 할머니는 항상 나를 살찌워야겠다고 생각하신다.

fat·ten·ing /'fæt'n-ɪŋ/ *adj* likely to make you fat ‖ 살이 찌게 하는: *I wish pizza weren't so fattening!* 나는 피자가 너무 살찌게 하지 않았으면 좋겠어!

fat·ty /'fæti/ *adj* containing a lot of fat ‖ 지방을 많이 함유하는. 지방질의. 기름진: *fatty foods* 기름진 음식

fat·u·ous /'fætʃuəs/ *adj* very silly or stupid ‖ 매우 바보 같거나 어리석은: *a fatuous remark* 어리석은 말

fau·cet /'fɔsɪt/ *n* a piece of equipment that you turn on and off to control the flow of water from a pipe ‖ 관에서 나오는 물의 흐름을 조절하기 위해 틀거나 잠그는 장치. 수도꼭지 —see picture at DRIP¹

fault¹ /fɔlt/ *n*

1 ▶BLAME 책임◀ responsibility for a mistake ‖ 실수에 대한 책임: *It's not my fault we missed the bus.* 우리가 버스를 놓친 것은 내 책임이 아니다.

2 at fault the state of being responsible for something bad that has happened ‖ 발생한 잘못된 일에 대해 책임이 있는: *It was the other driver who was at fault.* 잘못이 있는 사람은 상대방 운전자였다.

3 ▶PROBLEM 문제◀ a problem with something that stops it working correctly ‖ 사물이 정상적으로 작동하지 못하게 하는 문제. 고장: *a fault in the electrical system* 전기 시스템의 고장

4 find fault with to criticize something or someone and complain about him, her, or it ‖ 사물이나 사람을 비난하고 그에 대하여 불평을 하다. 흠을 잡다: *Why do you always have to find fault with my work?* 왜 내 작업에 항상 흠을 잡으셔야만 하는 겁니까?

5 through no fault of sb's own used in order to say that something bad that happened to someone was not caused by him/her ‖ 남에게 일어난 나쁜 일이 그 사람 때문이 아니라고 말하는 데에 쓰여. …의 책임[잘못]이 아닌데도: *Through no fault of their own, some students have trouble learning.* 그들의 잘못이 아닌데도 몇몇 학생은 학습에 애를 먹는다.

6 ▶NOT PERFECT 완전하지 않은◀ something that is wrong or not perfect ‖ 잘못되거나 완전하지 않은 것. 결함. 흠: *For all her faults* (=in spite of her faults) *I still love her.* 흠이 있음에도 불구하고 나는 여전히 그녀를 사랑한다.

7 ▶CRACK 갈라진 틈◀ a large crack in the rocks that form the Earth's surface ‖ 지구의 표면을 형성하는 바위의 큰 갈라진 틈. 단층(斷層): *the San Andreas fault* 산안드레아 단층

8 to a fault to a degree that is unnecessary or bad ‖ 불필요하거나 나쁠 정도로. 지나치게: *Mr. Blackburn is generous to a fault.* 블랙번 씨는 지나치게 관대하다.

fault² *v* [T] to find a mistake in something ‖ 어떤 것의 흠을 잡다: *We couldn't fault her singing.* 그녀의 노래는

흠잡을 데가 없었다.

fault·less /ˈfɔltlɪs/ *adj* having no mistakes; perfect ‖ 결점 없는; 완벽한: *a faultless performance* 완벽한 연주

fault·y /ˈfɔlti/ *adj* **1** not working correctly ‖ 제대로 작동하지 않는. 결함 있는: *faulty wires* 결함 있는 전선 **2** not correct ‖ 부정확한. 틀린. 잘못된: *faulty reasoning* 잘못된 추론

fau·na /ˈfɔnə/ *n* [U] TECHNICAL all the animals that live in a particular place or at a particular time in history ‖ 역사상 특정한 지역이나 특정한 시대에 살았던 동물상(相) —compare FLORA

faux pas /ˌfoʊ ˈpɑ/ *n* an embarrassing mistake in a social situation ‖ 사교상의 난처한 실수. 실례: *The other day I made a terrible faux pas.* 요전 날 나는 커다란 실례를 범했다.

fa·vor¹ /ˈfeɪvɚ/ *n* **1** something you do for someone to help or be kind to him/her ‖ 남에게 도움이나 친절을 베풀기 위해 하는 것. 호의: *Could you do me a favor and watch the baby for half an hour?* 부탁이 하나 있는데 반 시간 동안 아기를 봐줄 수 있습니까? / *Can I ask you a favor?* 부탁 하나 드려도 될까요? **2 in favor of** choosing one plan, idea, or system instead of another ‖ 다른 것 대신에 하나의 계획[생각, 시스템]을 선택하는: *Plans for a tunnel were rejected in favor of the bridge.* 터널 계획은 다리를 선택하는 바람에 거부되었다. **3** [U] support or approval for a plan, idea, or system ‖ 계획[생각, 시스템]의 지지나 찬성: *All the board members were in favor of the idea.* 모든 위원들은 그 생각을 지지했다. **4 in sb's favor** to someone's advantage ‖ 어떤 사람에게 유리하도록: *The vote was 60-59 in his favor.* 투표는 60대 59로 그가 유리했다. **5 in favor/out of favor** liked and approved of, or no longer liked and approved of ‖ 마음에 들어 또는 마음에 들지 않아: *Although he's out of favor, some people still read his books.* 비록 그는 대중의 사랑을 잃었지만 여전히 그의 책을 읽는 사람들도 있다. **6** a small gift that is given to guests at a party ‖ 파티에서 손님에게 주는 작은 선물. 기념품

fa·vor² *v* [T] **1** to prefer something more than other choices ‖ 다른 것보다 어떤 것을 더 선호하다. 찬성하다: *Blyth favors gun control laws.* 블라이스는 총기 규제법을 지지한다. **2** to unfairly treat one person or group better than another ‖ 한 사람이나 집단을 다른 사람이나 집단보다 불공정하게 더 나은 대우를 하다. 편애

하다: *tax cuts that favor the rich* 부자에게 유리한 세금 감면 **3** to provide the right conditions for something to happen ‖ 일이 일어나는 적합한 조건을 제공하다. …에 알맞다: *wind conditions that favor sailing* 요트를 타기에 알맞은 풍향 여건

fa·vor·able /ˈfeɪvərəbəl/ *adj* **1** making people like or approve of someone or something ‖ 사람들이 어떤 사람이나 사물을 좋아하거나 인정하게 만드는. 호감을 주는 : *Try to make a favorable impression.* 좋은 인상을 주도록 해라. **2** saying or showing that you approve of something or someone ‖ 사물이나 사람에 대하여 인정을 하거나 나타내는. 호의적인: *I've heard favorable reports about your work.* 나는 당신의 업무에 관한 호의적인 보고를 들었다. **3** likely to make something happen or succeed ‖ 일이 일어나거나 성공할 것 같은. 유망한: *a favorable economic environment* 밝은 경제 여건 - **favorably** *adv* —opposite UNFAVORABLE

fa·vor·ite¹ /ˈfeɪvrɪt, -vərɪt/ *adj* liked more than others of the same kind ‖ 같은 종류의 다른 것보다 더 좋아하는. 가장 좋아하는: *Who's your favorite actor?* 당신이 가장 좋아하는 배우는 누구입니까? ✗DON'T SAY "most favorite."✗ "most favorite"라고는 하지 않는다.

favorite² *n* **1** someone or something that you like more than any other one of its kind ‖ 같은 종류의 다른 것보다 더 좋아하는 사람이나 사물. 마음에 드는 사람[물건]: *I like all her books, but this one is my favorite.* 나는 그녀의 책을 전부 좋아하지만 이것은 특히 좋아하는 책이다. **2** someone who receives more attention and approval than is fair ‖ 정당한 것 이상으로 주목과 인정을 받는 사람. 편애 받는 사람. 총아(寵兒): *Teachers shouldn't have favorites.* 교사는 편애해서는 안 된다. **3** the team, person etc. that is expected to win a competition ‖ 경기에 우승하리라고 예상되는 팀이나 사람 등. 우승 후보: *The Yankees are favorites to win the World Series.* 양키즈 팀은 월드 시리즈의 우승 후보이다.

fa·vor·it·ism /ˈfeɪvrəˌtɪzəm/ *n* [U] the act of unfairly treating one person or group better than another ‖ 다른 사람이나 집단보다 한 사람이나 집단을 불공정하게 더 잘 대우하기. 편애. 편들기

fawn¹ /fɔn/ *v*

fawn on/over sb *phr v* [T] to praise someone and be friendly to him/her because you want something ‖ 무엇인가

F

를 바라고 남을 칭찬하며 다정하게 굴다. 비위를 맞추다. 알랑거리다: *All those people are fawning over her as if she's someone special!* 그 모든 사람들이 그녀가 특별한 사람인 것처럼 그녀에게 알랑거리고 있어!

fawn² *n* a young DEER ‖ 새끼 사슴

fax /fæks/ *n* **1 a)** a document that is sent in electronic form down a telephone line and then printed using a special machine ‖ 전화선을 통하여 전자 형태로 발송되어 특수 기계를 사용하여 인쇄된 문서. 팩스(문서): *Did you get my fax?* 내가 보낸 팩스를 받았냐? **b)** [U] the system of sending documents this way ‖ 이런 식으로 문서를 보내는 시스템. 팩스[모사 전송](시스템): *a letter sent by fax* 팩스로 보낸 편지 **2** also **fax machine** a machine used for sending and receiving faxes ‖ 팩스를 보내고 받는 데에 사용되는 기계. 팩시밀리 송수신기. 모사 전송기: *What's your fax number?* 너의 팩스 번호가 어떻게 되지? **– fax** *v* [T]

faze /feɪz/ *v* [T] INFORMAL to make someone feel nervous or confused ‖ 남을 초조하거나 혼란스럽게 하다: *Nothing ever seemed to faze Rosie.* 로지는 당황하게 하는 것은 아무것도 없는 것 같았다. **– fazed** *adj*

FBI *n* **the FBI** the Federal Bureau of Investigation; the US police department that is controlled by the government and is concerned with FEDERAL law rather than state law ‖ Federal Bureau of Investigation(미연방 수사국)의 약어; 정부의 통제를 받고 주법보다는 연방법에 관련된 미국 경찰 기구

fear¹ /fɪr/ *n* **1** [C, U] the feeling you get when you are afraid or worried that something bad will happen ‖ 나쁜 일이 일어날 것을 두려워하거나 걱정할 때의 감정. 무서움. 두려움. 공포: *a fear of heights/flying/spiders* 고소/비행/거미 공포증 / *Here, refugees live in fear of being sent back.* 이곳 난민들은 송환될까봐 두려워하며 살고 있다. / *the fear that the guy next to you will have a gun* 당신 옆 사람이 총을 소지할 두려움 / *parents' fears for their children's safety* 자녀들의 안전에 대한 부모의 걱정 **2 for fear of/for fear that** because you are worried that something will happen ‖ 일이 일어날 것을 걱정하여. …을 두려워하여: *She kept quiet, for fear of saying the wrong thing.* 그녀는 적절치 못한 말을 할까봐 두려워서 잠자코 있었다.

fear² *v* [T] **1** to feel afraid or worried that something bad will happen ‖ 나쁜 일이 일어나는 것을 무서워하거나 걱정하다: *Fearing a snowstorm, many people stayed home.* 눈보라를 두려워하여 많은 사람들이 집에 있었다. **2 fear the worst** to think that the worst possible thing has happened or will happen ‖ 최악의 일이 일어났거나 일어날 것으로 생각하다: *When they heard about Heidi's car crash, they feared the worst.* 그들이 하이디의 자동차 충돌 소식을 들었을 때 최악의 경우를 걱정했다. **3** to be afraid of someone because s/he is very powerful ‖ 강력해서 남을 두려워하다: *a dictator feared by his country* 국민이 두려워하는 독재자 **4 fear for sb** to be worried about someone who may be in danger ‖ 위험에 처할지도 모를 사람을 걱정하다: *Obviously, they left because they feared for their lives.* 분명히 그들은 자신들의 목숨을 염려하여 떠났다.

fear·ful /'fɪrfəl/ *adj* FORMAL **1** afraid ‖ 두려워하는: *Even doctors are fearful of getting the disease.* 의사들조차도 그 병에 걸릴까봐 두려워한다. **2** causing fear ‖ 두려움을 야기하는. 무시무시한: *a fearful noise* 소름 끼치는 소리 **– fearfully** *adv*

fear·less /'fɪrlɪs/ *adj* not afraid of anything ‖ 어떤 것도 두려워하지 않는: *a fearless soldier* 두려움을 모르는 병사 **– fearlessness** *n* [U]

fear·some /'fɪrsəm/ *adj* very frightening ‖ 몹시 무서운: *a fearsome sight* 무서운 광경

fea·si·ble /'fizəbəl/ *adj* possible, and likely to work ‖ 가능하고 수행할 것 같은. 실현 가능한: *a feasible plan* 실현 가능한 계획

feast¹ /fist/ *n* **1** a large meal for many people to celebrate a special occasion ‖ 특별한 때를 축하하기 위한 많은 사람용의 대규모 식사. 연회. 잔치: *a wedding feast* 결혼 피로연 **2** a very good large meal ‖ 성대한 식사. 성찬: *That was a real feast!* 그건 정말 성찬이었어! **3** a religious holiday ‖ 종교적인 축제일

feast² *v* **1** [I] to eat and drink a lot to celebrate something ‖ 어떤 것을 축하하려고 많이 먹고 마시다 **2 feast your eyes on** to look at something for a long time because you like it ‖ 어떤 것이 마음에 들어서 오랫동안 보다. 눈요기하다 **3 feast on sth** to eat a lot of a particular food with great enjoyment ‖ 아주 즐겁게 특정 음식을 많이 먹다: *feasting on fresh corn on the cob* 통째로 찐 신선한 옥수수를 잔뜩 먹기

feat /fit/ *n* something that someone does that shows strength, skill etc. ‖ 힘·기술 등을 보여 주는 사람이 하는 일. 공적. 위업. 재주: *an amazing feat of engineering* 놀라운 공학 기술 / *Getting your doctorate is no mean feat.* (=difficult to do) 박사 학위를 받는 것은 어려운 일이다.

feath·er¹ /ˈfɛðɚ/ *n* one of the light soft things that cover a bird's body ‖ 새의 몸을 덮고 있는 가볍고 부드러운 것 중의 하나. 깃털

feather² *v* [T] **feather your nest** to make yourself rich by dishonest methods ‖ 부정한 방법으로 부유하게 만들다. 부정 축재하다

feath·er·y /ˈfɛðəri/ *adj* **1** covered with feathers ‖ 깃털로 덮인 **2** soft and light ‖ 부드럽고 가벼운. 깃털 같은: *feathery snow* 깃털 같은 눈

fea·ture¹ /ˈfitʃɚ/ *n* **1** a part of something that you notice because it seems important, interesting, or typical ‖ 중요하거나 재미있거나, 또는 전형적으로 보이기 때문에 눈에 띄는 사물의 일부. 특징. 특색: *a report that compares the safety features of new cars* 새 차들의 안전상의 특징을 비교하는 보고서 **2** a special newspaper or magazine article, or a special treatment of a subject on radio or television ‖ 특별한 신문이나 잡지 기사, 또는 라디오나 텔레비전에서 특별히 취급한 주제. 특집 기사[프로]: *a feature on Johnny Depp in Sunday's paper* 일요일 신문에 난 조니 뎁에 관한 특집 기사 **3** a part of someone's face ‖ 사람 얼굴의 일부. 이목구비: *Her eyes are her best feature.* 그녀는 눈이 제일 예쁘다. **4** a movie ‖ 영화: *There's a double feature* (=two movies the same evening) *playing at the mall theater.* 쇼핑센터 영화관에서는 두 편의 영화를 동시 상영한다.

feature² *v* **1** [T] to show a particular person or thing in a film, magazine, show etc. ‖ 영화·잡지·쇼 등에서 특정한 사람이나 사물을 보여 주다. 출연시키다. 나오게 하다. 싣다: *a new movie featuring Meryl Streep* 메릴 스트립 주연의 새 영화 **2** [I] to be an important part of something ‖ 어떤 것의 중요한 부분이다. …의 특징을 이루다. …의 특색이 되다: *Violence features too strongly in many TV shows.* 폭력은 많은 텔레비전 쇼에서 아주 중요한 역할을 한다 **3** [T] to advertise a particular product ‖ 특정한 상품을 광고하다: *The supermarket's featuring a new ice cream.* 그 슈퍼마켓은 새 아이스크림을 광고하고 있다.

Feb·ru·ar·y /ˈfɛbyuˌɛri, ˈfɛbruˌɛri/, *written abbreviation* **Feb.** *n* the second month of the year ‖ 그 해의 두 번째 달. 2월 —see usage note at JANUARY

fe·ces /ˈfisiz/ *n* [plural] FORMAL solid waste material from the BOWELS ‖ 장에서 나오는 고형 배설물. 대변. 똥 – **fecal** /ˈfikəl/ *adj*

Fed /fɛd/ *n* **the Fed** INFORMAL ⇨ FEDERAL RESERVE SYSTEM

fed¹ *v* the past tense and PAST PARTICIPLE of FEED ‖ feed의 과거·과거 분사형

fed² *n* INFORMAL a police officer in the FBI ‖ FBI 수사관

fed·er·al /ˈfɛdərəl/ *adj* **1** relating to the central government of a country ‖ 국가의 중앙 정부의: *federal and state taxes* 연방세(稅)와 주세(州稅) **2** consisting of a group of states that control their own affairs but are controlled by a central government ‖ 행정 업무를 자체적으로 운영하지만 중앙 정부의 통제를 받는 일단의 주로 구성된. 연방의: *the Federal Republic of Germany* 독일 연방 공화국

Federal Bu·reau of In·ves·ti·ga·tion /ˌ… ˌ… … ˈ…/ *n* [singular] ⇨ FBI

F

fed·er·al·ism /ˈfɛdərəˌlɪzəm/ *n* [U] belief in or support for a FEDERAL system of government ‖ 정부의 연방 제도에 대한 신념이나 지지. 연방주의. 연방 제도 – **federalist** *n, adj*

Federal Reserve Sys·tem /ˌ… ˈ…ˌ… …/ *n* [singular] the main system of banks in the US, in which a group of 7 officials and 12 banks control the way the country's banks work ‖ 7명의 관리와 12개의 은행 집단이 미국의 은행 업무 방식을 통제하는 미국 은행의 주요 시스템. 미국 연방 준비 제도

fed·er·a·tion /ˌfɛdəˈreɪʃən/ *n* a group of countries, organizations, clubs, or people that have joined together to form a single group ‖ 하나의 집단을 이루려고 합친 일단의 국가[조직, 클럽, 사람]. 연합. 연맹. 동맹: *the American Federation of Teachers* 미국 교사 연맹 – **federate** /ˈfɛdəˌreɪt/ *v* [I]

fed up /ˌ. ˈ./ *adj* INFORMAL annoyed or bored, and wanting something to change ‖ 짜증나거나 싫증이 나서 뭔가 변화를 바라는. 진력이 난. 질린: *I'm really fed up with these boring business dinners.* 이 지루한 업무상 식사에는 정말 진력이 난다.

fee /fi/ *n* **1** an amount of money that you pay for professional services ‖ 전문

적인 활동에 지불하는 금액. 수수료. 보
수: *medical fees* 의료비 / *college fees* 대
학 수업료 **2** an amount of money that
you pay to do something ‖ 어떤 것을 하
기 위해 지불하는 돈. 요금: *video rental
fees* 비디오 대여료

fee·ble /'fibəl/ *adj* **1** extremely weak ‖
아주 약한. 가냘픈: *His voice sounded
feeble.* 그의 목소리는 가냘팠다. **2** a
feeble joke, excuse, argument etc. is
not very good ‖ 농담·변명·토론 등이 그
다지 효력이 좋지 않은. 설득력이 약한

fee·ble-mind·ed /'.. ,../ *adj* unable to
think clearly and decide what to do, or
showing this quality ‖ 생각을 명확하게
할 수 없거나 할 것을 결정할 수 없는, 또
는 이런 속성을 나타내는. 정신 박약의.
지능이 낮은

feed¹ /fid/ *v* **fed, fed, feeding 1** [T]
to give food to a person or animal ‖ 사람
이나 동물에게 음식을 주다. 먹이다: *Jimmy likes feeding acorns to the
squirrels.* 지미는 다람쥐에게 도토리를 먹
이는 것을 좋아한다. **2** [T] to provide
enough food for a group of people ‖ 일단
의 사람들에게 충분한 음식을 제공하다.
부양하다: *How can you feed a family on
$50 a week?* 일주일에 50달러로 가족을
어떻게 부양할 수 있겠어요? **3** [T] to give
a special substance to a plant to make it
grow ‖ 식물이 자라도록 특별한 물질을 주
다. 비료를 주다: *Feed your violets once
a month.* 한 달에 한 번 제비꽃에 비료를
주어라. **4** [T] to put something slowly
and continuously into something else ‖
무엇인가를 천천히 계속하여 다른 것 속에
넣다. 차츰차츰 넣다: *The tube was fed
into the patient's stomach.* 관은 환자의
위 속으로 조금씩 들어갔다. **5** to give
someone information or ideas ‖ 남에게
정보나 아이디어를 제공하다: *She's been
fed a lot of lies by her friends at school.*
그녀는 학교 친구들에게서 거짓말을 많이
들었다. **6 well-fed/under-fed/poorly-
fed etc.** having plenty of food or not
enough food ‖ 음식이 충분하거나 불충분
한. 영양이 충분한/불충분한/부족한 **7** [I]
a word meaning to eat, used about
animals or babies ‖ 동물이나 아기에 대
해 쓰이는 먹다라는 의미의 단어: *Frogs
feed at night.* 개구리는 밤에 먹이를 먹는
다.

feed on sth *phr v* [T] if an animal feeds
on a particular food, it usually eats that
food ‖ 동물이 특정한 음식을 먹고 산다.
상식하다: *Cows feed on grass.* 젖소는 풀
을 상식한다.

feed² *n* [U] food for animals ‖ 동물용 먹

이. 사료: *cattle feed* 소 사료

feed·back /'fidbæk/ *n* [U] advice,
criticism etc. about how good or useful
something is ‖ 어떤 것의 우수성이나 유용
성에 대한 충고나 비판 등. 반응. 의견:
*The teacher's been giving us helpful
feedback.* 그 선생님은 우리에게 유익한
충고를 해 오고 계신다. / *Can I get some
feedback on this artwork?* 이 예술 작품
에 대한 의견을 말씀해 주시겠어요?

feed·bag /'fidbæg/ *n* a bag put around
a horse's head, containing food ‖ 말의
목에 거는 사료 자루

feed·ing /'fidɪŋ/ *n* a meal eaten by a
baby ‖ 아기의 한 끼 식사: *It's time for
her noon feeding.* 우리 아가 정오 식사 시
간이다.

feel¹ /fil/ *v* **felt, felt, feeling**

1 ▶EMOTIONS 정서◀ [linking verb, I]
to experience a particular feeling or
emotion ‖ 특정한 감정이나 정서를 경험하
다. 느끼다: *We felt guilty for not asking
her to come with us.* 우리는 그녀에게 함
께 가자고 청하지 않은 것에 대해 죄책감
을 느꼈다. / *They didn't make us feel
very welcome.* 그들은 우리에게 대환영을
받는다는 느낌을 주지 못했다. / *I walked
through the door, and I felt as if/as
though I was walking into a foreign
country.* 나는 문으로 걸어 들어가면서 마
치 외국으로 걸어 들어가고 있는 것처럼
느꼈다. / *The Lees made me feel like
their own son.* 리 씨 가족은 나를 아들 같
은 기분이 들게 해주었다.

2 ▶PHYSICAL 육체적인◀ [linking verb]
to have a particular physical feeling ‖ 신
체적으로 특정한 느낌이 들다: *I feel
better today.* 오늘은 기분이 좋아요. / *Do
you feel cold?* 춥습니까? / *The ground
still feels damp.* 땅은 여전히 축축한 느낌
이 든다.

3 ▶OPINION 의견◀ [I, T] to have an
opinion based on your feeling rather
than on facts ‖ 사실보다는 감정에 근거한
의견이 있다. …이라고 생각하다: *How do
you feel about your new stepfather?* 새
의붓아버지를 어떻게 생각하니?

4 ▶TOUCH 만지다◀ [T] to touch
something with your fingers to find out
about it ‖ 어떤 것에 대해 알아내려고 손
가락으로 만지다: *Feel my forehead. Does
it seem hot?* 내 이마를 만져 봐. 열이 있
는 것 같니?

5 ▶NOTICE STH …을 알아채다◀ [T] to
notice something physical that is
happening to you ‖ 자신에게 일어나고 있
는 신체적인 일을 알아채다. 느끼다: *She
felt a bug crawling up her leg.* 그녀는 벌

레 한 마리가 다리 위로 기어오르는 것을 느꼈다. / *Just feel that fresh sea air!* 그 상쾌한 바다 바람 좀 느껴 봐!

6 feel the effects/benefits etc. of sth to experience the good or bad results of something ‖ 어떤 것의 좋거나 나쁜 결과를 경험하다. …의 영향/혜택을 받다: *We've started to feel the effects of the recession.* 우리는 불황의 영향을 받기 시작했다.

7 feel your way to move carefully with your hands in front of you because you cannot see well ‖ 잘 볼 수 없어서 조심스럽게 손으로 앞을 더듬으며 나아가다

8 feel the pinch to have problems because of lack of money ‖ 돈이 없어서 고생하다. 돈에 쪼들리다: *Small businesses are feeling the pinch of the recession.* 영세 기업은 불경기로 돈에 쪼들려 고생하고 있다.

SPOKEN PHRASES
---

9 feel like to want to have something or do something ‖ 어떤 것을 가지거나 하기를 원하다. …하고 싶다: *Do you feel like ordering a pizza?* 피자 주문하고 싶니? / *I feel like a cigarette.* 담배 피우고 싶다. (=feel like having a cigarette)

10 feel free used in order to say that you are happy if someone wants to do something ‖ 남이 어떤 것을 하기 원하면 화자(話者)는 기쁘다는 것을 말하는 데에 쓰여. 마음대로[서슴지 않고] …하다: *Please feel free to come by my office.* 부담 갖지 말고 내 사무실에 들르세요.

11 I know how you feel said in order to show your sympathy with someone ‖ 남에게 공감을 나타내는 데에 쓰여: *"I can't seem to do anything right today." "I know exactly how you feel."* "오늘은 아무 일도 제대로 못할 것 같아." "나도 네 기분 잘 알아."

feel for sb *phr v* [T] to feel sympathy for someone ‖ 남을 동정하다: *I really feel for you, Joel, but I don't know what to suggest.* 조엘, 정말 안됐구나. 하지만 뭐라 해야 할지 모르겠다.

feel sb ↔ **out** *phr v* [T] INFORMAL to find out what someone's opinions or feelings are without asking him/her directly ‖ 남의 의견이나 감정을 직접 물어 보지 않고 알아내다. 타진하다. 염탐하다: *Well, I could feel my Dad out about using the cabin.* 어쩌면 내가 오두막집을 사용하는 것에 대해서 아빠의 의향을 알아낼 수 있

을거야.

feel sb ↔ **up** *phr v* [T] SLANG to touch someone sexually ‖ 남을 성(性)적으로 만지다

feel up to sth *phr v* [T] INFORMAL to feel you can do a particular job ‖ 특정한 일을 할 수 있을 것 같은 생각이 들다: *I don't really feel up to going out tonight.* 나는 오늘 밤은 정말 외출하고 싶지 않다.

feel² *n* [singular] **1** the way something feels when you touch it ‖ 사물을 만질 때의 느낌. 감촉. 촉감: *the feel of the sand under our feet* 발밑에서 느껴지는 모래의 감촉 / *Wet soap has a greasy feel.* 젖은 비누는 미끈거리는 촉감이 있다. **2** a quality that something has that makes you feel a particular way about it ‖ 특정한 느낌이 들게 하는 사물이 지닌 성질. 느낌. 분위기: *The beach has a kind of lonely feel.* 그 해변은 좀 쓸쓸한 느낌이 든다. / *The house had a nice feel about it.* 그 집은 분위기가 괜찮았다. **3 have a feel for** INFORMAL to have a natural understanding of something and skill in doing it ‖ 어떤 것에 대한 천부적인 이해력과 수행 솜씨가 있다. 감각[센스]이 있다: *Pete has a real feel for music.* 피트는 음악에 대한 감각이 대단하다. **4 get the feel of** to become comfortable with something ‖ 어떤 것에 편안해지다. …에 익숙해지다: *You'll soon get the feel of the car.* 너는 그 차에 곧 익숙해질 거다.

feel·er /ˈfilɚ/ *n* **1 put out feelers** to start to try to discover what people think about something that you want to do ‖ 자신이 하고 싶어 하는 것에 대한 사람들의 생각을 애써 알려고 하다. 떠보다. 타진하다: *I'm putting out feelers to see if they have any jobs open.* 나는 그들에게 공석인 일자리가 있는지의 여부를 타진하고 있다. **2** INFORMAL one of the two long things on an insect's head that it uses to feel or touch things ‖ 물체를 느끼거나 더듬는 데에 사용하는 곤충의 머리에 길게 나 있는 두 개 중의 하나. 더듬이. 촉각

feel·ing /ˈfilɪŋ/ *n* **1** something that you feel such as anger, sadness, or happiness ‖ 분노[슬픔, 행복] 등의 느끼는 것. 느낌. 감정: *There's no reason for you to have these guilt feelings.* 당신은 이러한 죄책감을 가질 이유가 없다. / *a feeling of confidence* 자신감 —see also **hurt sb's feelings** (FEELINGS) **2** a belief or opinion about something ‖ 어떤 것에 대한 신념이나 의견: *What are your feelings on the drug problem?* 마약 문제에 대해서 당신은 어떻게 생각하십니까? / *I have a feeling she's lying to us.* 나는

그녀가 우리에게 거짓말을 하고 있다는 생각이 든다. / *Mothers sometimes have mixed feelings about going to work.* (=are not sure what they feel or think) 어머니들은 가끔 직장에 나가는 것에 착잡한 기분이 든다. **3** [singular, U] a general attitude among a group of people about a subject ‖ 어떤 주제에 대한 일단의 사람 사이의 일반적인 태도: *a strong anti-war feeling* 강렬한 반전 기류 **4** [C, U] something that you feel in your body such as pain, heat, cold etc., or your ability to feel this ‖ 고통[더위, 추위]등의 몸에서 느끼는 것, 또는 이것을 느끼는 능력. 감각. 촉감. 느낌: *I have this funny feeling* (=a strange feeling) *in my neck.* 내 목에서 이 이상한 느낌이 든다. / *He has no feeling in his legs.* 그는 다리에 감각이 없다. **5 with feeling** in a way that shows you understand or care very much about something ‖ 어떤 것에 대한 대단한 이해와 관심을 나타내어. 감정을 넣어. 열의 있게: *She plays the violin with great feeling.* 그녀는 아주 심취하여 바이올린을 연주한다. / *He spoke with deep feeling about the war.* 그는 그 전쟁에 대해 아주 열광적으로 말했다. **6 bad/ill feeling** anger, lack of trust etc. between people ‖ 사람 사이의 분노나 믿음의 결여 등. 반감. 악감정: *The divorce caused a lot of bad feeling between them.* 그 이혼으로 그들은 서로에게 안 좋은 감정만 더 쌓였다. **7 I know the feeling** SPOKEN said when you understand how someone feels because you have had the same feeling ‖ 같은 감정을 경험했기 때문에 남의 기분을 이해할 때에 쓰여. 그 기분을 안다: *"I'm too tired to work today." "I know the feeling."* "오늘은 너무 피곤해서 일할 수 없어." "나도 그 기분 알지."

feel·ings /'filiŋz/ *n* **hurt sb's feelings** to upset or offend someone, especially by saying something unfair or untrue about him/her ‖ 특히 부당하거나 진실하지 않은 말을 남을 당황하게 하거나 기분을 상하게 하여: *Don't say things like that! You really hurt her feelings.* 그런 말은 하지 마라! 정말이지 네가 그녀의 마음을 상하게 한단 말이야.

feet /fit/ *n* the plural of FOOT ‖ foot의 복수형

feign /feɪn/ *v* [T] FORMAL to pretend to have a particular feeling or to be ill, asleep etc. ‖ 특정한 감정이 있는[아픈, 잠자는] 체하다. 가장하다: *We feigned interest in Mr. Dixon's stamp collection.* 우리는 딕슨 씨의 우표 수집에 흥미있는

척했다.

feint /feɪnt/ *n* a movement or an attack that is intended to deceive an opponent ‖ 상대를 속이기 위한 동작이나 공격. 페인트

feist·y /'faɪsti/ *adj* APPROVING having a lot of energy and liking to argue ‖ 원기 왕성하고 논쟁하기 좋아하는. 팔팔한. 의욕이 넘치는: *a feisty 8-year-old girl* 발랄한 8살 소녀

fe·line /'filaɪn/ *n* TECHNICAL a cat or a member of the cat family ‖ 고양이나 고양잇과의 동물 **– feline** *adj*

fell¹ /fɛl/ *v* the past tense of FALL ‖ fall의 과거형

fell² *v* [T] **1** to cut down a tree ‖ 나무를 베어 넘어뜨리다 **2** to knock someone down with a lot of force ‖ 남을 완력으로 때려눕히다

fel·low¹ /'fɛloʊ/ *n* **1** INFORMAL a man ‖ 남자: *I have a fellow who cuts my grass.* 나는 잔디를 깎아주는 남자를 두고 있다. **2** a GRADUATE student who has a FELLOWSHIP in a university ‖ 대학에서 장학금을 받고 있는 대학원생 **3** a member of a society in a school or university ‖ 학교나 대학의 학회 회원

fellow² *adj* relating to people who do the same thing you do ‖ 같은 일을 하는 사람의. 동료의: *He traveled with some of his fellow workers/students.* 그는 동료 직원[학생] 몇 명과 여행했다.

fel·low·ship /'fɛloʊˌʃɪp, -lə-/ *n* **1** money given to a student to allow him/her to continue his/her studies ‖ 학생에게 학업을 계속하도록 주어지는 돈. 연구 장학금: *a graduate fellowship* 대학원생 연구 장학금 **2** a group with similar interests or beliefs ‖ 비슷한 관심사나 믿음을 가진 단체. 회. 조합: *a Christian youth fellowship* 기독교 청년 단체 **3** [U] a feeling of friendship resulting from shared interests or experiences ‖ 관심사나 경험의 공유에서 생기는 친밀한 느낌. 동료애. 우정. 유대감

fel·on /'fɛlən/ *n* a criminal who has COMMITTED a serious crime ‖ 중대한 범죄를 저지른 죄인. 중죄인: *a convicted felon* (=a criminal who is sent to prison) 유죄를 선고받은 중죄인

fel·o·ny /'fɛləni/ *n* LAW a serious crime such as murder ‖ 살인 등의 중대한 범죄. 흉악 범죄. 중죄

felt¹ /fɛlt/ *v* the past tense and PAST PARTICIPLE of FEEL ‖ feel의 과거·과거 분사형

felt² *n* [U] a thick soft material made of wool, hair, or fur that has been pressed flat ‖ 압착된 양모[털, 모피]로 만든 도톰하고 부드러운 물질. 펠트

felt tip pen /ˌ. ˈ. ./ *n* a pen that has a hard piece of felt at the end that the ink comes through ‖ 잉크가 나오는 끝이 딱딱한 펠트 조각으로 된 펜. 펠트 펜

fe·male¹ /ˈfiːmeɪl/ *n* a person or animal that belongs to the sex that can have babies or produce eggs ‖ 아이[새끼]를 갖거나 알을 낳을 수 있는 성에 속하는 사람이나 동물. 여성. 암컷

female² *adj* **1** belonging to the sex that can have babies or produce eggs ‖ 아이[새끼]를 갖거나 알을 낳을 수 있는 성에 속하는. 여성의. 암컷의: *a female horse* 암 말 **2** a female plant or flower produces fruit ‖ 식물이나 꽃이 열매를 맺는 —see usage note at MASCULINE

fem·i·nine /ˈfɛmənɪn/ *adj* **1** having qualities that are considered to be typical of women ‖ 여자에게 전형적인 것으로 생각되는 특성을 갖는. 여성의. 여성적인[다운]: *feminine clothes* 여성 의류 **2** TECHNICAL in grammar, a feminine noun or PRONOUN has a special form that means it relates to a female, such as "actress" or "her" ‖ 문법에서 명사나 대명사가 "actress"나 "her" 등의 여성과 관련됨을 의미하는 특수 형태를 취하는. 여성(형)의. 여성형 단어의 —compare MASCULINE

fem·i·nin·i·ty /ˌfɛməˈnɪnəti/ *n* [U] qualities that are considered to be typical of women ‖ 여성에게 전형적이라고 생각되는 특성. 여성적 기질[특질]. 여자다움 —compare MASCULINITY

fem·i·nism /ˈfɛməˌnɪzəm/ *n* [U] the belief that women should have the same rights and opportunities as men ‖ 여성도 남성과 똑같은 권리와 기회를 가져야 한다는 믿음. 남녀 평등[동권]주의. 페미니즘 – **feminist** *n, adj*

fence¹ /fɛns/ *n* **1** a structure made of wood, metal etc. that surrounds a piece of land ‖ 대지를 둘러싸고 있는 목재·금속 등으로 만들어진 구조물. 담(장). 울타리 **2 on the fence** not having decided something ‖ 어떤 것을 결정하지 않고 있는. 편에 들지 않은. 어정쩡한 태도를 취하는. 형세를 관망하는: *54 senators were in favor, 29 were opposed, and 17 were still sitting on the fence.* 54명의 상원 의원이 찬성했고, 29명은 반대, 17명은 여전히 관망 중이었다. **3** someone who buys and sells stolen goods ‖ 도난된 물품을 사고 파는 사람. 장물아비

fence² *v* **1** [T] to put a fence around something ‖ 무엇의 둘레에 울타리를 치

다. 담을 세우다[으로 막다] **2** [I] to fight with a sword as a sport ‖ 운동 경기로서 칼로 싸우다. 펜싱을 하다. 검술(시합)을 하다

fence sth ↔ in *phr v* [T] to surround a place with a fence ‖ 울타리[담]로 한 지역을 둘러싸다. …에 울타리를 치다 – **fenced-in** /ˌfɛnst ˈɪn/ *adj*

fence sb/sth ↔ off *phr v* [T] to separate one area from another with a fence ‖ 울타리[담]로 한 지역을 다른 지역으로부터 분리하다. 울타리[담]로 나누다[구분하다]: *We fenced off part of the backyard.* 우리는 뒷마당의 일부에 담을 쌓았다.

fenc·ing /ˈfɛnsɪŋ/ *n* [U] **1** the sport of fighting with a long thin sword ‖ 길고 가는 검으로 싸우는 운동 경기. 펜싱 **2** fences, or the material used for making them ‖ 울타리[담장], 또는 이것을 만드는 데에 쓰이는 재료. 울타리[담장](재료)

fend /fɛnd/ *v* **fend for yourself** to take care of yourself without help from other people ‖ 다른 사람의 도움 없이 자신을 돌보다. 스스로를 보살피다. 자활(自活)하다: *Now that the kids are old enough to fend for themselves, we're free to travel more.* 이제는 아이들이 스스로 자신들을 돌볼 만큼 충분히 나이가 들어서 우리는 자유롭게 더 자주 여행을 한다.

fend sb/sth off *phr v* [T] to defend yourself from something such as competition, an attack, or things you do not want to deal with ‖ 경쟁[공격, 다루고 싶지 않은 것] 등으로부터 자신을 방어하다. 막아내다. 물리치다. 받아 넘기다: *Mrs. Spector tried to fend off the other mugger.* 스펙터 부인은 다른 노상 강도를 막아내려고 애썼다. / *Henry did his best to fend off the journalists.* 헨리는 기자들을 뿌리치려고 안간힘을 썼다.

fend·er /ˈfɛndɚ/ *n* **1** the part of a car that covers the wheels ‖ 자동차의 바퀴를 덮는 부품. 바퀴 덮개 —see picture on page 943 **2** a curved piece of metal that covers the wheel on a bicycle ‖ 자전거의 바퀴를 덮는 휘어진 금속 부분. 바퀴 덮개. 흙받기

fer·ment¹ /fɚˈmɛnt/ *v* [I, T] if fruit, beer, or wine ferments, the sugar in it changes to alcohol ‖ 과일[맥주, 포도주] 내의 당분이 알코올로 변하다. 발효하다 [시 키 다] – **fermentation** /ˌfɚmənˈteɪʃən/ *n* [U] – **fermented** /fɚˈmɛntɪd/ *adj*

fer·ment² /ˈfɚmɛnt/ *n* [U] a situation of excitement or trouble in a country, especially caused by political change ‖

한 나라 내에서 특히 정치적 변동에 의해 야기된 흥분되거나 곤란한 상황. 정치적 동요[소요] 상태

fern /fɚn/ *n* a plant with green leaves shaped like large feathers, but no flowers ‖ 큰 깃털 모양의 녹색 잎이 달린, 꽃이 없는 식물. 고사리류

fe·ro·cious /fəˈroʊʃəs/ *adj* extremely violent or severe ‖ 매우 폭력적이거나 흑한. 격렬한. 난폭한. 사나운. 잔혹한: *There was a big ferocious dog chained inside the gate.* 대문 안에는 크고 사나운 개가 줄에 묶여 있었다. / *a ferocious Atlantic storm* 맹렬한 기세의 대서양 폭풍 **– ferociously** *adv*

fe·ro·ci·ty /fəˈrɑsəti/ *n* [U] the state of being extremely violent or severe ‖ 극히 난폭하거나 가혹함. 잔인. 흉포. 포악 (성): *Felipe was shocked by the ferocity of her anger.* 펠리페는 그녀가 포악하게 화내는 데에 충격을 받았다.

fer·ret¹ /ˈfɛrɪt/ *v* [I] INFORMAL to search for something, especially inside a box, drawer etc. ‖ 특히 상자·서랍 등의 속에서 어떤 것을 찾다. 이리 저리 뒤지다. 찾아 뒤적거리다: *Andy ferreted around in his desk for a pen.* 앤디는 펜을 찾기 위해 책상 서랍을 뒤졌다.

ferret sth ↔ **out** *phr v* [T] INFORMAL to succeed in finding something, especially information ‖ 특히 정보 등을 찾는 데에 성공하다. 발견해 내다. 찾아내다: *It took years of research to ferret out the truth.* 그 사실을 발견해 내기 위해 수년 동안 연구했다.

ferret² *n* a small animal with soft fur, used for hunting rats and rabbits ‖ 부드러운 털이 나 있고 쥐와 토끼를 사냥하는 데에 쓰는 작은 동물. 흰담비

fer·ris wheel /ˈfɛrɪs ˌwil/ *n* a very large wheel with seats on it for people to ride on in an AMUSEMENT PARK ‖ 놀이 동산에서 사람들이 타는 좌석이 달린 큰 바퀴. 페리스 관람차

fer·rous /ˈfɛrəs/ *adj* TECHNICAL containing iron, or relating to iron ‖ 철을 함유한, 또는 철의[에 관련된]: *ferrous metals* 철(을 함유한) 금속

fer·ry¹ /ˈfɛri/ *n* a boat that carries people, often with their cars, across a narrow area of water such as a river ‖ 사람을, 종종 그들의 차량과 함께 강 등의 수역을 건네주는 배. 나룻배. 연락선

ferry² *v* [T] to carry people or goods a short distance from one place to another ‖ 사람이나 물자를 한 장소에서 다른 곳으로 짧은 구간을 나르다. 수송하다: *a bus that ferries tourists from the*

hotel to the beach 관광객들을 호텔에서 해변으로 실어 나르는 버스

fer·tile /ˈfɚtl/ *adj* **1** fertile land or soil is able to produce a lot of plants — opposite INFERTILE ‖ 땅이나 흙이 작물을 많이 생산할 수 있는. 비옥한. 기름진 **2** fertile people or animals are able to produce babies ‖ 사람이나 동물이 아이[새끼]를 낳을 수 있는. 번식력이 있는. 다산인 —opposite INFERTILE **3** **fertile imagination** an imagination that is able to produce a lot of unusual ideas ‖ 특이한 생각을 많이 내놓을 수 있는 상상력. 창의적 상상력 **– fertility** /fɚˈtɪləti/ *n* [U]

fer·til·ize /ˈfɚtlˌaɪz/ *v* [T] **1** to put FERTILIZER on the soil to help plants grow ‖ 식물 성장을 돕도록 땅에 비료를 주다. 비료로 땅을 기름지게[비옥하게] 하다 **2** to make new animal or plant life begin to develop ‖ 동물이나 식물의 새 생명이 성장하기 시작하게 하다. 수정[수태]시키다: *a fertilized egg* 수정란 **– fertilization** /ˌfɚtləˈzeɪʃən/ *n* [U]

fer·til·iz·er /ˈfɚtlˌaɪzɚ/ *n* [C, U] a substance that is put on the soil to help plants grow ‖ 식물 성장을 돕도록 땅에 뿌려지는 물질. 비료. 거름

fer·vent /ˈfɚvənt/ *adj* believing or feeling something very strongly ‖ 어떤 것을 매우 강하게 믿거나 느끼는. 열렬한. 열심인: *Marion's a fervent believer in working hard.* 메리언은 열심히 일하는 것을 열렬하게 신봉하는 사람이다. **– fervently** *adv*

fer·vor /ˈfɚvɚ/ *n* [U] very strong belief or feeling ‖ 매우 강한 믿음이나 감정. 열렬. 열정: *religious fervor* 종교적 열정

fess /fɛs/ *v*

fess up *phr v* [I] SPOKEN to admit that you have done something wrong, although it is not serious ‖ 심하지는 않지만 어떤 일을 잘못했음을 인정하다. 실토하다. 고백[자인]하다: *Come on, fess up! Who drank all the milk?* 어서, 실토해! 누가 우유를 다 마셨지?

fest /fɛst/ *n* **beer/song/food fest etc.** an informal occasion when a lot of people do a fun activity together ‖ 많은 사람들이 함께 놀이를 하는 비공식 행사. 맥주/노래/음식 파티

fes·ter /ˈfɛstɚ/ *v* [I] **1** if a bad situation or a problem festers, it continues for too long because is has not been dealt with ‖ 나쁜 상황이나 문제가 처리되지 않아서 너무 오랫동안 지속되다. 고질이 되다. 마음에 맺히다. 심해지다. 악화되다: *Letting your anger fester will only make things worse.* 당신이 분노를 계속 터뜨려

봤자 상황을 더욱 악화시킬 뿐입니다. **2** if a wound festers, it becomes infected || 상처가 감염되다. 곪다. 화농하다

fes·ti·val /ˈfɛstəvəl/ n **1** an organized set of events such as musical performances or movies || 음악 공연이나 영화 등 조직화된 일련의 행사. 축제. 예술 공연제: *the Cannes film festival* 칸느 영화제 **2** a time of public celebration, especially for a religious event || 특히 종교적 행사를 위한 대중 축제일. 경축일. 축제일

fes·tive /ˈfɛstɪv/ adj happy or cheerful in a way that is suitable for celebrating something || 어떤 일을 축하하기에 알맞게 행복하거나 즐거운. 명절 기분의. 축제다운: *Hollie was in a festive mood at the office party.* 홀리는 사무실 파티에서 축제 분위기에 싸여 있었다.

fes·tiv·i·ties /fɛˈstɪvətiz/ [plural] things such as dancing, eating etc. that are done to celebrate a special occasion || 특별 행사를 축하하기 위해 행해지는 춤 추기·먹기 등의 일. 축제. 제전. 축제 행사[의식]

fes·toon /fɛˈstun/ v [T] to cover something with cloth, flowers etc., especially as a decoration || 특히 장식으로서 사물을 천·꽃 등으로 덮다. 꽃 장식을 두르다

fe·tal /ˈfitl/ adj relating to a FETUS || 태아에 관한. 태아의: *an instrument to measure fetal growth* 태아의 성장을 측정하는 기구

fetal po·si·tion /ˈ.. .,../ n a body position in which your body is curled up, and your arms and legs are pulled up against your chest || 몸을 (둥글게) 말아 올려 팔과 다리를 가슴에 끌어 모은 몸 자세. 태아의 자세

fetch /fɛtʃ/ v [T] INFORMAL **1** to be sold for a particular amount of money || 특정한 가격에 팔리다. 값이 …이 되다: *The tractor should fetch over $10,000 at public auction.* 그 트랙터는 일반 경매에서 1만 달러 이상의 가격이 나갈 것이다. **2** to go and get something, and bring it back || 가서 물건을 집어서 가져오다. 가져다주다. 가지고 오다: *Would you fetch me a glass of water from the kitchen?* 부엌에서 물 좀 한 잔 가져다 주시겠습니까?

fetch·ing /ˈfɛtʃɪŋ/ adj OLD-FASHIONED attractive || 매력적인. 관심을 끄는. 마음을 사로잡는

fete¹ /feɪt/ v [T] to honor someone by having a public celebration for him/her || 대중 축하 행사를 열어서 어떤 사람을

기리다. 잔치를 베풀어 환대하다: *The champions were feted from coast to coast.* 챔피언들은 전국에서 축하 행사로 환영받았다.

fete² n a special occasion to celebrate something || 어떤 일을 축하하는 특별 행사. 향연. 축제 행사. 잔치

fet·id /ˈfɛtɪd/ adj FORMAL having a very bad smell || 매우 고약한 냄새를 풍기는. 악취가 나는: *the black fetid water* 시커멓고 악취를 풍기는 오수

fet·ish /ˈfɛtɪʃ/ n **1** an unusual object or activity that gives someone sexual pleasure || 사람에게 성적인 쾌락을 주는 특이한 물체나 행위. 성적 자극물[행위]. 성적 대상물: *a leather fetish* 가죽 제품에 의한 성적 자극(물) **2** something that you are always thinking about, or spending too much time doing || 항상 생각하고 있거나 행하는 데 너무 많은 시간을 소모하는 것. 집착물. 맹목적 숭배물: *McBride has a real fetish about exercising every day.* 맥브라이드는 매일 운동하는 일에 몹시 집착하고 있다. **3** an object that is thought to have magical powers || 마력을 지녔다고 여겨지는 대상(물). 주물(呪物)

fet·ter /ˈfɛtɚ/ v [T] FORMAL to prevent someone from doing what s/he wants to do || 어떤 사람이 원하는 것을 하지 못하게 막다. 구속하다: *managers fettered by rules and regulations* 규칙과 규정에 의해 속박된 관리자들

fet·ters /ˈfɛtɚz/ n [plural] **1** FORMAL things that prevent someone from doing what s/he wants to do || 어떤 사람이 원하는 것을 하지 못하게 막는 것. 구속[속박](물) **2** OLD-FASHIONED chains that are put around a prisoner's feet || 죄수의 발에 두르는 사슬. 족쇄. 차꼬

fe·tus /ˈfitəs/ n TECHNICAL a young human or animal before birth || 태어나기 전의 어린 사람이나 동물. 태아 — compare EMBRYO

feud /fyud/ n an angry quarrel between two people or groups that continues for a long time || 두 사람이나 집단 간에 오랫동안 계속되어 온 불화. 반목. 숙원: *a bitter feud between the two neighbors* 두 이웃간의 모진 반목 **– feud** v [I]

feu·dal·is·m /ˈfyudə,lɪzəm/ n [U] a social system in the Middle Ages, in which people received land and protection from someone of higher rank when they worked and fought for him || 사람들이 상층 계급의 사람을 위해 일하고 싸울 때 그들로부터 토지와 보호를 받는, 중세 시대의 사회 제도. 봉건 제도. 봉건

주의 – **feudal** adj

fe·ver /'fivər/ n 1 [C, U] an illness in which you have a very high temperature ∥ 매우 높은 열이 나는 병. 열병. 고열: *Drink a lot of fluids, it'll help your fever go down.* 물을 많이 드세요, 열을 내리게 해줄 것입니다. 2 [U] a state in which a lot of people are excited about something in a crazy way ∥ 많은 사람들이 미친 듯이 어떤 일에 흥분되어 있는 상태. 극도의 흥분. 열광. 열풍. 광기: *lottery fever* (=excitement about winning money) 복권 열풍 / *When the TV crews arrived, the demonstration reached fever pitch.* (=an extreme level of excitement) 텔레비전 방송 기자들이 도착했을 때 시위는 가장 격렬해졌다. – **fevered** adj

fe·ver·ish /'fivərɪʃ/ adj 1 suffering from a fever ∥ 고열로 시달리는. 열이 있는 (듯한). 발열한 2 done extremely quickly by people who are very excited or worried ∥ 매우 흥분되거나 걱정스러워 하는 사람들에 의해 극히 빠르게 행해진. 열광적으로 빨리 하는. 미친 듯이[열에 들떠서] 하는: *working at a feverish pace* 신들린 듯이 빠른 속도로 일하는 – **feverishly** adv

few /fyu/ quantifier, n [plural] 1 **a few/the few** a small number of something ∥ 사물의 적은 수. 소수[소량]의…. 몇몇[약간]의…: *I've seen a few of those new cars around.* 나는 그 새 차 몇 대가 돌아다니는 것을 보았다. / *Let's wait a few minutes and see if Carrie gets here.* 몇 분 기다려서 캐리가 여기 오는가 보자. / *Don has seemed really happy these last few weeks.* (=the weeks just before this) 돈은 최근의 요 몇 주간 아주 행복해 보였다. / *You'll have to work hard over the next few months.* (=the months just after this time) 당신은 다음 몇 달에 걸쳐 열심히 일해야 할 것입니다. / *There are a few more things I'd like to talk about before we go.* 우리가 가기 전에 이야기하고 싶은 것이 몇 가지 더 있습니다. / *I've read a few of her books.* 나는 그녀의 책들 중 몇 권을 읽었다. / *Grant's one of the few people I know who can tell stories well.* 그랜트는 이야기를 잘하는 내가 아는 몇 사람 중의 한 명입니다. 2 **quite a few** a fairly large number of things or people ∥ 사물이나 사람의 꽤 많은 숫자. 상당수. 다수: *Quite a few people came to the meeting.* 상당수의 사람들이 회의에 참석했다. 3 not many ∥ 많지 않음. 거의 없음. 아주 적음. 극소수[량]: *There are few events*

that are as exciting as having a baby. 아이를 갖는 것만큼 흥분되는 사건은 거의 없다. 4 **be few and far between** to be rare ∥ 드물다. 희귀하다. 극히 드물다. 매우 적다: *Good jobs are few and far between these days.* 요즈음은 좋은 일자리가 극히 드물다. —see usage note at LESS¹

USAGE NOTE few, a few, little, and **a little**

Use **few** with plural countable nouns to mean "not many": *Few people said they'd help.* Use **a few** with plural countable nouns to mean "some": *A few people arrived late.* Use **little** with uncountable nouns to mean "not much": *There's usually little traffic early in the morning.* Use **a little** with uncountable nouns to mean "a small amount of something": *There was only a little ice cream left.*
few는 "많지 않은 수"를 뜻하며 복수 가산 명사와 함께 쓴다: 그들이 도울 거라고 말한 사람은 거의 없었다. **a few**는 "약간[다소]"을 뜻하며 복수 가산 명사와 함께 쓴다: 몇몇 사람이 늦게 도착했다. **little**은 "많지 않음"을 뜻하며 불가산 명사와 함께 쓴다: 보통 이른 아침에는 교통량이 거의 없다. **a little**은 "소량의 사물[조금]"을 뜻하며 불가산 명사와 함께 쓴다: 아이스크림이 아주 조금만 남아 있었다.

---

fez /fɛz/ n a small round red hat with a flat top ∥ 위가 납작한 작고 둥근 모자. 터키 모자

fi·an·cé /,fian'seɪ, fi'ɑnseɪ/ n the man whom you are going to marry ∥ 결혼할 남자. 약혼한 남자

fi·an·cée /,fian'seɪ, fi'ɑnseɪ/ n the woman whom you are going to marry ∥ 결혼할 여자. 약혼녀

fi·as·co /fi'æskoʊ/ n, plural **fiascoes** or **fiascos** [C, U] something that is done that is completely unsuccessful ∥ 완전히 실패로 끝난 일. 대실패. 완패. 참패: *Their attempt to compete in the software market has been a total fiasco.* 소프트웨어 시장에서 경쟁하려 했던 그들의 시도는 대참패로 끝났다.

fi·at /'fiæt, -ɑt, -ət/ n [C, U] FORMAL a command that is given by someone in authority without considering what other people want ∥ 권력을 잡은 사람에 의해 다른 사람들이 원하는 것을 고려하지 않고 내리는 명령. 독단적[강압적] 명령. 칙령 통치: *Too often he governed by fiat* *rather than by the law.* 그는 법률보다는 강압적인 명령으로 통치하는 일이 너무 많았다.

fib¹ /fɪb/ *n* INFORMAL a small, unimportant lie ‖ 사소하고 중요하지 않은 거짓말. 사소한[악의 없는] 거짓말: *You shouldn't tell fibs. It's not nice.* 너는 사소한 거짓말을 해서는 안 된다. 그것은 좋지 않아.

fib² *v* [I] SPOKEN to tell a small, unimportant lie ‖ 사소하고 중요하지 않은 거짓말을 하다. 사소한[악의 없는] 거짓말을 하다 **– fibber** *n*

fi·ber /'faɪbɚ/ *n* **1** [U] parts of plants that you eat but do not DIGEST, that help food to move through your body ‖ 먹어도 소화가 되지 않으며, 체내에서 음식물의 이동을 도와주는, 식물의 한 성분. 섬유질 [소]: *The doctor said I need more fiber in my diet.* 의사는 내가 식사에서 더 많은 섬유질을 섭취해야 한다고 말했다. **2** [U] the woody part of some plants that is used for making materials such as rope or cloth ‖ 밧줄이나 천 등의 소재를 만드는 데 쓰이는 일부 식물의 목질 부분. 섬유 조직 **3** a natural or artificial thread used for making cloth ‖ 천을 짜는 데 쓰이는 자연적이거나 인공적인 실. 섬유 (사): *cotton fibers* 면사(뭉치) / *polyester fibers* 폴리에스테르 사(絲) **– fibrous** /'faɪbrəs/ *adj*

fi·ber·glass /'faɪbɚˌglæs/ *n* [U] a light material made from small FIBERs of glass, used for making racing cars, small boats etc. ‖ 유리에서 뽑은 가는 섬유로 만들어져 경주용 차·소형 배 등을 만드는 데 쓰이는 가벼운 물질. 유리 섬유

fiber op·tics /ˌ.. '../ *n* [U] the use of long thin threads of glass to carry information in the form of light, especially on telephone lines ‖ 특히 전화선에서 정보를 빛의 형태로 전달하기 위해, 길고 가는 유리 섬유를 이용하는 것. 섬유 광학 **– fiber optic** *adj*

fick·le /'fɪkəl/ *adj* **1** someone who is fickle always changes his/her opinions or feelings about what s/he wants or likes ‖ 사람이 자신이 원하거나 좋아하는 것에 대한 생각이나 감정이 항상 변하는. 변덕스러운. 불안정한. 마음이 잘 바뀌는: *Every politician knows that voters are fickle.* 모든 정치인들은 유권자들이 변덕스럽다는 것을 알고 있다. **2** something that is fickle, such as the weather, often changes suddenly ‖ 날씨 등의 것이 종종 갑자기 변하는. 급변[돌변]하는

fic·tion /'fɪkʃən/ *n* **1** [U] books and stories about people and things that are

imaginary ‖ 상상(속)의 사람이나 사물에 대한 책과 이야기. 소설. 픽션: *A. A. Milne was a popular writer of children's fiction.* A. A. 밀느는 유명한 아동 소설 작가였다. —compare NONFICTION **2** something that someone wants you to believe is true, but that is not true ‖ 다른 사람이 사실이라고 믿어 주기를 바라지만 사실이 아닌 것. 허구. 가공. 꾸며낸 [지어낸] 이야기: *The newspaper story turned out to be a complete fiction.* 신문 기사의 내용은 완전히 날조된 것으로 드러났다.

fic·tion·al /'fɪkʃənəl/ *adj* fictional people or events are from a book or story, and are not real ‖ 사람이나 사건이 실재가 아닌 책이나 이야기에서 나오는. 지어낸. 허구[가공]의. 소설적인

fic·tion·al·ize /'fɪkʃənəˌlaɪz/ *v* [T] to tell the story of a real event, changing some details and adding imaginary characters ‖ 실제 사건의 줄거리에 약간의 세부 내용을 바꾸고 가공의 인물을 등장시켜 말하다. 소설화하다. 각색하다

fic·ti·tious /fɪk'tɪʃəs/ *adj* not true, or not real ‖ 사실이 아니거나 진짜가 아닌. 거짓의. 허구의. 날조된. 가공의: *Evans uses a fictitious name when he writes articles for the magazine.* 에반스는 잡지에 기고문을 쓸 때 가명을 쓴다.

fid·dle¹ /'fɪdl/ *v*

fiddle around *phr v* [I] to waste time by doing things that are not important ‖ 중요하지 않은 일을 하면서 시간을 낭비하다. 빈둥거리다. 꾸물거리다. 허송하다: *If you keep fiddling around we're going to be late!* 네가 계속해서 꾸물대면 우리는 늦을 거야!

fiddle around with sth *phr v* [T] to keep making changes to something in a way that annoys people ‖ 사람들이 짜증나게 계속 어떤 일에 변화를 주다. 계속 뜯어고치다[바꾸다]: *Why can't they stop fiddling around with the Social Security system?* 그들은 왜 계속 사회 보장 제도를 뜯어고치는 것일까?

fiddle with sth *phr v* [I] to keep moving something or touching something with your fingers because you are bored, nervous, or want to change something ‖ 지루해서, 초조해서, 어떤 것을 바꾸고 싶어서) 손가락으로 사물을 계속 움직이거나 만지다. 만지작거리다. 이리저리 계속 움직여대다: *Stop fiddling with your hair!* 네 머리 좀 그만 만지작거려라! / *Joshua's been fiddling with the TV controls again.* 조수아가 텔레비전 채널을 또 다시 이리저리 바꾸어대고 있다.

F

fiddle² *n* ⇨ VIOLIN, —see also **play second fiddle** (PLAY)

fid·dler /'fɪdlə/ *n* someone who plays the VIOLIN ‖ 바이올린 연주자

fi·del·i·ty /fə'dɛləti, faɪ-/ *n* [U] **1** loyalty to a person, organization, set of beliefs etc. ‖ 사람·조직·믿음 체계 등에 대한 충성. 충절. 정절: *Joan's fidelity to her husband has never been doubted.* 남편에 대한 조안의 정절은 결코 의심받지 않았다. —opposite INFIDELITY **2** FORMAL the quality of not changing something when you copy, record, or translate it ‖ 복사[녹음, 번역]할 때 어떤 것을 변화시키지 않는 성질. 정확[엄밀](함). 충실도

fidg·et /'fɪdʒɪt/ *v* [I] to keep moving your hands or feet, especially because you are bored or nervous ‖ 특히 지루하거나 초조해서 다리나 손을 계속 움직이다. 안절부절못하다. 초조해하다. (참지 못하고) 들썩거리다[손발을 떨어대다]: *children fidgeting in their seats* 자리에서 들썩거리는 아이들 – **fidgety** *adj*

field¹ /fild/ *n* **1** an area of land that is used for a special purpose, or that is covered in the same plants or substances ‖ 특별한 목적으로 쓰이고 있는 부지, 또는 같은 식물(군)이나 물질로 뒤덮인 구역. 대지. (들)판. 초지. 전답: *a corn field* (=where corn is grown) 옥수수밭 / *a football/baseball/soccer field* (=for playing football etc.) 미식축구[야구, 축구]장 / *an oil/coal/gas field* (=where oil etc. has been found) 석유[석탄, 가스] 산지[전] / *a snow/ice field* (=area covered with snow or ice) 눈밭[빙판] **2** a particular subject that people study ‖ 사람들이 연구하는 특정 분야. 영역. 전공[전문] 분야: *Professor Kramer is an expert in the field of ancient history.* 크레이머 교수는 고대사 분야 전문가이다. **3 the field** all the competitors, companies etc. that are involved in a particular activity ‖ 특정 활동에 관련된 모든 경쟁자·회사 등. 활동 범위[영역]. 참여[참가·출전]자(전체): *They now lead the field* (=are the most successful company) *in making powerful computer chips.* 그들은 강력한 컴퓨터 칩을 생산하는 분야에서 현재 선두를 달리고 있다. **4 field of view/vision** the area that you can see when looking through something, such as a camera ‖ 카메라 등을 통해서 볼 때 볼 수 있는 범위. 시계/시야 **5 magnetic/ gravitational/force field** an area where a strong natural force is felt or has an effect on things ‖ 강한 자연적 힘

이 느껴지거나 사물에 영향을 미치는 구역. 자기장(磁氣場)/중력장(重力場)/역장(力場)

field² *v* [T] **1** if you field a ball, you catch it after it has been hit ‖ 타격된 공을 잡다 **2 field a question** to answer a difficult question ‖ 어려운 질문에 대답하다. 질문에 (능란하게) 응답하다[잘 받아넘기다]: *The Mayor fielded a lot of tricky questions from the reporters.* 시장은 기자들의 까다로운 많은 질문을 잘 받아넘겼다.

field day /'. ./ *n* **1 have a field day** to have a chance to do something you want, especially a chance to criticize someone or something ‖ 원하는 것을 할 기회, 특히 다른 사람이나 사물을 비판할 기회를 갖다. 좋아하는[신나는] 일이 생기다[벌이다]. 무척 좋아하다[신나 하다]: *Any time there's a scandal in politics, the media have a field day with it.* 정치권에서 추문이 있을 때면 언제나 언론들은 쾌재를 부른다. **2** a day when students have outdoor sports competitions at school ‖ 학교에서 학생들이 야외 운동 경기 대회를 갖는 날. 운동회[체육 대회] 날

field·er /'fildə/ *n* one of the players who tries to catch the ball in baseball ‖ 야구에서 공을 잡아내는 선수들 중 하나. 야수. 외야수

field e·vent /'. ,./ *n* a sports activity such as jumping over BARs or throwing heavy things, that is part of an outdoor competition ‖ 장대 위를 뛰어넘거나 무거운 것을 던지는 등의 옥외 경기의 일부인 스포츠 활동. 필드 경기[종목]

field glass·es /'. ,./ *n* [plural] ⇨ BINOCULARS

field goal /'. ./ *n* the action of kicking the ball over the BAR or the GOAL for three points in football ‖ 미식축구에서 3점을 득점하기 위해 골대 위로 공을 차기. 필드골

field hock·ey /'. ,./ *n* [U] an outdoor game in which two teams of eleven players try to hit a ball with special sticks into their opponents' GOAL ‖ 11명의 선수로 된 두 팀이 특수한 스틱으로 공을 쳐서 상대편의 골문으로 넣는 옥외 경기. (필드) 하키

field house /'. ./ *n* a large building used for indoor sports events such as basketball ‖ 농구 등 옥내 스포츠 행사에 쓰이는 큰 건물. 실내 경기장[체육관]

field test /'. ./ *n* a test of a new product or system that is done outside the LABORATORY in real conditions ‖ 실험실 밖의 실제 조건에서 행해진 새 제품이

나 시스템의 시험. 실지[현장] 테스트: *Vegetables that can resist insects are doing well in field tests.* 병충해에 강한 채소들이 현장 테스트에서 좋은 성과를 보이고 있다. – **field-test** *v* [T]

field trip /'. ./ *n* an occasion when students go somewhere to learn about a particular subject ‖ 학생들이 특정 분야에 대해 배우기 위해 어떤 곳에 가는 행사. 현장 견학. 야외 조사[답사]여행: *We're going on a field trip to the Science Museum.* 우리는 과학 박물관에 견학을 간다.

field·work /'fildwɔk/ *n* [U] the study of scientific or social subjects that is done outside the school or LABORATORY ‖ 학교나 실험실 밖에서 행해지는 과학적 또는 사회적 분야의 연구. 야외 연구. 실지[현지] 조사: *I'll be doing archeological fieldwork over the summer.* 나는 여름 동안에 고고학 현지 조사를 할 것이다.

fiend /find/ *n* **1 sports/television etc.** **fiend** INFORMAL someone who likes doing something much more than other people do ‖ 다른 사람들이 하는 것 이상으로 어떤 일을 하기를 좋아하는 사람. 스포츠/텔레비전 광[중독자] 등: *Isaac turns into a football fiend during the Super Bowl.* 아이작은 수퍼볼 기간에는 미식축구 열광자로 변한다. **2** LITERARY an evil spirit, or someone who is very cruel ‖ 악령, 또는 매우 잔인한 사람. 악마. 마귀

fiend·ish /'findɪʃ/ *adj* **1** LITERARY very bad in a way that seems evil ‖ 악마로 여겨질 정도로 매우 나쁜. 흉포한. 잔혹한. 냉혹한: *a fiendish temper/plot* 잔혹한 성질[계획] **2** FORMAL very difficult ‖ 매우 어려운. 복잡한: *a fiendish puzzle* 매우 어려운 수수께끼

fierce /fɪrs/ *adj* **1** very angry, violent, and ready to attack ‖ 매우 화나고 폭력적이며 공격 태세인. 사나운. 격노한. 난폭한. 잔인한: *fierce dogs* 사나운 개들 **2** done with a lot of energy and strong feelings ‖ 많은 기운과 격한 감정으로 행해진. 격렬한. 맹렬한. 격심한: *a fierce debate between the political parties* 정당간의 격심한 논쟁 **3** fierce heat, cold, weather etc. is much more extreme than usual ‖ 더위·추위·날씨 등이 보통 때보다 더 극심한. 맹렬한. 격심한 – **fiercely** *adv*

fi·er·y /'faɪəri/ *adj* **1** involving fire, or on fire ‖ 불을 수반한, 또는 불이 붙은. 불꽃이 타오르는. 불같은. 불타는 듯한: *the fiery launch of the space shuttle* 불꽃을 뿜으며 발사되는 우주 왕복선 **2** making

people feel strong emotions such as anger, or showing these types of emotions ‖ 사람들에게 분노 등의 격한 감정을 들게 하는, 또는 이런 종류의 감정을 나타내는. 불같은. 격렬한. 맹렬한: *a fiery speech* 열변 / *a fiery temper* 불같은 성미

fi·es·ta /fi'ɛstə/ *n* a religious holiday in Spain or Latin America, with dancing, music etc. ‖ 스페인이나 남미에서 춤·음악 등이 수반되는 종교 축제일

fif·teen /ˌfɪf'tin/ *number* 15 ‖ 15 – **fifteenth** *number*

fifth¹ /fɪfθ/ *number* **1** 5th ‖ 5번째 **2** 1/5 ‖ 5분의 1 **3 feel like a fifth wheel** to feel that the people you are with do not want you to be there ‖ 같이 있는 사람들에게서 자신이 거기에 있는 것을 원하지 않음을 느끼다. 찬밥 대우를 받다. (자동차의 5번째 바퀴처럼) 있으나마나 하게 [쓸모없게] 여겨지다: *I felt like a fifth wheel with all those couples.* 나는 그 모든 부부들 사이에서 개밥에 도토리가 된 것처럼 느껴졌다.

fifth² *n* an amount of alcoholic drink equal to 1/5 of a gallon, sold in bottles ‖ 병에 담아 파는, 1갤론의 1/5에 해당하는 술의 양

fif·ty¹ /'fɪfti/ *number* **1** 50 ‖ 50 **2 the fifties a)** the years between 1950 and 1959 ‖ 1950에서 1959년 사이의 연대. 50년대 **b)** the numbers between 50 and 59, especially when used for measuring temperature ‖ 특히 온도 측정에 쓰일 때의 50과 59 사이의 수 – **fiftieth** /'fɪftiəθ/ *number*

fifty² *n* a piece of paper money worth $50 ‖ (액면가) 50달러짜리 지폐

fifty-fifty /ˌ.. '..'/ *adj, adv* SPOKEN **1** divided or shared equally between two people ‖ 두 사람 사이에 똑같이 나누어지거나 공유된. 반반의. 똑같이 분배된: *We should divide the profits fifty-fifty.* 우리는 이익을 반반으로 나누어야 한다. **2 a fifty-fifty chance** an equal chance that something will happen or not happen ‖ 어떤 일이 일어나거나 일어나지 않을 가능성이 반반임. 반반의 가능성[가망성]: *I think we have a fifty-fifty chance of winning.* 나는 우리가 승리할 가능성이 반반이라고 생각한다.

fig /fɪg/ *n* a small soft sweet fruit, often eaten dried, or the tree on which this grows ‖ 흔히 말려서 먹는 작고 부드러운 달콤한 과일, 또는 이 과일이 자라는 나무. 무화과(나무)

fig. the written abbreviation of FIGURE ‖ figure의 약어

fight¹ /faɪt/ *v* **fought, fought,**

fighting 1 [I, T] to use violence, guns, weapons etc. against someone or something ‖ 다른 사람이나 사물에 대해 폭력·총·무기 등을 사용하다. 무력을 쓰다 [행사하다, 휘두르다]. 싸우다. 격투하다: *Did your uncle fight in the war?* 너희 삼촌은 전쟁에 참전했었니? / *The country fought a three-year civil war.* 그 나라는 3년간의 내전을 치렀다. / *dogs fighting over a bone* 뼈다귀를 두고 싸우는 개들 **2** [I] to argue ‖ 말다툼하다. 의견 충돌을 벌이다: *Are the kids fighting again?* 애들이 또 다투고 있습니까? **3** [I, T] to try hard to get, change, or prevent something ‖ 어떤 것을 얻기[바꾸기, 막기] 위해 열심히 애를 쓰다. 투쟁하다. 분투하다: *He had to fight for the leadership.* 그는 지배권을 획득하기 위해 투쟁해야 했다. / *Senator Redkin is fighting the proposal.* 레드킨 상원의원은 그 동의안을 통과시키기 위해 분투하고 있다. **4** [I, T] ⇨ box² **5** [T] also **fight back** to try very hard not to show your feelings or not to do something you want to do ‖ 감정을 보이지 않기 위해 또는 하고 싶은 어떤 것을 하지 않기 위해 무척 애를 쓰다. 자제[억제]하다: *He fought the impulse to yell at her.* 그는 그녀에게 소리치고 싶은 충동을 참아냈다. **6 fight your way** to move through a group of people by pushing past them ‖ 사람들을 밀쳐가며 군중을 뚫고 나아가다: *We had to fight our way through the crowd.* 우리는 군중 속을 뚫고 가야 했다. **7 a fighting chance** a chance to achieve something by working very hard ‖ 매우 열심히 일해서 어떤 것을 달성할 수 있는 기회. 절호의[성공할] 기회: *We still have a fighting chance of winning.* 우리는 아직 승리할 수 있는 절호의 기회가 있다.

fight back *phr v* [I] to use violence or arguments against someone who has attacked you or argued with you ‖ 자신을 공격하거나 말다툼하고 있는 다른 사람에 대항해 무력이나 논쟁을 사용하다. 맞서 싸우다. 방어하다. 반격하다

fight sb/sth ↔ **off** *phr v* [T] **1** to use violence to keep someone or something away ‖ 사람이나 사물을 멀리 떼어 놓기 위해 무력을 사용하다. …을 (무력으로) 물리치다[물러가게 하다]. 격퇴시키다: *They managed to fight off their attackers.* 그들은 가까스로 습격자들을 물리쳤다. **2** to try hard to get rid of a feeling or illness ‖ 감정이나 병세를 없애기 위해 열심히 애를 쓰다. 물리치도록 싸우다. 퇴치시키다: *I've been fighting off*

a cold for days. 나는 며칠 동안 감기를 물리치려고 애써 왔다.

fight sth **out** *phr v* [T] to argue or use violence untila a disagreement is settled ‖ 불화[의견 충돌]가 해결될 때까지 말다툼을 벌이거나 폭력을 사용하다. 싸워서 해결하다[끝장을 보다]. 승부가 날 때까지 싸우다: *We left them alone to fight it out themselves.* 우리는 그들이 자기들끼리 싸워서 끝장을 내버려 두었다.

fight² *n* **1** an act of fighting between two people or groups ‖ 두 사람이나 집단 간의 싸우기. 싸움. 격투. 결투. 투쟁: *He's always getting into fights at school.* 그는 학교에서 항상 싸움을 한다. / *Who picked the fight?* (=started it) 누가 싸움을 걸었느냐? **2** a battle between two armies ‖ 두 군대 사이의 전투: *a fight for control of the islands* 섬의 지배권이 걸린 전투 **3** an argument ‖ 말싸움. 언쟁. 말다툼: *They've had a fight with the neighbors.* 그들은 이웃과 말다툼을 해 왔다. **4** [singular] the process of trying to achieve something difficult or prevent something ‖ 어려운 일을 달성하거나 어떤 것을 막으려고 애쓰는 과정. 투쟁. 분투: *the union's fight for better working conditions* 근로 조건의 개선을 위한 노조의 투쟁

fight·er /ˈfaɪtɚ/ *n* **1** someone who continues to try to do something although it is difficult ‖ 어려움에도 불구하고 계속해서 어떤 일을 하려고 애쓰는 사람. 전사. 투사 **2** ⇨ BOXER **3** also **fighter plane** a small, fast military plane that can destroy other planes ‖ 다른 항공기를 파괴할 수 있는 작고 빠른 군용 비행기. 전투기

fig·ment /ˈfɪgmənt/ *n* **a figment of sb's imagination** something you imagine to be real, but does not exist ‖ 실재하는 것이라 상상하지만 존재하지 않는 것. 상상[허구]의 산물. 공상. 환상: *The "friend" that the boy talks about is just a figment of his imagination.* 소년이 말하는 "친구"는 단지 그의 상상의 산물일 뿐이다.

fig·u·ra·tive /ˈfɪgyərətɪv/ *adj* a figurative word or expression is used in a different way from the usual one, to give you a picture in your mind ‖ 말이나 표현이 마음속에 구체적 형상을 주기 위해 통상의 뜻과 다르게 쓰이는. 비유[은유]적인. 표상[상징]하는 - **figuratively** *adv* —compare LITERAL

fig·ure¹ /ˈfɪgyɚ/ *n* **1** a number that represents an amount, especially an officially printed number ‖ 크기[양]를 나

타내는 숫자, 특히 공식적으로 인쇄된 숫자. 수치: *population figures* 인구 규모[총수] **2** the shape of a woman's body, used when describing how attractive it is ‖ 얼마나 매력적인지를 묘사할 때 쓰는 여성의 인체 형상. 몸매. 체형. 체격: *She has a great figure.* 그녀는 멋진 몸매를 가지고 있다. **3** a particular amount of money ‖ 특정한 액수의 돈. 금액. …자릿수 (금액): *a six-figure income* (=over $100,000) 여섯 자릿수 소득 **4** a number from 0 to 9, written as a sign rather than spelled with letters ‖ 문자로 철자된 대신 기호로 씌어진 0부터 9까지의 숫자 **5** someone with a particular type of character, position, appearance etc. ‖ 특정한 종류의 성격·지위·외모 등을 가진 사람. 인물. 인사. 인상. 모습. 용모: *an important political figure* 중요한 정계 인사 / *a sad figure dressed in old clothes* 헌 옷을 입고 슬픔이 잠긴 사람 **6** a drawing in a book that has a number on it to show what part of the book it relates to ‖ 책의 관련 부분을 나타내는 숫자가 적힌 책 속의 그림. 도해. 삽화 **7** a shape in mathematics ‖ 수학에서의 도형: *a six-sided figure* 6각형

figure[2] *v* [I] to be important or included in something ‖ 중요하거나 다른 것에 포함되다. (중요한 인물로서) 나타나다[표현되다]. 출연하다. 역할을 맡다: *The Kennedys figure in her recent book.* 케네디 가문이 그녀의 최근 저서에 나타난다.

SPOKEN PHRASES

1 [T] to have a particular opinion after thinking about a situation ‖ 상황에 대해 고려한 후에 특정한 견해를 갖다. …이라고 생각하다. 판단하다: *I figured* (that) *you'd need help moving, so I came over.* 나는 네가 이사하는 데 도움이 필요할 것 같아서 왔다. **2 that figures/it figures** said when you are annoyed because something bad you expected to happen does happen ‖ 예상했던 안 좋은 일이 일어나서 짜증이 났을 때 쓰여. 그럴 줄 미리 알다. 당연한 일이다. 예상했던 대로야: *"I forgot to bring my checkbook again." "That figures."* "또 수표장 가져오는 것을 잊었어." "예상했어." **3 go figure** said in order to show that you cannot believe something because it seems so strange ‖ 어떤 일이 아주 이상해 보여서 믿을 수 없다는 것을 나타내는 데에 쓰여. 글쎄다. 믿을 수 없다. 별일이다. 희한하다

figure on sth *phr v* [T] SPOKEN to include something in your plans ‖ 계획에 어떤 일을 포함시키다. 고려에 넣다. …을 대비해서 계획을 세우다: *With traffic so heavy, we'd better figure on an extra hour.* 교통 체증이 심하니까 한 시간 초과되는 것을 고려해야 할 것이다.

figure sb/sth ↔ **out** *phr v* [T] to understand someone or something after thinking about him, her, or it ‖ 다른 사람이나 사물에 대해 생각한 후에 이해하다. …을 알게 되다[깨닫다]. 이해하다: *I can't figure Betty out.* 나는 베티를 이해할 수 없다.

figure eight /ˌ.. ˈ./ *n* the pattern of the number 8, for example, in a dance ‖ 무용 등에서의 8자 형태. 8자 모양(의 도형). 8자형

fig·ure·head /ˈfɪgyɚˌhɛd/ *n* a leader who has no real power ‖ 실제 권력을 가지지 않은 지도자. 명목[표면]상의 우두머리

figure of speech /ˌ.. ˈ. ˈ./ *n* a word or expression that is used in a different way from the usual one, to give you a picture in your mind ‖ 마음속에 구체적 형상을 주기 위해 통상의 뜻과 다르게 사용된 단어나 표현. 비유[은유]적 표현: *"We died laughing" is a figure of speech.* "우리는 죽도록 웃었다"는 비유적 표현이다.

figure skat·ing /ˈ.. ˌ../ *n* a type of skating (SKATE) in which you move in patterns on the ice ‖ 얼음 위에서 여러 가지 형태를 그리며 움직이는 스케이트 종목. 피겨 스케이팅

fil·a·ment /ˈfɪləmənt/ *n* a very thin thread, especially the thin wire in a LIGHT BULB ‖ 매우 가는 줄, 특히 전구 안의 가는 철사. 필라멘트

filch /fɪltʃ/ *v* [T] INFORMAL to steal something small ‖ 하찮은 것을 훔치다. 좀도둑질을 하다

file[1] /faɪl/ *n* **1** a box or folded piece of heavy paper that is used in order to keep papers organized or separate from other papers ‖ 서류를 정리하거나 다른 서류로부터 분리하기 위해 쓰이는 두툼한 종이로 만든 상자나 접철로 된 것. 파일. 철(綴): *a desk cluttered with files* 파일들로 어질러진 책상 **2** a collection of information about a particular person or thing ‖ 특정 사람이나 일에 대해 정보를 수집해 놓은 것. 정보철. 서류 묶음: *The school keeps files on each student.* 학교는 각 학생들에 대한 서류 일체를 보관한다. **3** a collection of information in a computer that is kept under a

F

particular name ‖ 특정 이름을 붙여 저장하는 컴퓨터 내의 정보 묶음. (컴퓨터) 파일 **4 on file a)** kept in a file so that it can be used later ‖ 나중에 사용될 수 있게 파일로 보관된. 철이 된. 파일화된[로 만든]: *We'll keep your application on file for six months.* 우리는 당신의 지원서를 6개월 동안 파일로 보관할 것입니다. **b)** officially recorded ‖ 공식 기록된. 문서화[서류화]된. 공식 문서로 제시된[접수된]: *Your insurance claim has to be on file by April 1.* 당신의 보험금 청구는 4월 1일까지 접수되어야 합니다. **5** a metal tool with a rough surface that is used for making other surfaces smooth ‖ 다른 (물체의) 표면을 매끈하게 만드는 데 쓰이는 표면이 거친 금속 연장. 줄

file² *v* **1** [T] LAW to officially record something such as a complaint, law case etc. ‖ 진정·소송건 등의 일을 공식 기록화하다. 공식 접수시키다. 공식 문서화하다: *Some employees are filing a claim against the department.* 몇몇 종업원들이 담당 부서를 상대로 요구 사항을 제출한 상태이다. **2** [T] to keep papers with information on them in a particular place ‖ 정보가 기록된 서류를 특정 장소에 보관하다. 파일화하다. 정리[분류]하여 보관하다: *File the contracts alphabetically.* 계약서들을 알파벳순으로 파일로 철하시오. **3** [I] to walk in a line of people, one behind the other ‖ 사람들이 한 줄로 줄을 지어 걷다. 일렬로[종대로] 걷다[행진하다]: *The jury filed into the courtroom.* 배심원단이 일렬로 법정으로 걸어 들어왔다. **4** [T] to rub something with a metal tool to make it smooth or cut it ‖ 매끈하게 하거나 깎아내기 위해 사물을 금속 도구로 갈다. 줄로 갈다[깎다]. 줄질하다

file cab·i·net /'. ,..../ *n* ⇨ FILING CABINET

fil·et, fillet /fɪ'leɪ/ *n* a piece of meat or fish without bones ‖ 뼈 없는 고기나 생선의 살(토막). 뼈를 발라낸 고기[생선]

fil·i·bus·ter /'fɪlə,bʌstɚ/ *v* [I] to try to delay action in Congress by making very long speeches ‖ 매우 긴 연설을 해서 의회에서 의사 일정을 지연시키려 하다. 의사진행을 방해하다 – **filibuster** *n*

fil·i·gree /'fɪlə,gri/ *n* [U] delicate decoration made of gold or silver wire ‖ 금이나 은의 선(線)으로 만든 정교한 장식. 금[은]선 세공

filing cab·i·net /'.. ,..../ *n* a piece of office furniture with drawers for keeping reports, letters etc. ‖ 보고서·서한 등을 보관하기 위한 서랍 달린 사무가구. (서류 정리용) 파일 캐비닛

fil·ings /'faɪlɪŋz/ *n* [plural] very small pieces that come off a piece of metal when it is FILE*d* ‖ 줄로 금속을 갈 때 나오는 매우 작은 조각[가루]. 줄밥

fill¹ /fɪl/ *v* **1** [I, T] also **fill up** to become full of something, or to make something full ‖ 어떤 것으로 가득 차다, 또는 가득 채우다. 가득하게 하다: *The audience soon filled the theater.* 관중들이 곧 극장을 가득 메웠다. / *The bedroom was filled with smoke.* 침실이 담배 연기로 가득했다. **2** [T] also **fill in** to put something in a hole or crack in order to make a smooth surface ‖ 표면을 매끄럽게 하기 위해 구멍이나 갈라진 틈에 어떤 것을 집어넣다. …을 메우다 **3** [T] if a sound, smell, or light fills a place or space, you notice it because it is loud or strong ‖ 소리[냄새, 빛] 등이 어떤 장소나 공간에서 주목을 끌 만큼 크거나 강하다. 넘치다. 가득하다: *The smell of fresh bread filled the kitchen.* 갓 구운 빵 냄새가 부엌에 가득했다. **4 fill a need/demand etc.** to give people something they want or need ‖ 사람들이 원하거나 필요로 하는 것을 주다. 필요/요구 등을 충족시키다: *Daycare centers fill a need for working parents.* 탁아소는 일하는 부모의 필요 사항을 충족시켜 준다. **5 fill a job/position etc.** to find someone to do a job ‖ 일을 할 다른 사람을 찾아내다. 충원하다: *Anderson says he hopes to fill the position by spring.* 앤더슨은 봄까지 그 자리에 사람을 충원하기를 바란다고 한다. **6** [T] if an emotion fills you, you feel it strongly ‖ 감정 등을 강렬하게 느끼다. 마음이 …한 감정으로 가득차다. 가슴이 벅차다 **7 fill sb's shoes** to be able to do a job as well as the person who had it before you ‖ 전에 일했던 사람만큼 일을 잘 할 수 있다. …의 자리를 대신하다: *It will be difficult to fill Ms. Brower's shoes, but I'll try.* 브라우어 여사를 대신하기는 어렵겠지만 노력해 보겠습니다.

fill in *phr v* **1** [T **fill** sth ↔ **in**] to write all the necessary information in special spaces on a document ‖ 서류상의 특정난에 모든 필요한 정보를 쓰다. 서류에 기입하다: *In the next part of the test, fill in the blanks with the correct answers.* 시험지의 다음 부분의 공란에 정답을 써넣으세요. **2** [T **fill** sb ↔ **in**] to tell

fill out

someone about things that have happened recently ‖ 최근에 일어난 일에 대해 다른 사람에게 말해 주다. 최신 정보를 주다: *I'll fill you in on all the news later.* 내가 나중에 모든 소식을 네게 이야기해 줄게. **3** [I] to do someone's job or work because s/he is unable to do it ‖ 남이 일을 할 수 없어서 그 사람의 일·업무를 하다. 대행[대리]하다. 대신 일하다: *Could you fill in for Bob while he's sick?* 보브가 아픈 동안 대신 일을 좀 해줄 수 있어요?

fill sth ↔ **out** *phr v* [T] to write all the necessary information in special spaces on a document ‖ 서류상의 특정 난에 모든 필요한 정보를 쓰다. 서류의 빈칸을 채우다. (공란에 써 넣어) 서류를 작성하다: *Fill out the application form by Oct. 1.* 10월 1일까지 지원서 양식을 작성하시오.

fill up *phr v* **1** [T **fill** sth ↔ **up**] to put enough of a liquid or substance in a container to make it full ‖ 용기를 가득 채우기 위해 액체나 물질을 충분히 넣다. 가득 채우다: *Can I fill up your glass?* 잔에 가득 채워[따라] 드릴까요? **2** [I] to gradually become full of people, things, etc. ‖ 점차 사람·사물 등으로 가득 차게 되다. 채워지다: *After school, the swimming pool starts filling up with kids.* 학교가 파한 후 수영장은 아이들로 가득 차기 시작했다.

fill² *n* **have/eat your fill** to have or eat as much of something as you want or can deal with ‖ 원하거나 처리할 수 있을 만큼 어떤 것을 많이 갖거나 먹다. 양껏[흡족하게] 가지다/먹다: *I've had my fill of screaming kids today!* 나는 오늘 소란 피우는 아이들에게 오늘 시달릴 만큼 시달렸다!

fil·let¹ /fɪˈleɪ/ *v* [T] to remove the bones from a piece of meat or fish ‖ 고기나 생선에서 뼈를 제거하다. 뼈를 발라내다

fillet² *n* ⇨ FILET

fil·ling¹ /ˈfɪlɪŋ/ *n* **1** a small amount of metal that is put into a hole in your tooth to preserve the tooth ‖ 치아를 보존하기 위해 치아의 구멍에 집어넣는 조그마한 금속. 봉. 충전재 **2** [C, U] the food that is put inside food such as a PIE or SANDWICH ‖ 파이나 샌드위치 등의 음식물 속에 넣는 음식. 속. 소: *apple pie filling* 애플파이 속

filling² *adj* food that is filling makes your stomach feel full ‖ 음식이 위를 가득 차게 느끼게 하는. 배부르게 하는

fil·ly /ˈfɪli/ *n* a young female horse ‖ 어린 암말

film¹ /fɪlm/ *n* **1** [U] the material used in a camera for taking photographs or recording moving pictures ‖ 사진을 찍거나 동영상을 기록하기 위해 카메라에 쓰이는 물건. 필름: *I don't have any film for my camera.* 내 카메라에 필름이 하나도 없다. / *The coach has the game on film.* (=we made a movie of the game) 코치에게 그 경기를 녹화한 테이프가 있다. **2** ⇨ MOVIE **3** [U] the art or business of making movies ‖ 영화를 만드는 기술이나 사업. 영화술[사업]: *the film industry* 영화 산업 **4** [singular, U] a very thin layer of something on the surface of something else ‖ 다른 것의 표면에 있는 어떤 것의 아주 얇은 층. 피막: *a film of oil on the lake* 호수 위의 기름층

film² *v* [I, T] to use a camera to make a movie ‖ 영화를 만들기 위해 카메라를 쓰다. 영화를 찍다. 촬영하다: *The movie was filmed in China.* 그 영화는 중국에서 촬영되었다. —compare RECORD²

film·mak·er /ˈfɪlmˌmeɪkɚ/ *n* someone who makes movies ‖ 영화를 만드는 사람. 영화 제작자

film·strip /ˈfɪlmˌstrɪp/ *n* a short film that shows photographs, drawings etc. one at a time ‖ 사진·그림 등을 한 번에 하나씩 보여 주는 짧은 필름. 슬라이드 필름

film·y /ˈfɪlmi/ *adj* fine and thin ‖ 곱고 얇은. 매우 얇은. 박막(성)의: *a filmy skirt* 매우 얇은 치마

fil·ter¹ /ˈfɪltɚ/ *n* something that gas or liquid is put through to remove unwanted substances ‖ 가스나 액체를 통과시켜 그 속의 불필요한 물질을 거르는 것. 여과기[장치]. 필터: *a water filter* 정수장치[필터]

filter² *v* **1** [T] to clean a liquid or gas using a FILTER ‖ 필터를 사용하여 액체나 가스를 깨끗이 하다. 여과기로 거르다: *filtered drinking water* 정수된 마실 물 **2** [I] if people filter somewhere, they gradually move in that direction through a door, hall etc. ‖ 사람이 문·홀 등을 통해 어떤 방향으로 서서히 이동하다: *The audience began to filter into the hall.* 청중들이 강당으로 천천히 움직이기 시작했다. **3** [I] if information filters somewhere, people gradually hear about it ‖ 정보가 사람들에게 점차 알려지다. 서서히 흘러들다[알려지다]: *The news slowly filtered through to everyone in the office.* 그 소식이 사무실의 모든 사람들에게 서서히 알려졌다. **4** [I] if light or sound filters into a place, it can be seen or heard only slightly ‖ 빛이

나 소리가 아주 조금 보이거나 들리다. 새다. 새어 나오다: *Sunshine filtered through the curtains.* 햇빛이 커튼을 통해 새어 들어왔다.

filter sth ↔ **out** *phr v* [T] to remove something by using a FILTER ‖ 필터를 이용하여 어떤 것을 거르다

filth /fɪlθ/ *n* [U] **1** an extremely dirty substance ‖ 아주 더러운 물질. 오물: *Wash that filth off your shoes.* 네 구두의 그 오물을 닦아내라. **2** very rude or offensive language, stories etc. about sex ‖ 성에 관한 아주 무례하거나 모욕적인 말·이야기 등. 외설. 음담패설

filth·y¹ /'fɪlθi/ *adj* **1** extremely dirty ‖ 아주 더러운: *Doesn't he ever wash that jacket? It's filthy.* 그는 그 재킷을 세탁한 적이 없지? 더러워. **2** showing or describing sexual acts in a very rude or offensive way ‖ 성행위를 아주 무례하거나 불쾌하게 보여 주거나 서술하는. 상스러운. 추잡한: *a filthy joke* 추잡한 농담

filth·y² *adv* **1 filthy dirty** INFORMAL very dirty ‖ 매우 더러운 **2 filthy rich** DISAPPROVING extremely rich ‖ 엄청난 부자인

fin /fɪn/ *n* **1** one of the thin body parts that a fish uses to swim ‖ 헤엄치는 데 사용하는 물고기의 가느다란 부분. 지느러미 **2** a part shaped like this on a plane or car ‖ 비행기나 자동차에서 물고기의 지느러미처럼 생긴 부분. 수직 안정판. 후미 안정판 —see picture at AIRPLANE

fi·na·gle /fə'neɪgəl/ *v* [T] INFORMAL to get something that is difficult to get, by using unusual methods ‖ 정상적이 아닌 방법을 사용하여 얻기 어려운 사물을 얻다. …을 교묘하게 입수하다: *He managed to finagle himself a job.* 그는 어렵게 일자리를 하나 잡았다.

fi·nal¹ /'faɪnl/ *adj* **1** last in a series of actions, events, or parts of something ‖ 연속된 행동[사건, 부분]의 마지막의. 최후의: *the final chapter of the book* 그 책의 마지막 장 **2** unable to be changed or doubted ‖ 변경하거나 의심할 수 없는. 결정적인. 최종적인: *Is that your final decision?* 그것이 너의 최종적인 결정이니? / *No more cookies, and that's final!* 과자는 더 없어. 그것이 마지막이야!

final² *n* **1** the last and most important game, race or set of games etc. in a competition ‖ 시합에서 최종적인 가장 중요한 경기[경주, 일련의 경기들]. 결승전. 최종 라운드: *She skated very well in the final.* 그녀는 결승전에서 스케이트를 아주 잘 지쳤다. / *the NBA finals* NBA 결승전 **2** an important test that students take at the end of each class in HIGH SCHOOL or college ‖ 고등학교나 대학에서 각 과목을 다 배우고 난 후에 학생들이 치르는 중요한 시험. 학기말 시험: *How did your finals go?* 학기말 시험은 어땠니?

fi·nal·e /fɪ'næli, -'nɑ-/ *n* the last part of a piece of music or a performance ‖ 음악이나 공연의 마지막 부분. 마지막 연주곡. 최종 장면: *the grand finale* (=very impressive end) *of a Broadway musical* 브로드웨이 뮤지컬의 대단원

fi·nal·ist /'faɪnl-ɪst/ *n* one of the people or teams that reaches the last competition in a series of competitions ‖ 일련의 시합에서 최종 시합에 오른 사람이나 팀. 결승전 진출자

fi·nal·i·ty /faɪ'næləti, fə-/ *n* [U] the feeling or idea that something is finished and cannot be changed ‖ 어떤 것이 완성되어서 변경할 수 없는 느낌이나 생각. 최종적인 상태. 종국(終局): *the finality of death* 죽음의 결말

fi·nal·ize /'faɪnl,aɪz/ *v* [T] to finish the last part of a plan, business deal etc. ‖ 계획·사업·거래 등의 마지막 부분을 완결하다. 마무리하다: *Can we finalize the details tomorrow?* 우리 내일 세부 사항을 결말지을 수 있을까요?

fi·nal·ly /'faɪnl-i/ *adv* **1** after a long time ‖ 오랜 시간 뒤에. 마침내. 드디어: *After several delays, the plane finally took off at 6:00.* 여러 차례 연기한 뒤에야 비행기는 마침내 오전 6시에 이륙했다. **2** as the last of a series of things ‖ 연속된 사물 중에서 마지막으로. 끝으로. 최후로: *And finally, I'd like to thank my teachers.* 끝으로 저의 은사님들에게 감사를 드리고 싶습니다. **3** in a way that does not allow further change ‖ 더 이상의 변경을 허용하지 않게. 최종적으로: *It's not finally settled yet.* 그것은 아직 최종적으로 결말이 나지 않았다.

fi·nance¹ /fə'næns, 'faɪnæns/ *n* [U] the management of money, especially for a company or a government ‖ 특히 회사나 정부의 자금 관리. 재무. 재정: *She's an accountant in the Finance Department.* 그녀는 재무부의 회계관이다.

finance² *v* [T] to provide money for something ‖ 어떤 것에 자금을 제공하다. 출자하다. 돈을 융통해 주다: *publicly financed services* 공적 자금 융자 서비스

fi·nanc·es /fə'nænsɪz, 'faɪnænsɪz/ *n* [plural] **1** the money that a person, company etc. has ‖ 개인·회사 등이 가진 자금. 재원: *The school's finances are limited.* 그 학교의 재원은 제한되어 있다. **2** the way a person, company etc.

manages money ‖ 개인·회사 등이 돈을 관리하는 방식. 자금 회전. 재정 운용: *My finances are a mess.* 나의 재정 관리는 엉망이다.

fi·nan·cial /fə'nænʃəl, faɪ-/ *adj* relating to money or the management of money ‖ 금전이나 금전의 관리에 관련된. 재무의. 회계의. 금전상의: *a financial adviser* 회계 고문 – **financially** *adv*

financial aid /.,.. './ *n* [U] money that is given or lent to students at college to pay for their education ‖ 대학생들에게 학자금으로 주거나 빌려주는 돈. 학자금 융자

fin·an·cier /,faɪnæn'sɪr, fə,næn-, ,fɪnən-/ *n* someone who controls or lends large sums of money ‖ 큰 자금을 관리하거나 빌려 주는 직업인. 금융업자. 재무관. 재정가

fi·nanc·ing /'faɪnænsɪŋ/ *n* [U] money provided by a bank to help a person or business ‖ 개인이나 기업을 돕기 위해 은행이 제공하는 돈. 조달 자금

finch /fɪntʃ/ *n* a small wild bird with a short beak ‖ 짧은 부리를 가진 작은 야생 조류. 되새류

find¹ /faɪnd/ *v* **found, found, finding** [T]

1 ▶DISCOVER 발견하다◀ to discover or see something, either by searching for it or by chance ‖ 탐색을 하거나 우연히 사물을 찾아내거나 만나다: *I can't find my keys.* 나는 열쇠를 못 찾겠다. / *Scientists are trying to find a cure for AIDS.* 과학자들은 에이즈 치료법을 찾으려 애쓰고 있다. / *I found a $20 bill today!* 나는 오늘 20달러짜리 지폐를 우연히 발견했다!

2 ▶REALIZE 깨닫다◀ to discover or realize something, especially something you did not expect ‖ 특히 기대하지 않던 사물을 발견하거나 깨닫다: *We got home and found that the basement had flooded.* 우리는 집에 와서 지하실이 물에 잠긴 것을 알았다. / *I found it difficult/easy to understand her.* 나는 그녀를 이해하는 것이 어렵다/쉽다는 것을 깨달았다.

3 ▶FEEL 느끼다◀ to have a particular feeling or idea about something ‖ 사물에 대한 특정한 감정이나 견해를 가지다. 느끼다. 알아차리다: *I don't find any of this funny.* 나는 이것에서 아무런 재미도 느끼지 못하겠다.

4 ▶LEARN 배우다◀ to learn or know something by experience ‖ 경험으로 사물을 배우거나 알다: *I tried using oil, but I've found that butter works best.* 나는 기름을 써 보았으나 버터가 가장 효과가

있다는 것을 알았다.

5 be found to live or exist somewhere ‖ 어떤 지역에 살거나 존재하다: *This type of grass is found only in the swamp.* 이런 종류의 풀은 늪지에서만 산다.

6 ▶TIME/MONEY/ENERGY 시간/돈/에너지◀ to have enough of something to be able to do what you want to do ‖ 하고 싶은 것을 할 수 있을 만큼 사물이 충분히 있다: *When do you find the time to read?* 너는 언제 독서할 시간이 나니?

7 ▶ARRIVE 도달하다◀ to arrive in a place by discovering the way to get there ‖ 길을 찾아 목적지에 도달하다: *Can you find your way, or do you need a map?* 길을 찾을 수 있겠니, 아니면 지도가 필요하니?

8 find yourself somewhere to realize that you are doing something or have arrived somewhere without intending to ‖ 자기도 모르게 어떤 일을 하고 있거나 어디에 도달한 것을 깨닫다: *Suddenly I found myself back at the hotel.* 내가 호텔에 돌아와 있다는 것을 불현듯 깨달았다.

9 find sb to meet someone that you can begin a romantic relationship with ‖ 연애 관계를 시작할 수 있는 사람을 만나다: *Rob needs to find somebody to make him happy.* 로브는 자기를 행복하게 해 줄 사람을 만나야 한다.

10 find sb guilty/find sb not guilty LAW to officially decide that someone is guilty or not guilty of a crime ‖ 어떤 사람의 유죄나 무죄 여부를 공식적으로 결정하다. 유죄/무죄로 판정하다

find out *phr v* **1** [I, T **find sth ↔ out**] to learn information after trying to discover it, or by chance ‖ 발견하려고 애를 쓴 끝에 또는 우연히 정보를 알아내다: *We should find out more about the show before we reserve tickets.* 우리는 입장권을 예약하기 전에 그 쇼에 대해 더 알아봐야 한다. **2** [T **find sb ↔ out**] INFORMAL to discover that someone has done something wrong ‖ 남이 잘못된 짓을 한 것을 발견하다: *What happens if we get found out?* 우리가 발각되면 어떻게 될까?

find² *n* something very good or valuable that you discover by chance ‖ 우연히 발견한 아주 좋거나 가치 있는 사물: *That antique carpet of Janine's was a real find.* 재닌의 그 고풍스런 양탄자는 정말 좋은 발견물이었다.

find·ing /'faɪndɪŋ/ *n* [C usually plural] the information that someone has learned as a result of studies, work etc.

‖ 연구·작업 등의 결과로 알게 된 정보. 결과. 소견: *the newest research findings* 최신의 연구 결과

fine¹ /faɪn/ *adj* **1** expensive or of a very high quality ‖ 고가의 또는 품질이 아주 좋은. 최고급의: *fine clothes* 최고급 옷 / *Dickinson's finest poems* 디킨슨의 훌륭한 시 **2** very thin, or in small pieces or drops ‖ 매우 가늘거나 매우 작은 조각이나 방울의. 미세한. 고운: *a fine layer of dust* 미세한 먼지층 / *fine rain* 보슬비[이슬비] **3** involving differences, changes, or details that are difficult to notice ‖ 인식하기 힘든 차이[변화, 정밀함]를 포함한. 세밀한. 정교한: *the fine tuning on the radio* 라디오의 미세 조정 **4 a fine woman/man/person** a good person that you have respect for ‖ 존경하는 좋은 사람. 품위 있는 여자/남자/사람 **5 a fine line** a point at which one thing can easily become a very different thing ‖ 어떤 사물이 쉽게 아주 다른 사물로 될 수 있는 지점. 미묘한 경계선: *There's a fine line between genius and madness.* 천재와 광인은 종이 한 장 차이다.

SPOKEN PHRASES

6 a) good enough; all right ‖ 아주 좋은; 괜찮은: *"What do you want for lunch?" "A sandwich is fine."* "점심으로 무엇을 원하세요?" "샌드위치가 좋습니다." / *"More coffee?" "No, I'm fine, thanks."* "커피 더 드릴까요?" "아니요, 괜찮습니다." **b)** healthy 건강한: *"How are you?" "Fine, thanks."* "안녕하세요?" "잘 있습니다, 덕분에." **7 that's/it's fine** said when you agree to something ‖ 어떤 것에 동의할 때에 쓰여. 좋아: *"How about seeing a movie?" "That's fine by me."* "영화 보는 건 어때요?" "나는 좋아요." **8** said when you are angry with someone because s/he is not being reasonable ‖ 어떤 사람이 비합리적이어서 화를 낼 때 쓰여: *Fine then, I'll do it myself.* 좋아. 그렇다면 내가 직접 하겠다. **9** used when you think someone is attractive ‖ 남이 매력적이라고 생각할 때 쓰여: *There are a bunch of fine ladies out there.* 그 곳에는 한 그룹의 멋진 숙녀들이 나와 있다.

---

fine² *adv* SPOKEN **1** in a way that is satisfactory ‖ 만족스럽게. 잘. 훌륭하게: *"How's everything going?" "Fine."* "일은 다 잘 되어 갑니까?" "좋아요." / *The washer's working fine now.* 세탁기는 이제 잘 돌아가고 있다. **2 do fine** to be

good enough or to do something well enough ‖ 충분히 좋거나 어떤 일을 아주 잘 하다: *"I can't paint." "Come on, you're doing fine."* "나는 그림을 못 그리겠어." "기운 내, 너 지금 아주 잘 하고 있어."

fine³ *n* money that you have to pay as a punishment ‖ 벌로 지불해야 하는 돈. 벌금. 과료: *a library fine for returning books late* 책의 반납 지연에 대한 도서관의 연체료

fine⁴ *v* [T] to make someone pay money as a punishment ‖ 남에게 벌로 돈을 납부하게 하다. 벌금을 과하다.: *He was fined $50 for speeding.* 그는 속도위반으로 50달러의 벌금을 부과 받았다.

fine arts /ˌ. ˈ./ *n* **the fine arts** activities such as painting, music etc. that are concerned with making beautiful things ‖ 회화·음악 등과 같이 아름다운 작품을 만들어 내는 활동. 예술

fine·ly /ˈfaɪnli/ *adv* **1** in very thin or small pieces ‖ 매우 가늘거나 작게: *finely chopped onion* 잘게 썬 양파 **2** to a very exact degree ‖ 상당히 정확한 정도로. 정교하게: *finely tuned instruments* 미세하게 조정된 기구

fine print /ˌ. ˈ./ *n* [U] the part of a contract or other document that has important information, often written in small print ‖ 계약서 등의 문서에서 중요한 정보를 흔히 작은 글씨로 기록한 부분. 계약서 등의 작은 글자[주의 사항]

fi·nesse /fɪˈnɛs/ *n* [U] delicate and impressive skill ‖ 섬세하고 인상적인 기량. 뛰어난 솜씨: *dancers performing with finesse* 뛰어난 기량으로 공연을 하는 무용수들

fin·ger¹ /ˈfɪŋgɚ/ *n* **1** one of the four long thin parts at the end of your hand ‖ 손끝에 있는 네 개의 길고 가는 부분의 한 개. 손가락 —see picture at HAND¹ **2 not lift/raise a finger** to not make any effort to help someone with his/her work ‖ 자신의 작업으로 남을 도우려는 노력을 조금도 하지 않다. 손가락 하나 까딱 않다: *I do all the work – Frank never lifts a finger.* 나는 모든 일을 하고 있는데 프랭크는 손 하나 까딱 않는다. **3 keep/have your fingers crossed** SPOKEN said when you hope that something will happen the way you want ‖ 일이 원하는 대로 되기를 바랄 때에 쓰여. 소원대로 되기를 빌다: *I had a job interview today. Keep your fingers crossed!* 나 오늘 취업 면접을 봤어. 내 행운을 빌어 줘! **4 not put your finger on sth** INFORMAL to be unable to realize exactly what is wrong, different, or unusual about a situation ‖ 상황에 대해 잘못된[다른, 독특한] 것을 정확히 알 수가 없는. 정확하게 지적하지 못하는: *Something's different here, but I can't put my finger on what it is.* 여기에 뭔가 다른 것이 있는데 나는 그것이 무엇인지 지적할 수가 없다. **5 give sb the finger** SLANG to make a very rude sign at someone by holding up your middle finger ‖ 가운뎃손가락을 위로 치켜들어 남에게 무례한 손짓을 하다. 남에게 지독한 욕을 하다

finger² *v* [T] to touch or handle something with your fingers ‖ 사물을 손가락으로 만지거나 다루다

fin·ger·nail /ˈfɪŋgɚˌneɪl/ *n* the hard flat part that covers the top end of your finger ‖ 손가락의 위 끝을 덮고 있는 딱딱하고 납작한 부분. 손톱

fin·ger·print /ˈfɪŋgɚˌprɪnt/ *n* the mark made by the pattern of lines at the end of someone's finger ‖ 사람의 손가락 끝에 있는 줄무늬로 이루어진 자국. 지문

fin·ger·tip /ˈfɪŋgɚˌtɪp/ *n* **1** the end of a finger ‖ 손가락 끝 **2 have something at your fingertips** to have something easily available, especially knowledge or information ‖ 특히 지식이나 정보를 쉽게 이용할 수 있다. …에 정통하다

fin·ick·y /ˈfɪnɪki/ *adj* someone who is finicky only likes a few kinds of food, clothes, music etc. and is difficult to please ‖ 사람이 몇 가지의 음식·옷·음악 등만을 좋아해서 만족시키기 어려운. 지나치게 까다로운: *a finicky eater* 식성이 까다로운 사람

fin·ish¹ /ˈfɪnɪʃ/ *v* **1** [I, T] to come to the end of doing or making something, so it is complete ‖ 어떤 일을 하거나 만드는 마지막에 이르러 완성하다. 끝내다. 끝나다: *I'll just finish this, and then we'll go.* 내가 이것을 곧 끝내면 그때 우리는 갈 거야. / *Are you almost finished?* 거의 끝났니? / *One more point, then I'll finish.* 한 학점만 더 따면 나는 졸업이야. —opposite START¹ **2** [T] to eat or drink all the rest of something ‖ 남김없이 모두 먹거나 마시다: *Finish your dinner, or there's no dessert.* 음식을 다 먹어라. 그렇지 않으면 후식은 없다. **3** [I, T] to be in a particular position at the end of a race, competition etc. ‖ 경주·시합 등의 마지막 단계에서 특정한 위치에 있다: *She finished second in the marathon.* 그녀는 마라톤에서 2등을 했다. **4** [T] to give the surface of something a smooth appearance by painting, polishing etc. ‖

페인트칠·광택 내기 등을 하여 사물의 표면을 매끄럽게 하다. 마무리 칠을 하다

finish off *phr v* **1** [T **finish** sth ↔ **off**] to use or eat all of something ‖ 어떤 것을 모두 사용하거나 먹어버리다: *Who finished off the cake?* 누가 케이크를 다 먹어 치웠니? **2** [T **finish** sb/sth ↔ **off**] to kill a person or animal when he, she, or it is weak or wounded ‖ 사람이나 동물이 쇠약하거나 부상당했을 때 죽이다

finish up *phr v* **1** [I, T **finish** sth ↔ **up**] to eat or drink all the rest of something ‖ 남김없이 모두 먹어 치우거나 마셔 버리다: *Why don't you finish up the pie?* 파이를 모두 먹어 버리지 그러니? **2** [I,T **finish** sth ↔ **up**] to end an event, situation etc. by doing one final thing ‖ 마지막 한 가지를 하여 사건·상황 등을 끝내다. 마무리짓다: *Let me finish up the dishes first.* 내가 설거지부터 먼저 끝낼게.

finish with sb/sth *phr v* [T] **be finished with** to no longer need something that you have been using ‖ 죽 사용해 오던 것이 더 이상 필요하지 않다. 용무가 끝나다: *Are you finished with the scissors?* 이제 가위는 필요 없니?

finish² *n* **1** the end or last part of something ‖ 어떤 것의 끝이나 마지막 부분. 종결: *It was a close finish* (=a race in which competitors are very close at the end)*, but Jarrett won.* 경주 막바지에서 접전이었으나 자렛이 승리했다. **2** [C, U] the appearance of the surface of an object after it has been painted, polished etc. ‖ 페인트칠·광택 등을 낸 뒤의 물건 표면의 모습. 끝마무리한 모양: *a table with a glossy finish* 광택 처리로 마무리한 탁자

fin·ished /ˈfɪnɪʃt/ *adj* **1** at the end of an activity ‖ 활동의 마지막의. 막바지의: *I'm not quite finished.* 나는 끝나려면 멀었다. **2** completed ‖ 완성된: *the finished product* 완제품 **3** no longer able to do something successfully ‖ 더 이상 성공적으로 어떤 일을 할 수 없는. 절망적인: *If the bank doesn't loan us the money, we're finished.* 은행이 우리에게 그 돈을 대출해 주지 않으면 우리는 끝장이다.

finish line /ˈ.. ˌ./ *n* the line at the end of a race that a competitor must cross first in order to win ‖ 우승하기 위해서는 경주자가 먼저 통과해야 하는 경주의 결승점에 있는 선. 결승선

fi·nite /ˈfaɪnaɪt/ *adj* having an end or a limit ‖ 끝이나 한계가 있는. 유한(有限)의: *the Earth's finite resources* 지구의 유한한 자원

fir /fɚ/ *n* a tree with leaves shaped like needles that do not fall off in winter ‖ 겨울에도 떨어지지 않는 바늘같이 생긴 잎을 가진 나무. 전나무

Nancy lit the candles.

The newspapers caught fire.

fire¹ /faɪɚ/ *n* **1** [U] the flames, light, and heat produced when something burns ‖ 물체가 탈 때 발생하는 불꽃·빛·열. 불: *Fire destroyed part of the building.* 화재로 건물의 일부가 파손되었다. / *The house is on fire!* (=burning) 집에 불이 났어요! / *Some other buildings caught fire.* (=started to burn) 몇 개의 다른 건물들에 불이 붙었다. / *Rioters set fire to cars and stores.* (=deliberately made them burn) 폭도들은 차와 상점에 방화를 했다. **2** uncontrolled burning that destroys things ‖ 물체를 파괴하는 걷잡을 수 없는 불길. 화재: *a forest fire* 산불 / *Police are trying to find out who started the fire.* (=deliberately made it start) 경찰은 방화범을 찾기 위해 애쓰고 있다. / *It took firefighters two days to put out the fire.* (=stop it burning) 그 화재를 소방관들이 진화하는 데에 이틀이 걸렸다. **3** burning wood or coal that provides heat ‖ 불에 타서 열을 제공하는 나무나 석탄. 땔감: *Let's light a fire in the fireplace.* 벽난로(의 땔감)에 불을 지피자. **4** [U] shooting by guns ‖ 총을 쏘기. 발사. 사격: *Our camp was under fire.* (=being shot at) 우리의 막사는 공격을 받았다. / *Troops opened fire on* (=started shooting) *the rebels.* 군대는 반란자들에게 사격을 개시했다. **5 be/come under fire** to be criticized very strongly for something you have done ‖ 자신이 한 일 때문에 아주 맹렬히 비판을 받다: *The school district has come under fire for its sex education policy.* 그 학교는 성교육 정책으로 비난을 받았다.

fire² *v* **1** [T] to make someone leave his/her job ‖ 사람을 직장에서 떠나게 하다. 해고[파면]하다 **2** [I, T] to shoot bullets from a gun ‖ 총으로 탄환을 쏘다. 발사하다: *He fired the gun by mistake.* 그는 실수로 총을 쏘았다. / *Don't fire until I tell you.* 내가 명령할 때까지는 총을 쏘지 마라. **3** [T] also **fire up** to make someone very excited or interested in something ‖ 사람을 어떤 것에 매우 흥분하거나 흥미를 갖게 하다. 사람을 감격[흥분]시키다. 불타오르게 하다: *Jo's imagination was fired by her grandmother's stories.* 조의 상상력은 할머니의 이야기로 인해 불타올랐다. **4 fire away!** SPOKEN said in order to show that you are ready to answer someone's questions ‖ 남의 질문에 대답할 준비가 되어 있는 것을 나타내는 데에 쓰여. 질문을 시작하세요!

fire a·larm /'. .,./ *n* a thing that makes a loud noise to warn people of a fire in a building ‖ 건물 내의 화재를 사람들에게 경고하기 위해 큰 소리를 내는 물건. 화재 경보기

fire·arm /'faɪɚɑrm/ *n* a gun that can be carried ‖ 휴대할 수 있는 총. 소형 화기

fire·brand /'faɪɚbrænd/ *n* someone who tries to make people angry enough about a law, government etc. to change it ‖ 법률·정부 등에 대해 사람들을 몹시 분노하게 만들어 그것을 변화시키려고 애쓰는 사람. 선동자. 활동가

fire·crack·er /'faɪɚ,krækɚ/ *n* a small explosive that explodes loudly, usually used when celebrating a special day ‖ 보통 특별한 날을 기념할 때 사용되는, 큰 소리를 내며 폭발하는 소형 폭발물. 폭죽

fire de·part·ment /'. .,../ *n* an organization that works to prevent fires and stop them burning ‖ 화재를 예방하고 진화하는 업무를 하는 기관. 소방서

fire drill /'. ./ *n* the act of practicing what to do in order to leave a burning building safely ‖ 불이 난 건물에서 안전하게 탈출하는 행동 요령을 연습하는 행위. 화재 피난 훈련

fire en·gine /'. ,../ *n* a special large vehicle that carries people and equipment to stop fires burning ‖ 진화를 위해 인원과 장비를 운반하는 특별 대형 차량. 소방차

fire es·cape /'. .,./ *n* metal stairs on the outside of a building, that people can use in order to escape if there is a fire ‖ 화재 발생시 탈출하기 위해 사람들이 사용할 수 있는 건물 외부의 철제 계단. 비상계단

fire ex·tin·guish·er /'. .,.../ *n* a metal container with water or chemicals in it, used for stopping fires ‖ 화재 진압에 사용되는 물이나 화학제품이 들어 있는 금속제 용기. 소화기

fire·fight·er /'faɪəˌfaɪtə/ *n* someone whose job is to stop fires ‖ 화재 진압을 하는 직업인. 소방대원[관]

fire·fly /'faɪəflaɪ/ *n* a flying insect that produces a bright light at night ‖ 야간에 밝은 빛을 발산하는 날아다니는 곤충. 반딧불이

fire hy·drant /'. ,../ *n* a water pipe in a street, used for getting water to stop fires ‖ 화재 진압용 물을 얻는 데 쓰이는 거리의 수도관. 소화전(栓)

fire·man /'faɪəmən/ *n* a man whose job is to stop fires ‖ 화재 진압을 하는 직업인. 소방대원

fire·place /'faɪəpleɪs/ *n* the open place in a wall of a room where you can burn wood etc. to heat the room ‖ 난방하기 위해 장작 등을 태울 수 있는, 실내 벽의 터져 있는 공간. 벽난로

fire·proof /'faɪəpruf/ *adj* a building, piece of cloth etc. that is fireproof cannot be damaged very much by fire ‖ 건물·옷감 등이 불에 많이 손상되지 않는. 내화성의. 불연성의. 잘 타지 않는 - **fireproof** *v* [T]

fire·side /'faɪəsaɪd/ *n* the area close to a FIREPLACE or around a small fire ‖ 벽난로 가까운 장소나 작은 불 근처. 노변. 난롯가. 모닥불 가: *We were sitting by the fireside.* 우리는 난롯가에 앉아 있었다.

fire sta·tion /'. ,../ *n* a building where FIREFIGHTERS and their equipment stay until they are needed for stopping fires ‖ 화재 진압이 필요할 때까지 소방대원과 그 장비가 대기하고 있는 건물. 소방서

fire truck /'. ./ *n* ⇨ FIRE ENGINE

fire·wall /'faɪəwɔl/ *n* **1** a wall that stops a fire from spreading into another room ‖ 화재가 다른 방으로 번지는 것을 방지하는 벽. 방화벽 **2** a system to stop people from looking at particular information on the INTERNET ‖ 인터넷상의 특정 정보를 보지 못하게 하기 위한 (보안)시스템. 방화벽

fire·wood /'faɪəwʊd/ *n* [U] wood that is cut to be used on fires ‖ 불 때는 데 사용하기 위해 자른 나무. 장작

fire·works /'faɪəwəks/ *n* [plural] colorful explosives that people burn when celebrating a special day ‖ 특별한 날을 기념할 때 사람들이 태우는 다양한 색채의 폭발물. 불꽃(놀이): *a Fourth of July fireworks display* 7월 4일(미국 독립 기념일) 불꽃놀이

fir·ing line /'.. ,./ *n* **be on the firing line** to be in a position or situation in which you can be attacked or criticized ‖ 공격이나 비난을 받을 수 있는 위치나 상황에 있다: *As Communications Director, Harris is constantly on the firing line.* 통신국장으로서 해리스는 항상 비난을 받을 수 있는 지위에 있다.

fir·ing squad /'.. ,./ *n* a group of soldiers whose duty is to punish prisoners by shooting and killing them ‖ 죄수들을 총살하는 임무를 가진 일단의 군인들. 총살대

firm¹ /fəm/ *n* a business or small company ‖ 사업체나 영세 기업: *I'm supposed to work at my uncle's law firm this summer.* 나는 이번 여름에 삼촌이 운영하시는 법무 법인에서 근무하기로 되어 있다.

firm² *adj* **1** not completely hard, but not soft and not easy to bend or press ‖ 아주 딱딱하지는 않지만 부드럽지 않으며 쉽게 구부러지거나 눌러지지 않는. 단단한. 굳은: *a bed with a firm mattress* 단단한 매트리스가 있는 침대 / *Choose the ripest firmest tomatoes.* 가장 잘 익고 단단한 토마토를 골라라. **2 a firm grip/grasp/ hold** a tight, strong hold on something ‖ 어떤 것을 단단히 또는 세게 잡음. 꽉 잡음: *Roger took her hand in his firm grip.* 로저는 그녀의 손을 꼭 잡았다. **3** not likely to change ‖ 변할 것 같지 않은. 확고한: *East Germany was the Soviet Union's firmest ally in Eastern Europe.* 동독은 동구에서 소련의 가장 확고한 동맹국이었다. **4** showing that you are strong and have control ‖ 사람이 강하고 통제력이 있음을 나타내는. 단호한: *You'll just have to be firmer with him.* 너는 그에게 보다 더 단호한 태도를 취해야 하겠다.

firm³ *v*

firm sth ↔ up *phr v* [T] to make arrangements, ideas, or plans more definite and exact ‖ 협정(견해, 계획)을 보다 명백하고 정확하게 하다. 확정하다: *We hope to firm up the deal later this month.* 우리는 그 거래를 이달 하순에 확정짓기를 바란다.

firm·ware /'fəmwɛr/ *n* [U] TECHNICAL instructions to computers that are stored on CHIPS rather than in programs ‖ 프로그램 형태가 아닌 칩에 저장된 컴퓨터에 대한 명령어. 펌웨어

first¹ /fəst/ *determiner, adj* **1** before anyone or anything else ‖ 어느 누구나 다른 어떤 것보다도 먼저. 첫째의. 처음의: *Who would like to go first?* 누가 첫 번째

로 가고 싶니? / *Just try a little first to see if you like it.* 네가 그것을 좋아하는지 알아보게 먼저 조금만 해봐라. **2 at first** in the beginning ∥ 시초에. 처음에는: *At first I thought he was weird, but now I really like him.* 처음에 나는 그가 괴상하다고 생각했으나 지금은 정말 그를 좋아한다. **3 first (of all) a)** used when telling someone the first or most important thing in a series of statements ∥ 일련의 진술 중에 첫 번째나 가장 중요한 일을 남에게 말할 때에 쓰여. 무엇보다. 제일 먼저: *First of all, I need my car back so we can drive to Renee's.* 무엇보다 차를 돌려야만 우리는 레니의 집으로 갈 수 있다. **b)** before doing anything else ∥ 다른 무엇을 하기 전에. 우선: *First, let's look at the sales reports.* 우선 판매 보고서를 봅시다. **4 in the first place** before something happens that cannot be changed ∥ 바꿀 수 없는 일이 발생하기 이전에. 우선. 맨 먼저: *If you'd done things right in the first place, we wouldn't have problems now.* 처음에 네가 일을 제대로 했더라면 우리는 지금 문제가 없었을 거야. **5 first thing** SPOKEN as soon as you wake up or start work in the morning ∥ 아침에 깨자마자 또는 일을 시작하자마자. 무엇보다도 먼저: *I'll call you first thing tomorrow, okay?* 내일 제일 먼저 너에게 전화할게. 알았지? **6 first come, first served** used in order to say that only the first people to arrive, ask for something etc. will be given something ∥ 도착·청구 등을 먼저 하는 사람에게만 무엇이 주어진다는 것을 말하는 데에 쓰여. 선착순: *Free movie tickets are being given away on a first come, first served basis.* 무료 영화 입장권을 선착순으로 주고 있다. **7 first things first** used in order to say that something is important and must be dealt with before other things ∥ 어떤 일이 중요하여 다른 일보다 먼저 처리되어야 한다는 것을 말하려는 데에 쓰여. 중요한 일부터 먼저: *First things first: who is going to pick up Ryder from the airport?* 중요한 일부터 먼저 하자. 누가 공항에 가서 라이더를 데려올래? —see also **first/second/third string** (STRING¹), **in the first/second/third place** (PLACE¹)

series of things: *First, chop the onions.* / *First of all, I'd like to thank everyone for coming today.* Use **at first** to talk about what happened at the beginning of an event or situation: *We really liked the hotel at first, but then we saw the roaches.*

first와 first of all은 일련의 일 중에서 첫 번째 또는 가장 중요한 일에 대해 언급하기 위해 문장의 첫머리에 쓰인다: 우선 양파를 잘게 썰어라. / 무엇보다도 저는 오늘 오신 모든 분께 감사드리고 싶습니다. at first는 사건이나 상황의 초기에 발생한 일에 대해 말하기 위해 쓰인다: 우리는 처음에는 정말 그 호텔을 좋아했지만 거기서 바퀴벌레들을 보았다.

first² *n, pron* **1** 1st; someone or something that is before anyone or anything else ∥ 1st로도 철자함; 어느 누구나 다른 어떤 것보다 앞서 있는 사람이나 사물. 첫째[최초]의 사람[것]: *Who's first in line?* 줄에서 누가 선두냐? / *My uncle was the first in my family to go to college.* 삼촌은 우리 집안에서 대학에 간 첫 번째 사람이었다. / *the 1st of June* (=first day of June) 6월 1일 **2 that's a first** SPOKEN said when you are surprised that something different or unusual has happened ∥ 다르거나 신기한 일이 발생하여 놀랐을 때에 쓰여: *"Dad actually washed the dishes tonight." "That's a first."* "아빠가 오늘 저녁에 정말로 설거지를 하셨어." "생전 처음 보는 일이네." **3 come (in) first** to win a race or competition ∥ 경주나 경기에서 우승하다: *Bill came in first in the 100-yard dash.* 빌은 100야드 단거리 경주에서 1등을 했다.

first aid /ˌ. ˈ./ *n* [U] simple medical treatment that you give to someone who is injured until a doctor can help ∥ 의사의 도움을 받을 수 있을 때까지 부상자에게 처치하는 간단한 의학적 치료. 응급처치

first base /ˌ. ˈ./ *n* [singular] **1** in baseball, the first place a player must touch before s/he can gain a point ∥ 야구에서 선수가 득점하기 전에 닿아야 하는 첫 번째 장소. 1루 —see picture on page 946 **2 get to first base** SPOKEN an expression meaning to HUG or kiss someone in a sexual way, used especially by young people ∥ 특히 젊은이들이 쓰는 말로 상대방을 성적으로 껴안거나 키스하는 것을 의미하는 표현. 포옹[키스]하다

first class¹ /ˌ. ˈ./ n [U] the best and most expensive place to sit on a plane, train, or ship ‖ 비행기[열차, 선박] 등에서 가장 좋고 제일 비싼 좌석. 1등(석): *In first class they get free champagne.* 1등 석에는 무료로 샴페인이 나온다.

first-class² adj **1** much better than other things of the same type ‖ 같은 종류의 다른 사물보다 훨씬 좋은. 최고급의. 훌륭한: *a first-class educational system* 훌륭한 교육 제도 **2** using the FIRST CLASS on a plane, train, or ship ‖ 비행기[열차, 선박]의 1등 좌석을 이용하는. 1등석의: *two first-class tickets to Hawaii* 하와이행 1등석 2매 – **first class** adv: *flying first class* 일등석으로의 비행

first floor /ˌ. ˈ./ n the floor of a building that is at ground level; GROUND FLOOR ‖ 지면 높이와 같은 건물의 층. 1층; 倒 ground floor —see picture at ATTIC

first gear /ˌ. ˈ./ n [singular] the lowest GEAR in a car, bicycle, vehicle etc. ‖ 차·자전거·탈것 등의 최저 변속 기어. 1단 기어: *Put it in first gear and try again.* 기어를 1단에 넣고 다시 해봐.

first-hand /ˌfɚst'hænd/ adj, adv from your own experience ‖ 자신의 경험으로부터. 직접적으로 (얻은): *Garner knows firsthand how the media work.* 가너는 미디어가 어떻게 작용하는지를 경험을 통하여 알고 있다. / *firsthand knowledge* 직접 경험을 통해 얻은 지식

first la·dy /ˌ. ˈ./ n the wife of the President of the US ‖ 미국 대통령의 부인. 영부인

first·ly /ˈfɚstli/ adv ⇨ **first (of all)** (FIRST¹)

first name /ˈ. ./ n the name that is your own name, and that in English comes before your family's name ‖ 영어에서 성(姓) 앞에 오는 자신만의 이름: *My teacher's first name is Caroline.* 나의 선생님의 이름은 캐롤라인이시다. — compare LAST NAME, MIDDLE NAME —see usage note at NAMES

first name은 아는 사람들이 상대방에게 말을 할 때 사용하는 상대방의 이름이다. **last name**은 가족의 모든 구성원이 공유하는 성(姓)을 말한다. 어떤 사람들은 이름과 성 사이에 놓이는 **middle name**도 갖고 있다. 이 middle name은 보통 공문서에만 쓰인다.

first per·son /ˌ. ˈ../ n [singular] TECHNICAL in grammar, a form of a verb or PRONOUN that you use to show that you are the speaker. "I," "we," "me," and "us" are all first person pronouns, and "I am" is the first person singular of the verb "to be" ‖ 문법에서 자신이 화자임을 나타내기 위하여 쓰는 동사나 대명사의 한 형태. 1인칭. "I," "we," "me," "us"는 모두 1인칭 대명사이고 "I am"은 "be"동사의 1인칭 단수이다

first-rate /ˌ. ˈ./ adj extremely good ‖ 지극히 좋은. 일류의. 훌륭한: *a first-rate performance by the San Francisco Ballet* 샌프란시스코 발레단의 훌륭한 공연

fis·cal /ˈfɪskəl/ adj **1** relating to government taxes, debts and spending ‖ 정부의 세입·채무·세출에 관련된. 재정의: *the city's social and fiscal policies* 그 시의 사회 및 재정 정책 **2 fiscal year** a period of 12 months, used by a government or business to calculate its accounts ‖ 정부나 기업이 자신의 회계를 계산하는 데 쓰이는 12개월의 기간. 회계연도

fish¹ /fɪʃ/ n, plural **fish** or **fishes** [C, U] an animal that lives in water and uses its FINS and tail to swim ‖ 물에 살면서 지느러미와 꼬리로 헤엄을 치는 동물. 물고기: *How many fish did you catch?* 물고기를 얼마나 잡았니? / *We're having fish for supper tonight.* 우리는 오늘 저녁 식사로 생선을 먹을 거야.

fish² v **1** [I] to try to catch fish ‖ 물고기를 잡으려고 하다. 고기잡이하다: *Dad's fishing for salmon.* 아빠는 연어를 잡고 있다. **2** [I, T] to search for something in a bag, pocket etc. ‖ 가방·주머니 등에서 무엇을 찾아내다: *Sally fished her keys out of her purse and unlocked the door.* 샐리는 핸드백에서 열쇠를 찾아 문을 열었다. / *Then he started fishing around in his pocket for a quarter.* 그리고 나서 그는 25센트짜리 동전을 찾으려고 주머니 속을 뒤지기 시작했다. **3 be fishing for compliments** to be trying to make someone say nice things about you ‖ 남에게 자신에 대하여 좋은 말을 늘어놓게 하다

fish·bowl /ˈfɪʃboʊl/ *n* **1** a glass container that pet fish are kept in ‖ 애완용 물고기를 기르는 유리 용기. 어항 **2** a situation in which everyone else can see what you are doing ‖ 자신이 하고 있는 것을 다른 사람들이 모두 볼 수 있는 상황. 공중(公衆)에 노출되는 상황: *The president's entire family is forced to live in a fishbowl.* 대통령의 온 가족은 대중에 노출되어 살 수 밖에 없다.

fish·er·man /ˈfɪʃəmən/ *n* a man who catches fish as a job or a sport ‖ 직업이나 스포츠로 물고기를 잡는 사람. 어부. 낚시꾼

fish·er·y /ˈfɪʃəri/ *n* a part of the ocean that is used for catching fish as a business ‖ 사업으로서 물고기를 잡는 데 이용되는 대양의 일부. 어장

fish·ing /ˈfɪʃɪŋ/ *n* [U] the sport or job of catching fish ‖ 물고기를 잡는 스포츠 또는 직업. 낚시질. 어업: *Do you want to go fishing?* 낚시하러 갈래? **– fishing** *adj*

fishing pole /ˈ.. ./, **fishing rod** *n* a long thin pole with a long string and a hook tied to it, used for catching fish ‖ 고기잡이에 쓰이는, 긴줄에 낚시바늘이 달려 있는 길고 가는 막대. 낚싯대

fish·net /ˈfɪʃnɛt/ *n* [U] a material with a pattern of threads and small holes like a net ‖ 줄과 작은 구멍들이 망(網)과 같은 모양을 이루는 물건. 어망. 그물 모양의 직물: *fishnet stockings* 망사 스타킹

fish·tail /ˈfɪʃteɪl/ *v* [I] if a vehicle fishtails, it slides from side to side on the road, especially because the road is wet ‖ 특히 도로가 젖어서 차량 등이 도로의 한쪽에서 다른 쪽으로 미끄러지다

fish·y /ˈfɪʃi/ *adj* **1** INFORMAL seeming bad or dishonest ‖ 나빠 보이거나 정직하지 않아 보이는. 믿지 못할. 의심스러운. 수상한: *I bet Mark's up to something fishy.* (=doing something bad or dishonest) 나는 마크가 수상한 짓을 하고 있다고 확신한다. **2** tasting or smelling like fish ‖ 물고기와 같은 맛이나 냄새가 나는. 생선 같은. 비린내 나는

fis·sion /ˈfɪʃən/ *n* [U] TECHNICAL the process of splitting an atom to produce large amounts of energy or an explosion ‖ 대량의 에너지를 만들기 위해, 또는 폭발을 일으키기 위해 원자를 분열시키는 과정. 원자핵 분열 —compare FUSION

fis·sure /ˈfɪʃɚ/ *n* a deep crack in rock or the ground ‖ 바위나 지면의 깊이 갈라진 틈. 균열

fist /fɪst/ *n* a hand with all the fingers bent tightly in toward the PALM ‖ 모든 손

가락을 손바닥 쪽으로 단단히 굽힌 손. 주먹: *She clenched her fist and screamed, "I hate you!"* 그녀는 주먹을 꽉 쥐고 소리 질렀다. "나는 네가 싫어!"

fit¹ /fɪt/ **fit** or **fitted, fitted, fitting** *v* **1** [I, T] to be the right size and shape for someone ‖ 사람에게 크기와 모양이 알맞다. 꼭 맞다. 잘 어울리다: *The pants fit fine, but the jacket's too tight.* 바지는 잘 맞는데 재킷은 너무 꽉 낀다. / *I wonder if my wedding dress still fits me?* 내 웨딩드레스가 아직 나한테 맞는지 모르겠네? **2** [I] to be the right size, shape, or amount for a particular space, and not be too big or too much ‖ 특정한 공간에 대해 크기[모양, 양]가 알맞고 너무 크거나 너무 많지 않다. 적합하다. 합치하다: *You can't move the table there. It won't fit through the door.* 테이블을 거기로 옮길 수 없어. 문을 통과하지 못할 거야. / *Sorry, you can't all fit in the car.* 안됐지만 너는 그 차에 모든 것을 실을 수는 없어. / *I'm looking for the puzzle piece that fits here.* 나는 여기에 맞는 퍼즐 조각을 찾고 있다. **3** [T] to have enough space for people or things, or to put something in a place that has enough space ‖ 사람이나 물건이 들어갈 충분한 공간이 있다, 또는 충분한 공간이 있는 장소에 물체를 넣다: *Are you sure your truck will fit all this gear?* 네 트럭에 모든 장비들을 충분히 실을 수 있니? / *I can't fit any more stuff into this suitcase.* 이 여행가방에는 더 이상 어떤 물건도 들어가지 않는다. **4** [I, T] to be suitable or to seem to have the right qualities for something ‖ 어떤 것에 적합하거나 적절한 자질을 갖춘 것처럼 보이다: *We wanted an experienced journalist, and Watts fit the bill.* (=had the right experience) 우리는 경력 있는 언론인을 원했고 와트는 그 요구에 적합한 경력을 가졌다. / *A man fitting the police description* (=looking like it) *was seen running from the park.* 경찰이 묘사한 것과 일치하는 한 남자가 공원에서 도주하는 것이 목격되었다.

fit in *phr v* **1** [I] to be accepted by other people in a group because you have similar interests and attitudes ‖ 비슷한 관심과 태도를 가져서 집단 내의 다른 사람들로부터 받아들여지다. …과 적합하다[어울리다]. …에 적응하다: *The new*

fit
Jim's shirt doesn't fit him anymore.

students all had a hard time fitting in.
신입생 모두가 적응하는 데에 힘든 시간을
보냈다. **2** [T **fit** sb/sth ↔ **in**] to manage
to do something during a very busy time
‖ 매우 바쁜 시간 동안에 간신히 어떤 일
을 하다. (예정 등을) 맞추다. 정하다. 시
간을 내다: *Dr. Tyler can fit you in on
Monday at 3:30 p.m.* 타일러 박사는 월요
일 오후 3시 30분에 당신에게 시간을 낼
수 있습니다.

USAGE NOTE fit

Although both **fit** and **fitted** can be
used in the past tense, we usually use
fit: *The dress she was wearing really
fit her well.*
fit과 **fitted**는 모두 과거 시제로 쓰일
수 있지만 보통 **fit**을 쓴다: 그녀가 입고
있었던 드레스는 정말 그녀에게 잘 어울
렸다.

---

fit² *n* [singular] **1 have/throw a fit**
SPOKEN to become very angry and shout
a lot ‖ 매우 성내고 큰 소리를 지르게 되
다. 격분[격노]하다: *Mom's going to have
a fit when she sees what you've done.* 어
머니가 네가 한 일을 보면 격분하실 거다.
2 a short period of time when someone
stops being conscious and cannot
control his/her body ‖ 사람이 의식을 잃
고 자신의 몸을 통제할 수 없는 짧은 시간.
발작. 경련: *an epileptic fit* 간질 발작 **3** a
very strong emotion that you cannot
control ‖ 통제할 수 없는 매우 강한 감정.
격분. 흥분(상태): *a fit of rage* 발작적 격
노 **4** the way that something fits or is
suitable for a particular person, space
etc. ‖ 어떤 것이 특정한 사람·공간 등에
적합하거나 어울리는 방식. 적합성. 적응
성: *I thought they'd be too big, but the
shelves are a perfect fit.* 나는 선반이 너
무 클 것이라 생각했는데 꼭 맞다.

fit³ *adj* **1** having the qualities that are
suitable for something ‖ 어떤 것에 적합
한 성질을 가진. 알맞은. 적당한. 어울리
는: *You're in no fit state to drive.* 너는
운전하기에 부적절한 상태이다. —
opposite UNFIT **2 see fit to do sth** to
decide that it is suitable to do
something, even though most people
disagree ‖ 대다수의 사람들이 동의하지
않더라도 하는 것이 적당하다고 결정하다:
*The government has seen fit to start
testing more nuclear weapons.* 정부는
더 많은 핵무기 실험에 착수하는 것이 적
당하다는 결정을 내렸다. **3** healthy and
strong ‖ 건강하고 강한. 튼튼한. 몸 상태
가 좋은. 원기 왕성한: *physically fit* 신체

건강한

fit·ful /ˈfɪtfəl/ *adj* happening for short
and irregular periods of time ‖ 짧고 불규
칙적인 시간 간격을 두고 발생하는. 발작
적인. 단속적인. 변덕스러운: *a fitful
sleep* 오락가락하는 잠

fit·ness /ˈfɪtˈnɪs/ *n* [U] **1** the condition
of being healthy or strong enough to do
hard work or sports ‖ 힘든 일이나 스포
츠를 하기에 충분히 건강하거나 강한 상
태. 건강(상태): *Join a health club to
improve your fitness.* 건강을 증진하기 위
해 헬스클럽에 가입해라. **2** the quality of
being suitable for something, especially
a job ‖ 특히 직업 등에 적합한 자질. 적합
함. 적절함: *He isn't unsure of his fitness
for the priesthood.* 그는 자신이 사제직에
적합한지 확신이 서지 않았다.

fit·ted /ˈfɪtɪd/ *adj* fitted clothes are
designed so that they fit closely to
someone's body ‖ 옷 등이 몸에 꼭 맞게
디자인된. 꼭 맞는. 알맞은: *a fitted
jacket* 몸에 딱 맞는 재킷

fit·ting¹ /ˈfɪtɪŋ/ *adj* FORMAL right or
suitable ‖ 알맞거나 적합한. 적절한. 꼭
들어맞는. 안성맞춤인: *It seemed fitting
that it rained the day of his funeral.* 그
의 장례식 날에 비가 온 것은 잘 어울려
보였다.

fitting² *n* an occasion when you put on
clothes that are being made for you to
find out if they fit ‖ 옷이 맞는지를 확인하
기 위해 만들고 있는 옷을 입어 보는 일.
(가봉한 옷) 입혀 보기

five¹ /faɪv/ *number* **1** 5 ‖ 5 **2** five
o'clock ‖ 5시: *I get off work at five.* 나는
5시에 일을 마친다.

five² *n* a piece of paper money worth $5
‖ 5달러 짜리 지폐 한 장

five and ten /ˌ. . ˈ./, **five and
dime** *n* OLD-FASHIONED ⇨ DIME STORE

fix¹ /fɪks/ *v* [T]
1 ▶ REPAIR 수리하다 ◀ to repair
something that is broken or not working
‖ 고장 나거나 작동하지 않는 물건을 수리
하다. (물건을) 수리[수선]하다: *Do you
know anyone who can fix the sewing
machine?* 재봉틀을 수리할 수 있는 사람
을 아니?
2 ▶ PREPARE 준비하다 ◀ to prepare a
meal or drinks ‖ 식사 또는 음료수를 준
비하다: *Can you set the table while I
finish fixing dinner?* 내가 저녁 식사 준비
를 마치는 동안 너는 식탁을 차려 주겠
니?
3 ▶ ARRANGE 정하다 ◀ to make
arrangements for something ‖ 어떤 것을
계획하다. (날짜를) 정하다: *Let's fix a*

day to go to the gallery together. 함께 미술관에 갈 날짜를 정하자.

4 ▶HAIR/FACE 머리털/얼굴◀ to make your hair or makeup look neat and attractive ‖ 머리를 정돈하거나 화장을 하여 깔끔하고 매력적으로 보이게 하다. 정리하다. 다듬다: *Let me fix my hair first and then we can go.* 먼저 내 머리를 다듬고 나서 우리는 갈 수 있다.

5 ▶CAT/DOG 고양이/개◀ INFORMAL to do a medical operation on a cat or dog so that it cannot have babies ‖ 새끼를 가질 수 없도록 고양이나 개에게 의료 수술을 하다. 동물을 거세하다

6 ▶RESULT 결과◀ to make dishonest arrangements so that an election, competition etc. has the results that you want ‖ 선거·경기 등에서 원하는 결과를 얻기 위해 부정한 계획을 세우다. (일을 부정하게) 진행시키다. (남을) 매수하다: *If you ask me, the game was fixed.* 내 생각을 말하면, 그 게임은 미리 짜고 한 것이었다.

7 ▶INJURY 상처◀ INFORMAL to treat an injury on your body so that it is completely better ‖ 완전히 좋아지도록 신체의 부상을 치료하다. 치료하다: *The doctors don't know if they can fix my kneecap.* 그 의사들은 내 종지뼈를 고칠 수 있을는지 알지 못한다.

8 ▶PUNISH 처벌하다◀ SPOKEN to harm or punish someone because s/he has done something you do not like ‖ 자신이 좋아하지 않는 일을 한 사람을 해치거나 처벌하다. 벌하다. 혼내 주다: *I'll fix him! Just you wait!* 그 녀석을 혼내 줄게! 넌 두고 보거나 해!

fix up *phr v* [T] **1** [**fix** sth ↔ **up**] to make a place look attractive by doing small repairs, decorating it again, etc. ‖ 작은 수리를 하고 장식을 다시 함으로써 장소를 매력적으로 보이게 하다. 손질하다. 준비하다: *We're trying to get the house fixed up before Grandpa and Grandma come to visit.* 우리는 할아버지와 할머니가 찾아오시기 전에 집을 손질해 놓으려 하고 있다. **2** [**fix** sb ↔ **up**] INFORMAL to find a romantic partner for someone ‖ 어떤 사람을 위해 연애 상대를 찾다. 구해 주다. 소개시켜 주다: *Rachel keeps trying to fix me up with her brother.* 레이첼은 계속 나를 자기 오빠에게 소개시켜 주려고 한다.

fix² *n* **1** [singular] SLANG an amount of something, such as an illegal drug, that you think you need and want to use ‖ 필요하다고 생각되어 사용하기를 원하는 불법 마약 등의 양. (마약의) 주사(량). 어

떤 분량. 한 대. 한 잔: *I have to have my coffee fix in the morning!* 나는 아침에 커피 한 잔을 마셔야 한다! **2 be in a fix** to have a problem that is difficult to solve ‖ 해결하기 곤란한 문제가 생기다. 궁지[곤경, 난관]에 몰리다: *We're going to be in a real fix if we miss the last bus.* 우리가 마지막 버스를 놓친다면 정말 큰 어려움에 처하게 될 것이다.

fix·a·tion /fɪkˈseɪʃən/ *n* an unnaturally strong interest in or love for someone or something ‖ 사람 또는 사물에 대한 비정상적으로 강한 관심 또는 애정. 병적인 집착. 편집. 고착: *Brian has a fixation with/about motorcycles.* 브라이언은 오토바이에 대해 병적으로 집착을 한다. – **fixated** /ˈfɪkseɪtɪd/ *adj*

fixed /fɪkst/ *adj* **1** not changing or moving ‖ 변하지 않는 또는 움직이지 않는. 고정된: *A fixed number of tickets will be on sale the day of the show.* 정해진 수의 입장권이 쇼 당일 날 판매될 것이다. / *a fixed smile* 굳은 미소 **2 have fixed ideas/opinions** to have very strong opinions or ideas that often do not seem reasonable ‖ 흔히 합리적으로 보이지 않는 매우 강한 의견 또는 생각을 가지다. 고정 관념을 가지다: *Lloyd has fixed ideas about religion.* 로이드는 종교에 대해 고정 관념을 가지고 있다.

fix·ed·ly /ˈfɪksɪdli/ *adv* without looking at or thinking about anything else ‖ 다른 것을 보거나 생각하지 않고. 확고하게. 꼼짝 않고: *Grover was staring fixedly at the boat.* 그로버는 배를 뚫어지게 응시하고 있었다.

fix·ture /ˈfɪkstʃɚ/ *n* **1** [C usually plural] a piece of equipment that is attached inside a house, such as an electric light or a FAUCET ‖ 전등 또는 수도꼭지 등 집 내부에 부착된 설비. 고정물. 비품 **2 be a (permanent) fixture** to always be present, and unlikely to move or go away ‖ 항상 존재하고 이동하거나 사라질 것 같지 않다: *Goldie's Bar has been a fixture on University Avenue for nine years.* 골디의 술집은 9년째 대학가에 자리 잡고 있다.

fizz /fɪz/ *n* [singular] the BUBBLEs of gas in some types of drinks, or the sound they make ‖ 몇몇 음료수에 있는 가스 거품 또는 그 거품이 내는 소리. 거품(이 이는 음료). 쏴 하는 소리: *The soda in the fridge has lost its fizz.* 냉장고 속에 있는 소다수[탄산수]는 김이 빠져 버렸다. – **fizz** *v* [I] – **fizzy** *adj*

fiz·zle /ˈfɪzəl/ *v*

fizzle out *phr v* [I] to gradually stop

being interesting, and therefore stop happening ‖ 흥미가 점점 없어져서 일이 발생하지 않다. 용두사미로 끝나다. (시초는 좋으나) 실패하다[흐지부지되다]: *The party fizzled out before midnight.* 그 파티는 자정 전에 싱겁게 끝났다.

fjord /fyɔrd/ *n* a long narrow area of sea between high cliffs ‖ 높은 절벽 사이에 있는 길고 좁은 바다 지역. 피오르드. 협만(峽灣)

FL the written abbreviation of Florida ‖ Florida(플로리다 주)의 약어

flab /flæb/ *n* [U] INFORMAL soft loose fat on a person's body ‖ 신체의 물렁하게 늘어진 지방. 군살: *I need to get rid of some of this flab!* 나는 이 군살을 좀 빼야 해!

flab·ber·gast·ed /ˈflæbərˌgæstɪd/ *adj* INFORMAL extremely shocked or surprised ‖ 매우 충격받거나 놀란. 소스라치게 놀란. 당황스러운

flab·by /ˈflæbi/ *adj* INFORMAL having too much soft loose fat instead of strong muscles ‖ 단단한 근육 대신에 아주 물렁하고 축 늘어진 지방이 있는. (근육이) 축 늘어진[처진]: *Since I've stopped swimming my arms have gotten flabby.* 수영을 그만두었더니 내 팔근육이 축 늘어졌다.

flac·cid /ˈflæsɪd/ *adj* TECHNICAL soft and weak instead of firm ‖ 단단하지 않으며 물렁하고 약한. 축 늘어진. 무른. 연약한: *flaccid muscles* 물렁물렁한 근육

flag¹ /flæg/ *n* **1** a piece of cloth with a colored picture or pattern on it that represents a particular country or organization ‖ 특정 국가 또는 조직을 나타내는 채색한 그림이나 무늬가 있는 천. 기: *The crowd was cheering, waving Canadian flags.* 군중들은 캐나다 국기를 흔들며 환호하고 있었다. **2** a colored piece of cloth used as a signal ‖ 하나의 신호로 쓰이는 채색된 천. (신호의) 기: *The flag went down, and the race began.* 깃발이 내려지자 경주가 시작되었다.

flag² *v* **-gged, -gging** [I] to become tired, weak, or less interested in something ‖ 피로해지다[약해지다, 사물에 대한 흥미가 덜해지다]. 해이해지다. 쇠퇴하다: *After fighting for four years, the soldier's morale was beginning to flag.* 4년간의 전투 끝에, 병사의 사기가 떨어지기 시작하고 있었다. **– flagging** *adj*

flag sb/sth ↔ **down** *phr v* [T] to make the driver of a car, bus etc. stop by waving at him/her ‖ 자동차·버스 등의 운전사에게 손을 흔들어 정지시키다. 정지 신호를 보내다: *Rhoda flagged down a*

cab. 로다는 손을 흔들어 택시를 세웠다.

flag·pole /ˈflægpoʊl/ *n* a tall pole used for hanging flags ‖ 기를 매다는 데에 쓰는 긴 막대. 깃대

fla·grant /ˈfleɪgrənt/ *adj* shocking and not showing any respect for laws, truth, someone's feelings etc. ‖ 충격적이며 법률·사실·남의 감정 등에 대해 어떠한 존중도 보이지 않는. 악명 높은. 파렴치한: *The arrests are a flagrant violation of human rights.* 그 체포는 인권을 명백하게 위반한 것이다. **– flagrantly** *adv*

flag·ship /ˈflægˌʃɪp/ *n* the most important ship in a group of Navy ships, on which the ADMIRAL sails ‖ 제독이 지휘하는 해군 함대의 가장 중요한 군함. 기함

flag·stone /ˈflægstoʊn/ *n* a smooth flat piece of stone used for floors, paths etc. ‖ 마룻바닥·길거리 등에 쓰이는 매끈하고 평평한 돌. 판석(板石)

flail /fleɪl/ *v* [I, T] to wave your arms and legs in a fast but uncontrolled way ‖ 불규칙적으로 빠르게 팔·다리를 흔들다. (팔·다리 등을) 심하게 휘두르다

flair /flɛr/ *n* [singular, U] a natural ability to do something very well or to use your imagination ‖ 어떤 일을 매우 잘하거나 상상력을 사용하는 타고난 능력. 재능. 안목. 직감: *Carla's always had a flair for advertising.* 칼라는 항상 광고에 대한 안목이 있었다.

flak /flæk/ *n* [U] INFORMAL strong criticism ‖ 강한 비판. 잇단 비판. 격론: *Melissa knew she'd get/take a lot of flak for dating her boss.* 멜리사는 그녀의 상사와 데이트한 것에 대해 격렬한 비난을 받으리라는 것을 알았다.

flake¹ /fleɪk/ *v* [I] to break or come off in small thin pieces ‖ 작고 얇은 조각으로 부서지거나 벗겨져 떨어지다: *The paint on the door is starting to flake off.* 문의 페인트칠이 벗겨져 떨어지기 시작하고 있다.

flake out *phr v* [I] SPOKEN **1** do something strange or forgetful ‖ 이상한 짓이나 잊어버리기 쉬운 일을 하다. 머리가 약간 돌다. (약속을) 잊어버리다: *Kathy kind of flaked out on us today.* 캐시는 오늘 우리에게 약간 이상한 행동을 보였다. **2** to fall asleep ‖ 잠들다: *Karl was flaked out on the sofa.* 칼은 소파에서 잠들었다.

flake² *n* **1** SPOKEN someone who easily forgets things or who does strange things ‖ 사물을 쉽게 잊어버리거나 이상한 짓을 하는 사람. 괴짜: *Sometimes I'm such a flake.* 때때로 나는 정말 괴짜가 된다. **2** a small flat thin piece that breaks off of something || 물체에서 떨어진 작고 납작한 얇은 조각. 파편. 층: *chocolate flakes on a cake* 케이크 위의 초콜릿 조각 – **flaky** *adj*

flam·boy·ant /flæm'bɔɪənt/ *adj* **1** behaving in a loud, confident, or surprising way so that people notice you || 남들이 알 수 있도록 요란스레 [자신 있게, 놀라운 방식으로] 행동하는. 눈부신. 현란한. 이채를 띤: *flamboyant gestures* 현란한 제스처[몸짓] **2** noticeable because of being brightly colored, expensive, big etc. || 밝은 색깔로 되어 있어서 또는 비싸거나 커서 눈에 띄는. 찬란한. 호화스러운. 두드러진: *a flamboyant red sequined dress* 현란한 붉은 색의 시퀸(장식용 작은 원형 금속 조각)을 단 드레스 – **flamboyance** *n* [U]

flame¹ /fleɪm/ *n* [C, U] **1** hot bright burning gas that you see when something is on fire || 사물이 불타고 있을 때 볼 수 있는 뜨겁고 밝게 불타는 가스. 불꽃. 화염: *a candle flame* 양초 불꽃 **2 in flames** burning strongly || 강하게 불타는. 화염에 휩싸인: *By the time the firemen arrived, the house was in flames.* 소방대원이 도착했을 무렵 그 집은 화염에 휩싸여 있었다.

flame² *v* [I] **1** LITERARY to suddenly become red or bright || 갑자기 빨갛게 또는 밝게 되다. 빛나다. 확 붉어지다: *Her cheeks were flaming with embarrassment.* 그녀의 뺨은 당황해서 빨갛게 달아오르고 있었다. **2** SLANG to send someone a message on the INTERNET that is insulting, or that shows you are angry by being written only in CAPITALs || 남에게 모욕적인, 또는 대문자만을 써서 분노한 것을 나타내는 인터넷 메시지를 보내다

fla·men·co /flə'mɛŋkoʊ/ *n* [C, U] a very fast and exciting Spanish dance, or the music for this dance || 아주 빠르고 흥이 나는 스페인 춤, 또는 이러한 춤곡. 플라멩코

flam·ing /'fleɪmɪŋ/ *adj* very bright || 매우 밝은. (색이) 타는 듯이 붉은: *flaming red hair* 불타는 듯한 붉은 머리카락

fla·min·go /flə'mɪŋgoʊ/ *n* a tall tropical water bird with long thin legs, pink feathers, and a long neck || 길고 가는 다리·핑크빛 깃털·긴 목을 가진, 키가 큰 열대산 물새. 홍학

flam·ma·ble /'flæməbəl/ *adj* something that is flammable burns very easily || 사물이 매우 쉽게 불에 타는. 가연성의 — opposite NONFLAMMABLE —compare INFLAMMABLE

USAGE NOTE flammable, inflammable

Both of these words mean the same thing, but we usually use **flammable**. The negative of both of these words is **nonflammable**.
이 두 어휘는 모두 같은 의미이지만 보통 **flammable**을 쓴다. 이 두 어휘의 부정은 **nonflammable**이다.

flank¹ /flæŋk/ *n* **1** the side of a person's or animal's body between the RIBs and the HIP || 사람이나 동물의 몸통 측면의 늑골과 엉덩이 사이. 옆구리 **2** the side of an army in a battle || 전투에서 군대의 옆면. 측면: *The enemy attacked us on our left flank.* 적은 우리의 좌측면으로 공격했다.

flank² *v* **be flanked by** to have one person or thing standing on one side, and one on the other side || 사람이나 사물이 하나는 한쪽에 서 있고 다른 하나는 다른 쪽에 서 있다. …의 측면에 위치하다. …옆에 있다[서다]: *The President stepped onto the plane, flanked by bodyguards.* 대통령은 양 측면에 경호원을 대동한 채 비행기에 올랐다.

flan·nel /'flænl/ *n* [U] soft light cotton or wool cloth that is used for making warm clothes || 따뜻한 옷을 만드는 데에 쓰이는 부드럽고 가벼운 면 또는 모직물. 무명. 면포. 플란넬: *a flannel shirt* 플란넬 셔츠

flap¹ /flæp/ *v* **-pped, pping 1** [T] if a bird flaps its wings, it moves them up and down || 새 등이 날개를 위아래로 움직이다. 퍼덕거리다 **2** [I] if a piece of cloth, paper etc. flaps, it moves around quickly and makes a noise || 천·종이 등이 빠르게 여기저기 움직이며 소리를 내다. 펄럭이다: *The ship's sails flapped in the wind.* 그 배의 돛은 바람에 펄럭거렸다.

flap² *n* a piece of cloth or paper that is used in order to cover the opening of a pocket, envelope, or TENT || 주머니[봉투, 천막]의 열린 부분을 덮는 데에 쓰는 천 또는 종이 조각. 뚜껑

flap·jack /'flæpdʒæk/ *n* ⇨ PANCAKE

flare¹ /flɛr/ *v* **1** [I] also **flare up** to suddenly begin to burn very brightly || 갑자기 매우 밝게 불타기 시작하다. (불길이)확 타오르다: *rockets flaring above Cape Canaveral* 케이프커내버럴 상공에서 불꽃을 내뿜는 로켓 **2** [I] also **flare up** to suddenly become very angry or violent || 갑자기 매우 성내거나 난폭해지다. 발끈해지다. 분노를 터뜨리다:

Maddie's temper flared. 매디의 노여움이 폭발했다. **3** [I, T] to become wider at the bottom edge, or to make something do this || 아래 가장자리가 더 넓어지다, 또는 넓게 만들다. (나팔꽃 모양으로) 아래 쪽이 벌어지다[벌어지게 하다]: *a skirt that flares out* 나팔꽃 모양으로 벌어진 스커트

flare² *n* a very bright light used outdoors as a signal to show people where you are, especially because you need help || 특히 도움이 필요해서, 남에게 자신의 위치를 알리기 위한 신호로서 야외에서 쓰는 매우 밝은 불. 횃불. 조명탄

flare-up /ˈ. ./ *n* a situation in which something bad becomes a problem again, after not being a problem for a while || 한동안 문제가 되지 않다가 다시 문제화 되는 상황. (병 등의) 재발. (문제 등의) 갑작스런 표면화: *a flare-up of her arthritis* 관절염의 재발

flash¹ /flæʃ/ *v* **1** [I, T] to suddenly shine brightly for a short time, or to make something do this || 갑자기 잠시 동안 밝게 빛나다, 또는 빛나게 하다. 번쩍이다. 확 들어오다. 확 비추다: *Why did that guy flash his headlights at me?* 왜 저 사람이 나한테 전조등을 확 비추었지? **2** [I] to move very quickly || 매우 빠르게 움직이다. 휙 지나가다: *An ambulance flashed by/past.* 구급차가 휙 지나갔다. **3** [T] to show something suddenly and for a very short amount of time || 갑자기 아주 단시간 동안 사물을 보여 주다. 언뜻 보여 주다: *Sergeant Wicks flashed his badge.* 윅스 경사는 그의 배지를 언뜻 보여 주었다. **4** [I] if images, thoughts etc. flash through your mind, you suddenly remember or think about them || 이미지·생각 등이 갑자기 기억나다 또는 생각나다. 번득이다. 퍼뜩 떠오르다: *Memories of Hawaii flashed through/across my mind.* 하와이에 대한 추억이 내 마음에 번개처럼 떠올랐다. **5 flash a smile/glance/look** to smile or look at someone quickly || 남에게 재빨리 미소 짓거나 쳐다보다. 미소 짓다/눈짓을 보내다/남을 흘끗 보다 **6** [I, T] INFORMAL if a man flashes, he suddenly shows his sex organs in public to a woman || 남성이 자신의 성기를 갑자기 공개적으로 여자에게 보이다. 성기 등을 살짝 보이다

flash sth **around** *phr v* [T] to show a lot of people something that you have, in order to try to make them admire you || 남이 자신에게 감탄하도록 자신이 갖고 있는 것을 많은 사람들에게 보이다. (물건을)남에게 자랑 삼아 내보이다: *Smythe*

was there, flashing his cash around. 스마이스는 거기서 자신의 현찰을 자랑 삼아 내보이고 있었다.

flash² *n* **1** a sudden quick bright light || 갑작스럽고 순간적인 밝은 빛. 섬광. 번쩍임: *a flash of lightning* 번개의 번쩍임 **2** [C, U] a small light on a camera that you use when taking photographs when it is dark || 어두울 때 사진을 찍는 경우에 쓰이는 카메라의 작은 전등. 섬광 전구. 플래시: *Did the flash go off?* 플래시가 터졌니? **3 in/like a flash** very quickly || 아주 빠르게. 곧. 순식간에: *Wait right here. I'll be back in a flash.* 바로 여기에서 기다려. 곧 돌아올게.

flash·back /ˈflæʃbæk/ *n* a sudden memory of an event that you or a character in a book, play etc. experienced in the past || 자신이나 또는 책·연극 등의 등장인물이 과거에 경험했던 사건의 갑작스런 기억. 회상 장면. 사건의 재현

flash·card /ˈflæʃkɑrd/ *n* a card with a word or picture on it, used in teaching || 교수용으로 쓰이는, 단어나 그림이 있는 카드. 플래시 카드. 순간적으로 보여 주는 학습용 카드

flash·er /ˈflæʃɚ/ *n* INFORMAL a man who shows his sex organs to women in public || 대중 앞에서 여자에게 성기를 보여 주는 남자. 노출광(狂)

flash·light /ˈflæʃlaɪt/ *n* a small electric light that you carry in your hand || 손에 들고 다니는 조그만 전등. 손전등

flash·y /ˈflæʃi/ *adj* intended to be impressive || 인상적으로 보이기 위한. 야한. 현란한: *a flashy new sports car* 현란한 새 스포츠카

flask /flæsk/ *n* **1** a small flat container used for carrying alcohol in your pocket || 주머니에 술을 휴대하기 위해 쓰이는 작고 납작한 용기. 휴대용 술병. 플라스크 병 **2** a glass bottle with a narrow top used by scientists || 과학자들이 쓰는 상단이 좁은 유리병. (화학 실험용) 플라스크

flat¹ /flæt/ *adj* **1** smooth and level, without any hollow or raised areas || 우묵하거나 불룩 솟은 부분이 없이 평탄하고 수평인. 평탄한. 밋밋한: *The highway stays flat for the next 50 miles.* 이 간선 도로는 이제부터 50마일은 계속 평탄하다. / *a flat roof* 평평한 지붕 **2** a tire or ball that is flat does not have enough air inside it || 타이어나 공 등의 내부 공기가 충분하지 않은. 바람이 빠진. 납작해진. 펑크 난 **3** a drink that is flat does not taste fresh because it has no more BUBBLEs of gas || 더 이상 가스 거품이 없

어서 신선한 맛이 나지 않는. (술·음식
이) 김빠진. 맛이 없는 **4** a musical note
that is flat is played or sung slightly
lower than it should be ‖ 음이 원래보다
약간 더 낮게 연주되거나 불려지는. 반음
내린 —compare SHARP¹ **5 flat rate/fee
etc.** an amount of money that is paid
and that does not increase or decrease
‖ 인상이나 인하되지 않고 지불한 금액.
균일가/균일 요금

flat² *adv* **1** in a straight position or
stretched against a flat surface ‖ 평평한
표면에 대고 똑바른 또는 쭉 뻗은 자세로.
납작 엎드려서. 길게 누워: *I have to lie
flat on my back when I sleep.* 나는 잘
때 쭉 뻗은 자세로 드러누워야 한다. **2 10
seconds/two minutes etc. flat**
INFORMAL in exactly 10 seconds, two
minutes etc. ‖ 정확히 10초/2분에: *I was
out of the house in ten minutes flat.* 나는
정확하게 10분에 집에서 나왔다. **3 fall
flat** to not have the result that you
hoped or expected ‖ 소망했던 또는 예상
해던 결과가 없다. (계획·시도가) 완전히
실패로 끝났다. (놀람 등이) 효과[반응]
가 없다: *All of her jokes/plans fell flat.*
그녀의 모든 농담[계획]은 실패로 끝났다.
4 slightly lower than a musical note
should be sung or played ‖ 원래 노래 또
는 연주되는 음보다 약간 더 낮은. 반음
내린 **5 flat out** INFORMAL in a direct
way, or completely ‖ 직접적으로, 또는 완
전히: *Dolly flat out refused to go.* 돌리는
가는 것을 완강히 거부했다. **6 go/
work/move etc. flat out** to go etc. as
fast as possible ‖ 가능한 한 빨리 가다. 전
속력으로[전력을 다해] 가다/일하다/움직
이다: *We worked flat out to finish on
time* 우리는 제시간에 끝내기 위해 전력을
다해 일했다.

flat³ *n* **1** INFORMAL a TIRE that does not
have enough air inside it ‖ 내부에 공기가
충분하지 않은 타이어. 펑크 난[바람이 빠
진] 타이어 **2** a musical note that is one
half STEP lower than a particular note,
represented by the sign (♭) in written
music ‖ 악보에 ♭ 기호로 나타낸, 특정
음보다 반음 더 낮춘 음표. 내림(표)

flat·ly /ˈflætli/ *adv* **1** said in a definite
way that is not likely to change ‖ 변경될
것 같지 않게 분명하게 말하여. 단호히:
They flatly refused to help me. 그들은
단호하게 나를 돕는 것을 거절했다. **2**
without showing any emotion ‖ 어떠한
감정도 나타내지 않고. 덤덤하게: *"It's
hopeless,"* he said flatly. "희망이 없어"
라고 그는 덤덤하게 말했다.

flats /flæts/ *n* [plural] a type of

women's shoes with very low heels ‖ 굽
이 아주 낮은 여성용 구두의 일종. 굽이
낮은 숙녀화 —see picture at SHOE¹

flat·ten /ˈflætⁿn/ *v* [I, T] to make
something flat or to become flat ‖ 사물을
평평하게 하다, 또는 평평해지다: *The hills
flatten out near the coast.* 그 언덕은 해
안 가까이에서 평평해졌다.

flat·ter /ˈflætɚ/ *v* **1 be flattered** to be
pleased because someone has shown
you that s/he likes or admires you ‖ 남이
자신을 좋아하거나 칭송하고 있음을 보여
주어서 기뻐하다. 우쭐해지다. 치켜세워지
다: *I was flattered to be considered for
the job.* 나는 그 직무에 적임자로 고려되
어 우쭐해졌다. **2** [T] to praise someone
in order to please him/her, even though
you do not really mean it ‖ 실제로 의도
하는 바는 아니지만, 남을 기쁘게 하려고
칭찬하다. 아첨하다. 알랑거리다: *Don't
try to flatter me!* 나에게 아첨하려고 하지
마! **3** [T] to make someone look more
attractive, younger etc. than s/he really
is ‖ 실제보다 더 매력적이고 젊어 보이게
하다. 돋보이게 하다. 아름다워 보이게
하다: *It's not a very flattering
photograph.* 사진은 정말 실물보다 못하
다. **4 flatter yourself** to let yourself
believe that something good about
yourself is true, although it is not ‖ 비록
실제가 아니더라도 자신에 대한 좋은 일이
사실이라고 스스로 믿게 하다. 우쭐대다.
자만하다: *"I think you like me more than
you'll admit." "Don't flatter yourself."*
"네가 인정하는 것 이상으로 네가 나를 좋
아한다고 나는 생각한다." "자만하지 마
라." **– flatterer** *n*

flat·ter·y /ˈflætəri/ *n* [U] praise that
you do not really mean ‖ 진심이 아닌 칭
찬. 아첨. 겉치레 말: *Flattery will get
you nowhere!* (=will not help you get
what you want) 아부는 네가 얻고자 하는
것을 얻는 데에 아무런 도움이 되지 않을
거야!

flat·u·lence /ˈflætʃələns/ *n* [U] FORMAL
the condition of having too much gas in
your stomach ‖ 위(胃)에 가스가 너무 많
은 상태. 헛배부름. 고창(鼓脹)

flaunt /flɔnt, flɑnt/ *v* [T] to show your
money, success, beauty etc. in order to
make other people notice it ‖ 다른 사람
들이 알도록 자신의 돈·성공·아름다움 등
을 보여 주다. 과시하다: *Pam was
flaunting her diamonds at Gary's party.*
팸은 개리의 파티에서 그녀의 다이아몬드
를 과시했다.

fla·vor¹ /ˈfleɪvɚ/ *n* **1** the particular
taste of a food or a drink ‖ 음식이나 음료

의 독특한 맛: *We have 21 flavors of ice cream.* 우리는 21가지 맛의 아이스크림이 있다. **2** [U] the quality of tasting good ‖ 좋은 맛을 내는 성질. 풍미. 향미: *For extra flavor, add some red wine to the stew.* 추가적인 풍미를 내기 위해서 스튜에 적포도주를 약간 넣어라. **3** [singular] a particular quality or the typical qualities of something ‖ 사물의 독특한 성질 또는 전형적인 성질. 정취. 묘미: *His book gives us the flavor of life on a midwestern farm.* 그의 책은 우리에게 중서부 농가의 삶의 정취를 보여 준다.

flavor² *v* [T] to give something a particular taste or more taste ‖ 어떤 것에 독특한 맛 또는 더 진한 맛을 내다. 맛을 들이다

fla·vored /ˈfleɪvəd/ *adj* **strawberry-flavored/chocolate-flavored etc.** tasting like a STRAWBERRY, chocolate etc. ‖ 딸기·초콜릿 등과 같은 맛을 내는. 딸기 맛/초콜릿 맛의: *almond-flavored cookies* 아몬드 맛 쿠키

fla·vor·ing /ˈfleɪvərɪŋ/ *n* [C, U] a substance used for giving something a particular FLAVOR ‖ 독특한 맛을 내기 위해 쓰는 물질. 조미료. 향신료. 양념

flaw /flɔ/ *n* **1** a mark, or weakness that makes something not perfect ‖ 어떤 것을 완벽하지 못하게 만드는 자국, 또는 약점. 흠. 금. 균열: *a flaw in the table's surface* 테이블 표면의 균열 **2** a mistake in an argument, plan etc. ‖ 주장·계획 등의 잘못. 결함. 결점: *The design has a major flaw.* 그 디자인에는 중대한 결함이 있다.

flawed /flɔd/ *adj* spoiled by having mistakes, weaknesses, or damage ‖ 실수[약점, 손상]가 있어서 망가진. 결함이 있는. 금이 간: *The whole system is flawed.* 전체 시스템에 결함이 있다

flaw·less /ˈflɔlɪs/ *adj* perfect, with no mistakes, marks, or weaknesses ‖ 실수[자국, 약점]가 없이 완전한. 흠이 없는: *Burton's flawless performance as Hamlet* 버튼의 완벽한 햄릿 연기 / *Lena has flawless skin.* 레나는 피부에 흠이 없다. **– flawlessly** *adv*

flea /fli/ *n* a very small jumping insect that bites animals to drink their blood ‖ 동물의 피를 빨아먹는 아주 작으며 높이 뛰는 곤충. 벼룩

flea·bag /ˈflibæg/ *adj* INFORMAL cheap and dirty ‖ 값싸고 더러운. 싸구려. 초라한: *a fleabag hotel* 싸구려 호텔

flea col·lar /ˈ. ˌ../ *n* a collar, worn by dogs or cats, that contains chemicals to keep FLEAs away from them ‖ 개나 고양이가 다는, 벼룩을 없애기 위한 화학 물질이 들어 있는 목걸이. 벼룩 퇴치용 목걸이

flea mar·ket /ˈ. ˌ../ *n* a market, usually in the street, where old or used goods are sold ‖ 오래된 물건이나 중고 물품을 파는, 보통 길거리 시장. 벼룩시장

fleck /flɛk/ *n* a small mark or spot ‖ 작은 자국, 또는 점. 얼룩. 반점. 흔적: *brown cloth with flecks of red* 붉은 얼룩이 있는 갈색 천

flecked /flɛkt/ *adj* having small marks or spots ‖ 작은 자국 또는 반점이 있는. 얼룩진. 흔적이 있는: *red cloth flecked with white* 흰 얼룩이 있는 붉은 천

fledg·ling /ˈflɛdʒlɪŋ/ *adj* a fledgling country, organization etc. has only recently been formed ‖ 국가·조직 등이 최근에 형성된. 신생의. 신출내기. 풋내기: *a fledgling republic* 신생 공화국

flee /fli/ *v* **fled** /flɛd/, **fled, fleeing** [I, T] to leave somewhere very quickly in order to escape from danger ‖ 위험에서 벗어나기 위해 아주 급히 어떤 장소를 떠나다. 달아나다. 도피하다: *The president was forced to flee the country after the revolution.* 대통령은 혁명이 일어난 뒤 그 나라에서 도망쳐야 했다. / *thousands of people fleeing from the fighting* 전투에서 피신한 수천 명의 사람들

fleece¹ /flis/ *n* **1** the wool of a sheep ‖ 양털 **2** an artificial soft material used for making warm coats ‖ 따뜻한 코트를 만드는 데에 쓰이는 인조의 부드러운 물질. 양털 같은[인조] 솜털 **– fleecy** *adj*

fleece² *v* [T] INFORMAL to charge someone too much money for something, usually by tricking him/her ‖ 보통 남을 속여서 사물에 너무 많은 돈을 매겨 청구하다. (남에게서 돈·물건 등을) 사취하다. 빼앗다

fleet /flit/ *n* **1** a group of ships, or all the ships in a navy ‖ 일단의 선박, 또는 해군의 모든 함정. 함대 **2** a group of vehicles that are controlled or owned by one company ‖ 한 회사가 통제하거나 소유하는 일단의 차량들. (같은 소유자에 속하는) 전 차량. 보유 차량: *a fleet of trucks* 한 회사 소유의 모든 트럭들

fleet·ing /ˈflitɪŋ/ *adj* continuing for only a short time ‖ 잠시 동안만 지속하는. 덧없는. 순식간의: *a fleeting glance* 흘끗 보기

flesh¹ /flɛʃ/ *n* [U] **1** the soft part of the body of a person or animal between the skin and the bones ‖ 사람이나 동물의 신체에서 피부나 뼈 사이에 있는 부드러운 부위. 살. 고기 **2** the soft part of a fruit or vegetable that you eat ‖ 사람이 먹는

과일이나 야채의 부드러운 부분. 과육(果肉). 잎살 **3 see/meet sb in the flesh** if you see or meet someone in the flesh, you see or meet someone who you previously had only seen in pictures, in movies, etc. ‖ 이전에 사진·영화 등으로만 봤던 사람을 보거나 만나다. 직접[실물로] …을 보다/만나다: *He's more handsome in the flesh than on television.* 그는 텔레비전에서 보는 것보다 실물로 만나 보면 더 미남이다. **4 flesh and blood** someone who is part of your family ‖ 가족의 일부인 사람. 혈육: *He raised those kids like they were his own flesh and blood.* 그는 저 아이들을 자신의 혈육처럼 키웠다.

flesh² *v*

flesh sth ↔ **out** *phr v* [T] to add more details to something in order to improve it ‖ 어떤 것을 향상시키기 위해 세부사항들을 더 추가하다. 살을 붙이다. 구체화하다: *Try to flesh your essay out with a few more examples.* 몇 가지 사례를 추가하여 너의 수필을 구체화해 보아라.

flesh·y /ˈflɛʃi/ *adj* **1** having a lot of flesh ‖ 살이 많은. 살찐: *a round fleshy face* 둥글고 통통한 얼굴 **2** having a soft thick inner part ‖ 부드럽고 두꺼운 속 부분을 가진. 다육질(多肉質)의: *a plant with green fleshy leaves* 녹색 다육질 잎을 가진 식물

flew /flu/ *v* the past tense of FLY ‖ fly의 과거형

flex /flɛks/ *v* [T] to bend and move part of your body so that your muscles become tight ‖ 근육을 단단하게 하려고 신체의 일부분을 굽히고 움직이다. 굽히다. 수축시키다

flex·i·ble /ˈflɛksəbəl/ *adj* **1** a person, plan etc. that is flexible can change or be changed easily to suit any new situation ‖ 사람·계획 등이 어떤 새로운 상황에도 적합하도록 쉽게 변하거나 변경될 수 있는. 융통성이 있는: *a flexible style of management* 융통성 있는 경영 방식 **2** something that is flexible can bend or be bent easily ‖ 쉽게 구부릴 수 있거나 구부려지는. 구부릴 수 있는. 휘기 쉬운: *flexible plastic* 구부리기 쉬운 플라스틱 **– flexibility** /ˌflɛksəˈbɪləti/ *n* [U] —opposite INFLEXIBLE

flex·time /ˈflɛks-taɪm/ *n* [U] a system in which people can change the times at which they start and finish working ‖ 작업 시작·종료 시간을 근로자가 변경할 수 있는 체제. 플렉스 타임 제도. 근무 시간 자유 선택제

flick¹ /flɪk/ *v* [T] **1** to make something

move by hitting or pushing it quickly, especially with your thumb and finger ‖ 특히 엄지와 다른 손가락으로 빨리 때리거나 눌러서 사물을 움직이게 하다. 가볍게 치다. 휙 튀기다: *Barry flicked the ash from his cigarette.* 배리는 담배의 재를 털었다. **2** to shake something such as a whip or rope so that the end moves quickly away from you ‖ 채찍이나 로프 등의 끝이 빠르게 멀리 움직이도록 흔들다. 휙 휘두르다

flick² *n* **1** SPOKEN a movie ‖ 영화 (필름): *That was a great flick!* 그 영화는 정말 훌륭해! **2** a short, light, sudden movement or hit with your hand, a whip etc. ‖ 손·채찍 등으로 짧고 가볍고 갑작스럽게 움직이거나 치는 것

flick·er¹ /ˈflɪkɚ/ *v* [I] **1** to burn or move in a quick and unsteady way ‖ 빠르고 불규칙하게 타거나 움직이다. 차츰 꺼지다. 깜박이다. 어른거리다: *flickering candles* 가물거리는 촛불 **2** if an emotion or expression flickers on someone's face, it is there for only a short time ‖ 감정·표정 등이 짧은 시간 동안만 사람의 얼굴에 머무르다. 언뜻 가로지르다. 어른거리다: *A look of anger flickered across Andrea's face.* 분노의 표정이 안드리아의 얼굴에 언뜻 비쳤다.

flick·er² *n* **1** [singular] an unsteady light or movement ‖ 불안정한 불빛, 또는 움직임. 깜빡임: *the flicker of the old gas lamp* 낡은 가스등의 깜빡임 **2** **a flicker of interest/guilt etc.** a feeling or an expression on your face that only continues for a short time ‖ 잠시 동안만 지속되는 감정 또는 얼굴의 표정. 언뜻 내비친 관심/죄책감: *Not even a flicker of emotion showed on his face.* 일말의 감정의 동요도 그의 얼굴에는 나타나지 않았다.

fli·er /ˈflaɪɚ/ *n* **1** a sheet of paper advertising something ‖ 사물을 광고하는 종이 한 장. 전단. 삐라: *People from the theater are passing out fliers in the street.* 극장 사람들이 거리에서 전단을 배포하고 있다. **2** INFORMAL a pilot or someone who travels on a plane ‖ 비행기로 여행하는 조종사 또는 일반인. 비행사. 비행기 여행객 —see also FREQUENT FLIER

flight /flaɪt/ *n* **1** a trip in a plane or space vehicle, or a plane making a particular trip ‖ 비행기 또는 우주선으로 하는 여행, 또는 특별한 여행을 마련하는 비행기. 비행. 항공[우주] 여행: *What time is the next flight to Miami?* 마이애미행 다음 항공편은 몇 시입니까? / *I'm* *coming in on Flight 255 from Chicago.* 나는 시카고발 255항공기편으로 입국합니다. **2** [U] the act of flying through the air ‖ 공중을 나는 행위. 날기. 비행: *a bird in flight* 날고 있는 새 **3** a set of stairs between one floor and the next ‖ 한 층에서 다른 층 사이에 있는 일련의 계단. 층계: *She fell down a whole flight of stairs.* 그녀는 계단 위에서 아래로 굴러 떨어졌다. **4** [U] the act of avoiding a difficult situation by leaving or escaping ‖ 떠나거나 도피하여 어려운 상황을 피하는 행위. 탈출. 도주: *The movie ends with the family's flight from Austria in World War II.* 그 영화는 2차 대전 중 오스트리아에서 그 가족이 탈출하는 것으로 끝난다.

flight at·tend·ant /ˈ. .ˌ../ *n* someone who is responsible for the comfort and safety of the passengers on a plane ‖ 비행기 승객들의 편안함과 안전을 책임지는 사람. (여객기의) 객실 승무원

flight deck /ˈ. ./ *n* the place where the pilot sits to control the plane ‖ 비행기를 조종하기 위해 조종사가 앉는 장소. 조종실

flight·less /ˈflaɪtlɪs/ *adj* a bird that is flightless is unable to fly ‖ 새가 날 수가 없는

flight·y /ˈflaɪti/ *adj* someone who is flighty changes his/her ideas or activities a lot without finishing them or being serious about them ‖ 생각이나 활동 등을 끝마치거나 진지하게 하지 못하고 많이 변경하는. 변덕스러운

flim·sy /ˈflɪmzi/ *adj* **1** thin, light, and not strong ‖ 얇고 가벼워 강하지 않은. 약한. 무른: *flimsy cloth* 약한 천 **2** weak and not made very well ‖ 약하고 그다지 잘 만들어지지 않은. 부서지기 쉬운: *a flimsy table* 부서지기 쉬운 테이블 **3** a flimsy argument, excuse etc. is hard to believe ‖ 주장·변명 등이 믿기 어려운. 설득력이 없는. (근거 등이) 박약한: *The evidence against him is very flimsy.* 그에 불리한 증거는 설득력이 거의 없다.

flinch /flɪntʃ/ *v* [I] **1** to make a sudden small backward movement when you are hurt or afraid of something ‖ 다치거나 두려워서 갑자기 조금 뒤로 움직이다. 주춤하다: *He raised his hand, and the child flinched.* 그가 손을 들자 그 아이는 주춤했다. **2** to avoid doing something because you dislike it or are afraid of it ‖ 싫거나 두려워서 어떤 일을 하는 것을 피하다. 물러서다. 꽁무니를 빼다: *Ann told us, without flinching, exactly what she thought.* 앤은 물러서지 않고 그녀가

생각한 그대로 우리에게 말했다.

fling¹ /flɪŋ/ *v* **flung, flung, flinging** [T] **1** to throw or move something quickly with a lot of force ‖ 큰 힘으로 빠르게 물체를 던지거나 움직이다. 휙[거칠게] 던지다: *She flung her coat onto the bed and sat down.* 그녀는 침대에 코트를 휙 집어던지고 나서 주저앉았다. / *Sister Margaret marched across the room and flung the windows open.* 마가렛 수녀님은 방을 가로질러 가서는 창문을 활짝 열었다. **2** to move yourself or part of your body suddenly and with a lot of force ‖ 갑자기 큰 힘으로 온몸이나 신체 일부를 움직이다. 쑥 내뻗다[쳐들다]: *Val flung her arms around my neck.* 밸은 잽싸게 내 목을 껴안았다. / *"I'm bored," said Wade, flinging himself on the couch.* "지겨워"라고 웨이드는 말하면서 소파에 몸을 던졌다.

fling² *n* a short and not very serious sexual relationship ‖ 짧고 아주 심각하지 않은 성적 관계. 가벼운 방종: *I've had a few flings since Tom and I split up, but nothing serious.* 톰과 헤어진 뒤 나는 몇 번의 가벼운 이성 관계가 있었지만 심각한 수준은 아니었다.

flint /flɪnt/ *n* [C, U] a type of very hard black or gray stone that makes a small flame when you strike it with steel ‖ 강철과 부딪치면 작은 불꽃을 일으키는 아주 단단한 검은색이나 회색 돌의 일종. 부싯돌

flip¹ /flɪp/ *v* **-pped, -pping** [T] **1** to turn something over or put it into a different position with a quick sudden movement ‖ 빠르고 갑작스런 동작으로 사물을 다른 위치로 뒤집거나 놓다. 튀기다. …을 탁 치다. 튀겨 날리다: *Could you flip the lid of that box open for me?* 저 상자의 뚜껑을 탁 쳐서 열어 주겠니? / *You just flip a switch and the machine does everything for you.* 스위치를 찰칵 켜기만 해도 기계가 모두 뜻대로 작동한다. **2** to throw something flat such as a coin up so that it turns over in the air ‖ 납작한 동전 등을 공중에서 뒤집히게 위쪽으로 던지다. (일을 결정하려고) 동전을 손가락으로 튀겨 올리다 **3** *also* **flip out** [I] INFORMAL to suddenly become very angry or upset, or start behaving in a crazy way ‖ 갑자기 매우 화를 내거나 심란해지다, 또는 미친 듯이 행동하기 시작하다. 흥분

flip

하다. 정신이 이상해지다[미치다]: *Harry flipped out when he found out that I wrecked his motorcycle.* 해리는 내가 그의 오토바이를 파손한 것을 알고는 발끈했다.

flip for sb *phr v* [T] INFORMAL to suddenly begin to like someone very much ‖ 갑자기 어떤 사람을 아주 많이 좋아하기 시작하다. 열중하다: *Ben has really flipped for Amanda.* 벤은 아만다를 정말 무척 좋아한다.

flip sb ↔ **off** *phr v* [T] SLANG to make a rude sign at someone by holding up your middle finger ‖ 가운뎃손가락을 치켜세워 남에게 무례한 신호를 하다

flip through sth *phr v* [T] to look at a book, magazine etc. quickly ‖ 책·잡지 등을 빨리 쳐다보다. 대충 훑어보다

flip² *n* a movement in which you jump and turn over in the air, so that your feet go over your head ‖ 공중으로 뛰어올라 발이 머리 위로 오도록 공중에서 뒤집는 동작. 공중제비. 뒤집기

flip³ *adj* INFORMAL ⇨ FLIPPANT

flip-flop /'. ./ *n* an occasion when someone changes his/her decision ‖ 결정을 바꾸는 일. (의견·태도 등의) 급변

flip·pant /'flɪpənt/ *adj* not serious about something that other people think you should be serious about ‖ 남들은 진지해야 된다고 생각하는 것에 대하여 심각하지 않은. 경박한. 성의 없는: *a flippant answer to her question* 그녀의 질문에 대한 무성의한 답변

flip·per /'flɪpɚ/ *n* **1** a flat part on the body of some large sea animals, used for pushing themselves through water ‖ 물 속에서 자신을 밀어서 움직이는 데에 쓰이는 몇몇 몸집이 큰 바다 동물의 몸통에 달린 넓적한 부분. 지느러미발 **2** a large flat rubber shoe that you use in order to help you swim faster ‖ 보다 빠르게 수영하도록 도와주는 데에 쓰이는 크고 납작한 고무 신발. (잠수용) 오리발

flip side /'. ./ *n* [singular] **1** INFORMAL used when you describe the bad effects of something, after you have just described the good effects ‖ 어떤 일의 좋은 효과만 기술한 다음 나쁜 효과를 서술할 때에 쓰여. 반대편. 이면. 대응: *The flip side is that the medicine may cause hair loss.* 반면에 그 약은 탈모를 일으킬 수 있다. **2** the other side of a popular record ‖ 유행가 음반의 다른 한쪽 면. B면

flirt¹ /flɚt/ *v* [I] to behave toward someone as though you are sexually attracted to him/her, but not in a very serious way ‖ 아주 진지하게는 아니지만 성적으로 매혹하는 것처럼 행동하다. 집적거리다. 시시덕거리다: *He's always flirting with the women in the office.* 그는 사무실에서 늘 여성들과 시시덕거린다.

flirt with sth *phr v* [T] **1** to consider doing something, but not be very serious about it ‖ 별로 진지하지 않게 어떤 것 하기를 고려하다. (장난삼아) 가볍게 생각해 보다: *I've been flirting with the idea of moving to Greece.* 나는 막연하게 그리스로 이사 가는 것을 생각해오고 있다. **2 flirt with danger/disaster etc.** to take an unnecessary risk and not be worried about it ‖ 불필요한 위험을 무릅쓰면서 그것에 대해 걱정하지 않다. 생각[대책] 없이 위험/재앙 등을 무릅쓰다: *You're flirting with disaster if you don't get this car fixed.* 네가 이 차를 수리하지 않으면 대책 없이 참극을 무릅쓰는 셈이다.

flirt² *n* someone who likes to FLIRT ‖ 집적거리기를 좋아하는 사람. 바람둥이: *Dave is such a flirt!* 데이브는 굉장한 바람둥이야!

flir·ta·tion /flɚ'teɪʃən/ *n* **1** a short period of time during which you are interested in someone or something ‖ 사람 또는 사물에 단시간 동안 흥미를 가지는 것. 일시적인[단발성] 관심: *the artist's brief flirtation with photography* 사진에 대한 예술가의 일시적 관심 **2** [U] behavior that shows you are sexually attracted to someone, though not in a serious way ‖ 심각한 정도는 아니지만, 남에게 성적으로 매혹되었음을 나타내는 행동. 희롱. 바람. 불장난

flir·ta·tious /flɚ'teɪʃəs/ *adj* behaving in a way that tries to attract sexual attention, but not in a serious way ‖ 심각한 정도는 아니나 성적 관심을 끌려는 행동을 하는. 시시덕거리는. 경박한. 바람난

flit /flɪt/ *v* **-tted, -tting** [I] to move lightly or quickly from one place to another ‖ 한 장소에서 다른 장소로 가볍게 또는 신속하게 움직이다. 경쾌하게 돌아다니다. 휙휙[날개치며] 날다: *birds flitting from branch to branch* 이 가지에서 저 가지로 날아다니는 새들

float¹ /flout/ *v* **1** [I] to stay or move on the surface of a liquid or up in the air without sinking ‖ 가라앉지 않고 액체 표면이나 공기 중에 머물거나 움직이다. 뜨다. 부유하다: *Boats floated down the river.* 배들

float

은 그 강을 떠내려갔다. / *I watched a balloon float up into the sky.* 나는 기구 (氣球)가 하늘로 높이 뜨는 것을 보았다. **2** [T] to make something float ‖ 사물을 뜨게 하다 **3** [T] to sell SHARES in a company or business to the public for the first time ‖ 최초로 회사 또는 기업의 주식을 일반 대중에게 팔다. (주식·채권을) 발행하다 **4 float sb a loan** INFORMAL to allow someone to borrow money from you ‖ 남이 자신의 돈을 꾸는 것을 허용하다. 대출의 교섭을 하다. 대부를 하다: *I could float you a small loan.* 내가 너에게 소액을 꾸어줄 수 있다.

float² *n* **1** a large vehicle that is decorated to be part of a PARADE ‖ 퍼레이드의 일부분으로 장식된 대형 차량. 이동식 무대차. 장식 수레 **2** a SOFT DRINK that has ICE CREAM floating in it ‖ 아이스크림을 띄운 청량음료. 크림소다

flock¹ /flɑk/ *n* **1** a group of sheep, goats, or birds ‖ 양[염소, 새]들의 무리. 떼: *a flock of geese* 거위 떼 **2** a large group of the same type of people, or a group of people who regularly attend the same church ‖ 같은 유형의 사람들의 대집단, 또는 정기적으로 같은 교회에 나가는 일단의 사람들. 군중. 회중: *a flock of tourists* 한 무리의 관광객

flock² *v* [I] if people flock to a place, a lot of them go there ‖ 많은 사람들이 특정 장소로 가다. 떼 지어 가다[오다]: *People are flocking to that new Thai restaurant.* 사람들이 새 타이 식당으로 떼 지어 가고 있다.

flog /flɑg, flɔg/ *v* [T] to beat a person or animal with a whip or stick as a punishment ‖ 벌로 채찍이나 회초리로 사람이나 동물을 때리다. 매질하다 – **flogging** *n*

flood¹ /flʌd/ *v* **1** [I, T] to fill a place with water, or to become filled with water ‖ 물로 한 장소를 채우다, 또는 물로 가득차게 되다. 범람하다[시키다]. 가득하[게 하]다: *The river floods the valley every spring.* 그 강은 매년 봄 유역을 범람시킨다. / *The basement flooded and everything got soaked.* 지하실에 물이 가득차서 모든 것이 물에 젖었다. **2** [I, T] to arrive or go somewhere in large numbers or amounts ‖ 어딘가에 대다수 또는 대량으로 도착하거나 가다. 쇄도하다. 몰려오다: *Letters came flooding in.* 편지가 쇄도했다. / *We've been flooded with phone calls since her new book came out.* 그녀의 신간이 나온 뒤 우리에게 전화가 쇄도했다. **3 flood the market** to sell something in very large numbers

or amounts ‖ 아주 많은 수나 분량의 물건을 팔다. 시장을 석권하다: *The company is flooding the market with cheap imports.* 그 회사는 값싼 수입품으로 시장을 석권하고 있다.

flood² *n* **1** a very large amount of water that covers an area that is usually dry ‖ 대개 말라 있는 지역을 뒤덮는 엄청난 양의 물. 홍수: *The town was destroyed by floods.* 그 마을은 홍수로 파괴되었다. — see usage note at WEATHER **2 flood of** a very large number of things or people that arrive at the same time ‖ 동시에 도착한 엄청난 수의 사물 또는 사람. …의 쇄도[충만]: *a flood of complaints about last night's TV show* 어젯밤 텔레비전 쇼에 대해 쇄도하는 항의

flood·gate /ˈflʌdgeɪt/ *n* **1 open the floodgates** to suddenly make it possible for a lot of people to do something ‖ 갑자기 많은 사람들이 어떤 일을 하는 것을 가능하게 하다: *The new laws opened the floodgates to increased immigration.* 새로운 법들은 갑작스럽게 이민을 증가시켜 놓았다. **2** a gate used in order to control the flow of water from a large lake, river etc. ‖ 큰 호수·강 등의 물 흐름을 조절하는 데에 쓰이는 문. 수문

flood·light /ˈflʌdlaɪt/ *n* a very bright light, used at night to light the outside of buildings, sports fields etc. ‖ 야간에 건물의 외부·운동장 등을 비추기 위해 쓰이는 매우 밝은 전등. 투광 조명등

flood·lit /ˈflʌdˌlɪt/ *adj* lit at night by FLOODLIGHTs ‖ 밤에 투광 조명으로 비춰진

floor¹ /flɔr/ *n* **1** the flat surface on which you stand indoors ‖ 사람이 서 있는 실내의 평평한 표면. 바닥: *Ernie spilled his milk on the floor.* 어니는 마룻바닥에다 우유를 쏟았다. **2** one of the levels in a building ‖ 건물에서의 한 층: *My office is on the third floor.* 내 사무실은 3층에 있다. —see picture at ATTIC **3 ocean/forest floor** the ground at the bottom of the ocean or in a forest ‖ 바다나 숲의 밑바닥에 있는 땅. 해저/숲속의 지표면 **4 the floor a)** the part of a public or government building where people discuss things ‖ 사람들이 토론하는, 공공건물이나 청사의 장소. 회의장. 의원석: *an argument on the Senate floor* 상원 회의장에서의 논쟁 **b)** the people attending a public meeting ‖ 공적인 모임에 참석하는 사람들: *Are there any questions from the floor?* 여러분들 중에 질문 있습니까?

floor² *v* [T] **1** to surprise or shock

someone so much that s/he does not know what to say or do ‖ 무슨 말이나 행동을 해야 할지 모를 정도로 남을 깜짝 놀라게 하거나 충격을 주다. 당황시키다: *I was totally floored when I heard about her death.* 나는 그녀가 죽었다는 소식을 듣고 정말 충격받았다. **2** to make a car go very fast by pressing the PEDAL all the way down ‖ 가속 페달을 힘껏 아래로 밟아 차가 매우 빨리 달리게 하다. 차를 전 속력으로 몰다

floor·board /'flɔrbɔrd/ n **1** a board in a wooden floor ‖ 목재로 된 바닥의 판자. 마루널 **2** the floor in a car ‖ 자동차 바닥

floor·ing /'flɔrɪŋ/ n [U] a substance used for making or covering floors ‖ 마루를 만들거나 덮는 데에 쓰이는 물질

floor lamp /'. ./ n a lamp on the top of a tall pole that stands on the floor ‖ 마루에 세우는 긴 막대기 꼭대기에 달린 전등. 마루에 놓는 스탠드 —see picture at LAMP

floor-length /'. ./ adj long enough to reach the floor ‖ 마루에 닿을 정도로 긴: *a floor-length skirt* 마루까지 닿을 정도로 긴 스커트

floor plan /'. ./ n a drawing that shows the shape of a room or rooms in a building and the positions of things in it, as seen from above ‖ 위에서 보았을 때 건물내 하나 또는 여러 개의 방 모양과 그 안에 놓인 것들의 위치를 보여 주는 그림. 평면도

floo·zy /'fluzi/ n INFORMAL DISAPPROVING a woman whose sexual behavior is considered to be immoral ‖ 성적으로 부도덕하게 행동한다고 생각되는 여자. 방탕한 여자. 창녀

flop¹ /flɑp/ v **-pped, -pping** [I] **1** to move or fall in a heavy or awkward way ‖ 무겁거나 꼴사납게 움직이거나 떨어지다. 털썩 떨어지다[넘어지다, 주저앉다]: *Jan flopped onto the bed.* 잰은 침대에 벌렁 드러 누웠다. **2** INFORMAL if something such as a product, play, or plan flops, it is not successful ‖ 제품[연극, 계획]이 실패하다: *The musical flopped after its first week on Broadway.* 그 뮤지컬은 브로드웨이에서 한 주 동안 공연하고 난 후 완전히 실패해 버리고 말았다.

flop² n **1** INFORMAL a film, play, plan etc. that is not successful ‖ 성공하지 못한 영화·연극·계획 등. 실패작: *Dean's party was a flop.* 딘의 파티는 실패작이었다. **2** a heavy falling movement or the noise that it makes ‖ 무겁게 떨어지는 동작, 또는 떨어질 때 나는 소리. 털썩 떨어짐. 털

썩 떨어지는 소리: *He fell with a flop into the water.* 그는 물속으로 풍덩하고 떨어졌다.

flop·house /'flɑphaʊs/ n SLANG a cheap hotel, especially one that has many beds in one room ‖ 특히 한 방에 여러 개의 침대가 있는 값싼 호텔

flop·py /'flɑpi/ adj soft and hanging loosely down ‖ 부드럽고 느슨하게 아래로 드리워진. 축 늘어진. 헐렁헐렁한: *a floppy hat* 헐렁한 모자

floppy disk /,.. '. /, **floppy** n ⇨ DISKETTE

flo·ra /'flɔrə/ n [U] TECHNICAL all the plants in a particular place or of a particular period of time ‖ 특정한 장소나 시대의 모든 식물. 지방[시대] 특유의 식물군 —compare FAUNA

flo·ral /'flɔrəl/ adj made of or decorated with flowers ‖ 꽃으로 만들어지거나 장식된: *floral curtains* 꽃 무늬 커튼

flor·id /'flɔrɪd, 'flɑrɪd/ adj **1** LITERARY skin that is florid is red ‖ 피부가 붉은: *florid cheeks* 불그레한 뺨 **2** having too much decoration or detail ‖ 너무 많이 장식한 또는 너무 세세한: *florid language* 미사여구

flo·rist /'flɔrɪst, 'flɑr-/ n someone who owns or works in a store that sells flowers ‖ 꽃을 파는 가게를 소유한 사람 또는 꽃가게에서 일하는 사람

floss¹ /flɑs, flɔs/ n [U] ⇨ DENTAL FLOSS

floss² v [T] to clean between your teeth with DENTAL FLOSS ‖ 치실로 이 사이를 깨끗이 하다

flo·til·la /floʊ'tɪlə/ n a group of small ships ‖ 일단의 소형 배. 소형 선단

flounce /flaʊns/ v [I] to walk in a way that shows you are angry ‖ 화가 난 듯이 걷다: *She frowned and flounced out of the room.* 그녀는 얼굴을 찡그리며 화난 듯이 그 방을 나가버렸다.

floun·der¹ /'flaʊndɚ/ v [I] **1** to have great difficulty saying or doing something ‖ 어떤 것을 말하거나 행하는 데에 많은 어려움을 겪다: *The team was floundering in the first half of the season.* 그 팀은 시즌 전반기에 힘겨워하고 있었다. **2** to move awkwardly or with difficulty, especially in water, mud etc. ‖ 특히 물속이나 진흙 속 등에서 어색하게 또는 힘들게 움직이다. 허우적거리다

floun·der² n [C, U] a flat ocean fish, or the meat from this fish ‖ 납작한 바닷물고기, 또는 그 생선살. 도다리(살)

flour /flaʊɚ/ n [U] a powder made from grain, usually wheat, that is used for making bread, cakes etc. ‖ 빵·케이크 등

을 만드는 데에 쓰이는, 일반적으로 밀로 만든 가루. 밀가루

flour·ish¹ /ˈflɝɪʃ, ˈflʌrɪʃ/ v **1** [I] to grow or develop well ‖ 잘 자라거나 발전하다. 번영[번창, 번성]하다: *The plants flourished in the warm sun.* 그 식물들은 따뜻한 햇볕 속에서 무럭무럭 자랐다. / *The company has flourished since we moved the factory.* 회사는 우리가 공장을 이전하고 난 이후로 번창했다. **2** [T] to wave something in your hand in order to make people notice it ‖ 사람들이 알아 보도록 손에 든 것을 흔들다: *Eve ran in, flourishing her acceptance letter.* 이브는 자기의 합격 통지서를 흔들며 달려 들어왔다.

flour·ish² n **with a flourish** with a large confident movement that makes people notice you ‖ 사람들이 알아 보도록 크고 자신감 있는 동작으로. 과격한 몸짓으로: *He opened the door with a flourish.* 그는 요란하게 문을 홱 열어 젖혔다.

flout /flaʊt/ v [T] FORMAL to deliberately disobey a rule or law ‖ 고의로 규칙이나 법을 어기다

flow¹ /floʊ/ v [I] **1** if a liquid flows, it moves in a steady continuous stream ‖ 액체가 꾸준히 계속하여 흐르다: *The river flows past our cabin.* 강은 우리 오두막을 지나 계속 흐른다. **2** to move easily, smoothly, and continuously from one place to another ‖ 한 곳에서 다른 곳으로 술술·유연하게·계속 움직이다: *The cars flowed in a steady stream.* 자동차들은 끊임없이 꼬리를 물고 지나갔다. **3** if conversation or ideas flow, people talk or have ideas without being interrupted ‖ 대화나 생각이 방해받지 않고 계속 이어지다 **4** if clothing, hair etc. flows, it hangs loosely and gracefully ‖ 옷·머리카락 등이 축 늘어져 우아하게 드리워지다

flow² n **1** [C usually singular] a smooth steady movement of liquid ‖ 액체의 매끄럽고 끊임없는 움직임: *the body's flow of blood* 몸속의 혈류(血流) **2** [C usually singular] a continuous movement of something from one place to another ‖ 한 곳에서 다른 곳으로의 계속인 움직임: *the constant flow of traffic in the street* 거리에 끊임없이 이어지는 교통의 흐름 **3** [U] actions, words or ideas that are produced continuously ‖ 계속해서 나오는 행동[말, 생각]: *I had interrupted the flow of their conversation.* 나는 그들의 계속되는 대화를 끊었다. **4 go with the flow** SPOKEN to do what is easiest in your situation, and

not try to do something difficult ‖ 주어진 상황에서 가장 수월한 것을 하고 힘든 것은 하려고 하지 않다. 시류에 영합하다

flow chart /ˈ. ./, **flow di·a·gram** /ˈ. ,.../ n a drawing that uses shapes and ARROWs to show how a series of actions or parts of a system are connected with each other ‖ 도형과 화살표를 사용하여 일련의 행동이나 시스템의 부분들이 상호 어떻게 연계되는지를 보여주는 그림. 흐름도. 공정도

flow·er¹ /ˈflaʊɚ/ n **1** the colored part of a plant or tree that produces the seeds or fruit ‖ 씨앗이나 열매를 맺는 식물이나 나무의 색깔이 있는 부분. 꽃: *a bunch of flowers* 한 다발의 꽃 **2** a plant that is grown for the beauty of this part ‖ 꽃이 아름다워서 재배되는 식물. 화초: *a yard full of flowers* 화초가 가득한 뜰

flower² v [I] to produce flowers ‖ 꽃을 피우다

flow·er·bed /ˈflaʊɚˌbɛd/ n an area of ground in which flowers are grown ‖ 화초가 자라는 지역. 화단

flow·ered /ˈflaʊɚd/ adj decorated with pictures of flowers ‖ 꽃그림으로 장식된: *a flowered dress* 꽃무늬 드레스

flow·er·pot /ˈflaʊɚˌpat/ n a pot in which you grow plants ‖ 식물을 재배하는 단지. 화분

flow·er·y /ˈflaʊəri/ adj **1** decorated with pictures of flowers ‖ 꽃그림으로 장식된: *a flowery pattern* 꽃무늬 **2** flowery speech or writing uses complicated and rare words instead of simple clear language ‖ 연설이나 문장이 간단 명료한 말 대신에 복잡하고 생경한 단어를 쓰는. 미사여구를 쓴

flown /floʊn/ the PAST PARTICIPLE of FLY ‖ fly의 과거 분사형

flu /flu/ n **the flu** a common disease that is like a bad cold but is more serious ‖ 심한 감기와 비슷하지만 더욱 심각하고 흔한 병. 독감. 인플루엔자

flub /flʌb/ v **-bbed, -bbing** SPOKEN to make a mistake or do something badly ‖ 실수하다, 또는 어떤 일을 잘못하다: *I flubbed the geography test.* 나는 지리 시험을 잘못봤다.

fluc·tu·ate /ˈflʌktʃuˌeɪt/ v [I] to change very often, especially from a high level to a low one and back again ‖ 특히 높은 수준에서 낮은 수준으로 그리고 다시 그 반대로 매우 자주 변하다. 수시로 오르내리다: *Our output fluctuates between 20 and 30 units per week.* 우리의 생산고는 주당 20과 30단위 사이에서 오르내린다.

fluc·tu·a·tion /ˌflʌktʃuˈeɪʃən/ n the act

of fluctuating (FLUCTUATE) ‖ 자주 변하는 행위. 끊임없는 변화. 변동: *These plants are affected by fluctuations in temperature.* 이 식물들은 온도 변화에 영향을 받는다.

flue /flu/ *n* a pipe through which smoke or heat from a fire can pass out of a building ‖ 난방 기구에서 연기나 열이 건물 밖으로 빠져나갈 수 있는 관. 연도(煙道). 송기관

flu·en·cy /ˈfluənsi/ *n* [U] the ability to speak or write a language well ‖ 말을 잘 하거나 글을 잘 쓰는 능력. 유창함. 능변. 달필: *I wanted to gain fluency in English.* 나는 영어를 유창하게 구사하고 싶었다.

flu·ent /ˈfluənt/ *adj* **1** able to speak or write a language very well ‖ 말을 아주 잘 하거나 글을 잘 쓸 수 있는. 유창한: *Ted's fluent in six languages.* 테드는 6개 국어를 유창하게 구사한다. **2** speaking, writing, or playing a musical instrument confidently and without long pauses ‖ 자신 있게 오래 중단하는 일 없이 말하는[쓰는, 악기를 연주하는]. 거침없는 – **fluently** *adv* : *She speaks Spanish fluently.* 그녀는 스페인어를 유창하게 말한다.

fluff¹ /flʌf/ *n* [U] **1** soft light pieces of thread or wool that have come from wool, cotton, or other materials ‖ 양털·솜 또는 다른 물질에서 나온 부드럽고 가벼운 실이나 털조각. 보풀 **2** very soft fur or feathers, especially from a young animal or bird ‖ 어린 동물이나 새의 매우 부드러운 털이나 깃털

fluff² *v* [T] **1** also **fluff up/out** to make something soft appear larger by shaking or brushing it ‖ 부드러운 것을 흔들거나 솔질하여 보다 크게 보이게 하다. 부풀리다: *a bird fluffing out its feathers* 깃털을 부풀려 세우는 새 **2** INFORMAL to make a mistake or do something badly ‖ 실수하다, 어떤 일을 잘 못하다: *Ricky fluffed the catch and we lost the game.* 릭키가 공을 잡지 못해서 우리는 그 경기에 졌다.

fluff·y /ˈflʌfi/ *adj* made of or covered with something soft and light ‖ 부드럽고 가벼운 것으로 만들어지거나 뒤덮인: *a fluffy kitten* 솜털로 뒤덮인 새끼 고양이

flu·id¹ /ˈfluɪd/ *n* [C, U] a liquid ‖ 액체: *It is a clear fluid that smells of alcohol.* 그것은 알코올 냄새가 나는 투명한 액체이다. —see also FLUIDS

fluid² *adj* **1** having a moving, flowing quality like a liquid or gas ‖ 액체나 기체처럼 움직이고 흐르는 성질이 있는. 유동성의: *fluid movements* 흐르는 듯 부드러

운 동작 **2** likely to change or able to change ‖ 변할 듯한, 변할 수 있는. 유동적인: *Our plans for the project are still fluid.* 그 프로젝트에 대한 우리의 계획은 아직 유동적이다. – **fluidity** /fluˈɪdəti/ *n* [U]

fluid ounce /ˌ.. ˈ./, *written abbreviation* **fl. oz.** *n* a unit for measuring liquid, equal to 1/16 of a PINT or 0.0296 liters ‖ 파인트의 16분의 1이나 0.0296리터에 해당하는 액량 측정 단위

flu·ids /ˈfluɪdz/ *n* [plural] TECHNICAL water, juice, and other things you drink ‖ 물·주스·기타 마실 것: *Rest in bed, and drink lots of fluids.* 침대에서 쉬면서 물을 많이 마셔라.

fluke /fluk/ *n* INFORMAL something that only happens because of chance or luck ‖ 단지 우연이나 운(運) 덕분에 일어나는 것. 요행. 우연한 사건: *It was just a fluke that we both were in St. Louis at the same time.* 우리가 둘 다 같은 시간에 세인트루이스에 있었던 것은 단지 우연한 일이었다.

flung /flʌŋ/ *v* the past tense and PAST PARTICIPLE of FLING ‖ fling의 과거·과거 분사형

flunk /flʌŋk/ *v* [I, T] INFORMAL to fail a test or course, or to give someone a low grade so s/he does this ‖ 시험이나 과정이 실패하다, 또는 남에게 시험이나 과정이 실패할 정도로 낮은 점수를 주다. 낙제하다. 낙제시키다: *I flunked the history exam.* 나는 역사 시험에 낙제했다. / *Mrs. Harris flunked me in English.* 해리스 선생님은 영어 과목에서 나에게 낙제점을 주었다.

flunk out *phr v* [I] INFORMAL to be forced to leave a school or college because your work is not good enough ‖ 성적이 별로 좋지 않기 때문에 학교나 대학교를 그만두라고 강요당하다. 성적 불량으로 퇴학당하다: *Tim flunked out of Yale.* 팀은 예일 대학에서 퇴학당했다.

flun·ky, flunkey /ˈflʌŋki/ *n* INFORMAL DISAPPROVING someone who is always with an important person and treats him/her with too much respect ‖ 중요 인물과 늘 함께 있으며 그 사람을 지나치게 경대(敬待)하는 사람. 알랑쇠. 추종자

flu·o·res·cent /fluˈrɛsənt, flɔ-/ *adj* **1** a fluorescent light is a very bright electric light in the form of a tube ‖ 빛이 관(管) 형태의 등(燈)에서 매우 밝게 빛나는. 형광의 **2** fluorescent colors shine very brightly ‖ 색이 매우 밝게 빛나는. 형광색의

fluor·ide /ˈflɔraɪd/ *n* [U] a chemical

that helps to protect teeth against decay ‖ 치아가 썩는 것을 막는 데에 도움을 주는 화학 물질. 불화물(弗化物)

flur·ries /ˈfləːiz, ˈflʌriz/ *n* [plural] a small amount of snow that falls ‖ 내리는 소량의 눈: *Colder temperatures and flurries are expected tonight.* 오늘 밤은 기온이 점점 더 떨어지고 약간의 눈이 예상된다.

flur·ry /ˈfləːi, ˈflʌri/ *n* [singular] an occasion when there is suddenly a lot of activity for a short time ‖ 짧은 시간 동안 갑자기 활기가 넘치는 경우: *His arrival produced a flurry of excitement.* 그의 출현으로 한바탕 흥분이 일었다. —see also FLURRIES

flush¹ /flʌʃ/ *v* 1 [I, T] if you flush a toilet or it flushes, you make water go through it to clean it ‖ 변기를 청소하기 위해 물을 흘려보내다. 물이 왈칵 흐르다. (변기) 물을 버리다 2 [I] to become red in the face, especially because you are embarrassed or angry ‖ 당황하거나 화가 나서 얼굴이 붉어지다. 상기되다: *Billy flushed and looked down.* 빌리는 얼굴을 붉히며 아래를 내려다보았다. —see also FLUSHED 3 [T] also **flush out** to clean an area or place by forcing water or another liquid through it ‖ 물이나 다른 액체를 통과시켜 어떤 장소를 깨끗이 하다

flush sb ↔ **out** *phr v* [T] to make someone leave the place where s/he is hiding ‖ 숨어 있는 곳에서 남을 떠나게 하다. …을 좇아내다: *The animals were flushed out and captured.* 그 동물들은 내몰려서 포획되었다.

flush² *n* 1 [singular] the red color that appears on your face when you FLUSH ‖ 얼굴이 상기되었을 때 나타나는 붉은 빛. 홍조 2 **a flush of pride/embarrassment/happiness etc.** a sudden feeling of pride, embarrassment etc. ‖ 갑작스런 자존심·당혹감. 갑작스레 일어나는 자존심/당혹감/행복감: *He felt a strong flush of pride as he watched his daughter on stage.* 그는 무대 위의 딸을 보자 갑자기 강한 자부심을 느꼈다.

flush³ *adj* 1 if two surfaces are flush, they are at exactly the same level, so that the place where they meet is flat ‖ 두 표면의 높이가 꼭 같아서 만나는 부분이 평평한. 수평의. 같은 평면의: *Is that cupboard flush with the wall?* 그 찬장은 벽과 붙어 있느냐? 2 INFORMAL if someone is flush, s/he has plenty of money ‖ 사람이 돈을 많이 가진. 부유한. 유복한: *I'll buy dinner. I'm feeling flush*

right now. 내가 저녁 식사 살게. 난 바로 지금 부자가 된 듯한 느낌이야.

flush⁴ *adv* fitting together so that the place where two surfaces meet is flat ‖ 두 표면이 만나는 곳이 평평하여 서로 잘 맞아. …에 꼭 맞아: *Make sure that door fits flush into its frame.* 그 문이 문틀에 꼭 들어맞는지 확인해라.

flushed /flʌʃt/ *adj* 1 red in the face ‖ 얼굴이 붉은. 홍조를 띤: *You look a little flushed.* 너는 얼굴이 조금 붉게 보인다. 2 **flushed with excitement/success** excited or pleased in a way that is easy to notice ‖ 알아채기 쉽게 흥분하거나 기뻐하는. 흥분/성공으로 들뜬: *Jill ran in, flushed with excitement.* 질은 흥분하여 달려 들어왔다.

flus·tered /ˈflʌstəd/ *adj* feeling nervous and confused ‖ 초조하고 혼란스러운. 당황한. 안절부절못하는: *Jay got flustered and forgot what he was supposed to say.* 제이는 당황하여 말하려고 했던 것을 잊어버렸다.

flute /flut/ *n* a musical instrument shaped like a pipe, that you play by holding it across your lips and blowing into it ‖ 양 입술 사이에 대고 그 안에 바람을 불어 넣어 연주하는, 파이프 같이 생긴 악기. 플루트

flut·ist /ˈflutɪst/ *n* someone who plays the FLUTE ‖ 플루트를 연주하는 사람

flut·ter¹ /ˈflʌtə/ *v* 1 [I, T] if a bird or insect flutters, or flutters its wings, its wings move quickly and lightly up and down ‖ 새나 곤충이 날개를 재빨리 가볍게 위아래로 움직이다. 날개치다. 푸드득거리다: *moths fluttering around the light* 불빛 주위에서 푸드득거리는 나방들 2 [I] to wave or move gently in the air ‖ 공중에서 부드럽게 흔들리거나 움직이다. 펄럭이다. 휘날리다: *flags fluttering in the wind* 바람에 휘날리고 있는 깃발들 3 [I] if your heart or your stomach flutters, you feel very excited or nervous ‖ 심장이나 위장이 매우 자극되거나 민감해지다. 조마조마하다. 신경 과민이 되다

flut·ter² *n* [singular] a FLUTTERing movement ‖ 펄럭거리는 움직임: *a flutter of wings* 날갯짓

flux /flʌks/ *n* **be in (a state of) flux** to be changing a lot so that you cannot be sure what will happen ‖ 무엇이 일어날지 확신할 수 없을 정도로 많은 것이 변하고 있다: *The economy is in flux at the moment.* 경제는 지금 끊임없이 변하고 있다.

fly¹ /flaɪ/ *v* **flew, flown, flying**

1 ▶THROUGH AIR 공중을 관통하여◀ [I,

T] to move through the air, or to make something do this ‖ 공중을 가로지르며 움직이다, 또는 이런 식으로 움직이게 하다. 날다. 날리다: *We watched the birds flying overhead.* 우리는 머리 위로 날아가는 새를 바라봤다. / *flying a kite* 연날리기 / *The planes fly right over our house.* 그 비행기들은 우리집 바로 위로 날아간다.

2 ▶TRAVEL 여행◀ [I, T] to travel by plane, or to make a person or thing go somewhere by plane ‖ 비행기로 여행하다, 또는 비행기로 사람이나 물건을 어딘가에 보내다: *Fran flew to Paris last week.* 프랜은 지난주에 비행기로 파리에 갔다. / *Food and medicine are being flown into the area.* 식량과 의약품이 그 지역에 공수되고 있다.

3 ▶BE A PILOT 조종사가 되다◀ [I, T] to be the pilot of a plane ‖ 비행기 조종사가 되다. 조종하다: *Bill's learning to fly.* 빌은 조종사가 되기 위해 공부하고 있다. / *He flew helicopters in Vietnam.* 그는 베트남에서 헬기를 조종했다.

4 ▶MOVE 움직이다◀ [I] to move very quickly and often unexpectedly ‖ 매우 재빠르게, 종종 불쑥 움직이다: *Timmy flew down the stairs and out the door.* 티미는 갑자기 계단을 뛰어내려와 바깥으로 나가버렸다. / *The door suddenly flew open.* 그 문은 갑자기 홱 열렸다.

5 ▶TIME 시간◀ [I] INFORMAL if time flies, it seems to pass quickly ‖ 시간이 매우 빨리 지나가는 것 같다: *Is it 5:30 already? Boy, time sure does fly!* 벌써 5시 30분이야? 야, 시간이 화살처럼 지나가네! / *Last week just flew by.* 지난주는 금새 지나가 버렸다.

6 fly off the handle INFORMAL to become angry suddenly and unexpectedly ‖ 갑자기 느닷없이 화내다: *I've never seen her fly off the handle like that before.* 나는 그녀가 그처럼 느닷없이 화내는 것을 처음 보았다.

7 ▶FLY OVER STH 사물 위로 날리다◀ [T] to fly a plane over a large area ‖ 비행기를 넓은 지역 위로 날리다. 횡단하다: *the first woman to fly the Atlantic* 대서양을 횡단하는 첫 번째 여성

8 fly into a temper/rage to suddenly become very angry ‖ 갑자기 매우 화를 내다

fly² *n* **1** a small flying insect with two wings ‖ 두 개의 날개로 나는 작은 곤충. 파리: *There were flies all over the food.* 음식은 온통 파리들로 득실댔다. **2** the part at the front of a pair of pants that you can open ‖ 바지 앞쪽의 열 수 있는 부분. 지퍼: *Your fly is unzipped.* 당신 바지 지퍼가 열렸다. **3** a hook that is made to look like a fly, used for catching fish ‖ 물고기를 잡는 데에 쓰는 파리처럼 보이게 만든 갈고리. 제물낚시 —see also **be dropping like flies** (DROP¹)

fly-by-night /'. . ,./ *adj* INFORMAL a fly-by-night organization cannot be trusted and is not likely to exist very long ‖ 조직이 믿을 수 없고 오래 갈 것 같지 않은: *a fly-by-night insurance company* 믿지 못할 보험 회사

fly·er /'flaɪɚ/ *n* ⇨ FLIER

fly·ing¹ /'flaɪ-ɪŋ/ *n* [U] the activity of traveling by plane or of being a pilot ‖ 비행기로 여행하거나 조종하는 행위: *My brother-in-law enjoys flying.* 내 처남은 비행기 조종을 즐긴다.

flying² *adj* **1** able to fly ‖ 날 수 있는: *a type of flying insect* 일종의 날 수 있는 곤충 **2 with flying colors** if you pass a test with flying colors, you are very successful on it ‖ 대성공을 거두어 **3 get off to a flying start** to begin something such as a job or a race very well ‖ 직무나 경주 등 일의 시작을 잘하다. 순조롭게 출발하다

flying sau·cer /,..'../ *n* a space vehicle shaped like a plate, that some people believe carries creatures from another world; UFO ‖ 일부 사람들이 외계에서 온 생명체를 태우고 다닌다고 믿는 접시처럼 생긴 우주선. 비행접시; ㉿ UFO

fly·swat·ter /'flaɪ,swɑtɚ/ *n* a plastic square attached to a long handle, used for killing flies ‖ 파리를 잡는 데에 쓰이는 긴 손잡이가 달린 네모난 플라스틱. 파리채

FM *n* [U] frequency modulation; a system of broadcasting radio programs in which the rate of the radio wave varies ‖ frequency modulation(주파수 변조)의 약어; 라디오 주파수대가 변하는 라디오 프로그램을 방송하는 시스템 — compare AM

foal /foʊl/ *n* a very young horse ‖ 매우 어린 말. 망아지

foam¹ /foʊm/ *n* [U] **1** a lot of very small BUBBLEs on the surface of something ‖ 사물의 표면에 있는 다량의 아주 작은 거품. 포말: *white foam on the tops of the waves* 파도 끝 부분의 흰 포말 **2** a light solid substance filled with many very small BUBBLEs of air. ‖ 아주 작은 기포들로 가득

foam

찬 가벼운 고체 물질. 스티로폼: *foam packaging* 스티로폼 포장 – **foamy** *adj*

foam² *v* [I] **1** to produce foam ‖ 거품이 일다 **2 foam at the mouth** to be very angry ‖ 몹시 화내다. 격노하다

foam rub·ber /ˌ. '../ *n* [U] soft rubber full of air BUBBLEs that is used, for example, to fill PILLOWs ‖ 예를 들어 베개를 채우는 속 재료로 쓰이는 기포로 가득한 부드러운 고무. 발포 고무

fo·cal point /ˈfoʊkəl ˌpɔɪnt/ *n* someone or something that you pay the most attention to ‖ 가장 주의를 기울이는 상대 또는 사물. 중심. 초점. 주안점: *Television has become the focal point of most American homes.* 텔레비전은 대부분의 미국 가정의 중심이 되었다.

fo·cus¹ /ˈfoʊkəs/ *v* **1** [I, T] to pay special attention to a particular person or thing instead of others ‖ 다른 것 대신에 특정의 사람이나 사물에 특별한 주의를 기울이다 또는 기울이게 하다. 집중하다. 집중시키다: *Their attention was again focused on the strange noise.* 그들의 주의력은 다시 이상한 소리에 집중되었다. **2** [T] to change the position of the LENS on a camera, TELESCOPE etc., so you can see something clearly ‖ 물체를 선명하게 볼 수 있게 카메라·망원경 등의 렌즈의 위치를 변화시키다. 초점을 맞추다 **3** [I, T] if you focus your eyes or if your eyes focus, you are able to see something clearly ‖ 눈이 물체를 선명하게 볼 수 있다. 초점을[이] 맞추다[맞다]

focus² *n, plural* **focuses** *or* **foci** /ˈfoʊsaɪ/ **1** [singular] a situation or subject that people are interested in because it is important ‖ 중요하므로 사람들이 관심을 가지고 있는 상황이나 주제. 주안점. 중점: *The war has become the focus of worldwide attention.* 그 전쟁은 전세계의 주목을 받는 초점이 되었다. **2** special attention that you give to a particular person or subject ‖ 특정의 사람이나 주제에 기울이는 특별한 관심: *Our language school puts a special focus on speaking English as well as writing it.* 우리 어학 학교는 영어를 쓰는 것뿐만 아니라 말하는 데에도 특별히 초점을 맞추고 있다. **3 in focus/out of focus** if a photograph, camera etc. is in focus, the edges of the things you see are clear; if it is out of focus the edges are not clear ‖ 사진·카메라 등에서 피사체의 가장자리가 선명하다, 또는 희미하다. 초점이 맞아[또렷하게]/초점이 벗어나[희미하게] – **focused** *adj*

fod·der /ˈfɑdɚ/ *n* [C, U] food for farm animals ‖ 농장 동물의 먹이. 사료

foe /foʊ/ *n* LITERARY an enemy ‖ 적

fog¹ /fɑg, fɔg/ *n* [C, U] **1** thick cloudy air that is difficult for you to see through ‖ 관통해서 보기 힘든 짙고 뿌연 공기. 안개 **2 be in a fog** INFORMAL to be confused and unable to think clearly ‖ 혼란스러워 뚜렷하게 생각할 수 없다. 오리무중이다

fog², fog up *v* **-gged, -gging** [I, T] if glass fogs or becomes fogged, it becomes covered with very small drops of water so you cannot see through it ‖ 유리가 그것을 통해 볼 수 없게 아주 작은 물방울로 뒤덮이다. 흐릿해지다. 흐릿하게 하다

fog·bound /ˈfɑgbaʊnd, ˈfɔg-/ *adj* prevented from traveling or working because of thick FOG ‖ 짙은 안개로 인해 여행 또는 일을 못하게 된: *Kennedy airport was fogbound on Monday.* 케네디 공항은 월요일에 안개로 발이 묶였다.

fogey, fogy /ˈfoʊgi/ *n, plural* **fogeys** *or* **fogies** INFORMAL someone who is old-fashioned and who does not like change ‖ 시대에 뒤지고 변화를 좋아하지 않는 사람. 구식 사람: *Don't listen to Mr. Dee; he's just an old fogey.* 디 씨의 말을 따르지 마라. 그는 구시대적인 사람에 지나지 않아.

fog·gy /ˈfɑgi, ˈfɔgi/ *adj* **1** not clear because of FOG ‖ 안개 때문에 선명하지 않은: *a damp and foggy morning* 축축하고 안개가 끼어 흐린 아침 **2 I don't have the foggiest (idea)** SPOKEN said in order to emphasize that you do not know something ‖ 어떤 일에 대해 모른다는 것을 강조하는 데에 쓰여. 전혀 모르겠다: *"When's Barry coming back?" "I don't have the foggiest."* "배리는 언제 돌아 오지?" "나는 전혀 몰라." – **fogginess** *n* [U]

fog·horn /ˈfɑghɔrn, ˈfɔg-/ *n* a loud horn used by ships in a FOG to warn other ships of their position ‖ 안개가 끼었을 때 배가 자신의 위치를 다른 배에 알리기 위해 사용하는 소리가 큰 경적. 농무 경적

foi·ble /ˈfɔɪbəl/ *n* FORMAL a habit that someone has that is slightly strange or silly ‖ 사람이 지닌 약간 이상하거나 어리석은 습관. 성격의 사소한 약점. 결점

foil¹ /fɔɪl/ *n* **1** [U] metal sheets that are thin like paper, used for wrapping food ‖ 음식물을 싸는 데에 사용하는, 종이처럼 얇은 금속판. 포일 **2 (be) a foil to** to make the good qualities of someone or something more noticeable ‖ 사람이나

사물의 좋은 자질을 더욱 돋보이게 하다: *Newman's low singing voice is the perfect foil to Allen's tenor.* 저음으로 노래하는 뉴먼의 목소리는 알렌의 테너를 완벽하게 돋보이게 한다.

foil² *v* [T] if you foil someone's plans, you stop him/her from doing something ‖ 남의 계획을 막아서 일을 하지 못하게 하다. 좌절시키다

foist /fɔɪst/ *v*

foist sth **on/upon** sb *phr v* [T] to make someone accept something that s/he does not want ‖ 남에게 원하지 않는 것을 받아들이게 하다: *Marie is always trying to foist her religious beliefs on everyone.* 마리는 항상 자기의 종교적 신념을 모든 사람이 받아들이도록 노력하고 있다.

fold¹ /foʊld/ *v* **1** [T] to bend a piece of paper, cloth etc. so that one part covers another part ‖ 한 부분이 다른 부분을 덮도록 종이·천 등을 접다: *Slide the omelet toward the edge of the pan and fold it in half.* 오믈렛을 팬 가장자리로 밀어서 반으로 접어라. —opposite UNFOLD **2** [I, T] if something such as furniture folds or you fold it, you make it smaller by bending it or closing it ‖ 가구 등을 구부리거나 닫아서 보다 작게 만들다. 접다. 접히다: *Be sure to fold up the ironing board when you're finished.* 끝나면 반드시 다리미판을 접어라. **3 fold your arms** to bend your arms so they are resting across your chest ‖ 가슴에서 서로 교차하도록 두 팔을 구부리다. 팔짱을 끼다 **4** [I] also **fold up** if a business folds, it fails and is not able to continue ‖ 사업이 실패하여 계속할 수 없다. 망하다. 도산하다

fold sth **in** *phr v* [T] to gently mix another substance into a mixture when you are preparing food ‖ 음식을 준비할 때 다른 물질을 살살 섞어 혼합물이 되게 하다

fold² *n* **1** a line made in paper, cloth etc. when you fold one part of it over another ‖ 종이나 천 등의 한 부분을 다른 부분에 접쳐 접을 때 생기는 선. 접은 자국 **2** [C usually plural] the folds in material, skin etc. are the loose parts that hang over other parts of it ‖ 물체나 피부 등의 다른 부분에 걸쳐 있는 느슨한 부분. 주름 **3 the fold** the group of people you belong to or have the same beliefs as ‖ 자신이 속

해 있는 사람들의 무리, 같은 믿음을 가진 사람들의 무리: *Democrats have to find some way to make voters return to the fold.* (=vote Democrat again) 민주당원들은 유권자들이 민주당으로 되돌아오게 하는 어떤 방법을 모색해야 한다. **4** a small area where sheep are kept for safety ‖ 양들을 안전하게 보호하는 작은 지역. 양의 우리

fold·er /ˈfoʊldɚ/ *n* **1** a large folded piece of hard paper, in which you keep loose papers ‖ 철하지 않은 서류를 보관하는 데 쓰는 접혀진 크고 견고한 종이. 서류 끼우개 **2** a picture on a computer screen that shows you where a FILE is kept ‖ 파일이 보관된 곳을 보여주는 컴퓨터 스크린 위의 그림. 폴더

fo·li·age /ˈfoʊliɪdʒ/ *n* [U] the leaves of a plant ‖ 한 식물의 전체 잎

folk¹ /foʊk/ *adj* folk art, dance, knowledge etc. is traditional and typical of the ordinary people who live in a particular area ‖ 예술·춤·지식 등이 특정한 지역에 살고 있는 보통 사람들에게 전통적이고 전형적인. 민속의

folk² *n* [U] ⇨ FOLK MUSIC

folk·lore /ˈfoʊk-lɔr/ *n* [U] the traditional stories, customs etc. of the ordinary people of a particular area ‖ 특정 지역의 평범한 사람들의 전통적인 이야기·관습 등. 민속

folk mu·sic /ˈ. ˌ../ *n* [U] traditional music that is played by the ordinary people of a particular area ‖ 특정 지역의 평범한 사람들에 의해 연주되는 전통적인 음악. 민속 음악. 민요

folks /foʊks/ *n* **1** [plural] your parents or family ‖ 자신의 양친이나 가족: *I need to call my folks sometime this weekend.* 나는 이번 주말쯤 부모님을 찾아봐야 한다. **2** SPOKEN said when you are talking to a group of people in a friendly way ‖ 일단의 사람들에게 친근하게 말할 때에 쓰여. 여러분: *Howdy folks, it's good to see everyone here tonight!* 여러분 안녕하세요, 오늘 밤 여기에서 여러분들을 만나게 되어 기쁘요! **3** people ‖ 사람들: *Most folks around here are very friendly.* 이곳 사람들 대부분은 매우 친절하다.

folk·sy /ˈfoʊksi/ *adj* INFORMAL **1** friendly and informal ‖ 친근하고 격식을 차리지 않는. 허물없는. 소탈한: *As a town, Colville has a folksy charm.* 콜빌은 시골풍의 매력이 있는 마을이다. **2** in a style that is typical of country speech and customs ‖ 시골 특유의 말과 관습의 형태인. 민속적인: *a funny folksy radio show* 재미있는 민속적인 라디오 쇼

fol·li·cle /ˈfɑlɪkəl/ *n* one of the small holes in the skin that hair grows from ‖ 털이 자라는 피부의 작은 구멍의 하나. 모공(毛孔)

fol·low /ˈfɑloʊ/ *v*

1 ▶COME BEHIND 뒤에 오다◀ [I, T] to walk, drive etc. behind or after someone else ‖ 다른 사람 뒤에서 또는 이후에 걷거나 운전하다. 따라가다: *If you follow me, I'll show you to your room.* 나를 따라오면 네 방을 보여줄게. / *Go on ahead – Dan will follow later.* 먼저 가라. 댄이 뒤따라 갈 것이다.

2 ▶IN ORDER TO WATCH SB 남을 살펴보려고◀ [T] to go closely behind someone else in order to find out where s/he is going ‖ 남이 가고 있는 곳을 알아내려고 바짝 뒤쫓다. 미행하다: *Marlowe looked over his shoulder to make sure no one was following him.* 말로는 미행하는 사람이 없는지 확인하려고 어깨 너머로 보았다.

3 ▶HAPPEN AFTER 뒤이어 일어나다◀ [I, T] to happen or come immediately after something else ‖ 다른 것 바로 다음에 일어나거나 오다: *There was a shout from the garage followed by a loud crash.* 차고에서 큰 고함 소리가 난 직후 충돌 소리가 크게 났다. / *In the days/weeks/months that followed, Angie tried to forget about Sam.* 그 다음날[그 다음주, 그 다음달]에 앤지는 샘에 관해서 잊으려고 애썼다.

4 follow the instructions/rules/signs etc. to do something according to how the instructions, rules etc. say it should be done ‖ 올바른 지시·규칙 등에 따라서 어떤 것을 하다. 지시/규칙/표식을 따르다: *Did you follow the instructions on the box?* 상자에 쓰여진 지시를 따랐니?

5 ▶GO IN A DIRECTION 한 방향으로 가다◀ [T] to go in the same direction as something else ‖ 다른 것과 마찬가지로 동일한 방향으로 가다: *The road follows the river for the next six miles.* 그 길은 앞으로 6마일 내내 강을 따라 나 있다.

6 follow suit to do the same thing as someone else ‖ 다른 사람과 동일한 것을 하다. 선례를 따르다. 남을 흉내내다: *When Allied Stores reduced prices, other companies were forced to follow suit.* 얼라이드 스토어가 가격을 내리자 다른 회사들도 따라서 가격을 내리지 않을 수 없었다.

7 follow sb's example/lead etc. to do the same type of thing as someone else ‖ 다른 사람과 마찬가지로 동일한 형태의 것을 하다. 남의 본을 따르다: *Don't be nervous; just follow my lead and you'll be fine.* 걱정하지 마라. 나만 따라와. 그러면 너는 괜찮을 거야.

8 ▶BE INTERESTED 흥미가 있다◀ [T] to be interested in something, and pay attention to it ‖ 일에 흥미가 있어서 관심을 갖다: *Do you follow baseball at all?* 너는 도대체 야구에 관심이 있는 거냐?

9 follow (in) sb's footsteps to do something that someone else did before you ‖ 다른 사람이 자신의 앞에 했던 것을 따라 하다. 선례를 따르다: *Toshi followed in his father's footsteps and started his own business.* 토시는 아버지의 선례를 따라서 자신의 사업을 시작했다.

10 as follows used in order to introduce a list of names, instructions etc. ‖ 명단·지시 사항 등을 도입하는 데에 쓰여. 다음과 같이: *The winners are as follows : first place, Tony Gwynn; second place, ...* 수상자는 다음과 같습니다. 일등은 토니 그윈, 이등은 …

11 ▶UNDERSTAND 이해하다◀ [I, T] SPOKEN to understand something such as an explanation or story ‖ 설명이나 이야기 등을 이해하다: *Sorry, I don't follow you.* 미안하지만 당신이 하는 말을 이해하지 못하겠어요

12 it follows that used in order to show that something must be true as a result of something else that is true ‖ 사실인 다른 것의 결과로 어떤 것이 사실임에 틀림없다는 것을 나타내는 데에 쓰여. 결과로서[당연히] …이 되다: *Of course she drinks, but it doesn't follow that she's an alcoholic.* 물론 그녀가 술을 마시지만 그것이 곧 그녀가 알코올 중독자라는 말은 아니다.

13 ▶BELIEVE/OBEY 믿다/따르다◀ [T] to believe in or obey a particular set of religious or political ideas ‖ 특정한 종교적 또는 정치적 사상 체계를 믿거나 따르다: *They still follow the teachings of Gandhi.* 그들은 여전히 간디의 가르침을 따르고 있다.

follow sb ↔ **around** *phr v* [T] to keep following someone everywhere s/he goes ‖ 남이 가는 곳은 어디든 졸졸 따라다니다: *My little brother is always following me around.* 내 동생은 항상 나를 졸졸 따라다니고 있다.

follow sth ↔ **through** *phr v* [I, T] to do what needs to be done to complete something or make it successful ‖ 어떤 것을 완성하거나 성공으로 이끌기 위해 하지 않으면 안 되는 것을 하다. 해내다: *Harry was trained as an actor, but he never followed through with it.* 해리는

연기 수업을 받았지만 결코 그 길로 나아
가지는 못했다.

follow sth ↔ **up** *phr v* [I, T] to find out
more about something, or to do more
about something ‖ 일에 대해 더 찾아내거
나 하다. 철저히 구명하다[하다]: *Did Jay
ever follow up on that job possibility in
Tucson?* 제이는 투손에서 그 일자리를 잡
을 가능성을 철저히 조사해 본 적이 있느
냐?

fol·low·er /'faloʊɚ/ *n* someone who
believes in or supports a particular
leader or set of ideas ‖ 특정한 지도자나
사상 체계를 믿거나 지지하는 사람. 추종
자. 지지자

fol·low·ing¹ /'faloʊɪŋ/ *adj* **the
following day/year/chapter etc.** the
day, year etc. after the one you have
just mentioned ‖ 방금 언급한 다음의 날·
해 등. 다음날/이듬해/다음 장: *Neil
arrived on Friday, and his wife came
the following day.* 닐은 금요일에 도착했
고 그의 아내는 그 다음날 왔다.

following² *n* **1** a group of people who
support or admire someone such as a
performer ‖ 연주자 등을 지지하거나 찬양
하는 일단의 사람들. 신봉자. 숭배자. 팬:
*I was playing in clubs and I'd gotten a
following there.* 나는 클럽에서 연주를 했
는데 그곳에서 나의 팬이 생겼다. **2 the
following** the people or things that you
are going to mention next ‖ 다음에 언급
할 사람이나 물건: *Typical examples of
opposites include the following: small
and large, cold and hot ...* ‖ 반의어의 전
형적인 예는 다음과 같다. '작은'과 '큰',
'차가운'과 '뜨거운' …

following³ *prep* immediately after ‖ 직
후에. …의 후[뒤]에: *There will be time
for questions following the lecture.* 강의
후에 질문하는 시간이 있을 것이다.

follow-up /'.. ,./ *adj* done in order to
find out more or do more about
something ‖ 어떤 것을 더 알아보거나 하
기 위해 행한. 잇따른. 후속의: *He's on
drug treatments, with monthly follow-
up visits.* 그는 매달 방문 추적 관찰 치료
와 더불어 약물 치료를 받고 있다. —
follow-up *n* [U]

fol·ly /'fali/ *n* [C, U] FORMAL a very
stupid thing to do ‖ 매우 어리석은 짓: *It
would be sheer folly to buy another car
at this point.* 이 시점에서 차를 한 대 더
사는 것은 아주 어리석은 행동이 될 것이
다.

fo·ment /'foʊmɛnt, foʊ'mɛnt/ *v* [T]
FORMAL **foment war/revolution/
trouble etc.** to make people do

something that causes a lot of trouble in
a society ‖ 사람들에게 사회에 많은 물의
를 빚을 일을 하게 하다. 전쟁을 도발하다
/혁명을 조장하다/문제를 일으키다

fond /fand/ *adj* **1 be fond of** to like
someone or something very much ‖ 사람
이나 사물을 매우 좋아하다: *Mrs. Winters
is very fond of her grandchildren.* 윈터
스 부인은 손자·손녀를 매우 예뻐한다. **2
fond memory** a memory that makes
you happy when you think of it ‖ 생각할
때 행복하게 만드는 기억: *"I really have
fond memories of those times," Bentley
said.* "나는 정말 그 시절의 좋은 추억들이
있지."라고 벤틀리는 말했다. **3 be fond
of doing** sth to enjoy doing something,
and to do it often ‖ 어떤 것을 즐겨 자주
하다: *There's a story the old lady is fond
of telling.* 노부인이 말하기 좋아하는 이야
기가 있습니다. **4** a fond look, smile etc.
is a kind, gentle one that shows that you
like someone very much ‖ 표정·웃음 등
이 남을 좋아하는 것을 나타내어. 다정한.
온화한 — **fondness** *n* [U]

fon·dle /'fandl/ *v* [T] **1** to touch
someone or something in a gentle way ‖
사람이나 물건을 다정스레 만지다. 어루만
지다: *a little girl fondling her cat* 고양이
를 어루만지고 있는 어린 소녀 **2** to touch
someone's body in a sexual way ‖ 남의
몸을 성적으로 만지다. 애무하다. 껴안다:
*She accused Harper of fondling her in
the elevator.* 그녀는 하퍼가 엘리베이터에
서 자기를 성추행했다고 고소했다.

fond·ly /'fandli/ *adv* **1** in a way that
shows you like someone or something
very much ‖ 사람이나 사물을 매우 좋아한
다는 것을 나타내는 투로. 다정하게. 귀엽
게. 사랑스럽게: *Greta smiled fondly at
him from across the room.* 그레타는 방
건너편에서 그를 보고 다정하게 웃었다. **2
fondly remember/recall** to feel happy
when you remember what you liked
about a person or place ‖ 사람이나 장소
에 대해 좋아한 것을 기억하며 행복해하
다: *Mrs. Vance fondly remembers when
Sunnyvale was a city of gardens.* 밴스
부인은 즐거운 기분으로 서니베일이 정원
도시였을 때를 떠올린다.

font /fant/ *n* **1** TECHNICAL a set of
printed letters that is a particular size
and shape ‖ 특정한 크기와 모양의 활자
한 벌. 폰트 **2** a container for the water
used in the ceremony of BAPTISM ‖ 세례
식에서 사용하는 물을 담는 용기. 세례반
(洗禮盤)

food /fud/ *n* **1** [U] things that people
and animals eat ‖ 사람이나 동물이 먹는

것. 음식물: *What kind of food are you in the mood for tonight?* 오늘 밤은 무슨 음식을 먹고 싶니? **2** [C, U] a particular type of food ‖ 특정한 유형의 음식: *All he ever eats is junk food.* 그가 여태까지 먹은 모든 것은 정크 푸드[몸에 좋지 않은 음식]이다 / *a health food store* 건강식품 가게 **3 give sb food for thought** to make someone think carefully about something ‖ 남에게 어떤 것에 관해 주의 깊게 생각하게 하다

food bank /'. ./ *n* a place that gives food to people who need it ‖ 필요한 사람들에게 음식을 주는 곳. 음식 은행[배급소]

food chain /'. ./ *n* [singular] animals and plants considered as a group in which one animal is eaten by another animal, which is eaten by another etc. ‖ 한 동물이 다른 동물에게 먹히고 그것은 다시 다른 것들에게 먹히는 등의 한 그룹으로 간주되는 동물이나 식물. 먹이 사슬

food poi·son·ing /'. ,.../ *n* [U] an illness caused by eating food that contains harmful BACTERIA ‖ 해로운 박테리아가 들어 있는 음식을 섭취하여 일어나는 병. 식중독

food pro·ces·sor /'. ,.../ *n* a piece of electrical equipment for preparing food, that cuts or mixes it very quickly ‖ 아주 신속히 자르거나 섞는 음식 조리용 전기 기구. 만능 조리 용구 —see picture at KITCHEN

food stamp /'. ./ *n* [C usually plural] an official piece of paper that poor people can use instead of money to buy food ‖ 가난한 사람들이 음식을 사는 데 돈 대신에 사용할 수 있는 공적인 종잇조각. 식료품 쿠폰

fool¹ /ful/ *n* **1** a stupid person ‖ 멍청한 사람. 바보: *I felt like a fool, locking my keys in the car like that.* 나는 열쇠를 저렇게 자동차 안에 놔 두고 문을 잠근 내 자신이 바보같이 느껴졌다. **2 make a fool of yourself** to do something embarrassing in front of other people ‖ 다른 사람 앞에서 난처한 짓을 하다. 바보짓을 하다. 웃음거리가 되다: *You're drunk, and you're making a fool of yourself.* 너는 술이 취했고 웃음거리가 되고 있어.

fool² *v* **1** [T] to trick or deceive someone ‖ 남을 속이거나 기만하다: *Don't be fooled into buying more insurance than you need.* 속아서 필요 이상의 보험에 들지 않도록 해라. **2 you could have fooled me** SPOKEN said when you do not believe what someone has told you ‖ 남

이 말한 것을 믿지 않을 때 쓰여. 도저히 못 믿겠다. 설마: *"Your dad's upset about this too, you know." "Well, you could have fooled me!"* "네 아빠도 이것에는 역시 화가 나셨단 말이야." "글쎄, 도저히 믿지 못하겠는데!"

fool around *phr v* [I] **1** to spend time doing something that you enjoy ‖ 즐기는 것을 하면서 시간을 보내다: *We spent the day fooling around at the beach.* 우리는 해변에서 즐기면서 하루를 보냈다. **2** to behave in a silly way ‖ 어리석게 행동하다: *Stop fooling around with those scissors before you hurt yourself!* 다치기 전에 그 가위 장난 그만둬! **3** to have a sexual relationship with someone else ‖ 다른 사람과 성관계를 가지다. 놀아나다: *Matt thinks his wife is fooling around with someone.* 매트는 자기 아내가 다른 남자와 바람피우고 있다고 생각한다.

fool with sb/sth *phr v* [T] INFORMAL to do something that could be dangerous or could ruin something ‖ 위험스러울 수 있고 사물을 망쳐놓을 수도 있는 일을 하다: *A hacker had been fooling with the hospital computers.* 한 해커가 그 병원의 컴퓨터를 장난삼아 해킹해 오고 있었다.

fool·har·dy /'ful,hardi/ *adj* taking risks that are not necessary ‖ 불필요한 위험을 감행하는. 무모한. 터무니없는

fool·ish /'fulɪʃ/ *adj* **1** not sensible or wise ‖ 분별없는. 현명하지 않은. 지각없는: *It would be foolish of them to start fighting over this.* 그들이 이 문제로 싸우기 시작하는 것은 지각없는 일일 게다. **2** silly or stupid ‖ 어리석은. 멍청한: *a foolish young man* 바보 같은 젊은 남자 – **foolishly** *adv* – **foolishness** *n* [U]

fool·proof /'fulpruf/ *adj* a foolproof plan, method etc. is certain to be successful ‖ 계획·방법 등이 성공이 확실한

foot¹ /fʊt/ *n*

1 ▶BODY PART 신체 부위◀ *plural* **feet** the part of your body that you stand on and walk on ‖ 서 있거나 걸을 때 사용하는 신체 부위. 발 —see picture at BODY

2 ▶MEASUREMENT 측량◀ *written abbreviation* **ft.** *plural* **feet** *or* **foot** a unit for measuring length, equal to 12 INCHes or 0.3048 meters ‖ 12인치나 0.3048미터에 해당하는 길이 측정 단위

3 on foot if you go somewhere on foot, you walk there ‖ 걸어서. 도보로: *We set out on foot to explore the city.* 우리는 그 도시를 답사하기 위해 걸어서 출발했다.

4 the foot of the lowest part of something such as a mountain or tree, or the end of something such as a bed ‖ 산이나 나무 등의 가장 낮은 부분, 또는 침대 등의 끝. 기슭. 밑둥. 발치

5 be on your feet a) to be standing for a long time without sitting down ‖ 앉아 있지 않고 오랫동안 서 있다: *Waitresses are on their feet all day.* 웨이트리스는 하루 종일 서 있는다. **b)** to be healthy again after being sick ‖ 앓고 나서 다시 건강해지다: *It's good to see you on your feet again!* 다시 건강해진 너의 모습을 보니 좋구나!

6 get/rise/jump etc. to your feet to stand up after you have been sitting ‖ 앉아 있다가 일어서다: *The fans cheered and rose to their feet.* 그 팬들은 환호하며 일어섰다.

7 set foot in to go into a place ‖ 장소에 들어가다. …에 발을 들여놓다: *If that woman ever sets foot in this house, I'm leaving!* 그 여자가 이 집에 발을 들여놓는다면 난 떠날 거야!

8 put your foot down a) to say very firmly what someone must do or not do ‖ 남이 해야 하거나 하지 말아야 할 것을 매우 단호하게 말하다. 단호한 태도를 취하다: *Brett didn't want to go to the doctor, but Dad put his foot down.* 브레트는 진찰받으러 가고 싶어하지 않았지만 아빠의 태도는 단호했다. **b)** to make a car go faster ‖ 차를 보다 빨리 달리게 하다. 속도를 내다

9 put your feet up to relax and rest, especially by having your feet supported on something ‖ 특히 발을 어떤 것에 얹어 긴장을 풀고 쉬다

10 put your foot in your mouth to say something that is embarrassing, or that upsets someone ‖ 남을 난처하게 하거나 화나게 하는 말을 하다. 실언하다

11 have/keep both feet on the ground to be sensible and practical in the way you do things ‖ 일을 하는 면에서 분별 있고 실제적이다. 들떠 있지 않다. 현실적이다

12 get your foot in the door to get your first opportunity to work in a particular organization or industry ‖ 특정한 조직이나 업계에서 일할 첫 번째의 기회를 잡다. …에 첫발을 내딛다

13 have one foot in the grave HUMOROUS to be old ‖ 늙다. 곧 죽을 것 같다

14 -footed having a particular number or type of feet ‖ 특정한 수나 형태의 발을 가진: *a four-footed animal* 네발짐승 / *a flat-footed man* 평발인 남자

15 -footer being a particular number of feet in length ‖ 길이가 …피트인 것[사람]: *Our sailboat's a twenty-footer.* 우리 범선은 전장 20피트짜리이다.

foot² *v* **foot the bill** INFORMAL to pay for something ‖ 어떤 것의 값을 지불하다. 셈을 치르다: *The insurance company should foot the bill for the damage.* 보험 회사가 그 피해액을 지불할 것이다.

foot·age /ˈfʊtɪdʒ/ *n* [U] film that shows a particular event ‖ 특정한 사건을 보여주는 영화: *black-and-white footage of the 1936 Olympics* 1936년의 올림픽 흑백 기록 영화

foot·ball /ˈfʊtˌbɔl/ *n* **1** [U] a game in which two teams of eleven players carry, kick, or throw a ball into an area at the end of a field to win points ‖ 선수 열한 명으로 구성된 두 팀이 득점하기 위하여 공을 구장 끝 구역으로 들고가거나 차거나, 또는 던지는 게임. 미식 축구 — see picture on page 946 **2** the ball used in this game ‖ 이 게임에 사용된 공. 미식 축구공 —see also SOCCER

foot·bridge /ˈfʊtˌbrɪdʒ/ *n* a narrow bridge for people to walk over ‖ 사람들이 그 위로 걸어가게 만든 좁은 다리. 보행자용 다리. 횡단육 육교

foot·fall /ˈfʊtfɔl/ *n* LITERARY ⇨ FOOTSTEP

foot·hill /ˈfʊtˌhɪl/ *n* [C usually plural] one of the low hills at the bottom of a group of mountains ‖ 한 무리의 산의 아래쪽의 낮은 언덕의 하나. 산기슭의 작은 언덕[구릉]: *the foothills of the Rockies* 록키 산맥의 작은 구릉들

foot·hold /ˈfʊthoʊld/ *n* **1** a position from which you can start trying to get what you want ‖ 원하는 것을 얻기 위한 노력이 시작되는 위치. 기반. 터전. 거점: *The Republicans gained a foothold during the last elections.* 공화당원들은 지난 선거 기간에 기반을 다졌다. **2** a space where you can safely put your foot when climbing a rock ‖ 바위에 오를 때 발을 안전하게 디딜 수 있는 공간. 발판

foot·ing /ˈfʊtɪŋ/ *n* [U] **1** the conditions or arrangements under which something exists or operates ‖ 사물이 존재하거나 작용하는 조건이나 준비 사항. 안전한 발판. 기반: *Most of all, the city needs to get on a firm financial footing.* 무엇보다도 그 시는 확고한 재정적 기반에 올라서야만 한다. / *Talks were held in Geneva so that the two sides were on an equal footing.* (=had the same advantages and disadvantages) 양측이 동등한 입장에 놓이도록 회담은 제네바에서 개최되었다. **2** a firm hold with your feet on a surface || 어떤 표면에 단단히 발붙이는 것. 발붙임: *A local boy lost his footing and fell 200 feet down a steep bank.* 한 지역 소년이 실족하여 가파른 둑에서 200피트 아래로 떨어졌다.

foot·lights /'fʊtlaɪts/ *n* [plural] a row of lights along the front of the stage in a theater || 극장의 무대 앞을 따라 열을 이룬 광선. 각광

foot lock·er /'. ,../ *n* a large strong plain box for keeping your possessions in || 소지품을 보관해 두는 크고 튼튼하며 수수한 상자. 사물 트렁크

foot·loose /'fʊtlus/ *adj* **footloose and fancy free** able to do what you want and enjoy yourself because you are not responsible for anyone or anything || 어느 사람이나 사물에도 책임이 없기 때문에 원하는 것을 하며 즐길 수 있는. 마음대로의: *No, I'm not married – still footloose and fancy free.* 아니, 나 결혼 안 했어. 아직 마음 편하고 자유분방해.

foot·note /'fʊtˌnoʊt/ *n* a note at the bottom of the page in a book, that gives more information about something on that page || 책의 페이지에 나오는 사항에 대하여 더 많은 정보를 제공하는 페이지 하단의 기록. 각주. 주석

foot·path /'fʊtpæθ/ *n* a narrow path for people to walk along, especially in the country; TRAIL || 특히 시골에서, 사람들이 따라 걷게 된 좁은 길. 오솔길; ㈜ trail

foot·print /'fʊtˌprɪnt/ *n* a mark made by a foot or shoe || 발이나 신발에 의해 난 자국. 발자국: *a deer's footprints in the snow* 눈 위의 사슴 발자국

foot·rest /'fʊtrɛst/ *n* a part of a chair that you can raise or lower in order to support your feet when you are sitting down || 앉아 있을 때 발을 받칠 수 있도록 올리거나 낮출 수 있는 의자의 한 부분. 발판

foot·sie /'fʊtsi/ *n* **play footsie** INFORMAL to secretly touch someone's feet with your feet under a table, to show that you think s/he is sexually attractive || 상대에게 성적 매력을 느낀다는 것을 보여주기 위해 테이블 아래에서 자신의 발로 상대의 발을 은밀하게 건드리다. 시시덕거리다. 새롱거리다

foot·step /'fʊtstɛp/ *n* the sound of each step when someone is walking || 사람이 걸어갈 때 나는 발소리: *He heard someone's footsteps in the hall.* 그는 강당에서 누군가의 발소리를 들었다. —see also **follow (in) sb's footsteps** (FOLLOW)

foot·stool /'fʊtstul/ *n* a low piece of furniture used for supporting your feet when you are sitting down || 앉아 있을 때 발을 받치는 데에 쓰는 낮은 가구. 발판. 발 얹는 대

foot·wear /'fʊtˌwɛr/ *n* [U] things you wear on your feet, such as shoes or boots || 신발이나 부츠 등의 발에 신는 물건. 신발

foot·work /'fʊtˌwɚk/ *n* [U] skillful use of your feet when dancing or playing a sport || 춤출 때나 경기할 때의 솜씨 있는 발놀림

for¹ /fɚ; *strong* fɔr/ *prep*

1 ▶MEANT FOR SB 어떤 사람을 위해 의도된◀ intended to be given to or used by a particular person or group || 특정 사람이나 무리에게 주려고 한, 또는 그들이 사용하도록 한: *Save a piece of cake for Noah.* 노아를 위해 케이크 한 조각 남겨 둬. / *I've got some good news for you.* 네게 들려줄 좋은 소식이 있어. / *Leave those chairs out – they're for the concert.* 저 의자들을 밖에 놔두어라. 콘서트에 사용할 거니까.

2 ▶PURPOSE 목적◀ used in order to show the purpose of an object, action, etc. || 물체·행위 등의 목적을 나타내는 데에 쓰여: *a knife for cutting bread* 빵을 자르는 데 쓰는 칼 / *What did you do that for?* (=why did you do it?) 왜 그랬니? / *What's this gadget for?* (=what is its purpose?) 이 기기는 무엇에 쓰이는 겁니까? / *a space just large enough for the bed to fit into* 침대가 꼭 들어갈 수 있는 정도의 공간 / *The house is for sale.* (=available to be sold) 그 집은 팔려고 내놓았다.

3 ▶SB WANTS TO GET/DO STH 사람이 어떤 것을 얻기/하기를 원하다◀ in order to get or do something || 어떤 것을 얻거나 하기 위해: *Alison is looking for a job.* 앨리슨은 직장을 구하고 있다. / *We were waiting for the bus.* 우리는 버스를 기다리고 있었다. / *Let's go for a walk.* 산책하러 가자. / *For more information, write to this address.* 더 많은 정보를 원하시면 이 주소로 편지를 보내십시오.

4 ▶PLANNED TIME 계획된[예정된] 시간◀ used in order to show the time when something is planned to happen || 일이 일어나기로 계획된 때의 시간을 나타내는 데에 쓰여: *an appointment for 3:00* 3시에 있는 약속 / *It's time for dinner.* (=we're going to have dinner now) 저녁 식사할 시간이다.

5 ▶HELP 도와주다◀ in order to help someone || 남을 돕기 위해: *Let me lift* *that box for you.* 제가 그 상자를 들어 줄 게요. / *What can I do for you?* (=can I help you?) 무엇을 도와 드릴까요?

6 ▶PERIOD OF TIME 일정 시간◀ used in order to express a length of time ‖ 시간 의 길이를 나타내는 데에 쓰여: *I've known Kim for a long time.* 나는 김씨와 오랫동안 알고 지냈다. / *Bake the cake for 40 minutes.* 40분간 케이크를 구워라. —see usage note at SINCE²

7 ▶REASON 이유◀ because of or as a result of ‖ 어떤 것 때문에, 어떤 것의 결 과로: *I got a ticket for going through a red light.* 나는 빨간불일 때 통과해서 딱 지를 떼었다. / *The award for the highest sales goes to Pete McGregor.* 최고 판매 실적상은 피트 맥그리거에게 돌아갑니다.

8 ▶DIRECTION 방향◀ used in order to show where a person, vehicle etc. is going ‖ 사람·차 등이 가고 있는 곳을 나타 내는 데에 쓰여: *The plane for Las Vegas took off an hour late.* 라스베이거스행 비 행기가 한 시간 늦게 이륙했다. / *I was just leaving for church when the phone rang.* 내가 막 교회로 가려 할 때 전화벨 이 울렸다.

9 ▶DISTANCE 거리◀ used in order to express a distance ‖ 거리를 나타내는 데 에 쓰여: *We walked for miles.* 우리는 수 마일을 걸었다.

10 ▶AMOUNT/PRICE 양/가격◀ used in order to show a price or amount ‖ 가격 이나 양을 나타내는 데에 쓰여: *a check for $100* 100달러짜리 수표 / *an order for 200 copies* 200권의 주문 / *I'm not working for nothing/for free.* (=without being paid) 나는 공짜[무보수]로는 일하 지 않는다.

11 for breakfast/lunch/dinner used in order to say what you ate or will eat at breakfast, LUNCH etc. ‖ 아침, 점심 등으로 무엇을 먹었는지 또는 먹을 것인지 말하는 데에 쓰여. 아침/점심/저녁으로: *"What's for lunch?" "Hamburgers."* "점심에 뭘 먹니?" "햄버거." / *We had steak for dinner last night.* 우리는 어젯밤에 저녁 으로 스테이크를 먹었다.

12 for sb/sth to do sth used when discussing what is happening, what may happen, or what can happen ‖ 일어 나고 있는[일어날지도 모를, 일어날 수 있 는] 일을 논의할 때 쓰여: *It's unusual for it to be this cold in June.* 6월에 이렇게 추운 것이 이상하다. / *The plan is for us to leave on Friday morning and pick up Joe.* 계획은 우리가 금요일 아침에 떠나서 조를 자동차로 마중나가 태우는 것이다. / *The cat's too high up the tree for me to*

reach her. 그 고양이가 나무 위에 너무 높 이 있어서 나는 닿지도 않는다.

13 ▶FEELING TOWARD SOMEONE 어떤 사람에 대한 느낌◀ used in order to show which person a feeling relates to ‖ 느낌이 관련된 사람을 나타내는 데에 쓰여: *I'm really happy for you.* 나는 네 덕분에 정말 행복해. / *He has a lot of respect for his teachers.* 그는 선생님들에 대해 큰 존 경심을 갖고 있다.

14 for now used in order to say that a situation can be changed later ‖ 어떤 상 황이 나중에는 바뀔 수 있음을 말하는 데 에 쓰여. 당분간. 현재로서는: *Just put the pictures in a box for now.* 당분간 사 진들을 상자 속에 그냥 넣어 두어라.

15 work for/play for etc. to play a sport on a particular team, work at a particular company etc. ‖ 특정 팀에서 선 수로 뛰다, 특정 회사 등에서 일하다: *She worked for Exxon until last year.* 그녀는 작년까지 엑손 사에 근무했다. / *He plays for the Boston Red Sox.* 그는 보스턴 레드 삭스팀의 선수다.

16 ▶SUPPORT/AGREE 지지하다/동의하다 ◀ in favor of, supporting, or agreeing with someone or something ‖ 사람이나 사물에 찬성하여[지지하여, 동의하여]: *How many people voted for Mulhoney?* 멀허니에게 몇 명이 찬성 투표했습니까? / *I'm for getting a pizza, what about you?* 난 피자가 먹고 싶어, 넌 어떠니?

17 for all a) considering how little ‖ 별 것 아님을 고려하면: *For all the good I did, I shouldn't have tried to help.* 내가 한 좋은 일이 하찮은 것인걸 생각하면, 난 도우려고 애쓰지 말았어야 했다. **b)** considering how much or many ‖ 양이나 수가 얼마만큼 많은지 고려하면: *For all the plays she's seen, she's never seen Hamlet.* 그녀는 수많은 연극을 보았지만 햄릿을 본 적은 없다.

18 for all I know/care SPOKEN used in order to say that you really do not know or care ‖ 정말 모르거나 상관하지 않는다 고 말하는 데에 쓰여. 잘은 모르지만/… 내 알 바 아니지만: *He could be in Canada by now for all I know.* 잘은 모르 지만 그는 아마 지금 캐나다에 있을지 모 른다.

19 for Christmas/for sb's birthday etc. in order to celebrate Christmas, someone's BIRTHDAY etc. ‖ 크리스마스·생 일 등을 축하하여: *What did you get for your birthday?* 네 생일 선물로 무엇을 받 았니? / *We went to my grandmother's for Thanksgiving last year.* 우리는 작년 추수 감사절에 할머니 댁에 갔다.

20 ▶MEANING 의미◀ meaning or representing ‖ 의미하는 또는 나타내는: *What's the Spanish word for oil?* 스페인어로 기름이 무엇입니까?

21 ▶COMPARING 비교◀ when you consider a particular fact ‖ 특정 사실을 고려할 때: *Libby's very tall for her age.* 리비는 나이에 비해 키가 매우 크다.

22 if it hadn't been for/if it weren't for if something had not happened, or if a situation were different 일이 일어나지 않았다면, 또는 상황이 달랐다면: *If it weren't for Missy's help, we'd never get this job done.* 미시의 도움이 없었다면 우리는 결코 그 일을 끝마칠 수 없었을 것이다. —see usage note at AGO

USAGE NOTE for

Use verbs like "buy" or "make" without **for** only to talk about buying or making something for a person or animal: *He bought a new dish for his dog.* or *He bought his dog a new dish.* / *She made a dress for her daughter.* or *She made her daughter a dress.* If you talk about buying or making something for an object, you must use **for**: *I bought a new tablecloth for the table.* ✗DON'T SAY "I bought the table a new tablecloth."✗
사람이나 동물을 위해 무엇을 사거나 만들어 주는 것에 대하여 말할 때에는 **for** 없이 "buy"나 "make" 같은 동사를 쓴다: 그는 자신의 개에게 새 접시를 사 주었다. / 그녀는 딸에게 새 드레스를 만들어 주었다. 사물에 쓰이는 어떤 것을 사거나 만드는 것에 대하여 말할 때에는 반드시 **for**를 써야 한다: 나는 식탁에 쓸 새 식탁보를 샀다. 이 경우 "I bought the table a new tablecloth."라고는 하지 않는다.

---

for² *conjunction* LITERARY because ‖ 왜냐하면, …이므로. 그 까닭은

for·age /ˈfɔrɪdʒ, ˈfɑr-/ *v* [I] to go around searching for food or other supplies ‖ 음식이나 다른 물품을 찾아다니다: *animals foraging for food* 먹을 것을 찾아다니는 동물들

for·ay /ˈfɔreɪ, ˈfɑreɪ/ *n* **1** a short attempt at doing a particular job or activity ‖ 특정한 일이나 활동을 하려는 짧은 시도: *a brief foray into politics* 짧은 정계 진출 시도 **2** a short sudden attack by a group of soldiers ‖ 일단의 군인들에 의한 짧고 갑작스런 공격. 급습: *nightly forays into enemy territory* 적진으로의 야간 급습

for·bade /fɚˈbæd/ *v* the past tense of FORBID ‖ forbid의 과거형

for·bear /fɔrˈbɛr, fɚ-/ *v* **forbore** /-ˈbɔr/, **forborne** /-ˈbɔrn/ [I] FORMAL to not do something that you could do because you think it is wiser not to do it ‖ 하지 않는 것이 더 현명하다고 여겨 할 수 있는 것을 하지 않다. 삼가다: *They were silly games, which Thornton forbore to join.* 그것은 바보 같은 게임이었고, 손턴은 그 게임에 참여하지 않았다.

for·bear·ance /fɔrˈbɛrəns, fɚ-/ *n* [U] FORMAL the quality of being patient, having control over your emotions, and being willing to forgive someone ‖ 인내심이 있고, 감정을 조절하며, 남을 기꺼이 용서하는 성질. 인내. 자제. 관용: *I know what forbearance you have shown him.* 나는 네가 어떤 관용을 그에게 보였는지 알고 있다.

for·bid /fɚˈbɪd/ *v* **forbade** *or* **forbid**, **forbid** *or* **forbidden**, **forbidding** [T] **1** to order someone not to do something ‖ 남에게 어떤 것을 하지 말라고 명령하다. 금하다. 허락하지 않다: *I forbid you to see that man again.* 나는 네가 그 남자를 다시 만나는 것을 금한다. **2 God/Heaven forbid** SPOKEN said in order to emphasize that you hope that something will not happen ‖ 어떤 것이 일어나지 않기를 바라는 것을 강조하는 데에 쓰여. (…이라니) 당치도 않다: *God forbid you should have an accident.* 네가 사고를 당하는 일은 결코 없을 거야.

for·bid·den /fɚˈbɪdn/ *adj* **1** not allowed, especially because of an official rule ‖ 특히 공식적인 규칙 때문에 용인되지 않는. 금지된: *It's forbidden to smoke in the hospital.* 병원에서는 흡연이 금지되어 있다. **2** a forbidden place is one that you are not allowed to go to ‖ 장소가 들어갈 수 없는. 출입이 금지된: *This is a forbidden area to everyone but the army.* 이곳은 군인 이외의 사람에게는 출입이 금지된 지역이다.

for·bid·ding /fɚˈbɪdɪŋ/ *adj* looking frightening, unfriendly, or dangerous ‖ 무서워[적대적으로, 위험해] 보이는: *The mountains looked more forbidding as we got closer.* 우리가 가까이 다가설수록 그 산은 더욱 위험해 보였다.

force¹ /fɔrs/ *n*

1 ▶TRAINED GROUP 훈련된 무리◀ a group of people who have been trained to do military or police work ‖ 군대나 경찰 업무를 수행하도록 훈련된 일단의 사람. 군대. 경찰: *the Air Force* 공군 / *forces that are loyal to the rebels* 반군들

에게 충성스런 군대 / *Both of her sons are in the forces.* (=a country's military) 그녀의 두 아들은 군대에 있다.

2 ▶MILITARY ACTION 군사적 행동◀ [U] military action used as a way of achieving your aims ‖ 목적 달성을 위한 방법으로서 사용되는 군사적 행동: *The UN tries to limit the use of force in conflicts.* UN은 분쟁시 군사 행동을 제한하려고 노력하고 있다.

3 ▶VIOLENT ACTION 폭력적인 행동◀ [U] violent physical action used in order to get what you want ‖ 원하는 것을 얻기 위해 사용하는 폭력적인 물리적 행동. 폭력. 무력: *The police used force to break up the demonstration.* 경찰은 데모를 해산시키기 위해 무력을 사용했다.

4 ▶NATURAL POWER 자연적인 힘◀ a) [U] the natural power that is used or produced when one thing moves or hits another thing ‖ 하나의 사물이 움직이거나 다른 사물을 칠 때 사용되거나 생기는 자연적인 힘. 힘. 세기: *Waves were hitting the rocks with great force.* 파도가 세차게 바위를 때리고 있었다. / *The force of the explosion threw her backwards.* 폭발의 위력 때문에 그녀는 뒤로 튕겨져 나갔다. **b)** [C, U] a natural power that produces movement in another object ‖ 다른 물체의 움직임을 만들어 내는 자연적 힘: *natural forces, such as gravity* 중력 등의 자연적 힘

5 ▶SB/STH THAT INFLUENCES 영향을 미치는 사람/사물◀ something or someone that has a strong influence or a lot of power ‖ 강한 영향력이나 많은 힘을 가진 사람이나 사물. 영향력. 지배력. 효력: *Mandela was the driving force behind the changes.* (=the one who made them happen) 만델라는 그러한 변화를 가능케 한 원동력이었다. / *a powerful force for peace/change* (=one that makes peace or change more likely to happen) 평화[변화]를 가능케 하는 힘

6 ▶STRONG EFFECT 강한 효력◀ [U] the powerful effect of someone or something ‖ 사람이나 사물의 강력한 영향: *The force of public opinion stopped the new highway project.* 여론의 영향으로 새 고속도로 건설 계획이 무산되었다.

7 join/combine forces to work together to do something ‖ 어떤 것을 하기 위해 함께 일하다. 협력하다. 힘을 합치다: *Workers are joining forces with the students to protest the new bill.* 새 법안에 항의하기 위해 근로자들이 학생들과 연대하고 있다.

8 in force a) in a large group ‖ 대규모로, 큰 무리를 지어. 대거: *The mosquitoes are going to be out in force tonight!* 모기들이 오늘밤 대거 밖으로 나올 거야! **b)** if a law or rule is in force, it must be obeyed ‖ 법이나 규칙 등이 준수되어야 하는. 법적 효력이 있는

9 by/from force of habit because you have always done a particular thing ‖ 특정한 일을 항상 해 왔기 때문에. 습관적으로: *Ken puts salt on everything by force of habit.* 켄은 모든 음식에 습관적으로 소금을 뿌린다.

USAGE NOTE force, power, strength

Force is the natural power that something has: *The force of the wind knocked the fence down.* **Power** is the ability and authority that you have to do something, or the energy that is used in order to make something work: *Congress has the power to make laws. / Their home is heated by solar power.* **Strength** is the physical quality that makes you strong: *I don't have the strength to lift this.*

force는 사물이 지닌 자연력을 말한다: 바람이 세게 불어 담장을 쓰러뜨렸다. **power**는 어떤 것을 하지 않으면 안 되는 능력·권위, 또는 어떤 것을 작동시키려고 사용하는 에너지를 말한다: 의회는 입법권이 있다. / 그들의 집은 태양력으로 난방이 된다. **strength**는 사람을 강하게 만드는 신체적 성질을 말한다: 나는 이것을 들어 올릴 힘이 없다.

---

force² *v* [T] **1** to make someone do something s/he does not want to do ‖ 남에게 원치 않는 일을 하게 하다. 억지로 …을 시키다: *Nobody's forcing you to come, you know.* 널 억지로 오라고 하는 사람은 아무도 없단 말이야. / *I had to force myself to get up this morning.* 난 오늘 아침에 억지로 일어나야 했다. / *Bad health forced him into early retirement.* 그는 건강이 안 좋아서 조기 퇴직할 수밖에 없었다. / *A truck driver forced her off the road yesterday.* 트럭 운전사는 어제 그녀를 도로 밖으로 밀어냈다. **2** to use physical strength to move something ‖ 사물을 옮기기 위해 물리적인 힘을 사용하다: *Firefighters had to force the door.* (=open it using force) 소방관들은 힘으로 문을 열어야 했다. / *Burglars had forced their way into the garage.* 강도들은 차고를 부수고 들어갔다. **3 force the issue** to do something that makes it necessary for someone to make decisions or take action ‖ 사람이 결정을 하거나 조치를 취하는데 필요한 일을 하다. 밀어부치다. 강행하다: *Don't force the issue; give them time to decide.* 너무 밀어부치지 말고 그들에게 결정할 시간을 줘라.

forced /fɔrst/ *adj* **1** done because you must do something, not because of any sincere feeling ‖ 진지한 감정 때문이 아니라 일을 해야 하기 때문에 행해진. 강요된. 억지의. 의무적인: *"It looks nice," he said with forced cheerfulness.* "좋아 보여."라고 그는 억지로 쾌활한 척하며 말했다. **2** done suddenly and quickly because a situation makes it necessary ‖ 상황이 필요로 하기 때문에 갑작스럽고 신속하게 행해진. 긴급한: *The plane had to make a forced landing in a field.* 그 비행기는 들판에 불시착해야 했다.

force-feed /'. ./ *v* [T] to force someone to eat by putting food or liquid down his/her throat ‖ 목구멍에 음식물이나 액체를 집어넣어 남을 억지로 먹게 하다. 억지로 먹이다

force·ful /'fɔrsfəl/ *adj* powerful and strong ‖ 강력하고 힘센. 힘이 있는[넘치는]. 강력한: *a forceful personality* 강인한 성격 / *a forceful argument* 치열한 논쟁 **– forcefully** *adv*

for·ceps /'fɔrsəps, -sɛps/ *n* [plural] a medical tool used for picking up, holding, or pulling things ‖ 물건을 집어올리는[집는, 당기는] 데에 쓰이는 의학 도구. 핀셋. 겸자(鉗子)

forc·i·ble /'fɔrsəbəl/ *adj* done using physical force ‖ 완력을 사용하여 행한. 힘[우격]으로의. 강제의: *There aren't any signs of forcible entry into the building.* 건물에 강제로 들어온 흔적은 없다. **– forcibly** *adv* : *The demonstrators were forcibly removed from the embassy.* 시위자들은 대사관에서 강제로 쫓겨났다.

ford¹ /fɔrd/ *n* a place in a river that is not deep, so that you can walk or drive across it ‖ 강이 깊지 않아서 걷거나 운전해 건널 수 있는 곳. 여울

ford² *v* [T] to walk or drive across a river at a place where it is not too deep ‖ 깊지 않은 곳에서 강을 가로질러 도보나 자동차로 건너다

fore /fɔr/ *n* **come to the fore** to become important or begin to have influence ‖ 중요해지거나 영향력을 갖기 시작하다. 대두되다: *Environmental issues came to the fore in the 1980s.* 1980년대에 환경 문제가 대두되었다.

fore·arm /'fɔrɑrm/ *n* the lower part of the arm between the hand and the

elbow ‖ 손과 팔꿈치 사이에 있는 팔의 아랫부분. 팔뚝 **—see picture at** BODY

fore·bod·ing /fɔr'boʊdɪŋ/ *n* [U] a feeling that something bad will happen soon ‖ 나쁜 일이 곧 일어날 것이라는 느낌. 불길한 예감: *We waited for news of the men with a sense of foreboding.* 우리는 불길한 예감으로 그 남자들의 소식을 기다렸다.

fore·cast¹ /'fɔrkæst/ *n* a description of what is likely to happen in the future, based on information you have now ‖ 현재 갖고 있는 정보에 근거한 장차 일어날 것 같은 일에 대한 설명. 예측. 예상. 예보: *the weather forecast* 일기 예보 / *the company's sales forecast* 회사의 판매량 예측

forecast² **forecast** *or* **forecasted, forecast** *or* **forecasted, forecasting** *v* [T] to say what is likely to happen in the future, based on information you have now ‖ 현재 갖고 있는 정보를 근거로 하여 장차 일어날 것 같은 일에 대해 말하다. 예상[예측, 예보]하다: *Warm weather has been forecast for this weekend.* 이번 주말은 따뜻한 날씨가 예상된다.

fore·cast·er /'fɔrkæstɚ/ *n* someone who says what is likely to happen in the future, especially the person on television who explains the weather ‖ 미래에 일어날 것 같은 일에 대해 말하는 사람, 특히 텔레비전에서 날씨를 설명하는 사람. 예측자. 일기 예보관. 기상 캐스터

fore·close /fɔr'kloʊz/ *v* [I] TECHNICAL to take away someone's property because s/he cannot pay back the money that s/he has borrowed to buy it ‖ 재산을 구입하기 위해 빌린 돈을 갚을 수 없기 때문에 그 사람의 재산을 빼앗아가다. 저당물을 유질(流質)시키다 **– foreclosure** /fɔr'kloʊʒɚ/ *n* [U]

fore·fa·thers /'fɔr,fɑðɚz/ *n* [plural] the people who were part of your family a long time ago; ANCESTORs ‖ 오래 전에 가족의 일부였던 사람들. 조상. 선조; ⊞ ancestors

fore·fin·ger /'fɔr,fɪŋɡɚ/ *n* ⇨ INDEX FINGER

fore·front /'fɔrfrʌnt/ *n* **in/at/to the forefront** in the main or most important position ‖ 주요하거나 가장 중요한 위치에. 전면[선두]에: *Today, violence has come to the forefront of society's concerns.* 오늘날 폭력은 사회의 주요 관심사가 되었다.

fore·gone con·clu·sion /,fɔrɡɔn kən'kluʒən/ *n* **be a foregone**

conclusion to be certain to have a particular result ‖ 틀림없이 특정한 결과가 되다. 어떤 결과가 필연적이다: *The last three elections were all foregone conclusions.* 지난 세 번의 선거는 모두 필연적 결론이었다

fore·ground /'fɔrɡraʊnd/ *n* **the foreground** the nearest part of a scene in a picture or photograph ‖ 그림이나 사진 속 장면의 가장 가까운 부분. 전경 — opposite BACKGROUND

fore·head /'fɔrhɛd, 'fɔrɪd, 'farɪd/ *n* the part of the face above the eyes and below the hair ‖ 얼굴에서 눈 위와 머리카락이 나는 곳 사이의 부분. 이마 —see picture at HEAD¹

for·eign /'farɪn, 'fɔrɪn/ *adj* **1** not from your own country ‖ 자신의 나라에서가 아닌. 외국의: *a foreign accent* 이국의 억양 / *the foreign languages department* 외국어 학부 / *I don't like foreign cars.* 난 외제차를 좋아하진 않아. **2** involving or dealing with other countries ‖ 외국과 관계되거나 외국과 상대하는: *the Senate Foreign Relations Committee* 상원의 국제 관계 위원회 / *foreign aid workers* 해외 구호 요원 **3 foreign to** not familiar, or not typical ‖ 친숙하거나 전형적이지 않은. 생소한: *Their way of life was completely foreign to her.* 그들의 생활 방식은 그녀에게 너무나 생소했다 **4 foreign body/matter** TECHNICAL something that has come into a place where it does not belong ‖ 속한 곳이 아닌 곳으로 들어온 사물. 이물(질). 불순물: *foreign matter in someone's eye* 어떤 사람의 눈에 들어 있는 이물질

for·eign·er /'farənɚ, 'fɔr-/ *n* someone who is from a country that is not your own ‖ 타국 출신의 사람. 외국인

> **USAGE NOTE** foreigner
>
> It is not polite to call someone from another country a **foreigner** because this can sometimes mean that s/he is strange or different in a way that we do not like. You should say that someone is "from Canada/Japan/Russia etc." instead.
> 다른 나라에서 온 사람을 foreigner라고 부르는 것은 예의에 어긋난다. 왜냐하면 때때로 **foreigner**는 우리가 좋아하지 않는 면으로 이상하거나 다른 것을 뜻하기 때문이다. 따라서 대신에 "캐나다 / 일본 / 러시아 등에서 온" 사람이라고 해야 한다.

fore·leg /'fɔrlɛɡ/ *n* one of the two front legs of an animal that has four legs ‖ 네 발 짐승의 앞쪽 두 다리 중의 하나. 앞다리

fore·lock /'fɔrlɑk/ *n* a piece of hair that falls over an animal's or person's FOREHEAD ‖ 동물이나 사람의 이마 위로 내려오는 머리카락. 앞머리

fore·man /'fɔrmən/ *n* **1** someone who is the leader of a group of workers, for example, in a factory ‖ 예컨대 공장의 노동자들의 지도자격 인물. 감독. 십장 **2** the leader of a JURY ‖ 배심장(陪審長)

fore·most /'fɔrmoʊst/ *adj* the most famous or important ‖ 가장 유명하거나 중요한: *the foremost writer of her time* 그녀가 살던 시기의 가장 중요한 작가

fo·ren·sic /fə'rɛnsɪk, -zɪk/ *adj* **1** relating to methods for finding out about a crime ‖ 범죄에 관해 알아내는 방법과 관련된. 과학 수사의. 범죄 과학의: *a specialist in forensic science* 범죄 과학 [과학 수사]의 전문가 **2** relating to arguments about the law ‖ 법에 관한 논쟁과 관련된. 변론의: *politician's forensic skill* 정치인의 변론술 – **forensics** *n* [singular]

fore·play /'fɔrpleɪ/ *n* [U] sexual activity such as touching the sexual organs and kissing, before having sex ‖ 성관계를 갖기 전 성기를 만지거나 키스하는 등의 성적 행위. 전희

fore·run·ner /'fɔr,rʌnɚ/ *n* someone or something that is an early example or a sign of something that comes later ‖ 초기의 예 또는 나중에 올 어떤 것의 표시가 되는 사람이나 사물. 선구자. 징조: *a race that was the forerunner of the Grand Prix* 그랑프리의 전조가 되었던 경주

fore·see /fɔr'si/ *v* [T] to know that something will happen before it happens ‖ 일이 일어나기 전에 이미 알다. 예상[예견]하다: *No one could have foreseen such a disaster.* 아무도 그러한 재앙을 예상하지 못했을 것이다.

fore·see·a·ble /fɔr'siəbəl/ *adj* **1 for/in the foreseeable future** for as long as anyone can know about, or in a period of time anyone can know about ‖ 누구나 알 수 있는 기간 동안이나 그 기간 안에. 당분간. 가까운 미래에(는): *Leila will be staying here for the foreseeable future.* 레일라는 당분간 여기 머물 거야. / *House prices will not rise in the foreseeable future.* 집값은 당분간 오르지 않을 것이다. **2** relating to what you can expect to happen ‖ 일어나리라 예상할 수 있는 것과 관련된. 예견할 수 있는: *foreseeable problems* 예측 가능한 문제들

fore·shad·ow /fɔr'ʃædoʊ/ *v* [T]

LITERARY to be a sign of something that will happen in the future ‖ 미래에 일어날 일의 징조가 되다. 예시하다. 전조가 되다

fore·sight /'fɔrsaɪt/ *n* [singular, U] the ability to imagine what will probably happen, and to consider this in your plans for the future ‖ 일어날 수 있는 일을 예상하고, 이를 미래의 계획 속에서 고려할 수 있는 능력. 선견지명. 통찰력: *City planners were criticized for not having the foresight to build bus lanes.* 도시 계획자들은 버스 전용 차선의 설치에 대한 선견지명이 없다고 비난받았다. — compare HINDSIGHT

fore·skin /'fɔr,skɪn/ *n* a loose fold of skin covering the end of a man's PENIS ‖ 남자의 성기 끝을 감싸고 있는 느슨하게 접힌 피부. 음경의 포피(包皮)

for·est /'fɔrɪst, 'fɑr-/ *n* [C, U] a very large number of trees, covering a large area of land ‖ 땅의 넓은 부분에 걸쳐 있는 매우 많은 나무들. 숲. 삼림: *We'll keep fighting to save our ancient forests.* 우리는 원시림을 지키기 위해 계속 싸울 것이다.

fore·stall /fɔr'stɔl/ *v* [T] to prevent an action or situation by doing something first ‖ 먼저 어떤 일을 함으로써 행동이나 상황이 발생하는 것을 막다. 미연에 방지하다. 선수를 치다: *The National Guard was sent in, to forestall trouble.* 분쟁을 미연에 방지하기 위해 주방위군(州防衛軍) 이 파견되었다.

forest rang·er /'.. ,../ *n* someone whose job is to protect or manage part of a public forest ‖ 공공림을 보호하거나 관리하는 직업인. 삼림 감시인

for·est·ry /'fɔrəstri, 'fɑr-/ *n* [U] the science and practice of planting and taking care of forests ‖ 나무를 심고 삼림을 가꾸는 것에 관한 학문과 실제. 임학. 삼림 관리

fore·taste /'fɔrteɪst/ *n* **be a foretaste of** FORMAL to be a sign of something that is likely to happen in the future ‖ 장차 일어날 것 같은 일의 징조가 되다. 전조가 되다: *The latest violence is only a foretaste of what might come.* 최근의 폭력 사태는 단지 앞으로 일어날 일의 전조일 뿐이다.

fore·tell /fɔr'tɛl/ *v* [T] to say what will happen in the future, especially by using special magic powers ‖ 특히 특별한 마술적 힘을 사용하여 미래에 일어날 일에 대해 말하다. 장래를 예언하다

fore·thought /'fɔrθɔt/ *n* [U] careful thought or planning before you do something ‖ 어떤 일을 하기 전의 세심한

고려나 계획. 사전의 깊은 생각: *A long hiking trip will require more forethought.* 장기간의 하이킹 여행을 하려면 철저한 준비가 필요하다.

for·ev·er /fə'rɛvɚ, fɔ-/ *adv* **1** for all future time; always ‖ 미래의 모든 시간 동안. 영원히; 항상: *I'll remember you forever.* 난 널 영원히 기억할 거야. / *You can't avoid him forever.* 넌 그를 영원히 피하지 못할 거야. **2** SPOKEN for a very long time ‖ 매우 오랜 시간 동안. 오랫동안. 죽: *Greg will probably be a student forever.* 그레그는 아마 오랫동안 학생 신세일 것이다. / *With traffic this slow, it'll take forever* (=take a long time) *to get to Helen's.* 교통이 이렇게 지체되니 헬렌의 집까지 가려면 시간이 오래 걸리겠다. **3 be forever doing sth** SPOKEN to do something many times, especially something that annoys people ‖ 특히 사람들을 화나게 하는 일을 여러 차례 하다: *You're forever losing those gloves!* 너 그 장갑 계속 잃어버리는구나! **4 go on forever** to be extremely long or large ‖ 지극히 길거나 크다: *The train just seemed to go on forever.* 그 열차는 끝이 없어 보였다.

fore·warn /fɔr'wɔrn/ *v* [T] **1** to warn someone about something dangerous or unpleasant that will happen ‖ 남에게 일어날 위험이나 불쾌한 일을 경고하다: *We'd been forewarned about the dangers of traveling at night.* 우리는 야간 여행의 위험성에 대해 경고를 받아 왔다. **2 forewarned is forearmed** used in order to say that if you know about something before it happens, you can be prepared for it ‖ 어떤 일이 일어나기 전에 미리 알게 되면 그에 대해 준비할 수 있다고 말하는 데에 쓰여. 유비무환

fore·wom·an /'fɔr,wʊmən/ *n* **1** a woman who is the leader of a group of workers, for example in a factory ‖ 예컨대 공장에서, 일단의 노동자들의 우두머리 여성. 여자 반장 **2** a woman who is the leader of a JURY ‖ 배심원단의 여성 장(長). 여자 배심장

fore·word /'fɔrwɚd/ *n* a short piece of writing at the beginning of a book that introduces the book or the person who wrote it ‖ 책이나 저자를 소개하는 책 첫머리의 짧은 글. 서문. 머리말

for·feit¹ /'fɔrfɪt/ *v* [T] to give something up or have it taken away from you, because of a rule or law ‖ 규칙이나 법률로 인하여 어떤 것을 포기하거나 빼앗기다. 벌로서 잃다. 몰수당하다: *Students will have to live with their parents or* *forfeit their benefits.* 학생들은 부모와 함께 살아야 하거나 혜택을 박탈당하게 될 것이다.

forfeit² *n* something that is taken away from you or something that you have to do as a punishment or because you have broken a rule or law ‖ 처벌로서 또는 규칙이나 법률을 위반했기 때문에 빼앗기는 사물이나 반드시 해야 하는 일. 몰수[박탈](되는 것)

for·gave /fər'geɪv/ *v* the past tense of FORGIVE ‖ forgive의 과거형

forge¹ /fɔrdʒ/ *v* [T] **1** to illegally copy something such as a document, a painting, or money in order to make people think it is real ‖ 남들이 진짜로 여기도록 서류[그림, 돈] 등을 불법적으로 복제하다. 위조하다: *Most experts thought the picture had been forged.* 대부분의 전문가들은 그 그림이 위조되었다고 생각했다. **2** to develop a strong relationship with other people or groups ‖ 다른 사람들이나 무리와 강한 유대관계를 맺다: *A special alliance has been forged between the US and Canada.* 미국과 캐나다 사이에는 특별한 동맹 관계가 맺어졌다. **3** to make something from a piece of metal by heating and shaping it ‖ 금속 조각을 가열하고 형태를 주어 어떤 것을 만들어내다. 단조(鍛造)하다

forge ahead *phr v* [I] to make progress quickly ‖ 빠르게 진전하다: *A small number of people who take risks are forging ahead in business.* 위험을 감수하는 소수의 사람들이 사업에서 승승장구하고 있다.

forge² *n* a large piece of equipment that is used for heating and shaping metal objects, or the building where this is done ‖ 금속 물체를 가열하고 형태를 만드는 데에 사용되는 큰 설비, 또는 이러한 작업이 이루어지는 건물. 노(爐). 대장간. 철공장

forg·er /'fɔrdʒər/ *n* someone who illegally copies documents, money, paintings etc. and tries to make people think they are real ‖ 서류·돈·그림 등을 불법 복제하여 남들이 그것들을 진짜로 믿게 하려고 애쓰는 사람. 위조자

for·ger·y /'fɔrdʒəri/ *n* **1** a document, painting, or piece of paper money that has been illegally copied; FAKE ‖ 불법 복제된 서류[그림, 지폐]. 위조[모조]품;㈜fake **2** [U] the crime of illegally copying something ‖ 어떤 것을 불법적으로 복제하는 범죄. 위조(죄)

forget /fər'gɛt/ *v* **forgot, forgotten, forgetting 1** [I, T] to be unable to remember facts, information, or something that happened ‖ 일어났던 사실[정보, 일]을 기억할 수 없다. 생각나지 않다. 잊다: *I've forgotten what her name is.* 나는 그녀의 이름이 무엇인지 생각나지 않는다. / *Don't forget (that) Linda's birthday is Friday.* 린다 생일이 금요일이라는 걸 잊지 마. / *I'd forgotten all about our bet until Bill reminded me.* 나는 빌이 일깨워 줄 때까지 우리 내기에 대해 모두 잊어버리고 있었다. **✗**DON'T SAY "I am forgetting."**✗** "I'm forgetting."이라고는 쓰지 않는다 **2** [I, T] to not remember to do something that you should do ‖ 해야 할 일을 기억하지 못하다. 잊어버리다: *Who forgot to turn off the lights?* 누가 불 끄는 것을 잊어버렸니? / *David forgot (that) we had a meeting today.* 데이비드는 오늘 우리가 모임이 있다는 것을 잊어버렸다. / *Oh, I forgot the book.* (=I did not remember to bring it) 어머나, 책 가져오는 것을 깜빡했어. **3** [I, T] to stop thinking or worrying about someone or something ‖ 사람이나 사물에 대해 생각하거나 걱정하는 것을 그만두다. 어떤 일을 잊다[무시하다]: *You'll forget (that) you're wearing contact lenses after a while.* 조금 있으면 콘택트렌즈를 착용하고 있다는 사실을 잊어버리게 될 거야. / *I can't just forget about her. We were married for six years.* 나는 그녀에 대한 생각을 멈출 수가 없어. 우리는 6년간이나 결혼 생활을 했거든 **4** [I, T] to stop planning to do or get something, because it is no longer possible ‖ 더 이상 가능하지 않기 때문에 어떤 일을 하거나 얻으려는 계획을 포기하다. 체념하다: *If you don't finish your homework, you can forget about going skiing this weekend.* 너는 숙제를 끝까지 않으면 이번 주말에 스키장 가는 것을 포기해야 해.

SPOKEN PHRASES

5 forget it a) used in order to tell someone that something is not important ‖ 남에게 어떤 일이 중요하지 않다고 말하는 데에 쓰여. 잊어버려. 괜찮아: *"I'm sorry I broke your mug." "Forget it."* "네 컵을 깨서 미안해." "괜찮아." / *"Did you say something?" "No, forget it."* "뭐라고 했어?" "아니, 별 것 아니야." **b)** used in order to tell someone to stop asking or talking about something because it is annoying you ‖ 성가시니 어떤 일에 관해 묻거나 이야기하지 말라고 남에게 말하는 데에 쓰여. 그만해: *I'm not buying* *you that bike, so just forget it.* 난 너에게 그 자전거 사 주지 않을 거야. 그러니 그만해.

6 I forget NONSTANDARD said instead of "I have forgotten" ‖ "I have forgotten"대신에 쓰여. 잊어버렸어: *You know the guy we saw last week – I forget his name.* 우리가 지난주에 봤던 남자 있지. 그 사람 이름은 잊어버렸는데.

7 forget it/you! an impolite expression that is used in order to refuse to do something, or to say that something is impossible ‖ 어떤 일 하기를 거절하거나 어떤 일이 불가능하다고 말하는 데에 쓰이는 불손한 표현. 말도 안돼. 천만에: *Drive to the airport in this snow? Forget it.* 이렇게 눈이 오는데 공항까지 차를 운전하고 가라구? 말도 안돼. / *Forget you! I took out the garbage last week.* 천만의 말씀! 지난주에 내가 쓰레기 치웠잖아.

8 ...and don't you forget it! said in order to remind someone angrily about something important that should make him/her behave differently ‖ 다르게 처신해야 마땅한 중요한 일에 대해 화를 내며 남에게 일깨워 주는 데에 쓰여. 명심해. 알았지: *I'm your father, and don't you forget it!* 나는 네 아버지야. 그 사실을 잊지 마!

—see usage note at LEAVE¹

for·get·ful /fɚˈgɛtfəl/ *adj* often forgetting things ‖ 종종 사물을 망각하는. 잘 잊는: *Papa's getting forgetful in his old age!* 아빠는 나이가 들면서 점점 건망증이 심해지네! **– forgetfulness** *n* [U]

forget-me-not /ˈ...ˌ., ˌ./ *n* a plant with small blue flowers ‖ 작고 푸른 꽃이 피는 식물. 물망초

for·give /fɚˈgɪv/ *v* **forgave, forgiven** /fɚˈgɪvən/, **forgiving** [I, T] **1** to decide not to blame someone or be angry at him/her, although s/he has done something wrong ‖ 남이 나쁜 짓을 했지만 비난하거나 화내지 않기로 결정하다. 용서하다: *Can you ever forgive me?* 나를 정말 용서할 수 있겠니? / *If you tell Laurie, I'll never forgive you for it!* 로리에게 말한다면 나는 너를 결코 용서하지 않을 거야! / *"I'm sorry." "That's OK – you're forgiven."* (=I forgive you) "미안합니다." "괜찮습니다. 이미 잊었어요." / *If anything happened to the kids, I'd never forgive myself.* 아이들에게 무슨 일이 일어난다면 나는 결코 내 자신을 용서하지 못할 것이다. / *Maybe you can*

forgive and forget, but I can't. (=forgive someone and behave as if s/he had never done anything wrong) 너는 지난 일을 깨끗이 잊어버릴 수 있을지 모르겠지만 나는 잊어버릴 수 없어 **2 forgive me** SPOKEN said when you are going to say or ask something that might seem rude or offensive ‖ 무례하거나 기분 나쁠 수 있는 말을 하거나 요청할 때 쓰여. 죄송합니다만: *Forgive me for saying so, but yellow doesn't look good on you.* 이런 말씀 죄송합니다만 노란색은 당신에게 어울리지 않는 것 같습니다. **3 forgive a loan/debt** if a country forgives a LOAN, it says that the country that borrowed the money does not have to repay it ‖ 돈을 빌린 국가에게 차관을 갚을 필요가 없다고 선언하다. 빚을 탕감[면제]하다

for·give·ness /fɚˈgɪvnɪs/ *n* [U] FORMAL the act of forgiving someone ‖ 남을 용서하기

for·giv·ing /fɚˈgɪvɪŋ/ *adj* willing to forgive ‖ 기꺼이 용서하는. 관대한: *a forgiving person* 관대한 사람

for·go /fɔrˈgoʊ/ *v* [T] FORMAL to decide not to do or have something ‖ 어떤 일을 하거나 가지지 않기로 결심하다. 삼가다. 버리다: *Johnson was not likely to forgo his executive privileges.* 존슨은 이사의 특권을 버릴 것 같지 않았다.

for·got /fɚˈgɑt/ *v* the past tense of FORGET ‖ forget의 과거형

for·got·ten /fɚˈgɑtˈn/ *v* the PAST PARTICIPLE of FORGET ‖ forget의 과거 분사형

fork¹ /fɔrk/ *n* **1** a tool used for picking up and eating food, with a handle and three or four points ‖ 손잡이와 서너 개의 뾰족한 끝이 달린, 음식을 찍어서 먹는 데에 쓰는 도구. 포크: *knives, forks, and spoons* 칼과 포크 및 숟가락 **2** a place where a road or river divides into two parts ‖ 길이나 강이 두 부분으로 갈라진 곳. 분기점: *Turn left at the fork in the road.* 도로의 분기점에서 좌회전해라. **3** ⇨ PITCHFORK

fork² *v* **1** [I] if a road or river forks, it divides into two parts ‖ 길이나 강이 두 부분으로 갈라지다 **2** [T] to pick up, carry, or turn something over using a fork ‖ 포크를 사용하여 물건을 집다[옮기다, 뒤집다]: *Anna forked more potatoes onto her plate.* 애너는 포크로 더 많은 감자를 찍어 접시에 담았다.

fork sth **over/out/up** *phr v* [T] INFORMAL to spend a lot of money on something because you have to ‖ 어쩔 수 없이 어떤 일에 많은 돈을 쓰다. 돈을 지

불하다: *I had to fork over $150 for two front-row seats.* 나는 도리 없이 앞 열 두 좌석에 150달러를 지불했다.

forked /fɔrkt/ *adj* with one end divided into two or more parts ‖ 한쪽 끝이 둘 이상으로 갈라진: *a snake's forked tongue* 뱀의 갈라진 혀

fork·lift /'fɔrk,lɪft/ *n* a vehicle with special equipment on the front for lifting and moving heavy things, for example, in a factory ‖ 예를 들면 공장에서 무거운 물건을 들어올리거나 옮기기 위해 전면에 특수 장치를 한 차량. 지게차

for·lorn /fə'lɔrn, fɔr-/ *adj* LITERARY sad and lonely ‖ 슬프고 외로운. 비참한: *a forlorn line of refugees at the station* 정거장의 비참한 난민 행렬

form¹ /fɔrm/ *n* **1** one type of something, that exists in many different types; KIND ‖ 여러 다른 형태로 존재하는 사물의 한 유형; ⓟ kind: *Ryan likes movies and other forms of entertainment.* 라이언은 영화와 그 밖의 다른 종류의 오락을 좋아한다. / *Felicia died of the same form of cancer as her mother.* 펠리시아는 자기 어머니와 같은 종류의 암으로 죽었다. **2** [C, U] the way in which something exists, is presented, or appears ‖ 사물이 존재하는[제시되는, 나타나는] 방식. 모양. 형태: *You can get the vitamin C in tablet or liquid form.* 너는 정제나 액체 형태로 비타민 C를 섭취할 수 있다. / *notes written in outline form* 개요 형식으로 쓴 편지 / *Language practice can take the form of drills or exercises.* 언어 훈련은 반복 연습이나 실습의 형태를 취한다. **3** an official document with spaces where you have to provide information ‖ 정보를 적어 넣어야 하는 공란이 있는 문서. 서식. 용지: *an application form for college* 대학의 입학 원서 / *Please fill in the form clearly.* 용지에 명확히 기입하시오 **4** a shape, especially of something you cannot see clearly ‖ 특히 확실히 볼 수 없는 사물의 형태. 모습. 그림자: *dark forms behind the trees* 나무 뒤에 있는 어두운 모습 **5** TECHNICAL in grammar, a way of writing or saying a word that shows its number, tense etc. For example, "was" is a past form of the verb "to be" ‖ 문법에서 단어가 말이나 글 속에서 수(數)나 시제 등을 나타내도록 활용하는 방법. 어형. 예를 들면 "was"는 동사 "to be"의 과거형이다.

form² *v* **1** [I, T] to start to exist, or to make something start to exist; develop ‖ 존재하기 시작하다, 또는 어떤 것이 존재하기 시작하게 하다. 형성되다. 형성하다; 발달하다: *Ice was already forming on the roads.* 이미 도로가 결빙되고 있었다. / *the cloud of dust and gas that formed the universe* 우주를 형성한 자욱한 먼지와 기체 / *Reporters had already formed the impression* (=begun to think) *that Myers was guilty.* 기자들은 이미 마이어스가 유죄라고 생각하기 시작했으다. **2** [I, T] to come together in a particular shape or a line, or to make something have a particular shape ‖ 모여서 특별한 형태나 선이 되다, 또는 사물이 특별한 형태가 되게 하다: *Form the dough into a circle, then roll it out.* 반죽을 동그랗게 만든 다음 그것을 밀어서 펴라. / *The line forms to the right.* 그 줄이 오른쪽으로 형성되어 있다. / *Our house and the barn form a big "L."* 우리 집과 헛간은 큰 "L"자 모양을 이뤄낸다 **3** [T] to start a new organization, committee, relationship etc. ‖ 새 조직체·위원회·관계 등을 구성·조직하다: *They're forming a computer club at Joan's high school.* 조안의 고등학교에서는 컴퓨터 클럽을 조직하고 있다. / *Everett seemed unable to form close friendships.* 에브릿은 절친한 교우 관계를 맺지 못하는 것 같았다. **4** [T] to make something by combining two or more parts ‖ 둘 이상의 부분을 결합하여 어떤 것을 만들다: *One way to form nouns is to add the suffix "-ness."* 명사를 만드는 한 가지 방법은 접미사 "ness"를 덧붙이는 것이다. **5** [linking verb] to be the thing, or one of the things, that makes up something else ‖ 다른 것을 구성하는 물건이나 그런 물건들 중의 하나가 되다: *Rice forms a basic part of their diet.* 쌀은 그들의 주식이다. / *The Rio Grande forms the boundary between Texas and Mexico.* 리오그란데 강은 텍사스와 멕시코의 국경을 이룬다.

for·mal¹ /'fɔrməl/ *adj* **1** formal language, behavior, or clothes are used for official or serious situations, or for when you do not know the people you are with very well ‖ 언어[행동, 옷]가 공식적이거나 중요한 상황 또는 함께 어울리는 사람들을 잘 모를 때에 사용하는. 공식의. 정식의: *a formal letter* 공식 편지 / *Jack won't wear a tie, even on formal occasions.* 잭은 심지어 공식 행사에서도 넥타이를 매지 않을 것이다. / *Please, call me Sam. There's no need to be formal.* 저를 샘이라고 부르세요. 격식 차릴 필요가 없습니다. / *men's formal wear* (=clothes for important events, parties etc.) 남성 정장 **2** official or public ‖ 공식

적인, 공공의: *a formal announcement* 공식 발표 / *The council never took a formal position on the issue.* 그 위원회는 그 문제에 대해 결코 공식적인 입장을 취하지 않았다. **3 formal education/ training/qualifications** education in a subject or skill that you get in school rather than by practical experience ‖ 실제 경험보다 학교에서 받는 학과목이나 기술의 교육. 정규 교육/훈련/ 자격증: *Most priests have no formal training in counseling.* 대부분의 성직자는 카운슬링의 정규 훈련을 받지 않는다. **– formally** *adv* —opposite INFORMAL

formal² *n* **1** a dance at which you have to wear formal clothes ‖ 정장을 입어야만 하는 무도회. 정식 무도회 **2** an expensive and usually long dress that women wear on formal occasions ‖ 공식 행사 때 여자들이 입는 비싸고 보통 긴 드레스. 야회복

for·mal·de·hyde /fɚˈmældə,haɪd, fɚ-/ *n* [U] a strong-smelling liquid that can be mixed with water and used for preserving things such as parts of a body ‖ 물과 섞여 신체의 부위 등을 보존하는 데 쓰이는 냄새가 강한 액체. (소독·방부제용) 포름알데히드

for·mal·i·ty /fɔrˈmæləti/ *n* **1** [C usually plural] something formal or official that you must do as part of an activity or process, although it may not be important ‖ 비록 중요하지 않을 수 있지만 활동이나 과정의 일부로서 반드시 해야 하는 공식적인 또는 격식적인 것. 합법[관습]적인 행위[절차]. 형식 절차[수속]: *I'm just waiting for some legal* FORMAL*ities before moving out.* 나는 이사 가기 전 몇 가지 법적 절차의 처리를 기다리고 있는 중이다. / *Ms. Cox has to interview you, but it's just a formality.* 콕스 부인이 당신을 인터뷰해야 하지만 그건 단지 요식 행위일 뿐입니다. **2** [U] careful attention to the right behavior or language in FORMAL situations ‖ 공식적 상황에서 적합한 행위나 언어에 대해 신중한 주의를 쏟는 것. 격식 준수

for·mal·ize /ˈfɔrməˌlaɪz/ *v* [T] to make a plan or decision official and describe all its details ‖ 계획이나 결정을 공식화하고 모든 세부 내용을 기술하다. …을 정식 [공식]적인 것으로 하다. 공식 형태를 갖추다[로 작성하다]: *The contracts must be formalized within one month.* 계약은 한 달 내에 공식적으로 작성되어야 한다.

for·mat¹ /ˈfɔrmæt/ *n* **1** the way something such as a computer document, television show, or meeting is organized or arranged ‖ 컴퓨터 문서 [텔레비전 쇼, 회합] 등이 구성되고 배열되는 형식. 서식. 형태. 체제. 포맷: *The interview was written in a question and answer format.* 인터뷰 내용은 질문과 답변 형식으로 쓰여졌다. **2** the size, shape, design etc. in which something such as a book, magazine, or VIDEO is produced ‖ 책[잡지, 비디오] 등이 제작되는 크기·모양·디자인 등. 체제. 구성. 판형

format² *v* **-tted, -tting** [T] **1** TECHNICAL to organize the space on a computer DISK so that information can be stored on it ‖ 정보가 저장될 수 있도록 컴퓨터 디스크의 공간을 조직화하다. 포맷하다 **2** to arrange a book, document, page etc. according to a particular design or plan ‖ 특정 구도나 계획에 따라 책·문서·페이지 등을 구성하다. 체제[형식]를 갖추다. …의 서식[포맷]을 설정하다 **– formatting** *n* [U] **– formatted** *adj*

for·ma·tion /fɔrˈmeɪʃən/ *n* **1** [U] the process by which something develops into a particular thing or shape ‖ 사물이 특정한 것이나 형태로 발전되어 가는 과정. 형성[육성, 발달](과정). 전개(과정): *rules for the formation of the past tense* 과거 시제의 형성 규칙 / *the formation of the solar system* 태양계의 형성(과정) **2** [U] the process of starting a new organization or group ‖ 새로운 조직이나 집단이 시작되는 과정. 조직. 구성. 출범. 수립: *the formation of a democratic government* 민주 정부의 수립 **3** [C, U] something that is formed in a particular shape, or the shape in which it is formed ‖ 특정 형태로 형성된 것, 또는 그것이 형성된 모양. 형성[조형](물). 대형. 진용: *rock formations* 바위층 / *ducks flying in a "V" formation* V자형으로 날아가는 청둥오리 떼 / *soldiers marching in formation* (=in a special order) 대형을 이뤄 행진하는 군인들

form·a·tive /ˈfɔrmətɪv/ *adj* having an important influence on the way something develops ‖ 사물이 발전하는 방식에 중요한 영향을 미치는. 형성[조형, 발달]의. 형을 갖추게 하는[부여하는]: *a formative stage of his career* 그의 경력 형성 단계 / *a child's formative years* (=when his/her character develops) 아동의 인격 형성기

for·mer¹ /ˈfɔrmɚ/ *adj* having a particular position before, but not now ‖ 지금은 아니지만 예전에 특정한 지위를 가진. (현재) 이전의[먼저의]. 옛날[과거]의: *a reunion of former baseball players* 전직 야구 선수들의 재회 / *our former* *president* 우리의 전직 대통령

former² *n* **the former** FORMAL the first of two people or things that are mentioned ‖ 언급된 두 사람이나 두 가지 사물 중 첫 (번)째. 전자(前者): *The former seems more likely as a possibility.* 전자가 훨씬 가능성이 있어 보인다. — compare LATTER¹

for·mer·ly /ˈfɔrmɚli/ *adv* in earlier times ‖ 더 이른 시기에. 예전[이전]에(는). 원래. 한때: *New York was formerly New Amsterdam.* 뉴욕은 예전에는 뉴 암스테르담이었다.

for·mi·da·ble /ˈfɔrmədəbəl, fɔrˈmɪdə-/ *adj* **1** very powerful or impressive ‖ 매우 강력하고 인상적인. 무서운. 겁먹게 하는. 위협적인. 경이적인: *her formidable debating skills* 상대를 꼼짝 못하게 하는 그녀의 논쟁 수완 / *a formidable opponent* 강력한[무서운] 적 **2** difficult to deal with and needing a lot of skill ‖ 다루기 어렵고 많은 기술을 요하는. 만만찮은. 곤란한. 처리하기[무찌르기] 어려운: *the formidable task of working out a peace plan* 평화안을 구현해 내는 만만찮은 과제 – **formidably** *adv*

form·less /ˈfɔrmlɪs/ *adj* without a definite shape; not clear ‖ 명확한 형태가 없는. 정형[모양]이 없는. 형태를 이루지 못한; 분명하지 않은

form let·ter /ˈ. ˌ../ *n* a standard letter that is sent to many people, without any personal details in it ‖ 일체의 사적인 내용 없이 많은 사람들에게 보내지는 표준 서한. 공한. 공식 편지

for·mu·la /ˈfɔrmyələ/ *n, plural* **formulas** *or* **formulae** /ˈfɔrmyəli/ **1** a method or set of principles that you use in order to solve a problem or to make sure that something is successful ‖ 문제를 풀거나 또는 확실하게 어떤 것을 성공시키기 위해 사용하는 방법이나 일련의 원칙들. 비법. 방책. 타개책: *a formula for peace* 평화 타개책[원칙] / *There's no magic formula for a happy marriage.* 행복한 결혼 생활을 위한 마술적인 비법은 없다. **2** a series of numbers or letters that represent a mathematical or scientific rule ‖ 수학적 또는 과학적 법칙을 나타내는 일련의 숫자나 문자. 공식. …식 **3** a list of substances used in order to make something, showing the amounts of each substance to use ‖ 사물을 만들기 위해 쓰이며 (거기에) 사용될 각 물질의 양을 나타내는 목록. 처방(전). 제조법 **4** [C, U] a liquid food for babies that is similar to a woman's breast milk ‖ 여성의 젖과 유사한 유아용 유동식. 조

제분유. 이유식

for·mu·late /ˈfɔrmyəˌleɪt/ *v* [T] **1** to develop something such as a plan or set of rules and decide all the details of how it will be followed ‖ 계획이나 일련의 규칙 등을 개발해서 어떻게 순차적으로 수행할지 자세한 내용을 결정하다. 수립[형성]하다: *Local governments will be able to formulate their own policies.* 지방 정부는 각자 자신의 정책을 수립할 수 있을 것이다. **2** to think carefully about what you want to say, and say it clearly ‖ 말하고 싶은 것에 대해 주의 깊게 생각하고 분명히 말하다. 명확히[계통적으로] 나타내다: *Ricardo asked for time to formulate a reply.* 리카르도는 답변을 정리할 시간을 요청했다. – **formulation** /ˌfɔrmyəˈleɪʃən/ *n* [C, U]

for·ni·cate /ˈfɔrnəˌkeɪt/ *v* [I] OLD-FASHIONED DISAPPROVING to have sex with someone you are not married to ‖ 결혼한 상대자가 아닌 다른 사람과 성관계를 갖다. 혼외정사를 가지다. 간음[간통]하다 – **fornication** /ˌfɔrnəˈkeɪʃən/ *n* [U]

for·sake /fəˈseɪk, fɔr-/ *v* **forsook** /-ˈsʊk/, **forsaken** /-ˈseɪkən/, **forsaking** [T] FORMAL to leave someone, especially when s/he needs you ‖ 특히 다른 사람이 자신을 필요로 할 때 떠나다. 저버리다

for·swear /fɔrˈswɛr/ *v* [T] LITERARY to stop doing something, or to promise that you will stop doing something ‖ 어떤 일을 하기를 중단하다, 또는 어떤 일을 하기를 중단할 것을 약속하다. (맹세코) 그만두다[중단하다]

fort /fɔrt/ *n* a strong building or group of buildings used by soldiers or an army for defending an important place ‖ 요충지를 방어하기 위해 군인들이나 군대에 의해 쓰이는 견고한 구조물이나 건물군(群). 요새

forte /fɔrt, ˈfɔrteɪ/ *n* **be sb's forte** to be something that someone is good at doing ‖ 어떤 사람이 잘 할 수 있는 것이 되다. …의 장점[강점]이다: *Cooking isn't my forte.* 요리는 내 장기가 아니다.

forth /fɔrθ/ *adv* **go forth** LITERARY to go out or away from where you are ‖ 현재 위치에서 나아가거나 떠나가다. 전진하다. 앞으로 나아가다 —see also **back and forth** (BACK¹), **and so on/forth** (SO¹)

forth·com·ing /ˌfɔrθˈkʌmɪŋ/ *adj* FORMAL **1** happening or coming soon ‖ 곧 일어나거나 오는. 다가오는. 박두하는: *their forthcoming marriage* 그들의 다가오는 결혼식 **2** given or offered when needed ‖ 필요할 때 주어지거나 제공되는. 준비된. 당장 쓸 수 있는. 입수되는: *If*

*more money is not forthcoming, we'll
have to close the theater.* 더 많은 돈이
들어오지 않는다면 우리는 극장 문을 닫아
야 할 것이다. **3** willing to give
information about something ‖ 어떤 일에
대한 정보를 기꺼이 주는. 적극적으로 발
언하는. 자진하여 밝히는: *Jerry's not the
type to be forthcoming about his
problems.* 제리는 자신의 문제에 대해 쉽
게 터놓는 사람이 아니다.

forth·right /'fɔrθraɪt/ *adj* saying
honestly what you think, in a way that
may seem rude ‖ 자신이 생각하는 바를
무례해 보일 정도로 솔직히 말하는. 기탄
없는. 솔직한: *a forthright answer* 솔직한
대답

for·ti·eth /'fɔrtiɪθ/ *number* 40th ‖ 40번
째

for·ti·fi·ca·tion /ˌfɔrtəfə'keɪʃən/ *n* [U]
the process of making something
stronger ‖ 어떤 것을 강하게 만드는 과정.
강화. 무장[요새]화

for·ti·fi·ca·tions /ˌfɔrtəfə'keɪʃənz/ *n*
[plural] towers, walls etc. built around
a place in order to protect it ‖ 어떤 장소
를 방어하기 위해 그 주변에 세운 망루·성
벽 등. 성채. 요새. 방벽

for·ti·fy /'fɔrtəˌfaɪ/ *v* [T] **1** to build
towers, walls etc. around a place in
order to defend it ‖ 어떤 장소를 방어하기
위해 주위에 망루·성벽 등을 세우다. 요새
화하다. (성을 쌓아) 강화[보강]하다: *a
fortified city* 요새화된 도시 **2** FORMAL or
HUMOROUS to make someone feel
physically or mentally stronger ‖ 다른 사
람을 육체적이나 정신적으로 더 강하게 느
끼게 하다. 강화하다. 강건하게 하다. 기
운을 돋우다: *We fortified ourselves with
a beer before we went.* 우리는 시작하
기 전에 맥주로 우리 마음을 든든하게 무
장했다. **3** to make food or drinks more
healthy by adding VITAMINS to them ‖ 음
식 또는 음료수에 비타민을 첨가해 건강에
더 좋도록 만들다. 영양가를 높이다[강화
하다]. 영양분을 보강하다: *vitamin D
fortified milk* 비타민 D강화 우유

for·ti·tude /'fɔrtəˌtud/ *n* [U] courage
shown when you are in pain or having a
lot of trouble ‖ 고통스럽거나 많은 문제를
겪고 있을 때 나타나는 용기. 꿋꿋함. 인
내. 불굴의 정신[용기]

for·tress /'fɔrtrɪs/ *n* a large, strong
building used for defending an
important place ‖ 요충지를 방어하는 데
이용되는 크고 강한 건물. 요새(지). 견고
[안전]한 곳

for·tu·i·tous /fɔr'tuətəs/ *adj* FORMAL
lucky and happening by chance ‖ 운 좋

게 우연히 발생하는. 우연의. 행운의: *a
fortuitous discovery* 우연한 발견

for·tu·nate /'fɔrtʃənɪt/ *adj* lucky ‖ 행운
의. 운 좋은: *We were fortunate enough
to get tickets for the last show.* 우리는
운 좋게 마지막 쇼의 표를 구했다. / *It
was fortunate that the ambulance
arrived so quickly.* 구급차가 아주 빨리
도착해서 다행이었다. —opposite
UNFORTUNATE

for·tu·nate·ly /'fɔrtʃənɪtli/ *adv*
happening because of good luck ‖ 운이
좋아서 일어나는. 다행히도. 운 좋게: *We
were late getting to the airport, but
fortunately our plane was delayed.* 우리
는 공항에 늦게 도착했지만 다행히도 우리
비행기가 연발되었다.

for·tune /'fɔrtʃən/ *n* **1** a very large
amount of money ‖ 막대한 양의 돈. 재
산. 부: *Julia must've spent a fortune
on her wedding dress.* 줄리아는 웨딩 드
레스에 많은 돈을 썼음에 틀림없다. **2**
make a fortune to gain a very large
amount of money doing something ‖ 어
떤 일을 해서 막대한 양의 돈을 벌다. 한
밑천 잡다. 큰 재산을 만들다: *Someday
he's going to make a fortune in the
music business.* 그는 언젠가 음악 사업에
서 큰 돈을 벌게 될 것이다. **3** [U] luck ‖
행운. 운(수). 운명: *I had the good
fortune to have Mrs. Dawson as my
instructor.* 도슨 여사를 교사로 모신 것은
내게 큰 행운이었다. **4 tell sb's fortune**
to use special cards or look at
someone's hand in order to tell them
what will happen to him/her in the
future ‖ 사람들에게 미래에 일어날 일에
대해 말해 주기 위해 특별한 카드를 사용
하거나 그 사람의 손을 들여다보다. 운수
[운세]를 점치다. 운(명)을 예언하다

fortune cook·ie /'.. ˌ../ *n* a Chinese-
American cookie with a piece of paper
inside it that tells you what will happen
in your future ‖ 장래에 일어날 일을 적어
놓은 쪽지를 그 안에 넣은 중국계 미국인
의 과자. 행운의 과자. 점치는 과자

fortune tell·er /'.. ˌ../ *n* someone who
tells you what is going to happen to you
in the future ‖ 장래에 벌어질 일에 대해
말해 주는 사람. 점쟁이. 사주쟁이

for·ty /'fɔrti/ *number* **1** 40 ‖ 40 **2 the
forties a)** the years between 1940 and
1949 ‖ 1940년과 1949년 사이의 연대.
40년대 **b)** the numbers between 40
and 49, especially when used for
measuring temperature ‖ 특히 온도를 잴
때 사용되는 40에서 49 사이의 숫자. 40
도대 **– fortieth** *number*

fo·rum /ˈfɔrəm/ *n* an organization, meeting, report etc. in which people have a chance to publicly discuss an important subject ǁ 사람들이 중요한 의제에 대해 공개적으로 토론할 기회를 갖는 기구·회의·보고서 등. 포럼. 공개 토론의 장[토론회, 좌담회]: *a neighborhood forum for dealing with gang problems* 갱 문제를 다루기 위한 지역 토론회

for·ward[1] /ˈfɔrwəd/ *adv* **1** also **forwards** toward a place or position that is in front of you ǁ 전면에 있는 장소나 위치 쪽으로. 앞으로: *The truck was moving forward into the road.* 트럭은 도로 쪽으로 이동하고 있었다. / *He leaned forwards to hear what they were saying.* 그는 그들이 말하는 것을 듣기 위해 앞쪽으로 몸을 기울였다. **2** toward more progress, improvement, or development ǁ 더 좋은 진보[개선, 발전]를 향해. 더 낫게. 나은 쪽으로: *NASA's space project cannot go forward without more money.* NASA의 우주 계획은 더 많은 자금이 없으면 진척될 수 없다. **3** toward the future ǁ 장래를 향해. 금후. …이후. 장래: *The company must look forward (=make plans for the future) and use the newest technology.* 회사는 반드시 장래를 내다보고 최신 기술(력)을 이용해야 한다. —see also FAST FORWARD, **look forward to** (LOOK[1]) —opposite BACKWARD[1]

forward[2] *adj* **1 forward progress/ planning/thinking etc.** progress, plans, ideas etc. that are helpful in a way that prepares you for the future ǁ 장래에 대한 대비에 도움이 되는 발전·계획·고안 등. 진보적인[선견지명의, 앞서 나가는]. 발전/계획/생각 **2** closer to a person, place etc. that is in front of you ǁ 전면에 있는 사람·장소 등에 더 가까운. 앞쪽[앞면]에 있는(의): *Troops were moved to a forward position on the battlefield.* 부대는 전장의 전면(前面)으로 이동했다. **3** at the front part of a ship, car, plane etc. ǁ 배·차·비행기 등의 선수(船首)[선두·이물]의: *the forward cabin* 이물 쪽 선실

forward[3] *v* [T] to send a message or letter that you have received to the person it was intended for, usually at his/her new address ǁ 자신이 받은 전언이나 편지를 본래의 수취인에게 보통 새 주소지로 보내다. 전송(轉送)하다. 앞으로[새 주소로] 전달하다: *The Post Office should be forwarding all my mail.* 우체국은 내 모든 우편물을 (새 주소로) 전송(轉送)해 주어야 한다.

forward[4] *n* in basketball, one of two players whose main job is to SHOOT the ball at the other team's BASKET ǁ 농구에서 상대팀의 골대에 공을 넣는 것이 주임무인 2명의 선수 중 한 명. 전위. 포워드 —see picture on page 946

for·ward·ing ad·dress /ˌ… ˈ.., ˌ… ./ *n* an address you give to someone when you move so that s/he can send your mail to you ǁ 이사할 때 자신의 우편물을 받아서 전달해 주도록 어떤 사람에게 주는 주소. 새 우편 주소. 전송[전달]지 주소

forward-look·ing /ˈ.. ˌ../, **forward-thinking** *adj* thinking about and planning for the future in a positive way, especially by being willing to try new ideas ǁ 특히 기꺼이 새로운 생각을 적용해서 긍정적으로 장래를 생각하거나 계획하는. 장래를 내다본. 선견지명이 있는. 진보적인. 전진적인: *Forward-looking businessmen are already trying this new method.* 선견지명이 있는 사업가는 이미 이 새 방식을 적용하고 있다.

fos·sil /ˈfɑsəl/ *n* part of an animal or plant that lived millions of years ago, or the shape of one of these plants or animals that is now preserved in rock ǁ 수백만 년 전에 살았던 동물이나 식물의 일부, 또는 현재 바위 속에 보존된 이들 동·식물들 중 하나의 형태. 화석 – **fossil** *adj*

fossil fu·el /ˌ… ˈ.. ../ *n* [C, U] a FUEL such as gas or oil that has been formed from plants and animals that lived millions of years ago ǁ 수백만 년 전에 살았던 동·식물에서 만들어진 가스나 기름 등의 연료. 화석 연료

fos·sil·ize /ˈfɑsəˌlaɪz/ *v* [I, T] to become a FOSSIL by being preserved in rock, or to make something do this ǁ 바위 속에 보존되어서 화석이 되다, 또는 어떤 것을 이렇게 되게 하다. 화석화하다

fos·ter[1] /ˈfɑstɚ, ˈfɑ-/ *v* [T] **1** to help to develop an idea, skill, feeling etc. ǁ 생각·기술·감정 등을 개발하도록 돕다. …을 육성[조장]하다. 발전을 촉진하다: *Keely's interested in art, and we want to foster that somehow.* 킬리는 예술에 관심이 있는데 우리는 그것을 어떻게든 길러 주고 싶다. **2** to take care of someone else's child for a period of time without becoming his/her legal parent ǁ 법적인 부모가 되지 않고 다른 사람의 아이를 한동안 돌봐 주다. 기르다. 양육하다 —compare ADOPT

foster[2] *adj* **1 foster mother/father/ parents/family** the person or people who FOSTER a child ‖ 다른 사람의 아이를 기르는 사람(들). (수)양모/부/부모/가족 **2 foster child** a child who is fostered ‖ 다른 사람에 의해 양육되는 아이. 양자[녀](養子[女]) **3 foster home** a person's or family's home where a child is fostered ‖ 다른 사람의 아이를 양육하는 사람 또는 가족의 집. 양가(養家). 수양가정

fought /fɔt/ the past tense and PAST PARTICIPLE of FIGHT ‖ fight의 과거·과거분사형

foul¹ /faʊl/ v **1** [I, T] if a sports player fouls or is fouled, s/he does something in a sport that is against the rules ‖ 운동 선수가 시합 중에 규칙에 어긋난 어떤 일을 하다. 반칙을 하다[저지르다]. 규칙을 어기다: *Johnson was fouled trying to get to the basket.* 존슨은 골 밑을 파고들다가 반칙을 얻어냈다. **2** [T] to make something very dirty ‖ 어떤 것을 매우 더러워지게 하다. 불결하게[지저분하게] 하다. …을 오염시키다: *Clouds of orange smog are fouling the city's air.* 자욱한 주황색 스모그가 도시의 공기를 오염시키고 있다.

foul sth ↔ **up** *phr v* [I, T] INFORMAL to do something wrong or to ruin something by making a mistake ‖ 잘못된 일을 하거나 잘못해서 어떤 일을 망치다. 실수하다. 죄를 범하다. 엉망으로 만들다: *She's suing her doctor for fouling up her operation.* 그녀는 수술을 잘못한 의사를 상대로 소송을 제기하고 있다.

foul² *adj* **1** very dirty or not having a pleasant smell ‖ 매우 더럽거나 불쾌한 냄새가 나는. 불결한. 지저분한. 악취를 풍기는: *a pile of foul-smelling rotting garbage* 악취를 풍기며 썩어가는 쓰레기 더미 **2 foul language** rude and offensive words ‖ 무례하고 불쾌하게 하는 말. 천한[상스러운] 말(투) **3** LITERARY evil or cruel ‖ 사악하거나 잔인한. 악랄한. 비열한

foul³ *n* an action in a sport that is against the rules ‖ 스포츠에서 규칙에 어긋나는 행위. 위반. 반칙(행위)

foul play /ˌ. './ *n* [C, U] an activity that is dishonest and unfair, especially when it is violent or illegal ‖ 특히 폭력적이거나 불법적인 경우의, 부정직하거나 불공정한 행위. 부정[배신] 행위. 범죄: *They think that there was some kind of foul play involved in the man's death.* 그들은 그 남자의 죽음에 모종의 범죄가 관련되었다고 생각한다.

found¹ /faʊnd/ the past tense and PAST PARTICIPLE of FIND ‖ find의 과거·과거분사형

found² *v* [T] **1** to start an organization, town, or institution that is intended to continue for a long time ‖ 오랫동안 존속시킬 의도로 조직[을, 기구]을 출범시키다. 설립[창립, 창설]하다: *The college was founded in 1701.* 그 대학은 1701년에 설립되었다. **2 be founded on/upon** to base your ideas, beliefs etc. on something ‖ 사상·신념 등을 어떤 것에 기초를 두다. …에 근거를 두다. …에 입각하다. …을 기초로 세우다: *The US was founded on the idea of religious freedom.* 미합중국은 종교의 자유라는 사상을 기초로 세워졌다.

foun·da·tion /faʊnˈdeɪʃən/ *n* **1** an idea, fact, or system from which a religion, way of life etc. develops ‖ 종교·생활 방식 등이 발전해 나오는 사상[사실, 체계]. 기초. 토대. 근거: *The Constitution provided/laid the foundation for the American government.* 헌법은 미국 정부의 토대를 제공했다[마련했다]. **2** an organization that collects money to be used for special purposes ‖ 특별한 목적에 쓰일 자금을 모금하는 단체. 기구. 재단: *the National Foundation for the Arts* 국립 예술 재단 **3** the solid base that is built underground to support a building ‖ 건물을 지탱하기 위해 지하에 구축한 단단한 기반. 기초. 주춧돌. 토대. 하부 구조 **4** [C, U] the action of establishing an organization, city, or institution ‖ 조직[도시, 기관]을 설립하는 것. 창설. 창립. 건설. 건립 **5 without foundation** not true, reasonable, or able to be proved ‖ 사실이 아닌[합리적이 아닌, 증명될 수 없는]. 근거[기반] 없는: *Luckily my fears were without foundation.* 다행히도 내 두려움은 기우였다.

found·er /ˈfaʊndɚ/ *n* someone who establishes a business, organization, school etc. ‖ 사업·조직·학교 등을 설립한 사람. 설립[창설]자: *the founders of Brandon College* 브랜든 대학의 설립자

found·ing fa·ther /ˌ.. ˈ../ *n* **the Founding Fathers** the men who started the government of the US by writing the Constitution and the Bill of Rights ‖ 미국 헌법과 권리장전을 작성해서 미국 정부를 출범시킨 사람들. 미국 건국의 아버지들[건국 지도자들]

found·ry /ˈfaʊndri/ *n* a place where metals are melted and made into new parts for machines ‖ 금속을 녹여서 기계의 새 부품으로 만드는 곳. 주조소. 주물 공장

foun·tain /ˈfaʊntˈn/ *n* a structure that

sends water straight up into the air, built for decoration ‖ 물을 공중으로 똑바로 분출시키는 장식용 구조물. 분수: *Children were splashing and playing in the park fountain.* 아이들은 공원의 분수에서 물장구를 치면서 놀고 있었다. —see also DRINKING FOUNTAIN

four /fɔr/ *number, n* **1 4** ‖ 4 **2** four o'clock ‖ 4시: *I'll meet you at four.* 4시에 당신을 만날 것입니다. **3 on all fours** on your hands and knees ‖ 손과 무릎으로. 네 발로 기어서: *I came in and found Andy crawling around on all fours looking for something.* 내가 방안에 들어와 보니 앤디가 무언가를 찾으며 네 발로 기어 돌아다니고 있었다.

four-leaf clo·ver /ˌ. . ˈ../ *n* a CLOVER plant with four leaves instead of the usual three, that is considered to be lucky ‖ 보통 세 개 달린 잎 대신에 행운으로 생각되는 4개의 잎을 가진 클로버 풀. 네잎 클로버

four·teen /ˌfɔrˈtin/ *number* **14** ‖ 14 – **fourteenth** *number*

fourth /fɔrθ/ *number, n* **1** 4th ‖ 네번째 **2** 1/4; quarter ‖ 1/4(4분의1); 쿼터: 5 3/4 (=said as "five and three fourths" or "five and three quarters") 5 3/4("five and three fourths" 또는 "five and three quarters"라고 읽는다) **3** [singular] also **fourth gear** a high GEAR in a car, bicycle, vehicle etc. ‖ 자동차·자전거·차량 등의 고단 기어. 4단 기어: *Suddenly I realized I was still in fourth.* 갑자기 나는 아직도 4단 기어를 넣고 있다는 것을 깨달았다.

Fourth of Ju·ly /ˌ. . .ˈ./ *n* [singular] a US national holiday to celebrate the beginning of the United States as an independent nation ‖ 독립 국가로서 미합중국의 출범을 축하하는 미국의 국경일. 미국 독립 기념일

fowl /faʊl/ *n* a bird, especially one such as a chicken that is kept for its meat and eggs ‖ 특히 고기와 알을 얻기 위해 사육하는 닭 등의 조류. 가금(家禽)

FOX /fɑks/ *n* one of the main companies that broadcasts television programs in the US ‖ 미국 내에서 TV 프로그램을 방영하는 주요 방송사 중의 하나. 폭스 방송사

fox /fɑks/ *n* **1** a wild animal like a small dog with dark red fur, a pointed face and a thick tail ‖ 검붉은 털·뾰족한 얼굴·두꺼운 꼬리를 가진, 작은 개와 비슷한 야생 동물. 여우 **2** SPOKEN an attractive person ‖ 매력적인 사람: *He is such a fox!* 그는 대단히 매력적이다!

fox·trot /ˈfɑkstrɑt/ *n* a type of formal

dancing with quick movements, or the music for this dance ‖ 빠른 움직임의 공식 사교춤 종류, 또는 이 춤을 위한 음악. 폭스트롯(4박자의 사교춤)

fox·y /ˈfɑksi/ *adj* INFORMAL someone who is foxy is sexually attractive ‖ 사람이 성적으로 매력적인. 요염한

foy·er /ˈfɔɪɚ/ *n* a room or hall at the entrance of a house, hotel, theater etc. ‖ 집·호텔·극장 등의 입구에 있는 방이나 홀. 현관홀. 로비. 휴게실

fra·cas /ˈfrækəs, ˈfreɪ-/ *n* a short noisy fight involving a lot of people ‖ 많은 사람들이 가담한 짧고 소란스런 싸움. 싸움판. 야단법석. 난동: *She was arrested after the fracas at the bowling alley.* 그녀는 볼링장에서 난동을 부린 후 체포되었다.

frac·tion /ˈfrækʃən/ *n* **1** a very small amount of something ‖ 어떤 것의 아주 적은 양. 조금. 소량. 단편: *At Mo's Motors we're selling cars for a fraction of the manufacturer's price!* 모의 자동차 대리점에서는 공장가보다 저렴한 가격에 자동차를 판매하고 있습니다! **2** a number that is smaller than 1; 3/4 and 1/4 are fractions ‖ 1보다 작은 수. 분수; 4분의 3과 4분의 1은 분수이다. – **fractional** *adj* – **fractionally** *adv*

frac·tious /ˈfrækʃəs/ *adj* someone who is fractious gets angry very easily and tends to start fights ‖ 사람이 쉽게 화를 내고 싸움을 거는 일이 많은. 성을 잘 내는. 싸우기 좋아하는

frac·ture[1] /ˈfræktʃɚ/ *n* TECHNICAL a crack or break in something hard such as a bone or rock ‖ 뼈나 바위 등 단단한 물체에 난 금이나 깨진 부위. 골절. 파손. 파열

fracture[2] *v* [I, T] TECHNICAL to crack or break something hard such as a bone or rock ‖ 뼈나 바위 등 단단한 것을 금가게 하거나 깨뜨리다. 부러지다. 부러뜨리다. 골절[파손·파열]되다[시키다]: *He fractured his arm when he fell.* 그는 떨어져서 팔이 골절되었다.

frag·ile /ˈfrædʒəl/ *adj* **1** easily broken, damaged, or ruined ‖ 쉽게 부서지는[파손되는, 망가지는]. 깨지기 쉬운: *Be careful with that vase – it's very fragile.* 저 꽃병 조심하세요. 깨지기 쉽습니다. **2** able to be harmed easily ‖ 쉽게 손상 입을 수 있는. 약한. 연약한. 허약한: *Remember that chicks are fragile creatures and need to be treated with care.* 병아리들은 연약한 생명체여서 조심스럽게 취급해야 함을 명심해라. – **fragility** /frəˈdʒɪləti/ *n* [U]

frag·ment /ˈfrægmənt/ *n* **1** a part of

something, or a small piece that has broken off of something ‖ 사물의 일부, 또는 사물의 쪼개진 작은 조각. 단편. 파편: *Only fragments of the text have survived.* 텍스트(내용)의 단지 일부만 남았다. / *fragments of glass* 유리 조각[파편] **2** also **sentence fragment** a sentence that is not complete, often because it does not have a verb ‖ 종종 동사가 없어서 불완전한 문장. 단문(장) —**fragment** /fræɡˈmɛnt/ *v* [T]

frag·ment·ed /ˈfræɡ,mɛntɪd/ *adj* separated into many parts, groups, or events and not seeming to have a main purpose ‖ 많은 부분[집단, 사건]으로 분리되고 주된 목적이 없어 보이는. 조각조각 난. 분열된. 단편적인: *Our society seems to be becoming more fragmented.* 우리 사회는 더욱 분열되어 가고 있는 것처럼 보인다.

fra·grance /ˈfreɪɡrəns/ *n* [C, U] a pleasant smell ‖ 기분 좋은 냄새. 향기. 방향: *the sweet, spicy fragrance of the flowers* 달콤하고 강렬한 꽃향기 —see usage note at SMELL²

fra·grant /ˈfreɪɡrənt/ *adj* having a pleasant smell ‖ 기분 좋은 향을 가진. 냄새가 좋은. 향기로운: *a fragrant bouquet of red roses* 향기로운 빨간 장미 꽃다발

frail /freɪl/ *adj* thin and weak, especially because of being old ‖ 특히 늙어서 여위고 약한. 허약한. 연약한: *Grandpa looked tiny and frail in the hospital bed.* 병원 침대에 누워 계신 할아버지는 조그맣고 연약해 보였다.

frail·ty /ˈfreɪlti/ *n* [C, U] FORMAL the lack of strength, determination, or confidence ‖ 힘[결단력, 자신감]의 결여. 무름. 결점: *human frailties* 인간의 나약함

frame¹ /freɪm/ *n* **1** a firm structure that holds or surrounds something such as a picture, door, or window ‖ 그림[문·창문] 등을 고정하고 있거나 둘러싸고 있는 단단한 구조물. 틀. 테(두리). 액자: *I should put this graduation picture in a frame.* 나는 이 졸업 사진을 액자에 넣어야 한다. / *Wes leaned against the door frame.* 웨스는 문틀에 기대었다. **2** the main structure that supports something such as a house, piece of furniture, or vehicle ‖ 가옥[가구, 차량] 등을 지탱하는 주요 구조물. 토대. 뼈대. 프레임. 골조: *a bicycle frame* 자전거의 뼈대 / *a frame house* (=with a wooden frame) 목조 가옥 **3** LITERARY someone's body ‖ 사람의 신체. 체격. 골격. 몸(매): *her slender frame* 그녀의 호리호리한 몸매 **4 frame of mind** a particular attitude or feeling

that you have ‖ 사람이 갖고 있는 특정 태도나 감정. 마음[감정] 상태. 기분: *Melissa was in a good frame of mind when we visited.* 멜리사는 우리가 방문했을 때 기분이 좋은 상태였다. **5 frame of reference** all your knowledge, experiences etc. that influence the way you think ‖ 사람이 생각하는 방식에 영향을 미치는 그의 모든 지식·경험 등. (판단·분석의) 기준 체계. 준거 기준

frame² *v* [T] **1** to put a structure around something to support or hold it firmly ‖ 사물을 단단히 지지하거나 고정시키기 위해 그 주위에 구조물을 설치하다. 테를 두르다. 틀을 만들어 붙이다. 액자에 끼우다: *I have a Monet print that I want to get framed.* 나는 액자에 끼워 넣고 싶은 모네 그림의 복사본을 가지고 있다. **2** to try to make someone seem guilty of a crime by deliberately giving false information ‖ 고의로 거짓 정보를 제공해 어떤 사람이 죄를 지은 것처럼 보이게 하려 하다. 남에게 죄를 씌우다[누명을 씌우다]. 함정에 빠뜨리다: *Murphy claims he was framed by his partner.* 머피는 동료에 의해 누명을 쓰게 되었다고 주장한다. **3** FORMAL to organize the way you are going to say a question or statement ‖ 말하려고 하는 질문이나 진술 방식을 체계화하다. 체계를 세우다. 구상하다: *Frank thought carefully, framing his response.* 프랭크는 자신이 보일 반응을 머리를 짜내며 주의 깊게 생각했다.

frames /freɪmz/ *n* [plural] the metal or plastic part of a pair of GLASSES that surrounds each LENS ‖ 각각의 안경 렌즈를 둘러싸고 있는 금속이나 플라스틱 부분. 안경테 —see picture at CLASSES

frame·work /ˈfreɪmwɔk/ *n* **1** a set of rules, beliefs, knowledge etc. that people use when making a decision or planning something ‖ 사람들이 결정을 내리거나 어떤 일을 계획할 때 사용하는 규칙·신념·지식 등의 한 체계. 틀. 기준[준거] 체계: *We were working within the framework of our financial aims.* 우리는 재정적 목표의 틀 안에서 작업하고 있었다. **2** the main structure that supports a large thing such as a building or vehicle ‖ 건물이나 차량 등 큰 물체를 받치는 주요 구조물. 뼈대. 골격

fran·chise /ˈfræntʃaɪz/ *n* permission that a company gives to a person or group so that she, he, or it can sell the company's products or services ‖ 사람이나 집단이 회사의 상품이나 용역을 팔 수 있도록 해주는 허가. 독점 판매권. 프랜차이즈(권)

frank /fræŋk/ *adj* honest and direct in the way that you speak ‖ 말하는 방식이 정직하고 직접적인. 솔직한. 툭 터놓는. 거리낌 없는[숨김없는]: *Jane and I have always been frank with each other about our feelings.* 제인과 나는 항상 우리의 감정에 대해 서로에게 솔직해 왔다.

frank·fur·ter /'fræŋk,fətər/, **frank** /fræŋk/ *n* a long rounded piece of cooked meat, often eaten in a long round piece of bread; HOT DOG ‖ 흔히 길고 둥근 빵조각에 넣어 먹는 길고 둥글게 조리된 고기 조각. 핫도그. 핫도그 고기; 魚 hot dog.

frank·ly /'fræŋkli/ *adv* **1** used in order to show that you are saying what you really think about something ‖ 사물에 대해 실제로 생각하고 있는 바를 말하고 있음을 나타내는 데에 쓰여. 솔직히[숨김없이, 기탄없이] 말해서: *Frankly, I don't want to be near her if she's going to be moody.* 솔직히 말해서 그녀가 우울해질 거라면 그녀 가까이 있고 싶지 않다. **2** honestly and directly ‖ 솔직하고 직접적으로. 있는 그대로 말해. 터놓고: *Alphonso frankly told us his concerns.* 알폰소는 그의 걱정을 우리에게 터놓고 얘기했다.

fran·tic /'fræntɪk/ *adj* **1** extremely hurried and not very organized ‖ 매우 서두르며 조직화되지 않은. 열팡[광란]하는. 정신없는. 허둥지둥 하는: *The mall was full of frantic Christmas shoppers.* 쇼핑몰은 쇼핑에 정신없는 크리스마스 구매객들로 가득 찼다. **2** very worried, frightened, or anxious ‖ 매우 걱정하는[겁먹은, 조바심치는]. 안절부절못하는. 어쩔 줄 모르는·미칠 것 같은. 필사적인: *The police tried to calm the boy's frantic mother.* 경찰은 안절부절못하는 소년의 어머니를 진정시키기 위해 애썼다. – **frantically** *adv*

frat¹ /fræt/ *adj* INFORMAL belonging or relating to a FRATERNITY ‖ 학생들의 클럽에 속하거나 관련된. 학생 써클의: *a frat house* 학생 우애회원들이 (집단으로)사는 집

frat² *n* INFORMAL ⇨ FRATERNITY

fra·ter·nal /frə'tənl/ *adj* **1** friendly because you share the same interests with someone ‖ 어떤 사람과 똑같은 관심을 공유하고 있어서 친밀한. 형제 같은. 동지애[우애]의: *a fraternal organization* 우애회 조직[단체] **2** relating to brothers ‖ 형제와 관련된. 형제의. 형제다운: *fraternal love* 형제애

fra·ter·ni·ty /frə'tənəti/ *n* **1** also **fraternity house** /.'... ,./ a club at a college or university that has only male members ‖ 남자 회원들만 있는 전문대학이나 대학의 클럽. (남자 대학생) 우애회 —compare SORORITY **2** [U] a feeling of friendship among people who have the same interests, job, or nationality ‖ 같은 관심[직업, 국적]을 갖는 사람들 사이의 우정의 감정. 형제애. 우애

frat·er·nize /'frætə,naɪz/ *v* [I] to be friendly with someone who is not allowed to be your friend ‖ 친구 관계가 허용되지 않는 사람과 친하게 지내다. 허물없이 지내다. 친하게 교제하다: *Soldiers who fraternize with the enemy will be shot.* 적군과 내통하는 병사들은 총살될 것이다.

fraud /frɔd/ *n* **1** [C, U] the illegal action of deceiving people in order to gain money ‖ 금전을 취득하기 위해 사람을 기망하는 불법 행위. 사기 행위. 협잡. 부정 행위: *The police arrested him for tax fraud.* 경찰은 세금 포탈로 그를 체포했다. **2** someone who pretends to be someone else in order to gain money, friendship etc. ‖ 돈·우정 등을 획득하기 위해 다른 사람인 체하는 사람. 사기꾼

fraud·u·lent /'frɔdʒələnt/ *adj* intended to deceive people ‖ 다른 사람들을 속일 의도의. 사기의. 부정한. 가짜로 만든. 위조의: *the sale of fraudulent bonds* 위조 채권 판매 / *fraudulent statements* 거짓 진술 – **fraudulently** *adv*

fraught /frɔt/ *adj* **fraught with problems/danger/pain etc.** full of problems, danger, pain etc. ‖ 문제·위험·고통 등으로 가득 찬: *"I'm so sorry," he said in a voice fraught with emotion.* "정말 미안합니다."라고 그는 진심 어린 목소리로 말했다.

fray¹ /freɪ/ *v* [I] if a cloth or rope frays, its threads become loose because it is old or torn ‖ 천이나 밧줄이 낡거나 찢겨서 그 실들이 헐렁해지다. 닳다. 닳아서 해지다. 올이 풀리다

fray² *n* **the fray** a fight or argument ‖ 싸움이나 말다툼. 분쟁. 논쟁. 언쟁: *Then, two junior congressmen joined/entered the fray.* 그리고서 두 명의 젊은 의원들이 논쟁에 가담했다[뛰어들었다].

fraz·zled /'fræzəld/ *adj* INFORMAL confused, tired, and worried ‖ 혼란스러운·피곤한·걱정스런. 기진맥진한. 완전히 닳아서 해진

freak¹ /frik/ **1 bike/movie/health etc. freak** someone who is so interested in bikes, movies etc. that other people think s/he is strange ‖ 자전거·영화 등에 너무 관심이 많아 다른 사람들이 이상하게

생각하는 사람. 자전거/영화/건강 광(狂): *Pat is turning into a health freak.* (=she's become very interested in being healthy) 팻은 건강광으로 변해 가고 있다. **2** someone or something that looks very strange or behaves in an unusual way ‖ 매우 이상해 보이거나 보통과 다르게 행동하는 사람이나 사물. 기형(종). 변종. 돌연변이. 괴짜. 별종: *He looked at me as if I were some kind of freak.* 그는 내가 마치 어떤 종류의 별종이나 되는 것처럼 나를 바라봤다. **3 by some freak (of nature)** happening without any reason ‖ 아무 이유없이 일어나는. (자연의) 변덕[이변·이상 현상]으로: *By some strange freak it started snowing in August.* 기이한 이상 현상으로 8월에 눈이 내리기 시작했다.

freak² *adj* **freak accident/storm etc.** a very unusual accident, storm etc. ‖ 아주 특이한 사건·폭풍 등. 이변적 사건/폭풍

freak³ *v* [I, T] SPOKEN also **freak out** to suddenly become very angry, frightened, or anxious, or to make someone do this ‖ 갑자기 매우 화나게[겁이 나게, 걱정하게] 되다, 또는 어떤 사람을 이렇게 되게 하다. 안절부절못하게 되다[만들다]. 이성을 잃다[잃게 하다]: *Mom totally freaked when Dad wasn't home on time.* 엄마는 아빠가 제 시간에 집에 안 들어오자 안절부절못하셨다. / *Horror films always freak me out.* 공포 영화는 항상 겁이 나게 만든다.

freak·y /'friki/ *adj* SPOKEN strange and slightly frightening ‖ 이상하고 약간 겁이 나게 하는. 기묘한. 불길한: *That was a freaky movie!* 그것은 머리털이 곤두서는 영화였다.

freck·le /'frɛkəl/ *n* [C usually plural] a small brown spot on someone's skin, especially the face ‖ 사람의 피부, 특히 얼굴에 난 작은 갈색 반점. 주근깨. 기미: *a little girl with red hair and freckles* 빨강 머리에 주근깨가 있는 작은 소녀 – **freckled** *adj*

free¹ /fri/ *adj*
1 ▶NOT RESTRICTED 제한되지 않은◀ allowed to live, exist, or happen without being controlled or restricted ‖ 통제되거나 제한되지 않고 사는[존재하는, 일어나는] 것이 허용된. 구속[속박]받지 않는. 자유로운. 자유롭게[마음대로] 할 수 있는: *People should be free to choose their own religion.* 사람들은 자신의 종교 선택에서 자유로워야 한다. / *This is the country's first free election* (=not controlled by the government) *in 30 years.* 이번이 이 나라의 30년 만의 첫 자유선거이다.

2 ▶NO COST 무료의◀ not costing any money ‖ 돈이 전혀 들지 않는. 무료의. 공짜의. 무상의. 대가 없는: *I won free tickets for tonight's concert.* 나는 오늘 밤 음악회의 무료 관람권을 얻었다.

3 not having any of a particular substance ‖ 특정 물질이 전혀 없는. …이 없는. 무(無)… [이 들어가지을 첨가하지] 않은: *sugar-free bubble gum* 무설탕 풍선껌

4 ▶NOT BUSY 바쁘지 않은◀ not busy doing other things ‖ 다른 일을 하느라 바쁘지 않은. 한가한. 예정이 빈. 일이 없는: *If you're free next weekend do you want to go see a movie?* 다음 주 한가하시면 영화 보러 가시겠습니까?

5 ▶NOT BEING USED 사용되고 있지 않은◀ not being used at this time ‖ 현재 쓰이고 있지 않은. 비어 있는. 누구나 이용할 수 있는. 개방된: *Excuse me, is this seat free?* 실례합니다, 이 자리 비어 있습니까?

6 feel free SPOKEN used in order to tell someone that s/he is allowed to do something ‖ 어떤 사람에게 어떤 일을 해도 좋다고 말하는 데 쓰여. 자유롭게 …하다: *Feel free to ask me any questions after the class.* 부담 갖지 말고 수업 후 무슨 질문이든 해 보세요.

7 ▶NOT A PRISONER 죄수가 아닌◀ not a prisoner or SLAVE ‖ 죄수나 노예가 아닌. 자유의 몸인. 자유인의. 감금[구속]되어 있지 않은: *The UN demanded that the three American hostages be set free.* (=be given their freedom) UN은 세 명의 미국인 인질들이 석방되어야 한다고 요구했다.

8 free of/from sth without something, especially something bad or unpleasant ‖ 어떤 일, 특히 나쁜 일이나 불쾌한 일이 없는. …을 면한. …에서 벗어난. …이 제거된: *free of danger* 위험이 없는 / *free from disease* 질병이 없는

free² *v* [T] **1** to allow someone to leave a place where s/he has been forced to stay, such as a prison ‖ 어떤 사람에게 감옥 등 강제로 머무르게 했던 곳을 떠나게 허용하다. 자유롭게 하다. 석방하다: *Nelson Mandela was freed in 1990.* 넬슨 만델라는 1990년에 석방되었다. **2** to move someone or something that is trapped or stuck, or to make something loose ‖ 덫에 걸리거나 꼼짝 못하는 사람이나 사물을 움직이게 하다, 또는 사물을 풀리게 하다. 해방하다[시키다]. 움직이게 하다[빠져 나오게 하다]: *Firefighters* *helped free two men trapped in the burning car.* 소방수들이 불타는 차 속에 갇힌 두 남자가 빠져 나오게 도와주었다. **3** to help someone by removing something that is bad or unpleasant ‖ 나쁘거나 불쾌한 일을 제거해서 어떤 사람을 돕다. …을 없애 주다[치워 주다]. …을 제거해 풀어 주다: *The scholarship has freed her from having to work while she studies.* 장학금 덕분에 그녀는 학업 중 일을 해야 하는 부담에서 벗어났다. **4** also **free up** to help someone be able to do something or to make something be able to be used ‖ 어떤 사람이 어떤 일을 할 수 있게 돕다, 또는 어떤 것이 이용될 수 있게 하다. …에서 벗어나[자유롭게] 하다. …할 수 있게 해주다: *Hiring an assistant will free up your time to do other tasks.* 조수를 고용하면 당신은 자유롭게 다른 과제를 할 수 있게 될 것입니다.

free³ *adv* **1** without having to pay any money ‖ 돈을 전혀 지불할 필요 없이. 무료로. 공짜로. 대가 없이. 무상으로: *Students can visit the museum free of charge.* 학생들은 무료로 박물관을 관람할 수 있다. / *Kyle is fixing my car for free.* 카일이 무료로 내 차를 고치고 있다. **2** not being restricted or controlled by someone ‖ 어떤 사람에 의해 제한되거나 통제되지 않고. 자유롭게. 방해받지 않고. 마음대로. 제한 없이: *Lucille finally broke free* (=left a person, place, or situation that restricted her) *and started a new life in Oregon.* 루실은 마침내 자유롭게 풀려나 오레곤 주에서 새 인생을 시작했다 **3** not stuck or held in a particular place or position ‖ 특정 장소나 위치에 끼였거나 고정되어 있지 않고. 느슨하게. 풀려서. 헐거워져서: *He grabbed my wrist but I managed to struggle/pull free.* (=move to become free) 그는 내 손목을 붙잡았지만 나는 몸부림쳐서[당겨서] 가까스로 빠져나왔다.

free·bie, freebee /'fribi/ *n* INFORMAL something that you are given that you do not have to pay for, especially by a business, store etc. ‖ 돈을 지불할 필요 없이 특히 기업·가게 등이 주는 것. 공짜로 주는[받는] 것(사은품, 무료입장권 등)

free·dom /'fridəm/ *n* **1** [C, U] the right to do whatever you want without being restricted or controlled by someone else ‖ 다른 사람에 의한 제한이나 통제 없이 무엇이든 원하는 것을 할 수 있는 권리. 자유. 자주: *freedom of speech/religion etc.* (=the legal right to say what you want, choose your own religion etc.) 언

론[종교] 등의 자유 / *The government must respect our basic freedoms.* 정부는 우리의 기본적 자유를 존중해야 한다. **2** [U] the state of being free and allowed to do what you want ‖ 자유로운 상태·원하는 것을 하도록 허용되어 있는 상태. 해방(되어 있는 상태)·통제[간섭]받지 않는 상태: *My father thinks that kids have too much freedom these days.* 내 아버지는 요즈음 아이들이 너무 지나친 자유를 누린다고 생각하신다. **3 freedom from sth** the state of not being hurt or affected by something ‖ 어떤 것에 의한 상해나 영향을 받지 않게 된 상태. …으로부터의 자유. …이 없는[당하지 않는] 자유: *freedom from hunger* 기아로부터의 자유[해방]

freedom fight·er /'.. ,../ *n* someone who fights in a war against a dishonest government, army etc. ‖ 부정한 정부·군대 등에 대항하는 전쟁에서 싸우는 사람. 자유의 투사

free en·ter·prise /,. '../ *n* [U] the freedom for companies to control their own business without being limited by the government very much ‖ 정부에 의해 심하게 제한받지 않고 기업이 자신의 사업을 운영할 수 있는 자유. 자유 기업(제)

free-for-all /'. . ,./ *n* INFORMAL a fight or noisy argument that a lot of people join ‖ 많은 사람들이 가담하는 싸움이나 소란스러운 다툼. 집단적인 난투. 패싸움: *The argument in the bar turned into a free-for-all.* 술집에서 일어난 말다툼은 난투극으로 변했다.

free·hand /'frihænd/ *adj* drawn without any special tools, by using just your hands and a pen or pencil ‖ 특별 도구가 전혀 없이 단지 손과 펜 또는 연필로만 그린. 손으로 자유롭게[손으로만] 그린. 자재 화법의

free·lance /'frilæns/ *adj, adv* doing work for a company without being one of its regular workers ‖ 정규 직원 중 한 명이 되지 않고 회사를 위해 일하는. 자유 계약의. 자유직의: *She worked as a freelance journalist for 15 years.* 그녀는 자유 계약 기자로 15년간 일했다. – **freelancer** *n* – **freelance** *v* [I]

free·load /'friloud/ *v* [I] INFORMAL to eat other people's food, use their money etc. without giving them anything in return ‖ 아무것도 대가로 주지 않고 다른 사람의 음식을 먹고 다른 사람의 돈 등을 쓰다. 공짜로 얻어먹다[이용하다]. 기식하다. 무임승차하다 – **freeloader** *n*

free·ly /'frili/ *adv* **1** in a way that shows you are not afraid to express what you believe ‖ 믿는 바를 거리낌 없이 표현한다고 보여주듯이. 두려움[거리낌] 없이. 자유롭게: *We encourage our students to speak freely.* 우리는 학생들이 자유롭게 발언하도록 권장한다. **2** without any restrictions ‖ 어떤 제한도 없이. 장애[구애]받지 않고. 무제한으로: *People can now travel freely across the border.* 사람들은 이제 국경을 넘어 자유롭게 여행할 수 있다. **3 freely admit/acknowledge** to say that something is true, even though this is difficult ‖ 비록 (인정한다는 것이) 어렵지만 어떤 것이 사실이라고 말하다. 솔직하게 인정하다/시인하다: *I freely admit I made a bad choice.* 나는 선택을 잘못했다고 솔직히 인정한다. **4** generously or in large amounts ‖ 관대하게 또는 대량으로. 아낌없이: *a company that gives freely to local charities* 지역 자선 사업에 아낌없이 기부하는 회사

free mar·ket /ˌ. ˈ../ *n* [singular] a situation in which prices are not controlled by the government or any other powerful group ‖ 정부나 다른 모든 유력한 집단에 의해서 가격이 통제되지 않는 상황. 자유 시장 (경제)

free speech /ˌ. ˈ./ *n* [U] the act of saying or right to say anything you want to ‖ 원하는 것은 어떤 것이나 말하는 행위나 권리. 언론의 자유: *We are guaranteed the right to free speech in the US Constitution.* 우리는 미합중국 헌법 하에서 언론의 자유를 보장받고 있다.

free·think·er /ˌfriˈθɪŋkɚ/ *n* someone who does not accept official opinions or ideas, especially about religion ‖ 특히 종교에 대한 공식 견해나 생각을 받아들이지 않는 사람. (종교상의) 자유 사상가 – **free-thinking** *adj*

free throw /ˈ. ./ *n* an occasion in the game of basketball when a player is allowed to throw the ball without any opposition, because another player has FOUL*ed* him/her ‖ 농구 시합 중에 다른 팀의 선수가 반칙했기 때문에 선수가 아무런 방해없이 볼을 던지는 것이 허용되는 경우. 자유투. 프리 스로

free·ware /ˈfriwɛr/ *n* [U] computer SOFTWARE that is given away free ‖ 무료로 주어지는 컴퓨터 소프트웨어 프로그램. 프리웨어(프로그램)

free·way /ˈfriweɪ/ *n* a very wide road in a city on which cars can travel at a fast speed ‖ 자동차들이 빠른 속도로 갈 수 있는 도시 내의 아주 넓은 도로. 고속(화)도로

free·wheel·ing /ˌfriˈwilɪŋ·/ *adj*

INFORMAL having the quality of not worrying about rules or being responsible for something ‖ 규칙에 대해 걱정하지 않거나 어떤 것에 책임지지 않는 성질을 가진. 자유분방한. (규칙에) 얽매이지 않는. 제멋대로의: *a freewheeling lifestyle* 자유분방한 생활방식

free will /ˌ. ˈ./ *n* **do sth of your own free will** to do something because you want to and not because someone forces you to ‖ 남이 강요해서가 아니라 자신이 하고 싶어서 어떤 일을 하다. 자유의지로[자발적으로] …하다: *She's offered to go of her own free will.* 그녀는 자발적으로 가겠다고 제안했다.

freeze¹ /friz/ *v* **froze, frozen, freezing** **1** [I, T] if a liquid or thing freezes or something freezes it, it becomes solid and hard because it is so cold ‖ 날씨가 매우 추워서 액체나 사물이 굳어지고 단단해지다 또는 어떤 것이 그렇게 되게 하다. 얼다[얼리다]. 얼어붙(게 하)다: *Last winter it was so cold that the water pipes froze.* 지난 겨울 너무 추워서 수도관이 얼었다. **2** [I, T] to preserve food for a long time by keeping it very cold in a FREEZER ‖ 음식을 냉장고에 매우 차게 보관해서 장기간 보존하다. 냉동시키다[보관하다]. 얼려 보관하다: *Do you want to freeze some of these pies?* 이들 파이 몇 조각을 냉동 보관하시겠습니까? **3 it's freezing** SPOKEN said when the temperature is extremely cold ‖ 기온이 극히 추울 때 쓰여. (얼어붙을 정도로) 매우 춥다[추워지다] **4 be freezing** SPOKEN to feel very cold ‖ 매우 춥게 느끼다. 몹시 추워지다. 꽁꽁 얼어붙다: *Man, we were freezing out there in the car.* 이야, 우리는 저 밖의 차에서 추워서 꽁꽁 얼어 붙을 것 같았다. —see usage note at TEMPERATURE **5** [I] to suddenly stop moving and stay very quiet and still ‖ 갑자기 움직임을 멈추고 매우 조용하게 가만히 있다. 꼼짝하지 않고 있다. 얼어붙어 있다: *Officer Greer shouted, "Freeze!"* 그러자 경찰관은 "꼼짝 마!"라고 외쳤다. **6** [T] to officially prevent money from being spent, or prevent prices, wages etc. from being increased ‖ 공식적으로 돈의 소비를 막거나 가격·임금 등이 오르는 것을 막다. 동결시키다. 차단[제한]하다

freeze up *phr v* [I] to be unable to move, speak, or do anything because you are so nervous or frightened ‖ 너무 긴장되거나 겁이 나서 움직이지[말하지, 아무것도 하지] 못하다. 얼어붙어 …하지 못하다. 꼼짝 못하고 굳어지다: *He* *freezes up whenever she asks him a question.* 그는 그녀가 질문을 할 때마다 꼼짝 못하고 얼어붙는다.

freeze² n **1 price/wage freeze** an occasion when prices or wages are not allowed to be increased ‖ 가격이나 임금이 오르는 것이 허용되지 않는 경우. 가격/임금 동결 **2** a short period of time, especially at night, when the temperature is very low ‖ 특히 밤에 기온이 몹시 낮은 짧은 시기. 결빙기(結氷期). 혹한기(酷寒期)

freeze-dried /'. ./ adj freeze-dried food or drinks are preserved by being frozen and then dried very quickly ‖ 식품이나 음료수가 냉동된 후 급속 건조되어 보관되는. 동결 건조된: *freeze-dried coffee* 동결 건조 커피

freez·er /'frizɚ/ n a large piece of electrical equipment that is usually part of a REFRIGERATOR and is used for storing food at a very low temperature for a long time ‖ 보통 냉동 장치의 일부분으로 매우 낮은 온도에서 장시간 음식물을 저장하는 데 사용되는 대형 전기 장치. 냉동기[장치] —see picture at KITCHEN

freez·ing /'frizɪŋ/ n [U] **above/below freezing** above or below 32°F or 0°C, the temperature at which water freezes ‖ 물이 어는 온도인 화씨 32도 또는 섭씨 0도 위로 또는 아래로. 빙점 이상/이하로

freezing point /'.. ,./ n TECHNICAL the temperature at which a liquid freezes ‖ 액체가 어는 온도. 빙점

freight /freɪt/ n [U] **1** goods that are carried by train, plane, or ship ‖ 열차[비행기, 배]로 실어 나르는 화물 **2** ⇨ FREIGHT TRAIN

freight·er /'freɪtɚ/ n a plane or ship that carries goods ‖ 화물을 수송하는 비행기나 배. 화물 수송기. 화물선

freight train /'. ./ n a train that carries goods ‖ 화물을 수송하는 열차. 화물 열차

French¹ /frɛntʃ/ adj **1** relating to or coming from France ‖ 프랑스와 관련되거나 프랑스산의. 프랑스(산)의 **2** relating to the French language ‖ 프랑스어와 관련된. 프랑스어의

French² n **1** [U] the language used in France ‖ 프랑스에서 사용하는 언어. 프랑스어 **2 the French** [plural] the people of France ‖ 프랑스 사람들. 프랑스인[국민]

French bread /,. './ n [U] white bread that is shaped like a long stick ‖ 긴 막대 모양의 흰 빵. 바게트빵

French fry /'. ./ n [C usually plural] ⇨ FRIES

French toast /,. './ n [U] pieces of bread that are put into a mixture of egg and milk, then cooked in hot oil ‖ 계란과 우유의 혼합물에 넣었다가 뜨거운 기름에 요리한 빵. 프렌치 토스트

fre·net·ic /frə'nɛtɪk/ adj frenetic activity happens in a way that is fast, exciting, and not very organized ‖ 활동이 빠르고 열성적이며 그다지 조직적이지 않게 일어나는. 광란의. 열광적인: *the frenetic pace of life in the city* 도시에서의 정신없이 바쁜 삶

fren·zied /'frɛnzid/ adj frenzied activity is completely uncontrolled ‖ 활동이 전혀 통제되지 않는. 광적인. 격분한: *a frenzied attack* 광적인 공격

fren·zy /'frɛnzi/ n [singular, U] **1** the state of being very anxious, excited, and unable to control your behavior ‖ 매우 초조하고 흥분되어 자신의 행동을 통제할 수 없는 상태. 극도의 흥분. 열광. 광란: *In a frenzy of frustration, Matt threw rocks at the window.* 매트는 실패로 격분하여 창문에다 돌을 던졌다. **2 a frenzy of activity/preparation etc.** a period in which people do a lot of things very quickly ‖ 사람들이 많은 일들을 매우 빨리 하는 시기. 정신 없이 하는 활동/준비: *The house was a frenzy of activity as we got ready for the party.* 우리가 파티 준비를 할 때, 그 집은 정신 없이 번잡했다.

fre·quen·cy /'frikwənsi/ n **1** [U] the number of times that something happens within a particular period, or the fact that it happens a lot ‖ 어떤 것이 특정한 시기 안에 일어나는 횟수, 또는 많이 일어남. 빈도. 빈번. 자주 일어남: *We want to reduce the frequency of these bacterial infections in AIDS patients.* 우리는 에이즈 환자에게서 이러한 세균 감염의 빈도가 줄어들기를 원한다. **2** [C, U] the rate at which a sound or light WAVE pattern is repeated ‖ 소리나 빛의 파동 형태가 반복되는 비율. 주파수. 진동수

fre·quent¹ /'frikwənt/ adj happening very often ‖ 매우 자주 일어나는. 빈번한: *Her teacher is worried about her frequent absences from class.* 그녀의 선생님은 그녀의 잦은 결석에 대해 걱정하신다. —opposite INFREQUENT

fre·quent² /fri'kwɛnt, 'frikwənt/ v [T] to go to a particular place very often ‖ 특정한 장소에 매우 자주 가다: *a restaurant frequented by students* 학생들이 자주 출입하는 식당

frequent fli·er /,.. '../ n someone who

travels on planes very often, especially on a particular AIRLINE's planes ‖ 특히 특정 항공사의 비행기로 매우 자주 여행하는 사람. 항공 회사의 우수 고객 **–fre·quent·flier** adj

fre·quent·ly /ˈfrikwəntʲli/ adv very often ‖ 매우 자주. 여러 번. 빈번하게: *She has frequently promised to help me, but she hasn't yet.* 번번이 그녀는 나를 도와주겠다고 약속했지만 아직 한번도 도와주지 않았다.

fresh /frɛʃ/ adj

1 ▶ADDED/REPLACING 추가된/대체한◀ an amount or a thing that is fresh is added to or replaces what was there before ‖ 양이나 물건이 전에 있던 것에 추가되거나 대체한. 추가의. 새로운: *Do you want some fresh coffee?* 커피 좀 더 드시겠어요? / *fresh sheets for the bed* 새 침대 시트

2 ▶RECENT 최근의◀ recently done, made, or learned ‖ 최근에 한[만든, 배운]: *fresh news/information/data* 최근 뉴스[정보, 자료] / *a fresh attempt/approach/idea* (=a new way of doing something) 새로운 시도[접근, 생각]

3 ▶FOOD 음식◀ fresh food or flowers are in good condition because they have recently been produced, picked, or prepared ‖ 음식이나 꽃이 최근에 조리되거나 따거나 준비되어 좋은 상태에 있는. 신선한. 싱싱한: *I bought some fresh strawberries for dessert.* 나는 후식으로 먹을 신선한 딸기를 좀 샀다.

4 ▶CLEAN 깨끗한◀ looking, feeling, smelling, or tasting clean, cool, and nice ‖ 모습[느낌, 냄새, 맛] 등이 깨끗한[시원한, 좋은]: *a fresh breeze* 시원한 미풍 / *a fresh minty taste* 상쾌한 박하 맛

5 fresh air air from outside, especially away from a city where the air is cleaner ‖ 특히 도시를 벗어나서 쐬는 더 깨끗한 바깥 공기. 신선한 공기: *It's nice to get some fresh air.* 신선한 공기를 쐬러 되어 즐겁다.

6 be fresh out of sth SPOKEN used in order to say that you have just used or given away the last supply of something ‖ 지금 막 마지막 것을 사용했거나 줘버렸다고 말하는 데에 쓰여. 방금 동이 나다: *I'm sorry, we're fresh out of bagels. Would you like a muffin instead?* 죄송합니다만 베이글빵이 방금 다 떨어졌네요. 대신 머핀빵은 어떠세요?

7 fresh-made/fresh-cut etc. having just been made, cut etc. ‖ 방금 만든, 방금 자른: *fresh-squeezed orange juice* 방금 짜낸 오렌지 주스

8 ▶WATER 물◀ fresh water has no salt and comes from rivers and lakes ‖ 물이 소금기가 없고 강·호수에서 흘러나온. 민물[담수]의

9 make a fresh start to try doing something again by using a completely different method, especially because you want to succeed, be happy etc. ‖ 특히 성공·행복 등을 원하기 때문에 완전히 다른 방법을 사용해서 다시 어떤 것을 시도하다. 처음부터 새로 시작하다: *My mother and I left Chicago to try to make a fresh start* (=start a new life) *in California.* 어머니와 나는 캘리포니아에서 새로운 출발을 하기 위해서 시카고를 떠났다.

10 fresh in your mind/memory etc. recent enough to be remembered ‖ 기억할 수 있을 정도로 최근의. 기억이 생생한: *You might want to write about your trip while it's still fresh in your mind.* 기억이 아직 생생할 동안에 당신이 여행한 것에 대해 글을 쓰고 싶을 법도 한데.

fresh·en /ˈfrɛʃən/ v

freshen up phr v [I, T **freshen yourself up**] to wash your hands and face in order to feel comfortable ‖ 상쾌한 기분을 느끼려고 손과 얼굴을 씻다: *Would you like to freshen up before dinner?* 식사 전에 손을 깨끗이 씻으시겠습니까?

fresh·ly /ˈfrɛʃli/ adv very recently ‖ 아주 최근에. 갓. 새롭게: *freshly mown grass* 갓 깎은 잔디

fresh·man /ˈfrɛʃmən/ n a student in the first year of HIGH SCHOOL or college ‖ 고등학교나 대학의 1학년생. 신입생

fresh·wa·ter /ˈfrɛʃˌwɔtɚ, -ˌwɑtɚ/ adj relating to rivers or lakes rather than the ocean ‖ 바다가 아니라 강이나 호수에 관련된. 민물의. 담수의: *freshwater fish* 담수어[민물고기]

fret¹ /frɛt/ v [I, T] OLD-FASHIONED to worry about small or unimportant things, or to make someone do this ‖ 사소하거나 중요하지 않은 것에 대해 걱정하거나 누군가를 걱정시키다.

fret² n one of the raised lines on the long straight part of a GUITAR or similar instruments ‖ 기타나 그 유사 악기의 길게 쭉 뻗은 부분 위에 돋아 있는 선들 중의 하나. 프렛. 줄받이

fret·ful /ˈfrɛtfəl/ adj OLD-FASHIONED worried and complaining about small things ‖ 사소한 것에 걱정하고 불평하는. 안달하는. 짜증내는: *a fretful child* 짜증 잘 내는 아이

Freud·i·an /ˈfrɔɪdiən/ adj **1** relating to Sigmund Freud's ideas about the way the mind works ‖ 정신 작용법에 대한 프로이트의 사상과 관련됨. 프로이트(학설)의 **2 Freudian slip** something you say by mistake that shows a thought or feeling you did not mean to show, or did not know you had ‖ 보여줄 의도가 없거나 자신도 의식하지 못했던 생각이나 감정을 실수로 드러낸 것. 속마음이 드러난 실언. 무의식의 발로

fri·ar /ˈfraɪɚ/ *n* a man who belongs to a Roman Catholic group, whose members in past times traveled around teaching about religion and who were very poor ‖ 과거에 종교를 가르치며 두루 돌아다니던 매우 가난했던 로마 가톨릭 분파의 일원. 탁발(수도회의) 수도사. 수사(修士)

fric·tion /ˈfrɪkʃən/ *n* [U] **1** disagreement, angry feelings, or unfriendliness between people ‖ 사람들 사이의 의견의 불일치[화난 감정, 비우호적임]. 불화[마찰]. 알력: *The way housework is shared has been a source of friction between Cathy and Jerry.* 집안 일을 나누는 방식이 케시와 제리 사이에 불화의 원인이 되었다. **2** the rubbing of one surface against another ‖ 한 표면을 다른 표면에 대고 문지름. 마찰: *friction between tires and the road* 타이어와 도로 사이의 마찰

Fri·day /ˈfraɪdi, -deɪ/, *written abbreviation* **Fri.** *n* the sixth day of the week ‖ 한 주의 여섯 번째 날. 금요일 — see usage note at SUNDAY

fridge /frɪdʒ/ *n* INFORMAL ⇨ REFRIGERATOR

fried¹ /fraɪd/ *adj* **1** cooked in hot fat ‖ 뜨거운 유지(油脂)에 요리한. 기름으로 튀긴: *a fried egg* 계란 프라이 **2** SLANG very tired ‖ 매우 피로한. 지친: *My brain is fried today.* 내 머리는 오늘 완전히 녹초가 되었다.

fried² *v* the past tense and PAST PARTICIPLE of FRY ‖ fry의 과거·과거 분사형

friend /frɛnd/ *n* **1** someone whom you like very much and enjoy spending time with ‖ 대단히 좋아하고 같이 시간 보내기가 즐거운 사람. 친구: *I'm meeting a friend for lunch.* 나는 친구와 점심 약속이 있다. / *Tony's her best friend.* (=the friend she likes best) 토니는 그녀의 가장 절친한 친구이다. / *Lee's an old friend.* (=one you have known a long time) 리는 오랜 친구이다. **2 make/be friends (with)** to have someone as your friend ‖ 남과 친구가 되다. …과 친해지다: *We made friends with our neighbors right away.* 우리는 곧바로 이웃과 친해졌다. /

They've been friends with the Wilsons for years. 그들은 오랫동안 윌슨 씨네와 가깝게 지내 오고 있다. **3** someone who supports a theater, MUSEUM etc. by giving money or help ‖ 돈이나 도움을 주어서 극장이나 박물관 등을 지원하는 사람. 후원자: *You can become a friend of the art gallery for $100 a year.* 1년에 100달러를 내면 그 미술관의 후원자가 될 수 있다. **4 have friends in high places** to know important people who can help you ‖ 도와줄 수 있는 중요한 사람을 알다. 유력한 연줄을 가지고 있다

friend·ly /ˈfrɛndli/ *adj* **1** showing that you like someone and are ready to talk to him/her ‖ 남을 좋아하며 그 사람과 말할 용의가 있다는 것을 나타내는. 호의적인. 친절한. 다정한: *Diane's friendly to/with everyone.* 다이앤은 모든 사람들에게 다정다감하다. / *a friendly smile* 다정한 미소 —opposite UNFRIENDLY **2 -friendly a)** easy for people to use or be comfortable with ‖ 사람들이 사용하기 쉽거나 편리한. …에 적합한: *user-friendly computers* 사용자 우선 컴퓨터 / *a kid-friendly house* 아이에게 적합한 집 **b)** not damaging or harming something ‖ 어떤 것을 파손하거나 해를 끼치지 않는. 친화적인. 해롭지 않은: *environmentally friendly detergent* 환경 친화적인 세제 **3 friendly fire** bombs, bullets etc. that accidentally kill people who are fighting on the same side ‖ 같은 편에서 싸우고 있는 사람을 사고로 죽이는 폭탄·총알 등. 아군에 의한 폭격[공격] **–friendliness** *n* [U]

friend·ship /ˈfrɛndʃɪp/ *n* **1** a relationship between friends ‖ 친구 사이의 관계. 교우 관계. 교제: *Their friendship began in college.* 그들의 친구 관계는 대학 때 시작되었다. / *Our children have formed/developed a friendship with the Websters.* 우리 아이들은 웹스터 씨네와 친교를 맺었다[쌓아갔다]. / *a close friendship* 절친한 친구 사이 **2** [U] the feelings that exist between friends, and the way they behave with each other ‖ 친구 사이에 존재하는 감정·친구 간에 대하는 방식. 우정. 우호. 우애: *I was grateful for her friendship and support.* 나는 그녀의 우정과 지지에 감사했다.

fries /fraɪz/ *n* [plural] potatoes cut into long thin pieces and cooked in hot oil ‖ 길고 얇은 조각으로 잘라 뜨거운 기름에 조리한 감자. 감자 튀김

frieze /friz/ *n* a thin border along the top of a wall, usually decorated with pictures, patterns etc. ‖ 일반적으로 그림·무늬 등으로 장식된 벽의 상단을 따라 쳐진 얇은 경계선. 띠 모양 장식을 두른 부분

frig·ate /ˈfrɪgɪt/ n a small fast ship used especially for protecting other ships in a war ‖ 특히 전쟁에서 다른 배들을 보호하기 위해 사용하는 작고 빠른 배. 프리깃함. 호위함

fright /fraɪt/ n [singular, U] a sudden fear ‖ 갑작스러운 공포. 경악. 섬뜩함: *People screamed and ran away in fright.* 사람들은 소스라치게 놀라 비명을 지르면서 도망갔다.

fright·en /ˈfraɪtn/ v [T] **1** to make someone feel afraid ‖ 남을 두려워하게 만들다. …을 소스라치게[소름끼치게] 하다. …을 겁주다: *Libby was frightened by the loud thunder.* 리비는 큰 천둥소리에 깜짝 놀랐다. **2 frighten sb into sth/frighten sb out of sth** to force someone to do something or not to do something by making him/her afraid ‖ 남을 겁주어 강제적으로 어떤 것을 하거나 하지 못하게 하다. …을 위협하여 …을 시키다[못하게 하다]: *At least the heart attack has frightened him out of smoking.* 그는 심장 마비를 겪으며 적어도 담배 하나는 확실히 끊었다.

frighten sb/sth ↔ **away** phr v [T] to make a person or animal go away by making him, her, or it afraid ‖ 사람이나 동물을 겁주어 도망가게 만들다. 겁을 주어 …을 쫓아버리다: *Be quiet or you'll frighten away the birds.* 조용히 해라. 그렇지 않으면 새들이 놀라 날아갈 거야.

frighten sb ↔ **off** phr v [T] to make someone so nervous or afraid that s/he goes away and does not do something s/he was going to do ‖ 남을 매우 긴장시키거나 겁을 주어 마음이 멀어지게 하여 하고자 했던 일을 하지 못하게 만들다. …에게 겁을 주어 단념시키다: *A car alarm is usually enough to frighten off a burglar.* 자동차 도난 경보 장치는 대개 절도범을 놀라서 그만두게 하기에 충분하다.

fright·ened /ˈfraɪtnd/ adj feeling afraid ‖ 두려움을 느끼는. 깜짝 놀란. 겁이 난: *a frightened child* 겁먹은 아이 / *He's still too frightened to be able to sleep.* 그는 여전히 너무 겁을 먹어 잠을 잘 수가 없다.

fright·en·ing /ˈfraɪtnɪŋ/ adj making you feel afraid or nervous ‖ 두려움이나 긴장감을 느끼게 만드는. 깜짝 놀라게 하는. 두려운. 끔찍한: *a frightening experience* 끔찍한 경험 – **frighteningly** adv

fright·ful /ˈfraɪtfəl/ adj OLD-FASHIONED very bad or not nice ‖ 매우 나쁘거나 좋지 않은. 끔찍한: *There's been a frightful accident on the freeway.* 고속도로상에서 끔찍한 사고가 있었다.

frig·id /ˈfrɪdʒɪd/ adj **1** a woman who is frigid does not like having sex ‖ 여성이 성관계를 가지는 것을 좋아하지 않는. 성교를 싫어하는. 불감증의 **2** LITERARY not friendly ‖ 우호적이지 않은. 냉담한. 쌀쌀한: *She gave me a frigid look.* 그녀는 나를 냉담한 표정으로 바라보았다. **3** a place that is frigid is very cold ‖ 장소가 매우 추운. 극한[혹한]의 – **frigidity** /frɪˈdʒɪdəti/ n [U]

frill /frɪl/ n **1** a decoration on the edge of a piece of cloth, made of another piece of cloth with many small folds in it ‖ 많은 작은 주름을 가진 다른 천 조각으로 만든, 천의 가장자리 장식. 주름 장식 **2** additional features that are nice but not necessary ‖ 필요한 것은 아니지만 좋은 추가적인 특징. 기본을 초과한 것. 항공사 등의 과잉 서비스: *Southwest Airlines offers few frills.* 사우스웨스트 항공사는 지나치게 불필요한 서비스는 제공하지 않는다. —see also NO-FRILLS

frill·y /ˈfrɪli/ adj with many FRILLs ‖ 많은 주름 장식이 달린: *a frilly blouse* 주름 장식이 있는 블라우스

fringe¹ /frɪndʒ/ n **1 the political/ radical/lunatic etc. fringe** a small number of people whose ideas are more unusual or extreme than those of most other people ‖ 생각이 대부분의 다른 사람들에 비하여 독특하거나 극단적인 소수의 사람들. 비주류 정치인/급진파/과격파: *the environmental fringe* 소수의 환경 보호주의자 **2 on the fringes of sth** not completely involved in or accepted by a particular group ‖ 특정한 집단에 완전히 참여하지 않거나 받아들여지지 않은. …의 변두리[주위, 가장자리]에: *Cato lived on the fringes of society.* 카토는 사회의 주변인으로 살았다. **3** [C, U] a decoration on a curtain, piece of clothing etc., made of hanging threads ‖ 커튼·의복 등에 붙이는, 실을 늘어뜨려 만든 장식. 술장식: *a cowboy jacket with leather fringe* 가죽 술이 달린 카우보이 재킷 **4** the area along the edge of a place ‖ 한 장소의 가장자리 둘레의 지역. 변두리. 주변: *the eastern fringes of downtown Vancouver* 밴쿠버 시내의 동쪽 변두리 지역

fringe² adj not representing or involving many people, and expressing unusual ideas ‖ 많은 사람들을 대표하거

나 포함하지 않으며 일반적이지 않은 생각을 표현하는. 소수의. 비주류의: *a fringe group of political extremists* 소수 집단의 정치적 극단주의자들 / *a fringe presidential candidate* 군소 대통령 후보

fringe ben·e·fit /'. ,.../ *n* [usually plural] a service or advantage that you are given with your job in addition to pay ‖ 직업에서 봉급 이외에 추가적으로 지급받는 혜택이나 이익. 후생 복지 혜택. 부가 급부. 급여 외 이익: *Fringe benefits include a company car and health club membership.* 후생 복지 혜택에는 회사 차와 헬스 클럽 회원권이 포함된다.

fringed /frɪndʒd/ *adj* 1 decorated with a FRINGE ‖ 술로 장식된: *a large fringed shawl* 술로 장식된 커다란 숄 2 having something on the edge ‖ 가장자리에 어떤 것이 있는: *a palm-fringed beach* 야자수가 늘어선 해변

Fris·bee /'frɪzbi/ *n* [C, U] TRADEMARK a piece of plastic shaped like a plate, that people throw and catch as a game ‖ 사람들이 놀이로서 던지고 잡는 접시 모양의 플라스틱 판. 프리스비. 플라스틱 원반

frisk /frɪsk/ *v* [T] to search someone for hidden weapons, drugs etc. by passing your hands over his/her body ‖ 손으로 남의 몸을 더듬어 숨긴 무기·마약 등을 찾다. 몸수색을 하다

frisk·y /'frɪski/ *adj* full of energy, happiness, and fun ‖ 활력·행복·재미로 가득한. 쾌활한. 까불어대는: *a frisky little boy* 쾌활한 작은 소년

frit·ter¹ /'frɪtɚ/ *n* a thin piece of fruit, vegetable, or meat covered with a mixture of eggs and flour and cooked in oil ‖ 계란과 밀가루의 혼합물을 입혀서 기름에 튀긴 과일[야채, 고기]의 얇은 조각. 프리터. 튀김: *corn fritters* 옥수수 프리터 [튀김]

fritter²

fritter sth ↔ **away** *phr v* [T] to waste time, money, or effort on something that is not important ‖ 중요하지 않은 것에 시간[돈, 노력]을 낭비하다: *They fritter away their days hanging around at the mall.* 그들은 쇼핑몰에서 배회하며 하루 하루를 허송세월하고 있다.

fritz /frɪts/ *n* INFORMAL **be on the fritz** if something electrical is on the fritz, it is not working correctly ‖ 전기 제품이 정상적으로 작동하지 않고 있다. 고장 나다: *It could be that your printer's on the fritz.* 네 프린터가 고장 난 것일 수도 있다.

fri·vol·i·ty /frɪ'vɑləti/ *n* [C, U] behavior or activities that are not serious or sensible ‖ 진지하지 않거나 분별이 없는

행동이나 활동. 경솔[경박]한 언행: *childish frivolity* 어린애 같은 경솔한 행동

friv·o·lous /'frɪvələs/ *adj* 1 not sensible ‖ 분별이 없는. 경솔한. 경박한: *pretty, frivolous clothes* 예쁘지만 천박한 옷 2 not important or necessary ‖ 중요하거나 필수적이지 않은. 시시한. 하찮은: *a frivolous request* 사소한 부탁

frizz /frɪz/ *v* [T] INFORMAL to make your hair curl very tightly ‖ 머리카락을 아주 촘촘하게 말다. 곱슬곱슬하게 지지다

frizz·y /'frɪzi/ *adj* frizzy hair is very tightly curled ‖ 머리카락이 아주 촘촘하게 말린. 매우 곱슬곱슬한

fro /froʊ/ *adv* ⇨ TO AND FRO

frog /frɔg, frɑg/ *n* 1 a small animal with smooth skin that lives in or near water, makes a deep sound, and has long legs for jumping ‖ 저음의 (울음)소리를 내며 뛰기에 적합한 긴 다리를 가진, 물 속이나 물가에 사는 피부가 부드러운 작은 동물. 개구리 —compare TOAD 2 **have a frog in your throat** INFORMAL to have difficulty in speaking because your throat is dry ‖ 목이 건조해서 말하기 어렵다. 목소리가 쉬다[걸걸하다]

frol·ic /'frɑlɪk/ *v* [I] to play in an active, happy way ‖ 활발히고 즐겁게 놀다. 들떠서 떠들다. 장난치다 –**frolic** *n*

from /frəm; *strong* frʌm/ *prep* 1 ▶WHERE SB/STH STARTS 사람/사물이 출발하는 곳◀ starting at a particular place, position, or condition ‖ 특정한 장소[위치, 상태]에서 시작하는. …에서. …으로부터: *He drove all the way from Colorado.* 그는 콜로라도에서부터 줄곧 운전했다. / *I liked him from the first time I met him.* 나는 그를 처음 만났을 때부터 좋아했다. / *prices ranging from $80 to $250* 80달러에서 250달러 범위의 가격 2 ▶ORIGIN 기원◀ **a)** used in order to show the origin of someone or something ‖ 사람이나 사물의 기원을 나타내는 데에 쓰여. …에서부터. …으로: *I took the lines from a play.* 나는 그 말을 연극에서 인용했다. / *a doll made from grass* 풀로 만든 인형 / *Our speaker today is from the University of Montana.* 오늘 연설자는 몬태나 대학에서 오신 분입니다. / *"Where do you come from?" "I'm from Norway."* "어느 나라에서 왔습니까?" "노르웨이에서 왔습니다." **b)** sent or given by someone ‖ 남이 보내거나 준. …에(게)서 온[받은]: *Who is the present from?* 누구한테 받은 선물이니? / *I got a phone call from Ernie today.* 나는 오늘 어니로부터 온 전화를 받았다.

3 ▶MOVED/SEPARATED 이동된/분리된◀ used in order to show that things or people are moved, separated, or taken away ‖ 사물이나 사람들이 이동된[분리된, 빼앗긴] 것을 나타내는 데에 쓰여: *He pulled his shoes out from under the bed.* 그는 침대 밑에서 신발을 꺼냈다. / *I'll take that away from you if you hit him with it again!* 너 다시 한 번 그걸로 그를 때리면 그거 압수할 거야! / *She needs some time away from the kids.* (=time when she is not with them) 그녀에게는 아이들과 떨어져 있는 시간이 좀 필요하다. / *Subtract $40 from the total.* 총액에서 40달러를 빼라.

4 ▶DISTANCE/TIME 거리/시간◀ used in order to show distance or time ‖ 거리나 시간을 나타내는 데에 쓰여: *We live about 3 miles from Des Moines.* 우리는 디모인에서 대략 3마일 떨어진 거리에 살고 있다. / *It'll cost $400 to fly from Albuquerque to Atlanta.* 비행기로 알부케르케에서 애틀랜타까지 가는 데 400달러가 들 것이다. / *The morning class is from 9:00 to 11:00.* 오전반은 오전 9시부터 11시까지이다.

5 ▶POSITION 위치◀ used in order to show where you are when you see, watch, or do something ‖ 무엇을 보거나 유심히 살피거나 행할 때 자신이 있는 곳을 나타내는 데에 쓰여. …에서(떨어져): *There's a man watching us from behind that fence.* 한 남자가 그 담 뒤에서 우리를 지켜보고 있었다. / *We could see the house from the road.* 그 집은 길에서 보였다.

6 ▶RESULT 결과◀ because of, or as a result of ‖ …때문에, 또는 …의 결과로: *I got this cold from walking in the rain all day Sunday.* 일요일에 하루 종일 빗속을 걸어서 이 감기에 걸렸다. / *We could tell what he was thinking from the expression on his face.* 우리는 그의 얼굴 표정으로 그가 무슨 생각을 하고 있는지 알 수 있었다.

7 a week/2 months/5 years from now one week, 2 months etc. after the time when you are speaking ‖ 말하고 있는 시점 이후로 한 주·2달 등. 지금으로부터 한 주 후/2달 후/5년 후: *One month from now we'll be in Mexico!* 이제부터 한 달 후면 우리는 멕시코에 있을 거야!

8 from now on starting now and continuing into the future ‖ 지금 시작해서 앞으로 계속되는. 앞으로. 지금부터 (계속): *From now on, Richard will be working in the Sales Department.* 앞으로 리처드는 영업부에서 일할 것이다.

9 ▶STOP SOMETHING HAPPENING 일어나고 있는 것을 멈추다◀ used with verbs such as "keep," "stop," "protect," and "prevent" in order to show the action that is stopped or avoided ‖ 중단되거나 회피된 행동을 나타내기 위해 "keep", "stop", "protect", "prevent" 등의 동사와 함께 쓰여: *Winston's bad eyesight prevented him from driving.* 윈스턴은 시력이 안 좋아서 운전을 할 수 없었다.

10 ▶COMPARING 비교◀ used when comparing things ‖ 사물을 비교할 때 쓰여: *Frieda is very different from her sister.* 프리더는 언니[여동생]와 매우 다르다.

frond /frɑnd/ *n* a leaf of a FERN or PALM TREE ‖ 고사리류나 야자나무의 잎. 잘게 갈라진 잎

front

Amy walked
in front of the bus.

Vicky got in the front seat of the car.

front¹ /frʌnt/ *n*

1 the front a) the most forward part of something ‖ 사물의 맨 앞부분. 앞. 전방. 앞쪽: *Let's sit at the front of the bus.* 버스 맨 앞자리에 앉자. / *I can't remember the page number, but it's near the front of the book.* 몇 쪽인지는 기억할 수 없지만 책의 맨 앞부분 근처이다. **b)** the side or surface of something that is in the direction that it faces or moves ‖ 사물이 향하거나 움직이는 방향에 있는 쪽이나 표면. 정면. 앞면. 앞부분: *Go in at the front of the building.* 건물의 정면으로 들어가라. / *There's a dent in the front of my bike.* 내 자전거의 앞면에 움푹 들어간 자국이 있다. **c)** the most important side or surface of something, that you look at first ‖ 맨 먼저 쳐다보는 사물의 가장 중요한 쪽이나 표면: *On the front of the postcard was a picture of the Golden Gate Bridge.* 그림엽서의 앞쪽에는 금문교 그림이 있었다. —opposite

BACK¹

2 in front of sth a) near the side of something that is in the direction it faces or moves ‖ 향하거나 움직이는 방향에 있는 어떤 물건 쪽 가까이에. …의 앞에. …의 정면에: *a tree in front of the house* 집 앞에 있는 나무 한 그루 / *A car suddenly pulled out in front of my van.* 자동차 한 대가 갑자기 내 밴 앞으로 추월해 나갔다. **b)** near the entrance of a building ‖ 건물의 출입구 근처에. …앞에. 입구에: *Park in front of the theater.* 극장 앞에 주차해라. —opposite BEHIND¹
3 in front of sb a) ahead of someone, in the direction s/he is facing or moving ‖ 향하거나 움직이고 있는 방향으로 어떤 사람 앞에. …의 앞에[으로]: *There are about 50 people in front of us in line.* 우리 앞으로 약 50명의 사람들이 줄서 있다. **b)** facing a person or group ‖ 사람이나 집단을 마주하는: *Come up here in front of the class.* 교실의 이 앞으로 나와라. **c)** where someone can see or hear you ‖ 어떤 사람이 보거나 들을 수 있는 곳에서: *Don't say anything in front of the children.* 아이들 앞에서는 아무 말도 하지 마라.
4 in (the) front a) in the most forward or leading position; ahead ‖ 가장 앞쪽에 또는 선도하는 위치에; 앞에: *Watch the car in front!* 전방에 있는 차를 조심해! **b)** in the area nearest to the most forward part of something, or nearest to the entrance to a building ‖ 사물의 맨 앞쪽과 가장 가까운 곳에, 또는 건물 출입구와 가장 가까이에: *The club has two bars, one in the front and one in the back.* 그 클럽에는 맨 앞쪽과, 맨 뒤쪽에 하나씩 두 개의 술 판매대가 있다.
5 out front in the area near the entrance to the building that you are in ‖ 자신이 있는 건물의 출입구 가까운 곳에. 문[집] 밖에서: *Jim's waiting out front.* 짐은 문 밖에서 기다리고 있다.
6 in (the) front in the part of a car where the driver sits ‖ 차의 운전자가 앉는 부분에. 앞좌석에: *Can I sit in front with you?* 앞좌석에 같이 앉아도 될까요?
7 ▶WEATHER 날씨◀ TECHNICAL the place where two areas of air that have different temperatures meet each other ‖ 온도가 다른 두 개의 기단(氣團)이 서로 만나는 지점. 전선: *The weather report says a warm/cold front is coming.* 기상 예보에 따르면 온난[한랭] 전선이 다가오고 있다.
8 on the publicity/money/health etc. front in a particular area of activity ‖ 특정한 활동 분야에. 홍보/자금/건강 분야에: *We've had some new developments on the economic front.* 우리는 경제 분야에서 약간의 새로운 발전을 이루었다.
9 up front INFORMAL **a)** money that is paid up front is paid before work is done or goods are supplied ‖ 작업이 완료되거나 물건이 공급되기 전에 돈이 지불된. 선불로: *We need the money up front before we can do anything.* 우리는 어떤 일이든 하기 전에 돈을 선불로 받아야 한다. **b)** directly and clearly from the start ‖ 처음부터 직접적이고 분명하게: *She told him up front she wasn't interested in marriage.* 그녀는 결혼에 흥미가 없다고 처음부터 솔직히 그에게 말했다.
10 ▶ON YOUR BODY 신체에서◀ INFORMAL someone's chest, or the part of the body that faces forward ‖ 사람의 가슴, 또는 앞쪽으로 향하고 있는 신체 부위. 가슴 부위. 앞쪽: *Oh, I've just spilled milk down my front!* 이런, 방금 내 가슴에다 우유를 쏟아버렸네!
11 ▶BEHAVIOR 행동◀ a way of behaving that shows what you want people to see, rather than what you may feel ‖ 자신이 느끼는 것이 아니라 사람들이 보았으면 하는 것을 보여주는 행동 방식. 겉모습. 겉치레. 체면. 외관: *Parents should always present a united front* (=seem to agree with each other) *to their children.* 부모들은 항상 자녀들에게 서로 의견이 일치하는 것처럼 보여야 한다.
12 ▶POLITICAL PARTY 정당◀ used in the names of political parties or unofficial military organizations ‖ 정당의 명칭이나 비공식적 군대 조직에 쓰여. 전선: *the Quebec Liberation Front* 퀘벡 자유 전선
13 ▶WAR 전쟁◀ a line along which fighting takes place during a war ‖ 전쟁 중에 전투가 일어나는 곳을 따라 형성된 선. 최전방. 전선
front² *adj* **1** at, on, or in the front of something ‖ 무엇의 앞에: *the front door* 정문 / *tickets for front row seats* 앞줄 좌석 표 **2** legally doing business as a way of hiding a secret or illegal activity ‖ 비밀스럽거나 불법적인 활동을 은폐하는 방식으로서 합법적으로 사업을 하는. 위장의: *a front organization for drug dealing* 마약 거래를 위한 위장 조직
front³ *v* **1** [I, T] to face something ‖ 무엇을 마주하다: *a building fronting Lake Michigan* 미시간호를 마주하고 있는 건물 **2** [T] to lead something such as a

musical group by being the person that the public sees most ‖ 대중의 눈에 가장 잘 띄는 사람이 되어서 음악 그룹 등을 이끌다. 리더가 되다: *He's now fronting his own band.* 그는 지금 자신의 밴드를 이끌고 있다.

front for sb/sth *phr v* [T] to be the person or organization used for hiding the real nature of a secret or illegal activity ‖ 비밀이나 불법 활동의 실체를 숨기는 데에 사용되는 사람이나 조직이 되다. 앞잡이[위장물]가 되다: *The FBI suspected him of fronting for a smuggling ring.* FBI는 그를 밀수단의 앞잡이로 의심했다.

front·age /'frʌntɪdʒ/ *n* the part of a building or piece of land that is along a road, river etc. ‖ 도로·강 등을 따라 있는 건물이나 토지의 부분. 인접지. 임계지(臨界地)

fron·tal /'frʌntəl/ *adj* **1** toward the front of something ‖ 무엇의 앞쪽의: *a frontal attack* 정면 공격 **2** at the front part of something ‖ 무엇의 앞부분의: *the frontal lobe of the brain* 뇌의 전두엽

fron·tier /frʌn'tɪr/ *n* **1 the frontier** the area beyond the places that people know well, especially in the western US in the 19th century ‖ 특히 19세기 미국 서부에서 사람들이 잘 아는 지역을 벗어난 지역. 서부 변경: *the settlement of the Oklahoma frontier* 오클라호마 변경 지대의 정착지 **2** the limit of what is known about something ‖ 어떤 것에 관해 알려진 것의 한계. 극한. 최전선: *the frontiers of science* 과학의 최첨단 영역 **3** the border of a country, or the area near the border ‖ 어떤 나라의 국경, 또는 국경 인근 지역. 국경(지대)

front man /'. ./ *n* **1** someone who speaks for an organization, often an illegal one, but is not the leader of it ‖ 종종 불법적인 조직을 대변하지만 그 조직의 지도자는 아닌 사람. 간판 구실을 하는 인물. 표면에 내세우는 인물 **2** the leader of a JAZZ or ROCK band ‖ 재즈나 록 밴드의 리더

front·run·ner /'frʌnt,rʌnɚ/ *n* the person or thing that is most likely to succeed in a competition ‖ 시합에서 가장 우승 가능성이 높은 사람이나 것: *the frontrunner in the race for the Republican nomination* 공화당 대통령 후보 지명 경쟁에서 가장 유력한 후보

frost¹ /frɔst/ *n* **1** [U] ice that looks white and powdery and covers things that are outside when the temperature is very cold ‖ 흰 가루처럼 생겼으며 날씨가 아주 추울 때 바깥에 있는 물체를 덮는 얼음. 서리: *trees covered with frost* 서리로 덮인 나무들 **2** very cold weather, when water freezes ‖ 물이 어는 매우 추운 날씨. 혹한: *an early frost* 이른 추위

frost² *v* [T] **1** to cover a cake with FROSTING ‖ 당의(糖衣)로 케이크를 입히다 **2** to cover something with FROST, or to become covered with frost ‖ 어떤 것을 [이] 서리로 덮다[덮이다]

frost·bite /'frɔstbaɪt/ *n* [U] a condition that is caused by extreme cold, that makes your fingers, toes etc. swell, become darker, and sometimes drop off ‖ 혹한으로 인해 손가락·발가락 등이 붓거나 시커멓게 되고 때로 떨어져 나가기도 하는 상태. 동상 **– frostbitten** /'frɔst,bɪtʰn/ *adj*

frost·ing /'frɔstɪŋ/ *n* [U] a sweet substance that you put on cakes, made from sugar and liquid ‖ 설탕과 액체로 만든 케이크에 입히는 단 물질. 당의(糖衣)

frost·y /'frɔsti/ *adj* **1** very cold or covered with FROST ‖ 매우 춥거나 서리로 덮인. 얼 것 같은. 서리가 앉은: *a frosty morning* 서리가 내린 아침 / *frosty ground* 서리가 내린 땅 **2** unfriendly ‖ 비우호적인. 쌀쌀한. 냉담한: *a frosty greeting* 쌀쌀맞은 인사

froth¹ /frɔθ/ *n* [singular, U] a lot of BUBBLEs formed on top of a liquid ‖ 액체의 맨 위에 형성된 다량의 거품

froth² *v* [I] to make FROTH ‖ 거품을 일으키다. 거품이 일다: *When you open the bottle, the beer will froth for a few seconds.* 병을 따면 몇 초 동안 맥주 거품이 일 것이다.

froth·y /'frɔθi, -ði/ *adj* full of FROTH or covered with froth ‖ 거품이 가득하거나 거품으로 덮인: *frothy beer* 거품이 가득 이는 맥주

frown¹ /fraʊn/ *v* [I] to make an angry or unhappy expression by moving your EYEBROWs together, so that lines appear on your FOREHEAD ‖ 눈썹을 함께 움직여 이마에 주름살이 지도록 화나거나 기분 나빠하는 표정을 짓다. 눈살을 찌푸리다. 얼굴을 찡그리다: *Mel frowned and pretended to ignore me.* 멜은 눈살을 찌푸리며 나를 무시하는 체했다.

frown on/upon sth *phr v* [T] to disapprove of something ‖ 어떤 것을 인정하지 않다. 불찬성을 나타내다. 난색을 표시하다: *Even though divorce is legal, it's often frowned upon.* 이혼은 합법적이기는 하나 종종 빈축을 산다.

frown² *n* the expression on your face when you frown ‖ 눈살을 찌푸릴 때의 얼

굴 표정. 언짢은 얼굴. 화난 기색: *Marty looked at his grades with a frown.* 마티는 언짢은 얼굴로 자신의 점수를 보았다.

froze /frouz/ *v* the past tense of FREEZE ‖ freeze의 과거형

frozen¹ /'frouzən/ *v* the PAST PARTICIPLE of FREEZE ‖ freeze의 과거 분사형

frozen² *adj* **1** preserved by being kept at a very low temperature ‖ 매우 낮은 온도로 유지시켜 보존된. 냉장 보관된: *frozen peas* 냉장 보관된 완두콩 **2 be frozen (stiff)** SPOKEN to feel very cold ‖ 매우 춥게 느끼다. 얼어 붙을 정도로 춥다: *Can you turn up the heat? I'm frozen!* 온도 좀 높여 줄래? 추위 죽겠어! **3** made very hard or turned to ice because of the cold ‖ 추워서 아주 딱딱하게 되거나 얼음으로 변한. 추위로 언. 결빙한: *frozen ground* 언 땅 / *the frozen lake* 얼어 붙은 호수 **4 be frozen with fear/terror/fright** to be so afraid, shocked etc. that you cannot move ‖ 너무 무섭거나 충격 등을 받아 움직일 수 없는. 공포로 얼어붙은[꼼짝 못하는]: *The dog was under the bed, frozen with terror, throughout the thunder storm.* 그 개는 폭풍우가 치는 동안 내내 무서워서 침대 밑에서 꼼짝도 하지 못했다.

fru·gal /'frugəl/ *adj* **1** careful to only buy what is necessary ‖ 신중하게 단지 필요한 것만 사는. 검약하는. 절약하는: *Dan's a very frugal young man.* 댄은 매우 절약 정신이 강한 젊은이이다. **2** small in quantity and cost ‖ 양과 비용이 적은. 검소한. 간소한: *a frugal lunch of cheese and bread* 치즈와 빵의 간소한 점심 식사 **– frugally** *adv* **– frugality** /fru'gæləti/ *n* [U]

fruit /frut/ *n, plural* **fruit** or **fruits 1** [C, U] the part of a plant, tree, or bush that contains seeds and is often eaten as food ‖ 씨가 들어 있으며 종종 식품으로 먹는 식물·나무·관목의 부분. 과일. 열매: *Apples and bananas are Nancy's favorite fruits.* 사과와 바나나는 낸시가 가장 좋아하는 과일이다. / *Would you like a piece of fruit?* 과일 좀 드시겠어요? / *You should eat more fruit.* 너는 과일을 좀 더 먹어야 해. **2 the fruits of sth** the good results that you have from something you have worked hard at ‖ 열심히 일해서 어떤 것에서 얻은 좋은 결과. …의 성과: *It's nice to see Barry enjoying the fruits of all his hard work.* 온 힘을 기울여 열심히 일한 성과를 즐기고 있는 배리를 보니 기분 좋다. **—see also bear fruit** (BEAR¹)

fruit·cake /'frut˼keɪk/ *n* **1** [C, U] a

cake that has dried fruit in it ‖ 말린 과일이 들어 있는 케이크. 과일 케이크 **2** INFORMAL someone who seems to be mentally ill or behaves in a strange way ‖ 정신적으로 병든 듯하며 이상하게 행동하는 사람. 괴짜. 머리가 돈 사람

fruit fly /'. ./ *n* a small fly that eats and lays eggs on fruit ‖ 과일을 먹으며 과일에다 알을 까기도 하는 작은 파리. 과일파리. 초파리

fruit·ful /'frutfəl/ *adj* producing good results ‖ 좋은 결과를 내는. 결과가 좋은. 효과적인. 유익한: *a fruitful meeting* 유익한 모임

fru·i·tion /fru'ɪʃən/ *n* [U] FORMAL the successful result of a plan, idea etc. ‖ 계획·생각 등의 성공적인 결과. …의 달성[실현, 성취]: *After three years, many of the president's plans have finally come to fruition.* 삼년 후 대통령의 많은 계획들은 마침내 성취되었다.

fruit·less /'frutlɪs/ *adj* failing to produce good results, especially after much effort ‖ 특히 많은 노력을 기울인 후에 좋은 성과를 내지 못하는. 효과 없는. 헛된. 보람 없는: *a fruitless attempt to end the fighting* 싸움을 끝내려는 헛된 시도 **– fruitlessly** *adv*

fruit·y /'fruti/ *adj* tasting or smelling strongly of fruit ‖ 과일의 맛이나 향을 강하게 내는. 과일 맛[향]이 나는: *a fruity wine* 과일 맛이 그윽한 포도주

frump·y /'frʌmpi/ *adj* someone, especially a woman, who is frumpy wears old-fashioned clothes and looks unattractive ‖ 특히 여자가 구식 옷을 입으며 매력적으로 보이지 않는. 너절한 차림의. 칠칠치 못한

frus·trate /'frʌstreɪt/ *v* [T] **1** if something frustrates you, it makes you feel annoyed or angry because you are unable to do what you want ‖ 원하는 것을 할 수 없기 때문에 신경질 나거나 화나게 하다. 실망[좌절]시키다. 좌절감을 안겨주다: *It's the lack of money that really frustrates me.* 나를 정말로 좌절시키는 것은 돈이 부족하다는 것이다. **2** to prevent someone's plans, efforts, or attempts from succeeding ‖ 남의 계획[노력, 시도]이 성공하는 것을 막다. 망치다. 꺾다. 소용없게 하다: *His attempts to escape were frustrated by an alert guard.* 그의 탈출 시도는 방심하지 않는 교도관 때문에 수포로 돌아갔다.

frus·trated /'frʌstreɪtɪd/ *adj* feeling annoyed or angry because you are unable to do what you want to do ‖ 하고 싶은 일을 할 수 없어서 신경질 나거나 화

나는. 낙담한. 실패한. 좌절한: *Don't get so frustrated; learning a language takes time.* 너무 실망하지 마. 언어를 배우는 데는 시간이 걸려. / *He gets frustrated when he doesn't win.* 그는 지는 것을 못 견뎌 한다.

frus·trat·ing /'frʌstreɪtɪŋ/ *adj* making you feel annoyed or angry because you cannot do what you want to do ‖ 하고 싶은 일을 할 수 없기 때문에 신경질 나거나 화나게 하는. 실망시키는. 답답한: *They keep sending me the wrong forms – it's really frustrating.* 그들은 나한테 계속 잘못된 양식을 보내주고 있어. 정말 실망이야.

frus·tra·tion /frʌ'streɪʃən/ *n* [C, U] the feeling of being annoyed or angry because you are unable to do what you want to do ‖ 하고 싶은 일을 할 수 없어서 신경질 나거나 화나는 감정. 실망. 낙담: *Dave thumped the table with his fist in frustration.* 데이브는 실망하여 주먹으로 탁자를 탕 하고 쳤다.

fry /fraɪ/ *v* **fried, fried, frying** [I, T] to cook something in hot fat or oil, or to be cooked in hot fat or oil ‖ 뜨거운 유지방이나 기름에 요리하거나 요리되다. 튀기다: *Do you want me to fry some eggs?* 계란 프라이 좀 해줄까?

fry·er /fraɪɚ/ *n* [C] **1** a special piece of equipment for frying food ‖ 음식을 튀기는 데에 쓰는 특별한 기구. 튀김 요리 기구. 프라이팬 **2** a chicken that has been specially bred to be fried 특히 튀김용으로 사육된 닭. 튀김용 닭

fry·ing pan /'.. ,./ *n* a round pan with a flat handle, used for frying food ‖ 음식을 튀기는 데 쓰는 납작한 손잡이가 달린 둥근 팬. 프라이팬 —see picture at PAN¹

ft. the written abbreviation of FOOT ‖ foot 의 약어

fuch·sia /'fjuʃə/ *n* **1** [U] a bright pink colour ‖ 밝은 분홍색 **2** [C, U] a type of bush with hanging bell-shaped flowers in red, pink, or white 붉은색[분홍색, 흰색]의 종 모양의 꽃이 매달린 관목의 일종. 수령초

fud·dy-dud·dy /'fʌdi, ,dʌdi/ *n* [C] **-ies** INFORMAL someone who has old fashioned ideas and attitudes ‖ 고루한 생각과 태도를 가진 사람. 시대에 뒤진 사람: *That dress makes you look such an old fuddy-duddy!.* 그 옷을 입으니까 네가 완전히 구닥다리처럼 보여!

fudge¹ /fʌdʒ/ *n* [U] a soft creamy sweet food, usually made with chocolate ‖ 보통 초콜릿으로 만든 부드럽고 크림 같은 달콤한 음식. 퍼지

fudge² *v* [T] to avoid giving exact figures or facts, in order to deceive people ‖ 사람들을 속이기 위해 정확한 수치나 사실 제공을 회피하다. …을 둘러대다. 날조하다. 속이다: *I knew that the only way I could get the job was to fudge on my experience.* 그 일자리를 잡을 수 있는 유일한 방법은 경력을 속이는 것이라는 것을 나는 알고 있었다.

fu·el¹ /'fjuəl, fyul/ *n* [C, U] a substance such as coal, gas, or oil that can be burned to produce heat or energy ‖ 열이나 에너지를 생산하기 위해 태울 수 있는 석탄[가스, 기름] 등의 물질. 연료

fuel² *v* **1** [T] to make a situation worse or to make someone's feelings stronger ‖ 상황을 더욱 나쁘게 하거나 사람의 감정을 더욱 격하게 하다: *The attempts to end the strike only fueled tensions on both sides.* 파업을 종결시키려는 시도는 (노·사) 양측에 긴장감만 더욱 가중시켰다. **2** [I, T] also **fuel up** to take fuel into a vehicle, or to provide a vehicle with fuel ‖ 차량에 연료를 넣거나 공급하다

fuel oil /'../ a type of oil that is burned to produce heat or power ‖ 연소되어 열이나 동력을 내는 기름의 일종. 연료유. 중유(重油)

fu·gi·tive /'fyudʒətɪv/ *n* someone who is trying to avoid being caught, especially by the police ‖ 특히 경찰에 잡히지 않으려고 하는 사람. 도망자. 탈주자: *a fugitive from justice* 수배자

ful·crum /'fʊlkrəm, 'fʌl-/ *n* the point on which a BAR that is being used for lifting something turns or is supported ‖ 사물을 들어올릴 때 사용하는 막대기가 돌거나 지지되는 지점. 지레의 받침점. 지렛대 받침

ful·fill /fʊl'fɪl/ *v* [T] **1** if a hope, promise, wish etc. is fulfilled, the thing that you had hoped etc. happens or is done ‖ 희망·약속·바람 등이 이루어지거나 완성되다. 이행[실행]하다. 이루다. 성취하다: *The president finally fulfilled his election promise to cut taxes.* 대통령은 마침내 세금을 줄이겠다는 자신의 선거 공약을 이행했다. **2** if a need, demand, or condition is fulfilled, you get what you need or want ‖ 욕구[요구, 조건] 등의 필요하거나 원하는 것을 얻다. 충족[만족]시키다: *Do you know enough about computers to fulfill our requirements?* 우리의 자격 조건을 충족시킬 만큼 컴퓨터에 대해 충분히 알고 있습니까? **3** to make something become true or cause something to happen ‖ 어떤 것이 사실이 되게 하거나 일어나게 하다. 실현하다. 이

루다: *If Terry doesn't work harder, he'll never fulfill his ambition to be a doctor.* 만일 테리가 좀 더 열심히 공부하지 않으면 의사가 되겠다는 꿈은 결코 이루지 못할 것이다. **4 fulfill yourself** to feel satisfied because you are using all your skills and qualities || 자신의 모든 기술과 역량을 사용하고 있어서 만족감을 느끼다. …에 자신의 역량을 십분 발휘하다: *She fulfilled herself both as a mother and as a successful writer.* 그녀는 어머니로서 그리고 성공적인 작가로서 모두 자신의 역량을 십분 발휘했다.

ful·filled /fʊlˈfɪld/ *adj* satisfied with your life, job etc. because you feel that it is interesting, or useful and you are using all your skills || 흥미 있거나 유용하다고 느끼며 자신의 모든 기술을 사용하고 있다고 느끼기 때문에 삶·직업 등에 만족한. 충만한: *I just don't feel fulfilled.* 나는 단지 만족감을 느끼지 못하는 though.

ful·fill·ing /fʊlˈfɪlɪŋ/ *adj* a job, relationship etc. that is fulfilling makes you feel satisfied because it allows you to use all your skills and qualities || 일·관계 등이 자신의 모든 기술과 역량을 발휘하도록 하기 때문에 만족감을 느끼게 하는. 만족시키는: *A career in nursing can be one of the most fulfilling jobs anyone can have.* 간호하는 일은 직업 중에서 만족감을 가장 많이 느끼는 일들 가운데 하나라고 할 수 있다.

ful·fill·ment /fʊlˈfɪlmənt/ *n* [U] **1** the feeling of being satisfied after a successful effort || 성공적인 노력을 한 후 느끼는 만족감. 실현. 성취. 수행. 달성: *Ann's work gives her a real sense of fulfillment.* 앤은 자신의 일에서 아주 큰 성취감을 느낀다. **2** the act or state of meeting a need, demand, or condition || 필요[요구, 조건]를 충족시키는 행동이나 상태: *The offer of this contract depends upon the fulfillment of certain conditions.* 이 계약의 신청은 일정한 조건의 충족에 달려 있다.

full¹ /fʊl/ *adj*
1 ▶CONTAINER/ROOM/PLACE ETC. 용기/방/장소 등◀ holding or containing as much of something, or as many things or people as possible || 어떤 것의 많은 양, 또는 가능한 한 많은 사물이나 사람을 보유하거나 포함하는. 가득 찬. 빽빽이 찬: *Is your glass full?* 잔이 가득 채워져 있니? / *a box full of paper* 종이로 가득 찬 상자 —see picture at EMPTY¹
2 ▶COMPLETE 완전한◀ **a)** including all parts or details; complete || 모든 부분이나 세부 사항까지 포함한. 전부[전체]의

완전한: *Please write down your full name and address.* 완전한 성명과 주소를 적어 주세요. / *Because it was slightly damaged, I didn't have to pay the full price for it.* 약간 손상을 입었기 때문에 그것에 대한 값을 전부 지불할 필요는 없었다. **b)** being the highest level or greatest amount of something || 어떤 것의 가장 높은 수준이나 가장 많은 양인. 최대한의. 최고의: *You have our full support in whatever you decide to do.* 당신이 무엇을 하기로 결정하든지 우리는 최대한의 지원을 하겠다.
3 be full of a) to contain many things of the same kind || 같은 종류의 많은 것들이 들어 있다. …으로 가득 차다. …이 많다: *Eric's essay is full of mistakes.* 에릭의 수필은 실수투성이다. **b)** to feel or express a strong emotion || 강렬한 감정을 느끼거나 표현하다. …으로 충만[가득]하다: *Cathy is full of guilt about the death of her mother.* 캐시는 어머니의 죽음에 대해 자책감을 몹시 느낀다. **c)** to think or talk about only one subject all the time || 언제나 한 주제에 대해서만 생각하거나 말하다. …에 정신이 쏠리다. 전념[몰두]하다: *Tim is just so full of himself—he really makes me mad!* 팀은 너무 자기 생각만 해. 그애 때문에 정말 화가 나!
4 ▶FOOD 음식◀ having eaten so much food that you cannot eat any more || 더 이상 먹지 못할 정도로 음식을 많이 먹은. 배부른: *"Would you like some more soup?" "No thanks. I'm full."* "수프 좀 더 드시겠어요?" "아뇨. 고맙지만 저는 먹을 만큼 많이 먹었습니다."
5 ▶SPEED/HEIGHT ETC. 속도/높이 등◀ as large, fast, strong etc. as possible || 가능한 한 큰[빠른, 강한]. 최대[최고]의: *running at full speed* 최고 속도로의 주행
6 ▶CLOTHING 옷◀ a full skirt, pair of pants etc. is made with a lot of material and fits loosely || 치마나 바지 등을 옷감을 많이 써서 만들어 느슨하게 맞는. 헐렁한. 치수가 넉넉한
7 ▶BODY 몸◀ a full face, body etc. is rounded or large || 얼굴·몸 등이 둥글거나 큰. 풍만한. 통통한: *clothes for the fuller figure* 더 통통한 체격에 맞는 옷
8 ▶TASTE/SOUND ETC. 맛/소리 등◀ a full taste, sound, color etc. is strong and pleasant || 맛·소리·색깔 등이 강렬하고 마음에 드는. 감칠맛이 나는. 풍미가 가득한: *a full-bodied wine* 감칠맛이 도는 포도주
full² *n* **1 in full** if you pay an amount of

money in full, you pay the whole amount ∥ 전액을 지불하는. 전부[전액]의 [으로]: *The bill was marked "paid in full."* 그 청구서에는 "완불"이라고 적혀 있었다. **2 to the full** in the best or most complete way ∥ 가장 좋거나 가장 완전한 방식으로. 완전하게. 마음껏. 최대한으로: *Ronnie lived his life to the full.* 로니는 여한이 없는 삶을 누렸다.

full³ *adv* LITERARY directly ∥ 직접적으로. 정확히: *The sun shone full on her face.* 햇빛이 그녀의 얼굴에 정통으로 비췄다.

full-blood·ed /ˈfʊl ˌblʌdɪd/ *adj* (only before noun; no comparative) having parents, grandparents etc from only one race of people, esp a race that is not the main one in a particular society ∥ (명사 앞에서만 사용; 비교급 없음)유일한 하나의 인종, 특히 특정 사회에서 주류를 이루지 않는 인종 출신의 부모·조부모 등을 가진. 혈통이 순수한. 순종의: *There are very few full-blooded cherokees left.* 순수한 혈통의 체로키족은 거의 남아 있지 않다.

full-blown /ˌ. ˈ./ *adj* fully developed ∥ 완전히 발달한. 성숙한. 완전한. 발병 단계의: *full-blown AIDS* 발병한 에이즈

full-fledged /ˌfʊl ˈfledʒd./ *adj* completely developed, trained, or established ∥ 완전하게 발달된(훈련된, 확립된). 완전한. 제 몫을 하게 된. 어엿한: *a full-fledged lawyer* 어엿한 변호사

full-grown /ˌ. ˈ./ *adj* a full-grown animal, plant, or person has developed to his, her, or its full size and will not grow any bigger ∥ 동물[식물, 사람]이 완전한 크기로 성장해서 더 이상 자라지 않는. 다 자란. 완전히 성장[발육]한

full house /ˌ. ˈ./ *n* an occasion at a concert hall, sports field etc. when every seat has someone sitting in it ∥ 콘서트장·경기장 등의 모든 좌석에 사람들이 앉아 있는 경우. 대만원. 만원인 극장[경기장]

full-length /ˌ. ˈ./ *adj* **1 full-length mirror/photograph etc.** a mirror etc. that shows all of a person, from his/her head to his/her feet ∥ 거울 등이 사람의 머리에서 발끝까지 전체를 비추는. 전신 거울/사진 **2 full-length skirt/dress** a skirt etc. that reaches the ground ∥ 치마 등이 땅에 닿는. 발목까지 오는 치마/드레스 **3 full-length play/book etc.** a play etc. of the normal length ∥ 정상적인 길이의 연극 등. (완전) 무삭제 연극/서적

full moon /ˌ. ˈ./ *n* [singular] the moon when it looks completely round ∥ 완전하게 둥글게 보일 때의 달. 보름달

full·ness /ˈfʊlnɪs/ *n* [U] **in the fullness of time** FORMAL when the right time comes ∥ 적당한 때가 올 때. 때가 되어 [차서]: *I'm sure he'll tell us everything in the fullness of time.* 때가 되면 그는 우리에게 모든 것을 말할 거라고 확신한다.

full-scale /ˌ. ˈ./ *adj* **1** using all possible powers or forces ∥ 가능한 모든 권능이나 힘을 사용하는. 전력을 다하는. 총력을 기울인. 전면적인: *a full-scale inquiry into the disaster* 재해에 대한 철저한 조사 **2** a full-scale model, copy, picture etc. is the same size as the thing it represents ∥ 모형·복사물·사진 등이 실물과 같은 크기의

full-time /ˌ. ˈ./ *adj, adv* working or studying for the number of hours that work is usually done ∥ 일반적으로 일이 마감되는 시간 동안 내내 일하거나 공부하는. 전시간 근무[노동]의. 상근의: *Until she had a baby, Andrea worked full-time for an insurance company.* 아기가 생기기 전까지 안드레아는 보험 회사에서 정규직 근무를 했다. / *a full-time job* 정규직 —compare PART-TIME

ful·ly /ˈfʊli/ *adv* completely ∥ 완전히. 전적으로: *a fully trained nurse* 교육 과정을 완전히 이수한 간호사

fum·ble /ˈfʌmbəl/ *v* **1** [I, T] to drop the ball in a game of football ∥ 미식축구 경기에서 공을 떨어뜨리다. 펌블하다. 공을 놓치다 **2** [I] to move your fingers or hands awkwardly when you are looking for something or trying to do something ∥ 어떤 것을 찾거나 하려고 할 때 손가락이나 손을 서투르게 움직이다. 더듬(어 찾)다. 서투르게 만지다: *Gary fumbled for the light switch in the dark.* 게리는 어둠 속에서 전등 스위치를 더듬어 찾았다. – **fumble** *n*

fume /fyum/ *v* [I] to show that you are very angry, usually without saying anything ∥ 보통 아무 말 없이 매우 화난 것을 나타내다. 부아가 나다: *"Was he angry?" "Yeah, he was really fuming."* "그 사람 화났니?" "그래, 그는 정말 잔뜩 화나 있어."

fumes /fyumz/ *n* [plural] strong-smelling gas or smoke that is unpleasant to breathe in ∥ 숨쉬기에 불쾌한 역한 냄새가 나는 가스나 연기. 유독 가스. 매연: *gasoline fumes* 가솔린 매연

fu·mi·gate /ˈfyuməˌgeɪt/ *v* [T] to remove disease, BACTERIA, insects etc. from somewhere using chemical smoke or gas ∥ 화학적 연기나 가스를 사용해서 어떤 장소로부터 병·박테리아·곤충 등을

없애다. …을 훈증 소독하다 –**fumi·gation** /ˌfjuməˈɡeɪʃən/ *n* [U]

fun¹ /fʌn/ *n* [U] **1** pleasure, amusement, and enjoyment, or something that causes these ‖ 즐거움·재미·기쁨, 또는 이러한 것을 유발하는 것. 재미(있는 일): *Swimming is fun.* 수영은 재미있다. / *Did you have fun at Phil's party?* 필의 파티는 재미있었니? / *He's learning to speak Spanish, just for fun.* (=because he enjoys it) 그는 단지 재미로 스페인어 회화를 배우고 있다. / *It's no fun* (=not fun) *to be sick.* 아픈 것은 즐거운 일이 아니다. **2 make fun of sb/sth** to make unkind jokes about someone or something ‖ 사람이나 사물에 매정한 농담을 하다. …을 놀리다: *All the kids at school are making fun of Billy because he can't read.* 학교의 모든 아이들이 빌리가 책을 읽지 못한다고 놀리고 있다. **3 in fun** if you make a joke or say something about someone in fun, you do not intend it to be insulting ‖ 농담이나 누군가에 대한 말이 모욕하려는 의도가 없는. 농담으로. 장난삼아: *I'm sorry, I only said it in fun.* 미안해, 나는 단지 농담으로 말했을 뿐이야.

USAGE NOTE fun and funny

Use **fun** as a noun to talk about events and activities that are enjoyable, such as games and parties: *Let's go to the beach and have some fun!* Use **fun** as an adjective to say that something was enjoyable: *Going to the beach was fun.* **Funny** is an adjective that describes someone or something that makes us laugh: *Bob's jokes are really funny.* ✗DON'T SAY "Going to the beach was funny."✗

fun은 게임 및 파티 등의 즐길 만한 행사와 활동을 말하는 데에는 명사로 쓰인다: 해변으로 가서 좀 놀자! **fun**은 어떤 것이 즐길 만하다고 말하는 데에는 형용사로 쓰인다: 해변에 간 것은 재미있었다. **funny**는 웃기게 만드는 사람이나 사물을 묘사하는 형용사이다: 보브의 농담은 정말 웃긴다. "Going to the beach was funny."라고는 하지 않는다.

---

fun² *adj* **1** a fun activity or experience is enjoyable ‖ 활동이나 경험이 즐길 만한. 유쾌한. 즐거운: *It'll be a fun thing to do.* 그것을 하는 것은 재미있는 일이 될 것이다. **2** a fun person is enjoyable to be with ‖ 사람이 함께 있으면 즐거운: *Terry is always fun to be with.* 테리와 함께 있으면 항상 즐겁다.

func·tion¹ /ˈfʌŋkʃən/ *n* **1** the usual purpose of a thing, or the job that someone usually does ‖ 사물의 일반적인 목적, 또는 사람이 일반적으로 하는 일. 기능. 작용. 직무. 역할: *What's the exact function of this program?* 이 프로그램의 정확한 기능이 무엇입니까? / *A manager has to perform many different functions.* 관리자는 여러 다양한 직분을 수행해야 한다. **2** a large party or ceremonial event, especially for an important or official occasion ‖ 특히 중요하거나 공식적인 경우의 큰 파티나 기념 행사. 의식. 축전. 대집회: *The mayor has to attend all kinds of official functions.* 시장은 모든 종류의 공식적인 행사에 참석해야 한다.

function² *v* [I] to work in a particular way or in the correct way ‖ 특정하거나 정확하게 작동하다. 작용하다. 기능하다: *Can you explain exactly how this new system will function?* 이 새로운 시스템이 정확히 어떻게 작동되는지 설명해 줄 수 있니?

function as sth *phr v* [T] to be used or work as something ‖ 어떤 것으로 사용되거나 활동하다. 기능을 다하다. 구실을 하다: *The new space station will function as a laboratory in space.* 새로운 우주 정거장은 우주에서 연구소로의 기능을 수행할 것이다.

func·tion·al /ˈfʌŋkʃənəl/ *adj* designed to be useful rather than attractive ‖ 멋지게 보이는 것보다 유용성의 목적으로 설계된. 기능 위주의. 실용적인: *functional furniture* 기능성 가구 –**functionally** *adv*

function key /ˈ.. ˌ./ *n* TECHNICAL a key on the KEYBOARD of a computer that tells it to do something ‖ 어떤 것을 하라고 명령을 내리는 컴퓨터 키보드상의 키. 기능키

fund¹ /fʌnd/ *n* an amount of money that is kept for a particular purpose ‖ 특정한 목적을 위해 비축하여 둔 돈의 액수. 기금. 자금: *the school sports fund* 학생 스포츠 관련 기금 —see also FUNDS

fund² *v* [T] to provide money for an activity, organization, event etc. ‖ 활동·조직·행사 등을 위해 돈을 공급하다. …에 자금을 제공하다: *How are you going to fund this project?* 이 프로젝트에 소요되는 자금은 어떻게 마련할 생각입니까?

fun·da·men·tal¹ /ˌfʌndəˈmɛntəl/ *adj* **1** relating to the most basic and important parts of something ‖ 어떤 것의 가장 기본적이고 중요한 부분과 관련된. 기본적인. 근본적인: *He's promised to make some* *fundamental changes in the tax laws.* 그는 세법에 있어서 몇 가지 근본적인 개정을 이루겠다는 약속을 했다. **2** necessary for something to exist or develop ‖ 어떤 것이 존재하거나 발전하기 위해 필요한. 필수적인. 중요한: *Water is fundamental to life.* 물은 생명 유지에 필수적이다. **– fundamentally** *adv*: *two fundamentally different approaches to solving the problem* 그 문제를 푸는 근본적으로 다른 두 가지 접근법

fundamental² *n* **the fundamentals of sth** the most important ideas, rules etc. that something is based on ‖ 어떤 것의 기반이 되는 가장 중요한 생각·규칙 등. 근본 (원칙): *a class in the fundamentals of computer programming* 컴퓨터 프로그래밍 기초반

fun·da·men·tal·ist /ˌfʌndəˈmɛntəlɪst/ *n* someone who follows the rules of his/her religion very exactly and believes that no other religion is true ‖ 자신의 종교 원칙을 매우 정확하게 따르며 다른 어떤 종교도 진리가 아니라고 믿는 사람. 근본주의자 **– fundamentalist** *adj* **– fundamentalism** *n* [U]

fund·ing /ˈfʌndɪŋ/ *n* [U] an amount of money used for a special purpose ‖ 특수 목적에 사용되는 일정액의 돈. 자금. 재원

fund-raising /ˈ. ˌ../ *adj* fund-raising events collect money for a specific purpose ‖ 행사에서 구체적인 목적을 위해 돈을 모으는. 모금의

funds /fʌndz/ *n* [plural] the money needed to do something ‖ 어떤 것을 하는 데에 필요한 돈. 자금: *It's a good idea, but we don't have the funds to do it.* 그건 좋은 생각이지만 우리는 그것을 실행할 자금이 없다.

fu·ner·al /ˈfyunərəl/ *n* a ceremony, usually religious, for burying or burning a dead person ‖ 시신을 묻거나 화장시키는 주로 종교적인 의식. 장례식: *The funeral will be held on Thursday at St. Patrick's church.* 장례식은 성 페트릭 교회에서 목요일에 열릴 예정이다.

funeral home /ˈ.. ˌ../, **funeral parlor** /ˈ... ˌ../ *n* the place where a body is kept before a funeral and where sometimes the funeral is held ‖ 장례식 전에 시신이 보관되며 때로는 장례식이 거행되는 곳. 장례식장. 영안실

fun·gus /ˈfʌŋgəs/ *n, plural* **fungi** /ˈfʌndʒaɪ, -gaɪ/ *or* **funguses** **1** [C, U] a simple plant without leaves, such as MUSHROOMs and MOLD, that grows in dark warm slightly wet places ‖ 어둡고 따뜻하며 약간 축축한 곳에서 자라는 버섯

과 균류 등의 잎이 없는 단일체 식물. 균류. 곰팡이. 효모균 **2** [U] this type of plant, especially considered as a disease ‖ 특히 병으로 간주되는 이런 종류의 식물. 균상종. 해면종 **– fungal** /ˈfʌŋgəl/ *adj*

funk /fʌŋk/ *n* [U] a type of popular music with a strong beat that is based on JAZZ and African music ‖ 재즈와 아프리카 음악에 기초를 둔 강한 박자를 가진 대중 음악의 한 형태. 펑크 (음악)

funk·y /ˈfʌŋki/ *adj* INFORMAL **1** modern, fashionable, and interesting ‖ 현대적이고 최신식이며 흥미를 끄는. 멋진. 훌륭한. 파격적인: *Where did you get those funky boots?* 그 멋들어진 부츠 어디에서 샀니? **2** relating to the strong RHYTHM of FUNK music ‖ 펑크 음악의 강한 리듬과 관계된. 펑키의. 펑크 음악의

fun·nel¹ /ˈfʌnl/ *n* a tube with a wide top and a narrow bottom, used for pouring liquids or powders into a container ‖ 용기에 액체나 가루를 따르기 위해 사용하는 맨 위는 넓고 밑쪽은 좁은 관. 깔때기

funnel

fun·nel² *v* **1** [I, T] to pass or to put something through a funnel or a narrow space like a funnel ‖ 깔때기나 깔때기처럼 좁은 공간을 통해 어떤 것을 통과시키거나 넣다. 깔때기[좁은 통로]를[로] 지나다[내보내다]: *The crowd funneled through the narrow streets.* 군중들이 좁은 거리를 통해 지나갔다. **2** [T] to send things or money from different places to a particular place ‖ 다른 장소들로부터 어떤 특정한 장소로 물건이나 돈을 보내다. 어떤 곳에 집중시키다: *a policy of funneling the most talented students into special schools* 가장 능력이 뛰어난 학생들을 특수 학교로 모으는 정책

fun·nies /ˈfʌniz/ *n* **the funnies** a number of different CARTOONs (=funny pictures) printed together in newspapers or magazines ‖ 신문이나 잡지에 함께 인쇄되는 재미있는 각종 만화

fun·ni·ly /ˈfʌnəli/ *adv* ⇨ **oddly/ funnily enough** (ENOUGH¹)

fun·ny¹ /ˈfʌni/ *adj* **1** amusing you and making you laugh ‖ 즐거움을 주며 웃게 만드는. 우스운. 익살맞은: *I have to tell you what she said. It was so funny.* 그녀가 무슨 말을 했는지 네게 말해줄게. 정말 우스워. / *You'd enjoy that book, it's really funny.* 그 책은 정말 재미있어서 즐

겁게 읽을 거야. / *a funny joke* 우스운 농담 **2 strange or unexpected, and difficult to understand or explain** ‖ 이상하거나 예상치 못하여 이해하거나 설명하기 어려운. 기묘한: *What's that funny noise coming from upstairs?* 위층에서 나는 저 이상한 소음은 도대체 뭐야? **3 slightly ill** ‖ 조금 아픈. 메스꺼운: *I've felt a little funny all week, so I thought I'd take the day off.* 한 주 내내 몸이 약간 안 좋아서 그 날 쉴까 생각했다.

SPOKEN PHRASES

4 it's funny used in order to say that you do not understand something that seems strange or unexpected ‖ 이상하거나 예상 밖으로 보이는 일을 이해하지 못한다고 말할 때 쓰여. 이상하단 말이야: *It's funny – he looks so healthy but he's always getting sick.* 그는 매우 건강해 보이는데 항상 아프니 이상하단 말이야. **5 that's funny** said when you are surprised by something that has happened, that you cannot explain ‖ 설명할 수 없는 일이 발생하여 놀랐을 때에 쓰여. 그것 참 이상하다: *That's funny! She was here just a minute ago.* 그것 참 이상하네! 방금 전까지만 해도 그녀가 여기 있었는데. **6 the funny thing is** used in order to say what the strangest or most amusing part of a story or situation is ‖ 이야기나 상황의 어떤 부분이 가장 이상하거나 가장 재미있는지 말하는 데에 쓰여. 가장 이상한[웃기는] 점은…: *The funny thing is, I knew what was going to happen before I even got to the meeting.* 가장 이상한 점은 내가 회의에 가기도 전에 무슨 일이 일어날지 알았다는 거야. **7 very funny!** said when someone is laughing at you or making a joke that you do not think is funny ‖ 남이 화자(話者)를 비웃거나 재미있게 생각되지 않는 농담을 할 때에 쓰여. 우습군! 웃기는군!

—see usage note at FUN¹

funny² *adv* in a strange or unusual way ‖ 이상하거나 별난 방식으로. 기묘하게. 비정상적으로: *Judy's been acting kind of funny lately.* 주디는 최근에 기묘한 행동을 하고 있다.

funny bone /ˌ.. ˌ./ *n* [singular] the soft part of your elbow that hurts a lot when you hit it against something ‖ 무엇에 부딪쳤을 때 매우 아픈 팔꿈치의 부드러운 부분. 팔꿈치의 척골(尺骨)

fur /fɚ/ *n* **1** [U] the thick soft hair that covers the bodies of some animals such as dogs and cats ‖ 개·고양이 등의 동물의 몸을 덮고 있는 빽빽하고 부드러운 털 **2** [C, U] the fur-covered skin of an animal, used especially for making clothes, or a piece of clothing made from fur ‖ 특히 옷 제조에 쓰이는 털로 뒤덮인 동물 가죽, 또는 털로 된 의류 한 점: *Several valuable furs were stolen last night.* 어젯밤에 몇 개의 값비싼 모피를 도난당했다. / *a fur coat* 모피 코트

fu·ri·ous /ˈfyuriəs/ *adj* **1 very angry** ‖ 매우 화난: *Jim'll be furious with me if I'm late.* 내가 만약 늦는다면 짐은 매우 화를 낼 것이다. **2** done with a lot of uncontrolled energy or anger ‖ 자제할 수 없을 정도로 왕성한 기력이나 노여움으로 행한. 맹렬한: *He woke up to a furious pounding at the door.* 그는 맹렬히 문 두드리는 소리에 잠에서 깨어났다. – **furiously** *adv*

furl /fɚl/ *v* [T] to roll or fold something such as a flag or sail ‖ 깃발이나 돛 등을 말거나 접다 —see also UNFURL¹

fur·long /ˈfɚlɔŋ/ *n* OLD-FASHIONED a unit for measuring length, equal to 1/8 of a mile or 201 meters ‖ 1/8마일이나 201미터에 상당하는 길이의 단위

fur·nace /ˈfɚnɪs/ *n* a large container with a hot fire inside it, used for producing power or heat, or to melt metals and other materials ‖ 동력이나 열의 생산, 또는 금속과 다른 물질을 녹이는 데에 쓰이는, 내부에 뜨거운 불을 피우는 대형 용기. 용광로

fur·nish /ˈfɚnɪʃ/ *v* [T] **1** to put furniture and other things into a house or room ‖ 집이나 방안에 가구와 다른 물건들을 갖추다: *a room furnished with two beds* 2개의 침대가 비치된 방 **2** to supply something that is necessary for a special purpose ‖ 특정한 목적에 필요로 하는 것을 공급하다: *The company furnished us with a free copy of their catalog.* 그 회사는 우리에게 카탈로그 한 부를 무료로 제공했다. – **furnished** *adj*: *a furnished apartment* 가구 딸린 아파트

fur·nished /ˈfɚnɪʃt/ *adj* a room, house, etc. that is furnished, has furniture in it ‖ 방·집 등이 가구를 갖추고 있는: *a beautifully furnished room* 가구가 멋지게 비치된 방 / *We got a furnished apartment for $400 a month!* 우리는 가구를 갖춘 아파트를 월 400달러에 구했어! —opposite UNFURNISHED

fur·nish·ings /ˈfɚnɪʃɪŋz/ *n* [plural] the furniture and other things in a room, such as curtains, decorations etc. ‖ 가구 및 커튼이나 장식품 등의 기타 실내 용품. 비품

fur·ni·ture /'fɜnɪtʃə/ n [U] large movable objects such as chairs, tables, and beds, that you use in a room, office etc. ‖ 의자·탁자·침대 등의 방·사무실에서 사용하는, 움직일 수 있는 큰 물건. 가구. 비품: *Aunt Sara has a lot of antique furniture.* 사라 고모는 고가구를 많이 갖고 계신다. / *office furniture* 사무용 가구

fu·ror /'fyʊrɔr/ n [singular] a sudden expression of anger or excitement among a large group of people ‖ 대규모 사람들 사이에서 일어나는 화나 흥분의 갑작스런 표현. 격노. 격앙: *His decision to resign caused quite a furor.* 사직하겠다는 그의 결심은 상당한 분노를 야기했다.

fur·row¹ /'fɜoʊ, 'fʌroʊ/ n a long deep fold or cut in the surface of something such as skin or the ground ‖ 피부나 땅 등의 표면에 길고 깊게 팬 골. 주름살. 밭고랑: *The deep furrows made it hard to walk across the field.* 고랑이 깊게 패어 있어 들판은 지나기가 힘들었다.

furrow² v [T] to make a long deep fold or cut in the surface of something such as skin or the ground ‖ 피부나 땅 등의 표면에 길고 깊은 골을 내다: *Saks furrowed his brow.* 삭스는 이마에 주름살을 지었다. **– furrowed** adj

fur·ry /'fɜi/ adj covered with fur, or looking or feeling as if covered with fur ‖ 모피로 덮인, 또는 모피로 덮인 듯한 모습이나 느낌의: *furry material* 모피 직물 / *a furry little rabbit* 털이 복슬복슬한 작은 토끼

fur·ther¹ /'fɜðə/ adv 1 more than before ‖ 전보다 더. 그 이상으로: *I have nothing further to say.* 나는 더 이상 할 말이 없다. 2 a longer way in time or space ‖ 시간이나 공간상으로 더 멀리: *The records don't go any further back than 1960.* 그 기록은 1960년 이전까지 거슬러 올라가지는 않는다. / *Their home is further down the street.* 그들의 집은 그 길의 훨씬 아래쪽에 있다. 3 **take sth further** to do something at a more serious or higher level ‖ 보다 진지하거나 높은 수준으로 어떤 것을 하다: *Hallas decided not to take the court case any further.* 할라스는 더 이상의 법정 소송을 하지 않기로 결심했다. 4 FORMAL ⇨ FURTHERMORE —see usage note at FARTHER

further² adj additional ‖ 추가된. 그 이상의: *Are there any further questions?* 질문 더 있습니까?

further³ v [T] FORMAL to help something to succeed ‖ 성공하도록 어떤 것을 돕다. 진척시키다: *They hope that the strike will further their cause.* (=help them to succeed) 그들은 파업을 통해 자신들의 주장을 진척시키기를 바란다.

fur·ther·more /'fɜðə,mɔr/ adv FORMAL in addition to what has already been written or said ‖ 이미 써넣은 것이나 말한 것에 덧붙여. 게다가: *The house is far too small for us. Furthermore, it's not close enough to the city.* 우리에게 그 집은 너무 좁고 게다가 시내에서 가깝지도 않다.

fur·thest /'fɜðɪst/ adj, adv 1 to the greatest degree or amount, or more than before ‖ 가장 최대의 정도나 양의[으로], 전보다 더한[더하게]: *Smith's book has probably gone the furthest* (=done the most) *in trying to explain the causes of war.* 스미스의 책이 전쟁의 원인에 대한 설명을 시도한 책 중에서 아마도 최상일 것이다. 2 as far away as possible from a particular point in time, or from a particular place ‖ 특정한 시점이나 장소로부터 가능한 한 멀리 떨어진[떨어져]. 먼[멀리]: *the houses furthest from the town center* 도심으로부터 가장 멀리 떨어진 집들

fur·tive /'fɜtɪv/ adj behaving as if you want to keep something secret ‖ 어떤 것을 비밀로 하고 싶은 듯이 행동하는. 은밀한: *a furtive glance* 슬쩍 엿보기 – **furtively** adv

fu·ry /'fyʊri/ n 1 [C, U] a state or feeling of extreme anger ‖ 심한 분노의 상태나 감정. 격노. 격분: *She was filled with fury.* 그녀는 격분해 있었다. / *Hank left the meeting in a fury.* 행크는 노발대발하여 모임을 떠났다. 2 **the fury of the wind/sea/storm etc.** used in order to describe very bad weather ‖ 악천후를 설명하는 데에 쓰여. 격심한 바람[바다, 폭풍]: *After three hours, the fury of the storm began to pass.* 세 시간이 지나자 격렬한 폭풍이 지나가기 시작했다. 3 **a fury of** a state of great activity or strong feeling ‖ 격렬한 행동이나 격한 감정 상태: *After the interview, Joe went home in a fury of frustration.* 인터뷰가 끝난 후, 조는 큰 좌절감을 안고 집으로 돌아갔다.

fuse¹ /fyuz/ n 1 a short wire inside a piece of electrical equipment that melts if too much electricity passes through it ‖ 전류가 너무 많이 흐르면 녹는, 전기 장치 안에 있는 짧은 전선. 퓨즈: *The lights in the kitchen are all out. I think we* *must have blown a fuse.* (=melted the wire) 부엌의 전등이 다 나갔는데 틀림없이 퓨즈가 끊긴 것 같다. **2** a thing such as a string that is connected to a bomb and used for making it explode ‖ 폭탄에 연결되어 폭발시킬 때 사용되는 선. 도화선 **3** used in expressions relating to someone's temper ‖ 성미와 관계된 표현에 쓰여: *Randy finally blew a fuse* (=got angry very suddenly) *and screamed at us.* 랜디는 마침내 분노가 폭발하여 우리에게 소리쳤다. / *I think Martina has a short fuse* (=gets angry easily) *when she's dealing with kids.* 내가 생각하기에 마티나는 아이들을 돌볼 때 화를 잘 낸다.

fuse² *v* [I, T] **1** to join together and become one thing, or to join two things together ‖ 결합하여 하나가 되거나 두 개를 결합시키다. 융합하다. 융합시키다: *His novel fuses historical information with a romantic story.* 그의 소설은 낭만적 이야기에 역사적 정보를 융합시켰다. **2** TECHNICAL if metals, rocks etc. fuse together, they become melted and are joined together ‖ 금속·암석 등이 녹아서 결합되다. 융합되다. 융용되다

fuse·box /ˈfyuzbɑks/ *n* a metal box that contains the FUSEs for the electrical system in a building ‖ 건물의 전기 시스템용 퓨즈가 들어 있는 금속 상자. 퓨즈함

fu·se·lage /ˈfyusə,lɑʒ, -lɪdʒ, -zə-/ *n* the main part of a plane, in which people sit or goods are carried ‖ 사람이 앉거나 물건을 실을 수 있는 비행기의 주요 부분. 동체 —see picture at AIRPLANE

fu·sion /ˈfyuʒən/ *n* [C, U] **1** the action of combining things such as metals by heating them ‖ 열을 가하여 금속 등의 물질을 결합시키는 행위. 용융 **2** the combination of separate things, groups, or ideas, or the action of joining them ‖ 개별적인 것[그룹, 사상]의 결합, 또는 그 행위. 융합(시키기): *jazz-funk fusion* 재즈와 펑크의 융합 —compare FISSION

fusion cui·sine /ˈ.. ../, **fusion food** /ˈ..,./ *n* [U] a style of cooking in which new dishes are developed which include foods from several different parts of the world, for example China and Mexico ‖ 중국·멕시코 등 세계의 각기 다른 지역의 음식을 포함시켜 새로운 요리를 만들어 내는 요리법. 퓨전 음식[조리법]

fuss¹ /fʌs/ *n* **1** [singular, U] attention or excitement that makes something seem more serious or important than it is ‖ 어떤 것을 실제보다 더 심각하고 중요해 보이게 만드는 주목이나 흥분. 공연한

소란: *Hey, what's all the fuss about?* (=why are people so excited, angry, busy etc.) 이봐! 왜 이렇게 소란스러워! **2** **make a fuss/kick up a fuss** to complain or become angry about something that other people do not think is important ‖ 다른 사람들이 중요하게 여기지 않는 것에 대해서 불평을 하거나 화를 내다. 소란을 피우다: *Cory made a fuss in the restaurant because her meat was burned.* 코리는 자신의 고기가 탄 것 때문에 식당에서 야단법석을 떨었다. **3** **make a fuss over sb/sth** to pay too much attention to someone or something that you like ‖ 좋아하는 사람이나 사물에 지나친 관심을 쏟다: *You always make a fuss over Kenny – it's really embarrassing!* 너는 항상 케니라면 사족을 못쓰는데 정말이지 당혹스러워!

fuss² *v* [I] to complain or become upset ‖ 불평하거나 심란해하다. 안달하다. 야단법석하다: *Stop fussing! We'll be home soon!* 안달하지 마! 우리는 금방 집에 도착할 테니.

fuss over sb/sth *phr v* [T] to pay too much attention to someone or something that you like ‖ 좋아하는 사람이나 사물에 지나친 신경을 쓰다: *Grandma's always fussing over the kids.* 할머니는 항상 아이들에 대해 마음을 졸이신다.

fuss with sth *phr v* [T] to move or touch something again and again in a nervous way ‖ 신경질적으로 어떤 것을 자꾸 움직이거나 건드리다: *Stop fussing with your hair!* 머리 좀 만지작거리지 마!

fuss·y /ˈfʌsi/ *adj* too concerned or worried about things that are not very important ‖ 그다지 중요하지 않은 것에 대해 지나치게 걱정하거나 염려하는. 안달하는: *Kids are often fussy eaters* 아이들은 종종 음식에 대해 까다롭다.

fu·tile /ˈfyutl/ *adj* not effective or successful ‖ 효과적이거나 성공적이지 못한. 헛된. 공연한: *Janet ran after the thief in a futile attempt/effort to get her purse back.* 자넷은 자신의 지갑을 되찾기 위해서 도둑을 쫓아가 봤지만 헛수고였다. – **futility** /fyuˈtɪləti/ *n* [U]

fu·ton /ˈfutɑn/ *n* a soft flat MATTRESS that can be used as a bed or folded into a chair ‖ 침대 또는 접어서 의자로 쓰는 부드럽고 납작한 매트리스. (일본의)요

fu·ture¹ /ˈfyutʃɚ/ *n* **1** **the future** the time that will happen after the present ‖ 현재 다음에 오게 될 시간. 미래: *Do you have any plans for the future?* 장래에 대한 계획이 있니? **2** **in the future**

a) at some time in the future ‖ 미래의 어떤 시점에. 장차: *I'm hoping to go to Atlanta in the near/immediate future.* (=soon) 나는 조만간에 애틀랜타에 가고 싶어. **b)** the next time you do the same activity ‖ 똑같은 행동을 하는 다음번에: *In the future I'll be sure to reserve tickets.* 다음에는 꼭 티켓 예약을 할 거야. **3** what will happen to someone or something ‖ 사람이나 사물에 닥칠 것. 장래. 전도: *My parents have already planned out my whole future.* 나의 부모님은 이미 나의 모든 장래에 대한 계획을 세우셨다. **4** [singular, U] the possibility of being or becoming successful ‖ 성공하거나 성공적이 될 가능성. 가망: *Pickford feels confident about the company's future.* 픽포드는 회사의 미래에 대해 자신만만하다. **5 in future** used in order to warn someone or announce something about the future ‖ 미래에 대하여 남에게 경고하거나 어떤 것을 알려주는 데에 쓰여. 앞으로: *In future, you will need a note from your parents in order to leave campus for lunch.* 앞으로 점심시간에 교내에서 외출하기 위해선 부모님의 통지서가 필요할 것이다. **6 the future** TECHNICAL in grammar, the tense of a verb that shows that an action or state will happen or exist at a later time. It is often shown in English by the MODAL VERB "will" followed by a verb. In the sentence, "We will leave tomorrow," "will leave" is in the future tense ‖ 문법에서 행동이나 상태가 차후에 발생하거나 존재할 것을 나타내는 동사의 시제. 미래 시제. 영어에서는 종종 법조동사 "will" 로 나타내며 뒤에 본동사가 이어진다. "We will leave tomorrow (우리는 내일 떠납니다)."라는 문장에서 "will leave"는 미래 시제이다.

future² *adj* **1** likely to happen or exist during the time after the present ‖ 현재 이후의 시간에 발생하거나 존재할 것 같은. 미래의: *I'd like you to meet Pam, my future wife/mother-in-law etc.* (=someone who will be your wife etc.) 당신이 내 미래의 아내[장모님]가 될 팸을 만나 주면 좋겠다. / *We'll discuss that in future contract talks.* 그것은 앞으로 있을 계약 협상에서 논의하게 될 것이다. **2** TECHNICAL in grammar, being a tense of a verb that shows a future action or state ‖ 문법적으로 미래의 행동이나 상태를 나타내는 동사 시제의. 미래(형)의: *the future tense* 미래 시제 **3 for future reference** kept or remembered in order to be used again at a later time ‖ 후에 다시 사용할 수 있게 보존하거나 기억하는. 후일의 참고용으로: *Can I keep that article for future reference?* 미래에 참고하기 위해 그 기사를 내가 보관해도 되겠어요?

future per·fect /ˌ.. ˈ../ *n* **the future perfect** TECHNICAL in grammar, the tense of a verb that shows that an action will be completed before a particular time in the future. It is shown by the AUXILIARY VERBs "will have" followed by a PAST PARTICIPLE. In the sentence "I will have finished my finals by next Friday," "will have finished" is in the future perfect ‖ 문법에서 행동이 미래의 특정 시간 전에 완료될 것을 나타내는 동사의 시제. 미래 완료 시제. 조동사 "will have"로 나타내며 뒤에 과거 분사가 이어진다. "I will have finished my finals by next Friday (나는 기말 시험을 다음 주 금요일까지는 마칠 것이다)."라는 문장에서 "will have finished"는 미래 완료시제이다

fu·tur·is·tic /ˌfyutʃəˈrɪstɪk/ *adj* futuristic ideas, books, movies etc. describe what might happen in the future, especially because of scientific developments ‖ 생각·책·영화 등이 특히 과학 발전으로 미래에 발생할 수 있는 것을 묘사한. 미래의[에 관한]

fuzz /fʌz/ *n* [U] INFORMAL small soft thin hairs, or a similar material on fruit such as PEACHes ‖ 작고 부드러우며 가는 솜털, 또는 복숭아 등의 과일에 있는 비슷한 물질. 솜털. 잔털: *Kelly's baby has a light fuzz of black hair on her head.* 켈리의 아기는 머리에 검은 솜털이 났다.

fuzz·y /ˈfʌzi/ *adj* **1** not easy to understand or not having very clear details ‖ 이해하기 쉽지 않거나 아주 분명한 세부 사항이 없는. 흐릿한. 애매한: *Unfortunately all the photographs are a little fuzzy.* 불행히도, 모든 사진들이 조금 흐릿하다. / *I only have a fuzzy idea of what she looks like.* 나는 그녀의 외모에 대해 막연히 추정해 볼 뿐이다. **2** having a lot of very small thin hairs, fur etc. that look very soft ‖ 매우 부드러워 보이는 몹시 작고 가는 털이 많은. 보풀[솜털]로 덮인: *a fuzzy sweater* 보풀이 인 스웨터

fwy the written abbreviation of FREEWAY ‖ freeway의 약어

FYI the abbreviation of "for your information," used especially on MEMOs (=short business notes) ‖ 특히 메모에 쓰이는 "for your information (참고로)"의 약어

Gg

G, g /dʒi/ the seventh letter of the English alphabet ‖ 영어 알파벳의 일곱째 자

G¹ /dʒi/ *n* **1** [C, U] the fifth note in the musical SCALE of C, or the musical KEY based on this note ‖ 다 장조의 다섯째 음이나 이 음을 기조로 한 조. 사 음. 사 조 **2** TECHNICAL an amount of force that is equal to the Earth's GRAVITY ‖ 지구의 중력에 해당하는 힘. 중력의 가속도

G² *adj* the abbreviation for "general audience," used in order to show that a movie has been officially approved for people of all ages ‖ "general audience"의 약어로 영화가 모든 연령층의 사람들에게 공식적으로 허용된 것임을 나타내는 데에 쓰여. 연령 제한이 없는 영화의

GA the written abbreviation of Georgia ‖ Georgia (조지아 주)의 약어

gab /gæb/ *v* **-bbed, -bbing** [I] INFORMAL to talk continuously, usually about things that are not important ‖ 대개 중요하지 않은 것들에 대해 끊임없이 말하다. 수다 떨다. 잡담하다 **– gabby** *adj*

ga·ble /ˈgeɪbəl/ *n* the top part of a wall of a house where it joins with a pointed roof, making a shape like a TRIANGLE ‖ 삼각형의 모양을 한 뾰족한 지붕과 만나는 집 벽의 꼭대기 부분. 박공. 합각

gadg·et /ˈgædʒɪt/ *n* a small tool or machine that makes a particular job easier ‖ 특정한 일을 더 쉽게 하는 작은 도구나 기계: *an interesting little gadget for cutting tomatoes* 토마토를 자르는 데 쓰는 흥미로운 작은 도구 —see usage note at MACHINE¹

gaffe /gæf/ *n* an embarrassing mistake made in a social situation ‖ 사교적인 상황에서 저지른 당황스러운 실수. 사교상의 실수. 결례

gag¹ /gæg/ *v* **-gged, -gging 1** [I] to feel sick in a way that makes food come up from your stomach to your throat without coming out ‖ 음식이 밖으로 나오지는 않고 위에서부터 목구멍까지 올라오게 메스껍다. 구역질나다: *The smell from the garbage made me gag.* 쓰레기 냄새 때문에 나는 구역질이 났다. **2** [T] to tie someone's mouth with a piece of cloth so that s/he cannot make any noise ‖ 소리를 내지 못하게 천 조각으로 남의 입을 묶다. …에 말 못하게 재갈을 물리다

gag² *n* **1** INFORMAL a joke or funny story ‖ 농담이나 웃음을 자아내는 이야기. 개그. 익살 **2** a piece of cloth used in order to GAG someone ‖ 남에게 재갈을 물리게 하는 데 쓰는 천 조각. 하무

gagged /gægd/ *adj* having your mouth tied with a piece of cloth so that you cannot make any noise ‖ 소리 내지 못하도록 천 조각으로 입을 묶은. 재갈을 물린

gag·gle /ˈgægəl/ *n* a group of geese (GOOSE), or a noisy group of people ‖ 거위 떼나 소란스러운 사람들의 집단. 거위 무리. 시끄러운 무리

gag or·der /ˈ. ˌ../ *n* an order given by a court of law to prevent any public reporting of a case that is still being considered in the court ‖ 법원에서 아직 심리 중인 사건의 공개적인 보도를 금지하는 법원이 내리는 명령. 보도[공표] 금지령. 함구령

gai·e·ty /ˈgeɪəti/ *n* [U] OLD-FASHIONED the state of having fun and being cheerful ‖ 재미있고 즐거운 상태. 명랑. 들뜬 기분

gai·ly /ˈgeɪli/ *adv* OLD-FASHIONED in a happy cheerful way ‖ 행복하고 즐겁게. 유쾌하게. 명랑하게

gain¹ /geɪn/ *v* **1** [I, T] to get, win, or achieve something that is important, useful, or valuable ‖ 중요한[유익한, 가치 있는] 것을 얻다[획득하다, 달성하다]: *You can gain a lot of computer experience doing this job.* 이 일을 하면서 컴퓨터 체험을 상당히 할 수 있다. / *A small army gained control of enemy territory.* 소규모 군대가 적의 영토를 장악했다. —opposite LOSE **2 gain weight/speed** to increase in weight or speed ‖ 몸무게나 속도가 늘다: *Bea has gained a lot of weight since Christmas.* 비는 크리스마스 이후로 몸무게가 많이 늘었다. **3 gain access a)** to be able to enter a room or building ‖ 방이나 건물에 들어갈 수 있다: *Somehow the thief had gained access to his apartment.* 어떻든지 그 도둑은 그의 아파트 침입에 성공했다. **b)** to be allowed to see or use something ‖ 무엇을 보거나 쓰는 것이 허용되다: *Marston had difficulty gaining access to official documents.* 마스턴은 공문서를 열람하는 데에 어려움이 있었다.

gain on sb/sth *phr v* [T] to start getting closer to the person, car etc. that you are chasing ‖ 추적하고 있는 사람·차 등에 접근하기 시작하다. …에 따라붙다. 다가가다: *Hurry up! They're gaining on us!* 서둘러라! 그들이 우리를 따라붙고 있어!

USAGE NOTE gain, earn, and **win**

Use **gain** to talk about gradually getting more of something, such as an ability or quality: *You'll gain a lot of experience working here.* Use **earn** to talk about getting money by working: *She earns about $50,000 a year.* Use **win** to say that someone has gotten a prize in a competition: *Brian won first prize in the skating competition.*

gain은 능력이나 질 등을 점진적으로 얻는 것을 언급하는 데에 쓴다: 너는 여기서 일하면 많은 경험을 쌓게 될 것이다. **earn**은 일을 하여 돈을 버는 것을 언급하는 데에 쓴다: 그녀는 일년에 약 5만 달러를 번다. **win**은 누군가가 경기에서 상을 탄 것을 말하는 데에 쓴다: 브라이언은 스케이트 경주에서 1등 상을 탔다.

---

gain² *n* **1** [C, U] an increase in the amount or level of something ‖ 물건의 양이나 수준의 증가: *We were delighted by their recent gain in popularity.* 그들이 최근에 인기를 얻어서 우리는 기뻤다. / *weight gain* 체중의 증가 **2** an advantage or an improvement ‖ 이점이나 진보. 이익. 이득. 향상: *gains in medical science* 의학의 진보

gait /geɪt/ *n* [U] the way that someone walks ‖ 사람이 걷는 방식. 걸음걸이

gal /gæl/ *n* INFORMAL a girl or woman ‖ 소녀나 여성

ga·la /ˈgælə, ˈgeɪlə/ *n* an event at which a lot of people are entertained and celebrate a special occasion ‖ 많은 사람이 즐기며 특별한 때를 기념하는 행사. 축제 – **gala** *adj*

ga·lac·tic /gəˈlæktɪk/ *adj* relating to the GALAXY ‖ 은하계와 관련된. 은하계의

gal·ax·y /ˈgæləksi/ *n* any of the large groups of stars that are in the universe ‖ 우주에 있는 별의 큰 집단. 은하. 성운

gale /geɪl/ *n* a very strong wind ‖ 아주 강한 바람. 강풍: *Our back fence was blown down in the gale.* 우리 뒷담이 강풍에 쓰러졌다. —see usage note at WEATHER

gall /gɔl/ *n* **have the gall to do sth** to do something without caring that other people think you are being rude or unreasonable ‖ 자신의 행동이 무례하거나

비이성적이라는 다른 사람의 생각을 신경 쓰지 않고 어떤 것을 하다. 뻔뻔스럽게도 …하다: *She had the gall to say that I looked fat!* 그녀는 뻔뻔스럽게도 내가 뚱뚱해 보인다고 말했어!

gal·lant /ˈgælənt/ *adj* OLD-FASHIONED brave or kind and polite toward women ‖ 용감하거나 여성에게 친절하고 예의 바른. 씩씩한. 정중한: *a gallant soldier* 용감한 병사 – **gallantly** *adv* – **gallantry** *n* [U]

gall blad·der /ˈ. ˌ../ *n* the organ in your body that stores BILE ‖ 담즙을 저장하는 신체 기관. 담낭. 쓸개

gal·ler·y /ˈgæləri/ *n* **1** a room, hall, or building where people can look at famous paintings and other types of art ‖ 유명한 그림과 다른 종류의 예술 작품을 볼 수 있는 방[홀, 건물]. 미술관. 미술품진열관[실]: *I took Monique to the little art gallery on Ridge Street.* 나는 리지가(街)에 있는 작은 화랑으로 모니크를 데려갔다. **2** a small expensive store where people can look at and buy art ‖ 미술품을 구경하고 살 수 있는 소규모의 고가 상점. 화랑 **3** an upper floor like a BALCONY inside a hall, church, or theater, where people can sit ‖ 사람이 앉는 홀[교회, 극장] 내부의 발코니와 비슷한 상층. 최상층 관람석. 특별석

gal·ley /ˈgæli/ *n* **1** a kitchen on a ship or a plane ‖ 배나 비행기의 주방. 취사실. 조리실 **2** a long Greek or Roman ship that was rowed by SLAVEs ‖ 노예에게 노를 젓게 한 그리스나 로마의 기다란 배. 갤리선

gal·li·vant /ˈgælɪˌvænt/ *v* [I] INFORMAL OR HUMOROUS to go from place to place enjoying yourself ‖ 즐기며 이곳저곳을 가다. 놀러 다니다. 신나게 돌아다니다: *Oh, he's out gallivanting around town.* 아, 그는 밖에 나가 시내를 신나게 돌아다니고 있어.

gal·lon /ˈgælən/ *n* a unit for measuring liquid, equal to 4 QUARTs or 3.785 liters ‖ 4쿼터나 3.785리터에 해당하는 액체를 측정하는 단위. 갤런

gal·lop¹ /ˈgæləp/ *v* [I] if a horse gallops it runs as fast as it can ‖ 말이 가장 빠른 속도로 달리다. 질주하다

gal·lop² /ˈgæləp/ *n* [singular] the fastest speed that a horse can go, or the movement of a horse at this speed ‖ 말이 달릴 수 있는 가장 빠른 속도, 또는 이 속도로 말이 달리는 동작: *riding at a gallop* 전 속력으로 말을 몰기

gal·lop·ing /ˈgæləpɪŋ/ *adj* increasing or developing very quickly ‖ 매우 빠르게 증

가하거나 발달하는. 빨리 움직이는. 급속
히 진행하는: *galloping prices* 급속히 오
르는 물가

gal·lows /'gæloʊz/ *n, plural* **gallows** a
structure that is used for killing
criminals by hanging them ‖ 범죄자를 교
수형에 처해 죽이는 데에 사용되는 구조
물. 교수대

ga·lore /gə'lɔr/ *adj* in large amounts or
numbers ‖ 많은 양이나 수의. 충분한. 푸
짐한: *He had toys and clothes galore.* 그
는 장난감과 옷이 많았다. **✗**DON'T SAY "He
had galore clothes."**✗** "He had galore
clothes."라고는 하지 않는다.

ga·losh·es /gə'lɑʃɪz/ *n* [plural] OLD-
FASHIONED rubber shoes you wear over
your normal shoes when it rains or
snows ‖ 비나 눈이 올 때 일반 신발 위에
신는 고무 신발. 고무 덧신[장화]

gal·va·nize /'gælvə,naɪz/ *v* [T] to shock
someone so much that s/he realizes s/he
needs to do something to solve a
problem or improve the situation ‖ 남에
게 문제를 해결하거나 상황을 개선하기 위
해 어떤 일을 할 필요가 있다고 깨달을 정
도의 충격을 주다. …을 자극[격려]하여
…시키다: *News of the captain's death
galvanized the soldiers into action.* 선
장의 사망 소식이 병사들을 자극하여 행동
하게 만들었다.

gal·va·nized /'gælvə,naɪzd/ *adj*
galvanized metal has been treated in a
special way so that it does not RUST ‖ 금
속이 녹슬지 않도록 특수하게 처리한. 아
연 도금을 한

gam·bit /'gæmbɪt/ *n* something you do
or say in order to gain control in an
argument, conversation, or meeting ‖ 토
론[대화, 모임]에서 기선을 제압하기 위해
하는 행동이나 말. 선수. 초반의 수

gam·ble¹ /'gæmbəl/ *v* **1** [I] to risk
money or possessions because you
might win a lot more if a card game,
race etc. has the result you want ‖ 카드
놀이·경주 등에서 원하는 결과를 얻게 되
면 더 많은 것을 얻을 수 있다는 가능성
때문에 돈이나 재산을 모험삼아 걸다. 도
박하다. 모험[투기]을 하다: *Jack won
$700 gambling in Las Vegas.* 잭은 라스
베이거스에서 도박으로 700달러를 벌었
다. **2** [I, T] to do something risky
because you hope a particular result
will happen ‖ 특정한 결과가 일어나길 바
라는 까닭에 위험한 일을 하다. …에 운을
걸다. …을 기대하다: *We're gambling
on the weather being nice for our
outdoor wedding.* 우리는 야외 결혼에 좋
은 날씨를 기대하고 있다.

gamble sth ↔ **away** *phr v* [T] to lose
money or possessions by gambling ‖ 도
박으로 돈이나 재산을 잃다. …을 도박으
로 잃다: *Tom's wife gambled away
their car.* 톰의 아내는 도박으로 자기들의
차를 잃었다.

gamble² *n* [singular] an action or plan
that is risky because it might not be
successful ‖ 성공하지 않을 수도 있기 때
문에 모험적인 행동이나 계획. 도박. 투기
. 모험: *Buying an old car is a real
gamble, you know.* 너도 알다시피 낡은
차를 사는 것은 진짜 모험이다.

gam·bler /'gæmblər/ *n* someone who
GAMBLES, especially as a habit ‖ 특히 습
관적으로 도박을 하는 사람. 도박꾼

gam·bling /'gæmblɪŋ/ *n* [U] the activity
of risking money and possessions
because you might win a lot more if a
card game, race etc. has the result you
want ‖ 카드 놀이·경주 등에서 원하는 결
과를 얻게 되면 더 많은 것을 얻을 수 있
다는 가능성 때문에 돈이나 재산을 모험삼
아 거는 행위. 도박. 노름: *My parents
think gambling should be illegal.* 우리 부
모님은 도박은 불법이라고 생각하신다.

game¹ /geɪm/ *n* **1** an activity or sport
that people play for fun or in a
competition ‖ 사람들이 재미로 또는 시합
에서 하는 활동이나 스포츠. 놀이. 오락.
경기[시합]: *Do you know any good card
games?* 쓸 만한 카드 게임을 아니? **2** a
particular occasion when you play a
sport or activity ‖ 스포츠나 활동을 할 때
의 특별한 경우. 특별한 행사: *Who won
the football game last night?* 어젯밤 미
식축구에서 어느 팀이 이겼니? **3** one of
the parts of a competition, such as in
tennis or BRIDGE ‖ 테니스나 브리지 등의
시합의 한 부분. 한 판. 한 승부[게임] **4**
play games to behave in a dishonest or
unfair way because you want to annoy
or trick someone ‖ 남을 괴롭히거나 속이
고 싶어서 부정직하거나 부당하게 행동하
다. 무책임한 짓을 하다. …을 속이다:
*Stop playing games with me and tell me
the truth!* 나를 속이지 말고 사실을 말해
라! **5 be (just) a game** if something is
just a game to you, you do not consider
how serious or important it is ‖ 어떤 것
이 얼마나 심각하거나 중요한지 고려하지
않다. 단순한 게임일 뿐이다: *Marriage is
just a game to you, isn't it?* 너에게 결혼
은 단순한 게임일 뿐이지, 그렇지 않니? **6**
[U] wild animals and birds that are
hunted for food and as a sport ‖ 식량과
스포츠로서 사냥되는 들짐승과 들새들. 사
냥감. 표적 —see also GAMES —see

usage note at SPORT

game² *adj* willing to do something dangerous, new, or difficult ‖ 위험한[새로운, 어려운] 일을 하고자 하는. 할 용기 [투지]가 있는: *I'm game if you are.* 당신이라면 나는 기꺼이 한다. / *Who's game for trying bungee jumping?* 번지 점프를 누가 해 볼 거니?

game plan /'. ./ *n* a plan for achieving success, especially in business ‖ 특히 사업에서 성공하기 위한 계획. 사업 전략: *What's the game plan for next year?* 내년의 사업 전략은 뭡니까?

gam·er /'geɪmɚ/ *n* INFORMAL **1** someone who plays computer games ‖ 컴퓨터 게임을 하는 사람 **2** a person who is very good at a sport and helps their team to win games ‖ 스포츠를 매우 잘 하여 팀이 시합에 이기도록 돕는 사람

games /geɪmz/ *n* [plural] a variety of sports played at one large event ‖ 큰 행사에서 하는 다양한 스포츠 경기 (대회): *the Olympic Games* 올림픽 경기 대회

game show /'. ./ *n* a television program in which people play games or answer questions in order to win money and prizes ‖ 상금과 상을 타려고 게임을 하거나 문제에 답하는 텔레비전 프로그램. 게임[퀴즈] 프로그램

gam·ut /'gæmət/ *n* [singular] a complete range of possibilities ‖ 가능한 전체 범위. 전영역. 전반: *Riesling wines run the gamut from dry to sweet.* (=they include all the possibilities between two extremes) 리즐링 포도주는 달지 않은 포도주에서 단 포도주까지 다양하게 있다. / *She had experienced the whole/full gamut of emotions in the weeks before she left home.* 그녀는 집을 떠나기 몇 주 전에 별의별 감정을 다 경험했다.

gan·der /'gændɚ/ *n* **1** a male GOOSE ‖ 거위의 수컷 **2 have/take a gander at** INFORMAL to look at something ‖ 무엇을 쳐다보다. …을 한 번 슬쩍 보다: *Come here and have a gander at this!* 이리 와서 이것 좀 잠깐 봐라!

gang¹ /gæŋ/ *n* **1** a group of young people who often cause trouble and fight other similar groups ‖ 종종 문제를 일으키고 다른 유사 집단과 싸우는 젊은이 집단. 한 패. 패거리. 비행 소년 집단: *Two members from their gang were shot.* 그들 패거리의 두 명이 사살되었다. **2** a group of people such as young criminals or prisoners who work together ‖ 함께 일하는 젊은 범죄자나 죄수 등의 집단. 갱. 폭력단: *a gang of drug*

dealers 마약 밀매단

gang² *v*

gang up on sb *phr v* [T] to join a group in order to criticize or attack someone ‖ 어떤 사람을 비난하거나 공격하기 위해 집단에 합류하다. 집단으로 행동[공격]하다: *Mommy! Tell Ricky and Paula to stop ganging up on me!* 엄마! 리키와 파울라에게 나를 집단적으로 공격하지 말라고 말해 줘요!

gang·bust·ers /'gæŋ,bʌstɚz/ *n* **like gangbusters** INFORMAL very quickly and successfully ‖ 매우 빠르고 성공적으로. 맹렬하게. 기세 좋게: *The town is growing like gangbusters.* 그 도시는 급속히 성장하고 있다.

gang·land /'gæŋlænd/ *adj* **a gangland killing/shooting/murder** a violent action that happens because of organized crime ‖ 조직 범죄로 일어나는 난폭한 행동. 암흑가의 살인

gan·gling /'gæŋglɪŋ/, **gan·gly** /'gæŋgli/ *adj* unusually tall and thin and unable to move gracefully ‖ 유달리 키가 크고 마르며 우아하게 움직일 수 없는. 호리호리한. 키다리의: *a gangly teenager* 호리호리한 십대

gang·plank /'gæŋplæŋk/ *n* a board you walk on between a ship and the shore, or between two ships ‖ 배와 해안 사이나 두 배 사이 위의 걷는 판자. (배의) 건널 판자. 트랩

gan·grene /'gæŋgrin, gæŋ'grin/ *n* [U] the decay of the flesh on part of someone's body that happens when blood stops flowing to that area ‖ 특정 신체 부위에 피의 흐름이 막힐 때 그 부위의 살이 썩는 것. 괴저(壞疽). 탈저(脫疽)

gang·ster /'gæŋstɚ/ *n* a member of a group of violent criminals ‖ 난폭한 범죄자 집단의 일원. 갱단의 일원

gang·way /'gæŋweɪ/ *n* a large GANGPLANK ‖ 커다란 건널 판자

gap /gæp/ *n* **1** an empty space between two things or two parts of something ‖ 두 개의 물건이나 사물의 두 부분 사이의 빈 공간. 갈라진 틈. 공백: *Dana has a really big gap between her two front teeth.* 다나는 두 앞니 사이에 아주 커다란 틈이 벌어져 있다. / *a gap in the fence* 담장의 갈라진 틈 —see picture at ESCAPE¹ **2** a difference between two situations, groups, amounts etc. ‖ 두 상황·집단·양(量) 등 사이의 차이. 격차. 불균형: *a group trying to bridge the gap between college students and the local citizens* (=reduce the importance of the differences between them) 대학생과 지

역 주민 사이의 격차를 메우려는 집단 / a large age gap between Jorge and his sister 조지와 여동생 사이의 많은 연령차 3 something that is missing that stops something else from being good or complete ‖ 다른 것이 좋거나 완벽해지지 못하게 하는, 빠져 있는 부분. 부족. 결함: No new producers have yet filled the gap in the market. 새 생산업자들은 아직 시장의 부족을 메울 수 없었다. / His death left a gap in my life. 그의 죽음은 나의 인생에 결함을 남겼다. / a gap in her memory 그녀의 기억에서 끊긴 부분 4 a period of time in which nothing happens or nothing is said ‖ 아무 일도 일어나지 않거나 아무 말도 하지 않는 기간. 공백 (기간): an uncomfortable gap in the conversation 대화의 불편한 공백 5 a low place between two higher parts of a mountain ‖ 산의 두 개의 높은 곳 사이의 낮은 장소. 협곡. 골짜기

gape /geɪp/ v [I] **1** to look at something for a long time, usually with your mouth open, because you are very shocked ‖ 아주 놀라서 보통 입을 벌리고 오랫동안 무엇을 바라보다: Mother cried out and gaped at him in horror. 어머니는 비명을 지르고 두려움에 떨며 그를 바라보았다. **2** also **gape open** to come apart or open widely ‖ 갈라지거나 넓게 벌리다

gap·ing /ˈgeɪpɪŋ/ adj a gaping hole, wound, or mouth is very wide and open ‖ 구멍[상처, 입]이 매우 넓게 열린. 크게 벌어진

ga·rage /gəˈrɑʒ, gəˈrɑdʒ/ n **1** a building, usually connected to your house, where you keep your car ‖ 차를 보관하는 보통 집에 연결된 건물. 차고 — see picture on page 945 **2** a place where cars are repaired ‖ 자동차를 수리하는 곳. 자동차 정비소

garage sale /ˈ.. ./ n a sale of used clothes, furniture, toys etc. from people's houses, usually held in someone's garage ‖ 보통 차고에서 여는 집에서 나온 중고 의류·가구·장난감 등의 판매

garb /gɑrb/ n [U] LITERARY a particular style of clothing ‖ 특별한 유형의 의복. 복장. 옷차림

gar·bage /ˈgɑrbɪdʒ/ n **1** [singular, U] waste material such as old food, dirty paper, and empty bags, or the container this is put in ‖ 오래된 음식·더러운 종이·빈 가방 등의 폐기물, 또는 이것을 넣는 통. 쓰레기(통): Can somebody take out the garbage? 누가 쓰레기를 내다버릴 거니? / Stop leaving garbage all

over the house! 집안 구석구석에 있는 쓰레기를 남겨 놓지 마라! **2** INFORMAL statements or ideas that are silly or wrong; nonsense ‖ 어리석거나 잘못된 말이나 생각; 무의미한 말: You didn't believe that garbage about him being in love, did you? 너 사랑에 빠졌다는 그의 시시한 말을 믿지 않았지, 그렇지?

garbage can /ˈ.. ./ n a large container with a lid in which you put waste materials, usually kept outside; TRASH CAN ‖ 보통 밖에 보관하며 쓰레기를 넣는 뚜껑이 달린 큰 용기. 쓰레기통; 윤 trash can. —see picture on page 945

garbage col·lec·tor /ˈ.. .,../ n someone whose job is to remove waste from GARBAGE CANs ‖ 쓰레기통에서 쓰레기를 수거해 가는 직업인. 쓰레기 수거인. 환경 미화원

garbage dis·pos·al /ˈ.. .,../ n a small machine in a kitchen SINK that cuts food waste into small pieces ‖ 음식물 쓰레기를 작은 조각으로 써는 부엌 싱크대에 있는 작은 기계. 음식 찌꺼기 분쇄기

garbage man /ˈ.. ./ n ⇨ GARBAGE COLLECTOR

garbage truck /ˈ.. ./ n a large vehicle used for carrying waste that is removed from people's GARBAGE CANs ‖ 쓰레기통에서 수거한 쓰레기를 운반하는 데 쓰는 큰 차량. 쓰레기 수거차

gar·bled /ˈgɑrbəld/ adj confusing and not giving correct information ‖ 혼란스럽고 정확한 정보를 주지 않는. 왜곡된. 의미를 알 수 없는: The newspapers gave a garbled version of the story. 그 신문은 그 이야기를 왜곡해서 실었다.

gar·den /ˈgɑrdn/ n the part of someone's land used for growing flowers or vegetable and fruit plants ‖ 꽃이나 채소와 과수를 재배하는 데 쓰이는 어떤 사람의 땅의 일부. 뜰. 정원: Mom's planting a rose garden in the back yard. 엄마는 뒤뜰에 있는 장미 정원을 가꾸고 있다. —see also GARDENS

gar·den·er /ˈgɑrdnɚ/ n someone who does gardening as a job ‖ 직업으로 정원을 가꾸는 사람. 정원사

gar·den·ing /ˈgɑrdn-ɪŋ/ n [U] the activity or job of making a garden, yard etc. look pretty by growing flowers, removing WEEDs etc. ‖ 꽃을 재배하거나 잡초 등을 제거함으로써 정원·뜰 등을 예쁘게 가꾸는 활동이나 일. 원예: I'm hoping to do some gardening this weekend. 나는 이번 주말에 정원을 좀 손질하고 싶다.

gar·dens /ˈgɑrdnz/ n [plural] a public

park where a lot of flowers and unusual plants are grown ‖ 많은 꽃과 이상한 식물이 자라는 공원. 유원지: *the Japanese Tea Gardens in Golden Gate park* 골든게이트 공원에 있는 일본차 유원지

gar·gan·tu·an /gɑr'gæntʃuən/ *adj* extremely large ‖ 엄청나게 큰. 거대한: *a gargantuan bed* 거대한 침대

gar·gle /'gɑrgəl/ *v* [I] to move medicine or liquid around in your throat in order to make it stop feeling sore, or to clean the inside of your mouth ‖ 통증을 멈추게 하거나 입 안을 깨끗하게 하기 위해 목구멍 주위에서 약이나 액체를 우물거리다. 양치질하다. 입 안을 가시다 – **gargle** *n* [C, U]

gar·goyle /'gɑrgɔɪl/ *n* a stone figure shaped like the face of a strange creature, usually on the roofs of old buildings ‖ 보통 오래된 건물의 지붕에 이상한 생명체의 얼굴 같은 모양을 한 돌 형상. 이무깃돌

gar·ish /'gærɪʃ, 'gɛr-/ *adj* very brightly colored and unpleasant to look at ‖ 아주 밝은 빛깔을 띠며 보기에 불쾌한. 지나치게 화려한[꾸민]. 눈부신: *the garish carpet in the hotel lobby* 호텔 로비의 지나치게 화려한 카펫

gar·land /'gɑrlənd/ *n* a ring of flowers or leaves, worn for decoration or in special ceremonies ‖ 장식용이나 특별한 의식에 두르는 꽃이나 잎으로 만든 고리 모양의 것. 화환. 화관

gar·lic /'gɑrlɪk/ *n* [U] a small plant like an onion with a very strong taste, used in cooking ‖ 요리에 쓰며 아주 독한 맛이 나는 양파 같은 작은 식물. 마늘 —see picture on page 944

gar·ment /'gɑrmənt/ *n* FORMAL a piece of clothing ‖ 의류 한 점. 의류. 옷

gar·net /'gɑrnɪt/ *n* a dark red stone used in jewelry ‖ 보석에 쓰이는 어둡고 붉은 돌. 석류석. 가닛

gar·nish¹ /'gɑrnɪʃ/ *v* [T] 1 to decorate food with a small piece of a fruit or vegetable ‖ 음식을 과일이나 야채의 작은 조각으로 장식하다. 고명을 하다[곁들이다] 2 TECHNICAL also **gar·nish·ee** /'gɑrnə'ʃi/ to take money from someone's wages because s/he has not paid his/her debts ‖ 빚을 갚지 않아서 어떤 사람의 임금에서 돈을 가져가다. 채무자의 임금 등을 압류하다

garnish² *n* a small piece of a fruit or vegetable that you use to decorate food ‖ 음식을 장식하는 데 쓰는 과일이나 야채의 작은 조각. 고명. 곁들임

gar·ret /'gærɪt/ *n* LITERARY a small room

at the top of a house ‖ 집의 맨 꼭대기에 있는 작은 방. 다락방

gar·ri·son /'gærəsən/ *n* a group of soldiers who live in a particular area in order to defend it ‖ 특정 지역을 지키기 위해 그 지역에 사는 일단의 병사들. 주둔군. 수비대 – **garrison** *v* [T]

gar·ru·lous /'gærələs/ *adj* always talking too much ‖ 항상 너무 말이 많은. 수다스러운. 잘 지껄이는

gar·ter /'gɑrtɚ/ *n* 1 an ELASTIC (=material that stretches) band that is used for holding socks or STOCKINGs up ‖ 양말이나 스타킹을 고정시키는 데 사용되는 고무줄. 양말[스타킹] 대님. 고무 밴드 2 a band worn for decoration on the upper part of a woman's leg ‖ 여성의 다리 윗부분에 장식용으로 매는 밴드

garter snake /'.. ,./ *n* a harmless American snake with colored lines along its back ‖ 등을 따라 색선이 있는 미국산의 독이 없는 뱀. 가터뱀

gas¹ /gæs/ *n* 1 [U] also **gasoline** a liquid made from PETROLEUM, used for producing power in the engines of cars, planes etc. ‖ 자동차·비행기 등의 엔진에서 동력을 내는 데 사용되는, 석유에서 만든 액체. 휘발유. 가솔린: *We need to stop for gas* (=buy gas) *before we drive into the city.* 우리는 그 도시로 차를 몰고 들어가기 전에 휘발유를 넣어야 한다. 2 [C, U] a substance like air that is not liquid or solid, and usually cannot be seen ‖ 액체나 고체가 아니고 보통 볼 수 없는 공기 같은 물질. 기체: *hydrogen gas* 수소 기체 3 [U] a clear substance like air that is burned and used for cooking and heating ‖ 요리나 난방용으로 연소시켜서 사용하는 공기처럼 투명한 물질. 가스: *a gas stove* 가스 난로 4 [U] INFORMAL the condition of having air or gas in your stomach ‖ 위장에 공기나 가스가 차 있는 상태. (장내의) 가스. 방귀: *Eating too much fried food gives me gas.* 튀긴 음식을 너무 많이 먹으면 가스가 찬다. 5 **the gas** also **gas pedal** the part of a car that you press with your foot in order to make the car move faster; ACCELERATOR ‖ 차를 더 빠르게 움직이기 위해 발로 누르는 차의 부분. 가속 페달; ㉟ accelerator

gas² *v* [T] to poison or kill someone with gas ‖ 가스로 사람을 질식시키거나 죽이다. …을 독가스로 질식[중독]시키다

gas cham·ber /'. ,../ *n* a room that is filled with poisonous gas, used for killing people or animals ‖ 사람이나 동물을 죽이는 데 사용되는 유독 가스로 가득

찬 방. 가스(처형)실

gas·e·ous /'gæsiəs, 'gæʃəs/ *adj* like gas or in the form of gas ‖ 가스 같거나 가스 형태의. 가스(모양)의. 기체의

gash /gæʃ/ *n* a large deep cut in something ‖ 어떤 것의 크고 깊은 상처 – **gash** *v* [T]

gas·ket /'gæskɪt/ *n* a flat piece of rubber between two surfaces of a machine that prevents steam, oil etc. from escaping ‖ 증기·기름 등이 새어 나오는 것을 막는 기계의 두 표면 사이의 납작한 고무 조각. 개스킷

gas mask /'. ./ *n* a piece of equipment worn over your face that protects you from breathing poisonous gases ‖ 유독 가스를 들이마시지 않도록 얼굴에 쓰는 장비. 방독면

gas·o·line /,gæsə'lin, 'gæsə,lin/ *n* [U] ⇨ GAS¹

gasp /gæsp/ *v* [I] **1** to quickly breathe in a lot of air because you are having difficulty breathing normally ‖ 정상적으로 숨을 쉬기가 곤란해서 많은 공기를 재빨리 들이마시다. 헐떡거리다. 숨차다: *Kim crawled out of the pool, gasping for air/breath.* 킴은 숨을 헐떡거리며 수영장에서 기어 나왔다. **2** to make a short sudden noise when you breathe in, usually because you are surprised or shocked ‖ 보통 놀라거나 충격을 받아서 숨을 들이쉴 때 짧고 갑작스러운 소리를 내다: *"Oh no!" she gasped.* 그녀는 "아, 안 돼!" 라고 숨을 헐떡이며 말했다. – **gasp** *n*

gas sta·tion /'. ,../ *n* a place where you can buy gas for your car ‖ 차량용 휘발유를 사는 곳. 주유소

gas·sy /'gæsi/ *adj* uncomfortable because you have too much gas in your stomach ‖ 위장에 너무 많은 가스가 차 있어서 불쾌한. 가스가 가득 찬

gas·tric /'gæstrɪk/ *adj* TECHNICAL **1** relating to the stomach ‖ 위와 관련된. 위의: *gastric ulcers* 위궤양 **2 gastric juices** the acids in the stomach that break food into smaller parts ‖ 음식물을 더 작은 조각으로 부수는 위 속의 산. 위액

gas·tro·nom·ic /,gæstrə'nɑmɪk/ *adj* relating to cooking good food, or the pleasure of eating it ‖ 좋은 음식을 요리하는 것이나 좋은 음식을 먹는 즐거움과 관련된. 미식(美食)의. 식도락의: *the gastronomic delights of Chinatown* 차이나타운의 식도락의 즐거움

gas·works /'gæswəks/ *n* a factory that produces the gas used for heating and cooking ‖ 난방·요리용으로 쓰이는 가스를 생산하는 공장. 가스 공장[제조소]

gate /geɪt/ *n* **1** the part of a fence or outside wall that you can open and close like a door ‖ 문처럼 열고 닫을 수 있는 울타리나 외벽의 일부. 대문. 문: *Who left the gate open?* 누가 문을 열어 놓았니? **2** the part of an airport that passengers walk through when getting onto a plane ‖ 비행기에 탑승할 때 승객이 걸어 들어가는 공항의 입구. 게이트. 탑승구: *Flight 207 to Chicago will be leaving from gate 16.* 시카고행 207편은 16번 게이트에서 출발할 예정입니다.

gate

gate·crash /'geɪtˌkræʃ/ *v* [I, T] to go to a party or event that you have not been invited to ‖ 초대받지 않은 파티나 행사에 가다. 표 없이 입장하다 – **gatecrasher** *n*

gate·way /'geɪtˌweɪ/ *n* **1** an opening in a fence or outside wall that can be closed with a gate ‖ 문으로 닫을 수 있는 울타리나 외벽의 입구. 출입구 **2 the gateway to** a place such as a city that you go through in order to reach a much larger place ‖ 훨씬 더 큰 장소에 도달하기 위해 통과하는 도시 등의 장소. 통로. 관문: *St. Louis was once the gateway to the West.* 세인트루이스는 한때 서부의 관문이었다. **3** a connection between two different computer NETWORKs that helps them to work together ‖ 서로 다른 두 컴퓨터의 네트워크가 함께 작동할 수 있도록 돕는 연결(장치). 게이트웨이. 네트워크 접속 장치

gath·er /'gæðə/ *v* **1** [I] to come together and form a group ‖ 한데 모여 한 집단을 이루다. 모이다. 집합하다: *A crowd gathered around to watch the fight.* 군중이 싸움을 구경하기 위해 주위에 모여들었다. **2** [T] to believe that something is true based on what you have already seen or heard ‖ 자신이 이미 보거나 들은 것을 기반으로 하여 어떤 것이 사실이라고 믿다. …을 …에서 알다[추측하다]. 결론을 내리다: *From what I can gather/As far as I can gather* (=I think it is true that) *he never intended to sell the house.* 내 추측으로는[내가 추측하는 한에서는] 그는 결코 집을 팔 생각이 없었다. **3** [T] to gradually obtain information, ideas etc. ‖ 점진적으로 정보·아이디어 등을 얻다. …을 수집하다. 모으다: *I'm currently trying to gather new* *ideas for my next novel.* 나는 다음 소설을 위해 현재 새 아이디어를 수집하려 하고 있다. **4 gather force/speed/intensity etc.** to become stronger, faster, more INTENSE etc. ‖ 더 강해지다[빨라지다, 강렬해지다]: *The car gathered speed quickly as it rolled down the hill.* 그 차는 언덕을 굴러 내려오면서 속도가 더 빨라졌다. **5** [T] also **gather up** to collect or move similar things into one pile or place ‖ 유사한 것들을 하나의 더미나 장소로 모으거나 옮기다. …을 주워 모으다[쌓다]: *"Wait for me," said Anna, gathering up her books.* 애너는 책을 주워 모으면서 "기다려 줘," 라고 말했다.

gath·ered /'gæðəd/ *adj* having small folds produced by pulling the edge of a piece of cloth together ‖ 천 조각의 끝을 함께 잡아당겨서 생긴 작은 주름이 있는. 주름 잡힌: *a gathered skirt* 주름치마 – **gathers** *n* [plural]

gath·er·ing /'gæðərɪŋ/ *n* a group of people meeting together for a particular purpose ‖ 특정한 목적을 위해 함께 모이는 사람들의 집단. 모임. 회합: *a large gathering of Vietnam veterans* 대규모의 베트남 재향 군인회

gauche /goʊʃ/ *adj* awkward and uncomfortable with other people, and always saying or doing the wrong thing ‖ 다른 사람들과 어색하고 불편하여 항상 잘못된 말이나 행동을 하는. 버릇없는. 눈치 없는. 서투른. 투박스러운

gaud·y /'gɔdi/ *adj* clothes, decorations etc. that are gaudy are too bright and look cheap ‖ 옷·장식 등이 너무 밝고 싸게 보이는. 현란한. 야한

gauge¹ /geɪdʒ/ *n* **1** an instrument that measures the amount or size of something ‖ 물건의 양이나 크기를 측정하는 기구. 게이지. 계측기: *a car's gas gauge* 차의 연료 계측기 / *a depth gauge* 깊이 측정기 —see picture on page 943 **2** a standard by which something else is measured ‖ 다른 물건을 측정하는 기준. 척도. 규격[표준 치수]: *The amount of money you make is not the only gauge of your success.* 돈을 번 액수가 성공의 유일한 척도는 아니다. **3** the width or thickness of something such as a wire, a piece of metal, or the BARREL of a gun ‖ 철사[금속 조각, 총신] 등의 넓이나 두께. 게이지. 구경: *a twelve-gauge shotgun* 12구경의 엽총

gauge² *v* [T] **1** to judge what someone's feelings, intentions etc. are ‖ 남의 감정·의도 등이 어떤지를 판단하다. 평가하다:

It's difficult to gauge exactly how he's going to respond. 그가 어떻게 반응할 것인지 정확히 판단하기 어렵다. **2** to measure or judge something using a particular instrument or method ‖ 특정한 도구나 방법을 사용하여 사물을 측정하거나 판단하다. 재다: *Grades are still the best way to gauge a student's success.* 여전히 성적은 학생의 성공을 측정하는 가장 좋은 방법이다.

gaunt /gɔnt, gɑnt/ *adj* very thin and pale, especially because of illness or worry ‖ 특히 병이나 걱정 때문에 매우 마르고 창백한. 여윈. 수척한

gaunt·let /'gɔntlɪt, 'gɑnt-/ *n* **1 run the gauntlet** to be criticized or attacked by a lot of people ‖ 많은 사람에게 비판이나 공격을 받다. 혹평을 받다. 고난을 당하다: *There was no way to avoid running the gauntlet of media attention.* 대중매체의 혹독한 비평을 피할 방법이 없었다. **2 throw down the gauntlet** to invite someone to argue or compete with you ‖ 논쟁하거나 경쟁하기 위해 남을 초대하다. 도전하다 **3** a thick long GLOVE worn for protection ‖ 보호용으로 끼는 두껍고 긴 장갑

gauze /gɔz/ *n* [U] a very thin light cloth used for covering wounds and making clothes ‖ 상처를 싸매거나 옷을 만드는 데 쓰는 아주 얇고 가벼운 천. 거즈. 가제 – **gauzy** *adj*

gave /geɪv/ *v* the past tense of GIVE ‖ give의 과거형

gav·el /'gævəl/ *n* a small hammer that someone in charge of a law court, meeting etc. hits on a table to get people's attention ‖ 법정·모임 등을 책임지고 있는 사람이 사람들의 주의를 끌기 위해 탁자를 치는 작은 망치. (의장·판사·경매인 등이 쓰는) 작은 망치

gawk /gɔk/ *v* [I] to look at someone or something in a way that is rude, stupid, or annoying ‖ 무례하게[멍청하게, 짜증나는 듯이] 사람이나 사물을 바라보다. 멍청히 바라보다: *Lenny couldn't stop gawking at the car accident.* 레니는 차 사고를 멍청히 바라보지 않을 수 없었다.

gawk·y /'gɔki/ *adj* awkward in the way you move ‖ 움직이는 방식이 어색한. 서투른. 볼품없는: *a tall gawky teenager* 키가 크고 볼품없는 십대 아이

gay¹ /geɪ/ *adj* **1** sexually attracted to people of the same sex; HOMOSEXUAL ‖ 성(性)이 같은 사람에게 성적으로 끌리는. 동성애의; ⓟ homosexual: *Did you know that Ken is gay?* 켄이 동성애자인 것을 알았니? —compare LESBIAN **2** OLD-

FASHIONED bright and attractive ‖ 밝고 매력적인. 화려한: *a room painted in gay colors* 화려한 색깔로 칠한 방 **3** OLD-FASHIONED happy and cheerful ‖ 행복하고 쾌활한. 명랑한: *gay laughter* 명랑한 웃음

gay² *n* someone, especially a man, who is sexually attracted to people of the same sex; HOMOSEXUAL ‖ 동성(同性)의 사람에게 성적으로 끌리는 사람, 특히 남자. 동성애자. 게이; ㊤ homosexual: *a parade organized by gays and lesbians* 게이와 레즈비언들로 이루어진 행진

gaze¹ /geɪz/ *v* [I] to look at someone or something for a long time ‖ 한참 동안 사람이나 사물을 바라보다. 응시하다: *He sat for hours just gazing out the window.* 그는 창 밖을 바라보며 몇 시간 동안 앉아 있었다.

gaze² *n* [singular] a long steady look ‖ 오래 꾸준히 바라봄. 응시. 주시: *Molly felt uncomfortable under the teacher's steady gaze.* 몰리는 선생님이 계속 응시하여 불편함을 느꼈다.

ga·ze·bo /gəˈzibou/ *n* a small shelter in a garden or park that you can sit in ‖ 정원이나 공원에서 앉을 수 있는 작은 오두막. 전망대. 정자

ga·zelle /gəˈzɛl/ *n* an animal like a small DEER that moves very quickly and gracefully ‖ 아주 빠르고 우아하게 움직이는 작은 사슴처럼 생긴 동물. 가젤

G ga·zette /gəˈzɛt/ *n* a newspaper or magazine ‖ 신문이나 잡지

gear¹ /gɪr/ *n* **1** [C, U] the machinery in a vehicle that turns power from the engine into movement ‖ 엔진의 동력을 운동으로 전환시키는 차량의 기계. 기어. 전동 장치: *There's a weird noise every time I change gears.* (=go from one gear to another one) 기어를 바꿀 때마다 이상한 소음이 난다. **2** [U] special equipment, clothing etc. that you need for a particular activity ‖ 특정한 활동에 필요한 특별한 장비·옷 등. 용구. 의류: *camping gear* 캠핑 장비 **3** [U] a piece of machinery that does a particular job ‖ 특정한 일을 하는 기계 장치: *the landing gear on a plane* 비행기의 착륙 장치

gear² *v* [T] **1 be geared to** to be organized in order to achieve a particular purpose ‖ 특정한 목적을 달성하도록 조직되다. (…에) 맞게 조정되다: *All his training was geared to winning an Olympic gold medal.* 그의 모든 훈련은 올림픽 금메달을 획득하는 데에 맞추어졌다. **2 be geared up** to be prepared to do a particular activity ‖ 특정한 활동을 하도록 준비되다. …할 대비가 되다: *The*

factory's geared up to make 300 cars a day. 그 공장은 하루에 300대의 차를 제작할 채비가 되어 있다.

gear·box /ˈgɪrbɑks/ *n* a metal box that contains the GEARs of a vehicle ‖ 차량의 기어가 들어 있는 금속 상자. 변속기 상자. 기어 박스

gear shift /ˈ. ./ *n* a long stick with a handle that you move to change GEARs in a vehicle ‖ 차량의 기어를 변경하기 위해 움직이는 손잡이가 달린 긴 막대. 변속 레버. 기어 전환 장치 —see picture on page 943

GED *n* **the GED** General Equivalency Diploma; a DIPLOMA that can be studied for at any time by people who left HIGH SCHOOL without finishing ‖ General Equivalency Diploma(미국의 대학 입학 자격 검정 시험)의 약어; 고등학교를 졸업하지 않은 사람이 언제라도 공부할 수 있는 졸업증서

gee /dʒi/ *interjection* OLD-FASHIONED said when you are surprised or annoyed ‖ 놀라거나 화가 날 때 쓰여. 이런. 어머나. 아이참: *Aw, gee, Mom, I'm not ready to go to bed.* 아이참, 엄마, 잠을 잘 준비가 안 됐어요.

geek /gik/ *n* SLANG someone who is not popular because s/he wears strange clothes or does strange things ‖ 이상한 옷을 입거나 기괴한 짓을 하여 인기가 없는 사람. 괴짜. 기인 – **geeky** *adj*

geese /gis/ *n* the plural of GOOSE ‖ goose의 복수형

geez /dʒiz/ *interjection* ⇨ JEEZ

gee·zer /ˈgizɚ/ *n* SLANG an impolite word meaning an old man ‖ 나이든 사람을 뜻하는 무례한 말. 늙은이

Gei·ger count·er /ˈgaɪgɚ ˌkaʊntɚ/ *n* an instrument that finds and measures RADIOACTIVITY ‖ 방사능을 발견하고 측정하는 기구. 가이거 계수관(計數管). 방사능 측정기

gei·sha /ˈgeɪʃə, ˈgiʃə/ *n* a Japanese woman who is trained to dance, play music, and entertain men ‖ 춤과 음악 연주, 그리고 남자들을 즐겁게 해 주는 교육을 받은 일본 여성. 게이샤. 일본 기생

gel¹ /dʒɛl/ *n* [C, U] a thick wet substance like JELLY, used in beauty or cleaning products ‖ 미를 위해 또는 제품을 세척하는 데 쓰이는 젤리처럼 걸쭉하고 축축한 물질. 젤: *hair gel* 헤어 젤

gel² *v* **-lled, -lling** [I] **1** if a liquid gels, it becomes thicker ‖ 액체가 약간 딱딱해지다. 교질화하다 **2** if an idea or plan gels, it becomes clearer or more definite ‖ 생각이나 계획이 더욱 분명해지

거나 명백해지다. 뚜렷해지다. 구체화되다: *They were going to make a movie together, but the project never gelled.* 그들은 함께 영화를 제작할 예정이었지만 기획이 구체화되지 않았다. **3** if people gel, they begin to work together well as a group ‖ 사람들이 한 그룹으로서 함께 일을 잘 하기 시작하다. 힘을 합쳐 일을 잘 하다

gel·a·tin /ˈdʒɛlətən, -lətˈn/ *n* [U] a clear substance from boiled animal bones, used for making liquid food more solid ‖ 액체 음식물을 약간 고체화 시키는 데 쓰이는, 짐승의 뼈 등을 끓여서 얻은 투명한 물질. 젤라틴

geld·ing /ˈgɛldɪŋ/ *n* a male horse that has had its TESTICLEs removed ‖ 고환을 제거한 수컷 말. 거세된 수말

gem /dʒɛm/ *n* a jewel that is cut into a particular shape ‖ 특정 형태로 깎은 보석

Gem·i·ni /ˈdʒɛməˌnaɪ/ *n* **1** [singular] the third sign of the ZODIAC, represented by TWINs ‖ 쌍둥이로 상징되는 황도 12궁의 셋째 별자리. 쌍둥이자리 **2** someone born between May 21 and June 21 ‖ 5월 21일에서 6월 21일 사이에 태어난 사람. 쌍둥이좌 태생자

gen·der /ˈdʒɛndɚ/ *n* **1** [C, U] FORMAL the fact of being male or female ‖ 남성 또는 여성. 성. 성별: *A person cannot be denied a job because of age, race, or gender.* 사람은 나이, 인종 또는 성별로 인해 직업을 거부당할 수 없다. **2** [U] TECHNICAL a system in some languages for separating words into special groups of grammar ‖ 단어를 특별한 문법 그룹으로 분류하기 위한 일부 언어상의 체계. 성(性)

gene /dʒin/ *n* a part of a cell that controls the development of a quality that is passed on to a living thing from its parents ‖ 부모에게서 생명체에 전해지는 형질의 발현을 관장하는 세포의 한 부분. 유전(인)자

ge·ne·al·o·gy /ˌdʒini'ɑlədʒi/ *n* [C, U] the history of a family, or the study of family histories ‖ 가문의 역사, 또는 가문 역사에 대한 연구. 족보. 족보학 – **genealogical** /ˌdʒiniə'lɑdʒɪkəl/ *adj* – **genealogist** /ˌdʒini'ɑlədʒɪst/ *n*

gen·er·al¹ /ˈdʒɛnərəl/ *adj* **1** ▸NOT DETAILED◂ 상세하지 않은◂ describing only the main features of something, not the details ‖ 사물을 세부적으로가 아니라 주요한 특징만을 묘사한. 일반[대략, 전반]적인: *a general introduction to computers* 컴퓨터에 대한 개괄적 소개 / *I think I've got the general*

idea now. (=I understand the main points) 이제 대충 이해한 것 같다. **2 in general a)** usually, or in most situations ‖ 보통, 또는 대부분의 상황에. 일반적으로: *In general, the Republicans favor tax cuts.* 일반적으로 공화당원들은 세금 감면에 찬성한다. **b)** as a whole ‖ 전체적으로. 총괄적으로. 대체적으로: *I think people in general are against nuclear weapons.* 나는 대다수의 사람들이 핵무기에 반대한다고 생각한다. **3** ▸AS A WHOLE◂ 전체적으로◂ as a whole considering the whole of a thing, group, or situation, rather than its parts; OVERALL ‖ 부분보다 전체적인 사물[그룹, 상황]을 고려한. 전체적인. 대체적인; ⑨ overall: *The general condition of the car is good, but it does need new tires.* 자동차의 전체적인 상태는 양호하지만 타이어는 새 것이 필요합니다. / *The general standard of the students isn't very high.* 학생들의 전반적인 수준은 그리 높지 않다. **4** ▸FOR MOST PEOPLE◂ 대부분의 사람들에게◂ affecting or shared by everyone or most people ‖ 모든 사람들 또는 대부분의 사람들에게 영향을 끼치거나 공유되는. 사회 일반의. 보통의. 공통된: *How soon will the drug be available for general use?* 이 약이 언제쯤 상용화될 수 있을까요? **5** ▸NOT LIMITED◂ 제한되지 않는◂ not limited to one subject, service, product etc. ‖ 한 개의 주제·용역·제품 등에 국한되지 않는. 전문적이 아닌. 광범위한: *a general education* 일반 교육 —opposite SPECIALIZED **6 as a general rule** usually, or in most situations ‖ 보통, 또는 대부분의 상황에. 일반적으로: *As a general rule, you should call before visiting someone.* 일반적으로 어떤 사람을 방문하기 전에 전화해야만 한다. **7 the general public** the ordinary people in a society ‖ 사회에서의 보통 사람들. 일반 대중: *The AIDS ad is designed to educate the general public.* 에이즈 광고는 대중을 교육하기 위해 계획되었다.

general², General *n* an officer with a very high rank in the Army, Air Force, or Marines ‖ 육군[공군, 해군]의 매우 높은 계급의 관리. 장군. 대장

general e·lec·tion /ˌ... .'../ *n* an election in which all the people in a country who can vote elect a president, GOVERNOR, SENATOR etc. ‖ 투표할 수 있는 전 국민이 대통령·주지사·상원 의원 등을

선출하는 선거. 총선거

gen·er·al·i·ty /ˌdʒɛnəˈrælət̬i/ *n* a statement that does not mention facts, details etc. ‖ 진상·세부 사항 등을 언급하지 않은 진술. 일반론. 개설: *Can we stop talking in generalities and get to the point?* 일반적인 말은 그만하고 본론으로 들어갈까요?

gen·er·al·i·za·tion /ˌdʒɛnərələˈzeɪʃən/ *n* a statement that may be true in most situations, but is not true all of the time ‖ 대부분의 상황에서는 사실일 수 있지만 항상 그런 것은 아닌 진술. 일반화. 보편론: *You shouldn't make sweeping generalizations* (=say something is always true) *about other countries.* 다른 나라에 대해서 (어떤 것이 항상 옳다는) 절대적인 일반화를 해서는 안 된다.

gen·er·al·ize /ˈdʒɛnərəˌlaɪz/ *v* [I] **1** to make a statement about people, events, or facts without mentioning any details ‖ 어떤 상세한 언급 없이 사람[사건, 진상] 등에 대해 진술하다. 개괄[종합]하다. 일반론을 말하다: *It's difficult to generalize about a subject as big as American history.* 미국사와 같은 큰 주제를 일반화하기는 어렵다. **2** to form an opinion about something after considering only a few examples of it ‖ 단지 몇 개의 예시만 고려하고 나서 어떤 것에 대한 의견을 형성하다. 일반화[보편화]시키다: *It's not fair to generalize from a few cases that all politicians are dishonest.* 몇 개의 사례를 통해 모든 정치가들이 정직하지 않다고 일반화시키는 것은 공정하지 않다.

gen·er·al·ly /ˈdʒɛnərəli/ *adv* **1** considering something as a whole ‖ 어떤 것을 전체적으로 고려하는. 일반적으로. 대개는: *Her school work is generally very good.* 그녀의 학교 성적은 대체로 매우 좋다. **2** by or to most people ‖ 대부분의 사람들에 의해[에게]: *It's generally believed that the story is true.* 그 이야기가 사실이라고 대부분 믿는다. / *an agreement that is generally acceptable* 대부분의 사람들이 받아 들일 만한 합의 **3** usually, or most of the time ‖ 보통, 또는 대부분(의 경우): *Megan generally works late on Fridays.* 미간은 보통 금요일에는 늦도록 일을 한다. **4 generally speaking** used in order to introduce a statement that is true most of the time, but not always ‖ 대부분의 경우 사실이지만 항상 그런 것은 아닌 말을 시작하는 데에 쓰여. 일반적으로 말해서. 대개: *Generally speaking, movie audiences like happy endings.* 대개 영화 관객들은 해피 엔딩을 좋아한다.

general store /ˌ... ˈ./ *n* a store that sells a lot of different things, especially in a small town ‖ 특히 소도시에서 각종 물건을 파는 상점. 잡화점. 만물상

gen·er·ate /ˈdʒɛnəˌreɪt/ *v* [T] **1** to produce or make something ‖ 어떤 것을 생산하거나 만들다. 낳다. 발생시키다: *Our discussion generated a lot of new ideas.* 우리는 토론에서 새로운 아이디어를 많이 얻어냈다. **2** to produce energy such as heat or electricity ‖ 열이나 전기 등의 에너지를 생산하다

gen·er·a·tion /ˌdʒɛnəˈreɪʃən/ *n* **1** all the people who are about the same age, especially in a family ‖ 특히 가족 중 비슷한 나이의 모든 사람들. 세대. 동시대의 사람들: *Three generations of Monroes have lived in this house.* 먼로즈가(家)는 3대째 이 집에서 살아 왔다. / *the younger/older generation* 청년[노년]층 **2** the average period of time between someone's birth and the birth of his/her children ‖ 어떤 사람의 출생 시기와 그 사람 자녀의 출생 시기 간의 평균 기간. 1세대: *A generation ago, no one had home computers.* 1세대 전에는 집에 컴퓨터를 보유한 사람이 아무도 없었다. **3** a group of machines, products etc. at a similar stage of development ‖ 발전 단계가 비슷한 일단의 기계·제품 등. 세대: *the next generation of TV technology* 차세대의 텔레비전 기술 **4** [U] the process of producing something, or making something happen ‖ 어떤 것의 생산 과정, 또는 발생 과정. 생성. 발생. 발전: *the generation of electricity* 전기의 발생

generation gap /ˌ...ˈ. ˌ./ *n* [singular] the lack of understanding between GENERATIONs, caused by their different attitudes and experiences ‖ 세대 간에 서로 다른 태도·경험으로 인해 야기되는 이해의 부족. 세대 차이

Generation X /ˌ...ˌ ˈ./ *n* [U] INFORMAL the group of people who were born during the late 1960s and the early 1970s in the US ‖ 1960년대 후반에서 1970년대 초반에 미국에서 태어난 사람들. X세대

gen·er·a·tor /ˈdʒɛnəˌreɪt̬ə/ *n* a machine that produces electricity ‖ 전기를 생산하는 기계. 발전기

ge·ner·ic /dʒəˈnɛrɪk/ *adj* **1** a generic product does not have a special name to show that it is made by a particular company ‖ 제품이 특정 기업에서 생산했다는 것을 나타내는 특별한 명칭이 없는. 일반 명칭의. 상표 없는: *generic drugs*

G

일반 명칭의 약품 **2** relating to a whole group of things, rather than to one in particular ‖ 특정한 것이 아닌 전체적인 것과 관련된. 일반적인. 포괄적인: *Fine Arts is a generic term for subjects such as painting, music, and sculpture.* 예술은 회화·음악·조각 등의 부문에 대한 일반적 용어이다. – **generically** *adv*

gen·er·os·i·ty /ˌdʒɛnəˈrɑsəti/ *n* [C, U] willingness to give money, time etc. to help someone, or something you do that shows this ‖ 어떤 사람을 돕기 위해 돈·시간 등을 들이려는 마음이나 이러한 마음을 보여 주기 위해 하는 행동. 관대함. 아량. 관대한 행위: *Thank you for your generosity.* 배려해 주셔서 감사합니다.

gen·er·ous /ˈdʒɛnərəs/ *adj* **1** willing to give more money, time etc. to help someone than is expected ‖ 어떤 사람을 돕기 위해 돈·시간 등을 기대 이상으로 많이 들이려고 하는. 관대한. 너그러운. 인심 좋은: *It is very generous of you to help.* 도와주시다니 당신은 정말 인심이 좋으시네요. **2** larger than the usual amount ‖ 보통의 양보다 더 많은. 큰. 풍부한: *a generous slice of cake* 많은 조각의 케이크

gen·e·sis /ˈdʒɛnəsɪs/ *n* [singular] FORMAL the beginning of something ‖ 어떤 것의 시작. 기원. 발생

gene ther·a·py /ˌ. ˈ.../ *n* [U] a way of using GENES to treat diseases ‖ 질병을 치료하기 위해 유전자를 이용하는 방법. 유전자 요법

ge·net·ic /dʒəˈnɛtɪk/ *adj* relating to GENES or GENETICS ‖ 유전자나 유전학에 관련된. 유전(학)의 – **genetically** *adv*

genetic en·gi·neer·ing /ˌ.ˌ. ...ˈ../ *n* [U] the science of changing the GENES of a plant or animal to make it stronger or more healthy ‖ 식물이나 동물의 유전자를 보다 강하게 또는 건강하게 변형하는 과학. 유전자 공학

ge·net·ics /dʒəˈnɛtɪks/ *n* [plural] the study of how the qualities of living things are passed on through the GENES ‖ 생물체가 물려받은 유전 형질에 관한 연구. 유전학 – **geneticist** *n*

ge·nial /ˈdʒinyəl, -niəl/ *adj* cheerful, kind, and friendly ‖ 쾌활하고 친절하고 다정한. 상냥한

ge·nie /ˈdʒini/ *n* a magical spirit in old Arabian stories ‖ 아라비아의 옛날이야기 속의 마법의 영혼. 정령. 요정

gen·i·tals /ˈdʒɛnətlz/, **genitalia** /ˌdʒɛnəˈteɪlyə/ *n* [plural] TECHNICAL the outer sex organs ‖ 외부 생식기. 외음부 – **genital** *adj*

ge·nius /ˈdʒinyəs/ *n* [C, U] a very high level of intelligence or ability, or someone who has this ‖ 지능이나 능력의 매우 높은 수준, 또는 그러한 수준을 가진 사람. 비범한 재능. 천재. 귀재: *Sandra's a genius at crossword puzzles.* 산드라는 십자 퍼즐에 재능이 있다. / *Even the movie's title was a stroke of genius.* (=a very smart idea) 영화 제목조차 천재적인 발상이었다.

gen·o·cide /ˈdʒɛnəˌsaɪd/ *n* [U] the deliberate murder of a race of people ‖ 어떤 종족에 대한 계획적인 살인. 대량[집단] 학살. 몰살: *What the army did there was an act of genocide.* 군대가 그곳에서 저지른 것은 대량 학살이었다. – **genocidal** /ˌdʒɛnəˈsaɪdl/ *adj*

gen·o·type /ˈdʒɛnəˌtaɪp/ *n* all the GENES that are found in one type of living thing ‖ 한 종류의 생물체에서 발견되는 모든 유전자들. 유전자형

gen·re /ˈʒɑnrə/ *n* FORMAL a type of art, music, literature etc. that has a particular style or subject ‖ 특정한 형식이나 주제를 갖고 있는 미술·음악·문학 등의 유형. 장르. 양식: *the science fiction genre* 공상 과학 장르

gent /dʒɛnt/ *n* INFORMAL ⇨ GENTLEMAN

gen·teel /dʒɛnˈtil/ *adj* extremely polite because you belong to a high social class ‖ 상류층에 속해 있어서 매우 예의 바른. 우아한. 품위 있는 – **gentility** /dʒɛnˈtɪləti/ *n* [U]

gen·tile /ˈdʒɛntaɪl/ *n* someone who is not Jewish ‖ 유대인이 아닌 사람. 비(非)유대인 – **gentile** *adj*

gen·tle /ˈdʒɛntəl/ *adj* **1** careful in the way you behave, so that you do not hurt or damage anyone or anything ‖ 조심스럽게 행동하여 다른 사람이나 사물에 상처나 피해를 주지 않는. 친절한. 다정한. 온화한: *Be gentle with the baby, Michael.* 마이클, 아기한테 좀 다정하게 대해라. / *Mia's such a gentle person!* 미아는 정말 친절한 사람이야! **2** not strong, loud, or forceful ‖ 강하지 않고 소리가 크지 않은, 또는 강압적이지 않은. 순한. 조용한. 부드러운: *a gentle voice* 조용한 목소리 **3** a gentle wind or rain is soft and light ‖ 바람이나 비가 부드럽고 가벼운 **4** a gentle hill or slope is not very steep ‖ 언덕이나 경사가 가파르지 않은. 완만한 – **gentleness** *n* [U] – **gently** *adv*

gen·tle·man /ˈdʒɛntəlmən/ *n, plural* **gentlemen 1** a man who is polite and behaves well toward other people ‖ 공손하고 다른 사람에게 잘 대해 주는 사람. 신사: *Roland was a perfect gentleman* *last night.* 롤랜드는 어젯밤 완벽한 신사였어. **2** a polite word meaning a man whose name you do not know ‖ 이름을 모르는 남자를 의미하는 경어. 신사분. 남자분: *Can you show this gentleman to his seat?* 이 신사분에게 자리를 보여 주시겠어요? – **gentlemanly** *adj*

gen·tri·fi·ca·tion /ˌdʒɛntrəfəˈkeɪʃən/ *n* [U] the change that happens when people with more money go to live in an area where poor people have lived ‖ 부자들이 가난한 사람들이 거주하는 지역으로 이사하면서 발생하는 변화. 빈민가의 고급 주택지화

gen·try /ˈdʒɛntri/ *n* **the gentry** OLD-FASHIONED people who belong to a high social class ‖ 상류층에 속한 사람들. 신사계급. 귀족 아래 계급의 사람들

gen·u·flect /ˈdʒɛnyəˌflɛkt/ *v* [I] to bend one knee when in a church or a holy place, as a sign of respect ‖ 존경의 표시로 교회나 성지(聖地)에서 한쪽 무릎을 꿇다. 정중히 무릎 꿇다

gen·u·ine /ˈdʒɛnyuɪn/ *adj* **1** a genuine feeling or desire is one that you really have, not one that you only pretend to have; sincere ‖ 느낌이나 바람을 단지 가지고 싶은 체하지 않고, 실제로 가지고 있는; 진지한. 진실한. 거짓없는: *Mrs. Liu showed a genuine concern for Lisa's well-being.* 리우 씨는 리자의 행복에 대해 진실한 관심을 표했다. **2** something genuine really is what it seems to be; real ‖ 어떤 것이 보이는 그대로의. 진짜의 진품의. 모조품이 아닌: *a genuine diamond* 진짜 다이아몬드 – **genuinely** *adv*

ge·nus /ˈdʒinəs/ *n, plural* **genera** /ˈdʒɛnərə/ TECHNICAL a group of animals or plants that are closely related, but cannot BREED with each other ‖ 상호간에 교배할 수 없지만, 긴밀히 연관된 동물군이나 식물군. 종류. 부류

ge·o·gra·phi·cal /ˌdʒiəˈgræfɪkəl/, **ge·o·graph·ic** /ˌdʒiəˈgræfɪk/ *adj* relating to GEOGRAPHY ‖ 지리학과 관련된. 지리학(상)의. 지리적인: *geographical maps of the area* 그 지역의 지형 지도

ge·og·ra·phy /dʒiˈɑgrəfi/ *n* [U] the study of the countries of the world, including such things as oceans, rivers, mountains, cities, population, and weather ‖ 바다·강·산·도시·인구·날씨 등을 포함한 전 세계 국가들에 관한 연구. 지리학 – **geographer** *n*

ge·ol·o·gy /dʒiˈɑlədʒi/ *n* [U] the study of materials such as rocks, soil, and minerals, and the way they have

changed since the Earth was formed ‖ 암석·토양·광물 등의 물질에 관한 연구. 지구 생성 이후 변화해 온 과정. 지질학 – **geological** /ˌdʒiəˈlɑdʒɪkəl/, **geologic** /ˌdʒiəˈlɑdʒɪk/ *adj* – **geologist** /dʒiˈɑlədʒɪst/ *n*

ge·o·met·ric /ˌdʒiəˈmɛtrɪk/, **ge·o·met·ric·al** /ˌdʒiəˈmɛtrɪkəl/ *adj* **1** a GEOMETRIC shape or pattern has straight lines that form squares, circles etc. ‖ 형태나 무늬 등이 사각형·원형 등을 이루는 직선을 가진. 기하학적인. 기하학 양식의 **2** relating to GEOMETRY ‖ 기하학과 관련된. 기하학(상)의

ge·om·e·try /dʒiˈɑmətri/ *n* [U] the study in mathematics of the form and relationships of angles, lines, curves, shapes, and solid objects ‖ 각·직선·곡선·형태·체적의 형성과 그 관계에 관한 수학적 연구. 기하학

ge·ra·ni·um /dʒəˈreɪniəm/ *n* a common house plant with colorful flowers and large round leaves ‖ 꽃이 다채롭고 잎이 크고 둥근 흔한 화초. 제라늄

ger·bil /ˈdʒɚbəl/ *n* a small animal with soft fur and a long tail, that is often kept as a pet ‖ 애완동물로 기르기도 하는, 부드러운 털과 긴 꼬리가 있는 작은 동물. 게르빌루스쥐

ger·i·at·ric /ˌdʒɛriˈætrɪk/ *adj* **1** relating to GERIATRICS ‖ 노인병학과 관련된. 노인병의, 노인의: *a geriatric hospital* 노인병원 **2** INFORMAL too old or too weak to work well ‖ 일을 잘 할 수 없을 만큼 너무 늙거나 너무 약한. 낡은. 노쇠한: *A geriatric truck had stalled near the highway.* 낡은 트럭이 간선도로 옆에 멈춰 서 있었다.

ger·i·at·rics /ˌdʒɛriˈætrɪks/ *n* [U] the medical treatment and care of older people ‖ 노인을 의학적으로 치료하고 보살핌. 노인병학

germ /dʒɚm/ *n* **1** a very small living thing that can make you ill ‖ 병을 유발할 수 있는 아주 작은 생물. 미생물. 세균: *Cover your mouth when you cough so you won't spread germs.* 병균을 퍼뜨리지 않으려면 기침할 때 입을 가려라. **2** **the germ of an idea/hope etc.** the beginning of an idea etc. that may develop into something else ‖ 다른 것으로 발달시킬 수 있는 생각 등의 시작. 기원. 근원. 발아. 생각/희망의 싹트

Ger·man¹ /ˈdʒɚmən/ *adj* **1** relating to or coming from Germany ‖ 독일과 관련된. 독일에서 온. 독일의. 독일 출신의 **2** relating to the German language ‖ 독일어와 관련된. 독일어의

German² *n* **1** [U] the language used in Germany ‖ 독일에서 사용되는 언어. 독일어 **2** someone from Germany ‖ 독일인

German mea·sles /ˌ.. '../ *n* [plural] a disease that causes red spots on the body ‖ 몸에 붉은 반점이 생기는 병. 풍진 (風疹)

German shep·herd /ˌ.. '../ *n* a large dog that looks like a WOLF, often used by the police and for guarding property ‖ 종종 경찰이 재산을 지키기 위해 이용하는, 생김새가 늑대와 비슷한 큰 개. (독일종) 세퍼드

ger·mi·nate /'dʒɚməˌneɪt/ *v* [I, T] if a seed germinates or is germinated, it begins to grow ‖ 씨앗이 자라기 시작하다. 싹트(게 하)다. 발아하다[시키다] —**germination** /ˌdʒɚmə'neɪʃən/ *n* [U]

ger·ry·man·der·ing /'dʒɛriˌmændərɪŋ/ *n* [U] the action of changing the borders of an area before an election, so that one person or party has an unfair advantage ‖ 어떤 사람이나 정당이 불공정한 이점을 얻기 위해 선거 전 지역구를 변경하는 행위. 자기 당에 유리한 선거구 개정. 게리맨더링 —**gerrymander** *v* [I, T]

ger·und /'dʒɛrənd/ *n* TECHNICAL in grammar, a noun formed from the PRESENT PARTICIPLE of a verb, such as "reading" in the sentence "He enjoys reading" ‖ "He enjoys reading"의 문장에서 "reading"과 같이 문법에서 동사의 현재 분사 형태를 띤 명사. 동명사

ges·ta·tion /dʒɛ'steɪʃən/ *n* TECHNICAL [U] the process of a baby developing inside its mother's body, or the period when this happens ‖ 모체 안에서 아기가 자라는 과정, 또는 그 시기. 임신. 잉태 기간: *a nine-month gestation period* 9개월의 임신 기간

ges·tic·u·late /dʒɛ'stɪkyəˌleɪt/ *v* [I] to move your arms and hands to express something, especially while you are speaking ‖ 특히 말하는 동안 팔과 손을 움직이면서 어떤 것을 표현하다. 몸짓으로 나타내다[말하다]

ges·ture¹ /'dʒɛstʃɚ, 'dʒɛʃtʃɚ/ *n* **1** [C, U] a movement of your head, arm, or hand that shows what you mean or how you feel ‖ 당신이 의미하는 것 또는 어떻게 느끼는지를 보여주는 머리[팔, 손]의 움직임. 몸짓. 손짓. 제스처: *a rude gesture* 무례한 몸짓 **2** something you do or say to show that you care about someone or something ‖ 사람이나 사물에 대한 관심을 표현하기 위해 하는 행동, 또는 말. 표시. 표현: *a gesture of friendship/support* 우

정[지지]의 표시

gesture² *v* [I] to tell someone something by moving your arms, hands, or head ‖ 남에게 팔[손, 머리]을 움직여서 어떤 것을 말하다. 몸짓[손짓]을 하다. 제스처를 쓰다: *Tom gestured for me to move out of the way.* 톰은 나에게 그 길에서 비키라고 손짓했다.

get /gɛt/ *v* **got, gotten, getting**

1 ▶BUY/OBTAIN 사다/얻다◀ [T] to buy or obtain something ‖ 어떤 것을 사거나 얻다: *Could you get me some coffee from the machine?* 자판기에서 커피 좀 사다 줄래요? / *My mom got these earrings for a dollar.* 나의 어머니께서는 1달러에 이 귀고리를 구입하셨다. / *Jill knows a woman who can get the material for you.* 질은 너를 위해 그 자료를 입수할 수 있는 여자를 알고 있다.

2 ▶RECEIVE 받다◀ [T] to receive or be given something ‖ 어떤 것을 받거나 받게 되다: *How much money did you get from Grandma?* 할머니한테 돈을 얼마나 받았니? / *We haven't gotten any mail for three days.* 3일 동안 우리는 어떤 우편물도 받지 않았다. / *Did you get the job?* 직장 구했니?

3 have got ⇨ HAVE²: *I've got a lot of work to do.* 나는 해야 할 일이 많다.

4 ▶BECOME 되다◀ [linking verb] to change from one state, feeling etc. to another; become ‖ 어떤 상태·감정에서 다른 상태·감정으로 바뀌다. …으로 변하다; …으로 되다: *Vicky got really mad at him.* 비키는 그에게 정말 화가 났다. / *If I wear wool, my skin gets all red.* 나는 모직물의 옷을 입으면 피부가 온통 붉어진다. / *The weather had suddenly gotten cold.* 날씨가 갑자기 추워졌다. / *Mom told you that you'd get hurt if you did that!* 네가 그것을 하면 다칠 거라고 엄마가 말했잖니! —see usage note at BECOME

5 ▶CHANGE POSITION/STATE 위치/상태를 변화시키다◀ [I, T] to change or move from one place, position, or state to another, or to make something do this ‖ 어떤 장소[위치, 상태]가 다른 장소[위치, 상태]로 변하거나 움직이다, 또는 어떤 것을 이렇게 만들다: *How did the guy get into their house?* 그 사람이 어떻게 그들의 집에 들어갈 수 있었지? / *I can't get the milk open.* 우유를 딸 수가 없어. / *Everybody get down on the floor!* 모두들 마루로 내려와라! / *Can you get the bags out of the car for me?* 차에서 가방 좀 꺼내 줄 수 있으신가요?

6 ▶REACH A PLACE 장소에 도착하다◀

[I] to reach a particular place or position ‖ 특정 장소나 위치에 도달하다: *She got downstairs, and found that the room was full of smoke.* 그녀는 계단을 내려와서 방이 연기로 가득 차 있음을 발견했다. / *You might be disappointed when you get to the end of the book.* 책의 마지막 부분에 가면 너는 실망할지도 모른다.

7 ▶BRING/TAKE 데려오다[가져오다]/취하다◀ [T] to bring someone or something back from somewhere, or take something from somewhere ‖ 사람이나 물체를 어떤 장소에서 데려오거나 가져오다, 또는 어떤 장소에서 사물을 취하다: *Carrie, can you go upstairs and get me that book, please?* 캐리, 위층에 가서 그 책 좀 나한테 가져다 주실 수 있으세요? / *She got some money out of her purse.* 그녀는 지갑에서 돈을 조금 꺼냈다.

8 get sb/sth to do sth to make someone or something do something, or persuade someone to do something ‖ 사람이나 사물에게 어떤 것을 하게 하다, 또는 사람에게 어떤 것을 하도록 설득하다. …에게 …하게 시키다[설득하다]: *Bert couldn't get the light to work.* 버트는 일하기 위해 불을 켤 수 없었다. / *I tried to get Jill to come out tonight, but she was too tired.* 나는 질을 오늘 밤 나오게 하려고 노력했으나 그녀는 너무 피곤해했다.

9 get to do sth to have an opportunity to do something ‖ 어떤 것을 할 기회를 갖다. …하게 되다[할 수 있다]: *Tom got to drive a Porsche today.* 톰은 오늘 포르쉐를 운전할 수 있는 기회를 가졌다. / *I'm so tired. I didn't get to sit down all day.* 너무 피곤해. 하루 종일 앉을 수 없었거든.

10 get sth fixed/done etc. to fix something, finish something etc., or have someone else do this ‖ 어떤 것을 수리하다, 일 등을 끝마치다, 다른 사람이 이렇게 하게 시키다. 일을 수리하다[시키다]/끝마치[게 하]다: *I have to get the paper done by 9:00 tomorrow morning.* 나는 내일 아침 9시까지 그 논문을 끝마쳐야 한다. / *We'll have to get this room painted before they move in.* 그들이 이사 오기 전에 우리는 이 방의 페인트칠을 끝마쳐야 할 것이다.

11 ▶ILLNESS 질병◀ [T] to have an illness ‖ 병에 걸리다: *I got the flu when we were on vacation.* 우리는 방학 때 독감에 걸렸다.

12 get the feeling/idea etc. to start to feel, think etc. something ‖ 어떤 것을 느끼고 생각하기 시작하다. …의 느낌/생각이 들다[나다]: *I get the feeling you don't like her.* 당신이 그녀를 좋아하지 않는다는 느낌이 든다.

13 ▶MONEY 돈◀ [T] to earn a particular amount of money, or receive a particular amount of money by selling something ‖ 특정 금액을 벌다, 또는 어떤 것을 팔아 특정 금액을 받다: *How much can you get for a house this size?* 이만한 규모의 집을 팔면 얼마를 받을 수 있지?

14 get the bus/a flight etc. to travel somewhere on a bus, plane etc. ‖ 버스·비행기 등을 타고 어딘가 가다: *She managed to get a flight into Detroit.* 그녀는 간신히 디트로이트행 비행기를 탔다.

15 you/we/they get sth SPOKEN used in order to say that something happens or exists ‖ 어떤 것이 일어나거나 존재한다고 말하는 데에 쓰여: *We get a lot of rain around here in the summer.* 여름에 이 주변에는 폭우가 내린다.

16 ▶UNDERSTAND 이해하다◀ INFORMAL [T] to understand something ‖ 어떤 것을 이해하다: *Tracey didn't get the joke.* 트레이시는 농담을 이해하지 못했다. / *Oh, I get it now – you have to divide 489 by 3.* 아, 이제 알겠다. 너는 489를 3으로 나누어야 한다.

17 get going/moving SPOKEN to make yourself do something more quickly ‖ 어떤 것을 더 빨리 하도록 하다. 빨리[서둘러] 가게[움직이게] 하다: *We have to get going, or we'll be late!* 서두르지 않으면 우리는 늦을 것이야!

18 get to know/like etc. to gradually begin to know, like etc. someone or something ‖ 사람이나 사물을 점차 알고 좋아하기 시작하다: *As you get to know the city, I'm sure you'll like it better.* 당신이 그 도시에 대해 점차 알아갈수록, 그 도시를 더욱 좋아하게 될 거라고 확신한다.

19 get the door/phone SPOKEN to go to the door to see who is there, or answer the telephone ‖ 문에 누가 있는지 알아보기 위해, 또는 전화를 받기 위해 가다. 문을 열어 주다/전화를 받다: *Val, can you get the phone, please – I'm making dinner.* 발, 전화 좀 받아 주시겠어요? 저녁 준비하고 있어요.

20 ▶RADIO/TV 라디오/텔레비전◀ [T] to be able to receive a particular radio signal or television station ‖ 특정 라디오 시그널 또는 텔레비전 방송국을 수신할 수 있다: *Her TV doesn't get channel 24.* 그녀의 TV는 채널 24를 수신하지 못한다. —see also HAVE TO —see usage note at BECOME

get sth ↔ **across** *phr v* [T] to be able to make someone understand an idea or piece of information ‖ 남에게 생각 또는 정보를 이해시킬 수 있다. 이해되다. 통하다: *It was difficult to get my idea across to the committee.* 내 견해를 위원회에 이해시키는 것은 어려웠다.

get along *phr v* [I] **1** to have a friendly relationship with someone or a group of people ‖ 남 또는 일단의 사람들과 좋은 관계를 가지다. 잘 지내다: *Rachel doesn't get along with Cy at all.* 레이첼은 싸이와는 전혀 마음이 맞지 않는다. **2 get along without sb/sth** to be able to continue doing something without having someone or something to help ‖ 도와주는 사람이나 사물 없이 어떤 것을 계속 할 수 있다. …없이 해나가다[지내다]: *We'll have to get along without the car until the new part arrives.* 우리는 새 부품이 도착할 때까지 차 없이 지내야한다.

get around *phr v* **1** [T **get around** sth] to find a way of dealing with a problem, usually by avoiding it ‖ 보통 문제를 회피함으로써 문제를 처리할 방법을 찾다. (곤란 등을) 모면하다: *businesses looking for ways to get around the tax laws* 세법을 빠져나갈 방법을 찾고 있는 기업들 **2** [I] to move or travel to different places ‖ 다른 장소로 이동하거나 여행하다: *His new wheelchair lets him get around more easily.* 그의 새 휠체어로 그는 더욱 쉽게 이동한다. **3** [I] if news or information gets around, a lot of people hear about it ‖ 많은 사람들이 뉴스나 정보를 듣다. 널리 알려지다[퍼지다]: *If this news gets around, we'll have reporters calling us all day.* 만일 이 뉴스가 퍼지면 온종일 우리는 기자들의 전화를 받아야 할 것이다. **4** [T **get around** sb/sth] to solve a problem in an unusual and intelligent way ‖ 유별나고 재치 있는 방식으로 문제를 해결하다. 헤쳐 나가다: *We have to find some way to get around these difficulties.* 우리는 이 난관을 헤쳐 나갈 몇 가지 방법을 찾아야 한다. **5 sb gets around** SPOKEN used in order to say that someone has had sex with a lot of people ‖ 남이 많은 사람과 성관계를 가진 것을 말하는 데에 쓰여

get around to sth *phr v* [T] to do something you have been intending to do for a long time ‖ 오랫동안 하려고 의도했던 일을 하다. …할 기회[여유]가 생기다: *I meant to go to the bookstore, but I never got around to it.* 나는 서점에 가려고 했지만 결코 시간이 나지 않았다.

get at sth *phr v* [T] **1** to try to explain something, especially something difficult ‖ 특히 어려운 일을 설명하려고 하다: *Did you understand what he was getting at?* 그가 설명하려고 했던 것을 알겠니? **2 get at the meaning/facts etc.** to discover the meaning of something, the facts about something or someone etc. ‖ 사물의 의미 또는 사물이나 사람 등에 대한 사실을 알아채다. 의미/사실을 이해하다[파악하다]: *The judge asked a few questions to try to get at the truth.* 그 판사는 진실을 알기 위해 몇 가지 질문을 했다. **3** to be able to reach or find something easily ‖ 쉽게 사물에 닿거나 찾을 수 있다: *I could see the ring stuck under there, but I couldn't get at it.* 나는 그 아래에 처박혀 있는 반지를 볼 수는 있었지만 손이 닿지 않았다.

get away *phr v* [I] **1** to leave a place, especially when this is difficult ‖ 특히 떠나기 어려울 때 어떤 장소를 떠나다. 도망치다. 도피하다: *Barney had to work late, and couldn't get away until 9:00.* 바니는 늦게까지 일해야해서 9시까지 나갈 수 없었다. **2** to escape from someone who is chasing you ‖ 쫓아다니는 사람을 피하다. 도망치다. 회피하다: *The two men got away in a blue pickup truck.* 두 남자는 파란 소형 트럭을 타고 도망쳤다. **3** to go on vacation ‖ 휴가 길에 나서다. 휴가를 떠나다: *Are you going to be able to get away this summer?* 너는 이번 여름에 휴가를 떠날 수 있니?

get away with sth *phr v* [T] to not be noticed or punished when you have done something wrong ‖ 잘못을 저지른 경우 남의 눈에 띄지 않거나 벌 받지 않다. …의 벌을 모면하다: *The kid was kicking me, and his mother just let him get away with it!* 그 아이가 나를 발로 차고 있었는데, 아이 엄마는 그냥 혼내지 않고 내버려 뒀어!

get sb **back** *phr v* [T] also **get back at** sb to do something to hurt or embarrass someone who has hurt or embarrassed you ‖ 자신을 해치거나 난처하게 한 사람을 해치거나 난처하게 하기 위해 어떤 것을 하다. 앙갚음하다. 원수를 갚다: *Jerry's trying to think of ways to get back at her for leaving him.* 제리는 그를 떠난 그녀에게 앙갚음할 방법을 찾으려고 고심하고 있다.

get back to sth *phr v* [T] **1** to start doing something again after not doing it for a while ‖ 잠시 하지 않다가 다시 어떤 것을 하기 시작하다. (일 등에) 돌아가다. 복귀하다: *She found it hard to get back*

G

to work after her vacation. 그녀는 휴가가 끝나고 업무에 복귀하는 것이 힘들다는 것을 알았다. **2** to talk or write to someone at a later time because you are busy, or do not know how to answer his/her question‖바쁘거나 질문에 어떻게 답변해야 할지를 몰라서 나중에 남에게 말하거나 편지를 쓰다. 나중에 연락하다: *I'll try to get back to you later today.* 오늘 중으로 나중에 너에게 연락할게.

get behind *phr v* [I] to not do or pay as much of something as you should have by a particular time‖특정한 시간까지 해야 할 만큼의 일을 하지 못하거나 지불하지 못하다. 늦어지다. 지체하다. 밀리다: *They made people pay extra if they got behind on their rent.* 그들은 사람들이 집세를 밀릴 경우 추가 금액을 내게 했다.

get by *phr v* [I] **1** to have enough money to buy the things you need, but not more‖더 많이는 아니지만 필요한 물건을 사는 데 충분한 돈을 가지다. 그럭저럭 (용케) 살아가다: *He only earns just enough to get by.* 그는 그저 그럭저럭 꾸려나갈 정도만큼만 번다. **2 get by on $10/$200 etc.** to manage to spend only $10, $200 etc. during a particular amount of time‖특정한 시간 동안 겨우 10달러·200달러 등만을 쓰면서 지내다. 10달러/200달러로 겨우 살아가다: *families trying to get by on $800 a month* 한 달에 800달러로 살아가려는 가족들

get down *phr v* **1** [T **get** sth ↔ **down**] to write something down on paper, especially quickly‖어떤 것을 특히 재빨리 종이에 (받아) 적다: *Let me get your number down before I forget it.* 잊어버리기 전에 당신 번호를 받아 적을게요. **2** [T **get** sb **down**] INFORMAL to make someone feel unhappy‖남을 불행하게 느끼게 하다. 남을 우울하게 하다[낙담시키다]: *You can't let the illness get you down, or you won't get better.* 병 때문에 우울해져서는 안된다. 그렇지 않으면 너는 낫지 못한다 **3** [T **get** sth ↔ **down**] to be able to swallow food or drink‖음식이나 음료수를 삼킬 수 있다. 삼키다

get down to sth *phr v* [T] to finally start doing something that will take a lot of time or effort‖많은 시간 또는 노력이 소요되는 일을 마침내 시작하다. (일 등을 차분히) 착수하다. …에 진지하게 대처하다: *By the time we finally got down to work, it was already 10:00.* 마침내 우리가 작업에 착수했을 때는 이미 10시였다.

get in *phr v* **1** [I] to be allowed or able to enter a place‖장소에 들어가는 것이 허용되거나 들어갈 수 있다. …에 들어가다. 타다: *You can't get in to the club without an I.D. card.* 너는 신분증 없이는 그 클럽에 들어갈 수 없다. **2** [I] to arrive at a particular time or in a particular place‖특정한 시간에 또는 특정한 장소에 도착하다. 오다. 도착하다: *What time does the plane/bus get in?* 몇 시에 비행기[버스]가 도착합니까? / *Steve just got in a few minutes ago.* 스티브는 몇 분 전에 막 도착했다. **3** [T **get** sth **in**] to send or give something to a particular person, company etc.‖특정한 사람·회사 등에 사물을 보내거나 주다. 제출하다: *Make sure you get your homework in by Thursday.* 목요일까지 꼭 숙제를 제출해라.

get in on sth *phr v* [T] INFORMAL to become involved in something that other people are doing‖남들이 하고 있는 일에 참가하게 되다. 한몫 끼다. 참여하다: *The kids saw us playing ball and wanted to get in on the game.* 아이들은 우리가 공놀이하는 것을 보고 놀이에 끼고 싶어했다.

get into sth *phr v* [T] **1** to be accepted by a college or university‖단과 대학 또는 대학교에서 (입학을) 허가받다. 입학하다. 들어가다: *Liz got into the graduate program at Berkeley.* 리즈는 버클리 대학원 과정에 입학했다. **2** INFORMAL to begin to be interested in an activity or subject‖활동이나 과목 등에 흥미를 갖기 시작하다. 마음을 사로잡다. 열중하다: *When I was in high school I got into rap music.* 내가 고등학생이었을 때 나는 랩 음악에 빠졌다. **3** INFORMAL to begin to have a discussion about something‖사물에 대하여 토론하기 시작하다: *Let's not get into it right now. I'm tired.* 논의를 지금 바로 시작하지 말자. 피곤해.

get off *phr v* **1** [I, T] to finish working‖일을 끝마치다: *What time do you get off (work)?* 몇 시에 일을 끝마치니? **2** [I, T **get** sb **off**] to get little or no punishment for a crime, or to help someone escape punishment‖범죄에 대한 처벌을 적게 받거나 받지 않게 하다, 또는 남의 형벌을 피하도록 도와주다. 벌을 면하(게 하)다: *I can't believe his lawyers managed to get him off.* 그의 변호사들이 용케 그의 벌을 면하게 한 것을 믿을 수 없다. **3 where does sb get off doing sth** SPOKEN said when you think someone has done something to you that s/he does not have a right to do‖

권리가 없는 사람이 자신에게 어떤 것을 했다고 생각될 때에 쓰여. 감히 …가 …을 하다니. 도대체 …가 …을 할 수 있나: *Where does he get off telling me how to live my life?* 나에게 인생을 어떻게 살라고 가르치다니 그는 참으로 뻔뻔스럽구나.

get off on sth *phr v* [T] SLANG to be excited by someone or something, especially sexually ‖ 사람 또는 사물에 의해 특히 성적으로 흥분되다. 짜릿한 쾌감을 느끼다

get on *phr v* **1 get on with** sth to continue doing something after you have stopped doing it for a while ‖ 잠시 어떤 것 하는 것을 중단했다가 계속하다. (일 등을) 적척 진행시키다. 부지런히 이어서 하다: *Can't we just get on with the job, so we can go home on time?* 일을 좀 이어서 진행할 수 없을까? 그러면 우리는 정시에 집에 갈 수 있어. **2 be getting on (in years)** to be old ‖ 나이를 먹다

get onto sth *phr v* [T] to start talking about a particular subject ‖ 특정 주제에 대해 말하기 시작하다: *Then, we got onto the subject of women, and Craig wouldn't shut up.* 우리가 여성에 관한 주제로 이야기를 시작하자 그때부터 크레이그는 입을 다물지 않았다.

get out *phr v* **1** [I] to escape from a place ‖ 어떤 장소에서 탈출하다. 도망치다. 나가다: *How did the dog get out of the yard?* 그 개가 우리에서 어떻게 탈출했지? **2** [T **get** sth ↔ **out**] to produce or publish something ‖ 어떤 것을 생산하거나 발행하다. 산출하다. 출판하다: *We have to get the book out next month.* 우리는 다음달에 그 책을 발행해야 한다.

get out of sth *phr v* [T] **1** to not do something you have promised to do or are supposed to do ‖ 하기로 약속하거나 하기로 되어 있는 일을 하지 않다. …하지 않게 되다. 해야 할 일을 피하다: *She couldn't get out of the meeting, so she canceled our dinner.* 그녀는 회의를 피할 수가 없어서 우리와의 저녁 식사를 취소했다. **2 get pleasure/satisfaction out of** sth to feel happy or satisfied because of doing something ‖ 어떤 것을 해서 행복 또는 만족을 느끼다: *She gets a lot of pleasure out of acting.* 그녀는 연기를 함으로써 큰 기쁨을 느낀다.

get over *phr v* **1** [T] to become healthy again after being sick, or to feel better after an upsetting experience ‖ 아픈 뒤에 다시 건강해지다, 또는 당황스러운 경험 뒤에 기분이 나아지다. 극복하다. 이겨내다: *The doctor said it will take a couple weeks to get over the infection.* 전염병이 낫는 데는 2주일 정도 걸린다고 의사는 말했다. **2 get** sth **over with** to finish something you do not like doing as quickly as possible ‖ 하기 싫은 일을 가능한 한 빨리 마치다. (싫은 일 등을) 끝마치다. 완성하다: *"It should only hurt a little." "OK. Just get it over with."* "조금 다친 것뿐이야." "좋아. 빨리 나아야지." **3** sb **can't/couldn't get over** SPOKEN said when you are surprised, shocked, or amused by something ‖ 어떤 것에 놀라거나 충격을 받거나, 또는 즐거울 때에 쓰여. …에 몹시 놀라다: *I can't get over the way you look. You're so thin!* 나는 네 모습을 보고 매우 놀랐다. 너무 야위었어!

get through *phr v* **1** [T] to manage to deal with an unpleasant experience until it ends ‖ 불쾌한 경험이 끝날 때까지 용케 대처하다. 벗어나다. 타개[극복]해 나가다: *I was so embarrassed. I don't know how I got through the rest of the dinner.* 나는 아주 당황했다. 남은 저녁 식사를 어떻게 다 해치웠는지 모르겠다. **2** [I] to be able to talk to someone on the telephone without any problems ‖ 어떤 문제도 없이 남과 전화로 말할 수 있다. (전화 등으로) 연락이 되다. 전화 연결이 되다: *When she finally got through, the department manager wasn't there.* 마침내 그녀가 전화 연결이 되었을 때 부장은 자리에 없었다. **3** [I, T] if a law gets through Congress, it is officially accepted ‖ 법률안이 의회에서 공식적으로 가결되다. (법안 등을) 통과하다[시키다]

get through to sb *phr v* [T] to be able to make someone understand something difficult ‖ 남에게 어려운 것을 이해시킬 수 있다. …에게 납득시키다: *Ben tried to apologize a few times, but he couldn't get through to her.* 벤은 여러 차례 사과하려고 했지만 그녀를 납득시킬 수 없었다.

get to sb *phr v* [T] INFORMAL to upset or annoy someone ‖ 남을 기분 상하게 하거나 괴롭히다: *Don't let him get to you, honey. He's just teasing you.* 여보, 그 사람을 받아 주지 말아요. 그가 막 놀려 대고 있잖아요.

get together *phr v* [I] **1** to meet with someone or with a group of people ‖ 한 사람 또는 일단의 사람들과 만나다. 모이다: *Every time he got together with Murphy they argued.* 그는 머피와 만날 때마다 그들은 다투었다. **2** to start a romantic relationship with someone ‖ 남과 연애를 시작하다. …과 데이트하다 **3 get yourself together/get it together**

to begin to be in control of your life and your emotions ‖ 자신의 생활과 감정을 통제하기 시작하다. 자제하다. 억제하다: *It took a year for me to get myself together after she left.* 그녀가 떠난 뒤 내가 내 자신을 자제 할 수 있기까지 1년이 걸렸다.

get up *phr v* **1** [I,T **get** sb **up**] to wake up and get out of your bed, especially in the morning, or to make someone do this ‖ 특히 아침에 일어나 침대에서 나오다, 또는 남을 깨워서 일어나게 하다. 일어나(게 하)다. 기상하다[시키다]: *I have to get up at 6:00 tomorrow.* 나는 내일 오전 6시에 일어나야 한다. / *Could you get me up at 8:00?* 8시에 나를 깨워주겠니? **2** [I] to stand up ‖ 일어서다: *Corrinne got up slowly and went to the window.* 코린은 천천히 일어서더니 창문으로 갔다. **3 get it up** SLANG to be able to have an ERECTION ‖ 발기하게 할 수 있다. 발기시키다

get·a·way /ˈgɛtəˌweɪ/ *n* **make a getaway** to escape from a place or a bad situation, especially after doing something illegal ‖ 특히 불법적인 일을 한 뒤에 어떤 장소 또는 나쁜 상황에서 도피하다. 도주하다

get-to·geth·er /ˈ. .ˌ../ *n* a friendly informal meeting or party ‖ 친밀한 비격식적인 모임 또는 파티. 회합. 간담회: *a small get-together with some friends* 몇 몇 친구들과의 작은 모임

get·up /ˈgɛtʌp/ *n* INFORMAL strange or unusual clothes that someone is wearing ‖ 어떤 사람이 입고 있는 이상하거나 특이한 옷. 기묘한 복장

get-up-and-go /ˌ. . . ˈ./ *n* [U] INFORMAL energy and determination ‖ 힘과 결단력. 열의. 적극성: *He's lost a lot of his get-up-and-go.* 그는 열의를 많이 상실했다.

gey·ser /ˈgaɪzɚ/ *n* hot water and steam that suddenly rises into the air from a natural hole in the ground ‖ 지상의 천연 구덩이에서 공중으로 갑자기 솟아오르는 뜨거운 물과 증기. 간헐 온천

ghast·ly /ˈgæsfli/ *adj* extremely bad or unpleasant ‖ 지극히 나쁘거나 불쾌한. 무서운

ghet·to /ˈgɛtoʊ/ *n, plural* **ghettos** or **ghettoes** a crowded and poor part of a city ‖ 도시의 번잡하고 가난한 지역. 흑인 빈민가. 슬럼가

ghetto blast·er /ˈ.. ˌ../ *n* INFORMAL a large radio and TAPE DECK that you can carry around ‖ 들고 다닐 수 있는 대형 라디오와 녹음 재생 장치. 대형 휴대용 라디오 카세트

ghost /goʊst/ *n* the spirit of a dead person that some people believe they can see or feel ‖ 몇몇 사람들이 보거나 느낄 수 있다고 믿는 죽은 사람의 영혼. 망령. 유령: *They say the captain's ghost still haunts the waterfront.* 그들은 선장의 망령이 아직도 해안 지구에 출몰한다고 말한다. – **ghostly** *adj*

ghost sto·ry /ˈ. ˌ../ *n* a story you tell people late at night in order to frighten them ‖ 사람들을 놀라게 하려고 늦은 밤에 해 주는 이야기. 유령 이야기. 괴담

ghost town /ˈ. ./ *n* a town that is empty because most of its people have left ‖ 대부분의 사람들이 떠나 버려서 텅빈 도시. 유령 도시

ghoul /gul/ *n* an evil spirit in stories that eats dead bodies that it steals from graves ‖ 무덤에서 훔친 시체를 먹는다는 이야기 속의 악령. 식시귀(食屍鬼). 시체를 먹는 악귀 – **ghoulish** *adj*

GI /ˌdʒi ˈaɪ/ *n* Government Issue; a soldier in the US army ‖ Government Issue의 약어; 미군 병사

gi·ant¹ /ˈdʒaɪənt/, **giant-sized** /ˈ. ./ *adj* extremely large and much bigger than other things of the same type ‖ 동종의 다른 사물보다 대단히 크고 훨씬 비대한. 엄청나게 큰. 거대한: *a giant TV screen* 초대형 텔레비전 화면

giant² *n* **1** an extremely tall strong man in children's stories ‖ 동화에 나오는 대단히 키가 크고 힘이 센 남자. 거인 **2** a very successful or important person or company ‖ 아주 성공하거나 중요한 사람 또는 회사. 위대한 재능[지력, 권력]의 소유자. 거대 기업: *one of the giants of the music industry* 음악 산업의 거대 기업의 하나

gib·ber·ish /ˈdʒɪbərɪʃ/ *n* [U] things you say or write that have no meaning ‖ 의미 없이 말하거나 쓰는 것. 횡설수설

gibe /dʒaɪb/ *n* an unkind remark intended to make someone seem silly ‖ 남을 어리석어 보이게 만들 목적의 불친절한 말. 조롱. 우롱

gib·lets /ˈdʒɪblɪts/ *n* [plural] organs such as the heart and LIVER that you remove from a bird before cooking it ‖ 요리하기 전에 제거하는 새의 심장·간 등의 기관. 내장

gid·dy /ˈgɪdi/ *adj* **1** behaving in a silly, happy, excited way ‖ 어리석고 쾌활하고 흥분되어 행동하는. 들뜬. 충동적인: *Drinking champagne always makes me giddy.* 샴페인을 마시면 나는 항상 들뜬다. **2** ⇨ DIZZY

gift /gɪft/ *n* **1** something that you give to someone you like or want to thank; PRESENT ‖ 좋아하거나 감사하고픈 사람에게 주는 것. 선물; ⓤ present: *You didn't have to buy me a gift for my birthday!* 내 생일 선물까지 사주지 않아도 됐는데! **2** a natural ability to do something ‖ 일을 하는 타고난 능력. 재능. 재주: *Gary sure has a gift for telling stories!* 개리는 확실히 이야기하는 것에 재주가 있어!

CULTURE NOTE giving gifts

In the US and Canada, gifts are given to family members and close friends on special occasions such as Christmas and birthdays. If you are invited to someone's home as a guest, you should also bring a gift, such as flowers, a bottle of wine, or a box of candy. If you are invited to the home of a good friend, you can ask if s/he would like you to bring something for dinner, such as a dessert. Gifts are usually opened immediately and the person who gives the gift is thanked. It is polite to say how much you like the gift. If you receive a gift through the mail, it is polite to send a note to thank the person who gave it.

미국과 캐나다에서는 크리스마스와 생일 등의 특별한 날에 가족들과 가까운 친구들에게 선물을 준다. 손님으로 남의 집에 초대를 받는 경우 꽃이나 와인 한 병, 또는 사탕 한 상자 등을 선물로 가져가면 좋을 것이다. 만일 친한 친구 집에 초대를 받으면 저녁 식사용 디저트 같은 것을 가져가는 것이 어떨지를 물어 볼 수도 있다. 선물은 보통 즉시 열어보고 선물을 준 사람에게 감사의 인사를 한다. 선물이 얼마나 마음에 드는지를 표현하는 것이 예의이다. 우편으로 선물을 받은 경우에는 보낸 사람에게 감사하다는 편지를 보내는 것이 예의이다.

---

gift cer·tif·i·cate /'. .,...,/ *n* a special piece of paper that is worth a specific amount of money when it is exchanged at a store for goods ‖ 상점에서 상품과 교환되는 특정 금액의 가치가 있는 특별한 종잇조각. 상품권

gift·ed /'gɪftɪd/ *adj* **1** having the natural ability to do something very well ‖ 어떤 것을 매우 잘 하는 타고난 능력을 가진. 천부적인[탁월한] 재능을 지닌: *a gifted poet* 천부적인 재능이 있는 시인 **2** very intelligent ‖ 매우 지적인. 총명한. 영특한: *a special class for gifted children* 영재 아동을 위한 특별반

gift wrap¹ /'. ./ *n* attractive colored paper for wrapping presents in ‖ 선물을 포장하기 위한 예쁜 채색 종이. 선물용 포장 재료

gift wrap² *v* [T] to wrap a present with GIFT WRAP ‖ 선물용 포장 재료로 선물을 포장하다: *Would you like this gift wrapped?* 이 선물을 포장해 드릴까요?

gig /gɪg/ *n* INFORMAL a musical performance that is played for money to a small group of people ‖ 소수 집단의 사람들을 상대로 돈을 벌기 위해 연주하는 음악 공연. (일일) 재즈 연주회: *Tom's band has a gig at the Blues Bar next week.* 톰의 밴드는 다음주 블루스 바에서 재즈 연주회를 갖는다.

gig·a·byte /'gɪgə,baɪt/ *n* TECHNICAL one BILLION BYTEs ‖ 기가바이트

gi·gan·tic /dʒaɪ'gæntɪk/ *adj* extremely large ‖ 대단히 큰. 거대한. 막대한: *The company is gigantic and has offices all over the world.* 그 회사는 규모가 커서 전 세계에 지사를 갖고 있다.

gig·gle /'gɪgəl/ *v* [I] to laugh quietly because you think something is very funny, or because you are nervous ‖ 어떤 일이 너무 재미있다고 생각되거나 긴장해서 조용히 웃다. 킬킬 웃다. 참으면서 웃다: *I can't stop giggling!* 나는 킬킬대고 웃지 않을 수 없다! – **giggle** *n*

gild /gɪld/ *v* [T] to cover the surface of something with a thin layer of gold or gold paint ‖ 사물의 표면에 금 또는 금 페인트를 얇게 입히다. 금박을 입히다. 금도금을 하다

gill /gɪl/ *n* one of the organs on the side of a fish through which it breathes ‖ 물고기의 측면에 있는 호흡 기관의 하나. 아가미

gilt /gɪlt/ *adj* covered with a thin layer of gold or gold-colored paint ‖ 금 또는 금색 페인트를 얇게 입힌. 도금한. 금가루를 칠한 – **gilt** *n* [U]

gim·me /'gɪmi/ SPOKEN NONSTANDARD a short form of "give me" ‖ "give me"의 단축형: *Gimme that ball back!* 그 공을 나에게 돌려줘!

gim·mick /'gɪmɪk/ *n* INFORMAL a trick or something unusual that you use or do in order to make people notice someone or something ‖ 사람들이 어떤 사람이나 사물에 주목하도록 사용하거나 행하는 기교 또는 특이한 것. (선전용) 술책. 계략: *advertising gimmicks* 광고 전략 – **gimmicky** *adj*

gin /dʒɪn/ *n* [U] a strong alcoholic drink made from grain ‖ 곡물로 만든 독한 술. 진

gin·ger /'dʒɪndʒə/ n [U] a hot-tasting light brown root, or the powder made from this root, used in cooking ‖ 매운맛이 나는 연한 갈색 뿌리, 또는 이 뿌리로 만든 요리할 때 쓰는 가루. 생강. 생강 가루

ginger ale /'.. ,.. ,.. './ n [U] a SOFT DRINK with a GINGER taste ‖ 생강 맛이 나는 탄산성 청량음료

gin·ger·bread /'dʒɪndʒə,brɛd/ n [U] a type of cookie made with GINGER and sweet SPICES in it ‖ 생강과 달콤한 향신료를 넣은 과자 종류. 생강 과자빵: a gingerbread house/man (=made into the shape of a house or person) 집[사람] 모양 생강 과자빵

gin·ger·ly /'dʒɪndʒəli/ adv very slowly, carefully, and gently ‖ 매우 천천히·주의 깊게·부드럽게. 용의주도하게. 매우 신중하게: Gingerly, she cleaned the wound on her arm. 매우 신중히 그녀는 팔의 상처를 닦아냈다.

ging·ham /'ɡɪŋəm/ n [U] cotton cloth that has a pattern of small white and colored squares on it ‖ 흰색과 다른 색의 격자 무늬를 이루는 면직물. 줄무늬[체크무늬]의 평직 면포

gi·raffe /dʒə'ræf/ n a tall animal that has a very long neck and dark spots on its fur, and that lives in Africa ‖ 목이 아주 길고 털에 검은 반점이 있는 아프리카에 서식하는 키가 큰 동물. 기린

G

gird·er /'ɡədə/ n a strong beam made of iron or steel, used for supporting a roof, floor, or bridge ‖ 지붕[마룻바닥, 교량]을 지탱해 주는 데에 쓰이는 철 또는 강철로 만든 강한 금속재. 도리. 대들보

gir·dle /'ɡədl/ n a type of underwear that a woman wears to make her look thinner ‖ 여자가 날씬하게 보이려고 입는 속옷의 일종. (코르셋의 일종인) 거들

girl /ɡəl/ n 1 a female child ‖ 여자 아이: She's tall for a girl of her age. 그녀는 그 또래의 여자 아이에 비해서는 키가 크다. 2 a daughter ‖ 딸: Karen has a little baby girl. 카렌은 어린 딸이 하나 있다. 3 a word meaning "woman", considered offensive by some women ‖ "여성"을 의미하는 말로 일부 여성들에게는 모욕적으로 여겨지는 말: A nice girl like you needs a boyfriend. 너처럼 멋진 아가씨는 남자 친구가 필요해. **4 the girls** INFORMAL a woman's female friends ‖ 여성의 여자 친구들: I'm going to the movies with the girls from work. 직장 여자 동료들하고 영화 구경을 갈려고 해. 5 SPOKEN a way of speaking to a female animal, such as a horse or a dog ‖ 말이

나 개 등의 암컷 동물에게 말하는 투: Come here, girl! 야! 이리와.

girl·friend /'ɡəlfrɛnd/ n 1 a girl or woman with whom you have a romantic relationship ‖ 연애 관계를 맺고 있는 소녀나 여성. 연인. 애인: Seth is bringing his new girlfriend to Heidi's party. 세스는 하이디의 파티에 새로운 여자 친구를 데려 올 거야. 2 a woman's female friend ‖ 여성의 여자 친구

girl·hood /'ɡəlhʊd/ n [U] the time in a woman's life when she is very young ‖ 여자의 인생에서 아주 젊은 시절. 소녀 시절. 처녀 시절

Girl Scouts /'. ./ n an organization for girls that teaches them practical skills and helps develop their character ‖ 실질적인 기술을 가르치고 품성의 개발을 돕는 소녀들을 위한 단체. 소녀단. 걸스카우트 —compare BOY SCOUTS

girth /ɡəθ/ n [C, U] the distance around the middle of something ‖ 어떤 것의 가운데 둘레의 거리. 허리둘레: the girth of the tree's trunk 나무의 줄기 둘레

gist /dʒɪst/ n **the gist** the main idea or meaning of what someone had said or written ‖ 사람이 한 말이나 쓴 글의 주된 생각 또는 의미. 요지. 골자: Don't worry about all the details, just get the gist of it. (=understand the main ideas) 모든 세부 사항에 대해서는 걱정하지 말고 그것의 요지만을 파악해라.

give¹ /ɡɪv/ v **gave, given, giving**
1 ▶PROVIDE 제공하다◀ [T] to provide someone with something, or let someone have or do something ‖ 남에게 어떤 것을 제공하다, 또는 남에게 어떤 것을 가지거나 하게 하다. 주다. 제공하다: Dan gave me/him/her a ride to work. 댄은 나를[그를, 그녀를] 직장까지 태워가 주었다. / They gave the job to that guy from Texas. 그들은 텍사스에서 온 그 남자에게 일자리를 주었다. / I was never given a chance to explain. 나에게 설명할 기회가 전혀 주어지지 않았다.
2 ▶IN SB'S HAND 사람의 손에◀ [T] to put something in someone's hand or near him/her so that s/he can use it, hold it etc. ‖ 사람이 사용하거나 잡을 수 있도록 손이나 손 근처에 사물을 놓다. 건네주다: He gave the books to Carl. 그는 칼에게 책을 주었다. / Here, give me your coat. I'll hang it up for you. 자, 코트를 저에게 주세요. 제가 걸어 드리겠습니다.
3 ▶PRESENT 선물◀ [T] to provide someone with something as a present ‖ 선물로 남에게 어떤 것을 주다. (선물을) 주다: She gave Jen a CD for Christmas.

그녀는 크리스마스에 젠에게 CD를 선물했다.

4 ▶TELL SB STH 남에게 어떤 것을 말하다 ◀ [T] to tell someone information or details about something ‖ 어떤 것에 대한 정보나 세부 사항을 남에게 말하다. 전하다: *Would you give Kim a message for me?* 김에게 나의 메시지를 전해 주겠니? / *The police will ask him to give a description of the man.* 경찰은 그 남자의 인상착의를 말해 달라고 그에게 요구할 것이다. / *Let me give you some advice.* 몇 가지 충고를 해 드리겠습니다.

5 ▶PERFORM AN ACTION 행위의 실행 ◀ [T] a word used before some words that show action, meaning to do the action ‖ 행위를 나타내는 몇몇 단어 앞에 쓰여, (특정) 행위를 하는 것을 뜻하는 말: *The boy gave Lydia a big smile.* 그 소년은 리디아를 보고 방긋 웃었다. / *Yo Yo Ma gave a performance of pieces by Bach.* 요요마는 바흐의 곡을 연주했다. / *Give me a call* (=telephone me) *at 8:00.* 오전 8시에 저에게 전화해 주세요. / *Come on, give your Grandpa a hug.* 자, 할아버지 안아 드려야지.

6 give sb trouble/problems etc. to cause problems or make a situation difficult ‖ 문제를 일으키거나 상황을 어렵게 만들다: *The machines in the lab are giving us trouble.* 실험실의 기계가 문제를 일으키고 있다. / *Stop giving me a hard time!* (=stop criticizing me) 나를 그만 좀 비난해라!

7 ▶ILLNESS 병 ◀ [T] to infect someone with an illness, or make someone feel a particular way ‖ 남에게 질병을 감염시키다, 또는 남에게 특정한 느낌을 갖게 하다. 옮기다. 생기게[일으키게] 하다: *My husband gave me this cold.* 이번 감기는 남편한테 옮았다. / *The noise is giving me a headache.* 나는 소음 때문에 두통이 난다.

8 give sb/sth time to allow a person or situation to have time to think, act, or develop ‖ 사람 또는 상황에 생각[행동, 발전]할 시간을 갖게 하다. …에게 (…할) 시간을 주다: *Give her some time. She'll make the right decision.* 그녀에게 약간의 시간을 주어라. 그녀가 옳은 결정을 내릴 것이다.

9 ▶QUALITY/SHAPE ETC. 성질/모양 등 ◀ [T] to make someone or something have a particular quality, shape, look etc. ‖ 사람 또는 사물이 특정한 성질·모양·모습 등을 가지게 하다. 부여하다: *The color of the room gives it a warm cozy feeling.* 그 방의 색깔이 따뜻하고 아늑한 느낌을 준다.

10 give the impression/feeling to make someone have a particular idea or feeling about someone or something ‖ 남에게 어떤 사람 또는 사물에 대해 특정한 생각 또는 느낌을 갖게 하다. 인상/느낌을 주다: *He gave us the impression that the last few years had been hard for him.* 그는 우리에게 지난 몇 년간 어렵게 생활했다는 인상을 주었다.

11 ▶MONEY 돈 ◀ [T] to be willing to pay a particular amount of money for something ‖ 사물에 대한 특정 금액을 지불하려고 하다. 지불하다. 치르다: *I'll give you $75 for the oak desk.* 내가 오크 재목 책상 대금 75달러를 지불하겠다.

12 ▶BEND/STRETCH 휘다/늘어나다 ◀ [I] to bend, stretch, or break because of weight or pressure ‖ 중량 또는 압력으로 구부러지다[늘어나다, 깨지다]: *The leather will give slightly when you wear the boots.* 부츠를 신을 때 가죽이 약간 늘어날 것이다.

13 give or take used in order to show that a number or amount is not exact ‖ 수 또는 양이 정확하지 않음을 나타내는 데에 쓰여. …의 증감을 포함해서. 대략. 대충: *The show lasts about an hour, give or take five minutes.* 그 쇼는 5분 정도의 시간 차이를 감안하더라도 대략 한 시간 걸린다.

14 give a party to be the person who organizes a party ‖ 파티를 준비하는 사람이 되다. 파티를 열다

G

SPOKEN PHRASES

15 sb would give anything said in order to emphasize that you want something very much ‖ 어떤 것을 아주 몹시 원하는 것을 강조하는 데에 쓰여. (…을 위해서라면) 어떠한 희생도 치르겠다. 꼭 …하고 싶다: *I'd give anything to be able to get tickets to the R.E.M. concert.* 나는 R.E.M. 콘서트의 입장권을 살 수만 있다면 무슨일이든 하겠다.

16 don't give me that! said when someone has just said something that you know is not true ‖ 남이 방금 말한 것이 사실이 아님을 알 때에 쓰여. 그런 말은 믿을 수가 없어. 그런 말도 안 되는 소리는 하지 마라: *"I'm too tired." "Oh, don't give me that. You just don't want to come."* "난 너무 피곤해." "아, 그런 말도 안 되는 소리는 하지 마라. 너는 그냥 오고 싶지 않은 거야."

—see also GIVE AND TAKE, **give sb a**

(big) hand (HAND¹)

give away *phr v* **1** [T **give** sth ↔ **away**] to give someone something instead of selling it ‖ 판매하는 대신에 남에게 어떤 것을 주다. …을 선물로 주다. 거저 주다: *The store is giving away a toaster to the first 50 customers.* 그 상점은 선착순 50명의 고객에게 토스터를 공짜로 주고 있다. / *I gave my old clothes away to the Salvation Army.* 나는 구세군에 내 헌 옷을 주었다. **2** [T **give** sb/sth ↔ **away**] to do or say something that shows thoughts or feelings that should be secret ‖ 비밀로 해야 할 생각이나 감정을 드러내는 일을 하거나 말하다. 누설하다. 폭로하다: *He said he hadn't told her, but his face gave him away.* (=showed that he had told her) 그는 그녀에게 얘기하지 않았다고 말했지만 그의 얼굴에 얘기 했다고 쓰여 있었다. / *I was afraid that the kids would give the game away.* (=tell the secret) 나는 아이들이 비밀을 누설할 것 같아 두려웠다. —see also GIVEAWAY

give sth ↔ **back** *phr v* [T] to return something to the person who owns it or who owned it before you ‖ 사물을 그 소유자 또는 본인 이전의 소유자에게 돌려주다. 되돌려주다. 원상대로 회복하다: *Give me back my popcorn!* 내 팝콘을 돌려줘! / *Will you give the money back to Rich for me?* 내 대신 리치에게 그 돈을 돌려주겠니?

give in *phr v* [II] to agree to something you were unwilling to agree to before, especially after a long argument ‖ 특히 오랜 논의 끝에 전에 동의하지 않으려 했던 일에 동의하다. 따르다. 요구를 받아들이다: *Randy had been asking her out for months, so she finally gave in.* 랜디는 수개월 동안 그녀에게 데이트 신청을 했는데 마침내 그녀가 승낙했다.

give in to sth *phr v* [T] to stop being able to control a strong need or desire ‖ 강한 욕구나 욕망을 자제할 수 없게 되다. 굴복[항복]하다. 지다: *If you feel the need for a cigarette, don't give in to it.* 담배를 피우고 싶은 욕구를 느끼더라도 그 것에 굴복하지 마라.

give off *phr v* [T] to produce a smell, light, heat, a sound etc. ‖ 냄새·빛·열·소리 등을 만들다. 풍기다. 내다. 발하다: *People complain about the terrible smell that the factory gives off.* 사람들은 공장에서 나오는 고약한 냄새에 대해 불평을 한다.

give out *phr v* **1** [T **give** sth ↔ **out**] to give something to each of several people ‖ 여러 사람 각각에게 사물을 주다. 나누

어 주다. 분배하다: *She gave copies of the report out to the committee before the meeting.* 그녀는 회의가 열리기 전에 위원회에 보고서 사본을 배포했다. **2** [II] to stop working correctly ‖ 제대로 작동을 하지 않다. 멈추다: *My voice gave out half way through the song.* 내 목소리가 노래의 중간 부분에서 나오지 않았다.

give up *phr v* **1** [I,T **give** sth ↔ **up**] to stop trying to do something or working at something ‖ 일을 하려고 애쓰거나 일에 종사하는 것을 그만두다. 단념하다. 포기하다: *I looked everywhere for the keys - finally, I just gave up.* 나는 도처에서 열쇠를 찾았으나 결국은 그냥 포기하고 말았다. / *Vladimir has given up trying to teach her Russian.* 블라디미르는 그녀에게 러시아어를 가르치려는 것을 단념했다. **2** [T **give** sth ↔ **up**] to stop doing or having something ‖ 어떤 것을 하거나 가지는 것을 그만두다. 중단하다. 버리다: *She gave up her job, and started writing full time.* 그녀는 직장을 버리고 전업으로 글쓰기를 시작했다. **3** [T **give** sb ↔ **up**] to allow yourself or someone else to be caught by the police or enemy soldiers ‖ 자기 자신 또는 남이 경찰 또는 적군에 잡히는 것을 용인하다. 넘겨주다. 내주다: *The police appealed for the fugitive to give himself up.* 경찰은 도망자에게 자수할 것을 호소했다.

give up on sb *phr v* [T] to stop hoping that someone will change his/her behavior ‖ 남이 태도를 바꾸리라는 바람을 포기하다: *I'd been in trouble so many times that my parents had given up on me.* 부모님이 나를 포기해 버릴 정도로 여러 번 어려움에 처했었다.

give² *n* [U] the ability of a material to bend or stretch when it is under pressure ‖ 압력을 받으면 구부러지거나 늘어나는 물질의 성질. 굽음. 탄력성: *This skirt doesn't have a lot of give to it.* 이 치마는 신축성이 좋지 않다.

give and take /ˌ. . ˈ./ *n* [U] a situation in which two people or groups are each willing to let the other have or do some of the things they want ‖ 두 사람 또는 그룹이 상대가 원하는 것의 어느 정도를 소유하거나 행하는 것을 기꺼이 허용하는 상황. 대등한 거래. 쌍방의 타협: *In every successful marriage there is a certain amount of give and take.* 모든 성공적인 결혼 생활에는 상호간에 어느 정도의 양보가 있다.

give·a·way /ˈɡɪvəˌweɪ/ *n* **1 be a dead giveaway** to make it very easy for someone to guess something ‖ 남이 어떤 것을 아주 쉽게 추정하게 만들다. 결정적인 증거가 되다: *Vince was lying. His red face was a dead giveaway.* 빈스는 거짓말을 하고 있었다. 그의 상기된 얼굴이 틀림없는 증거였다. **2** a product, prize etc. that a store or company gives to its customers for free ‖ 상점이나 회사 등이 무료로 고객들에게 주는 상품·경품 등. 무료 증정품 **– giveaway** *adj* : *giveaway prices* 헐값

giv·en¹ /'gɪvən/ *adj* **1 any/a given** ... any particular time, idea, or thing that is being used as an example ‖ 일례로 사용되는 특정한 시간[생각, 것]의. 주어진. 소정의: *In any given year, over half of all accidents happen in the home.* 어느 해를 보든 모든 사고의 반 이상은 가정에서 발생한다. **2 a given** time, date etc. is one that has been fixed or agreed on ‖ 시간·날짜 등이 정해지거나 합의된. 정해진. 일정한: *How much electricity is used in any given period?* 일정한 기간을 측정해 보면 전기는 얼마나 사용됩니까?

given² *prep* if you consider ‖ 고려하면: *Given the number of people we invited, I'm surprised that so few came.* 우리가 초대한 사람 수를 생각하면 너무 소수가 온 것이 놀랍다.

given³ *v* the PAST PARTICIPLE of GIVE ‖ give의 과거 분사형

given⁴ *n* **a given** a basic fact that you accept as the truth ‖ 진실로써 받아들이는 기본적인 사실. 기지의 사실[상황]: *Sandra is always at least 15 minutes late; that's a given.* 산드라는 항상 적어도 15분은 늦는다. 그건 기정 사실이야.

given name /.. ,./ *n* ⇨ FIRST NAME

giz·mo /'gɪzmoʊ/ *n* ⇨ GADGET

giz·zard /'gɪzɚd/ *n* an organ near a bird's stomach that helps it break down food ‖ 음식을 분해하는 것을 돕는 새의 위 부근에 있는 기관. 모래주머니

gla·cial /'gleɪʃəl/ *adj* relating to ice or GLACIERS, or formed by glaciers ‖ 얼음 또는 빙하에 관련된, 빙하로 형성된. 얼음의. 빙하의: *glacial streams* 빙하의 흐름

gla·cier /'gleɪʃɚ/ *n* a large area of ice that moves slowly over an area of land ‖ 육지 지대 위로 서서히 움직이는 큰 얼음 지대. 빙하

glad /glæd/ *adj* **1** happy or satisfied about something good that has happened ‖ 일어난 좋은 일에 대해 행복하거나 만족한. 기쁜: *Mom's really glad (that) you could come home for Christmas.* 네가 크리스마스에 집에 올 수 있다니 엄마는 정말 기쁘다. ✗DON'T SAY

"She's a really glad person." ✗ "She's a really glad person."이라고는 하지 않는다 **2 be glad to do sth** to be willing to do something ‖ 기꺼이 무엇을 하다: *He said he'd be glad to help me.* 그는 기꺼이 나를 돕겠다고 말했다.

glade /gleɪd/ *n* LITERARY an area with very few trees inside a forest ‖ 숲 속의 나무가 아주 적게 있는 지역. 숲 속의 빈터

glad·i·a·tor /'glædi,eɪtɚ/ *n* a strong man who fought other men or animals as a public event in ancient Rome ‖ 고대 로마의 국가적 행사로 다른 남자들 또는 동물들과 싸운 강한 남자. 검투사

glad·ly /'glædli/ *adv* willingly or eagerly ‖ 기꺼이, 열심히: *"Would you drive Jenny to school today?" "Gladly."* "오늘 제니를 학교에 태워다 주시겠어요?" "기꺼이."

glam·or /'glæmɚ/ *n* [U] the quality of being attractive, exciting, rich, and successful ‖ 매력적이고 재미있으며 호화롭고 성공적인 특성. 황홀하게 하는 매력: *the glamor of Hollywood* 할리우드의 매력

glam·or·ize /'glæmə,raɪz/ *v* [T] to make something seem more attractive or exciting than it really is ‖ 사물을 실제보다 더 매력적이거나 재미있어 보이게 하다. 매혹적으로 하다. 매력을 더하다

glam·or·ous /'glæmərəs/ *adj* attractive, exciting, and relating to wealth and success ‖ 매력적이고 재미있으며 부유함과 성공에 관련된. 매력이 넘치는. 매혹적인: *On television she looked so beautiful and glamorous.* 텔레비전에서 그녀는 너무나 아름답고 매혹적으로 보였다.

glance¹ /glæns/ *v* [I] **1** to quickly look at someone or something ‖ 사람이나 사물을 재빨리 보다. 언뜻 보다: *He glanced at his watch.* 그는 시계를 흘끗 보았다. **2** to read something very quickly ‖ 어떤 것을 매우 빨리 읽다. 훑어보다: *Paul glanced through/at the menu and ordered a ham sandwich.* 폴은 메뉴를 훑어보더니 햄 샌드위치를 주문했다.

glance² *n* **1** a quick look that you give someone or something ‖ 사람 또는 사물을 재빨리 봄. 일견. 흘끗 보기: *She took/shot/threw a glance at the man behind her.* 그녀는 자기 뒤에 있는 남자를 흘끗 보았다. **2 at a glance** immediately ‖ 즉시. 곧: *I knew at a glance that something was wrong.* 나는 뭔가 잘못되었다는 것을 곧 알았다. **3 at first glance** when you see or think about something for the first time ‖ 첫 번째로 사물을 보거나 생각할 때. 첫눈에: *At first glance, the place seemed completely empty.* 첫눈에 그곳은 텅 비어 있는 것처럼 보였다.

gland /ɡlænd/ *n* an organ in the body that produces a liquid substance that the body needs, such as SWEAT or SALIVA ‖ 땀·침 등의 신체에 필요한 액상 물질을 생산하는 신체 기관. 선(腺) – **glandular** /ˈɡlændʒələ/ *adj*

glare /ɡlɛr/ *v* [I] **1** to angrily look at someone or something for a long time ‖ 장시간 사람이나 사물을 화가 나서 쳐다보다. 노려보다: *What's wrong with Kathy? She's been glaring at me all day.* 캐시에게 무슨 일이 있니? 하루 종일 나를 노려보고 있어. **2** to shine with such a bright light that it hurts your eyes ‖ 눈을 해칠 정도로 아주 밝은 빛이 비치다. 눈부시게 비치다: *Sunlight was glaring off the shiny hood of the car.* 햇빛이 반짝이는 자동차 보닛에 반사되어 눈부시게 비치고 있었다.

glar·ing /ˈɡlɛrɪŋ/ *adj* **1** shining a light that is too bright to look at ‖ 보기에는 너무 밝은 빛이 비치는. 눈부신. 번쩍번쩍하는: *the glaring white light from the explosion* 폭발에서 생기는 눈부신 백색광 **2** very bad and very noticeable ‖ 아주 나쁘고 매우 눈에 띄는. 역력한. 빤한: *glaring mistakes* 확연한 실수

glass /ɡlæs/ *n* **1** [U] a transparent material that is usually used for making windows and bottles ‖ 보통 창문과 병 등을 만드는 데에 쓰이는 투명한 물질. 유리: *Be careful! Don't cut yourself on the broken glass!* 조심해라! 깨진 유리에 베이지 말고! **2** a glass container without a handle that you use for drinking liquids ‖ 액체를 마시는 데에 사용하는 손잡이 없는 유리 용기. 유리잔: *Did you put the wine glasses on the table?* 식탁에 포도주 잔을 놓았니? **3** the amount of a drink contained in a glass ‖ 잔 하나에 담긴 음료의 양: *Would you like a glass of milk?* 우유 한 잔 드시겠어요? **4** [U] objects made of glass ‖ 유리로 만든 물체. 유리 제품: *an impressive collection of Venetian glass* 인상적인 베네치아제(製) 유리그릇 소장품 —see also GLASSES

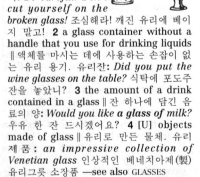

glass ceil·ing /ˌ. ˈ../ *n* the attitudes and practices that prevent women or people from minority groups from getting high level jobs ‖ 여자나 소수 민족의 고위직 획득을 저지하는 태도와 관행. 보이지 않는 차별[장벽]

glassed-in /ˌɡlæst ˈɪn·/ *adj* surrounded by a glass structure ‖ 유리 구조에 둘러싸인: *a glassed-in porch* 유리로 둘러싸인 현관

glass·es /ˈɡlæsɪz/ *n* [plural] two round pieces of glass in a FRAME that you wear in front of your eyes in order to see better ‖ 테에 동그란 두 개의 유리를 끼운, 더 잘 보이게 하기 위해 눈앞에 착용하는 것. 안경: *I need to buy a new pair of glasses.* 나는 새 안경을 하나 사야 한다.

glasses

glass·ware /ˈɡlæswɛr/ *n* [U] glass containers that you drink from ‖ 음료용 유리 용기

glass·y /ˈɡlæsi/ *adj* **1** smooth and shiny, like glass ‖ 유리처럼 매끄럽고 빛나는. 유리 같은: *the glassy surface of the lake* 거울 같이 잔잔한 호수 표면 **2** glassy eyes are shiny, do not move, and do not show any expression ‖ 눈이 빛나지만 움직이지도 않고 어떤 표정도 나타내지 않는. 무표정한. 흐리멍덩한

glaze¹ /ɡleɪz/ *v* **1** [I] also **glaze over** if your eyes glaze, they stop showing any expression because you are bored or tired ‖ 지루하거나 피로해서 눈이 아무런 표정도 나타내지 않다. 흐리멍덩하다 **2** [T] to cover clay pots, bowls etc. with a thin liquid in order to give them a shiny surface ‖ 표면을 반짝거리게 하려고 묽은 액체를 점토 항아리·사발 등에 바르다. 유약을 바르다 **3** [T] to put a liquid on fruit, cake, or meat so that it has a shiny attractive surface ‖ 반들거리는 보기 좋은 표면을 갖도록 과일[케이크, 고기]에 액체를 바르다 **4** [T] to put glass into a window frame ‖ 창틀에 유리를 끼워 넣다 – **glazed** *adj*

glaze² *n* **1** a thin liquid paint that is put on clay pots, bowls etc. to give them a shiny surface ‖ 점토 항아리·사발 등의 표면을 반들거리게 하기 위해 바르는 묽은 액체 염료. 유약 **2** [U] a liquid put on fruit, cake, or meat to give it an attractive shiny surface ‖ 보기 좋은 윤이 나는 표면을 만들려고 과일[케이크, 고기]에 바르는 액체

gleam¹ /ɡlim/ *v* [I] to shine, especially after being cleaned ‖ 특히 깨끗이 닦아서

반들거리다. 빛나다. 반짝이다: *Grandpa polished his shoes until they gleamed.* 할아버지는 구두를 반짝일 때까지 닦았다.

gleam[2] *n* **1** the slightly shiny quality that something is polished has when light shines on it ‖ 광택을 낸 물체에 빛이 비칠 때 살짝 반짝이는 성질. 빛남. 번쩍임. 섬광 **2 with a gleam in your eye** showing that you are amused, or that you are not telling someone something secret ‖ 즐겁다는 것을 나타내거나 비밀을 남에게 말하지 않으리라는 것을 나타내는: *"I bet you want to know what your birthday present is!" he said with a gleam in his eye.* "네 생일 선물이 무엇인지 알고 싶지!"라고 그는 눈을 반짝이며 말했다.

glean /glin/ *v* [T] to find out information, even though this is difficult and takes time ‖ 어렵고 시간이 걸릴지라도 정보 등을 찾다. 조금씩 수집하다. 하나씩 조사하다: *Several lessons can be gleaned from our experience so far.* 우리는 지금까지의 경험을 통해 몇 가지 교훈을 얻었다.

glee /gli/ *n* [U] a feeling of happy excitement and satisfaction ‖ 행복하고 흥분되며 만족스러운 감정. 큰 기쁨. 환희: *The kids shouted with glee when they saw Santa.* 아이들은 산타를 보자 환호했다. – **gleefully** *adv*

glen /glɛn/ *n* a deep narrow valley ‖ 깊고 좁은 계곡. 협곡. 골짜기

glib /glɪb/ *adj* **1** said without thinking about all the problems in something, or about how your remarks will affect someone ‖ 어떤 것의 모든 문제점이나 자신의 말이 남에게 어떤 영향을 미칠는지에 대한 생각 없이 말한. 재잘재잘 잘 지껄이는. 입이 가벼운: *The doctor made some glib remark, saying my headaches were just "stress."* 의사는 나의 두통은 스트레스성일 뿐이라고 하면서 몇 마디 가볍게 덧붙였다. **2** able to persuade people that what you are saying is true ‖ 말하고 있는 내용이 진실이라고 사람들을 설득할 수 있는. 그럴듯한. 구변 좋은: *a glib talker* 구변 좋은 사람 – **glibly** *adv*

glide /glaɪd/ *v* [I] to move smoothly and quietly, as if no effort were being made ‖ 조금도 애쓰지 않는 듯이 부드럽고 조용히 움직이다. 미끄러지듯이 움직이다: *We watched the sailboats glide across the lake.* 우리는 요트들이 미끄러지듯이 호수를 가로지르는 모습을 보았다. – **glide** *n*

glid·er /ˈglaɪdɚ/ *n* a plane without an engine ‖ 엔진 없는 비행기. 활공기. 글라이더

glid·ing /ˈglaɪdɪŋ/ *n* the sport of flying a GLIDER ‖ 글라이더로 나는 스포츠. 글라이더로 활공하기

glim·mer[1] /ˈglɪmɚ/ *n* **1 a glimmer of hope/doubt etc.** a small amount of hope, doubt etc. ‖ 극히 적은 희망·의심 등. 일말의 희망/의심 **2** a light that does not shine very brightly ‖ 아주 밝게 빛나지는 않는 불빛. 희미한[흐릿한] 빛

glimmer[2] *v* [I] to shine weakly with a pale light ‖ 희미한 빛으로 약하게 빛나다. 가물가물 비치다

glimpse[1] /glɪmps/ *n* **1** a look at someone or something that is quicker than you want it to be ‖ 바라던 것보다 더 짧게 다른 사람이나 사물을 보다. 힐끗[얼핏] 보기: *Dad only got/caught a glimpse of the guy who stole our car.* 아빠는 우리 차를 훔쳐간 남자를 얼핏 보았을 뿐이었다. **2** a short experience of something that helps you begin to understand it ‖ 어떤 것을 간신히 이해하는데 도움을 주는 짧은 체험. 넌지시[어렴풋이] 알아차리기: *a glimpse into the future* 미래에 대한 어렴풋한 예감

glimpse[2] *v* [T] to quickly look at someone or something ‖ 사람이나 사물을 재빨리 보다. 힐끗[얼핏] 보다: *Glimpsing Joe behind him, he turned around to say "hello."* 뒤따라오는 조를 얼핏 보고서 그는 돌아서서 "안녕"하고 인사했다.

glint[1] /glɪnt/ *v* [I] if something that is shiny or smooth glints, it flashes with a very small amount of light ‖ 윤이 나거나 매끈한 물체가 희미하게 빛을 내다. 반짝이다: *Her teeth glinted as she smiled.* 그녀가 웃자 치아가 반짝였다.

glint[2] *n* a small flash of light that shines off something smooth or shiny ‖ 매끈하거나 윤나는 물체에서 비치는 약한 불빛. 반짝임. 윤. 광택: *the glint of his gold watch* 번쩍거리는 그의 금시계

glis·ten /ˈglɪsən/ *v* [I] to shine because of being wet or oily ‖ 물기나 기름기 때문에 반짝이다. 번들거리다. 미끈거리며 윤이 나다: *His back was glistening with sweat.* 그의 등이 땀으로 번들거리고 있었다. – **glistening** *adj*

glitch /glɪtʃ/ *n* a small problem that prevents something from working correctly ‖ 사물이 제대로 작동하지 못하게 하는 사소한 문제. 자그마한 고장[결함]: *Company records were lost due to a computer glitch.* 회사의 기록 자료들이 컴퓨터 고장으로 멸실되었다.

glit·ter[1] /ˈglɪtɚ/ *v* [I] to shine with a lot of small flashes of light ‖ 많은 희미한 불빛들이 깜박이며 빛나다. 반짝거리다:

Fresh snow was glittering outside in the morning light. 밤새 내린 눈이 집 밖에서 아침 햇살에 반짝이고 있었다. – **glittering** *adj*

glitter² *n* 1 [singular] a lot of small flashes of light ‖ 수없이 깜박이는 작은 빛. 반짝이는 빛. 빛나는 광휘: *the glitter of her diamond ring* 그녀의 다이아몬드 반지의 광채 2 [U] very small pieces of shiny plastic or metal that you glue onto paper, cards etc. for decoration ‖ 종이· 카드 등에 장식용으로 붙이는 반짝이는 플라스틱이나 금속의 작은 조각. 반짝이 (장식)

gloat /glout/ *v* [I] to behave in an annoying way because you are proud of your success, or happy about someone else's failure ‖ 자신의 성공을 자랑스러워 하거나 다른 사람의 실패에 대해 기분 좋아져서 눈꼴시게 처신하다. 자랑스럽게 만족해하다. 유세하듯이 행동하다: *The baseball team was gloating over its victory.* 야구팀은 승리한 것에 대해 매우 흡족해하고 있었다.

glob /glab/ *n* INFORMAL a small amount of a soft substance or thick liquid ‖ 소량의 말랑한 물질이나 진한 액체 덩어리. 작은 [한]방울: *a glob of ketchup* 케첩 한 덩어리

glob·al /'gloubəl/ *adj* 1 affecting the whole world, or relating to the whole world ‖ 전 세계에 영향을 끼치는, 또는 전 세계에 관한. 세계적인. 지구상의: *the global problems of pollution, disease, and overpopulation* 전 세계적 문제인 오염·질병·인구 과잉 2 considering all the parts of a problem or a situation ‖ 문제나 상황의 모든 부분을 고려한. 전체적[포괄적]인. 광범위한: *a global study on the company's weaknesses* 회사의 취약점에 대한 광범위한 연구 – **globally** *adv*

global e·con·o·my /ˌ.. ...../ *n* [singular] the economic activity of the world considered as a whole ‖ 전체로서 간주한 세계의 경제 활동. 지구촌 경제

global warm·ing /ˌ.. '../ *n* [U] an increase in the world's temperature, caused by an increase of CARBON DIOXIDE around the earth ‖ 지구상의 이산화탄소의 증가로 인한 지구 기온의 상승. 지구 온난화

globe /gloub/ *n* 1 **the globe** the world ‖ 세계. 지구: *Our company has offices all over the globe.* 우리 회사는 전 세계에 지점을 가지고 있다. 2 an object shaped like a ball ‖ 공 모양의 물체. 구체. 둥근 물건 3 a round object that has a map of the earth painted on it ‖ 표면에 세계 지

도가 채색된 둥근 물체. 지구의(地球儀). 지구본

glob·u·lar /'glabyələ/ *adj* shaped like a ball or a drop of liquid ‖ 공이나 액체 방울 같은 모양의. 공 모양의. 구형(球型)의

glob·ule /'glabyul/ *n* a small drop of liquid or a melted substance ‖ 액체나 녹은 물질의 작은 방울. 소구(체)립(粒)

gloom /glum/ *n* [singular, U] 1 darkness that you can hardly see through ‖ 거의 관통해 볼 수 없는 어둠. 어둑어둑함: *A man was sitting alone in the gloom.* 한 남자가 어둠 속에 혼자 앉아 있었다. 2 a feeling of sadness, or having no hope ‖ 슬프거나 희망이 없는 느낌. 우울. 침울. 의기소침

gloom·y /'glumi/ *adj* 1 feeling sad because you do not have a lot of hope, or making you feel sad ‖ 희망이 많지 않기 때문에 우울하게 느끼는, 또는 우울하게 느끼게 하는. 우울한[하게 하는]. 울적한[하게 하는]: *a gloomy movie about a girl who dies of cancer* 암으로 죽은 소녀에 관한 우울한 영화 2 dark in a way that makes you feel sad ‖ 슬픈 기분이 들도록 어두운. 어둠침침한. 음울한: *the cold gloomy weather* 춥고 음울한 날씨 – **gloomily** *adv*

glo·ri·fied /'glɔrəˌfaɪd/ *adj* made to seem like something more important ‖ 더 중요한 것처럼 보이게 만들어진. 부풀려진. 미화된. 꾸며진: *My title is "Editorial Assistant," but I'm just a glorified secretary.* 내 직함은 "논설 보조"이지만, 단지 비서를 미화시킨 것일 뿐이다.

glo·ri·fy /'glɔrəˌfaɪ/ *v* [T] 1 to make someone or something seem more important or better than he, she, or it is ‖ 사람이나 사물을 실제보다 더 중요하거나 더 낫게 보이게 하다. 꾸며 보이다. 미화하다: *We must avoid glorifying the war.* 우리는 전쟁을 미화하는 짓은 피해야 한다. 2 to praise someone or something important, especially God ‖ 중요한 사람이나 사물, 특히 신을 찬양하다 – **glorification** /ˌglɔrəfə'keɪʃən/ *n* [U]

glo·ri·ous /'glɔriəs/ *adj* 1 deserving praise or honor ‖ 찬양이나 명예를 받을 만한. 영광스러운. 영예[명예]로운: *a glorious achievement* 영예로운 위업 2 beautiful and extremely nice ‖ 아름답거나 몹시 훌륭한;㉨wonderful: *It was a glorious day!* (=beautiful sunny weather) 눈부시게 화창한 날이었다! – **gloriously** *adv*

glo·ry¹ /'glɔri/ *n* 1 the importance, praise, and honor that people give someone they admire ‖ 사람들이 숭배하는 사람에게 부여하는 중시(重視)·찬사·명예. 찬미. 영광. 명예: *At 19 he won glory as an Olympic champion.* 19세에 그는 올림픽 챔피언의 영예를 안았다. / *Someone in the church shouted out "glory to God!"* 교회 안의 누군가가 "신에게 영광을!"이라고 소리쳤다. **2** an achievement that you are proud of ‖ 자랑스러워하는 업적. 명예[명성]가 되는 것: *Becoming a Supreme Court judge was the crowning glory* (=the final, most successful part) *of her legal career.* 대법원 판사가 된 것이 그녀의 법조 경력의 최고의 영예였다. **3** [C, U] a beautiful and impressive appearance ‖ 아름답고 인상적인 모습. 장관. 찬란함. 미관: *They spent $10 million on restoring the Grand Theater to its former glory.* 그들은 그랜드 씨어터를 예전의 훌륭한 모습으로 복원하기 위해 1천만 달러를 들였다.

glory² *v*

glory in sth *phr v* [T] to enjoy or be proud of the praise, attention, and success that you get ‖ 받게 된 찬사·관심·성공을 즐기거나 자랑스러워하다. 뽐내다. 자랑스러워하다: *The new mayor gloried in his victory.* 새로 당선된 시장은 승리를 기뻐했다.

gloss¹ /glɔs, glas/ *n* **1** [singular, U] a shiny attractive surface ‖ 반짝이며 눈길을 끄는 표면. 광택. 윤: *a new hair gel that adds gloss to even the dullest hair* 극심하게 푸석푸석한 머리에도 윤기를 더해 주는 새 헤어젤 **2** an explanation of a written word or expression ‖ 문장상의 단어나 표현에 대한 설명. 주(註). 주해. 주석. 해설

gloss² *v* [T] to provide an explanation for something that is written in a book ‖ 책에 씌어진 어떤 것에 대한 설명을 제시하다. …에 주를 달다. …을 주해[주석]하다

gloss over sth *phr v* to deliberately avoid talking about the details of a situation, fact etc. ‖ 상황·사실 등의 상세한 내용에 대해 이야기하기를 고의적으로 회피하다. …을 용케 발뺌하다. 요리조리 빠져 나가다: *The report glossed over the company's recent profit losses.* 보고서는 회사의 최근 수익 손실에 대해 얼버무리고 넘어갔다.

glos·sa·ry /ˈglasəri, ˈglɔ-/ *n* a list of special words and explanations of what they mean, written at the end of a book ‖ 책의 끝에 써놓은 특별한 어구와 그 어구에 대한 설명 목록. 용어 풀이[해설]

gloss·y /ˈglɔsi, ˈglasi/ *adj* **1** shiny and smooth ‖ 윤이 나고 매끈한. 광택이 있는. 반들반들한: *glossy healthy hair* 윤이 나고 건강한 모발 **2** a glossy magazine, book, or photograph is printed on shiny, good quality paper ‖ 잡지[책, 사진]가 광택이 나는 양질의 종이에 인쇄된. 광택지로 된

glove /glʌv/ *n* a piece of clothing worn on your hand, with separate parts to cover the thumb and each finger ‖ 엄지와 각 손가락을 감싸는 부분이 각각 달려 있는 손에 끼는 한 점의 의류. 장갑

glove

glove com·part·ment /ˈ. .,../,
glove box /ˈ. ./ *n* a place like a small cupboard in front of the passenger seat of a car, often used for storing road maps ‖ 종종 도로 지도의 보관에 쓰이는, 자동차 조수석 앞의 작은 선반 모양의 칸. 사물함 —see picture on page 943

glow¹ /gloʊ/ *v* [I] **1** to shine with a gentle steady light ‖ 온화한 빛이 계속 빛나다. 빛을 내다. 계속 똑같은 빛을 발하다: *The church walls glowed in the candlelight.* 교회의 벽면이 촛불로 빛났다. **2** to produce a red light and heat without flames ‖ 불꽃 없이 붉은 빛과 열을 내다. 작열하다: *A log fire was glowing in the fireplace.* 장작불이 난로 안에서 벌겋게 타고 있었다 **3** to look very happy and healthy ‖ 매우 행복하고 건강하게 보이다. 상기되다. 홍조를 띠다. 혈색이 좋다: *Jodie was glowing with pride as she looked at the baby.* 조디는 아기를 바라보면서 자랑스러움으로 상기되어 있었다.

glow² *n* [singular] **1** a gentle steady light, especially from something that is burning without flames ‖ 특히 불꽃이 없이 타고 있는 물체로부터 꾸준히 나오는 온화한 빛. 새빨간[붉은] 빛: *The sky was filled with an orange glow.* 하늘은 오렌지 빛으로 물들여져 있었다. **2** the slightly red appearance your face or body has when you exercise or feel very happy ‖ 운동을 하거나 매우 행복할 때 얼굴이나 몸에 나타나는 불그스레한 기운. 홍조. 상기. 달아오름: *the healthy glow in her cheeks* 그녀의 볼의 건강한 혈색

glow·er /ˈglaʊɚ/ *v* [I] to look at someone in an angry way ‖ 화나서 남을 바라보다. 노려보다. 언짢은 얼굴로 보다: *Donna glowered at her husband but*

said nothing. 도나는 남편을 노려보면서
도 아무 말도 하지 않았다. – **glowering**
adj

glow·ing /'gloʊɪŋ/ *adj* **1 glowing
report/description etc.** a report etc.
that is full of praise for someone or
something ‖ 사람이나 사물에 대한 찬사로
가득 찬 보고서 등. 격찬하는 보고서/생생
한 묘사 ‖ **2** looking very healthy and
attractive ‖ 매우 건강하고 매력적으로 보
이는. 상기된. 달아오른. 홍조를 띤 –
glowingly *adv*

glow·worm /'gloʊwɜrm/ *n* an insect
that gives out light from its body ‖ 몸
에서 빛을 발하는 곤충. 반딧불이류 곤충

glu·cose /'glukoʊs/ *n* [U] a natural
form of sugar that is in fruits ‖ 과일에 들
어 있는 천연의 당(糖). 포도당

glue¹ /glu/ *n* [C, U] a sticky substance
used for joining things together ‖ 물체를
접합시키는 데에 쓰이는 점착성(粘着性)
물질. 풀. 아교. 접착제

glue² *v* **glued, gluing** *or* **glueing** [T]
1 to join two things together using glue
‖ 풀을 써서 2개의 물체를 접합시키다. 접
착제를 바르다. 풀칠하다 **2 be glued to
sth** to look at something with all your
attention ‖ 주의를 온통 기울여 어떤 것을
바라보다. …에 열중하다. 넋을 잃고 빠
져들다: *The kids are glued to the TV set
all day long!* 아이들이 하루 종일 TV에
붙어서 떨어지지 않네!

glum /glʌm/ *adj* sad and quiet ‖ 슬프고
조용한. 침울한. 뚱한

glut¹ /glʌt/ *n* a large supply of
something that is more than you need ‖
사물의 필요 이상의 대량 공급. 공급 과
잉. 과다 공급: *a glut of oil on the
market* 시장에서의 유류 과잉 공급

glut² *v* **-tted, -tting** [T] **be glutted
with** to be supplied with too much of
something ‖ 어떤 것이 너무 많이 공급되
다. 넘쳐나다. 공급이 과잉되다: *an area
glutted with half-empty office buildings*
절반이 텅텅 빈 사무실 건물들로 넘쳐나는
지역

glut·ton /'glʌtʔn/ *n* **1** someone who
eats too much food ‖ 음식을 너무 많이 먹
는 사람. 대식[폭식]가 **2 a glutton for
punishment** someone who seems to
enjoy working very hard or doing
something unpleasant ‖ 열심히 일하거나
내키지 않는 일을 하는 것을 즐기는 듯한
사람. 궂은[어떤] 일도 마다하지 않는
사람

glut·ton·y /'glʌtʔn-i/ *n* [U] the bad
habit of eating and drinking too much ‖
너무 많이 먹거나 마시는 나쁜 습성. 폭

음. 폭식. 과식

glyc·er·in /'glɪsərɪn/ *n* [U] a sticky
colorless liquid used in making soap,
medicine, and EXPLOSIVEs ‖ 비누·의약품·
폭약 제조에 쓰이는 끈적이는 무색의 액
체. 글리세린

gm. the written abbreviation of GRAM ‖
gram의 약어

GMO *n* genetically modified organism; a plant or other living thing
whose GENEs have been changed by
scientists, especially in order to make it
less likely to get diseases or be harmed
by insects etc. ‖ genetically modified
organism(유전자 변형 개체)의 약어; 특히
질병에 덜 걸리고 병충해를 덜 입게 하려
고 과학자들이 유전자를 변형시킨 식물이
나 생물

gnarled /nɑrld/ *adj* rough and twisted
‖ 거칠고 꼬인. 울퉁불퉁한. 마디[옹이]투
성이의. 비틀린: *a gnarled branch* 옹이투
성이의 가지 / *gnarled fingers* 비틀린 손
가락들

gnash /næʃ/ *v* [T] **gnash your teeth**
LITERARY to move your teeth against
each other because you are angry or
unhappy ‖ 화가 나거나 불쾌해서 이를 서
로 맞부딪치다. 이를 갈다

gnat /næt/ *n* a small flying insect that
bites ‖ 물어뜯는 날아다니는 작은 곤충. 각
다귀

gnaw /nɔ/ *v* [I, T] to keep biting
something ‖ 어떤 것을 계속 물어뜯다. 갉
아먹다. 쏠다: *a dog gnawing on a bone*
뼈다귀를 물어뜯고 있는 개

gnaw at sb *phr v* [T] to make someone
feel worried or anxious ‖ 사람에게 걱정
이나 불안을 느끼게 하다. 괴롭히다. 고민
하게 하다: *Fear had been gnawing at
him all day.* 그는 공포로 하루 종일 시달
리고 있었다.

gnaw·ing /'nɔ-ɪŋ/ *adj* worrying or
painful, usually for a long time ‖ 보통 오
랫동안 걱정하거나 고통스러운: *a
gnawing fear/pain* 고통스러운 공포[고
통]

gnome /noʊm/ *n* a creature in
children's stories like a little old man,
who lives under the ground ‖ 지하에서
사는 난쟁이 노인 같은 동화 속의 가공 인
물. 땅의 요정. 작은[난쟁이] 도깨비

GNP *n* **the GNP** Gross National
Product; the total value of the goods
and services produced in a country,
including income from abroad ‖ Gross
National Product(국민 총생산)의 약어;
해외로부터의 소득을 포함하여 한 나라에
서 생산된 재화와 용역의 총 가치

go

Lucia has gone to Paris.

Lucia has been to Paris.

go¹ /gou/ *v* **went, gone, going** *third person singular* **goes**

1 ▶**LEAVE** 떠나다◀ [I] to leave the place where the speaker is in order to go somewhere else ‖ 다른 장소로 가기 위해 현재 화자가 있는 곳을 떠나다: *I wanted to go, but Craig wanted to stay.* 나는 떠나고 싶었지만, 크레이그는 남기를 원했다. / *It's late – we should be/get going.* 늦었어. 우리는 떠나야[출발해야] 해. —compare COME

2 ▶**VISIT** 방문하다◀ *past participle also* **been** [I] to visit a place and then leave it ‖ 한 장소를 방문한 후 그곳을 떠나다. 가다. 가보다: *Lucia has gone to Paris.* (=she is in Paris now) 루시아는 파리에 갔다. / *Lucia has been to Paris.* (=she has visited Paris in the past) 루시아는 파리에 가본 적이 있다. / *The doctor hasn't been here yet.* 의사는 아직 여기에 도착하지 않았다. / *Are you going to the game on Saturday?* 토요일에 시합을 보러 가시겠습니까?

3 ▶**TRAVEL/MOVE** 여행하다/이동하다◀ [I] to travel or move in a particular way, to a particular place, or for a particular distance ‖ 특정 수단으로[특정 장소로, 특정 거리만큼] 여행하거나 이동하다: *We can go by bus.* 우리는 버스로 갈 수 있다. / *We went home to eat dinner.* 우리는 저녁을 먹으러 집에 갔다. / *Where are you going?* 어디에 가니?

4 be going to do sth used in order to say that something will happen, or is supposed to happen in the future ‖ 장차 어떤 일이 일어나거나 일어나기로 되어 있다는 것을 말하는 데에 쓰여. …할 것이다. …하기로 되어 있다: *It looks like it's going to rain.* 비가 올 것 같다. —

compare GONNA —see usage note at GONNA

5 go shopping/swimming etc. to go somewhere in order to buy things, swim etc. ‖ 물건을 사거나 수영 등을 하기 위해 어딘가로 가다. 쇼핑/수영하러 가다: *Let's go running tomorrow morning.* 내일 아침에 달리기하러 가자.

6 go for a walk/swim etc. to spend some time walking, swimming etc. ‖ 걷기·수영하기 등에 일정 시간을 소비하다. 산책/수영하러 가다: *We went for a ride in the car after lunch.* 점심 식사 후 우리는 드라이브하러 갔다.

7 ▶**REACH** 도달하다◀ [I] to reach as far as a particular place, or lead to a particular place ‖ 특정 장소까지 도달하다, 또는 특정 장소까지 뻗어 있다. 펼쳐지다. 달하다. 미치다: *The roots of the tree go very deep.* 그 나무의 뿌리는 매우 깊이 뻗어 있다.

8 ▶**BELONG** 속하다◀ [I] to belong or fit in a particular place or position ‖ 특정 장소나 위치에 속하거나 들어맞다. …에 놓여지다: *"Where do the plates go?" "On the shelf."* "접시들을 어디에 둘까요?" "선반에요."

9 ▶**BECOME** 어떤 것이 되다◀ [linking verb] to become ‖ 어떤 것이 되다: *My hair's going gray.* 나는 흰머리가 생기고 있다. —see usage note at BECOME

10 ▶**BE IN A STATE** 어떤 상태에 있다◀ [linking verb] to be or remain in a particular state ‖ 특정한 상태이거나 특정한 상태로 여전히 있다. …한 채로 있다 [지내다]: *The mother bird will go hungry to keep the babies alive.* 어미 새는 새끼들을 먹여 살리기 위해 굶고 지낸다.

11 go to church/school etc. to regularly go to a church, school etc. ‖ 정기적으로 교회·학교 등에 가다: *Is Brett going to college next year?* 브렛은 내년에 대학에 갑니까?

12 ▶**GET RID OF** 제거하다◀ [I] to be bad enough to be made to leave or be thrown away ‖ 내버려지거나 치워 버리기에 충분할 만큼 나쁘다. 제거되다. 없어지다: *They knew that Parker had to go.* 그들은 파커가 해고당해야만 한다는 것을 잘 알고 있었다. / *"Do you want all these magazines?" "No, they can go."* "이 잡지들 전부 가지고 있을래?" "아니, 버려도 돼."

13 ▶**SPEND** 소비하다◀ [I] if money or time goes, it is spent ‖ 돈·시간이 소모되다: *The money goes to local charities.* 그 돈은 지역 자선 단체에 기부된다. / *I*

G

just don't know where the time goes! 나
는 대체 시간이 왜 이리 빨리 흐르는지 모
르겠어!

14 ▶**WORK CORRECTLY** 정상 작동하다◀
[I] INFORMAL if a machine goes, it works
in the way that it should ‖ 기계가 제대로
작동하다. 돌아가다. 작동하다: *I can't get
the car to go.* 차에 시동이 걸리지 않는다.

15 ▶**BE SOLD** 팔리다◀ [I] to be sold ‖
팔리다: *The painting should go for
$2000.* 그 그림은 2천 달러에 팔릴 것이
다.

16 ▶**NO LONGER WORK** 작동이 중단되
다◀ [I] to become weak and not work
correctly ‖ 약해져서 정상적으로 작동하지
않게 되다. 쇠약[쇠퇴]해지다: *He's old,
and his hearing is going.* 그는 늙었고 그
의 청력은 나빠지고 있다.

17 ▶**SOUND/SONG** 소리/노래◀ [T] to
make a particular sound, or have
particular words or music ‖ 특정한 소리
를 내다, 또는 특정한 어구나 음악 소리를
갖다. …이라고 씌어[되어] 있다: *Ducks
go "quack."* 오리는 "꽥"하는 소리를 낸
다. / *How does the song go?* 그 노래는 어
떻게 부릅니까?

18 ▶**HAPPEN** 일어나다◀ [I] to happen
or develop in a particular way ‖ 특정하
게 일어나거나 전개되다. 되어가다. 되다:
The play went well/fine (=happened in
the way it was intended to) *until the
last ten minutes.* 연극은 끝나기 10분 전
까지는 괜찮았다. / *Then everything went
wrong.* (=happened in the wrong way)
그러다가 모든 것이 엉망이 되었다.

19 ▶**MATCH** 조화되다◀ [I] to look or
taste good together ‖ 합해서 좋아 보이거
나 좋은 맛을 내다. 어울리다. 조화되다:
*Those colors don't go together very
well.* 그 색깔들이 아주 잘 어울리지는 않
는다. / *Does red wine go with chicken?*
적포도주는 닭고기와 어울립니까?

20 get going INFORMAL to start doing
something ‖ 무언가를 하기 시작하다: *It's
time to get going on the cleaning.* 청소
를 시작할 시간이다.

21 ready to go ready to start doing
something ‖ 무엇을 시작할 준비가 된:
*The builders are ready to go, but their
equipment isn't here yet.* 건축업자들은
준비가 끝났지만 그들의 장비가 채 이곳에
도착하지 않았다.

22 to go a) remaining before
something happens ‖ 일이 일어나기 전까
지 아직 남아 있는. …앞으로 다가온. …
이 지나면 일어나는: *Only two weeks to
go before we leave for South America!*
우리가 남아메리카로 출발할 날이 겨우 2

주 남았네! **b)** food that is to go is
bought from a restaurant and taken
away to be eaten ‖ 식당에서 음식을 사서
가지고 나가는. 사서 가져가는: *I'll have a
large order of fries to go, please.* 감자 튀
김을 대짜로 포장해주세요.

23 it (just) goes to show used in order
to emphasize what something proves or
shows ‖ 어떤 것이 입증하거나 보여주는
것을 강조하는 데에 쓰여. …하는 생생한
[좋은] 예[본보기]이다: *It just goes to
show that anything can happen in
America.* 그것은 미국에서는 무슨 일이든
일어날 수 있다는 것을 그대로 보여준다.

SPOKEN PHRASES

24 How's it going? said in order to
ask someone how s/he is ‖ 남에게 안부
를 묻는 데에 쓰여. 어떻게 지내?:
*"Hey, Jimmy, how's it going?" "All
right, I guess."* "이봐, 지미, 어떻게 지
내?" "좋아, 그런대로."

25 go and do sth to go somewhere in
order to do something ‖ 어떤 것을 하
기 위해 어딘가를 가다. 가서 …하다:
I'll go and pick up the car for you. 내
가 가서 너 대신 차를 가져올게.

26 [I] to make a particular movement
‖ 특정한 동작을 취하다: *He went like
this and knocked the lamp over.* 그가
이렇게 움직이더니 스탠드를 쳐서 넘어
뜨렸다.

27 [T] NONSTANDARD said when telling
someone what someone else has said
‖ 남에게 다른 사람이 한 말을 전할 때
에 쓰여. …이[가] 말하기를 …이라 했
다: *I asked her how she was, and she
goes, "Do you really care?"* 내가 그녀
에게 어떻게 지냈냐고 물었더니 그녀가
말하기를 "정말 관심있어 묻는 거예
요?" 했다.

28 [I] to pass liquid or solid waste
from your body ‖ 소변이나 대변을 체외
로 내보내다. 화장실에 가다. 용변을 보
다: *Mommy, I have to go!* 엄마, 나 화
장실에 가야 해요!

---

go about sth *phr v* [T] to do something
or begin doing something ‖ 어떤 것을 하
거나 하기 시작하다. 행하다. 착수하다: *I
don't know how to go about this.* 나는
이것을 어떻게 시작해야 할지 모르겠다.

go after sb/sth *phr v* [T] to try to get or
catch someone ‖ 다른 사람을 붙잡거나
따라잡으려 하다. 좇아가다. 따라가다. 뒤
좇다: *Go after him and tell him he has
to be home by 6:00.* 그를 뒤좇아가서 그
에게 6시까지 집에 돌아와야 한다고 말해

라.

go against sb/sth *phr v* [T] to do the opposite of what someone wants you to do, or be the opposite of what you want or believe in ‖ 남이 해주기 원하는 것과 반대로 하다, 또는 자신이 원하는 것이나 믿는 것의 반대가 되다. …에 거역하다[거스르다]. …에 반대하다. …과 대립하다. …에 맞지 않다: *He would never force her to go against her principles.* 그는 결코 그녀에게 그녀의 원칙에 위배되는 일을 억지로 시키려고 하지 않았다.

go ahead *phr v* [I] **1** SPOKEN said in order to politely let someone move in front of you, or to speak before you ‖ 정중하게 남을 자신보다 앞서 가게 하거나 먼저 말하게 하는 데에 쓰여. 먼저[앞서] …하다: *You can go ahead of me – I'm waiting for someone.* 먼저 가시지요. 나는 사람을 기다리고 있습니다. **2 go ahead and do sth** SPOKEN said when something you were possibly going to do is now definite ‖ 하려고 했던 것이 이제 명백해졌을 때에 쓰여. …하기로 결정을 보다: *Okay, I'll go ahead and call her today.* 좋아, 우선 오늘 그녀에게 전화해야지. **3** to begin or continue ‖ 시작하거나 계속하다. 착수하다. 진행하다: *Work on the new church will go ahead in May.* 새로운 교회를 짓는 공사는 5월에 착공할 것이다.

go along *phr v* [I] **1** to continue ‖ 계속하다: *I went along making the same mistakes for weeks.* 나는 수 주일 동안 똑같은 실수를 계속했다. **2** to agree with or support something ‖ 어떤 것에 찬성하거나 어떤 것을 지지하다: *You'll never get Mom to go along with it.* 너는 결코 어머니를 그것에 동의하게 할 수 없을 것이다.

go around *phr v* [I] **1 go around doing sth** to do something that other people do not approve of ‖ 다른 사람들이 용인하지 않는 것을 하다. …하고 다니다: *You can't go around lying to people all the time!* 항상 사람들에게 거짓말만 하고 다니면 안 돼! **2** if an illness goes around, many people get it ‖ 많은 사람이 병에 걸리다 **3** to be enough for everyone ‖ 모든 사람에게 충분하다. 골고루 돌아가다: *Are there enough glasses to go around?* 유리잔이 모두에게 돌아가기에 충분합니까?

go at sb/sth *phr v* [T] to start to do something, especially fighting or arguing, with a lot of energy ‖ 기력이 왕성하게 특히 싸움이나 말다툼을 시작하다. …에 맹렬히 뛰어들다[덤벼들다]: *The dogs went at each other as soon as we let go.* 개들은 우리가 놓아주자마자 서로에게 달려들었다.

go away *phr v* [I] **1** to leave a place or a person ‖ 장소나 사람을 떠나다. 가 버리다: *Go away! Leave me alone!* 저리 가! 나를 혼자 내버려둬! **2** to spend some time away from home ‖ 집을 떠나 한동안 지내다. 멀리 떠나 있다: *We're going away for two weeks in June.* 우리는 6월에 2주간 집을 떠나 있을 것이다. **3** to disappear or not happen any longer ‖ 사라지거나 더 이상 일어나지 않다. 가시다. 그치다: *My headache hasn't gone away.* 내 두통은 가시지 않았다.

go back on sth *phr v* [T] if you go back on a promise or agreement, you do not do what you promised to do ‖ 약속이나 동의한 것을 지키지 않다. 어기다. 취소하다

go back to sth *phr v* [T] **1** to do something again after having stopped doing it ‖ 어떤 것 하기를 한동안 중단한 후에 다시 하다. 되돌아가다. 다시 …하기 시작하다: *I can't study any more. I'll go back to it later.* 나는 더 이상 공부할 수 없다. 나중에 다시 하겠다. **2** to have been started or made at a particular time in the past ‖ 과거의 특정한 때에 시작되었거나 만들어지다. 거슬러 올라가다. …부터 기원이 시작되다: *His family history goes back to the 16th century.* 그의 가계 내력은 16세기로 거슬러 올라간다.

go by *phr v* **1** [I] to pass ‖ 지나가다. 흘러가다. 경과하다. 지나치다: *Two months went by before Winton called.* 2개월이 지난 뒤에 윈턴이 전화했다. **2** [I, T **go by** sth] to go to a place for a short time on your way to somewhere else ‖ 다른 곳으로 가는 도중에 잠시 어떤 장소에 가다. 잠깐 들르다. 경유하다: *We went by Greg's house before we came here.* 우리는 여기 오기 전에 그레그네 집에 잠간 들렀다. **3** [T **go by** sth] to use information, rules etc. to help you decide what to do ‖ 무엇을 할 것인지 결정하는데 도움을 받기 위해 정보·규정 등을 참고하다. …에 따라 행동하다. …에 의거해서 판단하다: *Don't go by that map. It's really old.* 그 지도대로 따라가지 마라. 그 지도는 아주 오래된 것이다.

go down *phr v* [I]
1 ▶FOR A PURPOSE 목적을 위해◀ SPOKEN to go to a place for a particular purpose ‖ 특정한 목적을 위해 한 장소에 가다: *We went down to Hudson's to buy a camera.* 우리는 카메라를 사러 허드슨 가게에 갔다.
2 ▶GO LOWER 하강하다◀ to go to a

G

lower floor of a building ‖ 건물의 저층으로 가다. 내려가다: *Go down and see who's at the door.* 내려가서 문 앞에 누가 왔는지 봐라.
3 ▸BECOME LESS 더 적어지다◂ **to** become lower or less in level, amount, size, quality etc. ‖ 수준·분량·크기·질 등에서 낮아지거나 줄어들다. 줄다. 내리다. 낮아지다. 나빠지다. 덜해지다: *The temperature went down to freezing last night.* 지난 밤 기온이 영하로 떨어졌다. / *The swelling in her knee didn't go down for days.* 그녀 무릎의 부기가 며칠 동안 가라앉지 않았다.
4 ▸GO UNDER 밑으로 들어가다◂ to sink below the level of a surface ‖ 표면 아래로 내려가다. 가라앉다: *He watched the sun go down over the ocean.* 그는 태양이 바다 너머로 지는 것을 바라보았다.
5 ▸GO SOUTH 남쪽으로 가다◂ to go south from the place where you are ‖ 현재 있는 곳에서 남쪽으로 가다: *We're going down to Florida for spring break.* 우리는 봄방학을 맞아 남쪽에 있는 플로리다에 갈 거다.
6 ▸REMEMBER 기억되다◂ to be remembered or recorded in a particular way ‖ 특정하게 기억되거나 기록되다: *This day will go down in history.* (=be remembered always) 이 날은 역사 속에서 늘 기억될 것입니다.
7 go down well/badly etc. to be liked, not liked etc. ‖ 마음에 들다, 마음에 들지 않다. 받아들여지다/받아들여지지 않다: *Robbie's jokes didn't go down very well with her parents.* 로비의 농담은 그의 부모들의 마음에 들지 않았다.
go for sb/sth *phr v* [T] **1 I could/would go for sth** SPOKEN to want or like something ‖ 어떤 것을 원하거나 좋아하다: *I could really go for a taco right now.* 나는 정말이지 지금 당장 타코를 먹었으면 좋겠다. **2 [go for** sb/sth] SPOKEN to choose a particular thing, or like a particular type of person ‖ 특정 사물을 선택하다, 또는 특정 유형의 사람을 좋아하다. …에 마음이 쏠리다[기울다]: *I think you should go for the gray suit.* 나는 당신이 틀림없이 회색 양복을 고르리라고 생각합니다. **3 go for it** SPOKEN said when you think someone should do or try something ‖ 남이 어떤 것을 하거나 시도해 봐야 한다는 생각이 들 때에 쓰여. 한번 해 봐: *Well, if you're sure you want to, go for it!* 자, 네가 정말 하고 싶다면, 한 번 해 봐! **4 [go for** sth] to try to get or win something ‖ 어떤 것을 얻거나 획

득하려고 애쓰다. …을 노리다: *a swimmer going for an Olympic record* 올림픽 기록을 노리는 수영 선수
go into sth *phr v* [T] **1** to start working in a particular profession or type of business ‖ 특정 직업이나 종류의 사업에서 일하기 시작하다. …에 진출하다[종사하다]: *Vivian wants to go into politics.* 비비안은 정계에 진출하기를 원한다. **2** to be used in order to make something work or happen ‖ 어떤 것을 가동시키거나 일어나게 하는 데에 쓰이다. …에 들어가다[투입되다]: *A lot of money has gone into building this house.* 이 집을 짓는 데에 많은 돈이 들어갔다. **3** to describe or explain something thoroughly ‖ 어떤 것을 철저히 묘사하거나 설명하다: *I don't want to go into details right now, but it was horrible.* 지금 당장은 상세히 말하고 싶지 않지만 그것은 끔찍했다. **4** if one number goes into another, it can divide it ‖ 한 숫자로 다른 숫자를 나누다. …으로 나누다. …이 …배 포함되다: *12 goes into 60 five times.* 60 나누기 12는 5이다.
go off *phr v* [I] **1** to explode ‖ 폭발하다. 터지다: *Fireworks went off all over the city that night.* 그날 밤 도시 전역에서 폭죽이 터졌다. **2** to make a loud noise ‖ 큰 소음을 내다. 울리다: *My alarm clock didn't go off.* 내 자명종이 울리지 않았다. **3** if a machine or light goes off, it stops working or stops shining ‖ 기계나 전등이 작동을 멈추거나 빛을 내지 않게 되다. 꺼지다. 전원이 나가다
go on *phr v* [I] **1** to continue without stopping or changing ‖ 중단이나 변동 없이 계속하다. 그대로 계속하다. 계속해서 …하다! *We can't go on fighting like this!* 우린 계속해서 이렇게 싸울 수는 없어! / *This guy went on and on* (=talked for a long time) *about himself all night.* 이 남자는 밤새도록 자신에 대해 계속 이야기했다. **2** to happen ‖ 일어나다. 벌어지다. 발생하다: *What's going on down there? Did something break?* 그 아래에 무슨 일이 벌어지고 있습니까? 뭐가 부서졌습니까? **3** to do something new when you have finished something else ‖ 다른 것을 끝내고 나서 새로운 것을 하다. (다음으로) 넘어가다: *Go on to question number 5 when you're done.* 다 끝마치면 5번 문항으로 넘어가시오. **4** if a machine or light goes on, it starts working or starts shining ‖ 기계나 전등이 작동을 시작하거나 빛을 내기 시작하다. 작동하다. 켜지다 **5** to continue talking or explaining something, after you have

stopped for a while ∥ 잠시 멈추었다가 어떤 것을 계속해서 말하거나 설명하다: *Go on, I'm listening.* 어서 계속해, 나 듣고 있잖아. / *After a minute, she stopped crying and went on with the story.* 잠시 후 그녀는 울음을 그치고 이야기를 계속했다. **6** if time goes on, it passes ∥ 시간이 경과하다. 흘러가다: *As time went on, he became more friendly.* 시간이 지나자 그는 좀 더 다정해졌다. **7** SPOKEN said in order to encourage someone to do something ∥ 남에게 어떤 것을 하도록 격려하는 데에 쓰여. 어서. 힘내. 자 해라: *Go on, have another drink.* 어서, 한 잔 더 마셔!

go out *phr v* [I] **1** to leave your house, especially in order to do something you enjoy ∥ 특히 즐기는 것을 하기 위해 집을 나서다. 밖으로 나가다. 외출하다: *Are you going out tonight?* 오늘 밤에 외출하십니까? / *We went out for dinner/lunch on Saturday.* 우리는 토요일에 저녁[점심]을 먹기 위해 외출했다. / *Can I go out and play now?* 이제 밖에 나가서 놀아도 돼요? **2** to have a romantic relationship with someone ∥ 남과 연애 관계를 갖다. 이성과 교제하다. 데이트하다: *Leah used to go out with Dan's brother.* 레아는 댄의 동생과 데이트하곤 했다. **3** if a light or fire goes out, it stops shining or burning ∥ 전등이나 불이 빛을 내지 않거나 타지 않게 되다. 불이 꺼지다. 불이 나가다 **4** to travel to a place that is far away, in order to live there ∥ 그곳에서 살려고 먼 곳으로 가다. 건너가다. 이민가다: *They've gone out to Malaysia to live.* 그들은 말레이시아에서 살려고 건너갔다.

go over *phr v* **1** [T] to look at something or think about something carefully ∥ 어떤 것을 주의 깊게 보거나 생각하다. 잘 살펴보다[검토하다]. 곱씹어 보다: *Jake went over his notes again before the test.* 제이크는 시험 전에 정리한 내용을 다시 살펴보았다. **2** [T] to search a place thoroughly ∥ 장소를 철저히 조사하다. 수색하다. 샅샅이 뒤지다: *The police will go over the area in the morning.* 경찰이 그 지역을 오전에 수색할 것이다. **3** ⇨ **go down well/badly etc.** (GO¹)

go through *phr v* **1** [T **go through** sth] to have a very upsetting experience or a period of time when a lot of bad things happen ∥ 매우 속상한 경험을 하거나 안 좋은 일이 많이 일어나는 시기를 거치다. 겪다. 경험[체험]하다: *She's just been through a divorce.* 그녀는 이제 막 이혼을 겪었다. **2** [T **go through** sth] to use

all of something ∥ 사물의 전부를 쓰다. 다 써버리다. 모두 해치우다: *Jeremy goes through at least a quart of milk every day!* 제레미는 매일 최소한 4분의 1갤런의 우유를 먹어 치운다! **3** [I,T **go through** sth] if a deal, agreement, or law goes through, it is officially accepted ∥ 계약[협정, 법률]이 공식적으로 인정되다. 승인[가결]되다. 통과하다: *My car loan has finally gone through.* 내 자동차 대출이 마침내 승인됐다. / *a law going through Congress* 의회에서 통과 중인 법률 **4** [T **go through** sth] to practice something from the beginning to the end ∥ 어떤 것을 처음부터 끝까지 복습하다. 전부 연습하다: *Let's go through the song one more time.* 노래를 처음부터 끝까지 한 번 더 연습해 봅시다. **5** [T **go through** sth] to look at something carefully, especially because you are looking for something ∥ 특히 어떤 것을 찾고 있기 때문에 어떤 것을 주의 깊게 바라보다. 자세히 조사[검토]하다: *She had to go through all her uncle's papers after he died.* 그녀는 삼촌이 죽은 후에 삼촌의 모든 서류를 자세히 조사해야 했다.

go to sth *phr v* [T] **1 go to a lot of trouble** to use a lot of effort to do something, especially for someone else ∥ 특히 남을 위해서 어떤 것을 하는 데에 많은 노력을 기울이다. 수고를 많이 하다: *Suki went to a lot of trouble to get us the tickets.* 수키는 우리에게 표를 구해주기 위해 많은 수고를 했다. **2 go to sleep/war etc.** to begin sleeping, fighting a war etc. ∥ 잠이 들거나 전쟁을 치르기 시작하다. 잠자리에 들다/전쟁에 돌입하다

go together *phr v* [I] to have a romantic relationship ∥ 연애 관계를 갖다. 교제하다. 사귀다: *Are Lizzie and Bud going together?* 리지와 버드는 사귀고 있습니까?

go under *phr v* [I] if a business goes under, it has serious problems and fails ∥ 사업체가 심각한 문제점이 있어서 망하다. 파산[도산]하다

go up *phr v* [I] **1 go up to** SPOKEN to walk toward someone or something until you are standing in front of him, her, or it ∥ 사람이나 사물 바로 앞에 서게 될 때까지 그쪽으로 걸어가다. 접근하다. 다가가다: *Andrea went up to him and asked him for directions.* 안드레아는 그에게 다가가서 길을 물었다. **2** to increase in number or amount ∥ 숫자나 양이 증가하다. 오르다. 상승하다: *Housing prices* *went up again last quarter.* 주택 가격이 지난 분기에 다시 올랐다. **3 to be built** ‖ 지어지다. 세워지다. 건설되다: *All of those houses have gone up in the past six months.* 저 모든 집들은 지난 6개월간에 지어졌다. **4 to explode or be destroyed by fire** ‖ 폭발하거나 화재로 파괴되다. 터지다. 불타서 없어지다[사라지다]: *The factory went up in flames before the firemen got there.* 그 공장은 소방대원들이 도착하기 전에 불길 속에 완전히 타버렸다.

go with sb/sth *phr v* [T] **1 to be included as part of something** ‖ 어떤 것의 일부로 포함되다. 어떤 것에 부속되다. 딸려 있다. …에 수반되다: *The car goes with the job.* 그 일자리는 자동차도 제공된다. **2 to choose something** ‖ 어떤 것을 선택하다: *I'd go with the green tie if I were you.* 내가 너라면 녹색 넥타이를 택하겠다.

go without *phr v* **1** [I, T **go without** sth] **to not have something you need or want** ‖ 필요하거나 원하는 것을 갖고 있지 않다. …이 없다. …없이 지내다: *We can go without a car in the city.* 우리는 도시에서 차 없이 지낼 수 있다. **2 it goes without saying (that)** used in order to say that something should be clear without needing to be said ‖ 어떤 것이 말할 필요도 없이 명백하다는 것을 나타내는 데에 쓰여. (…은) 말할 필요도 없다 [두말하면 잔소리이다]: *It goes without saying that artists should have the right of freedom of expression.* 예술가들에게 자유롭게 표현할 권리가 있어야 한다는 것은 두말할 나위도 없다.

USAGE NOTE go, gone, and been

Use **gone** as the usual past participle of **go**: *George has gone to Denver.* (=he is there now). Use **been** as the past participle with the sense of **go** that means "visit": *George has been to Denver.* (=he has visited Denver before, but is not there now)

보통은 **go**의 과거 분사로 **gone**을 쓴다: 조지는 덴버로 갔다. "방문하다"를 뜻하는 **go**의 의미를 가진 과거 분사로는 **been**을 쓴다: 조지는 덴버에 간 적이 있다.

---

go² *n* **1 make a go of sth** to try to make something such as a business or marriage successful ‖ 사업체나 결혼 등을 성공적으로 만들려 하다. …을 성공시키다. 잘 해나가다: *Do you think they'll make a go of it with their new*

restaurant. 그들이 새 레스토랑을 잘 해나갈 것으로 생각하십니까? **2 on the go** very busy or working all the time ‖ 매우 바쁘거나 줄곧 일하는. 일만 하는. 쉴 새 없이 활동하는

goad /goʊd/ *v* [T] **to make someone do something by annoying him/her until** s/he does it ‖ 남이 할 때까지 귀찮게 굴어서 어떤 것을 하게 하다. 국국 찔러서[부추겨서] …하도록 하다: *Troy's friends goaded him into asking Susan for a date.* 트로이의 친구들은 그를 부추겨서 수잔에게 데이트 신청을 하게 했다.

go·a·head /'. ,./ *n* **give sb the go-ahead** INFORMAL **to give someone permission to start doing something** ‖ 남에게 어떤 것을 시작하라고 허가를 하다. 개시[착수]를 인가하다. 진행 명령을 내리다: *The film was given the go-ahead and production starts next May.* 그 영화는 진행이 승인됐고 제작은 다음 5월에 시작한다.

goal /goʊl/ *n* **1 something that you hope to achieve in the future** ‖ 장차 달성하기를 바라는 것. 목적. 목표: *The company achieved its sales goal for the month.* 회사는 이 달의 판매 목표를 달성했다. **2 the action in a game or sport of making the ball go into a particular area to win a point, or the point won by doing this** ‖ 운동 시합이나 경기에서 점수를 얻기 위해 공이 특정 구역 안으로 들어가게 하기, 또는 이렇게 해서 올린 점수. 득점(행위). 골(인): *Ramos scored two goals for the US.* 라모스는 미국 팀에 2점을 올려 줬다. **3 the area into which a player tries to put the ball in order to win a point** ‖ 선수가 득점하기 위해 공을 넣으려고 하는 구역. 득점 장소. 골

goal·ie /'goʊli/ *n* INFORMAL ⇨ GOALKEEPER

goal·keep·er /'goʊl,kipɚ/, **goal-tend·er** /'goʊl,tɛndɚ/ *n* the player on a sports team who tries to stop the ball from going into the GOAL ‖ 공이 골에 들어가는 것을 막아내려 하는 스포츠 팀의 선수. 골키퍼

goal·post /'goʊlpoʊst/ *n* one of the two upright BARs, with another bar along the top or across the middle, that form the GOAL in games like SOCCER and football ‖ 상단 또는 중단에 가로쳐진 또 다른 봉과 함께 축구·미식축구 등의 경기에서 골대를 만드는 두 개의 수직 기둥 중의 하나. 골대. 골포스트 —see picture on page 946

goat /goʊt/ *n* **1 a common farm animal with horns and with long hair under its**

chin ‖ 뿔이 달렸고 턱 밑에 긴 수염이 난 흔한 사육 동물. 염소 **2 get sb's goat** INFORMAL to make someone very angry or annoyed ‖ 남을 매우 화나거나 성가시게 만들다

goat·ee /gou'ti/ *n* a small BEARD on the end of a man's chin ‖ 남자의 턱 끝에 조금 나 있는 턱수염. 염소 수염

gob /gab/ *n* [C] INFORMAL a mass of something wet and sticky ‖ 축축하고 끈적끈적한 덩어리: *There's gobs of gum on my chair.* 내 의자에 껌 덩어리가 붙어 있다.

gob·ble /'gabəl/ *v* INFORMAL **1** [T] also **gobble up** to eat something very quickly ‖ 어떤 것을 매우 빠르게 먹다. 급하게[게걸스럽게] 먹다 **2** [T] also **gobble up** to use a supply of something quickly ‖ 어떤 것의 공급량을 빠르게 소모하다. 다 써버리다. 다 먹어 치우다: *Taxes gobble up 25% of my income every year.* 세금이 매년 내 소득의 25%를 먹어 치우고 있다. **3** [I] to make a sound like a TURKEY ‖ 칠면조 같은 소리를 내다. 꼬르륵거리다

gob·ble·dy·gook, gobbledegook /'gabəldi,guk/ *n* [U] INFORMAL complicated language, especially in official letters, that you do not understand ‖ 특히 공문서에서 쓰는 이해할 수 없는 복잡한 말. 난해한 표현

go-be·tween /'. . ,./ *n* someone who takes messages from one person or group to another, because the two sides do not want to meet or cannot meet ‖ 사람이나 집단의 양측이 서로 만나기를 원치 않거나 만날 수 없기 때문에 한 쪽에서 다른 쪽으로 메시지를 전달해 주는 사람. 중개자. 중매인: *The lawyer will act as a go-between for the couple.* 변호사가 그 부부 사이에 중개자 역할을 할 것이다.

gob·let /'gablıt/ *n* a cup with a base and long stem but no handles ‖ 기단(基壇)과 긴 자루가 달렸지만 손잡이는 없는 컵. 와인 잔. 자루가 긴 잔

gob·lin /'gablın/ *n* a small and ugly creature in children's stories who likes to trick people ‖ 사람들에게 장난치기를 좋아하는 동화 속의 작고 추한 존재. 마귀. 악귀

gobs /gabz/ *n* [plural] INFORMAL a large amount of something ‖ 어떤 것의 많은 양. 엄청난 양. 한 무더기: *I'm sure old Mr. Kratten has gobs of money hidden in his house.* 나는 크래튼옹이 엄청난 돈을 자기 집에 숨겨 놓고 있다고 믿고 있다.

go-cart /'. ./ *n* a small car made of an open frame on four wheels, that people race for fun ‖ 네 바퀴 위에 덮개가 없고 뼈대만 갖춰 사람들이 재미로 경주를 하는 작은 차. 고카트

God /gad/ *n* [singular] **1** the spirit or BEING whom Christians, Jews, and Muslims pray to ‖ 크리스트교도, 유대교도, 회교도들이 기도하는 신령이나 절대자. 신. 창조주. 천주 **2 play God** to behave as if you have the power to do whatever you want ‖ 원하는 것은 무엇이나 할 수 있는 능력을 지닌 듯이 행동하다. 마치 신처럼[방자하게] 행동하다. 절대 권력을 휘두르다 **3 a God-given duty/right/talent etc.** a duty etc. received from God ‖ 신으로부터 받은 의무 등. 신이 부여한 의무/권리/재능

───── SPOKEN PHRASES ─────

4 God/oh God/my God a phrase said in order to add force to what you are saying when you are surprised, angry etc., that some people consider offensive ‖ 놀라거나 화가 난 경우 등에 말하고 있는 것에 힘을 더하는 데에 쓰이는, 혹자들은 무례하다고 생각하는 어구. 야단[큰일]났군. 아뿔싸. 이런 괘씸한 **5 I swear/hope/wish etc. to God** said in order to emphasize that you promise, hope etc. that something is true ‖ 어떤 일이 사실임을 약속·희망한다는 것을 강조하는 데에 쓰여. 신에게 맹세컨대/바라건대/소망하건대 **6 God (only) knows** said in order to show that you are annoyed because you do not know something or understand something ‖ 어떤 일을 모르거나 이해할 수 없기 때문에 괴롭다는 것을 나타내는 데에 쓰여. 아무도 모른다. (오직) 신만이 아신다: *God only knows where those kids are now!* 그 아이들이 지금 어디 있는지는 아무도 모른다! **7 what/how/where/who in God's name** said in order to add force to a question when you are surprised or angry ‖ 놀라거나 화가 났을 때 질문에 힘을 더하는 데에 쓰여. 도대체[대관절] 무엇을/어떻게/어디서/누가: *Where in God's name have you been?* 대체 너는 어디에 있었니? **8 honest to God** said in order to emphasize that you are not lying or joking ‖ 거짓말이나 농담하지 않는다는 것을 강조하는 데 쓰여. 신[하늘]에 맹세코 **9 God bless** said in order to show that you hope someone will be safe and happy ‖ 남이 안전하고 행복하기를 바란다는 것을 나타내는 데에 쓰여. 신의 축복을. 축복이 있기를. 신의

가호를: *Good night, and God bless.* 안녕히 주무세요, 그리고 신의 축복이 있기를.

god *n* **1** a male spirit or BEING who is believed to control the world, or a part of it ‖ 세상이나 그 일부분을 관장한다고 믿어지는 남성 신령이나 초월적 존재. 남성 신. 신화상의 남신 **2** someone or something that is given too much importance or respect ‖ 지나치게 중시되거나 존경을 받는 사람이나 사물. 신상. 우상. 신격화된 것[사람] —see also GODDESS

god·aw·ful /ˌ. '../ *adj* INFORMAL very bad or unpleasant ‖ 매우 나쁘거나 불쾌한. 지독한. 역한: *What is that god-awful smell?* 도대체 저 지독한 냄새는 무엇입니까?

god·child /'gɑdtʃaɪld/ *n, plural* **godchildren** a child that a GODPARENT promises to help, usually by teaching him/her religious values ‖ 보통 대부모(代父母)가 종교적 가치를 가르쳐서 돕겠다고 약속한 아이. 대자(代子)

god·dess /'gɑdɪs/ *n* **1** a female spirit or BEING who is believed to control the world, or part of it ‖ 세계 또는 그 일부분을 관장한다고 믿어지는 여성 신령이나 초월적 존재. 여성 신. 신화상의 여신 **2** a woman who is very beautiful or sexually attractive ‖ 매우 아름답거나 성적으로 매력적인 여성. 절세미인. 천하일색: *Hollywood movie goddess Marilyn Monroe* 할리우드 은막의 여신 마릴린 먼로

god·fa·ther /'gɑdˌfɑðɚ/ *n* **1** a male GODPARENT ‖ 남성 대부모. 대부(代父) **2** SLANG the leader of a criminal organization ‖ 범죄 조직의 지도자. 갱단의 두목

god-fear·ing /'. ˌ../ *adj* OLD-FASHIONED behaving according to the moral rules of a religion ‖ 종교의 도덕률에 따라 행동하는. 신앙심 깊은. 독실한

god-for·sak·en /'gɑdfɚˌseɪkən/ *adj* a godforsaken place is far away from where people live, and does not have anything interesting or cheerful in it ‖ 장소가 사람들이 사는 곳에서 멀리 떨어져서 흥미 있거나 즐거운 것이 아무것도 없는. 외진. 쓸쓸한. 황량한

god·less /'gɑdlɪs/ *adj* not showing respect for God or a god, or belief in God or a god ‖ 절대자나 신에 대한 존경이나 믿음을 보이지 않는. 신을 모독하는[믿지 않는]. 신에 불경하는

godlike, Godlike /'gɑdlaɪk/ *adj* having a quality like God or a god ‖ 절대자나 신 같은 특성을 가진. 신성한. 신 같은

god·ly /'gɑdli/ *adj* OLD-FASHIONED showing that you obey God by behaving according to the moral rules of a religion ‖ 종교적 도덕률에 따라 행동함으로써 신에게 복종함을 보이는. 신의 뜻에 순종하는

god·moth·er /'gɑdˌmʌðɚ/ *n* a female GODPARENT ‖ 여성 대부모. 대모(代母)

god·par·ent /'gɑdˌpɛrənt/ *n* someone who promises to help a child, usually by teaching him/her religious values ‖ 보통 종교적 가치를 가르침으로써 어린이를 돕겠다고 약속한 사람. 대부[모][代父母]

god·send /'gɑdsɛnd/ *n* [singular] something good that happens to you at a time when you really need it ‖ 정말 필요한 때에 일어나는 좋은 것. 뜻밖의 행운. 횡재

go·fer /'goufɚ/ *n* INFORMAL someone whose job is to get and carry things for other people ‖ 다른 사람을 위해 물건을 받고 전하는 직업인. 잔심부름꾼. 사환

go-get·ter /ˌ. '../ *n* INFORMAL someone who is very determined to succeed ‖ 성공하기를 단호히 결심한 사람. 수완가. 수단꾼

gog·gle-eyed /'gɑgəl ˌaɪd/ *adj* INFORMAL with your eyes wide open and looking at something that surprises you ‖ 눈을 크게 뜨고 자신을 놀라게 하는 것을 바라보는. 눈을 부릅뜬

gog·gles /'gɑgəlz/ *n* [plural] something that protects your eyes, made of two large round pieces of glass or plastic with an edge that fits against your skin ‖ 피부에 꼭 밀착되는 테가 달린 두 개의 크고 둥근 유리나 플라스틱 조각으로 만들어져, 눈을 보호하는 것. 큰 안경. 보안경: *skiing goggles* 스키용 안경

go·ing¹ /'gouɪŋ/ *n* [U] **1** the act of leaving a place ‖ 한 장소를 떠나기. 가기. 출발: *His going will be a great loss to the company.* 그가 떠나면 회사에 막대한 손실이 될 것이다. **2** the speed at which you travel or work ‖ 여행하거나 일하는 속도. 진행 속도. 진도. 진척 상황: *We made the trip in four hours, which is not bad going.* 우리는 네 시간 내에 여행을 마쳤는데 그리 느린 속도는 아니다.

going² *adj* **1 the going rate** the usual cost of a service, or the usual pay for a job ‖ 서비스의 통상 가격, 또는 일에 대한 통상 임금. 현행 비율[요금] **2** available, or able to be found ‖ 획득 가능한, 또는 찾아 낼 수 있는. 입수할 수 있는: *We* *think we make the best computers going.* 우리는 가장 좋은 컴퓨터를 (쉽게) 입수할 수 있다고 생각한다. **3 a going concern** a successful business || 성공적인 사업. 성업 중인 회사

going-o·ver /ˌ.. '../ n a thorough examination of something || 어떤 일의 철저한 조사: *My car needs a good going-over.* 내 차는 철저한 검사가 필요하다.

goings-on /ˌ.. './ n [plural] INFORMAL activities or events that you think are strange or interesting || 이상하거나 재미있다고 생각하는 활동이나 사건. 행위. 행실. 소행

gold¹ /goʊld/ n 1 [U] a valuable soft yellow metal that is used for making jewelry, coins etc. || 보석·주화 등을 제조하는 데 쓰이는 값이 나가며 딱딱하지 않은 노란 금속. 금 2 [C, U] a bright shiny yellow color || 밝게 빛나는 노란색. 금빛. 황금색

gold² *adj* 1 made of gold || 금으로 만든. 금의: *a gold necklace* 금 목걸이 2 having the color of gold || 금 색깔을 가진. 금빛의: *a gold dress* 금빛 드레스

gold dig·ger /'. ˌ../ n INFORMAL someone who marries someone else only for his/her money || 단지 돈을 위해 다른 사람과 결혼하는 사람

gold·en /'goʊldən/ adj 1 having a bright shiny yellow color || 밝게 빛나는 노란색을 띤. 금빛의. 황금색의: *golden hair* 금빛 머리카락. 금발 2 made of gold || 금으로 만든: *a golden crown* 금관 3 **golden age** the time when something was at its best || 어떤 것이 최고였던 때. 전성기. 황금시대: *the golden age of television* 텔레비전의 전성기 4 **a golden opportunity** a good chance to get something valuable, or to be very successful || 가치 있는 것을 얻거나 대단히 성공하게 될 좋은 기회. 황금 기회. 절호의 기회 5 **golden years** old age || 노년. 노후: *I want to enjoy my golden years.* 나는 노후를 즐기고 싶다.

gold·fish /'goʊld.fɪʃ/ n a small shiny orange fish often kept as a pet || 종종 애완동물로 키우는 작고 빛이 나는 오렌지색깔의 물고기. 금붕어

gold med·al /ˌ. '../ n a prize that is given to the winner of a race, competition etc., and that is usually made of gold || 경주·시합 등의 우승자에게 주는 보통 금으로 만든 상. 금메달

gold·mine /'goʊldmaɪn/ n 1 a business or activity that produces a lot of money || 많은 돈을 벌게 하는 사업이나 활동 2 a hole under the ground from which gold is taken || 금을 채굴하는 지하의 갱. 금광. 금갱

golf /gɑlf, gɔlf/ n [U] a game in which you hit a small white ball into a hole in the ground with a golf club, using as few hits as possible || 골프채로 조그맣고 하얀 공을 가능한 한 적은 횟수로 쳐서 땅에 있는 구멍에 집어넣는 게임. 골프 – **golfer** n

golf club /'. ./ n 1 a long wooden or metal stick used for hitting the ball in golf || 골프에서 공을 치는 데 사용되는 나무나 금속으로 만든 긴 막대. 골프채. 클럽 2 a group of people who pay to play golf at a particular place, or the land and buildings they use || 특정 장소에서 골프를 치기 위해 돈을 지불하는 사람들의 집단, 또는 그들이 사용하는 땅과 건물. 골프 클럽[모임]. 골프용 토지[건물]

golf course /'. ./ n an area of land on which you play golf || 골프를 치는 지역. 골프 코스. 골프장

gol·ly /'gɑli/ *interjection* OLD-FASHIONED said when you are surprised || 놀랐을 때 쓰여. 어머나. 저런

gon·do·la /'gɑndələ, gɑn'doʊlə/ n a long narrow boat, used on the CANALs of Venice || 베니스의 운하에서 쓰는 길고 좁은 배. 곤돌라

gon·do·lier /ˌgɑndə'lɪr/ n someone who rows a GONDOLA || 곤돌라를 젓는 사람. 곤돌라 사공

gone /gɔn, gɑn/ v the PAST PARTICIPLE of GO || go의 과거 분사형 —see usage note at GO¹

gon·er /'gɔnə/ n INFORMAL **be a goner** SPOKEN to be about to die, or in a lot of danger || 곧 죽거나 많은 위험에 처하다: *The car kept spinning, and I thought we were goners.* 차가 계속 빙빙 돌아서 이제 우리는 끝장이라고 생각했다.

gong /gɔŋ, gɑŋ/ n a round piece of metal that hangs in a frame and is hit with a stick to make a loud sound as a signal || 틀에 매달아 막대로 쳐서 큰 신호음을 내는 둥그런 금속판. 징

gon·na /'gɔnə, gənə/ SPOKEN NON-STANDARD a short form of "going to," used when talking about the future || 미래에 대해 말할 때에 쓰이는 "going to"의 단축형: *I'm gonna talk to her about it tomorrow.* 나는 내일 그것에 대해 그녀에게 말할 거야.

USAGE NOTE gonna and going to

Use **going to** in front of another verb to talk about something that will happen in the future: *I'm going to buy it later*. In INFORMAL speech, we often pronounce this as **gonna**: *I'm gonna buy it later*. Use **going to** to talk about a place you are traveling to: *I'm going to Montreal for the weekend*. ✗DON'T SAY "I'm gonna Montreal for the weekend."✗

다른 동사 앞에서 미래에 일어날 일을 말하는 데 **going to**를 쓴다: 그것은 나중에 살 거야. 비격식어에서는 **gonna**로 자주 발음한다: 그것은 나중에 살 거야. 여행하러 갈 장소를 말할 때 **going to**를 쓴다: 주말에 몬트리얼로 갈거야. "I'm gonna Montreal for the weekend."라고는 하지 않는다.

gon·or·rhe·a /ˌɡɑnəˈriə/ *n* [U] a disease of the sex organs that is passed from one person to another during sex; VD ‖ 성행위중 한 사람에게서 다른 사람에게 전염되는 성기의 질병. 임질; ⑲ VD

goo /ɡu/ *n* [U] ⇨ GOOP

good¹ /ɡʊd/ *adj* **better, best**

1 ▶HIGH IN QUALITY 질이 높은◀ of a high standard ‖ 수준 높은. 훌륭한: *His score on the test was very good*. 그의 시험 점수는 아주 좋았다. / *Thanks, Maria, you did a good job*. 고마워, 마리아, 너 참 잘했다. ✗DON'T SAY "You did good."SAY "You did well."✗ "You did good."이라고 하지 않고 "You did well."이라고 한다.

2 ▶SUITABLE 알맞은 ◀ useful or suitable for a particular purpose ‖ 특별한 목적에 유용하거나 알맞은: *It's a good day for going to the beach*. 해변에 가기에 알맞은 날이다.

3 ▶SKILLFUL 솜씨 좋은◀ smart or skillful ‖ 영리하거나 솜씨 좋은. 능숙한: *Andrea is very good at Cajun cooking*. 안드레아는 케이전 요리를 아주 잘 한다.

4 no good/not any good a) not likely to be useful or successful ‖ 유익하거나 성공할 것 같지 않은. 소용없는/좋지 않은: *It's no good trying to explain it to her, she won't listen!* 그녀에게 설명해 봐야 소용없어, 그녀는 듣지 않을 걸! **b)** bad ‖ 나쁜: *That movie isn't any good*. 그 영화는 형편없어.

5 ▶NICE 좋은◀ enjoyable and pleasant ‖ 즐겁고 유쾌한. 좋은. 훌륭한: *good weather* 좋은 날씨 / *It's good to see you again*. 당신을 다시 만나서 반가워요.

6 ▶HEALTHY 건강한◀ **a)** useful for your health or character ‖ 건강이나 품성에 좋은: *Watching so much TV isn't good for you*. 텔레비전을 그렇게 많이 시

청하는 것은 너에게 그다지 좋지 않아. **b)** healthy ‖ 건강한: *"How do you feel today?" "Better, thanks."* "오늘 기분 어때?" "좋아졌어, 고마워."

7 ▶ABLE TO BE USED 사용될 수 있는◀ in a satisfactory condition for use; not broken, damaged etc. ‖ 사용하기에 만족스러운 상태로; 깨어지거나 손상되지 않은 등: *There now, your dress is as good as new*. (=fixed so that it looks new again) 자, 봐라, 너의 드레스는 새 것이나 다름없다. / *The product guarantee is good for* (=can be used for) *three years*. 그 제품 보증은 3년 동안 유효하다.

8 ▶WELL-BEHAVED 품행이 좋은◀ a word meaning well-behaved, used especially about children ‖ 특히 어린이에 대해 써 품행이 착하란 뜻의 단어. 얌전한. 의젓한: *Sit here and be a good girl*. 여기에 앉아서 얌전히 굴어라.

9 ▶KIND 친절한◀ kind and helpful ‖ 친절하며 도움이 되는. 인정 많은: *It's good of you to come on such short notice*. 그렇게 시간 여유도 없이 통지한데도 와 주시다니 정말 자상하십니다.

10 as good as almost ‖ 거의. …과 같은. …이나 다름없는: *The work is as good as finished*. 그 일은 거의 끝났다.

11 a good deal (of sth) a lot ‖ 많은. 상당수의: *I spent a good deal of time preparing for this test*. 나는 이 시험을 준비하는 데 많은 시간을 보냈다.

12 ▶RIGHT 올바른◀ morally right ‖ 도덕적으로 올바른: *Billy Amos led a good life*. 빌리 아모스는 올바른 생활을 했다.

13 ▶LARGE/LONG 큰/긴◀ large in amount, size etc. ‖ 양이나 크기 등이 큰: *a good-sized car* 큰 차 / *They've been gone a good while*. (=a long time) 그들은 오랫동안 외출 중이다.

14 complete; thorough ‖ 완전한; 철저한: *The car needs a good wash*. 그 차는 철저한 세차가 필요하다.

15 be in sb's good graces to be liked and approved of by someone at a particular time ‖ 특정한 때에 남에게 사랑받거나 인정받다

16 good/oh good said when you are pleased that something has happened or has been done ‖ 일어나거나 끝마친 일에 대해 기뻐할 때 쓰여. 잘했어: *"I've finished." "Good, put your papers in the box."* "끝마쳤어요." "잘했어, 네 시험지를 그 상자에 넣어라."

17 that's/it's not good enough said

when you are not satisfied with someone or something ‖ 사람이나 사물에 만족하지 못할 때 쓰여. 그걸로는 충분하지 않아[부족해]

18 good luck used in order to say that you hope that someone is successful, or that something good will happen to him/her ‖ 남이 성공하는 것을 희망하거나 좋은 일이 일어날 것이라고 말하는 데 쓰여. 행운을 빌어

19 good God/grief/heavens etc. said in order to express anger, surprise, or other strong feelings. Saying "God" in this way is offensive to some people ‖ 분노나 놀람, 또는 다른 강한 감정을 표현하는 데 쓰여. 이렇게 "하느님"을 부르는 것은 어떤 사람에게는 기분을 상하게 한다. 아아, 하느님/이런/아유 (깜짝이야): *Good grief! Is it that late?* 세상에나! 그렇게 늦었나?

20 it's a good thing said when you are glad that something has happened ‖ 어떤 일이 일어난 것이 기뻤을 때 쓰여. 잘됐다. 다행이야: *It's a good thing you remembered to bring napkins.* 네가 냅킨 가져오는 것을 기억해서 다행이다.

21 Good for you! said when you are pleased with something someone has done ‖ 남이 한 일에 흡족할 때 쓰여. 잘했어! 잘됐어!

USAGE NOTE good and well

Use **good** as an adjective to talk about the quality of someone or something: *She's a good singer.* Use **well** as an adverb to talk about the way that something is done: *She sings very well.*
사람이나 사물의 성질에 대해 말할 때 형용사 **good**을 쓴다: 그녀는 좋은 가수이다. 일이 이루어진 방식에 대해 말할 때 부사 **well**을 쓴다: 그녀는 노래를 아주 잘 부른다.

---

good² *n* [U] **1** something that improves a situation or gives you an advantage ‖ 상황을 개선하거나 이점을 주는 것. 이익. 유익: *It'll do you a world of good* (=make you feel better) *to take a vacation.* 휴가를 다녀 오면 기분이 더 좋아질 것이다. **2 do no good** to not be of any use, or to have no effect on something ‖ 아무 소용이 없거나 어떤 일에 효과가 없다: *You can talk to her all you want, but it won't do any good.* 네가 하고 싶은 모든 말을 그녀에게 할 수는 있

겠지만 아무 효과도 없을 것이다. **3 make good on a promise/threat/claim etc.** to succeed in doing what you have said you would do ‖ 자신이 하겠다고 말했던 것을 하는 데 성공하다. 약속/위협/주장 등을[에 대해] 수행하다[달성하다]: *They're asking for more time to make good on their debts.* 그들은 빚을 갚는 데 더 많은 시간을 요구하고 있다. **4** behavior or actions that are morally right or follow religious principles ‖ 도덕적으로 옳거나 종교적 원칙을 따르는 행위나 행동. 선: *the battle between good and evil* 선과 악의 싸움 **5 for good** permanently ‖ 영원히. 영구적으로. 영영: *Is he really gone for good?* 그는 정말 영원히 가버린 것일까? **6 be up to no good** INFORMAL to be doing or planning to do something that is wrong or bad ‖ 잘못되거나 나쁜 일을 하고 있거나 계획하고 있다. 나쁜 일을 꾀하는 중이다 —see also GOODS

good af·ter·noon /ˌ ͵ˈ .ˈ/ *interjection* used in order to say hello to someone in the afternoon ‖ 오후에 남에게 인사하는 데에 쓰여. 안녕하세요

good·bye /gʊdˈbaɪ, gədˈbaɪ/ *interjection* said when you are leaving or being left by someone ‖ 자신이 또는 남이 떠날 때 쓰여. 안녕히 계[가]십시오: *Goodbye, Mrs. Anderson.* 안녕히 계[가]십시오, 앤더슨 부인 / *I just have to say goodbye to Erica.* 에리카에게 작별 인사해야 해.

good eve·ning /ˌ ˈ ./ *interjection* used in order to say hello to someone in the evening ‖ 저녁에 남에게 인사하는 데에 쓰여. 안녕하세요: *Good evening, ladies and gentlemen!* 안녕하십니까, 신사 숙녀 여러분! —compare GOOD NIGHT

good-for-noth·ing /ˈ . . ͵. ./ *n, adj* someone who is lazy or has no skills ‖ 게으르거나 기술이 전혀 없는 사람. 무가치한[쓸모없는] (사람). 건달의. 밥벌레의: *He's a lazy good-for-nothing.* 그는 아무 쓸모 없는 게으름뱅이다.

Good Fri·day /ˌ ˈ ./ *n* [C, U] the Friday before EASTER ‖ 부활절 전의 금요일. 성(聖) 금요일

good-hu·mored /ˌ ˈ ./ *adj* naturally cheerful and friendly ‖ 천성적으로 명랑하고 친절한. 쾌활한. 사근사근한

good-look·ing /ˌ ˈ ./ *adj* someone who is good-looking is attractive ‖ 사람이 매력적인. 잘생긴 —see usage note at BEAUTIFUL

good morn·ing /ˌ ˈ ./ *interjection* used in order to say hello to someone in

the morning ‖ 아침에 남에게 인사하는 데
에 쓰여. 안녕하세요. 좋은 아침: *Good
morning! Did you sleep well?* 안녕! 잘 잤
니?

good-na·tured /ˌ. '.../ *adj* naturally
kind and helpful, and not easily made
angry ‖ 천성적으로 친절하고 도움을 주며
쉽게 화를 내지 않는. 착한. 너그러운. 상
냥한 **- good-naturedly** *adv*

good·ness /'gʊdnɪs/ *n* [U] **1** SPOKEN
said when you are surprised or annoyed
‖ 놀라거나 짜증날 때 쓰여. 어머나. 저
런: *My goodness, you've lost a lot of
weight!* 저런, 너 몸무게가 많이 빠졌구나!
/ *For goodness' sake, will you be
quiet!* 제발, 조용히 좀 해! **2** the quality
of being good ‖ 착한 성질. 선함. 온순:
*Anne believed in the basic goodness of
people.* 앤은 사람이 기본적으로 선량하다
고 믿었다. **3** the best part of food that is
good for your health ‖ 음식물 중 건강에
가장 좋은 부분. (음식의) 자양분: *All the
goodness has been boiled out of these
carrots.* 이 당근에서 모든 자양분을 끓여
냈다.

good night /. './ *interjection* said
when you are leaving or being left by
someone at night, especially late at
night. ‖ 밤에 특히 밤늦게 본인이나 남이
떠날 때 쓰여: *Good night, Sandy. Be
careful driving home!* 샌디야, 잘 가라.
집에까지 운전 조심해! —compare GOOD
EVENING

goods /gʊdz/ *n* [plural] **1** things that
are produced in order to be sold ‖ 판매
되도록 생산되는 물건. 상품. 제품:
electrical goods 전기 제품 —see also
DRY GOODS **2** possessions that can be
moved, as opposed to houses, land etc.,
BELONGINGS ‖ 집이나 땅 등에 반대되는, 이
동할 수 있는 재산. 동산; ⑨ belongings

good·will /gʊd'wɪl/ *n* [U] kind feelings
toward or between people ‖ 사람들에 대
한 또는 사람들간의 친절한 감정. 호의.
선의. 친선: *The company gave our Little
League team $1000 as a goodwill
gesture.* (=something you do to show
you are kind) 그 회사는 친선의 표시로
우리 리틀 리그 팀에 1000달러를 제공했
다.

good·y¹ /'gʊdi/ *n* [C usually plural]
INFORMAL something that is attractive,
pleasant, or desirable, especially
something good to eat ‖ 매력적인[유쾌
한, 바람직한] 것으로 특히 먹기에 좋은
것. 맛있는 과자. 먹음직스러운 것: *We
brought lots of goodies for the picnic.* 우
리는 소풍에 많은 맛있는 것들을 가져갔
다.

goody² *interjection* said especially by
children when they are excited or happy
‖ 특히 아이들이 흥분하거나 행복할 때 쓰
여. 멋지다! 근사하다!: *Oh goody - we're
having ice cream!* 야 신난다. 우리 아이스
크림 먹을 거다!

goody-good·y /ˌ.. ˌ..., ˌ.. '. ./, **goody-
two-shoes** /ˌ.. '. ./ *n* DISAPPROVING
someone who likes to seem very good
and helpful in order to please his/her
parents, teachers etc. ‖ 부모님이나 선생
님 등을 기쁘게 하기 위해 아주 착하고 도
움을 주는 것처럼 보이기를 좋아하는 사
람. 착한[선량한] 체하는 사람

goo·ey /'gui/ *adj* INFORMAL **1** sticky,
soft, and usually sweet ‖ 끈끈하고 부드
럽고 보통 달콤한. 달고 쫀득쫀득한. 끈적
거리는: *gooey caramel* 달고 쫀득쫀득한
캐러멜 **2** expressing your love for
someone in a way that other people
think is silly ‖ 다른 사람이 어리석다고 생
각할 정도로 누군가에 대한 사랑을 표현하
는. 아주 감상적인. 센티멘털한: *I hate
gooey romantic movies!* 나는 아주 감상
적인 애정 영화는 싫어해!

goof¹ /guf/ *v* [I] INFORMAL to make a silly
mistake ‖ 어리석은 실수를 하다. 바보짓
을 하다: *Oops! I goofed.* 아차! 내가 실수
를 했어.

goof around *phr v* [I] INFORMAL to
spend time doing silly things ‖ 어리석은
일을 하는 데에 시간을 보내다. 빈둥거리
다: *We were just goofing around at the
mall.* 우리는 쇼핑센터에서 빈둥빈둥 시간
만 낭비하고 있었다.

goof off *phr v* [I] INFORMAL to waste
time or avoid doing any work ‖ 시간을
낭비하거나 어떤 일도 하기를 꺼리다. 일
을 게을리하다. 농땡이치다: *Jason's been
goofing off in class lately.* 요사이 제이
슨은 교실에서 농땡이 부려 왔다. **-
goof-off** /'. ./ *n*

goof² *n* INFORMAL **1** a silly mistake ‖ 어리
석은 실수 **2** someone who is silly ‖ 어리
석은 사람. 바보. 멍청이: *You big goof!* 이
바보 멍청아!

goof·y /'gufi/ *adj* INFORMAL stupid or
silly ‖ 우둔하거나 어리석은. 바보 같은.
얼빠진: *a goofy smile* 바보 같은 미소

goo-goo eyes /ˌ.. '. ./ *n* [plural]
HUMOROUS a silly look that shows you
love someone ‖ 누군가를 사랑한다는 것
을 보여주는 얼이 빠진 것 같은 눈빛. 홀린
듯한[넋 나간] 눈빛: *Look at them
making goo-goo eyes at each other.* 서
로에게 빠져서 홀린 듯이 바라보고 있는
저들을 봐.

goon /guːn/ *n* INFORMAL **1** a violent criminal who is paid to frighten or attack people ‖ 돈을 받고 사람을 위협하거나 공격하는 난폭한 범죄자. 깡패 **2** a silly or stupid person ‖ 어리석거나 우둔한 사람. 바보. 멍텅구리

goop /guːp/ *n* [U] INFORMAL a thick, slightly sticky substance ‖ 걸쭉하고 약간 끈적거리는 물질: *What's that goop in your hair?* 너의 머리에 끈적거리는 것이 무엇이니?

goose /guːs/ *n, plural* **geese 1** a common water bird that is similar to a duck but larger, and makes loud noises ‖ 오리와 비슷하나 몸집이 더 크며 큰 소리를 내는 흔한 물새. 거위 **2** [U] the meat from this bird ‖ 거위 고기

goose·bumps /ˈguːsbʌmps/, **goose pimples** /ˈ. ˌ../ *n* [plural] a condition in which your skin is raised up in small points because you are cold or afraid ‖ 춥거나 두려워서 피부가 조그만 점으로 도드라지는 증상. 소름

GOP *n* **the GOP** Grand Old Party; another name for the Republican party in US politics ‖ Grand Old Party(공화당)의 약어; 미국 정치에서 공화당의 별명

go·pher /ˈɡoʊfɚ/ *n* a North and Central American animal like a SQUIRREL with a short tail, that lives in holes in the ground ‖ 땅속의 굴에 살며 꼬리가 짧고 다람쥐처럼 생긴 북·중미산 동물. 땅다람쥐. 뒤쥐

gore¹ /ɡɔːr/ *v* [T] if an animal gores someone, it wounds him/her with its horns ‖ 동물이 뿔로 사람에게 상처를 내다. 사람을 뿔[뾰족한 것]로 받다[찌르다]

gore² *n* [U] blood that has flowed from a wound and become thicker and darker ‖ 상처에서 흘러나와 더 진하고 검게 된 피. 유혈. 응고된 피

gorge¹ /ɡɔːrdʒ/ *n* a deep narrow valley with steep sides ‖ 급경사면이 있는 깊고 좁은 골짜기. (산)골짜기

gorge² *v* **gorge yourself on/with sth** to eat until you are too full ‖ 완전히 배부를 때까지 먹다. 배불리[게걸스럽게] 먹다: *We were gorging ourselves on popcorn and hot dogs at the game.* 우리는 그 시합에서 팝콘과 핫도그를 배불리 먹고 있었다.

gor·geous /ˈɡɔːrdʒəs/ *adj* very beautiful or pleasant ‖ 매우 아름답거나 즐거운. 매력적인. 멋진. 유쾌한: *What a gorgeous sunny day!* 너무도 멋진 화창한 날이구나! / *I think Lizzie is gorgeous.* 리지는 대단한 미인이라고 생각한다.

go·ril·la /ɡəˈrɪlə/ *n* the largest type of APE (=animal like a monkey) ‖ 체구가 가장 큰 유인원(=원숭이처럼 생긴 동물). 고릴라

gor·y /ˈɡɔːri/ *adj* clearly describing or showing violence, blood, and killing ‖ 폭력·유혈·살인을 선명하게 묘사하거나 보여주는. 폭력의. 피투성이의: *a gory movie* 잔혹한 영화

gosh /ɡɑʃ/ *interjection* said when you are surprised ‖ 놀랐을 때 쓰여. 뭐라고. 아이쿠: *Gosh! I never knew that!* 뭐라고! 나는 그것을 전혀 몰랐어!

gos·ling /ˈɡɑzlɪŋ/ *n* a baby GOOSE ‖ 새끼 거위

gos·pel /ˈɡɑspəl/ *n* **1** also **Gospel** one of the four stories of Christ's life in the Bible ‖ 성경에 있는 예수의 생애에 관한 4복음서중 하나. 복음(서) **2** [U] also **gospel truth** /ˌ.. ˈ./ something that is completely true ‖ 완전히 사실인 것. 진리: *Don't take what Ellen says as gospel.* (=believe it to be completely true) 엘렌의 말을 진실이라고 믿지 마라. **3** [U] also **gospel music** /ˈ.. ˌ../ a type of Christian music, performed especially in African-American churches ‖ 특히 아프리카계 미국 교회에서 부르는 기독교 음악의 일종. 복음 성가

gos·sip¹ /ˈɡɑsəp/ *n* **1** [C, U] conversation or information about other people's behavior and private lives, often including unkind or untrue remarks ‖ 가끔 호의적이지 않거나 사실이 아닌 말이 포함되는, 다른 사람의 행동과 사생활에 대한 대화나 정보. 뜬소문. 쑥덕공론. 험담: *People love hearing gossip about movie stars.* 사람들은 영화배우에 관한 뜬소문을 듣기 좋아한다. **2** someone who likes talking about other people's private lives ‖ 다른 사람의 사생활에 대해 이야기하기를 좋아하는 사람. 수다쟁이

gossip² *v* [I] to talk or write gossip about someone or something ‖ 사람이나 사물에 대해 뜬소문을 말하거나 글을 쓰다. 가십거리로 쓰다. 험담을 퍼뜨리다. 잡담하다: *What are you gossiping about?* 무슨 수다를 떨고 있니?

got /ɡɑt/ *v* **1** the past tense of GET ‖ get의 과거형 **2** a PAST PARTICIPLE of GET ‖ get의 과거 분사형

USAGE NOTE got, gotten, have got, and **have**

Use **gotten** as the past participle of **get**: *He'd gotten up early that day.* / *Kim has gotten engaged!* ✗DON'T SAY

"Kim has got engaged!"✗ You can use **got** as a past tense instead of "became": *Kim just got engaged! You can use* **have** *to mean* "possess": *I've got a new bicycle.* Usually, however, we use **have**: *I have a new bicycle.*

get의 과거 분사로 **gotten**을 쓴다: 그는 그 날 일찍 일어났다. / 김이 약혼했어! ✗ "Kim has got engaged!"라고는 하지 않는다.✗ "became"대신에 **got**을 과거 시제로 쓸 수 있다: 김은 방금 약혼했어! **have got**은 "소유하다"의 의미로 쓸 수 있다: 나는 새 자전거를 가지고 있다. 그러나 보통은 **have**를 쓴다: 나는 새 자전거를 가지고 있다.

got·cha /ˈgɑtʃə/ *interjection* SPOKEN NONSTANDARD **1** a short form of "I've got you," said when you catch someone, or you have gained an advantage over him/her ‖ "I've got you"의 단축형. 남을 잡을 때, 또는 남보다 이점을 더 얻었을 때 쓰여. 잡았다!: *"Gotcha, Pete! You're it now."* (=you're the person who chases other people in a game) "잡았다, 피트! 이제 네가 술래야." **2** a word meaning "I understand" or "all right" ‖ "알았어" 또는 "좋아"라는 의미의 단어: *"First put this one here, and then tie them like this, OK?" "Gotcha."* "먼저 여기에 이것을 놓고 그리고 나서 이렇게 묶어라, 알았지?" "알았어."

got·ta /ˈgɑtə/ *v* SPOKEN NONSTANDARD a short form of "got to," used alone or with "have" ‖ 단독으로 또는 "have"와 함께 쓰는 "got to"의 단축형: *I gotta go now.* 지금 가야 해. / *You've gotta admit he plays really well.* 그가 정말 경기를 잘 한다는 것을 너는 인정해야 해. —see usage note at HAVE TO

got·ten /ˈgɑtʼn/ *v* the usual PAST PARTICIPLE of GET ‖ get의 일반적인 과거 분사형 —see usage note at GOT

gouge /gaʊdʒ/ *v* [T] **1** to make a deep hole or cut in the surface of something ‖ 물건의 표면에 깊은 구멍이나 도려낸 구멍을 만들다. …을 파다[새기다]. 파내다 **2** INFORMAL to charge someone too much money for something ‖ 남에게 어떤 것에 대해 너무 많은 돈을 청구하다. 바가지 씌우다: *Hotels are ready to gouge Olympic visitors by raising their prices.* 호텔은 가격을 인상함으로써 올림픽 관광객에게 바가지를 씌우려고 한다. – **gouge** *n*

gouge sth ↔ **out** *phr v* [T] to make a hole in something by removing material

that is on its surface ‖ 표면에 있는 물질을 제거함으로써 어떤 것에 구멍을 만들다. 도려내다

gou·lash /ˈguːlɑʃ, -læʃ/ *n* [C, U] a dish made of meat cooked in liquid with a hot tasting pepper ‖ 국물에 매운 맛이 나는 후추를 넣고 끓인 고기로 만든 요리. 굴라시. 스튜 요리

gourd /gɔrd, gʊrd/ *n* a large fruit with a hard shell that is sometimes used as a container ‖ 때때로 용기로 사용되는 딱딱한 껍질이 있는 큰 과일. 호리병박 열매

gour·met¹ /gʊrˈmeɪ, ˈgʊrmeɪ/ *adj* relating to very good food and drink ‖ 아주 좋은 음식과 음료의. 미식(가)의. 미식가를 위한: *a gourmet restaurant* 미식가의 식당 / *gourmet food* 맛있는 음식

gourmet² *n* someone who knows a lot about good food and drink, and who enjoys them ‖ 좋은 음식과 음료에 대해 많이 알고 즐기는 사람. 미식가. 식도락가

gout /gaʊt/ *n* [U] a disease that makes your toes, knees, and fingers hurt and swell ‖ 발가락·무릎·손가락이 아프고 부어오르는 병. 통풍

gov·ern /ˈgʌvərn/ *v* **1** [I, T] to officially control a country, state etc. and make all the decisions about things such as taxes and laws ‖ 나라·주 등을 공식적으로 지배하고 세금·법률 등에 대한 모든 결정을 하다. 다스리다. 통치하다: *The same party governed for thirty years.* 한 정당이 30년 동안 통치했다. / *The Socialists have governed the country well.* 그 사회주의자들이 나라를 잘 다스려 왔다. **2** [T] to control the way a system or situation works ‖ 제도나 상황이 돌아가는 방식을 통제하다. 좌우하다. 규제하다: *new rules governing immigration* 이민을 규제하는 새 법령들

gov·ern·ess /ˈgʌvərnɪs/ *n* a female teacher who lives with a family and teaches their children at home ‖ 가족과 함께 거주하며 그 가족의 자녀를 집에서 가르치는 여자 교사. 여자 가정교사

gov·ern·ment /ˈgʌvərmənt, ˈgʌvərnmənt/ *n* **1** also **Government** the group of people who govern a country, state etc. ‖ 나라·주 등을 통치하는 일단의 사람들. 정부. 통치 기관: *The government will send aid to the disaster area.* 정부는 재해 지역에 구호품을 보낼 것이다. **2** [U] the process of governing, or the system used for governing ‖ 통치 과정, 또는 통치를 위한 제도. 통치(행위). 통치 조직. 정치 체제: *a democratic government* 민주 정체 – **governmental** /ˌgʌvərnˈmɛntl/ *adj*

gov·er·nor, Governor /ˈgʌvənə, -və-/ *n* the person in charge of governing a US state ‖ 미국의 주를 통치하는 사람. 주지사: *the Governor of California* 캘리포니아 주지사 – **governorship** *n* [U]

gown /gaʊn/ *n* **1** a long dress worn by a woman on formal occasions ‖ 공식 행사에서 여성이 입는 긴 드레스. 야회복: *a silk evening gown* 실크 야회복 **2** a long loose piece of clothing worn for a special reason, for example by doctors, or by students at GRADUATION ‖ 특별한 이유로 예를 들어 의사나 졸업생이 입는 길고 낙낙한 옷. 제복. 가운: *a hospital gown* (=worn by someone who is sick in the hospital) (병원 환자가 입는) 병원 가운

GPA *n* grade point average; the average score that a student earns based on all of his/her grades, in which an A is 4 points, a B is 3, a C is 2, a D is 1, and an F is 0 ‖ grade point average(평점)의 약어; A는 4점, B는 3점, C는 2점, D는 2점, F는 0점으로 모든 성적을 환산한 값에 기초해 학생이 받는 평균 점수: *To be on the Honor Roll, students must have a GPA of at least 3.5.* 우등생이 되려면 학생은 평점이 적어도 3.5가 되어야 한다.

GPS *n* Global Positioning System; a system that uses radio signals from SATELLITEs to show your exact position on the Earth on a special piece of equipment, often used by the military or in cars and boats ‖ Global Positioning System(전 지구 위치 파악 시스템)의 약어; 종종 군대나 자동차·배에서 사용되는, 지구상에서 정확한 현 위치를 특수 장비에 나타내기 위해 인공위성으로부터의 무선 신호를 사용하는 시스템

grab¹ /græb/ *v* **-bbed, -bbing** [T] **1** to take hold of someone or something with a sudden or violent movement ‖ 갑작스럽거나 난폭한 동작으로 사람이나 물건을 잡다. 움켜쥐다. 잡아채다: *He grabbed my bag and ran off.* 그는 나의 가방을 잡아채서 달아났다. **2** INFORMAL to do something such as eat or sleep for a very short time ‖ 아주 짧은 시간 동안 먹거나 잠을 자는 등의 일을 하다. 가볍게 먹다[자다]: *I'll just grab a sandwich for lunch.* 점심 식사로 가볍게 샌드위치만 먹겠다. **3** INFORMAL to quickly take an opportunity to do something ‖ 어떤 일을 할 기회를 재빠르게 잡다. 거머쥐다: *Try to get there early and grab a seat.* 일찍 그곳에 가서 자리를 잡아봐라. / *Sylvia grabbed the chance to work in Italy.* 실비아는 이탈리아에서 일할 기회를 잡았다.

4 how does sth grab you? SPOKEN used in order to ask if someone would be interested in doing a particular thing ‖ 특정한 어떤 일을 하는 것에 관심이 있는지 여부를 묻는 데에 쓰여. 구미가 당깁니까?: *How does the idea of a trip to Hawaii grab you?* 하와이 여행에 구미가 당기세요?

grab at *phr v* [T] to quickly and suddenly put out your hand in order to take hold of something ‖ 어떤 것을 잡기 위해 빠르고 갑작스럽게 손을 내밀다. …을 낚아채다

grab² *n* **1 make a grab for/at** to suddenly try to take hold of something ‖ 갑자기 어떤 것을 잡으려고 하다. …을 홱 잡아채려 하다: *Parker made a grab for the knife.* 파커는 재빨리 칼을 잡았다. **2 be up for grabs** INFORMAL if a job, prize, opportunity etc. is up for grabs, it is available for anyone who wants to try to get it ‖ 일·상(賞)·기회 등이 그것을 얻고자 하는 모든 사람이 획득할 수 있는. 누구나 쉽게 입수할 수 있는. 선착순의. 조금만 애쓰면 잡히는: *There are still four tickets up for grabs for tonight's show.* 오늘밤 쇼를 위한 선착순 티켓 네 장이 아직 남아 있다.

grace¹ /greɪs/ *n* **1** [U] a smooth way of moving that appears natural, relaxed, and attractive ‖ 자연스럽고 느긋하며 매력적으로 보이는 부드럽게 움직이는 태도. 우아(함): *She moved with the grace of a dancer.* 그녀는 무용수처럼 우아하게 움직였다. **2** [U] polite and pleasant behavior ‖ 예의바르고 쾌활한 행동. 호의. 친절. 관용. 관대함: *At least he had the grace to admit he was wrong.* 최소한 그는 선뜻[깨끗하게] 자신이 틀렸다고 시인하는 관대함을 지녔다. **3** [U] also **grace period** more time that is added to the period you are allowed for finishing a piece of work, paying a debt etc. ‖ 일을 마치거나 빚을 갚는 등에 허용되는 기간에 추가되는 시간. 유예 기간: *The bill was supposed to be paid by Friday, but they're giving me a week's grace.* 그 청구서는 금요일까지 지불하는 것으로 되어 있었지만 그들은 나에게 일주일 간의 유예 기간을 주고 있다. **4 with good/bad grace** willingly and cheerfully, or in an unwilling and angry way ‖ 기꺼이·쾌히, 또는 내키지 않고 화가 나서. 자진해서/마지못해서: *Kevin smiled and accepted his defeat with good grace.* 케빈은 웃으며 기꺼이 패배를 받아들였다. **5 the grace of God** the kindness shown to people by God ‖ 신이 인간에게 보이는 호의. 신의

은총: *It was only by the grace of God that we weren't killed.* 우리가 죽지 않은 것은 단지 신의 은총 때문이었다. **6** [C, U] a prayer thanking God that you say before a meal ‖ 식사 전에 신에게 감사하는 기도. 식전의 감사 기도: *Who would like to say grace?* 누가 감사 기도를 올려 주시겠습니까? —see also **be in sb's good graces** (GOOD¹)

grace² *v* [T] **1 grace sb/sth with your presence** HUMOROUS said when someone arrives late, or when someone who does not often come to meetings or events arrives ‖ 누군가 늦게 도착했을 때, 또는 모임이나 행사에 자주 오지 않는 사람이 도착했을 때 쓰여. 참석함으로써 …을 빛내 주다[영광스럽게 하다]: *I'm so glad you've decided to grace us with your presence!* 참석하셔서 우리를 영광스럽게 해주신다니 정말 기쁩니다! **2** FORMAL to make a place or an object look more beautiful or attractive ‖ 장소나 물체가 더 아름답거나 매력적으로 보이게 하다. 아름답게 꾸미다[장식하다]: *His new painting now graces the wall of the dining room.* 그의 새 그림은 지금 식당의 벽을 아름답게 장식한다.

grace·ful /'greɪsfəl/ *adj* **1** moving in a smooth and attractive way, or having an attractive shape ‖ 부드럽고 매력적으로 움직이는, 또는 매력적인 형태를 가진. 우아한: *a graceful dancer* 우아한 무용수 / *graceful arched windows* 우아한 아치형 창문 **2** polite and exactly right for a situation ‖ 예의바르고 상황에 아주 적절한. 점잖은. 의젓한: *a graceful apology* 점잖은 사과 **– gracefully** *adv* **–** compare GRACIOUS

gra·cious /'greɪʃəs/ *adj* **1** behaving in a polite, kind, and generous way ‖ 예의바르고 친절하고 관대하게 행동하는. 정중한. 상냥한: *a gracious host* 친절한 주인 **2** having the type of expensive style, comfort, and beauty that only wealthy people can afford ‖ 부유층 사람만이 감당할 수 있는 값비싼 (생활)양식·안락함·미를 가진. 우아한. 운치 있는: *gracious living* 우아한 생활 **3 (goodness) gracious!** SPOKEN OLD-FASHIONED used in order to express surprise or to emphasize "yes" or "no" ‖ 놀람을 표현하거나 "예"나 "아니요"를 강조하는 데에 쓰여. 저런. 아차 **– graciously** *adv*

grad /græd/ *n* SPOKEN ⇨ GRADUATE¹

gra·da·tion /greɪˈdeɪʃən, grə-/ *n* FORMAL a small change in a set of changes, or one level in a number of levels of development ‖ 일련의 변화 단계에 있어

서 하나의 작은 변화, 또는 많은 발달 단계의 한 단계. 점진적 변화[이행]. 단계. 정도: *gradations of color from dark red to pink* 검붉은색에서 핑크색으로의 색의 점진적 변화

grade¹ /greɪd/ *n* **1** one of the 12 years you are in school in the US, or the students in a particular year ‖ 미국의 재학 기간인 12년의 하나, 또는 특정 연도의 학생들. 학년: *He's just finished third/fourth etc. grade.* 그는 3학년/4학년 (등)을 막 마쳤다. / *What grade are you in?* 몇 학년이니? **2** [C, U] a particular standard or level of quality that a product, material etc. has ‖ 제품이나 제재 등이 지니는 특정한 표준이나 품질의 수준. 등급. 계급: *Grade A milk/eggs/beef* A등급 우유/계란/쇠고기 **3** a number or letter that shows how well you have done at school, college etc ‖ 학교·대학 등에서 공부를 얼마나 잘 했는지를 보여주는 숫자나 문자. 성적. 평점: *Betsy always gets good grades.* 벳시는 항상 좋은 점수를 받는다. **4 make the grade** to succeed or reach the necessary standard ‖ 성공하다, 또는 필요한 기준에 도달하다. 규정된 목표에 이르다. 잘 해내다: *Only a few athletes make the grade in professional sports.* 소수의 운동선수만이 프로 스포츠에서 성공한다. **5** ⇨ GRADIENT

grade² *v* [T] **1** to separate things, or arrange them in order according to their quality or rank ‖ 질이나 등급에 따라 물건을 나누거나 배열하다. …을 등급으로 나누다: *eggs graded according to size* 크기에 따라 등급이 매겨진 계란 **2** to give a grade to an examination paper or to a piece of school work ‖ 시험지나 학교 숙제에 점수를 주다. 채점하다: *I spent the weekend grading tests.* 나는 시험지를 채점하면서 주말을 보냈다.

grade point av·er·age /. . ,../ *n* ⇨ GPA

-grad·er /'greɪdɚ/ *n* a child in a particular grade ‖ 특정한 학년의 아이. …학년 학생: *a cute little first-grader* 귀엽고 작은 초등학교 1학년생

grade school /'. ./ *n* ⇨ ELEMENTARY SCHOOL

gra·di·ent /'greɪdiənt/ *n* a degree of slope, especially in a road or railroad ‖ 특히 도로나 철도의 가파른 정도. 경사도. 기울기. 비탈. 사면: *a steep gradient* 가파른 경사

grad school /'. ./ *n* INFORMAL ⇨ GRADUATE SCHOOL

grad·u·al /'grædʒuəl/ *adj* **1** happening,

developing, or changing slowly over a long time ‖ 오랫동안 천천히 일어나고 있는[발달하는, 변화하는]. 점진적인: *gradual changes* 점진적인 변화 **2** a gradual slope is not steep ‖ 경사가 가파르지 않은. 완만한

grad·u·al·ly /'grædʒuəli, -dʒəli/ *adv* in a way that happens or develops slowly over time ‖ 오랜 시간 동안 천천히 일어나거나 발달하는 방식으로. 점진적으로: *Gradually, their marriage got better.* 점차 그들의 결혼 생활은 나아졌다.

grad·u·ate¹ /'grædʒuɪt/ *n* someone who has completed a course at a school, college, or university ‖ 학교[단과대학, 종합대학]의 과정을 이수한 사람. 졸업생: *a graduate of UCLA* UCLA 졸업생 – **graduate** *adj*

grad·u·ate² /'grædʒu,eɪt/ *v* [I] to obtain a degree from a college or university, or to complete your education at HIGH SCHOOL ‖ 단과대학이나 종합대학에서 학위를 따거나 또는 고등학교에서 교육을 마치다. 졸업하다: *Ruth has just graduated from Princeton.* 루스는 이제 막 프린스턴 대학을 졸업했다.

grad·u·at·ed /'grædʒu,eɪtɪd/ *adj* divided into different levels or sizes from lower to higher amounts or degrees ‖ 더 낮은 양이나 정도에서 더 높은 양이나 정도에 이르기까지 다른 수준이나 크기로 나눈. 눈금을 매긴. 등급을 매긴. 누진적인: *graduated rates of income tax* 소득 누진 세율 / *graduated measuring cups* 눈금 있는 계량컵

graduate school /'... ,./ *n* [C, U] a college or university where you can study for a MASTER'S DEGREE or a PH.D.., or the period of time when you do this ‖ 석사 학위나 박사 학위를 위해 공부하는 단과대학이나 종합대학, 또는 이러한 기간. 대학원(과정)

grad·u·a·tion /,grædʒu'eɪʃən/ *n* **1** [U] the time when you complete a university degree or HIGH SCHOOL education ‖ 대학 학위나 고등학교 교육을 마치는 시기. 졸업: *After graduation, Jayne went to nursing school.* 졸업 후 제인은 간호학교로 진학했다. **2** [U] a ceremony at which you receive a degree or DIPLOMA ‖ 학위나 졸업장을 받는 의식. 졸업식: *graduation speeches* 졸업식 연설

graf·fi·ti /grə'fiti/ *n* [U] rude, humorous, or political writing and pictures on the walls of buildings ‖ 건물 벽에 있는 난잡한[재미있는, 정치적인] 글과 그림. 낙서

graft¹ /græft/ *n* **1** [U] the practice of dishonestly using your position to get money or advantages ‖ 돈이나 이익을 얻기 위해 지위를 부정하게 이용하는 행위. 수뢰(受賂). 부당 이득: *politicians accused of graft* 수뢰 혐의가 있는 정치인 **2** a piece of healthy skin or bone taken from someone's body and put on a damaged part of his/her body ‖ 남의 신체에서 떼어내어 자신의 손상된 부위에 붙이는 건강한 피부나 뼛조각. 이식 조직. 이식편 **3** a piece cut from one plant and joined to another plant so that it grows where it is joined ‖ 접붙인 곳에서 자라도록 한 식물에서 잘라내어 다른 식물에 접붙인 부분. 접가지[눈]. 접지(椄枝)

graft² *v* [I, T] **1** to put a piece of skin or bone from one part of someone's body onto another part that has been damaged ‖ 신체의 한 부위에서 떼어낸 피부나 뼛조각을 손상된 다른 부위에 입히다. 이식하다: *Doctors grafted skin from Mike's arm onto his face where it was burned.* 의사들은 마이크 팔에서 떼어낸 피부를 불에 덴 그의 얼굴에 이식했다. **2** to join a part of a flower, plant, or tree onto another flower, plant, or tree ‖ 꽃[식물, 나무]의 일부를 다른 꽃[식물, 나무]에 접붙이다. 접붙이다. 접목하다

grain /greɪn/ *n* **1** [C, U] a seed or seeds of crops such as corn, wheat, or rice that are used for food, or the crops themselves ‖ 식량으로 사용되는 옥수수[밀, 쌀] 등의 농작물의 낟알이나 낟알들, 또는 농작물 그 자체. 곡물. 곡류: *five-grain cereal* 오곡으로 된 시리얼[곡물식] / *fields of grain* 곡물 밭 **2** a single, very small piece of something such as sand, salt etc. ‖ 모래·소금 등의 단일한 아주 작은 조각. 알. 알갱이 **3** **the grain** the lines or patterns you can see in things such as wood or rock ‖ 목재나 바위 등의 사물에서 볼 수 있는 선이나 무늬. 결: *Split the wood along the grain.* 나무를 결따라 쪼개라. **4** **go against the grain** if something that you must do goes against the grain, you do not like doing it because it is not what you would naturally do ‖ 자신이 해야 하는 일이 천성적으로 하고 싶어 하는 일이 아니기 때문에 하기 싫어하다. 성미에 맞지 않다. 못마땅하다 **5** **a grain of truth/doubt etc.** a small amount of truth etc. ‖ 조금의 진실 등. 티끌만큼의 진실/의심: *There's not a grain of truth in what she said.* 그녀가 한 말에는 진실이라고는 눈곱만큼도 없다. **6** **take sth with a grain of salt** to not completely believe what someone tells you, because you know that s/he often lies or is wrong ‖ 어떤 사람이 자주 거짓말을 하거나 틀리다는 것을 알기 때문에 그 사람이 한 말을 전적으로는 믿지 않다. 에누리해서 듣다

grainy

grainy   sharp

grain·y /ˈgreɪni/ *adj* a photograph that is grainy has a rough appearance, as if the images are made up of spots ‖ 사진 이미지가 점으로 구성된 것처럼 거친 모습을 띤. 사진의 입자가 거친. 선명하지 않은

gram /græm/ *n* written abbreviation **gm.** a unit for measuring weight, equal to 1/1000 of a kilogram or 0.035 OUNCES ‖ 1킬로그램의 1/1000 또는 0.035온스에 상당하는 무게를 측정하는 단위. 그램

gram·mar /ˈgræmɚ/ *n* **1** [U] the rules by which words change their form and are combined into sentences, or the study or use of these rules ‖ 단어들이 그 형태를 변화시켜 문장으로 결합되는 규칙, 또는 이 규칙에 대한 연구나 활용. 문법. 어법: *Mr. Watson, will you correct the grammar in my essay?* 왓슨 씨, 제 에세이의 어법을 바로 잡아 주시겠어요? **2** a particular description of grammar, or a book that describes grammar rules ‖ 문법에 대한 특별한 설명, 또는 문법 규칙을 기술한 책. 문법(책): *a good English grammar* 좋은 영문법 책

gram·mat·i·cal /grəˈmætɪkəl/ *adj* **1** relating to the use of grammar ‖ 문법의 활용과 관련된. 문법(상)의. 문법적인: *You're still making grammatical errors.* 너는 아직 문법상의 오류를 범하고 있어. ✗DON'T SAY "You're still making errors that are grammatical."✗ "You're still making errors that are grammatical." 이라고는 하지 않는다. **2** correct according to the rules of grammar ‖ 문법 규칙에 맞추어 올바른. 문법적으로 옳은. 문법에 맞는: *a grammatical sentence* 문법에 맞는 문장 - **gram·matically** *adv* —opposite UNGRAMMATICAL

Gram·my /ˈgræmi/ *n* a prize given in the US every year to the best song, the best singer etc. in the music industry ‖ 매년 미국 음악계에서 최고의 노래·최고의 가수 등에게 주는 상. 그래미상

grand¹ /grænd/ *adj* **1** higher in rank than others of the same kind ‖ 동종의 다른 것보다 순위가 높은. 최고의. 고위의. 중요한: *the grand prize* 대상, 최우수 상 **2** **grand total** the final total you get when you add up several numbers or amounts ‖ 여러 숫자나 양을 합산할 때 얻는 최종 합계. 총계 **3** OLD-FASHIONED very good or impressive ‖ 매우 좋거나 인상적인. 웅장한. 위엄 있는: *a grand old house* 웅장한 옛 집 - **grandly** *adv*

grand² *n* INFORMAL **1** [plural] **grand** 1000 dollars ‖ 1천 달러: *Bill only paid five grand for that car.* 빌은 겨우 5천달러 주고 그 차를 샀다. **2** ⇨ GRAND PIANO

grand·child /ˈgræntʃaɪld/ *n* the child of your son or daughter ‖ 아들이나 딸의 자식. 친손자. 외손자 —see picture at FAMILY

grand·dad /ˈgrændæd/ *n* INFORMAL ⇨ GRANDFATHER

grand·daugh·ter /ˈgrænˌdɔtɚ/ *n* the daughter of your son or daughter ‖ 아들이나 딸의 딸. (외)손녀 —see picture at FAMILY

gran·deur /ˈgrændʒɚ, -dʒʊr/ *n* [U] impressive beauty, power, or size ‖ 장엄함을 느끼게 하는 아름다움[힘, 크기]. 웅장함. 장대함: *the grandeur of the Pacific Ocean* 태평양의 장대함

grand·fa·ther /ˈgrænˌfɑðɚ/ *n* the father of your mother or father ‖ 어머니나 아버지의 아버지. (외)할아버지. (외)조부 —see picture at FAMILY

grandfather clock /ˈ... ./ *n* a tall clock in a wooden case that stands on the floor ‖ 바닥에 서 있는 나무 상자 속의 큰 시계. 그랜드파더 시계. 대형 괘종시계

gran·di·ose /ˈgrændiˌoʊs, ˌgrændiˈoʊs/ *adj* DISAPPROVING grandiose plans sound very important but are really not practical ‖ 계획이 아주 중요한 것 같지만 실제로는 실제적이 아닌. 웅대한

grand ju·ry /ˌ. ˈ../ *n* a group of people who decide whether someone who may be guilty of a crime should be judged in a court of law ‖ 범죄 혐의가 있는 사람이 법정에서 재판을 받아야 하는지를 결정하는 사람들의 집단. 대배심(원)

grand·ma /ˈgrændˌmɑ, ˈgræmɑ/ *n* INFORMAL ⇨ GRANDMOTHER

grand·moth·er /ˈgrændˌmʌðɚ/ *n* the mother of your mother or father ‖ 어머니나 아버지의 어머니. (외)조모. (외)할머니 —see picture at FAMILY

grand·pa /ˈgrændˌpɑ, ˈgræmpɑ/ *n* INFORMAL ⇨ GRANDFATHER

grand·par·ent /'grænd‚pɛrənt/ *n* the parent of your mother or father ‖ 어머니 나 아버지의 부모. (외)조부[모]. (외)할 아버지[할머니] —see picture at FAMILY

grand pi·an·o /‚. .'../ *n* the type of large piano often used at concerts ‖ 콘서트에서 자주 사용하는 대형 피 아노 종류. 그랜드 피 아노

grand piano

grand prix /‚grɑn 'pri/ *n* one of a set of international races, especially a car race ‖ 일련의 국제 경주, 특히 자동차 경주의 하나. 그랑프리(경주)

grand slam /‚. './ *n* **1** a hit in baseball that gets four points because it is a HOME RUN and there are players on all the bases ‖ 홈런을 쳤을 때 모든 베이 스에 주자가 있기 때문에 4점을 얻는 야구 의 타격. 만루 홈런 **2** the act of winning all of a set of important sports competitions in the same year ‖ 같은 해 에 일련의 중요한 스포츠 경기에서 모두 우승을 거두는 것. 그랜드 슬램

grand·son /'grændsʌn/ *n* the son of your son or daughter ‖ 아들이나 딸의 자 식. (외)손자 —see picture at FAMILY

grand·stand /'grændstænd/ *n* a large structure that has many rows of seats and a roof, where people sit to watch sports competitions or races ‖ 사람이 스 포츠 경기나 경주를 관람하기 위해 앉는, 많은 줄의 좌석과 지붕이 있는 큰 구조물. 특별 관람석 —compare BLEACHERS

gran·ite /'grænɪt/ *n* a very hard gray rock, often used in buildings ‖ 자주 건물 에 사용되는 아주 단단한 회색 바위. 화강 암

gran·ny /'græni/ *n* INFORMAL ⇨ GRANDMOTHER

gra·no·la /grə'noʊlə/ *n* [U] a breakfast food made from nuts, OATS, and seeds ‖ 견과·귀리·씨앗으로 만든 아침 식사. 조반 용 건강식

grant¹ /grænt/ *n* an amount of money given to someone by the government for a particular purpose ‖ 특정한 목적을 위 해 정부가 어떤 사람에게 주는 돈. 보조금: *a research grant for cancer treatment* 암 치료를 위한 연구 보조금

grant² *v* **1 take it for granted (that)** to believe that something is true without making sure; ASSUME ‖ 확실하지 않고 어 떤 것이 사실이라고 믿다. …을 당연한 것 이라고[의심의 여지가 없다고] 여기다; 윤 assume: *You shouldn't take it for*

granted that your parents will pay for college. 너는 부모님이 대학 등록금을 지 불하는 것을 당연한 것으로 여겨서는 안 된다. **2 take sb for granted** to expect that someone will always support you, and never thank him/her ‖ 어떤 사람이 항상 자신을 지지할 것이라 기대하고 그 사람에게 전혀 감사함을 표현하지 않다. 당연한 것으로[예사로] 알고 소홀히 하 다: *He's so busy with his work that he takes his family for granted.* 그는 일이 너무 바빠서 자기 가족을 소홀히 한다. **3** [T] FORMAL to give someone something that s/he has asked for or earned, especially official permission to do something ‖ 어떤 사람에게 요청했거나 받 을 만한 것, 특히 어떤 일을 할 수 있는 공 식적인 허가를 내주다. 수여[교부, 하사] 하다. 승낙하다: *Ms. Chung was granted American citizenship last year.* 정 씨는 작년에 미국 시민권을 받았다. **4 granted (that)** used in order to say that something is true, before you say something else about it ‖ 어떤 일에 대한 다른 말을 하기 전에 그것이 사실임을 말 하는 데에 쓰여. 맞았어. 분명해. 확실해: *Granted, he didn't practice much, but he played well anyway.* 맞았어, 그는 연습 을 많이 하지 않았음이 분명해, 그래도 여 하튼 잘했어.

gran·u·lat·ed /'grænyə‚leɪtɪd/ *adj* granulated sugar is in the form of small white grains ‖ 설탕이 작고 흰 낱알의 형 태로 되어 있는. 알갱이 모양의

gran·ule /'grænyul/ *n* a very small hard piece of something ‖ 어떤 것의 아 주 작고 딱딱한 조각. 과립. 작은 알갱이. 미립자: *instant coffee granules* 인스턴트 커피의 작은 알갱이 – **granular** /'grænyələ/ *adj*

grape /greɪp/ *n* a small round green or purple fruit that grows on a VINE and is often used for making wine ‖ 포도나무에 서 자라고 종종 포도주를 만드는 데 사용 되는 작고 둥근 초록색이나 자주색의 과 일. 포도 —see picture on page 944

grape·fruit /'greɪpfrut/ *n* a yellow bitter-tasting fruit, with thick skin like an orange ‖ 오렌지처럼 두꺼운 껍질이 있 는 노란색의 쓴 맛이 나는 과일. 그레이프 프루트 —see picture on page 944

grape·vine /'greɪpvaɪn/ *n* **1 hear sth on/through the grapevine** to hear news because it has been passed from one person to another in conversation ‖ 한 사람에게서 다른 사람에게로 대화로 전 해져서 소식을 듣다. …을 소문으로 듣다: *Sarah had heard through the grapevine*

graph 704

that Larry was getting the job. 사라는 래리가 직업을 구하고 있다는 소문을 들었다. **2** a plant that produces GRAPES ‖ 포도 열매를 맺는 식물. 포도 덩굴[나무]

graph

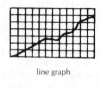

line graph

pie chart

bar graph

graph /græf/ *n* a drawing that shows how two or more sets of measurements are related to each other ‖ 둘 또는 둘 이상의 수치가 서로 어떻게 관련되는지를 나타내는 그림. 도표. 그래프: *a graph showing population growth over 50 years* 50년 동안의 인구 증가를 나타내는 도표

graph·ic /'græfɪk/ *adj* **1** relating to drawing or printing ‖ 그림이나 인쇄물과 관련된. 그림[도표]를 사용한. 도식적인. 그래픽(아트)의: *graphic illustrations* 그래픽 삽화 **2 a graphic account/description etc.** a very clear description of an event that gives a lot of details ‖ 많은 세부 사항을 설명해 주는 사건의 매우 명확한 묘사. 생생한[사실적인] 설명/묘사 — see also GRAPHICS

graph·i·cal·ly /'græfɪkli/ *adv* **1** clearly and with a lot of detail ‖ 명백하고 아주 상세하게. 생생하게. 그림을 보는 것같이: *She described the scene so graphically that we felt we were there.* 그녀가 그 장면을 아주 생생하게 묘사해서 우리는 현장에 있는 것처럼 느꼈다. **2** FORMAL using a graph ‖ 그래프를 써서. 그래프로(나타내어): *temperature changes shown graphically* 그래프로 나타낸 온도 변화

graphic de·sign /... './ *n* [U] the art of combining pictures, words, and decoration in the production of books, magazines etc. ‖ 책·잡지 등의 제작에 그림·단어·장식을 결합시키는 미술. 그래픽 디자인. 그래픽 아트를 이용한 디자인

graph·ics /'græfɪks/ *n* [plural, U] the activity of drawing pictures or designs, or the designs or pictures themselves ‖ 그림이나 디자인을 그리는 행위, 또는 디자인이나 그림 그 자체. 그래픽스[그래픽 아트]. 화상(畫像): *a graphics program for the computer* 컴퓨터 그래픽스 프로그램 / *a magazine with strong graphics* 삽화가 두드러진 잡지

graphics card /'... ,./ *n* a CIRCUIT BOARD that connects to a computer and allows the computer to show images, such as VIDEO images, on its screen ‖ 컴퓨터에 연결해서 비디오 이미지 등의 화상을 화면에 나타나게 해주는 회로판. 비디오 카드[보드]

graph·ite /'græfaɪt/ *n* [U] a soft black substance that is a type of CARBON and is used in pencils ‖ 일종의 탄소로 연필에 쓰이는 부드럽고 검은 물질. 흑연

grap·ple /'græpəl/ *v* [I] to fight or struggle with someone, holding him/her tightly ‖ 누구와 꽉 붙잡고 싸우거나 맞붙다. …과 맞붙어 싸우다. 격투하다: *A young man was grappling with the guard.* 한 젊은이가 그 경비원과 몸싸움을 벌이고 있었다.

grapple with sth *phr v* [T] to try hard to solve a difficult problem ‖ 어려운 문제를 풀기 위해 열심히 노력하다. …와 맞붙어 싸우다. 극복하려고 노력하다: *The Government has to grapple with the problem of unemployment.* 정부는 실업 문제와 맞싸워야 한다.

grasp¹ /græsp/ *v* [T] **1** to take and hold something firmly ‖ 무엇을 잡아서 꽉 쥐다. 움켜쥐다: *He stumbled a little and grasped Tanya's arm.* 그는 약간 비틀거리며 걷다가 타냐의 팔을 움켜 잡았다. **2** to completely understand something, especially a complicated fact or idea ‖ 복잡한 사실이나 생각을 완전히 이해하다. 파악하다: *They couldn't quite grasp the significance of the problem.* 그들은 그 문제의 중요성을 전혀 이해하지 못했다.

grasp at sth *phr v* [T] **1 sb is grasping at straws** used when someone keeps trying to stop a bad thing from happening, even though nothing s/he does will stop it ‖ 비록 아무 것도 멈추게 할 수 없더라도 나쁜 일이 일어나는 것을 중단시키려고 계속 노력할 때에 쓰여. 지푸라기라도 잡고 있다 **2** to eagerly try to reach something or to use an opportunity ‖ 어떤 것에 도달하거나 기회를 이용하려고 몹시 애를 쓰다. …을 잡으려[붙들려] 하다: *The public is grasping at these reforms because they believe schools have failed to do their job.* 대중은 학교가 본연의 업무에 실패했

다고 믿기 때문에 이들 개혁안에 매달리고 있다.

grasp² n [singular] **1** the ability to understand a complicated idea or situation ‖ 복잡한 사상이나 상황을 이해하는 능력. 이해(력). 파악: *a good grasp of world politics* 세계 정세에 대한 뛰어난 파악능력 / *ideas that are beyond their grasp* (=too difficult to understand) 이해의 범위를 넘어선 사상 **2** the possibility of being able to achieve or gain something ‖ 어떤 일을 성취하거나 얻을 수 있는 가능성. 손이 미치는 범위: *Control over the whole program was now within her grasp.* 당시 모든 프로그램에 대한 통제력이 그녀의 손아귀에 있었다. **3** a hold on something, or your ability to hold it ‖ 사물을 쥐기 또는 쥐는 능력. 꽉쥐기: *a firm grasp* 단단히 쥠

grasp·ing /ˈgræspɪŋ/ adj too eager to get money ‖ 너무도 돈을 가지고 싶어하는. 욕심 많은. 탐욕스러운: *a grasping man* 욕심 많은 남자

grass /græs/ n **1** [U] a very common plant with thin green leaves that grows across fields, parks, hills, and yards ‖ 들판·공원·언덕·마당에 걸쳐 자라는 얇은 녹색 잎을 가진 아주 흔한 식물. 잔디. 풀: *Please keep off the grass.* 잔디밭에 들어가지 마세요. / *a blade of grass* 풀잎 **2** [C, U] a particular type of grass ‖ 특정한 종류의 풀: *mountain grasses* 산 속의 목초 **3** [U] SLANG ➪ MARIJUANA

grass·hop·per /ˈgræsˌhɑpə/ n an insect that jumps with its long back legs and makes short loud noises ‖ 긴 뒷다리로 뛰며 짧고 큰 소리를 내는 곤충. 메뚜기. 여치류

grass·land /ˈgræslænd/ n [U] a large area of land covered with wild grass ‖ 야생목초로 덮인 넓은 지역의 땅. 목초지

grass roots /ˌ. ˈ./ n **the grass roots** the ordinary people in an organization rather than the leaders ‖ 지도자가 아닌 조직 내의 평범한 사람들. 일반인. 민중. 대중. 민초(民草) - **grass-roots** adj : *a grassroots campaign/movement* 대중 캠페인[민중 운동]

gras·sy /ˈgræsi/ adj covered with grass ‖ 풀로 뒤덮인. 풀이 많은[무성한]: *a grassy hill* 풀이 무성한 언덕

grate¹ /greɪt/ v **1** [T] to rub food such as cheese against a rough surface in order to break it into small pieces ‖ 잘게 부수기 위해 치즈 등의 음식을 거친 표면에 문지르다. 강판으로 …을 갈다 **2** [I] to make an unpleasant sound by rubbing against something else ‖ 다른 것에 대고 문질러 불쾌한 소리를 내다. 삐걱삐걱 소리나다 : *chalk grating against the blackboard* 흑판에 분필을 문지르는 소리 **3 grate on sb's nerves** INFORMAL to annoy someone often ‖ 남을 자주 짜증나게 하다. …의 신경을 건드리다. 불쾌감을 주다: *She really grates on my nerves.* 그녀는 정말 내 신경에 거슬린다.

grate

grater

grate² n the metal BARs or frame that holds wood, coal etc. in a FIREPLACE ‖ 벽난로에서 나무·석탄 등을 담는 금속 막대들, 또는 금속 틀. 벽난로의 받침쇠

grate·ful /ˈgreɪtfəl/ adj **1** feeling that you want to thank someone because of something kind that s/he has done ‖ 남이 한 친절한 행동 때문에 감사를 표하고 싶어 하는. 감사하는. 고마워하는: *Mona was grateful to Lorenzo for his support.* 모나는 로렌조가 자기를 지지해 준 것에 대해 고마워 했다. —opposite UNGRATEFUL **2 I/we would be grateful if …** used in formal situations or letters to make a request ‖ 요청을 하는 격식차린 상황이나 편지에 쓰여. …해 주신다면 감사하겠습니다: *I would be grateful if you would allow me to visit your school.* 제가 귀교(貴校)를 방문하는 것을 허락해 주신다면 감사하겠습니다.

grat·er /ˈgreɪtə/ n a kitchen tool used for grating (GRATE) food ‖ 음식을 가는 데에 쓰는 주방 기구. 강판 —see picture at GRATE¹

grat·i·fy /ˈgrætəˌfaɪ/ v [T] FORMAL **1 be gratified** to feel pleased and satisfied ‖ 기쁘고 만족하게 느끼다: *I was gratified to hear/know that they like my work.* 그들이 내 작품을 좋아한다는 것을 듣고[알고] 나는 기뻤다. **2 gratify a desire/need etc.** to do something so that you learn or get what you want ‖ 원하는 것을 배우거나 얻기 위해 어떤 일을 하다. 욕구/필요를 만족[충족]시키다 - **gratification** /ˌgrætəfəˈkeɪʃən/ n [U]

grat·i·fy·ing /ˈgrætəˌfaɪ-ɪŋ/ adj FORMAL pleasing and satisfying ‖ 즐거운·만족스러운. 흡족한. 기분 좋은: *It's gratifying to know that we helped Matt get his job.* 매트가 일자리를 구하는 데 우리가 도움이 되었다니 기쁘다.

grat·ing¹ /ˈgreɪtɪŋ/ n a metal frame with BARs across it, used for covering a window or a hole in the ground ‖ 창문에 덧대거나 땅에 난 구멍을 덮기 위해 쓰는

막대기가 가로질러져 있는 금속 틀. 쇠격
자

grating² *adj* a grating sound is
unpleasant and annoying ‖ 소리가 기분
나쁘고 짜증나는. 귀에 거슬리는. 신경을
건드리는: *a grating voice* 거슬리는 목소
리

gra·tis /'grætɪs, 'gra-/ *adj, adv* FORMAL
provided without payment; free ‖ 돈을
지불하지 않고 제공되는[어]. 무료의[로].
거저(의); 공짜의[로].

grat·i·tude /'grætə,tud/ *n* [U] the
feeling of being grateful ‖ 감사하는 마음:
*I would like to express my gratitude to
everyone who helped us.* 나는 우리를 도
와준 모든 분들께 감사의 마음을 전하고
싶다. —opposite INGRATITUDE

gra·tu·i·tous /grə'tuətəs/ *adj* said or
done without a good reason in a way
that offends someone ‖ 타당한 이유 없이
남을 화나게 하는 투로 말하거나 행동하
는. 원인[까닭]없는. 불필요한: *The
gratuitous killing of dolphins must be
stopped.* 이유 없이 돌고래를 죽이는 일은
중단되어야 한다.

gra·tu·i·ty /grə'tuəti/ *n* FORMAL ⇨ TIP¹

grave¹ /greɪv/ *n* **1** the place where a
dead body is buried ‖ 시체가 묻혀 있는
곳. 무덤. 묘소 **2 sb will turn/roll
over in the grave** used in order to say
that someone who is dead would
strongly disapprove of something that is
happening now ‖ 죽은 사람이 현재 일어
나고 있는 일을 강력히 반대하리라고 말하
는 데에 쓰여. 무덤 속에서 탄식할 것이
다: *Mozart would roll over in his grave
if he heard this music.* 모짜르트가 이 음
악을 들었다면 무덤 속에서 탄식했을 것이
다. **3 the grave** LITERARY death ‖ 죽음
—see also **dig your own grave** (DIG¹)

grave² *adj* **1** very serious and worrying
‖ 매우 심각하고 걱정스러운. 심상치[예사
롭지] 않은: *I have grave doubts about
his ability.* 나는 그의 능력에 대해 심히
의심을 하고 있다. **2** looking or sounding
very serious ‖ 매우 진지하게 보이거나 들
리는. 엄숙한. 장엄한: *Dr. Fromm looked
grave. "I have some bad news," he said.*
프롬 박사는 심각해 보였다. "나쁜 소식이
좀 있어."라고 그는 말했다. **– gravely**
adv

grav·el /'grævəl/ *n* [U] small stones
used in order to make a surface for
paths or roads ‖ 길이나 도로의 표면을 만
드는 데에 쓰이는 작은 돌. 자갈. 잔돌 –
graveled *adj*: *a graveled driveway* 자
갈이 깔린 집앞 진입로

grav·el·ly /'grævəli/ *adj* **1** a gravelly

voice sounds low and rough ‖ 목소리가
낮고 거칠게 나는. 목소리가 걸걸한 **2**
covered or mixed with GRAVEL ‖ 자갈로
덮이거나 자갈이 섞인. 자갈이 많은

grave·side /'greɪvsaɪd/ *n* **at the
graveside** beside a grave, especially
when someone is being buried there ‖ 특
히 누군가가 묻혀 있는 무덤 옆에

grave·stone /'greɪvstoʊn/ *n* a stone on
a grave that shows the name of the
dead person and the dates of his/her
birth and death ‖ 죽은 사람의 이름과 출
생·사망 날짜를 알려주는 무덤가에 있는
돌. 묘비

grave·yard /'greɪvyard/ *n* an area of
ground where people are buried, often
near a church ‖ 종종 교회 근처의, 사람들
이 묻혀 있는 구역의 땅. 묘지 —compare
CEMETERY

grav·i·tate /'grævə,teɪt/ *v* [I] **gravitate
to/toward** to be attracted to something
and move toward it, or become involved
with it ‖ 어떤 것에 끌려서 그 쪽으로 움직
이거나 그것과 관계를 맺게 되다. …에 끌
리 다: *Different types of students
gravitate toward different subjects.* 다양
한 부류의 학생들이 제각기 다른 과목에
마음을 끌게 된다.

grav·i·ta·tion /,grævə'teɪʃən/ *n* [U]
TECHNICAL the force that makes two
objects, such as PLANETS, move toward
each other because of their MASS ‖ 행성
등의 두 물체가 그들의 질량 때문에 서로
를 향해 움직이게 하는 힘. 인력. 중력

grav·i·ta·tion·al /,grævə'teɪʃənl/ *adj*
TECHNICAL related to GRAVITY ‖ 중력에 관
계된. 인력[중력]의. 중력 작용의: *the
Earth's gravitational pull* 지구의 인력

grav·i·ty /'grævəti/ *n* [U] **1** TECHNICAL
the force that makes objects fall to the
ground ‖ 물체를 땅에 떨어지게 하는 힘.
중력. 만유인력: *the laws of gravity* 중력
의 법칙 **2** FORMAL the seriousness or
importance of an event, situation etc. ‖
사건·상황 등의 심각성이나 중요성. 진지
함. 중대함

gra·vy /'greɪvi/ *n* [U] **1** SAUCE made
from the juice of cooked meat, flour,
and milk ‖ 육즙·밀가루·우유로 만든 소
스. 그레이비 **2** INFORMAL something good
that is more than you expected to get ‖
얻을 것으로 기대했던 것 이상의 좋은 것.
횡재. 쉽게 번 돈: *Once you've paid your
debts, the rest is gravy.* 일단 빚만 갚으
면 나머지는 횡재다.

gray¹ /greɪ/ *adj* **1** having a color of
black mixed with white, like rain clouds
‖ 비구름처럼 검은색에 흰색이 섞인 색을

가진. 회색의 **2** having gray hair ‖ 회색의 머리칼을 가진. 머리가 희끗희끗한: *Ryan turned gray when he was only 30.* 라이언은 겨우 30살 나이에 머리가 희끗해졌다. **3** if the weather is gray, the sky is full of clouds ‖ 하늘이 구름으로 가득한. 구름이 잔득 낀 **4 a gray area** a subject that is hard to deal with or understand because it does not have clear rules or limits ‖ 규칙이나 한계가 명확하지 않아 다루거나 이해하기 힘든 주제. 중간 영역. 애매한 부분

gray² *n* [U] a color made from black mixed with white ‖ 검정색에다 흰색을 섞은 색깔. 회색: *The suit comes in gray or red.* 그 정장은 회색이나 빨강색이 나온다.

gray³ *v* [I] if someone grays, his/her hair becomes gray ‖ 사람의 머리칼이 회색으로 되다. 희끗희끗해지다.

gray mat·ter /ˌ. ˈ../ *n* [U] INFORMAL your intelligence ‖ 지능. 지성. 두뇌

graze /greɪz/ *v* **1** [I, T] if an animal grazes or you graze it, it eats grass ‖ 동물이 풀을 먹다 또는 풀을 먹이다. 가축을 방목하다: *cattle grazing in the field* 들판에서 풀을 뜯고 있는 소 **2** [T] to touch something lightly while passing it, sometimes damaging it ‖ 때때로 손상을 주기도 하며, 어떤 사물을 지나치며 살짝 건드리다. 가볍게 스쳐 지나가다: *A bullet grazed his arm.* 총알이 그의 팔을 스쳐 지나갔다. **3** [T] to injure yourself by accidentally rubbing against something rough ‖ 우연히 거칠거칠한 사물에 스쳐 부상을 입다. (…에) 닿아[스쳐] 까지다: *Billy grazed his knee on the sidewalk when he fell.* 빌리는 넘어져 보도에 무릎이 까졌다. **– graze** *n*

grease¹ /gris/ *n* [U] **1** a thick oily substance that is put on the moving parts of a car or machine to make it run smoothly ‖ 자동차나 기계의 가동부분을 부드럽게 작동시키기 위해 치는 기름기 있는 끈적한 물질. 그리스. 윤활유 **2** soft fat from animals or vegetables ‖ 동물이나 야채의 부드러운 지방

grease² *v* [T] to put GREASE on something ‖ 어떤 것에 윤활유를 치다

greas·y /ˈgrisi, -zi/ *adj* covered in GREASE or oil, or full of grease ‖ 윤활유나 기름으로 덮인, 또는 윤활유로 꽉 찬. 기름 투성이의. 기름기가 도는. 번들거리는: *greasy food* 기름진 음식 / *greasy hair* 기름기가 번들거리는 머리칼

greasy spoon /ˌ.. ˈ./ *n* INFORMAL an old, slightly dirty restaurant that serves cheap food that is mainly fried (FRY) ‖ 주로 기름에 튀긴 싼 음식을 제공하는 오

래되고 약간 불결한 식당

great /greɪt/ *adj*

1 ▶USEFUL 유용한◀ INFORMAL very useful or suitable for something ‖ 어떤 것에 매우 유용하거나 적합한: *This stuff's great for getting stains out of clothes.* 이 물질은 옷의 얼룩을 빼는 데 유용하다.

2 ▶LARGE 큰◀ very large in size, amount, or degree ‖ 크기·양·정도가 매우 큰. 거대한. 다수[다량]의: *Willis caught a great big fish!* 윌리스가 엄청나게 큰 물고기를 잡았어! / *A great many people died.* 매우 많은 사람들이 죽었다.

3 ▶IMPORTANT 중요한◀ very important, successful, or famous ‖ 매우 중요한[성공적인, 유명한]. 위대한. 주목할 만한: *the great civilizations of the past* 과거의 위대한 문명 / *the greatest movie star of all time* 불멸의 위대한 영화 배우

4 a great deal a lot ‖ 많은: *He's traveled a great deal.* 그는 여행을 많이 했다.

5 (the) Great used in names to mean large or important ‖ 크거나 중요한 것을 의미하는 이름에 쓰여. 대왕. 대제: *Alexander the Great* 알렉산더 대왕 / *the Great Lakes* (미국과 캐나다 사이의) 5대호

6 great-grandmother/great-uncle etc. the grandmother etc. of one of your parents ‖ 부모 중 한 분의 할머니 등. 증조모/종조부

7 great-granddaughter/great-nephew etc. the GRANDDAUGHTER etc. of your child ‖ 자식의 손녀 등. 증손녀/조카(딸)의 아들

8 Greater used before the name of a city to mean the city and its outer areas ‖ 도시와 그 외곽 지역을 의미하는 도시명 앞에 쓰여. 교외를 포함한. 대(大)…: *Greater Seattle* 대(大)시애틀

───── SPOKEN PHRASES ─────

9 very good; excellent ‖ 매우 좋은; 뛰어난: *It's great to see you again!* 다시 만나게 되어 정말 기쁘다! / *We had a great time.* 우리는 아주 멋진 시간을 보냈다.

10 said when you are annoyed and think that something is not good at all ‖ 짜증이 나서 어떤 일이 전혀 좋게 생각되지 않을 때 쓰여: *"Your car won't be ready until next week." "Oh, great!"* "당신 차는 다음 주까지 준비되지 않을 겁니다." "오, 맙소사!"

– greatness *n* [U]

great·ly /'greıtli/ *adv* FORMAL extremely or very much || 대단히 또는 매우 많이. 아주. 훨씬: *The money you lent us was greatly appreciated.* 우리에게 빌려준 돈 대단히 고마웠어요. ✗DON'T SAY "The money was appreciated greatly."✗ "The money was appreciated greatly."라고는 하지 않는다.

greed /grid/ *n* [U] a strong desire to have more money, food, power etc. than you need || 필요 이상의 돈·음식·힘 등을 가지려는 강한 욕구. 탐욕

greed·y /'gridi/ *adj* wanting more money, food, power etc. than you need || 필요 이상의 돈·음식·힘 등을 바라는. 탐욕스러운: *Don't be so greedy – leave some cake for the rest of us!* 그렇게 너무 욕심 부리지 말고 우리한테 케이크 좀 남겨 줘! **– greedily** *adv* **– greediness** *n* [U]

Greek¹ /grik/ *adj* **1** relating to or coming from Greece || 그리스와 관련되거나 그리스 출신의. 그리스(산)의 **2** relating to the Greek language || 그리스어와 관련된. 그리스어의

Greek² *n* **1** [U] the language used in Greece || 그리스에서 쓰이는 언어. 그리스어 **2** someone from Greece || 그리스인

green¹ /grin/ *adj* **1** having the color of grass || 풀색을 가진. 초록색의: *green eyes* 초록색 눈 / *Go on – the light's green.* 어서 가라. 초록색 불이다. **2** covered with grass, trees, bushes etc. || 풀·나무·관목 등으로 덮인. 초목으로 덮인. 신록의. 푸릇푸릇한: *green fields* 푸른 들판 **3** fruit that is green is not yet ready to be eaten || 과일이 아직 먹을 준비가 안 된. 익지 않은. 덜 익은: *green bananas* 덜 익은 바나나 **4** relating to the environment || 환경에 관련된. 환경의: *green issues* 환경 문제 **5 be green with envy** to be very JEALOUS || 몹시 시샘하다. 질투하는 기색을 보이다 **6 give sb/sth the green light** to allow a PROJECT, plan etc. to begin || 기획·계획 등을 시작하도록 허락하다. 해도 좋다는 인가가 나다: *The board just gave us the green light to begin research.* 위원회는 이제 막 우리가 연구를 시작하게 허락했다. **7** INFORMAL young and lacking experience in a job || 젊고 일에 대한 경험이 부족한. 미숙한. 풋내기의: *The trainees are still pretty green.* 견습공들은 아직 경험이 매우 부족하다. **8 have a green thumb** to be good at making plants grow || 식물 재배에 능숙하다. 원예의 재능이 있다

green² *n* **1** [C, U] the color of grass and leaves || 풀과 나뭇잎의 색. 초록색 **2** the smooth flat area of grass around a hole on a GOLF COURSE || 골프 코스에서 홀 주위의 풀이 있는 매끄럽고 평평한 지역. 그린 —see also GREENS

green·back /'grinbæk/ *n* INFORMAL a dollar BILL || 달러 지폐. 미국의 지폐

green bean /'. ., ,. './ *n* a long thin green vegetable that is picked and eaten before the beans inside it grow || 안에 있는 콩이 다 자라기 전에 따서 먹는 길고 가느다란 초록색 야채. 초록막지강낭콩 —see picture at page 944

green card /'. ./ *n* a document that shows that a foreigner can live and work in the US. The card itself is no longer green || 외국인이 미국에서 살며 일할 수 있음을 나타내는 서류로, 이 카드 자체는 이제 녹색은 아님. 영주권

green·er·y /'grinəri/ *n* [U] green leaves and plants, often used as a decoration || 종종 장식용으로 쓰이는 초록색 잎과 식물. 신록의 초목

green·horn /'grinhɔrn/ *n* INFORMAL someone who lacks experience in a job and can be easily deceived || 일에 대한 경험이 부족하고 잘 속는 사람. 풋내기. 초심자. 속기 쉬운 사람

green·house /'grinhaʊs/ *n* a glass building in which you grow plants that need to be protected from the weather || 날씨로부터 보호해 주어야 하는 식물을 재배하는 유리 건물. 온실

greenhouse ef·fect /'. . .,./ *n* **the greenhouse effect** the gradual warming of the air around the Earth as a result of the sun's heat being trapped by POLLUTION || 태양열이 오염 때문에 갇혀서 지구의 대기가 점점 더워지는 현상. 온실 효과. 지구 온난화 현상

greenhouse effect
Sun
sun's rays
greenhouse gases
Earth

green on·ion /,. '../ *n* [C, U] a small white onion with long thin green leaves that you eat raw || 생으로 먹는 길고 얇은 초록색 잎을 가진 작고 흰 파. 골파

greens /grinz/ *n* [plural] **1** vegetables with large green leaves || 큰 초록색 잎을 가진 야채. 푸른 야채: *Eat your greens, they're good for you.* 야채를 먹어라. 야채가 몸에 좋다. **2** leaves and branches used for decoration, especially at Christmas || 특히 크리스마스 때 장식용으로 쓰이는 잎이나 나뭇가지

greet /grit/ *v* [T] **1** to say hello to

greet·ing /ˈgritɪŋ/ n 1 something that you say or do when you meet someone ‖ 어떤 사람을 만날 경우에 하는 말, 또는 행동. 인사: *The two men exchanged greetings.* (=said hello to each other) 두 사람은 서로 인사를 나누었다. 2 **birthday/Christmas etc. greetings** a message saying that you hope someone will be happy and healthy on his/her BIRTHDAY, at Christmas etc. ‖ 남의 생일이나 크리스마스 때 행복하고 건강하기를 바란다고 말하는 전언. 생일/성탄절 인사말

USAGE NOTE greetings

When you see someone you know, you can greet him/her informally by saying "Hi, how are you?" or more formally by saying "Hello, how are you?" You usually answer by saying "Fine, thanks, and you?" Asking "How are you?" is just a greeting. Do not answer this question by talking about your health or any problems you might have, unless you are talking to a good friend.

아는 사람을 만났을 때 격의 없이 "Hi, how are you?"나 보다 격식을 차려서 "Hello, how are you?"라고 인사할 수 있다. 그러면 상대방은 보통 "Fine, thanks, and you?"라고 대답한다. "How are you?"라고 묻는 것은 단순한 인사말이다. 친한 친구에게 말하는 것이 아니라면 자신에게 있을 수 있는 건강이나 어떤 문제에 대한 말로 이 질문에 대답하지 않도록 한다.

greeting card /ˈ.. ˌ./ n a card that you send to someone on his/her BIRTHDAY, at Christmas etc. ‖ 생일·크리스마스 등에 남에게 보내는 카드. 연하장. 생일[크리스마스] 카드

gre·gar·i·ous /grɪˈgɛriəs/ adj someone who is gregarious is friendly and enjoys being with other people; SOCIABLE ‖ 사람이 친절하고 다른 사람들과 함께 있는 것을 즐기는. 사교적인. 집단을 좋아하는; ㊌ sociable: *Kim's very gregarious.* 김씨는 매우 사교적이다.

grem·lin /ˈgrɛmlən/ n an imaginary evil spirit that is blamed for problems in machinery ‖ 기계류에 문제를 일으킨다는 상상 속의 악령. 눈에 보이지 않는 꼬마 마귀

gre·nade /grəˈneɪd/ n a small bomb that can be thrown by hand or fired from a gun ‖ 손으로 던지거나 총으로 발사할 수 있는 작은 폭탄. 수류탄. 척루탄

grew /gru/ v the past tense of GROW ‖ grow의 과거형

grey /greɪ/ adj ➪ GRAY¹

grey·hound /ˈgreɪhaʊnd/ n a thin dog with long legs that can run very fast, often used in races ‖ 흔히 경주에 쓰이는, 매우 빨리 달릴 수 있는 긴 다리를 가진 날씬한 개. 그레이하운드

grid /grɪd/ n 1 a pattern of straight lines that cross each other and form squares ‖ 서로 교차해 있으며 정사각형 형태를 이루는 일직선의 무늬. 격자무늬: *streets organized in a grid system* 바둑판 무늬 형태로 조성된 거리 2 the system of squares with numbers on them that are printed on a map so the exact position of any place can be found ‖ 어떤 장소라도 정확한 위치를 찾을 수 있게 지도상의 격자무늬 위에 숫자들이 인쇄되어 있는 체계. 위선·경선

grid·dle /ˈgrɪdl/ n an iron plate used for cooking food on top of a STOVE ‖ 레인지 상부의 음식을 요리하는 데에 쓰이는 철판. 번철

grid·i·ron /ˈgrɪdaɪən/ n INFORMAL a football field ‖ 미식 축구장

grid·lock /ˈgrɪdlɑk/ n [U] a situation in which the streets are so full of cars that the cars cannot move ‖ 도로가 차들로 꽉 차서 차들이 움직일 수 없는 상태. 교통 정체[마비]

grief /grif/ n [U] 1 extreme sadness, especially because someone you love has died ‖ 특히 자신이 사랑하는 사람이 죽어서 생기는 극단적인 슬픔. 비통. 애통. 큰 슬픔: *His grief was obvious from the way he spoke.* 그가 말하는 것으로 봐서 그가 애통해 한 것이 분명했다. 2 **give sb grief** INFORMAL to say something that annoys or causes trouble for someone ‖ 남을 짜증나게 하거나 남에게 문제를 일으키는 것을 말하다. 남에게 잔소리[꾸중]하다: *My mom's been giving me grief about not helping with my little sister.* 엄마는 누이동생을 도와주지 않는다고 나를 꾸중해 오신다. 3 **come to grief** to not be successful, or to be harmed in an accident ‖ 성공하지 못하다, 또는 사고로 피해를 입다. 실패하다. 재난을 만나다 —

see also **good grief** (GOOD)

griev·ance /'grivəns/ n [C, U] something that you complain about because you think it is unfair ‖ 부당하다고 생각하여 불평하는 것. 불만. 불평: *You ought to follow the correct grievance procedure.* (=the official way to make a complaint) 당신은 올바른 불만 처리 절차를 따라야 합니다.

grieve /griv/ v 1 [I, T] to feel extremely sad, especially because someone you love has died ‖ 특히 사랑하는 사람이 죽어서 극단적인 슬픔을 느끼다. 몹시 슬퍼하다. 애통해 하다 2 [T] FORMAL to make someone feel very unhappy ‖ 남을 매우 불행하게 느끼게 하다. 슬프게[비탄에 잠기게] 하다. 괴롭히다: *It grieves me to see him wasting his talents.* 재능을 낭비하고 있는 그를 보면 슬퍼진다.

griev·ous /'grivəs/ adj FORMAL very serious and likely to be harmful; severe ‖ 매우 심각하여 해로울 것 같은. 중대한. 지독한. 통탄할; 격심한: *a grievous error* 심각한 잘못 – **grievously** adv

grill¹ /grɪl/ v 1 [I, T] if you grill something, or if something grills, you cook it over a fire ‖ 불 위에서 조리하거나 조리되다. 석쇠에 구워지다[굽다] — compare BROIL 2 [T] INFORMAL to ask someone a lot of difficult questions for a long period of time ‖ 남에게 오랜 시간 동안 많은 어려운 질문을 하다. 호되게 심문하다. 다그치다: *Police are grilling the suspect now.* 경찰은 지금 피의자를 심문하고 있다.

grill² n 1 a flat metal frame with BARs across it that can be put over a fire so that food can be cooked on it ‖ 불 위에 놓고 그 위에서 음식을 구울 수 있는, 막대를 가로지른 납작한 금속 틀. 석쇠. 철판. 그릴 2 also **grille** a frame of metal bars used for protecting something such as a window or the front of a car ‖ 유리창이나 차의 앞부분 등을 보호하는 데에 쓰이는 금속 막대 틀. 쇠창살. 자동차의 엔진 방열판

grim /grɪm/ adj 1 making you feel worried and unhappy ‖ 걱정스럽고 불행하게 느끼게 만드는. 기분 나쁜. 섬뜩한: *grim news* 끔찍한 뉴스 / *We were running out of money and things were looking pretty grim.* 우리는 돈이 다 바닥나고 있었고 상황이 무척이나 어두워 보였다. 2 very serious, not smiling ‖ 웃지 않고 매우 심각한. 험상궂은. 엄격한: *a grim-faced judge* 준엄한 표정의 판사 / *their grim determination to reach the*

mountain top (=determination in spite of difficulties or danger) 산 정상에 오르기 위한 그들의 단호한 결의 3 a place that is grim is unattractive and unpleasant ‖ 장소가 끌리지 않고 불쾌한. 형편 없는 – **grimly** adv

grim·ace /'grɪməs/ v [I] to twist your face in an ugly way because you feel pain, do not like something, or are trying to be funny ‖ 고통스러워서[어떤 것을 좋아하지 않아서, 재미있게 하려고] 얼굴을 보기 흉하게 찡그리다. 얼굴을 찌푸리다. 우거지상을 하다: *Theo rolled around on the field grimacing with pain.* 테오는 고통으로 얼굴을 찡그리며 운동장 위에서 대굴대굴 굴렀다. – **grimace** n

grime /graɪm/ n [U] thick black dirt that forms a layer on surfaces ‖ 표면에 층을 형성하는 두꺼운 검은 때. 그을음

grim·y /'graɪmi/ adj covered in thick black dirt ‖ 두꺼운 검은 때로 덮인. 더러워진. 때가 묻은

grin¹ /grɪn/ v -nned, -nning [I] 1 to smile continuously with a very big smile ‖ 계속해서 미소를 크게 짓다. 활짝[방긋] 웃다: *Sally was grinning at Martin from across the room.* 샐리는 방 맞은편에 있는 마틴을 보고 방긋 웃고 있었다. 2 **grin and bear it** INFORMAL to accept a difficult situation without complaining because you cannot change it ‖ 자신의 상황을 바꿀 수 없어서 불평 없이 어려운 상황을 받아들이다. 억지로 웃으며 참다: *It won't be fun, but we'll have to grin and bear it.* 재미는 없겠지만 우리는 억지로 웃으며 참아야 한다.

grin² n a wide smile ‖ 환한 웃음. 방긋[싱글벙글] 웃음

grind¹ /graɪnd/ v **ground, ground, grinding** [T] 1 to crush something such as coffee beans into small pieces or powder, either in a machine or between two hard surfaces ‖ 기계나 두 개의 딱딱한 표면 사이에 넣어 커피 열매 등을 잘게 또는 가루로 부수다. …을 분쇄하다. 잘게 갈다[으깨다] 2 to cut food such as raw meat into small pieces by using a machine ‖ 기계를 사용하여 생고기 등의 음식을 잘게 자르다 3 to rub two hard surfaces against each other, especially to make one of them sharper or smoother ‖ 특히 두 개의 굳은 표면 중 한

grind

pepper mill

면을 더 날카롭게 또는 더 매끈하게 하기 위해 서로 맞대어 문지르다. …을 갈다: *Sam grinds his teeth at night.* 샘은 밤에 잘 때 이를 간다. / *grinding knives* 갈고 있는 칼 **4 grind to a halt** if something grinds to a halt, it slowly stops moving or stops being successful ‖ 천천히 움직임을 멈추거나 성공적인 상태가 끝나다. 끼익 소리를 내며 멈추다: *Traffic slowly ground to a halt.* 차가 천천히 끼익 소리를 내며 멈추었다. / *Production ground to a halt at five of the factories.* 5개의 공장에서 생산이 중단됐다.

grind² *n* [singular] INFORMAL work that makes you tired because it is physically hard or boring ‖ 육체적으로 힘들거나 지루해서 지치게 만드는 일: *It's Monday again – back to the grind.* 다시 힘들고 지루한 일과로 돌아가는 월요일이다.

grind·er /'graɪndɚ/ *n* a machine for GRINDing something ‖ 무엇을 가는 기계. 분쇄기. 연삭기. 숫돌: *a coffee grinder* 커피 분쇄기 / *a knife grinder* 칼 가는 기계

grind·ing /'graɪndɪŋ/ *adj* **grinding poverty** the state of being extremely poor ‖ 매우 가난한 상태. 가혹한 빈곤

grind·stone /'graɪndstoʊn/ *n* a large round stone that is turned like a wheel and is used for making tools sharp ‖ 도구를 날카롭게 만드는 데에 쓰이는 바퀴처럼 돌아가는 크고 둥근 돌. 맷돌. 회전식 숫돌 —see also **keep your nose to the grindstone** (NOSE¹)

grip¹ /grɪp/ *n* **1** [singular] a tight hold on something, or your ability to hold it ‖ 무엇을 단단히 붙잡기, 또는 붙잡는 힘. 꽉 붙잡음[쥠]. 쥐는 힘: *Get a firm grip on the rope, then pull.* 밧줄을 꽉 잡은 다음 당겨라. **2** [singular] power and control over a person, a situation, or your emotions ‖ 사람[상황, 감정]을 장악하는 힘과 통제. 지배력. 통솔력. 통제. 제어: *Come on, Dee, get a grip on yourself!* (=make an effort to control your emotions) 자, 디, 진정해! **3 come/get to grips with** to understand and deal with a difficult problem or situation ‖ 어려운 문제나 상황을 이해하고 대처하다. 직면하다. 맞닥뜨리다. …에 대처하다: *Eric still hasn't come to grips with his drug problem.* 에릭은 자신의 마약 문제에 아직 정면으로 대처하지 않았다. **4 be in the grip of** to be experiencing a very unpleasant situation ‖ 매우 불쾌한 상황을 경험하고 있다. …에 지배되다. …의 곤란한 상황에 있다: *a country in the grip of a bad winter* 추운 겨울 날씨로 꽁꽁 언 나라

grip² *v* **-pped, -pping 1** [I, T] to hold something very tightly ‖ 무엇을 매우 꽉 잡다. 단단히[세게] 붙잡다[쥐다] **2** [T] to have a strong effect on someone or something ‖ 사람이나 사물에 강한 영향력을 미치다. 사로잡다: *Unusually cold weather has gripped the northwest.* 이상 혹한(酷寒)이 서북부를 강타했다. **3** [T] if something grips a surface, it stays on without slipping ‖ 어떤 것이 미끄러지지 않고 그대로 있다. …을 (마찰로) 미끄러지지 않게 하다: *tires that grip the road* 도로에서 미끄러지지 않고 멈추는 타이어

gripe¹ /graɪp/ *v* [I] INFORMAL to complain about something continuously and in an annoying way ‖ 어떤 일에 관해 계속하여 짜증스럽게 불평하다. (…에 대해) 투덜대다: *Now what's Pete griping about?* 피트는 지금 무엇 때문에 투덜대는 거야?

gripe² *n* something that you keep complaining about ‖ 계속 불평하고 있는 것. 불평. 푸념: *The students' main gripe is the dorm food.* 학생들의 주요 불평거리는 기숙사의 음식에 관한 것이다.

grip·ping /'grɪpɪŋ/ *adj* very exciting and interesting ‖ 상당한 흥미와 관심이 있는. 주의[관심]를 끄는: *a gripping story* 매우 재미있는 이야기

gris·ly /'grɪzli/ *adj* extremely unpleasant because death or violence is involved ‖ 죽음이나 폭력이 관련되어서 몹시 불쾌한. 무서운. 험악한: *a grisly murder* 소름 끼치는 살인

grist /grɪst/ *n* **grist for the mill** something that is useful in a particular situation ‖ 특정한 상황에 유용한 것. …감 [거리]: *a baseball player whose love life is grist for the gossip mill* (=it gives people something to talk about) 이성 관계로 얘깃거리가 되는 야구 선수

gris·tle /'grɪsəl/ *n* [U] the part of a piece of meat that is not soft enough to eat ‖ 먹을 수 있을 만큼 연하지 않은 고기의 부분. 연골. 고기 속의 심

grit¹ /grɪt/ *n* [U] **1** very small pieces of stone ‖ 매우 작은 돌조각. 모래알 **2** INFORMAL determination and courage ‖ 결의·용기. 기개. 담력. 배짱: *He's a guy who plays ball with a lot of grit.* 그는 대담하게 야구를 하는 사람이다. – **gritty** *adj*

grit² *v* **grit your teeth** to use all your determination to continue doing something in spite of pain or difficulties

‖ 고통이나 역경에도 불구하고 어떤 일을 해나가려고 굳은 결의를 하다. 이를 악물고 견디다: *Just grit your teeth; the worst is almost over.* 이를 악물고 견뎌라. 최악의 상황은 거의 끝났다.

grits /grɪts/ *n* [plural] crushed grain that is cooked and often eaten for breakfast ‖ 요리해서 종종 아침 식사로 먹는 빻은 곡물

griz·zly bear /'grɪzli bɛr/, **grizzly** *n* a large brown bear that lives in the northwest of North America ‖ 북미 북서부에 사는 큰 갈색 곰. 회색 큰곰

groan /groʊn/ *v* [I] **1** to make a long deep sound because you are in pain, or are not happy about something ‖ 아프거나 어떤 것에 대해 기쁘지 않아 길고 낮은 소리를 내다. 신음하다. 불평하다: *Captain Marsh was holding his arm and groaning.* 마쉬 선장은 자신의 팔을 움켜잡고서 신음하고 있었다. / *Scott told a terrible joke, and everyone groaned.* 스콧이 형편없는 농담을 해서 모든 사람이 투덜거렸다. **2** to bend from carrying a heavy load ‖ 무거운 짐을 싣고 있어서 구부러지다. 휘어지다: *shelves groaning under hundreds of books* 수백 권의 책의 무게로 내려 앉은 선반 – **groan** *n* : *Loud groans came from the crowd.* 떠들썩한 불평이 군중 속에서 터져 나왔다.

gro·cer /'groʊsə, -ʃə/ *n* someone who owns a GROCERY STORE or is in charge of one ‖ 식료 잡화점을 소유하거나 관리하는 사람. 식료품 장수. 식료 잡화 상인

gro·cer·ies /'groʊsəriz, 'groʊʃriz/ *n* [plural] the food or other goods sold in a GROCERY STORE ‖ 식료 잡화점에서 팔리는 음식이나 기타 상품. 식료 잡화류

gro·cer·y store /'groʊsri ˌstɔr, -ʃri-/, **grocery** *n* a store that sells food and other things used in the home ‖ 가정에서 쓰는 음식이나 기타 물건을 파는 가게. 식료 잡화점

grog·gy /'grɑgi/ *adj* weak and unable to think clearly, because you are ill or tired ‖ 아프거나 지쳐서 약하고 명확하게 생각할 수 없는. 비틀거리는. 휘청거리는. 그로기의: *Bill was groggy after studying all night.* 빌은 밤새도록 공부한 후에 완전히 녹초가 되었다.

groin /grɔɪn/ *n* the part of your body where your legs join at the front ‖ 다리가 합쳐지는 신체의 앞부분. 서혜부(鼠蹊部). 사타구니 —see picture at BODY

groom¹ /grum/ *v* **1** [I, T] to take care of your appearance by keeping your hair and clothes clean and neat ‖ 머리나 옷을 깨끗하고 단정히 해서 용모를 신경 쓰다.

복장을 가다듬다. 깔끔하게 다듬다[손질하다]: *a well-groomed/badly-groomed young man* 몸단장을 잘 한[안 한] 젊은 남자 **2** [T] to prepare someone for an important job or position by training him/her ‖ 남을 훈련시켜 중요한 일이나 지위에 맞게 대비시키다. …을 …하도록 기르다: *Sharon's being groomed to take over the business.* 샤론은 그 사업을 떠맡기 위해 교육을 받고 있다. **3** [T] to take care of animals by cleaning and brushing them ‖ 동물을 씻기고 빗질하여 돌보다. …을 손질[솔질]하다 – **grooming** *n* [U]

groom² *n* **1** a man at the time he gets married, or just after he is married ‖ 결혼할 때나 결혼한 직후의 남자. 신랑 **2** someone whose job is to take care of horses ‖ 말을 돌보는 직업인. 말 사육 담당자. 마부

groove /gruv/ *n* **1** a thin line cut into a surface to hold something, or to make something move or flow where you want it to ‖ 어떤 것을 담기 위해, 또는 자신이 원하는 곳으로 움직이거나 흘러가게 하기 위해 표면에다 새긴 얇은 줄. 홈: *Plant the seeds in grooves about a foot apart.* 한 걸음 정도씩 띄워서 홈에다 씨앗을 심어라. **2** [singular] INFORMAL the way things should be done, so that it seems easy and natural ‖ 응당 일이 쉽고 자연스러워 보이도록 행해야 하는 방식. 관례. 관행: *It will take the players a while to get back in the groove.* 선수들이 최고조의 상태로 되돌아가기 위해서 잠시 시간이 걸릴 것이다.

groov·y /'gruvi/ *adj* INFORMAL a word meaning very good, fashionable, or fun, used especially in the 1960s ‖ 특히 1960년대에 쓰였던, 매우 좋은[최신식의, 재미있는]을 뜻하는 말. 멋진. 근사한. 매력적인

grope /groʊp/ *v* **1** [I] to try to find something you cannot see, using your hands ‖ 손을 사용해서 보이지 않는 것을 찾으려고 하다. 손으로 더듬다: *She groped in the dark for the flashlight.* 그녀는 어둠 속에서 손을 더듬어 손전등을 찾았다. **2 grope your way along/ across etc.** to go somewhere by feeling the way with your hands because you cannot see ‖ 볼 수 없어서 손으로 더듬어 어딘가로 가다 **3 grope for sth** to try hard to find the right words to say, or the right solution to a problem ‖ 적당한 말이나 문제의 정확한 해결책을 찾기 위해 애쓰다. 모색하다 **4** [T] INFORMAL to touch someone's body in a sexual way ‖

성적(性的)으로 남의 몸을 더듬다 -
grope n

gross¹ /grous/ adj 1 SPOKEN very
unpleasant to look at or think about ‖ 보
거나 생각하기에 매우 불쾌한. 기분 나쁜.
메스꺼운: *There was one really gross
part in the movie.* 영화에서 정말 역겨운
장면이 한 군데 있었다. / *"Yesterday the
dog threw up on the rug." "Oh, gross."*
"어제 그 개가 양탄자에 토했어." "아, 역
겨워." 2 a gross amount of money is the
total amount before any tax or costs
have been taken away ‖ 금액이 세금이나
비용을 제하기 전의 총액인: *gross
income/sales* 총수입[총 매상고] —
compare NET³ 3 a gross weight is the
total weight of something, including its
wrapping ‖ 무게가 포장을 포함한 총량의
4 wrong and unacceptable in a way that
is very extreme. ‖ 지나치게 잘못되어 받
아들일 수 없는. 극심한: *gross
inequalities in pay* 임금의 극심한 불평등
– **grossly** adv

gross² v [T] to earn an amount as a
total profit or as wages, before tax has
been taken away ‖ 세금을 제하기 전에
…의 총수익이나 총임금을 벌다: *the
year's biggest grossing movie* 당해 가장
큰 수익을 올린 영화

gross sb ↔ **out** phr v [T] SPOKEN to
make someone feel sick because of
something you say or do ‖ 말하거나 행동
한 것 때문에 남의 속을 울렁거리게 하다.
역겹게 하다: *Don't talk about your
operation! It grosses me out.* 너의 수술
에 대해 말하지 마! 속이 울렁거려.

gross na·tion·al prod·uct /ˌ. ˌ...
ˈ../ n [singular] ⇨ GNP

gro·tesque /grouˈtɛsk/ adj ugly or
strange in a way that is not natural or
makes you uncomfortable ‖ 부자연스럽
거나 불편하게 할 정도로 추하거나 이상
한. 그로테스크풍의. 괴상한: *drawings of
grotesque monsters* 기괴한 괴물 그림 –
grotesquely adv

grot·to /ˈgrɑtou/ n a small natural CAVE,
or one that someone has made ‖ 천연 또
는 인공의 작은 동굴

grouch¹ /grautʃ/ n INFORMAL someone
who is always complaining ‖ 항상 불평하
는 사람. 투덜대는 사람

grouch² v [I] INFORMAL to complain in a
slightly angry way ‖ 다소 화내는 투로 불
평하다. 토라지다

grouch·y /ˈgrautʃi/ adj feeling annoyed
and complaining a lot, especially
because you are tired ‖ 특히 피곤해서 짜
증스럽고 매우 불만스러운. 토라진. 언짢

ground¹ /graund/ n **the ground a)** the
surface of the earth ‖ 지구 표면: *The
ground is too wet to sit on.* 땅이 너무 젖
어서 앉을 수가 없다. **b)** the soil on and
under the surface of the earth ‖ 지구 표
면 위·아래의 토양. 토지. 땅: *The
ground's too hard to plant trees now.* 땅
이 지금 너무 굳어서 나무를 심을 수 없다.
1 ▶KNOWLEDGE 지식◀ [U] an area of
knowledge, ideas, experience etc. ‖ 지
식·사고·경험 등의 분야. 영역: *Scientists
are breaking new ground
(=discovering new ideas) in cancer
research.* 과학자들은 암 연구에 새로운
차원을 열어가고 있다.
2 ▶OPINIONS 의견◀ [U] the opinions
you have about something that people
disagree about ‖ 사람들과 일치하지 않
는. 어떤 것에 대한 개인적 견해: *There
has to be a way we can find some
common ground.* (=something that
everyone can agree about) 우리는 어떤
합일점을 찾아낼 방법이 있어야만 한다. /
*It isn't likely that the Mayor will give
ground.* (=change his/her opinions) 시장
이 의견을 바꿀 것 같지 않다.
3 **parade/sports/hunting etc. ground**
a piece of land used for a special
purpose ‖ 특별한 목적에 쓰이는 땅. 연병
장/운동장/사냥터
4 **get off the ground** to start being
successful ‖ 성공적으로 출발하다: *His
company hasn't really gotten off the
ground yet.* 사실상 그의 회사는 아직 제
대로 출범하지 못했다.
5 **gain/lose ground** to become more or
less successful or popular ‖ 보다 성공하
거나 더 많은 인기를 얻다 또는 보다 성공
하지 못하거나 인기를 잃게 되다. 진보하
다. 인기를 얻다/쇠퇴하다. 인기를 잃다:
*Republicans have been gaining ground
in recent months.* 공화당원들은 최근 몇
달 새 지지세를 얻어 오고 있다.
6 **hold/stand your ground** to refuse to
change your opinion in spite of
opposition ‖ 반대에도 불구하고 자신의 의
견을 바꾸지 않다. 입장을 지키다
7 ▶WIRE 전선◀ [singular] a wire that
connects a piece of electrical equipment
to the ground for safety ‖ 안전을 위해 전
기 기구를 땅에 연결한 선. 접지(선) —
see also GROUNDS, UNDERGROUND

USAGE NOTE ground

Use **on the ground** to say where
something is: *Sue's dropped her glove*

on the ground. Use **to the ground** to talk about downward movement: *Eddie was knocked to the ground.*

on the ground는 물건의 위치를 말하는 데에 쓰인다: 수는 장갑을 땅바닥에 떨어뜨렸다. **to the ground**는 아래쪽으로의 움직임을 말하는 데에 쓰인다: 에디는 땅바닥에 쓰러졌다.

ground² *v* [T] **1** to stop an aircraft or pilot from flying ‖ 비행기나 조종사의 비행을 막다. 이륙을 못하게 하다: *All planes are grounded due to snow.* 모든 항공기가 눈 때문에 이륙하지 못했다. **2 be grounded in** to be based on something ‖ 어떤 것에 근거하다: *a way of life grounded in your beliefs* 당신의 신념에 입각한 생활 방식 **3** INFORMAL to stop a child from going out with his/her friends as a punishment for doing something wrong ‖ 잘못을 저지른 벌로 아이에게 친구와의 외출을 금하다: *If you stay out that late again, you'll be grounded for a week.* 또 이렇게 늦게 들어 오면 일주일 동안 외출금지 된다. **4** to make a piece of electrical equipment safe by connecting it to the ground with a wire ‖ 전선을 땅에 연결시켜 전기 제품을 안전하게 하다. 접지(接地)하다

ground³ *adj* ground coffee, pepper etc. has been crushed into small pieces ‖ 커피·후추 등이 작은 조각으로 부숴진. 빻은. 가루로 만든

ground⁴ *v* the past tense and PAST PARTICIPLE of GRIND ‖ grind의 과거·과거분사형

ground beef /ˌ. './ *n* ⇨ HAMBURGER

ground·break·ing /'. ˌ../ *adj* involving new discoveries or new methods ‖ 새로운 발견이나 방법에 관한. 획기적인: *groundbreaking research in physics* 물리학의 획기적 연구

ground crew /'. ./ *n* the group of people who work at an airport and take care of the aircraft ‖ 공항에서 근무하며 항공기를 돌보는 일단의 사람들. 지상 근무원. 정비사

ground floor /ˌ. './ *n* **1** the part of a building that is on the same level as the ground ‖ 지면과 같은 높이에 있는 건물의 부분. 1층 —see picture at ATTIC **2 be/get in on the ground floor** to become involved in a plan or business activity from the beginning ‖ 계획 또는 사업 활동에 처음부터 관여하다. 유리한 입장을 차지하다

ground·hog /'graʊndˌhɔg/ *n* a small North American animal that has thick brown fur and lives in holes in the ground; WOODCHUCK ‖ 땅 속의 굴에 살며 빽빽한 갈색 털을 지닌 북미의 작은 동물 . 마멋 ; 畏 woodchuck

groundhog

Groundhog Day /'.. ˌ./ *n* February 2; according to American stories, the first day of the year that a GROUNDHOG comes out of its hole. If it sees its shadow, there will be six more weeks of winter; if it does not, good weather will come early ‖ 2월 2일. 성촉절(聖燭節); 미국의 동화에 따르면, 그 해 마멋이 굴에서 나오는 첫 날이다. 만일 마멋이 자신의 그림자를 보면 겨울이 6주 이상 지속되고 그림자를 보지 못한다면 좋은 날씨가 일찍 찾아온다고 한다

ground·less /'graʊndlɪs/ *adj* without any reason ‖ 어떤 까닭도 없는. 근거 없는: *groundless fears* 이유 없는 두려움 – **groundlessly** *adv*

ground rule /'. ./ *n* a rule or principle on which future action or behavior should be based ‖ 앞으로의 활동이나 품행의 근거가 되는 규칙이나 원칙. 행동의 기본 원칙: *First, they had to set the ground rules for the debate.* 먼저 그들은 토론을 위한 기본 원칙들을 세워야 했다.

grounds /graʊndz/ *n* [plural] **1** a large area of land or sea that is used for a particular purpose ‖ 특정 용도로 쓰이는 넓은 땅이나 바다: *burial grounds* 묘지 / *fishing grounds* 낚시터 **2** the land or gardens around a building ‖ 건물 주변의 땅이나 정원 **3** reasons for thinking that something is true or for doing something ‖ 어떤 것을 사실로 생각하거나 행하는 까닭: *Mark's drinking was grounds for divorce.* 마크의 음주가 이혼의 사유였다. **4** the small pieces of something that sink to the bottom of a liquid ‖ 액체의 바닥에 가라앉는 어떤 것의 작은 조각. 찌꺼기: *coffee grounds* 커피 찌꺼기

ground·swell /'graʊndswɛl/ *n* **1 a groundswell of support/enthusiasm** a sudden increase in how strongly people feel about something ‖ 어떤 것에 대하여 사람들이 느끼는 강도의 급격한 증대. 지지/열정의 고조 **2** [singular, U] the strong movement of the sea that continues after a storm or strong winds ‖ 폭풍이나 강풍 뒤에 계속되는 바다의 격렬한 움직임. 너울

ground·work /ˈgraundwɚk/ n [U] important work that has to take place before another activity can be successful ‖ 또 다른 작업을 성공적으로 수행하기에 앞서 해야 하는 중요한 작업. 기초[사전] 작업: *The groundwork for next year's conference will start soon.* 내년 회담을 위한 기초 작업을 곧 시작할 것이다.

group¹ /grup/ n **1** several people or things that are all together in the same place ‖ 같은 곳에 함께 있는 여러 사람들이나 사물들. 떼: *Everyone please get into groups of four.* 모두 4명씩 조를 짜 주세요. **2** several people or things that are connected with each other in some way ‖ 어떤 측면에서 서로 연관된 몇몇 사람이나 사물. 그룹. 단체: *a group of Native American writers* 아메리카 원주민 작가들의 모임 / *One woman in our group goes to night school.* 우리 모임의 여자 한 명이 야간학교를 다닌다. ✗DON'T SAY "One woman of our group."✗ "one woman of our group"이라고는 하지 않는다. **3** several companies that all have the same owner ‖ 주인이 동일한 몇 개의 기업. (기업) 그룹: *a book publishing group* 서적 출판 그룹 **4** a number of musicians or singers who perform together, usually playing popular music ‖ 보통 대중음악을 연주하는, 함께 공연하는 일단의 음악가나 가수. 그룹: *a rock group* 록 그룹

group² v [I, T] to come together to make a group, or to arrange people or things in a group ‖ 그룹을 결성하기 위해 모이다, 또는 사람들이나 사물들을 하나의 그룹으로 묶다. 무리를 짓다. 무리로 만들다: *The visitors grouped themselves around the statue.* 방문객들이 그 동상 주변에 모여 들었다. / *Birds can be grouped into several types.* 새는 몇 가지 종류로 그룹을 지을 수 있다.

group·ie /ˈgrupi/ n INFORMAL someone who follows ROCK musicians to their concerts, hoping to meet them ‖ 록 음악가를 만나기 바라면서 콘서트에 따라다니는 사람. 열광적인 록 팬

group·ing /ˈgrupɪŋ/ n a set of people, things, or organizations that have the same interests, qualities, or features ‖ 관심사[속성, 특징]가 같은 일단의 사람[사물, 단체]. 그룹: *social groupings* 사회 단체

group ther·a·py /ˌ. ˈ.../ n [U] a method of treating people with emotional or PSYCHOLOGICAL problems by bringing them together in groups to talk about their problems ‖ 정서적이나 심리적인 문제가 있는 사람들을 그룹에 참석시켜 자신들의 문제에 대해 대화를 나누게 함으로써 치료하는 방법. 집단 요법

grouse¹ /graus/ v [I] INFORMAL to complain ‖ 불평하다: *Tourists were grousing about the long lines.* 관광객들은 길게 줄서서 기다려야 하는 것을 불평하고 있었다.

grouse² n [C, U] a small fat bird that is hunted for food and sport, or the meat from this bird ‖ 식용 및 스포츠용으로 사냥하는 작고 통통한 새, 또는 그 고기. 뇌조(의 고기)

grove /grouv/ n **1** an area of land planted with a particular type of tree ‖ 특정한 종류의 나무를 심은 지역. 과수원: *a lemon grove* 레몬 과수원 **2** a small group of trees ‖ 작은 숲

grov·el /ˈgrɑvəl, ˈgrʌ-/ v [I] **1** to behave with too much respect toward someone because you want him/her to help or forgive you ‖ 도움이나 용서를 받고 싶어서 남에게 지나치게 정중하게 행동하다. 비굴하게 굴다: *I've apologized, I've even groveled to him.* 나는 사과했고 게다가 그에게 비굴하게 굴기까지 했다. **2** to lie or move flat on the ground because you are afraid of someone, or as a way of obeying ‖ 남을 두려워하여, 또는 복종의 방법으로 땅에 납작 엎드리거나 기다: *a dog groveling in front of its owner* 주인 앞에 엎드리고 있는 개

grow /grou/ v grew, grown, growing **1** ▶DEVELOP 발전하다◀ [I, T] to develop and become bigger or longer over time, or to make something do this ‖ 시간이 흘러서 발육하여 더 커지거나 길어지다, 또는 어떤 것을 커지거나 길어지게 하다: *Jamie's grown two inches this year.* 제이미는 올해 2인치가 자랐다. / *Are you growing a beard?* 너 수염 기르고 있니? / *Your hair's grown really long.* 네 머리카락 정말 길게 자랐구나.
2 ▶PLANTS 식물◀ [I, T] to exist and develop in a natural way, or to help plants do this ‖ 자연스럽게 생겨서 발육하다, 또는 식물이 발육하도록 돕다. 자라다. 기르다: *Not many plants can grow in the far north.* 극북(極北)에서는 많은 식물이 자라지 못한다. / *We're trying to grow roses this year.* 올해 우리는 장미를 재배하려 한다.
3 ▶INCREASE 증가하다◀ [I] to increase in amount, size, or degree ‖ 양[규모, 정도]이 증가하다: *A growing number of students are dropping out of college.* 대학을 중퇴하는 학생수가 증가하고 있다. /

a growing business 성장 산업

4 ▶BECOME ···이 되다◀ [linking verb] to become old, hot, worse etc. over a period of time ‖ 시간이 흘러서 늙고 뜨거워지며 악화되다: *We're growing older, Margaret.* 마가렛, 우리는 점차 늙어가고 있어.

5 grow to like/fear/respect etc. to gradually start to have an opinion or feeling about someone or something ‖ 사람이나 사물에 대하여 차츰 어떤 견해나 감정을 갖기 시작하다. 좋아하게 되다/두려워하게 되다/존경하게 되다: *I'm growing to like Dallas more.* 나는 차츰 댈러스가 더 좋아지고 있다.

6 ▶IMPROVE 향상되다◀ [I] to improve in ability or character ‖ 능력이나 특성이 향상되다: *Beth's really growing as a singer.* 베스는 가수로 잘 성장해가고 있다.

7 ▶BUSINESS 사업◀ [T] to make part of a business become larger or more successful ‖ 사업을 더욱 확장시키거나 성장시키다

grow apart *phr v* [I] if two people grow apart, their relationship becomes less close ‖ 두 사람의 관계가 가깝지 않게 되다. 멀어지다

grow into sb/sth *v* [T] **1** to develop over time and become a particular type of person or thing ‖ 시간이 흘러서 특정한 부류의 사람이나 사물이 되다. 성장하여 ···이 되다: *Gene's grown into a handsome young man.* 진은 멋진 젊은이로 성장했다. **2** if a child grows into clothes, s/he becomes big enough to wear them ‖ 아이가 옷이 맞을 만큼 충분히 자라다

grow on sb *phr v* [T] to gradually become more liked by someone ‖ 점점 남의 마음에 들게 되다. 점점 좋아하게 되다: *Their music's strange, but after a while it will grows on you.* 그들의 음악은 이상하지만 조금 있으면 점점 좋아하게 될 거야.

grow out of sth *phr v* [T] **1** to become too big to wear your old clothes ‖ 예전 옷을 입을 수 없을 만큼 성장하다 **2** to stop doing something as you get older ‖ 나이를 먹으면서 어떤 것을 하지 않다: *Sarah still sucks her thumb, but she'll grow out of it.* 사라는 아직 엄지손가락을 빨지만 자라면 하지 않을 것이다.

grow up *phr v* [I] **1** to develop from being a child to being an adult ‖ 아이에서 어른으로 성장하다: *I grew up in San Diego.* 나는 샌디에고에서 자랐다. **2 grow up!** SPOKEN said in order to tell

someone to behave more like an adult ‖ 남에게 보다 어른답게 행동하라고 말하는 데에 쓰여. 철 좀 들어라!

grow·er /ˈɡroʊɚ/ *n* a person or company that grows fruit, vegetables etc. in order to sell them ‖ 판매하려고 과일·야채 등을 재배하는 사람이나 기업. 재배자

grow·ing pains /ˈ.. ,./ *n* [plural] problems and difficulties that start at the beginning of a new activity, for example starting a business ‖ 사업 시작 등의 새로운 활동의 초기에 나타나는 문제와 어려움. (사업 등의) 초기의 고통

growl /ɡraʊl/ *v* **1** [I] to make a deep angry sound ‖ 나지막하게 화난 소리를 내다. 으르렁거리다: *dogs growling at a visitor* 방문객에게 으르렁대고 있는 개들 **2** [I, T] to say something in a low angry voice ‖ 화를 내며 낮은 목소리로 무엇을 말하다. 딱딱거리다: *"Go away!" he growled.* "가 버려!"라고 그는 쏘아붙였다. **– growl** *n*

grown¹ /ɡroʊn/ *adj* **grown man/woman** a phrase meaning an adult, used when you think someone is not behaving in an adult way ‖ 사람이 어른답게 굴지 못한다고 여겨질 때 쓰는 어른을 뜻하는 말: *I've never seen a grown man act like that!* 나는 저따위로 구는 어른은 한 번도 본 적이 없어!

grown² *v* the PAST PARTICIPLE of GROW ‖ grow의 과거 분사형

grown-up¹ /ˈ. ./ *n* a word meaning an adult, used especially by or to children ‖ 특히 아이들이나 어른이 아이들에게 쓰는, 어른을 뜻하는 말: *Ask a grown-up to help you.* 어른께 도와달라고 부탁을 드려라.

grown-up² *adj* fully developed as an adult ‖ 완전히 성인으로 자란. 성숙한, 어른이 된: *a grown-up son* 장성한 아들

growth /ɡroʊθ/ *n* **1** [singular, U] an increase or development in size, quality, amount, or importance ‖ 규모[질, 양, 중요도]의 증가나 발전. 성장: *Vitamins are necessary for healthy growth.* 비타민은 건강하게 성장하는 데에 필수적이다. / *the growth of modern technology* 현대 기술의 발전 / *population growth* 인구 증가 / *There's a growth of interest in African music.* 아프리카 음악에 대한 관심이 커지고 있다. **2** [U] the development of someone's character, intelligence, or emotions ‖ 사람의 인격[지성, 감성]의 발달. 성숙. 성장: *a job that provides opportunities for personal growth* 개인의 발전을 위한 기회를 제공하는 직업 **3**

something that grows in your body or on your skin, caused by a disease ‖ 병으로 인해, 몸이나 피부에 증식하는 것. 증식물. 종양 **4** [C, U] something that is growing ‖ 성장하는 것: *New growth is showing on the plants.* 그 식물이 새롭게 성장하는 것이 보인다.

grub¹ /grʌb/ *n* **1** [U] INFORMAL food ‖ 음식 **2** an insect when it is in the form of a soft white WORM ‖ 연약한 흰 벌레의 모습을 하고 있을 때의 곤충. 유충. 애벌레

grub² *v* **-bbed, -bbing** [I] INFORMAL to dig in order to get something ‖ 어떤 것을 얻기 위해 파다. 파헤치다: *pigs grubbing for roots* 흙을 파헤쳐 뿌리를 캐는 돼지들

grub·by /'grʌbi/ *adj* dirty ‖ 더러운: *grubby hands* 더러운 손

grudge¹ /grʌdʒ/ *n* a feeling of anger or dislike you have for someone who has harmed you ‖ 해를 입힌 사람에 대한 분노나 혐오의 감정. 원한. 악의: *Diane doesn't hold grudges.* (=stay angry with people) 다이앤은 원한을 담아두지 않는다. / *Aunt Alice bore a grudge against him for 25 years.* 앨리스 숙모는 25년 동안 그에게 원망을 품고 있었다.

grudge² *v* [T] ⇨ BEGRUDGE

grudg·ing /'grʌdʒɪŋ/ *adj* done or given without wanting to do so ‖ 그렇게 하고 싶지 않으면서 행하거나 주는. 마지못해 하는: *their grudging acceptance of the changes* 변화에 대한 그들의 마지못해 하는 수용

gru·el /'gruəl/ *n* [U] thin OATMEAL that was eaten in past times by poor or sick people ‖ 예전에 가난하거나 아픈 사람들이 먹었던 묽은 오트밀. 묽은 죽

gru·el·ing /'gruəlɪŋ/ *adj* very tiring ‖ 매우 피곤한. 지독한: *a grueling climb* 힘든 산행

grue·some /'grusəm/ *adj* very unpleasant to look at, and usually involving death or injury ‖ 보통 죽음이나 부상에 관련하여, 매우 보기 흉한. 무시무시한. 섬뜩한: *a gruesome accident* 끔찍한 사고

gruff /grʌf/ *adj* unfriendly or annoyed ‖ 무뚝뚝하거나 화가 난. 거친. 퉁명스러운: *a gruff answer* 퉁명스런 대답 **– gruffly** *adj*

grum·ble /'grʌmbəl/ *v* [I] to complain in a quiet but slightly angry way ‖ 나지막하지만 다소 화난 투로 불평하다. 투덜거리다: *Their school bus driver used to grumble about the noise.* 그들의 스쿨버스 기사는 (차 안에서) 시끄럽게 떠드는 것에 대해 불평하곤 했다.

grump·y /'grʌmpi/ *adj* having a bad

temper and tending to complain ‖ 성미가 고약하고 불평을 잘 하는. 심술을 잘 부리는 **– grumpily** *adv*

grunge /grʌndʒ/ *n* **1** INFORMAL dirt and GREASE; GRIME ‖ 더럽고 미끈미끈한 것. 지저분한 것; ㉤ grime: *What's all this grunge in the bathtub?* 욕조 안에 이 더럽고 미끈거리는 건 다 뭐지? **2** a style of music and fashion popular with young people in the early 1990s ‖ 1990년대 초 젊은이들에게 유행한 음악과 패션 스타일. 그런지 음악[패션]

grun·gy /'grʌndʒi/ *adj* INFORMAL dirty and sometimes smelling bad ‖ 더럽고 때때로 악취가 나는. 더러운. 불결한

grunt /grʌnt/ *v* **1** [I, T] to make short sounds or say only a few words, when you do not want to talk ‖ 말하기 싫을 때 외마디 소리를 내거나 몇 마디만 하다: *He just grunted hello and kept walking.* 그는 한 마디 인사만 하고 계속 걷기만 했다. **2** [I] to make short low sounds deep in your throat, like the sounds a pig makes ‖ 돼지가 내는 소리처럼, 목구멍 깊숙이에서 짧고 낮은 소리를 내다. 꿀꿀거리다 **– grunt** *n*

G-string /'. ./ *n* very small underwear that does not cover the BUTTOCKS ‖ 엉덩이를 가리지 않는 매우 작은 속옷

gua·ca·mo·le /ˌgwɑkə'mouleɪ/ *n* [U] a Mexican dish made with crushed AVOCADOs ‖ 으깬 아보카도로 만든 멕시코 음식

guar·an·tee¹ /ˌgærən'ti/ *v* [T] **1** to promise that something will happen or be done ‖ 어떤 일이 발생하거나 수행될 것을 약속하다: *We guarantee to provide you with the most up-to-date market information.* 우리는 당신에게 최신 시장 정보를 제공할 것을 약속합니다. **2** to make a formal written promise to repair or replace a product if it has a problem within a specific time ‖ 특정 기간 안에 하자가 발생하면 제품의 수리나 교환을 해 줄 것을 공식적으로 서면 보증하다: *All stereo parts are guaranteed against failure for a year.* 모든 스테레오 부품은 고장에 대하여 1년간 보증된다. **3** to make it certain that something will happen ‖ 어떤 것이 일어나리라는 것을 확실히 하다. 보장하다: *An education doesn't guarantee a good job.* 교육이 좋은 직업을 보장하지 않는다. **4 be guaranteed to do sth** to be certain to behave, work, or happen in a particular way ‖ 특정한 방식으로 행동하거나 일하거나, 또는 일어날 것이 확실하다. 반드시 …하다: *Buying something new is* *guaranteed to make you feel better.* 새 물건을 구입하면 틀림없이 네 기분이 좋아 질 것이다.

guarantee² *n* **1** a formal written promise to repair or replace a product without charging, if it has a problem within a specific time after you buy it ‖ 물품 구입 후 특정 기간 내에 하자가 생기 면 비용 없이 수리하거나 교환하겠다는 공 식적 서면 약속. 보증(서): *a two-year guarantee* 2년간의 보증서 / *Is the microwave still under guarantee?* (=protected by a guarantee) 그 전자레인 지는 아직 보증서에 의해 보호됩니까? **2** a formal promise that something will be done or will happen ‖ 어떤 것이 수행되 거나 발생될 것이라는 공적인 약속: *There's no guarantee that the books will be delivered this week.* (=it is not at all sure to happen) 금주에 책이 배달된다 는 보장이 없다.

guar·an·tor /ˌgærənˈtɔr, ˈgærəntɚ/ *n* LAW someone who promises that s/he will pay for something if the person who should pay for it does not ‖ 어떤 것에 대 한 지급 의무가 있는 사람이 지급하지 않 으면 대신 지급할 것을 약속하는 사람. 보 증인

guar·an·ty /ˈgærənti/ *n* LAW a formal promise, especially of payment ‖ 특히 지 불에 관련한 공적 약속. 보증

guard¹ /gɑrd/ *n*

1 ▶PROTECTOR 호위자◀ someone whose job is to guard people, places, or objects so that they are not attacked or stolen ‖ 사람[장소, 물건]이 공격받거나 도난당하지 않게 보호하는 직업인. 경비 원. 감시인: *security guards at the bank* 은행의 청원 경찰

2 ▶IN A PRISON 교도소에서◀ someone whose job is to prevent prisoners from escaping ‖ 죄수가 탈옥하는 것을 막는 직 업인. 교도관. 간수

3 be on guard/stand guard to be responsible for guarding a place or person for a specific time ‖ 특정 시간 동 안 장소나 사람을 지켜야 할 책임을 지다. 보초를 서다. 경호하다: *Hogan was on guard until midnight.* 호건은 자정까지 보초를 섰다.

4 catch/take sb off guard to surprise someone by doing something that s/he is not ready to deal with ‖ 무엇을 하여 대 처할 준비가 되어 있지 않은 사람을 놀라 게 하다. …의 방심을 틈타다. 허를 찌르 다: *The question caught the senator off guard.* 그 질문은 그 상원 의원의 허를 찔 렀다.

5 ▶EQUIPMENT 장비◀ something that covers and protects someone or something ‖ 사람이나 사물을 막아서 보호 하는 것. 방호구: *a hockey player's face guard* 하키 선수의 안면 보호대

6 be under (armed) guard to be guarded by a group of people with weapons ‖ 일단의 무기 소지자들의 경호 를 받다. 무장 호위를 받다

7 sb's guard the state of being ready to defend yourself against an attack ‖ 공격 에 맞서 자신을 방어할 수 있는 준비를 한 상태. 방어 자세: *She's not going to let her guard down.* (=relax because a threat is gone) 그녀는 긴장을 늦추지 않 으려 한다.

8 ▶SPORTS 스포츠◀ **a)** one of two players in basketball whose main job is to defend his/her BASKET ‖ 농구에서 골대 를 지키는 주임무를 띤 두 선수 중 한 사 람. 가드 —see picture on page 946 **b)** one of two football players who play on either side of the CENTER ‖ 미식축구에서 센터의 양 측면에서 경기를 하는 두 선수 중 한 사람. 가드

guard² *v* [T] to protect someone or something from being attacked or stolen, or to prevent a prisoner from escaping ‖ 공격이나 도난을 당하지 않도 록 사람이나 사물을 보호하다, 또는 죄수 의 탈옥을 막다. 보호하다. 감시하다: *They have a dog to guard their house.* 그들은 집 지키는 개를 키운다.

guard against sth *phr v* [T] to try to prevent something from happening by being careful ‖ 주의를 기울여 어떤 것이 발생하는 것을 막기 위해 애쓰다: *Exercise can help guard against a number of serious illnesses.* 운동은 여러 심각한 질 병을 예방하는 데 도움이 된다.

guard·ed /ˈgɑrdɪd/ *adj* careful not to say too much ‖ 말을 지나치게 많이 하지 않고 조심스러운. 신중한: *a guarded answer* 신중한 대답

guard·i·an /ˈgɑrdiən/ *n* **1** someone who is legally responsible for someone else, especially a child ‖ 다른 사람, 특히 어린이에 대한 법적 책임이 있는 사람. 보 호자. 감시인 **2** FORMAL a person or organization that tries to protect laws, moral principles, traditional ways of doing things etc. ‖ 법·윤리·무엇을 하는 전통적 방식 등을 수호하려는 사람이나 기 관. 수호자 **– guardianship** *n* [U]

guardian an·gel /ˌ... ˈ../ *n* an imaginary good spirit who protects a person ‖ 사람을 지켜주는 상상 속의 착한 천사. 수호천사

guard·rail /'gard-reil/ *n* a long metal BAR that keeps cars or people from falling over the edge of a road, boat, or high structure ‖ 도로[배, 고층 건물]의 가장자리로 자동차나 사람이 떨어지는 것을 방지하기 위한 긴 금속 막대기. 난간. 보조 레일

gua·va /'gwavə/ *n* a small tropical fruit with pink flesh and many seeds inside ‖ 분홍색 과육 속에 씨가 많이 들어 있는 작은 열대 과일. 구아바

gu·ber·na·to·ri·al /,gubənə'tɔriəl/ *adj* FORMAL relating to the position of being a GOVERNOR ‖ 주지사직과 관련된. 주지사의

guer·ril·la, guerilla /gə'rɪlə/ *n* a member of an independent fighting group that fights for political reasons and attacks the enemy in small groups ‖ 정치적 이유로 투쟁하며 소규모로 적을 공격하는 독자적인 전투 집단의 일원. 게릴라병: *guerrilla warfare* 게릴라전

guess¹ /gɛs/ *v* **1** [I, T] **a)** to try to answer a question or make a judgment without knowing all the facts ‖ 질문에 대답하려고, 또는 모든 사실을 알지 못한 채 판단하려고 애쓰다. 추측하다: *"How old is Ginny's son?" "I'd say 25, but I'm just guessing."* "지니의 아들은 몇 살이죠?" "25살일걸요. 그런데 단지 추측일 뿐이에요." **b)** to get the right answer to something in this way ‖ 추측하여 무엇의 정답을 얻다. 알아맞히다: *"Don't tell me; you got the job." "How did you guess?"* "당찮은 소리 마라. 너 직장 잡았잖아." "어떻게 알았니?" **2 keep sb guessing** to not tell someone what is going to happen next ‖ 다음에 일어날 일을 남에게 알리지 않다. …에게 기대를 갖게 하다

<hr>

SPOKEN PHRASES

3 I guess a) said when you suppose that something is true or likely ‖ 무엇이 사실이거나 가능성이 있을 때 쓰여: *His light's on, so I guess he's still up.* 불이 켜진 것으로 보아 그가 아직 깨어 있는 것 같다. **b)** used in order to show that you know about a situation because someone else has told you about it ‖ 다른 사람이 이미 말해 주어서 그 상황을 안다는 것을 나타내는 데에 쓰여: *I wasn't there, but I guess Mr. Radkin yelled at Jeannie.* 나는 그곳에 없었지만 라드킨 씨가 지니에게 고함친 것은 알아. **4 I guess so/not** used in order to say yes or no when you are not very sure ‖ 그다지 확신이 없을 때 예나 아니오로 말하는 데에 쓰

여: *"She wasn't happy?" "I guess not."* "그녀는 행복하지 않았습니까?" "그랬던 것 같아요." **5 guess what/ you'll never guess** said when you are about to tell someone something that will surprise him/her ‖ 놀랄 만한 일을 남에게 말하려 할 때에 쓰여: *You'll never guess what I bought!* 내가 뭘 샀는지 넌 절대로 모를걸!

guess² *n* **1** an attempt to guess something ‖ 어떤 것을 추측하려는 시도. 추측. 억측: *Just take a guess.* 추측해 봐! **2** an opinion you get by guessing ‖ 추측으로 생긴 견해. 짐작: *My guess is (that) Don won't come.* 내 짐작에 돈은 오지 않을 것 같다. **3 be anybody's guess** to be something that no one knows ‖ 어떤 것을 아무도 모르다: *Where he disappeared to was anybody's guess.* 그가 어디로 사라졌는지 아무도 몰랐다. **4 your guess is as good as mine** SPOKEN said in order to tell someone that you do not know any more than s/he does about something ‖ 무엇에 대하여 상대방이 알고 있는 이상은 알지 못한다고 말하는 데에 쓰여. 나도 잘 모르겠다

guess·ti·mate /'gɛstəmɪt/ *n* INFORMAL an attempt to judge a quantity by guessing it ‖ 추측에 의해 양을 판단하려는 시도. 추정. 어림짐작 **– guesstimate** /'gɛstə,meɪt/ *v* [I, T]

guess·work /'gɛswək/ *n* [U] a way of trying to find the answer to something by guessing ‖ 추측으로 무엇에 대한 답을 찾으려는 방법. 짐작. 추측: *Many of Carey's price estimates are based on guesswork.* 캐리의 추정으로 가격을 산정하는 일이 많다.

guest¹ /gɛst/ *n* **1** someone who is visiting or staying in someone else's home because s/he has been invited ‖ 초대받아 남의 집에 방문하거나 체류하는 사람. 손님: *We're having guests this weekend.* 우리는 이번 주말에 손님을 맞이할 예정이다. / *a dinner guest* 만찬 손님 **2** someone who is paying to stay in a hotel ‖ 돈을 내고 호텔에 묵는 사람. 투숙객 **3** someone who is invited to a restaurant, theater, club etc. by someone else who pays for him/her ‖ 대금을 지불하는 다른 사람에 의하여 식당·극장·클럽 등에 초대받은 사람: *Now, you and Anna are our guests this evening, all right?* 자, 당신과 애너는 오늘 저녁 우리 손님이에요, 알았죠? **4 be my guest** SPOKEN said when giving someone permission to do what s/he has asked to do ‖ 요청한 대로 하라고 남에게 허락을 할 때에 쓰여. 그러세요: *"Could I use your phone?" "Be my guest."* "전화기 좀 사용할 수 있을까요?" "그러세요."

guest² *adj* **1 guest speaker/artist/star** someone famous who is invited to speak on a subject or take part in a performance ‖ 어떤 주제에 관해 연설하거나 공연에 참여하도록 초대된 유명 인사. 초청 연사/예술인/스타 **2 for guests to use** ‖ 손님용의: *the guest room* 객실 / *guest towels* 손님용 수건

guff /gʌf/ *n* [U] SPOKEN stupid or annoying behavior or talk ‖ 어리석거나 짜증스러운 행동이나 말. 허튼 짓[소리]: *Don't take any guff from those guys.* 저자들의 어떤 허튼 언행도 받아들이지 마라.

guf·faw /gəˈfɔ/ *v* [I] to laugh loudly ‖ 큰 소리로 웃다. 깔깔 웃다 **– guffaw** *n*

guid·ance /ˈgaɪdns/ *n* [U] helpful advice about work, education etc. ‖ 일·교육 등에 대한 유익한 조언. 안내. 지도: *Francis had worked at a magazine, and gave me some guidance.* 프란시스는 잡지사에서 일했었기 때문에 나에게 약간의 조언을 해줬다.

guidance coun·sel·or /ˈ.. ˌ.../ *n* someone who works in a school to give advice to students about what subjects to study, and to help them with personal problems ‖ 학생들에게 공부해야 할 과목에 대한 조언을 해주고 개인적인 문제를 지닌 학생들을 도와주는 교직원. 상담 교사

guide¹ /gaɪd/ *n* **1** someone who shows you the way to a place, especially someone whose job is to show a place to tourists ‖ 특히 관광객에게 장소를 안내하는 직업을 가진, 어떤 장소로 가는 길을 안내하는 사람. 안내인. 가이드: *a tour guide* 여행 가이드[안내인] **2** a book that provides information about a particular subject or explains how to do something ‖ 특정 주제에 관한 정보를 제공하거나 어떤 것을 하는 방법을 설명하는 책. 안내서. 입문서: *a guide for new parents* 초보 부모를 위한 입문서 **3** something or someone that helps you decide what to do or how to do it ‖ 할 것이나 하는 방법을 결정하는 데에 도움을 주는 사물이나 사람: *A friend's experience isn't always the best guide for you.* 친구의 경험이 너에게 항상 최고의 길잡이는 아니다

guide² *v* [T] **1** to take someone to a place that you know very well and show it to him/her ‖ 매우 잘 알고 있는 곳에 남을 데려가 보여주다. 안내하다: *He offered to guide us around/through the city.* 그는 우리에게 도시 구경을 시켜주겠고 제안했다. **2** to help someone go somewhere or do something correctly ‖ 남이 정확히 어딘가로 가거나 무엇을 하도록 도와주다. 인도[유도]하다: *The pilot guided the plane to a safe landing.* 조종사는 비행기의 안전한 착륙을 유도했다. **3** to strongly influence someone ‖ 남에게 강하게 영향을 끼치다: *We hope you'll be guided by our advice.* 우리는 당신이 우리의 조언대로 따르기를 바랍니다. **—see usage note at** LEAD¹

guide·book /ˈgaɪdbʊk/ *n* a special book about a city or country that gives details about the place and its history ‖ 도시나 국가의 지리·역사에 대해 상술한 특별한 책. 여행안내서. 가이드북

guide·lines /ˈgaɪdlaɪnz/ *n* [plural] rules or instructions about the best way to do something ‖ 어떤 것을 하는 최선의 방법에 관한 규칙이나 지침. 가이드라인

guild /gɪld/ *n* an organization of people who share the same interests, skills, or profession ‖ 동일한 관심사[기술, 직업]를 공유하는 사람들의 기구. 조합. 협회: *the writers' guild* 작가 협회

guile /gaɪl/ *n* [U] FORMAL the use of smart but dishonest methods to deceive someone ‖ 명석하지만 다른 사람을 속이는 부정한 방법을 씀. 교활. 엉큼함

guile·less /ˈgaɪl-lɪs/ *adj* behaving in an honest way, without trying to deceive people ‖ 사람들을 속이려 하지 않고 정직하게 행동하는. 성실한. 간계가 없는

guil·lo·tine /ˈgɪləˌtin, ˈgiə-, ˌgɪəˈtin/ *n* a piece of equipment that was used in past times to cut off the heads of criminals ‖ 예전에 죄인의 목을 베기 위하여 쓰인 도구. 길로틴. 단두대 **– guillotine** *v* [T]

guilt /gɪlt/ *n* [U] **1** a strong feeling of shame and sadness that you have when you know or believe you have done something wrong ‖ 잘못했다는 것을 깨닫거나 확신할 때 느끼는 몹시 부끄럽고 슬픈 느낌. 가책: *Marta felt a sense of guilt about leaving home.* 마르타는 집을 떠나는 데 대해 죄책감을 느꼈다. **2 guilt trip** INFORMAL a feeling of guilt about something, when this is unreasonable ‖ 어떤 것에 대한 이치에 맞지 않는 자책감: *I wish my parents would stop laying a guilt trip on me about not going to college.* (=making me feel guilty) 나는 부모님이 내게 대학에 가지 않은 것에 대한 자책감이 들게 하지 않았으면 좋겠다. **3** the fact of having broken an official law or moral rule ‖ 공법이나 도덕 규범을 어긴 사실. 범죄: *The jury was sure of the defendant's guilt.* 배심원은 피고인의 죄를 확신했다. **4** the state of being responsible for something bad that has happened; FAULT ‖ 벌어진 나쁜 일에 대한 책임이 있는 상태. 책임; (유) fault: *Ron admitted that the guilt was his.* 론은 책임이 자신에게 있음을 인정했다. — opposite INNOCENCE

guilt·rid·den /ˈ. ˌ../ *adj* feeling so guilty about something that you cannot think about anything else ‖ 다른 것을 생각할 수 없을 만큼 무엇에 대하여 죄책감을 느끼는. 죄의식에 찬

guilt·y /ˈgɪlti/ *adj* **1** ashamed and sad because you know you have done something wrong ‖ 잘못을 저지른 것을 깨달아 부끄럽고 슬픈. 가책 받는. 죄의식이 드는: *I feel guilty about not inviting her to the party.* 나는 그녀를 파티에 초대하지 않은 것에 대하여 죄책감이 든다. **2** having done something that is a crime ‖ 죄를 범한: *He was found guilty of fraud.* 그는 사기죄로 판명되었다. — **guiltily** *adv* — **guiltiness** *n* [U] — opposite INNOCENT

USAGE NOTE guilty, ashamed, and **embarrassed**

Use **guilty** to say that someone is unhappy because s/he has done something that has harmed someone else: *He felt guilty about always working so late.* Use **ashamed** to say that someone feels disappointed with himself/herself about doing something that is wrong or unacceptable: *She was ashamed of having told her mother a lie.* Use **embarrassed** to say that someone is upset because s/he has done something that makes him/her seem silly: *He was embarrassed about the way he acted at the party.*

guilty는 사람이 남에게 해를 입히는 짓을 했기 때문에 불행하다는 것을 말하는 데에 쓰인다: 그는 늘 늦도록 일하는 것에 죄책감을 느꼈다. **ashamed**는 잘못된 것이나 마음에 들지 않는 일을 하는 데 대하여 스스로에게 느끼는 실망을 말하는 데에 쓰인다: 그녀는 어머니께 거짓말을 한 것이 부끄러웠다. **embarrassed**는 어리석어 보이는 짓을 하여 당혹스럽다고 말하는 데에 쓰인다: 그는 파티에서 자신이 한 행동에 난처해했다.

---

guin·ea pig /ˈgɪni ˌpɪg/ *n* **1** a small animal like a rat with fur, short ears, and no tail, that is often kept as a pet ‖ 종종 애완동물로 키우며, 털이 있고 귀는 짧으며 꼬리가 없는 쥐처럼 생긴 작은 동물. 기니피그 **2** INFORMAL someone who is used in a test to see how successful or safe a new product, system etc. is ‖ 새로운 상품·시스템 등이 얼마나 성공적이거나 안전한지 알아보기 위한 시험에 이용되는 사람. 시험 재료(가 되는 사람)

guise /gaɪz/ *n* FORMAL the way someone or something seems to be, which is meant to hide the truth ‖ 진실을 감추기 위해 의도된 사람이나 사물의 겉으로 보이는 면. 외관. 겉모양: *In/under the guise of being protectors, the army took over the government.* 보호자임을 가장하여 군은 정부를 접수했다.

gui·tar /gɪˈtɑr/ *n* a musical instrument with six strings, a long neck, and a wooden body, which you play by PLUCKing the strings ‖ 현을 퉁겨서 연주하는, 6개의 현·긴 목·목제 몸통으로 된 악기. 기타 — **guitarist** *n*

gulch /gʌltʃ/ *n* a narrow deep valley formed by flowing water, but usually dry ‖ 보통 물이 말라 있는, 흐르는 물에 의해 형성된 좁고 깊은 계곡. (깊고 험한) 작은 협곡

gulf /gʌlf/ *n* **1** a large area of ocean partly enclosed by land ‖ 육지로 둘러싸인 큰 바다의 일부분. 만(灣): *the Gulf of Mexico* 멕시코만 **2** a great difference and lack of understanding between two groups of people ‖ 두 집단의 사람들간의 큰 격차 및 이해 부족: *the wide gulf between the rich and the poor* 빈부의 현격한 격차 **3** a deep hollow place in the Earth's surface ‖ 지표면의 깊고 우묵한 장소. 깊은 틈

gulf
the Gulf of Mexico

gull /gʌl/ *n* ⇨ SEAGULL

gul·let /ˈgʌlɪt/ *n* INFORMAL ⇨ ESOPHAGUS

gul·li·ble /ˈgʌləbəl/ *adj* too ready to believe what other people say, and therefore easy to trick ‖ 다른 사람들의 말을 너무 쉽게 믿어 잘 속는. 속기 쉬운. 잘 넘어가는 — **gullibility** /ˌgʌləˈbɪləti/ *n* [U]

gul·ly /ˈgʌli/ *n* **1** a small narrow valley, formed by a lot of rain flowing down the side of a hill ‖ 언덕의 경사면으로 흘러내리는 많은 빗물로 인해 형성된 작고 좁은

계곡. 작은 협곡 **2** a deep DITCH ‖ 깊은 도랑

gulp¹ /gʌlp/ v **1** [T] also **gulp down** to swallow something quickly ‖ 재빨리 무엇을 삼키다. 꿀꺽 삼키다: *She gulped her tea and ran to catch the bus.* 그녀는 급히 차를 마시고 버스를 타기 위해 뛰었다. **2** [T] also **gulp in** to quickly take in large breaths of air ‖ 빠르고 크게 숨을 들이쉬다: *Steve leaned on the car and gulped in the night air.* 스티브는 차에 기대서 밤공기를 들이마셨다. **3** [I] to swallow suddenly because you are surprised or nervous ‖ 놀라거나 초조하여 침을 꿀꺽 삼키다: *Shula read the test questions, and gulped.* 슐라는 시험 문제를 읽고 초조함을 삼켰다[억눌렀다].

gulp sth ↔ **back** *phr v* [T] to stop yourself from expressing your feelings ‖ 감정 표현을 억제하다: *The boy was trying to gulp back his tears.* 소년은 눈물을 참느라 애쓰고 있었다.

gulp² n an act of swallowing something quickly ‖ 무엇을 재빨리 삼키는 행동. 꿀꺽 삼킴: *He drank his beer in one gulp.* 그는 단숨에 맥주를 들이켰다.

gum¹ /gʌm/ n **1** a sweet substance that you CHEW for a long time but do not swallow ‖ 오랫동안 씹지만 삼키지는 않는 달콤한 물질. 껌 **2** [C usually plural] the pink part inside your mouth that holds your teeth ‖ 이를 지탱하고 있는 입안의 핑크빛 부위. 잇몸 **3** [U] a sticky substance in the stems of some trees ‖ 어떤 나무 줄기에 들어 있는 끈끈한 물질. 수지 – **gummy** adj

gum² v

gum sth ↔ **up** *phr v* [T] INFORMAL to prevent something from working correctly by covering it with a sticky substance ‖ 어떤 것에 끈끈한 물질을 발라서 제대로 작동하지 않게 하다. 못 쓰게 하다: *How did this lock get so gummed up?* 이 자물쇠가 어쩌다 이렇게 못 쓰게 되었지?

gum·bo /ˈgʌmboʊ/ n [U] a thick soup made with meat, fish, and particular vegetables ‖ 고기·생선·특정한 야채로 만든 진한 수프. 검보스튜

gum·drop /ˈgʌmdrɑp/ n a small CHEWY candy ‖ 씹어 먹는 작은 사탕. 작은 젤리 과자

gump·tion /ˈgʌmpʃən/ n [U] INFORMAL the ability and determination to decide what needs to be done and to do it ‖ 해야 할 일을 결정하고 그것을 하려는 능력과 결심. 결단력: *At least Kathy has the gumption to get what she wants.* 적어도

캐시는 그녀가 원하는 것을 얻을 수 있는 결단력이 있다.

gun¹ /gʌn/ n **1** a weapon from which bullets or SHELLs (=LARGE METAL OBJECTS) are fired ‖ 탄알이나 포탄이 발사되는 무기. 총포 **2 big/top gun** INFORMAL someone who controls an organization, or who is the most successful person in a group ‖ 조직을 통제하거나 집단에서 가장 성공한 사람. 거물. 중요 인물 **3** a tool used in order to send out a liquid by pressure ‖ 압력으로 액체를 분사하는 데에 사용되는 도구. 분무기: *a spray gun* 분무기 **4 hired gun** INFORMAL someone who is paid to shoot someone else or to protect someone ‖ 돈을 받고 남을 저격하거나 경호하는 사람. 고용된 살인 청부업자[보디가드] —see also **jump the gun** (JUMP¹), **stick to your guns** (STICK¹)

gun² v **1** [T] INFORMAL to make the engine of a car go very fast by pressing the ACCELERATOR very hard ‖ 액셀러레이터를 매우 세게 밟아 차의 엔진을 가속시키다. 〈엔진을〉 고속 회전시키다. 속도를 갑자기 올리다 **2 be/go gunning for sb** to look for someone in order to criticize or harm him/her ‖ 비난하거나 해치기 위해 어떤 사람을 찾다: *After the meeting, Ken went gunning for Mike.* 모임을 가진 후 켄은 마이크를 찾아다니고 있었다.

gun sb ↔ **down** *phr v* [T] to shoot someone who cannot defend himself/herself ‖ 스스로를 방어할 수 없는 사람에게 총격을 가하다. 사살하다: *Bobby Kennedy was gunned down in a hotel.* 보비 케네디는 호텔에서 총격당했다.

gun·boat /ˈgʌnboʊt/ n a small military ship that is used near the coast ‖ 해안 근처에서 운항되는 소형 군함. (소형) 포함(砲艦)

gun·fire /ˈgʌnfaɪər/ n [U] the repeated firing of guns, or the noise made by this ‖ 연속 사격, 또는 연속 사격으로 인한 소음. 발포. 총성

gung-ho /ˌgʌŋ ˈhoʊ/ adj INFORMAL very eager, or too eager ‖ 열성적이거나 열광적인: *a gung-ho attitude* 열성적 태도

gunk /gʌŋk/ n INFORMAL a substance that is sticky and dirty ‖ 진득진득하고 더러운 물질. 진득진득[끈적끈적]한 것. 오물: *There's a bunch of gunk clogging the drain.* 한 덩어리의 오물이 하수관을 막고 있다.

gun·man /ˈgʌnmən/ n a criminal who uses a gun ‖ 총을 사용하는 범죄자. 무장 범인

gun·ner /ˈgʌnər/ n a soldier, sailor etc. whose job is to aim or fire a large gun ‖

큰 총포를 조준하거나 발포하는 것이 임무인 육군·해군 등의 병사. 조준수. 사수

gun·ny·sack /'gʌni,sæk/ n a large BURLAP bag used for storing and sending grain, coffee etc. ‖ 곡물·커피 등을 저장·운송하는 데에 쓰이는 큰 삼베 자루. 마대

gun·point /'gʌnpɔɪnt/ n at gunpoint while threatening people with a gun, or being threatened with a gun ‖ 총으로 위협하여, 또는 총으로 위협당하여: a bank robbed at gunpoint 총으로 위협받아 털린 은행

gun·pow·der /'gʌn,paʊdɚ/ n [U] an explosive substance in the form of powder ‖ 가루 형태의 폭발 물질. 화약

gun·run·ning /'gʌn,rʌnɪŋ/ n [U] the activity of taking guns into a country secretly and illegally ‖ 비밀리에 불법적으로 한 국가에 총포를 반입하는 행위. 총포의 밀수입 **– gunrunner** n

gun·shot /'gʌnʃɑt/ n 1 the sound made when a gun is fired ‖ 총포가 발사될 때 나는 소리. 총성. 포성 2 [U] the bullets fired from a gun ‖ 총포에서 발사된 탄환: a gunshot wound 총상

gup·py /'gʌpi/ n a small brightly colored tropical fish ‖ 밝은 색의 작은 열대어. 거피

gur·gle /'gɚgəl/ v [I] to make a sound like flowing water ‖ 물이 흐르는 듯한 소리를 내다. 꼴깍하는 소리를 내다: a baby gurgling in her crib 요람에서 꼴깍꼴깍하는 소리를 내는 아기 **– gurgling** adj **– gurgle** n

gu·ru /'guru, 'gʊru/ n 1 INFORMAL someone who knows a lot about a particular subject, and to whom people go for advice ‖ 특정 분야에 대해 많이 알아 사람들이 조언을 구하는 사람. 권위자. 전문가: a computer guru 컴퓨터 전문가 2 a Hindu religious teacher or leader ‖ 힌두교의 스승이나 지도자

gush¹ /gʌʃ/ v [I, T] 1 to flow or pour out quickly in large quantities ‖ 대량으로 세차게 흐르거나 쏟아져 나오다. 액체가[를] 세차게 분출하다[분출시키다]: water gushing out of a pipe 파이프에서 쏟아져 나오는 물 / a wound gushing blood 피가 솟구치는 상처 2 to express praise so strongly that people think you are not sincere ‖ 사람들이 진실하지 않다고 여길 정도로 극구 칭찬하다. (과장하여) 지껄여 대다

gush² n 1 a large quantity of liquid that suddenly flows from somewhere ‖ 어딘가에서 갑자기 흘러나오는 대량의 액체: a gush of oil 분출하는 기름 2 a gush of

relief/anxiety etc. a sudden feeling or expression of emotion ‖ 감정의 갑작스런 느낌이나 표현. 밀려오는 안도감/불안함의 분출

gush·er /'gʌʃɚ/ n INFORMAL an oil WELL where the flow of oil is suddenly so strong that it shoots into the air ‖ 기름의 유출이 갑자기 세차져 공중으로 솟구치는 유정. 분유정(噴油井)

gush·y /'gʌʃi/ adj too full of praise for someone or something, so that people think you are not sincere ‖ 사람들이 진실하지 않다고 여길 정도로 사람이나 사물에 대한 칭찬이 지나친. 감정을 과장하여 표현하는

gust¹ /gʌst/ n a sudden strong movement of wind, air, snow etc. ‖ 바람·공기·눈 등의 갑작스런 강한 움직임: A gust of wind blew our tent over. 돌풍이 불어 우리 텐트를 뒤집어 놓았다. **– gusty** adj —see usage note at WEATHER

gust² v [I] if wind gusts, it blows strongly with sudden short movements ‖ 바람이 일순간 급격히 불다

gus·to /'gʌstoʊ/ n [U] with gusto with eager enjoyment ‖ 아주 즐겁게: a band playing with gusto 홍겹게 연주하는 밴드

gut¹ /gʌt/ n INFORMAL 1 gut reaction/feeling etc. a reaction or feeling that you are sure is right, although you cannot give a reason for it ‖ 근거를 제시할 수는 없지만 옳다고 확신하는 반응이나 느낌. 직관적 반응/직관: My gut reaction is that it's a bad idea. 내 직관으로는 그것은 나쁜 생각이다. 2 the tube through which food passes from your stomach ‖ 위에서 음식물이 통과하는 관. 창자 —see also GUTS

gut² v **-tted, -tting** [T] 1 to completely destroy the inside of a building, especially by fire ‖ 특히 불이 나서 건물 내부를 완전히 파괴하다 2 to remove the organs from inside a fish or animal in order to prepare it for cooking ‖ 요리를 준비하기 위해 생선이나 동물의 내장을 제거하다

guts /gʌts/ n [plural] INFORMAL 1 the courage and determination you need to do something difficult or unpleasant ‖ 어렵거나 불쾌한 일을 하기 위해 필요한 용기와 결심. 배짱: Dickie didn't have the guts to say what he really thought. 디키는 자기가 정말로 생각하고 있는 것을 말할 용기가 없었다. 2 the organs inside your body ‖ 신체 내부 기관. 내장 3 hate sb's guts to hate someone very much ‖ 남을 몹시 증오하다

gut·sy /'gʌtsi/ adj INFORMAL brave and

determined ‖ 용감하고 결단력 있는: *a gutsy speech* 용기 있는 발언

gut·ter /'gʌtə/ *n* **1** the low place along the edge of a road, where water collects and flows away ‖ 물이 모여 흘러가는 길가를 따라 나 있는 낮은 부분. 도랑 **2** an open pipe at the edge of a roof for collecting and carrying away rain water ‖ 빗물을 모아 내보내는 지붕 가장자리의 뚫어진 관. 홈통 **3 the gutter** the bad social conditions of the lowest and poorest people in society ‖ 사회에서 가장 낮고 가난한 사람들의 좋지 않은 사회적 여건. 빈민가. 밑바닥 사회

gut·ter·al /'gʌtərəl/ *adj* a gutteral sound is produced deep in the throat ‖ 소리가 목 깊은 곳에서 나는. 후두음인

guy /gaɪ/ *n* **1** INFORMAL a man ‖ 남자. 녀석: *I'm going out with a few guys from work tonight.* 오늘 밤 직장 동료들과 함께 외출할 겁니다. / *Some guy wanted to talk to you.* 어떤 사내가 당신과 이야기하고 싶어했다. **2 you guys/those guys** SPOKEN said when talking to or about two or more people, both men and women ‖ 남성·여성에 상관없이 두 사람 이상을 언급할 때 쓰여: *We'll see you guys Sunday, okay?* 우리는 너희들을 일요일에 만날게, 알겠니? —compare Y'ALL

guz·zle /'gʌzəl/ *v* [I, T] INFORMAL to drink a lot of something eagerly and quickly ‖ 무엇을 갈망하여 빨리 많이 마시다. 폭음하다: *Marge was guzzling martinis because they were free.* 마지는 마티니가 공짜라 마구 들이켜고 있었다.

guz·zler /'gʌzlə/ *n* INFORMAL **gas guzzler** a car that uses too much gas ‖ 연료가 너무 많이 소비되는 차

gym /dʒɪm/ *n* **1** a special hall or room that has equipment for doing physical exercise ‖ 육체적 운동을 하기 위한 장비를 구비한 특별한 홀이나 방. 체육관 **2** [U] sports and exercises done indoors, especially as a school subject ‖ 특히, 학교 교과 과목으로 실내에서 하는 스포츠·운동. 체육: *gym class* 체육 수업

gym·na·si·um /dʒɪm'neɪziəm/ *n* ⇨ GYM

gym·nast /'dʒɪmnæst, -nəst/ *n* someone who does GYMNASTICS as a sport ‖ 운동으로 체조를 하는 사람. 체조 선수

gym·nas·tics /dʒɪm'næstɪks/ *n* [plural] **1** a sport involving physical exercises and movements that need skill and control, and that are often performed in competitions ‖ 종종 시합으로 하며, 기술과 컨트롤이 필요한 육체적 운동과 동작을 수반하는 스포츠. 체조 **2 mental/intellectual gymnastics** very quick and skillful thinking ‖ 매우 빠르고 능란하게 생각하기. 정신/지적 훈련

gy·ne·col·o·gy /ˌgaɪnə'kɑlədʒi/ *n* [U] the study and treatment of medical conditions and illnesses affecting only women ‖ 여성에게만 일어나는 의학적 증세와 질병에 관한 연구 및 치료. 부인과(의학) **– gynecologist** *n* **– gynecological** /ˌgaɪnəkə'lɑdʒɪkəl/ *adj*

gyp /dʒɪp/ *v* **-pped, -pping** [T] SPOKEN to trick or cheat someone ‖ 남을 기만하거나 속이다: *I got gypped out of $50!* 나는 50달러를 사취당했다!

gyp·sy /'dʒɪpsi/ *n* **1** a member of a group of people originally from northern India, who usually live and travel around in CARAVANS ‖ 보통 대상(隊商)으로 떠돌아다니면서 생활하는, 본래 북인도 출신의 일단의 사람들의 한 구성원. 집시 **2** someone who does not like to stay in the same place for a long time ‖ 오랫동안 한 곳에 머무는 것을 좋아하지 않는 사람. 방랑벽이 있는 사람

gy·rate /'dʒaɪreɪt/ *v* [I] to turn around fast in circles ‖ 원 모양으로 빠르게 회전하다. 선회하다: *dancers gyrating wildly* 열광적으로 빙빙 돌며 춤추고 있는 무희들 **– gyration** /dʒaɪ'reɪʃən/ *n* [C, U]

gy·ro·scope /'dʒaɪrəˌskoʊp/, **gy·ro** /'dʒaɪroʊ/ *n* a heavy wheel that spins inside a frame, and is used for keeping ships and aircraft steady ‖ 배·항공기를 일정하게 유지하기 위해 쓰이는 틀 내를 회전하는 육중한 바퀴 모양의 장치. 자이로스코프. 회전의(回轉儀)

Hh

H, h /eɪtʃ/ the eighth letter of the English alphabet ‖ 영어 알파벳의 여덟째 자

ha /hɑ/ *interjection* said when you have discovered something, or are proud of yourself ‖ 어떤 것을 발견하거나 자신이 자랑스러울 때 쓰여. 어마. 어유. 하. 아. 야: *Ha! I knew I was right.* 아! 나는 내가 옳다는 것을 알았다. —see also HA HA, — compare HUH

hab·er·dash·er·y /ˈhæbəˌdæʃəri/ *n* [C, U] OLD-FASHIONED a store or part of a store that sells men's clothing, or the clothes and hats sold there ‖ 남성 의류를 파는 가게나 그 가게의 일부, 또는 거기서 파는 옷과 모자. 남자용 복식품(점)

hab·it /ˈhæbɪt/ *n* **1** [C, U] something that you do regularly, and usually without thinking ‖ 규칙적으로 대개 별 생각 없이 하는 일. 습관. 버릇: *Jen had developed a/the habit of asking her sister for advice.* 젠은 여동생에게 조언을 구하는 습관이 생겼다. / *After he moved out, I was still cleaning his room out of habit.* (=because it was a habit) 그가 이사 간 뒤에 나는 여전히 습관적으로 그의 방을 청소하고 있었다. / *I've gotten in the habit of running every morning.* (=I've started running regularly) 나는 아침마다 조깅하는 버릇이 생겼다 / *Dad needs to change his eating/drinking habits.* (=what he eats or drinks, and when he does it) 아빠는 먹는[마시는] 습관을 고쳐야 한다. —compare CUSTOM **2** something you do regularly that annoys other people ‖ 일정하게 다른 사람을 성가시게 하는 행위. (나쁜) 버릇: *He has a habit of being late.* 그는 지각하는 버릇이 있다. / *I admit smoking is a bad habit of mine.* 흡연은 나의 나쁜 버릇이라고 나는 인정한다. **3 make a habit of doing sth** to start doing something very often ‖ 너무 자주 어떤 일을 하기 시작하다. …하는 버릇[습관]이 있다. 늘 …하다: *Don't make a habit of staying up late studying!* 너무 늦게까지 공부하는 버릇을 갖지 마라! **4 kick/break the habit** to stop doing something that is bad for your health, such as regularly taking drugs ‖ 규칙적으로 마약을 복용하는 등 건강에 나쁜 일을 하는 것을 그만두다. 나쁜 버릇을 고치다 **5** a set of long loose clothes worn by members of some religious groups ‖ 몇몇 종교 집단의 구성원이 입는 길고 느슨한 옷. (수녀 등의) 의복. 복장

hab·it·a·ble /ˈhæbətəbəl/ *adj* suitable for people to live in ‖ 사람이 살기에 알맞은. 살 수 있는 —opposite UNINHABITABLE

hab·i·tat /ˈhæbəˌtæt/ *n* the natural environment in which a plant or animal lives ‖ 식물이나 동물이 사는 자연 환경. 서식 환경. 서식지

hab·i·ta·tion /ˌhæbəˈteɪʃən/ *n* FORMAL **1** [U] the act of living in a place ‖ 어떤 장소에서 사는 행위. 거주: *There was no sign of habitation on the island.* 그 섬에는 거주의 흔적이 없었다. **2** a house or place to live in ‖ 사는 집이나 장소. 주소. 주거지

ha·bit·u·al /həˈbɪtʃuəl/ *adj* **1** happening as a habit, or often doing something because it is a habit ‖ 습관처럼 일어나는, 또는 어떤 것이 습관이기 때문에 그것을 자주 하는. 습관의. 습관적인. 상습적인. 상용하는: *his habitual smoking* 그의 습관적인 흡연 / *a habitual smoker* 습관적

인 흡연자 **2** usual or typical ‖ 일상적인, 전형적인. 특유의. 타고난: *her habitual bad temper* 그녀의 타고난 나쁜 성미 – **habitually** *adv*

hack¹ /hæk/ *v* **1** [I, T] to violently cut something into pieces ‖ 사물을 조각조각 난폭하게 자르다. 마구 자르다. 난도질하다: *All of the murder victims had been hacked to death.* 모든 살인 사건 피해자들은 난도질을 당해 죽었다. **2** [I] to cough very loudly and painfully ‖ 아주 크고 고통스럽게 기침을 하다. 마른기침[헛기침]을 몹시 하다: *She started hacking and gasping.* 그녀는 헛기침을 시작하면서 숨을 헐떡거리고 있다. **3** *sb* **can't hack it** INFORMAL used in order to say that someone cannot continue to do something difficult or boring ‖ 사람이 어렵거나 따분한 일을 계속할 수 없다는 것을 말하는 데에 쓰여. …이 …을 도저히 못 해내다

hack into sth *phr v* [T] to use a computer to enter someone else's computer system ‖ 다른 사람의 컴퓨터 시스템에 들어가기 위해 컴퓨터를 사용하다. 컴퓨터 시스템에 불법 침입하다: *Morris managed to hack into a federal computer network.* 모리스는 용케도 연방 컴퓨터망에 침입했다.

hack² *n* someone who writes low quality books, articles etc. ‖ 낮은 수준의 책·기사 등을 쓰는 사람. 통속 작가[예술가]

hack·er /ˈhækɚ/ *n* INFORMAL someone who uses computers a lot, especially in order to secretly use or change the information in another person's computer system ‖ 특히 타인의 컴퓨터 시스템의 정보를 몰래 사용하거나 변경하려고 컴퓨터를 많이 사용하는 사람. (비밀 정보를 캐내는) 컴퓨터 침입자. 해커 – **hacking** *n* [U]

hack·neyed /ˈhæknid/ *adj* a hackneyed phrase or statement is no longer interesting because it has been used too often ‖ 어구나 진술이 너무 자주 사용해서 더 이상 흥미가 없는. 진부한. 평범한

hack·saw /ˈhæksɔ/ *n* a small SAW (=cutting tool) used especially to cut metal ‖ 특히 금속을 절단하는 데에 쓰는 조그만 톱. 쇠톱

had /d, əd, həd; strong hæd/ *v* **1** the past tense and PAST PARTICIPLE of HAVE ‖ have의 과거·과거 분사형 **2 be had** to be tricked or made to look stupid ‖ 기만당하다 또는 어리석어 보이게 하다. 속다. 사기 당하다: *She had the feeling she'd been had.* 그녀는 사기 당한 느낌이었다.

had·dock /ˈhædək/ *n* [C, U] a common fish that lives in northern oceans, or the meat from this fish ‖ 북대양에 서식하는 보통의 물고기, 또는 이 물고기의 살. 대구의 일종

had·n't /ˈhædnt/ *v* the short form of "had not" ‖ "had not"의 단축형: *We hadn't been there long.* 우리는 거기 오래 있지 않았다.

hag /hæg/ *n* an impolite word meaning an ugly or old woman ‖ 못생기거나 늙은 여자를 무례하게 이르는 말. 추한 노파

hag·gard /ˈhægɚd/ *adj* having lines on your face and dark marks around your eyes because you are tired, sick, or worried ‖ 피곤[질병, 걱정]으로 인해 얼굴에 주름이나 눈 언저리에 검은 점이 있는. 초췌한. 수척한: *He was thin and haggard.* 그는 말라빠지고 초췌했다.

hag·gle /ˈhægəl/ *v* [I] to argue, especially about the amount of money you will pay for something ‖ 특히 어떤 것에 지불할 금액을 놓고 언쟁하다. (값을)끈질기게 깎다. 흥정[옥신각신]하다: *The car dealer and I were haggling over the price for an hour.* 자동차 판매원과 나는 1시간 동안 가격에 대해 끈질기게 실랑이하고 있었다.

hah /hɑ/ *interjection* ⇨ HA

ha ha /hɑ ˈhɑ/ *interjection* **1** used in writing to represent laughter ‖ 글에서 웃음을 나타내는 데에 쓰여. 하하 **2** SPOKEN said in order to show that you are annoyed and do not think something is funny ‖ 자신이 짜증이 나 있고 어떤 일을 재미있게 여기지 않음을 나타내는 데에 쓰여. 걸작이군. 재미있군: *Very funny, Tyrell, ha ha.* 아주 웃기는군, 티렐. 하하[걸작이야]

hail¹ /heɪl/ *v* **1** [T] to call out to someone in order to get his/her attention or to greet him/her ‖ 주의를 끌거나 인사하려고 남에게 소리쳐 부르다. 큰 소리로 부르다: *He tried hailing a taxi/cab, but it drove by.* 택시를 잡으려고 큰 소리로 불렀지만 지나가 버렸다. **2** [I] if it hails, frozen rain falls from the sky ‖ 비가 얼어서 하늘에서 떨어지다. 싸라기눈[우박]이 내리다[오다]

hail sb/sth **as** sth *phr v* [T] to publicly state how good someone or something is ‖ 사람 또는 사물이 얼마나 좋은지를 공개적으로 말하다. …을 열렬히 지지하다. 갈채를 보내다. 환호하며 맞이하다: *Their discovery was hailed as the most important event of the century.* 그들의 발견은 세기의 가장 중요한 사건이라고 열렬한 지지를 받았다.

hail from *phr v* [I] to come from a particular place ‖ 특정한 장소에서 오다. …출신이다: *The professor hailed from Massachusetts.* 그 교수는 매사추세츠 출신이었다.

hail² *n* **1** [U] small hard drops of frozen rain that fall from the sky ‖ 하늘에서 떨어지는 조그맣고 딱딱하게 언 빗방울. 싸라기눈. 우박 —see usage note at WEATHER **2 a hail of bullets/stones etc.** a lot of bullets, stones etc. that are shot or thrown at someone ‖ 남에게 쏘거나 던지는 많은 양의 총알·돌 등. 빗발치는 총탄/돌

hail·stone /ˈheɪlstoʊn/ *n* a small drop of hard frozen rain ‖ 단단하게 얼어버린 작은 빗방울. (한 알의) 싸라기눈. 우박

hail·storm /ˈheɪlstɔrm/ *n* a storm when a lot of HAIL falls ‖ 많은 우박이 내릴 때의 폭풍. 싸라기눈[우박]을 수반하는 폭풍

hair /hɛr/ *n* **1** [U] the things like thin threads that grow on your head ‖ 머리에서 자라는 가는 실 같은 물질. 머리카락: *Mike's the guy with the blond curly hair.* 마이크는 금발의 곱슬머리를 한 남자이다. / *She's tall and she has dark brown hair.* 그녀는 키가 크고 머리카락은 흑갈색이다. / *I used to have/wear my hair very long.* 나는 머리를 아주 길게 기르곤 했다. **2** [C, U] the things like thin threads that grow on a person's or animal's skin ‖ 사람 또는 동물의 피부에서 자라는 가는 실 같은 물질. 털: *an old blanket covered with cat hair* 고양이털로 덮인 낡은 담요 —compare FUR **3 let your hair down** INFORMAL to stop being serious and enjoy yourself ‖ 진지하지 않게 편히 즐기다. 느긋하게 쉬다. 마음 편하게 거동하다. 스스럼없이 지내다 **4 -haired** having a particular type of hair or fur ‖ 특별한 형태의 머리털이나 부드러운 털을 가진. 털이 있는. 털이 …한: *a long-haired cat* 털이 긴 고양이 **5** SPOKEN a very small amount or distance ‖ 매우 작은 양 또는 거리. 털끝만큼. 조금: *"Is this picture straight?" "Raise the right side just a hair."* "이 그림이 똑바로 되어 있습니까?" "오른쪽을 조금만 올리거라."

hair·ball /ˈhɛrbɔl/ *n* [C] a ball of hair that forms in the stomach of animals, such as cats, that LICK their fur ‖ 고양이 등 자신의 털을 핥는 동물의 위 속에 형성되는 머리카락 뭉치. 모구(毛球). 모발 결석

hair·brush /ˈhɛrbrʌʃ/ *n* a brush you use on your hair to make it look neat ‖ 단정하게 보이기 위해 머리카락에 사용하는 솔. 머리빗. 솔. 브러시

hair·cut /ˈhɛrkʌt/ *n* **1** the act of having your hair cut by someone ‖ 남에게 머리를 자르게 하는 행위. 이발: *I'm getting a haircut tomorrow.* 나는 내일 이발을 해야겠다. **2** the style your hair has when it is cut ‖ 이발할 때의 머리 스타일. 헤어스타일. 머리 모양: *They gave her a really short haircut.* 그들은 그녀에게 정말 짧은 머리 모양을 해 주었다.

hair·do /ˈhɛrdu/ *n, plural* **hairdos** INFORMAL a woman's HAIRSTYLE ‖ 여성의 머리 모양

hair·dress·er /ˈhɛrˌdrɛsɚ/ *n* someone who washes, cuts, and arranges people's hair ‖ 머리를 감겨주고 자르고 다듬어주는 사람. (특히 여성 머리의) 미용사

hair·dryer /ˈhɛrˌdraɪɚ/ *n* a machine that you sit under that blows out hot air, used for drying hair ‖ 그 아래 앉아서 머리를 말리는 데에 사용되는 뜨거운 바람을 분출하는 기계. 헤어드라이어

hair·line /ˈhɛrlaɪn/ *n* **1** the area around the top of your face where your hair starts growing ‖ 머리털이 자라기 시작하는 얼굴 맨 윗부분 둘레의 부위. (특히 이마의) 앞머리털이 난 언저리 **2 a hairline crack/fracture** a very thin crack in something hard such as a glass or bone ‖ 유리나 뼈 등의 딱딱한 물체에 난 매우 가는 금. (털 모양의) 잔금. 실금

hair·net /ˈhɛrnɛt/ *n* a thin net worn over your hair in order to keep it in place ‖ 머리털이 제자리에 있도록 머리 위에 쓰는 가는 망. 머리 (손질용) 망

hair·rais·ing /ˈ..../ *adj* frightening in an exciting way ‖ 흥분시킬 정도로 무서운. 머리털이 쭈뼛해지는[곤두서는]. 무시무시한: *a hair-raising adventure* 무시무시한 모험

hair·split·ting /ˈhɛrˌsplɪtɪŋ/ *n* [U] the act of paying too much attention to unimportant details and differences ‖ 중요하지 않은 세부 사항과 차이에 너무 많은 주의를 기울이는 행위. 하찮은 것을 꼬치꼬치 따짐. 궤변

hair spray /ˈ. ./ *n* [C, U] a sticky liquid that you put onto your hair in order to make it stay in place ‖ 머리를 고정시키려고 머리에 뿌리는 끈적끈적한 액체. 헤어스프레이

hair·style /ˈhɛrstaɪl/ *n* the particular style your hair has when it is cut, brushed, or arranged ‖ 머리를 자르거나 빗질하거나 다듬을 때의 특정한 머리 모양. 헤어스타일

hairstyles

bun · mustache · beard · bangs

braid · pigtails · ponytail

hair·y /'hɛri/ *adj* **1** having a lot of body hair ‖ 몸에 털이 많은. 털투성이의: *His arms and chest are really hairy.* 그의 팔과 가슴에는 정말 털이 많다. / *a hairy man* 털투성이의 남자 **2** INFORMAL a hairy situation makes people feel angry, worried, excited, or frightened ‖ 상황이 사람들로 하여금 화나게[걱정되게, 흥분되게, 무섭게] 하는. 싫은. 불쾌한. 곤란한. 위험한: *Tom and Linda are in a really hairy lawsuit right now.* 톰과 린다는 지금 정말로 지겨운 소송을 하는 중이다.

hal·cy·on /'hælsiən/ *adj* LITERARY **halcyon days/years/season etc.** the happiest, most peaceful time of someone's life, or a company's most successful time ‖ 사람의 일생에서 가장 행복하고 평화로운 기간, 또는 회사의 가장 성공적인 순간. 평온한 시기/시대/계절

hale /heɪl/ *adj* **hale and hearty** HUMOROUS healthy and full of energy ‖ 건강하고 힘이 충만한. 강건한[원기 왕성한]. 정정한

half¹ /hæf/ *determiner, adj* **1** ½ of an amount, time, distance, number etc. ‖ 양·시간·거리·수 등의 2분의 1의. 절반의: *The wall is half a mile long.* 그 벽의 길이는 반 마일이다. / *At least half the time was spent deciding what to do.* 무엇을 할지를 결정하는 데에 적어도 반 시간이 소비되었다. / *Cyndi was more than half an hour late.* 신디는 반 시간 이상 지각했다. **2 half the fun/time etc.** a lot of the fun, a lot of times etc. ‖ 아주 재미있는. 여러 번. 아주 신나는/누차[종종]: *Half the time she makes me so mad that I want to hit her.* 그녀는 종종 나를 미칠 정도로 화나게 해서 때려주고 싶다. **3 half a second/minute** a very short time ‖ 매우 짧은 시간. 아주 잠깐: *If you can wait half a second, I'll be ready to go.* 네가 잠깐만 기다릴 수 있다면 나는 갈 준비가 된다.

half² *number* ½ ‖ 2분의 1: *five and a half* (=5½) 5와 2분의 1

half³ *n, plural* **halves 1** one of two equal parts of something ‖ 사물의 동일한 두 부분 중의 하나. 절반: *Half of 10 is 5.* 10의 반은 5이다. / *Do you want the sandwich cut in half?* (=in two equal pieces) 샌드위치를 절반으로 잘라 드릴까요? / *Half of the rooms have double beds in them.* 방의 절반이 2인용 침대 방이다. ✗DON'T SAY "the half of the rooms."✗ "the half of the rooms"라고는 하지 않는다. / *Our profits increased in the second half of the year.* 우리의 수익은 연도 후반기에 증가했다. / *"How old is your daughter?" "She's two and a half."* "딸은 몇 살이니?" "그녀는 두 살 반이야." ✗DON'T SAY "two and one half."✗ "two and one half"라고는 하지 않는다. **2** one of two parts into which a sports event is divided ‖ 스포츠 경기가 나누어지는 두 부분 중의 하나. (시합의) 전반[후반]. …회: *The score was 21 to 10 at the end of the second half.* 점수는 2회 말에 21대 10이었다.

half⁴ *adv* **1** partly but not completely ‖ 부분적이지 완전하지는 않게. 불충분하게. 다소. 거의: *He shouldn't be allowed to drive. He's half blind!* 그에게는 운전이 허용되지 않는다. 그는 반소경이다! / *I half expected her to yell at me, but she laughed instead.* 나는 그녀가 나에게 소리 지를 것이라고 어느 정도 예상했으나 그녀는 그러기는커녕 웃었다. / *There were several half-empty coffee cups on the table.* 테이블에는 반쯤 비어 있는 커피 잔들이 여러 개 있었다. **2 half French/American etc.** having one parent who is French, American etc. ‖ 한 쪽 부모가 프랑스인·미국인 등 **3 not half bad** said when something that you expected to be bad is actually good ‖ 나쁠 것으로 예상했던 어떤 것이 실제로는 좋은 경우에 쓰여. 조금도 나쁘지 않다. 매우 좋다: *Murray told us he couldn't cook, but the dinner wasn't half bad.* 머레이는 우리에게 자기가 요리를 못 한다고 말했지만 저녁 식사는 전혀 나쁘지 않았다. **4 half and half** partly one thing and partly something else ‖ 한 가지의 일부와 다른 것의 일부로. 반반으로. 등분하여: *"Do you make it with milk or water?" "Half and half."* "그것을 우유로 만듭니까, 아니면 물로 만듭니까?" "반반으로 만듭니다."

half a doz·en /ˌ. . '../ *number* **1** also **a half dozen** six ‖ 6개. 반 다스: *half a dozen donuts* 도넛 6개 / *a half dozen eggs* 달걀 6개 **2** several ‖ 수차례의. 여러 번의: *"Where's Tom?" "I've already told you half a dozen times!"* "톰은 어디 있지?" "내가 이미 너에게 여러 번 말했잖아!"

half-and-half /ˌ. . '. './ *n* [U] a mixture of milk and cream, used in coffee ‖ 커피에서 사용되는 우유와 크림의 혼합물. 반반의 혼합물

half-baked /ˌ. '../ *adj* INFORMAL a half-baked idea, plan, or suggestion is not sensible or intelligent enough to be successful ‖ 생각[계획, 제안]이 충분히 성공할 만큼 사리에 맞지 않거나 총명하지 않은. 어설픈. 미숙한. 비현실적인

half-broth·er /'. . ,../ *n* a brother who is the child of only one of your parents ‖ 부모 중 한 쪽 부모만의 친자식인 형제. 배다른 형제

half-heart·ed /ˌ. '../ *adj* a half-hearted attempt is something that you do without really trying or wanting to be successful ‖ 시도가 진정으로 노력하지 않거나 성공하기를 원하지 않고 행하는. 마음이 내키지 않는. 건성으로 하는

half-life /'. ./ *n* the amount of time it takes for a RADIOACTIVE substance to lose half of its RADIOACTIVITY ‖ 방사성 물질의 방사능의 절반을 상실하는 데에 소요되는 시간의 양. 반감기(半減期)

half-mast /ˌ. '. / *adj* **fly/be at half-mast** if a flag flies or is at half-mast, it is lowered to the middle of its pole because someone important has died ‖ 중요한 사람이 죽어서 깃발을 깃대의 중간까지 내리다. (조의·조난을 나타내는) 반기의 게양에 내려서 게양하다

half note /'. ./ *n* a musical note equal to two QUARTER NOTEs ‖ 두 개의 사분 음표와 같은 음표. 이분 음표

half-sis·ter /'. . ,../ *n* a sister who is the child of only one of your parents ‖ 부모 중 한 쪽 부모만의 아이인 여자 형제. 의붓자매

half time /'. ./ *n* [U] a period of rest between two parts of a game such as football or basketball ‖ 축구나 농구 등의 경기에서 두 부분 사이의 휴식 시간. 중간 휴식. 하프 타임

half·way /ˌhæf'weɪ./ *adj, adv* **1** at the middle point between two places or two points ‖ 두 장소 또는 두 점 사이의 중간 지점에 있는. 중도의[에서]. 중간의[즘까지]: *Their boat was halfway across the lake when it started to rain.* 그들의 배는

비가 내리기 시작했을 때 호수를 가로지른 중간 지점에 있었다. / *We had reached the halfway mark/point of the trail.* 우리는 오솔길의 중간 지점에 도착했다. **2** in the middle of a period of time or an event ‖ 기간 또는 사건의 중간에 있는. 중간의[에서]: *I fell asleep halfway through the concert.* 나는 연주회 도중에 잠들었다. —see also **meet (sb) halfway** (MEET¹)

hal·i·but /'hæləbət/ *n* [C, U] a large flat sea fish, or the meat from this fish ‖ 크고 넓적한 바닷고기, 또는 그 고기의 살. 큰넙치(살)

hall /hɔl/ *n* **1** a passage in a house or building that leads to other rooms ‖ 집 또는 건물에서 다른 방으로 연결되는 통로. 복도: *The bathroom's just down the hall.* 화장실은 통로 바로 아래쪽에 있다. **2** a public building or large room that is used for important events such as meetings, concerts, and FORMAL parties ‖ 회의·연주회·공식 파티 등의 중요한 행사에 사용되는 공공 건물 또는 큰 방. 홀. 회관. 집회장: *Carnegie Hall* 카네기 홀

hal·le·lu·jah /ˌhælə'luyə/ *interjection* said in order to express thanks, or praise to God ‖ 신에게 감사함을 표시하거나 신을 찬양하는 데에 쓰여. 할렐루야

hall·mark /'hɔlmɑrk/ *n* **1** a quality, idea, or method that is typical of a particular person or thing ‖ 특정한 사람 또는 사물의 전형적인 성질[생각, 방식]. (현저한) 특징. 특질: *Discipline is the hallmark of this institution.* 규율은 이 기관의 현저한 특징이다. **2** an official mark put on silver, gold, or PLATINUM to prove that it is real ‖ 진품이라는 것을 증명하기 위해 은[금, 백금]에 넣은 공식 마크. (금은 제품의) 순도 검증 각인. 우량[보증] 마크

H

Hall of Fame /ˌ. . '. / *n* a list of famous sports players, or the building where their uniforms, sports equipment, and information about them are all shown ‖ 유명한 운동 선수들의 목록, 또는 그들의 운동복·운동 장비·그들에 관한 정보가 모두 전시된 건물. (스포츠계의) 명예의 전당

hal·lowed /'hæloud/ *adj* **1** made holy ‖ 신성하게 하는. 신성한. 거룩한. 신성시되는: *hallowed ground* 성지 **2** respected, honored, and important ‖ 존중되는·명예로운·중요한. 숭배되는: *the hallowed memories of our war heroes* 전쟁 영웅들에 대한 숭배되는 기억들

Hal·low·een /ˌhælə'win, ˌhɑ-/ *n* [U] a holiday on the night of October 31, when children wear COSTUMES, play tricks, and walk from house to house in order to get candy ‖ 어린이들이 캔디를 얻기 위해 특유한 복장을 하고, 속임수를 쓰면서 이집 저집으로 다니는 10월 31일 휴일 밤. 핼로윈. 만성절 전야

hal·lu·ci·nate /həˈluːsəˌneɪt/ v [I] to see, feel, or hear something that is not really there ‖ 실제로 그 자리에 없는 사물을 보다[느끼다, 들다]. 환각을 느끼다. 환각을 일으키게 하다

hal·lu·ci·na·tion /həˌluːsəˈneɪʃən/ n [C, U] something you see, feel, or hear that is not really there, or the experience of this, usually caused by a drug or mental illness ‖ 실제로 그 자리에 없는 것을 보고 느끼고 듣는 일, 또는 보통 마약 또는 정신병으로 인해 일어나는 이러한 경험. 환각. 환상. 망상: *Doctors now believe the medication was the cause of her hallucinations.* 현재 의사들은 약물 치료가 그녀의 망상의 원인이었다고 믿는다. – **hallucinatory** /həˈluːsənəˌtɔri/ *adj*

hal·lu·ci·no·gen·ic /həˌluːsənəˈdʒɛnɪk/ *adj* causing HALLUCINATIONS ‖ 환각을 일으키는. 환각제의

hall·way /ˈhɔlweɪ/ n ⇨ HALL

ha·lo /ˈheɪloʊ/ n, plural **halos** a golden circle that is painted above the head of a holy person in a religious painting ‖ 종교적인 그림에서 성인의 머리 위에 그려지는 금빛의 원. 성상(聖像)의 머리 둘레나 그 위쪽에 그려지는 원광(圓光). 후광

halt¹ /hɔlt/ v [I, T] to stop or make something stop ‖ 정지하거나 일을 정지시키다. 중지하다[시키다]. 그치(게 하)다: *The city council had halted repair work on the subway.* 시의회는 지하철 수리 작업을 중지시켰다.

halt² n a stop or pause ‖ 정지나 휴지. 중지. 멈춤: *Traffic suddenly came/ground to a halt.* (=stopped) 교통이 갑자기 정지되었다. / *The project was brought to a halt* (=ended) *due to lack of money.* 그 사업 계획을 자금 부족으로 중지시켰다.

hal·ter /ˈhɔltər/ n **1** also **halter top** a piece of women's clothing that ties behind the neck and does not cover the arms or back ‖ 목 뒤에 매는 팔이나 등이 가려지지 않는 여성용 의류. 홀터. 팔[등]이 노출된 여성복 **2** a rope or leather band fastened around a horse's head in order to lead it ‖ 말을 이끌기 위해 말의 머리 근처에 묶는 밧줄이나 가죽 띠. 고삐. 굴레

halt·ing /ˈhɔltɪŋ/ *adj* stopping a lot when you move or speak, especially because you are nervous ‖ 특히 긴장되어서 움직이거나 말할 때 많이 중지하는. (말이)막히는. 더듬거리는. 우물쭈물하는: *her halting voice* 그녀의 더듬거리는 목소리

halve /hæv/ v [T] **1** to reduce the amount of something by half ‖ 사물의 양을 절반으로 줄이다. 반감하다: *Food production was almost halved during the war.* 전시에 식량 생산이 거의 반으로 줄었다. **2** to cut something into two equal parts ‖ 사물을 동일하게 두 부분으로 자르다. 이등분하다: *Wash and halve the mushrooms.* 버섯을 씻어서 절반으로 잘라라.

halves /hævz/ n the plural of HALF ‖ half의 복수형

ham¹ /hæm/ n **1** [C, U] meat from the upper part of a pig's leg that is preserved with salt or smoke ‖ 소금이나 훈제로 저장하는 돼지 허벅지의 상단 부위의 고기. 햄: *a ham sandwich* 햄 샌드위치 —see usage note at MEAT **2** INFORMAL someone who behaves in a silly way in order to get a lot of attention ‖ 많은 주의를 끌려고 바보같이 행동하는 사람. (연기가 지나친) 서투른 배우. 과잉 연기: *Your nephew's such a ham!* 네 조카는 정말 과잉 연기를 하는구나!

ham² v INFORMAL **ham it up** to perform or behave with too much false emotion ‖ 지나친 거짓 감정으로 연기하거나 행동하다. 너무 과장해서 연기하다

ham·burg·er /ˈhæmˌbɚɡɚ/ n **1** [U] BEEF that is ground (GRIND) into very small pieces ‖ 아주 잘게 간 쇠고기: *a pound of hamburger* 햄버거 1파운드 **2** this type of beef cooked in a flat round shape and eaten between pieces of round bread ‖ 넓적하고 둥근 형태로 요리하여 둥근 빵 조각 사이에 넣어서 먹는 형태의 쇠고기. 햄버거

ham·let /ˈhæmlɪt/ n a very small village ‖ 아주 작은 마을. 촌락

ham·mer¹ /ˈhæmɚ/ n a tool with a heavy metal part on a straight handle, used for hitting nails into wood ‖ 나무에 못을 박는 데 사용하는 일직선의 손잡이에 무거운 금속 부분이 달린 연장. 망치

hammer² v **1** [I, T] to hit something with a hammer ‖ 물건을 망치로 두드리다 **2** [I] to hit something again and again, making a lot of noise ‖ 많은 소음을 내며 물건을 계속 두드리다. 땅땅 [쾅쾅] 두드리다: *They hammered on the door until I opened it.* 그들은 내가 문을 열 때까지 쾅쾅 두드렸다.

hammer sth **in/into** *phr v* [T] also **hammer** sth **home** to continue repeating something until people completely understand it ‖ 사람들이 완전히 이해할 때까지 일을 계속 반복하다. 주입시키다. 되풀이하여 역설하다: *Mom hammered the message into us: don't talk to strangers!* 낯선 사람에게는 말을 걸지 말라고 엄마는 우리에게 여러 번 되풀이해서 말씀하셨다.

hammer out sth *phr v* [T] to finally agree on a solution, contract etc. after arguing about details for a long time ‖ 장시간 세부 사항에 대해 논의한 뒤에 해결 방법·계약 등에 최종적으로 동의하다. 강구해 내다. 조정하다. 애써 …에 도달하다: *It took several days to hammer out an agreement.* 애써 합의에 도달하는 데 며칠 걸렸다.

ham·mock /'hæmək/ *n* a large piece of material or a net you can sleep on that hangs between two trees or poles ‖ 두 개의 나무나 막대에 매달아 그 위에서 잠을 잘 수 있는 큰 용구나 그물. 달아맨 그물 침대

hammock

ham·per¹ /'hæmpɚ/ *v* [T] to make someone have difficulty moving, doing something, or achieving something ‖ 남을 움직이기[일을 하기, 성취하기] 어렵게 하다. 저지하다. 방해하다: *The searches for the missing girl were hampered by the bad weather.* 실종 소녀에 대한 수색은 악천후로 난관에 부딪쳤다.

hamper² *n* 1 a large basket with a lid, used for holding dirty clothes until they can be washed ‖ 세탁할 수 있을 때까지 더러운 옷을 보관하는 데에 사용하는 뚜껑 달린 큰 바구니. 빨래 광주리 2 a basket with a lid, used for carrying food ‖ 음식물을 나르는 데에 사용하는 뚜껑 달린 바구니. 식료품 광주리

ham ra·di·o /ˌ. '.../ *n* [U] a legal method of sending and receiving messages by radio for fun, rather than officially ‖ 직무상이 아니라, 재미로서 무선 통신을 이용하여 전언을 주고받는 합법적인 방식. 햄 라디오

ham·ster /'hæmstɚ/ *n* a small animal with soft fur and no tail that is often kept as a pet ‖ 종종 애완동물로 기르는, 털이 부드럽고 꼬리가 없는 작은 동물. 햄스터

ham·string¹ /'hæmˌstrɪŋ/ *n* a TENDON behind your knee ‖ 무릎 뒤의 힘줄. 사람의 오금

hamstring² *v* [T] to make a person or group have difficulty doing or achieving something ‖ 사람이나 집단이 어떤 것을 하거나 성취하는 것을 곤란하게 하다. …을 무력하게 하다: *a government hamstrung by student protests* 대학생들의 항의로 무력화된 정부

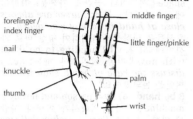

hand

forefinger / index finger — middle finger
nail — little finger/pinkie
knuckle — palm
thumb
wrist

hand¹ /hænd/ *n*

1 ▶BODY PART 신체 부위◀ the body part at the end of a person's arm that includes the fingers and thumb, used for picking up, holding, and touching things ‖ 물건을 집어 올리고 붙잡고 만지는 데에 쓰이는 손가락들과 엄지를 포함한 사람의 팔 끝에 있는 신체 부위. 손: *I write with my right/left hand.* 나는 오른손/왼손으로 글을 쓴다. / *Hold hands with your sister while we cross the street.* 우리가 길을 건너는 동안에는 네 여동생의 손을 잡아라. / *I took her hand and helped her down the stairs.* 나는 그녀의 손을 잡아서 그녀가 층계 내려가는 것을 도와주었다. / *Raise your hand* (=lift it up) *if you know the answer.* 답을 알면 손을 들어라. —see picture at BODY

2 right-handed/left-handed always using the right hand to do important things such as writing, using tools, holding things etc., or always using the left hand to do things ‖ 글쓰기·연장 사용하기·물건 들기 등과 같은 중요한 일을 하는 데 오른손을 항상 사용하는, 또는 일을 하기 위해 왼손을 항상 사용하는. 오른손잡이의/왼손잡이의

3 on the one hand... on the other hand used when comparing two different or opposite facts or ideas ‖ 두 개의 다른 또는 반대의 사실이나 생각을 비교할 경우에 쓰여. 한편으로는… 다른 한편으로는[반대로]: *The movie was scary, but on the other hand it made me laugh.* 그 영화는 무시무시했으나 또 한편으로는 나를 웃겼다. / *On the one hand, they work slowly, but on the other hand they always finish the job.* 한편으로 그들은 느리게 작업하지만 다른 면에서 말하면

그들은 항상 일을 완수한다.

4 on hand close and ready to be used when needed ‖ 필요할 때 쓸 수 있도록 가까이에 있고 준비된. 수중에: *Keep a supply of candles on hand in case of power cuts.* 정전이 될 경우에 대비하여 양초를 가까이에 준비해 두어라.

5 at hand FORMAL **a)** near in time or space ‖ 시간이나 공간에 가까운. 가까이에. 손이 닿는 곳에: *Nurses are always close at hand in case of emergency.* 간호사들은 비상시에 대비하여 항상 바로 가까이에 있다. **b)** needing to be dealt with now ‖ 지금 처리해야 하는: *Let's discuss the case at hand, shall we?* 그 현안을 논의할까요?

6 by hand a) by a person and not by a machine ‖ 기계에 의해서가 아니라 사람에 의한. 손으로: *Each porcelain doll was decorated by hand.* 각각의 자기(磁器) 인형들은 직접 손으로 장식되었다. **b)** delivered from one person to another, not through the mail ‖ 우편을 통하지 않고 한 사람에서 다른 사람에게로 배달된. 수교(手交)로. 인편으로

7 a hand help ‖ 도움: *Can you give/lend me a hand with this box? It's really heavy.* 이 상자를 옮기는 것을 도와줄 수 있겠니? 정말 무거워. / *Do you need a hand with the cooking?* 요리하는 데 도움이 필요하니?

8 have a hand in to be involved in doing or making something ‖ 어떤 것을 하거나 만드는 데에 관계하다: *Eddie has had a hand in the operation of the club.* 에디는 클럽 운영에 관여했다.

9 in sb's hands/in the hands of controlled by someone or taken care of by someone ‖ 남에게 조종되거나 맡겨져서. …의 수중에: *The schedule will be entirely in your hands.* 일정은 전적으로 너에게 맡겨질 것이다.

10 get/lay your hands on sth to find or obtain something ‖ 어떤 것을 찾거나 얻다. …을 수중에 넣다: *I read every book I could get my hands on at school.* 나는 학교에서 손에 넣을 수 있는 책은 모두 읽었다.

11 get out of hand to become impossible to control ‖ 통제할 수 없게 되다. 감당할 수 없게 되다: *The party was getting out of hand so someone called the police.* 그 파티는 감당할 수 없게 되어 누군가가 경찰을 불렀다.

12 hand in hand holding each other's hands ‖ 서로 다른 사람의 손을 잡고. 손에 손을 마주 잡고. 협력하여

13 in hand being dealt with now ‖ 지금 다루고 있는. 수중에 있는. 진행 중인: *We need to solve the matter in hand before we can solve other problems.* 다른 문제들을 해결하기 전에 지금 진행 중인 일을 해결해야 한다.

14 have your hands full to be very busy or too busy ‖ 매우 바쁘거나 너무 바쁘다: *You're going to have your hands full once you have the baby!* 너는 아기가 생기면 아주 바쁠 것이다.

15 give sb a (big) hand to CLAP loudly for a performer or speaker ‖ 연기자나 연사에게 큰 소리로 손뼉을 치다. 박수갈채를 받다

16 ▶WORKER 노동자◀ OLD-FASHIONED someone who works with his/her hands ‖ 손으로 작업을 하는 사람. 노동자. 장인

17 ▶CLOCK 시계◀ one of the long things that point to the numbers on a clock ‖ 시계의 숫자를 가리키는 긴 물건의 하나. 시계바늘

18 ▶CARDS 카드◀ the cards that you are holding in a game ‖ 게임에서 갖고 있는 카드. (가진) 패 —see also FIRSTHAND, LEFT-HAND, RIGHT-HAND, SECONDHAND, **shake hands (with sb)** (SHAKE¹), **wait on sb hand and foot** (WAIT¹)

hand² *v* [T] **1** to pass something to someone else ‖ 다른 사람에게 물건을 건네다: *Can you hand me a towel?* 나에게 수건을 건네 주겠니? **2 you have to hand it to sb** SPOKEN said when you are admiring something that someone has done ‖ 사람이 한 일을 칭찬할 때 쓰여. 남에게 손들다. 우수성을 인정하다: *I have to hand it to you, Claire: you sure know how to cook!* 클레어, 너에게 손들었어. 분명히 너는 요리법에 정통해!

hand sth ↔ **back** *phr v* [T] to give something back to the person it belongs to, or to the person who just gave it to you ‖ 사물을 소유자 또는 제공했던 사람에게 돌려주다: *Mr. Evans handed back our essays today.* 에반스 선생님은 오늘 우리가 쓴 작문들을 돌려줬다.

hand sth ↔ **down** *phr v* [T] **1** to give something to a younger relative, or to people who live after you ‖ 일을 젊은 친족 또는 자기 후손들에게 주다. 물려주다. 대대로 전하다: *traditions that were handed down from generation to generation* 세대에서 세대로 전해져 온 전통 **2** if a court of law hands down a decision or sentence, it officially announces a decision or punishment ‖ 법원이 판결이나 형벌을 공식적으로 말하다. 언도하다.

hand sth ↔ **in** *phr v* [T] to give

something to someone in a position of authority ‖ 어떤 것을 권한 있는 직위의 사람에게 주다. 제출하다: *Please hand in your application by September 30.* 9월 30일까지 신청서를 제출하세요.

hand sth ↔ **out** *phr v* [T] to give something to everyone who is part of a group or in a particular place ‖ 물건을 그룹의 일부 구성원이나 특정 장소에 있는 사람 모두에게 주다. 배부하다: *They were handing out free t-shirts at the club.* 그들은 클럽에서 무료로 티셔츠를 나눠주고 있었다.

hand over *phr v* **1** [T **hand** sb/sth ↔ **over**] to give someone or something to the person who wants to control him, her, or it ‖ 사람 또는 사물을 관리하기를 원하는 사람에게 주다. 남의 관리에 맡기다[넘기다]: *The thief was caught and handed over to the police.* 그 도둑놈은 체포되어 경찰에 넘겨졌다. **2** [I,T **hand** sth ↔ **over**] to give power or duties to someone else ‖ 다른 사람에게 권한이나 직무를 주다. 양도하다: *Cirallo will be handing over the chairmanship in June.* 씨랄로는 6월에 의장직을 인계한다.

hand·bag /ˈhændˌbæg/ *n* ⇨ PURSE¹

hand·book /ˈhændbʊk/ *n* a small book with instructions and information about a particular subject ‖ 특정한 주제에 대한 지식과 정보가 들어 있는 작은 책. 안내서. 편람: *an employee handbook* 직원 편람

hand·cuff /ˈhændkʌf/ *v* [T] to put HANDCUFFs on someone ‖ 어떤 사람에게 수갑을 채우다

hand·cuffs /ˈhændkʌfs/ *n* [plural] two metal rings joined by a chain, used for holding a prisoner's wrists together ‖ 죄수의 손목을 함께 묶는 데에 쓰이는 쇠줄로 연결된 두 개의 금속 고리. 수갑

hand·ful /ˈhændfʊl/ *n* **1** an amount that you can hold in your hand ‖ 손으로 잡을 수 있는 양. 한 움큼. 한 줌: *We were eating popcorn by the handful.* 우리는 한 줌씩 팝콘을 먹고 있었다. **2 a handful of** a small number of people or things ‖ 소수의 사람들이나 물건들. 소량. 소수: *Only a handful of people showed up.* 몇몇 사람만이 모습을 나타냈다. **3 a handful** INFORMAL someone, especially a child, who is difficult to control ‖ 감당하기 어려운 사람, 특히 아이. 성가신 사람. 골칫거리: *She's a real handful!* 그녀는 정말 골칫거리야!

hand·gun /ˈhændgʌn/ *n* a small gun you hold in one hand when you shoot ‖ 사격할 때 한 손으로 잡는 작은 총. 권총

hand·i·cap /ˈhændiˌkæp/ *n* **1** a condition in which you cannot use a part of your body or mind because it is damaged ‖ 손상되어서 심신의 일부를 사용할 수 없는 상태. (신체 · 정신) 장애 **2** something that makes a race or competition more difficult for stronger or more skillful competitors, so the players who are not so good have a better chance of winning ‖ 그다지 우수하지 않은 선수들이 더 나은 우승 기회를 갖도록, 더 강하거나 더 나은 기량의 경쟁자에게는 경주나 경기를 더 어렵게 하는 일. 핸디캡. 우열의 균형을 위해 우세[열세] 쪽에 주는 불리[유리]한 조건

hand·i·capped /ˈhændiˌkæpt/ *adj* **1** not able to use a part of your body or mind normally because it has been damaged ‖ 손상되어서 신체 또는 정신의 일부를 정상적으로 사용할 수 없는. 신체[정신] 장애가 있는. 불구의: *schools for mentally/physically handicapped children* 정신적[신체적] 장애가 있는 아이들을 위한 학교들 **2 the handicapped** people who are mentally or physically handicapped ‖ 정신적 또는 신체적으로 장애가 있는 사람들. 장애자 **3 be handicapped by** to have difficulties that are caused by a particular problem ‖ 특정한 문제로 인한 어려움이 있다: *Firefighters were handicapped by the strength of the wind.* 소방대원들은 강풍으로 인해 어려운 입장에 있었다.

USAGE NOTE handicapped

Using the word **handicapped** to talk about someone who cannot use a part of her/his body or mind normally may be considered offensive by some people. The word **disabled** is used by many people, but it is most polite to say **challenged** or **impaired**: *a special library entrance for the disabled / physically challenged / hearing impaired.* 신체나 정신의 일부를 정상적으로 사용할 수 있는 사람에 대해 말할 때 쓰이는 **handicapped**를 모욕적인 말로 여기는 사람들도 있다. **disabled**는 많은 사람들이 쓰는 말이지만 **challenged**나 **impaired**로 말하는 것이 가장 정중하다: 장애자[신체 장애자, 청각 장애자]를 위한 도서관의 특별 출입문

---

hand·i·work /ˈhændiˌwɔ˞k/ *n* [U] **1** something that someone does or makes ‖ 사람이 하거나 만드는 일. 소행. 짓: *The documentary is the handiwork of a*

H

respected director. 그 다큐멘터리는 한 훌륭한 감독의 솜씨이다. **2** skillful work that you do with your hands ‖ 손으로 하는 솜씨 좋은 작업. 수세공

hand·ker·chief /ˈhæŋkərtʃɪf, -,tʃif/ *n* a piece of cloth that you use for drying your nose or eyes ‖ 콧물이나 눈물을 닦는 데에 사용하는 한 장의 천. 손수건

han·dle¹ /ˈhændl/ *v* [T] **1** to deal with someone or something ‖ 사람 또는 사물을 처리하다. 다루다. 취급하다: *She couldn't handle the responsibility of being a doctor.* 그녀는 의사로서의 책임을 처리할 줄을 몰랐다. / *How did he handle himself* (=behave) *at the meeting?* 그는 회의에서 어떻게 처신했느냐? **2** to pick up, hold, or touch something ‖ 사물을 집어들다[붙잡다, 만지다]. 다루다: *Please handle this package with care.* 이 소포를 조심해서 다루세요. **3** to organize or be in charge of something ‖ 사물을 조직하거나 담당하다. 취급하다: *Ms. Lee handled all of our travel arrangements.* 이 여사가 우리의 여행 준비를 담당했다. **4** to buy, sell, or deal with particular products or services ‖ 특정 제품 또는 서비스를 구입[판매, 거래]하다. 장사하다. 취급하다: *Upton was charged with handling stolen goods.* 업턴은 장물 취급 혐의로 고발되었다.

handle² *n* **1** the part of a door, window, etc. that you hold in order to open it ‖ 문· 창문 등을 열기 위해 붙잡는 부분. 손잡이. 문고리 **2** the part of a tool, knife, pot etc. that you can hold to use or carry it ‖ 연장· 칼·단지 등을 사용하거나 나르기 위해 잡는 부분. 자루. 손잡이

handle

—handle

handle

han·dle·bars /ˈhændl,barz/ *n* [plural] the metal BARs above the front wheel of a bicycle or MOTORCYCLE, that you turn to control the direction you go in ‖ 가는 방향을 조종하기 위해 돌리는, 자전거나 오토바이의 앞바퀴 위에 있는 금속 막대. 핸들(바)

han·dler /ˈhændlɚ/ *n* someone who trains animals, especially dogs ‖ 동물, 특히 개들을 훈련시키는 사람. 조련사

hand lug·gage /ˈ. ,../ *n* [U] small bags that you carry with you when you travel, especially on a plane ‖ 여행하는 경우에, 특히 비행기 여행에 휴대하는 작은 가방들. 수화물

hand·made /,hændˈmeɪd/ *adj* made by a person and not a machine ‖ 기계가 아닌 사람의 손으로 만든. 수제의

hand-me-down /ˈ. . ,./ *n* a piece of clothing that has been worn by someone and then given to his/her younger relative ‖ 입었던 것을 자신의 어린 친척들에게 주는 옷. 물림 옷 **– hand-me-down** *adj*

hand·out /ˈhændaʊt/ *n* **1** money or food that is given to someone, usually because s/he is poor ‖ 보통 가난한 사람에게 주는 돈 또는 음식물. 동냥 (물품) **2** a piece of paper with printed or copied information, that is given to people in a class, meeting etc. ‖ 학급·회의 등에서 사람들에게 나눠주는, 정보가 인쇄되거나 복사되어 있는 종이. 배부용 인쇄물. 유인물

hand·picked /,hændˈpɪkt/ *adj* someone who is handpicked has been carefully chosen for a particular purpose ‖ 사람이 특정한 목적을 위해 신중히 선발된. 발탁한. 엄선한

hand·set /ˈhændsɛt/ *n* the part of a MOBILE PHONE that you hold in your hand ‖ 손에 휴대하는 이동 전화기의 한 부분. 송수화기

hands-free /,hændzˈfri/ *n* mobile phone equipment that allows you to speak to someone without having to hold the phone, either by having an EARPIECE or by having SPEAKERs in a car ‖ 차 내에 이어폰이나 스피커를 갖추어서 전화기를 들지 않고 통화할 수 있게 해주는 이동 전화 장비. 핸드 프리 장치

hand·shake /ˈhændʃeɪk/ *n* the action of taking someone's right hand and shaking it, usually done when people meet or leave each other ‖ 보통 사람들이 서로 만나거나 헤어질 때 하는, 오른손을 잡고 흔드는 행위. 악수

hands off /,. ˈ./ *interjection* said when warning someone not to touch something that is yours ‖ 자신의 물건을 건드리지 말라고 남에게 경고할 때에 쓰여. 손대지 마라: *Hands off my cookies!* 내 과자에 손대지 마!

hand·some /ˈhænsəm/ *adj* **1 a)** a man who is handsome is attractive ‖ 남성이 매력적인. 잘생긴. 수려한 **b)** a woman who is handsome looks healthy and strong in an attractive way ‖ 여성이 매혹적으로 건강하고 강한. 야무진. 위엄이 있는 —see usage note at BEAUTIFUL **2 a handsome gift/reward/profit** a gift etc. that is valuable or is a lot of money ‖ 가치 있는 또는 액수가 큰 선물 등. 푸짐한 선물/후한 보상/상당한 수익

hands·on /ˌ. ˈ./ *adj* **hands-on experience/training etc.** experience, training etc. that you get by doing something ‖ 어떤 것을 하여 얻은 경험·훈련 등. 실제 체험/훈련

hand·stand /ˈhændstænd/ *n* a movement in which you kick your legs up into the air so that you are upside down and supporting yourself on your hands ‖ 몸이 거꾸로 되도록 두 다리를 공중으로 차 올려 손으로 몸을 지탱하는 동작. 물구나무서기

hands up /ˌ. ˈ./ *interjection* **1** used when telling people to raise an arm if they can answer a question, want something etc. ‖ 질문에 대답할 수 있고 원하는 것 등이 있으면 사람들에게 손을 들라고 말할 때에 쓰여. 손을 들어라: *Hands up if you know the answer.* 답을 알면 손을 들어라. **2** said when threatening someone with a gun ‖ 총으로 남을 위협할 때에 쓰여. 손들어

hand·writ·ing /ˈhænd,raɪtɪŋ/ *n* [U] the way someone writes with his/her hand ‖ 사람이 손으로 글을 쓰는 방식. 필적. 서체: *His handwriting is so messy, I can hardly read it.* 그의 필적은 엉망이어서 나는 거의 읽을 수 없다.

hand·y /ˈhændi/ *adj* **1** useful, or simple to use ‖ 유용하거나 사용하기 간편한. 도움이 되는. 쓸모가 있는: *The extra key may come in handy.* (=be useful in the future) 예비 열쇠는 앞으로 쓸모가 있을지도 모른다. **2** INFORMAL near and easy to reach ‖ 도달하기에 가깝고 쉬운. 손 닿는 곳에 있는: *You should always keep a first aid kit handy.* 응급용 약품 세트를 항상 가까이에 두어야 한다. **3 be handy with sth** to be good at using something, especially a tool ‖ 특히 도구를 잘 다루다: *Terry's very handy with a needle and thread.* 테리는 바느질을 잘 한다.

hand·y·man /ˈhændi,mæn/ *n* someone who is good at making and repairing things ‖ 물건의 제조·수리에 능숙한 사람. 숙련공. 손재간꾼

hang up

hang¹ /hæŋ/ *v* **hung, hung, hanging**

1 [I, T] to put something somewhere so that its top part is fixed but its bottom part is free to move, or to be in this position ‖ 물건을 윗부분은 고정시키고 아랫부분은 자유롭게 움직이도록 어딘가에 놓다, 또는 그렇게 되어 있다. 걸다. 걸려 있다: *You can hang your coat in the closet.* 코트를 벽장 안에 걸어도 된다. / *paintings hanging on the wall* 벽에 걸려 있는 그림들 / *Thick curtains were hung at the windows.* 두꺼운 커튼이 창문에 쳐져 있다. **2 hang in there** INFORMAL to remain determined to succeed in a difficult situation ‖ 어려운 상황에서 여전히 성공하기로 결심한 상태로 있다. 버티다. 견디다: *Just hang in there, Midori, things will get better.* 미도리, 버텨 봐. 일은 잘 풀릴 거야. **3 hang in the balance** to be in a situation in which the result is not certain, and something bad may happen ‖ 결과가 불확실하고 나쁜 일이 생길지도 모르는 상황에 있다. 미정 상태에 있다: *The whole future of the airline is hanging in the balance.* 그 항공 회사의 장래는 미정 상태에 있다. **4 leave sb/sth hanging** to fail to finish something, or tell someone your decision about something ‖ 일을 완료하거나 일에 대한 결정을 남에게 말하는 데에 실패하다. 미결인 상태로 두다: *The investigation should not be left hanging.* 그 수사는 미제 상태로 두어서는 안 된다. **5 hang a right/left** SPOKEN said in order to tell the driver of a car to turn right or left ‖ 자동차 운전자에게 오른쪽이나 왼쪽으로 돌라고 말하는 데에 쓰여. 우회전/좌회전하다 **6** to stay in the air in the same place for a long time ‖ 장시간 대기 중의 같은 장소에서. 공중에 머물러 있다. 떠 있다: *Dark clouds hung over the valley.* 검은 구름이 계곡 위에 떠 있었다.

hang around *phr v* [I, T] INFORMAL **1** to stay in one place without doing very much, often because you are waiting for someone ‖ 종종 사람을 기다리느라 별로 하는 일 없이 한 자리에 머물다. 서성거리다: *I hung around for about an hour and then left.* 나는 약 한 시간을 서성거리다가 떠났다. **2 hang around with sb** to spend a lot of time with someone ‖ 남과 많은 시간을 보내다. 늘 …과 붙어 지내다

hang back *phr v* [I] to be unwilling to say or do something, often because you are shy ‖ 종종 수줍어서 말을 하거나 행동하기를 꺼려하다. 망설이다. 주춤거리다

hang on *phr v* [I] **1** INFORMAL to hold

something tightly ‖ 물건을 단단히 잡다: *Hang on, everybody, the road's pretty bumpy.* 꼭 잡으세요. 여러분, 도로가 매우 울퉁불퉁해요. **2 hang on!** SPOKEN said in order to tell someone to wait for you ‖ 기다리라고 남에게 말하는 데에 쓰여: *Hang on, I'll be with you in a minute!* 기다려, 곧 올게!

hang onto sb/sth *phr v* [T] SPOKEN to keep something ‖ 물건을 보관하다: *I'd hang onto that letter. You might need it later.* 내가 그 편지를 보관하겠다. 네가 나중에 필요할지도 모르니까.

hang out *phr v* [I] INFORMAL to spend a lot of time at a particular place or with particular people ‖ 특정한 장소에서, 또는 특정한 사람들과 많은 시간을 보내다. 자주 드나들다. 살다시피 하다: *kids hanging out at the mall* 쇼핑 센터에 자주 드나드는 아이들

hang up *phr v* **1** [I] to finish a telephone conversation by putting the telephone down ‖ 수화기를 놓아서 통화를 끝내다. 전화를 끊다: *She got mad and hung up on me.* (=put the phone down before I was finished speaking) 그녀는 화가 나서 내가 말을 끝내기 전에 전화를 끊었다. **2** [T **hang** sth ↔ **up**] to put something such as clothes on a hook or HANGER ‖ 고리나 옷걸이에 옷 등의 물건을 놓다. 걸다. 매달다

hang² *v* [I, T] to kill someone by dropping him/her with a rope around his/her neck, or to die in this way ‖ 남을 목에 밧줄을 걸어 죽이다, 또는 그런 방식으로 죽다. 교수(絞首)하다: *Clayton hanged himself in his prison cell.* 클레이턴은 그의 감방에서 목을 매 자살했다.

hang³ *n* **get the hang of** sth INFORMAL to learn how to do something ‖ 어떤 것을 하는 방법을 배우다. 터득하다: *Driving a car is hard at first, but you'll get the hang of it.* 자동차 운전은 처음에 어렵기는 하지만 너는 터득할 거야.

hang·ar /ˈhæŋɚ, ˈhæŋgɚ/ *n* a very large building where aircraft are kept ‖ 비행기를 보관하는 아주 큰 건물. 격납고

hang·er /ˈhæŋɚ/ *n* a thing for hanging clothes on, made of a curved piece of metal, wood, or plastic with a hook on it ‖ 고리가 달린 굽은 금속[나무, 플라스틱]으로 만든 옷을 거는 물건. 옷걸이

hanger-on /ˌ.. ˈ./ *n, plural* **hangers-on** someone who tries to spend a lot of time with important people for his/her own advantage ‖ 자신의 이득을 위해 중요 인사와 많은 시간을 보내려고 하는 사람. 추종자. 측근자

hang glid·ing /ˈ. ˌ../ *n* [U] the sport of flying using a large frame covered with cloth that you hold on to ‖ 천으로 덮은 큰 틀을 이용하여 그것에 매달려 나는 스포츠. 행글라이딩 **– hang glider** *n*

hang·ing /ˈhæŋɪŋ/ *n* [C, U] the action of killing someone by dropping him/her with a rope around his/her neck as a punishment ‖ 형벌로 사람의 목 둘레에 밧줄을 걸어 죽이는 행위. 교수형

hang·man /ˈhæŋmən/ *n* someone whose job is to kill criminals by hanging them ‖ 교수형으로 범죄자를 죽이는 직업인. 사형 집행인

hang·nail /ˈhæŋneɪl/ *n* a piece of dead skin that has become loose near the bottom of your FINGERNAIL ‖ 손톱 아래쪽의 늘어진 죽은 피부 조각. 손거스러미

hang·out /ˈhæŋaʊt/ *n* INFORMAL a place that you like to go to often, such as a BAR ‖ 술집 등의 즐겨 자주 가는 장소. 아지트. 소굴

hang·o·ver /ˈhæŋˌoʊvɚ/ *n* the feeling of sickness that someone has the day after s/he has drunk too much alcohol ‖ 술을 너무 많이 마신 다음날 겪게 되는 메스꺼운 느낌. 숙취

hang·up /ˈhæŋʌp/ *n* INFORMAL **have a hangup about** sth to feel worried or embarrassed about something in an unreasonable way ‖ 불합리하게 어떤 것에 대하여 걱정하거나 난처해 하다. …을 고민하다: *Cindy has a hangup about her nose.* 신디는 코에 대한 고민이 있다.

hank·er /ˈhæŋkɚ/ *v* INFORMAL

hanker after/for sth *phr v* [T] to have a very strong desire for something over a period of time ‖ 일정 기간에 걸쳐 어떤 것에 대하여 매우 강렬한 욕망을 가지다. 갈망하다. 항상 연연해 하다: *Julie's been hankering for some carrot cake.* 줄리는 홍당무 케이크를 먹고 싶어했다. **– hankering** *n*

hankie, hanky /ˈhæŋki/ *n* INFORMAL ⇨ HANDKERCHIEF

hanky-pan·ky /ˌhæŋki ˈpæŋki/ *n* [U] INFORMAL sexual or criminal behavior that is not very serious ‖ 그다지 심각하지 않은 성적 또는 범죄적인 행위. 부도덕한 행위. 부정(不貞). 간통

Ha·nuk·kah /ˈhɑnəkə/ *n* [U] an eight-day Jewish holiday in December ‖ 12월의 8일간의 유대교 휴일. 하누카. 신전 정화제

hap·haz·ard /ˌhæpˈhæzɚd/ *adj* happening or done in a way that is not organized or planned ‖ 조직되거나 계획되지 않고 일어나거나 이루어진. 되는대로

의. 무작정의 **- haphazardly** *adv*

hap·less /'hæpləs/ *adj* LITERARY unlucky ‖ 불운한. 불행한

hap·pen /'hæpən/ *v* [I] **1** if an event or situation happens, it starts, exists, and continues for a period of time, usually without being planned ‖ 보통 계획되지 않고 사건이나 상황이 시작되어 한동안 존속되다. 일어나다. 생기다: *It's impossible to say what will happen next year.* 내년에 어떤 일이 일어날지를 말한다는 것은 불가능하다 / *What happened last night, Roger?* 로저, 어젯밤에 무슨 일이 일어났니? / *When did the accident happen?* 언제 그 사고가 발생했니? **2** to be caused as the result of an event or action ‖ 사건이나 행위의 결과로 야기되다: *What happens if your parents find out?* (=what will they do as a result?) 만일 너의 부모님이 아신다면 어떤 일이 일어나겠니? / *Look, when I try to turn on the motor, nothing happens.* 이것 봐, 내가 모터를 가동시키려는 데 아무 일도 일어나질 않아. / *Let's wait and see what happens.* (=find out what the result is) 어떤 일이 일어나는지 관망하자. **3** to do or to have something by chance ‖ 우연히 어떤 것을 하거나 가지다: *I happened to see Hannah at the store today.* 나는 오늘 우연히 가게에서 한나를 만났다. **4 sb/sth happens to be** SPOKEN said when you are angry or annoyed, to add force to what you are saying ‖ 화가 나거나 성가실 때에 자신이 하는 말에 힘을 싣는 데에 쓰여. 마침[공교롭게도] …하다. 우연히 …하다: *That happens to be my foot that you just stepped on!* 네가 방금 밟은 것은 공교롭게도 내 발이야! **5 it (just) so happens** SPOKEN said when the thing you are about to say is slightly surprising, because it is related to what someone else has said ‖ 말하려는 일이 다른 사람이 말한 것과 연관되어서 다소 놀라울 때에 쓰여. 공교롭게도. 마침: *"We visited Miami last week." "Really? It just so happens our son lives in Miami."* "우리는 지난주 마이애미를 방문했어." "그래? 마침 우리 아들도 마이애미에 살고 있는데."

happen on/upon sb/sth *phr v* [T] to find something or meet someone by chance ‖ 사물을 우연히 발견하거나 사람을 우연히 만나다: *We just happened on the cabin when we were hiking one day.* 우리는 어느 날 하이킹을 갔었는데 우연히 오두막집을 발견했다.

happen to sb/sth *phr v* [T] **1** to be affected by something ‖ 어떤 것에 영향

받다. …이 닥치다: *I don't know what I'd do if anything happened to Jane.* (=if something hurt her, or she died) 만일 제인에게 무슨 일이 일어난다면 나는 어떻게 해야 할지 모르겠다. **2 what/whatever happened to …?** used in order to ask where something is or what someone is doing now ‖ 사물이 어디에 있는지 또는 사람이 지금 무엇을 하고 있는지 묻는 데에 쓰여. …는 어떻게 된 거야?: *What happened to my blue sweater?* 내 파란 스웨터는 어떻게 된 거야[어디 있지]? / *Whatever happened to Jenny Beale?* 제니 빌에게 무슨 일이 일어났나요?

> **USAGE NOTE happen, occur, take place,** and **happen to**
>
> Use **happen** especially to talk about past or future events that are accidents or that cannot be planned: *A funny thing happened on my way to school.* / *What will happen if you have to change jobs?* **Occur** is more formal, and is used in order to talk about a specific event that has already happened: *The explosion occurred about 5:30 a.m.* Use **take place** to talk about a planned event: *Their wedding will take place on Saturday.* Use **happen to** to say that a person or thing is affected by an event: *What happened to your car?* / *This is the second time this has happened to him.*
>
> **happen**은 특히 과거의 사고나 계획되지 않은 미래의 일을 언급하는 데에 쓴다: 재미있는 일이 내가 학교 가는 도중에 일어났다. / 직업을 꼭 바꾸어야 한다면 어떤 일이 일어날까? **occur**는 좀 더 격식 있는 말로서 이미 발생한 특별한 일을 언급하는 데에 쓰인다: 그 폭발은 오전 5시 30분에 일어났다. **take place**는 계획된 일을 언급하는 데에 쓰인다: 그들의 결혼식은 토요일에 거행될 것이다. 사람이나 물건이 사건으로 인해 영향을 받은 것을 언급하는 데에는 **happen to**를 쓴다: 네 자동차에 무슨 일이 생겼니? / 이 일이 그에게 일어난 것은 이번이 두 번째이다.

hap·pen·ing[1] /'hæpənɪŋ/ *adj* SLANG fashionable and exciting ‖ 최신 유행이면서 신나는: *a happening club* 신나는 최신식 클럽

happening[2] *n* something that happens, especially a strange event ‖ 일어난 일, 특히 이상한 일. 해프닝. 우발 사건

hap·pi·ly /'hæpəli/ *adv* **1** in a happy

way ‖ 행복하게. 즐겁게: *children playing happily in the pool* 수영장에서 즐겁게 놀고 있는 아이들 **2** *fortunately* ‖ 다행히 (도). 운 좋게: *Happily no one was hurt in the fire.* 다행히도 그 화재에서 아무도 다치지 않았다. **3** *very willingly* ‖ 아주 기꺼이: *I'll happily watch the kids for you while you're gone.* 네가 없는 동안 내가 기꺼이 아이들을 돌봐 주겠다.

hap·pi·ness /ˈhæpinɪs/ *n* [U] the state of being happy ‖ 행복한 상태. 행복. 기쁨

hap·py /ˈhæpi/ *adj* **1** having feelings of pleasure, often because something good has happened to you ‖ 종종 좋은 일이 생겨서 즐거운 기분이 드는. 기쁜: *You look happier today than yesterday.* 너는 어제보다 오늘은 더 즐거워 보인다. / *I am very happy for both of you.* 나는 너희 둘 덕분에 아주 행복하다. —opposite UNHAPPY **2** **be happy to do sth** to be willing to do something, especially to help someone else ‖ 특히 다른 사람을 돕기 위해 기꺼이 어떤 것을 하다: *I'll be happy to answer questions later.* 나는 나중에 기꺼이 질문에 대답하겠습니다. **3** a happy time, place etc. is one that makes you feel pleased ‖ 시간·장소 등이 사람을 즐겁게 하는. 행복한. 기쁜: *Those were the happiest years of my life.* 그 시절이 내 생애에서 가장 행복한 몇 해였다. **4** satisfied or not worried ‖ 만족한, 걱정 없는: *Amy was not very happy with their decision.* 에이미는 그들의 결정에 아주 만족하지는 않았다. **5 Happy Birthday/New Year etc.** used as a greeting, or to wish someone good luck on his/her BIRTHDAY or a special occasion ‖ 생일이나 특별한 때에 남에게 인사로, 또는 행운을 기원하는 데에 쓰여. 생일 축하합니다/새해 복 많이 받으세요

한다: 그들은 단순하게 사는 것에 만족하고 있다. **glad**는 발생한 일에 대해 즐거워하는 것을 뜻한다: 네가 올 수 있다면 나는 정말 기쁘다. 만일 즐거움은 물론이요, 재미까지 느낀다면 **ecstatic**이나 **elated**를 쓴다: 아이들은 여름 방학이 시작되자 기뻐서 날뛰었다.

happy-go-luck·y /ˌ.. ..ˈ../ *adj* not caring or worrying about what happens ‖ 발생하는 일에 대해 관심을 두지 않거나 걱정하지 않는. 낙천적인. 태평스러운

happy hour /ˈ.. ./ *n* [singular] a special time when a BAR sells drinks at a lower price ‖ 술집에서 염가로 술을 파는 특별한 시간.

ha·rangue /həˈræŋ/ *v* [T] to speak in an angry way, often for a long time, to try to persuade someone that you are right ‖ 자신이 옳다는 것을 남에게 설득하려고 종종 장시간 동안 성난 투로 말하다. 열변을 토하다 – **harangue** *n*

ha·rass /həˈræs, ˈhærəs/ *v* [T] to annoy or threaten someone again and again ‖ 남을 되풀이해서 괴롭히거나 위협하다. 집요하게 괴롭히다: *The police are accused of harassing Asian families.* 경찰은 아시아계 민족을 괴롭힌다고 비난받고 있다. / *Stop harassing me! I'll get it done!* 나를 괴롭히지 마라! 혼내 줄 거야!

ha·rassed /həˈræst, ˈhærəst/ *adj* anxious and tired because you have too many problems or too much to do ‖ 너무 많은 문제가 있거나 할 일이 너무 많아서 불안하고 지친. 잔뜩 시달린. 고민하는

ha·rass·ment /həˈræsmənt, ˈhærəs-/ *n* [U] behavior that is threatening or offensive to other people ‖ 다른 사람들에게 위협적이거나 공격적인 행동. 괴롭힘. 애먹임: *Tina accused her boss of sexual harassment.* (=offensive sexual behavior) 티나는 그녀의 사장의 성희롱을 비난했다.

har·bor¹ /ˈhɑrbɚ/ *n* [C, U] an area of water next to the land where the water is calm, so that ships are safe when they are inside it, and can be left there ‖ 바닷물이 잔잔해서 선박이 그 안에서 안전하게 있다가 떠날 수 있는 육지에 인접한 해상 지역. 항구

har·bor² *v* [T] **1** to protect someone by hiding him/her from the police ‖ 경찰로부터 몸을 숨겨서 남을 보호하다. 숨기다 **2** to keep hopes, bad thoughts, or fears in your mind for a long time ‖ 장시간 희망[나쁜 생각, 두려움]을 마음속에 품다: *Some parents still harbor suspicions about the principal.* 어떤 학부모들은 아

H

직도 교장에 대해 의구심을 품고 있다.

hard¹ /hɑːrd/ *adj*

1 ▶FIRM TO TOUCH 만지기에 단단한◀ firm and stiff, and difficult to cut, press down, or break ‖ 단단하고 뻣뻣하여 절단[압박, 파괴]하기 어려운. 딱딱한. 견고한: *I can't sleep on a hard mattress.* 나는 딱딱한 매트리스 위에서는 잠을 잘 수 없다. / *hard candy* 딱딱한 캔디 / *The plums are still too hard to eat.* 서양자두는 아직 너무 단단해서 먹을 수 없다. —opposite SOFT

2 ▶DIFFICULT 어려운◀ difficult to do or understand ‖ 행하거나 이해하기 어려운: *It was the hardest class he'd ever had.* 그것은 그가 지금껏 경험했던 가장 어려운 강의였다. / *It's hard to say* (=difficult to know) *when Glenn will be back.* 글렌이 언제 돌아올지는 말하기 어렵다. / *It is hard for me to understand why this happened.* 이런 일이 어째서 일어났는지를 이해한다는 것이 나에게는 어려운 일이다. —opposite EASY¹

3 ▶A LOT OF EFFORT 많은 노력◀ involving a lot of physical or mental effort ‖ 신체적 또는 정신적인 많은 노력이 포함된. 힘든: *I had a hard day at work.* 나는 직장에서 힘든 날을 보냈다. / *Mowing the lawn is hard work.* 잔디를 깎는 것은 힘든 일이다.

4 ▶NOT KIND 친절하지 않은◀ showing no kindness or sympathy ‖ 친절이나 동정을 보이지 않는. 가혹한. 무정한: *Mr. Katz is a hard man to work for, but he's fair.* 카츠 씨는 일에 있어서는 매정한 사람이지만 그는 공정하다.

5 be hard on sb INFORMAL **a)** to treat someone in a way that is unfair or too strict ‖ 남을 불공정하거나 너무 엄하게 대하다: *Don't be too hard on the children - they were only playing.* ‖ 아이들에게 너무 모질게 굴지 마라. 그들은 그저 놀고 있었을 뿐이니까. **b)** to cause someone a lot of problems 남에게 많은 문제를 일으키다. …에게 특히 힘들게 하다: *It's hard on her, having her husband in the hospital.* 남편이 병원에 입원한 것은 그녀를 힘들게 한다.

6 be hard on sth INFORMAL to have a bad effect on something ‖ 어떤 것에 나쁜 영향을 주다: *Those pills are pretty hard on your stomach.* 그 알약들은 너의 위장에 아주 나쁜 영향을 준다.

7 give sb a hard time INFORMAL **a)** to make someone feel embarrassed or uncomfortable, often by making jokes about him/her ‖ 남에게 종종 농담을 하여 당황스럽게 또는 불편하게 하다. 괴롭히다. 난처하게 하다: *The guys were giving him a hard time about missing the ball.* 그 녀석들은 공을 놓친 일로 그를 괴롭히고 있었다. **b)** to criticize someone a lot ‖ 남을 몹시 비난하다

8 find sth hard to believe to think that something is probably not true ‖ 어떤 일을 진실이 아닐 거라고 생각하다: *I find it hard to believe that no one saw the accident.* 아무도 사고를 목격하지 못했다고 믿기는 어려울 것이라고 생각한다.

9 ▶PROBLEMS 문제◀ full of problems ‖ 문제로 가득 찬. 험난한: *Poor Mary, she's had a hard life.* 불쌍한 메리, 그녀는 험난한 인생을 살았다.

10 do/learn sth the hard way to make a lot of mistakes or have a lot of difficulty before learning something ‖ 어떤 일을 배우기까지 많은 실수를 하거나 많은 어려움을 겪다. 경험으로 배우다: *Darcy said she had learned the hard way to watch what she said around reporters.* 다르시는 자기가 기자들에게 둘러싸여 말한 것을 관찰해 내느라고 숱한 고생을 했다고 말했다.

11 no hard feelings SPOKEN used in order to tell someone that you no longer feel angry with him/her ‖ 남에게 이제는 화내고 있지 않다는 것을 말하는 데에 쓰여. 언짢지 않은

12 ▶WATER 물◀ hard water has a lot of MINERALs in it ‖ 물이 무기질을 많이 함유하고 있는. 경질(硬質)인 —compare SOFT —**hardness** *n* [U]

hard² *adv* **1** using a lot of effort ‖ 많은 노력을 들여. 열심히. 부지런히: *She's working very hard.* 그녀는 매우 열심히 일하고 있다. / *You're not trying hard enough.* 너는 열심히 하려고 하지를 않는다. / *Come on, push harder!* 자, 좀 더 열심히 해라! **2** with a lot of force ‖ 큰 힘으로. 세게. 맹렬히: *It's raining hard outside.* 밖에는 비가 몹시 오고 있다. **3 be hard pressed/put/pushed to do sth** to have difficulty doing something ‖ 어떤 것을 하는 데에 어려움이 있다: *The painters will be hard pressed to finish by 6 o'clock.* 그 도장공들이 6시까지 완성하기는 곤란할 것이다. **4 take sth hard** to feel very upset about something ‖ 어떤 것에 대하여 매우 심란해 하다: *I didn't know that Joe would take the news so hard.* 나는 조가 그 소식에 그렇게 심란해 할 줄은 몰랐다. **5 laugh/cry hard etc.** to laugh, cry etc. a lot ‖ 많이 웃고 울다: *We were laughing so hard we couldn't breathe.* 우리는 숨을 쉴 수가 없을 정도로 너무 많이 웃었다.

USAGE NOTE hard and hardly

Use **hard** as an adverb to say that something is done using a lot of effort or force: *We studied hard for two weeks. / You have to push hard or it won't open.* Use **hardly** to mean "almost not": *I could hardly believe what she said. / I hardly know the guy. / There's hardly any difference between them.* ✗DON'T USE "hardly" with "not" or "no."✗
많은 노력이나 힘을 들여 이룬 일을 말하기 위한 부사로 **hard**를 쓴다: 우리는 2주 동안 열심히 공부했다. / 너는 세게 밀어야 한다. 그렇지 않으면 열리지 않을 것이다. "almost not(거의 아닌)"을 뜻할 때는 **hardly**를 쓴다: 나는 그녀가 말한 것을 거의 믿을 수 없었다. / 나는 그 녀석을 거의 알지 못한다. / 그들 사이에 차이는 거의 없다. "hardly"를 "not" 또는 "no"와 함께 써서는 안 된다.

hard-and-fast /ˌ. . ˈ.ˌ/ *adj* **hard-and-fast rules/regulations** rules that cannot be changed ‖ 변경할 수 없는 규칙

hard-back /ˈhɑrdbæk/ *n* a book that has a strong stiff cover ‖ 튼튼하고 딱딱한 표지를 가진 책. 표지가 딱딱한 책 — compare PAPERBACK

hard-ball /ˈhɑrdbɔl/ *n* [C, U] **play hardball** INFORMAL to do everything you can to prevent someone from succeeding ‖ 남의 성공을 막기 위해 할 수 있는 모든 일을 하다. (적을 물리치기 위해) 적극적인 행동을 취하다

hard-boiled /ˌ. ˈ./ *adj* **1** a hard-boiled egg has been boiled until it becomes solid ‖ 계란이 단단하게 삶겨진 **2** INFORMAL not showing your emotions, and not influenced by them in what you do ‖ 감정을 드러내지 않으며 하는 일에 감정의 영향을 받지 않는. 무정한

hard cash /ˌ. ˈ./ *n* [U] coins and bills ‖ 동전과 지폐. 현금

hard cop-y /ˌ. ˈ.ˌ/ *n* [U] information from a computer that is printed onto paper ‖ 종이에 인쇄된 컴퓨터 정보. 하드 카피(눈으로 읽을 수 있는 모양으로 기계 출력을 인쇄한 것)

hard-core /ˌhɑrdˈkɔr./ *adj* extreme, and unlikely to change ‖ 극단적이며 변경할 것 같지 않은. 요지부동인. 단호한: *hardcore opposition to abortion* 낙태에 대한 단호한 반대 / *a hardcore drug addict* 습관성 마약 중독자

hard cur·ren·cy /ˌ. ˈ.../ *n* [C, U] money that can be used in any country because it is from a country that has a strong ECONOMY ‖ 경제력이 막강한 국가의 것이기 때문에 어느 국가에서나 통용되는 돈. 국제적으로 교환 가능한 통화. 기축 통화

hard disk /ˌ. ˈ./, **hard drive** *n* a part that is fixed inside a computer, used for permanently keeping information ‖ 정보의 영구 보존에 사용되는, 컴퓨터 내부에 고정되어 있는 부분. 하드 디스크

hard drugs /ˌ. ˈ./ *n* [plural] very strong illegal drugs such as COCAINE ‖ 코카인 등의 불법적이며 매우 강력한 마약. 중독성 마약

hard·en /ˈhɑrdn/ *v* **1** [I, T] to become firm or stiff, or to make something do this ‖ 단단하거나 딱딱하게 되다, 또는 사물을 그렇게 만들다. 굳어지다[단단해지다]. 굳히다[단단하게 하다]: *The pottery has to harden before it's painted.* 도기류는 칠하기 전에 꼭 굳혀야 한다. **2** [I, T] to become less kind, less afraid, and more determined, or to make someone become this way ‖ 친절과 두려움이 덜하게 되고 더욱 단호해지다, 또는 사람을 그렇게 되게 하다. 무정[강인]해지다. 비정하게 하다: *Leslie's face hardened, and she turned away from him.* 레슬리의 얼굴은 굳어져서 그를 외면했다. / *a hardened criminal* 비정한 범인

hard hat /ˈ. ./ *n* a protective hat, worn by workers in places where buildings are being built ‖ 건물 공사장에서 작업자가 쓰는 보호용 모자. 안전모

hard-head·ed /ˌ. ˈ.ˌ/ *adj* able to make difficult decisions without being influenced by your emotions ‖ 감정의 영향을 받지 않고 어려운 결정을 할 수 있는. 냉정한

hard-heart·ed /ˌ. ˈ.ˌ/ *adj* not caring about other people's feelings ‖ 다른 사람들의 감정을 무시하는. 냉혹한. 몰인정한

hard-hit·ting /ˌ. ˈ.ˌ/ *adj* criticizing someone or something in a strong and effective way ‖ 사람이나 사물을 강력하고 효과적으로 비판하는. 신랄한

hard-line /ˌhɑrdˈlaɪn./ *adj* unwilling to change your extreme political opinions ‖ 극단적인 정치적 견해를 바꾸기를 꺼리는. 강경 노선의: *hardline conservatives* 강경한 보수주의자 — **hardliner** *n*

hard liq·uor /ˌ. ˈ.ˌ/ *n* [U] strong alcohol such as WHISKEY ‖ 위스키 등의 독한 술. 독주

hard·ly /ˈhɑrdli/ *adv* **1** almost not ‖ 거의 … 아니다: *I hardly know the people*

I'm working with. (=don't know them very well) 나는 같이 일하는 사람들을 거의 알지 못한다. / *I remember how we could hardly wait for Christmas when we were kids.* 우리가 아이들이었을 때 얼마나 크리스마스를 기다리느라 못 견뎌 했는지 생각이 난다. / *Hardly anyone* (=very few people) *goes to the old theater anymore.* 거의 아무도 그 낡은 극장에 가지 않는다. / *Katy is hardly ever* (=almost never) *at home.* 캐티는 좀처럼 집에 없다. **2** FORMAL used in order to say that something is not at all true, possible, surprising etc. ‖ 어떤 것이 전혀 진실성·가능성·놀라움 등이 없다고 말하는 데에 쓰여. 도저히 …이라고는 할 수 없다: *This is hardly the ideal time to buy a house.* 도저히 지금이 주택 구입에 더할 나위 없는 시기라고는 할 수 없다. —compare BARELY —see usage note at HARD²

hard-nosed /ˌ. ˈ./ *adj* not affected by emotions, and determined to get what you want ‖ 감정에 영향받지 않고 원하는 것을 얻는 데 단호한. 감상에 흐르지 않는. 비정한: *a hard-nosed negotiator* 감정에 좌우되지 않는 인질 협상가

hard of hearing /ˌ. . ˈ./ *adj* unable to hear well ‖ 잘 들을 수 없는. 귀가 어두운. 난청의

hard-pressed /ˌ. ˈ./ *adj* **1 sb will/would be hard-pressed to do sth** used in order to say that it will or would be difficult for someone to do something ‖ 사람이 어떤 것을 하기가 어려울 것이라고, 또는 어려울 수도 있을 거라고 말하는 데에 쓰여. 사람이 …을 하는 데에 쪼들릴 [시달릴] 것이다: *I think he'll be hard-pressed to repay the money.* 나는 그가 돈을 갚기로 쪼들릴 거라고 생각한다. **2** having a lot of money problems ‖ 돈 문제가 많은. 돈에 쪼들리는. 돈이 궁한. 가난한: *help for hard-pressed families with young children* 어린애가 딸려 돈에 쪼들리는 가족에 대한 도움

hard rock /ˌ. ˈ./ *n* [U] extremely loud ROCK music that uses a lot of electric instruments ‖ 전자 악기를 많이 사용하는 매우 시끄러운 록 음악. 하드록

hard sell /ˌ. ˈ./ *n* [singular] a way of selling something in which you try very hard to persuade someone to buy it ‖ 남에게 물건을 사도록 설득하기 위해 매우 열심히 노력하는 판매 방식. 적극적인[끈질긴] 판매[선전]법. 강매 (전술)

hard·ship /ˈhɑrdˌʃɪp/ *n* [C, U] something that makes your life difficult, especially the condition of having very little money ‖ 생활을 힘들게 하는 것, 특히 돈이 매우 궁핍한 상황. 고난. 곤궁. 역경. 고생: *Many families were suffering economic hardship.* 많은 가정이 경제적 어려움으로 고통받고 있었다. / *the hardships of daily life* 일상 생활의 고난

hard up /ˌ. ˈ./ *adj* INFORMAL not having something that you want or need, especially money or sex ‖ 원하거나 필요한 것, 특히 돈이나 성생활이 없는. …이 결핍된. 쪼들리는: *Scott was pretty hard up, so I gave him $20.* 스콧은 몹시 쪼들려서 나는 20달러를 주었다.

hard·ware /ˈhɑrdwɛr/ *n* [U] **1** computer machinery and equipment ‖ 컴퓨터 기기·장비. 컴퓨터 기계 설비. 하드웨어 —compare SOFTWARE **2** equipment and tools you use in your home and yard ‖ 집·작업장에서 사용하는 장비와 연장. 철물(류). 금속 제품: *a hardware store* (=where you can buy these things) 철물점

hard·wood /ˈhɑrdwʊd/ *n* [C, U] strong heavy wood used for making furniture, or a type of tree that produces this kind of wood ‖ 가구를 만드는 데에 쓰이는 강하고 무거운 목재, 또는 이런 목재를 생산하는 나무류. 경재(硬材)(목)

hard-work·ing /ˌ. ˈ../ *adj* working seriously with a lot of effort, and not wasting time; DILIGENT ‖ 많은 노력을 기울이고 시간 낭비 없이 열심히 일하는. 부지런히 일하는; ⓡ diligent: *a hard-working student* 열심히 공부하는 학생

har·dy /ˈhɑrdi/ *adj* strong and healthy and able to bear difficult conditions ‖ 강하고 건강하며 어려운 조건들을 참아낼 수 있는. 튼튼한. 억센. 강한. 내성이 좋은: *hardy plants* 내성이 강한 식물들

hare /hɛr/ *n* an animal like a rabbit, but larger, with longer ears and longer back legs ‖ 집토끼와 비슷하지만 몸집이 더 크고 귀와 뒷다리가 더 긴 동물. 산토끼

hare·brained /ˈhɛrbreɪnd/ *adj* not sensible or practical ‖ 지각이 없거나 실제적이지 않은. 경솔한. 무모한. 어리석은: *a harebrained scheme* 어리석은 계획

hare·lip /ˈhɛrˌlɪp/ *n* [singular, U] the condition of having a top lip that is divided into two parts ‖ 윗입술이 두 부분으로 나뉘어진 상태. 언청이

har·em /ˈhɛrəm, ˈhærəm/ *n* **1** the rooms in a Muslim home where the women live ‖ 회교도 가옥 내의 여자들이 사는 방. 회교도의 규방. 하렘 **2** the group of wives or women who lived with a rich or powerful man in some Muslim

societies in past times ‖ 과거에 회교도 사
회에서 부자나 권력자와 함께 사는 부인
들, 또는 그 여자들의 집단. 회교도의 처첩
들

hark /hɑrk/ v

hark back to phr v [I] to remember or
to remind people of things that
happened in the past ‖ 과거에 일어났던
일을 기억하거나 다른 사람들에게 상기시
키다. 지난 일을 회상[상기]하다: His
writing style harks back to Fitzgerald.
그의 문체는 피츠제럴드를 떠올리게 한다.

har·lot /ˈhɑrlət/ n LITERARY a
PROSTITUTE ‖ 매춘부

harm[1] /hɑrm/ n [U] 1 damage, injury,
or trouble caused by someone's actions
or by an event ‖ 사람의 행동이나 사건에
의해 초래된 손해[상해, 고통]. (위)해.
손상: chemicals that cause harm to the
environment 환경에 해를 끼치는 화학 약
품들 / I don't think a little wine does
you any harm. 소량의 포도주가 너에게
해가 된다고는 생각하지 않는다. / Trying
to lose weight can do more harm than
good. (=cause problems) 살을 빼려고 노
력하는 것은 좋은 효과보다 더 많은 해를
끼칠 수 있다. 2 **there's no harm in
doing sth** used in order to suggest that
doing something may be helpful or
useful ‖ 어떤 일을 하는 것이 도움이 되거
나 유익할 수도 있다는 것을 제시하는 데
에 쓰여. …하는 데에 해가 전혀 없다. …
한다고 나쁠 것은 없다: There's no harm
in asking. 물어 본다고 나쁠 것은 없다. 3
not mean any harm to have no
intention of hurting or upsetting anyone
‖ 다른 사람에게 상해를 입히거나 화나게
할 의도가 전혀 없다. 나쁜[불순한] 의도
가 없다: I was just kidding; I didn't
mean any harm. 나는 그저 농담했을 뿐
이야. 기분 상하게 할 의도는 전혀 없었어.
4 **no harm done** SPOKEN said in order to
tell someone that you are not upset by
what s/he has done or said ‖ 어떤 사람에
게 그 사람의 행동이나 말에 의해 화가 나
지 않았다는 것을 말하는 데에 쓰여. 아무
렇지도 않다. 괜찮다: "I'm sorry."
"That's OK; no harm done." "미안합니
다." "괜찮아요; 아무렇지도 않아요."

harm[2] v [T] to damage or hurt
something ‖ 사물을 손상시키거나 상해를
입히다. 해치다. 상하게 하다. 해롭게 하
다: Too much sun will harm your skin.
너무 많이 햇볕을 쬐면 피부에 손상을 준
다.

harm·ful /ˈhɑrmfəl/ adj causing harm,
or likely to cause harm ‖ 해를 끼치거나
해를 끼칠 것 같은. 해로운. 유해한: the

harmful effects of pollution 공해의 해로
운 영향

harm·less /ˈhɑrmlɪs/ adj 1 unable or
unlikely to hurt anyone or cause
damage ‖ 사람을 해칠 수 없거나 손해를
끼치지 않는, 또는 그럴 것 같지 않은. 무
해한. 해치지 않는: Don't worry, the dog
is harmless. 걱정 마라, 그 개는 물지 않
는다. 2 not likely to upset or offend
anyone ‖ 사람을 화나게 하거나 기분 상하
게 할 것 같지 않은. 악의 없는. 순진한:
harmless fun 악의 없는 장난 –
harmlessly adv

har·mon·i·ca /hɑrˈmɑnɪkə/ n a small
musical instrument that you play by
blowing into it and moving it from side
to side ‖ 바람을 불어 넣으며 좌우로 움직
여서 연주하는 작은 악기. 하모니카

har·mo·nize /ˈhɑrməˌnaɪz/ v [I] 1 to
work well or look good together ‖ 함께
일을 잘 하거나 서로 어울려 보이다. 일치
[조화]하다. 어울리다: clothes that
harmonize with her coloring 그녀의 피
부와 잘 어울리는 의상 2 to sing or play
music in HARMONY ‖ 화음을 맞춰 노래를
부르거나 연주하다. 화성으로 노래하다.
합창하다

har·mo·ny /ˈhɑrməni/ n 1 [U] a
situation in which people are friendly
and peaceful, and agree with each
other ‖ 사람들이 친밀하고 평화로우며 서
로 간에 의견이 일치하는 상태. 조화. 화
합. 일치: a city that lives/works in
racial harmony 인종 간의 화합 속에서
살아가는/일하는 도시 2 [C, U]
combinations of musical notes that
sound good together ‖ 함께(어울려) 좋은
소리를 내는 음표의 조합. 화음. 화성:
four-part harmony 4부(部)로 된 화음(악)
– **harmonious** /hɑrˈmoʊniəs/ adj

har·ness[1] /ˈhɑrnɪs/ n 1 [C, U] a set of
leather bands fastened with metal that
is used in order to control a horse and
attach it to a vehicle that it pulls ‖ 말을
제어하며 말이 끄는 마차를 연결하는 데에
쓰이는 금속으로 조여진 가죽 띠 세트. 마
구(馬具) 2 a set of bands that is used to
hold someone in a place, or to stop
him/her from falling ‖ 사람을 한 곳에 고
정시키거나 떨어지는 것을 막는 데에 쓰는
일련의 띠. 고정 장구[벨트]: a safety
harness 보호 장구

harness[2] v [T] 1 to control and use the
natural force or power of something ‖ 자
연적 힘이나 사물의 동력을 제어하고 이용
하다. 동력으로 이용하다: water
harnessed to generate electricity 전기를
발생시키기 위해 이용된 물 2 to fasten

two animals together, or to fasten an animal to something using a HARNESS || 두 마리의 동물을 함께 매다, 또는 마구를 써서 동물을 어떤 것에 묶다. 마구를 달다. 마구로 매다

harp¹ /hɑrp/ *n* a large musical instrument with strings stretched on a frame with three corners || 세 개의 모서리가 있는 틀에 줄을 팽팽이 늘여 맨 대형 악기. 하프 **– harpist** *n*

harp² *v*

harp on *phr v* [T] INFORMAL to talk about something again and again, in a way that is annoying or boring || 짜증나거나 지루하게 어떤 일에 대해 계속 반복해서 말하다. 끊임없이 되뇌이다. …을 되풀이하다: *They kept harping on the fact that she'd left her daughter alone.* 그들은 그녀가 자신의 딸을 혼자 내버려 두었다는 사실을 계속 되뇌었다.

har·poon /hɑr'pun/ *n* a weapon used for hunting WHALES || 고래잡이에 쓰이는 무기. 작살

harp·si·chord /'hɑrpsɪˌkɔrd/ *n* a musical instrument like a piano, used especially in CLASSICAL MUSIC || 특히 고전 음악에 쓰이는 피아노 같은 악기. 하프시코드. 건반 악기

har·row·ing /'hærouɪŋ/ *adj* a harrowing sight or experience is one that frightens, shocks, or upsets you very much || 광경이나 경험이 사람을 매우 두렵게[충격을 받게, 화가 나게] 하는. 고통을 주는. 괴롭히는. 참혹한

harsh /hɑrʃ/ *adj* **1** harsh conditions are difficult to live in and very uncomfortable || 환경이 살기 힘들고 매우 불편한. 혹독한. 가혹한. 황폐한: *harsh Canadian winters* 혹독한 캐나다의 겨울철 **2** unpleasant and too loud or too bright || 불쾌하며 너무 시끄럽거나 너무 밝은. 거슬리는. 자극적인. 조악(粗惡)한. 거친: *a harsh voice* (귀에 거슬리는) 거친 목소리 / *the harsh street lights* (지나치게) 눈을 자극하는 가로등불 **3** unkind, cruel, or strict || 불친절한, 잔인한, 엄격한. 모진. 사나운. 무자비한: *harsh criticism* 심한 비판 / *harsh unfair laws* 무자비하고 부당한 법 **– harshly** *adv* **– harshness** *n* [U]

har·vest¹ /'hɑrvɪst/ *n* [C, U] **1** the time when crops are gathered from the fields, or the act of gathering them || 농작물이 들판에서 거둬지는 때, 또는 농작물을 거둬들이기. 수확(추수)(기): *It was harvest time.* 추수철이었다. / *the wheat harvest* 밀 수확(기) **2** the size or quality of the crops || 수확물의 크기나 양. 수확

량. 산출량: *a good harvest* 풍작

harvest² *v* [T] to gather crops from the fields || 농작물을 들판에서 거둬들이다. 수확(추수)하다

has /z, s, həz, həz; *strong* hæz/ *v* the third person singular of the present tense of HAVE || have의 3인칭 단수 현재형

has-been /'. ./ *n* INFORMAL someone who was important or popular, but who has been forgotten || 중요하거나 유명한 사람이었으나 이제는 잊혀진 사람. 영향력[인기]을 잃은 사람

hash¹ /hæʃ/ *n* **1** [C, U] a dish made with cooked meat and potatoes || 조리된 고기와 감자로 만든 요리 **2** INFORMAL a drug similar to MARIJUANA, made from the HEMP plant || 대마(大麻) 식물로 만든, 마리화나와 비슷한 마약. 해시시

hash² *v*

hash sth **↔ out** *phr v* [T] to discuss something very thoroughly and carefully || 어떤 것을 매우 철저하고 주의 깊게 논의하다. 집중 토론하다: *Look, let's get together and hash this thing out.* 이봐요, 함께 모여서 이 일을 집중 토론해 봅시다.

hash browns /'. ./ *n* [plural] potatoes that are cut into very small pieces, pressed together, and cooked in oil || 잘게 잘라서 함께 으깨어 기름에 튀긴 감자(요리). 해시 브라운스

has·n't /'hæzənt/ *v* the short form of "has not" || "has not"의 단축형: *She hasn't seen Bruce in seven years.* 그녀는 지난 7년 동안 브루스를 보지 못했다.

has·sle¹ /'hæsəl/ *n* **1** [C, U] something that is annoying because it causes problems, or is difficult to do || 문제를 초래하거나 하기 힘들어서 짜증나게 하는 것. 혼란. 소동. 골칫[두통]거리: *Driving downtown is just too much hassle.* 도심을 운전하는 것은 엄청난 골칫거리이다. **2** an argument || 말다툼. 언쟁. 티격태격: *We always have this big hassle about who's going to pay.* 우리는 누가 돈을 낼 것인가를 놓고 항상 이렇게 크게 티격태격한다.

hassle² *v* INFORMAL [T] to ask someone again and again to do something, in a way that is annoying || 남에게 어떤 것을 해 달라고 계속 짜증스럽게 요구하다. 귀찮게 조르다. 끈질기게 요청하다: *Just stop hassling me, will you?* 나 좀 그만 졸라, 알았지?

haste /heɪst/ *n* [U] **1** great speed in doing something, especially because you do not have enough time || 특히 충분한 시간이 없어서 어떤 것을 빨리 하기. 신

속[급속]히 하기. 서두름. 허둥댐: *In her haste to get to the airport, Pam forgot the tickets.* 서둘러서 공항에 가다보니 팸은 비행기표를 깜박했다. **2 in haste** quickly or in a hurry ∥ 신속히 또는 서둘러서. 급히

has·ten /'heɪsən/ *v* **1** [T] to make something happen faster or sooner ∥ 어떤 것을 더 빠르거나 이른 시간에 일어나게 하다. 서두르게 하다. 재촉하다. 앞당기다: *The popularity of radio hastened the end of silent movies.* 라디오의 대중화가 무성 영화의 종식을 앞당겼다. **2 hasten to do sth** to do or say something quickly or without delay ∥ 어떤 것을 신속하게 또는 지체 없이 하거나 말하다. 서둘러서[급하게] …하다

hast·y /'heɪsti/ *adj* done in a hurry, especially with bad results ∥ 특히 안 좋은 결과가 나게 서둘러서 행해진. 성급한. 경솔한. 조급한: *a hasty decision* 성급한 결정 **- hastily** *adv* : *a hastily written speech* 급히 작성된 연설문

hat /hæt/ *n* **1** a piece of clothing that you wear on your head ∥ 머리에 쓰는 의류의 한 가지. 모자: *a big straw hat* 큰 밀짚모자 **2 keep sth under your hat** INFORMAL to keep information secret ∥ 정보를 비밀로 유지하다. 감추어 두다 **3 hats off to sb** INFORMAL used in order to praise someone ∥ 사람을 칭찬하는 데에 쓰여. (모자를 벗어) 경의를 표하다[경례하다]: *"Jane played great. Hats off to her,"* Sheehan said. "제인은 훌륭하게 해냈다. 그녀에게 경의를 표한다"라고 쉬한이 말했다.

hatch¹ /hætʃ/ *v* [I, T] **1** if an egg hatches or is hatched, it breaks and a baby bird, fish, or insect is born ∥ 알이 깨어져서 새끼 새[치어, 곤충]가 태어나다. 부화하다[되다]. 새끼를 까다. 알에서 까다 **2** also **hatch out** to break through an egg in order to be born ∥ 태어나기 위해 알을 깨뜨리다. 알을 깨고 부화하다

hatch² *n* a hole in a ship or aircraft, used for loading goods, or the door that covers it ∥ 배나 비행기에서 화물을 싣는 데에 쓰이는 구멍, 또는 그것을 막는 문. 창구(艙口). 승강구. 해치. 출입구. 비상구 —see picture at AIRPLANE

hatch·back /'hætʃbæk/ *n* a car with a door at the back that opens up ∥ 뒤쪽에 여는 문이 달린 자동차 —see picture on page 943

hatch·et /'hætʃɪt/ *n* **1** a small AXE with a short handle ∥ 짧은 손잡이가 달린 작은 도끼. 손도끼 **2 do a hatchet job on sb**

INFORMAL to criticize someone severely and unfairly in a newspaper or on television ∥ 신문이나 텔레비전에서 사람을 심하고 부당하게 비판하다. …을 혹평하다

hate¹ /heɪt/ *v* [T] **1** to dislike someone or something very much ∥ 어떤 사람이나 사물을 아주 싫어하다. 미워하다. 혐오하다. 증오하다: *She hated Eddie when he was drunk.* 그녀는 술에 취한 에디라면 질색했다. / *Tony hates it when people are late.* 토니는 사람들이 늦는 것을 아주 싫어한다. **2 I hate to think what/how** SPOKEN used when you feel sure that something would have a bad result ∥ 어떤 것이 나쁜 결과가 나올 수도 있다고 확실히 느낄 때에 쓰여. …을 생각도 하고 싶지 않다. …은 생각하기도 싫다: *I hate to think what would happen if Joe got lost.* 조가 실종되면 무슨 일이 일어날지는 생각하기도 싫다. **- hated** *adj* —see also **hate sb's guts** (GUTS)

hate² *n* [U] an angry feeling of wanting to harm someone you dislike ∥ 싫어하는 사람에게 해를 끼치고 싶어하는 분노의 감정. 혐오. 증오. 미움: *a look of hate* 증오의 표정

hate crime /'. ./ *n* [U] a crime that is COMMITTed against someone only because they belong to a particular race, religion etc ∥ 단지 사람들이 특정 인종·종교 등의 일원이기 때문에 가해지는 범죄. (인종·종교) 차별 범죄

hate·ful /'heɪtfəl/ *adj* very bad, unpleasant, or unkind ∥ 매우 나쁜, 불쾌한, 불친절한. 미운. 싫은. 지겨운. 밉살스런: *a hateful thought* 미워하는 마음

ha·tred /'heɪtrɪd/ *n* [U] FORMAL hate ∥ 미움. 증오. 혐오: *eyes full of hatred* 증오에 가득 찬 눈

haugh·ty /'hɔti/ *adj* proud and unfriendly ∥ 거만하게 뽐내며 불친절한. 오만한. 불손한. 얕잡아 보는. 깔보는 **- haughtily** *adv*

haul¹ /hɔl/ *v* **1** to carry or pull something heavy ∥ 무거운 것을 옮기거나 끌다. 운반하다. 수송하다: *trucks hauling cement* 시멘트를 수송하는 트럭 **2 haul ass** SLANG to hurry ∥ 서두르다. 재빠르게 행동하다. 급히 떠나다

haul off *phr v* [I] INFORMAL to take someone somewhere s/he does not want to go ∥ 사람을 가고 싶어하지 않는 어떤 곳으로 데려가다. 강제로 데려가다. 끌어가다. 연행해 가다: *getting hauled off to jail* 감옥으로 연행하기

haul² *n* **1** a large amount of illegal or stolen goods that are found by the police ‖ 경찰에 의해 발견된 대량의 불법 또는 훔친 물건들. 장물(의 양). 압류품: *a big drugs haul* 대량의 마약 압류품 **2 the long haul** the long time that it takes to achieve something difficult ‖ 어려운 일을 완수하는 데에 걸린 긴 시간. 오랜 기간. 장기간: *"We're in this for the long haul,"* said a government source. "우리는 장기간 여기에 매달려 있다"라고 정부 소식통이 말했다. **3 a long haul** a long distance to travel ‖ 여행하는 긴 거리. 장거리. 긴 여정: *It's a long haul, driving from here to Phoenix.* 여기서 피닉스까지 운전하는 것은 긴 여정이다.

haunch·es /'hɔntʃɪz, 'hɑntʃɪz/ *n* [plural] the part of your body at the back between your waist and legs ‖ 허리와 다리 사이에 있는 신체의 뒤쪽 부위. 엉덩이. 둔부: *They squatted on their haunches playing dice.* 그들은 엉덩이를 깔고 주저앉아 주사위 놀이를 했다.

haunt¹ /hɔnt, hɑnt/ *v* [T] **1** if the spirit of a dead person haunts a place, it appears there often ‖ 죽은 사람의 혼령이 한 장소에 자주 나타나다. …에 떠돌다. 출몰하다: *a ship haunted by ghosts of sea captains* 선장의 유령이 출몰하는 배 **2** if something haunts you, you keep remembering it or being affected by it, although you do not want this ‖ 자신은 원하지 않지만, 어떤 일이 계속 기억나거나 그것에 의해 영향을 받다. 끊임없이 마음속에 떠오르다[붙어 다니다]: *It's the kind of decision that comes back to haunt you later.* 그 결정은 나중에 너를 끊임없이 붙어 다니며 괴롭힐 것이다.

haunt² *n* a place that someone likes to go to often ‖ 사람이 자주 가기를 좋아하는 곳. 빈번하게 가는 곳. 늘 다니는 곳: *Dan went back to visit his favorite old haunts.* 댄은 그가 예전에 늘 다니던 곳을 찾아가기 위해 되돌아갔다.

haunt·ed /'hɔntɪd, 'hɑn-/ *adj* a place that is haunted is one where the spirits of dead people are believed to live ‖ 어떤 장소가 죽은 사람들의 혼령이 산다고 믿어지는. 유령이 자주 나오는[출몰하는]. 귀신이 사는: *a haunted house* 유령이 출몰하는 집

haunt·ing /'hɔntɪŋ, 'hɑn-/ *adj* sad, beautiful, and staying in your thoughts for a long time ‖ 사람의 마음속에 오랫동안 슬프고 아름답게 머무는. 끊임없이 마음속에 떠오르는. 좀처럼 잊혀지지 않는: *a haunting memory* 좀처럼 잊을 수 없는 기억 – **hauntingly** *adv*

have¹ /v, əv, həv; *strong* hæv/ *auxiliary verb*

PRESENT TENSE (현재 시제)

singular (단수)	*plural* (복수)
I **have**, I've	we **have**, we've
you **have**, you've	you **have**, you've
he/she/it **has**	
he's/she's/it's	they **have**, they've

PAST TENSE (과거 시제))

singular (단수)	*plural* (복수)
I **had**, I'd	we **had**, we'd
you **had**, you'd	you **had**, you'd
he/she/it **had**	
he'd/she'd/it'd	they **had**, they'd

PAST PARTICIPLE (과거 분사) **had**

PRESENT PARTICIPLE (현재 분사) **having**

NEGATIVE *short forms* (부정 단축형) **haven't, hasn't, hadn't**

1 used with the PAST PARTICIPLE of a verb to make the perfect tenses ‖ 완료 시제를 만들기 위해 동사의 과거 분사와 함께 쓰여: *Yes, I've read the book.* 예, 나는 그 책을 읽었습니다. / *Have you seen the new Disney movie?* 새 디즈니 영화 봤습니까? / *She had lived in Peru for 30 years.* 그녀는 페루에서 30년간 살았었다. / *Rick has not been honest with us.* 릭은 우리에게 솔직하지 않았다. **2** used with some MODAL VERBS and a PAST PARTICIPLE to make a past modal ‖ 과거 서법(敍法)을 만들기 위해 조동사 및 과거 분사와 함께 쓰여: *Carrie should have been nicer.* 캐리는 더 친절했어야 했다. / *I must've left my wallet at home.* 나는 지갑을 집에 놓고 나온 게 틀림없다. **3 had better** used in order to give advice, or to say what is the best thing to do ‖ 충고를 해 주거나 무엇을 하는 것이 가장 좋은지 말하는 데에 쓰여. …하는 편이 좋다[낫다]. …하지 않으면 안 된다: *You'd better take the popcorn off the stove or it'll burn.* 팝콘을 스토브에서 꺼내는 것이 좋을 것이다. 그렇지 않으면 타버릴 것이다. / *I'd better not go out tonight–I'm too tired.* 오늘 밤 외출하지 않는 게 좋겠다. 너무 피곤해. **4 have had it** SPOKEN **a)** said when someone or something is old, broken, or not good any longer ‖ 사람이나 사물이 낡은[고장 난, 더 이상 좋지 않은] 때에 쓰여. (수명이) 다하다. (폐기할) 때가 되다: *I think the car has had it. It wouldn't start this morning.* 그 차가 수명이 다 됐나봐. 오늘 아침에 시동이

걸리지 않았어. **b) I've had it with** said when you are so annoyed by someone or something that you do not want to deal with him, her, or it any longer ‖ 어떤 사람이나 사물 때문에 아주 화가 나서 더 이상 상대하고 싶지 않을 때에 쓰여. …을 끝내다. 그만두다: *I've had it with the noise here. I want to move!* 나는 여기 소음을 더 이상 못 참겠어. 이사가고 싶어!

have² *v* [T not in passive]

1 ▶FEATURES/QUALITIES 특징/성질◀ used when saying what someone or something looks like, or what qualities or features he, she, or it possesses ‖ 사람이나 사물이 어떻게 생겼는가 또는 어떤 성질이나 특징을 가지고 있는가를 말할 때에 쓰여. …을 가지고 있다. …하는 특징[성질]이 있다: *Rudy has brown eyes and dark hair.* 루디의 눈은 갈색이고 머리색은 검다. / *The stereo doesn't have a tape deck.* 그 스테레오 전축에는 테이프 덱이 없다. / *Japan has a population of over 120 million.* 일본은 인구가 1억 2천만 명이 넘는다.

2 ▶OWN OR USE 소유하거나 이용하다◀ to own something, or be able to use something ‖ 사물을 소유하다, 또는 사물을 이용할 수 있다: *Kurt had a nice bike, but it got stolen.* 커트는 좋은 자전거를 갖고 있었지만 도둑맞았다. / *The school doesn't have room for any more students.* 그 학교는 더 이상의 학생을 받을 공간이 없다. / *We don't have enough money for a washing machine.* 우리는 세탁기를 살 만큼 돈이 충분하지 않다. / *Dad, can I have the car tonight?* 아빠, 오늘 밤 제가 차를 써도 되요?

3 have got used instead of "have" to mean "possess" ‖ "소유하다"를 뜻하는 "have" 대신에 쓰여. 가지고 있다: *I've got four tickets to the opera.* 나는 그 오페라 표 4장을 가지고 있다.

4 ▶EAT/DRINK 먹다/마시다◀ to eat, drink, or smoke something ‖ 어떤 것을 먹다[마시다, 피우다]: *Do you want to come have a beer with us?* 와서 우리와 맥주 한 잔 하실래요? / *We're having steak for dinner tonight.* 우리는 오늘 밤 저녁 식사에 스테이크를 먹을 것입니다. / *What time do you usually have lunch/breakfast/dinner?* 점심[아침, 저녁]은 보통 몇 시에 먹습니까?

5 ▶EXPERIENCE/DO 경험하다/하다◀ to experience or do something ‖ 무엇을 경험하거나 하다: *I have a meeting in 15 minutes.* 나는 15분 후에 회의가 있습니다. / *The kids will have fun at the circus.* 아이들은 서커스를 보며 재미있게

보낼 것입니다. / *Her secretary had trouble/problems with the copy machine.* 그녀의 비서는 복사기 사용에 어려움[문제]을 겪었다.

6 ▶RECEIVE 받다◀ to receive something ‖ 어떤 것을 받다: *Jenny! You have a phone call!* 제니야! 전화 왔다! / *I'm sure he had help from his father on his homework.* 나는 그가 숙제하면서 아버지의 도움을 받았다고 확신한다.

7 ▶IN A POSITION/STATE 위치/상태에◀ to put or keep something in a particular position or state ‖ 어떤 것을 특별한 위치나 상태로 놓거나 유지하다: *He had his eyes closed.* 그는 눈을 감고 있었다. / *Why do you always have the TV on so loud?* 너는 왜 항상 텔레비전을 그렇게 크게 켜 놓고 있느냐?

8 may I have/can I have/I'll have SPOKEN said when you are asking for something ‖ 어떤 것을 요청할 때에 쓰여. 내가 가져도 갖게 되나/가질 수 있나/갖겠습니다: *I'll have two hot dogs to go, please.* 핫도그 2개 싸가지고 갈 수 있게 부탁합니다. / *Could I have that pencil, please?* 그 연필 내가 가져도 될까요?

9 ▶SELL/MAKE AVAILABLE 팔다/이용할 수 있게 하다◀ to sell something, or make it available for people to use ‖ 어떤 것을 팔다, 또는 사람들이 이용할 수 있게 해주다: *Do they have lawn mowers at Sears?* 시어스 백화점에서 잔디 깎는 기계를 팔고 있습니까? / *The other pool has a water slide.* 다른 풀장은 물미끄럼틀 시설을 갖추고 있습니다.

10 ▶FAMILY/FRIENDS ETC 가족/친구 등◀ to know or be related to someone ‖ 어떤 사람과 알거나 관련되어 있다: *She has six brothers.* 그녀는 6명의 남자 형제를 가지고 있다. / *Chris has a friend who lives in Malta.* 크리스는 몰타에 사는 친구가 있다.

11 ▶AMOUNT OF TIME 시간의 양◀ also **have got** to be allowed a particular amount of time to do something ‖ 어떤 것을 하도록 특정한 양의 시간이 허용되다: *You have 30 minutes to finish the test.* 시험 종료 30분 전입니다.

12 have time if you have time to do something, there is nothing else that you must do at that particular time ‖ 특정 시간에 해야 할 다른 일이 없다. 시간이 있다: *Do you have time to come and have a cup of coffee with us?* 와서 우리와 함께 커피 마실 시간이 있습니까?

13 ▶BE SICK/INJURED 아프다/상처 입다◀ to become sick with a particular illness, or be injured in a particular way

‖ 특정 질병으로 아프다, 또는 특별하게 상처를 입다. 병이 나다: *Sheila had the flu for a week.* 쉴러는 1주일간 독감으로 아팠다. / *He has a broken leg.* 그는 다리에 골절상을 입었다.

14 ▶**CARRY WITH YOU** 휴대하다◀ to be carrying something with you ‖ 사물을 가지고 다니다. 휴대[지참]하다: *Do you have your knife?* 칼 가진 거 있어요? / *How much money do you have on you?* (현재) 돈을 얼마나 가지고 있어요?

15 ▶**IDEA/THOUGHT** 사고/생각◀ to think of something, or realize something ‖ 어떤 것을 생각하다, 또는 인식하다. …에 대한 생각을 갖다: *Listen, I have an idea.* 들어 봐요, 내게 생각이 있어요.

16 have sth ready/done etc. to make something ready, or finish something ‖ 어떤 일을 준비하게 하다, 또는 끝내다. …을 준비되게/끝마치게 하다: *They promised to have it done by Friday.* 그들은 금요일까지 그것을 끝내기로 약속했다.

17 ▶**GIVE BIRTH** 낳다◀ to give birth ‖ 아이를 낳다. 출산하다: *Sasha had twins!* 사샤가 쌍둥이를 낳았어!

18 have your hair cut/have your house painted etc. to employ someone to cut your hair, paint your house etc. ‖ 어떤 사람을 고용해서 머리를 깎거나 집에 페인트칠 등을 하게 하다. 머리를 깎다/집에 페인트칠 하다

19 ▶**GUESTS** 손님◀ to be with someone, or be visited by someone ‖ 어떤 사람과 함께 있다, 또는 어떤 사람의 방문을 받다: *Sorry, I didn't realize you had guests.* 미안합니다, 손님이 있는지 몰랐습니다. / *Barry had an Australian guy with him.* 배리는 호주 남자와 같이 있었다.

20 have an influence/effect etc. to influence someone or something, or cause a particular effect ‖ 사람이나 사물에 영향을 미치다, 또는 특정한 효과를 일으키다. …에 영향/효과를 미치다: *Hungarian folk songs had a great influence on Bartok's music.* 헝가리 민요들은 바르톡의 음악에 큰 영향을 끼쳤다.

21 have nothing against used in order to say that you do not dislike someone or something ‖ 사람이나 사물을 싫어하지 않는다는 것을 말하는 데에 쓰여. 반대하는[싫어하는] 것이 없다: *I have nothing against hard work, but 80 hours a week is too much.* 나는 열심히 일하는 것에 반대하지 않지만 일주일에 80시간은 너무 많다. —see also **be had** (HAD) —see usage note at GOT

have on *phr v* [T] **1** [**have** sth **on**] to be wearing something ‖ 어떤 것을 입고 있다: *Marty had a blue shirt on.* 마티는 파란 셔츠를 입고 있었다. **2** [**have** sth **on** sb] to know about something bad someone has done ‖ 어떤 사람이 한 나쁜 일에 대해 알다. 혐의[용의]점을 찾다: *Do the police have anything on him?* 경찰은 그에게 어떤 혐의를 두고 있습니까?

ha·ven /'heɪvən/ *n* [C, U] a place where people go to be safe ‖ 사람들이 안전해지기 위해 가는 곳. 피난처. 안식처: *a haven for refugees* 난민들의 안식처

have·n't /'hævənt/ *v* the short form of "have not" ‖ "have not"의 단축형: *We haven't tried Indian food yet.* 우리는 아직 인도 음식을 먹어보지 않았다. ✗DON'T SAY "haven't to."✗ "haven't to"라고는 하지 않는다.

have to /'hæftə; *strong* 'hæftu/, **have got to** /v 'gɑtə, əv-, həv-/ *modal verb* **1** to be forced to do something because someone makes you do it, or because a situation makes it necessary ‖ 어떤 사람이 어떤 것을 하라고 시키거나 그것을 해야 할 상황이어서 억지로 어떤 것을 하게 되다. …해야 하다: *We don't have to answer their questions.* 우리는 그들의 질문에 대답해야 할 필요가 없다. / *Susan hates having to get up early.* 수잔은 아침에 일찍 일어나야 하는 것을 싫어한다. / *I've got to go now. I'm already late!* 이제 가야 해. 벌써 늦었네! **2** used when saying that it is important that something happens ‖ 어떤 일이 일어나는 것이 중요하다고 말할 때에 쓰여. 반드시 …해야 한다: *You'll have to be nice to Aunt Lynn.* 린 숙모님께 공손해야 한다. **3** used when telling someone how to do something ‖ 남에게 어떤 것을 하는 방법을 말할 때에 쓰여. (…을 따라서[…순으로]) …해야 하다: *First you have to take the wheel off.* 먼저 바퀴를 떼내어야 합니다. **4** used when saying that you are sure that something will happen or is true ‖ 어떤 일이 일어날 것이 또는 사실임이 확실하다고 말할 때에 쓰여. …에 틀림없다. (필시) …일 것이다: *He has to be stuck in traffic – he wouldn't be late otherwise.* 차가 막히는 게 틀림없다. 그렇지 않다면 그는 늦지 않을 것이다. —see study note on page 932

USAGE NOTE have to, have got to and must

Use all of these phrases to talk about what it is necessary to do. Use **have to** to say that something is necessary,

and you do not have a choice about it: *I have to study for my test. / We have to visit Grandma on Sunday.* Use **must** to say that something is necessary, and that you know it is a good idea: *I really must study harder. / We must visit Grandma sometime soon.* Use **have got** instead of **have to** or **must** in order to emphasize how important something is: *I've got to talk to him.* In informal speech, we often say **gotta** instead of **have got to**: *I gotta talk to him.* ✗DON'T USE "gotta" in written or formal English.✗ The past tense of **have to, have got to**, and **must** is **had to**: *I had to talk to him.*
이 구문들은 모두 필수적으로 해야 하는 것에 대해 말할 때 쓴다. **have to**는 어떤 것이 필수적이고 그에 대해 선택의 여지가 없음을 말하는 데에 쓴다: 나는 시험에 대비해서 공부해야 한다. / 우리는 일요일에 할머니를 찾아봐야 한다. **must**는 어떤 것이 필수적이고 그것이 좋은 생각임을 알고 있을 때 쓴다: 나는 정말로 더 열심히 공부해야 한다. / 우리는 조만간 할머니를 찾아뵈야 한다. **have got**은 어떤 것이 얼마나 중요한가를 강조하기 위해 **have to**나 **must** 대신에 쓴다: 나는 그에게 말해야 한다. 비격식 회화에서 종종 **have got to** 대신에 **gotta**를 쓴다: 나는 그에게 말해야 한다. "gotta"는 문어체나 격식체 영어에서는 쓰지 않는다. **have to, have got to, must** 의 과거 시제는 **had to** 이다: 나는 그에게 말해야만 했다.

hav·oc /'hævək/ *n* [U] a situation in which there is a lot of confusion and damage ‖ 매우 혼란스럽고 많은 피해를 입은 상태. 대파괴. 황폐. 대혼란. 대소동: *a bus strike that caused/created havoc in the city's streets* 도시의 교통에 대혼란을 초래한[일으킨] 버스 파업 / *The war will wreak havoc on the country's economy.* 전쟁은 국가 경제의 대혼란을 초래할 것이다.

hawk¹ /hɔk/ *v* [T] to try to sell goods by carrying them around and talking about them ‖ 상품을 들고 돌아다니며 설명하여 팔려 하다. 물건을 팔고 다니다. 행상하다 – **hawker** *n*

hawk² *n* a large wild bird that eats small birds and animals ‖ 작은 새나 동물을 (잡아)먹는 큰 야생의 새. 매

hay /heɪ/ *n* [U] a type of long grass that has been cut and dried, used as food for horses ‖ 베어서 건조하여 말의 먹이로 쓰

는 긴 풀의 일종. 꼴. 건초(용 목초)

hay fe·ver /'. ˌ../ *n* [U] a medical condition like a bad COLD, caused by breathing in POLLEN (=dust from plants) ‖ 꽃가루를 흡입하여 일어나는, 독감과 유사한 의학적 상태. 고초열. 꽃가루병

hay·ride /'heɪraɪd/ *n* an organized ride in a CART filled with HAY, usually as part of a social event ‖ 보통 사회적 행사의 일부로서 건초를 실은 수레를 줄지어 타는 것. 마차 (가장) 행렬

hay·stack /'heɪstæk/ *n* a large, firmly built pile of HAY ‖ 크고 단단하게 쌓아 놓은 건초더미

hay·wire /'heɪwaɪɚ/ *adj* **go haywire** INFORMAL to start working in completely the wrong way ‖ 완전히 잘못된 방식으로 작동하기 시작하다. 엉망이 되다. 뒤죽박죽이 되다. 이상[오류]을 일으키다: *My computer's going haywire again.* 내 컴퓨터가 다시 오작동하고 있다.

haz·ard¹ /'hæzɚd/ *n* **1** something that may be dangerous or cause accidents, problems etc. ‖ 위험할 수 있거나 사고·문제 등을 일으키는 것. 위험. 해로운[해치는] 것: *a health hazard* 건강을 해치는 것 / *the hazards of starting your own business* 자기의 사업을 시작하는 데에 따른 위험 **2 occupational hazard** a problem or risk that cannot be avoided in the job that you do ‖ 하고 있는 업무에서 피할 수 없는 문제나 위험. 직업상 위험 – **hazardous** *adj* : *hazardous waste from factories* 공장에서 나오는 유해 폐기물

haz·ard² *v* [T] to say something that is only a suggestion or guess ‖ 단지 제안이나 추측에 불과한 것을 말하다. (틀릴 수도 있지만) 과감[대담]하게 추측해 보다. 추정해서 말하다: *I don't know, but I could hazard a guess.* 나는 잘 모르지만 (과감하게) 추정해서 말할 수 있다.

haze /heɪz/ *n* [U] smoke, dust etc. in the air that is difficult to see through ‖ 관통해서 보기 힘든 대기 중의 연기·먼지 등. 아지랑이. 엷은 안개[연기](무리): *a gray haze of smoke over the mountains* 산 위의 자욱한 회색 연기

ha·zel /'heɪzəl/ *adj* eyes that are hazel are green-brown ‖ 눈이 녹갈색인. 담갈색의

ha·zel·nut /'heɪzəlˌnʌt/ *n* a sweet round nut ‖ 달콤하고 둥근 견과. 개암

haz·ing /'heɪzɪŋ/ *n* [C, U] the activity of making people who want to join a club or FRATERNITY do silly or dangerous things before they can join ‖ 클럽이나 우애회에 가입하고 싶어 하는 사람에게 가입

전에 바보스럽거나 위험한 것들을 시키는 행위. 가입 신고식 (행사)

haz·y /ˈheɪzi/ adj **1** air that is hazy is not clear because there is a lot of smoke, dust, or mist in it ‖ 공기 중에 연기[먼지, 안개]가 많이 있어서 맑지 않은. 흐린. 탁한: *a hazy sky* 흐린 하늘 **2** an idea, memory etc. that is hazy is not clear ‖ 생각·기억 등이 분명치 않은. 흐리멍덩한. 막연한. 혼란된. 모호한: *My memories of that night are a little hazy.* 그날 밤의 기억은 분명치 않다.

H-bomb /ˈeɪtʃ bɑm/ n ⇨ HYDROGEN BOMB

he /i; *strong* hi/ *pron* a male person or animal that has already been mentioned or is already known about ‖ 이미 언급되었거나 알고 있는 남성이나 동물의 수컷. 그(사람). 그것: *"Does Josh still live in New York?" "No, he lives in Ohio now."* "조쉬는 아직 뉴욕에 사나요?" "아니요, 그는 지금 오하이오에 삽니다." / *How old is he?* 그는 몇 살입니까? / *He's* (=he is) *my brother.* 그는 내 동생입니다.

head

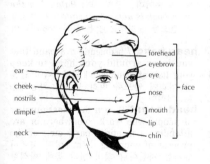

forehead
eyebrow
eye
ear
cheek
nostrils
nose]face
dimple
mouth
lip
neck
chin

head¹ /hɛd/ n
1 ▶TOP OF BODY 신체의 머리◀ the top part of your body that has your eyes, mouth etc. in it ‖ 눈·입 등이 있는 신체의 머리 부분: *He turned his head to kiss her.* 그는 고개를 돌려 그녀에게 키스했다.
—see also picture at BODY
2 ▶MIND 정신◀ your mind ‖ 정신. 생각. 마음. 두뇌. 머리. 지력. 지능: *Troy's head is filled with ideas.* 트로이의 머리는 아이디어로 가득 차 있다. / *a good head for math* 수학에 뛰어난 머리.
3 ▶LEADER 지도자◀ the leader or most important person in a group or organization ‖ 단체나 조직의 지도자나 가장 중요한 인사. 우두머리. 지배자. 수장. 리더: *the head of the biology*

department 생물학 과장 / *the head waiter* 수석 웨이터
4 ▶POSITION 위치◀ [singular] the top or front of something, or the most important part of it ‖ 어떤 것의 맨 위나 가장 선두, 또는 가장 중요한 부분. 첫머리. 수위. 수석: *Edgar sat proudly at the head of the table.* (=the end where the important people sit) 에드거는 탁자의 상석에 거만하게 앉았다.
5 ▶ON A TOOL 도구상의◀ the widest or top part of something such as a piece of equipment or a tool ‖ 장비나 도구 등의 가장 넓거나 끝 부분. 상부. 상단. 끝. 대가리: *a shower head* 샤워기 꼭지
6 ▶PLANT 식물◀ the top part of a plant with a lot of leaves ‖ 잎이 많이 달린 식물의 상단부. 결구(結球) 부분: *a head of lettuce/cabbage* 상추[양배추] 하나
7 use your head INFORMAL to think about something in a sensible way ‖ 어떤 것에 대해 현명하게 생각하다. 머리를 쓰다. 머리를 써서[깊게 생각해서](합리적으로)…하다: *You're not using your head!* 너는 머리를 쓰지 않고 있구나!
8 put your heads together INFORMAL to discuss a difficult problem together ‖ 어려운 문제를 함께 의논하다. 머리를 맞대고 서로 생각을 짜내다: *If we put our heads together we'll think of a way.* 우리가 머리를 맞대고 생각을 짜내면 방법이 보일 거야.
9 go over sb's head a) to be too difficult for someone to understand ‖ 너무 어려워서 이해할 수 없다. 이해하기에 너무 어렵다. …의 이해 범위를 넘다: *I could see that the discussion was going over their heads.* 나는 그 논의가 그들의 이해 범위를 넘어서는 것을 알 수 있었다. **b)** to ask a more important person to deal with something than the person you would normally ask ‖ 통상 (도움을) 청하던 사람보다 더 중요한 사람에게 어떤 것을 해결해 줄 것을 요청하다. 윗선을 대다. 상부에 도움을 청하다
10 get sth into your head INFORMAL to understand and realize something ‖ 어떤 것을 이해하고 깨닫다. …을 충분히 주지하다[깨닫다]: *I wish he'd get it into his head that school is important.* 나는 그가 학교가 중요하다는 사실을 깨닫기를 바란다.
11 keep/lose your head to behave reasonably or stupidly in a difficult situation ‖ 어려운 상황에서 현명하게 또는 멍청하게 행동하다. 정신을 차리다/냉정을 잃다
12 go to sb's head a) to make

someone feel more important than s/he really is ‖ 사람을 실제보다 더 중요하게 느끼게 하다. 자만하게 하다. 우쭐하게 느끼게 하다: *It's too bad Dave let his promotion go to his head.* 데이브가 그의 승진에 너무 우쭐해 하는 것은 아주 꼴불견이다. **b)** to make someone quickly feel slightly drunk ‖ 누군가를 바로 살짝 취한 느낌이 들게 하다. 취하게 만들다: *That beer went right to my head.* 그 맥주는 나를 바로 취하게 했다.

13 come to a head if a problem comes to a head, it becomes worse and you have to do something about it immediately ‖ 문제가 악화되어 그것에 대해 당장 조치를 취해야 하다. 샤태가 중대한 국면을 맞다. 위기에 빠지다: *The situation came to a head when the workers went on strike.* 노동자들이 파업으로 들어가자 상황은 위기에 빠졌다.

14 heads up! SPOKEN used in order to warn people that something is falling from above, or that something is being thrown to them ‖ 물체가 사람 위로 떨어지고 있거나 그들을 향해 던져졌음을 경고하는 데에 쓰여. 머리 들어! 조심해!

15 keep your head above water to only just be able to live or keep your business working when you have money problems ‖ 돈 문제를 겪으면서 겨우 생활이나 사업을 운영할 정도이다. 그럭저럭 겨우 해나가다

16 laugh/scream/shout your head off INFORMAL to laugh, scream etc. very much ‖ 아주 크게 웃다·비명을 지르다 등. (머리가 떨어져라) 크게 웃다/비명을 지르다/소리치다

17 head over heels in love loving someone very much ‖ 누군가를 무척 사랑하는. 홀딱 반한 —see also BIGHEADED, REDHEAD

head² *v* **1** [I, T] to go or make something go in a particular direction ‖ 특정 방향으로 가거나 어떤 것을 가게 하다. 나아가다. 향하다[향해 가게 하다]: *Where are you guys headed?* 너희들 어디로 가고 있니? / *a boat heading toward/for the shore* 해변을 향해 가는 배 / *Roz headed the car down the hill.* 로즈는 언덕 아래로 차를 몰았다. **2** [T] to be in charge of a government, organization, or group ‖ 정부[조직, 단체]에 대한 책임이 있다. …을 이끌다[지도하다]. 장(長)이 되다: *The commission was headed by Barry Kerr.* 위원회는 배리 커가 이끌고 있었다. / *Most single-parent families are headed by women.* 대부분의 편부모 가정은 여성들이 꾸려 나

가고 있다. **3 be heading/headed for** if you are heading for a situation, it is likely to happen ‖ 어떤 상황이 일어날 것 같다. …이 일어날 것이 확실하다[뻔하다]: *They're heading for trouble.* 그들은 곤란해질게 뻔하다. **4** [T] to be at the top of a list, a page, or a group of words ‖ 목록[페이지, 단어군]의 상단에 위치하다. …으로 시작되다. 첫머리에 나오다: *The longest list was headed "Problems."* 가장 긴 목록은 "Problems"란 단어로 시작되었다.

head sb/sth ↔ **off** *phr v* [T] to stop someone moving in a particular direction by moving in front of him/her ‖ 어떤 사람의 앞으로 가서 그 사람이 특정 방향으로 움직이지 못하게 막다. 길을 차단하다[끊다]. 진로를 방해하다[바꾸게 하다]: *The police headed them off at the cross street.* 경찰은 교차로에서 그들을 차단했다.

head·ache /ˈhɛdeɪk/ *n* **1** a pain in your head ‖ 머리의 통증. 두통: *I have a bad headache.* 나는 심한 두통이 있다. **2** INFORMAL an annoying or worrying problem ‖ 짜증나게 하거나 걱정시키는 문제. 두통거리. 골칫거리: *Balancing the checkbook is always a headache.* 수표장의 잔고를 유지하는 것은 항상 골칫거리다.

head·band /ˈhɛdbænd/ *n* a band that you wear around your head to keep your hair off your face ‖ 머리카락이 얼굴을 가리지 않도록 머리 둘레에 착용하는 띠. 머리띠

head count /ˈ. ./ *n* the exact number of people who work somewhere or are attending a meeting, party etc., or the process of counting them ‖ 어떤 곳에서 일하는 사람이나 회의·파티 등에 참석한 사람들의 정확한 숫자, 또는 그들을 세는 과정. 인원수[머릿수](조사). 인구(조사)

head·dress /ˈhɛd-drɛs/ *n* something that someone wears on his/her head for decoration on a special occasion ‖ 사람이 특별한 경우에 장식용으로 머리에 쓰는 것. 머리 장식: *a feathered headdress* 깃털로 된 머리 장식

head·first /ˌhɛdˈfɚst/ *adv* moving or falling forward with your head going first ‖ 머리 먼저 앞으로 움직이거나 떨어지게. 머리 먼저. 거꾸로. 곤두박질로: *He fell down the stairs headfirst.* 그는 계단에서 곤두박질쳐 떨어졌다.

head·gear /ˈhɛdgɪr/ *n* [U] hats and similar things that you wear on your head ‖ 머리에 쓰는 모자와 그와 유사한 것. 쓸 것. 머리 보호 장구. 헤드기어

head·hunt·er /ˈhɛdˌhʌntɚ/ *n* someone who finds people with the right skills and experience to do a particular job ‖ 특정 직업에 적합한 기술과 경험이 있는 인재를 찾아내는 사람. 인재 스카우트 담당자. 헤드 헌터

hea·ding /ˈhɛdɪŋ/ *n* the title written at the top of a piece of writing ‖ 글의 상단에 쓰인 제목. 표제

head·land /ˈhɛdlənd, -lænd/ *n* an area of land that sticks out from the coast into the ocean ‖ 해안에서 바다로 툭 튀어 나온 육지 지역. 곶. 갑(岬)

head·light /ˈhɛdlaɪt/ *n* one of the large lights at the front of a vehicle ‖ 차량의 전면에 있는 큰 전등의 하나. 전조등. 헤드라이트 —see picture on page 943

head·line /ˈhɛdlaɪn/ *n* 1 the title of a newspaper article, printed in large letters above the article ‖ 신문 기사 위에 큰 글자로 인쇄된 신문 기사의 제목. 큰 표제[제목] 2 **make headlines** to do something important, shocking, or new, so that newspapers, television shows etc. talk about you ‖ 중요한[충격적인, 새로운] 것을 해서 신문·TV 쇼 등에서 화제가 되다. 대서특필되다. 대대적으로 보도되다. 언론의 조명을 받다: *Johnson's announcement that he had AIDS made headlines.* 존슨이 에이즈에 걸렸다는 발표는 (언론에) 대서특필되었다.

head·long /ˈhɛdlɔŋ, ˌhɛdˈlɔŋ/ *adv* 1 without thinking carefully ‖ 주의 깊게 생각하지 않고. 황급히. 성급하게. 앞뒤 가리지 않고. 저돌적으로: *They rushed headlong into marriage.* 그들은 앞뒤 생각없이 결혼생활을 시작했다. 2 falling with your head going first ‖ 머리가 먼저 떨어지는. 거꾸로. 곤두박질로: *tumbling headlong down the slope* 비탈을 곤두박질치며 굴러 떨어짐

head·mas·ter /ˈhɛdˌmæstɚ/, **head·mis·tress** /ˈhɛdˌmɪstrɪs/ *n* a PRINCIPAL in a private school ‖ 사립학교 교장

head-on /ˌ. ˈ./ *adv* 1 **meet/hit head-on** if two vehicles meet or hit head-on, the front part of one vehicle comes toward or hits the front part of the other vehicle ‖ 두 대의 차량 중 한 차의 앞부분이 다른 차의 앞부분을 향해서 다가오거나 들이받다. 정면으로 만나다[마주치다]/충돌하다 2 to deal with someone or something in a direct and determined way ‖ 직접적이고 단호하게 사람이나 사물을 대하다. 정면으로[대놓고, 툭 까놓고] 다루다: *She intended to face her difficulties head-on.* 그녀는 자신의 어려

움을 정면으로 맞닥뜨리기로 했다. — **head-on** *adj* : *a head-on collision* 정면 충돌

head·phones /ˈhɛdfoʊnz/ *n* [plural] a piece of equipment that you wear over your ears to listen to a radio or recording ‖ 라디오나 녹음된 것을 듣기 위해 귀 위에 착용하는 장비. 헤드폰

head·quar·ters /ˈhɛdˌkwɔtɚz/ *n* [plural] 1 a building or office that is the center of a large organization, or the center of a particular activity ‖ 큰 조직의 중심이 되는 건물이나 사무실, 또는 특정 활동의 중심(지). 본부. 본사. 본서: *Republican Party headquarters* 공화당 중앙당(사) 2 also **HQ** the place from which military operations are controlled ‖ 군사 작전을 통제하는 곳. 작전 본부. 사령부

head·rest /ˈhɛdrɛst/ *n* the top part of a chair or seat that supports the back of your head ‖ 뒤통수를 받쳐 주는 의자나 좌석의 상부. 머리받이

head·room /ˈhɛd-rum/ *n* [U] the amount of space above your head inside a car ‖ 자동차 내부의 머리 위 공간의 크기. 머리와 천장 사이의 공간

head set /ˈhɛdsɛt/ *n* a set of HEADPHONES, often with a MICROPHONE attached ‖ 종종 마이크가 부착된 헤드폰 세트. 헤드 세트

heads /hɛdz/ *n* [plural] the side of a coin that has a picture of a head on it ‖ 동전에 인물상이 새겨져 있는 면. 동전의 앞면[쪽] —opposite TAILS

head start /ˌ. ˈ./ *n* the advantage you gain in a particular activity by starting before other people ‖ 다른 사람들보다 먼저 시작함으로써 특정 활동에서 얻는 이점. 유리한 시작. 선점(先占). 가선: *The younger children were given a head start in the race.* 더 어린 아이들은 경주에서 먼저 출발시켰다.

head·stone /ˈhɛdstoʊn/ *n* ➪ GRAVESTONE

head·strong /ˈhɛdstrɔŋ/ *adj* very determined to do what you want, even when other people advise you not to do it ‖ 다른 사람들이 하지 말라고 충고할 때조차도 단호하게 자신이 원하는 바를 하는. 완고한. 고집 센. 제 고집대로 하는: *a headstrong child* 고집 센 아이

head-to-head /ˌ. . ˈ./ *adj, adv* directly competing with another person or group ‖ 다른 사람이나 집단과 직접적으로 경쟁하는. 머리를 나란히 하고 경쟁하는. 대접전의. 앞서거니 뒤서거니[치열하게] 경쟁하는: *Courier companies are* *going head-to-head with the Post Office.* 택배 회사는 우체국과 치열한 경쟁을 벌이고 있다. / *head-to-head competition* 선두 다툼이 치열한 경기

head·way /'hɛdweɪ/ n **make headway a)** to make progress toward achieving something even when you have difficulties ‖ 어려울 때조차도 어떤 것을 완수하는 방향으로 나아가다. 어려움을 무릅쓰고 전진[진보]하다. 진척을 보이다: *They have made little headway in the peace talks.* 그들은 평화 회담에서 조금의 진척도 이루어 내지 못했다. **b)** to move forward ‖ 앞으로 나아가다. 전진하다: *a ship making headway through the channel* 해협을 뚫고 앞으로 나아가는 배

head·wind /'hɛd,wɪnd/ n a wind that blows directly toward you when you are moving ‖ 움직일 때 자신 쪽으로 곧장 불어오는 바람. 역풍. 맞바람

head·y /'hɛdi/ adj exciting in a way that makes you feel you can do anything ‖ 무엇이나 할 수 있다고 느끼게 흥분시키는. 들뜨게 하는. 위세 등등하게 하는: *the heady days of our youth* 의기 양양하던 우리의 젊은 시절

heal /hil/ v **1** [I] if a wound or broken bone heals, it becomes healthy again ‖ 상처나 부러진 뼈가 낫다. 치유되다. 아물다: *The scratch on her finger healed quickly.* 그녀의 손가락의 긁힌 상처는 빨리 아물었다. **2** [T] to cure someone who is ill, or make a wound heal ‖ 아픈 사람을 치료하거나 상처를 아물게 하다. 치유하다. 낫게 하다 **– healer** n

health /hɛlθ/ n [U] **1** the general condition of your body, and how healthy you are ‖ 신체에 대한 일반적 상태와 건강 정도. 건강. (몸의) 상태: *You should take better care of your health.* 당신은 자신의 건강을 더 잘 돌봐야 합니다. / *She's not in the best of health.* 그녀는 최상의 건강 상태가 아니다. / *a 68-year-old man in good health* 건강한 68세의 노인 **2** the state of being without illness or disease ‖ 아프거나 병들지 않은 상태. 건강(함). 건강함: *I wish you health and happiness.* 당신의 건강과 행복을 기원합니다. **3** how successful an ECONOMY, business, or organization is ‖ 경제[사업, 조직]의 성공적인 상태. 건전. 활력. 안정

health care /'. ,./ n [U] the service of taking care of the health of all the people in a country or area ‖ 국가나 한 지역 내 모든 사람들의 건강을 돌보는 서비스. 의료 서비스: *a health care plan* 의료 서비스 계획

health club /'. ./ n a place where

people go to exercise, that you have to pay to use ‖ 이용료를 지불하고 운동을 하러 가는 곳. 헬스클럽[장]

health food /'. ./ n [C, U] food that contains only natural substances ‖ 자연 성분만을 함유한 식품. 천연식품. 건강식품

health·ful /'hɛlθfəl/ adj likely to make you healthy ‖ 건강하게 해줄 것 같은. 건강에 좋은

health·y /'hɛlθi/ adj **1** physically strong and not likely to become ill ‖ 육체적으로 강하고 병에 걸릴 것 같지 않은. 건강한. 건강한. 몸에 이상이 없는: *a healthy baby girl* 건강한 여자 아이 — opposite UNHEALTHY **2** good for your body or your mind ‖ 신체나 정신에 좋은. 건강에 좋은. 바람직한: *a healthy diet/lifestyle* 건강에 좋은 식단[생활 양식] / *It's not healthy for her to depend on him like that.* 그녀가 그렇게 그에게 의지하는 것은 바람직하지 않다. / *We all have the right to a healthy workplace.* 우리는 모두 쾌적한 환경에서 일할 권리가 있다. **3** successful and likely to stay that way ‖ 성공적이며 그대로 유지할 것 같은. 건전한. 건실한: *a healthy economy/business/relationship* 건실한 경제[사업, 관계] **4** INFORMAL fairly large or noticeable ‖ 상당히 크거나 눈에 띄는. 대량의. 왕성한: *She seems to have a healthy appetite.* 그녀는 왕성한 식욕을 가진 것 같다. / *a healthy increase in sales* 판매액의 대폭 증가 / *Reed has a healthy respect for rattlesnakes.* 리드는 방울뱀을 상당히 경외시한다. **5** showing that you are healthy ‖ 건강함을 보여 주는. 건강해 보이는: *healthy skin* 건강해 보이는 피부 **– healthiness** n [U]

heap¹ /hip/ n **1** a large messy pile of things ‖ 사물을 대충 크게 쌓은 더미. 무더기. 퇴적물: *a heap of newspapers* 신문더미 / *His clothes lay in a heap by the bed.* 그의 옷들이 침대 옆에 무더기로 놓여 있었다. **2** INFORMAL an old car that is in bad condition ‖ 상태가 나쁜 낡은 차. 고물차

heap² v [T] **1** to put a lot of things on top of each other in a messy way ‖ 많은 사물을 아무렇게나 서로 겹쳐서 놓다. 쌓아 올리다. 겹쳐[무더기로] 쌓다: *magazines heaped on the table* 책상 위에 마구 쌓아 올려진 잡지들 **2 be heaped with** to have a lot of things on top of something ‖ 어떤 것 위에 많은 사물들이 올려져 있다. 수북이 쌓이다: *a plate heaped with food* 음식이 가득 담긴 접시

heap·ing /'hipɪŋ/ adj a heaping measurement of food is slightly more than the tool it is being measured with can hold ‖ 음식의 양이 그것을 담을 수 있다고 판단한 그릇보다 약간 더 많은. 수북한. 넘치는

hear

Mike didn't hear the phone because he was listening to music.

hear /hɪr/ v **heard, heard** /hɚd/, **hearing 1** [I, T] to know that a sound is being made, using your ears ‖ 귀를 이용해서 소리가 나고 있음을 알다. 소리를 듣다[소리가 들리다]: *I love to hear the baby laugh like that.* 나는 아이들이 그렇게 웃는 것을 듣기 좋아한다. / *Didn't you hear when I called you?* 내가 불렀을 때 듣지 못했습니까? **2** [T] to listen to music that is being played, what someone is saying etc. ‖ 연주되고 있는 음악·사람이 말하고 있는 것 등을 듣다. 주의해서 듣다. 경청하다: *I heard a great song on the radio.* 나는 라디오에서 정말 멋진 노래를 들었다. / *You should at least hear what she has to say.* 너는 최소한 그녀가 해야 하는 말은 들어야 한다. **3** [I, T] to be told or find out a piece of information ‖ 정보를 듣게 되거나 찾아내다. 전해 듣다. 소문으로 듣다[들어서 알다]: *Have you heard about the new project?* 새 계획에 대해서 들었습니까? / *"Mark's going to law school." "So I've heard."* (=said when you already know about something) "마크는 법대에 간답니다." "나도 그렇게 들었습니다." **4 hear a case** to listen to what is said in a court of law, and make a decision ‖ 법정에서 진술되는 것을 듣고 결정을 내리다. 사건을 심리하다: *The case will be heard on July 16.* 그 사건은 7월 16일에 심리된다. **5 (do) you hear (me)?** SPOKEN said when you are giving someone an order and want to be certain that s/he will obey you ‖ 남에게 명령을 내리고 그 사람이 그것에 복종할지 확인하고 싶을 때에 쓰여. 알아듣겠니? 알았니? 잘 들었니?: *Be home by ten, you hear?* 10시까지 집에 돌아와라, 알겠니? —see usage note at LISTEN

hear from sb *phr v* [T] to get news or information from someone, usually by letter ‖ 어떤 사람으로부터 보통 편지로 소식이나 정보를 듣다. 전해 듣다. …의 소식[소문]을 듣다: *Have you heard from Jane yet?* 벌써 제인에게서 소식 들었습니까?

hear of sb/sth *phr v* [T] **have heard of** to know that someone or something exists because you have been told about him, her, or it ‖ 사람이나 사물에 대해 전해 듣고서 그 사람이나 사물이 존재함을 알다. 들어서 알고 있다: *"Do you know a guy named Phil Merton?" "I've never heard of him."* "필 머튼이라는 이름의 남자 알아?" "전혀 못 들어 본 사람인데."

hear sb **out** *phr v* [T] to listen to all of someone's explanation for something, without interrupting ‖ 어떤 일에 대한 어떤 사람의 설명을 방해하지 않고 모두 듣다. 자초지종을 듣다. …의 말을 끝까지 듣다: *Look, I know you're mad, but at least hear me out.* 봐요, 당신이 화난 것은 알겠는데 최소한 내 말을 끝까지 들어 보세요.

hear·ing /ˈhɪrɪŋ/ *n* **1** [U] the sense that you use to hear sounds ‖ 소리를 듣기 위해 사용하는 감각. 청력. 청각: *My hearing's not as good as it used to be.* 내 청력이 예전만큼 좋지 않다. **2** a meeting of a court or special committee to find out the facts about a case ‖ 사건에 대한 사실을 알아내기 위한 법정이나 특별 위원회의 모임. 청문회. 심리

hearing aid /ˈ.. ./ *n* a small thing that makes sounds louder, that you put in your ear if you cannot hear well ‖ 잘 들을 수 없을 때 귀에 넣어 소리를 크게 해주는 작은 물건. 보청기

hearing im·paired /ˈ.. ,./ *adj* unable to hear well or hear at all ‖ 잘 들을 수 없거나 전혀 들을 수 없는. 청각[청력] 장애의. 난청의

hear·say /ˈhɪrseɪ/ *n* [U] something that you have heard about from other people but do not know to be true ‖ 다른 사람들에게서 들었지만 사실인지는 알지 못하는 것. 소문. 풍문. 전문. 들은 바: *This witness's testimony is based only on hearsay.* 이 증인의 증언은 단지 소문에 근거하고 있을 뿐이다.

hearse /hɚs/ *n* a large car for carrying a dead body in a COFFIN at a funeral ‖ 장례식에서 관에 든 시신을 운구하는 큰 차. 장의차. 영구차

heart /hart/ *n* **1** ▶BODY 신체◀ the organ inside a person's or animal's chest that pumps blood through the body ‖ 피를 온몸으로 뿜어 내보내는 사람이나 동물의 가슴 속의

H

장기. 심장. 염통: *He could feel his heart beating faster.* 그는 자신의 심장 박동이 더 빨라지는 것을 느낄 수 있었다.

2 ▶EMOTIONS 감정◀ [C, U] the part of you that is able to feel strong emotions such as love ‖ 사랑 등의 강한 감정을 느낄 수 있는 사람의 한 부분. 마음[가슴](속). 본심: *I knew in my heart that I wouldn't see her again.* 나는 다시는 그녀를 볼 수 없으리라는 걸 마음속으로 알았다. / *I was hoping with all my heart that you would win.* 나는 진심으로 네가 이기기를 바라고 있었다.

3 ▶SHAPE 형상◀ a shape used for representing love ‖ 사랑을 나타내기 위해 쓰이는 형상. 심장 모양. 하트형(의 것) —see picture at SHAPE

4 the heart of sth a) the main or most important part of something ‖ 사물의 주요 부문이나 가장 중요한 부분. 중심. 본질. 핵심: *We talked for hours before we got to the heart of the problem/matter.* 우리는 몇 시간 동안 이야기하고서야 문제의 본질에 도달했다. **b)** [singular] the middle or the busiest part of an area ‖ 어떤 지역의 한가운데나 가장 번화한 부분. 중앙부. 중심부: *a big hotel in the heart of the city* 도시의 중심부에 있는 큰 호텔

5 at heart if you are a particular type of person at heart, that is the type of person you really are ‖ 특정 유형의 사람이 실제로도 그러한 유형인. 마음속은. 진심은. 사실은: *I guess I'm just a kid at heart.* 난 사실 그저 어린애인 것 같애.

6 know/learn sth by heart to correctly remember all of something that you have been taught ‖ 배운 것을 모두 정확히 기억하다. 암기하다

7 ▶GAME 게임◀ a playing card with one or more red heart shapes on it ‖ 하나 이상의 빨간 하트 모양이 그려진 놀이용 카드. 하트 카드. 카드의 하트 패

8 sb's heart sank used in order to say that someone suddenly became very sad or disappointed ‖ 사람이 갑자기 매우 슬퍼지거나 실망하게 되었음을 말하는 데에 쓰여. 가슴이 내려앉다[무너지다, 메이다]. 의기소침해지다: *Bert's heart sank when he saw the mess in the house.* 집안이 난장판이 된 것을 보고 버트의 가슴은 무너져 내렸다.

9 do sth to your heart's content to do something as much as you want to ‖ 어떤 일을 원하는 만큼 많이 하다. …을 실컷[흡족하게, 원 없이, 마음껏] 하다: *Finish your homework, and then you can play video games to your heart's*

content. 숙제를 끝내라, 그러고 나면 비디오 게임을 실컷 해도 된다.

10 -hearted having a particular type of character ‖ 특정 유형의 성격을 가진. …한 마음의[을 가진]. 마음이 …한: *a kind-hearted man* 마음이 다정한 남자

11 take/lose heart to begin to have more hope, or to stop having hope ‖ 더 많은 희망을 갖기 시작하거나 희망을 갖기를 중단하다. 용기를 내다/낙담하다

SPOKEN PHRASES

12 not have the heart to do sth to be unable to do something because you do not want to upset someone ‖ 다른 사람을 화나게 하고 싶지 않아서 어떤 것을 할 수 없다. 용기가 없다. 감히 …하지 못하다: *I didn't have the heart to tell her she was wrong.* 나는 그녀가 틀렸다고 말할 용기가 없었다.

13 my/her etc. heart isn't in it if you do something when your heart isn't in it, you do not care about what you are doing ‖ 현재 하고 있는 것에 마음 쓰지 않다. 상관하지[개의치] 않다

14 have a heart said when you want someone to be kinder or more helpful ‖ 남이 더 친절하거나 더 도움을 주는 사람이 되기를 원할 때에 쓰여. 인정이 있다: *Have a heart – don't leave your dog in the car on a hot day.* 부탁입니다. 무더위에 개를 차 속에 남겨 두지 마세요.

15 a man/woman after my own heart SPOKEN said when you like someone because s/he is similar to you ‖ 어떤 사람이 자신과 비슷해서 좋아할 때에 쓰여. 마음에 맞는 남자/여자: *"Jill only drinks whiskey." "A woman after my own heart!"* "질은 위스키만 마신다." "딱 내 마음에 드는 여자군!"

16 my heart goes out to sb used in order to say that you feel sympathy for someone ‖ 어떤 사람에 대한 동정심을 느낀다는 것을 말하는 데에 쓰여. …에게 동정이 가다

—see also **cross my heart (and hope to die)** (CROSS[1])

heart·ache /ˈhɑrteɪk/ *n* [U] a strong feeling of sadness ‖ 격한 슬픔의 감정. 비탄. 마음의 고통

heart at·tack /ˈ. .../ *n* a serious medical condition in which a person's heart suddenly stops working ‖ 사람의 심장이 갑자기 작동을 멈춰버리는 심각한 의학적 상태. 심장마비[발작]. 심근경색

heart·beat /'hɑrt˺bit/ *n* the action or the sound of a heart pumping blood through the body ‖ 피를 몸 전체로 뿜어 내는 심장의 활동이나 소리. 심장 박동. 심장 뛰는 소리: *The doctor listened to my heartbeat.* 의사는 내 심장 박동 소리에 귀를 기울였다.

heart·break /'hɑrt˺breɪk/ *n* [U] a strong feeling of sadness and disappointment ‖ 슬픔과 실망의 격한 감정. 비탄. 비통.

heart·break·ing /'hɑrt˺ˌbreɪkɪŋ/ *adj* making you feel very upset ‖ 매우 심란하게 하는. 가슴이 찢어지듯 슬픈. 비통한 느낌이 들게 하는: *the heartbreaking sound of an animal in pain* 고통에 울부 짖는 동물의 가슴 아픈 울음소리

heart·bro·ken /'hɑrt˺ˌbroʊkən/ *adj* very sad because someone or something has disappointed you ‖ 어떤 사람이나 사물이 자신을 실망시켜서 매우 슬픈. 비탄에 잠긴. 깊이 상심한. 애끓는: *The kid was heartbroken.* 아이는 깊이 상심했다.

heart·burn /'hɑrt˺bɜn/ *n* [U] a slightly painful burning feeling in your stomach or chest caused by INDIGESTION ‖ 소화불량으로 인해 위장이나 가슴이 약간 아프고 얼얼한 느낌. 가슴앓이

heart di·sease /'. .ˌ./ *n* [U] a medical condition in which a person's heart has difficulty pumping blood ‖ 사람의 심장이 피를 뿜어내는 데에 어려움이 있는 의학적 상태. 심장병[질환]

heart·ened /'hɑrt˺nd/ *adj* feeling happier and more hopeful ‖ 더 행복하고 더 희망적인 느낌이 드는. 기운찬. 용기가 난. 격려[고무]된 **– hearten** *v* [T] — opposite DISHEARTENED

heart·en·ing /'hɑrt˺n-ɪŋ/ *adj* making you feel happier and full of hope ‖ 더 행복하게 느끼게 하며 희망으로 가득 차게 하는. 기운[용기]을 북돋는. 격려[고무]하는: *heartening news* 고무적인 뉴스 — opposite DISHEARTENING

heart fail·ure /'. .ˌ./ *n* [U] the failure of the heart to continue working, which causes death ‖ 심장이 계속 활동하지 못해 죽음을 초래할 수 있는 것. 심장마비

heart·felt /'hɑrtfɛlt/ *adj* felt very strongly and sincerely ‖ 매우 강하고 진정으로 느낀. 절실히 느낀. 깊이 감명한. 진정어린. 진심으로부터의: *heartfelt thanks* 진심에서 우러난 감사

hearth /hɑrθ/ *n* the part of the floor around a FIREPLACE ‖ 난로 주변의 바닥 부분. 노변(爐邊)

heart·i·ly /'hɑrtl-i/ *adv* **1** loudly and cheerfully ‖ 큰 소리로, 즐겁게. 열렬히.

열광적으로. 마음껏: *He laughed heartily.* 그는 호쾌하게 웃었다. **2** very much or completely ‖ 매우 많거나 완전하게. 몹시. 철저히: *I heartily agree with you.* 나는 완전히 너와 동감이다.

heart·land /'hɑrtlænd/ *n* **the heartland** the part of a country where most of the food is produced and where people live in a way that represents the basic values of that country ‖ 식량의 대부분이 생산되고 그 지역의 사람들이 그 나라의 기본 가치관을 대표하면서 사는 한 국가의 일부. 심장부. 중심지(역)

heart·less /'hɑrtlɪs/ *adj* cruel or not feeling any pity ‖ 잔인하거나 연민을 전혀 느끼지 않는. 무정한. 매정한. 냉혹한

heart·rend·ing /'hɑrtˌrɛndɪŋ/ *adj* making you feel great pity ‖ 엄청난 연민을 느끼게 하는. 가슴이 터질 것 같은. 비통한: *heartrending sobs* 가슴을 쥐어뜯는 듯한 흐느낌

heart·strings /'hɑrtˌstrɪŋz/ *n* **tug/pull on sb's heartstrings** to make someone feel a lot of pity or love ‖ 사람에게 많은 연민과 사랑을 느끼게 하다. …의 심금을 울리다

heart·throb /'hɑrtθrɑb/ *n* a famous person who many young people feel romantic love for ‖ 많은 젊은 사람들이 낭만적 사랑을 느끼는 유명 인사. 젊은이의 우상. 인기 스타: *1950s heartthrob and movie star – James Dean* 1950년대의 우상이자 은막의 스타인 제임스 딘

heart-to-heart /ˌ. . '. ./ *n* a conversation in which two people honestly express their feelings or opinions about something ‖ 두 사람이 어떤 것에 대해 진솔하게 자신의 감정이나 견해를 표현하는 대화. 마음을 터놓는 흉금을 털어놓는 대화 **– heart-to-heart** *adj*

heart·warm·ing /'hɑrtˌwɔrmɪŋ/ *adj* making you feel happy, calm, and hopeful ‖ 행복하고 안정되고 희망차게 해 주는. 마음이 따뜻해지는: *a heart-warming story* 마음이 따뜻해지는 이야기

heart·y /'hɑrti/ *adj* **1** very cheerful and friendly ‖ 매우 명랑하며 다정한. 활발한. 상냥한. 정성어린: *We were given a hearty welcome.* 우리는 따뜻한 환대를 받았다. **2** a hearty meal or APPETITE is very large ‖ 식사량이나 식욕이 매우 많은. 풍족[풍성]한. 넘치는. 왕성한

heat¹ /hit/ *n* **1** [U] warmth or hotness ‖ 따뜻함이나 열(기). 따스함. 온기: *heat generated by the sun* 태양에서 내뿜는 열 **2 the heat a)** very hot weather ‖ 매우

더운 날씨. 더위: *Cindy was constantly complaining about the heat.* 신디는 끊임 없이 더위에 대해 불평하고 있었다. **b)** the system in a house that keeps it warm ‖ 집안을 따뜻하게 유지해 주는 장 치. 난방 장치: *Can you turn the heat on/off?* 난방 장치 좀 켜[꺼] 주시겠어요? **c)** the heat that comes from this type of system, or from an OVEN or STOVE ‖ 난방 장치나 오븐 또는 난로에서 나오는 열(기). 열. 온도. 온기: *Lower the heat to 250°.* 온도를 250도로 낮추시오. **3 the heat of the moment/argument etc.** the period in a situation, argument etc. when you feel extremely angry or excited ‖ 어떤 상황·논쟁 등에서 극도로 화나거나 흥분됨을 느끼는 시기. 격렬한 때/토론의 최고조: *In the heat of the moment, I said some things I didn't mean.* 나는 매우 흥분하여 진심이 아닌 것들을 말해 버렸다. **4 take the heat** to deal with difficulties in a situation, especially by saying that you are responsible for them ‖ 특히 자신이 책임 진다고 말함으로써 상황의 어려움을 해결 하다. 위기를 받아들이다. 비난[책임]을 감수하다: *Coach Brown took the heat for the team's loss.* 브라운 코치는 팀의 패배 에 대해 책임을 졌다. **5** one of the parts of a sports competition from which the winners are chosen to go on to the next part ‖ 승자가 다음 경기 순서로 넘어가도 록 선발되는 스포츠 경기의 여러 시합 중 의 하나. (1)회전. 예선 **6 in heat** if a female animal is in heat, she is able to become PREGNANT ‖ 동물의 암컷이 새끼 를 밸 수 있는. 발정한. 암내를 풍기는

heat² *v* [I, T] also **heat up** to become warm or hot, or to make something warm or hot ‖ 따뜻하거나 뜨겁게 되다. 또는 사물을 따뜻하거나 뜨겁게 하다. 가 열하다. 데우다: *We could heat up some soup for dinner.* 저녁으로 수프를 좀 데워 먹으면 됩니다.

heat up *phr v* [I] if a situation, argument etc. heats up, the people involved in it become angrier and more excited ‖ 상황·논쟁 등의 관련자들이 더 화가 나고 더 흥분하게 되다. 격렬해지다. 고조되다

heat·ed /'hiːtɪd/ *adj* **1** kept warm by a HEATER ‖ 난방기에 의해 따뜻하게 유지된. 가열된. 데워진. 난방이 된: *a heated swimming pool* 온수 수영장 **2 heated argument/discussion etc.** an argument etc. in which people become very angry and excited ‖ 사람들이 매우 화가 나고 흥분이 되는 논쟁 등. 고조된

[격렬해진] 논쟁/논의

heat·er /'hiːtə/ *n* a machine used for heating air or water ‖ 공기나 물을 데우 기 위해 쓰이는 기계. 가열[난방]기(구). 난방 장치. 온수기

hea·then /'hiːðən/ *n* OLD-FASHIONED DISAPPROVING someone who does not belong to your religion ‖ 자신의 종교에 소속되지 않은 사람. 이교도 **– heathen** *adj*

heat wave /'. ./ *n* a period of unusually hot weather ‖ 유난히 더운 날씨가 더운 기간. 열파. 혹서 기간

heave¹ /hiːv/ *v* **1** [I, T] to pull, throw, or lift something with a lot of effort ‖ 많 은 노력을 기울여 사물을 끌어당기다[던지 다, 들어올리다]: *She heaved the box onto the back of the truck.* 그녀는 상자를 트럭 뒤에 실어 올렸다. **2 heave a sigh** to breathe out loudly, especially because you have stopped worrying about something ‖ 특히 어떤 것에 대한 걱정을 하지 않게 되어 소리를 내며 숨을 내쉬다. 한숨을 쉬다: *We all heaved a sigh of relief when it was over.* 우리 모 두는 그것이 끝나자 안도의 한숨을 내쉬었 다. **3** [I] if your chest heaves, it moves up and down quickly because it is difficult to breathe ‖ 숨쉬기가 힘들어서 가슴이 빠르게 오르내리다. 헐떡이다 **4** [I] INFORMAL ⇨ VOMIT¹

heave² *n* a strong pulling, pushing, or throwing movement ‖ 강하게 당김[밀침, 던짐]. 끌어[들어] 올리기. 던지기

heav·en /'hɛvən/ *n* **1** [U] also **Heaven** the place where God or the gods are believed to live, and where good people go after they die ‖ 창조주나 신들이 사는 곳이라 여겨지며 선한 사람들이 사후에 가 는 곳. 천국. 천당. 하늘(나라) **–** compare HELL **2** [U] INFORMAL a very good thing, situation, or place ‖ 아주 좋 은 것[상황, 장소]. 천당 같은 곳. 낙원. 더 없는 행복: *"How was your vacation?" "Oh, it was heaven!"* "휴가 어 땠어?" "아, 천국이었지!" **3 for heaven's sake** SPOKEN said when you are annoyed or angry ‖ 짜증이 나거나 화 가 났을 때에 쓰여. 제발. 부디. 아무조 록: *For heaven's sake, just shut up!* 제발 입 좀 닥쳐라! **4 heaven forbid** SPOKEN said in order to emphasize that you hope something will not happen ‖ 어떤 일이 일어나지 않았으면 하는 바람을 강조 하는 데에 쓰여. 맙소사. 그럴 리가 있나. 그런 일이 될 말인가: *And if–heaven forbid–he has an accident, what do I do then?* 그리고 만약, 그럴 리는 없겠지

만 그에게 사고가 난다면 그땐 나는 어떡
하지?

heav·en·ly /ˈhɛvənli/ *adj* **1** relating to
heaven ‖ 천국과 관련된. 천국의 **2** very
good or pleasing ‖ 매우 좋거나 즐겁게 하
는. 놀라운. 천국과 같은. 기쁨이 넘치는.
훌륭한: *a heavenly dessert* 훌륭한 후식

heavenly bod·y /ˌ… ˈ…/ *n* a star,
PLANET, or moon ‖ 별, 행성, 달. 천체

heavens /ˈhɛvənz/ *n* **1 (Good)
Heavens!** SPOKEN said when you are
surprised or slightly annoyed ‖ 놀라거나
약간 짜증이 났을 때에 쓰여. 어머나. 아
이구. 야단났군: *Good Heavens! Where
have you been?* 세상에! 지금까지 어디에
있었니? **2 the heavens** LITERARY the sky
‖ 하늘. 창공

heav·i·ly /ˈhɛvəli/ *adv* **1** in very large
amounts ‖ 아주 많은 양으로. 대량[다량]
으로. 많이: *He's been drinking heavily
recently.* 그는 최근에 엄청 마셔댔다. **2**
very or very much ‖ 매우 또는 매우 많이.
심하게. 크게: *The building was heavily
damaged by the fire.* 그 건물은 화재로
심하게 손상됐다. / *Our work is heavily
dependent on computers.* 우리 업무는
컴퓨터에 크게 의존한다. **3** someone who
breathes heavily is breathing very
loudly and slowly ‖ 사람이 매우 큰 소리
로 천천히 숨쉬는. 힘겹게[힘들게] 숨을
몰아쉬는. 괴로운 듯이 숨쉬는

heavy

heavy bags

heavy traffic

heav·y /ˈhɛvi/ *adj*
1 ▶THINGS 사물◀ weighing a lot ‖ 무게
가 많이 나가는. 무거운. 중량[비중]이 큰
[있는]: *Be careful lifting that box – it's
really heavy.* 그 상자 조심해서 들어. 정
말 무겁다. / *The suitcase feels heavier
than before.* 가방이 전보다 무거워진 느낌
이다.
2 ▶PEOPLE 사람◀ used in order to
politely describe someone who is fat ‖ 뚱
뚱한 사람을 정중하게 묘사하는 데에 쓰
여. 무거운. 몸집이 큰: *He's gotten very
heavy since we saw him last.* 우리가 지
난 번에 본 후로 그는 몸이 많이 불었다.
3 ▶AMOUNT 양◀ unusually large in

amount or quantity ‖ 유별나게 양이 많
은. 정도·규모가 큰[심한]. 막대한:
*Roads were closed due to heavy
rains/snow.* 도로는 폭우[폭설]로 폐쇄됐
다. / *Traffic is heavy on the 405
freeway.* 405번 고속도로에 교통 체증이
심하다.
4 ▶BUSY 바쁜◀ very busy and full of
activities ‖ 매우 바쁘고 활동으로 가득 찬.
촉박한. 빡빡한: *a heavy day/schedule*
바쁜 하루[일정]
5 heavy sleeper someone who does not
wake up very easily ‖ 쉽게 잠에서 깨지
않는 사람. 잠이 많은 사람. 깊은 잠을 자
는 사람
6 a heavy smoker/drinker someone
who smokes a lot or drinks a lot of
alcohol ‖ 담배를 많이 피우거나 술을 많이
마시는 사람. 골초/주당
7 ▶SERIOUS 심한◀ very complicated or
serious and involving a lot of mental
effort ‖ 매우 복잡하거나 심각하여 많은
정신적 노력을 요하는. 곤란한. 어려운.
중대한. 심원한. 힘드는. 지치게 하는: *a
heavy discussion* 격렬한 토론 / *For a
comedy that movie was heavy going.* 그
영화는 코미디물로서는 재미가 없었다.
8 heavy breathing breathing that is
slow and loud ‖ 느리고 소리가 큰 호흡.
깊은[무거운] 한숨
9 be heavy into sth SPOKEN
NONSTANDARD to be very involved in an
activity, especially one that is not good
for you ‖ 특히 좋지 않은 어떤 활동에 깊
이 관련되다. 깊이 빠져 있다[중독되다]:
Eric was real heavy into drugs. 에릭은
마약에 깊이 중독되었다.
10 a heavy load/burden a problem or
situation that is large or too difficult to
deal with ‖ 크거나 너무 어려워서 다루기
힘든 문제나 상황. 중대한[심각한, 과중
한] 부담/짐: *Three jobs! That's a heavy
load for just one person.* 세 가지 업무라
니! 그것은 한 사람에게는 너무 과중한 부
담이군.
11 with a heavy heart LITERARY feeling
very sad ‖ 매우 슬프게 느끼는. 울적한[우
울한] 마음으로 **– heaviness** *n* [U] —
compare LIGHT²

heavy-du·ty /ˌ… ˈ…/ *adj* **1** strong
enough to be used often or for hard
work without being damaged ‖ 손상됨이
자주 격한 작업에 사용할 만큼 충분히 강
한. 튼튼한. 강력한. 함부로 쓸 수 있는:
heavy-duty plastic gloves 튼튼한 고무
장갑 **2** SLANG said when you want to
emphasize how complicated, serious
etc. someone or something is ‖ 사람이나

사물이 얼마나 복잡하고 심각한가 등을 강조하고 싶을 때에 쓰여. 중대한. 진지한: *That was a heavy-duty conversation!* 진지한 대화였어!

heavy-hand·ed /,.. '../ *adj* strict, unfair, and not considering other people's feelings ‖ 엄격한·부당한·다른 사람의 감정을 고려하지 않는. 고압적인. 가혹한. 꼼짝 못하게 하는. 밀어부치는: *heavy-handed demands* 고압적인 요구

heavy in·dus·try /,.. '.../ *n* [U] industry that produces goods such as coal, steel, or chemicals, or large goods such as cars and machines ‖ 석탄[철강, 화학제품] 등의 재화, 또는 자동차·기계 등의 규모가 큰 재화를 생산하는 산업. 중공업

heavy met·al /,.. '../ *n* [U] a type of ROCK music with a strong beat that is played very loudly on electric GUITARs ‖ 전자 기타로 매우 요란하게 연주되는 강한 비트를 가진 록 음악의 한 형태. 헤비메탈

heav·y·weight /'hɛvi,weɪt/ *n* 1 someone who BOXes or WRESTLEs, and is in the heaviest weight group ‖ 권투나 레슬링을 하는 사람 중 가장 중량이 무거운 그룹에 속하는 사람. 헤비급 선수 2 someone who has a lot of power and experience in a particular business or job ‖ 특정한 사업이나 일에서 많은 힘과 경험을 가진 사람. 기업의 중요 인물. 실세. 유력자: *a debate between political heavyweights* 정치적 실세간의 토론

He·brew /'hibru/ *n* [U] the official language of Israel, also used in many other places by Jewish people ‖ 유대인들이 (이스라엘이 아닌) 많은 다른 곳에서 사용하기도 하는 이스라엘의 공식 언어. 히브리어 **– Hebrew, Hebraic** /hɪ'breɪɪk/ *adj*

heck /hɛk/ *interjection* 1 said in order to emphasize a question, or when you are annoyed ‖ 질문을 강조하거나 화가 날 때 쓰여. 도대체: *Who/what/where etc. the heck is that?* 저것이 도대체 누구야 [뭐야, 어디야]? / *Ah, heck! I've lost my glasses.* 아, 젠장! 안경을 잃어버렸어. 2 **What the heck!** said when you do something that you should not do ‖ 하지 말아야 할 것을 할 때 쓰여: "*Want another piece of pie?*" "*Yeah, what the heck!*" "파이 하나 더 먹을래?" "그러지 뭐 젠장!" —see also HELL

heck·le /'hɛkəl/ *v* [T] to interrupt and try to embarrass someone who is speaking or performing ‖ 연설하고 있거나 공연하고 있는 사람을 방해해서 당황하게 하려고 하다. 연설자 등에게 야유를 퍼붓다. 괴롭히다. 애먹이다 **– heckler** *n* **– heckling** *n* [U]

hec·tare /'hɛktɛr/ *n* a unit for measuring an area of land, equal to 10,000 square meters or 2.471 ACRES ‖ 1만 평방미터나 2.471에이커에 해당하는 면적을 재는 단위. 헥타르

hec·tic /'hɛktɪk/ *adj* very busy, hurried, and slightly exciting ‖ 매우 바쁘고 서두르며 약간 흥분한. 법석을 떠는: *It's been a really hectic week.* 정말 바쁜 주였다.

he'd /id; *strong* hid/ 1 the short form of "he would" ‖ "he would"의 단축형: *I'm sure he'd drive you there.* 그가 당신을 거기까지 태워줄 거라 확신한다. 2 the short form of "he had" ‖ "he had"의 단축형: *He'd never been a good dancer.* 그는 결코 좋은 무용수는 아니었다.

hedge¹ /hɛdʒ/ *n* 1 a row of bushes used as a border around a yard or between two yards ‖ 한 마당 둘레나 두 마당 사이의 경계로 사용되는 일렬로 된 관목. 울타리 2 **hedge against disaster/inflation etc.** something that helps avoid problems, losing a lot of money etc. ‖ 많은 돈을 잃는 등의 문제들을 피하는 데에 도움을 주는 것. 재난/인플레이션 등에 대한 대비책: *a hedge against financial risk* 재정적 위험의 대비책

hedge² *v* 1 to avoid giving a direct answer to a question ‖ 질문에 직접적인 대답을 하는 것을 피하다. 얼렁뚱땅 대답하다. 답변을 얼버무리다: *I got the feeling he was hedging.* 나는 그가 답변을 얼버무리고 있다는 느낌을 받았다. 2 **hedge your bets** to reduce your chances of failing by trying several different possibilities instead of one ‖ 하나 대신에 여러 가지 다른 가능성을 시도함으로써 실패의 가능성을 줄이다. 내기에서 여러 곳에다[양쪽에] 걸다

hedge against sth *phr v* [T] to protect yourself from having problems, losing a lot of money etc. ‖ 많은 금전을 잃는 등의 문제가 생기지 않게 자신을 보호하다. (위험 등에 대한) 방어책[대책]을 세우다: *A well-managed business will hedge against financial loss.* 제대로 운영되는 사업체는 재정적 손실에 대한 대책을 세운

he·do·nism /'hidn,ɪzəm/ *n* [U] the belief that pleasure is the most important thing in life ‖ 쾌락이 인생에서 제일 중요한 것이라는 믿음. 쾌락설. 쾌락주의 **– hedonist** *n* **– hedonistic** /,hidn'ɪstɪk/ *adj*

heed¹ /hid/ v [T] FORMAL to pay attention to someone's advice or warning ‖ 남의 충고나 경고에 주의를 기울이다. …에 주의[유의]하다

heed² n [U] FORMAL **take heed of/pay heed to** to pay attention to something and think about it seriously ‖ 어떤 것에 주의를 기울여 그것에 대해 심각하게 생각하다. …에 주의[유의]하다

heed·less /'hidlɪs/ adj LITERARY not paying attention to something important ‖ 중요한 것에 주의를 기울이지 않는. 부주의한. 경솔한. 조심성 없는

heel¹ /hil/ n **1** the back part of your foot ‖ 발의 뒷부분. (발)뒤꿈치 —see picture at BODY **2** the back raised part of a shoe, or the back part of a sock that is under your heel ‖ 구두의 높여진 뒷부분, 또는 발뒤꿈치 아래에 있는 양말의 뒷부분. 구두[양말]의 뒤축 **3 -heeled** having a particular type of heel ‖ 뒤꿈치가 특정한 형태를 가진. 뒤꿈치[뒤축]가 …한: a high-heeled shoe 뒤축이 높은 구두 **4 on the heels of** very soon after something ‖ 어떤 것 뒤에 곧바로: Christmas vacation came on the heels of our finals. 기말 고사가 끝난 후 바로 크리스마스 방학이었다. **5** the raised part of your hand near your wrist ‖ 손목 근처에 있는 손의 튀어나온 부분

heel² v heel! used in order to tell your dog to stay near you ‖ 자신의 개에게 자기 주위에 있으라고 말하는 데에 쓰여. (개를 향하여) 따라와!

heels /hilz/ n [plural] ⇨ HIGH HEELS

heft·y /'hɛfti/ adj **1** big or strong ‖ 크거나 강한. 건장한. 힘이 있는: a hefty man 건장한 남자 **2 a hefty price/sum etc.** a large amount of money ‖ 많은 액수의 돈. 고가/고액

heif·er /'hɛfɚ/ n a young female cow that has not yet given birth to a calf (=baby cow) ‖ 아직 새끼를 낳지 않은 어린 암소

height /haɪt/ n **1** [C, U] how tall someone or something is ‖ 사람이나 사물의 큰 정도. 키. 높이: Howard and Ben are about the same height. 하워드와 밴은 거의 키가 같다. / Sunflowers can grow to a height of 15 feet. 해바라기는 15피트 높이까지 자랄 수 있다. **2** a particular distance above the ground ‖ 지면 위로의 특정한 거리. 높이: The shelves were installed at

the wrong height. 그 선반들은 제 높이에 맞지 않게 설치되었다. **3 the height of a)** the period when something is the strongest, most intense, best etc. it can ever be ‖ 어떤 것이 이제까지 할 수 있었던(것 중) 가장 강하고 격렬하며 최고인 기간. 절정. 극치. 정점. 한창 때: the height of the oil crisis 석유 위기의 최고조기 **b)** the greatest degree or amount of something ‖ 어떤 것의 최대의 정도나 양: rich people living in the height of luxury 최고로 호사스럽게 살고 있는 부자들 —see also HEIGHTS

height·en /'haɪtˀn/ v [I, T] to increase or make something become increased ‖ 증대하거나 어떤 것을 증대시키다. 높아지다[높이다]: Taking the class has heightened my appreciation of modern art. 그 수업을 받아 현대 미술에 대한 나의 감상력은 향상되었다.

heights /haɪts/ n [plural] **1** a high position or place ‖ 높은 위치나 장소. 정점. 정상. 고지: I'm afraid of heights. 나는 고소 공포증이 있다. **2 to new heights** to an increased or more successful level ‖ 증가되거나 더욱 성공적인 수준으로. 더 높은 수준으로: Prices jumped to new heights on Wednesday. 수요일에 물가가 폭등했다.

hei·nous /'heɪnəs/ adj extremely bad ‖ 매우 나쁜. 극악[흉악]한: a heinous crime 흉악한 범죄

heir /ɛr/ n someone who will legally receive all of the money, property etc. of a person who has died ‖ 죽은 사람의 모든 돈·재산 등을 합법적으로 받게 되는 사람. 상속인

heir·loom /'ɛrlum/ n a valuable object that a family owns for many years ‖ 집안 사람들이 아주 오랫동안 소유한 가치 있는 물건. 가보

heist /haɪst/ n a BURGLARY ‖ 강도

held /hɛld/ the past tense and PAST PARTICIPLE of hold ‖ hold의 과거·과거 분사형

hel·i·cop·ter /'hɛlɪ,kaptɚ/ n a type of aircraft with metal blades on top of it that spin very fast ‖ 매우 빨리 도는 금속 날개가 맨 위에 달려 있는 항공기의 일종. 헬리콥터

hel·i·port /'hɛlə,pɔrt/ n an airport for HELICOPTERS ‖ 헬리콥터 용의 공항. 헬리콥터 이착륙장

he·li·um /'hiliəm/ n [U] a gas that is an

ELEMENT and that is lighter than air, often used in order to make BALLOONS float ‖ 종종 풍선을 띄우는 데 쓰는 공기보다 가벼운 원소인 가스. 헬륨

he'll /ɪl, il, hɪl; *strong* hil/ **1** the short form of "he will" ‖ "he will"의 단축형: *He'll be arriving later tonight.* 그는 오늘 밤 늦게 도착할 것이다. / *The law says he'll be punished for his crimes.* 그는 법에 따라 그가 저지른 죄에 대한 처벌을 받게 될 것이다. **2** the short form of "he shall" ‖ "he shall"의 단축형

hell /hɛl/ *n* **1** [singular] *also* **Hell** the place where bad people will be punished after they die, according to the Christian and Muslim religions ‖ 기독교와 이슬람교에 의하면 악한 사람이 사후에 처벌을 받게 되는 곳. 지옥 **2 be hell** to be very bad ‖ 매우 나쁘다: *Traffic was hell all the way home.* 집으로 가는 내내 교통 상황이 매우 좋지 않았다.

SPOKEN PHRASES

3 an impolite way to emphasize a question or statement ‖ 질문이나 말을 강조하기 위한 무례한 어법. 도대체. 대관절: *What the hell are you doing?* 도대체 뭐 하고 있는 거니? / *"Are you working late tonight?" "Hell, no!"* "오늘 밤 야근할 거니?" "아니, 천만에!" / *Get the hell out of here!* 여기서 당장 나가! / *It's hard as hell to hear anything in there.* 그곳에서 어떤 소리를 듣는다는 것은 대단히 어렵다. / *He's a hell of a salesman.* (=he's a good salesman) 그는 대단한 세일즈맨이다. **4 go to hell** an impolite phrase said when you are very angry with someone ‖ 자신이 남에게 대단히 화났을 때에 쓰는 무례한 어구. 뒈져버려. 꺼져 **5 for the hell of it** for no particular reason or purpose ‖ 특정한 이유나 목적 없이: *We just decided to drive up to Montreal for the hell of it.* 우리는 무작정 그냥 몬트리올까지 운전해 가기로 결정했다. **6 to hell with sb/sth** an impolite way of saying that you do not care about someone or something any longer ‖ 사람이나 사물에 대해서 더 이상 신경 쓰지 않는다고 말하는 무례한 어법. …을 없애버리다. 타도하다 **7 from hell** said when you think something is the worst it could be ‖ 어떤 것이 있을 수 있는 최악의 것이라 생각할 때에 쓰여. 최악의: *It was the vacation from hell.* 그 휴가는 최악이었다. **8 give sb hell** an impolite phrase meaning to tell someone angrily that s/he should not have done something ‖ 무엇을 하지 말았어야 했다고 남에게 화내어 말하려는 뜻의 무례한 어구. 남을 못 배기게 하다. 혼내 주다 **9 like hell** used for emphasizing what you are saying ‖ 자신이 말하고 있는 것을 강조하는 데에 쓰여. 결사적으로. 대단히: *I'd been really sick, and I looked like hell.* (=looked terrible) 나는 정말 아팠었고 끔찍한 몰골이었다. / *We're going to have to work like hell to get this done.* (=work very hard) 우리는 이것을 마치기 위해 대단히 열심히 일해야 할 것이다. **10 go through hell/put sb through hell** to experience a situation that is extremely bad, or to make someone do this ‖ 극히 나쁜 상황을 경험하거나 남이 극히 나쁜 상황을 겪게 하다: *My father's drinking problem must have put my mother through hell.* 나의 아버지의 알코올 중독 문제가 어머니에게 극히 나쁜 상황을 겪게 했음에 틀림 없다. **11 raise hell** an impolite phrase meaning to have fun in a loud and annoying way ‖ 시끄럽게 괴롭히며 즐기는 것을 뜻하는 무례한 어구. 야단법석을 떨다. 소동을 일으키다: *kids raising hell at 3:00 a.m.* ‖ 새벽 3시에 시끄럽게 놀고 있는 아이들 **12 all hell breaks loose** used in order to say that a situation suddenly becomes very bad, disorganized, or violent ‖ 상황이 갑자기 매우 나빠지는[무질서해지는, 격렬해지는] 것을 말하는 데에 쓰여. 큰 혼란이 일어나다

hel·lo /həˈloʊ, hɛˈloʊ, ˈhɛloʊ/ *interjection* **1** used when meeting someone or greeting someone ‖ 남을 만날 때나 남에게 인사할 때 쓰여. 안녕(하세요): *Hello, my name is Betty.* 안녕, 내 이름은 베티야. **2** said when answering the telephone or when starting a telephone conversation ‖ 전화를 받을 때나 전화 통화를 시작할 때 쓰여. 여보세요: *"Hello?" "Hello, is Chad there?"* "여보세요?" "여보세요, 채드 씨 계십니까?" **3** said when trying to get someone's attention ‖ 남의 주의를 끌려고 할 때 쓰여: *Hello? Is anybody here?* 이봐요? 여기에 아무도 없어요? **4 say hello** to have a quick conversation with someone ‖ 남과 잠깐 대화를 나누다. 인사를 나누다: *I'll drop by later and say hello.* 나중에 들러서 잠깐 얘기를 나눌게요.

helm /hɛlm/ *n* **1 at the helm** controlling a group or organization ‖ 단

체나 조직을 통솔하는. 키를 잡고 있는: *With Ms. Mathis at the helm, the company has grown by 20%.* 마티스 씨가 실권을 잡아서 그 회사는 20퍼센트의 성장을 이룩했다. **2** a wheel used for guiding a ship's direction ‖ 배의 방향을 조종하는 데 사용하는 바퀴 모양의 장치. 키(의 손잡이). 타륜

hel·met /ˈhɛlmɪt/ *n* a hard hat that covers and protects your head ‖ 머리를 덮어서 보호하는 딱딱한 모자. 헬멧: *a motorcycle helmet* 오토바이 헬멧 —see picture at MASK¹

help¹ /hɛlp/ *v* **1** [I, T] to make someone be able to do something more easily ‖ 사람이 더욱 쉽게 무엇을 할 수 있게 하다. …을 돕다. 거들다: *Do you want me to help you move that table?* 제가 저 탁자 옮기는 것을 도와드릴까요? / *Mom, can you help me with my homework?* 엄마, 제 숙제 하는 것 좀 도와줄래요? / *Is there anything I can do to help?* 내가 뭔가 도와줄 게 있니? **2** [I, T] to make it possible for something to become better, easier, or more developed ‖ 어떤 일이 더 좋아지게[용이해지게, 발전되게] 하다: *It might help to talk to someone about your problems.* 당신의 문제에 대해 남에게 말하는 것이 도움이 될 것이다. / *Brushing your teeth helps prevent cavities.* 양치질을 하면 충치를 예방하는 데 도움이 된다.

SPOKEN PHRASES

3 can't/couldn't help said when you are unable to stop doing something ‖ 어떤 일을 하는 것을 멈출 수 없을 때 쓰여. …하지 않을 수 없다[없었다]: *I just couldn't help laughing.* 나는 웃음을 멈출 수가 없었다. **4 I can't help it** said when you think something is not your fault ‖ 어떤 일이 자신의 잘못이 아니라고 생각할 때 쓰여. 나로서는 어찌할 도리가 없다: *I can't help it if she lost the stupid book!* 그녀가 그 시시한 책을 잃어버렸다면 나로서는 어쩔 도리가 없다! **5 help yourself** used when telling someone to take as much food or drink as s/he wants ‖ 남에게 원하는 만큼 음식이나 음료를 먹으라고 말할 때 쓰여. 마음껏[멋대로] 먹다: *Help yourself to anything in the fridge.* 냉장고에 있는 음식을 마음껏 드세요. **6 help!** said when you need someone to help you, especially because you are in danger ‖ 특히 자신이 위험에 처해 있어서 남의 도움이 필요할 때 쓰여. 도와주세요!

help out *phr v* [I, T **help** sb ↔ **out**] to help someone because s/he is very busy, has a lot of problems etc. ‖ 남이 매우 바쁘거나 많은 문제점 등을 가지고 있기 때문에 돕다. 거들다. 도와주다: *They did everything they could to help us out.* 그들은 우리를 돕기 위해 그들이 할 수 있는 모든 것을 했다.

USAGE NOTE help and assist

Assist is more formal than **help**. Use **help** to mean "make it easier for someone to do something": *Could you help me move this desk?* Use **assist** when someone has special skills to help someone do something: *Dr. Taylor assisted in the research of this article.*

assist는 **help**보다 더욱 격식을 차린 말이다. **help**는 "남이 어떤 일을 하는 데 보다 쉽게 해주다"의 의미로 쓴다: 이 책상을 옮기게 나를 좀 도와줄래? **assist**는 누군가가 어떤 일을 하는 데 도울 수 있는 특별한 기술을 가지고 있을 때 쓴다: 테일러 박사는 이 논문의 연구에 도움을 주었다.

---

help² *n* [U] **1** the action of helping someone ‖ 남을 돕는 행동. 도움. 원조. 조력: *Do you need any help washing the dishes?* 설거지하는 데 도움이 필요하니? **2** the quality of being useful ‖ 유용한 자질. 도움이 되는 것: *Unfortunately the instructions weren't a lot of help.* 불행하게도 그 사용 설명서는 큰 도움이 되지 못했다. **3** advice, treatment, money etc. that someone gives you in order to help you ‖ 남이 자신을 도와주기 위해 주는 충고·대우·돈 등: *Go get help, quickly!* 가서 도와달라고 그래, 빨리!

help·er /ˈhɛlpɚ/ *n* someone who helps another person ‖ 다른 사람을 도와주는 사람. 조력자. 조수. 가정부

help·ful /ˈhɛlpfəl/ *adj* **1** useful ‖ 유용한. 유익한. 도움이 되는: *The map was really helpful.* 그 지도는 정말 유용했다. **2** willing to help ‖ 기꺼이 돕는. 도와주는. 협조적인: *Everyone was so helpful and friendly.* 모든 사람들이 아주 협조적이었고 다정했다. – **helpfully** *adv*

help·ing¹ /ˈhɛlpɪŋ/ *n* the amount of food you are given or that you take ‖ 주어진 음식의 양, 또는 자신이 먹는 음식의 양. (음식물) 한 그릇. (일정한) 양: *Who wants another helping of apple pie?* 누구 사과 파이 한 접시 더 먹을 사람?

helping² *adj* **lend/give a helping hand** to help someone ‖ 누군가를 돕다

helping verb /'.. ,./ n TECHNICAL ⇨
AUXILIARY VERB

help·less /'hɛlplɪs/ adj unable to take
care of yourself or protect yourself || 스
스로를 돌보거나 보호할 수 없는. 어쩔 수
없는. 무력한: *The man lay helpless in
the street.* 그 남자는 거리에서 어쩔 바
를 몰랐다. – **helplessness** n [U] –
helplessly adv

hel·ter-skel·ter /,hɛltɚˈskɛltɚ/ adv
done in a disorganized, confusing, and
hurried way || 무질서하고 혼란스러우며
급하게 하여. 당황하여. 허둥지둥

hem[1] /hɛm/ n the folded and sewn edge
of a piece of clothing || 옷을 접어서 꿰맨
가장자리 부분. 옷단

hem[2] v **-mmed, -mming** [T] to fold
and sew the edge of a piece of clothing
|| 옷의 가장자리를 접어서 꿰매다. 단을
꿰매다

hem sb ↔ **in** n [T] to surround someone
so that s/he cannot move where s/he
wants || 사람이 가고 싶은 곳으로 이동할
수 없도록 둘러싸다. …을 속박하다[포위
하다]. 가두어 넣다: *It was really
scary – I was hemmed in by two cars
and a big truck on the freeway.* 고속도로
상에서 자동차 두 대와 큰 트럭 한 대에
둘러싸여 나는 몹시 겁이 났다.

hem·i·sphere /'hɛmə,sfɪr/ n one of the
halves of the earth, especially the
northern or southern parts above and
below the EQUATOR || 특히 적도 위·아래
의 북쪽이나 남쪽 지역인 지구의 반쪽 중
하나. 반구(체). 북[남]반구

hem·line /'hɛmlaɪn/ n the length of a
dress, skirt, or pants || 드레스[치마, 바
지]의 길이

hem·lock /'hɛmlɑk/ n [C, U] a very
poisonous plant, or the poison of this
plant || 매우 독성이 강한 식물, 또는 이 식
물의 독. 독미나리(의 독)

he·mo·glo·bin /'himə,gloʊbɪn/ n [U] a
red substance in the blood that carries
oxygen and iron || 산소와 철분을 운반하
는 혈액 속의 붉은 물질. 헤모글로빈. 혈
색소

he·mo·phil·i·a /,himəˈfɪliə, -ˈfilyə/ n
[U] a serious disease that usually
affects only men, in which the blood
does not become thick, so that he loses
too much blood after being cut or
wounded || 베이거나 상처가 난 후 혈액이
굳지 않아서 너무 많은 피를 상실하는 병
으로, 일반적으로 남자들에게만 영향을 미
치는 중병. 혈우병 – **hemophiliac**
/,himəˈfɪli,æk/ n

hem·or·rhage /'hɛmərɪdʒ/ n a serious

medical condition in which an area in
someone's body loses too much blood ||
사람의 신체 일부에서 너무 많은 피를 상
실하는 심각한 의학적 상태. 과다 출혈

hem·or·rhoids /'hɛmə,rɔɪdz/ n
[plural] painfully swollen BLOOD VESSELS
at the ANUS || 항문의 통증을 수반하는 부
풀어 오른 혈관. 치질. 치핵

hemp /hɛmp/ n [U] a plant used for
making strong rope, a rough cloth, and
the drug CANNABIS || 튼튼한 밧줄·거친
천·마리화나의 제조에 쓰이는 식물. 대마

hen /hɛn/ n a fully grown female bird,
especially a female chicken || 완전히 자
란 새, 특히 닭의 암컷. 암탉

hence /hɛns/ adv FORMAL for this
reason || 이러한 이유 때문에. 그러므로.
따라서: *The sugar from the grapes
remains in the wine, hence the sweet
taste.* 포도주에는 포도당이 들어 있어서
맛이 달콤하다.

hence·forth /'hɛnsfɔrθ, ,hɛnsˈfɔrθ/,
henceforward /hɛnsˈfɔrwɚd/ adv
FORMAL from this time on || 이 시간부터.
지금부터. 이제부터는: *Henceforth in this
book, these people will be called "The
Islanders."* 지금부터는 이 책에서 이 사람
들을 "섬사람들"로 부를 것이다.

hench·man /'hɛntʃmən/ n someone
who faithfully obeys a powerful person
such as a politician or a criminal || 정치
인이나 범죄자 등의 유력한 사람에게 충성
스레 복종하는 사람. 추종자. 똘마니. 심복

hep·a·ti·tis /,hɛpəˈtaɪtɪs/ n [U] a
serious disease of the LIVER || 간의 심각
한 병. 간염

her[1] /ɚ, hɚ; *strong* hɚ/ possessive adj
1 belonging to or relating to a female
person or animal that has been
mentioned or is known about || 언급되거
나 알고 있는 여자나 동물의 암컷에 속하
거나 관련된. 그녀[그 여자]의: *Maura
wants to know where her yellow
sweater is.* 모라는 그녀의 노란색 스웨터
가 어디에 있는지 알고 싶어한다. / *That's
her new car.* 그 차는 그녀의 새 차이다.
2 used when talking about a country,
car, ship etc. that has been mentioned
|| 언급된 나라·자동차·배 등에 대해 말할
때 쓰여. 그것의: *Her top speed is 110
miles per hour.* 그 차의 최고 속도는 시속
110마일이다.

her[2] pron **1** the object form of "she" ||
"she"의 목적격: *I've never seen your
boss. Is that her?* 나는 너희 사장을 본 적
이 없어. 저 여자가 네 사장이니? / *I gave
her $20.* 나는 그녀에게 20달러를 주었다.
—see usage note at ME **2** a country,

ship, car etc. that has been mentioned ‖ 언급된 나라·배·자동차 등

her·ald /'hɛrəld/ v [T] **1** to publicly praise someone or something ‖ 사람이나 사물을 공개적으로 칭찬하다. 칭송하다: *He was heralded as the poet of his generation.* 그는 당대의 시인으로서 칭송 받았다. **2** to be a sign that something is going to come or happen soon ‖ 어떤 일이 곧 닥치거나 일어날 것이라는 징조가 되다. …을 예고하다. 미리 알리다: *The development of the computer chip heralded a new age of technology.* 컴퓨터 칩의 발달은 새로운 과학기술 시대를 예고했다.

herb /əb/ n a plant used in cooking to give food more taste, or to make medicine ‖ 요리에서 음식에 맛을 더 내기 위해, 또는 약을 만들기 위해 사용되는 식물. 약초. 허브

herb·al /'əbəl/ adj relating to HERBs ‖ 허브와 관련된. 약초의: *herbal medicine* 한방약

herb·i·vore /'həbə,vɔr, 'əbə-/ n an animal that only eats plants ‖ 풀만을 먹는 동물. 초식 동물 —compare CARNIVORE

herd¹ /həd/ n a group of a particular type of animal that lives together ‖ 함께 모여 사는 특정 종류의 동물의 무리. 떼: *a herd of cattle* 소떼

herd² v [I, T] to form a group, or to make people or animals move together as a group ‖ 무리를 이루다, 또는 사람이나 동물들을 무리지어 함께 움직이게 하다. 떼를 짓다. 모으다: *The tour guide herded us onto the bus.* 그 여행 가이드는 우리를 버스로 모이게 했다.

here¹ /hɪr/ adv **1** in or to this place ‖ 이 장소에서[로]. 여기에[로]: *I'm going to stay here with Kim.* 나는 킴과 함께 여기에 머물 예정이다. / *How far is Canada from here?* 여기서 캐나다까지는 얼마나 멉니까? / *Remember, we came here on Dad's birthday.* 기억해 봐, 아빠 생일에 우리 여기에 왔었잖아. / *It's so dark out here.* 여기 바깥은 매우 어둡다. **2** if a period of time is here, it has begun ‖ 기간이 시작되어. 도래하여: *Spring is here!* 봄이 왔네! **3** at this point in a discussion or piece of writing ‖ 토론이나 글의 이 시점에서. 여기서: *The subject is too difficult to explain here, but I'll give you some books that will help you.* 그 주제는 여기서 설명하기에는 너무 어렵지만 당신에게 도움이 될 몇 권의 책을 드릴게요.

SPOKEN PHRASES

4 here you are/go said when you give someone something s/he has asked for ‖ 남이 요청한 것을 줄 때 쓰여. 자, 여기 있습니다: *"Could you bring me a glass of water, please?" "Here you are, sir."* "물 한 잔 갖다 주시겠습니까?" "네, 여기 있습니다." **5 here's** ... also **here he/she/it is** used in order to say that you have arrived somewhere, or that someone you have been waiting or looking for has arrived ‖ 자신이 어딘가에 도착했을 때, 또는 기다리거나 찾던 사람이 도착했다는 것을 말하는 데에 쓰여. 여기에 …이 왔다[있다]: *Here's the restaurant I was telling you about.* 내가 당신에게 말한 식당에 다 왔네요. / *Here you are – we've been looking everywhere for you.* 여기 계시는군요. 우리는 사방으로 당신을 찾아다니고 있었어요. **6 here comes**... said as the person or vehicle you have been waiting for is arriving ‖ 자신이 기다리고 있던 사람이나 탈것이 도착할 때 쓰여. …이 왔군: *Oh, here comes Sam now.* 오, 지금 샘이 오는군! / *Here comes the bus.* 버스가 오는군! **7 here goes** said before you do something exciting, dangerous, or new ‖ 흥분되는[위험한, 새로운] 것을 하기 전에 쓰여. 자, 간다. 자, 시작한다: *Are you ready? OK, here goes.* 준비됐니? 좋았어. 자, 시작한다. **8 here's to sb/sth** said when you are praising or thanking someone or something ‖ 사람이나 사물에 칭찬하거나 감사함을 표현할 때 쓰여. …에게 행운이 있기를. …을 위해 건배: *Here's to Jane for all her hard work!* 최선을 다해서 일한 제인에게 행운이 있기를!

here² interjection said when you offer something to someone ‖ 남에게 어떤 것을 제공할 때 쓰여. 여기 있습니다: *Here, use my pen.* 자, 여기 내 펜 써.

here·a·bouts /'hɪrə,bauts, ,hɪrə'bauts/ adv around or near the place where you are ‖ 자신이 있는 곳 둘레에 또는 근처에. 이 근처[부근]에(서): *Everyone hereabouts thinks he's guilty.* 여기 있는 모든 사람들은 그가 유죄라고 생각한다.

here·af·ter¹ /,hɪr'æftə/ adv FORMAL from this time or in the future ‖ 지금부터는, 또는 미래에. 이제부터. 향후. 장차

hereafter² n the hereafter life after you die ‖ 죽은 후의 삶. 내세: *Do you believe in the hereafter?* 당신은 내세가 있다고 믿습니까?

here·by /,hɪr'baɪ, 'hɪrbaɪ/ adv FORMAL

as a result of this statement ‖ 이 말의 결과로서. 이에 의하여. 이로써: *I hereby pronounce you man and wife.* 이로써 당신들은 부부가 되었음을 선언합니다.

he·red·i·tar·y /həˈrɛdəˌtɛri/ *adj* if a mental or physical quality, or a disease is hereditary, it is passed to a child from the GENES of his/her parents ‖ 정신적 또는 육체적 자질이나 병이 부모의 유전자에서 자식에게로 전해지는. 유전의. 유전하는: *Heart disease is often hereditary.* 심장병은 종종 유전된다.

he·red·i·ty /həˈrɛdəti/ *n* [U] the process of passing on a mental or physical quality from a parent's GENES to a child ‖ 정신적 또는 신체적 자질이나 병이 부모의 유전자에서 자식에게로 전해지는 과정. 유전

here·in /ˌhɪrˈɪn/ *adv* FORMAL in this place, situation, or piece of writing ‖ 이 장소[상황, 문서]에서. 이에 비추어

her·e·sy /ˈhɛrəsi/ *n* [C, U] a belief that a religious, political, or social group considers to be wrong or evil ‖ 어떤 종교[정치, 사회] 단체가 잘못되거나 사악한 것으로 여기는 신념. 이단. 이설

her·e·tic /ˈhɛrəˌtɪk/ *n* someone whose beliefs are considered to be wrong or evil ‖ 그릇되거나 사악하다고 간주되는 믿음을 가진 사람. 이단자. 이교도 – **heretical** /həˈrɛtɪkəl/ *adj*

here·with /ˌhɪrˈwɪθ, -ˈwɪð/ *adv* FORMAL with this letter or document ‖ 이 편지나 서류와 함께. 이것에 덧붙여서. 동봉하여

her·it·age /ˈhɛrətɪdʒ/ *n* [C, U] the traditional beliefs, values, customs etc. of a family or country ‖ 가족이나 국가의 전통적인 믿음·가치·관습 등. 유산. 전승: *Ireland's musical heritage* 아일랜드의 음악적 유산

her·met·i·cal·ly /hərˈmɛtɪkli/ *adv* TECHNICAL **hermetically sealed** very tightly closed so that no air can get in or out ‖ 공기가 출입할 수 없도록 매우 꽉 닫아. 밀폐[밀봉]하여 – **hermetic** *adj*

her·mit /ˈhɛmɪt/ *n* someone who prefers to live far away from other people ‖ 다른 사람들과 멀리 떨어져 살기 좋아하는 사람. 은둔자

her·ni·a /ˈhɛniə/ *n* [C, U] a medical condition in which an organ pushes through the skin or muscle that covers it; RUPTURE ‖ 신체 기관이 그것을 덮고 있는 피부나 근육을 빠져나오는 의학적 상태. 헤르니아. 탈장. ⓟ rupture

he·ro /ˈhɪroʊ/ *n, plural* **heroes** **1** someone who is admired for doing something very brave or good ‖ 매우 용

감하거나 좋은 일을 해서 존경받는 사람. 영웅. 위인: *He became a local hero for saving the child's life.* 그는 그 아이의 생명을 구해서 그 지방의 영웅이 되었다. **2** someone, especially a man or boy, who is the main character of a book, play, or movie ‖ 책[연극, 영화]에서 특히 남자나 소년 주인공 **3** also **hero sandwich** ⇨ SUB **3** —see also HEROINE

he·ro·ic /hɪˈroʊɪk/ *adj* **1** admired for being brave, strong, and determined ‖ 용감하고 강하며 의지가 강해 존경받는. 영웅의. 영웅다운. 훌륭한: *the people's heroic efforts in the fight for independence* 독립을 위해 싸우는 국민들의 영웅적 분투 **2** a heroic story, poem etc. has a HERO in it ‖ 이야기나 시 등에 영웅이 포함되어 있는. 영웅을 다룬

he·ro·ics /hɪˈroʊɪks/ *n* [plural] brave or impressive actions or words that someone does in order to seem impressive to other people ‖ 어떤 사람이 다른 사람들에게 잘 보이기 위해서 하는 용감하거나 인상적인 행동이나 말. 과장된 언행

her·o·in /ˈhɛroʊɪn/ *n* [U] a strong illegal drug made from MORPHINE ‖ 모르핀으로 만든 강력한 마약. 헤로인

her·o·ine /ˈhɛroʊɪn/ *n* a female HERO ‖ 여자 영웅. 여장부. 여걸

her·o·ism /ˈhɛroʊˌɪzəm/ *n* [U] very great courage ‖ 매우 대단한 용기. 용맹. 대담: *Firefighters were praised for their heroism.* 소방관들은 그들의 용맹함으로 칭찬을 받았다.

her·on /ˈhɛrən/ *n* a large wild bird with very long legs and a long beak, that lives near water ‖ 물가에 사는 매우 긴 다리와 긴 부리를 가진 큰 야조. 왜가리

her·pes /ˈhəpiz/ *n* [U] a very infectious disease that causes spots on the skin, especially on the face or GENITALS ‖ 피부, 특히 얼굴이나 생식기 위에 반점이 생기는 매우 전염성이 강한 병. 포진(疱疹)

her·ring /ˈhɛrɪŋ/ *n* [C, U] a long thin silver sea fish, or the meat from this fish ‖ 길고 가느다란 은빛의 바닷물고기, 또는 이 물고기의 살. 청어(고기)

hers /hɚz/ *possessive pron* the thing or things belonging to or relating to a female person or animal that has been mentioned or is known about ‖ 언급되거나 알고 있는 여성, 또는 동물의 암컷에 속하거나 관련된 것(들). 그녀의 것[소유물]: *That's my car. This is hers.* 저것은 내 차고 이것은 그녀의 차이다. / *Angela is a friend of hers.* 안젤라는 그녀의 친구이다. / *My boots are black. Hers are brown.*

내 부츠는 검은색이고 그녀의 것은 갈색이다.

her·self /əˈsɛlf; *strong* həˈsɛlf/ *pron* 1 the REFLEXIVE form of "she" ‖ "she"의 재귀 대명사형. 그녀 자신[스스로]: *Carol hurt herself.* 캐롤은 자해했다. / *She made herself a cup of coffee.* 그녀는 자신의 커피를 탔다. 2 the strong form of "she," used in order to emphasize the subject or object of a sentence ‖ "she"의 강조형으로, 문장의 주어나 목적어를 강조하는 데에 쓰여: *She went to the library herself to get the information.* 그 정보를 얻기 위해 직접 도서관에 갔다. / *It's true! Vicky told me herself.* 그건 사실이야! 비키가 본인이 나에게 말했어. 3 **(all) by herself a)** without help ‖ 도움 없이. 혼자 힘으로. 스스로: *My daughter made dinner all by herself.* 내 딸이 혼자 힘으로 저녁을 준비했다. **b)** alone ‖ 홀로. 자기 혼자서: *She went to the concert by herself.* 그녀 혼자 그 콘서트에 갔다. 4 **(all) to herself** for her own use ‖ 그녀 자신이 쓰기 위한. 자기 자신에게(만). 독점하여: *Alison had the whole house to herself that night.* 앨리슨은 그 날 밤에 집을 독차지했다. 5 **not be herself** SPOKEN if someone is not herself, she is not behaving or feeling the way she usually does, because she is sick or upset ‖ 아프거나 기분이 나빠서 그녀가 평소에 하던 식으로 행동하지 않거나 느끼지 않는. 평소 자신과 다르다: *Mom hasn't been herself lately.* 엄마는 최근에 평소와는 다르게 행동하신다.

hertz /həts/, *written abbreviation* **Hz** *n, plural* **hertz** a unit for measuring sound WAVEs ‖ 음파를 측정하는 단위

he's /iz; *strong* hiz/ 1 the short form of "he is" ‖ "he is"의 단축형: *He's my brother.* 그는 내 형이다. 2 the short form of "he has" ‖ "he has"의 단축형: *He's lost his keys.* 그는 열쇠를 잃어버렸다.

hes·i·tant /ˈhɛzətənt/ *adj* not willing to do or say something because you are uncertain or worried ‖ 확신하지 않거나 걱정되어 기꺼이 어떤 일을 하거나 말하려고 하지 않는. 망설이는. 주저하는. 꺼리는: *He was hesitant about admitting he was wrong.* 그는 자신이 잘못했다고 인정하는 것을 꺼려했다.

hes·i·tate /ˈhɛzəˌteɪt/ *v* [I] 1 to pause before doing or saying something because you are uncertain ‖ 확신하지 못하기 때문에 어떤 일을 하거나 말하기 전에 지체하다. 주저하다. 망설이다: *She hesitated before answering his question.* 그녀는 그의 질문에 대답하기 전에 우물쭈물했다. 2 **do not hesitate to do sth** SPOKEN FORMAL used in order to tell someone not to worry about doing something ‖ 어떤 일을 하는 것에 대해 남에게 걱정하지 말라고 말하는 데에 쓰여. 주저하지 말고 …해라: *Don't hesitate to call me if you need any help.* 도움이 필요하면 주저하지 말고 나에게 전화해라.

hes·i·ta·tion /ˌhɛzəˈteɪʃən/ *n* [U] the action of hesitating (HESITATE) ‖ 주저하는 행동. 망설임. 우유부단: *Without hesitation he said, "Yes!"* 그는 주저없이 "예!"라고 말했다.

het·er·o·ge·ne·ous /ˌhɛtərəˈdʒiniəs, -nyəs/, **heterogenous** *adj* FORMAL consisting of parts or members that are very different from each other ‖ 서로 매우 다른 부분이나 요소로 구성된. 이종의. 이질적인. 잡다한. 혼성의: *a heterogeneous population* 다양한 인종들로 이루어진 인구 **-heterogeneity** /ˌhɛtəroʊdʒəˈniəti/ *n* [U] —compare HOMOGENEOUS

het·er·o·sex·u·al /ˌhɛtərəˈsɛkʃuəl/ *n* someone who is sexually attracted to people of the opposite sex ‖ 이성에게 성적으로 끌리는 사람. 이성애자 **-heterosexual** *adj* **-heterosexuality** /ˌhɛtərəˌsɛkʃuˈæləti/ *n* [U] —compare BISEXUAL², HOMOSEXUAL

hew /hyu/ *v* **hewed, hewed** *or* **hewn** /hyun/, **hewing** [I, T] LITERARY to cut something with a cutting tool ‖ 자르는 도구로 무엇을 자르다

hew to sth *phr v* [T] to obey someone or do something according to the rules or instructions ‖ 규칙이나 지시에 의거하여 어떤 사람에게 복종하거나 어떤 일을 하다. …을 신봉하다. 지키다: *a country that hews to socialist principles* 사회주의 원칙을 신봉하는 나라

hex·a·gon /ˈhɛksəˌgɑn/ *n* a flat shape with six sides ‖ 육면을 가진 평평한 모양. 6각형. 6변형 **-hexagonal** /hɛksˈægənl/ *adj*

hey /heɪ/ *interjection* said in order to get someone's attention, or to show you are surprised or annoyed ‖ 남의 주의를 끌거나 남에게 깜짝 놀라거나 화난 것을 보여 주는 데에 쓰여. 어이. 이봐: *Hey, you! What are you doing?* 이봐, 당신! 뭐 하고 있어?

hey·day /ˈheɪdeɪ/ *n* the time when someone or something was most popular, successful, or powerful ‖ 사람이나 사물이 가장 인기 있는[성공적인, 힘이 있는] 때. 전성기. 절정. 한창 때: *the*

heyday of silent movies 무성 영화의 전
성기

HI the written abbreviation of Hawaii ‖
Hawaii(하와이 주)의 약어

hi /haɪ/ *interjection* INFORMAL hello ‖ 안
녕: *Hi! How are you?* 안녕! 잘 지내?

hi·a·tus /haɪˈeɪtəs/ *n* [C usually
singular] FORMAL a pause in an activity
‖ 활동의 중단. 휴지(기)

hi·ber·nate /ˈhaɪbəˌneɪt/ *v* [I] if an
animal hibernates, it sleeps all the time
during the winter ‖ 동물이 겨울 내내 잠
을 자다. 동면하다 – **hibernation**
/ˌhaɪbəˈneɪʃən/ *n* [U]

hiccup[1] /ˈhɪkʌp/ *n* 1 a sudden repeated
stopping of the breath, usually caused
by eating or drinking too fast ‖ 보통 너무
빨리 먹거나 마셔서 일어나는 갑작스럽게
반복되는 숨의 멈춤. 딸꾹질: *I have the
hiccups.* 나는 딸꾹질이 난다. 2 a small
problem or delay ‖ 작은 문제점이나 지
체. 대수롭지 않은 지장, 잠깐 동안의 지
체: *There's a slight hiccup in the
schedule for today.* 오늘 일정에 약간의
차질이 있다.

hiccup[2] *v* **-pped, -pping** [I] to have
HICCUPs ‖ 딸꾹질하다

hick /hɪk/ *n* DISAPPROVING someone who
lives in the country and is thought to be
uneducated or stupid ‖ 시골에 살며 교육
을 받지 못했거나 멍청하다고 생각되는 사
람. 시골뜨기, 촌놈

hick·ey /ˈhɪki/ *n* INFORMAL a slight
BRUISE (=dark mark on your skin) from
being kissed too hard ‖ 아주 세게 키스를
받아 생긴 약한 멍. 키스 자국

hick·o·ry /ˈhɪkəri/ *n* a North American
tree that produces nuts, or the hard
wood from this tree ‖ 견과를 맺는 북미산
나무, 또는 이 나무의 딱딱한 목재. 히코리
나무. 히코리 재목

hid /hɪd/ *v* the past tense of HIDE ‖ hide
의 과거형

hid·den[1] /ˈhɪdn/ *v* the PAST PARTICIPLE of
HIDE ‖ hide의 과거 분사형

hidden[2] *adj* 1 difficult to see or find ‖
보거나 찾기 힘든. 숨겨진. 숨은: *Marcia
kept her letters hidden in a box.* 마르시
아는 자기 편지를 상자 안에 숨겨 두었다.
2 not easy to notice or discover ‖ 알아보
거나 발견하기 쉽지 않은: *There may
have been a hidden meaning in what he
said.* 그가 말한 것에는 숨은 뜻이 있을지
도 모른다.

hide[1] /haɪd/ **hid, hid, hidden** *v* 1 [T]
to put something in a place where no
one else can see or find it ‖ 어떤 것을 아
무도 볼 수 없거나 찾을 수 없는 곳에 놓

다. …을 숨기다: *Jane hid the Christmas
presents in the closet.* 제인은 크리스마
스 선물을 벽장 속에 숨겼다. 2 [I] to go
to or stay in a place where no one can
see or find you ‖ 아무도 볼 수 없거나 찾
을 수 없는 곳에 가거나 머무르다. 숨다:
I'll hide behind the tree. 나는 나무 뒤에
숨어야지. 3 [T] to not show your
feelings to people, or to not tell
someone about something ‖ 사람들에게
자신의 감정을 보이지 않거나 어떤 일에
대해 남에게 말을 하지 않다: *Lee was
heartbroken, but hid her feelings.* 리는
비통했지만 자기의 감정을 숨겼다. 4 to
deliberately not tell people facts or
information ‖ 고의로 사람들에게 사실이
나 정보를 말하지 않다: *I'll talk to the
police – I have nothing to hide.* (=I
have not done anything wrong that I do
not want to talk about) 나는 숨기는 것이
아무것도 없다고 경찰관에게 말할 거야.

hide[2] *n* an animal's skin, especially
when it is removed to be used for
leather ‖ 특히 가죽으로 사용하기 위하여
벗겨낸 동물의 피부. 가죽. 수피(獸皮)

hide-and-seek /ˌ. . ˈ./ *n* [U] a
children's game in which one child
shuts his/her eyes while the other
children hide, and then tries to find
them ‖ 다른 아이들이 숨는 동안 한 아이
가 눈을 감고 있다가 숨은 아이들을 찾는
아이들의 놀이. 숨바꼭질

hide·a·way /ˈhaɪdəˌweɪ/ *n* a place
where you can go to hide or be alone ‖
숨으러 가거나 혼자 있을 수 있는 장소. 잠
복 장소. 은신처

hid·e·ous /ˈhɪdiəs/ *adj* extremely ugly
or unpleasant ‖ 매우 추하거나 불쾌한. 섬
뜩한. 무서운: *a hideous monster* 소름끼
치는 괴물 – **hideously** *adv*

hide·out /ˈhaɪdaʊt/ *n* a place where
you can hide ‖ 숨을 수 있는 장소. 은신
처. 잠복 장소

hid·ing /ˈhaɪdɪŋ/ *n* **go into hiding** to
hide yourself, often because you have
done something illegal or you are in
danger ‖ 종종 불법적인 일을 했거나 위험
에 처해 있기 때문에 숨다

hi·er·ar·chy /ˈhaɪəˌrɑrki/ *n* 1 [C, U] a
system of organization in which people
have higher and lower ranks ‖ 사람들이
보유한 지위의 높고 낮은 조직 제도. 계급
[계층]제 2 the most powerful members
of an organization ‖ 조직에서 가장 막강
한 구성원들. 지배층. 권력층 – **hier·
archical** /haɪəˈrɑrkɪkəl/ *adj*

hi·er·o·glyph·ics /ˌhaɪrəˈɡlɪfɪks/ *n* [U]
a system of writing that uses pictures to

represent words ‖ 단어를 표현하기 위해 그림을 이용하는 서법 체계. 상형 문자 표기법 – **hieroglyphic** *adj*

hi-fi /ˌhaɪ ˈfaɪ/ *adj* OLD-FASHIONED hi-fi equipment produces very clear sound ‖ 장치가 매우 선명한 소리를 내는. 하이파이(장치)의 – **hi-fi** *n*

high¹ /haɪ/ *adj*

1 ▶TALL 높은◀ having a top that is a long distance from its bottom ‖ 꼭대기가 밑바닥에서부터 먼 거리인. 높은: *Pike's Peak is the highest mountain in Colorado.* 파이크 피크는 콜로라도에서 가장 높은 산이다. / *a high wall* 높은 담 — opposite LOW¹ —compare TALL

2 ▶ABOVE GROUND 지면 위◀ being a long way above the ground ‖ 지면 위에서 먼 거리에 있는. 높은 곳의. 높은 곳에 있는: *We were looking down from a high window.* 우리는 높은 곳에 있는 유리창에서 아래를 내려다보고 있었다.

high

a high shelf   a tall tree

3 ▶MORE THAN USUAL 보통 이상◀ a high amount, number, or level is greater than usual ‖ 양[수, 수준]이 보통보다 더 큰. 풍부한. 비싼. 높은 수준의: *clothes selling at high prices* (=expensive prices) 고가로 파는 옷 / *achieving a higher level of productivity* 보다 높은 생산성의 달성

4 ▶RANK/POSITION 지위/신분◀ having an important or powerful position or rank ‖ 중요하거나 유력한 지위나 신분을 가진. 고귀한. 고위의. 상류의: *She was elected to high office last November.* 그녀는 지난 11월에 고위직으로 선출되었다. / *the highest levels of management* 고위층 경영진

5 ▶GOOD 좋은◀ very good ‖ 매우 좋은. 높은. 고등의. 뛰어난: *The boss has a high opinion of my work.* (=thinks my work is very good) 사장은 나의 작업을 높이 평가한다. / *Insist on high standards of quality and efficiency.* 뛰어난 품질 수준과 효율성을 강조해라.

6 ▶DRUGS 약◀ under the effects of drugs or alcohol ‖ 약이나 술의 효과를 경험하고 있는. 취한. (취하여) 기분 좋은:

He was so high on drugs that he didn't know what he was doing. 그는 마약에 흥건히 취해 자기가 무엇을 하고 있는지 알지 못했다. / *kids getting high on marijuana* 마리화나에 취해 황홀해하는 아이들

7 ▶CONTAINING A LOT 많이 포함한◀ containing a lot of a particular substance or quality ‖ 특정한 물질이나 자질을 많이 포함한. 고(高)…의. 다량으로 함유한: *Most candy bars are high in calories.* 대부분의 막대 사탕은 칼로리가 높다.

8 ▶SOUND/VOICE 소리/음성◀ near the top of the range of sounds that humans can hear ‖ 인간이 들을 수 있는 소리의 범위 중 가장 높은 곳 근처의. 높은. 날카로운. 음조가 높은: *singing the high notes* 높은 음조로 노래하기

9 -high having a particular height ‖ 특정한 높이를 가진. …높이의: *The grass was knee-high.* 풀이 무릎 높이까지 올라왔다.

10 high noon exactly 12 o'clock in the day ‖ 정각 낮 12시. 정오

high² *adv* **1** at or to a level high above the ground ‖ 지면 위 높은 위치에[로]. 높이. 높게. 위로: *kites flying high in the sky* 하늘 높이 날고 있는 연들 **2** at or to a high value, amount, rank etc. ‖ 높은 가치·양·지위에[로]. 비싸게. 많이. 고위직에: *Jenkins has risen high in the company.* 젠킨스는 회사에서 고위직에 올랐다. / *Ribas advised the graduating students to "aim high."* (=try to be successful) 리바스는 졸업하는 학생들에게 "큰 야망을 품어라"라고 조언했다. **3 look/search high and low** to look everywhere for someone or something ‖ 사람이나 사물을 찾기 위해 모든 곳을 둘러보다. 사방을 둘러보다/수색하다: *I searched high and low for the car keys.* 나는 자동차 열쇠를 찾기 위해 모든 곳을 살펴보았다. **4 be left high and dry** INFORMAL to be left without any help in a difficult situation ‖ 어려운 상황에서 어떠한 도움도 없이 방치되다

high³ *n* **1** the highest level, number, temperature etc. that has been recorded in a particular time period ‖ 특정한 기간 내에 기록된 가장 높은 수준·수·온도 등. 최고 기록. 최고치. 신기록: *The price of gold reached a new high yesterday.* 금값은 어제 새로이 최고치에 달했다. / *Highs of 40°C were recorded in the region last summer.* 작년 여름에 그 지역은 섭씨 40도라는 최고치를 기록했다. **2** a feeling of great excitement caused by success, drugs, alcohol etc. ‖

성공·마약·술 등으로 일어나는 대단
히 흥분된 감정. 취한[들뜬] 상태. 황홀
감. 도취경

high·brow /'haɪbraʊ/ adj a highbrow
book, movie etc. is very serious and
may be difficult to understand ‖ 책·영화
등이 매우 진지하고 이해하기에 어려울 것
같은. (소설·영화 등이) 지식인에게 알
맞은. 고상한 —compare LOWBROW

high chair /'. ./ n a tall chair that a
baby sits in to eat ‖ 아기가 음식을 먹기
위해 앉는 높은 의자. 어린이 식사용의 높
은 의자

high-class /ˌ. './ adj of good quality
and style, and usually expensive ‖ 질과
형태가 뛰어나며 보통 값비싼. 고급의. 상
류의: a high-class restaurant 고급 식당

higher ed·u·ca·tion /ˌ.. ..'../ n [U]
education at a college or university ‖ 단
과 대학이나 종합 대학에서의 교육. 고등
교육. 대학 교육

high fi·del·i·ty /ˌ. .'../ adj ⇨ HI-FI

high-grade /ˌ. './ adj of high quality
‖ 높은 질의. 양질의. 우수한: high-grade
motor oil 양질의 자동차 기름

high-hand·ed /ˌ. './ adj DISAPPROVING
using your authority in a way that is not
reasonable ‖ 자신의 권한을 부당하게 사
용하는. 위압적인. 고압적인. 독단적인

high heels /ˌ. './ n [plural] women's
shoes with a high HEEL (=raised part at
the back) ‖ 굽이 높은 여성용 구두. 하이
힐 – **high-heeled** adj —see picture at
SHOE¹

high jinks /'. ./ n [U] OLD-FASHIONED
noisy or excited behavior when people
are having fun ‖ 사람들이 놀고 있을 때의
시끄럽거나 들뜬 행동. 야단법석

high jump /'. ./ n **the high jump** a
sport in which you run and jump over a
bar that is raised higher after each
successful jump ‖ 매번 점프에 성공한 뒤
에 더 높이 올린 봉 위를 달리다가 뛰어
넘는 경기. 높이뛰기 – **high jumper** n

high·lands /'haɪləndz/ n [plural] an
area with a lot of mountains ‖ 산이 많은
지역. 고지. 산악 지방

high-lev·el /ˌ. './ adj involving
important people, especially in the
government ‖ 특히 정부에서, 중요한 사람
들이 포함된. 고위층의. 고관의: High-
level peace talks began this week. 고위
층의 평화 회담은 이번 주에 시작됐다.

high·light¹ /'haɪlaɪt/ v [T] **1** to make a
problem, subject etc. easy to notice so
people will pay attention to it ‖ 사람들이
문제·주제 등에 주목하도록 그것을 눈에
띄기 쉽게 만들다. …을 두드러지게 하다.

강조하다: The report highlights the
problem of inner-city crime. 그 보고서는
도심 빈민가의 범죄 문제를 강조하고 있
다. **2** to mark written words with a pen
or on a computer so you can see them
more easily ‖ 더 쉽게 볼 수 있도록 문자
를 펜으로, 또는 컴퓨터상에 표시를 하다.
형광펜으로 표시하다. (문자열을) 하이라
이트를 주다

highlight² n the most important or
exciting part of a movie, sports event
etc. ‖ 영화·스포츠 경기 등의 가장 중요하
거나 흥미진진한 부분. 명장면. 하이라이
트: a video of football highlights 미식 축
구 하이라이트를 담은 비디오

high·light·er /'haɪlaɪtɚ/ n a special
pen that you use to mark written words
so that you can see them more easily ‖
더 쉽게 볼 수 있도록 문자에 표시를 하는
데 사용하는 특수한 펜. 형광펜

high·ly /'haɪli/ adv **1** very ‖ 매우. 크게.
대단히: We had a highly successful
meeting. 우리는 매우 성공적인 모임을 가
졌다. **2** to a high level or degree ‖ 높은
수준이나 정도로. 높이 (평가되어). 값비
싸게: a highly paid attorney 수임료가 비
싼 변호사

high-mind·ed /ˌ. './ adj having high
moral standards or principles ‖ 높은 도
덕 수준이나 원칙을 가진. 고상한. 고결
한. 기품이 있는

High·ness /'haɪnɪs/ n **Your/His etc.**
Highness a royal title used when
speaking to a king, queen etc. ‖ 왕·여왕
등에게 말할 때 쓰는 국왕[여왕]의 칭호.
전하. 폐하

high-pitched /ˌ. './ adj a high-
pitched song or voice is higher than
most sounds or voices ‖ 노래나 목소리가
대부분의 소리나 목소리보다 더 높은. 음
락[음성]이 높은

high-pow·ered /ˌ. './ adj **1** very
powerful ‖ 매우 강력한. 고마력의. 고성
능의: a high-powered speedboat 고마력
의 고속 모터 보트 **2** very important or
successful ‖ 매우 중요하거나 성공적인.
유력한. 영향력이 큰: a high-powered
businessman 영향력이 큰 실업가

high-pres·sure /ˌ. './ adj **1** a high-
pressure job or situation is one in which
you need to work very hard to be
successful ‖ 일이나 상황이 성공하기 위해
서는 매우 열심히 일할 필요가 있는. 극도
의 긴장을 요하는 **2** having or using a lot
of pressure ‖ 압력이 많거나 많은 압력을
사용하는. 고압의: a high-pressure hose
고압 호스

high-pro·file /ˌ. './ adj attracting a

lot of attention from people ‖ 사람들로부터 많은 주목을 끄는. 눈에 띄는. 시선을 끄는: *a high-profile court case* 세간의 이목을 끄는 법정 소송

high-rise /'. ./ *n* a tall building ‖ 높은 건물. 고층 빌딩 – **high-rise** *adj*

high roll·er /ˌ. '../ *n* INFORMAL someone who spends a lot of money, especially by BETting on games, races etc. ‖ 특히 게임·경주 등에 내기 돈을 걸며 많은 돈을 쓰는 사람. 낭비가. 손이 큰 도박꾼

high school /'. ./ *n* [C, U] a school in the US and Canada for students over the age of 14 ‖ 14세 이상의 학생들을 위한 미국과 캐나다의 학교. 고등학교

high-spir·it·ed /ˌ. '.../ *adj* having a lot of energy and liking to have fun ‖ 힘이 넘치고 놀기를 좋아하는. 혈기 왕성한. 기운찬. 활기찬: *a high-spirited four-year-old boy* 활달한 네 살배기 남자 아이

high-strung /ˌ. '../ *adj* nervous, and easily upset or excited ‖ 긴장하고 쉽게 화내거나 흥분하는. 신경질적인. 예민한: *a high-strung horse* 예민한 말

high-tech /ˌ. '../ *adj* using the most modern information, machines etc. ‖ 최신의 정보·기계 등을 쓰는. 첨단 기술의. 하이테크의: *a new high-tech camera* 새로운 첨단 기술의 카메라

high tide /ˌ. './ *n* [C, U] the time when the sea is at its highest level ‖ 바닷물이 가장 높은 수위에 있는 때. 만조(때)

high·way /'haɪweɪ/ *n* a wide fast road that connects cities or towns ‖ 도시나 읍을 연결하는 넓은 고속용 도로. 고속도로

hi·jack /'haɪdʒæk/ *v* [T] **1** to take control of a plane, vehicle etc. illegally ‖ 비행기·탈것 등을 불법적으로 통제하다. 선박·항공기 등을 납치하다 **2** to take control of something ‖ 사물을 통제하다. 점거하다: *The protesters tried to hijack the meeting.* 항의자들은 그 모임을 점거하려 했다. – **hijacker** *n* – **hijacking** *n* [C, U]

hike¹ /haɪk/ *n* **1** a long walk in the country, mountains etc. ‖ 시골·산 등에서 오래 걷는 것. 하이킹. 도보 여행 **2** INFORMAL a large increase in something ‖ 큰 상승. 인상: *a huge tax hike* 큰 폭의 세금 인상 **3 take a hike** SPOKEN a rude way of telling someone to go away ‖ 남에게 가버리라고 말하는 무례한 말투. 저리 가. 씩 꺼져

hike² *v* **1** [I, T] to take a long walk in the country, mountains etc. ‖ 시골·산 등에서 오래 걷다. 도보 여행하다. 하이킹하다 **2** [T] also **hike** sth ↔ **up** to

increase the price of something by a large amount ‖ 어떤 것의 가격을 크게 올리다. 대폭 인상하다: *Gas stations hiked prices in response to the Gulf War.* 주유소는 걸프전의 영향으로 기름값을 대폭 인상했다.

hik·ing /'haɪkɪŋ/ *n* [U] an outdoor activity in which you take long walks in the mountains or country ‖ 산이나 시골에서 오래 걷는 야외 활동. 도보 여행

hi·lar·i·ous /hɪ'lɛriəs, -'lær-/ *adj* extremely funny ‖ 매우 웃기는. 아주 재미있는. 유쾌한: *I thought the movie was hilarious!* 나는 그 영화가 아주 재미있다고 생각했어! – **hilariously** *adv* – **hilarity** /hɪ'lærəti/ *n* [U]

hill /hɪl/ *n* **1** an area of high land, like a small mountain ‖ 작은 산처럼 높은 지역. 언덕. 구릉 (지대): *the hills in upstate New York* 뉴욕 북부 쪽의 구릉 지대 / *driving up a steep hill* 가파른 언덕을 올라가기 **2 over the hill** INFORMAL no longer young, or too old to do a job well ‖ 더 이상 젊지 않거나 너무 늙어서 일을 잘 하지 못하는. 한창 때[전성기]가 지난. 한물간. 나이 들어 퇴물이 된: *Larry can still play football – he's not over the hill yet.* 래리는 여전히 미식축구를 할 수 있어. 그는 아직 젊어. **3 the Hill**⇨ CAPITOL HILL – **hilly** *adj*

hill·bil·ly /'hɪlˌbɪli/ *n* someone who lives in the mountains and is thought to be uneducated or stupid ‖ 산 속에 살며 교육을 받지 못했거나 어리석다고 생각되는 사람. 두멧사람. 촌뜨기

hill·side /'hɪlsaɪd/ *n* the side of a hill ‖ 언덕의 경사면. 언덕 비탈. 산허리

hilt /hɪlt/ *n* **1 to the hilt** completely or extremely ‖ 완전히. 지극히. 철저하게: *a warship armed to the hilt* 완전 무장한 전함 **2** the handle of a sword or a large knife ‖ 검이나 큰 칼의 손잡이. 칼자루

him /ɪm; *strong* hɪm/ *pron* the object form of "he" ‖ "he"의 목적격: *Why don't you just ask him yourself?* 그에게 당신이 직접 물어보는 게 어때요? / *The cop ordered him out of the car.* 경찰관은 그에게 차에서 나오라고 지시했다. —see usage note at ME

him·self /ɪm'sɛlf; *strong* hɪm'sɛlf/ *pron* **1** the REFLEXIVE form of "he" ‖ "he"의 재귀형. 그 자신[스스로]: *Bill looked at himself in the mirror.* 빌은 거울 속의 자기 자신을 바라보았다. **2** the strong form of "he," used in order to emphasize the subject or object of a sentence ‖ 문장의 주어나 목적어를 강조하는 데에 쓰이는 "he"의 강조형: *It's* *true! He told me himself.* 그건 사실이야! 그 사람이 직접 나에게 말했어. **3 (all) by himself a)** without help ‖ 도움 없이. 혼자 힘으로. 스스로: *He tried to fix the car by himself.* 그는 혼자 힘으로 차를 고쳐 보려고 했다. **b)** alone ‖ 홀로. 자기 혼자서: *Sam was all by himself on the mountain trail.* 샘은 산길에 자기 혼자 있었다. **4 (all) to himself** SPOKEN for his own use ‖ 그 자신이 쓰기 위한. 자기 자신에게(만). 독점하여: *Ben had the house to himself for a week.* 벤은 일주일 동안 그 집을 독차지했다. **5 not be himself** if someone is not himself, he is not behaving or feeling as he usually does, because he is sick or upset ‖ 아프거나 기분이 나빠서 평소처럼 행동하지 않거나 느끼지 않다. 평소 자신과 다르다: *Andy hasn't been himself lately.* 앤디는 최근에 평소와는 다르게 행동한다.

hind /haɪnd/ *adj* **hind legs/feet** the back legs or feet of an animal ‖ 동물의 뒷다리나 뒷발

hin·der /'hɪndɚ/ *v* [T] to make it difficult for someone to do something ‖ 사람이 어떤 일을 하기 어렵게 만들다. …을 방해하다. 훼방: *The bad weather is hindering rescue efforts.* 악천후가 구조 작업에 방해가 되고 있다.

Hin·di /'hɪndi/ *n* [U] a language used in India ‖ 인도에서 쓰이는 언어. 힌디어

hind·quar·ters /'haɪnd,kwɔrtɚz/ *n* [plural] the back part of an animal ‖ 동물의 뒷부분. 동물의 뒷다리와 엉덩이

hin·drance /'hɪndrəns/ *n* someone or something that makes it difficult for you to do something ‖ 어떤 것을 하기 어렵게 만드는 사람이나 사물. 방해하는 사람[것]. 장애물: *He feels marriage would be a hindrance to his career.* 그는 결혼이 자기의 출세에 걸림돌이 될 거라고 느낀다.

hind·sight /'haɪndsaɪt/ *n* [U] the ability to understand something after it has happened ‖ 어떤 일이 발생한 후에 그것을 이해하는 능력. 때늦은[사후의] 지혜[판단]. 뒷궁리: *In hindsight, I think it was a terrible mistake.* 돌이켜보면 그것이 대단한 실수였다는 생각이 든다.

Hin·du /'hɪndu/ *n* someone who believes in Hinduism ‖ 힌두교를 믿는 사람. 힌두교도

Hin·du·ism /'hɪndu,ɪzəm/ *n* [U] the main religion in India, which includes belief in many gods and in REINCARNATION ‖ 많은 신을 믿고 윤회설에 대한 믿음을 포함하는, 인도의 주된 종교. 힌두교

hinge¹ /hɪndʒ/ *n* a metal part that joins two things together, such as a door and a frame, so that one part can swing open and shut ‖ 한 부분이 활짝 열렸다 닫혔다 할 수 있도록 문과 문틀의 두 부분을 함께 연결하는 금속 부분. 경첩 – **hinged** *adj*

hinge² *v*

hinge on/upon sth *phr v* [T] to depend on something ‖ 어떤 것에 의존하다. …에 달려 있다: *The success of the team hinges on how well Ripken plays.* 그 팀의 성공은 립켄이 얼마나 경기를 잘 하느냐에 달려 있다.

hint¹ /hɪnt/ *n* **1** something that you say or do that helps someone guess what you really want ‖ 자신이 진짜로 원하는 것이 무엇인지를 남이 추측하도록 도와주는 말이나 행동. 암시. 단서. 힌트: *I don't know the answer, can you give me a hint?* 답을 모르겠는데 나에게 힌트 좀 줄 수 있겠니? / *Sue has been dropping hints* (=giving hints) *about what she wants for her birthday.* 수는 생일에 바라는 것에 대해 암시를 주고 있다. **2 a hint of** sth a small amount of something ‖ 작은 양. 근소. 약간: *There was a hint of perfume in the air.* 공기에서 향내가 약간 났다. **3** a useful piece of advice on how to do something ‖ 어떤 것을 하는 방법에 대한 유용한 몇 마디의 충고. 간단한 유의 사항. 주의. 지침: *a book full of hints on gardening* 정원 가꾸기에 대한 지침이 가득한 책

hint² *v* [I, T] to say something that helps someone guess what you want, or what will happen ‖ 자신이 바라는 것이나 발생할 것을 추측하는 데에 도움이 되는 것을 남에게 말하다. (…을) 암시하다. 넌지시 알리다: *Archie hinted at the possibility that he was going to retire.* 아치는 자신이 은퇴할 수도 있다는 것을 넌지시 알렸다.

hin·ter·land /'hɪntɚ,lænd/ *n* [singular] **the hinterland** the inner part of a country, usually away from cities or the coast ‖ 일반적으로 도시나 해안에서 떨어진 한 나라의 내륙 지역

hip¹ /hɪp/ *n* one of the two parts on either side of your body, where your legs join your body ‖ 다리와 몸통이 연결되는 부분으로 신체의 양쪽에 있는 두 부분 중 하나. 엉덩이

hip² *adj* INFORMAL modern and fashionable ‖ 현대적이며 최신식인. 세련된. 멋있는. 최신 유행에 정통한: *a hip new comedy on NBC* NBC 방송국의 최신 스타일의 새로운 코미디

hip hop /'. ./ *n* [U] a kind of popular dance music with a regular heavy BEAT and spoken words ‖ 규칙적인 강한 박자와 대화조 가사로 된 일종의 대중 댄스 음악. 힙합 음악

hip·pie, hippy /'hɪpi/ *n* someone, especially in the 1960s and 1970s, who usually had long hair, opposed the standards of society, and took drugs for pleasure ‖ 특히 1960년대와 1970년대에 보통 긴 머리 스타일을 하고 사회 규범에 반대하며 쾌락을 얻기 위해 마약을 복용했던 사람. 히피(족)

hip·po·pot·a·mus /ˌhɪpə'pɑtəməs/, **hip·po** /'hɪpoʊ/ *n, plural* **hippopotamuses, hippopotami** /-'pɑtəmai/ a large African animal with a big head, fat body, and thick gray skin, that lives in and near water ‖ 물 속이나 물가에 살며 큰 머리·뚱뚱한 몸집·두꺼운 회색 피부를 가진 거대한 아프리카산 동물. 하마

hire /haɪɚ/ *v* [T] to employ someone to work for you ‖ 자신을 위해 일할 사람을 고용하다: *Peter got hired at the new factory.* 피터는 새로운 공장에 고용되었다.

his¹ /ɪz; *strong* hɪz/ *possessive adj* belonging to or relating to a male person or animal that has been mentioned or is known about ‖ 이미 언급되거나 알고 있는 남성이나 동물의 수컷에 속하거나 관련된. 그의: *Leo hates cleaning his room.* 레오는 자기 방 청소하는 것을 싫어한다.

his² *possessive pron* the thing or things belonging to or relating to a male person or animal that has been mentioned or is known about ‖ 언급되거나 알고 있는 남성이나 동물의 수컷에 속하거나 관련된 것(들). 그의 것: *I think he has my suitcase, and I have his.* 그가 내 가방을 가지고 있고 내가 그의 것을 가지고 있는 것 같다. / *Dave is a friend of his.* 데이브는 그의 친구 중 하나이다. / *My boots are black. His are brown.* 내 부츠는 검정색이고 그의 부츠는 갈색이다

His·pan·ic /hɪ'spænɪk/ *adj* from or relating to a country where Spanish or Portuguese is spoken ‖ 스페인어나 포르투갈어를 쓰는 나라 출신이나 그 나라와 관련된. 라틴 아메리카(산)의 – **Hispanic** *n*

hiss /hɪs/ *v* [I] to make a noise that sounds like "ssss" ‖ "쉿"처럼 들리는 소리를 내다. 쉿하는[새는] 소리를 내다: *I could hear steam hissing from the pipe.* 나는 파이프에서 쉬쉬대는 증기 소리를 들을 수 있었다. – **hiss** *n*

his·to·ri·an /hɪ'stɔriən/ *n* someone who studies or writes about history ‖ 역사에 대해 연구하거나 글을 쓰는 사람. 역사가. 사학자. 연대기 작가

his·tor·ic /hɪ'stɔrɪk, -'stɑr-/ *adj* a historic place or event is important as a part of history ‖ 장소나 사건이 역사의 일부분으로서 중요한. 역사상 유명[중요]한. 역사적인

his·tor·i·cal /hɪ'stɔrɪkəl, -'stɑr-/ *adj* **1** relating to the study of history ‖ 역사 연구와 관련된. 역사의[에 관한]. 역사적인: *a collection of historical documents* 역사적인 문헌의 수집 **2** historical events, people etc. really happened or existed in the past ‖ 사건·사람 등이 과거에 실제로 일어났거나 존재했던. 역사상 실재의: *Jesus is a historical figure.* 예수는 역사상 실재한 인물이다.

his·to·ry /'hɪstəri/ *n* **1** [U] all the things that happened in the past ‖ 과거에 일어난 모든 것들. 역사: *All through human history, wars have been fought over religion.* 인간의 모든 역사를 통해서 보면 전쟁은 종교와 관련되어 발발했다. **2** the study of history, especially the political, social, or economic development of a particular country ‖ 특히 특정 국가의 정치적[사회적, 경제적] 발전에 대한 역사 연구. 역사학: *a class in European history* 유럽사 강의 **3** a book about events that happened in the past ‖ 과거에 일어난 사건에 관한 책. 사서(史書): *a history of the Roman empire* 로마 제국 역사책 **4 have a history of sth** to have had illness, problems etc. in the past ‖ 과거에 병·문제 등을 가지고 있었다. …의 전력이 있다: *Paul has a history of heart disease.* 폴은 과거에 심장병을 앓은 병력이 있다. **5 make history/go down in history** to do something important that will be remembered ‖ 기억될 만한 중요한 일을 하다. 역사에 남을 중대한 일을 하다. 역사에 이름을 남기다

his·tri·on·ics /ˌhɪstri'ɑnɪks/ *n* [plural] DISAPPROVING behavior that is very emotional but is not sincere ‖ 매우 감정적이지만 진지하지 않은 행동. 꾸민 듯한 [연극 같은] 행동 – **histrionic** *adj*

hit¹ /hɪt/ *v* **hit, hit, hitting** [T]

1 ▶STRIKE 치다◀ to swing your hand, or something held in your hand, hard against someone or something ‖ 손이나 손에 쥐고 있는 것을 사람이나 사물을 향해 세

hit

차게 휘두르다. 때리다. 치다: *He hit the boy on the nose.* 그는 그 소년의 코를 때렸다. / *She swung the bat and hit the ball.* 그녀는 방망이를 휘둘러 공을 쳤다.
2 ▶CRASH 부딪치다◀ to crash into someone or something quickly and hard ‖ 사람이나 물건에 순식간에 세차게 부딪치다. 충돌하다: *The car was totalled after hitting a wall.* 그 자동차는 벽에 충돌해서 완전히 부서졌다. / *I hit my head on the table.* 탁자에 내 머리를 부딪쳤다.
3 ▶BAD EFFECT 나쁜 영향◀ to have a bad effect on someone or something ‖ 사람이나 사물에 나쁜 영향을 미치다. 영향을 주다. 타격을 입히다: *The economy has been hard hit by inflation.* 경제는 인플레이션으로 인해 큰 타격을 받았다.
4 ▶BULLET/BOMB 총알/폭탄◀ to wound someone or damage something with a bullet or bomb ‖ 총알이나 폭탄으로 사람에게 상처를 입히거나 사물에 손상을 입히다. 명중[적중]하다: *A bullet hit her in the thigh.* 총알은 그녀의 대퇴부를 맞혔다.
5 ▶REACH STH 도달하다◀ to reach a particular level, number, position etc. ‖ 특정한 수준·수·위치 등에 도달하다: *Unemployment has hit a new high, at 11.3%.* 실업률은 11.3퍼센트로 최고 기록을 갱신했다. / *We'll hit the exit in three miles.* 3마일만 가면 출구에 도달할 것이다.
6 hit it off (with sb) INFORMAL to like someone as soon as you meet him/her ‖ 어떤 사람을 만나자마자 좋아하다. (…과) 죽이 맞다. 잘 해나가다
7 ▶THINK OF 생각하다◀ if an idea, thought etc. hits you, you suddenly think of it ‖ 아이디어·생각 등이 갑자기 생각나다. 문득 떠오르다: *It suddenly hit me that he was just lonely.* 나는 그가 외로웠을 뿐이라는 생각이 문득 떠올랐다.
8 hit the roof/ceiling INFORMAL to become very angry ‖ 매우 화나게 되다. 격노하다. 길길이 뛰다: *Dad's going to hit the roof when he sees this mess!* 아빠가 이렇게 엉망이 된 것을 보면 화가 머리 끝까지 치밀어 오를 거야!
9 hit the road INFORMAL to start on a trip ‖ 여행을 시작하다. 출발하다
10 hit the hay/sack SPOKEN to go to bed ‖ 자러 가다. 잠자리에 들다
11 hit the spot SPOKEN if a food or drink hits the spot, it tastes good and is exactly what you want ‖ 음식이나 음료수가 맛이 좋고 정확하게 자신이 원하는 것이다. 더할 나위 없다. 만족스럽다 —see also **hit the bottle** (BOTTLE¹)

hit back *phr v* [I] to attack or criticize someone who is attacking or criticizing you ‖ 자신을 공격하거나 비판하는 사람을 공격하거나 비판하다. 보복하다. 반박하다: *Today the President hit back at his critics.* 오늘 대통령은 자신을 비판하는 사람들에게 반박했다.
hit on *phr v* [T] **1** [**hit on** sth] to have a good idea about something, often by chance ‖ 종종 우연히 어떤 것에 대한 좋은 생각을 하다. 묘안을 생각해 내다. 머리에 떠오르다: *I think Turner may have hit on a solution there.* 나는 터너가 거기에서 그 해결책을 생각해 냈을지도 모른다고 생각한다. **2** [**hit on** sb] INFORMAL to try to talk to someone who you are sexually interested in ‖ 성적으로 흥미를 느끼는 사람에게 말을 붙이려고 하다. 접근하다. 추근대다: *Men are always trying to hit on me at parties.* 남자들은 항상 파티에서 나에게 추근대려고 한다.
hit sb **up for** sth *phr v* [T] SPOKEN to ask someone for something ‖ 남에게 어떤 것을 부탁하다: *Mitch will probably try to hit you up for a loan.* 미치는 아마도 당신에게 돈을 빌려 달라고 부탁할 것이다.

USAGE NOTE hit, strike, and beat

Use **hit** as a general word to talk about most kinds of hitting: *Dave hit Peter. / The van hit the car in front of it.* **Strike** is more formal and means "to hit very hard": *She had been struck on the side of the head. / A car ran off the highway and struck a telephone pole.* **Beat** means "to hit someone or something many times": *The man was robbed and beaten.* You can **hit** or **strike** someone or something accidentally or deliberately, but you **beat** someone or something deliberately.
hit는 대부분의 종류의 치는 것에 대해 말하는 일반적인 단어로 쓰인다: 데이브는 피터를 때렸다. / 소형 트럭이 그 차의 앞부분을 들이받았다. **strike**는 더욱 격식 차린 말로서 "매우 세게 치다"의 뜻이다: 그녀는 머리 옆부분을 세게 맞았다. / 차 한 대가 고속도로를 벗어나 전신주를 들이받았다. **beat**는 "사람이나 물체를 여러 차례 때리다"의 뜻이다: 그 남자는 폭행 강도를 당했다. **hit**나 **strike**는 사람이나 물체를 우연히 또는 고의로 때리다의 뜻으로 쓸 수 있지만 **beat**는 사람이나 물체를 고의로 때릴 때에 쓸 수 있다.

hit² *n* [C usually singular] **1** a movie, song, play etc. that is very successful ‖ 매우 성공적인 영화·노래·연극 등. 성공. 히트(작품[곡]): *Her first novel was a big hit.* 그녀의 첫 소설은 대성공이었다. **2** the action of successfully striking something you are aiming at ‖ 목표로 하고 있는 것을 성공적으로 맞추는 행동. 명중. 적중: *The missile scored a direct hit.* 미사일이 정확하게 명중했다. **3 be a hit (with sb)** to be liked very much by someone ‖ 누군가에게 많은 사랑을 받다. …에게 크게 호평을 받다: *These brownies are always a hit with my guests.* 이 초콜릿 케이크는 내 손님들에게 항상 인기가 좋다. **4** a quick hard blow with your hand, or something in your hand ‖ 손이나 손에 든 것으로 빠르고 세차게 침. 타격

hit·and·miss /ˌ. . ˈ./, **hit·or·miss** *adj* INFORMAL done in a way that is not planned or organized well ‖ 그다지 계획적이거나 조직적이지 않게 행해지는. 일관성이 없는. 되는 대로의

hit·and·run /ˌ. . ˈ./ *adj* a hit-and-run accident is one in which the driver of a car hits someone and then drives away without stopping to help ‖ 자동차 운전자가 사람을 치고 나서 도와주기 위해 정차하지 않고 도망가 버리는. 뺑소니의

hitch¹ /hɪtʃ/ *v* **1** [I, T] INFORMAL to travel by asking for free rides in other people's cars; HITCHHIKE ‖ 다른 사람의 차에 무임승차를 부탁해서 여행하다. 히치하이크하다. 자동차 편승 여행을 하다; 逾 hitchhike: *We hitched a ride with a couple from Florida.* 우리는 플로리다에서 온 부부의 차를 얻어 탔다. **2** [T] to fasten something to something else ‖ 사물을 다른 것에 단단히 고정시키다. 연결하다: *Dad finished hitching the trailer on to the car.* 아빠는 트레일러를 자동차에 연결하는 것을 끝냈다. **3 get hitched** INFORMAL to get married ‖ 결혼하다

hitch sth **up** *phr v* [T] to pull a piece of clothing up ‖ 옷을 끌어올리다. 추켜올리다: *Bill hitched up his pants.* 빌은 바지를 추켜올렸다.

hitch² *n* a small problem that causes a delay ‖ 지체를 야기시키는 작은 문제. 장애. 지장. 고장: *The performance went off without a hitch.* (=with no problems) 그 공연은 아무 차질 없이 끝났다.

hitch·hike /ˈhɪtʃhaɪk/ *v* [I] to travel by asking for free rides in other people's cars ‖ 다른 사람의 차에 무임승차를 부탁

해서 여행하다. 히치하이크를 하다. 무료 편승 여행을 하다 – **hitchhiker** *n* – **hitchhiking** *n* [U]

hith·er /ˈhɪðɚ/ *adv* LITERARY or OLD-FASHIONED here, to this place ‖ 여기에, 이 장소로. 여기로. 이쪽(방향)으로: *Come hither!* 이리 오너라! **2 hither and thither/yon** in many directions ‖ 여러 방향으로. 여기저기로

hith·er·to /ˌhɪðɚˈtu, ˈhɪðɚˌtu/ *adv* FORMAL up until now ‖ 지금까지. 여태까지: *The Pilgrims were sailing to a hitherto unexplored land.* 미국의 최초의 이주자들은 지금까지 개척되지 않은 땅으로 항해하고 있었다.

hit man /ˈ. ./ *n* INFORMAL a criminal whose job is to kill someone ‖ 사람을 죽이는 게 직업인 범죄자. 청부 살인자

HIV *n* [U] Human Immunodeficiency Virus; a type of VIRUS that enters the body through the blood or sexual activity, and can cause AIDS ‖ Human Immunodeficiency Virus(인체 면역결핍 바이러스)의 약어; 혈액이나 성행위를 통해서 인체에 들어와서 에이즈를 유발할 수 있는 바이러스의 일종: *Brad tested HIV positive.* (=has HIV) 브래드는 HIV양성으로 판명되었다.

hive /haɪv/, **beehive** *n* a place where BEEs live ‖ 벌들이 사는 곳. 벌통. 벌집

hives /haɪvz/ *n* [U] a condition in which someone's skin swells and becomes red, usually because s/he is ALLERGIC to something ‖ 일반적으로 어떤 것에 알레르기 증상을 보여서 사람의 피부가 부풀어 오르거나 붉게 되는 증상. 발진. 두드러기

h'm, hmm /hm, hmh/ *interjection* a sound that you make to express doubt or disagreement ‖ 의문스럽다든지 동의하지 않음을 표현하기 위해 내는 소리. 흠. 흐음

hoard¹ /hɔrd/, **hoard up** *v* [T] to collect things in large amounts and keep them in a secret place ‖ 물건을 대량으로 수집하여 비밀 장소에 두다. …을 사재기하다. 매점하다: *Fearful citizens were hoarding food in case of war.* 두려움에 떠는 시민들은 전쟁에 대비하여 식량을 사재기하고 있었다. – **hoarder** *n*

hoard² *n* a group of valuable things that someone has hidden to keep it safe ‖ 안전하게 보관하기 위해 숨겨둔 일단의 값어치 있는 물건들. 비장물: *a hoard of gold* 사재기한 금

hoarse /hɔrs/ *adj* someone who is hoarse has a voice that sounds rough, often because of a sore throat ‖ 종종 목

이 아파서 목소리가 거칠게 나오는. 쉰(목소리의). 허스키한

hoax /hoʊks/ *n* a trick that makes someone believe something that is not true ‖ 사실이 아닌 것을 믿게 만드는 속임수. 속이기. 날조. 조작: *The bomb threat turned out to be a hoax.* 폭탄 위협은 허구임이 밝혀졌다. — **hoax** *v* [T]

hob·ble /'habəl/ *v* [I] to walk with difficulty, taking small steps, usually because you are injured ‖ 일반적으로 다쳐서 작은 보폭으로 힘들게 걷다. 절름거리다. 절름절름 걷다

hob·by /'habi/ *n* an activity that you enjoy doing in your free time ‖ 여유 시간에 즐기는 활동. 취미: *Do you have a hobby?* 너 취미 가지고 있니? / *I started painting as a hobby.* 나는 취미로 그림을 그리기 시작했다. —see usage note at SPORT

hob·nob /'habnab/ *v* -**bbed**, -**bbing** [I] INFORMAL to spend time talking to people who are more famous or more important than you ‖ 자신보다 더욱 유명하거나 중요한 사람들과 얘기하며 시간을 보내다. 유쾌하게 담소하다. 허물없이 어울리다: *Jeremy is always hobnobbing with the bosses.* 제레미는 항상 상사들과 허물없이 어울린다.

ho·bo /'hoʊboʊ/ *n, plural* **hoboes**, **hobos** INFORMAL someone who travels around and has no home or regular job; TRAMP ‖ 이리저리 여행하며 집이나 일정한 직업이 없는 사람. 떠돌이. 부랑자; ㊤ tramp

hock¹ /hak/ *n* **be in hock** INFORMAL to be in debt ‖ 빚을 지다

hock² *v* [T] INFORMAL ⇨ PAWN²

hock·ey /'haki/ *n* [U] **1** also **ice hockey** a sport played on ice in which players use long curved sticks to try to hit a hard flat round object into a GOAL ‖ 선수들이 길고 곡선형의 스틱으로 딱딱하고 납작한 둥근 물체를 골대 안으로 쳐서 넣는, 얼음 위에서 하는 운동. 아이스하키 **2** ⇨ FIELD HOCKEY

hodge·podge /'hadʒpadʒ/ *n* [singular] a lot of things put together with no order or arrangement ‖ 질서나 정리 없이 한데 많이 모아 놓은 것. 뒤범벅. 뒤죽박죽: *a hodgepodge of old toys* 뒤엉켜 있는 낡은 장난감들

hoe /hoʊ/ *n* a garden tool with a long handle, used for making the soil loose and for removing wild plants ‖ 흙을 푸석푸석하게 하고 잡초를 제거하는 데에 쓰이는 긴 손잡이가 달린 정원 용구. 괭이 — **hoe** *v* [I, T]

hog¹ /hɔg, hag/ *n* **1** a large pig that is kept for its meat ‖ 식용으로 사육되는 큰 돼지. 식용 돼지 **2** INFORMAL someone who keeps or uses all of something for himself/herself ‖ 모든 것을 혼자 차지하거나 쓰는 사람. 욕심꾸러기 **3 go (the) whole hog** INFORMAL to do something thoroughly or completely ‖ 철저하게 또는 완벽하게 어떤 일을 하다

hog² *v* -**gged**, -**gging** [T] INFORMAL to keep or use all of something for yourself ‖ 혼자 모든 것을 차지하거나 쓰다. 독차지하다: *Look at that guy hogging the road.* (=driving so that no one can pass) 아무도 지나가지 못하게 도로를 제멋대로 달리는 저 녀석 좀 봐.

ho-hum /ˌhoʊ 'hʌm/ *adj* INFORMAL disappointing or boring ‖ 실망스러운. 지루한: *The food was ho-hum.* 그 음식은 실망스러웠다.

hoist¹ /hɔɪst/ *v* [T] to raise or lift something, especially using ropes or a special machine ‖ 특히 밧줄이나 특별한 기계를 써서 물건을 올리거나 들다

hoist² *n* a piece of equipment used for lifting heavy things ‖ 무거운 것을 들어 올리는 데에 쓰는 장비

ho·key /'hoʊki/ *adj* INFORMAL expressing emotions in a way that seems old-fashioned, silly, or too simple ‖ 진부하게[어리석게, 너무 단순히] 감정을 표현하는: *a hokey love song* 진부한 사랑 노래

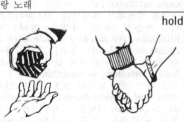

hold

hold your hand out   hold hands

hold¹ /hoʊld/ *v* **held**, **held**, **holding** **1** ▶IN YOUR HANDS/ARMS 손/팔에◀ [T] to have something firmly in your hands or arms ‖ 손이나 팔로 사물을 꽉 잡다: *Hold my purse for a minute.* 잠깐 내 지갑 좀 들고 있어 줘. / *She was crying, and I held her tight.* 그녀가 울어서 나는 꽉 안아주었다. —see also picture on page 947 **2** ▶KEEP STH IN POSITION 사물을 어떤 위치에 두다◀ [T] to hold or keep something in a particular position ‖ 어떤 것을 특정한 위치에 두거나 유지하다: *She held the piece of paper up so we could* *see it.* 우리가 볼 수 있게 그녀는 그 종이를 들어올렸다. / *Hold your hand out, and I'll give you a present.* 손을 내밀어 봐, 그러면 내가 선물을 줄게. / *Hold still* (=don't move) *so I can cut your hair!* 움직이지 마라, 그래야지 내가 네 머리를 자를 수 있어!

3 ▶HAVE SPACE FOR 사물을 위한 공간이 있다◀ [T] to have space for a particular amount of something ‖ 특정 양만큼의 공간이 있다: *The jug holds two gallons of liquid.* 그 병은 2갤런의 액체를 담을 수 있다.

4 ▶KEEP/CONTAIN 보관하다/포함하다◀ [T] to keep or contain something ‖ 사물을 보관하거나 포함하다: *All our files are now held on computer.* 우리의 모든 파일은 지금 컴퓨터에 보관되어 있다. / *the closet that held our winter clothes* 우리의 겨울옷이 들어 있는 옷장

5 ▶POSITION/RANK/JOB 지위/등급/직업 ◀ [T] to have a particular position, job, or level of achievement ‖ 특정한 지위[직업, 성취도]를 갖고 있다: *Dr. Werner holds a degree in Political Science.* 워너 박사는 정치학 학위를 소지하고 있다.

6 ▶ARRANGE TIME/PLACE 시간/장소를 배정하다◀ [T] to have a meeting, party etc. in a particular place or at a particular time ‖ 특정한 장소나 시간에 회의·파티를 열다: *The conference will be held in Las Vegas.* 그 회의는 라스베이거스에서 개최될 것이다.

7 hold hands if two people hold hands, they hold each other's hands ‖ 두 사람이 서로의 손을 잡다: *a couple walking on the beach, holding hands* 손을 잡고 해변을 거니는 한 쌍

8 ▶CONTINUE/NOT CHANGE 지속하다/변하지 않다◀ [I, T] to continue at a particular level, rate, or number, or to make something do this ‖ 특정 수준[비율, 숫자]이 유지되거나 유지되게 하다: *Hold your speed at fifty.* 속도 50을 유지하라. / *Housing prices have held at the current level for three months.* 주택 가격은 3개월간 현수준을 유지하고 있다.

9 hold it! SPOKEN used in order to tell someone to wait, or to stop doing something ‖ 남에게 기다리라고 말하거나 어떤 것 하기를 중단하라고 말하는 데에 쓰여. 기다려! 멈춰!: *Hold it a minute! I'm trying to explain it to you.* 잠시 기다려! 내가 너한테 설명해 줄 테니까.

10 ▶TELEPHONE 전화◀ [I] to wait until the person you have telephoned is ready to answer ‖ 통화하려는 사람이 받을 때까지 기다리다: *Mr. Penrose is on the other*

line. Can you hold? 펜로즈 씨는 다른 전화를 받고 계십니다. 기다리시겠어요?

11 hold sb's interest/attention to keep someone interested ‖ 남의 관심을 끌다: *She knows how to hold her students' interest.* 그녀는 학생들의 관심 끄는 방법을 안다.

12 hold sb responsible to think that someone is responsible for something bad that has happened ‖ 일어난 나쁜 일에 대해 남에게 책임이 있다고 생각하다: *Parents may be held responsible for their children's crimes.* 자녀들의 범죄는 부모에게 책임이 있다고 볼 수도 있다.

13 hold your own to succeed in a difficult situation, or to be good enough when compared to similar things ‖ 어려운 상황에서도 성공하다, 또는 비슷한 것과 비교해 볼 때 뒤지지 않다: *Tanner's art can hold its own alongside other American artists of his time.* 태너의 솜씨는 그 시대 다른 미국 예술가들 못지 않게 뛰어나다고 할 수 있다.

14 ▶HAVE A QUALITY 속성이 있다◀ [T] to have a particular quality ‖ 특정한 속성이 있다: *This new industry holds great promise for the future.* 이 새로운 산업은 대단히 전도유망하다.

15 ▶CAGE/PRISONER 우리/죄수◀ [T] to keep a person or animal in a place where he, she, or it cannot leave ‖ 도망가지 못하도록 사람이나 동물을 한 장소에 가두다: *Virginia Piper was kidnapped and held for two days.* 버지니아 파이퍼는 납치당해 이틀 동안 감금되었다. / *tigers held in cages* 우리 안에 갇힌 호랑이들

16 ▶SUPPORT WEIGHT 무게를 지탱하다 ◀ [I, T] to support the weight of something ‖ 사물의 무게를 지탱하다: *The branch held, and Nick climbed higher up the tree.* 나뭇가지가 그의 무게를 견뎌내 닉은 나무 위로 더 높이 올라갔다.

17 ▶THINK/BELIEVE 생각하다/믿다◀ FORMAL to think or believe something ‖ 어떤 것을 생각하거나 믿다: *My grandfather held the belief that women should not speak too often.* 나의 할아버지는 여자는 말이 많으면 안 된다고 믿었다. / *Pythagoras held that planets have souls.* 피타고라스는 행성이 영혼을 갖고 있다고 믿었다.

18 be left holding the bag to have to deal with problems that someone else has started ‖ 다른 사람이 시작한 문제를 해결해야 하다. 책임을 떠맡다: *Rogers went on vacation and left us holding the bag.* 로저스가 휴가를 떠나자 우리가 그

책임을 떠안았다.

19 hold true/good FORMAL to be true in particular situations ‖ 특정한 상황에서 사실이다. 유효하다. 들어맞다: *I think her statement holds true for older women.* (=is true about them) 나는 그녀의 이야기가 나이든 여자에게는 들어맞는다고 생각한다. —see also **hold your breath** (BREATH), **hold your horses!** (HORSE¹), **bite/hold your tongue** (TONGUE)

hold sth **against** *phr v* [T] to blame someone for something s/he has done ‖ 남이 한 일을 비난하다: *If the economy worsens, voters are likely to hold it against him when they vote in November.* 경기가 악화된다면, 11월 선거 때 유권자들이 그를 비난할 것 같다.

hold back *phr v* **1** [T **hold** sth ↔ **back**] to control something or make it stay in one place ‖ 사물을 제지하거나 한 장소에 머물게 하다. 막다: *The police couldn't hold the crowds back.* 경찰은 군중을 제지할 수 없었다. **2** [I,T **hold back** sth] to stop yourself from showing a particular feeling or saying something ‖ 특정한 감정을 드러내거나 어떤 것에 대해 언급하는 것을 그만두다. 숨기다: *He didn't hold back. He yelled at me for at least ten minutes.* 그는 참지 못했다. 적어도 10분 동안은 나에게 고함을 질렀다. / *I couldn't hold my laughter back any longer.* 나는 웃음을 더 이상 참을 수 없었다. **3** [T **hold** sb ↔ **back**] to prevent someone from developing or improving ‖ 남이 발전하거나 향상하는 것을 막다: *The housing market is still being held back by a weak economy.* 주택 시장이 불황으로 인해 여전히 침체되어 있다.

hold sth **down** *phr v* [T] **1** to keep something at a low level ‖ 낮은 수준으로 유지하다: *We're going to hold down these prices until the New Year.* 우리는 새해까지 이 가격을 유지하려 한다. **2 hold down a job** to keep your job ‖ 일을 계속하다: *We can't hire a guy who's never been able to hold down a job.* 우리는 한 가지 일을 꾸준히 한 경험이 없는 사람을 고용할 수는 없다.

hold forth *phr v* [I] to say what you think about something, loudly and for a long time ‖ 어떤 일에 대한 자신의 생각을 오랫동안 크게 말하다. 장황하게 이야기하다: *A guy at the bar was holding forth on why movies aren't as good as they used to be.* 그 술집에 있던 한 사람이 왜 영화가 예전만큼 좋지 않은가에 대하여 일장 연설을 늘어놓고 있었다.

hold off *phr v* [I] to delay doing something ‖ 지체하다: *We held off making the decision for a month.* 우리는 그 결정을 내리는 것을 한 달간 유보했다.

hold on *phr v* **1** SPOKEN said when you want someone to wait or stop talking, for example during a telephone call ‖ 예컨대, 전화 통화시에 남에게 기다리라고 하거나 말하는 것을 중단하라고 하고 싶을 때에 쓰여: *Yeah, hold on, Mike is right here.* 잠시만 기다리세요. 마이크 바로 바꿔 드리겠습니다. / *Hold on a minute/second. Let me put this in the car.* 잠시만 기다리세요. 차 안에 이것 좀 넣을게요. **2** to hold something tightly with your hand or arms ‖ 손이나 팔로 물체를 꽉 잡다: *I was so scared, I held on to the reins as tightly as I could.* 나는 너무 무서워서 내가 잡을 수 있는 한 세게 고삐를 꽉 잡았다. **3** to continue to do something difficult until it gets better ‖ 더 나아질 때까지 어려운 일을 계속하다. 참아내다: *The Rangers held on to win the game in the final period.* 레인저스 팀은 마지막 피리어드까지 잘 버티어 승리했다.

hold on to sth *phr v* [T] to keep something, especially something that someone else wants ‖ 특히 다른 사람이 원하는 것을 계속 갖고 있다: *I think you should hold on to it. After all, your mother gave it to you.* 결국 당신의 어머니께서 당신께 그것을 주셨으니까 내 생각엔 당신이 그것을 간직해야 한다고 생각한다.

hold out *phr v* [I] **1** if a supply of something holds out, there is still some of it left ‖ 어떤 것이 어느 정도 계속 남아 있다: *We talked for as long as the wine held out.* 우리는 포도주를 다 마실 때까지 이야기를 계속했다. **2** to continue to defend yourself, or keep on refusing to do something ‖ 계속해서 자신을 방어하거나 어떤 일 하는 것을 거부하다. 굴하지 않다. 저항하다: *The rebels are holding out in the south.* 반란군들은 남부에서 저항을 계속하고 있다. **3 hold out hope/the prospect etc.** to say that something may happen ‖ 어떤 일이 일어날 수도 있다고 말하다. 희망/가능성을 주다: *The doctors don't hold out much hope that she will live.* 의사들은 그녀가 살 것이라는 큰 희망을 주지 않는다.

hold out for sth *phr v* [T] to refuse to accept less than you have asked for ‖ 요구한 것 이하로는 받아들이지 않다. 끝까지 요구하다: *We expected him to hold out for more money, but he just signed* *the contract.* 우리는 그가 끝까지 더 많은 돈을 요구할 것으로 생각했지만, 그는 그 냥 계약서에 서명했다.

hold out on sb *phr v* [T] to refuse to tell someone something s/he wants or needs to know ‖ 남이 알고 싶어하는 것이 나 알아야 할 필요가 있는 것을 말하지 않다. 비밀로 하다. 숨기다: *You should have told me, instead of holding out on me for so long!* 너는 그렇게 오랫동안 숨기지 말고 나한테 말했어야 했어!

hold over *phr v* **1 be held over** if a concert, play, or movie is held over, it is shown for longer than was planned because it is very good ‖ 음악회[연극, 영화]가 아주 뛰어나서 계획했던 것보다 오래 공연되다. 연장 공연[상영]하다: *Come see "Pulp Fiction." Held over for the fifth week.* "펄프 픽션"을 관람하세요. 5 주째 연장 상영합니다. **2** [T **hold** sth **over** sb] to use something bad that you know about someone to control or threaten him/her ‖ 남에 대해 알고 있는 나쁜 일을 이용하여 그 사람을 좌지우지하거나 협박하다: *My brother held that secret over me until I was 30 years old.* 오빠는 그 비밀로 내가 30살이 될 때까지 나를 못살게 굴었다.

hold sb **to** sth *phr v* [T] to make someone do what s/he has promised to do ‖ 남에게 하기로 약속한 것을 하게 하다. 지키게 하다: *"He said he would do it." "Well, you'd better hold him to it."* "그가 그것을 하겠다고 했거든." "그래도 다시 한 번 그에게 확인하는 편이 좋아."

hold together *phr v* **1** [I,T **hold** sth **together**] if a group, family, organization etc. holds together or something holds it together, it stays together ‖ 집단·가족·조직 등이 함께 있거나 있게 하다: *The children are the only thing holding their marriage together.* 아이들은 그들의 결혼생활을 유지시켜 주는 유일한 요소이다. **2** [I] to remain whole, without breaking ‖ 끊기지 않고 전체를 유지하다. 이어지다: *I hope this bus holds together long enough to get us to Fresno.* 나는 우리가 프레스노까지 한 번에 가게 이 버스가 연장되기를 바란다.

hold up *phr v* **1** [T **hold** sb/sth ↔ **up**] to make someone or something late ‖ 사람이나 사물을 늦게 만들다. 지연시키다: *Sorry, I didn't mean to hold everybody up.* 죄송합니다, 모두를 지체시킬 의도는 아니었습니다. **2** [T **hold up** sth] to try to steal money from a store, bank etc. using a gun ‖ 총을 써서 상점·은행 등에

서 돈을 강탈하려 하다: *Brad's in jail for holding up a convenience store.* 브래드는 편의점을 털어서 수감되어 있다. **3** [I] to remain physically or emotionally strong ‖ 신체적 또는 정신적으로 강한 상태를 유지하다: *Nancy held up really well through all her family troubles.* 낸시는 그녀의 온갖 가족 문제에도 정말 잘 견뎌냈다.

hold² *n* **1** [singular] the action of holding something ‖ 사물을 잡는 행위. 잡기. 쥐기: *Take hold of the rope and we'll pull you up.* 밧줄을 잡아라 그러면 우리가 너를 끌어올릴게. **2 get a) hold of** to find someone or something for a particular purpose ‖ 특정한 목적으로 사람이나 물건을 찾다: *I need to get hold of Mark to ask him if he's coming to the party.* 나는 마크의 파티 참석 여부를 묻기 위해 그를 찾아야 한다. / *The kids don't seem to have a problem getting a hold of drugs.* 아이들은 마약을 입수하는 데에 문제가 없어 보였다. **3 on hold** waiting on the telephone before speaking to someone ‖ 남과 통화하기 전에 전화를 기다리는. 대기 중의: *I will have to put you on hold.* 끊지 말고 기다리세요. **4 have a hold over/on** sb to have power or control over someone ‖ 남에 대한 지배이나 통제력이 있다 **5 take hold** to start to have an effect on someone or something ‖ 사람이나 사물에 영향을 미치기 시작하다: *These new ideas are taking hold across the country.* 이 신개념은 전국에 걸쳐 영향을 미치기 시작하고 있다. **6** the part of a ship where goods are stored ‖ 배의 물건이 저장된 부분

hold·er /'houldɚ/ *n* **1** someone who has control of or owns a place, position, or thing ‖ 장소[지위, 물건] 등을 통제하거나 소유하는 사람. 보유[소지]자: *Only ticket holders will be admitted.* 표를 소지하신 분만 입장이 가능합니다. **2** something that holds or contains something else ‖ 다른 것을 고정시키거나 포함하는 것. …용기. …대: *a red candle holder* 붉은 촛대

hold·ing /'houldɪŋ/ *n* something that you own or rent, especially land or part of a company ‖ 특히 토지나 회사의 일부분 등의 자신이 소유하거나 빌린 것. 소유지. 차지. 소유 회사

hold·o·ver /'hould,ouvɚ/ *n* a feeling, idea, fashion etc. from the past that has continued to the present ‖ 과거에서 현재까지 계속되는 정서·생각·패션 등. 유물: *styles that are a holdover from the 60s*

60년대 풍의 스타일

hold·up /'hoʊldʌp/ n 1 a delay, especially one caused by traffic ‖ 특히 교통에 의한 지체 2 an attempt to rob someone, especially using a gun ‖ 특히 총을 이용한, 남을 강탈하려는 시도

hole¹ /hoʊl/ n 1 an empty or open space in something solid ‖ 고형물의 속이 비거나 뚫려 있는 곳. 구멍: We saw the dog digging a hole in the yard. 우리는 안마당에 구멍을 파고 있는 개를 보았다. / I have a hole in my sock. 내 양말에 구멍이 났다. 2 the home of a small animal ‖ 작은 동물의 집. 굴: a rabbit hole 토끼굴 3 one of the small holes in the ground that you try to hit the ball into in the game of GOLF ‖ 골프에서 공을 쳐서 넣는 지면의 작은 구멍들 중의 하나. 홀 4 a problem or fault in an idea, plan, or story, so that it can be proved wrong or does not make sense ‖ 잘못으로 입증되거나 이치에 맞지 않게 되는 관념[계획, 이야기] 상의 문제나 오류. 결점. 결함: The witness's testimony was full of holes. 목격자의 증언은 앞뒤가 전혀 맞지 않았다. 5 INFORMAL an unpleasant place to live in, work in etc. ‖ 살거나 일하기에 쾌적하지 못한 장소: I have to get out of this hole. 나는 이 험한 곳에서 벗어나야 한다. 6 be in the hole SPOKEN to owe money ‖ 빚을 지다: We're still $600 in the hole. 우리는 아직 600달러를 빚지고 있다.

hole² v

hole up phr v [I] to hide somewhere, or find shelter somewhere ‖ 숨다, 또는 은신처를 찾다: The rebels are still holed up in an army building. 반란군들은 여전히 막사 안에 은신해 있다.

hol·i·day /'hɑlə,deɪ/ n a day when you do not have to go to work, school etc. ‖ 직장이나 학교에 가지 않아도 되는 날. 휴일: Labor Day is a national holiday in America. 노동절은 미국의 국경일이다. — see usage note at VACATION

ho·li·ness /'hoʊlinɪs/ n 1 [U] the quality of being pure and holy ‖ 순수하고 신성함 2 Your/His Holiness a title used for talking to or about some religious leaders, especially the Pope ‖ 특히 교황 등의 종교 지도자와 말하거나 그 사람에 대해 말하는 데에 쓰는 경칭. 성하(聖下)

ho·lis·tic /hoʊ'lɪstɪk/ adj concerning the whole of something rather than its parts ‖ 부분이 아니라 전체에 관한. 전체의: a doctor interested in holistic medicine (=medicine that treats the whole person, not just the illness) 전인적 의학에 관심이 있는 의사

hol·ler /'hɑlɚ/ v [I, T] INFORMAL to shout loudly ‖ 크게 소리치다. 고함지르다: Dad hollered at me to hurry up. 아빠는 나에게 서두르라고 소리치셨다. — **holler** n

hol·low¹ /'hɑloʊ/ adj 1 having an empty space inside ‖ 안에 빈 공간이 있는. 속이 빈: a hollow tree 속이 빈 나무 2 feelings or words that are hollow are not sincere ‖ 감정이나 말이 성실하지 못한. 허울뿐인: His promises ring hollow. (=seem not sincere) 그의 약속은 공허하게 들린다. 3 hollow cheeks/eyes etc. cheeks, eyes etc. where the skin has sunk inward ‖ 움푹 들어간 볼, 눈 등

hollow² n 1 a hole in something, especially the ground, that is not very deep ‖ 특히, 지면의 그다지 깊지 않은 구멍 2 a small valley ‖ 작은 계곡: cows grazing in the hollow 골짜기에서 풀을 뜯어 먹고 있는 소들

hollow³ v

hollow sth ↔ **out** phr v [T] to remove the inside of something ‖ 사물의 속을 제거하다. 도려내다

hol·ly /'hɑli/ n [U] a small tree with dark shiny pointed green leaves and red berries (BERRY), often used as a decoration at Christmas ‖ 종종 크리스마스 장식으로 쓰이며 끝이 뾰족하고 광택이 나는 진초록 잎과 붉은 열매가 달리는 작은 나무. 서양호랑가시나무

Hol·ly·wood /'hɑli,wʊd/ n [singular] a city in California near Los Angeles, known as the center of the American movie industry ‖ 미국 영화 산업의 중심지로 알려진 캘리포니아 주 로스앤젤레스 근방의 도시. 할리우드

hol·o·caust /'hɑlə,kɔst, 'hoʊ-/ n 1 an event that kills many people and destroys many things ‖ 많은 사람을 죽이고 많은 것들을 파괴하는 사건. 대참사: a nuclear holocaust 핵 참사 2 the Holocaust the killing of millions of Jews by the Nazis in World War II ‖ 제2차 세계 대전 중 나치에 의한 수백만 명의 유대인 학살

hol·o·gram /'hoʊlə,græm, 'hɑ-/ n a special picture made with a LASER that looks as if it is not flat ‖ 평면이 아닌 것처럼 보이는, 레이저로 만드는 특별한 영상. 홀로그램

hol·ster /'hoʊlstɚ/ n a leather object that you use for carrying a gun ‖ 총을 소지하는 데 쓰이는 가죽 제품. 권총집

ho·ly /'hoʊli/ adj 1 relating to God or

religion; SACRED ‖ 신이나 종교에 관련된. 신성한. 성스러운; 㙮 sacred : *the holy city of Jerusalem* 성스러운 도시인 예루살렘 **2** very religious and morally pure ‖ 매우 종교적이고 도덕적으로 순수한: *a holy man* 성직자

Holy Land /'.. ,./ n [singular] the parts of the Middle East where the events in the Bible happened ‖ 성경상의 사건들이 있었던 중동 지역. 성지

hom·age /'hɑmɪdʒ, 'ɑ-/ n [singular, U] FORMAL something that you say or do to show respect for an important person ‖ 중요한 사람에게 존경을 표하거나 말함. 경의. 존경: *The visitors paid homage to the Queen.* 방문객들은 여왕에게 경의를 표했다.

home[1] /hoʊm/ n **1** [C, U] the place where you usually live, especially with your family ‖ 특히 가족과 함께 사는 장소. 집: *I'm sorry, Lisa is not at home now.* 죄송합니다. 리사는 지금 집에 없습니다. / *I've been living at home/living away from home for the past two years.* (=living with my parents/living in a different house from my parents) 나는 지난 2년간 집에서 살고 있다[집에서 나와 지내고 있다]. / *Neil is determined to leave home as soon as he is 18.* (=stop living with his parents) 닐은 18세가 되자마자 집을 떠날 결심을 하고 있다. **2 be/feel at home** to feel comfortable somewhere, or confident doing something ‖ 어떤 장소에 편안함을 느끼거나 어떤 일을 하는 데에 자신감이 있다: *It's hard to feel at home in a new place.* 새로운 장소에서 마음이 편키는 쉽지 않다. **3 the home of sth/be home to** the place where something lives or comes from ‖ 어떤 것이 살거나 유래한 장소: *Australia is the home of the kangaroo.* 오스트레일리아는 캥거루의 서식지이다. **4 make yourself at home** SPOKEN said in order to tell someone who is visiting that s/he should relax ‖ 방문객에게 편히 하라고 말하는 데에 쓰여. 편하게 생각하세요 **5** a place where people live who cannot take care of themselves, because they are very old, sick etc. ‖ 매우 늙고 병들어서 스스로를 돌볼 수 없는 사람들이 사는 장소. 양로원. 요양원 **6** also **home plate** the base that players must touch in baseball to gain a point ‖ 야구에서 점수를 얻기 위해 선수들이 밟아야 하는 베이스. 본루. 홈베이스 —see picture on page 946

home[2] *adv* **1** to or at the place where you live ‖ 살고 있는 장소로 또는 장소에.

집으로. 집에: *Hi, honey, I'm home.* 여보, 나 집에 왔어. / *When does Mike get home?* (=arrive at home) 마이크는 언제 집에 와요? / *What time did you go home?* (=go to your house) 몇 시에 집에 갔니? ✗DON'T SAY "go/get/arrive at home."✗ home 자체에 전치사 at의 뜻이 이미 들어 있으므로 "go/get/arrive at home"이라고는 하지 않는다. **2 take home** to earn a particular amount of money after tax has been taken away ‖ 세금 공제 후 특정액을 벌다. …의 실수령액을 벌다: *I take home about $200 a week.* 나는 일주일에 약 200 달러의 실수령액을 받는다. **3 hit/drive sth home** to make someone understand what you mean by saying it in a very clear and determined way ‖ 분명하고 단호하게 말하여 자신의 의도를 남에게 이해시키다: *The teacher drove the point home by doing an experiment.* 선생님은 실험을 하여 요점을 이해시켜 주셨다.

home[3] *adj* **1** relating to or belonging to your home or family ‖ 집이나 가족에 관련한 또는 속한. 집[가정]의: *My home town is Matamata.* 나의 고향은 마타마타입니다. / *What's your home address?* 당신의 집 주소는 어떻게 됩니까? / *I'm looking forward to some home cooking* (=meals cooked by your family) *over Christmas.* 나는 크리스마스에 가족들이 만들어 주는 음식이 몹시 기다려진다. **2** playing on your own sports field rather than an opponent's field ‖ 상대편의 경기장이 아닌 자신의 스포츠 경기장에서 경기하는. 홈그라운드의: *The home team is ahead by four runs.* 홈팀이 4점 앞서고 있다. —opposite AWAY[2]

home[4] *v*

home in on *phr v* [T] to aim exactly at something and move directly toward it ‖ 어떤 것을 정확히 겨냥해서 그 쪽으로 곧장 움직이다

home·boy /'hoʊmbɔɪ/ n SLANG ⇨ HOMEY[2]

home·com·ing /'hoʊm,kʌmɪŋ/ n **1** an occasion when someone comes back to his/her home after being away for a long time ‖ 오랜 시간 떠나 있다가 집으로 다시 돌아옴. 귀향. 귀가 **2** an occasion when former students return to their school or college ‖ 졸업한 학생들이 출신 학교나 대학교를 방문하는 행사. 모교 방문 행사

home·land /'hoʊmlænd/ n the country where you were born ‖ 태어난 국가. 고국. 조국

home·less /'hoʊmlɪs/ *adj* **1 the**

homeless people who do not have a place to live, and who often live in the streets ‖ 살 집이 없어 때때로 거리에서 지내는 사람들. 노숙자 **2** without a home ‖ 집 없는: *The war left a lot of people homeless.* 전쟁으로 집 없는 사람들이 많이 발생했다. – **homelessness** *n* [U]

home·ly /'hoʊmli/ *adj* a homely person is not very attractive ‖ 사람이 매력 없는. 못생긴 – **homeliness** *n* [U]

home·made /,hoʊm'eɪd/ *adj* made at home and not bought from a store ‖ 상점에서 사지 않고 집에서 만든: *homemade jam* 손수 만든 잼

home·mak·er /'hoʊm,meɪkɚ/ *n* someone who works at home cooking and cleaning, and does not have another job ‖ 다른 직업 없이 집에서 요리와 청소를 하는 사람. 전업 가사 담당자

home of·fice /,. '../ *n* an office you have in your house so that you can do your job at home ‖ 집에서 일할 수 있도록 집안에 갖춘 사무실. 자택 사무실

ho·me·op·a·thy /,hoʊmi'ɑpəθi/ *n* [U] a system of medicine in which someone who is sick is given very small amounts of a substance that has the same effects as the disease ‖ 그 질병과 동일한 효능을 일으키는 물질을 환자에게 극소량 투약하는 의료 요법. 동종요법 – **homeopathic** /,hoʊmiə'pæθɪk/ *adj*

home·page /'hoʊmpeɪdʒ/ *n* a place on the INTERNET where you can find information about a particular person, company etc. ‖ 특정인·특정 기업에 대한 정보를 찾을 수 있는 인터넷상의 장소. 홈페이지

hom·er /'hoʊmɚ/ *n* ⇨ HOME RUN – **homer** *v* [I]

home·room /'hoʊmrum/ *n* the room where students go at the beginning of the school day, or at the beginning of each SEMESTER ‖ 등교해서 처음에 또는 매 학기 초에 학생들이 가는 교실. 홈룸. 학급 지도 교실

home run /,. './ *n* a long hit in baseball that lets the player run around all the bases and get a point ‖ 야구에서 타자가 모든 베이스를 돌고 득점을 올릴 수 있도록 친 장타. 홈런

home·sick /'hoʊm,sɪk/ *adj* feeling sad because you are away from your home ‖ 집에서 멀리 떨어져 있어서 슬픈 감정을 느끼는. 향수병의: *On her first night at camp, Sheila felt very homesick for her family.* 캠프 첫날 밤 쉴라는 가족이 매우 그리웠다. – **homesickness** *n* [U]

home·stead /'hoʊmstɛd/ *n* a farm and the area of land and buildings around it, especially one that was originally given to someone by the government ‖ 특히 본래 정부가 준, 농장·토지·부속 건물. 농가. 자작 농장

home·ward /'hoʊmwɚd/ *adj* going towards home ‖ 집으로 향해 가는. 귀가의: *my homeward trip* 나의 귀향 여행 – **homeward** *adv*

home·work /'hoʊmwɚk/ *n* [U] **1** work for school that a student does at home ‖ 학생이 집에서 하는 학교 과제. 숙제 **2 sb has done his/her homework** someone has prepared well for something ‖ 누가 무엇을 잘 준비하다. 사전 준비를 잘 하다 —compare HOUSEWORK

hom·ey¹ /'hoʊmi/ *adj* comfortable and pleasant, like home ‖ 집처럼 편안하고 기분 좋은. 안락한: *The restaurant had a nice homey atmosphere.* 그 식당은 집처럼 아주 안락한 분위기였다.

homey² *n* SLANG a friend, or someone who comes from your area or GANG ‖ 친구, 또는 자기 지역이나 집단 출신의 사람. 친구. 동향 사람

hom·i·ci·dal /,hɑmə'saɪdl-, ,hoʊ-/ *adj* likely to murder someone ‖ 쉽게 남을 살해하는. 살인을 범하는 경향이 있는

hom·i·cide /'hɑmə,saɪd, 'hoʊ-/ *n* [C, U] the crime of murder ‖ 살인죄

ho·mo·ge·ne·ous /,hoʊmə'dʒiniəs, -nyəs/, **ho·mog·e·nous** /hə'mɑdʒənəs/ *adj* FORMAL consisting of parts or members that are all the same ‖ 모두 똑같은 부분이나 구성원으로 이루어진. 동종의 – **homogeneity** /,hoʊmoʊdʒə'niəti, -'neɪəti/ *n* [U] —compare HETEROGENEOUS

ho·mo·ge·nize /hə'mɑdʒə,naɪz/ *v* [T] FORMAL to change something so that its parts become more similar, or the whole of it is the same ‖ 어떤 것을 부분적으로 더 비슷하거나 전체적으로 똑같게 변화시키다. 동질이 되게 하다

ho·mo·gen·ized /hə'mɑdʒə,naɪzd/ *adj* homogenized milk has had its cream mixed in with the milk ‖ 우유가 크림이 골고루 섞인. 균질의

hom·o·nym /'hɑmə,nɪm/ *n* a word that sounds the same and is spelled the same as another word, but has a different meaning, for example, the noun "bear" and the *v* "bear" ‖ 예를 들어 명사 "bear" 및 동사 "bear"와 같이 발음과 철자는 같지만 뜻이 다른 단어. 동철 이의어

ho·mo·pho·bi·a /,hoʊmə'foʊbiə/ *n* [U] hatred and fear of HOMOSEXUALs ‖ 동성애

에 대한 혐오·공포. 동성애 공포증 –
homophobic *adj*

hom·o·phone /ˈhɑməˌfoʊn, ˈhoʊ-/ *n* a
word that sounds like another word,
but is different in spelling or meaning,
for example, "pair" and "pear" ‖ 예를
들어 "pair" 및 "pear" 와 같이 발음은 같
지만 철자와 뜻이 다른 단어. 동음 이의어

ho·mo·sex·u·al /ˌhoʊməˈsɛkʃuəl/ *adj*
sexually attracted to people of the same
sex ‖ 성적(性的)으로 동성인 사람들에게
매료된. 동성애의 – **homosexual** *n* –
homosexuality /ˌhoʊməˌsɛkʃuˈæləti/ *n*
[U] —compare BISEXUAL¹, GAY¹,
HETEROSEXUAL

hon·cho /ˈhɑntʃoʊ/ *n* INFORMAL an
important person who controls
something ‖ 어떤 것을 통제하는 중요한
인물. 책임자. 지도자: *The company's
head honchos are meeting next week.*
그 회사의 최고 책임자들은 다음주에 모일
예정이다.

hone /hoʊn/ *v* [T] **1** to improve a skill ‖
기술을 연마하다: *players honing their
skills* 기술을 연마하는 운동 선수들 **2** to
make a knife, sword etc. sharp ‖ 작은
칼·검 등을 날카롭게 하다. 갈다

hon·est /ˈɑnɪst/ *adj* **1** someone who is
honest does not lie, cheat, or steal ‖ 사
람이 거짓말하지[속이지, 강탈하지] 않는.
정직한 —opposite DISHONEST **2** truthful
and sincere ‖ 진실하고 성실한: *Give me
an honest answer.* 나에게 솔직히 대답해
줘. **3 honest/to be honest** SPOKEN said
to emphasize that what you are saying
is true ‖ 말하는 것이 사실임을 강조하는
데에 쓰여. 솔직히 말해서: *We didn't
think to do that, to be honest with you.*
당신에게 솔직히 말해서 우리는 그렇게 하
지 못한다고 생각했어요.

hon·est·ly /ˈɑnɪstli/ *adv* **1** SPOKEN said
when you want to make someone
believe what you have just said ‖ 방금 한
말을 남에게 믿게 만들고 싶을 때에 쓰여.
솔직히 말하면: *I honestly don't know
what's the best thing to do.* 나는 솔직히
말해서 어떻게 하는 것이 최선인지 모르겠
다. **2 in an honest way** ‖ 솔직하게:
*Walters spoke honestly about her
problems.* 월터스는 그녀의 문제에 대하여
솔직하게 얘기했다.

hon·es·ty /ˈɑnɪsti/ *n* [U] **1** the quality
of being honest ‖ 정직. 성실: *We never
doubted Frank's honesty.* 우리는 프랭크
가 정직하다는 것을 결코 의심하지 않았
다. **2 in all honesty** SPOKEN said when
you tell someone what you really think
‖ 진짜로 생각하는 것을 남에게 말할 때에

쓰여. 솔직히 말해서: *In all honesty, we
made a lot of mistakes.* 솔직히 말해서,
우리는 실수를 많이 했다.

hon·ey /ˈhʌni/ *n* [U] **1** a sweet sticky
substance made by BEES, used as food ‖
음식으로 쓰이는 벌이 만든 달콤하고 끈적
끈적한 물질. 꿀 **2** SPOKEN a name that
you call someone you love ‖ 사랑하는 사
람을 부를 때의 호칭. 얘. 자기. 여보

hon·ey·comb /ˈhʌniˌkoʊm/ *n* a
structure made by BEES to store HONEY
in ‖ 속에 꿀을 저장하기 위해 벌이 만든
구조물. 벌집

hon·ey·moon /ˈhʌniˌmun/ *n* a
vacation taken by two people who have
just been married ‖ 방금 결혼한 부부가
보내는 휴가. 신혼 여행: *Jen and Dave
are going to Alaska on their
honeymoon.* 젠과 데이브는 알래스카로
신혼여행을 갈 예정이다. – **honey-
mooner** *n*

hon·ey·suck·le /ˈhʌniˌsʌkəl/ *n* a
climbing plant with yellow or pink
flowers that smell sweet ‖ 달콤한 냄새가
나며 노란색이나 분홍색 꽃이 피는 덩굴
식물. 인동 (덩굴)

honk /hɑŋk, hɔŋk/ *v* [I, T] to make a
loud noise like a car horn or a GOOSE ‖
자동차의 경적이나 기러기처럼 큰 소리를
내다. 경적을 울리다. 기러기가 울다 –
honk *n*

hon·or¹ /ˈɑnɚ/ *n* **1** [U] the respect that
someone or something receives from
other people ‖ 사람이나 사물이 다른 사람
으로부터 받는 경의. 존경: *a ceremony in
honor of* (=to show respect to) *the
soldiers who died* 전몰 장병을 기리는 의
식 **2** [singular] something that makes
you feel proud and glad ‖ 자랑스럽고 기
쁘게 만드는 것. 영광: *It's an honor to
meet you.* 만나 뵙게 되어서 영광입니다.
3 [U] strong moral beliefs and
standards of behavior that make people
respect and trust you ‖ 사람들이 존경하
고 신뢰할 수 있게 하는 강한 도덕 관념·
행동의 기준. 도의심. 지조: *He's a man
of honor.* 그는 지조 있는 사람이다. **4**
something that is given to someone to
show him/her that people respect and
admire what s/he has done ‖ 남이 한 일
에 존경과 칭송을 표하기 위해 사람들이
주는 것. 상. 훈장 **5 Your Honor** used
when speaking to a judge ‖ 판사에게 말
할 때에 쓰여. 판사님 —compare
DISHONOR¹

honor² *v* [T] **1** to treat someone with
special respect ‖ 남을 특별히 존중하여
대하다. 예우하다: *Morgan was honored*

at a retirement dinner. 모건은 은퇴 만찬으로 예우받았다. **2** to feel very proud and glad ‖ 매우 자랑스럽고 기쁘게 여기다. 영광으로 여기다: *I'm honored to meet you.* 당신을 만나 뵙게 되어 영광입니다. **3** honor a contract/agreement etc. to do what you have agreed to do in a contract etc. ‖ 계약 등에서 하기로 동의한 것을 행하다. 계약/협정을 지키다 **4** honor a check to accept a check as payment ‖ 보수를 수표로 받다

hon·or·a·ble /'ɑnərəbəl/ *adj* morally correct, and deserving respect and admiration ‖ 도덕적으로 옳고 존경과 칭송을 받을 만한. 고결한. 훌륭한. 존경할 만한: *an honorable man/action* 훌륭한 사람[행동] **– honorably** *adv —* opposite DISHONORABLE

hon·or·ar·y /'ɑnəˌrɛri/ *adj* **1** given to someone as an honor ‖ 남에게 명예로 준. 명예상의: *an honorary degree* 명예학위 **2** someone who has an honorary position does not receive payment for his/her work ‖ 사람의 지위가 일에 대한 보수를 받지 않는. 명예직의

honor roll /'.. ,./ *n* a list of the best students in a school ‖ 우등생 명단: *Did you make the honor roll?* 우등생 명단 만드셨어요?

hon·ors /'ɑnəz/ *n* [plural] **with honors** if you finish high school or college with honors, you get one of the highest grades ‖ 고등학교나 대학교에서 우수한 성적을 얻어. 우등으로

hood /hʊd/ *n* **1** the part of a coat that you pull up to cover your head ‖ 끌어당겨서 머리를 덮는 코트의 부분. 두건 **2** the metal cover over the engine on a car ‖ 자동차의 엔진 위의 금속 덮개. 보닛 **3** SLANG ⇨ NEIGHBORHOOD **4** INFORMAL ⇨ HOODLUM

hood·ed /'hʊdɪd/ *adj* having a HOOD or wearing a hood ‖ 두건이 있는. 두건을 쓴: *a hooded jacket* 후드 달린 재킷

hood·lum /'hudləm, 'hʊd-/ *n* OLD-FASHIONED a young person who does bad, often illegal things ‖ 종종 불법적인 나쁜 짓을 하는 젊은이. 불량배. 깡패

hoof /hʊf/ *n, plural* **hoofs** *or* **hooves** the hard foot of an animal such as a horse ‖ 말 등의 동물의 딱딱한 발. 발굽

hook¹ /hʊk/ *n* **1** a curved object that you hang things on ‖ 물건을 거는 구부러진 물체. 갈고리: *a coat hook* 코트걸이 **2** a curved piece of metal with a sharp point that you use for catching fish ‖ 낚시에 사용하는 끝이 날카롭고 구부러진 금속 조각. 낚싯바늘 **3** let sb off the hook

to decide not to punish someone for something s/he did wrong ‖ 잘못한 것에 대해 남을 처벌하지 않기로 결심하다. 용서하다: *I'll let you off the hook today, but don't be late again.* 오늘은 용서해 줄 테니 다시는 늦지 말아라. **4** off the hook if a telephone is off the hook, the part of the telephone that you speak into is not on its base, so no one can call you ‖ 수화기가 수화기 받침 위에 놓이지 않아서 아무도 전화할 수 없는. 수화기가 잘못 놓여

hook² *v* [T] **1** to fasten or hang something onto something else ‖ 무엇을 다른 것에 고정시키거나 걸다: *Hook the rope over the nail.* 밧줄을 못에 걸어라. **2** INFORMAL to catch a fish with a hook ‖ 낚싯바늘로 고기를 낚다: *Ben hooked a four-pound bass.* 벤은 4파운드짜리 농어를 낚았다.

hook sth ↔ **up** *phr v* [T] to connect a piece of electronic equipment to another piece of equipment ‖ 전기 제품을 또 다른 장치에 연결하다: *Are the speakers hooked up?* 스피커가 연결됐습니까?

hooked /hʊkt/ *adj* **1** shaped like a hook ‖ 갈고리 모양의: *a hooked nose* 매부리코 **2** be hooked on INFORMAL **a)** to be unable to stop taking a drug; ADDICTED ‖ 마약 복용을 그만두지 못하다. 중독되다; ㊎ addicted **b)** to like something a lot ‖ 어떤 것을 매우 좋아하다: *Gina's hooked on old movies.* 지나는 옛날 영화에 푹 빠져 있다.

hook·er /'hʊkə/ *n* INFORMAL ⇨ PROSTITUTE

hook·y /'hʊki/ *n* INFORMAL **play hooky** to stay away from school without permission ‖ 허락 없이 학교를 빼먹다: *The kids were caught playing hooky at the mall.* 아이들은 학교를 무단결석하다 쇼핑센터에서 잡혔다.

hoo·li·gan /'hulɪgən/ *n* a noisy violent person who tries to make people fight and deliberately damages things ‖ 싸움을 걸거나 고의로 기물을 파손하는 시끄럽고 난폭한 사람. 불량배. 훌리건

hoop /hup/ *n* a circular piece of wood, metal, plastic etc. ‖ 나무·금속·플라스틱 등으로 된 원형 물체. 고리. 테: *hoop earrings* 동그란 귀고리 / *a basketball hoop* (=what you throw the ball through) (공을 넣는 농구대의) 링

hoops /hups/ *n* [U] INFORMAL basketball ‖ 농구: *The guys are out shooting hoops.* (=playing basketball) 사람들이 밖에서 농구를 하고 있다.

hoo·ray /hʊ'reɪ/ *interjection* shouted when you are very excited and happy

about something ‖ 어떤 것에 대해 매우
흥분되고 기쁠 때에 외치어. 만세

hoot¹ /hut/ n **1** the sound made by an
OWL or a ship's horn ‖ 올빼미나 배의 경
적이 내는 소리 **2 be a hoot** SPOKEN to
be a lot of fun ‖ 아주 재미있다: *The
show was a hoot!* 그 쇼는 재미있었어! **3
not give a hoot** SPOKEN to not care or
be interested in something ‖ 어떤 것에
대해 신경 쓰지 않거나 관심이 없다: *I
don't give a hoot what they think.* 나는
그들이 생각하는 것에 대해 관심이 없다.

hoot² v [I, T] **1** if an OWL or a ship's
horn hoots, it makes a loud clear noise
‖ 올빼미나 배의 경적이 크고 명료한 소리
를 내다. 울다. 울리다 **2** to shout or
laugh loudly because you think
something is funny or stupid ‖ 사물이 재
미있거나 우스꽝스럽게 생각되어 소리지
르거나 크게 웃다: *The crowd was
hooting and whistling.* 관중들은 크게 소
리지르며 휘파람을 불고 있었다.

hooves /huvz, hʊvz/ n the plural of
HOOF ‖ hoof의 복수형

hop¹ /hɑp/ v **-pped, -pping** [I] **1** to
move by making short quick jumps ‖ 짧
고 빠르게 뛰다. 깡충 뛰다: *rabbits
hopping along* 깡충깡충 뛰고 있는 토끼
2 INFORMAL to get into, onto, or out of
something, such as a vehicle ‖ 자동차 등
에 타다[올라가다, 내리다]: *Hop in and
I'll give you a ride.* 타세요. 제가 태워다
드릴게요. / *Richie hopped on his bike.*
리치는 자전거에 올라탔다.

hop² n **1** a short jump ‖ 깡충 뜀 **2 short
hop** INFORMAL a short trip by plane ‖ 비
행기로 하는 단거리 여행

hope¹ /hoʊp/ v [I, T] to want something
to happen or be true ‖ 어떤 것이 일어나
거나 사실이기를 바라다: *I hope (that)
you feel better soon.* 나는 네가 곧 나아지
기를 바란다. / *He's hoping to take a trip
to Africa next year.* 그는 내년에 아프리
카로 여행할 수 있기를 바라고 있다. /
"Will Grandma be there?" "I hope so."
(=I hope this will happen) "할머니께서
그곳에 계실까요?" "그러길 바래요." /
*"Do you think it's going to rain?" "I
hope not!"* (=I hope this will not
happen) "비 올 것 같니?" "안 왔으면 좋
겠어!"

USAGE NOTE hope to and hope that

Use **hope to** to talk about something
that you or someone else wants to do,
and **hope that** to talk about what
you hope will happen: *Michelle hopes*

*to go to college. / I hope that Michelle
can go to college.*
hope to는 본인 또는 다른 사람이 하
고 싶어하는 것을 말하는 데에 쓰이고
hope that은 본인이 일어나기를 바란
다고 말하는 데에 쓰인다: 미쉘은 대학
에 가고 싶어한다. / 나는 미쉘이 대학에
갈 수 있기를 바란다.

hope² n **1** [singular, U] the feeling that
good things can or will happen ‖ 좋은 일
이 일어날 수 있거나 일어날 것이라는 느
낌. 희망: *a new treatment that gives
hope to cancer patients* (=makes them
have hope) 암 환자에게 희망을 주는 새로
운 치료법 **2** something that you hope
will happen ‖ 일어나길 바라는 것: *Andy
had hopes of competing in the
Olympics.* 앤디는 올림픽 경기에 참가하고
싶어했다. **3 in the hope that/of** if you
do something in the hope that you will
get a particular result, you do it even
though you cannot be sure of this result
‖ 특정 결과가 나온다는 확신은 없지만 기
대를 갖고. …을 기대하여 **4 don't get
your hopes up** SPOKEN used in order to
tell someone that something s/he is
hoping for is not likely to happen ‖ 남에
게 그 사람이 바라는 일이 일어날 것 같지
않다고 말하는 데에 쓰여. 기대하지 마라
5 [C, U] a chance that something good
will happen ‖ 좋은 일이 일어날 가능성.
가망: *There was no hope of escape.* 탈출
할 가망이 없었다.

hope·ful /ˈhoʊpfəl/ adj **1** believing that
what you want is likely to happen ‖ 원하
는 일이 일어날 것이라고 믿는. 희망에 찬:
*We're hopeful about our chances of
winning.* 우리는 승리의 가능성을 낙관하
고 있다. **2** making you feel that what
you want is likely to happen ‖ 원하는 일
이 일어날 것 같은 느낌을 갖게 하는. 희망
적인: *There are hopeful signs that an
agreement will be reached.* 합의가 이뤄
질 희망적인 조짐이 보인다. –
hopefulness n [U]

hope·ful·ly /ˈhoʊpfəli/ adv **1** a word
used at the beginning of a sentence
when saying what you hope will
happen, which some people consider
nonstandard ‖ 원하는 일이 일어나리라고
말할 때에 문장 맨 처음에 쓰이는 말로, 혹
자는 이것을 비표준적인 용법으로 간주한
다. 바라건대: *Hopefully the letter will
come Monday.* 바라건대 편지가 월요일에
도착하면 좋겠다. **2** in a hopeful way ‖ 희
망적으로: *"Can we go to the zoo
tomorrow?" he asked hopefully.* 내일 동

물원 가실래요?라고 그는 희망을 갖고 물
었다.

hope·less /'houp-lɪs/ *adj* **1** without
any chance of success or improvement
∥ 성공이나 발전의 기회가 없는. 가망이
없는: *a hopeless situation* 가망이 없는
상황 **2** INFORMAL unable or unwilling to
do something correctly ∥ 어떤 것을 제대
로 할 능력이나 의지가 없는. 무능한: *He's
hopeless at fixing stuff.* 그는 물건을 수리
에는 젬병이다. **3** feeling no hope, or
showing this ∥ 아무 희망이 없음을 느끼거
나 나타내는. 희망이 없는. 절망적인: *a
hopeless look on her face* 그녀의 얼굴에
드리워진 절망적인 표정 **– hopelessly**
adv **– hopelessness** *n* [U]

hop·scotch /'hɑpskɑtʃ/ *n* [U] a game
in which children jump on squares
drawn on the ground ∥ 아이들이 땅 위에
그린 사각형 위에서 뛰는 게임. 돌차기 놀
이

horde /hɔrd/ *n* a large crowd moving in
a noisy uncontrolled way ∥ 시끄럽고 통
제받지 않으면서 이동하는 큰 무리. 다수.
떼: *hordes of tourists* 수많은 관광객 무리

ho·ri·zon /hə'raɪzən/ *n* **the horizon**
the place where the land or ocean
seems to meet the sky ∥ 지표나 대양이
하늘과 만난 것처럼 보이는 지점. 지평선.
수평선: *a ship on the horizon* 수평선 위
의 배

horizons /hə'raɪzənz/ *n* [plural] the
limit of your ideas, knowledge, and
experience ∥ 사고·지식·경험의 한계. 범
위. 지평: *I took an evening class to
broaden my horizons.* 나는 시야를 넓히
기 위해 야간 수업을 받았다.

hor·i·zon·tal /ˌhɔrə'zɑntəl, ˌhɑr-/ *adj*
flat and level ∥ 납작하고 평평한. 수평의:
a horizontal surface 수평면 **–
horizontally** *adv* —compare VERTICAL
—see picture at VERTICAL

hor·mone /'hɔrmoʊn/ *n* a substance in
the body that influences its growth,
development, and condition ∥ 성장·발
육·건강 상태에 영향을 미치는 체내 물질.
호르몬 **– hormonal** /hɔr'moʊnl/ *adj*

horn /hɔrn/ *n* **1** a hard pointed part
that grows on the heads of cows, goats
etc., or the substance this is made of ∥
소·염소 등의 머리에서 자라는 딱딱하고
뾰족한 부분, 또는 이것을 구성하는 물질.
뿔. 각질(角質) 물질 **2** the thing in a
car, truck etc. that you push to make a
sound as a warning ∥ 자동차·트럭 등에
있는 눌러서 경고음을 내는 물체. 경적:
Ernie blew his horn (=made a noise
with his horn) *at the boys in the street.*
어니는 길거리에 있는 소년들에게 경적을
울렸다. —see picture on page 943 **3 a)**
a metal musical instrument that is wide
at one end, which you play by blowing
∥ 입으로 불어서 연주하는 한쪽 끝이 넓은
금관악기. 호른: *the French horn* 프렌치
호른 **b)** INFORMAL ⇨ TRUMPET[1]

hor·net /'hɔrnɪt/ *n* a large black and
yellow insect that can sting you ∥ 침을
쏠 수 있는 검고 노란 큰 곤충. 말벌

hor·o·scope /'hɔrə,skoʊp, 'hɑr-/ *n* a
description of your character and things
that will happen to you, based on the
position of the stars and PLANETs when
you were born ∥ 탄생시의 별·행성의 위
치에 근거하여 성격 및 앞으로 닥칠 일을
설명하는 것. 점성술

hor·ren·dous /hə'rɛndəs, hɔ-/ *adj* **1**
frightening and terrible ∥ 소름끼치고 무
시무시한. 끔찍한: *a horrendous
experience* 끔찍한 경험 **2** extremely bad
∥ 매우 좋지 않은: *a horrendous meal* 형
편없는 식사

hor·ri·ble /'hɔrəbəl, 'hɑr-/ *adj* **1** very
unpleasant and often frightening ∥ 매우
불쾌하고 종종 소름끼치는. 끔찍한: *a
horrible accident* 끔찍한 사고 **2** very
bad, unpleasant, or rude ∥ 매우 나쁜[불
쾌한, 무례한]: *horrible manners* 무례한
태도 **– horribly** *adv*

hor·rid /'hɔrɪd, 'hɑrɪd/ *adj* ⇨ HORRIBLE

hor·rif·ic /hɔ'rɪfɪk, hə-/ *adj* very
frightening and upsetting ∥ 매우 소름끼
치고 당황스러운. 오싹한. 끔찍한: *horrific
violence* 끔찍한 폭행

hor·ri·fied /'hɔrə,faɪd, 'hɑr-/ *adj*
feeling shocked or upset ∥ 충격적이고 당
황스러운. 오싹한. 기가 막힌: *We were
horrified to see how sick he looked.* 우
리는 그가 얼마나 아파 보이는지 보고 기
가 막혔다. **– horrifying** *adj* **– horrify**
v [T]

hor·ror /'hɔrə, 'hɑrə/ *n* [C, U] a strong
feeling of shock and fear, or someone or
something that makes you feel this ∥ 큰
충격·두려움, 또는 이런 충격·두려움을 느
끼게 하는 사람이나 사물. 전율. 공포. 무

horn

horn

sound the horn

서운 사람[것]: *I watched in horror as Ramsey hit her.* 나는 램지가 그녀를 때릴 때 무서워 떨면서 보았다. / *the horrors of war* 전쟁에 대한 두려움

hors d'oeu·vre /ɔr ˈdəv/ *n* a small amount of food that is served before the main meal ‖ 주요리 전에 제공되는 약간의 음식. 오르되브르. 전채

horse¹ /hɔrs/ *n* **1** a large strong animal that people ride on and use for pulling heavy things ‖ 사람들이 올라 타고 무거운 것을 끄는 데에 쓰이는 크고 튼튼한 동물. 말 **2 hold your horses!** SPOKEN said when you want someone to wait or to stop doing something ‖ 남에게 기다리거나 무엇을 하지 않기를 바랄 때에 쓰여. 잠깐 기다려! 서두르지 마!

horse² *v*

horse around *phr v* [I] INFORMAL to play in a rough and silly way ‖ 거칠고 어리석게 놀다. 법석 떨다: *Stop horsing around and get back to work!* 그만 법석 떨고 일하거라!

horse·back /ˈhɔrsbæk/ *n* **1 horseback riding** the activity of riding a horse for pleasure ‖ 재미로 말을 타는 행위. 승마 **2 on horseback** riding a horse ‖ 말을 탄

horse·play /ˈhɔrs-pleɪ/ *n* [U] rough noisy play, usually involving more than one child ‖ 보통 한 아이 이상이 거칠고 떠들썩하게 행동함. 야단법석

horse·pow·er /ˈhɔrsˌpaʊɚ/, *written abbreviation* **hp** *n, plural* **horsepower** a unit for measuring the power of an engine ‖ 엔진의 동력 측정 단위. 마력

horse·shoe /ˈhɔrʃʃu, ˈhɔrs-/ *n* a curved piece of iron that is attached to the bottom of a horse's foot to protect it ‖ 말의 발바닥을 보호하기 위해 붙이는 구부러진 금속 조각. 편자

horti·cul·ture /ˈhɔrtəˌkʌltʃɚ/ *n* [U] the practice or science of growing plants ‖ 식물 재배 활동이나 연구. 원예(학) – **horticultural** /ˌhɔrtəˈkʌltʃərəl/ *adj*

hose¹ /hoʊz/ *n* **1** [C, U] a long tube that can bend, used for putting water onto a garden, allowing liquids or air to flow through an engine etc. ‖ 정원에 물을 주거나 엔진 등에 액체나 공기를 흐르게 하는 데에 쓰이는 구부릴 수 있는 긴 관. 호스 **2** [plural] ⇨ PANTYHOSE

hose² *v*

hose sth ↔ **down** *phr v* [T] to use a HOSE to put water on something, for example in order to clean it ‖ 예를 들어 깨끗이 하려고 호스를 써서 어떤 것에 물

을 끼얹다: *They came in every week to hose down the floors of the prison cells.* 그들은 교도소 감방 바닥을 물청소하기 위해 매주 왔다.

ho·sier·y /ˈhoʊʒəri/ *n* [U] clothing such as socks and STOCKINGs ‖ 양말·스타킹 등의 의류

hos·pice /ˈhɑspɪs/ *n* a special hospital where people who are dying are cared for ‖ 죽어가는 사람들을 돌보는 특수 병원. 말기 환자를 위한 병원

hos·pi·ta·ble /hɑˈspɪtəbəl, ˈhɑspɪ-/ *adj* friendly, welcoming, and generous to visitors ‖ 방문객들에게 친절하고 환영하며 후한. 환대하는: *The local people were really hospitable to us.* 그 지역 사람들은 정말 우리에게 친절했다. —compare INHOSPITABLE

hos·pi·tal /ˈhɑspɪtl/ *n* [C, U] a building where sick or injured people receive medical treatment ‖ 병들거나 다친 사람들이 치료를 받는 건물. 병원: *Rick's dad is still in the hospital.* (=being cared for in a hospital) 릭의 아버지는 아직 입원 중이다.

hos·pi·tal·i·ty /ˌhɑspəˈtæləti/ *n* [U] friendly behavior toward visitors ‖ 방문객에게 대한 친절한 행동. 환대: *the hospitality of the inn's owners* 여관 주인의 환대

hos·pi·tal·ize /ˈhɑspɪtlˌaɪz/ *v* [T] to put someone into a hospital for medical treatment ‖ 남을 치료를 위해 병원에 입원시키다: *Two people were hospitalized with stab wounds.* 두 사람이 칼에 찔린 상처로 입원을 했다. – **hospitalization** /ˌhɑspɪtləˈzeɪʃən/ *n* [U]

host¹ /hoʊst/ *n* **1** the person at a party who invited the guests and organized the party ‖ 손님을 초대하고 파티를 준비한 사람. 파티의 주인 **2** someone who introduces the guests on a television or radio show ‖ 텔레비전이나 라디오 쇼에서 초대 손님을 이끌어 나가는 사람. 사회자: *a game show host* 게임 쇼 사회자 **3** a country or organization that provides the space, equipment etc. for a special event ‖ 특별 행사에 장소·장비 등을 제공하는 국가나 조직. 주최국. 주최측: *the host city for the next Olympic Games* 다음 올림픽 개최 도시 **4 a (whole) host of** a large number of ‖ 다수의. 많은: *a host of possibilities* 많은 가능성

host² *v* [T] to be the HOST of an event ‖ 행사의 주인이 되다. …을 주최하다: *What country is hosting the next World Cup?* 다음 월드컵은 어느 나라가 주최합니까?

hos·tage /ˈhɑstɪdʒ/ *n* someone who is

kept as a prisoner by an enemy, so that the other side will do what the enemy demands ‖ 적이 요구하는 것을 상대측이 하도록 적에게 포로로 잡혀 있는 사람. 인질. 볼모: *Three nurses were taken/held hostage* (=caught and used as hostages) *by the terrorists.* 세 명의 간호사가 테러리스트에 의해 인질로 잡혔다.

hos·tel /'hɑstl/ *n* a cheap place for young people to stay when they are away from home ‖ 젊은이들이 집을 떠나 있을 때 묵는 값이 싼 곳. 유스 호스텔

host·ess /'houstɪs/ *n* 1 the woman at a party who invited the guests and organized the party ‖ 손님을 초대하고 파티를 준비하는 파티의 여성. 여자 주인[주최자] 2 a woman who takes people to their seats in a restaurant ‖ 레스토랑에서 손님을 그들의 좌석으로 안내해 주는 여성. 호스티스

hos·tile /'hɑstl, 'hɑstaɪl/ *adj* 1 very unfriendly and ready to fight or argue with someone ‖ 매우 비우호적이고 남과 싸우려고 하거나 논쟁하려고 하는. 적의를 가진. 적대적인: *a hostile crowd throwing rocks* 돌을 던지는 적대적인 군중 2 opposing a plan or idea very strongly ‖ 계획이나 생각에 아주 강력히 반대하는. 대립[적대]하는: *One senator was hostile to the proposed law.* 한 상원 의원이 제안된 법률에 강경하게 반대했다. 3 belonging to an enemy ‖ 적에게 속해 있는. 적의: *hostile territory* 적지

hostile take·over /ˌ.. '.../ *n* a situation in which a company starts to control a smaller one because the smaller one does not have enough power or money to stop it ‖ 한 회사가 지배를 막을 충분한 힘이나 돈이 없는 작은 회사를 지배하기 시작하는 상황. 적대적[비우호적] 인수

hos·til·i·ties /hɑ'stɪlətiz/ *n* [plural] FORMAL acts of fighting ‖ 전투 행위. 전쟁. 교전: *efforts to end the hostilities in the region* 그 지역에서 전쟁을 종식시키려는 노력

hos·til·i·ty /hɑ'stɪləti/ *n* [U] 1 unfriendly and angry feelings or behavior ‖ 비우호적이고 성난 감정이나 행동. 적의. 적대: *Jessie has so much hostility toward men!* 제시는 남성들에게 너무 적대적이야! 2 strong opposition to a plan or idea ‖ 계획이나 생각에 대한 강한 반대: *There's too much hostility to the changes for us to go ahead.* 우리가 앞으로 전진하기 위한 변화에 너무 많은 반대가 있다.

hot /hɑt/ *adj* **-tter, -ttest** 1 high in temperature ‖ 온도가 높은. 뜨거운. 더운: *The soup's really hot.* 그 수프는 정말 뜨겁다. / *the hottest day of the year* 그 해의 가장 더운 날 / *Your forehead feels hot.* 네 이마가 뜨겁게 느껴진다. —see usage note at TEMPERATURE 2 having a burning taste; SPICY ‖ 타는 듯한 맛이 있는. 매운. 얼얼한; ㉦ spicy : *hot salsa* 매운 살사(소스) 3 INFORMAL very good, popular, or exciting ‖ 매우 좋은[인기 있는, 흥미 있는]. 잘 팔리는. 수요가 많은: *a hot new singer* 인기 있는 신인 가수 / *the hottest item* (=thing that sold the most) *at the software exposition* 소프트웨어 전시회에서 가장 잘 팔린 상품 4 likely to cause trouble or arguments ‖ 문제나 논쟁을 일으키기 쉬운. 물의를 빚는: *Studio bosses decided her video was too hot to handle.* (=too much trouble to deal with) 영화사 사장들은 그녀의 비디오가 너무 문제가 많아서 다룰 수 없다고 판단했다. / *Fishing rights have become a hot topic/issue* (=subject that people are arguing about) *in the race for Governor.* 어업권이 주지사 선거에서 물의를 빚고 있는 쟁점이 되었다. 5 **not so hot** SPOKEN not very good ‖ 그다지 좋지 않은: *I'm not feeling so hot.* 나는 그다지 좋지 않은 느낌이 든다. 6 SLANG goods that are hot have been stolen ‖ 물건이 도난당한. 부정하게 입수한. 장물의: *a hot car* 도난 차량 7 **be hot at sth** to be very good at doing something ‖ 어떤 것을 하는 것에 아주 능하다. …을 썩 잘 하다: *I wasn't too hot at math.* 나는 수학을 그리 잘하지 못했다.

hot air /ˌ. './ *n* [U] INFORMAL things someone says that sound important, but really are not ‖ 중요한 것처럼 들리지만 실제로는 그렇지 않은 사람들의 말. 쓸데없는[실없는] 이야기. 허풍

hot air bal·loon /ˌ. '. ˌ../ *n* a very large BALLOON made of cloth and filled with hot air, used for carrying people in the air ‖ 공중에서 사람을 운반하는 데에 사용되는 천으로 만들어 더운 공기를 가득 채운 아주 큰 풍선. 열기구

hot·bed /'hɑtˈbɛd/ *n* a place where a lot of a particular type of activity happens ‖ 특정한 형태의 활동이 많이 일어나는 장소. 온상: *colleges that were hotbeds of dissent during the 1960s* 1960년대에 반대 의견의 온상이었던 대학

hot but·ton /'. ˌ../ *n* something that makes people react with strong opinions ‖ 사람들을 강력한 의견으로 반응하게 하

는 것. 큰 반향을 부르는 것[문제]: *An issue such as abortion pushes all the hot buttons*. 낙태 같은 문제는 큰 반향을 일으킨다.

hot·cake /ˈhɑtˌkeɪk/ *n* **1 sell/go like hotcakes** SPOKEN to sell very quickly and in large amounts ‖ 매우 빠르게 많이 팔리다. 날개 돋친 듯이[불티나게] 팔리다 **2** ⇨ PANCAKE

hot dog /'. ./ *n* a long SAUSAGE (=tube-shaped piece of cooked meat), eaten in a long bun (=type of bread) ‖ 긴 빵 속에 넣어 먹는 (튜브 모양으로 조리된) 긴 소시지. 핫도그

hot dog

ho·tel /hoʊˈtɛl/ *n* a large building where people pay to stay for a short time ‖ 사람이 잠시 동안 체류하기 위해 돈을 지불하는 큰 건물. 호텔

hot flash /ˌ. ˈ./, **hot flush** *n* a sudden hot feeling that women have during MENOPAUSE ‖ 폐경기에 여성이 느끼는 갑작스러운 열감(熱感)

hot·head·ed /ˌhɑtˈhɛdɪd/ *adj* getting angry or excited easily and doing things too quickly, without thinking ‖ 쉽게 화를 내거나 흥분하여 생각하지 않고 너무 빨리 어떤 것을 하는. 성급한. 조급한. 성마른 **– hothead** /ˈhɑthɛd/ *n*

hot·line /ˈhɑtˌlaɪn/ *n* a special telephone number that people can call for quick help with questions or problems ‖ 궁금증이나 문제가 있는 사람들이 신속한 도움을 요청할 수 있는 특별 전화 번호. 긴급 직통 전화. 전화 상담 서비스: *a suicide hotline* 자살 전화 상담 서비스

hot·ly /ˈhɑtli/ *adv* **1 hotly debated/disputed etc.** discussed or argued about very angrily ‖ 매우 격분하여 토론하거나 논쟁하는. 맹렬히 토론/논쟁하는: *a hotly debated issue* 맹렬한 논쟁거리 **2 hotly contested/fought** fought or COMPETEd for in an extremely strong way ‖ 극도로 강력하게 싸우거나 경쟁하는. 맹렬히 겨루는/싸우는: *the hotly contested race for Governor* 치열한 주지사 선거전

hot plate /'. ./ *n* a small piece of equipment with a flat heated top, used for cooking food ‖ 평평한 표면이 달궈져 음식을 요리하는 데 쓰는 작은 기구. 요리용 철판

hot po·ta·to /ˌ. .ˈ../ *n* INFORMAL a subject or problem that no one wants to deal with, because any decision would make a lot of people angry ‖ 어떤 결정이 많은 사람을 화나게 할 수 있기 때문에 아무도 다루고 싶어 하지 않는 주제나 문제. 다루기 곤란[불쾌, 위험]한 문제. 뜨거운 감자: *The issue of prayer in schools became a political hot potato in the 1980s.* 교내 기도 문제는 1980년대에 정치적으로 민감한 문제가 되었다.

hot rod /'. ./ *n* INFORMAL a car that you have put a powerful engine into ‖ 강력한 엔진을 장착한 자동차. 개조 자동차

hot seat /'. ./ *n* INFORMAL **be in the hot seat** to be forced to deal with a difficult or unpleasant situation, especially in politics ‖ 특히 정치상으로, 어렵거나 불쾌한 상황을 억지로 다루게 되다. 곤경에 처하다

hot·shot /ˈhɑt-tʃɑt/ *n* INFORMAL someone who is very successful and confident ‖ 매우 성공적이고 자신 있는 사람. 적극적이고 유능한 사람. 수완가 **– hotshot** *adj* : *a hotshot lawyer* 적극적이고 유능한 변호사

hot spot /'. ./ *n* **1** a place where there is likely to be trouble, fighting etc. ‖ 문제·싸움 등이 도사리고 있는 장소. 분쟁 지역: *Soldiers were moved to hot spots along the border.* 병사들은 국경을 따라 분쟁 지역으로 이동하였다. **2** an area on a computer screen that you CLICK on in order to make other pictures, words etc. appear ‖ 다른 그림·단어 등을 나타나게 하기 위하여 클릭하는 컴퓨터 화면상의 부분. 핫스폿

hot-tem·pered /ˌ. ˈ../ *adj* tending to become angry very easily ‖ 아주 쉽게 화를 내는 경향이 있는. 욱하는 성질의. 성미가 급한

hot tub /'. ./ *n* a heated bathtub that several people can sit in ‖ 여러 사람이 들어앉을 수 있는 덥혀진 욕조. 온수 욕조

hot-wa·ter bot·tle /ˌ. ˈ.. ˌ../ *n* a rubber container filled with hot water, used for keeping part of your body warm ‖ 신체 부위를 따뜻하게 유지시키는 데 사용하는 뜨거운 물을 가득 채운 고무 용기. 열탕 주머니. 탕파

hot-wire /ˈhɑtˌwaɪɚ/ *v* [T] INFORMAL to start the engine of a vehicle without a key, by using the wires of the IGNITION system ‖ 점화 장치의 전선을 이용하여 열쇠 없이 자동차 엔진에 시동을 걸다

hound¹ /haʊnd/ *v* [T] to keep following someone and asking him/her questions in an annoying or threatening way ‖ 남을 계속 따라다니면서 귀찮게 또는 위협적으로 질문을 하다. 끈질기게 괴롭히다:

She's constantly hounded by reporters.
그녀는 기자들에게 끈질기게 괴롭힘을 당했다.

hound² *n* a dog used for hunting ‖ 사냥하는 데 쓰이는 개. 사냥개

hour /auɚ/ *n* **1** a period of 60 minutes ‖ 60분의 시간. 한 시간: *It takes two hours to get here from the city.* 그 도시에서 여기에 도착하는 데 2시간이 걸린다. / *I'll be home in an hour.* 한 시간 안에 집에 도착할 것이다. / *a ten-hour trip* (=one that is ten hours long) 10시간에 걸친 여행 ✗DON'T SAY "a ten hours trip."✗ "a ten hours trip"이라고는 하지 않는다. **2** the distance you can travel in an hour ‖ 한 시간 안에 여행할 수 있는 거리. 한 시간 (걸리는) 거리: *The lake is an hour from Hartford.* 그 호수는 하트포드에서 한 시간 거리에 있다. **3** [singular] a time of day when a new hour starts ‖ 새로운 시간이 시작되는 하루 중의 시간. 정각. 정시: *Classes begin on the hour.* (=exactly at 1 o'clock, 2 o'clock etc.) 수업은(정확히 1시·2시 등) 정시에 시작한다. **4** a period of time in the day when a particular activity always happens ‖ 특정한 활동이 항상 일어나는 하루의 시간: *Opening hours are from 9:00 a.m. to 8:00 p.m.* 개점 시간은 아침 9시부터 오후 8시까지 입니다. / *I'll go to the store on my lunch hour.* 점심 시간에 상점에 갈 것이다. **5** a particular time of the day or night ‖ 낮이나 밤의 특정한 시간: *The subway doesn't run at this hour of the night.* 지하철은 이런 심야에는 운행되지 않는다. **6** an important time in history or in your life ‖ 역사상 또는 인생에서의 중요한 시간: *You were there in my hour of need.* (=when I needed help) 내가 도움을 필요로 하는 순간에 너는 그곳에 있었다. —see also HOURS

hour·glass /'auɚglæs/ *n* a glass container for measuring time, in which sand moves from the top half to the bottom in exactly one hour ‖ 모래가 상층 중간에서 바닥까지 정확히 한 시간에 이동하는, 시간 측정용 유리 용기. 모래시계

hour·ly /'auɚli/ *adj, adv* **1** happening or done every hour or once an hour ‖ 매 시간 또는 1시간에 한 번 발생하거나 행해지는. 매 시간의. 한 시간마다의: *Trains from Boston arrive hourly.* 보스턴에서 오는 열차가 한 시간마다 도착한다. / *an hourly news bulletin* 1시간 단위의 뉴스 속보 **2 hourly pay/fees etc**. the amount you earn or charge for every hour you work ‖ 작업 시간당 벌거나 지불받는 액수. 시간당 급여/요금

hours /auɚz/ *n* [plural] **1** the period of time when a store or business is open ‖ 상점이나 기업이 문을 열어 놓는 시간. 영업 시간: *The mall's opening hours are from 9 a.m. till 9 p.m.* 그 쇼핑센터의 영업 시간은 아침 9시부터 오후 9시까지이다. / *visiting hours* (=the time when you can visit) *at the hospital* 그 병원의 면회[문병] 시간 / *The inventory will be done after hours.* (=when the store is closed) 가게의 영업을 끝낸 후에 재고 조사를 한다. **2 hours before/earlier/ after/later** two or more hours before or after something happens ‖ 무엇이 일어나기 전이나 후의 두 시간 또는 두 시간 이상의 시간. 몇 시간 전에/앞서/후에/지나서: *A bomb exploded in the airport just hours before the President's arrival.* 대통령이 도착하기 바로 몇 시간 전에 공항에서 폭탄이 폭발했다. **3** INFORMAL a long time ‖ 긴 시간: *She spends hours on the phone.* 그녀는 전화하며 몇 시간을 보낸다. **4 at all hours** at any time during the day and night ‖ 밤·낮 동안 어느 때나. 언제든지: *They're up with that baby at all hours.* 그들은 밤낮할 것 없이 그 아이와 함께 깨어 있다.

house¹ /haus/ *n, plural* **houses** /'hauziz/ **1** a building that you live in, especially one that is intended to be used by one family ‖ 사람이 거주하는, 특히 한 가족이 사용하도록 되어 있는 건물. 주택. 집: *I'm going over to Dean's house.* 나는 딘의 집으로 (건너)갈 것이다. **2** all the people who live in a house ‖ 집에 사는 모든 사람. 가족: *Be quiet, or you'll wake the whole house!* 조용히 해라, 그렇지 않으면 온 가족을 깨우겠어! **3** a building used for a particular purpose or to keep a particular thing in ‖ 특정 목적이나 특정 물건을 보관하기 위해서 사용되는 건물: *the Opera House* 오페라 하우스 / *a hen house* 닭장 **4 a)** one of the groups of people who make the laws of a state or country ‖ 주(州) 또는 국가의 법을 제정하는 일단의 사람들 중의 한 명. 의원: *The President will speak to both houses of Congress on Thursday.* ‖ 대통령은 목요일에 의회의 상·하원 의원들에게 연설할 것이다. **b) the House** ⇨ HOUSE OF REPRESENTATIVES **5 publishing/ fashion house** a company that produces books or designs clothes ‖ 책을 출판하거나 옷을 디자인하는 회사. 출판사 /패션 회사 **6** the part of a theater where people sit, or the people in it ‖ 극장에서 사람들이 앉는 곳, 또는 극장 안의 사람들. 극장. 관중. 청중: *We had a full* *house for the play.* 그 연극은 대성황이었다. **7 be on the house** SPOKEN if drinks or meals in a restaurant are on the house, they are free ‖ 식당의 음료나 음식이 무료이다. 주인이 부담하다

house² /haʊz/ v [T] **1** to provide someone with a place to live ‖ 누구에게 살 곳을 제공하다. …에게 거처할 곳을 주다. …을 묵게 하다: *a program to house the homeless* 집 없는 사람들에게 살 곳을 주는 프로그램 **2** if a building houses something, it is kept there ‖ 건물에 무엇을 보관하다. 건물이 …의 보호 장소가 되다: *The new building will house the college's art collection.* 그 신축 건물에는 대학 미술 수집품을 소장할 것이다.

house ar·rest /ˌ. .ˈ./ n **be under house arrest** to not be allowed to leave your house by the government ‖ 정부가 자기 집을 떠나는 것을 허용하지 않다. 가택 연금되어 있다

house·boat /ˈhaʊsboʊt/ n a special boat that you can live in ‖ 안에서 거주할 수 있는 특별한 배. 숙박 시설을 갖춘 배

house·bound /ˈhaʊsbaʊnd/ adj unable to leave your house, especially because you are sick or old ‖ 특히 병이 나거나 늙어서 집을 떠날 수 없는. 집에 틀어박혀 있는. 두문불출의

house·bro·ken /ˈhaʊsˌbroʊkən/ adj an animal that is housebroken has been trained not to empty its bowels or BLADDER in the house ‖ 동물이 집 안에서 대소변을 보지 않도록 훈련된

house·hold¹ /ˈhaʊshoʊld, ˈhaʊsoʊld/ adj **1** relating to a house and the people in it ‖ 집과 집안사람들과 관련된. 가족[가정]의. 가정용의: *household chores* 가사 **2 be a household name/word** to be famous or known about by many people ‖ 많은 사람들에게 유명하거나 알려지다. 잘 알려져 있다

household² n all the people who live together in one house ‖ 한 집에 함께 사는 모든 사람들. 가족. 세대

house hus·band /ˈ. ˌ.../ n a married man who works at home doing the cooking, cleaning etc. ‖ 요리·청소 등의 집안일을 하는 결혼한 남자. 가사를 전업으로 하는 남편

house·keep·er /ˈhaʊsˌkipɚ/ n someone whose job is to do the cooking, cleaning etc. in a house or hotel ‖ 집이나 호텔에서 요리·청소 등을 하는 직업인. 가정부. 관리인

house·keep·ing /ˈhaʊsˌkipɪŋ/ n [U] the work that you do at home, such as cooking and cleaning ‖ 요리와 청소 등의 가정에서 하는 일. 살림살이. 가사

House of Rep·re·sent·a·tives /ˌ. . ..ˈ...ˈ../ n [singular] the larger of the two groups of people who are part of the government and who make the laws in countries such as the US and Australia ‖ 미국과 호주 등의 나라에서 정부의 한 기관으로 법을 제정하는 사람들의 두 집단 중에 더 큰 집단. 하원 —compare SENATE

house·plant /ˈhaʊsplænt/ n a plant that is grown indoors for decoration ‖ 장식용으로 실내에서 재배하는 식물. 실내용 화초

house-sit /ˈ. ./ v [I] to take care of someone's house while s/he is away ‖ 부재중에 남의 집을 돌보다. …의 집을 봐주다 – **house sitter** n

house·wares /ˈhaʊswɛrz/ n things used in the home, such as plates and lamps ‖ 접시와 램프 등의 가정에서 사용되는 물건. 가정용품

house·warm·ing /ˈhaʊsˌwɔrmɪŋ/ n a party that you give to celebrate moving into a new house ‖ 새집으로 이사 간 것을 축하하기 위해 여는 파티. 집들이

house·wife /ˈhaʊswaɪf/ n, plural **housewives** /-waɪvz/ a married woman who works at home doing the cooking, cleaning etc. ‖ 요리·청소 등의 집안일을 하는 결혼한 여자. 전업주부 — see also HOMEMAKER

house·work /ˈhaʊswɚk/ n [U] the work that you do to take care of a house ‖ 집을 돌보기 위해 하는 일. 가사. 집안일 —compare HOMEWORK

hous·ing /ˈhaʊzɪŋ/ n **1** [U] buildings that people live in ‖ 사람들이 사는 건물. 집. 주택: *a shortage of good housing* 좋은 주택의 부족 **2** [U] the work of providing houses for people to live in ‖ 사람들에게 거주하기 위한 주택을 공급하는 일. 주택 공급: *a housing program* 주택 공급 프로그램 **3** a protective cover for a machine ‖ 기계용 보호 덮개: *the engine housing* 엔진 덮개

housing de·vel·op·ment /ˈ.. .ˌ.../ n a number of houses built in the same area ‖ 같은 지역에 지어진 다수의 집. 주택 단지(團地)

housing proj·ect /ˈ.. ˌ../ n a group of houses or apartments for poor families, usually built with money from the government ‖ 보통 정부의 돈으로 짓는 빈곤(층) 세대를 위한 일단의 집이나 아파트. (저소득층을 위한) 공영 주택 (단지)

hov·el /ˈhʌvəl, ˈhɑ-/ n a small dirty place where someone lives ‖ 사람이 사는 작고 더러운 곳. 오두막집

hov·er /ˈhʌvɚ/ v [I] **1** to stay in one place in the air while flying ‖ 비행 중에 공중의 한 지점에 머무르다. 맴돌다: *A helicopter hovered above the crowd.* 헬리콥터 한 대가 군중 위를 맴돌았다. **2** to stay around one place, especially because you are waiting for something ‖ 특히 무엇을 기다리고 있기 때문에 한 장소 주위에 머무르다. 근방을 배회하다. 서성거리다: *Richard was hovering by the door, hoping to talk to me.* 리차드는 나에게 말하고 싶어하며 문 옆에서 서성거리고 있었다.

how /haʊ/ adv, conj **1** used in order to ask about or explain the way to do something, or the way something happened ‖ 무엇에 대하여 묻거나 어떤 것을 하는 방법이나 어떤 것이 일어난 방법을 설명하는 데에 쓰여. 어떤 방법으로. 어떻게: *How do you spell your name?* 네 이름은 어떻게 철자하니? / *How do I get to K-Mart from here?* 여기서 K-마트까지 어떻게 가야 합니까? / *The advisor can show you how to apply for the loan.* 그 상담원이 대출 신청 방법을 당신에게 알려줄 겁니다. **2** used in order to ask about the amount, size, or degree of something ‖ 물건의 양[크기, 정도]에 대해 묻는 데에 쓰여. 얼마만큼. 어느 정도. 얼마나: *How old is Debbie?* 데비는 몇 살이니? / *How tall do you think Mario is?* 마리오는 키가 얼마나 된다고 생각하니? / *How much is that car?* (=what does it cost?) 그 차는 얼마입니까? **3** used in order to ask about someone's health ‖ 남의 건강에 대해 묻는 데에 쓰여: *How is your mother doing?* 네 어머니 건강이 어떠시니? **4** used in order to ask someone his/her opinion, or about his/her experience of something ‖ 남의 의견이나 어떤 것에 대한 경험에 대해 묻는 데에 쓰여. 어떤 모양[상태, 형편]으로: *"How do I look?" "Great!"* "어때 보여요?" "멋져!" / *How was your vacation?* 휴가는 어땠어? **5** used in order to ask what someone or something looks like, behaves like, or the way something is expressed ‖ 사람이나 사물이 어떤 모습인지[어떻게 행동하는지, 무엇이 어떻게 표현되는지]를 묻는 데에 쓰여: *How does that song go?* 그 노래를 어떻게 하죠[하더라]? / *How does she act with other children?* 그녀는 다른 아이들과 함께 어떻게 지냅니까? **6** used before an adjective or adverb to emphasize it ‖ 강조하기 위해 형용사나 부사 앞에 쓰여: *I can't even remember how many times I've seen "Star Wars."* 나는

영화 "스타워즈"를 얼마나 많이 보았는지 기억조차 할 수 없어. / *Did he tell you how boring it was?* 그 일이 얼마나 지루했는지 그가 네게 말했니?

SPOKEN PHRASES

7 How are you?/How's it going? used when asking if someone is well and happy ‖ 사람이 건강하고 행복한지를 물을 때 쓰여. 안녕하십니까?/어떻게 지내십니까?: *"Hi, Kelly. How are you doing?" "Fine, thanks."* "안녕 켈리. 어떻게 지내니?" "잘 지내, 고마워." / *So, how's it going at work?* 그럼, 일은 어떻게 돼 가니? **8 how about...?** used when making a suggestion about what to do ‖ 할 일에 대해 제안할 때 쓰여. …하는 것은 어떠니[어떻습니까]?: *I'm busy tonight, but how about tomorrow?* 오늘 밤은 바쁜데, 내일은 어떠니? **9 how come?** used when asking why something has happened ‖ 어떤 일이 일어난 까닭을 물을 때 쓰여. 어찌하여. 왜?: *"I can't come to the dance." "How come?"* "나는 춤을 추러 갈 수 없어." "왜?" **10 how do you know?** used when asking why someone is sure about something ‖ 누군가가 어떤 일에 대해 확신하는 까닭을 물을 때 쓰여. (당신이) 어떻게 압니까?: *"I'm sure she's nice." "How do you know? You haven't met her."* ‖ "나는 그녀가 멋있다고 확신해." "네가 어떻게 알아? 그녀를 만난 적도 없잖아." **11 how can sb do sth?** said when you are surprised, shocked, or angry, or when you disapprove of something ‖ 놀라거나 충격받거나 화났을 때, 또는 어떤 것에 동의하지 않을 때 쓰여. (도대체) …이 어떻게 …을 할 수 있을까?: *How could you say a mean thing like that to her?* ‖ 너는 어떻게 그녀에게 그런 야비한 말을 할 수 있니? **12 how do you do?** FORMAL said when you meet someone for the first time ‖ 누군가를 처음 만났을 때 쓰여. 처음 뵙겠습니다

how·dy /ˈhaʊdi/ SPOKEN used in order to say "hello" in an informal, usually humorous way ‖ 격의 없이 보통 익살스럽게 "안녕"이라고 말하는 데에 쓰여

how·ev·er¹ /haʊˈɛvɚ/ adv **1** used in order to add an idea or fact that is surprising or seems like the opposite of what you have just said ‖ 자신이 방금 말한 것과 반대로 보이거나 놀라운 생각, 또는 사실을 첨가하는 데에 쓰여. 그럼에도

불구하고. 한편. 그렇지만. 그러나: *The clouds were very thick; however, we managed to land the plane smoothly.* 구름이 매우 짙었지만 우리는 용케도 비행기를 순조롭게 착륙시켰다. / *I love tomatoes. I don't, however, like tomato soup.* 나는 토마토를 좋아해. 그러나 토마토 수프는 좋아하지 않아. **2 however long/serious/slowly etc.** used before adjectives and adverbs to show that it does not matter how long, serious etc. something is or how slowly etc. it happens ‖ 어떤 것이 얼마나 길고 심각한지 또는 얼마나 천천히 일어나는지 문제가 되지 않는다는 것을 나타내기 위해 형용사나 부사 앞에 쓰여. 아무리 길어도/심각해도/느려도: *We'll have to keep working, however difficult the job gets.* 그 일이 아무리 어렵다 할지라도 우리는 계속해서 일을 해야 할 것이다. / *I want that car, however much it costs.* 아무리 많은 비용이 들더라도 나는 그 차를 원한다.

however² *conjunction* in whatever way ‖ 어떤 식으로든지: *However you do it, I'm sure it will be good.* 어떤 식으로 그 일을 하든 유익할 것이라고 확신한다.

howl /haʊl/ *v* [I] **1** to make a long loud crying sound like a dog or a WOLF ‖ 개나 늑대처럼 길고 큰 울음소리를 내다. 울부짖다 **2** if the wind howls, it makes a loud high sound as it blows ‖ 바람이 불면서 크고 높은 소리를 내다. 바람이 윙윙거리다 **3** to make a loud shouting or crying sound ‖ 크게 소리치거나 우는 소리를 내다. 큰 소리로 웃다. 아우성치다: *an audience howling with laughter* 크게 웃으며 아우성치는 청중 **– howl** *n*

HQ *n* the abbreviation of HEADQUARTERS ‖ headquarters의 약어

hr. *n, plural* **hrs.** the written abbreviation of HOUR ‖ hour의 약어

HTML *n* [U] hypertext markup language; a computer language used for Producing pages of writing and pictures that can be put on the Internet ‖ hypertext markup language(하이퍼텍스트 마크업 언어)의 약어; 인터넷에 올릴 수 있는 글·사진으로 된 페이지를 작성하는 데 쓰이는 컴퓨터 언어.

http *n* [U] hypertext transfer protocol; a set of standards that controls how computer documents that are written in HTML connect to each other ‖ hypertext transfer protocol(하이퍼텍스트 전송 규약)의 약어; HTML로 쓰여진 컴퓨터 문서의 상호 연계 방식을 제어하는 일련의 기준

hub /hʌb/ *n* **1** the central part of an area, system etc. that all the other parts are connected to ‖ 다른 모든 부분과 관련되어 있는 구역이나 시스템의 중심 부분. 중심. 중핵: *the hub of a transit system* 운송 체계의 중심 **2** the central part of a wheel ‖ 바퀴의 중심 부분. 허브. 바퀴통

hub·bub /ˈhʌbʌb/ *n* [singular, U] INFORMAL many noises heard at the same time ‖ 한꺼번에 들리는 많은 소음. 왁자지껄. 소동: *the hubbub of the crowd* 군중의 왁자지껄함

hub·cap /ˈhʌbkæp/ *n* a metal cover for the center of a wheel on a vehicle ‖ 자동차 바퀴의 중심에 쓰이는 금속 덮개. 휠캡 —see picture on page 943

hud·dle¹ /ˈhʌdl/ *v* [I, T] also **huddle together/up** if a group of people huddle together, they gather very closely together ‖ 일단의 사람들이 아주 가까이에 함께 모이다. 빽빽이 모이다[모으다]: *homeless people huddled around/over fires* 불 주위에 모여든 집 없는 사람들

huddle² *n* a group of people or things that are HUDDLEd ‖ 떼지어 모인 사람이나 사물의 집단. 빽빽이 모인 군중. 뒤죽박죽 (으로 쌓인 물건)

hue /hyu/ *n* LITERARY a color or type of color ‖ 색깔이나 색깔의 유형. 색조. 빛깔: *a golden hue* 금빛

huff¹ /hʌf/ *n* **in a huff** feeling angry ‖ 화나는. 발끈[버럭] 화를 내어: *Ray got mad and left in a huff.* 레이는 성질이 나서 발끈 화를 내고 나갔다.

huff² *v* INFORMAL **huff and puff** to breathe out in a noisy way, especially because you are tired ‖ 특히 피곤해서 거칠게 숨을 내쉬다. 숨을 헐떡이다. 거칠게 호흡하다: *At the end of the hike, we were all huffing and puffing.* 하이킹이 끝날 무렵에 우리는 모두 숨을 헐떡이고 있었다.

huff·y /ˈhʌfi/ *adj* INFORMAL in a bad temper ‖ 성미가 고약한. 성 잘 내는. 골난: *Don't get huffy with me.* 나에게 화를 내지 마라.

hug¹ /hʌg/ *v* **-gged, -gging** [T] **1** to put your arms around someone and hold him/her tightly to show love or friendship ‖ 사랑이나 우정을 표현하기 위해 팔로 남을 꽉 껴안다. 포옹하다 **2** to move along the side, edge, top etc. of

hug

something, staying very close to it ‖ 무엇에 매우 가까이 있으면서 그것의 측면·가장자리·꼭대기 등을 따라 움직이다. 접근하여 움직이다: *a boat hugging the coast* 해안에 인접하여 항해하고 있는 배

hug² *n* the act of hugging (HUG) someone ‖ 누군가를 안는 행동. 껴안음. 포옹: *Give me a hug before you go.* 가기 전에 나를 한 번 안아 줘.

huge /hyudʒ/ *adj* very big ‖ 매우 큰: *a huge house* 대저택 – **hugely** *adv*

huh /hʌ/ *interjection* **1** said when you have not heard or understood a question ‖ 질문을 못 듣거나 이해하지 못했을 때 쓰여. 뭐라고: *"What do you think, Bob?" "Huh?"* "네 생각은 어때, 보브?" "뭐라고?" **2** said at the end of a question to ask for agreement ‖ 동의를 요구하는 질문의 끝에 쓰여. 그렇지? 안 그래?: *Not a bad restaurant, huh?* 그리 나쁜 식당은 아니지, 그렇지?

hulk /hʌlk/ *n* **1** an old ship, plane, or vehicle that is no longer used ‖ 더 이상 사용되지 않는 낡은 배[비행기, 탈것] **2** a large heavy person or thing ‖ 크고 무거운 사람이나 물건. 몸집이 육중한 사람. 부피가 큰 물건

hull¹ /hʌl/ *n* the main part of a ship ‖ 배의 주요 부분. 선체

hull² *v* [T] to take off the outer part of rice, grain, seeds etc. ‖ 쌀·곡물·씨앗 등의 겉껍질을 벗기다

hul·la·ba·loo /ˈhʌləbəˌlu, ˌhʌləbəˈlu/ *n* INFORMAL excited talk, newspaper stories etc., especially about something surprising or shocking ‖ 특히 놀랍거나 충격적인 일에 대한 흥분된 말·신문 기사 등. 와글와글. 소란: *a huge hullabaloo over his new book* 그의 새 책에 대한 큰 반향

hum /hʌm/ *v* **-mmed, -mming** **1** [I, T] to sing a tune by making a continuous sound with your lips closed ‖ 입술을 다물고 계속 소리를 내서 노래를 부르다. 콧노래를 부르다: *If you don't know the words, just hum it.* 가사를 모른다면 콧노래만 불러라. **2** [I] to make a low continuous sound ‖ 낮은 소리를 계속해서 내다. 중얼[웅얼]거리다: *What's making that humming noise?* 그 중얼거리는 소리는 무엇이냐? **3** [I] if a place is humming, it is very busy and full of activity ‖ 장소가 아주 분주하고 활력으로 가득하다. …이 활기가 있다 – **hum** *n* [singular]

hu·man¹ /ˈhyumən/ *adj* **1** belonging to or relating to people ‖ 사람들에게 속하거나 사람들과 관련된. 사람[인간]의: *the*

human voice 사람의 목소리 / *NASA said the accident was a result of human error.* (=a mistake made by a person not a machine) 나사[미국 항공 우주국]는 그 사고가 인간이 저지른 실수의 결과였다고 발표했다. **2** human weaknesses, emotions etc. are typical of ordinary people ‖ 일반적인 사람들의 전형인 나약함·감정 등의. 인간성의. 인간의 감정에 관한: *human nature* (=the good and bad qualities that are typical of people) 인간의 본성 **3** *sb is only human* used in order to say that someone should not be blamed for what s/he has done ‖ 누군가가 저지른 일에 대해 비난받아서는 안 된다고 말하는 데에 쓰여. …은 한낱 인간일 뿐이다 —compare INHUMAN

human², human being /ˌ.. ˈ../ *n* a person ‖ 사람. 인간

hu·mane /hyuˈmeɪn/ *adj* treating people or animals in a way that is kind, not cruel ‖ 사람이나 동물을 잔인하지 않고 친절하게 대하는. 인간미가 있는. 자비로운 – **humanely** *adv* —opposite INHUMANE

hu·man·ism /ˈhyuməˌnɪzəm/ *n* [U] a system of beliefs that tries to solve human problems through science rather than religion ‖ 종교보다는 과학을 통하여 인간의 문제를 해결하려는 신념 체계. 인문[인본]주의 – **humanistic** /ˌhyuməˈnɪstɪk/ *adj* – **humanist** /ˈhyumənɪst/ *n*

hu·man·i·tar·i·an /hyuˌmænəˈtɛriən/ *adj* concerned with improving bad living conditions and preventing unfair treatment of people ‖ 열악한 생활 여건을 개선하고 사람들에 대한 부당한 대우를 방지하는 일과 관계된. 인도주의의 – **humanitarianism** *n* [U] – **humanitarian** *n*

hu·man·i·ties /hyuˈmænət̬iz/ *n* **the humanities** subjects you study that are related to literature, history, art etc. rather than mathematics or science ‖ 수학이나 과학보다 문학·역사·예술 등에 관련된 것을 연구하는 학과. 인문 과학

hu·man·i·ty /hyuˈmænət̬i/ *n* [U] **1** kindness, respect, and sympathy toward other people ‖ 다른 사람들에 대한 친절·존경·동정심. 인간애[미]. 인정: *a man of great humanity* 인간미가 넘치는 사람 —opposite INHUMANITY **2** people in general ‖ 일반적인 사람들. 인류. 인간: *the danger pollution poses to humanity* 공해가 인류에게 야기하는 위험 —see also HUMANKIND **3** the state of being human ‖ 인간으로서의 상태. 인간

성. 인간의 속성

hu·man·ize /'hyumə,naɪz/ v [T] to make a system more pleasant for people ‖ 제도를 사람들이 더 기분 좋게 만들다. …을 보다 인도적으로 만들다: *attempts to humanize the prison* 교도소를 인도적 분위기화하려는 시도

hu·man·kind /'hyumən,kaɪnd/ n [U] people in general ‖ 일반적인 사람들. 인류. 인간 —see also HUMANITY, —see usage note at MAN¹

hu·man·ly /'hyumənli/ adv **humanly possible** able to be done using all your skills, knowledge, time etc. ‖ 모든 기술·지식·시간 등을 사용하여 행해질 수 있는. 인력으로 할 수 있는: *It's not humanly possible* (=impossible) *to finish the building by next week.* 다음주까지 그 건물을 완성하는 것은 인력으로는 불가능하다. / *We did everything humanly possible to save people from the fire.* 우리는 화재에서 사람들을 구하기 위해 인간의 힘으로 할 수 있는 모든 일을 했다.

human race /,.. './ n **the human race** all people, considered as a single group ‖ 하나의 집단으로 본 모든 사람들. 인류. 인간

human re·sourc·es /,.. '.../ n [plural] the department in a company that deals with employing, training, and helping people ‖ 사람을 채용하고 훈련하며 돕는 일을 다루는 회사 내의 부서. 인사부

human rights /,.. './ n [plural] the basic rights that every person has to be treated in a fair, equal way without cruelty, especially by his/her government ‖ 모든 사람은 특히 정부에 의한 잔혹 행위 없이 공정하고 동등하게 대우받아야 한다는 기본적인 권리. (기본적인) 인권

hum·ble¹ /'hʌmbəl/ adj **1** APPROVING not considering yourself or your ideas to be as important as other people's ‖ 자신이나 자신의 생각을 다른 사람이나 그 사람의 생각만큼 중요하게 생각하지 않는. 겸손한. 열등감을 느끼는 **2** relating to a low social class or position ‖ 낮은 사회적 계급이나 지위와 관련된. 비천한. 초라한. 보잘것없는: *the senator's humble beginnings on a farm in Iowa* 아이오와 한 농장에서의 그 상원 의원의 보잘것없는 시작 —**humbly** adv

humble² v [T] to make someone realize that s/he is not as important, good, kind etc. as s/he thought ‖ 누군가에게 본인이 생각했던 것만큼 중요하고 좋고 친절하지

않다는 것을 깨닫게 하다. 겸손해[초라해]지게 하다: *I felt humbled after the interview.* 나는 인터뷰한 후에 초라함을 느꼈다. —**humbling** adj

hum·drum /'hʌmdrʌm/ adj boring, ordinary, and having very little variety ‖ 지루하고 일상적이며 그다지 변화가 없는. 단조로운: *a humdrum job* 단조로운 일

hu·mid /'hyumɪd/ adj air that is humid feels warm and wet ‖ 공기가 따뜻하고 축축하게 느껴지는. 습한. 눅눅한 —see usage note at TEMPERATURE

hu·mid·i·fier /hyu'mɪdə,faɪə/ n a machine that makes the air in a room less dry ‖ 방 안의 공기를 덜 건조하게 하는 기계. 가습기 —**humidify** v [T]

hu·mid·i·ty /hyu'mɪdəṭi/ n [U] the amount of water that is contained in the air ‖ 공기 중에 함유되어 있는 물의 양. 습도: *The humidity will be lower tomorrow.* 습도는 내일 더 낮아질 것이다.

hu·mil·i·ate /hyu'mɪli,eɪt/ v [T] to make someone feel ashamed or embarrassed by making him/her seem stupid or weak ‖ 어리석거나 나약해 보이게 하여 남을 부끄럽게 하거나 당황하게 하다. 굴욕감을 주다. 창피를 주다: *Mrs. Banks humiliated me in front of the whole class.* 뱅크스 선생님은 학급 전원 앞에서 나에게 창피를 주었다. —**humiliation** /,hyumɪli'eɪʃən/ n [C, U] —**humiliated** /hyu'mɪli,eɪtɪd/ adj

hu·mil·i·at·ing /hyu'mɪli,eɪtɪŋ/ adj making you feel ashamed or embarrassed ‖ 부끄럽게 하거나 당황하게 하는. 굴욕적인. 창피한: *a humiliating experience* 굴욕적인 경험

hu·mil·i·ty /hyu'mɪləṭi/ n [U] APPROVING the quality of not being too proud about yourself ‖ 자신에 대해 너무 자랑스러워하지 않는 성질. 겸손. 겸허

hu·mor¹ /'hyumə/ n [U] **1** the ability to laugh at things and think that they are funny ‖ 무엇을 보고 웃으며 그것을 재미있다고 생각하는 능력. 유머에 대한 이해력[감각]: *Dale has no sense of humor at all.* (=cannot understand when something is funny) 데일은 유머 감각이 전혀 없다. **2** the quality in something that makes it funny and makes people laugh ‖ 어떤 것을 재미있게 만들어 사람들을 웃기는 특성. 유머. 해학. 익살: *There's a lot of humor in his songs.* 그의 노래에는 많은 해학이 담겨 있다. **3 good humor** a cheerful friendly attitude to people and events ‖ 사람·사건에 대해 유쾌하고 친근한 태도. 좋은 기분

humor² *v* [T] to do what someone wants so s/he will not become angry or upset ‖ 누군가가 화나거나 기분 나빠지지 않도록 그 사람이 원하는 일을 하다. 비위를 맞추다. 즐겁게 해 주다: *Just humor me and listen, please.* 제발 내 비위 좀 건드리지 말고 그냥 내 말 좀 들어 줘.

hu·mor·ist /'hyumərɪst/ *n* someone, especially a writer, who tells jokes and funny stories ‖ 농담과 재미있는 이야기를 하는 사람, 특히 작가. 해학적인 사람. 유머 작가

hu·mor·less /'hyumɚlɪs/ *adj* too serious and not able to laugh at things that are funny ‖ 너무 진지하여 재미있는 사물을 보고 웃을 수 없는. 유머 감각이 없는

hu·mor·ous /'hyumərəs/ *adj* funny and enjoyable ‖ 재미있고 즐거운. 유머러스한. 해학적인: *a humorous account of her trip to Egypt* 그녀의 이집트 여행에 대한 유머러스한 설명 **– humorously** *adv*

hump /hʌmp/ *n* **1 be over the hump** to have finished the most difficult part of something ‖ 사물의 가장 어려운 부분을 마치다. 고비를 넘기다. 난관[위기]을 벗어나다 **2** a round shape that rises above a surface ‖ 표면 위로 솟은 둥근 모양. 낮고 둥근 언덕 **3** a raised part on the back of a person or animal ‖ 사람이나 동물의 등에 튀어나온 부분. 혹: *a camel's hump* 낙타의 혹

hunch¹ /hʌntʃ/ *n* a feeling that something is true or that something will happen, even if you do not have any facts or proof about it ‖ 그에 대한 어떤 사실이나 증거가 없더라도, 무엇이 사실이거나 일어날 것이라는 느낌. 예감. 육감: *I had a hunch that you'd call today.* 당신이 오늘 전화하리라는 예감이 들었다.

hunch² *v* [I] to bend down and lean forward so that your back forms a curve ‖ 등이 곡선이 되도록 아래로 굽혀서 앞으로 기울이다. 몸을 구부리다 **– hunched** *adj*

hunch·back /'hʌntʃbæk/ *n* OFFENSIVE someone who has a large raised part on his/her back ‖ 등부위가 많이 튀어나온 사람. 곱사등이. 등이 굽은 사람

hun·dred¹ /'hʌndrɪd/ *number* **1** 100 ‖ 100: *a hundred years* 100년 / *two hundred miles* 200마일 **2 hundreds of sth** a very large number of something ‖ 어떤 것의 아주 큰 수. 수백의 …. 많은 …: *Hundreds of people marched in protest.* 수백 명의 사람이 항의하면서 행진했다. **3 a hundred times** SPOKEN a phrase meaning many times, used when

you are annoyed ‖ 화가 날 때 쓰이는, 여러 번을 의미하는 어구. 무수히. 여러 번: *I've told you a hundred times to turn off the lights!* 불을 끄라고 당신에게 여러 번 얘기 했잖아요! **4 a/one hundred percent** completely ‖ 완전히. 100퍼센트로: *I agree one hundred percent.* 완전히 동의한다. **5 give a hundred percent** to do everything you can in order to achieve something ‖ 일을 완수하기 위해 할 수 있는 모든 일을 하다. 최선을 다하다: *Everyone on the team gave a hundred percent.* 팀원 모두가 최선을 다했다. **– hundredth** /'hʌndrɪdθ/ *number*

hundred² *n* a piece of paper money worth $100 ‖ 100달러짜리 지폐

hun·dred·weight /'hʌndrɪd,weɪt/, *written abbreviation* **cwt.** *n* a measure of weight equal to 100 pounds or 45.36 kilograms ‖ 100파운드나 45.36킬로그램에 해당하는 무게의 단위

hung /hʌŋ/ the past tense and PAST PARTICIPLE of HANG ‖ hang의 과거·과거분사형

hun·ger¹ /'hʌŋgɚ/ *n* [U] **1** the feeling that you want or need to eat ‖ 먹고 싶거나 먹을 필요성을 느끼는 감정. 굶주림. 기아. 공복: *babies crying from hunger* 굶주려서 울고 있는 아기들 ✗DON'T SAY "I have hunger."SAY "I am hungry."✗ "I have hunger."라고 하지 않고. "I am hungry."라고 한다. **2** a severe lack of food, especially for a long period of time ‖ 특히 오랜 기간 동안의 심각한 식량 부족. 기근: *people dying from hunger* 기근으로 죽어가고 있는 사람들 —compare THIRST

hunger² *v* [I] **hunger for sth** to want something very much ‖ 무엇을 아주 몹시 원하다. 갈망하다. 열망하다: *an actor hungering for success* 성공을 열망하는 배우

hunger strike /'.. ,./ *n* a situation in which someone refuses to eat, in order to protest about something ‖ 어떤 것에 대해 항의하기 위해 먹기를 거부하는 상황. 단식 투쟁

hung ju·ry /,. '../ *n* [singular] a JURY that cannot agree about whether someone is guilty of a crime ‖ 범죄에 대한 유죄 여부에 대해 일치하지 않는 배심. 불일치[평결 불능] 배심

hung o·ver /,. '../ *adj* feeling sick because you drank too much alcohol the previous day ‖ 전날 너무 많은 술을 마셔서 몸이 좋지 않은. 숙취의

hun·gry /'hʌŋgri/ *adj* **1** wanting to eat

something ‖ 무엇을 먹기 원하는. 배고픈. 허기진: *I'm hungry, let's eat!* 배고파, 식 사하자! / *If you get hungry, there's some turkey in the fridge.* 배가 고프면 냉장고에 칠면조 고기가 좀 있으니까 먹 어. **2 go hungry** to not have enough food to eat ‖ 먹을 충분한 음식이 없다. 굶 주리고 있다: *Many people in our city go hungry day after day.* 우리 도시의 많은 사람들이 하루하루를 굶주리고 있다. **3 be hungry for sth** to want something very much ‖ 무엇을 대단히 원하다. 열망하다. 갈망하다: *Rick was hungry for a chance to work.* 릭은 일할 기회를 몹시 원했다. **– hungrily** *adv* —compare THIRSTY

hung up /ˌ. ˈ./ *adj* INFORMAL worrying too much about someone or something ‖ 사람이나 사물에 대해 너무 많이 걱정하 는: *You shouldn't get all hung up over him, it's not worth it!* 너는 그에 대해 지 나치게 걱정해서도 안 되고, 그럴 가치도 없어!

hunk /hʌŋk/ *n* **1** a thick piece of something that has been taken from a bigger piece ‖ 큰 조각에서 떼어낸 물건의 두툼한 조각. 큰 덩어리: *a hunk of bread* 빵 덩어리 **2** INFORMAL an attractive man who has a strong body ‖ 튼튼한 신체를 가진 매력적인 남자. 건장한 남자

hun·ker /ˈhʌŋkɚ/ *v* [I]

hunker down *phr v* [I] **1** INFORMAL to not do things that may be risky, so that you are safe and protected ‖ 안전하게 보 호되도록 위험성이 있는 일을 하지 않다. 몸을 사리다: *People are hunkering down and waiting for the economy to get better.* 사람들은 몸을 사리며 경제가 나아지기를 기다리고 있다. **2** to sit on your heels with your knees bent in front of you; SQUAT ‖ 앞으로 무릎을 구부리고 쭈그리고 앉다; 伷 squat

hunt¹ /hʌnt/ *v* **1** [I, T] to chase animals in order to catch and kill them ‖ 동물을 잡거나 죽이기 위해 추격하다. 사냥[수렵] 하다. 좇다: *Tigers hunt at night.* 호랑이 는 밤에 사냥한다. **2** to look for someone or something very carefully ‖ 사람이나 사물을 아주 주의 깊게 찾다. 샅샅이 뒤지 다. 사냥하러 다니다: *Police are still hunting for the murderer.* 경찰은 아직 살인범을 추적하고 있다.

hunt sb/sth ↔ down *phr v* [T] to find an enemy or criminal after searching hard ‖ 열심히 수색한 후에 적이나 범죄자 를 찾아 내다. …을 추적하여 (붙)잡다: *a plan to hunt down fathers who don't pay child support* 아이의 부양비를 주지 않는 아버지를 찾아내려는 계획

hunt² *n* **1** a careful search for someone or something ‖ 사람이나 물건을 주의깊게 찾기. 수색: *The hunt for the missing child continues today.* 실종된 아이에 대 한 수색이 오늘 계속된다. **2** an occasion when people chase animals in order to catch and kill them ‖ 사람들이 동물을 잡 거나 죽이기 위해 동물을 추적하는 일. 사 냥. 수렵

hunt·er /ˈhʌntɚ/ *n* a person or animal that hunts wild animals ‖ 야생 동물을 사 냥하는 사람이나 동물. 사냥꾼. 수렵가

hunt·ing /ˈhʌntɪŋ/ *n* [U] **1** the act of chasing animals in order to catch and kill them ‖ 동물을 잡거나 죽이기 위해 동 물을 추적하는 행위. 사냥. 수렵 **2 job-hunting/house-hunting etc.** the activity of looking for a job, a house to live in etc. ‖ 직업이나 살 집 등을 찾는 행 위. 구직/집 구하기 **– hunting** *adj*

hur·dle¹ /ˈhɚdl/ *n* **1** a problem or difficulty that you must deal with before you can do something else ‖ 다른 일을 할 수 있기 전에 처리해야 될 문제나 어려 움. 장애: *the final hurdle in buying a house* 주택 매입에 있어서의 마지막 장애 **2** a type of small fence that a person or a horse jumps over during a race ‖ 경주 하는 동안 사람이나 말이 뛰어넘는 일종의 작은 울타리. 장애물. 허들

hurdle² *v* [T] to jump over something while you are running ‖ 달리면서 사물을 뛰어넘다. 허들을 뛰어넘다 **– hurdler** *n*

hurl /hɚl/ *v* [T] **1** to throw something using a lot of force ‖ 많은 힘을 사용하여 물건을 던지다. 세게 던지다. 내던지다: *He hurled a brick through/out the window.* 그는 창문(을) 통해[밖으로] 벽 돌을 세게 던졌다. **2 hurl insults/abuse etc. at sb** to shout at someone in a loud and angry way ‖ 큰 소리로 화 내서 남에게 소리치다. 모욕적인 말/욕설을 퍼 붓다 **3** SPOKEN ⇨ VOMIT¹

hur·ray /həˈreɪ, hʊˈreɪ/, **hurrah** /hʊˈrɑ/ *interjection* OLD-FASHIONED ⇨ HOORAY

hur·ri·cane /ˈhɚˌkeɪn, ˈhʌr-/ *n* a storm that has very strong fast winds ‖ 매우 강하고 빠른 바람을 동반하는 폭 풍우. 대폭풍. 허리케인 —compare TORNADO, —see usage note at WEATHER

hur·ried /ˈhɚid, ˈhʌrid/ *adj* done more quickly than usual ‖ 평소보다 더 빠르게 행동하는. 허둥대는. 급히 서두르는: *We ate a hurried breakfast and left.* 우리는 서둘러 아침 식사를 하고 떠났다. **– hurriedly** *adv*

hur·ry¹ /ˈhɚi, ˈhʌri/ *v* [I, T] to do

something or go somewhere more quickly than usual, or to make someone or something do this ‖ 평상시보다 더 빨리 일을 하거나 어디로 가다, 또는 사람이나 사물이 이렇게 하도록 하다. 서두르(게 하)다. 급히 하다. 재촉하다: *Their mother hurried the children across the road.* 아이들 어머니는 아이들이 서둘러 길을 건너게 했다. / *We will have to hurry if we don't want to miss the start of the movie.* 영화가 시작되는 것을 놓치고 싶지 않으면 우리는 서둘러야 할 것이다.

hurry up *phr v* **1 hurry up!** SPOKEN said in order to tell someone to do something more quickly ‖ 남에게 어떤 것을 더 빨리 하라고 말하는 데에 쓰여. 서둘러! **2** [I,T **hurry** sb/sth **up**] to do something or go somewhere more quickly than usual, or to make someone or something do this ‖ 평소보다 더 빨리 어떤 것을 하거나 어디로 가다, 또는 사람이나 사물이 이렇게 하도록 하다. 서두르(게 하)다. 급히 하다. 재촉하다: *I tried to hurry the kids up so they wouldn't be late for school.* 학교에 지각하지 않도록 아이들을 서두르게 했다. / *I wish the bus would hurry up and get here.* 나는 버스가 평소보다 더 빨리 여기 도착하기를 바란다.

hurry² *n* **1 be in a hurry** to need to do something, go somewhere etc. more quickly than usual ‖ 평소보다 더 빨리 어떤 것을 하거나 어디로 가다. 서두르다. 황급히 …하다: *I can't talk now, I'm in a hurry.* 지금 이야기할 수 없어, 서둘러야 해. **2 (there's) no hurry** SPOKEN said in order to tell someone that s/he does not have to do something quickly or soon ‖ 남에게 어떤 것을 빨리 또는 바로 할 필요가 없다고 말하는 데에 쓰여. 급할 거 없어: *You can pay me back next week, there's no hurry.* 다음 주에 갚아도 돼, 서두를 필요 없어. **3 not be in any hurry/be in no hurry** to be able to wait because you have a lot of time in which to do something ‖ 어떤 것을 할 시간이 많아서 기다릴 수 있다. 서두르지[급하지] 않다: *Take your time, I'm not in any hurry.* 천천히 해라, 나는 급하지 않아. **4 what's (all) the hurry?** SPOKEN said when you think someone is doing something too quickly ‖ 남이 어떤 것을 너무 빨리 하고 있다는 생각이 들 때 쓰여. 뭐가 그리 급하니? 서두르지 마!

hurt¹ /hɚt/ *v* **hurt, hurt, hurting 1** [T] to injure yourself or someone else, especially not very seriously ‖ 특히 아주 심하지는 않지만 자기 자신이나 다른 사람

을 다치게 하다. 아프게 하다: *She hurt her knee playing volleyball.* 그녀는 배구를 하다가 무릎을 다쳤다. / *Sammy! Don't throw sand, you might hurt somebody!* 새미야! 모래를 던지지 마라, 사람 다칠라! **2** [I, T] to feel pain or cause pain in a part of your body ‖ 신체 일부의 아픔을 느끼거나 느끼게 하다: *My feet really hurt after all that walking!* 그렇게 많이 걷고 나니 다리가 정말 아팠어! / *It hurts my knees to run.* 달려서 무릎이 아파. **3** [I, T] to make someone feel very upset or unhappy ‖ 사람을 매우 기분 나쁘게 또는 불행하게 느끼게 하다. 감정을 상하게 하다: *I'm sorry, I didn't mean to hurt your feelings.* 미안하지만 너의 감정을 상하게 할 의도는 아니었어. **4** [T] to have a bad effect on someone or something ‖ 사람이나 사물에 나쁜 영향을 미치다. …을 해치다. 손상시키다: *Will this hurt my chances of getting the job?* 이것 때문에 취직할 기회를 놓치게 될까? **5 it won't/doesn't hurt to do sth** SPOKEN said when you think someone should do something ‖ 남이 어떤 것을 해야 한다고 생각될 때 쓰여. …을 하는 것이 해가 되지는 않을 것이다[이로울 것이다]: *It won't hurt him to clean his room.* 그의 방을 청소하는 것이 그에게 이로울 것이다. **6 be hurting** INFORMAL to feel upset or unhappy about something ‖ 어떤 것에 대해 기분 나빠하거나 불행해 하다. 괴로워하다 **– hurt** *n* [C, U] —see usage note at WOUND²

hurt² *adj* **1** suffering pain or injury ‖ 고통이나 상처로 괴로워하는. 다친. 부상한: *It's okay, nobody got hurt.* 괜찮아요, 아무도 다치지 않았어요. / *Kerry was badly/seriously/slightly hurt in a skiing accident.* 케리는 스키 사고로 몹시 다쳤다[중상이었다, 경상이었다]. **2** very upset or unhappy ‖ 매우 기분 나쁘거나 불행한. 상처를 입은: *I was very hurt by what you said.* 당신이 한 말에 상처를 입었다. ✗YOU SAY "seriously/badly/slightly hurt" about an injury, but "very hurt" when someone upsets you. 상처에 대해 "seriously/badly/slightly hurt"라고 하나, 누군가 당신을 기분 나쁘게 했을 때는 "very hurt"라고 한다.✗

hurt·ful /ˈhɚtfəl/ *adj* making you feel upset or unhappy ‖ 자기를 기분 나쁘게 하거나 불행하게 하는. 감정을 상하게 하는. 해로운

hur·tle /ˈhɚtl/ *v* [I] to move or fall very fast ‖ 매우 빠르게 움직이거나 떨어지다. 돌진하다. 고속으로 움직이다: *cars hurtling down the freeway at 90 miles* *per hour* 시속 90마일로 고속도로를 질주하는 차들

hus·band /ˈhʌzbənd/ *n* the man that a woman is married to ‖ 여자가 결혼을 한 상대 남자. 남편

hush[1] /hʌʃ/ *v* SPOKEN said in order to tell someone to be quiet, or to comfort a child who is crying ‖ 남에게 조용하라고 말하는 데에, 또는 울고 있는 아이를 달래는 데에 쓰여. 조용히 하다[조용하게 하다]

hush sth **up** *phr v* [T] to prevent people from knowing about something dishonest ‖ 사람들이 부정직한 어떤 일에 대해 알지 못하게 하다. …을 은폐하다: *The bank tried to hush the scandal up.* 그 은행은 그 추문을 은폐하려고 했다.

hush[2] *n* [singular] a peaceful silence ‖ 평화로운 침묵. 고요: *A hush fell over the room.* (=everyone suddenly became quiet) 방 안이 고요해졌다.

hushed /hʌʃt/ *adj* quiet ‖ 조용한: *hushed voices* 조용한 목소리

hush-hush /ˌ. ˈ./ *adj* INFORMAL secret ‖ 비밀의. 극비의

husk /hʌsk/ *n* [C, U] the dry outer part of some grains, nuts, corn etc. ‖ 곡식류·견과·옥수수 등의 마른 껍질 —see picture at PEEL[2]

husk·y[1] /ˈhʌski/ *adj* APPROVING 1 a husky voice is deep and sounds rough ‖ 목소리가 낮고 거칠게 들리는. (목소리가) 쉰 2 a husky man is big and strong ‖ 사람이 몸집이 크고 강한. 튼튼한. 건장한 – **huskily** *adv* – **huskiness** *n* [U]

husky[2] *n* a dog with thick hair, often used for pulling SLEDs over the snow ‖ 가끔 눈 위에서 썰매를 끄는 데에 쓰이는 털이 많은 개

hus·tle[1] /ˈhʌsəl/ *v* 1 [T] to make someone move quickly, often by pushing him/her ‖ 가끔 남을 밀어서 빨리 움직이게 하다. 떠밀다. 재촉하여 이동시키다: *Jackson was hustled into his car by bodyguards.* 보디가드가 잭슨을 차 안에 밀어 넣었다. 2 [I] to hurry in doing something or going somewhere ‖ 서둘러서 무엇을 하거나 어디로 가다. 서두르다. 급히 해치우다: *We've got to hustle, or we'll be late!* 우리는 서둘러야 해, 그렇지 않으면 늦어! 3 [I, T] INFORMAL to cheat someone to get money etc. ‖ 돈 등을 얻기 위해 남을 속이다. …을 부정하게[억지로] 손에 넣다

hustle[2] *n* 1 **hustle and bustle** busy and noisy activity ‖ 바쁘고 시끄러운 활동. 서두름. 밀치락달치락하기. 혼잡. 붐빔 2 INFORMAL a way of getting money

that is illegal and dishonest ‖ 불법적이고 부정직한 돈을 얻는 방법. 사기

hus·tler /ˈhʌslɚ/ *n* someone who gets money in a way that is illegal and dishonest ‖ 불법적이고 부정하게 돈을 얻는 사람. 사기꾼. 협잡꾼

hut /hʌt/ *n* a small house with only one or two rooms ‖ 하나나 두 개의 방만 있는 작은 집. 오두막. 임시 가옥

hutch /hʌtʃ/ *n* a small wooden box in which you can keep rabbits ‖ 토끼를 기르는 작은 나무 상자. 토끼 우리

hy·brid /ˈhaɪbrɪd/ *n* 1 an animal or plant that is produced from parents of different breeds or types ‖ 다른 품종이나 종류의 모체로부터 나온 동물이나 식물. 잡종. 혼혈아[종] 2 something that is a mixture of two or more things ‖ 둘 또는 둘 이상의 물질이 혼합된 것. 혼성물. 합성물: *The car is a hybrid that can run on gas or batteries.* 그 차는 휘발유나 배터리로 운행할 수 있는 하이브리드 승용차이다. – **hybrid** *adj*

hy·drant /ˈhaɪdrənt/ *n* ⇨ FIRE HYDRANT

hy·drau·lic /haɪˈdrɔlɪk/ *adj* moved or operated by the pressure of water or other liquids ‖ 수압이나 기타 액체의 압력으로 움직이거나 작동하는: *hydraulic brakes* 유압 브레이크 – **hydraulically** *adv*

hy·drau·lics /haɪˈdrɔlɪks/ *n* [plural] the study of how to use water pressure to produce power ‖ 동력을 생산하기 위해 수압을 이용하는 방법에 관한 연구. 수역학

hy·dro·e·lec·tric /ˌhaɪdroʊɪˈlɛktrɪk/ *adj* using water power to produce electricity ‖ 전기를 생산하기 위해 물의 힘을 이용하는. 수력 전기의[발전의]: *a hydroelectric dam* 수력 발전 댐

hy·dro·gen /ˈhaɪdrədʒən/ *n* [U] a gas that is an ELEMENT and is lighter than air, and that becomes water when it combines with OXYGEN ‖ 원소로서 공기보다 더 가볍고 산소와 결합할 때 물이 되는 기체. 수소

hydrogen bomb /ˈ... ˌ./ *n* an extremely powerful NUCLEAR bomb ‖ 매우 강력한 핵폭탄. 수소 폭탄

hy·dro·plane /ˈhaɪdrəˌpleɪn/ *v* [I] if a car hydroplanes, it slides on a wet road ‖ 차가 물기 있는 도로에서 미끄러지다. 노면에서 미끄러지는 현상을 일으키다

hy·e·na /haɪˈinə/ *n* a wild animal like a dog that makes a loud sound like a laugh ‖ 웃음소리 같은 큰 소리를 내는 개와 비슷한 야생 동물. 하이에나

hy·giene /ˈhaɪdʒin/ *n* [U] the practice

of keeping yourself and the things around you clean in order to prevent diseases ‖ 질병을 예방하기 위해 자신과 주변의 물건을 청결하게 유지하는 습관. 위생: *Hygiene is very important when preparing a baby's food.* 아기 음식을 준비할 때 위생은 매우 중요하다.

hy·gi·en·ic /haɪ'dʒɛnɪk, -'dʒinɪk/ *adj* clean and likely to prevent diseases from spreading ‖ 깨끗하며 질병이 퍼지는 것을 예방하기에 적당한. 건강에 좋은. 위생적인

hymn /hɪm/ *n* a song of praise to God ‖ 하나님을 찬양하는 노래. 성가. 찬송가

hym·nal /'hɪmnəl/ *n* a book of HYMNs ‖ 찬송가집. 성가집

hype¹ /haɪp/ *n* [U] attempts to make people think something is good or important by talking about it a lot on television, the radio etc. ‖ 텔레비전·라디오 등에서 많이 이야기함으로써 어떤 물건을 좋거나 중요한 것이라고 생각하게 하려는 시도. 과대광고: *the media hype surrounding Spielberg's new movie* 스필버그의 새 영화를 둘러싼 미디어의 과대광고

hype² *v* [T] also **hype** sth ↔ **up** to try to make people think something is good or important by advertising or talking about it a lot on television, the radio etc. ‖ 텔레비전·라디오 등에서 광고하거나 많이 이야기함으로써 사람들이 어떤 물건을 좋거나 중요한 것이라고 생각하게 하려고 노력하다. 과대광고하다: *The author has been hyped as the next Raymond Chandler.* 그 작가는 제2의 레이먼드 챈들러로 과대광고되어 왔다.

hyped up /ˌ. './ *adj* INFORMAL very excited or anxious about something ‖ 어떤 것에 매우 흥분하거나 초조해 하는: *They're all hyped up about getting into the playoffs.* 그들은 플레이오프전을 시작한 것에 대해 모두 흥분했다.

hy·per /'haɪpə/ *adj* INFORMAL extremely excited or nervous ‖ 매우 흥분하거나 긴장한

hy·per·ac·tive /ˌhaɪpə'æktɪv/ *adj* someone, especially a child, who is hyperactive is too active, and not able to keep still or quiet for very long ‖ 특히 어린이가 너무 활동적이고, 아주 오랫동안 가만히 또는 조용히 있을 수 없는. 지나치게 활동적인. 과민한. 주의 산만한 – **hyperactivity** /ˌhaɪpəæk'tɪvəti/ *n* [U]

hy·per·bo·le /hɪ'pɜbəli/ *n* [U] a way of describing something by saying that it is much bigger, smaller, heavier etc. than it really is ‖ 실제의 사물보다 훨씬 더 크

다·작다·무겁다는 등의 말로써 사물을 묘사하는 방법. 과장(법)

hy·per·link /'haɪpə,lɪŋk/, **hy·per·text link** /ˌhaɪpətɛkst 'lɪŋk/ *n* a special picture or word on a computer screen that you CLICK on in order to move quickly to a place where you can find more information ‖ 더 많은 정보를 얻을 수 있는 장소로 신속히 이동하려고 클릭을 하는 컴퓨터 화면 위의 특별한 그림 또는 말. 하이퍼 링크. 하이퍼텍스트를 연결하는 링크 구조

hy·per·sen·si·tive /ˌhaɪpə'sɛnsətɪv/ *adj* very easily offended or made upset ‖ 매우 쉽게 화내거나 기분 상해 하는. 과민한. 과민증의

hy·per·ten·sion /ˌhaɪpə'tɛnʃən, 'haɪpə,tɛnʃən/ *n* [U] TECHNICAL a medical condition in which someone's BLOOD PRESSURE is too high ‖ 어떤 사람의 혈압이 너무 높은 의학적인 상태. 고혈압

hy·per·ven·ti·late /ˌhaɪpə'vɛntl,eɪt/ *v* [I] to breathe too quickly because you are very excited or upset ‖ 너무 흥분하거나 화가 나서 아주 빨리 호흡하다

hy·phen /'haɪfən/ *n* a mark (-) used in writing to join words or parts of words ‖ 단어들 또는 단어의 일부분을 연결하기 위해 글에서 사용하는 부호(-). 하이픈(-)

USAGE NOTE hyphens

Use a hyphen (-) to join two or more words that are used as an adjective in front of a noun: *a two-car garage / a ten-year-old boy.* You can also say: *a garage for two cars / a boy who is ten years old*

명사 앞에서 형용사로 사용되는 둘 이상의 단어들을 연결시키기 위해서 하이픈 (-)을 쓴다: 자동차 두 대용 차고 / 10세 소년. 또한 다음과 같이 말할 수 있다: 자동차 두 대가 들어가는 차고 / 열 살 난 소년

---

hy·phen·ate /'haɪfə,neɪt/ *v* [T] to join words or parts of words with a HYPHEN ‖ 하이픈으로 단어들 또는 단어들의 일부를 연결하다. …을 하이픈으로 잇다 – **hyphenated** *adj*

hyp·no·sis /hɪp'noʊsɪs/ *n* [U] a state similar to sleep in which someone's thoughts and actions can be influenced by someone else, or the act of producing this state ‖ 사람의 생각·행동이 다른 사람에 의해 영향을 받을 수 있는 수면 상태와 유사한 상태, 또는 이러한 상태를 일으키는 행위. (인위적인) 최면 상태. 최면(술): *He remembered details of* *the crime under hypnosis.* 그는 최면 상태에서 범죄의 세부 사항을 생각해 냈다.

hyp·not·ic /hɪpˈnɑtɪk/ *adj* **1** making someone feel tired, especially because sound or movement is repeated ‖ 특히 소리 또는 동작이 반복되어서 사람에게 피로를 느끼게 하는. (사람이) 최면술에 걸리기 쉬운. 잠이 오게 하는 **2** relating to HYPNOSIS ‖ 최면 상태와 관련된. 최면 상태의 – **hypnotically** *adv*

hyp·no·tize /ˈhɪpnəˌtaɪz/ *v* [T] to produce a sleep-like state in someone, so that you can influence his/her thoughts or actions ‖ 사람의 생각 또는 행위에 영향을 줄 수 있도록 사람을 수면 유사 상태로 만들다. …에 최면술을 걸다 – **hypnotism** /ˈhɪpnəˌtɪzəm/ *n* [U] – **hypnotist** /ˈhɪpnətɪst/ *n*

hy·po·chon·dri·ac /ˌhaɪpəˈkɑndriˌæk/ *n* someone who worries all the time about his/her health, even when s/he is not sick ‖ 사람이 아프지 않은데도 건강에 대해 항상 걱정하는 사람. 심기증 환자 – **hypochondriac** *adj* – **hypochondria** /ˌhaɪpoʊˈkɑndriə/ *n* [U]

hy·poc·ri·sy /hɪˈpɑkrəsi/ *n* [U] DISAPPROVING the act of saying you have particular beliefs, feelings etc., but behaving in a way that shows you do not really have these beliefs etc. ‖ 특정한 믿음·감정 등을 가지고 있다고 말하지만, 실제로는 이러한 믿음 등을 가지고 있지 않은 것처럼 하는 행위. 위선(적 행위). 가장: *the hypocrisy of divorced politicians talking about family values* 가족의 가치에 대하여 말하고 있는 이혼한 정치인의 위선적 행위

hyp·o·crite /ˈhɪpəˌkrɪt/ *n* someone who pretends to believe something or behave in a good way when really s/he does not ‖ 실제로는 그렇지 않은 경우에 어떤 것을 믿는 척하거나 착하게 행동하는 척하는 사람. 위선자. 착한 체하는 사람 – **hypocritical** /ˌhɪpəˈkrɪtɪkəl/ *adj*

hy·po·der·mic /ˌhaɪpəˈdəmɪk/ *n* an instrument with a hollow needle used for putting drugs into someone's body through the skin ‖ 피부를 통해 사람의 신체에 약을 투입하는 데에 쓰는 속이 빈 바늘이 있는 기구. 피하 주사기 – **hypodermic** *adj* —compare SYRINGE

hy·pot·e·nuse /haɪˈpɑtˀnˌus/ *n* TECHNICAL the longest side of a TRIANGLE that has a RIGHT ANGLE ‖ 직각이 있는 삼각형의 가장 긴 옆면. 직각 삼각형의 빗변

hy·po·ther·mi·a /ˌhaɪpəˈθəmiə/ *n* [U] TECHNICAL a serious medical condition in which someone's body temperature becomes very low, caused by extreme cold ‖ 극심한 추위로 인해 사람의 체온이 아주 낮아지는 심상치 않은 의학적 상태. 저체온

hy·poth·e·sis /haɪˈpɑθəsɪs/ *n, plural* **hypotheses** an idea that is suggested as an explanation of something, but that has not yet been proved to be true ‖ 어떤 것에 대한 설명으로 제시되었지만 아직 사실로 증명되지 않은 생각. 가설. 전제 – **hypothesize** /haɪˈpɑθəˌsaɪz/ *v* [T]

hy·po·thet·i·cal /ˌhaɪpəˈθɛtɪkəl/ *adj* based on a situation that is not real but that might happen ‖ 사실은 아니지만 일어날 가능성이 있는 상황에 기초한. 가설의[적]. 가정적인: *Students were given a hypothetical law case to discuss.* 학생들에게는 논의하기 위한 가설적인 법률 사건이 주어졌다. – **hypothetically** *adv*

hys·ter·ec·to·my /ˌhɪstəˈrɛktəmi/ *n* [C, U] a medical operation to remove a woman's UTERUS ‖ 여자의 자궁을 제거하기 위한 의학적인 수술. 자궁 절제 수술

hys·ter·i·a /hɪˈstɛriə, -ˈstɪriə/ *n* [U] extreme excitement, anger, fear etc. that you cannot control ‖ 억제할 수 없는 극단적인 흥분·분노·공포 등. 병적 흥분 상태. 히스테리증(症)

hys·ter·i·cal /hɪˈstɛrɪkəl/ *adj* **1** INFORMAL extremely funny ‖ 지극히 재미있는. 아주 우스운: *Robin Williams' act was hysterical!* 로빈 윌리암스의 연기에 배꼽이 빠졌다! **2** unable to control your behavior or emotions because you are very upset, afraid, excited etc. ‖ 너무나 심란하고 두렵고 흥분이 되어서 행동이나 감정을 억제할 수 없는. 분별이 없어진. 광란의. 히스테리를 일으키기 쉬운 – **hysterically** *adv*

hys·ter·ics /hɪˈstɛrɪks/ *n* [plural] **1** a state of being unable to control your behavior or emotions because you are very upset, afraid, excited etc. ‖ 너무 심란하고 두렵고 흥분이 되어서 행동이나 감정을 억제할 수 없는 상태. 히스테리 발작. 히스테리: *She went into hysterics when she found out her husband had died.* 그녀는 남편이 죽었다는 것을 알았을 때 히스테리를 일으켰다. **2** be in hysterics INFORMAL to be laughing and not be able to stop ‖ 웃음을 멈출 수가 없다. 발작적인 웃음을 터뜨리다

I, i /aɪ/ **1** the ninth letter of the English alphabet ‖ 영어 알파벳의 아홉째 자 **2** the ROMAN NUMERAL for 1 ‖ 1의 로마 숫자

I /aɪ/ *pron* used as the subject of a verb when you are the person speaking ‖ 자신이 화자(話者)일 때 동사의 주어로 쓰여: *I saw Mike yesterday.* 나는 어제 마이크를 보았다. / *I've been playing softball.* 나는 소프트볼을 해오고 있다. / *I'm really hot.* 나는 정말 더워. / *My husband and I are going to Mexico.* 내 남편과 나는 멕시코로 간다. ✗DON'T SAY "I and my husband."✗ "I and my husband"라고는 하지 않는다.

IA the written abbreviation of Iowa ‖ Iowa(아이오와 주)의 약어

ice¹ /aɪs/ *n* **1** [U] water that has frozen into a solid state ‖ 고체 상태로 얼어버린 물. 얼음: *Do you want some ice in your drink?* 음료수에 얼음 좀 넣어드릴까요? / *Drive carefully, there's ice on the roads.* 운전 조심해, 도로가 결빙됐어. **2 break the ice** to begin to be friendly to someone by talking to him/her ‖ 사람에게 말을 걸어 친숙해지기 시작하다. 썰렁한 분위기를 누그러뜨리다. 서먹서먹한 침묵을 깨다: *Stan tried to break the ice by asking her where she was from.* 스탠은 그녀에게 어디 출신이냐고 물으면서 서먹한 분위기를 깨려고 애썼다.

ice² *v* **1** [I, T] to put ice on a part of your body that is injured ‖ 신체의 다친 부위에 얼음을 놓다 **2** [T] ⇨ FROST²

ice
ice/ice cubes

ice over/up *phr v* [I] to become covered with ice ‖ 얼음으로 덮이게 되다. 얼어붙다: *The lake iced over during the night.* 호수는 밤 사이에 얼어붙었다.

icicle

ice·berg /ˈaɪsbɔːg/ *n* an extremely large piece of ice floating in the sea ‖ 바다에 떠다니는 아주 큰 얼음 덩어리. 빙산

ice·break·er /ˈaɪsˌbreɪkɚ/ *n* **1** something you say or do to make someone less nervous ‖ 사람을 덜 긴장시키려 하려는 말 또는 행동. 긴장 또는 어색함을 누그러뜨리는 말[사람·행위] **2 a** ship that can sail through ice ‖ 얼음을 뚫고 항해할 수 있는 선박. 쇄빙선

ice cap /'. ./ *n* an area of thick ice that always covers the North and South Poles ‖ 북극과 남극을 항상 덮고 있는 두꺼운 얼음 지역. 만년설

ice-cold /ˌ. '././ *adj* extremely cold ‖ 지극히 차가운. 얼음처럼 차가운: *ice-cold drinks* 얼음처럼 차가운 음료

ice cream /'. ./ *n* [U] a frozen sweet food made of milk or cream and sugar, usually with fruit, nuts, chocolate etc. added to it ‖ 보통 과일·견과·초콜릿 등을 첨가해서 우유나 크림과 설탕으로 만든 단 맛의 냉동 음식. 아이스크림

ice cream cone /'. . ,./ *n* a hard thin cookie shaped like a CONE, that you put ice cream in ‖ 속에 아이스크림을 넣은 원뿔 모양의 딱딱하고 얇은 과자. 아이스크림콘: *a vanilla ice cream cone* 바닐라 아이스크림콘 —see picture at CONE

ice cube /'. ./ *n* a small block of ice that you put in cold drinks ‖ 차가운 음료에 넣는 작은 얼음 덩어리. 네모진 얼음덩이

ice hock·ey /'. ,../ *n* [U] ⇨ HOCKEY

ice pack /'. ./ *n* a bag of ice used for keeping something cold ‖ 사물을 차게 유지하는 데 쓰이는 얼음주머니

ice skate¹ /'. ./ *v* [I] to slide on ice wearing ICE SKATEs ‖ 빙상 스케이트화를 신고 얼음 위를 미끄러지다. 스케이트를 타다 **–ice skater** *n* **–ice skating** *n* [U]

ice skate² *n* [C usually plural] one of two special boots with metal blades on the bottom that let you slide quickly on ice ‖ 얼음 위에서 신속하게 미끄러지게 하는, 밑바닥에 금속 날이 있는 두 짝의 특수한 신발 중 하나. 스케이트화

i·ci·cle /ˈaɪsɪkəl/ *n* a thin pointed stick of ice that hangs down from something such as a roof ‖ 지붕 등에서 아래로 매달려 있는 가늘고 뾰족한 얼음 막대. 고드름 —see picture at ICE¹

ic·ing /ˈaɪsɪŋ/ *n* [U] **1** ⇨ FROSTING **2 icing on the cake** something that makes a good situation even better ‖ 좋은 상황을 더욱 좋게 만드는 것. 첨가물. 두 배의 기쁨[최고]: *I love the new job – the extra money is just icing on the cake!* 나는 새 직업이 좋다. 부수입이 그야말로 더 없이 좋아!

ick·y /ˈiki/ *adj* SPOKEN very unpleasant to look at, taste, or feel ‖ 보는[맛보는,

느끼는] 것이 매우 불쾌한. 싫은: *The soup tasted icky.* 그 수프는 아주 맛이 없다.

i·con /'aɪkɑn/ *n* **1** a small picture on a computer screen that makes the computer do something when you use the MOUSE to choose it ‖ 마우스를 써서 선택하여 컴퓨터가 어떤 일을 하게 하는 컴퓨터 화면 상의 작은 그림. 아이콘 **2** someone or something famous, that people think represents an important idea ‖ 중요한 견해를 대표한다고 사람들이 생각하는 유명한 사람 또는 사물: *The peace symbol is an icon of the sixties.* 평화의 상징은 60년대의 아이콘이다. **3** also **ikon** a picture or figure of a holy person ‖ 성인의 그림 또는 형상. 성상(聖像)

ic·y /'aɪsi/ *adj* **1** extremely cold ‖ 지극히 차가운. 얼음 같은[처럼 차가운]: *an icy wind* 얼음같이 차가운 바람 **2** covered in ice ‖ 얼음으로 덮인: *an icy road* 얼음으로 덮인 도로 **3** unfriendly and frightening ‖ 우호적이지 않고 놀라게 하는. 매정한. 쌀쌀한. 냉담한: *an icy stare* 쌀쌀한 눈초리 **– icily** *adv* **– iciness** *n* [U]

I'd /aɪd/ **1** the short form of "I had" ‖ "I had"의 단축형: *I'd never met Kurt before today.* 오늘 이전에는 커트를 만난 적이 없었다. **2** the short form of "I would" ‖ "I would"의 단축형: *I'd love to come!* 나는 정말 가고 싶다!

ID¹ *n* [C, U] identification; something that shows your name, address, the date you were born etc., usually with a photograph ‖ identification(신분증·신분 증명 서류)의 약어; 보통 사진과 함께 성명·주소·생년월일 등을 보여주는 물건: *May I see some ID, please?* 신분증 좀 보여주시겠습니까?

ID² the written abbreviation of Idaho ‖ Idaho(아이다호 주)의 약어

i·de·a /aɪ'diə/ *n* **1** a plan or suggestion, especially one you think of suddenly ‖ 특히 갑자기 생각한 계획 또는 제안. 의도. 의향: *Where did you get the idea for the book?* 너는 어디서 그 책에 대한 착상을 하게 되었니? / *Going to the beach is a good idea!* 해변에 가는 것은 훌륭한 계획이다. / *I have an idea – let's get Dad a set of golf clubs.* 생각이 있는데. 대드에게 골프채 한 세트 해주자. **2** [C, U] understanding or knowledge of something ‖ 사물에 대한 이해 또는 지식. 인식. 어림: *The book gives you a pretty good idea of what it was like to grow up during the Depression.* 그 책은 불황 기간 중 어떤 업종이 성장했는지에 대한 아

주 좋은 지식을 제공해 준다. / *Can you give me a rough idea* (=a not very exact understanding) *of how much it will cost?* 그 가격이 얼마나 될지 내게 대략 알려줄 수 있니? / *Roman had no idea* (=did not know) *where Celia had gone.* 로만은 실리아가 어디에 갔는지를 몰랐다. / *I explained it twice, but she didn't seem to get the idea.* (=did not understand). 나는 그것을 두 번이나 설명했으나 그녀는 이해하지 못한 듯했다. **3** [C, U] the aim or purpose of doing something ‖ 어떤 일을 하는 목표 또는 목적: *The idea of the game is to hit the ball into the holes.* 경기의 목표는 공을 때려 홀에 넣는 것이다. **4** an opinion or belief ‖ 견해 또는 믿음: *Bill has some strange ideas about religion.* 빌은 종교에 대해 좀 이상한 견해를 가지고 있다. / *Somewhere he's gotten the idea* (=begun to believe) *that I'm in love with him.* 내가 그를 사랑하고 있다는 것을 그는 대충 믿기 시작했다.

i·de·al¹ /aɪ'diəl/ *adj* **1** being the best that something could possibly be ‖ 사물이 될 수 있는 한의 최선이 되는. 이상적인. 더할 나위 없는: *an ideal place for a picnic* 피크닉하기에 더할 나위 없는 장소 **2** perfect, but not likely to exist ‖ 완벽하지만 존재할 것 같지 않은. 이상적인: *In an ideal world no one would ever get sick.* 이상적인 세계에서는 아무도 병에 걸리는 일은 없을 것이다.

ideal² *n* **1** a principle or standard that you would like to achieve ‖ 성취하고 싶은 원칙 또는 기준. 이상. 이념: *the ideal of perfect equality* 완전 평등의 이상 **2** a perfect example of something ‖ 사물의 완벽한 사례. 전형

i·de·al·ism /aɪ'diə,lɪzəm/ *n* [U] the belief that you should live according to your high standards or principles, even if it is difficult ‖ 어렵더라도 높은 기준이나 원칙에 따라 살아야 한다는 신념. 이상주의

i·de·al·ist·ic /,aɪdiə'lɪstɪk/ *adj* APPROVING believing in principles and high standards, even if they cannot be achieved in real life ‖ 실제 생활에서는 달성할 수 없더라도 원칙과 높은 기준을 신뢰하는. 이상주의적인. 비현실적인: *In the movie, Stewart is an idealistic young senator.* 영화에서 스튜어트는 이상주의적인 젊은 상원의원이다. **– idealist** /aɪ'diəlɪst/ *n*

i·de·al·ize /aɪ'diə,laɪz/ *v* [T] to imagine that something is perfect or better than it really is ‖ 어떤 것이 실제보다 완벽하게

나 더 낫다고 생각하다. 이상화하다: *The show idealizes family life.* 그 쇼는 가족 생활을 이상적인 것으로서 다루고 있다. – **idealization** /aɪˌdiələˈzeɪʃən/ *n* [C, U] – **idealized** /aɪˈdiəˌlaɪzd/ *adj*

i·de·al·ly /aɪˈdiəli/ *adv* **1** in a way that you would like things to be, even if it is not possible ‖ 가능하지는 않더라도 사물 이 그렇게 되었으면 하고 바라는 대로. 이 상적으로: *Ideally I'd like to work at home.* 바라는 바로는 집에서 근무하고 싶 다. **2** perfectly ‖ 완전하게. 더할 나위 없 이. 완벽하게: *Don is ideally suited for the job.* 돈은 더할 나위 없이 그 직무에 적 합하다.

i·den·ti·cal /aɪˈdɛntɪkəl, ɪ-/ *adj* exactly the same ‖ 정확하게 동일한. 아주 똑같 은: *Your shoes are identical to mine.* 너 의 구두는 내 것과 아주 똑같다. / *William and David are identical twins.* (=two babies that are born together and look the same) 윌리암과 데이비드는 일란성 쌍둥이다. – **identically** *adv*

i·den·ti·fi·a·ble /aɪˌdɛntəˈfaɪəbəl, ɪ-/ *adj* able to be recognized ‖ 알아볼 수 있 는. 동일함을 증명할 수 있는

i·den·ti·fi·ca·tion /aɪˌdɛntəfəˈkeɪʃən, ɪ-/ *n* [U] **1** official documents that prove who you are ‖ 자신이 누구인지를 증명하 는 공적인 문서. 신분증명서: *You can use a passport as identification.* 너는 여권을 신분증명서로 사용할 수 있다. **2** the act of recognizing someone or something ‖ 사람이나 사물을 확인해보는 행위. 신원의 확인: *The bodies have been brought to the hospital for identification.* 그 시체는 신원 확인을 위해 병원으로 이송되었다.

i·den·ti·fy /aɪˈdɛntəˌfaɪ, ɪ-/ *v* [T] to recognize and name someone or something ‖ 사람이나 사물을 인식하고 이 름을 대다. 확인하다. 식별하다: *Can you identify the man who robbed you?* 너에 게 강도질한 남자를 알아볼 수 있니?

identify with *phr v* [T] **1** [**identify with** sb] to be able to share or understand the feelings of someone else ‖ 다른 사람 의 감정을 공유하거나 이해할 수 있다. 공 감[투합]하다. 일체감을 가지다: *It was easy to identify with the novel's main character.* 소설의 주인공과 같은 심정이 되는 것은 쉬웠다. **2** be identified with to be closely connected with an idea or group of people ‖ 사람의 생각 또는 집단 과 긴밀하게 연관되다. 관계하게 되다. 결 부되다: *The Peace Corps will always be identified with Kennedy.* 평화봉사단은 항상 케네디와 결부될 것이다.

i·den·ti·ty /aɪˈdɛntəti, ɪ-/ *n* **1** [C, U] who someone is ‖ 정체. 본체. 신원: *The identity of the killer is still unknown.* 살 인범의 정체는 아직 모른다. **2** [U] the qualities someone has that make him/her different from other people ‖ 다 른 사람과 차별화하는 자신만이 가지는 성 질. 개성. 독자성: *Many people's sense of identity comes from their job.* 많은 사 람들의 독자적인 의식은 그들의 직업에서 나온다.

i·de·o·log·i·cal /ˌaɪdiəˈlɑdʒɪkəl, ˌɪdiə-/ *adj* based on a particular set of beliefs or ideas ‖ 특정한 체계의 신념 또는 관념 에 기초한. 공론의. 관념적인. 이데올로기 에 관한 – **ideologically** *adv*

i·de·ol·o·gy /ˌaɪdiˈɑlədʒi, ˌɪdi-/ *n* [C, U] a set of beliefs or ideas, especially political beliefs ‖ 신념이나 관념 특히 정 치적인 신념의 체계. 이데올로기

id·i·o·cy /ˈɪdiəsi/ *n* [C, U] something that is extremely stupid ‖ 지나치게 우둔 한 일. 백치(같은 언행). 바보짓

id·i·om /ˈɪdiəm/ *n* a group of words that have a special meaning that is very different from the ordinary meaning of the separate words ‖ 개별적인 단어들의 보통의 의미와는 아주 다른 특별한 의미를 가지는 단어군. 숙어 – **idiomatic** /ˌɪdiəˈmætɪk/ *adj*

id·i·o·syn·cra·sy /ˌɪdiəˈsɪŋkrəsi/ *n* an unusual habit or way of behaving that someone has ‖ 사람이 갖고 있는 유별난 습관이나 태도. 개인의 특이한 성질. 성향 – **idiosyncratic** /ˌɪdioʊsɪnˈkrætɪk/ *adj*

id·i·ot /ˈɪdiət/ *n* a stupid person or someone who has done something stupid ‖ 어리석은 사람 또는 어리석은 짓 을 한 사람. 멍청이. 천치 – **idiotic** /ˌɪdiˈɑtɪk/ *adj*

i·dle¹ /ˈaɪdl/ *adj* **1** not working or being used ‖ 작동하지 않거나 쓰이지 않는: *a tractor sitting idle in the field* 들에 세워 두고 놀리는 트랙터 **2** OLD-FASHIONED lazy ‖ 게으른 **3** having no useful purpose ‖ 유용한 목적이 없는. 무익한: *idle gossip* 무의미한 잡담 – **idleness** *n* [U] – **idly** *adv*

i·dle² *v* [I] if an engine idles, it runs slowly because it is not doing much work ‖ 엔진이 많은 일을 하지 않으므로 천천히 가동하다. (기계가) 헛돌다. (엔진 이) 공회전하다

i·dol /ˈaɪdl/ *n* **1** someone or something that you admire very much ‖ 아주 많이 칭송하는 사람이나 사물. 숭배 받는 사람 [것]. 우상: *a teen idol* 10대 우상 **2** an image or object that people pray to as a god ‖ 사람들이 신으로서 (모시어) 기도하

는 상(像), 또는 물체. 신상(神像)

i·dol·a·try /aɪˈdɑlətri/ *n* [U] the practice of praying to IDOLs ‖ 우상에 기도하는 관례. 우상 숭배 – **idolatrous** *adj* – **idolater** *n*

i·dol·ize /ˈaɪdl̩ˌaɪz/ *v* [T] to admire someone so much that you think s/he is perfect ‖ 사람을 완전하다고 생각하여 아주 많이 칭송하다. 우상을 숭배하다. 맹목적으로 숭배하다: *She idolizes her mother.* 그녀는 자신의 어머니를 맹목적으로 숭배한다.

i·dyl·lic /aɪˈdɪlɪk/ *adj* very happy and peaceful ‖ 매우 행복하고 평화로운. 한가로운

i.e. /ˌaɪ ˈi/ a written abbreviation used when you want to explain the exact meaning of something ‖ 사물의 정확한 의미를 설명하려고 할 때 쓰이는 약어. 즉 …이다: *The movie is only for adults, i.e. those over 18.* 그 영화는 성인용, 즉 18세 이상용이다.

if¹ /ɪf; *weak* əf/ *conjunction* **1** used in order to talk about something that might happen ‖ 일어날지도 모르는 일에 대해 말하는 데 쓰여. 만약 …이면: *If I call her now, she should still be at home.* 내가 지금 그녀에게 전화하면 아직 집에 있을 거야. / *We'll have to go on Monday instead, if it snows today.* 만일 오늘 눈이 오면 대신에 월요일에 가야 하겠다. ✗DON'T SAY "if it will snow."✗ "if it will snow"라고는 하지 않는다. **2** used in order to mean "whether," when you are asking or deciding something ‖ 어떤 것을 묻거나 결정할 때 "whether"를 뜻하는 데에 쓰여. …인지 어떤지. …이건 아니건: *Would you mind if I used your phone?* 전화 좀 써도 괜찮겠니? **3** used when you are talking about something that always happens ‖ 항상 일어나는 일에 대해 말할 때 쓰여. …할 때는 (언제든지): *If I don't go to bed by 11:00, I feel terrible the next day.* 11시까지 잠자리에 들지 않을 때면, 다음날 나는 힘들어요. **4** said when you are surprised, angry, or upset because something has happened or is true ‖ 어떤 일이 일어났거나 사실이기 때문에 놀라거나 화날 때, 또는 심란한 경우에 쓰여. 설령 …일지라도: *I'm sorry if I upset you.* 걱정을 끼쳐드렸다면 미안합니다. / *I don't care if he is your brother – he's acting like an idiot.* 그가 너의 남동생이더라도 나는 개의치 않는다. 그는 백치처럼 행동하니까. **5 if I were you** used in order to give advice to someone ‖ 남에게 충고를 하는 데에 쓰여. 내가 너라면: *If I were you, I'd call him instead of writing to him.* 내가 너라면 그에게 편지를 쓰는 대신에 전화하겠다. — see also **even if** (EVEN¹), **as if/though** (AS²), **if only** (ONLY¹)

if² *n* **1** INFORMAL a condition or possibility ‖ 조건 또는 가능성: *There are still too many ifs to know if this will succeed.* 이것의 성공 여부를 알기 위해서는 여전히 너무나 많은 조건들이 있다. **2 no ifs, ands, or buts** if you want something done with no ifs, ands, or buts, you want it done quickly, without any arguing ‖ 어떤 일에 대해 옥신 각신 하지 않고 신속히 끝나기를 바라는. 구구한 변명[이유, 구실, 핑계] 없이

if·fy /ˈɪfi/ *adj* INFORMAL an iffy situation is one in which you do not know what will happen ‖ 상황이 어떻게 될지를 알지 못하는. 애매한. 불확실한: *The weather looks iffy today.* 오늘의 날씨는 불확실하게 보인다.

ig·loo /ˈɪglu/ *n* a round house made from blocks of hard snow and ice ‖ 딱딱한 눈과 얼음덩이로 만든 둥근 집. 이글루

ig·nite /ɪgˈnaɪt/ *v* FORMAL **1** [T] to start a dangerous situation, angry argument etc. ‖ 위험한 상황·격렬한 논쟁 등을 시작하다: *actions that could ignite a civil war* 내란을 일으킬 수 있는 조치 **2** [I, T] to start burning, or to make something do this ‖ 불타기 시작하다, 또는 어떤 것을 불타게 하다. 불이 붙다[…에 불을 붙이다]. …을 태우다

ig·ni·tion /ɪgˈnɪʃən/ *n* **1** [singular] the electrical part of an engine in a car that makes it start working ‖ 자동차 엔진을 가동하기 시작하게 하는 전기 장치 부분. (내연 기관의) 점화 장치: *Put the key in the ignition.* 점화 장치에 키를 넣어라. — see picture on page 943 **2** [U] FORMAL the act of making something start to burn ‖ 어떤 것이 불붙기 시작하게 하는 것. 점화. 발화

ig·no·min·i·ous /ˌɪgnəˈmɪniəs/ *adj* FORMAL making you feel ashamed or embarrassed ‖ 수치감 또는 당혹감을 일으키게 하는. 수치스러운. 창피한: *an ignominious defeat* 불명예스러운 패배

ig·no·rance /ˈɪgnərəns/ *n* [U] DISAPPROVING lack of knowledge or information about something ‖ 어떤 것에 대한 지식 또는 정보의 부족. 무지: *We talked about how racism comes from ignorance and fear.* 우리는 인종적 편견이 무지와 공포에서 어떻게 비롯되는지에 대해 이야기했다.

ig·no·rant /ˈɪgnərənt/ *adj* not knowing facts or information that you should know ‖ 사람이 알아야 할 사실 또는 정보를 알지 못하는. 무지한: *students who are ignorant of geography* 지리(학)에 무지한 대학생들

ig·nore /ɪgˈnɔr/ *v* [T] to not pay any attention to someone or something ‖ 사람이나 사물에 관심을 전혀 기울이지 않다. 무시하다. 묵살하다: *Jeannie ignored me all night!* 지니가 밤새 나를 못 본 체 했어! / *The school board has ignored our complaints.* 학교 위원회는 우리의 항의를 무시해 왔다.

i·gua·na /ɪˈgwɑnə/ *n* a large tropical American LIZARD ‖ 열대 아메리카산의 큰 도마뱀. 이구아나 도마뱀

i·kon /ˈaɪkɑn/ *n* ⇨ ICON

IL the written abbreviation of Illinois ‖ Illinois(일리노이 주)의 약어

I'll /aɪl/ the short form of "I will" ‖ "I will"의 단축형: *I'll be there in a minute.* 거기에 금방 갈게.

ill¹ /ɪl/ *adj* **1** suffering from a disease or not feeling well; SICK ‖ 병으로 고통 받는 또는 기분이 좋지 않은. 병든. 기분이 언짢은; ㉠ sick: *The doctor said Patty was seriously/critically ill.* (=extremely ill) 의사는 패티의 병세가 심각하다고[위독하다고] 말했다. **2** bad or harmful ‖ 나쁜, 해로운. 못된. 사악한. 불친절한: *Has he suffered any ill effects from the treatment?* 그는 치료 후 어떤 부작용을 겪고 있습니까? **3 ill at ease** nervous or embarrassed ‖ 긴장한, 당혹한. 불안한. 안절부절 못하는

ill² *adv* **1** badly or not pleasantly ‖ 나쁘게, 언짢게. 사악하게. 불충분하게. 부적당하게: *We were ill-prepared for the cold weather.* 우리는 추운 날씨에 대한 대비가 부족했다. **2 can ill afford (to do sth)** to not be able to do something because it would make your situation more difficult ‖ 상황을 더욱 어렵게 하므로 어떤 일을 할 수가 없다. …할 여유가 없다: *Congress can ill afford to raise taxes so close to an election.* 선거가 너무 임박해 의회는 세금을 인상할 수가 없다.

ill³ *n* a bad thing, especially a problem or something that makes you worry ‖ 나쁜 일, 특히 사람을 걱정하게 하는 문제 또는 일. 악. 고난: *the social ills caused by poverty* 가난으로 빚어진 사회악

ill-ad·vised /ˌ. .ˈ./ *adj* not sensible or not wise ‖ 분별없는 또는 현명하지 않은. 사려 없는. 경솔한

il·le·gal¹ /ɪˈligəl/ *adj* not allowed by the law ‖ 법에 의해 허용되지 않는. 불법[위법]의: *Did you know it is illegal to park your car here?* 이 곳에 주차하는 것이 불

법인지 알았나요? / *illegal drugs* 불법 마약 **– illegally** *adv* —opposite LEGAL

illegal² *n* also **illegal immigrant/alien** someone who comes into a country to live or work without official permission ‖ 공식 허가 없이 살거나 일하기 위해 입국한 사람. 불법 이민자. 불법 체류 외국인

il·leg·i·ble /ɪˈlɛdʒəbəl/ *adj* difficult or impossible to read ‖ 읽기 어렵거나 불가능한. 판독[독해]하기 어려운: *illegible handwriting* 읽기 어려운 필적 **– illegibly** *adv*

il·le·git·i·mate /ˌɪləˈdʒɪtəmɪt/ *adj* **1** born to parents who are not married to each other ‖ 서로 결혼을 하지 않은 부모에게서 태어난. 서출의. 적출(嫡出)이 아닌: *an illegitimate child* 사생아[서자] **2** not allowed by the rules ‖ 규칙에 의해 허용되지 않는. 불법[위법]의. 비합법적인: *an illegitimate use of public money* 공적 자금의 불법 사용 **– illegitimacy** /ˌɪləˈdʒɪtəməsi/ *n* [U]

ill-equipped /ˌ. .ˈ./ *adj* not having the necessary equipment or skills for something ‖ 어떤 것에 대한 필요한 장비 또는 기술을 갖추지 않은. 능력[장비, 설비]이 불충분한. 준비가 부실한: *The hospitals there are dirty and ill-equipped.* 그곳의 병원들은 불결하고 시설이 부실하다.

ill-fat·ed /ˌ. ˈ../ *adj* not likely to have a good result ‖ 좋은 결과를 갖게 될 것 같지 않은. 불운[불행]한. 불운[불행]을 가져오는

il·lic·it /ɪˈlɪsɪt/ *adj* not allowed by the law, or not approved of by society ‖ 법에 의해 허용되지 않는, 또는 사회에 의해서 용인되지 않는. 부정한. 불법의: *an illicit love affair* 용납되지 않는 정사(情事) **– illicitly** *adv*

il·lit·er·ate /ɪˈlɪtərɪt/ *adj* not able to read or write ‖ 읽거나 쓸 수 없는. 문맹의. 무식한. 교양이 없는 **– illiteracy** /ɪˈlɪtərəsi/ *n* [U]

ill-man·nered /ˌ. ˈ../ *adj* FORMAL not polite ‖ 공손하지 않은. 버릇없는. 무례한

ill·ness /ˈɪlnɪs/ *n* [C, U] a disease of the body or mind, or the state of having a disease or sickness ‖ 신체나 정신의 질병, 또는 질병을 가지거나 아픈 상태. 병. 불쾌: *mental illness* 정신병 / *a serious illness* 중병 —see usage note at DISEASE

il·log·i·cal /ɪˈlɑdʒɪkəl/ *adj* not sensible or reasonable ‖ 분별없는, 불합리한. 비논리적인. 부조리한

ill-treat /ˌ. ˈ./ *v* [T] to be cruel to someone ‖ 사람에게 잔인하(게 대하)는.

학대하다: *The prisoners were beaten and ill-treated.* 그 죄수들은 구타당하고 학대받았다. – **ill-treatment** *n* [U]

il·lu·mi·nate /ɪˈluməˌneɪt/ *v* [T] to make a light shine on something ‖ 어떤 것 위에 빛을 비추어 밝게 하다. …을 비추다[조명하다]. 밝게 하다: *The room was illuminated by candles.* 그 방은 촛불로 밝아졌다. – **illuminated** *adj*

il·lu·mi·nat·ing /ɪˈluməˌneɪtɪŋ/ *adj* FORMAL making something easier to understand ‖ 어떤 것을 이해하기 더욱 쉽게 하는. 비추는. 조명하는. 밝히는: *an illuminating lecture on physics* 물리학의 이해를 돕는 강의

il·lu·mi·na·tion /ɪˌluməˈneɪʃən/ *n* [U] FORMAL the light provided by a lamp, fire etc. ‖ 등·불꽃 등에서 나오는 빛. 조명

il·lu·sion /ɪˈluʒən/ *n* **1** something that seems to be different from what it really is ‖ 실제와 다르게 보이는 사물. 환영(幻影). 환각: *The design of the room gave an illusion of space.* 그 방의 디자인은 공간적인 착각을 일으켰다. **2** an idea or belief that is false ‖ 잘못된 생각 또는 믿음. 오해. 착각. 망상: *Terry is under the illusion that* (=wrongly believes that) *he's going to pass the test.* 테리는 시험에 합격할 것이라는 망상에 빠져 있다. / *We have no illusions about the hard work that lies ahead.* 우리는 앞에 놓인 어려운 과업에 대하여 망상을 갖고 있지 않다.

il·lu·so·ry /ɪˈlusəri, -zəri/ *adj* FORMAL false, but seeming to be true or real ‖ 거짓된, 하지만 사실이나 실제처럼 보이는. 환영의. 착각의. (가치·내용에 대해) 속이는[홀리는]

il·lus·trate /ˈɪləˌstreɪt/ *v* [T] **1** to explain or make something clear by giving examples ‖ 실례를 들어서 사물을 설명하거나 분명하게 하다. 설명하다. 예증[예시]하다: *The charts will help to illustrate this point.* 도표는 이 점을 설명하는 데 도움이 될 것이다. **2** to draw, paint etc. pictures for a book ‖ 책에 들어가는 그림을 그리고 채색 등을 하다. 도해[삽화]를 넣다: *a children's book illustrated by Dr. Seuss* 슈스 박사가 도해[삽화]를 그린 아동도서 – **illustrative** /ɪˈlʌstrətɪv, ˌɪləˈstreɪtɪv/ *adj*

il·lus·tra·tion /ˌɪləˈstreɪʃən/ *n* **1** a picture in a book ‖ 책 속의 그림. 삽화. 도해: *watercolor illustrations* 수채화 삽화 **2** an example that helps you understand something ‖ 어떤 것의 이해를 돕는 예. 실례. 예증. 설명. 해설: *an*

illustration of how big the planets are, in comparison to Earth 지구와 비교해서 그 행성의 크기가 어떤지에 관해 예시한 그림

il·lus·tra·tor /ˈɪləˌstreɪtɚ/ *n* someone whose job is to draw pictures for a book, magazine etc. ‖ 책·잡지 등에 그림을 그리는 직업인. 삽화가

il·lus·tri·ous /ɪˈlʌstriəs/ *adj* FORMAL very famous and admired by a lot of people ‖ 매우 유명하고 많은 사람들이 감탄하는. 걸출한. 뛰어난

ill will /ˌ ˈ / *n* [U] unfriendly feelings for someone ‖ 남에 대한 반감. 나쁜 감정. 적의. 원한. 혐오감

I'm /aɪm/ the short form of "I am" ‖ "I am"의 단축형: *I'm not sure where he is.* 나는 그가 어디 있는지 확실히 모른다. / *Hello, I'm Donna.* 여보세요, 저는 도나입니다.

im·age /ˈɪmɪdʒ/ *n* **1** the opinion that people have about someone or something, especially because of the way he, she, or it is shown on television, in newspapers etc. ‖ 특히 사람이나 사물이 텔레비전·신문 등에 나타나는 태도 때문에 사람이나 사물에 대하여 일반인들이 갖고 있는 견해. (매스컴에 의한) 일반 개념. 인상. 이미지: *The President will have to improve his image if he wants to be re-elected.* 대통령이 재선을 바란다면 그의 이미지를 개선해야 할 것이다. **2** a picture that you can see through a camera, on a television, in a mirror etc. ‖ 카메라를 통해·텔레비전 상에서·거울 속에서 볼 수 있는 그림. 상(像): *a baby looking at his image in the mirror* 거울 속의 자기 모습을 보고 있는 아기 **3** a picture that you have in your mind ‖ 마음속에 가지고 있는 그림. 심상(心像): *She had a clear image of how he would look in 20 years.* 그녀는 20년 후에 그 남자가 어떤 모습일지에 대한 뚜렷한 이미지를 가졌다. **4** a word, picture, or phrase that describes an idea in a poem, book, movie etc. ‖ 시·책·영화 등에서 생각을 묘사하는 단어·그림·어구. 상징. 전형. 구현

im·age·ry /ˈɪmɪdʒri/ *n* [U] the use of words, pictures, or phrases to describe ideas or actions in poems, books, movies etc. ‖ 시·책·영화 등에서 생각 또는 행동을 묘사하는 단어·그림·어구의 사용. 형상. 묘사. 표현: *the disturbing imagery of Bosch's paintings* 보슈의 그림이 주는 불온한 이미지

i·mag·i·na·ble /ɪˈmædʒənəbəl/ *adj* able to be imagined ‖ 상상할 수 있는. 생각할

수 있는. 가능한: *I had the worst/best day imaginable.* 나는 상상할 수 있는 최악[최고]의 날을 겪었다.

i·mag·i·nar·y /ɪˈmædʒəˌnɛri/ *adj* not real, but imagined ‖ 실제는 아닌 상상의. 가상의: *Many children have imaginary friends.* 많은 아이들은 가상의 친구들이 있다. —compare IMAGINATIVE

i·mag·i·na·tion /ɪˌmædʒəˈneɪʃən/ *n* [C, U] the ability to form pictures or ideas in your mind ‖ 마음에 그림 또는 개념을 구성하는 능력. 상상(력). 구상력(構想力): *Teachers encouraged the students to use their imaginations in solving the problem.* 교사들은 그 문제를 푸는 데 상상력을 발휘하라고 학생들을 격려했다. / *Sheila realized that her fears had all been in her imagination.* (=were not true) 쉴라는 그녀의 공포가 모두 상상에 불과했다는 것을 깨달았다. —compare FANTASY

i·mag·i·na·tive /ɪˈmædʒənətɪv/ *adj* **1** able to think of new and interesting ideas ‖ 새롭고 흥미 있는 아이디어를 생각할 수 있는. 상상의. 상상력이 풍부한: *an imaginative writer* 상상력이 풍부한 작가 **2** containing new and interesting ideas ‖ 새롭고 흥미 있는 생각을 포함한. 상상으로 채워진. 상상력으로 만들어 낸: *an imaginative story* 상상으로 가득찬 이야기 **– imaginatively** *adv* —compare IMAGINARY

i·mag·ine /ɪˈmædʒɪn/ *v* [T] **1** to form pictures or ideas in your mind ‖ 마음에 그림 또는 개념을 형성하다. 상상하다. 마음에 그리다: *Imagine that you're lying on a beach somewhere.* 어딘가의 해변에 네가 누워 있다고 상상해 봐. / *Bobby couldn't imagine why she had lied to him.* 보비는 그녀가 왜 자기에게 거짓말을 했는지를 상상할 수 없었다. **2** to have a false or wrong idea about something ‖ 어떤 것에 대하여 거짓된 또는 잘못된 생각을 가지다. …이라고 (잘못)상상하다: *No one is out there, you're just imagining things.* 밖에 아무도 없는데 네가 잘못 생각한 거야. **3** to think that something may happen or may be true ‖ 일이 일어날 수도 있거나 사실일 수도 있다고 생각하다. 추측하다. 가정하다: *I imagine Kathy will be there tomorrow.* 캐시가 내일 거기 올 거라고 짐작한다.

im·bal·ance /ɪmˈbæləns/ *n* [C, U] a lack of balance between two things, so they are not equal or correct ‖ 동등하거나 똑바르게 되지 않은 두 물건 사이의 균형의 결함. 불균형. 불안정: *a trade imbalance* 무역 불균형 **– imbalanced** *adj*

im·be·cile /ˈɪmbəsəl/ *n* someone who is extremely stupid ‖ 아주 우둔한 사람. 바보

im·bibe /ɪmˈbaɪb/ *v* [I, T] FORMAL to drink something, especially alcohol ‖ 특히 술 등을 마시다. 들이마시다. 흡수하다

im·bue /ɪmˈbyu/ *v*

imbue sb/sth **with** *phr v* [T] to make someone feel an emotion very strongly, or to make something contain a strong emotion ‖ 사람에게 매우 강하게 감정을 느끼게 하다, 또는 사물이 강렬한 감정을 지니도록 하다. 불어넣다. 주입시키다: *songs imbued with a romantic tenderness* 로맨틱한 부드러움을 불어넣은 노래

im·i·tate /ˈɪməˌteɪt/ *v* [T] to do something in exactly the same way as someone or something else ‖ 다른 사람이나 사물과 완전히 똑같은 방식으로 어떤 일을 하다. …을 모방하다[흉내 내다]: *The tape was made with an actor imitating his voice.* 그 테이프는 그의 목소리를 흉내 내는 배우를 써서 제작되었다. **– imitative** *adj* **– imitator** *n* —compare COPY²

im·i·ta·tion¹ /ˌɪməˈteɪʃən/ *n* **1** [C, U] a copy of someone's speech, behavior etc., or the act of copying ‖ 남의 말·행동 등의 모방, 또는 그 모방하는 행위. 모방(행동). 흉내 내기: *Harry does an excellent imitation of Elvis.* 해리는 엘비스를 훌륭하게 흉내 낸다. / *Children learn by imitation.* 아이들은 모방에 의해서 배운다. **2** a copy of something ‖ 사물의 복제. 모조[위조]품. 가짜. 복사물: *It's not an antique; it's an imitation.* 그것은 골동품이 아니라 모조품이다.

imitation² *adj* imitation leather/wood/ivory etc. something that looks real, but that is a copy ‖ 진짜처럼 보이나 모조품인 물건. 모조 가죽/나무/상아

im·mac·u·late /ɪˈmækyəlɪt/ *adj* **1** very clean and neat ‖ 매우 깨끗한·산뜻한. 더러워지지 않은: *an immaculate house* 깨끗한 집 **2** perfect and without any mistakes ‖ 완벽한. 어떤 실수도 없는. 흠 없는. 결점이 없는: *dancing with immaculate precision* 실수 없는 정확한 춤 **– immaculately** *adv*

im·ma·te·ri·al /ˌɪməˈtɪriəl/ *adj* not important in a particular situation ‖ 특정한 상황에서 중요하지 않은. 하찮은

im·ma·ture /ˌɪməˈtʃʊr, -ˈtʊr/ *adj* **1** DISAPPROVING not behaving in a sensible way that is correct for your age ‖ 나이에 맞게 분별 있게 행동하지 않는. 미숙한.

유치한: *Stop being so childish and immature!* 그렇게 어린애처럼 유치하게 행동하지 마라! **2** not fully formed or developed ‖ 완전히 형성되거나 발달하지 않은. 미완성의. 미숙한 **– immaturity** *n* [U]

im·me·di·a·cy /ɪˈmidiəsi/ *n* [U] the quality of seeming to be important and urgent, and directly relating to what is happening now ‖ 중요하고 긴급하게 보이며 현재 발생하고 있는 것과 직접적으로 관련된 성질. 직접[즉시](성). 긴급성

im·me·di·ate /ɪˈmidiɪt/ *adj* **1** happening or done at once with no delay ‖ 지체 없이 즉시 발생하거나 이루어진. 즉석의. 즉시의: *Police demanded the immediate release of the hostages.* 경찰은 인질의 즉각적인 석방을 요구했다. **2** existing now, and needing to be dealt with quickly ‖ 현재 존재하고 신속한 처리가 필요한. 당면한. 목전의. 바로(전[후]의): *Our immediate concern was to stop the fire from spreading.* 우리의 당면한 관심은 화재의 확산을 막는 것이었다. **3** near something or someone in time or place ‖ 시간 또는 장소에 있어서 사물이나 사람에 가까운. 머지않은. 인접한: *We have no plans to expand the business in the immediate future.* 우리는 가까운 장래에 사업을 확장할 계획이 없다. **4 immediate family** your parents, children, brothers, and sisters ‖ 부모·자녀·형제·자매. 육친

im·me·di·ate·ly /ɪˈmidiɪtli/ *adv* **1** at once and with no delay ‖ 즉시·지체 없이. 곧 : *Mandy answered the phone immediately.* 맨디는 즉시 전화를 받았다. **2** very near to something in time or place ‖ 시간 또는 장소에 있어서 어떤 것에 매우 가까이에. 바로(접하여): *We left immediately afterwards.* 우리는 그 뒤에 곧 떠났다. / *They live immediately above us.* 그들은 우리 바로 위층에 산다.

im·mense /ɪˈmɛns/ *adj* extremely large ‖ 지극히 큰. 거대한. 굉장한. 대단한: *an immense palace* 거대한 궁전 **– immensity** *n* [U]

im·mense·ly /ɪˈmɛnsli/ *adv* very much ‖ 아주 많게. 무한히. 굉장히. 몹시. 매우: *I enjoyed your party immensely.* 나는 네 파티에서 매우 즐거웠다.

im·merse /ɪˈmɚs/ *v* [T] **1 be immersed in sth/immerse yourself in sth** to be completely involved in something ‖ 완전히 어떤 일에 관련되다. …에 열중[몰두, 몰입]하다: *Grant is completely immersed in his work.* 그랜트는 그의 작업에 완전히 몰두해 있다. **2** to put something completely in a liquid ‖ 어떤 것을 액체에 완전히 담그다. 가라앉히다 **– immersion** /ɪˈmɚʒən/ *n* [U]

im·mi·grant /ˈɪməɡrənt/ *n* someone who enters another country to live there ‖ 거주하기 위해 다른 나라에 입국하는 사람. 이민. 이주자. 입국자: *an immigrant from Russia* 러시아에서 온 이민자 — compare EMIGRANT

im·mi·grate /ˈɪməˌɡreɪt/ *v* [I] to enter another country in order to live there ‖ 거주하기 위해 다른 나라에 들어가다. 이주해 오다. 이주하다 —compare EMIGRATE —see usage note at EMIGRATE

im·mi·gra·tion /ˌɪməˈɡreɪʃən/ *n* [U] **1** the process of entering another country in order to live there ‖ 거주 목적으로 다른 나라에 입국하는 절차. 이주. 이민. 입국 **2** the place in an airport, at a border etc. where officials check your documents, such as your PASSPORT ‖ 여권 등의 문서를 공무원이 확인하는 공항·국경 등의 장소. (출)입국 관리 사무(소[카운터])

im·mi·nent /ˈɪmənənt/ *adj* happening or likely to happen very soon ‖ 발생하고 있거나 조만간 곧 발생할 것 같은. 절박한. 급박한. 임박한: *We believe that an attack is imminent.* 우리는 공격이 임박해 있다고 믿는다. / *The city is not in imminent danger.* 그 도시는 절박한 위험에 처해 있지는 않다. **– imminently** *adv*

im·mo·bile /ɪˈmoʊbəl/ *adj* not moving, or not able to move ‖ 움직이지 않는, 또는 움직일 수 없는. 정지된. 부동의

im·mor·al /ɪˈmɔrəl, ɪˈmɑr-/ *adj* morally wrong, and not accepted by society ‖ 도덕적으로 잘못되어 사회에서 용인되지 않는. 부도덕한. 음란한. 외설적인: *immoral sexual acts* 외설적인 성행위 **– immorality** /ˌɪməˈræləti, ˌɪmɔr-/ *n* [U]

im·mor·tal /ɪˈmɔrtl/ *adj* **1** living or continuing always ‖ 언제나 살아 있거나 계속되는. 불멸의. 불사의. 영원한: *your immortal soul* 당신의 불멸의 영혼 **2** an immortal poem, song etc. is so famous that it will never be forgotten ‖ 시·노래 등이 유명하여 결코 잊혀지지 않을. 불후(不朽)의: *the immortal writings of Charles Dickens* 찰스 디킨스의 불후의 작품 **– immortality** /ˌɪmɔrˈtæləti/ *n* [U]

im·mov·a·ble /ɪˈmuvəbəl/ *adj* impossible to move, change, or persuade ‖ 움직일 수 없는, 변경할 수 없는, 설득할 수 없는. 부동의. 고정된. 확고한

im·mune /ɪˈmyun/ *adj* **1** not able to be

affected by a disease or illness ‖ 병에 의한 영향을 받지 않을 수 있는. 면역(성)의. 면역이 된. 면역 항체를 지닌: *Pregnant women should make sure they are immune to German measles.* 임신부들은 자신들이 풍진에 면역 항체가 있는지를 확인해야 한다. **2 not affected by** unpleasant things that affect people, organizations etc. in similar situations ‖ 유사한 상황에서 다른 사람·조직 들에 영향을 주는 불쾌한 일에 의해서 영향을 받지 않는. 면제된. 면한: *The company seems to be immune to economic pressures.* 그 회사는 경제적 압력의 영향을 받지 않는 듯하다. / *The Governor is popular, but not immune from criticism.* 그 지사는 유명하지만 비판을 면할 수는 없다.

immune sys·tem /.ˈ. ˌ../ *n* the system by which your body protects itself against disease ‖ 신체가 질병에 대항해 스스로 방어하는 체계. 면역 시스템

im·mun·i·ty /ɪˈmyunəti/ *n* [U] **1** the state or right of being IMMUNE to laws or punishment ‖ 법률 또는 형벌에서 영향을 받지 않는 상태 또는 권리. 면제. 면책(특권): *Congress granted immunity* (=gave immunity) *to both men.* 의회는 두 남자에게 면책을 허용했다. **2** the state of being IMMUNE to diseases or illnesses ‖ 질병에 면역이 되어 있는 상태. 면역(성). 항체: *The patient's immunity is low.* 그 환자는 면역성이 낮다.

im·mu·ni·za·tion /ˌɪmyənəˈzeɪʃən/ *n* [C, U] the act of immunizing (IMMUNIZE) someone ‖ 사람에게 면역성을 주는 행위. 면역(법). 면역 조치: *the immunization of babies in the U.S. against hepatitis B* B형 간염에 대한 미국 내 아기들의 면역 조치

im·mu·nize /ˈɪmyəˌnaɪz/ *v* [T] to protect someone from disease by giving him/her a VACCINE ‖ 사람에게 백신을 투여해서 병으로부터 방어하다. 면역성을 주다: *Have you been immunized against cholera?* 너는 콜레라에 대한 면역이 되어 있니?

im·mu·ta·ble /ɪˈmyutəbəl/ *adj* FORMAL never changing, or impossible to change ‖ 절대 변하지 않는, 또는 변경이 불가능한. 변치 않는. 불변의

imp /ɪmp/ *n* a child who behaves badly, but in a funny way ‖ 못됐지만 장난스럽게 행동하는 아이. 개구쟁이. 악동

im·pact¹ /ˈɪmpækt/ *n* **1** the effect that an event or situation has on someone or something ‖ 사건 또는 상황이 사람 또는 사물에 대해 미치는 영향. 영향(력). 효과. 감화: *Every decision at work has an impact on profit.* 작업시의 모든 결정이 수익에 영향을 미친다. / *the environmental impact of the three new housing developments* 3대 신규 주택 개발에 대한 환경적 영향 **2** the force of one object hitting another ‖ 하나의 물체가 다른 물체를 때리는 힘. 충격(력). 충돌: *The impact of the crash made the car flip over.* 충돌의 충격으로 인해 자동차가 튕겨져서 뒤집어졌다. **3 on impact** at the moment when one thing hits another ‖ 한 사물이 다른 것을 치는 순간에. 부딪치는 순간에. 충격으로: *a missile that explodes on impact* 충돌 순간에 폭발하는 미사일

im·pact² /ɪmˈpækt/ *v* [I, T] to have an important or noticeable effect on someone or something ‖ 사람 또는 사물에 중요하거나 눈에 띄는 영향력을 미치다. 강한 충격[영향]을 주다: *The growth of the airport has impacted the city's economy.* 공항의 성장은 그 도시 경제에 괄목할 만한 영향을 주었다.

im·pair /ɪmˈpɛr/ *v* [T] to damage something or make it less good ‖ 사물을 손상시키거나 덜 좋게 만들다. 해치다. 상하게 하다: *Her sight was impaired as a result of the disease.* 질병의 결과로 그녀의 시력은 손상되었다. – **impairment** *n* [U]

im·paired /ɪmˈpɛrd/ *adj* **1** damaged, less strong, or less good ‖ 손상된·덜 강한·덜 좋은. 망가진. 고장 난. 나빠진: *Radio reception was impaired after the storm.* 폭풍이 지나간 후 라디오 수신이 제대로 안 되었다. / *impaired vision* 나빠진 시력 **2 hearing/visually impaired etc.** someone who is hearing impaired or visually impaired cannot hear, see etc. very well or at all ‖ 어떤 사람이 듣고 보는 것 등을 제대로 또는 전혀 할 수 없는. 청각/시각 장애의

im·pale /ɪmˈpeɪl/ *v* [T] to push a sharp pointed object through something or someone ‖ 사물 또는 사람에게 날카롭고 뾰족한 물체를 밀어 넣다. …을 (꿰)찌르다[꽂다]. …을 고정시키다

im·part /ɪmˈpɑrt/ *v* [T] FORMAL **1** to give information, knowledge etc. to someone ‖ 남에게 정보·지식 등을 주다. 알리다. 전하다: *He accused the universities of failing to impart moral values.* 그는 대학들이 도덕적 가치를 가르치지 않는다고 비난했다. **2** to give a particular quality to something ‖ 어떤 것에 특정한 성질을 주다. …을 …에게 주다. 나누어 주다: *Burned butter imparts a bitter flavor to* *the sauce.* 불에 탄 버터는 소스에 쓴 맛을 준다.

im·par·tial /ɪmˈpɑrʃəl/ *adj* not giving special attention or support to any one person or group ‖ 어떤 한 사람이나 집단에 특별한 배려나 지원을 하지 않는. 공정한. 편견이 없는: *impartial advice* 편견이 없는 충고 / *impartial observers of the election* 공정한 선거 참관인들 – **impartially** *adv* – **impartiality** /ɪmˌpɑrʃiˈæləti/ *n* [U]

im·pass·a·ble /ɪmˈpæsəbəl/ *adj* impossible to travel along or through ‖ 따라서 또는 통과해 나아갈 수 없는. 지나갈 수 없는. 통행할 수 없는: *Some streets are impassable because of the snow.* 몇몇 거리는 눈 때문에 통행할 수 없다.

im·passe /ˈɪmpæs/ *n* [singular] a situation in which it is impossible to continue with a discussion or plan because the people involved cannot agree ‖ 관련자들이 의견일치를 볼 수 없기 때문에 의논이나 계획을 계속 진행할 수 없는 상황. 곤경. 막다른 골목: *Discussions about pay have reached an impasse.* 임금에 대한 토의는 교착상태에 빠졌다.

im·pas·sioned /ɪmˈpæʃənd/ *adj* full of strong feelings and emotion ‖ 강렬한 느낌과 감정이 가득한. 감격한. 열렬한. 정열이 깃든. 열정적인: *an impassioned speech* 열정적인 연설

im·pas·sive /ɪmˈpæsɪv/ *adj* not showing any emotions ‖ 감정을 전혀 나타내지 않는. 침착한. 무감동의. 냉담한: *His face was impassive as the judge spoke.* 판사가 말할 때 그의 얼굴은 무표정했다. – **impassively** *adv*

im·pa·tient /ɪmˈpeɪʃənt/ *adj* 1 annoyed because of delays or mistakes that make you wait ‖ 지연 또는 실수로 사람을 기다리게 해서 화난. 참을 수 없는. 견디지 못하는. 짜증을 내는. 성급한: *After an hour's delay, the airline passengers were becoming impatient.* 한 시간이 지연된 후 항공기 승객들은 짜증을 내기 시작하고 있었다. / *Rob's teacher seems very impatient with some of the slower kids.* 로브의 선생님은 몇몇 둔한 아이들에게 매우 짜증 나 있는 듯이 보인다. 2 very eager for something to happen, and not wanting to wait ‖ 어떤 일이 일어날 것을 매우 열망하면서 기다리는 것을 원하지 않는. …을 초조하게 기다리는. 몹시 …하고 싶어 하는: *Gary was impatient to leave.* 게리는 (자리를) 뜨고 싶어 안달하였다. – **impatience** *n* [U] –

impatiently *adv*

im·peach /ɪmˈpitʃ/ *v* [T] LAW to say that a public official is guilty of a serious crime ‖ 공무원이 중죄에 대해 유죄라고 말하다. 탄핵하다 – **impeachment** *n* [U]

im·pec·ca·ble /ɪmˈpɛkəbəl/ *adj* completely perfect and impossible to criticize ‖ 철저하게 완벽한·비난할 수 없는. 결함[나무랄 데]없는. 죄가 없는: *She has impeccable taste in clothes.* 그녀는 의상에 완벽한 심미안을 갖고 있다. – **impeccably** *adv*

im·pede /ɪmˈpid/ *v* [T] FORMAL to make it difficult for someone or something to make progress ‖ 사람 또는 사물이 전진하는 것을 어렵게 하다. 방해하다. 훼방놓다: *Rescue attempts were impeded by storms.* 구조하기 위한 시도가 폭풍으로 지체되었다.

im·ped·i·ment /ɪmˈpɛdəmənt/ *n* 1 a fact or event that makes action difficult or impossible ‖ 활동을 곤란하게 하거나 불가능하게 하는 사실, 또는 사건. 방해. 장애(물): *The country's debt has been an impediment to development.* 국가의 채무가 발전을 가로막아 왔다. 2 a physical problem that makes speaking, hearing, or moving difficult ‖ 말하는[듣는, 움직이는] 것을 어렵게 하는 육체적 문제. 언어[청각, 신체]장애: *a speech impediment* 언어 장애

im·pel /ɪmˈpɛl/ **-elled, -elling** *v* [T] FORMAL to make you feel very strongly that you must do something ‖ 사람이 어떤 일을 해야 한다고 매우 강렬하게 느끼게 하다. 압박하여[재촉하여, 억지로] … 하게 하다: *He felt impelled to explain why he had acted the way he did.* 그는 왜 그런 식으로 행동했는지를 설명해야 한다는 느낌을 받았다.

im·pend·ing /ɪmˈpɛndɪŋ/ *adj* likely to happen soon ‖ 곧 일어날 것 같은. 임박한. 절박한: *the impending legal battle* 당면한 법적 분쟁

im·pen·e·tra·ble /ɪmˈpɛnətrəbəl/ *adj* 1 impossible to get through, see through, or get into ‖ 관통할 수 없는, 투과해볼 수 없는, 뚫고 들어갈 수 없는. 꿰뚫을 수가 없는: *impenetrable fog* 앞을 내다볼 수 없는 안개 2 very difficult or impossible to understand ‖ 이해하기가 매우 어렵거나 불가능한. (사물이) 불가해한. 헤아릴 수 없는: *impenetrable scientific language* 이해하기 힘든 과학 용어

im·per·a·tive¹ /ɪmˈpɛrətɪv/ *adj* FORMAL 1 extremely important and urgent ‖ 지극히 중요하고 긴급한. 피할 수 없는. 필수

의. 의무적인. 긴요한: *It's imperative that you leave immediately.* 너는 무슨 일이 있어도 즉시 출발해야 한다. **2** TECHNICAL an imperative verb expresses a command ‖ 명령을 표현하는 명령법 동사

imperative² *n* **1** something that must be done urgently ‖ 긴급하게 행해져야 하는 일. 의무. 필요. 긴급한 일. 불가피한 임무: *Reducing air pollution has become an imperative.* 대기 오염을 줄이는 것은 긴급한 당면과제가 되었다. **2** TECHNICAL the form of a verb that expresses a command. In the sentence "Do it now!" the verb "do" is in the imperative ‖ 명령을 나타내는 동사형. "Do it now!"라는 문장에서 "do"는 명령법의 동사이다

im·per·cep·ti·ble /ˌɪmpəˈsɛptəbəl/ *adj* impossible to notice ‖ 인식할 수 없는. 지각할 수 없는. 감지될 수 없는. 미세한. 근소한: *an almost imperceptible change* 거의 감지할 수 없는 변화 –**imperceptibly** *adv*

im·per·fect¹ /ɪmˈpəfɪkt/ *adj* not completely perfect ‖ 철저하게 완전하지 않은. 미완성의. 불완전한. 불충분한: *an imperfect legal system* 불완전한 법률 제도 –**imperfectly** *adv*

imperfect² *n* [singular] TECHNICAL the form of a verb that shows an incomplete action in the past, that is formed with "be" and the PAST PARTICIPLE. In the sentence "We were walking down the road" the verb phrase "were walking" is in the imperfect ‖ be동사와 과거 분사로 구성되는 과거의 불완전한 행위를 나타내는 동사형. 미완료 시제. 반과거. 미완료[반과거]형의 동사. "We were walking down the road"라는 문장에서 동사구 "were walking"은 미완료 시제[반과거]이다

im·per·fec·tion /ˌɪmpəˈfɛkʃən/ *n* [C, U] the state of being IMPERFECT, or something that is imperfect ‖ 불완전한 상태, 또는 미완성의 일. 불완전. 결함. 흠: *human imperfection* 인간의 단점 / *There may be slight imperfections in the cloth.* 옷감에 약간의 흠이 있을 수 있다.

im·pe·ri·al /ɪmˈpɪriəl/ *adj* relating to an EMPIRE or to the person who rules it ‖ 제국 또는 제국을 통치하는 사람과 관련된. 제국의. 황제의

im·pe·ri·al·ism /ɪmˈpɪriəˌlɪzəm/ *n* [U] USUALLY DISAPPROVING a political system in which one country controls a lot of other countries ‖ 한 나라가 많은 다른 나라를 통치하는 정치적 체제. 제국주의 – **imperialist** *n* – **imperialist,**

imperialistic /ɪmˌpɪriəˈlɪstɪk/ *adj*

im·per·il /ɪmˈpɛrəl/ *v* [T] FORMAL to put something or someone in danger ‖ 사물 또는 사람을 위험에 처하게 하다. 위태롭게 하다. 위험에 빠뜨리다

im·per·son·al /ɪmˈpəsənəl/ *adj* not showing any feelings of sympathy, friendliness etc. ‖ 동정·우정 등의 감정을 전혀 나타내지 않는. 인간미가 없는. 냉정한: *an impersonal letter* 사무적인 편지 – **impersonally** *adv*

im·per·so·nate /ɪmˈpəsəˌneɪt/ *v* [T] **1** to pretend to be someone else by copying his/her appearance, voice etc., in order to deceive people ‖ 사람을 속이려고 외모·음성 등을 모방하여 다른 사람으로 가장하다. 흉내 내다. …의 (대)역을 하다: *They were arrested for impersonating police officers.* 그들은 경찰관 행세를 한 혐의로 체포되었다. **2** to copy someone's voice and behavior in order to make people laugh ‖ 사람을 웃기려고 다른 사람의 목소리와 행동을 모방하다. 흉내 내다. …으로 분장하다: *a comedian who impersonates politicians* 정치인을 흉내 내는 코미디언 – **impersonator** *n* – **impersonation** /ɪmˌpəsəˈneɪʃən/ *n* [U]

im·per·ti·nent /ɪmˈpət̬n-ənt/ *adj* rude and not respectful, especially to an older person ‖ 특히 연장자에게 무례하고 존경하지 않는. 건방진. 불손한: *asking impertinent questions* 불손한 질문하기 – **impertinence** *n* [U]

im·per·vi·ous /ɪmˈpəviəs/ *adj* **1** not affected or influenced by something ‖ 어떤 것의 작용이나 영향을 받지 않는. 둔감한. …을 느끼지 못하는: *He seemed impervious to the noise around him.* 그는 주변의 소음에 둔감한 듯이 보였다. **2** not allowing anything to pass through ‖ 아무 것도 통과를 허용하지 않는. 통과시키지 않는. 불침투성의. 새지 않는: *Clothing must be impervious to cold and rain for the climbers to survive.* 등반자의 생존을 위해서 등산복은 반드시 추위와 빗물을 차단해야 한다.

im·pet·u·ous /ɪmˈpɛtʃuəs/ *adj* tending to do things quickly, without thinking ‖ 생각 없이 신속하게 어떤 일을 하는 경향이 있는. 충동적인. 성급한. 경솔한: *an impetuous decision to get married* 결혼하려는 성급한 결정 / *She is impetuous and stubborn.* 그녀는 충동적이고 완고하다. – **impetuously** *adv*

im·pe·tus /ˈɪmpətəs/ *n* [U] **1** an influence that makes something happen, or happen more quickly ‖ 어떤 일을 발생

하게 하거나 더 신속히 발생하게 하는 영
향력. 힘. 반동력. 자극. 유인: *The
Surgeon General has provided the
impetus for health prevention programs.*
공중위생국장은 건강 예방 프로그램을 촉
진시켜 왔다. **2** TECHNICAL a force that
makes an object start moving, or keeps
it moving ‖ 물체를 움직이기 시작하게 하
거나 계속 움직이게 하는 힘. 기동력. 운
동력

im·pinge /ɪmˈpɪndʒ/ *v*
impinge on/upon sth *phr v* [T] FORMAL
to have an effect, often an unwanted
one, on someone or something ‖ 사람이
나 사물에 종종 바람직 하지 않은 영향을
주다. 악영향을 미치다: *International
politics have impinged on decisions
made in Congress.* 국제 정치 관계는 의
회를 통과한 결정에 악영향을 미쳤다.

imp·ish /ˈɪmpɪʃ/ *adj* behaving like an
IMP ‖ 개구쟁이처럼 행동하는. 장난꾸러기
의: *an impish laugh* 장난기 있는 웃음 –
impishly *adv*

im·plac·a·ble /ɪmˈplækəbəl/ *adj* very
determined to continue opposing
someone or something ‖ 단호하게 사람
또는 사물을 계속 반대하는. 앙심깊은. 무
자비한. 냉혹한: *an implacable enemy* 무
자비한 적 – **implacably** *adv*

im·plant¹ /ɪmˈplænt/ *v* [T] **1** to put
something into someone's body by a
medical operation ‖ 의료 수술로 신체에
어떤 것을 끼워 넣다. 이식하다: *Doctors
implanted a new lens in her eye.* 의사들
은 그녀의 안구에 새로운 수정체를 이식했
다. **2** to influence someone so that s/he
believes or feels something strongly ‖ 어
떤 것을 강렬하게 믿거나 느끼게 사람에게
영향을 주다. (마음에) 심다. 불어넣다:
*the patriotism implanted in him by his
father* 그의 아버지가 그에게 심어준 애국
심

im·plant² /ˈɪmplænt/ *n* something that
has been put into someone's body in a
medical operation ‖ 의료 수술로 사람의
신체에 삽입되는 것. 임플란트. 보형물:
silicon breast implants 실리콘 유방 보형
물

im·plau·si·ble /ɪmˈplɔːzəbəl/ *adj*
difficult to believe and not likely to be
true ‖ 믿기 어렵고 사실일 것 같지 않은.
미심쩍은: *an implausible excuse* 미심쩍
은 변명

im·ple·ment¹ /ˈɪmpləˌmɛnt/ *v* [T] if you
implement a plan, process etc., you
begin to make it happen ‖ 계획·과정 등
이 수행되도록 시작하다. 실행[이행]하다:
When will Congress implement its

welfare reforms? 의회는 언제 그 복지 개
혁을 실시할 것입니까? – **implemen-
tation** /ˌɪmpləmənˈteɪʃən/ *n* [U]

im·ple·ment² /ˈɪmpləmənt/ *n* a large
tool or instrument with no motor ‖ 모터
없는 큰 도구나 기구. 용구. 비품:
farming implements 농기구

im·pli·cate /ˈɪmplɪˌkeɪt/ *v* [T] to show
that someone is involved in something
wrong ‖ 어떤 사람이 나쁜 일에 관련되어
있음을 나타내다. …을 …에 말려들게 하
다. 관련[연루]시키다: *The witness
implicated two other men in the
robbery.* 그 증인은 다른 두 남자가 강도
사건에 연루되어 있음을 시사했다.

im·pli·ca·tion /ˌɪmplɪˈkeɪʃən/ *n* **1** a
possible effect or result of a plan, action
etc. ‖ 계획·행위 등의 가능한 영향이나 결
과: *What are the implications of a
disaster in the nuclear power industry?*
핵 발전 산업에서 재해의 결과는 무엇입니
까? **2** [C, U] something you do not say
directly but that you want people to
understand ‖ 직접적으로 언급하지는 않
지만 사람들이 이해하기를 바라는 것. 함
축. 언외의 뜻. 암시: *I don't like the
implication that I was lying.* 내가 거짓
말하고 있었다는 식의 말투가 싫다. **3** [U]
the act of making a statement that
suggests that someone has done
something wrong or illegal ‖ 어떤 사람이
잘못되거나 불법적인 행위를 한 것을 시사
하는 말을 하는 행위. 연루. 관련. 밀접한
관계: *the implication of the bank
president in the theft* 은행장의 절도 사건
연루

im·plic·it /ɪmˈplɪsɪt/ *adj* **1** suggested or
understood but not stated directly ‖ 직접
적으로 언급되지는 않고 시사되거나 이해
된. 무언의. 암묵의. 함축적인: *There was
implicit criticism in the principal's
statement.* 교장의 말 가운데에는 암묵적
인 비난이 들어 있었다. **2** complete and
containing no doubts ‖ 완전하고 의심을
품지 않은. 절대[무조건]적인. 맹목적인:
*an implicit faith in her husband's
faithfulness* 남편의 충실성에 대한 그녀의
절대적인 신뢰 **3 be implicit in** FORMAL to
be a central part of something, without
being stated ‖ 언급되지 않은 채 어떤 일
의 중심 부분이 되다. 잠재[내재]되어 있
다: *Risk is implicit in owning a business.*
사업체를 소유하는 데에는 위험성이 내재
되어 있다. – **implicitly** *adv* —compare
EXPLICIT

im·plode /ɪmˈploʊd/ *v* [I] to explode
inward ‖ 안쪽으로 폭발하다. 내측에 파열
하다

im·plore /ɪmˈplɔr/ v [T] FORMAL to ask for something in an emotional way; BEG ∥ 감정에 호소하는 방법으로 어떤 것을 요구하다. 간청[애원]하다. 탄원하다; ⓨbeg: *Joan implored him not to leave.* 조앤은 그에게 떠나지 말라고 애원했다.

im·ply /ɪmˈplaɪ/ v [T] to suggest that something is true without saying or showing it directly ∥ 직접적으로는 말하거나 나타내지 않고 어떤 것이 사실이라고 시사하다. 함축하다. …의 뜻을 내포하다: *He implied that the money hadn't been lost, but was stolen.* 그는 그 돈이 분실되지 않고 도난당했다고 넌지시 나타냈다. —compare INFER

im·po·lite /ˌɪmpəˈlaɪt/ adj not polite ∥ 예의바르지 못한. 버릇 없는. 무례한: *It would be impolite not to call her back and say "thank you."* 그녀에게 "고맙다"고 답례 전화를 하지 않는 것은 예의바르지 못한 것이다.

im·port¹ /ˈɪmpɔrt/ n 1 [C, U] the business of bringing products into one country from another in order to be sold, or the products that are sold ∥ 제품을 판매하기 위해서 다른 나라에서 한 나라로 제품을 들여오는 사업, 또는 판매되는 제품. 수입. 수입품: *Car imports have risen recently.* 최근에 자동차 수입이 증가해 왔다. —compare EXPORT¹ 2 FORMAL importance or meaning ∥ 중요(성), 또는 의미. 취지. 진의: *a matter of import* 중요한 문제

im·port² /ɪmˈpɔrt/ v [T] to bring something into a country from abroad in order to sell it ∥ 어떤 것을 팔기 위해 해외에서 어떤 나라로 그것을 들여오다. 수입하다: *oil imported from the Middle East* 중동에서 수입한 석유 –**importer** n —compare EXPORT²

im·por·tance /ɪmˈpɔrtns, -pɔrtns/ n [U] 1 the quality of being important ∥ 중요한 성질. 중요성. 중대성: *the importance of regular exercise* 규칙적인 운동의 중요성 / *political issues of great importance* 대단히 중요한 정치적 문제 2 the reason why something is important ∥ 어떤 일이 중요한 이유: *Explain the importance of the Monroe Doctrine in a 750 word essay.* 750자 소론으로 몬로 독트린의 중요성을 설명하시오.

im·por·tant /ɪmˈpɔrtnt, -ˈpɔrtnt/ adj 1 having a big effect or influence ∥ 큰 영향 또는 효과가 있는. 중요한: *important questions* 중요한 문제 / *It's important to explain things carefully to the patient.* 환자에게 상태를 정성들여 꼼꼼히 설명하

는 것은 중요하다. 2 having a lot of power or influence ∥ 큰 세력과 영향을 가진. 유력한. 저명한: *an important senator* 유력한 상원의원 –**importantly** adv —opposite UNIMPORTANT

im·por·ta·tion /ˌɪmpɔrˈteɪʃən/ n [U] the business of bringing goods from another country to sell in your country ∥ 자기 나라에서 팔기 위해 다른 나라에서 상품을 가져오는 사업. 수입

im·pose /ɪmˈpoʊz/ v 1 [T] to introduce a rule, tax, punishment etc. and force people to accept it ∥ 규칙·세금·형벌 등을 도입하여 사람에게 받아들이도록 강요하다. …을 …에게 지우다. 부과하다: *Many countries imposed economic sanctions on South Africa during apartheid.* 많은 국가들이 인종 차별 정책 기간 중에 남아프리카 공화국에 경제적 제재를 가했다. 2 [T] to force someone to have the same ideas, beliefs etc. as you ∥ 남에게 억지로 자신과 같은 견해·신념 등을 갖도록 하다. 강요하다. 간섭하다: *parents imposing their values on their children* 자녀들에게 자신들의 가치관을 강요하는 부모들 3 [I] to unreasonably ask or expect someone to do something ∥ 어떤 일을 하도록 남에게 당치않게 요구하거나 기대하다. 부담을 주다. 폐를 끼치다: *I didn't ask you, because I didn't want to impose.* 나는 너에게 부담을 주고 싶지 않았기에 부탁하지 않았다.

im·pos·ing /ɪmˈpoʊzɪŋ/ adj large and impressive ∥ 크고 인상적인. 으리으리한. 두드러진: *an imposing building* 으리으리한 건물

im·po·si·tion /ˌɪmpəˈzɪʃən/ n something that someone unreasonably expects or asks you to do for him/her ∥ 자신을 위해 남에게 어떤 일을 할 것을 부당하게 기대하거나 요구하는 일. 부담. 부과하기: *They stayed for a month? What an imposition!* 그들이 한 달이나 머물렀다고? 웬 부담이야! 2 [U] the introduction of something such as a rule, tax, or punishment ∥ 규칙[세금, 형벌] 등의 일을 과(課)하기. 부과. 지우기: *the imposition of taxes on cigarettes* 담배에 대한 세금의 부과

im·pos·si·ble /ɪmˈpɑsəbəl/ adj 1 not able to be done or to happen ∥ 실행될 수 없거나 발생할 수 없는. 불가능한. 할 수 없는: *It's impossible to sleep with all this noise.* 이 모든 소음속에서 잠자기란 불가능하다. 2 extremely difficult to deal with ∥ 처리하기에 지극히 어려운. …하기 어려운[무리한]: *an impossible situation* 어려운 상황 3 behaving in an unreasonable and annoying way || 분별 없고 짜증나게 행동하는. 견딜[참을]수 없는. 손댈 수 없는: *You're impossible; you change your mind every day.* 너는 어쩔 도리가 없구나. 매일 변덕을 부리니. **-impossibly** *adv* **-impossibility** /ɪm‚pɑsə'bɪləti/ *n* [C, U]

im·pos·ter /ɪm'pɑstɚ/ *n* someone who pretends to be someone else in order to trick people || 사람을 속이려고 다른 사람인 체하는 사람. 사기꾼. 사칭자. 가짜…

im·po·tent /'ɪmpətənt/ *adj* **1** unable to take effective action because you do not have enough power, strength, or control || 충분한 세력[힘, 지배력]이 없어서 효과적인 조치를 취할 수 없는. …를 전혀 할 수 없는. 무력한: *an impotent city government* 무력한 시 정부 **2** a man who is impotent is unable to have sex because he cannot have an ERECTION || 발기가 되지 않아서 성행위를 할 수 없는. 성교 불능의 **-impotence** *n* [U]

im·pound /ɪm'paʊnd/ *v* [T] LAW if the police or law courts impound your possessions, they take them and keep them until you claim them || 소유자가 청구할 때까지 경찰이나 법원이 남의 소유물을 빼앗아 보관하다. 압수[몰수]하다

im·pov·er·ished /ɪm'pɑvərɪʃt/ *adj* very poor || 매우 가난한. 가난해진. 빈곤에 빠진. 메마른. 불모의

im·prac·ti·cal /ɪm'præktɪkəl/ *adj* **1** an impractical plan, suggestion etc. is not sensible because it would be too expensive or difficult || 계획·제안 등이 너무 비싸거나 어려워서 합리적이지 못한. 비현실적인. 실행 불가능한 **2** not good at dealing with ordinary practical matters || 일상의 현실적인 문제를 처리하기에 좋지 않은. 실용적[실제적]이 아닌 **-impractically** *adv* **-impracticality** /ɪm‚præktɪ'kæləti/ *n* [U]

im·pre·cise /‚ɪmprɪ'saɪs/ *adj* not exact || 정확하지 않은. 모호한: *John's directions were imprecise.* 존의 지시는 애매했다. **-imprecisely** *adv* **-imprecision** /‚ɪmprɪ'sɪʒən/ *n* [U]

im·preg·na·ble /ɪm'prɛgnəbəl/ *adj* very strong and unable to be entered || 매우 견고하고 들어갈 수 없는. 난공불락의: *an impregnable fort* 난공불락의 요새

im·preg·nate /ɪm'prɛg‚neɪt/ *v* [T] FORMAL **1** to make a substance spread completely through something, or to spread completely through something || 어떤 물질이 어떤 것에 완전히 퍼지게 하다, 또는 어떤 것에 완전히 퍼지다. 포화시키다. 스며들게 하다: *paper*

impregnated with perfume 향수가 스며 있는 종이 **2** to make a woman or female animal PREGNANT || 여성 또는 암컷 동물을 임신[수태]시키다. …에 수정시키다

im·press /ɪm'prɛs/ *v* [T] **1** to make someone feel admiration and respect || 남에게 감탄과 존경을 느끼게 하다. …에게 감명을 주다. 인상을 갖게 하다. 감동시키다: *She dresses like that to impress people.* 그녀는 사람들에게 감동을 주려고 그 같은 옷을 입고 있다. / *We were impressed by the size of his art collection.* 우리는 그가 수집한 미술 작품의 규모에 깊은 인상을 받았다. **2** to make the importance of something clear to someone || 남에게 어떤 것의 중요성을 분명히 알게 하다. 명심하게 하다. 심어 주다: *My parents impressed on me the value of an education.* 나의 부모님은 나에게 교육의 가치를 인식 시켰다.

im·pres·sion /ɪm'prɛʃən/ *n* **1** the opinion or feeling you have about someone or something because of the way she, he, or it seems || 사람 또는 사물에 대하여 겉으로 보이는 모습 때문에 사람들이 갖는 견해 또는 감정. 인상: *What were your first impressions of New York?* 뉴욕에 대한 너의 첫 인상은 어떠했니? / *I get the impression that something's wrong here.* 나는 여기서 뭔가 잘못이라는 인상을 받는다. / *It's important to make a good impression at your interview.* 인터뷰에서 좋은 인상을 주는 것이 네게 중요하다. **2 be under the impression (that)** to think that something is true when it is not true || 어떤 일이 사실이 아닐 때 그것이 사실이라고 생각하다. (잘못하여) …이라고 믿다. 착각하게 되다: *I was under the impression that Marcie was coming to dinner too.* 나는 마시도 저녁 식사에 올 거라고 착각했다. **3** the act of copying the speech or behavior of a famous person in order to make people laugh || 사람들을 웃기려고 유명인사의 말이나 행동을 모방하는 행위. 흉내. 연기: *Rich Little did a great impression of Nixon.* 리치 리틀은 닉슨의 흉내를 정말 잘 냈다. **4** the mark left by pressing something into a soft surface || 사물을 부드러운 표면 속으로 눌러서 남은 표시. 자국. 흔적

im·pres·sion·a·ble /ɪm'prɛʃənəbəl/ *adj* easy to be influenced || 영향 받기 쉬운. 민감한. 감수성이 예민한: *The girls are at an impressionable age.* 그 소녀들은 감수성이 예민한 연령이다.

im·pres·sion·is·tic /ɪm‚prɛʃə'nɪstɪk/

adj based on a general feeling of what something is like rather than on details ∥ 상세한 묘사보다 오히려 사물의 형상에 대한 일반적인 느낌에 기초한. 인상적인. 인상에 의한: *an impressionistic account of the events* 인상적인 사건의 설명

im·pres·sive /ɪmˈprɛsɪv/ *adj* causing admiration ∥ 감동을 일으키는. 깊은 감명을 주는. 인상적인. 감동적인: *an impressive performance on the piano* 감동적인 피아노 연주 **- impressively** *adv*

im·print[1] /ˈɪmˌprɪnt/ *n* the mark left by an object that has been pressed into or onto something ∥ 어떤 것의 속이나 위에 물체를 눌러서 남은 표시. 자국. 흔적: *the imprint of her thumb on the clay* 점토 위에 남겨진 그녀의 엄지손가락 자국

im·print[2] /ɪmˈprɪnt/ *v* **be imprinted on your mind/memory** if something is imprinted on your mind or memory, you can never forget it ∥ 어떤 것을 마음이나 기억 등에서 결코 잊을 수 없다. …을 마음/기억에 새기다[각인시키다]

im·pris·on /ɪmˈprɪzən/ *v* [T] to put someone in prison or to keep him/her in a place s/he cannot escape from ∥ 누군가를 교도소에 가두거나 도망갈 수 없는 장소에 잡아두다. 구속하다. 투옥하다: *The government imprisoned the leader of the rebellion.* 정부는 반란 주모자를 투옥했다. **- imprisonment** *n* [U]

im·prob·a·ble /ɪmˈprɑbəbəl/ *adj* **1** not likely to happen or to be true ∥ 일어날 것 같지 않은, 또는 사실일 것 같지 않은. 믿어지지 않는: *It is highly improbable that you will find sharks in these waters.* 네가 이 해역에서 상어를 발견한다는 것은 거의 있을 수 없다. **2** surprising and slightly strange ∥ 놀랍고 약간 이상한. 희한한: *an improbable partnership* 희한한 제휴 **- improbably** *adv* **- improbability** /ɪmˌprɑbəˈbɪləti/ *n* [C, U]

im·promp·tu /ɪmˈprɑmptu/ *adj* done or said without any preparation or planning ∥ 어떤 준비 또는 계획 없이 행해지거나 언급된. 즉석의. 급히 장만한. 임시변통의: *an impromptu speech* 즉석 연설 **- impromptu** *adv*

im·prop·er /ɪmˈprɑpɚ/ *adj* **1** unacceptable according to professional, moral, or social rules of behavior ∥ 직업적[도덕적, 사회적] 행동 규범에 따라 받아들일 수 없는. 그릇된. 타당치 않은. 부적절한: *Many cases of "stomach flu" result from improper cooking of food.* "위장의 탈"이 나는 많은 경우는 음식물의

조리를 부적절하게 한 결과이다. **2** illegal or dishonest ∥ 불법적인. 부정직한. 변칙적인. 온당하지 않은: *The bank's director made an improper use of funds held by the bank.* 그 은행의 행장은 은행이 보유중인 자금을 부정하게 사용했다. **- improperly** *adv* : *improperly dressed* 부적절하게 [노출이 심하게] 입은

im·pro·pri·e·ty /ˌɪmprəˈpraɪəti/ *n* [C, U] FORMAL behavior or an action that is unacceptable according to moral, social, or professional standards ∥ 도덕적[사회적, 직업적] 기준에 따라 받아들일 수 없는 행동이나 행위. 부적당. 잘못. 무례(한 행위)

im·prove /ɪmˈpruv/ *v* [I, T] to become better, or to make something better ∥ 더 나아지다, 또는 어떤 것을 더 나아지게 하다. …을 개선하다. …을 향상시키다: *exercises to improve muscle strength* 근력(筋力)을 강화하는 운동 / *Your math skills have improved this year.* 금년에 너의 수학실력은 나아졌다. **- improved** *adj*

improve on/upon sth *phr v* [T] to do something better than before, or make it better ∥ 어떤 일을 전보다 더 잘하거나 어떤 일을 더 좋아지게 하다. 능가하다. …보다 좋게 하다: *No one's been able to improve on her Olympic record.* 아무도 그녀의 올림픽 기록을 갱신할 수가 없었다.

im·prove·ment /ɪmˈpruvmənt/ *n* **1** [C, U] an act of improving, or the state of being improved ∥ 개선 행위, 또는 개선된 상태. 개선. 향상: *There's certainly been an improvement in Danny's behavior.* 대니의 행동은 확실히 향상되고 있다. / *Your German is getting better, but there's still room for improvement.* (=the possibility of more improvement) 너의 독일어는 점점 향상되고 있지만 아직 개선될 여지가 남아 있다. **2** a change or addition that makes something better ∥ 어떤 것을 더 낫게 하는 변화 또는 추가 개량 공사. 개수(改修) 공사: *home improvements* 주택 개수 공사

im·pro·vise /ˈɪmprəˌvaɪz/ *v* **1** [I, T] to make or do something without any preparation, using what you have ∥ 준비 없이 자기가 갖고 있는 것을 사용해서 어떤 것을 만들거나 하다. 즉석에서 하다. 임시변통으로 만들다: *I left my lesson plans at home, so I'll have to improvise.* 수업 계획서를 집에 두고 와서 임시변통으로 만들어야겠다. **2** [I] to perform music, sing, etc. from your imagination ∥ 상상력으로 음악·노래 등을 공연하거나 연주하다. 즉흥적으로 작곡[연주]하다: *Jazz* *musicians are good at improvising.* 재즈 음악가들은 즉흥적인 연주에 능하다. –

improvisation /ɪm,prɑvə'zeɪʃən/ *n* [C, U]

im·pu·dent /'ɪmpyədənt/ *adj* rude and not showing respect ‖ 무례하고 존경심을 보이지 않는. 사리 분별이 없는. 경박한 – **impudence** *n* [U]

im·pulse /'ɪmpʌls/ *n* **1** a sudden desire to do something without thinking about the results ‖ 결과는 생각하지 않고 어떤 일을 하려는 갑작스런 욕구. 충동: *She resisted the impulse to hit him.* 그녀는 그를 때리고 싶은 충동을 억제했다. / *I bought this shirt on impulse, and now I don't like it.* 나는 이 셔츠를 충동구매했는데 지금은 좋아하지 않는다. **2** TECHNICAL a short electrical signal sent in one direction along a wire or nerve, or through the air ‖ 전선 또는 신경을 따라, 또는 대기를 통해 한 방향으로 보낸 짧은 전기 신호. 충격. 임펄스

im·pul·sive /ɪm'pʌlsɪv/ *adj* tending to do things without thinking about the results, or showing this quality ‖ 결과에 대한 생각 없이 어떤 일을 하곤 하는, 또는 이러한 성질을 나타내는. 충동적인. 일시적 감정에 사로잡힌: *an impulsive shopper* 충동적인 구매자 / *an impulsive decision* 일시적인 감정에 사로잡힌 결정 – **impulsively** *adv*

im·pu·ni·ty /ɪm'pyunəti/ *n* [U] **with impunity** without risk of punishment ‖ 형벌의 위험 없이. 벌을 받지 않고. 무사히: *We cannot let them break laws with impunity.* 우리는 그들이 처벌 받지 않고 법률을 위반하게 놔둘 수는 없다.

im·pure /ɪm'pyʊr/ *adj* mixed with other substances ‖ 다른 물질과 섞인. 불순한. 순수하지 않은: *impure drugs* 다른 것이 섞인 약

im·pu·ri·ty /ɪm'pyʊrəti/ *n* [C, U] a part of an almost pure substance that is of a lower quality, or the state of being IMPURE ‖ 거의 순수한 물질 속에 섞여 있는 순도가 낮은 부분, 또는 불순한 상태. 불순(물): *minerals containing impurities* 불순물을 함유한 광물질

IN the written abbreviation of Indiana ‖ Indiana(인디애나 주)의 약어

in¹ /ɪn; weak ən, n/ *prep* **1** used with the name of a container, place, or area to show where something is ‖ 어떤 것의 위치를 나타내기 위해 용기[장소, 지역]의 이름과 같이 쓰여. …안에[에서, 의]: *The paper is in the top drawer in the desk.* 그 종이는 책상의 맨 위 서랍 안에 (들어) 있다. / *I was still in bed at 11:30.* 나는

11시 30분에 잠자리에 여전히 있었다. / *cows standing in a field* 들에 서 있는 암소들 / *He lived in Boston/Spain for 15 years.* 그는 15년간 보스톤[스페인]에 살았다. / *Grandpa's in the hospital.* (=because he is sick or injured) 할아버지는 입원 중이시다. **2** used with the names of months, years, seasons etc. to say when something happened ‖ 어떤 일이 발생한 때를 말하기 위해 월, 년, 계절 등의 이름과 같이 쓰여: *We bought our car in April.* 우리는 4월에 자동차를 구입했다. / *In 1969 the first astronauts landed on the moon.* 1969년에 우주인이 달에 최초로 착륙했다. / *In the winter, we use a wood stove.* 겨울에 우리는 나무를 땔 때는 난로를 사용한다. **3** during a period of time ‖ 일정 기간 동안. …사이에. …동안에: *We finished the whole project in a/one week.* 우리는 일주일 내에 전체 사업 계획을 완료했다. **4** at the end of a period of time ‖ 일정 기간의 끝에. …내에. …지나서: *Gerry should be home in an hour.* 게리는 한 시간 내에 집에 가야 한다. / *I wonder if the business will still be going in a year.* 나는 1년 후에도 사업이 여전히 잘될지 의문이다. **5** included as part of something ‖ 사물의 일부로서 포함된: *One of the people in the story is a young doctor.* 그 이야기에 나오는 사람들 중의 한 사람은 젊은 의사이다. / *In the first part of the speech, he talked about the environment.* 그 연설의 첫 부분에서 그는 환경에 대해 언급했다. **6 not done sth in years/months/weeks** if you have not done something in years etc., you have not done it for that amount of time ‖ 일정한 시간 동안 어떤 일을 한 적이 없는. …을 수년/수개월/수주일 동안 하지 못한: *I haven't been to the circus in years!* 나는 수년간 서커스(공연)에 가 본 적이 없다. **7** using a particular kind of voice, or a particular way of speaking or writing ‖ 특정한 성질의 목소리를 사용하여, 또는 특별한 방식의 말 또는 글을 사용하여. …(으)로: *"I'm afraid," Violet said in a quiet voice.* "나는 무서워"라고 바이올렛은 조용한 목소리로 말했다. / *Their parents always talk to them in Italian.* 그들의 부모는 항상 그들에게 이태리어로 말한다. / *Do not write in pen on this test.* 이 시험에서는 펜으로 쓰지 말아라. **8** working at a particular kind of job ‖ 특정한 종류의 직업에 종사하는. …에 종사[소속]하고. …을 하고: *She's in advertising.* 그녀는 광고업에 종사하고 있다. **9** arranged in a particular way, often to form a group or shape ‖ 종종 집

단 또는 형상을 이루기 위해 특정 방식으로 배열된. …으로. …의: *Stand against the wall in a line.* 벽에 기대어 한 줄로 서라. / *He had made a bowl in the shape of a heart.* 그는 하트[심장] 모양의 사발을 만들었다. / *Put the words in alphabetical order.* 단어들을 알파벳순으로 놓아라. **10** used in order to show the connection between two ideas or subjects ‖ 두 개의 생각 또는 주제 사이의 연관을 나타내는 데에 쓰여: *I was never interested in sports as a kid.* 나는 아이였을 때 스포츠에는 관심이 조금도 없었다. **11** used before the bigger number when you are talking about a relationship between two numbers ‖ 두 숫자 사이의 관계에 대하여 말할 때 보다 큰 숫자 앞에 쓰여: *1 in 10 women* (=of all women) *have the disease.* 여자 10명 중 1명은 질병이 있다. **12 in shock/ horror etc.** used in order to describe a strong feeling someone has when s/he does something ‖ 사람이 어떤 일을 할 경우에 가지는 강한 감정을 묘사하는 데에 쓰여. 충격으로/겁을 내어: *She looked at me in shock as I told her how everything had gone wrong.* 모든 일이 얼마나 잘못되었는지를 내가 그녀에게 말하자 그녀는 충격으로 나를 바라보았다. **13 in all** used when giving a total amount ‖ 전체 분량을 제시하는 경우에 쓰여. 모두(해서): *Lots of my cousins came to the party. I think there were 25 of us in all.* 많은 내 사촌들이 파티에 왔다. 모두 합해 25명이었다고 생각된다.

in² *adj, adv* **1** so as to be contained inside or surrounded by something ‖ 어떤 것에 의해 안에 담겨지거나 또는 둘러싸이도록. 안에. 안으로: *She pushed the box towards me so that I could put my money in.* 내가 돈을 넣을 수 있도록 그녀는 그 상자를 나에게 밀었다. **2** inside a building, especially the one where you live or work ‖ 특히 거주하거나 근무하는 건물 안에: *Ms. Robinson isn't in yet this morning.* 로빈슨 씨는 오늘 아침 아직 (들어)오지 않았다. / *You're never in when I call.* 내가 전화할 때 너는 언제나 집에 없다. **3** if a plane, bus, train, or boat is in, it has arrived at the airport, station etc. ‖ 비행기・버스・기차・선박이 공항・정류장 등에 도착하여. 들어와: *What time does his bus get in?* 그의 버스는 몇 시에 도착하니? **4** given or sent to a particular place in order to be read or looked at ‖ 읽거나 보게 하려고 특정 장소에 제출하거나 보내는. 제출되어: *Your final papers have to be in by Friday.* 너의 최종 논문

은 금요일까지 제출되어야 한다. **5** if you write, paint, or draw something in, you write it etc. in the correct place ‖ 어떤 것을 적절한 곳에 쓰다・칠하다・그리다. …(안)에: *Fill in the blanks, using a number 2 pencil.* 2번 연필을 사용해서 공란을 채워라. **6** if clothes, colors, etc. are in, they are fashionable ‖ 옷・색상 등이 유행하는: *Long hair is in again.* 긴 머리가 다시 유행한다. **7** if a ball is in during a game, it is inside the area where the game is played ‖ 경기 동안에 경기가 진행되고 있는 지역 안에 공이 있는 **8 be in for sth** if someone is in for something unpleasant, it is about to happen to him/her ‖ 불쾌한 일이 어떤 사람에게 발생하려고 하는. …에 말려들어 있다[들 것 같다]. …을 당하지 않을 수 없게 되다: *She's in for a shock if she thinks we're going to help her pay for it.* 그 빚을 상환하는 데 우리가 도움을 줄 것이라는 것을 그녀가 알게되면 충격을 받게 될 것이 뻔하다. **9 be in on sth** to be involved in doing, talking about, or planning something ‖ 어떤 일을 하는[말하는, 계획하는] 데 관계된. …에 참여한: *The movie asks questions about who was in on the plan to kill Kennedy.* 그 영화는 케네디 암살 계획에 누가 관여했는가에 대한 의문을 제기한다. **10** if the TIDE comes in or is in, the ocean water is at its highest level ‖ 대양의 수위가 가장 높은. (조수가) 밀물인 경우에 **11 in joke** an in joke is one that is only understood by a small group of people ‖ 농담이 소수 집단의 사람들에 의해서만 이해되는

in・a・bil・i・ty /ˌɪnəˈbɪləti/ *n* [singular, U] a lack of the ability, skill etc. to do something ‖ 어떤 일을 하기 위한 능력・기술 등의 부족. 불능. 무능(력): *an inability to work quickly* 신속한 작업 불능

in・ac・ces・si・ble /ˌɪnəkˈsɛsəbəl/ *adj* difficult or impossible to reach ‖ 도달하기 어렵거나 불가능한. 도달할 수 없는. 얻기 어려운: *roads that are inaccessible in winter* 겨울에는 접근하기 어려운 도로

in・ac・cu・ra・cy /ɪnˈækyərəsi/ *n* [C, U] a mistake, or a lack of correctness ‖ 실수, 또는 정확성의 결여. 부정확(한 점): *There were several inaccuracies in the report.* 보고서에는 몇몇의 부정확한 점이 있었다.

in・ac・cu・rate /ɪnˈækyərɪt/ *adj* not completely correct ‖ 완전히 정확하지 않은. 부정확한[확실하지 않은]. 틀린: *an inaccurate description* 정확하지 않은 묘

사 – **inaccurately** *adv*

in·ac·tion /ɪnˈækʃən/ *n* [U] lack of action ‖ 활동의 부족. 무위. 나태. 휴지 (休止): *The city council was criticized for its inaction on the parking problem.* 시의회는 주차 문제에 관해 아무일도 하지 않고 있다고 비난받았다.

in·ac·tive /ɪnˈæktɪv/ *adj* not doing anything or not working ‖ 아무 일도 하지 않거나 움직이지 않는. 활동하지 않는: *inactive members of the club* 클럽의 활동하지 않는 회원들 / *The rate of heart disease among inactive men* (=men who do not exercise) *is much higher than in active men.* 운동하지 않는 사람의 심장병 비율이 운동하는 사람의 경우보다 아주 높다 – **inactivity** /ˌɪnækˈtɪvəti/ *n* [U]

in·ad·e·qua·cy /ɪnˈædəkwəsi/ *n* **1** [U] a feeling that you are unable to deal with situations because you are not as good as other people ‖ 자신이 다른 사람들만큼 뛰어나지 못해서 상황을 처리할 수 없다는 느낌. 부적당. 부적절: *Not having a job can cause strong feelings of inadequacy.* 직업이 없다는 것은 강한 무능(無能)감을 야기할 수 있다. **2** [C, U] the fact of not being good enough for a particular purpose, or something that is not good enough ‖ 특정한 목적에 충분할 정도로 좋지는 않다는 사실, 또는 충분하게 좋지는 않은 사물. 부족. 부적당[불충분]한 점: *the inadequacy of safety standards in the coal mines.* 석탄 광산 내 안전 기준의 미비한 점 / *The airlines don't want the public to know about the system's inadequacies.* 항공사들은 일반인들이 시스템의 부적설성에 대해 아는 것을 원치 않는다.

in·ad·e·quate /ɪnˈædəkwɪt/ *adj* not good enough for a particular purpose ‖ 특정한 목적에 충분히 좋지 않은. 불충분한. 부적당한: *inadequate health care services* 불충분한 보건 진료 서비스 – **inadequately** *adv*

in·ad·mis·si·ble /ˌɪnədˈmɪsəbəl/ *adj* FORMAL not allowed ‖ 허용되지 않는. 용인할 수 없는: *Some of the evidence was inadmissible in court.* 일부 증거는 법정에서 인용(認容)되지 않았다.

in·ad·vert·ent·ly /ˌɪnədˈvɚtntli/ *adv* without intending to do something ‖ 어떤 일을 하려는 의도가 없는. 부주의하게. 무심코. 우연히: *She inadvertently hit the brakes.* 그녀는 무심코 브레이크를 걸었다. – **inadvertent** *adj*

in·ad·vis·a·ble /ˌɪnədˈvaɪzəbəl/ *adj* an inadvisable decision is not sensible; UNWISE ‖ 결정 등이 현명하지 못한. 권할 수 없는. 부적당한; ⊞ unwise: *It's inadvisable to take medicine without asking your doctor.* 의사와 상의도 않고 약을 먹는 것은 현명하지 못한 것이다.

in·al·ien·a·ble /ɪnˈeɪlyənəbəl/ *adj* FORMAL an inalienable right cannot be taken away from you ‖ 권리 등을 빼앗을 수 없는. 양도할 수 없는

in·ane /ɪˈneɪn/ *adj* extremely stupid or without much meaning ‖ 아주 어리석은 또는 많은 의미가 없는. 무의미한. 공허한: *inane jokes* 무의미한 농담

in·an·i·mate /ɪnˈænəmɪt/ *adj* not living ‖ 살아 있지 않은. 죽은: *Rocks are inanimate objects.* 바위는 무생물이다.

in·ap·pro·pri·ate /ˌɪnəˈproʊpriɪt/ *adj* not suitable or correct for a particular purpose or situation ‖ 특정한 목적 또는 상황에 대하여 적합하거나 알맞지 않은. 부적당한. 어울리지 않는: *Martin's behavior at the funeral was inappropriate.* 장례식에서 마틴의 행동은 적절치 못했다. – **inappropriately** *adv*

in·ar·tic·u·late /ˌɪnɑrˈtɪkyəlɪt/ *adj* not able to express yourself or speak clearly ‖ 자신을 명확히 표현할 수 없는, 또는 분명히 말을 못하는. 말로 표현 못하는: *His grief made him inarticulate.* 그는 슬픔으로 인해서 말을 제대로 못했다.

in·as·much as /ˌɪnəzˈʧʌm əz/ *conjunction* FORMAL used in order to begin a phrase that explains the rest of your sentence by showing the limited way that it is true ‖ 사실인 것을 한정적으로 나타냄으로써 나머지 문장을 설명하는 어구를 시작하는 데에 쓰여. …이므로. …하므로: *She's guilty, inasmuch as she knew what the other girls were planning to do.* 그녀는 다른 소녀들이 무엇을 하려고 했는지를 알고 있었기 때문에 유죄이다.

in·au·di·ble /ɪnˈɔdəbəl/ *adj* too quiet to be heard ‖ 너무 조용해서 들리지 않는. 들리지 않는. 알아들을 수 없는: *Her reply was inaudible.* 그녀의 대답은 알아들을 수 없었다. – **inaudibly** *adv*

in·au·gu·rate /ɪˈnɔgyəˌreɪt/ *v* [T] **1** to have an official ceremony in order to show that someone is beginning an important job ‖ 사람이 중요한 일을 시작하려고 한다는 것을 나타내기 위해 공식적인 의식을 가지다. 취임시키다: *The President is inaugurated in January.* 대통령은 1월에 취임식을 가진다. **2** to open a new building or start a new service with a ceremony ‖ 신축 건물을 개방하다, 또는 의식과 더불어 새로운 서비스를 시작

하다. 개회[개통, 낙성]식을 하다. 정식으로 발족하다 – **inaugural** /ɪˈnɔgyərəl/ *adj* – **inauguration** /ɪˌnɔgyəˈreɪʃən/ *n* [C, U]

in·aus·pi·cious /ˌɪnɔˈspɪʃəs/ *adj* FORMAL seeming to show that the future will be unlucky || 미래가 불길할 것을 나타내는 듯한. 불길한: *an inauspicious start to our trip* 불길한 우리 여행의 출발

in·be·tween /ˌ.ˈ./ *adj* INFORMAL in the middle of two points, sizes, etc. || 두 개의 지점·크기 등의 중간에 있는. 중간적인. 중간의: *She's at that in-between age, neither a girl nor a woman.* 그녀는 소녀도 아니고 여성도 아닌 그 중간의 나이에 있다.

in·born /ˌɪnˈbɔrn·/ *adj* an inborn quality or ability is one that you have had naturally since birth || 성질이나 능력이 태어날 때부터 선천적으로 갖고 있는 것인. 천부의. 선천적인: *an inborn sense of justice* 타고난 정의감

in·box /ˈɪnbaks/ *n* a place on a computer which stores the E-MAIL messages that you have received || 수신된 이메일 메시지를 저장하는 컴퓨터 내의 장소. 인박스

in·bred /ˌɪnˈbrɛd·/ *adj* **1** having developed as a natural part of your character || 성격의 선천적인 일부로서 개발된. 타고난. 천부의: *an inbred sense of respect* 타고난 배려심 **2** produced by the breeding of closely related members of a family, which often causes problems || 종종 문제를 일으키는, 밀접하게 연관된 가족 구성원 사이의 생식에 의해 낳은. 근친 교배의: *an inbred genetic defect* 근친 교배로 인한 유전적인 결함 – **inbreeding** /ˈɪnˌbridɪŋ/ *n* [U]

Inc. /ɪŋk, ɪnˈkɔrpəˌreɪtɪd/ the written abbreviation of INCORPORATED || incorporated의 약어: *General Motors Inc.* 제너럴 모터스 주식회사

in·cal·cu·la·ble /ɪnˈkælkyələbəl/ *adj* too many or too great to be measured || 측정하기에 너무 많거나 너무 큰. 막대한. 무수한 : *The scandal has done incalculable damage to the college's reputation.* 그 스캔들은 그 대학의 명성을 크게 손상시켰다.

in·can·des·cent /ˌɪnkənˈdɛsənt/ *adj* giving a bright light when heated || 가열되면 밝은 빛을 내는. (빛이) 고온에 의해 생기는 – **incandescence** *n* [U]

in·can·ta·tion /ˌɪnkænˈteɪʃən/ *n* [C, U] a set of special words that someone uses in magic, or the act of saying these words || 마술에서 쓰이는 일련의 특별한

말, 또는 이런 말을 하는 행위. 주문(을 외기). 마술

in·ca·pa·ble /ɪnˈkeɪpəbəl/ *adj* unable to do something or to feel a particular emotion || 어떤 일을 할 수 없거나 특별한 감정을 느끼지 못하는. …을 할[느낄] 능력 없는: *Debbie is incapable of being sympathetic.* 데비는 동정이라는 것을 모른다. – **incapably** *adv*

in·ca·pac·i·tate /ˌɪnkəˈpæsəˌteɪt/ *v* [T] to make someone too sick or weak to live or work normally || 너무 아프거나 약하여 정상적으로 생활하거나 일하기 어렵게 만들다. …을 무능[부적격]하게 하다: *He was incapacitated for a while after the operation.* 그는 수술 후에 잠시 동안 아무 일도 할 수 없었다.

in·ca·pac·i·ty /ˌɪnkəˈpæsəti/ *n* [U] lack of ability, strength, or power to do something, especially because you are sick || 특히 아파서 어떤 것을 할 능력[힘, 체력]이 부족한. 무력. 무능. 부적격

in·car·cer·ate /ɪnˈkɑrsəˌreɪt/ *v* [T] FORMAL to put someone in a prison || 남을 교도소에 가두다. 투옥[감금]하다 – **incarceration** /ɪnˌkɑrsəˈreɪʃən/ *n* [U]

in·car·nate /ɪnˈkɑrnɪt, -ˌneɪt/ *adj* the devil/evil etc. incarnate someone who is considered to be the human form of evil etc. || 악령 등이 인간의 형태를 한 것으로 여겨지는 존재. 악마/악의 화신

in·car·na·tion /ˌɪnkɑrˈneɪʃən/ *n* **1** a time before or after the life you are living now when, according to some religions, you were alive in the form of a different person or animal || 몇몇 종교에서 믿는 다른 사람 또는 동물의 형태로 살았던, 현세 삶의 이전 또는 이후의 시간. 전생. 전세. 내세 **2 be the incarnation of goodness/evil etc.** to represent perfect goodness etc. in the way you live || 사람이 사는 방식에서 완전한 선(善) 등을 나타내다. 선/악 등의 전형이 되다

in·cen·di·ar·y /ɪnˈsɛndiˌɛri/ *adj* **1** incendiary bomb/device etc. a bomb etc. designed to cause a fire || 화재를 일으키기 위해 고안된 폭탄 등. 소이탄/방화장치 **2** an incendiary speech or piece of writing is intended to make people angry and is likely to cause trouble || 말 또는 글 등이 사람을 화나게 할 의도가 있고 문제를 일으키는 경향이 있는. 선동적인. 자극적인

in·cense¹ /ˈɪnsɛns/ *n* [U] a substance that has a pleasant smell when you burn it || 태울 때 좋은 냄새가 나는 물질. 향. 방향

in·cense² /ɪnˈsɛns/ *v* [T] to make

someone extremely angry ‖ 남을 아주 화
나게 하다. 격분시키다: *I was incensed by
his racist attitudes!* 나는 그의 인종 차별
적 태도에 격분했어!

in·cen·tive /ɪnˈsɛntɪv/ *n* [C, U]
something that encourages you to work
harder, start new activities etc. ‖ 일을
더 열심히 하도록 또는 새로운 활동 등을
시작하도록 고무시키는 것. 유인. 자극.
동 기 : *The government provides
incentives for new businesses.* 정부는 신
규 사업을 위한 장려금을 제공하고 있다.

in·cep·tion /ɪnˈsɛpʃən/ *n* [singular]
FORMAL the start of an organization or
institution ‖ 조직 또는 기구의 시작. 개
시 . 시초: *He has worked for the
company since its inception in 1970.* 그
는 1970년 창립 초기부터 회사에 근무했
다.

in·ces·sant /ɪnˈsɛsənt/ *adj* without
stopping ‖ 멈추지 않는. 끊임없는. 그칠
새 없는: *the incessant traffic noise* 끊임
없는 교통 소음 **– incessantly** *adv*

in·cest /ˈɪnsɛst/ *n* [U] illegal sex
between people who are closely part of
the same family ‖ 같은 가족의 가까운 구
성원들 간의 허용되지 않는 성행위. 근친
상간(죄)

in·ces·tu·ous /ɪnˈsɛstʃuəs/ *adj* relating
to INCEST ‖ 근친상간과 관련된. 근친상간
의 . 근친상간 죄를 저지른 **–
incestuously** *adv*

inch¹ /ɪntʃ/, *written abbreviation* **in.** *n,*
plural **inches** **1** a unit for measuring
length, equal to 1/12 of a foot or 2.54
centimeters ‖ foot(피트)의 12분의 1 또
는 2.54센티미터에 상당하는 길이의 측정
단위 **2 every inch** all of someone or
something ‖ 모든 사람 또는 사물. 완전
히 . 구석구석. 모든 점에서: *Pictures
cover every inch of wall space.* 벽의 모
든 공간이 그림으로 덮여 있다. **3 inch by
inch** very slowly or by a small amount
at a time ‖ 한 번에 매우 천천히, 또는 작
은 분량으로. 조금씩: *The area was
searched inch by inch for landmines.* 지
뢰들을 찾기 위해 그 지역이 샅샅이 수색
되었다. **4 not give/budge an inch** to
refuse to change your opinions at all ‖
자신의 의견을 조금도 바꾸려 하지 않다.
한 치도 물러서지 않다: *At first Will
refused to give an inch in the argument.*
처음에 윌은 토론에서 한 발짝도 양보하기
를 거부했다.

inch² *v* [I, T] to move very slowly and
carefully, or to move something this
way ‖ 매우 천천히·신중하게 움직이다, 또
는 이런 방식으로 사물을 움직이다. 조금

씩 움직이다: *I got a glass of wine and
inched my way across the crowded
room.* 나는 와인 잔을 들고 사람이 가득한
방을 천천히 가로질러 나아갔다.

in·ci·dence /ˈɪnsədəns/ *n* [singular]
FORMAL the number of times something
happens ‖ 어떤 것의 발생 횟수. 발생(의
정도[범위, 율]): *an increased incidence
of heart attacks* 증가된 심장마비 발생율

in·ci·dent /ˈɪnsədənt/ *n* something
unusual, serious, or violent that
happens ‖ 발생한 특별한[심각한, 폭력적
인] 일. 사건. 생긴 일: *Any witnesses to
the incident should speak to the police.*
그 사건의 증인은 누구라도 경찰에게 진술
해야 한다.

in·ci·den·tal /ˌɪnsəˈdɛntl/ *adj*
happening or existing in connection
with something else that is more
important ‖ 더욱 중요한 다른 일에 연관
되어 발생하거나 존재하는. …에 부수하여
일어나는. 따르기 마련인. 부수적인:
*Keep a record of your incidental
expenses on your trip.* 여행 중에 생긴
부수적인 비용을 기록해 나가라.

in·ci·den·tal·ly /ˌɪnsəˈdɛntli/ *adv* used
when giving additional information, or
when changing the subject of a
conversation ‖ 추가적인 정보를 줄 때, 또
는 대화 주제를 바꿀 때에 쓰여. 첨언하
면. 말이 난 김에 말인데. 그런데:
*Incidentally, Jenny's coming over
tonight.* 그런데, 오늘밤에 제니가 올 거야.

in·cin·er·ate /ɪnˈsɪnəˌreɪt/ *v* [T] to burn
something in order to destroy it ‖ 파괴하
기 위해 어떤 것을 태우다. 소각하다 **–
incineration** /ɪnˌsɪnəˈreɪʃən/ *n* [U]

in·cin·er·a·tor /ɪnˈsɪnəˌreɪtə/ *n* a
machine that burns things at very high
temperatures ‖ 아주 높은 온도로 물체를
태우는 기계. 소각로. 화장로

in·cip·i·ent /ɪnˈsɪpiənt/ *adj* FORMAL
starting to happen or exist ‖ 발생하거나
존재하기 시작하는. 초기의. 발단의

in·ci·sion /ɪnˈsɪʒən/ *n* TECHNICAL a cut
that a doctor makes in someone's body
during an operation ‖ 의사가 수술 중 사
람의 신체에 내는 칼로 절개한 자국

in·ci·sive /ɪnˈsaɪsɪv/ *adj* incisive words,
remarks etc. are very direct and deal
with the most important part of a
subject ‖ 말·진술 등이 매우 직접적이고
주제의 가장 중요한 부분을 다루는. 신랄
한. 통렬한. 날카로운

in·ci·sor /ɪnˈsaɪzə/ *n* one of your eight
front teeth that have sharp edges ‖ 8개
의 앞니 중 하나로 끝이 날카로운 이빨. 앞
니

in·cite /ɪn'saɪt/ v [T] to deliberately make someone feel so angry or excited that s/he does something bad ‖ 고의로 남을 화나게 하거나 흥분하게 해서 나쁜 일을 하게 만들다. 자극하다. 불러일으키다. 고무하다: *One man was jailed for inciting a riot.* 한 남자가 폭동을 선동하여 투옥되었다.

in·cli·na·tion /ˌɪnklə'neɪʃən/ n 1 [C, U] the desire to do something ‖ 어떤 것을 하려는 욕구. 의향. 기분: *I didn't have the time or inclination to go with them.* 나는 그들과 같이 갈 시간이나 의향이 없었다. 2 [C, U] a tendency to think or behave in a particular way ‖ 특정하게 생각하거나 행동하려는 경향. 성향. 기호: *his inclination to act violently* 그의 난폭한 행동 성향

in·cline¹ /ɪn'klaɪn/ v [I, T] to slope at a particular angle, or make something do this ‖ 특정한 각도로 기울다, 또는 물체를 이렇게 만들다. 경사지[게 하]다

in·cline² /'ɪnklaɪn/ n a slope ‖ 경사면: *a steep incline* 가파른 경사면

in·clined /ɪn'klaɪnd/ adj 1 **be inclined to agree/believe/think etc.** to have a particular opinion, but not have it very strongly ‖ 매우 강하진 않지만 특별한 견해를 갖고 있다. 동의하고/믿고/생각하고 싶어지다: *I'm inclined to agree with you, but I don't really know.* 나는 너에게 동의하고 싶지만 정말 모른다. 2 wanting to do something ‖ 어떤 일을 하길 바라는. 마음이 내키는: *My client is not inclined to speak with reporters.* 나의 의뢰인은 기자들과 이야기하기를 원하지 않는다. 3 likely or tending to do something ‖ 어떤 일을 할 것 같은 또는 하는 경향이 있는. 쉽게 …해지는 (경향이 있는): *He's inclined to get upset over small things.* 그는 작은 일에도 쉽게 당황하는 경향이 있다.

in·clude /ɪn'klud/ v [T] 1 if a group or set includes something or someone, it has that person or thing as one of its parts ‖ 한 집단 또는 세트가 그것의 일부분으로서 사물이나 사람을 가지다. 포함하다: *The price includes your flight, hotel, and car rental.* 그 가격에는 항공료·호텔 요금·차 임대료가 포함된다. 2 to make someone or something part of a larger group or set ‖ 사람이나 사물을 보다 큰 그룹 또는 세트의 일부분으로 만들다. 포함시키다: *Is my name included on the list?* 내 이름이 명부에 들어 있습니까? / *Try to include Rosie more in your games, Sam.* 샘, 너 노는 데에 로지를 더 끼워 줘라. —opposite EXCLUDE

in·clud·ing /ɪn'kludɪŋ/ prep used in order to show that someone or something is part of a larger group or set that you are talking about ‖ 사람 또는 사물이 언급하고 있는 보다 큰 그룹 또는 세트의 일부라는 것을 나타내는 데에 쓰여. …을 포함한[하여]: *There were 20 people in the room, including the teacher.* 방에는 교사를 포함하여 20명이 있었다. / *We only paid $12 for dinner, including the tip.* 우리는 팁을 포함하여 저녁 식사 대금으로 12달러를 지불했을 뿐이다. —opposite EXCLUDING

in·clu·sion /ɪn'kluʒən/ n 1 [U] the action of including someone or something in a larger group or set, or the fact of being included in one ‖ 보다 큰 그룹 또는 세트에 사람이나 사물을 포함하는 행위, 또는 하나에 포함되어 있는 사실. 포함. 함유. 포괄: *Here's the list of books we're considering for inclusion on the reading list.* 우리가 독서 목록에 포함시키려고 검토 중인 도서 목록이 여기 있다. 2 someone or something that is included ‖ 포함된 사람 또는 물체. 함유물

in·clu·sive /ɪn'klusɪv/ adj including all the possible information, parts, numbers etc. ‖ 모든 가능한 정보·부분·숫자를 포함한. 일체를 포함한. 포괄적인: *an all inclusive guide to the restaurants in Manhattan* 맨해튼의 레스토랑에 대한 총괄적인 안내서

in·cog·ni·to /ˌɪnkɑg'nitoʊ/ adv if a famous person does something incognito, s/he is hiding who s/he really is ‖ 유명 인사 등이 실제로 자신이 누구인지를 숨기고. 익명으로

in·co·her·ent /ˌɪnkoʊ'hɪrənt/ adj 1 badly explained and unable to be understood ‖ 서투르게 설명되어 이해할 수 없는. 앞뒤가 맞지 않는. 지리멸렬한: *a dull incoherent speech* 지루하고 논리에 맞지 않는 연설 2 not talking clearly ‖ 분명히 말하지 않는. 횡설수설하는. 허튼소리 하는: *The two women were incoherent after their ordeal.* 그 두 여자는 호된 시련 뒤에 횡설수설했다. — **incoherently** adv

in·come /'ɪnkʌm, 'ɪŋ-/ n [C, U] the money that you earn from working or making INVESTMENTS ‖ 일하거나 투자해서 벌어들이는 돈. 수입. 소득: *a good/high/low income* 상당한[고, 저] 소득 —see usage note at PAY²

income tax /'.. ˌ./ n [U] tax paid on the money you earn ‖ 소득액에 대해 지급한 세금. 소득세

in·com·ing /ˈɪnˌkʌmɪŋ/ adj 1 **incoming call/letter/fax** a telephone call, letter, or FAX that you receive ‖ 걸려오는 전화/편지/팩스 2 coming toward a place, or about to arrive ‖ 한 장소로 들어오는, 또는 도착하려 하는. 들어오는. 들어온: the incoming tide 밀물

in·com·mu·ni·ca·do /ˌɪnkəˌmyunɪˈkadoʊ/ adj, adv not allowed or not wanting to communicate with anyone ‖ 누구와도 의사소통이 허용되지 않는 또는 원하지 않는. …와 연락이 끊겨[끊긴]

in·com·pa·ra·ble /ɪnˈkɑmpərəbəl/ adj so impressive, beautiful etc. that nothing or no one is better ‖ 너무 인상적이고 아름다워서 어떤 사물이나 사람도 이보다 더 좋지 않은. 비할 데 없는. 비교가 안되는. 빼어난: her incomparable beauty/talents 그녀의 비길 데 없는 아름다움[재능] – **incomparably** adv

in·com·pat·i·ble /ˌɪnkəmˈpætəbəl/ adj too different to be able to work together well or have a good relationship ‖ 함께 일을 잘 할 수 있거나 좋은 관계를 가질 수 있기에는 너무나 다른. 양립하지 않는. 조화되지 않는. 호환성이 없는: The software is incompatible with the operating system. 그 소프트웨어는 운영 체제와는 호환성이 없다. / Tony and I have always been incompatible. 토니와 나는 항상 서로 통하지 않는다. – **incompatibility** /ˌɪnkəmˌpætəˈbɪləti/ n [U]

in·com·pe·tence /ɪnˈkɑmpətəns/ n [U] lack of ability or skill to do your job ‖ 일을 하는 능력이나 기술의 부족. 무능(력). 무자격. 부적당: The doctor is being charged in court with incompetence. 그 의사는 무자격으로 법정에 고발된 상태이다.

in·com·pe·tent /ɪnˈkɑmpətənt/ adj not having the ability or skill to do your job ‖ 일을 하는 능력이나 기술을 갖지 못한. 무능한. 부적당한: a totally incompetent waitress 매우 서투른 웨이트리스 – **incompetent** n

in·com·plete /ˌɪnkəmˈplit/ adj not having all its parts or not finished yet ‖ 모든 부분들을 갖추지 못한, 또는 아직 완성하지 못한. 불완전한. 불충분한: an incomplete sentence 불완전한 문장 / The report is still incomplete. 그 보고서는 아직 불완전하다.

in·com·pre·hen·si·ble /ˌɪnkɑmprɪˈhɛnsəbəl/ adj impossible to understand ‖ 이해하기 불가능한. 이해할 수 없는. 불가해한: incomprehensible legal language 이해할 수 없는 법률 용어

in·con·ceiv·a·ble /ˌɪnkənˈsivəbəl/ adj too strange or unusual to seem real or possible ‖ 너무나 이상하거나 유별나서 실제적이거나 가능한 것으로 보이지 않는. 믿기 어려운. 생각조차 못한: It was inconceivable that such a quiet man could be violent. 그렇게 얌전한 남자가 폭력적일 수 있다는 것은 상상할 수 없는 일이었다. – **inconceivably** adv

in·con·clu·sive /ˌɪnkənˈklusɪv/ adj not leading to any decision or result ‖ 어떠한 결정이나 결과를 이끌지 않는. 결론에 이르지 못하는. 결정적이 아닌: Our experiments are inconclusive. 우리의 실험은 결정적인 것이 아니다. / inconclusive evidence (=not proving anything) 결정적이지 못한 증거 – **inconclusively** adv

in·con·gru·ous /ɪnˈkɑŋgruəs/ adj seeming to be wrong or unusual in a particular situation ‖ 특정한 상황에서 잘 못되거나 유별나게 보이는. 일치하지 않는. 부조리한: Her quiet voice seemed incongruous with her hard face. 그녀의 차분한 목소리는 그녀의 험상궂은 얼굴과 어울리지 않아 보였다. – **incongruity** /ˌɪnkənˈgruəti/ n [C, U] – **incongruously** /ɪnˈkɑŋgruəsli/ adv

in·con·se·quen·tial /ˌɪnkɑnsəˈkwɛnʃəl/ adj FORMAL not important; INSIGNIFICANT ‖ 중요하지 않은. 사소한 ⓟ insignificant: an inconsequential role in a soap opera 멜로 드라마에서의 비중없는 역할 – **inconsequentially** adv

in·con·sid·er·ate /ˌɪnkənˈsɪdərɪt/ adj not caring about other people's needs or feelings ‖ 다른 사람의 요구나 감정에 대해서 개의치 않는. 배려하지 않는. (남을 헤아리는) 마음이 없는: It was really inconsiderate of you not to call and say you'd be late. 네가 전화해서 늦는다고 말하지 않은 것은 정말 사려 깊지 못한 행동이었다. – **inconsiderately** adv — opposite CONSIDERATE

in·con·sist·en·cy /ˌɪnkənˈsɪstənsi/ n 1 [C, U] information or a statement that cannot be true if the rest of the information or statement is true, or the state of being INCONSISTENT in this way ‖ 정보나 진술의 나머지 부분이 사실이면, 정보나 진술이 사실일 리가 없는, 또는 이런 식으로 모순된 상태. 불일치. 모순. 모순된 일[행위, 말]: The police became suspicious because of the inconsistencies in her statement. 경찰은 그녀의 진술이 모순되기 때문에 그녀를 의심하게 되었다. 2 [U] the quality of changing your ideas too often or of doing something differently each time, so that people do not know what you think or want ‖ 생각이나 원하는 것이 무엇인지 사람들이 알 수 없을 만큼 생각을 너무 자주 바꾸거나 시시각각으로 다르게 행하는 성질. 비일관성. 일관적이지 못함. 불일치. 무정견: *The team's inconsistency last season disappointed many fans.* 지난 시즌 그 팀의 모순된 행동은 많은 팬들을 실망시켰다. —opposite CONSISTENCY

in·con·sist·ent /ˌɪnkən'sɪstənt/ *adj* **1** two ideas or statements that are inconsistent are different and cannot both be true ‖ 두 개의 생각 또는 진술이 다르고 두 개 모두가 사실일 수 없는. 일치하지 않는. 앞뒤가 맞지 않는. 모순된: *We're getting inconsistent results from the lab tests.* 우리는 실험실 테스트에서 모순된 결과를 얻고 있다. **2** not doing things in the same way each time, or not following an expected principle or standard ‖ 매번 같은 방식으로 일을 하지 않는, 또는 예상된 원칙이나 기준에 따르지 않는. 일관성이 없는. 변덕스러운: *I'm not being inconsistent! This is a different situation.* 내가 변덕스러운 것이 아니다! 이것은 상황이 다른 거야. / *What they have done is inconsistent with the agreement that they made with us.* 그들이 한 행위는 우리와 체결한 계약에 모순된다. **– inconsistently** *adv* —opposite CONSISTENT

in·con·sol·a·ble /ˌɪnkən'soʊləbəl/ *adj* so sad that you cannot be comforted ‖ 너무나 슬퍼서 위로받을 수 없는. 슬픔에 잠긴. 낙심한. 낙담한: *His widow was inconsolable.* 그의 미망인은 슬픔에 잠겼다.

in·con·spic·u·ous /ˌɪnkən'spɪkyuəs/ *adj* not easily seen or noticed ‖ 쉽게 보이거나 눈에 띄지 않는. 두드러지지 않은. 눈을 끌지 않는: *I sat in the corner, trying to be as inconspicuous as possible.* 나는 가능한 한 눈에 띄지 않으려고 구석에 앉았다. —opposite CONSPICUOUS

in·con·ti·nent /ɪn'kɑntˤnənt, -tənənt/ *adj* unable to control your BLADDER or BOWELs ‖ 방광 또는 장을 제어할 수 없는. 자제[억제]할 수 없는. 실금의 **– incontinence** *n* [U]

in·con·tro·vert·i·ble /ˌɪnkɑntrə'-vətˤəbəl/ *adj* an incontrovertible fact is definitely true ‖ 사실 등이 명백히 맞는. 틀림없는. 명백한. 논의할 여지없는: *The police have incontrovertible evidence that he committed the crime.* 경찰은 그가 범행을 저질렀다는 명백한 증거를 가지고 있다. **– incontrovertibly** *adv*

in·con·ven·ience[1] /ˌɪnkən'vinyəns/ *n* [C, U] something that causes you problems or difficulties, or the state of having problems or difficulties ‖ 문제 또는 곤란을 초래한 일, 또는 문제나 난관이 있는 상태. 귀찮은[불편한] 일. 불편[부자유, 폐]: *We apologize for any inconvenience caused by the delay to the bus service.* 버스 운행의 지연으로 야기된 불편 사항에 대해 사과드립니다.

inconvenience[2] *v* [T] to cause problems or difficulties for someone ‖ 남에게 문제 또는 어려움을 일으키다. …에게 폐[불편]을 끼치다: *"I'll drive you home." "Are you sure? I don't want to inconvenience you."* "집에 태워다 줄게." "정말이니? 나는 폐를 끼치고 싶지 않은데."

in·con·ven·ient /ˌɪnkən'vinyənt/ *adj* causing problems or difficulties, especially in an annoying way ‖ 특히 성가시게 문제나 어려움을 일으키는. 불편한. 폐가 되는. 형편이 나쁜: *I hope I haven't called at an inconvenient time.* 불편한 시간에 전화한 것이 아니었으면 좋겠네요. **– inconveniently** *adv*

in·cor·po·rate /ɪn'kɔrpəˌreɪt/ *v* [T] **1** to include something as part of a group, system etc. ‖ 집단·시스템 등의 일부로서 사물을 포함하다. …을 …에 통합[편입, 합병]하다. 받아들이다. 짜넣다: *Several safety features have been incorporated into the car's design.* 여러 가지의 안전성을 고려한 요소들이 자동차 디자인에 반영되었다. **2** to form a CORPORATION ‖ 법인을 구성하다. …을 법인[단체 조직]으로 만들다. 주식[유한 책임] 회사로 하다. **– incorporation** /ɪnˌkɔrpə'reɪʃən/ *n* [U]

In·cor·po·rat·ed /ɪn'kɔrpəˌreɪtɪd/, *written abbreviation* **Inc.** *adj* used after the name of a company in the US to show that it is a CORPORATION 유한 책임 회사임을 나타내기 위해 미국 회사의 이름 뒤에 쓰여

in·cor·rect /ˌɪnkə'rɛkt/ *adj* not correct; wrong ‖ 정확하지 않은. 올바르지 않은. 적당하지 않은. 틀린; 잘못된: *incorrect spelling* 틀린 철자법 **– incorrectly** *adv*

in·cor·ri·gi·ble /ɪnˈkɔrədʒəbəl, -'kɑr-/ *adj* someone who is incorrigible is bad in some way and cannot be changed ‖ 사람이 어떤 점에서 나쁘고 바뀔 수 없는. 고칠 수[구제할 수] 없는. 어쩔 수 없는. 상습의. 뿌리 깊은: *an incorrigible liar* 어쩔 수 없는 거짓말쟁이

in·cor·rupt·i·ble /ˌɪnkə'rʌptəbəl/ *adj*

too honest to be persuaded to do anything that is wrong ‖ 잘못된 일을 하도록 설득하기에는 너무나 정직한. 부패하지[타락하지] 않은. 청렴한. 결백한: *an incorruptible judge* 청렴한 판사

in·crease¹ /ɪnˈkris/ *v* [I, T] to become larger in number, amount, or degree or make something do this ‖ 수[양, 정도]면에서 더 커지다, 또는 더 크게 만들다. 늘[리]다. 증대[증가]하다[시키다]: *The price of gas has increased by 4%.* 가스 요금이 4% 인상되었다. / *City populations are steadily increasing.* 도시 인구가 꾸준히 증가하고 있다. / *Smoking increases your chances of getting cancer.* 흡연은 암에 걸릴 가능성을 높인다. **– increasing** *adj* : *increasing concern about job security* 직업 안정성에 대해 높아지는 우려 **—opposite** DECREASE¹

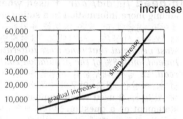

increase

in·crease² /ˈɪŋkris/ *n* [C, U] a rise in number, amount, or degree ‖ 수[양, 정도]의 증가. 증대. 증가: *There's been a huge increase in profits.* 수익이 엄청나게 증가했다. / *Crime in the city is on the increase.* (=increasing) 그 도시의 범죄는 증가 추세에 있다. **—opposite** DECREASE²

in·creased /ɪnˈkrist/ *adj* larger or more than before ‖ 전보다 더욱 커지거나 많아진. 증가한. 증대된: *an increased awareness of environmental issues* 증대된 환경 문제에 대한 인식

in·creas·ing·ly /ɪnˈkrisɪŋli/ *adv* more and more ‖ 더욱더. 점점 더: *It's becoming increasingly difficult to find employment.* 일자리를 찾는 것이 더욱더 어려워지고 있다.

in·cred·i·ble /ɪnˈkrɛdəbəl/ *adj* **1** extremely good, large, or impressive ‖ 매우 좋은[큰, 인상적인]. 엄청난. 놀랄 만한: *They serve the most incredible food there.* 그들은 그곳에서 가장 좋은 음식을 제공한다. / *an incredible bargain* 대폭 염가 판매 **2** very hard to believe ‖ 매우 믿기 어려운. 믿어지지 않는: *It's*

incredible how much you remind me of your father. 너를 보면 네 아버지 모습이 아주 많이 떠올라 정말 놀랍다.

in·cred·i·bly /ɪnˈkrɛdəbli/ *adv* extremely ‖ 엄청나게: *It's incredibly beautiful here in the spring.* 이곳의 봄은 믿을 수 없을 만큼 아름답다.

in·cred·u·lous /ɪnˈkrɛdʒələs/ *adj* showing that you are unable or unwilling to believe something ‖ 어떤 것을 믿을 수 없거나 믿으려 하지 않음을 나타내는. 의심하는. 의심하는 듯한: *"They don't have a phone?" asked one incredulous woman.* "그 사람들은 전화도 없나요?"라고 한 여자가 의심하는 듯이 물었다. **– incredulously** *adv* **– incredulity** /ˌɪnkrɪˈduləti/ *n* [U]

in·cre·ment /ˈɪnkrəmənt, ˈɪŋ-/ *n* an amount by which a value, number, or amount of money increases ‖ 가치[숫자, 액수]가 증가하는 양. 증가(량): *an annual salary increment of 2.9%* 연봉 2.9% 증가 **– incremental** /ˌɪnkrəˈmɛntl/ *adj*

in·crim·i·nate /ɪnˈkrɪməˌneɪt/ *v* [T] to make someone seem guilty of a crime ‖ (남에게) 죄를 씌우다: *He refused to incriminate himself by answering questions.* 그는 질문에 대답함으로써 자신이 죄가 있다는 것을 부인했다. **– incriminating** *adj* : *incriminating evidence* 죄가 될 만한 증거 **– incrimination** /ɪnˌkrɪməˈneɪʃən/ *n* [U]

in·cu·bate /ˈɪŋkyəˌbeɪt/ *v* [I, T] if a bird incubates its egg or if an egg incubates, it is kept warm under a bird's body until it HATCHes (=the baby bird comes out) ‖ 새가 알이 부화될 때까지 자신의 몸으로 따뜻하게 하다. 알을 품다. 알을[알이] 부화하다 **– incubation** /ˌɪŋkyəˈbeɪʃən/ *n* [U]

in·cu·ba·tor /ˈɪŋkyəˌbeɪtə/ *n* **1** a machine for keeping eggs warm until the young birds HATCH (=come out) ‖ 새끼 알이 부화될 때까지 알을 따뜻하게 유지하는 기계. 부화기 **2** a machine used by hospitals for keeping very small or weak babies alive ‖ 아주 작거나 약한 아기들의 생명을 유지하기 위해 병원에서 쓰는 기계. 인큐베이터

in·cul·cate /ˈɪnkʌlˌkeɪt, ɪnˈkʌlˌkeɪt/ *v* [T] FORMAL to make someone accept an idea by repeating it to him/her often ‖ 남에게 어떤 생각을 자주 반복적으로 말해서 받아들이게 하다. (생각을) 심어 주다

in·cum·bent¹ /ɪnˈkʌmbənt/ *n* a word meaning someone who has previously been elected to an official position, used during elections ‖ 현 선거 기간에 쓰여, 지난번에 공직에 당선된 사람을 뜻하는 단어. 현직자. 재직자. 현역 의원: *The election will be tough for the incumbents on the city council.* 시의회 현직 의원들에게는 이번 선거가 힘겨울 것이다.

incumbent² *adj* FORMAL **it is incumbent on/upon sb to do sth** if it is incumbent upon you to do something, it is your duty or responsibility to do it ‖ 누군가에게 어떤 일 하는 것에 대한 의무나 책임이 있다

in·cur /ɪnˈkɚ/ *v* **-rred, -rring** [T] to have something bad, such as a punishment or debt, happen because of something you have done ‖ 저지른 일로 인해서 처벌이나 빚 등의 좋지 않은 일이 생기다. 초래하다: *The oil company incurred a debt of $5 million last year.* 그 정유회사는 작년에 5백만 달러의 빚을 졌다.

in·cur·a·ble /ɪnˈkyʊrəbəl/ *adj* impossible to cure or stop ‖ 치료하거나 중단시키기 불가능한. 고칠 수 없는. 불치의: *an incurable disease* 불치병 / *He's an incurable romantic.* (=he will never stop being romantic) 그는 못말리는 낭만주의자다. **- incurably** *adv* —opposite CURABLE

in·cur·sion /ɪnˈkɚʒən/ *n* FORMAL a sudden attack or arrival into an area that belongs to other people ‖ 다른 사람의 영역 안으로의 갑작스런 공격이나 도래. 침략. 급습

in·debt·ed /ɪnˈdɛtɪd/ *adj* **be indebted to** to be very grateful to someone for the help s/he has given you ‖ 도와준 것에 대해서 남에게 매우 감사해 하다: *I am indebted to my friend Catherine, who edited my manuscript.* 내 원고를 편집해 준 친구 캐서린이 너무 고맙다. **- indebtedness** *n* [U]

in·de·cent /ɪnˈdisənt/ *adj* **1** indecent behavior, clothes, or actions are likely to offend or shock people because they are against social or moral standards, or because they involve sex ‖ 행동[옷, 동작]이 사회적 또는 도덕적 기준에 반하거나 성적인 것을 포함하기 때문에 사람들을 불쾌하게 하거나 놀라게 하기 쉬운. 점잖지 못한. 꼴사나운: *You can't wear a skirt that short - it's indecent!* 너는 그렇게 짧은 치마를 입어선 안돼. 꼴사나워! / *indecent photographs* 야한 사진들 **2 indecent exposure** LAW the crime of deliberately showing your sex organs in a public place ‖ 공공장소에서 의도적으로

성기를 노출시키는 범죄. 공연(公然) 음란죄 **- indecency** *n* [C, U] —compare DECENT

in·de·ci·sion /ˌɪndɪˈsɪʒən/ *n* [U] the state of not being able to make decisions ‖ 결정을 내릴 수 없는 상태. 우유부단. 망설임: *After a week of indecision, we agreed to buy the house.* 일주일간을 망설인 끝에 우리는 그 집을 사기로 했다.

in·de·ci·sive /ˌɪndɪˈsaɪsɪv/ *adj* **1** unable to make decisions ‖ 결정을 내릴 수 없는. 우유 부단한. 결단성 없는: *He was criticized for being a weak indecisive leader.* 그는 결단성이 없는 약한 지도자라는 비난을 받았다. **2** not having a clear result; INCONCLUSIVE ‖ 분명한 결과가 없는. 결말이 나지 않는. 결정적이 아닌; ㉤ inconclusive: *an indecisive battle* 승패의 결말이 나지 않는 싸움 **- indecisiveness** *n* [U]

in·deed /ɪnˈdid/ *adv* **1** used when adding more information to a statement ‖ 어떤 진술에 더 많은 정보를 추가할 때에 쓰여. 사실은. 사실대로 말하자면: *Most people at that time were illiterate. Indeed, only 8% of the population could read.* 그 당시 대부분의 사람들은 문맹이었다. 사실은 전체 인구의 8%만이 읽을 수 있었다. **2** used when emphasizing a statement or a question ‖ 어떤 진술이나 질문을 강조할 때에 쓰여. 정말로. 참으로: *"Vernon is one of the best pilots around." "Yes, indeed."* "버논은 주변에 있는 최고 조종사 중 한 명이야." "정말 그래."

in·de·fen·si·ble /ˌɪndɪˈfɛnsəbəl/ *adj* too bad to be excused or defended ‖ 너무나 나빠서 변명하거나 방어할 수 없는. 변명의 여지가 없는. 방어할 수 없는: *indefensible behavior* 변명의 여지가 없는 행동

in·de·fin·a·ble /ˌɪndɪˈfaɪnəbəl/ *adj* difficult to describe or explain ‖ 묘사하거나 설명하기 어려운. 정의[설명]할 수 없는: *For some indefinable reason she felt afraid.* 그녀는 뭔가 설명할 수 없는 이유로 두려움을 느꼈다.

in·def·i·nite /ɪnˈdɛfənɪt/ *adj* **1** an indefinite action or period of time has no definite end arranged for it ‖ 행동이나 기간의 끝이 정해져 있지 않은. 부정의: *He was away in Alaska for an indefinite period.* 그는 무기한으로 알래스카에 떠나 있었다. **2** not clear or definite; VAGUE ‖ 명확하거나 분명하지 않은. 불명확한. 막연한; ㉤ vague: *Our plans are still indefinite.* 우리 계획은 여전히 분명하지 않다.

in·def·i·nite·ly /ɪnˈdɛfənɪtli/ *adv* for a period of time without an arranged end ‖ 정해 놓은 끝이 없는 기간 동안에. 무기한으로: *I'll be staying here indefinitely.* 나는 여기에 무기한으로 머무를 거야.

in·del·i·ble /ɪnˈdɛləbəl/ *adj* impossible to remove or forget; PERMANENT ‖ 제거하거나 잊기 불가능한. 지울 수 없는. 씻어버릴 수 없는; 영 permanent: *indelible ink* 지워지지 않는 잉크 / *The movie left an indelible impression on her.* (=she could not forget it) 그 영화는 그녀에게 잊을 수 없는 인상을 남겼다. **–indelibly** *adv*

in·del·i·cate /ɪnˈdɛlɪkɪt/ *adj* slightly impolite or offensive ‖ 약간 정중하지 못하거나 거슬리는. 상스러운. 거친: *an indelicate question* 무례한 질문 **– indelicately** *adv*

in·dem·ni·fy /ɪnˈdɛmnəˌfaɪ/ *v* [T] LAW to promise to pay someone if something s/he owns becomes lost or damaged, or if s/he is injured ‖ 소유한 물건을 잃거나 손해가 발생했을 때, 또는 사람이 다쳤을 때에 손해를 본 사람에게 지불을 약속하다. 보상[배상, 변상]하다

in·dem·ni·ty /ɪnˈdɛmnəti/ *n* LAW **1** [U] protection in the form of a promise to pay for any damage or loss ‖ 어떠한 손해나 상실에 대한 지불 약속 형태의 보호. 보상. 배상. 변상 **2** money that is paid to someone for any damages, losses, or injury ‖ 어떠한 손해[상실, 부상]에 대해 지불되는 돈. 보상[배상, 변상]금

in·dent /ɪnˈdɛnt/ *v* [T] to start a line of writing closer to the middle of the page than the other lines ‖ 글의 한 행을 다른 행들보다 페이지의 중앙 쪽으로 더 가깝게 하여 시작하다. 들여 쓰다

in·den·ta·tion /ˌɪndɛnˈteɪʃən/ *n* **1** a space at the beginning of a line of writing ‖ 글의 한 행의 처음에 있는 빈 공간 **2** a cut or space in the edge of something ‖ 사물의 가장자리에 있는 절단면이나 빈 공간

in·de·pend·ence /ˌɪndɪˈpɛndəns/ *n* [U] **1** the freedom and ability to make your own decisions and take care of yourself without having to ask other people for help, money, or permission ‖ 다른 사람에게 도움[돈, 허락]을 요청할 필요 없이 자기가 직접 결정을 내리고 자기 자신을 돌보는 자유와 능력. 자립. 독립: *The apartments allow older people to keep their independence, while having medical care available.* 그 아파트에서는 노인들이 의료 서비스를 받으면서 독립적인 생활을 유지할 수 있다. **2**

political freedom from control by another country ‖ 다른 국가의 통제로부터의 정치적 자유. 자주. 독립: *The United States declared its independence in 1776.* 미국은 1776년에 독립을 선언했다.

Independence Day /..ˈ.. ./ *n* [U] ⇨ FOURTH OF JULY

in·de·pend·ent /ˌɪndɪˈpɛndənt/ *adj* **1** confident, free, and not needing to ask other people for help, money, or permission to do something ‖ 다른 사람에게 어떤 일을 하기 위해 도움[돈, 허락]을 요청할 필요 없이 자신감 있고 자유로운. 독립한. 독립심이 강한: *I feel so much more independent now that I'm working.* 나는 이제 일을 하기 때문에 훨씬 더 독립적인 느낌이 든다. **2** not controlled by another government or organization ‖ 다른 정부나 조직의 통제를 받지 않는. 독립한. 자주의: *India became an independent nation in 1947.* 인도는 1947년에 독립국이 되었다. / *a European army independent of NATO* 나토에서 독립한 유럽군 **3** not influenced by other people ‖ 다른 사람의 영향을 받지 않는. 자주적인. 독자적인: *an independent report on the experiment* 그 실험에 대한 독자적인 보고서 **–independently** *adv*

in·depth /ˌ. ˈ./ *adj* **in-depth study/report** a study or report that is very thorough and considers all the details ‖ 매우 철저하고 모든 세부 사항을 고려한 연구나 보고서. 심층적인[철저한] 연구[보고서]

in·de·scrib·a·ble /ˌɪndɪˈskraɪbəbəl/ *adj* too good, strange, frightening etc. to be described ‖ 너무 좋아[이상하여, 두려워] 묘사할 수 없는. 형언할 수 없는: *My joy at seeing him was indescribable.* 그를 만나는 즐거움은 말로 다 표현할 수 없었다.

in·de·struct·i·ble /ˌɪndɪˈstrʌktəbəl/ *adj* impossible to destroy ‖ 파괴할 수 없는. 불멸의: *The tank was built to be indestructible.* 이 탱크는 파괴할 수 없도록 만들어졌다.

in·de·ter·mi·nate /ˌɪndɪˈtəmənɪt/ *adj* impossible to find out or calculate exactly ‖ 정확히 알아내거나 계산하기 불가능한. 확실하지 않은. 불확실한: *a dog of indeterminate breed* 품종을 정확히 모르는 개 한 마리 **–indeterminacy** /ˌɪndɪˈtəmənɪsi/ *n* [U]

in·dex¹ /ˈɪndɛks/ *n, plural* **indexes** *or* **indices** /ˈɪndəˌsiz/ **1** an alphabetical list at the end of a book, that lists all the names, subjects etc. in the book and the pages where you can find them ‖ 책에 들어 있는 모든 이름과 주제 등을 벌여 놓은, 책 뒤의 알파벳 순서로 된 목록과 그것을 찾아볼 수 있는 페이지. 색인. 목록 **2** a set of cards with information, or a DATABASE in alphabetical order ‖ 정보가 담긴 일련의 카드, 또는 알파벳 순의 데이터 베이스. 카드식[데이터베이스] 색인 **3** a standard or level you can use for judging or measuring something by ‖ 사물을 판단하거나 측정할 때 쓸 수 있는 기준이나 수준. 지수

index² v [T] to make an INDEX for something ‖ 어떤 것을 위한 색인을 만들다. 색인을 달다. 색인에 넣다 – **indexation** /ˌɪndɛkˈseɪʃən/ n

index card /'.. ˌ./ n a small card for writing information on, used especially for INDEXes ‖ 특히 색인 용도로 쓰이는 정보를 적는 작은 카드. 색인 카드

index fin·ger /'.. ˌ../ n the finger next to the thumb; FOREFINGER ‖ 엄지 옆에 있는 손가락. 집게손가락. 검지; forefinger —see picture at HAND¹

In·di·an¹ /'ɪndiən/ adj **1** ⇨ NATIVE AMERICAN **2** relating to or coming from India ‖ 인도와 관련되거나 인도 출신의. 인도(산)의

Indian² n **1** ⇨ NATIVE AMERICAN **2** someone from India ‖ 인도 출신의 사람. 인도인

Indian O·cean /ˌ... '../ n the Indian Ocean the ocean between Africa in the west, India in the north, and Australia in the east ‖ 서쪽으로는 아프리카, 북쪽으로는 인도, 동쪽으로는 호주가 있는 대양. 인도양

Indian sum·mer /ˌ... '../ n a period of warm weather in the fall ‖ 가을에 보이는 한 동안의 따뜻한 날씨. 인디언 써머

in·di·cate /'ɪndəˌkeɪt/ v [T] **1** to show that something exists or is likely to be true ‖ 어떤 것이 존재하거나 사실일 수 있음을 나타내다. 암시하다. 비추다: *Research indicates that women live longer than men.* 조사는 여자가 남자보다 더 오래 산다는 것을 보여준다. **2** to point at something ‖ 어떤 것을 가리키다. 지시[지적]하다: *Indicating a chair, he said, "Please, sit down."* 그는 의자를 가리키며 "앉으세요."라고 말했다. **3** to say or do something that shows what you want or intend to do ‖ 원하거나 하려는 것을 나타내는 어떤 것을 말하거나 하다. 알리다. 표현하다: *He indicated that he had no desire to come with us.* 그는 우리와 함께 갈 마음이 없다고 말했다.

in·di·ca·tion /ˌɪndəˈkeɪʃən/ n [C, U] a

sign that something exists or is likely to be true ‖ 어떤 것이 존재하거나 사실일 듯한 표시. 암시. 징조: *Did Rick ever give any indication that he was unhappy?* 릭이 너한테 자신이 불행했다는 암시를 준 적이 있었니?

in·dic·a·tive /ɪnˈdɪkətɪv/ adj **be indicative of** to show that something exists or is likely to be true ‖ 어떤 것이 존재하거나 사실일 가능성이 있음을 나타내다. …을 표시[지시, 암시]하다: *His reaction is indicative of how frightened he is.* 그의 반응은 그가 얼마나 두려워하는지를 보여준다.

in·di·ca·tor /'ɪndəˌkeɪtɚ/ n an event, fact etc. that shows that something exists, or shows you the way something is developing ‖ 어떤 것이 존재하거나 발전하는 모습을 나타내는 사건·사실 등. 지표: *All the main economic indicators suggest that business is improving.* 모든 주요 경제 지표들은 경기가 활성화되고 있음을 나타낸다.

in·di·ces /'ɪndəˌsiz/ n a plural of INDEX ‖ index의 복수형

in·dict /ɪnˈdaɪt/ v [I, T] LAW to officially charge someone with a crime ‖ 죄가 있는 사람에게 공식적으로 죄를 묻다. 기소하다. 기소되다 – **indictable** /ɪnˈdaɪtəbəl/ adj

in·dict·ment /ɪnˈdaɪtmənt/ n **1 be an indictment of** to be a very clear sign that a system, method etc. is very bad or wrong ‖ 시스템·방법 등이 매우 나쁘거나 잘못됐다는 아주 분명한 표시를 하다. 비난[공격]하다: *It is an indictment of TV today that it doesn't make people think.* 오늘날 TV가 비난받는 것은 사람들을 생각하도록 만들지 못하기 때문이다. **2** LAW an official written statement saying that someone has done something illegal, or the act of making this statement ‖ 남이 불법 행위를 했다는 것을 가리키는 공식적인 문서, 또는 이러한 진술을 하는 행위. 기소(장)

in·dif·fer·ence /ɪnˈdɪfrəns/ n [U] lack of interest or concern ‖ 흥미나 관심의 부족. 무관심. 냉담: *I am amazed at the local government's indifference to the homeless people in our city.* 나는 우리 도시에 있는 노숙자들에 대한 지방 정부의 무관심에 놀라움을 금할 수 없다.

in·dif·fer·ent /ɪnˈdɪfrənt/ adj not interested in someone or something, or not having any feelings or opinions about him, her, or it ‖ 사람이나 사물에 대한 흥미가 없거나 어떠한 감정이나 의견도 가지고 있지 않은. 무관심한. 냉담한:

The industry seems indifferent to environmental concerns. 산업계는 환경 문제에 대해서는 무관심한 듯 보인다.

in·dig·e·nous /ɪnˈdɪdʒənəs/ *adj* indigenous plants, animals etc. have always lived or grown naturally in the place where they are ‖ 식물·동물 등이 현재 있는 곳에서 자연스럽게 항상 살아왔거나 자라온. 토종인. 토착적인: *plants indigenous to the Amazon region* 아마존 지역 원산종의 식물

in·di·gest·i·ble /ˌɪndɪˈdʒɛstəbəl, -daɪ-/ *adj* food that is indigestible is difficult for the stomach to deal with ‖ 음식이 위에서 처리되기 어려운. 소화하기 힘든 – see also DIGEST¹

in·di·ges·tion /ˌɪndəˈdʒɛstʃən, -daɪ-/ *n* [U] the pain caused by eating food that your stomach has difficulty DIGESTing ‖ 소화시키기 힘든 음식물을 먹어서 위에 생기는 고통. 소화불량

in·dig·nant /ɪnˈdɪgnənt/ *adj* angry because you feel you have been insulted or unfairly treated ‖ 모욕을 당했거나 부당하게 취급받았다고 느껴서 화가 난. 분개한. 성난: *Indignant nurses said the hospital cared more about money than health care.* 분개한 간호사들은 병원이 환자들의 병보다 돈을 더 중요하게 여긴다고 말했다. – **indignantly** *adv*

in·dig·na·tion /ˌɪndɪgˈneɪʃən/ *n* [U] the feeling of being INDIGNANT ‖ 분개한 상태의 감정. 분개. 의분: *Rich's indignation at not being chosen for the team was obvious.* 그 팀에 선택받지 못한 리치의 분개는 노골적이었다.

in·dig·ni·ty /ɪnˈdɪgnəti/ *n* [C, U] a situation that makes you feel very ashamed and not respected ‖ 매우 부끄럽고 존중받지 못한다고 느끼게 하는 상황. 모욕. 수모: *They suffered the indignity of being tied up like animals.* 그들은 동물처럼 묶이는 수모를 당했다.

in·di·rect /ˌɪndəˈrɛkt, -daɪ-/ *adj* **1** not directly caused by something or relating to it ‖ 직접적으로 어떤 것에 의해 일어난 것이 아니거나 관련이 없는. 간접적인: *The accident was an indirect result of the heavy rain.* 그 사고는 폭우에 따른 간접적인 결과였다. **2** not using the straightest or most direct way to get to a place ‖ 어떤 장소에 이르는 가장 곧은 길이나 직접적인 길을 이용하지 않는. 우회하는: *an indirect route* 우회로 **3** suggesting something without saying it directly or clearly ‖ 어떤 것을 직접적으로 또는 분명히 말하지 않고 암시하는. 에둘러서 말하는: *He never mentioned my work, which I felt was an indirect criticism of its quality.* 그는 내 작품에 대해서 한 마디도 언급하지 않았는데, 나는 그것을 작품의 질에 대한 암시적인 비판으로 느꼈다. – **indirectly** *adv*

indirect ar·ti·cle /ˌ... ˈ.../ *n* ⇨ ARTICLE

indirect ob·ject /ˌ... ˈ../ *n* TECHNICAL in grammar, the person or thing that received something as the result of the action of the verb in a sentence. In the sentence "Pete gave me the money," "me" is the indirect object ‖ 문법에서 한 문장 내의 동사의 행위에 따른 결과로써 사물을 받는 사람이나 사물. 간접 목적어. "피트가 나에게(me) 그 돈을 주었다."라는 문장에서 "나에게(me)"는 간접 목적어이다.

indirect speech /ˌ... ˈ./ *n* TECHNICAL ⇨ REPORTED SPEECH

in·dis·creet /ˌɪndɪˈskrɪt/ *adj* careless about what you say or do, so that you let people know too much ‖ 말하거나 하는 것에 대해서 부주의하여 다른 사람들이 너무 많이 알게 하는. 무분별한. 경솔한: *Try to stop him from saying anything indiscreet.* 그가 경솔한 말을 하지 못하게 해라.

in·dis·cre·tion /ˌɪndɪˈskrɛʃən/ *n* [C, U] an action, remark, or behavior that shows bad judgment and is usually considered socially or morally unacceptable ‖ 형편없는 판단력을 나타내면서 대체로 사회적으로나 도덕적으로 받아들일 수 없다고 고려되는 동작[말, 행동]. 무분별(한 행위). 경솔(한 짓): *his embarrassing sexual indiscretions* 당혹스럽게 하는 그의 성적인 추태 / *youthful indiscretion* 젊은 혈기로 저지른 경솔한 행동

in·dis·crim·i·nate /ˌɪndɪˈskrɪmənɪt/ *adj* without considering whom or what you should choose, or without thinking about how he, she, or it will be affected ‖ 누구를 또는 무엇을 선택할 것인지를 고려하지 않거나, 그 사람 또는 그것이 어떤 영향을 미칠 것인지에 대해서도 생각하지 않는. 무차별의. 무계획적인: *indiscriminate acts of violence* 무차별적인 폭력 행위

in·dis·pen·sa·ble /ˌɪndɪˈspɛnsəbəl/ *adj* someone or something that is indispensable is so important or useful that you cannot manage without him, her, or it ‖ 사람이나 사물이 매우 중요하거나 유용하여 그 사람이나 사물 없이는 운영할 수 없는. 없어서는 안 될. 필수 불가결한: *The information he provided was indispensable to our research.* 그

가 제공한 정보는 우리의 연구에 없어서는 안 될 것이었다.

in·dis·pu·ta·ble /ˌɪndɪˈspyuʊʃəbəl/ *adj* a fact that is indisputable must be accepted because it is definitely true ‖ 어떠한 사실이 명백한 진실이기 때문에 받아들여야만 하는. 논란의 여지가 없는. 부정할 수 없는 **– indisputably** *adv*

in·dis·tinct /ˌɪndɪˈstɪŋkt/ *adj* not able to be seen, heard, or remembered very clearly ‖ 아주 뚜렷이 보이지[들리지, 기억되지] 않는. 뚜렷하지 않은. 희미한: *indistinct voices in the next room* 옆방에서 나는 희미한 목소리 **– indistinctly** *adv*

in·dis·tin·guish·a·ble /ˌɪndɪˈstɪŋgwɪʃəbəl/ *adj* things that are indistinguishable are so similar that you cannot see any difference between them ‖ 사물이 아주 흡사해서 별 차이를 느끼지 못하는. [구별]분간할 수 없는: *This material is indistinguishable from real silk.* 이 원단은 진짜 비단과 구별할 수가 없다.

in·di·vid·u·al[1] /ˌɪndəˈvɪdʒuəl/ *adj* **1** considered separately from other people or things in the same group ‖ 같은 집단 내에 있는 다른 사람이나 사물과 따로 분리되어 고려되는. 개개의. 별개의: *Each individual drawing is slightly different.* 개개인의 그림마다 약간씩 차이가 있다. **2** belonging to or intended for one person rather than a group ‖ 한 집단보다는 한 사람에게 속하거나 한 사람을 위해 의도된. 개인의. 개인적인: *Individual attention must be given to each student.* 학생 한 사람 한 사람마다 개인적인 관심을 가져야 한다.

individual[2] *n* one person, considered separately from the rest of the group or society that s/he lives in ‖ 살고 있는 집단이나 사회의 나머지로부터 따로 떼어 고려되는 한 사람. 개인: *the rights of the individual* 개인의 권리

in·di·vid·u·al·ism /ˌɪndəˈvɪdʒuəlɪzəm/ *n* the belief or practice of allowing people to do things in their own way without being influenced by other people ‖ 사람들이 타인에게 영향을 받지 않고 자신의 방식대로 일을 하도록 하는 신념이나 관습. 개인주의 **– individualist** *n* **– individualistic** /ˌɪndəˌvɪdʒuəˈlɪstɪk/ *adj*

in·di·vid·u·al·i·ty /ˌɪndəˌvɪdʒuˈæləti/ *n* [U] the quality that makes someone or something different from all others ‖ 사람이나 사물을 모든 다른 사람들이나 사물들과 다르게 만드는 성질. 개성. 특성: *His*

individuality shows in his art work. 그의 개성이 그의 예술 작품에 드러난다.

in·di·vid·u·al·ly /ˌɪndəˈvɪdʒuəli, -dʒəli/ *adv* separately, not together in a group ‖ 한 집단 전체가 아니라 분리해서. 개별적으로. 개인적으로: *Mr. Wong met with each employee individually.* 웡 씨는 각 사원을 개별적으로 만났다.

in·di·vis·i·ble /ˌɪndəˈvɪzəbəl/ *adj* not able to be separated or divided into parts ‖ 분리하거나 부분으로 나눌 수 없는. 분리할 수 없는. 불가분의 **– indivisibly** *adv*

in·doc·tri·nate /ɪnˈdɑktrəˌneɪt/ *v* [T] to teach someone to accept a particular set of beliefs and not consider any others ‖ 남에게 다른 어떤 것도 고려하지 말고 일련의 특정한 신념만을 받아들이도록 가르치다. (신념을) 가르치다[심어주다]: *Schools may not indoctrinate children with religious beliefs.* 학교는 아이들에게 종교적 신조를 주입시켜서는 안 된다. **– indoctrination** /ɪnˌdɑktrəˈneɪʃən/ *n* [U]

in·do·lent /ˈɪndələnt/ *adj* FORMAL lazy ‖ 게으른. 나태한 **– indolently** *adv* **– indolence** *n* [U]

in·dom·i·ta·ble /ɪnˈdɑmətəbəl/ *adj* **indomitable spirit/courage etc.** FORMAL determination, courage etc. that can never be defeated ‖ 결코 꺾이지 않는 결의·용기 등. 불굴의 정신/용기

in·door /ˈɪndɔr/ *adj* used or happening inside a building ‖ 건물 안에서 사용되거나 발생하는. 옥내의. 실내용의: *an indoor swimming pool* 실내 수영장 — opposite OUTDOOR

in·doors /ˌɪnˈdɔrz/ *adv* into or inside a building ‖ 건물 안쪽으로 또는 안에서. 옥내[실내]로[에서]: *It's raining – let's go indoors.* 비가 온다. 실내로 들어가자. / *He stayed indoors all morning.* 그는 아침 내내 실내에 있었다. —opposite OUTDOORS

in·duce /ɪnˈdus/ *v* FORMAL **1** [T] to make someone decide to do something ‖ 남에게 어떤 것을 하도록 결심하게 하다. 설득하여 …하게 하다: *What induced you to spend so much money on a car?* 무엇이 네가 차에 그렇게 많은 돈을 쓰도록 만들었니? **2** [T] to cause a particular physical condition ‖ 특정한 몸 상태가 되게 하다. 야기하다. 유발하다: *This drug may induce drowsiness.* 이 약은 졸음을 유발할지도 모른다. **3** [I, T] to make a woman give birth to her baby by giving her a special drug ‖ 임산부에게 특별한 약을 주어 아기를 낳게 하다. 분만 촉진하

in·duce·ment /ɪn'dusmənt/ *n* [C, U] something that you are offered to persuade you to do something ‖ 어떤 것을 하도록 설득하기 위해 제공되는 것. 유인(책). 장려금: *He was given $10,000 as an inducement to leave the company.* 그는 퇴사 장려금으로 만 달러를 받았다.

in·duct /ɪn'dʌkt/ *v* [T] to officially introduce someone into a group or organization, especially the army, navy etc. ‖ 특히 육군·해군 등에서 사람을 공식적으로 단체나 조직에 받아들이다. 가입시키다. 입대시키다 **- inductee** /ɪn,dʌk'ti/ *n*

in·duc·tion /ɪn'dʌkʃən/ *n* [C, U] the act or ceremony of officially introducing someone into a group or organization, especially the army, navy etc. ‖ 특히 육군·해군 등에서 사람을 공식적으로 단체나 조직에 받아들이는 행위나 의식. 입대[입회]식

in·dulge /ɪn'dʌldʒ/ *v* **1** [I, T] to let yourself do or have something you enjoy, especially something that is considered bad for you ‖ 자기가 즐기는 것, 특히 나쁜 것으로 간주되는 것을 맘껏 하거나 가지다. 탐닉하다. 실컷 즐기다: *I sometimes indulge in a cigarette at a party.* 나는 가끔 파티에서 담배 한 대를 즐긴다. **2** [T] to let someone do or have whatever s/he wants, even if it is bad for him/her ‖ 남에게 설령 그것이 나쁘더라도 원하는 것은 무엇이든 하거나 갖게 하다. 제멋대로 하게 하다: *Ralph indulges his dogs terribly.* 랠프는 자기 개들을 너무 제멋대로 내버려 둔다.

in·dul·gence /ɪn'dʌldʒəns/ *n* **1** [U] the habit of eating too much, drinking too much etc. ‖ 너무 많이 먹고 너무 많이 술을 마시는 등의 습관. 탐닉. 제멋대로 함: *a life of indulgence* 탐닉적인 삶 **2** something that you do or have for pleasure, not because you need it ‖ 필요해서가 아니라 쾌락을 위해 하거나 가지는 것. 도락. 좋아하는 것: *Chocolate is my only indulgence.* 초콜릿은 내가 유일하게 즐기는 것이다.

in·dul·gent /ɪn'dʌldʒənt/ *adj* allowing someone to do or have whatever s/he wants, even if it is bad for him/her ‖ 남에게 설령 그것이 나쁘더라도 원하는 것은 무엇이든 하거나 갖게 하는. 관대한. 응석을 받아주는: *indulgent parents* 아이의 응석을 받아주는 부모 **- indulgently** *adv*

in·dus·tri·al /ɪn'dʌstriəl/ *adj* **1** relating to industry or the people working in industry ‖ 산업이나 산업에서 일하는 사람들에게 관련된. 산업[공업]의. 산업[공업]에 종사하는: *industrial waste* 산업 폐기물 **2** having many industries, or industries that are well developed ‖ 여러 산업이나 잘 발달된 산업을 갖고 있는. 산업[공업]적인: *an industrial region* 공업지역 **- industrially** *adv*

in·dus·tri·al·ist /ɪn'dʌstriəlɪst/ *n* the owner of a factory, industrial company etc. ‖ 공장·공업 회사 등의 소유주. 산업자본가. 실업가

in·dus·tri·al·ize /ɪn'dʌstriə,laɪz/ *v* [I, T] if a country or place is industrialized or if it industrializes, it develops a lot of industry ‖ 국가나 지역이 많은 산업을 발전시키다. 산업화되다[하다] **- industrialization** /ɪn,dʌstriələ'zeɪʃən/ *n* [U]

industrial park /.,... './ *n* an area of land that has offices, businesses, small factories etc. on it ‖ 사무실·사업체·작은 공장 등이 있는 일정한 지역. 공업 단지

in·dus·tri·ous /ɪn'dʌstriəs/ *adj* FORMAL tending to work hard ‖ 일을 열심히 하려는 경향이 있는. 근면한. 부지런한: *an industrious young woman* 근면한 젊은 여자 **- industriously** *adv*

in·dus·try /'ɪndəstri/ *n* **1** [U] the production of goods, especially in factories ‖ 특히 공장에서의 제품의 생산. 산업: *The country's economy is supported by industry.* 그 나라의 경제는 제조업으로 뒷받침된다. **2** a particular type of trade or service that produces things ‖ 물건을 생산해 내는 특정한 형태의 업계나 용역. 제조업. 각 부분의 …업(業): *the clothing industry* 의류업

in·e·bri·at·ed /ɪ'nibri,eɪtɪd/ *adj* FORMAL drunk ‖ 술 취한 **- inebriation** /ɪ,nibri'eɪʃən/ *n* [U]

in·ed·i·ble /ɪn'ɛdəbəl/ *adj* not suitable for eating ‖ 먹기에 적합하지 않은. 먹을 수 없는: *inedible mushrooms* 식용할 수 없는 버섯

in·ef·fec·tive /,ɪnə'fɛktɪv/ *adj* not achieving the correct effect or result ‖ 올바른 효과나 결과를 달성하지 못하는. 효과[효력] 없는: *an ineffective treatment for this disease* 이 병에는 효력이 없는 치료 **- ineffectiveness** *n* [U]

in·ef·fec·tu·al /,ɪnə'fɛktʃuəl/ *adj* not achieving what someone or something is trying to do ‖ 사람이나 사물이 하고자 하는 것을 달성하지 못하는. 효과적이 아닌. 무력한. 무능한: *an ineffectual leader* 무

능한 지도자 **-ineffectually** *adv*

in·ef·fi·cient /ˌɪnəˈfɪʃənt/ *adj* not working well and wasting time, money, or energy ‖ 잘 작동하지 않고 시간[돈, 정력]을 낭비하는. 비능률적인: *an inefficient use of good farm land* 기름진 농지의 비효율적인 활용 **-inefficiently** *adv* **-inefficiency** *n* [C, U]

in·el·e·gant /ɪnˈɛləgənt/ *adj* not graceful or well done ‖ 우아하거나 잘하지 못한. 우아하지[세련되지] 않은: *Her writing is sloppy and inelegant.* 그녀의 글은 감상적이며 세련되지 못하다.

in·el·i·gi·ble /ɪnˈɛlədʒəbəl/ *adj* not allowed to do or have something ‖ 일을 하거나 가지도록 허락받지 못한. 자격 없는. 부적격의: *Non-citizens are ineligible to vote in the election.* 비시민권자들은 선거에서 투표할 자격이 없다. **-ineligibility** /ɪnˌɛlədʒəˈbɪləti/ *n* [U]

in·ept /ɪˈnɛpt/ *adj* having no skill ‖ 솜씨가 없는. 서투른. 무능한: *an inept driver* 서투른 운전자 **-ineptitude** /ɪˈnɛptəˌtud/ *n* [U]

in·e·qual·i·ty /ˌɪnɪˈkwɑləti/ *n* [C, U] an unfair situation, in which some groups in society have less money or influence, or fewer opportunities than others ‖ 사회에서 어떤 집단이 다른 집단보다 돈[영향력, 기회]이 더 적은 불공평한 상황. 불평등. 불공평: *There are many inequalities in our legal system.* 우리의 법률 제도에는 불평등한 부분이 많이 있다.

in·eq·ui·ty /ɪnˈɛkwəti/ *n* [C, U] FORMAL lack of fairness, or something that is unfair ‖ 공정함의 결여나 불공정한 것. 불공정. 불공평: *gross inequities* (=something very clearly unfair) *in the distribution of aid* 원조의 분배에 있어서의 심한 불공정

in·ert /ɪˈnɚt/ *adj* **1** TECHNICAL not producing a chemical reaction when combined with other substances ‖ 다른 물질과 결합했을 때 화학적 반응을 일으키지 않는. 불활성의: *inert gases* 불활성 기체 **2** not moving ‖ 움직이지 않는. 활동력이 없는: *He checked her inert body for signs of life.* 그는 살아있는지 보기 위해 그녀의 움직이지 않는 몸을 살폈다.

in·er·tia /ɪˈnɚʃə/ *n* [U] **1** TECHNICAL the force that keeps an object in the same position or keeps it moving until it is moved or stopped by another force ‖ 물체를 동일한 자세로 계속 유지하거나 다른 힘에 의하여 움직이거나 중지될 때까지 계속 움직이게 하는 힘. 관성 **2** a tendency for a situation to stay unchanged for a long time ‖ 어떤 상황이 오랫동안 변하지

않고 있으려는 경향. 불활성. 타성: *the problem of inertia in large bureaucracies* 타성에 젖은 거대한 관료집단의 문제 **3** a feeling that you do not want to do anything at all ‖ 어떤 것도 전혀 하고 싶지 않은 감정. 무력감

in·es·cap·a·ble /ˌɪnəˈskeɪpəbəl/ *adj* FORMAL impossible to avoid ‖ 피할 수 없는. 불가피한: *The effects of the war are inescapable.* 그 전쟁의 영향을 피할 수 없다. **-inescapably** *adv*

in·es·sen·tial /ˌɪnəˈsɛnʃəl/ *adj* FORMAL not necessary ‖ 필요하지 않은. 없어도 되는

in·es·ti·ma·ble /ɪnˈɛstəməbəl/ *adj* FORMAL too much or too great to be calculated ‖ 계산하기에는 너무 많거나 큰. 헤아릴 수 없는 **-inestimably** *adv*

in·ev·i·ta·ble /ɪˈnɛvətəbəl/ *adj* **1** certain to happen and impossible to avoid ‖ 확실히 일어나며 피하기 불가능한. 피할 수 없는. 필연적인: *Death is inevitable.* 죽음은 필연적인 것이다. **2 the inevitable** something that is certain to happen ‖ 확실히 일어나는 것. 피할 수 없는[필연적인] 것: *Finally, the inevitable happened and he lost his job.* 마침내 불가피한 일이 생겨 그는 직장을 잃었다. **-inevitability** /ɪˌnɛvətəˈbɪləti/ *n* [U]

in·ev·i·ta·bly /ɪnˈɛvətəbli/ *adv* as was certain to happen ‖ 확실히 일어나는 것으로서. 필연적으로. 반드시: *Inevitably, there were a few mistakes.* 부득이 하게 실수가 몇 가지 있었다. / *People inevitably gain some weight as they get older.* 사람들은 나이가 들면서 어쩔 수 없이 살이 찐다.

in·ex·act /ˌɪnɪɡˈzækt/ *adj* not exact ‖ 정확하지 않은. 엄밀[정밀]하지 않은: *Psychology is an inexact science.* (=you cannot measure things exactly in it) 심리학은 엄밀하지 못한 학문이다.

in·ex·cus·a·ble /ˌɪnɪkˈskyuzəbəl/ *adj* inexcusable behavior is too bad to be excused ‖ 행위가 너무나 나빠서 용서가 안 되는. 용서[변명]할 수 없는 **-inexcusably** *adv*

in·ex·haust·i·ble /ˌɪnɪɡˈzɔstəbəl/ *adj* a supply that is inexhaustible exists in such large amounts that it can never be used up ‖ 공급량이 다 사용할 수 없을 만큼 많은. 무진장의: *Warton seems to have an inexhaustible supply of energy.* 와턴은 지칠 줄 모르는 정력적인 사람 같다. **-inexhaustibly** *adv*

in·ex·o·ra·ble /ɪnˈɛksərəbəl/ *adj* FORMAL an inexorable process cannot be stopped ‖ 진행을 막을 수 없는. 변경할 수 없는. 불변의: *the inexorable aging of the body* 막을 수 없는 신체의 노화 – **inexorably** *adv*

in·ex·pen·sive /ˌɪnɪkˈspɛnsɪv/ *adj* low in price ‖ 값이 싼. 저렴한: *an inexpensive vacation* 돈이 적게 드는 휴가 – **inexpensively** *adv*

in·ex·pe·ri·enced /ˌɪnɪkˈspɪriənst/ *adj* not having much experience or knowledge ‖ 경험이나 지식이 많지 않은. 미숙한. 서투른: *an inexperienced driver* 서투른 운전자 – **inexperience** *n* [U]

in·ex·pli·ca·ble /ˌɪnɪkˈsplɪkəbəl/ *adj* too unusual or strange to be explained or understood ‖ 너무 유별나고 이상해서 설명하거나 이해할 수 없는. 불가해한. 불가사의한: *the inexplicable disappearance of the young man* 그 젊은이의 불가사의한 실종 – **inexplicably** *adv*

in·ex·tri·ca·bly /ˌɪnɪkˈstrɪkəbli/ *adv* FORMAL things that are inextricably connected or related cannot be separated from each other ‖ 사물이 서로 연결되거나 관련되어 분리할 수 없는. 밀접하게. 복잡하게 얽히어: *Smoking and lung cancer are inextricably linked.* 흡연과 폐암은 서로 아주 밀접하게 관련되어 있다. – **inextricable** *adj*

in·fal·li·ble /ɪnˈfæləbəl/ *adj* 1 always right, and never making mistakes ‖ 항상 옳으며 결코 실수를 하지 않는. 오류가 없는: *Many Catholics consider the Pope to be infallible.* 많은 가톨릭 신자들은 교황을 절대 무류(無謬)하다고 간주한다. 2 always having the intended effect ‖ 항상 의도된 효과를 얻는. (효능 등이) 확실한. 틀림없이 듣는: *an infallible cure for hiccups* 딸꾹질의 특효약 – **infallibility** /ɪnˌfæləˈbɪləţi/ *n* [U]

in·fa·mous /ˈɪnfəməs/ *adj* well known for being bad or evil ‖ 나쁘거나 사악함으로 잘 알려진. 악명 높은: *an infamous criminal* 악명 높은 범죄자 – **infamously** *adv* —compare FAMOUS

in·fa·my /ˈɪnfəmi/ *N* [U] the state of being evil or of being well known for evil things ‖ 악한 상태나 악한 것으로 잘 알려져 있는 상태. 사악. 악명. 불명예

in·fan·cy /ˈɪnfənsi/ *n* [singular, U] 1 the period in a child's life before s/he can walk or talk ‖ 아이의 삶에서 걷거나 말할 수 있기 전의 기간. 유아기: *Their son died in infancy.* 그들의 아들은 유아기에 죽었다. 2 **in its infancy** something that is in its infancy is just starting to be developed ‖ 어떤 것이 막 발전하기 시작하고 있는. 초기(단계)에: *The project is*

still in its infancy. 그 프로젝트는 아직 초기 단계이다.

in·fant /ˈɪnfənt/ *n* FORMAL a baby, especially one that cannot walk ‖ 특히 걸을 수 없는 아기. 유아

in·fan·tile /ˈɪnfənˌtaɪl, -təl/ *adj* 1 infantile behavior seems silly in an adult because it is typical of a child ‖ 행동이 전형적인 어린이의 모습이어서 어른에게 어리석어 보이는. 어린애 같은. 유치한: *his infantile jokes* 그의 유치한 농담들 2 affecting very small children ‖ 아주 어린 아이들에게 영향을 미치는: *infantile illnesses* 유아병

in·fan·try /ˈɪnfəntri/ *n* [U] soldiers who fight on foot ‖ 걸으면서 싸우는 군인들. 보병(부대)

in·fat·u·at·ed /ɪnˈfætʃuˌeɪţɪd/ *adj* having unreasonably strong feelings of love for someone ‖ 남에게 무작정 사랑의 강한 감정을 가지는. 홀딱 빠진[반한]: *He's infatuated with her.* 그는 그녀에게 홀딱 빠졌다. – **infatuation** /ɪnˌfætʃuˈeɪʃən/ *n* [C, U]

in·fect /ɪnˈfɛkt/ *v* [T] 1 to give someone a disease ‖ 남에게 질병을 주다. 병을 옮기다. 감염[전염]시키다: *a young man infected with the AIDS virus* 에이즈 바이러스에 감염된 한 젊은 남자 2 to make food, water etc. dangerous and able to spread disease ‖ 음식·물 등을 위험하게 하고 질병을 퍼뜨릴 수 있게 하다. 오염시키다: *a bacteria that can infect fruit* 과일을 오염시킬 수 있는 박테리아 3 if a feeling that you have infects other people, it makes them begin to feel the same way ‖ 어떠한 감정을 다른 사람들도 똑같이 느끼기 시작하게 하다. 영향을 주다. 감화하다: *Lucy's enthusiasm soon infected the rest of the class.* 루시의 열정에 그 반의 나머지 학생들도 곧 활기를 띠었다.

in·fect·ed /ɪnˈfɛktɪd/ *adj* 1 a wound that is infected has harmful BACTERIA in it that prevent it from getting better ‖ 상처가 호전되는 것을 막는 해로운 박테리아를 가지고 있는. 감염[전염]된: *an infected finger* (=a finger with an infected wound) 감염된 손가락 2 food, water etc. that is infected contains BACTERIA that spread disease ‖ 음식·물 등이 질병을 퍼뜨리는 박테리아를 함유하고 있는. 오염된: *water infected with cholera* 콜레라에 오염된 물 3 if a computer or DISK is infected, the information in or on it has been changed or destroyed by a computer VIRUS ‖ 컴퓨터나 디스크가 컴퓨터 바이러

스에 의해 내부의 정보가 변형되거나 파괴
된. (바이러스에) 감염된

in·fec·tion /ɪnˈfɛkʃən/ n [C, U] a
disease or sickness in a part of your
body caused by BACTERIA or a VIRUS ‖ 박
테리아나 바이러스로 인한 자신의 신체 일
부의 질병이나 아픔. 감염. 전염(병):
*Wash the cut thoroughly to protect
against infection.* 감염을 막기 위해서 상
처를 철저히 씻어라. / *an ear infection* 귀
전염병

in·fec·tious /ɪnˈfɛkʃəs/ adj 1 an
infectious disease can be passed from
one person to another ‖ 질병이 한 사람
에게서 다른 사람에게로 옮길 수 있는. 전
염성인. 전염병의 2 someone who is
infectious has a disease that could be
passed to other people ‖ 사람이 다른 사
람들에게로 옮길 수 있는 질병을 가지고
있는. 전염병 환자의 3 infectious feelings
or laughter spread quickly from one
person to another ‖ 감정이나 웃음이 한
사람에게서 다른 사람에게로 빠르게 퍼지
는. 남에게 옮기 쉬운. 전염성인

in·fer /ɪnˈfɚ/ v **-rred, -rring** [T]
FORMAL to begin to have an opinion that
something is probably true because of
information that you have learned ‖ 얻은
정보 때문에 어떤 것이 아마도 사실일 거
라는 의견을 가지기 시작하다. 추론[추정]
하다: *What can you infer from the
available data?* 너는 이용할 수 있는 자
료에서 무엇을 추론할 수 있니? —
compare IMPLY

in·fer·ence /ˈɪnfərəns/ n a belief or
opinion you have, based on information
that you already know ‖ 이미 알고 있는
정보에 근거하여 갖고 있는 신념이나 의
견. 추론. 추정: *You'll have to draw
your own inferences from the evidence.*
(=decide what you think is true) 너는 그
증거에서 네가 직접 추론을 이끌어내야 할
거야.

in·fe·ri·or¹ /ɪnˈfɪriɚ/ adj not good, or
not as good in quality, value, or skill as
someone or something else ‖ 질[가치,
솜씨]이 다른 사람이나 사물만큼 좋지 않은.
열등한. 하등의: *Larry always makes me
feel inferior.* 래리를 보면 나는 항상 열등
감을 느낀다. / *Her work is inferior to
mine.* 그녀의 작품은 내 것보다 못하다.
– **inferiority** /ɪnˌfɪriˈɑrəti, -ˈɔr-/ n [U]
—opposite SUPERIOR¹

inferior² n someone who has a lower
position or rank than you in an
organization ‖ 어떤 조직에서 자신보다 더
낮은 지위나 계급의 사람. 손아랫사람. 하
급자. 후배 —opposite SUPERIOR²

in·fer·no /ɪnˈfɚnoʊ/ n LITERARY a very
large and dangerous fire ‖ 아주 거대하고
위험한 불. 화염: *a raging inferno*
(=an extremely violent fire) 집어삼킬 듯
한 불

in·fer·tile /ɪnˈfɚtl/ adj 1 an infertile
person or animal cannot have babies ‖
사람이나 동물이 아기나 새끼를 가질 수
없는. 생식력이 없는. 불임의 2 infertile
land or soil is not good enough to grow
plants in ‖ 땅이나 흙이 식물이 자라는 데
에 족할 만큼 좋지 않은. 메마른. 불모의
– **infertility** /ˌɪnfɚˈtɪləti/ n [U]

in·fest /ɪnˈfɛst/ v [T] if insects, rats
etc. infest a place, they are there in
large numbers and usually cause
damage ‖ 곤충·쥐 등이 한 장소에 많은
수가 있으면서 대체로 피해를 일으키다.
들끓다. 출몰[횡행]하다: *an old carpet
infested with fleas* 벼룩이 들끓는 낡은
카펫 – **infestation** /ˌɪnfɛˈsteɪʃən/ n [C,
U]

in·fi·del /ˈɪnfədl, -ˌdɛl/ n OLD-FASHIONED
a disapproving word for someone who
does not believe in what you consider to
be the true religion ‖ 자신이 진실한 종교
로 여기는 것을 믿지 않는 사람에 대하여
비난하는 말. 이교도. 이단자

in·fi·del·i·ty /ˌɪnfəˈdɛləti/ n [C, U] an
act of being unfaithful to your wife or
husband by having sex with someone
else ‖ 다른 사람과 성관계를 가져 아내나
남편에게 충실하지 못한 행위. 부정(不貞)

in·field /ˈɪnfild/ n [singular] the part of
a baseball field inside the four bases ‖
네 개의 누(壘) 안에 있는 야구장의 지역.
내야 – **infielder** n

in·fight·ing /ˈɪnˌfaɪtɪŋ/ n [U]
unfriendly competition and disagreement among members of the
same group or organization ‖ 같은 집단이나 조
직의 구성원간의 비우호적인 경쟁과 의견
차이. 내분. 암투: *political infighting* 정
치적 암투

in·fil·trate /ɪnˈfɪlˌtreɪt, ˈɪnfɪl-/ v [I, T]
to join an organization or enter a place,
especially in order to find out secret
information about it or to harm it ‖ 특히
비밀 정보를 알아내거나 해를 입히려고 어
떤 조직에 가입하거나 장소에 들어가다.
침투[침입, 잠입]하다: *The police have
made several attempts to infiltrate the
Mafia.* 경찰은 몇 차례 마피아 조직에 침
투하려고 했다. – **infiltrator** n –
infiltration /ˌɪnfɪlˈtreɪʃən/ n [U]

in·fi·nite /ˈɪnfənɪt/ adj very great or
without limits ‖ 매우 거대하거나 한계가
없는. 막대한. 무한한: *a teacher with*

infinite patience 대단한 인내심이 있는 교사 / *an infinite universe* 무한한 우주

in·fi·nite·ly /ˈɪnfənɪtli/ *adv* very much ‖ 대단히: *This stove is infinitely better/worse than the other one.* 이 난로는 다른 난로보다 월등히 더 낫다[못하다]

in·fin·i·tes·i·mal /ˌɪnfɪnəˈtɛsəməl/ *adj* extremely small ‖ 매우 작은. 극소한. 미소한: *infinitesimal changes in temperature* 온도의 미소한 변화 — **infinitesimally** *adv*

in·fin·i·tive /ɪnˈfɪnəṭɪv/ *n* TECHNICAL in grammar, the basic form of a verb, used with "to." In the sentence "I forgot to buy milk," "to buy" is an infinitive ‖ 문법에서 "to"와 함께 쓰이는 동사의 기본형태. 부정사. "I forgot to buy milk"라는 문장에서 "to buy"는 부정사이다

in·fin·i·ty /ɪnˈfɪnəṭi/ *n* **1** [U] a space or distance without limits or an end ‖ 한계나 끝이 없는 공간이나 거리. 무한. 무궁 **2** TECHNICAL a number that is larger than all others ‖ 다른 모든 수보다 더 큰 수. 무한대

in·firm /ɪnˈfəm/ *adj* FORMAL weak or ill, especially because of being old ‖ 특히 나이가 들었기 때문에 약하거나 아픈. 허약한. 노쇠한: *Aunt Louise has become old and infirm.* 루이즈 이모는 늙고 노쇠해졌다.

in·fir·ma·ry /ɪnˈfəməri/ *n* FORMAL a place where sick people can receive medical treatment, especially in a place such as a school ‖ 특히 학교 등의 장소에서 아픈 사람들이 의학적 치료를 받을 수 있는 곳. 진료소. 양호실

in·fir·mi·ty /ɪnˈfəməṭi/ *n* [C, U] FORMAL bad health or a particular illness ‖ 건강치 못함, 또는 특정한 질병. 허약. 질환

in·flame /ɪnˈfleɪm/ *v* [T] LITERARY to make someone have strong feelings of anger, excitement etc. ‖ 남에게 화·흥분 등의 강한 감정을 가지게 하다. 화나게 하다. 흥분시키다

in·flam·ma·ble /ɪnˈflæməbəl/ *adj* inflammable materials or substances will start to burn very easily ‖ 재료나 물질이 아주 쉽게 타기 시작하는. 불붙기[불타기] 쉬운. 인화성의: *Gasoline is highly inflammable.* 휘발유는 인화성이 매우 강하다. —opposite NONFLAMMABLE — compare FLAMMABLE —see usage note at FLAMMABLE

in·flam·ma·tion /ˌɪnfləˈmeɪʃən/ *n* [C, U] swelling and soreness on or in a part of your body, which is often red and hot to touch ‖ 종종 만지면 붉어지거나 따끔거

리는 신체 부위의 속이나 겉의 부기와 쑤심. 염증 — **inflamed** *adj*

in·flam·ma·to·ry /ɪnˈflæməˌtɔri/ *adj* FORMAL an inflammatory speech, piece of writing etc. is likely to make people angry ‖ 연설·글 등이 사람들을 화나게 할 듯한. 자극적[선동적]인

in·flat·a·ble /ɪnˈfleɪt̬əbəl/ *adj* an inflatable object has to be filled with air before you can use it ‖ 물체가 사용하기에 앞서서 공기로 채워져야만 하는. 부풀릴 수 있는. 팽창성의: *an inflatable mattress* 팽창시킬 수 있는 매트리스

inflate

in·flate /ɪnˈfleɪt/ *v* **1** [I, T] to fill something with air or gas, so that it becomes larger, or to make something do this ‖ 사물이 공기나 기체로 채워서 더 커지다, 또는 사물을 이렇게 만들다. 부풀다. 부풀리다: *The machine quickly inflates the tires.* 그 기계는 타이어에 바람을 신속히 넣는다. **2** [T] to make something larger in size, amount, or importance ‖ 사물의 크기[양, 중요성]를 확대하다. 팽창시키다. 과장하다: *a policy that inflates land prices* 토지 가격을 상승시키는 정책 —opposite DEFLATE

in·flat·ed /ɪnˈfleɪt̬ɪd/ *adj* **1** greater or larger than is reasonable ‖ 합당한 이상으로 크거나 거대한. 과장된. 자만한: *He has an inflated opinion of his own importance.* 그는 자기 자신이 아주 대단한 사람이라는 자만한 생각을 가지고 있다. **2** filled with air or gas ‖ 공기나 기체로 가득 찬. 부푼. 부푼: *an inflated balloon* 팽창한 풍선

in·fla·tion /ɪnˈfleɪʃən/ *n* [U] **1** a continuing increase in prices or the rate at which prices increase ‖ 물가나 물가 상승 비율의 계속적인 상승. 통화 팽창. 인플레이션: *the Mexican government's efforts to control inflation* 인플레이션을 규제하려는 멕시코 정부의 노력 **2** the process of filling something with air or gas ‖ 사물을 공기나 기체로 채우는 과정. 부풀리기. 팽창

in·fla·tion·a·ry /ɪnˈfleɪʃəˌnɛri/ *adj* relating to or causing price increases ‖

물가 상승에 관련되거나 물가 상승을 일으키는. 통화 팽창의. 인플레이션의: *inflationary wage increases* 인플레이션을 유발하는 임금 인상

in·flex·i·ble /ɪnˈflɛksəbəl/ *adj* **1** impossible to influence or change ‖ 영향을 미치거나 변경하기 불가능한. 불변의: *a school with inflexible rules* 변경할 수 없는 규칙을 가진 학교 **2** inflexible material is stiff and will not bend ‖ 재료가 딱딱하고 구부러지지 않는. 구부릴 수 없는. 경직한 – **inflexibility** /ɪnˌflɛksəˈbɪləti/ *n* [U]

in·flict /ɪnˈflɪkt/ *v* [T] to make someone suffer something unpleasant ‖ 남에게 불쾌한 것으로 고통받게 하다. …을 …에게 가하다[입히다]: *the damage inflicted on/upon the enemy* 적에게 입힌 피해 – **infliction** /ɪnˈflɪkʃən/ *n* [U]

in·flu·ence¹ /ˈɪnfluəns/ *n* **1** [C, U] the power to have an effect on the way someone or something develops, behaves, or thinks ‖ 사람이나 사물이 발전[행동, 생각]하는 방식에 효과를 미치는 힘. 영향(력): *Vince used his influence with the union to get his nephew a job.* 빈스는 조카의 일자리를 마련하려고 노조에 영향력을 행사했다. **2** someone or something that has an effect on other people or things ‖ 다른 사람들이나 사물들에 효과를 미치는 사람이나 사물. 영향을 미치는 사람[것]: *Alex's parents always thought that I was a good/bad influence on him.* 알렉스의 부모님은 항상 내가 알렉스에게 좋은[나쁜] 영향을 미치는 사람이라고 생각하셨다. **3 under the influence** drunk or feeling the effects of a drug ‖ 취하거나 약의 효과를 느끼는. 술 취하여. 약 기운이 돌아

influence² *v* [T] to have an effect on the way someone or something develops, behaves, or thinks ‖ 사람이나 사물이 발전[행동, 생각]하는 방식에 효과를 미치다. 영향을 미치다: *I don't want to influence your decision.* 나는 네 결정에 영향을 미치고 싶지 않다. / *He lets his brother influence him too much.* 그는 형이 자기에게 너무 많은 영향을 미치게 내버려 둔다.

in·flu·en·tial /ˌɪnfluˈɛnʃəl/ *adj* having a lot of influence ‖ 많은 영향력을 미치는. 영향력 있는. 유력한: *an influential politician* 유력한 정치인 – **influentially** *adv*

in·flu·en·za /ˌɪnfluˈɛnzə/ *n* [U] FORMAL ⇨ FLU

in·flux /ˈɪnflʌks/ *n* [C usually singular] the arrival of large numbers of people or things ‖ 다수의 사람이나 사물의 도래. 유입. 쇄도: *an influx of cheap imported goods* 값싼 수입품의 유입

in·fo /ˈɪnfoʊ/ *n* [U] INFORMAL ⇨ INFORMATION

in·fo·mer·cial /ˈɪnfoʊˌmɚʃəl/ *n* a long television advertisement that is made to seem like a regular program ‖ 일반 프로그램처럼 보이게 만든 긴 텔레비전 광고. 인포머셜. 정보 광고

in·form /ɪnˈfɔrm/ *v* [T] to formally tell someone about something ‖ 사람에게 어떤 것에 대해 공식적으로 말하다. 알리다. 알려 주다. 통지하다: *Please inform us of any progress.* 진전 상황을 우리에게 알려 주세요.

inform against/on sb *phr v* [T] to tell the police, an enemy etc. about what someone has done ‖ 경찰·적 등에게 남이 한 일에 대해서 알리다. 고자질하다. 밀고하다

in·for·mal /ɪnˈfɔrməl/ *adj* **1** relaxed and friendly ‖ 긴장을 풀고 친근한. 비공식의. 격식을 차리지 않는: *an informal meeting* 비공식적인 회의 **2** suitable for ordinary situations or conversations ‖ 일반적인 상황이나 대화에 알맞은. 구어체의: *an informal letter to your family* 가족에게 보내는 대화체 편지 – **informally** *adv* – **informality** /ˌɪnfɔrˈmæləti/ *n* [U]

in·form·ant /ɪnˈfɔrmənt/ *n* someone who gives secret information to the police, a government department etc. ‖ 비밀 정보를 경찰·정부 부처 등에 제공하는 사람. 정보원. 밀고자: *a CIA informant* CIA(중앙 정보국) 정보원

in·for·ma·tion /ˌɪnfɚˈmeɪʃən/ *n* [U] **1** facts or details that tell you something about a situation, person, event etc. ‖ 상황·사람·사건 등에 대한 것을 말해 주는 사실이나 세부 사항. 정보: *I need some more information about/on this machine.* 나는 이 기계에 대한 정보가 더 많이 필요하다. / *Goodwin was able to provide several new pieces of information.* 굿윈은 몇 가지 새로운 정보를 제공할 수 있었다. **2** a telephone service that you can call to get someone's telephone number ‖ 남의 전화번호를 얻기 위해 전화를 걸 수 있는 전화 서비스. 전화 안내 서비스

information su·per·high·way /ˌ…ˌ…ˈ…ˌ…/ *n* [singular] the system of computer connections that people anywhere in the world can use in order to electronically send or obtain information, pictures, sounds etc. ‖ 세계

도처에 있는 사람들이 정보·그림·소리 등을 전자적으로 보내거나 얻기 위해서 사용할 수 있는 컴퓨터 연결 체계. 정보 고속 도로

information tech·nol·o·gy /... ,.. .'.../, **IT** *n* [U] the use of electronic processes, especially computers, for gathering information, storing it, and making it available ‖ 정보의 수집·저장·이용을 위한 전자 공정, 특히 컴퓨터의 활용. 정보 기술. 정보 공학

in·form·a·tive /ɪnˈfɔrmətɪv/ *adj* providing many useful facts or ideas ‖ 유용한 사실이나 생각을 많이 제공하는. 유익한: *a very informative book* 매우 유익한 책 **– informatively** *adv*

in·formed /ɪnˈfɔrmd/ *adj* having a lot of knowledge or information about a particular subject or situation ‖ 특정한 주제나 상황에 대해서 많은 지식이나 정보를 가지고 있는. 견문이 넓은. 박식한: *Women should be able to make an informed choice about contraception.* 여자는 피임에 대해서 많은 정보를 얻은 후에 선택을 할 수 있어야 한다. / *well-informed voters* 선거 관련 정보에 밝은 유권자들 **—opposite** UNINFORMED

in·form·er /ɪnˈfɔrmɚ/ *n* ⇨ INFORMANT

in·fo·tain·ment /ˌɪnfoʊˈteɪnmənt/ *n* [U] television programs that present news and other types of information in an entertaining way ‖ 뉴스와 다른 종류의 정보를 오락적으로 제공하는 텔레비전 프로그램. 정보성 오락 프로그램

in·frac·tion /ɪnˈfrækʃən/ *n* [C, U] FORMAL an act of breaking a rule or law ‖ 규칙이나 법을 어기는 행위. 위반. 침해

in·fra·red /ˌɪnfrəˈrɛd/ *adj* infrared light produces heat but cannot be seen ‖ 빛이 열은 발생하지만 볼 수 없는. 적외선의 — compare ULTRAVIOLET

in·fra·struc·ture /ˈɪnfrəˌstrʌktʃɚ/ *n* the basic systems that a country or organization needs in order to work in the right way ‖ 한 국가나 조직이 제대로 일을 하기 위해서 필요한 기본적인 체계. 기반(시설): *Japan's economic infrastructure* 일본의 경제 기반

in·fre·quent /ɪnˈfrikwənt/ *adj* not happening often ‖ 자주 일어나지 않는. 드문. 드물게 일어나는. 이따금 하는: *one of our infrequent visits to Uncle Edwin's house* 에드윈 삼촌 집에 어쩌다 한 번 방문한 것 **– infrequently** *adv*

in·fringe /ɪnˈfrɪndʒ/ *v* [T] to do something that is against the law or that limits someone's legal rights ‖ 법에 저촉되거나 다른 사람의 권리를 제한하는 것을

하다. 어기다. 위반[침해]하다: *The new law infringes on our basic right to freedom of speech.* 새 법률은 언론의 자유에 대한 우리의 기본권을 침해한다. **– infringement** *n* [C, U]

in·fu·ri·ate /ɪnˈfyʊriˌeɪt/ *v* [T] to make someone very angry ‖ 다른 사람을 매우 화나게 만들다. 격노하게 하다. 격분[격앙]시키다: *He really infuriates me!* 그는 정말 나를 격분시키고 있구나!

in·fu·ri·at·ing /ɪnˈfyʊriˌeɪtɪŋ/ *adj* very annoying ‖ 매우 화나게 하는. 격분[격노]하게 하는: *an infuriating delay of four hours* 격분케 하는 4시간의 지체[지연] **– infuriatingly** *adv*

in·fuse /ɪnˈfyuz/ *v* 1 [T] to fill someone or something with a particular feeling or quality ‖ 사람이나 사물을 특별한 감정이나 성질로 채우다. 특질을 불어넣다[주입시키다]. 고취시키다: *The coach has managed to infuse the team with new enthusiasm.* 코치는 가까스로 팀에 새로운 열의를 불어넣었다. 2 [I, T] to put a substance such as tea in very hot water, so that its taste passes into the water ‖ 차 등의 물질을 아주 뜨거운 물에 넣어 그 맛이 물 속에 전해지다. 달여지다[달이다]. 우러나다[우리다] **– infusion** /ɪnˈfyuʒən/ *n* [C, U]

in·ge·nious /ɪnˈdʒinyəs/ *adj* 1 an ingenious plan, idea, etc. works well and is the result of intelligent thinking and new ideas ‖ 계획·생각 등이 효과를 잘 발휘하며 총명한 사고와 새로운 생각의 결과인. 정교한. 독창적인. 착상이 좋은 2 an ingenious person is very good at inventing things, thinking of new ideas etc. ‖ 사람이 사물을 고안하고 새로운 아이디어 등을 생각하는 데에 아주 뛰어난. 독창성이 풍부한. 재간이 있는. 솜씨 좋은 **– ingeniously** *adv*

in·ge·nu·i·ty /ˌɪndʒəˈnuəti/ *n* [U] skill at inventing things, thinking of new ideas etc. ‖ 사물을 고안하고 새로운 아이디어 등을 생각하는 능력. 창의력. 발명[고안]의 재간

in·gest /ɪnˈdʒɛst/ *v* [T] TECHNICAL to eat something ‖ 어떤 것을 먹다. 섭취하다 **– ingestion** *n* [U]

in·grained /ɪnˈɡreɪnd, ˈɪnɡreɪnd/ *adj* 1 ingrained attitudes or behavior are firmly established and difficult to change ‖ 태도나 행동이 확고하게 정립되어서 변화하기 어려운. 뿌리 깊은. 깊이 배어든 2 ingrained dirt is under the surface of something and difficult to remove ‖ 때가 물건의 속에 있어 제거하기 어려운. 속까지 배어든

in·gra·ti·ate /ɪn'greɪʃiˌeɪt/ v **ingratiate yourself (with)** DISAPPROVING to try to get someone's approval by doing things to please him/her, expressing admiration etc. ‖ 어떤 사람을 즐겁게 하기 위한 일을 하거나 존경심을 표시하는 것 등에 의해 인정을 받으려 하다. 환심을 사다. 비위를 맞추다. 마음에 들게 하다: *a politician trying to ingratiate himself with the voters* 유권자들의 환심을 사려 하는 정치인 – **ingratiating** *adj* – **ingratiatingly** *adv*

in·grat·i·tude /ɪn'grætəˌtud/ n [U] the quality of not being grateful for something ‖ 어떤 것에 감사하지 않는 특성. 망은(忘恩). 배은망덕. 감사하는 마음이 없음 – **ingrate** /'ɪngreɪt/ n

in·gre·di·ent /ɪn'gridiənt/ n **1** one of the things that goes into a mixture from which a type of food is made ‖ 한 종류의 음식을 만드는 혼합물에 들어가는 것들 중의 하나. 성분. 요소. 재료. 원료: *Flour, water, and eggs are the main ingredients.* 밀가루, 물, 계란이 주재료이다. **2** a quality that helps to achieve something ‖ 어떤 것을 달성하는 데에 도움이 되는 특성. 중요한 요소. 구성 분자: *Imagination and hard work are the ingredients of success.* 상상력과 열심히 일하는 것이 성공의 주요 요소이다.

in·hab·it /ɪn'hæbɪt/ v [T] to live in a particular place ‖ 특정 장소에 살다. 거주[서식]하다: *a forest inhabited by bears and moose* 곰과 북미 큰사슴이 서식하는 숲 – **inhabitable** *adj*

in·hab·it·ant /ɪn'hæbətənt/ n one of the people who live in a particular place ‖ 특정 장소에 사는 사람들 중의 한 명. 거주자[민]. 주민: *the inhabitants of large cities* 대도시 거주자

in·hale /ɪn'heɪl/ v [I, T] to breathe in air, smoke, or gas ‖ 공기[연기, 가스]를 흡입하다. 마시다. 들이쉬다. 빨아들이다: *Try not to inhale the fumes from the glue.* 접착제의 냄새를 들이마시지 않도록 하시오. – **inhalation** /ˌɪnhə'leɪʃən/ n [C, U]

in·hal·er /ɪn'heɪlɚ/ n a plastic tube containing medicine that someone, especially someone with ASTHMA, breathes in order to make his/her breathing easier ‖ 특히 천식에 걸린 사람이 숨을 쉽게 쉴 수 있도록 흡입하는, 약품이 들어 있는 플라스틱 관. (의료용) 흡입기[호흡기]

in·her·ent /ɪn'hɪrənt, -'hɛr-/ *adj* a quality that is inherent in something is a natural part of it and cannot be separated from it ‖ 사물의 특성이 자연적인 부분이어서 분리될 수 없는. 본래 갖추어져 있는. 고유의. 타고난. 선천적인: *a problem that is inherent in the system* 시스템[체제] 내의 고유한[본래부터 있던] 문제 – **inherently** *adv*

in·her·it /ɪn'hɛrɪt/ v **1** [I, T] to receive something from someone after s/he has died ‖ 죽은 사람에게서 어떤 것을 물려받다. 상속하다[받다]. 유산을 받다: *I inherited the house from my uncle.* 나는 삼촌에게서 그 집을 상속받았다. **2** [T] to get a quality, type of behavior, appearance etc. from one of your parents ‖ 부모 중의 한 명에게서 특성·행동 양식·외모 등을 받다. 이어받다. 물려받다: *Tony inherited his father's nose.* 토니는 제 아버지의 코를 물려받았다.

in·her·i·tance /ɪn'hɛrɪtəns/ n [C, U] money, property etc. that you receive from someone after s/he has died ‖ 죽은 사람에게서 받는 돈·재산 등. 상속 재산[물건]. 상속[계승]된 것

in·hib·it /ɪn'hɪbɪt/ v [T] **1** to prevent something from growing or developing in the usual or expected way ‖ 어떤 것이 통상적 또는 예상했던 방식대로 자라거나 발전하는 것을 막다. …을 억제하다[억누르다, 저지하다]. 금지하다: *new treatments to inhibit the spread of the disease* 질병의 확산을 막는 새 치료법 **2** to make someone feel embarrassed or less confident, so s/he cannot do or say what s/he wants to ‖ 어떤 사람을 당황하게 하거나 자신감을 떨어뜨려서 원하는 바를 하거나 말할 수 없게 하다. 하지 못하게 하다. 방해하다. 가로막다: *Fear of criticism may inhibit a child's curiosity.* 비난에 대한 두려움이 아이들의 호기심을 억누르는지도 모른다.

in·hib·it·ed /ɪn'hɪbɪtɪd/ *adj* not confident or relaxed enough to express how you really feel or do what you really want to do ‖ 실제로 느끼는 바를 표현하거나 실제 하고 싶은 바를 할 만큼 충분히 자신이 있거나 편안하지 않은. 억제된. 방해된. 내성적인. 쉽게 …하지 못하는: *Julie's too inhibited to talk about sex.* 줄리는 너무 내성적이어서 성에 대해 이야기하지 못한다. —opposite UNINHIBITED

in·hi·bi·tion /ˌɪnhɪ'bɪʃən, ˌɪnə-/ n [C, U] a feeling of worry or embarrassment that stops you from expressing how you really feel or doing what you really want to do ‖ 실제 느끼는 바를 표현하거나 하고 싶은 것을 하지 못하게 막는 걱정이나 당혹감. 억제. 억압. 방해. 금지: *She soon* *loses her inhibitions* (=stops feeling worried etc.) *when she's had a few glasses of wine.* 그녀는 포도주를 몇 잔 마시자 곧 조심스러움이 가셨다.

in·hos·pi·ta·ble /ˌɪnhɑ'spɪtəbəl/ *adj* **1** not friendly, welcoming, or generous to visitors ‖ 방문자에게 친절하지[환영하지, 관대하지] 않은. 무뚝뚝한. 쌀쌀한 **2** difficult to live or stay in because of severe weather conditions or lack of shelter ‖ 가혹한 기상 조건이나 피난처가 부족해서 거주하거나 머물기 어려운. 거주하기[머무르기] 부적당한. 살 만하지 못한: *an inhospitable climate* 거주하기에 부적당한 기후 **– inhospitably** *adv*

in-house /ˌɪn'haʊs·/ *adj, adv* within a company or organization rather than outside it ‖ 회사나 조직의 외부보다 내부의[에서]. 조직 안의[에서]. 사내의[에서]: *an in-house training department* 사내 교육 부(서)

in·hu·man /ɪn'hyumən/ *adj* **1** very cruel and without any normal feelings of pity ‖ 매우 잔인하며 정상적인 동정심이 전혀 없는. 냉혹한. 잔혹한. 무정한. 인정머리 없는: *inhuman punishment* 냉혹한 처벌 **2** lacking any human qualities in a way that seems strange or frightening ‖ 기이하거나 무서워 보일 정도로 인간적 특성이 전혀 없는. 비인간적인. 인간이 아닌. 동물의: *an inhuman scream* 동물적인 비명

in·hu·mane /ˌɪnhyu'meɪn/ *adj* treating people or animals in a cruel and unacceptable way ‖ 사람이나 동물을 잔인하고 용납할 수 없게 대하는. 비인도[비인간]적인. 몰인정한. 박정한: *inhumane living conditions* 비인간적인 생활 조건 **– inhumanely** *adv*

in·hu·man·i·ty /ˌɪnhyu'mænəti/ *n* [C, U] extreme cruelty or an act of cruelty ‖ 극도의 잔인성이나 잔인한 행위. 잔혹. 비정. 몰인정. 무자비. 비인도적 행위: *the inhumanities of war* 전쟁의 잔혹성

in·im·i·ta·ble /ɪ'nɪmətəbəl/ *adj* too good for anyone else to copy ‖ 너무 훌륭해서 다른 어떤 사람도 복제할 수 없는. 흉내 낼[모방할] 수 없는: *Sinatra sings in his own inimitable style.* 시나트라는 모방할 수 없는 그만의 스타일로 노래한다.

i·ni·tial[1] /ɪ'nɪʃəl/ *adj* happening at the beginning; first ‖ 처음에 일어나는. 최초의. 초기의; 처음의: *the initial stages of the disease* 질병의 초기 단계들 **– initially** *adv*

initial[2] *n* the first letter of a name ‖ 이름의 첫 글자. 머리글자. 이니셜: *a suitcase with the initials S.H. on it* 머리글자 S.H.가 새겨진 가방

initial[3] *v* [T] to write your INITIALs on a document ‖ 서류에 이름의 첫 글자를 쓰다. 머리글자를 써넣다. 머리글자를 써서 서명[동의]하다: *Could you initial this form for me, please?* 이 양식에 서명을 해 주시겠어요?

i·ni·ti·ate /ɪ'nɪʃiˌeɪt/ *v* [T] **1** FORMAL to arrange for something important to start ‖ 중요한 것이 시작되도록 준비하다. …을 시작[개시]하다. 착수하다: *The prison has recently initiated new security procedures.* 그 교도소는 최근 새로운 보안 조치를 시작했다. **2** to introduce someone into an organization, club etc., usually with a special ceremony ‖ 사람을 조직·클럽 등에 대개는 특별 의식과 함께 소개하다. …에 입회[가입]시키다: *students initiated into the school's honor society* 학교의 명예 학생 모임에 가입한 학생들 **– initiation** /ɪˌnɪʃi'eɪʃən/ *n* [C, U]

i·ni·tia·tive /ɪ'nɪʃətɪv/ *n* **1** [U] the ability to make decisions and take action without waiting for someone to tell you what to do ‖ 자신의 할 일에 대해 다른 사람이 시키기를 기다리지 않고 결정을 내려서 행동을 취하는 능력. 결단력. 주도(권): *Try using your own initiative.* (=doing something without being told what to do) 네 스스로의 주도권을 행사해 봐라. **2** a plan or process that has been started in order to achieve a particular aim or to solve a particular problem ‖ 특정 목표를 달성하거나 특정 문제를 풀기 위해 시작되어 온 계획이나 진행. 발안(發案). 주도 사업[계획]: *state initiatives to reduce spending* (재정)지출을 줄이기 위한 주정부 주도 계획 **3 take the initiative** to be the first one to take action to achieve a particular aim or solve a particular problem ‖ 특정 목표를 달성하거나 특정 문제를 해소하기 위해 행동을 취하는 첫 번째(사람)가 되다. 선제[선도]하다. 선수치다. 주도권을 잡다

in·ject /ɪn'dʒɛkt/ *v* [T] **1** to put a liquid, especially a drug, into your body by using a special needle ‖ 액체 특히 약물을 특수 주사기를 이용해 신체에 투입하다. 주입[주사]하다. 주사를 놓다: *The rat has been injected with a new drug.* 그 쥐는 계속 신약 주사를 맞았다. **2** to improve something by adding an important thing or quality to it ‖ 중요한 것이나 특성을 더해서 어떤 것을 개선하다. 불어넣다. 고취시키다. 도입[투입]하다: *remarks that injected some humor into the situation* 그 상황에 약간의 유머

를 섞은 발언

in·jec·tion /ɪnˈdʒɛkʃən/ *n* **1** [C, U] an act of putting a liquid, especially a drug, into your body by using a special needle ‖ 특별한 주사기로 액체, 특히 약물을 신체에 삽입하기. 주입. 주사: *The nurse gave me an injection.* 간호사가 나에게 주사를 놓았다. **2** an addition of an important thing or quality to something in order to improve it ‖ 어떤 것을 개선하기 위해 중요한 것이나 특성을 추가하기. 고취. 도입. 투입: *The business received a cash injection of $20,000.* 그 사업체에 2만 달러의 현금이 투입되었다.

in·junc·tion /ɪnˈdʒʌŋkʃən/ *n* LAW an official order given by a court that stops someone from being allowed to do something ‖ 사람이 어떤 일을 하도록 허용되어 있는 것을 중단시키는 법원의 공식 명령. 금지[강제] 명령

in·jure /ˈɪndʒɚ/ *v* [T] to hurt a person or animal ‖ 사람이나 동물을 다치게 하다. 해치다. 상처를 입히다: *She was badly injured in the accident.* 그녀는 그 사고로 심하게 부상당했다. **– injured** *adj* **– injurious** /ɪnˈdʒʊriəs/ *adj* —see usage note at WOUND²

in·ju·ry /ˈɪndʒəri/ *n* [C, U] physical harm or damage that is caused by an accident or attack, or a particular example of this ‖ 사고나 공격으로 입은 신체적 해나 손상, 또는 이러한 특례. 부상. 손상. 상해: *serious injuries to the head and neck* 머리와 목에 입은 심한 부상

in·jus·tice /ɪnˈdʒʌstɪs/ *n* [C, U] a situation in which people are treated very unfairly ‖ 사람들이 아주 불공정하게 대우 받는 상황. 부정[불법] 행위. 부당(함). 불공평: *a history of injustices against Black people* 흑인들을 부당하게 대우한 역사

ink /ɪŋk/ *n* [U] a colored liquid used for writing, printing etc. ‖ 필기·인쇄 등에 사용되는 색깔 있는 액체. 잉크

ink·ling /ˈɪŋklɪŋ/ *n* **have an inkling** to have a slight idea about something ‖ 어떤 것에 대해 약간의 생각을 갖다. 어렴풋이 감지하다. 암시를 받다: *We had no inkling that he was leaving.* 우리는 그가 떠나는 것을 전혀 알지 못했다.

in·laid /ˈɪnleɪd, ɪnˈleɪd/ *adj* having a thin layer of a material set into the surface for decoration ‖ 장식용으로 표면에 얇은 층의 물질을 입힌. 박아 넣은. 상감 세공한. 박(箔)이 입혀진: *a wooden box inlaid with gold* 금박이 입혀진 나무 상자

in·land¹ /ˈɪnlənd/ *adj* an inland area, city etc. is not near the coast ‖ 지역·도시 등이 해안에서 가깝지 않은. 내륙[내지, 오지]의

in·land² /ɪnˈlænd, ˈɪnlænd, -lənd/ *adv* in a direction away from the coast and toward the center of a country ‖ 해안에서 멀리 떨어진 방향으로·나라의 중심 방향을 향해. 내륙[내지, 오지]에[으로]: *driving inland* 내륙 쪽으로 운전하기

in·laws /ˈ. ./ *n* [plural] INFORMAL your relatives by marriage, especially the mother and father of your husband or wife ‖ 혼인 관계에 의한 친척, 특히 남편이나 아내의 모친과 부친. 장인. 장모. 시부모. 사돈. 시가. 처가의 친척: *We're spending Christmas with my in-laws.* 우리는 사돈 댁과 크리스마스를 보낼 예정이다.

in·lay /ˈɪnleɪ/ *n* [C, U] a material that has been set into the surface of another material as a decoration, or the pattern made by this ‖ 장식으로 다른 재질의 표면에 박아진 재료, 또는 이것으로 만들어진 문양. 상감. 박(箔). 상감 무늬

in·let /ˈɪnlɛt, ˈɪnlət/ *n* **1** a narrow area of water reaching from the sea or a lake into the land, or between islands ‖ 바다나 호수에서 내륙으로 이르는 좁은 수역, 또는 섬 사이의 해역. 후미. 작은 만. 해협 **2** the part of a machine through which liquid or gas flows in ‖ 액체나 가스가 흘러 들어가는 기계의 부분. 주입구

in-line skate /ˌ. . ˈ./ *n* a special boot with a single row of wheels fixed under it ‖ 한 줄의 바퀴가 밑에 장착된 특수 신발. 인라인 스케이트 —compare ROLLER SKATE

in·mate /ˈɪnmeɪt/ *n* someone who is kept in a prison or in a hospital for people with mental illnesses ‖ 교도소에 갇혀 있거나 정신 병원에 수용되어 있는 사람. 피수용자

inn /ɪn/ *n* a small hotel, especially one that is not in a city ‖ 작은 여관, 특히 도시에 있지 않은 것. 여인숙. 여관

in·nards /ˈɪnɚdz/ *n* [plural] INFORMAL **1** the parts inside your body, especially your stomach ‖ 신체 내의 장기, 특히 위. 내장. 위장 **2** the parts inside a machine ‖ 기계 내부 부품. 내부 기구[구조]: *the innards of the computer* 컴퓨터의 내부 (구조)

in·nate /ˌɪˈneɪt/ *adj* an innate quality has been part of your character since you were born ‖ 특성이 태어난 이후로 성격의 일부분이 되어온. 성질이 타고난. 천성의. 선천적인: *an innate sense of fun*

타고난 유머 감각 **- innately** *adv*

in·ner /'ɪnə/ *adj* **1** on the inside or close to the center of something ∥ 사물의 내부에 있거나 중심에 가까운. 안의. 속의: *the inner ear* 내이(內耳) — opposite OUTER **2** inner feelings, thoughts, meanings etc. are secret and not expressed ∥ 감정·생각·의미 등이 비밀스러우며 표현되지 않는. 내밀한. 숨어 있는. 속에 있는 **3 inner circle** the few people in an organization, political party etc. who control it or share power with its leader ∥ 조직·정당 등을 통제하고 지도자와 권력을 나눠 갖는 그 내부의 소수의 사람. 핵심[측근] 그룹[세력]. 권력 중추

inner cit·y /ˌ.. '../ *n* the part of a city that is near the middle, especially the part where the buildings are in a bad condition and the people are poor ∥ 도시의 중심 근처 지역, 특히 건물 상태가 불량하고 사람들이 가난한 지역. 도심 빈민가 지구: *Crime in our inner cities seems to be getting worse.* 도심 빈민가 범죄가 더욱 악화되고 있는 것 같다. **– inner city** *adj* : *an inner city school* 도심 빈민가 학교

in·ner·most /'ɪnəˌmoʊst/ *adj* **1** your innermost feelings, desires etc. are the ones you feel most strongly and keep private ∥ 감정·욕구 등이 매우 강하게 느껴지고 비밀로[사적으로] 지켜지는. 내밀한. 깊숙이 숨겨진 **2** FORMAL farthest inside ∥ 맨 안쪽의. 가장 내부의[깊은]. 가장 깊숙한 —opposite OUTERMOST

inner tube /'.. ./ *n* the rubber tube that is filled with air inside a tire ∥ 타이어 안에 있는, 공기로 채워진 고무관. 타이어의 (속)튜브

in·ning /'ɪnɪŋ/ *n* one of the nine playing periods in a game of baseball ∥ 야구 경기에서 아홉 번의 경기 시간 중의 하나. 회(回). 이닝

inn·keep·er /'ɪnˌkipə/ *n* OLD-FASHIONED someone who owns or manages an INN ∥ 여인숙을 소유하거나 운영하는 사람. 여인숙[여관] 주인

in·no·cence /'ɪnəsəns/ *n* [U] **1** the fact of not being guilty of a crime ∥ 범죄에 대해 유죄가 아닌 상태. 무죄. 결백: *How did they prove her innocence?* 그들은 그녀의 결백을 어떻게 입증했습니까? **2** the state of not having much experience of life, especially experience of bad or complicated things ∥ 인생의 경험, 특히 나쁘거나 복잡한 일들에 대한 경험이 많지 않은 상태. 순진. 천진난만: *a child's innocence* 아이들의 순진무구함

in·no·cent /'ɪnəsənt/ *adj* **1** not guilty of a crime ∥ 범죄에 대해 죄가 없는. 무죄의. 죄를 짓지 않은. 결백한: *Nobody would believe that I was innocent.* 아무도 내가 결백하다는 것을 믿으려 하지 않았다. / *He was found innocent of murder by the jury.* (=they decided he was innocent) 배심원단은 살인에 대해 그에게 무죄 평결을 내렸다. **2** not having much experience of life, especially so that you are easily deceived ∥ 삶에 대한 경험이 많지 않은, 특히 그래서 쉽게 속는. 순진한. 천진난만한: *I was 13 years old and very innocent.* 나는 13살이었고 아주 순진했다. **3** done or said without intending to harm or offend anyone ∥ 다른 사람에게 해를 끼치거나 불쾌하게 할 의도 없이 행하거나 말한. 무해한. 해롭지 않은. 악의 없는: *an innocent remark* 악의 없는 발언 **– innocently** *adv*

in·noc·u·ous /ɪˈnɑkyuəs/ *adj* not offensive, dangerous, or harmful ∥ 무례하지[위험하지, 해롭지] 않은. 거슬리지 않는. 불쾌감을 주지 않는: *an innocuous but boring movie* 해롭지는 않지만 지루한 영화 **– innocuously** *adv*

in·no·va·tion /ˌɪnəˈveɪʃən/ *n* [C, U] the introduction of new ideas, methods, or inventions, or the idea, method, or invention itself ∥ 새로운 생각[방법, 고안]의 도입, 또는 생각[방법, 고안] 그 자체. 새로운 것의 도입[채용]. 쇄신. 혁신(적인 것): *recent innovations in computing* 최근의 컴퓨터 작업의 혁신 / *The west coast has been the center of innovation in the computer industry.* 서해안이 컴퓨터 산업에서 혁신의 중심이 되어 왔다. **– innovate** /'ɪnəˌveɪt/ *v* [I] **– innovative** *adj* **– innovator** *n*

in·nu·en·do /ˌɪnyuˈɛndoʊ/ *n*, *plural* **innuendoes** *or* **innuendos** [C, U] an indirect remark about sex or about something bad that someone has done, or the act of making this type of remark ∥ 성이나 다른 사람이 행한 나쁜 일에 대한 간접적인 표현, 또는 이런 종류의 말을 하는 행위. 암시. 넌지시 비춤. 빗대어 말함: *nasty innuendos about Laurie and the boss* 로리와 사장에 대한 추잡한[악의 있는] 비꼼

in·nu·mer·a·ble /ɪˈnumərəbəl/ *adj* too many to be counted ∥ 너무 많아 헤아릴 수 없는. 셀 수도 없이 많은. 엄청나게 많은. 무수한: *innumerable stars* 무수한 별들

in·oc·u·late /ɪˈnɑkyəˌleɪt/ *v* [T] to protect someone against a disease by introducing a weak form of it into

his/her body‖사람의 신체에 약한 병원체
를 주입해서 질병으로부터 보호하다. 접종
조치를 하다. 예방 접종을 하다: *Children
should be inoculated against measles.*
아이들은 홍역에 대한 예방 접종을 해야
한다. – **inoculation** /ɪˌnɑkyəˈleɪʃən/ *n*
[C, U]

in·of·fen·sive /ˌɪnəˈfensɪv/ *adj*
unlikely to offend anyone‖다른 사람을
침해할 것 같지 않은. 무해한. 악의 없는.
거슬리지 않는. 불쾌감을 주지 않는: *a
quiet inoffensive man* 조용하고 불쾌감을
주지 않는 남자

in·op·por·tune /ɪnˌɑpɚˈtun, ˌɪnɑ-/ *adj*
FORMAL not suitable or not good for a
particular situation‖특정 상황에 적합하
지 않거나 좋지 않은. 시기[계제]가 적절
치 못한[나쁜]. 부적당[부적절]한: *They
arrived at an inopportune moment.* 그들
은 상황이 나쁜 때에 도착했다.

in·or·di·nate /ɪnˈɔrdn-ɪt/ *adj* FORMAL
much greater than is reasonable‖합당
한 것보다 훨씬 더 큰. 지나친. 과도한.
터무니없는: *an inordinate amount of
work* 과도한 업무량 – **inordinately**
adv

in·or·gan·ic /ˌɪnɔrˈgænɪk/ *adj* not
consisting of anything that is living‖살
아 있는 어떤 것으로도 이루어지지 않은.
무생물의: *inorganic matter* 무생물(체) –
inorganically *adv*

in·pa·tient /ˈɪnpeɪʃənt/ *n* someone who
stays in a hospital at least one night for
medical treatment‖의학적 치료를 위해
최소한 하룻밤을 병원에 머무는 사람. 입
원환자 —compare OUTPATIENT

in·put /ˈɪnput/ *n* [singular, U] **1** ideas,
advice, money, or effort that you put
into a job, meeting etc. in order to help
it succeed‖일·회의 등이 성공하도록 들
이는 생각[충고, 돈, 노력] 등. 투입(량).
(…의) 제공: *Students are allowed input
into what they learn in class.* 학생들은
수업 시간에 적극적으로 참여할 수 있다.
2 information that is put into a
computer‖컴퓨터에 입력되는 정보. 입력
(데이터) **3** electrical power that is put
into a machine for it to use‖기계를 사용
하기 위해 공급하는 전력. 공급 전력. 입
력 에너지 —compare OUTPUT

in·quest /ˈɪnkwɛst/ *n* LAW an official
process to find out the cause of a
sudden or unexpected death, especially
if there is a possibility that the death is
the result of a crime‖갑작스럽거나 예기
치 않은 사망의 원인, 특히 그 사망이 범죄
의 결과일 가능성이 있는지를 규명하는 공
무상의 과정. 검시(檢屍)

in·quire /ɪnˈkwaɪɚ/ *v* [I, T] FORMAL to
ask someone for information‖어떤 사람
에게 정보를 얻으려고 묻다. 문의하다. 알
아보다: *I am writing to inquire about
your advertisement in the New York
Post.* 뉴욕 포스트 신문에 난 당신의 광고
에 대해 문의하기 위해 편지를 씁니다. –
inquirer *n* —see usage note at ASK

inquire into sth *phr v* [T] to ask
questions in order to get more
information about something or to find
out why something happened‖어떤 것
에 대한 더 많은 정보를 얻거나 왜 그 일
이 일어났는가를 밝히기 위해 질문하다.
…에 대해 조사하다. 심문하다: *The
investigation will inquire into the
reasons for the disaster.* 그 조사를 통해
참사에 대한 원인을 규명할 것이다.

in·quir·ing /ɪnˈkwaɪərɪŋ/ *adj* wanting
to find out more about something‖어떤
것에 대해 더 많이 찾고 싶어하는. 탐구심
[호기심]이 있는. 캐기 좋아하는: *Dad
taught us to have inquiring minds.*
(=taught us to ask questions about
things) 아버지는 우리에게 탐구 정신을
갖도록 가르치셨다. – **inquiringly** *adv*

in·quir·y /ɪnˈkwaɪəri, ˈɪŋkwəri/ *n* **1** a
question you ask in order to get
information‖정보를 얻기 위해 물어보는
질문. 탐문. 문의: *We're getting a lot of
inquiries about our new train service.*
우리는 새 열차 서비스에 대한 많은 문의
를 받고 있다. **2** [C, U] the act of asking
questions in order to get information
about something or to find out why
something happened, or the series of
meetings in which this is done‖어떤 것
에 대한 정보를 얻거나 일어난 이유를 밝
히기 위해 질문하기, 또는 이것이 행해지
는 일련의 회합. 조사 (활동). 심문 (과
정): *There will be an official inquiry
into the incident.* 그 사건에 공식 조사가
이루어질 것이다.

in·qui·si·tion /ˌɪnkwəˈzɪʃən/ *n*
[singular] FORMAL a series of questions
that someone asks in a threatening or
unpleasant way‖어떤 사람이 위협적으
로 또는 불쾌하게 물어보는 일련의 질문.
공식 조사. 문초. 엄한 심문

in·quis·i·tive /ɪnˈkwɪzətɪv/ *adj*
interested in a lot of different things and
wanting to find out more about them‖
많은 다른 사물들에 관심을 갖고 그것들에
대해 더 많이 알고 싶어 하는. 호기심 많
은. 캐묻기 좋아하는: *a cheerful
inquisitive little boy* 명랑하고 호기심 많
은 작은 소년

in·roads /ˈɪnroʊdz/ *n* **make inroads**

into/on to become more and more successful, powerful, or popular and so take away power, trade, votes etc. from a competitor or enemy ‖ 점점 더 성공하게[강력하게, 인기 있게] 되어서 경쟁자나 적으로부터 권력·거래·표를 빼앗다. 침해[잠식]하다. 감소시키다: *Their new soft drink is already making huge inroads into the market.* 그들의 새 음료수는 이미 시장을 크게 잠식해 들어가고 있다.

ins and outs /ˌ. . ˈ./ *n* [plural] all the exact details of a complicated situation, system, problem etc. ‖ 복잡한 상황·체계·문제 등의 모든 정확한 세부 내용. 세부 지식. 총체적 내용: *I'm still learning the ins and outs of my new job.* 나는 아직 새 직업에 대한 모든 지식을 배우고 있습니다.

in·sane /ɪnˈseɪn/ *adj* **1** INFORMAL completely stupid or crazy, often in a way that is dangerous ‖ 종종 위험할 정도로 완전히 어리석거나 미친. 제 정신이 아닌. 실성한. 머리가 돈. 광기어린: *You must've been totally insane to go with him!* 그와 같이 가다니 너는 머리가 돈 것이 틀림없다! / *an insane idea* 제 정신이 아닌 생각 **2** someone who is insane is permanently and seriously mentally ill ‖ 사람이 영구적이고 심각하게 정신적으로 병든. 정신 이상의. 정신병자의 – **insanely** *adv*

in·san·i·ty /ɪnˈsænəti/ *n* [U] **1** very stupid actions that may cause you serious harm ‖ 심각한 해를 초래할지 모르는 매우 어리석은 행동. 미친 짓. 무모함. 광기: *the insanity of war* 전쟁의 광기 **2** the state of being seriously mentally ill ‖ 심각하게 정신적으로 병들어 있는 상태. 정신 이상. 착란. 발광. 미침

in·sa·ti·a·ble /ɪnˈseɪʃəbəl/ *adj* always wanting more and more of something ‖ 언제나 점점 더 많은 것을 원하는. 만족할 줄 모르는. 탐욕스런: *an insatiable appetite* 만족할 줄 모르는[끝없는] 식욕

in·scribe /ɪnˈskraɪb/ *v* [T] to cut, print, or write words on something, especially on the surface of a stone or coin ‖ 사물 위에, 특히 돌이나 동전의 표면에 단어를 새기다[인쇄하다, 쓰다]: *a tree inscribed with the initials J.S.* 머리글자 J.S.가 새겨진 나무 – **inscription** /ɪnˈskrɪpʃən/ *n*

in·scru·ta·ble /ɪnˈskruːtəbəl/ *adj* not easily understood, because you cannot tell what someone is thinking or feeling ‖ 어떤 사람의 생각이나 감정을 알 수 없어서 쉽게 이해할 수 없는. 알아내기 어려운. 불가사의한·신비한: *an inscrutable smile* 이해할 수 없는 미소 – **inscrutably** *adv*

in·sect /ˈɪnsɛkt/ *n* a small creature such as an ANT or a fly, with six legs and a body divided into three parts ‖ 다리가 6개이고 몸이 세 부분으로 나뉘어진 개미나 파리 등의 작은 생명체. 곤충

in·sec·ti·cide /ɪnˈsɛktəˌsaɪd/ *n* [U] a chemical substance used for killing insects ‖ 곤충을 죽이는 데에 쓰이는 화학 물질. 살충제

in·se·cure /ˌɪnsɪˈkyʊr/ *adj* **1** not feeling confident about yourself, your abilities, your relationships etc. ‖ 자기 자신·자신의 능력·자신의 관계 등에 대해 자신감을 느끼지 않는. 불안한. 초조한. 걱정스러운. 염려되는: *She's very shy and insecure.* 그녀는 매우 부끄럼을 타고 불안해 한다. **2** not safe or not protected ‖ 안전하지 않거나 보호되지 않은. 위험한. 안전치 못한. 불안정한: *She feels that her position in the company is insecure.* (=she may lose her job) 그녀는 회사 내에서 자신의 지위가 불안정하다고 느낀다. – **insecurity** *n* [U] – **insecurely** *adv*

in·sem·i·na·tion /ɪnˌsɛməˈneɪʃən/ *n* [U] the act of putting SPERM into a female's body in order to make her have a baby ‖ 여성이 아이를 갖도록 몸 안에 정자를 삽입하는 행위. (인공) 수정(受精): *the artificial insemination of cattle* (=done by medical treatment, not sex) 소의 인공 수정

in·sen·si·tive /ɪnˈsɛnsətɪv/ *adj* **1** not noticing other people's feelings, and not realizing that something that you do will upset them ‖ 다른 사람의 감정을 알아차리지 못하며 자신이 하고 있는 일이 그들을 화나게 할 수 있음을 인식하지 못하는. 눈치가 없는. 감각이 둔한: *Sue asked several insensitive questions about Carla's recent divorce.* 수는 칼라의 최근 이혼에 대해 눈치도 없이 몇 가지 질문을 했다. **2** not affected by physical effects or changes ‖ 육체적 효과나 변화에 영향 받지 않는. 반응이 없는. 둔감한. 무감각한: *Some people are more insensitive to pain than others.* 어떤 사람들은 다른 사람들보다 고통에 대해 더 무감각하다. – **insensitively** *adv* – **insensitivity** /ɪnˌsɛnsəˈtɪvəti/ *n* [U]

in·sep·a·ra·ble /ɪnˈsɛpərəbəl/ *adj* **1** people who are inseparable are always together and are very friendly with each other ‖ 사람들이 항상 같이 있고 서로 아주 친한. 항상 붙어 다니는. 떨어질 수 없는. 절친한. 둘도 없는: *When they were* *younger, the boys were inseparable.* 그 소년들은 어린 시절에 늘 붙어 다녔다. **2** unable to be separated or not able to be considered separately ∥ 분리될 수 없거나 따로 생각될 수 없는. 따로 떼어낼 수 없는. 불가분의: *The patient's mental and physical problems are inseparable.* 환자의 정신과 육체의 문제는 따로 떼어낼 수 없다. **- inseparably** *adv*

in·sert¹ /ɪnˈsɚt/ *v* [T] to put something inside or into something else ∥ 사물을 다른 사물이나 속으로 집어넣다. …을 삽입하다[끼우다]. 끼워[꽂아] 넣다: *Insert the key in/into the lock.* 열쇠를 자물통에 끼우시오. **- insertion** /ɪnˈsɚʃən/ *n* [C, U]

insert

in·sert² /ˈɪnsɚt/ *n* **1** something that is designed to be put inside something else ∥ 다른 것 안에 넣게 고안된 것. 삽입물: *Dan wears special inserts in his shoes to make him look taller.* 댄은 더 커보이게 하기 위해 신발 속에 특수 삽입물을 넣어 신는다. **2** printed pages that are put inside a newspaper or magazine in order to advertise something ∥ 어떤 것을 광고하기 위해 신문이나 잡지 안에 삽입되는 인쇄된 페이지. 삽입 광고물. 전단

in·side¹ /ɪnˈsaɪd, ˈɪnsaɪd/ *prep, adv* **1** in a container, room, building etc. ∥ 용기·방·건물 등의 속에. 안쪽[에] 있는: *He opened the box to find two kittens inside.* 그가 상자를 열자 고양이 새끼 두 마리가 그 안에 있었다. / *Go/come inside* (=into the house) *and get your jacket.* —opposite OUTSIDE¹ 집안에 들어가서[들어와서] 웃옷을 가져 와라[가라]. **2** if you have a feeling or thought inside you, you feel or think it but do not always express it ∥ 감정이나 생각을 느끼거나 생각하지만 항상 표현하지는 않는. 마음속으로. 내심: *You never know what's happening inside his head.* 너는 그의 머리 속에서 무슨 일이 벌어지는지 결코 모른다. / *Don't keep the anger inside.* 분노를 마음속에 담아두지 마세요. **3** used in order to emphasize that what is happening in a country or organization is only known by people who live there ∥ 나라나 조직 내에서 일어나고 있는 일이 그 안에 사는 사람들에게만 알려지는 것을 강조하는 데에 쓰여. 내부[자체]적으로. 내부에 있는: *People inside the organization have told us that changes are happening.* 변화가 일

고 있다고 조직 내부 사람들이 우리에게 말했다. **4** in less time than ∥ …보다 적은 시간 내에. …시간 안에. …이내에: *We'll be there inside of an hour.* 우리는 1시간 내에 거기에 도달할 것이다.

in·side² *n* **1 the inside** the inner part of something ∥ 사물의 내부. 안쪽: *The inside of the house was nicer than the outside.* 그 집의 내부는 외부보다 더 근사했다. **2 inside out** with the usual outside parts on the inside ∥ 통상 바깥 부분이 안쪽에 있는. 뒤집어서. 거꾸로: *Your shirt is on inside out.* 너 셔츠를 뒤집어 입었어. **3 know/learn sth inside out** to know everything about a subject ∥ 한 주제에 대해 모든 것을 알다. 안팎으로[철저히, 완전히, 샅샅이, 모조리 다] 알다/배우다: *She knows the business inside out.* 그녀는 그 사업을 속속들이 안다. —opposite OUTSIDE

in·side³ *adj* **1** on or facing the inside of something ∥ 사물의 내부에 있거나 향하고 있는. 안쪽의. 내면의: *the inside pages of a magazine* 잡지의 속 페이지들 **2 inside information/the inside story** information that is known only by people who are part of an organization, company etc. ∥ 조직·회사 등의 구성원들만 알고 있는 정보. 내부의[내부적인] 정보/이야기[내막]

in·sid·er /ɪnˈsaɪdɚ/ *n* someone who has a special knowledge of a particular organization because s/he is part of it ∥ 구성원이기 때문에 특정 조직[단체]에 대한 특별한 지식을 갖고 있는 사람. 내부 사람. 내부 소식통. 내막을 아는 사람

in·sid·i·ous /ɪnˈsɪdiəs/ *adj* happening gradually without being noticed, but causing great harm ∥ 눈에 띄지 않고 점진적으로 발생하지만 큰 해를 끼치는. 은연중[몰래] 벌어지는[해치는]. 모르는 새 작용하는. 잠행성의: *the insidious effects of breathing polluted air* 오염된 공기 호흡의 잠재적인 영향 **- insidiously** *adv*

in·sight /ˈɪnsaɪt/ *n* [C, U] the ability to understand something clearly, or an example of this ∥ 사물을 분명하게 이해하는 능력, 또는 이의 실례. 통찰(력). 식견. 간파: *The article gives us a real insight into Chinese culture.* 그 기사는 중국 문화에 대한 우리의 안목을 크게 높여 준다.

in·sig·ni·a /ɪnˈsɪgniə/ *n, plural* **insignia** a BADGE or other object that shows what official or military rank someone has, or which group or organization s/he belongs to ∥ 관리나 군인이 무슨 계급을 가지고 있는지, 또는 어떤 집단이나 조직에 속해 있는지 보여주는

배지나 다른 물체. 휘장. 기장

in·sig·nif·i·cant /ˌɪnsɪgˈnɪfəkənt/ *adj* too small or unimportant to consider or worry about ‖ 고려하거나 걱정하기에는 너무 작거나 중요하지 않은. 하찮은. 대수롭지 않은. 사소한: *an insignificant change in the unemployment rate* 실업률의 사소한 변화 **- insignificantly** *adv* **- insignificance** *n* [U]

in·sin·cere /ˌɪnsɪnˈsɪr/ *adj* pretending to be pleased, sympathetic etc., but not really meaning what you say ‖ 기뻐거나 동정하는 척 행동하지만 실제로는 자신이 말하는 바를 뜻하지 않는. 성실치 못한. 성의 없는. 거짓의. 지어낸: *an insincere smile* 억지웃음 **- insincerely** *adv* **- insincerity** /ˌɪnsɪnˈsɛrəti/ *n* [U]

in·sin·u·ate /ɪnˈsɪnyuˌeɪt/ *v* [T] to say something that seems to mean something unpleasant, without saying it directly ‖ 직접적으로 말하지 않고 불쾌함을 의미하는 듯한 things 암시하다. 빗대다. 넌지시 비치다: *Are you insinuating that she didn't deserve the promotion?* 당신은 지금 그녀가 승진할 자격이 없었다고 빗대는 것입니까? **- insinuation** /ɪnˌsɪnyuˈeɪʃən/ *n* [C, U]

in·sip·id /ɪnˈsɪpɪd/ *adj* not interesting, exciting, or attractive ‖ 재미있지[흥미롭지, 매력적이지] 않은. 따분한. 지루한. 맛없는. 풍미 없는: *the movie's insipid story* 그 영화의 지루한 줄거리 / *his insipid voice* 그의 따분한 목소리 / *the insipid taste of weak tea* 맛이 없는 연한 게 탄 차 **- insipidly** *adv*

in·sist /ɪnˈsɪst/ *v* [I] **1** to say firmly and again and again that something is true, especially when other people think it may not be true ‖ 특히 다른 사람들이 사실이 아닐 거라 생각할 때 어떤 것이 사실이라고 확고하게 반복해서 말하다. 강력히 주장하다[우기다]. 강조[역설]하다: *Mike insisted that Joelle would never have gone by herself.* 마이크는 죠엘이 결코 그녀 혼자서 가지는 않았을 거라고 주장했다. **2** to demand that something should happen ‖ 어떤 일이 일어나야 한다고 요구하다. 고집하다. 강력히 요구하다. …할 것을 우기다: *I insisted that he leave.* 나는 그가 떠나야 한다고 요구했다. / *They're insisting on your resignation.* 그들은 당신의 사임을 강하게 고집하고 있습니다. **—see usage note at** RECOMMEND

in·sist·ence /ɪnˈsɪstəns/ *n* [U] the act of INSISTing that something should happen ‖ 어떤 일이 일어나야 한다고 주장하기. 강조. 역설. 강요. 억지(부리기): *He came, but only at my insistence.* 그

는 왔지만 단지 내 강요에 의해서였다.

in·sist·ent /ɪnˈsɪstənt/ *adj* INSISTing that something should happen ‖ 어떤 일이 일어나야 한다고 주장하는. 고집하는. 끈덕진. 집요한. 고집 센: *She's very insistent that we should all be on time.* 그녀는 우리 모두가 제 시간에 도착해야 한다고 매우 고집을 부린다. **- insistently** *adv*

in so far as, insofar as /ˌɪnsoʊˈfɑr əz/ *conjunction* FORMAL to the degree that something affects another thing ‖ 어떤 것이 다른 것에 영향을 미치는 정도까지. …하는 한에서[에 있어서는]. (…의)정도[범위]까지는: *Insofar as sales are concerned, the company is doing very well.* 판매(량)에 관한 한 그 회사는 매우 잘 하고 있다.

in·so·lent /ˈɪnsələnt/ *adj* rude and not showing any respect ‖ 무례하며 어떠한 존경심도 보이지 않는. 거만한. 오만한. 모욕적인: *He was suspended for being insolent to the principal.* 그는 교장에게 무례했다는 이유로 정학당했다. **- insolence** *n* [U] **- insolently** *adv*

in·sol·u·ble /ɪnˈsɑlyəbəl/ *adj* **1** an insoluble substance does not DISSOLVE when you put it into a liquid ‖ 물질을 액체 속에 집어넣을 때 녹지 않는. 용해되지 않는. 불용성의 **2** also **insolvable** impossible to explain or solve ‖ 설명하거나 해결하기 불가능한. 해결[해명]할 수 없는. 풀 수 없는: *a number of seemingly insoluble conflicts in the region* 그 지역 내의 일견 해결할 수 없을 것 같은 많은 갈등

in·sol·vent /ɪnˈsalvənt/ *adj* FORMAL not having enough money to pay what you owe ‖ 빚진 것을 갚을 충분한 돈을 가지고 있지 않은. 지불 능력이 없는. 파산한. 파산(자)의 **- insolvency** *n* [U]

in·som·ni·a /ɪnˈsɑmniə/ *n* [U] the condition of not being able to sleep ‖ 잠이 들지 못하는 상태. 불면증 **- insomniac** /ɪnˈsɑmniˌæk/ *n*

in·spect /ɪnˈspɛkt/ *v* [T] **1** to examine something carefully ‖ 사물을 주의 깊게 검사하다. …을 정밀하게 조사하다. 점검하다: *Inspect the car for dents before you buy it.* 자동차를 사기 전에 자동차의 흠집을 잘 점검하시오. **2** to make an official visit to a building, organization etc. to check that everything is satisfactory and that rules are being obeyed ‖ 모든 것이 만족스럽고 규정이 준수되고 있는지 확인하기 위해 건물·조직 등을 공식적으로 방문하다. …을 정식으로 검사[조사]하다. 시찰[감사]하다: *The* *building is regularly inspected by the fire department.* 그 건물은 소방 당국에 의해 정기적으로 검사받고 있다.

in·spec·tion /ɪnˈspɛkʃən/ *n* [C, U] the act of carefully checking an object's condition, or an organization, in order to be sure that it is obeying rules ‖ 규정이 준수되고 있는지를 확인하기 위해 사물의 상태나 조직을 주의 깊게 점검하기. 면밀한 조사. 정밀 검사. 시찰. 검열. 감사: *The restaurant is due for a health inspection this month.* 그 식당은 이번 달에 (공중)위생 검사를 받기로 되어 있다. / *a close inspection of the soldiers' living areas* 군인들의 숙영지에 대한 면밀한 검열

in·spec·tor /ɪnˈspɛktɚ/ *n* **1** an official whose job is to INSPECT something ‖ 사물을 검사하는 공무원. 조사[검사, 감사]관. 감독관: *a health inspector* 위생 검사관[공무원] **2** a police officer of middle rank ‖ 중간 계급의 경찰관. 경위

in·spi·ra·tion /ˌɪnspəˈreɪʃən/ *n* [C, U] **1** something or someone that encourages you to do or produce something good ‖ 훌륭한 것을 하거나 만들어 낼 수 있게 고무하는 사물이나 사람. 영감. 영감[감화]을 주는 것[사람]: *Dante was the inspiration for my book on Italy.* 단테는 이탈리아에 관한 내 책에 영감을 준 사람이었다. / *Her hard work and imagination should be an inspiration to everyone.* 그녀의 근면함과 상상력은 모든 사람에게 귀감이 되어야 한다. **2** a good idea ‖ 좋은 생각[계획]. 좋은 착상. 명안: *I've had an inspiration – let's go to the lake!* 내게 좋은 생각이 떠올랐다. 호수로 가자! **– inspirational** *adj*

in·spire /ɪnˈspaɪɚ/ *v* [T] **1** to encourage someone to do or produce something good ‖ 훌륭한 것을 하거나 만들어 내도록 사람을 고무시키다. 고취하다. 분발하게 하다. 고무하여 …할 마음이 생기게 하다: *We were inspired by the coach's pre-game pep talk.* 우리는 경기 전에 감독님이 격려를 해주어 고무되었다. **2** to make someone have a particular feeling ‖ 어떤 사람이 특별한 감정을 갖게 하다. 품게 하다. 불어넣다: *The captain inspires confidence in his men.* 대장은 그의 부하들에게 자신감을 불어넣어 준다. **– inspiring** *adj*

in·spired /ɪnˈspaɪɚd/ *adj* having very exciting special qualities ‖ 매우 감동시키는 특별한 특성을 지닌. 영감을 받은. 직관적인. 예지력을 가진: *Abraham Lincoln was an inspired leader.* 아브라함 링컨은 예지력을 가진 지도자였다.

in·sta·bil·i·ty /ˌɪnstəˈbɪləṭi/ *n* [U] the state of being uncertain and likely to change suddenly ‖ 불안정하며 갑자기 변하기 쉬운 상태. 불안정. 변하기 쉬움: *the political instability in the region* 그 지역의 정치적 불안 상태

in·stall /ɪnˈstɔl/ *v* [T] **1** to put a piece of equipment somewhere and connect it so that it is ready to be used ‖ 장비가 사용될 수 있도록 위치에 집어넣고 그것을 연결하다. (장치를) 가설[설치]하다: *The school is installing a new furnace.* 학교는 새로운 난로를 설치하고 있다. **2** to put someone in an important job or position, especially with a ceremony ‖ 어떤 사람을 특히 의식을 거쳐 중요한 업무나 지위에 두다. 임명하다. 취임시키다: *The college is installing a new chancellor.* 그 대학은 새로운 총장을 임명할 예정이다. **– installation** /ˌɪnstəˈleɪʃən/ *n* [C, U]

in·stall·ment /ɪnˈstɔlmənt/ *n* **1** one of a series of regular payments that you make until you have paid all the money you owe ‖ 모든 빚진 돈을 갚을 때까지 여러 번에 걸쳐 정기적으로 지불하는 돈의 1회분. 할부금. 할부 불입금: *I'm paying for the car in monthly installments.* 나는 매달 할부로 차값을 내고 있다. **2** one of the parts of a story that appears as a series in a magazine, newspaper etc. ‖ 잡지·신문 등에 연속물로서 연재되는 기사 중의 한 부분. 1회분

in·stance /ˈɪnstəns/ *n* **1 for instance** for example ‖ 예를 들어[면]. 실례로: *You can't depend on her. For instance, she arrived an hour late for an important meeting yesterday.* 너는 그녀에게 의지해서는 안 돼. 예를 들면 그녀는 어제 중요한 회의에 1시간이나 늦게 도착했어. **2** an example of a particular fact, event etc. ‖ 특정 사실·사건 등의 실례. 보기. 예. 경우: *reports on instances of police brutality* 경찰의 가혹 행위에 대한 사례 보도

in·stant¹ /ˈɪnstənt/ *adj* **1** happening or produced immediately ‖ 즉시 일어나거나 생겨나는. 즉각적인. 즉시의. 곧바로의: *The movie was an instant success.* 그 영화는 바로 성공했다. **2** instant food, coffee etc. is in the form of powder and is prepared by adding hot water ‖ 식품·커피 등이 가루 형태로 되어 있고 뜨거운 물을 부어서 준비되는. 인스턴트의. 즉석의

instant² *n* **1** [C usually singular] a moment in time ‖ 시간의 한 순간. 바로 …하는 찰나. 즉각: *I didn't believe her* *for an instant.* 나는 한 순간 그녀를 믿지 않았다. **2 this instant** SPOKEN now, without delay ‖ 지체 없이 지금(당장). 바로. 즉시: *Come here this instant!* 지금 당장 이리와!

in·stan·ta·ne·ous /ˌɪnstənˈteɪniəs/ *adj* happening immediately ‖ 즉시 발생하는. 순간적으로 생기는[벌어지는]. 즉시[즉각]적인: *an instantaneous reaction to the drug* 약[마약]에 대한 즉각적인 반응 – **instantaneously** *adv*

in·stant·ly /ˈɪnstəntli/ *adv* immediately ‖ 곧. 즉각. 즉시에. 바로. 당장에. 그 자리에서: *He was killed instantly.* 그는 즉사했다.

instant re·play /ˌ.. ˈ../ *n* the immediate repeating of an important moment in a sports game on television by showing the film again ‖ 텔레비전에 방영되는 스포츠 경기에서 장면을 다시 보여주어 중요한 순간을 즉시 반복하기. 즉시[순간] 재생

in·stead /ɪnˈstɛd/ *adv* **1 instead of** in place of someone or something ‖ 다른 사람이나 사물 대신에. …하는 대신에. …하기는 커녕[하지 않고]: *I'll have lamb instead of beef.* 나는 소고기 대신에 양고기를 먹겠다. / *Why don't you do something, instead of just talking about it!* 너희들 그저 그것에 대해 말만 할 게 아니라 어떻게든 해보는 게 어때! **2** in place of someone or something that has just been mentioned ‖ 바로 직전에 거론된 사람이나 사물 대신에. (그)대신(에). 그보다는. 오히려: *I can't go, but Lilly could go instead.* 나는 갈 수 없지만 릴리가 대신 갈 수 있다.

in·step /ˈɪnstɛp/ *n* the raised part of your foot between your toes and your ANKLE, or the part of a shoe that this is under ‖ 발가락과 발목 사이에 있는 발의 위로 도드라진 부분, 또는 이 부분이 밑에 있는 신발 부분. 발등(부위)

in·sti·gate /ˈɪnstəˌgeɪt/ *v* [T] to make something start to happen, especially to start something that will cause trouble ‖ 어떤 일이 발생하기 시작하게 하다, 특히 문제를 초래하게 될 어떤 일을 시작하다. 선동[교사]하다. 부추기어[선동하여] 일으키다: *Gang leaders were accused of instigating the riot.* 깡패 두목들은 폭동을 선동한 죄로 소되었다. – **instigator** *n* – **instigation** /ˌɪnstəˈgeɪʃən/ *n* [U]

in·still /ɪnˈstɪl/ *v* [T] to teach someone a way of thinking or behaving over a long time ‖ 어떤 사람에게 오랜 기간에 걸쳐 생각하거나 처신하는 방식을 가르치다. 서서히 스며들게 하다. 주입시키다: *We tried to instill good manners into all our children.* 우리는 아이들 모두에게 훌륭한 예절을 가르치려고 노력했다.

in·stinct /ˈɪnstɪŋkt/ *n* [C, U] a natural tendency or ability to behave or react in a particular way, without having to learn it or think about it ‖ 배우거나 생각할 필요 없이 특정한 방식으로 행동하거나 반응하는 자연적 경향이나 능력. 본능. 타고난 충동[성향]: *a lion's instinct to hunt* 사자의 사냥 본능

in·stinc·tive·ly /ɪnˈstɪŋktɪvli/ *adv* reacting to something because of INSTINCT ‖ 본능 때문에 어떤 것에 반응하는. 직관적으로. 본능적으로: *He heard a crash and instinctively turned his head.* 그는 충돌하는 소리를 듣고 본능적으로 고개를 돌렸다. – **instinctive** *adj*

in·sti·tute¹ /ˈɪnstəˌtut/ *n* an organization that has a particular purpose, such as scientific or educational work ‖ 과학적 또는 교육적 업무 등의 특별한 목적을 가진 조직. 협회. 학회. 기관: *research institutes* 연구 기관

institute² *v* [T] FORMAL to introduce or start a system, rule, legal process etc. ‖ 체제, 규칙, 법적 절차 등을 도입하거나 시작하다. 설립[설치, 제정, 제기]하다. 열다. 개시하다: *The President agreed to institute welfare reforms.* 대통령은 복지[사회 보장] 개선안을 추진하는데 동의했다.

in·sti·tu·tion /ˌɪnstəˈtuʃən/ *n* **1** a large organization that has a particular purpose, such as scientific, educational, or medical work ‖ 과학적[교육적, 의학적] 업무 등의 특정 목적을 가진 큰 조직. 기관. 단체. 협회. 학회. 원(院). 소(所). 회(會): *one of the most advanced medical institutions in the world* 세계에서 최첨단 의학 연구소 중의 하나 **2** an established system or custom in society ‖ 사회 내의 정립된 체계나 관습. 관례. 제도: *the institution of marriage* 혼인 제도 **3** the act of introducing or starting a system, rule, legal process etc. ‖ 체제·규칙·법적 절차 등을 도입하거나 시작하기. 제정. 수립. 설립. 창설: *the institution of a new law* 새로운 법의 제정 – **institutional** *adj* —see also MENTAL INSTITUTION

in·sti·tu·tion·al·ized /ˌɪnstəˈtuʃənlˌaɪzd/ *adj* **1 institutionalized violence/racism/corruption** violence etc. that has happened for so long in an organization or society that it has become accepted as normal ‖ 조직이나 사회 내에서 너무 오랫동안 일어나서 일반 적인 것으로 받아들여지게 된 폭력 등. 제 도화된 폭력/인종 차별/부패 **2** someone who has become institutionalized has lived for a long time in a prison, hospital for people who are mentally ill etc. and cannot now live normally in society ‖ 사람이 교도소나 정신 병원 등에 서 오랫동안 살아서 이제 사회 속에서 정 상적으로 살 수 없는. 사회에 적응할 수 없는. 수용 기관[시설]에 길들여진[적응 된]

in·struct /ɪnˈstrʌkt/ v [T] **1** to officially tell someone what to do ‖ 어떤 사람에게 해야 할 일을 공식적으로 말하다. 지시[명 령]하다. 지시[명령, 지령]하여 …시키 다: *I've been instructed to wait here until Mr. Borman arrives.* 저는 보만 씨 가 여기 도착할 때까지 기다리라고 지시 받았습니다. **2** to teach someone or show him/her how to do something ‖ 어떤 사 람에게 어떤 것을 하는 방법을 가르치거나 보여주다. 지도[교육]하다. 알려주다: *She's instructing the class in oil painting.* 그녀는 유화반을 지도하고 있다.

in·struc·tion /ɪnˈstrʌkʃən/ n **1** [C usually plural] information or advice that tells you how to do something, especially printed material that explains how to use a piece of equipment, machine etc. ‖ 어떤 것을 하는 방법을 알 려주는 정보나 충고, 특히 장비·기계 등의 사용 방법을 설명하는 인쇄물. 설명[안내, 지침](서): *Follow the instructions on the back of the box.* 상자 뒷면의 지시를 따르시오. / *Don't forget to read the instructions.* 설명서를 꼭 읽으세요. / *He gave us instructions on/about how to fix the toilet.* 그는 우리에게 화장실 고치 는 방법에 대해 설명해 주었다. **2** [U] teaching that you are given in a particular skill or subject ‖ 특정 기술이 나 과목에서 받는 가르침. 지도. 교육: *He's under instruction to become a pilot.* 그는 조종사가 되기 위한 교육을 받 고 있다. **– instructional** adj

in·struc·tive /ɪnˈstrʌktɪv/ adj giving useful information ‖ 유용한 정보를 주는. 교육상 유익한. 교육적인: *a very instructive book on grammar* 문법에 대 한 매우 유익한 책

in·struc·tor /ɪnˈstrʌktɚ/ n someone who teaches a particular subject, sport, skill etc. ‖ 특정 과목·운동·기술 등을 가 르치는 사람. 교사. 지도자. 강사. 교관: *a ski instructor* 스키 강사

in·stru·ment /ˈɪnstrəmənt/ n **1** a tool used in work such as science or medicine ‖ 과학이나 의학 등의 업무에 사 용되는 도구. 기구. 기기. 기계: *medical instruments* 의료 기구 **2** an object such as a piano, horn, VIOLIN etc., used for producing musical sounds ‖ 피아노·호 른·바이올린 등 음악 소리를 내는 데에 쓰 이는 사물. 악기 **3** a piece of equipment for measuring and showing distance, speed etc. ‖ 거리·속도 등을 측정해서 나 타내는 장비. 계기. 계측 장비: *a pilot examining her instruments* 계기(판)를 점검하는 조종사

in·stru·men·tal /ˌɪnstrəˈmɛntl/ adj **1** **be instrumental in** to be important in making something happen ‖ 어떤 일의 발생에 중요한 역할을 하다. 도움이 되다. 쓸모가 있다. 원인[수단]이 되다: *a clue that was instrumental in solving the mystery* 미스터리를 해결하는 데 도움이 되었던 단서 **2** instrumental music is for instruments, not voices ‖ 음악이 음성이 아니라 악기용으로 된. 기악의. 악기의

in·sub·or·di·nate /ˌɪnsəˈbɔrdn-ɪt/ adj refusing to obey someone who has a higher rank than you in the army, navy etc. ‖ 육군·해군 등에서 계급이 높은 사람 에게 복종하기를 거부하는. 항명하는 **– insubordination** /ˌɪnsəˌbɔrdnˈeɪʃən/ n [U]

in·sub·stan·tial /ˌɪnsəbˈstænʃəl/ adj not solid, large, strong, or satisfying ‖ 단단하지[크지, 강하지, 만족스럽지] 않은. 부실한. 무른. 약한. 빈약한: *The evidence against him was insubstantial.* (=not good enough) 그에게 불리한 증거 는 부실했다.

in·suf·fer·a·ble /ɪnˈsʌfərəbəl/ adj very annoying or unpleasant ‖ 매우 화가 나거 나 불쾌한. 견딜[참을] 수 없는: *insufferable rudeness* 참을 수 없는 무례 함 **– insufferably** adv

in·suf·fi·cient /ˌɪnsəˈfɪʃənt/ adj not enough ‖ 충분하지 않은. 불충분한. 모자 라는. 부족한: *insufficient supplies of food* 부족한 식량 보급 **– insufficiently** adv **– insufficiency** n [singular, U]

in·su·lar /ˈɪnsələ, ˈɪnsyə-/ adj FORMAL not interested in anything except your own group, country, way of life etc. ‖ 자 신의 집단·국가·생활 방식 등 외에는 어떤 것에도 관심 없는. 편협한. 도량이 좁은 **– insularity** /ˌɪnsʊˈlærəti/ n [U]

in·su·late /ˈɪnsəˌleɪt/ v [T] **1** to cover or protect something so that electricity, sound, heat etc. cannot get in or out ‖ 사물을 덮거나 보호해서 전기·소리·열 등 이 들어오거나 나갈 수 없게 하다. 절연

[방음, 단열]하다. 절연[방음, 단열]재로 싸 다 [덮 다]: *The pipes should be insulated so they don't freeze.* 파이프를 얼지 않도록 단열재로 싸야 한다. **2** to protect someone from unpleasant experiences or unwanted influences ‖ 사람을 불쾌한 경험이나 원하지 않는 영향으로부터 보호하다. 격리[분리, 고립]시키다. 단절시키다: *college students insulated from the hardships of real life* 실생활의 어려움으로부터 단절된 대학생들

in·su·la·tion /ˌɪnsəˈleɪʃən/ *n* [U] **1** the material used in order to INSULATE something, especially a building ‖ 사물, 특히 건물을 절연·단열·방음하기 위해 이용되는 재료. 절연[단열, 방음]재. 보온재: *Insulation can save money on heating bills.* 보온 단열재는 난방비를 절약할 수 있게 한다. **2** the act of insulating something or the state of being insulated ‖ 사물을 격리·분리·고립시키기, 또는 그 상태. 단절(상태)

in·su·lin /ˈɪnsələn/ *n* [U] a substance produced naturally by your body that allows sugar to be used for energy ‖ 인체에서 자연적으로 생성되어 당분이 에너지원으로 이용되게 해주는 물질. 인슐린. 췌장 호르몬

in·sult¹ /ɪnˈsʌlt/ *v* [T] to say or do something that offends someone, by showing that you do not respect him/her ‖ 어떤 사람에게 존중하지 않음을 드러내어 기분 상하게 하는 말이나 행동을 하다. 모욕하다. 창피주다: *I was insulted when he refused to shake my hand.* 그가 내 악수를 거절했을 때 나는 모욕감을 느꼈다. – **insulting** *adj*

in·sult² /ˈɪnsʌlt/ *n* a rude or offensive remark or action ‖ 무례하거나 기분 상하게 하는 발언이나 행위. 모욕적 언동. 무례한 짓[말]: *shouting insults at the police* 경찰에게 모욕적인 말로 소리치기 —see also **add insult to injury** (ADD)

in·sur·ance /ɪnˈʃʊrəns/ *n* **1** [U] an arrangement with a company in which you pay it money each year and it pays the costs if anything bad happens to you or your property, such as having an illness or an accident ‖ 매년 (일정한) 돈을 특정 회사에 납부하여 질병이나 사고 등 나쁜 일이 자신이나 재산상에 일어나면 회사가 그 비용을 보상하는 계약 관계. 보험. 보험 계약[방식]: *Do you have insurance on/for your car?* 당신은 자동차 보험에 들어 있습니까? **2** [U] the business of providing insurance ‖ 보험을 제공하는 사업. 보험업[회사]: *My cousin works in insurance.* 내 사촌은 보험회사에서 근무한다. **3** [singular, U] protection against something bad happening ‖ 나쁜 일이 일어나는 것에 대한 보호(책). 보호[예방] 수단[장치]: *We bought an alarm as insurance against burglary.* 우리는 도난 방지용으로 경보기를 샀다.

in·sure /ɪnˈʃʊr/ *v* **1** [I, T] to buy or provide insurance ‖ 보험을 사거나 제공하다. 보험에 들다. 보험 계약을 하다: *My house is insured against fire.* 내 집은 화재 보험이 들어 있다. / *This painting is insured for $5000.* 이 그림은 5천 달러 보험에 들어 있다. / *Many companies won't insure young drivers.* 다수의 회사들이 젊은 운전자들에게 보험 계약을 해주지 않으려 한다. **2** [T] to protect yourself against something bad happening ‖ 나쁜 일이 일어나는 것에 대비해 자신을 보호하다. 예방[방호]하다. 보장하다: *We've done everything we can to insure that the project succeeds.* 우리는 그 계획의 성공을 보장하기 위해 할 수 있는 모든 것을 다 했다.

in·sur·gent /ɪnˈsɝdʒənt/ *n* one of a group of people fighting against the government of their own country ‖ 자국의 정부에 대항해 싸우는 일단의 사람들의 하나. 반란자. 반란군 병사. 폭도 – **insurgency** *n* [U] – **insurgent** *adj*

in·sur·mount·a·ble /ˌɪnsɚˈmaʊntəbəl/ *adj* a difficulty or problem that is insurmountable is too large or too difficult to deal with ‖ 어려움이나 문제가 다루기에 너무 크거나 너무 어려운. 넘을 수 없는. 이겨낼[극복할] 수 없는

in·sur·rec·tion /ˌɪnsəˈrɛkʃən/ *n* [C, U] an attempt by a group of people within a country to take control using force and violence ‖ 국가 내 일단의 사람들이 무력과 폭력을 사용해서 통치권을 잡으려는 시도. 반란. 반역. 폭동: *an armed insurrection led by the army* 육군에 의해 주도된 무장 반란 – **insurrectionist** *n*

in·tact /ɪnˈtækt/ *adj* not broken, damaged, or spoiled ‖ 깨지거나[손상되거나, 망가지지] 않은. 온전한. 원형대로의. 손대지 않은: *The package arrived intact.* 소포는 손상되지 않고 도착했다.

in·take /ˈɪnteɪk/ *n* [singular] **1** the amount of food, FUEL etc. that is taken in by someone or something ‖ 사람이나 사물이 섭취[흡입]한 식품·연료 등의 양. 섭취[흡입, 주입]량: *I've been told to lower my intake of fat and alcohol.* 나는 지방과 알코올 섭취량을 줄이라는 말을 들었다. **2** the number of people allowed to enter a school, profession etc. ‖ 학교·전 문직 등에 입학이나 진출이 허용된 사람들의 숫자. 채용[수용](인원)수: *the yearly intake of students* 연간 입학생수

in·tan·gi·ble /ɪnˈtændʒəbəl/ *adj* an intangible quality or feeling cannot be clearly felt or described, although you know it exists ‖ 성질이나 느낌이 비록 존재하는 것은 알아도 분명히 느껴지거나 묘사될 수 없는. 만질 수[만져서 느낄 수] 없는. 실체가 없는. 무형의 – **intangibly** *adv*

in·te·ger /ˈɪntədʒɚ/ *n* TECHNICAL a whole number ‖ 정수(整數)

in·te·gral /ˈɪntəgrəl, ɪnˈtɛgrəl/ *adj* forming a necessary part of something ‖ 사물의 필수적인 부분을 형성하는. 불가결한. 없어서는 안 될. 필수의: *an integral part of the contract* 계약의 필수적인 부분 – **integrally** *adv*

in·te·grate /ˈɪntəˌgreɪt/ *v* 1 [I, T] to end the practice of separating people of different races in a place or institution; DESEGREGATE ‖ 다른 인종의 사람들을 한 장소나 시설에 분리하는 관행을 종식시키다. 통합하다[시키다]. 인종 차별을 없애다[하지 않다]; ⚑ desegregate: *Many cities transported children long distances in order to integrate schools.* 많은 도시들이 학교를 통합시키기 위해 아이들을 장거리 통학시켰다. 2 [I, T] to join in the life and customs of a group or society, or to help someone do this ‖ 집단이나 사회의 생활과 관습에 동참하다. 또는 다른 사람을 이렇게 하도록 돕다. 융합[융화]하다[시키다]. 동화하다[시키다]: *It will take time for new members to integrate into the group.* 새 회원이 단체에 융화하는 데 시간이 걸릴 것이다. 3 [T] to combine two or more things in order to make an effective system ‖ 효율적인 체계를 만들기 위해 둘 이상의 것을 조합하다. 통합하다. 집적하다[시키다]: *This software integrates moving pictures with sound.* 이 프로그램은 동화상을 소리와 통합시킨다. – **integration** /ɪntəˈgreɪʃən/ *n* [U] – **integrated** /ˈɪntəˌgreɪtɪd/ *adj* —compare SEGREGATE

in·teg·ri·ty /ɪnˈtɛgrəti/ *n* [U] 1 the quality of being honest and having high moral principles ‖ 솔직하고 높은 도덕적 원칙을 가지고 있는 특성. 고결. 성실. 정직. 청렴(성): *a man of integrity* 고결한 사람 2 FORMAL the state of being united as one complete thing ‖ 하나의 완전한 것으로 통합되어 있는 상태. 완전한 상태. 무결(성). 흠 없는 상태. 통합(성): *the integrity of the economic system* 경제 체

제의 통합(성)

in·tel·lect /ˈɪntəlˌɛkt/ *n* [C, U] the ability to understand things and think intelligently ‖ 사물을 이해하고 지적으로 생각하는 능력. 지성. 이지(理智). 지적 능력: *a man of superior intellect* 지적 능력이 뛰어난 사람

in·tel·lec·tu·al¹ /ˌɪntəlˈɛktʃuəl/ *adj* concerning the ability to think and understand ideas and information ‖ 개념과 정보를 생각하고 이해하는 능력에 관한. 지적인. 지력[지성, 지능]의: *the intellectual development of children* 아이들의 지능 개발 – **intellectually** *adv*

intellectual² *n* someone who is intelligent and who thinks about complicated ideas ‖ 지적이며 복잡한 사상에 대해 생각하는 사람. 지식인. 식자(識者)

in·tel·li·gence /ɪnˈtɛlədʒəns/ *n* [U] 1 the ability to learn, understand, and think about things ‖ 사물에 대해 배우고 이해하고 생각하는 능력. 지력. 지성. 이해력. 지능: *a child of average intelligence* 평균 지능을 가진 아이 2 information about the secret activities of other governments, or the group of people who gather this ‖ 다른 (나라) 정부의 비밀 활동에 대한 정보, 또는 이것을 수집하는 사람들의 집단. 첩보[정보](부)

in·tel·li·gent /ɪnˈtɛlədʒənt/ *adj* having a high level of ability to learn, understand, and think about things ‖ 사물에 대해 배우고 이해하고 생각하는 능력이 높은 수준인. 총명한. 높은 지능을 갖춘. 지성[이해력] 있는 – **intelligently** *adv*

in·tel·li·gi·ble /ɪnˈtɛlədʒəbəl/ *adj* able to be understood ‖ 이해될 수 있는. 잘 이해되는. 뜻이 분명한 – **intelligibly** *adv* —opposite UNINTELLIGIBLE

in·tend /ɪnˈtɛnd/ *v* 1 [T] to have something in your mind as a plan or purpose ‖ 어떤 것을 계획이나 목적으로서 마음속에 지니다. …할 작정이다. …하려고 생각하다. …하고 싶다: *She never really intended to marry him.* 실제로 그녀는 그와 결혼할 의도가 전혀 없었다. 2 **be intended for sb/sth** to be provided or designed for someone or something ‖ 사람이나 사물을 위해 제공되거나 고안되다. …을 위해 꾀하다[의도하다]. …에[…을 대상으로] 맞춘: *a program intended for the families of deaf children* 청각 장애 아동 가정을 위한 프로그램 – **intended** *adj*

in·tense /ɪnˈtɛns/ *adj* 1 having a very strong effect, or felt very strongly ‖ 매우 strong effect, or felt very strongly ‖ 매우

강한 효과를 갖는, 또는 매우 강하게 느끼는. 강력한. 격렬한. 극심한. 극도의: *the intense heat of the desert* 사막의 극심한 열기 **2** making you do a lot of work, think hard etc. ‖ 많은 일을 하게 하거나 열심히 생각하게 하는. 열심인. 분투하는: *They finished in three days after an intense effort.* 그들은 열심히 노력한 끝에 3일 내에 끝마쳤다. **3** serious and having very strong feelings or opinions ‖ 진지하며 매우 강한 감정이나 견해를 갖는. 격렬한. 강렬한. 열렬한: *an intense young woman* 열성적인 젊은 여성 **– intensely** *adv*

in·ten·si·fi·er /ɪnˈtɛnsəˌfaɪɚ/ *n* TECHNICAL in grammar, a word that changes the meaning of another word, phrase, or sentence, in order to make its meaning stronger or weaker ‖ 문법상 다른 단어[구, 문장]의 뜻을 더욱 강하게 또는 약하게 하기 위해 그것들의 의미를 바꿔주는 단어. 강조어 **—see study note on page 937**

in·ten·si·fy /ɪnˈtɛnsəˌfaɪ/ *v* [I, T] to increase in strength, size, or amount etc., or to make something do this ‖ 강도[크기, 수량] 등에서 증가하다, 또는 어떤 것이 이렇게 하게 하다. 한층 더 강해지다[강해지게 하다]. 격렬해지다[하게 하다]: *Spices will intensify the flavor.* 향신료는 맛에 풍미를 더한다. / *The smell intensified as it grew hotter.* 점점 더 뜨거워짐에 따라 냄새가 강해졌다. **– intensification** /ɪnˌtɛnsəfəˈkeɪʃən/ *n* [U]

in·ten·si·ty /ɪnˈtɛnsəti/ *n* [U] the quality of being felt very strongly or of having a strong effect ‖ 매우 강하게 느껴지거나 강한 효과를 갖는 특성. 강렬[격렬](함). 강도(强度): *the intensity of his anger* 그의 격렬한 분노

in·ten·sive /ɪnˈtɛnsɪv/ *adj* involving a lot of activity, effort, or attention in order to achieve something ‖ 어떤 것을 달성하기 위해 많은 활동[노력, 주의]을 포함하는. 강한. 철저한. 집중적인: *The class is four weeks of intensive study.* 그 반은 4주간의 집중 코스 학습반이다. **– intensively** *adv*

intensive care /.ˌ.. ˈ./ *n* [U] a department in a hospital that treats people who are very seriously ill or injured ‖ 매우 심하게 아프거나 상처 입은 사람들을 치료하는 병원의 진료 부서. 중환자 담당 부서

in·tent¹ /ɪnˈtɛnt/ *n* **1** FORMAL what you intend to do ‖ 하려고 하는 것. 의향. 의도. 의사. 목적. 의미. 취지: *The intent was to keep the area safe.* 취지는 그 지역을 안전하게 유지하는 것이었다. **2 to/for all intents and purposes** almost completely, or very nearly ‖ 거의 완전히, 또는 거의 다. 어느 면으로 보나. 사실상: *Their marriage was over for all intents and purposes.* 그들의 결혼 생활은 사실상 끝장났다.

intent² *adj* **1 be intent on (doing) sth** to be determined to do something ‖ 어떤 것을 하기로 결심하다. …을 (하기로) 결심[결의]하고 있다: *Alan is intent on going to Spain this summer.* 앨런은 이번 여름에 스페인에 갈 결심이다. **2** giving careful attention to something ‖ 어떤 것에 주의 깊은 관심을 주는. 열중한. 여념이 없는. 골몰하는: *an intent look* 응시 (凝視)

in·ten·tion /ɪnˈtɛnʃən/ *n* [C, U] something that you plan to do ‖ 하려고 계획한 것. 의도. 의향. 의지. …할 작정: *I have no intention of retiring anytime soon.* 나는 조만간 곧 은퇴할 의사가 없다.

in·ten·tion·al /ɪnˈtɛnʃənəl/ *adj* done deliberately ‖ 고의적으로 한. 고의의. 의식[계획]적인: *an intentional attempt to mislead the public* 대중을 오도하려는 고의적 시도 **– intentionally** *adv* **—** opposite UNINTENTIONAL

in·ter /ɪnˈtɚ/ *v* **-rred, -rring** [T] FORMAL to bury a dead body ‖ 시체를 묻다. 매장하다. 장사지내다

in·ter·act /ˌɪntəˈrækt/ *v* [I] **1** to talk to other people and work together with them ‖ 다른 사람들에게 말하고 그들과 함께 일하다. …과 교류하다. 서로 어울려 지내다[어울리다]: *Craig hasn't learned how to interact with the other kids.* 크레이그는 다른 아이들과 어울려 지내는 법을 배우지 못했다. **2** if two or more things interact, they have an effect on each other ‖ 두 가지 이상의 것이 서로 영향을 미치다. 상호 작용하다: *How will the drug interact with other medicines?* 그 약이 다른 약과 어떻게 상호 작용할까요?

in·ter·ac·tion /ˌɪntəˈrækʃən/ *n* [C, U] the activity of talking with other people and working together with them ‖ 다른 사람들과 함께 이야기하고 일하는 활동. 교류. 함께 어울리기: *social interaction between teenagers* 10대들 간의 사회적 교류

in·ter·ac·tive /ˌɪntəˈræktɪv/ *adj* **1** involving communication between a computer, television etc. and the person using it ‖ 컴퓨터·텔레비전 등과 그것을 사용하는 사람 사이의 통신에 관한. 상호 대화식의. 쌍방향의: *an interactive*

software program for children 아동용 쌍
방향 소프트웨어 프로그램 **2** involving
people talking and working together ‖
함께 이야기하고 일하는 사람간의. 상호간
의

in·ter·cede /ˌɪntəˈsid/ *v* [I] to talk to
someone in authority or do something in
order to prevent something from
happening ‖ 책임을 맡은 사람에게 이야
기하거나 일이 일어나는 것을 막기
위해 무엇을 하다. (…을) 탄원[중재, 조
정]하다: *Hansen interceded on our
behalf.* (=for us) 한센이 우리를 대신해서
중재했다. – **intercession** /ˌɪntəˈsɛʃən/
n [U]

in·ter·cept /ˌɪntəˈsɛpt/ *v* [T] to stop
someone or catch something that is
going from one place to another ‖ 한 곳
에서 다른 곳으로 가는 사람을 정지시키거
나 사물을 잡다. 도중에서 막다[가로채다,
빼앗다, 붙잡다]. 방해하다: *O'Neill
intercepted the ball.* 오닐이 공을 가로챘
다. – **interception** /ˌɪntəˈsɛpʃən/ *n* [C,
U]

in·ter·change /ˈɪntəˌtʃeɪndʒ/ *n* a place
where two HIGHWAYs or FREEWAYs meet
‖ 두 개의 간선도로나 고속도로가 만나는
지점. 나들목. 인터체인지

in·ter·change·a·ble /ˌɪntəˈtʃeɪn-
dʒəbəl/ *adj* things that are interchangeable can be used instead of each
other ‖ 사물이 서로를 대신해 사용될 수
있는. 교환[교체]할 수 있는. 서로 대체할
수 있는: *a toy with interchangeable
parts* 부품을 교체할 수 있는 장난감 –
interchangeably *adv*

in·ter·com /ˈɪntəˌkɑm/ *n* a
communication system by which people
in different parts of a building, aircraft
etc. can speak to one another ‖ 건물이나
항공기 내 서로 다른 지점에 있는 사람들
이 서로 말할 수 있게 해주는 통신 기
기. 내부 통화 장치. 인터콤: *An
announcement came over the intercom
telling everyone to get out of the
building.* 모든 사람들에게 건물 밖으로 나
가라고 말하는 방송이 인터콤으로 들려왔
다.

in·ter·con·ti·nen·tal /ˌɪntəˌkɑn-
təˈnɛntl, -ˌkɑntˈnˈɛntl/ *adj* happening
between or going from one CONTINENT
(=africa, asia, europe etc.) to another ‖
대륙간의 또는 아프리카, 아시아, 유럽 등
의 대륙에서 다른 대륙으로 가는. 대륙
을 잇는. 대륙간에 행해지는: *an
intercontinental flight* 대륙간 비행

in·ter·course /ˈɪntəˌkɔrs/ *n* [U]
FORMAL the act of having sex ‖ 성교하는

행위. 성교. 섹스

in·ter·de·pend·ent /ˌɪntədɪˈpɛndənt/
adj depending on or necessary to each
other ‖ 서로에게 의지하거나 서로를 필요
로 하는. 상호 의존의. 상호 결속의: *the
interdependent group of countries
called the European union* 유럽 연합이라
불리는 상호 결속 국가군 – **inter-
dependence** *n* [U]

in·ter·est¹ /ˈɪntrɪst/ *n* **1** [singular, U] a
feeling that makes you want to pay
attention to something and find out
more about it ‖ 어떤 것에 대해 관심을 기
울이고 더 많이 알고 싶어 하게 하는 감정.
관심. 호기심. 흥미: *We share an
interest in music.* 우리는 음악에 대한 관
심을 공유한다. / *Kelly lost interest
(=stopped showing an interest) halfway
through the movie.* 켈리는 영화의 절반
정도 가서 흥미를 잃었다. **2** a subject or
activity that you enjoy studying or doing
‖ 공부하거나 행하는 것을 즐기는 분야나
활동. 관심사. 흥밋거리. 흥미의 대상:
What sort of interests do you have? 당신
의 관심사는 무엇입니까? **3** [U] **a)**
money that you must pay for borrowing
money ‖ 돈을 빌리기 위해 지불해야 하는
돈. 이자 **b)** money that a bank pays you
when you keep your money there ‖ 돈을
은행에 보관할 때 은행이 지불하는 돈. 이
자 **4** [U] a quality of something that
attracts your attention and makes you
want to know more about it ‖ 관심을 끌
고 더 많이 알고 싶어 하게 하는 사물의
특징. 호기심[흥미]을 끄는 것. 흥(취)을
북돋움[북돋는 것]: *a tourist guide to
local places of interest* 지방 명소에 대한
여행 안내 **5 be in sb's interest** to be
an advantage to someone ‖ 어떤 사람에
게 유리한 점이 되다. 이익[이점, 이득]이
되다

interest² *v* [T] to make someone want
to pay attention to something and find
out more about it ‖ 사람이 어떤 것에 관
심을 기울이고 더 많은 것을 알고 싶어 하
게 하다. 흥미[관심]를 갖게 하다. 호기심
을 품게 하다[북돋우다, 불러일으키다]: *I
have some books that might interest
you.* 나는 네가 호기심을 가질 만한 책 몇
권을 가지고 있다.

in·ter·est·ed /ˈɪntrɪstɪd, ˈɪntəˌrɛstɪd/
adj **1** giving a lot of attention to
something because you want to find out
more about it ‖ 어떤 것에 대해 더 많은
것을 알고 싶어서 많은 관심을 기울이는.
…에 흥미[관심]를 가진. 호기심을 품은:
Peter is interested in Mexican politics.
피터는 멕시코 정치에 관심을 가지고 있

다. **2** eager to do or have something ‖ 어떤 것을 하거나 갖기를 열망하는. …하고 싶어하는. 흥미를 갖고 …하기를 원하는: *Lisa is interested in studying law.* 리사는 법률 공부를 하고 싶어한다.

in·ter·est·ing /ˈɪntrɪstɪŋ, ˈɪntəˌrɛstɪŋ/ *adj* unusual or exciting in a way that keeps your attention ‖ 계속 관심을 가질 만큼 특이하고 흥미로운. 관심을 끄는. 호기심을 일으키는: *a very interesting idea/book/person* 매우 흥미로운 생각[책, 사람] – **interestingly** *adv*

in·ter·face /ˈɪntəˌfeɪs/ *n* TECHNICAL the HARDWARE and SOFTWARE needed for a computer to do things such as print documents, use a MOUSE etc. ‖ 문서를 인쇄하고 마우스를 사용하는 등의 일을 하는 데 필요한 컴퓨터의 하드웨어와 소프트웨어. 인터페이스

in·ter·fere /ˌɪntəˈfɪr/ *v* [I] to deliberately get involved in a situation when you are not wanted or needed ‖ 자신을 원하거나 필요로 하지 않는 상황에 고의적으로 개입하다. …에 간섭하다. 참견하다: *It's better not to interfere in their arguments.* 그들의 말다툼에 참견하지 않는 것이 좋다.

interfere with sth *phr v* [T] **1** to prevent something from happening in the way it was planned ‖ 어떤 일이 계획대로 일어나는 것을 막다. 방해하다. 훼방놓다: *Don't let sports interfere with your schoolwork.* 운동이 네 학교 공부를 방해하지 않게 해라. **2** to spoil the sound or picture of a radio or television broadcast ‖ 라디오나 텔레비전 방송의 소리나 화상을 망치다. 전파를 방해[간섭]하다

in·ter·fer·ence /ˌɪntəˈfɪrəns/ *n* [U] **1** an act of interfering (INTERFERE) ‖ 간섭하는 행위. 개입. 참견. 훼방. 방해: *I resented his interference in my personal life.* 나는 그가 내 사생활에 간섭하는 것을 분개했다. **2** in sports, the act of illegally preventing another player from doing something ‖ 운동 경기에서 다른 선수의 플레이를 반칙해서 막기. 방해 행위. 저지 **3** unwanted noise, a spoiled picture etc. on the radio, telephone, or television ‖ 라디오[전화, 텔레비전]의 원치 않은 소음이나 찌그러진 화상 등. 잡음. 전파 방해

in·ter·fer·on /ˌɪntəˈfɪrɑn/ *n* [U] a chemical substance that is produced by your body to fight against VIRUSES that cause disease ‖ 질병을 일으키는 바이러스에 대항하기 위해 몸에서 생성되는 화학 물질. 인터페론

in·ter·im¹ /ˈɪntərəm/ *adj* an interim report, payment, agreement etc. is used or accepted for a short time until a final one is made ‖ 보고·지불·계약 등이 최종적으로 마무리되기 전에 짧은 기간 동안 사용되거나 받아들여지는. 일시적인. 임시의. 잠시의. 중간의

interim² *n* **in the interim** in the period of time between two events ‖ 두 사건 사이의 일정 시간에. 그 동안에. …하는 사이에[중간에]: *There are two parts to the tour, so the visitors will need a place to rest in the interim.* 시찰[관람]은 두 부분으로 되어 있습니다. 그래서 방문자들은 중간에 쉴 곳이 필요할 것입니다.

in·te·ri·or¹ /ɪnˈtɪriə/ *n* the inner part or inside of something ‖ 사물의 안쪽이나 내부. 실내: *a car with brown leather interior* 갈색 가죽으로 실내 장식된 자동차 —opposite EXTERIOR¹

interior² *adj* inside or indoors ‖ 내부의 또는 실내의. 안(쪽)의. 옥내의: *an interior decorator* 실내 장식가 —opposite EXTERIOR²

interior de·sign /.,.. .'./ *n* [U] the job or skill of choosing and arranging furniture, paints, art etc. for the inside of houses, buildings etc. ‖ 주택·건물 등의 내부를 위한 가구·그림·예술품 등을 선택하고 배치하는 일이나 기술. 실내 장식

in·ter·ject /ˌɪntəˈdʒɛkt/ *v* [I, T] FORMAL to interrupt what someone is saying with a sudden remark ‖ 갑작스런 발언으로 어떤 사람이 말하는 것에 참견하다. 불쑥 발언하다[의견을 말하다]. 말참견하다

in·ter·jec·tion /ˌɪntəˈdʒɛkʃən/ *n* in grammar, a word or phrase that is used in order to express surprise, shock, pain etc. In the sentence "Ouch! That hurt!", "ouch" is an interjection ‖ 문법에서 놀람·충격·고통 등을 표현하기 위해 사용되는 단어나 구문. 감탄사. "Ouch! That hurt!" 문장에서 "ouch"는 감탄사이다.

in·ter·lock·ing /ˌɪntəˈlɑkɪŋ/ *adj* connected firmly together ‖ 서로 단단하게 결합된. 서로 얽힌. 포개진. 맞물린. 엇걸린: *the Olympic symbol of interlocking circles* 서로 엇걸린 원들로 된 올림픽 상징 기호 – **interlock** *v* [I, T]

in·ter·lop·er /ˈɪntəˌloupə/ *n* someone who enters a place where s/he should not be ‖ 있어서는 안 될 곳에 들어가는 사람. (불법) 침입자[침범꾼]

in·ter·lude /ˈɪntəˌlud/ *n* a period of time between activities or events ‖ 활동이나 행사 사이의 일정 시간. 휴식[휴게] 시간. 막간: *a brief interlude of peace* *before the fighting began again* 전투가 다시 시작되기 전 막간의 짧았던 평온한 시기

in·ter·mar·ry /ˌɪntəˈmæri/ *v* [I] if people from different races, religions etc. intermarry, someone from one group marries someone from another group ‖ 인종·종교 등이 다른 한 집단 출신 사람이 다른 집단 출신 사람과 결혼하다. …간에 결혼하다 **– intermarriage** /ˌɪntəˈmærɪdʒ/ *n* [U]

in·ter·me·di·ar·y /ˌɪntəˈmidiˌɛri/ *n* someone who tries to help two other people or groups to agree with one another ‖ 두 사람이나 집단이 서로 합의하도록 도우려는 사람. 중재[중개, 매개]자

in·ter·me·di·ate /ˌɪntəˈmidiɪt/ *adj* done or happening between two other stages, levels etc. ‖ 두 개의 서로 다른 단계·수준 등의 사이에서 행해지거나 일어나는. 중간의. 중급의: *an intermediate Spanish class* 중급 스페인어반

in·ter·mi·na·ble /ɪnˈtəmənəbəl/ *adj* very boring and taking a lot of time ‖ 매우 지루하며 많은 시간이 걸리는. 그칠 줄 모르는. 지루하게도 긴: *interminable delays* 한없는 지연 **– interminably** *adv*

in·ter·mis·sion /ˌɪntəˈmɪʃən/ *n* a short period of time between the parts of a play, concert etc. ‖ 연극·음악회 등의 사이의 짧은 시간. 막간. 휴식[휴게] 시간

in·ter·mit·tent /ˌɪntəˈmɪtˈnt/ *adj* happening at some times but not regularly or continuously ‖ 정기적 또는 계속적으로는 아니지만 한동안 일어나는. 간헐적[단속적]인: *clouds and intermittent rain* 구름이 끼고 간헐적으로 내리는 비 **– intermittently** *adv*

in·tern¹ /ˈɪntən/ *n* 1 someone who has almost finished training as a doctor and is working in a hospital ‖ 의사로서의 수련을 거의 마치고 병원에 근무하는 사람. 수련의. 인턴 2 someone, especially a student, who works for a short time in a particular job in order to gain experience ‖ 특정한 직무 경험을 얻기 위해 짧은 기간 동안 일하는 사람, 특히 학생. 인턴 사원

in·tern² /ɪnˈtən/ *v* [T] to put someone in prison, especially for political reasons ‖ 특히 정치적 이유로 어떤 사람을 교도소에 수감하다. 구속[억류, 구금]하다 **– internment** *n* [C, U]

in·ter·nal /ɪnˈtənl/ *adj* 1 inside something such as your body rather than outside ‖ 신체 등의 외부가 아니라 내부의. 체내의: *a lot of internal bleeding*

다량의 내출혈 2 within a particular country, company, organization etc. ‖ 특정 국가·회사·조직 등의 내부의: *an internal flight from Denver to Chicago* 덴버발 시카고행 국내선 **– internally** *adv* —opposite EXTERNAL

Internal Rev·e·nue Serv·ice /ˌ…ˈ…ˌ…/ *n* [singular] ⇨ IRS

in·ter·na·tion·al /ˌɪntəˈnæʃənəl/ *adj* concerning more than one nation ‖ 일개국 이상이 관계된. 국제적인: *an international agreement* 국제 협약 **– internationally** *adv*

In·ter·net /ˈɪntəˌnɛt/ *n* **the Internet** also **the Net** a system of connected computers that allows computer users around the world to exchange information ‖ 전 세계적으로 컴퓨터 사용자들이 정보 교환을 가능하게 하는 접속된 컴퓨터 시스템. 인터넷: *Are you on the Internet yet?* 아직도 인터넷 하니?

CULTURE NOTE The Internet

The Internet is a system of many computers all around the world that allows people to communicate with each other and share information. Through **the Internet** you can find information about almost anything you can think of. You can read information from books and magazines that are **on line** (=available electronically instead of on paper). You can also use **the Internet** to send **e-mail** (=electronic mail), which is a way of sending letters and documents very quickly using a computer. The **World Wide Web** is what makes it possible for you to see and use the information on **the Internet** in an easy way.

Internet은 사람들이 상호 의사 소통하고 정보를 공유할 수 있게 하는 전 세계적인 컴퓨터 시스템이다. **Internet**을 통해서 우리가 생각할 수 있는 거의 대부분의 것에 대한 정보를 찾을 수 있다. (종이 대신 전자적으로 이용 가능한) **on line**상의 책과 잡지를 통해서도 정보를 읽을 수 있다. 또한 우리는 컴퓨터를 이용하여 아주 신속히 편지와 서류를 보내는 방식인 **e-mail**을 보내는 데도 **Internet**을 이용할 수 있다. **World Wide Web**은 **Internet**상에서 쉽게 정보를 보고 이용하는 것을 가능하게 해준다.

Internet bank·ing /ˈ… ˌ…/ *n* [U] a service provided by banks so that people can find out information about their bank account, pay bills etc. using the Internet ‖ 사람들이 인터넷을 이용해 은행 계좌·청구서 결제 등에 대한 정보를 알 수 있도록 은행이 제공하는 서비스. 인터넷 뱅킹

Internet pro·to·col /'. ,.../, written abbreviation **IP** n TECHNICAL a set of rules that describe how and in what form electronic information should be sent on the Internet ‖ 인터넷 상에서 전자 정보를 전송하는 방법과 양식을 규정하는 일련의 규칙. 인터넷 프로토콜

in·ter·nist /'ɪntənɪst/ n a doctor who treats people using medicines etc., rather than by using SURGERY ‖ 수술이 아니라 약 등으로 사람들을 치료하는 의사. 내과 전문의 —compare SURGEON

in·tern·ship /'ɪntən,ʃɪp/ n the period of time when an INTERN works, or the particular job s/he does ‖ 인턴으로 일하는 기간이나 인턴이 하는 특정한 일. 인턴 기간. 인턴직: an internship in a law firm 법무 법인에서의 인턴 기간

in·ter·per·son·al /,ɪntə'pəsənl/ adj involving relationships between people ‖ 사람들 사이의 관계에 관련된. 대인 관계의

in·ter·plan·e·tar·y /,ɪntə'plænə,tɛri/ adj happening or done between the PLANETs ‖ 행성 간에 발생하거나 일어나는. 행성 간의

in·ter·play /'ɪntə,pleɪ/ n [U] the way that two people or things affect each other ‖ 두 사람이나 사물이 상호 영향을 미침. 상호 작용: the interplay of light and color in her films 그녀의 필름들에서의 빛과 색의 상호 작용

in·ter·pose /,ɪntə'poʊz/ v [T] FORMAL to put something between two other things, people etc., usually to stop something ‖ 보통 무엇을 중단시키기 위해 두 사물·사람 등의 사이에 어떤 것을 넣다. 사이에 끼우다. 개입시키다: a neutral group interposed between the warring sides 분쟁을 하는 양측을 중재하는 중립 그룹

in·ter·pret /ɪn'təprɪt/ v 1 [I, T] to change words spoken in one language into another ‖ 한 가지 언어로 한 말을 다른 언어로 바꾸다. 통역을 하다: Gina spoke enough Spanish to be able to interpret for me. 지나는 나에게 통역을 할 수 있을 만큼 스페인어를 구사했다. —compare TRANSLATE 2 [T] to explain or decide on the meaning of an event, statement etc. ‖ 사건·진술의 의미를 해석하거나 판단하다: His silence was interpreted as guilt. 그의 침묵은 유죄의 뜻으로 해석되었다.

in·ter·pre·ta·tion /ɪn'təprə,teɪʃən/ n [C, U]an explanation for an event, someone's actions etc. ‖ 사건·남의 행동 등에 대한 설명. 해석: one scientist's interpretation of the data 그 데이터에 대한 한 과학자의 해석

in·ter·pret·er /ɪn'təprətə/ n someone who changes the spoken words of one language into another ‖ 한 언어로 한 말을 다른 언어로 바꾸는 사람. 통역자 —compare TRANSLATOR

in·ter·ra·cial /,ɪntə'reɪʃəl/ adj between different races of people ‖ 다른 인종간의: an interracial marriage 다른 인종간의 결혼

in·ter·re·lat·ed /,ɪntəri'leɪtɪd/ adj many things that are interrelated all have an effect on each other ‖ 여러 가지가 상호 모든 면에서 영향을 미치는. 상호 관련된

in·ter·ro·gate /ɪn'tɛrə,geɪt/ v [T] to ask someone a lot of questions, sometimes in a threatening way ‖ 때로는 협박 투로 남에게 많은 질문을 하다. 심문하다: Police are interrogating the suspect now. 경찰은 현재 피의자를 심문중이다. – **interrogation** /ɪn,tɛrə'geɪʃən/ n [C, U] – **interrogator** /ɪn'tɛrə,geɪtə/ n – see usage note at ASK

in·ter·rupt /,ɪntə'rʌpt/ v 1 [I, T] to stop someone from speaking by suddenly saying or doing something ‖ 갑자기 어떤 말이나 행동을 하여 남의 말을 막다: I'm sorry, I didn't mean to interrupt you. 죄송합니다. 저는 당신의 말을 방해할 생각은 아니었습니다. / We'd only said a few words when Brian interrupted. 브라이언이 끼어들었을 때 우리는 겨우 몇 마디밖에 나누지 못했다. 2 [T] to stop a process or activity for a short time ‖ 잠시 진행이나 행동을 중단하다: The war interrupted the supply of oil. 전쟁으로 유류 공급이 잠시 중단되었다. – **interruption** /,ɪntə'rʌpʃən/ n [C, U]

in·ter·sect /,ɪntə'sɛkt/ v [I, T] if two lines, roads etc. intersect, they meet or go across each other ‖ 두 선·도로 등이 서로 만나거나 가로지르다. 교차하다

in·ter·sec·tion /'ɪntə,sɛkʃən, ,ɪntə'sɛkʃən/ n the place where two roads, lines etc. meet and go across each other ‖ 두 도로·선 등이 서로 만나거나 가로지르는 지점. 교차로

in·ter·sperse /,ɪntə'spəs/ v [T] to mix something together with something else

‖ 사물을 다른 것과 함께 섞다: *Music videos were interspersed with interviews.* 뮤직 비디오는 틈틈이 인터뷰가 삽입되어 있었다.

in·ter·state¹ /'ɪntəˌsteɪt/ *n* a road that goes between states ‖ 주간(州間) 도로

interstate² *adj* between or involving different states in the US ‖ 미국의 다른 주(州) 사이의, 또는 다른 주에 관련된. 주간의: *interstate trade* 주(州)간의 거래

in·ter·twined /ˌɪntə'twaɪnd/ *adj* twisted together or closely related ‖ 서로 얽히거나 긴밀히 연관된: *several intertwined stories* 긴밀히 얽힌 몇 가지 이야기

in·ter·val /'ɪntəvəl/ *n* **1** a period of time between two events, activities etc. ‖ 두 사건·행위 사이의 시간. (시간상의) 사이. 간격: *The Bijou Theater opened again after an interval of five years.* 비쥬 극장은 5년의 공백이 있은 후 재개관했다. **2 at daily/weekly/monthly etc. intervals** every day, week, month etc. ‖ 매일, 매주, 매월 **3 at regular intervals** with the same amount of time or distance between each thing, activity etc ‖ 각 사물·행위 등의 사이에 같은 시간이나 거리를 두고. 일정한 간격으로: *Water your plants at regular intervals.* 정기적으로 식물에 물을 주어라. **4 at intervals of** with a particular amount of time or distance between things, activities etc. ‖ 사물·행위 등의 사이에 특정 시간이나 거리를 두고. …간격으로: *at intervals of six feet* 6피트 간격으로

in·ter·vene /ˌɪntə'vin/ *v* [I] **1** to do something to try to stop an argument, problem, war etc. ‖ 논쟁·문제·전쟁 등을 중단시키려는 노력을 하다. 개입하다. 중재하다: *The police had to intervene in the march to stop the fighting.* 경찰은 싸움을 중지시키기 위해 그 행진에 개입해야 했다. **2** to happen between two events, especially in a way that interrupts or prevents something ‖ 특히 어떤 것을 방해하거나 막으며 두 사건 사이에 일어나다: *They had planned to get married, but the war intervened.* 그들은 결혼할 계획이었으나 전쟁이 발발했다. — **intervening** *adj*

in·ter·ven·tion /ˌɪntə'vɛnʃən/ *n* [C, U] the act of intervening (INTERVENE) ‖ 중재하는 행위. 중재. 개입

in·ter·view¹ /'ɪntəˌvyu/ *n* **1** an occasion when someone famous is asked questions about his/her life, opinions etc. ‖ 유명 인사가 자신의 생활·견해 등에 관한 질문을 받는 상황. 회견.

인터뷰: *Michael Jackson gave an interview to Barbara Walters.* (=he answered her questions) 마이클 잭슨은 바바라 월터스의 인터뷰에 응했다. **2** [C, U] a formal meeting in which someone is asked questions, usually to find out if s/he is good enough for a job ‖ 일반적으로 일에 대한 적임 여부의 파악을 위해 질문을 받는 공식 회합. 면접

interview² *v* [T] to ask someone questions during an INTERVIEW ‖ 인터뷰 동안 남에게 질문을 하다. 회견하다. 면접하다 — **interviewer** *n*

in·ter·weave /ˌɪntə'wiv/ *v* **interwove** /-'wouv/, **interwoven** /-'wouvən/, **interweaving** [T] if two or more ideas or situations are interwoven, they are too closely related to be separated easily ‖ 두 가지 이상의 생각이나 상황이 아주 긴밀히 연관되어 쉽게 분리되지 않다: *The histories of the two countries are closely interwoven.* 양국의 역사는 긴밀히 연관되어 있다.

in·tes·tate /ɪn'tɛˌsteɪt/ *adj* LAW **die intestate** to die without a WILL ‖ 유언 없이 죽다

in·tes·tine /ɪn'tɛstɪn/ *n* the long tube that takes food from your stomach out of your body ‖ 위에서 내려온 음식물을 몸 밖으로 배출하는 긴 관. 장 — **intestinal** *adj*

in·ti·ma·cy /'ɪntəməsi/ *n* a state of having a close personal relationship with someone ‖ 남과 친밀한 개인적 관계가 있는 상태. 절친함. 친교: *the intimacy of good friends* 절친한 좋은 친구 사이

in·ti·mate¹ /'ɪntəmɪt/ *adj* **1** having a very close relationship with someone ‖ 남과 매우 가까운 사이인. 친밀한: *She only told a few intimate friends that she was pregnant.* 그녀는 임신했다는 사실을 몇 명의 절친한 친구에게만 말했다. **2** relating to very private or personal matters ‖ 매우 사적인 또는 개인적인 문제에 관한. 일신상의. 개인적인: *the intimate nature of the doctor's relationship with a patient* 의사와 환자와의 관계의 사적인 특성 **3** FORMAL relating to sex ‖ 성에 관련된. 성적인: *The virus can only be transmitted through intimate contact.* 그 바이러스는 성적 접촉을 통해서만 전염이 가능하다. — **intimately** *adv*

in·ti·mate² /'ɪntəˌmeɪt/ *v* [T] FORMAL to make someone understand what you mean without saying it directly ‖ 직접적으로 말하지 않고 자신의 의도를 남에게 이해시키다. 암시하다. 넌지시 알리다 —

intimation /ˌɪntəˈmeɪʃən/ *n* [C, U]

in·tim·i·date /ɪnˈtɪmə.deɪt/ *v* [T] to make someone afraid, often by using threats, so that s/he does what you want ‖ 자신이 원하는 것을 하도록 종종 협박하여 남을 두려워하게 하다. 위협하다 – **intimidation** /ɪnˌtɪməˈdeɪʃən/ *n* [U]

in·tim·i·dat·ed /ɪnˈtɪmə.deɪtɪd/ *adj* feeling worried or frightened because you are in a difficult situation ‖ 어려운 상황에 처하여 걱정하거나 무서워하는. 벌벌 떠는: *Ben felt intimidated by the older boys.* 벤은 자신보다 나이 많은 소년들에게 벌벌 떨었다.

in·tim·i·dat·ing /ɪnˈtɪmə.deɪtɪŋ/ *adj* making you feel worried and less confident ‖ 걱정스럽고 더 자신 없게 하는. 겁먹게 하는: *Interviews can be an intimidating experience.* 인터뷰는 떨리는 경험일 수 있다.

in·to /ˈɪntə; *before vowels* ˈɪntu; *strong* ˈɪntu/ *prep* **1** in order to be inside something or in a place ‖ 사물의 내부나 어떤 장소 안에 있으려고. …안에[으로]: *Charlie went into the kitchen.* 찰리는 부엌으로 들어갔다. / *The child had fallen into the water.* 그 아이는 물속으로 빠졌었다. **2** involved in a situation or activity ‖ 상황이나 행위에 관련되어: *He decided he would try to go into business for himself.* (=start his own business) 그는 자신의 사업을 해볼 결심을 했다. / *Don't get into trouble, and be home by 10:00!* 말썽 피우지 말고 10시까지 집에 들어와라! **3** in a different situation or physical form ‖ 다른 상황이나 물리적인 형태로: *Make the bread dough into a ball.* (=the shape of a ball) 빵 반죽을 공 모양으로 만들어라. / *I couldn't get into the Art History class, so I'm taking photography.* 나는 예술사 강의를 수강하지 못해서 사진 촬영술을 수강하고 있다. **4** to a point where you hit something, usually causing damage ‖ 보통 손상을 야기하며 사물을 부딪친 지점으로. …에 부딪쳐: *The car had run into a tree.* 자동차가 돌진하여 나무에 부딪혔다. **5 be into sth** SPOKEN to like and be interested in something ‖ 어떤 것을 좋아하고 관심을 갖다. 열중하다: *I was into ice skating when I was 10.* 나는 10살 때 아이스 스케이팅에 빠졌다. **6** in a particular direction ‖ 특정 방향으로: *Look into my eyes.* 내 눈을 보아라 **7** at or until a particular time ‖ 특정 시간에 또는 특정 시간까지: *We talked into the night.* 우리는 저녁까지 이야기했다.

in·tol·er·able /ɪnˈtɑlərəbəl/ *adj* too difficult, unpleasant, or painful for you to bear ‖ 참기에는 너무나 힘들거나 불쾌하거나 고통스러운. 애타는 견딜 수 없는: *an intolerable pain in my back* 내 허리의 참을 수 없는 고통 – **intolerably** *adv*

in·tol·er·ant /ɪnˈtɑlərənt/ *adj* not willing to accept ways of thinking and behaving that are different from your own ‖ 자신의 것과 다른 사고·행동 방식을 받아들이려 하지 않는. 관용이 없는. 편협한: *He's very intolerant of other people's political opinions.* 그는 다른 사람들의 정견에 매우 편협하다. – **intolerance** *n* [U]

in·to·na·tion /ˌɪntəˈneɪʃən, -toʊ-/ *n* [C, U] the rise and fall in the level of your voice ‖ 목소리 높이의 상승 및 하강. 억양. 음조

in·tox·i·cat·ed /ɪnˈtɑksə.keɪtɪd/ *adj* **1** drunk ‖ 술 취한: *He was intoxicated at the time of the accident.* 그는 사고 당시에 술에 취한 상태였다. **2** happy and excited because of success, love, power etc. ‖ 성공·사랑·권력 등으로 행복하고 흥분한. 들뜬 – **intoxicating** *adj*

in·tox·i·ca·tion /ɪnˌtɑksəˈkeɪʃən/ *n* [U] the state of being drunk ‖ 술 취한 상태. 술 취함

in·trac·ta·ble /ɪnˈtræktəbəl/ *adj* FORMAL very difficult to control, manage, or solve ‖ 통제하기[다루기, 해결하기] 매우 힘든: *intractable problems* 해결하기 힘든 문제들

in·tra·mu·ral /ˌɪntrəˈmyʊrəl/ *adj* intended for the students of one school ‖ 한 학교의 학생들을 위한. 교내의: *intramural sports* 교내 스포츠

in·tra·net /ˈɪntrənɛt/ *n* a computer network used for exchanging or seeing information within a company, which works in the same way as the Internet ‖ 인터넷과 유사하게 작동하는, 회사 내 정보의 교환이나 열람에 쓰이는 컴퓨터 네트워크. 인트라넷

in·tran·si·gent /ɪnˈtrænsədʒənt, -zə-/ *adj* FORMAL not willing to change your opinions or behavior ‖ 견해나 행동을 바꾸려 하지 않는. 타협하지 않는 – **intransigence** *n* [U]

in·tran·si·tive verb /ˌ…ˈ… ˈ./ *n* TECHNICAL in grammar, an intransitive verb has a subject but no object. In the sentence, "They arrived early," "arrive" is an intransitive verb ‖ 문법에서 주어는 취하지만 목적어는 취하지 않는 동사. 자동사. "They arrived early."의 문장에서 "arrive"는 자동사이다. —compare

TRANSITIVE VERB —see study note on page 942

in·tra·ve·nous /ˌɪntrəˈviːnəs/ *adj* within or connected to a VEIN (=a tube that takes blood to your heart) ‖ 정맥 내의 또는 정맥과 관련된: *an intravenous injection* 정맥 주사 **– intravenously** *adv*

in·trep·id /ɪnˈtrepɪd/ *adj* LITERARY willing to do dangerous things or go to dangerous places ‖ 위험한 일을 하거나 위험한 장소에 가려고 하는. 두려움을 모르는

in·tri·ca·cy /ˈɪntrɪkəsi/ *n* **1** [U] the state of containing a lot of parts or details ‖ 많은 요소나 세목을 포함한 상태. 복잡함: *the intricacy of the plot* 복잡한 줄거리 **2 the intricacies of sth** the complicated details of something ‖ 사물의 복잡한 세부: *the intricacies of Bach's music* 바흐 음악의 복잡한 요소들

in·tri·cate /ˈɪntrɪkɪt/ *adj* containing a lot of parts or details ‖ 많은 요소나 세목을 포함한. 복잡한: *an intricate pattern in the rug* 양탄자의 복잡한 무늬

in·trigue¹ /ɪnˈtriːg/ *v* [T] to interest someone a lot, especially by being strange or mysterious ‖ 특히 이상하거나 신비하여 남의 흥미를 몹시 끌다: *I was intrigued by her story.* 나는 그녀의 이야기에 흥미를 느꼈다.

in·trigue² /ˈɪntriːg, ɪnˈtriːg/ *n* [C, U] the practice of making secret plans to harm or deceive someone ‖ 남을 해치거나 속이려고 비밀 계획을 짜는 일. 음모: *a book about political intrigue* 정치 음모에 관한 책

in·tri·guing /ɪnˈtriːgɪŋ/ *adj* very interesting because it is strange or mysterious ‖ 이상하거나 신비하기 때문에 매우 흥미로운. 재미있는: *an intriguing idea* 흥미로운 생각 **– intriguingly** *adv*

in·trin·sic /ɪnˈtrɪnzɪk, -sɪk/ *adj* being part of the basic nature or character of someone or something ‖ 사람이나 사물의 본질적 특성이나 성격의 일부인. 고유한. 본질적인: *The art has an intrinsic value that is not connected to how much it is worth.* 예술은 값으로 매길 수 없는 본질적 가치를 지니고 있다. **– intrinsically** *adv*

in·tro /ˈɪntroʊ/ *n* INFORMAL the introduction to a song, television program etc. ‖ 노래·텔레비전 프로그램 등의 도입부

in·tro·duce /ˌɪntrəˈduːs/ *v* [T] **1** if you introduce someone to another person, you tell them each other's name for the first time ‖ 처음으로 만나는 두 사람의 이름을 알려주다. 소개하다: *Alice, may I introduce you to Megan?* 앨리스, 미간에게 너를 소개해도 될까? **2** to make a change, plan, etc. happen or exist for the first time ‖ 처음으로 변화·계획 등이 일어나거나 생기게 하다: *The company has introduced a new insurance plan.* 그 회사는 새로운 보험 안을 내놓았다. **3 introduce sb to sth** to show someone something or tell him/her about it for the first time ‖ 사물을 처음에 남에게 보여주거나 말하다: *He introduced us to Thai food.* 그는 태국 음식을 우리에게 처음 소개시켜 줬다. **4** to speak at the beginning of a television program, public speech etc. to say what will happen next ‖ 텔레비전 프로그램·대중 연설 등의 첫머리에서 다음에 있게 될 일에 대해 말하다. 예고하다

in·tro·duc·tion /ˌɪntrəˈdʌkʃən/ *n* **1** [C, U] the act of making a change, plan etc. happen or exist for the first time ‖ 처음으로 변화·계획 등이 일어나거나 생기게 하는 행위. 도입. 소개: *the introduction of personal computers into the schools* 학교에의 개인 컴퓨터의 도입 **2** the act of telling two people each other's names when they first meet ‖ 처음 만났을 때 두 사람이 서로의 이름을 말하는 행위. 소개 **3** a written or spoken explanation at the beginning of a book or speech ‖ 책이나 연설 첫머리에서 설명한 글이나 말. 서론. 서설

USAGE NOTE introductions

When you are introduced to someone, you usually shake hands with that person and say, "Hello, it's nice to meet you." In an informal situation, you can say, "Hi, nice to meet you." In a formal situation, you say, "How do you do?" When you introduce people to each other, you say, "This is…" You introduce each person: *"Ron, this is Jan Brown. Jan, this is Ron Jackson."* In an informal situation, you can say, "Do you know my daughter/friend/wife Kate?" In a formal situation, you say, "May I introduce you to my daughter/friend/ wife Kate?"

당신이 어떤 사람에게 소개될 때, 당신은 보통 그 사람과 악수하면서, "안녕하세요. 뵙게 되어 반갑습니다."라고 한다. 비공식석상에서는 "안녕, 만나서 반가워."라고 할 수 있고 공식석상에서는

"처음 뵙겠습니다."라고 한다. 당신이 사람들을 서로에게 소개시킬 경우에는 "이 사람은 ….”라고 개개인을 소개한 다: "론, 이분은 얀 브라운입니다. 얀, 이분은 론 잭슨입니다." 비공식석상에서 는, "내 딸[친구, 아내], 케이트 알지?" 라고 할 수 있고, 공식석상에서는 "당신 을 내 딸[친구, 아내] 케이트에게 소개 해도 괜찮겠습니까?"라고 한다.

in·tro·duc·to·ry /ˌɪntrəˈdʌktəri/ *adj* **1** concerning the beginning of a book, speech, course etc. ‖ 책·연설·과정 등의 처음에 관한. 서두의. 서론의: *the introductory chapter* 서장(序章) **2 introductory offer** a special low price to encourage you to buy something new ‖ 새로운 것의 구매를 장려하기 위한 특별 염가

in·tro·spec·tive /ˌɪntrəˈspɛktɪv/ *adj* thinking deeply about your own thoughts and feelings ‖ 자신의 사고와 감정에 대해 깊이 생각하는. 내성적인 – **introspection** /ˌɪntrəˈspɛkʃən/ *n* [U]

in·tro·vert·ed /ˈɪntrəˌvɚtɪd/ *adj* thinking a lot about your own problems, interests etc. and not wanting to be with other people ‖ 자신의 문제·관심 등에 대해 많이 생각하며 다른 사람들과 함께 있고 싶어하지 않는. 내성적인 – **introvert** *n* —compare EXTROVERTED

in·trude /ɪnˈtrud/ *v* [I] to go into a place or get involved in a situation where you are not wanted ‖ 자신을 반기지 않는 장소에 들어가거나 상황에 개입되다. 억지로 밀고 들어가다. 침입하다: *newspapers that intrude into/on people's private lives* 사람들의 사생활을 침해하는 신문들.

in·trud·er /ɪnˈtrudɚ/ *n* someone who enters a building or area where s/he is not supposed to be ‖ 있어서는 안 되는 건물이나 지역에 들어온 사람. 침입자

in·tru·sion /ɪnˈtruʒən/ *n* [C, U] the act of intruding, or something that intrudes on or interrupts something ‖ 침입하는 행위, 또는 사물을 침범하거나 방해하는 것. 침입[방해](하기): *He resented her intrusion into his work time.* 그는 자신의 작업 시간을 그녀가 방해해서 불쾌하게 생각했다. – **intrusive** /ɪnˈtrusɪv/ *adj*

in·tu·i·tion /ˌɪntuˈɪʃən/ *n* [C, U] the ability to understand or know that something is true based on your feelings rather than facts, or an example of this ‖ 사실보다는 자신의 느낌에 근거하여 진실성을 파악하거나 아는 능력, 또는 이런 예. 통찰(력). 직관(력): *My intuition*

told me not to trust Reynolds. 나는 레이놀즈를 믿어선 안 된다고 직관적으로 알았다.

in·tu·i·tive /ɪnˈtuətɪv/ *adj* based on feelings rather than facts ‖ 사실보다 느낌에 근거하는. 직관적인. 직관적으로 인식하는: *an intuitive understanding of the problem* 문제의 직관적 이해 – **intuitively** *adv*

In·u·it /ˈɪnuɪt/ *n* **the Inuit** [plural] a group of people who live in ARCTIC places such as northern Canada, Greenland, Alaska, and Eastern Siberia ‖ 북부 캐나다·그린란드·알래스카·동시베리아 등의 북극 지역에 사는 일단의 사람들. 이누잇 – **Inuit** *adj*

in·un·date /ˈɪnənˌdeɪt/ *v* [T] **1 be inundated with/by sth** to receive so much of something that you cannot deal with all of it ‖ 모두 처리할 수 없을 만큼 어떤 것을 대단히 많이 받다. …이 쇄도하다: *We were inundated with requests for tickets.* 우리에게 티켓 요청이 쇄도하였다. **2** FORMAL to flood a place ‖ 장소를 물에 잠기게 하다. 범람시키다 – **inundation** /ˌɪnənˈdeɪʃən/ *n* [C, U]

in·vade /ɪnˈveɪd/ *v* **1** [I, T] to enter a place using military force ‖ 군사력을 이용하여 어떤 장소에 들어가다. 침입하다. …을 침략하다: *Germany invaded Poland in 1939.* 독일은 1939년에 폴란드를 침략했다. **2** [T] to go into a place in large numbers ‖ 많은 수가 어떤 장소로 들어가다. 우르르 몰려들다: *Every Christmas Jerusalem is invaded by tourists.* 매년 크리스마스마다 예루살렘에는 관광객들이 밀어닥친다. – **invader** *n*

in·val·id¹ /ɪnˈvælɪd/ *adj* not legally or officially acceptable ‖ 법적으로 또는 공식적으로 받아들여지지 않는. 효력이 없는: *an invalid bus pass* 무효 버스표

in·va·lid² /ˈɪnvələd/ *n* someone who needs to be cared for because s/he is ill, injured, or very old ‖ 병이 들어서[다쳐서, 몹시 늙어서] 보살핌이 필요한 사람. 병자. 병약자 – **invalid** *adj*

in·val·i·date /ɪnˈvæləˌdeɪt/ *v* [T] **1** to make a document, ticket etc. no longer legally acceptable ‖ 서류·표 등을 법적으로 인정되지 않게 만들다. 법적 효력을 없애다 **2** to show that something such as a belief, explanation etc. is wrong ‖ 신념·해설 등이 틀렸다는 것을 보여 주다. …의 잘못을 증명하다: *New research has invalidated the theory.* 새로운 연구는 그 이론이 잘못되었다는 것을 증명했다. – **invalidity** /ˌɪnvəˈlɪdəti/ *n* [U]

in·val·u·a·ble /ɪnˈvælyəbəl, -yuəbəl/

adj extremely useful ‖ 매우 유용한: *Your advice has been invaluable.* 당신의 조언은 매우 귀중했습니다.

in·var·i·a·bly /ɪnˈvɛriəbli, -ˈvær-/ *adv* always, without changing ‖ 항상, 변함없이: *They invariably go to Florida on their vacation.* 그들은 휴가 중에 항상 플로리다에 간다. **– invariable** *adj*

in·va·sion /ɪnˈveɪʒən/ *n* [C, U] **1** an occasion when an army enters a country using military force ‖ 군사력을 이용하여 군대가 한 국가로 들어가는 경우. 침략 **2** the arrival of people or things at a place where they are not wanted ‖ 환영받지 못하는 곳에 사람들이나 사물이 도래함. 밀어닥침. 쇄도: *the yearly invasion of mosquitoes* 해마다 있는 모기의 습격 **3 invasion of privacy** a situation in which someone tries to find out about someone else's personal life, in a way that is upsetting and often illegal ‖ 사람이 당황스럽고 불법적인 방법으로 다른 사람의 사생활을 알려고 하는 상황. 프라이버시[사생활] 침해 **– invasive** /ɪnˈveɪsɪv/ *adj*

in·vent /ɪnˈvɛnt/ *v* [T] **1** to make, design, or produce something for the first time ‖ 처음으로 무엇을 만들다[고안하다, 생산하다]. 발명하다: *Who invented the light bulb?* 전구를 누가 발명했습니까? **2** to think of an idea, story etc. that is not true, usually to deceive people ‖ 보통 사람들을 속이기 위해 사실이 아닌 개념·이야기 등을 생각해 내다. 날조하다. 꾸며내다

in·ven·tion /ɪnˈvɛnʃən/ *n* [C, U] **1** the act of inventing something, or the thing that is invented ‖ 무엇을 발명하는 행위, 또는 발명한 것. 발명(품): *The fax machine is an amazing invention.* 팩스기는 놀라운 발명품이다. **2** an idea, story etc. that is not true ‖ 사실이 아닌 생각·이야기 등. 날조. 허구

in·ven·tive /ɪnˈvɛntɪv/ *adj* able to think of new and interesting ideas ‖ 새롭고 흥미있는 개념을 생각해 낼 수 있는. 창의력이 풍부한: *an inventive cook* 창의성이 풍부한 요리사 **– inventiveness** *n* [U]

in·ven·tor /ɪnˈvɛntɚ/ *n* someone who has invented something ‖ 사물을 발명한 사람. 발명가

in·ven·to·ry /ˈɪnvənˌtɔri/ *n* **1** [U] all the goods in a store ‖ 상점 안의 모든 물건. 재고 **2** a list of all the things in a place ‖ 어떤 장소에 있는 모든 물건의 목록. 상품 목록. 재고 품목: *The store will be closed on Friday to take inventory.* (=make a list of its goods) 그 상점은 재고 목록을 작성하기 위해 금요일에 문을 닫을 것입니다.

in·verse /ɪnˈvɚs, ˈɪnvɚs/ *adj* TECHNICAL **in inverse proportion/relation etc. to** getting larger as something else gets smaller, or getting smaller as something else gets larger ‖ 다른 것이 작아지면 커지거나 다른 것이 커지면 점점 작아져. …에 반비례하여 **– inversely** *adv* **– inverse** *n*

in·vert /ɪnˈvɚt/ *v* [T] FORMAL to put something in the opposite position, especially by turning it upside down ‖ 어떤 것을 반대로 특히 위아래를 거꾸로 하여 놓다. 뒤집다 **– inversion** /ɪnˈvɚʒən/ *n* [C, U]

in·vest /ɪnˈvɛst/ *v* **1** [I, T] to give money to a company, bank etc., or to buy something, in order to get a profit later ‖ 나중에 수익을 얻기 위해 회사·은행 등에 돈을 위탁하거나 무엇을 사다. 투자하다: *investing in stocks and bonds* 주식 및 채권에의 투자 **2** [T] to use a lot of time or effort to make something succeed ‖ 무엇인가를 성공시키기 위해 시간이나 노력을 상당히 들이다 **– investor** *n*

in·ves·ti·gate /ɪnˈvɛstəˌgeɪt/ *v* [I, T] to try to find out the truth about a crime, accident etc. ‖ 범죄·사건 등의 진실을 알려고 애쓰다. 조사하다. 수사하다: *The police are investigating the fraud charges.* 경찰은 사기 고소건을 수사 중이다. **– investigator** *n*

in·ves·ti·ga·tion /ɪnˌvɛstəˈgeɪʃən/ *n* an official attempt to find out the reasons for something, such as a crime or scientific problem ‖ 범죄나 과학적 문제 등의 것에 대한 원인을 알아내려는 공식적인 시도. 수사. 탐사: *an investigation into the plane crash* 비행기 추락에 대한 조사 **– investigative** /ɪnˈvɛstəˌgeɪtɪv/ *adj*

in·vest·ment /ɪnˈvɛstmənt/ *n* **1** [C, U] the money that you give to a company, bank etc. in order to get a profit later, or the act of doing this ‖ 나중에 수익을 얻기 위해 회사·은행 등에 위탁하는 돈, 또는 이러한 행위. 투자(금): *a $5000 investment in stocks* 5000달러의 증권 투자 **2** something that you buy or do because it will be more valuable or useful later ‖ 나중에 더 가치 있거나 유용할 것이기 때문에 사거나 하는 것. 투자물: *We bought the house as an investment.* 우리는 투자 대상으로 그 집을 구입했다.

in·vet·er·ate /ɪnˈvɛtərɪt/ *adj* having done something over a long time, and not likely to stop ‖ 오랜 시간에 걸쳐 멈추지 않고 무엇을 하는. 상습적인. 만성의: *an inveterate liar* 상습적인 거짓말쟁이

in·vig·o·rat·ing /ɪnˈvɪgəˌreɪtɪŋ/ *adj* making you feel more active and healthy ‖ 보다 활기차고 건강한 느낌이 들게 하는. 기운 나게 하는: *an invigorating swim* 기분을 상쾌하게 하는 수영 – **invigorate** *v* [T] – **invigorated** *adj*

in·vin·ci·ble /ɪnˈvɪnsəbəl/ *adj* too strong to be defeated or destroyed ‖ 패배하거나 파괴되지 않을 만큼 아주 강한. 정복할 수 없는. 무적의: *Bubka is invincible in the pole vault.* 부브카는 장대높이뛰기에서 천하무적이다. – **invincibly** *adv*

in·vis·i·ble /ɪnˈvɪzəbəl/ *adj* not able to be seen ‖ 보이지 않는: *organisms that are invisible without using a microscope* 현미경을 사용하지 않고는 볼 수 없는 유기체 – **invisibly** *adv* – **invisibility** /ɪnˌvɪzəˈbɪləti/ *n* [U]

in·vi·ta·tion /ˌɪnvəˈteɪʃən/ *n* a request to someone that invites him/her to go somewhere or do something, or the card this is written on ‖ 남을 어떤 장소로 오거나 무엇을 하도록 청하는 부탁, 또는 이 부탁이 기재된 카드. 초대[초청](장): *Did you get an invitation to the wedding?* 그 결혼식 청첩장 받았죠?

in·vite¹ /ɪnˈvaɪt/ *v* [T] **1** to ask someone to come to a party, meal, wedding etc. ‖ 파티·식사·결혼식 등에 남을 오라고 요청하다. 초청하다. 초대하다: *I invited the Rosens to dinner next Friday.* 나는 다음 금요일 저녁 식사에 로젠스 씨 가족을 초대했다. **2 invite trouble/criticism etc.** to make trouble, criticism etc. more likely to happen to you ‖ 문제·비판 등이 더 일어날 수 있게 하다. 문제/비판을 초래하다

invite sb **along** *phr v* [T] to ask someone to come with you when you go somewhere ‖ 어디에 갈 때 함께 가자고 남에게 부탁하다: *You can invite one of your friends along.* 당신은 친구 한 명에게 함께 가자고 부탁해도 된다.

invite sb **in** *phr v* [T] to ask someone to come into your home, usually when they are standing at the door ‖ 보통 누가 문 앞에 서 있을 때에 집안으로 들어오라고 권하다

invite sb **over** *phr v* [T] to ask someone to come to your home for a party, meal etc. ‖ 파티·식사 등을 위해 남에게 집으로 오라고 청하다: *I invited the Blackmers over for a meal.* 나는 블랙머스 씨 가족을 식사에 초대했다.

USAGE NOTE invite

Invite is usually used only to talk about the fact that you have been asked to go somewhere: *I've been invited to Barbara's party.* When you invite someone, say, "Would you like to come to my party?"

invite는 보통 자신이 어떤 장소로 오라고 부탁받은 사실을 언급할 때만 사용된다: 나는 바바라의 파티에 초대받았어. 자신이 남을 초대할 경우에는 **come**을 써서 "내 파티에 오시겠어요?"라고 한다.

in·vite² /ˈɪnvaɪt/ *n* INFORMAL an invitation ‖ 초대(장)

in·vit·ing /ɪnˈvaɪtɪŋ/ *adj* an inviting sight, smell etc. is attractive and makes you want to do something ‖ 경치·냄새 등이 마음을 끌어서 무엇을 하고 싶게 만드는. 매력적인. 솔깃한: *The lake looked inviting.* (=made me want to swim in it) 그 호수는 (수영을 하고 싶게) 매력적으로 보였다. – **invitingly** *adv*

in·voice /ˈɪnvɔɪs/ *n* a list that shows how much you owe for goods, work etc. ‖ 상품·작업 등의 빚진 양을 나타내는 목록표. 송장 – **invoice** *v* [T]

in·voke /ɪnˈvoʊk/ *v* [T] FORMAL **1** to use a law, principle etc. to support your opinions or actions ‖ 견해나 행위를 뒷받침할 수 있게 법·원칙 등을 이용하다. 법 등을 행사하다. 발동하다 **2** LITERARY to ask for help from someone, especially a god ‖ 특히 신에게 도움을 요청하다. 기원하다. 호소하다

in·vol·un·tar·y /ɪnˈvɑlənˌtɛri/ *adj* an involuntary movement, reaction etc. is one that you make suddenly without intending to ‖ 동작·반응 등이 그럴 의도 없이 갑자기 이뤄지는. 무의식적인 – **involuntarily** /ɪnˌvɑlənˈtɛrəli/ *adv*

in·volve /ɪnˈvɑlv/ *v* [T] **1** to include or affect someone or something ‖ 사람이나 사물을 포함하거나 영향을 주다. 끌어넣다. 연루시키다: *a riot involving 45 prisoners* 45명의 죄수들이 연루된 폭동 **2** to ask or allow someone to take part in something ‖ 남에게 어떤 것에 참여하기를 권하거나 허락하다: *We're trying to involve as many of the parents as possible in the PTA.* 우리는 육성회에 가능한 한 많은 부모님들이 참여할 수 있게 애쓰고 있다. **3** to include something as a necessary part or result of something else ‖ 다른 것의 필수적인 부분이나 결과로 어떤 것을 포함하다. …을 필연적으로

포함하다: *Taking the job involves moving to Texas.* 그 일자리를 잡으려면 텍사스로 이사가야 한다.

in·volved /ɪnˈvɑlvd/ *adj* **1** taking part in an activity or event ‖ 행위나 사건에 참여한: *More than 50 nations were involved in the war effort.* 50개국 이상이 전쟁에 대한 협력에 참여하였다. **2** difficult to understand because it is complicated or has a lot of parts ‖ 복잡하거나 요소가 많아서 이해하기 어려운. 복잡한. 뒤얽힌: *a long involved answer* 길고 복잡한 답 **3 be involved with sb** to be having a sexual relationship with someone ‖ 남과 성관계를 갖고 있다

in·volve·ment /ɪnˈvɑlvmənt/ *n* [U] the act of taking part in an activity or event ‖ 행위나 사건에 참가하는 행위. 관련. 연루

in·ward¹ /ˈɪnwəd/ *adj* **1** felt in your own mind, but not expressed to other people ‖ 다른 사람들에게 표현하지 않고 마음으로 느끼는. 마음속의: *Her calm face hid her inward fear.* 그녀의 차분한 얼굴이 마음속의 두려움을 덮어 가렸다. ✗DON'T SAY "Her fear was inward."✗ "Her fear was inward."라고는 하지 않는다. **2** on or toward the inside of something ‖ 사물의 내부의 또는 내부를 향한 – **inwardly** *adv* : *Ginny was inwardly disappointed that she hadn't seen him at the party.* 지니는 파티에서 그를 보지 못해서 속으로 실망했다.

inward² *inwards* *adv* toward the inside ‖ 안으로 —opposite OUTWARD²

i·o·dine /ˈaɪəˌdaɪn, -ˌdɪn/ *n* [U] a chemical that is often used on wounds to prevent infection ‖ 종종 상처에 감염을 막기 위해 쓰이는 화학 물질. 요오드

i·on /ˈaɪən, ˈaɪɑn/ *n* TECHNICAL an atom that has been given a positive or negative force ‖ 양성 또는 음성의 에너지를 갖는 원자. 이온

i·o·ta /aɪˈoʊtə/ *n* [singular] **not one/an iota of sth** not even a small amount of something ‖ 어떤 것이 조금도 없는: *There's not an iota of truth in what he says.* 그가 하는 말엔 일말의 진실도 없다.

IOU *n* INFORMAL an abbreviation for "I owe you"; a note that you sign to say that you owe someone some money ‖ "I owe you"의 약어; 자신이 남에게 얼마간의 돈을 빚지고 있다고 말하기 위해 서명하는 각서. 약식 차용증

IPA *n* [singular] the International Phonetic Alphabet; a system of signs that represent the sounds made in speech ‖ the International Phonetic Alphabet(국제 음성 기호)의 약어; 말할 때 나는 소리를 나타내는 신호 체계

IQ *n* Intelligence Quotient; the level of someone's intelligence, with 100 being the average level ‖ Intelligence Quotient(지능 지수)의 약어; 100을 평균 수준으로 한, 사람의 지능 수준

IRA *n* Individual Retirement Account; a special bank account in which you can save money for your RETIREMENT without paying tax on it until later ‖ Individual Retirement Account(개인 퇴직금 계좌)의 약어; 은퇴 후까지도 세금을 내지 않고 은퇴를 위해 돈을 적금할 수 있는 특수한 은행 적금 계좌

i·ras·ci·ble /ɪˈræsəbəl/ *adj* FORMAL becoming angry easily ‖ 화를 쉽게 내는. 성마른

i·rate /ˌaɪˈreɪt/ *adj* extremely angry ‖ 매우 화난. 격노한 – **irately** *adv*

ir·i·des·cent /ˌɪrəˈdɛsənt/ *adj* showing colors that seem to change in different lights ‖ 조명을 달리하면 색이 변하는 듯한. 조명에 따라 색깔이 달리 보이는 – **iridescence** *n* [U]

i·ris /ˈaɪrɪs/ *n* **1** the round colored part of your eye ‖ 눈의 둥글고 색깔을 띤 부분. 홍채 —see picture at EYE¹ **2** a tall plant with purple, yellow, or white flowers and long thin leaves ‖ 자주색[노란색, 흰색] 꽃이 피며 길고 가는 잎을 가진 키 큰 식물. 아이리스

I·rish¹ /ˈaɪrɪʃ/ *adj* relating to or coming from Ireland ‖ 아일랜드와 관련되거나 아일랜드에서 온. 아일랜드 (산)의

Irish² *n* **the Irish** [plural] the people of Ireland ‖ 아일랜드인

irk /ək/ *v* [T] to trouble or annoy someone ‖ 남을 괴롭히거나 짜증나게 하다. …을 지치게[진저리나게] 하다

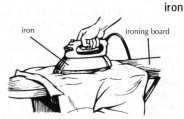

iron

iron · ironing board

i·ron¹ /ˈaɪən/ *n* **1** an object that is heated and that you push across a piece of clothing to make it smooth ‖ 가열하여 왔다갔다 밀어서 옷을 매끈하게 하는 물건. 다리미 **2** [U] a common heavy metal that is used in making steel ‖ 강철을 만드는 데에 사용되는 흔한 중금속. 철

iron² *v* [T] to make your clothes smooth using an iron ‖ 다리미를 이용해서 옷을 매끈하게 만들다. …을 다리미질하다: *Can you iron my shirt for me?* 내 셔츠를 다려 줄 수 있어요?

iron sth ↔ **out** *phr v* [T] to solve a small problem or difficulty ‖ 작은 문제나 어려움을 해결하다. …을 원활하게 하다. 장애물을 없애다: *Jim and Sharon are ironing out their differences.* 짐과 샤론은 그들의 의견 차이를 해결하고 있는 중이다.

iron³ *adj* 1 made of iron ‖ 철로 된. 철의. 철제의: *iron bars on the gate* 문 위의 철봉들 2 very firm or strict ‖ 매우 단단하거나 엄격한. 쇠처럼 강한(단단한): *He ruled the country with an iron fist.* (=in a very strict and powerful way) 그는 그 나라를 철권 통치했다.

Iron Cur·tain /ˌ.. '../ *n* **the Iron Curtain** a name used in past times for the border between the Communist countries of eastern Europe and the rest of Europe ‖ 동유럽의 공산주의 국가와 나머지 유럽 (민주주의) 국가 사이의 국경에 대해 예전에 사용하던 명칭. 철의 장막

i·ron·ic /aɪˈrɑnɪk/ *adj* 1 using words that are the opposite of what you really mean in order to be amusing, or show that you are annoyed ‖ 재미있게 하기 위해, 또는 화가 난 것을 보여 주기 위해 진정 의미하는 것과 반대되는 말을 사용하는. 비꼬아 말하는. 빈정대는 2 an ironic situation is unusual or amusing because something strange or unexpected happens ‖ 이상하거나 뜻밖의 일이 일어나기 때문에 상황이 평범하지 않거나 재미있는. 상황이 얄궂은[기이한] – **ironically** *adv*

i·ron·ing /ˈaɪ˞nɪŋ/ *n* [U] the activity of making clothes smooth with an iron ‖ 다리미로 옷을 매끈하게 하기. 다리미질

ironing board /ˈ... ./ *n* a narrow board on which you make your clothes smooth with an iron ‖ 다리미로 옷을 매끈하게 하는 데에 쓰는 좁은 판. 다리미판 —see picture at IRON²

i·ro·ny /ˈaɪrəni/ *n* [U] 1 the use of words that are the opposite of what you really mean in order to be amusing, or show that you are annoyed ‖ 재미있게 하기 위해, 또는 화가 나 있는 것을 보여 주기 위해 진정 의미하는 것과 반대되는 말을 사용함. 반어. 빈정댐. 비꼼. 풍자 2 the part of a situation that is unusual or amusing because something strange happens, or the opposite of what is expected happens ‖ 이상한 일이 일어나

거나 예상했던 것과 반대로 일어나기 때문에 평범하지 않거나 재미있는 상황. 얄궂은 상황. 기이한 상황: *The irony is that the drug was supposed to save lives.* 얄궂은 것은 그 약은 원래 목숨을 구해야 했었다는 점이다.

ir·ra·tion·al /ɪˈræʃənəl/ *adj* not reasonable or not based on good reasons ‖ 합리적이지 못하거나 합당한 이유에 근거하지 않은. 이치에 어긋나는. 불합리한: *an irrational fear of spiders* 거미에 대한 막연한 공포 – **irrationally** *adv* – **irrationality** /ɪˌræʃəˈnæləţi/ *n* [U]

ir·rec·on·cil·a·ble /ɪˌrɛkənˈsaɪləbəl/ *adj* so different that it is impossible to reach an agreement ‖ 너무 달라서 합의에 이르기가 불가능한. 타협할 수 없는. 조화되지 않는: *irreconcilable opinions* 서로 융화될 수 없는 의견들 – **irreconcilably** *adv*

ir·re·fut·a·ble /ˌɪrɪˈfyuţəbəl/ *adj* FORMAL an irrefutable statement, argument etc. cannot be proved wrong ‖ 진술·논쟁 등이 잘못되었다고 증명할 수 없는. 반박[논파]할 수 없는

ir·reg·u·lar /ɪˈrɛgyələ˞/ *adj* 1 having a shape, surface etc. that is not even or smooth ‖ 모양·표면 등이 고르거나 매끄럽지 않은. 가지런하지 않은. 울퉁불퉁한: *a face with irregular features* 울퉁불퉁한 용모의 얼굴 2 not happening at regular times or at the usual time ‖ 규칙적으로 또는 정상적으로 일어나지 않는. 불규칙한. 변칙적인: *an irregular heartbeat* 불규칙한 심장 박동 3 not following the usual pattern in grammar ‖ 문법에서 일반적인 유형을 따르지 않는. 불규칙의: *an irregular verb* 불규칙 동사 – **irregularity** /ɪˌrɛgyəˈlærəţi/ *n* [C, U] – **irregularly** /ɪˈrɛgyələ˞li/ *adv*

ir·rel·e·vance /ɪˈrɛləvəns/, **ir·rel·e·van·cy** /ɪˈrɛləvənsi/ *n* [U] a lack of importance in a particular situation ‖ 특정한 상황에서 중요성의 부족. 부적절

ir·rel·e·vant /ɪˈrɛləvənt/ *adj* not useful in or relating to a particular situation, and therefore not important ‖ 특정한 상황에 도움이 되지 않거나 관련되지 않아서 중요하지 않은. 부적절한. 관계가 없는: *His age is irrelevant if he can do the job.* 그가 그 일을 할 수 있다면 그의 나이는 상관 없다. – **irrelevantly** *adv*

ir·rep·a·ra·ble /ɪˈrɛpərəbəl/ *adj* so bad that it cannot be repaired or made better ‖ 너무 나빠서 수리하거나 개선할 수 없는. 고칠 수 없는. 치료할 수 없는

– **irreparably** *adv*

ir·re·place·a·ble /ˌɪrɪˈpleɪsəbəl/ *adj* too special, valuable, or rare to be replaced by anything else ‖ 너무 특별하여[가치가 있어서, 희귀하여] 다른 것으로 대체할 수 없는. 대신할 수 없는. 둘도 없는: *an irreplaceable work of art* 둘도 없는 예술 작품

ir·re·press·i·ble /ˌɪrɪˈprɛsəbəl/ *adj* full of energy and happiness that is too strong to be controlled ‖ 너무 강력해서 조절될 수 없는 활력과 행복으로 가득한. 억제[감당]할 수 없는. 참기 어려운: *Nathan's excitement was irrepressible.* 네이선은 흥분을 가라앉히기 어려웠다.

ir·re·proach·a·ble /ˌɪrɪˈproʊtʃəbəl/ *adj* FORMAL so good that you cannot criticize it ‖ 너무 좋아 비판할 수 없는. 나무랄 데 없는. 결점이 없는: *Her behavior was irreproachable.* 그녀의 행동은 나무랄 데 가 없었다.

ir·re·sist·i·ble /ˌɪrɪˈzɪstəbəl/ *adj* **1** so attractive or desirable that you cannot stop yourself from wanting it ‖ 너무 매력 있거나 호감이 가서 그것에 대한 마음을 멈출 수 없는. 저항할 수 없는. 이겨낼 수 없는. 억누를 수 없는: *The dessert looks irresistible.* 그 후식은 안 먹고는 못 배기 게 맛있어 보인다. **2** too strong or powerful to be stopped ‖ 너무 견고하거 나 강력하여 멈출 수 없는: *an irresistible force* 불가항력 – **irresistibly** *adv*

ir·re·spec·tive of /ˌɪrɪˈspɛktɪv əv/ *prep* used in order to show that a particular fact does not affect a situation at all ‖ 특정한 사실이 상황에 전 혀 영향을 미치지 못하는 것을 나타내는 데에 쓰여. …에 관계[상관]없이: *Anyone can play, irrespective of age.* 나이와 관 계없이 누구든지 놀[경기할] 수 있다.

ir·re·spon·si·ble /ˌɪrɪˈspɑnsəbəl/ *adj* doing things that are careless without thinking about the possible results ‖ 일 어날 수 있는 결과에 대한 고려 없이 경솔 하게 어떤 것을 하는. 책임을 지지 않는. 무책임한: *It was irresponsible of John to leave the kids alone.* 존이 아이들만 남 기고 혼자 가 버린 것은 무책임한 행동이 었 다 . – **irresponsibly** *adv* – **irresponsibility** /ˌɪrɪˌspɑnsəˈbɪləti/ *n* [U]

ir·rev·er·ent /ɪˈrɛvərənt/ *adj* not showing respect for religion, customs etc. ‖ 종교·관습 등을 존중하지 않는. 불손 한. 무례한 – **irreverence** *n* [U] – **irreverently** *adv*

ir·re·ver·si·ble /ˌɪrɪˈvɜsəbəl/ *adj* impossible to change something back to the way it was before ‖ 무엇을 이전의 방 식으로 되돌릴 수 없는. 역행시킬 수 없 는. 돌이킬 수 없는: *irreversible brain damage* 돌이킬 수 없는 뇌손상

ir·rev·o·ca·ble /ɪˈrɛvəkəbəl/ *adj* not able to be changed or stopped ‖ 변화되 거나 멈추어질 수 없는. 돌이킬 수 없는. 변경할 수 없는: *an irrevocable decision* 변경할 수 없는 결정 – **irrevocably** *adv*

ir·ri·gate /ˈɪrəˌɡeɪt/ *v* [T] to supply water to land or crops ‖ 땅이나 농작물에 물을 공급하다. …에 물을 대다. 관개하다

ir·ri·ga·tion /ˌɪrəˈɡeɪʃən/ *n* [U] the act of supplying water to land or crops ‖ 땅이 나 농작물에 물을 공급하는 행위. 관개. 관수. 물 대기

ir·ri·ta·ble /ˈɪrətəbəl/ *adj* easily annoyed or made angry ‖ 쉽게 짜증내거 나 화를 내는. 성마른: *He's always irritable in the morning.* 그는 아침에는 항상 짜증을 낸다. – **irritably** *adv* – **irritability** /ˌɪrətəˈbɪləti/ *n* [U]

ir·ri·tant /ˈɪrətənt/ *n* FORMAL **1** something that makes you feel angry or annoyed ‖ 화나거나 짜증나게 하는 것 **2** a substance that makes part of your body painful and sore ‖ 신체 부위를 아프 고 쓰리게 하는 물질

ir·ri·tate /ˈɪrəˌteɪt/ *v* [T] **1** to make someone angry or annoyed ‖ 남을 화나 거나 짜증나게 하다: *The way she yells at her kids really irritates me.* 그녀가 자기 아이들에게 고함치는 모습은 정말 나를 화 나게 한다. **2** to make a part of your body painful and sore ‖ 신체 부위를 아프 고 쓰리게 하다. 자극하다: *Wool irritates my skin.* 양모는 내 피부를 따끔거리게 한 다.

ir·ri·tat·ing /ˈɪrəˌteɪtɪŋ/ *adj* annoying ‖ 짜증나는. 화나게 하는: *an irritating habit of always being late* 항상 지각하는 짜증나는 습관 – **irritatingly** *adv*

ir·ri·ta·tion /ˌɪrəˈteɪʃən/ *n* **1** [C, U] the feeling of being annoyed, or something that makes you feel this way ‖ 짜증나는 감정, 또는 이렇게 느끼게 하는 것. 짜증. 성 남. 화나게 함: *the irritation of constant traffic noise outside* 바깥의 계 속되는 교통 소음에 대한 짜증 **2** [U] a painful, sore feeling on a part of your body ‖ 신체 부위의 아프고 쓰린 느낌. 자 극. 통증

IRS *n* **the IRS** the Internal Revenue Service; the government organization in the US that deals with taxes ‖ the Internal Revenue Service(국세청)의 약 어; 세금을 취급하는 미국의 정부 기관

is /z, s, əz; *strong* ɪz/ the third person

singular of the present tense of BE ‖ be
의 3인칭 단수 현재형

Is·lam /ˈɪzlam, ɪzˈlam, ˈɪslam/ *n* [U] the
religion that was started by Muhammed
and whose holy book is the Koran ‖ 코란
을 성서로 하는 마호메트가 창시한 종교.
이슬람교. 회교 – **Islamic** /ɪzˈlamɪk, ɪs-
/ *adj*

is·land /ˈaɪlənd/ *n* a piece of land
completely surrounded by water ‖ 완전
히 물로 둘러싸인 육지. 섬: *a hotel
development on the island* 그 섬의 호텔
개발

is·land·er /ˈaɪləndɚ/ *n* someone who
lives on an island ‖ 섬에 사는 사람. 섬사
람

isle /aɪl/ *n* LITERARY an island ‖ 섬

is·n't /ˈɪzənt/ *v* the short form of "is
not" ‖ "is not"의 단축형: *That isn't the
same car I saw yesterday.* 그것은 내가
어제 보았던 차와 같은 차가 아니다.

i·so·late /ˈaɪsəˌleɪt/ *v* [T] **1** to make or
keep one person or thing separate from
others ‖ 한 사람이나 사물을 다른 사람
[것]들과 떼어 놓게 하거나 떼어 두다. …
을 격리시키다. 분리시키다. 고립시키다:
The town was isolated by the floods. 그
읍은 홍수로 고립되었다. **2** to prevent a
country, political group etc. from
getting support from other countries or
groups ‖ 어떤 나라·정치 단체 등이 타국
이나 단체의 지원을 받는 것을 막다

i·so·lat·ed /ˈaɪsəˌleɪtɪd/ *adj* **1** far away
from other things ‖ 다른 것들에서 멀리
떨어진. 고립된. 외딴: *an isolated farm*
외딴 농장 **2** feeling alone or separated
from other people ‖ 외롭다고 느끼는, 또
는 다른 사람들로부터 격리된: *Newly
retired people can often feel isolated
and useless.* 최근에 은퇴한 사람들은 종
종 외롭고 쓸모없다는 기분이 들 수 있다.
3 an isolated case/example etc. a
case, example etc. that happens only
once ‖ 단지 한 번만 일어나는 경우·예 등.
단발적인 경우/예: *an isolated case of
the disease* 단발성의 질병

i·so·la·tion /ˌaɪsəˈleɪʃən/ *n* [U] **1** the
state of being separate from other
places, things, or people ‖ 다른 장소[물
건, 사람]와 떨어져 있는 상태. 고립. 격
리. 분리: *the city's geographical
isolation* (=its location far away from
other cities) 그 도시의 지리적 고립 **2 in
isolation** separately ‖ 개별적으로. 분리
하여: *These events cannot be examined
in isolation from one another.* 이들 사건
들은 서로 분리하여 조사할 수 없다. **3** a
feeling of being lonely ‖ 외로운 느낌. 고

독. 고립감

ISP *n* TECHNICAL Internet service
provider; a business that connects
people's computers to the Internet ‖
Internet service provider(인터넷 서비스
공급자)의 약어; 일반인들의 컴퓨터를 인
터넷에 연결시켜 주는 사업(체)

is·sue¹ /ˈɪʃu/ *n* **1** a subject or problem
that people discuss ‖ 사람들이 토의하는
주제나 문제. 쟁점: *We should raise the
issue* (=begin to discuss it) *at our next
meeting.* 우리는 다음 회의에서 그 쟁점을
제기[토의]해야 한다. **2** a magazine,
newspaper etc. printed for a particular
day, week, month, or year ‖ 특정한 날
[주, 달, 해]에 인쇄된 잡지·신문 등. …호
[판]: *the new issue of Sports Illustrated*
스포츠 일러스트레이티드지의 최신호 **3
at issue** FORMAL being discussed or
considered ‖ 논쟁 중인, 고려 중인: *Only
the nurse's contract was at issue.* 그 간
호사와의 계약만이 고려 중에 있었다. **4
make an issue (out) of sth** to argue
about something ‖ 무엇에 대해 논쟁하다.
…을 문제로 삼다: *There's no need to
make an issue out of this!* 이것에 대해
논쟁을 벌일 필요는 없어! **5 take issue
with** to disagree or argue with someone
about something ‖ 무엇에 대해 남과 의견
이 맞지 않거나 논쟁하다: *He took issue
with Mayor Farrell's statement.* 그는 파
렐 시장의 성명과 의견을 달리했다.

is·sue² *v* [T] **1** to officially make a
statement or give a warning ‖ 공식적으
로 성명을 발표하거나 경고를 발하다. …
을 공포하다. 발령하다: *a statement
issued by the White House* 백악관이 발표
한 성명 **2** to officially provide or
produce something ‖ 사물을 공식적으로
제공하거나 생산하다. …을 지급[배급]하
다: *Every player was issued with a new
uniform.* 모든 선수가 새 유니폼을 지급받
았다.

isth·mus /ˈɪsməs/ *n* a narrow piece of
land with water on both sides, that
connects two larger areas of land ‖ 두
개의 큰 지역을 연결하며 양쪽에 물이 있
는 좁은 땅. 지협

IT *n* [U] ⇨ INFORMATION TECHNOLOGY

it /ɪt/ *pron* [used as a subject or object]
1 a thing, situation, person, or idea that
has been mentioned or is known about
‖ 언급되거나 알려진 사물[상황, 사람, 생
각]. 그것: *"Did you bring your
umbrella?" "No, I left it at home."* "우산
가져왔니?" "아니, 집에 두고 왔는데." /
"Where's the bread?" "It's (=it is) *on the
shelf."* "빵 어디에 있니?" "선반 위에 있

어." / *You two are married? I can't believe it.* 당신 두 사람 서로 결혼한 사이에요? 믿어지지 않네요. **2** the situation that someone is in now ‖ 사람이 지금 처해 있는 상황: *It's fun at school right now.* 학교에서는 바로 지금이 재미있는 때다. / *How's it going, Bob?* (=How are you?) 지내기가 어때, 보브? **3** used as the subject or object of a sentence when the real subject or object is later in the sentence ‖ 진주어나 진목적어가 문장의 뒷부분에 있을 때 문장의 주어나 목적어로 쓰여: *It costs less to drive than to take the bus.* 버스를 타는 것보다 자가운전하는 것이 비용이 덜 든다. **4** used with the verb "be" to talk about the weather, time, distance etc. ‖ 날씨·시간·거리 등을 언급하는 데에 "be"동사와 함께 쓰여: *It's raining again.* 다시 비가 오고 있다. / *It's only a few miles from here to the beach.* 여기에서 해변까지는 몇 마일밖에 안 된다. / *I forgot that it was her birthday.* 나는 그 날이 그녀의 생일이라는 것을 깜박했다. / *I was surprised that it was only 3:00.* 시간이 겨우 3시라는 것을 알고 나는 깜짝 놀랐다. **5** used in order to emphasize one piece of information in a sentence ‖ 문장에서 한 가지 정보를 강조하는 데에 쓰여: *I don't know who took your book, but it wasn't me.* 나는 누가 네 책을 가져갔는지는 모르지만 나는 가져가지 않았다. / *It must have been Ben* (=not any other person) *because nobody else was here.* 다른 사람은 아무도 여기에 없었기 때문에 그것은 틀림없이 벤이었다. / *It was yesterday* (=not any other day) *that we went to the Chinese restaurant.* 우리가 중국 식당에 간 것은 바로 어제였다. **6** used as the subject of the words "seem," "appear," "look," and "happen" ‖ "seem" "appear" "look" "happen"과 같은 단어의 주어로 쓰여: *It looks like Henry's not going to be able to come to lunch.* 헨리는 점심 식사하러 올 수 있을 것 같지 않아 보인다. **7 it's me/John/a pen etc.** used in order to give the name of a person or thing when it is not already known ‖ 미처 알고 있지 못할 때 사람이나 사물의 이름을 말하는 데에 쓰여. 나야/존이야/펜이야: *"What's that?" "It's a pen."* "그거 뭐냐?" "펜이야." / *"Who's on the phone?" "It's Jill."* "누가 통화하고 있니?" "질이야." **8** used in order to talk about a child or animal when you do not know what sex s/he is ‖ 성별을 알지 못할 때 아이나 동물을 언급하는 데에 쓰여: *"Marilyn had a baby." "Is it a boy or girl?"* "마릴린이 아기를 낳

았어." "사내애니 계집애니?" —see also **that's it** (THAT¹)

I·tal·ian¹ /ɪˈtælyən/ *adj* **1** relating to or coming from Italy ‖ 이탈리아와 관련되거나 이탈리아에서 온. 이탈리아(산)의 **2** relating to the Italian language ‖ 이탈리아어와 관련된. 이탈리아어의

I·tal·ian² *n* **1** [U] the language used in Italy ‖ 이탈리아에서 사용되는 언어. 이탈리아어 **2** someone from Italy ‖ 이탈리아 출신의 사람. 이탈리아인

i·tal·i·cize /ɪˈtæləˌsaɪz/ *v* [T] to put or print written words in ITALICS ‖ 이탤릭체로 글씨를 쓰거나 인쇄하다

i·tal·ics /ɪˈtælɪks, aɪ-/ *n* [plural] a type of printed letters that lean to the right ‖ 오른쪽으로 기운 활자체의 한 형태. 이탤릭체. 사체(斜體): *This example is printed in italics.* 이것은 이탤릭체로 인쇄된 예이다.

itch¹ /ɪtʃ/ *v* **1** [I, T] to have an unpleasant ITCH ‖ 불쾌하게 가렵다, 근질근질하다: *My back is itching.* 내 등이 가렵다. **2 be itching to do sth** INFORMAL to want to do something very much ‖ 몹시 무엇을 하고 싶어하다: *Ian's been itching to try out his new bike.* 이안은 새 자전거를 타고 싶어서 안달하고 있다.

itch² *n* **1** an unpleasant feeling on your skin that makes you want to rub it with your nails ‖ 손톱으로 긁고 싶게 만드는 피부의 불쾌한 느낌. 가려움. 근질거림 **2** INFORMAL a strong desire to do or have something ‖ 무엇을 하거나 가지려는 강한 욕구. 참을 수 없는 욕망. 갈망: *an itch for travel* 여행하고 싶은 강한 욕구 – **itchy** *adj* – **itchiness** *n* [U]

it'd /ˈɪtəd/ **1** the short form of "it would" ‖ "it would"의 단축형: *It'd be easier if we both did it.* 만일 우리 둘이 그것을 한다면 보다 쉬울 것이다. **2** the short form of "it had" ‖ "it had"의 단축형: *It'd been raining since Sunday.* 일요일 이후로 계속 비가 내리고 있었다.

i·tem /ˈaɪtəm/ *n* **1** a single thing in a set, group, or list ‖ 세트[그룹, 목록]에서 낱낱의 것. 항목. 조항. 품목: *There are over 20 items on the menu.* 메뉴에는 20가지가 넘는 종류가 있다. **2** a piece of news in the newspaper or on television ‖ 신문이나 텔레비전에서 뉴스의 하나: *I saw an item about the kidnapping in the paper.* 나는 신문에서 유괴 사건에 관한 한 기사를 보았다. **3 be an item** INFORMAL to be having a sexual or romantic relationship with someone ‖ 남과 성적인 관계나 연애 관계를 맺고 있다

i·tem·ize /ˈaɪtəˌmaɪz/ *v* [T] to write

down all of the parts of something in a list ‖ 목록에 사물의 모든 요소들을 적다. …을 항목[조목] 별로 적다 **- itemized** *adj*

i·tin·er·ant /aɪ'tɪnərənt/ *adj* FORMAL traveling from place to place ‖ 이리저리 돌아다니는. 순회하는. 편력하는

i·tin·er·ar·y /aɪ'tɪnə,rɛri/ *n* a plan of a trip, usually including the places you want to see ‖ 보통 자신이 보고 싶어하는 장소를 포함한 여행 계획. 여정. 여행 일정표

it'll /'ɪtl/ the short form of "it will" ‖ "it will"의 단축형: *It'll be nice to see Martha again.* 마사를 다시 만나면 기쁠 것이다.

it's /ɪts/ **1** the short form of "it is" ‖ "it is"의 단축형: *It's snowing!* 눈이 오고 있어! **2** the short form of "it has" ‖ "it has"의 단축형: *It's been snowing all day.* 하루 종일 눈이 오고 있다.

its /ɪts/ *possessive, adj* belonging or relating to a thing, situation, person, or idea that has been mentioned or is known about ‖ 이미 언급되거나 알려진 물건[상황, 사람, 생각]에 속하거나 관련된. 그(것의): *The tree has lost all of its leaves.* 나무는 그 잎이 다 떨어졌다.

it·self /ɪt'sɛlf/ *pron* **1** the REFLEXIVE form of "it" ‖ "it"의 재귀형: *The cat was licking itself.* 그 고양이는 자기 자신을 혀로 핥고 있었다. **2 in itself** only the thing mentioned, and not anything else ‖ 다른 것이 아니고 언급한 것만으로. 그 자체로: *We're proud you finished the race. That in itself is an accomplishment.* 네가 그 경주를 마쳤다니 우리는 정말 자랑스럽다. 그것은 그 자체로 하나의 업적이다.

it·sy-bit·sy /,ɪtsi 'bɪtsi-/, **it·ty-bit·ty** /,ɪti 'bɪti-/ *adj* INFORMAL very small ‖ 매우 작은. 조그마한

IUD *n* intrauterine device; a small plastic or metal object placed in a woman's UTERUS to prevent her from having a baby ‖ intrauterine device(자궁 내 피임 기구)의 약어; 임신을 방지하기 위해 여성의 자궁 내에 넣어 두는 작은 플라스틱이나 금속 물체

IV *n* the abbreviation of "intravenous"; medical equipment that is used for putting liquid directly into your body ‖ "intravenous"의 약어; 신체에 직접 액체를 주입하는 데에 사용하는 의료 장치. 점적 기구. 링거 주사

I've /aɪv/ the short form of "I have" ‖ "I have"의 단축형: *I've seen you somewhere before.* 나는 전에 당신을 어딘가에서 본 적이 있다.

i·vo·ry /'aɪvəri/ *n* **1** [C, U] the hard smooth yellow-white substance from an ELEPHANT's tooth, or something made from this substance ‖ 코끼리의 이빨에서 얻은 딱딱하고 매끄러운 황백색 물질, 또는 이 물질로 만든 것. 상아. 상아 제품 **2** [u] a pale yellow-white color ‖ 옅은 황백색. 상아색. 아이보리색 **- ivory** *adj*

ivy /'aɪvi/ *n* [U] a climbing plant with dark green shiny leaves ‖ 짙은 초록색의 윤이 나는 잎을 가진 덩굴성 식물. 담쟁이덩굴 —see also POISON IVY

ivy

Ivy League /,.. './ *adj* relating to a small group of old respected colleges in the north east of the US ‖ 미국의 동북부에 있는 일부 오래된 명문 대학들과 관련된. 아이비 리그의: *an Ivy League graduate* 아이비 리그 대학의 졸업생 **- Ivy League** *n* [singular]

Jj

J, j /dʒeɪ/ the tenth letter of the English alphabet ‖ 영어 알파벳의 열째 자

jab /dʒæb/ v [I, T] to quickly push something pointed into something else, or toward it ‖ 뾰족한 것을 다른 것에 또는 다른 것 쪽으로 속히 밀어 넣다. …을 꽉 찌르다: *The nurse jabbed a needle into his arm.* 그 간호사는 그의 팔에 주사 바늘을 찔러 넣었다. – **jab** *n*

jab·ber /'dʒæbɚ/ v [I] to talk quickly, in an excited way, and not very clearly ‖ 흥분한 투로 불분명하게 재빨리 지껄이다.

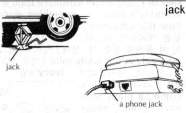

jack

jack

a phone jack

jack¹ /dʒæk/ n **1** a piece of equipment used for lifting something heavy, such as a car, and supporting it ‖ 자동차 등의 무거운 것을 들어올려 지탱하는 데에 쓰이는 장비. 잭 **2** an electronic connection for a telephone or other electronic machine ‖ 전화기나 다른 전자 기계의 전자 접속부. 잭. 플러그 구멍

jack² v

jack sb/sth ↔ **up** *phr v* [T] **1** to lift something heavy using a JACK ‖ 잭을 사용해서 무거운 것을 들어올리다: *Dad jacked the car up so I could change the tire.* 아빠는 내가 타이어를 갈 수 있게 자동차를 잭으로 들어올렸다. **2** to increase prices, sales etc. by a large amount ‖ 가격·매출 등을 크게 올리다: *Stores have jacked up their prices since July.* 가게들은 7월 이후로 가격을 크게 올렸다.

jack·al /'dʒækəl/ n a wild animal like a dog that lives in Africa and Asia ‖ 아프리카와 아시아에 사는 개같이 생긴 야생 동물. 자칼

jack·ass /'dʒækæs/ n **1** SPOKEN an impolite word meaning an annoying stupid person ‖ 짜증나게 어리석은 사람을 무례하게 이르는 말. 바보. 얼간이 **2** a male DONKEY ‖ 수탕나귀

jack·et /'dʒækɪt/ n **1** a short light coat ‖ 짧고 가벼운 웃옷. 재킷 **2** the part of a SUIT that covers the top part of your body ‖ 몸의 상반신을 덮는 양복 부분. 양복 상의 **3** ⇨ DUST JACKET

jack·ham·mer /'dʒæk,hæmɚ/ n a large powerful tool used for breaking hard materials such as the surface of a road ‖ 노면 등의 굳은 물질을 부수는 데에 쓰이는 크고 강력한 도구. 착암기

jack-in-the-box /'. . . . ,./ n a toy shaped like a box from which a figure jumps out when the box's lid is lifted ‖ 뚜껑을 열 때 물체가 튀어 올라오는 상자처럼 생긴 장난감. 깜짝[도깨비] 상자

jack knife /'. ./ n ⇨ POCKET KNIFE

jack·knife /'dʒæknaɪf/ v [I] if a truck or train with two or more parts jackknifes, the back part swings toward the front part ‖ 두 개 이상의 부분으로 구성된 트럭이나 열차의 뒷부분이 앞부분 쪽으로 방향 회전하다. 연결부에서 급각도로 꺾이다

jack-of-all-trades /,. . . '. ./ n [singular] someone who can do many different types of jobs ‖ 많은 다른 종류의 일을 할 수 있는 사람. 만물박사

jack-o-lan·tern /'dʒæk ə ,læntɚn/ n a PUMPKIN with a face cut into it, usually with a light inside, made at HALLOWEEN ‖ 할로윈 축제 때 만드는 것으로 보통 (속을 파내어) 안에 불을 넣는, 얼굴을 조각한 호박. 호박등

jack·pot /'dʒækpɑt/ n **1** a very large amount of money that you can win in a game ‖ 게임에서 탈 수 있는 거액의 돈 **2 hit the jackpot a)** to win a lot of money ‖ 많은 돈을 타다 **b)** to be very successful or lucky ‖ 매우 성공하거나 운이 좋다. 대성공[히트]하다: *The movie "Total Recall" hit the jackpot.* "토탈 리콜"이라는 영화는 대히트했다.

Ja·cuz·zi /dʒə'kuzi/ n TRADEMARK ⇨ HOT TUB

jade /dʒeɪd/ n [U] a usually green stone used for making jewelry and ORNAMENTs ‖ 보석 및 장식품을 만드는 데에 쓰이는 보통 초록색의 돌. 비취. 옥

jad·ed /'dʒeɪdɪd/ adj not interested in or excited by things because you have seen or done them too much ‖ 너무 많이 봤거나 너무 많이 해서 어떤 것에 재미나 흥미를 느끼지 못하는. 지겨운. 넌더리나는

jag·ged /'dʒægɪd/ adj having a rough uneven edge with a lot of sharp points ‖

가장자리가 날카로운 부분이 많고 거칠거칠하며 울퉁불퉁한. 들쭉날쭉한: *jagged rocks* 뾰족뾰족 날이 선 바위들

jag·uar /ˈdʒægwɑr/ n a large wild cat with black spots from Central and South America ‖ 중앙 아메리카 및 남아메리카 산의 검은 얼룩무늬가 있는 큰 야생 고양이. 재규어

jail¹ /dʒeɪl/ n [C, U] a place where someone is sent to be punished for a crime; prison ‖ 죄를 지은 사람이 벌을 받도록 보내지는 곳; 감옥: *overcrowded jails* 초만원인 감옥들 / *He was in jail for 15 years.* 그는 15년 동안 수감되어 있었다.

jail² v [T] to put someone in JAIL ‖ 남을 투옥하다

jailer, jailor /ˈdʒeɪlɚ/ n someone whose job is to guard a prison or prisoners ‖ 교도소나 죄수를 지키는 직업인. 교도관. 간수

ja·lop·y /dʒəˈlɑpi/ n INFORMAL a very old car in bad condition ‖ 상태가 좋지 않은 매우 낡은 차. 고물[구식] 자동차

jam¹ /dʒæm/ v **-mmed, -mming 1** [T] to push someone or something using a lot of force, especially into a small place ‖ 사람이나 물체를 특히 좁은 장소에 많은 힘을 가하여 밀어 넣다. 채워 넣다. 쑤셔 넣다: *Mr. Braithe jammed the letters into his pockets and left.* 브라이드 씨는 자기 주머니에 편지를 쑤셔 넣고 가버렸다. **2** [I, T] also **jam up** if a machine jams up or if you jam it, it stops working because something is stuck inside it ‖ 기계가 안에서 걸려서 작동하는 것을 멈추다. (막혀서) 움직이지 않다[움직이지 못하게 하다]: *Every time I try to use the Xerox machine it jams.* 내가 복사기를 사용하려고 할 때마다 걸려서 멈춘다. **3** [T] to fill a place with a lot of people or things, so that nothing can move ‖ 움직일 수 없을 정도로 장소를 많은 사람이나 물건으로 채우다. 꽉 채우다: *The roads were jammed with cars.* 그 도로는 자동차로 꽉 막혀 있었다. **4** [I] to play music for fun with a group of people without practicing first ‖ 먼저 연습하지 않고 일단의 사람들과 재미로 음악을 연주하다. 즉흥적으로 연주하다

jam² n **1** [U] a thick sticky sweet substance made from fruit, usually eaten on bread ‖ 보통 빵에다 발라 먹는 과일로 만든 걸쭉하고 찐득찐득하여 달콤한 물질. 잼: *strawberry jam* 딸기잼 **2** also **traffic jam** a situation in which there are so many cars on the road that you cannot move ‖ 움직이지 못할 정도로

너무 많은 차가 도로에 있는 상황. 교통 체증[정체]: *Sorry I'm late – I got stuck in a jam.* 늦어서 미안. 교통 체증으로 꼼짝 못했어. **3 be in a jam/get into a jam** to be or become involved in a difficult or bad situation ‖ 어렵거나 나쁜 상황에 처하거나 빠지다. 궁지에 빠지다: *Sarah, I'm in a jam – could you do me a favor?* 새라, 어쩔 수 없어서 그러는데 부탁 좀 들어 줄래? **4** a situation in which something is stuck somewhere ‖ 무엇이 어딘가에 막힌 상황: *a jam in the fax machine* 팩스기의 종이 걸림

jamb /dʒæm/ n the side post of a door or window ‖ 문이나 창문의 측면 기둥. 문설주

jam·bo·ree /ˌdʒæmbəˈri/ n a big noisy party or celebration ‖ 크고 왁자지껄한 파티나 축제

jammed /dʒæmd/ adj impossible to move because of being stuck ‖ 꼭 끼어서 움직일 수 없는. 꼼짝 못하는: *The stupid door's jammed again.* 그 망할 놈의 문은 또 꼼짝 않는다.

jam-packed /ˌ. ˈ./ adj INFORMAL completely full of people or things ‖ 사람이나 물체들로 완전히 가득찬. 꽉찬: *a cereal jam-packed with vitamins* 비타민이 가득 들어 있는 시리얼

jam ses·sion /ˈ. ˌ../ n an occasion when people meet to play music together for fun ‖ 사람들이 재미로 함께 음악을 연주하기 위해 모이는 행사. 즉흥 재즈 연주회. 잼 세션

Jane Doe /ˌdʒeɪn ˈdoʊ/ n [singular] a name used in legal forms, documents etc. when a woman's name is not known ‖ 여성의 이름이 밝혀지지 않은 경우 법률적인 상투적 문구나 문서 등에 쓰는 이름. 제인 도

jan·gle /ˈdʒæŋgəl/ v [I, T] to make a noise that sounds like metal objects hitting against each other ‖ 금속류이 서로 부딪치는 듯한 시끄러운 소리를 내다. 쩽그랑거리다: *keys jangling in his pocket* 그의 주머니에서 쩽그랑거리고 있는 열쇠

jan·i·tor /ˈdʒænətɚ/ n someone whose job is to clean and take care of a large building ‖ 큰 건물을 청소하고 관리하는 직업인. 건물 잡역부[관리인]: *the school janitor* 학교 관리인

Jan·u·ar·y /ˈdʒænyuˌɛri/, *written abbreviation* **Jan.** n the first month of the year ‖ 한 해의 첫 번째 달. 1월

USAGE NOTE January

When you use a month without a

date, say "in January/February" etc. If you use it with a date, write "on January 9/10/11" etc. and say "on January ninth/tenth/eleventh" etc. ‖ 날짜 없이 달(月)을 말할 경우는 "in January/February"등으로 쓰며 날짜와 함께 달을 표기할 경우는 "on January 9/10/11"처럼 쓰고 "on January ninth/tenth/eleventh"처럼 말한다.

Jap·a·nese¹ /ˌdʒæpəˈniz/ *adj* **1** relating to or coming from Japan ‖ 일본과 관련되거나 일본에서 온. 일본(출신)의 **2** relating to the Japanese language ‖ 일본어와 관련된. 일본어의

Japanese² *n* **1** [U] the language used in Japan ‖ 일본에서 쓰는 언어. 일본어 **2** **the Japanese** [plural] the people of Japan ‖ 일본 사람들. 일본 국민

jar¹ /dʒɑr/ *n* **1** a rounded glass container with a lid, used for storing food ‖ 식품 저장에 쓰이는 뚜껑이 달린 둥근 유리 용기. 병. 단지 —see picture at CONTAINER **2** the amount of food contained in a jar ‖ 병에 담긴 식품의 양: *half a jar of peanut butter* 땅콩버터 반 병

jar² *v* **-rred, -rring** **1** [I, T] to shake or hit something with enough force to damage it or make it become loose ‖ 손상을 주거나 헐겁게 만들기에 충분한 힘을 가해 무엇을 흔들거나 치다. 삐걱거리다 [삐걱거리게 하다]: *Alice jarred her knee when she jumped off the wall.* 앨리스는 담에서 뛰어 내릴 때 무릎을 삐끗했다. **2** [I, T] to shock someone, especially by making an unpleasant noise ‖ 특히 불쾌한 소리를 내서 남을 깜짝 놀라게 하다, 또는 깜짝 놀라다: *The alarm jarred her awake.* 그녀는 자명종 소리에 깜짝 놀라 깼다. **3** [I] to be very different in style and therefore look strange or unsuitable ‖ 모양이 너무 달라서 이상하거나 어울리지 않게 보이다: *a modern building that jars with the historic surroundings* 역사적인 주변 환경과 어울리지 않는 현대식 건물

jar·gon /ˈdʒɑrgən/ *n* [U] technical words and phrases that are difficult to understand unless you work in a particular profession ‖ 특정 직업에 종사하지 않으면 이해하기 어려운 단어나 구. 전문어: *medical jargon* 의학 용어

jaun·dice /ˈdʒɔndɪs, ˈdʒɑn-/ *n* [U] a medical condition in which your skin and the white part of your eyes become yellow ‖ 피부나 눈의 흰자위가 노랗게 되는 의학적 상태. 황달

jaun·diced /ˈdʒɔndɪst, ˈdʒɑn-/ *adj* **1** tending to judge people, things, or situations in a negative way ‖ 사람[사물, 상황]을 부정적으로 판단하는 경향이 있는. 편견을 가진. 비뚤어진: *a jaundiced view of the world* 비뚤어진 세계관 **2** suffering from JAUNDICE ‖ 황달에 걸린

jaunt /dʒɔnt, dʒɑnt/ *n* a short trip for pleasure ‖ 즐기기 위한 짧은 여행. 소풍

jaun·ty /ˈdʒɔnti, ˈdʒɑnti/ *adj* showing that you feel confident and cheerful ‖ 자신감 있고 쾌활하다는 것을 나타내는. 명랑한. 경쾌한 – **jauntily** *adv*

jav·e·lin /ˈdʒævəlɪn, -vlɪn/ *n* **1** [U] a sport in which you throw a SPEAR (=a long pointed stick) as far as you can ‖ 던질 수 있는 한 멀리 창을 던지는 스포츠. 투창 **2** the stick used in this sport ‖ 투창에 사용되는 창

jaw /dʒɔ/ *n* **1** one of the two bones that form your mouth and that have all your teeth ‖ 입을 형성하며 모든 이가 박혀 있는 두 개의 뼈 중 하나. 턱: *a broken jaw* 부러진 턱 **2** **sb's jaw dropped** used in order to say that someone looked very surprised or shocked ‖ 어떤 사람이 매우 놀라거나 충격을 받은 것같이 보였다고 말하는 데에 쓰여. 놀라서 입을 딱 벌렸다: *Sam's jaw dropped when Katy walked into the room.* 케이티가 방안으로 걸어 들어오자 샘은 놀라서 입을 딱 벌렸다.

jaws /dʒɔz/ *n* [plural] the mouth of an animal or person ‖ 동물이나 사람의 입: *the powerful grip of the lion's jaws* 무는 힘이 강력한 사자의 입

jay·walk·ing /ˈdʒeɪˌwɔkɪŋ/ *n* [U] the action of walking across a street in an area that is not marked for walking ‖ 횡단보도 표시가 없는 지역에서 도로를 건너는 행위. 무단 횡단 – **jaywalker** *n*

jazz¹ /dʒæz/ *n* [U] **1** a type of popular music that usually has a strong beat and parts for performers to play alone ‖ 일반적으로 강한 비트와 연주자가 독자적으로 연주하는 부분들이 들어 있는 일종의 대중음악. 재즈 **2** **and all that jazz** SPOKEN and things like that ‖ 그와 같은 것들. … 따위 . 등등 : *I'm sick of rules, responsibilities, and all that jazz.* 규칙과 책임 등등의 것들에 신물이 난다.

jazz² *v*

jazz sth ↔ **up** *phr v* [I, T] to make something more exciting and interesting ‖ 어떤 것을 더욱 재미있고 흥미 있게 만들다: *We need a few pictures to jazz up the walls.* 벽을 치장하기 위해 몇 점의 그림이 필요하다.

jazzed /dʒæzd/ *adj* SPOKEN excited ‖ 흥분한: *I'm really jazzed about going to*

New York. 나는 뉴욕에 가는 것에 대해 몹시 흥분해 있다.

jazz·y /'dʒæzi/ *adj* **1** bright, colorful, and easily noticed ‖ 밝고 화려하고 쉽게 눈에 띄는. 요란한: *a jazzy tie* 색깔이 화려한 넥타이 **2** similar to the style of JAZZ music ‖ 재즈 음악 스타일과 비슷한. 재즈풍의

jeal·ous /'dʒɛləs/ *adj* **1** feeling angry or unhappy because someone else has a quality, thing, or ability that you wish you had ‖ 자신이 가지고 싶어했던 자질 [물건, 능력]을 남이 가져서 화나거나 불만스럽게 느끼는. 시기하는: *Diane was jealous of me because I got better grades.* 다이앤은 내가 더 나은 점수를 받아서 나를 시샘했다. **2** feeling angry or unhappy because someone you love is paying attention to another person, or because another person is showing too much interest in someone you love ‖ 자신이 사랑하는 사람이 남에게 관심을 쏟고 있거나 자신이 사랑하는 사람에게 남이 많은 관심을 보이고 있기 때문에 화나거나 불만스럽게 느끼는. 질투하는: *It used to make me jealous when he danced with other women.* 그가 다른 여자와 춤을 출 때 나는 질투심을 느끼곤 했다.

USAGE NOTE jealous and envious

If someone is **jealous**, s/he feels angry or unhappy because s/he cannot have something that someone else has: *Bill was jealous of his brother's success. / The older kids were jealous of the attention the new baby was getting.* If someone is **envious**, s/he wants to have the qualities or things that someone else has: *Linda was envious of Marcy's new car.*

jealous는 남이 가지고 있는 것을 가질 수 없어서 화나거나 불만스럽게 느끼는 것을 말한다: 빌은 자기 형의 성공을 시샘했다. / 손위 애들은 새로 태어난 아기에게 관심이 쏠리는 것을 질투했다. **envious**는 남이 지닌 자질이나 물건을 가지고 싶어하는 것을 말한다: 린다는 마시의 새 차를 부러워했다.

---

jeal·ous·y /'dʒɛləsi/ *n* [C, U] the feeling of being JEALOUS ‖ 질투하는 감정. 시기. 시샘. 투기

jeans /dʒinz/ *n* [plural] a popular type of pants made from DENIM ‖ 데님으로 만든 대중적인 바지의 한 형태. 진바지

Jeep /dʒip/ *n* TRADEMARK a type of car made to travel over rough ground ‖ 울퉁불퉁한 땅을 달리기 위해 만들어진 자동차의 일종. 지프

jeer /dʒɪr/ *v* [I, T] to shout, speak, or laugh in order to annoy or frighten someone you dislike ‖ 싫어하는 사람을 괴롭히거나 겁을 주려고 소리치다[말하다, 웃다]. 조소하다. 야유하다. 비아냥거리다: *The crowd jeered at the speaker.* 청중들은 연설자에게 야유했다. **– jeer** *n* **– jeering** *adj: jeering laughter* 조소

jeez /dʒiz/ *interjection* said in order to express sudden feelings such as surprise, anger, or shock ‖ 놀람[분노, 충격] 등의 갑작스러운 감정을 표현하는 데에 쓰여. 이런. 어머나. 빌어먹을

Je·ho·vah's Wit·ness /dʒɪˌhoʊvəz 'wɪtˌnɪs/ *n* a member of a religious organization that believes in every word of the Bible and will not fight in a war ‖ 성경의 모든 구절을 믿고 전쟁에서 싸우려 하지 않는 종교 단체의 한 신도. 여호와의 증인 신자

Jell-O, jello /'dʒɛloʊ/ *n* [U] TRADEMARK a soft solid substance made from GELATIN and sweet fruit juice ‖ 젤라틴과 달콤한 과즙으로 만든 말랑말랑한 고형 물질. 젤오 —see picture at DESSERT

jel·ly /'dʒɛli/ *n* [U] a thick sticky sweet substance made from fruit but having no pieces of fruit in it, usually eaten on bread ‖ 일반적으로 빵에 얹어 먹는 것으로, 과일로 만들었지만 그 속에 과일 조각이 들어 있지 않은 걸쭉하고 찐득찐득하며 달콤한 물질. 젤리: *a peanut butter and jelly sandwich* 땅콩 버터와 젤리를 바른 샌드위치

jel·ly·fish /'dʒɛliˌfɪʃ/ *n* a round transparent sea animal with long things that hang down from its body ‖ 몸체에 축 늘어진 긴 촉수들이 달린 둥글고 투명한 바다 동물. 해파리

jeop·ard·ize /'dʒɛpəˌdaɪz/ *v* [T] to risk losing or destroying something that is valuable or important ‖ 가치 있거나 중요한 것을 잃거나 파괴할 위험에 처하게 하다. …을 위태롭게 하다: *Junot was too worried about jeopardizing his career to say anything.* 주노트는 자기의 출세가 위태롭게 될 것을 너무 걱정한 나머지 아무 말도 하지 못했다.

jeop·ard·y /'dʒɛpədi/ *n* [U] **in jeopardy** in danger of being lost or destroyed ‖ 잃거나 파괴되는 위험에 빠져: *The latest killings could very well put the whole peace process in jeopardy.* 최근의 암살 사건은 모든 강화(講和) 과정을 매우 위험에 빠지게 할 수 있었다.

J

jerk¹ /dʒɚk/ *v* **1** [I, T] to move with a

quick movement, or to make something move this way ‖ 재빠른 동작으로 움직이거나 움직이게 하다. (…을) 홱 움직이다: *Her head jerked up when Matt walked into the room.* 매트가 방안으로 걸어들어왔을 때 그녀는 머리를 홱 쳐들었다. **2** [I, T] to pull something suddenly and quickly ‖ 어떤 것을 갑자기 재빠르게 잡아당기다: *Tom jerked open the door.* 톰은 문을 홱 잡아당겨 열었다.

jerk sb **around** *phr v* [T] INFORMAL to deliberately annoy someone by causing difficulties ‖ 곤란함을 야기시켜 일부러 남을 괴롭히다

jerk² *n* **1** INFORMAL someone who is stupid or very annoying ‖ 멍청하거나 매우 짜증나는 사람. 멍청이. 바보: *What a jerk!* 이런 바보 같으니라구! **2** a quick movement, especially a pulling movement ‖ 특히 잡아당기는 재빠른 동작. 홱 잡아당기기: *He pulled the cord with a jerk.* 그는 그 끈을 홱 잡아당겼다. **– jerky** *adj*

jerk·y /ˈdʒɚki/ *n* [U] pieces of dried meat, usually with a salty or SPICY taste ‖ 보통 짭짤하거나 양념맛이 나는 말린 고깃조각. 육포

jer·sey /ˈdʒɚzi/ *n* [U] a shirt worn as part of a sports uniform ‖ 운동복의 일부로서 입는 셔츠

jest /dʒɛst/ *n* **1 in jest** intending to be funny ‖ 재미있게 하려고. 장난으로: *The criticisms were said in jest.* 그 비난은 농담으로 한 것이었다. **2** a joke ‖ 농담

jest·er /ˈdʒɛstɚ/ *n* a man employed in past times to entertain important people with jokes, stories etc. ‖ 예전에 농담·이야기 등으로 요인들에게 즐거움을 주도록 고용된 사람. 어릿광대

Je·sus /ˈdʒizəs/, **Jesus Christ** /ˌ./ *n* the man on whose life and teachings Christianity is based ‖ 기독교의 근간이 되는 삶과 교훈을 준 사람. 예수

jet¹ /dʒɛt/ *n* **1** a fast plane with a jet engine ‖ 제트 엔진을 단 빠른 비행기. 제트기 **2** a narrow stream of gas, liquid etc. that is forced out of a small hole, or the small hole this comes from ‖ 작은 구멍에서 좁고 세차게 빠져나오는 한 줄기의 가스·액체, 또는 이것이 빠져 나오는 작은 구멍. 분류. 분출. 분사구: *a strong jet of water* 세찬 한 줄기의 물

jet² *v* **-tted, -tting** [I] INFORMAL to travel in a JET ‖ 제트기로 여행하다: *He jetted in from Paris yesterday.* 그는 어제 파리에서 제트기로 도착했다.

jet en·gine /ˌ. ˈ../ *n* an engine that forces out a stream of hot air and gases,

used in planes ‖ 비행기에 사용하는 뜨거운 공기와 가스를 세차게 분출시키는 엔진. 제트 엔진

jet lag /ˈ. ./ *n* [U] the feeling of being very tired after traveling a long distance in a plane ‖ 비행기로 장거리 여행을 한 후의 매우 피곤한 느낌. 시차증(時差症) **– jet-lagged** *adj*

jet-pro·pelled /ˌ. .ˈ./ *adj* using a jet ENGINE for power ‖ 동력으로 제트 엔진을 사용하는. 제트 추진식의 **– jet propulsion** /ˌ. .ˈ../ *n* [U]

jet set /ˈ. ./ *n* [singular] rich and fashionable people who travel a lot ‖ 여행을 많이 하는 유복한 상류층의 사람들. 제트족(族) **– jet setter** *n*

jet·ti·son /ˈdʒɛtəsən, -zən/ *v* [T] **1** to decide not to use an idea, plan, object etc. ‖ 생각·계획·물체 등을 이용하지 않기로 결정하다: *Jones & Co. had to jettison the project for lack of funds.* 존즈 앤 코 회사는 자금 부족으로 그 계획안을 포기해야만 했다. **2** to throw something from a plane or moving vehicle ‖ 비행기나 움직이고 있는 탈것에서 어떤 것을 던지다. 버리다: *The pilot accidentally jettisoned some of their fuel.* 그 조종사는 뜻하지 않게 그들의 연료 일부를 배출시켰다.

jet·ty /ˈdʒɛti/ *n* **1** a wide wall built out into the water, as protection against large waves ‖ 큰 파도에 대비한 방호용으로 물 밖으로 내달아 지은 넓은 벽. 둑. 방파제 **2** ⇨ WHARF

jew·el /ˈdʒuəl/ *n* a small valuable stone, such as a DIAMOND ‖ 다이아몬드 등의 작고 값진 돌. 보석

jew·eled /ˈdʒuəld/ *adj* decorated with valuable stones ‖ 값진 보석으로 장식한

jew·el·er /ˈdʒuələ/ *n* someone who buys, sells, makes, or repairs jewelry ‖ 보석을 사는[파는, 만드는, 수리하는] 사람. 보석상. 보석 세공인

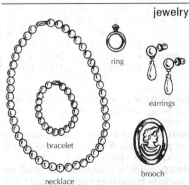

jewelry

ring

earrings

bracelet

necklace

brooch

jew·el·ry /'dʒuəlri/ *n* [U] small decorations you wear that are usually made from gold, silver, and jewels, such as rings and NECKLACEs ‖ 보통 금·은·보석으로 만들어 착용하는 반지나 목걸이 등의 작은 장신구들. 보석류. 장신구류

jew·els /'dʒuəlz/ *n* [plural] jewelry or decorations that are made with valuable stones ‖ 값진 보석으로 만든 보석류나 장신구류

Jew·ish /'dʒuɪʃ/ *adj* belonging to a group of people whose religion is Judaism, or to a family that in ancient times lived in the land of Israel ‖ 일단의 유대교도나 고대 이스라엘 지역에 살았던 종족에 속하는. 유대인[유대교도]의 – **Jew** *n*

jibe¹ /dʒaɪb/ *n* ⇨ GIDE

jibe² *v* [I] if two statements, actions etc. jibe with each other, they agree or make sense together ‖ 두 가지의 말이나 행동 등이 서로 일치하거나 부합되다: *Your statement to the police does not jibe with the facts.* 경찰에게 한 당신의 진술은 사실과 일치하지 않는다.

jif·fy /'dʒɪfi/ *n* SPOKEN **in a jiffy** very soon ‖ 바로 곧. 즉시: *I'll be back in a jiffy.* 곧 돌아오겠다.

jig /dʒɪg/ *n* a type of quick dance, or the music for this dance ‖ 빠르게 추는 춤의 한 종류, 또는 이 춤을 위한 음악. 지그 춤 (곡)

jig·ger /'dʒɪgɚ/ *n* a unit for measuring alcohol, equal to 1.5 OUNCEs ‖ 1.5온스에 상당하는 알코올의 측정 단위. 지거

jig·gle /'dʒɪgəl/ *v* **-ggled, -ggling** [I, T] to move from side to side with short quick movements, or to make something do this ‖ 짧고 재빠르게 좌우로 움직이다, 또는 움직이게 하다: *Don't jiggle my arm while I'm pouring!* 내가 (물을) 따를 때 내 팔을 흔들지 마라!

jig·saw puz·zle /'dʒɪgsɔ ,pʌzəl/ *n* a picture cut up into many small pieces that you try to fit together for fun ‖ 재미로 서로 끼워 맞추는 여러 작은 조각들로 자른 그림. 조각 그림

jigsaw puzzle

jilt /dʒɪlt/ *v* [T] to suddenly end a relationship with someone ‖ 어떤 사람과의 관계를 갑자기 끝내다. 버리다: *His girlfriend jilted him.* 그의 여자 친구는 그를 차버렸다. – **jilted** *adj*

jin·gle¹ /'dʒɪŋgəl/ *v* [I, T] to shake small metal objects together so that they produce a noise, or to make this noise ‖ 소리를 내기 위해 작은 금속 물체들을 함께 흔들다, 또는 이러한 소리를 내다. 딸랑딸랑 소리나다. …을 딸랑딸랑 울리다: *He jingled his keys in his pocket.* 그는 자기 주머니 속의 열쇠를 딸랑거렸다.

jin·gle² *n* **1** a short song used in television and radio advertisements ‖ 텔레비전 및 라디오 광고에 사용되는 짧은 노래. 시엠송: *I can't get the jingle from that beer ad out of my head.* 나는 그 맥주 광고에 나오는 시엠송을 머리에서 떨쳐 버릴 수 없다. **2** the noise of something jingling (JINGLE) ‖ 무엇이 딸랑거리는 소리

jinx /dʒɪŋks/ *n* [singular] someone or something that brings bad luck, or a period of bad luck that results from this ‖ 불운을 가져오는 사람이나 사물, 또는 이러한 사람이나 사물에서 생기는 불운의 기간. 재수 없는 사람[것]. 불운의 시기

jinxed /dʒɪŋkst/ *adj* often having bad luck, or making people have bad luck ‖ 종종 불운을 가지고 있는, 또는 사람들에게 불운을 가져 오게 하는. 재수 없는: *We must be jinxed, we've lost every game!* 매번 게임에서 지는 것을 보니 우리는 분명히 재수가 없는 거야!

jit·ters /'dʒɪtɚz/ *n* **the jitters** the feeling of being nervous and anxious, especially before an important event ‖ 특히 중요한 일을 앞두고 초조하고 염려되는 느낌. 불안감. 안절부절못함: *I always get the jitters before I go on stage.* 나는 무대에 오르기 전에는 항상 불안해진다.

jit·ter·y /'dʒɪtəri/ *adj* worried and nervous ‖ 걱정하고 초조해하는. 불안한. 안절부절못하는: *The recession has made consumers jittery.* 불경기는 소비자들을 불안하게 만들었다.

jive¹ /dʒaɪv/ *v* [T] SLANG to try to make someone believe something that is not true ‖ 남에게 사실이 아닌 것을 믿게 만들려고 하다. 속이다: *You're jiving me!* 너 나를 속이고 있어!

jive² *n* **1** a very fast type of dance, often performed to fast JAZZ music ‖ 종종 빠른 재즈 음악에 맞추어 추는 매우 빠른 춤의 한 종류. 자이브 춤 **2** [U] SLANG statements that you do not believe are true ‖ 사실이라고 믿지 않는 말. 허튼 소리. 터무니없는 말: *Don't you go giving me any of that jive!* 나에게 그런 터무니없는 말은 아예 하지 마라!

job /dʒab/ *n*

1 ▶WORK 일◀ work that you do regularly in order to earn money ‖ 돈을

벌기 위해 정기적으로 하는 일. 직업: *I got a part-time/full-time job as a waitress.* 나는 웨이트리스로 시간직[상근직]을 얻었다. / *She applied for a job at the bank.* 그녀는 은행 일자리에 지원했다. / *He quit/left his job so he could go back to school.* 그는 학교로 되돌아가기 위해 일을 그만두었다.

2 on the job while doing work or at work || 일하고 있거나 작업 중인 동안. 근무 중인: *Our reporters are on the job now.* 우리의 리포터들은 지금 일하는 중이다. / *All our employees get on-the-job training.* 우리 종업원 모두는 현장 연수를 받는다.

3 ▶DUTY 의무◀ a particular duty or responsibility that you have || 자신이 지닌 특정한 의무나 책임: *It's my job to take care of my little brother.* 내 남동생을 돌보는 것은 내 의무이다. / *It's Jim's job as secretary of the club to communicate with the members.* 회원들과 연락하는 것은 그 클럽 서기로서의 짐의 의무이다.

4 ▶IMPROVE STH 어떤 것을 개선하다◀ something you do to fix or improve something || 무엇을 고치거나 개선하기 위해 하는 것. 작업. 수술: *The car needs a paint job.* 그 차는 도색이 필요하다. / *a nose job* (=an operation to change the shape of your nose) 코 성형 수술

5 ▶STH YOU MUST DO 해야 하는 것◀ a piece of work you must do, usually without being paid || 보통 보수 없이 해야 하는 일: *I have a lot of odd jobs* (=different things) *to do on Saturday.* 나는 토요일에 해야 할 일이 여러 가지 있다.

6 ▶KIND OF THING 사물의 종류◀ also **jobby** SPOKEN used in order to say that something is of a particular type || 어떤 것이 특정 종류의 것임을 말하는 데에 쓰여: *His new computer's one of those little portable jobs.* 그의 새 컴퓨터는 저런 작은 휴대용 중의 하나이다.

7 do a nice/great etc. job to do something very well || 어떤 일을 매우 잘 하다: *Tina did a nice job on your makeup.* 티나가 네 화장을 잘 해주었다.

8 Good job! SPOKEN said when you are proud that someone has done something well || 남이 어떤 것을 잘 해서 만족스러울 때에 쓰여. 잘했어! 훌륭해!: *"Guess what? I passed the test!" "Good job!"* "무슨 일이 있는지 알아? 나 시험에 합격했어!" "훌륭해!"

9 do the job INFORMAL to make something have the result that you want or need || 자신이 원하거나 필요로 하는

결과를 얻을 수 있게 만들다. 목적을 달성하다: *A little more glue should do the job.* 풀칠 조금 더하면 다 된다.

10 ▶CRIME 범죄◀ INFORMAL a crime such as robbing a bank || 은행 강도 등의 범죄

USAGE NOTE job, work, occupation, position, trade, career, and profession

Use **work** as a general word to talk about what you do everyday in order to earn money: *I have to go to work.* Your **job** is the particular type of work that you do: *Jeff just got a job as a waiter.* **Occupation** is a formal word for **job** that is used on official forms: *Please state your name, address, and occupation.* **Position** is a formal word that is used when a **job** is advertised in the newspaper. **Position** is also used by someone who is answering the advertisement: *I am writing to apply for the position of Teaching Assistant.* A **trade** is a job that you do with your hands and that needs skill: *She's an electrician by trade.* A **career** is a professional **job** that you do for most of your life, or for a long time: *Her political career began 20 years ago.* A **profession** is a **career** that you need a lot of formal training to do: *He decided to enter the medical profession.*

work는 돈을 벌기 위해 매일 하는 일을 언급하기 위한 일반적인 말로 쓰인다: 나는 일하러 가야 한다. **job**은 자신이 하는 특정한 형태의 일을 의미한다: 제프는 이제 막 웨이터 일자리를 구했다. **occupation**은 공식 서식에 사용되는 **job**에 대한 격식 차린 말이다: 당신의 이름, 주소, 그리고 직업을 말하세요. **position**은 **job**(일자리)이 신문에 광고될 때에 사용되는 격식 차린 말이다. **position**은 또한 광고에 대한 응답자가 사용하는 말이다: 나는 보조 교사의 일자리에 지원하기 위해 이력서를 쓰고 있다. **trade**는 손으로 하는 기술이 필요한 일을 말한다: 그녀의 직업은 전기 기술자이다. **career**는 인생의 대부분의 시간 동안, 또는 오랫동안 하는 전문적인 일을 뜻한다: 그녀의 정치인으로서의 경력은 20년 전에 시작됐다. **profession**은 일하는 데에 정식 훈련이 많이 필요한 **career**(일)이다: 그는 의료업에 입문하기로 결정했다.

---

jock /dʒɑk/ *n* INFORMAL a student who plays a lot of sports || 운동을 많이 하는

학생. (학생인) 운동 선수

jock·ey¹ /'dʒɑki/ *n* someone who rides horses in races ‖ 경마에서 말을 모는 사람. 기수

jockey² *v* [T] **jockey for position** to try to be in the best position or situation ‖ 가장 좋은 위치나 상황에 있으려고 하다

jock·strap /'dʒɑkstræp/ *n* a piece of underwear that men wear when playing sports to support their sex organs ‖ 남성들이 자신들의 성기를 보호하려고 운동할 때 입는 속옷. 남자 선수의 국부 보호대

joc·u·lar /'dʒɑkyəlɚ/ *adj* FORMAL joking or humorous ‖ 웃기는, 익살스러운 – **jocularity** /ˌdʒɑkyə'lærəti/ *n* [U]

jog¹ /dʒɑg/ *v* **-gged, -gging 1** [I] to run slowly and in a steady way, especially for exercise ‖ 특히 운동삼아 느린 속도로 꾸준히 달리다. 조깅하다: *Julie jogs every morning.* 줄리는 매일 아침 조깅한다. **2 jog sb's memory** to make someone remember something ‖ 남에게 무엇을 기억나게 하다. 기억을 일깨우다: *This picture might jog your memory.* 이 사진이 당신의 기억을 일깨울지 모른다. **3** [T] to knock or push something lightly by mistake ‖ 어떤 것을 실수로 가볍게 치거나 밀다: *Someone jogged my elbow and I dropped the plate.* 누군가가 팔꿈치를 쳐서 나는 접시를 떨어뜨렸다.

jog² *n* [singular] a slow steady run, especially for exercise ‖ 특히 운동삼아 천천히 그리고 꾸준히 달리기. 조깅: *Let's go for a jog.* 조깅하러 가자.

jog·ging /'dʒɑgɪŋ/ *n* [U] the activity of running as a way of exercising ‖ 운동삼아서 달리는 행위. 조깅: *Let's go jogging before breakfast.* 아침 식사 전에 조깅하러 가자. **– jogger** *n*

john /dʒɑn/ *n* SPOKEN a toilet ‖ 화장실

John Doe /ˌdʒɑn 'doʊ/ *n* [singular] a name used in legal forms, documents etc. when a man's name is not known ‖ 남성의 이름이 알려져 있지 않을 때 법률적인 상투적 문구나 문서 등에 쓰는 이름. 존 도

join /dʒɔɪn/ *v* **1** [T] also **join in** to begin to take part in an activity that other people are involved in ‖ 다른 사람이 관여하고 있는 활동에 참가하기 시작하다. 참가하다: *joining a political campaign* 정치 운동에의 참여 **2** [I, T] to become a member of an organization, society, or group ‖ 기관[사회, 단체]의 회원이 되다. …에 가입하다. 입회하다: *He joined a health club to get in shape.* 그는 체형을 관리하기 위해 헬스클럽에 가입했다. / *It doesn't cost anything to join.* 가입에는 아무런 비용도 들지 않는다. **3** [T] to do something together with someone else ‖ 남과 함께 어떤 일을 하다: *Why don't you join us for dinner?* 우리와 함께 저녁 식사하시지 그래요? / *Please join with me in welcoming tonight's speaker.* 오늘밤 연사를 저와 함께 환영해 주세요. **4** [I, T] to connect or fasten things together, or to be connected ‖ 사물을 서로 연결시키거나 묶다, 또는 연결되다: *the place where the pipes join.* 파이프가 연결된 곳 **5 join the club!** SPOKEN said when you and other people are in the same situation ‖ 자신과 다른 사람이 같은 상황에 처해 있을 때에 쓰여. 나도 마찬가지야!: *You can't find a job? Join the club!* 일자리를 구할 수 없으십니까? 나도 마찬가지예요! **6 join hands** if two or more people join hands, they hold each other's hands ‖ 두 명 이상의 사람들이 서로의 손을 잡다. 손잡다. 제휴하다

joint¹ /dʒɔɪnt/ *adj* **1** involving two or more people or groups, or owned or shared by them ‖ 둘 이상의 사람이나 단체가 연루된[소유한, 공유한]. 공동의. 공유의. 연대의: *They have to reach a joint decision.* 그들은 공통된 결론에 도달해야만 한다. / *a joint bank account* 공동 은행 계좌 / *"Who cooked dinner?" "It was a joint effort."* (=we did it together) "누가 식사 준비를 했어요?" "우리가 함께 했어요." **2 joint resolution** LAW a decision or law agreed by both houses of the US Congress and signed by the President ‖ 미국 의회의 상·하 양원이 승인하고 대통령이 서명한 결정이나 법률. 공동 결의 – **jointly** *adv*: *The two of you will be jointly responsible for the project.* 당신들 두 사람은 그 계획사업에 대해 공동 책임을 져야 한다.

joint² *n* **1** a part of the body where two bones meet, that can bend ‖ 두 뼈가 만나는 굽힐 수 있는 신체 부위. 관절(부): *the knee joint* 무릎 관절 **2** SLANG a place, especially a BAR, club, or restaurant ‖ 특히 술집·클럽·식당: *a fast-food joint* 패스트푸드점 **3** SLANG a MARIJUANA cigarette ‖ 마리화나 담배 **4** a place where two things or parts of an object are joined together ‖ 두 가지나 물체의 두 부분이 결합되는 곳. 이음매: *One of the pipe joints was leaking.* 파이프의 이음매의 한 부분

joint

이 새고 있었다. **5 out of joint** a bone that is out of joint has been pushed out of its correct position ‖ 뼈가 정상적인 위치에서 밀려난. 관절이 빠진. —see also **put sb's nose out of joint** (NOSE¹)

joint ven·ture /ˌ. ˈ../ *n* a business arrangement in which two or more companies work together to achieve something ‖ 두 개 이상의 회사들이 공동으로 일을 하여 어떤 것을 달성하려는 사업 협정. 합작 사업: *The two computer giants announced a joint venture in Malaysia.* 두 개의 거대한 컴퓨터 회사는 말레이시아에서의 합작 사업을 발표했다.

joke¹ /dʒoʊk/ *n* **1** something funny that you say or do to make people laugh ‖ 사람들을 웃기려고 말하거나 행동하는 재미있는 것. 농담. 익살스러운 언동. 장난: *We stayed up telling jokes until two a.m.* 우리는 우스갯소리를 하며 새벽 2시까지 자지 않고 있었다. **2** INFORMAL a situation that is so silly or unreasonable that it makes you angry ‖ 화나게 만드는 너무 바보 같거나 불합리한 상황: *What a joke that meeting was.* 그 모임은 정말 어처구니 없는 것이었다. **3 take a joke** to be able to laugh at a joke about yourself ‖ 자신에 대한 농담을 웃어넘길 수 있다. 농담으로 받아들이다: *Come on – can't you take a joke?* 이봐, 농담으로 받아들일 수 없겠니?

joke² *v* [I] to say things that are intended to be funny ‖ 웃기려는 의도로 어떤 것을 말하다. 농담을 하다. 우스갯소리를 하다: *Owen's always joking about something.* 오웬은 항상 무언가에 대해 우스갯소리를 하고 있다. **– jokingly** *adv*

jok·er /ˈdʒoʊkɚ/ *n* someone who makes a lot of jokes ‖ 농담을 많이 하는 사람. 재담꾼. 익살꾼

jol·ly /ˈdʒɑli/ *adj* happy and cheerful ‖ 행복하고 쾌활한. 명쾌한. 기분 좋은

jolt¹ /dʒoʊlt/ *n* **1** a sudden rough or violent movement ‖ 거칠거나 격렬한 갑작스런 동요. 급격한 동요: *We felt a big jolt, and then things started shaking.* 우리는 큰 요동을 느꼈고 그러자 물건들이 흔들리기 시작했다. **2** a sudden shock ‖ 갑작스런 충격: *a jolt of electricity* 전기 충격 / *It was kind of an emotional jolt for me.* 그것은 내게 일종의 정신적인 충격이었다.

jolt² *v* **1** [I, T] to move suddenly and roughly, or to make someone or something do this ‖ 갑자기 거칠게 움직이다, 또는 사람이나 사물을 그렇게 만들다. 뒤흔들리다. 뒤흔들다: *an earthquake that jolted southern California* 캘리포니아 남부를 강타한 지진 **2** [T] to give someone a sudden shock ‖ 남에게 갑작스러운 충격을 주다: *companies jolted by the tax changes* 세제(稅制)의 변화로 충격을 받은 회사

jos·tle /ˈdʒɑsəl/ *v* [I, T] to push or knock against someone in a crowd ‖ 군중 속에서 남을 떠밀거나 부딪치다. 밀치다: *Spectators jostled for a better view.* 구경꾼들은 전망이 더 좋은 곳을 차지하려고 서로 밀쳐댔다.

jot /dʒɑt/ *v* **-tted, -tting**

jot sth ↔ **down** *phr v* [T] to write something quickly ‖ 무엇을 재빨리 쓰다. …을 간단히 적다. 메모하다: *Let me just jot down your phone number.* 당신의 전화번호만 적을게요.

jour·nal /ˈdʒɚnl/ *n* **1** a written record that you make of the things that happen to you each day ‖ 매일 일어나는 일들에 대한 기록. 일기. 일지 **2** a magazine or newspaper for people who are interested in a particular subject ‖ 특정한 주제에 흥미를 가지고 있는 사람들을 위한 잡지나 신문: *The Wall Street Journal* 월 스트리트 저널 / *a medical journal* 의학 잡지

jour·nal·is·m /ˈdʒɚnlˌɪzəm/ *n* [U] the job or activity of writing reports for newspapers, magazines, television, or radio ‖ 신문[잡지, 텔레비전, 라디오] 기사 작성의 업무나 활동. 저널리즘. 문필업

jour·nal·ist /ˈdʒɚnl-ɪst/ *n* someone who writes reports for newspapers, magazines, television, or radio ‖ 신문[잡지, 텔레비전, 라디오] 기사를 쓰는 사람. 저널리스트. 기자

jour·ney /ˈdʒɚni/ *n* a trip from one place to another, especially over a long distance ‖ 특히 장거리의, 한 장소에서 다른 장소로의 여행 —see usage note at TRAVEL²

jo·vi·al /ˈdʒoʊviəl/ *adj* friendly and cheerful ‖ 다정하고 쾌활한. 명랑한. 즐거운: *a jovial face* 명랑한 얼굴

jowls /dʒaʊlz/ *n* [plural] loose skin on someone's lower jaw ‖ 아래턱의 늘어진 피부. 턱살

joy /dʒɔɪ/ *n* [C, U] great happiness and pleasure, or something that gives you this feeling ‖ 큰 행복과 즐거움, 또는 이런 감정을 주는 것. 기쁨(을 주는 것): *She laughed with joy at the news.* 그녀는 그 소식을 듣고 기뻐서 웃었다.

joy·ful /ˈdʒɔɪfəl/ *adj* very happy, or likely to make people very happy ‖ 매우 행복한, 또는 사람들을 매우 행복하게 할

것 같은. 기쁨에 넘치는. 기쁜 듯한:
joyful laughter 기쁨에 넘치는 웃음 –
joyfully *adv*

joy·ous /'dʒɔɪəs/ *adj* LITERARY full of
happiness, or likely to make people
happy ‖ 행복으로 가득한, 또는 사람들을
행복하게 할 것 같은. 즐거운. 기쁨에 넘
치는. 기쁜 듯한: *a joyous song* 즐거운
노래 – **joyously** *adv*

joy·ride /'dʒɔɪraɪd/ *n* a fast dangerous
drive in a car, often after someone has
stolen it for fun ‖ 종종 사람이 재미로 훔
친 차로 위험스럽게 빨리 운전하는 것. 난
폭 운전. 폭주 – **joyriding** *n* [U] –
joyrider *n*

joy·stick /'dʒɔɪ,stɪk/ *n* a handle that
you use in order to control something
such as an aircraft or a computer game
‖ 항공기나 컴퓨터 게임 등을 조종하기 위
해 사용하는 손잡이. 조종간(桿)

Jr. *adj* the written abbreviation of
JUNIOR ‖ junior의 약어

ju·bi·lant /'dʒubələnt/ *adj* extremely
happy and pleased because you have
been successful ‖ 자신이 성공했기 때문에
매우 행복하고 기쁜. 환희에 넘친. 환성을
지르는: *a jubilant smile* 환희에 넘친 웃음
– **jubilation** /,dʒubə'leɪʃən/ *n* [U]

Ju·da·ism /'dʒudi,ɪzəm, -deɪ-, -də-/ *n*
[U] the Jewish religion based on the Old
Testament, the Talmud, and later
teachings of the RABBIs ‖ 구약·탈무드와
랍비의 만년의 가르침에 근거한 유대인의
종교. 유대교

judge¹ /dʒʌdʒ/ *n* **1** the official in control
of a court who decides how criminals
should be punished ‖ 범죄자들을 어떻게
처벌할 것인가를 결정하는 재판을 지휘하
는 관리. 재판관. 판사 **2** someone who
decides on the result of a competition ‖
시합의 결과를 판정하는 사람. 심판: *a
panel of judges at the Olympics* 올림픽의
심판단 **3** someone who has a natural
ability or the knowledge and experience
to give an opinion about something ‖ 어
떤 일에 대한 의견을 제시하는 천부적인
능력이나 지식과 경험을 가진 사람. 감정
가. 품평가. 평론가: *a good judge of
character* 성격을 잘 판단하는 사람

judge² *v* **1** [I, T] to form or give an
opinion about someone or something
after thinking about all the information
‖ 모든 정보를 생각해본 후에 사람이나 사
물에 대한 의견을 형성하거나 내다. 판단
하다. 평가하다: *Employees should be
judged on the quality of their work.* 종
업원들은 그들의 업무의 질을 평가받아야
만 한다. / *Judging by her clothes, I'd*

say she's rich. 옷 입은 것으로 판단하건
대 그녀는 부자이다. **2** [T] to decide in
court whether someone is guilty of a
crime ‖ 어떤 사람이 유죄인지 법정에서
결정하다. …을 재판하다 **3** [I, T] to
decide the result in a competition ‖ 시합
의 결과를 판정하다. 심판하다: *Who's
judging the pie-eating contest?* 파이 먹
기 대회에 누가 심판을 보고 있니? **4** [I,
T] to form an opinion about someone in
an unfair or criticizing way ‖ 남에 대하
여 불공정하거나 비평하는 투의 의견을 가
지다. …을 비판[비난]하다: *I just want
Mom to stop judging me.* 나는 엄마가 나
에 대해 불평을 좀 그만 했으면 좋겠어.

judg·ment /'dʒʌdʒmənt/ *n* **1** [C, U] an
opinion that you form after thinking
about something ‖ 어떤 일에 대해 생각해
본 후에 가지는 의견. 견해. 판단: *It's
time to make your own judgments
about what to do.* 무엇을 해야 할지에 대
해서 당신 자신이 판단해야 할 때이다. /
*People were right in their judgment of
him.* 그에 대한 사람들의 판단은 옳았다.
2 [U] the ability to make decisions
about situations or people ‖ 상황이나 사
람에 대해 결정하는 능력. 판단력. 비판
력: *She seems to have pretty good
judgment.* 그녀는 꽤 뛰어난 판단력을 가
지고 있는 것처럼 보인다. **3** [C, U] an
official decision given by a judge or a
court of law ‖ 판사나 법정에 의해 선고된
공식적인 결정. 판결 **4 judgment call** a
decision you have to make yourself
because there are no fixed rules in a
situation ‖ 상황에 정해진 규칙이 없기 때
문에 스스로 해야 하는 결정. 개인적 의견
[해석]

judg·men·tal /dʒʌdʒ'mɛntl/ *adj* too
quick to form opinions and criticize
other people ‖ 의견을 형성하고 다른 사람
을 비판하는 데에 지나치게 성급한. 성급
한 판단의

Judgment Day /'.. ,./ *n* the day at
the end of the world when everyone is
judged by God, according to some
religions ‖ 몇몇의 종교에서, 모든 사람이
신의 심판을 받는 세계 종말의 날. 최후의
심판일

ju·di·cial /dʒu'dɪʃəl/ *adj* relating to a
court of law, judges etc. ‖ 법정·재판관
등과 관련된. 재판의. 재판관의. 재판에
의한: *the judicial system* 사법 제도

ju·di·ci·ar·y /dʒu'dɪʃi,ɛri, -ʃəri/ *n* **the
judiciary** FORMAL all the judges in a
country who, as a group, form part of
the system of government ‖ 정부 조직의
일부를 이루는 단체로서의 한 나라의 모든

J

재판관들. 사법부. 사법권

ju·di·cious /dʒuˈdɪʃəs/ *adj* FORMAL sensible and careful ‖ 분별력이 있고 주의 깊은. 현명한: *a judicious use of money* 돈의 현명한 사용

jug /dʒʌg/ *n* a large deep container for liquids that has a narrow opening and a handle ‖ 주둥이가 좁고 손잡이가 달린 액체를 담는 데 쓰는, 크고 깊은 용기. 주전자 —see picture at CONTAINER

jug·gle /ˈdʒʌgəl/ *v* 1 [I, T] to keep three or more objects moving through the air by throwing them and catching them very quickly ‖ 세 개 이상의 물체를 공중으로 던지고 받기를 매우 빠르게 계속해서 하다. 저글링하다 2 [T] to try to fit two or more jobs, activities etc. into your life ‖ 삶 속에 두 가지 이상의 일이나 활동 등을 조화시키려고 노력하다. 양립시키다: *It's hard trying to juggle work and children.* 일과 아이들을 양립시키려 하는 것은 어렵다. – **juggler** *n*

juggle

jug·u·lar /ˈdʒʌgyələ/ *n* 1 **go for the jugular** INFORMAL to criticize or attack someone very strongly ‖ 남을 매우 강하게 비판하거나 공격하다. 급소를 찌르다 2 the large VEIN in your neck that takes blood from your head to your heart ‖ 머리에서 심장으로 피를 보내는 목에 있는 큰 정맥. 경정맥

juice /dʒus/ *n* 1 [C, U] the liquid that comes from fruit and vegetables, or a drink made from this ‖ 과일과 야채에서 나오는 액체, 또는 이것으로 만든 음료. 과즙. 야채즙. 주스: *a glass of orange juice* 오렌지 주스 한 잔 2 [U] the liquid that comes out of meat when it is cooked ‖ 요리할 때 고기에서 나오는 액체. 육즙 3 [U] INFORMAL electricity ‖ 전기

juic·y /ˈdʒusi/ *adj* 1 containing a lot of juice ‖ 많은 주스를 함유하는. 즙이 많은: *a juicy peach* 즙이 많은 복숭아 2 **juicy gossip/details** INFORMAL interesting or shocking information ‖ 재미있거나 충격적인 정보. 호기심을 자극하는 소문/자세한 이야기 – **juiciness** *n* [U]

juke box /ˈdʒuk bɑks/ *n* a machine in BARs and restaurants that plays music when you put money in it ‖ 술집·식당 안에 있는, 돈을 넣으면 음악이 나오는 기계. 주크박스. 자동 전축

Ju·ly /dʒʊˈlaɪ, dʒə-/, *written abbreviation* **Jul.** *n* the seventh month of the year ‖ 그 해의 일곱 번째 달. 7월 —see usage note at JANUARY

jum·ble /ˈdʒʌmbəl/ *n* [singular] a messy mixture of things ‖ 뒤죽박죽으로 물건이 섞임. 뒤범벅. 잡동사니: *a jumble of clothes on the floor* 마루 위에 뒤범벅이 된 옷 – **jumble** *v* [T]

jum·bo /ˈdʒʌmboʊ/ *adj* larger than other things of the same type ‖ 같은 종류의 다른 것보다 더 큰. 특대의: *a jumbo jet* 점보 제트기

jump¹ /dʒʌmp/ *v*
1 ▶UP 위로◀ [I, T] to push yourself suddenly up in the air using your legs, or to go over something doing this ‖ 다리를 이용하여 자신을 갑자기 공중으로 밀어 올리다, 또는 그렇게 하여 물건을 넘다. 뛰다. 뛰어넘다: *Several fans tried to jump onto the stage.* 몇몇 팬이 무대 위로 뛰어 오르려고 했다. / *kids jumping up and down on the bed* 침대에서 위 아래로 풀쩍풀쩍 뛰고 있는 아이들 —see picture on page 947
2 ▶DOWN 밑으로◀ [I] to let yourself drop from a place that is above the ground ‖ 지상의 높은 곳에서 자신을 떨어지게 하다. 뛰어내리다: *During the fire, two people jumped out of a window.* 화재가 났을 때 두 사람이 창문에서 뛰어내렸다.
3 ▶MOVE FAST 빠르게 움직이다◀ [I] to move quickly or suddenly in a particular direction ‖ 특정한 방향으로 재빨리 또는 갑자기 움직이다: *Paul jumped up to answer the door.* 폴은 벌떡 일어서서 방문객을 맞으러 나갔다.
4 ▶IN SURPRISE/FEAR 놀라서/두려워서◀ [I] to make a sudden movement because you are surprised or frightened ‖ 놀라거나 두려워서 갑자기 움직이다. 움찔하다. 덜컥하다: *The sudden ring of the telephone made us jump.* 갑작스런 전화벨 소리에 우리는 움찔했다.
5 ▶INCREASE 증가하다◀ [I] to increase suddenly and by a large amount ‖ 갑자기 엄청나게 증가하다. 급증하다. 폭등하다: *Profits jumped 20% last month.* 이익이 지난 달에 20% 급증했다.
6 jump down sb's throat INFORMAL to suddenly speak angrily to someone ‖ 갑자기 남에게 화를 내며 말하다: *All I did was ask a question, and he jumped down my throat!* 내가 한 것이라고는 질문 하나 한 것뿐인데 그는 나한테 막 화를 냈어!
7 jump to conclusions to form an opinion about something before you have all the facts ‖ 모든 사실을 알기 전

에 어떤 일에 대한 견해를 가지다. 성급하게 결론을 내리다: *Don't jump to conclusions when you don't know the facts!* 사실을 모르면서 성급히 결정을 내리지 마!

8 jump the gun to start doing something too soon ‖ 일을 너무 빨리 시작하다. 성급하게 시작하다

jump at sth *phr v* [T] to eagerly accept the chance to do something ‖ 어떤 일을 할 기회를 기꺼이 받아들이다: *Ruth jumped at the chance to study at Harvard.* 루스는 하버드 대학에서 공부할 기회를 기꺼이 받아들였다.

jump on sb *phr v* [T] INFORMAL to criticize or punish someone, especially unfairly ‖ 특히 불공평하게 남을 비판하거나 책망하다. 맹렬히 비난하다: *Dad jumps on Jeff for every little mistake.* 아빠는 사소한 실수에도 제프를 몹시 야단치신다.

jump² *n* **1** an act of pushing yourself suddenly up into the air using your legs ‖ 다리를 이용하여 자신을 갑자기 공중으로 밀어올리기. 뛰기. 뛰어오르기. 도약 **2** an act of letting yourself drop from a place that is above the ground ‖ 지상의 높은 곳에서 자신을 떨어지게 하는 행위. 뛰어내리기: *a parachute jump* 낙하산으로 뛰어내리기 **3** a sudden large increase in an amount or value ‖ 양이나 가치의 갑작스러운 엄청난 증가. 폭등. 급증: *a jump in prices* 물가의 폭등 **4 get a jump on** to gain an advantage by doing something earlier than usual or earlier than someone else ‖ 평소보다 또는 다른 사람보다 일찍 어떤 일을 하여 이득을 보다. 남보다 한 발 앞서다. …을 앞지르다: *I want to get a jump on my Christmas shopping.* 크리스마스 쇼핑을 남보다 먼저 하고 싶다.

jump·er /ˈdʒʌmpɚ/ *n* a dress without SLEEVES usually worn over a shirt ‖ 셔츠 위에 걸쳐 입는 소매 없는 옷

jumper ca·ble /ˈ.. ˌ../ *n* [C usually plural] one of two thick wires used in order to send electricity from a car BATTERY that works to one that has stopped working ‖ 작동되는 차 배터리에서 작동을 멈춘 배터리로 전기를 보내는 데에 사용되는 굵은 두 전선 중 하나. 점퍼 케이블

jump rope /ˈ. ./ *n* a long piece of rope that children use for jumping over ‖ 어린이가 뛰어넘는 놀이에 사용하는 긴 줄. 줄넘기 줄

jump-start /ˈ. ./ *v* [T] **1** to do something to help a process or activity start working better or more quickly ‖ 과정이나 활동을 더 좋게 또는 더 빨리 시작하도록 돕는 일을 하다. 활성화하다: *the government's efforts to jump-start the economy* 경제를 활성화하려는 정부의 노력 **2** to start a car whose BATTERY has lost power by connecting it to the battery of a car that works ‖ 배터리의 에너지를 상실한 차를 작동하는 차의 배터리에 연결하여 시동을 걸다

jump·suit /ˈdʒʌmpsut/ *n* a single piece of clothing like a shirt attached to a pair of pants, worn especially by women ‖ 특히 여성이 입는, 바지에 셔츠가 붙은 한 벌의 옷. 상하가 붙은 여성복

jump·y /ˈdʒʌmpi/ *adj* worried or excited because you are expecting something bad to happen ‖ 나쁜 일이 일어나리라고 예상되어 걱정되거나 흥분하는. 신경과민인. 안달하는

junc·tion /ˈdʒʌŋkʃən/ *n* a place where one road, track etc. meets another one ‖ 도로·궤도 등이 다른 도로·궤도와 마주치는 곳. 교차점: *a railroad junction* 철도의 교차점

junc·ture /ˈdʒʌŋktʃɚ/ *n* **at this juncture** SPOKEN FORMAL at this point in an activity or time ‖ 활동이나 시간의 이 시점에서. 이 중대한 시기에. 이때에

June /dʒun/, *written abbreviation* **Jun.** *n* the sixth month of the year ‖ 그 해의 여섯 번째 달. 6월 —see usage note at JANUARY

jun·gle /ˈdʒʌŋgəl/ *n* [C, U] a thick tropical forest with many large plants that grow very close together ‖ 큰 식물들이 빽빽이 우거져 자라는 열대의 무성한 삼림. 밀림(지대). 정글

Jun·ior /ˈdʒunyɚ/, *written abbreviation* **Jr.** *adj* used after the name of a man who has the same name as his father ‖ 아버지와 같은 이름을 가진 아들의 이름 뒤에 쓰여. 2세: *William Jones Jr.* 윌리엄 존스 2세 —compare SENIOR

junior¹ *n* **1** a student in the third year of HIGH SCHOOL or college ‖ 고등학교나 대학의 3학년생 **2 be two/five/ten years sb's junior** to be two, five etc. years younger than someone else ‖ 남보다 두 살·다섯 살 등이 적다. …보다 두/다섯/열 살 어리다 —compare SENIOR¹

junior² *adj* younger or of a lower rank ‖ 나이가 어리거나 계급이 낮은: *a junior partner* 후배 동료 —compare SENIOR²

junior col·lege /ˌ.. ˈ../ *n* [C, U] a college where students take a course of study that continues for two years ‖ 학생이 2년 동안 계속되는 학습 과정을 이수하

는 대학. 전문대학

junior high school /ˌ.. '. ˌ./, **junior high** /ˌ.. './ n [C, U] a school in the US and Canada for students who are aged between 12 and 14 or 15 ‖ 12세에서 14세 또는 15세 사이의 학생이 다니는 미국과 캐나다의 학교. 중학교

junk /dʒʌŋk/ n [U] old or unwanted things that have no use or value ‖ 소용이나 가치가 없는 오래되거나 불필요한 물건. 쓰레기. 폐품: *an attic filled with junk* 폐품들로 가득 찬 다락방

junk·ket /'dʒʌŋkɪt/ n a trip that is paid for by government money ‖ 정부 돈으로 지불되는 여행. 관비 여행

junk food /'. ./ n [U] INFORMAL food that is not healthy because it has a lot of fat or sugar ‖ 지방이나 당분이 많이 들어 있어서 몸에 좋지 않은 음식. 정크 푸드

junk·ie /'dʒʌŋki/ n 1 INFORMAL someone who takes dangerous drugs and is dependent on them ‖ 위험한 마약을 복용하며 그것에 의존하는 사람. 마약 상습자 2 HUMOROUS someone who likes something so much that s/he seems to need it ‖ 없으면 안 될 정도로 어떤 것을 매우 좋아하는 사람. 마니아. 심취자: *My dad's a TV junkie.* 나의 아빠는 텔레비전 중독자이다.

junk mail /'. ./ n [U] letters that advertisers send to people ‖ 광고주가 사람들에게 보내는 우편물. 정크 메일

junk·yard /'dʒʌŋk.yard/ n **a)** a business that buys old cars, broken furniture etc. and sells the parts of them that can be used again ‖ 낡은 차·부서진 가구 등을 사서 다시 쓸 수 있는 그 부품을 파는 사업. 고물업 **b)** the place where this business keeps the things it collects ‖ 고물업을 하는 사람이 모아 놓은 물건을 보관하는 장소. 고물 집적소

jun·ta /'hʊntə, 'dʒʌntə/ n a military government that has gained power by using force ‖ 무력을 사용하여 권력을 잡은 군사 정부

Ju·pi·ter /'dʒupətɚ/ n [singular] the largest PLANET that is the fifth farthest from the sun ‖ 태양에서 다섯 번째로 멀리 떨어져 있는 가장 큰 행성. 목성

jur·is·dic·tion /ˌdʒʊrɪs'dɪkʃən/ n [U] the right to use official authority to make legal decisions ‖ 합법적인 결정을 하기 위해 공식적인 권한을 사용할 권리. 재판권. 사법권. 관할권: *a matter outside the court's jurisdiction* 법원의 관할권 밖의 문제

ju·ror /'dʒʊrɚ/ n a member of a JURY ‖ 배심원단의 한 사람. 배심원

ju·ry /'dʒʊri/ n 1 a group of 12 people who listen to details of a case in court and decide whether someone is guilty or not ‖ 법정에서 사건의 상세한 진술을 듣고 어떤 사람이 유죄인지 무죄인지를 결정하는 12명으로 구성된 집단. 배심원단 2 a group of people chosen to judge a competition ‖ 콘테스트를 심사하기 위해 선발된 심사원단

just¹ /dʒʌst/ adv 1 exactly ‖ 꼭. 정확히: *My brother looks just like my dad.* 내 동생은 아빠를 꼭 닮았다. 2 only ‖ 단지. …뿐: *I just play the piano for fun.* 나는 재미로 피아노를 연주할 뿐이다. / *It happened just a few weeks ago.* 그것은 바로 몇 주 전에 발생했다. / *Can you wait five minutes? I just have to iron this.* (=it's the last thing I have to do) 5분만 기다려 줄래? 이것만 다리면 돼. 3 if something has just happened, it happened only a short time before ‖ 조금 전에: *I just got back from Marilyn's house.* 나는 매릴린 집에서 조금 전에 돌아왔다. 4 **just about** almost ‖ 거의: *She calls her grandfather just about every day.* 그녀는 거의 매일 자기 할아버지에게 전화를 한다. / *I'm just about finished.* 나는 거의 끝마쳤다. 5 **be just about to do sth** to be going to do something soon ‖ 곧 어떤 일을 하려고 하다: *We were just about to go riding when it started raining.* 우리가 막 말을 타려 할 때 비가 오기 시작했다. 6 **be just doing sth** to be starting to do something ‖ 어떤 일을 하기 시작하다: *I'm just making dinner now.* 나는 지금 막 식사를 준비하고 있다. 7 **just before/after etc.** only a short time before, after etc. ‖ 조금 전 또는 후에: *Theresa got home just before us.* 테레사는 우리가 도착하기 바로 전에 집에 도착했다. 8 **(only) just** if something just happens, it does happen, but it almost did not ‖ 어떤 일이 거의 일어나지 못할 뻔 했지만 일어나는. 간신히. 가까스로: *Kurt only just made it home before the storm.* 커트는 폭풍이 오기 전에 가까스로 집에 도착했다. 9 **just as** equally as ‖ 꼭 …처럼: *The $250 TV is just as good as the $300 one.* 그 250달러짜리 텔레비전은 300달러짜리 텔레비전만큼 좋다. 10 **sth is just around the corner** used in order to say that something will happen or arrive soon ‖ 어떤 일이 곧 일어나거나 도래하리라는 것을 말하는 데에 쓰여. 곧 …이다: *Summer is just around the corner.* 여름이 바로 눈앞에 다가왔다.

SPOKEN PHRASES

11 used for politely asking or telling someone something ‖ 예의바르게 남에게 어떤 것을 묻거나 말하는 데에 쓰여: *Could I just use your phone for a minute?* 잠시 전화 좀 써도 되겠습니까? **12 just a minute/second** said in order to ask someone to wait for a short time ‖ 남에게 잠깐 동안 기다리라고 부탁하는 데에 쓰여: *Just a second – I can't find my keys.* 잠시만 기다려. 열쇠를 못 찾겠어. **13** used in order to emphasize something that you are saying ‖ 하는 말을 강조하기 위해 쓰여. 정말: *I just couldn't believe what she was saying.* 그녀가 말하는 것을 정말이지 믿을 수가 없었어요. / *Just shut up and listen!* 닥치고 듣기나 해! **14 it's just that** used in order to explain the reason for something when someone thinks there is a different reason ‖ 상대방이 다른 이유가 있다고 여길 때 어떤 일에 대한 이유를 설명하는 데에 쓰여. 그저[단지] …이다: *He's not ugly. It's just that he's too short for me.* 그는 못생긴게 아니야. 단지 나에 비해 너무 작아서 그렇지. **15 just now** a short time before now ‖ 바로 전에. 방금: *Your mother called just now.* 네 어머니가 바로 전에 전화하셨어. **16 would just as soon** if you would just as soon do something, you would prefer to do it ‖ 어떤 일을 하는 것이 좋겠다: *I'd just as soon go with you, if that's okay.* 괜찮다면 너와 동행하면 좋겠다. **17 it's just as well** said when it is lucky that something has happened in the way it did, because if not, there may have been problems ‖ 일이 일어났던 식으로 일어나지 않으면 곤란할 뻔 했는데 그렇게 되어 다행일 때 쓰여. …은 천만다행이다: *It's just as well Scott didn't go to the party, because Lisa was there.* 리사가 거기에 있었기 때문에 스콧이 그 파티에 가지 않은 것은 천만다행이다. **18 just because** used in order to say that although one thing is true, it does not mean that something else is true ‖ 한 가지가 사실이더라도 다른 일까지 사실임을 의미하지 않는다는 것을 말하는 데에 쓰여: *Just because you're older than me doesn't mean you can tell me what to do!* 단지 당신이 나보다 나이가 많다고 해서 당신이 나에게 어떤 것을 하라고 명령할 수 있다는 뜻은 아니야!

USAGE NOTE just, already, and **yet**

In formal or written English, you must use these words with the present perfect tense: *I've already seen him. / The bell has just rung. / Have you eaten yet? However, in informal speech, we often use these words with the simple past tense: I already saw him. / The bell just rang. / Did you eat yet?*
격식 차린 영어나 문어체 영어에서 이 단어들은 현재 완료 시제와 함께 써야 한다: 나는 이미 그를 보았다. / 종이 방금 울렸다. / 벌써 먹었니? 그러나 비격식의 대화에서는 종종 이 단어들이 단순 과거 시제와 함께 쓰인다: 나는 이미 그를 보았다. / 종이 방금 울렸다. / 벌써 먹었니?

just² *adj* morally right and fair ‖ 도덕적으로 옳고 공정한. 정당한: *a just punishment* 정당한 처벌 —opposite UNJUST

jus·tice /ˈdʒʌstɪs/ *n* [U] **1** fairness in the way people are treated ‖ 사람의 대우 면에서의 공정성. 정의: *Children have a strong sense of justice.* 어린이들은 강한 정의감이 있다. **2** the system by which people are judged in courts of law and criminals are punished ‖ 사람이 법정에서 재판받고 범죄자가 처벌받는 제도. 재판. 사법: *the criminal justice system* 형사 사법 제도 **3 do sb/sth justice** to treat or represent someone or something in a way that is fair and shows his, her, or its best qualities ‖ 사람이나 사물을 공평하게 다루거나 재현하며 최적의 특성을 보여주다. (사람·물건을) 실물대로 나타내다: *This picture doesn't do you justice.* 이 사진은 당신이 제대로 나오지 않았다.

Justice of the Peace /ˌ.. . . ˈ./ *n* FORMAL an official who judges offenses that are not serious, performs marriages, etc. ‖ 중하지 않은 범죄를 재판하고 결혼 등을 공증해 주는 공무원. 치안 판사

jus·ti·fi·a·ble /ˌdʒʌstəˈfaɪəbəl/ *adj* done for good reasons ‖ 정당한 사유에서 행한. 이치에 맞는: *justifiable decisions* 정당한 결정 **–justifiably** *adv*

jus·ti·fi·ca·tion /ˌdʒʌstəfəˈkeɪʃən/ *n* [C, U] a good and acceptable reason for doing something ‖ 어떤 일을 하는 데에 대한 정당하고 받아들일 수 있는 이유. 정당성: *There is no justification for terrorism.* 테러 행위는 정당성이 없다.

J

jus·ti·fied /ˈdʒʌstəˌfaɪd/ *adj* having an acceptable explanation or reason ‖ 받아들일 수 있는 설명이나 이유가 있는. 정당한 (이유가 있는): *Your complaints are certainly justified.* 너의 불만은 분명 정당하다. —opposite UNJUSTIFIED

jus·ti·fy /ˈdʒʌstəˌfaɪ/ *v* [T] to give an acceptable explanation for something, especially when other people think it is unreasonable ‖ 특히 다른 사람들이 불합리하게 생각할 때 어떤 일에 대한 받아들일 수 있는 설명을 하다. 정당화하다: *How can you justify spending so much money on a coat?* 코트에 그렇게 많은 돈을 쓴 것을 너는 어떻게 정당화할거니?

jut /dʒʌt/ *v* **-tted, -tting** [I] also **jut out** to stick up or out farther than the other things in the same area ‖ 같은 지역에서 다른 것보다 튀어 나오다. 돌출하다: *a point of land that juts out into the ocean* 바다로 튀어나온 육지의 돌출부

ju·ve·nile /ˈdʒuvənl, -ˌnaɪl/ *adj* **1** LAW relating to young people who are not yet adults ‖ 아직 성인이 아닌 젊은이의. 청소년의: *juvenile crime* 청소년 범죄 **2** typical of a child rather than an adult ‖ 성인보다는 어린이에게 전형적인. 어린아이 같은. 유치한: *a juvenile sense of humor* 유치한 유머 감각 **– juvenile** *n*

juvenile de·lin·quent /ˌ... .ˈ../ *n* a child or young person who behaves in a criminal way ‖ 범법적으로 행동하는 어린이나 청소년. 비행 소년[소녀]

jux·ta·pose /ˈdʒʌkstəˌpouz, ˌdʒʌkstəˈpouz/ *v* [T] FORMAL to put things that are different together, especially in order to compare them ‖ 특히 비교하기 위해 다른 물건들을 함께 놓다. 병렬하다 **– juxtaposition** /ˌdʒʌkstəpəˈzɪʃən/ *n* [C, U]

J

Kk

K, k /keɪ/ the eleventh letter of the English alphabet ‖ 영어 알파벳의 열한째 자

K /keɪ/ *n* **1** the abbreviation of 1000 ‖ 1000의 약어: *He earns $50K a year.* 그는 일 년에 5만 달러를 번다. **2** the abbreviation of KILOBYTE ‖ kilobyte 의 약어

ka·bob /kə'bɑb/ *n* small pieces of meat and vegetables cooked on a stick ‖ 꼬치에 꿰어 요리한 고기와 야채의 작은 조각. 카보브. 산적의 일종

ka·lei·do·scope /kə'laɪdə,skoup/ *n* a tube with mirrors and pieces of colored glass at one end, that shows colored patterns when you look through and turn it ‖ 한쪽 끝에 거울과 채색 유리 조각이 달린 관으로, 그 관을 들여다 보다 보면서 돌리면 채색 문양들을 보여주는 것. 만화경

kan·ga·roo /,kæŋgə'ru/ *n* an Australian animal that has large strong back legs for jumping and carries its babies in a pocket of skin on its front ‖ 뛰는 데 사용하는 크고 강한 뒷다리가 있고 앞쪽의 가죽 주머니에 새끼를 담고 다니는 호주산 동물. 캥거루

ka·put /kə'pʊt/ *adj* SPOKEN broken ‖ 고장난. 쓸모가 없는: *The lawnmower's gone kaput.* 잔디 깎는 기계가 고장 나 버렸다.

kar·at /'kærət/ *n* a unit for measuring how pure a piece of gold is ‖ 금의 순도를 측정하는 단위. 캐럿. 금의 순도 단위 — see also CARAT

ka·ra·te /kə'rɑti/ *n* [U] the Asian sport of fighting in which you use your hands and feet to hit and kick ‖ 손과 발을 써서 때리고 차는 아시아의 격투 경기. 가라데

kar·ma /'kɑrmə/ *n* [U] **1** INFORMAL the feeling you get from a person, place, or action ‖ 사람[장소, 행동]에서 얻는 느낌. 분위기: *This house has a lot of good/bad karma.* 이 집은 분위기가 아주 좋다[나쁘다]. **2** the force that is produced by the things you do in your life and that will influence you in the future, according to some religions ‖ 몇몇 종교상에서, 일생 동안 자신이 행동한 일에 의해 조성되어 미래에 자신에게 영향을 미치는 힘. 업보. 인과응보

kay·ak /'kaɪæk/ *n* a CANOE (=type of boat) usually for one person, that is enclosed and has a hole for that person to sit in ‖ 막혀 있고 사람이 안에 들어가 앉을 수 있는 구멍이 있는 보통 1인용의 카누. 카약

kayak
paddle

keel¹ /kil/ *n* **on an even keel** steady and without any sudden changes ‖ 안정되어 아무런 갑작스러운 변동도 없는. 균형을 유지하여

keel² *v*

keel over *phr v* [I] to fall over sideways ‖ 옆으로 뒤집히다. 전복하다

keen /kin/ *adj* **1** a keen sense of smell, sight, or hearing is an extremely good ability to smell etc. ‖ 후각[시각, 청각]이 지극히 냄새를 잘 맡는 등의 능력이 있는. 민감한. 예민한 **2** someone with a keen mind can understand things quickly ‖ 사람의 정신이 어떤 것을 빨리 이해할 수 있는. 기민한. 빈틈없는 **3** very interested in something or eager to do it ‖ 어떤 것에 매우 흥미를 갖거나 그것을 하고 싶어 하는. 열심인. 열중한. …을 갈망하는: *Most people are keen to do a job well.* 대부분의 사람들은 일을 잘 하기 위해 열중한다. — **keenly** *adv*

keep¹ /kip/ *v* **kept, kept, keeping**
1 ▶NOT GIVE BACK 돌려주지 않다◀ [T] to have something and not give it back to the person who owned it before ‖ 이전에 소유했던 사람에게 돌려주지 않고 물건을 가지다. 자기 것으로 하다. 보유하다: *You can keep the book. I don't need it now.* 네가 그 책을 가지고 있어도 돼. 나는 지금 그 책이 필요 없거든.

2 ▶NOT LOSE 잃지 않다◀ [T] to continue to have something and not lose it or get rid of it ‖ 물건을 잃어버리거나 없애지 않고 계속해서 가지고 있다. 보관하다: *I kept the letter for 35 years.* 나는 35년 동안 그 편지를 보관했다. / *They're keeping the house in Colorado and selling this one.* 그들은 이 집을 팔고 콜로라도에 있는 그 집을 계속해서 보유할 것이다.

3 ▶CONTINUE IN STATE 상태를 유지하다◀ [I, T] to make someone or something continue to be in a particular state or condition ‖ 사람이나 사물을 특별한 상태나 조건에 계속해서 있게 하다. 계

속[유지]하다: *This blanket should help you keep warm*. 이 담요는 당신을 따뜻하게 하는 데에 도움을 줄 것이다. / *Her son kept her waiting for an hour*. 그녀의 아들은 한 시간 동안 그녀를 기다리게 했다.

4 keep (on) doing sth to continue doing something, or repeat an action many times ‖ 어떤 일을 계속하거나 한 행동을 여러 번 반복하다. …을 그대로 계속하다: *If he keeps on growing like this, he'll be taller than Dad*. 그가 이렇게 계속해서 자라면 아빠보다 키가 더 클 것이다. / *Rod kept calling them, but they weren't home*. 로드가 계속 전화를 걸었으나 그들은 집에 없었다.

5 ▶STAY IN A PLACE 장소에 머물다◀ [T] to make someone or something stay in a particular place ‖ 사람이나 사물을 특정한 장소에 머물게 하다. …에 (붙)잡아두다. 유치[구류]하다: *They kept him in jail for two weeks*. 그들은 2주 동안 그를 교도소에 수감했다.

6 ▶DELAY 지체 시키다◀ [T] to delay someone, or stop someone from doing something ‖ 사람을 지체시키거나 어떤 것을 하지 못하게 하다. 남을 늦어지게 하다. …하지 못하게 하다: *I don't know what's keeping her. It's 8:00 already*. 무엇 때문에 그녀가 지체하고 있는지 모르겠다. 벌써 8시이다. / *Keep those kids out of my yard!* 저 아이들을 내 뜰에 들어오지 못하게 하라!

7 keep a record/diary etc. to regularly write down information in a particular place ‖ 특정한 곳에 규칙적으로 정보를 적다. 기록하다/일기를 쓰다: *Keep a record of the food you eat for one week*. 일주일 동안 먹는 음식 일지를 작성하시오.

8 keep going SPOKEN used in order to tell someone to continue doing something ‖ 남에게 어떤 일을 계속하라고 말하는 데에 쓰여. 계속 해[버티어] 나가다: *Keep going, you're doing fine*. 계속해, 너 아주 잘 하고 있어.

9 keep it down SPOKEN said when you want someone to be quiet ‖ 남이 조용하기를 바랄 때에 쓰여. 조용히 하다. 소리를 낮추다: *Keep it down. I'm trying to watch TV*. 조용히 해라, 텔레비전 보려고 하잖니.

10 keep your promise to do what you have promised to do ‖ 하기로 약속했던 일을 하다. 약속을 지키다

11 keep (sth) quiet to not say anything in order to avoid complaining, telling a secret, or causing problems ‖ 불평하는

것을 피하거나 비밀을 누설하지 않기 위해 또는 문제를 일으키지 않으려고 아무 말도 하지 않다. 침묵을 지키다: *Let's keep quiet about this until someone asks us*. 누군가가 우리에게 묻기 전까지 이 일에 대해 입을 다물고 있자.

12 keep a secret to not tell anyone about a secret that you know ‖ 자신이 알고 있는 비밀에 대해 누구에게도 말하지 않다. 비밀을 지키다

13 keep sb posted to continue to tell someone the most recent news about someone or something ‖ 남에게 사람이나 사물에 대한 가장 최근 소식을 계속해서 알리다. 근황[소식]을 전하다: *Be sure to keep us posted about how you're doing*. 네가 어떻게 지내는지 꼭 우리에게 알려줘.

14 ▶FOOD 음식◀ [I] if food keeps, it stays fresh enough to still be eaten ‖ 음식이 아직 먹을 수 있을 만큼 신선하여 유지되다. (음식이)오래가다[보존되다]: *That yogurt won't keep much longer*. 그 요구르트는 그리 오래가지 못할 거다.

keep at sth *phr v* [T] to continue working hard at something ‖ 계속해서 어떤 일을 열심히 하다. 끈기 있게[계속해서] …하다: *Just keep at it until you get it right*. 그것을 제대로 알 때까지 계속해서 공부 해라.

keep after sb *phr v* [T] to tell someone to do something again and again until s/he does it ‖ 실행할 때까지 남에게 반복해서 어떤 것을 하라고 말하다. 끈질기게 [끊임없이] 말하다: *My mother kept after me to practice*. 어머니는 나에게 연습하라고 계속해서 말했다.

keep away *phr v* [I,T **keep** sth/sb ↔ **away**] to avoid going somewhere or seeing someone, or to make someone do this ‖ 어떤 곳에 가는 일이나 누구를 만나는 것을 피하다, 또는 남을 이렇게 하게 하다. …을 피하다[피하게 하다]: *Keep away from my children!* 내 아이한테서 떨어져! / *Mom kept us away from school for a week*. 엄마는 우리를 일주일 간 학교에 가지 못하게 했다.

keep sth ↔ **down** *phr v* [T] **1** to control something in order to prevent it from increasing ‖ 어떤 것이 증가하는 것을 막기 위해 통제하다. …을 억제하다: *They promised to keep the rents down*. 그들은 집세를 올리지 않기로 약속했다. **2** to stop yourself from VOMITing something ‖ 어떤 것을 토하지 않다. 삼키다: *I couldn't keep any food down all week*. 일주일 내내 어떤 음식도 삼킬 수 없었다.

keep from *phr v* [T] **1** [**keep** sth **from**

sb] to not tell someone something that you know ‖ 남에게 자신이 알고 있는 것을 말하지 않다. …에게 …을 숨기다: *He kept Angie's death from his family for 3 days.* 그는 엔지의 죽음을 삼일 동안 그의 가족에게 말하지 않았다. **2 keep (sb/sth) from doing sth** to prevent someone or something from doing something ‖ 사람이나 사물이 어떤 일 하는 것을 막다. 삼가다: *It was hard to keep from telling him to shut up.* 그에게 입을 다물라는 말을 억제하기가 힘들었다. / *Put foil over the pie to keep it from burning.* 타지 않도록 파이에 포일을 씌워라.

keep sth **off** *phr v* [T] to prevent something from affecting or damaging something else ‖ 사물이 다른 것에 영향이나 손상을 끼치는 것을 막다. 차단하다: *Wear a hat to keep the sun off your head.* 햇볕을 머리에 쬐지 않게 모자를 써라.

keep sb **on** *phr v* [T] to continue to employ someone ‖ 계속 남을 고용하다: *We keep some of our Christmas workers on.* 우리는 크리스마스 일꾼 몇 명을 계속 일을 하게 한다.

keep out *phr v* **1 Keep Out!** used on signs to tell people that they are not allowed into a place ‖ 사람들에게 어떤 장소에 들어가는 것이 허용되지 않음을 알리는 표지에 쓰여. 출입금지! **2** [T **keep** sb/sth **out**] to prevent someone or something from getting into a place ‖ 사람이나 사물이 어떤 장소에 들어오지 못하게 하다. …을 막아내다: *a coat that keeps the rain out* 방수 코트

keep out of sth *phr v* [T] to not become involved with something ‖ 어떤 것에 관련되지 않다. …에 가담하지 않다. …을 피하다: *My father's advice was to "keep out of trouble."* 아버지의 충고는 "말썽을 피하라"는 것이었다.

keep to *phr v* **1** [T **keep to** sth] to continue to do, use, or talk about one thing and not change ‖ 계속 한 가지만을 행하거나 쓰고, 또는 그에 대해 말하면서 바꾸지 않다. 고수하다. 벗어나지 않다: *Keep to the main roads. They're better.* 간선 도로를 벗어나지 마라. 그 도로들이 훨씬 좋아. **2 keep** sth **to yourself** to not tell anyone else something that you know ‖ 자신이 알고 있는 것을 아무에게도 말하지 않다. …을 비밀로 해두다[간직하다]: *Kim kept Gina's secret to herself.* 킴은 지나의 비밀을 혼자 간직했다. **3 keep to yourself** to not do things that involve other people, because you want

to be alone ‖ 혼자 있고 싶어서 다른 사람과 관련된 일을 하지 않다. 혼자 있다. 남과 교제하지 않다: *Nina kept to herself at the party.* 니나는 파티에서 혼자 있었다.

keep up *phr v* **1** [T **keep** sth ↔ **up**] to prevent something from going to a lower level ‖ 사물이 더 낮은 수준으로 가지 않게 막다. 계속하다. 유지하다: *keeping up high standards of health care* 건강 관리를 높은 수준으로 유지하기 **2** [I, T **keep** sth ↔ **up**] to continue doing something, or to make something continue ‖ 어떤 일을 계속하거나 어떤 일이 계속되게 하다: *Keep up the good work!* 계속해서 잘 해라! **3** [I] to move as fast as someone else ‖ 다른 사람만큼 빨리 움직이다. 뒤떨어지지 않도록 따라가다. 속도[보조]를 맞추다: *Hey, slow down, I can't keep up!* 야, 속도 좀 늦춰, 난 못 따라가겠어! **4** [I] to learn as fast or do as much as other people ‖ 다른 사람만큼 빨리 배우거나 많은 일을 하다: *Davey isn't keeping up with the rest of the class in reading.* 데이비는 읽기 수업에서 나머지 학생들을 따라가지 못한다. **5** [I] to continue to learn about a subject ‖ 한 분야를 계속해서 배우다: *It's hard to keep up on/with changes in computer technology.* 컴퓨터 기술의 변화를 따라가는 것은 어렵다. **6** [T **keep** sb **up**] to prevent someone from sleeping ‖ 사람을 잠들지 못하게 하다. (자지 않고)깨어 있게 하다: *The racket next door kept us up all night.* 옆집의 소음으로 우리는 밤새도록 잠을 못 잤다.

keep[2] *n* **1 earn your keep** to do a job in order to pay for the basic things you need such as food, clothing etc. ‖ 음식이나 옷 등의 기본적으로 필요한 것의 값을 치르기 위해 일을 하다. 생활비를 벌다 **2 for keeps** a phrase meaning always, used especially by children ‖ 특히 어린이가 쓰는 항상이라는 뜻의 어구

kee·ping /ˈkipɪŋ/ *n* [U] **1 for safe keeping** in order to avoid losing something ‖ 물건의 분실을 피하기 위해. 안전하게 보관하기 위해: *I'll put the tickets here for safe keeping.* 안전하게 보관하기 위해 표를 여기에 둘게. **2 in keeping/out of keeping** suitable or not suitable for a particular occasion or purpose ‖ 특정한 경우나 목적에 적합한 또는 적합하지 않은. (…과) 조화되어/어긋나서: *a silly joke out of keeping with the solemn occasion* 엄숙한 상황에 어울리지 않는 어리석은 농담

keep·sake /ˈkipseɪk/ *n* a small object

that reminds you of someone ‖ 남을 회상
시키는 작은 물건. 기념품. 유품

keg /kɛg/ *n* a large container with
curved sides and a flat top and bottom,
used for storing beer ‖ 맥주 저장에 쓰이
는, 옆은 곡선 모양이며 위와 밑바닥은 평
평한 모양의 큰 용기. (나무)통

ken·nel /'kɛnl/ *n* a place where dogs
are cared for while their owners are
away, or the CAGE where they sleep ‖ 개
의 주인이 떠나 있는 동안 개를 돌봐주는
곳, 또는 개가 잠자는 우리. 애완용 동물
보관소. 개집

kept /kɛpt/ *v* the past tense and PAST
PARTICIPLE of KEEP ‖ keep의 과거·과거 분
사형

ker·nel /'kɚnl/ *n* **1** the center part of a
nut or seed, usually the part you can
eat ‖ 대개 먹을 수 있는 부분인, 견과나 씨
앗의 중심 부분. (과실의) 인(仁). 종자.
낟알 **2** something that forms the most
important part of a statement, idea,
plan etc. ‖ 진술·아이디어·계획 등의 가장
중요한 부분을 형성하는 것. 핵심. 요점:
*There may be a kernel of truth in what
he says.* 그가 한 말에 진실의 핵심이 있을
지도 모른다.

ker·o·sene /'kɛrəˌsin, ˌkɛrə'sin/ *n* [U]
a type of oil that is burned for heat and
light ‖ 열과 빛을 내기 위하여 태우는 기름
의 한 종류. 등유. 등불용 석유

ketch·up /'kɛtʃəp, 'kæ-/ *n* [U] a thick
liquid made from TOMATO*es* ‖ 토마토로
만든 진한 액체. 케첩

ket·tle /'kɛtl/ *n* a metal container used
for boiling and pouring water ‖ 물을 끓
이고 붓는 데에 쓰이는 금속 용기. 솥. 주
전자

key¹ /ki/ *n* **1** a specially shaped piece of
metal that you put into a lock in order
to lock or unlock a door, start a car etc.
‖ 문을 잠그거나 열고 자동차의 시동 등을
걸기 위해 자물쇠에 꽂는 특수한 형태의
금속. 열쇠. 키 **2 the key** the part of a
plan, action, etc. that everything else
depends on ‖ 다른 모든 것이 걸려 있는
계획·조치 등의 부분. 비결. 실마리:
Exercise is the key to a healthy body.
운동은 건강한 신체의 비결이다. **3** the
part of a musical instrument or a
machine such as a computer that you
press with your fingers to make it work
‖ 악기나 컴퓨터 등의 기계를 작동시키기
위해 손가락으로 누르는 부분. 키. 건(鍵)
4 a set of seven musical notes that have
a particular base note, or the quality of
sound these notes have ‖ 특정한 기본 음
표를 가진 일련의 일곱 음표, 또는 이러한

음표가 가진 소리의 특성. (장단의) 조
(調). 으뜸음: *the key of G* 사조

key² *adj* very important and necessary
for success or to understand something
‖ 성공하거나 사물을 이해하는 데 매우 중
요하고 필수적인. 중요한. 중대한. 핵심적
인: *a key witness* 중요한 목격자

key³ *v*

key sth ↔ **in** *phr v* [T] to put
information into a computer by using a
KEYBOARD ‖ 키보드를 사용하여 컴퓨터에
정보를 입력하다

key·board /'kibɔrd/
n a row or several
rows of keys on a
machine such as
a computer, or a
musical instrument
such as a piano ‖ 컴퓨
터 등의 기계나 피아노
등의 악기에 있는 한
줄 또는 여러 줄의 키.
건반. 자판. 키보드

keyboard

keyed up /ˌ. './ *adj* worried or excited
‖ 걱정하거나 흥분한. 매우 긴장한: *We
were all very keyed up about the test.*
우리는 모두 그 시험에 대해 긴장했다.

key·hole /'kihoʊl/ *n* the hole in a lock
that you put a key in ‖ 열쇠를 꽂는 자물
쇠의 구멍. 열쇠 구멍

key·note /'kinoʊt/ *adj* **keynote
speaker/speech** the most important
speaker at an official event, or the
speech that s/he gives ‖ 공식 행사에서의
가장 중요한 연사 또는 그 연사가 하는 연
설. 기조 연사/연설

key ring /'. ./ *n* a metal ring that you
keep keys on ‖ 열쇠를 끼워 두는 금속 고
리. 열쇠 고리

kg. *n* the written abbreviation of
KILOGRAM ‖ kilogram의 약어

kha·ki /'kæki/ *n* [U] **1** a dull pale
green-brown or yellow-brown color ‖ 탁
하고 옅은 녹갈색 또는 황갈색. 카키색 **2**
cloth of this color, especially when worn
by soldiers ‖ 특히 군인이 입는 이 색깔의
옷. 카키색 옷[제복, 군복] **–khaki** *adj*

kha·kis /'kækiz/ *n* [plural] pants that
are made from KHAKI ‖ 카키색 옷감으로
만든 바지

kick¹ /kɪk/ *v* **1** [T] to hit something with
your foot ‖ 발로 사물을 차다. 걷어차다:
She kicked the pile of books over. 그녀
는 책더미를 발로 차서 넘어뜨렸다. / *Stop
kicking me!* 나를 차지 마! **2** [I, T] to
move your legs as if you are kicking
something ‖ 어떤 것을 차는 것처럼 다리
를 움직이다: *a baby kicking its legs* 발길

K

질 하는 아기 **3 kick the habit** to stop doing something, such as smoking, that is a harmful habit ‖ 해로운 습관인 흡연 등을 그만두다. 좋지 않은 습관을 버리다 **4 I could kick myself** SPOKEN said when you

are annoyed because you have made a mistake or missed an opportunity ‖ 실수를 하거나 기회를 놓쳐서 괴로울 때에 쓰여. 자책하다. …의 행동을 후회하다: *I could have kicked myself for saying that.* 나는 그런 말을 한 것을 후회했다. **5 kick the bucket** HUMOROUS to die ‖ 죽다. 뒈지다

kick around *phr v* [T] **1** [**kick sth ↔ around**] to think about something a lot or get people's opinions about it before making a decision ‖ 어떤 일에 대해 많이 생각하거나 결정을 내리기 전에 다른 사람들의 의견을 얻다. 숙고[토의]하다: *Doug's been kicking around an idea for the slogan.* 더그는 표어에 대해 심사숙고해 오고 있다. **2** [**kick sb ↔ around**] to treat someone badly or unfairly ‖ 남을 불친절하거나 부당하게 다루다. 사람을 가혹하게 다루다. 학대하다: *He won't be kicking me around anymore!* 그는 이제는 나에게 함부로 대하지 않을 거야!

kick back *phr v* [I] INFORMAL to relax ‖ 쉬다. 휴식을 취하다: *Here. Kick back and have a beer.* 이봐. 쉬면서 맥주 한잔 하지.

kick in *phr v* **1** [I] INFORMAL to begin to have an effect ‖ 효과가 나타나기 시작하다. 효과[기능]를 발휘하다. 듣다: *Those pills should kick in any time now.* 그 약은 지금쯤 효과를 발휘해야 된다. **2** [T **kick sth ↔ in**] to kick something so hard that it breaks ‖ 사물을 심하게 차서 부서지다. 밖에서 차 부수고 들어가다: *The police had to kick the door in.* 경찰은 문을 차 부수고 들어가야 했다.

kick off *phr v* [I,T **kick sth ↔ off**] INFORMAL to start, or to make an event start ‖ 시작하다. 또는 행사를 시작시키다. 개시하다: *The festivities will kick off with a barbecue dinner.* 그 축제는 바비큐 식사로 시작된다.

kick sb ↔ out *phr v* [T] INFORMAL to make someone leave a place ‖ 남을 자리에서 떠나게 하다. …을 쫓아내다. 해고[해임]하다

kick² *n* **1** an act of hitting something with your foot ‖ 물건을 발로 차는 행위.

걷어차기. 발길질: *If the gate won't open, just give it a good kick.* (=kick it hard) 정문이 열리지 않으면 그냥 세게 걷어차라. **2** INFORMAL a strong feeling of excitement or pleasure ‖ 흥분이나 즐거움의 강한 감정. 스릴. 쾌감. 자극: *Alan gets a real kick out of skiing.* 앨런은 스키에서 정말 짜릿한 흥분을 맛본다. / *She started stealing for kicks.* 그녀는 스릴을 느끼기 위해 도둑질을 시작했다. **3 be on a health/wine/swimming etc. kick** INFORMAL to have a new interest that you are very involved in ‖ 자신이 이제 막 관계하는 일에 새로운 관심을 가지다. 건강/포도주/수영에 열중하고 있다

kick·back /ˈkɪkbæk/ *n* [C, U] INFORMAL money that you pay secretly or dishonestly for someone's help; BRIBE ‖ 남의 도움을 바라고 은밀하거나 부정직하게 지불하는 돈. 뇌물; ⑳ bribe

kick·off /ˈkɪk-ɔf/ *n* [C, U] the time when a game of football starts, or the first kick that starts it ‖ 미식 축구 경기가 시작하는 때, 또는 경기를 시작하는 첫 번째 킥. 킥오프. 시합 개시[재개]: *Kickoff is at 3:00.* 축구 시합 시작은 3시이다.

kick-start /ˈ. ./ *v* [T] to start a MOTORCYCLE using your foot ‖ 발을 사용하여 오토바이의 시동을 걸다. 오토바이를 킥 스타트를 밟아 시동을 걸다

kid¹ /kɪd/ *n* **1** INFORMAL a child ‖ 아이. 어린이: *How many kids do you have?* 당신은 아이들이 몇이나 있습니까? **2** INFORMAL a young person ‖ 젊은이: *college kids* 대학생들 **3 kid stuff** INFORMAL something that is very easy or boring ‖ 아주 쉽거나 따분한 일. 어린 아이 같은 짓[언행]. 아주 간단한 일 **4** [C, U] a young goat, or the leather made from its skin ‖ 새끼 염소, 또는 새끼 염소 가죽

kid² *v* **-dded, -dding** INFORMAL **1** [I, T] to say something that is not true, especially as a joke ‖ 특히 농담으로 사실이 아닌 말을 하다. 농담하다. 놀리다: *Don't get mad, I was just kidding.* 화 내지 마, 난 그냥 농담한 거야. **2** [T] to make yourself believe something that is untrue or unlikely ‖ 사실이 아니거나 가능성이 없는 일을 자신에게 믿게 하다. 자신을 속이다: *Don't kid yourself; she'll never change.* 네 자신을 속이지 마라; 그녀는 결코 변하지 않을 거다. **3 no kidding** SPOKEN used in order to ask someone if what s/he says is true, or to show that you already know it is true ‖ 남에게 말하는 것이 사실인지를 묻거나, 또는 그 말이 사실이라고 이미 알고 있음

을 보여주는 데에 쓰여. 정말? 설마!: *"You lived in Baltimore? I did, too." "No kidding."* "너는 볼티모어에 살았다며? 나도 그랬는데." "농담 마."

kid³ *adj* **kid brother/sister** INFORMAL your brother or sister who is younger than you ‖ 자신보다 어린 남동생이나 여동생

kid·do /'kɪdoʊ/ *n* SPOKEN said when talking to a child or friend ‖ 어린이나 친구에게 말할 때에 쓰여. 어린이. 젊은이. 얘. 이봐. 어이: *Okay, kiddo, it's time to go.* 됐어, 얘야, 갈 시간이야.

kid·nap /'kɪdnæp/ *v* **-pped, -pping** [T] to take someone away illegally and demand money for returning him/her ‖ 남을 불법으로 데려가서 그 사람을 돌려주는 대가로 돈을 요구하다. 납치하다. 유괴하다 – **kidnapper** *n* – **kidnapping** *n* [C, U]

kid·ney /'kɪdni/ *n* one of the two organs in the body that separate waste liquid from blood and make URINE ‖ 혈액 속에서 노폐물을 걸러내어 오줌을 만드는 신체 내부의 두 기관 중의 하나. 신장

kidney bean /'.. ./ *n* a dark red bean, shaped like a KIDNEY ‖ 신장처럼 생긴 검붉은 콩. 강남콩

kid·ult /'kɪdʌlt/ *n* an adult who likes to play games or buy things that most people consider more suitable for children. This word comes from a combination of the words 'KID' and 'adult' ‖ 대부분의 사람들이 아이들에게 더 어울린다고 여기는 게임을 하거나 물건 사기를 좋아하는 성인으로 'kid'와 'adult'의 합성어. 키덜트. 어린이 취향의 성인

kill¹ /kɪl/ *v* **1** [I, T] to make a living thing die ‖ 생물을 죽게 하다. 죽이다. 살해하다. 사살[도살]하다: *First she killed her husband, then she killed herself.* 먼저 그녀는 자기의 남편을 죽인 뒤, 스스로 목숨을 끊었다. / *These chemicals can kill.* 이 화학 약품들은 생명을 해칠 수 있다. **2** [T] to make something stop, end, or finish ‖ 어떤 일을 그만두다[끝내다, 마치다]. …을 멈추다[없애다]: *Nothing that the doctor gives me kills the pain.* 의사가 내게 준 어떤 것도 통증을 없애지 못한다. **3 sb will kill sb** SPOKEN used in order to say that someone will get very angry at someone else ‖ 누군가가 다른 사람에게 아주 화를 낼 것이라고 말하는 데에 쓰여. …이 …을 죽이려 들다[죽일 듯이 화내다]: *My wife will kill me if I don't get home soon.* 내 아내는 내가 바로 귀가하지 않으면 나에게 무척 화를 낼 것이다. **4 sth is killing me** SPOKEN used in order to say that a part of your body is hurting a lot ‖ 신체 일부가 대단히 아프다는 것을 말하는 데에 쓰여. …이 몹시[죽을 듯이] 아프다: *My head is killing me.* 머리가 깨질듯이 아프다. **5 kill time** INFORMAL to do something that is not very interesting while you are waiting for something to happen ‖ 어떤 일이 발생하기를 기다리는 동안 별로 재미없는 일을 하다. 시간을 죽이다. 무의미한 시간을 보내다. 소일하다 **6 kill two birds with one stone** to achieve two things with one action ‖ 한 번의 행동으로 두 가지 일을 달성하다. 일석이조의 결과를 얻다

kill sb/sth ↔ off *phr v* [T] to cause the death of a lot of people, animals, or plants ‖ 많은 사람[동물, 식물]의 죽음을 야기하다. 전멸[절멸]시키다: *What killed off the dinosaurs?* 무엇이 공룡을 멸종시켰습니까?

kill² *n* [singular] an animal killed by another animal, especially for food ‖ 특히 먹이용으로, 다른 동물이 죽인 동물. 사냥감. 먹이감: *The lion dragged its kill into the bushes.* 그 사자는 먹잇감을 덤불 속으로 끌고 갔다.

kill·er¹ /'kɪlɚ/ *n* a person, animal, or thing that kills or has killed ‖ 죽이거나 죽여 온 사람[동물, 것]. 살인자. 도살자. 죽음에 이르게 하는 것: *The police are still looking for the girl's killer.* 경찰은 아직 그 소녀의 살인자를 찾고 있다. – **killer** *adj* : *a killer disease* 죽음에 이르게 하는 병

killer² *adj* SLANG extremely good, extremely difficult to deal with, extremely impressive etc. ‖ 매우 좋거나 다루기 매우 어렵거나 매우 인상적인 등. 환상적인. 끔짝 못하게 하는: *He's working a killer schedule.* 그는 매우 살인적인 일정을 수행하고 있다.

kill·ing /'kɪlɪŋ/ *n* **1** a murder ‖ 살인. 살해: *a series of brutal killings* 잔인한 연쇄 살인 **2 make a killing** INFORMAL to make a lot of money very quickly ‖ 많은 돈을 아주 빨리 벌다. 횡재[큰 벌이]하다

kiln /kɪln/ *n* a special OVEN for baking clay pots, bricks etc. ‖ 진흙 항아리·벽돌 등을 굽는 특수한 가마. 노(爐)

ki·lo /'kiloʊ, 'kɪ-/ *n* ⇨ KILOGRAM

ki·lo·byte /'kɪlə,baɪt/ *n* a unit for measuring computer information, equal to 1024 BYTE*s* ‖ 1024바이트에 상당하는 컴퓨터 정보를 측정하는 데에 쓰는 단위. 킬로바이트

kil·o·gram /'kɪlə,græm/ *n* a unit for measuring weight, equal to 1000 grams ‖ 1000그램에 상당한 무게의 측정 단위.

K

킬로그램
ki·lo·me·ter /kɪˈlɑmətɚ, ˈkɪləˌmitɚ/ *n* a unit for measuring length, equal to 1000 meters ‖ 1000미터에 상당한 길이의 측정 단위. 킬로미터

kil·o·watt /ˈkɪləˌwɑt/ *n* a unit for measuring electrical power, equal to 1000 WATTs ‖ 1000와트에 상당한 전력의 측정 단위. 킬로와트

kilt /kɪlt/ *n* a type of thick PLAID skirt, traditionally worn by Scottish men ‖ 스코틀랜드 남자들이 전통적으로 입는 두꺼운 격자무늬 스커트의 일종. 킬트

ki·mo·no /kəˈmoʊnoʊ/ *n* a loose piece of clothing with wide SLEEVES, traditionally worn in Japan ‖ 일본에서 전통적으로 입는 소매가 넓은 헐렁한 옷. 기모노

kin /kɪn/ *n* [plural] **1** next of kin FORMAL your most closely related family ‖ 자신과 가장 밀접하게 연관된 가족. 친척. 집안[일가] 사람 **2** OLD-FASHIONED your family ‖ 자신의 가족. 혈족. 인척. 일족

kind¹ /kaɪnd/ *n* **1** a type or sort of person or thing ‖ 사람이나 사물의 유형이나 종류: *What kind of pizza do you want?* 어떤 피자를 좋아하니? / *We sell all kinds of hats.* 우리는 모든 종류의 모자를 판다. **2** kind of SPOKEN **a)** slightly, or in some ways ‖ 약간 또는 다소. 어느 정도. 얼마간: *You must be kind of disappointed.* 너는 약간 실망한 게 틀림없구나. **b)** used when you are explaining something and want to avoid giving the details ‖ 사물을 설명하면서 상세한 정보 제공을 피하고 싶을 때에 쓰여. 거의 …하는 편인: *I kind of made it look like the post office had lost his letter.* 아무래도 그 우체국이 그의 편지를 잃어버린 것 같았다. **3** a kind of (a) SPOKEN used in order to say that your description of something is not exact ‖ 사물에 대한 자신의 묘사가 정확하지 않다고 말하는 데에 쓰여. 일종의 … 같은 것[사람]: *a reddish-brown color* 불그레한 갈색 비슷한 색깔 **4** of a kind of the same type ‖ 같은 종류의: *Each vase is handmade and is one of a kind.* (=the only one of its type) 각 꽃병은 수제품이고 한 가지 종류 뿐이다. **5** in kind by doing the same thing that has just been done to or for you ‖ 자신에게 또는 자신을 위해 행해진 바로 그 것과 같은 일을 함으로써. 같은 방법으로: *The US should respond in kind if other countries do not trade fairly.* 다른 나라가 무역을 공정하게 하지 않으면 미국은 똑같이 대해야 한다.

kind² *adj* helpful, friendly, and caring toward other people ‖ 다른 사람에게 도움을 주는·우호적인·배려하는. 친절한. 호의적인: *Thank you for your kind invitation.* 당신의 친절한 초대에 감사합니다. / *That was very kind of you.* 당신의 호의에 너무 감사했습니다. ✗DON'T SAY "That was very kindly"✗ "That was very kindly" 라고는 하지 않는다.

kind·a /ˈkaɪndə/ SPOKEN NONSTANDARD a short form of "kind of" ‖ "kind of" 의 단축형: *I'm kinda tired.* 나는 좀 피곤하다.

kin·der·gar·ten /ˈkɪndɚˌgɑrt̩n, -ˌgɑrdn/ *n* a class for young children, usually aged five, that prepares them for school ‖ 학교 갈 준비를 하는 보통 5세의 어린 아동을 위한 반. 유치원

kind-heart·ed /ˌ. ˈ..../ *adj* kind and generous ‖ 친절하고 관대한. 인정 많은. 마음씨 고운: *a kind-hearted woman* 마음씨가 고운 여자

kin·dle /ˈkɪndl/ *v* **1** [I, T] to start burning, or to make something start burning ‖ 타기 시작하다 또는 물체를 타기 시작하게 하다. 타다. 피우다. 때다. 점화하다: *They taught us how to kindle a fire.* 그들은 우리에게 불을 붙이는 법을 가르쳐 주었다. **2** kindle excitement/interest etc. to make someone excited, interested etc. ‖ 남을 흥분시키다·재미있게 하다 등. 흥분/관심을 자극하다[충동질하다]

kin·dling /ˈkɪndlɪŋ/ *n* [U] small pieces of dry wood, leaves etc. that you use for starting a fire ‖ 불을 일으키는 데에 쓰이는 마른 장작·잎 등의 작은 조각. 불쏘시개

kind·ly¹ /ˈkaɪndli/ *adv* **1** in a kind way; generously ‖ 친절하게; 관대히. 다정하게. 인정 있게: *Mr. Thomas has kindly offered to let us use his car.* 토마스 씨는 친절하게도 우리에게 자기 차를 사용하도록 제안했다. **2** SPOKEN a word meaning "please," often used when you are annoyed ‖ 괴로울 때에 가끔 쓰여 '제발'이라는 뜻의 단어. 제발. 미안하지만: *Would you kindly go away?* 미안하지만 가 주시겠습니까? **3** not take kindly to sth to be annoyed or upset by something that someone says or does ‖ 남이 말하거나 행동하는 것에 심란해지거나 기분 나빠지다. …을 자진해서[기꺼이] 받아들이지 않다: *He didn't take kindly to my remark about his brother.* 그는 자기 동생에 관한 내 말을 기분좋게 받아들이지 않았다.

kindly² *adj* kind and caring about other people; SYMPATHETIC ‖ 다른 사람에게 친

kitchen

Labels: cabinet, coffee maker, burner, food processor, stove, sink, dishrack, oven, dishwasher, freezer, refrigerator, broom, microwave

절하고 배려하는. 인정 있는; @
sympathetic: *a kindly woman* 친절한 여
자

kind·ness /'kaɪndnɪs/ *n* [C, U] kind
behavior, or a kind action ‖ 친절한 태도
나 친절한 행동. 다정함. 인정: *kindness
to animals* 동물에 대한 따뜻한 마음씨 /
*It would be a kindness to tell him the
truth.* 그에게 사실대로 말하는 것이 인지
상정(人之常情)이다.

kin·dred /'kɪndrɪd/ *adj* **a kindred
spirit** someone who thinks and feels the
way you do ‖ 생각과 느낌이 자신의 취향
과 같은 사람. 마음이 맞는 사람

kin·folk /'kɪnfoʊk/, **kinfolks** *n*
[plural] OLD-FASHIONED your family ‖ 자
신의 가족. 친척. 친족. 일족. 동족

king /kɪŋ/ *n* **1** a man from a royal
family who rules a country ‖ 나라를 다스
리는 왕족 출신의 남자. 왕. 국왕. 군주:
the King of Spain 스페인의 국왕 / *King
Edward* 에드워드 왕 **2** someone who is
considered to be the most important or
best member of a group ‖ 한 집단에서 가
장 중요하거나 뛰어나다고 생각되는 사람.
가장 대표적인 인물. 거물. …왕: *the
king of rock'n'roll* 로큰롤의 황제

king·dom /'kɪŋdəm/ *n* **1** a country
ruled by a king or queen ‖ 왕이나 여왕에
의해 통치되는 나라. 왕국 **2 the
animal/plant/mineral kingdom** one of
the three parts into which the natural
world is divided ‖ 자연계를 구분한 세 부
분 중의 하나. 동물/식물/광물계(界)

king·fish·er /'kɪŋˌfɪʃər/ *n* a small
brightly colored wild bird that eats fish
from rivers and lakes ‖ 강과 호수에서 물
고기를 잡아 먹는 작고 색깔이 밝은 야생
새. 물총새

king·pin /'kɪŋˌpɪn/ *n* the most
important person in an organized group
‖ 조직화된 집단에서 가장 중요한 사람.
중심 인물. 두목. 우두머리: *a drug
kingpin* 마약 밀매단 두목

king-size /'. ./, **king-sized** *adj* very
large, and usually the largest of its type
‖ 보통 같은 종류 중에서 가장 큰. 특대의:
a king-size bed 특대형 침대

kink /kɪŋk/ *n* **1** a twist in something
that is normally straight ‖ 보통 곧은 물
건의 꼬임. 얽힘. 비틀림: *The hose has a
kink in it.* 호스에는 꼬인 데가 있다. **2
work out the kinks** to solve all the
problems in a plan, situation etc. ‖ 계
획·상황 등의 모든 문제를 해결하다

kink·y /'kɪŋki/ *adj* INFORMAL **1** someone
who is kinky or who does kinky things
has strange ways of getting sexual
excitement ‖ 사람이 성적 흥분을 얻는 이
상한 방법을 가진. 변태적인. 비정상적인
2 kinky hair has very tight curls ‖ 머리털
이 매우 촘촘하게 구부러진. 곱슬곱슬한

ki·osk /'kiɑsk/ *n* a small building
where you can buy things such as
newspapers or tickets ‖ 신문이나 표 등의
물건을 팔 수 있는 작은 건물. 가판대. 매
점

kiss¹ /kɪs/ *v* **1** [I, T]
to touch someone
with your lips as a
greeting, or to show
love ‖ 인사나 애정의
표시로 남에게 입술을
맞추다. 입 맞추다. 키
스하다: *She kissed
me on the cheek.* 그녀
는 나의 뺨에 키스했다.
/ *Matt kissed her goodnight and left*

kiss

K

the room. 매트는 잘 자라고 키스하고 그녀 방을 나갔다. **2 kiss sth goodbye** SPOKEN used in order to say that someone will lose his/her chance to get or do something ‖ 남이 어떤 것을 얻거나 할 기회를 잃어버릴 거라고 말하는 데에 쓰여. …과는 끝나다[이별이다]: *If you don't work harder you can kiss medical school goodbye.* 더 열심히 공부하지 않으면 너는 의과대학과는 끝장이 될 수 있다.

kiss² *n* the action of touching someone with your lips as a greeting, or to show love ‖ 인사나 애정의 표시로 입술을 다른 사람에게 맞추는 행위. 입맞춤. 키스: *Come here and give me a kiss.* 이리 와서 나한테 키스해라.

kit /kɪt/ *n* **1** a set of tools, equipment etc. that you use for a particular purpose or activity ‖ 특정한 목적이나 행위에 쓰이는 한 세트의 도구·장비 등. 용구[부품](세트): *a first-aid kit* 구급용품(세트) **2** something that you buy in parts and put together yourself ‖ 부품으로 사서 스스로 조립하는 것. (모형 비행기 등의)조립용품 한 벌: *He made the model from a kit.* 그는 조립 세트로 모형을 만들었다.

kitch·en /'kɪtʃən/ *n* the room where you prepare and cook food ‖ 음식을 준비하고 조리하는 장소. 부엌

kite /kaɪt/ *n* a toy that you fly in the air on the end of a long string, made from a light frame covered in paper or plastic ‖ 가벼운 틀에 종이나 플라스틱을 씌워서 만들어 끝에 긴 끈을 달아 공중으로 날리는 장난감. 연

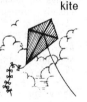

kite

kitsch /kɪtʃ/ *n* [U] kitsch decorations, movies etc. seem to be cheap and without style, and often amuse people because of this ‖ 장식·영화 등이 천박하고 스타일이 없어 보이며 종종 이러한 이유로 사람들을 즐겁게 해주는 것. 저속한[시시한] 예술. 천박하게 장식한 것 – **kitsch, kitschy** *adj*

kit·ten /'kɪt̮n/ *n* a young cat ‖ 새끼 고양이

kit·ty /'kɪt̮i/ *n* [C usually singular] **1** SPOKEN also **kittycat** a word meaning a cat, used by children or when calling to a cat ‖ 아이들이 고양이를 부를 때 쓰는 고양이라는 뜻의 단어. 새끼 고양이. 야옹이: *Here, kitty kitty!* 야옹아, 야옹아 이리 와! **2** INFORMAL the money that people have collected for a particular purpose

‖ 사람들이 특정 목적을 위해 모은 돈. 공동 적립금[출자금]

kitty-cor·ner /'.. ,../ *adv* INFORMAL on the opposite corner of a street from a particular place ‖ 특정 장소에서 길 반대편 모퉁이로. 대각선상에: *His store is kitty-corner from the bank.* 그의 가게는 은행에서 대각선상에 있다.

ki·wi /'kiwi/, **kiwi fruit** /'.. ./ *n* a soft green fruit with small black seeds and a thin brown skin ‖ 작고 검은 씨와 얇은 갈색 껍질이 있는 연질(軟質)의 녹색 과일. 키위

Kleen·ex /'klinɛks/ *n* [C, U] TRADEMARK a piece of soft thin paper, used especially for blowing your nose ‖ 특히 코를 풀 때에 쓰는 부드럽고 얇은 종이. 클리넥스. 화장지

klep·to·ma·ni·ac /,klɛptə'meɪni,æk/ *n* someone who has a mental illness in which s/he has an uncontrollable desire to steal things ‖ 물건을 훔치려는 욕망을 자제할 수 없는 정신적 질병이 있는 사람. 병적 도벽자

klutz /klʌts/ *n* INFORMAL someone who often drops things, falls easily etc. ‖ 무엇을 종종 떨어뜨리거나 잘 넘어지는 사람. 바보. 솜씨 없는 사람 – **klutzy** *adj*

km *n* the written abbreviation of KILOMETER ‖ kilometer의 약어

knack /næk/ *n* [singular] INFORMAL a natural ability to do something well ‖ 어떤 것을 잘 할 수 있는 천부적 재능. 요령: *Harry has the knack of making friends wherever he goes.* 해리는 어디를 가든지 친구를 사귀는 재능이 있다. —see usage note at ABILITY

knap·sack /'næpsæk/ *n* a bag that you carry on your back ‖ 등에 짊어질 수 있는 가방. 배낭

knead /nid/ *v* [T] to press a mixture of flour and water many times with your hands ‖ 밀가루와 물의 혼합물을 손으로 여러 번 짓누르다. 반죽하다. 섞어 이기다: *Knead the bread dough for three minutes.* 3분간 빵 만들 밀가루를 반죽하세요.

knee¹ /ni/ *n* **1** the joint that bends in the middle of your leg ‖ 다리 중간의 구부러지는 관절. 무릎 —see picture at BODY **2** the part of your pants that covers your knee ‖ 바지의 무릎을 덮는 부분. 무릎 부분: *His jeans had holes in both knees.* 그의 청바지 양 무릎에 구멍이 났다. **3 bring sb/sth to their knees a)** to defeat a country or group of people in a war ‖ 전쟁에서 국가나 사람들 집단을 패배시키다. 남을 굴복시키다 **b)** to have

K

such a bad effect on an organization, activity etc. that it cannot continue ‖ 조직·행위 등에 심한 악영향을 미쳐 그것이 지속할 수 없게 하다. …을 굴복[파탄]시키다

knee² v [T] to hit someone with your knee ‖ 무엇을 무릎으로 차다: *Victor kneed him in the stomach.* 빅터는 그의 배를 무릎으로 찼다.

knee·cap /'niːkæp/ n the bone at the front of your knee ‖ 무릎 앞쪽 뼈. 슬개골 (膝蓋骨). 종지뼈

knee-deep /ˌ. '.·/ adj 1 deep enough to reach your knees ‖ 무릎까지 닿을 만큼 깊은. 무릎까지 빠지는[깊이의]: *knee-deep in mud* 무릎 깊이까지 오는 진흙 2 INFORMAL greatly affected by something that you cannot avoid ‖ 피할 수 없는 어떤 것에 의해 크게 영향을 받은. (곤란 등에) 깊이 빠져든. 휩쓸린. 휘말린: *Ralph lost his job, and we ended up knee-deep in debt.* 랄프가 직장을 잃어서, 우리는 결국 빚에 쪼들리게 되었다.

knee-high /ˌ. '.·/ adj tall enough to reach your knees ‖ 무릎에 닿을 만큼 높은. 무릎까지 오는[높이의]: *knee-high grass* 무릎까지 오는 풀

knee-jerk /'. ./ adj DISAPPROVING relating to the reactions someone always has to particular questions or situations, without thinking about them first ‖ 어떤 사람이 특정 질문이나 상황에 대해 우선 생각하지 않고 항상 가지는 반응에 관련된. 무조건 반사하는: *a knee-jerk reaction* 무조건 반사 작용 / *a knee-jerk liberal* 무조건적인 자유주의자

kneel /niːl/, **kneel down** v **knelt** /nelt/ or **kneeled, knelt** or **kneeled, kneeling** [I] to be in or move into a position where your body is resting on your knees ‖ 몸이 무릎 위에 얹힌 자세로 있거나 그 자세로 들어가다. 무릎을 꿇다: *She knelt down on the floor to pray.* 그녀는 기도하기 위해 바닥에 무릎을 꿇었다. —see picture on page 947

knew /nuː/ v the past tense of KNOW ‖ know의 과거형

knick·ers /'nɪkəz/ n [plural] old-fashioned loose pants that are short and fit tightly at the knees ‖ 짧고 무릎에서 꽉 끼는 옛날에 유행한 헐렁한 반바지

knick-knack /'nɪk næk/ n INFORMAL a small object used as a decoration ‖ 장식으로 사용하는 작은 물체. 작은 장신구

knife¹ /naɪf/ n, plural **knives** a tool used for cutting or as a weapon, consisting of a metal blade attached to a handle ‖ 손잡이에 금속 날이 붙어 있는, 자르는 용도나 무기로 쓰이는 도구. 칼: *a knife and fork* 칼과 포크

knife² v [T] to STAB someone ‖ 사람을 찌르다. …을 칼로 찌르다[베다]: *They got into a fight, and Raul was knifed in the stomach.* 그들은 싸우기 시작했고, 라울은 배를 칼에 찔렸다.

knight¹ /naɪt/ n in the Middle Ages, a man with a high rank who fought while riding a horse ‖ 중세 시대에 말을 타며 싸운 지위가 높은 사람. 기사

knight² v [T] to give someone a KNIGHTHOOD ‖ 아무에게 기사 작위를 수여하다: *He was knighted in 1977.* 그는 1977년에 기사 작위를 수여받았다.

knight·hood /'naɪthʊd/ n [C, U] a special title or rank that is given to someone by the King or Queen in Britain ‖ 영국에서 왕이나 여왕이 어떤 사람에게 수여하는 특별한 직함이나 지위. 기사의 신분[작위]

knit /nɪt/ v **knitted** or **knit, knitted** or **knit, knitting** [I, T] 1 to make clothes out of YARN (=thick thread) using special sticks to weave or tie the stitches together ‖ 천을 한데 짜거나 엮기 위해 특별한 막대를 이용하여 두꺼운 실로 옷을 만들다. (털실·천을) 뜨다: *She's knitting me a sweater.* 그녀는 나에게 줄 스웨터를 짜고 있다. 2 to join people, things, or ideas more closely, or to be closely connected ‖ 사람[사물, 생각]을 보다 긴밀히 결합시키다 또는 빈틈없이 연결되다. 접합[밀착]하다[시키다]: *The broken bone should knit together smoothly.* 부러진 뼈는 부드럽게 접합시켜야 한다. / *a tightly knit family* 사이가 매우 돈독한 가족 3 **knit your brows** to show you are worried, thinking hard etc. by moving your EYEBROWS together ‖ 눈썹을 함께 움직여서 걱정하거나 힘들게 생각하고 있음을 보이다. 이맛살을 찌푸리다

knit·ting /'nɪtɪŋ/ n [U] something that is being KNITted ‖ 뜨개질하는 것. 뜨개질. 편물(제품): *Margaret keeps her knitting in a canvas bag.* 마가렛은 그녀의 편물을 캔버스 가방 안에 담아둔다.

knitting nee·dle /'.. ,../ n one of the two long sticks that you use to KNIT something ‖ 무엇을 뜨개질 할 때 사용하는 두 개의 긴 막대 중의 하나. 뜨개바늘 —see picture at NEEDLE¹

knit·wear /'nɪtwɛr/ n [U] knitted clothing ‖ 털실로 짠 의류. 니트웨어. 편물 의류: *a knitwear shop* 편물 의류점

knives /naɪvz/ n the plural of KNIFE ‖ knife의 복수형

K

knob /nɑb/ *n* a round handle that you turn or pull to open a door or drawer, turn on a radio etc. ‖ 문이나 서랍을 열기 위해 또는 라디오 등을 켜기 위해 돌리거나 당기는 둥근 손잡이

knob·by /'nɑbi/ *adj* with hard parts that stick out from under the surface of something ‖ 어떤 것의 표면 아래에서 불거져 나온 딱딱한 부분을 가진. 울퉁불퉁한. 혹 모양의: *knobby knees* 툭 불거진 무릎

knock

knock   knock over

knock¹ /nɑk/ *v* **1** [I] to hit a door or window with your closed hand in order to attract someone's attention ‖ 남의 주의를 끌기 위해 주먹을 쥐고서 문이나 창문을 치다. 똑똑 두드리다. 노크하다: *I've been knocking at/on the door for five minutes.* 나는 5분 동안 문을 두드리고 있었다. **2** [I, T] to hit someone or something with a quick hard hit, so that he, she, or it moves or falls down ‖ 사람이나 사물을 빠르고 강하게 쳐서 움직이거나 떨어지게 하다. 가격하다: *Don't knock my beer over.* 내 맥주 넘어뜨리지 마세요. / *Scott Payton got knocked down by a truck.* 스콧 페이턴은 트럭에 치였다. / *The ball was knocked loose, and Benjamin grabbed it.* 공이 약하게 맞아서 벤자민은 공을 잡았다. / *A car knocked into a pole in the parking lot.* 자동차가 주차장에 있는 지주대를 들이받았다. **3 knock sb unconscious** to hit someone so hard that s/he becomes unconscious ‖ 누가 의식을 잃을 만큼 세게 때리다. …을 때려 의식을 잃게 만들다

SPOKEN PHRASES

4 Knock it off! SPOKEN used in order to tell someone to stop doing something because it is annoying you ‖ 자신을 괴롭히므로 남에게 하는 짓을 그만두라고 말하는 데에 쓰여. 그만 둬. 조용히 해 **5** [T] to criticize someone or something ‖ 사람이나 사물을 비판하다. 트집잡다: *"I hate this job." "Don't knock it – lots of people would like to have it."* "나는 이 일이 싫어요." "트집

잡지 말아라. 많은 사람들은 이런 직업을 갖고 싶어 한단다." **6 knock some sense into sb** to make someone learn to behave in a more sensible way ‖ 누군가에게 보다 현명하게 행동하는 법을 배우게 하다. 교훈을 주다: *Maybe getting arrested will knock some sense into him.* 아마 그가 체포당해 보면 분별있는 행동을 하게 될 것이다. **7 knock on wood** an expression that is used after a statement about something good, in order to prevent your luck from becoming bad ‖ 좋은 일에 대해 얘기한 후 행운이 불운으로 변하는 것을 막기 위해 쓰이는 표현. 귀신은 물러가라: *I haven't had a cold all winter, knock on wood.* 나는 겨울 내내 감기에 걸리지 않았다, 귀신은 물러가라.

knock sth ↔ **back** *phr v* [T] to drink a large amount of alcohol very quickly ‖ 많은 양의 술을 매우 빨리 마시다. 죽 들이켜다: *We knocked back a bottle of tequila in an hour.* 우리는 한 시간 내에 데킬라 술 한 병을 단숨에 들이켰다.

knock sth ↔ **down** *phr v* [T] INFORMAL to reduce the price of something ‖ 어떤 것의 값을 내리다. 인하하다: *The new stove we bought was knocked down from $800 to $550.* 우리가 구입한 새 난로 가격이 800달러에서 550달러로 인하되었다.

knock off *phr v* INFORMAL **1** [I] to stop working ‖ 하는 일을 멈추다. 중지하다: *It's late; let's knock off for the day.* 늦었으니 오늘은 그만 합시다. **2** [T **knock** sth ↔ **off**] to reduce the price of something by a particular amount ‖ 특정 금액만큼 어떤 것의 가격을 내리다. …을 빼다[감하다]: *I got him to knock $10 off the regular price.* 나는 그에게 정가에서 10달러를 깎아 주도록 했다.

knock out *phr v* [T] **1** [**knock** sb ↔ **out**] to make someone become unconscious, especially by hitting him/her ‖ 특히 누군가를 때려서 의식을 잃게 하다. (…을) 기절시키다: *He knocked out his opponent in the fifth round.* 그는 5라운드에서 상대방을 케이오시켰다. **2** [**knock** sb/sth ↔ **out**] to defeat a person or team in a competition so that he, she, or it cannot continue to be in it ‖ 경기에서 다음 시합을 계속 할 수 없게 사람이나 팀을 패배시키다. …을 물리치다: *Indiana knocked Kentucky out of the tournament.* 인디애나는 토너먼트에서 켄터키를 탈락시켰다.

K

3 knock yourself out INFORMAL to work very hard ‖ 매우 열심히 일하다. 크게 노력하다[힘쓰다]: *I really knocked myself out to finish the essay on time.* 나는 제시간에 에세이를 끝마치려고 정말로 심혈을 기울였다.

knock sb/sth ↔ **over** *phr v* [T] to hit someone or something so hard that he, she, or it falls down ‖ 사람이나 물건을 넘어지도록 세게 때리다. 치어 넘어뜨리다. 쳐서 쓰러뜨리다: *Scott knocked the lamp over.* 스콧은 램프를 넘어뜨렸다.

knock sb ↔ **up** *phr v* [T] SLANG to make a woman PREGNANT ‖ 여자를 임신시키다

knock² *n* **1** the sound of something hard hitting a hard surface ‖ 딱딱한 표면을 세게 치는 어떤 소리. 노크하는 소리: *a loud knock at the door* 문을 두드리는 큰 소리 **2** the action of something hard hitting your body ‖ 신체를 세게 때리는 행위. 구타. 타격: *a knock on the head* 머리에 대한 가격 **3 take a knock** INFORMAL to have some bad luck or trouble ‖ 약간의 불운이나 어려움을 겪다. 타격을 입다: *Lee's taken quite a few hard knocks lately.* 리는 최근에 대단히 심각한 타격을 입었다.

knock·down-drag-out /ˌ...'. ./ *adj* using all kinds of methods to win, sometimes including violence ‖ 이기기 위해 때때로 폭력을 포함한 모든 종류의 방법을 사용하는. 가차 없는. 철저한: *a knockdown-drag-out election campaign* 이전투구(泥田鬪狗)의 선거 운동

knock·er /'nɑkɚ/ *n* a piece of metal on an outside door that you use to KNOCK loudly ‖ 크게 노크하기 위해 사용하는 문밖의 금속 조각. 문 두드리는 고리쇠

knock·on /'. ./ *adj* **have a knock-on effect** to start a process in which each part is directly influenced by the one before it ‖ 각 부분이 이전에 일어난 것에 직접 영향을 받는 과정이 일어나다. 연쇄 반응을 일으키다: *The price rises will have a knock-on effect throughout the economy.* 가격 상승은 경제 전반에 연쇄 효과를 가져올 것이다.

knock·out /'nɑk-aʊt/ *n* **1** an act of hitting your opponent so hard in BOXING that s/he cannot get up again ‖ 권투에서 상대방이 다시 일어날 수 없도록 매우 세게 치는 행위. 때려눕히기. 녹아웃. 케이오 **2** INFORMAL someone who is very attractive ‖ 매우 매력적인 사람. 매력덩어리. 멋진 사람[것]: *Barbara is a real knockout.* 바바라는 정말 매력덩어리이다.

knoll /noʊl/ *n* a small round hill ‖ 작고 둥근 언덕

knot¹ /nɑt/ *n* **1** a place where two ends or pieces of rope, string etc. have been tied together ‖ 밧줄·끈 등의 양 끝이나 두 조각을 서로 묶은 곳. 매듭: *Her Brownie troop is learning how to tie knots.* 그녀의 브라우니 단(團)은 매듭짓는 법을 배우고 있다. **2** many hairs, threads etc. that are twisted together ‖ 서로 엉킨 많은 머리카락·실 등. 엉클어짐 [얽힘]: *My hair always ends up in knots.* 내 머리카락은 결국엔 항상 엉킨다. **3** a unit for measuring the speed of a ship, equal to 6080 feet per hour or about 1853 meters per hour ‖ 시간당 6080피트나 대략 1853미터에 상당하는 배의 속도 측정 단위. 노트 **4** a hard round place in a piece of wood where a branch once joined the tree ‖ 한때 가지가 나무에 연결되어 있던, 재목의 딱딱하고 둥근 부위. 마디. 옹이 **5** a small group of people standing close together ‖ 서로 가깝게 서있는 소집단의 사람들. 무리. 떼 **6** a tight painful place in a muscle, or a tight uncomfortable feeling in your stomach ‖ 근육이 뭉치고 통증이 있는 부분, 또는 위가 답답하고 불편한 느낌. 혹. 결절. 뭉침. 엉킴: *My stomach is in knots.* 위가 엉킨 듯이 답답하다. **7 tie the knot** INFORMAL to get married ‖ 결혼하다

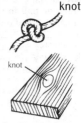
knot
knot

knot² *v* **-tted, -tting 1** [T] to tie together two ends or pieces of rope, string etc. ‖ 밧줄·끈 등의 양 끝이나 두 조각을 한데 묶다. (끈 등을) 매다. 매듭을 짓다 **2** [I, T] if hairs, threads etc. knot or something knots them, they become twisted together ‖ 머리카락·실 등이 함께 얽히다[얽히게 하다]

knot·ty /'nɑti/ *adj* **knotty wood** contains a lot of knots ‖ 나무에 많은 마디가 있는. 마디가 많은. 옹이투성이의

know¹ /noʊ/ *v* **knew, known, knowing**

1 ▶HAVE INFORMATION 정보를 가지다 ◀ [I, T] to have information about something ‖ 어떤 것에 대한 정보를 갖다. 알다. 알고 있다: *Do you know the answer?* 답을 알고 계신가요? / *She knows a lot about rare coins.* 그녀는 희귀한 동전에 대해 많이 안다. / *We don't know what we're supposed to be doing.* 우리는 우리가 해야 하는 것이 무엇인지 모른다. / *Martin didn't know that Ricky*

was coming. 마틴은 리키가 오고 있는 것을 몰랐다. / *He wants to know* (=wants to be told) *what happened.* 그는 무슨 일이 일어났는지 알고 싶어 한다.

2 ▶BE SURE 확신하다◀ [I, T] to be sure about something ‖ 어떤 것에 대해 확신하다: *I knew she didn't like him.* 나는 그녀가 그를 좋아하지 않는다고 확신했다. / *Barry didn't know what to say.* 베리는 무슨 말을 해야 할 지 몰랐다.

3 ▶BE FAMILIAR WITH …와 친숙하다◀ [T] to be familiar with a person, place, system etc. ‖ 사람·장소·체계 등에 친숙하다. …에 익숙하다. 잘 알다. 정통하다: *I knew Hilary in high school.* 나는 고등학교 때 힐러리를 알았다. / *She knew the city well because she grew up there.* 그녀는 그 도시에서 성장했기 때문에 그곳을 매우 잘 압니다. / *He said he'd like to get to know us better.* (=would like to know more about us) 그는 우리를 더 잘 알게 되기를 바란다고 말했다.

4 ▶REALIZE 깨닫다◀ [T] to realize or understand something ‖ 무엇을 깨닫거나 이해하다: *I don't think he knows how stupid he sounds.* 나는 그의 말이 얼마나 어리석게 들리는지 그가 알 거라고 생각하지 않는다. / *I know exactly how you feel!* 나는 너의 느낌이 어떠한지 정확히 안다.

5 ▶RECOGNIZE 인지하다◀ [T] to be able to recognize someone or something ‖ 사람이나 사물을 인지할 수 있다. 알아차리다: *She knew it was Gail by her voice.* (=she recognized Gail because of her voice) 그녀는 그 목소리로 게일임을 알았다.

6 know better to be old or experienced enough to avoid making mistakes ‖ 실수하는 것을 피할 만큼 충분히 나이 들거나 경험이 있다. (…할 정도로) 어리석지는 않다. 잘 알고 있다: *Ben should have known better than to tell his mother.* 벤은 그의 어머니에게 말 할 만큼 어리석지 않았어야 했다.

7 know your way around to be familiar with a place, organization, system etc. so that you can use it effectively ‖ 효율적으로 이용할 수 있을 만큼 장소·조직·체계 등에 익숙하다

8 know full well/know perfectly well used in order to emphasize that someone realizes or understands something ‖ 누군가가 어떤 것을 깨닫거나 이해하고 있음을 강조하는 데에 쓰여. 완벽하게[완전하게] 알다: *You know perfectly well what I mean.* 너는 내가 뜻하는 바를 매우 잘 안다.

— SPOKEN PHRASES —

9 you know a) said when you cannot quickly think of what to say next ‖ 다음에 무엇을 말해야 할지 빨리 생각나지 않을 때 쓰여. 그, 저. 음: *It has, you know, cherry pie filling.* 그것은 음, 체리 파이로 속이 꽉 차 있어. **b)** said when you are trying to explain something by giving more information ‖ 더 많은 정보를 제시하여 무엇을 설명하려고 할 때 쓰여. 다시 말해: *I have some clothes for Matthew, you know, for the baby, if Carrie wants them.* 만약 캐리가 옷을 얻기 바란다면, 나는 매튜를 위한, 다시 말해서 아기를 위한 옷을 몇 벌 갖고 있어. **c)** said when you begin talking about a subject ‖ 한 주제에 대해 말하기 시작할 때 쓰여. 아시다시피. 있잖아: *You know, I worked in Arizona before I came here.* 알다시피, 내가 여기에 오기 전에는 애리조나에서 일했어. **d)** said in order to check if someone understands what you are saying ‖ 자신이 말하고 있는 것을 다른 사람이 이해하는지 (여부를) 확인하는 데 쓰여: *I feel like New Mexico is really my home, you know?* 나는 뉴멕시코가 정말 내 고향같이 느껴져. 알지?

10 I know a) used in order to agree with someone ‖ 누군가와 의견을 같이 하는 데에 쓰여. 맞아: *"Trey's shoes are so ugly!" "I know, aren't they awful?"* "트레이의 신발은 정말 보기 흉해!" "맞아, 끔찍하지 않아?" **b)** said when you suddenly have an idea or think of the answer to a problem ‖ 갑자기 생각이 떠오를 때 또는 문제에 대한 답이 생각날 때 쓰여: *I know, let's ask Mr. McMillan for help.* 그렇지, 맥밀란 씨께 도움을 청하자.

11 as far as I know said when you think something is true, but you are not sure ‖ 확신하지는 않지만 어떤 것이 사실이라고 생각할 때 쓰여. 내가 아는 한. 내가 알기로는: *As far as I know, Gail left at 6:00.* 내가 아는 한 게일은 6시에 떠났어.

12 you never know used in order to say that you are not sure about what will happen ‖ 무엇이 일어날지 확신이 없음을 말하는 데에 쓰여. 아마도. 어쩌면: *You never know. You might be lucky and win!* 어쩌면 네가 운이 좋아서 이길지도 모르지!

—see also **how do you know** (HOW)
know of sb/sth *phr v* [T] **1** to have been

told about or have read about someone or something, but not know much about it ‖ 많이 알지는 못하지만 사람이나 사물에 대해 듣거나 읽어 왔다. …을 알고 있다 : *Do you know of any good restaurants around here?* 이 근처에 어디 좋은 식당 알고 있어요? **2 not that I know of** used in order to say that the answer to a question is "no," but that there may be other facts you do not know about ‖ 질문에 대한 대답은 "아니오"이지만, 자신이 알지 못하는 다른 사실이 있을지도 모른다고 말하는 데에 쓰여. 내가 아는 한 …은 아니다 : *"She was married before, wasn't she?" "Not that I know of."* "그녀는 전에 결혼했었지, 그렇지 않니?" "내가 아는 한, 결혼하지 않았어."

know² *n* **in the know** having a position in which you know more about something than most people ‖ 대부분의 사람들보다 무엇에 대해 더 잘 아는 위치를 가진. 사정에 밝은. 정통한 : *Those in the know say that gas prices will go up next month.* 사정에 밝은 사람들은 휘발유 가격이 다음달 상승할 것이라고 말한다.

know-how /'. ./ *n* [U] INFORMAL practical ability or skill ‖ 실제적인 능력이나 기술. 전문적 지식. 일의 요령

know·ing /'nouɪŋ/ *adj* showing that you know all about something ‖ 어떤 것에 대해 모두 알고 있음을 나타내는. 아는 체하는. 알고 있는 : *Glenn gave her a knowing look when she came in late.* 글렌은 그녀가 늦게 들어왔을 때 그녀에게 (무언가를) 알고 있다는 표정을 지었다.

know·ing·ly /'nouɪŋli/ *adv* **1** in a way that shows you know all about something ‖ 무엇에 대해 모두 알고 있음을 나타내는 식으로. 알고 있다는 듯이[아는 체하고]. 빈틈없이 : *Brenda smiled knowingly at me.* 브렌다는 나에게 알고 있다는 듯이 씩 웃었다. **2** deliberately ‖ 고의로 : *He'd never knowingly hurt you.* 그는 결코 일부러 네 기분을 상하게 하지는 않았어.

know-it-all /'..,./ *n* INFORMAL someone who behaves as if s/he knows everything ‖ 모든 것을 아는 듯 행동하는 사람. 아는 체하는 사람

K knowl·edge /'nɑlɪdʒ/ *n* [U] **1** the information and understanding that you have gained through learning or experience ‖ 배움이나 경험을 통해 얻은 정보나 이해. 지식 : *His knowledge of American history is impressive.* 미국 역사에 대한 그의 지식은 인상적이다. **2** what someone knows or has

information about ‖ 어떤 것에 대해 알거나 가진 정보. 알려진 것. 정보 : *To the best of my knowledge, none of the staff has complained.* (=I think this is true, although I may not have all the facts) 틀림없이 어떤 직원도 불평하지 않았다. / *The decision to attack was made without my knowledge.* (=without my knowing about it) 공격 결정은 내가 모르는 채 내려졌다. / *"Is she really leaving?" "Not to my knowledge."* (=I do not think this is true, based on what I know) "그녀가 정말 떠나나요?" "내가 아는 한 사실이 아닐 텐데요."

knowl·edge·a·ble /'nɑlɪdʒəbəl/ *adj* knowing a lot ‖ 많이 알고 있는. 지성이 있는. 총명한. 박식한 : *Steve's very knowledgeable about politics.* 스티브는 정치학에 대해 매우 박식하다.

known¹ /noʊn/ *v* the PAST PARTICIPLE of KNOW ‖ know의 과거 분사형

known² *adj* known about, especially by many people ‖ 특히 많은 사람들에게 어떤 것에 대해 알려져 있는. 알려진. 유명한 : *a known criminal* 소문난 범죄자

knuck·le¹ /'nʌkəl/ *n* one of the joints in your fingers ‖ 손가락 관절 중 하나. 손가락 마디[관절] —see picture at HAND¹

knuckle² *v*

knuckle down *phr v* [I] INFORMAL to suddenly start working hard ‖ 갑자기 일을 열심히 하기 시작하다. 열심히[힘차게] 하다 : *You just have to knuckle down and do it.* 너는 그저 열심히 그것을 해야 한다.

knuckle under *phr v* [I] INFORMAL to accept someone's authority or orders without wanting to ‖ 원하지 않지만 누군가의 권위나 명령을 받아들이다. …에 굴복하다 : *She refused to knuckle under to company regulations.* 그녀는 회사 규정에 따르는 것을 거부했다.

KO *n* the abbreviation of KNOCKOUT ‖ knockout의 약어

ko·a·la /koʊˈɑlə/, **koala bear** /.'.. ,./ *n* an Australian animal like a small bear that climbs trees and eats leaves ‖ 나무를 타고 나뭇잎을 먹는 작은 곰처럼 생긴 호주산 동물. 코알라

Ko·ran /kəˈræn, -ˈrɑn/ *n* **1 the Koran** the holy book of the Muslim religion ‖ 회교의 경전. 코란 **2** a copy of this book ‖ 이 책 한 권

Ko·re·an¹ /kəˈriən/ *adj* **1** relating to or coming from Korea ‖ 한국과 관련되거나 한국에서 온. 한국의. 한국 출신의 **2** relating to the Korean language ‖ 한국어와 관련된. 한국어의

Korean² *n* **1** [U] the language used in Korea ‖ 한국에서 쓰이는 언어. 한국어 **2** someone from Korea ‖ 한국 출신의 사람. 한국인

ko·sher /'koʊʃɚ/ *adj* **1** kosher food is prepared according to Jewish law ‖ 음식이 유대교의 율법에 따라 준비된. (음식이) 적법한 **2** kosher restaurants or stores sell food prepared in this way ‖ 식당이나 상점이 이러한 방식에 따라 준비된 식품을 파는. 정결한 식품을 파는 **3** INFORMAL honest and legal, or socially acceptable ‖ 정직한[합법적인, 사회적으로 용인되는]. 순수한. 정결한: *Are you sure their offer is kosher?* 그들의 제안이 합법적인 것이라고 확신하세요?

kow·tow /'kaʊtaʊ/ *v* [I] INFORMAL to be too eager to please or obey someone who has more power than you ‖ 자신보다 더 힘을 가진 사람을 지나치게 기쁘게 해주고 싶어 하거나 복종하려 하다. 비굴하게 아부하다: *Be polite, but don't kowtow to him.* 그에게 공손해라. 하지만 비굴하게 굴지는 말아라.

Krem·lin /'krɛmlɪn/ *n* **the Kremlin** the government of Russia and the former USSR, or the buildings that are this government's offices ‖ 러시아와 옛 소련 정부 또는 이 정부 청사. (옛) 소련 정부. 크렘린 궁전

KS the written abbreviation of Kansas ‖ Kansas(캔자스 주)의 약어

ku·dos /'kudoʊs, -doʊz/ *n* [U] admiration and respect that you get for being important or doing something important ‖ 중요해지거나 중요한 일을 해서 받는 칭찬과 존경. 영광·명성

kung fu /ˌkʌŋ 'fu/ *n* [U] a Chinese method of fighting in which you attack people with your feet and hands ‖ 발과 손으로 사람을 공격하는 중국의 격투 방법. 쿵후

kW *n* the written abbreviation of KILOWATT ‖ kilowatt의 약어

KY the written abbreviation of Kentucky ‖ Kentucky(켄터키 주)의 약어

L

L, l /εl/ **1** the twelfth letter of the English alphabet ‖ 영어 알파벳의 열두째 자 **2** the ROMAN NUMERAL (=number) for 50 ‖ 로마 숫자의 50

LA the written abbreviation of Louisiana ‖ Louisiana(루이지애나 주)의 약어

lab /læb/ *n* INFORMAL ⇨ LABORATORY

label[1] /'leɪbəl/ *n* **1** a piece of paper or cloth that is attached to something and has information about that thing printed on it ‖ 어떤 것에 대한 정보를 인쇄하여 그 위에 붙이는 종이나 천 조각. 라벨: *a label on a wine bottle* 포도주 병에 붙은 라벨 / *Always read the instructions on the label.* 라벨에 쓰인 지시 사항을 항상 읽으시오. **2** a famous name that represents the company that is selling a product ‖ 제품의 판매 회사를 대표하는 유명한 이름. 상표. 브랜드: *a clothing designer's label* 의상 디자이너의 상표 **3** a word or phrase that is used in order to describe someone or something ‖ 사람이나 사물을 묘사하는 데에 쓰는 단어나 어구. 칭호: *As a writer, he's proud of his "liberal" label.* 그는 작가로서 "자유주의자"라는 호칭을 자랑스러워 한다.

label

label[2] *v* [T] **1** to attach a LABEL to something, or to write information on something ‖ 어떤 것에 라벨을 부착하거나 그 위에 정보를 쓰다. 라벨을 붙이다: *Make sure your charts are clearly labeled.* 네 차트에 반드시 분명하게 라벨을 붙여라. **2** to use a particular word or phrase in order to describe someone ‖ 어떤 사람을 묘사하기 위해서 특정한 단어나 어구를 사용하다. 꼬리표를 달다. …고 부르다: *Teachers labeled the child a "slow learner."* 선생님들은 그 아이를 "지진아"로 분류했다.

la·bor[1] /'leɪbɚ/ *n* **1** [C, U] work, especially work using a lot of physical or mental effort ‖ 특히 육체적 또는 정신적 노력을 많이 하는 일. 노동. 노고. 노무. 일. 과업: *farm labor* 농장 일 / *manual labor* (=physical work) 육체노동 **2** [U] all the people who work in an industry or country ‖ 한 산업이나 국가에서 일하는 모든 사람들. 노동자: *The auto industry needs skilled labor.* (=trained workers) 자동차 업계는 숙련된 노동자가 필요하다. **3** [U] the process of a baby being born, or the period when this happens ‖ 아기가 태어나는 과정이나 이것이 발생하는 기간. 산고. 출산. 분만(시간): *Sandra was in labor for 17 hours.* 샌드라는 17시간 동안 산고를 겪었다.

labor[2] *v* **1** [I] to work very hard ‖ 매우 열심히 일하다. 노동하다: *farmers laboring in the fields* 들에서 열심히 일하는 농부들 **2** [I, T] to try to do something that is difficult ‖ 어려운 것을 하려고 시도하다. 노력[주력]하다. 애쓰다: *He labored over the report for hours.* 그는 몇 시간동안 그 보고서에 매달렸다.

lab·o·ra·to·ry /'læbrə,tɔri/ *n* a room or building in which a scientist does special tests and RESEARCH ‖ 과학자가 특별한 실험과 연구를 하는 방이나 건물. 실험실. 연구실[소]

labor camp /'.. ,./ *n* a place where prisoners are forced to do hard physical work ‖ 죄수들이 강제로 힘든 육체노동을 하는 곳. 강제 노동 수용소

Labor Day /'.. ,./ *n* a national holiday in the US and Canada on the first Monday in September, to show support for workers ‖ 9월 첫 번째 월요일에 노동자에 대한 성원을 나타내는, 미국과 캐나다의 국경일. 노동절

la·bor·er /'leɪbərɚ/ *n* someone whose job involves a lot of physical work ‖ 많은 육체노동을 필요로 하는 직업인. (육체)노동자. 인부

la·bo·ri·ous /lə'bɔriəs/ *adj* needing to be done slowly, and with a lot of effort ‖ 천천히 그리고 많은 노력을 들여 수행할 필요가 있는. 고된. 고심한. 공들인: *the laborious process of examining all the data* 모든 자료를 조사하는 고된 과정

labor u·nion /'.. ,./ *n* an organization that represents workers in a particular industry, usually to discuss wages and working conditions with employers ‖ 일반적으로 임금과 근로 조건에 대해 고용주와 협의하기 위한 특정한 업계의 근로자들을 대표하는 조직. 노동조합

Lab·ra·dor /'læbrə,dɔr/ *n* a large dog with black or yellow fur, often used for guiding blind people ‖ 종종 맹인 안내에 이용되는 검거나 노란 털을 가진 큰 개. 래

브라도(안내견)

lab·y·rinth /ˈlæbə,rɪnθ/ *n* ⇨ MAZE

lace¹ /leɪs/ *n* [U] a type of fine cloth with patterns of very small holes in it ‖ 아주 작은 구멍들이 무늬를 이루는 얇은 천의 일종. 레이스: *white lace on a wedding dress* 웨딩드레스에 단 하얀 레이스 —see also LACES

lace² *v* [T] also **lace up** to fasten clothes or shoes by tying their LACES ‖ 끈을 묶어서 옷이나 신발을 조이다. …을 끈으로 졸라매다. 묶다: *Paul laced up his boots.* 폴은 부츠의 끈을 졸라맸다.

lac·er·ate /ˈlæsə,reɪt/ *v* [T] to badly cut or tear the skin ‖ 피부를 심하게 베거나 찢다. 째다. 깊은 상처를 입히다 – **laceration** /,læsəˈreɪʃən/ *n*

lac·es /ˈleɪsɪz/ *n* [plural] strings that are pulled through special holes in clothing or shoes in order to fasten them ‖ 옷이나 신발을 동여매도록 특별히 마련된 구멍 사이로 조이는 줄. 끈 —see picture at SHOE¹

lack¹ /læk/ *n* [singular, U] the state of not having something or not having enough of something ‖ 어떤 것을 가지고 있지 않거나 충분히 가지고 있지 않은 상태. 부족. 결핍. 결여: *The project was canceled for lack of money.* (=because there was not enough) 그 프로젝트는 자금 부족으로 취소되었다. / *a total lack of interest* 전혀 흥미가 없음

lack² *v* [T] to not have something or enough of something ‖ 어떤 것을 가지고 있지 않거나 충분히 가지고 있지 않다. 부족하다. 모자라다: *Unfortunately, he lacks confidence.* 불행히도 그는 자신감이 없다.

lack·ing /ˈlækɪŋ/ *adj* **1 be lacking in** to not have enough of a particular thing or quality ‖ 특정한 것이나 성질을 충분히 가지고 있지 않다. 부족하다. 모자라다: *No one said she was lacking in determination.* 그녀가 결단력이 부족하다고 말하는 사람은 아무도 없었다. **2** not existing or available ‖ 존재하지 않거나 이용 가능하지 않은. …이 없는[빠진]: *Information about the cause of the crash was lacking.* 충돌의 원인에 대한 정보가 빠져있었다.

lack·lus·ter /ˈlæk,lʌstɚ/ *adj* not very exciting or impressive ‖ 아주 흥미롭거나 인상적이지 않은. 열의[활기]가 없는. 신통치 않은: *a lackluster performance* 맥빠진 공연

la·con·ic /ləˈkɑnɪk/ *adj* tending to use only a few words when you talk ‖ 말할 때 단지 몇 마디만을 사용하는 경향이 있

는. 말이 적은. 무뚝뚝한

lac·quer /ˈlækɚ/ *n* a clear substance painted on wood or metal to give it a hard shiny surface ‖ 표면을 견고하고 빛나게 만들기 위해 나무나 금속 위에 칠한 투명한 물질. 래커. 도료. (옻)칠 – **laquered** *adj* : *a lacquered box* 래커 칠을 한 상자

lac·y /ˈleɪsi/ *adj* decorated with LACE, or looking like lace ‖ 레이스로 장식한 또는 레이스처럼 보이는. 레이스 (모양)의: *black lacy underwear* 검은 레이스가 달린 속옷 / *lacy flowers* 레이스 모양의 꽃

lad /læd/ *n* OLD-FASHIONED a boy or young man ‖ 소년 또는 젊은이

lad·der /ˈlædɚ/ *n* **1** a piece of equipment used for climbing up to high places, consisting of two long BARs connected with RUNGs (=steps) ‖ 가로장으로 연결된 두 개의 긴 막대로 이루어진, 높은 장소에 오르기 위해

사용되는 장비. 사다리 **2** the jobs you have to do in an organization in order to gradually become more powerful or important ‖ 점점 더 막강해지거나 중요한 사람이 되기 위해서 한 조직 내에서 해야 하는 일들. (출세의)길[수단]. (지위의)단계: *Stevens worked his way to the top of the corporate ladder.* 스티븐스는 열심히 일해 회사의 최고 지위에 올랐다.

lad·en /ˈleɪdn/ *adj* carrying or loaded with a lot of something ‖ 어떤 것을 많이 지니거나 실은. (짐을) 적재한[지고 있는]. 시달리고 있는: *Grandma walked in, laden with presents.* 할머니는 선물을 들고 걸어 들어오셨다.

la·dies' room /ˈ.. ,./ *n* a room in a public building with toilets for women ‖ 여성용 변기가 있는 공공건물 안의 공간. 여자 화장실 —see usage note at TOILET

la·dle /ˈleɪdl/ *n* a deep spoon with a long handle ‖ 긴 손잡이가 있는 움푹한 수저 모양의 것. 국자 – **ladle** *v* [T]: *ladling soup into bowls* 수프를 국자로 그릇에 떠 담기

la·dy /ˈleɪdi/ *n* **1** a word meaning a woman, used in order to be polite ‖ 정중하게 사용되는 여자를 뜻하는 단어. 숙녀. 부인: *Good afternoon, ladies.* 숙녀 여러분, 안녕하세요. / *a sweet old lady* 상냥한 노부인 **2** SPOKEN OFFENSIVE said when talking to a woman you do not know ‖ 모르는 여자에게 말할 때에 쓰여. 아줌마: *Hey, lady, get out of the way!* 이봐요 아

줌마, 저리 비켜요!

la·dy·bug /ˈleɪdiˌbʌg/ *n* a small round BEETLE (=insect) that is red with black spots ‖ 검은 점이 있는 작고 둥글며 빨간 딱정벌레. 무당벌레

lag¹ /læg/ *v* **-gged, -gging** [I] **lag behind** to move or develop more slowly than other things or people ‖ 다른 사물이나 사람보다 더 천천히 움직이거나 발전하다. 뒤처지다. 뒤떨어지다: *Many small firms are lagging behind their larger rivals.* 많은 소규모 회사들이 자신들보다 큰 경쟁 업체들에게 뒤처지고 있다.

lag² *n* a delay between two events ‖ 두 사건들 사이의 지연. 지연. 지체 —see also JET LAG

la·goon /ləˈgun/ *n* an area of ocean that is not very deep, and is nearly separated from the ocean by rocks, sand, or CORAL ‖ 아주 깊지는 않으며 바위[모래, 산호]로 바다에서 거의 분리된 바다의 한 지역. 석호. 초호

laid /leɪd/ *v* the past tense and PAST PARTICIPLE of LAY ‖ lay의 과거·과거 분사형

laid-back /ˌ. ˈ./ *adj* relaxed and not seeming to worry about anything ‖ 긴장을 풀고서 어떤 것도 걱정하지 않는 듯한. 마음 편한. 느긋한: *He's easy to talk to, and very laid-back.* 그는 말하기가 쉽고 편한 사람이다.

lain /leɪn/ *v* the PAST PARTICIPLE of LIE ‖ lie의 과거 분사형

lair /lɛr/ *n* the place where a wild animal hides and sleeps ‖ 야생 동물이 숨거나 잠자는 장소. 굴: *a wolf's lair* 늑대굴

lake /leɪk/ *n* a large area of water surrounded by land ‖ 육지로 둘러싸인 물이 괴인 큰 지역. 호수. …호: *We're going swimming in the lake.* 우리는 호수로 수영하러 갈 거야. / *Lake Michigan* 미시간 호

lamb /læm/ *n* [C, U] a young sheep, or the meat of a young sheep ‖ 어린 양, 또는 어린 양의 고기 —see usage note at MEAT

lam·bast /læmˈbeɪst, ˈlæmbeɪst/ *v* [T] to severely criticize someone or something ‖ 사람이나 사물을 심하게 비판하다. 몹시 꾸짖다. 혹평하다: *The governor lambasted state workers for wasting money.* 주지사는 돈을 낭비한다고 주 공무원들을 몹시 질책했다.

lame¹ /leɪm/ *adj* **1** unable to walk easily because your leg or foot is injured ‖ 다리나 발을 다쳐서 쉽게 걸을 수 없는. 다리를 저는. 절름발이의 **2** INFORMAL too silly or stupid to believe ‖ 믿기에는 너무 우습거

나 어리석은. 설득력이 없는. 어설픈: *a lame excuse* 설득력이 없는 변명

lame² *v* [T] to make a person or animal LAME ‖ 사람이나 동물을 다리를 절게 하다

lame duck /ˌ. ˈ./ *n* someone in an official position, such as a president, who is powerless because his/her period in office will soon end ‖ 임기가 곧 끝나기 때문에 대통령 등의 공직에 무력하게 있는 사람. (임기가 남아 있는)낙선 의원[대통령]

la·ment¹ /ləˈmɛnt/ *v* [I, T] to express feelings of great sadness or disappointment about something ‖ 어떤 일에 대한 큰 슬픔이나 실망감을 표현하다. …을 슬퍼하다. 비탄[후회]하다

lament² *n* something such as a song that expresses great sadness ‖ 큰 슬픔을 표현하는 노래 등의 것. 애가. 만가. 비가

lam·en·ta·ble /ləˈmɛntəbəl/ *adj* very disappointing ‖ 매우 실망스러운. 통탄[한탄]할. 형편없는: *her lamentable performance at the tennis match* 그녀가 테니스 시합에서 보여 준 형편없는 모습

lam·i·nate /ˈlæməˌneɪt/ *v* [T] to cover paper or wood with a thin layer of plastic in order to protect it ‖ 종이나 나무를 보호하기 위해서 얇은 비닐 층으로 덮다. 박층[박판]을 씌우다 – **laminated** *adj*

lamp

lamp   desk lamp

gas lamp   light bulb   floor lamp

lamp /læmp/ *n* an object that produces light by using electricity, oil, or gas ‖ 전기[기름, 가스]를 이용해서 빛을 내는 물체. 등: *a desk lamp* 책상 등

lam·poon /læmˈpun/ *v* [T] to write about someone such as a politician in a funny way that makes him/her seem stupid ‖ 정치인 등을 어리석어 보이게 하려고 재미있게 글을 쓰다. 놀리다. 빈정거리다. 풍자하다 – **lampoon** *n*

lamp·shade /ˈlæmpˌʃeɪd/ *n* a decorative

cover put over the top of a lamp in order to make the light less bright ‖ 빛을 덜 밝게 하려고 등의 꼭대기에 얹은 장식용 덮개. 전등갓

lance /læns/ *n* a long thin pointed weapon used in past times by soldiers on horses ‖ 말을 탄 군인들이 과거에 사용한 길고 가늘며 끝이 뾰족한 무기. 창

land¹ /lænd/ *n* **1** [U] the ground, especially when owned by someone and used for buildings or farming ‖ 특히 어떤 사람이 소유한 건물이나 농사용으로 사용되는 땅. 토지: *A mall is being built on the land near the lake.* 쇼핑센터가 호수 근처의 부지에 건축되고 있다. / *5000 acres of agricultural land* 5000에이커의 농지 **2** [U] the solid dry part of the Earth's surface ‖ 지구 표면의 단단하고 마른 부분. 뭍. 육지: *Frogs live on land and in the water.* 개구리는 수륙에서 서식한다. **3** LITERARY a country or place, especially one with a particular quality ‖ 특히 특정한 성질을 가진 나라나 장소. 지역. 나라: *a faraway land* 먼 나라 —see usage note at EARTH

land² *v* **1** [I, T] if a plane lands, or if a pilot lands a plane, the plane moves down until it is safely on the ground ‖ 비행기가, 또는 조종사가 비행기를, 안전하게 도달할 때까지 하강하다[시키다]. 착륙[상륙]하다[시키다]: *My flight landed in Chicago an hour late.* 내가 탄 비행기가 한 시간 늦게 시카고에 착륙했다. **2** [I] to fall or come down onto something after moving through the air ‖ 공중에서 움직인 후에 어떤 것 위에 떨어지거나 내려앉다. 떨어지다: *Chris slipped and landed on his back.* 크리스는 미끄러져서 뒤로 넘어졌다. **3** [I] to arrive somewhere in a boat, plane etc. ‖ 배·비행기 등으로 어딘가에 도착하다. …에 닿다. 상륙[착륙]하다: *The Pilgrims landed on Cape Cod in 1620.* 최초의 이주자들은 1620년에 케이프 코드 반도에 상륙했다. **4** [T] to put someone or something on land from a plane or boat ‖ 사람이나 사물을 비행기나 배에서 육지에 내려 놓다. 하선시키다: *They landed 1200 troops on the beach.* 그들은 1200명의 군대를 해변에 상륙시켰다. **5** [T] INFORMAL to finally succeed in getting a particular job, contract, or deal ‖ 마침내 특정한 일자리[계약, 거래]를 얻는 데 성공하다. 획득하다: *Kelly's landed a job with a big law firm.* 켈리는 큰 법률 회사에 취직하게 되었다.

land·fill /'lændfɪl/ *n* a place where waste is buried in large amounts ‖ 쓰레기가 대량으로 묻히는 곳. 쓰레기 매립지

land·ing /'lændɪŋ/ *n* **1** the floor at the top of a set of stairs ‖ 이어진 계단 꼭대기의 평평한 곳. 층계참 **2** the action of arriving on land, or of making something such as a plane or boat come onto land ‖ 육지에 도착하거나 비행기나 배 등을 육지에 도달하게 하는 행위. 상륙. 착륙. 착수 —compare TAKEOFF

landing gear /'.. ,./ *n* [U] an aircraft's wheels and wheel supports ‖ 항공기의 바퀴와 바퀴 지지대. 착륙[착수]장치 —see picture at AIRPLANE

landing pad /'.. ,./ *n* the area where a HELICOPTER comes down to earth ‖ 헬리콥터가 지상에 착륙하는 구역. 착륙장

landing strip /'.. ,./ *n* a special road on which a plane lands, especially not at an airport ‖ 특히 공항이 아닌 곳에서 비행기가 착륙하는 특별한 도로. 활주로 —compare RUNWAY

land·la·dy /'lænd,leɪdi/ *n* a woman who owns a building or other property and rents it to people ‖ 건물이나 다른 부동산을 소유하고 그것을 사람들에게 임대하는 여자. 안[여]주인. 여자 지주[집주인]

land·locked /'lændlɑkt/ *adj* surrounded by land ‖ 육지에 둘러싸인. 바다와 접해 있지 않은: *a landlocked country* 내륙국

land·lord /'lændlɔrd/ *n* someone who owns a building or other property and rents it to other people ‖ 건물이나 다른 부동산을 소유하고 그것을 다른 사람들에게 임대하는 사람. 건물주. 지주

land·mark /'lændmɑrk/ *n* **1** something that helps you recognize where you are, such as a famous building ‖ 현재 위치를 인식할 수 있게 도와주는 유명한 건물 등의 것. (주요) 표지물[장소] **2** one of the most important events, changes, or discoveries that influences someone or something ‖ 사람이나 사물에 영향을 미친 가장 중요한 사건[변화, 발견] 중의 하나. 획기적인 사건: *a scientific landmark* 과학상의 획기적인 대 발견

land·own·er /'lænd,oʊnɚ/ *n* someone who owns a large amount of land ‖ 거대한 크기의 토지를 소유한 사람. 지주

land·scape¹ /'lændskeɪp/ *n* **1** a view across an area of land, including hills, forests, fields etc. ‖ 언덕·숲·들 등을 포함하는 일정한 지역을 망라하는 경치. 경관. 풍경: *the sandy landscape of the desert* 사막의 모래벌판 풍경 —compare SCENERY **2** a photograph or painting of a landscape ‖ 풍경의 사진이나 그림. 풍경

화[사진]. 산수화

landscape² *v* [T] to arrange where the plants should grow in a park, yard, or garden ‖ 공원·뜰·정원에서 식물이 자라는 구역을 배열하다. 조경하다

land·slide /ˈlændˌslaɪd/ *n* **1** the sudden falling of a lot of soil and rocks down the side of a hill, cliff, or mountain ‖ 많은 흙과 바위가 언덕[절벽, 산]사면 아래로 갑작스럽게 떨어짐. 산사태: *Part of Highway 101 is blocked by a landslide.* 101번 고속도로의 일부가 산사태로 막혀 있다. **2** a victory in which a person or political party wins a lot more votes than the others in an election ‖ 선거에서 한 사람이나 정당이 다른 사람이나 정당보다 훨씬 많이 득표하는 승리. 압승: *Reagan won by a landslide in 1984.* 레이건은 1984년 선거에서 압도적으로 승리했다.

lane /leɪn/ *n* **1** one of the parts of a main road that is divided by painted lines ‖ 페인트 선으로 분할된 대로의 여러 부분 중의 하나. 차선: *driving in the fast/slow lane* (=in the lane that is farthest left or farthest right) 고속[저속용] 차선에서의 운전 **2** a narrow country road ‖ 좁은 시골길 **3** one of the narrow areas that a pool or race track is divided into ‖ 수영장이나 경주 트랙의 분할된 좁은 영역 중의 하나. 레인

lan·guage /ˈlæŋgwɪdʒ/ *n* **1** a system of speaking, and usually writing, used by people in one country or area ‖ 한 나라나 지역의 사람들이 사용하는 말과 보통은 글의 체계. 국어. …어: *the English language* 영어 / *"Do you speak any foreign languages?" "Yes, I speak French."* "외국어 말할 줄 아는 것 있어요?" "네, 불어를 할 줄 압니다." **✗**DON'T SAY "I speak French language."**✗** "I speak French language." 라고는 하지 않는다. **2** [U] the system of written and SPOKEN words that people use to communicate ‖ 사람들이 의사소통할 때 사용하는 글과 말의 체계. 언어. 말: *language skills* 언어 능력 **3** [C, U] TECHNICAL a system of commands and instructions used for operating a computer ‖ 컴퓨터를 작동할 때 사용하는 명령·지시 체계. 컴퓨터 언어 **4** [C, U] the way that something such as poetry or music expresses feelings ‖ 시나 음악 등에서 감정을 표현하는 방식. 문체. 말투 **5** [U] INFORMAL words and phrases that most people consider to be OFFENSIVE; swearing ‖ 대부분의 사람들이 불쾌하게 여기는 단어·어구. 상스러운 말. 욕; 욕

설: *Watch your language!* (=stop swearing!) 욕 좀 그만해라!

language lab·o·ra·to·ry /ˈ.. ˌ..../ *n* a room in a school or college where students can listen to TAPEs of a foreign language and practice speaking it ‖ 학교나 대학에서 학생들이 외국어 테이프를 듣고 말하는 것을 연습할 수 있는 교실. 어학 실습실

lan·guid /ˈlæŋgwɪd/ *adj* moving slowly and weakly, but in an attractive way ‖ 천천히·힘없이 움직이지만 매력적인 모습인. 나른한. 노곤한. 맥 없는 – **languorous** /ˈlæŋgərəs/ *adj* —compare LISTLESS

lan·guish /ˈlæŋgwɪʃ/ *v* [I] to be prevented from developing, improving, or being dealt with ‖ 발전[개선, 처리]되지 않고 막히다. 활기를 잃다. 쇠약해지다: *a case that has languished for years in the courts* 법원에서 몇 년간 질질 끌려온 한 사건

lank·y /ˈlæŋki/ *adj* someone who is lanky is very tall and thin ‖ 사람이 키가 매우 크고 마른. 빼빼마른. 호리호리한

lan·tern /ˈlæntən/ *n* a type of lamp you can carry, that usually has a metal frame and glass sides ‖ 보통 금속 틀에 옆면들은 유리로 된, 휴대 가능한 일종의 등. 랜턴. 제등(提燈). 초롱

lap¹ /læp/ *n* **1** the upper part of your legs when you are sitting down ‖ 앉아 있을 때 다리의 윗부분. 무릎: *sitting on Grandma's comfortable lap* 할머니의 편안한 무릎 위에 앉기 **2** a single trip around a race track or between the two ends of a pool ‖ 육상 트랙의 둘레나 수영장의 양 끝 사이를 한 번 돌기. 한 바퀴: *Patty swims 30 laps a day.* 패티는 하루에 30번 왕복 수영한다.

lap² *v* **-pped, -pping 1** [I, T] if water laps something or laps against something, it touches something with small waves ‖ 물이 어떤 것을 작은 파도로 치다. …을 찰싹찰싹 치다. …에 철썩 철썩 부딪치다: *the sound of the lake lapping against the shore* 호숫가에 철썩철썩 부딪치는 호수의 (물결)소리 **2** [T] also **lap up** to drink using quick movements of the tongue ‖ 혀를 빨리 움직여 마시다. 핥아먹다: *a cat lapping milk* 우유를 핥아먹는 고양이

lap sth ↔ **up** *phr v* [T] DISAPPROVING to enjoy or believe something without criticizing or doubting it at all ‖ 전혀 비판하거나 의심하지 않고 무엇을 즐기거나 믿다. 곧이곧대로[열심히] 듣다: *She's flattering him and he's just lapping it* *up*! 그녀가 그에게 아첨을 하고 있는 건데 그는 그것을 곧이 곧대로 듣고 있네!

la·pel /ləˈpɛl/ *n* the front part of a coat or JACKET that is attached to the collar and folds back on both sides ‖ 옷깃에 부착되어서 뒤로 접힌 외투나 재킷의 양쪽 앞부분. (양복 상의의) 접은 깃

lapse¹ /læps/ *n* **1** a short period of time when you forget something, do not pay attention, or fail to do something you should ‖ 어떤 것을 잊는[주의를 기울이지 않는, 해야 할 것을 하지 못하는] 짧은 기간. 일순간의 잘못[과실, 실수]: *a memory lapse* 기억 착오 **2** the period of time between two events ‖ 두 사건 사이의 기간. 경과. 추이: *a lapse of 5 years* 5년의 경과

lapse² *v* [I] to end, especially because an agreed time limit is finished ‖ 특히 합의된 시간 제한이 완료되어 끝나다. 실효[소멸]하다: *a book on which the copyright has lapsed* 저작권이 실효된 책

lapse into sth *phr v* [T] **1** to start behaving or speaking in a very different way, especially one that is more normal or usual for you ‖ 특히 자신에게는 보다 정상적이거나 일상적이지만 아주 특이하게 행동하거나 말하기 시작하다. (자연스럽게) …하게 되다: *Without thinking, he lapsed into French.* 그는 생각하지 않고 바로 불어로 말하기 시작했다. **2** to become very quiet, less active, or unconscious ‖ 매우 조용해지다[덜 활동적이 되다, 의식을 잃게 되다]. (어떤 상태로)빠지다[들어가다, 되다]: *She lapsed into silence.* 그녀는 침묵 속에 빠졌다. / *a country lapsing back into recession* 다시 경기 침체 국면으로 빠져드는 국가

lap·top /ˈlæptɑp/ *n* a small computer that you can carry with you ‖ 가지고 다닐 수 있는 작은 컴퓨터. 휴대용 컴퓨터. 노트북

lar·ce·ny /ˈlɑrsəni/ *n* [C, U] LAW the action or crime of stealing something ‖ 물건을 훔치는 행위나 범죄. 절도(죄)

larch /lɑrtʃ/ *n* [C, U] a tree with bright green leaves shaped like needles that fall off in winter ‖ 겨울에 떨어지는 바늘 모양의 연녹색 잎을 가진 나무. 낙엽송

lard /lɑrd/ *n* [U] the thick white fat from pigs, used in cooking ‖ 요리에 쓰이는 진득하고 하얀 돼지 지방. 비계(를 정제한 기름)

large /lɑrdʒ/ *adj* **1** big, or bigger than usual in size, number, or amount ‖ 크기[수, 양]에서 보통의 것보다 크거나 더 큰. 큰. 거대한: *I'd like a large pepperoni pizza, please.* 페퍼로니 피자 큰 사이즈로

하나 주세요. / *What's the largest city in Canada?* 캐나다에서 가장 큰 도시는 어느 도시입니까? —opposite SMALL, —see usage note at BIG **2 at large** in general ‖ 일반적으로. 전반[전체]적으로: *The risk is to American society at large.* 위험은 미국 사회 전반에 있다. **3 be at large** to not yet be caught by the police ‖ 아직 경찰에 잡히지 않다. 자유롭다. 도피 중이다: *Police say the murderer is still at large.* 경찰은 그 살인자가 아직 도피 중이라고 말한다. **4 larger than life** more attractive, exciting, or interesting than other people or things ‖ 다른 사람이나 사물보다 더 매력적이고 재미있거나 또는 흥미 있는. 과장된 **5 by and large** used in order to say that something is generally true or usually happens, but not always ‖ 어떤 일이 일반적으로 사실이거나 대체로 발생하지만 항상 그러한 것은 아님을 말하는 데에 쓰여. 전반적으로. 대체로: *By and large, the decisions are all made by the students.* 대체로 그 결정들은 모두 학생들에 의해 이루어진다. —**largeness** *n* [U]

large·ly /ˈlɑrdʒli/ *adv* mostly or mainly ‖ 대부분. 주로. 대개: *The delay was largely due to bad weather.* 주로 악천후 때문에 지연되었다.

large-scale /ˌ. ˈ./ *adj* involving a lot of people, effort, money, supplies etc. ‖ 많은 사람들·노력·돈·물품 등을 포함하는. 광범위한. 대규모의: *large-scale unemployment* 대규모의 실업

lark /lɑrk/ *n* a small wild brown bird that sings and has long pointed wings ‖ 노래를 부르며 길고 뾰족한 날개를 가진 야생의 작은 갈색 새. 종달새

lar·va /ˈlɑrvə/ *n, plural* **larvae** /ˈlɑrvi/ a young insect with a soft tube-shaped body, that will become an insect with wings ‖ 날개가 있는 곤충이 될, 물컹거리는 관 모양의 몸을 가진 어린 곤충. 유충. 애벌레

lar·yn·gi·tis /ˌlærənˈdʒaɪtɪs/ *n* [U] an illness in which your throat and LARYNX are swollen, making it difficult for you to talk ‖ 목구멍과 후두가 부어올라 말하기 힘들게 만드는 질병. 후두염

lar·ynx /ˈlærɪŋks/ *n* TECHNICAL the part of your throat from which your voice is produced ‖ 목소리가 발성되는 목구멍의 부위. 후두

las·civ·i·ous /ləˈsɪviəs/ *adj* DISAPPROVING showing a very strong sexual desire ‖ 아주 강한 성적인 욕구를 보이는. 음탕한. 호색적인

la·ser /ˈleɪzɚ/ *n* a piece of equipment

that produces a powerful narrow beam of light, or the beam of light itself ‖ 강력한 가는 광선을 방출하는 장비 또는 광선 그 자체. 레이저: *laser surgery* 레이저 외과 수술

laser point·er /ˈ.. ˌ../ *n* a small piece of equipment that produces a LASER BEAM (=powerful narrow beam of light) that you hold in your hand and use to point at things on a map, board etc. so that other people will pay attention to them ‖ 손에 쥐고 레이저 광선을 방출해 사람들이 주의를 기울이도록 지도·칠판 등에 있는 내용을 가리키는데 사용하는 소형 장비. 레이저 포인터

lash[1] /læʃ/ *v* **1** [T] to hit someone very hard with a whip, stick etc. ‖ 채찍·막대기 등으로 사람을 매우 세게 때리다. 채찍질하다. 후려갈기다 **2** [T] to tie something tightly to something else using a rope ‖ 밧줄을 이용해서 무엇을 다른 것에 단단히 매다. (잡아)매다 **3** [I, T] to hit sharply against something ‖ 어떤 것에[을] 세차게 부딪치다[때리다]: *waves lashing the rocks* 바위에 세차게 부딪치는 파도

lash out *phr v* [I] **1** to suddenly speak loudly and angrily ‖ 갑자기 큰 소리로 화를 내며 말하다. 비난을 퍼붓다. 심하게 욕하다: *George lashed out at him, screaming abuse.* 조지는 욕을 해대면서 그를 심하게 비난했다. **2** to suddenly try to hit someone with a lot of violent uncontrolled movements ‖ 몹시 폭력적이고 자제력 없이 갑자기 사람을 때리려 하다. 세게[심하게] 때리다

lash[2] *n* **1** a hit with a whip, especially as a punishment ‖ 특히 처벌로서 채찍으로 때림. 채찍질 **2** ⇨ EYELASH

las·so /ˈlæsoʊ/ *n* a rope with one end tied in a circle, used for catching cattle and horses ‖ 소와 말을 잡기 위해 쓰이는 한쪽 끝이 둥글게 묶인 밧줄. 올가미 밧줄 – **lasso** *v* [T]

last[1] /læst/ *determiner, adj* **1** most recent ‖ 가장 최근의. 요전의. 지난: *Did you go to the last football game?* 저번 축구 경기를 보러 갔었니? / *I saw Tim last night/week/Sunday.* 나는 지난밤[주, 일요일]에 팀을 보았다. / *The last time we went to that restaurant, I got sick afterward.* 우리가 지난번에 그 식당에 갔던 이후로 나는 아팠다. —compare NEXT[1] **2** at the end, after everyone or everything else ‖ 끝에 또는 다른 모든 사람이나 모든 것 다음에. 최후의. 마지막의: *The last part of the song is sad.* 그 노래의 마지막 부분은 슬프다. / *He's the last person I'd ask for help.* (=I do not want to ask him) 그는 내가 가장 도움을 받고 싶지 않은 사람이다. **3** remaining after all others have gone ‖ 다른 것들이 모두 사라진 후에 남아 있는. 최후로 남은. 마지막의: *Chris is always the last person to leave a party.* 크리스는 항상 마지막에 파티장을 떠난다. / *my last cigarette* 나의 마지막 남은 담배 **4 on its last legs** likely to fail or break ‖ 실패하거나 부서질 듯한. 거의 망가져서. 거덜 나서: *The truck was on its last legs.* 트럭은 거의 망가졌다. **5 have the last word** to make the last statement in an argument, which gives you an advantage ‖ 논쟁에서 우위에 서게 하는 결정적인 진술을 하다

last[2] *adv* **1** most recently before now ‖ 현재 이전의 가장 최근에. 바로 전에. 전번에: *When I last saw her she was pregnant.* 지난번 보았을 때 그녀는 임신 중이었다. **2** after everything or everyone else ‖ 다른 모든 것이나 모든 사람 다음에. 최후에. 마침내: *Harris is going to speak last.* 해리스가 마지막으로 말할 것이다. **3 last but not least** said when making a final statement, to show that it is just as important as your other statements ‖ 다른 말만큼 중요하다는 것을 나타내기 해 마지막 말을 할 때 쓰여. 마지막이지만 못지않게 중요한: *... and last but not least, I'd like to thank my mother.* 그리고 마지막으로 말하지만 못지않게 중요한 말로서, 어머니께 감사를 드리고 싶습니다.

last[3] *n, pron* **1 the last** the person or thing that comes after all the others ‖ 다른 모든 사람[것] 이후에 오는 사람[것]. 최후의 사람[것]: *Joe was the last of nine children.* (=he was born last) 조는 구 남매 중 막내였다. / *Les was the last to go to bed that night.* 레즈는 그날 밤 가장 늦게 잠자리에 들었다. **2 the day/week/year before last** the day, week etc. before the one that has just finished ‖ 막 지나간 날·주의 그 전 날·주 등. 그저께/지지난 주/재작년 **3 the last I/we ...** INFORMAL used when telling someone the most recent news that you know ‖ 남에게 자신이 알고 있는 가장 최근의 소식을 말할 때 쓰여. 마지막으로 내가/우리가 …했을 때: *The last we heard, Paul was in Cuba.* 우리가 마지막으로 들은 이야기로는, 폴이 쿠바에 있다고 한다. / *The last I talked to her, she seemed fine.* 마지막으로 그녀와 이야기했을 때 그녀는 괜찮아 보였다. **4 the last of** the remaining part of something ‖ 어떤 것의

남아 있는 부분. …의 마지막(부분): *We ate the last of that bread yesterday.* 우리는 어제 그 빵의 나머지를 먹었다.

last⁴ *v* [I] **1** to continue for a particular length of time ‖ 특정한 기간 동안 계속되다. 이어지다. 지속되다: *Jeff's operation lasted 3 hours.* 제프의 수술은 3시간 동안 계속되었다. **2** to continue to be effective, useful, or in good condition ‖ 효과적이거나 유용하거나 좋은 상태가 지속되다. 오래가다: *Most batteries will last for up to 8 hours.* 대부분의 배터리는 8시간까지 지속된다. **3** to be involved in a situation for a long time, especially when it is difficult ‖ 특히 어려울 때 오랫동안 어떤 상황에 개입되어 있다. 지속되다: *I doubt their relationship will last.* 나는 그들의 관계가 계속 지속될지 의심스럽다.

last-ditch /ˌ. ˈ./ *adj* **last-ditch effort/attempt etc.** a final attempt to achieve something before it becomes impossible to do ‖ 어떤 일을 하는 것이 불가능해지기 전에 그것을 성취하려는 마지막 시도. 필사적인 노력/시도

last·ing /ˈlæstɪŋ/ *adj* continuing for a long time ‖ 오랫동안 계속되는. 영속[지속]적인. 영구적인: *a lasting peace agreement* 영구적인 평화 협약

last·ly /ˈlæstli/ *adv* FORMAL used when telling someone the last thing in a series of statements ‖ 일련의 말 중에서 남에게 마지막 말을 할 때 쓰여. 끝으로. 마지막으로: *And lastly, we ask you all to be patient.* 그리고 마지막으로 여러분 모두 인내심을 가지시기를 부탁드립니다.

last name /ˌ. ˈ./ *n* your family's name, which in English comes after your other names ‖ 영어에서 본인의 다른 이름 뒤에 오는 가문명. 성(姓) —compare FIRST NAME, MIDDLE NAME —see usage note at NAMES

latch¹ /lætʃ/ *n* a small metal BAR used for fastening a door, gate, window etc. ‖ 문·출입구·창문 등을 잠글 때 사용하는 작은 금속 막대. 걸쇠. 빗장

latch² *v*

latch onto sth *phr v* [T] INFORMAL if you latch onto an idea, style, phrase etc. you think it is so good, important etc. that you start using it too ‖ 어떤 생각·양식·어구 등이 아주 좋거나 중요하게 생각되어 그것을 지나치게 이용하기 시작하다. …에 집착하다. …을 자기 것으로 하다

late¹ /leɪt/ *adj* **1** arriving, happening, or done after the expected time ‖ 예상 시간 이후에 도착[발생, 완성]하는. (뒤)늦은:

Sorry I'm late. I got stuck in traffic. 늦어서 미안해. 교통이 막혀서. / *Peggy was late for school.* 페기는 학교에 지각했다. / *a late breakfast* 늦은 조반 **2** near the end of a period of time ‖ 일정한 기간이 끝날 무렵의. 후기의. 말기의: *a house built in the late 19th century* 19세기 후반에 지어진 집 / *working until late at night* 밤늦게까지 일하기 **3** happening at night, especially when most people are asleep ‖ 특히 대부분의 사람들이 잠든 밤에 일어나는. 밤이 깊은. 심야의: *I watched the late show on TV.* 나는 TV에서 심야 쇼를 봤다. **4** paid or given back after the arranged time ‖ 정해진 시간 이후에 되갚거나 돌려받은. 연체의: *Oh no, my library books are late.* 아니 이럴 수가, 내 도서관 책 반납이 연체되었네. **5** FORMAL dead ‖ 죽은. 작고한. 고(故)…: *Mrs. Clausen's late husband* 클로슨 부인의 작고한 남편

late² *adv* **1** after the usual or expected time ‖ 일반적인 또는 예상된 시간 이후에. 늦게. 늦어서: *Most restaurants stay open late on Fridays.* 대부분의 식당은 금요일에는 늦게까지 영업을 한다. / *I probably won't be home until late.* 나는 아마도 늦게까지 집에 들어가지 못할 것이다. / *Our flight arrived 2 hours late.* 우리가 탄 비행기가 2시간 늦게 도착했다. **2** near the end of a period of time ‖ 일정한 기간이 끝날 무렵에. 늦게. 늦게까지: *late in the afternoon* 오후 늦게 / *taking a walk late at night* 밤늦게 산책하기

late·ly /ˈleɪtli/ *adv* recently ‖ 최근에. 요즈음. 요사이: *Lately I've been really busy.* 최근에 나는 정말로 바빴다.

USAGE NOTE lately and recently

Use both of these words with the present perfect tenses to talk about something that began in the recent past and continues until now: *Lately I've been thinking about buying a new car.* / *Recently I've been thinking about buying a new car.* You can also use **recently** with the past tense to talk about a particular action in the recent past: *She recently got married.* ✗DON'T SAY "She lately got married."✗ 이들 두 단어는 최근의 과거에 시작하여 현재까지 계속되는 것에 대해 이야기할 때 현재 완료 시제와 함께 사용한다: 요즈음 나는 새 차를 살까 생각 중이다./ 최근에 나는 새 차를 살까 생각 중이다. **recently**는 최근의 과거의 특정 행동에 대해 이야기할 때 과거 시제와 함께

L

사용할 수도 있다: 그녀는 최근에 결혼 했다. "She lately got married." 라고는 하지 않는다.

la·tent /'leɪtnt/ adj present but not yet noticeable, active, or completely developed ‖ 실재하지만 아직 눈에 띄지 않는[활동하지 않는, 완전히 발달되지 않은]. 숨어 있는. 잠재성의: a latent disease 잠복성 질병

lat·er¹ /'leɪtɚ/ adv **1** after the present time or a time you are talking about ‖ 현재 시간이나 말하고 있는 때 이후에. 나중에. 추후에. …후에: I'll see you later. 나중에 보자. / They met in July, and two months later they were married. 그들은 7월에 만나 2개월 후에 결혼했다. **2 later on** at some time in the future, or after something else ‖ 미래의 어떤 시간에 또는 다른 일 이후에. 나중에. 후반부에: Later on in the movie the hero gets killed. 영화의 후반부에서 남자 주인공은 죽는다.

later² adj **1** coming in the future, or after something else ‖ 앞으로 다가올 또는 다른 것 이후의. 더 늦은. 더 나중의: This will be decided at a later time/date. 이것은 좀 더 있다가 결정될 것이다. / information in a later chapter 뒷장에 있는 정보 **2** more recent ‖ 보다 최근의: Later models of the car are much improved. 그 차의 보다 최근 모델은 훨씬 개선되었다. ✗DON'T SAY "models that are later."✗ "models that are later." 라고는 하지 않는다.

lat·er·al /'læt̮ərəl/ adj TECHNICAL relating to the side of something, or movement to the side ‖ 어떤 것의 옆이나 옆으로의 움직임과 관련된. 옆의. 측면의

lat·est¹ /'leɪt̮ɪst/ adj the most recent or the newest ‖ 가장 최근의 또는 가장 새로운. 최근의. 최신(식)의: What's the latest news? 가장 최근의 뉴스가 뭐니? / the latest fashions 최신 (유행)패션 —see usage note at NEW

latest² n **at the latest** no later than the time mentioned ‖ 언급된 시간보다 더 늦지 않게. 늦어도: I want you home by 11 at the latest. 늦어도 11시까지는 집에 들어와야 돼.

la·tex /'leɪtɛks/ n [U] a thick white liquid used for making products such as rubber, glue, and paint, and produced artificially or by some plants ‖ 고무·접착제·도료 등의 제품을 만들기 위해 사용되며 인공적으로 또는 어떤 식물에서 생산되는 진한 흰색 액체. 유액(乳液). 라텍스

lath·er¹ /'læðɚ/ n [singular, U] a lot of small white BUBBLEs produced by rubbing soap with water ‖ 비누에 물을 묻혀 비벼서 생긴 많은 작고 하얀 거품. 비누거품

lather² v [I, T] to produce a LATHER, or cover something with lather ‖ 비누거품을 만들거나 무엇을 비누거품으로 덮다. 거품이 일다. …에 비누거품을 칠하다

Lat·in¹ /'læt̮n/ adj **1** relating to or coming from Mexico, Central America, or South America ‖ 멕시코[중미, 남미]와 관련되거나 그곳에서 온. 라틴계의. 라틴계 민족의 **2** relating to the Latin language ‖ 라틴어와 관계된. 라틴어의

Latin² n [U] an old language that is now used mostly for legal, scientific, or medical words ‖ 지금은 대개 법률[과학, 의학] 용어로 사용되는 옛 언어. 라틴어

La·ti·na /lə'tinə/ n a woman in the US whose family comes from a country in LATIN AMERICA ‖ 가족이 라틴 아메리카 국가 출신인 미국 거주 여성. 재미 라틴 아메리카계 여성

Lat·in A·mer·i·ca /ˌlæt̮n ə'mɛrɪkə/ n the land including Mexico, Central America, and South America ‖ 멕시코·중미·남미를 포함하는 지역. 라틴 아메리카 —**Latin American** adj

La·ti·no /lə'tinoʊ/ n a man in the US whose family comes from a country in LATIN AMERICA. In the plural, Latinos can mean a group of men and women, or just men ‖ 가족이 라틴 아메리카 국가 출신인 미국에 거주하는 남성. 복수형인 Latinos는 한 무리의 남성과 여성, 또는 단지 남성들만을 의미하기도 한다. 재미 라틴 아메리카계 남성

lat·i·tude /'læt̮ə,tud/ n **1** [C, U] TECHNICAL the distance north or south of the equator, measured in degrees ‖ 각도로서 측정된 적도에서 북쪽·남쪽의 거리. 위도 —compare longitude —see picture at AXIS **2** [U] freedom to do or say what you like ‖ 좋아하는 것을 하거나 말하는 자유. 자유(범위). 허용 정도: Students now have greater latitude in choosing their classes. 학생들은 이제는 보다 자유롭게 자신들의 수업을 선택한다.

la·trine /lə'trin/ n an outdoor toilet at a camp or military area ‖ 캠프장이나 군사 지역에 있는 야외 화장실. 간이 화장실

lat·te /'lɑteɪ/ n [C, U] coffee with hot milk in it, or a cup of this type of coffee ‖ 뜨거운 우유가 들어 있는 커피, 또는 이런 종류의 커피 한 잔. 라떼(커피)

lat·ter¹ /'læt̮ɚ/ n **the latter** FORMAL the second of two people or things that are mentioned ‖ 언급된 두 사람이나 사물 중

에서 두 번째. 후자: *Either glass or plastic would be effective, but the latter (=plastic) weighs less.* 유리나 플라스틱 어느 것이나 효과적이겠지만 후자가 무게 가 덜 나간다. —compare FORMER²

latter² *adj* **1** FORMAL being the last person or thing that has just been mentioned ‖ 방금 언급한 마지막 사람이 나 사물인. 마지막의. 끝의: *Of the phrases "go crazy" and "go nuts," the latter term is used less frequently.* "미치다"와 "돌다"라는 어구 중에서 마지막 용어의 사용 빈도가 낮다. **2** closer to the end of a period of time ‖ 일정한 기간의 마지막에 더 가까운. 나중의. 후반의: *the latter part of the 19th century* 19세기 후반부

laud·a·ble /ˈlɔdəbəl/ *adj* FORMAL deserving praise or admiration ‖ 칭찬이나 찬양을 받을 만한. 칭찬할 만한

laugh¹ /læf/ *v* **1** [I] to make a sound with your voice, usually while smiling, because you think something is funny ‖ 무엇이 우스워서 보통 미소를 지으면서 소리를 내다. 웃다: *How come no one ever laughs at my jokes?* 어떻게 아무도 내 농담에 웃지 않을 수 있지? / *Then Tom's pants fell down and we all burst out laughing.* 그때 톰의 바지가 흘러내리자 우리는 모두 웃음을 터뜨렸다. **2 laugh in sb's face** to show that you do not respect someone or will not obey him/her ‖ 남을 존중하지 않거나 남에게 복종하지 않겠다는 것을 나타내다. 면전에서 비웃다: *I told him he had to leave, but he just laughed in my face.* 나는 그가 떠나야 한다고 그에게 말했지만 그는 내 면전에서 비웃기만 했다.

laugh at sb/sth *phr v* [T] to make unkind or funny remarks about someone because s/he does or says something stupid ‖ 남이 멍청한 어떤 일을 하거나 말을 하여 그 사람에 대해서 심술궂거나 우스운 말을 하다. 비웃다: *Mommy, all the kids at school were laughing at me!* 엄마, 학교의 모든 애들이 나를 비웃고 있어요!

laugh sth ↔ **off** *phr v* [T] to joke about something in order to pretend that it is not very serious or important ‖ 어떤 일이 그다지 심각하거나 중요하지 않다는 척하기 위해서 그것에 대해 농담을 하다. 웃어 넘기다: *She laughed off their insults.* 그녀는 그들의 모욕적인 말들을 웃어 넘겼다.

laugh² *n* **1** the sound you make when you laugh ‖ 웃을 때 내는 소리. 웃음(소리): *a big hearty laugh* 마음껏 웃는 큰

웃음 **2 have the last laugh** to finally be successful after someone has criticized or defeated you ‖ 남에게 비판·패배당한 이후에 마침내 성공하다. 결국 이기다[성공하다]

laugh·a·ble /ˈlæfəbəl/ *adj* impossible to be treated seriously because of being so silly, bad, or difficult to believe ‖ 아주 어리석어[형편없어, 믿기 어려워서] 진지하게 다루기 불가능한. 우스운. 터무니없는

laugh·ing·stock /ˈlæfɪŋˌstɑk/ *n* someone who has done something so silly or stupid that people laugh unkindly at him/her ‖ 사람들이 심술궂게 비웃을 정도로 아주 바보스럽거나 멍청한 짓을 한 사람. 웃음거리. 조소의 대상

laugh·ter /ˈlæftɚ/ *n* [U] the action of laughing, or the sound of people laughing ‖ 웃는 동작이나 사람들이 웃는 소리. 웃음(소리): *a roar of laughter from the audience* 청중으로부터 터져나온 한바탕 웃음소리

launch¹ /lɔntʃ, lɑntʃ/ *v* [T] **1** to start something new, such as an activity, plan, or profession ‖ 활동[계획, 직업] 등의 새로운 것을 시작하다. 진출하다. 착수하다: *the movie that launched his acting career* 그의 연기 인생을 시작하게 한 영화 **2** to send a weapon or a space vehicle into the sky or into space ‖ 무기나 우주선을 하늘이나 우주로 보내다. 발사하다 **3** to put a boat or ship into the water ‖ 보트나 배를 물 속에 넣다. 띄우다. 진수시키다

launch into sth *phr v* [T] to suddenly start describing something or criticizing something ‖ 갑자기 어떤 일을 묘사하거나 비판하기 시작하다. (…)하기 시작하다: *He launched into the story of his life.* 그는 갑자기 자기 인생 이야기를 하기 시작했다.

launch² *n* an occasion at which a new product is shown or made available ‖ 신제품을 선보이거나 이용할 수 있게 하는 때. 출시

launch pad /ˈ. ./ *n* the area from which a space vehicle, ROCKET etc. is sent into space ‖ 우주선·로켓 등을 우주로 보내는 장소. 발사대

laun·der /ˈlɔndɚ, ˈlɑn-/ *v* [T] **1** to put stolen money into legal businesses or bank accounts in order to hide it or use it ‖ 훔친 돈을 숨기거나 사용하기 위해 합법적인 사업체나 은행 계좌에 넣다. 돈세탁하다. 출처를 숨기다 **2** FORMAL to wash clothes ‖ 옷을 빨다. 빨래[세탁]하다

laun·dro·mat /ˈlɔndrəˌmæt, ˈlɑn-/ *n* a place where you pay money to wash your clothes in machines ‖ 기계로 옷을 빨기 위해서 돈을 지불하는 곳. 빨래방.

laun·dry /'lɔndri, 'lɑn-/ *n* [U] clothes, sheets etc. that need to be washed, or that have already been washed ‖ 빨래할 필요가 있거나 이미 빨래를 한 옷·침대보 등. 빨래. 세탁물: *I have to do the laundry.* (=wash clothes, sheets etc.) 나는 빨래를 해야 돼.

lau·re·ate /'lɔriɪt, 'lɑr-/ *n* someone who has been given an important prize ‖ 중요한 상을 받은 사람. 수상자: *a Nobel laureate* 노벨상 수상자

lau·rel /'lɔrəl, 'lɑr-/ *n* a small tree with smooth shiny dark green leaves that do not fall off in winter ‖ 겨울에 떨어지지 않는 매끈하고 광택 있는 암록색 잎을 가진 작은 나무. 월계수

la·va /'lɑvə, 'lævə/ *n* [U] **1** hot melted rock that flows from a VOLCANO ‖ 화산에서 흘러나오는 고열의 용융된 바위. 용암 **2** this rock when it becomes cold and solid ‖ 식어서 단단해진 이런 바위. 용암

lav·a·to·ry /'lævə,tɔri/ *n* FORMAL the room a toilet is in ‖ 변기가 설치된 실내. 변소. 화장실. 세면장 —see usage note at TOILET

lav·en·der /'lævəndɚ/ *n* a plant with purple flowers that have a strong pleasant smell ‖ 기분 좋은 강한 냄새가 나는 보라색 꽃을 가진 식물. 라벤더

lav·ish[1] /'lævɪʃ/ *adj* very generous and often expensive or complicated ‖ 매우 관대하고 종종 비싸거나 복잡한. 마음이 후한[아끼지 않는]. 사치스러운: *lavish gifts* 사치스러운 선물 / *He is lavish with his praise.* 그는 칭찬을 아끼지 않는다.

lav·ish[2] *v*
lavish sth **on** sb *phr v* [T] to give someone a lot of something good ‖ 어떤 사람에게 좋은 것을 많이 주다. …에게 …을 아낌없이 주다: *They lavish a lot of attention on their children.* 그들은 자녀들에게 아낌없는 관심을 쏟고 있다.

law /lɔ/ *n* **1** [singular, U] the system of rules that people in a country, city, or state must obey ‖ 한 국가[도시, 주]에 사는 사람들이 준수해야 할 규칙의 체계. 법. 법률: *Drunk driving is against the law.* (=illegal) 음주 운전은 법률 위반이다. / *breaking the law* (=doing something illegal) 법을 어김 **2** a rule that people in a particular country, city, or local area must obey ‖ 특정한 국가[도시, 지역]에 사는 사람들이 준수해야 할 규칙. 법률. 법령. 조례: *The city is trying to pass a new law allowing overnight parking.* 그 시는 밤샘 주차를

허용하는 새로운 조례를 통과시키려고 하고 있다. **3 the law** the police ‖ 경찰: *Is he in trouble with the law?* 그 사람 경찰과 문제 있어요? **4 law and order** a situation in which people respect the law, and crime is controlled by the police, the prison system etc. ‖ 사람들이 법률을 존중하고 경찰·교정(矯正) 제도 등에 의해 범죄가 통제되는 상황. 법과 질서. 치안 유지: *The national guard was sent in to restore law and order.* 주 방위군이 법과 질서를 회복하기 위해 파견되었다. **5** a statement that describes and explains how something works ‖ 어떤 것이 어떻게 작동하는지를 묘사하고 설명하는 말. 법칙. 원리: *the law of gravity* 중력의 법칙 / *the economic law of supply and demand* 수요와 공급의 경제 법칙

law·a·bid·ing /'. ,.../ *adj* respectful of the law and obeying it ‖ 법률을 존중하고 준수하는. 준법적인

law·ful /'lɔfəl/ *adj* FORMAL considered by the government or law courts to be legal ‖ 정부나 법원이 합법적인 것으로 간주하는. 합법적인. 적법의 —opposite UNLAWFUL

law·less /'lɔlɪs/ *adj* FORMAL not obeying the law, or not controlled by law ‖ 법을 준수하지 않거나 법의 통제를 받지 않는. 비합법적인. 무법의

lawn /lɔn/ *n* an area of ground around a house or in a park that is covered with grass ‖ 잔디로 덮인 집 주위나 공원 내의 구역. 잔디(밭) —see picture on page 945

lawn mow·er /'lɔn ,mouɚ/ *n* a machine that you use to cut the grass ‖ 잔디를 깎기 위해 사용하는 기계. 잔디 깎는 기계

law·suit /'lɔsut/ *n* a problem or complaint that someone brings to a court of law to be settled, especially for money ‖ 사람이 법원에 해결을 제기하는, 특히 금전상의 문제나 불평거리. 소송. 고소

law·yer /'lɔyɚ/ *n* someone whose job is to advise people about laws, write formal agreements, or represent people in court ‖ 사람들에게 법에 관한 조언을 하는[공식 계약서를 작성하는, 법정에서 사람들을 대리하는] 직업인. 변호사

lax /læks/ *adj* not strict or careful about standards of behavior, work, safety etc. ‖ 행동·일·안전 등의 기준에 관해서 엄격하거나 주의 깊지 않은. 느슨한. 해이한. 미온적인: *lax security for the building* 그 건물의 허술한 보안 - **laxity** *n* [U]

lax·a·tive /'læksətɪv/ *n* a medicine or

something that you eat that makes your bowels empty easily ‖ 장이 쉽게 비도록 먹는 약이나 그와 같은 것. 하제(下劑). 완하제(緩下劑) – **laxative** *adj*

lay

Pam laid her dress out on the bed.

Pam lay down on the bed.

lay¹ /leɪ/ *v* **laid, laid, laying** 1 [T] to put someone or something carefully into a particular position ‖ 사람이나 사물을 특정한 위치에 조심스럽게 놓다. 두다. 눕히다: *Guests can lay their coats on the bed.* 손님들은 자기의 외투를 침대 위에 놓아 둘 수 있다. / *Martha laid the baby down.* 마서는 아기를 눕혔다. 2 **lay bricks/carpet/cable etc.** to put or attach something in the correct place, especially onto something flat or under the ground ‖ 사물을 알맞은 자리에, 특히 평평한 것이나 지면 아래에 놓거나 부착하다. 벽돌을 쌓다/카펫을 깔다/전선을 가설하다: *laying down a new bedroom carpet* 새 침실 카펫을 바닥에 깔기 3 [I, T] if a bird, insect etc. lays eggs, it produces them from its body ‖ 새·곤충 등이 몸에서 알을 생산하다. (알을)낳다 4 **lay a finger/hand on sb** to hurt someone, especially to hit him/her ‖ 특히 남을 때려서 해치다. 남에게 손을 대다: *If you lay a hand on her, I'll call the police.* 만약 네가 그녀에게 손을 대면 난 경찰을 부를 거야. 5 **lay blame/criticism/emphasis etc** FORMAL to blame, criticize, emphasize etc. ‖ 비난하다, 비판하다, 강조하다 6 **lay yourself open to blame/criticism etc.** to do something that makes you likely to be blamed, criticized etc. ‖ 비난·비판 등을 받게 될 일을 하다. 비난/비판을 초래하다 —compare LIE¹

lay sth ↔ **down** *phr v* [T] to officially state rules, methods etc. that someone must obey or use ‖ 사람이 준수하거나 사용해야 할 규칙·방법 등을 공식적으로 공표하다. 규정하다. 정하다: *strict safety regulations laid down by the government* 정부가 제정한 엄격한 안전 규정

lay into sb *phr v* [T] INFORMAL to attack someone physically or criticize him/her angrily ‖ 남을 육체적으로 공격하거나 화를 내며 비판하다. 세게 때리다. 몹시 비난하다: *You should have heard Dad laying into Tommy.* 아빠가 토미를 호되게 꾸짖는 것을 네가 들었어야 했는데.

lay off *phr v* 1 [T **lay** sb ↔ **off**] to stop employing someone, especially when there is not much work to do ‖ 특히 할 일이 많지 않을 때 인력 고용을 중단하다. 일시 해고하다: *Jerry's just been laid off again.* 제리는 이제 막 다시 일시 해고를 당했다. 2 [I,T **lay off** sth/sb] SPOKEN to stop doing, having, or using something that is bad or annoying ‖ 나쁘거나 성가신 것을 하거나 가지거나 사용하기를 멈추다. 그만두다. 끊다. 가만히 두다: *Don't you think you should lay off alcohol for a while?* 한동안 술을 끊어야 한다고 생각하지 않니? / *Just lay off (=stop criticizing) – I don't care what you think!* 그런 소리 그만 해라. 네 생각 따위는 신경 안 써!

lay sth ↔ **on** *phr v* [T] to provide food, entertainment etc. in a very generous way ‖ 아주 후하게 음식·오락 등을 제공하다. …을 주다[제공하다]. 한 턱 내다: *Lola really laid on a great meal for us.* 롤라는 우리에게 정말로 근사한 식사를 대접했다.

lay sb/sth ↔ **out** *phr v* [T] 1 to spread something out ‖ 어떤 것을 펴다: *Pam laid her dress out on the bed.* 팸은 침대 위에 드레스를 펼쳐 놓았다. 2 INFORMAL to spend a lot of money ‖ 많은 돈을 쓰다: *We've just laid out $500 on a new fridge.* 우리는 좀 전에 새 냉장고에 500달러를 썼다.

lay up *phr v* [T] **be laid up (with)** to have to stay in bed because you are ill or injured ‖ 아프거나 다쳐서 침대에 있어야 하다. (…으로) 드러눕다: *He's laid up with a broken collarbone.* 그는 쇄골이 부러져서 드러누워 있다.

USAGE NOTE lay, lie, and lie

Lay means "to put something somewhere": *Just lay the papers on the desk.* The other forms of this verb are **laid, laid,** and **laying**. **Lie** has two different meanings. Use one meaning of **lie** to talk about someone or something that is flat on a surface: *He likes to lie on his stomach and read the paper. / Don't leave your socks lying on the floor!* The other forms of this verb are **lain** and **lying**. The other meaning of **lie** is

"to say something that is not true":
Are you lying to me? The other forms
of this verb are **lied** and **lying.**

lay는 "사물을 어딘가에 놓다"를 의미
한다: 그 서류들은 책상에 그냥 놓아라.
이 동사의 다른 형태로는 **laid, laid,
laying**이 있다. 표면 위에 납작하게 있
는 사람이나 사물을 언급하는 데에는
lie의 두 가지 다른 의미 중 한 가지를
사용한다: 그는 배를 깔고 엎드려서 신
문 읽기를 좋아한다. / 바닥에 양말을 놔
두지 마라! **lain**과 **lying**이 이 동사의
다른 시제형이다. **lie**의 다른 의미는
"사실이 아닌 것을 말하다"이다: 너 나
한테 거짓말하는 거야? **lied**와 **lying**이
이 동사의 다른 시제형이다.

lay² v the past tense of LIE ‖ lie의 과거형

lay³ *adj* not trained in a particular
profession or subject ‖ 특정한 직업이나
분야에 대해서 훈련받지 않은. 비전문가
의. 문외한의. 평신도의: *a lay preacher*
평신도 설교자

lay·a·way /'leɪəˌweɪ/ n [U] a method of
buying goods in which the goods are
kept by the seller for a small amount of
money until the full price is paid ‖ 완불
될 때까지 소액을 받고 판매자가 물건을
보관하는 물건 구입 방식. 상품 예약 구입
법

lay·er¹ /'leɪɚ/ n **1** an
amount of a
substance that covers
all of a surface ‖ 표면
전체를 덮는 물질의
양: *a layer of dust on
the desk* 책상 위에 뒤
덮인 먼지 **2** some-
thing that is placed on
or between other things ‖ 다른 사물 위나
사이에 놓인 것. 층. 켜. 겹: *several
layers of clothing* 몇 겹의 옷

layer² v [T] to put something down in
layers ‖ 사물을 층으로 놓다. 층지게 하
다: *macaroni layered with cheese* 치즈
위에 곁들인 마카로니

lay·man /'leɪmən/ n someone who is
not trained in a particular subject or
type of work ‖ 특정 주제나 특정 종류의
일에 대해서 훈련받지 않은 사람. 비전문
가. 문외한. 평신도: *a book on
astronomy written for the layman*
(=people in general) 일반인을 위해 쓴 천
문학 서적

lay-off /'. ./ n the act of stopping a
worker's employment because there is
not enough work ‖ 충분한 일이 없어서
근로자의 고용 상태를 정지시키는 행동.

일시 해고: *lay-offs in the steel industry*
강철업계의 일시 해고

lay·out /'leɪaʊt/ n **1** the way things are
arranged in a particular area or place ‖
사물이 특정한 구역이나 장소에 배정되는
방식. 배치. 설계: *changes in the office
layout* 사무실 배치의 변화 **2** the way in
which writing and pictures are
arranged on a page ‖ 글과 그림이 페이지
위에 배열되는 방식. 지면 배정. 레이아웃

lay·o·ver /'leɪˌoʊvɚ/ n a short stay
somewhere between parts of a trip ‖ 여
행 도중에 어딘가에 잠시 머무름. 단기 체
재. 잠깐 들르는 곳

lay·per·son /'leɪˌpɚsən/ n a word
meaning a LAYMAN that is used when
the person could be a man or a woman
‖ 남자·여자를 공통적으로 가리킬 때에 사
용하는 layman을 뜻하는 단어. 비전문가.
문외한. 평신도

laze /leɪz/ v [I] to relax and enjoy
yourself without doing very much ‖ 그다
지 하는 일 없이 긴장을 풀고서 즐기다. 빈
둥거리다. 게으름피우다: *Jeff spent the
morning just lazing in the yard.* 제프는
뜰에서 그저 빈둥거리며 아침을 보냈다.

la·zy /'leɪzi/ *adj* **1** not liking and not
doing work or physical activity ‖ 일이나
육체 활동을 좋아하지도 않고 하지도 않
는. 게으른. 나태한: *the laziest boy in the
class* 그 반에서 가장 게으른 소년 **2** a
lazy time is spent relaxing ‖ 긴장을 풀고
서 시간을 보내는. 나른한. 빈둥거리는:
lazy summer afternoons 나른한 여름의
오후들 **3** moving slowly ‖ 천천히 움직이
는. 느린. 굼뜬. 꾸물거리는: *a lazy river*
느릿느릿 흐르는 강물

lb. n the written abbreviation of POUND ‖
pound의 약어

leading a horse

The stairs lead to
the back door.

lead¹ /lid/ v led, led, leading
1 ▶GUIDE 안내하다◀ [T] to guide a
person or animal to a place, especially
by going with or in front of the person
or animal ‖ 특히 함께 또는 앞장을 서서
사람이나 동물을 어떤 장소로 안내하다.
인도하다. 이끌다: *Aid workers led the*

refugees to safety. 구호원들은 난민들을 안전한 곳으로 안내했다. / *Carl led his horse into the judging ring.* 칼은 말을 승자를 결정하는 경마장으로 끌고 갔다.

2 ▶GO IN FRONT 앞에 가다◀ [I, T] to go in front of a group of people or vehicles || 일단의 사람들이나 탈것들의 앞에서 가다. 선두에 서다. 앞장서 가다: *The high school band is leading the parade.* 고등학교 밴드가 행렬의 선두에 서서 가고 있다.

3 ▶DOOR/ROAD/WIRE 문/길/전선◀ [I] if a door, road etc. leads to somewhere, you can get there by using it || 문·길 등을 이용해 어딘가에 다다르다. …에 이르다. …으로 통하다: *The second door leads to the principal's office.* 두 번째 문은 교장실로 통한다.

4 ▶CONTROL 통제하다◀ [T] to be in charge of something, especially an activity or a group of people || 특히 활동이나 일단의 사람들을 책임지다. 지휘[인솔]하다. 주도하다: *Who is leading the investigation?* 누가 그 수사를 지휘하고 있나요?

5 ▶WIN 이기다◀ [I, T] to be winning a game or competition || 경기나 경쟁을 이기고 있다. 앞서 있다: *At half-time, Green Bay was leading 12-0.* 전반전에서 그린 베이가 12대 0으로 앞서고 있었다.

6 ▶CAUSE STH …을 야기하다◀ [T] to be the thing that makes someone do something or think something || 남에게 무엇을 하거나 생각하게 하는 요소가 되다. …에 이르게 하다: *What led you to study geology?* 어떻게 해서 지질학을 공부하게 됐니? / *Rick led me to believe* (=made me believe) *he was going to return the money.* 릭은 돈을 돌려줄 것처럼 나에게 믿게 했어.

7 lead a normal/dull etc. life to have a normal, boring etc. type of life || 평범한·따분한 인생을 보내다

8 ▶SUCCESS 성공하다◀ [I, T] to be more successful than other people, companies, or countries in a particular activity or area of business || 특정한 활동이나 사업 영역에서 다른 사람들[회사들, 국가들]보다 더 성공적이다. 앞지르다. 능가하다. 1위를 차지하다: *The US leads the world in coal production.* 미국은 석탄 생산에서 세계 최고이다.

9 lead the way a) to guide someone in a particular direction || 특정한 방향으로 남을 안내하다. 앞장서다. 안내하다 **b)** to be the first to do something good or successful || 좋거나 성공적인 것을 하는 첫 번째가 되다. 맨 앞을 가다. 일등이다:

The Japanese led the way in using robots in industry. 일본은 산업에 로봇을 이용하는 데에 있어서 선두를 달렸다.

10 ▶CONVERSATION 대화◀ [I, T] to direct a conversation or discussion so that it develops in the way you want || 대화나 토론을 원하는 쪽으로 전개되도록 이끌다. …으로 화제를 끌고 가다: *She finally led the topic around to pay raises.* 그녀는 마침내 주제를 임금 인상 쪽으로 끌고 갔다.

lead off sth *phr v* [T] to begin an event by doing something || 어떤 것을 하여 행사를 시작하다. …을 개시하다: *They led off the concert with a Beethoven Overture.* 그들은 베토벤 서곡으로 콘서트를 시작했다.

lead sb **on** *phr v* [T] to make someone believe something that is not true || 사실이 아닌 것을 남에게 믿게 하다. (남을) 꾀다: *He said it would only cost $15, but I think he was leading me on.* 그는 15달러만 들 거라고 말했지만 그가 나를 꾀려 했던 것 같다.

lead to sth *phr v* [T] to make something happen or exist as a result of something else || 다른 것의 결과로서 어떤 일이 발생하거나 존재하게 하다. 도달하다. 이르다: *Opening the new lumber mill has led to the creation of 200 jobs.* 새로운 목재소가 문을 열어 200개의 일자리가 생겼다.

lead up to sth *phr v* [T] **1** to come before something and be a cause of it || 어떤 일의 앞에 와서 그것의 원인이 되다. …의 도화선이 되다: *events leading up to the trial* 재판의 도화선이 되는 사건들 **2** to gradually introduce a subject into a conversation || 점차로 어떤 주제를 대화 속으로 끌어들이다. …으로 화제를 끌고 가다: *remarks leading up to a request for money* 돈을 요구하는 쪽으로 끌고 가는 말

USAGE NOTE lead, guide, and direct

Lead means "to show the way by going first": *He led us down the mountain.* **Guide** means "to show the way and explain things": *She guides tourists around the White House.* **Direct** means "to explain to someone how to get somewhere": *Could you direct me to the station?* **lead**는 "선두로 가서 길을 안내하다"를 뜻한다: 그는 선두에서 우리의 하산을 인도했다. **guide**는 "길을 안내하고 상황을 설명하다"를 뜻한다: 그녀는 관광

객에게 백악관 주변을 구경시켜 주었다. **direct**는 "어딘가에 이르는 방법을 남에게 설명하다"를 뜻한다: 역으로 가는 길 좀 가르쳐 주시겠어요?

lead² *n* **1** [singular] the position or situation of being in front of or better than everyone else in a race or competition ‖ 경주나 경쟁에서 다른 모든 사람들보다 앞서 있거나 더 잘하는 입장이나 상황. 선두. 우세: *Lewis is still in the lead.* 루이스가 여전히 선두를 유지하고 있다. / *Joyner has taken the lead.* (=moved into the front position in a race) 조이너가 선두로 나섰다. / *The US has taken the lead* (=is more advanced than others) *in space technology.* 미국은 우주 기술에서 선도적 역할을 해 왔다. **2** the distance, number of points etc. by which one competitor is ahead of another ‖ 한 경쟁자가 다른 경쟁자를 앞서는 거리·점수 등. 이긴 양[시간, 거리]. 리드: *The Bulls have a 5-point lead over the Celtics at halftime.* 하프타임에 불스가 5점 차로 셀틱을 리드하고 있다. **3** a piece of information that may help you to make a discovery or find the answer to a problem ‖ 발견을 하거나 문제에 대한 답을 찾는 데에 도움이 될 수도 있는 정보. 단서. 실마리: *Do the police have any leads in the robbery?* 경찰은 그 강도 사건에 대한 어떠한 단서라도 가지고 있나요? **4** the main acting part in a play, movie etc., or the main singer etc. in a musical group ‖ 연극·영화 등에서의 주역이나 뮤지컬 단체에서의 주역 가수 등. 주연 (배우). 주인공: *Who has the lead in the school play?* 학교 연극에서 누가 주인공 역할을 하니? / *the lead guitarist* 수석 기타 연주자

lead³ /lɛd/ *n* [U] **1** a soft gray-blue metal that melts easily ‖ 쉽게 녹는 연한 회청빛이 도는 금속. 납 **2** [C, U] the substance in a pencil that makes the marks when you write ‖ 글을 쓸 때 자국을 남기는 연필 속의 물질. 연필심

lead·er /ˈlidɚ/ *n* **1** the person who directs or controls a team, organization, country etc. ‖ 팀·조직·국가 등을 지휘하거나 통제하는 사람. 지도자: *Most world leaders will attend the conference.* 대부분의 세계 지도자들이 그 회담에 참석할 것이다. **2** the person, organization etc. that is better than all the others in a race or competition ‖ 경주나 경쟁에서 다른 모든 사람[것]보다 더 잘하는 사람·조직 등. 선두 주자: *leaders in the field of medical science* 의학 분야의 선두 주자들

lead·er·ship /ˈlidɚˌʃɪp/ *n* **1** [U] the quality of being good at leading a team, organization, country etc. ‖ 팀·조직·국가 등을 잘 이끄는 자질. 지도성: *America needs strong leadership.* 미국은 강력한 지도력이 필요하다. **2** [U] the position of being the leader of a team, organization etc. ‖ 팀·조직 등의 지도자의 위치. 지도자의 지위[신분]: *The bill was passed when the Senate was under Dole's leadership.* 돌 의원이 상원을 이끌 때 그 법안은 통과되었다. **3** [singular] the people who lead a country, organization etc. ‖ 국가·조직 등을 이끄는 사람들. 지도부

lead·ing /ˈlidɪŋ/ *adj* **1** best, most important, or most successful ‖ 최고의 [가장 중요한, 가장 성공적인]. 1급[1류]의: *a leading athlete* 최고의 운동 선수 **2 a leading question** a question asked in a way that makes you give a particular answer ‖ 특정한 대답을 하게 만드는 식으로 하는 질문. 유도 심문

leaf¹ /lif/ *n, plural* **leaves 1** one of the flat green parts of a plant that are joined to its stem or branches ‖ 줄기나 가지에 붙어 있는 식물의 납작한 녹색 부분의 하나. 잎(사귀) **2** a part of the top of a table that can be added to make the table larger ‖ 더 크게 하기 위해 덧붙일 수 있는 책상의 맨 윗부분 **3** [U] gold or silver in a very thin sheet ‖ 아주 얇은 종이 같은 금이나 은. 금속 박 —see also **turn over a new leaf** (TURN¹)

leaf² *v*

leaf through sth *phr v* [T] to turn the pages of a book quickly, without reading it carefully ‖ 책장을 주의 깊게 읽지 않고 속히 넘기다. 책을 훑어보다

leaf·let /ˈliflɪt/ *n* a small piece of printed paper that gives information or advertises something ‖ 정보를 주거나 어떤 것을 광고하는 작은 인쇄물. 전단

leaf·y /ˈlifi/ *adj* having a lot of leaves ‖ 많은 잎을 가지고 있는. 잎이 많은[우거진]: *green leafy vegetables* 푸른 잎채소

league /lig/ *n* **1** a group of sports teams or players who play games against each other to see who is best ‖ 누가 최고인지 판가름하려고 서로 경기를 하는 일단의 스포츠 팀이나 선수들. 경기 연맹. 리그: *Our team finished second in the league this year.* 우리 팀은 올해 리그에서 2위로 끝났다. **2** a group of people or countries that have joined together because they have similar aims, political beliefs etc. ‖ 유사한 목표·정치적 신념 등을 가져서 함께 가맹한 일

단의 사람들이나 국가들. 동맹[연맹](참가자[국]): *the League of Nations* 국제 연맹 **3 not in the same league/out of sb's league** not having the same abilities or qualities as someone or something else ‖ 어떤 사람이나 사물과 동등한 능력이나 자질을 가지고 있지 않은. 수준이 다른. 같은 부류가 아닌: *He knows a lot more than I do—he's way out of my league.* 그는 내가 아는 것보다 훨씬 더 많이 알고 있다. 그는 나와는 수준이 다르다.

leak¹ /lik/ *v* **1** [I, T] to let a liquid or gas in or out of a hole or crack ‖ 액체나 기체를 구멍이나 틈 안이나 밖으로 흐르게 하다. 새게 하다. 새다: *Somebody's car must be leaking oil.* 누군가의 차에서 오일이 새는 게 분명하다 / *The roof's leaking!* 지붕이 새잖아! **2** [I] to pass through a hole or crack ‖ 구멍이나 틈으로 통과하다. 새다: *Gas was leaking out of the pipes.* 가스가 파이프에서 새어나오고 있었다. **3** [T] to deliberately give secret information to a newspaper, television company etc. ‖ 신문사·방송사 등에 비밀 정보를 고의적으로 주다. 누설하다: *Details of the President's speech were leaked to reporters.* 대통령 연설의 세부 사항이 기자들에게 누설되었다. —**leakage** *n* [U]

leak out *phr v* [I] if secret information leaks out, a lot of people find out about it ‖ 많은 사람들이 비밀 정보에 대해서 알게 되다. 새다. 누설되다

leak² *n* **1** a small hole that lets liquid or gas flow into or out of something ‖ 액체나 기체를 사물 안이나 밖으로 흐르게 하는 작은 구멍. 새는 곳[구멍]: *a leak in the water pipe* 수도관의 새는 곳 **2** a situation in which someone has secret information ‖ 남이 비밀 정보를 가지고 있는 상황. 누설: *leaks about a secret deal* 비밀 거래에 관한 누설 **3 take/have a leak** SLANG to URINATE ‖ 오줌을 누다

leak·y /'liki/ *adj* having a hole or crack so that liquid or gas can pass through ‖ 구멍이나 틈이 있어서 액체나 기체가 통과할 수 있는. 새는: *a leaky faucet* 물이 새는 수도꼭지

lean¹ /lin/ *v* **1** [I] to move or bend your body in a particular position ‖ 특정한 위치로 몸을 움직이거나 구부리다: *Celia leaned forward and whispered to Angie.* 셀리아는 몸을 앞으로 구부려 앤지에게 속삭였다. **2** [I] to support

lean

yourself or be supported in a position that is not straight or upright ‖ 곧거나 똑바르지 않은 자세를 유지하거나 유지되다. 기대다: *Brad was leaning on/against a wall.* 브래드는 벽에 의지하고 [기대고] 있었다. **3** [T] to put something in a sloping position against something else ‖ 사물을 다른 사물에 비스듬한 상태로 놓다. 기대어 놓다: *Dad leaned the ladder against the wall.* 아빠는 사다리를 벽에 기대어 놓았다.

lean on sb/sth *phr v* [T] to get support and encouragement from someone ‖ 남에게서 지지와 격려를 얻다. 의지하다: *I know I can always lean on my friends.* 나는 친구들에게 항상 의지할 수 있다는 것을 알아.

lean toward sth *phr v* [T] to tend to agree with or support a particular set of opinions, beliefs etc. ‖ 특정한 의견·신념 등에 동의하거나 지지하는 경향이 있다. 기울어지다. 치우치다: *Most of the church's members lean toward the political right.* 대부분의 교회 신도들은 정치적 우파 쪽으로 치우쳐 있다.

lean² *adj* **1** thin in a healthy and attractive way ‖ 건강해 보이고 매력적으로 보이게 날씬한: *lean and athletic* 호리호리하고 강건한 **2** lean meat does not have much fat on it ‖ 고기가 지방이 많지 않은. 비계가 적은. 살코기인 **3** difficult as a result of bad economic conditions or lack of money ‖ 나쁜 경제 상황이나 돈이 부족한 탓에 힘든: *a lean year for the business* 사업상 고난의 한 해 **4** a lean organization, company etc. uses only as much money and as many people as it needs ‖ 조직·회사 등이 필요한 만큼의 돈과 사람들만을 쓰는. 낭비가 없는

lean·ing /'liniŋ/ *n* a tendency to prefer or agree with a particular set of beliefs, opinions etc. ‖ 특정한 신념이나 의견 등을 선호하거나 동의하는 경향. 성향. 기호: *socialist leanings* 사회주의자적 성향

leap¹ /lip/ *v* **leaped** or **leapt** /lɛpt/, **leaped** or **leapt, leaping** [I] **1** to jump high into the air or over something ‖ 공중이나 사물 위로 높이 뛰다. 뛰어오르다. 도약하다: *a dog leaping over a puddle* 물웅덩이를 뛰어넘는 개 한 마리 —see picture on page 947 **2** to move very quickly and with a lot of energy ‖ 매우 빠르고 힘차게 움직이다. 날쌔게 움직이다: *Jon leaped up to answer the phone.* 존은 전화를 받으려고 날쌔게 움직였다.

leap at sth *phr v* [T] to accept an

opportunity very eagerly ‖ 매우 열망하며 기회를 받아들이다. 기꺼이 응하다. 재빨리 잡다: *I leapt at the chance to go to India.* 나는 인도에 갈 기회에 선뜻 응했다.

leap² *n* **1** a big jump ‖ 크게 뜀. 도약. 약진 **2 by/in leaps and bounds** very quickly ‖ 매우 빠르게. 급속히. 척척: *Your English is improving in leaps and bounds.* 네 영어 실력이 몰라보게 향상되고 있다.

leap·frog /'lipfrɑg/ *n* [U] a children's game in which someone bends over and someone else jumps over him/her ‖ 한 사람이 몸을 구부리면 다른 사람이 그 위를 넘는, 아이들이 하는 게임. 등짚고 넘기 – **leapfrog** *v* [I, T]

leap year /'. ./ *n* a year when February has 29 days instead of 28, which happens every four years ‖ 4년마다 발생하는, 2월이 28일이 아니라 29일인 해(年). 윤년

learn /lən/ *v* **1** [I, T] to gain knowledge of a subject or of how to do something, through experience or study ‖ 경험이나 연구를 통해 어떤 주제에 관한 지식이나 어떤 것을 하는 방법을 배우다. 알다 · … 을 배우다: *Lisa's learning Spanish.* 리사는 스페인어를 배우고 있다. / *I'd like to learn (how) to sew.* 나는 바느질하는 법을 배우고 싶다. / *We've been learning about electricity in school.* 우리는 학교에서 전기에 관해 배워오고 있다. **2** [T] to get to know something so well that you can easily remember it ‖ 어떤 것을 너무 잘 알아서 쉽게 그것을 기억할 수 있다. … 을 외다(기억하다): *Have you learned your lines for the play?* 당신은 연극 대사를 외우셨습니까? **3** [I, T] FORMAL to find out information, news etc. by hearing it from someone else ‖ 다른 사람에게 들어서 정보·뉴스 등을 알다. (들어서) 알다: *We only learned about the accident later.* 우리는 그 후에 그 사건에 대해 듣고 알았다. **4 learn sth the hard way** to understand something by learning from your mistakes and experiences ‖ 실수·경험으로 배워 무엇을 이해하다. 어렵게 배우다: *I learned the hard way that bicycle helmets are necessary.* 나는 자전거 헬멧이 필요하다는 것을 어렵게 배웠다. **5 learn your lesson** to suffer so much after doing something wrong that you will not do it again ‖ 잘못된 일을 한 후 너무 많은 고생을 해서 다시는 그런 일을 하지 않게 되다. 경험으로 배우다(알다). 경험으로 뼈저리게 느끼다: *I didn't punish him because I thought he had learned his lesson.* 나는 그가 경험으로 뼈저리게 느꼈다고 생각했기 때문에 그를 처벌하지 않았다. – **learner** *n*: *a fast learner* 학습 속도가 빠른 사람

USAGE NOTE learn, teach, and show

Both **teach** and **learn** are used about things that take time to be able to do. **Learn** means to study or practice so that you can know facts or know how to do something: *Bev's learning how to drive.* **Teach** means to explain to someone what to do or how to do it, over a period of time: *Who taught you how to dance?* **Show** means to use actions to explain how to do something: *Let me show you how the stove works.*

teach와 **learn**은 둘 다 시간을 들여야 할 수 있는 것에 대해 쓰인다. **learn**은 사실이나 어떤 일을 하는 방법을 알기위해 공부하거나 연습하는 것을 뜻한다: 베브는 운전을 배우고 있다. **teach**는 일정 시간 동안 남에게 해야 할 것 또는 하는 방법을 설명하는 것을 뜻한다: 너에게 춤추는 법을 누가 가르쳐 줬니? **show**는 어떤 것을 하는 방법을 설명하기 위해 동작을 사용 하는 것을 뜻한다: 난로를 작동시키는 법을 당신에게 보여 드릴게요.

---

learn·ed /'lənɪd/ *adj* FORMAL having a lot of knowledge because you have read and studied a lot ‖ 많이 읽고 공부를 많이 하여 많이 알고 있는. 박학한

learn·ing /'lənɪŋ/ *n* [U] knowledge gained through reading and study ‖ 독서·연구로 얻은 지식. 학문. 학식

learning dis·a·bil·i·ty /'.. ..,.../ *n* a mental problem that affects a child's ability to learn ‖ 아동의 학습 능력에 영향을 미치는 정신적 문제. 학습 장애

lease¹ /lis/ *n* **1** a legal agreement that allows you to use a building, property etc. when you pay rent ‖ 임대료를 지불하면 건물·부동산 등의 사용을 허가하는 법적 합의. 임대차 계약: *a two-year lease on the apartment* 아파트 2년 임대 계약 **2 a new/fresh lease on life** the feeling of being healthy, active, or happy again after being sick or unhappy ‖ 아프거나 불행한 후 다시 건강하게[활동적이게, 행복하게] 되는 기분. 회복됨. 다시 찾은 삶[행복]

lease² *v* [T] to use or let someone use buildings, property etc. when s/he pays rent ‖ 임대료를 지불하고 건물·부동산 등

을 사용하거나 임대료를 받고 남에게 건물·부동산을 사용하게 하다. 임대[임차]하다: *The offices have been leased to a new company.* 그 사무실은 새로운 회사에게 임대되었다.

leash /liʃ/ *n* a piece of rope, leather etc. fastened to a dog's collar in order to control the dog ‖ 개를 통제하기 위해 개의 목걸이에 채우는 밧줄·가죽 등. (개 등을 매어두는) 가죽 끈

least¹ /list/ *determiner, pron* [the superlative of "little" "little"의 최상급] **1 at least a)** not less than a particular number or amount ‖ 특정한 수나 양보다는 적지 않은. 최소한. 적어도: *The thunderstorm lasted at least two hours.* 심한 뇌우가 적어도 2시간 동안 지속되었다. **b)** used when mentioning an advantage to show that a situation is not as bad as it seems ‖ 상황이 보이는 만큼 나쁘지 않다는 것을 보여주기 위해 이점을 언급할 때에 쓰여: *Well, at least you got your money back.* 적어도 당신은 당신의 돈을 돌려 받았습니다. **c)** said when you want to correct or change something you have just said ‖ 방금 말한 것을 정정하거나 바꾸기 바랄 때 쓰여: *His name is Jerry. At least, I think it is.* 그의 이름은 제리입니다. 적어도 저는 그렇게 생각합니다. **d)** even if nothing else is said or done ‖ 아무것도 말하거나 행하지 않을지라도. 최소한: *Will you at least say you're sorry to her?* 최소한 그녀에게 미안하다고 말은 해야지? **2 the least sb could do** said when you think someone should do something to help someone else ‖ 다른 사람을 돕기 위해 남이 어떤 일을 해야 한다고 생각할 때에 쓰여. 적어도 …은 […을]할 수도 있다[해야 한다]: *The least he could do is help you clean up.* 그는 적어도 너를 도와 청소해야 한다. **3 to say the least** used in order to show that something is more serious than you are actually saying ‖ 어떤 것이 실제로 말하는 것보다 더 심각하다는 것을 보여주는 데에 쓰여. 줄잡아 말하더라도. 적어도: *Mrs. Caferelli was upset, to say the least.* 적어도 카페렐리 부인은 당황했다. **4 the smallest number or amount** ‖ 가장 작은 수나 적은 양. 최소의: *Even the least amount of the poison can kill you.* 그 독은 최소량만으로도 목숨을 앗아 갈 수 있다. —see study note on page 931

least² *adv* **1** less than anything or anyone else ‖ 다른 어떤 사물이나 사람보다 적게. 가장 적게: *It always happens when you least expect it.* 당신이 거의 기대하지 않을 때 항상 그 일은 일어난다. / *I'm the least experienced person on the team.* 내가 팀에서 가장 경험이 적다. **2 least of all** especially not ‖ 특히 어떤 것이 아닌. 가장 …아니다: *I don't like any of them, least of all Debbie.* 나는 그들 중 어느 누구도 좋아하지 않고, 그 중 특히 데비는 가장 좋아하지 않는다.

leath·er /'lɛðɚ/ *n* [U] animal skin that has been treated to preserve it, and is used for making shoes etc. ‖ 신발 등을 만드는 데에 쓰이는, 보존 처리된 짐승의 피부. 가죽: *a leather belt* 가죽벨트

leath·er·y /'lɛðəri/ *adj* hard and stiff like LEATHER ‖ 가죽처럼 단단하고 뻣뻣한. 가죽 같은. 질긴: *leathery hands* 거친 손

leave¹ /liv/ *v* **left, left, leaving**
1 ▶GO AWAY 사라지다◀ [I, T] to go away from a place or person ‖ 한 장소나 사람으로부터 멀리 가다. 떠나다. 출발하다: *Nick doesn't want to leave California.* 닉은 캘리포니아에서 떠나기를 바라지 않는다. / *When are you leaving for Calgary?* (=leaving the place you are in now to go to Calgary) 언제 캘거리로 떠날 거니? / *I feel a little lonely now the kids have all left home.* (=are no longer living at home) 아이들이 모두 집을 떠나서 지금 약간 외롭습니다.
2 leave sb alone SPOKEN used in order to tell someone to stop annoying or upsetting someone else ‖ 누군가가 다른 사람을 귀찮게 하거나 화나게 하는 것을 그만두라고 말하는 데에 쓰여. 가만히 두다. …에게 간섭하지 않다: *Just stop asking questions and leave me alone.* 질문 좀 그만하고 나를 혼자 내버려 두세요.
3 leave sth alone SPOKEN used in order to tell someone to stop touching something ‖ 어떤 것을 만지지 말라고 남에게 말하는 데에 쓰여. 내버려[그대로] 두다. 건드리지 않다: *Timmy! Leave that alone, you'll break it!* 티미! 건드리지 마, 그거 깨뜨릴라.
4 ▶STAY IN POSITION/STATE 위치/상태를 유지하다◀ [T] to make or let something stay in a particular state, place, or position when you are not there ‖ 부재 중일 때 특정한 상태[장소, 위치]로 있게 하거나 그대로 내버려 두다. …을 그대로 두다: *Why did you leave the windows open?* 당신은 왜 창문을 열어 두었습니까?
5 ▶PUT STH IN A PLACE 사물을 어느 장소에 두다◀ [T] to put something in a place for someone ‖ 누군가를 위해 물건을 어떤 장소에 두다. …에 두다: *Just leave the map on the table.* 그냥 지도를

탁자 위에 놓아 두세요. / *Please leave a message and I'll get back to you.* 메시지를 남겨 주시면 회답하겠습니다.

6 ▶FORGET 잊다◀ [T] to forget to take something with you when you leave a place ‖ 어떤 곳에서 떠나면서 무엇을 갖고 가는 것을 잊다. 두고 가다: *I think I left my keys in the car.* 나는 차 안에 열쇠를 두고 온 것 같다.

7 ▶REMAIN 남기다◀ [T] to remain after everything else has been taken away ‖ 그 밖의 모든 것을 가져간 후 남아 있다. …을 남기다: *Is there any coffee left?* 커피 남은 것 있어요?

8 ▶NOT DO STH 어떤 일을 하지 않다◀ [T] to not do something until later ‖ 나중까지 어떤 일을 하지 않다: *Can we leave the ironing for tomorrow?* 우리가 내일까지 다림질을 하지 않아도 괜찮습니까?

9 ▶HUSBAND/WIFE 남편/아내◀ [I, T] to stop living with your husband or wife ‖ 남편이나 아내와 사는 것을 중지하다. 버리다. 버리고 가다: *Tammy's husband left her last year.* 태미의 남편은 작년에 그녀를 떠났다.

10 ▶LET SB DECIDE 결정하게 하다◀ [T] to let someone decide something or be responsible for something ‖ 누군가가 어떤 일을 결정하게 하다, 또는 어떤 일에 책임을 지게 하다. 맡기다. 위임하다: *Leave the details to me; I'll arrange everything.* 세부적인 것을 저에게 맡겨 주시면 제가 모든 것을 준비하죠.

11 ▶GIVE AFTER DEATH 사후에 주다◀ [T] to give something to someone after you die ‖ 죽은 후 누군가에게 어떤 것을 주다. …을 남기고 죽다: *She left a lot of money to her son.* 그녀는 아들에게 많은 돈을 남기고 죽었다.

12 leave it at that SPOKEN to not say or do anything more about a situation ‖ 상황에 대해 더 이상 어떤 것도 말하거나 행동하지 않다. 그 정도로 해두다: *He's not going – let's just leave it at that.* 그는 가지 않을 거야. 더 이상 얘기하지 말자.

13 leave a mark/stain etc. to make a mark etc. that remains afterwards ‖ 표시 등이 계속 남아있게 만들다. 흔적/얼룩을 남기다

14 leave a lot to be desired to be very unsatisfactory ‖ 매우 불만족스럽다: *Your work in this class leaves a lot to be desired.* 이 수업에서의 너의 학업은 개선의 여지가 아주 많다.

15 from where sb left off from the place where you stopped ‖ 멈춘 장소로부터. 중지[중단]한 곳에서부터: *Tomorrow*

we'll start the reading from where we left off. 내일은 우리가 중단한 곳부터 읽기 시작하겠다.

16 leave sb in the lurch INFORMAL to not help someone when you should stay and help him/her or when you promised to help ‖ 남을 머물러서 도와주어야 할 때 또는 도와주기로 약속했을 때에 돕지 않다. …을 궁지에 버려두다. 저버리다

leave sb/sth **behind** *phr v* [T] to forget to take something with you when you leave a place, or to not take something on purpose ‖ 장소를 떠날 때 물건을 갖고 오는 것을 잊어버리다, 또는 고의로 가져오지 않다. …을 남겨두다[놓아두다]: *Did you leave your umbrella behind in the restaurant?* 너 식당에 우산 두고 왔지?

leave sb/sth **out** *phr v* [T] **1** to not include someone or something in a group, list, activity etc. ‖ 그룹[목록, 행위] 등에서 사람이나 사물을 포함하지 않다. …을 제외하다[빼다]: *The stew will still taste okay if we leave out the wine.* 그 스튜는 우리가 와인을 넣지 않아도 여전히 맛있을 것이다. **2 be/feel left out** to feel as if you are not accepted or welcome in a social group ‖ 사교 단체에서 인정을 받거나 환영을 받지 못하는 듯한 느낌이 들다. 소외감[따돌림 당하는 느낌]을 받다: *I always felt left out when I played with my sister and her friends.* 나는 내 여동생 및 그녀의 친구들과 함께 놀 때면 항상 소외감을 느꼈다.

USAGE NOTE leave and forget

Use **leave** to say that you have not brought something with you that you need: *I left my umbrella at home.* You can also use **forget** in this way: *I forgot my umbrella at home.* However, in written or formal English, it is better to say: *I forgot to bring my umbrella.*
leave는 자신이 필요한 것을 가져오지 않았다고 말할 때 쓰인다: 나는 우산을 집에 두고 왔다. **forget**도 이런 식으로 쓸 수 있다: 나는 집에서 우산을 깜빡 놓고 왔다. 하지만 글이나 격식체의 영어에서는 이렇게 말하는 것이 더 낫다: 나는 우산 가져오는 것을 깜빡했다.

---

leave² *n* [U] **1** time that you are allowed to spend away from your work because you are ill, have had a baby etc. ‖ 아프고 아이를 가지는 등의 이유로 일에서 벗어날 수 있게 허락된 시간. (유급) 휴가(기간): *How much sick leave have you taken?* 얼마간의 병가를 받았습

ni까? **2 leave of absence** a period of time that you are allowed to spend away from work for a particular purpose ‖ 특정한 목적으로 일에서 벗어나 보낼 수 있게 허락된 기간. (유급) 휴가 —see usage note at VACATION

leaves /livz/ *n* the plural of LEAF ‖ leaf 의 복수형

lech·er·ous /'lɛtʃərəs/ *adj* a lecherous man is always thinking about sex ‖ 남자 가 항상 성행위에 대해 생각하는. 음란한

lec·tern /'lɛktən/ *n* a high desk that you stand behind when you give a speech ‖ 연설할 때 연사 앞에 놓인 높은 책상. 연설용 탁자

lec·ture¹ /'lɛktʃə/ *n* **1** a long talk to a group of people about a particular subject ‖ 특정 주제에 대해 일단의 사람들 에게 하는 긴 연설. 강의: *She's giving a lecture on modern art.* 그녀는 현대 미술 에 대해 강의 중이다. **2** a long serious talk that criticizes someone or warns him/her about something ‖ 남을 비판하 거나 어떤 것에 대해 남에게 경고하는 길 고 진지한 말. 훈계. 잔소리: *My parents gave me another lecture about my school work.* 나의 부모님은 나의 학업 성 적에 대해 또 다른 훈계를 하셨다.

lecture² *v* **1** [T] to talk angrily or seriously to someone in order to criticize or warn him/her ‖ 남을 비판하 거나 경고하기 위해 그 사람에게 화내거나 심각하게 말하다. 훈계하다: *I wish you'd stop lecturing me about smoking.* 내가 담배 피우는 것에 대한 훈계를 그만 해 주 셨으면 좋겠네요. **2** [I] to teach a group of people about a particular subject, especially at a college ‖ 특히 대학에서, 특정 주제를 일단의 사람들에게 가르치다. 강의하다

led /lɛd/ *v* the past tense and PAST PARTICIPLE of LEAD ‖ lead의 과거·과거 분 사형

ledge /lɛdʒ/ *n* **1** a narrow flat surface like a shelf that sticks out from the side of a building ‖ 건물 측면에 돌출한 선반과 같이 좁고 평평한 표면. (선반 모양의) 수 평 돌기: *a window ledge* 창문 선반 **2** a narrow flat surface of rock that is parallel to the ground ‖ 지면과 평행한 암 석의 좁고 평평한 표면. 바위 턱

ledg·er /'lɛdʒə/ *n* a book in which a bank, business etc. records the money received and spent ‖ 은행·기업 등에서 돈의 출납을 기록하는 장부. (회계) 원장. 대장

leech /litʃ/ *n* a small soft creature that attaches itself to an animal in order to drink its blood ‖ 동물에 들러붙어 그 피를 빨아먹는 흐물흐물한 작은 생물. 거머리

leek /lik/ *n* a vegetable with long straight green leaves, that tastes like onion ‖ 양파와 같은 맛을 내는 길고 곧은 초록색 잎이 있는 식물. 부추

leer /lɪr/ *v* [I] to look at someone in an unpleasant way that shows that you think s/he is sexually attractive ‖ 어떤 사 람이 성적으로 매력적이라고 생각하는 불 쾌한 태도로 그 사람을 바라보다. 선정적 인[추파의] 눈초리로 보다. 곁눈질하다 – **leer** *n*

leer·y /'lɪri/ *adj* worried and unable to trust someone or something ‖ 사람이나 사물을 걱정하고 믿지 못하는. 조심스러 운. 의심 많은: *The girl was leery of strangers.* 그 소녀는 낯선 사람을 경계했 다.

lee·way /'liweɪ/ *n* [U] freedom to do things in the way you want to ‖ 원하는 방식으로 어떤 것을 하는 자유: *Students have some leeway in what they can write about.* 학생들은 작문 주제에 대해 자유롭다.

left¹ /lɛft/ *adj* **1** on the side of your body that contains your heart ‖ 심장이 들어 있는 신체 좌측의. 왼쪽의: *He broke his left leg.* 그의 왼쪽 다리가 부러졌다. **2** on, by, or in the direction of your left side ‖ 왼쪽 방향의 위에[옆에, 안에]: *the first house on the left side of the street* 거리 왼편의 첫 번째 집 —opposite RIGHT¹

left² *adv* toward the left side ‖ 왼쪽으로: *Turn left at the next street.* 다음 거리에 서 왼쪽으로 돌아라. —opposite RIGHT²

left³ *n* **1** the left side or direction ‖ 좌측 이나 왼쪽 방향: *It's the second door on your left.* 당신 왼쪽의 두 번째 문입니다. **2 the left** in politics, the left are people who believe that the government has a duty to pay for social services and to limit the power of businesses ‖ 정치학에 서, 정부는 사회 복지에 대한 비용을 지불 해야 할 의무가 있으며 재계의 힘을 제한 해야 한다고 믿는 사람들. 좌파 — opposite RIGHT³

left⁴ *v* the past tense and PAST PARTICIPLE of LEAVE ‖ leave의 과거·과거 분사형

left field /ˌ. './ *n* **1 in/from left field** INFORMAL unusual or strange compared to the way that people usually behave ‖ 사람들이 보통 행동하는 방식과 비교하여 독특하거나 이상한. 색다른. 뜻밖의. 예기 치 않은: *Some of his ideas are way out in left field.* (=very strange) 그의 생각중 일부는 아주 색다르다. **2** [singular] the area in baseball in the left side of the

OUTFIELD ‖ 야구에서 외야의 좌측 지역. 좌익. 좌익수의 수비 위치

left·hand /'. ./ *adj* on the left side of something ‖ 사물의 왼쪽에 있는. 왼쪽의. 좌측의: *the top left-hand drawer* 왼쪽 제일 윗 서랍

left·hand·ed /,. '../ *adj* **1** someone who is left-handed uses his/her left hand to do most things ‖ 대부분의 일을 왼손으로 하는. 왼손잡이의 **2** done with the left hand ‖ 왼손으로 한. 왼손에 의한. 왼손을 쓴: *a left-handed punch* 왼손 편치 **3** made to be used with the left hand ‖ 왼손을 사용하도록 만들어진. 왼손 잡이용의: *a left-handed iron* 왼손잡이용 다리미 – **left-handed** *adv* —see picture at RIGHT-HANDED

left·o·vers /'lɛft,ouvəz/ *n* [plural] food that remains at the end of a meal and is kept to be eaten later ‖ 식사 후 남아서 후에 먹기 위해 보관하는 음식. 잔반

left-wing /'. ./ *adj* supporting the political aims of groups such as Socialists and Communists ‖ 사회주의자·공산주의자 등 집단의 정치적 목적을 지지하는. 좌파의: *a left-wing newspaper* 좌파 신문 – **left-wing** /,. './ *n* – **left-winger** /,. '../ *n*

leg /lɛg/ *n*

1 ▸BODY PART◂ 신체 부위◂ either of the two long parts of your body that you use to stand or walk, or a similar part on an animal or insect ‖ 서거나 걷기 위해 사용하는 두 개의 긴 신체 부위, 또는 동물이나 곤충의 비슷한 부위. 다리: *How did you hurt your leg?* 너는 어쩌다 다리를 다쳤니? —see picture at BODY

2 ▸FURNITURE◂ 가구◂ one of the upright parts that supports a piece of furniture ‖ 가구를 지탱하는 곧추선 부분의 하나. 다리: *a table leg* 탁자 다리

3 ▸PANTS◂ 바지◂ the part of your pants that covers your leg ‖ 다리를 덮는 바지의 부분

4 ▸FOOD◂ 음식◂ [C, U] the leg of an animal eaten as food ‖ 음식으로 먹는 동물의 다리: *roast leg of lamb* 구운 양(羊) 다리

5 ▸TRIP/RACE ETC.◂ 여행/경주 등◂ a part of a long trip, race, process etc. that is done one part at a time ‖ 한 번에 한 부분을 수행하는 장기 여행·경주·과정 등의 한 부분. 한 구간: *the last leg of our vacation* 방학의 끝자락

6 -legged having a particular number or type of legs ‖ 특정한 개수나 형태의 다리를 가진. 다리가 …인: *a three-legged cat* 다리가 세 개인 고양이

7 leg room space in which to put your legs comfortably when you are sitting in a car, theater etc. ‖ 자동차·극장 등에 앉을 때 편안하게 다리를 놓는 공간

8 not have a leg to stand on INFORMAL to be in a situation where you cannot prove or legally support what you say ‖ 말하는 것을 증명하거나 법적으로 지지할 수 없는 상황에 있다. 성립되지 않는다. 입증할 수 없다 —see also **on its last legs** (LAST¹)

leg·a·cy /'lɛgəsi/ *n* **1** a situation that exists as a result of things that happened at an earlier time ‖ 과거에 발생한 일의 결과로서 존재하는 상황. 유산. 유물: *a legacy of good government* 선정(善政)의 유산 **2** money or property that you receive from someone after s/he dies ‖ 남이 죽은 후 그에게서 물려받은 돈이나 재산. 유산

le·gal /'ligəl/ *adj* **1** allowed, ordered, or approved by law ‖ 법에 의해 허가된 [명령된, 승인된]. 합법적인. 적법한: *a legal agreement* 법적 동의 —opposite ILLEGAL¹ **2** relating to the law ‖ 법과 관련된. 법률(관계)의: *the legal system* 법체제 / *If you don't pay soon, we'll be forced to take legal action.* (=go to court) 당신이 빠른 시일 내에 지불하지 않는다면, 우리는 어쩔 수 없이 법적 조치를 취할 것입니다. – **legally** *adv*: *You can't legally buy alcohol until you're 21.* 당신은 21세가 될 때까지 법적으로 술을 살 수 없습니다. – **legality** /lɪ'gælət̮i/ *n* [U]

le·gal·ize /'ligə,laɪz/ *v* [T] to make something legal that was not legal before ‖ 전에 합법적이지 않았던 것을 합법적인 것으로 만들다. 합법화[적법화]하다: *a campaign to legalize marijuana* 마리화나를 합법화하려는 운동 – **legalization** /,ligələ'zeɪʃən/ *n*

leg·end /'lɛdʒənd/ *n* **1** [C, U] an old well-known story, often about brave people or adventures, or all stories of this kind ‖ 종종 용감한 사람들이나 모험에 대한 오래되고 유명한 이야기, 또는 이러한 종류의 모든 이야기. 전설: *the legend of King Arthur.* 아서 왕의 전설 **2** someone who is famous and admired for being extremely good at doing something ‖ 어떤 일을 매우 능숙하게 하여 유명하고 존경받는 사람. 전설적 인물: *Elvis Presley, the rock and roll legend.* 로큰롤의 전설적 인물, 엘비스 프레슬리

leg·end·ar·y /'lɛdʒən,dɛri/ *adj* **1** famous and admired ‖ 유명하고 존경받는. 전설의. 전설적인. 전설상의: *the* *legendary baseball player Ty Cobb* 전설적 야구 선수 타이 코브 **2** talked or read about in LEGENDS ‖ 전설상에서 이야기되거나 읽혀지는. 전설에 남을 만한

leg·gings /'lɛgɪŋz/ *n* [plural] women's pants that stretch to fit the shape of the body ‖ 체형에 맞게 늘어나는 여성의 바지. 레깅스

leg·gy /'lɛgi/ *adj* having long legs ‖ 긴 다리를 가진. 다리가 호리호리한

leg·i·ble /'lɛdʒəbəl/ *adj* written or printed clearly enough for you to read ‖ 읽기에 충분할 만큼 명확히 쓰이거나 인쇄된. 읽기 쉬운. 읽을 수 있는: *His writing was barely legible.* 그의 글은 간신히 판독할 수 있었다. **—legibly** *adv* — opposite ILLEGIBLE

le·gion /'lidʒən/ *n* a large group of soldiers or people ‖ 군인이나 사람의 큰 무리. 군대. 군중

leg·is·late /'lɛdʒə,sleɪt/ *v* [I] to make a law about something ‖ 어떤 것에 대한 법을 만들다. 법률을 제정하다: *plans to legislate against abortion* 낙태 금지법 제정 계획

leg·is·la·tion /,lɛdʒə'sleɪʃən/ *n* [U] **1** a law or set of laws ‖ 법률이나 법체계: *human rights legislation* 인권 법률 **2** the act of making laws ‖ 법률 제정 행위. 입법 행위

leg·is·la·tive /'lɛdʒə,sleɪtɪv/ *adj* relating to laws or to making laws ‖ 법이나 입법에 관련된. 법적으로[법률로] 정해진. 입법상의: *a legislative assembly* 입법부 / *legislative measures to control illegal drugs* 불법 마약을 통제하기 위한 법적 조치들

leg·is·la·tor /'lɛdʒɪ,sleɪtə/ *n* an elected government official who is involved in making laws ‖ 입법에 관여하는 선출된 정부 관료. 입법자. 입법부 의원

leg·is·la·ture /'lɛdʒə,sleɪtʃə/ *n* an institution that has the power to make or change laws ‖ 법을 제정하거나 개정하는 권력을 가진 기관. 의회. 입법부. 입법기관: *the Ohio state legislature* 오하이오 주 의회

leg·it /lɪ'dʒɪt/ *adj* SPOKEN ⇨ LEGITIMATE

le·git·i·mate /lə'dʒɪtəmɪt/ *adj* **1** correct, allowable, or operating according to the law ‖ 법에 따라 올바른[허용되는, 작용하는]. 합법의. 적법의: *legitimate business activities* 합법적인 사업 활동 **2** fair, correct, or reasonable according to accepted standards of behavior ‖ 인정되는 행동의 기준에 따라 공평한[올바른, 합리적인]. 이치에 맞는. 논리적인: *a legitimate question* 적절한

질문 **3** legitimate children are born to parents who are legally married to each other ‖ 자식들이 상호 합법적으로 결혼한 부모 밑에서 태어난. 적출(자)인 — **legitimacy** *n* [U] —opposite ILLEGITIMACY

lei·sure /'liʒə/ *n* [U] **1** time when you are not working or studying and can relax and do things you enjoy ‖ 일하거나 공부하지 않고 쉬면서 좋아하는 것을 할 수 있는 시간. 여가(시간). 틈: *How do you spend your leisure time?* 당신은 여가 시간을 어떻게 보내십니까? **2 at sb's leisure** as slowly as you want and when you want ‖ 원하는 만큼 천천히·원하는 때에. 한가한[편리한] 때에. 느긋하게: *Read it at your leisure.* 느긋하게 그것을 읽어라.

lei·sure·ly /'liʒəli/ *adj* moving or done in a relaxed way ‖ 편안하게 움직이거나 행동하는. 한가로운. 느긋한: *a leisurely walk around the park* 공원 주변의 한가로운 산책

lem·on /'lɛmən/ *n* [C, U] **1** a yellow fruit that has a sour-tasting juice ‖ 신맛의 과즙을 갖는 노란색 과일. 레몬 —see picture on page 944 **2** INFORMAL something that does not work correctly ‖ 제대로 작동하지 않는 것. 불량품: *This car's a real lemon.* 이 자동차는 정말 고물이다.

lem·on·ade /,lɛmə'neɪd/ *n* [U] a drink made with LEMON juice, sugar, and water ‖ 레몬 주스·설탕·물로 만든 음료. 레모네이드

lend /lɛnd/ *v* **lent, lent, lending 1** [T] to let someone borrow something that you own, which s/he will give back to you later ‖ 자기 소유의 물건을 나중에 되돌려 받기로 하고 어떤 사람에게 빌려주다. 대여하다: *Could you lend me your bike?* 당신의 자전거를 제게 빌려주실 수 있으십니까? —see picture at BORROW **2** [T] if a bank lends money, it lets someone borrow it if s/he pays it back with an additional amount of money ‖ 이자와 더불어 돈을 상환한다는 조건으로 은행이 남에게 돈을 빌려주다. 대출하다: *Our bank lends money at low interest rates.* 우리 은행은 저금리로 돈을 대출해 준다. **3 lend (sb) a hand** to help someone do something, especially something that needs physical effort ‖ 특히 육체적인 힘이 필요할 때 어떤 사람이 하는 일을 돕다. …을 돕다: *Lend me a hand with this box.* 이 상자 나르는 것 좀 도와주세요. **4 lend itself to** to be suitable to be used in a particular way ‖

특정하게 사용하기에 적합하다. …에 알맞다[도움이 되다]: *The story lends itself to a lot of pictures.* 그 이야기는 많은 영화에 적합하다. **5** [T] FORMAL to give something, especially an event, a particular quality ‖ 특히 행사에 특성을 부여하다. …에 주다. 첨가하다. 덧붙이다: *The music lent a little elegance to the event.* 음악이 그 행사를 우아하게 만들었다. **– lender** *n*

USAGE NOTE lend, borrow, and loan

Use **lend** when you let someone use something that s/he will give back to you: *I can lend you a pen if you don't have one.* Use **borrow** when you use something that belongs to someone else, that you will give back to him/her: *Could I borrow your pen for a minute?* Use **loan** to say that a bank or a person is lending money to someone: *I asked the bank manager if he could loan me $1000.* You also use **loan** when a museum, art gallery etc. borrows a work of art: *The paintings have been loaned to the Smithsonian for an exhibition.* In informal speech, we often use **loan** instead of **lend**: *Could you loan me your pen?* However, you should always use **lend** in written or formal English.

lend는 자신에게 되돌려 줄 물건을 어떤 사람이 사용할 수 있게 할 때에 쓰인다: 당신이 펜이 없다면 제가 펜을 빌려 줄 수 있습니다. **borrow**는 되돌려줘야 할 다른 사람의 물건을 사용할 때에 쓰인다: 잠시 당신의 펜을 빌려도 되겠습니까? **loan**은 은행이나 개인이 어떤 사람에게 돈을 빌려주는 것을 말하는 데에 쓰인다: 나는 은행 지점장에게 1000달러를 대출해 줄 수 있는지 물었다. 또한 **loan**은 박물관·화랑 등에서 미술품을 빌릴 때에도 쓰인다: 그 그림들은 전시회를 위해 스미스소니언에 대여되었다. 비격식 구어체에서, 우리는 종종 **loan**을 **lend** 대신 사용하기도 한다: 당신의 펜을 빌려주실 수 있으십니까? 하지만, 문어체나 격식체의 영어에서는 항상 **lend**를 써야 한다.

---

length /lɛŋkθ, lɛnθ/ *n* **1** [C, U] the measurement of something from one end to the other ‖ 사물의 한쪽 끝에서 다른 쪽 끝까지의 측정(치). 길이: *The length of the room is five feet.* 방의 길이는 5피트이다. / *a whale 3 meters in length* 길이가 3미터인 고래 —see

picture at HEIGHT. **2** [C, U] the amount of time that you spend doing something or that something continues for ‖ 어떤 일을 하는 데에 걸리는 시간 또는 어떤 것이 지속되는 시간의 양. 기간: *the length of your stay in the hospital* 당신의 병원 입원 기간 **3** [C, U] the amount of writing in a book, or the amount of time that a movie, play etc. continues for ‖ 책 속의 글의 양, 또는 영화·연극 등이 지속되는 시간. 글의 길이[분량]. 상영[공연] 시간: *We thought the length of the play was fine.* 우리는 연극의 공연 시간이 괜찮았다고 생각했다. **4 go to great lengths to do sth** to be willing to use a lot of different methods to achieve something you want ‖ 원하는 것을 얻기 위해 온갖 방법을 사용하려 하다. 무슨 짓이라도 하다. 어떤 노고[고생]도 마다하지 않다: *She went to great lengths to help us.* 그녀는 우리를 돕기 위해 온갖 방법을 다 동원했다. **5 at length** for a long time ‖ 오랫동안. 장황하게. 충분히. 상세히: *She spoke at length on the dangers of smoking.* 그녀는 흡연의 위험에 대해 장황하게 말했다. **6** a piece of something that is long and thin ‖ 길고 가는 물건. 긴 것: *two lengths of rope* 두 개의 밧줄

length·en /ˈlɛŋkθən/ *v* [I, T] to make something longer or to become longer ‖ 사물을 더 길게 하다 또는 더 길어지다. 늘이다. 연장하다. 늘어나다: *I need this dress lengthened.* 나는 이 드레스 길이를 늘여야겠다.

length·wise /ˈlɛŋkθwaɪz/, **length·ways** /ˈlɛŋkθweɪz/ *adv* in the direction or position of the longest side ‖ 가장 긴 쪽의 방향이나 위치로. 세로로. 길게: *Fold the cloth lengthwise.* 천을 길게 접어라.

length·y /ˈlɛŋkθi/ *adj* continuing for a long time ‖ 오랫동안 계속되는. 장황한. 매우 긴: *a lengthy speech/process/interview* 긴 연설[절차, 인터뷰]

le·ni·ent /ˈliniənt, ˈlinyənt/ *adj* not strict in the way you punish someone or control his/her behavior ‖ 다른 사람을 벌주거나 다른 사람의 행동을 통제하는 방식이 엄하지 않은. 너그러운. 관대한. 인정이 많은: *Her parents are too lenient.* 그녀의 부모님은 너무 너그러우시다. **– leniency** *n* [U]

lens /lɛnz/ *n* **1** a piece of curved glass or plastic that makes things look bigger or smaller ‖ 사물을 더 크게 또는 더 작게 보이게 하는 곡선형 유리나 플라스틱 조각. 렌즈: *He wore glasses with thick* *lenses.* 그는 렌즈가 두 꺼운 안경을 썼다. / *a telescope lens* 망원경 렌 즈 —see also picture at GLASSES **2** the clear part inside your eye that FOCUSes so you can see things clearly ‖ 사물을 선명 하게 볼 수 있도록 초 점을 맞추는 눈 속의 투명한 부분. 수정체

lens
contact lens

lens

Lent /lɛnt/ *n* the 40 days before Easter, when some Christians stop eating particular things or stop particular habits ‖ 일부 기독교인들이 특정한 음식 먹기를 중단하거나 특정한 습관을 멈추는, 부활절 전의 40일간. 사순절(四旬節)

lent *v* the past tense and PAST PARTICIPLE of LEND ‖ lend의 과거·과거 분사형

len·til /'lɛntəl/ *n* a small round seed like a bean, dried and used for food ‖ 식 용으로 말려서 쓰는, 콩 모양의 작고 둥근 씨. 렌즈콩(씨)

Le·o /'liou/ *n* **1** [singular] the fifth sign of the ZODIAC, represented by a lion ‖ 사 자로 상징되는 황도 12궁의 다섯째 별자 리. 사자자리 **2** someone born between July 23 and August 22 ‖ 7월 23일에서 8 월 22일 사이에 태어난 사람. 사자좌 태생 자

leop·ard /'lɛpəd/ *n* a large and strong wild cat with yellow fur and black spots, from Africa and southern Asia ‖ 노란 털 과 검은 반점이 있는 아프리카와 남아시아 산의 크고 강한 야생 고양이. 표범

le·o·tard /'liə,tard/ *n* a tight-fitting piece of woman's clothing that covers the body from the neck to the top of the legs, worn especially while exercising ‖ 특히 운동할 때 입는 목부터 다리 윗부분 까지를 덮는 꼭 끼는 여성복. 리어타드

lep·er /'lɛpə/ *n* someone who has LEPROSY ‖ 나병 환자

lep·ro·sy /'lɛprəsi/ *n* [U] an infectious disease in which someone's skin becomes hard and is gradually destroyed ‖ 피부가 딱딱해지면서 점차 파 괴되는 전염병. 나병(癩病) – **leprous** /'lɛprəs/ *adj*

les·bi·an /'lɛzbiən/ *n* a woman who is sexually attracted to other women; HOMOSEXUAL ‖ 다른 여자에게 성적으로 끌 리는 여성. 여자 동성애자. 레즈비언; ㊌ homosexual —see also GAY

less¹ /lɛs/ *determiner, pron* [the comparative of "little" "little"의 비교급] **1** a smaller amount ‖ 더 적은 양: *The job*

involves much less stress than my last one. 그 일은 지난번 일보다 스트레스를 덜 받는다. / *Skimmed milk has less fat than whole milk.* 탈지유는 전유(全乳)보 다 지방이 덜 함유되어 있다. / *She spends less of her time playing tennis now.* 그녀는 현재 테니스를 치는 데에 시 간을 덜 쏟는다. **2 no less than** used in order to emphasize that an amount or number is large ‖ 양이나 수가 크다는 것 을 강조하는 데에 쓰여. …만큼이나: *It took no less than nine policemen to hold him down.* 그를 제압하는 데에 경찰이 아 홉 명이나 필요했다 **3 nothing less than** used in order to emphasize how serious or important something is ‖ 어떤 것이 얼 마나 심각하거나 중요한지를 강조하는 데 에 쓰여. 바로[아주] …이다: *He demands nothing less than perfection.* 그는 매우 완벽함을 요구한다.

less² *adv* [the comparative of "little"] **1** not so much, or to a smaller degree ‖ 아 주 많지 않은 또는 더 작은 정도로. 더 적 게: *I'm trying to exercise more and eat less.* 나는 더 많이 운동하고 더 적게 먹으 려고 노력 중이다. —compare MORE¹ **2 less and less** continuing to become smaller in amount or degree ‖ 양이나 정 도가 계속해서 더 적어지는. 점점 감소하 여[적게]: *We seem to be spending less and less time together.* 우리가 함께 보내 는 시간이 점점 줄어드는 것 같다. —see study note on page 931

USAGE NOTE less and fewer

Use **less** before an uncountable noun: *You get more food for less money at Shop 'n' Save.* Use **fewer** before a countable noun: *There are fewer trees in the neighborhood now.* **less**는 불가산 명사 앞에 쓴다: 당신은 Shop 'n' Save가게에서 적은 돈으로 더 많은 식품을 살 수 있습니다. **fewer**는 가산 명사 앞에 쓴다: 현재 이 동네에는 전보다 나무가 적다.

---

less·en /'lɛsən/ *v* [I, T] to become less, or to make something become less ‖ 적 어지거나 적어지게 하다. 줄다. 줄이다. 감하다: *A low-fat diet can lessen the risk of heart disease.* 저지방 식단은 심 장병의 위험을 줄일 수 있다. – **lessening** *n* [U] —compare REDUCE

less·er /'lɛsə/ *adj* **1** FORMAL not as large or important as something else, or not as much as something else ‖ 다른 것 보다 크거나 중요하지 않은, 또는 양이 많 지 않은. 보다 작은[적은]. 시시한. 뒤떨

L

어진: *A lesser man* (=someone not as strong or brave) *would have quit before now.* 약자는 이전에 그만뒀을 것이다. **2 the lesser of two evils** the less harmful or unpleasant of two bad choices ‖ 두 개의 나쁜 선택 중 덜 해롭거나 덜 불쾌한 것 **– lesser** *adv*

les·son /ˈlesən/ *n* a period of time in which someone is taught a particular subject or how to do something ‖ 특정 학과나 어떤 것을 하는 방법을 배우는 시간. 수업: *Hannah is taking guitar lessons.* 한나는 기타 교습을 받고 있다. —see also **teach sb a lesson** (TEACH)

let /let/ *v* **let, let, letting 1** [T] to allow someone to do something, or allow something to happen ‖ 다른 사람이 어떤 일 하는 것을 허락하다, 또는 어떤 일이 발생하는 것을 허용하다. …하게 해주다: *I wanted to go but my mother wouldn't let me.* 나는 가고 싶어 했지만 어머니는 허락하지 않으셨다. / *Let the other car go past before you turn.* 네가 방향을 바꾸기 전에 다른 차를 먼저 지나가게 해라. / *Let me finish this, then we can go.* 내가 이것을 끝마치면 우리는 갈 수 있습니다. / *He let Chris have one of his CDs.* 그는 크리스가 자신의 시디 한 장을 갖도록 허락했다. **2 let go** to stop holding something ‖ 어떤 것을 잡아 두지 않다. 자유롭게 해주다: *Marlon let go of the horse, and it ran away.* 말론이 놓아주자 말은 달아났다. **3 let sb go a)** to allow someone to be free after s/he has been kept somewhere ‖ 어딘가에 갇혀 있던 사람을 자유롭게 해주다. 놓아주다. 석방하다: *The police let her go after two hours.* 경찰은 2시간 후 그녀를 풀어줬다. **b)** a phrase meaning to dismiss someone from his/her job, used in order to avoid saying this directly ‖ 누군가를 직장에서 해고시키다라는 뜻의 어구로 이것을 직접적으로 말하는 것을 피하는 데에 쓰여: *I'm afraid we have to let you go.* 당신을 해고해야 할 것 같습니다. **4 let sb know** to tell someone something ‖ 남에게 어떤 것을 말하다. …에게 알려주다: *Could you let me know when you're done?* 당신이 언제 일을 끝낼지 알 수 있을까요? **5 let alone** used in order to say that one thing is not true or does not happen, so another thing cannot possibly be true or happen ‖ 한 가지가 사실이 아니거나 발생하지 않아 나머지 한 가지도 사실이거나 발생할 가능성이 없다고 말하는 데에 쓰여. …은 말할 것도 없이: *Davey can't even crawl yet, let alone walk!* 데이비는 걸음은 말할 것도 없고 아

직 길 수도 없어! **6 let sth go** to decide not to react to or annoying that someone has said or done ‖ 다른 사람이 말하거나 행동한 나쁜 일이나 화나는 일에 반응하지 않기로 결심하다. 그냥 넘어가다: *We'll let it go this time, but don't be late again.* 이번에는 그냥 넘어가지만 다시는 늦지 마라. **7 let me tell you** SPOKEN said in order to emphasize that something is true ‖ 어떤 것이 사실임을 강조하는 데에 쓰여: *It was a really great party, let me tell you.* 정말 대단한 파티였어, 진짜야. **8 let sb/sth be** to stop annoying someone, asking questions, or trying to change things ‖ 다른 사람을 괴롭히거나 질문을 하거나 어떤 것을 변화시키려고 하지 않다. 상관하지 않다. 내버려 두다: *Your mother's had a hard day, so just let her be.* 네 어머니는 힘든 하루를 보내셨으니까 그냥 내버려 둬.

SPOKEN PHRASES

9 let's the short form of "let us," used when you want to suggest that someone do something with you ‖ "let us"의 단축형으로, 자신과 함께 어떤 것을 하자고 어떤 사람에게 제안하고 싶을 때에 쓰여: *Come on, let's dance!* 어서, 춤추자! / *I'm hungry, let's eat.* 배고파요, 식사합시다. **10 let's see a)** said when you are going to try to do something ‖ 어떤 것을 해 보려고 할 때 쓰여: *Let's see if/whether Andy's home.* 앤디가 집에 있는지 보자. **b)** said when you pause because you cannot remember or find something ‖ 어떤 것을 기억할 수 없거나 찾을 수 없어서 잠깐 생각할 때에 쓰여: *Now let's see, where did I put it?* 음 가만 있자, 그걸 어디에 두었더라? **c)** said when you want someone to show you something ‖ 다른 사람이 자신에게 어떤 것을 보여 주기 바랄 때에 쓰여: *"I got a new dress." "Really? Let's see."* "나 새로운 드레스 샀어." "정말? 어디 보자." **11 let me do sth** said when you are offering to help someone ‖ 다른 사람에게 도와주겠다고 제안할 때에 쓰여. …해 줄게: *Let me carry that for you.* 내가 저것을 들어줄게. **12 let's hope** said when you hope something is true or will happen ‖ 어떤 것이 사실이거나 일어나기를 바랄 때에 쓰여: *Let's hope they get here before it snows.* 눈이 오기 전에 그들이 여기 도착하기를 바라자.

let sb ↔ **down** *phr v* [T] to make someone feel disappointed because you have not done what you promised ‖ 약속했던 일을 하지 않아서 다른 사람을 실망시키다. …을 실망시키다. 기대를 저버리다: *You won't let me down, will you?* 너는 나를 실망시키지 않을 거야, 그렇지? —see also LETDOWN

let sb ↔ **in** *phr v* [T] **1** to open the door of a house or building so that someone can come in ‖ 다른 사람이 들어올 수 있도록 집이나 건물의 문을 열다. …을 안으로 들이다[들여보내다]. 통과시키다: *She unlocked the door to let him in.* 그녀는 그가 들어올 수 있도록 문을 열었다. **2 let sb in on sth** to tell someone a secret ‖ 다른 사람에게 비밀을 말하다. …에게 (비밀을) 털어놓다: *I'll let you in on a little secret.* 내가 조그만 비밀을 네게 알려줄게.

let sb ↔ **into** sth *phr v* [T] to allow someone to come into a house or building ‖ 다른 사람이 집이나 건물에 들어오는 것을 허락하다: *Maria wouldn't let Billy into her house.* 마리아는 빌리를 그녀의 집에 들이지 않으려 했다.

let sb ↔ **off** *phr v* [T] to not punish someone, or to not make him/her do something s/he was supposed to do ‖ 어떤 사람을 처벌하지 않다, 또는 어떤 사람이 하게 되어 있는 것을 시키지 않다. (형벌을) 면제하다. 눈감아 주다: *I'll let you off this time, but don't do it again.* 내가 이번엔 혼내지 않을 테니, 다시는 그러지 마라.

let on *phr v* [I] to behave in a way that shows you know a secret ‖ 비밀을 알고 있다고 나타내듯이 행동하다. 비밀을 누설하다: *Don't let on (that) you know!* 당신이 알고 있는 비밀을 누설하지 마!

let out *phr v* **1** [T **let** sb ↔ **out**] to allow someone to leave a building, room etc. ‖ 다른 사람이 건물·방 등을 떠나게 허락하다. …을 나가게 하다. 해방시키다: *Let the dog out, please.* 개를 내보내 주세요. **2** [I] if a school, college, movie etc. lets out, the people attending it can leave ‖ 학교·대학·영화 등에 참석했던 사람들이 떠날 수 있다. 끝나다: *School lets out at 3:30.* 학교는 3시 30분에 파한다. **3** [T **let** sth ↔ **out**] to allow light, air etc. to escape from a place ‖ 한 장소에서 불빛·공기 등이 새어 나가게 하다. 유출시키다: *Close the door – you're letting all the heat out.* 문을 닫으세요. 열이 모두 빠져 나가고 있어요. **4 let out a scream/ cry etc.** to make a sound, especially a loud one ‖ 소리를, 특히 크게 내다. 비명/

소리 등을 내다[지르다]: *Suddenly, Ben let out a yell and jumped up.* 갑자기, 벤은 소리치며 벌떡 일어났다.

let up *phr v* [I] if rain or snow lets up, it stops or there is less of it ‖ 비나 눈이 멈추거나 줄다. 멎다. 약해지다 —see also LETUP

let·down /ˈlɛtdaʊn/ *n* [singular] INFORMAL something that makes you feel disappointed because it is not as good as you expected ‖ 기대했던 만큼 좋지 않아 실망스럽게 하는 것. 환멸. 실망: *The movie was a real letdown!* 그 영화는 정말 실망스러웠어!

le·thal /ˈliːθəl/ *adj* able to kill someone ‖ 사람을 죽일 수 있는. 치명적인: *a lethal dose of heroin* 치사량의 헤로인

le·thar·gic /ləˈθɑːrdʒɪk/ *adj* having no energy, so that you feel lazy or tired ‖ 나른함이나 피곤함을 느낄 만큼 기운이 없는. 무기력한 **– lethargy** /ˈlɛθərdʒi/ *n* [U]

let's /lɛts/ ⇨ **let's** (LET)

let·ter /ˈlɛtər/ *n* **1** a written message that you put into an envelope and send to someone by mail ‖ 봉투에 넣어 다른 사람에게 우편으로 보내는 글로 쓴 서신. 편지: *Mollie wrote a letter to her friend Gail.* 몰리는 친구 게일에게 편지를 썼다. **2** one of the signs in writing that represents a sound in speech ‖ 말할 때의 소리를 나타내는 글로 된 기호의 하나. 문자: *There are 26 letters in the English alphabet.* 영어 알파벳에는 26개의 문자가 있다 **3 (do sth) to the letter** to do exactly what you are told to do ‖ 하라고 지시받은 것을 정확히 하다. 지시대로[글자 그대로](하다): *He followed their instructions to the letter.* 그는 그들의 지시대로 따랐다.

let·ter·head /ˈlɛtərˌhɛd/ *n* the name and address of a person or business printed at the top of a piece of paper ‖ 종이 상단에 인쇄된 개인이나 회사의 이름과 주소

let·tuce /ˈlɛtɪs/ *n* [C, U] a round green vegetable with large thin leaves, eaten raw in SALADs ‖ 커다랗고 얇은 잎이 있으며 익히지 않고 샐러드로 먹는 둥근 초록색 야채. (양)상추 —see picture on page 944

let·up /ˈlɛtʌp/ *n* [singular, U] an end to an activity, or a decrease in activity ‖ 행위의 종지(終止), 또는 활동의 감소. 정지. 감소: *There has been no letup in the requests for help.* 도움의 요청이 끊이지 않고 있다.

leu·ke·mia /luˈkimiə/ *n* [U] a serious

disease that affects the blood and that can cause death ‖ 혈액에 영향을 미쳐 죽음을 야기할 수 있는 심각한 질병. 백혈병

lev·ee /ˈlɛvi/ n a special wall that is built to stop a river from flooding ‖ 강의 범람을 막기 위해 세운 특별한 벽. 제방

lev·el¹ /ˈlɛvəl/ n 1 the amount, degree, or number of something, as compared to another amount, degree, or number ‖ 다른 것과 비교되는 양[정도, 수]. 수준. 정도. 단계: *There were **high levels of** radiation after the explosion.* 폭발 후 고농도의 방사능이 존재했다. / *We can expect the temperature to stay at these levels until Friday.* 우리는 금요일까지 기온이 이 수준을 유지할 것으로 예상한다. 2 the height or position of something in relation to the ground or another thing ‖ 지면이나 다른 것과 관련하여 어떤 것의 높이나 위치. 수준. 위치: *Check the water level in the radiator.* 냉각기의 물높이를 확인해라. / *All the pictures were hung at eye level.* (=at the same height as people's eyes) 모든 그림은 눈높이에 걸려 있었다. 3 a standard of skill or ability in a particular subject, sport etc. ‖ 특정 주제·스포츠 등의 기술이나 능력 수준: *reading exercises designed for every level of student* 모든 수준의 학생들에 맞게 고안된 읽기 연습 / *Few athletes can compete at this level.* 이 수준에서 경쟁할 수 있는 선수는 거의 없다. 4 a particular position in a system that has different ranks ‖ 상이한 계급이 있는 체제에서의 특정 지위: *high-level talks* (=discussions between important people) 고위급 회담 5 a floor in a building that has several floors ‖ 층이 여러 개인 건물 내의 한 층. …층: *Housewares is on Level 3.* 가정용품은 3층에 있다. 6 a tool used for checking if a surface is flat ‖ 표면이 평평한지를 검사하는 데에 쓰이는 도구. 수준기 —see also SEA LEVEL

level² adj 1 flat, with no surface higher than the rest ‖ 평평하며 표면이 나머지 것보다 높지 않은. 수평의. 같은 높이의: *The floor was level but the walls sloped inward.* 바닥은 평평하나 벽은 안쪽으로 기울었다. 2 at the same height or position as something else ‖ 다른 것과 같은 높이나 위치의: *My head was level with his chin.* 내 머리는 그의 턱 높이였다.

level³ v [T] 1 to knock something down to the ground and destroy it ‖ 어떤 것을 지면으로 쓰러뜨려 파괴하다. 무너뜨리다. 때려눕히다: *An earthquake leveled*

several buildings in the city. 지진은 그 도시에 있는 여러 개의 건물을 파괴했다. 2 **level a charge against sb** to say that you think someone has done something wrong; ACCUSE ‖ 자신이 생각하기에 남이 잘못됐다고 말하다. 비난을 남에게 돌리다; 윤 accuse

level off/out phr v [I] to stop going up or down, and continue at the same height or amount ‖ 올라가거나 내려가지 않고 계속해서 동일한 높이나 양에 머물다. 수평으로 되다. 안정되다. 변동하지 않다: *The plane climbed to 20,000 feet, then leveled off.* 그 비행기는 20,000피트로 고도를 올린 후 수평 비행했다. / *Oil prices have leveled off at $25 a barrel.* 유가는 배럴당 25달러로 안정되었다.

level with sb phr v [T] INFORMAL to speak honestly with someone and tell him/her what you really think ‖ 남에게 솔직히 자신이 실제로 생각하는 것을 말하다. 털어놓다. (…에게) 사실을 말하다

level-head·ed /ˌ.. ˈ../ adj calm and sensible in making decisions ‖ 결정하는 데 침착하고 분별 있는. 온건한. 분별 있는

lev·er /ˈlɛvɚ, ˈli-/ n 1 a long metal BAR that you use to lift something by putting one end under the object and pushing the other end down ‖ 한쪽 끝의 위에 물건을 놓고 다른 한쪽 끝을 눌러서 물건을 들어올리는 데에 쓰는 긴 금속 막대기. 지레 2 a stick or handle on a machine that you move to make the machine work ‖ 기계를 작동시키려고 움직이는 막대나 손잡이 —**lever** v [T]

lev·er·age¹ /ˈlɛvərɪdʒ, ˈli-/ n [U] 1 influence that you use to make people do what you want ‖ 남에게 자신이 원하는 것을 시키기 위해 사용하는 영향력. 세력: *Small businesses have less leverage in dealing with banks.* 소규모 기업들은 은행과 거래하는 데 영향력이 적다. 2 the action, use, or power of a LEVER ‖ 지레의 작용[사용, 힘]

leverage² v [T] to buy INVESTMENTs using money you have borrowed ‖ 차입금을 써서 투자물을 구입하다. 차입금으로 투기하다

lev·i·tate /ˈlɛvəˌteɪt/ v [I] to rise and float in the air as if by magic ‖ 마술에 의한 것처럼 공중에 올라가 부양하다. 공중에 떠오르다 —**levitation** /ˌlɛvəˈteɪʃən/ n [U]

lev·i·ty /ˈlɛvəti/ n [U] FORMAL the quality of telling jokes and having fun instead of being serious ‖ 진지하지 않고 농담하며 즐거워함. 경솔. 경박

lev·y¹ /ˈlɛvi/ v [T] **levy a tax/charge etc.** to officially make someone pay a tax etc. ‖ 공식적으로 남에게 세금 등을 내게 하다. 세금/요금을 징수하다[부과하다]

levy² n an official demand for someone to pay a tax ‖ 남에게 세금을 내라는 공식적인 요구. 징세

lewd /lud/ adj using rude words or behaving in a way that makes someone think of sex ‖ 남에게 성행위를 연상시키는 무례한 말이나 행동을 하는. 음란한. 외설스러운: *lewd comments* 음란한 말

lex·i·con /ˈlɛksɪˌkɑn/ n all the words used in a language or a particular profession, or a book containing lists of these words ‖ 어떤 언어나 특정 직업에 쓰이는 모든 단어, 또는 이러한 단어 목록이 있는 책. 용어(집). 사전: *a lexicon of cooking terms* 요리 용어집 – **lexical** /ˈlɛksɪkəl/ adj

li·a·bil·i·ty /ˌlaɪəˈbɪləti/ n **1** [U] the state of being responsible for something, especially for injury or damage ‖ 어떤 것에 대해, 특히 상해나 손해의 책임이 있는 상태. 책임. 의무: *The company has admitted liability for the accident.* 그 회사는 그 사고에 대해 책임이 있음을 인정했다. **2** [singular] something that makes it difficult to do something, or that causes problems for you ‖ 어떤 일 하는 것을 어렵게 만드는 것, 또는 문제를 일으키는 것. 짐. 장애: *Johnson was a real liability to the team.* 존슨은 팀에 정말 골칫거리였다. — compare ASSET

li·a·ble /ˈlaɪəbəl/ adj **1 be liable to do sth** to be likely to do something or likely to behave in a particular way ‖ 어떤 일을 하는 경향이 있거나 특정하게 행동하려 하다. …하기 쉽다. 걸핏하면 …하다. …할 듯하다: *She's liable to watch programs that aren't good for her.* 그녀는 자신에게 좋지 않은 프로그램을 시청하는 경향이 있다. / *The car's liable to overheat on long trips.* 장기 여행에서는 자동차가 과열되기 쉽다. **2** legally responsible for the cost of something ‖ 어떤 것의 비용에 대해 법적인 책임이 있는: *The university was not held liable for the damage done by its students.* 대학은 그 대학 학생들이 입힌 손해에 대해 책임이 없었다.

li·aise /liˈeɪz/ v [I] to exchange information with someone who works in a different office or job, so that everyone knows what is happening ‖ 발생하는 일을 모든 사람이 알기 위해 다른 사무실이나 일자리에서 일하는 사람과 정보를 교환하다. (…과) 연락을 취하다

li·ai·son /liˈeɪˌzɑn/ n **1** a sexual relationship between two people who are not married ‖ 결혼하지 않은 두 사람 사이의 성적 관계. 간통. 밀통 **2** [singular, U] a working relationship between two groups, companies etc. ‖ 두 집단·회사 간의 일하는 관계. 연락. 교섭

li·ar /ˈlaɪə/ n someone who tells lies ‖ 거짓말을 하는 사람. 거짓말쟁이

lib /lɪb/ n INFORMAL ⇨ LIBERATION

li·bel¹ /ˈlaɪbəl/ n [C, U] the illegal act of writing or printing something about someone that is not true, and that would make people have a bad opinion of him/her ‖ 남에 대해 사실이 아닌 것과 사람들이 그 사람에 대해 좋지 않은 견해를 갖게 할 수 있는 것을 쓰거나 인쇄하는 불법적 행위. 명예훼손(죄): *He is suing the magazine for libel.* 그는 명예훼손으로 그 잡지를 고소한 상태다. —compare SLANDER

libel² v [T] to write or print a LIBEL against someone ‖ 다른 사람에 대한 명예훼손문을 쓰거나 인쇄하다. 문서로 명예훼손하다 – **libelous** adj

lib·er·al¹ /ˈlɪbrəl, -bərəl/ adj **1** willing to understand or respect the different behavior, ideas etc. of other people ‖ 다른 사람의 서로 다른 행동·생각 등을 기꺼이 이해하거나 존중하는. 편견이 없는. 마음이 넓은. 관대한. 관용[인습]에 얽매이지 않는: *a liberal attitude toward sex* 섹스에 대한 자유스러운 태도 **2** supporting changes in political, social, or religious systems that allow people more freedom to do what they want ‖ 사람들이 원하는 바를 할 수 있게 더 많은 자유를 허용하는 정치[사회, 종교] 체제의 변화를 지지하는. 자유주의의. 진보적인: *a liberal democracy* 자유 민주주의 **3** FORMAL generous ‖ 관대한. 후한. 아끼지 않는. …에 인색하지 않은. 선뜻 잘 주는: *a liberal donation to charity* 아낌없는 자선 기부

liberal² n someone with LIBERAL opinions or principles ‖ 자유스러운 견해나 원칙을 가진 사람. 자유[진보]주의자. 자유사상가

liberal arts /ˌ.. ˈ./ n [plural] subjects that increase someone's general knowledge, rather than teach technical skills ‖ 전문적 기술을 가르치기보다 사람의 일반 지식을 증대시키는 과목들. 교양과목

lib·er·al·is·m /ˈlɪbrəˌlɪzəm/ n [U] opinions or principles that support

L

changes in politics, religion etc. ‖ 정치·종교 등의 변화를 지지하는 견해나 원칙. 자유[진보]주의

lib·er·al·ize /'lɪbrə,laɪz/ v [T] to make a system, law, or moral attitude less strict ‖ 체제[법, 도덕적 태도]를 덜 엄격하게 하다. 완화하다. 관대하게 풀다

lib·er·al·ly /'lɪbrəli/ adv in large amounts; generously ‖ 많은 양으로. 아낌없이. 후하게. 풍부[넉넉]하게; 관대하게

lib·er·ate /'lɪbə,reɪt/ v [T] **1** to make someone free from feelings or situations that make his/her life difficult ‖ 어떤 사람을 힘들게 하는 감정이나 상황에서 자유롭게 해주다. 풀어주다. 해방하다: *In the 1930s, electricity liberated farmers from many hard chores.* 1930년대에 전기는 농부들을 많은 힘든 일로부터 자유롭게 해주었다. **2** to free a place and the people in it from political or military control ‖ 정치나 군사 통제로부터 한 장소나 그 안의 사람들을 자유롭게 해주다. 해방시키다. 억압에서 풀어주다: *The city was liberated by the Allies in 1944.* 그 도시는 1944년 연합군에 의해 해방되었다. **– liberator** n

lib·er·at·ed /'lɪbə,reɪt̬ɪd/ adj free to do the things you want, and not controlled by rules or other people ‖ 규칙이나 다른 사람에 의해 통제받지 않고 원하는 것을 자유롭게 하는. 해방된

lib·er·a·tion /,lɪbə'reɪʃən/ n [U] the state of being LIBERATED ‖ 해방된 상태. 해방

lib·er·ty /'lɪbət̬i/ n **1** [C, U] the freedom to do what you want without having to ask permission from people in authority ‖ 권력자에게 허가를 청할 필요 없이 원하는 것을 할 수 있는 자유: *principles of liberty and democracy* 자유와 민주주의라는 원칙 / *civil liberties* (=the things you have a legal right to do) 시민의 자유 **2 be at liberty to do sth** to have permission to do something ‖ 어떤 것을 할 수 있는 허가를 갖다. …해도 되는 상태이다. …을 할 권리가 있다: *I'm not at liberty to say where he is at the moment.* 나는 그가 지금 어디에 있는지 말할 수 없습니다. **3 take the liberty of doing sth** to do something without asking permission, because you do not think it will upset or offend anyone ‖ 아무도 화나게 하거나 기분 상하게 할 거라고 생각하지 않기 때문에 허가 요청 없이 어떤 일을 하다. 자유롭게 …하다. 구애받지 않고 …하다: *I took the liberty of helping myself to a piece of cake.* 나는 부담 없이 케이크 한 조각을 먹었다. **4**

take liberties with sth to make unreasonable changes in something such as a piece of writing ‖ 글 등을 무분별하게 바꾸다. 제멋대로[함부로] 바꾸다

li·bi·do /lɪ'bidoʊ/ n [C, U] TECHNICAL someone's desire to have sex ‖ 성교를 하고 싶어 하는 사람의 욕구. 성충동. 성욕. 리비도

Li·bra /'librə/ n **1** [singular] the seventh sign of the ZODIAC, represented by a SCALE ‖ 저울로 상징되는 황도 12궁의 일곱번째 별자리. 천칭(天秤)자리 **2** someone born between September 23 and October 23 ‖ 9월 23일부터 10월 23일 사이에 태어난 사람. 천칭좌 태생자

li·brar·i·an /laɪ'brɛriən/ n someone who works in a library ‖ 도서관에서 일하는 사람. 사서(司書). 도서관원

li·brar·y /'laɪ,brɛri/ n a room or building containing books that you can read there or borrow ‖ 그 자리에서 읽거나 빌릴 수 있게 책을 보유하고 있는 실내나 건물. 도서관. 도서실. 서재. 서고

lice /laɪs/ n the plural of LOUSE ‖ louse의 복수형

li·cense¹ /'laɪsəns/ n **1** an official document that gives you permission to own something or do something ‖ 어떤 것을 소유하거나 할 수 있는 허가를 부여하는 공식 증서. 면허(증[장]). 인가[허가](서[증]): *a driver's license* 운전면허증 **2** [U] FORMAL freedom to do or say whatever you think is best ‖ 최선이라 생각하는 것은 무엇이든 하거나 말하는 자유. (지나친) 자유. 방종. 방자

license² v [T] to give official permission for someone to own or do something ‖ 다른 사람이 어떤 것을 소유하거나 할 수 있게 공식적으로 허가하다. …을 인가하다. 면허를 주다: *He is licensed to carry a gun.* 그는 총기 소지 면허가 있다.

license plate /'.. ,./ n a sign with numbers and letters on it at the front and back of your car ‖ 차의 앞과 뒤에 부착된 숫자와 문자가 쓰인 표지. (자동차) 번호판 —see picture on page 943

li·chen /'laɪkən/ n [C, U] a gray, green, or yellow plant that spreads over the surface of trees and stones ‖ 나무와 돌의 표면을 덮고 있는 회색[녹색, 노란색] 식물. 지의(地衣)(류) —compare MOSS

lick¹ /lɪk/ v [T] **1** to move your tongue across the surface of something in order to eat it, taste it etc. ‖ 어떤 것을 먹기·맛보기 등을 위해 혀로 그 표면을 핥다: *Judy's dog jumped up to lick her face.* 주디의 개는 펄쩍 뛰어올라 그녀의 얼굴을

활았다. **2** INFORMAL to defeat an opponent or solve a problem ∥ 적을 패배시키거나 문제를 해결하다. 이기다. 능가하다. 해치우다: *"It looks like we have the fire licked," said Chief Grafton.* "화재가 진화된 것 같군"이라고 그 래프턴 소방대장이 말했다. **3 lick your lips** INFORMAL to feel eager or excited because you are expecting something ∥ 어떤 것에 대한 기대로 열망이나 흥분을 느끼다

lick

lick² *n* **1** [C usually singular] an act of LICKing something with your tongue ∥ 혀로 어떤 것을 핥는 행위. 핥기: *Can I have a lick of your ice cream cone?* 네 아이스크림콘을 한 입 먹을 수 있어? **2 a lick of paint** INFORMAL a small amount of paint ∥ 소량의 페인트. 한 번 바를[칠할] 양의 페인트 **3 not do a lick of work** INFORMAL to not do any work at all ∥ 어떤 일도 전혀 하지 않다. 전혀 일하지 않다. 일을 조금도 하지 않다

lick·e·ty-split /ˌlɪkəti ˈsplɪt/ *adv* OLD-FASHIONED very fast ∥ 매우 빠르게. 전속력으로. 재빨리

lick·ing /ˈlɪkɪŋ/ *n* [singular] INFORMAL the act of hitting someone as a punishment ∥ 벌로 다른 사람을 때리는 행위. 매질. 체벌

lic·o·rice /ˈlɪkərɪs/ *n* [U] a strong-tasting sweet black substance used in candy and medicine ∥ 과자와 약에 쓰이는 단 맛이 강한 흑색 물질. 감초

lid /lɪd/ *n* **1** a cover for a pot, box, or other container ∥ 항아리[상자, 기타 용기]의 덮개. 뚜껑: *Where's the lid for this jar?* 이 항아리 뚜껑이 어디 있어요? — see picture at PAN¹ **2 keep/put a lid on** INFORMAL to control a situation so that it does not become worse ∥ 상황을 통제해서 더 이상 나빠지지 않게 하다. …을 억제 [단속]하다: *putting a lid on government spending* 정부 지출을 통제하기 **3** ⇨ EYELID

lie¹ /laɪ/ *v* **lay, lain, lying** [I] **1 a)** to be in a position in which your body is flat on the floor, a bed etc. ∥ 신체가 바닥·침대 등에 평평한 자세로 있다. 눕다. 드러눕다: *We lay on the beach for a couple of hours.* 우리는 두어 시간 동안 해변에 누워 있었다. **b)** also **lie down** to put yourself in this position ∥ 누운 자세를 취하다. (드러)눕다: *I'm going upstairs to lie down.* 나는 드러누우러 위

층에 간다. **2** to be in a particular place or position ∥ 특정 장소나 위치에 있다. 놓여[위치해] 있다. …에 존재하다[자리잡고 있다]: *The town lies to the east of the lake.* 그 읍은 호수의 동쪽에 자리하고 있다. / *Letters and bills were lying on the kitchen table.* 편지와 청구서들이 부엌 탁자 위에 놓여 있었다. **3** used in order to say where something such as a reason or answer can be found ∥ 이유나 해답 등을 어디서 찾을 수 있는가를 말하는 데에 쓰여. …에 있다. …에서 찾을[얻을] 수 있다: *The solution lies in alternative sources of power.* 해결책은 대체 동력원에서 찾을 수 있다. **4** to remain in a particular condition or place ∥ 특정 조건이나 장소에 남아 있다. …인 채로 있다. …에 놓여 있다: *The letters lay hidden in her attic for forty years.* 그 편지들은 40년 동안 그녀의 다락방에 숨겨진 채로 남아 있었다. **5 lie low** to remain hidden because you do not want someone to find you ∥ 다른 사람이 찾아내는 것을 원하지 않아서 숨어 지내다. 눈에 띄지 않게 피하다[숨다] **6 lie ahead** if something lies ahead, it is going to happen in the future ∥ 어떤 일이 미래에 일어날 예정이다. 앞길에 가로놓여[대기하고] 있다. 앞에 전개되다: *There are difficulties that lie ahead.* 앞날에 어려움이 놓여 있다. **7 lie in wait (for sb/sth)** to remain hidden in order to attack someone or something ∥ 다른 사람이나 사물을 공격하기 위해 숨은 채로 있다. 매복하다 — see also **not take sth lying down** (TAKE¹) —see picture at LAY¹ —see usage note at LAY¹

lie around *phr v* **1** [I, T] to be left out of the correct place, so that things look messy ∥ 올바른 위치에서 벗어나 있어서 물건들이 뒤죽박죽으로 보이다. 아무렇게나[제멋대로] 놓여 있다[딩굴고 있다]. 여기 저기[어지럽게] 널려 있다: *Books and papers were lying around everywhere.* 책과 종이들이 도처에 널려 있었다. **2** [I] to spend time relaxing, especially by lying down ∥ 긴장을 풀고서 특히 누워서 시간을 보내다. 빈둥빈둥 누워 지내다. 게으름을 피우다: *We just lay around on the beach the whole time.* 우리는 해변에서 내내 그냥 누워 빈둥거리며 지냈다.

lie behind sth *phr v* [T] to be the true reason for an action, decision etc. ∥ 행동·결정 등의 진짜 이유가 되다. 배후에 있다: *I wonder what really lay behind her decision to quit her job.* 나는 그녀가 직장을 그만두기로 결정한 진짜 숨은 이유

가 무엇이었는지 궁금하다.

lie² *v* **lied, lied, lying** [I] to tell someone a lie ‖ 남에게 거짓말을 하다: *I was pretty sure she was lying to me about where she'd been that night.* 나는 그녀가 그날 밤 있었던 곳에 대해 거짓말 하고 있음을 확신했다.

lie³ *n* something that you say or write that you know is not true ‖ 사실이 아닌 줄 알면서 말하거나 쓰는 것. 거짓말. 허언: *Mom spanked her for telling lies.* 엄마는 그녀가 거짓말을 했다고 엉덩이를 때 렸다.

lie de·tect·or /'. .,../ *n* a machine used by the police to find out if someone is lying ‖ 거짓말 하는지를 알아내려고 경찰이 사용하는 기계. 거짓말 탐지기

lien /lin, 'liən/ *n* TECHNICAL a legal right to take someone's property if s/he does not pay a debt ‖ 남이 빚을 상환하지 않으면 그 재산을 취할 수 있는 법적 권리. 유치권. 담보권

lieu /lu/ *n* FORMAL **in lieu of** instead of ‖ …대신에: *property given in lieu of payment* 지불금 대신에 받은 재산

lieu·ten·ant, Lieutenant /lu'tɛnənt/ *n* an officer who has a middle rank in the Army, Navy, Air Force, or Marines ‖ 육군[해군, 공군, 해병대]에서 중간 계급을 가진 장교. 중위

life /laɪf/ *n, plural* **lives**
1 ▶PERIOD OF LIFE 일생◀ [C, U] the period of time between someone's birth and death ‖ 사람의 출생과 죽음 사이의 시간. 일생. 생애. 평생: *Charles lived in New York City all his life.* 찰스는 평생을 뉴욕시에서 살았다. / *It was one of the happiest days of my life.* 그것은 내 인생의 가장 행복한 날들 중 하나였다. / *He became a father late in life.* (=when he was fairly old) 그는 만년에 아버지가 되었다.
2 ▶BEING ALIVE 살아있음◀ [C, U] the state or quality of being alive ‖ 살아 있는 상태나 특성. 생명(현상). 목숨: *a baby's first moments of life* 아기 탄생의 첫 순간 / *Firemen risked their lives* (=did something during which they could have been killed) *to save the children.* 소방수들은 목숨을 걸고 아이들을 구했다.
3 ▶WAY OF LIVING 사는 방식◀ [C, U] all the experiences and activities that are typical of a particular way of living ‖ 특정 생활 방식의 전형적인 모든 경험과 활동. 생활. 삶: *Life in L.A. is exciting.* LA에서의 생활은 흥미진진하다. / *country life* 전원 생활 / *He's spent most of his working life* (=time spent working)

with one company. 그는 직장 생활의 대부분을 한 회사에서 보냈다. / *the American way of life* 미국식 생활 방식 / *This is the life, Joan!* (=what we are doing is the most enjoyable way to live) 이것이 인생이다, 조안!
4 ▶EXPERIENCES 경험◀ the type of experience that someone has during his/her life ‖ 사람이 사는 동안 겪은 일종의 경험. 인생(살이). 삶: *Tia had a full and happy life.* 티아는 충만하고 행복한 삶을 보냈다. / *I'm hoping to win the lottery and live a life of luxury!* 나는 복권에 당첨되어 호화로운 삶을 살기를 바라고 있어! / *Then he started telling me his whole life story.* (=all the things that happened in his life) 그러고 나서 그는 인생살이를 모두 이야기하기 시작했다.
5 ▶LIVING THINGS 생명체◀ [U] living things such as people, animals, or plants ‖ 사람[동물, 식물] 등 살아 있는 것. 생명이 있는 것. 생물: *Do you think there is life on other planets?* 당신은 다른 행성에 생명체가 있다고 생각하십니까? / *studying the island's plant life* 섬의 식생군(植生群) 연구
6 private/sex/social etc. life activities in your life that are private, relate to sex, are done with friends etc. ‖ 인생에 있어서 사적이거나 성과 관련되거나 친구들과 함께 한 활동. 사생활/성생활/사회생활
7 ▶MOVEMENT 운동◀ [U] activity or movement ‖ 활동이나 움직임. 원기. 생기. 활력(소): *There were no signs of life in the house.* 그 집에는 인기척이 없었다. / *Katie was young and full of life.* (=very cheerful and active) 케이티는 젊고 활기로 가득찼었다.
8 quality of life the level or quality of health, success, and comfort in someone's life ‖ 사람의 생활에서 건강·성공·안락함의 수준이나 질. 삶의 질
9 ▶EXISTENCE 존재◀ [U] human existence, and all the things that can happen during someone's life ‖ 인간 존재와 사람의 일생 동안 일어날 수 있는 모든 것. 인생(살이). 세상(살이): *Life can be hard sometimes.* 세상살이는 때로 힘들 수 있다.
10 ▶PRISON 감옥◀ [U] also **life in prison** ⇨ LIFE SENTENCE
11 ▶WORKING/EXISTING 작용/존속◀ [singular] the period of time that something continues to work or exist ‖ 사물이 계속 작용하거나 존속하는 기간. 수명. 존속[활동, 유효] 기간: *long-life batteries* 수명이 긴 배터리

12 (in) real life what really happens rather than what only happens in stories or someone's imagination ‖ 이야기나 사람의 상상 속에서만 일어나는 것이 아닌 실제로 일어나는 것. 실생활(에서)
13 bring sth to life/come to life to make something more exciting, or to start to become more exciting ‖ 어떤 것을 더욱 흥분되게 하다, 또는 더 흥분되기 시작하다. 활기를 띠게 하다/활기를 띠다

SPOKEN PHRASES
---

14 Not on your life! used in order to say that you will definitely not do something ‖ 어떤 것을 결코 하지 않을 것이라고 말하는 데에 쓰여. 결코 아니야! 그런 일은 절대 없을 거야!
15 Get a life! said when you are annoyed with someone because you think s/he is boring ‖ 어떤 사람이 지루하게 생각되어 그 사람에게 짜증났을 때에 쓰여. 정신 좀 차려!
16 for the life of me said when you cannot do something even when you try very hard ‖ 아주 열심히 노력했을 때조차도 어떤 일을 할 수 없을 때에 쓰여. 아무리 해도[전력을 다했어도](…) 않다): *I can't remember her name for the life of me!* 아무리 해도 그녀의 이름을 기억해 낼 수 없구나!
17 that's life said when something bad has happened that you must accept ‖ 감수할 수밖에 없는 안 좋은 일이 일어났을 때에 쓰여. 어쩔 수 없다
18 life is too short said when telling someone that something is not important enough to worry about ‖ 어떤 일이 걱정할 만큼 중요하지 않다고 남에게 말할 때에 쓰여. (걱정하기엔) 인생이 너무 짧다. 잊어버리는 게 낫다

life·boat /ˈlaɪfboʊt/ *n* a small boat that is used for helping people who are in danger on the ocean ‖ 바다에서 위험에 빠진 사람들을 돕는 데에 쓰는 작은 배. 구명보트[정]
life buoy /ˈ. ./ *n* a large ring that you can throw to someone in the water, so that s/he will float ‖ 물에 빠진 사람에게 던져서 그 사람이 떠 있도록 하는 큰 원형체. 구명(용) 튜브
life ex·pect·an·cy /ˈ. .,.../ *n* the length of time that a person or animal is expected to live ‖ 사람이나 동물이 살 수 있을 것으로 기대되는 시간의 길이. 기대수명
life·guard /ˈlaɪfgɑrd/ *n* someone whose job is to help swimmers who are in

danger at the beach or a pool ‖ 해변이나 풀장에서 위험에 빠진 수영자들을 돕는 직업인. 인명 구조원
life in·sur·ance /ˈ. .,../ *n* [U] a type of insurance that someone buys so that when s/he dies, his/her family will receive money ‖ 어떤 사람이 자신이 죽었을 때 가족이 돈을 받을 수 있도록 드는 보험의 일종. 생명보험
life jack·et /ˈ. ,../ *n* a piece of equipment that you wear around your chest so that you float in the water ‖ 물에서 뜰 수 있도록 가슴 둘레에 착용하는 장비. 구명조끼
life·less /ˈlaɪflɪs/ *adj* **1** lacking interest, excitement, or activity ‖ 흥미[활기, 활동]가 결여된. 기운[활력]이 없는. 맥 빠진: *a lifeless party* 맥 빠진 파티 **2** dead or seeming to be dead ‖ 죽은 또는 죽은 것처럼 보이는. 생명이 없는
life·like /ˈlaɪflaɪk/ *adj* very much like a real person or thing ‖ 실제 사람이나 사물과 아주 많이 닮은. 살아 있는 듯한. 실물과 똑같은. 생동감 있는: *a very lifelike statue* 실물과 아주 흡사한 상(像)
life·line /ˈlaɪflaɪn/ *n* something that someone depends on completely ‖ 사람이 전적으로 의지하는 것. 생명선. 구명밧줄: *She isn't able to leave the house, so the phone is her lifeline.* 그녀는 집을 떠날 수 없기 때문에 전화는 그녀의 생명선이다.
life·long /ˈlaɪflɔŋ/ *adj* continuing all through your life ‖ 일생을 통해 계속되는. 일생 동안의. 평생의: *a lifelong friend* 평생 친구
life·sav·er /ˈlaɪfˌseɪvər/ *n* **1** someone or something that helps you in a very important way ‖ 매우 긴요하게 도와주는 사람이나 사물. 궁지[곤경, 위기]에서 구해주는 사람[것]. 인명 구조자 **2 Lifesaver** TRADEMARK a small ring-shaped hard candy ‖ 작은 고리 모양의 단단한 사탕. 라이프세이버 사탕
life sen·tence /ˌ. ˈ../ *n* the punishment of sending someone to prison for the rest of his/her life ‖ 사람을 남은 여생 동안 감옥에 보내는 형벌. 종신형. 무기 징역
life-size /ˈ. ./, **life-sized** *adj* a life-size model, picture etc. is the same size as the person or object it represents ‖ 모형·그림 등이 그것이 나타내는 사람이나 물체와 같은 크기인. 실물[실제] 크기의
life·style /ˈ. ./ *n* the way that someone lives, including his/her work and activities, and what things s/he owns ‖ 일·활동·소유하는 것을 포함한 사람이 사

L

는 방식. 생활 방식[양식]: *Getting married can mean a sudden change in your lifestyle.* 결혼하는 것은 생활 방식의 갑작스런 변화를 의미할 수 있다.

life sup·port sys·tem /'. ., ,../ *n* medical equipment that keeps someone alive who is extremely sick ‖ 심하게 아픈 사람을 살아 있게 해 주는 의료 장비. 생명 유지 장치

life-threat·en·ing /'. ,.../ *adj* a life-threatening illness can kill you ‖ 병이 죽음을 초래할 수 있는. 생명[목숨]을 위협하는. 목숨이 걸려 있는

life·time /'laiftaim/ *n* the period of time during which someone is alive ‖ 사람이 살아 있는 동안의 시간. 일생. 생애

life vest /'. ./ *n* ➪ LIFE JACKET

lift¹ /lɪft/ *v* **1** [T] to take something in your hands and raise it or move it higher ‖ 사물을 손으로 잡아서 올리거나 더 높이 옮기다. …을 들다. 들어[끌어]올리다: *Can you help me lift this box and put it in the car?* 이 상자를 들어서 차 안에 넣게 도와줄래? —see picture on page 947 **2** [I, T] also **lift up** to move something up into the air, or to move up into the air ‖ 사물을 공중으로 들어올리다, 또는 공중으로 올라가다. 높이 들다 [들어올리다]. 위로 향하다: *Lift up your feet so I can sweep the floor.* 내가 바닥을 쓸 수 있게 발을 위로 들어주세요. **3** [T] to remove a rule or law that prevents someone from doing something ‖ 사람이 하려는 일을 막는 규정이나 법을 제거하다. 철폐[폐지]하다. 그만두다. 해제하다: *The US has lifted trade restrictions with the country.* 미국은 그 나라와의 통상 제한 규정을 철폐했다. **4** [I] if clouds or FOG lifts, it disappears ‖ 구름이나 안개가 사라지다. 걷히다. 없어지다 **5** [T] INFORMAL to steal something ‖ 물건을 훔치다. 슬쩍 집어가다

lift² *n* **1 give sb/sth a lift** to make someone feel happier, or to make something more likely to be successful ‖ 사람을 더 행복하게 느끼게 하다, 또는 사물을 보다 성공적이 되게 하다. 기분·기운을 북돋우다[고양시키다]. 밝아지게 하다. 유망하게 하다: *The end of the war is expected to give the economy a lift.* 종전은 경제에 상승효과를 줄 것으로 기대된다. **2 give sb a lift** to take someone somewhere in your vehicle ‖ 사람을 자동차로 어떤 곳에 데리고 가다. 남을 태워주다. 차로 데려다주다 **3** a movement in which something is lifted or raised ‖ 사물을 들거나 올리는 동작

lift-off /'. ./ *n* [C, U] the moment when a space vehicle leaves the ground and rises up into the air ‖ 우주선이 지상을 떠나 공중으로 올라가는 때. 이륙. 발사

lig·a·ment /'lɪɡəmənt/ *n* a band of strong material in your body that joins your bones together ‖ 인체의 뼈들을 서로 결합시켜 주는 질긴 물질의 띠. 인대

light¹ /laɪt/ *n*

1 ▶LIGHT TO SEE 보는 빛◀ [U] the energy from the sun, a lamp etc. that allows you to see things ‖ 사물을 볼 수 있게 해주는 태양·등불 등에서 나오는 에너지. 빛. 광선: *Light was streaming in through the window.* 빛이 창문으로 흘러 들어 오고 있었다. / *The light in here isn't very good.* 여기는 빛이 밝지 않다.

2 ▶ELECTRIC LIGHT 전깃불◀ something such as a lamp that produces light using electricity ‖ 전기를 이용해 빛을 내는 등불 등의 것. 전등(불): *Can you turn the lights on/off for me?* 전등 좀 켜[꺼] 주실래요?

3 ▶TRAFFIC 교통◀ one of a set of red, green, and yellow lights that are used for controlling traffic ‖ 교통 통제에 사용되는 적·녹·황색 전등 세트의 하나. (교통)신호등: *Turn left at the lights.* 신호등에서 좌회전하시오. / *Moore drove straight through a red light.* 무어는 빨간 신호등을 그대로 통과했다.

4 a light something such as a match that starts a cigarette burning ‖ 담뱃불을 붙이는 성냥 등의 것. 불. 성냥[라이터]불: *Excuse me, do you have a light?* 실례합니다, 불 좀 있어요?

5 bring sth to light/come to light to make something known, or to become known ‖ 어떤 것을 알려지게 하다, 또는 알려지다. …을 밝은 데에 드러내다[폭로하다]/드러나다: *New information about the case has come to light.* 그 사건에 대한 새 정보가 드러났다.

6 in light of sth after considering something; because of ‖ 어떤 것을 고려한 후에. …의 관점[견지]에서. …에 비추어; …때문에: *In light of the low profits, we will have to make budget cuts.* 저조한 수익을 고려해서 우리는 예산을 삭감해야 할 것이다.

7 see sth in a new/different light to understand something in a new or different way ‖ 사물을 새롭거나 다른 방식으로 이해하다. …을 새로운/전혀 다른 시각으로 보다

8 shed/throw/cast light on sth to provide new information about something so it is easier to understand ‖ 사물을 더 쉽게 이해하도록 새로운 정보

를 제공하다. …을 분명하게 해주다. …에 (해결의) 실마리를 던지다
9 a light at the end of the tunnel something that gives you hope that a bad situation will end soon ‖ 나쁜 상황이 곧 끝날 것이란 희망을 주는 것. 터널 저 편에 보이는 빛. 겨우 보이기 시작한 밝은 징조: *Kids often drop out of school because they can't see a light at the end of the tunnel.* 아이들은 희망의 여지를 찾을 수 없어서 종종 학교를 그만둔다.
10 see the light to finally realize and understand something ‖ 마침내 어떤 것을 깨달아 이해하다. 사리를 알게 되다. 납득하다: *Maybe Gus will see the light and do what's good for the team.* 아마 거스는 사리 판단을 잘해서 팀을 위해 좋은 일을 할 것이다.

light² adj
1 ▶COLOR 색깔◀ pale and not dark ‖ 옅으며 진하지 않은. 빛깔이 연한: *a light blue dress* 연한 청색 드레스 —compare DARK¹
2 ▶WEIGHT 중량◀ not weighing very much ‖ 무게가 많이 나가지 않는. 무겁지 않은. 가벼운: *Your backpack's lighter than mine.* 너의 배낭은 내 것보다 가볍다. —compare HEAVY
3 ▶FORCE 힘◀ not having much force or power ‖ 세기나 힘이 크지 않은. 약한. 부드러운: *a light wind* 약한 바람
4 ▶CLOTHES 의상◀ thin and not very warm ‖ 얇으며 별로 덥지 않은. 가벼운, 가뿐한: *a light sweater* 가벼운 스웨터
5 ▶IN A ROOM/HOUSE 방/집에◀ having plenty of light in it, especially from the sun ‖ 빛, 특히 햇빛이 많이 드는. 방[집]이 환한. 채광이 좋은: *The house was light and airy.* 그 집은 볕이 잘 들고 바람이 잘 통한다.
6 ▶FOOD 식품◀ having less fat or fewer CALORIEs than usual, or not having a strong taste ‖ 보통보다 지방이 적거나 칼로리가 낮은, 또는 맛이 강하지 않은. 담백한. 저칼로리의. 저지방의: *light cream cheese* 저지방 크림치즈 / *a light wine* 순한 포도주 —see also LITE
7 ▶NOT SERIOUS 심각하지 않은◀ not serious in meaning or style ‖ 의미나 형식이 심각하지 않은. 가벼운. 딱딱하지 않은. 오락적인: *a light comedy on TV* TV에 방영되는 가벼운 코미디물
8 it is light used in order to say that there is enough light outside to see by ‖ 사물을 보기에 바깥에 빛이 충분하다는 것을 말하는 데에 쓰여. 밝다. 환하다: *It was still light when we got home.* 우리가 집에 도착했을 때도 여전히 환했다.

9 ▶SMALL AMOUNT 소량◀ small in amount or degree ‖ 양이나 정도가 적은. 가벼운. 소량의. 약한. 심하지 않은: *Traffic was lighter than usual today.* 오늘 교통량은 평소보다 적었다.
10 make light of sth to joke about something or to treat it as if it were not important ‖ 어떤 것에 대해 농담하다, 또는 중요치 않은 것처럼 대하다. …을 경시[무시]하다. 얕잡아보다

light³ v lit or lighted, lit or lighted, lighting 1 [I, T] to start burning, or to make something do this ‖ 불이 붙다, 또는 사물에 불을 붙이다. 점화하다[시키다]. 타다[타게 하다]: *Dad is trying to light a fire in the fireplace.* 아버지는 난로에 불을 붙이려고 하신다. —see picture at FIRE¹ **2** [T] to give light to something ‖ 어떤 것에 빛을 비추다. 밝게 하다. 조명하다: *The room was lit by two lamps.* 두 개의 전등이 그 방을 비추었다.

light up *phr v* **1** [I, T] to become bright or to make something bright ‖ 밝아지다, 또는 어떤 것을 밝게 하다. 밝히다: *The fireworks lit up the night sky.* 불꽃놀이가 밤하늘을 밝혔다. **2** [I] if your face or eyes light up, you show that you are pleased or excited ‖ 얼굴이나 눈에 기쁨과 흥분을 나타내다. 명랑해지다. 밝게 활짝 피다 **3** [I] INFORMAL to light a cigarette ‖ 담뱃불을 붙이다

USAGE NOTE lit and lighted

Use **lit** as the past participle of **light**: *Dean had already lit the candles.* Use **lighted** as an adjective before a noun: *a lighted candle.*
light의 과거 분사로서 **lit**을 쓴다: 딘은 이미 촛불을 밝혔다. **lighted**는 명사 앞의 형용사로서 쓴다: 불이 붙은 초.

---

light⁴ *adv* **travel light** to travel without carrying too many of your possessions ‖ 소지품을 너무 많이 소지하지 않고 여행하다. 간단한 차림으로[짐 없이] 여행하다
light bulb /'. ./ *n* the glass object in a lamp that produces light ‖ 빛을 내는 전등의 유리 물체. (백열) 전구 —see picture at LAMP
light·ed /'laɪtɪd/ *adj* used before some nouns to mean "lit" ‖ "lit"을 의미하기 위해 일부 명사 앞에 쓰여. 불이 켜진[붙은]. 밝혀진: *a lighted cigarette/match/lamp* 불이 붙은[켜진] 담배[성냥, 등(燈)]
light·en /'laɪtⁿn/ *v* **1** [T] to reduce the amount of work, worry, debt etc. that someone has ‖ 사람이 가진 일·걱정·빚 등의 양을 줄이다. 가볍게 하다. 덜어주

STUDY NOTES

This special section contains helpful information about the most common usage problems for students of English, plus five picture pages that show vocabulary in context.

- **Adjective word order** *page 930*
- **Capitalization** *page 930*
- **Comparatives** *page 931*
- **Modal verbs** *page 932*
- **Numbers** *page 934*
- **Phrasal verbs** *page 936*
- **Intensifiers** *page 937*
- **Prepositions** *page 938*
- **Quantity** *page 940*
- **Verbs** *page 942*
- **Pictures** *beginning page 943*

STUDY NOTES adjective word order

- When you use more than one adjective to describe a noun, the adjectives are usually in the following order:

1. what something is like
2. what color it is
3. what type of thing it is:

	QUALITY/SIZE	TEMPERATURE	FEATURE/SHAPE	COLOR	TYPE	NOUN
a	beautiful		new	white	wool	*sweater*
a	long	hot	dry		summer	*day*
a	big		square	green	wooden	*box*
a	nice	cold				*glass of milk*
	delicious	warm	fresh		homemade	*bread*

Comparatives (like **better**) and superlatives (like **best**) are used before all the other adjectives in a group:
It was the most beautiful white wool sweater I've ever seen.
Do you want the smaller yellow metal box or the bigger green wooden one?

STUDY NOTES capitalization

- The first word of a sentence is capitalized in English: *How are you today?*

- The names of people, places, and things that are trademarks are capitalized:
  Mary Johnson / Los Angeles, California / Pepsi-Cola

- In titles of books, movies, essays etc., capitalize the first word, the last word, and most of the other words. Do not capitalize prepositions (*of, by, at* etc.), the determiners *a, an,* and *the,* or the conjunctions *and, but, so, yet, or, for,* and *nor*:
  The Call of the Wild / Money, Banking, and the Economy

- Words like *college, high school,* and *place* are capitalized when they are part of a name:
  I'm in college.
  BUT
  I go to City College.
  Do you know a good place to have lunch?
  BUT
  There's a good restaurant near Walton Place.

- In titles of professions, words are also capitalized when they are part of a name:
  I'm going to see the doctor.
  BUT
  I'm going to see Dr. Taylor / Doctor Taylor.

- In titles of family members, words are capitalized when you are using that word as a name:
  My grandma is 83 years old.
  BUT
  Can I have some milk, Grandma?

STUDY NOTES comparatives

- The COMPARATIVE and SUPERLATIVE forms of adjectives and adverbs show an increase in quality, quantity, or degree. Comparatives are formed in three ways:

by adding **-er** and **-est** to the end of short words, like this:

All of the girls' presents are big.
*Anita's present is **bigger than** Jody's.*
*Melissa's present is **bigger than** both*
   Anita's and Jody's.
*Melissa's present is **the biggest** of the three.*

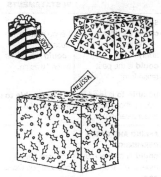

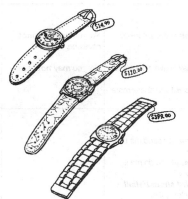

by adding **more** and **most** or **less** and **least** before longer words, like this:

*The watch with the leather band is **more***
   ***expensive than** the child's watch.*
*The watch with the leather band is **less***
   ***expensive than** the gold watch.*
*The gold watch is **the most expensive**.*
*The child's watch is **the least expensive**.*

by using a different word, like these comparatives of **good**:

*Brad's work is **the worst** of the three.*
*Jamie's work is **better than** Brad's, but*
   ***worse than** Jerome's.*
*Jerome's work is **the best**.*

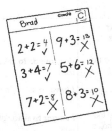

STUDY NOTES modal verbs

The verbs in the charts below are modal verbs. They are used as auxiliary verbs with another verb to change its meaning in some way. This list tells you what the modal verbs mean and how to use them.

	IN STATEMENTS	IN QUESTIONS	IN NEGATIVE STATEMENTS
SHOWING ABILITY **can** is used for talking about an ability or skill. **could** is the past tense form.	*Deena **can** speak Russian.* *I **could** ride a bike when I was six.*	***Can** Deena speak Russian?* ***Could** you ride a bike when you were little?*	*Deena **can't/cannot** speak Russian.* *I **couldn't/could not** ride a bike until I was seven.*
be able to is used for talking about actions or achievements.	*Pete **was able to** get there on time.*	***Was** Pete **able to** get there on time?*	*Pete **wasn't/was not** able to get there on time.*
ASKING AND GIVING PERMISSION **could** and **may** are more polite than **can**. may is more formal than **could** or **can**. Use **could** in this way only in questions.	*You **can** have a cookie if you want.* *You **may** have a cookie if you like.*	***Can** I have a cookie?* ***May** I have a cookie?* ***Could** you speak more clearly?*	*No, you **can't/cannot** have one.* *No, you **may not** have one.*
MAKING REQUESTS AND SUGGESTIONS **could** is more polite than **can**.	*I **can** help, if you want.* *We **could** barbecue some chicken.*	***Can** you hand me that pen?* ***Could** you do me a favor?*	
Use **should** or **shall** with *I* and *we* to make suggestions.	*We **should** get that door fixed.*	*What **should/shall** we do tonight?* should is now used much more than shall in questions.	
SHOWING THAT SOMETHING IS NECESSARY **need to** means that something is necessary. **have to** means that something is necessary, and that you have no choice about doing it. **must** is used by people in authority. **have got to** is a stronger way to say this. Never use **have got to** in questions or negative statements.	*Perry **needs to** talk to us.* *I **have to** ask my mom first.* *I've **got to** leave right now.* *We **had to** wait a long time.* *Paige, you **must** come wash your hands.*	***Does** Perry **need to** talk to us?* ***Do** you **have to** ask your mom first?* ***Do** you **have to** leave right now?* ***Did** you **have to** wait a long time?* ***Do** I **have to** wash my hands, Dad?* must is not used in questions very often.	*Perry **doesn't need to** talk to us.* *I **don't have to** ask my mom first.* *I **don't have to** leave right now.* *We **didn't have to** wait a long time.* *You **don't have to** wash your hands.* don't need to and don't have to are the only modal verbs you can use to say that something is not necessary.

STUDY NOTES modal verbs

	IN STATEMENTS	IN QUESTIONS	IN NEGATIVE STATEMENTS
GIVING COMMANDS **be to** is stronger than **must**.	*You **must** tell them everything you know.* *You **are to** tell them everything you know.*		*You **mustn't/must not** tell them anything.* *You **are not to** tell them anything.*
GIVING ADVICE **should** is the most common modal verb for giving advice. **ought to** is a little stronger than **should**. **must** is used in order to emphasize that something is a good idea.	*You **should** hang the painting there.* *Reggie **ought to** try to find a different job.* *You **must** try some of this cake.* *I really **must** go to the dentist's.*	***Should** I hang the painting here?* ***Should** Reggie try to find a different job?* ought to and must are almost never used in questions.	*You **shouldn't/should not** hang the painting there.* *Reggie **shouldn't/should not** try to find a different job.* *You **shouldn't/should not** leave without trying this cake.* **ought not to** is fairly formal, and is not used very often. **must not** and **mustn't** are not used very often for giving advice.
SHOWING THAT SOMETHING IS ALMOST CERTAIN, OR IS IMPOSSIBLE	*She **must be** sick, because she hasn't been to work.* *Craig **must have** forgotten his keys.*		*She **can't be** sick, because I saw her at the mall.* *Craig **can't have** forgotten his keys, because the house is locked.*
SHOWING THAT SOMETHING IS POSSIBLE	*I **might/may** take chemistry next semester.* *They **could be** lost.*	***Could** they be lost?*	*I **might not/may not** take chemistry next semester.*
TALKING ABOUT THE FUTURE	*Kathy **will** be there tomorrow.* *The weatherman said it **would** rain tomorrow.*	***Will** Kathy be there tomorrow?*	*Kathy **won't/will not** be there tomorrow.* *The weatherman said it **wouldn't/would not** rain tomorrow.*
TALKING ABOUT THE PAST Use **used to** to talk about states, situations, or actions in the past. Use **would** only for talking about past actions.	*I **used to** have a car, but now I don't.* *We **would** often go camping when we were younger.*	***Did** you **use to** have a car?*	*I **didn't use to** have a car, but now I do.*

STUDY NOTES numbers

수의 쓰기 및 읽기

수는 상황에 따라 다르게 읽는다

"A"와 "ONE"

- 구어에서는 "one"(one hundred)이 아니라 "a"(a hundred)를 쓴다: *My watch cost a hundred dollars.*/*There were about a hundred people at the wedding.* 그러나 수학에서는 "one"(one hundred, one fourth)을 쓴다: *One fourth plus one fourth is* (OR *equals*) *one half.*/*One plus one is*(OR *equals*) *two.*
- 일반적으로 사물 중의 한 개를 말할 때는 "one"대신에 "a"를 쓴다: *I need a nail.*/*I have a sister.* 그러나 단 하나만 필요하다고 강조할 때나 숫자에 대한 질문에 대답할 때는 "one"을 쓴다: *I only need one nail, not two.*/*"How many brothers and sisters do you have?" "I have one sister and two brothers."*

날짜 (✗ 표시는 틀리거나 비표준적인 사례임)

- 미국에서는 월·일·년 순으로 날짜를 표기한다: *July 1, 1999*(개인 편지나 상용 편지에서)/*7/1/99*(문서에서). 말할때는 "July first, nineteen ninety-nine"이나 "the first of July, nineteen ninety-nine으로 읽고, 글 속에서는 *I'm leaving on July 1st.* 또는 *I'm leaving on July 1.*로 쓴다. 이 들 둘다 *"I'm leaving on July first."*로 읽지만 ✗*July 1st, 1999.*✗라고는 쓰지 않는다.
- 연도 표기 중의 셋째 자리 숫자가 0 이면 "Zero"가 아니라 "oh"라고 읽는다:*1904*(=nineteen oh four). 10, 20 등으로 시작되는 연도는 다음과 같이 읽는다: *2001*(=twenty oh one 또는 two thousand one)/ *2010*(=twenty ten 또는 two thousand ten)/ *2021*(=twenty twenty-one 또는 two thousand twenty-one)

강의실, 호텔, 아파트 호수

- 두 자리 수는 일반적인 수처럼 읽는다: *room 21*(=room twenty-one)/*apartment 12*(=apartment twelve)
- 세 자리 수는 첫째 자리 숫자를 읽고 남은 두 자리 숫자를 하나의 수로 읽는다: *English 221*(=English two twenty-one)/*apartment 518*(=apartment five eighteen).

  예외: 둘째 자리 숫자가 0 이면 각 자리 숫자를 따로 따로 읽는다: *English 203*(=English two oh three)/*apartment 708*(=apartment seven oh eight). 100, 200, 300 등의 수는 자연수로 읽는다: *room 100*(=room one hundred)
- 네 자리 수는 숫자를 둘 씩 짝을 지어 읽는다: *English 2220*(=English twenty-two twenty)/*apartment 1146*(=apartment eleven forty-six)

  예외: 셋째 자리 숫자가 0 이면 마지막 두 자리 숫자는 각각 읽는다: *English 2102*(English twenty-one oh two)/*apartment 1305*(=apartment thirteen oh five). 1000, 2000, 3000 등의 수는 자연수로 읽는다: *room 1000*(=room one thousand)

주소

주소는 수를 읽는 것과 같은 방식으로 읽지만 몇 몇 예외가 있다
- 다섯 자리 수의 집 주소는 각 자리 숫자를 따로 따로 읽는다: *20619 W. 182nd St.*(=two oh six one nine west a hundred and eighty-second street)
- 세 자리 수의 우편 사서함 번호는 각 자리 숫자를 따로 따로 읽는다: *Box 150*(=box one five oh)
- 우편번호도 각 자리 숫자를 따로 따로 읽는다: *98119*(=nine eight one one nine)/*02134*(=oh two one three four)/*10011*(=one oh oh one one)

전화번호

- 전화번호는 각 자리 숫자를 따로 따로 읽는다:*The number for information is 555-1212.*(five five five one two one two)/*area code 206*(=two oh six)

"OH" and "ZERO"

- 수학에서는 특히 0 이 정수일 때 보통 "oh" 대신에 "zero"를 쓴다: *0.05%*(=zero point zero five percent 또는 point zero five percent)
- 운동 경기의 득점에 대해서는 "zero"나 "nothing"으로 읽는다: *The final score was 18-0.*(=eighteen (to) zero)/*They had a 2-0 lead at half time.*(=two (to) nothing 또는 two (to) zero) 비격식체에서는 또한 "zip"과 "zilch"로도 쓴다: *We beat them 35-0 !*(thirty-five zip 또는 thirty-five zilch)

STUDY NOTES numbers

HOW MANY		ORDER	FRACTIONS		USING THESE NUMBERS IN SENTENCES
IN NUMERALS	IN WORDS	IN A LIST	IN NUMERALS	IN WORDS	
1	one	first	1	a whole	Two halves make a whole.
2	two	second	1/2	a/one half	Cut the pie in half.
3	three	third	1/3	a/one third	Cut the pie in thirds.
4	four	fourth	1/4	a/one fourth OR a/one quarter	Cut the pie in fourths/ quarters.
5	five	fifth	1/5	a/one fifth	Cut the pie in fifths.
6	six	sixth	1/6	a/one sixth	Cut the pie in sixths.
7	seven	seventh	1/7	a/one seventh	Cut the pie in sevenths.
8	eight	eighth	1/8	an/one eighth	Cut the pie in eighths.
9	nine	ninth	1/9	a/one ninth	
10	ten	tenth	1/10	a/one tenth	
11	eleven	eleventh	1/11	an/one eleventh	
12	twelve	twelfth	1/12	a/one twelfth	
13	thirteen	thirteenth	1/13	a/one thirteenth	My kids are in their teens. (between 13 and 19 years old)
14	fourteen	fourteenth	1/14	a/one fourteenth	
15	fifteen	fifteenth	1/15	a/one fifteenth	
16	sixteen	sixteenth	1/16	a/one sixteenth	
17	seventeen	seventeenth	1/17	a/one seventeenth	
18	eighteen	eighteenth	1/18	an/one eighteenth	
19	nineteen	nineteenth	1/19	a/one nineteenth	
20	twenty	twentieth	1/20	a/one twentieth	Jack is in his twenties. (between 20 and 29 years old)
21	twenty-one	twenty-first	1/21	a/one twenty-first	
22	twenty-two	twenty-second	1/22	a/one twenty-second	
30	thirty	thirtieth	1/30	a/one thirtieth	It's in the thirties. (between 30 and 39 degrees in temperature)
40	forty	fortieth	1/40	a/one fortieth	
50	fifty	fiftieth	1/50	a/one fiftieth	
60	sixty	sixtieth	1/60	a/one sixtieth	I was born in the sixties. (between 1960 and 1969)
70	seventy	seventieth	1/70	a/one seventieth	
80	eighty	eightieth	1/80	a/one eightieth	
90	ninety	ninetieth	1/90	a/one ninetieth	
100	a/one hundred	hundredth	1/100	a hundredth/ one one hundredth	
			2/100	two hundredths/ two one hundredths	
200	two hundred	two hundredth	1/200	a/one two hundredth	
1000	a/one thousand	thousandth	1/1000	a/one thousandth	
100,000	a/one hundred thousand		1/100,000	a/one hundred thousandth	
1,000,000	a/one million	millionth	1/1,000,000	a/one millionth	

STUDY NOTES phrasal verbs

WHAT A PHRASAL VERB IS

Verbs like **get to**, **pull off**, and **come down on** are very common in English. These are called phrasal verbs, and they include a verb and one or more prepositions or adverbs.

- When these words are used together, they mean something different from what they mean when they are used separately. For example, **get** usually means to receive something, and **to** usually shows direction. However, to **get to** someone means "to upset or annoy someone."

- This dictionary makes it easy for you to understand and use phrasal verbs. They are listed under the main verb so that it is easy to find them. For example, **get to** is listed under **get**, after the meanings of the main verb. The phrasal verb in the example sentence is always in *dark letters* so you can see clearly how it is used in a sentence:

- The entry for **get to** shows that in informal speech and writing, you can say

  Don't let him **get to** you, honey.

  instead of

  Don't let him **annoy** you, honey.

> **get to** sb *phr v* [T] INFORMAL to upset or annoy someone: *Don't let him get to you, honey. He's just teasing you.*

THE GRAMMAR OF PHRASAL VERBS

Phrasal verbs can be INTRANSITIVE or TRANSITIVE(see Study Note on p. 942). When they are intransitive, this dictionary shows them like this:

> **look out** *phr v* [I] to pay attention to what is happening around you: *Look out! You almost hit the cat.*

When phrasal verbs are transitive, they can be very difficult to use. To help you use them correctly, this dictionary shows whether the DIRECT OBJECT is a person or a thing, and where the object can be used in the sentence.

- The abbreviation **sb** means that the object is a person:

> **take after** sb *phr v* [T] to look or behave like another member of your family: *Jenny takes after her dad.*

- The abbreviation **sth** means that the object is a thing:

> **plow into** sth *phr v* [T] to hit something hard with a car, truck etc.: *A train derailed and plowed into two houses.*

- The abbreviation **sb/sth** means that the object can be a person or a thing:

> **think of** sb/sth *phr v* [T] **1** to produce a new idea, suggestion etc.: *Can you think of anything better to do?* **2** to remember a name or fact: *I can't think of his name now.* **3** to show that you want to treat other people well: *Bill's always thinking of others.*

- When the object can only follow the preposition or adverb, the entry looks like this:

> **run up** sth *phr v* [T] to make a debt, cost, price etc. greater: *We ran up a huge phone bill.*

- When the object can only follow the verb, the entry looks like this:

> **follow** sb **around** *phr v* [T] to keep following someone everywhere s/he goes: *My little brother is always following me around.*

STUDY NOTES phrasal verbs

- When the object can follow either the verb or the preposition or adverb, the entry uses the symbol ↔ and looks like this:

> **bring** sth ↔ **out** *phr v* [T] **1** to make something become easier to notice, see, taste etc.: *The red paint **brings out** the red in the curtains..*

- Sometimes a phrasal verb can have two objects. These phrasal verbs are shown like this:

> **hit** sb **up for** sth *phr v* [T] SPOKEN to ask someone for something: *Mitch will probably try to **hit you up for** a loan.*

STUDY NOTES intensifiers

- Some adverbs, like **very**, **fairly**, and **extremely** can be used in order to change the meaning of a word, phrase, or sentence.
They can make the meaning stronger:
   *They live **very** close to the beach.* (=more than just close)
Or, they can make the meaning less strong:
   *They live **fairly** close to the beach.* (not really close, but definitely not far)

In the chart below, the meaning of the group of words gets stronger as you move from top to bottom:

WORD GROUP	MEANING	EXAMPLES
pretty (INFORMAL)	to some degree, but not too much	*I'm **pretty** tired.*
kind of (INFORMAL)		*They're **kind of** busy.*
sort of (INFORMAL)		*It made me **sort of** curious.*
fairly		*It's a **fairly** expensive restaurant.*
a little (**bit**)		*The hamburgers are a **little** burned.*
really	more than just	*He's a **really** nice guy.*
very		*I think it's **very** pretty.*
quite		*It's **quite** useful to know that.*
rather (FORMAL)		*We have a **rather** long list.*
quite	more than expected	*In fact, the wine was **quite** nice.*
amazingly		*Nina is **amazingly** smart.*
surprisingly		*Bats can fly **surprisingly** fast.*
incredibly		*You've been **incredibly** kind.*
remarkably		*The sound is **remarkably** clear.*
awfully (INFORMAL)	very much	*He's **awfully** cute.*
extremely		*Erin's **extremely** shy.*
completely	as much as possible	*The snake is **completely** harmless.*
totally		*Wait, I'm **totally** confused.*
absolutely		*I'm **absolutely** sure.*
entirely		*This is an **entirely** different case.*
utterly (FORMAL)		*Dr. Lallas is **utterly** wrong.*

Answers to the questions on pages 938 and 939

1	in/on	6	on/beside	12	on
2	in/on	7	in/near	11	on/on
3	over	8	between	10	in
4	above/over	9	beside/between	15	in front of
5	under/beside	13	behind	16	toward
6	on/beside	14	between	17	out of

STUDY NOTES prepositions

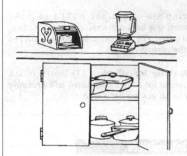

The casseroles are **in** the cupboard **on** the top shelf.

The blender is **on** the counter.

Fill in the blanks with _in_ or _on_.

1. "Where are your pans?"
   "They're _____ the cupboard under the counter_____ the bottom shelf."

2. The bread is _____ the breadbox _____ the counter.

There are cobwebs **over** everything in the house.

There's an old chandelier **above/over** the big table.

Fill in the blanks with _over_ or _above_.

3. There are old sheets _____ the furniture.

4. There's a spider hanging down _____ the chair.

There's a campground **below** the hill, **beside** the river **near** the bridge.
There's a bridge **over** the river.
Cars are **on** the bridge, driving **over** it.
The river flows **through** the valley **under** the bridge **past** the campground.
There's a rowboat **on** the river and someone is fishing **in** the river.

Fill in the blanks with the correct preposition.

5. There's a tent _____ the tree _____ the river.

6. A boy is walking _____ a log _____ the river.

7. A beaver is swimming _____ the river _____ the bank.

STUDY NOTES prepositions

One candlestick is **beside** the vase.
The picture frames are **between** the other candlestick and the clock.

Fill in the blanks with *beside* or *between*.

8. The clock is right in the middle, _____ the vase and the picture frames.

9. The vase is _____ the clock, _____ it and a candlestick.

Shawn and Terry live **in** this house.
They live **on** East 135th Street.
They live **on** the corner of East 135th and Ferndale Avenue.
They live **in** a city.

Fill in the blanks with *in*, *on*, or *at*.

10. "Where do you live?"
    "I live _____ a small town in Iowa."

11. "Where is that Mexican restaurant you like?"
    "It's _____ Larch Way, _____ the corner of Larch Way and 130th."

12. We live _____ 20033 7th Avenue West.

The truck is **in front of** the station wagon.
The convertible is **between** the truck and the motorcycle.
All the other vehicles are **behind** the motorcycle.

Fill in the blanks with *in front of*, *behind*, or *between*.

13. The station wagon is _____ the truck.

14. The truck is _____ the station wagon and the convertible.

15. The motorcycle is _____ the convertible.

A woman is coming **out of** the bookstore. Two teenagers are going **into** the shoe store. A group of children are walking **toward** the toy store. A man is walking **away from** it.

Fill in the blanks with *out of*, *into*, *toward*, or *away from*.

16. A mother is walking _____ the shoe store with her kids.

17. An old man is coming _____ the toy store.   Answers are on page 937

NOUNS THAT SHOW QUANTITY

COUNTABLE NOUNS

(no grammar code)

- Words like **egg** and **cup** are COUNTABLE nouns because they are separate things that can be counted:

an egg   *a cup*

two eggs   *two cups*

- These nouns have plural forms, and can be used with **a** or **an** when they are singular.

UNCOUNTABLE NOUNS

(grammar code [U])

- Words like **lemonade** and **aluminum** are UNCOUNTABLE nouns because they are substances that cannot be counted:

There's some   *a can made of*
lemonade left.   *aluminum*

- These nouns do not have plural forms, and they cannot be used with **a** or **an**. Many other nouns that are not physical substances are also uncountable, such as **music, laughter, knowledge, swimming,** and **marriage**.

NOUNS THAT ARE BOTH COUNTABLE AND UNCOUNTABLE

(grammar code [C,U])

- Some nouns, such as **jam** and **lipstick**, can be countable in one meaning and uncountable in another. When they are countable, they can be used in their plural forms; when they are uncountable, they cannot. For example:

jam [C,U]
a nice thick layer of jam   *lots of different jams*

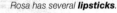

lipstick [C,U]
Rosa is putting on her lipstick.   *Rosa has several lipsticks.*

PLURAL NOUNS

(grammar code [plural])

Some nouns, such as **pants** and **manners**, are used only in their plural form, with a plural verb:

*My **pants are** too small.*

*His **manners were** really bad.*

Sometimes these nouns do not look like plurals, such as the plural noun **media**:
*The **media are** now interested in her story.*

SINGULAR NOUNS

(grammar code [singular])

Some nouns, such as **feel, collapse, electorate,** and **Neptune** are only used in their singular form, with a singular verb.
They can be used with **a**, **an**, or **the**, or without any determiner at all:

*Silk has a wonderful **feel**.*

*Floods caused **the collapse** of the bridge.*

*The idea is not popular with **the electorate**.*

***Neptune** is far away from the Sun.*

STUDY NOTES quantity

TALKING ABOUT QUANTITIES

The sentences on the left show which words to use with COUNTABLE nouns in order to show quantity, and the sentences on the right show which words to use with UNCOUNTABLE nouns.

ALL

HOW MANY? (for countable nouns) | **HOW MUCH? (for uncountable nouns)**

- **Every class** was full.
  All (**of**) the classes were full.

- **Most of** the kids in my class take the bus.

- Use **a lot of** with the object of a sentence:
  I have **a lot of** relatives in Ohio.

- Use **many** (**of**) with the subject of a sentence:
  Many of my relatives live in Ohio.
  Many roads are full of litter.

- Use **many** in questions:
  Do you have **many** relatives in Idaho?

- Use **many** or **a lot of** in negative statements:
  I don't have **many** relatives in Idaho.
  I don't have **a lot of** relatives in Idaho.
  (INFORMAL)

- It will take **several** days to complete.

- I've read **some of** his short stories. We need to buy **some** new towels.

- Use **some** (**of**) in questions when you expect the answer to be yes:
  Can I use **some of** your paper clips?

- Use **a few** in positive statements, and **few** or **not many** in negative statements:
  A few people did show up.
  Not many people showed up.
  Few visitors came that year.

- Use **any** in negative statements, and in questions when you do not know if the answer will be yes or no:
  They never had **any** children.
  Are there **any** gas stations near here?

- The camera broke, so we have **no** pictures of the picnic – **none** at all.
  None of the schools in the area has a pool.

- **All** (**of**) the money will go in Audrey's account.

- We worked in the lab **most of** the time.

- Use **a lot of** with the object of a sentence:
  They wanted **a lot of** money for the guitar.

- Use **much** (**of**) with the subject of a sentence:
  Much of our money is gone.
  Much work remains to be done. (FORMAL)

- Use **much** in questions:
  Is there **much** money left?

- Use **much** or **a lot of** in negative statements:
  There isn't **much** money left.
  There isn't **a lot of** money left. (INFORMAL)

- **Some of** your stuff just fell off the table.
  There's **some** glue here if you need it.

- Use **some** (**of**) in questions when you expect the answer to be yes:
  Do you want **some** carrot cake?

- Use **a little** in positive statements, and **little** or **not much** in negative statements:
  There's **a little** work left to do.
  There's **not much** work left to do.
  The bill has **little** support in Congress.

- Use **any** in negative statements, and in questions when you do not know if the answer will be yes or no:
  No one paid **any** attention to them.
  Is there **any** coffee left?

- This tax makes **no** sense, **none** at all.
  None of their stock was on sale yet.

942

STUDY NOTES verbs

TRANSITIVE VERBS

(grammar code [T])

- **fix** and **thank** are both TRANSITIVE verbs. This means that they must be followed by a noun or noun phrase as a DIRECT OBJECT. If you take away the direct object, the sentence no longer makes sense. So we can say:

Alicia **thanked** Mr. Quintero.
Darren **was fixing** his bike.

Alicia   thanked   Mr. Quintero.
[subject] [verb]   [object]

Darren   was fixing his bike.
[subject] [verb]   [object]

- In this dictionary, transitive verbs are shown like this:

fix¹ /fɪks/ *v* [T]
1 ▶REPAIR◀ to repair something broken or not working: *Do you know*

INTRANSITIVE VERBS

(grammar code [I])

- **bounce** and **argue** are both INTRANSITIVE verbs. This means that their meaning is complete without a DIRECT OBJECT. So we can say:

The ball **bounced**.
Kate and Rob **were arguing**.

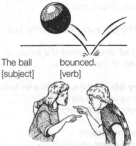

The ball   bounced.
[subject]   [verb]

Kate and Rob were arguing.
[subject]   [verb]

- In this dictionary, intransitive verbs are shown like this:

ar·gue /ˈɑrgyu/ *v* 1 [I] to disagree with someone, usually by talking or shouting in an angry way, or getting upset: *Mom and Dad always*

VERBS THAT ARE BOTH INTRANSITIVE AND TRANSITIVE

(grammar code [I,T])

- Many verbs like **speak** and **see** can be both [T] (TRANSITIVE) and [I] (INTRANSITIVE). In this dictionary, these verbs are shown like this:

speak /spik/ *v* spoke, spoken, speak·ing 1 ▶TALK TO SB◀ [I] to talk to someone about something or have a conversation: *Hello, can I speak to*

3 ▶LANGUAGE◀ [T] to be able to talk in a particular language: *My brother*

see /si/ *v* saw, seen, seeing 1 ▶USE EYES◀ [I, T] to use your eyes to notice people or things: *I can't see without my*

LINKING VERBS

(grammar code [linking verb])

- Some verbs like **become** do not have an [I] or a [T] after them in some or all of their meanings. These are called LINKING VERBS. These verbs must be followed by another word for their meaning to be complete, but the word can be a noun, an adjective or an adverb. These nouns, adjectives, and adverbs always tell us something about the subject of a sentence. In this dictionary, linking verbs are shown like this:

be·come /bɪˈkʌm/ *v* became, become, becoming 1 [linking verb] to begin to be something, or to develop in a particular way: *The weather had become warmer. / In 1960 Kennedy became the first Catholic president. / It is becoming harder to find good housing*

Other linking verbs are **appear, be, feel, look, remain,** and **seem.**

cars

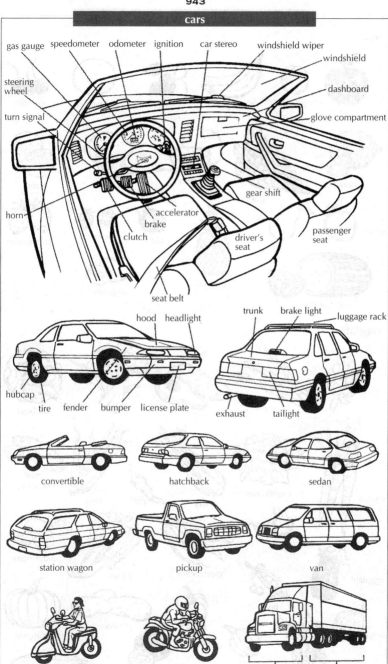

gas gauge speedometer odometer ignition car stereo windshield wiper
windshield
steering wheel
dashboard
turn signal
glove compartment
gear shift
horn
accelerator
brake
clutch
passenger seat
driver's seat
seat belt

hood headlight
trunk brake light luggage rack
hubcap
tire fender bumper license plate
exhaust tailight

convertible hatchback sedan

station wagon pickup van

scooter motorcycle cab trailer
truck

fruit and vegetables

fruit

apple apricot bananas blueberries cantaloupe cherries

coconut grapes grapefruit lemon orange

peach pear plum raspberries strawberries

watermelon pineapple tangerine

vegetables

   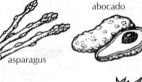

artichoke abocado broccoli

asparagus cabbage

carrots cauliflower celery chili corn cucumber

garlic mushrooms

eggplant green beans lettuce

peas potatoes pumpkin

onion pepper

radishes squash tomato zucchini

houses

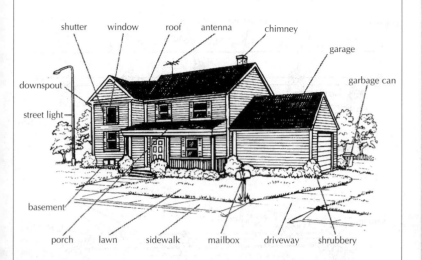

shutter window roof antenna chimney garage garbage can

downspout

street light

basement

porch lawn sidewalk mailbox driveway shrubbery

balcony

apartment building

townhouse/brownstone

ranch house

baseball

outfielder · shortstop · second base · pitcher · infielder · outfield · infield · first base · third base · batter · catcher · home plate · umpire

football

end zone · goalpost · goal line · yard line · linebackers · defense · sideline · line men · offense · receiver · quarterback · running backs

basketball

dunk · guard · free throw line · forward · center

verbs of movement

push

pull

jump

leap

put down

pick up

walk

jog

run

crouch

kneel

lift

carry

hold

다. 경감[완화]하다: *The new computers were supposed to lighten our work load.* 새 컴퓨터가 우리의 작업 부담을 덜어줄 것이라 생각되었다. **2** [I, T] to become brighter, or make something become brighter ‖ 밝아지다, 또는 어떤 것을 밝게 하다. 환해지다[환하게 하다]. 빛나다[빛나게 하다] **3 lighten up!** SPOKEN used in order to tell someone not to be so serious about something ‖ 남에게 어떤 것에 대해 너무 심각해하지 말라고 말하는 데에 쓰여. 기운 내! 걱정 마! 가볍게 생각해! 웃어 넘겨!: *Hey, lighten up, it was just a joke!* 야, 웃어넘겨, 그냥 농담이었어! **4** [I, T] to reduce the weight of something ‖ 사물의 무게를 줄이다. 덜어주다. 가볍게 해주다

light·er /ˈlaɪtə/ *n* a small object that produces a flame to light a cigarette ‖ 담뱃불을 붙이는 불꽃을 내는 작은 물건. 라이터

light-head·ed /ˌ. ˈ../ *adj* not able to think clearly or move steadily because you are sick or have drunk too much alcohol ‖ 아프거나 술을 너무 많이 마셔서 분명하게 생각하거나 안정되게 움직일 수 없는. 머리가 어지러운. 현기증이 나는

light-heart·ed /ˌ. ˈ../ *adj* **1** cheerful and happy ‖ 활기차고 행복한. 쾌활[명랑]한. 근심[걱정]이 없는 **2** not intended to be serious ‖ 심각해질 의도가 없는. 마음 편한. 태평한. 낙천적인

light·house /ˈlaɪthaʊs/ *n* a tower with a bright light that warns ships of danger ‖ 선박들에게 위험을 경고하는 밝은 등불이 있는 탑. 등대

light·ing /ˈlaɪtɪŋ/ *n* [U] the lights that light a room, building etc., or the quality of the light ‖ 방·건물 등을 밝히는 빛, 또는 이 빛의 특성. 조명. 조명 효과: *soft/bright/dim lighting* 부드러운[밝은, 희미한] 조명

light·ly /ˈlaɪtli/ *adv* **1** with only a small amount of weight or force ‖ 오직 소량의 무게나 힘으로. 가볍게. 가뿐하게. 살며시: *He kissed the child lightly on the head.* 그는 아이의 머리에 가볍게 입을 맞추었다. **2** using or having only a small amount of something ‖ 사물의 소량만을 이용하거나 가지고. 약간. 소량으로. 살짝: *Sprinkle sugar lightly over the cake.* 설탕을 케이크 위에 살짝 뿌리시오. **3 not take sth lightly** to treat something in a serious way ‖ 어떤 일을 심각하게 대하다. 예사롭지 않게 처리하다[받아들이다]. …을 가볍게 여기지 않다: *A bomb threat is not to be taken lightly.* 폭파 위협을 가볍게 받아들여서는 안 된다

light·ning¹ /ˈlaɪtnɪŋ/ *n* [U] a bright flash of light in the sky that happens during a storm ‖ 폭풍우 때 일어나는 하늘에서의 밝은 섬광. 번개(불). 벼락: *a tall oak tree that was struck by lightning* 벼락을 맞은 커다란 참나무

lightning

lightning² *adj* extremely fast or sudden ‖ 매우 빠르거나 갑작스러운. 번개 같은. 전광석화의. 전격적인: *a lightning attack by the army* 육군에 의한 전격적인 공격

light·weight¹ /ˈlaɪtˌweɪt/ *adj* **1** weighing less than average ‖ 무게가 평균보다 적게 나가는. 가벼운. 경량의. 표준 중량 이하의: *a lightweight jacket* 가벼운 재킷 **2** not needing much thinking or skill to understand or do ‖ 이해하거나 행하는 데 많은 생각이나 기술이 필요치 않은. 진지하지 않은. 내용이 가벼운: *a lightweight novel* 가벼운 소설

lightweight² *n* someone who is not important enough to have any influence, or who does not have enough intelligence ‖ 어느 정도 영향력을 가질 만큼 중요치 않거나 충분한 지능을 갖지 않은 사람. 시시한 사람. 하수(下手). 멍청한[미련한] 사람: *a political/intellectual lightweight* 정계의 약자[지적 열등자]

light year /ˈ. ./ *n* the distance that light travels from the sun in one year ‖ 빛이 태양으로부터 1년간 이동하는 거리. 광년(光年)

lik·a·ble /ˈlaɪkəbəl/ *adj* likable people are nice, and are easy to like ‖ 사람이 멋있고 쉽게 좋아할 수 있는. 마음에 드는. 호감이 가는

like¹ /laɪk/ *prep* **1** similar in some way to something else ‖ 어떤 면에서 다른 것과 유사한. …과 닮아[유사하여, 비슷하게]. (마치)…같이[처럼]: *The lamp was round - like a ball.* 그 등은 공처럼 둥글었다. / *You two are behaving like children.* 너희 둘은 마치 어린애들처럼 행동하고 있다. / *I'd love to have a car like yours.* 나는 네 것과 비슷한 차를 갖고 싶다. / *Ken looks like his brother.* 켄은 그의 형과 닮았다. / *Was the movie anything like the book?* (=was it similar in any way?) 그 영화 말이야 책과 좀 비슷했냐? / *There's nothing like* (=nothing better than) *Mom's chicken soup!* 어머니가 끓여 준 닭고기수프만한 것은 없다. **2** typical of a particular person or thing ‖ 특정 사람이나 사물에

전형적인. …의 특성을 나타내어. …답게:
It's not like Dad to be late. (=it is
unusual that Dad is late) 늦으시다니 아
버지답지 않어! **3** NONSTANDARD such as
‖ …등. …과 같은(것의): *Foods like
spinach and broccoli are high in iron.* 시
금치나 브로콜리 같은 식품은 철분 함유량
이 높다. **4 what is sb/sth like?** used
when asking someone to describe
something or to give his/her opinion ‖ 다
른 사람에게 사물을 묘사해 달라거나 견해
를 물을 때에 쓰여. 어떻게 생각해[생겼
어]?: *What's the new house like?* 새 집
은 어때?

SPOKEN PHRASES

5 like this said when showing
someone how something is or was
done ‖ 다른 사람에게 사물이 어떠한가
또는 어떻게 행해졌는지 보일 때에 쓰
여. 이렇게. 이처럼. 이같이: *She had
her arms around his neck, like this.* 그
녀는 팔을 그의 목에, 이렇게 감았다. **6
more like** said when giving someone
a number or amount that is more
correct than the one s/he has
mentioned ‖ 다른 사람이 언급한 수나
양보다 더 정확한 것을 그 사람에게 제
시할 때에 쓰여. 그보다는. 더 정확하게
는. 오히려 …에 가까운: *"He's been in
there for 15 minutes!" "More like half
an hour."* "그는 15분 동안 거기에 있
었어!" "더 정확하게는 30분일 걸."

—see also **something like** (SOMETHING)
—see usage note at AS

like² *adv* SPOKEN **1 I'm like/he's
like/Bob's like etc.** NONSTANDARD **a)**
used in order to tell someone the exact
words someone used ‖ 남에게 다른 사람
이 썼던 그대로의 말을 전해주는 데에 쓰
여. 나는 이렇게/그는 이렇게/보브는 이
렇게 …이라고 하다: *I asked him if he
thought Liz was cute, and he's like,
yeah, definitely.* 내가 그에게 리즈를 귀엽
게 생각하는지 물었더니 그는 물론 당연하
지 이렇게 말했다. **b)** said when
describing an event, feeling, or person,
when it is difficult to do this exactly or
when you use a noise instead of a word
‖ 사건[감정, 사람] 등을 묘사할 때, 정확
히 묘사하기 힘들거나 단어 대신 소리를
쓸 때에 쓰여. …은 말이야 …하다. 말하
자면[이를테면] … 같다: *I'm like, ooh!* (=I
was really surprised) 내가 그래서, 어! 했
지. / *We were like, oh no!* (=we realized
something was wrong) 안 돼! 우리는 이
런 분위기였지. / *Their music has like,*

weird lyrics. (=weird is not the best
word, but I cannot think of a better one)
그들의 음악은 뭐랄까 괴상한 시 같아. **2**
said when you pause because you do
not know what to say, you are
embarrassed etc. ‖ 무슨 말을 할지 알 수
없거나 당황해서 (말을) 멈추었을 때에 쓰
여. 아. 저. 어떻게: *Do you think you
could, like, just lend me $25?* 당신은 혹
시, 저, 25달러 좀 빌려줄 수 있어요? **3**
said in order to give an example ‖ 실례
를 제시하는 데에 쓰여. (비근한) 예로.
실제로. 실례로: *The problem is that
sushi is so expensive. Like last week I
paid $40 for a meal.* 문제는 스시가 너무
비싸다는 것이다. 실제로 지난주 나는 한
끼 식사에 40달러를 냈다. **4** said when
what you are saying is not exact ‖ 말하
고 있는 것이 정확하지 않은 때에 쓰여. 아
마. 대략. 대충. 거의: *It was like 9
o'clock and she still wasn't home.* 그게
아마 9시쯤이었고 그녀는 여전히 집에 돌
아오지 않았었다. **5** said in order to
emphasize something ‖ 어떤 것을 강조하
는 데에 쓰여. 정말. 영락없이. 꼭: *That's
like so stupid.* 그것은 영락없는 바보짓이
다.

like³ *v* [T] **1** to enjoy something, or
think that someone or something is nice
or pleasant ‖ 어떤 것을 즐기다, 또는 사
람이나 사물이 멋있거나 유쾌하다고 생각
하다. 좋아하다. 마음에 들다. 호의[호감]
를 가지다: *Do you like oranges?* 오렌지
좋아하십니까? / *I like Billy a lot.* 나는 빌
리가 꽤 마음에 든다. / *I really like
swimming in the ocean.* 나는 바다에서
헤엄치기를 정말 좋아한다. / *Pam doesn't
like to walk home late at night.* 팸은 밤
늦게 집에 걸어오는 것을 좋아하지 않는
다. / *Mom doesn't like it when we make
a lot of noise.* 어머니는 우리가 소란피우
는 것을 좋아하시지 않는다. —opposite
DISLIKE¹ **2** to think that it is good to do
something in a particular way, so that
you do it regularly; prefer ‖ 특정한 방식
으로 어떤 것을 하는 것이 좋다고 생각하
여 규칙적으로 그렇게 하다. …하기를 좋
아하다. …하고 싶다; …하기를 선호하다:
Jim likes to get to the airport early. 짐은
공항에 일찍 도착하는 것을 좋아한다. /
*How do you like your hamburger
cooked?* 햄버거를 어떻게 요리할 줄까?

SPOKEN PHRASES

3 used in order to ask politely for
something, to ask someone to do
something, or to offer someone
something ‖ 정중히 어떤 것을 간청하

거나 남에게 어떤 것을 해 달라고 요청하거나 남에게 어떤 것을 제안하는 데에 쓰여. …해 주기를 바라다[원하다]. … **임을 좋아하다 : I'd like a cheeseburger, please.** 치즈버거로 부탁합니다. / **We would like you to be there if you can.** 우리는 가능하다면 자네가 거기에 가주기를 바란다. / **He'd like to know how much it will cost.** 그는 비용이 얼마가 들지 알고 싶어 합니다. / **Would you like some more coffee?** 커피 좀 더 드시겠습니까? **4 How do you like…?** said when you want to know someone's opinion about something ‖ 어떤 것에 대한 다른 사람의 의견을 알고 싶을 때에 쓰여. 어떻게 생각하십니까? 어떻든가요?: **"How did you like the movie?" "It was okay."** "영화 어땠어요?" "좋았어요." **5 not like the sound of sth** to be worried because of something you have heard or read ‖ 듣거나 읽은 것 때문에 걱정되다. …이 마음에 걸리다. …을 들으니 좋지 않다[좋지 않게 느껴지다]: **I don't like the sound of that weather report** 그 일기 예보가 마음에 걸린다. **6 (whether you) like it or not** used in order to tell someone that something unpleasant will happen and cannot be changed ‖ 다른 사람에게 불쾌한 일이 벌어질 것이며 그것을 바꿀 수 없다고 말하는 데에 쓰여. 좋든 싫든. 좋아하건 말건: **You're going to the dentist, like it or not!** 너는 치과에 가야 해. 좋든 싫든!

like⁴ conjunction NONSTANDARD **1** as if ‖ 마치 …처럼: **He acted like he owned the place.** 그는 마치 그 자리가 자기 것인양 행동했다. **2 like I said/told you/was saying** said when you are repeating something you have already said ‖ 이미 말했던 것을 반복할 때에 쓰여. 내가 말했듯이/말한 대로: **Like I said, we'll probably be there around ten.** 내가 말한 대로 우리는 아마 10시쯤 거기 도착할 겁니다. **3 in the same way as** ‖ …과 같은 방식으로. …한 대로. …과 같이. …처럼: **Do it like I told you to.** 내가 너에게 하라고 한 대로 해라.

like⁵ adj FORMAL **1** similar in some way ‖ 어느 면에서 유사한. 같은. 동일한. 비슷한: **two people of like mind** (=who think in a similar way) 비슷한 생각을 가진 두 사람 **2 -like** typical of or similar to something ‖ 어떤 것에 특유한 또는 유사한. …다운[같은]: **moving with cat-like grace** 고양이같이 우아하게 움직이기

like⁶ n **sb's likes and dislikes** all the things someone likes and does not like ‖ 사람이 좋아하는 것과 싫어하는 모든 것들. 취향. 기호

like·li·hood /ˈlaɪkliˌhʊd/ n [singular, U] **1** how likely something is to happen ‖ 일이 일어날 가능성. 개연성. 공산. 가망 : **Clean water decreases the likelihood of disease.** 깨끗한 물이 질병의 가능성을 줄인다. **2 in all likelihood** almost definitely ‖ 거의 확실하게. 아마도. 십중팔구

like·ly /ˈlaɪkli/ adj, adv probably or almost definitely ‖ 아마 또는 거의 확실하게. …할 것 같은[같게]. 확실한 듯한[하게]: **It's likely to rain tomorrow.** 내일 비가 올 것 같다. **– likely** adv: **I'd very likely have done the same thing as you did.** 나는 십중팔구 네가 했던 것과 똑같이 했을 것이다.

like·mind·ed /ˌ ˈ .../ adj two or more people who are like-minded have similar interests or opinions ‖ 둘 이상의 사람이 유사한 관심이나 의견을 가진. 같은 마음[취미]의. 같은 의견을 가진

lik·en /ˈlaɪkən/ v

liken sb/sth to sb/sth phr v [T] FORMAL to describe someone or something as similar to someone or something else ‖ 사람이나 사물을 다른 사람이나 사물과 유사한 것으로 묘사하다. …을 …에 비기다[비유하다]: **The writer likens marriage to slavery.** 그 작가는 결혼을 노예 생활에 비유하다.

like·ness /ˈlaɪknɪs/ n **1** [U] the quality of being similar in appearance to something else ‖ 겉모습이 다른 것과 유사한 특성. 닮음. 비슷함. 유사함 **2** the image of someone in a painting or photograph ‖ 그림이나 사진 속의 사람의 모습. 화상. 초상: **It's a good likeness of Eva.** 그것은 에바와 꼭 닮은 초상이다.

like·wise /ˈlaɪk-waɪz/ adv **1** FORMAL in the same way ‖ 똑같이. 마찬가지로. 역시. 또한: **The dinner was amazing; likewise, the concert.** 저녁 식사는 훌륭했어요. 마찬가지로 연주회도 그렇고요. **2** SPOKEN said in order to return someone's greeting or polite remark ‖ 다른 사람의 인사나 정중한 말에 답하는 데에 쓰여. 마찬가지다. 동감이다: **"It's great to see you here." "Likewise."** "여기서 당신을 만나니 반갑습니다." "마찬가지입니다."

lik·ing /ˈlaɪkɪŋ/ n **1 have a liking for sth** to like or enjoy something ‖ 어떤 것을 좋아하거나 즐기다. …을 애호하다. 기호를 갖다: **She has a liking for chocolate**

cake. 그녀는 초콜릿 케이크를 좋아한다.
2 take a liking to sb INFORMAL to like someone you have just met ‖ 방금 만난 사람을 좋아하다. …가 마음에 들다

li·lac /ˈlaɪlɑk, -lək/ *n* **1** a small tree with pale purple and white flowers ‖ 연자주색과 하얀색의 꽃이 피는 작은 나무. 라일락 **2** [U] a pale purple color ‖ 연자주색 **– lilac** *adj*

lilt /lɪlt/ *n* [singular] the pleasant rise and fall in the sound of someone's voice or a piece of music ‖ 사람의 목소리나 음악 작품 소리의 기분 좋은 오르내림. 경쾌하고 활발한 가락[억양, 곡, 노래]

lil·y /ˈlɪli/ *n* a plant with large, usually bell-shaped white flowers ‖ 크고 보통 종 모양의 하얀 꽃이 피는 식물. 백합

li·ma bean /ˈlaɪmə ˌbin/ *n* a pale green flat bean ‖ 연녹색의 납작한 콩. 리마콩

limb /lɪm/ *n* **1** a large branch of a tree ‖ 나무의 큰 가지 **2 go out on a limb** to do something alone and without help or support ‖ 혼자서 도움이나 지원 없이 어떤 일을 하다. 위태로운 다리를 건너다. 위험한 상황을 각오하다: *I'm glad it worked because I'd gone out on a limb to try it.* 나는 위험한 상황에서 그것을 하려고 했기 때문에 해낸 것이 기쁘다. **3** FORMAL an arm or leg ‖ 팔이나 다리

lim·bo /ˈlɪmboʊ/ *n* **be in limbo** to be in an uncertain situation because you are waiting for something ‖ 어떤 것을 기다리고 있기 때문에 불확실한 상황에 있다. 불안정하다. 과도기에 있다: *I'm kind of in limbo until I know which college I'm going to.* 내가 어느 대학에 갈지를 알 때까지는 불안정하다[막연하다].

lime /laɪm/ *n* **1** [C, U] a bright green fruit with a sour taste, or the tree this grows on ‖ 신맛이 나는 선명한 녹색 과일, 또는 이 과일이 자라는 나무. 라임나무(열매) **2** [U] a white powdery substance used in making CEMENT ‖ 시멘트를 만드는 데에 사용되는 하얀 가루로 된 물질. 석회

lime·light /ˈlaɪmlaɪt/ *n* **the limelight** attention from the public ‖ 대중에게 받는 주목. 세상의 이목. 각광

lim·er·ick /ˈlɪmərɪk/ *n* a humorous short poem with five lines ‖ 5행의 해학적인 짧은 시. 5행 희시(戲詩)

lim·it¹ /ˈlɪmɪt/ *n* **1** the greatest amount, number etc. that is allowed or is possible ‖ 허용되거나 가능한 최대의 양·수 등. 한계(점[선]): *There is a limit on/to the amount of time we have.* 우리가 가진 시간에는 한도가 있다. / *a 65 mph speed limit* 제한 속도 시속 65마일

/ *Our finances are stretched to the limit.* (=we do not have any more money to spend) 우리의 재정은 한계에 다다랐다. **2** the border or edge of something ‖ 어떤 것의 경계나 가장자리. 경계(선). 범위. 구역: *A fence marks the limit of the school fields.* 담장은 교내의 경계를 표시한다. **3 off limits** beyond the area where someone is allowed to go ‖ 통행이 허용되는 지역을 넘어서. 출입 금지 구역: *The beach is off limits after midnight.* 그 해변은 자정 이후에는 출입 금지이다. **4 within limits** within the time, using the effort etc. that is reasonable and acceptable ‖ 시간이나 노력 등을 들이는 데에 있어서 합리적이고 받아들일 수 있는 범위 안에. 어느 한도 내에서. 적당하게. 지나치지 않게

limit² *v* [T] **1** to prevent an amount, number etc. from increasing beyond a particular point ‖ 양·수 등이 특정 지점을 넘어서 증가하는 것을 방지하다. 제한하다: *The economy will be limited to a 4% growth rate.* 경제는 4% 성장률로 제한될 것이다. **2** to allow someone to use only a particular amount of something ‖ 남에게 어떤 것의 특정량만을 사용하게 하다. …에 한계를 설정하다: *He's been limited to one hour of TV per night.* 그는 밤에 텔레비전을 한 시간만 시청할 수 있다. **3 be limited to** to exist or happen only in a particular place or group ‖ 특정 장소나 집단에서만 존재하거나 발생하다. 한정되다: *The damage was limited to the roof.* 지붕만 피해를 입었다. **– limiting** *adj*

lim·i·ta·tion /ˌlɪmɪˈteɪʃən/ *n* **1** [U] the act of limiting something ‖ 어떤 것을 제한하는 행위. 제한. 한정: *the limitation of nuclear testing* 핵 실험의 제한 **2** a limit on what you are able to do or how good something can be ‖ 사람이 할 수 있는 것이나 사물의 성능에 대한 한계. 제약: *Computers have their limitations.* 컴퓨터는 그 한계가 있다.

lim·it·ed /ˈlɪmɪtɪd/ *adj* not very great in amount, number, degree etc. ‖ 양·수·정도 등에 있어서 매우 크지 않은. 한정된: *a family living on a limited income* 한정된 수입으로 살고 있는 가족 **—opposite** UNLIMITED

lim·o /ˈlɪmoʊ/ *n* INFORMAL ⇨ LIMOUSINE

lim·ou·sine /ˈlɪməˌzin, ˌlɪməˈzin/ *n* a big expensive car ‖ 크고 값이 비싼 차. 호화 대형 자동차. 리무진

limp¹ /lɪmp/ *adj* without strength or firmness ‖ 힘이나 단단함이 없는. 축 늘어진. 흐느적거리는. 유연한: *The dog's* *body went limp as the drug took effect.* 그 개의 몸은 약이 효과를 발생하자마자 축 늘어졌다.

limp² *v* [I] to walk with difficulty because one leg is hurt ‖ 한쪽 다리를 다쳐서 힘들게 걷다. 다리를 절다: *He limped to the chair and sat down.* 그는 다리를 절면서 의자로 가서 앉았다.

limp³ *n* the way someone walks when s/he is LIMP*ing* ‖ 사람이 절뚝거리며 걷는 모습. 절뚝거림: *The man we're looking for walks with a limp.* 우리가 찾고 있는 남자는 절뚝절뚝 걷는다.

linch·pin /ˈlɪntʃˌpɪn/ *n* **the linchpin of** someone or something that a system depends on, so that it will not work without him, her, or it ‖ 그 사람이나 사물이 없으면 작동되지 않는, 한 시스템이 의존하는 사람이나 사물. 가장 중요한 사람. 대들보: *My uncle was the linchpin of the family.* 나의 삼촌은 가족 중에서 가장 중요한 사람이었다.

line¹ /laɪn/ *n*

1 ▶LONG THIN MARK 길고 가는 자국◀ a long thin mark on a surface, especially one that has been drawn ‖ 특히 표면 위에 그려진 길고 가느다란 자국. 선: *She drew a line on the map to show him how to get to the museum.* 박물관에

line

They're standing in line to buy tickets.

가는 방법을 그에게 보여주려고 그녀는 지도 위에 선을 그었다. —see also DOTTED LINE

2 ▶LIMIT/BORDER 한계/경계◀ a long thin mark used in order to show a limit or border ‖ 한계나 경계를 나타내는 데에 쓰이는 길고 가느다란 표시. 경계선. 한도: *Carol fell as she crossed the finish line.* (=the line that marks the end of a race) 캐롤은 결승선을 넘자마자 쓰러졌다. / *the dividing line between the lanes on the road* 도로 위의 차선 사이에 있는 분할선

3 be/stand/wait in line to stand in a row of people who are waiting for something ‖ 어떤 것을 기다리는 사람들의 줄에 서다. 줄서 있다/줄서다/줄서서 기다리다: *We stood in line for two hours for tickets.* 우리는 표를 사려고 두 시간 동안이나 줄서서 기다렸다.

4 ▶ROW 열◀ a row of people or things ‖ 한 줄로 선[된] 사람이나 사물: *toys arranged in a line on the floor* 바닥에 일렬로 배열된 장난감들

5 ▶DIRECTION 방향◀ a direction something travels, or the imaginary path between two points in space ‖ 사물이 이동하는 방향, 또는 공간상 두 지점 사이의 가상의 길. 진행 방향. 진로: *Light travels in a straight line.* 빛은 직선으로 나아간다.

6 ▶SKIN 피부◀ a very small fold in the skin; WRINKLE ‖ 피부의 아주 작은 주름; ㈜ wrinkle: *tiny lines around his eyes* 그의 눈가에 있는 아주 작은 주름들

7 county/state line the border between two counties (COUNTY) or states in the US ‖ 미국에서 두 개의 군이나 주 사이의 경계. 군/주 경계선

8 ▶WAY 방법◀ a way of thinking about or doing something ‖ 어떤 것에 대해 생각하거나 실행하는 방식: *This meeting will be organized along the same lines* (=in the same way) *as the last one.* 이번 회의는 지난번과 같은 방식으로 구성될 것이다.

9 in line/out of line happening or behaving in the correct or expected way, or not happening or behaving in this way ‖ 바르거나 예상된 방식의 사건이나 행동인, 또는 이 같은 방식의 사건이나 행동이 아닌. 일치하여/일치되지 않는[관행에 맞지 않는]: *The company's actions are in line with the state laws.* 그 회사의 조치는 주(州) 법률과 일치한다. / *I thought what Kenny said was way out of line!* 케니가 말한 내용은 터무니없다고 나는 생각했다.

10 ▶TELEPHONE 전화◀ a telephone wire, or the connection between two telephones ‖ 전화선, 또는 두 전화 사이의 연결: *The line was bad, so we hung up and tried again.* 전화 연결 상태가 나빠서 우리는 전화를 끊고 다시 해보았다. —see usage note at TELEPHONE

11 ▶PRODUCTS 제품◀ a particular type of goods ‖ 상품의 특정한 유형: *The new line of shoes should sell really well.* 신제품 구두는 정말 잘 팔릴 것이다.

12 be first/next in line for sth to be very likely to be the next person to get something ‖ 어떤 것을 얻을 다음 사람이 될 가능성이 크다. …의 첫 번째/차기 후보[주자]가 되다: *I'm sure Carl is next in line for a raise.* 칼이 다음번에 임금 인상될 거라고 나는 확신한다.

13 ▶SHAPE 모양◀ the outer shape of something long or tall ‖ 길거나 높은 사물의 외형. 윤곽: *The building has beautiful lines.* 그 건물은 윤곽이 아름답다.

14 ▶SPORTS 스포츠◀ a row of players with a particular purpose in a sport ‖ 스포츠에서 특정 목적을 가진 선수들의 열: *the Bears' defensive line* 베어스 팀의 수비진[라인]

15 ▶COMPANY 회사◀ a company that provides a system for moving goods by road, water, or air ‖ 육상[해상, 항공]편으로 상품을 이동시키기 위한 체계를 제공하는 회사. 운수 회사: *a large shipping line* 거대한 운송 회사

16 the line ⇨ CLOTHESLINE

17 ▶FAMILY 가족◀ the people that existed before you in your family ‖ 가족에서 자기 이전에 존재한 사람들. 가계(家系). 혈통: *She comes from a long line of politicians.* 그녀는 오랜 정치인 가문 출신이다.

18 ▶WORDS 말◀ a line of words in a poem, play, film, or song ‖ 시[연극·영화, 노래]에서의 한 줄의 말. 한 행(行). 대사

19 ▶FISHING 낚시◀ a strong thin piece of string you use to catch fish ‖ 고기를 잡을 때 사용하는 강하고 가느다란 줄. 낚싯줄 —see also ON LINE, **somewhere along the line/way** (SOMEWHERE)

line² *v* [T] **1** to cover the inside of a piece of material, a container etc. with another material or substance ‖ 다른 재료나 물질로 재료·용기 등의 안을 덮다. …에 안감을 대다[받치다]: *We lined the box with newspapers.* 우리는 신문지로 상자 안을 붙였다. / *a lined skirt* 안감을 댄 치마 **2** to form rows along the edge of something ‖ 어떤 것의 가장자리를 따라 열을 짓다. …을 따라 늘어서다. 늘어서게 하다: *a wide road lined with trees* 나무들이 늘어선 널따란 도로

line up *phr v* **1** [I,T **line** sb/sth ↔ **up**] to make a row, or arrange people or things in a row ‖ 줄을 세우다, 또는 사람이나 사물을 한 줄로 배열하다. 정렬하다[시키다]: *OK class, line up by the door.* 자 여러분, 문 옆으로 정렬하세요. / *We lined the jars up on the shelf.* 우리는 선반에 단지들을 정렬했다. **2** [T **line** sb/sth ↔ **up**] to organize the activities that will happen at an event ‖ 행사에서 일어날 활동을 조직하다. 준비하다. 확보하다: *They've lined up some dancers for the show.* 그들은 그 쇼에 나올 몇몇 무용수들을 확보했다.

lin·e·age /ˈlɪnɪɪdʒ/ *n* [C, U] the way in which members of a family are related to other members who lived in past times ‖ 가족 구성원이 과거에 살았던 다른 구성원과 관련된 방식. 혈통. 가계

lin·e·ar /ˈlɪnɪə/ *adj* **1** consisting of lines, or in the form of a straight line ‖ 선들로 구성되었거나 직선의 형태인. 직선 모양의: *a linear drawing* 일직선 긋기 **2** related to length ‖ 길이에 관한: *linear measurements* 길이의 측정

line·back·er /ˈlaɪnˌbækə/ *n* [C, U] in football, a player on the DEFENSE who stands behind the TACKLEs and ENDs ‖ 미식축구에서 태클과 엔드 후방에 위치한 수비 선수. 라인배커 —see picture on page 946

lined /laɪnd/ *adj* **1** a skirt, coat etc. that is lined has a piece of material covering the inside ‖ 치마·외투 등에 안쪽을 덮는 재료가 있는. 안감을 댄: *a fur-lined coat* 부드러운 털로 안감을 댄 외투 **2** lined paper has straight lines printed on it ‖ 종이에 직선이 인쇄돼 있는. 괘선이 있는

line·man /ˈlaɪnmən/ *n* in football, one of the players who face each other in a line and try to stop the other team or to help their own team to move forward ‖ 미식축구에서, 라인에서 서로 맞서서 상대 팀을 막거나 자기 팀의 전진을 도우려는 선수. 라인맨 —see picture on page 946

lin·en /ˈlɪnən/ *n* [U] **1** sheets, TABLECLOTHs etc. ‖ 시트·테이블보 등. 리넨 제품: *bed/table linen* 리넨 침대[탁자]보 **2** cloth used for making good quality summer clothes ‖ 우수한 품질의 여름옷을 만드는 데에 쓰이는 옷감. 아마 직물

lin·er /ˈlaɪnə/ *n* **1** a large ship for carrying people ‖ 사람을 수송하는 큰 선박. 정기선 **2** a thick layer of material that can be attached to the inside of a piece of clothing to make it warmer ‖ 보온용으로 의류의 안쪽에 덧붙일 수 있는 두꺼운 옷감. 안감

lin·er notes /ˈ.. ˌ./ *n* [plural] the writing on the case of a CD, record etc. that tells about the performers and music on it ‖ 공연자와 음악에 대해 설명하는 CD·음반 등의 케이스에 있는 글

line·up /ˈlaɪnʌp/ *n* **1** a group of people arranged in a row by the police so that a person who saw a crime can try to recognize the criminal ‖ 범죄를 목격한 사람이 범인을 기억해낼 수 있도록 경찰이 한 줄로 정렬시킨 사람들의 집단. 용의자들의 열 **2** a set of events, programs, performers etc. that are arranged to follow each other ‖ 서로 순서를 정해 편

성된 일단의 행사·프로그램·연주자 등. 구성: *The lineup of performers included Tony Curtis and Diana Ross.* 공연자 구성에는 토니 커티스와 다이애나 로스가 포함되었다. —see also STARTING LINEUP

lin·ger /'lɪŋɡɚ/ v [I] **1** to stay somewhere longer or to take longer to do something than usual ‖ 어딘가에 더 오래 머물거나 어떤 일을 하는 데 평소보다 오래 걸리다. 꾸물거리다. 더디다. 처지다: *We like to linger over breakfast on Saturday morning.* 우리는 토요일 아침에는 여유를 부리며 아침 식사 하기를 좋아한다. **2** also **linger on** to be slow to disappear ‖ 느리게 사라지다. 잔존하다. 좀처럼 없어지지 않다: *The smell of smoke lingered for a week after the party.* 파티 후에도 일주일간 연기 냄새가 남아 있었다.

lin·ge·rie /ˌlɑnʒəˈreɪ, ˌlɑndʒə-/ n [U] women's underwear ‖ 여성용 속옷. 란제리

lin·ger·ing /'lɪŋɡərɪŋ/ adj continuing a long time ‖ 오랜 시간 계속되는. 꾸물거리는. 질질[오래] 끄는: *a long lingering kiss* 오랫동안 하는 키스

lin·go /'lɪŋɡoʊ/ n INFORMAL **1** words used only by a group of people who do a particular job or activity ‖ 특정한 직무나 활동을 하는 사람들의 집단에 의해서만 사용되는 말. 전문 용어: *medical lingo* 의학 전문 용어 **2** a language ‖ 언어

lin·guist /'lɪŋɡwɪst/ n **1** someone who studies LINGUISTICS ‖ 언어학을 연구하는 사람. 언어학자 **2** someone who speaks several languages well ‖ 여러 언어를 잘 말하는 사람. 수개 국어에 능한 사람

lin·guis·tic /lɪŋˈɡwɪstɪk/ adj relating to language, words, or LINGUISTICS ‖ 언어[말, 언어학]에 관련된. 언어의: *a child's linguistic development* 아동 언어 발달

lin·guis·tics /lɪŋˈɡwɪstɪks/ n [U] the study of languages, including their structures, grammar, and history ‖ 언어의 구조·문법·역사를 포함한 언어의 연구. 언어학

lin·i·ment /'lɪnəmənt/ n [C, U] an oily liquid you rub on your skin when your muscles are sore or stiff ‖ 근육이 쑤시거나 뻣뻣할 때 피부에 문질러 바르는 유성(油性)의 액체. 바르는 약. 도찰제

lin·ing /'laɪnɪŋ/ n [C, U] a piece of material covering the inside of something such as a box, a coat etc. ‖ 상자·외투 등의 안을 덮는 재료. 안감: *a jacket with a silk lining* 실크 안감을 댄 재킷

link¹ /lɪŋk/ v [T] **1** to make a connection between two or more situations, events, or people ‖ 둘이나 그 이상의 상황[사건, 사람들] 사이를 연결 짓다. 연결하다. 관련시키다: *Lung cancer has been linked to smoking cigarettes.* 폐암은 흡연과 관련된 것으로 여겨져 왔다. **2** also **link up** to connect computers, communication systems, etc. so that sound, pictures, or information can be shared among them ‖ 소리[화상, 정보]가 서로 공유될 수 있도록 컴퓨터·통신 시스템 등을 연결하다. 결합하다: *Our computers are linked to the central system.* 우리 컴퓨터는 중앙 시스템에 연결되어 있다. **3** to join one place to another ‖ 한 장소를 다른 장소에 잇다. 연결하다: *a highway linking two major cities* 두 주요 도시를 연결하는 고속도로 **4** **link arms** to bend your arm and put it through someone else's bent arm ‖ 팔을 구부려서 다른 사람의 굽은 팔 사이로 끼어 넣다. 팔을 끼다

link² n **1** a relationship or connection between two or more events, people, or ideas ‖ 둘 이상의 사건[사람들, 생각] 사이의 관계나 연관성. 유대. 관련: *Latin is the link between all of the Romance languages.* 라틴어는 모든 로맨스어와 관련되어 있다. / *He has links with the Socialist party.* 그는 사회당과 관련되어 있다. / **2** one of the rings that makes up a chain ‖ 쇠사슬을 구성하는 고리의 하나. 고리 —see picture at CHAIN¹ **3** also **linkup** a connection between two places that allows people to travel or communicate between them ‖ 상호간에 오가거나 통신이 가능한 두 장소 사이의 연결. 링크. 연결. 연계. 접속: *a telephone/satellite link* 전화[위성] 연결 —see also CUFF LINK

link·age /'lɪŋkɪdʒ/ n **1** [C, U] a LINK or connection between two things ‖ 두 사물 사이의 연결이나 연관. 결합. 연합. 연쇄 **2** [U] a situation in which one country agrees to do something only if another country does something as well ‖ 다른 나라가 마찬가지로 어떤 것을 하는 경우에만 자기 나라도 어떤 것을 하는 데 동의하는 상황. 연관 외교

link·ing verb /'.. ˌ./ n TECHNICAL in grammar, a verb that connects the subject of a sentence to its COMPLEMENT. In the sentence, "She seems friendly," "seems" is a linking verb ‖ 문법에서 문장의 주어를 보어에 연결시키는 동사. 연결 동사. "She seems friendly."라는 문장에서 "seems"는 연결 동사이다. —see study note on page 942

li·no·le·um /lɪˈnoʊliəm/ n [U] smooth

shiny material that is used for covering floors ‖ 마루를 까는 데 사용되는 부드럽고 광택이 있는 바닥재. 리놀륨

lint /lɪnt/ *n* [U] soft light pieces of thread or wool that come off cotton, wool, or other material ‖ 면[양모, 기타 직물]에서 떨어져나오는 부드럽고 가벼운 실이나 털실 조각. 실보푸라기

li·on /'laɪən/ *n* a large African and Asian wild cat, the male of which has long thick hair around his neck ‖ 수컷의 목 주위에 긴 갈기가 더부룩하게 나 있는 몸집이 큰 아프리카·아시아산 야생 고양이과의 동물. 사자

li·on·ess /'laɪənɪs/ *n* a female lion ‖ 암사자

lip /lɪp/ *n* **1** one of the two soft parts around your mouth ‖ 입가의 말랑한 두 부분 중 하나. 입술: *a kiss on the lips* 입술 키스 —see picture at HEAD[1] **2** the edge of a container that will hold liquid ‖ 액체를 담은 용기의 가장자리: *the lip of the cup* 컵의 가장자리 **3 my lips are sealed** SPOKEN said when promising someone that you will not tell a secret ‖ 비밀을 말하지 않을 것이라고 남에게 약속할 때에 쓰여. 내 입은 봉해졌다. 입 밖에 내지 않는다 **4 -lipped** with lips of a particular type ‖ 특정한 형태의 입술을 가진: *a thin-lipped woman* 입술이 얇은 여인 **5 pay/give lip service** to say that you support or agree with something, without doing anything to prove this ‖ 증명할 어떠한 행동도 하지 않고 어떤 것을 지원하거나 동의한다고 말하다. 말뿐인 호의를 보이다: *They're only paying lip service to pollution prevention.* 그들은 말로만 오염 방지에 대해 떠들고 있다.

lip gloss /'. ./ *n* [C, U] a substance that women use to make their lips very shiny ‖ 여성이 입술을 매우 윤이 나게 하는 데에 사용하는 물질. 립글로스

lip-read /'lɪp rɪd/ *v* [I, T] to watch someone's lips move in order to understand what s/he is saying, especially because you cannot hear ‖ 특히 들을 수 없어서, 사람이 말하는 것을 이해하려고 입술의 움직임을 보다. 남의 말을 독순술(讀脣術)[입술 모양]로 이해하다 **– lip-reading** *n* [U]

lip·stick /'lɪp,stɪk/ *n* [C, U] a colored substance that women put on their lips, or a small tube containing this ‖ 여성이 입술에 바르는 색깔이 있는 물질, 또는 이 것을 담은 작은 통. 립스틱. 입술연지

lip synch /'lɪp,sɪŋk/ *v* [I] to pretend to sing by moving your lips at the same time as a recording is being played ‖ 녹

음된 것을 틀어 놓고 동시에 입술을 움직여 노래하는 척하다. 립싱크하다

liq·ue·fy /'lɪkwə,faɪ/ *v* [I, T] to become liquid, or to make something become liquid ‖ 액체화되다, 또는 어떤 것을 액체화되게 하다. 액화[용해]하다[시키다]

li·queur /lɪ'kə, lɪ'kʊə/ *n* [C, U] a sweet alcoholic drink usually drunk after a meal ‖ 보통 식사 후에 마시는 달콤한 술. 리큐어

liq·uid /'lɪkwɪd/ *n* [C, U] a substance such as water, that is not solid or a gas, but that can flow and be poured ‖ 고체나 기체가 아닌, 흐르거나 따를 수 있는 물 등의 물질. 액체 **– liquid** *adj* : *liquid soap* 물비누 —see also FLUID

liq·ui·date /'lɪkwə,deɪt/ *v* **1** [I, T] to close a business or company and sell its goods in order to pay a debt ‖ 사업체나 회사를 폐쇄하고 부채를 갚기 위해 남은 상품을 팔다. (파산한 기업의) 재산[부채]을 청산하다 **2** [T] INFORMAL to kill someone ‖ 사람을 죽이다. 없애 버리다 **– liquidation** /,lɪkwɪ'deɪʃən/ *n* [C, U]

liq·uor /'lɪkə/ *n* [U] a strong alcoholic drink such as WHISKEY ‖ 위스키 등의 독한 술. 증류주

liquor store /'.. ,./ *n* a store where alcohol is sold ‖ 술을 파는 가게. 주류 판매점

lisp /lɪsp/ *v* [I, T] to pronounce the "s" sound like "th," so the word "sing" sounds like "thing" ‖ "s"음을 "th"음처럼 발음해, "sing"이란 단어를 "thing"처럼 발음하다. 혀 짧은 소리로 발음하다 **– lisp** *n*

list[1] /lɪst/ *n* a set of names, things, numbers etc. that are written one below the other so you can remember them ‖ 기억할 수 있게 다른 항목 아래 쓰여진, 일련의 이름·물건·숫자 등. 목록. 명부: *Make a list of the equipment you'll need.* 앞으로 필요한 장비 목록을 작성해라. / *Butter wasn't on the shopping list.* 버터는 쇼핑 목록에는 없었다. ✗DON'T SAY "in the list."✗ "in the list"라고는 하지 는다.

list[2] *v* [T] to write a list, or to mention things one after the other ‖ 목록을 작성하다, 또는 잇따라서 어떤 것을 언급하다. …을 기재하다. …의 일람표를 만들다: *All the players must be listed on the scoresheet.* 모든 선수들은 득점 기입표에 기재되어야 한다.

lis·ten /'lɪsən/ *v* [I] **1** to pay attention to what someone is saying or to something that you hear ‖ 남이 말하는 것이나 자신이 듣는 것에 주의를 기울이다. 듣다. 귀

를 기울이다: *Have you listened to any of these tapes yet?* 이 테이프 중에서 어느 것이라도 전에 들어본 적이 있니? / *Are you listening to me?* 내 말 듣고 있니? **2** SPOKEN used in order to tell someone to pay attention to what you are saying ‖ 자신이 하고 있는 말에 주의를 기울이라고 남에게 말하는 데에 쓰여. 주목. 들어보세요: *Listen, can I call you back later?* 있잖아요. 제가 나중에 다시 전화해도 될까요? **3** to pay attention and accept what someone tells you ‖ 주의를 기울여 남이 말하는 것을 받아들이다. 따르다: *I told him it was dangerous, but he wouldn't listen.* 나는 그에게 그것은 위험하다고 말했으나 그는 말을 들으려 하지 않았다.

listen for sth/sb *phr v* [T] to pay attention so that you are sure you will hear a sound ‖ 소리를 확실히 들으려고 주의를 기울이다. 귀를 기울이다: *I was listening for Bill's car in the street.* 나는 거리에서 빌의 자동차 소리를 들으려고 귀를 기울이고 있었다.

listen in *phr v* [I] to listen to what someone is saying without him/her knowing it ‖ 남이 말하는 것을 몰래 듣다. 도청하다. 엿듣다: *I think someone's listening in on the other phone.* 누군가가 다른 전화로 엿듣고 있는 것 같아.

listen up *phr v* [I] SPOKEN used in order to get people's attention so they will hear what you are going to say ‖ 자신이 말하려는 것을 사람들이 듣도록 주의를 기울이게 하는 데 쓰여. 잘 듣다: *OK people, listen up. I'm only going to say this once.* 자, 여러분, 잘 들으세요. 이번 한 번만 말할 겁니다.

USAGE NOTE listen and hear

Use both of these words to talk about sounds. **Listen** means "to pay attention to a sound or to what someone says": *She never listens to what I say.* **Hear** usually means "to know that a sound is being made": *Couldn't you hear the doorbell?* You can also use **hear** to talk about listening to music, or to ask if someone understands you: *Would you like to hear my new CD?* / *Make sure you come home at 6:00, do you hear me?*

이들 두 말은 소리에 대해 말하는 데 모두 사용 가능하다. **listen**은 "소리에 귀를 기울이거나 남이 말하는 내용에 주의를 기울이다"라는 의미이다: 그녀는 내

말에 전혀 귀를 기울이지 않는다. **hear**는 보통 "소리가 나고 있다는 것을 알다"라는 의미이다: 초인종 소리를 못 들었니? 또한 음악을 듣거나 다른 사람이 자신의 말을 이해했는지를 물을 때도 **hear**를 사용한다: 내 새 CD를 듣고 싶니? / 6시에는 틀림없이 와야 한다. 알겠지?

lis·ten·er /'lɪsənɚ/ *n* **1** someone who listens, especially to the radio ‖ 특히 라디오를 듣는 사람. 청취자 **2 good listener** someone who listens in a sympathetic way to other people ‖ 다른 사람의 말을 공감하며 듣는 사람. 열심히 듣는 사람

lis·ting /'lɪstɪŋ/ *n* a printed or written list ‖ 인쇄되거나 쓰여진 목록. 일람표. 명부: *movie listings* 영화 일람표

list·less /'lɪstlɪs/ *adj* feeling tired and uninterested in doing things ‖ 일을 하는 데 싫증을 느끼고 흥미가 없는. 마음이 내키지 않는. 무관심한

list price /ˌ. './ *n* a price for a product that is set by the company that makes it ‖ 제조 회사에 의해 정해진 제품 가격. 정가. 생산자 희망 소비자 가격

lit¹ /lɪt/ *v* the past tense and PAST PARTICIPLE of LIGHT ‖ light의 과거·과거 분사형

lit² *adj* having light or burning ‖ 빛이 나거나 타고 있는. 불타는: *a well-lit room* 조명이 잘된 방 / *a lit cigarette* 타고 있는 담배

lit·a·ny /'lɪtˀn-i/ *n* **a litany of** sth a long list of problems, questions, complaints etc. ‖ 길게 나열된 문제·질문·불만 등. 장황한 설명: *a litany of economic problems* 경제 문제에 대한 장황한 이야기

lite /laɪt/ *adj* NONSTANDARD having fewer CALORIEs than usual ‖ 보통보다 적은 칼로리를 함유한. 저칼로리의: *lite beer* 저알코올 맥주

li·ter /'litɚ/, *written abbreviation* **l** *n* a unit for measuring liquid, equal to 2.12 PINTs or 0.26 gallons ‖ 2.12파인트 또는 0.26갤런에 해당하는 액체 측정 단위. 리터

lit·er·a·cy /'lɪtərəsi/ *n* [U] the ability to read and write ‖ 읽고 쓰는 능력

lit·er·al /'lɪtərəl/ *adj* relating to the most basic or original meaning of a word, statement, book etc. ‖ 어휘·말·책 등의 가장 기본적이거나 본래의 의미에 관한. 문자 그대로인. 원문에 충실한: *a literal interpretation of the Bible* 성경의 원문에 충실한 해석 —compare

FIGURATIVE

lit·er·al·ly /ˈlɪtərəli/ *adv* **1** according to the most basic meaning of a word or expression ‖ 어휘 또는 표현의 가장 기본적인 의미에 따라. 축어적으로. 문자 그대로: *There are literally millions of students in these programs.* 이 프로그램에는 문자 그대로 수백만 명의 학생이 나온다. **2** SPOKEN used in order to emphasize something you have just said ‖ 방금 말한 사항을 강조하는 데에 쓰여. 실제로. 완전히. 아주: *The place was literally crawling with cops.* (=there were a lot of police officers there) 그 곳은 실제로 경찰관들이 득실거렸다. **3 take sb/sth literally** to think that a word or statement is LITERAL when it is not ‖ 어휘 또는 말이 (실제는) 그렇지 않은 경우에 문자 그대로 받아들이다: *Lou was joking, but Sara took it literally.* 루는 농담을 하고 있었지만, 새라는 그것을 문자 그대로 받아들였다.

lit·er·ar·y /ˈlɪtəˌrɛri/ *adj* **1** relating to literature ‖ 문학에 관련된. 문학의 **2** typical of writing used in literature rather than in ordinary writing and talking ‖ 일상적으로 쓰고 말하는 것보다는 문학에서 사용되는 전형적인 글쓰기의. 문어적(文語的)인

lit·er·ate /ˈlɪtərɪt/ *adj* **1** able to read and write ‖ 읽고 쓸 줄 아는 **2** well educated ‖ 잘 교육받은. 학식 있는 — opposite ILLITERATE

lit·er·a·ture /ˈlɪtərətʃə, ˈlɪtrə-/ *n* [U] **1** books, plays etc. that are considered very good and that people have liked for a long time ‖ 아주 훌륭한 것으로 간주되어 사람들이 오랫동안 좋아해 온 서적·연극 등. 문학. 문예 작품: *the great classics of English literature* 영문학의 위대한 고전 **2** printed information designed by a company or organization to sell you something or give you advice ‖ 어떤 것을 팔거나 권고하기 위해 회사나 조직이 고안하여 인쇄한 정보. (팸플릿·전단 등의) 인쇄물

lithe /laɪð/ *adj* able to bend and move your body easily and gracefully ‖ 신체를 쉽고 우아하게 굽히고 움직일 수 있는. 유연한

lit·i·gate /ˈlɪtəˌgeɪt/ *v* [I, T] LAW to take a legal case to a court of law ‖ 법률 사건을 법원에 제기하다. 소송하다

lit·i·ga·tion /ˌlɪtəˈgeɪʃən/ *n* [U] the process of taking a legal case to a court of law ‖ 법원에 법률 사건을 제기하는 과정. 소송. 고소

lit·mus test /ˈlɪtməs ˌtɛst/ *n* a single

action, situation, or quality that allows you to measure someone's attitude, beliefs etc. ‖ 어떤 사람의 태도·신념 등을 가늠할 수 있는 단일 조치[상황, 특질]. (일반적으로) 결정적인 테스트: *The elections will be a litmus test of the political mood in the US.* 그 선거는 미국의 정치적 분위기에 대한 시금석(試金石)이 될 것이다.

lit·ter¹ /ˈlɪtə/ *n* **1** [U] pieces of waste paper etc. that people leave on the ground in public places ‖ 공공장소의 땅바닥에 사람들이 버려둔 휴지조각. 쓰레기 **2** a group of baby animals born at the same time to one mother ‖ 동시에 한 어미에게서 태어난 새끼 동물들. 한 배의[한 배에 난] 새끼들

litter² *v* **1** [I, T] to leave pieces of waste paper etc. on the ground in a public place ‖ 공공장소의 땅바닥에 휴지조각을 버리다. 어지르다. 흩어놓다. 더럽히다: *The sign says: Please Do Not Litter.* 표지판에는 이런 글이 써있다. 쓰레기를 버리지 마시오. **2** [T] if a lot of things litter a place, they are spread all over it in a messy way ‖ 많은 물건들을 지저분하게 사방으로 널려있게 하다. 흩뜨리다: *The floor was littered with clothes.* 마룻바닥에는 옷가지들이 흩어져 있었다.

lit·ter·bug /ˈlɪtəˌbʌg/ *n* DISAPPROVING someone who LITTERs ‖ 쓰레기를 마구 버리는 사람

lit·tle¹ /ˈlɪtl/ *adj* **1** small in size ‖ 크기가 작은: *a little house* 작은 집 **2 a little bit** not very much ‖ 그리 많지 않은. 조금. 소량의: *It will only hurt a little bit.* 조금 아플 것이다. / *Can I have a little bit of* (=a small amount of) *milk in my coffee, please?* 커피에 우유를 조금 넣어 주시겠어요? **3** short in time or distance ‖ 시간이나 거리상 짧은. 잠깐: *I'll wait a little while and then call again.* 조금 있다 다시 전화할게. / *Anna walked a little way down the road with him.* 안나는 그와 함께 길을 조금 걸어 내려왔다. **4** young and small ‖ 어리고 작은. 어린(애의): *a little boy* 어린 소년 **5** not important ‖ 중요하지 않은. 하찮은. 사소한: *He gets angry over little things.* 그는 사소한 일에 화를 낸다. **6** used in order to emphasize the adjective in a sentence ‖ 문장에서 형용사를 강조하는 데에 쓰여: *She owns a nice little restaurant in the city.* 그녀는 시내에 멋지고 아담한 레스토랑을 갖고 있다.

little² *quantifier* **less, least 1** only a small amount of something ‖ 어떤 것이 아주 소량인. 적은: *Little is known about* *the planet.* 그 행성에 대해 알려진 바가 거의 없다. / *I have very little money right now, but he has even less.* 나는 지금 아주 적은 돈이나마 있지만 그는 (나보다도) 훨씬 덜 갖고 있다. **2 a little** a small amount ‖ 작은 분량. 조금. 약간: *I only know a little Spanish.* 나는 스페인어를 조금 알 뿐이다. / *She told him a little about it.* 그녀는 그것에 관하여 그에게 조금 말했다. / *Would you like a little more cake?* 케이크를 조금 더 드시겠습니까? / *I explained a little of the family's history.* 나는 가족사에 관해서 조금 설명했다. **3** a short time or distance ‖ 짧은 시간이나 거리: *He must be a little over 60.* (=slightly older than 60) 그는 60세를 조금 넘은 것이 틀림없다. / *Phoenix is a little under 50 miles from here.* (=slightly fewer than 50 miles) 피닉스는 여기에서 50마일 좀 못 되는 거리에 있다. —see usage note at FEW

little³ *adv* **1** not much or only slightly ‖ 많지 않거나 그저 약간의. 다소. 조금: *He moved the table a little closer to the wall.* 그는 테이블을 벽 쪽으로 좀 더 가까이 옮겼다. / *I was a little afraid of the dog.* 나는 개를 좀 무서워했다. / *She goes out very little.* 그녀는 좀처럼 외출하지 않는다. —compare LESS², LEAST² **2 little by little** gradually ‖ 점차로. 점점: *Little by little, she became more confident.* 조금씩 그녀는 더욱 자신을 갖게 되었다.

little fin·ger /ˌ.. '../ *n* the smallest finger on your hand ‖ 손에서 가장 작은 손가락. 새끼손가락 —see picture at HAND¹

Little League Base·ball /ˌ..ˌ. '../ *n* TRADEMARK a group of baseball teams for children ‖ 어린이 야구팀의 집단. 소년 야구 리그

lit·ur·gy /'lɪtədʒi/ *n* [C, U] prayers, songs etc. that are said in a particular order in a religious ceremony ‖ 종교 의식의 특정 순서에서 쓰이는 기도문·노래 등. 교회 의식[전례](문) **– liturgical** /lɪ'tədʒɪkəl/ *adj*

liv·a·ble, liveable /'lɪvəbəl/ *adj* suitable to live in ‖ 살기에 적합한. 살기 좋은: *The apartment isn't fancy but it's livable.* 그 아파트는 고급은 아니지만 살기에는 편하다.

live¹ /lɪv/ *v* **1** [I] to be alive or to continue to stay alive ‖ 살아 있다, 또는 계속 살아 있다. 생존하다[해 있다]: *My grandmother lived to be 88.* 나의 할머니는 88세까지 생존하셨다. / *Pythagoras lived a century before Socrates.* 피타고라스는 소크라테스보다 한 세기 앞서 살았다. **2** [I] to have your home in a particular place ‖ 특정 장소에 집을 가지다. 거주하다: *"Where do you live?" "I live in Boston."* "어디에 사니?" "보스톤에 살아." / *The Reyes family live on White Oak Avenue.* 레이즈 가족은 화이트 오크 가(街)에 살고 있다. **3** [I, T] to have a particular type of life, or to live in a particular way ‖ 특정한 삶의 형태를 가지다, 또는 특정한 방식으로 살다. 살아가다. 지내다: *We can live comfortably on the money that I earn.* 우리는 내가 번 돈으로 편히 살 수 있다. / *children living in poverty* 가난하게 살고 있는 아이들 **4 live together** to live with another person in a sexual relationship without being married ‖ 결혼하지 않은 상태로 다른 사람과 성적인 관계를 가지며 함께 살다. 동거하다: *Mark and I have been living together for two years.* 마크와 나는 2년 동안 동거해 오고 있다. **5** [I] to keep yourself alive by doing a particular thing or eating a particular food ‖ 특정한 일을 하거나 특정한 음식을 먹고 살아가다. 먹고 살다. 생활하다. 살림을 꾸리다: *These animals live on insects.* 이 동물들은 곤충을 잡아먹고 산다.

live for sb/sth *phr v* [T] to be the most important thing in your life ‖ 삶에서 가장 중요한 일이 되다. …을 보람으로 여기다. …을 낙으로 기다리다: *She lives for ballet.* 그녀는 발레를 삶에서 가장 중요한 것으로 여긴다.

live off sth/sb *phr v* [T] to get your food or money from someone or something ‖ 사람이나 사물로부터 음식 또는 돈을 얻다. …에게 기식하다. …으로(만) 살다: *He's living off money from his investments.* 그는 투자에서 나오는 돈으로 생활하고 있다.

live sth **down** *phr v* [T] **not live** sth **down** to not be able to make people forget about something bad or embarrassing you have done ‖ 이전에 저지른 나쁘거나 난처한 일을 사람들이 잊어버리게 할 수 없다. …을 떨쳐버릴 수 없다. 씻어버릴 수 없다: *You'll never live this evening down!* 너는 오늘밤 일을 사람들의 기억에서 결코 지워버릴 수 없을 것이다!

live on *phr v* [I] to continue to exist ‖ 계속 존재하다. 계속 살다: *She will live on in our memories.* 그녀는 우리의 기억 속에 계속 살아 있을 것이다.

live through sth *phr v* [T] to experience difficult or dangerous conditions and continue living ‖ 어렵거나 위험한 상황을 경험하면서 계속 살다. 살아남다. 견디어

내다: *Don didn't expect to live through the war.* 돈은 전쟁에서 살아 남으리라 기대하지 못했다.

live up to sth *phr v* [T] to do something as well, or be as good as someone expects ‖ 어떤 것을 다른 사람이 기대한 만큼 잘 하거나 그만큼 좋다. …에 따라 행동하다. 부응하다: *Charles could never live up to his father's expectations.* 찰스는 아버지의 기대에 결코 부응할 수가 없었다.

live with *phr v* [T] **1** [**live with** sth] to accept a difficult situation even when it continues for a long time ‖ 장시간 계속되는데도 어려운 상황을 받아들이다. 감내[감수]하다: *living with pain* 고통을 감내하기 **2** [**live with** sb] to live with another person, especially in a sexual relationship without being married ‖ 특히 결혼하지 않고 성적인 관계를 가지며 다른 사람과 같이 살다. 같이 지내다. 동거하다: *Tim's living with a girl he met in college.* 팀은 대학에서 만난 여자와 동거하고 있다.

live² /laɪv/ *adj* **1** not dead or artificial; LIVING ‖ 죽지 않은 또는 인공적이지 않은. 살아 있는. 산. 진짜의; ⓐ living: *He fed the snake live rats.* 그는 살아 있는 쥐들을 뱀에게 먹이로 주었다. —compare DEAD¹ **2** broadcast as an event happens ‖ 사건의 발생과 동시에 방송하는. 생방송인. 실황인: *a live broadcast of the Rose Parade* 로즈 퍼레이드의 실황 방송 **3** performed for people who are watching ‖ 보고 있는 사람을 위해 연주되는. 라이브[실황] 음악의: *The Dew Drop Inn has live music every weekend.* 듀 드롭 인에서는 매 주말에 라이브 음악을 연주한다. **4** having electricity flowing through it ‖ 어떤 것을 따라 전기가 흐르는. 전기가 통하는: *a live wire* 전기가 통하고 있는 전선 **5** ready to explode ‖ 폭발할 준비가 된. 장전이 된: *a live bomb* 실폭탄 —see also **real live** (REAL¹)

live³ /laɪv/ *adv* **1** broadcast sth live to broadcast something at the same time that it happens ‖ 일의 발생과 동시에 방송하다. 생방송하다. 실황으로 방송하다: *We'll be broadcasting the program live from Washington.* 그 프로그램을 워싱턴으로부터 생방송으로 보내드리겠습니다. **2** performing in front of people ‖ 사람들 앞에서 연주하여. 라이브[실황] 연주로: *I'd love to see the band play live!* 그 밴드가 라이브 연주하는 것을 정말 보고 싶다!

live·li·hood /ˈlaɪvliˌhʊd/ *n* [C, U] the way you earn money in order to live ‖ 살

기 위하여 돈을 버는 방법. 생계(의 수단). 살림: *Farming is their livelihood.* 농사는 그들의 생계 수단이다.

live·ly /ˈlaɪvli/ *adj* **1** very active and cheerful ‖ 매우 활동적이며 쾌활한. 활발한. 활기찬. 원기[생기]있는: *a lively group of children* 활기찬 한 무리의 어린이들 **2** very exciting and interesting ‖ 매우 흥미진진하고 재미있는. 박진감 있는: *a lively debate* 흥미진진한 토론 – **liveliness** *n* [U]

liv·en /ˈlaɪvən/ *v*

liven up *phr v* [I, T **liven** sth **up**] to become more exciting, or to make something more exciting ‖ 더 흥미진진해지거나 어떤 것을 더 흥미진진하게 하다. 활발[쾌활]하게 되다[하다]: *Better music might liven the party up.* 아마 더 좋은 음악이 파티에 더욱 활기를 불어 넣을 것이다.

liv·er /ˈlɪvɚ/ *n* **1** a large organ in your body that cleans your blood ‖ 혈액을 깨끗이 하는 신체의 큰 장기. 간 **2** [U] the liver of an animal used as food ‖ 음식물로 쓰이는 동물의 간

lives /laɪvz/ *n* the plural of LIFE ‖ life의 복수형

live·stock /ˈlaɪvstɑk/ *n* [U] animals that are kept on a farm ‖ 농장에서 사육하는 동물. 가축류

liv·id /ˈlɪvɪd/ *adj* **1** extremely angry; FURIOUS ‖ 극도로 화난. 격노한; ⓐ furious: *Dad will be livid when he finds out!* 아버지가 아시면 몹시 화내실 거야! **2** a livid BRUISE is blue and black ‖ 멍 등이 검푸른. 납빛인 **3** pale because you are angry ‖ 화가 나서 창백한. 하얗게 질린

liv·ing¹ /ˈlɪvɪŋ/ *adj* **1** alive now ‖ 현재 살아 있는. 생명이 있는. 생존하는: *She is one of our greatest living writers.* 그녀는 생존하는 우리의 가장 위대한 작가들 중의 한 사람이다. —opposite DEAD¹ **2** existing or being used now ‖ 현재 존재하거나 쓰이고 있는. 당대의. 현존하는: *a living language* 현재 쓰이고 있는 언어 **3** living things anything that lives, such as animals, plants, and people ‖ 동물·식물·사람 등의 살아 있는 것. 생물. 생명체

living² *n* **1** the way that you earn money ‖ 돈을 버는 방식. 생계 수단: *What does he do for a living?* 그의 직업이 무엇입니까? / *It's hard to make a living* (=earn enough money) *as an actor.* 배우로서 생계를 꾸려 나가기는 힘들다. **2** [U] the way that someone lives his/her life ‖ 사람이 삶을 사는 방식. 생활 방식: *Martha has always believed in* *healthy living.* 마사는 건강한 생활 방식에 대한 믿음을 항상 지녀 왔다. **3 the living** all the people who are alive ‖ 살아 있는 모든 사람들. 생존하는 사람들. 산자 —see also COST OF LIVING

living room /'.. ,./ *n* the main room in a house, where you relax, watch television etc. ‖ 휴식을 취하고 텔레비전을 보는 등의 집 안의 주요한 방. 거실

living will /,.. './ *n* a document that explains what legal and medical decisions should be made for you if you are too sick to make them yourself ‖ 질병이 너무 중해서 스스로 결정을 내리지 못할 경우 어떤 법률적·의학적인 결정을 내려야 하는지 설명하는 문서. 사망 선택 유언. 사망 희망서

liz·ard /'lɪzəd/ *n* a REPTILE that has rough skin, four short legs, and a long tail ‖ 거친 피부와 짧은 네 다리 그리고 긴 꼬리를 가진 파충류. 도마뱀

-'ll /l, əl/ the short form of "will" or "shall" ‖ "will" 또는 "shall"의 단축형: *He'll be here soon.* 그는 곧 이리 올 거다.

lla·ma /'lɑmə/ *n* a large South American animal with thick hair like wool and a long neck ‖ 양털처럼 빽빽한 털과 긴 목을 가진 몸집이 큰 남미산 동물. 라마

Ln. the written abbreviation of LANE ‖ lane의 약어

load¹ /loud/ *n* **1** a large quantity of something that is carried by a person, a vehicle etc. ‖ 사람·차량 등에 의해 운송되는 물체의 큰 용량. 적하. 짐. 적재량: *a ship carrying a full load of fuel and supplies* 연료와 물품을 가득 실어 운송하는 선박 **2 carload/truckload etc.** the largest amount or number that a car etc. can carry ‖ 자동차 등이 운송할 수 있는 최대 용량 또는 수효. 자동차 한 대 분/트럭 한 대분: *a busload of kids* 버스 한 대분의 어린이들 **3** the amount of work that a machine or a person has to do ‖ 기계 또는 사람이 해야 하는 일의 분량. 작업량. 부담량: *a heavy work load* 과중한 작업량 **4** a quantity of clothes that are washed at the same time ‖ 동시에 세탁되는 옷의 양: *Can you do a load of clothes later today?* 오늘 늦게 세탁기 한 대분의 옷을 세탁할 수 있겠어요?

---SPOKEN PHRASES---

5 a load of sth/loads of sth a lot of something ‖ 많은 사물: *Don't worry, there's loads of time.* 걱정하지 마라. 시간은 많아. **6 get a load of sb/sth** said when you want someone to notice something funny or surprising ‖ 재미있거나 놀라운 일에 누군가가 주목해 주기를 원할 때 쓰여. …을 (잘) 보다[듣다]. 평가하다: *Get a load of that guy in the silver pants!* 은색 바지를 입은 저 녀석 좀 봐!

load² *v* **1** [I, T] also **load up** to put a load of something on or into a vehicle ‖ 어떤 짐을 차량에 넣거나 싣다. 적재하다. 잔뜩 쌓다: *He loaded up the car with camping gear.* 그는 차에 캠핑 장비를 가득 실었다. **2** [T] to put bullets into a gun, film into a camera etc. ‖ 총에 탄환을 재다. 카메라에 필름을 넣다 **3** [T] to put a program into a computer ‖ 컴퓨터에 프로그램을 입력하다. 전송[로드]하다

load sb/sth ↔ **down (with)** *phr v* [T] to make someone carry too many things or do too much work ‖ 사람에게 너무 많은 물건을 나르게 하거나 너무 많은 일을 시키다. (짐·책임 등을) 걸머지게 하다. 부담을 주다. …으로 짓눌리다: *I was loaded down with luggage.* 나는 많은 짐을 드느라 애를 먹었다.

load up on sth *phr v* [T] to get a lot of something ‖ 많은 것을 얻다: *People were loading up on bottled water.* 사람들은 병에 든 물을 양껏 마시고 있었다.

load·ed /'loudɪd/ *adj* **1** containing bullets, film etc. ‖ 탄환·필름 등이 들어 있는. 필름이 든. 장전된: *Is the camera loaded?* 그 카메라는 필름이 들어 있니? / *a loaded gun* 장전된 총 **2** carrying a load of something ‖ 어떤 짐을 나르는: *a loaded truck* 짐을 실은 트럭 **3** INFORMAL very rich ‖ 매우 부유한. 돈이 많은. 부자인: *His grandmother is loaded.* 그의 할머니는 돈이 많다. **4 loaded question** a question that is unfair because it makes you give a particular answer ‖ 특정한 대답을 하게 하는 불공정한 질문. 유도(적인) 질문 **5 loaded with** full of a particular quality, or containing a lot of something ‖ 특정한 성질로 가득한. 또는 무엇을 많이 포함하고 있는: *a cake loaded with nuts* 견과류가 많이 든 케이크 **6** INFORMAL very drunk ‖ 매우 취한. 만취한

loaf¹ /louf/ *n*, *plural* **loaves** bread that is shaped and baked in one large piece ‖ 하나의 큰 덩어리 형태로 구운 빵 —see picture at BREAD

loaf² *v* [I] INFORMAL to waste time in a lazy way when you should be working ‖ 일하고 있어야 할 때 게으르게 시간을 허비하다. …을 게으름 피우며 하다. 빈둥거리다: *He spends his days loafing* *around the house.* 그는 집에서 빈둥거리면서 낮 시간을 보낸다.

Loaf·er /ˈloʊfɚ/ *n* TRADEMARK a flat leather shoe without LACES ‖ 매는 끈이 없는 뒷굽이 낮은 가죽 신발. 간편화. 로퍼 —see picture at SHOE¹

loan¹ /loʊn/ *n* **1** an amount of money that you borrow from a bank ‖ 은행에서 빌리는 금액. 대출금. 융자: *We'll take out a loan to buy the car.* 우리는 자동차를 사기 위해 대출을 받아야겠다. **2 on loan** being borrowed ‖ 차용하여. 대부[차입]하여. 대출 받은: *The book is on loan from the library.* 그 책은 도서관에서 빌린 것이다. **3** [singular] the act of lending something ‖ 어떤 것을 빌려 주는 행위. 대여. 대출

loan² *v* [T] to lend someone something, especially money ‖ 물건, 특히 돈을 남에게 빌려 주다: *Can you loan me $20 until Friday?* 금요일까지 나에게 20달러를 빌려줄 수 있겠니? —see usage note at LEND

loan shark /ˈ. ./ *n* DISAPPROVING someone who lends money to people and charges a very high rate of INTEREST ‖ 사람들에게 돈을 빌려 주고 아주 높은 이자율을 부과해 받는 사람. 사채업자. 고리대금업자

loath /loʊθ, loʊð/ *adj* **be loath to do sth** FORMAL to be unwilling to do something ‖ 어떤 것을 하는 것이 내키지 않다. …하기가 싫다[꺼림칙하다]: *I was loath to leave her alone.* 나는 그녀를 혼자 남겨 두는 것이 내키지 않았다.

loathe /loʊð/ *v* [T] to hate someone or something ‖ 사람 또는 사물을 몹시 싫어하다. 질색하다. 혐오하다 – **loathing** *n* [C, U]

loath·ing /ˈloʊðɪŋ/ *n* [singular, U] a very strong feeling of hatred ‖ 아주 강한 증오의 감정. 혐오: *The more he called me 'Sugar', the more my loathing for him increased.* 그가 나를 '자기야'라고 부르면 부를수록 그가 더욱 혐오스러워졌다.

loath·some /ˈloʊðsəm, ˈloʊθ-/ *adj* very unpleasant; DISGUSTING ‖ 아주 불쾌한. 미운. 지긋지긋한. 메스꺼운; 趣 disgusting

loaves /loʊvz/ *n* the plural form of LOAF ‖ loaf의 복수형

lob /lɑb/ *v* **-bbed, -bbing** [T] to throw or hit a ball so that it moves slowly in a high curve ‖ 공을 높이 곡선을 그리며 완만하게 움직이게 던지거나 치다

lob·by¹ /ˈlɑbi/ *n* **1** a large hall inside the entrance of a building ‖ 건물 출입구 안쪽의 커다란 홀. 로비: *waiting in the hotel lobby* 호텔 로비에서 기다리기 **2** a group of people who try to persuade the government to change or approve a particular law ‖ 특정 법률을 개정하거나 승인하도록 정부를 설득하려고 하는 사람들의 집단. 압력 단체. 원외 활동단: *the environmental lobby* 환경 보호를 호소하는 압력 단체

lob·by² *v* [I, T] to try to persuade the government to change a particular law ‖ 특정 법률을 개정하기 위해 정부를 설득하려고 하다. 의안을 청원 운동으로 통과시키려고 하다: *a group lobbying for/against the law* 법률에 찬성[반대] 운동을 하고 있는 집단 – **lobbyist** *n*

lobe /loʊb/ *n* ⇨ EARLOBE

lob·ster /ˈlɑbstɚ/ *n* [C, U] an ocean animal with eight legs, a shell, and two large CLAWs, or the meat of this animal ‖ 8개의 다리·껍데기·두 개의 커다란 집게발을 가진 해양 동물, 또는 이 동물의 살. 바닷가재(살)

lo·cal¹ /ˈloʊkəl/ *adj* **1** relating to a particular place or area, especially the place you live in ‖ 특히 거주하고 있는 특정한 장소나 지역에 관련된. 장소[지역]의. 특정한 장소[위치]의: *a good local hospital* 훌륭한 지역 병원 / *reading the local paper* (=a newspaper for the place you live) 지역 신문 구독 / *It costs a quarter to make a local call.* (=a telephone call to someone in the same area as you) 시내 전화를 하는 데는 25센트가 든다. **2** TECHNICAL affecting a particular part of your body ‖ 신체의 특정한 부위에 영향을 미치는. 일부분의. 국부[국소]적인: *a local anesthetic* 국부 마취

lo·cal² *n* **the locals** the people who live in a particular place ‖ 특정한 장소에 거주하는 사람들. 그 지방 사람. 지역 주민: *I asked one of the locals for directions.* 나는 그 지방 주민 중의 한 사람에게 길을 물었다.

lo·cale /loʊˈkæl/ *n* FORMAL the place where something happens ‖ 무슨 일이 발생한 장소. 현장. 무대. 장면. 배경: *The novel is set in a tropical locale.* 그 소설은 열대를 배경으로 설정되어 있다.

lo·cal·i·ty /loʊˈkæləti/ *n* FORMAL a small area of a country, city etc. ‖ 군·시 등의 작은 지역. 장소. 한 구획.

lo·cal·ized /ˈloʊkəˌlaɪzd/ *adj* FORMAL only within a small area ‖ 작은 지역 내에만. 국지적인. 한 지방에 한정시킨: *localized pain* 국부적 통증

lo·cal·ly /ˈloʊkəli/ *adv* in or near the area where you are or the area you are talking about ‖ 현재 있는 지역이나 언급

하고 있는 지역 내에 또는 그 부근에. …근처에: *Do you live locally?* 근방에 사십니까?

lo·cate /'loʊkeɪt/ *v* **1** [T] to find the exact position of something ‖ 어떤 것의 정확한 위치를 알아내다. 소재를 파악하다: *Divers have located the shipwreck.* 잠수부는 난파선의 위치를 알아냈다. **2 be located** to be in a particular place or position ‖ 특정한 장소 또는 위치에 있다. …에 위치하다[자리잡다]: *The bakery is located in the middle of town.* 그 제과점은 시내 중심가에 위치하고 있다. **3** [I, T] to come to a place and start a business there ‖ 어떤 장소에 와서 사업을 시작하다. 개업하다. 가게를 차리다: *The company located its offices in New Jersey when rents went up in New York.* 그 회사는 뉴욕의 임대료가 상승했을 때 뉴저지 주에 사무실을 차렸다.

lo·ca·tion /loʊ'keɪʃən/ *n* **1** a particular place or position ‖ 특정한 장소 또는 위치: *a map showing the location of the school* 학교 위치를 나타내고 있는 지도 **2** [C, U] a place where a movie is filmed, away from the STUDIO ‖ 스튜디오에서 멀리 떨어져서 영화를 촬영하는 장소. 야외 촬영(지). 로케이션: *scenes shot on location in Montana* 몬타나 주의 야외 촬영지에서 찍은 장면

lock¹ /lɑk/ *v* **1** [I, T] to be fastened with a lock, or to fasten something with a lock ‖ 자물쇠로 채워지다, 또는 무언가를 자물쇠로 채우다. (자물쇠로[를]) 잠기다[잠그다]: *Lock the door when you leave.* 나갈 때 문을 잠가라. —opposite UNLOCK **2 lock sth up/away/in etc.** to put something in a safe place and fasten it with a lock ‖ 무엇을 안전한 장소에 넣고 자물쇠로 채우다. (자물쇠를 채워) 숨기다/간수하다/보관하다: *He locked the money in a safe.* 그는 금고에 돈을 넣고 자물쇠를 채웠다. **3** [I] to become set in one position and be unable to move ‖ 한 위치에 고정되어 움직일 수 없다. 고정[고착]하다. 맞물리다: *The brakes locked and we skidded.* 제동 장치가 말을 안 들어 우리는 옆으로 미끄러졌다.

lock sb in *phr v* [T] to prevent someone from leaving a place by locking the door ‖ 문을 잠가서 사람이 장소를 떠나는 것을 막다. (남을) 가두다

lock into sth *phr v* **be locked into** to be unable to change a situation ‖ 상황을 바꿀 수 없다: *The company is locked into a three-year contract with PARCO.* 그 회사는 PARCO와 체결한 3년간의 계약을 변경할 수 없다.

lock sb out *phr v* [T] to prevent someone from entering a place by locking the door ‖ 문을 잠가서 사람이 어떤 장소에 들어오는 것을 막다. 들어지 않다. 못 들어오게 하다

lock up *phr v* **1** [T **lock sb up**] INFORMAL to put someone in prison ‖ 사람을 감옥에 가두다. 감금하다 **2** [T **lock sth ↔ up**] to make a building safe by locking all the doors ‖ 모든 문을 잠가서 건물을 안전하게 하다. 문단속하다

lock² *n* **1** a thing that keeps a door, drawer etc. fastened or shut and is usually opened with a key ‖ 문·서랍 등을 잠그거나 닫혀 있게 하며 보통 열쇠로 여는 물건. 자물쇠: *There's no lock on the door.* 문에 자물쇠가 없다. **2 lock, stock, and barrel** including every part of something ‖ 어떤 것의 모든 부분을 포함하는. 모조리. 완전히. 전부: *They sold everything, lock, stock, and barrel.* 그들은 모든 것을 죄다 팔았다. **3 under lock and key** kept safely in something that is locked ‖ 잠겨진 어떤 것에 안전하게 보관되어. 단단히 보관[보존]되어 **4** a small number of hairs on your head that hang together ‖ 늘어뜨린 머리채 중 몇가닥의 머리털. 타래. (한 타래의) 늘어뜨린 머리 **5** a special area on a river where the water level can go up or down to raise or lower boats ‖ 선박을 올리거나 내리기 위해 수위를 높게 또는 낮게 할 수 있는 강의 특별 구역. 수문. 갑문

lock·er /'lɑkɚ/ *n* a small cupboard with a lock where you leave books, clothes etc., especially at school or when you are playing sports ‖ 특히 학교에서 또는 운동을 할 때 책·옷 등을 넣어 두는 자물쇠가 달린 작은 장. 로커. 사물함

locker room /'.. ,./ *n* a room where you change your clothes and leave them in a LOCKER ‖ 옷을 갈아입고 그 갈아입은 옷을 사물함에 넣어 두는 방. 탈의실

lock·et /'lɑkɪt/ *n* a piece of jewelry like a small round box in which you put a picture of someone, worn on a chain around your neck ‖ 다른 사람의 사진을 넣어 목걸이에 달아매는 작고 둥근 상자 모양의 보석류. 펜던트

lock·smith /'lɑk,smɪθ/ *n* someone who makes and repairs locks ‖ 자물쇠를 만들고 수리하는 사람. 자물쇠 장수[수리인]

lo·co·mo·tive /,loʊkə'moʊtɪv/ *n* a train engine ‖ 기관차

lo·cust /'loʊkəst/ *n* an insect similar to a GRASSHOPPER that flies in large groups and often destroys crops ‖ 큰 무리를 지어 날아다니며 종종 농작물을 망가뜨리는

여치 비슷한 곤충. 메뚜기

lodge[1] /ladʒ/ v **1** [I] to become stuck somewhere ‖ 어딘가에 달라붙게 되다. 박히다. 꽂히다. 막히다. 걸리다: *He had a fish bone lodged in his throat.* 그는 목에 생선 가시가 걸렸다. —opposite DISLODGE **2 lodge a complaint/protest etc.** to officially complain, protest etc. about something ‖ 어떤 것에 대하여 공식적으로 불평·항의 등을 하다. 진정서/항의서를 제출 하 다 : *He has lodged a formal complaint with the club.* 그는 클럽에 정식으로 불만을 제기했다. **3** [I] to pay someone rent in order to live in a room in his/her house ‖ 남의 집 방에 살려고 임대료를 지불하다. 하숙하다

lodge[2] n **1** a building in the country where people can stay for a short time, especially in order to do a particular activity ‖ 특히 특정한 활동을 하기 위해 사람들이 잠시 머물 수 있는 시골의 건물. 오두막집. 산장: *a ski/hunting lodge* 스키 [사냥] 산장 **2** a local meeting place for some organizations ‖ 몇몇 조직을 위한 지방 집회장. (비밀 결사 등의) 지부[집회소]: *the Masonic lodge* 프리메이슨 (Freemason)의 집회소

loft /lɔft/ n **1** a raised level in a BARN where HAY is kept ‖ 건초를 보관하는 헛간의 위층 **2** a raised area above the main part of a room, usually used for sleeping, or an apartment with one of these ‖ 주로 잠자는 데 쓰이는, (큰)방 위로 돋우어 올린 장소, 또는 그런 곳이 있는 아파트. (고미)다락(방). 지붕 밑 방

loft·y /ˈlɔfti/ adj **1** showing high standards or high moral qualities ‖ 높은 수준 또는 높은 도덕적 특성을 나타내는. 지위 높은. 고결한. 고상한: *lofty ideals* 숭고한 이상 **2** LITERARY high ‖ (아주) 높은. 우뚝 솟은

log[1] /lɔg, lag/ n **1** a thick piece of wood cut from a tree ‖ 나무에서 자른 목재의 두꺼운 조각. 통나무. 장작 **2** an official record of events on a ship or plane ‖ 선박이나 항공기에서 벌어지는 사항의 공식적인 기록. 항해[항공] (업무)일지 —see also **sleep like a log** (SLEEP[1])

log[2] v **-gged, -gging 1** [T] to make an official record of events, facts etc., especially on a ship or plane ‖ 특히 선박 또는 항공기에서 벌어지는 일·사실 등의 공식적인 기록을 하다. (정식으로) …을 항해 일지[항공 일지]에 기록하다 **2** [I, T] to cut down trees ‖ 나무를 잘라내다. 벌채하다 – **logger** n

log off/out phr v [I] to stop using a computer or computer system by typing (TYPE) a special word ‖ 특정한 단어를 타자하여 컴퓨터 또는 컴퓨터 시스템의 사용을 끝내다. 로그 오프/아웃하다

log on/in phr v [I] to start using a computer or computer system by typing (TYPE) a special word ‖ 특정한 단어를 타자하여 컴퓨터 또는 컴퓨터 시스템의 사용을 시작하다. 로그 온/인하다

log cab·in /ˌ. ˈ../ n a small house made of LOGs ‖ 통나무로 만든 작은 집. 통나무집

log·ger·heads /ˈlɔgəˌhɛdz, ˈla-/ n **be at loggerheads** to disagree very strongly with someone ‖ 다른 사람과 아주 심하게 의견이 맞지 않다. (남과) 맞다툼하다. 싸우다: *The two Senators have been at loggerheads for years.* 그 두 상원의원은 수년간 다투어 왔다.

log·ging /ˈlɔgɪŋ, ˈla-/ n [U] the industry of cutting down trees for LUMBER, paper etc. ‖ 목재·종이 등에 쓰이는 나무를 벌채하는 산업. 벌목 반출(업)

log·ic /ˈladʒɪk/ n [U] **1** a set of sensible and correct reasons ‖ 분별있고 올바른 이유 체계. 논리. 이론: *There is no logic in releasing criminals just because the prisons are crowded.* 교도소가 만원이란 이유만으로 범죄인을 석방하는 것은 논리에 맞지 않다. **2** the science or study of thinking carefully about something, using formal methods ‖ 정형화된 방법을 써서 사물에 대해 주의 깊게 사고하는 학문이나 연구 분야. 논리학

log·i·cal /ˈladʒɪkəl/ adj **1** seeming reasonable and sensible ‖ 합리적이고 분별력이 있어 보이는. 조리에 닿는. 타당한: *It's the logical place to build a new supermarket.* 새 슈퍼마켓을 신축하기에는 합당한 장소이다. —opposite ILLOGICAL **2** based on the rules of LOGIC ‖ 논리(학)의 법칙에 기초한. 논리적인: *a logical conclusion* 논리적인 결론 – **logically** adv

lo·gis·tics /loʊˈdʒɪstɪks, lə-/ n **the logistics of sth** the practical organizing that is needed to make a complicated plan or activity successful ‖ 복잡한 계획이나 활동을 성공적으로 만드는 데에 필요한 실제적인 구성. (업무의) 상세한 계획 – **logistical** adj – **logistically** adv

log·jam /ˈlɔgdʒæm, ˈlag-/ n a lot of problems or other things that are preventing something from being done ‖ 일이 성취되는 것을 막는 많은 문제점이나 기타 사항들. 봉쇄. 정체: *a logjam of work* 업무의 정체(停滯)

lo·go /ˈloʊgoʊ/ n a small design that is

the official sign of a company or organization ‖ 회사나 조직의 공식 표지인 작은 디자인. 의장 문자. 로고

loin·cloth /'lɔɪnklɔθ/ *n* a piece of cloth that men in some hot countries wear around their loins ‖ 몇몇 더운 나라의 남자들이 아랫배에 두르는 천 조각. (열대 지방 사람의) 허리감개

loins /lɔɪnz/ *n* [plural] LITERARY the part of the body below your waist where the sexual organs are ‖ 성기가 있는 허리 아래의 신체 부위. 아랫배. 국부

loi·ter /'lɔɪtə/ *v* [I] to stand in a public place without having a reason to be there ‖ 있을 이유도 없이 공공 장소에 서 있다. 어슬렁거리다. 헤매다 **– loitering** *n* [U]

loll /lɑl/ *v* [I] **1** to hang down in a loose or relaxed way ‖ 느슨하게 또는 이완되어 늘어지다: *The dog's tongue **lolled** out of its mouth.* 그 개의 혀가 입 밖으로 축 늘어졌다. **2** to sit or lie in a lazy or relaxed way ‖ 나른하게 또는 느긋하게 앉거나 눕다. 맥없이 앉다[눕다]

lol·li·pop /'lɑli,pɑp/ *n* a hard candy made of boiled sugar on the end of a stick ‖ 끓인 설탕으로 만들어 막대 끝에 붙인 딱딱한 캔디. 막대 사탕

lone /loʊn/ *adj* LITERARY being the only person or thing in a place, or the only person or thing that does something ‖ 어떤 장소에 단 한 사람이나 한 물건만 있는, 또는 어떤 것을 하는 단 한 사람이나 한 사물만이 있는. 단 하나의. 유일한: *a lone figure standing in the snow* 눈 속에 서 있는 단 하나의 모습 / *Thea was the lone voice against the idea.* 시어는 그 생각에 반대하는 유일한 목소리였다.

lone·ly /'loʊnli/ *adj* **1** unhappy because you are alone ‖ 혼자이기 때문에 즐겁지 않은. 쓸쓸한. 외로운: *She was very lonely after her husband died.* 그녀는 남편이 죽은 뒤에 매우 고독했다. **2** LITERARY far from where people live ‖ 사람이 사는 곳에서 멀리 떨어진. 외진. 벽지의. 고립된: *a lonely country road* 외진 시골 도로 **– loneliness** *n* [U]

lon·er /'loʊnə/ *n* someone who wants to be alone or who has no friends ‖ 혼자 있고 싶어하거나 친구가 없는 사람. 개인주의자. 독불장군

lone·some /'loʊnsəm/ *adj* ⇨ LONELY

long¹ /lɔŋ/ *adj*
1 ▶MEASUREMENT 측정◀ measuring a great length, distance, or time ‖ 긴 길이[거리, 시간]를 나타내는. 긴. 장거리의. 오래 걸리는: *There was a long line at the bank.* 은행의 대기 줄이 길었다. / *It's*

a long walk home from here. 여기서 집까지는 오래 걸어야 한다. / *The meeting was long and boring.* 그 회의는 길고 지루했다. / *It takes a long time to drive to work.* 직장까지 차를 몰고 가는 데 오래 걸린다. **—opposite** SHORT¹

2 ▶PARTICULAR LENGTH/TIME 특정한 길이/시간◀ having a particular length or continuing for a particular amount of time ‖ 특정한 길이를 가지는 또는 특정한 시간 동안 계속하는. …의 길이인/…시간의: *The snake was at least 3 feet long.* 그 뱀의 길이는 적어도 3피트는 되었다. / *How long is the movie?* 그 영화는 상영 시간이 얼마나 되니?

3 ▶SEEMING LONG 길어 보이는◀ INFORMAL seeming too long in time or distance because you are tired, bored etc. ‖ 피곤하고 지루하기 때문에 시간이나 거리가 아주 길어 보이는: *It's been a long day.* 긴 하루였다.

4 long hours a large amount of time ‖ 많은 시간. 장시간: *She spent long hours working at the computer.* 그녀는 컴퓨터 작업을 하면서 장시간을 보냈다.

5 ▶BOOK/LIST/NAME ETC. 책/목록/이름 등◀ a long book, list etc. has a lot of pages, details etc. ‖ 책·목록 등이 페이지가 많고 내용이 세세한. 항목이 많은. 내용이 풍부한

6 long weekend three days, including Saturday and Sunday, when you do not have to go to work or school ‖ 직장이나 학교에 가지 않아도 되는 경우의 토요일·일요일을 포함한 3일간. 긴 주말

7 in the long run when something is finished, or at a later time ‖ 일이 완료된 때, 또는 나중에. 결국(에는): *All our hard work will be worth it in the long run.* 결국에는 우리가 애쓴 모든 일은 그만한 가치가 있을 것이다.

8 ▶CLOTHES 의류◀ long dresses, pants, sleeves etc. cover all of your arms or legs ‖ 드레스·바지·소매 등이 팔·다리를 모두 덮는. 긴

long² *adv* **1** for a long time ‖ 오랫동안: *Have you been waiting long?* 오래 기다렸니? **2 long before/after** for a long time before or after a particular time or event ‖ 특정 시간 또는 사건 전이나 후의 장시간 동안. …의 오래 전/오랜 후: *The farm was sold long before you were born.* 그 농장은 네가 태어나기 훨씬 전에 팔렸다. **3 for long** for a long time ‖ 오랫동안: *Have you known the Garretts for very long?* 아주 오랫동안 가렛씨 가족과 알고 지냈니? **4 as long as** if ‖ …이라면. …인 한. …인 이상: *You can go as long* *as you're back by four o'clock.* 4시까지 돌아온다면 너는 가도 된다. **5 no longer** used in order to show that something happened in the past, but does not happen now ‖ 과거에 일이 발생하였으나 지금은 일어나지 않는 것을 나타내는 데에 쓰여. 이미[더 이상] … 아니다: *Mr. Allen no longer works for the company.* 알렌 씨는 더 이상 그 회사에 근무하지 않는다. **6 so long** SPOKEN goodbye ‖ 안녕. 잘 있어. 또 만나. **7 before long** soon ‖ 곧: *It will be Christmas before long.* 머지 않아 크리스마스이다.

long³ *v* [I] FORMAL to want something very much ‖ 무엇을 아주 몹시 원하다. 간절히 바라다: *The children longed to get outside.* 아이들은 몹시 밖에 나가고 싶어 했다.

long·dis·tance /ˌ. '../ *adj* **1** a long-distance telephone call is to a place that is far away ‖ 멀리 떨어져 있는 장소에 전화를 거는. 장거리 전화의 **2** traveling, running etc. between two places that are far away from each other ‖ 여행·달리기 등을 할 때 두 장소가 서로 멀리 떨어진. 장거리의: *long-distance flights* 장거리 비행 – **long·distance** *adv*

long-drawn-out /ˌ. ˌ. '../ *adj* continuing for a longer time than is necessary ‖ 필요 이상으로 오래 계속되는. 너무 오래 끄는. 지연되는: *a long-drawn-out discussion* 오래 끄는 토의

lon·gev·i·ty /lɑnˈdʒɛvəti, lɔn-/ *n* [U] FORMAL long life ‖ 긴 수명. 장수

long·hand /ˈlɔŋhænd/ *n* [U] writing full words by hand rather than using a machine such as a computer ‖ 컴퓨터 등의 기계를 이용하는 것이 아니라 손으로 모든 단어를 쓰는 것. 수기(手記) — compare SHORTHAND

long·ing /ˈlɔŋɪŋ/ *n* [singular, U] a strong feeling of wanting someone or something very much ‖ 사람이나 사물을 몹시 원하는 강렬한 감정. 동경. 갈망: *a longing for peace* 평화에 대한 갈망 – **longingly** *adv*

lon·gi·tude /ˈlɑndʒə,tud/ *n* [C, U] a position on the Earth measured in degrees east or west of an imaginary line from the top of the Earth to the bottom ‖ 지구의 꼭대기에서 밑바닥까지의 가상의 선으로 동쪽이나 서쪽을 각도로 측정한 지구상의 위치. 경도(經度). 경선 – **longitudinal** /ˌlɑndʒəˈtudnəl/ *adj* – compare LATITUDE —see picture at AXIS

long johns /ˈ. ./ *n* [plural] warm underwear that covers your legs ‖ 다리를 덮는 따뜻한 속옷. 긴 내의

long jump /ˈ. ./ *n* [U] a sport in which you jump as far as possible ‖ 가능한 한 멀리 뛰는 경기. 멀리뛰기

long-last·ing /ˌ. '../ *adj* continuing for a long time ‖ 오랫동안 계속되는. 장기간에 걸친: *the long-lasting effects of child abuse* 아동 학대의 장기간에 걸친 영향

long-lived /ˌlɔŋ ˈlaɪvd·/ *adj* living or existing for a long time ‖ 오래 살거나 존재하는. 장수하는. 오래 계속하는

long-lost /ˈ. ./ *adj* lost or not seen for a long time ‖ 오랫동안 실종되거나 보이지 않는. 장기간 행방불명의: *a long-lost friend* 오랫동안 보지 못한 친구

long-range /ˌ. '../ *adj* **1** relating to a time that continues far into the future ‖ 미래로 멀리 이어지는 시간과 관련된. 장기적인. 원대한: *long-range development plans* 장기 개발 계획 **2** covering a long distance ‖ 장거리에 미치는. 장거리(용)의: *a long-range missile* 장거리 미사일

long-run·ning /ˌ. '../ *adj* having existed or happened for a long time ‖ 장기간 존재해 왔거나 발생해 온. 장기의. 장기간 계속되는: *a long-running show on Broadway* 브로드웨이에서 장기간 계속되는 쇼

long·shore·man /ˌlɔŋˈʃɔrmən, ˈlɔŋˌʃɔrmən/ *n* someone whose job is to load and unload ships ‖ 배에 짐을 싣거나 내리는 직업인. 항만 노동자. 부두 하역부

long shot /ˈ. ./ *n* INFORMAL **1** someone or something with very little chance of success ‖ 성공할 가망이 거의 없는 사람이나 사물. 거의 승산이 없는 사람[것]: *This plan is a real long shot.* 이 계획은 정말 승산이 거의 없다. **2 not by a long shot** not at all or not nearly ‖ 전혀 또는 거의 … 아닌. 단연[결코] …아닌: *This isn't over, not by a long shot.* 이것은 결코 끝나지 않았다.

long-stand·ing /ˌ. '../ *adj* having continued or existed for a long time ‖ 오랫동안 계속되거나 존속해 온. 오래 계속되는. 오래된: *a long-standing agreement between the two countries* 양국 간의 오래된 협정

long-suf·fer·ing /ˌ. '.../ *adj* patient in spite of problems or unhappiness ‖ 문제나 불행에도 불구하고 인내하는. 잘 견디어 내는. 참을성 많은

long-term /ˌ. '../ *adj* continuing for a long period of time into the future ‖ 미래의 오랜 기간 동안 계속되는. 장기의. 먼 장래의: *The long-term effects of the drug are not known.* 그 약의 장기적인 효과는 알려져 있지 않다. —see also **in the**

long/short term (TERM) —compare
SHORT-TERM

long·time /'lɔŋtaɪm/ *adj* having existed
for a long time, or having had a
particular position for a long time ‖ 오랫
동안 존속한, 또는 오랫동안 특정한 위치
에 있는. 예로부터의. 오랫동안의: *her
longtime boyfriend* 그녀의 오랜 남자 친
구 / *a longtime goal* 오랜 목표

long-wind·ed /ˌ ˈ...ˈ.../ *adj* continuing to
talk for too long in a way that is boring
‖ 지루하며 너무 길게 이야기를 계속 하
는. 장황한: *a long-winded speech* 장황한
연설

look¹ /lʊk/ *v* **1** [I] to turn your eyes
toward something so that you can see it
‖ 볼 수 있게 어떤 것 쪽으로 눈을 돌리다.
보다. 바라보다: *I didn't see it. I wasn't
looking.* 나는 그것을 알아차릴 수 없었어.
보지 않고 있었거든. / *Patrick looked
down at his shoes.* 패트릭은 자기의 구두
를 내려다보았다. —see picture at WATCH¹
2 [I] to try to find someone or
something using your eyes ‖ 눈으로 사람
이나 물건을 찾으려고 하다. …을 찾다.
…을 찾기 위해 보다: *I've looked
everywhere for the money.* 그 돈을 찾으
려고 모든 곳을 뒤졌다. / *Have you
looked in here?* 이곳을 살펴봤니? / *Brad
was looking for you last night.* 브래드가
어젯밤에 당신을 찾고 있었어. **3** [linking
verb] to seem to be something,
especially by having a particular
appearance ‖ 특히 특정한 모양을 가져서
어떤 것처럼 보이다. …인 것 같다: *You
look nice/good in that dress.* 그 드레스를
입으니 멋져[좋아] 보인다. / *He looks
like he hasn't slept for days.* 그는 며칠
동안 잠을 자지 않은 것 같다. / *Gina and
Ron looked very happy.* 지나와 론은 매
우 행복해 보였다. **4 -looking** having a
particular type of appearance ‖ 특정한
외형을 가진. …처럼[해] 보이는: *That
was a funny-looking dog!* 그 개 웃기게
생겼어! / *healthy-looking children* 건
강해 보이는 아이들 **5 look sb in the eye**
to look directly at someone in order to
show that you are not afraid of him/her
‖ 어떤 사람을 두려워하지 않는다는 것을
보여주기 위해 똑바로 쳐다보다. …을 빤
히 쳐다보다

SPOKEN PHRASES

6 Look... said when you are annoyed
and you want to emphasize what you
are saying ‖ 짜증이 나서 하고 있는 말
을 강조하고 싶을 때에 쓰여. 이봐. 어
이: *Look, I'm very serious about this.*

이봐, 나는 이 문제가 심각하다고. **7** [T]
said in order to make someone notice
something ‖ 남에게 어떤 것을 주목시
키는 데에 쓰여. …을 보세요: *Look how
tall he's gotten!* 그의 키가 얼마나 큰지
봐라! / *Mom, look what I made!* 엄마,
내가 만든 것을 보세요! **8 (I'm) just
looking** used in a store in order to tell
someone who works there that you do
not need help ‖ 상점에서 일하는 사람
에게 도움이 필요없다는 것을 말하는 데
에 쓰여. 둘러보는 겁니다. 그냥 구경하
는 중입니다: *"Can I help you?" "No
thanks, I'm just looking."* "도와 드릴까
요?" "괜찮습니다. 그냥 구경하는 거예
요."

—see usage note at SEE

look after sb/sth *phr v* [T] to take care
of someone or something ‖ 사람이나 사
물을 돌보다. 보살피다: *We look after
Rodney's kids after school.* 우리는 방과
후에 로드니의 아이들을 돌본다.

look ahead *phr v* [I] to think about
what will happen in the future ‖ 앞으로
무슨 일이 일어날 것인지에 대해 생각하
다. 장래를 내다보다: *We need to look
ahead and plan for next year.* 우리는 앞
을 내다보고 내년도의 계획을 세울 필요가
있다.

look around *phr v* [I,T **look around**
sth] to see, study, read etc. many
different things in order to find
something or to learn about something
‖ 무엇을 발견하기 위해 또는 무엇에 대해
알기 위해 많은 다른 것들을 보고 연구하
며 읽다. 둘러보다. 훑어보다: *We have 3
or 4 hours to look around the city.* 우리
는 그 도시를 둘러볼 시간이 서너 시간 정
도 있다.

look at sth *phr v* [T] **1** to read
something quickly ‖ 빨리 무엇을 읽다. …
을 (바라)보다: *Jane was looking at a
magazine while she waited.* 제인은 기다
리는 동안에 잡지를 보고 있었다. **2** to
study and consider something in order
to decide what to do ‖ 무엇을 할 것인지
를 결정하기 위해 어떤 것을 연구하고 검
토하다. 검사하다: *The doctor looked at
the cut on her head.* 그 의사는 그녀의 머
리 상처를 검사했다. **3** SPOKEN said when
you are using something or something as
an example of a situation ‖ 사람이나 사
물을 상황의 일례로 사용할 때 쓰여. …을
(예로서) 봐라: *We need insurance! Look
at what happened to Tom when he
didn't have any.* 우리는 보험이 필요해!
보험이 없을 때에 톰에게 일어났던 일을

생각해 봐라.

look back *phr v* [I] to think about something that happened in the past ‖ 과거에 일어난 일에 대해 생각하다. 회상 [회고]하다: *Looking back (on it), I see my mistake.* (그것에 대해) 다시 생각해 보니 내 잘못을 알겠다.

look down on *sb/sth phr v* [T] to think that you are better than someone or something else ‖ 자신이 남이나 다른 것 보다 더 낫다고 생각하다. 업신여기다. 깔 보다: *Ted seems to look down on poor people.* 테드는 가난한 사람들을 깔보는 것 같다.

look for *sb/sth phr v* [T] **1** to try to find a particular type of thing or person that you need or want ‖ 자신이 필요로 하거나 원하는 특별한 종류의 사물이나 사람을 발 견하려고 하다. …을 찾다: *How long have you been looking for a job?* 얼마나 오랫 동안 일자리를 찾아왔습니까? **2 be looking for trouble** INFORMAL to be behaving in a way that makes it likely that problems will happen ‖ 문제가 발생 할 가능성이 있게 행동하고 있다. 말썽이 될 일을 하고 있다. 문제를 자초하고 있 다: *You're looking for trouble if you argue with her.* 그녀와 논쟁한다면, 너는 문제를 자초하고 있는 것이다.

look forward to *sth phr v* [T] to be excited and happy about something that is going to happen ‖ 일어날 일에 대해 흥 분하고 기뻐하다. 기대하다. 학수고대하 다: *We're really looking forward to skiing in Tahoe.* 우리는 타호에서 스키 타 는 것을 정말 학수고대하고 있다.

look into *sth phr v* [T] to try to find out the truth about something ‖ 무엇에 대한 사실을 알아내려고 하다. 조사하다: *The FBI will look into the cause of the fire.* 미국 연방 수사국이 화재의 원인을 조사할 것이다.

look on *phr v* **1** [I] to watch something, without being involved in it ‖ 어떤 것에 관여하지 않고 그것을 지켜보다. 구경하 다. 방관하다: *The crowd looked on as the two men fought.* 두 남자가 싸울 때 많은 사람들이 구경했다. **2** [T **look on** sth] also **look upon** to think about something in a particular way ‖ 어떤 것 에 대해 특정하게 생각하다: *My family looks on divorce as a sin.* 내 가족은 이 혼을 죄악으로 여긴다.

look out *phr v* [I] to pay attention to what is happening around you ‖ 자기 주 변에 일어나는 일에 주목하다. 조심하다: *Look out! You almost hit the cat.* 조심해 라! 너는 하마터면 고양이를 칠 뻔했다.

look *sth/sb* ↔ **over** *phr v* [T] to examine something or someone quickly ‖ 사물이 나 사람을 빨리 검사하다. 살피다. 점검하 다. 죽 훑어보다: *Can you look this letter over for me before I send it?* 내가 편지를 보내기 전에 죽 훑어봐 주시겠습니 까?

look through *phr v* [T] **1** [**look through** sth] to look for something in a pile of papers, a drawer, someone's pockets etc. ‖ 서류 더미·서랍·남의 주머니 등에서 물건을 찾다. …을 자세히 조사하다. 샅샅 이 찾다: *Her mother was looking through her stuff.* 그녀의 어머니는 그녀 의 소지품을 샅샅이 뒤지고 있었다. **2 look right through** sb to pretend that you have not seen someone ‖ 남을 못 본 척하다

look up *phr v* **1** [I] if a situation is looking up, it is becoming better ‖ 상황 이 더 좋아지고 있다. 잘 되어 가다. 나아 지고 있다: *Things are looking up since I found a job.* 내가 일자리를 얻은 후로 일 이 잘 되어 가고 있다. **2** [T **look** sth ↔ **up**] to try to find information in a book, on a computer etc. ‖ 책·컴퓨터 등에서 정보를 발견하려고 하다. …을 찾아보다: *If you don't know the word, look it up in the dictionary.* 그 단어를 모르면 사전 에서 찾아보아라. **3** [T **look** sb ↔ **up**] to visit someone you know, especially when you go to the place where s/he lives for another reason ‖ 특히 다른 이유 로 아는 사람이 사는 장소에 가게 되어 그 사람을 방문하다. …을 찾아가다: *Don't forget to look up my parents when you're in Boston.* 네가 보스턴에 가게 되 면 잊지 말고 내 부모님을 찾아 뵈라.

look up to *sb phr v* [T] to admire and respect someone ‖ 어떤 사람을 칭찬하며 존경하다: *He looks up to his older brother.* 그는 자기 형을 존경한다.

look² *n* **1** [C usually singular] an act of looking at something ‖ 사물을 보는 행위. 보기: *Let me take a look at that map again.* 내가 다시 한 번 그 지도를 볼게. **2** an expression that you make with your eyes or face to show how you feel ‖ 자신 의 느낌이 어떠한지를 나타내기 위해 눈이 나 얼굴에 짓는 표정: *She gave me an angry look.* 그녀는 나를 화난 표정으로 보았다. **3** the appearance of someone or something ‖ 사람이나 물건의 외관. 모습. 모양: *I don't like the look of that bruise – maybe you should see a doctor.* 그 멍든 모습이 좋지 않네. 의사의 진찰을 받아봐야 할 것 같아. —see also LOOKS

look·a·like /'lʊkə,laɪk/ n INFORMAL someone who looks very similar to someone else, especially someone famous ‖ 특히 유명한 사람과 매우 비슷하게 생긴 사람. 매우 닮은 사람: *a Madonna lookalike* 마돈나와 닮은 사람

look·out /'lʊk-aʊt/ n **1 be on the lookout** to continually watch a place or pay attention to a situation because you are looking for someone or something ‖ 사람이나 사물을 찾고 있어서 끊임없이 장소를 지켜보거나 상황을 주시하다. 경계하고 있다. 망보고 있다: *Be on the lookout for snakes!* 뱀을 경계해라! **2** someone whose duty is to watch carefully for danger, or the place where s/he does this ‖ 위험에 대해 주의 깊게 경계하는 것이 임무인 사람, 또는 이런 일을 하는 장소. 망보는 사람. 감시인. 망보는 곳

looks /lʊks/ n [plural] how beautiful or attractive someone is ‖ 사람의 아름다움이나 매력의 정도. 생김새. 용모: *Stop worrying about your looks.* 네 용모에 대해서 걱정 그만해라.

loom¹ /lum/ v [I] **1** to appear as a large unclear threatening shape ‖ 크고 불명확하게 위협적인 모양으로 나타나다. 어렴풋이 나타나다: *The mountain loomed in front of us.* 산이 우리 앞에 흐릿하게 우뚝 서 있었다. **2** if a problem or difficult situation looms, it is likely to happen soon ‖ 문제나 어려운 상황이 곧 일어날 것 같다. 급박한[좋지 않은] 형세가 되다: *economic changes that loom ahead* 곧 닥쳐올 경제 변화 **3 loom large** to seem important, worrying, and difficult to avoid ‖ 중대하고 우려스러우며 피하기 어려워 보이다. 기분 나쁘게 닥치다. 덮치다: *Fear of failure loomed large in his mind.* 실패의 두려움이 그의 마음에 엄습했다.

loom² n a frame or machine used for weaving cloth ‖ 천을 짜는 데에 사용되는 틀이나 기계. 베틀. 직기

loon·y /'luni/ adj INFORMAL extremely silly or crazy ‖ 매우 어리석거나 미친

loop¹ /lup/ n **1** a shape like a curve or a circle, or a line, piece of wire, string etc. that has this shape ‖ 곡선이나 원 모양, 또는 이런 모양을 한 선·철사 조각·실 등. 고리. 코[고리] 모양을 한 것: *belt loops* (=cloth loops used for holding a belt on pants) 벨트 고리 **2 be out of the loop** to not be part of a group of people that make decisions ‖ 결정을 하는 일단의 사람들의 일원이 되지 않다. 실세에 속하지 못하다. 중추에서 벗어나다: *Gaynor says he was out of the loop when the order was given.* 게이너는 명령을 받았을 당시 자신은 실세가 아니었다고 말한다.

loop² v [I, T] to make a LOOP or to make something into a loop ‖ 고리(모양)을 만들다, 또는 어떤 것을 고리(모양)으로 만들다

loop·hole /'luphoʊl/ n a small mistake in a law or rule that makes it possible to legally avoid doing what the law says ‖ 법률에서 언급한 것을 합법적으로 피할 수 있는 법이나 규칙상의 작은 실수. 빠져나갈 구멍. 허점: *tax loopholes* 세금을 포탈할 구멍

loose¹ /lus/ adj

1 ▶NOT FIRMLY ATTACHED◀ not firmly attached to something ‖ 무엇에 단단히 부착되어 있지 않은. 느슨한. 헐렁한: *The buttons on my shirt are coming loose.* 내 셔츠의 단추가 느슨해지고 있다.

2 ▶NOT TIED/FASTENED◀ not tied or fastened very tightly ‖ 아주 꽉 매어 있지 않거나 고정되어 있지 않은: *My shoe laces are loose.* 나의 구두 끈이 풀려 있다.

3 ▶CLOTHES◀ 의복 ▶ loose clothes are big and do not fit tightly on your body ‖ 옷이 크고 몸에 꼭 맞지 않는. 헐렁한

4 ▶NOT CONTROLLED◀ 통제를 받지 않는 ◀ free from being controlled in a CAGE, prison, or institution ‖ 우리[감옥, 제도]의 통제를 받는 상태에서 벗어난. 자유로운. 풀려난: *Two of the prisoners broke loose from the guards.* 두 명의 죄수가 교도관을 따돌리고 탈옥했다. / *Don't let your dog loose on the beach.* 개를 해변에 풀어 놓지 마라.

5 a loose translation/interpretation something that has been translated etc. in a way that is not exact ‖ 정확하지 않게 번역된 것. 부정확한 번역/통역: *My French isn't very good, but I can give you a loose translation.* 나는 프랑스어가 아주 능숙하지 못하지만 대충은 번역해 줄 수 있다.

6 loose ends parts of something such as work or an agreement that have not yet been completed ‖ 아직 완성되지 않은 일이나 협정 등의 일부. 미결[미처리] 사항: *I have to tie up a few loose ends before we go away.* 우리가 떠나기 전에 나는 몇 가지 미결 사항을 매듭지어야 한다.

7 loose cannon someone who cannot be trusted because s/he says or does things you do not want him/her to ‖ 원하지 않는 말이나 행동을 하기 때문에 신뢰

할 수 없는 사람. 요주의 인물. 위험한 사람

8 ▶NOT MORAL 부도덕한 ◀ OLD-FASHIONED behaving in an immoral way ‖ 부도덕하게 행동하는. 무절제한. 방탕한: *a loose woman* 품행이 나쁜 여자 – **loosely** *adv*

loose² *n* **on the loose** if a criminal is on the loose, s/he has escaped from prison ‖ 범죄자가 감옥에서 탈출한. 탈옥하여 도주 중인

loose-leaf /'luslif/ *adj* having pages that can be put in or taken out easily ‖ 페이지를 쉽게 넣거나 뺄 수 있게 되어 있는. 루스리프식의: *a loose-leaf notebook* 루스리프식의 노트

loos·en /'lusən/ *v* [I, T] to become less tight or less firmly attached to something, or to make something do this ‖ 어떤 것에 밀착이나 부착되는 강도가 약해지다, 또는 그렇게 되게 하다. 헐거워[느슨해]지다. …을 늦추다[풀다]: *He loosened his tie.* 그는 넥타이를 조금 풀었다. / *The screws in the shelf had loosened.* 선반의 나사가 느슨해졌다.

loosen up *phr v* **1** [I] to become more relaxed and feel less worried ‖ 보다 이완되고 걱정이 덜해지다. 긴장이 풀리다: *Claire loosened up after a few drinks.* 클레어는 몇 잔 마시자 긴장이 풀렸다. **2** [I, T] if your muscles loosen up, or if you loosen them up, they stop feeling stiff ‖ 근육이 뻣뻣해짐을 느끼지 않게 되다. 근육이 풀리다. 근육을 풀다

loot¹ /lut/ *v* [I, T] to steal things, especially from stores that have been damaged in a war or RIOT ‖ 특히 전쟁이나 폭동으로 피해를 입은 상점에서 물건을 훔치다. 약탈하다 – **looting** *n* [U] – **looter** *n*

loot² *n* [U] goods that are stolen by thieves or taken by soldiers who have won a battle ‖ 도둑이 훔쳐간, 또는 전투에서 이긴 병사가 가져간 물건. 약탈품. 전리품

lop /lɑp/ *v* **-pped, -pping** [T] also **lop off** to cut part of something off ‖ 물건의 일부를 잘라내다. 쳐내다

lope /loup/ *v* [I] to run easily using long steps ‖ 긴 발걸음으로 쉽게 달리다. 깡충깡충 뛰다 – **lope** *n*

lop·sid·ed /'lɑp,saɪdɪd/ *adj* having one side that is heavier, larger, or lower than the other side ‖ 한 쪽이 다른 쪽보다 더 무거운[큰, 낮은]. 한쪽으로 기울어진: *The cake was lopsided when it came out of the oven.* 그 케이크는 오븐에서 나올 때 한쪽으로 기울어졌다.

Lord /lɔrd/ *n* **1** also **the Lord** a title used for God or Jesus Christ ‖ 하나님 또는 예수 그리스도에 사용되는 칭호 **2 good/oh/my Lord!** SPOKEN said when you are surprised, worried, or angry ‖ 놀라거나 걱정되거나, 또는 화가 날 때 쓰여. 어이쿠! 어머! 저런!

lord *n* a man who has a particular position in the ARISTOCRACY ‖ 귀족 사회에서 특별한 지위를 가진 사람. 귀족

lore /lɔr/ *n* [U] knowledge and TRADITIONs that people learn from other people rather than from books ‖ 책보다는 다른 사람들에게서 배운 지식과 전통. 구전

lose /luz/ *v* **lost, lost, losing**
1 ▶NOT HAVE 가지지 않다◀ [I] to stop having something important that you need ‖ 필요한 중요한 것을 갖지 못하게 되다. …을 잃다. 상실하다: *Michelle lost her job.* 미셸은 직장을 잃었다. / *We lost a lot of money on that deal.* 우리는 그 거래에서 많은 돈을 잃었다.

2 ▶NOT FIND 발견하지 못하다◀ [T] to be unable to find someone or something ‖ 사람 또는 사물을 발견할 수 없다: *Danny's always losing his keys.* 대니는 노상 열쇠를 잃어 버린다.

3 ▶NOT WIN 이기지 못하다◀ [I, T] to not win a game, argument, war etc. ‖ 경기·논쟁·전쟁 등을 이기지 못하다. 지다: *We lost to the Red Sox, 5-0.* 우리는 레드삭스 팀에게 5대 0으로 졌다. / *Sanders lost the election by 371 votes.* 샌더스는 371표 차로 선거에 패했다.

4 ▶HAVE LESS 적게 가지다◀ [T] to have less of something than before ‖ 전보다 사물을 적게 가지다. 줄이다: *I need to lose weight.* 나는 체중을 줄여야 한다. / *She's lost a lot of blood.* 그녀는 피를 많이 흘렸다.

5 lose your sight/memory/voice etc. to stop being able to see, remember things, talk etc. ‖ 사물을 보지 못하다·기억하지 못하다·말하지 못하다 등. 시력/기억력/음성 등을 상실하다

6 ▶STOP HAVING A QUALITY 성질을 가지지 못하다◀ [T] to no longer have a particular quality, belief, attitude etc. ‖ 특정한 성질·믿음·태도 등을 더 이상 가지고 있지 않다: *The kids were losing interest in the game.* 아이들이 그 경기에 흥미를 잃고 있었다. / *Jake lost his temper/cool* (=became angry) *and started shouting.* 제이크는 화가 나서 소리 치기 시작했다.

7 lose an arm/eye etc. to have a serious injury in which your arm etc. is cut off ‖ 팔 등이 절단되는 심한 상처를 입다. 팔/눈을 잃다

8 lose your balance to become unsteady, especially so that you fall ‖ 특히 넘어질 정도로 불안정해지다. 평형을 잃다. 비틀거리다

9 lose your husband/mother etc. if you lose your husband etc., he dies ‖ 남편 등이 죽다. 남편을 잃다/어머니를 여의다: *Janet lost the baby.* (=the baby died before being born) 재닛은 아이가 유산됐다.

10 lose your life to die ‖ 죽다. 목숨을 잃다: *5000 soldiers lost their lives.* 5000명의 군인이 목숨을 잃었다.

11 ▶WASTE 낭비하다◀ [T] to waste time or opportunities ‖ 시간이나 기회를 낭비하다: *She lost no time in changing jobs.* 그녀는 직업을 바꾸면서 시간을 허비하지 않았다. / *You lost your chance!* 너는 기회를 잃었어!

12 lose sb INFORMAL to confuse someone when explaining something to him/her ‖ 사물을 설명할 때 사람을 혼란시키다. 못 듣다. 이해하지 못하다: *You've lost me. Can you repeat that?* 듣지 못했어요. 다시 한 번 말해 줄래요?

13 have nothing to lose to be in a situation in which you can attempt to do something because you may be successful, and you will not be in a worse situation if you fail ‖ 성공할 가능성이 있기 때문에 무엇을 시도할 수 있는 상황에 있으며, 실패한다 해도 더 나쁜 상황에 처하지 않게 되다. 잃을 것이 아무 것도 없다. 밑져야 본전이다

14 lose touch (with) a) to not speak, see, or write to someone for so long that you do not know where s/he is ‖ 오랫동안 어떤 사람과 이야기하지[만나지, 소식을 전하지] 못해서 그 소재를 모르다. (…과) 연락하지 않다. 연락이 두절되다[끊기다]: *I've lost touch with all my high school friends.* 나는 모든 고등학교 친구들과 연락이 끊긴 채 지냈다. **b)** to not know the most recent information about a particular place, situation, event etc. ‖ 특정한 장소·상황·사건 등에 대한 가장 최근의 정보를 모르다

15 lose it SPOKEN **a)** to suddenly start shouting, laughing, or crying a lot because you think something is very bad, funny, or wrong ‖ 무엇이 매우 나쁘거나 웃기거나, 또는 잘못되어 있다고 생각해서 갑자기 소리를 지르거나 웃거나, 또는 심하게 울기 시작하다. 자제력을 잃다. 감정을 못 이기다: *I saw him hit the child and I lost it.* 나는 그가 아이를 때리

는 것을 보고 화를 내었다. **b)** to become crazy ‖ 미치다: *You're losing it, Mabel.* 마벨, 너는 미쳤어.

16 lose your head INFORMAL to stop being calm, so that you do the wrong thing ‖ 침착하지 못해서 일을 그르치다. 흥분하다: *I lost my head and started yelling.* 나는 흥분하여 소리를 지르기 시작했다.

17 lose heart to become disappointed and unhappy ‖ 실망하여 즐겁지 않다. 낙담하다: *The team lost heart after they lost their fifth game.* 그 팀은 다섯 번째 경기에 패배한 후 낙담했다.

18 lose sight of to forget about the most important part of something you are doing ‖ 자신이 하고 있는 일의 가장 중요한 부분을 잊다. …을 잊어버리다. …의 핵심을 놓치다: *We can't lose sight of our goals.* 우리는 우리의 목표를 잊을 수 없다.

19 lose your touch to stop having a special ability or skill ‖ 특별한 능력이나 기술을 더 이상 갖지 못하다. 기량이 퇴보하다

lose out *phr v* [I] to not get something important such as a job because someone else gets it ‖ 다른 사람이 선점하여 직업 등의 중요한 일을 얻지 못하다. 실패하다. 손해 보다: *He lost out on a scholarship because his grades were low.* 그는 성적이 낮아서 장학금을 받지 못했다.

USAGE NOTE lose, miss, lost, missing, and **disappear**

Use **lose** if you cannot find something: *I think I've lost my wallet.* Use **miss** if you do not attend a class, meeting etc. that you regularly go to: *Bill's been sick and has missed several days of work.* Use **lost** to describe someone who does not know where s/he is, or someone or something that you cannot find: *Will the parents of the lost girl please come to the information desk?* Use **missing** to describe someone or something that you have been looking for, especially when the situation is serious: *the missing jewels / Detectives are searching for two missing boys, aged 10 and 12.* Use **disappear** when the way in which someone or something has been lost seems very strange; *My favorite pen seems to have disappeared. / Two soldiers disappeared over the*

weekend. ✗DON'T SAY "the disappeared pen/soldiers."✗
lose는 물건을 발견할 수 없을 때 쓴다: 지갑을 잃어버린 것 같다. **miss**는 규칙적으로 가는 수업·모임 등에 참석할 수 없을 때 쓴다: 빌은 몸이 아파서 며칠을 결근했다. **lost**는 어디 있는지 모르는 사람, 또는 찾을 수 없는 사람이나 사물을 묘사하는 데에 쓴다: 여자아이를 잃어버리신 부모님은 안내소로 와주시겠습니까? **missing**은 특히 상황이 심각할 때 찾고 있는 사람이나 사물을 묘사하는 데에 쓴다: 분실한 보석 / 형사들이 10세와 12세인 실종된 두 소년을 찾고 있다. **disappear**는 사람이나 사물을 잃어버린 방식이 매우 이상할 때 쓴다: 가장 좋아하는 펜이 없어진 것 같다. / 두 명의 군인이 주말 동안에 실종되었다. / "the disappeared pen/soldiers." 라고는 하지 않는다.

los·er /ˈluzɚ/ *n* **1** someone who does not win ‖ 이기지 못한 사람. 패자(敗者): *a bad/sore loser* (=someone who becomes too upset when s/he loses) 진 것을 깨끗이 인정하지 못하는 패자 **2** someone who is never successful in life, work, or relationships ‖ 인생이나 일, 또는 관계에서 결코 성공적이지 못한 사람. 실패자. 낙오자: *Pam's boyfriend is such a loser!* 팸의 남자 친구는 인생 낙오자야!

loss /lɔs/ *n* **1** [C, U] the fact of not having something any longer, or the action of losing something ‖ 어떤 것을 더 이상 소유하지 않은 사실, 또는 잃어버린 행위. 잃음. 분실. 상실. 손실: *The loss of their home was a shock to the family.* 자기네 집을 잃은 것은 그 가족에게 충격이었다. / *weight loss* 체중 감소 **2** [C, U] money that has been lost by a company, government, person, etc. ‖ 회사·정부·사람 등이 잃어버린 돈. 손실액: *The coal industry made a loss of $2 million last year.* 석탄업계는 작년에 2백만 달러의 손실을 입었다. **3** an occasion when you do not win a game ‖ 경기를 이기지 못한 경우. 패배: *3 wins and 4 losses so far this season* 이번 시즌 현재 3승 4패 **4** [C, U] the death of someone ‖ 사람의 죽음. 사상(자수): *Troops suffered heavy losses* (=many deaths) *in the first battle.* 부대는 첫 번째 전투에서 막대한 인명 손실을 입었다. **5** [singular, U] the sadness you feel or disadvantage you have because someone or something leaves ‖ 사람이나 사물이 떠나서 느끼는 슬픔이나 갖게 되는 불이익. 상실(감): *She felt a great sense of loss when her son left home.* 그녀는

아들이 집을 떠날 때 커다란 상실감을 느꼈다. **6 be at a loss** to not know what you should do or say ‖ 무슨 행동이나 말을 해야 할지 모르다. 당황하다. 어찌할 바를 모르다: *I'm at a loss to know what to do.* 나는 무슨 일을 해야 할지 몰라서 당황스럽다. **7 it's his/your loss** SPOKEN said when you think someone is stupid for not taking a good opportunity ‖ 어떤 사람이 좋은 기회를 잡지 못해서 어리석다고 생각할 때에 쓰여: *Well, if he doesn't take the job, it's his loss.* 글쎄, 그가 그 직장을 잡지 않으면 본인만 손해지.

lost¹ /lɔst/ *adj* **1** not knowing where you are or how to find your way ‖ 자신의 위치 또는 길을 찾는 법을 모르는. 길을 잃은: *We got lost driving around the city.* 우리는 도시를 차로 돌아보다가 길을 잃었다. **2** unable to be found ‖ 찾을 수 없는. 잃은. 분실한: *a lost dog* 잃어버린 개 **3** wasted ‖ 허비된: *lost opportunities* 놓친 기회 **4 be/feel lost** to not feel confident or able to take care of yourself ‖ 자신감을 느낄 수 없거나 자신을 돌볼 수 없다. 자신감이 없다. 어찌할 바를 모르다: *I'd be lost without all your help.* 너의 도움이 없으면 나는 자신 없어. **5** destroyed, ruined, or killed ‖ 파멸한[파괴된, 살해된]: *200 men were lost in battle.* 200명의 군인이 전사했다. **6 be lost on sb** if humor or intelligent thinking is lost on someone, s/he cannot understand it or does not want to accept it ‖ 유머나 지적인 사고를 이해할 수 없거나 그것을 받아들이고 싶어하지 않다. …에 효과가 없다. …에게 이해가 안 가다: *The joke was lost on him.* 그 농담은 그에게 이해가 안 갔다. **7 Get lost!** SPOKEN used in order to tell someone rudely to go away ‖ 남에게 무례하게 가버리라고 말하는 데에 쓰여. 꺼져버려! **8 lost cause** something that has no chance of succeeding ‖ 성공할 가망성이 없는 것. 가망 없는 계획[노력] —see usage note at LOSE

lost² *v* the past tense and PAST PARTICIPLE of LOSE ‖ lose의 과거·과거 분사형

lost-and-found /ˌ. . ˈ./ *n* an office used for keeping things that people have lost until their owners can get them ‖ 사람들이 잃어버린 물건을 찾아갈 때까지 보관하는 사무소. 분실물 보관소

lot /lɑt/ *n* **1 a lot** also **lots** INFORMAL **a)** a large amount, quantity, or number of something ‖ 사물의 많은 양[수량, 수]. 많음. 다량. 다수: *A lot of people at work have the flu.* 직장의 많은 사람들이 독감

에 걸려 있다. / *Mrs. Ruiz has lots of money.* 루이즈 여사는 돈이 많다. / *A lot of times* (=usually or often) *we just sat and talked.* 대개 우리는 그냥 앉아서 이야기했다. **b)** much || 많이. 훨씬: *You'll get there a lot quicker if you drive.* 운전해서 가면 훨씬 더 빨리 그곳에 도착할 것이다. —see usage note at MUCH¹ —see picture on page 941 **2 have a lot on your mind** to have many problems you are thinking about || 생각하고 있는 많은 문제가 있다. 많은 생각거리가 있다 **3** an area of land used especially for building on || 특히 건축용으로 사용되는 땅의 구역. 대지. 부지 —see also PARKING LOT

lo·tion /ˈloʊʃən/ *n* [C, U] a liquid mixture that you put on your skin in order to make it soft or to protect it || 피부를 부드럽게 하거나 또는 보호하기 위해 바르는 액체 혼합물. 로션. 세정제(洗淨劑): *suntan lotion* 선탠 로션

lot·ter·y /ˈlɑtəri/ *n* a game of chance in which people buy tickets in order to try to win a lot of money || 사람들이 많은 돈에 당첨되기 위해 표를 사서 운에 맡기는 게임. 복권

loud¹ /laʊd/ *adj* **1** making a lot of noise; not quiet || 많은 소음을 내는. 시끄러운; 조용하지 않은: *The TV's too loud!* 텔레비전이 너무 시끄럽구나! **2** loud clothes are too brightly colored || 옷이 지나치게 밝은 색깔을 띤. 야한. 화려한 **– loudly** *adv*

loud² *adv* loudly || 시끄럽게. 큰소리로: *Can you talk a little louder please?* 좀 더 큰소리로 말해 주실래요? —see also **out loud** (OUT¹)

loud-mouth /ˈ. ./ *n* someone who talks too much, too loudly, and often in an offensive way || 너무 많이·너무 큰소리로·종종 공격적으로 말하는 사람. 허풍선이. 말이 많은 사람 **– loud-mouthed** *adj*

loud·speak·er /ˈlaʊdˌspikɚ/ *n* a piece of equipment that makes messages loud enough to be heard in a store, office, or station || 상점[사무실, 역]에서 들을 수 있을 만큼 크게 말을 전하는 기구. 확성기

lounge¹ /laʊndʒ/ *n* a public room in a hotel or airport, where people can relax, sit down, or drink || 사람들이 쉬거나 앉거나 마실 수 있는, 호텔이나 공항의 공공장소. 휴게실. 대합실. 로비. 라운지

lounge² *v* [I] to stand or sit in a lazy way || 느릿느릿 서거나 앉다. 빈둥거리다. 어슬렁거리다: *We were lounging by the pool.* 우리는 수영장 옆에서 어슬렁거리고 있었다.

louse¹ /laʊs/ *n, plural* **lice** a very small insect that lives on the skin and hair of animals and people || 동물과 사람들의 피부와 머리털에 사는 아주 작은 벌레. 이

louse² *v*

louse up *phr v* [I, T **louse** sth ↔ **up**] to make a mistake or do something badly, especially so that it affects other people || 특히 다른 사람들에게 영향을 줄 만큼 실수를 하거나 일을 잘못하다. …을 망치다. …을 엉망으로[못쓰게] 만들다: *Why are you blaming me? You loused up!* 왜 나를 비난하는 거야? 네가 망쳤잖아!

lous·y /ˈlaʊzi/ *adj* INFORMAL very bad or unimportant || 매우 나쁘거나 중요하지 않은. 비참한. 형편없는: *I've had a lousy day!* 형편없는 하루였어!

lov·a·ble /ˈlʌvəbəl/ *adj* easy to love || 사랑하기 쉬운. 사랑스러운. 귀여운: *a lovable child* 사랑스러운 아이

love¹ /lʌv/ *v* **1** [T] to like something very much, or enjoy doing something very much || 무엇을 매우 좋아하거나 어떤 것을 하기를 대단히 즐기다: *Tom loves to read.* 톰은 독서를 대단히 좋아한다. / *Mom really loved her new dress.* 엄마는 자신의 새 드레스를 정말 좋아했다. **2** [T] to care very much about someone or something that is very special to you || 자신에게 매우 특별한 사람이나 사물에 대해 대단히 관심을 갖다. 사랑하다: *I love you very much.* 나는 당신을 매우 사랑합니다. / *He loves his country.* 그는 조국을 사랑한다. **3 I would love to/I'd love to** SPOKEN said when you really want to do something || 무엇을 정말 하고 싶을 때 쓰여: *I'd love to come with you but I have work to do.* 나는 당신과 함께 정말로 가고 싶지만 할 일이 있어요.

love² *n* **1** [U] a strong romantic feeling for someone || 어떤 사람에 대한 강한 연애 감정. 사랑. 연정: *I fell in love with her the first time we met.* 우리가 처음 만났을 때 나는 그녀와 사랑에 빠졌다. **2** [U] the strong feeling of caring very much about someone or something || 사람이나 사물에 대해 대단히 배려하는 강한 감정. 사랑. 애정. 호의. 관심: *a mother's love for her child* 자식에 대한 어머니의 사랑 **3** [C, U] something that you like very much, or that you enjoy doing very much || 대단히 좋아하는 것, 또는 매우 하기를 즐기는 것: *his love of music/nature/singing etc.* 음악[자연, 노래 등]에 대한 그의 사랑 **4** someone who you have romantic feelings about || 연애 감정을 갖게 하는 사람. 애인. 연인. 사랑하는 사람: *Mike was my first love.* 마이크는 나의 첫사랑이었다. **5 make love** to have sex with someone you love romantically ‖ 낭만적으로 사랑하는 사람과 성관계를 가지다. 성행위를 하다 **6 love/lots of love/all my love** INFORMAL written at the end of a letter to a friend, parent, husband etc. ‖ 친구·부모님·남편 등에게 보내는 편지의 마지막에 쓰여. 사랑[애정]을 담아. 안녕히: *Take care. Lots of love, Dad.* 잘 지내거라. 사랑하는 아빠가.

love af·fair /ˈ. .,./ *n* a romantic sexual relationship ‖ 연애적인 성적 관계. 정사 (情事): *a secret love affair* 은밀한 정사

love·ly /ˈlʌvli/ *adj* very nice, beautiful, or enjoyable ‖ 매우 멋있는[아름다운, 즐거운]. 굉장히 예쁜[훌륭한]. 유쾌한: *Thank you for a lovely evening.* 즐거운 저녁 시간을 마련해 주셔서 감사합니다.

lov·er /ˈlʌvɚ/ *n* **1** a sexual partner, usually someone who you are not married to ‖ 보통 결혼하지 않은 섹스 파트너. 정부(情夫). 애인: *I think my wife has a lover.* 내 아내에게 애인이 있는 것 같아. **2** someone who enjoys something very much ‖ 무엇을 매우 즐기는 사람. 애호가: *a chocolate lover* 초콜릿 애호가

love seat /ˈ. ./ *n* a small SOFA for two people ‖ 2인용 작은 소파

love·sick /ˈlʌvˌsɪk/ *adj* sad because the person you love is not with you or does not love you ‖ 사랑하는 사람이 자신과 같이 있지 않거나 자신을 사랑하지 않아서 슬픈. 상사병의. 사랑에 번민하는

love tri·an·gle /ˈ. .,../ *n* a situation in which one person is romantically involved with two other people ‖ 한 사람이 다른 두 사람과 연애 관계에 있는 상황. 삼각 관계

lov·ing /ˈlʌvɪŋ/ *adj* very caring ‖ 상당히 배려하는. 애정이 깊은: *a wonderful, loving husband* 멋있고 애정이 깊은 남편

low¹ /loʊ/ *adj* **1** not high, or not far above the ground ‖ 지상에서 높지 않거나 멀리 떨어지지 않은. 낮은: *These shelves are a little too low for me.* 이 선반은 나에게 좀 너무 낮다. / *a low ceiling* 낮은 천장 / *low clouds* 낮은 구름 **2** small in degree or amount ‖ 정도나 양이 낮은[적은]: *a low temperature* 낮은 온도 / *new low prices* 새로운 저가 **3** bad, or below an acceptable standard ‖ 나쁜, 또는 받아들일 수 있는 수준 이하의. 낮은: *a low grade in math* 낮은 수학 점수 / *a low opinion of his work* 그의 업무에 대한 낮은 평가 **4** if a supply is low, you have used almost all of it ‖ 모든 공급이 거의 바닥난. 공급이 부족한: *We're running/getting low on gas.* 우리는 휘

발유가 떨어져 간다. **5** unhappy ‖ 불행한: *Kerry's been pretty low lately.* 케리는 최근에 매우 불행했다. **6 a low voice**, sound etc. is quiet or deep ‖ 목소리·소리 등이 조용하거나 낮은. 저음의. 작은 **7** lights that are low are not bright ‖ 빛이 밝지 않은. 약한 —opposite HIGH¹

low² *adv* in a low position or at a low level ‖ 낮은 위치나 낮은 수준에서. 낮게. 낮은 곳으로: *The sun sank low on the horizon.* 해가 지평선 아래로 가라앉았다. / *He scored low on the SAT.* 그는 SAT (미국의 대학 진학 능력 기초 시험)에서 낮은 점수를 받았다. —opposite HIGH²

low³ *n* a low price, level, degree etc. ‖ 낮은 가격·수준·정도 등. (온도·숫자 등의) 최저치: *Prices dropped to an all-time low.* (=the lowest they have ever been) 가격은 사상 최저치까지 떨어졌다. / *Tomorrow's low will be 25°*F. 내일의 최저 기온은 화씨 25°가 될 전망입니다.

low·brow /ˈloʊbraʊ/ *adj* a lowbrow book, movie etc. is not serious or not of very good quality ‖ 책·영화 등이 진지하지 않거나 아주 좋은 품질이 아닌. 질이 낮은. 저속한

low-cal /ˌloʊˈkæl/ *adj* INFORMAL low-cal food or drinks do not have many CALORIEs ‖ 음식이나 음료가 많은 칼로리를 함유하지 않은. 저칼로리의

low-down /ˈloʊdaʊn/ *n* **get the lowdown on sb/sth** INFORMAL to be given the important facts about someone or something ‖ 사람이나 사물에 관한 중요한 사실을 제공받다. 진상이나 내막을 알게 되다

low-end /ˈ. ./ *adj* INFORMAL not the most expensive or not of the best quality ‖ 가장 비싸지 않거나 질이 좋지 않은. 값싼. 질이 낮은: *low-end home computers* 값싼 가정용 컴퓨터

low·er¹ /ˈloʊɚ/ *adj* being the bottom part of something, or at the bottom of something ‖ 어떤 것의 바닥쪽에 있는, 또는 어떤 것의 바닥의. 하부[하위]의: *I injured my lower back.* 나는 허리를 다쳤다. / *the lower floors of the building* 그 건물의 아래층

lower² *v* **1** [I, T] to become less, or to reduce something in amount, degree, strength etc. ‖ 적어지다, 또는 사물의 양·정도·힘 등을 줄이다. 내려가다[낮추어지다]. …을 내리다[낮추다]: *We're lowering prices on all our products!* 우리는 모든 제품 가격을 낮추고 있다! / *Please lower your voice!* (=speak more quietly) 목소리를 줄여 주세요! **2** [T] to move something down ‖ 무엇을 아래로

움직이다. …을 내리다: *The flag was lowered at sunset.* 깃발은 해질녘에 내려 졌다.

lower·case /ˌ. ˈ./ *n* [U] letters written in their small form, such as a, b, c etc. ‖ a·b·c 등의 소문자로 쓴 문자. 소문자 (활자) —compare CAPITAL¹, UPPERCASE

low-fat /ˌ. ˈ./ *adj* low-fat food, cooking etc. has or uses very little fat ‖ 음식·요 리 등이 지방을 아주 적게 함유하거나 사 용하는. 저지방의

low-key /ˌ. ˈ./ *adj* not intended to attract a lot of attention ‖ 많은 주목을 끌 려는 의도가 아닌. 삼가는. 억제된: *The reception was very low-key.* 그 환영회는 아주 조촐하게 치러졌다.

low-life /ˈ. ./ *adj* INFORMAL bad and usually involved in crimes ‖ 나쁘며 대개 범죄와 관련된. 몹쓸. 비열한. 범죄자의: *a bunch of low-life criminals* 한 무리의 저질 범죄자들

low·ly /ˈloʊli/ *adj* low in rank or importance ‖ 지위나 중요성이 낮은. 비천 한. 초라한

low-ly·ing /ˌ. ˈ./ *adj* 1 low-lying land is not much higher than the level of the ocean ‖ 땅이 해면보다 그리 높지 않은. 저 지의 2 not very high ‖ 그리 높지 않은. 낮 게 낀: *low-lying fog* 낮게 낀 안개

loy·al /ˈlɔɪəl/ *adj* never changing your feelings for a particular person, set of beliefs, or country ‖ 특정한 사람이나 믿 음 체계, 또는 나라에 대한 감정이 결코 변 하지 않는. 충성스러운. 성실[충실]한: *a loyal friend* 충직한 친구 —opposite DISLOYAL

loy·al·ty /ˈlɔɪəlti/ *n* 1 [U] the quality of being LOYAL to a particular person, set of beliefs, or country ‖ 특정한 사람이나 믿음 체계, 또는 나라에 충실한 성질. 충 성. 헌신: *The company demands loyalty from its workers.* 그 회사는 근로자에게 헌신을 요구한다. 2 [C usually plural] a feeling of wanting to help and encourage someone or something ‖ 사람 이나 사물을 도와주거나 격려해 주고 싶은 감정. 충성심: *political loyalties* 정치적 충성심

loz·enge /ˈlɑzəndʒ/ *n* a small candy that has medicine in it ‖ 약이 들어 있는 작은 사탕. 약용 박하 드롭스

LP *n* long playing record; a record that plays for about 25 minutes on each side ‖ long playing record(장시간용 음반)의 약어; 각 면에 약 25분간의 연주 분량이 (녹음되어) 있는 음반

LPG *n* [U] liquefied petroleum gas; a type of liquid FUEL that is burned to produce heat or power ‖ liquefied petroleum gas(액화 석유 가스)의 약어; 연소되어 열이나 동력을 내는 액화 연료의 일종

LSD *n* [U] an illegal drug that makes people HALLUCINATE ‖ 사람들에게 환각을 일으키게 하는 마약. 엘에스디

lube /lub/ *v* [T] INFORMAL to LUBRICATE the parts of a car's engine ‖ 자동차의 엔 진 부분에 기름을 치다. 윤활유를 바르다

lu·bri·cant /ˈlubrəkənt/ *n* [C, U] a substance such as oil that is used on things that rub together, making them move more smoothly and easily ‖ 더 부 드럽고 쉽게 움직이도록 서로 맞닿는 물건 에 사용되는 기름 등의 물질. 윤활유

lu·bri·cate /ˈlubrə,keɪt/ *v* [T] to put a LUBRICANT on something ‖ 어떤 것에 윤활 유를 치다 – **lubrication** /ˌlubrəˈkeɪʃən/ *n* [U]

lu·cid /ˈlusɪd/ *adj* 1 clearly expressed and easy to understand ‖ 명백하며 표현 되어 이해하기 쉬운. 명쾌한: *a lucid and interesting article* 명쾌하고 흥미있는 기사 2 able to think clearly and understand what is happening around you ‖ 자기 주변에서 일어나는 일을 명백 하게 생각할 수 있으며 이해할 수 있는. 명 석한. 바른 정신의. 이성적인: *He was rarely lucid during his long illness.* 그는 오랜 병고를 겪는 동안 거의 제정신이 아 니었다.

luck¹ /lʌk/ *n* [U] 1 success or something good that happens by chance ‖ 우연히 일 어나는 성공이나 좋은 일. 운. 재수: *Have you had any luck finding a new roommate?* 혹시 새 룸메이트를 찾았습니 까? / *Wish me luck!* 내게 행운을 빌어줘! / *Good luck with your interview!* 면접 잘 봐라! 2 the way in which good or bad things happen to people by chance ‖ 좋 거나 나쁜 일이 우연히 사람에게 일어나는 기회: *I've had bad luck all day. I missed the bus, was late for work, and I lost my keys.* 나는 온종일 재수가 없었다. 버스를 놓치고 직장에 지각하고 열쇠를 잃 어버렸다. 3 **be in luck** to be able to do or get something that you want ‖ 자신이 원하는 것을 할 수 있거나 구할 수 있다. 운이 좋다: *You're in luck – there's one ticket left!* 표가 한 장 남았는데, 당신 운 이 좋네요! 4 **be out of luck** to not be able to do or get something you want ‖ 자신이 원하는 것을 하거나 구할 수 없다. 운이 나쁘다: *We're out of luck – the park is closed.* 우리는 운이 없다. 공원이 문을 닫았어. 5 **just my luck!** SPOKEN said when you are disappointed but not surprised that something bad has happened ‖ 나쁜 일이 일어났다는 사실에 실망스럽지만 놀라지는 않을 때 쓰여. 글 렀구나[김샜어]!: *Just my luck! The guys just left.* 글렀군! 그 녀석들이 방금 떠났으 니. **6 better luck next time** SPOKEN said when you hope that someone will be more successful the next time s/he tries to do something ‖ 다음번에 하고자 하는 일이 더 성공하기를 바랄 때 쓰여. 다 음 기회에는 운이 더 좋기를 —see also **tough!/tough luck!** (TOUGH[1])

USAGE NOTE luck and lucky

Use the noun **luck** without an adjective to mean the good things that happen to you by chance: *Winning the game was just a matter of luck. / With luck, you'll find the right job.* You can use "have" with **luck**, but only if a word such as an adjective or determiner comes before **luck**: *He's had a lot of bad luck lately. / We didn't have any luck getting tickets.* Use **lucky** to describe a situation that is good by chance, or someone who always has good luck: *We're lucky we haven't gone out of business like some other small companies.* ✗DON'T SAY "we have luck."✗
우연히 일어난 좋은 일을 뜻하는 데에는 형용사 없이 명사 **luck**을 쓴다: 경기를 이긴 것은 단지 운이 좋아서였다. / 운이 좋으면 너는 적당한 직장을 구할 것이 다. 형용사나 한정사 등의 단어가 **luck** 앞에 오면 **luck**과 함께 "have"를 쓸 수 있다: 그는 최근에 많은 불행을 겪었다. / 우리는 운이 없게도 표를 구하지 못했 다. 우연히 좋은 상황이나 항상 행운이 있는 사람을 나타내는 데는 **lucky**를 쓴 다: 우리는 다른 일부 영세 업체들처럼 망하지 않아서 다행이다. "we have luck."이라고는 하지 않는다.

---

luck[2] v

luck out *phr v* [I] INFORMAL to be lucky ‖ 운이 좋다: *We lucked out and found someone who spoke English.* 우리는 운이 좋게도 영어를 구사하는 사람을 발견했다.

luck·y /ˈlʌki/ *adj* **1** having good luck; fortunate ‖ 운이 좋은. 다행한. 재수 좋 은; 행운인: *He's lucky to still be alive.* 그 는 다행히도 아직 살아 있다. / *"I just got the last bus." "That was lucky!"* "나는 막 마지막 버스를 탔어." "운 좋았군!" **2 I'll be lucky if** SPOKEN said when you think something is very unlikely ‖ 어떤 일이 그다지 일어날 것 같지 않다고 생각

될 때 쓰여. …이라면 천만 다행이다. … 은 잘 안 될 듯하다: *I'll be lucky if I can pay my bills this month.* 이번 달에 공과 금을 지불하면 다행이야. **– luckily** *adv* : *Luckily, no one was hurt.* 다행히도 아무 도 다치지 않았다. —opposite UNLUCKY — see usage note at LUCK[1]

lu·cra·tive /ˈlukrətɪv/ *adj* FORMAL making you earn a lot of money ‖ 많은 돈을 벌게 하는. 수지맞는. 돈벌이가 되 는: *lucrative job opportunities* 돈벌이가 되는 일의 기회

lu·di·crous /ˈludɪkrəs/ *adj* silly, wrong, and unreasonable; RIDICULOUS ‖ 어리석으 며 잘못되고 비이성적인. 터무니없는. 바 보 같은; ⑤ ridiculous: *The newspaper has printed some ludicrous stories.* 그 신문은 아주 터무니없는 기사를 실었다.

lug /lʌg/ *v* **-gged, -gging** [T] INFORMAL to pull or carry something that is very heavy ‖ 매우 무거운 것을 끌거나 나르다: *We lugged our suitcases up to our room.* 우리는 여행 가방을 방까지 끌고 갔다.

lug·gage /ˈlʌgɪdʒ/ *n* [U] the bags etc. carried by people who are traveling; BAGGAGE ‖ 여행하고 있는 사람들이 들고 가는 가방 등. 수화물; ⑤ baggage

lu·gu·bri·ous /ləˈgubriəs/ *adj* LITERARY very sad and serious ‖ 매우 슬프고 심각 한. 울적한. 가련한

luke·warm /ˌlukˈwɔrm/ *adj* **1** a liquid that is lukewarm is only slightly warm ‖ 액체가 약간만 따뜻한. 미지근한 —see usage note at TEMPERATURE **2** not showing very much interest or excitement ‖ 많은 관심이나 열의를 보이 지 않는. 미온적인. 냉담한: *a lukewarm response* 냉담한 반응

lull[1] /lʌl/ *v* [T] **1** to make someone feel calm or sleepy ‖ 남을 차분하게 또는 졸리 게 하다. 달래다. 어르다. 재우다: *Singing softly, she lulled us to sleep.* 부 드럽게 노래하면서 그녀는 우리를 잠들게 했다. **2** to make someone feel so safe and confident that you can easily deceive him/her ‖ 사람을 쉽게 속일 수 있 을 정도로 안전하고 확신에 찬 느낌이 들 게 하다. …을 (속여서) 안심시켜 …하게 하다: *She was lulled into believing that there was no danger.* 그녀는 속아넘어가 위험이 없다고 믿었다.

lull[2] *n* a short period when there is less activity or noise than usual ‖ 평소보다 활동이나 소음이 적을 때의 짧은 기간. 소 강 상태. 일시적 잠잠함: *a lull in the conversation* 대화의 일시적 중단

lul·la·by /ˈlʌləˌbaɪ/ *n* a song that you sing to children in order to make them calm and sleepy ‖ 아이들을 달래고 재우기 위해서 부르는 노래. 자장가

lum·ber¹ /'lʌmbər/ n [U] trees that are cut down and used as wood for building ‖ 베어 넘어뜨려 건축용 재목으로 사용되는 나무. 목재

lumber² v [I] **1** to move in a slow, awkward way, usually because you are heavy ‖ 보통 몸무게가 많이 나가 천천히 어색하게 움직이다. 육중하게 움직이다[걷다]: *The bear lumbered towards us.* 그 곰은 우리를 향해 육중하게 다가왔다. **2 get/be lumbered with** to get a job or duty that you do not want ‖ 자신이 원하지 않는 일이나 임무를 얻다. 귀찮은 일을 떠맡다: *I get lumbered with the work he doesn't want.* 나는 그가 원치 않는 일을 떠맡았다.

lum·ber·ing /'lʌmbərɪŋ/ n [U] ⇨ LOGGING

lum·ber·jack /'lʌmbər,dʒæk/ n someone whose job is to cut down trees for wood ‖ 재목용으로 나무를 베어 넘어뜨리는 직업인. 벌목꾼. 벌채 인부

lu·mi·nar·y /'lumə,nɛri/ n someone who is famous and respected because of his/her knowledge or skills ‖ 지식이나 기술 때문에 유명하고 존경받는 사람. 권위자. 선각자

lu·mi·nous /'lumənəs/ adj able to shine in the dark without being lit ‖ 점화되지 않고 어둠 속에서 빛나는. 야광의: *luminous paint* 야광 페인트

lump¹ /lʌmp/ n **1** a small piece of something solid that does not have a definite shape ‖ 정해진 형태가 없는 딱딱한 작은 조각. 덩어리: *a lump of clay* 한 덩어리의 진흙 —see picture at PIECE¹ **2** a hard swollen area on someone's skin or in his/her body ‖ 사람의 피부나 몸에 단단하게 부어오른 곳. 혹. 부스럼 **3 a lump in your throat** the tight feeling in your throat that happens when you want to cry ‖ 울고 싶을 때 생기는 목구멍의 당기는 느낌. 목이 멤

lump² v [T] to put two or more different people or things together and consider them as a single group ‖ 둘 이상의 다른 사람이나 사물을 한데 묶어서 단일한 집단으로 생각하다. 일괄하여 다루다. 총괄하다: *Do you think I can lump these ideas into one paragraph?* 당신은 이 생각들을 한 단락으로 묶을 수 있다고 생각합니까?

lump sum /ˌ. './ n an amount of money given in a single payment ‖ 단번에 지불하는 돈의 액수. 일시불. 총액

lump·y /'lʌmpi/ adj having LUMPs and therefore not smooth ‖ 덩어리가 있어서

부드럽지 않은. 덩어리가 많은. 울퉁불퉁한: *a lumpy mattress* 울퉁불퉁한 매트리스

lu·na·cy /'lunəsi/ n [U] actions or behavior that seem very stupid and unreasonable ‖ 아주 어리석고 비이성적으로 보이는 행동이나 태도. 기묘한[미친] 행동. 바보짓

lu·nar /'lunər/ adj relating to the moon ‖ 달과 관련된. 달의: *a lunar eclipse* 월식

lu·na·tic /'lunə,tɪk/ n someone who behaves in a crazy, stupid, or very strange way ‖ 미치거나 어리석거나, 또는 매우 이상하게 행동하는 사람. 미치광이 – **lunatic** adj

lunch /lʌntʃ/ n [C, U] a meal eaten in the middle of the day, or that time of day ‖ 한낮에 먹는 식사, 또는 하루의 그 시간. 점심 (시간): *What do you want for lunch?* 점심으로 뭘 먹고 싶니? / *When do you usually eat lunch?* 보통 언제 점심을 먹니? / *We've already had lunch.* 우리는 벌써 점심을 먹었다. / *Dad usually goes jogging at lunch.* 아빠는 보통 점심 때 조깅을 한다. —see usage note at MEAL TIMES

lunch·eon /'lʌntʃən/ n [C, U] FORMAL ⇨ LUNCH

lunch·time /'lʌntʃtaɪm/ n [C, U] the time in the middle of the day when people usually eat LUNCH ‖ 사람들이 보통 점심 식사를 하는 때인 한낮의 시간. 점심 시간: *Is it lunchtime yet?* 벌써 점심 시간이니?

lung /lʌŋ/ n one of two organs in the body used for breathing ‖ 숨을 쉬는 데에 사용되는 신체의 두 기관 중의 하나. 폐

lunge /lʌndʒ/ v [I] to make a sudden forceful movement toward someone or something ‖ 사람이나 사물을 향해 갑작스럽고 힘이 넘치는 동작을 하다. 돌진하다. (…을) 뻗다: *Greg lunged forward to grab her arm.* 그레그는 그녀의 팔을 잡기 위해 앞으로 손을 쭉 내밀었다. – **lunge** n

lurch /lɜrtʃ/ v [I] to walk or move in an unsteady, uncontrolled way ‖ 불안정하고 멋대로 걷거나 움직이다. 비틀거리다: *He lurched drunkenly towards us.* 그는 술에 취해 우리 쪽으로 비틀거리며 걸어왔다. – **lurch** n —see also **leave sb in the lurch** (LEAVE¹)

lure¹ /lʊr/ v [T] to persuade someone to do something by making it seem attractive, exciting etc.; TEMPT ‖ 무엇을 매력적이고 흥미로워 보이게 하여 그것을 하도록 남을 설득하다. 유혹하다. 꾀어내다; ⓟ tempt: *Another company tried to* *lure him over by offering more money.* 또 다른 회사가 더 많은 돈을 제안하여 그를 유혹했다.

lure² *n* **1** something that attracts people, or the quality of being able to do this ‖ 사람들을 끌어당기는 것, 또는 사람들을 끌어당길 수 있는 성질. 유혹. 매력: *the lure of power and money* 권력과 돈의 유혹 **2** an object used in order to attract animals or fish so that they can be caught ‖ 동물이나 물고기를 잡을 수 있게 그것을 유인하는 데에 사용되는 물체. 미끼

lu·rid /ˈlʊrɪd/ *adj* DISAPPROVING deliberately shocking and involving sex or violence ‖ 의도적으로 충격적이며 섹스나 폭력이 뒤얽힌. 끔찍한. 야단스러운. 야한: *the lurid details of the murder* 살인 사건의 끔찍한 내용

lurk /lɚk/ *v* [I] to wait somewhere secretly, usually before doing something bad ‖ 보통 나쁜 일을 하기 전에 어딘가에서 은밀하게 기다리다. 숨어 기다리다[잠복하다]. 어슬렁거리다: *men lurking in the alley* 골목에서 어슬렁거리는 남자들

lus·cious /ˈlʌʃəs/ *adj* **1** extremely good to eat ‖ 먹기에 아주 좋은. 맛있는: *luscious ripe strawberries* 맛있게 익은 딸기 **2** INFORMAL very sexually attractive ‖ 매우 성적으로 매력적인. 관능적인

lush¹ /lʌʃ/ *adj* having lots of very green and healthy plants or leaves ‖ 짙은 초록색의 건강한 식물이나 잎이 많은. 우거진

lush² *n* INFORMAL someone who drinks too much alcohol ‖ 너무 많은 술을 마시는 사람. 술고래. 고주망태

lust¹ /lʌst/ *n* [C, U] DISAPPROVING a very strong feeling of sexual desire, or a strong desire for something such as power or money ‖ 강하게 느끼는 성욕이나 권력이나 돈 등에 대한 강한 욕구. 욕정. 권세[금전]욕

lust² *v*

lust after/for sb/sth *phr v* [T] DISAPPROVING **1** to have a strong feeling of sexual desire for someone ‖ 누군가에게 강한 성적 욕망을 가지다. 욕정이 타오르다 **2** to want something very much because you do not have it yet ‖ 아직 가지지 않아서 어떤 것을 몹시 원하다. 열망[갈망]하다: *politicians lusting for power* 권력을 갈망하는 정치인들

lus·ter /ˈlʌstɚ/ *n* [singular, U] an attractive shiny appearance ‖ 보기 좋게 윤이 나는 외관. 광택. 윤기: *the luster of her long dark hair* 그녀의 길고 검은 머리카락의 윤기 – **lustrous** /ˈlʌstrəs/ *adj*

lust·y /ˈlʌsti/ *adj* strong and healthy; powerful ‖ 강하고 건강한. 기운이 넘치는. 원기 왕성한; 강력한: *The baby gave a lusty cry.* 그 아기는 우렁찬 울음소리를 냈다. – **lustily** *adv*

Lu·ther·an /ˈluθərən/ *adj* relating to the Protestant church whose members follow the ideas of Martin Luther ‖ 신도들이 마틴 루터의 사상을 따르는 개신교와 관련된. – **Lutheran** *n*

lux·u·ri·ant /lʌgˈʒʊriənt, lʌkˈʃʊ-/ *adj* healthy and growing thickly and strongly ‖ 건강하며 빽빽하고 강하게 자라는. 무성한. 울창한

lux·u·ri·ate /lʌgˈʒʊriˌeɪt, lʌkˈʃʊ-/ *v*

luxuriate in sth *phr v* [T] to relax and enjoy the pleasure you feel ‖ 긴장을 풀고 자신이 느끼는 쾌감을 즐기다. …을 탐닉[만끽]하다: *She luxuriated in the hot bath.* 그녀는 온수욕을 실컷 즐겼다.

lux·u·ri·ous /lʌgˈʒʊriəs, lʌkˈʃʊ-/ *adj* very comfortable, beautiful, and expensive ‖ 매우 안락하며 아름답고 비싼. 사치스러운. 호화스러운: *a luxurious room in a hotel on the coast* 해변가 호텔의 호화로운 방

lux·u·ry /ˈlʌkʃəri, ˈlʌgʒəri/ *n* **1** luxury car/hotel/vacation etc. a luxury car etc. is of the highest standard ‖ 최고 수준의 자동차 등. 호화스러운 자동차/호텔/휴가 **2** something expensive that you want but do not need ‖ 자신이 원하는 것이지만 필요하지 않은 비싼 것. 사치품: *We can't afford the luxury of a new car.* 우리는 사치품인 새 차를 살 여유가 없다.

Ly·cra /ˈlaɪkrə/ *n* [U] TRADEMARK a cloth that stretches, used especially for making tight-fitting sports clothes ‖ 특히 꼭 끼는 운동복을 만드는 데에 쓰는 늘어나는 천. 라이크라

ly·ing /ˈlaɪ-ɪŋ/ *v* the PRESENT PARTICIPLE of LIE ‖ lie의 현재 분사형

lynch /lɪntʃ/ *v* [T] if a crowd of people lynches someone, they illegally hang him/her as a punishment ‖ 군중들이 처벌로서 사람을 불법적으로 매달다. …을 린치[사형(私刑)]를 가하여 죽이다. 교수형에 처하다 – **lynching** *n*

lynch·pin /ˈlɪntʃˌpɪn/ *n* ⇨ LINCHPIN

lyr·i·cal /ˈlɪrɪkəl/ *adj* expressing strong emotions in a beautiful way ‖ 아름답게 강한 감정을 표현하는. 서정적인: *lyrical music/poetry* 서정 음악[서정시]

lyr·i·cist /ˈlɪrəsɪst/ *n* someone who writes LYRICS ‖ 가사를 쓰는 사람. 작사자

lyr·ics /ˈlɪrɪks/ *n* [plural] the words of a song ‖ 노랫말. 가사

Mm

M, m /ɛm/ **1** the thirteenth letter of the English alphabet ‖ 영어 알파벳의 열셋째 자 **2** the ROMAN NUMERAL (=number) for 1000 ‖ 로마 숫자의 1000

m *n* **1** the written abbreviation of "meter" ‖ "meter"의 약어 **2** the written abbreviation of "million" ‖ "million"의 약어 **3** the written abbreviation of "male" ‖ "male"의 약어 **4** the written abbreviation of "mile" ‖ "mile"의 약어 **5** the written abbreviation of "married" ‖ "married"의 약어 **6** the written abbreviation of "medium", used especially in clothes ‖ 특히 옷에 쓰여 "medium"의 약어

M.A. *n* Master of Arts; a university degree in a subject such as history or literature that you can get after you have your first degree ‖ Master of Arts(문학 석사)의 약어; 첫 번째 학위를 딴 이후에 얻을 수 있는 역사나 문학 등의 과목의 대학 학위 —compare M.S.

MA the written abbreviation of Massachusetts ‖ Massachusetts(매사추세츠 주)의 약어

ma /mɑ, mɔ/ *n* OLD-FASHIONED mother ‖ 어머니

ma'am /mæm/ *n* SPOKEN used in order to speak politely to a woman when you do not know her name ‖ 이름을 모르는 여자에게 정중하게 말하는 데에 쓰여. 아주머니, 사모님: *Excuse me, ma'am.* 실례합니다, 아주머니

mac /mæk/ *n* SPOKEN used in order to speak to a man when you do not know his name ‖ 이름을 모르는 남자에게 말하는 데에 쓰여. 이보게. 자네: *Hey, mac! Is that your car?* 이보게! 저게 자네 차인가?

ma·ca·bre /məˈkɑbrə, məˈkɑb/ *adj* strange, frightening, and relating to death or injury ‖ 이상하고 무서우며 죽음이나 부상과 관련된. 으스스한. 소름끼치는. 죽음의: *a macabre tale* 섬뜩한 이야기

mac·a·ro·ni /ˌmækəˈroʊni/ *n* [U] a type of PASTA in the shape of small curved tubes, that you cook in boiling water ‖ 끓는 물에서 요리하는 작고 굽은 관 모양의 파스타의 일종. 마카로니

Mace /meɪs/ *n* TRADEMARK a chemical that some people carry to defend themselves, which makes your eyes and skin sting painfully if it is SPRAYed in your face ‖ 일부의 사람들이 자신을 방어하려고 가지고 다니는, 남의 얼굴에 뿌리면 눈과 피부를 고통스럽게 따끔거리게 하는 화학 물질. 최루 신경가스

Mach /mɑk/ *n* [U] a unit for measuring the speed of a plane in relation to the speed of sound ‖ 음속과 관련하여 비행기의 속도를 측정하는 단위. 마하

ma·che·te /məˈʃɛti, -ˈtʃɛ-/ *n* a large knife with a broad heavy blade, used as a tool for cutting or as a weapon ‖ 절단용 도구나 무기로 사용되는 넓고 무거운 칼날을 가진 큰 칼. 벌채용 칼

ma·chine¹ /məˈʃin/ *n* a piece of equipment that uses power such as electricity to do a particular job ‖ 특정한 일을 하려고 전기 등의 동력을 사용하는 장비. 기계: *a sewing machine* 재봉틀 / *The machines in the lab were running all night.* 연구실의 기계들은 밤새 돌아가고 있었다.

USAGE NOTE machine, appliance, device, gadget, and **tool**

Machine is a general word for a piece of equipment that uses electricity or another form of power: *We've just bought a new sewing machine.* An **appliance** is a large **machine** that is used in the home: *Now, save 30% off all appliances, including refrigerators and dishwashers!* A **device** is a piece of equipment that is usually small and usually electronic, that does a special job: *A seismograph is a device that measures earthquake activity.* A **gadget** is a small piece of equipment that makes a particular job easier to do: *Have you seen this new gadget for opening wine bottles?* A **tool** is a small object that is used for making and repairing things, and that usually does not use electricity: *We keep most of the tools in the garage.*
machine은 전기나 다른 형태의 동력을 사용하는 장비를 뜻하는 일반적인 단어이다: 우리는 지금 막 새 재봉틀을 샀다. **appliance**는 가정에서 사용하는 큰 **machine**(기계)이다: 냉장고와 자동 세척기를 포함해서 모든 가정용 기구를 지금 30% 할인합니다! **device**는 특수한 일을 하는 대체로 작은 전자 장비이다: 지진계는 지진 활동을 측정하는 장

치이다. **gadget**는 특정한 일을 더 쉽게 할 수 있게 하는 작은 장비이다: 포도주 병을 따는 이 새로운 고안품을 봤어? **tool**은 대체로 전기를 사용하지 않으며 물건을 만들거나 수리할 때 사용하는 작은 도구이다: 우리는 대부분의 도구를 차고에 보관한다.

machine² v [T] to make or shape something, especially metal parts for something, using a machine ‖ 기계를 사용해 특히 사물의 금속 부분을 만들거나 형태를 잡다. …을 기계로 만들다

ma·chine gun /ˈ. ˌ./ n a gun that fires a lot of bullets very quickly ‖ 많은 총알을 매우 빠르게 발사하는 총. 기관총

machine-read·a·ble /.ˌ. ˈ...ˌ/ adj able to be understood and used by a computer ‖ 컴퓨터로 이해하고 사용할 수 있는. 컴퓨터로 처리[해독]할 수 있는: *machine-readable text* 컴퓨터로 처리 가능한 문서

ma·chin·er·y /məˈʃinəri/ n [U] 1 machines, especially large ones ‖ 특히 거대한 기계들. 기계(류): *agricultural machinery* 농업용 기계 / *The machinery in the factory is controlled by computers.* 공장에 있는 기계들은 컴퓨터로 조작된다. 2 the parts inside a machine that make it work ‖ 기계를 작동시키는 기계 내부의 부품. 기계 장치 3 an official system or set of processes for organizing or achieving something ‖ 어떤 일을 조직하거나 성취하기 위한 공식적인 체계나 일련의 과정들. 기구. 조직. 절차: *The machinery of the law works slowly.* 법의 절차는 천천히 효력을 발휘한다.

ma·chin·ist /məˈʃinist/ n someone who operates or makes machines ‖ 기계를 조작하거나 제작하는 사람. 기계 운전자[제작공]

ma·cho /ˈmɑtʃoʊ/ adj INFORMAL a man who is macho has qualities such as strength that are typical of men, but is not sensitive or sympathetic ‖ 남자가 남성의 전형적인 특질인 힘 등을 지니고 있으나 민감하거나 동정적이지 않은. 남자다운. 남성적인

mack·er·el /ˈmækərəl/ n [C, U] a common sea fish, that has a strong taste, or the meat from this fish ‖ 매우 비린내가 나는 흔한 바닷물고기, 또는 이 물고기의 살. 고등어

mac·ro·cos·m /ˈmækrə‚kɑzəm/ n a large complicated system such as the whole universe or a society, considered as a single unit ‖ 하나의 단위로 간주되는 전 우주나 한 사회 등의 거대하고 복잡한 체계. 대우주. 대세계. 전체. 총체 — compare MICROCOSM

mad /mæd/ adj **-dder, -ddest 1** INFORMAL angry ‖ 화가 난. 성난: *You make me so mad!* 너 정말 나를 화나게 하는구나! / *Lisa was really mad at me for telling.* 리사는 고자질한 것 때문에 나에게 정말로 골이 나 있어. **2 do sth like mad** INFORMAL to do something as quickly as you can ‖ 가능한 한 빨리 어떤 일을 하다. 미친 듯이[맹렬히] …하다: *Carlos was writing like mad at the end of the exam.* 카를로스는 시험이 끝날 즈음에 미친 듯이 답안을 작성하고 있었다. **3** behaving in a wild way, without thinking about what you are doing ‖ 행동하고 있는 것에 대해 생각하지 않고 무모하게 행동하는. 미친 듯한. 무분별한: *We made a mad dash for* (=ran wildly towards) *the door.* 우리는 문을 향해 미친 듯이 돌진했다. **4 power-mad/ money-mad etc.** only interested in or only thinking about power, money etc. ‖ 오로지 권력·돈 등에 대해서만 관심이 있거나 생각을 하는. 권력/돈 등에 너무 집착하는: *a power-mad dictator* 권력에만 몰두하는 독재자

mad·am /ˈmædəm/ n **1** used in order to speak politely to a woman when you do not know her name ‖ 이름을 모를 때 여자에게 정중하게 말하는 데에 쓰여. 부인. 사모님: *May I help you, madam?* 사모님, 무엇을 도와드릴까요? / *Dear Madam* (=used at the beginning of a business letter to a woman when you do not know her name) 사모님 귀하 **2** a woman who is in charge of a group of PROSTITUTES ‖ 일단의 매춘부들을 책임지고 있는 여자. 여자 포주

mad·den·ing /ˈmædn-ɪŋ, ˈmædnɪŋ/ adj very annoying ‖ 매우 짜증나는. 부아가 치미는. 괘씸한: *maddening behavior* 괘씸한 행동

made¹ /meid/ v the past tense and PAST PARTICIPLE of MAKE ‖ make의 과거·과거분사형

made² adj **1 be made of** to be built from or consist of something ‖ 어떤 것으로 만들어지거나 구성되다. …으로 만들다: *The frame is made of silver.* 그 틀은 은으로 만들어졌다. **2 be made for** to be perfectly suitable for a particular person, group, or situation ‖ 특정한 사람·단체·상황에 완벽하게 적합하다. …에 꼭 알맞다. (서로) 잘 어울리다: *I think Anna and Juan were made for each other.* 나는 애나와 후안이 서로 잘 어울렸

다고 생각한다. **3 sb has (got) it made** used in order to say that someone is sure of success or happiness ‖ 남이 확실하게 성공하거나 행복한 상태라고 말하는 데 쓰여. 대성공하다. 선망하는 삶을 이루다: *You have a wonderful family, plenty of money – you've got it made!* 당신은 멋진 가정과 충분한 돈을 가지고 있어 정말 남 부러울 게 없군요!

mad·house /'mædhaʊs/ *n* a place that is very busy and noisy ‖ 매우 바쁘고 시끄러운 장소. 붐비는[혼란한] 장소: *The airport is a madhouse at Christmas.* 공항은 성탄절에 시끌벅적하다.

mad·ly /'mædli/ *adv* **1 madly in love** very much in love ‖ 사랑에 폭 빠져 **2** in a wild way ‖ 거칠게. 미친 듯이. 맹렬히: *Allen was beating madly on the door.* 앨런은 문을 미친 듯이 두드리고 있었다.

mad·man /'mædmæn, -mən/ *n* **like a madman** in a wild uncontrolled way ‖ 거칠고 통제되지 않은 모습으로. 미친 사람처럼: *He drives like a madman.* 그는 미친 사람처럼 운전한다.

mad·ness /'mædnɪs/ *n* [U] very stupid and often dangerous behavior ‖ 매우 어리석고 종종 위험한 행동. 광기. 미친 짓: *It would be absolute madness to try to cross the desert on your own.* 혼자서 사막을 횡단하려는 것은 절대적으로 미친 짓일 것이다.

Ma·don·na /mə'dɑnə/ *n* a picture or figure of Mary, the mother of Jesus Christ ‖ 예수 그리스도의 어머니인 성모 마리아의 그림이나 인물상. 성모 마리아상 [그림]

mael·strom /'meɪlstrəm/ *n* a situation full of events that you cannot control or strong emotions that make people feel confused or frightened ‖ 통제할 수 없는 사건들로 가득 찬 상황이나 사람들을 혼란스럽거나 두렵게 느끼게 하는 격한 감정. 대혼란. 큰 동요. 격동: *Forbes was pulled into the maelstrom of newspapers and TV attention.* 포브즈지 (誌)는 신문과 텔레비전의 대격동에 휘말려들었다.

mae·stro /'maɪstroʊ/ *n* someone who can do something very well, especially a musician ‖ 어떤 것을 매우 잘 할 수 있는 사람, 특히 음악인. 대가. 거장

ma·fi·a /'mɑfiə/ *n* **the Mafia** a large organization of criminals who control many illegal activities ‖ 많은 불법적인 활동을 조종하는 거대한 범죄 조직. 마피아

mag·a·zine /ˌmæɡə'zin, 'mæɡəˌzin/ *n* **1** a large thin book usually with a large picture on the cover, that is sold weekly or monthly and contains articles, photographs etc. ‖ 주간이나 월간으로 팔리며 기사·사진 등을 포함하는, 대체로 표지에 큰 사진이 있는 크기가 크면서 얇은 책. 잡지: *a fashion magazine* 패션 잡지 **2** the part of a gun that holds the bullets ‖ 총알을 (보충용으로) 재어 두는 총의 일부분. 탄창

ma·gen·ta /mə'dʒɛntə/ *n* [U] a dark purple-red color ‖ 짙은 붉은 자주색. 심홍색 – **magenta** *adj*

mag·got /'mæɡət/ *n* the LARVA (=young insect) of a fly that lives in decaying food or flesh ‖ 부패하는 음식이나 육질에 사는 파리의 유충. 구더기

mag·ic /'mædʒɪk/ *n* [U] **1** a secret power used for controlling events or doing impossible things, by saying special words or doing special actions ‖ 특별한 말을 하거나 특별한 행동을 함으로써, 일어나는 일을 통제하거나 불가능한 일을 하는 데 사용되는 비밀스런 힘. 불가사의한 힘. 마력: *a witch's magic* 마녀의 마력 **2** the skill of doing tricks that look like magic, or the tricks themselves ‖ 마술처럼 보이는 기교를 부리는 솜씨나 기교 그 자체. 마법. 마술. 요술: *Dad always did a magic show at my birthday parties.* 아빠는 항상 내 생일 잔치에 마술 쇼를 하셨다. **3** an attractive quality that makes someone or something interesting or exciting ‖ 사람이나 사물의 관심을 끌거나 마음 설레게 하는 매력적인 성질. 저항할 수 없는 매력: *These old stories still retain their magic.* 이 옛이야기들은 여전히 묘한 매력을 지니고 있다.

mag·i·cal /'mædʒɪkəl/ *adj* **1** very enjoyable and exciting, in a strange or special way ‖ 이상하거나 특별하게 매우 즐겁고 흥분되는. 매력적인. 황홀한: *a magical evening beneath the stars* 별빛 아래의 황홀한 밤 **2** containing magic, or done using magic ‖ 마술을 포함한, 또는 마술을 이용해서 행한. 마술적인. 마법의: *magical powers* 마법의 힘 – **magically** *adv*

ma·gi·cian /mə'dʒɪʃən/ *n* someone who performs magic tricks and makes things appear and disappear ‖ 마술을 부리고 사물을 나타냈다 사라지게 하는 사람. 마술사. 마법사

mag·is·trate /'mædʒɪˌstreɪt, -strɪt/ *n* someone who judges less serious crimes in a court of law ‖ 법원에서 덜 중대한 범죄를 재판하는 사람. 하급 판사. 치안 판사

mag·nan·i·mous /mæɡ'nænəməs/ *adj* kind and generous toward other people

∥다른 사람들에 대해 친절하고 관대한. 도량[아량]이 넓은 – **magnanimity** /ˌmæɡnə'nɪməti/ n [U]

mag·nate /'mæɡneɪt, -nɪt/ n **steel/oil/shipping etc. magnate** a wealthy and powerful person in the steel etc. industry ∥강철 등의 산업에서 부유하고 힘이 있는 사람. 유력자. 대사업가. 거물. …왕. 강철/석유/선박의 왕

mag·ne·si·um /mæɡ'niziəm, -ʒəm/ n [U] a light silver-white metal that is often used in medicine and to make other metals ∥흔히 의약품에 사용되며 다른 금속을 만드는 데 쓰이는 가벼운 은백색의 금속. 마그네슘

mag·net /'mæɡnɪt/ n

magnet

1 a piece of iron or steel that can make other metal objects move toward it ∥다른 금속체를 자기 쪽으로 움직이게 할 수 있는 철이나 강철 조각. 자석. 자철광 2 a person or place that attracts many other people or things ∥많은 다른 사람들이나 사물을 끌어당기는 사람이나 장소. 마음을 끄는 사람[장소, 것]: *The city has become a magnet for many new industries.* 그 도시는 많은 새로운 산업을 자석처럼 끌어들였다. – **magnetize** /'mæɡnə,taɪz/ v [T]

mag·net·ic /mæɡ'nɛtɪk/ adj 1 having the power of a MAGNET ∥자석의 힘을 가지고 있는. 자석의. 자기의: *There's a magnetic strip on the back so that you can hang it up.* 그것을 걸 수 있도록 뒤에 자석 띠가 있다. 2 **magnetic personality** a quality that someone has that makes other people feel strongly attracted to him/her ∥다른 사람들에게 강하게 끌림을 느끼게 하는 어떤 사람이 지닌 자질. 매력적인[있는] 인물 3 **magnetic tape/disk etc.** TAPE etc. that uses MAGNETs to record and store information, for example in a computer system ∥컴퓨터 시스템의 실례에서처럼 정보를 기록하고 저장하기 위해 자기를 이용하는 테이프 등. 자기테이프/디스크

mag·net·ism /'mæɡnə,tɪzəm/ n [U] 1 a quality that makes other people feel attracted to you ∥다른 사람들이 자신에게 마음이 끌림을 느끼게 하는 자질. 마음을 끄는 힘. 매력: *Her magnetism is a great asset in her career on television.* 그녀의 묘한 매력은 방송 활동에 있어 큰 자산이다. 2 the qualities of a MAGNET ∥자석의 성질. 자성. 자력

mag·nif·i·cent /mæɡ'nɪfəsənt/ adj very impressive because of being big, beautiful etc. ∥크고 아름다워서 매우 감동적인. 장엄한. 웅장한: *a magnificent painting/sunset* 장엄한 그림[일몰] – **magnificence** n [U]

mag·ni·fy /'mæɡnə,faɪ/ v [T] 1 to make something appear larger than it is ∥사물을 실제보다 더 크게 보이게 하다. 확대하다: *A microscope magnifies the image so you can see the cells.* 현미경은 세포를 볼 수 있도록 상(像)을 확대한다. 2 to make something seem more important or worse than it really is ∥어떤 것을 실제보다 더 중요하게 보이게 하거나 더 나쁘게 보이게 하다. 과장하다: *The reports tend to magnify the risks involved.* 그 기사는 관련된 위험을 과장하는 경향이 있다. – **magnification** /ˌmæɡnəfə'keɪʃən/ n [C, U]

magnifying glass /'.... ,./ n a round piece of glass with a handle, that magnifies (MAGNIFY) things when you look through it ∥이것을 통해 보면 사물을 확대되는, 손잡이가 달린 둥근 유리 조각. 확대경. 돋보기

mag·ni·tude /'mæɡnə,tud/ n [U] 1 how large or important something is ∥어떤 것이 얼마나 크거나 중요한지의 정도. 중대함. 방대함: *I hadn't realized the magnitude of the problem.* 나는 그 문제의 중대성을 깨닫지 못했다. 2 TECHNICAL how strong an EARTHQUAKE is, or how bright a star is ∥지진이 얼마나 강한지 또는 별이 얼마나 밝은지의 정도. 진도. 광도

mag·no·lia /mæɡ'noʊlyə/ n a tree with large white, yellow, pink, or purple sweet-smelling flowers ∥흰[노란, 분홍, 자주]색의 향긋한 냄새가 나는 큰 꽃이 피는 교목. 목련

mag·pie /'mæɡpaɪ/ n a wild bird with black and white feathers and a loud cry ∥검은색과 흰색 깃털이 나 있고 울음소리가 큰 야생의 새. 까치

ma·hog·a·ny /mə'hɑɡəni/ n [C, U] a tropical American tree, or the hard dark wood of this tree ∥열대 미국산 나무, 또는 이 나무의 단단하고 짙은 목재. 마호가니

maid /meɪd/ n a female servant, especially in a large house ∥특히 큰 집에서의 여자 하인. 하녀. 식모

maid·en¹ /'meɪdn/, **maid** n LITERARY a young woman or girl who is not married ∥결혼하지 않은 젊은 여자나 소녀. 아가씨. 처녀

maiden² adj **maiden flight/voyage** the

first trip that a plane or ship makes ‖ 비행기나 배가 하는 첫 번째 여행. 처녀 비행/항해

maiden name /ˌ.. ˈ./ *n* the family name that a woman had before she got married and began using her husband's name ‖ 여성이 결혼해서 남성의 성을 사용하기 시작하기 전에 가졌던 성(姓). 결혼 전의 성.

maid of hon·or /ˌ. . ˈ../ *n* the main BRIDESMAID in a wedding ‖ 결혼식에서 주된 신부 들러리

mail¹ /meɪl/ *n* **1 the mail** the system of collecting and delivering letters, packages etc. ‖ 편지·소포 등을 수집하고 배달하는 체계. 우편 (제도): *I just put the letter in the mail.* 나는 방금 편지를 우편으로 부쳤다. / *What time does the mail come?* 몇 시에 우편이 옵니까? **2** [U] the letters, packages etc., that are delivered to a particular person or at a particular time ‖ 특정한 사람에게 또는 특정한 시간에 배달되는 편지·소포 등. 우편물: *They sent his mail to the wrong address.* 그들은 그의 우편물을 잘못된 주소로 보냈다. —see also AIRMAIL

mail² *v* [T] to send a letter, package etc. to someone ‖ 남에게 편지·소포 등을 보내다. 우송하다. 우편으로 보내다: *I'll mail it to you tomorrow.* 내일 너에게 그것을 우편으로 보낼게.

mail·box /ˈmeɪlbɑks/ *n* **1** a box outside your house or in a POST OFFICE where your letters are delivered or collected ‖ 편지가 배달되거나 수집되는, 옥외 또는 우체국 내에 있는 상자. 우편함 —see picture on page 945 **2** a special box in the street or at a POST OFFICE where you mail letters ‖ 거리나 우체국에 있는 편지를 부치는 특별한 통. 우체통

mail·ing /ˈmeɪlɪŋ/ *n* [C, U] the act of sending a large number of letters, advertisements etc. at the same time, or the total number of letters that you send ‖ 동시에 막대한 수의 편지·광고물 등을 부치는 행위, 또는 부치는 편지의 총수. 우송(량)

mail·ing list /ˈ.. ˌ./ *n* a list of people's names and addresses that a company keeps in order to send information or advertisements to them ‖ 정보나 광고물을 보내기 위해서 회사가 보유하는 사람들의 이름과 주소 목록. 이메일 주소록. 우송용 회원 명부

mail·man /ˈmeɪlmæn, -mən/ *n* a man who delivers mail to people's houses ‖ 사람들의 집에 우편물을 배달하는 사람. 우편집배원

mail or·der /ˈ. ˌ../ *n* [U] a method of selling in which you buy goods from a company that sends them by mail ‖ 회사에서 우편으로 보내는 상품을 사는 판매 방법. 통신 판매: *a mail order catalog* 통신 판매용 카탈로그

maim /meɪm/ *v* [T] to wound or injure someone very seriously and often permanently ‖ 남을 매우 심하게·종종 영구적으로 상처를 입히거나 다치게 하다. 중상을 입히다. 불구로 만들다: *The accident maimed her for life.* 그 사고로 그녀는 평생 불구가 되었다.

main¹ /meɪn/ *adj* **1** bigger or more important than all other things, ideas etc. of the same kind ‖ 같은 종류 중에서 다른 모든 물건·생각 등보다 더 크거나 더 중요한. 주요한. 주된: *the main meal of the day* 오늘의 주식 / *the main points of his speech* 그의 연설의 주요 논점 **2 the main thing** SPOKEN used in order to say what the most important thing is in a situation ‖ 어떤 상황에서 가장 중요한 것이 무엇인지를 말하는 데에 쓰여. 중요한 것. 주된 점: *As long as you're not hurt, that's the main thing.* 어쨌든 네가 다치지 않은 것이 중요하다.

main² *n* a large pipe carrying water or gas that is connected to people's houses by smaller pipes ‖ 더 작은 관으로 사람들의 집에 연결되어 물이나 가스를 나르는 커다란 관. 본관: *a broken water/gas main* 부서진 수도[가스] 본관

main·frame /ˈmeɪnfreɪm/ *n* a large computer that can work very fast and that a lot of people can use at the same time ‖ 매우 빠르게 일할 수 있으며 동시에 많은 사람들이 사용할 수 있는 커다란 컴퓨터. 본체. 대형 법용 컴퓨터

main·land /ˈmeɪnlænd, -lənd/ *n* **the mainland** the main area of land that forms a country, as compared to islands near it that are also part of that country ‖ 인접하여 역시 한 나라의 일부가 되는 섬에 비교되는 것으로, 한 국가를 형성하는 주요 영토. (연안의 섬·반도에 대하여) 본토. 대륙

main·ly /ˈmeɪnli/ *adv* **1** used in order to show that something is true of most members of a group ‖ 한 집단의 대부분의 구성원들에게는 어떤 것이 사실이라는 것을 나타내는 데에 쓰여. 대개는. 대부분은: *The workforce mainly consists of men.* 인력은 대부분 남자들로 구성되어 있다. **2** used in order to show that something is generally true ‖ 어떤 것이 일반적으로 사실이라는 것을 나타내는 데에 쓰여. 주로: *I bought the answering* *machine mainly for business reasons.* 나는 주로 사업상의 이유로 자동 응답기를 샀다. ✗DON'T SAY "Mainly I bought the answering machine..."✗"Mainly I bought the answering machine... "이라고는 하지 않는다.

main·stay /ˈmeɪnsteɪ/ *n* the most important part of something that makes it possible for it to work correctly or to continue to exist ‖ 어떤 것이 제대로 작동하거나 계속 존재하게 할 수 있도록 하는 어떤 것의 가장 중요한 부분. 대들보: *Farming is still the mainstay of our country's economy.* 농업은 여전히 우리 나라 경제의 대들보이다.

main·stream /ˈmeɪnstrim/ *n* **the mainstream** the beliefs and opinions that represent the most usual way of thinking about or doing something, or the people who have these beliefs and opinions ‖ 어떤 일에 대한 가장 통상적인 사고 방식이나 행동 양식을 대표하는 신념과 견해, 또는 이러한 신념과 견해를 가지고 있는 사람들. 주류. 대세: *His beliefs are very much those of the mainstream.* 그의 신념은 주류를 이루는 신념 바로 그것들에 다름 아니다. — **mainstream** *adj*

main·tain /meɪnˈteɪn/ *v* [T] **1** to make something continue in the same way or at the same standard as before ‖ 어떤 것을 이전과 같은 방식이나 같은 기준으로 계속하게 하다. 유지[지속]하다: *We have always maintained good relations with our customers.* 우리는 항상 고객들과 좋은 관계를 유지해 오고 있다. **2** to keep something in good condition by taking care of it ‖ 어떤 것을 돌보아서 좋은 상태로 유지하다. 정비하다: *It costs a lot of money to maintain a big house.* 큰 집을 유지하는 데는 많은 돈이 든다. **3** to strongly express an opinion or attitude ‖ 의견이나 태도를 강하게 표현하다. 주장하다. 견지하다: *I've always maintained that any changes in the law will hurt the poor more than the rich.* 법이 조금이라도 바뀌면 부자보다는 빈자가 더 어려울 것이라고 나는 항상 주장해 왔다 **4** to provide someone with the things he, she, or it needs, such as money or food ‖ 돈이나 음식 등의 필요한 것을 어떤 사람에게 제공하다. 부양하다. 뒷바라지하다: *He's too poor to maintain a wife and children.* 그는 너무나 가난해서 아내와 자식들을 부양할 수 없다.

main·te·nance /ˈmeɪntˀn-əns/ *n* [U] the work that is necessary to keep something in good condition ‖ 어떤 것을 좋은 상태로 유지하기 위해 필요한 작업.

보수. 관리: *car maintenance* 자동차 정비

ma·jes·tic /məˈdʒɛstɪk/ *adj* looking very big and impressive ‖ 아주 크고 인상적으로 보이는. 위엄 있는. 존엄한: *a majestic view of the lake* 호수의 장엄한 경치 – **majestically** *adv*

maj·es·ty /ˈmædʒəsti/ *n* **1** [U] the quality of being impressive and beautiful ‖ 인상적이며 아름다운 성질. 위엄. 존엄함: *the majesty of the Great Pyramids* 대피라미드의 웅장함 **2 Your/Her/His Majesty** used when talking to or about a king or queen ‖ 왕이나 여왕에게 말하거나 그들에 대해 말할 때 쓰여. 폐하

ma·jor¹ /ˈmeɪdʒɚ/ *adj* very large or important, especially when compared to other things or people of a similar kind ‖ 특히 비슷한 종류의 다른 사물이나 사람들과 비교할 때 매우 크거나 중요한. 중요[주요]한. 큰[많은] 쪽의: *The car needs major repairs.* 그 차는 대폭적인 수리가 필요하다. / *a major operation* 대수술 ✗DON'T SAY "major than." SAY "more important than" or "bigger than."✗ "major than"이라고는 하지 않고 "more important than"이나 "bigger than"이라고 한다. —compare MINOR¹ **1**

ma·jor² *n* **1** the main subject that you study at a college or university ‖ 단과 대학이나 종합 대학에서 공부하는 주요 과목. 전공 (과목): *His major is history.* 그의 전공은 역사이다. —compare MINOR² **2** also **Major** an officer who has a middle rank in the Army, Air Force, or Marines ‖ 육군[공군, 해병대]에서 중간 지위를 가진 장교. 소령

ma·jor³ *v*

major in sth *phr v* [T] to study something as your main subject at a college or university ‖ 단과 대학이나 종합 대학에서 주요 과목으로서 무엇을 공부하다. 전공하다: *I'm majoring in biology.* 난 생물학을 전공하고 있어.

ma·jor·i·ty¹ /məˈdʒɔrəti, -ˈdʒɑr-/ *n* **1** [singular] most of the people or things in a particular group ‖ 특정한 집단 내의 대부분의 사람들이나 사물. 대부분. 대다수: *The majority of Americans do not want advertisements to be shown before a movie.* 대다수의 미국인들은 본영화 전에 상영되는 광고를 원하지 않는다. **2** [C usually singular] the difference between the number of votes gained by the winning party or person in an election and the number gained by other parties or people ‖ 선거에서 승리한 당이나 사람

이 얻은 득표수와 다른 당이나 사람들이 얻은 득표수 사이의 차이. 득표차: *a majority of 500 votes* 500표의 차이 — compare MINORITY²

majority² *adj* happening as a result of the decision of most members of a group ‖ 한 집단 구성원들의 대부분이 결정한 결과로서 발생하는. 대다수의: *a majority decision/ruling* 대다수의 결정 [판정]

major-league /'.. ,./ *adj* INFORMAL important or having a lot of power ‖ 중요하거나 많은 힘을 가지고 있는. 초일류의. 최고의: *a major-league player in Michigan politics* 미시간 정계에서 영향력 있는 정치인

Major Leagues /,.. './, **Majors** *n* [plural] the group of teams that make up the highest level of American professional baseball ‖ 미국 프로 야구에서 최상위 수준을 형성하는 팀들의 집단. 메이저 리그

ma·jor·ly /'meɪdʒɚli/ *adv* SPOKEN NONSTANDARD very or extremely ‖ 매우, 극도로. 몹시: *My parents weren't majorly upset about the dent in the car.* 부모님은 차가 찌그러진 것에 대해서 그렇게 화내지는 않으셨다.

make¹ /meɪk/ *v* **made, made, making**
1 ▶PRODUCE STH 어떤 것을 생산하다◀ [T] to produce something by working or doing something ‖ 어떤 것을 작동시키거나 함으로써 어떤 것을 생산하다. 만들다. 제작하다: *I'll make the cake, and you make dinner.* 난 케이크를 만들 테니, 넌 저녁밥을 지어라. / *Grandma made dolls for us.* 할머니는 우리에게 인형을 만들어 주셨다. / *The toy says "Made in Taiwan" on it.* 장난감에는 "대만산"이라고 쓰여 있다. / *The scissors slipped, and she made a hole in the cloth.* 가위가 미끄러져 그녀는 천에 구멍을 냈다.
2 ▶DO STH 어떤 일을 하다◀ [T] used before some nouns to show that someone does the action of the noun ‖ 일부 명사 앞에 쓰여 어떤 사람이 그 명사가 의미하는 행동을 함을 나타내는 데 쓰여. 하다. 행동하다: *They made a mistake on the electricity bill.* 그들은 전기 요금을 잘못 청구했다. / *Roger made a good suggestion.* 로저는 좋은 제안을 했다. / *Do you want to make an appointment with the doctor?* 진료 예약을 원합니까?
3 ▶CAUSE 어떤 일을 일으키다◀ [T] to cause a particular state or situation to happen ‖ 특정한 상태나 상황이 발생하게 하다. …을 일으키다. 야기시키다:

Everything he says makes her mad. 그가 하는 모든 말은 그녀를 화나게 한다. / *That button makes the machine stop.* 그 버튼이 기계를 멈추게 한다. / *Look at the mess you made!* 네가 어질러 놓은 것 좀 봐라! / *What made you decide to become a lawyer?* 어떻게 해서 변호사가 될 결심을 하게 되었어요? ✗DON'T SAY "What made you to decide to become a lawyer?"✗ "What made you to decide to become a lawyer?"라고는 하지 않는다.
4 ▶FORCE 억지로 시키다◀ [T] to force someone to do something ‖ 남에게 어떤 일을 하도록 억지로 시키다. …을 시키다 [하게 하다]: *I wasn't hungry, but I made myself eat something.* 나는 배고프지 않았지만 억지로 뭔가를 먹었다. / *The police made them stand up against the wall.* 경찰은 그들을 벽에 붙여 세웠다.
5 ▶EARN MONEY 돈을 벌다◀ [T] to earn or get money ‖ 돈을 벌거나 얻다: *Irene makes about $60,000 a year.* 아이린은 일년에 6만 달러 정도를 번다. / *You can make a lot of money working with computers.* 컴퓨터로 일하면 많은 돈을 벌 수 있다.
6 ▶NUMBER 수◀ [linking verb] to be a particular number or amount when added together ‖ 함께 더했을 때 특정한 수나 양이 되다. (합계가) …이 되다: *2 and 2 make 4.* 2 더하기 2는 4이다. / *If you include us, that makes eight people for dinner.* 우리를 포함하면 저녁 식사에는 총 8명이 된다.
7 make a phone call to talk to someone using the telephone ‖ 전화를 이용해 어떤 사람에게 말하다. 전화를 걸다
8 make time to leave enough time to do something ‖ 어떤 일을 하려고 충분한 시간을 남기다. 시간을 내다: *Don't forget to make time to visit Grandpa this week.* 이번 주에 할아버지께 방문할 시간 내는 것 잊지 마라.
9 ▶BE SUITABLE 알맞다◀ [linking verb] to have the qualities that are necessary for a particular job, use, or purpose ‖ 특정한 일[사용, 목적]에 필요한 특성을 지니다. …에 적합하다. (결국) …이 되다: *John will make a good father.* 존은 좋은 아버지가 될 것이다. / *Her idea would make a good book.* 그녀의 아이디어는 좋은 책이 될 것이다.
10 make believe to pretend that something is true, especially as a game ‖ 특히 놀이로서 어떤 것이 사실인 체하다. …흉내를 내다: *The kids make believe they're cowboys.* 아이들은 카우보이인 척 한다.

11 make it a) to arrive somewhere ‖ 어딘가에 도착하다. 시간에 대다: *We made it to the station just as the bus was leaving.* 버스가 막 떠나려고 할 때 우리는 역에 간신히 도착했다. **b)** to be able to go to an event, meeting etc. ‖ 행사·모임 등에 갈 수 있다. 참석하다: *I'm sorry I can't make it to your play.* 네 경기에 갈 수 없어서 미안해. **c)** to be successful in a particular business or activity ‖ 특정한 사업이나 활동에서 성공적이다. 성공하다: *He's made it big* (=was very successful) *in Hollywood.* 그는 할리우드에서 크게 성공했다. **d)** to live after a serious illness or injury, or to deal with a very difficult situation ‖ 심각한 병이나 부상을 겪은 후에 살다, 또는 아주 어려운 상황을 처리하다. 잘해내다: *Mom made it through the operation all right.* 엄마는 수술을 무사히 잘 견디셨다.

12 make a difference to cause a change, especially one that improves a situation ‖ 특히 상황을 개선시키는 변화를 일으키다. 변화를 가져오다: *The tax cuts will make a big difference in my salary.* 세금 감면으로 내 월급에도 큰 변화가 생길 것이다.

13 make the bed to pull the sheets and BLANKETs over a bed to make it look neat when you are not sleeping in it ‖ 자지 않을 때 말끔하게 보이게 침대 위의 침대보나 담요를 정리하다. 이불을 개다

14 that makes two of us SPOKEN used in order to say that you feel the same way that someone else does ‖ 다른 사람이 느끼는 것과 똑같이 느낀다고 말하는 데에 쓰여. 나도 마찬가지다: *"I'm so tired!" "Yeah, that makes two of us."* "난 정말 피곤해!" "그래, 나도 마찬가지야."

15 make or break to cause either great success or failure ‖ 큰 성공 아니면 실패를 초래하다. 운명[성패]을 좌우하다: *The first year can make or break a new business.* 새 사업은 첫 해가 성패를 좌우할 수 있다.

16 make do to manage to do something using the things you already have, even though they are not exactly what you want ‖ 이미 가지고 있는 것이 정확히 원하는 것은 아닐지라도 그것들을 이용해 어떤 일을 겨우 해나가다. 그럭저럭 견디다[버티다]: *We'll have to make do with these old clothes.* 우리는 이 낡은 옷으로 어떻게든 버텨야만 해. —see also **be made of** (MADE²), **make sure** (SURE¹), **make a (big) difference/make all the difference** (DIFFERENCE), **make love** (LOVE²) **make sense** (SENSE¹), **make the**

best of sth (BEST³), **make/be friends (with)** (FRIEND), **make up your mind** (MIND¹)

make for sth *phr v* [T] to have a particular result or effect ‖ 특정한 결과나 효과를 가지다. 기여하다. 조장하다: *His laziness makes for a lot of work for the rest of us.* 그의 게으름 때문에 나머지 우리들이 더 많은 일을 하게 된다. —see also **be made for** (MADE²)

make sth **of** sb/sth *phr v* [T] **1** to have a particular opinion about someone or something, or a particular way of understanding something ‖ 사람이나 사물에 대한 특정한 의견, 또는 어떤 것을 이해하는 특정한 방식을 가지다. …을 …이라고 생각하다: *What do you make of* (=what is your opinion of) *Robert's new idea?* 로버트의 새로운 아이디어를 어떻게 생각해요? **2 make the most of** to use an opportunity in a way that gives you as much advantage as possible ‖ 가능한 한 많은 이익을 얻는 방식으로 기회를 이용하다. …을 최대한 활용하다: *I want to make the most of the time I have left in Europe.* 나는 유럽에서 떠나 있는 시간을 최대한 활용하고 싶다. **3 make much of** to treat a situation or person as if he, she, or it is extremely important ‖ 상황이나 사람을 지극히 중요한 것처럼 다루다. …을 중(요)시하다: *He doesn't like us to make too much of his birthday.* 그는 우리가 자기 생일에 대해 너무 수선떠는 것을 좋아하지 않는다. —see also **make a fool of yourself** (FOOL¹)

make off with sth *phr v* [T] to steal something ‖ 어떤 것을 훔치다. …을 갖고 달아나다: *They made off with our TV.* 그들은 우리의 TV를 훔쳐서 달아났다.

make out *phr v* **1** [T **make** sth ↔ **out**] to be able to hear, see, or understand something ‖ 어떤 것을 보거나 듣거나 이해할 수 있다. 분간하다. 판별[판독]하다: *I can't make out what the sign says.* 나는 그 기호가 무슨 의미인지 이해할 수가 없다. **2 make a check out to sb** to write a check so that the money is paid to a particular person, company, store etc. ‖ 특정한 사람·회사·상점 등에 돈이 지불되도록 수표를 끊다. … 앞으로 수표를 발행하다: *Make the check out to Ms. Linda Wright.* 린다 라이트 씨 앞으로 수표를 발행하세요. **3 make out (that)** INFORMAL to say that something is true when it is not ‖ 어떤 일이 사실이 아닐 때 사실이라고 말하다. …인 듯이 말하다. (…이라고) 주장하다: *Brian was making out he had won all the prizes.* 브라이언

M

은 자신이 모든 상을 다 탄 것처럼 말하고 있었다. **4 How did sb make out...?**SPOKEN used in order to ask if someone did something well ‖ 남이 어떤 일을 잘 했는지 묻는 데에 쓰여. …이 … 을 어떻게 해냈어?: *"How did you make out in the interview?" "I think it went well."* "면접은 잘 봤어?" "잘 본 것 같아." **5** [I] SPOKEN to kiss and touch someone in a sexual way ‖ 성적으로 어떤 사람에게 입맞춤을 하고 만지다. 애무하다 **6 make out like a bandit** SPOKEN to get a lot of money or gifts, win a lot etc. ‖ 많은 돈이나 선물을 얻거나 당첨 등이 되다. 큰돈을 벌다: *My nephew makes out like a bandit every Christmas.* 내 조카는 성탄절마다 많은 선물을 받는다.

make sth ↔ **over** *phr v* [T] to change something ‖ 어떤 것을 고치다. 고쳐 만들다: *The basement has been made over into a playroom.* 지하실은 놀이방으로 개조되었다.

make up *phr v* **1** [T **make** sth ↔ **up**] to invent the words of a poem or story or the music for a song ‖ 시[이야기, 노래 가사]를 만들어 내다. 창작하다: *"What are you singing?" "I don't know, I just made it up."* "무슨 노래를 부르고 있니?" "나도 몰라. 내가 그냥 만들었어." **2** [T **make** sth ↔ **up**] to invent a story, explanation etc. in order to deceive someone ‖ 남을 속이려고 이야기·설명 등을 만들어 내다. 지어내다. 날조하다: *Ron made up an excuse so his mother wouldn't be mad.* 론이 핑계를 꾸며내서 그의 어머니는 화를 내지 않으셨다. **3** [T **make up** sth] to combine together to form a substance, group, system etc. ‖ 물질·집단·체계 등을 형성하려고 함께 결합하다. 구성[형성]하다: *Chapter 5 is about the rocks and minerals that make up the earth's outer layer.* 5장은 지구의 지각을 구성하는 암석과 광물질에 대해 다룬다. / *Women make up 60% of our employees.* 여성이 우리 직원의 60%를 차지한다. **4** [T **make** sth ↔ **up**] to work at times when you do not usually work, because you have not done enough work at some other time ‖ 다른 때에 충분히 일을 하지 않아서 보통 일이 없을 때에 일하다. 보충하다: *I have to leave early, but I'll make up the time/work tomorrow.* 나는 일찍 떠나야 하지만 내일 그 시간[일]을 보충할 것이다. **5 make it up to sb** to do something good for someone because you feel responsible for something bad that happened to

him/her ‖ 남에게 발생한 나쁜 일에 책임을 느껴서 그 사람에게 좋은 일을 하다. 보상하다: *I'm sorry I forgot! I promise I'll make it up to you.* 잊어서 미안해! 나중에 정말로 보상해 줄게. **6** [I] to become friends with someone again, after you have had an argument ‖ 다투고 난 후에 다시 친구가 되다. 화해하다: *Have you two made up?* 너희 둘 화해했니?

make up for sth *phr v* [T] **1** to make a bad situation or event seem better ‖ 나쁜 상황이나 사건을 더 좋아 보이게 하다. 만회하다: *I bought her flowers to try to make up for the nasty things I said.* 내가 한 불쾌한 말을 만회할 요량으로 나는 그녀에게 꽃을 사주었다. **2** to have so much of one quality that it does not matter that you do not have others ‖ 다른 자질을 가지고 있지 않는 것이 문제가 되지 않을 정도로 하나의 자질을 아주 많이 가지고 있다. 메우다. 벌충[보상]하다: *Jay lacks experience, but he makes up for it with hard work.* 제이는 경험이 부족하지만 열심히 일해서 그것을 벌충한다. **3 make up for lost time** to do something very quickly because you started too late or something made you work too slowly ‖ 어떤 일을 늦게 시작했거나 어떤 이유로 일을 질질 끌었기 때문에 (그것을 보충하기 위해) 매우 빨리 어떤 일을 하다. 지체된 시간을 만회[벌충]하다: *I've been reading a lot at night to make up for lost time.* 지체된 시간을 만회하기 위해 난 밤에 책을 많이 읽어 오고 있었다.

USAGE NOTE make and do

Although there are no fixed rules about when to use **make** and when to use **do**, we tend to use **make** to talk about producing things, and **do** to talk about actions: *Who made your dress? / We need to make plans for our trip. / I'll make you a drink. / Could you do me a favor? / Thanks for all you've done to help. / It's my turn to do the dishes.*
make를 사용할 때와 **do**를 사용할 때에 관한 고정된 규칙은 없지만, 사물을 생산하는 것에 대해서 말할 때는 **make**를, 동작에 대해서 말할 때는 **do**를 사용하는 경향이 있다: 누가 네 드레스를 만들었니? / 우리는 여행 계획을 세울 필요가 있다. / 내가 마실 것 한 잔 만들어 줄게. / 부탁 하나 들어 줄래요? / 도와주셔서 정말 감사합니다. / 이번엔 내가 설거지할 차례다.

make² *n* **1** a product made by a particular company ‖ 특정한 회사가 만든 제품. …제. 브랜드: *"What make is your car?" "It's a Chevy."* "네 차는 어느 회사 차종이니?" "시보레야." **2 be on the make** DISAPPROVING to be trying hard to get something such as money or sex ‖ 돈이나 섹스 등을 얻기 위해 열심히 노력하다. 성공[출세, 돈벌이] 등에 열을 올리다. 섹스의 상대를 찾고 있다

make-be·lieve /ˌ. .ˈ.ˌ./ *n* [U] a state of imagining or pretending that something is real ‖ 어떤 것이 실제라고 상상하거나 가장하는 상태. 지어내기. 가장. 거짓: *Don't be afraid, honey – the monster is only make-believe* 애야, 무서워할 것 없어. 괴물은 가공의 것에 불과해.

mak·er /ˈmeɪkɚ/ *n* **1** a person or company that makes something or does something ‖ 어떤 것을 만들거나 어떤 일을 하는 사람이나 회사. 제작자. 제조업체: *The maker of the drug is studying new ways to use it.* 그 약의 제조업체는 새로운 사용 방법을 연구하고 있다. / *a dress maker* 드레스 제작자 **2 decision maker/peace maker etc.** someone who is good at or responsible for making decisions, stopping arguments etc. ‖ 결정내리기·분쟁 해소 등을 잘하거나 책임을 지고 있는 사람. 의사 결정권자 /중재자

make·shift /ˈmeɪkˌʃɪft/ *adj* made for temporary use when you need something and there is nothing better available ‖ 어떤 것이 필요한 데 거기에 이용할 만한 더 나은 것이 전혀 없을 때 임시로 사용하기 위해 만든. 임시변통의: *a makeshift table made from boxes* 상자로 만든 임시변통용 탁자

make·up /ˈmeɪk-ʌp/ *n* **1** [U] substances such as powder, creams, and lipstick that some people, usually women or actors, put on their faces ‖ 보통 여자나 배우들이 얼굴에 바르는 분·크림·립스틱 등의 물질. 화장품: *I waited for Ginny to put on her makeup.* 나는 지니가 화장하는 것을 기다렸다. **2** all the parts, members, or qualities that make up something ‖ 어떤 것을 이루는 모든 부분[구성원, 특성]. 구성. 구조: *We haven't yet been told what the makeup of the new government will be.* (=who the members will be) 새 정부의 구성이 어떻게 될지 우리는 아직 들은 바가 없다.

mak·ing /ˈmeɪkɪŋ/ *n* **1** the process or business of making something ‖ 어떤 것을 만드는 과정이나 일. 제조. 제작: *The making of the movie took four years.* 그 영화 제작은 4년이 걸렸다. / *the art of rug making* 양탄자 제작 기술 **2 in the making** in the process of being made or produced ‖ 만들어지거나 생산되는 과정에 있는. 제작[진행] 중인: *The deal was 11 months in the making.* 그 거래는 11개월째 진행 중에 있었다.

mak·ings /ˈmeɪkɪŋz/ *n* [plural] **have the makings of** to have the qualities or skills needed to become a particular type of person or thing ‖ 특정한 유형의 사람이나 사물이 되기 위해 필요한 특성이나 기술을 가지고 있다. …이 될 소질[능력, 자질]이 있다: *Sandy has the makings of a good doctor.* 샌디는 좋은 의사가 될 소질이 있다.

mal·a·dy /ˈmælədi/ *n* FORMAL **1** an illness ‖ 병 **2** something that is wrong with a system or organization ‖ 체제나 조직에서 잘못된 것. 병폐. 악폐

mal·aise /mæˈleɪz/ *n* [U] a feeling of anxiety, and a lack of confidence and satisfaction ‖ 불안감, 그리고 자신감과 만족감의 부족. 초조. 불쾌감

ma·lar·i·a /məˈlɛriə/ *n* [U] a disease common in hot countries that is caused by the bite of an infected MOSQUITO ‖ 감염된 모기에 물려서 발생하는, 열대 국가에서 흔한 질병. 말라리아 **– malarial** *adj*

male /meɪl/ *adj* **1** belonging to the sex that cannot have babies ‖ 아이를 가질 수 없는 성(性)에 속하는. 남성[남자]의. 수컷의: *a male lion* 숫사자 **2** typical of this sex ‖ 남성[남자]의 전형적인. 남성적인. 남자다운: *a male voice* 남성적인 목소리 **– male** *n* —see usage note at MASCULINE

male chau·vin·ist /ˌmeɪl ˈʃoʊvənɪst/, **male chauvinist pig** /ˌ. ˌ.... ˈ./ *n* a man who believes that men are better than women ‖ 남자가 여자보다 더 우월하다고 믿는 남자. 남성 우월[중심]주의자 **– male chauvinism** *n* [U]

ma·lev·o·lent /məˈlɛvələnt/ *adj* FORMAL showing a desire to harm other people ‖ 다른 사람들을 해치고 싶어하는 바람을 나타내는. 악의 있는. 심술궂은 **– malevolence** *n* [U]

mal·func·tion /mælˈfʌŋkʃən/ *n* a fault in the way a machine works ‖ 기계 작동 방식에서의 잘못. 기능 장애. 오작동: *a malfunction in the computer system* 컴퓨터 시스템의 오작동 **– malfunction** *v* [I]

mal·ice /ˈmælɪs/ *n* [U] the desire to harm or upset someone ‖ 남을 해치거나 화나게 하려는 욕구. 악의. 적의: *Corran wasn't acting out of malice.* (=did not desire to harm someone) 코란은 악의에서 그런 것은 아니었다.

M

ma·li·cious /məˈlɪʃəs/ *adj* showing a desire to harm or upset someone ‖ 남을 해치거나 화나게 하려는 욕구를 나타내는. 악의적인. 심술궂은: *malicious gossip* 험담 – **maliciously** *adv*

ma·lign /məˈlaɪn/ *v* [T] FORMAL to say or write unpleasant and untrue things about someone ‖ 남에 대해 불쾌하고 사실이 아닌 것을 말하거나 쓰다. 중상[비방]하다. 헐뜯다: *He's been much maligned by the press.* 언론은 그를 심하게 비방했다.

ma·lig·nant /məˈlɪɡnənt/ *adj* **1** TECHNICAL a malignant TUMOR (=a group of growing cells) contains CANCER and may kill someone ‖ 종양이 암으로 이루어져서 사람을 죽일 수도 있는. 악성인 **2** FORMAL showing hatred and a strong desire to harm someone ‖ 증오와 남을 해치려는 강한 욕구를 나타내는. 악의[적의]에 찬: *a malignant grin* 악의에 찬 조소 – **malignancy** *n* [U] —compare BENIGN

mall /mɔl/ *n* a very large building with a lot of stores in it ‖ 많은 상점들이 입점해 있는 아주 큰 건물. 쇼핑몰

mal·lard /ˈmælərd/ *n* a type of common wild duck ‖ 흔한 야생 오리의 일종. 청둥오리

mal·le·a·ble /ˈmæliəbəl/ *adj* **1** something that is malleable is easy to press, pull, or bend into a new shape ‖ 어떤 것이 압착하거나 늘리거나 구부려서 새로운 형태로 만들기 쉬운. 두드려 펼 수 있는. 조형[변형]이 쉬운: *a malleable metal* 변형이 쉬운 금속 **2** someone who is malleable is easily influenced or changed by people ‖ 사람이 다른 사람들에 의해 쉽사리 영향을 받거나 변하는. 줏대가 없는. 유순한

mal·let /ˈmælɪt/ *n* a wooden hammer ‖ 나무 망치

mal·nour·ished /ˌmælˈnɜʊʃt, -ˈnʌrɪʃt/ *adj* ill or weak because of not eating enough food, or because of not eating good food ‖ 충분한 음식을 먹지 않았거나 좋은 음식을 먹지 않아서 아프거나 허약한. 영양실조의

mal·nu·tri·tion /ˌmælnuˈtrɪʃən/ *n* [U] illness or weakness as a result of being MALNOURISHED ‖ 영양실조 상태의 결과로서의 질병이나 허약함. 영양실조

mal·prac·tice /ˌmælˈpræktɪs/ *n* [C, U] the act of failing to do a professional duty, or of making a mistake while doing it ‖ 전문적인 임무를 수행하는 데 실패하는 것이나 그것을 하면서 실수를 하는 행위. 직무상의 과실

malt /mɔlt/ *n* **1** [U] grain, usually BARLEY, that is used for making beer, WHISKEY etc. ‖ 맥주·위스키 등을 만드는 데 사용하는 곡물로서 보통 보리. 엿기름. 맥아 **2** a drink made from milk, malt, ICE CREAM, and something such as chocolate ‖ 우유·엿기름·아이스크림·초콜릿 등의 것으로 만든 마실 것. 맥아주

malt·ed /ˈmɔltɪd/, **malted milk** /ˌ..ˈ./ *n* ⇨ MALT

mal·treat /mælˈtrit/ *v* [T] FORMAL to treat an animal or person cruelly ‖ 동물이나 사람을 잔인하게 다루다. 학대[혹사]하다 – **maltreatment** *n* [U]

ma·ma /ˈmɑmə/ *n* INFORMAL ⇨ MOTHER¹

ma·ma's boy /ˈ.. ˌ./ *n* INFORMAL a boy or man that people think is weak because his mother is too protective of him ‖ 어머니가 과보호를 해서 사람들이 약하다고 생각하는 소년이나 남자. 마마보이

mam·mal /ˈmæməl/ *n* the group of animals including humans that drink milk from their mother's breasts when they are young ‖ 어릴 때 어머니나 어미의 유방에서 젖을 먹는, 사람을 포함한 동물의 집단. 포유동물

mam·moth /ˈmæməθ/ *adj* very large ‖ 아주 큰. 거대한: *a mammoth job* 막대한 일

man¹ /mæn/ *n, plural* **men**
1 ▶MALE 남성◀ an adult male human ‖ 성인 남자: *What did the man look like?* 그 남자 어떻게 생겼었니? / *We met a Polish man and his wife.* 우리는 한 폴란드 남자와 그의 아내를 만났다.
2 ▶ALL PEOPLE 모든 사람들◀ [U] all people, both male and female, considered as a group ‖ 한 집단으로 간주되는 남성과 여성 양쪽의 모든 사람들. 사람. 인간: *one of the worst disasters in the history of man* 인간의 역사에서 최악의 재난 중의 하나 / *All men must die.* 모든 인간은 죽기 마련이다. ✗DON'T SAY "all the men."✗ "all the men"이라고는 하지 않는다.
3 ▶SOLDIER/EMPLOYEE 병사/고용인◀ [C usually plural] a man who works for an employer such as a builder, or who has a low rank in the Army, Navy etc. ‖ 건축업자 등의 고용주를 위해 일하는 사람, 또는 육군·해군 등에서 낮은 계급을 가진 사람. 직원. 아랫사람. 부하. 병사: *Call the men to meet here at 11:00 for an important announcement.* 중요한 발표가 있으니 직원들을 11시에 이곳에 모이도록

전화해라.

4 ▶GAMES 놀이◀ one of the pieces you use in a game such as CHESS ‖ 체스 등의 놀이에서 사용하는 말 중의 하나. 말

5 ▶WHAT SB LIKES 사람이 좋아하는 것◀ used in order to say that a man likes, or likes doing, a particular thing ‖ 남자가 특정한 것을 좋아하거나 특정한 일하기를 좋아한다고 말하는 데에 쓰여. …하는 남자. …광: *a gambling man* 도박꾼 / *He's a meat and potatoes man.* (=likes eating food like meat and potatoes) 그는 고기와 감자라면 사족을 못 쓴다.

6 the man in the street the average person, who represents the general opinion of many people ‖ 많은 사람들의 일반적인 의견을 대표하는 평균적인 사람. 보통 사람. 일반 시민: *What the man in the street wants is a reduction in taxes.* 일반 사람들이 원하는 것은 세금 인하이다.

7 be/become man and wife FORMAL to be or become married ‖ 결혼하다

8 SPOKEN used in order to speak to someone, especially an adult male ‖ 특히 성인 남성에게 말하는 데에 쓰여. 이봐. 자네!: *Hey, man! How're you doing?* 어이, 자네? 요즘 어떻게 지내나?

9 my man SPOKEN said by some men when talking to a male friend ‖ 일부 남자들이 남성 친구에게 말할 때 쓰여. 친구야

USAGE NOTE man, mankind, people, humankind

Man can mean "people in general": *Man has always tried to understand the stars.* **Mankind** means "all people, considered as a group": *It was the richest country in the history of mankind.* However, many people think that using **man** and **mankind** in this way is wrong because it seems not to include women. Therefore, it is more usual to use **people** to mean "people in general" and **humankind** instead of **mankind**: *People have always tried to understand the stars. / It was the richest country in the history of humankind.*
man은 "일반 대중"을 의미한다: 인간 (man)은 항상 별을 알아보려고 노력해 왔다. **mankind**는 "한 집단으로 간주되는 모든 사람들"을 의미한다: 그 국가는 인류(mankind) 역사에서 가장 부유한 국가였다. 하지만 많은 사람들은 **man** 과 **mankind**를 이런 식으로 사용하는 것은 여자를 포함하지 않는 것 같아서

잘못이라고 생각한다. 그러므로 "일반 대중"을 의미하는 **people**과 **mankind** 대신에 **humankind**를 사용하는 것이 더 일반적이다: 인간(people)은 항상 별을 알아보려고 노력해 왔다. / 그 국가는 인류(humankind) 역사에서 가장 부유한 국가였다.

---

man² *v* **-nned, -nning** [T] to use or operate a vehicle, piece of equipment etc. ‖ 차량·장비 등을 사용하거나 작동하다. …에 인원을 배치시키다. 탑승시키다: *the astronauts who manned the first spacecraft* 최초의 우주선에 탑승했던 우주 비행사들 —see also MANNED

man³ *interjection* used in order to emphasize what you are saying ‖ 말하는 바를 강조하는 데에 쓰여. 이런. 이거: *Oh man! I'm going to be really late.* 이런! 정말 늦겠는걸.

man·a·cle /ˈmænəkəl/ *n* an iron ring on a chain that is put around the hand or foot of a prisoner ‖ 죄수의 손이나 발에 채우는 사슬에 달린 철 고리. 수갑. 족쇄

man·age /ˈmænɪdʒ/ *v* [I, T] **1** to succeed in doing something difficult, such as dealing with a problem, living in a difficult situation ‖ 문제를 해결하거나 어려운 상황에서 생존하는 등의 어려운 일을 해내는 데 성공하다. 그럭저럭[용케] 해내다: *It was heavy, but I managed to get it up the stairs.* 무거웠지만 나는 가까스로 그것을 들고 계단을 오를 수 있었다. / *I don't know how we'll manage* (=how we'll buy the things we need) *now that Keith's lost his job.* 키스가 직장을 잃었으니 이제 어떻게 살아가야 할지 모르겠다. **2** to direct or control a business and the people who work in it ‖ 사업체와 거기에서 일하는 사람들을 감독하거나 통제하다. 경영[관리]하다: *I spent 16 years managing a hotel in Wilmington.* 나는 윌밍턴에 있는 한 호텔을 관리하며 16년을 보냈다. **3** SPOKEN HUMOROUS to do something that causes problems ‖ 문제를 일으키는 일을 하다. 어리석게도[불행하게도] …하다: *The kids managed to spill paint all over the carpet.* 아이들이 카펫에 온통 페인트를 엎질러 놓고 말았다.

man·age·a·ble /ˈmænɪdʒəbəl/ *adj* easy to control or deal with ‖ 통제하거나 다루기 쉬운. 조작[관리]할 수 있는: *My hair's more manageable since I had it cut.* 내 머리는 자른 이후로 손질하기가 편하다.

man·age·ment /ˈmænɪdʒmənt/ *n* **1** [U]

the act or process of controlling and organizing the work of a company or organization and the people who work for it ‖ 회사나 조직의 업무와 거기서 일하는 사람들을 통제하고 조직하는 행위나 과정. 경영. 관리: *He studied Business Management.* 그는 경영학을 공부했다. **2** [singular, U] the people who are in charge of controlling and organizing a company or organization ‖ 회사나 조직을 통제하고 조직하는 책임을 맡고 있는 사람들. 경영진: *The management has agreed to talk with our union.* 경영진은 우리 노조와 협상하는 데 동의했다. / *There are several jobs open at management level.* 관리직에 비어 있는 자리가 몇 개 있다.

man·ag·er /'mænɪdʒɚ/ n someone who directs the work of something such as a business, a sports team, an actor etc. ‖ 사업체·스포츠 팀·배우 등의 업무를 관리하는 사람. 지배인. 감독. 매니저: *That meal was terrible–I want to speak to the manager!* 음식이 형편없었어요. 지배인 좀 불러줘요! / *the manager of the Boston Red Sox* 보스턴 레드 삭스 감독

man·a·ge·ri·al /ˌmænəˈdʒɪriəl/ adj relating to the job of being a manager ‖ 관리인이 하는 일과 관련된. 경영[관리]상의: *good managerial skills* 훌륭한 경영[관리] 기술

Man·da·rin /'mændərɪn/ n [U] the official language of China ‖ 중국의 공식적인 언어. 표준[북방] 중국어

man·date /'mændeɪt/ n FORMAL **1** the right or power that a government has to do something, given by the people in an election ‖ 선거에서 국민들에 의해 부여된, 정부가 어떤 일을 해야 할 권한이나 권력. 위임. 권한 부여: *The party has been given a mandate to raise taxes.* 그 정당은 세금을 인상하는 권한을 부여받았다. **2** an official command given to a person or organization to do something ‖ 사람이나 조직에게 어떤 일을 하도록 내리는 공식적인 지시. 명령. 지령 – **mandate** v [T]

man·da·to·ry /'mændəˌtɔri/ adj something that is mandatory must be done ‖ 어떤 일이 반드시 행해져야 하는. 의무적인. 강제적인: *mandatory safety inspections* 의무적인 안전 점검

mane /meɪn/ n the long hair on the back of a horse's neck, or around the face and neck of a male lion ‖ 말의 목덜미나 숫사자의 얼굴과 목 주위의 긴 털. 갈기

ma·neu·ver¹ /məˈnuvɚ/ n a skillful movement or carefully planned action, especially to avoid something or go around it ‖ 특히 어떤 것을 피하거나 우회하기 위한 능숙한 움직임이나 주의 깊게 계획된 동작. …하는 기술적 동작[요령]: *basic skiing maneuvers* 기초 스키타기 요령 —see also MANEUVERS

ma·neu·ver² v [I, T] to move or turn skillfully, or to move or turn something skillfully ‖ 능숙하게 움직이거나 돌다, 또는 사물을 능숙하게 움직이거나 돌리다. 교묘히 움직이다. 솜씨 있게 다루다[조작하다]: *It was hard to maneuver the piano through the door.* 그 문으로 피아노를 통과시키느라 애를 먹었다. / *The car behind me was so close, I didn't have room to maneuver.* 내 뒤로 차가 너무 가깝게 있어서 나는 어떻게 해볼 여지가 없었다.

ma·neu·ver·a·ble /məˈnuvərəbəl/ adj easy to move or turn ‖ 움직이거나 돌리기에 쉬운. 조작[운전]할 수 있는: *a very maneuverable car* 매우 운전하기 쉬운 차 – **maneuverability** /məˌnuvrəˈbɪləti/ n [U]

ma·neu·vers /məˈnuvɚz/ n [plural] a military exercise like a battle used for training soldiers ‖ 병사 훈련을 위한 실전 같은 군사 훈련. 대연습. 기동훈련

mange /meɪndʒ/ n [U] a skin disease of animals that makes them lose small areas of fur ‖ 군데군데 털이 빠지는 동물의 피부병. 가축의 옴 – **mangy** adj

man·ger /'meɪndʒɚ/ n a long open container that horses, cows etc. eat from ‖ 말·소 등이 먹이를 먹는 길고 덮개가 없는 통. 여물통. 구유

man·gle /'mæŋgəl/ v [T] to damage something badly by crushing or twisting it ‖ 어떤 것을 찌부러뜨리거나 비틀어 몹시 손상을 입히다. …을 짓이기다. 엉망으로 만들다: *The car was badly mangled in the accident.* 그 자동차는 사고로 몹시 찌그러졌다.

man·go /'mæŋgoʊ/ n a sweet juicy tropical fruit with a large seed ‖ 큰 씨가 들어 있으며 달콤한 즙이 많은 열대 과일. 망고

man·grove /'mæŋgroʊv/ n a tropical tree that grows in or near water and grows new roots from its branches ‖ 물 속이나 물가에서 자라며 그 가지에서 새 뿌리가 자라는 열대성 식물. 맹그로브

man·han·dle /'mænˌhændl/ v [T] to move someone or something roughly, using force ‖ 완력을 사용하여, 사람이나 사물을 난폭하게 움직이다. …을 거칠게 다루다: *She complained that she had* *been manhandled by the police.* 그녀는 경찰이 자신을 함부로 대했다고 불평했다.

man·hole /'mænhoʊl/ *n* a hole on the surface of a road covered by a lid, that people go down to examine pipes, wires etc. ‖ 사람들이 관이나 전선 등을 검사하기 위해 내려가는, 뚜껑이 덮인 도로면의 구멍. 맨홀

man·hood /'mænhʊd/ *n* [U] **1** the qualities that people think a man should have ‖ 사람들이 남자라면 갖춰야 한다고 생각하는 자질. 남자다움: *He feels the remark is an insult to his manhood* 그는 그 말이 자신의 남자다움에 대한 모욕이라고 느낀다. **2** the state of being a man rather than a boy ‖ 소년이라기보다는 남성인 상태. 남자임. 어른임: *The tribe performs special ceremonies when the boys reach manhood.* 그 종족은 소년들이 성인이 될 때 특별한 의식을 치른다.

man·hunt /'mænhʌnt/ *n* an organized search, usually for a criminal ‖ 보통 범죄자에 대한 조직적인 수사. 범인 수색[추적]

ma·ni·a /'meɪniə/ *n* **1** a very strong desire for something or interest in something, that changes your behavior ‖ 자신의 행동을 바꿀 만한, 매우 강한 욕구나 흥미. 열광. 열중. …열: *a mania for driving fast cars* 자동차 스피드에의 열광 **2** TECHNICAL a type of mental illness in which someone is extremely excited and active ‖ 사람이 극단적으로 흥분하고 활동적이 되는 정신병의 일종. 조병(躁病)

ma·ni·ac /'meɪniˌæk/ *n* INFORMAL **1** someone who is not responsible and behaves in a stupid or dangerous way ‖ 책임 능력이 없고 어리석거나 위험하게 행동하는 사람. 미치광이: *He drives like a maniac.* 그는 미치광이처럼 운전한다. **2** someone who has such a strong desire for something that it makes him/her very dangerous ‖ 자신을 큰 위험에 빠드리게 만드는 것에 몹시 강렬한 욕구를 지닌 사람. 광적인 애호가. …광: *a dangerous sex maniac* 위험스러운 섹스광

ma·ni·a·cal /mə'naɪəkəl/ *adj* behaving like you are crazy ‖ 미친 듯이 행동하는. 광적인. 정신 이상의: *maniacal laughter* 미친 사람처럼 웃는 웃음

man·ic /'mænɪk/ *adj* behaving in a very excited and often anxious way ‖ 매우 흥분하고 종종 걱정스럽게 행동하는. 열광적인: *We were feeling really manic after the exam.* 우리는 시험이 끝난 후 대단히 광적인 흥분을 느끼고 있었다.

man·i·cure /'mænɪˌkyʊr/ *n* [C, U] a treatment for the hands and FINGERNAILs that includes cleaning, cutting etc. ‖ 청결·깎기 등을 포함한 손과 손톱을 위한 처리. 미조술(美爪術). 손(톱) 손질[다듬기] – **manicure** *v* [T] – **manicurist** *n*

man·i·fest¹ /'mænəˌfɛst/ *v* [T] FORMAL to become easy to see ‖ 보기 쉽게 되다. 분명하게 보여 주다. 명시하다: *The disease can manifest itself in many ways.* 그 병은 여러 방식으로 나타날 수 있다.

manifest² *adj* FORMAL plain and easy to see ‖ 또렷하고 보기 쉬운. 명백한. 분명한. 일목요연한: *a manifest error in his judgment* 그의 명백한 오판 – **manifestly** *adv*

man·i·fes·ta·tion /ˌmænəfə'steɪʃən/ *n* [C, U] a very clear sign that a particular situation or feeling exists ‖ 특정한 상황이나 느낌이 존재한다는 매우 명백한 징후. 표현. 표명: *These latest riots are a clear manifestation of growing unhappiness.* 최근의 이들 폭동들은 늘어나는 불만의 명백한 표출이다.

man·i·fes·to /ˌmænə'fɛstoʊ/ *n* a written statement by a group, especially a political group, saying what it thinks and intends to do ‖ 특히 정치 단체에 의한 자신들의 이상과 강령에 대해 표명한 성명서. 선언(문): *the Communist manifesto* 공산당 선언

man·i·fold /'mænəˌfoʊld/ *adj* FORMAL many, and of different kinds ‖ 여러 가지의. 서로 다른 종류의. 다양한. 갖가지의: *The problems facing the government are manifold.* 그 정부가 직면하고 있는 문제들은 다양하다.

ma·nil·a en·ve·lope /mə,nɪlə 'ɛnvəloʊp/ *n* an envelope made of strong brown paper ‖ 질긴 갈색 종이로 만든 봉투. 마닐라지로 만든 봉투

ma·nip·u·late /mə'nɪpyəˌleɪt/ *v* [T] **1** to make someone do exactly what you want by deceiving or influencing him/her ‖ 남을 속이거나 영향을 주어 자신이 원하는 대로 남이 하도록 만들다. 조종하다. 조작하다: *I don't like the way he manipulates people.* 나는 그가 사람들을 조종하는 방식을 좋아하지 않는다. **2** to skillfully handle, control, or move something ‖ 어떤 것을 능숙하게 다루다[조종하다, 움직이다] – **manipulation** /mə,nɪpyə'leɪʃən/ *n* [U]

ma·nip·u·la·tive /mə'nɪpyələtɪv/ *adj* good at controlling or deceiving people to get what you want ‖ 자신이 원하는 것

man·kind /ˌmænˈkaɪnd/ n [U] all humans, considered as a group ∥ 한 집단으로 간주되는 모든 인간들. 인류: *the worst war in the history of mankind* 인류 역사상 최악의 전쟁 —see usage note at MAN¹

man·ly /ˈmænli/ adj having qualities such as strength or courage that are considered to be typical of a man ∥ 남자의 전형으로 여겨지는 힘이나 용기 등의 자질을 가진. 남자다운. 용기 있는. 강건한 **– manliness** n [U]

man-made /ˌ. ˈ./ adj made of substances such as plastic that are not natural ∥ 플라스틱 등의 비천연적인 물질로 만든. 인조의. 인공의: *man-made fibers* 인조[합성] 섬유

manned /mænd/ adj controlled or operated by people ∥ 사람에 의해 조정되거나 작동되는. 유인(有人)의: *a manned space flight* 유인 우주 비행 —opposite UNMANNED

man·ne·quin /ˈmænəkən/ n a model of a human body used for showing clothes ∥ 옷을 전시하는 데 쓰는 인체 모형. 마네킹

man·ner /ˈmænɚ/ n 1 [singular] FORMAL the way in which something is done or happens ∥ 어떤 것이 행해지거나 발생하는 양식. 방법. 방식. 투: *The disease is usually treated in this manner.* 그 병은 보통 이러한 방식으로 치료된다. 2 [singular] the way in which someone talks or behaves with other people ∥ 사람이 다른 사람들과 얘기하거나 행동하는 방식. 태도: *Caleb has a pleasant manner.* 캘렙의 태도는 남을 기분 좋게 한다. 3 **all manner of** FORMAL many different kinds of things or people —see also MANNERS ∥ 사물이나 사람들의 여러 다른 종류의. 온갖 부류[종류]의

man·nered /ˈmænɚd/ adj 1 **well-mannered/bad-mannered** polite or not polite to other people ∥ 타인에게 정중하게 대하거나 정중하지 않은. 예의 바른/예의 없는: *a bad-mannered old man* 예의 없는 노인 2 DISAPPROVING relating to behavior that seems unnatural because it is only done to impress people ∥ 단지 사람들을 감동시킬 목적으로 이루어졌기 때문에 자연스러워 보이지 않는 행동과 관련된. 부자연스러운. 꾸민 듯한: *a mannered way of talking* 부자연스러운 [꾸민 듯한] 말투

man·ner·ism /ˈmænəˌrɪzəm/ n [C, U] a way of speaking, behaving, moving etc. that is typical of a particular person or group of people ∥ 특정한 사람이나 일단의 사람들에게 전형적인 말투·행동 방식·거동 등. 버릇: *Some of his mannerisms are exactly like his father's.* 그의 몇 가지 버릇은 자기 아버지의 버릇과 똑같다.

man·ners /ˈmænɚz/ n [plural] polite ways of behaving in social situations ∥ 사회 활동 중의 정중한 행동 방식. 예의범절: *Her children have such good manners.* 그녀의 아이들은 예의범절이 매우 훌륭하다.

man·nish /ˈmænɪʃ/ adj a woman who is mannish looks or behaves like a man ∥ 여자가 남자처럼 보이거나 행동하는. 남자 같은. 남성적인

man·or /ˈmænɚ/ n a large country house with a large area of land around it ∥ 주위에 너른 토지가 딸린 시골의 저택. 장원(莊園)

man·pow·er /ˈmænˌpaʊɚ/ n [U] all the workers available to do a particular type of work ∥ 특정한 종류의 업무를 처리하는 데에 이용할 수 있는 모든 일꾼들. 인력. 일손. 인적 자원: *We don't have enough manpower right now to start the project.* 우리는 바로 지금 그 프로젝트를 시작할 충분한 인력이 없다.

man·sion /ˈmænʃən/ n a very large house ∥ 매우 큰 집. 대저택

man·slaugh·ter /ˈmænˌslɔtɚ/ n [U] LAW the crime of killing someone without intending to ∥ 의도하지 않고 사람을 (우발적으로) 죽이는 범죄. 살인(죄) —compare MURDER¹

man·tel /ˈmæntl/, **mantelpiece** /ˈmæntlˌpis/ n the shelf above a FIREPLACE ∥ 벽난로 위의 선반

man·tle /ˈmæntl/ n 1 **take on/assume/wear the mantle of** to accept or have a particular duty or responsibility ∥ 특정한 의무나 책임을 받아들이거나 가지다. …의 책임을 맡다: *He assumed the mantle of leadership when the Prime Minister died.* 그는 수상이 죽었을 때 지도자의 임무를 맡았다. 2 **a mantle of snow/darkness etc.** LITERARY something that covers a surface or area ∥ 표면이나 지역을 덮은 것. 설원/어둠의 장막 3 TECHNICAL the part of the inside of the earth that surrounds its center ∥ 지구 중심을 둘러싸고 있는 지구 내부의 부분. 맨틀

man·tra /ˈmɑntrə/ n a repeated word or sound used as a prayer or to help people MEDITATE ‖ 기도로서 사용되거나 사람들이 명상하는 데에 도움을 주기 위한 반복적인 말이나 소리. 만트라. 주문(呪文). 진언(眞言)

man·u·al¹ /ˈmænyuəl/ *adj* **1** involving the use of the hands ‖ 손의 사용과 관련된. 손의. 손으로 만든. 수공의: *manual skills* 손 기술 **2** using human power or skill, not electricity, machines etc. ‖ 전기나 기계 등이 아닌 인간의 힘이나 기술을 이용하는. 수동식의: *a manual pump* 수동식 펌프 — **manually** *adv*

manual² *n* a book that gives instructions about how to do something such as use a machine ‖ 기계 사용 등의 방법에 대한 지침을 주는 책. 입문서. 설명서. 안내서: *a computer manual* 컴퓨터 설명서

manual la·bor /ˌ... ˈ../ *n* [U] work done with your hands that does not need a lot of skill ‖ 많은 기술을 요하지 않는 손으로 하는 일. 육체 노동

man·u·fac·ture¹ /ˌmænyəˈfæktʃər/ *v* [T] to use machines to make goods, usually in large numbers ‖ 보통 대량으로 제품을 만들기 위해 기계를 사용하다. 기계로 대량 제작[제조]하다: *I work for a company that manufactures aircraft engine parts.* 나는 항공기 엔진 부품을 제조하는 회사에서 일한다.

manufacture² *n* [U] FORMAL the process of making goods usually in large numbers ‖ 보통 대량으로 제품을 만드는 과정. 제조. 대량 생산

man·u·fac·tur·er /ˌmænyəˈfæktʃərə/ *n* a company that makes goods usually in large numbers ‖ 보통 대량으로 제품을 만드는 회사. 제조 회사. 제조업자: *the world's largest shoe manufacturer* 세계 최대 신발 제조 회사

man·u·fac·tur·ing /ˌmænyəˈfæktʃərɪŋ/ *n* [U] the process of making goods in factories ‖ 공장에서 제품을 만드는 과정. 제조(업).

ma·nure /məˈnʊə/ *n* [U] waste matter from animals that is put into the soil to produce better crops ‖ 농작물을 더 많이 생산하기 위해 토양에 첨가해 넣는 동물의 배설물. 거름. 퇴비

man·u·script /ˈmænyəˌskrɪpt/ *n* **1** a book or piece of writing before it is printed ‖ 출판 전의 책이나 글. 원고: *She sent a 350 page manuscript to the publisher.* 그녀는 출판사에 350쪽 분량의 원고를 보냈다. **2** an old book written by hand before printing was invented ‖ 인쇄술이 발명되기 이전의 손으로 쓴 낡은 책. 사본. 필사본: *an ancient Chinese*

manuscript 고대 중국어 필사본

man·y /ˈmɛni/ *quantifier, pron* **more, most** **1** used in formal English and in questions or negatives to mean a large number of people or things ‖ 격식 차린 영어와 의문문 또는 부정문에서 다수의 사람이나 사물을 나타내는 데에 쓰여. 많은: *Many animals do not eat meat.* 많은 동물들은 고기를 먹지 않는다. / *How many people are in your class?* 너희 반은 학생이 몇 명이니? / *There aren't many (=are not many) tickets left.* 남아 있는 표가 많지 않다. / *Many of our teachers are Japanese.* 우리 선생님 중 다수가 일본 사람이다. / *I've eaten too many doughnuts (=more than you should) already!* 나는 이미 도넛을 너무 많이 먹었어! / *Why did you bring so many (=such a large number of) pencils?* 너는 왜 그렇게 많은 연필을 가져왔니? **2 as many** the same number ‖ 같은 수: *There weren't as many people at the meeting as we had hoped.* 우리가 기대했던 것만큼 모임에 사람들이 많이 오지는 않았다. **3 a good/great many** FORMAL a large number ‖ 많은 수. 아주/대단히 많은: *A great many men died in that battle.* 수많은 남자들이 그 전투에서 죽었다. —see usage note at MUCH¹ —see study note on page 940

map¹ /mæp/ *n* a drawing of an area or country showing rivers, roads, cities etc ‖ 강·길·도시 등을 나타내는 한 지역이나 국가의 그림. 지도: *a map of Texas* 텍사스의 지도

map² *v* **-pped, -pping** [T] to make a map of a particular area ‖ 특정한 지역의 지도를 만들다: *a device used to map the ocean floor* 해저의 지도를 만들기 위해 사용된 장치

map sth ↔ **out** *phr v* [T] to plan something carefully ‖ 어떤 것을 주의 깊게 계획하다. 꼼꼼히 계획을 세우다: *The UN mapped out a plan to rebuild the country.* 유엔은 그 나라의 재건 계획을 세웠다.

ma·ple /ˈmeɪpəl/ *n* [C, U] a tree in northern countries that has leaves with many points, or the wood from this tree ‖ 북쪽 나라들에서 자라는 잎이 여럿으로 갈래진 나무, 또는 이 나무의 목재. 단풍나무(재목)

mar /mɑr/ *v* **-rred, -rring** [T] to make something less attractive or enjoyable; SPOIL ‖ 어떤 것을 매력이나 재미가 덜하게 만들다. 매력을 약화시키다. 손상[훼손]하다; ㊉ spoil: *The table had been marred by cigarette burns.* 그 테이블은 담뱃불에

타서 외관이 훼손되었다.

mar·a·thon¹ /ˈmærə,θɑn/ *n* a race in which competitors run 26 miles and 385 yards ‖ 선수들이 26마일 385야드를 뛰는 경주. 마라톤

marathon² *adj* continuing for a very long time ‖ 매우 오랫동안 계속하는. 몹시 오래 걸리는. 매우 긴: *a marathon session of Congress* 의회의 매우 긴 회기

ma·raud·ing /məˈrɔdɪŋ/ *adj* searching for something to kill, steal, or destroy ‖ 죽이려고[훔치려고, 파괴하려고] 어떤 것을 찾는. 약탈하려고 돌아다니는: *marauding soldiers* 약탈하는 병사들

mar·ble /ˈmɑrbəl/ *n* **1** [U] a hard white rock that can be polished and used for building, STATUES etc. ‖ 윤을 내서 건물과 조상(彫像)에 사용되는 단단한 흰색의 돌. 대리석: *a marble floor* 대리석 바닥 **2** a small colored glass ball ‖ 작고 색깔 있는 유리 구슬

March /mɑrtʃ/, *written abbreviation* **Mar.** *n* the third month of the year ‖ 한 해의 셋째 달. 3월 —see usage note at JANUARY

march

Their marching band marched in the parade.

march¹ *v* [I] **1** to walk with firm regular steps like a soldier ‖ 군인처럼 굳건하고 규칙적인 걸음으로 걷다. 행진하다. 행군하다: *The Union army marched across the field.* 영국 군대는 들판을 가로질러 행진했다. **2** to walk quickly because you are angry or determined ‖ 화나거나 결심이 서서 빨리 걷다. 당당히[신속히] 걷다: *She marched out of the room without looking at us.* 그녀는 우리들을 보지도 않고 방에서 휙 걸어 나갔다. **3** to walk somewhere in a large group to protest about something ‖ 어떤 것에 항의하기 위해 무리를 지어 어딘가로 걸어 가다. 시위 행진하다: *The group plans to march on the White House next week.* 그 단체는 다음주에 백악관으로 시위 행진을 할 작정이다.

march² *n* **1** an organized event in which many people walk together to protest about something ‖ 어떤 것에 항

의하기 위해 많은 사람들이 함께 걷는 조직적인 행사. 시위 행진: *a civil rights march* 시민권을 위한 시위 행진 **2** the act of walking with firm regular steps like a soldier ‖ 군인처럼 굳건하고 규칙적인 걸음으로 걷는 행동. 행군. 행진 **3** a piece of music with a regular beat for soldiers to MARCH to ‖ 군인들이 맞춰서 행군하는 규칙적인 박자로 된 악곡. 행진곡

march·ing band /ˈ.. ,./ *n* a group of musicians who march while they play instruments ‖ 행진하면서 악기를 연주하는 일단의 음악인. 악대

Mar·di Gras /ˈmɑrdi ,grɑ/ *n* [singular] the day before Lent, or the music, dancing etc. that celebrate this day ‖ 사순절 전날, 또는 이 날을 축하하는 음악·춤 등

mare /mɛr/ *n* a female horse or DONKEY ‖ 암말이나 암탕나귀

mar·ga·rine /ˈmɑrdʒərɪn/ *n* [U] a yellow food often used instead of butter ‖ 흔히 버터 대신에 사용하는 노란색 식품. 마가린

mar·gin /ˈmɑrdʒɪn/ *n* **1** the empty space at the side of a printed page ‖ 인쇄된 페이지의 가장자리의 빈 공간. 여백: *I wrote some notes in the margin.* 나는 여백에 조금 메모를 했다. **2** the difference in the number of votes, points etc. that exists between the winners and the losers of an election or competition ‖ 선거나 시합에서 승자와 패자 사이에 벌어진 득표수나 점수 차이: *The democrats won by a wide margin.* (=by a lot of votes) 민주당은 많은 표 차이로 승리했다. **3 margin of error** the degree to which a calculation can be wrong without affecting the final results ‖ 계산이 최종 결과에 영향을 주지 않고 틀릴 수 있는 정도. 오차 범위 **4** ⇨ PROFIT MARGIN

mar·gin·al /ˈmɑrdʒənl/ *adj* small in importance or amount ‖ 중요도나 분량에 있어서 적은. 보잘것없는. 하찮은: *Doctors only had marginal success in fighting the virus.* 의사들은 단지 그 바이러스를 퇴치하는 데에 미미한 성공을 거두었을 뿐이다. **– marginally** *adv*

mar·i·jua·na /ˌmærəˈwɑnə/ *n* [U] a drug in the form of dried leaves that people smoke ‖ 말린 잎의 형태로 사람들이 피우는 마약. 마리화나

ma·ri·na /məˈrinə/ *n* an area of water where people pay to keep their boats ‖ 배를 대놓기 위해 사람들이 돈을 지불하는 수역. 항구. 정박지. 계류장

mar·i·nate /ˈmærə,neɪt/, **mar·i·nade**

/ˌmærəˈneɪd, ˈmærəˌneɪd/ v [T] to put meat or fish in a mixture of oil, wine, SPICEs etc. before you cook it ‖ 요리하기 전에 고기나 생선을 기름·포도주·향신료 등의 혼합물에 담그다. 고기·생선 등을 매리네이드에 담그다 — **marinade** n

ma·rine¹ /məˈrin/ adj relating to the sea ‖ 바다와 관련된. 바다의: *marine life* 해양 생물

marine² n someone who is in the MARINES ‖ 미국 해병대에 있는 사람. 미국 해병대원

mar·i·ner /ˈmærənɚ/ n LITERARY a sailor ‖ 선원. 뱃사람

Ma·rines /məˈrinz/, **Marine Corps** /ˌ. ˌ./ n [U] the military organization of the US consisting of soldiers who work on ships ‖ 선상에서 근무하는 군인들로 구성된 미국 군사 조직. 미국 해병대

mar·i·o·nette /ˌmæriəˈnɛt/ n a toy that looks like a person, animal etc. that is moved by pulling strings attached to its body ‖ 몸에 달린 줄을 당겨 움직이게 되는 사람·동물 모양의 장난감. 꼭두각시 — compare PUPPET

mar·i·tal /ˈmærətl/ adj relating to marriage ‖ 결혼과 관련된. 결혼의: *marital problems* 결혼 생활의 문제

mar·i·time /ˈmærəˌtaɪm/ adj **1** relating to the sea or ships ‖ 바다나 배와 관련된. 해상의: *maritime trade* 해상 무역 **2** near the sea ‖ 바다 근처의. 해안의: *the maritime provinces* 해안 지방

mark¹ /mɑrk/ v [T] **1** to make a sign, shape, or word using a pen or pencil ‖ 펜이나 연필을 사용해서 기호[모양, 단어]를 만들다. …에 표를 하다. 표시하다: *Check the envelopes that are marked "urgent" first.* 우선 "긴급"이라고 표시된 봉투를 점검해라. **2** to show where something is ‖ 사물이 있는 곳을 나타내다: *The grave is marked by a stone cross.* 그 무덤은 돌 십자가로 표시되어 있다. **3** to represent the fact that something has happened or is true ‖ 어떤 일이 일어났거나 참이라는 사실을 나타내다. …을 기념하다: *This year marks the company's 50th anniversary.* 올해로 그 회사는 창립 50주년을 맞이한다. **4** if a teacher marks a test, paper etc., s/he corrects mistakes and gives it a grade ‖ 선생님이 시험지·보고서 등의 틀린 것을 바로잡아 주고 점수를 매기다. 답안을 채점하다 **5** to make a mark on something in a way that spoils or damages it ‖ 망치거나 훼손하는 식으로 어떤 것 위에 표시를 하다. 자국을 내다. 상처를 남기다: *The heels of his boots had marked the*

floor. 그의 부츠의 뒤축이 마룻바닥에 자국을 남겼다.

mark sth ↔ **down** phr v [T] to reduce the price of things that are being sold ‖ 판매 중인 물건의 가격을 내리다: *All items in the store have been marked down for one week only.* 가게에 있는 모든 물건들은 단 일주일 동안만 계속 값을 내렸다. —see also MARKDOWN

mark sth ↔ **up** phr v [T] to increase the price of an item in order to sell it for more than you paid for it ‖ 구매액 이상으로 판매하려고 물건의 가격을 올리다: *We could mark the prices up a little and still be competitive.* 우리는 가격을 조금 올렸는데에 아직 경쟁력이 있다. —see also MARKUP

mark² n

1 ▶DIRTY SPOT 더러운 곳◀ a spot or small dirty area on something that spoils its appearance ‖ 사물의 외관을 손상시키는 얼룩이나 작고 더러운 부분. 자국. 얼룩: *What are these black marks on the couch?* 소파에 이 검은 얼룩들은 뭐냐?

2 ▶DAMAGE 손상◀ a small area of something or on someone that has been damaged ‖ 사물이나 사람이 손상을 입은 작은 부분. 자국. 흉터. 멍: *He had teeth marks (=marks made by teeth) on his arm.* 그의 팔에는 이빨 자국이 있었다.

3 ▶WRITING 쓰기◀ a sign or shape that is written or printed ‖ 손으로 쓰거나 인쇄된 표시나 모양: *She made a mark on the map to show where her house was.* 그녀는 자기 집이 있는 곳을 알려주려고 지도에 표시를 했다.

4 make your mark to become successful or famous ‖ 성공하거나 유명해지다. 이름을 떨치다: *Muis made his mark as a leader, journalist, and novelist.* 무이스는 지도자이자 언론인이자 소설가로 이름을 떨쳤다.

5 a mark of a sign that something is true or exists ‖ 어떤 것이 사실이거나 존재한다는 표시. …의 징표[징조]: *We'd like to give you this gift as a mark of our respect.* 우리는 존경의 표시로서 이 선물을 드리고 싶습니다.

6 off the mark/wide of the mark not correct ‖ 맞지 않는. 빗나간. 예상이 틀린. 엉뚱한: *My estimate was way off the mark.* 내 예상은 완전히 빗나갔다.

7 on your mark, get set, go! SPOKEN said in order to start a race ‖ 경주를 시작하는 데에 쓰여. 제자리, 준비, 출발!

8 a particular type of car, machine etc. ‖ 차·기계 등의 특정한 형: *a Lincoln*

Mark V V 형 링컨차

mark·down /'markdaʊn/ *n* a reduction in the price of something ‖ 사물의 가격 인하: *Huge markdowns on all stock!* 재고 전 제품 대폭 가격 인하!

marked /markt/ *adj* very easy to notice ‖ 알아보기 매우 쉬운. 두드러진. 현저한: *There has been a marked increase in crime in the last year.* 작년에 눈에 띄게 범죄가 늘어났다. – **markedly** /'mark-ɪdli/ *adv*

mark·er /'markə/ *n* **1** an object, sign etc. that shows the position of something ‖ 어떤 것의 위치를 나타내는 물체나 표시: *a marker at the edge of the football field* 미식축구 구장의 외곽의 표지 **2** a large pen with a thick point ‖ 끝이 굵고 큰 펜. 매직펜류

mar·ket¹ /'markɪt/ *n*
1 ▶PLACE TO SELL 판매 장소◀ an area outside where people buy and sell goods, food etc. ‖ 사람들이 물건·음식 등을 사고파는 옥외 지역. 시장: *We buy all our vegetables from the farmer's market.* 우리는 농산물 시장에서 야채를 몽땅 산다. —compare SUPERMARKET
2 the market ▷ STOCK MARKET
3 on the market available for someone to buy ‖ 사람이 살 수 있는. 팔려고 내놓은: *That house has been on the market for a year now.* 저 집은 지금 1년째 팔려고 내놓고 있다.
4 ▶COUNTRY/AREA 나라/지역◀ a particular country or area where a company sells its goods ‖ 회사가 상품을 파는 특정한 나라나 지역. 시장: *Is China the company's biggest overseas market?* 중국이 그 회사의 가장 큰 해외 시장입니까?
5 ▶BUYERS 구매자◀ the number of people who want to buy something ‖ 어떤 것을 사려고 하는 사람의 수. 구입자수: *The market for used cars in the US seems to be getting smaller.* 미국에서 중고차 수요는 점점 줄어드는 것 같다.
6 be in the market for to be interested in buying something ‖ 어떤 것을 사는 데 흥미를 느끼다. …을 사려고 하다: *Are you in the market for a new boat?* 새 보트를 사고 싶으냐?
7 a buyer's/seller's market a time when it is better for buyers because prices are low, or better for sellers because prices are high ‖ 가격이 낮아 구매자에게 유리한 때, 또는 가격이 높아 판매자에게 유리한 때. 매수인/매도인 시장

market² *v* [T] to try to persuade someone to buy something by advertising it in a particular way ‖ 특정한 방식으로 광고하여 상품을 사람에게 설득시키려고 하다. 판매를 촉진시키다: *The game is being marketed as a learning toy.* 그 게임은 학습용 장난감으로 판매 촉진되고[광고되고] 있다. – **marketer** *n*

mar·ket·a·ble /'markɪtəbəl/ *adj* marketable goods, skills etc. are easy to sell ‖ 제품·기술 등이 팔기 쉬운. 잘 팔리는. 시장성이 있는 – **marketability** /,markɪtə'bɪləti/ *n* [U]

mar·ket·ing /'markɪtɪŋ/ *n* [U] the activity of deciding how to advertise a product, what price to charge for it etc., or the type of job in which you do this ‖ 제품의 광고 방법이나 가격 책정 등을 결정하는 활동, 또는 이러한 것을 하는 일. 마케팅: *new marketing strategy* 새로운 마케팅 전략 / *Reed works in marketing.* 리드는 마케팅에 종사한다.

mar·ket·place /'markɪt,pleɪs/ *n* **1 the marketplace** the business of buying and selling goods in competition with other companies ‖ 다른 회사들과 경쟁하며 물건을 사고파는 사업. 상업[실업, 재]계 **2 ▷** MARKET¹

mark·ing /'markɪŋ/ *n* [C usually plural] the colored shapes, patterns etc. on something such as an animal ‖ 동물 등의 색깔 있는 모양이나 무늬 등. 동물의 반점. 무늬: *a cat with black and gray markings* 검정과 회색의 반점이 있는 고양이

marks·man /'marksmən/ *n* someone who can shoot a gun very well ‖ 총을 매우 잘 쏘는 사람. 사격의 명수

mark·up /'mark-ʌp/ *n* an increase in the price of something ‖ 사물의 가격 인상: *The usual markup is 20%.* 통상적인 가격 인상은 20퍼센트이다.

mar·ma·lade /'marmə,leɪd/ *n* [U] a jam made with fruit such as oranges ‖ 오렌지 등의 과일로 만든 잼. 마멀레이드

ma·roon¹ /mə'run/ *n* [U] a very dark red-brown color ‖ 매우 짙은 적갈색. 밤색 – **maroon** *adj*

maroon² *v* **be marooned** to be left in a place where there are no people or from which you cannot escape ‖ 사람이 없거나 도망갈 수 없는 곳에 남겨지다. 고립되다: *The sailors were marooned on an island for 14 weeks.* 그 선원들은 14주 동안 섬에 고립되었다.

mar·quee /mar'ki/ *n* a large sign above a theater that gives the name of the movie or play ‖ 영화나 연극의 제목을 나타내는 극장 위의 큰 간판

mar·riage /'mærɪdʒ/ *n* **1** the relationship between two people who are married || 결혼한 두 사람 사이의 관계. 부부 관계. 결혼 생활: *a long and happy marriage* 오래도록 행복한 결혼 생활 **2** [U] the state of being married || 결혼해 있는 상태. 결혼: *He is not interested in marriage.* 그는 결혼에 흥미가 없다.

mar·riage·a·ble /'mærɪdʒəbəl/ *adj* OLD-FASHIONED suitable for marriage || 결혼에 적당한, 혼기의

mar·ried /'mærɪd/ *adj* having a husband or a wife || 남편이나 아내가 있는. 결혼한: *Are you married or single?* 기혼입니까, 미혼입니까? —see also MARRY

mar·row /'mæroʊ/ *n* the soft substance in the hollow center of bones || 뼈 가운데의 속이 빈 부분에 있는 부드러운 물질. 골수

mar·ry /'mæri/ *v* **1** [I, T] to become someone's husband or wife || 누군가의 남편이나 아내가 되다. …과 결혼하다: *When are you going to get married?* 언제 결혼할 거죠? / *Tony is married to my sister.* 토니는 내 누이와 결혼했다. ✗DON'T SAY "married with."✗ "married with"라고는 하지 않는다. **2** [T] to perform the ceremony at which two people get married || 두 사람이 결혼을 하는 의식을 거행하다. …의 결혼식을 주례하다: *Rabbi Feingold will marry us.* 라비 페인골드는 우리 결혼식을 주례할 것이다.

marry into sth *phr v* [T] to join a family by marrying someone who belongs to it || 남과 결혼하여 그 사람이 속해 있는 가족의 일원이 되다

Mars /marz/ *n* [singular] a small red PLANET, fourth from the sun || 태양에서 네 번째의 작은 붉은 행성. 화성

marsh /marʃ/ *n* [C, U] an area of low ground that is soft and wet || 땅이 무르고 습한 낮은 지역. (저)습지. 늪지대 – **marshy** *adj*

mar·shal¹ /'marʃəl/ *n* the officer in charge of a city's police or fire fighting department || 시의 경찰서나 소방서를 책임 맡고 있는 공무원. 경찰서장. 소방서장: *the fire marshal* 소방서장

marshal² *v* [T] **marshal your arguments/forces etc.** to organize your facts, people etc. so that they are most effective || 더욱 효과적이 되도록 사실이나 사람 등을 조직화하다. 논의/세력을 정돈[결집]하다

marsh·mal·low /'marʃˌmɛloʊ/ *n* [C, U]

a soft white food made of sugar || 설탕으로 만든 부드럽고 흰 음식. 마시멜로

mar·su·pi·al /mar'supiəl/ *n* an animal such as a KANGAROO that carries its babies in a pocket of skin on its body || 몸의 피부 주머니에 새끼를 넣고 다니는 캥거루 등의 동물. 유대류(有袋類)

mart /mart/ *n* an abbreviation of MARKET || market의 약어

mar·tial /'marʃəl/ *adj* related to war or the army || 전쟁이나 군대에 관련된. 전쟁의. 군의

martial art /ˌ.. './ *n* a sport such as KARATE in which you fight using your hands and feet || 손과 발을 이용해 싸우는 가라테 등의 운동. 무술. 무도

martial law /ˌ.. './ *n* [U] a situation in which the army controls a city, country etc. || 군대가 도시·국가 등을 통제하는 상황. 계엄령

Mar·tian /ˌmarʃən/ *n* an imaginary creature from Mars || 화성의 상상속의 생물. 화성인

Mar·tin Lu·ther King Day /ˌmartʾn ˌluθɚ 'kɪŋ ˌdeɪ/ *n* an American holiday on the third Monday in January to remember the day that Martin Luther King Jr. was born || 마틴 루터 킹 목사가 태어난 날을 기리기 위한 1월 셋째 주 월요일의 미국 공휴일. 킹 목사 탄신일

mar·tyr¹ /'martɚ/ *n* **1** someone who tries to make people feel sympathy by talking about how difficult his/her life is || 자신의 삶이 얼마나 힘든지에 대해서 말하여 사람들에게 동정을 사려는 사람 **2** someone who dies for his/her religious or political beliefs, and whose death makes people believe more strongly in those beliefs || 자신의 종교적 또는 정치적 신념을 위해 죽음으로써 사람들이 더욱 강하게 믿게 만드는 사람. 순교자. 열사. 의사

martyr² *v* **be martyred** to become a MARTYR by dying for your religious or political beliefs || 자신의 종교적 또는 정치적 신념을 위해 죽어서 순교자가 되다

mar·tyr·dom /'martɚdəm/ *n* [U] the death or suffering of a MARTYR || 순교자의 죽음이나 고통

mar·vel¹ /'marvəl/ *v* [I, T] to feel surprise and admiration for the quality of something || 어떤 것의 특성에 놀라고 경탄하다: *We marveled at the technology involved in creating such a tiny computer.* 우리는 그처럼 작은 컴퓨터를 만들어 내는 일에 관련된 기술에 경탄했다.

marvel² *n* something or someone that

makes you MARVEL ‖ 놀라거나 경탄하게 만드는 사물이나 사람. 놀라운 것[사람]. 경이. 불가사의: *Laser surgery is one of the marvels of modern medicine.* 레이저 수술은 현대 의학의 경이 중 하나이다.

mar·vel·ous /'mɑrvələs/ *adj* extremely good, enjoyable, and sometimes surprising ‖ 매우 좋고 즐거우며 때때로 놀라운. 훌륭한. 감탄스러운: *a marvelous book by Sue Grafton* 수 그라프턴이 쓴 경탄스러운 책

Marx·is·m /'mɑrkˌsɪzəm/ *n* [U] a political system based on Karl Marx's ideas that explains the changes in history as the result of the struggle between social classes ‖ 사회 계급간의 투쟁의 결과로 역사가 변한다고 설명하는 칼 마르크스의 사상에 기초한 정치적 체계. 마르크시즘. 마르크스주의

Marx·ist /'mɑrksɪst/ *adj* relating to MARXISM ‖ 마르크스주의와 관련된. 마르크스주의의 – **Marxist** *n*

masc the written abbreviation of MASCULINE ‖ masculine의 약어

mas·car·a /mæ'skærə/ *n* [U] a dark substance that you use to color your EYELASHes ‖ 속눈썹에 색을 내는 데에 사용하는 어두운 색깔의 물질. 마스카라

mas·cot /'mæskɑt/ *n* an animal that represents a sports team or organization, and brings good luck ‖ 스포츠 팀이나 조직을 대표하며 행운을 가져다 준다는 동물. 마스코트

mas·cu·line /'mæskyəlɪn/ *adj* 1 having qualities that are considered to be typical of men ‖ 남성의 전형으로 여겨지는 특성이 있는. 사내다운. 힘센. 씩씩한: *a masculine voice* 남성다운 목소리 2 TECHNICAL in grammar, a masculine noun or pronoun has a form that means it relates to a male, such as "widower" or "him" ‖ 문법에서 명사나 대명사가 "widower" 또는 "him" 등의 남성과 관련된 것을 의미하는 형태의. 남성의 — compare FEMININE

USAGE NOTE masculine, feminine, male, female

Use **masculine** to talk about things that people think are typical of men: *a masculine voice*. Use **feminine** to talk about things that people think are typical of women: *a feminine voice*. Use **male** and **female** to describe the sex of a person or animal: *Is your cat male or female?*

masculine은 사람들이 남성의 전형이라고 생각하는 것을 언급하는 데에 쓰인

다: 남성다운 목소리. **feminine**은 사람들이 여성의 전형이라고 생각하는 것을 언급하는 데에 쓰인다: 여성스러운 목소리. **male**과 **female**은 사람이나 동물의 성(性)을 나타내는 데에 쓰인다: 네 고양이는 수컷이냐 암컷이냐?

mas·cu·lin·i·ty /ˌmæskyə'lɪnəʈi/ *n* [U] qualities that are considered to be typical of men ‖ 남성의 전형이라고 생각되는 특성. 남자다움 — compare FEMININITY

mash /mæʃ/ *v* [T] to crush something, such as food that has been cooked, until it is soft ‖ 요리한 음식 등을 부드러워질 때까지 짓이기다: *Mash the potatoes in a bowl.* 사발에 있는 감자를 으깨어라.

mask

helmet
mask
ski mask
face
mask
hospital mask

mask¹ /mæsk/ *n* 1 something that covers all or part of your face in order to protect or hide it ‖ 얼굴의 전부나 일부를 보호하거나 숨기려고 가리는 것. 마스크: *a ski mask* 스키용 마스크 / *The doctor wore a mask over his mouth and nose.* 의사는 입과 코를 가리는 마스크를 썼다. 2 something that covers your face and has another face painted on it ‖ 얼굴을 덮는 채색된 별도의 얼굴 모양의 것. 가면. 탈: *a Halloween mask* 할로윈 때 쓰는 가면

mask² *v* [T] keep something from being seen, heard, noticed etc ‖ 어떤 것을 보이지 않게·들리지 않게·눈에 띄지 않게 하다. 숨기다. 가리다: *The horrible smell was barely masked by the cheap perfume.* 그 지독한 냄새는 값싼 향수를 써서 간신히 없앴다.

masked /mæskt/ *adj* wearing a MASK ‖ 가면을 쓴

mask·ing tape /'mæskɪŋ ˌteɪp/ *n* [U] a special type of TAPE, made of paper ‖ 종이로 만든 특별한 형태의 테이프. 보호테이프

mas·och·ism /'mæsəˌkɪzəm/ *n* [U] sexual behavior in which you get pleasure from being hurt ‖ 고통을 느껴서 희열을 얻는 성적 행위. 마조히즘. 피학대 음란증 – **masochistic** /ˌmæsəˈkɪstɪk/ *adj*

ma·son /ˈmeɪsən/ *n* **1** someone whose job is cutting stone into pieces to be used in buildings ‖ 돌을 건물에 쓸 수 있게 조각으로 자르는 직업인. 석공. 석수 **2 Mason** a man who belongs to a secret society, in which each member helps the other members to become successful ‖ 각 회원이 다른 회원이 성공하도록 도와주는 비밀 단체에 속한 사람. 프리메이슨

ma·son·ry /ˈmeɪsənri/ *n* [U] brick or stone from which a building or wall is made ‖ 건물이나 벽을 구성하는 벽돌이나 돌

mas·quer·ade¹ /ˌmæskəˈreɪd/ *n* a dance or party where people wear MASKs and unusual clothes ‖ 사람들이 가면을 쓰고 독특한 옷을 입고 추는 춤이나 파티. 가장 무도(회)

masquerade² *v* [I] to pretend to be someone or something else ‖ 다른 사람이나 사물인 체하다

Mass /mæs/ *n* **1** [C, U] the main religious ceremony in the Roman Catholic Church ‖ 로마 가톨릭 교회의 주요 종교 의식. 미사 (의식) **2** a piece of music written to be played at a Mass ‖ 미사 때 연주하도록 씌어진 악곡. 미사곡

mass¹ *n* **1** a large amount or quantity of something ‖ 사물의 많은 분량이나 양. 다수. 대량: *The train wreck was a mass of twisted steel.* 파손된 열차는 찌그러진 강철투성이였다. **2** [singular] a large crowd ‖ 많은 사람들: *A mass of people were marching in the street.* 많은 사람들이 거리에서 행진을 하고 있었다. **3** [U] TECHNICAL the amount of material in something ‖ 사물 속에 있는 물질의 양. 질량: *the mass of a star* 별의 질량 —see also MASSES

mass² *adj* involving or intended for a large number of people ‖ 많은 수의 사람을 포함하거나 겨냥한. 대량의. 대규모의: *mass communication* 매스컴, 대량 전달

mass³ *v* [I, T] to gather together in a large group, or to make people or things do this ‖ 큰 무리로 함께 모이다, 또는 사람이나 사물을 큰 무리로 모이게 하다. 한 덩어리가 되다. …을 한 덩어리로 하다

massacre¹ /ˈmæsəkəʳ/ *n* the act of massacring (MASSACRE) people ‖ 사람을 대량으로 학살하는 행위. 대량 살육. 대학살: *a bloody massacre* 피비린내 나는 대량 학살

massacre² *v* [T] to kill a lot of people, especially people who cannot defend themselves ‖ 특히 스스로 방어할 수 없는 사람들을 대량으로 죽이다. 대량 학살하다: *In the middle ages whole villages were massacred by the king's soldiers.* 중세에는 온 마을이 왕의 군인들에게 대량 학살당했다.

mas·sage¹ /məˈsɑʒ, -ˈsɑdʒ/ *n* [C, U] the action of pressing and rubbing someone's body with your hands to reduce pain or make him/her relax ‖ 고통을 줄이거나 긴장을 풀려고 손으로 사람의 몸을 누르고 문지르는 행동. 마사지. 안마: *Larry gave me a massage to help my back.* 래리는 나를 위해 내 등을 마사지해 주었다.

massage² *v* [T] to give someone a MASSAGE ‖ 어떤 사람을 마사지해 주다

massage par·lor /ˈ. ˌ./ *n* **1** a place where people pay to have sex ‖ 사람들이 돈을 내고 성관계를 하는 곳. 사창가 **2** a place where people pay to have a MASSAGE ‖ 사람들이 돈을 내고 마사지를 받는 곳. 안마 시술소

mass·es /ˈmæsɪz/ *n* **the masses** [plural] all the ordinary people in a society ‖ 사회의 모든 보통 사람들. 일반 대중. 서민: *music that appeals to the masses* 일반 대중의 흥미를 끄는 음악

mas·seur /mæˈsɜʳ, mə-/ *n* someone who gives MASSAGEs ‖ 마사지를 해주는 사람. 마사지사. 안마사

mas·seuse /mæˈsuz, mə-/ *n* a woman who gives MASSAGEs ‖ 마사지를 해주는 여자. 여자 마사지사[안마사]

mas·sive /ˈmæsɪv/ *adj* **1** very large, heavy, or powerful ‖ 매우 큰[무거운, 강력한]: *massive oil reserves beneath the ocean* 해저에 매장되어 있는 대량의 석유 / *a massive dog* 덩치가 매우 큰 개 **2** causing a lot of damage ‖ 많은 손상을 일으키는. 치명적인: *Carl had a massive heart attack at the age of 52.* 칼은 52세의 나이에 치명적인 심장 마비를 일으켰다. — **massively** *adv*

mass me·di·a /ˌ. ˈ.../ *n* **the mass media** all the people and organizations that provide information and news for the public ‖ 대중을 위해 정보와 뉴스를 제공하는 모든 사람들 및 조직. 매스 미디어. 대중 매체

mass mur·der·er /ˌ. ˈ.../ *n* someone who has murdered a lot of people ‖ 많은 사람들을 학살한 사람. 대량 학살범

mass·pro·duce /ˌ. .ˈ./ *v* [T] to make a large number of goods using machinery so that each one can be sold cheaply ‖ 개개의 제품이 저렴하게 팔릴 수 있도록 기계를 사용하여 대량으로 물건

M

을 만들다. 대량 생산하다. 양산하다: *The computers will be mass-produced in Korea.* 그 컴퓨터들은 한국에서 대량 생산될 것이다. – **mass production** /,. .'./ *n* [U]

mass-pro·duced /,. .'./ *adj* made in large numbers using machinery so that each object can be sold cheaply ∥ 각각의 제품이 저렴하게 팔릴 수 있도록 기계를 사용하여 대량으로 만든. 대량 생산하는. 양산하는: *manufacturers of mass-produced cars* 자동차를 대량 생산하는 제조 회사들

mast /mæst/ *n* a tall pole on which the sails of a ship are hung ∥ 배의 돛을 다는 높은 기둥. 돛대. 마스트

mas·ter¹ /'mæstɚ/ *n* **1** OLD-FASHIONED a man who has authority over servants or animals ∥ 하인이나 동물에 대한 권한을 가진 사람. 주인. 소유자. 임자: *the master of the house* 그 집의 주인 / *the dog's master* 그 개의 주인 **2** someone who is very skillful at doing a particular job, activity etc. ∥ 특정한 일·활동 등을 하는 데에 매우 숙련된 사람. 정통자. 대가. 거장: *a master of kung fu* 쿵후의 대가 **3** a document, record etc. from which other copies are made ∥ 다른 복사본을 만드는 원서류·기록 등. 원물. 원본

master² *v* [T] to learn something so well that you understand it completely and have no difficulty with it ∥ 완전히 이해하여 어려움이 없을 정도로 어떤 것을 매우 잘 배우다. 숙달하다. 터득하다. 마스터하다: *It only took him a few months to master French.* 그가 프랑스어를 마스터하는 데에 불과 몇 달 안 걸렸다.

master³ *adj* **1** master copy/list/tape etc. the original copy, list etc. from which other copies are made ∥ 다른 복사본을 만드는 원본·원본 명부 등. 원본/원본 명부/원본 테이프 **2** master plumber/chef etc. someone who is very skillful at doing a particular job ∥ 특정한 일을 하는 데에 매우 숙련된 사람. 일류 배관공/요리사 **3** most important or main ∥ 가장 중요한. 주된: *the master bedroom* 주(主)침실

mas·ter·ful /'mæstɚfəl/ *adj* skillfully done, made, or dealt with ∥ 능숙하게 한[만든, 다룬]. 훌륭한: *a masterful performance* 훌륭한 공연

master key /,. './ *n* a key that will open all the doors in a building ∥ 건물 안에 있는 모든 문을 열 수 있는 열쇠. 만능 열쇠. 마스터 키

mas·ter·mind¹ /'mæstɚ,maɪnd/ *n* [singular] someone who organizes a complicated plan, especially a criminal plan ∥ 특히 범행 계획 등의 복잡한 계획을 세우는 사람. 주모[주동]자: *Corran was the mastermind behind the hijacking.* 코랜이 비행기 공중 납치의 주모자였다.

mastermind² *v* [T] to think of and organize a complicated plan ∥ 복잡한 계획을 생각하여 준비하다.

Master of Arts /,... . './ *n* ⇨ M.A.

master of cer·e·mo·nies /,... . '..../ *n* ⇨ EMCEE

Master of Sci·ence /,... . './ *n* ⇨ M.S.

mas·ter·piece /'mæstɚ,pis/ *n* a work of art, piece of writing, music etc. that is of the highest quality compared to others of its kind ∥ 같은 종류의 다른 작품들과 비교하여 최고의 질을 가진 미술품·문학 작품·음악 작품 등. 명작. 걸작

master's de·gree /'.. ,./, **master's** *n* a university degree that you can get by studying for two years after your first degree ∥ 학사 학위를 취득한 후 2년 동안 공부해서 얻을 수 있는 대학의 학위. 석사 학위

mas·ter·y /'mæstəri/ *n* [U] **1** complete control of a situation or complete understanding of a subject ∥ 한 가지 상황이나 주제에 대한 완전한 통제나 이해. 지배. 숙달. 정통: *Early explorers could not match the Inuit mastery of the seas.* 초기 탐험가들은 이뉴잇족의 바다의 제해권에 맞설 수가 없었다. **2** thorough understanding or great skill ∥ 철저한 이해 또는 뛰어난 기술. 정복. 우월

mas·tur·bate /'mæstɚ,beɪt/ *v* [I, T] to rub your sexual organs in order to get sexual pleasure ∥ 성적인 만족을 얻기 위해 자신의 성기를 문지르다. 자위행위를 하다 – **masturbation** /,mæstɚ'beɪʃən/ *n* [U]

mat /mæt/ *n* **1** a small piece of thick material that covers part of a floor ∥ 바닥의 일부분을 덮는 두꺼운 물질로 된 작은 조각. 매트. 돗자리 **2** a large piece of thick soft material used in some sports for people to fall on ∥ 넘어지는 사람들을 위해 몇몇 스포츠에서 사용되는 두껍고 부드러운 물질로 된 넓은 조각. 매트

mat·a·dor /'mætə,dɔr/ *n* someone who fights and tries to kill a BULL during a BULLFIGHT ∥ 투우를 하면서 황소와 싸워서 죽이려는 사람. 투우사

match¹ /mætʃ/ *n* **1** a short wooden stick that produces a flame when it is rubbed against a rough surface ∥ 거친 표면에 대고 문지르면 불꽃이 일어나는 짧은 나무 막대기. 성냥: *a box of matches* 성냥 한

통 / *He lit a match so we could see.* 그
가 성냥불을 켜서 우리는 볼 수가 있었다.
2 a game or sports event ‖ 게임이나 스포
츠 경기. 시합: *a tennis match* 테니스 시
합 **3** [singular] something that is the
same color or pattern as something else
‖ 다른 종류의 물건과 동일한 색깔과 무늬
가 있는 물건. 서로 잘 어울리는 것:
*These shoes are **a perfect match** for the
hat.* 이들 신발은 그 모자와 아주 잘 어울
린다. **4 be no match for** to be much
less strong, fast etc. than an opponent
‖ 상대보다 강도·빠르기 등이 훨씬 못 미
치다. 상대가 되지 못하다: *Our defense
was no match for theirs.* 우리의 수비는
그들에게 상대가 되지 못했다.

match² *v* **1** [I, T] if
one thing matches
another, or if two
things match, they
look good together
because they have a
similar color, pattern
etc. ‖ 하나의 물건이 다
른 것과, 또는 두 개의
물체가 색상이나 무늬
가 비슷하여 서로 좋아
보이다. (…과) 조화되
다. (…에) 어울리다:

match

These socks
don't match.

*We found carpet to match the curtains
in this room.* 우리는 이 방에 있는 커튼과
어울리는 카펫을 찾았다. **2** [I, T] to be
the same or look the same as something
else ‖ 다른 것과 같거나 같아 보이다. 일치
하다: *The story she told about the
accident doesn't match her husband's
story.* 그 사고에 대해 그녀가 한 이야기는
그녀의 남편이 한 얘기와 일치하지 않는
다. / *Do these socks match?* 이들 양말은
짝이 맞느냐? **3** [T] to find something
that is similar or related to something
else ‖ 다른 것과 비슷하거나 관련된 것을
찾다. …을 짝짓다: *Match the words on
the left with the meanings on the right.*
오른쪽의 단어와 의미가 비슷한 단어를 왼
쪽 단어에서 찾으시오. **4** [T] to be of the
same quality or amount as someone or
something else ‖ 다른 사람이나 사물과
질이나 양이 같다. 필적하다: *No one can
match Rogers' speed on the football
field.* 미식축구 경기장에서 로저의 스피드
를 따라잡을 수 있는 사람은 아무도 없다.
5 [T] to provide something that is
suitable for a particular situation ‖ 특정
한 상황에 알맞은 것을 제공하다: *We'll
try to help you find a job to match your
skills.* 우리가 너를 도와 네 기술에 어울리
는 일자리를 찾아 볼게.

match up *phr v* [I] **1** to belong with or
fit together with something ‖ 어떤 것에
속하거나 어떤 것과 서로 어울리다: *The
edges of the cloth don't match up.* 천의
가장자리가 서로 어울리지 않는다. **2** to
be of a similar level or of similar quality
as something ‖ 어떤 것과 같은 수준 또는
같은 질이다. 필적하다. 대응하다: *If the
product doesn't match up to our
standards, we don't sell it.* 만일 그 제품
이 우리의 기준에 미치지 못한다면 우리는
팔지 않는다.

match·book /ˈmætʃbʊk/ *n* a small
piece of thick folded paper containing
paper matches ‖ 종이 성냥이 들어 있는
두툼하게 접힌 작은 종잇조각. 성냥첩

match·box /ˈmætʃbɑks/ *n* a small box
containing matches ‖ 성냥이 들어 있는
작은 상자. 성냥통

match·ing /ˈmætʃɪŋ/ *adj* having the
same color, style, pattern etc. as
something else ‖ 다른 것과 같은 색상·스
타일·무늬 등을 가진. 조화되는. 어울리
는: *a sapphire necklace with matching
earrings* 귀걸이와 어울리는 사파이어 목
걸이

match·less /ˈmætʃlɪs/ *adj* FORMAL
better than all other things of the same
kind ‖ 같은 종류의 모든 다른 것보다 나
은. 상대가 없는. 무쌍의

match·mak·er /ˈmætʃˌmeɪkɚ/ *n*
someone who is always trying to find
suitable people for his/her friends to
have romantic relationships with ‖ 친구
들을 위해 연애 관계를 갖기에 적합한 사
람을 늘 물색 중인 사람. 중매쟁이 –
matchmaking *n* [U]

mate¹ /meɪt/ *n* **1** one of a pair of objects
‖ 한 쌍의 물건 중 한쪽. 짝: *I can't find
the mate to this glove.* 이 장갑의 한 짝을
찾을 수 없다. **2** HUMOROUS someone's
wife, husband, or sexual partner ‖ 한 사
람의 아내[남편, 성적인 상대]. 배우자.
배필: *He's still searching for the perfect
mate.* 그는 아직도 완벽한 배필을 찾고 있
다. **3** the sexual partner of an animal ‖
동물의 성적인 상대. 짝 —see also
CLASSMATE, ROOMMATE

mate² *v* **1** [I] if animals mate they have
sex to produce babies ‖ 동물이 새끼를 낳
기 위해 교미하다. 짝짓기하다: *Most birds
mate in the spring.* 대부분의 새들은 봄에
짝짓기 한다. **2** [T] to put animals
together so that they will have sex and
produce babies ‖ 교미해서 새끼를 낳으려
고 동물들을 한데 모으다. 짝짓기하게 하
다

ma·te·ri·al¹ /məˈtɪriəl/ *n* **1** [C, U] cloth

M

used for making things like clothes, curtains etc. ‖ 옷·커튼 등과 같은 것을 만드는 데에 사용하는 천. 복지. 옷감. 직물: *Mom bought some velvet material for the dress.* 엄마는 드레스를 만들려고 벨벳 옷감을 좀 샀다. —see usage note at CLOTH **2** [C, U] things such as wood, plastic, paper etc. from which things can be made ‖ 물건을 만들 수 있는 나무·플라스틱·종이 등의 것. 재료. 원료: *building materials* 건축 자재 **3** [U] information or ideas used in books, movies etc. ‖ 책·영화 등에 사용되는 정보나 아이디어. 제재. 자료. 소재: *The director added some new material to the play.* 감독은 그 연극에 몇 가지 새로운 아이디어를 추가했다.

material² *adj* **1** relating to someone's money, possessions, living conditions etc. ‖ 사람의 돈·소유물·생활 여건과 관련된. 물질적인: *the material comforts that money can buy* 돈으로 살 수 있는 물질적인 안락 **2** relating to the real world or to physical objects, rather than religious or SPIRITUAL things ‖ 종교적이거나 정신적인 것보다는 현실 세계나 물질적인 대상에 관련된. 세속적인: *the material world* 세속적인 세계 **3** LAW very important and needing to be considered when making a decision ‖ 어떤 결정을 할 때 고려해야 할 매우 중요하고 필요한. 중요한. 요긴한. 필수의: *a material witness for the defense* 피고측의 중요한 증인

ma·te·ri·al·ism /məˈtɪriəˌlɪzəm/ *n* [U] DISAPPROVING the belief that getting money and possessions is the most important thing in life ‖ 돈과 부를 얻는 것이 인생에서 가장 중요하다는 신념. 물질 만능주의 **– materialist** *adj* **– materialistic** /məˌtɪriəˈlɪstɪk/ *adj*

ma·te·ri·al·ize /məˈtɪriəˌlaɪz/ *v* [I] **1** if a possible event or plan materializes, it happens ‖ 가능한 사건이나 계획이 실현되다: *His dream of building a hospital failed to materialize.* (=did not happen) 병원을 짓겠다는 그의 꿈은 실현되지 않았다. **2** to appear suddenly in a way that is strange or unexpected ‖ 이상스럽거나 뜻밖에 갑자기 나타나다: *A man materialized from the shadows.* 어둠 속에서 한 남자가 갑자기 모습을 드러냈다.

ma·ter·nal /məˈtɚnl/ *adj* **1** typical of the way a mother feels or acts ‖ 전형적으로 어머니가 느끼거나 행동하는 식의. 어머니의. 어머니다운: *maternal feelings* 모성 감정 **2 maternal grandfather/ aunt etc.** your mother's grandfather,

aunt etc. ‖ 자신의 외조부/외숙모 — compare PATERNAL

ma·ter·ni·ty /məˈtɚnəti/ *adj* relating to a woman who is PREGNANT, or who has had a baby, or to the time when she is pregnant ‖ 임신한 여자[아기를 낳은 여자, 여자가 임신했을 때]와 관련된. 임부[산부]의. 임신 기간의: *maternity clothes* 임신복

maternity leave /.'... ,./ *n* [U] time that a woman is allowed away from her job when she has a baby ‖ 여성이 아기를 가졌을 때 자기의 일을 쉬도록 허용되는 때. 출산 휴가

maternity ward /.'... ,./ *n* a department in a hospital where a woman is cared for after having a baby ‖ 아기를 가진 여성을 돌보는 병원의 분과. 산부인과 병동

math /mæθ/ *n* [U] INFORMAL the study or science of numbers and of the structure and measurement of shapes ‖ 수와 도형의 구조와 측정에 대한 연구나 학문. 수학

math·e·mat·i·cal /ˌmæθˈmætɪkəl/ *adj* related to or using mathematics ‖ 수학과 관련되거나 수학을 사용하는. 수학의. 수학적인: *a mathematical equation* 수학 방정식

math·e·ma·ti·cian /ˌmæθəməˈtɪʃən/ *n* someone who studies or teaches mathematics ‖ 수학을 연구하거나 가르치는 사람. 수학자

math·e·mat·ics /ˌmæθˈmætɪks, ˌmæθə-/ *n* [U] FORMAL ⇨ MATH

mat·i·née /ˌmætˈnˈeɪ/ *n* a performance of a play or movie in the afternoon ‖ 오후에 하는 연극이나 영화 공연. 마티네

ma·tri·arch /ˈmeɪtriˌɑrk/ *n* a woman who leads or controls a family or social group ‖ 가족이나 사회 단체를 이끌거나 지배하는 여자. 가장의 아내. 수령격의 여자 —compare PATRIARCH **– matriarchal** /ˌmeɪtriˈɑrkəl/ *adj*

ma·tri·archy /ˈmeɪtriˌɑrki/ *n* [C, U] a social system that is led or controlled by women ‖ 여자에 의해 이끌어지거나 지배되는 사회 제도. 가모장제(家母長制)

ma·tric·u·late /məˈtrɪkyəˌleɪt/ *v* [I] FORMAL to officially start a course of study at a university ‖ 대학의 학업 과정을 공식적으로 시작하다. 대학에 입학하다. 대학생이 되다 **– matriculation** /məˌtrɪkyəˈleɪʃən/ *n*

mat·ri·mo·ny /ˈmætrəˌmoʊni/ *n* [U] FORMAL the state of being married ‖ 결혼한 상태. 부부[결혼] 생활 **– matrimonial** /ˌmætrəˈmoʊniəl/ *adj*

ma·tron /ˈmeɪtrən/ *n* **1** a woman who is in charge of women and children in a school or prison ‖ 학교나 교도소에서 여성 및 아이들을 관리하는 여자. 여자 교도관. 여자 감독자 **2** LITERARY an older married woman ‖ 나이 많은 기혼 여성

ma·tron·ly /ˈmeɪtrənli/ *adj* used when politely describing a woman who is slightly older and fatter than what is considered attractive ‖ 매력적이라고 여겨지기보다는 다소 나이가 많고 좀 뚱뚱한 여성을 정중하게 묘사할 때에 쓰여. (중년 여성이) 품위가 있는

matt, mat, matte /mæt/ *adj* matt paint, color, or photographs are not shiny ‖ 페인트[색깔, 사진]가 광택이 나지 않는

mat·ted /ˈmætɪd/ *adj* matted hair or fur is twisted and stuck together ‖ 머리털이나 털이 서로 꼬여 들러붙은. 엉킨. 헝클어진

mat·ter¹ /ˈmætɚ/ *n*

1 ▶SUBJECT/SITUATION 주제/상황◀ a subject or situation that you have to think about or deal with, often one that causes problems ‖ 종종 문제를 일으키는, 생각해야 하거나 다루어야 할 주제나 상황. 문제: *Several important matters were discussed at the meeting.* 몇 가지 중요한 문제점들이 회의에서 논의되었다. / *Whether he is guilty is a matter for the jury to decide.* 그의 유죄 여부는 배심원단이 결정해야 할 문제이다. / *financial matters* 재정적 문제 / *It will only make matters worse if you complain.* 당신이 불평하면 문제는 더욱 악화만 될 것이다.

2 sth is a matter of money/principle etc a decision or situation that involves money etc. ‖ 돈 등이 연관된 결정이나 상황. 돈의/원칙의 문제이다: *The planning is finished. Now it's just a matter of money and time.* 계획 수립은 끝났다. 이제 단지 돈과 시간의 문제이다.

3 sth is a matter of opinion used in order to say that people have different opinions about something ‖ 사람들이 어떤 것에 대한 상이한 의견을 지니고 있는 것을 말하는 데에 쓰여. 견해의 문제이다. 견해 차이이다

4 a matter of seconds/days/inches etc. only a few seconds, days, inches etc. ‖ 단지 몇 초·며칠·몇 인치 등: *The bullet missed him by a matter of inches.* 총알은 단지 몇 인치 차이로 그를 비껴갔다.

5 no matter how/where/what etc. said when a situation does not change even though things happen that could

change it ‖ 상황을 바꿀 수 있었던 일이 일어나더라도 상황이 바뀌지 않을 때에 쓰여. 비록 …일지라도: *No matter how hard she tried, she couldn't get the door open.* 비록 그녀가 열심히 애써봤지만 문을 열지는 못했다.

6 for that matter said when what you have said about one thing is also true about another ‖ 한 가지에 대해 말한 것이 다른 것에 대해서도 역시 사실일 때에 쓰여. 그것에 대해서는 마찬가지로: *I don't like him or, for that matter, his girlfriend either!* 나는 그를 좋아하지 않는데 그의 여자 친구도 마찬가지로 싫어!

7 ▶SUBSTANCE/THINGS 물질/사물◀ [U] **a)** TECHNICAL the material that everything in the universe is made of ‖ 이 세상에서 만들어진 모든 물질 **b)** things of a particular kind or for a particular use ‖ 특정한 종류나 용도의 물건: *waste/vegetable matter* 폐기물[식물] / *reading matter* 읽을거리

8 it's only/just a matter of time used in order to say that something will definitely happen even though you cannot say exactly when ‖ 비록 언제인지는 정확히 말할 수 없어도 어떤 일이 틀림없이 일어날 것이라고 말하는 데에 쓰여. 단지 시간 문제다: *It's only a matter of time, until he is too old to live alone.* 그가 너무 늙어 혼자 살아갈 수 없기 까지는 단지 시간의 문제이다.

9 a matter of life and death a very dangerous or serious situation ‖ 매우 위험하거나 심각한 상황. 사활이 걸린 문제

—————— SPOKEN PHRASES ——————

10 what's the matter? used in order to ask someone why s/he is upset, angry etc. ‖ 왜 기분이 엉망인지·화가 났는지 남에게 묻는 데에 쓰여. 무슨 일이야?: *What's the matter? Why are you crying?* 무슨 일이야? 왜 울고 있어?

11 as a matter of fact said when giving a surprising or unexpected answer to a question or statement ‖ 질문이나 성명에 놀랍거나 예상 밖의 대답을 할 때에 쓰여. 실제로는. 사실은: *"Have you ever been to Paris?" "As a matter of fact I just came from there."* "파리에 가본 적이 있느냐?" "사실은 막 파리에서 왔어."

12 there's something/nothing the matter with said when there is or is not a problem with something ‖ 어떤 것에 문제가 있거나 문제가 없을 때에 쓰여. 이상이 있다/없다: *There's*

something the matter with the TV – the picture is bad. 텔레비전에 이상이 있어. 화면이 좋지 않아.

matter² *v* [I] **1** to be important, or to have an effect on what happens ‖ 중요하다, 일어나는 일에 영향이 있다: *Money is the only thing that matters to him.* 그에게 중요한 것은 돈뿐이다. / *"Does it matter which road I take?" "No, it's the same distance."* "내가 어느 도로를 택하는가가 중요한가요?" "아니, 거리는 같아." **2 it doesn't matter** SPOKEN **a)** used in order to say that you do not care which one of two things you have ‖ 두 개 중 어떤 것도 개의치 않는다고 말하는 데에 쓰여. 아무거나 상관없다: *"Do you want tea or coffee?" "Oh, it doesn't matter."* "홍차를 드실래요, 커피를 드실래요?" "아무거나 상관없어요." **b)** used in order to tell someone you are not angry or upset ‖ 남에게 화나거나 심란하지 않다고 말하는 데에 쓰여. 괜찮아: *"I'm sorry – I didn't realize you were eating dinner." "It doesn't matter!"* "미안해. 나는 네가 식사를 하고 있는지 몰랐어." "괜찮아."

matter-of-fact /ˌ.. . '../ *adj* showing no strong emotions when you are talking about something ‖ 어떤 것에 대해 말할 때 두드러진 감정을 보이지 않는다. 사실대로의. 평범한. 무미건조한: *The doctor was very matter-of-fact when he explained the problem.* 그 의사는 그 문제를 설명할 때 매우 무덤덤했다. – **matter-of-factly** *adv*

mat·ting /'mætɪŋ/ *n* [U] strong rough material used for covering a floor ‖ 바닥을 덮는 데에 사용하는 질기고 거칠거칠한 물질. 돗자리. 깔개. 매트

mat·tress /'mætrɪs/ *n* the soft part of a bed that you lie on ‖ 사람이 눕는, 침대의 푹신한 부분. 매트리스: *a king-size mattress* 킹사이즈의 매트리스

ma·ture¹ /məˈtʃʊr, məˈtʊr/ *adj* **1** behaving in a reasonable way like an adult ‖ 어른같이 합리적으로 행동하는. 성숙한: *She's young, but she's very mature for her age.* 그녀는 어리지만 나이에 비해 매우 성숙하다. **2** fully grown or developed ‖ 완전히 자라거나 발달된. 완전히 발육한. 잘 익은. 숙성한: *Meat from mature animals is often tough.* 완전히 자란 동물의 고기는 종종 질기다. / *mature wine* 숙성된 포도주 —opposite IMMATURE

mature² *v* [I] **1** to become fully grown or developed ‖ 완전히 자라거나 충분히 발달하다: *The fly matures in only seven days.* 파리는 7일 만에 성충이 된다. **2** to begin to behave in a reasonable way like an adult ‖ 성인처럼 합리적으로 행동하기 시작하다. 성숙하다: *Pat's matured a lot since going to college.* 패트는 대학에 들어가고 난 이후로 많이 성숙해졌다. **3** if a BOND or POLICY matures, it becomes ready to be paid ‖ 채권이나 보험 증권의 지불 준비가 되다. 만기가 되다

ma·tu·ri·ty /məˈtʃʊrəti, -ˈtʊr-/ *n* [U] **1** the quality of behaving in a sensible way like an adult ‖ 성인처럼 이성적으로 행동하는 자질. 성숙. 원숙: *He has a lot of maturity for a fifteen year old.* 그는 15살 나이에 비해 상당히 성숙하다. **2** the time when a person, animal, or plant is fully grown or developed ‖ 사람[동물, 식물]이 완전히 자라거나 충분히 발육된 때. 성숙기. 원숙기: *Rabbits reach maturity in only five weeks.* 토끼들은 5주 만에 다 자란다. **3** TECHNICAL the time when a financial arrangement is ready to be paid ‖ 금융 협정의 지불 준비가 되어 있는 때. 만기. 지급기일

maud·lin /'mɔdlɪn/ *adj* talking or behaving in a sad and silly way; SENTIMENTAL ‖ 슬프고 어리석게 말하거나 행동하는. 눈물이 헤픈. 감상적인; ㈜ sentimental

maul /mɔl/ *v* [T] to injure someone by tearing his/her flesh ‖ 남의 피부를 찢어 다치게 하다. 상처를 입히다

mau·so·le·um /ˌmɔsəˈliəm, -zə-/ *n* a large stone building containing many graves or built over a grave ‖ 많은 무덤이 들어 있거나 하나의 무덤 위에 지은 큰 석조 건물. 웅장한 무덤. 능묘

mauve /moʊv/ *n* [U] a pale purple color ‖ 담자색(淡紫色) – **mauve** *adj*

mav·er·ick /'mævərɪk/ *n* someone who thinks or behaves in a way that is surprising and different from most people ‖ 대부분의 사람들과는 경이적이며 유별난 방식으로 생각하거나 행동하는 사람. 독불장군: *a political maverick* 정치적 독불장군 – **maverick** *adj*

mawk·ish /'mɔkɪʃ/ *adj* showing too much emotion in a way that is embarrassing ‖ 난처할 정도로 감정을 지나치게 드러내는. 별나게 감상적인 – **mawkishly** *adv*

max¹ /mæks/ *n* [U] **1** SPOKEN at the most ‖ 많아야: *It'll cost $50 max.* 비용은 많아야 50달러가 될 것이다. **2** the written abbreviation for MAXIMUM ‖ maximum의 약어 **3 to the max** SLANG to the greatest degree possible ‖ 가능한 한 최고도로. 완

전히. 극도로

max² v

max out *phr v* **max out (on sth)** SLANG to have or do too much of something so that you are tired or bored ‖ 지치거나 지겨울 정도로 어떤 것을 너무 많이 가지거나 하다. 최고점에 달하다. 한계에 이르다: *No more chocolate. I maxed out on it last night.* 초콜릿은 이제 그만. 나는 어제 저녁 초콜릿을 지겨울 정도로 잔뜩 먹었어.

max·im /ˈmæksɪm/ *n* a well-known phrase that shows how to behave in a reasonable way ‖ 합리적으로 처신하는 방법을 보여 주는 잘 알려진 문구. 격언. 금언: *"A penny saved is a penny earned" is a maxim.* "한 푼 절약하는 것이 한 푼 버는 것이다"라는 말은 격언이다.

max·i·mize /ˈmæksəˌmaɪz/ *v* [T] to increase something as much as possible ‖ 어떤 것을 가능한 한 증대하다. 최대로 하다: *We want to maximize the services available to our customers.* 우리는 우리의 고객에게 가능한 한 최고의 서비스를 하고 싶다. —opposite MINIMIZE

max·i·mum¹ /ˈmæksəməm/ *adj* being the largest that is possible, allowed, or needed ‖ 가능한 한[허용되는 한, 필요한 한] 가장 큰. 최대의. 최고의: *The car has a maximum speed of 125 mph.* 그 차는 최고 속도가 시속 125마일이다. —opposite MINIMUM¹

maximum² *n* the largest number, amount etc. that is possible, allowed, or needed ‖ 가능한 한[허용되는 한, 필요한 한] 가장 큰 수나 양 등. 최고. 최대(한). 최대량: *"How much tax will I have to pay?" "20% is the maximum you could pay."* "내가 내야 할 세금이 얼마입니까?" "최대 20%를 내야 할 것입니다." —opposite MINIMUM²

May /meɪ/ *n* the fifth month of a year ‖ 한 해의 다섯 번째 달. 5월 —see usage note at JANUARY

may *modal verb* **1** used in order to talk about what was, is, or will be possible ‖ 무엇이 가능했는지[가능한지, 가능할지]를 언급하는 데에 쓰여. …일[이었을]지도 모른다: *It may snow tonight.* 오늘 밤 눈이 올지도 모른다. / *This may not be enough money.* 이것으로 돈이 충분하지 않을지 모르겠다. ✗DON'T SAY "mayn't"✗ "mayn't"라고는 하지 않는다. **2 may I** SPOKEN used in order to politely ask if you can do or have something ‖ 어떤 것을 하거나 가질 수 있는지 정중하게 묻는 데에 쓰여: *May I borrow your pen?* 네 펜을 좀 빌릴 수 있을까? / *May I have some more coffee?* 커피 좀 더 마실 수 있을까

요? **3** FORMAL used in order to allow someone to do something ‖ 남에게 무엇을 하도록 허락하는 데에 쓰여. …을 해도 좋다: *You may start writing on your test forms now.* 지금 시험지를 작성하기 시작해도 좋다. **4 may as well** ⇨ **might as well**(MIGHT¹) -compare MIGHT¹ -see usage note at PERHAPS -see study note on page 932

may·be /ˈmeɪbi/ *adv* **1** used in order to say that something may be true or may happen, but that you are not sure ‖ 어떤 것이 사실이거나 일어날지 모르지만 확신할 수는 없다는 것을 말하는 데에 쓰여. 아마. 혹시. 어쩌면: *Maybe Anna's stuck in traffic.* 아마도 애너는 교통 체증으로 꼼짝없이 갇혔을 것이다. / *There were 300 or maybe 400 people there.* 그곳에는 아마 300 또는 400명 정도 있었다. / *Maybe I'll wear my blue suit.* 아마도 나는 파란색 옷을 입을 거야. **2** used in order to make a suggestion ‖ 제의를 하는 데에 쓰여. …하면 어떨까: *Maybe Jeff could help you.* 제프가 너를 도와주면 어떨까. —see usage note at PERHAPS

May Day /ˈ. ./ *n* [C, U] the first day of May, when LEFT-WING political parties have celebrations, and when people traditionally celebrate the arrival of spring ‖ 좌익 정치 단체가 축제를 열며, 사람들이 전통적으로 봄이 오는 것을 축하하는 5월의 첫째 날. 노동절. 메이 데이

may·day /ˈmeɪdeɪ/ *n* a radio signal used in order to ask for help when a ship or plane is in danger ‖ 배나 비행기가 위험에 처해 있을 경우 도움을 요청하는 데에 쓰이는 무선 신호. 메이데이

may·hem /ˈmeɪhɛm/ *n* [U] an extremely confused situation in which people are very frightened or excited ‖ 사람들이 매우 겁먹거나 흥분된 극단적으로 혼란한 상태. 대혼란. 소동: *There was complete mayhem after the explosion.* 폭발 후에 대혼란이 있었다.

may·on·naise /ˈmeɪəˌneɪz, ˌmæneɪz/ *n* [U] a thick white SAUCE made of egg and oil, often eaten on sandwiches (SANDWICH) ‖ 종종 샌드위치에 얹어 먹는 계란과 식용유로 만든 진한 흰 소스. 마요네즈

may·or /ˈmeɪə, mɛr/ *n* someone who is elected to lead the government of a town or city ‖ 읍이나 시의 행정을 이끌도록 선출된 사람. 시장. 읍장. 면장

maze /meɪz/ *n* **1** a specially designed system of paths that is difficult to find your way through, or something like this drawn on paper ‖ 통로를 찾기 어렵

M

게 특별히 디자인된 길
의 편성, 또는 종이에
그린 이와 같은 것. 미
로: *We got lost in the
maze.* 우리는 미로 속
에서 길을 잃었다. **2** a
place that is difficult
to find your way
through ‖ 통로를 찾기
어려운 장소. 미궁: *a
maze of dark hallways* 미궁 같은 어두운
통로 **3** something that is complicated
and difficult to understand ‖ 이해하기 복
잡하고 어려운 것. 혼란: *a maze of
government rules* 행정 규정의 혼선

maze

M.B.A. *n* Master of Business
Administration; a GRADUATE degree that
teaches you the skills you need to be in
charge of a business ‖ Master of
Business Administration(경영학 석사)의
약어; 사업 관리에 필요한 기술을 가르치
는 석사 학위

Mc·Coy /məˈkɔɪ/ *n* **the real McCoy**
INFORMAL something that is real and not
a copy ‖ 모조품이 아닌 진짜의 것. 진품:
*Paste jewels cost hundreds less than the
real McCoy.* 인조 보석은 진짜 보석보다
값이 100달러 더 싸다.

M.D. *n* the abbreviation of Doctor of
Medicine ‖ Doctor of Medicine의 약어

MD the written abbreviation of
Maryland ‖ Maryland(메릴랜드 주)의 약
어

ME the written abbreviation of Maine ‖
Maine(메인 주)의 약어

me /mi/ *pron* **1** the object form of "I" ‖
"I"의 목적격: *Cathy called me last night.*
캐시는 어젯밤 나에게 전화했다. / *My
parents gave me a necklace for my
birthday.* 부모님은 내 생일날 목걸이를
주셨다. **2 me too** SPOKEN said when you
agree with someone ‖ 남에게 동의할 때
에 쓰여. 나도 마찬가지야: *"I'm hungry!"
"Me too."* "배고파 죽겠어!" "나도 마찬가
지야." **3 me neither** SPOKEN said when
you agree with a negative statement
someone has just made ‖ 남이 이미 한
부정적인 말에 동의할 때에 쓰여. 나도 아
니다: *"I don't like fruitcake." "Me
neither."* "나는 과일 케이크를 좋아하지
않아." "나도 좋아하지 않아."

USAGE NOTE me, him, her, us, and
them

In informal speech, we often use
object pronouns after "as," "than,"
and "be" when making comparisons:
He's a better player than me. / She's

not as tall as him. In written or
formal English, use subject pronouns:
*He's a better player than I. / She's not
as tall as he.*
비격식적인 말에서, 비교를 할 때 "as",
"than" 및 "be" 뒤에 대명사의 목적격
이 종종 사용된다: 그는 나보다 더 나은
선수이다. / 그녀는 그만큼 키가 크지 않
다. 문어체나 격식을 차린 영어에서는
대명사의 주격을 사용한다: 그는 나보다
더 훌륭한 선수이다. / 그녀는 그만큼 키
가 크지 않다.

mead·ow /ˈmɛdoʊ/ *n* a field with wild
grass and flowers ‖ 야생의 풀과 꽃이 자
라는 들판. 초원. 목초지

mea·ger /ˈmigɚ/ *adj* very small in
amount ‖ 양이 매우 적은. 근소한. 빈약
한: *a meager breakfast* 변변찮은 아침 식
사

meal /mil/ *n* a particular time when
you eat food, or the food that is eaten
then ‖ 음식을 먹는 특정한 시간, 또는 그
때 먹는 음식. 식사(시간): *Would you like
wine with your meal?* 식사하면서 포도주
좀 마실래요? / *It's important to eat
regular meals.* 식사를 규칙적으로 하는
것이 중요하다. —see also CORNMEAL,
OATMEAL

meal·time /ˈmiltaɪm/ *n* the usual time
for eating a meal ‖ 보통 식사하는 시간.
일상적인 식사 시간

USAGE NOTE meal times

The first meal of the day is
breakfast, which is eaten in the
morning just after getting up. **Lunch**
is the meal that is eaten around 12:00
p.m. **Dinner** is the main meal of the
day, usually eaten in the evening
between 5:30 and 7:30 p.m. A
dinner can also be a special meal:
*Thanksgiving Dinner / Sunday
dinner.* **Supper** is a light or informal
evening meal. **Brunch** is a meal
eaten fairly late in the morning.
잠에서 막 깬 뒤 아침에 먹는 하루의 첫
식사는 **breakfast**이다. **lunch**는 낮
12시 경에 먹는 식사이다. **dinner**는 보
통 저녁 5시 30분과 7시 30분 사이에
먹는 하루의 주요한 식사이다. **dinner**
에는 특별한 음식을 먹을 수 있다: 추수
감사절 정찬/일요일 정찬. **supper**는 가
볍거나 격식을 차리지 않은 저녁 식사이
다. **brunch**는 꽤 늦은 아침에 먹는 식
사이다.

meal·y-mouthed /ˌmili ˈmaʊðd/ *adj*

not brave or honest enough to say clearly what you think‖ 생각하는 것을 분명히 말할 만큼 충분히 용감하거나 정직하지 않은. 완곡하게[에둘러] 말하는. 듣기 좋게 말하는

mean¹ /min/ *v* **meant, meant, meaning** [T] **1** to express or mean a particular meaning or message‖ 특정한 의미나 메시지를 표현하거나 가지다. …을 의미하다: *"What does the word 'Konbanwa' mean?" "It means 'Good Evening.'"* "'Konbanwa'라는 단어는 무슨 뜻이냐?" "'Good Evening'이라는 뜻이다." / *The red light means "stop."* 적색등은 "정지"를 뜻한다. ✗DON'T SAY "is meaning."✗ "is meaning"이라고는 하지 않는다. **2** to intend a particular meaning when you say something‖ 무엇을 말할 때 특정한 의미를 의도하다: *I didn't mean to sound like I was mad.* 내가 미쳤다는 식의 소리를 들으려고 한 것은 아니었다. / *I said Monday but I meant Tuesday.* 나는 화요일로 생각했지만 월요일이라고 말했다. ✗DON'T SAY "I am meaning."✗ "I am meaning"이라고는 하지 않는다. **3** to have a particular result‖ 특정한 결과를 낳다. …하게 되다. …이라는 결과가 되다: *It's snowing, which means that it will take longer to get there.* 눈이 와서 거기에 도착하는 데 더 오래 걸릴 것이다. ✗DON'T SAY "which is meaning."✗ "which is meaning"이라고는 하지 않는다. **4 mean to do sth** to intend to do something‖ 어떤 것을 하려고 작정하다: *I've been meaning to ask you something.* 나는 당신에게 무언가 물어볼 참이었다. / *He says he didn't mean for her to get hurt.* 그는 그녀를 다치게 할 생각은 아니었다고 말한다. **5 sb/sth means a lot (to sb)** used in order to say that someone or something is very important or special to someone‖ 사람이나 사물이 남에게 매우 중요하거나 특별하다고 말하는 데에 쓰여. 매우 소중하다: *It would mean a lot to your father if you offered to help.* 만일 당신이 도와준다면 당신 아버지에게는 아주 귀중한 일이 될 것이다. **6 mean business** to be very serious about something such as a threat‖ 위협 등의 것에 대해서 매우 진지하다. (장난이 아니고) 진심이다: *You have to be strict about the rules so they know you mean business.* 당신이 진심이라는 것을 그들이 알도록 당신은 그 규칙을 엄격히 지켜야 한다. **7 sth was meant to be** used in order to say that you think a situation was certain to happen‖ 어떤 상황이 발생하는 것을 피할

수 없었다고 여기는 것을 말하는 데에 쓰여. 불가항력이었다: *I'm sure this marriage was meant to be.* 나는 이 결혼이 불가항력이었다고 확신한다.

SPOKEN PHRASES

8 I mean a) said when you stop to think about what to say next‖ 다음에 할 말을 생각하기 위해 멈출 때에 쓰여. 즉. 요컨대. 바꾸어 말하면: *She's just so nice. I mean, she's a really gentle person.* 그녀는 정말 멋있어. 그러니까 그녀는 정말 다정한 사람이야. **b)** said when you want to quickly change what you have just said‖ 자신이 방금 말한 것을 재빨리 번복하고 싶을 때에 쓰여. 아니…: *She plays the violin, I mean the viola.* 그녀는 바이올린, 아니 비올라를 연주한다. **9 I mean it!** said in order to emphasize what you are saying when you are very angry‖ 매우 화났을 때 하고 있는 말을 강조하는 데에 쓰여. 명심하라구. 진심이야. 농담이 아냐: *Don't ever say that word again, and I mean it!* 그 말을 다시는 하지 마, 명심하라구! **10 (Do) you mean …?** said when you want to check that you understand something‖ 자신이 이해하고 있는 것을 확인하고 싶을 때에 쓰여. …이라는 말이냐?: *You mean you want me to call you, or will you call me?* 내가 너에게 전화를 하라는 거냐, 네가 내게 전화를 하겠다는 거냐? **11 (Do) you know what I mean?** said in order to ask someone if s/he understands you‖ 남에게 자신의 말을 이해하고 있는지 묻는 데에 쓰여. 내 말 알겠어?: *I want to go somewhere different on vacation. You know what I mean?* 나는 휴가 때 색다른 곳으로 가고 싶어. 내 말 알겠어? **12 I know what you mean** said in order to show that you understand someone‖ 남의 말을 이해한다는 것을 나타내는 데에 쓰여. 무슨 말인 줄 안다: *"I'm so tired of his complaining." "I know what you mean."* "그의 불평에 너무 지쳤어." "이해해." **13 what do you mean? a)** said when you do not understand someone‖ 남의 말을 이해하지 못할 때에 쓰여. …은 무슨 말이야? **b)** said when you are very surprised and annoyed by something someone has done‖ 남이 한 일이 몹시 놀랍거나 짜증스러울 때에 쓰여. …이라니 도대체 무슨 말이야?: *What do you mean, you sold the car?* 그 차를 팔았다니 도대체 무슨 말이야?

mean² *adj* **1** unkind or nasty ‖ 불친절한, 불쾌한: *Why do you say such mean things to me?* 왜 너는 나에게 그런 불쾌한 일들을 말하는 거야? **2** cruel and having a bad temper ‖ 잔인하고 성질이 나쁜. 고약한. 심술궂은: *a mean old man* 고약스러운 노옹(老翁) **3** INFORMAL very good ‖ 매우 좋은. 훌륭한: *Ray plays a mean game of tennis.* 레이는 테니스를 잘 한다. **4 no mean** used in order to say that something is very good, or that someone does something very well ‖ 사물이 아주 좋거나 남이 어떤 것을 상당히 잘 한다고 말하는 데에 쓰여. 비할 데 없는. 대단한: *It was no mean achievement for a woman to become a doctor in 1920.* 1920년에 여성이 의사가 된다는 것은 대단한 성과였다. **5** average ‖ 평균의. 보통의. 평범한: *The mean temperature in Akron was 18.2°F this month.* 이번 달 아크론의 평균 기온은 화씨 18.2도였다.

mean³ *n* TECHNICAL an average amount, figure, or value ‖ 평균량, 평균 수치, 평균값. 평균: *The mean of 7, 9, and 14 is 10.* 7과 9와 14의 평균은 10이다. —see also MEANS

me·an·der /mi'ændər/ *v* [I] to move slowly and turn many times ‖ 천천히 움직이고 여러 번 방향을 바꾸다. 꼬불꼬불 [굽이쳐] 흐르다: *a meandering stream* 굽이쳐 흐르는 시내 – **meanderings** *n* [plural]

mean·ing /'minɪŋ/ *n* **1** [C, U] the thing or idea that a word, phrase, or sign represents ‖ 단어[구, 기호]가 나타내는 것이나 의미. 뜻: *I don't understand the meaning of this word.* 나는 이 단어의 뜻을 알지 못한다. **2** [C, U] the idea that someone intends to express when s/he says something, writes a book, makes a film etc. ‖ 사람이 말을 할 때·책을 쓸 때·영화를 제작 할 때에 나타내고자 하는 생각. 취지. 의도: *There seemed to be very little meaning in the film's violence.* 그 영화의 폭력 장면은 거의 의미가 없는 것 같았다. / *The poem could have two meanings.* 그 시는 두 가지 진의를 담고 있었다. **3** [U] the quality that makes something seem important and valuable ‖ 어떤 것을 중요하고 값져 보이게 만드는 자질. 중요성. 진가. 의의: *Until today, I hadn't realized the full meaning of what had happened.* 오늘까지도 나는 벌어진 일에 대한 완전한 의미를 깨닫지 못했다. **4 not know the meaning of** used in order to say that someone has no understanding of a particular situation or feeling ‖ 사람이 특정한 상황이나 감정을 이해하지 못하거나 말하는 데에 쓰여: *Those kids don't know the meaning of hard work.* 그 아이들은 근면의 뜻을 이해하지 못한다.

mean·ing·ful /'minɪŋfəl/ *adj* **1** serious, useful, or important ‖ 심각한, 유용한, 중요한. 의미 있는. 의미심장한: *a meaningful relationship* 중요한 관계 / *You need a meaningful sample for the experiment to work.* 너에게는 작업 실험을 할 유용한 견본이 필요하다. / *Congress hasn't made any meaningful changes to the bill.* 의회는 그 법안에 대한 어떤 의미 있는 개정을 이루어내지 못했다. **2** easy to understand ‖ 이해하기 쉬운: *The data isn't very meaningful to anyone but a scientist.* 그 자료는 과학자를 제외하고 일반인이 이해하기에 그리 쉽지 않다. **3 a meaningful look/smile etc.** a look that clearly expresses the way someone feels ‖ 사람이 느끼는 바를 분명히 나타내는 표정. 의미심장한 표정/미소

mean·ing·less /'minɪŋlɪs/ *adj* without any purpose or meaning that you can understand or explain ‖ 이해하거나 설명할 수 있는 어떤 목적이나 의미가 없는. 무의미한. 가치 없는: *Her whole life felt meaningless.* 그녀의 일생이 무의미하게 느껴졌다.

means /minz/ *n* [plural] **1** a method, system, object etc. that is used as a way of doing something ‖ 어떤 것을 하는 방책으로 쓰이는 방법·시스템·목적 등. 수단. 방법: *We'll use any means we can to raise the money.* 우리는 임금을 올리기 위해 우리가 할 수 있는 어떠한 방법이든 사용할 것이다. / *She took up photography as a means of earning a living.* 그녀는 생활비를 버는 수단으로 사진 찍는 일을 시작했다. / *The oil is transported by means of* (=using) *a pipeline.* 그 기름은 송유관을 통해 수송된다. **2 by all means** said in order to emphasize that someone should do or is allowed to do something ‖ 남이 어떤 것을 해야 하거나 해도 좋다는 것을 강조하는 데에 쓰여. 꼭. 반드시. 좋다마다: *By all means, drink while you are exercising.* 반드시 운동 중에 음료수를 마셔라. **3 by no means** FORMAL not at all ‖ 조금도. 전혀: *The results are by no means certain.* 그 결과들은 전혀 확실하지 않다. **4 a means to an end** something that you do or use only to achieve a result ‖ 오직 결과를 얻기 위해 하거나 사용하는 것. 목적 달성을 위한 한 가지 수단: *Bev always says her job is* *just a means to an end.* 베브는 늘 자기의 일이 목적 달성을 위한 수단에 불과하다고 말한다. **5** the money or things that you have that make it possible for you to buy or do things ‖ 어떤 것을 사거나 할 수 있는 수중에 지닌 돈이나 물건. 재력. 돈. 재산: *They don't have the means to buy a car.* 그들은 차를 살 만한 돈이 없다. / *a man of means* (=who is rich) 부자

meant /ment/ *v* the past tense and PAST PARTICIPLE of MEAN ‖ mean의 과거·과거 분사형

mean·time /'miːntaɪm/ *n* **in the meantime** until something happens, or in the time between two events ‖ 어떤 일이 일어날 때까지, 또는 두 가지 일이 일어나는 사이에. 그때까지. 이럭저럭 하는 동안에. 그 동안에: *We want to buy a house, but in the meantime we're renting the apartment.* 우리는 집을 사고 싶지만 그 동안에 아파트에 세를 살려고 한다.

mean·while /'miːnwaɪl/ *adv* while something else is happening, or in the time between two events ‖ 다른 일이 일어나고 있는 동안에, 두 가지 일이 일어나는 사이에. 그 동안에: *Chris was gone for hours; meanwhile, she got some work done.* 크리스는 몇 시간 동안 외출한 동안 일을 꽤 했다.

mea·sles /'miːzəlz/ *n* **the measles** an infectious illness in which you have a fever and small red spots on your face and body ‖ 열이 나고 얼굴과 몸에 작은 붉은 반점이 생기는 전염성 질병. 홍역

mea·sly /'miːzli/ *adj* INFORMAL too small in amount or value ‖ 양이나 가치가 너무 적은. 아주 조금의: *I only won a measly $5.* 나는 겨우 5달러밖에 못 받았다.

meas·ur·a·ble /'meʒərəbəl/ *adj* **1** able to be measured ‖ 측정할 수 있는. 잴 수 있는: *A manager should set measurable goals.* 경영자는 측정 가능한 목표를 세워야 한다. **2** important or large enough to have an effect ‖ 영향을 미칠 만큼 충분히 중요하거나 큰: *The changes have not achieved any measurable results.* 그 변화는 어떤 중요한 성과도 올리지 못했다. – **measurably** *adv*

meas·ure¹ /'meʒɚ/ *n* **1** an official action that is intended to deal with a problem ‖ 문제를 처리하려고 하는 공식적인 행동. 조치. 방책: *Congress passed a measure to control spending today.* 오늘 의회는 지출을 조정하기 위한 법안을 통과시켰다. **2 a measure of sth** enough to be noticed, but not a large amount ‖ 많이는 아니지만 충분히 알 수 있는. 어느 정도의: *He ought to be treated with a*

measure of respect. 어느 정도의 존경심을 가지고 그를 대해야 한다. **3 take measures** to use your authority in order to do whatever is necessary to achieve an aim ‖ 목적 달성에 필요한 것은 무엇이든 하려고 자신의 권력을 사용하다. 조치를 취하다: *We have taken measures to limit smoking to one area in the building.* 우리는 건물 내에서의 흡연을 한 구역으로 제한하는 조치를 취했다. **4 be a measure of sth** FORMAL to be a sign of the importance, strength etc. of something ‖ 어떤 것의 중요성·세기 등의 신호이다. …의 척도이다 **5** [C, U] a system for measuring the weight, length etc. of something, or the unit of weight, length etc. that is used ‖ 어떤 것의 무게·길이 등의 측정을 위한 체계, 또는 무게나 길이 등에 쓰이는 단위. 도량형. 도량 단위: *The Richter scale is a measure of the strength of earthquakes.* 리히터 척도는 지진의 강도를 측정하는 단위이다. / *The pint is a liquid measure.* 파인트는 액량을 측정하는 단위이다. **6 for good measure** in addition, so that what you do or give is enough ‖ 하거나 주는 것이 충분할 만큼 더하여. 덤으로. 넉넉하게: *Add a little more salt for good measure.* 소금을 추가로 조금 더 넣어라.

measure

measuring cup   measuring tape

measure² *v* **1** [T] to find the size, length, or amount of something ‖ 어떤 것의 크기[길이, 양]를 알아내다. 재다. 측정하다: *Let's measure the wall to see if the bookshelves will fit.* 책장이 꼭 맞을지 알아보기 위해 벽의 치수를 재보자. / *Measure one cup of flour and add it to the mixture.* 밀가루 한 컵을 재어 혼합물에 첨가해라. **2** [T] to judge the importance or value of something ‖ 어떤 것의 중요성이나 가치를 판단하다. 평가하다: *It's difficult to measure educational success.* 교육의 성공을 평가하는 것은 어렵다. **3** [linking verb] to be a particular size, length, or amount ‖ 특정한 크기[길이, 양]이다: *The table measures four feet by six feet.* 그 탁자의 크기는 가로 4

피트, 세로 6피트이다.

measure sb/sth **against** *phr v* [T] to judge someone or something by comparing him, her, or it to another person or thing ‖ 사람이나 사물을 다른 사람이나 사물과 비교하여 판단하다: *All managers should be measured against the same standard.* 모든 관리자들은 같은 기준으로 비교하여 평가되어야 한다.

measure up *phr v* [I] to be good enough to do a particular job or to reach a particular standard ‖ 특정한 일을 하거나 특정한 기준에 이를 정도로 충분히 좋다. 일정한 표준에 들어맞다. 달하다: *The steak didn't measure up to his expectations.* 그 스테이크는 그의 기대에 미치지 못했다.

meas·ure·ment /ˈmɛʒɚmənt/ *n* [C, U] the length, height, value etc. of something, or the act of measuring this ‖ 사물의 길이·높이·가치 등, 또는 이것들을 재는 행위. 측정[계량](치수): *We had to make/take a lot of measurements for the new carpet.* 우리는 새 양탄자의 치수를 여러 번 재어야 했다.

meat /mit/ *n* [U] the flesh of animals and birds eaten as food ‖ 음식으로 먹는 동물이나 새의 고기: *I don't eat much meat.* 나는 고기를 많이 먹지 않는다. — see also **dead meat** (DEAD¹)

USAGE NOTE meat

The meat from some animals has a different name from the animal itself. For example, the meat from a **cow** is **beef**. The meat from a **pig** is **pork** or **ham**. The meat from a **calf** (a young cow) is **veal**. But the meat from a **lamb** is **lamb**, and for birds and fish we use the same word for the meat and the animal: *They raise chickens and ducks on their farm. / Should we have chicken or duck for dinner?*

어떤 동물의 고기는 동물 자체의 이름과는 다른 명칭을 가지고 있다. 예를 들면 **cow**(소)의 고기는 **beef**이다. **pig**(돼지)의 고기는 **pork** 또는 **ham**이다. **calf**(송아지)의 고기는 **veal** 이다. 그러나 **lamb**(양)의 고기는 **lamb** 그대로이며 새나 물고기에 대해서도 동물과 그 고기에 동일한 단어를 사용한다: 그들은 농장에서 chicken(닭)과 duck(오리)들을 기른다. / 우리는 저녁에 chicken(닭고기)나 duck(오리 고기)를 먹나요?

---

meat·ball /ˈmitˌbɔl/ *n* a type of food made of very small pieces of meat pressed together into a ball and cooked ‖ 매우 작은 고기 조각을 공 모양으로 꽉 뭉쳐서 요리하여 만든 음식의 일종. 미트볼

meat·loaf /ˈmitloʊf/ *n* [C, U] a dish made from a meat mixture and baked in the shape of a LOAF ‖ 덩어리 모양으로 고기를 섞어서 구워 만든 음식. 미트로프

meat·y /ˈmiti/ *adj* containing a lot of meat or tasting strongly of meat ‖ 고기가 많이 들어간, 고기 맛이 강한: *a meaty stew* 고기가 많이 들어간 스튜

mec·ca /ˈmɛkə/ *n* [singular] **1** a place that many people want to visit for a particular reason ‖ 많은 사람들이 특정한 이유로 방문하고 싶어하는 장소. 동경의 장소. 목표의 땅. 메카: *Florence is a mecca for art students.* 플로렌스는 미술학도들에게 동경의 장소이다. **2 Mecca** a city in Saudi Arabia which many Muslims visit because it is holy to them ‖ 이슬람교도에게 신성한 곳이기 때문에 많은 이슬람교도들이 방문하는 사우디 아라비아에 있는 한 도시. 메카

me·chan·ic /mɪˈkænɪk/ *n* someone whose job is to repair vehicles and machinery ‖ 탈것과 기계류를 수리하는 직업인. 수리공: *an auto mechanic* 자동차 정비공 —see also MECHANICS

me·chan·i·cal /mɪˈkænɪkəl/ *adj* **1** relating to machines, or using power from a machine ‖ 기계와 관련된, 기계의 힘을 이용한. 기계의. 기계에 의한: *mechanical engineering* 기계 공학 / *a mechanical toy* 기계 장치의 장난감 **2** done or said without thinking, as if you were a machine ‖ 마치 기계처럼 생각 없이 행동하거나 말하는. 기계적인: *a mechanical answer* 기계적인 대답 **— mechanically** *adv*

me·chan·ics /mɪˈkænɪks/ *n* [U] **1** the science that deals with the effects of forces on objects ‖ 물체에 가해지는 힘의 영향을 다루는 과학. 역학 **2 the mechanics of (doing) sth** the way in which something works or is done ‖ 무엇이 작동하거나 다루어지는 방법. 기술: *the mechanics of the stock market* 주식 시장의 기법

mech·a·nism /ˈmɛkəˌnɪzəm/ *n* **1** the part of a machine that does a particular job ‖ 특정한 일을 하는 기계의 부분. 기계 장치: *a car's steering mechanism* 자동차의 조종 장치 **2** a way in which something works or the process by which it is done ‖ 어떤 것이 작동하는 방법이나 이루어지는 과정. 구조. 체제: *the mechanisms of the brain* 뇌의 구조 / *a* *mechanism for controlling the flow of traffic* 교통의 흐름을 관리하는 체제

mech·a·nize /'mɛkə,naɪz/ *v* [I, T] to change a process so that machines do it instead of people ‖ 공정을 사람 대신에 기계가 하도록 바꾸다. …을 기계화하다

mech·a·nized /'mɛkə,naɪzd/ *adj* done by machines, or using machines ‖ 기계로 하거나 이용하는. 기계화된: *a highly mechanized factory* 고도로 기계화된 공장 / *farming techniques that are completely mechanized* 완전히 기계화된 농업 기술

med·al /'mɛdl/ *n* a round flat piece of metal given as a prize to someone who has won a competition or who has done something brave ‖ 시합에서 승리한 사람이나 용감한 일을 한 사람에게 상으로 주는 둥글고 납작한 금속 조각. 메달. 훈장: *an Olympic gold medal* 올림픽의 금메달

med·al·ist /'mɛdl-ɪst/ *n* someone who has won a MEDAL in a competition ‖ 시합에서 메달을 수상한 사람: *the 1996 silver medalist* 1996년의 은메달 수상자

me·dal·lion /mə'dælyən/ *n* a piece of metal like a large coin, worn as jewelry on a chain around the neck ‖ 목 주위에 건 쇠줄에 장신구로 달린 큰 동전 같은 금속 조각. 큰 메달

med·dle /'mɛdl/ *v* [I] DISAPPROVING to try to influence a situation that does not concern you ‖ 자신과 관련이 없는 상황에 영향을 주려 하다. 간섭하다. 참견하다: *meddling in other countries' affairs* 다른 나라의 일에 대한 간섭 – **meddler** *n*

med·dle·some /'mɛdlsəm/ *adj* tending to become involved in other people's private lives when they do not want you to ‖ 타인들이 원하지 않을 때 그들의 사생활에 관여하려는 경향이 있는. 쓸데없이 참견하는. 간섭을 좋아하는

me·di·a /'midiə/ *n* **1** [plural] television, radio, and newspapers ‖ 텔레비전, 라디오, 신문. 매스 미디어: *There's been a lot of media coverage* (=information on television, in newspapers etc.) *of the President's visit.* 대통령의 방문에 관한 매스컴에 의한 보도가 많이 있었다. **2** the plural of MEDIUM ‖ medium의 복수형 — see also MASS MEDIA

me·di·an /'midiən/ *n* **1** something that divides a road or HIGHWAY, such as a thin piece of land ‖ 조붓한 땅 등의 도로나 간선도로를 나누는 것. 고속도로의 중앙 분리대 **2** TECHNICAL the middle number in a set of numbers that are arranged in order ‖ 순서대로 배열된 일련의 숫자들 중 중간 숫자. 중앙값

me·di·ate /'midi,eɪt/ *v* [I, T] to try to help two groups, countries etc. to stop arguing and make an agreement ‖ 두 집단·나라 등이 논쟁을 끝내고 합의하도록 도우려 하다. …을 조정[중재]하다: *The court had to mediate between Hassel and his neighbors.* 그 법정은 하셀과 그의 이웃들 간의 중재를 해야만 했다. / *mediating a marriage dispute* 결혼 분쟁의 조정 – **mediator** *n* – **mediation** /,midi'eɪʃən/ *n* [U]

Med·i·caid /'mɛdɪ,keɪd/ *n* [U] a system by which the government helps to pay the cost of medical treatment for poor people ‖ 정부가 가난한 사람들을 위해 의료비를 지원하는 제도. 의료 보장 제도

med·i·cal /'mɛdɪkəl/ *adj* relating to medicine and the treatment of disease or injury ‖ 의학 및 질병이나 부상의 치료에 관련된. 의학[의술, 의료]의: *medical school* 의과 대학 / *families who cannot afford medical care* 치료 받을 여유가 없는 가족들 / *The man was taken to St. Luke's hospital for medical treatment.* 그 남자는 치료를 위해 성 누가 병원으로 호송되었다. – **medically** *adv*

Med·i·care /'mɛdɪ,kɛr/ *n* [U] a system by which the government helps to pay for the medical treatment of old people ‖ 정부가 노인들의 치료를 위한 의료비를 지원하는 제도. 노인 건강 보험 제도

med·i·cat·ed /'mɛdɪ,keɪtɪd/ *adj* containing medicine ‖ 약을 함유한. 약제를 넣은. 약용의: *medicated soap/shampoo* 약용 비누[샴푸]

med·i·ca·tion /,mɛdɪ'keɪʃən/ *n* [C, U] medicine given to people who are ill ‖ 아픈 사람들에게 투여하는 약물. 투약. 약물 치료: *Has the medication helped?* 그 약물 치료가 도움이 됐니? / *He's on medication for his heart.* 그는 심장병 때문에 약물 치료를 받고 있다.

me·dic·i·nal /mə'dɪsənəl/ *adj* helping to cure illness or disease ‖ 병이나 질환을 치료하는 데에 도움이 되는. 약효가 있는: *Cough drops should be used for medicinal purposes only.* 기침약은 오로지 치료용으로만 사용되어야 한다.

med·i·cine /'mɛd-əsən/ *n* **1** [C, U] a substance used for treating illness ‖ 병을 치료하는 데에 쓰이는 물질. 약: *Remember to take your medicine.* 약을 복용하는 것을 잊지 마라. / *Medicines should be kept away*

medicine

capsules

pills　　　syrup

from children. 약은 아이들의 손이 닿지 않는 곳에 두어야 한다. **2** [U] the treatment and study of illnesses and injuries ‖ 병과 부상의 치료와 연구. 의학: *She plans to study medicine at Harvard.* 그녀는 하버드 대학에서 의학을 공부하기로 계획하고 있다.

me·di·e·val /ˌmɪdˈivəl, ˌmɛ-, ˌmi-/ *adj* relating to the MIDDLE AGES ‖ 중세와 관련 된. 중세의: *medieval poetry* 중세의 시 (詩)

me·di·o·cre /ˌmidiˈoʊkɚ/ *adj* neither good nor bad ‖ 좋지도 나쁘지도 않은. 보통의. 평범한: *a mediocre book* 평범한 책 / *The food at the cafe was mediocre.* 그 카페의 음식은 그저 그랬다. – **mediocrity** /ˌmidiˈɑkrəti/ *n* [U]

med·i·tate /ˈmɛdəˌteɪt/ *v* [I] to make yourself feel calm by being silent and still, and thinking only about one thing such as a sound or a simple religious idea ‖ 침묵과 정적으로 평온한 느낌이 들게 하여 소리나 단순한 종교적 사상 등의 한 가지에 대해서만 생각하다. 명상[묵상] 하다 – **meditation** /ˌmɛdəˈteɪʃən/ *n* [U]

med·i·ta·tive /ˈmɛdəˌteɪtɪv/ *adj* thinking deeply and seriously about something, or showing that you are doing this ‖ 무엇에 대해 깊고 심각하게 생각하는, 또는 이렇게 하는 것을 보이는. 묵상에 잠기는. 묵상적인. 사색적인: *He was in a meditative mood.* 그는 사색적인 분위기에 잠겨 있었다.

Med·i·ter·ra·ne·an¹ /ˌmɛdətəˈreɪniən/ *adj* relating to or coming from the Mediterranean ‖ 지중해와 관련된. 지중해 출신의. 지중해(산)의

Mediterranean² *n* **the Mediterranean** the areas of land surrounding the Mediterranean Sea (=sea between northern Africa and southern Europe), and the islands in it ‖ (북아프리카와 남유럽 사이에 있는 바다 인) 지중해를 둘러싸고 있는 육지 및 그 섬들. 지중해 연안

me·di·um¹ /ˈmidiəm/ *adj* of middle size or amount ‖ 크기나 양이 중간 정도인: *"What size do you wear?" "Medium."* "어떤 사이즈의 옷을 입느냐?" "중간 사이즈요." / *Cook the soup over medium heat for 30 minutes.* 중간 불에서 30분간 수프를 요리해라. / *a man of medium height* 보통 키의 사내

medium² *n* **1** *plural* **media** a way of communicating or expressing something ‖ 어떤 것을 전달하거나 표현하는 방식. 매체. 전달 수단: *The Internet is a powerful advertising medium.* 인터넷은

강력한 광고 매체이다. **2** *plural* **media** the material, paints etc. that an artist uses ‖ 예술가가 사용하는 물건이나 그림물감 등. 제작 재료. 매체물: *This sculptor's favorite medium is wood.* 이 조각가가 즐겨 쓰는 재료는 나무이다. **3** *plural* **mediums** someone who claims to speak to dead people and receive messages from them ‖ 죽은 사람들에게 말하고 그들로부터 메시지를 받는다고 주장하는 사람. 영매(靈媒). 무당

medium-sized /ˈ... ../, **medium-size** *adj* not small, but not large either ‖ 작지도 크지도 않은. 중형의: *medium-sized apples/cars* 중간 크기의 사과[중형차] / *a medium-size business* 중형 기업

med·ley /ˈmɛdli/ *n* **1** tunes from different songs that are played one after the other as a single piece of music ‖ 다른 곡들이 하나의 곡으로서 연이어 연주되는 곡조. 혼성곡. 메들리: *a medley of folk songs* 포크송 메들리 **2** a mixture of things or people ‖ 사물이나 사람들의 혼합. 잡동사니ㆍ잡다한 사람들의 모임: *a vegetable medley* 야채 혼합

meek /mik/ *adj* very quiet and gentle, and not willing to argue ‖ 논쟁하려 하지 않고 매우 조용하고 온화한. 온순한 – **meekly** *adv* – **meekness** *n* [U]

meet¹ /mit/ *v* **met, met, meeting**
1 ▶SEE SB FOR THE FIRST TIME 처음으로 누군가를 보다◀ [I, T] to see and talk to someone for the first time, or to be introduced to someone ‖ 처음으로 누구를 보고 말하다, 또는 누구에게 소개되다. 만나다: *Mike and Sara met in college.* 마이크와 사라는 대학교에서 만났다. / *"Do you know Rick Jones?" "I've never met him."* "릭 존스를 아세요?" "그를 만난 적이 없어요."

2 ▶BE IN THE SAME PLACE 같은 장소에 있다◀ [I, T] to come to the same place as someone else because you have arranged to find him/her there ‖ 그곳에서 아무를 만나기로 약속했기 때문에 그 사람과 같은 장소로 가다. 만나러 가다: *Let's meet for lunch tomorrow.* 내일 점심 때 봅시다. / *I'll meet you at the bank.* 은행에서 뵙겠습니다.

3 (it's) nice to meet you SPOKEN said when you meet someone for the first time ‖ 처음으로 누구를 만날 때에 쓰여. 만나서 반갑습니다: *"Paul, this is Jack." "Nice to meet you."* "폴, 이쪽은 잭이야." "만나서 반가워."

4 (it was) nice meeting you SPOKEN used when saying goodbye to someone you have just met for the first time ‖ 처

음 만난 사람에게 헤어지는 인사말을 할 때에 쓰여. 만나서 반가웠어

5 ▶MEETING 모임◀ [I] to be together in the same place in order to discuss something ‖ 어떤 것을 토론하기 위해 같은 장소에 모이다. 회합[회의]하다: *What time does the committee meet?* 그 위원회의 모임은 몇 시입니까?

6 meet a need/demand etc. to have or do enough of what is needed, or be good enough to reach a particular standard ‖ 필요한 것을 충분히 갖거나 하다, 또는 특정 기준에 도달하기에 충분히 좋다. 만족시키다. 부합하다: *She didn't meet all of the requirements for the job.* 그녀는 그 일자리에 필요한 모든 조건들을 충족시키지 못했다.

7 ▶SB ARRIVING 도착한 사람◀ [T] to be at an airport, station etc. when someone arrives ‖ 누군가가 도착할 때 공항·역 등에 있다. 마중 나가다. 맞이하다: *I'm going to meet John's plane.* 공항에 존을 마중 나가겠습니다.

8 ▶JOIN 합류하다◀ [I, T] to join together at a particular place ‖ 특정 장소에서 합류하다. …과 교차하다[만나다]. 접속하다: *the place where two roads meet* 두 개의 길이 만나는 장소

9 meet sth head-on to deal with a problem without trying to avoid it ‖ 문제를 피하려 하지 않고 처리하다. 잘 대처하다

10 meet (sb) halfway to do some of the things that someone wants, if s/he does some of the things you want ‖ 남이 자신이 원하는 것의 일부를 해주면 그 사람이 원하는 것의 일부를 해주다. …과 타협하다: *Democrats plan to meet the governor halfway on welfare cuts.* 민주당원들은 복지비를 줄이는 것에 대해 주지사와 타협할 계획이다.

meet up *phr v* [I] to meet someone informally in order to do something together ‖ 격식 없이 함께 어떤 것을 하기 위해 누구를 만나다: *Let's meet up after the game.* 경기 끝나고 만나자.

meet with sb/sth *phr v* [T] **1** to have a meeting with someone ‖ 누구와 모임을 갖다. …과 회담하다: *The President met with European leaders today in Paris.* 대통령은 오늘 파리에서 유럽 정상들과 회담했다. **2** to get a particular reaction or result ‖ 특별한 반응이나 결과를 얻다. 비난·환대 등을 받다. …에 부닥치다: *His proposal met with some criticism.* 그의 제안은 다소 비난을 받았다.

meet² *n* a sports competition ‖ 운동 경기 (대회): *a swim meet* 수영 대회

meet·ing /'mitɪŋ/ *n* **1** an organized gathering of people for the purpose of discussing something ‖ 어떤 것에 대해 토론하는 것을 목적으로 하는 사람들의 조직화된 모임. 회의. 회합: *There's a faculty meeting this afternoon.* 오늘 오후에 직원 회의가 있습니다. **2 a meeting of the minds** a situation in which people agree about something ‖ 사람들이 어떤 것에 대해 동의하는 상황. 합의

meeting house /'.. ,./ *n* a building where Quakers go to WORSHIP ‖ 퀘이커 교도들이 예배하러 가는 건물. 예배당. 교회당

meg·a /'mɛgə/ *adj* SLANG very big, impressive, and enjoyable ‖ 매우 크고 인상적이며 유쾌한. 멋진. 최고의: *What a mega party!* 대단한 파티야!

meg·a·byte /'mɛgə,baɪt/ *n* a unit for measuring computer information equal to a million BYTES ‖ 백만 바이트에 상당하는 컴퓨터 정보 측정 단위. 메가바이트

meg·a·lo·ma·ni·a /,mɛgəlou'meɪniə/ *n* [U] the belief that you are extremely important and powerful ‖ 자신이 매우 중요하고 강력하다는 믿음. 과대망상증 – **megalomaniac** /,mɛgəlou'meɪni,æk/ *adj*

meg·a·phone /'mɛgə,foun/ *n* a thing like a large horn, that you talk through when speaking to a crowd in order to make your voice sound louder ‖ 대중에게 말할 때, 목소리를 크게 하기 위해 대고 말하는 큰 나팔 같은 것. 메가폰. 확성기

meg·a·ton /'mɛgə,tʌn/ *n* a measure of the power of an explosive that is equal to that of a million TONS of TNT (=a powerful explosive) ‖ TNT의 백만톤에 상당하는 폭발력 단위. 메가톤

mel·an·chol·y¹ /'mɛlən,kɑli/ *adj* sad, or making you feel sad ‖ 슬픈, 슬프게 만드는. 우울한: *a melancholy look* 우울한 표정

melancholy² *n* [U] LITERARY a feeling of sadness ‖ 슬픈 감정. 우울

meld /mɛld/ *v* to mix or combine two or more different things together ‖ 두 개 이상의 서로 다른 것들을 섞거나 결합하다. …을 혼합하다: *a record that melds many different styles of music* 다양한 스타일의 음악이 수록된 음반

me·lee /'meɪleɪ, meɪ'leɪ/ *n* a confusing, noisy and sometimes violent situation ‖ 혼란스럽고 소란하고 때로는 난폭한 상황. 난투: *Several people were hurt in the melee.* 몇몇 사람들은 난동 중에 다쳤다.

mel·low¹ /'mɛlou/ *adj* **1** pleasant and smooth in sound or taste ‖ 소리나 맛이

기분 좋고 부드러운. 익은·달콤한:
mellow jazz 부드러운 재즈 / *a mellow
wine* 향기로운 와인 **2** gentle or calm
because of age or experience ‖ 나이나 경
험으로 점잖거나 차분한. 원숙한. 온화한:
Tim's more mellow now that he's older.
팀은 나이가 들어서 지금 더 원숙하다.
mellow², mellow out v [I, T] to
become more relaxed and calm, or to
make someone do this ‖ 더 편안하고 차
분해지다, 또는 남을 이렇게 만들다. 원숙
하게 하다. 원만해지다: *She's mellowed
over the years.* 그녀는 세월이 흐르면서
원숙해졌다.

me·lod·ic /məˈlɑdɪk/ *adj* **1** having a
pleasant tune or a pleasant sound like
music ‖ 음악처럼 기분 좋은 곡조나 소리
를 가진. 노래하는 듯한[듯이 아름다운]:
a sweet melodic voice 감미롭고 아름다운
목소리 **2** relating to the main tune in a
piece of music ‖ 한 곡 안에서 주선율의:
*the melodic structure of Beethoven's
symphonies* 베토벤 교향곡의 주(主)선율
구성

me·lo·di·ous /məˈloʊdiəs/ *adj* having a
pleasant tune or a pleasant sound like
music ‖ 음악처럼 기분 좋은 곡조나 소리
를 가진. 선율적인. 음악적인: *a
melodious voice* 선율적인 목소리

mel·o·dra·ma /ˈmɛləˌdrɑmə/ *n* [C, U] a
story or play with many exciting events
in which people's emotions are shown
very strongly ‖ 사람들의 감정이 매우 강
하게 표출되는 흥미로운 사건이 많은 이야
기 또는 연극. 멜로드라마

mel·o·dra·mat·ic /ˌmɛlədrəˈmætɪk/
adj having and showing emotions that are
strong and unreasonable ‖ 강렬하면서
비현실적인 감정을 갖거나 나타내는. 멜
로드라마식의·신파조의: *Stop being
melodramatic!* 신파조는 집어치워!

mel·o·dy /ˈmɛlədi/ *n* **1** [C, U] a song or
tune ‖ 노래 또는 곡조 **2** the main tune in
a complicated piece of music ‖ 복잡한 곡
의 주선율

mel·on /ˈmɛlən/ *n* [C, U] one of several
types of large sweet juicy fruits with
hard skins and flat seeds ‖ 껍질이 단단하
고 납작한 씨가 있으며 달콤한 과즙이 있
는 큰 여러 과일 중 하나. 멜론

melt /mɛlt/ *v* **1** [I, T] to change
something from solid to liquid by
heating ‖ 어떤 것을 가열하여 고체에서 액
체로 변화시키다. 변하다. 용해하다: *The
snow's melting.* 눈이 녹고 있다. / *Melt
the butter, and add the chopped onion.*
버터를 녹인 후 양파 저민 것을 넣어라. **2**
[I] to suddenly feel love or sympathy ‖

갑자기 사랑이나 동정을 느끼다. 감동하
다. 누그러지다: *Whenever I hear his
voice, I just melt.* 그의 목소리를 들을 때
마다 나는 그냥 마음이 누그러진다. **3
melt in your mouth** if food melts in
your mouth, it is smooth and tastes
extremely good ‖ 음식이 입 안에서 연하
게 되어서 아주 맛있다. 음식이 (입안에
서 녹을 듯이) 매우 맛있다

melt away *phr v* [I] to disappear
quickly and easily ‖ 빠르고 쉽게 사라지
다. (녹아서) 없어지다: *He began to
exercise regularly, and the weight
melted away.* 그는 규칙적으로 운동하기
시작하면서 몸무게가 급속히 빠졌다.

melt·down /ˈmɛltdaʊn/ *n* [C, U] a very
dangerous situation in which the
material in a NUCLEAR REACTOR melts
and burns through its container ‖ 핵반응
으로 안의 원료가 녹아서 노벽을 뚫고 연
소하는 매우 위험한 상황. (원자로의) 노
심(爐心)

melting pot /ˈ.. ./ *n* a place where
people from different races, countries,
or social classes come and live together
‖ 다른 인종[국가·사회 계층]의 사람들이
들어와 함께 사는 장소. 도가니: *The US is
often called a melting pot.* 미국을 흔히
인종의 도가니라고 말한다.

mem·ber /ˈmɛmbɚ/ *n* **1** someone who
has joined a particular club, group, or
organization ‖ 특정 클럽·집단·조직에 참
가한 사람. 회원: *Are you a member of
the French club?* 당신은 프랑스어 클럽의
회원이십니까? / *Two of the band
members quit yesterday.* 어제 밴드 멤버
두 명이 그만두었다. **2** one of a group of
similar people or things ‖ 비슷한 사람 또
는 사물의 한 무리 중 하나. 일종: *Cats
and tigers are members of the same
species.* 고양이와 호랑이는 동종의 동물
이다.

mem·ber·ship /ˈmɛmbɚˌʃɪp/ *n* **1** [C,
U] the state of being a member of a
club, group, organization, or system ‖
클럽·집단·조직·체제의 일원인 상태. 회원
의 지위: *I forgot to renew my
membership in the sailing club.* 나는 항
해 클럽 회원 자격 갱신을 깜빡했다. **2**
[singular] all the members of a club,
group, or organization ‖ 클럽[집단,
조직]의 전(全) 회원. 총회원: *The
membership will vote for a chairman
tonight.* 모든 회원들은 오늘 밤 의장을 선
출할 것이다.

mem·brane /ˈmɛmbreɪn/ *n* [C, U] a
very thin substance similar to skin that
covers or connects parts of the body ‖ 신

체의 기관들을 덮거나 연결하는 피부같은 매우 얇은 물질. 세포막: *a membrane in the ear that helps us hear* 들을 수 있게 해주는 귀의 고막

me·men·to /məˈmɛntoʊ/ *n* a small object that you keep to remind you of someone or something ‖ 사람이나 사물을 회상할 수 있게 하는 작은 물건. 기념품: *a memento of my college days* 내 대학 시절의 추억거리

mem·o /ˈmɛmoʊ/ *n* a short official note to another person in the same company ‖ 같은 회사 내의 다른 사람에게 보내는 짧은 공식 편지. 메모

mem·oirs /ˈmɛmwɑrz/ *n* [plural] a book written by a famous person about his/her life and experiences ‖ 유명 인사가 자신의 생활·경험에 대하여 쓴 책. 회고록. 자서전

mem·o·ra·bil·i·a /ˌmɛmərəˈbɪliə, -ˈbil-/ *n* [plural] things that you keep or collect because they relate to a famous person, event, or time ‖ 유명한 사람[사건, 시기]과 관련 되어서 보존하거나 수집한 것. 수집품: *Kennedy memorabilia* 케네디 대통령의 유품들

mem·o·ra·ble /ˈmɛmrəbəl/ *adj* worth remembering ‖ 기억할 가치가 있는. 기억할 만한: *Brando's memorable performance in "On the Waterfront"* 영화 "워터프론트"에서 브랜도의 인상적인 연기 / *a memorable weekend* 잊지 못할 주말 **– memorably** *adv*

mem·o·ran·dum /ˌmɛməˈrændəm/ *n* FORMAL ➪ MEMO

me·mo·ri·al¹ /məˈmɔriəl/ *adj* made or done in order to remind people of someone who has died ‖ 죽은 사람을 기리기 위해 만들거나 행한. 기념의. 추도의: *a memorial service for my grandfather* 나의 할아버지를 위한 추도식

memorial² *n* a public structure with writing on it that reminds people of someone who has died ‖ 죽은 사람을 기리기 위한 글을 써 놓은 공공 구조물. 기념비. 기념관: *the Lincoln memorial* 링컨 기념관 / *The wall was built as a memorial to soldiers who died in Vietnam.* 그 벽은 베트남에서 전사한 군인들을 추도하기 위해 세워졌다.

Memorial Day /.ˈ... ˌ./ *n* [U] a US national holiday on the last Monday in May, to remember soldiers killed in wars ‖ 전사한 군인들을 추도하기 위한 5월의 마지막 월요일인 국경일. 현충일

mem·o·rize /ˈmɛməˌraɪz/ *v* [T] to learn and remember words, music, or other information ‖ 말·음악·여타 정보를 알고

기억하다. …을 외우다. 기억하다: *You all should have your lines memorized by Friday.* 너희는 모두 금요일까지 자신의 대사를 외워야 한다.

mem·o·ry /ˈmɛmri, -məri/ *n* **1** [C, U] the ability to remember things, places, experiences etc. ‖ 사물·장소·경험 등을 기억하는 능력. 기억력: *My memory isn't as good as it used to be.* 나의 기억력은 예전만큼 좋지 않다. / *Could you draw the map from memory?* (=by remembering it) 기억해 내서 지도를 그릴 수 있으세요? **2** something that you remember from the past about a person, place, or experience ‖ 사람·장소·경험에 대해 과거로부터 기억하고 있는 것. 추억: *I have a lot of happy memories of that summer.* 나는 그 여름의 행복한 추억이 많다. / *That sound brings back memories of my childhood.* (=makes me remember it) 그 소리는 내 어린 시절 기억을 불러일으킨다. —compare SOUVENIR **3** [U] the amount of space that can be used for storing information on a computer ‖ 정보가 저장될 수 있는 컴퓨터상의 공간의 크기. 메모리(용량): *30 megabytes of memory* 30메가바이트의 메모리 **4** the part of a computer in which information can be stored ‖ 컴퓨터에 정보가 저장될 수 있는 부분. 기억장치 **5 in memory of** for the purpose of remembering someone who has died ‖ 죽은 사람을 기억하기 위해. …의 기념으로서: *She started a scholarship fund in memory of her husband.* 그녀는 남편을 기리기 위해 장학 기금을 마련했다.

men /mɛn/ *n* the plural of MAN ‖ man의 복수형

men·ace¹ /ˈmɛnɪs/ *n* **1** something or someone that is dangerous or extremely annoying ‖ 위험하거나 매우 짜증나게 하는 사물이나 사람. 골칫거리: *That man is a menace to society!* 그 남자는 사회의 위험 인물이다! / *The mosquitoes are a menace at this time of year.* 연중 이맘때는 모기가 골칫거리이다. **2** [U] a threatening quality or manner ‖ 위협적인 속성이나 태도. 협박: *There was menace in her voice* 그녀의 음성은 위협적이었다.

menace² *v* [T] FORMAL to threaten someone or something with danger or harm ‖ 위험이나 해악을 가하겠다고 사람이나 사물을 위협하다. 협박하다

men·ac·ing /ˈmɛnɪsɪŋ/ *adj* making you expect something dangerous or bad; THREATENING ‖ 위험하거나 나쁜 것을 예상하게 하는. 위협적인. 협박을 가하는; ㉤

menagerie

threatening: *a menacing laugh* 위협적인 웃음

me·nag·er·ie /mə'nædʒəri, -ʒə-/ n a collection of animals kept privately or for people to see ‖ 사적으로 소유하거나 사람들이 볼 수 있게 수집한 동물들. (특히 구경거리인) 야수[진기한 동물]들

mend¹ /mɛnd/ v 1 [T] to repair a tear or hole in a piece of clothing ‖ 옷의 해진 곳이나 구멍을 수선하다. …을 고치다: *You'd better mend that shirt.* 너 그 셔츠를 수선해야겠다. 2 **mend your ways** to improve the way you behave after behaving badly for a long time ‖ 오랫동안 해온 나쁜 행동 방식을 개선하다. (태도를) 고치다

mend² n **be on the mend** INFORMAL to be getting better after an illness ‖ 병이 나아지다. 낫다

me·ni·al /'miniəl, -nyəl/ adj menial work is boring and needs no skill ‖ (작업 등이) 지루하고 아무런 기술이 필요 없는. 단조롭고 지루한

men·o·pause /'mɛnə,pɔz/ n [U] the time when a woman stops menstruating (MENSTRUATE) ‖ 여성의 월경이 중단되는 시기. 폐경기

me·no·rah /mə'nɔrə/ n a special CANDLESTICK, used in Jewish ceremonies ‖ 유대교 의식에 사용되는 특별한 촛대. 가지달린 촛대

men's room /'. ./ n a room in a public place with toilets for men ‖ 공공장소의 남성용 변기가 있는 방. 남자 화장실 – see usage note at TOILET

men·stru·ate /'mɛnstru,eɪt, -streɪt/ v [I] TECHNICAL when a woman menstruates every month, blood flows from her body ‖ 매달 여성의 몸에서 출혈이 일어나다. 월경하다 – **menstruation** /,mɛnstru'eɪʃən, mɛn'streɪʃən/ n [U] – **menstrual** /'mɛnstruəl, -strəl/ adj

men·tal /'mɛntəl/ adj 1 relating to the mind, or happening in the mind ‖ 마음과 관련된. 마음에서 일어나는. 정신의. 지능의: *your mental abilities* 당신의 지능 / *a mental illness* 정신병 / *I made a mental note* (=made an effort to remember) *to call Julie.* 나는 줄리에게 전화할 것을 기억해 두었다. 2 SLANG crazy ‖ 미친: *That guy's mental!* 저 놈은 미쳤어! – **mentally** adv : *mentally ill* 정신적으로 병든

mental health /,.. '.'/ adj relating to the treatment of mental illnesses ‖ 정신병을 치료하는. 정신 건강의: *mental health workers/programs* 정신 건강 치료사[프로그램]

mental in·sti·tu·tion /'.. ..,../ n a hospital for people who are mentally ill ‖ 정신적인 병이 있는 사람을 위한 병원. 정신 병원

men·tal·i·ty /mɛn'tæləti/ n [U] a particular type of attitude or way of thinking ‖ 특정한 형태의 태도나 사고 방식. 정신적 경향·사물을 보는 관점: *an aggressive mentality* 공격적 성향

men·thol /'mɛnθɔl, -θɑl/ n [U] a substance that smells and tastes like MINT, used in medicine, candy, and cigarettes ‖ 약·사탕·담배에 쓰이는 박하 같은 향과 맛이 나는 물질. 멘톨. 박하뇌 – **mentholated** /'mɛnθə,leɪtɪd/ adj

men·tion¹ /'mɛnʃən/ v [T] 1 to say or write about something in a few words ‖ 몇 마디 말로 어떤 것에 대해 말하거나 쓰다. …에 대하여 언급하다: *Yes, Sheila did mention to me that her brother was ill.* 그래요, 실라가 내게 자기 오빠가 아프다고 말했어요. / *Cooper wasn't mentioned in the article.* 쿠퍼는 기사에서 언급되지 않았어요. 2 **don't mention it** SPOKEN used in order to politely say that there is no need for someone to thank you ‖ 감사해 할 필요가 없다는 것을 남에게 정중하게 말하는 데에 쓰여. 천만에 말씀: *"Thanks for helping me out." "Don't mention it."* "도와주셔서 고맙습니다." "천만에요." 3 **not to mention** said when you are adding a piece of information that emphasizes what you have been saying ‖ 지금까지 말해온 것을 강조하는 정보를 덧붙일 때에 쓰여. …은 말할 것도 없고: *He already has two houses and two cars, not to mention the boat.* 그는 이미 보트는 말할 것도 없고 집 두 채와 자동차 두 대를 갖고 있다.

mention² n [C, U] the act of mentioning someone or something in a conversation or piece of writing ‖ 대화 또는 문장에서 사람이나 사물을 언급하는 행위. 언급·진술: *Any mention of the accident upsets her.* 사고에 관한 어떤 언급도 그녀를 화나게 했다. / *He's had a couple of mentions in the newspaper.* 그는 신문에 몇 번 언급된 적이 있었다. / *The report made no mention of any profit figures,* 그 보고서에는 수익 계수에 대한 아무런 언급도 없었다.

men·tor /'mɛntɔr, -tə/ n an experienced person who advises and helps a less experienced person ‖ 경험이 보다 적은 사람에게 조언하고 도와주는, 경험이 많은 사람. 충실한 조언자

men·u /'mɛnyu/ n 1 a list of all the kinds of food that are available for a meal in a restaurant ‖ 식당에서 식사가 가능한 음식의 모든 종류를 나열한 목록. 메뉴. 식단표: *Let's see what's on the menu.* 메뉴에 뭐가 있나 보자. **2** a list of things that you can choose from or ask a computer to do, that is shown on the screen ‖ 컴퓨터 화면에 나타나 선택할 수 있거나 작업 지시를 할 수 있는 것들의 목록(표). (컴퓨터) 메뉴

menu bar /'.. ./ *n* a bar across the top of a computer SCREEN that contains several PULL-DOWN MENUs, for example 'File', 'View', 'Help' etc. ‖ '파일', '보기', '도움말' 등 몇몇 풀다운 메뉴가 들어 있는 컴퓨터 화면 상단을 가로지르는 막대. 메뉴 바

me·ow /mi'aʊ/ *n* the crying sound that a cat makes ‖ 고양이가 내는 울음소리. 야옹 – **meow** *v* [I]

mer·ce·nar·y[1] /'mɚsə,nɛri/ *n* someone who fights for any country who pays him/her ‖ 봉급을 주는 어떤 국가를 위해 싸우는 사람. 용병

mercenary[2] *adj* only concerned with making money ‖ 오직 돈버는 데만 관심 있는. 돈만 바라는

mer·chan·dise /'mɚtʃən,daɪz, -,daɪs/ *n* [U] goods that are for sale in stores ‖ 상점 판매용 물품. 상품: *We've ordered the merchandise from a company in San Diego.* 우리는 샌디에이고에 있는 회사에 제품을 주문했다.

mer·chant[1] /'mɚtʃənt/ *n* someone who buys and sells large quantities of goods ‖ 많은 양의 재화를 사고파는 사람. (도매) 상인

merchant[2] *adj* relating to trade in large quantities of goods ‖ 대량의 물건 거래에 관련된. 무역의: *a merchant vessel* (=ship) 상선

mer·ci·ful /'mɚsɪfəl/ *adj* kind to people rather than being cruel ‖ 사람들에게 모질지 않고 친절한. 자비로운

mer·ci·ful·ly /'mɚsɪfli/ *adv* fortunately, because a situation could have been much worse ‖ 상황이 더 악화될 수 있었는데 운이 좋게. 다행히도: *Mercifully, I managed to stop the car just in time.* 다행히도 나는 용케 제때에 차를 멈춰 세웠다.

Mer·cu·ry /'mɚkyəri/ *n* [singular] the smallest PLANET, nearest the sun ‖ 태양의 가장 가까운 곳에 있는 가장 작은 행성. 수성(水星)

mer·cu·ry *n* [U] a liquid silver-white metal that is used in THERMOMETERs ‖ 온도계에 쓰이는, 은백색의 액상 금속. 수은

mer·cy /'mɚsi/ *n* **1** [U] kindness, pity,

and a willingness to forgive ‖ 친절·연민·기꺼이 용서하려는 마음. 자비: *Three of the attackers apologized and asked for mercy.* 공격자들 중 3명은 사과하여 자비를 구했다. **2 at the mercy of** unable to do anything to protect yourself from someone or something ‖ 어떤 사람이나 사물로부터 자신을 보호하기 위한 어떠한 일도 할 수 없는. …의 처분대로: *The houses near the forest fire are at the mercy of the winds.* 산불이 난 근처의 집들은 바람에 운명이 맡겨져 있다.

mercy kill·ing /'.. ,./ *n* ⇨ EUTHANASIA

mere /mɪr/ *adj* **1** used in order to emphasize how small or unimportant someone or something is ‖ 사람이나 사물이 얼마나 작은지 또는 하찮은지를 강조하는 데에 쓰여. 단지 …에 불과한. 겨우 … 일 뿐인: *She was a mere two years younger than the Princess.* 그녀는 그 공주보다 겨우 두 살 더 적을 뿐이었다. **2** used in order to say that something small or unimportant has a big effect ‖ 작거나 하찮은 것이 대단한 영향력을 갖고 있음을 말하는 데에 쓰여. 아주 사소한[말도 안 되는] …으로도: *The mere thought that he might be hurt made her want to cry.* 그가 다칠지도 모른다는 엉뚱한 생각이 그녀를 울고 싶도록 만들었다.

mere·ly /'mɪrli/ *adv* **1** used in order to emphasize that something is exactly what you say it is, not better or worse, not more or less, etc; just ‖ 어떤 것이 더 좋거나 나쁘지도·더 많거나 적지도 않고 말한 그대로임을 강조하는 데에 쓰여. 단지. 오직: *I'm not making criticisms, merely suggestions.* 나는 비판하는 게 아니야. 단지 제안하는 것일 뿐이야. **2** used in order to emphasize that something or someone is small or unimportant, compared to someone or something else; only ‖ 사물이나 사람이 다른 사물이나 사람과 비교해서 작거나 하찮다는 것을 강조하는 데에 쓰여. 단지[오로지] …이 (라)기보다; 오직: *We want more from work than merely a paycheck.* 우리는 직업에서 단지 돈보다는 그 이상의 것을 원한다.

merge /mɚdʒ/ *v* **1** [I, T] to combine or join together to form one thing ‖ 하나가 되도록 서로 결합하거나 합치다. 합병[병합]하다: *The two unions merged to form a larger one.* 두 개의 노조는 보다 큰 노조가 되기 위해 합병했다. **2 merge into sth** to seem to disappear into something and become part of it ‖ 어떤 것 안으로 사라져 그 부분이 된 것처럼 보이다. …에 흡수되다: *a point where the* *mountains merged into the sky* 산과 하늘이 맞닿은 지점 **3** if traffic merges, the cars from two roads come together onto the same road ‖ 두 개의 도로에서 나온 자동차가 동일한 도로로 함께 가다. 합류되다

merg·er /'mɝdʒɝ/ *n* the act of joining together two more companies or organizations to form one larger one ‖ 두 개 이상의 기업이나 조직이 합쳐져 보다 큰 하나가 되는 것. 합병

me·rid·i·an /mə'rɪdiən/ *n* the line drawn from the NORTH POLE to the SOUTH POLE to show the positions of places on a map ‖ 지도상의 지점을 나타내기 위해 북극에서 남극까지 그어진 선. 경선(經線). 자오선

me·ringue /mə'ræŋ/ *n* [C, U] a light sweet food made by baking a mixture of sugar and the white parts of eggs ‖ 설탕과 계란 흰자위를 섞은 것을 구워 만든 말랑말랑하고 달콤한 음식. 머랭과자

mer·it[1] /'mɛrɪt/ *n* **1** one of the good qualities or features of something or someone ‖ 사물이나 사람의 좋은 속성이나 특징의 하나. 장점: *Living downtown has its merits.* 도심에서 사는 데는 좋은 점들이 있다. **2** [U] FORMAL a good quality that makes something deserve praise or admiration ‖ 칭찬이나 존경을 받을 만하게 하는 좋은 특성. 가치. 우수함: *a book of great merit* 가치가 매우 큰 책

merit[2] *v* [T] FORMAL to deserve something ‖ 어떤 것을 받을 만하다. …할 가치가 있다: *The play merits the awards it's won.* 그 연극은 수상할 만 했다.

mer·maid /'mɝmeɪd/ *n* a woman in stories who has a fish's tail instead of legs ‖ 다리 대신 물고기의 꼬리를 가진, 동화속에 등장하는 여자. (여자) 인어

mer·ry /'mɛri/ *adj* happy and having fun ‖ 행복하고 즐거운. 명랑한. 쾌활한: *Merry Christmas!* (=used in order to tell someone you hope s/he has a good Christmas) 크리스마스를 축하합니다. 메리 크리스마스!

merry-go-round /'.. ,./ *n* a machine at a FAIR that turns around and around, and has model animals and seats for children to sit on ‖ 유원지에서 아이들이 앉을 수 있는 동물 모형의 좌석을 갖추고 둥글게 회전하는 놀이기구. 회전목마

mesh[1] /mɛʃ/ *n* [U] a piece of material made of threads or wires that have been woven together like a net ‖ 실이나 철사를 서로 엮어 그물처럼 만든 것. 그물코 [망]: *a wire mesh screen* 철사 그물망 체

mesh[2] *v* [I] **1** if two or more ideas, qualities, people etc. mesh, they go well together ‖ 둘 이상의 사상·속성·사람 등이 서로 잘 어울리다. 잘 맞다: *Their two management styles never meshed successfully.* 그들이 다른 경영 스타일은 결코 성공적으로 맞출 수 없었다. **2** TECHNICAL if two parts of an engine or machine mesh, they fit closely together ‖ 엔진이나 기계의 두 부분이 서로 꼭 맞물리다. 들어맞다

mes·mer·ize /'mɛzmə,raɪz/ *v* [T] to make someone become completely interested in something ‖ 어떤 사람을 어떤 것에 완전히 빠져들게 하다. 매료시키다: *The video game kept the kids mesmerized for hours.* 아이들은 몇 시간 동안 그 비디오 게임에 빠졌다. — **mesmerizing** *adj*

mess[1] /mɛs/ *n* **1** [singular, U] a place or a group of things that is not organized or arranged neatly ‖ 말끔하게 정리 또는 정돈되지 않은 장소 또는 일단의 물건. 엉망인[어지러진] 상태: *This house is a mess!* 이 집은 엉망이야! / *The kids made a mess in their room again.* 아이들이 그들의 방을 또다시 어질러 놓았다. **2** [singular] INFORMAL a situation in which there are a lot of problems and difficulties, especially as a result of mistakes or people not being careful ‖ 특히 실수 또는 부주의한 사람으로 인해 많은 문제와 어려움이 있는 상황. 혼란 상태. 곤경: *His personal life was a mess.* 그의 사생활은 엉망이었다. / *I'm sorry, I've really made a mess of things.* 죄송해요, 제가 다 망쳐 놨어요. **3** INFORMAL someone who behaves or thinks in a disorganized way ‖ 어수선하게 행동하거나 생각하는 사람. 지저분한 녀석·무기력한 사람: *I'd been crying for hours – I was a mess.* 나는 몇 시간 동안 울었고 무기력해졌다. **4** a room in which members of the military eat and drink together ‖ 군인들이 모여 먹고 마시는 방. 식당

mess[2] *v*

mess around *phr v* INFORMAL **1** [I] to play or do silly things when you should be working or paying attention ‖ 일하거나 집중해야 할 때 놀거나 어리석은 짓들을 하다. 빈둥거리다. 꾸물대다: *Stop messing around and do your homework!* 빈둥거리지 말고 숙제해라! **2** [T **mess** sb **around**] to make someone angry by lying, or by not giving him/her something s/he wants ‖ 거짓말을 하거나, 또는 원하는 것을 주지 않아서 남을 화나게 하다. 부아를 돋우다: *Don't mess me* *around. Tell me where she went!* 나를 화나게 하지 말고 그녀가 어디로 갔는지 말해!

mess around with sb/sth *phr v* [T] INFORMAL **1** [**mess around with** sth] to play with something or make small changes to it ‖ 어떤 것을 갖고 놀다, 어떤 것에 작은 변화를 주다. 장난삼아 잠깐 해 보다. 만지작거리다: *I told you not to mess around with my camera!* 내 카메라 갖고 놀지 말라고 그랬지! **2** [**mess around with** sb] to have a sexual relationship with someone, especially someone who is married ‖ 남과 특히 기혼자와 성관계를 갖다. (이성과) 함부로 관계하다

mess up *phr v* INFORMAL **1** [T] to spoil something or make it dirty and disorganized ‖ 어떤 것을 망치거나 더럽게 어질러 놓다. 망쳐 놓다. 난잡하게 해 놓다: *I hope I haven't messed up your big plans.* 내가 너의 야심찬 계획을 망치지 않았기를 바란다. / *Who messed up my clean kitchen?* 누가 내 깨끗한 부엌을 어질러 놨어? **2** [I,T **mess** sth ↔ **up**] to make a mistake or do something badly ‖ 실수하거나 어떤 일을 잘 못하다. …을 망치다. 엉망을 만들다: *"How did you do on the test?" "Oh, I really messed up."* "시험 어땠어?" "오, 아주 망쳤어." —see also MESSED UP

mess with sb/sth *phr v* [T] **1** [**mess with** sth] to deal with something or use something that you do not understand ‖ 잘 모르는 것을 다루거나 사용하다. 끙끙대며 사용하다[다루다]: *You don't have to mess with any gears; the car's automatic.* 어떤 장치도 끙끙대며 손댈 필요 없다, 차가 자동식이니까. **2** [**mess with** sb] to annoy or argue with someone ‖ 남을 괴롭히거나 남과 다투다. 건드리다. 시비 걸다: *I'm not in a bad mood, just don't mess with me.* 나 지금 기분 안 좋으니까 건드리지 마.

mes·sage /ˈmɛsɪdʒ/ *n* **1** a small amount of written or spoken information that you pass from one person to another ‖ 어떤 사람으로부터 다른 사람에게 전달되는, 글이나 말로 된 소량의 정보. 메시지. 전갈: *"Janet just called." "Did she leave a message?"* "재닛한테 방금 전화 왔었어." "메시지 남겼어?" / *Sorry, Tony's not home yet. Can I take a message?* (=used during phone calls) 미안한데, 토니 아직 집에 안 왔거든 전할 말 있니? **2** [singular] the main idea or the most important idea in a movie, book, speech etc. ‖ 영화·책·연설

의 주요 생각 또는 가장 중요한 개념. 교훈. 의도: *The movie has a clear message: don't take drugs.* 그 영화는 마약을 하지 말라는 분명한 메시지를 담고 있다. **3 get the message:** INFORMAL to understand what someone means or what s/he wants you to do ‖ 남의 뜻이나 남이 해주기 바라는 것을 이해하다. 뜻을 납득하다[알아듣다]: *Hopefully he got the message and will stop bothering me!* 그가 뜻을 납득하고 나를 괴롭히지 않았으면 좋겠어!

message board /ˌ.. ./ *n* a place on a WEBSITE where you can read or leave messages ‖ 메시지를 읽거나 남길 수 있는 웹사이트 상의 장소. 자유 게시판

messed up /ˌ. ˈ../ *adj* INFORMAL if someone is messed up, s/he has a lot of emotional problems ‖ 사람이 정신적으로 많은 문제를 가진. 신경이 쇠약해진: *Fred's all messed up from the divorce.* 프레드는 이혼으로 신경이 쇠약해졌다.

mes·sen·ger /ˈmɛsəndʒɚ/ *n* someone who takes messages to other people ‖ 남에게 메시지를 전하는 사람. 메신저

mess hall /ˈ. ./ *n* a large room where soldiers eat ‖ 군인들이 식사하는 큰 방. (공장·군대 등 집단의) 식당

mes·si·ah /məˈsaɪə/ *n* **the Messiah** Jesus Christ in the Christian religion, or the leader sent by God to save the world in the Jewish religion ‖ 크리스도교에서의 예수 그리스도, 또는 유대교에서 세계를 구하기 위해 신이 보낸 지도자. 메시아. 구세주

Messrs. /ˈmɛsɚz/ *n* FORMAL the written plural of Mr. ‖ Mr.의 복수형

mess·y /ˈmɛsi/ *adj* **1** dirty, or not arranged in an organized way ‖ 더럽거나, 가지런하게 정돈되지 않은. 지저분한. 엉망인: *a messy desk* 지저분한 책상 **2** a messy situation is complicated and unpleasant to deal with ‖ 상황이 다루기 복잡하고 불쾌한. 난처하게 하는. 귀찮은: *a messy divorce* 혼란스러운 이혼

met /mɛt/ *v* the past tense and PAST PARTICIPLE of MEET ‖ meet의 과거·과거분사형

me·tab·o·lism /məˈtæbəˌlɪzəm/ *n* [C, U] the chemical processes in your body that change food into the energy you need for working and growing ‖ 몸 안에서 음식물을 일과 성장에 필요한 에너지로 바꾸는 화학적 과정. (신진)대사 − **metabolic** /ˌmɛtəˈbɑlɪk/ *adj*

met·al /ˈmɛtl/ *n* [C, U] a hard, usually shiny substance such as iron, gold, or steel ‖ 철[금, 강철]등의 단단하고 보통 광

(光)이 나는 물질. 금속

met·al de·tect·or /ˈ.. .,../ *n* a machine used for finding metal, especially one used at airports for finding weapons ‖ 특히 공항에서 무기 검색에 사용되는 금속 탐지용 기계. 금속 탐지기

me·tal·lic /məˈtælɪk/ *adj* made of metal, or similar to metal in color, appearance, or taste ‖ 금속으로 만든, 또는 색[모양, 맛]이 금속과 비슷한. 금속(제, 성)의: *a car painted metallic blue* 금속 광택이 나는 파란색을 칠한 자동차

met·al·lur·gy /ˈmɛtl̩,ərdʒi/ *n* [U] the scientific study of metals and their uses ‖ 금속과 그 쓰임에 대한 과학적인 연구. 야 금 학 (冶 金 學) - **metallurgical** /,mɛtəˈlərdʒɪkəl/ *adj* - **metallurgist** /ˈmɛtl̩,ərdʒɪst/ *n*

met·a·mor·pho·sis /,mɛtəˈmɔrfəsɪs/ *n, plural* **metamorphoses** /-fəsiz/ [C, U] the process in which something changes into a completely different form ‖ 사물이 완전히 다른 형태로 변화하는 과정. 변형. 변태: *a caterpillar's metamorphosis into a butterfly* 나비가 되는 애벌레의 변태

met·a·phor /ˈmɛtə,fɔr/ *n* [C, U] a way of describing something by comparing it to something else that has similar qualities, without using the words "like" or "as." "A river of tears" is a metaphor ‖ 사물을 묘사할 때 "처럼" 또는 "같이"란 단어를 사용하지 않고 비슷한 성질을 갖는 다른 것에 비유하는 방법. 은유. "눈물의 강"은 은유적 표현이다 - **metaphorical** /,mɛtəˈfɔrɪkəl/ *adj* - **metaphorically** *adv*

met·a·phys·i·cal /,mɛtəˈfɪzɪkəl/ *adj* relating to a study of PHILOSOPHY that is concerned with trying to understand and describe what REALITY is ‖ 본질이 무엇인지 이해하고 설명하려는 데 관심이 있는 철학과 관련된. 형이상학의 - **metaphysics** *n* [U] - **metaphysically** *adv*

mete /mit/ *v*

mete sth ↔ **out** *phr v* [T] FORMAL to give someone a punishment ‖ 남에게 벌을 주다

me·te·or /ˈmitiər/ *n* a small piece of rock or metal that produces a bright burning line in the sky when it falls from space into the earth's ATMOSPHERE ‖ 우주 공간에서 지구 대기권으로 떨어지면서 밝게 불타는 궤적을 그리는 작은 암석 또는 금속 조각. 유성(流星). 별똥별

me·te·or·ic /,mitiˈɔrɪk, -ˈar-/ *adj* happening very suddenly and usually continuing for only a short time ‖ 매우 갑자기 발생해서 아주 잠깐 지속되는. 일시적인. 급속한: *his meteoric rise to fame* 잠깐 반짝하고 떠오른 그의 인기

me·te·or·ite /ˈmitiə,raɪt/ *n* a small METEOR that has landed on the earth's surface ‖ 지구 표면에 떨어진 작은 운석. 유성

me·te·or·ol·o·gy /,mitiəˈralədʒi/ *n* [U] the scientific study of weather ‖ 날씨의 과학적 연구. 기상학 - **meteorologist** *n*

meter /ˈmitər/ *n* **1** *written abbreviation* **m.** a unit for measuring length, equal to 100 centimeters or 39.37 inches ‖ 100센티미터 또는 39.37인치에 상당하는 길이 측정 단위. 미터 **2** a piece of equipment that measures the amount of gas, electricity, time etc. you have used ‖ 사용한 가스·전기·시간 등의 양을 측정하는 장비류. 계량기: *The cab driver looked at the meter and said, "$5.70, please."* 택시 기사는 미터기를 보고 "5달러 70센트입니다."라고 말했다. —see also PARKING METER **3** [C, U] the way that the words of a poem are arranged into a pattern of weak and strong beats ‖ 시의 어구가 약·강박의 규칙적 형태로 배열되는 방식. 운율

meter maid /ˈ.. ,./ *n* OLD-FASHIONED a woman whose job is to check that cars are not parked illegally ‖ 불법 주차를 단속하는 여성 직업인. 여성 주차 위반 단속인

meth·a·done /ˈmɛθə,doʊn/ *n* [U] TECHNICAL a drug that is often given to people who are trying to stop taking HEROIN ‖ 흔히 헤로인을 끊으려는 사람에게 주는 약. 메타돈

meth·ane /ˈmɛθeɪn/ *n* [U] a gas with no color or smell, which can be burned to give heat ‖ 열을 내기 위해 태우는 무색무취의 가스. 메탄

meth·od /ˈmɛθəd/ *n* a planned way of doing something ‖ 어떤 일을 하는 계획된 방식. 방법: *This is the simplest method of payment.* 이것은 가장 간단한 지불 방법이다. / *Her teaching methods are unusual.* 그녀의 교습 방법은 특이하다.

meth·od·i·cal /məˈθadɪkəl/ *adj* done in a careful and well organized way, or always doing things this way ‖ 신경 써서 잘 정돈된 또는 항상 이런 식으로 일하는. 정연한. 꼼꼼한: *They made a methodical search of the building.* 그들은 그 건물에 대해 철저한 수색을 했다. / *a methodical woman* 꼼꼼한 여자 - **methodically** *adv*

Meth·od·ist /'mɛθədɪst/ *adj* relating to the Protestant church whose members follow the ideas of John Wesley ‖ 교인들이 존 웨슬리의 사상을 따르는 프로테스탄트 교회의. 감리교의 **– Methodist** *n*

meth·od·ol·o·gy /ˌmɛθəˈdɑlədʒi/ *n* [C, U] the set of methods and principles used when studying a particular subject or doing a particular type of work ‖ 특정한 과목을 공부하거나 또는 특정한 일을 할 때 사용되는 일단의 방법과 원칙. 방법론: *the methodology used in genetic research* 유전자 연구 방법론 **– methodological** /ˌmɛθədəˈlɑdʒɪkəl/ *adj*

me·tic·u·lous /məˈtɪkyələs/ *adj* very careful about details, and always trying to do things correctly ‖ 세부적인 것에 관해 매우 주의 깊고 어떤 것을 항상 정확하게 하려는. 세심한: *The hospital keeps meticulous records.* 그 병원은 꼼꼼하게 기록을 보관하고 있다. **– meticulously** *adv*

met·ric /'mɛtrɪk/ *adj* using the metric system, or relating to it ‖ 미터법을 사용하는, 또는 미터법에 관한. 미터(법)의: *metric tons* 미터 톤

metric sys·tem /'.. ˌ../ *n* [singular] the system of weights and measures based on the kilogram and the meter ‖ 킬로그램과 미터에 기초한 무게와 치수를 재는 법. 미터법

me·tro /'mɛtroʊ/ *adj* relating to or belonging to a very large city ‖ 매우 큰 도시에 관한 또는 그에 속해 있는. 대도시(권)의: *the metro area* 대도시권역

me·trop·o·lis /məˈtrɑpəlɪs/ *n* a very large city, or the most important city of a country or area ‖ 매우 큰 도시 또는 국가나 지역의 가장 중요한 도시. 주요[중심] 도시: *Las Vegas is America's fastest growing metropolis.* 라스베이거스는 미국에서 가장 빠르게 성장하는 대도시이다. **– metropolitan** /ˌmɛtrəˈpɑlət̮n/ *adj*

met·tle /'mɛt̮l/ *n* [U] LITERARY courage and determination ‖ 용기, 결단력

Mex·i·can[1] /'mɛksɪkən/ *adj* relating to or coming from Mexico ‖ 멕시코에 관한 또는 멕시코 출신의. 멕시코(인)의

Mexican[2] *n* someone from Mexico ‖ 멕시코인

mez·za·nine /'mɛzəˌnin, ˌmɛzəˈnin/ *n* the floor or BALCONY just above the main floor in a theater, hotel, store etc. ‖ 극장·호텔·상점 등의 주요층 바로 위에 있는 층이나 발코니. (바닥과 천장 사이의) 중(中)이층

mg. the written abbreviation of MILLIGRAM ‖ milligram의 약어

MI the written abbreviation of Michigan ‖ Michigan(미시간 주)의 약어

mice /maɪs/ *n* the plural of MOUSE ‖ mouse의 복수형

mi·crobe /'maɪkroʊb/ *n* an extremely small living creature that cannot be seen without a MICROSCOPE ‖ 현미경 없이는 볼 수 없는 극히 작은 생명체. 미생물

mi·cro·bi·ol·o·gy /ˌmaɪkroʊbaɪˈɑlədʒi/ *n* [U] the scientific study of very small living things ‖ 극히 작은 생물에 관한 과학적 연구. 미생물학 **– microbiologist** *n*

mi·cro·chip /'maɪkroʊˌtʃɪp/ *n* ⇨ CHIP[1]

mi·cro·cosm /'maɪkrəˌkɑzəm/ *n* a small group, society etc. that has the same qualities as a much larger one ‖ 보다 큰 것과 동일한 성질을 갖는 소집단·사회 등. 소우주. 축소판: *San Jose's mix of people is a microcosm of America.* 다양한 사람들이 섞여 사는 새너제이는 미국의 축소판이다. **—compare** MACROCOSM

mi·cro·fiche /'maɪkroʊˌfiʃ/ *n* [C, U] a sheet of MICROFILM that can be read using a special machine, especially at a library ‖ 특히 도서관에서 특별한 기계를 사용하여 읽을 수 있는 마이크로필름 한 장. 마이크로피시

mi·cro·film /'maɪkrəˌfɪlm/ *n* [C, U] film used for making very small photographs of important documents, newspapers, maps etc. ‖ 중요한 서류·신문·지도 등을 매우 작은 사진으로 찍는 데 쓰이는 필름. 마이크로필름

mi·cro·or·ga·nism /ˌmaɪkroʊˈɔrgəˌnɪzəm/ *n* an extremely small living creature that cannot be seen without a MICROSCOPE ‖ 현미경 없이는 볼 수 없는 극히 작은 생명체. 미생물

mi·cro·phone /'maɪkrəˌfoʊn/ *n* a piece of electrical equipment for making your voice sound louder, that you hold in front of your mouth when you are singing, giving a speech etc. ‖ 노래나 연설을 할 때 입 앞쪽에 대면 목소리를 증폭시키는 전기 장치. 마이크

mi·cro·proc·es·sor /ˌmaɪkroʊˈprɑsɛsɚ/ *n* the main CHIP in a computer that controls most of its operations ‖ 컴퓨터의 대부분의 기능을 통제하는 메인 칩. 마이크로프로세서

mi·cro·scope /'maɪkrəˌskoʊp/ *n* a scientific instrument that makes extremely small things appear large enough to be seen ‖ 매우 작은 것을 눈에 보일 만큼 크게 보이게 하는 과학 도구. 현미경

mi·cro·scop·ic /ˌmaɪkrəˈskɑpɪk/ *adj* **1**

extremely small ‖ 극히 작은: *microscopic animals/organisms* 아주 작은 동물[미생물] **2** using a MICROSCOPE ‖ 현미경을 사용하는: *a microscopic examination* 현미경 검사

mi·cro·wave /'maɪkrə,weɪv/ *n* **1** also **microwave oven** a type of OVEN that cooks food very quickly by using MICROWAVEs instead of heat ‖ 열 대신 극초단파를 사용하여 음식을 매우 빨리 조리하는 오븐. 전자레인지 —see picture at KITCHEN **2** a very short electric wave used especially for cooking food, sending radio messages, and in RADAR ‖ 특히 음식 조리·무선 통신·레이더에 사용되는 파장이 매우 짧은 전파. 마이크로파. 극초단파

mid·air /,mɪd'ɛr/ *n* **in midair** in the air or sky ‖ 공중에, 중천에: *The plane exploded in midair.* 그 비행기는 공중에서 폭발했다.

mid·day /'mɪd-deɪ/ *n* [U] the middle of the day, around 12:00 p.m.; NOON ‖ 오후 12시경의 한낮. 정오; 㳄 noon —compare MIDNIGHT

Billy   Tom   Chris
Tom is in the middle.
middle

mid·dle¹ /'mɪdl/ *n* **1** **the middle** **a)** the center part of a thing, place, or position ‖ 사물[장소, 위치]의 중간 부분. 한가운데. 중앙: *Why's your car parked in the middle of the road?* 왜 네 차가 길 한복판에 주차되어 있지? / *Tom's the guy in the middle.* 톰은 가운데 있는 사내이다. **b)** the part that is between the beginning and the end of a story, event, period etc. ‖ 이야기·사건·기간 등의 처음과 끝 사이 부분. 중간 부분: *I fell asleep in the middle of class.* 나는 수업 도중에 잠들었다. / *Who'd call us in the middle of the night?* 한밤중에 우리에게 전화했던 사람이 누구지? **2** **be in the middle of doing something** to be busy doing something ‖ 어떤 일을 하느라 바쁘다. 한창 때[…]하는 중]이다: *Can I call you back later? I'm right in the middle of cooking dinner.* 제가 나중에 전화 드려도 될까요? 제가 지금 저녁 준비 중이거든요.

middle² *adj* **1** nearest to the center of something ‖ 사물의 중심에 가장 근접한. 한가운데의. 중앙의: *Do you mind if we sit in the middle row?* 우리가 중간 열에 앉아도 괜찮으시겠습니까? / *The middle lane was blocked off because of an accident.* 사고 때문에 가운데 차선이 막혔다. **2** half way through an event, action, or period of time, or between the beginning and the end ‖ 사건[행사, 기간]의 중간쯤에, 또는 시작과 끝의 사이에. 도중에. 중간에: *I missed the middle act of the play.* 나는 연극의 중간 막[장면]을 놓쳤다.

middle-aged /,... '../ *n* belonging or relating to the period of your life when you are about 40 to 60 years old ‖ 생애 중에 나이가 약 40세에서 60세까지 시기에 속하거나 관계된. 중년의: *a middle-aged woman* 중년의 여성 – **middle age** *n* [U]

Middle Ag·es /,... '../ *n* **the Middle Ages** the period in European history between the 5th and 15th centuries A.D. ‖ 유럽사에서 5세기에서 15세기 사이의 기간. 중세 (시대)

Middle A·mer·i·ca /,mɪdl ə'mɛrɪkə/ *n* [U] **1** ⇨ MIDWEST **2** Americans who are neither rich nor poor, who usually have traditional values ‖ 보통 전통적 가치관을 갖고 있고 부유하지도 가난하지도 않은 미국인. 미국의 평균적 중산 계급: *Cars that attract Middle America – people who are looking for comfort and value.* 편안함과 유용성을 찾는 미국 중산층의 관심을 끄는 자동차

middle class /,.. '../ *n* **the middle class** the social class that includes people who are neither rich nor poor ‖ 부유하지도 가난하지도 않은 사람들이 속

한 사회 계층. 중산층: *a tax reduction for the middle class* 중산층에 대한 감세 – **middle-class** *adj* —see usage note at CLASS¹

Middle East /ˌ.. '.../ *n* **the Middle East** the part of Asia that is between the Mediterranean Sea and the Arabian Sea, including countries such as Turkey and Iran ‖ 터키·이란 등의 국가가 속한, 지중해와 아라비아해 사이에 위치한 아시아 지역. 중동 – **Middle Eastern** *adj*

middle fin·ger /ˌ.. '../ *n* the longest finger in the middle of the five fingers on your hand ‖ 손에서 다섯 손가락의 가운데에 위치한 가장 긴 손가락. 중지 — see picture at HAND¹

mid·dle·man /'mɪdl,mæn/ *n* someone who buys things in order to get a profit by selling them to someone else ‖ 남에게 팔아 이윤을 얻기 위해 물건을 사는 사람. 중간 상인. 중개인

middle name /ˌ.. '../ *n* the name that, in English, comes between your first name and your family name ‖ 영어에서 이름과 성(姓) 사이에 오는 이름. 중간 이름 —see usage note at NAMES

middle-of-the-road /ˌ.. .. '.../ *adj* middle-of-the-road ideas, opinions etc. are not extreme, so many people agree with them ‖ 생각·의견이 극단적이지 않아 많은 사람들이 동의하는. 중도의. 온건한: *a politician that appeals to middle-of-the-road voters* 온건한 유권자에게 호소하는 정치인

middle school /'.. ,./ *n* a school in the US for students between the ages of 11 and 14 ‖ 11세에서 14세 사이의 학생을 위한 미국의 학교. 중학교

midg·et /'mɪdʒɪt/ *n* a very small person ‖ 매우 작은 사람. 꼬마. 난쟁이

mid·life crisis /ˌmɪdlaɪf 'kraɪsɪs/ *n* the worry and lack of confidence that some people feel when they are about 40 or 50 years old ‖ 사람들이 40대나 50대가 되면 느끼는 걱정과 자신감의 결여. 중년의 위기

mid·night /'mɪdnaɪt/ *n* [U] 12 o'clock at night, or 0:00 a.m. ‖ 밤 12시 또는 오전 0시. 자정. 한밤중: *I fell asleep a little after midnight.* 나는 자정이 좀 지나서야 잠들었다. —compare MIDDAY

mid·riff /'mɪdrɪf/ *n* the part of the body between your chest and your waist ‖ 가슴과 허리 사이의 신체 부분. 상복부

midst /mɪdst/ *n* **in the midst of** in the middle of something such as an event, situation, place, or group ‖ 사건[상황, 장소, 집단] 등의 한가운데에. 중앙에. 한복판에: *a reason for hope in the midst of a war* 전쟁 한가운데서 희망을 갖는 이유

mid·term /'mɪdtəm/ *n* **1** an examination that students take in the middle of a SEMESTER ‖ 학생들이 학기 중간에 치르는 시험. 중간 시험: *When are your midterms?* 너 언제 중간 시험을 치니? **2** [U] the middle of the period when an elected government has power ‖ 선출된 정부가 권력을 갖고 있는 시기의 중간. 중간기 – **midterm** *adj*

mid·way /ˌmɪd'weɪ/ *adj, adv* at the middle point between two places, or in the middle of a period of time or an event ‖ 두 장소 사이의 중간 지점의[에], 또는 기간이나 사건 가운데의[에]. 도중의[에]: *There's a gas station midway between here and Fresno.* 이곳과 프레즈노 도중에 주유소가 있다. / *He went silent midway through his speech.* 그는 그의 연설 도중에 침묵했다.

mid·week /ˌmɪd'wik·/ *adj, adv* on one of the middle days of the week, such as Tuesday, Wednesday, or Thursday ‖ 화[수, 목]요일 등 주중의 하루의[에]. 주중(週中)의[에]: *midweek classes* 주중 수업 / *I can see you midweek.* 나는 너를 주중에 볼 수 있어.

Mid·west /ˌmɪd'wɛst/ *n* **the Midwest** the central area of the US ‖ 미국의 중부 지역. 중서부 – **Midwestern** /mɪd'wɛstən/ *adj*

mid·wife /'mɪdwaɪf/ *n* a specially trained nurse, usually a woman, whose job is to help women when they are having a baby ‖ 대개 여자로, 임신한 여성을 돕는 일을 하며 특별히 훈련된 간호사. 산파. 조산사

miffed /mɪft/ *adj* INFORMAL annoyed ‖ 화가 난. 분개하는. 불끈하는

might¹ /maɪt/ *modal v* **1** used in order to talk about what was, is, or might be possible ‖ 과거에 있을 수 있었던 것[현재에 있을 수 있는 것, 앞으로 있을 수 있는 것]에 대해 말하는 데에 쓰여. …이었을지도[일지도] 모른다. 아마 …일 것이다: *I might be wrong, but I'm almost positive she said that.* 나는 틀릴지도 모르지만, 그녀가 그것을 말했다고 거의 확신하고 있다. / *I might not be able to go – my son is sick.* 나는 내 아들이 아파서 갈 수 없을지도 몰라요. / *She might have tried calling, but I've been out.* 그녀가 전화를 걸었을지도 모르나 나는 외출중이었다. **2** used in CONDITIONAL sentences to show possibility ‖ 가능성을 나타내기 위해 조건문에 쓰여: *If Hawaii is too expensive, we might go to Florida.* 만일 하와이가 너무

돈이 많이 든다면, 우리는 플로리다로 갈 수도 있다. **3** used instead of "may" when reporting what someone said or thought ‖ 누군가 한 말이나 생각을 전할 때 "may" 대신 쓰여: *This morning I thought it might rain, so I brought an umbrella.* 오늘 아침 나는 비가 올 것이라고 생각해서 우산을 가져왔다. **4 might as well** SPOKEN used in order to say that you will do something even though you are not very interested in it or excited about it ‖ 어떤 것에 관심이 많지 않거나 흥미가 없어도 무엇을 할 거라고 말하는 데에 쓰여. (…하느니) …하는 편이 좋다[낫다]: *I might as well go with you. I don't have anything else to do.* 달리 할 일이 없으니 차라리 너와 함께 가는 편이 낫겠다. **5** FORMAL used in order to give advice ‖ 충고를 하는 데에 쓰여: *You might try calling the manager of the store.* 너는 상점 지배인에게 전화하는 편이 낫겠다. / *You might want to get your blood pressure checked.* 너는 혈압 검사를 받는 것이 나을 것이다.

might² *n* [U] LITERARY strength and power ‖ 힘, 권력: *She tried with all her might to push him away.* 그녀는 온힘으로 그를 밀어내려 했다.

might·y¹ /'maɪti/ *adj* strong and powerful ‖ 강하고 힘 있는. 강력한: *mighty warriors* 강한 전사들

mighty² *adv* INFORMAL very ‖ 매우. 몹시. 아주: *That chicken smells mighty good, Jenny.* 제니, 그 닭고기는 냄새가 아주 좋아.

mi·graine /'maɪgreɪn/ *n* an extremely bad HEADACHE ‖ 극심한 두통

mi·grant /'maɪgrənt/ *n* a person, bird, or animal that regularly moves from one area or country to another ‖ 한 지역이나 국가에서 다른 지역이나 국가로 정기적으로 이동하는 사람[새, 동물]. 이주자. 철새: *migrant workers hired during the war* 전쟁 중에 고용된 이주 노동자들 —compare EMIGRANT, IMMIGRANT

mi·grate /'maɪgreɪt/ *v* [I] **1** if birds or animals migrate, they travel to a different part of the world, especially in the fall and spring ‖ 새 또는 동물이 특히 가을과 봄에 세계의 다른 지역으로 이동하다. 철따라 정기적으로 이주하다 **2** to go to another area or country for a short time, usually in order to find a place to live or work ‖ 보통 거주하거나 일할 장소를 찾아 단기간 동안 다른 지역이나 국가로 가다. 이주하다: *farmworkers who migrate from state to state, harvesting crops* 추수를 하면서 주에서 주로 이주하

는 농장 노동자들 —compare EMIGRATE, IMMIGRATE —see usage note at EMIGRATE

mi·gra·tion /maɪˈgreɪʃən/ *n* the action of a large group of birds, animals, or people moving from one area or country to another ‖ 큰 무리의 새[동물, 사람들]가 한 지역이나 국가에서 다른 지역이나 국가로 이동하는 행위. 이주. 이동: *the yearly migration of geese* 매년마다의 기러기의 이동 — **migratory** /'maɪgrə,tɔri/ *adj*

mike /maɪk/ *n* INFORMAL ⇨ MICROPHONE

mild /maɪld/ *adj* **1** not too severe or serious ‖ 너무 심하거나 심각하지 않은. 가벼운: *a mild case of flu* 가벼운 유행성 감기 / *mild criticism* 가벼운 비판 **2** not strong-tasting or hot-tasting ‖ 맛이 강하거나 맵지 않은. (음식 등이) 순한. 부드러운: *mild cheddar cheese* 순한 맛의 체더 치즈 / *a mild green chili* 맵지 않은 푸른 (칠리) 고추 **3** if the weather is mild, it is not too cold or wet and not too hot ‖ 기후가 너무 춥거나 습하지 않으며 너무 덥지 않은. (기후 등이) 온화한·포근한 **4** if a soap or beauty product is mild, it is gentle to your skin, hair etc. ‖ 비누·미용 제품이 피부·머리카락 등에 독하지 않은. 자극성이 적은.

mil·dew /'mɪldu/ *n* [U] a very small white or gray FUNGUS (=plant without leaves) that grows on walls, leather, and other surfaces in warm, slightly wet places ‖ 따뜻하고 약간 습한 장소에서 벽·가죽·다른 것의 표면 위에서 자라는 매우 작고 하얗거나 회색의 균. 곰팡이 — **mildew** *v* [I]

mild·ly /'maɪldli/ *adv* **1** slightly ‖ 약간. 조금: *McKee was only mildly interested.* 맥키는 단지 약간 흥미가 있었다. **2 to put it mildly** SPOKEN said when you are saying something unpleasant in the most polite way that you can ‖ 할 수 있는 한 최대한으로 공손하게 불쾌한 것을 말할 때 쓰여. 조심스레 말하자면: *Well, to put it mildly, I don't think Greg likes you very much.* 조심스레 말하자면, 나는 그레그가 당신을 많이 좋아한다고 생각하지 않습니다. **3** in a gentle way ‖ 온화하게. 부드럽게: *"Perhaps," he answered mildly.* "아마도,"하고 그는 부드럽게 대답했다.

mile /maɪl/ *n* **1** a unit for measuring distance, equal to 1760 yards or 1609 meters ‖ 1760야드 또는 1609미터에 상당하는 거리 측정 단위. 마일: *The city is about 15 miles north of here.* 그 도시는 여기서 북쪽으로 약 15마일 거리에 있다. / *Mark jogs at least 5 miles a day.* 마크

는 하루에 적어도 5마일은 조깅한다. **2 miles** INFORMAL a very long distance ‖ 매우 먼 거리: *We walked for miles without seeing anyone.* 우리는 사람을 아무도 만나지 못한 채 아주 먼 거리를 걸었다. **3 talk a mile a minute** SPOKEN to talk very quickly without stopping ‖ 멈추지 않고 매우 빨리 말하다. 계속 지껄여대다 **4 be miles away** SPOKEN to not be paying attention to what is happening around you ‖ 주위에서 일어나는 일에 주의를 기울이지 않고 있다. 다른 일을 생각하다: *Sorry, I was miles away. What did you say?* 미안하지만, 다른 일을 생각했어. 뭐라고 했지?

mile·age /ˈmaɪlɪdʒ/ *n* **1** [singular, U] the number of miles that a car has traveled since it was new ‖ 신품 출고 이래 차가 주행한 마일수. 총 마일수. 마일리지: *a used car with low mileage* 주행 마일수가 적은 중고차 **2** [U] the number of miles a car travels using each gallon of gasoline ‖ 차가 가솔린 1갤런당 주행하는 마일수. 연비: *Our car gets really good mileage.* (=a lot of miles per gallon) 우리 차는 정말 연비가 높다. **3 get a lot of mileage out of sth** to make something be as useful for you as it can be ‖ 무엇을 할 수 있는 한 유용하게 하다. …을 충분히 이용하다: *I've gotten a lot of mileage out of that old joke.* 나는 그 오래된 농담을 충분히 이용했다.

mile·stone /ˈmaɪlstoʊn/ *n* a very important event in the development of something ‖ 어떤 것의 발달 단계에서 매우 중요한 사건. 중대한[획기적] 사건: *Winning the election was a milestone in his political career.* 선거의 승리는 그의 정치가로서의 경력에 매우 중요한 사건이었다.

mi·lieu /milˈyu, mɪlˈyʊ/ *n, plural* **milieus** [C, U] FORMAL all the things and people that surround you and influence you ‖ 주변을 둘러싸고 있으면서 영향을 미치는 모든 것과 사람들. 주위. 환경: *Always consider the writer's social and political milieu.* 항상 작가의 사회적·정치적 환경을 고려해라.

mil·i·tant¹ /ˈmɪlətənt/ *adj* willing to use force or violence ‖ 힘이나 폭력을 꺼리지 않고 사용하려고 하는. 공격[호전]적인: *Militant groups were still protesting against the new law.* 투쟁적인 단체들은 여전히 새로운 법에 대해 항의하고 있었다. **– militancy** *n* [U]

militant² *n* someone who uses violence to achieve social or political change ‖ 사회적, 또는 정치적 변화를 달성하기 위해

폭력을 쓰는 사람. 투사

mil·i·ta·ris·m /ˈmɪlɪtəˌrɪzəm/ *n* [U] the belief that a country should increase its army, navy etc. and use them to get what it wants ‖ 일국이 자국의 육군·해군 등을 증강하고 그들이 원하는 것을 얻기 위해 군을 사용해야 한다는 신념. 군국주의 **– militaristic** /ˌmɪlɪtəˈrɪstɪk/ *adj*

mil·i·tar·y¹ /ˈmɪləˌtɛri/ *adj* used by the Army, Navy, or Air Force, or relating to war ‖ 육군[해군, 공군]에서 쓰이는, 또는 전쟁에 관한. 군(용)의. 군사의: *military aircraft* 군용 항공기 / *a military base in Greece* 그리스의 군사 기지 / *My brother was sent to military academy.* (=military school) 내 남동생은 군사 학교에 보내졌다. **– militarily** /ˌmɪləˈtɛrəli/ *adv*

military² *n* [C usually singular] the military organizations of a country, such as the army and navy ‖ 육군·해군 등 일국의 군사 조직. 군(대): *My father is in the military.* 나의 아버지는 군대에 계신다.

mil·i·tate /ˈmɪləˌteɪt/ *v*
militate against sth *phr v* [T] FORMAL to prevent something from happening or from being likely to happen ‖ 무엇이 발생하거나 발생할 수 있는 것을 막다. …에 불리하게 작용하다: *factors that militated against her becoming a political leader* 그녀가 정치 지도자가 되는 데에 불리한 영향을 미치는 요인들

mi·li·tia /məˈlɪʃə/ *n* a group of people trained as soldiers who are not members of the permanent army ‖ 상설 군대의 구성원은 아니지만 군인으로 훈련받은 일단의 사람. 시민군. 민병: *a militia of 300,000* 300,000명의 민병

milk¹ /mɪlk/ *n* [U] **1** a white liquid that people drink, which is usually produced by cows or goats ‖ 보통 젖소나 염소가 생산하는, 사람들이 마시는 하얀 액체. 우유: *a glass of milk* 우유 한 잔 / *Would you like milk in your coffee?* 커피에 우유 넣을까요? **2** a white liquid produced by female animals and women for feeding their babies ‖ 동물의 암컷과 여성이 그들의 아기나 새끼를 먹이기 위해 생산하는 하얀 액체. 젖

milk² *v* [T] **1** to take milk from a cow or goat ‖ 젖소나 염소로부터 젖을 짜다 **2 milk sb/sth for sth** INFORMAL to get all the money, advantages etc. that you can from a person, thing, or situation ‖ 사람[사물, 상황]에게서 얻을 수 있는 모든 돈·이익 등을 얻다. …에서 단물을 빨아먹다. 우려내다: *I'm going to milk her* *for every penny she has.* 나는 그녀가 가진 모든 돈을 우려낼 것이다.

milk·man /'mɪlkmæn/ *n* someone who delivers milk to houses each morning ‖ 매일 아침 집으로 우유를 배달하는 사람. 우유 배달인

milk·shake /'mɪlkʃeɪk/ *n* a drink made from milk and ICE CREAM ‖ 우유와 아이스크림으로 만든 음료. 밀크셰이크: *a chocolate milkshake* 초콜릿 밀크셰이크

milk·y /'mɪlki/ *adj* **1** if water or a liquid is milky, it is not clear and looks slightly white, like milk ‖ 물이나 액체가 투명하지 않고 우유처럼 약간 희게 보이는. 뿌연 **2** milky skin is white and smooth ‖ 피부가 하얗고 부드러운. 우유 같은. 젖빛인

Milky Way /ˌ..ˈ./ *n* **the Milky Way** the pale white band made up of large numbers of stars that you can see across the sky at night ‖ 밤하늘을 가로질러서 볼 수 있는, 수많은 별들로 구성된 엷은 횐색의 띠. 은하(수)

mill[1] /mɪl/ *n* **1** a large machine used for crushing food such as corn, grain, or coffee into a powder ‖ 옥수수[곡물, 커피]등의 식품을 가루로 부수는 데에 쓰이는 큰 기계. 제분기 **2** a building where materials such as paper, steel, or cotton cloth are made ‖ 종이[강철, 면포] 등의 소재가 만들어지는 건물. 공장 **3** a small tool or machine used especially for crushing pepper or coffee ‖ 특히 후추나 커피를 분쇄하는 데에 쓰이는 작은 도구나 기계. 분쇄기

mill[2] *v* [T] to crush grains in a MILL ‖ 곡물을 제분기로 빻다. …을 제분하다 —see picture at GRIND[1]

mill around *phr v* [I] INFORMAL if a lot of people are milling around, they are moving around a place and do not seem to have a particular purpose ‖ 많은 사람들이 특정한 목적이 없는 것처럼 한 장소를 이리저리 돌아다니다. 떼지어 어슬렁거리다: *Tourists were milling around the streets.* 관광객들은 거리를 이리저리 몰려다니고 있었다.

mil·len·ni·um /məˈlɛniəm/ *n, plural* **millennia** **1** a period of time equal to 1000 years ‖ 일천년에 상당하는 기간. 천년(간) **2** the time when a new 1000 year period begins ‖ 새 천년이 시작되는 시점: *projects planned for the start of the new millennium* 새 천년의 시작에 맞춰 계획된 사업(계획) —**millennial** *adj*

mil·li·gram /'mɪləˌgræm/, *written abbreviation* **mg.** *n* a unit for measuring weight, equal to 1/1000th of a gram ‖ 일천분의 일 그램에 상당하는 무게 측정 단위. 밀리그램

mil·li·li·ter /'mɪləˌlitɚ/ *n* a unit for measuring liquids, equal to 1/1000th of a liter or .00212 of a PINT ‖ 일천분의 일 리터 또는 0.00212 파인트에 상당하는 액체 계량 단위. 밀리리터

mil·li·me·ter /'mɪləˌmitɚ/ *written abbreviation* **mm.** *n* a unit for measuring length, equal to 1/1000th of a meter or 0.03937 inches ‖ 일천분의 일 미터 또는 0.03937인치에 상당하는 길이 측정 단위. 밀리미터

mil·li·ner·y /'mɪləˌnɛri/ *n* [U] OLD-FASHIONED women's hats, or the activity of making these hats ‖ 여성 모자, 또는 이 모자를 만드는 활동. 여성 모자류. 여성 모자업 —**milliner** /'mɪlənɚ/ *n*

mil·lion /'mɪlyən/ *number* **1** 1,000,000 ‖ 일백만: *$350 million* 3억 5천만 달러 / *4 million people* 4백만 명의 사람들 ✗DON'T SAY "4 million of people."✗ "4 million of people"이라고는 하지 않는다. **2** also **millions** an extremely large number of people or things ‖ 사람들이나 사물의 굉장히 많은 수. 다수. 무수: *I've heard that excuse a million times.* 나는 그 변명을 무수히 들었다. **3** not/never **in a million years** SPOKEN said in order to emphasize how impossible or unlikely something is ‖ 어떤 것이 얼마나 불가능하거나 있을 것 같지 않은지를 강조하는 데에 쓰여. 절대 …아닌[없는]: *I never would have guessed in a million years!* 나는 절대 알아내지 못했을 거야! **4** **look/feel like a million dollars** INFORMAL to look very attractive or feel very happy and healthy ‖ 아주 매력적으로 보이거나 아주 행복하고 건강하게 느끼다. 최고로 보이다/최고처럼 느끼다 **5** **one in a million** the best of all possible people or things ‖ 있을 수 있는 모든 사람들이나 사물 중 최고: *My wife is one in a million!* 내 아내는 최고야! —**millionth** /'mɪlyənθ/ *number*

mil·lion·aire /ˌmɪlyəˈnɛr/ *n* someone who is very rich and has at least one million dollars ‖ 최소한 100만 달러나 지니고 있는 아주 부유한 사람. 백만장자

mime[1] /maɪm/ *n* an actor who performs without using words, or a performance in which no words are used ‖ 말하지 않고 연기하는 연기자, 또는 말을 하지 않고 하는 공연. 무언 배우. 무언극

mime[2] *n* [I, T] to perform using actions and movements instead of using words ‖ 말 대신 행동과 움직임을 이용하여 연기하다. 말없이 무언극을 하다. …을 무언으로 연기하다: *She stretched out her* *arms, miming a swimmer.* 헤엄치는 사람을 흉내 내며 그녀는 두 팔을 뻗었다.

mim·ic¹ /ˈmɪmɪk/ *v* **mimicked, mimicked, mimicking** [T] **1** to copy the way someone speaks, moves, or behaves, usually to make people laugh ‖ 보통 사람들을 웃기기 위해 남이 말하는 [움직이는, 행동하는] 투를 모방하다. …을 흉내 내다: *Lily mimicked Sue's Southern accent.* 릴리는 수의 남부 억양을 흉내 냈다. **2** to have the same behavior, appearance, or qualities as someone or something else ‖ 다른 사람이나 사물과 같은 행동[외모, 성질]을 갖다. …과 흡사하다: *a computer that mimics human abilities, such as walking and speaking* 걷고 말하는 등 인간과 흡사한 능력이 있는 컴퓨터 – **mimicry** *n* [U]

mimic² *n* a person or animal that is good at MIMICing someone or something else ‖ 다른 사람이나 사물의 흉내를 잘 내는 사람이나 동물

mince /mɪns/ *v* **1** [T] to cut food into extremely small pieces ‖ 음식을 매우 작은 조각으로 자르다. …을 잘게 썰다. 다지다: *Mince the onion and garlic.* 양파와 마늘을 곱게 다져라. **2 not mince words** to say exactly what you think, even if this may offend people ‖ 남의 감정을 상하게 할지라도 자신이 생각하는 것을 그대로 말하다. 숨김없이 분명히 말하다: *He's a brash New Yorker who doesn't mince words.* 그는 거리낌없이 직설적으로 말하는 무례한 뉴욕 사람이다. **3** [I] to walk, using very small steps and moving your hips a lot ‖ 아주 작은 보폭으로 엉덩이를 많이 흔들며 걷다. 뽐내며 종종걸음으로 걷다: *models mincing down/along the runway* (패션쇼의) 무대를 뽐내며 걷는 모델들

mince·meat /ˈmɪnsmit/ *n* [U] a sweet mixture of apples, dried fruit, and SPICEs, but no meat, used in PIEs ‖ 고기를 넣지 않은 파이에 쓰이는, 사과·말린 과일·향료를 달콤하게 섞은 혼합물. 민스미트. 민스파이의 재료

mind¹ /maɪnd/ *n*
1 ▶BRAIN 머리◀ your thoughts, or the part of your brain used for thinking and imagining things ‖ 생각, 또는 무엇을 사고하고 상상하는 데 쓰이는 두뇌 부분. 정신. 머리: *What kind of plans did you have in mind?* (=what plans were you thinking about) 자네는 어떤 계획들을 생각하고 있었나? / *What's on your mind?* (=what are you thinking about) 무엇을 생각하니?

2 change your mind to change your opinions or decision about something ‖ 무엇에 대한 견해나 결정을 바꾸다. 생각을 바꾸다: *If you change your mind and want to come, give us a call.* 네 마음이 변해서 오고 싶으면 우리에게 전화해.

3 make up your mind to decide something, or become very determined to do something ‖ 무엇을 결정하다, 또는 어떤 것을 하기로 매우 굳게 마음먹다: *Have you made up your mind which college you want to go to?* 가고 싶은 대학을 결정했니?

4 come/spring to mind if something comes to mind, you suddenly think of it ‖ 무엇을 갑자기 생각하다. 머리에 문득 떠오르다

5 state of mind the way you are feeling, such as how happy or sad you are ‖ 얼마나 행복한지 또는 슬픈지 등을 느끼는 상태. 마음의 상태

6 cross/enter your mind if something crosses your mind, you think about it for a short period ‖ 잠시 어떤 것을 생각하다. 뇌리를 스치다: *It never crossed my mind that she might be unhappy.* 난 그녀가 불행할지 모른다는 생각은 단 한번도 해 본 적이 없었다.

7 -minded having a particular attitude or believing that a particular thing is important ‖ 특정한 태도를 가진 또는 특정한 것이 중요하다고 믿는. …한 마음을 가진: *He was a mean, narrow/closed-minded old man.* (=he did not accept other ideas and opinions) 그는 비열하고 좁은[닫힌] 마음을 가진 노인이다. / *politically-minded students* 술수에 능한 학생

8 keep/bear sth in mind to remember something ‖ 무엇을 기억하다. 외고 있다. 명심하다: *Keep in mind that the bank will be closed tomorrow.* 내일 은행이 문 닫는 것을 명심해라.

9 have a lot on your mind to be unable to think clearly because you are very busy or have a lot of problems ‖ 매우 바쁘거나 문제가 많아서 똑똑히 생각할 수 없다. 머릿속이 꽉 차다[복잡하다]

10 out of your mind INFORMAL crazy ‖ 미친. 정신이 나간: *Are you out of your mind?* 너 정신 나갔어?

11 go out of your mind/lose your mind INFORMAL to start to become mentally ill or to behave in a strange way ‖ 정신적으로 병들거나 이상하게 행동하기 시작하다. 정신이 이상해지다[나가다]: *I have so much to do, I feel like I'm going out of my mind.* 나는 할 일이 너무

많아서 돌아버릴 것 같아.

12 no one in his/her right mind INFORMAL no one who is sensible ‖ 지각이 없는 사람. 현명하지 못한 사람. 제정신이 아닌 사람: *No woman in her right mind would walk alone at night around here.* 정신이 온전한 여자는 누구도 밤에 이 부근을 혼자서 걷지 않을 것이다.

13 your mind goes blank INFORMAL if your mind goes blank, you suddenly cannot remember something ‖ 머리가 텅 비어서 갑자기 어떤 것을 기억해 낼 수 없다. 정신이 아득해지다: *As soon as Mr. Daniels asked me for the answer, my mind went blank.* 다니엘 씨가 나에게 대답을 요구하자마자 내 머릿속이 갑자기 아득해졌다.

14 put your mind to to decide to do something and use a lot of effort in order to succeed ‖ 무엇을 하기로 결심하고 성공하기 위해 많은 노력을 하다. 주의를 집중하다. 온 마음을 다 쏟아넣다: *You can win if you just put your mind to it.* 만일 네가 그것에 총력을 기울인다면 너는 이길 수 있을 것이다.

15 have/keep an open mind to be willing to accept other ideas and opinions ‖ 다른 생각과 의견을 기꺼이 받아들이려고 하다. 마음을 터놓다. 열린 마음을 가지다

16 take your mind off sth to make you stop thinking about something ‖ 어떤것에 대한 생각을 멈추게 하다. 걱정거리를 잊게 하다: *Dad needs a vacation to take his mind off work.* 아빠는 일에 대한 걱정을 잊기 위해 휴가가 필요하시다. —see also ONE-TRACK MIND **blow sb's mind** (BLOW¹), **slip your mind** (SLIP¹)

mind² *v* **1** [I, T] to feel annoyed, worried, or angry about something ‖ 무엇에 대해 성가시게[걱정되게, 화가 나게] 느끼다. 신경을 쓰다. 싫어하다. 꺼리다: *It's not my job, but I don't mind doing it.* 그건 내 일이 아니지만 하는 것이 싫진 않아. / *Do you think she'd mind if we didn't come?* 만약 우리가 오지 않았더라면 그녀가 언짢아했을 거라고 생각하니?

2 mind your manners/language OLD-FASHIONED to behave or speak in a polite way ‖ 예의바르게 행동하거나 말하다. 몸가짐/말을 주의하다

SPOKEN PHRASES

3 do you mind/would you mind used in order to politely ask if you can do something, or if someone will do something for you ‖ 예의바르게 무엇을 할 수 있는지 또는 남이 일을 해 줄 것

인지를 묻는 데에 쓰여. …해 주지 않으시겠습니까. …해도 괜찮습니까: *Do you mind if I use your phone?* 제가 당신의 전화를 사용해도 괜찮겠습니까? / *Would you mind waiting here a minute?* 여기서 잠시만 기다려 주시겠습니까? **4 I wouldn't mind doing sth** said when you would like to do something ‖ 무엇을 하기 바랄 때 쓰여. …하고 싶다: *I wouldn't mind living in Minneapolis.* 나는 미니애폴리스에서 살고 싶다. **5 mind your own business** to not try to find out what other people are doing ‖ 다른 사람들이 하는 일을 알려고 하지 않다. 남의 일에 간섭하지 않다. 관심 갖지 않다: *"So, did he kiss you?" "Mind your own business!"* "그래서, 그가 너한테 키스했니?" "참견하지 마!"

mind·bog·gling /'maɪndˌbagəlɪŋ/ *adj* INFORMAL strange or complicated, and difficult to imagine or believe ‖ 이상하거나 복잡하여 상상하거나 믿기 어려운. 깜짝 놀랄 만한: *a mind-boggling amount of money* 어마어마한 액수의 돈

mind·ful /'maɪndfəl/ *adj* behaving in a way that shows you remember a rule or fact ‖ 규칙이나 사실을 기억한다는 것을 보여 주며 행동하는. …에 신경을 쓰는. 유념[유의]하는: *Mindful of the guide's warning, they returned before dark.* 가이드의 경고에 유의하여 그들은 날이 저물기 전에 돌아왔다.

mind·less /'maɪndlɪs/ *adj* so simple that you do not have to think carefully about what you are doing ‖ 하고 있는 일이 너무 단순해서 주의 깊게 생각할 필요가 없는. 머리를 쓰지 않아도 되는. 단순한: *Stuffing envelopes is mindless work.* 봉투들을 채우는 것은 단순한 일이다. — **mindlessness** *n* [U]

mine¹ /maɪn/ *possessive pron* the thing or things belonging to or relating to the person who is speaking ‖ 말하는 사람에 속하거나 관련된 것이나 것들. 내 것: *That's her car. This is mine.* 저것이 그녀의 차이고 이것은 제 차입니다. / *He didn't have a pencil so I let him borrow mine.* 그가 연필을 갖고 있지 않아서 내 것을 빌려 주었다. / *Theresa's coat is black. Mine is blue.* 테레사의 코트는 검정색이고 내 것은 파란색이다.

mine² *n* **1** a type of bomb that is hidden below the surface of the ground or in the water, which explodes when someone or something touches it ‖ 지표면 밑이나 물 속에 숨겨 놓아 사람이나 물

체가 닿으면 폭발하는 폭탄의 일종. 지뢰. 수뢰 **2** a deep hole or series of holes in the ground from which gold, coal etc. is dug ‖ 금·석탄 등을 채굴하는 땅 속의 깊은 구멍이나 갱도들. 광산. 채굴갱: *He's worked in the coal mines all his life.* 그는 평생 동안 석탄 광산에서 일했다.

mine³ *v* **1** [I, T] to dig into the ground in order to get gold, coal etc. ‖ 금·석탄 등을 얻기 위해 땅을 파다. …을 채굴[채굴]하다: *men mining for gold* 금을 채굴하는 사람들 **2** [T] to hide bombs under the ground or in the water ‖ 땅 밑이나 물 밑에 폭탄을 숨기다. 지뢰[기뢰]를 매설하다: *The entire field was mined by the enemy.* 적이 모든 전장에 지뢰를 매설해 놓았다.

mine·field /'maɪnfild/ *n* an area of land that has mines hidden in it ‖ 지뢰가 매설된 지역

min·er /'maɪnɚ/ *n* someone who works in a mine ‖ 광산에서 일하는 사람. 광부: *a coal miner* 석탄 광부

min·er·al /'mɪnərəl/ *n* a natural substance such as CALCIUM, iron, coal, or salt, that is present in some foods and in the earth ‖ 몇몇 식품과 땅 속에 들어 있는 칼슘[철, 석탄, 염분] 등의 천연 물질. 광물. 미네랄: *Milk is full of valuable vitamins and minerals.* 우유에는 유익한 비타민과 미네랄이 가득 들어 있다.

mineral wa·ter /'... ,../ *n* water that comes from under the ground and contains MINERALs ‖ 땅 밑에서 나오는 미네랄을 함유한 물. 광천수

min·gle /'mɪŋgəl/ *v* **1** [I] to meet and talk with a lot of different people at a social event ‖ 사교 행사에서 많은 사람들을 만나고 대화하다. 교제하다. 어울리다: *Reporters mingled with movie stars at the awards ceremony.* 기자들은 시상식에서 영화배우들과 어울렸다. **2** [I, T] if two or more smells, sounds, feelings etc. mingle or are mingled, they combine with each other ‖ 둘 이상의 냄새·소리·느낌 등을 서로 합치다[합쳐지다]. 섞다[섞이다]: *anger mingled with disappointment and fear* 실망과 두려움이 뒤섞인 분노

min·i /'mɪni/ *adj* INFORMAL very small; MINIATURE ‖ 매우 작은. 소형의; 畲 miniature: *mini bottles of shampoo* 아주 작은 샴푸병들

min·i·a·ture¹ /'mɪniətʃɚ, 'mɪnɪtʃɚ/ *adj* very small ‖ 매우 작은. 소형인. 축소인: *a miniature doll house* 매우 작은 인형의 집

miniature² *n* **1** something that has the same appearance as someone or something, but is much smaller ‖ 어떤 사람이나 물체와 같은 모양이지만 훨씬 작은 것. 축소(모)형: *This painting is a miniature of the one in the museum.* 이 그림은 박물관에 있는 것의 축소형이다. **2 in miniature** exactly the same as someone or something else, except much smaller ‖ 훨씬 더 작다는 것을 제외하고는 다른 사람이나 사물과 아주 똑같은. 축소판의: *She has her mother's face in miniature.* 그녀의 얼굴은 자기 어머니의 축소판이다.

miniature golf /,... './ *n* [U] a GOLF game, played for fun, in which you hit a small ball through passages, over small bridges and hills etc. ‖ 재미삼아 작은 다리와 언덕 등의 위로 난 통로로 작은 공을 치는 골프 경기. 미니 골프

min·i·mal /'mɪnəməl/ *adj* extremely small in amount or degree and therefore not worth worrying about ‖ 양이나 정도가 매우 적어서 걱정할 가치가 없는. 최소한(의): *The new operation causes a minimal amount of pain to the patient.* 그 새로운 수술은 환자의 고통을 최소한으로 줄여 준다. – **minimally** *adv*

min·i·mize /'mɪnə,maɪz/ *v* [T] to make the degree or amount of something as small as possible ‖ 사물의 정도나 양을 가능한 한 최소로 하다. 최소화하다: *To minimize the risk of getting heart disease, eat well and exercise daily.* 심장병에 걸릴 위험을 최소화하기 위해서는 잘 먹고 매일 운동하세요. —opposite MAXIMIZE

min·i·mum¹ /'mɪnəməm/ *adj* the minimum number, amount, or degree is the smallest that it is possible to have ‖ 수[양, 정도]가 가능한 한 가장 적은. 최소[최저](한도)인: *$30,000 is the minimum price that we would accept.* 우리가 수락할 수 있는 최저가는 30,000달러이다. / *You will need to make a minimum payment of $50 a month.* 당신은 한 달에 최소 50달러를 지급해야 할 것이다. —opposite MAXIMUM¹

minimum² *n* the smallest number, amount, or degree that it is possible to have ‖ 가질 수 있는 최소한의 수[양, 정도]. 최저 한도: *Jim works a minimum of* (=at least) *50 hours a week.* 짐은 일주일에 적어도 50시간은 일한다. / *Costs were kept to a minimum.* (=as small as possible) 비용은 최소한도로 유지되었다. —opposite MAXIMUM²

minimum wage /ˌ... '.'/ n [U] the lowest amount of money that can legally be paid per hour to a worker ‖ 노동자에게 한 시간당 법적으로 지급될 수 있는 최저 금액. 최저 임금: *I'm only earning minimum wage, but it's a fun job.* 나는 단지 최저 임금만 받지만, 일이 재미있어.

min·ing /'maɪnɪŋ/ n [U] the industry of digging gold, coal etc. out of the ground, or the action of digging for gold etc. ‖ 땅에서 금·석탄 등을 채굴하는 산업, 또는 금 등의 채굴 행위. 광업. 채광: *coal mining in Oklahoma* 오클라호마의 탄광업 / *mining companies* 광산 회사

min·i·se·ries /'mɪniˌsɪriz/ n [plural] a television DRAMA that is divided into several parts and shown on different nights ‖ 몇 개의 부분으로 나뉘어 여러 날 밤에 걸쳐 방영되는 텔레비전 드라마. 미니시리즈

min·i·skirt /'mɪniˌskɚt/ n a very short skirt ‖ 매우 짧은 치마. 미니스커트

min·is·ter¹ /'mɪnəstɚ/ n 1 a religious leader in some Christian churches ‖ 몇몇 크리스트교회의 종교 지도자. 성직자 — compare PRIEST 2 a politician who is in charge of a government department ‖ 정부 부처를 담당하는 정치가. 장관. 각료: *a meeting of European ministers* 유럽 각료 회의

minister² v

minister to sb/sth phr v [T] FORMAL to give help to someone or something ‖ 사람이나 사물에 도움을 주다. …에 도움이 되다: *doctors who minister to the needs of their patients* 환자가 필요로 하는 것을 보살펴 주는 의사들

min·is·te·ri·al /ˌmɪnə'stɪriəl/ adj relating to a minister, or done by a minister ‖ 성직자에 관한. 또는 성직자에 의해 행해진. 성직자의. 성직자로서의: *ministerial decisions* 성직자로서의 결정

min·is·try /'mɪnəstri/ n 1 [U] the profession of being a church leader, or the work done by a religious leader ‖ 교회 지도자로서의 직업, 또는 종교 지도자가 수행하는 업무. 목사[성직자](의 직무): *Our son entered/joined the ministry two years ago.* (=became a minister) 우리 아들은 2년 전에 목사가 되었다. 2 a government department ‖ 정부 부처. 내각. 각료: *the Defense Ministry* 국방부

min·i·van /'mɪniˌvæn/ n a large vehicle with seats for six or more people ‖ 6인 또는 그 이상을 위한 좌석이 마련된 큰 차. 미니밴

mink /mɪŋk/ n [C, U] a small animal with soft brown fur, or the valuable fur from this animal ‖ 부드러운 갈색 털을 가진 작은 동물, 또는 이 동물의 값비싼 털. 밍크(모피)

min·now /'mɪnoʊ/ n a very small fish that lives in rivers, lakes etc. ‖ 강·호수 등에 사는 매우 작은 물고기. 연준모치. 잉엇과의 작은 물고기

mi·nor¹ /'maɪnɚ/ adj small and not very important or serious ‖ 작고 그다지 중요하지 않거나 심각하지 않은. 보다 작은. 적은. 대수롭지 않은. 사소한: *We made a few minor changes to the plan.* 우리는 계획에 몇 가지 사소한 변화를 주었다. / *It's only a minor injury.* 그것은 대수롭지 않은 상처일 뿐이다. ✗DON'T SAY "minor than."✗ "minor than" 이라고는 하지 않는다. —opposite MAJOR¹

minor² n 1 LAW someone who is not old enough to be considered legally responsible for his/her actions, usually someone under the age of 18 ‖ 자신의 행동에 대해 법적으로 책임이 있는 것으로 간주될 만큼 나이가 들지 않은 사람. 보통 18세 이하인 자. 미성년자 2 the second main subject that you study at college for your degree ‖ 대학에서 학위를 위해 공부하는 두 번째 전공 과목. 부전공 (과목[과정]): *"What's your minor?" "Math."* "부전공은 뭐지요?" "수학입니다." —compare MAJOR²

minor³ v

minor in sth phr v [T] to study a second main subject as part of your college degree ‖ 대학 학위 과정의 일부로 부전공 과목을 공부하다. …을 부전공하다: *I'm minoring in African Studies.* 나는 부전공으로 아프리카학을 공부하고 있습니다.

mi·nor·i·ty¹ /mə'nɔrəti, maɪ-, -'nɑr-/ adj relating to a group of people who do not have the same opinion, religion, race etc. as most of the larger group that they are in ‖ 소속된 더 큰 집단의 대다수와 의견·종교·인종 등이 같지 않은 일단의 사람들과 관련된. 소수의. 소수 집단의: *help for minority groups* 소수 집단에 대한 원조 / *minority students* 소수 민족의 학생들

minority² n 1 a group of people of a different race or religion than most people in a country, or someone in one of these groups ‖ 한 나라의 다수의 사람들과 다른 인종 또는 종교를 가진 사람들 집단, 또는 이들 집단 중 하나에 소속된 사람. 소수파[민족, 종교](사람·신도): *job opportunities for minorities and women* 소수 민족과 여성들을 위한 취업 기회 2 [singular] a small part of a larger group of people or things ‖ 사람 또는 사물의 더 큰 집단 중 작은 일부. 소수(파). 과반수 이하: *Only a minority of the committee voted against the new rule.* 위원회의 오직 소수만이 새 규칙에 반대 투표했다. **3 be in the minority** to be less in number than any other group ‖ 숫자상으로 어떤 다른 그룹보다 적다. 소수(파)이다. 소수(그룹)에 속하다: *Male teachers are very much in the minority at public schools.* 공립 학교에 남자 교사들은 아주 적다. — compare MAJORITY¹

Minor Leagues /ˌ.. ˈ./ *n* [plural] the groups of teams that form the lower levels of American professional baseball ‖ 미국 프로 야구의 하위 단계를 이루는 팀들의 집단. 마이너 리그

min·strel /ˈmɪnstrəl/ *n* **1** a singer or dancer who pretended to be a black person and who performed in shows in the early part of the 20th century ‖ 20세기 초기에 흑인으로 분장하고 쇼에서 공연했던 가수나 무용수. 민스트럴 **2** a singer or musician in the Middle Ages ‖ 중세의 가수나 음악가. 음유 시인

mint¹ /mɪnt/ *n* **1** a candy with a sweet hot taste ‖ 달고 화한 맛이 나는 사탕. 박하사탕: *an after dinner mint* 식후에 먹는 박하사탕 **2** [U] a plant with sweet hot-tasting leaves used in cooking and making medicine ‖ 요리와 약품 제조에 사용되는 달고 화한 맛이 나는 잎이 달린 식물. 박하(잎) —see also PEPPERMINT, SPEARMINT **3 a mint** INFORMAL a large amount of money ‖ 많은 액수의 돈. 떼돈. 어마어마한 돈: *Bill made a mint when he sold his company.* 빌은 자신의 회사를 팔아서 어마어마한 돈을 벌었다. **4** a place where coins are officially made ‖ 동전이 공식적으로 주조되는 곳. 화폐 주조소. 조폐국

mint² *adj* **in mint condition** looking new and in perfect condition ‖ 신형이고 완벽한 상태로 보이는. 새 것 같은: *a 1957 Chevy in mint condition* 새 차나 마찬가지인 1957년산 시보레차

mint³ *v* [T] to make a coin ‖ 화폐를 주조하다

mint·y /ˈmɪnti/ *adj* tasting or smelling of MINT ‖ 박하 맛이 나거나 향이 나는: *minty mouthwash* 박하 향이 나는 구강 청정제

mi·nus¹ /ˈmaɪnəs/ *prep* **1** used in mathematics when you SUBTRACT one number from another ‖ 수학에서 다른 수에서 한 수를 뺄 때 쓰여. 뺀. 마이너스: *17 minus 5 is 12 (17-5=12)* 17에서 5를 빼면 12이다. **2** INFORMAL without

something that would normally be there ‖ 정상적으로는 그 자리에 있어야 할 것이 없는 (채로). …이 상실된[빠진, 없는]: *He came back from the fight minus a couple of front teeth.* 그는 앞니 두 개가 빠진 채로 싸움에서 돌아왔다.

minus² *n* **1** ⇨ MINUS SIGN **2** something bad about a situation ‖ 상황에 대해 나쁜 것. 불리(한 점). 손실: *There are pluses and minuses to living in a big city.* 대도시에 사는 것은 유리한 점과 불리한 점이 있다. —compare PLUS⁴

minus³ *adj* **1 A minus/B minus etc.** a mark used in a system of marking a student's work. "A minus" is lower than "A," but higher than "B plus" ‖ 학생들의 학업 성적을 채점하는 체계에 사용되는 부호. "A마이너스"는 "A"보다 낮지만 "B플러스"보다 높다. A⁻/B⁻ —compare PLUS³ **2 minus 5/20/30 etc.** less than zero, especially less than zero degrees in temperature ‖ 영 미만의, 특히 기온이 0도보다 낮은. 영하의. 빙점 이하의. 영하 5/20/30도: *At night the temperature can go as low as minus 30.* 밤에는 기온이 영하 30도로 낮게 내려갈 수 있다.

min·us·cule /ˈmɪnəˌskyul/ *adj* extremely small ‖ 아주 작은: *a minuscule amount of food* 대단히 적은 양의 음식

minus sign /ˈ.. ˌ./ *n* a sign (-) showing that a number is less than zero, or that the second of two numbers is to be SUBTRACTed from the first ‖ 숫자가 영보다 작은 것, 또는 두 수 중 두 번째가 첫 번째로부터 차감되는 것을 나타내는 기호. 마이너스(-) 기호[부호]

min·ute¹ /ˈmɪnɪt/ *n* **1** a period of time equal to 60 seconds ‖ 60초와 같은 시간(주기). 분: *Ethel's train arrives in fifteen minutes.* 에텔의 기차는 15분 후 도착한다. / *It's three minutes to 4:00.* (=three minutes before 4:00) 4시 3분 전이다. **2** a very short period of time ‖ 매우 짧은 시간. 순간. 잠깐: *For a minute I thought he was serious.* 순간, 나는 그가 심각하다고 생각했다. / *I'll be ready in a minute.* 나는 곧 준비될 것이다. **3 wait/just a minute** SPOKEN **a)** used in order to ask someone to wait a short period of time for something ‖ 남에게 무엇을 위해 잠시 동안 기다리라고 요청하는 데에 쓰여. 잠깐. 잠시(기다려요): *"Are you coming with us?" "Yes, just a minute."* "지금 오고 있니?" "그래, 잠깐 기다려." **b)** used when you do not agree with someone or do not think that s/he is doing or saying something that is right

‖ 다른 사람에게 동의하지 않거나 그 사람의 행동이나 말이 옳다고 생각하지 않을 때 쓰여. 잠깐만요. 기다려 봐요: *Wait a minute here! I can't believe you think that $20 is a fair price!* 잠깐만요! 20달러가 공정한 가격이라고 생각하다니 믿을 수 없군요! **4 the minute (that)** as soon as ‖ …하자마자. …하는 순간: *I knew it was Jill the minute I heard her voice.* 나는 그녀의 목소리를 듣는 순간 질이라는 것을 알았다. **5 last minute** at the last possible time, just before something must be done or completed ‖ 어떤 것이 끝나거나 완료되기 바로 직전의 최종 순간에. 임박하여. 막판에: *Frank changed his mind at the last minute and decided to come with us after all.* 프랭크는 막판에 마음을 바꿨고 결국 우리와 함께 가기로 결정했다. / *a few last minute arrangements* 막판의 몇 가지 타협 **6 any minute (now)** very soon ‖ 아주 조만간. 지금 당장에라도. 언제라도: *She should get here any minute now.* 그녀는 지금 당장에라도 여기에 도착해야 한다.

mi·nute² /maɪˈnut/ *adj* **1** extremely small ‖ 극히 작은. 미세[미소]한: *Her handwriting is minute–I can't read what the note says.* 그녀의 글씨는 너무 작아서, 그 메모에 뭐가 씌어져 있는지 읽을 수가 없다. **2** paying attention to the smallest things or parts ‖ 가장 작은 것이나 부분까지 주의를 기울이는. 면밀한. 세심한: *Johnson explained the plan in minute detail.* 존슨은 상세한 세부 내용까지 그 계획을 설명했다.

min·utes /ˈmɪnɪts/ *n* [plural] an official written record of what is said at a meeting and what decisions are made there ‖ 회의에서 언급된 것과 결정된 것의 공식적 문서 기록. 회의[의사]록. 비망록

mir·a·cle /ˈmɪrəkəl/ *n* **1** something lucky that happens, that you did not think was possible ‖ 가능하다고 생각하지 않았던 일이 운 좋게 일어나는 것. 기적. 경이(驚異). 놀랄 만한 행운: *It's a miracle (that) you weren't killed!* 네가 죽지 않았다니 기적이다! **2** an action or event that is impossible according to the ordinary laws of nature, believed to be done or caused by God ‖ 통상의 자연 법칙에 의해서는 불가능하며 신에 의해 행해지거나 일어난다고 믿어지는 활동 또는 사건. 이적(異蹟). 불가사의(한 일). 초자연적인 신비한 일: *the miracles of Jesus* 예수의 이적

mi·rac·u·lous /mɪˈrækyələs/ *adj* completely unexpected and very lucky ‖ 예상 밖으로 아주 운이 좋은. 기적적인.

놀랄 만한. 경이적인: *The doctors thought she might die, but she made a miraculous recovery.* 의사들은 그녀가 죽을 것으로 생각했지만 그녀는 기적적으로 회복했다. – **miraculously** *adv*

mi·rage /mɪˈrɑʒ/ *n* a strange effect caused by hot air in a desert, in which you can see things when they are not actually there ‖ 사막에서 뜨거운 공기에 의해 생겨, 실제로 그 자리에 없는 것들을 볼 수 있는 기묘한 효과. 신기루. 환영

mire¹ /maɪr/ *v* **be mired (down) in a)** to be in a very difficult situation ‖ 매우 어려운 상황에 처하다. 곤경[궁지]에 빠지다: *an economy mired in recession* 불황에 빠진 경제 **b)** to be stuck in deep mud ‖ 깊은 진흙에 빠지다. 진창[수렁]에 빠져 꼼짝 못하게 되다: *The car's wheels became mired in mud and snow.* 차바퀴가 진흙과 눈 속에 빠져 꼼짝 못하게 되었다.

mire² *n* **1** [singular, U] a very difficult situation ‖ 매우 어려운 상황. 곤경. 궁지: *The company sank deeper into the mire of debt.* 회사는 빚의 수렁으로 더 깊이 빠져들었다. **2** [U] LITERARY deep mud ‖ 깊은 진창. 늪. 수렁

mir·ror¹ /ˈmɪrə/ *n* **1** a piece of special flat glass that you can look at and see yourself in ‖ 자신을 비쳐보거나 들여다볼 수 있는 특수한 평면 유리(조각). 거울. 반사경: *the bathroom mirror* 욕실의 거울 / *a rearview mirror* (=a mirror in a car, for looking at the area behind you) 자동차의 백미러 **2 mirror image** a system or pattern that is almost exactly the same as another one ‖ 다른 것과 거의 정확하게 똑같은 체제나 양식. 닮은꼴[물건]. 복제판[형]: *Some experts believe that this economic recession is a mirror image of the events leading up to the Great Depression in the 1930s.* 어떤 전문가들은 이번 경기 후퇴가 1930년대 대공황의 전조가 되는 사건들의 복제판이라고 믿는다.

mirror² *v* [T] to represent or be very similar to something else ‖ 다른 어떤 것을 나타내거나 그것과 매우 유사하다. 비추다. 반영하다: *The election results mirrored public opinion.* 선거 결과는 여론을 반영했다.

mirth /mɜθ/ *n* [U] LITERARY happiness and laughter ‖ 행복감과 웃음. 환희. 유쾌함

mis·ad·ven·ture /ˌmɪsədˈvɛntʃə/ *n* [C, U] bad luck or an accident ‖ 불운 또는 (우발) 사고. 재난. 불행

mis·ap·pre·hen·sion /ˌmɪsˌæprɪˈhɛnʃən/ *n* FORMAL a mistaken belief or a wrong understanding of something ‖ 어떤 것에 대한 그릇된 믿음이나 잘못된 이해. 오해. 잘못 생각하기: *I was under the misapprehension that the work would be completed by Friday.* 나는 그 작업이 금요일까지는 완료될 것으로 잘못 생각했다.

mis·ap·pro·pri·ate /ˌmɪsəˈproupriˌeɪt/ *v* [T] FORMAL to dishonestly take something, especially money, that a company, organization etc. has trusted you to keep safe ‖ 회사·단체 등이 안전하게 보관 되어 있다고 믿은 것, 특히 돈을 부정직하게 취하다. 횡령[착복]하다. …을 오용[악용]하다: *One of the partners in the firm misappropriated company funds.* 회사의 공동 경영자 중 한 명이 회사 기금을 횡령했다. – **misappropriation** /ˌmɪsəˌproupriˈeɪʃən/ *n* [U]

mis·be·have /ˌmɪsbɪˈheɪv/ *v* [I] to behave badly ‖ 못되게 행동하다. 버릇없는 짓을 하다. 말썽을 부리다[피우다]: *Anne's being punished for misbehaving in class.* 앤은 학급에서 말썽을 피웠다고 벌을 받고 있다. – **misbehavior** /ˌmɪsbɪˈheɪvyɚ/ *n* [U]

misc. the written abbreviation of MISCELLANEOUS ‖ miscellaneous의 약어

mis·cal·cu·late /ˌmɪsˈkælkyəˌleɪt/ *v* [I, T] **1** to make a mistake in calculating the number, length, cost etc. of something ‖ 어떤 것의 숫자·길이·비용 등의 계산에 실수를 하다. 잘못 계산하다. 오산하다: *We miscalculated the time it would take to drive to Long Island.* 우리는 롱아일랜드까지 운전하는 데에 걸리는 시간을 잘못 계산했다. **2** to make a mistake when you are judging a situation ‖ 상황을 판단할 때 잘못을 범하다. 잘못 판단[짐작]하다. 판단 착오를 일으키다[범하다]: *I think politicians have miscalculated the strength of public feeling about the tax issue.* 나는 정치가들이 세금 문제에 대한 대중 정서의 강도를 잘못 판단했다고 생각한다.

mis·cal·cu·la·tion /ˌmɪsˌkælkyəˈleɪʃən/ *n* **1** a mistake made in calculating the number, length, cost etc. of something ‖ 어떤 것의 숫자·길이·비용 등의 계산에서 범한 실수. 오산. 계산 착오: *The builders made a huge miscalculation in the cost of repairs to the building.* 건축 시공자는 빌딩 보수 비용 산정에서 큰 착오를 일으켰다. **2** a wrong judgment about a situation ‖ 상황에 대한 잘못된 판단. 오판. 판단 착오: *A slight miscalculation by either country could lead to war.* 양국가의 사소한 오판이 전쟁으로 이어질 수 있다.

mis·car·riage /ˈmɪsˌkærɪdʒ, ˌmɪsˈkærɪdʒ/ *n* [C, U] **1** the act of accidentally giving birth to a baby too early for him/her to live ‖ 뜻하지 않게 너무 일찍 출산해서 아기가 살 수 없는 것. 유산: *Did you hear that Sharon had a miscarriage?* 샤론이 유산했다는 것 들었어 ? —compare ABORTION **2 miscarriage of justice** a situation in which someone is wrongly punished by a court of law for something s/he did not do ‖ 어떤 사람이 저지르지 않은 일에 대해 법정이 잘못 처벌한 상황. 오심(誤審). 오판

mis·car·ry /ˌmɪsˈkæri/ *v* [I] to accidentally give birth to a baby too early for him/her to live ‖ 뜻하지 않게 아기를 너무 일찍 출산해서 아기가 살 수 없다. 유산하다

mis·cel·la·ne·ous /ˌmɪsəˈleɪniəs/ *adj* made up of many different things or people that do not seem to be related to each other ‖ 서로 관련이 없는 듯한 여러 다른 사물이나 사람들로 이루어진. 갖가지 잡다한. 잡동사니의. 형형색색의: *a miscellaneous assortment of books* 갖가지 잡다하게 모아놓은 책들

mis·chief /ˈmɪstʃɪf/ *n* [U] bad behavior, especially by children, that causes trouble or damage but no serious harm ‖ 심각한 해가 되지 않는 문제나 손해를 초래하는, 특히 아이들의 못된 행동. 말썽. 짓궂은 행동: *He's always getting into mischief.* (=behaving in a way that causes trouble) 그는 항상 말썽을 부리고 있다. / *I knew those kids were up to some mischief.* (=doing or planning to do something that will cause trouble) 나는 그 아이들이 어떤 장난을 칠 궁리를 하고 있다는 것을 알았다.

mis·chie·vous /ˈmɪstʃəvəs/ *adj* liking to have fun by playing tricks on people or doing things to annoy or embarrass them ‖ 사람들에게 속임수를 쓰거나 그들을 화나게 또는 당황하게 하는 일을 하며 즐기기를 좋아하는. 장난치기 좋아하는. 짓궂은. 말썽을 부리는: *a mischievous child* 짓궂은 아이

mis·con·cep·tion /ˌmɪskənˈsɛpʃən/ *n* [C, U] an idea that is wrong or untrue, but that people still believe ‖ 잘못되거나 사실이 아니지만 사람들이 여전히 믿는 생각. 잘못된 생각. 오해. 오인: *At first, there was a misconception that only gay people could get AIDS.* 처음에는 단

지 동성애자만이 에이즈에 걸린다는 잘못
된 인식이 있었다

mis·con·duct /ˌmɪsˈkɑndʌkt/ n [U]
FORMAL bad or dishonest behavior by
someone in a position of authority or
trust‖ 권위나 신뢰받는 위치에 있는 사람
의 그릇되거나 부정직한 행동. 비행. 부정
[불법] 행위: *an investigation into police
misconduct* 경찰의 불법 행위에 대한 조
사

mis·con·strue /ˌmɪskənˈstru/ v [T]
FORMAL to not understand correctly
what someone has said or done‖ 다른
사람이 말하거나 한 것을 정확하게 이해하
지 못하다. …의 뜻을 잘못 해석하다. 곡
해하다: *The research results have been
misconstrued.* 연구 결과는 잘못 해석되었
다.

mis·deed /ˌmɪsˈdid/ n FORMAL a wrong
or illegal action‖ 잘못되거나 불법적인 행
동. 나쁜 짓. 비행. 범죄 행위

mis·de·mean·or /ˌmɪsdɪˈminɚ/ n LAW
a crime that is not very serious‖ 아주 심
하지 않은 범죄. 경범죄

mis·di·rect /ˌmɪsdəˈrɛkt/ v [T] FORMAL
to use your efforts, emotion, or abilities
in a way that is wrong or unsuitable‖ 잘
못되거나 부적합하게 노력[감정, 능력]을
쓰다. 방향을 잘못 잡다. 잘못 지도하다
[가르치다]: *misdirected anger* 그릇된 분
노 **– misdirection** /ˌmɪsdəˈrɛkʃən/ n
[U]

mi·ser /ˈmaɪzɚ/ n DISAPPROVING
someone who hates spending money
and likes saving it‖ 돈 쓰기를 싫어하고
저축하기를 좋아하는 사람. 수전노. 구두
쇠 **– miserly** adj

mis·er·a·ble /ˈmɪzərəbəl/ adj **1** very
unhappy, especially because you are
lonely or sick‖ 특히 외롭거나 아파서 몹
시 불행한. 비참한. 불쌍한. 고생스러운:
*She's at home feeling miserable with the
flu.* 그녀는 불쌍하게도 독감으로 집에만
있다. **2** very bad in quality‖ 속성이 아주
나쁜. 형편없는. 한심한. 지독한. 심한:
miserable weather 지독한 날씨 **–
miserably** adv

mis·er·y /ˈmɪzəri/ n [U] great suffering
or unhappiness‖ 큰 고통 또는 불행. 비
참. 고난: *the misery of life in the
refugee camps* (피)난민 수용소의 비참한
생활

mis·fit /ˈmɪsˌfɪt/ n someone who does
not seem to belong in the place where
s/he lives or works, because s/he is very
different from the other people there‖
어떤 사람이 다른 사람들과 매우 달라서
거주하거나 일하는 곳에 속하지 않는 듯한

사람. 환경에 잘 맞지 않는[적응을 못하
는] 사람. 부적임[부적격]자

mis·for·tune /mɪsˈfɔrtʃən/ n [C, U] bad
luck, or something that happens to you
as a result of bad luck‖ 불운, 또는 불운
의 결과로 일어난 것. 불행. 재난. 불행
[불운]한 일: *We had the misfortune of
being in a hotel in Boston when the
snow storm hit.* 우리는 눈보라가 강타했
을 때 보스턴의 한 호텔에 묵었던 불운한
경험이 있었다.

mis·giv·ing /mɪsˈgɪvɪŋ/ n [C, U] a
feeling of doubt or fear about what
might happen or about whether
something is right‖ 어떤 것이 일어날 가
능성이 있는지, 또는 어떤 것이 옳은지 여
부에 대한 회의나 두려움의 감정. 걱정.
불안. 염려. 의혹. 불신(감): *I knew he
had some misgivings about letting me
use his car.* 나는 그가 자신의 차를 내게
쓰게 한 데 대해 불안해함을 알았다.

mis·guid·ed /mɪsˈgaɪdɪd/ adj **1**
intended to be helpful but actually
making a situation worse‖ 도움을 주고
자 하는 의도였지만 실제로는 상황을 악화
시키는. 빗나간. 잘못된. 엉뚱한: *The
song is a misguided attempt to turn
popular music into poetry.* 그 노래는 대
중음악을 시로 바꾸려 한 잘못된 시도이
다. **2** wrong because of being based on
a wrong understanding of a situation‖
상황에 대한 잘못된 이해를 바탕으로 해서
잘못된. 잘못 인도된. 오도된. 잘못 인식
한. 오류의: *The belief that communism
must be opposed was misguided.* 공산주
의에 반대해야 한다는 믿음은 오도된 것이
었다.

mis·han·dle /ˌmɪsˈhændl/ v [T] to deal
with a situation badly, or not skillfully‖
상황을 잘못되게 또는 엉터리로 처리하다.
…의 취급[처리]을 잘못하다. 거칠게 다
루다[학대하다]: *University officials are
being criticized for mishandling the
student protest.* 대학교 직원들은 학생들
의 항의를 잘못 처리한 것에 대해 비난 받
고 있다.

mis·hap /ˈmɪshæp/ n [C, U] a small
accident or mistake that does not have a
very serious effect‖ 아주 심한 영향을 끼
치지 않는 작은 사고나 실수. 불행한 사
건. 재난

mis·in·form /ˌmɪsɪnˈfɔrm/ v [T] to give
someone information that is incorrect or
untrue, either deliberately or
accidentally‖ 어떤 사람에게 고의적으로
또는 우연히 부정확하거나 사실이 아닌 정
보를 주다. 잘못된 정보를 전하다[가르쳐
주다]. 오보하다: *The public has been*

misinformed about the nature of our work. 대중은 우리 업무의 특성에 대해 잘 못된 정보를 받아 왔다.

mis·in·ter·pret /ˌmɪsɪnˈtɚprɪt/ *v* [T] to not understand the correct meaning of something that someone says or does ‖ 다른 사람이 말하거나 하는 것의 정확한 의미를 이해하지 못하다. 잘못 해석[설명] 하 다 . 오 해 하 다 : *I think she misinterpreted my joke – I didn't mean to upset her.* 나는 그녀가 내 농담을 오해 했다고 생각한다. 나는 그녀의 화를 돋울 의도가 아니었다. – **misinterpretation** /ˌmɪsɪnˌtɚprəˈteɪʃən/ *n* [C, U]

mis·judge /ˌmɪsˈdʒʌdʒ/ *v* [T] **1** to form a wrong or unfair opinion about a person or situation ‖ 사람이나 상황에 대 해 잘못되거나 부당한 의견을 형성하다. 잘못 판단하다. 오해하다. 판단 착오를 일으키다: *The White House has badly misjudged Congress's support for his bill.* 백악관은 의회가 그의 법안을 지지한 것에 대해 심각하게 오해를 했다. **2** to guess an amount, distance etc. wrongly ‖ 양·거리 등을 잘못 추정하다. 견적[어 림]을 잘못하다: *Don misjudged the turn and wrecked his car.* 돈은 자동차를 돌릴 곳을 잘못 판단해서 차를 박살냈다. – **misjudgment** *n* [C, U]

mis·lay /ˌmɪsˈleɪ/ *v* **mislaid** /-ˈleɪd/, **mislaid, mislaying** [T] ⇨ MISPLACE

mis·lead /ˌmɪsˈlid/ *v* **misled** /-ˈlɛd/, **misled, misleading** [T] to make someone believe something that is not true by giving him/her false or incomplete information ‖ 다른 사람에게 거짓 또는 불완전한 정보를 제공해서 사실 이 아닌 것을 믿게 하다. 오해하게 하다. 속이다. 오도하다: *I wasn't trying to mislead anyone, I just didn't know all the facts.* 나는 누구도 속이려고 하지 않 았다. 단지 모든 사실들을 알지 못했을 뿐 이다.

mis·lead·ing /ˌmɪsˈlidɪŋ/ *adj* likely to make someone believe something that is not true ‖ 사실이 아닌 것을 믿게할 가능 성이 있는. 오해하게 하는. 현혹하는: *It is illegal to put misleading information into an advertisement.* 오해의 소지가 있 는 정보를 광고에 싣는 것은 불법이다. – **misleadingly** *adv*

mis·man·age /ˌmɪsˈmænɪdʒ/ *v* [T] to deal with something you are in charge of in a way that is not effective or organized ‖ 맡은 일을 효과적 또는 조직 적으로 처리하지 못하다. …의 관리[경영] 를 잘못하다. 실수하다: *This project's been completely mismanaged from the*

beginning. 이 계획사업은 처음부터 완전 히 잘못 관리되었다. – **mismanage- ment** *n* [U]

mis·match /ˈmɪsmætʃ/ *n* a combination of things or people that are not equal in quality, strength, ability, or looks ‖ 특성 [힘, 능력, 모양]이 같지 않은 사물이나 사 람의 조합. 부조화. 부적당한[어울리지 않 는] 짝[조합, 구성]: *Saturday's game was a complete mismatch.* (=one team was much better than the other) 토요일 시합은 서로 전혀 상대가 되지 않는 것이 었다. – **mismatched** *adj*

mis·no·mer /ˌmɪsˈnoʊmɚ/ *n* a wrong or unsuitable name ‖ 잘못되거나 부적합 한 이름. 잘못된 호칭. 오칭(誤稱): *The police chief said it would be a misnomer to call their actions "big drug raids."* 경 찰서장은 자신들의 작전을 "대대적 마약 단속"이라고 부르는 것은 잘못된 명명이라 말했다.

mis·sog·y·nist /mɪˈsɑdʒənɪst/ *n* FORMAL a man who hates women ‖ 여자를 싫어 하는 남자. 여자 혐오(주의)자 – **misogyny** *n* [U] – **misogynistic** /mɪˌsɑdʒəˈnɪstɪk/ *adj*

mis·place /ˌmɪsˈpleɪs/ *v* [T] to put something somewhere and then forget where you put it ‖ 사물을 어떤 곳에 놓아 두고서 놓아둔 위치를 잊어버리다. …을 잘못 놓다. …을 어디에 두고 잊어버리 다: *I've misplaced my glasses again.* 나 는 또 내 안경을 (어디 두었는지) 잊어 버 렸다.

mis·placed /ˌmɪsˈpleɪst/ *adj* misplaced feelings of trust, love etc. are unsuitable because the person that you have these feelings for does not deserve them ‖ 신 뢰·사랑 등의 감정이 그것들을 받을 가치 가 없다고 생각하는 사람에게 주어져서 부 적합한. 잘못 짚은. 잘못 쏟은[부여한, 바 쳐진]: *a misplaced sense of loyalty* 잘못 된 충성심

mis·print /ˈmɪsˌprɪnt/ *n* a mistake in a book, magazine etc. ‖ 책·잡지 등에서의 실수. 오자. 오기. 오식

mis·quote /ˌmɪsˈkwoʊt/ *v* [T] to make a mistake in reporting what someone else has said or written ‖ 다른 사람이 말 하거나 쓴 것을 알리는 데에서 잘못을 범 하다. 잘못 인용하다: *The governor's speech was misquoted in the newspapers.* 주지사의 연설은 신문에 잘 못 인용 보도됐다.

mis·read /ˌmɪsˈrid/ *v* **misread** /-ˈrɛd/, **misread, misreading** [T] **1** to make a judgment about a situation or person that is wrong ‖ 상황이나 사람에 대해 잘

못된 판단을 내리다. …을 …으로 이해하다[오해하다]. 잘못 해석하다: *Fischer misread her silence as anger.* 피셔는 그녀의 침묵을 그녀가 화난 것으로 잘못 이해했다. **2 to read something in the wrong way** ‖ 어떤 것을 잘못 읽다. 착각하다: *Did you misread the date on the letter?* 편지의 날짜를 잘못 읽었습니까? **– misreading** *n* [C, U]

mis·rep·re·sent /ˌmɪsrɛprɪˈzɛnt/ *v* [T] to deliberately give a wrong description of someone's opinions or of a situation, especially in order to get an advantage for yourself ‖ 특히 자신의 이득을 얻기 위해 다른 사람의 의견이나 상황에 대해 고의로 틀리게 기술하다. …을 (…으로) 거짓으로 전하다. (고의로) 부정확하게 나타내다: *Some of these ideas about welfare reform have been misrepresented in the press.* 복지 제도 개혁안에 대한 이러한 구상들의 일부가 언론에서 왜곡하여 보도되었다. **– misrepresentation** /mɪsˌrɛprɪzənˈteɪʃən/ *n* [C, U]

miss¹ /mɪs/ *v* **1** [T] to not go somewhere or do something, especially when you want to but cannot ‖ 특히 자신이 원하지만 할 수 없을 때 어떤 곳에 가지 않거나 어떤 일을 하지 않다. …을 놓치다[하지 못하다].

miss

Lucia just missed the bus.

…에 빠지다: *Sorry I have to miss your barbecue.* 미안, 네 바비큐 파티에 빠질 수밖에 없어. / *He'd never miss the chance/opportunity to go to Acapulco!* 그는 결코 아카폴코에 가는 찬스[기회]를 놓치지 않을 것이다! **2** [T] to not arrive in time for something ‖ 어떤 일에 맞게 제 시간에 도착하지 못하다. …을 놓치다. (늦게 도착해) …하지 못하다: *By the time we got there, we'd missed the beginning of the movie.* 우리가 도착했을 때에는 영화가 시작된 뒤였다. **3** [T] to feel sad because you are not with a particular person, or because you no longer have something or are no longer doing something ‖ 특정의 사람과 같이 있지 못해서, 또는 더 이상 어떤 것을 갖지 못하거나 어떤 일을 더 이상 하지 못해서 슬픔을 느끼다. 그리워하다. 섭섭하게 여기다: *I've missed you so much!* 나는 네가 정말 보고 싶었어! / *Do you miss living in the city?* 도시의 삶을 그리워하십니까? **4** [I, T] to not hit or catch something ‖ 어떤 것을 맞추지 못하거나 잡지 못하다. 거

냥한 것을 놓치다. 빗맞히다. 헛치다: *She fired at the target but missed.* 그녀는 과녁에 대고 쐈지만 빗맞혔다. / *Jackson missed an easy catch and the A's scored.* 잭슨은 쉬운 것을 틀려서 A를 맞았다. **5** [T] to not see, hear, or notice something ‖ 어떤 것을 보거나 듣거나 알아채지 못하다. …을 빠뜨리다[빼먹다]. …을 놓치다: *Jody found an error that everyone else had missed.* 조디는 다른 모든 사람들이 놓친 실수를 찾아냈다. **6** [T] to notice that something or someone is not in the place you expect him, her, or it to be ‖ 다른 사람이나 사물이 있으리라 예상했던 자리에 있지 않음을 알아채다. 없는[잃은] 것을 알아채다: *I didn't miss my key until I got home.* 나는 집에 도착했을 때까지 열쇠가 없는 것을 알아채지 못했다. **7 miss the boat** INFORMAL to fail to take an opportunity that will give you an advantage ‖ 이득을 줄 기회를 차지하지 못하다. …을 놓치다. …을 얻지 못하다: *You'll be missing the boat if you don't buy these shares now.* 이들 주식을 지금 사지 않으면 당신은 기회를 놓치게 될 것입니다. —see usage note at LOSE

miss out *phr v* [I] to not have the chance to do something that you enjoy ‖ 즐기는 어떤 일을 할 기회를 갖지 못하다. …을 놓치다. …하지 못해 아쉬워하다: *You're the one who'll miss out if you don't come.* 당신은 오지 않으면 아쉬워할 겁니다. / *She got married very young, and now she feels she's missing out on life.* 그녀는 매우 어려서 결혼했고 지금은 인생에 대해 아쉬움을 느낀다.

miss² *n* **1 Miss Smith/Jones etc.** used in front of the family name of a woman who is not married in order to speak to her politely, to write to her, or talk about her ‖ 결혼하지 않은 여자에게 정중히 말을 하거나 글을 쓰거나 또는 그 여자에 대해 이야기할 때, 그 여자의 성(姓) 앞에 쓰여. 아가씨. …양. 스미스/존스 양 **2** a failed attempt to hit, catch, or hold something ‖ 어떤 것을 치기[잡기, 쥐기]에 실패한 시도. 빗맞힘. 놓침. 실수 **3** used in order to speak politely to a young woman when you do not know her name ‖ 이름을 모르는 젊은 여성에게 정중하게 이야기하는 데에 쓰여. 아가씨: *Excuse me, miss, you've dropped your umbrella.* 실례합니다, 아가씨. 우산을 떨어뜨렸습니다. **4 Miss Italy/Ohio/World etc.** used before the name of a country, city etc. that a woman represents in a beauty competition ‖ 미인 선발 대회에서 여성이 대표하는 나라·

시 등의 이름 앞에 쓰여. 미스 이탈리아/오하이오/월드

mis·shap·en /ˌmɪsˈʃeɪpən, ˌmɪˈʃeɪ-/ *adj* not the normal or natural shape ‖ 정상적 또는 자연스러운 모양이 아닌. 모양이 흉한. 기형의: *He was born with a misshapen spine.* 그는 척추 기형으로 태어났다.

mis·sile /ˈmɪsəl/ *n* **1** a weapon that can fly over long distances and that explodes when it hits something ‖ 장거리를 날아갈 수 있고 물체에 명중했을 때 폭발하는 무기. 미사일. 유도탄 **2** FORMAL an object that is thrown at someone in order to hurt him/her ‖ 해를 끼치기 위해 사람에게 던지는 물체. 무기로서 던져지는 모든 것

miss·ing /ˈmɪsɪŋ/ *adj* **1** someone or something that is missing is not in the place where you would normally expect him, her, or it to be ‖ 사람이나 사물이 통상 있으리라 기대한 장소에 있지 않은. 실종된. 행방불명된. 분실된. …에 없는: *Police are still searching for the missing child.* 경찰은 아직도 실종된 아이를 찾고 있다. / *a kid with his two front teeth missing* 앞니 두 개가 없는 아이 **2** not included, although it ought to have been ‖ 포함되어야 함에도 되어 있는. …에서 빠진[결여된]. 제외된. 생략된: *Why is my name missing from the list?* 왜 명단에서 내 이름이 빠져 있지요? —see usage note at LOSE

mis·sion /ˈmɪʃən/ *n* **1** an important job that someone has been given to do ‖ 어떤 사람에게 하도록 주어진 중요한 일. 임무. 사명: *Our mission was to blow up the airport.* 우리 임무는 공항을 폭파하는 것이었다. **2** a group of people who go to another country for a particular purpose ‖ 특정 목적을 위해 타국에 가는 일단의 사람들. 사절단: *a Canadian trade mission to Japan* 일본에 파견된 캐나다 무역 대표단 **3** a special trip made by a space vehicle or military plane ‖ 우주선이나 군용기에 의한 특수 비행 임무. 탐사 비행: *a mission to Mars* 화성 탐사 임무[비행] **4** the work of a MISSIONARY, or a building where s/he does this work ‖ 선교사의 활동, 또는 이 사업을 하는 건물. 전도[포교]. 포교소 **5** something that you feel you must do because it is your duty ‖ 의무이기에 반드시 해야 한다고 느끼는 것. 사명. 천직. 과업: *She feels her mission in life is to help poor people.* 가난한 사람들을 돕는 것이 자신의 일생의 사명이라고 그녀는 생각한다.

mis·sion·ar·y /ˈmɪʃəˌnɛri/ *n* someone who has gone to a foreign country in order to teach people about Christianity ‖ 사람들에게 기독교에 대해 가르치기 위해 외국에 간 사람. 선교사. 전도[포교]자

mis·spell /ˌmɪsˈspɛl/ *v* [T] to spell a word incorrectly ‖ 단어를 틀리게 철자하다. 철자를 잘못 쓰다 **–misspelling** *n* [C, U]

mis·step /ˈmɪs-stɛp/ *n* a mistake, especially one that offends or upsets people ‖ 실수, 특히 다른 사람을 불쾌하게 하거나 화나게 하는 것. 과실: *political missteps* 정치적 과오

mist¹ /mɪst/ *n* [C, U] a light cloud low over the ground that makes it difficult for you to see very far ‖ 지상에 낮게 깔려 멀리 보기 어렵게 만드는 엷은 구름. 안개. 운무. 연무: *Heavy mists followed the rain.* 비온 후 짙은 안개가 끼었다.

mist² *v* [I, T] to become covered with very small drops of water, or to make something do this ‖ 매우 작은 물방울들로 덮이다, 또는 어떤 것을 이렇게 하게 하다. 안개가 끼다[로 덮다]. 안개로 흐려지다[가리다]: *The windows are all misted up/over.* 창문 전체가 뿌옇게 흐려졌다.

mis·take¹ /mɪˈsteɪk/ *n* **1** something that has been done in the wrong way, or an opinion or statement that is incorrect ‖ 잘못 된 것, 또는 틀린 의견이나 진술. 잘못[된 생각[행위]]. 실수. 오류: *Ivan's work is full of spelling mistakes.* 이반의 저서는 철자 오류 투성이다. / *I think you've made a mistake – I ordered fish, not beef.* 나는 네가 실수했다고 생각해. 나는 쇠고기가 아니라 생선을 주문했어. **2** something you do that you later realize was not the right thing to do ‖ 나중에 깨닫고 보니 자기가 잘못했다고 느껴지는 어떤 일. 후회스러운 일. 실수. 잘못: *Marrying him was a big mistake.* 그와 결혼한 것은 큰 실수였다. / *I made the mistake of giving him my phone number.* 나는 그에게 내 전화번호를 알려주는 실수를 저질렀다. **3 by mistake** without intending to do something ‖ 어떤 일을 할 의도가 없이. 실수로. 잘못하여: *Someone must have left the door open by mistake.* 누군가 실수로 문을 열어 두었음이 틀림없다. —see usage note at ERROR

mis·take² *v* **mistook, mistaken, mistaking** [T] to understand something wrongly ‖ 어떤 일을 틀리게 이해하다. 잘못 알다[생각하다]: *He'd mistaken the address and gone to the wrong house.* 그는 주소를 잘못 알고 다

른 집으로 갔었다.

mistake sb/sth **for** sb/sth *phr v* [T] to think that one person or thing is someone or something else‖사람이나 사물을 다른 사람이나 다른 사물로 생각하다. …을 …으로 잘못 생각하다[알다]. 오인하다: *I mistook him for his brother.* 나는 그를 그의 형으로 잘못 알았다.

mis·tak·en /mɪˈsteɪkən/ *adj* wrong about something‖어떤 일에 대해 틀린. 잘못된. 잘못 생각한: *I had the mistaken idea that it would be quicker to take the bus.* 나는 버스를 타는 것이 더 빠를 것이라고 잘못 생각했다. - **mistakenly** *adv*

mis·ter /ˈmɪstɚ/ *n* **1** ⇨ MR. **2** SPOKEN said in order to speak to a man when you do not know his name‖이름을 모르는 남성에게 말하는 데에 쓰여. …씨. …님. 선생: *Hey mister, is this your wallet?* 여보세요 선생, 이거 당신 지갑아닙니까?

mis·tle·toe /ˈmɪsəlˌtoʊ/ *n* [U] a plant with small round white fruit that is often used as a decoration at Christmas‖종종 크리스마스에 장식용으로 쓰이는 작고 둥근 흰 열매가 열리는 식물. 겨우살이(의 일종)

mis·took /mɪˈstʊk/ *v* the past tense of MISTAKE‖mistake의 과거형

mis·treat /mɪsˈtrit/ *v* [T] to treat a person or animal cruelly‖사람이나 동물을 잔인하게 다루다. 학대하다. 혹사하다: *The hostages said they had not been mistreated.* 인질들은 학대당하지 않았다고 말했다. - **mistreatment** *n* [U]

mis·tress /ˈmɪstrɪs/ *n* a woman that a man has a sexual relationship with even though he is married to someone else‖남성이 다른 사람과 결혼했음에도 성적 관계를 맺고 있는 여성. 정부. 첩

mis·tri·al /ˈmɪstraɪl/ *n* a TRIAL during which a mistake in the law is made, so that a new trial has to be held‖판결이 잘못되어 재판을 새로 열어야 하는 재판. 무효심리

mis·trust /mɪsˈtrʌst/ *n* [U] the feeling that you cannot trust someone or his/her reasons for behaving in a particular way‖특정하게 행동하기 때문에 어떤 사람이나 그 사람의 분별력을 신뢰할 수 없는 느낌. 불신. 의혹: *We both have a deep mistrust of politicians.* 우리 둘은 정치인들을 깊이 불신하고 있다. - **mistrustful** *adj* - **mistrust** *v* [T]

mist·y /ˈmɪsti/ *adj* **1** misty weather is weather with a lot of mist‖안개가 많이 낀 날씨의. 안개로 뒤덮인 **2** LITERARY full of tears‖눈물이 가득하게 고인. 눈물이

고여 흐려진. 눈물로 흐릿한[뿌예진]: *her eyes became misty* 눈물로 뿌예진 그녀의 눈

mis·un·der·stand /ˌmɪsʌndɚˈstænd/ *v* **1** [I, T] to think that something means one thing when in fact it means something different‖사물이 실제로는 다른 것을 의미할 때에 어떤 것을 의미한다고 생각하다. 오해하다. 잘못 해석[생각]하다: *I think you misunderstood what I was trying to say.* 내가 말하려고 했던 것을 네가 오해했다고 생각한다. **2** [T] to fail to recognize someone's true character or qualities‖다른 사람의 진정한 성격이나 특성을 파악하는 데 실패하다. 진가를 못 알아보다: *Why am I always misunderstood by people who work with me?* 나는 왜 항상 같이 일하는 사람들로부터 진가를 인정받지 못하지?

mis·un·der·stand·ing /ˌmɪsʌndɚˈstændɪŋ/ *n* **1** [C, U] a failure to understand a question, situation, or instruction‖질문[상황, 지시]을 이해하는 데 실패함. 오해. 잘못된 해석[생각]: *I think there's been a misunderstanding about what time we were supposed to meet.* 나는 우리가 만나기로 했던 시간에 대해 오해가 있었다고 생각한다. **2** an argument or disagreement that is not very serious‖아주 심하지는 않은 말다툼이나 불화. 분쟁: *We've had our misunderstandings in the past, but we're good friends now.* 우리는 과거에 약간 불화가 있었지만 지금은 사이좋은 친구다.

mis·use¹ /ˌmɪsˈyuz/ *v* [T] to use something in the wrong way or for the wrong purpose‖어떤 것을 잘못된 방식이나 나쁜 목적으로 이용하다. …을 오용[남용]하다. 악용하다: *an attempt to prevent the telephones at work from being misused for personal calls* 업무용 전화가 사적인 통화에 남용되는 것을 막으려는 시도

mis·use² /ˌmɪsˈyus/ *n* [C, U] the use of something in the wrong way or for the wrong purpose‖어떤 것을 잘못된 방식이나 나쁜 목적으로 사용하기. 오용. 남용. 악용: *a misuse of power* 권력의 남용

mite¹ /maɪt/ *n* **1** a very small insect that lives in plants, CARPETs etc.‖식물·카펫 등에 사는 아주 작은 벌레. 진드기: *dust mites* (집)먼지 진드기 **2** a small child, especially one you feel pity for‖특히 동정심을 느끼게 하는 작은 아이. 꼬마

mite² *adv* INFORMAL a small amount‖소량으로. 조금. 약간: *She's a mite shy.* 그녀는 약간 수줍어한다.

mit·i·gate /ˈmɪtəˌgeɪt/ v [T] FORMAL to make a situation or the effects of something less unpleasant, harmful, or serious || 어떤 일의 상황이나 효과를 덜 불쾌하게[해롭게, 심각하게] 하다. 완화시키다. 누그러뜨리다. 경감하다: *Only foreign aid can mitigate the terrible effects of the war.* 오직 외국의 원조만이 전쟁의 참혹한 피해를 줄일 수 있다. – **mitigation** /ˌmɪtəˈgeɪʃən/ n [U]

mitt /mɪt/ n **1** a type of leather GLOVE used for catching a ball in baseball || 야구에서 공을 잡는 데 쓰이는 가죽 장갑의 한 종류. 미트. 야구 장갑 **2** a GLOVE made of thick material, worn to protect your hand || 손을 보호하기 위해 끼는 두터운 재질로 만든 장갑. 보호용 장갑: *an oven mitt* 오븐용 장갑

mit·ten /ˈmɪtn/ n a type of GLOVE that has one part that covers your fingers and a separate part for your thumb || 네 손가락을 한데 넣는 부분과 엄지손가락만 따로 넣는 부분이 있는 장갑의 일종. 벙어리장갑

mix¹ /mɪks/ v **1** [I, T] if you mix two or more substances or if they mix, they combine to become a single substance || 두 가지 이상의 물질을 단일 물질로 되도록 결합하다. 섞(이)다. 혼합하다: *You can't mix oil and water.* 기름과 물은 섞을 수 없습니다. / *Mix the butter and sugar together, then add the milk.* 버터와 설탕을 함께 섞은 다음 우유를 넣어라. **2** [I, T] to combine two or more different activities, ideas, groups of things etc. || 두 가지 이상의 서로 다른 활동·생각·사물의 집단 등을 혼합하다. 섞어서 만들다. …을 …과 섞다: *This record mixes jazz with rock.* 이 레코드는 재즈를 록 음악과 섞어서 만들었다. **3** [I] to enjoy meeting, talking, and spending time with other people, especially people you do not know very well || 다른 사람들, 특히 아주 잘 알지 못하는 사람들과 만나기[이야기하기, 시간 보내기]를 즐기다. 남과 교제하다[사귀다]. 잘 어울리다. 사이좋게 지내다: *Charlie doesn't mix well with the other children.* 찰리는 다른 아이들과 잘 어울리지 않는다.

mix up phr v [T] **1** [**mix sb/sth ↔ up**] to make the mistake of thinking that someone or something is another person or thing || 사람이나 사물을 다른 사람이나 사물로 생각하는 실수를 하다. 혼동하다. 착각하다. 잘못 알다: *It's easy to mix him up with his brother; they look so much alike.* 두 사람이 너무나 많이 닮아서 그는 형과 혼동되기 쉽다. **2**

[**mix sth ↔ up**] to change the way things have been arranged so that they are no longer in the same order || 사물이 배열된 방식을 바꿔 더 이상 같은 순서로 있지 않게 하다. 뒤죽박죽 섞다. 뒤섞다: *Don't mix up those papers, or we'll never find the ones we need.* 저 서류들을 뒤섞지 마라, 그렇지 않으면 우리가 필요한 것을 결코 찾지 못할 것이다. **3** [**mix sb up**] INFORMAL to make someone feel confused || 어떤 사람을 혼란스럽게 만들다. 혼란[혼동]시키다. 혼을 빼놓다. 정신을 어지럽게 하다: *They kept asking me questions and trying to mix me up.* 그들은 나에게 계속 질문을 하여 나를 혼란시키려 했다. —see also MIXED UP, MIX-UP

mix² n **1** [C, U] a combination of substances that you mix together to make something || 어떤 것을 만들기 위해 서로 섞은 물질의 혼합물. 혼합된 것. 믹스: *cake mix* 케이크 믹스 **2** [singular] the particular combination of things or people that form a group || 한 집단을 형성하는 사물이나 사람의 특정 혼합(상태). 잡다하게 섞인 것[상태]. 뒤죽박죽. 혼란: *There was a strange mix of people at Larry's party.* 래리의 파티에는 특이한 사람들이 뒤섞여 있었다.

mixed /mɪkst/ adj **1** consisting of many different types of things, people, ideas etc. || 많은 서로 다른 종류의 사물·사람·생각 등으로 이루어진. 잡다한. 뒤섞인. 혼합된. 혼성의: *a mixed diet of fruit and vegetables* 과일과 채소의 혼합 식단 / *We had mixed feelings (=felt both happy and sad) about moving so far away.* 우리는 그렇게 멀리 이사 가는 데 대해 마음이 착잡했다. **2 a mixed blessing** something that is good in some ways but bad in others || 어떤 면에서는 좋지만 다른 면에서는 나쁜 것. 상반된[모순된] 축복. 이해가 엇비슷한 것: *Having the kids at home for the summer is always a mixed blessing – I miss the time alone.* 여름 동안 아이들이 집에 있는 것은 항상 좋기도 하고 나쁘기도 하다. 나는 혼자 있는 시간이 그립기 때문이다. **3 a mixed bag** a group of things or people that are all very different from each other || 서로 전혀 다른 사물이나 사람의 집단. 잡탕. 뒤범벅. 잡동사니

mixed mar·riage /ˌ. ˈ../ n [C, U] a marriage between two people from different races or religions || 서로 다른 인종이나 종교 출신의 두 사람 간의 결혼. 다른 인종[종교] 간의 결혼

mixed up /ˌ. ˈ./ adj **1 be mixed up in something/be mixed up with**

someone to be involved with a bad or dishonest situation or person ‖ 나쁘거나 부정한 상황 또는 사람과 관련되다. 연루되다. 어울리다. …에/…과 관련되다: *kids getting mixed up with gang members* 갱단 단원들과 어울리고 있는 아이들 **2** confused ‖ 혼동된. 머리가 혼란된. 착각을 일으킨: *I got mixed up and went to the wrong restaurant.* 나는 착각을 일으켜 다른 레스토랑에 갔다. —see also **mix up** (MIX¹), MIX-UP

mix·er /ˈmɪksɚ/ *n* **1** a piece of equipment used for mixing different substances together ‖ 서로 다른 물질을 혼합하는 데 쓰이는 기구. 혼합기. 교반기. 믹서기: *a food mixer* 음식 혼합기 **2** a drink that can be mixed with alcohol ‖ 술과 섞일 수 있는 음료수. 칵테일용 음료수: *Use the orange juice as a mixer.* 오렌지 주스를 칵테일용 음료수로 써라.

mix·ture /ˈmɪkstʃɚ/ *n* **1** [C, U] a single substance made by mixing two or more different substances together ‖ 두 개 이상의 서로 다른 물질을 함께 혼합해서 만들어지는 단일 물질. 혼합물. 합성품: *Pour the cake mixture into a pan and bake it for 45 minutes.* 케이크 혼합물을 팬에 붓고 45분 동안 구우시오. **2** [singular] a combination of two or more people, things, feelings, or ideas that are different ‖ 서로 다른 둘 이상의 사람[사물, 감정, 생각]들의 조합. 혼합(된 것). 뒤섞임. 착잡: *I listened to his excuse with a mixture of amusement and disbelief.* 나는 재미와 불신의 뒤섞인 감정으로 그의 변명을 들었다.

mix-up /ˈ. ./ *n* INFORMAL a mistake that causes confusion about details or arrangements ‖ 세부 내용이나 준비에 혼동을 일으키는 실수. 오류. 혼란. 착오: *There was a mix-up at the station and Eddie got on the wrong bus.* 버스 정류장에서 혼동하여 에디는 버스를 잘못 탔다. —see also **mix up** (MIX¹), MIXED UP

ml. the written abbreviation of MILLILITER ‖ milliliter의 약어

mm. the written abbreviation of MILLIMETER ‖ millimeter의 약어

MN the written abbreviation of Minnesota ‖ Minnesota(미네소타 주)의 약어

MO the written abbreviation of Missouri ‖ Missouri(미주리 주)의 약어

moan¹ /moʊn/ *v* **1** [I] to make the sound of a moan ‖ 신음 소리를 내다. 끙끙거리다. 신음하다: *An injured soldier moaned in the bed next to mine.* 부상당한 병사가 내 옆 침대에서 신음 소리를 내

었다. **2** [I, T] to complain in an annoying way, especially in an unhappy voice ‖ 짜증나는 투로, 특히 불만스러운 목소리로 불평하다. 불평[불만]을 말하다. 한탄하다: *Stop moaning about your problems and get to work!* 네 문제에 대한 불평은 그만 하고 일을 시작해라! – **moaner** *n*

moan² *n* a long low sound expressing pain or sadness ‖ 고통이나 슬픔을 표현하는 길고 낮은 소리. 신음(소리). 끙끙 앓는 소리

moat /moʊt/ *n* a deep wide hole, usually filled with water, that is dug around a building such as a castle as a defense ‖ 방호물로서 성 등의 건물 주위에 파놓은, 보통 물로 채워진 깊고 넓은 구덩이. 호. 해자(垓子)

mob¹ /mɑb/ *n* **1** a large noisy crowd, especially one that is angry and violent ‖ 특히 분노한 폭력적인 대규모의 소란스런 군중. 폭도 **2** **the Mob** INFORMAL ⇨ MAFIA

mob² *v* **-bbed, -bbing** [T] to move forward and form a crowd around someone in order to express admiration or to attack him/her ‖ 어떤 사람에게 경의를 표시하거나 또는 그를 공격하기 위해 그의 주변으로 떼를 지어 다가가다. 떼지어 몰려들다[야유하다]. 떼를 지어 습격하다: *She's mobbed by her fans wherever she goes.* 그녀는 가는 곳마다 팬들이 떼를 지어 몰려들었다.

mo·bile¹ /ˈmoʊbəl/ *adj* able to move or be moved quickly and easily ‖ 빠르고 쉽게 이동하거나 이동될 수 있는. 움직이기 쉬운. 기동성의. 기동성이 있는. 고정되지 않은: *a mobile phone* 이동전화기 / *I'm much more mobile now that I have a car.* 나는 차가 있어서 현재 훨씬 더 기동성이 있다. – **mobility** /moʊˈbɪləti/ *n* [U] —opposite IMMOBILE

mo·bile² /ˈmoʊbil/ *n* a decoration made of small objects tied to string and hung up so that they move when air blows around them ‖ 줄에 묶여 높이 매달려서 주변에 바람이 불 때 움직이는 작은 물체로 만든 장식(물). 모빌

mobile home /ˌ.. ˈ./ *n* a type of house made of metal that can be pulled by a large vehicle and moved to another place ‖ 대형 차량으로 견인되어 다른 장소로 이동될 수 있는 금속제 유형의 가옥. 이동 주택

mo·bi·lize /ˈmoʊbəˌlaɪz/ *v* [I, T] to gather together or be brought together in order to work to achieve something difficult ‖ 어려운 일을 달성하도록 작업하

기 위해 함께 모으거나 모아지다. (전시) 동원하다. 집결시키다: *Forces have been mobilized to defend the capital.* 병력이 수도를 방어하기 위해 집결되었다. —

mobilization /ˌmoʊbələˈzeɪʃən/ *n* [C, U]

mob·ster /ˈmɑbstər/ *n* INFORMAL a member of the Mafia ‖ 마피아의 단원. 갱 조직원. 폭도

moc·ca·sin /ˈmɑkəsən/ *n* a flat comfortable shoe made of soft leather ‖ 부드러운 가죽으로 만든 (굽이) 납작한 간 편화. 모카신. 뒤축 없는 신

mock¹ /mɑk/ *v* [I, T] to laugh in an unkind way at someone or something and try to make him, her, or it seem stupid or silly, especially by copying his or her actions or speech ‖ 사람이나 사물 에 대해 무례하게 웃고 특히 남의 행동이 나 말을 모방해서 사람이나 사물을 멍청하 거나 바보같이 보이게 하려고 하다. 비웃 다. 조롱하다. 업신여기다. 흉내 내서 놀 리다: *Wilson mocked Joe's southern accent.* 윌슨은 조의 남부 사투리를 놀려 댔다. – **mockingly** *adv* —compare **make fun of sb/sth** (FUN¹)

mock² *adj* not real, but intended to be very similar to a real situation, substance etc. ‖ 진짜가 아니지만 실제 상 황·물체 등과 매우 흡사하도록 의도된. 가 짜의. 모조의. 거짓의. 가장의: *law students arguing cases in mock trials* 모 의 재판에서 사건을 심리하는 법대생들

mock·er·y /ˈmɑkəri/ *n* **1** [U] the act of laughing at someone or something and trying to make him, her, or it seem stupid or silly ‖ 어떤 사람이나 사물을 비 웃고 바보 같거나 멍청하게 보이도록 하는 행동. 조롱. 조소. 말봄 **2** [singular] something that you expect to be a good example of what it is, but instead is completely useless or ineffective ‖ 어떤 것의 실체에 대한 좋은 실례가 될 것으로 기대했으나 대신에 완전히 쓸모없고 효력 없는 것. 엉터리. 흉내만 낸 것. 조소거 리. 놀림감: *The trial made a mockery of justice.* (=the trial was expected to produce justice, but it did not) 그 재판은 정의를 조소거리로 만들었다.

mock·ing·bird /ˈmɑkɪŋˌbərd/ *n* an American bird that copies the songs of other birds ‖ 다른 새들의 소리를 모방하 는 미국산 새. 흉내지바뀌

mo·dal verb /ˌmoʊdl ˈvərb/, **modal** *n* TECHNICAL in grammar, a verb that is used with other verbs to change their meaning by expressing ideas such as possibility, permission, or intention. In English, the modals are "can," "could,"

"may," "might," "shall," "should," "will," "would," "must," "ought to," "have to," and "had better" ‖ 문법에서 다른 동사와 함께 쓰여, 가능성[허가, 의 도] 등의 생각을 표현해서 그 의미를 바꾸 는 동사. 조동사. 영어에서 조동사는 "can", "could", "may", "might", "shall", "should", "will", "would", "must", "ought to", "have to", "had better"가 있 다. —see study note on page 932

mode /moʊd/ *n* FORMAL a particular way or style of behaving, living, or doing something ‖ 행동하는[생활하는, 어 떤 일을 하는] 특정한 방법 또는 유형. 방 식. 양식. 관행: *a very efficient mode of transportation* 매우 효율적인 수송 방식

mod·el¹ /ˈmɑdl/ *n* **1** someone whose job is to show clothes, hair styles etc. by wearing them and being photographed ‖ 어떤 의상을 입거나 헤어스타일을 하고 사진을 찍게 하여 그것을 보여 주는 직업 인. 모델: *a top fashion model* 최고 패션 모델 **2** a small copy of something such as a vehicle, building, or machine, especially one that can be put together from separate parts ‖ 특히 각 부분품으 로 조립될 수 있는 차량[건물, 기계] 등의 작은 모사품. 모형. 견본. 원형: *a toy store with a large selection of models* 견 본품을 대규모로 모아 놓은 장난감 가게 **3** someone who is employed by an artist or photographer in order to be painted or photographed ‖ 미술가나 사진작가가 그림을 그리거나 사진 찍기 위해 고용한 사람. 모델 **4** a particular type or design of a vehicle, machine, weapon etc. ‖ 차 량·기계·무기 등의 특정 종류나 양식. 형 (型). 기종. 모델: *Ford has two new models coming out in October.* 포드사는 10월에 2종의 신형 모델을 출시한다. **5** a person or thing that is a perfect example of something good and is therefore worth copying ‖ 훌륭한 것의 완벽한 예로서 모방할 가치가 있는 사람이 나 사물. 모범[본보기] 기준이 되는 것[사 람]: *Shelly's essay is a model of care and neatness.* 셸리의 작문은 사려 깊고 깔끔함의 표본이다.

model² *adj* **1 model airplane/train/ car etc.** a small copy of a plane etc., especially one that can be put together from separate parts ‖ 특히 각 부품으로 조립될 수 있는 비행기 등의 작은 모사품. 모형 비행기/열차/자동차 **2 model wife/employee/prison/school etc.** a person or thing that is a perfect example of its type ‖ 각 유형의 완벽한 예 가 되는 사람이나 사물. 모범 아내/총업원

/교도소/학교

model³ v 1 [I, T] to have a job in which you show clothes, hair styles etc. by wearing them and being photographed ‖ 의상·헤어스타일 등을 입거나 하고, 사진 촬영되어 그것을 보여 주는 직업을 갖다. 모델로 일하다 2 [I, T] to have a job in which you are employed by an artist or photographer in order to be painted or photographed ‖ 미술가나 사진작가가 그림을 그리거나 사진을 찍을 때 그 대상으로 고용되는 직업을 갖다. 모델로 일하다 3 [T] to copy a system or way of doing something ‖ 어떤 일을 하는 체제나 방식을 모방하다. 본뜨다. 흉내 내다. …을 따라 하다: *Their education system is modeled on the French one.* 그들의 교육 체계는 프랑스 교육 체계를 모방하였다. 4 **model yourself on** to try to be like someone else because you admire him/her ‖ 다른 사람을 존경해서 그 사람을 닮으려 하다. …을 따라하다: *James had always modeled himself on his hero, Martin Luther King.* 제임스는 항상 그의 영웅인 마틴 루터 킹 목사를 닮으려고 했다. 5 [T] to make small objects from materials such as wood or clay ‖ 나무나 점토 등의 재료로 작은 대상물을 만들다. 축소 모델[모형]을 만들다.

mod·el·ing /ˈmɑdl-ɪŋ/ n [U] 1 the work of a model ‖ 모델 업무. 모델로 일하기: *a career in modeling* 모델로서의 경력[직업] 2 the activity of making model ships, planes, cars etc. ‖ 모형 배·비행기·자동차 등을 만드는 활동. 모형 제작술[업]

mo·dem /ˈmoʊdəm/ n a piece of electronic equipment that allows information from one computer to be sent along telephone wires to another computer ‖ 정보가 한 컴퓨터에서 전화선을 따라 다른 컴퓨터로 보내지게 하는 전자 장비. 모뎀

mod·er·ate¹ /ˈmɑdərɪt/ adj 1 neither very big nor very small, neither very hot nor very cold, neither very fast nor very slow etc. ‖ 매우 크거나 매우 작지도 않은, 매우 덥거나 매우 춥지도 않은, 매우 빠르거나 매우 느리지도 않은 등. 적당한. 알맞은. 중간 정도의. 보통의: *students of moderate ability* 중간 정도 능력의 학생들 / *a moderate temperature* 온화한 기후 2 having opinions or beliefs, especially about politics, that are not extreme and that most people consider reasonable or sensible ‖ 특히 정치에 대해, 극단적이 아니고 대부분의 사람들이 합리적이거나 분별있게 생각하는 의견이

나 신념을 가진. 온건한. 중도의. 균형감 있는: *a senator with moderate views* 온건한 견해를 가진 상원의원

mod·er·ate² /ˈmɑdəˈreɪt/ v [I, T] to make something less extreme or violent, or to become this ‖ 어떤 것을 덜 극단적이고 폭력적이 되게 하다, 또는 이렇게 되다. 온화[온건]하게 하다[되다]. 완화[가감]하다[되다]: *To lose weight, moderate the amount of food you eat.* 살을 빼기 위해서 식사량을 절제해야 한다.

mod·er·ate³ /ˈmɑdərɪt/ n someone whose opinions or beliefs, especially about politics, are not extreme and are considered reasonable or sensible by most people ‖ 특히 정치에 대한 의견이나 신념이 극단적이지 않고 대부분의 사람들에 의해 합리적 또는 분별 있는 것으로 생각되는 사람. 온건한 사람. 온건[중도]주의자

mod·er·ate·ly /ˈmɑdərɪtli/ adv fairly but not very ‖ 상당하지만 대단치는 않게. 알맞게. 적당히. 온건하게. 절도를 지켜: *a moderately successful company* 적당히 성공적인 기업

mod·er·a·tion /ˌmɑdəˈreɪʃən/ n [U] 1 in moderation if you do something in moderation, you do not do it too much ‖ 어떤 일을 너무 지나치게 하지 않게. 알맞게. 적당히: *You've got to learn to drink in moderation.* 너는 술을 적당히 마시는 법을 배워야 한다. 2 FORMAL control of your behavior, so that you keep your actions, feelings, habits etc. within reasonable or sensible limits ‖ 행동을 통제해서 행동·감정·습관 등이 이성적이고 분별 있는 한계를 지키도록 하는 것. 온건. 온화. 절제. 절도

mod·er·a·tor /ˈmɑdəˌreɪtɚ/ n someone whose job is to control a discussion or argument and to help people reach an agreement ‖ 토론이나 논쟁을 조절하고 사람들이 합의에 도달하게 돕는 직업인. 중재자. 조정자

mod·ern /ˈmɑdɚn/ adj 1 belonging to the present time or the most recent time ‖ 현재나 가장 최근 시기에 속하는. 현대의. 요즈음의. 지금의: *modern American history* 미국 현대사 / *modern medical techniques* 현대 의학 기술 2 using or willing to use very recent ideas, fashions, or ways of thinking ‖ 아주 최근의 생각[유행, 사고 방식]을 쓰거나 쓰려 하는. 현대적인. 새로운. 최신의: *The school is very modern in its approach to sex education.* 그 학교는 성교육에 대한 접근에서 매우 현대적이다. – **modernity** /mɑˈdɚnəti, -ˈdɛr-/ n [U] —see usage note at NEW

mod·ern·ize /'madə,naɪz/ v [T] to change something, using new things or methods so that it is more suitable to be used in the present time ‖ 현재 시기에 이용되기에 더 적합하게, 새로운 물건이나 방법을 써서 사물을 변화시키다. …을 현대화[근대화]하다. 현대식으로 하다: *We're modernizing the whole house, starting with a new bathroom.* 우리는 목욕탕을 새로 바꾸는 것을 시작으로 집안 전체를 현대화하고 있다. – **modernization** /,madənə'zeɪʃən/ n [C, U]

mod·est /'madɪst/ adj 1 APPROVING unwilling to talk proudly about your abilities and achievements ‖ 자신의 능력이나 업적에 대해 자랑스럽게 얘기하려 하지 않는. 겸손한. 삼가는. 자랑하지 않는. 점잖은: *He's very modest about his success.* 그는 자신의 성공에 대해 매우 겸손하다. 2 not very big in size, quantity, value etc. ‖ 크기·양·가치 등에서 그다지 크지 않은. 심하지[많지, 크지, 높지] 않은. 적당한, 적절한: *a modest salary* 많지 않은[적당한] 봉급 3 APPROVING shy about showing your body or attracting sexual interest ‖ 신체를 보이거나 성적 관심을 끄는 데에 부끄러워하는. 정숙한. 얌전한. 품위 있는 – **modestly** adv — opposite IMMODEST

mod·es·ty /'madəsti/ n [U] APPROVING 1 the quality of being MODEST about your abilities or achievements ‖ 능력이나 업적에 대해 겸손한 성질. 겸손. 겸양. 삼가함 2 the quality of being MODEST about your body ‖ 신체에 대해 삼가하는 특성. 정숙. 얌전

mod·i·cum /'madɪkəm/ n FORMAL a modicum of a small amount of something, especially a good quality ‖ 특히 우수한 특성을 가진 소량의 사물. 근소(한 양). 약간: *Even children need a modicum of privacy.* 아이들일지라도 어느 정도의 사생활은 필요하다.

mod·i·fi·ca·tion /,madəfə'keɪʃən/ n 1 a small change made in something, in order to improve it ‖ 개선하기 위해 어떤 것에 이루어진 작은 변경. (부분적인) 변경. 수정: *We've made a few modifications to the original design.* 우리는 본래의 디자인에 약간의 일부 수정을 했다. 2 [U] the act of modifying (MODIFY) something, or the process of being modified ‖ 어떤 일을 수정하는 행위, 또는 수정되는 과정. 개량. 변형. 수식

mod·i·fi·er /'madə,faɪə/ n TECHNICAL in grammar, an adjective, adverb, or phrase that gives additional information about another word. In the sentence "The dog is barking loudly," "loudly" is a modifier ‖ 문법에서, 다른 단어에 추가 정보를 제공하는 형용사[부사, 어구]. 수식어[어구, 절]. 한정어[어구, 절] "The dog is barking loudly"라는 문장에서 "loudly"는 수식어이다.

mod·i·fy /'madə,faɪ/ v [T] 1 to make small changes to something in order to improve it ‖ 개선하려고 어떤 일에 약간의 수정을 하다. …을 부분 수정하다: *The car's been modified to use less fuel.* 그 자동차는 연료를 적게 사용하도록 개조되었다. 2 TECHNICAL to act as a MODIFIER ‖ 수식어로 작용하다. …의 뜻을 한정하다

mod·u·lar /'madʒələ/ adj based on MODULEs or made using modules ‖ 모듈에 기초한, 또는 모듈을 사용하여 만든. 모듈의. 모듈식의. 조립식의: *modular furniture* 조립식 가구

mod·u·late /'madʒə,leɪt/ v [T] TECHNICAL to change the sound of your voice or another sound ‖ 자신의 목소리 또는 다른 소리를 바꾸다. 변조시키다. 조절[조정]하다 – **modulation** /,madʒə'leɪʃən/ n [U]

mod·ule /'madʒul/ n 1 one of several separate parts that can be combined to form a larger object, such as a machine or building ‖ 기계나 건물 등의 더 큰 물체를 형성하기 위해서 결합될 수 있는 여러 가지 각각의 부품 중의 한 개. (공업 제품 등의) 규격화된 구성[조립] 단위. 모듈 2 a part of a SPACECRAFT that can be separated from the main part and used for a particular purpose ‖ 주요부에서 분리되어 특정한 목적에 사용될 수 있는 우주선의 일부. 모듈

mo·hair /'mouhɛr/ n [U] expensive wool made from ANGORA ‖ 앙고라 염소로 만든 값비싼 털. 모헤어(직)

Mo·ham·med /mou'hæməd/ ⇨ MUHAMMAD

moist /mɔɪst/ adj slightly wet, in a pleasant way ‖ 기분 좋게 약간 축축한: *Make sure the soil is moist before planting the seeds.* 씨앗을 심기 전에 꼭 땅을 축축하게 해라. / *a moist chocolate cake* 촉촉한 초콜릿 케이크 —compare DAMP

moist·en /'mɔɪsən/ v [I, T] to become MOIST, or to make something do this ‖ 축축해지거나 어떤 것을 축축하게 하다: *Moisten the clay with a little water.* 약간의 물을 섞어 찰흙을 축축하게 해라.

mois·ture /'mɔɪstʃə/ n [U] small

amounts of water that are present in the air, in a substance, or on a surface ‖ 공기 중·물체 내·표면 위에 있는 소량의 물. 습기. 수분: *The desert air contains hardly any moisture.* 사막의 공기는 습기를 거의 포함하고 있지 않다.

mois·tur·iz·er /ˈmɔɪstʃəˌraɪzɚ/ *n* a creamy liquid you put on your skin to keep it soft ‖ 피부를 부드럽게 유지시키기 위해 피부에 바르는 크림 형태의 액체. 피부 로션[크림]

mo·lar /ˈmoʊlɚ/ *n* one of the large teeth at the back of the mouth, used for crushing food ‖ 음식물을 부수는 데 사용하는 입 뒤쪽에 있는 큰 치아 중의 하나. 어금니

mo·las·ses /məˈlæsɪz/ *n* [U] a thick dark sweet liquid that is obtained from raw sugar plants when they are being made into sugar ‖ 설탕을 만들 때 사탕수수나무에서 얻은 진하고 검은 달콤한 액체. 당밀. 당액

mold¹ /moʊld/ *n* **1** [U] a green or black FUNGUS (=plant without leaves) that grows on old food and on walls or objects that are in warm, slightly wet places ‖ 오래된 음식물과 따뜻하고 약간 습기 있는 장소에 있는 담벼락이나 물체에서 자라는 푸른 색이나 검정 색의 잎이 없는 식물인 균류. 곰팡이 **2** a hollow container that you pour liquid into, so that when the liquid becomes solid, it takes the shape of the container ‖ 액체를 부어넣어서 고체가 되면 용기의 모양과 같은 형태를 얻는 속이 빈 용기. 거푸집. 틀. 주형(鑄型)[형(型)]: *a candle mold shaped like a star* 별 모양의 형태로 된 틀에 부어서 만든 양초

mold

mold² *v* [T] **1** to shape a solid substance by pressing or rolling it or by putting it into a MOLD ‖ 압력을 가하거나 회전시켜서 또는 틀에 집어넣어 고체 물질을 만들다. …을 틀에 넣어[굳혀서] …을 만들다. 주조하다: *a figure of a man molded out of clay* 점토를 틀에 넣어 만든 사람의 형상 **2** to influence the way someone's character or attitudes develop ‖ 어떤 사람의 성격이나 태도 발달의 방식에 영향을 주다. (사람이 인격·성격 등을) …에 입각하여 만들다. …에 영향을 주어서 (…으로) 하다: *His character has been molded more by his experiences than by his education.* 그의

성격은 교육에 의하기보다는 그의 경험에서 더 많은 영향을 받아 이루어졌다.

mold·ing /ˈmoʊldɪŋ/ *n* [C, U] a thin decorative line of stone, wood, plastic etc. around the edge of something such as a wall, car, or piece of furniture ‖ 벽[자동차, 가구] 등의 가장자리 근처에 있는 돌·나무·플라스틱 등의 가는 장식 선. 쇠시리. 몰딩

mold·y /ˈmoʊldi/ *adj* covered with MOLD ‖ 곰팡이로 덮인. 곰팡이 슨: *moldy bread* 곰팡이 슨 빵

mole /moʊl/ *n* **1** a small dark brown mark on the skin that is often slightly higher than the skin around it ‖ 주위의 피부보다는 종종 약간 더 높게 도드라진, 피부의 작고 짙은 갈색의 점. 사마귀. 검은 점 **2** a small animal with brown fur that cannot see very well and lives in holes in the ground ‖ 아주 잘 볼 수가 없고 땅속 굴에 사는 갈색 털을 가진 작은 동물. 두더지 **3** someone who works for an organization, especially a government, while secretly giving information to its enemy ‖ 조직 특히 정부를 위해 근무하면서도 적에게 정보를 몰래 제공하는 사람. (잠입) 스파이. 잠복 내통자

mole·cule /ˈmɑləˌkyul/ *n* the smallest unit into which any substance can be divided without losing its own chemical nature, usually consisting of two or more atoms ‖ 보통 둘 또는 그 이상의 원자로 구성되어 있으면서 자신의 화학적 성질을 상실하지 않고 분리될 수 있는 물질의 최소 단위. 분자 – **molecular** /məˈlɛkyələ/ *adj*

mo·lest /məˈlɛst/ *v* [T] to attack or harm someone by touching him/her in a sexual way or trying to have sex with him/her ‖ 성적으로 사람을 만지거나 사람과 성행위를 가지려고 함으로써 다른 사람을 공격하거나 위해를 가하다. 성적으로 희롱하다. …에게 외설적인 행동이나 말을 하다: *Tina was molested by her uncle when she was 13.* 티나는 13세 때 그녀의 삼촌한테 성희롱을 당했다. – **molester** *n* – **molestation** /ˌmoʊlɛˈsteɪʃən, ˌmɑ-/ *n* [U]

mol·li·fy /ˈmɑləˌfaɪ/ *v* [T] FORMAL to make someone feel less angry and upset about something ‖ 어떤 일에 대하여 남이 성을 덜 내거나 덜 당황하게 하다. 누그러뜨리다. 달래다. 진정시키다

mol·lusk /ˈmɑləsk/ *n* a type of sea or land animal, for example a SNAIL or CLAM, with a soft body covered by a hard shell ‖ 예를 들어 달팽이나 조개류 같이

딱딱한 껍데기로 덮여 있는 부드러운 몸통을 가진 바다나 육지의 동물의 일종. 연체동물

molt /moʊlt/ v [I] when a bird or animal molts, it loses hair, feathers, or skin so that new hair, feathers, or skin can grow ‖ 새 또는 동물 등이 머리털[깃털, 피부]을 벗고 새로운 머리털[깃털, 피부]이 자라나다. 털갈이하다. 탈피하다. 갈다

mol·ten /ˈmoʊltˀn/ adj molten metal or rock has been made into a liquid by being heated to a very high temperature ‖ 매우 높은 온도로 가열되어 금속 또는 바위 등이 액체로 되는. 용해된. 녹은

mom /mɑm/ n INFORMAL mother ‖ 엄마: Can I go to David's house, Mom? 엄마, 나 데이비드 집에 가도 돼요?

mo·ment /ˈmoʊmənt/ n 1 a very short period of time ‖ 매우 짧은 시간 동안. 순간. 찰나. 단시간: I'll be back in a moment. 곧 돌아오겠습니다. / Your food will be ready in a moment. 음식이 곧 준비됩니다. 2 a particular point in time ‖ 특정한 시점. 한때: At that moment, the door opened and Danny walked in. 그때 문이 열려서 데니는 걸어 들어갔다. / I knew it was you the moment (that) I heard your voice. 네 목소리를 듣는 순간 너란 것을 알았다. 3 **at the moment** now ‖ 지금 : We're living in an apartment at the moment, but we'll be moving into our house in six weeks. 우리는 지금 아파트에 잠깐 살고 있지만 6주 후에 우리 집으로 이사할 것이다. 4 **for the moment** used in order to say that something is happening now but will probably change in the future ‖ 어떤 일이 지금 발생하고 있지만 장래에는 아마도 변경될 것이라고 말하는 데에 쓰여. (지금) 당장은. 우선은: The rain has stopped for the moment. 지금은 비가 그쳤다. 5 [C usually singular] a particular period of time when you have a chance to do something ‖ 어떤 일을 하는 기회를 가진 특정한 기간. 시기. 기회. 호기: It was her big moment (=her chance to show other people how skilled she is); she took a deep breath and began to play. 그것은 그녀에게 역량을 발휘할 좋은 기회였다. 그녀는 숨을 깊이 들이쉬고는 연극을 시작했다. —compare MINUTE¹

mo·men·tar·i·ly /ˌmoʊmənˈtɛrəli/ adv 1 for a very short time ‖ 잠시 (동안). 잠깐: Jason was momentarily stunned by the explosion. 제이슨은 그 폭발로 잠시 실신했다. 2 very soon ‖ 바로 곧. 즉각: I'll be with you momentarily. 내가 즉시

너에게 가겠다.

mo·men·tar·y /ˈmoʊmənˌtɛri/ adj continuing for a very short time ‖ 아주 짧은 시간 동안 계속되는. 순간의. 찰나의. 일시적인: a momentary silence 일순간의 침묵

mo·men·tous /moʊˈmɛntəs, mə-/ adj a momentous event, occasion, decision etc. is very important, especially because of the effects it will have in the future ‖ 특히 장래에 영향을 주기 때문에 사건·일·결정 등이 매우 중요한. (사물이) 중대한: the momentous changes in Central Europe 중부 유럽의 중대한 변화

mo·men·tum /moʊˈmɛntəm, mə-/ n [U] 1 the force that makes a moving object keep moving ‖ 움직이고 있는 물체를 계속 움직이게 하는 힘. 탄력. 타성: The rock gained/gathered momentum (=moved faster and faster) as it rolled down the hill. 그 바위는 언덕에서 굴러 내리면서 탄력이 붙었다. 2 the ability to keep increasing, developing, or being more successful ‖ 계속 증가·발전하게 하거나 더욱 성공하게 하는 능력. 기세. 여세: The business did very well at first but now it seems to be losing momentum. 그 사업은 처음에는 매우 잘 나갔는데 지금은 여세를 상실하는 듯이 보인다.

mom·ma /ˈmɑmə/ n SPOKEN mother ‖ 엄마

mom·my /ˈmɑmi/ n SPOKEN a word meaning mother, used especially by a child or when speaking to a child ‖ 특히 어린이에 의해서 또는 어린이에게 말할 때 사용되는 어머니를 의미하는 말. 엄마

mon·arch /ˈmɑnək, ˈmɑnɑrk/ n a king or queen ‖ 왕 또는 여왕. 세습적 군주

mon·ar·chy /ˈmɑnəki/ n 1 [U] the system in which a country is ruled by a king or queen ‖ 한 나라가 왕이나 여왕에 의해 통치되는 체제. 군주제[정치] 2 a country that is ruled by a king or queen ‖ 왕이나 여왕에 의해 통치되는 나라. 군주국

mon·as·ter·y /ˈmɑnəˌstɛri/ n a building or group of buildings in which MONKs live ‖ 수도사가 사는 건물이나 일단의 건물들. 수도원

mo·nas·tic /məˈnæstɪk/ adj relating to MONKs or a MONASTERY ‖ 수도사 또는 수도원에 관계된. 수도사의. 수도원의

Mon·day /ˈmʌndi, -deɪ/, written abbreviation **Mon.** n the second day of the week ‖ 주중[일주일]의 둘쨋날. 월요일 —see usage note at SUNDAY

mon·e·tar·y /ˈmɑnəˌtɛri/ adj relating to

money, especially all the money in a particular country ‖ 돈 특히 특정 국가의 모든 화폐에 관련된. (한 나라의) 화폐의. 통화의: *a monetary system based on the value of gold* 금 가치에 기초를 둔 통화 제도

mon·ey /ˈmʌni/ *n* [U] **1** what you earn by working and use in order to buy things, usually in the form of coins or pieces of paper with their value printed on them ‖ 보통 표면에 그것의 가치가 인쇄된 동전 또는 지폐의 형태로, 일해서 받고 물건을 사는 데에 쓰는 것. 통화. 화폐. 돈: *How much money do you have?* 돈을 얼마나 갖고 있니? / *That car must have cost a lot of money.* 그 자동차는 분명히 많은 돈이 들 거야. / *We're trying to save enough money for a trip to Europe.* 우리는 유럽 여행을 위해서 충분한 돈을 저축하려고 애쓰고 있다. / *Zach's making a lot of money* (=earning money or making a profit) *selling his paintings.* 자크는 그림을 팔아서 큰돈을 벌고 있다. / *I left my wallet at home – do you have enough money on you* (=carry money with you) *to pay for the meal?* 지갑을 집에 두고 왔어. 식사비용을 낼 충분한 돈을 가지고 있니? / *She's making about $40,000 a year, which is pretty good money.* (=good wages for your work) 그녀는 연봉 약 4만 달러를 버는데 그것은 꽤 괜찮은 급료이다. **2** wealth ‖ 부(富). 재산: *Money isn't everything.* 재산이 전부가 아니다. / *Fred lost all his money when he was forced to close his business.* 프레드는 어쩔 수 없이 폐업을 하게 되었을 때 그의 모든 재산을 잃었다. / *I think he made his money on the stock market.* 내 생각에 그는 주식 시장에서 돈을 벌었다. **3 get your money's worth** to think that something you have paid to do or see was worth the price that you paid ‖ 어떤 일을 하거나 보는 데 지불한 값이 그 값만큼의 가치가 있었다고 생각하다. 지불한 돈만큼의 대가를 얻어서 만족하다: *The tickets were expensive, but we felt that we got our money's worth.* 입장권은 비쌌으나 우리가 지불한 만큼의 대가는 얻었다고 느꼈다.

SPOKEN PHRASES

4 kind of money a phrase meaning a lot of money, used when you think something costs too much, when someone earns a lot more than other people etc. ‖ 어떤 일이 너무 많은 비용이 든다고 생각할 때, 어떤 사람이 다른

사람보다 돈을 더 많이 버는 등의 경우에 쓰여서 큰돈을 의미하는 어구: *They wanted $5000, and I just don't have that kind of money.* 그들은 5천 달러를 원했는데 나는 그렇게 많은 돈을 지금 갖고 있지 않다. / *People with that kind of money* (=rich people) *don't need to work.* 그렇게 많은 돈을 가진 부자들은 일할 필요가 없다. **5 pay good money for** to spend a lot of money on something ‖ 어떤 일에 많은 돈을 소비하다. …에 많은 돈을 지불하다: *I paid good money for that sofa, so it should last.* 나는 그 소파에 많은 돈을 지불했으므로 그것은 오래 써야 한다. **6 there's money (to be made)** used in order to say that you can get a lot of money from a particular activity or from buying and selling something ‖ 특별한 활동으로 또는 어떤 것을 사고팔아서 많은 돈을 벌 수 있다는 것을 말하려는 데에 쓰여. …은 돈이 된다. 수지가 맞다: *There's a lot of money in selling antiques.* 골동품 판매는 큰 돈벌이가 된다. **7 for my money** used when giving your opinion about something, to emphasize that you believe it strongly ‖ 어떤 일에 대하여 의견을 말할 때, 또는 어떤 일을 강렬하게 믿는다는 것을 강조하는 데에 쓰여. 나의 의견으로는. 안성맞춤의. 마음에 드는: *For my money, the Chicago Bears are one of the best teams in the league.* 내 생각으로는 시카고 베어스가 리그에서 최고 팀 중의 하나라고 생각한다. **8 money talks** used in order to say that people who have money can usually get whatever they want ‖ 돈이 있는 사람은 대개 그들이 원하는 것은 무엇이나 얻을 수 있다는 것을 말하는 데에 쓰여. 돈이 말해 준다. 돈만 있으면 귀신도 부릴 수 있다. 돈이 힘을 쓴다. **9 be (right) on the money** used when something is perfect or exactly right for the situation ‖ 어떤 일이 완벽할 때 또는 상황에 정확히 맞을 경우에 쓰여. 완벽하다: *Her solution was right on the money – the clients loved it.* 그녀의 해법은 완벽했다. 고객들은 그것을 아주 좋아했다. **10 money is no object** used in order to say that you can spend as much money as you want to on something ‖ 어떤 일에 바라는 만큼 많은 돈을 쓸 수 있음을 말하는 데에 쓰여. 금액은 문제가 아니다. 돈은 불문 [상관없음]: *Choose whatever you like, money is no object.* 네가 좋아하는 것은 무엇이든 선택해라. 돈은 걱정 말고.

money mar·ket /'.. ,../ *n* the banks and other financial institutions that buy and sell BONDs, CURRENCY (=paper money) etc. ‖ 채권·지폐 등을 사고파는 은행 및 기타 금융 기관. 화폐 시장

money or·der /'.. ,../ *n* a special type of check that you buy and send to someone so that s/he can exchange it for money ‖ 구입하여 다른 사람에게 보내면 그(것을 받은) 사람이 돈으로 바꿀 수 있는 특별한 수표 유형. 환. 우편환

mon·grel /'maŋgrəl, 'mʌŋ-/ *n* a dog that is a mix of several breeds of dog ‖ 여러 품종의 개를 교배한 개. 잡종(개)

mon·i·ker /'manıkɚ/ *n* INFORMAL someone's name or NICKNAME ‖ 남의 인명이나 별명

mon·i·tor¹ /'manətɚ/ *n* **1** a piece of equipment that looks like a television and that shows information or pictures, especially on a computer ‖ 특히 컴퓨터에서 정보나 그림을 보여 주며 텔레비전같이 생긴 장치. 모니터 **2** a child who is chosen to help a teacher in some way ‖ 어떤 면으로든 선생님을 돕기 위해 선출된 아동. 반장. 학급 위원: *The blackboard monitor cleans the boards.* 칠판 담당 학급 위원은 칠판을 닦는다.

mon·i·tor² *v* [T] to carefully watch, listen to, or examine something over a period of time, to check for any changes or developments ‖ 어떤 변경 또는 발전을 확인하기 위해 일정 기간에 걸쳐 어떤 일을 주의 깊게 보거나 듣거나 조사하다. 감시하다. 검토하다. 관찰[기록, 탐지]하다 : *Army intelligence has been monitoring the enemy's radio broadcasts.* 육군 첩보 부대는 적의 라디오 방송을 방수[청취]해 오고 있다. / *Doctors are monitoring the patient's condition.* 의사들은 환자의 상태를 체크하고 있다.

monk /mʌŋk/ *n* a man who is a member of a group of religious men who live together in a MONASTERY (=special building) ‖ 수도원에 같이 사는 종교인 집단의 구성원인 남자. 수도사

mon·key¹ /'mʌŋki/ *n* **1** a type of active animal that lives in hot countries and has a long tail, that it uses with its hands to climb trees ‖ 열대 지방에 살며 긴 꼬리를 가지고 나무를 올라가는 데 손을 사용하는 활동적인 유형의 동물. 원숭이 **2 monkey business** behavior that may cause trouble or be dishonest ‖ 분쟁을 일으키거나 부정직하게 할 수도 있는 행동. 속임수. 협잡. 불성실한 행위. 장난: *The boys are awfully quiet – I think they're up to some monkey business.* 그 소년들은 지독히 조용하다. 나는 그들이 어떤 장난을 치려 한다고 생각한다. **3 make a monkey out of sb** to make someone seem stupid ‖ 어떤 사람을 바보처럼 보이게 하다. 조롱하다. …을 웃음거리로 만들다

monkey² *v*

monkey around *phr v* [I] INFORMAL to behave in a stupid or careless way ‖ 바보같이 또는 경솔하게 행동하다. 장난치며 놀다: *They were monkeying around in the playground and one of them got hurt.* 그들은 운동장에서 장난치며 놀고 있었는데 그 중 한 명이 다쳤다.

monkey (around) with sth *phr v* [T] to touch or use something, usually when you do not know how to do it correctly ‖ 보통 정확히 작동 방법을 모를 때 어떤 것을 만지거나 사용하다. 만지작거리다: *You'll break the TV if you don't stop monkeying with it.* 텔레비전을 만지작거리는 걸 그만두지 않으면 고장내고 말 거야.

monkey wrench /'.. ,./ *n* a tool that is used for holding or turning things of different widths, especially NUTs ‖ 폭이 다른 물건 특히 너트를 잡거나 돌리는 데 사용되는 연장. 멍키 스패너

mon·o /'manoʊ/ *n* [U] INFORMAL an infectious illness that makes you feel weak and tired for a long time ‖ 오랫동안 허약하고 피곤함을 느끼게 하는 전염성 질환. 전염성 단핵증(바이러스에 의한 급성 질환)

mon·o·chrome /'manə,kroʊm/ *adj* having, using, or appearing in only black, white, and gray ‖ 흑색·백색·회색만을 갖거나 사용하거나 또는 흑·백·회색에만 나타나는. 단색의. 흑백의: *a monochrome computer monitor* 흑백 컴퓨터 모니터

mo·nog·a·my /mə'nagəmi/ *n* [U] the custom or practice of being married to only one person at one time ‖ 한 번에 한 사람하고만 결혼하는 관습이나 관행. 일부일처혼. 단혼 – **monogamous** /mə'nagəməs/ *adj*

mon·o·gram /'manə,græm/ *n* a design made from the first letters of someone's names, that is put on things such as shirts or writing paper ‖ 셔츠나 필기 용지 등에 새긴 사람 이름의 첫 글자로 만든 디자인. 모노그램. 결합 문자 – **monogrammed** *adj*

mon·o·lith·ic /,manl'ıθɪk/ *adj* **1** a monolithic organization, political system etc. is very large and difficult to change ‖ 조직·정치 체제 등이 매우 크고 변경하기 어려운. 획일적 구조를 가진. 완전히 통일된 **2** very large, solid, and impressive ‖ 매우 크고 단단하며 인상적인: *a monolithic building* 튼튼한 구조를 가진 건물 – **monolith** /'mɑnəlɪθ/ *n*

mon·o·logue, monolog /'mɑnl,ɔg, -,ɑg/ *n* a long speech by one character in a play, movie, or television show ‖ 연극·영화·텔레비전 쇼의 한 주인공에 의한 긴 대화. 독백

mon·o·nu·cle·o·sis /,mɑnoʊ,nukli'oʊ-sɪs/ *n* [U] ⇨ MONO

mo·nop·o·lize /mə'nɑpə,laɪz/ *v* [T] to have complete control over something, especially a type of business, so that other people cannot get involved ‖ 다른 사람은 참여할 수 없게 어떤 일을 특히 사업의 유형을 완전 지배하다. (상품·사업 등을) 독점[전매]하다: *The tobacco industry is monopolized by a few large companies.* 담배 산업은 소수의 거대 회사들에 의해 독점되고 있다. – **monopolization** /mə,nɑpələ'zeɪʃən/ *n* [U]

Mo·nop·o·ly /mə'nɑpəli/ *n* [U] TRADEMARK a game using artificial money in which you try to get more money and property than your opponents ‖ 모조 화폐를 사용하여 상대방보다 더 많은 돈과 재산을 획득하려고 하는 게임. 모노폴리. 주사위를 사용하는 탁상 게임의 일종

mo·nop·o·ly *n* the control of all or most of a business activity ‖ 전체 또는 대개의 사업 활동의 지배. 독점. 전매: *The government broke up Bell Telephone's monopoly on telephone services.* 정부는 전화 서비스에 대한 벨 전화회사의 독점을 깨뜨렸다. – **monopolistic** /mə,nɑpə'lɪstɪk/ *adj*

mon·o·rail /'mɑnə,reɪl/ *n* [C, U] a type of railroad that uses a single RAIL, or the train that travels on this type of railroad ‖ 단일 궤도를 사용한 철로의 유형, 또는 이러한 유형의 철로를 달리는 열차. 모노레일. 단궤(單軌)열차

mon·o·tone /'mɑnə,toʊn/ *n* [singular] a sound that continues on the same note without getting any louder or softer ‖ 더 커지거나 부드러워지지 않고 동일한 음조로 이어지는 소리. 단조로움. 단조로운 음: *He spoke in a monotone.* 그는 단조롭게 말했다.

mo·not·o·nous /mə'nɑt̮n-əs/ *adj* boring because there is no variety ‖ 변화가 없어서 지루한. 단조로운: *a monotonous job* 단조로운 일 –

monotony *n* [U] – **monotonously** *adv*

mon·soon /mɑn'sun/ *n* the season when it rains a lot in India and other southern Asian countries, or the rain or wind that happens during this season ‖ 인도와 기타 남아시아 국가에 비가 많이 오는 계절, 또는 이 계절 동안에 발생하는 비 또는 바람. 계절풍. 우기

mon·ster /'mɑnstər/ *n* **1** an imaginary large ugly frightening creature ‖ 상상의 크고 추한 소름끼치는 생물. 괴물: *a sea monster* 바다 괴수(怪獸) **2** someone who is cruel and evil ‖ 잔인한 사람. 극악무도한 사람: *Only a monster could kill an innocent child.* 잔인한 사람만이 순진한 어린이를 살해할 수 있었다. **3** an object, animal etc. that is unusually large ‖ 보통 커다란 물체·동물 등. 거대한 동물[식물, 것]: *That dog's a real monster!* 그 개는 정말로 괴물같이 크다! – **monster** *adj*

mon·stros·i·ty /mɑn'strɑsət̮i/ *n* something large that is very ugly, especially a building ‖ 매우 보기 흉한 거대한 사물, 특히 건물. 기괴한[거대한] 것

mon·strous /'mɑnstrəs/ *adj* **1** very wrong, immoral, or unfair ‖ 매우 나쁜 [부도덕한, 불공정한]. 무시무시한. 소름끼치는. 지독한: *a monstrous crime* 극악무도한 범죄 **2** unusually large ‖ 유별나게 큰. 거대한. 엄청난: *a monstrous piece of pie* 엄청나게 큰 파이 조각 / *a monstrous truck* 엄청나게 큰 트럭 – **monstrously** *adv*

mon·tage /mɑn'tɑʒ, moʊn-/ *n* **1** [U] an art form in which a picture, movie etc. is made from parts of different pictures etc. that are combined to form a whole ‖ 서로 다른 그림 등의 단편으로 하나의 전체 그림을 구성하려고 조합하여 제작한 그림·영화 등의 미술 형식. 몽타주(기법) **2** a picture, movie etc. made using this process ‖ 이러한 과정을 통해서 제작된 그림·영화 등. (화면의 합성이나 2중 인화로) 하나의 영상을 만드는 것

month /mʌnθ/ *n* **1** one of the 12 periods of time that a year is divided into ‖ 1년을 12로 나눈 기간 중 하나. 달: *the month of May* 5월 / *He's starting college at the end of this month.* 그는 이달 말부터 대학을 다니기 시작한다. / *last/next month* (=the month before or after this one) 지난[다음] 달 **2** any period of time equal to about four weeks ‖ 약 4주에 해당하는 기간. 한 달: *Jeff is away for two months.* 제프는 2달간 자리를 비운다. / *We'll be back a* *month from today/tomorrow/Friday*. (=a month after today, etc.) 우리는 오늘 [내일, 금요일]부터 1달 후에 돌아올 것이다.

month·ly /ˈmʌnθli/ *adj* **1** happening or done every month ‖ 매달 발생하거나 이루어지는. 매달의. 월 1회의. 월간의: *a monthly meeting* 월 1회의 모임 **2** relating to a single month ‖ 한 달의. 1개월에 걸친: *his monthly rate of pay* 그의 1개월분의 납부 — **monthly** *adv*

mon·u·ment /ˈmɑnyəmənt/ *n* **1** a building or other large structure that is built to remind people of an important event or famous person ‖ 중대한 사건이나 유명인사를 사람들이 회상하기 위해 지은 건물 또는 기타 큰 구조물. 기념탑[비, 상, 관]: *a monument to soldiers killed in the war* 전쟁 중 전사한 군인들을 위한 기념비 **2 be a monument to** to be a very clear example of what can happen as a result of a particular quality ‖ 특별한 속성의 결과로 발생할 수 있는 것에 대한 매우 분명한 사례가 되다. 전형[화신]이 되다: *The huge empty office buildings are a monument to bad planning.* 그 거대한 빈 사무실용 건물은 형편없는 설계의 전형적인 사례이다.

mon·u·men·tal /ˌmɑnyəˈmɛntl̩/ *adj* **1** a monumental achievement, piece of work etc. is very important and has a lot of influence ‖ 성취·일 등이 매우 중요하고 큰 영향력을 가진. 기념비적인: *Darwin's monumental work on evolution* 진화에 관한 다윈의 불멸의 업적 **2** extremely large, bad, good, impressive etc. ‖ 매우 크고 나쁘고 좋고 인상적인. 대단한: *monumental stupidity* 엄청난 어리석음

moo /mu/ *n* the sound that a cow makes ‖ 암소가 내는 소리. 음매 — **moo** *v* [I]

mooch /mutʃ/ *v* [T] INFORMAL to get something by asking someone to give it to you instead of paying for it yourself ‖ 대가를 치르지 않고 남에게 어떤 것을 달라고 청해서 얻다. 구걸하다. (보시를) 청하다. 우려내다. 등쳐먹다: *Tim's always mooching my cigarettes.* 팀은 항상 내 담배를 얻어 피운다.

mood /mud/ *n* **1** the way you feel at a particular time, or the way a group of people feel ‖ 특정한 때에 사람이 느끼는 상태, 또는 일단의 사람들이 느끼는 상태. 기분. 심정. 분위기: *You're certainly in a good/bad mood today.* 너는 오늘 확실히 기분이 좋다[언짢다]. / *The mood after the game was one of extreme*

gloom. 경기 후의 분위기는 지극히 우울한 분위기였다. **2 be in the mood** to want to do something or feel that you would enjoy doing something ‖ 어떤 일 하기를 바라거나 어떤 일 하는 것을 즐기고 싶어하다. …할 마음이 되어 있다. …할 기분이다: *Are you in the mood for a walk?* 걷고 싶니?

mood·y /ˈmudi/ *adj* **1** having MOODs that change often and quickly, especially angry or bad moods ‖ 특히 화를 내거나 기분이 좋지 않아 자주·신속하게 기분이 바뀌는. 변덕스러운: *a moody teenager* 변덕스러운 10대 **2** making people feel particular MOODs ‖ 사람들에게 특정한 기분을 느끼게 하는. 시무룩한. 침울한: *moody music* 우울한 음악

moon¹ /mun/ *n* **1 the moon** the round object that can be seen shining in the sky at night ‖ 밤에 하늘에서 밝게 볼 수 있는 둥근 물체. 달 **2** [singular] the shape of this object as it appears at a particular time ‖ 특정한 시간에 나타나는 이 물체의 형상. 달: *There's no moon tonight.* (=it cannot be seen) 오늘 밤에는 달이 안 보인다. / *a full moon* (=the moon appearing as a full circle) 보름달 **3** a large round object that moves around PLANETs other than the earth ‖ 지구 이외의 행성 근처에서 운행하는 커다란 둥근 물체. 위성: *Saturn has several moons.* 토성은 여러 개의 위성을 가지고 있다. — see also **once in a blue moon** (ONCE¹) — see picture at ORBIT¹

moon² *v* [I, T] INFORMAL to bend over and show your uncovered BUTTOCKs to someone as a rude joke ‖ 무례한 장난으로 몸을 굽혀서 벌거벗은 엉덩이를 남에게 보이다. 엉덩이를 드러내다

moon over sb/sth *phr v* [T] INFORMAL to spend your time thinking about someone or something that you love ‖ 사랑하는 사람 또는 사물에 대해 생각하면서 시간을 보내다. 곰곰이 …하면서 시간을 보내다: *She's been mooning over his photograph for hours.* 그녀는 몇 시간 동안 그의 사진을 보면서 멍하니 시간을 보내고 있다.

moon·beam /ˈmunbim/ *n* a beam of light from the moon ‖ 달에서 나오는 한 줄기 빛. 달빛

moon·less /ˈmunlɪs/ *adj* without the moon showing in the sky ‖ 하늘에 달이 보이지 않는: *a cloudy moonless night* 구름 낀, 달이 없는 밤

moon·light¹ /ˈmunlaɪt/ *n* [U] the light of the moon ‖ 달빛

moonlight² *v* [I] INFORMAL to have a

second job in addition to your main job ‖ 본업에 추가로 제2의 직업을 가지다. (야간의) 아르바이트를 하다. 겹치기로 일하다: *Clayton's been moonlighting as a security guard.* 클레이턴은 야간에 경비로 아르바이트를 하고 있다. – **moonlighting** *n* [U] – **moonlighter** *n*

moon·lit /'mun,lɪt/ *adj* made brighter by the light of the moon ‖ 달빛으로 더 밝은. 달빛에 비친: *a beautiful moonlit night* 아름다운 달 밝은 밤

moor /mʊr/ *v* [I, T] to fasten a ship or boat to the land or the bottom of the sea, lake etc. with a rope or chain ‖ 밧줄이나 쇠사슬로 선박 또는 소형 배를 육지나 해저(海底)·호수 등에 매어두다. 계류하다. 정박하다[시키다]

moor·ing /'mʊrɪŋ/ *n* the place where a ship or boat MOORs ‖ 선박이나 소형 배가 정박하는 장소. 정박지. 계류소

moose /mus/ *n* a large wild North American, European, or Asian animal with large ANTLERs (=flat horns that look like branches) and a head like a horse ‖ 가지진 넓적한 뿔과, 말과 같은 머리를 가진 북미[유럽, 아시아]산의 큰 야생 동물. 무스. 큰사슴

moot /mut/ *adj* 1 question or point that is moot is one that has not yet been decided, and about which people have different opinions ‖ 질문이나 요점이 아직 결정되지 않고 사람들이 그것에 대해 각기 다른 견해를 가진. 논쟁 중인. 미해결의: *Whether these laws will really reduce violent crime is a moot point.* 이 법률이 실제로 강력 범죄를 감소시킬 것인지에 대해서는 의문이다. 2 a situation or possible action that is moot is no longer likely to happen or exist, or is no longer important ‖ 상황이나 가능한 조치가 더 이상 발생하거나 존재할 것 같지 않거나 또는 더 이상 중요하지 않은: *Questions about planning the project are moot, because there is no money to finance it.* 거기에 출자할 자금이 없기 때문에 그 사업 계획에 대한 의문은 이미 중요한 것이 아니다.

mop¹ /mɑp/ *n* 1 a thing for washing floors, made of a long stick with threads of thick string or a piece of SPONGE fastened to one end ‖ 굵은 줄의 실이 달린 긴 막대 또는 한쪽 끝에 스펀지를 고착시킨 마루를 닦는 물건. 대걸레 2 INFORMAL a large amount of thick messy hair ‖ 많은 분량의 굵고 엉성한 머리털. 머리털의 뭉치: *a mop of curly hair* 곱슬더벅머리

mop² *v* **-pped, -pping** [T] 1 to wash a floor with a wet MOP ‖ 젖은 대걸레로 마루를 닦다 2 to remove liquid from a surface by rubbing it with a cloth or something soft ‖ 천이나 부드러운 것으로 문질러서 표면에서 액체를 제거하다. 훔치다: *Earl mopped the sweat from his face.* 얼은 얼굴의 땀을 닦았다.

mop sth ↔ **up** *phr v* [T] to clean liquid off a surface using a mop, cloth, or something soft ‖ 대걸레[천, 부드러운 것]를 사용하여 표면의 액체를 깨끗이 닦아내다. 훔쳐내다: *Can you mop up the milk you've spilled?* 네가 흘린 우유를 훔쳐내겠니?

mope /moʊp/ *v* [I] to pity yourself and feel sad, without making any effort to be more cheerful ‖ 더 활기를 띠려는 노력을 하지 않고 자신을 동정하고 슬퍼하다. 우울해지다. 의기소침하다: *Don't just sit there moping – go out and play!* 의기소침해서 거기 그렇게 앉아 있지만 말고 나가서 놀아라!

mope around *phr v* [I, T] to do nothing because you are sad and you pity yourself ‖ 슬프고 자신이 측은해서 아무것도 하지 않다. 풀이 죽어서 …을 정처없이 걸어다니다. 헤매다: *Since Jerry left, she's just been moping around the house.* 제리가 떠나서 그녀는 그저 집 주변을 헤매고 있었다.

mo·ped /'moʊpɛd/ *n* a vehicle like a bicycle with a small engine ‖ 작은 엔진이 부착된 자전거 비슷한 차량. 모터 달린 자전거

mor·al¹ /'mɔrəl, 'mɑrəl/ *adj* 1 relating to the principles of what is right and wrong, and the difference between good and evil ‖ 무엇이 옳고 그른지 그리고 선(善)과 악(惡)의 차이가 무엇인지에 대한 원칙에 관한. 도덕(상)의. 선악의 판단에 관한: *Terry refused to join the army for moral reasons.* 테리는 도덕상의 이유로 입대를 거부했다 / *a woman of high moral standards* 도덕 수준이 높은 여자 / *a moral responsibility/duty to help the poor* 가난한 사람을 돕는 도의적 책임[의무] —opposite IMMORAL 2 **moral support** encouragement that you give by expressing approval or interest, rather than by giving practical help ‖ 실제적인 도움을 주기보다는 인정 또는 관심을 나타내어서 보내 주는 격려. 정신적인 원조 3 **moral victory** a situation in which you show that your beliefs are right and fair, or that you are the most skillful, even if you do not win the argument, game etc. ‖ 자신의 신념이 옳고 공정하다는 것, 또는 비록 논쟁·경기

등에서 이기지는 못했더라도 자신의 능력이 최고라는 것을 나타내는 상황. 정신적 승리 **4** always behaving in a way that is based on strong principles about what is right and wrong ‖ 항상 무엇이 옳고 그른지에 대한 강한 원칙에 근거하여 행동하는. 사람의 도리에서 벗어나지 않는. 도덕적인. 정숙한: *a moral man* 품행이 방정한 사람

moral² *n* a practical lesson about how to behave, that you learn from a story or from something that happens to you ‖ 이야기 또는 자신에게 일어난 일로부터 배운, 어떻게 행동할 것인가에 대한 실제적인 교훈. 우의(寓意): *The moral of the story is that crime doesn't pay.* 그 이야기의 교훈은 범죄가 이롭지 않다는 것이다. —see also MORALS

mo·rale /mə'ræl/ *n* [U] the level of confidence and positive feelings a person or group has, especially a group that works together, belongs to the same team etc. ‖ 특히, 함께 일하거나 같은 팀 등에 속한 개인이나 집단이 가지고 있는 신뢰감과 자신감의 수준. 사기. 기세: *Rumors of job losses are bad for morale.* 실업에 대한 소문들은 사기에 좋지 않다.

mor·al·ist·ic /ˌmɔrə'lɪstɪk, ˌmɑr-/ *adj* having very strong and fixed beliefs about what is right and wrong and about how people should behave ‖ 무엇이 옳고 그른지 그리고 사람이 어떻게 행동해야 하는지에 대한 매우 강하고 확고한 신념을 가진. 도학적인. 교훈적인 – **moralist** /'mɔrəlɪst, 'mɑ-/ *n*

mo·ral·i·ty /mə'ræləti/ *n* [U] **1** beliefs or ideas about what is right and wrong and about how people should behave ‖ 무엇이 옳고 그른지 그리고 사람이 어떻게 행동해야 하는지에 대한 신념 또는 견해. 도덕적임. 덕성: *declining standards of morality* 낮아지는 도덕 기준 **2** the degree to which something is right or acceptable ‖ 어떤 것이 옳고 또는 받아들일 수 있는지에 대한 정도. 도덕성: *a discussion on the morality of the death penalty* 사형 제도의 도덕성에 관한 논의

mor·al·ize /'mɔrəˌlaɪz, 'mɑr-/ *v* [I] DISAPPROVING to tell other people your ideas about right and wrong behavior and about how people should behave ‖ 옳고 그른 행동과 사람들이 어떻게 행동해야 하는지에 대한 자신의 견해를 다른 사람들에게 말하다. 도덕적 관점에서 말하다. 설교하다

mor·al·ly /'mɔrəli, 'mɑr-/ *adv* **1** according to moral principles about what is right and wrong ‖ 무엇이 옳고 그른지에 대한 도덕적인 기준에 따라서. 도덕적으로. 도덕적인 의미로: *It wasn't actually against the law, but it was morally wrong.* 그것은 법에는 실제적으로 위반되지 않았으나 도덕적으로 그릇된 것이었다. **2** in a way that is good and right ‖ 선악의 관점에서. 도덕적인 의미로: *the difficulty of behaving morally in a corrupt society* 부패 사회에서 올바르게 행동하기 어려움

mor·als /'mɔrəlz, 'mɑr-/ *n* [plural] principles or standards of good behavior, especially in matters of sex ‖ 특히 성적 문제에서의 좋은 행동의 원칙 또는 기준. 품행. (남녀간의) 행실: *His book reflects the morals and customs of the time.* 그의 책에는 그 시대의 성도덕과 관행이 반영되어 있다.

mo·rass /mə'ræs/ *n* [singular] **1** a complicated and confusing situation that is very difficult to get out of ‖ 벗어나기 매우 어려운 복잡하고 혼란스러운 상태. 곤경. 곤궁. 난국: *California's economic morass* 캘리포니아의 경제 난국 **2** a complicated amount of information ‖ 이해하기 어려운 정보: *a morass of details* 이해하기 어려운 세부 사항

mor·a·to·ri·um /ˌmɔrə'tɔriəm, ˌmɑr-/ *n* [C usually singular] an official announcement stopping an activity for a period of time ‖ 일정 기간 활동을 정지하라는 공적인 선언. 일시 정지: *a moratorium on nuclear weapons testing* 핵무기 실험의 일시 정지

mor·bid /'mɔrbɪd/ *adj* having a strong and unhealthy interest in unpleasant subjects, especially death ‖ 불쾌한 주제 특히 죽음에 대한 강하고 불건전한 관심을 가진. (정신이) 병적인. 병적으로 과민한: *a morbid interest in fatal diseases* 불치병에 대한 병적인 관심 – **morbidly** *adv*

more¹ /mɔr/ *adv* **1** used before many adjectives and adverbs that have two or more SYLLABLEs in order to make the COMPARATIVE form ‖ 비교급을 만들기 위해 음절이 둘 이상인 많은 형용사·부사의 앞에 쓰여. 더 많이[크게]: *My meal was more expensive than Dan's.* 나의 식사는 댄의 것보다 더 비쌌다. / *You'll have to be more careful next time.* 너는 다음 번에는 더욱 주의를 기울여야 하겠다. / *The students will feel much more confident if they work in groups.* 학생들은 집단 내에서 활동하면 더 많은 자신감을 갖게 될 것이다. / *The troops were becoming more and more tired as the* *weeks went on.* 그 부대 병사들은 몇 주가 지나면서 더욱 더 지쳐가고 있었다. — opposite LESS² **2** happening a greater number of times or for longer ‖ 더 많은 횟수로 또는 더 오래 발생하는. …보다 이상으로. 조금 더: *I promised Mom I'd help her more with the housework.* 나는 가사 일을 조금 더 도와 드리겠다고 어머니에게 약속했다. / *We see our grandchildren more than we used to.* 우리는 전보다 더 자주 손자를 만난다. / *He goes out a lot more now that he has a car.* 그는 자동차가 있으니까 빈번하게 외출한다. —opposite LESS¹ **3 not...any more** used in order to show that something that used to happen or be true does not happen or is not true now ‖ 발생해 왔거나 사실이었던 것이 이제는 일어나지도 않고 사실도 아닌 것을 나타내는 데에 쓰여. 이제[더 이상]…하지 않다[아니다]: *Sarah doesn't live here any more.* 사라는 이제 여기에 살지 않는다. —see also ANY², ANYMORE, **once more** (ONCE¹) —see study note on page 931

USAGE NOTE more

Use **more** as the opposite of both "less" and "fewer": *I think I'll need more money. / There were more people there than yesterday.* If an adjective has more than one syllable, you should usually use **more** instead of a COMPARATIVE form of the adjective: *He's more intelligent than the others.* ✗DON'T SAY "intelligenter."✗

"less"와 "fewer"의 반대말로 **more**가 쓰인다: 내 생각에 나는 돈이 더 필요할 것이다. / 거기에는 어제보다 더 많은 사람들이 있었다. 만일 형용사가 1음절 이상이라면 보통 형용사의 비교급보다는 **more**를 써야 한다: 그는 다른 사람들보다 더 영리하다. "intelligenter"라고는 하지 않는다.

---

more² *quantifier* [the comparative of "many" and "much" "many"와 "much"의 비교급] **1** a greater amount or number ‖ 양이 더 많거나 수가 더 큰: *There were more accidents on the highways this year than last year.* 금년에는 작년보다 고속도로에서 더 많은 사고가 발생했다. / *They haven't been gone more than 2 or 3 days.* 그들은 이삼일 이상을 가지 않고 있다. / *These days, more and more people travel long distances in their jobs.* 오늘날, 더 많은 사람들이 업무상으로 장거리 여행을 한다.

2 an additional number or amount ‖ 추가한 수 또는 양. 그 이상의. 더 많은: *Would you like some more coffee?* 커피를 좀 드릴까요? / *I have to make a few more phone calls.* 나는 전화를 몇 번 더 해야 돼. / *We had 5/12/20 more people at the meeting than we expected.* 그 회의에는 우리가 예상했던 것보다 5[12, 20]명의 사람들이 더 왔다. **3 more or less** almost ‖ 거의. 대체로. 사실상: *This report says more or less the same thing as the other one.* 이 보고서는 다른 것과 대체로 같은 내용이 쓰여 있다.

more·o·ver /mɔr'ouvɚ/ *adv* FORMAL a word meaning "in addition to this," that is used in order to add information to something that has just been said ‖ 방금 말한 것에 정보를 추가하는 데에 쓰여 "이것에 추가하여"란 의미를 가진 어휘. 게다가. 더욱이. 더구나: *A new design would not be acceptable, and, moreover, would delay the project even further.* 새 디자인은 받아들일 수 없는데다가 그 프로젝트를 한 층 더 지체시킬 것이다.

mo·res /'mɔreɪz/ *n* [plural] FORMAL the customs, social behavior, and moral values of a particular group ‖ 특정한 집단의 관습·사회적 행동·도덕적 가치. (사회의) 관례: *American social mores* 미국인의 사회적 관습

morgue /mɔrg/ *n* a building or room where dead bodies are kept before they are buried or burned ‖ 사체를 매장하거나 화장하기 전에 보관하는 건물, 또는 방. 영안실. 시체 안치소

Mor·mon /'mɔrmən/ *adj* relating to a religious organization called The Church of Jesus Christ of Latter-Day Saints, that has strict moral rules such as not allowing its members to drink alcohol and coffee ‖ 교도들에게 술·커피를 금지하는 등 엄격한 도덕적 계율을 갖고 있는 말일 성도 예수 그리스도교라고 부르는 종교 조직에 관한. 모르몬교(도)의 – **Mormon** *n* – **Mormonism** *n* [U]

morn·ing /'mɔrnɪŋ/ *n* **1** [C, U] the early part of the day, especially from when the sun rises until the middle of the day ‖ 특히 해가 솟아서 하루의 중간까지의 하루의 앞부분. 아침. 오전: *I got a letter from Wayne this morning.* 나는 오늘 오전 웨인한테서 편지 한 통을 받았다. / *The freeway is usually jammed in the morning.* 고속도로는 보통 아침에는 막힌다. **2 (Good) Morning** SPOKEN said in order to greet someone when you meet him/her in the morning ‖ 아침에 사람을 만났을 때 남에게 인사하는 데에 쓰

여. 안녕하세요: *Morning, Rick.* 릭, 안녕
하세요.

morning sick·ness /ˈ.. ˌ../ *n* [U] a
feeling of sickness that some women
have when they are going to have a
baby ‖ 임신하게 될 때 일부 여성들이 겪
는 구토의 느낌. (입덧 같은) 아침의 구토
증

mo·ron /ˈmɔrɑn/ *n* someone who is
very stupid ‖ 매우 우둔한 사람. 바보 –
moronic /məˈrɑnɪk/ *adj*

mo·rose /məˈroʊs/ *adj* unhappy, silent,
and having a bad temper ‖ 불만스럽고
조용하며 나쁜 성미를 지닌. 시무룩한. 기
분이 언짢은 – **morosely** *adv*

mor·phine /ˈmɔrfin/ *n* [U] a powerful
drug used for stopping pain ‖ 통증을 멈
추게 하는 데에 쓰이는 강력한 약. 모르핀

morph·ing /ˈmɔrfɪŋ/ *n* [U] a computer
method that is used in order to make
one image gradually change into a
different one ‖ 한 이미지를 서서히 전혀
다른 이미지로 변화시키는 데에 쓰이는 컴
퓨터 그래픽 기법. 모핑 – **morph** *v* [I,
T]

Morse code /ˌmɔrs ˈkoʊd/ *n* [U] a
system of sending messages in which
the alphabet is represented by short
and long signals of sound or light ‖ 소리
나 빛의 짧고 긴 신호로 알파벳을 나타내
어 메시지를 발신하는 방식. 모스식 (전
신) 부호

mor·sel /ˈmɔrsəl/ *n* a small piece of
food ‖ 소량의 음식 조각. 한 입. 한 조각:
a morsel of bread 빵 한 조각

mor·tal¹ /ˈmɔrtl/ *adj* **1** not living for
ever ‖ 영원히 살지 않는. 죽을 운명의:
mortal creatures 죽음을 면할 수 없는 생
명체 —opposite IMMORTAL **2 mortal
injuries/blow/danger etc.** injuries etc.
that will cause death or are likely to
cause death ‖ 죽음을 초래하거나 죽음을
초래하기 쉬운 부상 등. 치명적인 부상/타
격/위험 **3 mortal fear/terror/dread**
extreme fear ‖ 극심한 공포. 극도의 두려
움/공포/불안 – **mortally** *adv*

mortal² *n* **1 lesser/ordinary/mere
mortals** HUMOROUS an expression
meaning ordinary people, as compared
with people who are more important or
more powerful ‖ 더 중요하거나 세력 있는
사람과 비교하여 보통 사람을 의미하는 표
현. 덜 중요한/평범한/비정한 인간 **2**
LITERARY a human ‖ 인간

mor·tal·i·ty /mɔrˈtæləti/ *n* [U] **1** also
mortality rate the number of deaths
during a particular period of time
among a particular group of people or

from a particular cause ‖ 특정한 집단 중
에서 또는 특정한 원인으로 특정 기간 동
안 사망한 사람의 수. 사망률: *a decrease
in the infant mortality rate* (=the rate
at which babies die) 유아 사망률의 감소
2 the condition of being human and
having to die ‖ 사람으로 태어나 죽어야
하는 사정. 죽을 운명

mor·tar /ˈmɔrtə/ *n* **1** a heavy gun that
fires explosives in a high curve ‖ 높은 곡
선을 그리면서 폭약을 발사하는 중포(重
砲). 박격포 **2** [U] a mixture of LIME,
sand, and water, used in building for
joining bricks or stones together ‖ 벽돌
또는 돌을 함께 접합하기 위해 건축에 사
용되는 석회·모래·물의 혼합물. 모르타르

mor·tar·board /ˈ.. ˌ./ *n* a cap with a
flat square top that you wear when you
GRADUATE from a HIGH SCHOOL or
university ‖ 고등학교나 대학을 졸업할 때
에 쓰는 꼭대기가 평평한 사각형 모자. 사
각모

mort·gage¹ /ˈmɔrgɪdʒ/ *n* **1** an
agreement in which you borrow money
from a bank in order to buy a house,
and pay back the money over a period
of years ‖ 주택을 구입하기 위해 은행에서
융자를 받아 수년 뒤에 자금을 상환하는
계약. 저당: *We've taken out a mortgage*
(=borrowed money for a mortgage) *on a
new house.* 우리는 새 집을 저당 잡히고
융자를 받았다. **2** the amount of money
lent on a mortgage ‖ 저당으로 빌린 금액:
a mortgage of $100,000 저당 차용액 10
만 달러

mortgage² *v* [T] to borrow money by
giving someone, usually a bank, the
right to own your house, land, or
property if you do not pay back the
money he, she, or it lent you within a
certain period of time ‖ 만일 일정한 기간
내에 빌린 돈을 상환하지 못할 경우에 나
의 주택[토지, 재산]의 소유권을 다른 사
람 대개 은행에 양도함으로써 자금을 빌리
다. 저당 잡히다. 담보로서 양도하다: *We
mortgaged the house to pay for Sarah's
college education.* 우리는 사라의 대학 등
록금을 마련하려고 집을 저당 잡혔다.

mor·ti·cian /mɔrˈtɪʃən/ *n* someone
whose job is to arrange funerals and
prepare bodies before they are buried ‖
장례식을 준비하고 매장 전에 시신을 수습
하는 직업인. 장의사

mor·ti·fy /ˈmɔrtəˌfaɪ/ *v* **be mortified** to
feel extremely embarrassed or ashamed
‖ 매우 당황하거나 부끄러움을 느끼다. …
으로[에 의해] 굴욕감을 느끼다. 분함을
느끼다: *I was mortified by my father's*

behavior. 나는 아버지의 행동으로 굴욕감을 느꼈다. — **mortifying** *adj* — **mortification** /ˌmɔrtəfə'keɪʃən/ *n* [U]

mor·tu·ar·y /'mɔrtʃu,ɛri/ *n* the place where a body is kept before a funeral and where the funeral is sometimes held || 장례식 이전에 시신을 보관하고 때로는 장례식이 행해지는 장소. 장의실. 시체 안치소. 영안실

mo·sa·ic /mou'zeɪ-ɪk/ *n* [C, U] a pattern or picture made by fitting together small pieces of colored stone, glass etc. || 채색된 돌·유리 등의 작은 조각을 함께 끼워 맞춰 만든 무늬 또는 그림. 모자이크: *a Roman stone mosaic floor* 고대 로마 양식의 돌 모자이크 바닥

mosaic

mo·sey /'mouzi/ *v* [I] INFORMAL to walk somewhere in a slow relaxed way || 천천히 느긋하게 어딘가로 걸어가다. 어슬렁거리며 걷다. 발을 끌면서 걷다: *I guess I'll mosey on down to the store now.* 내 생각에 지금 가게까지 발을 질질 끌면서 걸어갈 것 같다.

mosey along *phr v* [I] to leave || 떠나다: *It's getting late; we'd better mosey along.* 늦어서 급히 떠나는 것이 좋겠다.

Mos·lem /'mazləm, 'mas-/ *n* ⇨ MUSLIM

mosque /mask/ *n* a building where Muslims go to have religious services || 회교도가 예배하러 가는 건물. 회교 사원

mosquito net /.'.. ./ a net which is placed over a bed as a protection against mosquitos || 모기에 대한 방어책으로 침대 위에 설치하는 그물. 모기장

mos·qui·to /mə'skitou/ *n* a small flying insect that bites and sucks the blood of people and animals, making you ITCH and sometimes spreading diseases || 사람·동물을 물고 피를 빨아서 가렵게 하고 때로는 질병을 확산시키는 작은 날아다니는 곤충. 모기

moss /mɔs/ *n* [U] a small flat green or yellow plant that looks like fur and often grows on trees and rocks || 털처럼 생긴, 종종 나무·바위에서 자라는 푸르거나 노란 색의 작고 납작한 식물. 이끼 — **mossy** *adj*

most¹ /moust/ *adv* **1** used before many adjectives and adverbs that have two or more SYLLABLEs in order to make the SUPERLATIVE form || 최상급을 만들기 위해 2음절 이상의 많은 형용사와 부사 앞에 쓰여. 가장. 최상으로: *I think Anna is one of the most beautiful women I know.* 내 생각에 애너는 내가 아는 가장 아름다운 여자 중의 한 명이다. / *I forgot to tell you the most important thing!* 네게 말할 가장 중요한 것을 깜빡했어! / *This style of management is most frequently used in Japan.* 이 경영 방식은 일본에서 가장 흔히 사용된다. **2** more than anything else || 다른 어떤 것보다 많이. 매우. 대단히: *She liked the dark beer most.* 그는 흑맥주를 가장 좋아했다. / *I was angry at her, but, most of all I felt sad that the marriage was over.* 나는 그녀에게 화가 났지만 무엇보다도 결혼 생활이 끝장났다는 것이 슬펐다. **3** SPOKEN NONSTANDARD almost || 거의: *We eat at Joe's most every weekend.* 우리는 거의 주말마다 조의 집에서 식사를 한다. —see study note on page 931

most² *quantifier* [the superlative of "many" and "much" || "many"와 "much"의 최상급] **1** almost all of a particular group of people or things || 사람이나 사물의 특정한 집단의 거의 모두. 대부분의: *Most of the kids I know have parents who are divorced.* 내가 아는 대다수 어린이들의 부모는 이혼했다. / *Most computers have two disk drives.* 대다수의 컴퓨터는 디스크 드라이브를 두 개 갖고 있다. **2** more than anyone or anything else || 다른 어떤 사람 또는 물건보다 많은. (수에 대하여) 가장 많은: *Ricardo's restaurant gives you the most food for your money.* 리카도의 식당은 네가 지불한 돈에 비해서 가장 많은 음식을 제공한다. / *Diane had the most to say of all of us.* (=she said more than everyone else) 다이앤은 우리 중에서 가장 많은 말을 했다. **3** the largest number or amount of something || 사물의 최대 수 또는 분량. 최대의. 최고의. 가장 많은. 큰: *He spent most of his time in Milwaukee.* 그는 밀워키에서 가장 많은 시간을 보냈다. / *How can we get the most power from the engine?* 어떻게 하면 우리가 엔진에서 최대의 동력을 얻을 수 있을까? **4** at (the) most used in order to say that a number or amount will not be larger than you say || 어떤 수·분량이 말한 것보다는 크지 않을 것이라는 것을 말하는 데에 쓰여. 고작. 많아야. …에 지나지 않는: *The book should cost $10 or $12 at the most.* 그 책은 10달러나 기껏해야 12달러 정도 할 것이다. **5** for the most part used in order to say that something is generally true or usually happens, but not always || 어떤 것이 일반적으로 사실이거나 일상적으로

발생하지만 항상 그렇지는 않다는 것을 말하는 데에 쓰여. 주로. 대개. 보통: *Everyone was talking except for Grandpa who, for the most part, was silent.* 보통 침묵을 지키시던 할머니를 제외하고는 모두들 말하고 있었다. **6 make the most of sth** to get the most advantage that is possible from a situation ‖ 어떤 상황에서 가능한 한 최대의 이득을 얻다. (기회·시간·재능 등을) 최대한으로 활용하다: *You'll have to make the most of the small amount of information you have.* 너는 네가 가지고 있는 소량의 정보를 최대한으로 활용해야 할 것이다.

most·ly /'moustli/ *adv* in most cases, or most of the time ‖ 대개의 경우나 대부분의 시간에. 대부분. 거의 모두: *Mostly, he travels by car or in his own plane.* 대개 그는 그의 자동차나 전용 비행기로 여행한다. / *The room was full of athletes, mostly football players.* 그 방은 운동 선수들, 특히 대부분 축구 선수들로 가득했다. ✗DON'T SAY "mostly all," "mostly everybody," etc. SAY "almost all," "almost everybody," etc.✗ "mostly all"·"mostly everybody"라고 하지 않고 "almost all"·"almost everybody"라고 한다.

mo·tel /mou'tɛl/ *n* a hotel for people traveling by car, with a place for the car near each room ‖ 각각의 방 가까이에 주차 공간이 딸려 있는 자동차 여행자를 위한 호텔. 모텔

moth /mɔθ/ *n* an insect similar to a BUTTERFLY that usually flies at night, especially toward lights ‖ 보통 밤에, 특히 불빛을 향해 날아가는 나비와 유사한 곤충. 나방

moth·ball[1] /'mɔθbɔl/ *n* a small ball made of a strong-smelling chemical, used for keeping MOTHs away from clothes ‖ 옷에서 옷좀나방을 쫓기 위해 쓰는 강한 냄새가 나는 화학제품으로 만든 작은 공 모양의 것. 좀약. 둥근 방충제

mothball[2] *v* [T] INFORMAL to close a factory or operation, and keep all its equipment or plans for a long time without using them ‖ 공장을 폐쇄하거나 작업을 중단하여 그 모든 장비 또는 계획을 장기간 사용하지 않고 두다. (공장 등을) 폐쇄한 채로 보존하다: *Our Denver factory is now mothballed.* 우리의 덴버 공장은 지금 폐쇄하여 장기 보존 상태에 있다.

moth-eat·en /'. ,../ *adj* **1** clothing that is moth-eaten has holes eaten in it by moths ‖ 옷좀 나방이 먹어서 옷에 구멍이 난. (옷이) 좀먹은 **2** old and in bad condition ‖ 낡고 상태가 나쁜: *a moth-eaten old chair* 낡고 오래된 의자

moth·er[1] /'mʌðɚ/ *n* **1** a female parent ‖ 여성 부모. 어머니: *My mother said I have to be home by 9:00.* 나의 어머니는 내가 9시까지는 집에 와야 한다고 말씀하셨다. / *Mother, can I have some ice cream?* 어머니, 제가 아이스크림 좀 먹어도 될까요? / *a mother hen and her chicks* 암탉과 그 병아리 —see picture at FAMILY **2** SPOKEN something that is very large ‖ 매우 큰 사물. 최대: *a real mother of a car* 아주 큰 자동차 **3** SPOKEN something that is a very good or very bad example of its type ‖ 그 유형의 아주 좋은 또는 아주 나쁜 사례의 것: *I woke up with the mother of all hangovers.* 나는 숙취가 너무 심해 잠을 깼다.

mother[2] *v* [T] to take care of and protect someone in the way that a mother does ‖ 어머니가 하는 방식으로 다른 사람을 돌보고 보호하다. 과보호로 돌보다: *Tom resented being constantly mothered by his wife.* 톰은 그의 부인이 어머니처럼 사건건건 과보호로 돌보는 것에 화가 났다.

moth·er·board /'mʌðɚ,bɔrd/ *n* TECHNICAL the main CIRCUIT BOARD inside a computer ‖ 컴퓨터 내의 주(主) 회로기판. 머더보드

moth·er·hood /'mʌðɚ,hʊd/ *n* [U] the state of being a mother ‖ 어머니가 되어 있는 상태. 모성. 어머니의 특성

mother-in-law /'.. ../ *n* the mother of your husband or wife ‖ 남편이나 처의 어머니. 시어머니. 장모 —see picture at FAMILY

moth·er·ly /'mʌðɚli/ *adj* typical of a kind or concerned mother ‖ 다정하거나 염려하는 어머니의 전형인. 어머니다운. 자애로운: *I remember Mrs. Sederman as a motherly woman who always had a cookie for us.* 나는 시더만 부인을 우리에게 항상 쿠키를 만들어주셨던 어머니 같은 분으로 기억한다.

Mother Na·ture /,.. '../ *n* [U] an expression used in order to talk about the force that controls and organizes the Earth, its weather, and the living creatures and plants on it ‖ 지구·지구의 날씨·지구상의 생물·식물을 통제하고 조직하는 힘에 대해 말하는 데에 쓰는 표현. 자연

mother-of-pearl /,.. '../ *n* [U] a pale-colored smooth shiny substance on the inside of some shells, used for making buttons, jewelry etc. ‖ 단추·보석

등을 만드는 데에 쓰이는 일부 조개의 안쪽에 있는 은백색의 매끄럽고 빛나는 물질. 진주층[모]

Mother's Day /'.. ,./ *n* a holiday in honor of mothers, celebrated in the US and Canada on the second Sunday of May ‖ 5월의 두 번째 일요일에 미국과 캐나다에서 거행되는 어머니들을 기리는 휴일. 어머니의 날

mo·tif /mou'tif/ *n* an idea, subject, or pattern that is regularly repeated and developed in a book, movie, work of art etc. ‖ 책·영화·예술 작품 등에서 규칙적으로 반복되고 전개되는 생각[주제, 형식]. 모티프. 동기

mo·tion¹ /'mouʃən/ *n* **1** [U] the process of moving, or the way that someone or something moves ‖ 움직이는 과정, 또는 사람이나 사물이 움직이는 방식. 운동. 움직임: *the gentle rolling motion of the ship* 배의 부드러운 좌우로의 흔들림 **2** a single movement of your head, hand etc. ‖ 머리·손 등의 한 번 움직임. 동작. 몸짓. 손짓: *He made a motion with his hand, as if to tell me to keep back.* 그는 나에게 물러서 있으라는 듯이 손짓을 했다. **3** a proposal that is made formally at a meeting and then decided on by voting ‖ 회의에서 공식적으로 작성되어 투표로 결정하는 제안. 동의. 발의. 제의: *The motion to increase the club's membership charges was passed/ carried by 15 votes to 10.* 클럽의 회비를 증액시키자는 제의는 15대 10의 표 차이로 가결되었다. **4 in slow motion** if something on television or in the movies is shown in slow motion, it is shown more slowly than usual so that all the actions can be clearly seen ‖ 텔레비전이나 영화에서 모든 동작들을 분명히 볼 수 있도록 보통 때보다 더 천천히 보여 주는. 느린 화면[동작]으로: *Let's look at that touchdown in slow motion.* 느린 화면으로 터치다운 장면을 보도록 합시다. **5 go through the motions** to do something because you have to do it, without being very interested in it ‖ 그다지 흥미는 없지만, 해야 하기 때문에 하다. 마지못해 …하다. …하는 시늉을 하다: *I thought they had a great marriage, but he says they've just been going through the motions for years.* 나는 그들이 결혼 생활을 잘한다고 생각했었지만 그는 자신들이 수년동안 그저 그런 척 해왔다고 말한다.

motion² *v* [I, T] to give someone directions or instructions by moving your head, hand etc. ‖ 머리·손 등을 움직여서 남에게 방향이나 지시 사항을 알리다. 몸짓[손짓]으로 신호하다: *The police officer motioned for me to stop the car.* 그 경찰관은 나에게 차를 세우라고 손짓을 했다.

mo·tion·less /'mouʃənlɪs/ *adj* not moving at all ‖ 전혀 움직이지 않는. 정지한. 가만히 있는

motion pic·ture /,.. '../ *n* ⇨ MOVIE

mo·ti·vate /'moutə,veɪt/ *v* [T] to be the reason that someone is willing or eager to do something ‖ 사람이 어떤 일을 기꺼이 하려 하거나 하기를 열망하는 이유가 되다. …에게 동기[자극]를 주다: *Every one of his actions is motivated by a desire for more power.* 그의 모든 행동은 더 많은 권력욕에 의해 자극을 받는다.

mo·ti·vat·ed /'moutə,veɪtɪd/ *adj* **1** very eager to do or achieve something ‖ 어떤 일을 하거나 성취하기를 열망하는. …하려는 의욕이 있는. 매우 적극적인: *an intelligent and highly motivated student* 지적이고 의욕이 넘치는 학생 **2** done for a particular reason ‖ 특정한 이유 때문에 행한. …의 동기가 있는: *The police believe the attack was racially motivated.* (=done because someone hates other races) 경찰은 그 공격이 인종적인 동기에서 비롯되었다고 생각한다. / *a politically motivated decision* (=done to gain an advantage in politics) 정치적 이유가 있는 결단

mo·ti·va·tion /,moutə'veɪʃən/ *n* **1** [U] eagerness and willingness to do something ‖ 어떤 것을 하고자 하는 열망·의지. 자발성. 적극성: *Jack is smart, but he lacks motivation.* 잭은 똑똑하지만 열의가 부족하다. **2** the reason why you want to do something ‖ 어떤 일을 하고 싶어하는 이유. 자극. 동기 부여: *the motivation for the lawsuit* 그 소송의 유인

mo·tive /'moutɪv/ *n* the reason that makes someone do something, especially when this reason is kept hidden ‖ 특히 그 이유가 숨겨져 있을 때에 남에게 어떤 것을 하게 하는 이유. 동기: *We believe that the motive for the murder was jealousy.* 우리는 그 살인의 동기가 질투였다고 믿는다.

mot·ley /'matli/ *adj* **a motley crew/bunch/assortment etc.** a group of people or other things that do not seem to belong together, especially people or things that you do not approve of ‖ 특히 좋게 보이지 않는 사람들이나 사물로 함께 속하는 것 같지 않은 일단의 사람들이나 다른 사물들. 수상쩍은 무리[떼]/잡다한 잡동사니

mo·tor¹ /ˈmoʊtɚ/ *n* the part of a machine that makes it work or move by changing power into movement ‖ 동력을 운동으로 바꾸어서 기계를 작동하게 하거나 움직이게 하는 기계의 일부분. 모터. 원동기: *The drill is powered by a small electric motor.* 이 드릴은 작은 전기 모터로 움직인다. —compare ENGINE

motor² *adj* using power provided by an engine ‖ 엔진이 제공하는 힘을 사용하는. 모터[원동기]로 움직이는: *a motor vehicle* 동력차

mo·tor·bike /ˈmoʊtɚˌbaɪk/ *n* a MOTORCYCLE, often a small one ‖ 종종 작은 오토바이. (소형) 오토바이

mo·tor·cade /ˈmoʊtɚˌkeɪd/ *n* a group of cars and other vehicles that travel together and surround a very important person's car ‖ 함께 이동하며 중요인사의 차량을 둘러싸는 일단의 차량과 다른 탈 것. 자동차 퍼레이드

mo·tor·cy·cle /ˈmoʊtɚˌsaɪkəl/ *n* a fast, usually large, two-wheeled vehicle with an engine ‖ 엔진과 보통 두 개의 큰 바퀴가 달려 있는 빠른 차(車). 오토바이 —see picture on page 943

motor home /ˌ.. ˈ./ *n* a large vehicle with beds, a kitchen etc. in it, used for traveling; RV ‖ 여행용으로 쓰이며 침대·부엌 등이 있는 큰 차(車). 이동 주택차; 麼 RV — compare MOBILE HOME

motor home

mo·tor·ist /ˈmoʊtərɪst/ *n* FORMAL someone who drives a car ‖ 차를 운전하는 사람. 자동차 운전자

mo·tor·ized /ˈmoʊtəˌraɪzd/ *adj* having an engine, especially when something does not usually have an engine ‖ 특히 어떤 사물에 엔진이 없는 것이 보통일 경우에 엔진을 가지고 있는. 모터[동력 장치]를 단[설치한]: *a motorized wheelchair* 모터가 달린 휠체어

mo·tor·mouth /ˈmoʊtɚˌmaʊθ/ *n* INFORMAL someone who talks too much ‖ 지나치게 많은 말을 하는 사람. 수다쟁이. 떠버리

motor scoot·er /ˈ.. ˌ../ *n* ⇨ SCOOTER

motor ve·hi·cle /ˌ.. ˈ.../ *n* FORMAL a car, bus, truck etc. ‖ 자동차·버스·트럭 등. 동력차

mot·tled /ˈmɑtld/ *adj* covered with patterns of light and dark colors of different shapes ‖ 다른 모양의 옅고 짙은 색깔의 무늬들로 덮인. 얼룩덜룩한. 반점이 있는: *a mottled brown snake* 얼룩덜룩한 갈색 뱀

mot·to /ˈmɑtoʊ/ *n* a short statement that expresses the aims or beliefs of a person, school, or institution ‖ 사람[학교, 기관]의 목표나 신념을 표현하는 짧은 말. 좌우명. 표어: *The school motto is "Never lose hope."* 그 학교의 교훈은 "절대로 희망을 잃지 마라"이다.

mound /maʊnd/ *n* **1** a pile of dirt, stones, sand etc. that looks like a small hill ‖ 작은 언덕처럼 보이는 한 무더기의 흙·돌·모래 등. 둔덕. 언덕 **2** a large pile of something ‖ 사물의 큰 더미: *a mound of papers* 서류 더미

mount¹ /maʊnt/ *v* **1** [I] also **mount up** to gradually increase in size or amount ‖ 크기나 양에서 점진적으로 증가하다. 늘다. 상승하다: *His debts continued to mount up.* 그의 부채가 나날이 늘어났다. **2** [T] to plan, organize, and begin an event or a course of action ‖ 행사나 행동의 절차를 계획·조직·시작하다. 준비[개시]하다: *mounting an attack on the enemy camp* 적진에 공격을 개시하기 **3** [I, T] FORMAL to get on a horse, bicycle etc. ‖ 말·자전거 등에 오르다. 타다. 태우다: *She mounted the horse and rode off.* 그녀는 말을 타고 달렸다. **4** [T] FORMAL to go up something such as a set of stairs ‖ 일련의 계단 등을 오르다: *Reporters shouted as Mayor Bradley mounted the steps of City Hall.* 기자들은 브래들리 시장이 시청의 계단을 오를 때 고함을 질렀다. **5** [T] to be attached to something and supported by it ‖ 사물에 부착되어 그것의 지탱을 받다. 끼우다. 붙이다. 박아 넣다: *I mounted his picture on a piece of stiff paper.* 나는 그의 사진을 빳빳한 종이 위에 붙였다.

mount² *n* **1 Mount** part of the name of a mountain ‖ 산 이름의 일부분. …산: *Mount Everest* 에베레스트 산 **2** LITERARY an animal, especially a horse, that you ride on ‖ 타는 동물, 특히 말

moun·tain /ˈmaʊntn/ *n* **1** a very high hill ‖ 아주 높은 언덕. 산: *climbing a mountain* 산에 오르기 **2** a very large pile or amount of something ‖ 어떤 것의 아주 큰 더미나 양. 산더미처럼 쌓인 것: *a mountain of work to do.* 산더미처럼 쌓인 해야 할 일 **3 make a mountain out of a molehill** to treat a problem as if it were very serious when in fact it is not ‖ 사실은 그렇지 않은데 아주 심각한 것처럼 문제를 다루다. 사소한 사건을 크게 떠들어대다. 침소 봉대하(여 말하)다

mountain bike /ˈ.. ˌ./ *n* a strong bicycle with wide thick tires ‖ 폭이 넓고 굵은 바퀴가 달린

두꺼운 타이어를 가진 튼튼한 자전거. 산
악 자전거

moun·tain·eer·ing /ˌmaʊntˈnˈɪrɪŋ/ n
[U] an outdoor activity in which you
climb mountains ‖ 산에 오르는 야외 활
동. 등산 - **mountaineer** n

mountain goat /ˈ.. ./ n an animal
that looks like a goat and lives in the
western mountains of North America ‖
염소처럼 생긴, 북미의 서부 산악 지대에
서 서식하는 동물. 야생 염소의 일종

mountain li·on /ˈ.. ˌ../ n ⇨ COUGAR

moun·tain·ous /ˈmaʊntˈn-əs/ adj
having a lot of mountains ‖ 많은 산을 가
지고 있는. 산이 많은. 산악성의: a
mountainous region of Europe 유럽의 산
악 지역

moun·tain·side /ˈmaʊntˈnˌsaɪd/ n the
side of a mountain ‖ 산의 사면. 산허리.
산등성이

moun·tain·top /ˈmaʊntˈnˌtɑp/ n the
top part of a mountain ‖ 산꼭대기. 산의
정상

Mount·ie /ˈmaʊnti/ n INFORMAL a
member of the national police force of
Canada ‖ 캐나다 경찰의 일원. 캐나다 기
마 경찰 대원

mount·ing /ˈmaʊntɪŋ/ adj gradually
increasing or becoming worse ‖ 점차 증
가하거나 악화되는: The Senator can
hardly ignore the mounting criticism. 그
상원의원은 점차 거세지는 비판을 도저히
무시할 수가 없다.

mourn /mɔrn/ v [I, T] to feel very sad
because someone has died, and show
this in the way you behave ‖ 사람이 죽어
서 매우 슬퍼하고 이것을 행동으로 나타내
보이다. 애도하다. 애통해하다: The whole
country mourned Kennedy's death. 전국
이 케네디의 죽음을 애도했다. / The old
woman still mourns for her son, 30
years after his death. 그 노부인은 30년
이 지난 지금까지 아들의 죽음을 애통해
한다.

mourn·er /ˈmɔrnɚ/ n someone who
attends a funeral, especially a relative
of the dead person ‖ 장례식에 참석하는
사람으로, 특히 죽은 사람의 친척. 조문[문
상]객

mourn·ful /ˈmɔrnfəl/ adj very sad ‖ 매
우 슬픈. 구슬픈. 슬픔에 잠긴: slow
mournful music 느리며 구슬픈 음악

mourn·ing /ˈmɔrnɪŋ/ n [U] 1 great
sadness because someone has died ‖ 어
떤 사람이 죽어서 대단히 슬픔. 비탄. 애
도: People wore black as a sign of
mourning. 사람들은 애도의 표시로 검은
옷을 입었다. 2 be in mourning to be

very sad because someone has died ‖ 어
떤 사람이 죽어서 매우 슬프다. 애도하다.
비통해하다: She's still in mourning for
her son. 그녀는 여전히 아들의 죽음을 비
통해 하고 있다.

mouse /maʊs/ n 1 a small object
connected to a computer, that you move
with your hand and press to give
commands to the computer ‖ 손으로 움
직이고 눌러서 컴퓨터에 명령을 할 수 있
도록 컴퓨터에 연결된 작은 물체. 마우스
2 plural **mice** a small animal like a rat
with smooth fur, a long tail, and a
pointed nose, that lives in buildings or
in fields ‖ 건물이나 들에 살며 부드러운
털·긴 꼬리·뾰족한 코를 가진 쥐처럼 생긴
작은 동물. 생쥐

mouse po·ta·to /ˈ. ˌ../ n, plural
mouse potatoes INFORMAL someone
who spends a lot of time playing on a
computer. This word developed form
the word 'COUCH POTATO' which means
someone who spends a lot of time
watching television. ‖ 컴퓨터를 실행하면
서 많은 시간을 보내는 사람을 말하며 텔
레비전을 보면서 많은 시간을 보내는 사람
을 뜻하는 'couch potato'에서 유래. 컴퓨
터광[중독자]

mousse /mus/ n [C, U] 1 a cold sweet
food made from a mixture of cream,
eggs, and fruit or chocolate ‖ 크림·계란·
과일이나 초콜릿을 섞어서 만든 차갑고 달
콤한 음식. 무스: chocolate mousse 초콜
릿 무스 2 a slightly sticky substance
that you put in your hair to make it
look thicker or to hold it in place ‖ 숱이
더 많아 보이게 하거나 위치를 고정시키기
위해 머리에 바르는 약간 끈적한 물질. 무
스

mous·tache /ˈmʌstæʃ, məˈstæʃ/ n ⇨
MUSTACHE

mous·y /ˈmaʊsi, -zi/ adj 1 mousy hair
is a dull brownish-gray color ‖ 머리카락
이 연한 갈색 빛이 도는 회색의. 쥐색의 2
a mousy girl or woman is small, quiet,
uninteresting, and unattractive ‖ 소녀나
여자가 작고 조용하며 흥미를 느끼게 하지
않고 매력이 없는

mouth[1] /maʊθ/ n 1 the part of your
face that you put food into, or that you
use for speaking ‖ 음식을 집어넣거나 말
할 때 사용하는 얼굴의 한 부위. 입 —see
picture at HEAD[1] 2 keep your mouth
shut INFORMAL to not say anything ‖ 아
무 말도 하지 않다. 입을 다물고 있다: I
was getting really mad, but I kept my
mouth shut. 나는 정말로 화가 치밀었지만
입을 다물고 있었다. 3 open/shut your

mouth to start to speak, or to stop speaking ‖ 말하기 시작하거나 멈추다. 입을 열다/다물다: *Everything was fine until you opened your mouth!* 네가 입을 열기 전까지는 모든 것이 다 좋았어! **4** an opening, entrance, or way out ‖ 열린 곳·입구·출구. 출입구. 어귀: *the mouth of a river* (=where it joins the sea) 강어귀 / *the mouth of a jar* 단지의 주둥이 **5 big mouth** INFORMAL someone who is a big mouth or has a big mouth often says things that s/he should not say ‖ 말해서는 안 되는 것을 종종 말하는 사람. 수다쟁이. 비밀 누설자 **6 make your mouth water** if food makes your mouth water, it looks so good you want to eat it immediately ‖ 음식이 아주 맛있어 보여서 즉시 먹고 싶어지다. 군침을 돌게 하다 — see also MOUTH-WATERING **7 open-mouthed/wide-mouthed etc.** with an open, wide etc. mouth ‖ 입을 크게 벌린 —see also **shoot your mouth off** (SHOOT¹)

mouth² /mauð/ *v* [T] **1** to move your lips as if you are saying words, but without making any sound ‖ 소리는 내지 않고 말을 하는 것처럼 입술을 움직이다. 입 모양으로 말하다: *When the teacher wasn't looking, Carter looked at me and mouthed "Don't laugh."* 선생님이 보지 않을 때 카터는 나를 보고서 "웃지 마"라고 입 모양으로 말했다. **2** to say things that you do not really believe or that you do not understand ‖ 정말로 믿지 않거나 이해하지 못하는 것을 말하다. 입으로만[형식적으로] 말하다: *people mouthing "politically correct" attitudes* "정치적으로 올바른" 태도에 대해 입으로만 떠들어 대는 사람들

mouth off *phr v* [I] INFORMAL to talk angrily or rudely to someone ‖ 남에게 화를 내며 또는 무례하게 말하다: *He was suspended for mouthing off to the principal.* 그는 교장에게 무례하게 말하다가 정학을 당했다.

mouth·ful /ˈmauθfʊl/ *n* **1** an amount of food or drink that you put into your mouth at one time ‖ 한번에 입에 넣을 수 있는 음식이나 음료의 양. 한 입 (분량): *I'm too full to eat another mouthful.* 난 너무 배불러서 한 입도 더 못 먹겠다. **2 a mouthful** INFORMAL a long word or phrase that is difficult to say ‖ 말하기 어려운 긴 단어나 구. 장황한 말: *Her real name is quite a mouthful, so we just call her Dee.* 그녀의 진짜 이름은 너무 길고 어려워서 우리는 그냥 디라고 부른다.

mouth·piece /ˈmauθpis/ *n* **1** the part of a musical instrument, telephone etc. that you put in your mouth or next to your mouth ‖ 입에 물거나 입 옆에 대는 악기·전화기 등의 일부분. 입에 대는 부분. 전화기의 송화구 **2** a person, newspaper etc. that expresses the opinions of a government or a political organization, especially without ever criticizing these opinions ‖ 특히 그 견해에 대한 아무 비판 없이 정부나 정치 조직의 견해를 그대로 표방하는 사람·신문 등. 대변자: *Pravda used to be the mouthpiece of the Communist Party.* 프라브다는 과거에 공산당의 대변자였다.

mouth·wash /ˈmauθwɑʃ, -wɔʃ/ *n* [C, U] a liquid used in order to make your mouth smell fresh or to get rid of an infection in your mouth ‖ 입을 상쾌하게 하거나 입 안의 감염체를 제거하는 데에 쓰이는 액체. 구강 청정제

mouth·wa·ter·ing /ˈ. ,.../ *adj* food that is mouth-watering looks or smells extremely good ‖ 음식이 매우 맛있어 보이거나 아주 좋은 냄새가 나는. 군침이 도는

mov·a·ble /ˈmuvəbəl/ *adj* able to be moved ‖ 움직일 수 있는: *toy soldiers with movable arms and legs* 팔과 다리를 움직일 수 있는 장난감 병정 —opposite IMMOVABLE

move¹ /muv/ *v*
1 ▶CHANGE POSITION 위치를 바꾸다◀ [I, T] to change from one place or position to another, or to make something do this ‖ 한 장소나 위치에서 다른 장소나 위치로 바꾸다, 또는 어떤 것을 이렇게 만들다. 움직이다. 이동하다[시키다]: *I saw the dog's leg move, so I knew he was alive.* 나는 개의 다리가 움직이는 것을 보고 살아 있다는 걸 알았다. / *He moved the chair into the corner of the room.* 그는 의자를 방구석으로 옮겼다. / *She could hear someone moving around in Gail's room.* 그녀는 게일의 방에서 누군가가 돌아다니는 소리를 들을 수 있었다.
2 ▶NEW PLACE 새로운 장소◀ [I, T] to go to a new place to live, work, or study, or to make someone do this ‖ 살기[일하기, 공부하기] 위해서 새로운 장소로 가다, 또는 누군가를 이렇게 하도록 하다. 이사[이전]하다[시키다]: *They moved to Atlanta in May.* 그들은 5월에 애틀랜타로 이사 갔다. / *The company is moving into larger offices next year.* 그 회사는 내년에 더 큰 사무실로 이전한다. / *They're moving Carrie into a different class next year.* 그들은 내년에

캐리를 다른 반으로 옮길 것이다.

3 ▶FEEL EMOTION 감정을 느끼다◀ [T] to make someone feel a strong emotion, especially sadness or sympathy ‖ 특히 남이 슬픔이나 동정의 강한 감정을 느끼게 하다. 감동시키다: *The story moved me to tears.* (=made me cry) 그 이야기는 나를 울렸다.

4 ▶PROGRESS 전 진 하 다 ◀ [I] to progress or change in a particular way ‖ 특정한 방향으로 전진하거나 변하다. 전 진[진보]하다. 진전되다: *He moved easily from teaching into admin- istration.* 그는 쉽게 교직에서 행정직으로 옮겼다.

5 get moving SPOKEN used in order to say that someone needs to hurry ‖ 사람이 서두를 필요가 있다고 말하는 데에 쓰여. 서두르다: *If you don't get moving, you'll miss the bus.* 서두르지 않으면 넌 버스를 놓칠 거야.

6 ▶START DOING STH 어떤 일을 하기 시작하다◀ [I] to start doing something in order to achieve something ‖ 무언가를 성취하기 위해서 어떤 일을 하기 시작하 다. 행동하다. 움직임을 보이다: *We'll have to move quickly if we want to give the report at the conference.* 회의에서 보고를 하고 싶다면 우린 빨리 행동에 옮겨야 한다. / *The Senate has not yet moved on* (=not done anything as a result of) *the suggestions from the committee.* 상원은 위원회의 제안에 아직 조치를 취하지 않았다.

7 ▶MEETING 회의◀ [I] FORMAL to make an official suggestion at a meeting ‖ 회의 에서 공식적인 제안을 하다. 동의[제의]하 다: *Dr. Reder moved that the proposal be accepted.* 리더 박사는 그 제안을 받아들여야 한다고 제의했다.

8 ▶CHANGE ARRANGEMENTS 일정을 바꾸다◀ [T] to change the time or order of something ‖ 어떤 것의 시간이나 순서를 바꾸다: *We'll have to move the party to another day.* 우린 파티를 다른 날로 옮겨야 하겠다.

9 ▶GO FAST 빨리 가다◀ [I] INFORMAL to travel very fast ‖ 아주 빨리 이동하다: *That truck was really moving.* 그 트럭은 정말로 빨리 달리고 있었다.

move away *phr v* [I] to go to a new home in a different area ‖ 다른 지역의 새로운 집으로 가다. 이사 가다: *They sold the house and moved away to a town in Ohio.* 그들은 집을 팔고 오하이오의 한 읍으로 이사 갔다.

move in *phr v* [I] **1** to start living in a new house ‖ 새 집에 살기 시작하다. 이사 오 다 : *We just moved in to the apartment yesterday.* 우리는 어제 이 아파트로 막 이사 왔다. **2** to start living with someone in the same house ‖ 같은 집에서 남과 살기 시작하다. 들어와 살다: *Jack asked Caroline to move in with him.* 잭은 캐롤라인에게 자기 집으로 들어와 살라고 말했다. **3** to begin to control a situation using your power or high rank ‖ 권력이나 높은 지위를 이용해 상황을 통제하기 시작하다. …을 공격하다. 공작하다. 압력을 가하다: *huge companies moving in on small businesses* 소규모 사업체에 압력을 가하는 거대 회사들

move off *phr v* [I] to leave a place ‖ 한 장소를 떠나다: *As we moved off in the car, Mom stood waving goodbye.* 우리가 차를 타고 떠날 때 엄마는 손을 흔들며 서 있었다.

move on *phr v* [I] **1** [I] to leave a place where you have been staying in order to continue on a trip ‖ 여행을 계속하기 위해 머물러 있던 장소를 떠나다. 다음 장소로 이동하다: *After three days we decided it was time to move on.* 3일 후에 우리는 이제 떠날 때라고 결정했다. **2** to start talking or writing about a new subject in a speech, book, discussion etc. ‖ 연설·책·토론 등에서 새로운 주제에 대해 이야기하거나 쓰기 시작하다. …으로 넘어가다: *I'd like to move on now to the subject of education.* 전 이제 교육 문제로 넘어가고 싶습니다. **3** to progress, improve, or become more modern as time passes ‖ 시간이 흐름에 따라 진보하다[개선되다, 더 현대적이 되다]. 진전하다[되다]: *The music business has certainly moved on since the days of vinyl records.* 음악 업계는 비닐 레코드 시절 이후로 장족의 발전을 했다.

move out *phr v* [I] to leave the house where you are living in order to go to live somewhere else ‖ 다른 곳에서 살기 위해 살고 있는 집을 떠나다. 이사 가다: *We have to move out by next Friday.* 우리는 다음 주 금요일까지 이사 가야 한다.

move over *phr v* [I] to change position in order to make room for someone or something else ‖ 다른 사람이나 사물을 위한 공간을 만들기 위해 위치를 바꾸다. 자리를 (옆으로) 옮기다: *Move over a little so I can sit down.* 내가 앉을 수 있도록 자리를 조금 옮겨라.

move up *phr v* [I] to get a better job than the one you had before ‖ 이전에 가졌던 일자리보다 더 좋은 일자리를 얻다. 승진하다: *She's been moved up to the managerial level.* 그녀는 관리직으로 승

진했다.

move² *n* **1** something that you decide to do in order to achieve something or make progress ‖ 어떤 것을 성취하거나 진전시키기 위해 하기로 결정한 것. 조치. 수단. 방법: *"I called Tom to say I don't want to see him again." "Good move!"* "나는 톰에게 전화해서 다시는 그를 보고 싶지 않다고 말했어." "잘 한 일이야!" / *The White House says the Premier's statement is a move towards peace.* 백악관은 그 수상의 성명이 평화를 위한 조치라고 말한다. / *Brian won't make the first move* (=be the first one to do something to change a situation) *because he says he didn't start the argument.* 브라이언은 자기가 그 논쟁을 시작하지 않았다고 말하기 때문에 먼저 행동을 취하지는 않을 것이다. **2** an action in which someone moves in a particular direction, especially in order to attack someone or to escape ‖ 특히 남을 공격하거나 피하려고 특정한 방향으로 움직이는 동작. 움직임. 이동: *Grodin made a move toward the door.* 그로딘은 문 쪽으로 이동했다. / *They watched us but made no move to stop us.* 그들은 우리를 지켜봤지만 우리를 막을 어떠한 움직임도 취하지 않았다. **3 be on the move** to be going or traveling to different places all the time ‖ 항상 다른 장소로 가거나 이동 중에 있다. 바쁘게 활동하는 중이다. 분주하다: *He was constantly on the move, visiting customers all over the state.* 그는 끊임없이 분주하게 전국에 있는 고객들을 방문하러 다녔다. **4 get a move on** SPOKEN said when you want someone to hurry ‖ 남이 서두르기를 원할 때에 쓰여. 서둘러라: *Get a move on, or we'll be late!* 서둘러, 그렇지 않으면 우린 늦을 거야! **5** the process of leaving the place where you live or work and going to live or work somewhere else ‖ 살거나 일하는 장소를 떠나 다른 곳으로 살거나 일하러 가는 과정. 이사. 이전: *The move to the new house took three days.* 새 집으로의 이사는 3일이 걸렸다. **6** the act of changing the position of one of the objects in a game, or the time when a particular player does this ‖ 놀이에서 대상 중의 하나의 위치를 바꾸는 행위나 특정한 경기자가 이것을 하는 때. 말을 쓰기 [두기]. 말을 쓸 차례: *It's your move.* 네가 둘 차례야.

move·ment /ˈmuvmənt/ *n* **1** [C, U] a change in the place or position of something or someone ‖ 사물이나 사람의 장소나 위치의 변화. 움직임. 운동. 이동: *I noticed a sudden movement behind the curtain.* 나는 커튼 뒤의 갑작스런 움직임을 알아차렸다. **2** a group of people who share the same ideas or beliefs and work together to achieve a particular aim ‖ 특정한 목표를 성취하려고 같은 생각이나 신념을 공유하고 함께 일하는 일단의 사람들. 운동 조직[세력]: *the anti-war movement* 반전 운동 세력 **3** a change or development in people's attitudes or behavior ‖ 사람들의 태도나 행동의 변화나 발전. 추이. 추세: *a movement away from traditional values* 전통적 가치관에서 벗어 나려는 추세 **4** one of the main parts into which a piece of music such as a SYMPHONY is divided ‖ 교향곡 등의 음악 작품이 분할되는 주요 부분 중의 하나. 악장 **5** the moving parts of a piece of machinery, especially a clock ‖ 기계, 특히 시계 부품 중의 움직이는 부분. 움직이는 부품. 기계 장치

mov·er /ˈmuvə/ *n* **1** someone whose job is to help people move from one house to another ‖ 사람들이 한 집에서 다른 집으로 이사하는 것을 돕는 직업인. 이삿짐 운송업자 **2 mover and shaker** an important person who has power and influence over many things in a situation ‖ 어떤 상황에서 발생하는 일에 대해 힘과 영향력을 가지는 중요한 사람. 유력자. 거물

mov·ie /ˈmuvi/ *n* a story that is told using sound and moving pictures; FILM ‖ 소리와 활동사진을 이용해 전달하는 이야기. 영화. 屢 film.

mov·ies /ˈmuviz/ *n* **the movies** the theater where you go to watch a movie ‖ 영화를 보러 가는 극장. 영화관: *Do you want to go to the movies with us?* 우리랑 같이 영화 보러 갈래?

movie star /ˈ.. ,./ *n* a famous movie actor or actress ‖ 유명한 남자나 여자 영화배우. 영화 스타

mov·ing /ˈmuvɪŋ/ *adj* **1** making you feel strong emotions, especially sadness or sympathy ‖ 특히 슬픔이나 동정의 강한 감정을 느끼게 하는. 감동적인. 감동시키는: *a moving story* 감동적인 이야기 **2** changing from one position to another ‖ 한 위치에서 다른 위치로 바꾸는. 움직이는. 움직이게 하는: *Oil the moving parts of this machine regularly.* 이 기계의 움직이는 부품에 규칙적으로 기름을 칠하세요. **– movingly** *adv*

moving van /ˈ.. ,./ *n* a large vehicle used for moving furniture from one house to another ‖ 한 집에서 다른 집으로 가구를 옮기는 데에 쓰이는 커다란 차

량. 이삿짐 트럭

mow /moʊ/ v **mowed, mowed** or **mown** /moʊn/, **mowing** [I, T] to cut grass or crops with a machine ‖ 기계로 풀이나 농작물을 자르다. 베다. 깎다: *When are you going to mow the lawn?* 언제 잔디를 깎을래?

mow sb ↔ **down** *phr v* [T] to kill people or knock them down, especially in large numbers ‖ 특히 대규모로 사람들을 죽이거나 쓰러뜨리다. 대량 살육하다: *soldiers mowed down by enemy guns* 적의 총탄에 쓰러진 병사들

mow·er /'moʊə/ n a machine that you use to cut grass ‖ 풀을 깎기 위해 사용하는 기계. 풀 베는 기계

MPEG /'ɛm pɛg/ n [C] Motion Picture Expert Group; a way in which sound and VIDEO material can be presented on the Internet ‖ Motion Picture Expert Group(동화상 전문가 그룹)의 약어; 시청각물이 인터넷 상에서 구현될 수 있는 방식.

mpg the written abbreviation of "miles per gallon"; used when describing the amount of GASOLINE used by a car ‖ "miles per gallon"의 약어; 차가 사용하는 휘발유의 양을 기술할 때 쓰여: *a car that gets 35 mpg* 갤런당 35마일을 달리는 차

mph the written abbreviation of "miles per hour"; used when describing the speed of a vehicle ‖ "miles per hour"의 약어; 차량의 속도를 기술할 때 쓰여: *driving along at 60 mph* 시속 60마일로의 주행

MP3 /'ɛm pi 'θri/ n a type of computer FILE which contains music. MP3 files are COMPRESSed (=made smaller) so that they can more easily be sent from computer to computer using the Internet. ‖ 압축되어 있어서 인터넷을 이용해 컴퓨터에서 컴퓨터로 보다 쉽게 전송할 수 있는 음악이 들어 있는 컴퓨터 파일의 한 종류. 엠피쓰리(파일)

MP3 play·er /ˌ.. ˈ. ˌ../ n a piece of electronic equipment or computer SOFTWARE that allows you to play and listen to MP3 FILEs ‖ MP3 파일을 재생하여 들을 수 있게 하는 전자 장비나 컴퓨터 프로그램. MP3 플레이어

Mr. /'mɪstə/ n **1 Mr. Smith/Jones etc.** used in front of the family name of a man to speak to him politely, to write to him, or to talk about him ‖ 정중하게 말을 건네기[쓰기, 이야기하기] 위해 남자의 성 앞에 쓰여. 스미스/존스 씨 **2** a title used when speaking to a man in an official position ‖ 공직에 있는 남성에게

말할 때 쓰는 칭호: *Mr. Chairman* 회장님 / *Mr. President* 대통령 각하

MRI n [C, U] TECHNICAL magnetic resonance imaging; a way of producing a picture of the inside of your body without cutting it open, by using radio waves and strong MAGNETIC FIELDs ‖ magnetic resonance imaging(자기공명영상)의 약어; 무선 전파와 강한 자기장을 이용해서 인체를 절개하지 않고 내부의 사진을 얻을 수 있는 방법

Mrs. /'mɪsɪz/ n **Mrs. Smith/Jones etc.** used in front of the family name of a woman who is married to speak to her politely, to write to her, or to talk about her ‖ 정중하게 말을 건네기[쓰기, 이야기하기] 위해 기혼 여성의 성 앞에 쓰여. 스미스/존스 부인

M.S., M.Sc. n Master of Science; a university degree in science that you can earn after your first degree ‖ Master of Science(이학 석사)의 약어; 학사 학위 이후에 받을 수 있는 이공계의 대학 학위 —compare M.A.

MS the written abbreviation of Mississippi ‖ Mississippi(미시시피 주)의 약어

Ms. /mɪz/ n **Ms. Smith/Jones etc.** used in front of the family name of a woman who does not want to call herself "Mrs." or "Miss" ‖ "Mrs."나 "Miss"라 불리는 것을 싫어하는 여자의 성 앞에 쓰여. 스미스/존스 씨

MT the written abbreviation of Montana ‖ Montana(몬태나 주)의 약어

Mt. the written abbreviation for MOUNT ‖ mount의 약어: *Mt. Everest* 에베레스트 산

much¹ /mʌtʃ/ adv **more, most 1** used before COMPARATIVES and SUPERLATIVES to mean a lot ‖ 많다는 것을 뜻하기 위해 비교급과 최상급 앞에 쓰여. 훨씬: *Wayne looked much older than the last time I saw him.* 웨인은 내가 지난 번 봤을 때보다 훨씬 더 나이 들어 보였다. / *Dad's feeling much better now.* 아빠는 지금 기분이 훨씬 더 나아지셨다. / *The fair this year was much more fun than last year.* 금년 박람회는 작년보다 훨씬 더 재미있었다. **2 too much/so much/very much/how much etc.** used in order to show the degree to which someone does something or something happens ‖ 사람이 어느 정도로 무엇을 하는지 또는 어느 정도로 어떤 것이 발생하는지를 나타내는 데에 쓰여. 너무 많이/아주 많이/ 매우 많이/얼마나 많이: *Thank you very much!* 대단히 감사합니다! / *I know how* *much he likes Ann.* 나는 그가 앤을 얼마나 많이 사랑하는지 안다. / *He's feeling so much better today that he went out for a walk.* 그는 오늘 기분이 훨씬 더 나아져서 산책하러 나갔다. **3 not much a)** only a little, only to a small degree etc. ‖ 겨우 조금, 단지 약간의 정도만. 그렇게 많이 …하지 않는: *She isn't much younger than me.* 그녀는 나보다 그렇게 많이 어리지 않다. / *Rob didn't like the movie very much.* 롭은 그 영화를 그렇게 많이 좋아하지는 않았다. **b)** used in order to say that something does not happen very often ‖ 어떤 것이 그다지 자주 발생하지 않는다고 말하는 데에 쓰여. 그렇게 자주 …하지 않는: *We don't go out much since the baby was born.* 우리는 아기가 태어난 이후로 외출을 그다지 많이 못한다. **4 much less** used in order to say that one thing is even less true or less possible than another ‖ 하나가 다른 하나보다 사실성이나 가능성이 훨씬 덜 하다는 것을 말하는 데에 쓰여. 훨씬 더 적은[적게]. 더군다나 더 아닌: *He doesn't have enough money to buy new shoes, much less a new car.* 그는 새 신발을 살 돈도 충분하지 않은데 더군다나 새 차는 말할 것도 없다.

USAGE NOTE much, very, a lot, and many

Use **much** with adjectives that come from the PASSIVE form of verbs: *The painting is much admired.* **Very** is used in the same way with ordinary adjectives: *The painting is very beautiful.* Use **much** with uncountable nouns in negative sentences and in questions: *These plants aren't getting much sunlight.* / *How much money do we have?* Use **a lot** or **many** with countable nouns: *She knows a lot of people.* / *There weren't many cars on the road.*

much는 동사의 수동형에서 나온 형용사와 함께 사용한다: 그 그림은 대단히 호평 받는다. very는 일반 형용사와 함께 같은 식으로 사용된다: 그 그림은 매우 아름답다. much는 부정문과 의문문에서 불가산 명사와 함께 쓴다: 이 식물들은 햇빛을 많이 못 받고 있다. / 우리가 가진 돈이 얼마나 되지? a lot이나 many는 가산 명사와 함께 쓴다: 그녀는 많은 사람들을 안다. / 도로에는 차량이 많지 않았다.

---

much² *quantifier* **1** used in spoken questions and negatives and in formal or written English to mean a lot of something ‖ 어떤 것이 많다는 것을 의미하기 위해 구어적 의문문과 부정문 및 격식체나 문어체 영어에서 쓰여. 많은: *Was there much traffic?* 교통량이 많았니? / *We don't have much time.* 우리는 시간이 많지 않다. / *The storm is bringing rain to much of the state.* 많은 지역에 폭풍이 비를 몰고 오고 있다. **2 how much** used in order to ask about the amount or cost of something ‖ 어떤 것의 양이나 비용에 대해 묻는 데에 쓰여. 얼마(나 많이): *How much is that green shirt?* (=what does it cost) 저 녹색 셔츠 얼마예요? / *She didn't know how much milk was left.* 그녀는 우유가 얼마나 남았는지 몰랐다. **3 so much/too much** used in order to talk about an amount that is very large, especially one that is too large ‖ 아주 큰 양, 특히 대단히 큰 양에 대해서 말하는 데에 쓰여. 아주 많이. 대단히 많이: *I have so much reading to do for tomorrow. I'll never get it done.* 나는 내일까지 읽어야 할 게 너무 많아. 절대 다 못 읽을 거야. / *He says the government has spent too much money on weapons.* 정부가 무기에 과대한 비용을 지출해 왔다고 그는 전한다. **4 not much** used in order to say that something is not important, interesting etc. ‖ 어떤 것이 중요하지도 흥미롭지도 않다고 말하는 데에 쓰여. 별로 …아닌: *"What's been happening with you this week?" "Not much."* (=nothing that is interesting or important) "이번 주에 네게 무슨 일이 있었니?" "별 일 없었어." **5 so much for** SPOKEN said when something that seemed useful or important before, does not seem that way now ‖ 전에는 유용하거나 중요해 보였던 것이 이제는 그렇게 보이지 않을 때에 쓰여. …에 대해서는 그만큼 (해두다). (결국) …이란 그런 것: *He didn't listen to me, but he won anyway. So much for my good advice!* 그는 내 말을 듣지 않았지만 어쨌든 이겼다. 내 좋은 충고는 결국 그저 그런 것이었지! **6 be too much for** to be too hard for someone ‖ 누군가에게 너무 어렵다. …에게 무리다[힘겹다]: *Climbing stairs is too much for me since the operation.* 수술을 한 이후로는 계단을 오르는 것이 내게 너무 벅차다.

muck /mʌk/ *n* [U] something such as dirt, mud, or another sticky substance ‖ 흙먼지[진흙, 다른 끈적한 물질] 등의 것. 때. 오물: *shoes covered in thick black muck* 검은 때로 찌든 신발

mu·cus /'myukəs/ *n* [U] a liquid produced by parts of your body such as your nose ‖ 코 등의 신체 부위에서 생성되는 액체. 점액. 콧물 – **mucous** *adj*

mud /mʌd/ *n* [U] **1** wet earth that is soft and sticky ‖ 부드럽고 끈적한 젖은 흙. 진흙: *The kids tracked mud all over the carpet.* 아이들은 카펫에 온통 진흙 발자국을 남겼다. **2 sb's name is mud** SPOKEN said when people are annoyed at someone because s/he has caused trouble ‖ 어떤 사람이 말썽을 일으켜서 그 사람에게 사람들이 짜증났을 때에 쓰여. 남의 평판[신용]이 땅에 떨어지다

mud·dle¹ /'mʌdl/ *v*

muddle through/on *phr v* [I] to continue doing something even though it is confusing or difficult ‖ 비록 어떤 것이 혼란스럽거나 어렵더라도 그것을 계속하다. 그럭저럭 해나가다

muddle² *n* a state of confusion or a lack of order ‖ 혼란한 상태나 질서의 부족. 혼란(상태). 뒤죽박죽: *papers in a muddle on the floor* 바닥에 널브러져 있는 서류들

mud·dy¹ /'mʌdi/ *adj* covered with mud or containing mud ‖ 진흙으로 덮여 있거나 진흙을 함유하는. 진흙(투성이)의. 진창의: *muddy boots* 진흙이 덕지덕지 붙은 부츠 / *muddy water* 흙탕물

muddy² *v* [T] **1 muddy the issue/waters** to make a situation more complicated or more confusing than it was before ‖ 상황을 전보다 더 복잡하게 나 더 혼란스럽게 하다. 논점을 흐리다/사태를 더욱 혼란시키다 **2** to make something dirty with mud ‖ 무엇을 진흙으로 더럽히다. 진흙투성이로 만들다

mud·guard /'mʌdgɑrd/ *n* a piece of rubber that hangs behind the wheel of a vehicle to prevent mud from getting on the vehicle ‖ 진흙이 탈것에 붙는 것을 방지하기 위해 탈것의 바퀴 뒤에 거는 고무 조각. 흙받기

mud·pack /'mʌdpæk/ *n* a soft mixture containing clay that you spread over your face and leave there for a short time to improve your skin ‖ 피부를 좋게 하기 위해 얼굴에 펴서 바르고 잠시 그대로 두는, 진흙이 함유된 부드러운 혼합물. 머드 팩

mud·slide /'mʌdslaɪd/ *n* a lot of very wet mud that has slid down the side of a hill ‖ 언덕의 사면 아래로 미끄러져내린 매우 축축한 많은 진흙. 진흙사태

mud·sling·ing /'mʌd,slɪŋɪŋ/ *n* [U] the practice of saying bad things about someone so that other people will have a bad opinion of him/her ‖ 남에 대해서 나쁜 말을 해서 다른 사람들이 그 사람에 대해서 안 좋은 생각을 가지게 하는 행위.

중상. 비방 – **mudslinger** *n*

muff /mʌf/ *v* [T] INFORMAL to do something badly or make a mistake so that something is not successful ‖ 어떤 것을 잘못하거나 실수를 해서 어떤 것이 성공하지 못하다. 그르치다. 실수하다: *Fonseca muffed the catch.* 폰세카는 공을 놓쳐 버렸다.

muf·fin /'mʌfən/ *n* a small, slightly sweet type of bread that often has fruit in it ‖ 종종 안에 과일이 들어 있는 작고 약간 단 빵의 일종. 머핀: *a blueberry muffin* 블루베리 머핀

muf·fle /'mʌfəl/ *v* [T] to make a sound less loud or clear ‖ 소리를 작거나 덜 분명하게 하다. 소리를 죽이다. 약하게 하다: *Thick curtains muffled the traffic noise.* 두꺼운 커튼이 교통 소음을 줄였다.

muf·fled /'mʌfəld/ *adj* muffled voices or sounds cannot be heard clearly ‖ 목소리나 소리가 분명하게 들리지 않는. 잘 들리지 않는. 우물거리는: *He could barely hear Lisa's muffled voice.* 그는 리사의 우물거리는 목소리를 겨우 알아들을 수 있었다.

muf·fler /'mʌflɚ/ *n* **1** a piece of equipment on a vehicle that makes the noise from the engine quieter ‖ 엔진 소음을 더 조용하게 하는 탈것에 부착된 장비. 소음기 **2** OLD-FASHIONED ⇨ SCARF¹

mug¹ /mʌg/ *n* a large cup with straight sides and a handle used for drinking coffee, tea etc., or a large glass with a handle used for drinking beer ‖ 커피·차 등을 마시는 데에 쓰이는 옆면이 반듯하고 손잡이가 달린 큰 잔이나 맥주를 마시는 데에 쓰이는 손잡이가 달린 큰 유리잔. 머그잔

mug² *v* **-gged, -gging** [T] to attack someone and take his/her money ‖ 남을 공격해서 그 사람의 돈을 빼앗다. (노상) 강도질하다: *She was mugged and her purse stolen.* 그녀는 강도를 당해 지갑을 강탈당했다. – **mugging** *n* [U]

mug·ger /'mʌgɚ/ *n* someone who attacks someone else to take his/her money ‖ 돈을 빼앗기 위해 다른 사람을 공격하는 사람. (노상) 강도 —see usage note at THIEF

mug·ging /'mʌgɪŋ/ *n* [C, U] an attack on someone in which they are robbed in a public place ‖ 공공장소에서 사람을 강탈하며 공격하는 행위. (노상) 강도질: *Robberies and muggings are common in this area.* 강도질과 노상 강탈은 이 지역에서 흔한 일이다.

mug·gy /'mʌgi/ *adj* INFORMAL muggy weather is unpleasant because it is too

warm and HUMID ‖ 너무 덥고 습기가 많
아서 날씨가 불쾌한. 무더운. 후텁지근한
- **mugginess** *n* [U] —see usage note
at TEMPERATURE

mug·shot /'mʌɡʃɑt/ *n* INFORMAL a
photograph of a criminal's face taken by
the police ‖ 경찰이 찍은 범인 얼굴 사진.
수배 사진

Mu·ham·mad /mou'hæməd/ a PROPHET
who taught ideas on which Islam is
based ‖ 이슬람교의 근간이 되는 사상을
가르친 예언자. 마호메트

mulch /mʌltʃ/ *n* [singular, U] decaying
leaves that you put on the soil to
improve its quality and to protect the
roots of plants ‖ 토질을 개선시키고 식물
뿌리를 보호하기 위해 흙 위에 덮는 부식
한 나뭇잎. 까는 짚. 뿌리 덮개

mule /myul/ *n* an animal that has a
DONKEY and a horse as parents ‖ 부모가
당나귀와 말인 동물. 노새

mull /mʌl/ *v* [T] to heat wine or beer
with sugar and SPICEs ‖ 포도주나 맥주를
설탕과 향료를 넣어 데우다

mull sth ↔ **over** *phr v* [T] to think
about something carefully ‖ 어떤 것에 대
해서 주의 깊게 생각하다. 곰곰이 생각하
다: *I mulled over his
offer for a day or two and then accepted
it.* 나는 그의 제안을 하루 이틀쯤 심사숙
고한 다음에 받아들였다.

mul·lah /'mʌlə/ *n* a religious leader or
teacher in Islam ‖ 이슬람교의 종교적 지
도자나 스승. 물라

mul·ti·col·ored /'mʌltɪˌkʌləd/ *adj*
having many different colors ‖ 여러 다양
한 색깔들을 가지는. 다색의. 다채로운: *a
multicolored shirt* 알록달록한 셔츠

mul·ti·cul·tur·al /ˌmʌltiˈkʌltʃərəl, -ti-/
adj involving people or ideas from many
different countries, races, religions etc.
‖ 많은 다른 국가·인종·종교 출신의 사람
들이나 사상을 포함하는. 다문화적인: *The
US is a multicultural society.* 미국은 다
문화 사회이다. - **multiculturalism** *n*
[U]

mul·ti·lat·er·al /ˌmʌltɪˈlætərəl/ *adj*
involving several different countries,
companies etc. ‖ 여러 개의 다른 국가·회
사 등을 포함하는. 다자간의: *a
multilateral agreement to stop the
fighting* 전투를 중단시키기 위한 다자간
협약 —compare BILATERAL, UNILATERAL

mul·ti·me·di·a /ˌmʌltɪˈmidiə, -ti-/ *adj*
using a mixture of sounds, words,
pictures etc. to give information,
especially on a computer program ‖ 특
히 컴퓨터 프로그램 상에서 정보를 제공하

기 위해 소리·문자·사진 등을 혼합해 사용
하는. 혼합[멀티] 미디어의 -
multimedia *n* [U]

mul·ti·na·tion·al /ˌmʌltɪˈnæʃənl/ *adj* **1**
a multinational company has offices,
businesses etc. in several different
countries ‖ 회사가 여러 개의 다른 국가들
에 사무실·사업체 등을 가지고 있는. 다국
적 기업의 **2** involving people from
several different countries ‖ 여러 개의
다른 국가들 출신의 사람들을 포함하는.
다국적의: *a multinational peace-keeping
force* 다국적 평화 유지군

mul·ti·ple¹ /'mʌltəpəl/ *adj* including or
involving many parts, people, events
etc. ‖ 많은 부분·사람들·사건 등을 포함하
거나 관련시키는. 다수의. 다양한: *He
suffered multiple injuries to his legs.* 그
는 다리 여러 군데에 부상을 입었다.

multiple² *n* a number that can be
divided by a smaller number or an exact
number of times ‖ 더 작은 수로 나눌 수
있는 수나 곱한 수(로 나누어 나머지가 남
지 않는 수). 배수: *20 is a multiple of 4
and 5.* 20은 4와 5의 배수이다.

multiple choice /ˌ... './ *adj* a
multiple choice test or question shows
several possible answers and you must
choose the correct one ‖ 시험이나 문제가
몇 개의 가능한 답을 제시하여 정답을 선
택해야 하는. 객관식의

mul·ti·plex /'mʌltɪˌplɛks/ *n* a movie
theater that has several rooms in which
different movies are shown ‖ 서로 다른
영화를 상영하는 여러 개의 상영관을 가지
고 있는 영화관. 복합 상영관

mul·ti·pli·ca·tion /ˌmʌltəpləˈkeɪʃən/ *n*
[U] **1** a method of calculating in which
you MULTIPLY numbers ‖ 수를 곱해서 계
산하는 방법. 곱셈 **2** FORMAL a large
increase in the SIZE, amount, or number
of something ‖ 어떤 것의 크기[양, 수]의
커다란 증가. 증대: *the multiplication of
the white blood cells* 백혈구의 급격한 증
가 —compare DIVISION

mul·ti·plic·i·ty /ˌmʌltəˈplɪsəti/ *n* [C, U]
FORMAL a large number or great variety
of things ‖ 사물의 많은 수나 매우 다양함.
다수. 다양성: *a multiplicity of views on
the issue* 그 쟁점에 대한 다양한 관점

mul·ti·ply /'mʌltəˌplaɪ/ *v* [I, T] **1** to
increase greatly, or to make something
do this ‖ 크게 증가하거나 증가시키다. 늘
다. 늘리다. 증대하다[시키다]: *The
company's problems have multiplied
over the past year.* 그 회사의 문제들은
지난 한 해 동안 크게 증가해 왔다. **2** to
do a calculation in which you add one

number to itself or a particular number of times ‖ 하나의 수를 그 자체의 수나 특정한 배수만큼 더하는 계산을 하다. 곱 (셈)하다: *4 multiplied by 5 is 20.* (=4 x 5=20) 4 곱하기 5는 20이다. —compare DIVIDE

mul·ti·pur·pose /ˌmʌltɪ'pəpəs·, -ti-/ *adj* having many different uses or purposes ‖ 다른 용도나 목적을 많이 가지고 있는. 다목적의. 다용도의: *a multipurpose room* 다용도실

mul·ti·ra·cial /ˌmʌltɪ'reɪʃəl, -ti-/ *adj* including or involving many different races of people ‖ 많은 다른 인종을 포함하거나 관련시키는. 다민족의. 다인종의

multi-task·ing /ˈ.. ˌ../ *n* [U] 1 a computer's ability to do more than one job at a time ‖ 한 번에 한 가지 이상의 일을 하는 컴퓨터의 능력 2 the ability to do different types of work at the same time ‖ 동시에 서로 다른 종류의 일을 하는 능력

mul·ti·tude /ˈmʌltəˌtud/ *n* FORMAL **a multitude of** a very large number of things or people ‖ 사물이나 사람의 매우 많은 수. 다수: *Poems often have a multitude of interpretations.* 시는 종종 다양한 해석을 낳는다.

mum·ble /ˈmʌmbəl/ *v* [I, T] to say something too quietly or not clearly enough, so that other people cannot understand you ‖ 다른 사람들이 자신의 말을 알아듣지 못할 정도로 너무 조용하게 또는 명확하지 못하게 말하다. 중얼거리다: *He mumbled his name and I had to ask him to repeat it.* 그가 이름을 우물우물 말해서 나는 그에게 다시 한 번 말해 달라고 부탁해야 했다.

mum·bo-jum·bo /ˌmʌmbou 'dʒʌmbou/ *n* [U] INFORMAL something that is difficult to understand or that makes no sense ‖ 이해하기 어렵거나 말이 안 되는 것. 뜻 모를[무의미한] 말: *She was telling me some New Age mumbo-jumbo about crystals.* 그녀는 나에게 수정에 대한 뉴에이지적인 뜻 모를 이야기를 늘어놓고 있었다.

mum·mi·fy /ˈmʌməˌfaɪ/ *v* [T] to preserve a dead body as a MUMMY ‖ 시체를 미라로 보존하다. 미라로 만들다

mum·my /ˈmʌmi/ *n* a dead body that has been preserved and often wrapped in cloth, especially in ancient Egypt ‖ 특히 고대 이집트에서 종종 천으로 싸서 보존된 시체. 미라

mumps /mʌmps/ *n* [U] an infectious illness in which your throat swells and becomes painful ‖ 목구멍이 부어올라 고통스럽게 되는 감염성 질병. 유행성 이하선염

munch /mʌntʃ/ *v* [I, T] to eat something in a noisy way ‖ 어떤 것을 시끄럽게 먹다. 우적우적[아작아작] (베어) 먹다: *The rabbit munched happily on its lettuce.* 토끼는 만족스럽게 상추를 아작아작 베어 먹었다.

munch·ies /ˈmʌntʃiz/ *n* [plural] INFORMAL **1 have the munchies** to feel hungry, especially for food such as cookies or POTATO CHIPs ‖ 특히 쿠키나 감자 튀김 등의 음식을 몹시 먹고 싶어 하다 **2** foods such as cookies or POTATO CHIPs that are served at a party ‖ 파티에서 제공되는 쿠키나 감자 튀김 등의 음식. 스낵 과자[음식]

mun·dane /mʌn'deɪn/ *adj* DISAPPROVING ordinary and not interesting or exciting; dull ‖ 평범하며 재미있거나 흥미롭지 않은. 흔한; 지루한: *a mundane life in the suburbs* 교외에서의 따분한 생활 – **mundanely** *adv*

mu·nic·i·pal /myu'nɪsəpəl/ *adj* relating to the government of a town or city ‖ 읍이나 시의 관청과 관련된. 지방 자치체[시, 읍]의

mu·nic·i·pal·i·ty /myuˌnɪsə'pæləti/ *n* a town or city that has its own government ‖ 스스로 관청을 가지고 있는 읍이나 시. (읍·시 등의) 지방 자치체

mu·ni·tions /myu'nɪʃənz/ *n* [plural] military supplies such as bombs and large guns ‖ 폭탄과 대포 등의 군수 물자. 군수품. 군용 물자 – **munition** *adj*

mu·ral /ˈmyʊrəl/ *n* a painting that is painted on a wall ‖ 벽에 그린 그림. 벽화

mur·der¹ /ˈmədə/ *n* **1** [C, U] the crime of deliberately killing someone ‖ 고의적으로 남을 죽이는 범죄. 살인(죄): *a man charged with the murder of two young girls* 어린 두 소녀 살해죄로 기소된 한 남자 / *4600 murders were committed in the US in 1975.* 1975년에 미국에서 4600건의 살인이 자행되었다. **2 get away with murder** INFORMAL to not be punished for doing something wrong, or to be allowed to do anything you want ‖ 잘못된 행위에 대해 처벌받지 않다, 또는 원하는 것은 무엇이든 하도록 허락받다. 나쁜 짓이 들키지[벌 받지] 않고 넘어가다. 하고 싶은 대로 하다: *Those kids of theirs get away with murder!* 그 집 아이들은 아주 제멋대로라니까! **3** SPOKEN used in order to say that something is very difficult or unpleasant ‖ 어떤 것이 매우 힘들거나 불쾌하다고 말하는 데에 쓰여. 매우 골치 아픈 일:

Traffic was murder this morning! 오늘 아침 교통은 지옥이었다!

murder² *v* [T] to kill someone deliberately and illegally ‖ 남을 고의적이고 불법적으로 죽이다. 살인[살해]하다: *He murdered his wife in a jealous rage.* 그는 질투심에 불타 아내를 살해했다. — **murderer** *n*

mur·der·ous /ˈmɜːdərəs/ *adj* very dangerous or violent and likely to kill someone ‖ 아주 위험하거나 폭력적이며 남을 죽일 듯한. 살인적인. 흉악한: *murderous gangs* 흉악한 폭력배

murk·y /ˈmɜːki/ *adj* dark and difficult to see through ‖ 꿰뚫어 보기에는 어둡고 힘든. 흐릿한. 탁한: *murky water* 탁한 물

mur·mur¹ /ˈmɜːmɚ/ *v* [I, T] to say something in a soft quiet voice ‖ 무엇을 부드럽고 조용한 목소리로 말하다. 소곤거리다. 속삭이다: *He softly murmured her name.* 그는 그녀의 이름을 부드럽게 속삭였다. — **murmuring** *n* [C, U]

murmur² *n* a soft quiet sound made by someone's voice ‖ 어떤 이의 음성으로 내는 부드럽고 조용한 소리. 속삭임. 중얼거림: *She answered in a low murmur.* 그녀는 아주 속삭이듯이 대답했다.

Mur·phy's law /ˌmɜːfɪz ˈlɔː/ *n* [C] INFORMAL a tendency for bad things to happen whenever it is possible for them to do so ‖ 안 좋은 일들이 그럴 가능성이 있을 때마다 언제든 일어나는 경향. 머피의 법칙

mus·cle /ˈmʌsəl/ *n* **1** [C, U] one of the pieces of flesh inside your body that join bones together and make your body move ‖ 뼈들을 서로 결합시키고 몸을 움직이게 하는 신체 내부의 살 조각의 하나. 근육: *Weight lifting will strengthen your arm muscles.* 웨이트 트레이닝은 팔 근육을 강화시킬 것이다. **2 military/political etc. muscle** military etc. power or influence ‖ 군사적인 것 등의 힘이나 영향력. 군사력/정치력 **3** [U] physical strength and power ‖ 체력과 힘. 근력. 완력: *It takes muscle to move a piano.* 피아노를 옮기려면 많은 힘이 필요하다. **4 not move a muscle** to not move at all ‖ 전혀 움직이지 않다. 미동도 하지 않다. 눈 하나 깜짝 않다

mus·cu·lar /ˈmʌskyələ/ *adj* **1** having a lot of big muscles ‖ 큰 근육을 많이 가지고 있는. 근육질의: *strong muscular arms* 강한 근육질의 팔 **2** related to or affecting the muscles ‖ 근육과 관련되거나 근육에 영향을 미치는. 근육성의: *a muscular disease* 근육성 질병

muse /myuz/ *v* [I] FORMAL to imagine or think a lot about something ‖ 어떤 것에 대해서 많이 상상하거나 생각하다. 심사숙고하다. 곰곰이 생각하다: *new college graduates musing on/over what the future might hold* 어떤 미래가 펼쳐질지 상상하고 있는 갓 대학을 졸업한 학생들 — **musing** *n*

mu·se·um /myuˈziəm/ *n* a building where important objects are kept and shown to the public ‖ 중요한 물건들을 보관하고 일반 대중에게 전시하는 건물. 박물관. 미술관. 기념관: *an art museum* 미술관

mush /mʌʃ/ *n* [singular, U] DISAPPROVING a soft food that is part solid and part liquid ‖ 일부분은 고체이고 일부분은 액체인 부드러운 음식. 죽 모양의 걸쭉한 것: *I can't eat this mush!* 나는 이 죽 못 먹어!

mush·room¹ /ˈmʌʃrum/ *n* a FUNGUS (=plant without leaves) that has a stem and a round top, of which some types can be eaten and some are poisonous ‖ 어떤 종류는 먹을 수 있고 어떤 종류는 독성이 있어 먹을 수 없는, 줄기와 둥근 갓을 가진 균류. 버섯 —see picture on page 944

mushroom² *v* [I] to grow in size or numbers very quickly ‖ 크기나 수가 매우 빨리 커지다. 급격히 퍼지다[증가하다]: *The city's population has mushroomed to over one million.* 그 도시의 인구는 백만 명 이상으로 급격히 팽창했다.

mushroom cloud /ˈ.. ˌ./ *n* a large cloud shaped like a MUSHROOM that is caused by a NUCLEAR explosion ‖ 핵폭발로 인해 생기는 버섯처럼 생긴 커다란 구름. 버섯구름

mush·y /ˈmʌʃi/ *adj* **1** DISAPPROVING very emotional ‖ 매우 감성적인. 감상적인. 눈물을 잘 흘리는: *mushy love stories* 감상적인 사랑 이야기들 **2** soft and wet ‖ 부드럽고 축축한. 죽 같은. 흐늘흐늘한: *mushy old potatoes* 물컹물컹한 오래된 감자들

mu·sic /ˈmyuzɪk/ *n* [U] **1** the arrangement of sounds made by musical instruments or voices ‖ 악기나 목소리로 내는 소리의 배열. 음악: *What kind of music do you like?* 너는 어떤 음악을 좋아하니? / *My favorite piece of music is Bach's "Magnificat."* 내가 제일 좋아하는 음악 작품은 바흐의 "마그니피캇[성모의 노래]"이야. **2** the art of writing or playing music ‖ 음악을 쓰거나 연주하는 기술. 음악. 작곡[연주]법: *music lessons* 음악 교습 **3** a set of written marks representing music, or the paper that this is written on ‖ 음악을 표현하는 일련의 쓰여진 기호나 이것이 쓰여진 종이. 악보: *Jim plays the piano well, but he can't read music.* 짐은 피아노는 잘 치지만 악보는 읽지 못한다. **4 put on some music** to turn on a radio etc. to listen to music ‖ 음악을 듣기 위해 라디오 등을 틀다. 음악을 틀다 **5 face the music** to admit that you have done something wrong and accept punishment ‖ 잘못된 짓을 저질렀다고 인정하고 처벌을 받아들이다. 자기 행동의 결과를 깨끗이 받아들이다: *If he took the money, he'll have to face the music.* 만약 그가 돈을 가져갔다면 그는 그 책임을 져야 할 것이다.

mu·si·cal¹ /'myuzɪkəl/ *adj* **1** relating to music or consisting of music ‖ 음악과 관련되거나 음악으로 구성된. 음악의. 음악적인: *musical instruments* 악기 **2** good at playing or singing music ‖ 음악을 연주하거나 노래를 부르는 데에 뛰어난. 음악에 뛰어난: *I wasn't very musical as a child.* 나는 어렸을 때 음악에는 별로 재주가 없었다. – **musically** *adv*

musical² *n* a play or movie that uses songs and music to tell a story ‖ 이야기를 전달하기 위해 노래와 음악을 사용하는 연극이나 영화. 뮤지컬

mu·si·cian /myu'zɪʃən/ *n* someone who plays a musical instrument very well or as a job ‖ 악기를 아주 잘 연주하거나 직업으로서 연주하는 사람. 연주를 잘 하는 사람. 음악가. 작곡가

musk /mʌsk/ *n* [U] a strong smelling substance used for making PERFUME ‖ 향수를 만드는 데 사용되는 냄새가 강한 물질. 사향 – **musky** *adj*

mus·ket /'mʌskɪt/ *n* a type of gun used in past times ‖ 과거에 사용했던 총의 일종. 머스킷총

Mus·lim /'mʌzləm, 'mʊz-, 'mʊs-/ *n* someone whose religion is Islam ‖ 종교가 이슬람교인 사람. 회교도 – **Muslim** *adj*

muss /mʌs/, **muss up** *v* [T] INFORMAL to make someone's hair, clothes etc. messy ‖ 남의 머리·옷 등을 엉망으로 만들다. 헝클어뜨리다. 짓구겨 놓다

mus·sel /'mʌsəl/ *n* [C, U] a small sea animal with a black shell and a soft body that can be eaten ‖ 검은 껍질과 먹을 수 있는 부드러운 육질을 가진 작은 바다 동물. 홍합

must¹ /məst; *strong* mʌst/ *modal verb* **1** *past form* **had to** used in order to say that something is necessary because of a rule, or because it is the best thing to do ‖ 어떤 것이 규칙이기 때문에, 또는 그것이 할 수 있는 최선의 것이기 때문에 필요하다고 말하는 데에 쓰여. …해야 한다: *All passengers must wear seatbelts.* 모든 승객은 안전띠를 착용해야 한다. / *You must not allow your dog out without a leash.* 개줄 없이 개를 밖에 풀어 놓아서는 안 된다. / *It's getting late, I really must go.* 점점 더 늦어져서 나는 정말로 가봐야 해. **2** *past form* **must have** used in order to say that something is very likely to be true ‖ 어떤 것이 아주 사실일 듯하다고 말하는 데에 쓰여. …일 것이다. …임에 틀림없다: *George must be almost eighty years old now.* 조지는 이제 거의 팔순일 것이다. / *That car must have been doing* (=traveling) *90 miles an hour!* 저 차는 틀림없이 시속 90마일로 달리고 있었을 거야! **3** used in order to suggest that someone do something ‖ 남에게 어떤 것을 하라고 제안하는 데에 쓰여. (꼭) …해주기 바라다. …해주면 좋겠다: *You must see Robin Williams' new movie. It's really funny.* 로빈 윌리엄스의 새 영화 꼭 봐봐. 정말 재미있어. —see usage note at HAVE TO —see study note on page 932

must² /mʌst/ *n* **a must** INFORMAL something that you must do or must have ‖ 해야만 하거나 가져야만 하는 것. 꼭 필요한 것: *If you visit Florida, going to Disney World is a must.* 플로리다에 방문한다면 디즈니 월드는 꼭 가봐야 할 곳이야.

mus·tache /'mʌstæʃ, mə'stæʃ/ *n* hair that grows on a man's upper lip ‖ 남성의 윗입술 위에 자라는 털. 콧수염 —see picture at HAIRSTYLE

mus·tang /'mʌstæŋ/ *n* a small wild horse ‖ 몸집이 작은 야생의 말

mus·tard /'mʌstəd/ *n* [U] **1** a yellow SAUCE usually eaten with meat ‖ 대체로 고기와 함께 먹는 노란 소스. 겨자 **2** a hot-tasting seed or the yellow powder made from it, used in making mustard ‖ 겨자를 만들 때 사용하는 매운 맛이 나는 씨나 그것으로 만든 노란 가루. 겨자씨 [가루]

mus·ter¹ /'mʌstə/ *v* **1 muster (up) courage/support etc.** to find or gather as much courage etc. as you can in order to do something difficult ‖ 어려운 일을 하기위해 할 수 있는 한 많은 용기 등을 불러 일으키거나 모으다. 용기를 내다/지원을 얻다: *I'm still trying to muster up the courage to speak to her.* 난 그녀에게 말을 건넬 용기를 내려고 여전히 노력 중이다. **2** [T] to gather a group of people such as soldiers into one place ‖ 군인 등의 일단의 사람들을 한 장소로 모으다. 소집하다. 집합시키다: *mustering an army* 군대 소집

muster² *n* **pass muster** to be accepted as good enough for a particular job ‖ 특정한 일에 충분히 적합한 것으로 받아들이다. 검열에 합격하다. 표준에 도달하다

must·n't /'mʌsnt/ *modal v* OLD-FASHIONED the short form of "must not" ‖ "must not"의 단축형: *You mustn't forget to tell her what I said.* 너는 내가 한 말을 그녀에게 잊지 말고 꼭 해야 해.

must·y /'mʌsti/ *adj* having a wet unpleasant smell ‖ 축축하고 불쾌한 냄새가 나는. 곰팡이 슨. 곰팡내 나는: *musty old books* 곰팡내 나는 낡은 책들

mu·ta·ble /'myutəbəl/ *adj* FORMAL able or likely to change ‖ 변할 수 있거나 변할 것 같은. 변하기 쉬운. 변덕스러운 – **mutability** /ˌmyutə'bɪləti/ *n* [U] — opposite IMMUTABLE

mu·tant /'myutnt/ *n* an animal or plant that is different from others of the same kind because of a change in its GENES ‖ 유전자의 변화 때문에 같은 종류의 다른 것들과 달라진 동물이나 식물. 돌연변이체 – **mutant** *adj*

mu·tate /'myuteɪt/ *v* [I] if an animal or plant mutates, it becomes different from others of the same kind because of a change in its GENES ‖ 동물이나 식물이 유전자의 변화 때문에 같은 종류의 다른 것들과 달라지다. 돌연변이하다 – **mutation** /myu'teɪʃən/ *n* [C, U]

mute¹ /myut/ *v* [T] to make a sound quieter ‖ 소리를 더 조용하게 하다. 소리를 죽이다[약하게 하다]: *The thick walls muted the sounds of the city.* 두꺼운 벽이 도시의 소음을 줄여 주었다.

mute² *n* someone who cannot or will not speak ‖ 말할 수 없거나 말하지 않으려는 사람. 벙어리. 답변을 거부하는 피의자 – **mute** *adj* – **mutely** *adv*

mut·ed /'myutɪd/ *adj* **1 muted criticism/response etc.** criticism etc. that is not strong or forceful ‖ 강하거나 강력하지 않은 비판 등. 약화된 비판/반응 **2** quieter than usual ‖ 보통보다 더 조용한. 약한: *the muted sound of snoring from the next room* 옆방에서 들려오는 평소보다 조용한 코고는 소리 **3** a muted color is less bright than usual ‖ 색깔이 보통보다 덜 밝은. 부드러운

mu·ti·late /'myutlˌeɪt/ *v* [T] to damage someone or something severely, especially by removing part of it ‖ 특히 그 일부를 제거해서 사람이나 사물을 심하

게 손상시키다. 절단하다: *bodies mutilated in the explosion* 폭발로 절단된 신체들 – **mutilation** /ˌmyutl'eɪʃən/ *n* [C, U]

mu·ti·nous /'myutn-əs/ *adj* not satisfied with the behavior of someone in authority, and refusing to obey his/her orders ‖ 권력자의 행동이 불만족스러워 그 사람의 명령에 따르기를 거부하는. 폭동의. 반란을 일으키는: *mutinous soldiers* 반란을 일으킨 병사들

mu·ti·ny /'myutn-i/ *n* [C, U] a situation in which people, especially soldiers or SAILORS, refuse to obey someone in authority and try to take control for themselves ‖ 특히 병사나 선원이 권력자에게 복종하기를 거부하고 스스로 통제하려고 시도하는 상황. (선상) 반란. 폭동: *a mutiny on the ship* 선상 반란 – **mutiny** *v* [I]

mutt /mʌt/ *n* INFORMAL a dog that does not belong to a particular breed ‖ 특정한 종에 속하지 않는 개. 잡종 개. 똥개

mut·ter /'mʌtər/ *v* [I, T] to speak in a quiet voice, especially when you are complaining about something but do not want other people to hear you ‖ 특히 어떤 것에 대해서 불평은 하지만 다른 사람들이 듣는 것을 원하지 않을 때 조용한 목소리로 말하다. 중얼[투덜]거리다: *He walked away muttering about how the world was going crazy.* 그는 세상이 얼마나 미쳐 가고 있는지에 대해 투덜거리며 걸어가 버렸다.

mut·ton /'mʌtn/ *n* [U] the meat from a sheep ‖ 양고기

mu·tu·al /'myutʃuəl/ *adj* **1** a feeling or action that is mutual is felt or done by two or more people toward one another ‖ 감정이나 동작을 둘 이상의 사람들이 서로에게 느끼거나 행한. 상호간의: *A good marriage is marked by mutual respect.* 상호간의 존중이 좋은 결혼 생활의 조건이다. **2** shared by two or more people ‖ 둘 이상의 사람들이 공유하는. 공통의: *We were introduced by a mutual friend.* (=someone we both know) 우리는 양쪽을 다 아는 친구에게 서로 소개를 받았다. **3 the feeling is mutual** SPOKEN said when you have the same feeling about someone as s/he has toward you ‖ 남이 자신에 대해 가지는 것과 같은 감정을 자신이 그 사람에게 가질 때 쓰여. 내 감정도 똑같다: *"You really drive me crazy sometimes!" "The feeling is mutual!"* "가끔 너는 정말로 나를 미치게 해!" "너도 마찬가지야!" – **mutuality** /ˌmyutʃu'æləti/ *n* [U]

mutual fund /'... ,./ *n* a company through which you can buy SHAREs of other companies || 다른 회사들의 주식을 그를 통해서 살 수 있는 회사. 투자 신탁 회사

mu·tu·al·ly /'myutʃuəli, -tʃəli/ *adv* 1 done, felt, or experienced by two or more people || 둘 이상의 사람들이 행하거나 느끼거나 경험한. 상호간에: *a mutually rewarding business arrangement* 상호간에 이익이 되는 사업 협정 2 **mutually exclusive** if two ideas, beliefs etc. are mutually exclusive, they cannot both exist or be true at the same time || 두 개의 사상·신념 등이 동시에 둘 다 존재하거나 사실일 수 없는. 상호 배타적인

Mu·zak /'myuzæk/ *n* [U] TRADEMARK recorded music that is played continuously in airports, offices etc. || 공항·사무실 등에서 계속해서 틀어 주는 녹음된 음악. 영업용 배경 음악

muz·zle¹ /'mʌzəl/ *n* 1 the nose and mouth of an animal such as a dog or horse || 개나 말 등의 동물의 코와 입. 주둥이 2 the end of the BARREL of a gun || 총열의 끝. 총구 3 something that you put over a dog's mouth so it cannot bite someone || 사람을 물지 못하게 개의 입에 씌운 것. 입마개. 재갈

muzzle² *v* [T] 1 to prevent someone from speaking freely or from expressing his/her opinions || 사람이 자유롭게 말하거나 의견을 표현하는 것을 막다. 입을 (틀어)막다. 말 못하게 하다: *an attempt to muzzle the press* 언론을 억압하려는 시도 2 to put a MUZZLE over a dog's mouth so that it cannot bite someone || 사람을 물지 못하게 개의 입에 재갈을 씌우다. 재갈을 물리다

my /maɪ/ *possessive, adj* belonging or relating to the person who is speaking || 말하고 있는 사람에게 속하거나 관련된. 나의: *I'd like you to meet my mother.* 당신이 제 어머니를 만났으면 합니다. / *That's my car over there.* 저쪽에 있는 차가 내 차다. / *I tried not to let my feelings show.* 나는 내 감정을 내보이지 않으려고 노력했다.

my·op·ic /maɪ'ɑpɪk, -'ou-/ *adj* 1 TECHNICAL ⇨ NEARSIGHTED 2 unwilling or unable to think about the future results of an action || 어떤 행위에 대한 미래의 결과에 대해서 기껍게 생각하려 들지 않거나 생각할 수 없는. 근시안적인: *a myopic view of crime prevention* 범죄 예방에 대한 근시안적인 견해 – **myopia** /maɪ'oupiə/ *n* [U]

myr·i·ad /'mɪriəd/ *n* LITERARY a very large number of something || 어떤 것의 매우 많은 수. 무수(한 사람[것]): *a myriad of stars in the sky* 하늘의 무수한 별들 – **myriad** *adj*

my·self /maɪ'sɛlf/ *pron* 1 the REFLEXIVE form of "me" || "me"의 재귀형. 나 자신 [스스로]: *I burned myself on the stove.* 나는 난로에 화상을 입었다. / *I made myself a cup of coffee.* 나는 스스로 커피 한 잔을 만들어 먹었다. 2 the strong form of "me," used in order to emphasize the subject or object of a sentence || "me"의 강조형으로서 문장의 주어나 목적어를 강조하는 데에 쓰여. 나 자신[스스로]: *I went to the grocery store myself to buy it.* 내 자신이 직접 그것을 사기 위해 식료품점에 갔다. 3 **(all) by myself a)** without help || 도움 없이. 혼자 힘으로: *Look, Mommy – I tied my shoes all by myself!* 엄마, 보세요. 제 혼자 힘으로 신발 끈을 묶었어요! **b)** alone || 홀로. 혼자서: *I went to the movie by myself.* 나는 혼자서 영화를 보러 갔다. 4 **(all) to myself** for my own use || 내 자신의 사용을 위해서. 나 자신을 위해서: *I had the whole swimming pool to myself today.* 나는 오늘 수영장 전부를 나 혼자 사용했다. 5 **not be myself** SPOKEN said when you are not behaving or feeling as you usually do, because you are sick or upset || 아프거나 화가 나서 평소대로 행동하거나 느끼지 않을 때 쓰여. 제 정신이 아닌: *I'm sorry for what I said – I'm not myself these days.* 내가 한 말 미안해. 내가 요즘 제 정신이 아니야.

mys·te·ri·ous /mɪ'stɪriəs/ *adj* 1 strange and difficult to explain or understand || 이상하며 설명하거나 이해하기 어려운. 신비한. 불가사의한: *a mysterious illness for which the doctors could not find a cause* 의사들이 원인을 찾아낼 수 없었던 원인 불명의 병 2 not saying much about something, because you want it to be a secret || 비밀로 하고 싶어서 어떤 것에 대해서 많이 말하지 않는. 비밀로 하는. 잠자코 있는: *John and Randi are being very mysterious about something – do you think they might be engaged?* 존과 랜디는 뭔가 매우 수상한 데가 있어. 그들이 약혼했을 거라고 생각하니? – **mysteriously** *adv*

mys·ter·y /'mɪstəri/ *n* 1 something that is difficult to explain or understand || 설명하거나 이해하기 어려운 것. 신비로운[불가사의한] 것: *The location of the stolen money remains a mystery.* 훔친 돈의 행방이 묘연하다. 2 a story, especially about a murder, in which events are not explained until the end ‖ 사건이 결말지어질 때까지는 밝혀지지 않는, 특히 살인에 대한 이야기. 추리 소설: *the Sherlock Holmes mystery stories* 셜록 홈즈 추리 소설 **3** [U] a quality that makes someone or something seem strange, interesting, and difficult to explain or understand ‖ 사람이나 사물을 이상하고 흥미로우며 설명하거나 이해하기 어려워 보이게 하는 특성. 신비. 불가사의: *old legends full of mystery* 신비로움으로 가득한 오랜 전설들

mys·ti·cal /ˈmɪstɪkəl/, **mystic** /ˈmɪstɪk/ *adj* relating to religious or magical powers that people cannot understand ‖ 사람들이 이해할 수 없는 종교적 또는 마법적 힘과 관련된. 신비주의의. 불가해한: *the mystical experiences of the Navajo religion* 나바호족 종교의 신비주의적 경험 **– mystically** *adv*

mys·ti·cism /ˈmɪstəˌsɪzəm/ *n* [U] a religious practice in which someone tries to gain knowledge about God and truth by praying and thinking very seriously ‖ 사람이 아주 진지하게 기도하고 생각해서 신과 진리에 대해 알려고 노력하는 종교적 실천. 신비주의 **– mystic** /ˈmɪstɪk/ *n*

mys·ti·fy /ˈmɪstəˌfaɪ/ *v* [T] to make someone feel confused and unable to explain or understand something ‖ 다른 사람을 혼동스럽게 하거나 어떤 것을 설명하거나 이해할 수 없게 하다. 어리둥절하게 하다: *a case that mystified the police* 경찰을 의혹에 빠지게 한 사건 **– mystifying** *adj*

mys·tique /mɪˈstik/ *n* [U] FORMAL the quality that makes something seem mysterious, special, or interesting ‖ 어떤 것을 신비롭게[특별하게, 흥미롭게] 보이게 하는 특성. 신비한 분위기. 신비성: *the mystique of Hollywood in the 1940s* 1940년대 할리우드의 신비성

myth /mɪθ/ *n* **1** [C, U] an ancient story, especially one that explains a natural or historical event, or this type of story in general ‖ 특히 자연적이거나 역사적인 사건을 설명하는 고대의 이야기, 또는 이런 종류의 이야기의 총칭. 신화: *the Greek myths that deal with the creation of the world* 세상의 창조에 대해 다루는 그리스 신화 **2** an idea or story that many people believe, but that is not true ‖ 많은 사람들이 믿지만 사실이 아닌 생각이나 이야기. (근거 없는) 사회 통념. 속설: *the myth that older workers are not productive* 나이 든 노동자가 비생산적이라는 (잘못된) 사회 통념

myth·i·cal /ˈmɪθɪkəl/ *adj* **1** relating to MYTH ‖ 신화와 관련된. 신화의. 신화적인: *mythical creatures such as the Minotaur* 미노타우로스 등의 신화속의 인물 **2** not real or true, but only imagined ‖ 진짜나 사실이 아니며 단지 상상에 불과한. 상상[가공]의. 사실무근인: *the mythical Wild West of popular fiction* 통속 소설 속에 나타난 허무맹랑한 미국 서부 개척시대 이야기

my·thol·o·gy /mɪˈθɑlədʒi/ *n* [C, U] ancient MYTHs in general, or the beliefs that they represent ‖ 고대신화를 총칭한 것, 또는 신화가 표현하는 믿음. 신화 (체계): *stories from Greek mythology* 그리스 신화 이야기 **– mythological** /ˌmɪθəˈlɑdʒɪkəl/ *adj*

Nn

N, n /ɛn/ the fourteenth letter of the English alphabet ‖ 영어 알파벳의 열넷째 자

N the written abbreviation of NORTH or NORTHERN ‖ north나 northern의 약어

n the written abbreviation of NOUN ‖ noun의 약어

'n' /n, ən/ *conjunction* a short form of AND ‖ and의 단축형: *rock 'n' roll music* 로큰롤 음악

N/A the written abbreviation of "not applicable"; used on a form to show that you do not need to answer a particular question ‖ "not applicable(해당 사항 없음)"의 약어; 서식에서 특정 질문에 답변할 필요가 없음을 표시하는 데에 쓰여

nab /næb/ *v* **-bbed, -bbing** [T] INFORMAL to catch someone doing something illegal ‖ 불법적인 짓을 하는 사람을 잡다. (붙)잡다. 체포하다: *You'd be surprised who gets **nabbed** for riding without a ticket.* 너는 누가 표 없이 타다 붙잡혔는지를 알면 놀랄 것이다.

nag¹ /næg/ *v* **-gged, -gging** [I, T] **1** to complain continuously to someone in order to get him/her to do something ‖ 남에게 어떤 것을 해 달라고 끊임없이 불평하다. 계속 잔소리하여 …하게 하다[시키다]. 성가시게 졸라대다: *Shawna has been **nagging** me to fix the kitchen sink.* 쇼나는 내게 부엌 싱크대를 고쳐 달라고 졸라댔다. **2** to be annoyed, worried, or upset about something again and again over a period of time ‖ 일정 기간에 걸쳐 반복하여 어떤 것으로 짜증나다[걱정하다, 속상해 하다]. 끊임없이 시달리다[애를 먹다]: *White has been **nagged** by various injuries throughout the season.* 화이트는 시즌 내내 여러 가지 부상으로 시달렸다.

nag² *n* INFORMAL someone who NAGs continuously ‖ 끊임없이 귀찮게 잔소리하는 사람

nag·ging /'nægɪŋ/ *adj* making you worry or feel pain all the time ‖ 항상 걱정하거나 고통을 느끼게 하는. 계속적으로 괴롭히는: *a nagging headache* 지속적인 두통

nail¹ /neɪl/ *n* **1** a thin pointed piece of metal with a flat end, that you push into a piece of wood etc. using a hammer ‖ 납작한 대가리가 달려 있으며 망치를 사용하여 나무 등에 박는 가늘고 뾰족한 금속 조각. 못 **2** the hard flat part that covers the top end of your fingers and toes ‖ 손가락과 발가락의 끝 부위를 덮는 딱딱하고 납작한 부분. 손톱. 발톱: *Taryn's trying hard to stop biting her nails.* 타린은 손톱을 깨물지 않으려고 열심히 노력하고 있다. —see picture at HAND¹ —see also **fight (sb/sth) tooth and nail** (TOOTH)

nail

nail² *v* [T] **1** to fasten something to something else with a nail ‖ 못으로 사물을 다른 사물에 고정시키다. 못을 박다. 못질하여 붙이다: *The windows were **nailed** shut.* 창문들은 열리지 않게 못질이 되어 있었다. **2** INFORMAL to catch someone who has done something wrong and prove that s/he is guilty ‖ 나쁜 짓을 한 사람을 붙잡아 유죄임을 증명하다. 범죄자를 체포[검거]하다: *They finally managed to **nail** the guy who killed those girls.* 그들은 마침내 그 소녀들을 살해한 사내를 검거해 냈다. **3** INFORMAL to do something exactly right, or to be exactly correct ‖ 어떤 것을 정확하게 하다, 또는 꼭 맞다. 명중[성공]시키다: *Taylor **nailed** a jump shot with 1.1 seconds left in the game.* 테일러는 경기에서 1.1초를 남겨 두고 점프 슛을 성공시켰다. **4** INFORMAL to hit something or someone ‖ 사물이나 사람을 때리다. 치다: *Somebody drove through a stop light and **nailed** her.* 누군가가 정지 신호를 무시하고 운전해서 그녀를 쳤다.

nail sb/sth ↔ **down** *phr v* [T] **1** to fasten something with nails ‖ 못으로 사물을 고정시키다. 못박아 붙이다 **2** to reach a final and definite decision about something ‖ 어떤 것에 대해 최종적이고 명확한 결정을 내리다. 최종 확정하다: *It will take some more work before the agreement is **nailed** down.* 협정이 최종 타결되기 전에 처리할 일이 몇 가지 더 있다.

nail·brush /'neɪlbrʌʃ/ *n* a small stiff brush used for cleaning your nails ‖ 손톱을 다듬을 때 쓰는 작고 뻣뻣한 솔. 손톱솔

nail file /ˈ. ./ *n* a thin piece of metal with a rough surface, used for shaping your nails ‖ 손톱의 모양을 내는 데에 사용하는 표면이 거친 얇은 금속 조각. 손톱 다듬는 줄

nail pol·ish /ˈ. ˌ../ *n* [U] colored or clear liquid that women paint on their nails to make them look attractive ‖ 여성이 매력적으로 보이도록 손톱에 칠하는 색깔이 있거나 투명한 액체. 매니큐어(용 에나멜)

na·ive /nɑˈiv/ *adj* lacking experience, so that you believe most people are honest and kind and that good things will happen to you ‖ 경험이 없어서 대부분의 사람이 정직하고 친절하며 좋은 일이 자기에게 일어날 것이라고 믿는. 순진한. 고지식한: *Perhaps it was naive, but I never regretted giving him my phone number.* 어쩌면 순진했었는지 모르지만 나는 그에게 전화번호를 준 일을 결코 후회하지 않았다. **– naively** *adv* **– naivety, naiveté** /nɑˈivəˌteɪ, nɑˌivˈteɪ/ *n* [U]

na·ked /ˈneɪkɪd/ *adj* **1** not wearing any clothes; NUDE ‖ 옷을 전혀 입지 않은. 벌거벗은. 나체의; ㊤ nude **2 with the naked eye** without an instrument such as a MICROSCOPE to help you see ‖ 관찰을 도와주는 현미경 등의 기구 없이. 육안[나안]으로 **– nakedness** *n* [U] **– nakedly** *adv*

name¹ /neɪm/ *n* **1** the word that someone or something is called or known by ‖ 사람이나 사물이 불리거나 식별되는 말. 이름. 명칭. 호칭. 성명: *Hi, what's your name?* 안녕, 이름이 뭐야? / *Peter is his first name, and Nolan is his last name.* 피터는 그의 이름이고 놀란은 성이다. / *What's the name of the street the school is on?* 그 학교가 있는 거리의 이름이 뭐야? **2 a big/famous/household name** INFORMAL someone who is famous ‖ 유명한 사람. 거물/유명인/명문가 **3** [singular] the opinion that people have about a person, company etc.; REPUTATION ‖ 사람들이 사람·회사 등에 대해 갖는 의견. 평판. 세평. 명성; ㊤ reputation: *He has given baseball a bad name.* (=made people have a bad opinion about it) 그는 야구를 악평했다. / *Carl returned to Bay City to clear his good name.* (=make people have a good opinion of him again) 칼은 명성을 되찾기 위해 베이 시로 돌아왔다. **4 be in sb's name** to officially belong to someone ‖ 공식적으로 누군가에게 속하다. …명의[소유]로 되다: *The house is in my wife's*

name. 그 집은 나의 아내 명의로 되어 있다. **5 the name of the game** the most important thing or quality in a particular activity ‖ 특정 활동에서 가장 중요한 것이나 특성. 불가결한 일. 본질: *Beating the competition is the whole name of the game.* 경기를 이긴다는 것이 가장 중요한 것이다. **6 (do sth) in the name of science/religion etc.** to use science, religion etc. as the reason for doing something, even if it is wrong ‖ 설령 그것이 잘못됐다 하더라도 어떤 일을 하는 근거로 과학·종교 등을 이용하다. (…을) 과학/종교의 이름으로[을 빌려서](하다)

USAGE NOTE names

Use someone's first name when you know him/her, unless s/he is quite a lot older than you are: *What do you think, Pat?* Use someone's title and last name in formal situations, or in order to show respect for someone who is quite a lot older than you are: *Professor Taylor, could I make an appointment to see you? / How are your grandchildren, Mr. Fox?* You can use titles such as Doctor and Professor alone, without a name: *What's wrong with me, Doctor?* However, the titles "Mr.," "Ms.," "Mrs.," and "Miss" can only be used if you are also saying someone's last name: *Hello, Mrs. Radnor! / Will Mrs. Fran Radnor please come to the information desk?* ✗DON'T SAY "Hello, Mrs.!" or "Hello, Mrs. Fran!"✗ Last names are not used alone, except by people who know each other very well. ✗DON'T SAY "Hello, Radnor!"✗ 아는 사람이 자신보다 나이가 훨씬 많지 않을 때에는 이름을 써서 부른다: 어떻게 생각해, 팻? 공식적 상황이나 자신보다 훨씬 나이 많은 사람에 대한 존중을 나타내기 위해 직함이나 성(姓)을 써서 부른다: 테일러 교수님, 면담 약속을 할 수 있을까요? / 폭스 씨, 손자·소녀들은 잘 있습니까? Doctor·Professor 등의 호칭은 이름 없이 단독으로 사용할 수 있다: 내게 무슨 이상이 있습니까, 의사 선생님? 그러나 "Mr."·"Ms."·"Mrs."·"Miss" 호칭은 사람의 성(姓)을 함께 말할 때에만 쓸 수 있다: 안녕하세요, 래드너 여사님! / 프랜 래드너 부인은 안내 창구로 와 주시겠습니까? "Hello, Mrs.!" 또는 "Hello, Mrs. Fran!"이라고는 하지 않는다. 성(姓) 호

칭은 서로 아주 잘 아는 사람들 외에는 단독으로 쓰이지 않는다. "Hello, Radnor!"라고는 하지 않는다.

name² *v* [T] **1** to give someone or something a particular name ‖ 사람이나 사물에 특정한 이름을 지어주다. 이름을 붙이다. 명명하다: *Sarah named the baby Henry, after his grandfather.* (=gave him the same name as his grandfather) 사라는 아기의 할아버지 이름을 따서 아기에게 헨리라고 이름지어 주었다. / *The stadium was named for Brady, who provided the money.* (=it was given the name of someone who was related in some way to the thing being named) 그 경기장은 돈을 제공한 브래디의 이름을 땄다. **2** to say what the name of someone or something is ‖ 사람이나 사물의 이름이 무엇인지 말하다. 이름을 부르다[대다]: *Can you name this song?* 이 노래의 제목을 댈 수 있어요? / *The police have not yet named the murder victim.* 경찰은 아직 살인 희생자의 이름을 발표하지 않았다. **3** to officially choose someone for a particular job ‖ 특정한 일에 사람을 공식적으로 선택하다. 지명[임명]하다: *Roy Johnson was named as the new manager.* 로이 존슨이 새 매니저로 임명되었다. **4 you name it** SPOKEN said after a list of things to mean that there are many more that you could mention ‖ 거론 가능한 것이 훨씬 더 많다는 것을 의미하기 위해 사물의 목록 뒤에 쓰여. 그 밖에 무엇이든지. 전부: *Beer, whiskey, wine – you name it and I've got it!* 맥주, 위스키, 포도주, 말만 해. 다 있으니까! **5 name names** to give the names of people who have done something wrong or illegal to someone in authority ‖ 권한 있는 사람에게 잘못이나 불법을 저지른 사람의 이름을 대다. 공범자의 이름을 불다

name-cal·ling /ˈ. ͵../ *n* [U] the act of saying or shouting rude words at someone ‖ 남에게 무례한 말을 하거나 소리치기. 욕설. 매도

name-drop /ˈneɪmdrɑp/ *v* **-pped, -pping** [I] DISAPPROVING to mention famous people's names and pretend that you know them so people will admire you ‖ 사람들이 우러러보도록 유명한 사람의 이름을 언급하고 그들을 잘 아는 것처럼 행동하다 – **namedropping** *n* [U]

name·less /ˈneɪmlɪs/ *adj* **1** not known by a name; ANONYMOUS ‖ 이름이 알려지지 않은. 이름을 모르는. 익명의; ⓐ

anonymous: *a gift from a nameless businessman* 익명의 사업가가 보낸 선물 **2** having no name ‖ 이름 없는. 무명의: *millions of nameless stars* 수백만 개의 이름 없는 별들

name·ly /ˈneɪmli/ *adv* used in order to make it clear exactly what or who you are talking about ‖ 정확히 무엇이나 누구에 대해 말하는지를 분명히 하는 데에 쓰여. 즉. 다시 말하면: *The movie won two Oscars, namely "Best Actor" and "Best Director."* 그 영화는 두 개의 오스카상, 즉 "최고 남우 주연상"과 "최고 감독상"을 받았다.

name·sake /ˈneɪmseɪk/ *n* **sb's namesake** someone or something that has the same name as someone or something else ‖ 어떤 사람이나 사물과 같은 이름을 가진 사람이나 사물. 이름이 같은[여타의 이름을 딴] 사람[것]

name tag /ˈ. ./ *n* a small sign with your name on it that you attach to your clothes so that people at a party, meeting etc. know who you are ‖ 파티·모임 등에 있는 사람들이, 자신이 누구인지 알도록 옷에 부착하는 이름이 적힌 작은 표. 이름표. 명찰

nan·ny /ˈnæni/ *n* a woman whose job is to take care of a family's children, usually in the children's own home ‖ 보통 어린애의 집에서 가족의 아이들을 돌보는 여성 직업인. 유모

nan·o·tech·nol·o·gy /ˈnænoʊtɛkˈnɑlədʒi/ *n* [U] TECHNICAL an area of science which involves developing and making extremely small but very powerful machines ‖ 아주 작지만 매우 강력한 기계의 개발과 제조에 관련된 과학 영역. 나노기술

nap¹ /næp/ *n* a short sleep during the day ‖ 낮에 잠깐 자는 잠. 낮잠: *Dad usually takes a nap in the afternoon.* 아빠는 오후에 보통 낮잠을 주무신다.

nap² *v* **-pped, -pping 1** [I] to sleep for a short time during the day ‖ 낮 동안에 짧은 시간 동안 자다. 잠시 졸다. 낮잠 자다 **2 be caught napping** INFORMAL to not be ready when something happens, although you should have been ready ‖ 미리 준비되어 있어야 함에도 일이 일어났을 때 준비되어 있지 않다. 방심하다. 허를 찔리다

na·palm /ˈneɪpɑm/ *n* [U] a thick liquid made from GASOLINE that is used in bombs ‖ 휘발유로 만들어 폭탄에 사용되는 진한 액체. 네이팜. 인화성 소이제

nape /neɪp/ *n* [singular] the back of your neck ‖ 목 뒷부위. 목덜미

nap·kin /'næpkɪn/ *n* a small piece of cloth or paper used for cleaning your mouth or hands when you are eating ‖ 식사할 때 입이나 손을 깨끗이 하는 데에 사용되는 작은 천이나 종이. 냅킨

narc¹ /nɑrk/ *n* INFORMAL a police officer who deals with catching people who use and sell illegal drugs ‖ 마약을 사용하고 파는 사람을 잡는 일을 담당하는 경찰관. 마약 단속관[수사관]

narc² *v* [I] SLANG to tell the police about something illegal that someone is doing, especially when it involves drugs ‖ 어떤 사람이 특히 마약과 관련되어 하고 있는 불법적인 일을 경찰에 말하다. 마약 범죄를 밀고하다

nar·cis·sis·m /'nɑrsə,sɪzəm/ *n* [U] FORMAL too much admiration for your own appearance or abilities ‖ 자기 자신의 외모나 능력에 대한 지나친 감탄. 자기 도취증. 나르시시즘 **– narcissistic** /,nɑrsə'sɪstɪk/ *adj* **– narcissist** /'nɑrsəsɪst/ *n*

nar·cot·ic /nɑr'kɑtɪk/ *n* [C usually plural] a type of drug that takes away pain and makes you feel sleepy, which may be used in hospitals but is usually illegal ‖ 병원에서는 사용될 수 있지만 보통 불법인, 통증을 없애고 잠이 오게 하는 약의 일종. 마취제. 마약: *The pair were arrested for possession of narcotics.* 그 부부는 마약 소지 혐의로 체포되었다. **– narcotic** *adj*

nar·rate /'næreɪt, næ'reɪt/ *v* [T] if someone narrates a movie or television program, s/he describes or explains what is happening in the pictures ‖ 영화나 TV의 화면에서 벌어지는 일에 대해 묘사하거나 설명하다. 내레이터를 맡다. 해설을 덧붙이다: *a documentary narrated by Robert Redford* 로버트 레드포드가 내레이션을 한 기록 영화

nar·ra·tion /næ'reɪʃən/ *n* [C, U] FORMAL **1** the act of telling what happens in a story ‖ 이야기 상에서 일어나는 일을 말하기. 이야기하기. 서술: *The narration switches from the past to the present and back again.* 이야기는 과거와 현재를 오가며 펼쳐진다. **2** a spoken description or explanation during a play, movie etc. ‖ 연극이나 영화 중의 말로 하는 묘사나 설명. 해설. 내레이션

nar·ra·tive /'nærətɪv/ *n* [C, U] FORMAL a description of events that is told as a story ‖ 이야기로 말해지는 사건의 묘사. 이야기: *a narrative that is set during the Civil War* 남북 전쟁 기간 중으로 배경이 설정된 이야기 **– narrative** *adj*

nar·ra·tor /'næ,reɪtɚ/ *n* someone who tells the story in a movie, book etc. ‖ 영화나 책 등에서 이야기를 말하는 사람. 내레이터. 해설자. 화자

narrow

a narrow street   a wide street

nar·row¹ /'næroʊ/ *adj* **1** only measuring a small distance from side to side ‖ 측면에서 측면까지의 거리가 아주 작게 측정되는. 폭이 좁은. 좁고 긴: *a long narrow street* 길고 폭이 좁은 거리 **—opposite** WIDE¹ **2** DISAPPROVING too limited, and not allowing other possibilities ‖ 너무 제한되고 다른 가능성을 허용하지 않는. 한정된. 편협한: *I am disappointed by the narrow viewpoint given by the author.* 나는 작가가 제시하는 편협한 견해에 실망했다. **3 win/lose etc. by a narrow margin** to win, lose etc. by a small amount ‖ 작은 차이로 이기거나 지다. 간신히 이기다/지다 **4 narrow defeat/victory etc.** a defeat, victory etc. that you only just lose or win ‖ 아슬아슬한 패배/승리 **5 narrow escape** a situation in which you only just avoid danger or trouble ‖ 가까스로 위험이나 어려움을 피하는 상황. 구사일생 **– narrowly** *adv* **– narrowness** *n* [U]

nar·row² *v* [I, T] **1** to become more narrow, or to make something do this ‖ 더 좁아지다, 또는 어떤 것을 좁히다: *The road narrows here.* 길은 여기서 좁아진다. / *She narrowed her eyes and frowned.* 그녀는 눈을 가늘게 뜨며 눈살을 찌푸렸다. **2** also **narrow down** to become less in number, range etc., or to make something do this ‖ 수나 범위 등이 더 적어지다, 또는 어떤 것을 이렇게 되게 하다. 줄다. 줄이다: *There were over 800 entries, and it was hard to narrow down the list of finalists.* 참가자가 800명이 넘어서 최종 참가자 명단을 좁혀 나가는 것은 어려운 일이었다.

nar·row³ *n* ⇨ **the straight and narrow** (STRAIGHT)

narrow-mind·ed /' .. ,../ *adj* not willing to accept ideas or beliefs that are new and different ‖ 새롭고 다른 사상이나 신념을 받아들이려고 하지 않는. 편

협한

na·sal /ˈneɪzəl/ adj 1 a nasal sound or voice comes mostly through your nose ‖ 소리나 목소리가 대부분 코를 통해 나오는. 콧소리[비음]의. 코먹은 소리의: a high nasal voice 높은 콧소리 2 relating to the nose ‖ 코에 관련된. 코의: the nasal cavity 비강(鼻腔) – **nasally** adv

nas·ty /ˈnæsti/ adj 1 having a bad appearance, smell, or taste ‖ 형편없는 모습[냄새, 맛]을 가진. 더러운. 불결한: a nasty looking apartment 몹시 불결해 보이는 아파트 2 unkind and unpleasant ‖ 불친절하고 불쾌한. 심술궂은. 고약한. 비열한: a nasty thing to say 심한 말 / a nasty old man 심술궂은 노인 3 very severe, painful, or unpleasant ‖ 매우 심한[고통스러운, 언짢은]. 험악한. 심각한: a nasty cut on his hand 그의 손의 심하게 벤 상처 / nasty weather 험악한 날씨 4 morally bad or offensive; OBSCENE ‖ 도덕적으로 부정하거나 방종한. 음란[음탕]한. 추잡한; ㉕ obscene: a nasty mind 추잡한 마음 – **nastiness** n [U] – **nastily** adv

na·tion /ˈneɪʃən/ n 1 a word meaning a country and its people, used especially when considering its political and economic structures ‖ 국가와 그 국민을 의미하는 말로서 특히 정치·경제 구조를 고려할 때 쓰여. 나라. 국가. 국민: The President is addressing the nation tomorrow. 대통령은 내일 대국민 담화를 발표한다. / the richest nation in the world 세계에서 가장 부유한 나라 2 a large group of people of the same race and speaking the same language ‖ 같은 인종이고 동일 언어를 말하는 사람의 큰 집단. 민족. 종족: the Cherokee nation 체로키 종족 —see usage note at RACE¹

na·tion·al¹ /ˈnæʃənl/ adj 1 relating to a whole nation rather than to part of it or to other nations ‖ 국가의 일부나 다른 국가들에 관련되기보다 한 국가 전체에 관한. 국가의[적인]. 전국(민)적인: the national news 국내 뉴스 / an issue of national importance 국가적으로 중요한 문제 —compare INTERNATIONAL 2 typical of a particular nation ‖ 특정 국가에 전형적인. 국민의[적인]. 국민 특유의: national dress 민족 의상

national² n someone who is a citizen of one country but is living in another country ‖ 한 나라의 시민이지만 다른 나라에 살고 있는 사람. 해외 동포. 교포: a Korean national living in the US 미국에 사는 한국인 교포 —compare ALIEN², CITIZEN

national an·them /ˌ... ˈ../ n the official song of a nation that is sung or played at public occasions ‖ 공공의 행사에서 불려지거나 연주되는 한 국가의 공식적인 노래. 국가(國歌)

na·tion·al·ism /ˈnæʃənlˌɪzəm/ n [U] 1 the belief that your country is better than any other country ‖ 자신의 나라가 다른 어떤 나라보다도 더 낫다는 신념. 국가주의. 국수주의 2 the desire of people who have the same race or who speak the same language etc. to have their own country ‖ 같은 인종이며 같은 언어를 사용하는 사람들이 자기 나라를 가지려는 욕구. 민족주의: the rise of nationalism in Eastern Europe 동유럽에서의 민족주의의 대두

na·tion·al·ist /ˈnæʃənl-ɪst/ adj wanting to become politically independent, or wanting to remain this way ‖ 정치적으로 독립하기를 원하는, 또는 독립 상태로 남아있기를 바라는. 민족 독립주의(자)의. 민족 자결주의(자)의: African nationalist movements 아프리카 민족 자결주의 운동 – **nationalist** n

na·tion·al·is·tic /ˌnæʃənəˈlɪstɪk/ adj believing that your country is better than other countries ‖ 자신의 나라가 다른 나라들보다 더 낫다고 믿는. 국가[국수]주의적인: a nationalistic speech 국수주의적인 연설

na·tion·al·i·ty /ˌnæʃəˈnæləti/ n [C, U] the legal right of belonging to a particular country; CITIZENSHIP ‖ 특정한 나라에 속하는 법적 권리. 국적; ㉕ citizenship: a man who has British nationality 영국 국적을 가진 남자 ✗DON'T SAY "My nationality is Mexican/Swedish etc." SAY "I come from Mexico/Sweden etc."✗ "My nationality is Mexican/Swedish etc."라고는 하지 않고 "I come from Mexico/Sweden etc."라고 한다.

na·tion·al·ize /ˈnæʃənəˌlaɪz/ v [T] if a government nationalizes an organization, industry etc., it buys it in order to take control of it ‖ 정부가 조직체나 산업 등을 국유[국영]화하다 —compare PRIVATIZE, SOCIALIZE

na·tion·al·ly /ˈnæʃənl-i/ adv by or to everyone in a nation ‖ 국가의 모든 사람에 의해 또는 에게. 국민으로서. 전국적으로: a series of nationally televised debates 전국적으로 방영된 일련의 토론

national mon·u·ment /ˌ... ˈ.../ n a building or a special place that is protected by the government for people to visit ‖ 사람들이 방문하도록 국가가 보

호하는 건물이나 특별한 장소. 국정 기념물

national park /ˌ… ˈ./ n a large area of beautiful land that is protected by the government for people to visit ‖ 사람들이 방문하도록 국가가 보호하는 경관이 훌륭한 넓은 지역. 국립공원: *Yellowstone National Park* 옐로스톤 국립공원

national se·cu·ri·ty /ˌ… .ˈ…/ n [U] the idea that a country must protect its citizens, especially by having a strong army, or the state of having this protection ‖ 국가가 특히 강한 군대를 보유해서 시민을 보호해야 한다는 생각, 또는 이렇게 보호되는 상태. 국가 안전 (보장): *The US Army says that releasing the document would damage national security.* 미군은 그 문서를 공표하면 국가 안보를 해칠 것이라고 말한다.

na·tion·wide /ˌneɪʃənˈwaɪd./ adj happening or existing in every part of a nation ‖ 한 나라의 모든 지역에서 일어나거나 존재하는. 전국적인. 전국에 걸친: *nationwide price increases* 전국적인 가격 인상 / *The brewery employs about 3000 people nationwide.* 그 맥주 회사는 전국적으로 약 3000명을 고용하고 있다. – **nationwide** adv

na·tive¹ /ˈneɪtɪv/ adj **1** **native country/land etc.** the place where you were born ‖ 태어난 곳. 고국. 본국. 모국: *The Pope is visiting his native Poland.* (=Poland is where he was born) 교황은 자신의 고국인 폴란드를 방문하고 있다. **2** **native Californian/New Yorker etc.** someone who was born in California etc. ‖ 캘리포니아 등에서 태어난 사람. 캘리포니아/뉴욕 토박이 **3** **native language/tongue** the language you spoke when you first learned to speak ‖ 처음 말하기를 배웠을 때 썼던 언어. 모국어 **4** growing, living, or produced in a particular area ‖ 특정한 지역에서 자라는[사는, 생산된]. …특산의. …원산의: *a plant native to Ecuador* 에콰도르 원산의 식물 **5** **native speaker** someone who speaks the language s/he learned as a baby ‖ 아기 때부터 배웠던 언어를 말하는 사람. 모국어를 말하는 사람. 원어민: *Practice your German with native speakers.* 원어민과 함께 독어를 연습하라. —opposite NON-NATIVE

native² n **1** **a native of** someone who was born in a particular place ‖ 특정한 지역에서 태어난 사람. …태생인 사람. 출신(자): *She's a native of southern Brazil.* 그녀는 남부 브라질 출신이다. **2** [C usually plural] OFFENSIVE a member of a race who lived in Africa, South

America etc. before the Europeans arrived ‖ 유럽인이 도착하기 전에 아프리카·남아메리카 등에 살았던 인종의 한 사람. 토착민. 원주민

Native A·mer·i·can /ˌ… .ˈ…/ n someone who belongs to one of the tribes who were living in North America before the Europeans arrived ‖ 유럽인이 도착하기 전에 북아메리카에 살고 있었던 종족 중 하나에 속한 사람. 아메리카 원주민[인디언] – **Native American** adj

NATO /ˈneɪtoʊ/ n [singular] the North Atlantic Treaty Organization; a group of countries in North America and Europe that give military help to each other ‖ 북대서양 조약 기구(나토)의 약어; 서로 군사적 협력을 하는 북아메리카와 유럽 국가들의 집단

nat·u·ral¹ /ˈnætʃərəl/ adj **1** normal or usual, and what you would expect in a particular situation ‖ 정상적이거나 일반적이며 특정 상황에서 예상할 수 있는 것의. 자연적인. 당연한: *It's only natural to have doubts before your wedding.* (=it is completely normal) 결혼식 전에 회의가 드는 것은 아주 당연하다. / *It's not natural for a four-year-old to be so quiet.* 4살짜리가 그렇게 조용한 것은 정상이 아니다. —opposite UNNATURAL **2** not caused, made, or controlled by people ‖ 사람에 의해 생기지[만들어지지, 제어되지] 않는. 자연의. 천연의. 야생의: *earthquakes and other natural disasters* 지진과 다른 자연 재해 / *natural fibers like cotton* 면화와 같은 천연 섬유 **3** having a particular skill or ability without being taught ‖ 배우지 않고 특정한 기술이나 능력이 있는. 타고난. 선천적인: *a natural athlete* 타고난 운동 선수 **4** not looking or sounding unusual ‖ 이상하게 보이거나 들리지 않는. 자연스런. 꾸밈[가식] 없는: *Was he really that nervous? He acted natural enough.* 그가 정말 그렇게 긴장했어? 자연스럽기 그지없었어. – **naturalness** n [U]

natural² n **be a natural** to be very good at doing something without being taught ‖ 배우지 않고서도 어떤 것을 하는 데 매우 능숙하다. 적격[천부적]이다: *Look how he swings that bat – he's a complete natural!* 그가 저 방망이를 어떻게 휘두르는가를 보라. 그는 완전히 천부적이다!

natural gas /ˌ… ˈ./ n [U] gas used for cooking or heating that is taken from under the earth or ocean ‖ 지하나 해저에서 채굴한 요리용이나 난방용 가스. 천연 가스

natural his·to·ry /,... '.../ *n* [U] the study of plants, animals, and minerals ‖ 식물·동물·광물의 연구. 박물학[지]

nat·u·ral·ist /'nætʃrəlɪst/ *n* someone who studies plants, animals, and other living things ‖ 식물·동물과 다른 생물을 연구하는 사람. 박물학자

nat·u·ral·ize /'nætʃrə,laɪz/ *v* [T] to make someone a citizen of a country that s/he was not born in ‖ 사람을 태어나지 않은 나라의 시민으로 만들다. 귀화시키다. 시민권을 주다 – **naturalization** /,nætʃrələ'zeɪʃən/ *n* [U]

nat·u·ral·ly /'nætʃrəli/ *adv* **1** in a way that you would expect ‖ 기대한 대로. 예상대로. 당연히: *Students naturally make mistakes when translating another language.* 학생들은 다른 언어를 번역할 때 당연히 실수를 한다. **2** SPOKEN used in order to agree with what someone has said, or to answer "of course" to a question ‖ 남이 말한 것에 동의하거나 질문에 "물론"이라고 대답하는 데에 쓰여: *"Are you excited to be home?" "Naturally."* "집으로 돌아오니 좋습니까?" "물론입니다." **3** as a natural feature or quality ‖ 자연적인 특징이나 특성으로. 나면서부터. 선천적으로: *naturally curly hair* 선천적인 곱슬머리 / *Golf seemed to come naturally to him.* (=he was good at it without being taught) 골프는 그의 선천적으로 타고난 소질 같았다. **4** in a manner that is no different from usual ‖ 평소와 전혀 다르지 않게. 자연스럽게. 꾸밈없이: *Speak naturally into the microphone, please.* 마이크를 통해 자연스럽게 말하세요.

natural re·sourc·es /,... '.../ *n* [plural] all the land, minerals, energy etc. that exist in a country ‖ 한 나라에 존재하는 모든 토지·광물·에너지 등. 천연자원

natural se·lec·tion /,... .'../ *n* [U] TECHNICAL the process by which only the plants and animals that are suitable to their environment will continue to live ‖ 환경에 적합한 식물과 동물만이 계속해서 사는 과정. 자연 도태. 적자생존

na·ture /'neɪtʃɚ/ *n* **1** [U] everything that exists in the world that is not made or controlled by humans, such as animals, plants, weather etc. ‖ 동물·식물·기후 등 인간에 의해 만들어지거나 지배되지 않은 세상에 존재하는 모든 것. 자연(계): *We like camping; it makes us feel closer to nature.* 우리는 캠핑을 좋아한다. 캠핑은 우리에게 자연에 좀 더 가까워진 느낌이 들게 한다. **2** [C, U] the

character or particular qualities of someone or something ‖ 사람이나 사물의 성격이나 특정한 성질. 본질. 본성. 천성. 기질: *She is a trusting person by nature.* 그녀는 천성적으로 남을 잘 믿는다. / *The nature of my work requires a lot of traveling.* 내 일은 특성상 여행을 아주 많이 한다. **3** a particular type of thing ‖ 특정한 유형의 것. 종류. 성질: *He provided support of a political/financial nature.* 그는 정치적[재정적]인 지원을 제공했다. **4 let nature take its course** to allow events to happen without doing anything to change the results ‖ 결과를 변화시키려는 어떤 것도 하지 않고 사건이 일어나도록 내버려 두다. 자연[운명]에 맡기다: *The medicine didn't work, so we let nature take its course.* 그 약도 듣지 않아서 우리는 운명에 맡겼다. —see also SECOND NATURE

nature re·serve /'.. .,./ *n* an area of land in which animals and plants are protected ‖ 동물과 식물이 보호되는 지역. 자연 보호구(역)

naught /nɔt/ *n* [U] OLD-FASHIONED nothing ‖ 없음. 무(無). 영(零): *All their plans came to naught.* (=failed) 그들의 모든 계획이 수포로 돌아갔다.

naugh·ty /'nɔti/ *adj* a naughty child behaves badly and is rude or does not obey adults ‖ 아이가 못되게 굴며 무례하거나 어른 말을 안 듣는. 버릇없는. 장난꾸러기의 – **naughtiness** *n* [U] – **naughtily** *adv*

nau·se·a /'nɔziə, 'nɔʒə, 'nɔʃə/ *n* [U] FORMAL the feeling you have when you think you are going to VOMIT ‖ 토할 것 같을 때 가지는 느낌. 구토. 메스꺼움. 멀미

nau·se·at·ed /'nɔzi,eɪtɪd/ *adj* feeling NAUSEA ‖ 구역질나는. 메스꺼운: *When I was pregnant I felt nauseated all the time.* 임신했을 때 나는 항상 구역질났다. – **nauseate** *v* [T]

nau·se·at·ing /'nɔzi,eɪtɪŋ/ *adj* making you feel NAUSEA ‖ 구역질나게 하는. 토할 것 같은: *the nauseating smell of cigar smoke* 토할 것 같은 시가 연기 냄새

nau·seous /'nɔʃəs, -ʒəs/ *adj* **1** NONSTANDARD ⇨ NAUSEATED **2** making you feel NAUSEA ‖ 구역질나게 하는. 메스꺼운: *nauseous odors* 구역질나는 악취 – **nauseously** *adv*

nau·ti·cal /'nɔtɪkəl/ *adj* relating to ships or sailing ‖ 선박이나 항해에 관련된. 해사(海事)의 – **nautically** *adv*

na·val /'neɪvəl/ *adj* relating to the navy ‖ 해군의: *a naval battle* 해전

na·vel /ˈneɪvəl/ *n* FORMAL ⇨ BELLY BUTTON

nav·i·ga·ble /ˈnævɪgəbəl/ *adj* deep and wide enough for ships to travel on ‖ 배가 다닐 수 있을 만큼 깊고 넓은. 항행이 가능한: *Part of the St. Lawrence River is navigable.* 세인트로렌스 강의 일부는 배가 다닐 수 있다.

nav·i·gate /ˈnævə,geɪt/ *v* **1** [I, T] to find the way to a place, especially by using maps ‖ 특히 지도를 이용하여 어떤 장소에 이르는 길을 찾다. (운전자의) 길 안내를 하다: *Rick usually drives and I navigate.* 릭이 보통 운전하고 나는 길 안내를 한다. **2** [T] to sail all the way across or along an area of water ‖ 수역(水域)을 가로지르거나 따라서 죽 항해하다. 항행하다 **3** to find your way around on a particular WEBSITE, or to move from one website to another ‖ 특정 웹사이트로 이리저리 길을 찾아가거나 한 웹사이트에서 다른 웹사이트로 옮겨 다니다. 웹사이트를 찾아가다. 웹서핑하다

nav·i·ga·tion /ˌnævəˈgeɪʃən/ *n* [U] **1** the science of planning the way along which you travel from one place to another ‖ 한 장소에서 다른 장소로 가는 길을 계획하는 학문. 항해술[학]. 항법: *a compass and other navigation instruments* 나침반과 다른 항해술 도구 **2** the act of sailing a ship or flying a plane along a particular line of travel ‖ 특정 항로를 따라 배나 비행기로 항행하기. 항해. 비행: *Navigation along this canal should be easy.* 이 운하를 따라 항해하는 것은 쉽다. **– navigational** *adj*

nav·i·ga·tor /ˈnævə,geɪtə/ *n* the officer on a ship or aircraft who plans the way along which it travels ‖ 다니는 길을 계획하는 선박이나 항공기의 책임자. 항해[항법]사

na·vy /ˈneɪvi/ *n* **1** the part of a country's military forces that is organized for fighting a war at sea ‖ 바다에서 전쟁을 치르기 위해 조직된 한 나라 군사력의 일부. 해군: *My dad was 20 when he joined the navy.* 아빠는 해군에 입대했을 때 20살이었다. **2** the war ships belonging to a country ‖ 한 나라에 속하는 모든 전함[군함]: *the need for a larger navy* 해군력 증강의 필요성 **3** ⇨ NAVY BLUE

navy blue /ˌ.. ˈ./ *adj* very dark blue ‖ 진한 감색의 **– navy blue** *n* [U]

NBC *n* National Broadcasting Company; one of the national television and radio companies in the US ‖ National Broadcasting Company(전미 방송 회사)

의 약어; 미국의 전국적인 텔레비전·라디오 방송 회사 중의 하나

NC the written abbreviation of North Carolina ‖ North Carolina(노스캐롤라이나 주)의 약어

NCAA *n* National Collegiate Athletic Association; the organization that is in charge of sports at American colleges and universities ‖ National Collegiate Athletic Association(전미 대학 체육 협회)의 약어; 미국 대학의 스포츠를 담당하는 조직체

NCO *n* Noncommissioned Officer; a soldier such as a CORPORAL or SERGEANT ‖ Noncommissioned Officer(육군 하사관)의 약어; 하사나 중사 등의 병사

ND the written abbreviation of North Dakota ‖ North Dakota(노스다코타 주)의 약어

NE **1** the written abbreviation of NORTHEAST ‖ Northeast의 약어 **2** the written abbreviation of Nebraska ‖ Nebraska(네브래스카 주)의 약어

near¹ /nɪr/ *adv, prep* **1** only a short distance from someone or something ‖ 사람이나 사물로부터 약간 떨어져. 가까이에. 가까운 장소[범위]에[로]: *Don't go too near the road.* 도로에 너무 가까이 가지 마라. / *I'd like to live nearer the ocean.* 나는 바다와 더 가까운 곳에 살고 싶다. **2** close in time to a particular event ‖ 특정한 행사에 시간적으로 가까이 임박하여: *She got more and more nervous as the wedding drew near.* (=became closer in time) 결혼식이 임박하자 그녀는 더욱더 초조해졌다. / *The construction work is now near completion.* 그 건설 공사는 현재 완공을 눈앞에 두고 있다. **3 nowhere near** not at all close to a particular quality or state ‖ 특정한 특성이나 상태에 전혀 가깝지 않다. 전혀 …아니다: *The new jazz station is nowhere near as good as the old one.* 새로운 재즈 방송 채널은 옛날 것보다 전혀 좋지 않다. / *We're nowhere near finished.* 우리는 끝내려면 아직 멀었다. **4 near perfect/impossible etc.** INFORMAL almost perfect, impossible etc.; nearly ‖ 거의 완벽한·불가능한; 거의: *a near perfect test score* 거의 완벽한 시험 점수

USAGE NOTE near and **close**

Use **near** and **close** to talk about short distances. **Close** is usually followed by the word "to," but **near** is not: *There's a new supermarket*

near our house. / We live close to the bus stop. We also use **close** to talk about something that is not far away in time: *It's close to your bedtime, kids.*
짧은 거리를 말하기 위해 **near**와 **close**를 쓴다. **close**는 보통 "to" 단어가 수반되나 **near**는 그렇지 않다: 우리 집 가까이에 새 슈퍼마켓이 있다. / 우리는 버스 정류장 가까이에 산다. 또한 시간적으로 멀리 떨어지지 않은 것을 말하기 위해 **close**를 쓴다: 얘들아, 잘 시간 다 됐다.

near² *adj* **1** only a short distance from someone or something ‖ 사람이나 사물에서 약간 떨어진. 가까운: *The nearest town (=the town that is the closest) is 20 miles away.* 가장 가까운 도시가 20마일 떨어져 있다. **2** very close to having a particular quality or being a particular thing ‖ 특정한 특성을 갖거나 특정한 것이 되는 데에 가까운. (거의) …에 근접한[닮은]: *His explanation is as near to the truth as we'll get.* 그의 설명은 우리가 얻을 수 있는 한에서는 진실에 거의 가까웠다. / *Honestly, it was a near miracle.* 솔직히 말하면 그것은 기적에 가까웠다. **3 in the near future** at a time that is not very far in the future ‖ 그리 멀지 않은 미래의 시간에. 가까운 장래에. 임박한 미래에: *We will have a new teacher joining us in the near future.* 우리는 머지않아 우리와 함께 할 새 선생님을 맞을 거다. **4 near miss** a situation in which something almost hits something else ‖ 사물이 다른 것을 거의 칠[맞출, 충돌할] 뻔한 상황. 이상(異常) 접근. 위기일발: *Two planes had a near miss above the airport today.* 두 비행기가 오늘 공항 상공에서 거의 충돌할 뻔했다.

near·by /ˌnɪrˈbaɪ/ *adj* not far away ‖ 멀리 떨어지지 않은. 근처의. 바로 가까이의: *We used to go swimming in a nearby lake.* 우리는 근처의 호수로 수영하러 가곤 했다. **– nearby** *adv*

near·ly /ˈnɪrli/ *adv* almost, but not completely or exactly ‖ 완전하거나 정확하지는 않지만 거의. 대략. 대체로: *This isn't nearly as hard as the last test.* 이것은 지난 시험만큼 결코 어렵지 않다. / *Frozen vegetables are nearly always cheaper than fresh ones.* 냉동 야채는 싱싱한 야채보다 대체로 항상 더 싸다.

near·sight·ed /ˈnɪrˌsaɪtɪd/ *adj* unable to see things clearly unless they are close to you ‖ 사물이 가까이에 있지 않으면 분명하게 볼 수 없는. 근시의. 근시안

적인 **– nearsightedness** *n* [U]

neat /nit/ *adj* **1** SPOKEN very good or pleasant ‖ 매우 훌륭하거나 기분 좋은. 솜씨 있는. 멋진: *The fireworks were really neat – I've never seen so many different kinds!* 불꽃놀이가 정말 멋졌는데 나는 그렇게 다양한 종류를 본 적이 없어! **2** carefully arranged and not messy ‖ 꼼꼼히 정리되고 지저분하지 않은. 정돈된. 말끔한. 말쑥한: *She wears her hair in a neat braid.* 그녀는 머리를 가지런히 땋았다. / *They keep their house neat and clean.* 그들은 자기 집을 말끔하고 깨끗하게 정돈해 둔다. **3** a neat person does not like his/her things or house to be messy ‖ 사람이 자신의 물건이나 집이 지저분해지는 것을 좋아하지 않는. 깨끗한 것을 좋아하는. 말끔한 **4** simple and effective ‖ 단순하고 효과적인. 산뜻한. 기막힌: *a neat solution to the problem* 그 문제에 대한 기막힌 해결책 **– neatly** *adv* **– neatness** *n* [U]

nec·es·sar·i·ly /ˌnɛsəˈsɛrəli/ *adv* **1 not necessarily** used in order to say that something is not certain, even if it might be reasonable to expect it to be ‖ 설령 그렇게 예상하는 것이 타당할지라도 확실하지 않다고 말하는 데에 쓰여. 반드시[필수적으로] …은 아니다: *Expensive restaurants do not necessarily have the best food.* 고급 식당이라고 해서 반드시 가장 좋은 음식을 구비하는 것은 아니다. **2** in a way that has to happen and cannot be avoided ‖ 반드시 일어나고 피할 수 없게. 부득이. 할 수 없이. 필연적으로: *Income tax laws are necessarily complicated.* 소득세법은 필연적으로 복잡하다.

nec·es·sar·y /ˈnɛsəˌsɛri/ *adj* **1** needed in order for you to do something or have something; ESSENTIAL ‖ 사람이 어떤 것을 하거나 갖기 위해 필요한. …에 없어서는 안 될. 필수의; ⚓ essential: *Don't call me unless it's absolutely necessary.* 절대적으로 필요하지 않는 한 나에게 전화하지 마라. / *Will you make all the necessary arrangements?* 당신은 필요한 모든 준비를 할 생각입니까? / *It may be necessary to operate on your knee.* 어쩌면 당신의 무릎을 수술해야 할지도 모르겠습니다. **2 a necessary evil** something bad or unpleasant that you have to accept in order to achieve what you want ‖ 원하는 것을 성취하기 위해 받아들여야 하는 나쁘거나 불쾌한 일. 필요악: *Parking fees are a necessary evil in the region's fight against air pollution.* 주차 요금은 그 지역의 공해와의 투쟁에서 필요악이다.

ne·ces·si·tate /nə'sɛsə,teɪt/ v [T] FORMAL to make it necessary for you to do something ∥ 사람이 어떤 것을 하는 데 필수적이게 하다. …을 필요로 하다. 피할 수 없게 하다: *The new law necessitated a change in the health and safety guidelines.* 새 법으로 건강 및 안전 지침상의 변경이 불가피했다.

ne·ces·si·ty /nə'sɛsəti/ n 1 something that you need to have or that must happen ∥ 갖출 필요가 있거나 반드시 일어나야 하는 것. 필수품. 필요 불가결한[절대 필요한] 것[일]: *A car is a necessity for this job.* 자동차는 이 직업에 필수품이다. / *Election reforms are an absolute necessity.* 선거 개혁은 절대 필요한 일이다. 2 [U] the fact of something being necessary ∥ 어떤 것이 필수적이라는 사실. 필요성. 불가결함. 절대 필요함: *the necessity of eating well* 잘 먹어야 할 필요성 3 of necessity in a way that you cannot avoid ∥ 피할 수 없는 방식으로. 필연적으로. 불가피하게: *A doctor must, of necessity, make decisions that no one else can.* 의사는 불가피하게 다른 누구도 할 수 없는 결정을 해야 한다.

neck¹ /nɛk/ n 1 the part of your body that joins your head to your shoulders ∥ 머리에서 양 어깨를 잇는 몸의 부위. 목: *Swans have long slender necks.* 백조는 길고 가느다란 목을 갖고 있다. —see picture at HEAD¹ 2 the part of a piece of clothing that goes around your neck ∥ 목을 두르는 옷의 일부. 옷깃. 목 부분 3 the narrow part of a bottle ∥ 병의 좁은 부분. 병목 4 be up to your neck in sth INFORMAL to be in a very difficult situation, or to be very busy doing something ∥ 매우 어려운 상황에 처해 있거나 어떤 일을 하느라 매우 바쁘다. …에 목까지 잠겨 있다[깊이 빠져 있다]. …에 몰두하고 있다: *Mason is up to his neck in debt.* 메이슨은 빚 더미에 치여 있다. 5 -neck, -necked having a particular type of neck ∥ 특별한 유형의 목을 가진. 목이 …인: *a V-neck sweater* 브이넥 스웨터 / *a long-necked bottle* 목이 긴 병 6 neck and neck INFORMAL if two people, teams etc. are neck and neck in a competition, they both have an equal chance of winning ∥ 두 사람이나 팀 등이 시합에서 승리할 가능성이 둘 다 대등한. 막상막로. 엇비슷하게 7 in this neck of the woods INFORMAL in this area or part of the country ∥ 나라의 이 지역이나 지방에서: *What are you doing in this neck of the woods?* 이 곳에서 무엇하고 있는 거야?

neck² v [I] OLD-FASHIONED SLANG if two people neck, they kiss for a long time in a sexual way ∥ 두 사람이 오랫동안 성적으로 키스하다. 목을 껴안고 애무하다 – **necking** n [U]

neck·lace /'nɛk-lɪs/ n a piece of jewelry that hangs around your neck ∥ 목에 거는 장신구. 목걸이: *a pearl necklace* 진주 목걸이 —see picture at JEWELRY

neck·line /'nɛk-laɪn/ n the shape made by the edge of a woman's dress, shirt etc. around or below the neck ∥ 여성의 드레스·셔츠 등의 목둘레나 아래쪽 가장자리에 만들어진 모양. 목선. 네크라인: *a low neckline* 깊게 파인 목선

neck·tie /'nɛktaɪ/ n FORMAL ⇨ TIE²

nec·tar /'nɛktɚ/ n [U] 1 thick juice made from some fruits ∥ 일부 과일로 만들어진 진한 주스. 과즙: *peach nectar* 복숭아 과즙 2 the sweet liquid that BEES collect from flowers ∥ 벌이 꽃에서 채집하는 달콤한 액체. 꿀

nec·ta·rine /,nɛktə'rin/ n a round juicy yellow-red fruit that has a large rough seed and smooth skin ∥ 크고 거친 씨와 부드러운 껍질을 가진 둥글고 즙이 많은 황적색의 과일. 승도복숭아

née /neɪ/ adj used in order to show the family name that a woman had before she was married ∥ 여성이 결혼하기 전에 가졌던 성(姓)을 나타내는 데에 쓰여. 구성(舊姓)의. 혼전(婚前) 성은 …인: *Lorna Brown, née Wilson* 로나 브라운, 구성 월슨

need¹ /nid/ v [T] 1 to feel that you must have or do something, or that something is necessary ∥ 반드시 어떤 것을 갖거나 해야 함을 느끼거나 어떤 것이 필수적이라고 느끼다. …이 필요하다. …을 필요로 하다. …할 필요[의무]가 있다: *I need a vacation.* 나는 휴가가 필요하다. / *The roast needs to cook a little longer.* 그 고기는 좀 더 오래 구울[조리]할 필요가 있다. / *You need a background in computer programming for this job.* 너는 이 일을 하려면 컴퓨터 프로그래밍 분야의 경험이 필요하다. / *David, I need you to go to the store for some milk.* 데이비드, 너 우유 좀 사러 가게에 갔다 와 야겠다. 2 to have to do something ∥ 어떤 일을 해야 한다. …하지 않으면 안 된다. …할 필요가 있다: *You need to make reservations for Yosemite campgrounds.* 요세미티 야영지를 이용하려면 예약해야 합니다. / *Do we need to dress up for the party?* 그 파티는 정장차림을 해야 합니까? / *You don't need to* *fill in any forms*. 당신은 어떤 양식도 기입할 필요가 없습니다. **3 sb does not need sth** SPOKEN used in order to say that something will make someone's life more difficult ‖ 어떤 것이 사람의 삶을 더 힘들게 만들 거라는 점을 말하는 데에 쓰여. …은 굳이 필요 없다: *"He's always questioning everything I do." "Yeah, you don't need that."* "그는 항상 내가 하는 모든 일에 토를 달아." "맞아, 그럴 필요가 없는데 말야." —see study note on page 932

need² *n* **1** [singular] a situation in which something must be done, especially to improve the situation ‖ 특히 상황을 개선시키기 위해 어떤 일이 반드시 행해져야 하는 상황. …의 필요(성). 필수적임: *There is an urgent need to improve teaching standards.* 교습 기준을 개선시킬 급한 필요성이 있다. / *the need for stricter safety regulations* 더욱 엄격한 안전 규정에 대한 필요성 / *We will work all night if need be.* (=if it is necessary) 우리는 필요하다면 밤새 일할 것이다. **2 be in need of** to need attention, help, money etc. ‖ 관심·도움·돈 등을 필요로 하다: *a large population in need of doctors* 의사가 필요한 다수의 인구 **3** [C usually plural] what someone needs to have in order to live a normal healthy life ‖ 사람이 정상적이며 건전한 삶을 살기 위해 가질 필요가 있는 것. 필요한[소용되는] 것. 욕구. 요구. 수요: *a school that meets the educational needs of the deaf* 청각 장애인의 교육적 욕구를 충족시켜 주는 학교 **4** [U] the state of not having enough food or money ‖ 충분한 음식이나 돈을 가지지 않은 상태. 빈곤. 궁핍: *We're collecting donations for families in need.* 우리는 빈곤 가정을 위한 기부금(품)을 모으고 있다.

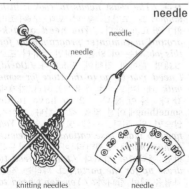

knitting needles   needle

nee·dle¹ /'nidl/ *n* **1** a small thin piece of steel used for sewing, that has a point at one end and a hole at the other end ‖ 한쪽 끝이 뾰족하고 다른 끝에 구멍이 있어 바느질하는 데 쓰이는 작고 가느다란 강철 조각. 바늘 —see also picture at SEW **2** the sharp hollow metal part on the end of a SYRINGE ‖ 주사기 끝에 날카롭고 속이 빈 금속 부분. 주삿바늘 **3** a small thin pointed leaf, especially from a PINE tree ‖ 특히 소나무에서 나는 작고 가늘며 뾰족한 잎. 솔잎. 침엽(針葉) **4** a long thin stick used in knitting (KNIT) ‖ 뜨개질에 쓰이는 길고 가는 꼬챙이. 뜨개[대]바늘. 코바늘 **5** the very small pointed part in a RECORD PLAYER that picks up sound from the records ‖ 레코드 플레이어에서 레코드판의 소리를 재생하는 매우 작고 날카로운 부분. 레코드 바늘 **6 it's like looking for a needle in a haystack** used in order to say that something is almost impossible to find ‖ 어떤 것이 찾기에 불가능함을 말하는 데에 쓰여. 가망이 없는 것을 찾다. (건초 더미 속의 바늘 찾기같이) 찾는 데 헛수고하다

needle² *v* [T] INFORMAL to deliberately annoy someone by making a lot of unkind remarks or stupid jokes ‖ 많은 매정한 발언이나 바보 같은 농담으로 사람을 의도적으로 화나게 하다. 자극하여 …시키다. 놀리다. 괴롭혀 몰아대다: *She's always needling Jim about his weight.* 그녀는 항상 짐의 몸무게에 대해 놀려댄다.

need·less /'nid-lıs/ *adj* **1 needless to say** used when you are telling someone something that s/he probably already knows or expects ‖ 다른 사람이 이미 알거나 예상할 것 같은 일을 말할 때 쓰여. 말할 나위[필요]도 없이. 물론. 당연히: *Needless to say, with four children we're always busy.* 말할 것도 없이, 네 명의 아이들로 인해 우리는 항상 바쁘다. **2** not necessary, and often easily avoided ‖ 필요하지 않으며 종종 쉽게 기피되는. 불필요한. 쓸데없는: *Why take needless risks?* 왜 쓸데없는 위험을 무릅쓰려 합니까? – **needlessly** *adv*

nee·dle·work /'nidl,wɚk/ *n* [U] the activity or art of sewing, or things made by sewing ‖ 바느질이나 바느질 기술. 또는 바느질로 만들어진 것

need·y /'nidi/ *adj* **1** having very little food or money ‖ 음식이나 돈이 거의 없는. 가난한. 빈곤[빈궁]한: *a needy family* 가난한 가정 **2 the needy** people who do not have enough food or money

‖ 충분한 음식이나 돈이 없는 사람들. 빈곤[가난]한 사람들

ne·gate /nɪˈgeɪt/ v [T] FORMAL **1** to prevent something from having any effect ‖ 어떤 것이 효력을 갖는 것을 막다. …을 무효로 하다. 취소하다: *The decision would effectively negate last year's Supreme Court ruling.* 그 결정은 지난해 대법원의 판결을 효과적으로 무효화시킬 것이다. **2** to state that something does not exist or is not true; DENY ‖ 어떤 것이 존재하지 않거나 사실이 아니라고 말하다. …을 부정[부인]하다; 윤 deny − **negation** /nɪˈgeɪʃən/ n [U]

neg·a·tive¹ /ˈnɛgətɪv/ adj **1** having a bad or harmful effect ‖ 나쁘거나 해로운 효과를 갖는. 부정적인. 나쁜 영향을 미치는: *Raising taxes could have a negative effect on the economy.* 세금 인상은 경제에 부정적 영향을 끼칠 수 있다. **2** considering only the bad qualities of a situation, person etc. ‖ 상황·사람 등의 오직 나쁜 특성만을 고려하는. 부정적인. 적대적인. 비판적인: *She's being very negative about school lately.* 그녀는 최근에 학교에 대해 매우 부정적이다. **3** saying or meaning no ‖ 부정을 말하거나 의미하는. 부정[반대]의. 거부[거절]하는: *a negative answer* 부정적 답변 — compare AFFIRMATIVE **4** a medical or scientific test that is negative does not show any sign of what was being looked for ‖ 의학적 또는 과학적 실험이 찾고 있던 것의 아무 흔적도 보이지 않는. 음성(반응)의: *Their test for phosphates came out/up negative.* 인산염이 있는지에 대한 그들의 실험은 음성으로 나왔다. **5** TECHNICAL having the type of electrical charge that is carried by ELECTRONs, shown by a (−) sign on a BATTERY ‖ 건전지에 음의 기호(−)로 표시되어, 전자에 의해 운반되는 전하의 유형을 띤. 음전하를 가진. 음극의. 마이너스의 **6** TECHNICAL a negative number or quantity is lower than zero. (−) is the negative sign ‖ 숫자나 크기가 0보다 낮은. 기호는 (−). 음수의. 마이너스 수[양]의 − **negatively** adv —opposite POSITIVE

negative² n **1** a statement or expression that means no ‖ 부정을 의미하는 말이나 표현. 부정하는 말[대답, 태도] **2** a piece of film that shows dark areas as light and light areas as dark, from which a photograph is printed ‖ 어두운 영역을 밝게, 밝은 영역을 어둡게 나타내어 사진이 인화되는 필름의 한 조각. 음화

negative

ne·glect¹ /nɪˈglɛkt/ v [T] **1** to not pay enough attention to someone or something, or to not take care of him, her, or it very well ‖ 사람이나 사물에 충분한 주의를 기울이지 않다, 또는 잘 돌보지 않다. 무시[경시]하다. 등한시[태만]하다: *Each year, 700,000 children are abused or neglected.* 매년 70만 명의 아이들이 학대당하거나 방치된다. **2** to not do something or forget to do it, often because you are lazy or careless ‖ 종종 게으르거나 부주의해서 어떤 일을 하지 않거나 하는 것을 잊어버리다. …을 소홀히[게을리] 하다. 하지 않고 두다. 방치하다: *The manufacturer had neglected to warn users about the possible health risks.* 제조업체는 건강상의 위험 가능성에 대해 사용자에게 경고하는 것을 게을리 했다. / *Four security guards were accused of neglecting their duties.* 4명의 안전 요원이 직무를 태만히 한 죄로 기소됐다. − **neglected** adj

neglect² n [U] **1** failure to take care of something or someone well ‖ 사물이나 사람을 잘 돌보지 못함. 무시. 경시. 등한시. 태만. 소홀: *I'm afraid my house plants are suffering from neglect!* 내 집의 화초들이 방치되어 손상을 입지 않는지 걱정된다. **2** the condition something or someone is in when he, she, or it has not been taken care of ‖ 사물이나 사람이 돌봐지지 않는 상태. 무관심. 소홀한 취급. 방치: *inner cities in a state of neglect* 방치 상태에 놓인 도심의 빈민가

ne·glect·ful /nɪˈglɛktfəl/ adj FORMAL not taking care of something very well, or not giving it enough attention ‖ 어떤 것을 잘 돌보지 않는, 또는 충분한 주의를 쏟지 않는. 태만한. 소홀한. 부주의한. 무관심한: *He had been neglectful of his work.* 그는 자신의 일에 태만했다. / *We have been too neglectful of educating the new generation.* 우리는 새로운 세대의 교육에 너무 소홀해 왔다.

neg·li·gee /ˌnɛglɪˈʒeɪ, ˈnɛglɪˌʒeɪ/ n a very thin pretty piece of clothing that a woman wears over a NIGHTGOWN ‖ 여성이 잠옷 위에 입는 매우 얇고 예쁜 옷 종류. 네글리제. 여성용 실내복

neg·li·gence /ˈnɛglɪdʒəns/ n [U] the failure to do something that you are responsible for in a careful enough way, so that something bad happens or may happen ‖ 책임지고 있는 일을 충분히 주의를 기울여 하지 않아 안 좋은 일이 일어나

거나 일어날지 모르는 상태. 태만. 소홀. 부주의. 무관심: *They're suing the doctor for negligence.* 그들은 그 의사를 업무상 과실로 제소한 상태이다.

neg·li·gent /'nɛglɪdʒənt/ *adj* not being careful enough about something that you are doing, so that serious mistakes are made ‖ 하고 있는 일에 대해 충분한 주의를 기울이지 않아 심각한 실수가 발생한. 게을리 하는. 태만한. 부주의한. 둔한한. 무관심한. 소홀한: *The company had been negligent in its safety procedures.* 회사는 안전 조치에 소홀했었다. - **negligently** *adv*

neg·li·gi·ble /'nɛglɪdʒəbəl/ *adj* too slight or unimportant to have any effect ‖ 어떤 영향을 미치기에는 너무 사소하거나 중요하지 않은. 무시해도 좋은. 하찮은. 시시한: *There is negligible damage to the car.* 자동차에 가해진 손상은 무시할 만한 것이다. - **negligibly** *adv*

ne·go·tia·ble /nɪ'goʊʃəbəl/ *adj* 1 prices, agreements etc. that are negotiable can be discussed and changed ‖ 가격·협정 등이 논의·조정될 수 있는. 협상할 수 있는. 교섭할 여지가 있는: *Is the salary negotiable?* 봉급 조정이 가능합니까? 2 a road that is negotiable can be traveled along ‖ 도로를 따라서 지나갈 수 있는. 통행[통과]할 수 있는 3 TECHNICAL a check that is negotiable can be exchanged for money ‖ 수표가 돈으로 교환될 수 있는. 양도[유통, 매매]할 수 있는

ne·go·ti·ate /nɪ'goʊʃi,eɪt/ *v* 1 [I, T] to discuss something in order to reach an agreement ‖ 합의에 도달하기 위해 어떤 것을 논의하다. 교섭하다. 담판[협의, 협상]하다: *UN representatives are trying to negotiate a ceasefire.* UN 대표단은 정전을 이끌어 내려고 노력하고 있다. 2 [T] to succeed in getting past or over a difficult place on a road, path etc. ‖ 도로·길 등의 어려운[험한] 지점을 지나가거나 뛰어넘는 데 성공하다. 통과하다. 뚫고 나아가다: *an old man carefully negotiating the steps* 계단을 조심스럽게 지나가는 노인

ne·go·ti·a·tion /nɪ,goʊʃi'eɪʃən/ *n* [C usually plural, U] official discussions between two groups who are trying to agree on something ‖ 어떤 것에 동의하려고 하는 두 집단 간의 공식 논의. 교섭. 협상. 협의: *Johnson and Co. has entered into negotiations with City Hall over its bid to build the new freeway.* 존슨 앤드 코 사는 새 고속도로 건설 입찰에 대해 시

청과 협상에 들어갔다. / *He was offered the job after some negotiation over the salary.* 그의 약간의 봉급 협상 후 그 일을 제안받았다.

Ne·gro /'nigroʊ/ *n* OLD-FASHIONED OFFENSIVE a Black person ‖ 흑인. 검둥이

neigh /neɪ/ *v* [I] to make a loud sound like a horse ‖ 말과 같은 큰 소리를 내다. 말 울음소리를 내다 - **neigh** *n*

neigh·bor /'neɪbɚ/ *n* 1 someone who lives in a house or apartment very near you ‖ 자기 바로 근처의 집이나 아파트에 사는 사람. 이웃(사람): *The Nelsons are our next-door neighbors.* (=they live in the house next to ours) 넬슨네는 우리 바로 옆집의 이웃이다. 2 someone who is sitting or standing next to you ‖ 자기 바로 옆에 앉거나 서 있는 사람. 옆사람: *Write down your name and then pass the paper to your neighbor.* 이름을 쓰고 나서 그 종이를 옆사람에게 넘기세요. 3 a country that has a border with another country ‖ 다른 나라와 국경이 맞닿은 나라. 이웃나라 - **neighbor** *adj* : *the neighbor kids* 이웃(집) 아이들 / *my neighbor lady* 내 이웃집 아가씨

neigh·bor·hood /'neɪbɚ,hʊd/ *n* 1 a small area of a town, or the people who live there ‖ 시의 작은 지역, 또는 그 곳에 사는 사람들. 동네 (사람들): *a nice neighborhood in Boston* 보스턴에서의 좋은 동네 / *a neighborhood school* 보통의 공립 학교 / *Are there any good restaurants in the neighborhood?* (=in this area of town) 이 동네에 좋은 식당이 있습니까? 2 **in the neighborhood of** either a little more or a little less than a particular number or amount ‖ 특정 수나 양보다 다소 많거나 적은. 대략…. 약…. …의 내외: *Do you have any stereos costing in the neighborhood of $300?* 3백 달러 정도 가격의 전축이 있습니까?

neigh·bor·ing /'neɪbərɪŋ/ *adj* near the place where you are or the place you are talking about ‖ 현재 있는 곳이나 언급하고 있는 곳 근처의. 인접한. 인근의. 근처에 있는[사는]: *There's a good bus service to neighboring towns.* 인접한 시로 연결되는 버스 편이 잘 되어 있다.

neigh·bor·ly /'neɪbɚli/ *adj* friendly and helpful toward your NEIGHBORs ‖ 이웃에 친절하고 도움을 주는. 이웃사람다운. 다정한. 우호적인 - **neighborliness** *n* [U]

nei·ther¹ /'niðɚ, 'naɪ-/ *determiner, pron* not one or the other of two people or things ‖ 두 명의 사람이나 두 가지 사

물 중에서 한쪽이나 다른 쪽도 아닌. 이쪽도 저쪽도 아닌. 어느 쪽도 아닌: *Neither of them was hungry, but they had a cup of coffee.* 그들 중 누구도 배가 고프지 않았지만 커피 한 잔을 마셨다. / *Neither leader would admit to being wrong.* 어느 쪽 지도자도 잘못됐음을 인정하지 않을 것이다. —compare EITHER², NONE¹ —see usage note at EITHER²

neither² *adv* used in order to agree with a negative statement that someone has made, or to add a negative statement to one that has just been made ‖ 어떤 사람이 한 부정적 발언에 동의하거나 방금 한 말에 부정적인 말을 덧붙이는 데에 쓰여. …도 또한 …아니다. (…아니듯) …도 아니다: *"I don't like herb tea." "Neither do I."* "나는 허브 차를 좋아하지 않아." "나도 그래." / *Bill can't sing at all, and neither can his brother.* (=both Bill and his brother can't sing) 빌은 전혀 노래할 줄 모르고 그의 동생도 역시 못한다. / *"I haven't seen Greg in a long time." "Me neither."* "나는 그레그를 오랫동안 못 봤어." "나도 그래." —compare **me either** EITHER³

neither³ *conjunction* **neither…nor…** used when mentioning two statements, facts, actions etc. that are not true or possible ‖ 두 가지 진술·사실·행동 등이 사실이 아니거나 가능하지 않음을 언급할 때 쓰여. 어느 쪽도 …아니다. 이쪽도 저쪽도 …아니다: *Neither his mother nor his father spoke English.* 그의 어머니와 아버지 중 어느 쪽도 영어를 못한다. —see usage note at EITHER¹

ne·on /ˈniɑn/ *n* [U] a gas that is an ELEMENT and that produces a bright light when electricity is passed through it ‖ 원소의 하나이며 전기가 통과될 때 밝은 빛을 내는 기체. 네온

neon light /,.. ˈ./ *n* a glass tube filled with NEON that produces a bright, usually colored light when electricity is passed through it ‖ 전기가 통과될 때 밝은, 보통 색깔 있는 빛을 내는 네온 가스를 채운 유리관. 네온(전)등

neph·ew /ˈnɛfyu/ *n* the son of your brother or sister, or the son of your husband's or wife's brother or sister ‖ 형제나 자매의 아들, 또는 남편이나 부인의 형제 자매의 아들. (남자) 조카 —compare NIECE —see picture at FAMILY

nep·o·tism /ˈnɛpə,tɪzəm/ *n* [U] the practice of giving the best jobs to members of your family when you are in a position of power ‖ 권력 있는 지위에 있을 때 가족의 일원에게 가장 좋은 자리

를 주는 관행. 친족 등용. 족벌주의. 정실 (情實)

Nep·tune /ˈnɛptun/ *n* [singular] the eighth PLANET from the sun ‖ 태양으로부터 여덟 번째 행성. 해왕성

nerd /nɚd/ *n* INFORMAL someone who is not fashionable and does not know how to behave in social situations ‖ 유행을 따르지 못하고 사회적 상황에서 어떻게 행동할지 모르는 사람. 멍청이. 괴짜. 얼간이: *a computer nerd* (=someone who is only interested in computers and does not know how to behave with people) 컴퓨터(에만 빠져 있는) 괴짜 – **nerdy** *adj*

nerve /nɚv/ *n* **1** [U] the ability to stay calm in a dangerous, difficult, or frightening situation ‖ 위험한[어려운, 겁 먹게 하는] 상황에서 냉정을 잃지 않는 능력. 용기. 담력. 정신력: *It takes a lot of nerve to give a speech in front of so many people.* 아주 많은 사람들 앞에서 연설하려면 많은 용기가 필요하다.

2 have the nerve to do sth INFORMAL to be rude without being ashamed or embarrassed about it ‖ 어떤 것에 창피해하거나 당황하지 않고 무례하다. 뻔뻔스럽게도[감히] …하다. 배짱 좋게[비위 좋게] …하다: *He had the nerve to criticize my cooking.* 그는 감히 내 요리를 비판했다.

3 one of the thin parts like threads inside your body that help control your movements, and along which your brain sends and receives feelings of heat, cold, pain etc. ‖ 사람의 동작을 통제하게 하고 두뇌가 이것을 따라 열·추위·고통 등의 느낌을 주고받는 인체 내의 실 같은 가느다란 부분의 하나. 신경(섬유[조직])

4 hit/touch/strike a nerve to do or say something that makes someone angry or upset because it relates to a subject that is important to him/her ‖ 남에게 중요한 주제와 관련된 것을 하거나 말해서 그 사람을 화나거나 속상하게 하다. 남의 신경을[아픈 곳을] 건드리다[자극하다]. 신경에 거슬리게 하다: *I accidentally hit a raw nerve by asking him about his wife.* 나는 뜻하지 않게 그에게 아내에 대해 물어서 그의 아픈 곳을 건드렸다.

nerve-rack·ing /ˈnɚv ,rækɪŋ/ *adj* very worrying or frightening ‖ 심하게 걱정하거나 겁을 먹은. 어쩔 줄 모르는. 안절부절못하는: *a nerve-racking drive through a snowstorm* 조마조마한 눈보라 속의 운전

nerves /nɚvz/ *n* [plural] INFORMAL **1** the feeling of being nervous because you are worried or a little frightened ‖ 걱정되거나 약간 겁이 나서 긴장된 느낌. 신경과민. 흥분. 초조: *What's wrong? You're a bundle of nerves.* (=extremely worried or frightened) 왜 그래? 왜 그렇게 안절부절못해. **2 get on sb's nerves** INFORMAL to annoy someone, especially by doing something again and again ‖ 특히 어떤 것을 반복적으로 해서 사람을 짜증나게 하다. 신경을 건드리다. 남의 화를 돋우다. 화나게 하다: *Joyce's complaining is getting on my nerves.* 조이스의 불평이 내 신경을 건드리고 있다.

nerve-wrack·ing /'nɚv ˌrækɪŋ/ *n* ⇨ NERVE-RACKING

nerv·ous /'nɚvəs/ *adj* **1** worried or frightened about something, and unable to relax ‖ 어떤 것에 대해 걱정되거나 겁이 나서 긴장을 풀 수 없는. 떨리는. 불안한: *Sam's nervous about taking his driving test again.* 샘은 다시 치르는 운전면허 시험에 바짝 얼어 있다. / *The way she was watching him made him nervous.* 그를 쳐다보는 그녀의 모습이 그를 불안하게 하였다.
2 often becoming worried or frightened and easily upset ‖ 종종 걱정되거나 겁이 나서 쉽게 화를 내는. 신경질적인. 신경과민의. 흥분하기 쉬운: *a thin nervous man* 마르고 신경질적인 남자 / *All the pressure to do well in college has made her a nervous wreck.* (=someone who is too anxious all the time) 대학에서 (공부를)잘 하려는 모든 압박감이 그녀를 신경과민이 되게 했다.
3 relating to the nerves in your body ‖ 인체 내 신경에 관련된. 신경성의. 신경이 있는[을 포함한]: *a nervous disorder* 신경성 질환 – **nervously** *adv* – **nervousness** *n* [U]

nervous는 곧 일어날 일에 대해 걱정·두려움을 느낄 때 쓴다: 잭은 모든 사람 앞에서 말하는 것이 겁났다. **concerned** 역시 "걱정스러운" 것을 의미하지만 특히 특정 문제에 대해 걱정될 때 쓰인다: 우리는 우리 시의 노숙자 수에 대해 우려하고 있다. **anxious**는 안 좋은 일이, 특히 아는 사람에게 일어났거나 일어날 것을 걱정할 때 쓴다: 그녀의 부모는 그 날 밤 그녀가 집에 돌아오지 않자 걱정했다.

nervous break·down /ˌ.. '../ *n* a mental illness in which someone becomes extremely anxious and tired and cannot live and work normally ‖ 사람이 매우 걱정하고 지쳐서 정상적으로 살거나 일할 수 없게 되는 정신 질환. 신경쇠약. 노이로제

nervous sys·tem /'.. ˌ../ *n* the system of nerves in your body, through which you feel pain, heat etc. and control your movements ‖ 고통·열 등을 느끼고 동작을 제어하는 인체 내의 신경 체계. 신경계(통)

nest¹ /nɛst/ *n* **1** a hollow place made or chosen by a bird to lay its eggs in and to live in ‖ 새가 알을 낳거나 서식하기 위해 만들거나 선택한 빈 공간. 둥지. 둥우리 **2** a place where insects or small animals live ‖ 곤충이나 작은 동물들이 사는 곳. 서식지[처]. 둥지. 보금자리: *a hornets' nest* 말벌집 **3** INFORMAL your parents' house ‖ 부모의 집: *children leaving the nest to go off to college* 부모의 곁을 떠나 대학에 가는 자녀들

nest² *v* [I] to build or use a NEST ‖ 둥지를 짓거나 둥지로 쓰다. 둥지를 틀다. 둥지로 사용하다: *owls nesting in a tree hole* 나무 구멍 속에 둥지를 튼 올빼미

nest egg /'. ./ *n* an amount of money that you save to use later ‖ 나중에 사용하기 위해 아껴 둔 금액. 예비금. 저축. 비상금

nes·tle /'nɛsəl/ *v* **1** [I, T] to move into a comfortable position by pressing against someone or something ‖ 다른 사람이나 사물에 밀착해서 편안한 자세로 움직이다. 바싹 대다. 다가붙다. 기분 좋게[편안하게] 드러눕다[앉다]: *The girl was still in her arms, her head nestled on Heather's chest.* 소녀는 헤더의 가슴에 머리를 기댄 채 팔에 안겨 가만히 있었다. **2** [I] to be in a position that is protected from wind, rain etc. ‖ 바람·비 등으로부터 보호되는 위치에 자리하다. 아늑하게 자리잡다. 보금자리에 깃들다: *a village nestled among the hills* 구릉 사이에 아

늑하게 자리한 마을

net

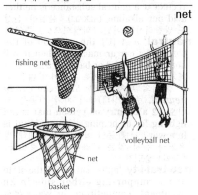

fishing net

hoop

volleyball net

net

basket

net¹ /nɛt/ n **1** [C, U] a material made of strings, wires, or threads woven across each other with regular spaces between them ‖ 사이 공간을 일정하게 두고 서로 엇갈리게 짜여진 줄[철사, 실]로 만들어진 소재. 그물. 망(網): *a fishing net* 어망(漁網) **2** [C usually singular] a net used in particular games ‖ 특정 경기에 사용되는 그물망. 네트: *I can't play tennis; I'm always hitting the ball into the net.* 나는 테니스를 못 친다. 나는 항상 공을 네트에 걸리게 친다. **3 the Net** ⇨ INTERNET

net² v **-tted, -tting** [T] **1** to earn a particular amount of money as a profit after paying taxes ‖ 세금 납부 후 특정 금액을 이익으로 벌다. 순이익[순소득]을 올리다: *Last year, they netted $52,000.* 지난해 그들은 5만 2천 달러의 순이익을 올렸다. —compare GROSS² **2** to catch a fish in a net ‖ 그물로 고기를 잡다

net³ adj **1** a net amount of money is the amount that remains after things such as taxes etc. have been taken away ‖ 세금 등이 공제된 후 남아 있는 금액의. 순(純)…. 정(正)…: *a net profit of $500,000* 50만 달러의 순이익 —compare GROSS¹ **2 net weight** the weight of something without its container ‖ 용기를 제외한 사물의 무게. 실중량 **3 net result** the final result, after all the effects are known ‖ 모든 효과가 드러난 후의 최종 결과: *The net result of the policy was higher prices in the stores.* 그 정책의 최종 결과는 상점에서의 가격 상승이었다.

net·iquette /ˈnɛtiket/ n [U] INFORMAL the commonly accepted rules for polite behaviour when communicating with other people on the Internet ‖ 인터넷상에서 타인들과 통신할 때 일반적으로 예절

을 갖춘 행위로 인정되는 규칙. 네티켓

net·i·zen /ˈnɛtəzən/ n SLANG someone who uses the Internet, especially someone who uses it in a responsible way. This word comes from a combination of the words 'net', meaning 'the Internet', and 'citizen' ‖ 인터넷 이용자, 특히 책임있게 이용하는 사람으로 '인터넷'을 뜻하는 'net'와 'citizen'의 합성어. 네티즌

net·tle¹ /ˈnɛtl/ n [C, U] a wild plant with rough leaves that sting you ‖ 사람을 찌르는 거친 잎을 가진 야생 식물. 쐐기풀

nettle² v [T] to annoy someone ‖ 사람을 짜증나게 하다. 안달나게[화나게] 하다: *Al realized he had nettled Eileen, and went silent.* 앨은 자신이 에일린을 화나게 했다는 것을 깨닫고 입을 다물었다.

net·work¹ /ˈnɛtwɜrk/ n **1** a group of radio or television stations that broadcasts many of the same programs in different parts of the country ‖ 다수의 똑같은 프로그램을 한 나라의 여러 다른 지역에 방송하는 라디오나 TV 방송국 집단. 방송망. 네트워크(방송):

network

a computer network

the four biggest TV networks 4대 거대 TV 방송망[네트워크] **2** a system of lines, tubes, wires, roads etc. that cross each other and are connected to each other ‖ 서로 교차하고 서로 연결된 선·관·전선·도로 등의 체계. …망(網). 망상 조직: *the freeway network* 고속도로망 **3** a set of computers that are connected to each other so that they can share information ‖ 서로 연결되어 정보를 공유할 수 있는 컴퓨터들의 집단. 네트워크 **4** a group of people, organizations etc. that are connected or that work together ‖ (서로) 연결되거나 함께 일하는 사람·조직 등의 집단. 연락망. 연관. 연계. 관계. 망: *Trina had developed a good network of business contacts.* 트리나는 사업상의 인맥을 많이 넓혀 놓았다.

network² v **1** [T] to connect several computers together so that they can share information ‖ 여러 대의 컴퓨터를 함께 연결해서 정보를 공유할 수 있게 하다. 네트워크화하다[로 연결하다] **2** [I] to meet other people who do the same type of work in order to share information, help each other etc. ‖ 정보를 공유하거나 서로 돕기 위해 같은 직종의 일을 하는 다른 사람들을 만나다. 연계 관계를 맺다[갖

N

다]. 인맥을 쌓다

net·work·ing /ˈnɛtˌwəkɪŋ/ *n* [U] the practice of meeting other people who do the same type of work, in order to share information, help each other etc. ‖ 정보를 공유하거나 서로 돕는 등의 일을 위해 같은 직종의 일을 하는 사람들을 만나는 행위. 인맥 쌓기

neu·rol·o·gy /nʊˈrɑlədʒi/ *n* [U] the scientific study of the NERVOUS SYSTEM and the diseases that are related to it ‖ 신경계와 그와 관련된 질환에 대한 과학적 연구. 신경학 – **neurological** /ˌnʊrəˈlɑdʒɪkəl/ *adj* – **neurologist** /nʊˈrɑlədʒɪst/ *n*

neu·ro·sis /nʊˈroʊsɪs/ *n* a mental illness that makes someone worried or frightened in an unreasonable way ‖ 사람을 까닭없이 걱정하거나 겁이 나게 하는 정신적 질병. 정신 신경증. 신경 쇠약. 노이로제

neu·rot·ic /nʊˈrɑtɪk/ *adj* 1 unreasonably anxious or afraid ‖ 까닭없이 불안하거나 두려운. 신경과민의. 항상 걱정하는: *My aunt is neurotic about cleanliness.* 내 숙모님은 결벽증이 있다. 2 relating to a NEUROSIS ‖ 신경증과 관련된. 노이로제에 걸린: *neurotic disorders* 신경증 – **neurotically** *adv* – **neurotic** *n*

neu·ter¹ /ˈnutə/ *adj* TECHNICAL in English grammar, a neuter pronoun such as "it" relates to something that has no sex, or does not show the sex of the person or animal that it relates to ‖ 영문법에서 "it" 등의 대명사가 성이 없거나 관련된 사람이나 동물의 성이 드러나지 않는 것과 관련된. 중성의

neuter² *v* [T] to remove part of the sex organs of a male animal so that it cannot produce babies ‖ 수컷 동물의 생식기 부분을 제거해서 새끼를 낳을 수 없게 하다. …을 거세하다 —compare SPAY

neu·tral¹ /ˈnutrəl/ *adj* 1 not supporting either side in an argument, competition, or war ‖ 논쟁[경쟁, 전쟁]에서 어느 쪽도 지지[지원]하지 않는. 중립의. 불편부당의. 편애하지 않는: *The paper was praised for its neutral reporting of the elections.* 그 신문은 선거의 중립 보도로 찬사를 받았다. / *Switzerland was neutral during World War II.* 스위스는 2차 대전 중 중립을 지켰다. 2 a neutral color such as gray or brown is not strong or bright ‖ 회색이나 갈색 등의 색이 진하거나 밝지 않은. 중간색의. 흐릿한. 무색의 3 TECHNICAL a neutral wire has no electrical CHARGE ‖ 전선이 전하를

띠지 않는. (전기적으로) 중성인 4 TECHNICAL a neutral substance is neither acid nor alkaline (ALKALI) ‖ 물질이 산성도 알칼리성도 아닌. (화학적으로) 중성의

neutral² *n* 1 [U] the position of the GEARs of a car or machine when it will not move forward or backward ‖ 차나 기계가 전방이나 후방으로 움직이지 않을 때의 기어의 위치. 중립: *Start the car in neutral.* 중립(상태)에서 차의 시동을 거시오. 2 a country or person that is not fighting for or helping a country that is in a war ‖ 전쟁 중인 어떤 나라를 위해 싸우거나 돕지 않는 나라나 사람. 중립국. (국외) 중립자

neu·tral·i·ty /nuˈtræləti/ *n* [U] the state of not supporting either side in an argument, competition, or war ‖ 논쟁[경쟁, 전쟁]에서 어느 쪽도 지지하지 않는 상태. 중립(상태[정책])

neu·tral·ize /ˈnutrəˌlaɪz/ *v* [T] 1 to prevent something from having any effect ‖ 사물이 어떤 영향을 끼치는 것을 막다. 중화하다. …의 효과를 없애다. 상쇄하다: *Higher taxes will neutralize increased wages.* 세금 인상이 봉급 인상 효과를 상쇄시킬 것이다. 2 TECHNICAL to make a substance chemically NEUTRAL ‖ 물질을 화학적으로 중성으로 만들다. 중화시키다 – **neutralization** /ˌnutrələˈzeɪʃən/ *n* [U]

neu·tron /ˈnutrɑn/ *n* a part of an atom that has no electrical CHARGE ‖ 전하를 띠지 않는 원자의 한 부분. 중성자

nev·er /ˈnɛvə/ *adv* 1 not at any time, or not once ‖ 어느 때도 아닌, 또는 단 한 번도 아닌. 조금도[전혀, 결코] …않다[아니다]. 지금까지[앞으로도, 어느 때건] 한 번도 …않다: *I've never been to Hawaii.* 나는 하와이에 한 번도 가 본 적이 없다. / *We waited until 11:00, but they never came.* 우리는 11시까지 기다렸지만 그들은 끝내 오지 않았다. / *I never thought I'd pass the class.* 내가 그 수업을 이수하리라고는 조금도 생각하지 못했다. / *I never knew* (=I did not know until now) *that you played the guitar!* 나는 네가 기타를 연주했다는 것을 전혀 몰랐다. 2 **never mind** SPOKEN used in order to tell someone that something was not important or that you do not want to say something again ‖ 남에게 어떤 것이 중요하지 않다거나 다시 말하고 싶지 않다고 말하는 데에 쓰여. 신경 쓰지 마. 잊어버려: *"What did you say?" "Never mind, it doesn't matter."* "뭐라고 말했니?" "신경 쓰지 마, 중요하지 않아." 3 **you never know** SPOKEN used in order to say that something that seems unlikely could happen ‖ 일어날 것 같지 않은 일이 발생할 수도 있다고 말하는 데에 쓰여. 앞일[사람 일]은 (결코) 모른다: *You never know, maybe you'll be lucky and win the lottery.* 그건 모르는 일이다. 네가 운이 좋아 복권이라도 당첨될지.

nev·er·the·less /ˌnɛvəðəˈlɛs/ *adv* in spite of what has just been mentioned ‖ 바로 전에 언급된 것에도 불구하고. 그럼에도 불구하고. 그렇다고 해도. 그렇기는 하지만: *I know he's telling the truth. Nevertheless, I don't trust him.* 나는 그가 사실을 말하고 있는 것을 안다. 그럼에도 불구하고 나는 그를 못 믿겠다.

new

old

new

new /nu/ *adj* **1** recently made, built, invented, or developed ‖ 최근에 만들어진[지어진, 발명된, 개발된]. 새로운. 새로 나타난[된]: *I went to see Mel Gibson's new movie.* 나는 멜 깁슨의 새[신작] 영화를 보러 갔다. / *Can the new drugs help her?* 신약이 그녀에게 도움이 될 수 있을까요? / *the new nations of Eastern Europe* 동유럽의 신흥 국가들 **2** recently bought ‖ 최근에 구매한. 새로 산: *Do you like my new dress?* 내 새 옷[새로 산 옷] 어때? **3** not used or owned by anyone before ‖ 전에 다른 사람이 사용했거나 소유하지 않았던. 신품의. 새것의: *A used car costs a lot less than a new one.* 중고차가 새 차보다 훨씬 싸다. / *a brand new CD player* (=completely new) 최신품 CD 플레이어 **4** not experienced by someone before ‖ 전에 사람들이 경험하지 않은. 처음 보는[겪는, 듣는]. 새로 온[가본, 경험하는]: *Do you like your new teacher?* 새[새로 온] 선생님 좋아요? / *Eve decided to move to a new town and start over.* 이브는 새로운 도시로 가서 다시 시작하기로 결심했다. / *We had fruit there that was completely new to me.* (=I had never seen it before) 우리는 거기서 나에게는 난생 처음인 과일을 먹었다. **5** having recently arrived in a place, or started a different job or activity ‖ 어떤 장소에 최근에 도착했거나 다른 일이나 활동을 시작한. 신임의. 신입의. 익숙하지

[해 보지] 않은: *Are you a new student here?* 여기 새로 온[입학한] 학생이세요? / *It's hard being the new kid on the block.* (=the newest person in a job, school etc.) 새로운 곳의 새내기가 되는 것은 힘들다. **6** recently discovered ‖ 최근에 발견된. 신종의: *Scientists have identified a new herpes-type virus.* 과학자들은 신종의 헤르페스 종 바이러스를 확인했다. **7 what's new?** SPOKEN used as a friendly greeting to ask what is happening in someone's life ‖ 다른 사람의 생활에 일어나는 일을 묻는 친밀한 인사로 쓰여. 별일[새로운 일] 있어요? – **newness** *n* [U]

USAGE NOTE new, recent, modern, current, up-to-date, and **latest**

Use **new** to talk about something that has existed for only a short time: *Have you read Alice Walker's new book?* Use **recent** to talk about something, especially an event, that happened a short time ago: *He won a medal in the recent Olympics.* Use **modern** to describe things that exist now, especially in order to emphasize that they are different from earlier things of the same kind: *modern machinery / modern teaching methods.* Use **current** to describe something that exists now but that may change: *the current economic crisis.* Use **up-to-date** to describe the newest knowledge, information, way of doing things etc.: *an up-to-date computer system.* Use **latest** to talk about the newest thing in a series of similar things: *the latest issue of Time magazine.*

new는 오직 단기간 동안만 존재해 온 것에 대해 말할 때 쓴다: 앨리스 워커의 새 책[신작] 읽어 봤어요? **recent**는 얼마 전에 일어났던 일, 특히 사건에 대해 말할 때 쓴다: 그는 최근에 열린 올림픽에서 메달을 땄다. **modern**은 현재 존재하고 있는 것을 묘사하며, 특히 그것들이 이전의 같은 종류의 것과 다르다는 것을 강조하기 위해 쓴다: 현대적인 기계 / 현대적[새로 고안된] 교수법. **current**는 현재 존재하지만 변할지 모르는 것을 묘사하기 위해 쓴다: 현재의 경제 위기. **up-to-date**는 가장 최신의 지식·정보·일하는 방식 등을 나타내기 위해 쓴다: 최신의[최신 기술로 된] 컴퓨터 시스템. **latest**는 일련의 비슷한 것들 중에서 가장 최신의 것에 대해 말하는 데 쓴다: 타임지의 최신호

New Age /ˌ. ˈ.ˌ/ *adj* relating to a set of beliefs about religion, medicine, and ways of life that are not part of traditional Western religions ‖ 전통적인 서구 종교의 일부가 아닌, 신앙·의약·생활 방식에 관한 일련의 사상에 관련된. 뉴에 이지(문화)의

new·bie /'nubi/ *n* INFORMAL someone who has just started doing something, especially using the Internet or computers ‖ 특히 인터넷이나 컴퓨터 이 용 등을 이제 막 시작한 사람. 뉴비. 초심 자

new·born /'nubɔrn/ *n* a baby that has only recently been born ‖ 아주 최근에 출 생한 아기. 신생아. 갓난아기 — **newborn** /ˌnu'bɔrn·/ *adj*

new·com·er /'nuˌkʌmɚ/ *n* someone who has recently arrived somewhere or recently started a particular activity ‖ 어 딘가에 최근에 도착했거나 최근에 특정 활 동을 시작한 사람. 갓 온[새로 온] 사람. 신출내기. 풋내기: *a newcomer to the real estate business* 부동산 업계의 신출 내기

new·fan·gled /ˈnuˌfæŋɡəld/ *adj* DISAPPROVING newfangled ideas, machines etc. have been recently invented but seem complicated or unnecessary ‖ 아이디어·기계 등이 최근 에 개발되었지만 복잡하거나 불필요해 보 이는. 신식인. 신기한. 유행의: *newfangled ideas about raising children* 자녀 양육에 대한 신식 사고

new·ly /'nuli/ *adv* very recently ‖ 아주 최근에. 방금. (이제) 막: *a newly married couple* 이제 막 결혼한 부부

new·ly·weds /'nuliˌwedz/ *n* [plural] a man and a woman who have recently gotten married ‖ 최근에 결혼한 남자와 여자. 신혼 부부

news /nuz/ *n* **1** [U] information about something that has happened recently ‖ 최근에 일어난 일에 대한 정보. 뉴스. 소 식: *Have you heard* (=received) *any news about your job application?* 구직 신청을 한 데에서 어떤 연락이라도 받았습 니까? / *I have some good/bad news for you.* 당신에게 몇 가지 좋은[나쁜] 소식이 있습니다. / *an interesting piece of news* 흥미 있는 소식거리 **2** [U] reports of recent events in the newspapers or on the radio or television ‖ 신문지상의 또는 라디오나 TV 방송상의 최근 사건 보도. 뉴 스. 기사. 보도 사항: *There is more news of fighting in the area.* 그 지역 내 전투에 대한 더 많은[상세한] 보도가 있습 니다. / *a news story/report/item on the*

plane crash 항공기 추락에 대한 뉴스 기 사[보도, 거리] / *I usually watch CNN for national and international news.* 나는 국내외 뉴스를 (보기) 위해 보통 CNN을 본다. / *Reports about the disabled rarely make the news.* (=are rarely reported in newspapers etc.) 장애인에 대한 기사 는 거의 보도되지 않는다. **3 the news** a regular television or radio program that gives you reports of recent events ‖ 최신 사건에 대해 보도하는 TV나 라디오의 정 규 프로그램. 뉴스 방송[보도]: *Did you see/hear that story on the news?* 뉴스에 서 그 기사 보았어요[들었어요]? **4 that's news to me** SPOKEN said when you are surprised or annoyed because you have not been told something earlier ‖ 그 이전에 어떤 일을 듣지 못해 서 놀라거나 화가 났을 때 쓰여. 그거 놀 랍군. 처음 듣는 걸: *The meeting's been canceled? That's news to me.* 회의가 취 소됐어요? 처음 듣는데요. **5 news blackout** a period of time when particular pieces of news are not allowed to be reported ‖ 특정 보도 사항 들이 보도가 허용되지 않는 기간. 보도 관 제[통제](기간)

news a·gen·cy /ˈ. ˌ…/ *n* a company that supplies reports on recent events to newspapers, radio, and television ‖ 신문 ·라디오·TV에 최신 사건 기사를 공급하는 회사. 통신사

news bul·le·tin /ˈ. ˌ…/ *n* a very short news program about something important that has just happened, that is broadcast suddenly in the middle of a television or radio program ‖ 텔레비전이 라디오 프로그램 중간에 방금 일어난 중요 한 일에 대하여 갑자기 방송하는 매우 짧 은 뉴스 (보도) 프로그램. 임시 특보. 속 보

news·cast /'nuzkæst/ *n* a news program on the radio or television ‖ 라 디오나 텔레비전의 뉴스 프로그램. 뉴스 방송[프로]

news·cast·er /'nuzˌkæstɚ/ *n* someone who reads the news on the radio or television ‖ 라디오나 텔레비전에서 뉴스 를 보도하는 사람. 뉴스 방송자[진행자]. 앵커

news·group /'nuzgrup/ *n* a discussion group on the Internet, with a place where people with a shared interest can exchange messages ‖ 공통의 관심을 가진 사람들이 메시지를 교환할 수 있는 장소를 가진, 인터넷 상의 토론 집단. 뉴스그룹

news·let·ter /'nuzˌlɛtɚ/ *n* a short written report of news about a club, organization, or particular subject that is sent regularly to people ‖ 클럽[조직, 특정 주제]에 대해 짧게 기록해 사람들에게 정기적으로 보내는 소식 보고서. 소식지. 사보. 회보. 연보. 월보: *our church newsletter* 우리 교회의 소식지[주보, 월보]

news·pa·per /'nuz,peɪpɚ/ *n* **1** a set of large folded sheets of paper containing news, pictures, advertisements etc., that is printed and sold daily or weekly ‖ 기사·사진·광고 등을 게재해 매일 또는 주 단위로 인쇄되어 팔리는, 크게 접힌 한 부 의 종이 뭉치. 신문: *the local newspaper* 지역 신문 / *an interesting article in the newspaper* 신문지상의 흥미 있는 기사 **2** [U] sheets of paper from old newspapers ‖ 오래된 신문의 종잇장들. 신문지: *We just use newspaper for packing dishes.* 우리는 접시를 싸는 데 그냥 신문지를 쓴다.

news·print /'nuz,prɪnt/ *n* cheap paper used mostly for printing newspapers on ‖ 주로 신문을 인쇄하는 데 쓰이는 값싼 종이. 신문 용지

news·stand /'nuzstænd/ *n* a place on a street where newspapers are sold ‖ 거리에서 신문을 판매하는 곳. 신문 가판대 [가두 판매대]

news·wor·thy /'nuz,wɚði/ *adj* important or interesting enough to be reported as news ‖ 뉴스로 보도될 만큼 중요하고 흥미로운. 뉴스[보도] 가치가 있는. 뉴스[기사]거리가 되는: *newsworthy events* 뉴스거리가 되는 사건

new·sy /'nuzi/ *adj* a newsy letter is from a friend or relative and contains a lot of news about him/her ‖ 편지가 친구나 친척에게서 받은 것이며 그들에 대한 많은 소식이 들어 있는

newt /nut/ *n* a small animal with a long body, four legs, and a tail, that lives in water ‖ 긴 몸통·네 다리·꼬리가 달려 있고 물에서 서식하는 작은 동물. 소형 도롱뇽

New Tes·ta·ment /ˌ. '.../ *n* **the New Testament** the part of the Bible that is about Jesus Christ's life and what he taught ‖ 예수 그리스도의 일생과 그의 가르침에 대한 성경의 부분. 신약성서 — compare OLD TESTAMENT

new wave /ˌ. './ *n* people who are trying to introduce new ideas in music, movies, art, politics etc. ‖ 음악·영화·예술·정치 등에 새로운 사상을 도입하고자 하는 사람들. 새물결. 신조류. 뉴웨이브 – **new wave** *adj*

New World /ˌ. './ *n* **the New World** a word meaning North, Central, and South America, used when talking about the time that Europeans first discovered these areas ‖ 북미·중미·남미를 의미하는 말로, 유럽인들이 처음 이 지역을 발견한 시대에 대해 말할 때 쓰여. 신대륙. 신세계: *Columbus' arrival in the New World* 콜럼버스의 신대륙 도착

New Year /ˌ. './, **New Year's** *n* the time when you celebrate the beginning of the year ‖ 한 해의 시작을 축하하는 때. 신년. 새해. 정초: *Happy New Year!* 새해 복 많이 받으세요! / *Have you made any New Year's resolutions?* (=promises to improve yourself) 신년 결심은 하셨습니까?

new year /ˌ. './ *n* **the new year** the year after the present year, especially the months at the beginning of it ‖ 올해의 다음해, 특히 그 해가 시작하는 달들. 새해. 정초: *We're opening three new stores in the new year.* 우리는 새해에 세 개의 새 점포를 개점합니다.

New Year's Day /ˌ. '. './ *n* [singular, U] a holiday on January 1, the first day of the year in Western countries ‖ 서구 국가들에서 그 해의 첫 날인 1월 1일 공휴일. 정월 초하루

New Year's Eve /ˌ. '. './ *n* [singular, U] a holiday on December 31, the last day of the year in Western countries ‖ 서구 국가들에서 그 해의 마지막 날인 12월 31일 공휴일. 섣달 그믐날

next¹ /nɛkst/ *determiner, adj* **1** the next day, time, event etc. is the one that happens after the present one ‖ 날짜·시간·사건 등이 현재의 것 뒤에 오는 것인. (바로)다음의. 뒤따르는: *The next flight leaves in 45 minutes.* 다음 항공편은 45분 후에 출발합니다. / *They returned to New York the next day.* 그들은 다음날 뉴욕으로 돌아갔다. / *Next time* (=when this happens again) *be more careful.* 다음(번)에는 더 주의하세요. / *Why don't we have lunch next week?* 우리 다음 주에 점심 식사 할까요? / *I'll see you next Monday.* 다음(주) 월요일 날 봅시다. ✗DON'T SAY "the next Monday/month/year etc."✗ "the next Monday/month/year"등 이라고는 하지 않는다. **2** the next place is the one closest to where you are now ‖ 장소가 현재 있는 곳에서 가장 가까운. 바로 옆의. 이웃의: *Turn left at the next corner.* 다음 모퉁이에서 좌회전하세요. / *the people at the next table* 바로 옆 탁자에 있는 사람들 **3** the next person or thing in a list, series etc. is the one you deal with after the present one ‖ 목록·연속된 것 등에서 사람이나 사물이 현재의 것 다음에 다루게 되는. 다음[이번] 차례의. 오는[다음]…: *Can I help the next person, please?* 다음 번 사람은 제가 도울 수 있을까요? / *Read the next two chapters by Friday.* 그 다음의 두 단원을 금요일까지 읽으세요. **4** slightly bigger, heavier etc. than the one you have ‖ (현재)가진 것보다 약간 더 크거나 무거운. 크기·무게가 한 등급 위의: *Can I try the the next size up?* (=a slightly bigger size) 한 치수 큰 사이즈를 입어 볼 수 있을까요? / *I'd like to exchange this shirt for the next biggest/smallest size.* 이 셔츠를 한 치수 큰/작은 사이즈로 바꾸고 싶습니다. **5 the next best thing** the thing or situation that is almost as good as the one you really want ‖ 거의 실제로 원하는 것만큼 좋은 것이나 상황. 차선(책). 두 번째의 것: *Visiting Victoria, in Canada, is the next best thing to being in England.* 캐나다 빅토리아 시 관광이 영국에 가는 것 다음으로 하고 싶은 것이다.

next² *adv* **1** immediately afterward ‖ 즉시 후에. (바로)다음에(는): *What should we do next?* 다음에는 무엇을 해야 합니까? / *First, write your name at the top of the page. Next, read the instructions.* 먼저 페이지 상단에 이름을 쓰세요. 다음으로 지시 사항을 읽어 보세요. **2 next to** very close to someone or something, with nothing in between ‖ 중간에 아무 것도 없이 사람이나 사물에 아주 가까운. …에 이웃해. …의 옆에. …과 나란히: *I sat next to a really nice lady on the plane.* 나는 비행기에서 정말 멋진 숙녀 옆에 앉았다. / *Your glasses are there, next to the phone.* 당신 안경은 저기 전화기 옆에 있습니다. **3 next to nothing** very little ‖ 매우 적게. 거의 없이. 없는 것이나 마찬가지로: *I actually bought the car for next to nothing.* (=very little money) 나는 실제로 돈을 거의 안 들이고 그 차를 샀다. **4 next to impossible** very difficult ‖ 매우 어려운. 거의 불가능한. 불가능에 가까운: *It's next to impossible to get tickets for the game.* 그 시합의 입장권을 구하기란 불가능에 가깝다.

next³ *pron* the person or thing in a list, series etc. that comes after the person or thing you are dealing with now ‖ 현재 다루고 있는 사람이나 사물의 다음에 오는 목록·연속물 속의 사람 또는 사물. 다음 (사람[것]). 다음 차례[번]: *Carrots. Milk. What's next on the shopping list?* 당근, 우유, 쇼핑 목록에서 다음은 뭐죠? /

Pauline was next in line. 폴린이 줄에서 다음 차례였다.

next door /ˌ. ˈ./ *adv* **1** in the room, building etc. that is next to yours ‖ 옆에 있는 방·건물 등에. 옆(집)에[에서]: *The Simpsons live next door.* 심슨 씨 가족은 옆집에 산다. **2 next door to** next to a building ‖ 건물의 바로 옆에. 옆 건물[방, 집]에: *Our apartment is right next door to the post office.* 우리 아파트는 우체국 바로 옆에 있다.

next-door /ˌ. ˈ./ *adj* relating to the room, building etc. that is next to yours ‖ 옆에 있는 방·건물 등에 관련된. 옆(집, 방, 건물)의: *I'd like you to meet my next-door neighbor, Lara Hughes.* 내 이웃인 라라 휴즈 씨와 인사하세요.

next of kin /ˌ. . ˈ./ *n, plural* **next of kin** LAW the person or people who are most closely related to you, and who are still alive ‖ 가장 가까운 인척 관계에 있고 아직 살아 있는 사람(들). 근친(자). 가장 가까운 친척: *The victim will not be named until her next of kin are informed.* 희생자는 그녀의 근친자가 알게 되어야 비로소 이름이 밝혀질 것이다.

NFC *n* National Football Conference; a group of teams that is part of the NFL ‖ National Football Conference(전미 미식 축구 협의회)의 약어; NFL을 이루는 팀들의 집단 —see also AFC

NFL *n* National Football League; the organization that is in charge of professional football in the US ‖ National Football League(전미 미식축구 연맹)의 약어; 미국 내 프로 미식축구를 관장하고 있는 조직

NH the written abbreviation of New Hampshire ‖ New Hampshire(뉴햄프셔주)의 약어

NHL *n* National Hockey League; the organization that is in charge of professional HOCKEY in the US and Canada ‖ National Hockey League(전미 하키 연맹)의 약어; 미국과 캐나다의 프로 하키 경기를 관장하고 있는 조직

nib·ble /ˈnɪbəl/ *v* [I, T] to eat a small amount of food with a lot of very small bites ‖ 아주 조금씩 자주 물어뜯어서 소량의 음식을 먹다. 조금씩 갉아먹다[뜯어 먹다]: *a rabbit nibbling on a carrot* 당근을 갉아 먹고 있는 토끼 – **nibble** *n*

nice /naɪs/ *adj* **1** good, pleasant, attractive, or enjoyable ‖ 좋은[기분 좋은, 매력적인, 즐길 만한]. 즐거운. 유쾌한. 멋진: *Did you have a nice time at the beach?* 해변에서 좋은 시간 보냈어요?

/ *That's a nice sweater.* 그거 멋진 스웨터네요. / *I'm going to take a nice hot shower.* 나는 기분 좋게 뜨거운 물로 샤워할 겁니다. / *Come on inside where it's nice and warm.* 아늑하고 따뜻한 안으로 들어오세요. / *You look nice today.* 오늘 멋있어 보이네요. **2** friendly or kind ‖ 다정한, 친절한. 인정 많은: *They're all very nice people.* 그들은 모두 매우 친절한 사람들입니다. / *It was nice of you to visit me in the hospital.* 친히 제 병문안을 와 주셨군요. / *Be nice to your little sister!* 네 여동생에게 따뜻하게 대해 줘라! **3** nice weather is warm and sunny ‖ 날씨가 따뜻하고 햇빛이 비치는. 날씨가 좋은: *It's really nice out today.* 오늘 바깥 날씨가 너무 좋다.

SPOKEN PHRASES
---

4 it is nice/it would be nice said when you think something is good or when you wish you could do something ‖ 어떤 것이 좋다고 생각할 때 또는 어떤 것을 할 수 있기를 바랄 때 쓰여. …이 좋다/…하면 좋을 것이다/…하기를 바란다: *It's nice (that) your family visits you so often.* 가족이 너를 그렇게 자주 방문하니 좋다. / *It'd be nice to go to Spain some day.* 언젠가 스페인에 가면 좋겠다. **5 (it's) nice to meet you** a polite phrase used when you meet someone for the first time ‖ 사람을 처음으로 만났을 때 쓰이는 정중한 어구. 만나서 반갑(습니)다 **6 (it was) nice meeting you** a polite phrase used when you say goodbye after meeting someone for the first time ‖ 사람을 처음으로 만난 후에 작별 인사할 때 쓰이는 정중한 어구. 만나서 반가웠(습니)다 **7 Nice going/move/one!** said as a joke when someone makes a mistake or does something wrong ‖ 다른 사람이 실수하거나 잘못을 할 때 농담으로 쓰여. 잘 한다/잘 하는 짓이야/ 한 건 했군!: *"I just spilled my coffee!" "Nice going!"* "방금 내 커피를 쏟았어!" "잘 한다!"

– niceness *n* [U]

USAGE NOTE nice

Use **nice** when you are speaking in order to show that you like someone or something: *We had a nice time at the party.* However, many teachers think that it is better to use a more specific adjective in formal and
---

written English: *They have a beautiful house.* / *He tells interesting stories.*

nice는 사람이나 사물을 좋아한다는 것을 나타내기 위해 말할 때에 쓴다: 우리는 그 파티에서 즐겁게 놀았다. 그러나 많은 교사들은 격식체·문어체 영어에서는 더욱 구체적인 형용사를 사용하는 것이 더 낫다고 생각한다: 그들은 아름다운 집을 가지고 있다. / 그는 흥미로운 이야기를 들려 준다.

nice-look·ing /ˌ. '../ *adj* fairly attractive ‖ 꽤 매력적인. 잘 생긴. 예쁜: *He's a really nice-looking guy.* 그는 정말 잘 생긴 남자다.

nice·ly /ˈnaɪsli/ *adv* **1** in a satisfactory, pleasing, or skillful way; WELL ‖ 만족스럽게[기분 좋게, 솜씨 있게]. 멋지게. 훌륭하게. 세련되게. 능숙하게; 쭢 well: *Belinda is always so nicely dressed.* (=wearing attractive clothes) 벨린다는 항상 옷을 맵시있게 차려 입는다. / *His arm is healing nicely.* 그의 팔은 말끔하게 치유되고 있다. **2** in a polite or friendly way ‖ 예절 바르게, 친절하게: *I hope you thanked Mrs. Chang nicely.* 나는 네가 창 여사에게 예의 바르게 감사 표시를 했기를 바란다.

ni·ce·ty /ˈnaɪsəti/ *n* a small and exact detail or difference ‖ 작고 정확한 세부 사항이나 차이점. 세밀한[미묘한] 점. 정확성. 정밀성: *legal niceties* 법적 정확성

niche /nɪtʃ/ *n* **1** a job or activity that is perfect for the skills, abilities, and character that you have ‖ 사람이 가진 기술·능력·성격에 꼭 맞는 일이나 활동. 적합한[안성맞춤의] 일[것]. 적소: *After many years, she found her niche as a fashion designer.* 수년이 지나서 그녀는 패션 디자이너라는 자신에게 꼭 맞는 일을 찾아냈다. **2** a small hollow place in a wall, often used for holding STATUEs ‖ 종종 조각상을 보관하는 데 쓰이는 벽에 난 작은 공간. 벽감(壁龕). 벽의 움푹 들어간 곳

nick¹ /nɪk/ *n* **1 in the nick of time** just before it is too late or before something bad happens ‖ 너무 늦기 직전이나 나쁜 일이 일어나기 바로 전에. 때마침. 제 때에: *The doctor arrived just in the nick of time.* 의사가 때맞추어 바로 도착했다. **2** a very small cut on the surface or edge of something ‖ 사물의 표면이나 가장자리에 매우 작게 깎인 곳. 흠집. 깨진[상처 난] 곳

nick² *v* [T] to accidentally make a small cut on the surface or edge of something

N

‖ 어쩌다가 사물의 표면이나 가장자리에 작은 흠집을 내다. …에 새김눈[칼자국, 흠]을 내다: *I nicked my chin when I was shaving.* 나는 면도하면서 턱을 베었다.

nick·el /'nɪkəl/ *n* **1** a coin used in the US and Canada worth 5 cents (=1/20 of a dollar) ‖ 미국과 캐나다에서 쓰이는 (1달러의 1/20인) 5센트짜리 동전. 니켈 **2** [U] a hard silver-white metal that is an ELEMENT and is used for making other metals ‖ 원소의 하나이고 다른 금속을 만드는 데 쓰이는 단단한 은백색의 금속. 니켈

nickel-and-dime /ˌ.. . './ *adj* INFORMAL not large, important, or effective enough ‖ 충분히 크지[중요하지, 효과적이지] 않은. 사소한. 그저 그런: *We face problems that can't be solved with nickel-and-dime solutions.* 우리는 그저 그런 해결책으로는 풀 수 없는 문제들에 직면해 있다.

nick·name¹ /'nɪkneɪm/ *n* a silly name or a shorter form of someone's real name, usually given by friends or family ‖ 보통 친구나 가족이 붙여주는, 우스운 이름이나 실제 이름을 줄인 형태. 별명. 애칭: *His nickname was "Elephant" because of his ears.* 그의 별명은 그의 귀 때문에 붙은 "코끼리"였다.

nickname² *v* [T] to give someone a NICKNAME ‖ 남에게 별명을 붙이다. …을 별명[애칭]으로 부르다

nicotine /'nɪkəˌtin/ *n* [U] a dangerous substance in tobacco ‖ 담배에 들어 있는 위험 물질. 니코틴

niece /nis/ *n* the daughter of your brother or sister, or the daughter of your husband's or wife's brother or sister ‖ 형제나 자매의 딸, 또는 남편이나 부인의 형제나 자매의 딸. 조카딸 — compare NEPHEW —see picture at FAMILY

nif·ty /'nɪfti/ *adj* INFORMAL very good, fast, or effective ‖ 매우 좋은[빠른, 효과적인]. 재빠른. 재치 있는: *John taught me a nifty little card trick.* 존은 간단하고 멋진 카드 속임수를 나에게 가르쳐 주었다.

nig·gling /'nɪɡlɪŋ/ *adj* not very important, but continuing to annoy someone ‖ 그리 중요하지는 않지만 어떤 사람을 계속해서 귀찮게 하는. 좀스럽게 괴롭히는. 지나치게 신경쓰는: *a niggling doubt* 지나친 의심

nigh /naɪ/ *adv, prep* LITERARY **1** near ‖ 가까이에 **2 well nigh/nigh on** almost ‖ 거의: *Edna was well nigh fifty when at last she married.* 에드나가 마침내 결혼

했을 때는 거의 50이 다 되었다.

night /naɪt/ *n* **1** [C, U] the dark part of each 24-hour period, when the sun cannot be seen ‖ 하루 24시간 중 해를 볼 수 없는 어두컴컴한 때. 밤. 야간: *a store that is open all night* 24시간 문을 여는 가게 / *You can see the stars really clearly here at night.* 밤에는 여기에서 정말 선명하게 별을 볼 수 있다. **2** [C, U] the evening ‖ 저녁: *Some friends are coming over tomorrow night.* 몇몇 친구들이 내일 저녁에 올 예정이다. / *Mom had to go to the hospital last night.* 어머니는 어제 저녁 병원에 가야 했다. / *I fly back to New Orleans on Thursday night.* 나는 목요일 밤에 뉴올리언즈로 비행기를 타고 돌아간다. / *We had a good night out.* 우리는 외출해서 저녁을 즐겁게 보냈다. (=when you go to a restaurant, party etc.) ✗DON'T SAY "this night." say "tonight."✗ "tonight"이라고 하며 "this night"이라고는 하지 않는다. **3** [C, U] the time when most people are sleeping ‖ 대부분의 사람이 잠자는 때. 밤(중): *The baby cried all night long.* 그 아기는 밤새도록 울었다. / *I woke up in the middle of the night.* 나는 한밤중에 잠에서 깨었다. / *What you need is a good night's sleep.* (=to sleep well all night) 당신에게 필요한 것은 하룻밤의 숙면이다. **4 night after night** every night for a long period ‖ 오랜 기간 동안 매일 밤. 밤마다: *He goes out drinking night after night.* 그는 밤마다 술 마시러 나간다. **5 night and day/day and night** all the time ‖ 내내. 밤낮 없이. 쉴 새 없이: *The store is guarded day and night.* 그 가게는 밤낮 없이 지켜진다. —see also DAY, NIGHTS, TONIGHT²

night·club /'naɪtˌklʌb/ *n* a place where people can drink and dance that is open late at night ‖ 밤 늦게까지 영업을 하며 사람들이 술 마시고 춤출 수 있는 곳. 나이트클럽

night·fall /'naɪtfɔl/ *n* [U] LITERARY the time in the evening when the sky becomes darker; DUSK ‖ 하늘이 보다 어두컴컴해지는 저녁 때. 해질녘. 일몰; ⑨ dusk

night·gown /'naɪtˌɡaʊn/, **night·ie** /'naɪti/ *n* a piece of loose clothing, like a dress, that women wear in bed ‖ 잠자리에서 여성들이 입는 드레스 같은 헐렁한 옷. 잠옷

night·in·gale /'naɪtⁿˌɡeɪl, 'naɪtɪŋ-/ *n* a small European wild bird that sings very beautifully, especially at night ‖ 특히 밤에 매우 아름답게 우는 유럽산의 작

은 들새. 나이팅게일

night·life /ˈnaɪtˌlaɪf/ *n* [U] entertainment in places where you can dance, drink etc. in the evening ‖ 밤에 춤추고 술 마실 수 있는 곳에서의 즐기기. 밤의 유흥: *Las Vegas is famous for its nightlife.* 라스베이거스는 밤의 유흥으로 유명하다.

night light /ˈ. ./ *n* a small, not very bright light, often put in a child's BEDROOM to stop him/her from being afraid ‖ 아이들이 무서워하지 않도록 침실에 놓아두는 작고 그리 밝지 않은 등. 철야 등

night·ly /ˈnaɪtli/ *adj, adv* happening every night ‖ 매일 밤에 일어나는. 밤마다(의): *the nightly news* 밤 뉴스 / *The restaurant is open nightly.* 그 식당은 밤마다 문을 연다.

night·mare /ˈnaɪtˌmɛr/ *n* **1** a very frightening dream ‖ 매우 무서운 꿈. 악몽: *Years after the accident I still have nightmares about it.* 그 사고 후 수년이 지났지만 아직까지도 나는 그것에 대한 악몽을 꾼다. **2** a person, thing, situation etc. that is very bad or very difficult to deal with ‖ 다루기에 매우 고약하거나 어려운 사람·사물·상황 등: *It was a nightmare driving home in the snow.* 눈 속에서 집에까지 운전해 간 것은 악몽 같은 경험이었다. **– nightmarish** *adj*

night owl /ˈ. ./ *n* INFORMAL someone who enjoys being awake or working late at night ‖ 밤 늦도록 깨어 있거나 일하기를 즐기는 사람. 올빼미족

nights /naɪts/ *adv* regularly or often at night ‖ 밤에 규칙적으로 또는 자주. 밤에는 언제나. 밤마다: *Juan works nights.* 후앙은 밤마다 일한다.

night school /ˈ. ./ *n* [U] classes taught at night, for people who work during the day ‖ 낮에 일하는 사람들을 위해 밤에 가르치는 학교. 야학. 야간 학교: *I'm studying Spanish at night school.* 나는 야학에서 스페인어를 배우고 있다.

night·stand /ˈnaɪtstænd/, **night ta·ble** /ˈ. ˌ../ *n* a small table beside a bed ‖ 침대 옆의 작은 탁자

night·time /ˈnaɪt-taɪm/ *n* [U] the time during the night when the sky is dark ‖ 하늘이 어둑어둑한 밤 동안의 때. 밤중. 야간 **—opposite** DAYTIME

nil /nɪl/ *n* [U] nothing or zero ‖ 아무것도 없음. 영. 무(無): *His chances of winning the election are almost nil.* (=not likely) 그가 선거에서 이길 가능성은 거의 전무하다.

nim·ble /ˈnɪmbəl/ *adj* **1** able to move

quickly, easily, and skillfully; AGILE ‖ 재빠르고 쉽고 능숙하게 움직일 수 있는. 날렵한. 민첩한. ⟨凾⟩ agile: *nimble fingers* 재빠른 손가락 / *a nimble climber* 날렵한 등반자 **2 a nimble mind/wit etc.** an ability to think quickly or understand things easily ‖ 어떤 것을 재빠르게 생각하거나 쉽게 이해하는 능력. 영리한. 이해[눈치]가 빠른

nim·by /ˈnɪmbi/ *n plural* **nimbies** not in my backyard; someone who does not want a particular activity or building near their home ‖ not in my backyard(님비(족))의 약어; 자신의 집 근처에서의 특정 활동이나 건축을 원하지 않는 사람

nin·com·poop /ˈnɪŋkəmˌpup/ *n* OLD-FASHIONED someone who has done something stupid; IDIOT ‖ 어리석은 짓을 한 사람. 바보. 멍청이; ⟨凾⟩ idiot

nine /naɪn/ *number* **1** 9 ‖ 9 **2** 9 o'clock ‖ 9시: *I have to be in the office by nine.* 나는 9시까지는 사무실에 가야 한다.

nine·teen /ˌnaɪnˈtin/ *number* 19 ‖ 19 **– nineteenth** *number*

nine-to-five /ˌ. . ˈ./ *adj, adv* from 9:00 a.m. until 5:00 p.m.; the hours that most people work in an office ‖ 오전 9시부터 오후 5시까지; 대부분의 사람들이 사무실에서 일하는 시간. 월급쟁이로(일하는): *You work nine-to-five, right?* 너는 (오전 9시에서 오후 5시까지)월급쟁이로 일하지, 맞지? / *a nine-to-five job* 월급쟁이 직(업)

nine·ty /ˈnaɪnti/ *number* **1** 90 ‖ 90 **2 the nineties a)** the years between 1990 and 1999 ‖ 1990년과 1999년 사이의 해. 1990년대 **b)** the numbers between 90 and 99, especially when used for measuring temperature ‖ 특히 온도를 측정하는 데 사용되는 90과 99 사이의 숫자. 90도대 **3 be in my/his/their etc. nineties** to be aged between 90 and 99 ‖ 90과 99 사이의 나이이다. 90대이다 **– ninetieth** /ˈnaɪntiɪθ/ *number*

ninth /naɪnθ/ *number* **1** 9th ‖ 아홉째 **2** 1/9 ‖ 9분의 1

nip¹ /nɪp/ **-pped, -pping** *v* **1** [I, T] to bite someone or something with small sharp bites, or to try to do this ‖ 날카롭게 조금씩 사람이나 사물을 물다, 또는 이렇게 하려고 하다. 물어뜯다: *This stupid dog keeps nipping at my ankles.* 이 멍청한 개가 내 발목을 계속 물어뜯고 있다. **2 nip sth in the bud** to prevent something from becoming a problem by stopping it as soon as it starts ‖ 어떤 일

을 시작하자마자 멈추게 하여 문제가 되는 것을 막다. …을 초기에 잡다. 싹 단계에서 꺾다. 미연에 방지하다

nip² *n* **1** a small sharp bite, or the action of biting someone or something ‖ 작고 날카롭게 물기. 사람 또는 사물을 무는 행위. 물어뜯기 **2 nip and tuck** equally likely to happen or not happen ‖ 일어나거나 일어나지 않을 가능성이 똑같은. (경주에서) 막상막하로. 치열하게 경합하여: *I made it to the airport, but it was nip and tuck.* 나는 공항에 시간에 대어 갔지만 아슬아슬했다.

nip·ple /ˈnɪpəl/ *n* **1** the dark raised circle in the middle of a woman's breast, that a baby sucks in order to get milk ‖ 아기들이 모유를 먹기 위해 빠는, 여성의 유방 중앙에 도드라져 내민 거무스름한 원형 부분. 여성의 젖꼭지 — compare TEAT **2** one of the two dark raised circles on a man's chest ‖ 남자 가슴에 거무스름하고 도드라져 내민 두 개의 원형 중 하나. 남자의 젖꼭지 **3** the small piece of rubber on the end of a baby's bottle ‖ 아기 젖병의 끝에 달린 작은 고무 조각. 고무 젖꼭지 **4** something shaped like a nipple, for example on a machine ‖ 기계 등에서의 젖꼭지 모양의 것

nip·py /ˈnɪpi/ *adj* weather that is nippy is cold enough that you need a coat ‖ 코트가 필요할 정도로 날씨가 추운. 살을 에는 듯이 추운

nit /nɪt/ *n* the egg of a LOUSE (=small insect) ‖ 이·벼룩 등의 알. 서캐

nit·pick·ing /ˈnɪt.pɪkɪŋ/ *n* [U] the act of criticizing people about unimportant details ‖ 그리 중요하지 않은 사항에 대해 사람을 비평하는 행위. 헐뜯기. 흠잡기 – **nitpicking** *adj*

ni·trate /ˈnaɪtreɪt/ *n* [C, U] a chemical compound that is mainly used for improving the soil that crops are grown in ‖ 곡물을 재배하는 토양을 개량하는 데 주로 쓰이는 화학적인 혼합물. 질산염[비료]

ni·tro·gen /ˈnaɪtrədʒən/ *n* [U] a gas that is an ELEMENT and is the main part of the earth's air ‖ 지구 공기의 대부분을 차지하는 원소인 가스. 질소

nitty-grit·ty /ˈnɪti ˌɡrɪti, ˌnɪti ˈɡrɪti/ *n* **the nitty-gritty** INFORMAL the basic and practical facts and details of an agreement or activity ‖ 계약이나 활동의 기본적·실제적인 요소와 내용. 사물의 핵심. 요체: *Let's get down to the nitty-gritty and work out the cost.* 본론으로 들어가 비용을 산정하자.

nit·wit /ˈnɪt.wɪt/ *n* INFORMAL a silly stupid person ‖ 어리석고 멍청한 사람. 멍청이. 바보

NJ the written abbreviation of New Jersey ‖ New Jersey(뉴저지 주)의 약어

NM the written abbreviation of New Mexico ‖ New Mexico(뉴멕시코 주)의 약어

no. *plural* **nos.** the written abbreviation of NUMBER ‖ number의 약어

no¹ /noʊ/ *adv* **1** SPOKEN said in order to give a negative reply to a question, offer, or request ‖ 물음[제안, 요청]에 부정적인 대답을 하는 데 쓰여. 아니. 싫어: *"Is she married?" "No, she's not."* "그녀는 결혼했니?" "아니, 안 했어." / *"Do you want some more coffee?" "No, thanks."* "커피 좀 더 마실래?" "아니, 괜찮아." / *I asked Dad if I could have a dog, but he said no.* 나는 아버지에게 개를 길러도 되는지 물어보았지만 안 된다고 말씀하셨다. **2** SPOKEN said when you disagree with a statement ‖ 남의 말에 동의하지 않을 때 쓰여. 그렇지 않다. 그런 게 아니라: *"Gary's weird." "No, he's just shy."* "게리는 괴상한 녀석이야." "아니야, 그는 단지 부끄럼을 타는 거야." **3** SPOKEN said when you do not want someone to do something ‖ 남이 어떤 일을 하는 것을 원하지 않을 때 쓰여. 안돼: *No, Jimmy, don't touch that.* 안돼, 지미, 그거 손대지 마. —opposite YES

no² *determiner* **1** not any, or not at all ‖ 어떤 또는 조금의 …도 아닌: *I'm sorry, there are no more tickets available.* 죄송합니다만 더 이상 표가 없습니다. / *He has no control over his children.* 그는 자신의 아이들을 전혀 통제하지 못한다. / *There's no reason to be afraid.* 두려워할 이유가 없다. / *I'm no fool.* (=I am not stupid) 나는 바보가 아니야. **2** used on a sign in order to show that something is not allowed ‖ 어떤 것이 허용되지 않음을 나타내기 위해 표지판에 쓰여. …반대. 금지. 사절: *No smoking* 금연 / *No parking* 주차 금지 —see also **in no time** (TIME¹)

USAGE NOTE no and not

Use **no** before nouns to mean "not any," or to say that something is not allowed: *He has no job and no money.* / *a "no smoking" sign.* You can also use **no** in order to agree with negative questions: *"It's not raining, is it?" "No, it isn't."* Use **not** in order to make a verb negative: *I'm not going camping.* When the word "all" and words that begin with "every-"

are the subject of a sentence, use **not** to make the subject negative: *Not all of the students finished the test. / Not everyone likes horror movies.* You can also use **not** before names, pronouns, adverbs of frequency, and prepositions: *"George and Diane are getting a divorce." "Not them!" / "Do you watch sports on TV?" "Not very often." / It's open on Saturday, but not on Sunday.*

no는 명사 앞에서 "어떤 …도 아닌"을 뜻하거나 어떤 것이 허용되지 않는다고 말하는 데에 쓴다: 그는 일자리도 돈도 없다. / "금연" 표지(판). **no**는 또한 부정적인 질문에 동의하기 위해 쓴다: "비가 안 오지, 그렇지?" "그래, 오지 않아." 동사를 부정형으로 만드는 데에 **not**을 쓴다: 나는 캠핑 안 갈 거야. "all"이란 단어와 "every"로 시작하는 단어가 문장의 주어일 때 **not**은 주어를 부정하기 위해 사용한다: 모든 학생들이 그 시험을 끝낸 것은 아니다. / 모든 사람들이 공포 영화를 좋아하는 것은 아니다. **not**은 또한 이름이나 대명사, 빈도 부사나 전치사 앞에 사용할 수 있다: "조지와 다이앤은 이혼을 할 거야." "안 돼, 그들은!" / "텔레비전에서 스포츠 경기를 보냐?" "그리 자주는 아냐." / 그곳은 토요일에는 문을 열지만 일요일은 안 연다.

no³ *n* a negative answer or decision ‖ 부정적인 대답이나 결정. 부인. 거부. 불찬성: *Her answer was a definite no.* 그녀의 대답은 분명한 거절이었다.

no·bil·i·ty /noʊˈbɪləti/ *n* **1 the nobility** the group of people in particular countries who have the highest social class ‖ 특정 국가에서 최고의 사회 계급을 가진 사람들의 집단. 귀족 (계급) **2** [U] the quality of being NOBLE ‖ 고귀한 자질. 고결함

no·ble¹ /ˈnoʊbəl/ *adj* **1** morally good or generous in a way that should be admired ‖ 존경받는 것이 마땅할 정도로 도덕적으로 훌륭하거나 관대한. 고결한. 고상한. 숭고한: *a noble young man* 고상한 젊은이 / *a noble achievement* 숭고한 업적 **2** belonging to the NOBILITY ‖ 귀족에 속한. 귀족의: *noble families* 귀족 가문 **– nobly** *adv*

no·ble², **no·ble·man** /ˈnoʊbəlmən/, **no·blewom·an** /ˈnoʊbəlˌwʊmən/ *n* someone who belongs to the NOBILITY ‖ 귀족에 속하는 사람. 귀족

nobody¹ /ˈnoʊˌbʌdi, -ˌbɑdi/ *pron* ⇨ NO ONE, —see usage note at ANYONE

nobody² *n* someone who is not important, successful, or famous ‖ 중요하지[성공적이지, 유명하지] 않은 사람. 하찮은 사람[별것 아닌] 사람: *I feel like a nobody!* 내가 하찮은 사람처럼 느껴져!

no-brain·er /ˈ. ˌ.ˈ/ *n* [C usually singular] SLANG something that you do not have to think about, because it is easy to understand ‖ 이해하기 쉬워서 생각해 볼 필요가 없는 것. 용이한[알기 쉬운] 것: *an action movie that's a real no-brainer* 정말 가볍게 볼 수 있는 액션 영화

noc·tur·nal /nɑkˈtɚnl/ *adj* **1** TECHNICAL nocturnal animals are active at night ‖ 동물이 밤에 활동하는. 야행성의 **2** FORMAL happening at night ‖ 밤에 일어나는. 밤의. 야간의

nod /nɑd/ *v* **-dded, -dding 1** [I, T] to move your head up and down, especially to show that you agree with or understand something ‖ 특히 어떤 일을 동의하거나 이해한다는 것을 나타내기 위해 머리를 위 아래로 움직이다. 머리를 끄덕이다: *The committee nodded their heads in agreement.* 그 위원회는 찬성의 표시로 그들의 머리를 끄덕였다. / *"Are you having fun?" he asked. Jill smiled and nodded.* "재미있니?"라고 그는 물었다. 질은 웃으며 고개를 끄덕였다. **2** to move your head up and down once toward someone or something, in order to greet someone or to give him/her a sign to do something ‖ 남에게 인사하거나 무엇을 하라는 신호를 하려고 사람이나 사물 쪽을 향해 고개를 끄덕이다. 인사하다. 끄덕여 알리다[신호하다]: *I nodded to the waiter and asked for the bill.* 나는 웨이터에게 머리를 끄덕여 계산서를 요청했다. / *"Sally's in there," Jim said, nodding toward the door.* 짐은 문 쪽을 향해 머리를 끄덕이며 "샐리는 저기 있어"라고 말했다.

nod off *phr v* [I] to begin to sleep, often without intending to ‖ 종종 의도하지 않은 잠을 자기 시작하다. 꾸벅꾸벅 졸다: *His speech was so boring I kept nodding off.* 그의 연설은 너무 지루해서 나는 계속 꾸벅꾸벅 졸았다. **– nod** *n*

node /noʊd/ *n* **1** a place where lines in a network, GRAPH etc. meet or join ‖ 네트워크나 그래프 등의 선이 서로 만나거나 합쳐지는 곳. 접속점 **2** ⇨ LYMPH NODE

no-fault /ˌ. ˈ. ˈ./ *adj* **1** no-fault car insurance will pay for the damage done in an accident, even if you caused the accident ‖ 자동차 보험에서 비록 자신이 사고를 일으켰다 하더라도 사고로 발생한

손해를 보상하는. 무과실 보험의 **2 a no-fault** DIVORCE does not blame either the husband or the wife ‖ 이혼에서 남편이나 아내 모두 다 책임을 지지 않는. 쌍방 모두 결혼 해소의 책임을 지지 않는. 협의 이혼의

N

no-frills /ˌ. ˈ.ˌ./ *adj* without any features that are not completely necessary; basic ‖ 불필요한 특성은 전혀 없는. 꼭 필요한 것만의; 기본적인: *a no-frills airline* 불필요한 서비스를 제공하지 않는 항공사

noise /nɔɪz/ *n* [C, U] a sound or sounds that is too loud, annoying, or not intended ‖ 너무 큰[짜증나게 하는, 자연적으로 나는] 소리(들). 소음. 잡음. 시끄러움: *the noise of the traffic* 교통 소음 / *What was that cracking noise?* 그 날카로운 소리는 뭐냐? / *The washing machine is making a weird noise.* 그 세탁기는 기묘한 소리를 내고 있다. / *There was a lot of noise outside.* 바깥이 무척 시끄러웠다.

USAGE NOTE noise and sound

Use **sound** to talk about something that you hear: *I love the sound of birds singing.* **Noise** means "loud unpleasant sounds": *Could you kids stop making so much noise?*

sound는 듣고 있는 것에 대해 말하는 데에 쓰인다: 나는 새가 지저귀는 소리를 좋아한다. **noise**는 "불쾌하게 큰 소리"를 의미한다: 얘들아 너희들 그렇게 시끄럽게 굴지 않을 수 없니?

---

noise·less·ly /ˈnɔɪzlɪsli/ *adv* not making any sound ‖ 어떠한 소리도 내지 않는. 소리 없이. 조용하게: *walking noiselessly* 조용하게 걷기 — **noiseless** *adj*

noise pol·lu·tion /ˈ. .ˌ../ *n* [U] very loud continuous noise in the environment that is harmful to people ‖ 환경 속에서 사람에게 유해한 매우 크고 지속적인 소음. 소음 공해

nois·y /ˈnɔɪzi/ *adj* making a lot of noise, or full of noise ‖ 많은 소음을 내거나 소음으로 가득한. 떠들썩한. 시끄러운. 소란한: *a group of noisy kids* 시끄럽게 떠드는 한 무리의 아이들 / *a noisy restaurant* 왁자지껄한 식당 — **noisily** *adv* — **noisiness** *n* [U]

no·mad /ˈnoʊmæd/ *n* a member of a tribe that travels from place to place, usually to find fields for his/her animals ‖ 보통 가축을 위한 초지를 찾아서 이곳저곳으로 이동하는 종족의 일원. 유목민 —

nomadic /noʊˈmædɪk/ *adj*

no-man's land /ˈ. .ˌ./ *n* [singular, U] land that no one owns or controls, especially between two opposing armies ‖ 특히 대치하고 있는 군대 사이에 있는 아무도 소유하거나 지배하지 않는 땅. 중간무인] 지대

no·men·cla·ture /ˈnoʊmən,kleɪtʃɚ/ *n* [C, U] FORMAL a system of naming things ‖ 사물을 명명하는 체계. 용어 체계. 용어법. 명명법

nom·i·nal /ˈnɑmənl/ *adj* **1 nominal leader/head etc.** someone who has the title of leader etc. but does not actually do that job ‖ 지도자 등의 칭호는 가졌지만 실제 그 직무는 수행하지 않는 사람. 명목상의 지도자/우두머리 **2 nominal price/fee/sum etc.** a small amount of money ‖ 적은 액수의 돈. 얼마 안 되는 가격/요금/합계액

nom·i·nal·ly /ˈnɑmənl-i/ *adv* officially described as something or as doing something, although the truth may be different ‖ 비록 사실은 다를 수 있지만, 공식적으로는 어떤 것이라고, 또는 어떤 것을 하는 것이라고 묘사되는. 명목상으로(는): *The President nominally commands the armed forces.* 대통령은 명목상으로 군 통수권이 있다.

nom·i·nate /ˈnɑmə,neɪt/ *v* [T] **1** to officially choose someone so that s/he can be one of the competitors in an election, competition etc. ‖ 선거·시합 등의 경쟁자의 한 사람이 될 수 있도록 누군가를 공식적으로 선택하다. 후보자로 추천[지명]하다: *Ferraro was the first woman to be nominated for the job of vice president.* 페라로는 부통령직에 지명된 최초의 여성이었다. **2** to choose someone for a particular job or position ‖ 특정 직무나 직위에 맞는 사람을 선택하다. …의 직위에 임명하다: *Margaret was nominated (as) club representative.* 마가렛은 클럽의 대표로 임명되었다.

nom·i·na·tion /ˌnɑmɪˈneɪʃən/ *n* [C, U] **1** the act of officially choosing someone to be a competitor in an election, competition etc., or the official choice ‖ 어떤 사람을 선거·시합 등의 경쟁자로 공식적으로 선택하는 행위, 또는 공식적인 선택. 지명. 추천: *Clinton got the Democratic nomination for President.* 클린턴은 민주당의 대통령 후보 지명을 받았다. **2** the act of choosing someone for a particular job, or the person chosen ‖ 특정 직무에 맞는 사람을 선택하는 행위, 또는 선택된 사람. 임명(자): *the nomination of O'Connor to the United*

States Supreme Court 오코너의 미연방 최고 법원 판사에의 임명

nom·i·nee /ˌnɑməˈni/ *n* someone who has been NOMINATEd for a prize, duty etc. ‖ 상·의무 등에 지명된 사람. 지명[추천, 임명]된 사람: *Oscar nominee Winona Ryder* 오스카상의 후보 위노나 라이더

non·ag·gres·sion /ˌnɑnəˈgrɛʃən/ *n* [U] the state of not fighting or attacking ‖ 싸우거나 공격하지 않는 상태. 불침략. 불가침: *a nonaggression pact/treaty* (=a country's promise not to attack) 불가침 조약[협정]

non·al·co·hol·ic /ˌnɑnælkəˈhɔlɪk/ *adj* a nonalcoholic drink does not have any alcohol in it ‖ 마실 것에 알코올 성분이 전혀 들어 있지 않는

non·cha·lant /ˌnɑnʃəˈlɑnt/ *adj* calm and not seeming interested in or worried about anything ‖ 차분하고 어떤 것에도 흥미 있거나 염려하는 듯하지 않은. 무관심한. 태연한. 무심한. 냉정한: *young men trying to appear nonchalant* 무관심한 척하려고 애쓰는 젊은 남자들 – **nonchalance** *n* [U] – **nonchalantly** *adv*

non·com·bat·ant /ˌnɑnkəmˈbætˈnt/ *n* someone in the army, navy etc. who does not do any fighting during a war, such as an army doctor ‖ 군의관 등의 전쟁 중에 어떤 전투도 하지 않는 육군·해군 등의 소속원. 비전투원

non·com·mit·tal /ˌnɑnkəˈmɪtl/ *adj* not giving a definite answer, or not willing to express your opinions ‖ 확실한 대답을 하지 않거나 자신의 의견을 표현하려 하지 않는. 모호한. 이도저도 아닌: *The lawyer was noncommittal about Jones' chances of going to prison.* 변호사는 존스가 감옥에 갈 가능성에 대해 정확한 대답을 하지 않았다. – **noncommittally** *adv*

non·con·form·ist /ˌnɑnkənˈfɔrmɪst/ *n* someone who deliberately does not accept the beliefs and customs that most people in a society accept ‖ 사회의 다수가 받아들이는 신념과 관습을 고의로 받아들이지 않는 사람. 관행을 따르지 않는 사람. 이단자: *a political nonconformist* 정치적인 이단자

non·dair·y /ˌ'...'/ *adj* containing no milk, and used instead of a product that contains milk ‖ 우유를 함유하지 않고 우유가 함유된 제품 대신에 사용되는: *non-dairy whipped topping* 비유제품으로 거품을 낸 토핑

non·de·nom·i·na·tion·al /ˌ...'...'.../ *adj* not related to a particular religion or religious group ‖ 특정한 종교나 종파에 관련되지 않은. 무종파의: *a non-denominational chapel* 무종파의 예배당

non·de·script /ˌnɑndɪˈskrɪpt/ *adj* not having any noticeable or interesting qualities ‖ 눈에 띄거나 흥미 있는 특성을 전혀 가지고 있지 않은. 뚜렷하게 나타낼 수 없는. 막연한: *a nondescript man in a plain gray suit* 평범한 회색 양복을 입은 특징이 없는 남자

none¹ /nʌn/ *quantifier, pron* **1** not any of something ‖ 어떤 것이 조금도 아닌[없는](것). 아무것도 아닌[없는](것): *"Can I have some more pie?" "Sorry, there's none left."* "파이 좀 더 먹어도 될까?" "미안하지만, 조금도 남아 있지 않아." **2** not one person or thing ‖ 단 한 사람이나 물건도 아닌[없는]. 어떤 것[사람]도 아닌[없는]: *None of my friends has a car.* 내 친구들 중 누구도 차를 가지고 있지 않다. / *Any decision is better than none at all.* 어떠한 결정도 전혀 없는 것보다는 낫다. **3 none other than** used in order to emphasize a fact when you are surprised that it is true ‖ 진짜라는 것에 깜짝 놀란 경우에 그 사실을 강조하는 데 쓰여. 바로[다름 아니라] …인: *Her uncle is none other than the President.* 그녀의 삼촌은 다름 아닌 대통령이다. —see usage note at EITHER² —see study note on page 940

none² *adv* **1 none the worse/wiser etc.** not any worse than before, not knowing any more than before etc. ‖ 전보다 조금도 더 나빠지지 않은, 전보다 조금도 더 많이 알지 않는. 전혀 더 나빠지지/더 알게 되지 않는: *The cat's none the worse for having stayed out all night.* 고양이가 밤새 바깥에 있다고 해서

더 나빠지지는 않는다. **2 none too soon/likely etc.** not at all soon, not at all likely etc. ‖ 결코 너무 빠르지 않은, 절대 그럴 것 같지 않은: *The ambulance arrived none too soon.* 앰뷸런스는 꼭 알맞은 때에 도착했다.

non·en·ti·ty /nɑn'ɛntəti/ *n* someone who has no importance, power, or ability ‖ 중요성·힘·능력이 없는 사람. 보잘것없는 사람

none·the·less /ˌnʌnðə'lɛs/ *adv* FORMAL in spite of what has just been mentioned; NEVERTHELESS ‖ 바로 직전에 언급된 것에도 불구하고. 그럼에도 불구하고. 그런데도; ⑨ nevertheless: *It won't be as fast as a supercomputer, but it will do the job nonetheless.* 그것은 슈퍼 컴퓨터만큼 빠르지는 않겠지만 그럼에도 불구하고 그 일을 해낼 것이다.

non·e·vent /'nɑnɪˌvɛnt, ˌnɑnɪ'vɛnt/ *n* INFORMAL an event that is disappointing and much less exciting or interesting than you expected ‖ 기대했던 것보다 실망스럽고 훨씬 자극이나 재미가 덜한 사건. 겉보기만 그럴듯한 일: *The concert was a total nonevent.* 그 콘서트는 소문난 잔치에 불과했다.

non·ex·ist·ent /ˌnɑnɪg'zɪstənt/ *adj* not existing at all in a particular place or situation ‖ 특정한 장소나 상황에 전혀 존재하지 않는. 실재하지 않는: *Airplanes were practically nonexistent in those days.* 비행기는 그 당시 실제로 존재하지 않았다.

non·fat /ˌnɑn'fæt/ *adj* nonfat milk, YOGURT etc. has no fat in it ‖ 우유나 요구르트 등에 지방이 들어 있지 않은. 탈지한

non·fic·tion /ˌnɑn'fɪkʃən/ *n* [U] articles, books etc. about real facts or events, not imagined ones ‖ 상상이 아니라 실제 사실이나 사건에 대한 글이나 책 등. 논픽션(작품) **–nonfiction** *adj* — compare FICTION

non·flam·ma·ble /ˌnɑn'flæməbəl/ *adj* difficult or impossible to burn ‖ 타기 어렵거나 불가능한. 타지 않는. 불연성의 — opposite INFLAMMABLE, FLAMMABLE

non·in·ter·ven·tion /ˌnɑnɪntɚ'vɛnʃən/ *n* [U] the refusal of a government to become involved in the affairs of other countries ‖ 정부가 다른 나라의 문제에 개입되는 것을 거절하는 것. 불개입. 내정 불간섭

no-no /'noʊnoʊ/ *n* INFORMAL something that is not allowed, or not socially acceptable ‖ 허용되지 않거나 사회적으로 용인되지 않는 것. 금기: *My parents think sex before marriage is a definite no-no.* 내 부모님들은 혼전 성관계는 절대 금기라고 생각한다.

no-non·sense /ˌnoʊ'nɑnsɛns-/ *adj* very practical, direct, and unwilling to waste time ‖ 매우 실제적이며 직접적이고 시간을 낭비하려 하지 않는. 현실적인. 경제적인. 실용적인. 효율적인: *a no-nonsense attitude toward work* 일에 대한 현실적인 태도

non·pay·ment /ˌnɑn'peɪmənt/ *n* [U] failure to pay bills, taxes, or debts ‖ 청구 금액·세금·빚의 지불의 불이행. 미불. 미지급

non·plussed /ˌnɑn'plʌst/ *adj* so surprised that you do not know what to say or do ‖ 너무 놀라서 무엇을 하거나 말해야 할지 모르는. 어찌해야 할 줄 모르는: *I was momentarily nonplussed by his news.* 나는 그의 소식을 듣고 순간적으로 깜짝 놀라 어리둥절해졌다.

non·prof·it /ˌnɑn'prɑfɪt/ *adj* a nonprofit organization, school, hospital etc. uses the money it earns to help people instead of making a profit, and therefore does not have to pay taxes ‖ 단체·학교·병원 등이 수익을 올리는 대신에 버는 돈을 사람을 돕는 데에 사용해서 세금을 내지 않아도 되는. 비영리적인

non·pro·lif·er·a·tion /ˌnɑnprəˌlɪfə'reɪʃən/ *n* [U] the act of limiting the number of NUCLEAR or chemical weapons that are being made across the world ‖ 전세계적으로 만들어지고 있는 핵무기나 화학 무기의 수를 제한하기. 핵 확산 방지

non·re·fund·a·ble /ˌ. .'...-/ *adj* if something you buy is non-refundable, you cannot get your money back after you have paid for it ‖ 구매하는 사물이 값을 지불한 후에는 다시 돌려받을 수 없는. 환불받을 수 없는: *non-refundable airline tickets* 환불받을 수 없는 비행기표

non·re·new·a·ble /ˌ. .'...-/ *adj* non-renewable types of energy such as coal or gas cannot be replaced after they have been used ‖ 석탄이나 가스등 에너지 종류가 사용된 후 다시 재사용할 수 없는. 재생 불가능한

non·sense /'nɑnsɛns, -səns/ *n* [U] **1** ideas, statements, or opinions that are not true or that seem very stupid ‖ 사실이 아니거나 매우 어리석어 보이는 생각·말·의견. 말도 안 되는 것. 허튼소리. 난센스: *"This dress makes me look fat." "Nonsense, you look great!"* "난 이 드레스를 입으면 뚱뚱해 보여." "말도 안돼, 아주 예뻐 보여!" **2** behavior that is stupid and annoying ‖ 어리석고 짜증나게 하는

행동. 터무니없는 행위[수작]: *I'm not putting up with any more of your nonsense!* 당신의 어리석은 행동에 더 이상 참을 수가 없어! **3** speech or writing that has no meaning or cannot be understood ‖ 무의미하거나 이해되지 않는 말이나 글. 무의미한[알아들을 수 없는] 것 [일]: *Children often make up nonsense songs.* 아이들은 종종 알아들을 수 없는 노래를 지어내곤 한다. –

nonsensical /nɑnˈsɛnsɪkəl/ *adj*

non se·qui·tur /ˌnɑn ˈsɛkwɪtɚ/ *n* FORMAL a statement that does not seem related to the statements that were made before it ‖ 이전에 한 진술과 관계가 없는 것으로 보이는 진술. 불합리한 추론. 그릇된 결론

non·smok·er /ˌnɑnˈsmoʊkɚ/ *n* someone who does not smoke ‖ 담배를 피우지 않는 사람. 비흡연자 —opposite SMOKER

non·smok·ing /ˌnɑnˈsmoʊkɪŋ/ *adj* a nonsmoking area, building etc. is one where people are not allowed to smoke ‖ 지역·건물 등이 사람들이 담배를 피우는 것이 허용되지 않는. 금연의

non·stand·ard /ˌnɑnˈstændɚd/ *adj* TECHNICAL nonstandard words, expressions, or pronunciations are usually considered to be incorrect by educated speakers of a language ‖ 단어 [표현, 발음]가 그 언어를 쓰는 교양 있는 사람들에게 일반적으로 틀린 것으로 여겨지는. 말 등이 표준이 아닌. 비표준의 — compare STANDARD²

non·stick /ˌnɑnˈstɪk/ *adj* nonstick pans have a special surface inside that food will not stick to ‖ 냄비가 음식이 눌어붙지 않게 안쪽에 특수한 표면을 가진. 냄비가 눌어붙지 않는

non·stop /ˌnɑnˈstɑp/ *adj, adv* without stopping or without a stop ‖ 멈추지 않거나 중단 없이. 무정차의[로]: *Dan worked nonstop for 12 hours.* 댄은 12시간 동안 쉬지 않고 계속 일했다. / *a nonstop flight to New York* 뉴욕행 직행편(便) 비행기

non·ver·bal /ˌnɑn ˈvɚbəl/ *adj* not using words ‖ 말을 사용하지 않는: *non-verbal communication* (몸짓 등의) 비언어적 의사 소통 – **non-verbally** *adv*

non·vi·o·lence /ˌnɑnˈvaɪələns/ *n* [U] the practice of opposing a government without fighting, for example by not obeying laws ‖ 법을 지키지 않는 등으로써 싸움 없이 정부에 대한 반대를 실행하기. 비폭력 (주의): *an environmental group with a policy of nonviolence* 비폭력 정책을 가진 환경 단체

non·vi·o·lent /ˌnɑnˈvaɪələnt/ *adj* not using or not involving violence ‖ 폭력을 사용하지 않거나 포함하지 않은. 비폭력 (주의)의: *nonviolent protests against the government* 정부에 대한 비폭력 항의 / *nonviolent mental patients* 폭력적이지 않은 정신병자

noo·dle /ˈnudl/ *n* [C usually plural] a long thin piece of soft food made from flour, water, and usually eggs, that is cooked by being boiled ‖ 끓여서 조리하는, 밀가루·물·보통 계란으로 만든 길고 가느다란 연질(軟質)의 음식. 면. 국수: *chicken noodle soup* 치킨 누들 수프

nook /nʊk/ *n* **1** a small, quiet, safe place ‖ 작고 조용하며 안전한 장소. 구석진[외진] 곳. 벽지: *a shady nook* 그늘진 구석진 곳 **2 every nook and cranny** every part of a place ‖ 한 장소의 모든 부분. 구석구석: *We've searched every nook and cranny for that key.* 우리는 그 열쇠를 찾아 구석구석을 다 뒤졌다.

noon /nun/ *n* 12 o'clock in the middle of the day; MIDDAY ‖ 하루의 정중앙에 위치한 낮 12시. 정오; ⑨ midday: *Lunch will be right at noon.* 점심 식사는 정각 낮 12시에 먹을 것이다. / *the noon meal* 정오의 식사

no one /ˈ. ./ *pron* not anyone ‖ 아무도 …아님[없음]: *I tried calling last night but no one was home.* 나는 어제 저녁 계속 전화했지만 아무도 집에 없었다. / *No one could remember her name.* 아무도 그녀의 이름을 기억할 수 없었다. —see usage note at ANYONE

noose /nus/ *n* a circle of a rope that becomes tighter as it is pulled, used for hanging people as a punishment ‖ 징벌로서 사람을 교수형시키는 데 쓰는, 당기면 죄어지는 원형으로 된 밧줄. 올가미. 고를 낸 매듭 —compare LASSO

nope /noʊp/ *adv* SPOKEN no ‖ 아니: *"Aren't you hungry?" "Nope."* "배고프지 않니?" "아니."

no·place, no place /ˈnoʊpleɪs/ *adv* INFORMAL ➪ NOWHERE, —see usage note at ANYONE

nor /nɚ; *strong* nɔr/ *conjunction* **1 neither … nor** used in order to show that not one of a set of facts, people, qualities, actions etc is true ‖ 일련의 사실·사람·자질·행동 중 어느 하나도 사실이 아님을 나타내는 데 쓰여. …도 아니고 또한 …도 아니다: *My mother's family were neither rich nor poor.* 내 외가댁은 부유하지도 가난하지도 않았다. / *Neither Matt nor Julie nor Mark said anything.* 매트와 줄리, 그리고 마크 모두 다 아무 말

도 하지 않았다. **2** used after a negative statement, meaning "and not," "or not," "neither," or "not either" ‖ "그리고 …아니다." "또는 …아니다." "…도 또한 …도 아니다." "어느 쪽도 …아니다."를 의미하는 부정적인 말 뒤에 쓰여: *He wasn't at the meeting, nor was he at work yesterday.* 그는 어제 그 회의에 참석하지도 않았고 근무하지도 않았다.

norm /nɔrm/ *n* the usual way of doing something, or the acceptable way of behaving ‖ 어떤 것을 하는 일반적인 방식이나 수용 가능한 행동 양식. 표준. 기준. 규범. 모범: *the values, norms, and traditions of North American families* 북미 가정의 가치관과 규범, 그리고 전통 / *Working at home is becoming the norm for many employees.* 재택 근무는 많은 근로자들에게 일반화되고 있다.

nor·mal /ˈnɔrməl/ *adj* usual, typical, or expected ‖ 통상적인[전형적인, 예상된]. 표준의. 정상의. 정규의: *Greg just isn't acting like his normal self.* 그레그는 평소의 자신처럼 행동하지 않고 있다. / *normal everyday life* 매일의 일상적인 삶 —opposite ABNORMAL

nor·mal·i·ty /nɔrˈmæləti/, **nor·mal·cy** /ˈnɔrməlsi/ *n* [U] a situation in which everything happens in the usual way ‖ 모든 것이 평소대로 일어나는 상황. 정상임. 정상 상태

nor·mal·ize /ˈnɔrməˌlaɪz/ *v* [I, T] to become normal again, or to make a situation become normal again ‖ 다시 정상으로 되다. 또한 상황을 다시 정상적으로 되게 하다. 정상화되다[하다]: *In March 1944 Russia normalized relations with Italy.* (=became friendly again after a period of disagreement) 1944년 3월 러시아는 이탈리아와의 관계를 정상화했다. – **normalization** /ˌnɔrmələˈzeɪʃən/ *n* [U]

nor·mal·ly /ˈnɔrməli/ *adv* **1** usually ‖ 일상적으로. 보통: *I normally go to bed around eleven.* 나는 보통 11시쯤에 잔다. **2** in the usual expected way ‖ 일반적으로 예상된 방식으로. 정상적[표준적]으로: *Try to relax and breathe normally.* 긴장을 풀고 정상적으로 호흡해 봐라.

north¹, North /nɔrθ/ *n* [singular, U] **1** the direction toward the top of the world, or to the left of someone facing the rising sun ‖ 지구의 꼭대기 쪽을 향한 방향, 또는 떠오르는 태양을 마주한 사람의 왼쪽 방향. 북. 북쪽: *Which way is north?* 어느 쪽이 북쪽이냐? **2 the north** the northern part of a country, state etc. ‖ 한 나라·주(州) 등의 북쪽 지역. 북

부 (지방): *Rain will spread to the north later today.* 비는 오늘 늦게 북부 지방으로 확장됩니다. **3 the North** the part of the US east of the Mississippi River and north of Washington, D.C. ‖ 미국의 미시시피 강 동쪽과 워싱턴 D.C.의 북쪽 지역. 북부 **4 up North** in or to the North of the US ‖ 미국 북부 지방에[으로]: *Douglas comes from somewhere up North.* 더글러스는 북부 모처 출신이다.

north² *adj* **1** in, to, or facing north ‖ 북쪽에 있는[을 향한, 을 대면한]. 북쪽의: *a town 20 miles north of Salem* 샐럼으로부터 20마일 북쪽의 도시 / *the north end of the field* 들판의 북쪽 끝 **2 north wind** a wind that comes from the north ‖ 북쪽에서 불어오는 바람. 북풍

north³ *adv* **1** toward the north ‖ 북쪽을 향한. 북(쪽)으로: *Go north on I-5 to Portland.* 포틀랜드까지 5번 고속도로상에서 북쪽으로 가라. / *The window faces north.* 창문은 북쪽으로 나 있다. **2 up north** in the north or to the north ‖ 북쪽에[으로]: *The Simpsons are moving up north in May.* 심프슨 가족은 5월에 북쪽으로 이사 갈 것이다.

USAGE NOTE north/south/east/ west of and in the north/south/ east/west of

Use **north/south/east/west of** as an adjective phrase to describe where a place is in relation to another place: *Chicago is south of Milwaukee.* Use **in the north/south/east/west of** as a noun phrase to say which part of a place you are talking about: *The mountains are in the north of the province.* However, you must use **northern, southern, eastern,** or **western** with the name of a place: *They have a cabin in northern Ontario.* ✗DON'T SAY "in the north of Ontario."✗

north/south/east/west of는 다른 장소와 관련해서 한 장소를 설명하는 형용사구로서 쓴다: 시카고는 밀워키의 남쪽에 있다. **in the north/south/ east/west/of**는 자신이 말하고 있는 곳이 어느 지역인가를 말하기 위해 명사구로 사용한다: 그 산맥은 그 지방의 북쪽에 있다. 그러나 **northern [southern, eastern, western]**은 어떤 장소의 이름과 함께 사용해야 한다. 그들은 북부 온타리오에 오두막집을 가지고 있다. "in the north of Ontario" 라고는 하지 않는다.

North A·mer·i·can /ˌ. .ˈ.../ *n* one of the seven CONTINENTs, that includes land between the Arctic Ocean and the Caribbean Sea ‖ 북극해와 카리브해 사이의 땅을 포함한, 일곱 대륙 중 하나. 북아메리카 대륙 – **North American** *adj*

north·bound /ˈnɔrθbaʊnd/ *adj* traveling or leading toward the north ‖ 북쪽으로 여행하거나 이르는. 북쪽으로 가는. 북행의: *northbound traffic* 북쪽으로 가는 교통 / *the northbound lanes of the freeway* 고속도로의 북행 차선

north·east¹ /ˌnɔrθˈist/ *n* [U] **1** the direction that is exactly between the north and the east ‖ 정확히 북쪽과 동쪽 사이의 방향. 북동 **2 the Northeast** the northeast part of a country, state etc. ‖ 한 나라·주(州) 등의 북동 지역. 북동 지방 – **northeastern** *adj*

northeast² *adj, adv* in, from, or toward the northeast ‖ 북동에[에서, 으로]. 북동의: *traveling northeast* 북동쪽으로의 여행 / *a northeast wind* 북동풍

north·er·ly /ˈnɔrðəli/ *adj* **1** in or toward the north ‖ 북쪽에, 북쪽을 향한. 북(쪽)의. 북으로의: *sailing in a northerly direction* 북쪽 방향으로의 항해 **2** a northerly wind comes from the north ‖ 바람이 북쪽에서 불어오는. 북풍의

north·ern /ˈnɔrðən/ *adj* in or from the north part of an area, country, state etc. ‖ 한 지역·나라·주(州) 등의 북부 지역에 또는 지역으로부터. 북(쪽)의: *northern California* 북부 캘리포니아 — see usage note at NORTH³

north·ern·er, **Northerner** /ˈnɔrðənə/ *n* someone who comes from the NORTHERN part of a country or the northern HEMISPHERE ‖ 한 나라의 북부 지방이나 북반구에서 온 사람. 북부[북국] 사람

Northern Lights /ˌ.. ˈ./ *n* [plural] bands of colored lights that are seen in the night sky in the most northern parts of the world ‖ 지구의 가장 북쪽 지방의 밤하늘에서 볼 수 있는 색깔이 있는 빛의 띠. 북극광

north·ern·most /ˈnɔrðən,moʊst/ *adj* farthest north ‖ 최 북 단 의 : *the northernmost tip of Maine* 메인 주(州)의 최북단

North Pole /ˌ.. ˈ./ *n* **the North Pole** the most northern point on the surface of the earth, or the area around it ‖ 지표면의 가장 북쪽 지점, 또는 그 주변 지역. 북극 (지방)

north·ward /ˈnɔrθwəd/ *adj, adv* toward the north ‖ 북으로 향하는[향하

여]. 북향의[에]

north·west¹ /ˌnɔrθˈwɛst/ *n* **1** the direction that is exactly between north and west ‖ 정확히 북쪽과 서쪽 사이의 방향. 북서 **2 the Northwest** the northwest part of a country, state etc. ‖ 한 나라·주(州) 등의 북서 지역. 북서부 – **northwestern** *adj*

northwest² *adj, adv* in, from, or toward the northwest ‖ 북서에[쪽에서, 쪽으로]. 북서의: *driving northwest* 북서쪽으로의 운전 / *a northwest wind* 북서풍

nose¹ /noʊz/ *n*

1 ▶FACE 얼굴◀ the part of a person's or animal's face used for smelling and breathing through ‖ 냄새 맡고 숨을 쉬는 데에 쓰이는 사람이나 동물 얼굴의 한 부분. 코: *Someone punched him and broke his nose.* 누군가가 그를 주먹으로 때려 코뼈를 부러뜨려 놓았다. / *the dog's cold wet nose* 개의 차갑고 축축하게 젖은 코 / *Don't pick your nose.* (=clean it with your finger) 코를 후비지 마라. —see picture at HEAD¹

2 sb's nose is running if someone's nose is running, liquid is slowly coming out of it because s/he has a cold ‖ 사람의 코가 감기에 걸려서 콧물이 서서히 흘러나오다. 콧물이 줄줄 흐르다

3 (right) under sb's nose so close to someone that s/he should notice, but does not ‖ 아주 가까워서 다른 사람이 알아차려야 하지만 그렇지 못하는. 남의 코 앞에서. 눈앞에서: *The man escaped right under the noses of the guards.* 그 남자는 경비원의 바로 코앞에서 도망쳤다.

4 stick/poke your nose into sth INFORMAL to show too much interest in private matters that do not concern you ‖ 자신과 관련이 없는 남의 사적인 문제에 너무 많은 관심을 보이다. 쓸데없는 일에 필요 이상으로 참견하다: *Jana's always sticking her nose into other people's business.* 재나는 항상 다른 사람의 일에 쓸데없이 참견하고 있다.

5 put sb's nose out of joint INFORMAL to annoy someone by attracting everyone's attention away from him/her ‖ 남으로부터 모든 사람의 관심을 빼앗아 남을 괴롭히다. 남을 밀어내어 그 자리를 차지하다. 남이 받고 있던 후원[헌신]을 가로채다

6 ▶PLANE 비행기◀ the pointed front end of a plane, rocket etc. ‖ 비행기·로켓 등의 뾰족한 앞부분의 끝

7 red-nosed/long-nosed etc. having a nose that is red, long etc. ‖ 붉은 코나 긴 코 등을 가진

8 on the nose INFORMAL exactly ‖ 정확하게. (목표에) 딱 맞게: *Tanya guessed the price right on the nose.* 타냐는 그 가격을 정확하게 맞추었다.

9 turn your nose up (at sth) to refuse to accept something because you do not think it is good enough for you ‖ 사물이 자신에게 충분히 좋다고 생각하지 않아서 받아들이기를 거절하다. …을 경멸하다[비웃다]: *Five years ago, lawyers were turning their noses up at bankruptcy work.* 5년 전에는 변호사들이 파산 업무를 맡는 것에는 콧방귀도 뀌지 않았다.

10 keep your nose to the grindstone to continue working very hard, without stopping to rest ‖ 쉬지 않고 매우 열심히 계속해서 일하다. 죽어라고 일만 하다 – see also **blow your nose** (BLOW¹), **pay through the nose** (PAY¹)

nose² *v* [I, T] move forward slowly and carefully ‖ 천천히·조심스럽게 앞으로 움직이다. 천천히 전진하다: *The boat nosed out into the lake.* 그 보트는 호수 안으로 천천히 전진해 갔다.

nose around/about *phr v* [I] to try to find out private information about someone or something ‖ 사람이나 사물에 대한 사적인 정보를 찾아내려 하다. 염탐하다. …을 캐묻다: *Why were you nosing around my office?* 당신은 왜 내 사무실 주위를 살피고 있었죠?

nose·bleed /'noʊzblid/ *n* **have a nosebleed** to have blood coming out of your nose ‖ 코에서 피가 나오다. 코피가 나다

nose·dive /'noʊzdaɪv/ *n* **1 take a nosedive** to suddenly become less in amount, price, rate etc. ‖ 갑자기 양·가격·비율 등이 줄어들다. 가격 등이 폭락하다: *The company's profits took a nosedive last year.* 그 회사의 수익은 작년에 급감했다. **2** a sudden steep drop by a plane, with its front end pointing toward the ground ‖ 비행기의 뾰족한 앞 끝이 지면을 향한 갑작스런 수직 하강. 항공기의 수직 강하 – **nosedive** *v* [I]

nose job /'. ./ *n* INFORMAL a medical operation on someone's nose in order to improve its appearance ‖ 코의 모습을 고치기 위해 하는 의료 시술. 코의 성형 수술

no-show /'. ./ *n* INFORMAL someone who does not go to an event that s/he has promised to go to ‖ 간다고 약속한 행사에 가지 않은 사람. 예약 미이행자. 좌석을 예약해 놓고 나타나지 않은 사람 – **no-show** *v* [I, T]

nos·tal·gia /nɑ'stældʒə, nə-/ *n* [U] the slightly sad feeling you have when you remember happy events from the past ‖ 과거에 행복했던 일을 회상할 때 가지는 약간 슬픈 감정. 향수(鄕愁). 그리움: *nostalgia for his life on the farm* 그의 농장에서의 생활에 대한 향수 – **nostalgic** *adj* – **nostalgically** *adv*

nos·tril /'nɑstrəl/ *n* one of the two holes at the end of your nose, through which you breathe ‖ 숨을 쉬는, 코의 끝부분에 있는 두 개의 구멍 중 하나. 콧구멍 —see picture at HEAD¹

nos·y /'noʊzi/ *adj* always trying to find out private information about someone or something ‖ 항상 사람이나 사물에 대한 사적인 정보를 캐내려고 하는. 참견하기 좋아하는. 꼬치꼬치 캐묻는: *Our neighbors are really nosy.* 우리 이웃들은 정말 남의 일에 참견하기 좋아한다. – **nosiness** *n* [U]

not /nɑt/ *adv* **1** used in order to make a word, statement, or question negative ‖ 단어[진술, 질문]를 부정적으로 만드는 데에 쓰여. …아니다[않다]: *Most stores are not open until 9:30 a.m.* 대부분의 가게들은 오전 9시 30분까지는 문을 열지 않는다. / *Is anyone not coming to the party?* 누구 파티에 오지 않을 사람 있어? / *I don't (=do not) smoke.* 나는 담배를 피우지 않는다. —compare NO¹ **2** used instead of a whole phrase, to mean the opposite of what has been mentioned before it ‖ 이전에 언급됐던 것의 반대를 뜻하기 위해 전체 구문 대신에 쓰여: *No one knows if the story is true or not.* (=or if it is not true) 아무도 그 얘기가 사실인지 아닌지 알지 못한다. / *"Is Mark still sick?" "I hope not."* (=I hope he is not still sick) "마크는 아직 아프니?" "그렇지 않기를 바래." —compare SO¹ **3** used in order to make a word or phrase have the opposite meaning ‖ 단어나 구가 반대의 의미를 갖게 하는 데에 쓰여: *Not a lot/not much* (=little) *is known about the disease.* 그 병에 관해서는 거의 알려진 바가 없다. / *Most of the hotels were not very expensive/not that great/not too bad.* (=slightly cheap, slightly bad, or acceptable) 대부분의 호텔들은 그리 비싸지[그리 좋지, 그리 나쁘지] 않았다. **4 not only ... (but) also** in addition to being or doing something ‖ 무엇이거나 무엇을 하는 것에 더하여. …뿐만 아니라 …도 또한: *She's not only funny, she's also smart.* 그녀는 재미있을 뿐만 아니라 영리하기까지 하다. **5 not a/not one** not any person or thing; none ‖ 어떤 사람이

나 사물도 …않다; 아무(것)도 …않다: *Not one of the students knew the answer.* 단 한 명의 학생도 답을 알지 못했다. / *Look! Not a cloud in the sky!* 봐라! 하늘에 구름 한 점 없어! **6 not bad!** SPOKEN said when you are proud of a small achievement ‖ 작은 업적에 대해 자랑스러워 할 때 쓰여. 나쁘지 않은데. 잘했군!: *"See, I got a B+ on my test!!" "Not bad!"* "봐, 시험에서 B+ 받았어!!" "야, 잘했는데!" **7 not that** ... used before a negative sentence ‖ 부정문 앞에 쓰여. …이라는 것은 아니다. …이기 때문이 아니다: *Sarah has a new boyfriend – not that I care.* 사라에게 새 남자 친구가 생겼어, 내가 알 바는 아니지만. **8 …not!** SLANG said when you mean the opposite of what you have just been saying ‖ 자신이 막 말한 것에 반대되는 것을 뜻할 때 쓰여. 아니야!: *Yeah, she's pretty – not!* 그래, 그녀는 정말 예뻐. 아니야! —see usage note at NO²

no·ta·ble /ˈnoʊtəbəl/ *adj* important, interesting, or unusual enough to be noticed ‖ 눈에 띌 정도로 중요한[흥미 있는, 특별한]. 주목할 만한. 현저한. 탁월한. 유명한: *It's their worst team ever, with the notable exception of Rawlings.* (=he is the only good player) 롤링스는 확실하게 예외이지만 그 팀은 그들의 사상 최악의 팀이다.

no·ta·bly /ˈnoʊtəbli/ *adv* **1** especially; particularly ‖ 특별히. 유명[중요]하게; 특히: *Some politicians, most notably the President, refused to comment.* 몇몇 정치인들, 특히나 대통령은 논평하기를 거절했다. **2** in a way that is noticeable ‖ 눈에 띄게. 명백히. 현저히: *a notably successful project* 확실히 성공적인 계획

no·ta·rize /ˈnoʊtəˌraɪz/ *v* [T] to have a NOTARY PUBLIC make a document official ‖ 공증인에게 서류를 공증하게 하다

no·ta·ry pub·lic /ˌnoʊtəri ˈpʌblɪk/, **notary** *n* someone who has the legal power to make a signed document official ‖ 서명된 서류를 공증하는 법적인 권한을 가진 사람. 공증인

no·ta·tion /noʊˈteɪʃən/ *n* [C, U] a system of written marks or signs used for representing musical sounds, mathematical problems, or scientific ideas ‖ 음악적 소리[수학 문제, 과학 개념]를 나타내는 데에 사용되는 표시나 기호의 체계. 표기[표시]법

notch¹ /nɑtʃ/ *n* **1** a V-shaped cut in a surface or edge ‖ 표면이나 가장자리에 새긴 V자형의 새김. 새김눈. 눈금: *Cut a notch near one end of the stick.* 막대기의 한쪽 끝 가까이에 눈금을 새겨라. **2** a level of achievement or a social position ‖ 성취도나 사회적 지위의 수준. 단계. 정도. 등급: *Losing the game brought the team down a few notches.* 그 경기에 져서 그 팀은 순위가 조금 내려갔다.

notch² *v* [T] to cut a V-shaped mark into something ‖ 사물에 V자형의 표시를 새기다. 눈금을 새기다[새겨 기록하다]

note¹ /noʊt/ *n* **1** a short informal letter ‖ 비공식적인 짧은 편지. 쪽지(편지): *I wrote Tina a note to thank her for helping.* 나는 티나에게 도와 줘서 고맙다고 쪽지(편지)를 썼다. **2** something that you write down in order to remind you of something ‖ 사물을 기억하기 위해 적어 놓은 것. 메모: *She made a note of my new address.* 그녀는 내 새 주소를 메모했다. **3** a particular musical sound or PITCH, or the sign in written music that represents this ‖ 특정한 음악적 소리나 고저, 또는 이것을 나타내는 악보의 기호. 음조. 음색. 음표 **4 take note (of sth)** to pay careful attention to something ‖ 어떤 것에 매우 주의를 기울이다. …에 주의[주목]하다: *Take note of the instructions at the top of the page.* 그 페이지 상단의 지시에 주의하시오. **5 a note of anger/sadness etc.** a particular quality or feeling that you notice in a particular person or situation ‖ 특정한 사람이나 상황에서 느끼는 특정한 특성이나 감정. 화난/슬픈(듯한) 기색: *The movie ended on a note of hope.* 그 영화는 희망적인 분위기로 끝났다. **6 of note** important or famous ‖ 중요한. 유명한. 저명[고명]한: *a writer of note* 저명한 작가 —see also NOTES

note² *v* [T] **1** to notice or pay careful attention to something ‖ 어떤 것을 알아차리거나 어떤 것에 주의를 기울이다. 유의하다. 주의하다: *Please note that the museum is closed on Monday.* 그 박물관은 월요일에 문 닫는다는 것을 유의하세요. **2** also **note down** to write something down so you will remember it ‖ 기억하기 위해서 어떤 것을 적다. 메모하다: *He noted my telephone number.* 그는 내 전화 번호를 메모했다.

note·book /ˈnoʊtbʊk/ *n* **1** a book of plain paper in which you can write notes ‖ 메모를 할 수 있는 공책. 메모장. 노트 **2** a small computer that is about the size of a book ‖ 대략 책 크기 만한 작은 컴퓨터. 노트북 컴퓨터

not·ed /ˈnoʊtɪd/ *adj* well-known; famous ‖ 잘 알려진. 저명한; 유명한: *a* *noted author* 유명한 저자

note·pa·per /ˈnoʊtˌpeɪpɚ/ *n* [U] paper used for writing letters or notes on ‖ 편지나 메모를 적기 위해 사용하는 종이. 편지지. 메모 용지

notes /noʊts/ *n* [plural] information that a student writes down during a class, from a book etc. so s/he will remember it ‖ 학생이 수업 중에 책 등으로부터 기억하기 위해 적어 놓는 정보. 필기: *Did you take any notes* (=write them) *in history class?* 역사 수업 중에 필기 좀 했냐? —see also **compare notes (with sb)** (COMPARE¹)

note·wor·thy /ˈnoʊtˌwɚði/ *adj* FORMAL important or interesting enough to deserve your attention ‖ 충분히 주의를 기울일 만하게 중요하거나 흥미 있는. 주목할 만한. 현저한. 두드러진: *a noteworthy event* 주목할 만한 사건

noth·ing¹ /ˈnʌθɪŋ/ *pron* **1** not anything; no thing ‖ 아무것도 …아니다[않다]; 조금도 …않다: *There's nothing in the bag.* 가방 안에는 아무것도 없다. / *I had nothing else* (=nothing more) *to do, so I went to bed.* 나는 할 것이 아무것도 없어서 자러 갔다. / *Nothing you say will change what he thinks.* 당신이 말하는 어떤 것도 그의 생각을 바꿀 수는 없을 것이다. / *There's nothing left to eat.* (=there was something but it is gone) 먹을 것이 아무것도 남아 있지 않다. / *I have nothing against New York,* (=I have no reason for not liking it) *I just don't want to live there.* 뉴욕을 싫어할 이유가 내게는 없고 그냥 거기서 살고 싶지 않을 뿐이다. **2** something that you do not consider to be important or interesting ‖ 중요하거나 흥미 있다고 생각하지 않는 것. 가치 없는 것. 별것 아닌 것: *I have nothing to wear tonight!* 오늘 밤 입을 것이 없어! / *"What did you say?" "Oh, nothing."* "뭐라고 했어?" "응, 아무것도 아냐." **3** zero ‖ 영. 무(無): *The Red Sox won the game three nothing.* (=the Red Sox had 3; the other team had no points) 레드 삭스 팀은 그 경기를 3대 0으로 이겼다. **4 for nothing a)** without having a purpose or a good reason ‖ 목적이나 합당한 근거 없이. 아무 이유[까닭] 없이. 헛되이: *I did all that work for nothing. The teacher didn't even look at it.* 나는 그 모든 과제물을 하느라 헛수고만 했다. 선생님은 그것을 쳐다보지도 않으셨다. **b)** without paying or being paid ‖ 돈을 지불하지 않거나 받지 않고. 거저. 무료로: *My dad said he'd fix it for nothing.* 아버지는 그것을 공짜로 수리해 주겠다고

말했다. **5 have nothing to do with a)** if something has nothing to do with a fact or situation, it is not related to that fact or situation ‖ 일이 어떤 사실이나 상황과 상관이 없다: *"He's mad because of what I said, isn't he?" "No, that has nothing to do with it."* "그는 내가 말한 것 때문에 화가 단단히 났지, 그렇지?" "아냐, 네가 말한 것과는 아무 상관이 없어." **b)** if someone has nothing to do with a situation or person, he or she is not involved in it or with him/her ‖ 어떤 사람이 상황이나 다른 사람과 관계가 없다: *"What happened?" "I don't know. I had nothing to do with it."* "어떻게 됐어?" "모르겠어. 나는 그것과 아무 관계가 없었어." **6 nothing special** having no very good or very bad qualities ‖ 특별히 좋거나 나쁜 특성이 전혀 없는. 그저 그런: *The story was nothing special, but the pictures were beautiful.* 줄거리는 뭐 특별한 것 없는 그저 그런 것이었지만 영상은 아름다웠다. **7 nothing but** only ‖ 오직. 단지: *We've had nothing but rain for two weeks now.* 지금까지 2주 동안 오직 비만 왔다.

SPOKEN PHRASES

8 nothing much SPOKEN very little ‖ 매우 적은. 거의 없는: *"Hi Judy! What's new?" "Oh, nothing much."* "안녕 주디! 좋은 일 있어?" "뭐, 별로." **9 it was nothing** used when someone thanks you, in order to say that you did not mind helping ‖ 남이 당신에게 도와 준 것에 고맙다고 할 때 아무 일 아닌 듯 말하는 데에 쓰여. 별일[대단한 것]이 아니었다: *"Thanks a lot!" "It was nothing."* "대단히 고마워!" "별일 아니었는데 뭐." **10** NONSTANDARD anything ‖ 어떤 것. 아무것: *I never said nothing about taking you swimming.* 나는 너를 수영장에 데려가겠다는 어떤 말도 한 적이 없다. **11 nothing doing** SPOKEN OLD-FASHIONED used in order to say that you refuse to do something ‖ 어떤 것을 하는 것을 거절한다고 말하는 데에 쓰여. 안돼. 싫어

---

nothing² *adv* **1 be nothing like** to have no qualities that are similar to someone or something else ‖ 다른 사람이나 사물과 유사한 특성이 전혀 없다. …과는 전혀 다르다: *We have hills at home, but they're nothing like the mountains here!* 우리가 사는 곳에도 산이 있지만 그것들은 여기 산들과는 전혀 다르다. **2 be nothing less than/**

nothing short of if something is nothing less than or nothing short of a particular quality, then it has that quality ‖ 사물이 특정 특성보다 조금도 덜 하지 않게 또는 모자라지 않게 바로 그 특성을 갖고 있다. 바로 …이다. 절대로 [아주] …이다: *She thought his ideas were nothing less than ridiculous.* 그녀는 그의 생각이 아주 터무니없다고 생각했다.

noth·ing·ness /'nʌθɪŋnɪs/ *n* [U] the state of complete emptiness where nothing exists ‖ 아무것도 존재하지 않는 완전히 텅 빈 상태. 무(의 상태). 없음

no·tice¹ /'noʊtɪs/ *v* [I, T] to see, feel, or hear someone or something ‖ 사람이나 사물을 보다[느끼다, 듣다]. 알아차리다. 깨닫다: *She noticed that I was getting nervous.* 그녀는 내가 불안해지고 있음을 알아차렸다. / *I said "hello," but she didn't notice.* 나는 "안녕"하고 인사했지만 그녀는 알아차리지 못했다.

notice² *n* **1** a written or printed statement that gives information or a warning to people ‖ 사람들에게 정보나 주의를 주는 글로 씌어지거나 인쇄된 공고. 고시. 통지. 게시: *Put the notice up here so everyone can see it.* 모든 사람이 공고를 알아볼 수 있게 여기에 게시해라. **2** [U] information or a warning about something that will happen ‖ 일어날 일에 대한 정보나 경고. 통고. 통보: *You must give the bank three days'/two weeks'/a month's notice before closing the account.* 당신은 계좌 해지 전 삼 일 [2주, 한 달 전]에 은행에 통고해야 한다. **3 not take any notice/take no notice** to pay no attention to someone or something ‖ 사람이나 사물에 주의를 기울이지 않다. 유의[주목]하지 않다: *Don't take any notice of her, she's just angry.* 그녀에게 신경 쓰지 마라, 그녀는 그저 화가 나 있을 뿐이다. **4 at short notice/at a moment's notice** without much warning, so that you have only a short time to do something ‖ 많은(시간 동안의) 예고가 없이 오직 단시간 내에 일 해야 하는. 당장에[급히]/곧바로[즉시, 즉각]: *You can't expect us to leave at a moment's notice!* 당장 떠나라면 우리가 바로 떠날 줄 알았냐! **5 until further notice** from now until another change is announced ‖ 지금부터 다른 변화가 통지되기까지. 당분간. 추후 통지가 있을 때까지: *The store will be closed until further notice.* 그 가게는 (추후 통지가 있을 때까지) 당분간 문을 닫을 것이다.

no·tice·a·ble /'noʊtɪsəbəl/ *adj* easy to notice ‖ 알아차리기 쉬운. 남의 눈을 끄는. 뚜렷한. 두드러진. 현저한: *There's been a noticeable improvement in your work.* 네가 하는 일이 눈에 띄게 좋아졌다. **– noticeably** *adv*

no·ti·fi·ca·tion /,noʊtəfə'keɪʃən/ *n* [C, U] FORMAL an act of officially informing someone about something ‖ 어떤 일에 대해 남에게 공식적으로 알리는 행위. 알림. 통지. 통고. 최고(催告)

no·ti·fy /'noʊtə,faɪ/ *v* [T] FORMAL to tell someone something formally or officially; INFORM ‖ 남에게 격식을 차려서 또는 공식적으로 어떤 것을 말하다. 보고 [통지, 통보]하다; 伊 inform: *Have you notified the police?* 경찰에 신고했느냐?

no·tion /'noʊʃən/ *n* an idea, belief, or opinion about something, especially one that you think is wrong ‖ 어떤 것에 대한 생각[믿음, 의견], 특히 틀렸다고 생각되는 것. 견해. 신념

no·to·ri·e·ty /,noʊtə'raɪəti/ *n* [U] the state of being famous for doing something bad ‖ 나쁜 일을 하는 것으로 유명한 상태. 악평. 악명

no·to·ri·ous /noʊ'tɔriəs/ *adj* famous for something bad ‖ 나쁜 일로 유명한. 악명 높은. 악평이 자자한: *The city is notorious for rainy weather.* 그 도시는 비가 많은 날씨로 유명하다. / *a notorious criminal* 악명 높은 범죄자 **– notoriously** *adv*

not·with·stand·ing /,nɑt'wɪθ'stændɪŋ/ *prep* FORMAL if something is true notwithstanding something else, it is true even though the other thing has happened ‖ 비록 다른 것이 발생했었음에도 불구하고 사실인. …에도 불구하고: *Their friendship notwithstanding, the two Senators have very different ideas.* 친구 사이임에도 불구하고 그 두 상원 의원은 매우 다른 생각을 가지고 있다.

noun /naʊn/ *n* in grammar, a word or group of words that represents a person, place, thing, quality, action, or idea. In the sentence "Pollution is a problem in some cities," "pollution," "problem," and "cities" are nouns ‖ 문법에서 사람·장소·사물·특성·행위·생각을 나타내는 단어나 단어군. 명사. *"Pollution is a problem in some cities"*의 문장에서 *"pollution" "problem"*과 *"cities"*는 명사이다.

nour·ish /'nɑrɪʃ, 'nʌrɪʃ/ *v* [T] **1 well-nourished/under-nourished** having had enough food or not enough food to eat to keep you healthy ‖ 건강을 유지하기에 충분한 또는 충분하지 않은 음식을 섭취하는. 영양 상태가 좋은/좋지 않은: *a well-nourished baby* 영양 상태가 좋은 아기 **2** to give a person or plant the food that is needed in order to live, grow, and be healthy ‖ 사람이나 식물이 살아가는 데[성장하는 데, 건강을 유지하는 데]에 필요한 음식을 공급하다. …에 영양분을 주다

nour·ish·ing /'nɔʊʃɪŋ, 'nʌr-/ *adj* food that is nourishing makes you strong and healthy ‖ 음식이 몸을 강하고 건강하게 만드는. 영양[자양]이 되는. 영양분이 많은: *a nourishing meal* 영양분이 많은 음식

nour·ish·ment /'nɔʊʃmənt, 'nʌr-/ *n* [U] FORMAL food that is needed so you can live, grow, and be healthy ‖ 사람이 살아가는[성장하는, 건강을 유지하는] 데에 필요한 음식물. 영양(물). 자양물

nov·el¹ /'nɑvəl/ *n* a long written story in which the characters and events are usually imaginary ‖ 등장인물과 사건이 보통 상상으로 길게 씌어진 이야기. 장편 소설: *a novel by Hemingway* 헤밍웨이의 장편 소설

novel² *adj* new, different, and unusual ‖ 새롭고 다르며 독특한. 기발한. 희한한: *a novel idea* 참신한 생각

nov·el·ist /'nɑvəlɪst/ *n* someone who writes NOVELs ‖ 장편 소설을 쓰는 사람. 소설가

nov·el·ty /'nɑvəlti/ *n* **1** something new and unusual that attracts people's attention and interest ‖ 사람들의 주목과 흥미를 끄는 새롭고 독특한 것. 희한한 사건[일]. 신기한 존재[경험]: *Cars are still a novelty on the island.* 자동차는 그 섬에서 아직 신기한 존재이다. **2** [U] the quality of being new, different, and unusual ‖ 새롭고 다르며 독특한 특성. 신기함. 참신함: *the novelty of using E-mail* 이메일을 사용하는 참신함 **3** a small cheap object often bought as a present ‖ 종종 선물로 구매된 작고 값싼 물건. 값싼 상품

No·vem·ber /noʊ'vɛmbər, nə-/, *written abbreviation* **Nov.** *n* the eleventh month of the year ‖ 한 해의 열한 번째 달. 11월 —see usage note at JANUARY

nov·ice /'nɑvɪs/ *n* someone who has only begun learning a skill or activity ‖ 기술이나 활동을 방금 배우기 시작한 사람. 미숙자. 초심자. 신출내기. 풋내기

now¹ /naʊ/ *adv* **1** at the present time ‖ 현재에. 지금. 오늘날에는: *Seattle is now one of the computer industry's major centers.* 시애틀은 현재 컴퓨터 산업의 주요 중심지 중 하나이다. / *Judy should have been home by now.* (=before now) 주디는 지금쯤에는 집에 들어왔어야 했다. / *Mom says we have to be home by 9:00 from now on.* (=starting now and continuing into the future) 어머니는 우리가 앞으로 9시까지 집에 들어와야 한다고 말한다. / *For now* (=for a short time), *Jim will be in charge of marketing.* 당분간 짐이 마케팅 부문을 관리하게 될 것이다. **2** immediately ‖ 곧. 지체 없이. 즉각: *You'd better go now – you're late.* 늦었으니 당신은 즉시 가는 게 낫겠다. / *Call her right now, before she leaves.* 그녀가 떠나기 전에 지금 당장 그녀에게 전화해라. **3** used when you know or understand something because of something you have just seen, just been told etc. ‖ 방금 보거나 들은 것 때문에 어떤 것을 알거나 이해할 때 쓰여. 이제는. 이제서야: *"I've just been talking to the landlord." "So, now do you see why I'm worried?"* "나는 방금 집 주인에게 말해 봤어." "그래, 이제는 내가 왜 걱정하는지 알겠어?" **4 (every) now and then** used in order to say that something happens sometimes but not always ‖ 사물이 항상은 아니고 때때로 일어난다고 말하는 데에 쓰여. 종종. 이따금: *He sees her every now and then at church.* 그는 그녀를 교회에서 자주 본다.

SPOKEN PHRASES

5 said when you pause because you cannot think what to say or when you want to get someone's attention ‖ 무슨 말을 할지 생각할 수 없어서 잠시 쉴 때, 또는 남의 이목을 끌기 원할 때 쓰여. 그런데. 그래서. 그럼. 자: *Now, what did you say your name was?* "어, 당신 이름이 뭐라고 했더라?" / *OK now. Watch me.* 됐어. 자, 나를 봐. **6 now you tell me!** said when you are annoyed because someone has just told you something s/he should have told you before ‖ 다른 사람이 더 일찍 자신에게 말했어야 하는 것을 방금 말해서 화가 났을 때 쓰여. 그걸 이제야 말하는 거야! **7 now now** said in order to try to make someone feel better when s/he is sad ‖ 남이 슬플 때 남의 기분을 좋게 해 주려고 하는 데에 쓰여. 그렇지. 이봐. 자자: *Now now, don't cry.* 자, 자, 울지 마.

---

now², now that *conjunction* because or after something has happened ‖ 일이 일어나서 또는 일이 일어난 후에. …이니

까. …이므로: *Now that I've bought the skirt, I don't like it.* 나는 그 치마를 사긴 했지만 마음에 들지 않는다.

now·a·days /'nauə,deız/ *adv* in the present, compared to what happened in past times ‖ 과거에 발생한 것에 비해, 현재에는. 오늘날에는. 요즈음에는: *People tend to live longer nowadays.* 오늘날에는 사람들이 (옛날보다) 더 오래 사는 경향이 있다.

no·where /'nouwɛr/ *adv* **1** not any place ‖ 아무 데도[어디에도] …없다[않다]: *There's nowhere to put anything in our new apartment.* 우리의 새 아파트에는 아무 데도 무엇을 놓을 자리가 없다. / *There are plants on the island that grow nowhere else.* (=in no other place) 그 섬에는 다른 어떤 곳에서도 자라지 않는 식물이 있다. —see usage note at ANYONE **2 get nowhere** to have no success, or make no progress ‖ 성공하지 못하거나 아무런 진전이 없다. 아무 성과도 얻지 못하다: *The committee is getting nowhere with the report.* 위원회는 그 보고서에 관한 아무런 성과도 얻지 못하고 있다. **3 be nowhere to be seen/found** to be impossible to find ‖ 찾을 수 없다. 어디에서도 찾을 수/발견할 수 없다: *The book I needed to finish my paper was nowhere to be found.* 논문을 마무리하는 데에 필요한 책은 어디에서도 찾을 수 없었다. **4 nowhere near a)** far from a particular place ‖ 특정한 곳에서 먼. …과 거리가 먼: *Buffalo is in New York State, but it's nowhere near New York City.* 버팔로 시는 뉴욕 주에 있지만 뉴욕 시와는 거리가 멀다. **b)** not at all ‖ 전혀 …이 아닌. …는 당치도 않은: *They've sold a lot of bikes, but nowhere near as many as they needed to.* 그들은 자전거를 많이 팔았지만 필요한 만큼 그렇게 많이 팔지는 못했다. **5 out of nowhere** happening or appearing suddenly and unexpectedly ‖ 갑자기·예상치 않게 발생하거나 나타나는. 갑자기. 불쑥: *The car came out of nowhere and just missed hitting her.* 그 차가 갑자기 나타나서 그녀를 칠 뻔했다.

nox·ious /'nakʃəs/ *adj* FORMAL harmful or poisonous ‖ 유해하거나 유독한. 해로운: *a noxious gas* 유독 가스

noz·zle /'nazəl/ *n* a short tube attached to the end of a pipe or HOSE that controls the flow of liquid coming out ‖ 파이프나 호스의 끝에 달려 액체가 흘러나오는 것을 조절하는 짧은 튜브. 주둥이 (부분). 노즐

NPR National Public Radio; a company in the US that broadcasts radio programs without advertisements ‖ National Public Radio(전미 공공 방송 협회)의 약어; 광고 없이 라디오 프로그램만 방송하는 미국의 회사

-n't /ənt/ *adv* the short form of NOT ‖ not의 단축형: *He isn't* (=is not) *here.* 그는 여기에 없다. / *She can't* (=cannot) *see him.* 그녀는 그를 볼 수 없다. / *I didn't* (=did not) *do it.* 나는 그것을 하지 않았다. —see usage note at NOT

nu·ance /'nuɑns/ *n* [C, U] a very slight difference in meaning, color, or feeling ‖ 의미[색깔, 감정]의 매우 미묘한 차이. 뉘앙스 – **nuanced** *adj*

nu·cle·ar /'nukliər/ *adj* **1** relating to or involving the use of nuclear weapons ‖ 핵무기의 사용과 관련되거나 포함하는. 핵무기의: *nuclear war* 핵전쟁 **2** using nuclear power, or relating to nuclear energy ‖ 원자력을 이용하거나 핵 에너지와 관련된. 원자력의: *a nuclear submarine* 핵잠수함 **3** relating to the NUCLEUS (=central part) of an atom ‖ 원자의 핵과 관련된. 원자핵의: *nuclear physics* 핵물리학

nuclear arm /,… '.../ *n* [C usually plural] ⇨ NUCLEAR WEAPON

nuclear dis·ar·ma·ment /,… .'.../ *n* [U] the activity of getting rid of NUCLEAR WEAPONs ‖ 핵무기를 제거하려는 활동. 핵군축

nuclear en·er·gy /,… '.../ *n* [U] the power that comes from splitting atoms, used for making electricity and the explosive part of some bombs ‖ 전기와 몇몇 폭탄의 폭발하는 부분을 만드는 데 쓰는 분열된 원자에서 나오는 힘. 원자력. 핵에너지

nuclear fam·i·ly /,… '.../ *n* a family that has a father, mother, and children ‖ 아빠·엄마·아이들로만 된 가족. 핵가족 —compare EXTENDED FAMILY

nuclear pow·er /,… '.../ *n* [U] power, usually in the form of electricity, produced from NUCLEAR ENERGY ‖ 원자력으로부터 생산된 보통 전기 형태의 힘. 원자력

nuclear re·ac·tion /,… .'.../ *n* a process in which the central part of an atom splits and forms new substances and produces a lot of energy ‖ 원자의 중심 부분이 분열해서 새로운 물질을 만들어 내고 많은 에너지를 생산하는 과정. 핵반응

nuclear re·ac·tor /,… .'.../ *n* a large machine that produces NUCLEAR ENERGY ‖ 원자력을 생성해 내는 큰 기계. 원자로

nuclear weap·on /ˌ... ˈ../ *n* a very powerful weapon that uses NUCLEAR ENERGY to destroy large areas ‖ 넓은 지역을 파괴하기 위해 원자력을 사용하는 매우 강력한 무기. 핵무기

nu·cle·us /ˈnukliəs/ *n, plural* **nuclei** /-kliaɪ/ **1** the central part of an atom, made up of PROTONs and NEUTRONs ‖ 양성자와 중성자로 이루어진 원자의 중심 부분. 원자핵 **2 the nucleus of sth** the central or most important part of something ‖ 사물의 중심이나 가장 중요한 부분. …의 핵(심): *Photographs by Adams, Weston, and Lange form the nucleus of the collection.* 아담스와 웨스톤 그리고 랭게가 찍은 사진들이 수집품의 중심을 이룬다. **3** the central part of a cell ‖ 세포의 중심 부분. 세포핵

nude¹ /nud/ *adj* not wearing any clothes; NAKED ‖ 아무 옷도 입지 않은. 벌거벗은. 나체의; ⑨ naked

nude² *n* **1 in the nude** without wearing any clothes ‖ 아무 옷도 입지 않고. 나체로: *sleeping in the nude* 발가벗고 잠자기 **2** a painting or STATUE of someone who is not wearing clothes ‖ 옷을 입지 않은 사람의 그림이나 상(像). 나체화[상]

nudge /nʌdʒ/ *v* [T] to push someone or something gently, especially with your elbow ‖ 특히 팔꿈치로 사람이나 사물을 가볍게 찌르다: *Ken nudged me and said, "Look, there's Cindy."* 켄은 팔꿈치로 나를 쿡 찌르며 "저기 봐. 신디가 있어"라고 말했다. **– nudge** *n*

nu·dist /ˈnudɪst/ *n* someone who believes it is natural and healthy not to wear clothes ‖ 옷을 입지 않는 것이 자연스럽고 건강하다고 믿는 사람. 나체주의자 **– nudist** *adj*

nu·di·ty /ˈnudəti/ *n* [U] the state of not wearing any clothes ‖ 아무 옷도 입지 않은 상태. 나체. 알몸

nug·get /ˈnʌgɪt/ *n* a small rough piece of a valuable metal found in the earth ‖ 땅에서 발견되는 값비싼 금속의 작고 거친 덩어리. 귀금속 등의 덩어리: *a gold nugget* 금괴

nui·sance /ˈnusəns/ *n* [C usually singular] someone or something that annoys you or causes problems ‖ 자신을 괴롭히거나 문제를 일으키는 사람이나 물건. 귀찮은 존재. 성가신 사람: *Jon is making a nuisance of himself, always phoning Rachel late at night.* 존은 항상 저녁 늦게 레이첼에게 전화를 걸어 귀찮게 굴고 있다.

nuke¹ /nuk/ *v* [T] INFORMAL **1** to attack a place using NUCLEAR WEAPONs ‖ 한 장소를 핵무기를 이용해서 공격하다. 핵공격을 가하다 **2** SPOKEN to cook food in a MICROWAVE ‖ 전자레인지로 음식을 요리하다

nuke² *n* INFORMAL ⇨ NUCLEAR WEAPON

null and void /ˌnʌl ən ˈvɔɪd/ *adj* LAW having no effect ‖ 효과가 없는. 무효의: *The court declared the contract to be null and void.* (=not legal, and therefore completely without an effect) 법원은 그 계약이 무효라고 선고했다.

nul·li·fy /ˈnʌlɪˌfaɪ/ *v* [T] LAW to state officially that something will have no legal effect ‖ 사물이 법적인 영향력을 미치지 못한다고 공식적으로 언명하다. (계약을 법률상)무효로 하다. 파기하다: *The new government nullified the 1964 treaty.* 새 정부는 1964년에 체결된 조약을 파기했다.

numb¹ /nʌm/ *adj* **1** unable to feel anything ‖ 아무 것도 느낄 수 없는. 감각을 잃은. 마비된: *My feet are getting numb from the cold.* 내 발은 추위로 마비되고 있다. **2** unable to think, feel, or react in a normal way ‖ 정상적으로 생각할 수[느낄 수, 반응할 수] 없는. 무감각해진. 멍해진: *She was numb with grief after her mother's death.* 그녀는 어머니가 죽고 난 후 슬픔으로 멍해졌다. **– numbness** *n* [U] **– numbly** *adv*

numb² *v* [T] to make someone unable to feel anything ‖ 남을 아무것도 느낄 수 없게 하다. 감각을 잃다. 마비시키다: *The cold wind numbed my face.* 내 얼굴은 차가운 바람으로 마비되었다.

num·ber¹ /ˈnʌmbɚ/ *n*

1 ▶SIGN 기호◀ a word or sign that represents an amount or quantity ‖ 수량을 나타내는 단어나 기호. 수. 숫자: *Choose a number between one and ten.* 1부터 10 사이의 숫자를 선택하시오. / *Add the numbers 7, 4, and 3.* 7과 4 그리고 3의 숫자를 더하시오. / *a round number* (=a number ending in 0, such as 10, 20 etc.) 십의 배수 / *an even number* (=2,4,6,8 etc.) 짝수 / *an odd number* (=1,3,5,7 etc.) 홀수

2 ▶ON A PHONE 전화기 상의◀ a set of numbers that you press on a telephone when you are calling someone ‖ 누군가에게 전화를 걸 때 누르는 전화기 상의 일련의 숫자. 전화번호: *I think I dialed the wrong number.* 제가 전화번호를 잘못 누른 것 같습니다. / *He gave me his work/home number.* 그는 나에게 자신의 직장/집 전화번호를 주었다. —see usage note at TELEPHONE

3 ▶IN A SERIES 일련으로◀ a sign used

in order to show the position of something in an ordered set, list, series etc. ‖ 순차적인 세트·목록·시리즈 등에서 사물의 위치를 보여주는 데에 쓰이는 표시. (번호가 붙어 있는 것의) …번[호]: *Look at question number five.* 5번 문제를 보시오. / *What's his room number?* 그는 몇 호실이냐?

4 ▶FOR RECOGNIZING PEOPLE/THINGS 사람/사물을 분간하기 위해◀ a set of numbers used in order to name or recognize someone or something ‖ 사람이나 사물을 부르거나 분간하는 데에 쓰이는 일련의 숫자. 일련 번호: *a social security number* 사회 보장 번호 / *the serial number on the car's engine* 그 자동차 엔진의 일련 번호

5 ▶AMOUNT 수량◀ [C, U] an amount of something that can be counted ‖ 셀 수 있는 것의 수량. 인원[개]수. 총원[수]: *There are a large/great/small number of cars on the road today.* 오늘 도로에 자동차가 많이[대단히 많이, 적게] 있다. / *The number of smokers is decreasing.* 흡연자수는 줄어들고 있다. / *A number of* (=several) *people have complained to the company.* 많은 사람들이 그 회사에 불만을 말해 왔다.

6 number one INFORMAL the best or most important person or thing in a group ‖ 집단 내의 최고로 또는 가장 중요한 사람이나 사물: *The fans shouted, "We're number one!"* 팬들은 "우리가 최고 야!"라고 소리 쳤다. / *California continues to be the number one travel destination in the US.* 캘리포니아는 계속해서 미국 내에서 최고의 여행지가 되고 있다.

7 ▶MUSIC 음악◀ a piece of popular music, a song, a dance etc. that forms part of a larger performance ‖ 보다 큰 공연의 일부를 이루는 대중 음악·노래·춤 등. 상연[연주]물. 곡목 —see study note on page 934

USAGE NOTE number

When we use **numbers** in a sentence, we usually use a plural verb: *Twenty bottles of wine were drunk at the party.* However, when we give an opinion about the amount itself, we use a singular verb: *Twenty bottles of wine is too much for the party.*
문장에서 **numbers**를 사용할 때는 보통 복수 동사를 사용한다: 그 파티에서 사람들은 포도주 20병을 마셨다. 그러

나, 수량 자체에 대한 의견을 말할 때는 단수 동사를 사용한다: 그 파티에 포도주 20병은 너무 많다.

number² *v* [T] **1** to give a number to something that is part of a set or list ‖ 세트나 목록의 부분인 것에 숫자를 매기다. 숫자를 붙이다: *Number the items from one to ten.* 그 품목들에 1부터 10까지 번호를 매겨라. **2** if people or things number a particular amount, that is how many there are ‖ 사람들이나 사물이 얼마나 많은지 특정 수량으로 숫자화하다. …을 세다[헤아리다]. (총계) …으로 숫자를 확인하다[읽다]: *The crowd numbered around 20,000.* 군중은 대략 2만 명 정도로 헤아려졌다. **3 sb's/sth's days are numbered** used in order to say that someone or something cannot live or continue much longer ‖ 사람이나 사물이 더 오래 살거나 계속될 수 없다고 말하는 데에 쓰여. 수명[연한]이 제한돼 있다[얼마 남지 않다]: *These injuries mean his days as a player are numbered.* 이들 부상은 선수로서의 그의 생명이 다했다는 것을 의미한다.

number crunch·er /ˈ.. ˌ../ *n* INFORMAL **1** a computer designed to work with numbers and calculate results ‖ 수치를 연산하고 결과를 산출하기 위해 고안된 컴퓨터. 고속[대형] 컴퓨터 **2** someone who works using numbers, such as an ACCOUNTANT ‖ 회계사 등 수를 사용해 일하는 사람. 수치 계산하는 사람 —**number-crunching** *n* [U]

nu·mer·al /ˈnumərəl, ˈnumrəl/ *n* a written sign that represents a number, such as 5, 22 etc. ‖ 5, 22 등 수를 나타내는 필기 기호. 숫자. 수사 —**numeral** *adj*

nu·mer·i·cal /nuˈmɛrɪkəl/ *adj* expressed in numbers, or relating to numbers ‖ 수로 표시되는, 또는 수에 관련된. 수의[를 가진]: *Are the pages in numerical order?* (=numbered 1, 2, 3 etc.) 페이지들이 숫자 순으로 되어 있어요? —**numerically** *adv*

num·er·ous /ˈnumərəs/ *adj* FORMAL many ‖ 많은. 다수의. 수많은: *We discussed the plans on numerous occasions.* 우리는 다각도로 그 계획을 토의했다.

nun /nʌn/ *n* a woman who is a member of a group of Christian women who live together in a CONVENT (=special building) ‖ 수도원에 함께 모여 사는 여자 기독교도 단체의 한 구성원. 수녀 —

compare MONK

nup·tial /'nʌpʃəl/ *adj* FORMAL relating to marriage ‖ 결혼과 관련된. 결혼(식)의

nup·tials /'nʌpʃəlz/ *n* [plural] FORMAL a wedding ‖ 결혼식

nurse¹ /nɚs/ *n* someone whose job is to take care of people who are ill or injured, usually in a hospital ‖ 보통 병원에서 아프거나 다친 사람들을 보살피는 직업인. 간호사

nurse² *v* **1** [T] to take care of people who are ill or injured ‖ 아프거나 다친 사람을 돌보다. 간호[병구완]하다 **2** [T] to rest when you have an illness or injury so you will get better ‖ 병이 들었거나 다쳤을 때 회복되기 위해 쉬다. 치료[요양]하다: *He's nursing a sprained ankle.* 그는 삔 발목을 치료하고 있다. **3** [I, T] ⇨ BREAST-FEED

nursery /'nɚsəri/ *n* **1** a place where plants and trees are grown and sold ‖ 식물과 나무가 재배되고 팔리는 곳. 묘목장 **2** OLD-FASHIONED a young child's room ‖ 어린 아이의 방. 육아실 **3** a place where young children are taken care of for a short time while their parents are shopping, in church etc. ‖ 부모가 쇼핑·교회 등에 갈 때 잠시 아이들을 보살펴 주는 곳. 탁아소

nursery rhyme /'... ˌ./ *n* a short well-known song or poem for children ‖ 아이들을 위한 짧고 잘 알려진 노래나 시. 동요. 자장가

nursery school /'... ˌ./ *n* a school for children from three to five years old ‖ 3세에서 5세까지의 아이들을 위한 학교. 보육원 —compare KINDERGARTEN

nurs·ing /'nɚsɪŋ/ *n* [U] the job of taking care of people who are ill, injured, or very old ‖ 병든[다친, 늙은] 사람들을 돌보는 일. 간호

nursing home /'.. ˌ./ *n* a small private hospital for people who are too old or injured to take care of themselves ‖ 너무 늙거나 다친 사람들이 스스로를 요양하는 작은 사설 병원. (사설) 요양원[양로원]

nur·ture¹ /'nɚtʃɚ/ *v* [T] FORMAL **1** to feed and take care of a child, plant etc. while it is growing ‖ 아이·식물 등이 자라는 동안 키우고 돌보다. 양육하다. 키우다: *children nurtured by loving parents* 애정 있는 부모가 키운 아이들 **2** to help a plan, idea, feeling etc. develop ‖ 계획·생각·감정 등이 발전하도록 돕다. 양성[육성, 조성]하다: *nurturing new democracies in the Third World* 제3세계에서의 새로운 민주주의 육성[지도](하기)

nurture² *n* [U] FORMAL the help, education, care etc. that is given to a child who is growing and developing ‖ 성장 발육하는 아이에게 주어지는 도움·교육·보살핌 등. 양육. 양성. 지도

nut /nʌt/ *n* **1** a large seed that you can eat that usually grows in a hard brown shell ‖ 보통 딱딱한 갈색의 껍질 속에서 자라는 먹을 수 있는 큰 씨앗. 견과 (堅果): *a cashew nut* 캐슈 너트 **2** INFORMAL someone who is crazy or behaves strangely ‖ 미치거나 이상하게 행동하는 사람. 괴짜. 정신병자 **3** a small piece of metal with a hole in the middle that is screwed onto a BOLT to fasten things together ‖ 사물을 서로 고정시키기 위해 볼트에다 돌려 끼우는, 중앙에 구멍이 있는 작은 금속 조각. 너트. 암나사 **4** INFORMAL someone who is extremely interested in a particular activity ‖ 특정한 활동에 대단한 흥미를 보이는 사람. …광: *a golf nut* 골프광 **5** [C usually plural] SLANG ⇨ TESTICLE **6 the nuts and bolts of sth** the practical details of a subject, plan, job etc. ‖ 주제·계획·일 등의 실제적인 세부 내용. 기본. 기초. 구조. 짜임새 —see also NUTS

nut·crack·er /'nʌtˌkrækɚ/ *n* a tool for cracking the shells of nuts ‖ 견과의 껍질을 까는 도구. 호두까기

nu·tri·ent /'nutriənt/ *n* a chemical or food that helps plants, animals, or people to live and grow ‖ 식물[동물, 사람]들이 살아가고 성장하는 것을 돕는 화학 성분이나 영양분. 영양제[물]: *Plants take nutrients from the soil.* 식물들은 토양에서 영양분을 섭취한다. **- nutrient** *adj*

nu·tri·tion /nu'trɪʃən/ *n* [U] the process of getting the right type of food for good health and growth ‖ 건강과 성장에 좋은 적절한 종류의 영양분을 얻는 과정. 영양 보급[섭취]. 영양 작용[과정] **- nutritional** *adj* : *nutritional information on food packages* 식품 포장 용기상의 영양 성분 정보 **- nutritionally** *adv*: *a nutritionally balanced diet* 영양상으로 균형을 이룬 식단

nu·tri·tious /nu'trɪʃəs/ *adj* food that is nutritious has a lot of substances that your body needs to stay healthy and grow ‖ 몸이 건강을 유지하고 성장하는 데에 필요한 물질을 많이 함유한. 영양이 되는. 자양분이 많은

nuts /nʌts/ *adj* INFORMAL crazy, silly, or angry ‖ 미친, 어리석은, 화난: *My sister will go nuts* (=become very angry) *when she finds out I wrecked her car.* 누나[언니]는 내가 자기 차를 망가뜨린 것을 알면 몹시 화를 낼 것이다.

nut·shell /ˈnʌtˌʃɛl/ *n* **1 (to put it) in a nutshell** INFORMAL used in order to show that you are going to give the main facts about something in a way that is short and clear ‖ 짧고 명확하게 사물에 대해 주요한 사실을 제시하려고 함을 나타내는 데에 쓰여. 아주 간단히 (말하면). 단 한 마디로 **2** the hard outer part of a nut ‖ 견과의 딱딱한 외피[껍질]

nut·ty /ˈnʌti/ *adj* **1** tasting like nuts ‖ 견과 같은 맛의: *a nutty flavor* 견과의 맛 **2** INFORMAL crazy ‖ 미친: *a nutty idea* 미친 생각

nuz·zle /ˈnʌzəl/ *v* [I, T] **1** to gently rub your face or head against someone in a loving way ‖ 사랑스럽게 자신의 얼굴이나 머리를 남에게 부드럽게 비비다: *a new mother gently nuzzling her baby's head* 아기의 머리에다 부드럽게 볼을 비비고 있는 갓 아기를 낳은 엄마 **2** if an animal nuzzles someone or nuzzles up against someone, it gently rubs its nose against him/her ‖ 동물이 사람에게 코를 부드럽게 비비다. 코로 부벼대다

NV the written abbreviation of Nevada ‖ Nevada(네바다 주)의 약어

NW the written abbreviation of NORTHWEST ‖ northwest의 약어

NY the written abbreviation of New York ‖ New York(뉴욕 주)의 약어

ny·lon /ˈnaɪlɑn/ *n* [U] a strong artificial material that is used for making plastic, cloth, rope etc. ‖ 플라스틱·천·밧줄 등을 만드는 데에 사용되는 질긴 인공 섬유. 나일론: *a nylon parka* 나일론(천) 파카

ny·lons /ˈnaɪlɑnz/ *n* [plural] a piece of clothing that women wear on their legs, that is very thin and made of NYLON ‖ 여성들이 다리에 신는, 매우 얇은 나일론제의 의류. 여성용 나일론 스타킹

nymph /nɪmf/ *n* one of the spirits of nature who appears in the form of a young girl, in ancient Greek and Roman stories ‖ 고대 그리스와 로마 신화에 어린 소녀의 형상으로 나타나는 자연의 정령 가운데 하나. 요정

nym·pho·ma·ni·ac /ˌnɪmfəˈmeɪniˌæk/ *n* a woman who wants to have sex often, usually with a lot of different men ‖ 보통 수많은 다른 남성들과 자주 성관계를 갖기를 원하는 여성. 여성 색정광 – **nymphomania** /ˌnɪmfəˈmeɪniə/ *n* [U]

Oo

O, o /oʊ/ **1** the fifteenth letter of the English alphabet ‖ 영어 알파벳의 열다섯째 자 **2** SPOKEN zero ‖ 제로. 영: *room 203* (=two o three) 203호 실

o' /ə/ *prep* NONSTANDARD a way of writing "of" as it is often said in speech. ‖ 대화에서 종종 쓰이는 문어체의 "of"의 표기 방법 중 하나: *a cup o' coffee* 커피 한 잔

oaf /oʊf/ *n* a stupid or awkward person, especially a man or boy ‖ 특히 남자나 소년을 가리키는 어리석은 사람. 바보. 멍청이

oak /oʊk/ *n* [C, U] a large tree that is common in northern countries, or the hard wood of this tree ‖ 북반구 국가에 흔히 있는 큰 나무, 또는 이 나무의 견고한 재목. 오크나무(재목)

oar /ɔr/ *n* a long pole with a wide blade at one end, used for rowing a boat ‖ 배를 젓는 데에 사용되는 한쪽 끝에 넓은 물갈퀴가 있는 긴 장대. 노

o·a·sis /oʊˈeɪsɪs/ *n*, *plural* **oases** /oʊˈeɪsiz/ a place with trees and water in a desert ‖ 사막의 나무와 물이 있는 장소. 오아시스

oasis

oath /oʊθ/ *n* **1** a formal and serious promise ‖ 공식적이고 진지한 약속. 맹세. 서약: *He swore an oath* (=gave a promise) *to support the Constitution.* 그는 헌법을 수호하기로 맹세했다. **2 be under oath** to have made an official promise to tell the truth in a court of law ‖ 법정에서 진실을 말할 것을 공식적으로 약속했다. 선서한 상태에다

oat·meal /ˈoʊtˌmil/ *n* [U] crushed OATS that are boiled and eaten for breakfast, or used in cooking ‖ 아침 식사용으로 삶아 먹거나 요리할 때에 쓰는 빻은 귀리. 오트밀

oats /oʊts/ *n* [plural] a grain that is eaten by people and animals ‖ 사람과 동물이 식용하는 곡식. 귀리

o·be·di·ence /əˈbidiəns, oʊ-/ *n* [U] doing what you are supposed to do, according to a law or to someone in authority ‖ 법률이나 권위 있는 사람을 좇아 해야만 하는 일을 하기. 복종. 준수: *He acted in obedience to the law.* 그는 법률에 따라 행동했다.

o·be·di·ent /əˈbidiənt, oʊ-/ *adj* always obeying laws, rules, or people in authority ‖ 법률이나 규칙, 또는 권위 있는 사람에게 항상 복종하는. 순종하는. 충실한: *an obedient dog* 충직한 개 – **obediently** *adv* —opposite DISOBEDIENT

o·bese /oʊˈbis/ *adj* extremely fat ‖ 매우 살찐. 뚱뚱한. 비만한 – **obesity** *n* [U] —see usage note at FAT

o·bey /əˈbeɪ, oʊ-/ *v* [I, T] to do what you are supposed to do, according to the law or to what someone in authority says ‖ 법률이나 권위 있는 사람이 말하는 것에 따라 해야만 하는 일을 하다. 복종하다. 따르다: *Children should be taught to obey the law.* 어린이들은 법률을 지키도록 가르침을 받아야 한다. / *The sergeant yells an order and the men obey immediately.* 중사가 큰 소리로 명령을 내리면 사병들은 즉시 따른다. —opposite DISOBEY

o·bit·u·ar·y /əˈbɪtʃuˌɛri, oʊ-/ *n* a report in a newspaper about the life of someone who has just died ‖ 고인(故人)의 삶에 대한 신문지상의 보도. 사망기사. 부고

ob·ject¹ /ˈɑbdʒɪkt, ˈɑbdʒɛkt/ *n* **1** a thing that you can see, hold, or touch ‖ 볼[잡을, 만질] 수 있는 것. 물체. 물건: *Cubes, balls, and other objects were set out for the students to draw.* 학생들이 그리도록 정육면체 및 구(球)와 다른 물체들이 놓여 있었다. **2** [singular] the purpose of a plan, action, or activity ‖ 계획[행동, 활동]의 목적: *The object of this game is to score points by kicking the ball into the goal.* 이 게임의 목적은 공을 골 안으로 차 넣어 득점하는 것이다. **3 an object of desire/pity etc.** someone or something that you desire, pity etc. ‖ 바라거나 동정하는 등의 사람이나 사물. 욕망/동정의 대상 **4** TECHNICAL in grammar, the person or thing that is affected by the action of the verb in a sentence. In the sentence "Sheila closed the door," "door" is the object ‖ 문법에서, 문장의 동사의 동작에 의해서 영향을 받는 사람이나 사물. 목적어. "Sheila closed the door"라는 문장에서 "door"는 목적어이다

ob·ject² /əbˈdʒɛkt/ *v* [I] to say that you

do not like or approve of something ‖ 어떤 것을 좋아하지 않거나 인정하지 않는다고 말하다. 반대하다. 이의를 말하다: *He objected to Bianchi's suggestion, saying it would cost too much.* 그는 그것이 비용이 너무 많이 든다고 말하면서 비안치의 제안을 반대했다.

ob·jec·tion /əb'dʒɛkʃən/ *n* a reason you give for not approving of an idea or plan ‖ 생각이나 계획을 승인하지 않는 이유. 반대하는 이유: *Does anyone have any objections to Mr. Ducin's proposal?* 두신씨의 제안에 누구 이의 있는 분 계십니까? / *Several Senators made/raised/voiced objections to the bill.* (=they objected) 몇몇 상원 의원들이 그 법안에 이의를 제기했다.

ob·jec·tion·a·ble /əb'dʒɛkʃənəbəl/ *adj* unpleasant and likely to offend people; OFFENSIVE ‖ 불쾌하고 사람들의 기분을 상하게 할 듯한. 못마땅한; 冊 offensive

ob·jec·tive¹ /əb'dʒɛktɪv/ *n* something that you are working hard to achieve ‖ 열심히 일하여 달성하려는 것. 목적. 목표: *The company's **main objective** is to increase sales overseas.* 그 회사의 주요 목표는 해외에서의 매출액을 늘리는 일이다.

objective² *adj* **1** not influenced by your own feelings, beliefs, or ideas ‖ 자신의 감정이나 신념, 또는 생각에 영향을 받지 않는. 객관적인: *an objective opinion from the judge* 판사가 내린 객관적 의견 **2** FORMAL not imagined; real ‖ 상상이 아닌; 실제의 **– objectively** *adv* **– objectivity** /ˌɑbdʒɛk'tɪvəti/ *n* [U] — compare SUBJECTIVE

ob·li·gate /'ɑblə,geɪt/ *v* [T] **1** to make someone feel that s/he has to do something, because it is right, a duty etc. ‖ 정당하고 의무이기 때문에 남에게 어떤 일을 하지 않으면 안 된다고 느끼게 하다. 의무를 지우다: *The city was obligated to make drastic spending cuts.* 그 시는 경비를 대폭 삭감해야 할 의무를 느꼈다. **2 be/feel obligated** to do something only because someone has done something nice for you ‖ 단지 상대방이 자신에게 좋은 일을 했기 때문에 어떤 일을 하다. 의무가 있다/의무감을 느끼다: *I hope he doesn't feel obligated to wear the shirt just because I gave it to him.* 내가 그에게 셔츠를 주었다고 해서 그가 그 셔츠를 입어야 한다고는 생각하지 않기를 바란다.

ob·li·ga·tion /ˌɑblə'geɪʃən/ *n* [C, U] a moral or legal duty to do something ‖ 일을 할 도덕적 또는 법적 의무. 책임. 책무: *Every father has an **obligation to** take care of his child.* 모든 아버지는 자녀를 돌봐야할 의무가 있다.

o·blig·a·to·ry /ə'blɪgə,tɔri/ *adj* FORMAL having to be done because of a law, rule etc.; COMPULSORY ‖ 법·규칙 등 때문에 해야만 하는. 의무적인. 강제적인; 冊 compulsory

o·blige /ə'blaɪdʒ/ *v* **1** [T] FORMAL to make someone feel that it is necessary to do something, especially because it is right, a duty etc. ‖ 특히 옳거나 의무이기 때문에 남에게 어떤 것을 할 필요성을 느끼게 하다. 의무를 지우다. 강제하다: *Doctors are obliged to keep their patients' records secret.* 의사들은 환자들의 진료기록을 비밀로 해야 한다. **2 I/we would be obliged if** used in formal letters to ask someone to do something for you ‖ 남에게 자신을 위해 일을 해줄 것을 부탁하는 격식적인 편지에 쓰여. …하면 감사하겠습니다: *I would be obliged if you could send me a copy of the contract as soon as possible.* 가능한 한 빨리 그 계약서 사본을 저에게 보내 주시면 감사하겠습니다. **3** [I, T] to do something that someone has asked you to do ‖ 남에게 부탁 받은 일을 하다. 호의[은혜]를 베풀다. 고맙게 …해주다: *He asked to borrow my car, and I was happy/glad to oblige.* 그가 나의 차를 빌려 달라고 부탁해서 나는 기꺼이 빌려 주었다.

o·blig·ing /ə'blaɪdʒɪŋ/ *adj* willing and eager to help ‖ 기꺼이 남을 도와주고 싶어하는. 친절한: *a cheerful and obliging woman* 쾌활하고 친절한 여성 **– obligingly** *adv*

o·blique /ə'blik, ou-/ *adj* not expressed in a direct way ‖ 직접적으로 표현하지 않는. 간접적인. 완곡한. 에두른: *oblique references to his drinking problem* 그의 음주 문제에 관한 간접적인 언급

ob·lit·er·ate /ə'blɪtə,reɪt/ *v* [T] to destroy something completely ‖ 사물을 완전히 파괴하다: *Large areas of the city were obliterated during World War II.* 제2차 세계 대전 동안에 그 도시의 광범위한 지역이 파괴되었다. **– obliteration** /ə,blɪtə'reɪʃən/ *n* [U]

ob·liv·i·on /ə'blɪviən/ *n* [U] FORMAL **1** the state of being completely forgotten ‖ 완전히 잊혀진 상태. 망각: *Old movie stars who have **faded into** oblivion.* 세상에서 잊혀진 왕년의 영화배우들 **2** the state of being unconscious or of not knowing what is happening ‖ 의식이 없는 상태나 일어나고 있는 일을 모르는 상

태. 무의식. 인사불성: *He spent the night drinking himself into oblivion.* 그는 인사불성이 될 정도로 술을 마시며 밤을 보냈다.

ob·liv·i·ous /əˈblɪviəs/ *adj* not knowing about or not noticing something happening around you; UNAWARE ‖ 주변에서 일어나는 일을 모르거나 알아채지 못하는. 염두에 없는; ⓕ unaware: *Maxwell walked on, completely oblivious to/of the danger.* 맥스웰은 위험을 전혀 알아차리지 못하고 계속 걸어갔다.

ob·long /ˈɑblɔŋ/ *adj* having a shape that is longer than it is wide ‖ 폭보다는 길이가 더 긴 모양을 한. 직사각형의: *an oblong mirror* 직사각형의 거울 – **oblong** *n*

ob·nox·ious /əbˈnɑkʃəs/ *adj* extremely unpleasant or rude ‖ 매우 불쾌하거나 무례한: *obnoxious behavior* 매우 불쾌한 행동 / *Robin gets so obnoxious when she's drunk.* 로빈은 취하면 매우 무례해진다. – **obnoxiously** *adv*

o·boe /ˈoʊboʊ/ *n* a wooden musical instrument shaped like a narrow tube, that you play by blowing into it ‖ 불어서 연주하는 좁은 관 모양의 목제 악기. 오보에

ob·scene /əbˈsin, ɑb-/ *adj* **1** dealing with sex or violence in a way that is offensive and shocking ‖ 성(性)이나 폭력을 불쾌하거나 충격적으로 다루는. 외설한. 음란한. 음탕한: *obscene photographs/language* 음란한 사진/말 **2** extremely immoral or unfair ‖ 매우 부도덕하거나 불공정한: *obscene wealth* 매우 부도덕한 재산

ob·scen·i·ty /əbˈsɛnəti/ *n* **1** [C usually plural] a sexually offensive word or action ‖ 성적으로 불쾌감을 주는 말이나 행동. 음탕한 언행: *kids shouting obscenities* 욕설을 외쳐대는 아이들 **2** [U] offensive language or behavior involving sex, especially in a book, play etc. ‖ 특히 책이나 연극 등에서의 성(性)에 관련된 불쾌감을 주는 말이나 행동. 외설. 음란: *laws against obscenity* 외설에 반대하는 법률

ob·scure¹ /əbˈskyʊr/ *adj* **1** unclear or difficult to understand ‖ 불명확하거나 이해하기 어려운. 불명료한. 애매한: *Jarrett didn't like the plan for some obscure reason.* 자레트는 뭔가 애매모호한 이유로 그 계획을 좋아하지 않았다. **2** known about only by a few people ‖ 단지 몇 사람만 아는. 무명의. 잘 알려지지 않은: *an obscure poet* 무명 시인

obscure² *v* [T] **1** to prevent something

from being seen ‖ 어떤 것을 보이지 않게 하다. 가리다. 감추다: *Clouds obscured the hills in the distance.* 구름이 멀리 있는 언덕을 가렸다. **2** to make something difficult to know or understand ‖ 어떤 것을 알거나 이해하기 어렵게 하다. 애매하게 하다: *legal language that seems to obscure meaning* 뜻이 난해해 보이는 법률어

ob·scu·ri·ty /əbˈskyʊrəti/ *n* **1** [U] the state of not being known or remembered ‖ 알려지거나 기억되지 않는 상태. 무명: *O'Brien retired from politics and died in obscurity.* 오브라이언 씨는 정치에서 은퇴하여 조용히 지내다가 죽었다. **2** [C, U] something that is difficult to understand, or the quality of being difficult to understand ‖ 이해하기 어려운 것, 또는 이해하기 어려움

ob·serv·a·ble /əbˈzɜvəbəl/ *adj* able to be seen or noticed ‖ 보이거나 알아챌 수 있는

ob·serv·ance /əbˈzɜvəns/ *n* [U] **1** the celebration of a religious or national event ‖ 종교적 또는 국가적인 행사의 축하. 축하 행사: *the observance of Yom Kippur* 속죄의 날의 축하 행사 **2** the practice of obeying a law or rule ‖ 법이나 규칙을 지키는 일. 준수

ob·serv·ant /əbˈzɜvənt/ *adj* good or quick at noticing things ‖ 어떤 것을 잘 또는 바로 알아채는. 관찰력이 날카로운: *An observant guard reported that there were three boxes missing.* 관찰력이 날카로운 감시인이 세 상자가 분실되었다고 보고했다.

ob·ser·va·tion /ˌɑbzɜˈveɪʃən, -sɚ-/ *n* **1** [C, U] the act or process of carefully watching someone or something, or one of the facts you learn from doing this ‖ 사람이나 사물을 주의 깊게 관찰하는 행위나 과정, 또는 이렇게 하여 배우는 사실들 중의 하나. 관찰(에 의한 지식): *Scientists are making careful observations of the meteor's path through space.* 과학자들은 우주를 통과하는 유성의 궤도를 주의깊게 관찰하고 있다. / *The patient is under close observation.* (=being continuously watched) 그 환자는 주의깊게 관찰되고 있다. **2** a remark about something that you have noticed ‖ 알아챈 일에 대한 언급. 의견. 소견: *He made several humorous observations about the state of our local theaters.* 그는 지방 극장의 실태에 대한 몇 가지 익살스러운 소견을 말했다.

ob·serv·a·to·ry /əbˈzɜvəˌtɔri/ *n* a

special building from which scientists watch the moon, stars, weather etc. ‖ 과학자들이 달·별·날씨 등을 관찰하는 특수 건물. 관측소. 천문대

ob·serve /əb'zɜːv/ *v* [T] **1** to watch someone or something carefully ‖ 사람이나 사물을 주의깊게 관찰하다: *Advertisers observed consumers' buying habits.* 광고업자들은 소비자들의 구매 습관을 관찰했다. **2** to obey a law, agreement, or religious rule ‖ 법률[협정, 종교적 규율]을 지키다. 따르다. 준수하다: *Both sides are observing the ceasefire.* 양측은 정전을 준수하고 있다. **3** FORMAL to see or notice something in particular ‖ 특별히 어떤 것을 보거나 알아차리다. 깨닫다: *Doctors observed that the disease only occurs in women over 50.* 의사들은 그 질병이 오직 50세 이상의 여성들에게만 발병한다는 것을 알았다. **4** FORMAL to say what you have noticed about something ‖ 어떤 것에 대하여 알아챈 것을 말하다. 의견을 말하다

ob·serv·er /əb'zɜːvə/ *n* **1** someone whose job is to watch a situation, system, business etc. carefully in order to report any changes or illegal actions or to say what will happen in the future ‖ 어떤 변화나 불법적인 행동을 보고하거나 장차 일어날 일을 말하기 위해 조심스럽게 상황·시스템·사업을 관찰하는 직업인. 관찰자: *International observers criticized the use of military force in the region.* 국제적인 감시자들이 그 지역의 군사력 사용을 비난했다. **2** someone who sees or notices something ‖ …을 보거나 알아챈 사람. 목격자

ob·sessed /əb'sɛst/ *adj* thinking about someone or something all the time, so that you cannot think of anything else ‖ 다른 것을 생각할 수 없도록 사람이나 사물을 항상 생각하는. 사로잡힌. 홀린: *William is obsessed with making money.* 윌리엄 씨는 돈 버는 일에 혈안이 되어 있다. **– obsess** *v* [I, T]

ob·ses·sion /əb'sɛʃən/ *n* something that you cannot stop thinking or worrying about ‖ 어떤 것에 대한 생각이나 걱정을 그만둘 수 없는 것. 강박 관념. 망상: *an unhealthy obsession with sex* 섹스에 대한 건전하지 못한 집착

ob·ses·sive /əb'sɛsɪv/ *adj* thinking too much about someone or something so that you do not think about other things enough ‖ 다른 것을 충분히 생각할 수 없도록 사람이나 사물을 너무 많이 생각하거나 걱정하는. 강박 관념의. 집착하는: *She has an obsessive*

need to control everything. 그녀는 모든 것을 지배하려는 강박적인 욕구가 있다. **– obsessively** *adv*

ob·so·lete /ˌɑbsə'liːt/ *adj* no longer useful or needed because something newer and better has been made ‖ 더 새롭고 좋은 것이 만들어져서 더 이상 유용하거나 필요하지 않은. 쓸모없어진. 한물간: *Our computer system will soon be obsolete.* 우리의 컴퓨터 시스템은 곧 쓸모없어질 것이다. **– obsolescence** /ˌɑbsə'lɛsəns/ *n* [U]

obstacle

an obstacle in the road　　causing an obstruction

ob·sta·cle /'ɑbstɪkəl/ *n* **1** something that makes it difficult for you to succeed ‖ 성공하기 어렵게 만드는 것. 장애: *Sylvia has had to overcome the obstacles of racism and sexism at work.* 실비아는 직장에서 인종주의와 성차별의 난관을 극복해야 했다. **2** something that blocks your way, so that you must go around it ‖ 돌아가도록 길을 막는 것. 장애물: *an obstacle in the road* 도로의 장애물

obstacle course /'... ˌ./ *n* a line of objects that a runner must jump over, go under etc. ‖ 경주자가 뛰어넘거나 밑으로 가야 하는 등의 일련의 물체들. 장애물 경주 코스

ob·stet·rics /əb'stɛtrɪks, ɑb-/ *n* [U] the part of medical science that deals with the birth of children ‖ 아이의 출산을 다루는 의학의 분야. 산과학(産科學) **– obstetrician** /ˌɑbstə'trɪʃən/ *n*

ob·sti·nate /'ɑbstənɪt/ *adj* DISAPPROVING determined not to change your opinions, ideas, behavior etc.; STUBBORN ‖ 자기의 의견·생각·행동 등을 바꾸려 하지 않는. 고집 센. 완고한; ㊰ stubborn **– obstinacy** *n* [U]

ob·struct /əb'strʌkt/ *v* [T] **1** to block a road, path, passage, or someone's view of something ‖ 도로[길, 통로, 사물에 대한 남의 전망]를 막다: *The new airport terminal partially obstructs the view from the tower.* 신 공항 터미널은 타워에서 보는 시야를 일부 가로막고 있다. / *The truck was on its side, obstructing two* *lanes of traffic.* 그 트럭은 옆으로 있어 차선 두 개를 막고 있었다. **2 to try to prevent someone from doing something by making it difficult** ‖ 어렵게 만들어 남이 일을 못하게 하다. 방해하다: *Federal officers accused Robbins of obstructing their investigation.* 연방 경찰은 자신들의 수사를 방해했다고 로빈스 씨를 비난했다. **– obstructive** *adj*

ob·struc·tion /əb'strʌkʃən/ *n* **1** [C, U] something that blocks a road, passage, tube etc., or the fact of blocking a road etc. ‖ 도로·통로·튜브 등을 막는 것, 또는 도로 등을 막음. 장애물. 장애: *The accident caused an obstruction on the freeway.* 그 사고로 고속도로가 막혔다. **2** [U] the act of preventing something from happening ‖ 일이 일어나지 못하게 함. 방해: *Kane could be charged with obstruction of justice for refusing to cooperate with authorities.* 케인은 사법 당국에 협조를 거부하여 사법 방해죄의 혐의를 받을 수 있었다. —see picture at OBSTACLE

ob·tain /əb'teɪn/ *v* [T] FORMAL to get something that you want ‖ 원하는 것을 얻다. 입수하다. 획득하다: *Information about passports can be obtained from the embassy.* 여권에 대한 정보는 대사관에서 얻을 수 있다.

ob·tain·a·ble /əb'teɪnəbəl/ *adj* able to be obtained ‖ 입수할 수 있는. 손에 넣을 수 있는

ob·tru·sive /əb'trusɪv/ *adj* noticeable in an unpleasant way ‖ 불쾌하게 눈에 띄는. 몹시 두드러진. 주제넘게 나서는. 돌출한: *The signs are obtrusive, blocking one of the city's most beautiful views.* 그 간판이 돌출되어 도시의 가장 아름다운 전망 중의 하나를 가로막고 있다. / *The waitresses were friendly but never obtrusive.* 그 웨이트리스는 친절하나 결코 주제넘게 나서지는 않았다. —opposite UNOBTRUSIVE

ob·tuse /əb'tus, ab-/ *adj* **1** FORMAL stupid or slow to understand something ‖ 어떤 것을 이해하는 데에 둔하거나 느린. 무딘 **2 obtuse angle** TECHNICAL an angle between 90 and 180 degrees ‖ 90도와 180도 사이의 각. 둔각(鈍角)

ob·vi·ous /'abviəs/ *adj* easy to notice or understand ‖ 알아채거나 이해하기 쉬운. 명백한. 빤한: *an obvious mistake* 명백한 잘못 / *Kyman is the obvious choice for team captain.* 카이만이 팀 주장으로 선출되는 것은 뻔하다. / *It was obvious that he was lying.* 그가 거짓말하고 있는 것이 분명했다.

ob·vi·ous·ly /'abviəsli/ *adv* used when something is easily noticed or understood, or when you expect that other people already know the thing you have just said ‖ 사물이 쉽게 눈에 띄거나 이해될 때 또는 방금 말한 것을 남이 이미 알고 있다고 생각할 때에 쓰여. 확실히: *Obviously, we won't have time to finish.* 분명 우리는 마무리 할 시간이 없을 것이다. / *She was obviously feeling terrible.* 그녀는 분명히 무서워하고 있었다.

oc·ca·sion /ə'keɪʒən/ *n* **1** a time when something happens ‖ 일이 발생하는 시간. 때. 경우: *I met with him on several occasions.* 나는 여러 번 그를 만났다. **2** an important event or ceremony ‖ 중요한 행사나 의식. 특별한 행사: *We're saving the champagne for a special occasion.* 우리는 특별한 행사를 위하여 샴페인을 비축하고 있다. / *Larsky rose to the occasion* (=achieved something difficult) *and scored the winning goal.* 라스키는 위기에서 수완을 발휘하여 결승골을 얻어냈다. **3** [singular] a suitable time, or reason to do something ‖ 적절한 시간, 또는 일을 하는 이유. 기회: *Veteran's day is the occasion when we remember people who died in war.* 재향군인의 날은 우리가 전쟁에서 죽은 사람들을 추모하는 때이다. **4 on occasion** sometimes but not often ‖ 자주는 아니지만 때때로. 이따금: *He has a drink on occasion.* 그는 때때로 술을 마신다.

oc·ca·sion·al /ə'keɪʒənl/ *adj* happening sometimes but not often ‖ 자주는 아니지만 때때로 일어나는. 가끔의. 이따금의: *strong winds and occasional rain* 강한 바람과 이따금 내리는 비

oc·ca·sion·al·ly /ə'keɪʒənl-i/ *adv* sometimes, but not regularly or often ‖ 규칙적이거나 자주는 아니지만 때때로. 가끔. 이따금: *Stir the soup occasionally and add the milk before serving.* 수프를 가끔 젓고 대접하기 전에 우유를 타라.

oc·cult /ə'kʌlt/ *n* **the occult** the knowledge and study of magic and spirits ‖ 마술과 유령에 대한 지식과 연구. 비술(祕術). 초자연 현상 **– occult** *adj*

oc·cu·pan·cy /'akyəpənsi/ *n* [U] FORMAL someone's use of a building or other space for living or working in ‖ 살거나 일하기 위해 건물이나 다른 공간을 사용함. 점유. 점거

oc·cu·pant /'akyəpənt/ *n* FORMAL someone who lives in a building, room etc., or who is in it at a particular time ‖ 건물·방 등에 사는 사람, 또는 특정한 때에 그곳에 있는 사람. 거주자. 점유자: *a* *letter addressed to the occupant* 거주자에게 보낸 편지

oc·cu·pa·tion /ˌɑkyə'peɪʃən/ *n* **1** FORMAL a job or profession; EMPLOYMENT ‖ 일 또는 직업; ㊦ employment: *Please state your name and occupation.* 이름과 직업을 말씀해 주세요. —see usage note at JOB **2** [U] the act of entering a place and getting control of it, especially by military force ‖ 특히 군사력으로 어떤 장소에 침투하여 그곳을 장악하는 행위. 점령 **3** FORMAL something that you spend time doing, especially for pleasure ‖ 특히 재미로 시간을 보내는 일. 심심풀이: *One of my childhood occupations was collecting baseball cards.* 내 어린 시절의 심심풀이중 하나는 야구 카드를 수집하는 것이었다.

oc·cu·pa·tion·al /ˌɑkyə'peɪʃənəl/ *adj* relating to your job ‖ 직업의

oc·cu·pied /'ɑkyə,paɪd/ *adj* **1** being used ‖ 사용되는. 사용 중: *All the beds in the youth hostel were already occupied.* 유스호스텔의 침상은 이미 모두 사용 중이었다. **2** busy doing or thinking about something ‖ 어떤 것을 하거나 생각하느라 바쁜. 여념이 없는. 정신이 팔린: *I brought along some toys to keep the kids occupied.* 나는 아이들이 가지고 놀도록 몇 개의 장난감을 가지고 갔다.

oc·cu·py /'ɑkyə,paɪ/ *v* [T] **1** to live, work etc. in a particular place ‖ 특정한 장소에서 살거나 일하다. 차지하다: *Salem Press occupies the seventh floor of the building.* 살렘 프레스는 그 건물의 7층을 쓰고 있다. **2** if something occupies you or your time, you are busy doing it ‖ 어떤 일을 하느라 바쁘다: *Fishing occupies most of my spare time.* 나는 대부분의 여가시간에 낚시 하느라 바쁘다. **3** to fill a particular amount of space ‖ 특정 공간을 채우다: *Family photos occupied almost the entire wall.* 가족사진이 거의 벽 전체를 차지했다. **4** to enter a place and get control of it, especially by military force ‖ 특히 군사력으로 장소에 침투하여 장악하다. 점령[점유]하다

oc·cur /ə'kɚ/ *v* **-rred, -rring** [I] FORMAL **1** to happen, especially without being planned first ‖ 특히 처음부터 계획되지 않고 일어나다. 생기다: *Earthquakes occur without any warning signs.* 지진은 어떤 조짐도 없이 발생한다. **2** to exist or be present in a particular place ‖ 특정한 장소에 존재하다 또는 있다: *The disease mainly occurs in young children.* 그 병은 주로 나이 어린 아이들에게 발생한다. —see usage note at HAPPEN

occur to sb *phr v* [T] to suddenly come into your mind ‖ 갑자기 마음에 떠오르다: *I washed it in hot water – it never occurred to me to check the label.* 라벨을 확인하는 것을 잊어버리고 그걸 뜨거운 물에 세탁했어.

o·cean /'oʊʃən/ *n* **1 the ocean** the great quantity of salt water that covers most of the Earth's surface ‖ 대부분의 지구의 표면을 덮고 있는 엄청난 양의 소금물. 해양. 대양 **2** a particular area of salt water somewhere on Earth ‖ 지구상의 특정 지역의 소금물. …양(洋): *the Indian Ocean* 인도양 **– oceanic** /ˌoʊʃi'ænɪk/ *adj*

o·cean·og·ra·phy /ˌoʊʃə'nɑgrəfi/ *n* [U] the scientific study of the ocean ‖ 해양에 대한 과학적인 연구. 해양학 **– oceanographer** *n*

o'clock /ə'klɑk/ *adv* **one/two/three etc. o'clock** one of the times when the clock shows the exact hour as a number from 1 to 12 ‖ 시계가 1에서 12까지의 숫자로 정확한 시각이 보여주는 시간들 중의 하나. 한/두/세 시

OCR *n* [U] optical character recognition; computer software that recognizes letters of the alphabet, so that you can put paper documents onto a computer ‖ optical character recognition(광학식 문자 인식)의 약자; 종이 문서를 컴퓨터에 입력시킬 수 있도록 알파벳 문자를 인식하는 컴퓨터 소프트웨어

oc·ta·gon /'ɑktə,gɑn/ *n* a flat shape with eight sides and eight angles ‖ 8변과 8각을 가진 편평한 모양. 8각형. 8변형 **– octagonal** /ɑk'tægənəl/ *adj* —see picture at SHAPE

Oc·to·ber /ɑk'toʊbɚ/, *written abbreviation* **Oct.** *n* the tenth month of the year ‖ 그 해의 열 번째 달. 10월 —see usage note at JANUARY

oc·to·pus /'ɑktəpəs/ *n, plural* **octopuses** *or* **octopi** /'ɑktəpaɪ/ a sea creature with a soft body and eight TENTACLEs (=arms) ‖ 몸이 물렁하고 발이 8개 달린 바다 생물. 문어

octopus

tentacle

OD *v* [I] SLANG to take too much of a dangerous drug; OVERDOSE ‖ 위험한 약물을 너무 많이 복용하다. 과다 복용하다; ㊦ overdose

odd /ɑd/ *adj* **1** different from what is expected; strange ‖ 예상한 것과 다른. 의

외의; 이상한: *It's odd that she hasn't phoned by now.* 그녀가 지금까지 전화를 하지 않았다니 이상하다. / *an odd guy* 이 상한 사람 **2 odd jobs** small jobs of different kinds that someone does, especially fixing or cleaning things ‖ 특 히 수리·청소 등 사람이 하는 여러 종류의 사소한 일. 부업. 뜨내기일: *The boys are earning money doing odd jobs for the neighbors.* 소년들은 이웃을 위해 잡일을 하면서 돈을 벌고 있다. **3** an odd number cannot be divided by 2 ‖ 수(數)가 2로 나뉘지 않는. 홀수의: *1, 3, 5, 7, etc. are odd numbers* 1, 3, 5, 7 등은 홀수들이다. — compare EVEN² **4** separated from its pair or set ‖ 한 쌍 또는 한 벌에서 분리된. 한[외] 짝의: *an odd sock* 양말 한 짝 **5 20-odd/30-odd etc.** INFORMAL a little more than 20, 30 etc. ‖ 20, 30 등보다 많은. 20/30 남짓 —see also ODDS

odd·i·ty /ˈɑdəti/ *n* a strange or unusual person or thing ‖ 이상하거나 유별난 사람 이나 사물. 괴짜

odd·ly /ˈɑdli/ *adv* in a strange or unusual way ‖ 이상하게 또는 유별나게 —see also **strangely/oddly/funnily enough** ENOUGH

odds /ɑdz/ *n* [plural] **1** how likely it is that something will or will not happen, often expressed as a number ‖ 종종 숫자로 표현되는, 일이 일어나거나 일어나지 않을 가망. 가능성. 확률: *The odds are about 1 in 12 that a boy will be colorblind.* 사내아이가 색맹이 될 가능성은 약 12분의 1이다. **2 at odds (with sb)** disagreeing with someone ‖ 남과 사이가 나쁜. 불화하여: *Briggs found himself at odds with his colleagues at NASA.* 브리그는 미국 항공 우주국의 동료들과 사이가 좋지 않았다. **3** difficulties that make a good result seem very unlikely ‖ 좋은 결과를 내기가 몹시 힘들어 보이는 어려움. 곤란: *Our team won the title against all the odds.* (=in spite of difficulties) 온갖 어려움을 무릅쓰고 우리 팀은 선수권을 차지했다.

odds and ends /ˌ. . ˈ./ *n* [plural] INFORMAL various small things, usually ones that have little value ‖ 보통 가치가 거의 없는 여러 가지 작은 물건들. 잡동사니

ode /oʊd/ *n* a long poem that is written in order to praise a person or thing ‖ 사람이나 사물을 칭송하기 위해 쓰인 장시(長詩). 오드. 송시(頌詩)

o·di·ous /ˈoʊdiəs/ *adj* FORMAL very bad or unpleasant ‖ 아주 싫거나 불쾌한: *an odious greedy little man* 혐오스럽고 욕심이 많은 작은 남자

o·dom·e·ter /oʊˈdɑmətər/ *n* an instrument in a vehicle that records the distance it travels ‖ 이동하는 거리를 기록하는 차량의 계기. 주행 거리계 —see picture on page 943

o·dor /ˈoʊdər/ *n* a smell, especially an unpleasant one ‖ 특히 불쾌한 냄새. 악취 —see usage note at SMELL²

o·dor·less /ˈoʊdərlɪs/ *adj* not having a smell ‖ 냄새가 없는. 무취의: *an odorless gas* 무취 기체

od·ys·sey /ˈɑdəsi/ *n* LITERARY a long trip ‖ 긴 여행

OECD *n* **the OECD** the Organization for Economic Cooperation and Development; a group of rich countries who work together to develop trade and economic growth ‖ the Organization for Economic Cooperation and Development(경제 협력 개발 기구)의 약어; 통상 개발과 경제 성장을 위해 함께 일하는 부유한 나라들의 기구

of /əv, ə; *strong* ʌv/ *prep* **1** used in order to show a quality or feature that someone or something has ‖ 사람이나 사물이 가진 자질이나 특징을 나타내는 데에 쓰여: *I love the color of his shirt.* 나는 그의 셔츠 색깔을 좋아한다. / *the size of the building* 그 건물의 크기 / *It was stupid of me to say that.* 내가 그렇게 말하다니 어리석었다. **2** used in order to show that something is a part of something else ‖ 어떤 사물이 다른 사물의 일부인 것을 나타내는 데에 쓰여: *The first part of the story is funny.* 그 이야기의 첫 부분은 재미있다. / *the tips of your fingers* 네 손가락들의 끝부분들 **3** used in order to show that something belongs to or relates to someone or something ‖ 사물이 어떤 사람이나 사물에 속하거나 관련되어 있는 것을 나타내는 데에 쓰여: *He gave her an old shirt of his.* 그는 그녀에게 자신의 낡은 셔츠를 주었다. / *a friend of Bobby's* 보비의 친구 **4** used with words that show a particular type of group ‖ 특정한 유형의 집단을 나타내는 말과 함께 쓰여: *a pack of cigarettes* 한 갑의 담배 / *a bunch of grapes* 한 송이의 포도 / *a herd of elephants* 한 무리의 코끼리 **5** used in order to show an amount or measurement ‖ 양이나 치수를 나타내는 데에 쓰여: *a cup of coffee* 한 잔의 커피 / *lots of room* 널찍한 공간 / *a drop of water* 물 한 방울 **6** used in order to show that someone or something is from a larger group of similar people or things ‖ 사람이나 사물이 비슷한 사람이나

사물로 된 큰 집단 출신이라는 것을 나타내는 데에 쓰여. …출신의: *That's one of her best poems.* 그것은 그녀의 가장 좋은 시 중의 하나이다. / *members of a rock group* 록 그룹의 구성원[멤버]들 / *a familiar brand of coffee* 잘 알려진 커피 상표 **7** used in dates ‖ 날짜에 쓰여: *the 23rd of January, 2003* 2003년 1월 23일 **8** SPOKEN used when you are giving the time to mean before ‖ 전(前)이라는 뜻으로 시간을 나타낼 때에 쓰여: *It's ten of five.* (=ten minutes before 5:00) 5시 10분 전이다. **9** used when giving the name of something ‖ 사물에 이름을 붙일 때에 쓰여. …이라는. …의: *the city of New Orleans* 뉴올리언스 시 / *the game of chess* 체스 게임 **10** used when giving the reason for or the cause of something ‖ 사물의 이유나 원인을 댈 때에 쓰여: *She died of cancer.* 그녀는 암으로 죽었다. **11** used in order to say what something shows ‖ 사물이 나타내는 것을 말하는 데에 쓰여: *a picture of his family* 그의 가족 사진 / *a map of the world* 세계 지도 **12** used in order to say what something is about or what type of thing it is ‖ 사물이 무엇에 대한 것인지, 또는 어떤 유형의 것인지를 말하는 데에 쓰여. …에 대한. …의: *Do you know the story of Tom Thumb?* 엄지손가락 톰에 대한 이야기를 아느냐? / *the problem of crime in schools* 교내 범죄에 관한 문제 **13** used in order to show direction or distance ‖ 방향이나 거리를 나타내는 데에 쓰여. …의. …으로부터: *I live just north of here.* 나는 여기에서 바로 북쪽에 산다. / *The school is within a mile of the park.* (=it is less than a mile from the park) 그 학교는 그 공원에서 1마일 내에 있다. **14** used after nouns describing actions to show to whom the action is done or who did the action ‖ 동작을 묘사하는 명사 뒤에서 동작이 누구에게 미치는지, 또는 동작을 누가 했는지 나타내는 데에 쓰여: *the testing of river water for chemicals* 강물의 화학 약품 실험 / *the crying of a child* 울고 있는 아이 **15** LITERARY made from ‖ 어떤 것으로 만들어진. …으로 된: *a dress of pure silk* 순수 비단으로 만든 옷 **16** written, made, produced etc. by ‖ 누군가가 쓰고, 만들고, 제작한: *the early plays of Shakespeare* 셰익스피어 초기의 희곡들 **17** used in order to say where someone lives ‖ 사람이 사는 곳을 말하는 데에 쓰여: *the people of Malaysia* 말레이시아 국민 —see also **of course** (COURSE¹)

off¹ /ɔf/ *adv* **1** away from or out of a

place or position ‖ 장소나 위치에서 떨어져: *She waved goodbye as she drove off.* 그녀는 차로 떠나면서 손을 흔들어 작별인사를 했다. / *My button fell off!* 내 단추가 떨어졌어! / *The bus stopped, and she got off.* 버스가 서자 그녀가 내렸다. **2** **turn/shut sth ↔ off** to make a machine or light stop working by pushing a button ‖ 단추를 눌러서 기계나 불이 작동을 멈추게 하다. 끄다: *Turn the lights off when you leave.* 떠날 때 불을 꺼라. / *Does the machine shut itself off?* 그 기계는 저절로 꺼집니까? **3** lower in price ‖ 가격을 더 낮춰. 할인하여: *You get 10%/15% off if you buy $100 worth of groceries.* 100달러어치의 식료품을 사면 10%[15%] 할인해 줍니다. **4** far in distance or long in time ‖ 거리가 멀거나 시간이 길어: *Spring is still a long way off.* 봄은 아직 멀다. / *mountains way off in the distance* 멀리 떨어져 있는 산들 **5** not at work or school because you are sick or on vacation ‖ 병이나 휴가 중이어서 직장이나 학교에 없어. 쉬어: *I'm taking the day/week off.* 나는 하루를/일주일을 쉬고 있다. **6** **off and on/on and off** for short periods of time, but not regularly ‖ 정기적은 아니지만 짧은 기간 동안. 때때로. 단속적으로: *I worked as a secretary off and on for three years.* 나는 3년 동안 비서로 일하다 말다 했다. —see also WELL-OFF

off² *adj* **1** removed or no longer connected ‖ 제거된, 더 이상 결합되지 않은. 떨어져 나간. 끊긴: *old paint cans with their lids off* 뚜껑이 없는 낡은 페인트 통 **2** a machine, light, or other piece of equipment that is off is not operating or not working ‖ 기계나 전등이나 다른 기구가 작동되지 않는: *Why are all the lights off?* 모든 전등이 왜 꺼졌습니까? —opposite ON³ **3** not at work or school because you are sick or on vacation ‖ 병이나 휴가 중이어서 직장이나 학교에 없는. 쉬는: *I'm off tomorrow, but I'll see you the next day.* 나는 내일 쉬지만 모레는 너를 만나겠다. **4** not correct or not of good quality ‖ 정확하지 않거나 좋은 품질이 아닌: *His calculations are off by 20%.* 그의 계산은 20%가 틀렸다. **5** an event that is off will not happen even though it has already been planned ‖ 행사가 계획된 일일지라도 거행되지 않는. 취소된: *The wedding is off. Scott and Liz had another fight.* 결혼식이 취소되었어. 스코트와 리즈가 또 싸웠어. —compare ON³ **6** **have an off day/week etc.** SPOKEN to have a day, week etc. when you are not doing something as well as you usually do ‖ 평소에 하듯이 무엇을 하지 않으며 하루·일주일을 보내다. 하루/일주일의 휴가를 얻다 **7 off season** the time in the year when a place or a business is not as busy as it usually is ‖ 장소나 사업이 평상시처럼 바쁘지 않은 그 해의 시기. 비수기. 시즌오프

off³ *prep* **1** not on something, or not touching something ‖ 어떤 것 위에 있지 않은, 어떤 것에 접하지 않은. 떨어져: *Get your feet off the couch!* 소파에서 네 발을 치워라! / *I'm taking the picture off the wall.* 나는 벽에서 그림을 떼어낼 거야. **2** away from a particular place ‖ 특정한 장소에서 떨어져: *The boat was seen just off* (=a short distance from) *the coast of Florida.* 그 보트는 플로리다 해안에서 좀 떨어진 곳에서 보였다. **3** if a room, road, building etc. is off a particular place, it is very near that place ‖ 방·도로·건물 등이 특정 장소 바로 가까이 떨어진: *Oak Hills – isn't that off Route 290?* 오크 힐스. 그건 290번 지방도로 바로 근처에 있지 않니?

off⁴ *v* [T] SLANG to kill someone ‖ 남을 죽이다

off·beat /ˌɔfˈbit/ *adj* INFORMAL unusual and not what people expect ‖ 유별나며 사람이 예상하는 것이 아닌. 색다른: *an offbeat style of comedy* 색다른 형태의 코미디

off·col·or /ˌ ˈ.../ *adj* offensive, especially in a sexual way ‖ 특히 성적으로 상스러운. 음탕한: *an off-color joke* 음탕한 농담

of·fend /əˈfɛnd/ *v* **1** [T] to make someone angry or upset ‖ 남을 화나게 하거나 기분을 상하게 하다. 감정을 해치다: *Several people were offended by Blaine's joke.* 몇몇 사람들이 블레인의 농담에 기분이 상했다. **2** [I] FORMAL to do something that is a crime ‖ 죄가 되는 일을 하다. 죄를 범하다

of·fend·er /əˈfɛndəʳ/ *n* someone who is guilty of a crime ‖ 죄를 범한 사람. 범죄자

of·fense¹ /əˈfɛns/ *n* **1** a crime ‖ 범죄: *Drinking and driving is a serious offense.* 음주 운전은 중대한 범죄이다. / *He was charged with committing several burglary offenses.* 그는 여러 차례 강도죄를 범하여 기소되었다. **2 no offense** SPOKEN said in order to show that you hope what you are saying will not offend someone ‖ 자신이 하는 말이 남의 기분을 해치지 않기 바라는 것을 나타내는 데에 쓰여. 악의는 없다[아니다]:

No offense, but your sister isn't very smart. 악의에서 하는 말은 아니지만 네 누이는 그리 영리하지 않아. **3 take offense/cause offense** to feel OFFENDed or to OFFEND someone ‖ 기분이 상하다, 남을 기분 나쁘게 하다. 화내다/화나게 하다: *Many women took offense at the tone of his speech.* 많은 여성들이 그의 연설 어조에 화를 냈다.

of·fense² /ˈɔfɛns/ *n* [U] the players in a game such as football, whose main job is to try to get points ‖ 득점을 하려는 것이 주임무인 미식축구 등의 경기의 선수. 공격진 – **offensive** *adj* —see picture on page 946

of·fen·sive¹ /əˈfɛnsɪv/ *adj* **1** used or intended for attacking ‖ 공격에 쓰이는, 공격을 노린. 공격용의: *offensive weapons* 공격용 무기 —opposite DEFENSIVE¹ **2** very rude and likely to upset people ‖ 매우 무례하고 남을 기분 나쁘게 할 것 같은. 불쾌감을 주는: *offensive jokes* 불쾌감을 주는 농담 – **offensively** *adv* – **offensiveness** *n* [U]

offensive² *n* **1** an attack made on a place by an army ‖ 군대가 어떤 장소에 가한 공격 **2 be on the offensive** to attack or criticize people ‖ 사람을 공격하거나 비난하다

of·fer¹ /ˈɔfəʳ, ˈɑfəʳ/ *v* **1** [T] to say that you are willing to give something to someone, or to hold something out to someone so that s/he can take it ‖ 남에게 어떤 것을 기꺼이 주겠다고 말하다, 어떤 것을 받아들일 수 있도록 남에게 제안하다. 제공하다. 권하다: *They've offered us $175,000 for the house.* 그들은 그 집 값으로 우리에게 17만 5천 달러를 제안했다. / *I was about to offer them some cookies.* 나는 그들에게 몇 개의 과자를 권하려는 참이었다. **2** [I, T] to say that you are willing to do something ‖ 무엇을 기꺼이 하겠다고 말하다. 뜻을 나타내다. 표명하다: *She didn't even offer to help.* 그녀는 도와주겠다는 말조차 하지 않았다.

offer² *n* **1** a statement that you are willing to give something to someone or to do something for someone ‖ 기꺼이 무엇을 남에게 주거나 기꺼이 남을 위해 무엇을 하겠다는 말. 제공. 제안: *Thanks for your offer of help.* 도와주신다고 하니 감사합니다. **2** something that is offered, especially an amount of money ‖ 특히 제안된 돈의 액수. 제시 금액: *He made me an offer of $50 for the bike.* 그는 나에게 자전거 값으로 50달러를 요구했다.

of·fer·ing /'ɔfrɪŋ, 'ɑ-/ *n* something you give someone, especially God ‖ 남, 특히 신에게 바치는 것. 공물(供物). 제물(祭物)

off·hand¹ /,ɔf'hænd-/ *adj* not giving people much time or attention when you are talking to them ‖ 사람들에게 말할 때 많은 시간이나 관심을 쏟지 않은. 무례한: *an offhand manner* 무례한 태도

offhand² *adv* immediately, without time to think ‖ 즉시, 생각할 시간 없이: *I can't give you an answer offhand – I'll have to check my notes.* 곧바로 대답할 수는 없고 메모를 확인해 봐야겠다.

of·fice /'ɔfɪs, 'ɑ-/ *n* **1** a room with a desk, telephone etc. in it where you do your work ‖ 일을 하는 곳인 책상이나 전화 등이 있는 방. 사무실: *the manager's office* 매니저의 사무실 **2** the building of a company or organization where people work ‖ 사람들이 일하는 회사나 조직체의 건물. 회사: *Are you going to the office today?* 너는 오늘 회사에 갈거니? **3** [C, U] an important job or position, especially in government ‖ 특히 정부의 중요한 일이나 직위. 관직. 공직: *She's been in office for too long.* 그녀는 너무 오랫동안 공직에 있었다. / *He holds the office of secretary.* 그는 비서직을 맡고 있다

of·fi·cer /'ɔfəsɚ, 'ɑ-/ *n* **1** someone who has a position of authority in the army, navy etc. ‖ 육군이나 해군 등에서 권위 있는 지위를 가진 사람. 지휘관. 장교 **2** a policeman ‖ 경찰관: *What's the problem, officer?* 경찰관 아저씨, 무슨 일이죠? / *Officer O'Leary* 오리어리 경찰관 **3** someone who has an important position in an organization ‖ 조직체에서 중요한 지위를 가진 사람. 임원. 간부 —see also CEO

이다: 이 클럽은 장교와 그들의 부인용이다. **official**은 권한 있는 직위를 가진 기업체나 정부 기관의 사람이다: 한 공장 임원은 100명의 근로자가 해고되리라고 발표했다. **authorities**는 조직체, 특히 정부 기관의 결정권을 지닌 사람들을 말한다: 당국자는 그 추락 사고의 원인은 알 수 없다고 말했다.

of·fi·cial¹ /ə'fɪʃəl/ *adj* approved of or done by someone in authority, especially the government ‖ 특히 정부의 권위 있는 사람이 인정하거나 행한. 공식의: *an official investigation* 공식 조사

official² *n* someone who has a responsible position in an organization ‖ 조직에서 책임 있는 지위를 가진 자. 임원. 중역: *a union official* 노동조합 임원 —see usage note at OFFICER

of·fi·cial·ly /ə'fɪʃəli/ *adv* **1** publicly and formally ‖ 공개적으로·공식적으로: *The new bridge was officially opened this morning.* 그 신축 교량은 오늘 아침에 공식적으로 개통되었다. **2** according to what you say publicly, even though this may not be true ‖ 사실이 아닐지라도 공개적으로 말한 내용에 따라. 표면상으로는: *Officially, he's on vacation, but actually he's in the hospital.* 표면상으로는 그는 휴가 중이지만 실은 그는 입원 중이다.

of·fi·ci·ate /ə'fɪʃiˌeɪt/ *v* [I] FORMAL to perform special duties, especially at a religious ceremony ‖ 특히 종교 의식에서 특별 임무를 수행하다. (사제·목사의) 역할을 하다

of·fi·cious /ə'fɪʃəs/ *adj* DISAPPROVING someone who is officious is always telling other people what to do ‖ 항상 다른 사람에게 무엇을 하라고 말하는. 참견[간섭]을 잘 하는

off·ing /'ɔfɪŋ/ *n* **be in the offing** to be about to happen ‖ 머지않아 일어날 듯하다: *I heard that there might be a promotion in the offing for you.* 나는 네가 가까운 장래에 승진될 것이라고 들었다.

off-ramp /'. ./ *n* a road for driving off A HIGHWAY or FREEWAY ‖ 주요 간선도로 또는 고속도로에서 (일반도로로) 나가는 도로. 출구 차선 —opposite ON-RAMP

off·set /,ɔf'sɛt, 'ɔfsɛt/ *v* offset, offset, offsetting [T] if something offsets another thing, it has an opposite effect so that the situation remains the same ‖ 어떤 것이 다른것과 상황이 똑같이 유지되도록 반대 효과를 가지다. 상쇄하다. 메우다: *The cost of the flight was* *offset by the cheapness of the hotel.* 항공 요금은 저렴한 호텔 비용으로 인해 상쇄되었다.

off·shoot /'ɔfʃut/ *n* an organization, system of beliefs etc. that has developed from a larger or earlier one ‖ 보다 크거나 더 이른 것에서 발전된 조직·신념 등의 체계. 분파. 파생물: *The business was an offshoot of IBM.* 그 사업체는 IBM에서 갈라져 나간 것이었다.

off·shore /ˌɔfˈʃɔr/ *adj, adv* in the water, at a distance from the shore ‖ 해안에서 떨어진 곳[물 속]에서. 앞바다에서. 앞바다의: *America's offshore oil reserves* 미국의 해양 석유 매장량 / *The ship is anchored offshore.* 그 선박은 앞바다에 정박해 있다.

off·spring /'ɔfˌsprɪŋ/ *n, plural* **offspring** 1 someone's child or children ‖ 어떤 사람의 아이 또는 아이들. 자식. 자손 2 an animal's baby or babies ‖ 동물의 새끼 또는 새끼들

off·stage /ˌɔfˈsteɪdʒ/ *adv* 1 just behind or to the side of a stage in a theater ‖ 극장의 무대 바로 뒤 또는 그 옆에서. 무대 밖에서. 안 보이는 데서: *There was a loud crash offstage.* 무대 뒤에서 부서지는 요란한 소리가 났다. 2 when an actor is not acting ‖ 배우가 연기를 하지 않을 때. 사생활에서: *What does the book tell us about Olivier's life offstage?* 그 책은 올리버의 사생활에 대한 어떤 이야기를 우리에게 해줍니까?

off-the-rec·ord /ˌ. . '. '../ *adj* an off-the-record remark is not supposed to be made public ‖ 발언 등이 공개 되지 않기로 되어 있는. 비공개의 — **off-the-record** *adv*

off-the-wall /ˌ. . '. ./ *adj* INFORMAL a little strange or unusual ‖ 약간 이상하거나 유별난. 기발한. 상식 밖의: *an off-the-wall TV show* 틀에 박히지 않은 텔레비전 쇼

of·ten /'ɔfən, 'ɔftən/ *adv* many times; frequently ‖ 여러 번. 종종. 대개; 자주: *That was fun! We should do it more often!* 그것은 재미있었어! 그것을 더 자주 해야겠어! / *How often do you come to New Orleans?* 뉴올리언스에 얼마나 자주 오십니까?

o·gle /'oʊgəl/ *v* [I, T] to look at someone in an OFFENSIVE way that shows you think s/he is sexually attractive ‖ 남이 성적으로 매력이 있다고 생각하는 것을 나타내는 무례한 태도로 다른 사람을 쳐다보다. 추파를 던지다. 곁눈질하다

o·gre /'oʊgɚ/ *n* 1 someone who seems cruel and frightening ‖ 잔인하고 무시무시하게 보이는 사람 2 a large ugly person in children's stories who eats people ‖ 사람을 잡아먹는 동화에 나오는 커다랗고 추한 사람. (동화 등의) 사람 잡아먹는 도깨비

OH the written abbreviation of Ohio ‖ Ohio(오하이오 주)의 약어

oh /oʊ/ *interjection* 1 used in phrases in order to express strong emotions or to emphasize what you think about something ‖ 강한 감정을 나타내거나 무엇에 대하여 생각하는 내용을 강조하려고 구(句)에 쓰여. 오. 저런: *"I didn't get the job." "Oh, that's too bad."* "나는 직업을 구하지 못했어." "저런, 안됐군." / *Oh no! I've lost my wallet!* 오 이런! 내 지갑을 잃어버렸어! 2 said in order to make a slight pause, especially before replying to a question or giving your opinion on something ‖ 특히 어떤 것에 대한 질문에 대답하기 전이나 의견을 말하기 전에 잠시 멈추는 데에 쓰여. 응: *"What time are you going to lunch?" "Oh, I haven't decided yet."* "몇 시에 점심 먹으러 갈 거니?" "응, 아직 결정하지 않았어."

ohm /oʊm/ *n* a unit for measuring electrical RESISTANCE ‖ 전기 저항을 측정하는 단위. 옴

oil¹ /ɔɪl/ *n* 1 [U] a smooth thick dark liquid that is burned to produce heat or used for making machines run easily ‖ 열을 내기 위해 태우거나 기계를 쉽게 작동시키는 데에 쓰이는 매끄럽고 진한 검은 액체. 기름. 오일: *motor oil* 모터 오일 2 [U] a thick dark liquid from under the ground, from which oil and GASOLINE are made; PETROLEUM ‖ 기름과 휘발유를 제조하는 것으로 지하에서 뽑아낸 걸쭉한 검은 액체. 원유. 석유; ㉤ petroleum. 3 [C, U] a smooth thick liquid made from plants or animals, used in cooking or for making beauty products ‖ 조리용 또는 제품의 윤택을 내는 데 쓰이는 동식물로 만든 매끄럽고 진한 액체. 식용유. 광택제: *olive oil* 올리브 기름 —see also OILS

oil² *v* [T] to put oil into or onto something ‖ 어떤 것에 기름을 바르다[치다. 먹이다]

oiled /ɔɪld/ *adj* covered with oil ‖ 기름으로 덮인. 기름을 친[바른]

oil paint·ing /'. . ,../ *n* [C, U] a picture painted with paint that contains oil, or all of these kinds of paintings considered as art ‖ 기름을 함유하고 있는 도료로 그린 그림, 또는 예술로 간주되는 이들 종류의 모든 그림. 유화

oils /ɔːlz/ *n* [plural] paints that contain oil ‖ 기름을 포함하고 있는 도료. 유화 물감

oil slick /'. ./ *n* a layer of oil floating on water ‖ 물 위에 떠 있는 기름 층. 유막(油膜). 기름띠

oil·y /'ɔːli/ *adj* **1** covered with oil, or containing a lot of oil ‖ 기름으로 덮인, 또는 많은 기름을 포함하고 있는. 기름[유질]의. 기름기가 많은: *an oily fish* 기름투성이의 물고기 **2** looking or feeling like oil ‖ 기름처럼 보이거나 느껴지는: *an oily liquid* 기름처럼 보이는 액체

oink /ɔɪŋk/ *n* the sound that a pig makes ‖ 돼지가 내는 소리. 돼지 울음소리. 꿀꿀 **- oink** *v* [I]

oint·ment /'ɔɪntˌmənt/ *n* [C, U] a soft oily substance that you rub into your skin, especially as a medical treatment ‖ 특히 의료용으로 피부에 바르는 연질의 기름기 많은 물질. 연고

OJ *n* [U] SPOKEN orange juice ‖ 오렌지 주스

OK¹, okay /oʊˈkeɪ/ *adj* SPOKEN **1** not ill, injured, unhappy etc. ‖ 아프지 않은·다치지 않은·불행하지 않은 등. 몸의 상태가 좋은: *Do you feel OK now?* 이제 괜찮니? **2** satisfactory or acceptable ‖ 만족스럽거나 받아들일 수 있는: *Does my hair look OK?* 내 머리가 보기에 괜찮니? **3** used in order to ask if you can do something, or to tell someone that s/he can do something ‖ 무엇을 할 수 있는 지를 묻거나 또는 남이 무엇을 할 수 있다고 말하는 데에 쓰여. 좋은. 문제 없는. 상관 않는: *"Is it OK if I leave early?" "Yes, that's OK."* "내가 일찍 떠나도 문제없니?" "그래, 상관없어." / *I'll go first, okay?* 내가 먼저 갈게, 괜찮지? **- OK** /ˌoʊˈkeɪ/, **okay** *adv* : *Is your computer working OK?* 네 컴퓨터는 작동이 잘 되고 있니? — see usage note at YES

OK², okay *interjection* **1** said when you start talking, or continue to talk after a pause ‖ 말을 시작할 때 또는 잠시 쉬었다가 말을 계속할 때 쓰여. 그런데. 그리고: *OK, can we go now?* 그런데 우리 지금 갈 수 있니? **2** said when you agree with someone ‖ 남에게 동의할 때 쓰여. 알았다. 알았어. 그래: *"We'd better be there by four." "Okay."* "우리는 4시까지 거기 가는 것이 좋겠어." "알았어."

OK³, okay *v* [T] INFORMAL to say officially that you will agree to something or allow it to happen ‖ 어떤 것에 동의하거나 무엇이 일어나는 것을 허용한다는 것을 공식적으로 말하다. …을 승인[찬성]하다: *Are you sure the bank will OK the loan?* 그 은행이 대출을 승인할 것이라고 너는 확신하니?

OK⁴, okay *n* INFORMAL **give the OK/get the OK** to give or get permission to do something ‖ 어떤 일을 하는 것에 허가를 해주거나 허가를 받다: *I got the OK to leave early.* 나는 일찍 떠나도 된다는 허락을 받았다.

OK⁵ the written abbreviation of Oklahoma ‖ Oklahoma(오클라호마 주)의 약어

old /oʊld/ *adj* **1** having lived or existed for a long time ‖ 오랫동안 살거나 존재하는. 나이 든. 오래 된: *an old man* 노인 / *We sell old and new books.* 우리는 고서와 신간을 팔고 있다. —see picture at NEW **2** having been used a lot ‖ 많이 사용해 온. 낡은: *an old pair of shoes* 헌 구두 한 짝 **3** having a particular age ‖ 특정한 나이를 가진. …세[살]의: *Our dog is three years old.* 우리 개는 세 살이다. / *my ten-year-old daughter* 나의 10살 된 딸 / *How old is Kenny?* 케니는 몇 살이니? **4 old house/job/teacher etc.** INFORMAL a house etc. that you had before but do not have now ‖ 전에 가졌으나 지금은 가지고 있지 않은 집 등. 구[예전의, 과거의] 가옥/직업/교사: *I saw your old girlfriend last night.* 나는 어젯밤에 네 옛날 여자 친구를 봤다. **5 good old/poor old etc. sb** SPOKEN used in order to talk to or about someone you know and like ‖ 알고 있고 좋아하는 사람에게 대하여 말하는 데에 쓰여. 좋은 녀석/불쌍한 녀석: *"Keith drove me home." "Good old Keith!"* "케이드가 집에까지 나를 태워다 주었어." "좋은 녀석 케이드!" **6** experienced, heard, or seen many times before; familiar ‖ 전에 여러 차례 경험한[들은, 본]. 익숙한; 친숙한: *I'm tired of listening to the same old music all the time.* 나는 언제나 똑같은 잘 아는 음악을 듣는 데 싫증이 났다. **7 an old friend/enemy etc.** a friend etc. that you have known for a long time ‖ 오랫동안 알아온 친구 등. 오랜 친구/적 **8 the old** old people ‖ 노인 —compare ANCIENT, ELDERLY —see usage note at ELDER

USAGE NOTE old and elderly

Use **old** to talk about the age of things or people: *How old are your children? / How old is your car?* Use **elderly** to be more polite when talking about people who are very old: *an elderly gentlemen in his 80s.*

사물 또는 사람의 나이에 대해 말하는 데에 **old**를 쓴다: 너의 아이들은 몇 살이니? / 너의 차는 출고 된지 몇년 되었니? 아주 나이가 많은 사람에 대해 말할 때 더 정중한 쓰임을 위해 **elderly**를 쓴다: 80대의 노신사

old·en /'ouldən/ adj LITERARY **in olden days/times** a long time ago ‖ 오래 전에. 옛날에

old-fash·ioned /ˌ. '.../ adj not modern and considered no longer fashionable ‖ 현대적이지 않은·더 이상 유행하는 것이라 생각되지 않는. 시대에 뒤떨어진. 고풍의. 옛날에 유행한: *old-fashioned ideas* 시대에 뒤떨어진 고리타분한 생각

old·ie /'ouldi/ n INFORMAL someone or something that is old, especially a song or movie ‖ 특히 노래나 영화의 오래된 사람 또는 사물

Old Tes·ta·ment /ˌ. '.../ n **the Old Testament** the part of the Bible that is about the time before the birth of Christ ‖ 예수 탄생 이전 시대에 대한 성경의 일부. 구약성서

old-tim·er /ˌ. '../ n INFORMAL **1** an old man ‖ 노인 **2** someone who has been in a particular job, place etc. for a long time ‖ 오랫동안 특정한 직업·장소 등에 있는 사람. 고참

Old World /ˌ. './ n **the Old World** Europe, and parts of Asia and Africa ‖ 유럽과 아시아·아프리카의 일부. 구세계 – **Old World** adj —compare NEW WORLD

ol·ive /'ɑlɪv/ n **1** a small black or green fruit, eaten as a vegetable or used for making oil ‖ 야채로 먹거나 기름을 짜는 데 사용하는 검거나 푸른 작은 과일. 올리브 열매 **2** [U] also **olive green** a dull pale green color ‖ 흐릿하고 엷은 푸른 색깔. 올리브색. 황록색 – **olive** adj

O·lym·pic Games /əˌlɪmpɪk 'geɪmz, ou-/, **Olympics** n [plural] an international sports event held every four years ‖ 4년마다 개최되는 국제 스포츠 행사. 올림픽 대회 – **Olympic** adj

om·buds·man /'ɑmbʊdzmən/ n someone who deals with complaints made by ordinary people against the government, banks, insurance companies etc. ‖ 정부·은행·보험 회사 등에 대한 일반 사람들의 불평을 처리하는 사람. 고충 처리 담당자

ome·let, omelette /'ɑmlɪt/ n eggs beaten together and cooked, often with other foods added ‖ 함께 휘저은 달걀에 종종 다른 음식물을 추가해서 요리한 것. 오믈렛: *a cheese omelet* 치즈 오믈렛

o·men /'oumən/ n a sign of what will happen in the future ‖ 장래에 발생할 것의 신호. 전조. 조짐. 예감: *a good/bad omen* 좋은/나쁜 징조

om·i·nous /'ɑmənəs/ adj making you feel that something bad is going to happen ‖ 어떤 나쁜 일이 일어날 것 같은 느낌이 들게 하는. 불길한. 심상치 않은: *ominous black clouds* 심상치 않은 검은 구름 – **ominously** adv

o·mis·sion /ou'mɪʃən, ə-/ n **1** [U] the act of not including or doing something ‖ 어떤 것을 포함하거나 행하지 않는 행위. 생략. 누락: *He's angry about the omission of his name from the list.* 그는 명단에서 자기의 이름을 누락시킨 데 대해 화가 나 있다. **2** something that has been OMITted ‖ 생략한 것: *The report is full of mistakes and omissions.* 그 보고서는 잘못된 것과 빠뜨린 것투성이다.

o·mit /ou'mɪt, ə-/ v **-tted, -tting** [T] to not include something, either deliberately or because you forgot to do it ‖ 고의로 또는 어떤 것을 하는 것을 잊어버려서 어떤 것을 포함하지 않다. …을 생략하다: *We decided to omit the third paragraph.* 우리는 셋째 단락을 생략하기로 결정했다.

om·nip·o·tent /ɑm'nɪpətənt/ adj FORMAL able to do everything ‖ 모든 것을 할 수 있는. 전능의 – **omnipotence** n [U]

om·ni·scient /ɑm'nɪʃənt/ adj FORMAL knowing everything ‖ 모든 것을 알고 있는. 전지(全知)의. 박식한 – **omniscience** n [U]

on¹ /ɔn, ɑn/ prep **1** touching, being supported by, or hanging from ‖ …에 접하여[지탱되어, 매달려]: *I got mud on my pants.* 내 바지에 진흙이 묻었다. / *pictures hanging on the wall* 벽에 걸려 있는 그림들 / *She was sitting on the bed.* 그녀는 침대에 앉아 있었다. **2 in a** particular place or area of land ‖ 특정한 장소에 또는 육지의 한 지역에서: *The answer is on page 44.* 그 답은 44쪽에 있다. / *Henry grew up on a farm.* 헨리는 농장에서 성장했다. / *My brother lives on Brady Road.* 나의 동생은 브래디로드에 산다. **3** at the side of something such as a road or river ‖ 도로나 강 등의 옆에: *a restaurant on the river* 강변의 레스토랑 / *cars parked on the road* 도로에 주차한 차 **4** at some time during a particular day ‖ 특정일 동안의 어느 때에. (시간적으로) …에[때에]: *The ad was in the* *newspaper on Monday.* 그 광고는 월요일 자 신문에 났다. / *It happened on my birthday.* 그것은 내 생일날에 발생했다. / *On May 10th Jo had a baby girl.* 5월 10일 날, 조는 딸아이를 낳았다. **5** being broadcast by a television or radio station ‖ 텔레비전이나 라디오 방송국에 의해 방송되는: *I heard it on the radio.* 나는 그것을 라디오로 들었다. / *The movie's on HBO tonight.* 그 영화는 오늘밤 HBO 방송에서 한다 **6** about a particular subject ‖ 특정한 주제에 대하여. …에 대한: *a book on China* 중국에 대한 책 **7** used in order to show who or what is affected by an action ‖ 누가 또는 무엇이 행동의 영향을 받는지를 나타내는 데에 쓰여: *a new tax on imported wine* 수입된 와인에 대한 새로운 세금 / *The divorce was hard on Jill.* 질에게 이혼은 힘든 것이었다. / *medical testing done on rats* 쥐에게 실시된 의학적인 실험 **8** used in order to say what has been used for doing something or to say what has made something happen ‖ 어떤 것을 하는 데 무엇이 쓰여졌는지 또는 무엇이 어떤 것을 발생하게 했는지를 말하는 데에 쓰여. …으로. …(때문)에: *Did you do these graphs on a computer?* 컴퓨터로 이 그래프를 그렸니? / *I cut myself on a piece of glass.* 나는 유리 조각에 베었다. **9** in a particular direction ‖ 특정한 방향으로. …에 향하여[대하여]: *The Mayor was sitting on my right.* (=on the right side of me) 그 시장은 내 오른편에 앉아 있었다. **10** in a vehicle such as a bus, plane, train etc. ‖ 버스·비행기·기차 등의 운송 수단으로: *I got a ticket on the last bus.* 나는 마지막 버스표를 구했다. **11 on a trip/vacation etc.** during a trip etc. ‖ 여행 등의 동안에. 여행/휴가 중에: *They met on a trip to Spain.* 그들은 스페인 여행 중에 만났다. **12** part of a team or group that works together ‖ 같이 일하는 팀 또는 집단의 일원. …의 일원으로[인]: *Are you on the soccer team?* 너는 그 축구 팀의 일원이니? **13 have/carry sth on you** to have something with you now ‖ 현재 어떤 것을 가지고 있다: *Do you have a pen on you?* 지금 너는 펜을 가지고 있니? **14** SPOKEN used in order to say that someone is paying for something ‖ 사람이 어떤 것의 값을 지불할 것이라고 말하는 데에 쓰여: *Dinner's on me, tonight.* 오늘 저녁은 내가 산다. **15** INFORMAL if something bad happens on someone, it happens when s/he is not expecting it ‖ 예상하지 못하고 있을 때 어떤 사람에게 나쁜 일이 발생하는:

You can't just quit on me! 너는 지금 나를 자르지 못해! **16** INFORMAL taking a medicine or drugs ‖ 내복약 또는 마약을 복용하는: *She's on antibiotics.* 그녀는 항생 물질을 복용하고 있다.

on² *adv* **1** continuing without stopping ‖ 중지하지 않고 계속하는: *"I'm not sure if…." "Go on, what were you going to say?"* "저, 확신할 수는 없는데." "계속해, 무슨 말을 하려고 하느냐?" / *The peace talks dragged on* (=continued slowly) *for months.* 평화 회담은 수개월째 지지부진했다. **2** forward or ahead, toward a particular place ‖ 앞으로, 특정한 장소를 향해: *We were tired from the climb, but Steve wanted to go on.* 우리는 등반하느라 지쳤지만 스티브는 전진하기를 원했다. **3** continuing into the future ‖ 장래에 계속하는. 줄곧: *From that day on he hasn't drunk any alcohol.* 그 날 이후 줄곧 그는 어떤 술도 입에 대지 않았다. **4** if you have a piece of clothing on, you are wearing it ‖ 옷을 입고 있는. 몸에 지니고 [신고, 쓰고, 걸치고] 있는: *Put your coat on, it's cold out.* 네 코트를 입어라. 밖이 춥다. **5** operating or working ‖ 작동하고 있는. (기계 등이)움직이고 있는: *Could you turn/switch on the lights, please?* (=push the button that makes them work) 전깃불 좀 켜 주시겠어요? —opposite OFF¹ **6** into a vehicle such as a bus, plane, or train ‖ 버스[비행기, 기차] 등의 운송 수단에 타는: *I got on at Vine Street.* 나는 바인 거리에서 탔다. **7** ⇨ **off and on/on and off** (OFF¹) —see also HEAD-ON, **later on** (LATER¹)

on³ *adj* **1** if a film or television show is on, it is being broadcast or shown ‖ 영화나 텔레비전 쇼가 방송되거나 보여지는: *The local news will be on in a minute.* 지역 뉴스는 잠시 후에 계속됩니다. / *What's on at the Rialto Theater tonight?* 오늘밤 리알토 극장에서는 무슨 공연이 있습니까? **2** operating or working ‖ 작동하는. (기계 등이) 움직이는: *The fax machine isn't on.* 팩스가 작동하지 않는다. —opposite OFF² **3** if an event is on, it will happen ‖ 행사 등이 있을 예정인: *There's a Jazz Festival on at the lake this weekend.* 이번 주말에 호숫가에서는 재즈 페스티벌이 있을 예정이다.

once¹ /wʌns/ *adv* **1** on one occasion, or at one time ‖ 한 번. 1회: *"Have you been to Texas?" "Yes, but only once."* "텍사스에 가본 적이 있니?" "그래, 하지만 딱 한 번 가봤어." / *He told me once he didn't like Thai food.* 그는 태국 음식을 좋아하지 않는다고 나에게 한 번 말했

다. / *He tried skiing once before but he didn't like it.* 그는 전에 한 번 스키를 타 보려고 했지만 좋아하지는 않았다. **2 once a week/year etc.** one time every week, year etc. as a regular activity ‖ 규칙적인 활동으로서 매주·매년 등에 한 번. 일주일/일년에 한 번: *She goes to the gym once a week.* 그녀는 일주일에 한 번 체육관에 간다. **3 (every) once in a while** sometimes, but not often ‖ 자주는 아니지만 때때로. 이따금: *My uncle sends us money every once in a while.* 나의 삼촌은 이따금 우리에게 돈을 보낸다. **4 once more** one more time; again ‖ 한 번 더; 다시: *I'll call him once more, but then we have to leave.* 내가 그에게 한 번 더 전화를 하고 나서 우리는 출발해야겠다. **5 at once a)** at the same time ‖ 동시에. 한꺼번에: *I can't do two things at once!* 나는 동시에 두 가지 일을 할 수 없어! **b)** FORMAL immediately or without waiting ‖ 즉시, 기다리지 않고. 곧. 당장에: *Everybody knew at once how serious the situation was.* 모두들 상황이 얼마나 심각한지를 즉시 알았다. **6 all at once** suddenly ‖ 갑자기. 별안간: *All at once, the room went quiet.* 갑자기 그 방은 조용해졌다. **7** in the past, but not now ‖ 지금은 아니지만 과거에. 이전에. 일찍이: *He must have been good-looking once.* 그는 분명히 옛날에는 미남이었을 것이다. **8 for once** SPOKEN used in order to say that something should happen more often ‖ 어떤 것이 더 자주 발생해야 한다고 말하는 데에 쓰여. 한 번뿐. 한 번만은: *"Where's Mark?" "He's washing the dishes, for once."* "마크가 어디 있니?" "그는 이번 뿐이지만, 설거지를 하고 있다." **9 once and for all** definitely and finally ‖ 단호하게·최종적으로. 끝으로 한 번만 더 (말하여). 딱 잘라서: *Let's settle this once and for all.* 이것을 최종적으로 해결하자. **10 once upon a time** a phrase meaning a long time ago, used in children's stories ‖ 동화에 사용되는 오래 전을 의미하는 어구. 먼 옛날에 **11 once in a blue moon** very rarely ‖ 극히 드물게: *He comes to see us once in a blue moon.* 그는 아주 가끔 우리를 찾아온다.

once² *conjunction* from the time something happens ‖ 어떤 것이 일어난 때로부터. 한 번[일단] …하면. …하자마자: *Once you try this, you'll never want to stop.* 일단 이것을 해보면, 너는 결코 중지하고 싶지 않을 것이다.

once·o·ver /ˈ. ˌ../ *n* INFORMAL **give sb/sth the once-over** to look at or examine someone or something quickly ‖ 신속히 사람 또는 사물을 보거나 살펴보다. …을 대충 훑어보다: *Ollie gave the car the once-over and decided not to buy it.* 올리는 그 자동차를 대충 훑어보고 나서 사지 않기로 결정했다.

on·com·ing /ˈɔn.kʌmɪŋ, ˈɑn-/ *adj* **oncoming car/traffic etc.** a car etc. that is coming toward you ‖ 다가오고 있는 자동차/대면 통행. 접근하는 자동차/대면 통행

one¹ /wʌn/ *number* **1** 1 ‖ 1 **2** one o'clock ‖ 1시: *I have a meeting at one.* 나는 1시에 회의가 있다.

one² *pron* **1** someone or something that has been mentioned or is known about ‖ 언급되거나 알려진 사람 또는 사물. (그것의) 한 사람. 하나: *"Do you have a bike?" "No, but I'm getting one for my birthday."* "너 자전거 있니?" "아니, 그런데 내 생일날 한 대 얻을 거다." / *"Do you know where those books are?" "Which ones?"* "그 책들이 어디 있는지 아니?" "어느 책들?" / *"Which candy bar do you want?" "This/that one."* "어떤 막대 캔디를 갖고 싶니?" "이[저] 캔디 바." / *Jane's the one with the red hair.* 머리가 빨간 사람이 바로 제인이다. **2 one by one** if people do something one by one, first one person does it, then the next etc. ‖ 한 사람이 먼저 무엇을 하고 나서 다음 사람 등이 하다. 한 사람[하나]씩 차례로: *One by one, the passengers got off the bus.* 승객들은 한 사람씩 차례로 버스에서 내렸다. **3 one after the other/one after another** if events or actions happen one after the other, they happen without much time between them ‖ 사건이나 행동 등이 많은 시간의 간격이 없이 일어나다. 차례차례로. 잇따라. 번갈아: *He's had one problem after another this year.* 그에게는 금년에 잇따라 문제가 발생했다. **4 (all) in one** used in order to say that something has many functions or works in many ways ‖ 사물이 많은 기능을 갖추고 있거나 여러 방식으로 작동한다는 것을 말하는 데에 쓰여. 하나로[혼자서] 모두를 겸하여: *This is a TV, radio, and VCR all in one.* 이것은 하나로, 텔레비전·라디오·VCR을 전부 겸하고 있다. **5** FORMAL **a)** people in general ‖ 일반적인 사람들. 누구나: *One must be careful to keep exact records.* 누구나 정확한 기록을 유지하도록 유의해야 한다. **b)** used in order to mean "I" ‖ "나"를 의미하는 데 쓰여: *One is tempted to ignore the whole problem.* 나는 모든 문제를 묵살하고 싶은 기분이 든다. **6 have had one too many** INFORMAL to have drunk too much alcohol ‖ 너무 많이 술을 마시다. 만취하다

one³ *determiner* **1** a word meaning a particular person or thing, used especially when there are others of the same kind ‖ 특히 같은 종류의 다른 것들이 있을 때 사용되는 특정한 사람이나 사물을 의미하는 어휘. 한 사람, 하나: *One reason I like the house is because of the big kitchen.* 내가 그 집을 좋아하는 한 가지 이유는 부엌이 크기 때문이다. / *One of the children is sick.* 아이들 중 한 명이 아프다. ✗DON'T SAY "One of the children are sick."✗ "One of the children are sick."처럼 복수형을 받지는 않는다. **2 one day/afternoon etc. a)** a particular day etc. in the past ‖ 과거의 특정한 날 등. (과거의) 어느 날/어느(날) 오후: *There was one week in April last year when we had two feet of snow.* 2피트의 눈이 왔던 때는 지난해 4월의 한 주였다. **b)** any day etc. in the future ‖ 미래의 어떤 일자 등: *Let's go shopping one Saturday when we're less busy.* 아무 토요일이나 우리가 덜 바쁠 때 쇼핑 가자. **3** only ‖ 오로지. 오직 하나의. 유일한: *My one worry is that she will decide to leave college.* 나의 유일한 걱정은 그녀가 대학을 자퇴하기로 결정할 것이라는 것이다. **4** SPOKEN used in order to emphasize your description of someone or something ‖ 사람이나 사물의 설명을 강조하는 데에 쓰여: *That is one cute kid!* 저 애는 정말 귀여운 아이야!

one⁴ *n* a piece of paper money worth $1 ‖ 1달러의 지폐

one an·oth·er /ˌ. .ˈ./ *pron* FORMAL ⇨ EACH OTHER: *The two men shook hands and thanked one another.* 그 두 남자는 악수를 하고 서로에게 감사함을 표시했다. —see usage note at EACH OTHER

one·lin·er /ˌ. ˈ../ *n* a very short joke ‖ 매우 짧은 농담

one-night stand /ˌ. . ˈ./ *n* INFORMAL an occasion when two people have sex, but do not intend to meet each other again ‖ 두 사람이 성관계를 갖지만 서로 다시 만날 의도가 없는 경우. 하룻밤만의 정사

one-of-a-kind /ˌ. . . ˈ./ *adj* special because no one else or nothing else is like him, her, or it ‖ 사람이나 사물이 그 어떤 사람이나 사물과도 같지 않아서 특별한. 유일한: *one-of-a-kind handmade carpets* 세상에 둘도 없는 수제(手製)양탄자

one-on-one /ˌ. . ˈ./ *adv* between only you and one other person ‖ 오직 한 사람과 다른 한 사람 사이에. 1대1로: *We're working one-on-one with the students to help them.* 우리는 그들을 돕기 위해 학생들과 1대1로 작업하고 있다.

on·er·ous /ˈɑnərəs, ˈoʊ-/ *adj* FORMAL difficult and tiring ‖ 힘들고 지치게 하는. 성가신. 짐이 되는: *onerous duties* 부담이 되는 의무

one-sid·ed /ˌ. ˈ../ *adj* **1** considering or showing only one side of a question, subject etc. in a way that is unfair ‖ 불공평한 방식으로 문제·주제 등의 한 쪽 (면)만을 고려하거나 나타내는. 편파적인. 한 쪽으로 치우친: *a one-sided view of the problem* 그 문제에 대한 편파적인 견해 **2** an activity or competition that is one-sided is one in which one person or team is much stronger than the other ‖ 활동·시합 등에서 한 사람이나 한 팀이 다른 쪽보다 훨씬 더 강한. 일방적인. 차가 크게 나는: *a one-sided football game* 일방적으로 한 쪽이 우세한 축구 경기

one·time /ˈwʌntaɪm/ *adj* former ‖ 전의. 한때. 일찍이: *Mitchell, a onetime carpenter, is now a successful writer.* 한때 목수였던 미첼은 지금은 성공한 작가이다.

one-to-one /ˌ. . ˈ./ *adj* **1** between only two people ‖ 단 두 사람 사이의. 일대 일의: *tuition on a one-to-one basis* 일대 일 원칙의 교습 **2** matching one other person, thing etc. exactly ‖ 정확하게 다른 하나의 사람·사물 등과 일치되는. 일대 일로 대응하는: *a one-to-one correspondence between sound and symbol* 소리와 기호의 일 대 일의 대응

one-track mind /ˌ. . ˈ./ *n* have a one-track mind to think about only one thing all the time ‖ 언제나 한 가지 일에 대해서만 생각하는: *All you ever talk about is baseball! You have a one-track mind.* 네가 말하는 모든 것은 늘 야구에 관한 것 뿐이야! 너는 한 가지만 아는 사람이야.

one-up·man·ship /ˌwʌnˈʌpmən.ʃɪp/ *n* [U] attempts to make yourself seem better than other people ‖ 자기 자신을 남들보다 더 낫게 보이게 하려는 시도. 한 발[한 수] 앞서기

one-way /ˌ. ˈ./ *adj* **1** moving or allowing movement in only one direction ‖ 오로지 한 방향으로만 움직이거나 이동을 허용하는. 일방통행의. 편도의: *one-way traffic* 일방통행 / *a one-way street* 일방통행 거리 **2** a one-way ticket is for taking a trip from one place to another but not back again ‖ 표가 한 장소에서 다른 장소로 여행은 하지만 다시

돌아오기 위한 것이 아닌. 편도의 —see also ROUND-TRIP

on·go·ing /ˈɒnˌɡəʊɪŋ, ˈɑn-/ *adj* continuing ‖ 계속하고 있는. 진행 중인: *ongoing discussions* 진행 중인 토론

on·ion /ˈʌnyən/ *n* [C, U] a round white yellow or red vegetable with many layers, that has a strong taste and smell ‖ 강한 맛과 냄새가 나는 (껍질이) 많은 층을 가진 둥그렇고 희면서 노랗거나 빨간 야채. 양파 —see picture on page 944

on-line, online /ˌ. ˈ./ *adj, adv* **1** directly connected to or controlled by a computer ‖ 컴퓨터에 또는 컴퓨터로 직접 연결되거나 통제되는. 온라인의. 온라인으로: *an on-line printer* 온라인 프린터 **2** connected to many other computers, especially computers that are on the INTERNET ‖ 많은 다른 컴퓨터 특히 인터넷에 접속되어 있는 컴퓨터에 연결된: *All of our local schools will be/go on line by the end of the year.* 우리 지역의 모든 학교들은 금년 말까지는 인터넷으로 연결될 것이다. —see culture note at INTERNET

online auc·tion /ˌ.. ˈ../ *n* a type of WEBSITE in which you can sell things to the person who offers you the highest price ‖ 자신에게 최고 가격을 제시하는 사람에게 물건을 팔 수 있는 유형의 웹 사이트. 온라인 경매(사이트)

online bank·ing /ˌ.. ˈ../ *n* [U] ⇨ INTERNET BANKING

on·look·er /ˈɒnˌlʊkɚ, ˈɑn-/ *n* someone who watches something happening without being involved in it ‖ 관여되어 있지 않고 어떤 일의 발생을 지켜보는 사람. 방관자. 구경꾼

on·ly¹ /ˈoʊnli/ *adv* **1** not more than a particular amount, number, age etc., especially when this is unusual ‖ 특히 보통이 아닌 때에 특정한 분량·수·연령 등보다 많지 않은. 오로지 …에 한하여. 단지 …만. 다만 …뿐: *Tammy was only 9 months old when she learned to walk.* 태미가 걸음마를 배웠을 때는 겨우 9개월에 지나지 않았었다. / *That TV only costs $55!* 저 텔레비전은 겨우 55달러 나간다. **2** nothing or no one except the person or thing mentioned ‖ 언급한 사람이나 사물을 제외하고는 아무(것)도 없이. 오직: *You're only wearing a T-shirt. No wonder you're cold.* 너 혼자만 티셔츠를 입고 있잖아, 그러니까 네가 추운 것은 당연하지. / *This parking lot is for restaurant customers only.* 이 주차장은 식당 고객 전용입니다. **3** in one place, situation, or way and no other, or for one reason and no other ‖ 다른 것이 아

닌 한 장소[상황, 방식]로만, 또는 다른 이유가 아닌 한 이유로만: *You can only get to the lake with a four-wheel-drive vehicle.* 너는 4륜 구동 차량으로는 호수까지만 갈 수 있다. / *You're only doing this because you think he'll pay you for it!* 네가 이것을 하고 있는 이유는 단지 그가 너에게 돈을 지불할 것이라고 생각하기 때문이잖아. **4** not better, worse, or more important than someone or something ‖ 어떤 사람이나 사물보다 더 좋지[나쁘지, 중요하지] 않은. 고작. 다만: *Steph's only the assistant manager.* 스테프는 고작 부지배인이다. / *I was only kidding.* 나는 그저 농담이었다. **5 not only…(but)** used in order to say that something is even better, worse, or more surprising than what you have just said ‖ 어떤 것이 방금 말한 것보다 더욱 좋다는[나쁘다는, 더 놀랍다는] 것을 말하는 데에 쓰여. …뿐만 아니라 (…역시): *Math is not only easy for her, it's fun.* 수학은 그녀에게는 쉬울 뿐만 아니라 재미있기도 하다. **6** FORMAL no earlier than a particular time ‖ 특정한 시간보다 더 이르지 않게. 겨우…. 불과…: *Congress passed the law only last year.* 의회는 바로 지난해에 그 법률을 통과시켰다. **7 only just a)** a very short time ago ‖ 매우 짧은 시간 바로 전에. 방금. 지금 막: *We're only just beginning the treatment.* 우리는 지금 막 치료를 시작하고 있다. **b)** almost not; hardly ‖ 거의 …아니다[않다]. 간신히. 겨우: *There's only just room here for two people.* 여기는 겨우 두 사람이 들어갈 수 있는 공간이 있다. **8 if only a)** used in order to give a reason for something, and say that it is not a good one ‖ 어떤 것에 대한 이유를 제시하면서 그 어떤 것이 달가운 것은 아니란 것을 말하는 데에 쓰여. 오직 …하기만 하면 (좋으련만): *Just call her, if only to say you're sorry.* 그녀에게 그냥 전화해서, 네가 미안하다는 말을 하기만 하면 좋으련만. **b)** used in order to express a strong wish ‖ 강한 소망을 나타내는 데에 쓰여: *If only I could have gone to the funeral.* 내가 장례식에 갈 수 있었더라면 좋았을 텐데. **9 only too** very or completely ‖ 매우 완전히. 아주: *He was only too ready to earn some more money.* 그는 약간의 돈을 더 벌기 위한 준비가 잘 되어 있었다.

USAGE NOTE only

The meaning of a sentence can change depending on where you use **only**. Always put **only** just before the word that it describes: *Only John saw the lion.* (=no one except John saw the lion) / *John only saw the lion.* (=he saw it, but he did not do anything else to it, such as take a photograph of it) / *John saw only the lion.* (=the lion was the only animal he saw)

only를 어디에 쓰는지에 따라서 문장의 의미가 바뀔 수 있다. 항상 설명하는 어휘 바로 앞에 **only**를 쓴다: 존만이 그 사자를 보았다. / 존은 그 사자를 보기만 했다. / 존은 그 사자만을 보았다.

only² *adj* **1** with no others of the same kind ‖ 같은 종류의 다른 것은 없는. 유일한. …뿐: *She's the only person I know who doesn't like chocolate.* 그녀는 초콜릿을 좋아하지 않는 내가 아는 유일한 사람이다. / *Walking is the only exercise I get.* 걷기는 내가 하는 유일한 운동이다. **2** an only child does not have any brothers or sisters ‖ 아이가 형제나 자매가 없는. 독자의. 외아들[외동딸]인 **3 the only thing is**… SPOKEN used before you begin to talk about something that might be a problem ‖ 문제가 될지 모르는 것에 대하여 말하기 시작하기 전에 쓰여. 단 한 가지 곤란한 점은…: *I'd like to come see you, the only thing is my car's being fixed.* 나는 너를 보러 가고 싶지만 단 한 가지 곤란한 점은 내 차가 지금 수리 중이라는 거야.

only³ *conjunction* except that; but ‖ 어떤 것을 제외하고는; …만 없다면: *We were going to go fishing, only it started raining.* 비가 오기 시작하지 않았다면 우리는 낚시하러 갔을 것이다.

on-ramp /'. ./ *n* a road for driving onto a HIGHWAY or FREEWAY ‖ (일반 도로에서) 주요 간선도로나 고속도로로 들어가는 도로. 온램프 —opposite OFF-RAMP

on-rush /'ɔnrʌʃ, 'an-/ *n* [singular] a strong movement forward ‖ 전진하는 강한 움직임. 돌진. 돌격: *a sudden onrush of water* 갑작스런 물의 분류(奔流)

on-set /'ɔnsɛt, 'an-/ *n* **the onset of** the beginning of something ‖ 어떤 것의 시작. 개시. 출발. 착수: *the onset of a bad cold* 독감의 징후

on-slaught /'ɑnslɔt, 'ɔn-/ *n* a very strong attack ‖ 매우 강한 공격. 맹공격

on-to /*before consonants* 자음 앞에서 'ɔntə, 'an-; *before vowels and strong* 모음과 강형 앞에서 'ɔntu, 'an-/ *prep* **1** used with verbs showing movement, to mean in or on a particular place ‖ 동작을 나타내는 동사와 함께. 특정 장소의 안

이나 위를 의미하는 데 쓰여. …의 위에: *The cat jumped onto the kitchen table.* 그 고양이는 식탁 위에 뛰어올랐다. / *How did he get onto the roof?* 그는 어떻게 지붕 위에 올라갔니? / *When you turn onto River Road, you'll see the church.* 리버로드 쪽으로 돌면 교회가 보일 것이다. **2 be onto sb** INFORMAL to know who did something wrong or illegal ‖ 나쁜 짓이나 불법을 저지른 자를 알다: *He was scared. He knows we're onto him.* 그는 겁을 먹었어. 자신이 저지른 짓을 우리가 알고 있다는 것을 그는 알고 있어.

o·nus /'ounəs/ *n* **the onus** the responsibility for something ‖ 어떤 것에 대한 책임. 부담. 의무: *The onus is on the company to provide safety equipment.* 회사에 안전 장비를 제공할 책임이 있다.

on·ward¹ /'ɔnwəd, 'an-/, **onwards** *adv* **1 from**…**onward** beginning at a particular time and continuing into the future ‖ 특정한 시간에 시작하여 미래로 계속 이어지는. …부터 계속: *European History from 1900 onward* 1900년 이후의 유럽의 역사 **2** forward ‖ 앞으로. 나아가서: *The ship moved onward through the fog.* 그 선박은 안개를 뚫고 나아갔다.

on·ward² *adj* **1** moving forward or continuing ‖ 앞으로 움직이거나 계속하는. 전진적인: *the onward journey* 계속되는 여행 **2** developing over a period of time ‖ 일정 기간에 걸쳐 발전하는. 향상하는: *the onward march of scientific progress* 과학 발달의 진전

oo·dles /'udlz/ *n* [plural] INFORMAL a large amount of something ‖ 어떤 것의 큰 분량. 다량. 풍부함: *oodles of fun* 큰 재미

oops /ups, ups/ *interjection* said when someone has fallen, dropped something, or made a small mistake ‖ 사람이 넘어지거나 어떤 것을 떨어뜨리거나 작은 실수를 했을 때에 쓰여. 이런. 아차. 아이쿠: *Oops! I spilled the milk!* 이런! 우유를 엎질렀어!

ooze¹ /uz/ *v* [I, T] **1** if a liquid oozes from something or if something oozes a liquid, liquid flows from it very slowly ‖ 액체가 어떤 것에서 아주 천천히 흘러나오다. 스며[새어] 나오다: *Blood was oozing from the cut* 피가 벤 상처에서 흘러나오고 있었다. **2** INFORMAL to show a lot of a particular quality ‖ 특정한 성질을 많이 나타내다. 발산하다[시키다]. 스며나오[게 하]다: *Leo's voice oozed sarcasm.* 레오의 목소리에서 빈정거림이 배어 나왔다.

ooze² *n* [U] very soft mud, especially at

the bottom of a lake or river ‖ 특히 호수
나 강 바닥에 있는 아주 부드러운 진흙

o·pal /ˈoʊpəl/ *n* [C, U] a white stone
used in jewelry that has other colors in
it that show when light shines on it ‖ 빛
을 비추었을 때 다른 색깔을 띄는, 보석박
힌 장신구류에 사용되는 하얀 보석. 단백
석. 오팔

o·paque /oʊˈpeɪk/ *adj* **1** not
transparent ‖ 투명하지 않은. 불투명한 **2**
hard to understand ‖ 이해하기 어려운.
불명료한 —compare TRANSPARENT

OPEC /ˈoʊpɛk/ *n* [U] Organization of
Petroleum Exporting Countries; an
organization of countries that produce
and sell oil, which sets the price of the
oil ‖ Organization of Petroleum
Exporting Countries(석유 수출국 기구)의
약어; 석유를 생산·판매하는 국가들의 기
구로 석유 가격을 결정함

open

o·pen¹ /ˈoʊpən/ *adj*

1 ▶OPEN 열린◀ not closed ‖ 닫지 않은.
열려 있는: *Who left the window open?* 누
가 창문을 열어 놓았니? / *I can barely
keep my eyes open, I'm so tired.* 나는 간
신히 눈을 뜰 수 있다. 나는 아주 지쳤다.
/ *A book lay open on the table.* 책 한 권
이 테이블 위에 펼쳐져 있었다.

2 ▶STORES/BANKS ETC. 가게/은행 등◀
ready for business, and letting
customers come in ‖ 영업을 준비하고 고
객을 들이는. 영업중인: *We're open until
six o'clock.* 우리는 6시까지 영업한다. /
Are the bars still open? 술집들이 아직 영
업하고 있니?

3 ▶PUBLIC USE 공용(公用)◀ ready or
available to be used by the public ‖ (일
반)대중들이 사용하도록 준비되거나 가능
한: *When is the new library going to be
open?* 그 새 도서관은 언제 개관합니까?
/ *The pool is only open to the public in
the summer.* 그 수영장은 여름에 일반에
게 개장할 뿐이다.

4 ▶NOT RESTRICTED 제한되지 않은◀
available to anyone, so that anyone can
take part ‖ 누구나 이용할 수 있어서 누구
라도 참여할 수 있는. 개방되어 있는: *Few

*jobs were open to women before World
War I.* 제1차 세계 대전 이전에는 극히 소
수의 직업만이 여성에게 개방되어 있었다.
/ *an open meeting* 공개 회의

5 ▶NOT ENCLOSED 둘러싸이지 않은◀
not enclosed or covered by buildings,
walls etc. ‖ 건물·벽 등에 의해 가로막히거
나 가려지지 않은. 탁 트인. 전망이 좋은:
driving in the open country 탁 트인 시
골 길의 드라이브 / *an open fire* 노천 (장
작)불

6 ▶NOT SECRET 비밀스럽지 않은◀ not
hiding anything ‖ 아무것도 숨기지 않은.
숨김없는: *Ralph looked at her with open
admiration.* 랄프는 숨김없는 찬사를 하면
서 그녀를 바라보았다.

7 ▶WILLING TO LISTEN 듣고자 하는◀
willing to listen to other people ‖ 다른 사
람에게 기꺼이 귀를 기울이는. 열린 마음
의. 편견이 없는: *Keep an open mind*
(=listen without judging) *until you've
heard everyone's ideas.* 모든 사람의 생
각을 들을 때까지 편견을 갖지 마라. /
*We're open to suggestions on how to
improve our service.* 우리는 어떻게 하면
우리의 서비스를 개선할 수 있을 것인가에
관한 제안을 받아들일 용의가 있다.

8 ▶HONEST 정직한◀ honest and not
wanting to hide anything ‖ 정직하고 어
떤 것이라도 숨기려고 하지 않는. 솔직한:
*My husband and I try to be open with
each other.* 나의 남편과 나는 서로 솔직하
려고 노력한다.

9 be open to criticism/discussion etc.
able to be criticized, discussed etc. ‖ 비
판받을 수 있는·논의될 수 있는 등. 비판/
논의의 소지가 있다: *Her comments were
open to misunderstanding.* 그녀의 논평
은 오해의 소지가 있었다.

10 ▶NOT DECIDED 결정되지 않은◀ not
finally decided ‖ 최종적으로 결정되지 않
은. 미정[미결]의: *The location of the
peace talks is still an open question.* 평
화 회담의 장소는 아직 미정이다. / *We'll
leave the discussion open until more
information is available.* 우리는 더 많은
정보를 이용할 수 있을 때까지 그 토의를
미결인 채로 남겨 두겠다.

11 keep your eyes/ears open SPOKEN
to keep looking or listening so that you
will notice anything that is important ‖
중요한 것을 인식하도록 계속해서 지켜보
거나 듣다. 눈여겨 지켜보다/귀를 기울여
듣다

12 welcome/greet sb with open arms
to greet someone with happiness and
excitement ‖ 즐거움과 흥분으로 사람을
맞이하다. 진심으로 환영/응대하다: *The

European visitors were welcomed by local people with open arms. 유럽의 방문자들은 지역민들로부터 진심어린 환대를 받았다.

open² *v* also **open up 1** [I, T] to become open, or to make something open ‖ 열리다, 열다: *Dan's opening his birthday presents.* 댄은 생일 선물을 열어보고 있다. / *Open up the window.* 창문을 열어라 / *a door that opens automatically* 자동으로 열리는 문 **2** [I] if a store, bank, or public building opens at a particular time, it begins to allow people inside at that time ‖ 상점·은행·공공건물이 특정한 시간에 사람들을 안에 들어오게 허용하기 시작하다. 개점하다: *What time does the bookstore open on Sundays?* 그 서점은 일요일에는 몇 시에 개점하니? **3** [I, T] to start, or to make something do this ‖ 시작하다, 시작되다: *The restaurant opens next month.* 그 식당은 다음달에 개점한다. / *a new play opening on Broadway* 브로드웨이에서 개막할 새 연극 / *He opened up a checking account at First National Bank.* 그는 퍼스트 내셔널 은행에 당좌 예금 계좌를 개설했다. **4** [I, T] to spread something out, or become spread out ‖ 어떤 것을 펼치다, 또는 펼쳐지다: *I can't open my umbrella.* 우산을 펼칠 수가 없다. / *The roses are starting to open up.* 장미가 꽃을 피우기 시작했다. / *Open your books to page 153.* 책 153쪽을 펴라. **5** [T] to make something available to be used or visited ‖ 어떤 곳을 이용하거나 방문할 수 있게 하다: *They're plowing the snow to open up the roads.* 그들은 길을 트기 위해 눈을 밀어제치고 나아가고 있다. / *Parts of the White House will be opened to the public.* 백악관의 일부가 일반에 공개될 것이다. **6 open fire (on)** to start shooting at someone or something ‖ 사람이나 사물에 사격을 개시하다

open into/onto sth *phr v* [T] to lead directly into a place ‖ 직접적으로 어떤 장소에 이르다. …으로 통하다: *The kitchen opens onto the back yard.* 부엌은 뒤뜰로 통한다.

open up *phr v* **1** [I] to stop being shy and say what you really think ‖ 부끄러워 하지 않고 자신이 실제 생각하고 있는 것을 말하다. 마음을 터놓다: *Once Ann gets to know you, she'll open up.* 앤이 일단 너를 알게 되기만 하면 그녀는 생각을 거리낌 없이 말할 것이다. **2** [I,T **open** sth ↔ **up**] to become available or possible, or to make something available or

possible ‖ 이용할 수 있거나 가능해지다, 또는 이렇게 만들다: *Education opens up all kinds of opportunities.* 교육은 모든 종류의 기회를 잡을 수 있게 한다.

USAGE NOTE open, close, turn on, and turn off

Use **open** and **close** to talk about objects such as doors, windows, or boxes: *Let's open a window; it's warm in here.* Use **turn on** and **turn off** to talk about water or gas, or about things that use electricity: *Turn on the TV; there's a good show on now.* 출입문·창문·상자 등의 물체에 대해 말하는 데에는 **open**과 **close**를 쓴다: 창문을 열자, 실내가 덥다. 수도·가스·전기를 사용하는 물건에 대해 말할 때는 **turn on**과 **turn off**를 사용한다: 텔레비전을 켜라. 지금 재미있는 쇼를 한다.

---

open³ *n* **(out) in the open** **a)** outdoors ‖ 옥외[야외]에서: *It's fun to eat out in the open.* 야외에 나와서 식사하는 것은 즐겁다. **b)** not hidden or secret ‖ 숨김이나 비밀이 없는. 주지(周知)하는. 공공연한: *The truth is finally out in the open.* 진실은 마침내 드러난다.

open-air /ˌ.. '../ *adj* outdoor ‖ 야외의: *open-air concerts* 야외 콘서트

open-and-shut case /ˌ.. .ˌ. '../ *n* something such as a law case that is very easy to prove ‖ 증명하기가 아주 용이한 소송 사건 등의 일. 간단히 해결할 수 있는[아주 단순한] 일[사건]

open-end-ed /ˌ.. '../ *adj* without a fixed ending time ‖ 지정된 만기가 없는. (기간 등이) 제한이 없는: *an open-ended job contract* 기간의 제한이 없는 근무 계약

o·pen·er /ˈoʊpənɚ/ *n* **1** a tool or machine used in order to open letters, bottles, or cans ‖ 편지·병·캔을 여는 데에 쓰는 도구나 기계. 따개. 따는 도구: *an electric can opener* 전기 캔 따개 **2** the first of a series of things such as sports competitions ‖ 스포츠 경기 등의 시리즈의 첫 번째의 것: *the opener against the Celtics* 셀틱스 팀을 상대로 한 개막전

open-heart sur·gery /ˌ.. .ˌ. '../ *n* [U] a medical operation in which doctors operate on someone's heart ‖ 의사가 사람의 심장을 수술하는 의학적인 수술. 심장 절개 수술

open house /ˌ.. '../ *n* **1** an occasion when a school or business allows the public to come in and see the work that is done there ‖ 학교나 기업이 일반에게 성취한 과업을 참관하게 허용하는 일. 일반 공개일. 수업 참관일 **2** a party that you can come to or leave at any time during a particular period ‖ 특정 기간 동안 아무 때나 오거나 갈 수 있는 파티. 공개 파티: *an open house from 2-6 p.m.* 오후 2시에서 6시 사이의 공개 파티

o·pen·ing¹ /'oʊpənɪŋ/ *n* **1** an occasion when a new business, building etc. is ready for use ‖ 새로운 사업·건물 등이 이용할 준비가 된 경우. 개시. 개막: *the opening of the new art gallery* 신축 미술관의 개관 **2** the beginning of something ‖ 어떤 것의 시작. 개시. 서두: *The chairman made a speech at the opening of the conference.* 의장은 회의의 서두에 연설을 했다. **3** a job or position that is available ‖ 이용할 수 있는 직업이나 직위. 빈자리. 공석. 결원: *Are there any openings for gardeners?* 정원사 중에 결원이 있습니까? **4** a hole or space in something ‖ 어떤 것에 있는 구멍이나 공간. 틈: *an opening in the fence* 울타리의 틈 **5** an opportunity to do or say something ‖ 무엇을 하거나 말할 기회. 호기: *He waited for an opening to ask his question.* 그는 질문할 기회를 기다렸다.

opening² *adj* first or beginning ‖ 첫 번째의. 시작의. 개시의. 서두의: *the President's opening remarks* 대통령의 서두 발언 / *Are you going to opening night?* (=the first night of a new play, movie etc.) 너 초연(初演)의 밤에 갈 거니?

o·pen·ly /'oʊpənli/ *adv* honestly and not secretly ‖ 정직하게·숨김없이. 공공연히. 공개적으로: *They talk openly about their problems.* 그들은 자신들의 문제점에 대해 숨김없이 말했다.

open-mind·ed /ˌ.. '../ *adj* willing to consider and accept new ideas, opinions etc. ‖ 새로운 생각·견해 등을 고려하고 수용하려고 하는. 받아들이기 쉬운. 마음이 넓은. 편견이 없는: *My doctor isn't very open-minded about new treatments.* 나의 의사는 새 치료법에 대해서 잘 받아들이려고 하지 않는다. **– open-mindedness** /ˌ.. '../ *n* [U]

o·pen·ness /'oʊpənɪs/ *n* [U] **1** the quality of being honest and not keeping things secret ‖ 솔직하고 일을 비밀로 하지 않는 성질. 솔직성: *the openness of a small child* 작은 아이의 솔직성 **2** the quality of being willing to accept new ideas or people ‖ 새로운 사상이나 사람을 기꺼이 받아들이려는 성질. 개방성. 관대: *Her openness to suggestions makes her*

easy to work with. 제안에 대한 그녀의 개방성은 그녀가 남들과 더불어 일하는 것을 용이하게 한다.

open-plan /ˌ.. '../ *adj* an open-plan office, school etc. does not have walls dividing it into separate rooms ‖ 사무실·학교 등이 각각의 방으로 분리하는 벽이 없는. 칸막이가 없는. 오픈 플랜식의

open sea·son /ˌ.. '../ *n* [singular] **1** the time each year when it is legal to kill particular animals or fish as a sport ‖ 스포츠로 특정한 동물이나 물고기를 매년 합법적으로 죽일 수 있는 시기. 수렵[어렵]기[허가 기간]: *open season for deer* 사슴 수렵기 **2** HUMOROUS a time during which someone or something is criticized a lot ‖ 사람이나 사물이 크게 비판 받는 시기. …을 자유롭게 비판할 수 있는 시기: *It's been open season on the President since he made his budget speech.* 대통령이 예산 연설을 한 이후로 대통령에 대한 강한 비판이 있어 왔다.

op·er·a /'ɑprə, 'ɑpərə/ *n* [C, U] a musical play in which all of the words are sung, or these plays considered as a form of art ‖ 모든 말을 노래로 하는 음악극, 또는 예술 형식으로 간주되는 음악극들. 가극. 오페라(형식, 예술) **– operatic** /ˌɑpə'rætɪk/ *adj*

op·er·a·ble /'ɑprəbəl/ *adj* **1** able to be treated by a medical operation ‖ 의학적인 수술로 치료될 수 있는. 수술이 가능한: *The cancer is operable.* 그 암은 수술이 가능하다. **2** working and ready to use ‖ 작동되어 사용하도록 준비된. 조작[사용]할 수 있는: *an operable machine* 조작할 수 있는 기계 **—opposite** INOPERABLE

op·er·ate /'ɑpəˌreɪt/ *v* **1** [I, T] if a machine operates or you operate it, it works or you make it work ‖ 기계 등이 [을] 작동하다[시키다]. 움직이다. 조종[작용]하다: *He doesn't know how to operate the equipment.* 그는 그 장비를 작동시키는 방법을 모른다. / *The machine seems to be operating smoothly.* 그 기계는 원활하게 작동되고 있는 것으로 보인다. **2** [I] to cut open someone's body in order to remove or fix a part that is damaged ‖ 상처 부위를 제거하거나 치료하기 위해 신체를 절개하다. 수술을 하다: *Doctors operated on him for appendicitis.* 의사는 그에게 맹장 수술을 했다. **3** [I, T] to organize and manage a business or activity ‖ 기업이나 활동을 조직하고 운영하다. 경영하다: *large banks that operate nationwide* 전국적으로 운영하는 큰 은행들 / *an agreement to build and operate a cellular phone network* 휴

대폰 네트워크의 설치·운영 협약 **4** [I, T] to have a particular effect, or to do something in a particular way ‖ 특정한 효과를 가지다, 또는 어떤 일을 특정한 방식으로 하다. …에 영향을 미치다. 효과적으로 작용하다: *How does the new security system operate?* 새로운 보안 시스템은 어떻게 작용을 합니까? / *The computer network will operate as an information resource for all universities in the state.* 컴퓨터 네트워크는 주(州)의 모든 대학교에 대한 정보 자료로서 활용될 것이다.

operating sys·tem /'.... ,../ *n* a system in a computer that helps all the programs to work ‖ 모든 프로그램의 운영을 돕는 컴퓨터 시스템. 오퍼레이팅 시스템. 운영 체계

op·er·a·tion /ˌɑpəˈreɪʃən/ *n* **1** the process of cutting into someone's body to fix or remove a part that is damaged ‖ 상처 부위를 치료하거나 제거하려고 신체를 절개하는 과정. 수술: *a knee operation* 무릎 수술 / *Mom had to have an operation on her back.* 어머니는 허리 수술을 받아야 했다. **2** a set of planned actions or activities for a particular purpose ‖ 특정한 목적을 위해 계획된 조치나 활동: *a rescue operation* 구조 활동 **3** [U] the way the parts of a machine or system work together ‖ 기계나 시스템의 부분이 함께 작용하는 방식. 작동. 운전: *Wear protective glasses when the machine is in operation.* 기계가 운전 중일 때는 보안경을 착용해라. **4** [C, U] a business or company, or the work of a business ‖ 기업이나 회사 또는 기업의 일. 운영. 업무. 영업: *The company's overseas operations are expanding.* 그 회사의 해외 업무가 확장되고 있다. / *Their delivery service has been in operation* (=been working) *for ten years.* 그들의 배달 서비스는 10년 동안 운영되어 왔다. **5** TECHNICAL an action done by a computer ‖ 컴퓨터에 의해 이루어진 활동. 작동. 연산: *a machine performing millions of operations per second* 초당 수백만 개의 연산을 수행하는 기계 **6** [U] the way something such as a law has an effect or achieves a result ‖ 법률 등이 효과를 가지거나 결과를 성취하는 방식. 시행. 실시: *a close look at the operation of the tax laws* 세법의 시행에 대한 상세한 검토

op·er·a·tion·al /ˌɑpəˈreɪʃənl/ *adj* **1** working and ready to be used ‖ 작동되어 사용하도록 준비되어 있는. 사용[조업, 운전]이 가능한: *The new airport will soon be operational.* 그 신공항은 곧 이용이 가능하게 될 것이다. **2** relating to the operation of a business, government etc. ‖ 기업·정부 등의 운영에 관한. 경영[운영]상의: *operational costs* 운영비 – **operationally** *adv*

op·er·a·tive /ˈɑpərətɪv/ *adj* working or having an effect ‖ 작용하거나 영향을 미치는. 효력[효험]이 있는: *The law will become operative in a month.* 그 법률은 1개월 뒤에 시행될 것이다.

op·er·a·tor /ˈɑpəˌreɪtɚ/ *n* **1** someone who works on a telephone SWITCHBOARD ‖ 전화 교환대에서 근무하는 직업인. 전화 교환원: *Ask the operator to help you with the call.* 전화하는 것을 도와달라고 교환원에게 요청해라. —see usage note at TELEPHONE **2** someone who operates a machine or piece of equipment ‖ 기계나 장비를 조작하는 사람. 기사. 조작자. 운전자: *a computer operator* 컴퓨터 운영자

oph·thal·mol·o·gy /ˌɑfθəlˈmɑlədʒi, -θəˈmɑ-, ˌɑp-/ *n* [U] TECHNICAL the medical study of the eyes and diseases that affect them ‖ 눈과 눈에 영향을 미치는 질병에 관한 의학적 연구(분야). 안과학 – **ophthalmologist** *n*

o·pin·ion /əˈpɪnyən/ *n* **1** [C, U] your ideas or beliefs about a particular subject ‖ 특정한 주제에 관한 자신의 생각이나 신념. 개인적 견해[의견]: *What's your opinion on nuclear testing?* 핵 실험에 관한 너의 견해는 무엇이냐? / *In my opinion, getting a divorce is too easy.* 내 의견으로는 이혼하는 것이 너무 쉽다. / *people who aren't afraid to express/give their opinions* 자신의 의견을 개진하는 것을 두려워하지 않는 사람들 **2** judgment or advice from a professional person about something ‖ 어떤 것에 대한 전문가의 판단이나 충고. 감정. 전문적인 의견: *We got a second opinion* (=we asked two people) *before replacing the furnace.* 난로를 교체하기 전에 우리는 또다른 사람에게 의견을 구했다. **3 have a high/low/good etc. opinion of** to think that someone or something is very good or very bad ‖ 사람 또는 사물이 매우 좋거나 매우 나쁘다고 생각하다. …에 대해 상당히 좋게[나쁘게] 생각하다: *The management seems to have a high opinion of her work.* 경영진은 그녀의 업무에 대해 상당히 인정하는 듯이 보인다. **4** [U] what people in general think about something ‖ 어떤 일에 대하여 일반인들이 생각하는 내용. 일반적인 의견:

Public opinion is strongly in favor of changing the election system. 여론은 선거 제도를 바꾸는 것에 강력하게 찬성하고 있다. —see usage note at VIEW¹

o·pin·ion·at·ed /ə'pɪnyə,neɪt̬ɪd/ *adj* DISAPPROVING expressing very strong opinions about things ‖ 어떤 것에 대한 매우 강한 의견을 표시하는. 의견을 고집하는. 완고한: *an opinionated letter* 자기 주장을 고집하는 편지

opinion poll /.'.. ,./ *n* ⇨ POLL¹

o·pi·um /'oupiəm/ *n* [U] an illegal drug made from POPPY seeds ‖ 양귀비 씨앗으로 만든 마약. 아편

o·pos·sum /ə'pasəm, 'pasəm/ *n* an American animal that looks like a large rat and can hang from trees by its tail ‖ 큰 쥐처럼 생기고 꼬리로 나무에 매달릴 수 있는 미국산 동물. 주머니쥐

op·po·nent /ə'pounənt/ *n* **1** someone who tries to defeat another person in a competition, game etc. ‖ 경기·게임 등에서 다른 사람을 패배시키려고 하는 사람. 적수. 상대: *His opponent is twice as big as he is.* 그의 적수는 그보다 두 배나 크다. **2** someone who disagrees with a plan, idea etc. ‖ 계획·의견 등에 동의하지 않는 사람. 반대자: *opponents of federal aid to education* 연방 정부의 교육 지원에 대한 반대자들

op·por·tune /,apə'tun/ *adj* FORMAL **an opportune moment/time/place etc.** a time etc. that is suitable for doing something ‖ 어떤 것을 하는 데 적합한 때 등. 형편이 좋은 적절한 때/시간/장소

op·por·tun·ist /,apə'tunɪst/ *n* DISAPPROVING someone who uses every chance to gain power or advantages over others ‖ 다른 사람보다 앞서 권력이나 이득을 얻으려고 모든 기회를 이용하는 사람. 기회주의자 **– opportunistic** /,apə'tu'nɪstɪk/ *adj* **– opportunism** /,apə'tu,nɪzəm/ *n* [U]

op·por·tu·ni·ty /,apə'tunət̬i/ *n* **1** an occasion when it is possible for you to do something ‖ 어떤 일을 하는 것이 가능한 경우. 기회. 호기: *I haven't had an opportunity to think about this yet.* 나는 아직 이것에 관해 생각해 볼 기회가 없었다. / *The meeting will give you the/an opportunity to introduce yourself to the team.* 그 모임은 너 자신을 그 팀에 소개하는 기회를 제공할 것이다. / *I'd like to take this opportunity to thank everyone who helped me.* 저는 이 기회를 빌어 저를 도와주셨던 여러분에게 감사드리고 싶습니다. **2** a chance to get a job ‖ 직업을 얻는 기회: *There are good*

opportunities for graduates in your field. 너와 같은 분야의 졸업생들에게는 구직을 할 좋은 기회가 많다. —compare CHANCE¹ —see usage note at CHANCE¹

op·pose /ə'pouz/ *v* [T] to disagree strongly with an idea or action ‖ 어떤 생각이나 행동에 강하게 불찬성하다. 반대 [대립]하다: *A local group opposes the plan for environmental reasons.* 한 지역 단체가 환경적인 이유로 그 계획에 반대한다.

op·posed /ə'pouzd/ *adj* **1** disagreeing strongly with someone or something, or feeling strongly that someone or something is wrong ‖ 사람이나 사물과 강하게 의견이 안맞는, 또는 사람이나 사물이 틀렸다고 강하게 느끼는. 반대의. 적대적인: *I'm opposed to the death penalty.* 나는 사형에 반대한다. **2 as opposed to** used in order to show that two things are different from each other ‖ 두 가지가 서로 다르다는 것을 나타내는 데에 쓰여. …과는 대조적으로: *The group gave out 300 food boxes this year, as opposed to 200 last year.* 그 단체는 작년의 200개와는 대조적으로 올해는 300개의 식품 상자를 배포했다.

op·pos·ing /ə'pouzɪŋ/ *adj* **1** opposing teams, groups etc. are competing, arguing etc. with each other ‖ 팀·그룹 등이 서로 경쟁하거나 논쟁하는. 대립하는 **2** opposing ideas, opinions etc. are completely different from each other ‖ 사고·견해 등이 서로 완전히 다른. 정반대의

op·po·site¹ /'apəzɪt, -sɪt/ *adj* **1** completely different ‖ 완전히 다른. 정반대의: *I thought the music would relax me, but it had the opposite effect.* 나는 그 음악이 나를 편하게 해 주리라고 여겼는데 정반대의 효과가 났다. / *Ray started walking in the opposite direction.* 레이는 반대 방향으로 걷기 시작했다. **2** facing something or directly across from something ‖ 어떤 것을 향하고 있는, 또는 어떤 것을 똑바로 가로지르는. 마주보고 있는. 맞은편의: *a building on the opposite side of the river* 강 맞은편 건물 / *Louise and I work at opposite ends of* (=on different sides of) *the city, so it's hard to meet.* 루이스와 나는 도시의 반대쪽에서 일하기 때문에 만나기 어렵다.

opposite² *prep, adv* if one thing or person is opposite another, they are facing each other ‖ 한 사물이나 사람이 다른 것과 서로 마주보고: *Put the piano opposite the sofa.* 피아노를 소파 맞은편

에 놓아라. / *He's moved into the house opposite.* 그는 맞은편 집으로 이사했다.

opposite³ *n* a person or thing that is completely different from someone or something else ‖ 다른 사람이나 사물과 완전히 다른 사람이나 사물. 정반대의 사람[것]: *Hot and cold are opposites.* 뜨겁고 찬 것은 반의어이다. / *David loves to read, but Mike's the opposite.* 데이비드는 독서하는 것을 좋아하지만 마이크는 정반대이다.

op·po·si·tion /ˌɑpəˈzɪʃən/ *n* [U] strong disagreement with, or protest against something ‖ 어떤 것에 대한 강한 반대나 항의: *the residents' opposition to plans for a new highway* 새로운 간선도로 계획에 대한 주민들의 반대

op·press /əˈprɛs/ *v* [T] to treat people in an unfair and cruel way ‖ 부당하고 잔인하게 사람들을 대하다. 억압하다

op·pressed /əˈprɛst/ *adj* treated unfairly or cruelly ‖ 부당하거나 잔인하게 대우받는. 억압받는: *oppressed minority groups* 억압받는 소수 그룹 / *the poor and the oppressed* (=people who are oppressed) 빈곤층과 피압제민

op·pres·sion /əˈprɛʃən/ *n* [U] the act of OPPRESSing people, or the state of being oppressed ‖ 사람들을 억압하는 행동, 또는 억압받는 상태. 억압. 압제: *People are demanding an end to the oppression.* 사람들은 억압의 종식을 요구하고 있다.

op·pres·sive /əˈprɛsɪv/ *adj* **1** cruel and unfair ‖ 잔인하고 부당한. 압제적인. 포학한: *an oppressive military government* 포학한 군사 정권 **2** making you feel uncomfortable ‖ 불편하게 하는: *oppressive heat* 찌는 듯한 더위

op·pres·sor /əˈprɛsə/ *n* a person or group that OPPRESSes people ‖ 사람들을 억압하는 사람이나 집단. 억압자. 압제자

opt /ɑpt/ *v* [I, T] to choose one thing instead of another ‖ 다른 것 대신에 한 가지를 선택하다: *We've opted for a smaller car.* 우리는 소형차를 선택했다. / *More high school students are opting to go to college.* 보다 많은 고등학생들이 대학 진학을 선택하고 있다.

opt out *phr v* [I] to decide not to join in a group or system ‖ 어떤 단체나 체제에 합류하지 않기로 결정하다. 빠지다. 탈퇴하다: *Several countries may opt out of NATO.* 몇몇 국가들이 NATO에서 탈퇴할지도 모른다.

op·tic /ˈɑptɪk/ *adj* relating to the eyes ‖ 눈에 관련된. 눈의: *the optic nerve* 시신경

op·ti·cal /ˈɑptɪkəl/ *adj* relating to the

way light is seen, or relating to the eyes ‖ 빛이 보이는 방식과 관련된, 또는 눈과 관련된. 광학의. 눈의: *an optical instrument* 광학 기기 – **optically** *adv*

optical il·lu·sion /ˌ… …ˈ…/ *n* a picture or image that tricks your eyes and makes you see something that is not actually there ‖ 눈을 속여 실제 그곳에 있지 않은 것을 보게 하는 그림이나 영상. 착시

op·ti·cian /ɑpˈtɪʃən/ *n* someone who makes GLASSES ‖ 안경을 제조하는 사람. 안경 제조업자

op·ti·mism /ˈɑptəˌmɪzəm/ *n* [U] a tendency to believe that good things will happen ‖ 좋은 일이 일어날 것이라고 믿는 성향. 낙천주의: *At the moment, there is optimism about the country's economic future* 지금 국가 경제의 미래에 대한 낙관론이 대두되어 있다. —opposite PESSIMISM

op·ti·mist /ˈɑptəˌmɪst/ *n* someone who believes that good things will happen ‖ 좋은 일이 일어날 것이라고 믿는 사람. 낙관론자 —opposite PESSIMIST

op·ti·mis·tic /ˌɑptəˈmɪstɪk/ *adj* believing that good things will happen in the future ‖ 앞으로 좋은 일이 일어날 것이라고 믿는. 낙천적인: *Tom's optimistic about finding a job.* 톰은 구직에 대해 낙천적이다. – **optimistically** *adv* —opposite PESSIMISTIC

op·ti·mum /ˈɑptəməm/ *adj* best or most suitable for a particular purpose ‖ 특정 목적에 최고이거나 최적인: *the optimum diet for good health* 건강을 위한 최고의 식단

op·tion /ˈɑpʃən/ *n* **1** a choice you can make in a particular situation ‖ 특정한 상황에서 할 수 있는 선택: *Consider all your options carefully.* 당신의 모든 선택에 신중을 기해라. / *If these talks fail, war may be the only option we have left.* 이 회담이 실패한다면, 전쟁이 우리에게 남은 유일한 선택일 수 있다. / *Dropping out of school is not an option.* (=you cannot do it) 학교를 중퇴하는 것은 선택 사항이 아니다. **2 keep/leave your options open** to wait before making a decision ‖ 결정을 하기 전에 기다리다. 선택을 보류하다: *Leave your options open until you have the results of the test.* 시험 결과가 나오기까지는 선택을 보류해라. **3** the right to buy or sell something in the future ‖ 장차 사거나 팔 권리. 옵션: *You can't rent the piano, with an option to buy.* 당신은 나중에 구입한다는 옵션으로 피아노를 임차할 수 있습니다.

op·tion·al /'ɑpʃənl/ *adj* something that is optional is something you do not need to do or have, but can choose if you want it ‖ 원하면 선택할 수는 있지만 의무적으로 어떤 것을 하거나 갖출 필요가 없는. 임의의. 자유 선택의: *A sun roof is optional in this car.* 선 루프는 이 자동차의 선택 사양입니다.

op·tom·e·trist /ɑp'tɑmətrɪst/ *n* someone who examines people's eyes and orders GLASSES for them ‖ 사람들의 눈을 검사하여 그들을 위한 안경을 처방하는 사람. 검안사 – **optometry** /ɑp'tɑm-ətri/ *n* [U]

op·u·lent /'ɑpyələnt/ *adj* decorated in an expensive way ‖ 값비싸게 장식한. 호화로운: *an opulent hotel* 호화로운 호텔 – **opulence** *n* [U]

OR the written abbreviation of Oregon ‖ Oregon(오리건 주)의 약어

or /ɚ; *strong* ɔr/ *conjunction* **1** used between two possibilities or before the last in a series of possibilities ‖ 두 개의 가능성 사이에, 또는 일련의 가능성들의 최종 요소 앞에 쓰여. 또는. …이든지: *Would you like pie, cake, or some ice cream?* 파이나 케이크 아니면 아이스크림 좀 드시겠습니까? / *Is she coming back with Nancy or with her aunt?* 그녀는 낸시하고 돌아올 건가요, 고모하고 돌아올 건가요? / *Tickets cost $4 or $5.* (=they cost around $5, but you are not sure exactly how much) 표는 4달러나 5달러이다. / *You can use either milk or cream in the sauce.* 너는 소스에 우유나 크림을 사용할 수 있다. / *I'll see him this afternoon, or else I'll call him tomorrow.* 나는 오늘 오후에 그를 만나든가, 그렇지 않으면 내일 그에게 전화할 것이다. –compare EITHER¹

2 or anything/something SPOKEN or something that is similar to what you have just mentioned ‖ 또는 방금 말한 것과 비슷한 것. 뭔가: *Do you want to go out for a drink or anything?* 술이나 한 잔 하러 나갈래?

3 used after a negative verb when you mean not one thing and not another thing ‖ 전자(前者)도 후자도 아니라는 의미로 동사의 부정형 뒤에 쓰여. …도 …도 아니라: *They don't go to movies or plays.* 그들은 영화도 연극도 보러 가지 않는다.

4 used in order to warn or advise someone ‖ 남에게 경고하거나 충고하는 데에 쓰여. 그렇지 않으면: *Hurry or you'll miss your plane.* 서둘러, 그렇지 않으면 비행기를 놓칠 거야. / *We can't go*

over 65, or else we'll get a speeding ticket. 우리는 65마일 이상으로 갈 수 없어, 그렇지 않으면 속도 위반 딱지를 떼게 된다. / *Don't be late, or else...* (=used as a threat) (위협적으로) 늦지 마라. 그렇지 않으면….

5 or so used with a number, time, distance etc. to show that it is not exact ‖ 수·시간·거리 등이 정확하지 않다는 것을 나타내는 데에 쓰여. …정도. …쯤: *There's a gas station a mile or so down the road.* 그 도로를 1마일쯤 내려가면 주유소가 있다.

6 used before a word or phrase that explains what has been said before ‖ 앞서 말한 것을 설명하는 단어나 구 앞에 쓰여. 말하자면. 즉: *biology, or the study of living things* 생물학, 바꾸어 말하면 생물에 관한 연구

7 used in order to explain why something happened or why something must be true ‖ 무엇이 발생하거나 사실임에 틀림없는 까닭을 설명하는 데에 쓰여: *She must be tired, or she wouldn't have yelled at us.* 그녀는 지친 것이 틀림없어. 그렇지 않으면 우리에게 고함치지 않았을 거야.

o·ral¹ /'ɔrəl/ *adj* **1** spoken not written ‖ 문자로 쓰지 않고 말로 한. 구두의: *an oral report* 구두 보고 **2** relating to the mouth ‖ 입에 관련된. 입의: *oral hygiene* 구강 위생

oral² *n* a test in a university in which questions and answers are spoken rather than written ‖ 대학에서 질문과 대답을 글로 쓰는 대신 말로 하는 시험. 구술 시험

or·ange /'ɔrɪndʒ, 'ɑr-/ *n* [U] **1** a round fruit that has a sweet-tasting juice and a thick skin that you do not eat ‖ 달콤한 과즙과 먹을 수 없는 두꺼운 껍질이 있는 둥근 과일. 오렌지 —see picture on page 944 **2** the color of an orange ‖ 오렌지색. 주황색 – **orange** *adj*

o·rang·u·tang /ə'ræŋə,tæŋ/, *also* **o·rang·u·tan** /ə'ræŋə,tæn/ *n* a large APE (=animal like a monkey) that has long arms and long orange hair ‖ 긴 팔과 주황색의 긴 털이 있는 큰 원숭이. 오랑우탄

or·a·tor /'ɔrətɚ, 'ɑr-/ *n* someone who makes speeches and is good at persuading people ‖ 연설하여 사람들을 잘 설득하는 사람. 연설자. 웅변가 – **oration** /ɔ'reɪʃən, ə-/ *n*

or·a·to·ry /'ɔrətɔri, 'ɑr-/ *n* [U] the skill or art of making public speeches ‖ 대중 연설을 하는 기술이나 기교. 웅변술

or·bit¹ /'ɔrbɪt/ *n* the path traveled by an object that is moving around a larger object ‖ 더 큰 물체의 주위를 도는 물체의 이동 경로. 궤도: *the Moon's orbit around the Earth* 지구 주위의 달의 궤도 – **orbital** *adj*

orbit
Earth
orbit
Moon

orbit² *v* [I, T] to travel in a circle around a larger object ‖ 보다 큰 물체의 주위를 원형으로 이동하다. 궤도를 따라 돌다. 선회하다: *a satellite that orbits the Earth* 지구를 선회하는 인공위성

or·chard /'ɔrtʃəd/ *n* a place where fruit trees are grown ‖ 과수를 기르는 장소. 과수원

or·ches·tra /'ɔrkɪstrə/ *n* a large group of musicians who play CLASSICAL MUSIC on different instruments ‖ 여러 악기들로 고전음악을 연주하는 대형 집단의 음악가들. 오케스트라. 관현악단 – **orchestral** /ɔr'kɛstrəl/ *adj*

orchestra pit /'... ,./ *n* the place at the front of a theater next to the stage and below the main floor, where the ORCHESTRA sits to play during a musical theater performance ‖ 극장 전면 무대 옆이며, 공연 동안 관현악단이 앉아서 연주하는 주 무대의 아래 위치. 무대 앞 맨 바닥 좌석

or·ches·trate /'ɔrkɪ,streɪt/ *v* [T] to organize an important event or a complicated plan, especially secretly ‖ 특히 비밀스럽게, 중요한 행사나 복잡한 계획을 조직하다. 교묘히 획책하다: *a rebellion orchestrated by the army* 군이 획책한 반란

or·ches·tra·tion /,ɔrkɪ'streɪʃən/ *n* [C, U] the way a piece of music is arranged for an ORCHESTRA, or the act of arranging it ‖ 한 곡의 음악을 관현악단 연주용으로 편곡하는 방식이나 그 행위. 관현악 편성[편곡]

or·chid /'ɔrkɪd/ *n* a tropical, often brightly colored, flower with three PETALS ‖ 꽃잎이 세 개이며 주로 밝은 색깔인 열대 꽃. 난초

or·dain /ɔr'deɪn/ *v* [T] to officially make someone a religious leader ‖ 공식적으로 남을 종교 지도자로 만들다. …을 사제로 임명하다 —see also ORDINATION

or·deal /ɔr'dil/ *n* a terrible or painful experience ‖ 무섭거나 고통스러운 경험. 고난: *School can be an ordeal for children with learning problems.* 학습 장애가 있는 아이들에게 학교는 지옥이 될

수도 있다.

or·der¹ /'ɔrdə/ *n* **1 in order (for sb/sth) to do sth** so that something can happen or so that someone can do something ‖ 일이 발생할 수 있도록 someone can do 할 수 있도록 혹은 누가 무엇을 할 수 있도록. …하기 위해. …할 목적으로: *In order for you to graduate next year, you'll have to go to summer school.* 네가 내년에 졸업하기 위해서는 여름 학기에 다녀야 한다. / *Sunlight is needed in order for this chemical process to take place.* 이러한 화학 작용이 일어나는 데에는 햇빛이 필요하다.

These names are in alphabetical order.

2 ▶ARRANGEMENT 정렬◀ [C, U] the way that several things are arranged, organized, or put on a list ‖ 몇몇 사물이 배열된[구성된, 목록에 올려진] 방식. 순서. 차례: *names written in alphabetical order* 알파벳순으로 적힌 이름들 / *Are these pictures in order?* (=arranged in a particular order) 이 사진들은 순서대로 되어 있나요? / *Some of the book's pages were out of order.* (=not correctly arranged) 그 책의 몇몇 쪽은 순서가 잘못되어 있었다. / *I need to put the files in order.* (=organize them) 나는 그 파일들을 정돈해야 한다.

3 ▶GOODS/MEAL 상품/음식◀ a request for goods from a company or for food in a restaurant, or the goods or food that you ask for ‖ 기업의 상품에 대한 요청이나 식당에서의 음식 요청, 또는 그 요청하는 상품이나 음식. 주문. 주문품: *The school's just placed an order for more books.* 그 학교는 방금 더 많은 책을 주문했다. / *Has anyone taken your order?* (=written down what you want in a restaurant) (식당에서) 주문하셨나요? / *I'll have an order of fries and a coke.* 나는 감자튀김과 콜라를 주문하겠어요.

4 ▶NO CRIME/TROUBLE 범죄/분쟁이 없음◀ [U] a situation in which people obey rules and respect authority ‖ 사람들이 규칙을 준수하고 권위를 존중하는 상황. 질서. 치안: *Police are working hard to maintain law and order in the area.* 경찰은 그 지역의 법과 질서를 유지하기 위해 열심히 일한다.

5 ▶COMMAND 명령◀ a command given by someone in authority ‖ 권위 있는 사람이 내린 명령. 지령. 지시: *Captain Marshall gave the order to* *advance.* 마셜 대위는 전진하라고 명령했다. / *He refused to obey the judge's order.* 그는 판사의 명령에 따르기를 거부했다.

6 out of order a phrase meaning not working, used especially on signs ‖ 특히 표지에 쓰이는 작동하지 않는다는 뜻의 문구. 고장이 난: *The photocopier is out of order again.* 그 복사기는 또 고장 났다.

7 in order legal and correct ‖ 적법하고 올바른. 정상적인: *Your passport seems to be in order* 당신의 여권은 적법한 것 같습니다.

8 ▶POLITICS ETC. 정치 등 ◀ the political, social, or economic situation at a particular time ‖ 특정한 시기의 정치적·사회적·경제적 상황: *the present economic order* 현재 경제 상황

9 on the order of sb/sth similar in some way to someone or something ‖ 어떤 면에서 어떤 사람이나 사물과 비슷한: *a car that averages on the order of 35 miles per gallon* 연비가 갤런당 평균 35마일 정도의 자동차 —see also **in short order** (SHORT¹)

order² *v* **1** [I, T] to ask for goods or services ‖ 물건이나 용역을 주문하다: *"What did you order?" "Spaghetti."* "뭘 주문했어?" "스파게티." / *I've ordered a new table for the kitchen.* 나는 새 식탁을 주문했다. **2** [T] to command someone to do something ‖ 누구에게 무엇을 하라고 명령하다: *The judge ordered the jury not to discuss the trial.* 판사는 배심원단에게 재판에 대하여 토론하지 말라고 명령했다. **3** [T] to arrange something in a particular way ‖ 특정한 방식으로 무엇을 정돈하다: *a list of names ordered alphabetically* 알파벳순으로 나열된 명단

USAGE NOTE order and command

Use **order** for most situations when someone who is in a position of authority tells other people to do something: *The governor ordered an investigation into the shootings.* Use **command** when it is someone in the military who is telling other people to do something: *The general commanded his troops to fire.* **order**는 권한이 있는 사람이 다른 사람들에게 무엇을 하라고 말하는 대부분의 상황에 쓰인다: 지사는 총격 사건에 대한 수사를 지시했다. **command**는 군인이 다른 사람들에게 무엇을 하라고 말하는 때에 쓰인다: 장군은 부대에 사격 명령을 내렸다.

---

or·der·ly¹ /ˈɔrdəli/ *adj* **1** arranged or organized in a neat way ‖ 말끔하게 정돈되거나 조직된. 단정한: *an orderly desk* 정돈된 책상 ‖ 평온하거나 올바르게 행동하는: *an orderly crowd* 질서 정연한 군중 —opposite DISORDERLY

orderly² *n* someone who does unskilled jobs in a hospital ‖ 병원에서 특별한 기술이 필요 없는 일을 하는 사람. 잡역부

or·di·nal num·ber /ˌɔrdn-əl ˈnʌmbər/ *n* one of the numbers such as first, second, third etc. that show the order of things ‖ 첫째·둘째·셋째 등의 사물의 순서를 나타내는 숫자들 중의 하나. 서수 —compare CARDINAL NUMBER

or·di·nance /ˈɔrdn-əns/ *n* a law of a city or town that does not allow an activity or that restricts an activity ‖ 어떤 행동을 용인하지 않거나 제한하는 시나읍의 법. 조례. 규정: *parking ordinances* 주차 규정

or·di·nar·i·ly /ˌɔrdnˈɛrəli/ *adv* usually ‖ 보통. 대개. 통상: *I don't ordinarily go to movies in the afternoon.* 대체로 나는 오후에는 영화 보러 가지 않는다. / *Ordinarily, he doesn't repair trucks, just cars.* 보통 그는 자동차만 수리하고 트럭은 수리하지 않는다.

or·di·nar·y /ˈɔrdnˌɛri/ *adj* **1** average, usual, or not different ‖ 평균의, 보통의, 다르지 않은: *laws written in language that ordinary people can understand* 일반인들이 이해할 수 있는 말로 기록된 법령 / *A videophone costs much more than an ordinary telephone.* 화상 전화는 일반 전화보다 비용이 훨씬 더 든다. / *ordinary items like toothpaste and soap* 치약과 비누 같은 일상용품 **2** not special in any way ‖ 어떤 면에서도 특별하지 않은. 평범한: *It was just an ordinary working day.* 그저 평상시와 다름없는 근무하는 날이었다. **3 out of the ordinary** very different from what is usual ‖ 보통의 것과 상당히 다른. 이상한. 비정상의: *I didn't notice anything out of the ordinary when I came home.* 나는 집에 왔을 때 어떤 이상한 점도 알아채지 못했다.

or·di·na·tion /ˌɔrdnˈeɪʃən/ *n* [C, U] the act or ceremony making someone a religious leader ‖ 어떤 사람을 종교 지도자로 만드는 행위 또는 그 의식. 성직 수임식(授任式). 목사 안수식 —see also ORDAIN

ore /ɔr/ *n* [C, U] rock or earth from which metal can be obtained ‖ 금속을 얻을 수 있는 암석이나 토양. 광석

or·gan /ˈɔrgən/ *n* **1** part of the body of

an animal or plant that has a particular purpose ‖ 특정한 용도가 있는 동물이나 식물의 각 기관(器官). 장기: *the heart, liver, and other internal organs* 심장, 간 및 다른 내장들 **2** a large musical instrument like a piano, with large pipes to make the sound, or an electric instrument that makes similar sounds ‖ 소리를 내는 큰 파이프가 달린 피아노처럼 큰 악기, 또는 이와 비슷한 소리를 내는 전자 악기. 오르간. 전자 오르간

or·gan·ic /ɔr'gænɪk/ *adj* **1** living, or related to living things ‖ 살아 있는, 또는 살아 있는 것에 관련된. 생물의. 유기체의: *organic matter* 유기 화합물 / *organic chemistry* 유기 화학 —opposite IN-ORGANIC **2** using farming methods that do not use chemicals, or produced by these methods ‖ 화학 약품을 쓰지 않는 농사법을 이용하는, 또는 이러한 방식으로 생산되는. 유기농법의: *organic vegetables* 유기농 야채 —**organically** *adv*

or·ga·nism /'ɔrgə,nɪzəm/ *n* a living thing ‖ 살아 있는 것. 생물. 유기체: *a microscopic organism* 미생물

or·gan·ist /'ɔrgənɪst/ *n* someone who plays the ORGAN ‖ 오르간 연주자

or·ga·ni·za·tion /ˌɔrgənə'zeɪʃən/ *n* **1** a group such as a club or business that has been formed for a particular purpose ‖ 특정한 목적을 위해 편성된 클럽이나 기업 등의 단체: *a charity organization* 자선 단체 / *an organization of Christian students* 그리스도교 학생 단체 **2** [U] the act of planning and arranging things effectively ‖ 사물을 효율적으로 계획하고 정리하는 행위. 편성. 구성: *She was responsible for the organization of the fund-raising campaign.* 그녀는 기금 모음 운동 편성의 책임을 맡고 있었다. **3** [U] the way in which the different parts of a system are arranged and work together ‖ 한 시스템의 각 부문들이 정돈이 되어 함께 어우러져 작동하는 모양. 조직: *the social organization of twelfth century Europe* 12세기 유럽의 사회 조직 —**organizational** *adj*

or·ga·nize /'ɔrgə,naɪz/ *v* **1** [T] to plan or arrange something ‖ 무엇을 계획하거나 정리하다: *Who's organizing the New Year's party?* 누가 새해 파티를 기획하고 있지? / *Organize your ideas on paper before you write your essay.* 수필을 쓰기 전에 종이에 너의 생각을 정리해라. **2** [I, T] to form a UNION (=an organization that protects workers' rights) or persuade people to join one ‖ 노동조합을

결성하거나 노동조합에 가입하라고 사람들을 설득하다

or·ga·nized /'ɔrgə,naɪzd/ *adj* **1** planned or arranged in an effective way ‖ 효율적으로 계획되거나 정리된: *The meeting's always well organized when Donita's in charge.* 도니타가 책임을 맡으면 항상 회의의 준비가 잘 되어 있다. **2** an organized activity is arranged for and done by many people ‖ 활동이 다수에 의해 마련되고 치러지는. 조직화된. 조직적인: *organized sports* 조직적인 스포츠 / *organized religion* 조직화된 종교

organized crime /ˌ... './ *n* [U] a large and powerful organization of criminals ‖ 범죄자들의 대규모의 강력한 조직. 범죄 조직

or·ga·niz·er /'ɔrgə,naɪzər/ *n* someone who organizes an event or group of people ‖ 행사나 일단의 사람들을 조직하는 사람. 조직자: *Last year the organizers of the event sent out 3000 invitations.* 작년에 그 행사의 주최자들은 초대장을 3000장 발송했다.

or·gasm /'ɔr,gæzəm/ *n* [C, U] the moment when you have the greatest sexual pleasure during sex ‖ 성교 중 성적 쾌감이 가장 큰 순간. 오르가슴

or·gy /'ɔrdʒi/ *n* a wild party with a lot of eating, drinking, and sexual activity ‖ 많이 먹고 마시며 성행위가 따르는 난잡한 파티. 난교[섹스] 파티

O·ri·ent /'ɔriənt/ *n* **the Orient** OLD-FASHIONED the eastern part of the world, especially China and Japan ‖ 세계의 동부, 특히 중국과 일본. 아시아. 동양

o·ri·ent /'ɔri,ɛnt/ *v* [T] **1** to make someone familiar with a place or situation ‖ 사람을 어떤 장소나 상황에 적응시키다: *It takes a while to orient yourself in a new city.* 새로운 도시에서 네 자신을 적응시키려면 잠시 시간이 걸린다. **2** to find someone's position using a map etc. ‖ 지도 등을 이용하여 사람의 위치를 확인하다

O·ri·en·tal /ˌɔri'ɛntl/ *adj* **1** relating to Asia ‖ 아시아에 관련된. 동양의: *Oriental culture* 동양 문화 **2** a word used for describing someone from Asia, that is sometimes considered offensive ‖ 때때로 모욕적인 것으로 간주되는, 아시아 출신의 사람을 말하는 데에 쓰이는 단어. 동양인의 —compare ASIAN

o·ri·en·ta·tion /ˌɔriən'teɪʃən/ *n* **1** [C, U] the beliefs, aims, or interests that a person or group chooses to have ‖ 어떤 사람이나 단체가 갖기로 선택한 신념[목표, 관심]: *the group's right-wing*

o·ri·ent·ed /ˈɔːriˌɛntɪd/ *adj* giving attention to a particular type of person or thing ‖ 특정 유형의 사람이나 사물에 관심을 쏟는: *male-oriented movies like "Die Hard"* "다이하드"와 같은 남성 지향의 영화들 / *a service oriented towards the needs of business people* 사업가들이 필요로 하는 것을 대상으로 한 서비스

o·ri·gin /ˈɔrədʒɪn, ˈɑr-/ *n* the situation or place from which something comes, or where it began to exist ‖ 무엇이 유래하거나 생기기 시작한 상황이나 장소. 기원. 근원: *a word of Latin origin* 라틴 기원의 단어 / *Scientists believe the origin of the disease is an illness common in monkeys.* 과학자들은 그 질병의 기원은 원숭이에게 흔한 병에 있다고 믿는다. — see also ORIGINS

o·rig·i·nal¹ /əˈrɪdʒənl/ *adj* **1** first or earliest ‖ 최초의, 가장 이른: *The house still has its original stone floor.* 그 집에는 여전히 원래의 석재 마루가 있다. / *Our original plan was too expensive.* 우리의 당초 계획은 너무 사치스러웠다. **2** completely new and different ‖ 완전히 새롭고 다른. 독창적인: *Students had to invent an original design for a chair.* 학생들은 독창적인 디자인의 의자를 창안해야 했다. **3** not copied, or not based on something else ‖ 베끼지 않거나 다른 것에 근거하지 않은. 원래의: *an original screenplay* 영화 각본 원본

original² *n* a painting, document etc. that is not a copy ‖ 복사본이 아닌 그림·서류 등. 원작. 원서

o·rig·i·nal·i·ty /əˌrɪdʒəˈnæləti/ *n* [U] the quality of being completely new and different ‖ 완전히 새롭고 다른 특성. 독창성: *the originality of her performance* 그녀의 공연의 독창성

o·rig·i·nal·ly /əˈrɪdʒənl-i/ *adv* in the beginning ‖ 처음에. 원래는. 당초에는: *Her family originally came from Thailand.* 그녀의 가족은 애초 태국에서 건너 왔다. / *Originally, we hoped to be finished by June.* 처음에 우리는 6월까지 끝나기를 바랐다.

o·rig·i·nate /əˈrɪdʒəˌneɪt/ *v* [I] FORMAL to start to develop in a particular place or from a particular situation ‖ 특정한 장소나 상황에서 발전하기 시작하다. …에서 생기다. 기원하다: *The custom of having a Christmas tree originated in Germany.* 크리스마스트리를 하는 풍습은 독일에서 시작되었다.

or·i·gins /ˈɔrədʒɪnz, ˈɑr-/ *n* [plural] the country, race, or class from which someone comes ‖ 사람의 출신 국가나 인종, 또는 계층. 태생. 혈통. 가문: *He's proud of his Italian origins.* 그는 자신이 이탈리아 혈통인 것을 자랑스럽게 여긴다.

o·ri·ole /ˈɔriˌoʊl, ˈɔriˌəl/ *n* a wild bird that is black with a red and a yellow stripe on its wing ‖ 날개에 빨갛고 노란 줄무늬가 있는 검은 들새. 오리올

or·na·ment /ˈɔrnəmənt/ *n* an object that you keep in your house because it is beautiful rather than useful ‖ 쓸모 있다기보다는 아름답기 때문에 집에 두는 물건. 장식물: *Christmas ornaments* 크리스마스 장식품

or·na·men·tal /ˌɔrnəˈmɛntl/ *adj* designed to decorate something ‖ 무엇을 장식하기 위해 고안된. 장식용의: *ornamental vases* 장식용 화병

or·nate /ɔrˈneɪt/ *adj* having a lot of decoration ‖ 장식이 많은. 지나치게 장식한: *ornate furniture* 화려한 가구 – **ornately** *adv*

or·ne·ry /ˈɔrnəri/ *adj* HUMOROUS behaving in an unreasonable and angry way ‖ 분별없고 화난 듯이 행동하는. 성미 고약한

or·ni·thol·o·gy /ˌɔrnəˈθɑlədʒi/ *n* [U] the scientific study of birds ‖ 새에 대한 과학적 연구. 조류학 – **ornithologist** *n*

or·phan¹ /ˈɔrfən/ *n* a child whose parents are dead ‖ 부모를 여읜 아이. 고아

orphan² *v* [T] **be orphaned** to become an ORPHAN ‖ 고아가 되다

or·phan·age /ˈɔrfənɪdʒ/ *n* a place where ORPHANed children live ‖ 고아들이 사는 곳. 고아원

or·tho·don·tist /ˌɔrθəˈdɑntɪst/ *n* a DENTIST who makes teeth straight when they have not been growing correctly ‖ 이가 바르게 자라지 않을 때 똑바로 만들어 주는 치과 의사. 치열 교정 의사 – **orthodontics** *n* – **orthodontic** *adj*

or·tho·dox /ˈɔrθəˌdɑks/ *adj* **1** officially accepted, or considered to be normal by most people ‖ 공식적으로 용인되는, 또는 대부분의 사람이 표준이라고 생각하는. 정통의. 옳다고 인정된: *orthodox methods of treating disease* 정통적인 질병 치료법

2 following the traditional beliefs of a religion ‖ 종교의 전통적 믿음을 따르는. 정통파의: *an orthodox Jew* 정통파 유대교 신자 – **orthodoxy** *n* [C, U]

Orthodox Church /ˌ... './ *n* **the Orthodox Church** one of the Christian churches in eastern Europe and parts of Asia ‖ 동유럽과 아시아 일부 지역의 그리스도교회의 일파. 동방 정교회

or·tho·pe·dics /ˌɔrθəˈpidɪks/ *n* [U] the area of medicine that deals with bones ‖ 뼈를 다루는 의학 분야. 정형 외과학 – **orthopedic** *adj*

Os·car /ˈɑskə/ *n* one of the prizes given each year to the best movies, actors etc. in the movie industry ‖ 매년 영화계에서 최고의 영화·배우 등에게 수여되는 상들 중 하나. 오스카: *an Oscar for best director* 아카데미 최고 감독상

os·ten·ta·tious /ˌɑstənˈteɪʃəs/ *adj* DISAPPROVING designed or done in order to be impressive to other people ‖ 다른 사람들에게 잘 보이려고 기획되거나 행해진. 과시하는: *ostentatious furniture* 과시용 가구 / *an ostentatious lifestyle* 허세부리는 생활 방식 – **ostentation** *n* [U]

ostracize /ˈɑstrəˌsaɪz/ *v* [T] to behave in a very unfriendly way toward someone and not allow him/her to be part of a group ‖ 남에게 매우 불친절하게 굴며 한 집단의 일원이 되는 것을 허락하지 않다. 추방하다. 배척하다 – **ostracism** /ˈɑstrəˌsɪzəm/ *n* [U]

os·trich /ˈɑstrɪtʃ, ˈɔ-/ *n* a very large African bird with long legs, that runs very quickly but cannot fly ‖ 긴 다리로 매우 빨리 달리지만 날지는 못하는 매우 큰 아프리카 새. 타조

oth·er[1] /ˈʌðə/ *determiner, adj* **1** used in order to mean one or more of the rest of a group of people or things, when you have already mentioned one person or thing ‖ 한 사람이나 사물을 이미 언급했을 때, 일단의 사람이나 사물의 나머지 가운데 하나나 그 이상을 뜻하는 데에 쓰여. 그 밖의. 또 다른: *Nora's home, but the other girls are at school.* 노라는 집에 있지만 다른 소녀들은 학교에 있다. / *Here's one sock, where's the other one?* 여기 양말 한 짝이 있는데 다른 한 짝은 어디에 있지? **2** used in order to mean someone or something that is different from, or exists in addition to, the person or thing you have already mentioned ‖ 이미 언급한 사람이나 사물과는 다르거나 그것에 추가되는 사람이나 사물을 나타내는 데에 쓰여. 다른. 이외의: *He shares an apartment with three other guys.* 그는

세 명의 다른 사람들과 아파트를 함께 쓴다. / *I'm busy now; could we talk some other time?* 제가 지금 바쁜데 우리 다른 시간에 얘기할까요? / *a cottage on the other side of the lake* (=on the side opposite you) 호수 반대편에 있는 별장 / *Everyone else seemed to be going the other way.* (=in a different direction, especially an opposite direction) 다른 모든 사람들은 반대로 가고 있는 것처럼 보였다. **3 the other day/morning etc.** SPOKEN recently ‖ 근래에. 요전날/요전날 아침: *I talked to Ted the other day.* 요전날 테드에게 말했다. **4 other than** except ‖ …을 제외하고: *I know she has brown hair, but other than that I don't remember much about her.* 나는 머리카락이 갈색이라는 것은 알지만 그것을 제외하고는 그녀에 대해 생각나는 것이 별로 없다. **5 every other day/week etc.** on one of every two days, weeks etc. ‖ 이틀·2주 등마다 한 번으로. 격일로/격주로: *Her husband cooks dinner every other day.* 그녀의 남편은 격일로 저녁을 짓는다. **6 in other words** used in order to express an idea or opinion in a way that is easier to understand ‖ 보다 이해하기 쉽게 생각이나 의견을 표현하는 데에 쓰여. 다시 말하면: *There are TV sets in 68.5 million homes; in other words, 97 percent of the population watch TV.* 가정에 육천팔백오십만 대의 텔레비전 수상기가 있다. 다시 말하면 인구의 97퍼센트가 텔레비전을 시청한다. —compare ANOTHER —see also EACH OTHER, **on the one hand...on the other hand** (HAND[1])

USAGE NOTE other, others, and another

Use all of these words to mean "more people or things of the same type." **Other** is a determiner that is used with plural nouns: *Do you have any other shoes to wear?* **Others** is a plural pronoun: *Besides these shoes, do you have any others?* **Another** is a singular pronoun, or a determiner that is used with a singular noun: *Besides these shoes, I have another pair.* / *Finish that hot dog first, then maybe you can have another.*
이 단어들은 모두 "같은 부류의 여분의 사람이나 사물"의 뜻으로 쓰인다. **other**는 복수 명사와 함께 쓰이는 한정사이다: 신을 다른 신발이 있니? **others**는 복수 대명사이다: 이 신발 말고 다른 신발들도 있어요? **another**는 단수 대명사 또는 단수 명사와 함께 쓰

이는 한정사이다: 이 신발 말고, 나는 신발이 한 켤레 더 있다. / 우선 저 핫도그를 먹어라. 그리고 나면 아마 하나 더 먹을 수 있을 거야.

other² *pron* **1** one or more people or things that form the rest of a group that you are talking about ‖ 언급하고 있는 집단의 나머지를 구성하는 하나나 그 이상의 사람이나 사물. 나머지 사람[사물]: *We ate one pizza and froze the other.* 우리는 피자를 하나는 먹고 나머지 하나는 얼렸다. / *John's here; where are the others?* (=the other people) 존은 여기 있는데 나머지 사람들은 어디에 있지? / *Some stereos are better than others.* 몇몇 스테레오는 다른 것들보다 더 좋다. **2** **someone/something etc. or other** used when you cannot be certain or definite about what you are saying ‖ 말하는 것에 대해 확신하거나 확정할 수 없을 때에 쓰여. 누군가/무언가: *We'll get the money somehow or other.* 우리는 어떻게 해서든지 그 돈을 구할 거야.

oth·er·wise /ˈʌðɚˌwaɪz/ *adv* **1** a word meaning "if not," used when there will be a bad result if something does not happen ‖ 만일 어떤 일이 발생하지 않는다면 나쁜 결과가 생길 때에 쓰여. "만일 아니라면"을 뜻하는 단어. 그렇지 않으면: *You'd better get the tickets now; otherwise, there may not be any left.* 너는 지금 표를 사는 편이 낫겠다. 그렇지 않으면 하나도 남지 않을지도 몰라. **2** except for what has just been mentioned ‖ 방금 언급한 것을 제외하고. 그 이외에는: *The sleeves are long, but otherwise the dress fits.* 소매가 길지만 그 이외에는 옷이 잘 맞는다. **3** in a different way ‖ 다른 방식으로. 다르게: *Adam was ready to buy the house, but his wife decided otherwise.* 아담은 그 집을 구입할 준비를 했지만 그의 아내는 달리 결정했다.

ot·ter /ˈɑtɚ/ *n* a small animal that can swim, has brown fur, and eats fish ‖ 헤엄을 치고 털은 갈색이며 물고기를 잡아먹는 작은 동물. 수달

ouch /aʊtʃ/ *interjection* said when you feel sudden pain ‖ 갑작스런 아픔을 느낄 때에 쓰여. 아야. 아이쿠: *Ouch! That hurt!* 아야! 아파요!

ought to /ˈɔtə; *strong* ˈɔtu/ *modal verb* **1** used in order to make a suggestion ‖ 제안을 하는 데에 쓰여. …해야 하다: *You ought to take a day off.* 너는 하루 쉬어야 한다. **2** used in order to say that someone should do something because

it is right ‖ 사람이 어떤 일이 옳기 때문에 그 일을 해야 한다고 말하는 데에 쓰여. … 하는 것이 당연하다: *He ought to apologize to her.* 그는 그녀에게 마땅히 사과해야 한다. / *We ought not to be eating such high fat food.* 우리는 그런 고지방 음식을 먹어서는 안 된다. **3** used in order to say that you expect something to happen or be true ‖ 어떤 일이 발생하거나 사실일 거라는 예상을 말하는 데에 쓰여. …임에 틀림없다. …일 듯하다: *The weather ought to be nice there in October.* 그곳의 10월 날씨는 좋을 듯하다. —see study note on page 932

ounce /aʊns/, *written abbreviation* **oz.** *n* **1** a unit for measuring weight equal to ¹/₁₆ of a pound or 28.35 grams ‖ 16분의 1파운드나 28.35그램에 상당하는 중량 측정 단위. 온스 **2** a unit for measuring the weight of a liquid, equal to ¹/₁₆ of a PINT or 29.574 MILLILITERS ‖ 16분의 1파인트나 29.574 밀리리터에 상당하는 액체의 중량 측정 단위. 액량 온스 **3** **an ounce of truth/sense etc.** a small amount or a particular quality ‖ 적은 양이나 특정한 자질. 일말의 진실/분별력: *Don't you have even an ounce of sense?* 너는 일말의 분별력도 없니?

our /ɑr; *strong* aʊɚ/ *possessive, adj* belonging or relating to the person who is speaking and one or more other people ‖ 말하는 사람과 한 명이나 그 이상의 다른 사람들에게 속하거나 관련된. 우리의: *We don't have curtains on our windows.* 우리 창문에는 커튼이 없다. / *Our daughter is at college.* 우리 딸은 대학에 다닌다.

ours /aʊɚz, ɑrz/ *possessive, pron* the thing or things belonging or relating to the person who is speaking and one or more other people ‖ 말하는 사람과 한 명이나 그 이상의 다른 사람에게 속하거나 관련된 사물이나 사물들. 우리의 것: *"Whose car is that?" "It's ours."* "저건 누구 차니?" "우리 차야." / *They have their tickets, but ours haven't come yet.* 그들은 자신들의 표를 받았으나 우리 것은 아직 오지 않았다.

our·selves /aʊɚˈsɛlvz, ɑr-/ *pron* **1** the REFLEXIVE form of "we" ‖ "we"의 재귀형. 우리 자신을[에게]: *We cook for ourselves.* 우리는 우리가 먹으려고 요리를 한다. **2** the strong form of "we," used in order to emphasize the subject or object of a sentence ‖ 문장의 주어나 목적어를 강조하는 데 쓰이는 "we"의 강형(強形). 우리 스스로: *We started this business ourselves.* 우리 자신이 직접 이

사업을 시작했다. **3 (all) by ourselves a)** without help ‖ 도움 없이. 우리 힘으로: *Amy and I made supper all by ourselves.* 에이미와 나는 우리 힘으로 저녁 식사를 만들었다. **b)** alone ‖ 우리 외에는 아무도 없이. 우리만: *Dad left us by ourselves for an hour.* 아버지는 한 시간 동안 아무도 없이 우리만 남겨두셨다. **4 to ourselves** not having to share with other people ‖ 다른 사람들과 공유하지 아도 되는. 우리가 독점적으로: *After Mom leaves, we'll have the house to ourselves.* 엄마가 떠난 후, 우리는 이 집을 독차지할 거야.

oust /aʊst/ *v* [T] to force someone out of a position of power ‖ 권좌에서 누군가를 끌어내다. 내쫓다. 축출하다

oust·er /'aʊstər/ *n* [C usually singular] the act of removing someone from a position of power ‖ 권좌에서 누군가를 물러나게 하는 행위. 추방

out¹ /aʊt/ *adj, adv* **1** away from the inside of a place or container ‖ 장소나 용기 안에 없는. 밖의. 밖에[으로]: *Close the door on your way out.* 나가는 길에 문을 닫아라. / *All his tools were out of their box on the floor.* 그의 연장은 모두 연장통에서 마루 위로 나와 있었다. **2** away from the place where you usually are, such as home or work ‖ 집이나 직장 등의 평소 있는 장소에서 떨어진. 벗어나서. 이탈해서: *Ms. Jackson is out right now. She'll be back at 1:00.* 잭슨 씨는 지금은 외출 중이십니다. 그녀는 1시에 돌아올 겁니다. / *He asked me out for dinner tonight.* (=invited me to dinner) 그는 나를 오늘 밤 저녁 식사에 초대했다. **3** away from a place ‖ 장소에서 떨어진: *The sign said "Keep Out."* 게시문에는 "출입 금지"라고 써 있었다. **4** outside ‖ 밖의. 밖으로: *Why don't you go out and play?* 밖에 나가서 놀지 그러니? **5** in or to a place that is far away or difficult to get to ‖ 멀리 떨어지거나 가기 어려운 장소에 또는 장소로: *Do you want me to come out and get you?* 내가 나가서 너한테 갈까? / *He's moved out to Arizona.* 그는 애리조나로 이사갔다. **6** completely or carefully ‖ 완전하게, 주의 깊게: *Clean out the cupboard before you put the dishes in.* 그릇들을 넣기 전에 찬장을 철저히 닦아라. / *I'm worn out.* (=very tired) 나는 매우 피곤해요. **7** if power, electricity etc. is out, it is not working correctly, or not on ‖ 동력·전기 등이 제대로 작동하지 않거나 켜지지 않는. 꺼진. 꺼져서: *The electricity was out for an hour last night.* 전기가 간밤에 한 시간

동안 나갔다. / *OK, kids. Put the lights out.* 자, 얘들아. 불을 꺼라. **8** not having power any more ‖ 더 이상 힘이 없는: *The only way to lower taxes is to vote the Democrats out!* 세금을 내리는 유일한 방법은 민주당 의원들을 투표로 낙선시키는 거야! **9** used in order to say that something has appeared ‖ 사물이 나타났다는 것을 말하는 데에 쓰여: *The sun wasn't out at all today.* 햇빛이 오늘은 전혀 비치지 않았다. / *leaves coming out on the trees* 나무 위에 싹터 나오고 있는 나뭇잎들 **10 out loud** done in a way so that people can hear your voice ‖ 사람들이 목소리를 들을 수 있게 하여. 크게 소리내어: *parents reading out loud to their kids* 자녀에게 책을 크게 읽어 주는 부모 **11** if a number or amount is out, it is not correct ‖ 수나 양이 정확하지 않아. 틀려: *My calculations are way out!* 내 계산이 전혀 맞지를 않아! **12** available to be bought ‖ 구입이 가능한: *Morrison has a new book out this month.* 모리슨은 이 달에 새 책을 출간했다. **13** SPOKEN not possible ‖ 불가능한: *"Where should we go?" "Well, skiing's out because it costs too much."* "우리 어디로 갈까?" "글쎄, 스키는 너무 비용이 많이 들어서 불가능해." **14 be out for sth/be out to do sth** INFORMAL to intend to do or get something ‖ 어떤 것을 하거나 얻으려고 하다: *Don't listen to Danny – he's just out to get attention.* 대니 말을 듣지 마. 그는 단지 관심을 끌려는 거야. **15** INFORMAL **a)** asleep ‖ 잠들어: *Billy was out like a light by 6:00.* 빌리는 6시까지 깊은 잠에 빠졌다. **b)** not conscious ‖ 정신을 잃어: *You must have hit him pretty hard. He's out cold.* 네가 그를 상당히 세게 때렸음에 틀림없다. 그는 정신을 잃고 있다. **16** a player in a game who is out is no longer allowed to play, or has lost one of his/her chances to get a point ‖ 선수가 경기에서 더 이상 경기할 수 없게 되거나 득점의 기회를 한 차례 놓쳐. 아웃이 되어 **17** clothes or styles that are out are no longer fashionable ‖ 옷이나 스타일이 더 이상 유행하지 않는 **18** someone who is out has told people that s/he is a HOMOSEXUAL ‖ 사람이 동성애자임을 공표한 **19** if the tide is out, the ocean is at its lowest level ‖ 바다가 가장 낮은 높이에 있는. 조수가 빠져

out² *prep* **1** from inside something, or through something ‖ 사물의 안에서, 또는 사물을 통하여. 밖으로: *She pulled out a $20 bill.* 그녀는 20달러짜리 지폐를 꺼냈다. / *He was looking out the window at* *the beach.* 그는 창 밖으로 해변을 바라보고 있었다. **2 out of a)** from a particular place or time ‖ 특정한 장소나 시간에서. …으로부터: *I took the books out of the box.* 나는 상자에서 책들을 꺼냈다. / *a nail sticking out of the wall* 벽에 튀어 나와 있는 못 / *It was one of the best movies to come out of the 1980s.* 그것은 1980년대에 나온 최고의 영화 중 하나였다. **b)** from a larger group of the same kind ‖ 같은 부류의 더 큰 집단으로부터. …중에: *Three out of four dentists recommend the toothpaste.* 네 명 중 세 명의 치과 의사가 그 치약을 추천했다. / *Kathy was chosen out of all the kids in her class.* 캐시는 학급 내의 모든 아이들 중에서 뽑혔다. **c)** having none of something that you had before ‖ 전에 있었던 것이 하나도 없는. 떨어진: *We're almost out of gas.* 우리는 기름이 거의 바닥이 났다. / *The car was completely out of control.* 그 자동차는 완전히 통제 불능이었다. **d)** used in order to show what something is made from ‖ 어떤 것으로 만들어진 것인가를 나타내는 데에 쓰여. …을 재료로 하여: *a box made out of wood* 나무로 만든 상자 **3 out of it** INFORMAL not able to think clearly because you are very tired, drunk etc. ‖ 매우 피곤하거나 취하여 똑바로 생각할 수 없는: *I'm really out of it today.* 나 오늘은 정말이지 정신이 멍하다. **4 out of the way a)** a place that is out of the way is far from any towns ‖ 장소가 어떤 도시에서나 멀리 떨어진. 외진 곳에: *an out of the way motel* 시내에서 멀리 떨어진 모텔 **b)** finished ‖ 끝난: *Good. Now that's out of the way, we can start working.* 좋아. 이제 그게 끝났으니 우리는 일을 시작할 수 있어.

out³ *n* **an out** INFORMAL an excuse for not doing something ‖ 무엇을 하지 않는 데에 대한 변명. 구실. 핑계: *I'm busy Sunday, so that gives me an out.* 나는 일요일에 바쁜데 그것이 핑계거리가 된다.

out⁴ *v* [T] to publicly say that someone is HOMOSEXUAL when that person wants it to be a secret ‖ 사람이 비밀로 하고 싶을 때에 동성애자임을 공공연하게 말하다. 동성애자임을 공표하다

out·age /ˈaʊtɪdʒ/ *n* a period of time when a service, especially the electricity supply, is not provided ‖ 특히, 전기 공급 서비스가 제공되지 않는 시간. 정전: *a power outage* 정전(停電)

out-and-out /ˌ. . ˈ./ *adj* having all the qualities of a particular type of person or thing; complete ‖ 특정한 사람이나 사물의 온갖 특성을 갖고 있는. 완벽한. 철저한: *an out-and-out lie* 새빨간 거짓말

out·bid /aʊtˈbɪd/ *v* **outbid, outbid, outbidding** [T] to offer more money than someone else for something that you want to buy ‖ 사고 싶은 것을 남보다 더 많은 돈을 제시하다. (경매에서) 남보다 비싼 값을 부르다

out·break /ˈaʊtbreɪk/ *n* the start or sudden appearance of something bad such as a war or disease ‖ 전쟁이나 질병 등 좋지 않은 것의 시작이나 돌연한 출현: *an outbreak of malaria* 말라리아의 발생

out·burst /ˈaʊtbɜrst/ *n* a sudden powerful expression of strong emotion ‖ 격한 감정의 갑작스런 강력한 표출. 분출. 폭발: *an angry outburst* 분노의 폭발

out·cast /ˈaʊtkæst/ *n* someone who is not accepted by other people and is forced to live away from them ‖ 다른 사람들에게 인정받지 못하고 그들로부터 멀리 떨어져 살도록 강요당하는 사람. 버림받은 사람. 추방자: *a social outcast* 사회의 부랑자

out·class /aʊtˈklæs/ *v* [T] to be much better than someone else at doing something ‖ 무엇을 하는 데에 다른 사람보다 훨씬 더 낫다: *Baltimore outclassed the Mets in the first game of the World Series.* 볼티모어는 월드 시리즈 첫 경기에서 메츠보다 더 뛰어났다.

out·come /ˈaʊtkʌm/ *n* [singular] the final result of a meeting, process etc. ‖ 회의·과정 등의 최종 결과. 성과: *We were eager to know what the outcome of the experiment would be.* 우리는 그 실험의 결과가 어떻게 될지 무척 알고 싶어했다.

out·crop·ping /ˈaʊtˌkrɑpɪŋ/ *n* a rock or group of rocks that sticks out from the surface of the ground ‖ 지표면에서 튀어나온 바위나 일단의 바위들. 노출부

out·cry /ˈaʊtkraɪ/ *n* [singular] an angry protest by a lot of people ‖ 많은 사람들의 성난 항의. 격렬한 항의[요구]: *The killings led to a public outcry for new gun restrictions.* 그 살인 사건은 새로운 총기 규제에 대한 일반 시민의 강력한 요구로 이어졌다.

out·dat·ed /ˌaʊtˈdeɪtɪd/ *adj* **1** no longer useful or modern ‖ 더 이상 유용하거나 현대적이지 않은. 시대에 뒤진. 구식의: *outdated computers* 구식 컴퓨터 **2** no longer effective ‖ 더 이상 유효하지 않은. 기한이 지난: *an outdated map* 갱신되지 않은 지도

out·dis·tance /aʊtˈdɪstəns/ *v* [T] to go faster or farther than someone else in a race ‖ 경주에서 다른 사람보다 더 빨리 또

는 더 멀리 가다. …을 월등히 앞서다

out·do /aʊt'du/ v [T] to be better or more successful than someone else ‖ 다른 사람보다 더 낫거나 더 성공적이다. …보다 뛰어나다. …을 능가하다: *My brothers are always trying to outdo each other.* 나의 형제들은 항상 서로를 이기려고 애쓰고 있다.

out·door /'aʊtdɔr/ adj happening, existing, or used outside and not in a building ‖ 건물 내부가 아닌 외부에서 발생하거나 존재하거나 사용되는. 옥외의. 야외의: *outdoor activities* 야외 활동 / *an outdoor swimming pool* 옥외 수영장 — compare INDOOR

out·doors /aʊt'dɔrz/ adv outside, not inside a building ‖ 건물 안쪽에서가 아니라 밖에서. 옥외[야외]에서[로]: *I prefer working outdoors.* —compare INDOORS 나는 야외에서 일하는 것을 선호한다.

out·er /'aʊtə/ adj 1 on the outside of something ‖ 어떤 것의 바깥쪽의. 밖의. 바깥 면의: *Peel off the outer leaves of lettuce.* 상추의 겉잎을 벗겨라. 2 far from the middle of something ‖ 어떤 것의 중심에서 멀리 떨어진. 외곽의: *an outer office* 건물 외곽의 사무실 — opposite INNER

out·er·most /'aʊtə,moʊst/ adj farthest from the middle ‖ 중심에서 가장 멀리 떨어진. 가장 바깥쪽의: *the outermost planets* 가장 바깥쪽의 행성 —opposite INNERMOST

outer space /ˌ.. ˈ./ n [U] the space outside the Earth's air where the stars and PLANETs are ‖ 별들과 행성들이 있는 지구의 대기 밖 공간. 우주 (공간)

out·field /'aʊtfild/ n [singular] the part of a baseball field that is farthest from the player who is BATTing ‖ 타석에 들어선 선수로부터 가장 먼 야구장의 일부. 외야 – **outfielder** n —see picture on page 946

out·fit¹ /'aʊt,fɪt/ n 1 a set of clothes worn together ‖ 같이 입은 한 벌의 옷. 의상 한 벌: *I love your outfit!* 네 의상 정말 마음에 든다! 2 INFORMAL a group of people who work together as an organization ‖ 한 조직으로서 함께 일하는 일단의 사람들. 단체. 부대. 회사: *When did you join this outfit?* 이 단체에 언제 가입했나요?

outfit² v -tted, -tting [T] to provide someone with a set of clothes or equipment for a special purpose, such as camping ‖ 남에게 캠핑 등의 특별한 목적을 위해 한 벌의 옷이나 장비를 제공하다. …에게 채비를 차려 주다

out·fit·ter /'aʊt,fɪtə/ n a person or business that OUTFITs people for a particular activity ‖ 특별한 활동을 위해 사람들에게 채비를 차려주는 사람이나 사업체. 장신구[운동구]상. (여행) 용품상

out·go·ing /'aʊtˌgoʊɪŋ/ adj 1 wanting to meet and talk to new people, or showing this quality; friendly ‖ 새로운 사람들을 만나 이야기하고 싶어하거나 이러한 특성을 나타내는; 붙임성 있는. 사교적인. 외향적인: *Sally is really outgoing and easy to talk to.* 샐리는 정말 외향적이라 말을 걸기가 편하다. / *an outgoing personality* 외향적인 성격 2 **the outgoing president/CEO etc.** someone who is finishing a job as president etc. ‖ 대통령 등의 직을 끝마치는 사람. 퇴임하는 대통령/최고 경영자 3 going out from or leaving a place ‖ 한 장소에서 나가거나 떠나는: *outgoing phone calls* 외부로 거는 전화

out·grow /aʊt'groʊ/ v [T] 1 to grow too big for something ‖ 어떤 것에 맞기에는 너무 크게 자라다. …보다 크게 성장하다. …에 들어가지 못할 정도로 커지다: *Kara's already outgrown her shoes.* 카라는 벌써 발이 커서 신발이 작아졌다. 2 to no longer enjoy something you used to enjoy ‖ 예전에 즐기던 것을 더 이상 즐기지 않다. (성장해서) …에서 벗어나다. …이 쓸모없게 되다

out·growth /'aʊtgroʊθ/ n a natural result of something ‖ 어떤 것의 자연적인 결과. 파생물. 부산물: *Pollution is an outgrowth of industry.* 오염은 산업의 부산물이다.

out·house /'aʊthaʊs/ n a small building outside the house, in which there is a toilet ‖ 변기가 있는 집 밖의 작은 건물. 옥외 변소

out·ing /'aʊtɪŋ/ n a short enjoyable trip for a group of people ‖ 일단의 사람들이 즐기는 짧은 여행. 나들이. 소풍: *a Sunday outing to the park* 일요일의 공원으로의 나들이

out·land·ish /aʊt'lændɪʃ/ adj strange and unusual ‖ 이상하고 유별난. 기이한. 희한한: *outlandish clothes* 희한한 옷

out·last /aʊt'læst/ v [T] to continue to exist or do something longer than someone else ‖ 계속 존재하거나 다른 사람보다 더 오래 일을 하다. …보다 오래 견디다[살다]: *The whole point of the game is to outlast your opponent.* 경기의 관건은 상대방보다 오래 견디는 것이다.

out·law¹ /'aʊtlɔ/ v [T] to say officially that something is illegal ‖ 일이 불법이라고 공식적으로 말하다. 금지하다: *Gam-*

bling was outlawed here in 1980. 도박은 이곳에서 1980년에 금지되었다.

outlaw² *n* OLD-FASHIONED a criminal who is hiding from the police ‖ 경찰로부터 숨어 있는 범죄자. 무법자. 상습적 범죄자

out·lay /'aʊtˌleɪ/ *n* [C, U] an amount of money that is spent for a particular purpose ‖ 특정한 목적을 위해 지출되는 액수. 지출(액). 경비: *Even after a huge outlay on the new building, the progress was slow.* 신축 건물에 막대한 지출액을 쓰고도 진척이 느렸다.

out·let /'aʊtlɛt, -lɪt/ *n* **1** a place on a wall where you can connect electrical equipment to the electricity supply ‖ 전기 용품을 전기 전력원에 연결할 수 있는 벽 위의 자리. 콘센트 **2** a store that sells things for less than the usual price ‖ 일반적인 가격 이하로 물건을 파는 상점. 할인점: *a clothes outlet* 의류 할인점 **3** a way of expressing or getting rid of strong feelings ‖ 강한 감정을 표현하거나 제거하는 방식. 배출구. 표출의 수단: *I use judo as an outlet for stress.* 나는 스트레스 해소 방법으로 유도를 한다. **4** a way out through which something such as a liquid or gas can flow ‖ 액체나 기체 등이 통과해서 흘러나갈 수 있는 길. 출구. 배출구

outlet mall /'.. ˌ./ *n* a large specially built area which is usually outside but still near to a town or city, where there are a lot of shops that sell popular products for less than the usual price. ‖ 대중적인 상품들을 일반 가격 이하로 파는 점포들이 많이 있는, 보통 시나 도시 근처의 변두리에 특별히 건축된 넓은 지역. 아웃렛 몰

out·line¹ /'aʊtlaɪn/ *n* **1** the main ideas or facts about something without all the details ‖ 모든 세부 사항이 없는 어떤 것에 대한 주된 생각이나 사실. 개요. 요점: *Here is an outline of the company's plan.* 이것이 회사 계획의 개요입니다. **2** a line around the edge of something that shows its shape ‖ 어떤 것의 모양을 나타내는 가장자리 주위의 선. 윤곽

out·line² *v* [T] **1** to describe the main ideas or facts about something, but not all the details ‖ 어떤 것에 대해 자세하게 기술하지 않고 주된 생각이나 사실을 기술하다. …을 약술하다. …의 개요[요점]를 말하다: *He gave us a five page memo outlining his theory.* 그는 자신의 이론을 요약한 5쪽 분량의 서류를 우리에게 제출했다. **2** to draw or put a line around the edge of something to show its shape ‖ 사물의 모양을 나타내기 위해 그것의 가장자

리 주위에 선으로 그리거나 선을 긋다. …의 윤곽을 그리다: *I've outlined the names on the cards in silver.* 나는 카드에 쓰여진 이름에 은색으로 윤곽을 그렸다.

out·live /aʊt'lɪv/ *v* [T] to live longer than someone else ‖ 다른 사람보다 더 오래 살다. 살아남다

out·look /'aʊtlʊk/ *n* **1** your general attitude to life and the world ‖ 인생과 세상에 대한 일반적인 태도. 견해. …관: *Nels has a very positive outlook on life.* 넬스는 매우 긍정적인 인생관을 가지고 있다. **2** what is expected to happen in the future ‖ 미래에 발생할 것으로 기대되는 것. 예상. 전망: *The long-term outlook for the computer industry remains fairly bright.* 컴퓨터 산업에 대한 장기적 전망은 상당히 밝다.

out·ly·ing /'aʊtˌlaɪ-ɪŋ/ *adj* far from cities, people etc. ‖ 도시들·사람들 등으로부터 멀리 떨어진. 외진[외딴]. 변경의: *There may be some frost in outlying areas.* 외곽 지역에 서리가 좀 내리는지도 모른다.

out·ma·neu·ver /ˌaʊtmə'nuvɚ/ *v* [T] to gain an advantage over someone by using skillful movements or plans ‖ 능숙한 동작이나 계획을 이용해서 남보다 이득을 얻다. …에게 책략으로 이기다

out·mod·ed /aʊt'moʊdɪd/ *adj* ⇨ OUTDATED

out·num·ber /aʊt'nʌmbɚ/ *v* [T] to be more in number than another group ‖ 다른 집단보다 수적으로 더 많다. …보다 수적으로 우세하다: *Men outnumber women in Congress.* 의회에서 남자가 여자보다 수가 더 많다.

out of bounds /ˌ. . '../ *adj* **1** not inside the official playing area in a sports game ‖ 스포츠 경기에서 공식적인 경기 지역의 내부가 아닌. 아웃된. 선 밖으로 나간: *The referee said the ball was out of bounds.* 심판은 공이 아웃되었다고 말했다. **2** not allowed or acceptable ‖ 허용되지 않거나 받아들여질 수 없는. 범위를 벗어난: *Some topics, such as sex, are out of bounds for discussion.* 성 등의 일부 주제는 토론의 대상이 될 수 없다. — **out of bounds** *adv* ‖ 아웃되어. 선 밖으로 나가. 장외로: *The ball was knocked out of bounds.* 친 공은 선 밖으로 나갔다[아웃되었다].

out-of-date /ˌ. . '../ *adj* ⇨ OUTDATED

out-of-state /ˌ. . '../ *adj, adv* from, to, or in another state ‖ 다른 주에서 온[다른 주로, 다른 주에]. 타주(他州)의. 주외(州外)의: *out-of-state license plates* 타주의 자동차 번호판 / *I could have gone out-of-*

state for college. 나는 대학에 가기 위해 다른 주로 갈 수 있었다.

out-of-the-way /ˌ. . . '. './ *adj* far from cities and people and often difficult to find ‖ 도시들과 사람들로부터 멀리 떨어져서 종종 찾기 어려운. 외딴. 벽촌의: *They met in an out-of-the-way hotel.* 그들은 외진 곳에 있는 호텔에서 만났다.

out·pa·tient /ˈaʊtˌpeɪʃənt/ *n* someone who goes to the hospital for treatment but does not stay there ‖ 치료를 받으러 병원에 가지만 그곳에 머무르지는 않는 사람. 외래 환자 —compare INPATIENT

out·per·form /ˌaʊtpəˈfɔrm/ *v* [T] to do something better than other things or people ‖ 다른 것이나 사람들보다 일을 더 잘하다. …을 능가하다: *Mart Stores continued to outperform other large retailers.* 할인점들은 다른 큰 도매상들을 계속 앞질렀다.

out·place·ment /ˈaʊtˌpleɪsmənt/ *n* [U] a service that a company provides to help its workers find other jobs when it cannot continue to employ them ‖ 회사가 직원을 계속 고용할 수 없을 때 그 직원이 다른 직장을 찾게 도움을 주는 활동. 재취업[전직] 알선

out·post /ˈaʊtpoʊst/ *n* a small town or group of buildings in a place that is far away from big cities ‖ 대도시에서 멀리 떨어진 장소에 있는 작은 도시나 일단의 건물들. 변경의 식민지[거류지]

out·pour·ing /ˈaʊtˌpɔrɪŋ/ *n* a large amount of something that is produced suddenly, such as strong emotions, ideas, or help ‖ 강한 감정[생각, 도움] 등이 갑자기 생성되는 대량의 것. (감정의) 분출[토로]. 쇄도: *an outpouring of help from the public* 대중들의 쇄도하는 원조

out·put /ˈaʊtpʊt/ *n* [C, U] the amount of work, goods etc. produced by someone or something ‖ 사람이나 사물이 생산한 작업·물건 등의 양. 생산량. 산출량: *Economic output is down 10% this year.* 올해 경제 생산량은 10% 감소된다. —compare INPUT

out·rage¹ /ˈaʊtreɪdʒ/ *n* [C, U] a feeling of great anger or shock, or something that causes this ‖ 막대한 화나 충격의 감정, 또는 이것을 일으키는 것. 격분. 무도한 행위: *a deep sense of moral outrage* 뼈저린 모욕감 – *"This is an outrage – they owe me at least another $350!"* "이건 말도 안 돼. 그들은 나한테 적어도 350 달러는 더 빚이 있다고!"

outrage² *v* [T] to make someone feel very angry or shocked ‖ 사람을 매우 화나게 하거나 충격을 받게 하다. 격분하게

하다. 아연실색케 하다: *Shorman's comments outraged leaders of the African-American community.* 셔먼의 발언은 흑인계 미국 사회의 지도자들을 격분시켰다. – **outraged** *adj*

out·ra·geous /aʊtˈreɪdʒəs/ *adj* very shocking and offensive ‖ 매우 충격적이고 기분을 상하게 하는. 터무니없는. 심한: *an outrageous comedy show* 말도 안 되는 코미디 쇼 – **outrageously** *adv*

out·reach /ˈaʊtritʃ/ *n* [U] the practice of trying to help people with particular problems, especially through an organization ‖ 특히 조직을 통해 특정한 문제를 가진 사람들을 도우려고 애쓰는 행위. 봉사 활동: *the church's community outreach program* 교회의 지역 사회 봉사 활동 프로그램

out·right¹ /ˈaʊtraɪt/ *adj* **1** complete and total ‖ 완전하고 전적인: *an outright refusal to sell the house* 주택 매매에 대한 단호한 거부 **2** clear and direct ‖ 분명하고 직접적인. 철저한. 노골적인: *an outright lie* 새빨간 거짓말

out·right² /aʊtˈraɪt, ˈaʊtraɪt/ *adv* **1** not trying to hide your feelings; OPENLY ‖ 감정을 숨기려고 애쓰지 않아. 거리낌 없이. 솔직하게; 匣 openly: *Nadine laughed outright at the suggestion.* 나딘은 그 제안에 터놓고 비웃었다. **2** completely ‖ 완벽하게. 완전히: *My parents own their home outright, after having worked hard to pay it off.* 나의 부모님은 열심히 일해서 할부금을 다 갚고 나서 집을 완전히 소유하셨다.

out·run /aʊtˈrʌn/ *v* [T] **1** to run faster or further than someone ‖ 남보다 더 빨리 또는 더 멀리 달리다. …을 앞지르다 **2** to develop more quickly than something else ‖ 다른 것보다 더 빠르게 성장하다. …의 범위를 넘다. …을 상회하다: *Social needs have outrun the state's ability to provide help.* 사회적 요구는 도움을 제공할 국가의 능력 범위를 상회해 왔다.

out·set /ˈaʊtsɛt/ *n* **at/from the outset** at or from the beginning of an event or process ‖ 사건이나 과정의 처음에 또는 처음부터. 최초에. 시작부터: *The rules were agreed at the outset of the game.* 게임 규칙은 게임 처음에 동의되었다.

out·shine /aʊtˈʃaɪn/ *v* [T] to be much better at something than someone else ‖ 다른 사람보다 일에서 훨씬 더 낫다. …보다 훌륭하다

out·side¹ /ˌaʊtˈsaɪd, ˈaʊtsaɪd/, **outside of** *prep* **1** out of a particular building or room, but still near it ‖ 특정한 건물이나 방을 벗어나 있지만 여전히 그 가까이에

있는. …의 밖에: *He left an envelope outside my door*. 그는 내 문 밖에 봉투 하나를 남겼다. —opposite INSIDE¹ **2** beyond the limits of a city, country etc. ‖ 도시·국가 등의 경계선을 넘어: *Perry lives just outside of Billings, Montana*. 페리는 몬태나 주 빌링스 경계선 바로 너머에 산다. **3** beyond the limits of a situation, activity etc. ‖ 상황·활동 등의 경계를 넘어. …을 제외하고. …이외에: *She's crying, but outside of that, I don't know anything*. 그녀가 울고 있다는 것을 제외하고는 나는 아무것도 모른다. / *Teachers can't control what students do outside school*. 교사들은 학생들이 학교 밖에서 하는 일을 통제할 수 없다.

outside² *adv* **1** not inside any building ‖ 어떠한 건물의 내부도 아닌. 바깥쪽으로 [에]: *Mom, can I go outside and play?* 엄마, 밖에 나가서 놀아도 돼요? / *No, it's dark outside*. 안 돼, 밖이 어둡잖아. **2** not in a room or building, but close to it ‖ 방이나 건물의 내부는 아니지만 그곳에 가까이에. 밖에(서): *Wait outside; I want to talk to him alone*. 밖에서 기다려라. 나는 그와 단독으로 말하고 싶다.

outside³ *n* **1** the outer part or surface of something ‖ 사물의 바깥 부분이나 표면. 바깥쪽. 바깥면: *They painted the outside of the building pink*. 그들은 그 건물의 바깥면을 분홍색으로 칠했다. —opposite INSIDE² **2** the area of land around something such as a building ‖ 건물 등 그 주변의 부지. 외부. 밖: *From the outside the house looked very nice*. 외부에서 보면 그 집은 매우 멋있게 보였다. **3 on the outside** used in order to describe the way someone or something appears to be ‖ 사람이나 사물이 (겉으로) 드러나는 방식을 묘사하는 데에 쓰여. 외관상. 겉으로: *Their marriage seemed so perfect on the outside*. 그들의 결혼 생활은 외관상으로는 아주 완벽해 보였다.

out·sid·er /aʊtˈsaɪdɚ/ *n* someone who does not belong to a particular group, organization etc. ‖ 특정한 집단·조직 등에 속하지 않은 사람. 국외자(局外者). 아웃사이더: *Corran is a Washington outsider who has never been in office before*. 코란은 전에 한 번도 공직에 오른 적이 없는 워싱턴 정가의 국외자이다.

out·skirts /ˈaʊtskɚts/ *n* [plural] the parts of a city or town that are farthest from the center ‖ 중심으로부터 가장 먼 도시나 읍의 일부분. 외곽. 변두리: *He lived on the outskirts of town*. 그는 도시의 변두리에 살았다.

out·smart /aʊtˈsmɑrt/ *v* [T] to gain an advantage over someone using tricks or your intelligence ‖ 속임수나 지능을 이용해 남보다 더 이득을 얻다. …보다 한 수 더 높다. …을 이기다: *He was mad because he had been outsmarted by his brother*. 그는 동생에게 당해서 화가 났다.

out·sourc·ing /ˈaʊtsɔrsɪŋ/ *n* [U] the practice of using workers from outside a company, or of buying supplies, parts etc. from another company instead of producing them yourself ‖ 회사 외부의 근로자를 이용하는 행위, 또는 직접 생산하는 대신에 다른 회사로부터 물품·부품 등을 구입하는 행위. 외주. 외부 조달

out·spo·ken /aʊtˈspoʊkən/ *adj* expressing your opinions honestly even if they shock or offend other people ‖ 다른 사람들에게 충격을 주거나 기분을 상하게 하더라도 자신의 의견을 솔직하게 표현하는. 거리낌없이 말하는. 솔직한: *an outspoken critic of the program* 그 프로그램에 대해 기탄없이 말하는 비평가 – **outspokenness** *n* [U]

out·stand·ing /aʊtˈstændɪŋ/ *adj* **1** better than anyone or anything else; excellent ‖ 다른 어떤 사람이나 사물보다 더 나은; 훌륭한. 뛰어난. 걸출한: *an outstanding performance* 훌륭한 공연 **2** not yet done, paid, or solved ‖ 아직 행해지지[지불되지, 해결되지] 않은. 미결정[결제]의. 미해결의: *an outstanding debt* 미불 채무

out·stretched /ˌaʊtˈstrɛtʃt/ *adj* reaching out to full length ‖ 완전한 길이로 뻗은. 펼친. 편. 내민: *I took hold of his outstretched arm*. 나는 그의 활짝 벌린 팔을 잡았다.

out·strip /aʊtˈstrɪp/ *v* [T] to be larger, greater, or better than someone or something else ‖ 어떤 사람이나 사물보다 더 크다[훌륭하다, 좋다]. …을 능가하다. …보다 뛰어나다: *The gains will outstrip the losses*. 수익이 손실을 웃돌 것이다.

out·ward¹ /ˈaʊtwɚd/ *adj* **1** relating to how people, things etc. seem to be rather than how they are ‖ 사람·사물 등이 어떠한가보다는 오히려 그것들이 어떻게 보이는가와 관련되는. 외관의. 표면상의: *Amy answered with a look of outward calm*. 에이미는 겉으로는 침착한 표정으로 대답했다. **2** going away from a place or toward the outside ‖ 한 장소에서 멀어져 가거나 바깥쪽을 향하는. 밖으로 가는[향하는]: *The outward flight was bumpy*. 외국행 비행기는 갑자기 덜컹거렸다. —compare INWARD¹

out·ward², **outwards** *adv* toward the outside ‖ 바깥쪽을 향해. 바깥쪽으로. 밖

으로: *The door opens outward.* 그 문은 바깥쪽으로 열린다. —compare INWARD²

out·ward·ly /'aʊt'wədli/ *adv* according to how people, things etc. seem to be rather than how they are inside ‖ 사람·사물 등의 내면보다는 오히려 겉모습에 따라. 외관상. 표면상: *Outwardly he seems to be very happy.* 그는 겉으로는 매우 행복해 보인다.

out·weigh /aʊt'weɪ/ *v* [T] to be more important or valuable than something else ‖ 다른 것보다 더 중요하거나 가치가 있다. …보다 중대하다[뛰어나다]. …의 결점을 메우기에 충분하다: *The advantages far outweigh the disadvantages.* 장점은 그 약점을 상쇄하고도 충분히 남는다.

out·wit /aʊt'wɪt/ *v* **-witted, -witting** [T] ⇨ OUTSMART

o·val /'oʊvəl/ *n* a shape like a circle, but longer than it is wide ‖ 원 같지만 한쪽 길이가 폭보다 더 긴 모양. 타원형 – **oval** *adj* —see picture at SHAPE

o·va·ry /'oʊvəri/ *n* the part of a female that produces eggs ‖ 난자를 생산하는 여성의 (신체) 부위. 난소 – **ovarian** /oʊ'vɛriən/ *adj*

o·va·tion /oʊ'veɪʃən/ *n* FORMAL if people give someone an ovation, they CLAP their hands to show approval ‖ 사람들이 어떤 사람에게 찬성한다는 것을 나타내기 위해 손뼉을 침. 열렬한 환영. 대단한 갈채: *The performance received a standing ovation.* 그 공연은 기립 박수를 받았다. —compare ENCORE

ov·en /'ʌvən/ *n* a piece of equipment that food is cooked inside, shaped like a metal box with a door on it ‖ 음식이 안쪽에서 요리되는 문이 달린 금속 상자 모양의 기구. 오븐 —see picture at KITCHEN

over

The truck is driving over the bridge.
The ferry is going across the river.

o·ver¹ /'oʊvə/ *prep* **1** above or higher than something, without touching it ‖ 사물을 건드리지 않고 그것보다 위에나 더 높이. …에서 떨어져서 위(쪽)에: *I leaned over the desk.* 나는 책상 위로 기댔다. / *The sign over the door said "No Exit."* 문 위쪽의 표지판에는 "출구 없음"이라고 쓰여 있었다. / *The ball went way over (=a long way above) my head.* 공은 내 머리 위를 훌쩍 넘어 날아갔다. —opposite UNDER¹ —compare ABOVE¹, ACROSS¹ —see also picture at ABOVE¹ **2** moving across the top of something, or from one side of it to the other ‖ 사물의 꼭대기를 가로질러 움직이거나 한쪽에서 다른 쪽으로 움직이는. …을 가로질러서. 건너서: *We walked over the hill.* 우리는 언덕을 가로질러 걸었다. / *The boy leaped over the stream.* 소년은 시내를 뛰어넘었다. —compare ACROSS¹ **3** on something or someone so that he, she, or it is covered ‖ 사물이나 사람을 덮을 수 있도록 그 위에. …(의 위)를 덮어서: *Put this blanket over him.* 그에게 이 담요를 덮어 줘라. —opposite UNDER¹ **4** more than a particular amount, number, or age ‖ 특정한 양[수, 나이] 이상으로. …을 넘어서. … 이상: *He told me he spent over $1000 last week.* 그는 지난주에 천 달러 이상을 썼다고 나에게 말했다. / *a game for children over seven* 7세 이상 어린이용 놀이 **5 over on** on the opposite side of something from where you are ‖ 지금 있는 것의 반대편에. …의 저편[건너편]에 [으로]: *Jamie lives over on Wicker Ave.* 제이미는 위커 거리의 건너편에 산다. **6** during ‖ … 동안. 내내: *I saw Julie over the summer.* 나는 줄리를 여름 내내 보았다. **7** down from the edge of something ‖ 사물의 가장자리로부터 아래로: *Hang the towel over the back of the chair.* 수건을 의자 뒤에 걸쳐 놔라. **8 be/get over sth** to feel better after being sick or upset ‖ 아프거나 화가 난 이후에 기분이 더 나아진다. 이겨내다. 극복하다: *He's mad, but he'll get over it.* 그는 화나 있지만 곧 진정할 거야. **9** about or concerning something ‖ 사물에 대해서 또는 관해서: *They had an argument over who would take the car.* 그들은 누가 차를 탈 것인지를 놓고 논쟁했다. **10** using the telephone or a radio ‖ 전화기나 무전기를 사용하여. …을 통하여: *The salesman explained it to me over the phone.* 영업 사원은 전화로 그것을 나에게 설명했다. —see also **all over** (ALL²)

over² *adv* **1** down from an upright position ‖ 똑바른 위치에서 아래로. 넘어

저서. 젖혀져서: *Kate fell over and hurt her ankle.* 케이트는 넘어져서 발목을 다쳤다. / *I saw him push the bike over.* 나는 그가 자전거를 밀어 넘어뜨리는 것을 보았다. **2** used in order to show where someone or something is ‖ 사람이나 사물이 어디 있는지를 나타내는 데에 쓰여. 이쪽으로. 저쪽에[으로]: *I'm over here!* 나 여기 있어! / *There's a mailbox over on the corner.* 저쪽 구석에 우체통이 있다. **3** to or in a particular place ‖ 특정한 장소로 또는 장소에: *We drove over to Macon County to the fair.* 우리는 박람회를 보러 메이콘 군으로 차를 몰고 갔다. / *The weather's awful. Why don't you stay over?* (=in my house) 날씨가 아주 나쁘니 저희 집에 머무르지 그래요? **4** above ‖ 위(쪽)에: *You can't hear anything when the planes fly over.* 비행기가 위로 날아갈 때는 어떤 소리도 안 들린다. **5** again ‖ 다시. 되풀이하여: *I got mixed up and had to start over.* 나는 혼란스러워져서 다시 시작해야 했다. / *She sings the same song over and over (again).* (=repeatedly) 그녀는 같은 노래를 반복해서 부른다. **6 think/talk sth over** to think or talk about something carefully or thoroughly before deciding what to do ‖ 무엇을 할지 결정하기 전에 사물에 대해서 주의 깊게 또는 철저하게 생각하거나 말하다. …에 대해서 곰곰이[자세히] 생각하다[말하다]: *Think it over, and give us your answer tomorrow.* 잘 생각하시고 내일까지 답변을 주세요. **7** so that another side is showing ‖ 다른 쪽이 보이도록. 뒤집어서: *He rolled over and went to sleep.* 그는 몸을 뒤척이더니 잠이 들었다. **8** from one person or group to another ‖ 한 사람이나 집단에서 다른 사람이나 집단으로. 한쪽에서 다른 쪽으로: *The land was handed over* (=given) *to the government.* 그 땅은 정부에 양도되었다. **9** more or higher than a particular amount, number, or age ‖ 특정한 양[수, 나이] 이상이나 더 높이. 넘어서. 초과하여: *"Did you guess the right number?" "No, I was over by two."* (=the number I guessed was two higher) "옳은 수를 맞혔니?" "아니, 2를 초과했어." / *a game for children aged six and over* 6세 이상 어린이용 놀이

over³ *adj* **1** finished ‖ 끝마친. 끝난: *The game's over – Dallas won.* 경기는 종료되었고 댈러스가 승리했다. **2 get sth over with** to do something unpleasant so that you do not have to worry about it any more ‖ 더 이상 걱정할 필요가 없도록 불쾌한 것을 하다. (싫은 것을) 끝마치다:

Well, call her and get it over with. 그냥 그녀에게 전화해서 화해해라.

o·ver·all¹ /ˈoʊvɚˌɔl/ *adj* including everything ‖ 모든 것을 포함하는. 종합적인. 전반적인: *The overall cost of the trip is $500.* 여행의 총경비는 500달러이다.

o·ver·all² /ˌoʊvɚˈɔl/ *adv* **1** generally ‖ 일반적으로. 전반적으로: *Overall, the situation looks good.* 전반적으로 상황은 좋아 보인다. **2** including everything ‖ 모든 것을 포함하여. 전부. 일반적으로: *Inflation is growing at 3% a year overall.* 인플레이션은 일반적으로 연간 3%의 증가 추세에 있다.

overalls

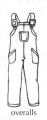
overalls

coveralls

o·ver·alls /ˈoʊvɚˌɔlz/ *n* [plural] heavy cotton pants with a piece that covers your chest, held up by two bands that go over your shoulders ‖ 어깨 위로 넘기는 두 개의 띠로 지지되는 가슴을 덮는 부분이 있는 무거운 면바지. 작업 바지[복]

o·ver·awed /ˌoʊvɚˈɔd/ *adj* feeling great respect or fear ‖ 큰 경의나 공포를 느끼는. 위압[압도]당하는: *Laura was overawed by the size of the house.* 로라는 그 집 규모에 압도당했다.

o·ver·bear·ing /ˌoʊvɚˈbɛrɪŋ/ *adj* always trying to control other people without considering their feelings or needs; DOMINEERING ‖ 다른 사람들의 감정이나 욕구를 고려하지 않고 항상 그들을 통제하려고 하는. 고압적인. 거만한; ㈜ domineering

o·ver·board /ˈoʊvɚˌbɔrd/ *adv* **1** over the side of a ship into the water ‖ 배의 측면을 넘어 물 속으로. 배 밖으로. 배에서 물 속으로: *He fell overboard by accident.* 그는 사고로 배에서 물로 떨어졌다. **2 go overboard** INFORMAL to do or say something that is too extreme for a particular situation, for example by being too emotional or expensive ‖ 예를 들어 너무 감정적으로 또는 비싼 것으로, 특정 상황에 대해 지나치게 극단적인 행동이나 말을 하다. 극단으로 흐르다: *She managed to find a nice present, without going overboard.* 그녀는 너무 과도하지 않은 괜찮은 선물을 간신히 찾았다.

o·ver·bur·dened /ˌoʊvɚˈbɚdnd/ adj carrying or doing too much ‖ 너무 많이 나르거나 행하는. 과중한. 지나친: overburdened freeways 차량이 너무 많은 고속도로 / the overburdened court system 과도한 부담의 사법 제도

o·ver·cast /ˈoʊvɚˌkæst/ adj dark because of clouds ‖ 구름 때문에 어두운. 잔뜩 흐린. 우중충한: a gray overcast sky 회색빛으로 잔뜩 흐린 하늘

o·ver·charge /ˌoʊvɚˈtʃɑrdʒ/ v [I, T] to charge someone too much money for something ‖ 남에게 사물에 대한 너무 많은 돈을 청구하다. (…에게) 부당한 값을 청구하다

o·ver·coat /ˈoʊvɚˌkoʊt/ n a long thick warm coat ‖ 길고 두꺼우며 따뜻한 웃옷. 외투

o·ver·come /ˌoʊvɚˈkʌm/ v 1 [T] to succeed in controlling a feeling or problem ‖ 감정이나 문제를 통제하는 데에 성공하다. …을 극복하다[억누르다]: I'm trying to overcome my fear of flying. 난 비행의 공포감을 극복하려고 애쓰고 있어. 2 be overcome (by sth) to be made weak, unconscious, or unable to control your feelings ‖ 약해지거나 의식을 잃거나 감정을 통제할 수 없게 되다. (…에) 압도되다: She was overcome by smoke. 그녀는 연기에 의식을 잃었다. 3 [I, T] to fight and win against someone or something ‖ 사람이나 사물에 대항해서 싸워 이기다. (…을) 정복하다: Antiaircraft guns were used to overcome the enemy. 대공포는 예전에 적을 물리치곤 했다.

o·ver·com·pen·sate /ˌoʊvɚˈkɑmpənˌseɪt/ v [I] to try to correct a weakness or mistake by doing too much of the opposite thing ‖ 정반대의 일을 너무 많이 함으로써 약함이나 실수를 고치려 하다. 과잉 보상하다. 지나치게 수정하다 – **overcompensation** /ˌoʊvɚˌkɑmpənˈseɪʃən/ n [U]

o·ver·crowd·ed /ˌoʊvɚˈkraʊdɪd/ adj filled with too many people or things ‖ 너무 많은 사람들이나 사물로 가득 찬. 초만원인. 북적대는: an overcrowded classroom 과밀 학급

o·ver·do /ˌoʊvɚˈdu/ v [T] to do or use too much of something ‖ 어떤 것을 너무 많이 하거나 사용하다. …을 지나치게 하다. 무리하다: When exercising you have to be careful not to overdo it. 너는 운동할 때 무리하지 않도록 주의해야 한다.

o·ver·done /ˌoʊvɚˈdʌn/ adj cooked too much ‖ 너무 많이 요리한. 너무 구운[익힌]: an overdone steak 너무 구운 스테이크

o·ver·dose /ˈoʊvɚˌdoʊs/ n too much of a drug taken at one time ‖ 약을 한 번에 지나치게 많이 복용함. 과다 복용: He died from a heroin overdose. 그는 헤로인을 과다 복용해서 사망했다. – **overdose** v [I]

o·ver·draw /ˌoʊvɚˈdrɔ/ v [T] to have spent more money than the amount you have in the bank ‖ 은행에 가지고 있는 액수보다 더 많은 돈을 지출하다. 초과 인출하다

o·ver·due /ˌoʊvɚˈdu/ adj 1 not done or happening when expected; late ‖ 예상한 때 행해지거나 발생하지 않은. 지체된. (지급) 기한이 지난. 연체된; 늦은: an overdue library book 연체된 도서관 책 2 be overdue (for sth) to have needed something done for a long time ‖ 오랫동안 어떤 일이 행해질 필요가 있어 왔다. (…이) 전부터의 현안이다: Salary increases are long overdue. 봉급 인상은 오랫동안 미루어져 있는 상태이다.

o·ver·eat /ˌoʊvɚˈit/ v [I] to eat too much, or more than is healthy ‖ 너무 많이, 또는 건강에 알맞은 양 이상을 먹다. 과식하다

o·ver·es·ti·mate /ˌoʊvɚˈɛstəˌmeɪt/ v 1 [I, T] to think that something is larger, more expensive, or more important than it really is ‖ 어떤 것이 실제보다 더 크거나 비싸거나 중요하다고 생각하다. (…을) 지나치게 많이[높게] 견적하다[되다] 2 [T] to think that someone is more skillful, intelligent etc. than s/he really is ‖ 사람이 실제보다 더 솜씨가 좋고 지적이라고 생각하다. …을 과대평가하다 — opposite UNDERESTIMATE

o·ver·ex·tend /ˌoʊvɚɪkˈstɛnd/ v [T] to try to do too much or use too much of something, causing problems ‖ 문제를 일으키는 것을 너무 많이 하거나 너무 많이 사용하려고 하다. 무리하다. …을 과도하게 (사용)하다: Even with extra people working, they're overextending themselves. 심지어 임시직 사람들도 무리해서 일하고 있다. – **overextended** adj

o·ver·flow¹ /ˌoʊvɚˈfloʊ/ v [I, T] 1 if a liquid or river overflows, it goes over the edges of the container or place where it is ‖ 액체나 강이 그것이 있는 용기나 장소의 가장자리를 넘어가다. 흘러넘치다. 범람하다: a sink overflowing with water 물이 흘러넘치는 싱크대 2 if people overflow a place, there are too many of them to fit into it ‖ 한 장소를 채우기에는 사람들이 너무 많다. 넘쳐 나오다. 만원이 되어 더 못 들어가다

o·ver·flow²
/'ouvəˌflou/ *n* [C, U]
the people, water etc.
that cannot be
contained in a place
because it is already
full ‖ 이미 꽉 차 있기
때문에 한 장소에 수용
할 수 없는 사람들·물
등. 넘친 물. 초과 인
원: *the overflow of people from the
concert* 콘서트에서 넘쳐 나온 사람들

overflow

o·ver·grown /ˌouvə'groun-/ *adj*
covered with plants that have grown
without being controlled ‖ 통제되지 않고
자란 식물로 뒤덮인. 우거진. 무성한: *a
yard overgrown with weeds* 잡초가 무
성한 뜰

o·ver·hand /'ouvəˌhænd/ *adj, adv*
thrown with your arm above the level of
your shoulder ‖ 팔을 어깨 높이 위로
던지는. 손을 위로 올렸다가 던지는[던
져]: *an overhand pitch* 손을 위로 올렸다
가 던지기

o·ver·hang /ˌouvə'hæŋ/ *v* [I, T] to
hang over something or stick out above
it ‖ 어떤 것 위에 걸려 있거나 그것 위로
튀어나오다. …의 위에 걸리다[돌출하다]:
tree branches overhanging the path 길
위까지 뻗어져 나온 나뭇가지들 –
overhang /'ouvəˌhæŋ/ *n*

o·ver·haul /ˌouvə'hɔl, 'ouvəˌhɔl/ *v* [T]
to repair or change all the parts of a
machine, system etc. that need it ‖ 기
계·시스템 등의 모든 부품을 필요에 의해
수리하거나 바꾸다. …을 정비[정밀 검사]
하다 – **overhaul** /'ouvəˌhɔl/ *n*

o·ver·head¹ /ˌouvə'hɛd·/ *adj, adv*
above your head ‖ 머리 위의 또는 머리
위에. 상공의[에]. 높이: *A plane flew
overhead.* 비행기 한 대가 머리 위로 날아
갔다. / *an overhead light* 천장에 매달린
등

o·ver·head² /'ouvəˌhɛd/ *n* money that
you spend for rent, electricity etc. to
keep a business operating ‖ 사업체를 계
속 운영하기 위해 임대료·전기료 등에 지
출하는 돈. 경상비. 고정비. 간접비

o·ver·hear /ˌouvə'hɪr/ *v* [T] to hear by
accident what other people are saying
when they do not know that you are
listening ‖ 다른 사람들이 말하는 것을 그
들이 알 수 없게 우연히 듣다. …을 우연
히 엿듣다: *I overheard some people
saying that the food was bad.* 나는 몇몇
사람들이 음식이 맛 없다고 말하는 것을
우연히 엿들었다. —compare EAVESDROP

o·ver·joyed /ˌouvə'dʒɔɪd/ *adj*
extremely happy because something
good has happened ‖ 좋은 일이 발생해서
매우 행복한. 대단히 기쁜: *We were
overjoyed to hear that they are getting
married.* 우리는 그들이 결혼한다는 소식
을 듣고 매우 기뻤다.

o·ver·kill /'ouvəˌkɪl/ *n* [U] INFORMAL
more of something than is necessary or
desirable ‖ 어떤 것이 필요하거나 바람직
한 것보다 더 많음. 과잉: *Starting
Christmas advertising in August seems
like overkill.* 8월에 성탄절 광고를 시작하
는 것은 좀 지나쳐 보인다.

o·ver·land /'ouvəˌlænd/ *adj, adv*
across land, not by sea or air ‖ 배편이나
항공편이 아닌 육지를 가로질러. 육로로
[로]: *traveling overland to Ayers Rock*
에어스 록까지의 육로 여행

o·ver·lap /ˌouvə-
'læp/ *v* **-pped, -
pping** [I, T] **1** if two
or more things
overlap, part of one
thing covers part of
another thing ‖ 두 개
나 그 이상의 사물에서
하나의 일부분이 또 다
른 하나의 일부분을 덮

overlap

overlapping roof tiles

다. 겹치다[겹쳐지다]. 포개다[포개지다]:
a pattern of overlapping circles 원이 겹
쳐지는 형태 **2** if two subjects, activities,
ideas etc. overlap, they share some but
not all of the same parts or qualities ‖ 두
개의 주제·활동·생각 등이 같은 부분이나
특성의 전부는 아니지만 그 일부를 공유하
다. …과 부분적으로 일치하다[되다] –
overlap /'ouvəˌlæp/ *n* [C, U]

o·ver·load /ˌouvə'loud/ *v* [T] **1** to load
something with too many things or
people ‖ 어떤 것에 너무 많은 사물이나 사
람들을 싣다. 과적하다. 초과 승차시키다:
*Don't overload the washing machine
with clothes.* 세탁기에 옷을 너무 많이 넣
지 마라. **2** to give someone too much
work to do ‖ 남에게 할 일을 너무 많이 주
다. 지나치게 부담시키다 **3** to damage an
electrical system by causing too much
electricity to flow through it ‖ 너무 많은
전기를 통하게 해서 전기 장치를 손상시
키다. …에 과부하를 걸다 – **overload**
/'ouvəˌloud/ *n* [C, U]

o·ver·look /ˌouvə'luk/ *v* [T] **1** to not
notice something or to not realize how
important it is ‖ 어떤 것을 알아채지 못하
거나 그것이 얼마나 중요한지 깨닫지 못하
다. …을 못 보고 넘어가다. 간과하다:
*It's easy to overlook mistakes when
reading your own writing.* 자신이 직접

쓴 글을 읽을 때는 실수를 못 보고 넘어가기가 쉽다. **2** to forgive someone's mistake, bad behavior etc. ‖ 남의 실수·잘못된 행동 등을 용서하다. …을 관대히 봐주다. 눈감아 주다: *I'm willing to overlook what you said this time.* 난 이번에는 네가 한 말을 기꺼이 눈감아 주겠다. **3** to have a view of something from above ‖ 위에서 어떤 것을 보다. …을 내려다보다. …이 내려다보이다: *a room overlooking the beach* 해변이 내려다보이는 방

o·ver·ly /'ouvɚli/ *adv* too much, or very ‖ 너무 많이, 또는 매우. 지나치게. 과도하게: *We weren't overly impressed with the movie.* 우리는 그 영화를 그다지 감명 깊게 보지 않았다.

o·ver·night¹ /,ouvɚ'naɪt/ *adv* **1** for or during the night ‖ 밤 동안. 밤새도록. 밤 새껏: *She's staying overnight at a friend's house.* 그녀는 친구 집에서 밤새도록 머무르고 있다. **2** INFORMAL suddenly ‖ 갑자기. 하룻밤 사이에: *You can't expect to lose the weight overnight.* 몸무게가 하룻밤 사이에 빠지리라고 기대해서는 안 된다.

o·ver·night² /'ouvɚ,naɪt/ *adj* continuing all night ‖ 밤새 계속되는. 밤을 새는. 철야의: *an overnight flight to Japan* 일본행 야간 비행

o·ver·pass /'ouvɚ,pæs/ *n* a structure like a bridge that allows one road to go over another road ‖ 하나의 길에서 또 다른 길로 넘어갈 수 있게 하는 다리 같은 구조물. 육교

o·ver·pop·u·lat·ed /,ouvɚ'pɑpyə,-leɪtɪd/ *adj* having too many people ‖ 너무 많은 사람들이 있는. 인구 과잉의: *an overpopulated city* 인구 과잉 도시 – **overpopulation** /,ouvɚ,pɑpyə'leɪʃən/ *n* [U]

o·ver·pow·er /,ouvɚ'pauɚ/ *v* [T] to defeat someone because you are stronger ‖ 더 강해서 남을 패배시키다. (힘으로) 눌러버리다[제압하다]

o·ver·pow·er·ing /,ouvɚ'pauɚɪŋ/ *adj* very strong; INTENSE ‖ 매우 강한. 압도적인. 우세한; ㈜ intense: *an overpowering smell* 참을 수 없는 냄새

o·ver·priced /,ouvɚ'praɪst/ *adj* too expensive ‖ 너무 비싼. 값이 너무 비싸게 매겨진

o·ver·rat·ed /,ouvɚ'reɪtɪd/ *adj* something or someone that is overrated is not as good or important as some people think ‖ 사물이나 사람이 일부 사람들이 생각하는 것만큼 좋거나 중요하지 않은. 과대평가된: *I think rave music is* overrated. 내 생각에 격찬받고 있는 음악은 과대평가된 것 같아. – **overrate** *v* [T] —compare UNDERRATED

o·ver·re·act /,ouvɚri'ækt/ *v* [I] to react to something with too much anger or surprise, or by doing more than is necessary ‖ 너무 많은 분노나 놀라움으로 또는 필요한 것 이상의 행동을 해서 어떤 것에 반응하다. 과잉 반응하다: *The fight started when Mark made a joke about Wayne, and Wayne overreacted.* 그 싸움은 마크가 웨인에 대한 농담을 하자 웨인이 과잉 반응을 해서 시작되었다. – **overreaction** /,ouvɚri'ækʃən/ *n* [C, U]

o·ver·ride /,ouvɚ'raɪd/ *v* [T] **1** to change someone's decision because you have the authority to do so ‖ 그렇게 할 권한이 있어서 남의 결정을 바꾸다. 뒤엎다. 무효로 하다: *Congress has overridden the President's veto.* 의회는 대통령의 거부권을 무효로 만들었다. **2** to be more important than something else ‖ 다른 것보다 더 중요하다. …을 능가하다. …에 우선하다: *The state of the economy seems to override other political and social questions.* 경제 상황은 다른 정치적·사회적 문제보다 더 시급한 것 같다.

o·ver·rid·ing /,ouvɚ'raɪdɪŋ/ *adj* more important than anything else ‖ 다른 어떤 것보다 더 중요한. 가장 중요한. 최우선의: *Security is of overriding importance.* 보안이 가장 중요한 문제이다.

o·ver·rule /,ouvɚ'rul/ *v* [T] to officially change someone's order or decision because you think that it is wrong ‖ 남의 명령이나 결정이 잘못되었다고 생각하여 공식적으로 바꾸다. 뒤엎다. 기각하다: *"Objection overruled," said Judge Klein.* "이의를 기각합니다"라고 클라인 판사가 말했다.

o·ver·run /,ouvɚ'rʌn/ *v* **1** [T] to spread over a place quickly and in great numbers, harming that place ‖ 어떤 장소에 빠르고 막대한 수로 퍼져서 그 장소를 해치다. 들끓다. 우거지다: *a town overrun with tourists* 관광객들로 북적되는 도시 **2** to continue beyond a limit ‖ 한계를 넘어 계속하다. …을 넘어서다[초과하다]: *The meeting overran by half an hour.* 회의는 30분이나 초과했다. – **overrun** /'ouvɚ,rʌn/ *n*

o·ver·seas /,ouvɚ'siz/ *adj, adv* to or in a foreign country that is across the ocean ‖ 바다를 가로질러 외국의 또는 외국으로. 해외의[로]: *I'm going to study overseas.* 나는 유학을 갈 거야. / *an overseas tour* 해외 여행

o·ver·see /,ouvɚ'si/ *v* [T] to watch a

group of workers to be sure that a piece of work is done correctly; SUPERVISE ‖ 일이 제대로 되는지 확인하기 위해 일단의 근로자를 지켜보다. 감독하다: 통 supervise: *Bentley is overseeing the project.* 벤틀리는 그 프로젝트를 감독하고 있다. **– overseer** /ˈouvəˌsiə/ *n*

o·ver·shad·ow /ˌouvəˈʃædou/ *v* [T] to make someone seem less important by being more successful than s/he is ‖ 어떤 사람보다 더 성공해서 그 사람을 덜 중요해 보이게 하다. …의 빛을 잃게 하다. …의 그림자로 가리다: *He felt constantly overshadowed by his older brother.* 그는 항상 형의 그림자에 가려진다고 느꼈다.

o·ver·shoot /ˌouvəˈʃut/ *v* [I, T] to miss a TARGET or a place where you wanted to stop or turn, by going too far past it ‖ 너무 멀리 지나쳐 가서 과녁을 빗나가거나 정지 또는 방향 전환을 할 곳을 놓치다. 빗나가게 쏘다. 지나쳐 가다: *I overshot the turn, and had to go back.* 나는 돌아야 할 지점을 지나쳐서 되돌아가야 했다.

o·ver·sight /ˈouvəˌsaɪt/ *n* [C, U] a mistake that you make by not noticing something or by forgetting to do something ‖ 어떤 것을 알아채지 못하거나 할 것을 잊어버려서 저지른 실수. 간과. 부주의(한 실수): *We apologize for the oversight; your refund will be mailed to you immediately.* 저희의 부주의한 실수를 사과드립니다. 환불금은 즉시 우편으로 보내 드리겠습니다.

o·ver·sim·pli·fy /ˌouvəˈsɪmpləˌfaɪ/ *v* [I, T] to make a problem or situation seem more simple than it really is, by ignoring important facts ‖ 중요한 사실을 무시함으로써 문제나 상황을 실제보다 더 단순하게 보이게 하다. (…을) 너무 순화하다 **– oversimplification** /ˌouvəˌsɪmpləfəˈkeɪʃən/ *n* [C, U]

o·ver·sleep /ˌouvəˈslip/ *v* [I] to sleep for longer than you intended ‖ 의도했던 것보다 더 오래 자다. 늦잠 자다

o·ver·state /ˌouvəˈsteɪt/ *v* [T] to talk about something in a way that makes it seem more important, serious etc. than it really is; EXAGGERATE ‖ 어떤 것에 대해서 실제보다 더 중요하며 심각하게 보이게 하는 식으로 이야기하다. …을 과장하여 말하다; 통 exaggerate: *I don't believe I'm overstating the danger of hiking alone.* 혼자 등산하는 것의 위험성을 내가 과장해서 말하고 있다고는 생각하지 않는다. —opposite UNDERSTATE

o·ver·step /ˌouvəˈstɛp/ *v* [T] to go beyond an acceptable limit ‖ 받아들일 수 있는 한계를 넘어가다. …의 한도를 넘다: *Wilson has clearly overstepped his authority.* 윌슨은 명백히 자신의 권한을 남용했다.

o·vert /ouˈvət, ˈouvət/ *adj* FORMAL done or shown in public or in an open way ‖ 공공연히 또는 드러내놓고 행동하거나 보여 주는. 공공연한. 명백한: *overt discrimination* 공공연한 차별 **– overtly** *adv*

o·ver·take /ˌouvəˈteɪk/ *v* [T] **1** to have a sudden and unexpected effect on someone ‖ 사람에게 갑작스럽고 예기치 못한 효과를 미치다. …에게 닥치다[갑자기 일어나다]: *He was overtaken by exhaustion.* 그는 갑자기 극도의 피로가 엄습해 왔다. **2** to develop or increase more quickly than someone else ‖ 다른 사람보다 더 빨리 발전하거나 증가하다. …을 따라잡다. 추월하다

over-the-counter /ˌ… ˈ…/ *adj* over-the-counter drugs can be bought without a PRESCRIPTION (=written order) from a doctor ‖ 약이 의사의 처방전 없이 살 수 있는

o·ver·throw /ˌouvəˈθrou/ *v* [T] to remove a leader or government from power by force ‖ 지도자나 정부를 강제로 권좌에서 축출하다. 타도하다. 전복시키다: *Rebel forces have made an attempt to overthrow the government.* 반란군은 정부를 전복시키려는 시도를 자행했다. **– overthrow** /ˈouvəˌθrou/ *n* [U]

o·ver·time /ˈouvəˌtaɪm/ *n* [U] time that you work on your job in addition to your usual working hours ‖ 평소 근무 시간에 추가하여 직장에서 일을 하는 시간. 규정외 노동 시간. 초과 근무: *Are you going to work any overtime this weekend?* 너 혹시 이번 주말에 초과 근무를 할 거야?

o·ver·ture /ˈouvətʃə, -ˌtʃʊr/ *n* **1** a piece of music written as an introduction to a longer musical piece, especially an OPERA ‖ 특히 오페라 같은 더 긴 음악 작품의 도입부로 작곡한 음악. 서곡. 전주곡 **2** also **overtures** an attempt to be friendly with a person, group, or country ‖ 사람[집단, 국가]과 친해지려는 시도. 예비 교섭. 제안: *Neither country is willing to make peace overtures to the other.* 양국 어느 국가도 상대 국가에게 강화를 기꺼이 제의하지 않는다.

o·ver·turn /ˌouvəˈtən/ *v* **1** [I, T] if something overturns or you overturn it, it turns upside down or falls over on its side ‖ 어떤 것이 거꾸로 뒤집히거나 거꾸

로 굴러 떨어지다. …을 뒤엎다. …이 뒤집히다. 전복되다: *The truck had overturned.* 트럭이 전복되었다. / *The kids overturned the table while they were playing.* 아이들은 놀면서 탁자를 쓰러뜨렸다. **2 overturn a ruling/ verdict/law** to change a decision made by a court so that it becomes the opposite of what it was before ‖ 법정에서 내린 판결을 바꾸어서 이전의 것과 반대가 되다. 판결/평결/법률을 뒤집다

o·ver·view /'oʊvɚ,vyu/ *n* a short description of a subject or situation that gives the main ideas without explaining all the details ‖ 어떤 주제나 상황에 대해서 모든 세부 사항을 설명하지 않고 주요 논점만을 제공하는 짧은 기술(記述). 개요. 개관: *an overview of the history of the region* 이 지역 역사의 개관

o·ver·weight /,oʊvɚ'weɪt/ *adj* too heavy or too fat ‖ 너무 무겁거나 너무 뚱뚱한. 비만의. 과체중의: *I'm ten pounds overweight.* 난 10파운드 과체중이다. — see usage note at FAT

o·ver·whelm /,oʊvɚ'wɛlm/ *v* [T] if a feeling overwhelms someone, s/he feels it very strongly ‖ 사람이 어떤 감정을 매우 강하게 느끼다. …을 압도하다[짓누르다]: *Gary was overwhelmed with sadness.* 게리는 슬픔에 잠겼다. – **overwhelmed** *adj*

o·ver·whelm·ing /,oʊvɚ'wɛlmɪŋ/ *adj* **1** affecting someone very strongly ‖ 사람에게 매우 강하게 영향을 미치는. 압도적인. 저항할 수 없는: *Shari felt an overwhelming urge/need to cry.* 샤리는 울고 싶은 억제할 수 없는 충동[욕구]를 느꼈다. **2** extremely large or great ‖ 매우 크거나 거대한. 엄청난. 압도적인: *an overwhelming number/majority* 엄청난[압도적인] 수/득표차 – **overwhelmingly** *adv*

o·ver·worked /,oʊvɚ'wɚkt/ *adj* working too much and for too long ‖ 너무 많이·너무 오랫동안 일하는. 과로한: *an overworked teacher* 과로한 교사 – **overwork** *n* [U]

o·ver·wrought /,oʊvɚ'rɔt/ *adj* very upset, nervous, and worried ‖ 매우 심란하고 초조하고 걱정하는. 잔뜩 긴장한. 지나치게 흥분한

ow /aʊ/ *interjection* said in order to show that something hurts you ‖ 어떤 것이 아프게 한다는 것을 나타내는 데에 쓰여. 으으. 아야: *Ow! That hurt!* 아야! 아프잖아!

owe /oʊ/ *v* [T] **1** to have to pay someone because s/he has allowed you to borrow money ‖ 남에게 돈을 빌렸기 때문에 그 사람에게 갚아야 하다. …에게 빚지다: *Bob owes me $20.* 보브는 나한테 20달러의 빚이 있다. **2** to feel grateful to someone, or to feel that you should do something for someone because s/he has done something for you ‖ 남이 자신을 위해 어떤 일을 해주어서 그 사람에게 감사하게 느끼거나 그 사람을 위해 어떤 것을 해주어야 한다고 느끼다. …에게 은혜를 입다[신세를 지다]: *Jane will watch the kids – she owes me a favor anyway.* 제인이 아이들을 돌볼 거야. 그녀는 어쨌든 나에게 신세를 진 게 있거든.

owing to /'.. ../ *prep* because of ‖ …때문에. …덕분에. …탓으로: *Work on the building has stopped, owing to lack of money.* 그 건축 공사는 자금 부족으로 중단되었다.

owl /aʊl/ *n* a bird that hunts at night and has large eyes and a loud call ‖ 밤에 사냥하며 큰 눈과 큰 울음소리를 지닌 새. 올빼미. 부엉이 —see also NIGHT OWL

own¹ /oʊn/ *determiner, pron* **1** belonging to or done by a particular person and no one else ‖ 그 밖의 다른 사람이 아닌 특정한 사람에게 속하거나 그 사람이 한. 자기 자신의. 자기 자신이 하는: *She wants her own room.* 그녀는 자기 자신의 방을 원한다. / *You have to learn to make your own decisions.* 너는 너 스스로 결정하는 법을 배워야 한다. / *He decided to start a business of his own.* 그는 자신의 사업을 시작하기로 결정했다. **2 (all) on your own a)** alone ‖ 홀로. 혼자: *Rick is home on his own.* 릭은 혼자서 집에 있다. **b)** without help ‖ 도움 없이. 혼자 힘으로. 자기 스스로: *Did you make that all on your own?* 너 혼자 힘으로 그것을 만들었니?

own² *v* [T] to legally have something because you bought it or have been given it ‖ 어떤 것을 샀거나 받았기 때문에 그것을 법적으로 가지다. …을 소유하다: *He owns two houses in Utah.* 그는 유타 주에 집 두 채를 소유하고 있다.

own up *phr v* [I] to admit that you have done something wrong ‖ 잘못된 일을 했다고 인정하다. 인정[자인]하다: *He'll never own up to his mistakes.* 그는 결코 자신의 실수를 인정하지 않을 것이다.

own·er /'oʊnɚ/ *n* someone who owns something ‖ 사물을 소유하고 있는 사람. 소유자. 주인: *the owner of the dog* 그 개의 주인 / *a home owner* 집 주인 – **ownership** *n* [U]

ox /aks/ *n, plural* **oxen** /'aksən/ a

male cow that has had part of its sex organs removed ‖ 생식기의 일부분이 제거된 수소. 황소

ox·ide /'ɑksaɪd/ *n* [C, U] TECHNICAL a chemical compound of an ELEMENT and oxygen ‖ 원소와 산소로 구성된 화학 합성물. 산화물

ox·i·dize /'ɑksə,daɪz/ *v* [I, T] TECHNICAL to combine with oxygen, especially when this causes RUST, or to make something do this ‖ 산소와 결합하여 특히 녹이 슬다, 또는 녹슬게 하다. (…을) 산화하다[시키다]

ox·y·gen /'ɑksɪdʒən/ *n* [U] a gas in the air that has no color, smell, or taste, and that all plants and animals need in order to live ‖ 색[냄새, 맛]이 없으며 모든 식물과 동물이 사는 데에 필요한 공기 중의 기체. 산소

oxygen bar /'... ,./ *n* a bar where you pay to breathe pure oxygen, or oxygen that has a pleasant smell, so that you can relax and have more energy ‖ 긴장을 풀고 더 많은 에너지를 가질 수 있도록 순수 산소나 기분 좋은 향이 나는 산소를 흡입하는 데에 돈을 지불하는 바. 산소바

oys·ter /'ɔɪstə/ *n* [C, U] a small sea animal that has a shell and can produce a jewel called a PEARL, or the meat of this animal ‖ 껍질이 있으며 진주라고 불리는 보석을 만들어 낼 수 있는 작은 바다 동물, 또는 이 동물의 살. 굴

oz. the written abbreviation of OUNCE or ounces ‖ ounce나 ounces의 약어

o·zone lay·er /'ouzoun ,leɪə/ *n* [singular] a layer of gases that prevents harmful RADIATION from the sun from reaching the Earth ‖ 태양으로부터 해로운 복사 에너지가 지구에 도달하는 것을 막는 가스층. 오존층

Pp

P, p /pi/ the sixteenth letter of the English alphabet ‖ 영어 알파벳의 열여섯째 자

p. *plural* **pp.** the written abbreviation of PAGE and PAGES ‖ page와 pages의 약어

PA¹ the written abbreviation of Pennsylvania ‖ Pennsylvania(펜실베이니아 주)의 약어

PA² *n* [C usually singular] public address system; electronic equipment that makes someone's voice loud enough to be heard by a large group of people ‖ public address system(대중 연설 장비[확성 장치])의 약어; 사람의 음성을 많은 군중들이 들을 수 있게 크게 확성하는 전자 장비

pa /pɑ/ *n* OLD-FASHIONED father ‖ 아버지. 아빠

PAC /pæk/ *n* [singular] political action committee; an organization that tries to influence politicians so that they support the group's aims, for example by voting in a particular way ‖ political action committee(정치 활동 위원회)의 약어; 예를 들어 특정하게 투표함으로써 정치가들에게 영향을 주어 집단의 목표를 지지하게 하려는 단체

pace¹ /peɪs/ *n* **1** [singular] the speed or rate at which something happens or at which you do something such as move, work etc. ‖ 어떤 일이 발생하거나 동작·작업 등을 하는 속도나 빠르기: *We were walking at a steady/slow pace.* 우리는 일정한[느린] 속도로 걷고 있었다. / *He likes to work at his own pace.* 그는 자신에 맞는 속도로 일하기를 좋아한다. **2 keep pace (with)** to move or change as fast as something or someone else ‖ 다른 사물이나 사람만큼의 빠르기로 움직이거나 변하다. …과 보조[속도]를 맞추다. …에 뒤지지 않게[나란하게] 나아가다[하다]: *Supply has to keep pace with increasing demand.* 공급은 늘어나는 수요와 보조를 맞추어야 한다.

pace² *v* [I, T] **1** to walk backward and forward when you are waiting or worried about something ‖ 어떤 것을 기다리거나 걱정하면서 앞뒤로 걷다. 왔다 갔다 하다. 서성거리다: *Darren paced back and forth in the waiting room.* 대린은 대기실에서 서성거렸다. **2 pace yourself** to do something at a steady speed so you do not get tired too quickly ‖ 너무 빨리 피곤해지지 않도록 일정한 속도로 어떤 일을 하다. 자신에게 맞는 속도로 …하다. 속도[빠르기]를 자신에 맞게 조절하다

pace·mak·er /'peɪsˌmeɪkɚ/ *n* a very small machine that is attached to someone's heart to help it beat regularly ‖ 사람의 심장이 규칙적으로 뛰도록 돕기 위해 부착되는 아주 작은 기계. 심장 박동 조절 장치

pace·set·ter /'peɪsˌsɛtɚ/ *n* someone or something that sets an example for others ‖ 다른 사람이나 사물들의 모범(사례)를 세우는 사람이나 사물. 주도[지도]자. 선두주자: *The pacesetter for high-speed trains is the French TGV.* 고속 열차의 선두주자는 프랑스의 TGV[테제베]이다.

Pacific O·cean /pəˌsɪfɪk 'oʊʃən/ *n* **the Pacific** the large ocean between Asia and Australia in the west, and North and South America in the east ‖ 서쪽으로 아시아와 호주, 동쪽으로 남·북아메리카 사이에 있는 큰 대양. 태평양

Pacific Rim /.ˌ.. './ *n* **the Pacific Rim** the land and islands that are around the edges of the Pacific Ocean, especially in Asia ‖ 태평양의 가장자리 주변의, 특히 아시아에 있는 육지와 섬들(의 때). 환태평양 지역

pac·i·fi·er /'pæsəˌfaɪɚ/ *n* a rubber object that a baby sucks on so that s/he does not cry ‖ 갓난아이가 울지 않게 (입에 물고) 빨게 하는 고무 제품. 유아용 고무 젖꼭지

pac·i·fism /'pæsəˌfɪzəm/ *n* [U] the belief that all wars and forms of violence are wrong ‖ 모든 전쟁과 모든 형태의 폭력이 나쁘다는 신념. 평화[반전]주의. 반전 비폭력 사상 **- pacifist** *n*

pac·i·fy /'pæsəˌfaɪ/ *v* [T] to make someone calm and quiet after s/he has been angry or upset ‖ 남이 분노하거나 화가 난 다음에 차분하고 잠잠해지게 하다. …을 달래다. 진정시키다: *a father pacifying a crying child* 우는 아이를 달래는 아버지

pack¹ /pæk/ *v* **1** [I, T] also **pack up** to put things into boxes, SUITCASEs, bags etc. in order to take or store them somewhere ‖ 물건을 다른 곳에 가져가거나 보관하기 위해 상자·옷가방·가방 등에 집어넣다. 싸다. 챙기다. 꾸리다. …에 넣

다: *I never pack until the night before a trip.* 나는 절대 여행 전날 밤까지는 짐을 꾸리지 않는다. / *Juanita packed up the glassware.* 화니타는 유리그릇들을 쌌다. / *Can you pack the kids' lunches?* 아이들 도시락을 싸줄 수 있어요? **2** [I, T] if a crowd of people packs a place, there are so many of them that the place is too full ‖ 어떤 장소에 너무 많은 사람들이 있어서 그 장소가 꽉 차다. 몰려들다. 빽빽이 들어가다. 만원이 되다: *Thousands of people packed the stadium.* 수천 명의 사람들이 경기장을 메웠다. **3** [T] to cover, fill, or surround something closely with material to protect it ‖ 사물을 보호하기 위해 소재로 빈틈없이 덮다[채우다, 둘러싸다]. …을 묶다[포장하다, 씌우다]: *Pack some newspaper around the bottles.* 병 주위를 신문지로 감싸라. **4** [T] to press soil, snow etc. down firmly ‖ 흙·눈 등을 단단하게 압착하다. 굳히다. 다지다: *The packed snow crunched under our feet.* 우리가 굳어진 눈 위를 걷자 자박자박 소리가 났다.

pack sb/sth ↔ **in** *phr v* [T] INFORMAL to attract a lot of people, or to try to put a lot of people or things somewhere ‖ 많은 사람들을 끌어들이거나 많은 사람 또는 물건들을 어떤 곳에 두려고 하다. 다수를 불러들이다. 가득 채우다: *Bryan Adams' concerts always pack them in.* 브라이언 아담스의 콘서트는 항상 많은 관객을 모은다.

pack sth **into** sth *phr v* [T] to fit a lot of something into a space, place, or period of time ‖ 많은 것을 공간[장소, 일정 시간]에 맞춰 넣다. …에 맞게 짜 넣다. 빽빽이 채우다: *We packed a lot of travel into our vacation.* 우리는 휴가에 많은 여행 일정을 짜 넣었다.

pack sb/sth **off** *phr v* [T] INFORMAL to send someone away quickly in order to get rid of him/her ‖ 사람을 없애기 위해 신속히 보내 버리다. (짐을 싸서) 쫓아버리다. 서둘러서 내보내다: *Our folks packed us off to camp every summer.* 우리 부모님은 매 여름마다 우리들을 서둘러서 캠프로 보내 버렸다.

pack up *phr v* [I] INFORMAL to finish work ‖ 일을 끝내다. 끝내서 짐을 싸다. 그만두다: *I think I'll pack up and go home early.* 나는 일을 끝내고 집에 일찍 갈 생각이다.

pack² *n* **1** a small container that holds a set of things ‖ 한 벌의 물건을 담는 작은 용기. 한 상자. 꾸러미. 그릇: *a pack of cigarettes/cards/gum* 담배 한 갑[카드 한 벌, 껌 한 통] —see picture at CONTAINER

2 a group of wild animals that live and hunt together ‖ 같이 살면서 함께 사냥하는 야생 동물들의 집단. 한 떼. 무리: *a wolf pack* 늑대 떼[무리] **3** a group of people ‖ 사람들의 집단. 떼. 패(거리). 일당: *a pack of reporters yelling questions* 질문을 외쳐대는 일단의 기자들 **4** several things wrapped or tied together to make them easy to sell, carry, or send ‖ 팔기[운반하기, 보내기] 쉽게 하기 위해 함께 포장되거나 묶인 몇 개의 물건. 꾸러미. 다발. 단위로 싼 것. 팩: *a gift pack of beauty products* 미용제품의 선물 꾸러미 / *a six-pack of beer* 여섯 병[캔]들이 맥주 상자 **5** ⇨ BACKPACK¹

pack·age¹ /ˈpækɪdʒ/ *n* **1** the box, bag etc. that food is put in for selling ‖ 식품이 판매용으로 들어 있는 상자·봉지 등. 꾸러미. 한 단위로 포장된 것. 세트: *a package of peanut butter cookies* 땅콩버터 쿠키 꾸러미

package

2 something packed into a box, wrapped in paper, especially for mailing ‖ 특히 우편으로 부치기 위해 상자에 꾸려지거나 종이로 포장된 것. 소포 **3** a set of related things or services that are sold or offered together ‖ 함께 판매되거나 제공되는 물건이나 용역의 한 묶음. 일체형의 것. 패키지 상품: *a new software package* 새로운 소프트웨어 패키지 / *a package tour to the Southwest* (=including room, meals etc.) 미국 남서부 패키지 여행 상품

package² *v* [T] **1** to put something in a special package, especially to be sold ‖ 특히 물건을 팔도록 특수 꾸러미에 넣다. 패키지로 만들다. 일괄해서 포장하다. 일체형으로[세트로] 만들다: *candy packaged in cellophane bags* 셀로판 봉지에 포장된 사탕 **2** to try to make an idea, person etc. seem interesting or attractive so that people will like it or buy it ‖ 사람들이 좋아하거나 사도록 아이디어·사람 등을 흥미 있거나 매력적으로 보이게 하다. 포장하다: *a new band packaged to appeal to teenage girls* 10대 소녀들의 관심을 끌기 위해 포장된 새로운 밴드[머리띠]

pack·ag·ing /ˈpækɪdʒɪŋ/ *n* [U] **1** bags, boxes etc. that contain a product that is sold in a store ‖ 상점에서 팔리는 제품을 담는 봉지·상자 등. 용기. 포장지[재]: *Putting apples in packaging seems*

completely unnecessary. 사과를 포장 상
자에 넣는 것은 매우 불필요해 보인다. **2**
a way of making something seem
attractive or interesting to people so
that they will buy it ‖ 사물을 사람들에게
매력적으로 또는 흥미 있게 보이게 해서
사도록 하는 방식. 포장: *the packaging of
a best-selling novel* 베스트셀러 소설의
포장

packed /pækt/ *adj* **1** extremely full of
people or things ‖ 사람이나 사물이 극도
로 꽉 찬. 혼잡한. 빽빽한. 입추의 여지가
없는: *The theater was packed.* 극장은 초
만원이었다. / *a box packed full of books*
책으로 가득 찬 상자 **2** if you are packed,
you have put everything you need into
boxes or cases before going on a trip ‖
여행을 가기 전에 필요한 모든 것을 상자
나 가방에 담아 넣은. 짐을 꾸린[싼]. 채
비가 끝난: *OK, I'm all packed.* 좋아, 나는
(짐을 싸고)모든 준비가 끝났다.

pack·er /ˈpækɚ/ *n* someone whose job
is to pack goods that are to be moved or
sold ‖ 운송되거나 팔릴 상품들을 포장하는
직업인. 짐 꾸리는 사람. 포장업자

pack·et /ˈpækɪt/ *n* **1** a small envelope
containing a group of things ‖ 일단의 물
건들을 담고 있는 작은 봉투. 봉지: *a
packet of carrot seeds* 당근 씨앗 봉지 —
see picture at CONTAINER **2** TECHNICAL a
unit of electronic information sent over
a computer network ‖ 컴퓨터 네트워크를
통해 전송되는 전자 정보의 단위. 패킷

pack·ing /ˈpækɪŋ/ *n* [U] **1** the act of
putting things into cases or boxes so
that you can send or take them
somewhere ‖ 물건을 다른 곳으로 보내거
나 가지고 갈 수 있도록 가방이나 상자에
담기. 포장. 짐 꾸리기: *I usually do my
packing the night before I leave.* 나는 보
통 떠나기 전날 밤 짐을 꾸린다. **2** paper,
plastic, cloth etc. used for packing
things ‖ 물건의 포장에 쓰이는 종이·플라
스틱·천 등. 포장재(료)

packing case /ˈ.. ../ *n* a large strong
wooden box in which things are packed
in order to be sent somewhere or stored
‖ 물건이 다른 곳에 보내지거나 보관되기
위해 포장되는 크고 튼튼한 목재 상자. 포
장 상자

pack rat /ˈ. ./ *n* INFORMAL someone
who collects and stores things that s/he
does not really need ‖ 실제로 필요하지
않은 것들을 모으거나 보관하는 사람. 허
섭스레기 수집가

pact /pækt/ *n* a formal agreement
between two groups, nations, or people
‖ 두 집단[국가, 사람] 간의 공식적 합의.

조약. 협정. 약속. 계약: *The two
countries will sign a non-aggression
pact.* 두 나라는 불가침 조약을 체결할 것
이다.

pad¹ /pæd/ *n* **1** a thick piece of soft
material used for protecting something
or making it more comfortable ‖ 어떤 것
을 보호하거나 보다 안락하게 하는 데에
쓰는 부드러운 재질의 두꺼운 조각. 덧대
는 것. 패드. 보호대: *the knee and
shoulder pads that football players
wear* 미식축구 선수들이 착용하는 무릎·
어깨 보호대 / *Ken slept on a foam pad
on the floor.* 켄은 마룻바닥에 놓인 발포
패드 위에서 잤다. **2** many sheets of
paper fastened together, used for
writing letters, drawing pictures etc. ‖
편지쓰기·그림 그리기 등에 이용되는 많은
매수의 종이를 함께 묶은 것. 필기첩. 용
지철: *a memo pad* 메모장

pad² *v* **-dded, -dding 1** [T] to protect
something, shape it, or make it more
comfortable by covering or filling it with
soft material ‖ 어떤 것을 부드러운 소재
로 덮거나 채워서 보호하다[모양을 내다,
보다 안락하게 하다]. 완충재[패드]를 넣
다[대다]. 속을 채우다: *Doug padded a
box for the kitten to sleep in.* 더그는 새
끼 고양이가 잠자도록 상자에 패드를 넣어
주었다. **2** [I] to walk softly and quietly ‖
부드럽고 조용하게 걷다. 살그머니[소리를
죽이고] 걷다: *a cat padding across the
floor* 마루 위를 살금살금 가로질러 걷는
고양이 **3** [T] INFORMAL to add something
unnecessary to a document or speech to
make it longer, or to a price to make it
higher ‖ 글이나 연설을 더 늘리거나 가격
을 올리기 위해 불필요한 것을 추가하
다. 길게 늘이다. 날조하여 불리다: *They
realized that their lawyer was padding
the court fees.* 그들은 변호사가 수임료를
부풀리고 있다는 것을 깨달았다.

pad·ding /ˈpædɪŋ/ *n* [U] material that
fills or covers something to make it
softer or more comfortable ‖ 어떤 것을
보다 부드럽거나 안락하게 만들기 위해 채
우거나 덮는 소재. 속. 심. 채워 넣는 재
료: *The padding is coming out of the car
seat.* 자동차 좌석에서 심이 삐져나오고
있다.

pad·dle¹ /ˈpædl/ *n* **1** a short pole with
a wide flat end, used for moving a small
boat along ‖ 작은 보트를 젓는 데 쓰이는,
끝이 넓고 평평한 짧은 장대. 노 —
compare OAR —see picture at KAYAK **2**
an object used for hitting the ball in
PING-PONG, consisting of a round flat top
on a short handle ‖ 탁구에서 짧은 손잡이

에 윗면이 둥글고 평평하게 되어 공을 치
는 데 쓰이는 물체. (탁구) 라켓

paddle² *v* [I, T] to move a small boat
through water, using a PADDLE ‖ 노를 사
용하여 작은 배가 물을 헤쳐 가게 하다. 노
를 저어 나아가다[가게 하다]: *We
paddled across the lake to the beach.* 우
리는 호수를 가로질러 물가까지 노를 저었
다. —see also DOG PADDLE

pad·dock /'pædək/ *n* a small enclosed
field in which horses are kept ‖ 말을 사
육하는 작고 울타리가 처진 목초지. 작은
방목지

pad·dy /'pædi/, **rice paddy** *n* a field
in which rice is grown in water ‖ 벼가 물
에서 자라는 들판. 논. 무논

pad·lock /'pædlɑk/ *n*
a small metal lock
that hangs, that you
can put on a door,
bicycle etc. ‖ 문·자전
거 등에 채울 수 있게
달아매는 작은 금속제
자물통. 맹꽁이자물쇠
– **padlock** *v* [T]

padlock

pa·dre /'pɑdreɪ, -dri/
n INFORMAL a priest, especially one in
the army ‖ 특히 군대에 있는 신부. 종군
사제. 군목

pa·gan /'peɪgən/ *n* someone who does
not believe in any of the main religions
of the world, but believes instead in
many gods ‖ 세계의 주요한 종교는 어느
것도 믿지 않고 대신에 많은 신들을 믿는
사람. 이교도. 다신교도 – **pagan** *adj*

page¹ /peɪdʒ/ *n* **1** one side of a sheet of
paper in a book, newspaper, etc., or
the sheet itself ‖ 책·신문 등의 종이 낱장
의 한쪽 면, 또는 종잇장 자체. 페이지.
쪽. (인쇄물의) 한 장: *Do the exercises
on page 10 for homework.* 숙제로 10페
이지의 연습 문제를 하시오. / *The story
was on the front page of every
newspaper.* 그 이야기는 모든 신문의 전
면을 장식했다. / *There's a page missing
from this comic book.* 이 만화책의 한 페
이지가 빠져 있다. **2** a young person who
works in a government office for a short
time in order to gain experience ‖ 경험
을 쌓기 위해 단기간 정부 부처에서 일하
는 젊은이. 견습생. 인턴

page² *v* [T] **1** to call someone's name in
a public place, especially using a
LOUDSPEAKER ‖ 공공장소에서 특히 확성기
를 써서 다른 사람의 이름을 부르다. (장
내 안내 방송으로) 사람 찾는 방송을 하
다: *We couldn't find Jan at the airport,
so we had her paged.* 우리는 공항에서

잰을 찾을 수 없어서 그녀를 찾는 안내 방
송을 했다. **2** to call someone using a
BEEPER (=small machine that receives
messages) ‖ 호출기를 이용해 사람을 호출
하다. 무선호출하다

pag·eant /'pædʒənt/ *n* **1** a public show
or ceremony that usually shows an
event in history ‖ 보통 역사적 사건을 보
여주는 대중 공연이나 축하 의식. 야외극.
가장 행렬 **2** a competition for young
women in which their beauty and other
qualities are judged ‖ 젊은 여성들의 미
와 기타 품성들이 평가되는 경연. 미인대
회

pag·eant·ry /'pædʒəntri/ *n* [U]
impressive ceremonies or events,
involving many people wearing special
clothes ‖ 특수 의상을 입은 많은 사람들이
참가하는 인상적인 의식이나 행사. 화려한
행렬. 공식 행사[의식]: *the pageantry of
a royal wedding* 왕실 결혼식의 화려한
행렬[장관]

pag·er /'peɪdʒɚ/ *n* ⇨ BEEPER

pa·go·da /pə'goudə/ *n* an Asian TEMPLE
that has several levels, with a decorated
roof at each level ‖ 여러 개의 층이 있고
각 층마다 장식된 지붕이 있는 아시아식
사원 건물. 탑

paid /peɪd/ *v* the past tense and PAST
PARTICIPLE of PAY ‖ pay의 과거·과거 분사
형

pail /peɪl/ *n* a container with a handle,
used for carrying liquids or by children
when playing on the beach; BUCKET ‖ 액
체를 운반하는 데 쓰거나 아이들이 해변에
서 놀이할 때 쓰는 손잡이가 달린 용기.
통. 양동이; ⑲ bucket: *We picked two
pails of blackberries.* (=enough to fill
two pails) 우리는 두 통 분량의 검은산딸
기를 땄다.

pain¹ /peɪn/ *n* **1** [C, U] the feeling you
have when part of your body hurts ‖ 신
체 부위가 다쳤을 때 갖는 느낌. 고통. 아
픔. 통증: *Soldiers lay groaning in pain*
(=feeling pain) *on the ground.* 군인들은
고통 속에서 신음하며 땅에 누워 있었다.
/ *The drugs don't do much to relieve
her pain.* (=make it hurt less) 그 약들이
그녀의 고통을 완화시켜 주지는 못한다. /
Wes has a pain in his lower back. 웨스
는 허리에 통증이 있다. **2 be a pain in
the ass/butt** SPOKEN an impolite
expression meaning to be extremely
annoying ‖ 심하게 짜증남을 의미하는 무
례한 표현. 싫은 사람[것]이다. 골칫거리
이다 **3 be a pain (in the neck)** SPOKEN
to be very annoying ‖ 아주 짜증나다. 성
가시다: *This pan is great to cook with,*

but it's a pain to wash. 이 냄비는 요리하기에는 좋지만 씻기에는 성가시다. **4** [C, U] emotional or mental suffering ‖ 감정적 또는 정신적 고통. 괴로움. 고뇌. 비탄: *the pain children feel when their parents divorce* 부모가 이혼했을 때 자녀들이 느끼는 괴로움 —see also PAINS

pain² *v* [T] FORMAL to make someone feel unhappy ‖ 사람을 불행하게 느끼게 하다. 남에게 아픔[고통]을 주다. 괴롭히다: *It pains me to see my mother growing old.* 내 어머니가 늙어가는 것을 보면 가슴이 아프다.

pained /peɪnd/ *adj* worried and upset ‖ 걱정스러우며 감정이 상한. 아파하는. 괴로운. 화난: *a pained look on his face* 그의 괴로운 얼굴 표정

pain·ful /'peɪnfəl/ *adj* **1** making you feel physical pain ‖ 육체적인 고통을 느끼게 하는. 아픈. 고통스런. 통증을 수반하는: *a painful injury* 고통스런 상처 **2** making you feel very unhappy ‖ 매우 불행하게 느끼게 하는. 괴로운. 가슴 아픈: *painful memories of the war* 가슴 아픈 전쟁의 기억들 **3** very bad and embarrassing for other people to watch, hear etc. ‖ 다른 사람들이 지켜보거나 듣기에 아주 나쁘고 당혹스런. 곤란한. 고통스런: *The acting in the movie was so bad, it was painful to watch.* 그 영화의 연기는 너무 형편없어서 정말 봐줄 수가 없었다.

pain·ful·ly /'peɪnfəli/ *adv* **1** with pain, or causing pain ‖ 아프게, 또는 통증을 일으키게. 고통스럽게. 괴롭게. 가슴 아프게: *Mike walked slowly and painfully to the door.* 마이크는 천천히 고통스럽게 문까지 걸어 갔다. / *People can be painfully cruel to each other.* 사람들은 서로에게 고통스러울 정도로 잔인할 수 있다. **2** **painfully obvious/clear etc.** a fact or situation that is painfully obvious etc., is so easy to notice that it is embarrassing ‖ 사실이나 상황을 너무 쉽게 알아볼 수 있어서 당황스러운. 너무나도[안쓰러울 정도로] 명백한/분명한: *It was painfully clear that Lynn would never be a ballet dancer.* 린이 발레 무용수가 결코 되지 못할 것이라는 게 너무나도 분명했다. **3** needing a lot of effort, or causing a lot of trouble ‖ 많은 노력이 필요한, 또는 많은 문제를 초래하는. 감내하기 힘들게. 지독하게: *Rebuilding the bridge was a painfully slow process.* 다리를 재건설하는 것은 지독히 느리게 진척되었다. **4** in a way that makes you sad or upset ‖ 슬프거나 화나게 할 정도로. 괴로울[가슴 아플] 정도로. 슬프게도: *I was painfully*

aware that she didn't like me. 나는 그녀가 나를 좋아하지 않는다는 것을 슬프게도 잘 알고 있었다.

pain·kill·er /'peɪn,kɪlɚ/ *n* a medicine that reduces or removes pain ‖ 통증을 줄이거나 없애는 약. 진통제

pain·less /'peɪnlɪs/ *adj* **1** without pain, or causing no pain ‖ 고통 없는, 또는 통증을 일으키지 않는. 아픔이 없는. 무통의: *Giving blood is a nearly painless process.* 헌혈하는 것은 거의 고통 없는 과정이다. **2** INFORMAL needing no effort or hard work ‖ 노력이나 힘든 작업이 필요하지 않는. 어렵지 않은. 힘이 안 드는: *a painless way to learn Spanish* 스페인어를 배우는 쉬운 방법

pains /peɪnz/ *n* [plural] **1** **take pains** to make a special effort to do something well ‖ 어떤 일을 잘 하기 위해 특별한 노력을 하다. 애쓰다. 수고를 아끼지 않다. 고통을 감내하며 하다: *Bonnie always takes pains to have a nice Thanksgiving dinner.* 보니는 항상 훌륭한 추수감사절 정찬을 먹기 위해 수고를 아끼지 않는다. **2** **be at pains to do sth** to be very careful to do something ‖ 어떤 일을 하기 위해 매우 조심하다. …하고자 무척 애쓰다: *The two leaders were at pains to avoid an argument.* 두 지도자는 논쟁을 피하기 위해 무척 애썼다.

pains·taking /'peɪnz,teɪkɪŋ, 'peɪn,steɪ-/ *adj* very careful and thorough ‖ 매우 조심스럽고 철저한. 애쓴. 고심한. 공들인: *painstaking research* 공을 들인 연구 – **painstakingly** *adv*

paint¹ /peɪnt/ *n* [U] a liquid that you put on a surface to make it a particular color ‖ 특정 색을 내도록 표면에 바르는 액체. 페인트. 도료. 안료. 물감: *a can of yellow paint* 노란색 페인트 통 / *The kitchen needs a fresh coat of paint.* (=layer of paint) 부엌에 페인트칠을 새로 할 필요가 있다. —see also PAINTS

paint

paint² *v* [I, T] **1** to put paint on a surface ‖ 표면에 페인트를 칠하다: *What color are you painting the house?* 집을 무슨 색으로 페인트칠하고 있니? **2** to make a picture of someone or something using paint ‖ 물감을 써서 사람이나 사물의 그림을 그리다. 그림물감으로 그리다: *Who painted your wife's portrait?* 부인의 초상화를 누가 그렸습니까? / *She likes to paint in watercolors.* 그녀는 수채화 그리기를 좋아한다. **3 paint a picture of sth** to describe something in a particular way ‖ 어떤 것을 특정하게 묘사하다. …을 (생생하게)표현하다. 기술하다: *The letters paint an interesting picture of her life.* 그 편지는 그녀의 일생을 흥미롭게 표현한다.

paint·box /ˈpeɪntˌbɑks/ *n* a special box with dry blocks of colored paint in it ‖ 안에 고체 물감들이 들어 있는 특수한 상자. 그림물감통

paint·brush /ˈpeɪntˌbrʌʃ/ *n* a special brush used for painting pictures or to paint rooms etc. ‖ 그림을 그리거나 방을 칠하는 등에 쓰이는 특별한 붓. 페인트용 솔[붓]. 화필. 그림붓

paint·er /ˈpeɪntɚ/ *n* **1** someone who paints pictures. ARTIST ‖ 그림을 그리는 사람. 화가; 英 artist: *a landscape painter* 풍경화가 **2** someone whose job is painting houses, rooms etc. ‖ 집·방 등에 페인트칠을 하는 직업인. 칠장이. 도장공: *a house painter* 집칠 페인트공

paint·ing /ˈpeɪntɪŋ/ *n* **1** a painted picture ‖ 채색된 그림. 유화. 수채화. 회화: *a painting of a mountain landscape* 산악 풍경화 **2** [U] the act of making a picture using paint ‖ 물감을 써서 그림 그리기. 채색: *Monet's style of painting* 모네의 화풍 **3** [U] the act of covering a wall, house etc. with paint ‖ 페인트로 벽·집 등을 칠하기. 도장[채색]하기: *We spent Saturday painting the bedrooms.* 우리는 침실에 페인트를 칠하면서 토요일을 보냈다.

paints /peɪnts/ *n* [plural] a set of small tubes or blocks of paint of different colors, used for painting pictures ‖ 그림을 그리는 데 쓰이는 서로 다른 색 물감의 작은 튜브나 덩어리의 세트. 그림물감 세트: *a set of oil paints* 유화물감 한 세트

paint thin·ner /ˈ. ˌ../ *n* [U] a liquid that you add to paint to make it less thick ‖ 페인트를 묽게 하기 위해 추가하는 용액. 페인트 희석제

pair¹ /pɛr/ *n, plural* **pairs** *or* **pair** **1** something made of two parts that are joined and used together ‖ 합쳐서 함께 사용하는 두 개의 부분으로 만들어진 것. 한 자루[벌, 개]: *a pair of scissors* 가위 한 자루 / *two pairs of jeans* 청바지 두 벌 **2** two things of the same kind that are

used together ‖ 함께 사용되는 같은 종류의 두 개의 물건. 한 쌍[켤레]. 한 조: *a pair of socks/earrings* 양말 한 켤레[귀걸이 한 쌍] / *She has 12 pairs of shoes!* 그녀는 구두 12켤레를 가지고 있어! **3** two people who are standing or doing something together ‖ 함께 서 있거나 어떤 일을 함께 하는 두 사람. 한 쌍의 남녀. 부부. 2인 1조: *a pair of dancers* 한 쌍의 무용수 / *Work in pairs* (=in groups of two) *on the next exercise.* 다음 운동에서는 짝을 이뤄 하세요. —see usage note at COUPLE¹

pair², **pair up** *v* [I, T] to form or be put into groups of two ‖ 둘씩 그룹을 형성하거나 나뉘다. 둘씩 쌍이 되다. 쌍[짝]을 짓다: *We were paired with partners in French class.* 우리는 불어 시간에 짝과 쌍을 이루었다.

pair off *phr v* [I, T] to come together or bring two people together ‖ 두 사람이 함께 모이거나 두 사람을 함께 맺어주다. 둘씩 쌍[짝]을 이루다[이루게 하다]: *The guests paired off for the first dance.* 손님들은 첫 댄스를 위해 둘씩 짝을 지었다.

pa·ja·mas /pəˈdʒɑməz, -ˈdʒæ-/ *n* [plural] a pair of loose pants and a loose shirt that you wear in bed ‖ 침실에서 입는 한 벌의 헐렁한 바지와 셔츠. 잠옷. 파자마

pal¹ /pæl/ *n* OLD-FASHIONED a close friend ‖ 친한 친구. 동무. 동료: *a college pal* 대학 동창

pal² *v* **-lled, -lling** OLD-FASHIONED

pal around *phr v* [I] to go places and do things with a friend ‖ 친구와 같이 이곳저곳에 가서 여러 가지 일을 하다. 친구와 어울리다. 친하게 지내다: *Rob and Dave have been palling around with each other for years.* 로브와 데이브는 오랫동안 서로 어울려 지내 왔다.

pal·ace /ˈpælɪs/ *n* a large house where a king or queen officially lives ‖ 왕이나 여왕이 공식적으로 사는 큰 저택. 궁전. 대궐: *Buckingham Palace* 버킹엄 궁전

pal·at·a·ble /ˈpælətəbəl/ *adj* **1** an idea, suggestion etc. that is palatable is acceptable ‖ 아이디어·제안 등이 받아들일 만한. 마음에 드는. 구미에 맞는: *It's the only health care proposal that is palatable to the voters.* 유권자들의 마음에 드는 것은 오직 건강 보험안뿐이다. **2** having an acceptable taste ‖ 인정할 만한 맛을 가진. 맛좋은. 입맛에 맞는: *a palatable wine* 입맛에 맞는 포도주

pal·ate /'pælɪt/ *n* **1** the top inside part of the mouth ‖ 입의 안쪽 윗부분. 구개. 입천장 **2** FORMAL someone's ability to taste things ‖ 어떤 것을 맛보는 사람의 능력. 맛의 감별력. 미각: *Each course was a delight to the palate.* 각각의 요리가 미각을 즐겁게 했다.

pa·la·tial /pə'leɪʃəl/ *adj* very large and beautifully decorated ‖ 매우 크고 아름답게 장식된. 궁궐 같은. 웅장한. 호화로운: *a palatial hotel* 호화로운 호텔

pale¹ /peɪl/ *adj* **1** having a much lighter skin color than usual, because you are sick, frightened etc. ‖ 아프고 겁에 질린 등의 이유로 평소보다 훨씬 더 엷은 피부색을 가진. 창백한. 핏기가 없는. 파리한: *Jan looked tired and pale.* 잰은 피곤하고 창백해 보였다. **2** lighter than the usual color ‖ 통상의 색보다 엷은. 엷은: *pale green walls* 엷은 녹색의 벽

pale² *v* [I] **1 pale into insignificance** to seem much less important when compared to something else ‖ 다른 것과 비교했을 때 훨씬 덜 중요해 보이다. 중요성이 약해지다[미약해지다]: *All our troubles paled into insignificance when we heard about the war.* 우리가 그 전쟁에 대해 들었을 때 우리의 모든 문제가 하찮게 여겨졌다. **2 pale in/by comparison** to seem less important, good etc. when compared to something else ‖ 다른 것과 비교했을 때 덜 중요하고 덜 좋아 보이다. …에 비해서/비교하면 못해 보이다: *This year's profits pale in comparison to last year's.* 올해의 수익은 작년에 비해 못해 보인다. **3** if you pale, your face becomes much whiter than usual, because you are sick, frightened etc. ‖ 아프고 겁에 질린 등의 이유로 사람의 얼굴이 평소보다 훨씬 더 하얗게 되다. 창백해지다: *Myra paled at the sight of the blood on the floor.* 마이라는 바닥의 핏자국을 보고 얼굴이 창백해졌다.

pa·le·on·tol·o·gy /ˌpeɪliən'tɑlədʒi, -liən-/ *n* [U] the study of FOSSILs (=ancient animals and plants that have been preserved in rock) ‖ 화석에 관한 연구. 고생물학 **–paleontologist** *n*

pal·ette /'pælɪt/ *n* a board with a curved edge and a hole for the thumb, on which a painter mixes colors ‖ 가장자리가 곡선형이고 엄지손가락용 구멍이 있어 화가가 그 위에서 물감을 혼합하는 판. 팔레트. 조색판(調色板)

pal·i·mo·ny /'pæləˌmoʊni/ *n* [U] money that someone must pay regularly to a former partner, when they have lived together for a long time without being married ‖ 결혼하지 않은 상태로 오랫동안 같이 살아온 이전 동거인에게 정기적으로 지불해야 하는 돈. 별거 수당

pall¹ /pɔl/ *n* **1** a low dark cloud of smoke, dust etc. ‖ 낮게 깔린 짙고 자욱한 연기·먼지 등. (연기의) (장) 막 **2** [singular] something that spoils an event or occasion that should have been happy ‖ 유쾌했어야 할 행사나 특별한 때를 망치는 것. (분위기를) 암울하게 하는 것. 암운(暗雲): *The drug scandal cast a pall over* (=spoiled the happy feelings at) *the Olympics.* 약물 복용 사건은 올림픽 경기에 찬물을 끼얹었다.

pall² *v* [I] to become uninteresting or unpleasant ‖ 흥미없거나 즐겁지 않게 되다. 시시해지다. 매력이 없어지다: *The excitement of the new job began to pall after a while.* 새로운 일에 대한 흥분도 얼마 후에는 시들해지기 시작했다.

pall·bear·er /'pɔlˌbɛrɚ/ *n* someone who helps to carry a COFFIN (=a box with a dead body inside) at a funeral ‖ 장례식에서 관의 운반을 돕는 사람. 관을 메는 사람. 운구인(運柩人)

pal·lid /'pælɪd/ *adj* looking pale and unhealthy ‖ 창백하고 건강하지 않게 보이는. 핼쑥한. 파리한: *pallid skin* 파리한 피부색

pal·lor /'pælɚ/ *n* [singular] a pale unhealthy color of your skin or face ‖ 피부나 얼굴의 창백하고 건강하지 못한 색. 나쁜 안색. 창백함

palm¹ /pɑm/ *n* **1** the inside surface of your hand between the base of your fingers and your wrist ‖ 손가락 뿌리와 손목 사이에 있는 손의 안쪽 표면(부). 손바닥: *She held out the sea shell in the palm of her hand.* 그녀는 손바닥에 있는 조개 껍질을 앞으로 내밀었다. —see picture at HAND¹ **2** ⇨ PALM TREE

palm² *v* [T]

palm sth ↔ **off** *phr v* [T] to persuade someone to accept or buy something, especially by deceiving him/her ‖ 특히 사람을 속여서 어떤 것을 받아들이거나 사도록 설득하다. …이라고 속이다. 속여서 팔아먹다: *He tried to palm off the jewelry as antiques.* 그는 싸구려 장신구를 골동품으로 속여서 팔려 했다.

palm read·er /'. ,../ n someone who tells you about your character or about what will happen to you by looking at your hand ‖ 손을 보고서 성격이나 미래에 벌어질 일에 대해 알려주는 사람. 손금쟁이. 수상가

Palm Sun·day /,. '../ n the Sunday before Easter in Christian religions ‖ 기독교에서 부활절 전 일요일. 종려 주일

palm tree /'. ./ n a tall tropical tree with large pointed leaves at its top, that grows near beaches or in deserts ‖ 해변 근처나 사막에서 자라며 꼭대기에 크고 뾰족한 잎이 달린 키 큰 열대성 나무. 야자나무

pal·pa·ble /'pælpəbəl/ adj FORMAL easily and clearly noticed ‖ 쉽고 분명하게 인식되는. 뚜렷한. 뻔한. 눈에 확 띄는: a palpable lie 뻔 한 거짓말 – **palpably** adv

pal·pi·ta·tions /,pælpə'teɪʃənz/ n [plural] irregular or extremely fast beating of your heart ‖ 심장이 불규칙하거나 매우 빠르게 뛰는 것. 동계(動悸). 가슴이 떨림. 심계항진

pal·try /'pɔltri/ adj too small to be useful or important ‖ 너무 작아서 유용하거나 중요치 않은. 시시한. 하찮은: a paltry pay raise 쥐꼬리만한 봉급 인상

pam·per /'pæmpɚ/ v [T] to give someone too much care and attention ‖ 다른 사람에게 너무 많은 배려와 관심을 쏟다. 지나치게 소중히 하다. 애지중지하다: She pampers her son too much. 그녀는 아들을 너무 끔찍이 위한다.

pam·phlet /'pæmflɪt/ n a very thin book with paper covers, giving information about something ‖ 어떤 것에 대한 정보를 제공하는, 종이 표지가 있는 아주 얇은 책자. 팸플릿. 소책자: a pamphlet about evening classes at the college 대학 야간반에 대한 팸플릿

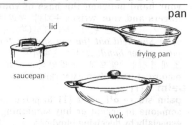

pan

lid

frying pan

saucepan

wok

pan¹ /pæn/ n 1 a round metal container used for cooking, usually with a handle ‖ 보통 손잡이가 달려 요리할 때 쓰는 금속제의 둥근 용기. 냄비. 팬: Melt the butter in a heavy pan, and stir in the flour. 큰 냄비에 버터를 녹인 다음 밀가루에 휘저으세요. 2 a metal container for baking things, or the food that this contains ‖ 음식을 굽는 금속 용기나 거기에 든 음식. 굽기에 쓰이는 통[판]: a pan of sweet rolls baking in the oven 오븐 속에서 구워지고 있는 달콤한 롤빵 한 판 3 a container with low sides, used for holding liquids ‖ 액체를 담는 데 쓰이는 옆면이 낮은 용기. 기름받이

pan² v -nned, -nning 1 [T] INFORMAL to strongly criticize a movie, play etc. in a newspaper or on television or radio ‖ 신문이나 TV 또는 라디오 방송에서 영화·연극 등을 강하게 비판하다. 혹평하다: The critics panned his first play. 비평가들은 그의 첫 번째 연극을 혹평했다. 2 [I, T] to move a camera while taking a picture or follow a moving object with a camera ‖ 사진을 촬영하면서 카메라를 움직이거나 이동하는 물체를 카메라로 따라가다. 카메라를 좌우[상하]로 움직이며 찍다: The camera panned across the crowd. 카메라가 군중을 가로지르며 촬영했다.

pan for sth phr v to wash soil in a pan in order to separate gold from it ‖ 금을 분리하기 위해 흙을 통 속에서 씻다. 선광냄비로 씻어서 일다

pan out phr v [I] to happen or develop in the expected way ‖ 예상한 대로 일어나거나 전개되다. 잘 되어가다. 성공하다: If this trip doesn't pan out, I might go to Indonesia instead. 이번 여행이 계획대로 안 되면, 나는 대신에 인도네시아로 갈지 모른다.

pan·a·ce·a /,pænə'siə/ n something that people think will make everything better or cure any illness ‖ 모든 것을 더 좋게 해주거나 어떤 질병이든 치료해 줄 거라고 사람들이 믿는 것. 만병통치약. 모든 문제의 해결책: Money is not a panacea for the problems in our schools, but it can help. 돈이 우리 학교 문제의 모든 해결책은 아니지만 도움은 될 것이다.

pa·nache /pə'næʃ, -'nɑʃ/ n [U] a way of doing things that is exciting and makes them seem easy ‖ 어떤 일을 흥미롭고 수월해 보이게 하는 것. 당당한 태도. 관록. 품격. 기백: Mr. Seaton danced with panache. 시튼 씨는 아주 격있게 춤을 추었다.

pan·cake /'pænkeɪk/ n a flat round type of bread made from flour, milk, and eggs, that is cooked in a pan and eaten for breakfast ‖ 밀가루·우유·계란으로 만들며 팬에서 구워 아침 식사용으로 먹는 납작하고 둥근 빵 종류. 팬케이크

pan·cre·as /'pæŋkriəs/ *n* a GLAND in your body that helps your body to use the food you eat ‖ 먹은 음식을 인체가 활용할 수 있게 도와주는 인체 내의 분비샘. 췌장. 이자 – **pancreatic** /ˌpæŋkri'ætɪk/ *adj*

pan·da /'pændə/ *n* a large black and white animal similar to a bear, that lives in China ‖ 중국에 서식하며 곰과 유사한 흑백색의 큰 동물. 판다(곰)

pan·de·mo·ni·um /ˌpændə'mouniəm/ *n* [U] a situation in which there is a lot of noise and confusion because people are angry, frightened, excited etc. ‖ 사람들이 화가 나고 겁에 질리고 흥분되어서 아주 소란스럽고 혼란스러운 상황. 대혼란. 혼돈. 아수라장. 무법천지: *There was pandemonium after UCLA won the football game.* UCLA가 미식축구 시합에서 승리하자 대혼란이 일어났다.

pan·der /'pændə/ *v*

pander to sth/sb *phr v* [T] to give someone what s/he wants, even though you know it is not good for him/her ‖ 그 사람에게 좋지 않은 줄 알면서도 그 사람이 원하는 것을 주다. 영합하다: *I won't read newspapers that pander to people's interest in sex and scandal.* 나는 성과 추문에 대한 사람들의 관심에 영합하는 신문은 읽지 않겠다.

pane /peɪn/ *n* a piece of glass in a window or door ‖ 유리창이나 문의 한 장의 유리. 창유리(한 장)

pan·el¹ /'pænl/ *n* **1** a group of people who are chosen to discuss something, decide something, or answer questions ‖ 어떤 일을 토론 또는 결정하거나 질문에 답하도록 선택된 일단의 사람들. 토론회 [퀴즈 프로] 참석자(단). 패널: *A panel of experts was there to give advice on gardening.* 일단의 전문가들이 정원 관리에 대한 조언을 해주기 위해 그 자리에 있었다. **2** a sheet of wood, glass, etc. that fits into a frame to form part of a door, wall, or ceiling ‖ 문[벽, 천장]의 일부를 이루는 틀에 맞춘 한 장의 목재·유리 등. 천장널. 창판자[유리]: *an oak door with three panels* 널빤지 3장으로 된 참나무 문짝 **3 instrument/control panel** the place in a plane, boat etc. on which the instruments or controls are fixed ‖ 비행기·배 등에서 계기나 제어 장치가 부착된 곳. 계기/제어판

panel² *v* [T] to cover or decorate something such as a wall with flat pieces of wood, glass etc. ‖ 납작한 판자·유리 등으로 벽 등을 덮거나 장식하다. 판자[유리]를 대다[끼우다]: *an oak-*

paneled room 참나무 판자로 장식된 방

pan·el·ing /'pænl-ɪŋ/ *n* [U] wood in long pieces that is used for covering walls etc. ‖ 벽 등을 덮는 데 쓰이는 긴 나무 조각. 널빤지: *pine paneling* 소나무 널빤지

pan·el·ist /'pænl-ɪst/ *n* a member of a PANEL, especially on a radio or television program ‖ 특히 라디오나 텔레비전 프로그램의 토론회 참석자. 토론자

pang /pæŋ/ *n* a sudden strong and unpleasant feeling ‖ 갑작스런 강하고 불쾌한 느낌. 고통. 격통: *hunger pangs* 허기의 고통 / *She had pangs of guilt over the way she had treated Pete.* 그녀는 피트를 대했던 자신의 태도에 대해 죄책감을 느꼈다.

pan·han·dle /'pæn,hændl/ *v* [I] to ask for money in the streets; BEG ‖ 거리에서 돈을 요구하다. 구걸하다; ⒫ beg – **panhandler** *n*

pan·ic¹ /'pænɪk/ *n* [C, U] a sudden feeling of fear or anxiety that makes you do things without thinking carefully about them ‖ 주의 깊게 생각하지 않고 어떤 일을 하게 하는 갑작스런 공포감이나 걱정. 공황(상태). 당황. 놀람: *People ran into the streets in a panic when the earthquake hit.* 지진이 강타하자 사람들은 놀래서 거리로 뛰쳐나왔다. / *There was panic on Wall Street as prices fell.* 주가가 하락하자 월스트리트는 공황에 빠졌다.

panic² *v* **panicked, panicked, panicking** [I, T] to suddenly feel so frightened that you do things without thinking clearly, or to make someone feel this way ‖ 갑자기 몹시 두려워져서 정신 없이 허둥거리며 행동을 하다, 또는 사람을 이렇게 느끼게 하다. 당황하다. 당황하게 하다. 공황(상태)에 빠지다: *Office workers panicked when fire broke out in the building.* 건물에 화재가 발생하자 사무실 직원들은 공포에 사로잡혔다. / *Don't shout – you'll panic the horses.* 소리치지 마라. 말들을 놀라게 할라. – **panicky** *adj*

panic-strick·en /'.. ˌ../ *adj* so frightened that you cannot think clearly ‖ 너무 겁을 먹어서 똑똑히 생각할 수 없는. 공황 상태에 빠진. 허둥대는: *I remember the panic-stricken look on her face.* 나는 공황 상태에 빠진 그녀의 얼굴 표정을 기억한다.

pan·o·ram·a /ˌpænə'ræmə, -'rɑ-/ *n* a view over a wide area of land ‖ 넓은 지역에 걸친 광경. 전경: *a panorama of the Rocky Mountains* 로키 산맥의 전경

– **panoramic** *adj*

pan·sy /'pænzi/ *n* **1** a small flat brightly colored garden flower ‖ 납작하고 밝은 색을 띤 정원용 작은 꽃. 팬지. 서양제비꽃 **2** SPOKEN an insulting word for a man who seems weak ‖ 약해 보이는 남성에 대한 모욕적인 말. 여성적인 남성. 동성애자 남성

pant /pænt/ *v* [I] to breathe quickly with short noisy breaths, especially after exercising or because it is hot ‖ 특히 운동한 후나 날이 더워서 짧고 요란스런 호흡으로 빠르게 숨쉬다. 숨을 헐떡이다: *a dog panting in the heat* 더위로 숨을 헐떡이는 개

pan·the·ism /'pænθi,ɪzəm/ *n* [U] the religious idea that God is present in all natural things in the universe ‖ 우주의 모든 자연물에 신이 존재한다는 종교 사상. 범신론

pan·ther /'pænθɚ/ *n* a large wild black cat that is good at hunting ‖ 사냥에 뛰어난 크고 검은 야생 고양이. 퓨마. 아메리카표범

pant·ies /'pæntiz/ *n* [plural] a piece of women's underwear that covers the area between the waist and the top of the legs ‖ 허리와 다리 위쪽 사이의 부위를 덮는 여자의 속옷. 팬티

pan·to·mime /'pæntə,maɪm/ *n* [C, U] a method of performing using only actions and not words, or a play performed using this method ‖ 오직 행동만을 사용하고 말은 하지 않는 공연의 방법, 또는 이런 방법을 사용해 공연하는 극. 무언극. 팬터마임

pan·try /'pæntri/ *n* a small room near the kitchen where food, dishes etc. are kept ‖ 음식·접시 등을 보관하는 부엌 옆의 작은 방. 식료품실. 식기실

pants /pænts/ *n* [plural] a piece of clothing that covers you from your waist to your feet and has separate parts for each leg ‖ 허리에서 다리까지를 덮고 각 다리 부분은 분리된 의류. 바지: *Jason needs a new pair of pants for school.* 제이슨은 학교에 입고 갈 새 바지가 필요하다.

pants leg /'. ./, **pant leg** *n* the part of a pair of pants that covers one leg ‖ 한쪽 다리를 덮는 바지 한 벌의 일부

pant·suit /'pæntsut/ *n* a women's suit consisting of a JACKET and matching pants ‖ 재킷과 (그것과) 어울리는 바지로 구성되는 여성의 정장

pan·ty·hose /'pænti,hoʊz/ *n* [plural] a very thin piece of women's clothing that covers the legs from the feet to the waist, usually worn with dresses or skirts ‖ 보통 드레스나 치마와 같이 입는, 발에서 허리까지의 다리를 감싸는 매우 얇은 여성의 의류. 팬티스타킹

pan·ty·lin·er /'pænti,laɪnɚ/ *n* a very thin SANITARY NAPKIN ‖ 매우 얇은 생리대

pa·pa /'pɑpə/ *n* OLD-FASHIONED ⇨ FATHER¹

pa·pa·cy /'peɪpəsi/ *n* **the papacy** the position and authority of the POPE ‖ 교황의 지위와 통치권. 교황권

pa·pal /'peɪpəl/ *adj* relating to the POPE ‖ 교황과 관련된. 로마 교황의

pa·pa·ya /pə'paɪə/ *n* [C, U] a sweet juicy tropical fruit with many small seeds inside it ‖ 속에 조그만 씨가 많이 들어 있으며 즙이 많은 달콤한 열대 과일. 파파야

pa·per¹ /'peɪpɚ/ *n* **1** [U] thin sheets used for writing or drawing on, wrapping things in etc. ‖ 글을 쓰거나 그림을 그리고 물건을 포장하는 등에 쓰이는 얇은 낱장. 종이: *a piece of writing paper* 필기 용지 한 장 / *a paper plate* 종이접시 **2** a newspaper ‖ 신문: *Have you seen today's paper?* 오늘 신문 봤니? / *an ad in the local paper* (=the newspaper for the area you live in) 지역 신문에 난 광고 **3** a piece of writing that is done as part of a class ‖ 수업의 일부로 쓴 한 편의 글. 과제물. 리포트: *My history paper is due tomorrow.* 나의 역사 과제물은 내일이 마감이다. **4 on paper** if an idea seems good on paper, it seems good or true but has not been tested in a real situation yet ‖ 아이디어가 좋거나 사실로 보이지만 실제 상황에서는 아직 시험되지 않은. 서류[이론]상은: *It looks good on paper, but I still don't think it will work.* 이론상으로는 좋아 보이지만 나는 아직 그것이 잘 될 것이라고 생각하지 않는다. **5** a piece of writing or a speech by someone who has studied a particular subject ‖ 특정한 주제를 연구한 사람의 논문이나 발표(문): *She's giving a paper on global warming at the conference.* 그녀는 그 회의에서 지구 온난화에 관한 논문을 발표 한다. **6** [C, U] ⇨ WALLPAPER¹ —see also PAPERS

paper² *v* [T] to decorate the walls of a room by covering them with WALLPAPER ‖ 벽지로 방의 벽을 덮어서 장식하다. 벽지를 바르다

pa·per·back /'peɪpɚ,bæk/ *n* a book with a stiff paper cover ‖ 빳빳한 종이 표지를 가진 책. 문고본[보급판] 책: *Her novel's just come out in paperback.* 그녀의 소설은 문고본으로 막 출판됐다. —

compare HARDBACK

paper boy /'.. ,./ n a boy who delivers newspapers to people's houses ‖ 사람들의 집에 신문을 배달하는 소년

paper clip /'.. ,./ n a small piece of curved wire used for holding sheets of paper together ‖ 종이 낱장들을 함께 집는 데 사용되는 작고 굽은 철사 조각. 종이 집게. 클립

paper girl /'.. ,./ n a girl who delivers newspapers to people's houses ‖ 사람들의 집에 신문을 배달하는 소녀. 신문 배달 소녀

pa·pers /'peɪpəz/ n [plural] important or official documents or letters, such as your will or your PASSPORT ‖ 유언장이나 여권 등의 중요하거나 공식적인 문서 또는 편지. 서류. 공문서

pa·per·weight /'peɪpəˌweɪt/ n a small heavy object that you put on top of papers so that they stay on a desk ‖ 문서가 책상 위에 그대로 있도록 문서 맨 위에 놓아두는 작고 무거운 물체. 서진(書鎭). 문진(文鎭)

pa·per·work /'peɪpəˌwɜk/ n [U] work such as writing letters or reports, or putting information on forms, especially when done as part of a job ‖ 특히 일의 일부로서 하는 편지나 보고서를 쓰거나 서류를 작성하는 등의 업무. 문서 업무. 사무 처리: *I have a lot of paperwork to do tonight.* 나는 오늘 밤에 서류 작업 할 게 많다.

pa·pier-mâ·ché /ˌpeɪpə məˈʃeɪ/ n [U] a soft substance made from a mixture of paper, water, and glue, which becomes hard when it dries ‖ 종이·물·아교를 혼합해서 만든 것으로 마르면 굳어지는 부드러운 물질. (골판지 제조용의) 걸쭉한 종이 반죽

Pap smear /'pæp smɪr/ n a medical test that takes cells from a woman's CERVIX and examines them for signs of CANCER ‖ 여자의 자궁 경관에서 세포를 떼어내서 자궁암의 징조를 검사하는 의학적인 시험. 팹 테스트

par /pɑr/ n [U] **1 be on a par (with)** to be of the same standard as something else ‖ 다른 것과 같은 수준에 있다. …과 같은 반열에 두다. …과 동등해지다: *Bruce thinks shopping is on a par with going to the dentist.* (=is as bad as going to the dentist) 브루스는 쇼핑과 치과에 가는 것이 오십보 백보라고 생각한다. **2 not be up to par/be below par** to be less good than usual ‖ 보통보다 좋지 않다. 정상[평균, 원상]을 밑돌다: *Beth is still not up to par after her operation.* 베스는

수술 후 아직 건강이 회복되지 않고 있다.

3 par for the course to be what you would normally expect to happen ‖ 당연하게 일어날 것으로 기대하는 것이 되다. 당연한 과정이 되다. 예사로운 일이다: *"Lisa was late again." "That's par for the course."* "리사는 또 지각했다." "그건 예사로운 일이다."

par·a·ble /'pærəbəl/ n a short simple story that teaches a moral or religious lesson ‖ 도덕적 또는 종교적인 교훈을 주는 짧고 간단한 이야기. 우화

par·a·chute¹
/'pærəˌʃut/ n a large piece of cloth that is attached to your back to make you fall through the air slowly when you jump out of a plane ‖ 비행기에서 뛰어내릴 때 공중에서 천천히 떨어지도록 등에 부착하는 커다란 천. 낙하산

parachute

parachute² v **1** [I] to jump from a plane using a PARACHUTE ‖ 낙하산을 이용하여 비행기에서 뛰어내리다. 낙하산으로 내려오다: *Soldiers parachuted into the field during the night.* 군인들이 야간에 들판으로 낙하했다. **2** [T] to drop something from a plane with a parachute ‖ 어떤 것에 낙하산을 매어 비행기에서 떨어뜨리다. 낙하산으로 투하하다: *We can parachute supplies to the troops.* 우리는 병사들에게 낙하산으로 보급품을 공수할 수 있다.

pa·rade¹ /pəˈreɪd/ n **1** a public celebration when musical bands, decorated vehicles etc. move down the street ‖ 악대·장식된 차량 등이 거리를 따라 움직이는 공공의 축하 행사. 축제 행진 [행렬]: *The city has a parade every Fourth of July.* 그 시는 매년 7월 4일마다 퍼레이드를 벌인다. **2** a military ceremony in which soldiers stand or march together so that they can be examined ‖ 검열을 받을 수 있게 군인들이 함께 정렬하거나 행진하는 군사 의식. 열병[분열]식

parade² v **1** [I] to march together to celebrate or protest something ‖ 어떤 것을 축하하거나 항의하기 위해 함께 행진하다. 줄을 지어[시위하며] 행진하다: *Peace demonstrators paraded toward the Capitol Building.* 평화 시위대가 의사당을 향해 행진했다. **2** [I] to walk around an area in order to attract attention ‖ 주의를 끌려고 어떤 지역을 돌아다니다. 뽐내

고 [과시하고] 다니다: *A couple of teenage girls were parading around the pool in their bikinis.* 10대 소녀 두세 명이 비키니 차림으로 수영장 주위를 자랑하듯이 돌아다니고 있었다. **3** [T] to show a particular quality or possession in order to make people notice you ‖ 사람들이 자신에게 주의를 기울이도록 특정한 특성이나 소유물을 보여주다. …을 남에게 과시하다: *Sara tends to parade her money in front of her friends.* 사라는 친구들 앞에서 자신의 돈을 자랑하는 경향이 있다. **4** [T] to show someone to the public, especially in order to prove that you have control or power over him/her ‖ 특히 어떤 사람에 대한 지배력이나 권력이 있다는 것을 증명하려고 일반 대중 앞에 그 사람을 나타내 보이다. (강제로) 행진 [정렬, 집합]시키다: *The prisoners were paraded in front of the TV cameras.* 그 포로들은 텔레비전 카메라 앞에 (강제로) 모습이 드러내졌다.

par·a·digm /ˈpærəˌdaɪm/ *n* FORMAL a model or typical example of something that explains an idea or process very clearly ‖ 생각이나 과정을 아주 분명하게 설명하는 모범적이거나 전형적인 예. 실례: *The Holocaust is a paradigm of evil.* 유대인 대학살은 악의 전형적인 실례이다. **– paradigmatic** /ˌpærədɪgˈmætɪk/ *adj*

par·a·dise /ˈpærəˌdaɪs, -ˌdaɪz/ *n* **1** [U] a place or situation that is as pleasant or beautiful as possible ‖ 최고로 즐겁고 멋진 장소나 상황. 천국. 낙원: *Hawaii is often referred to as a natural paradise.* 하와이는 종종 천혜의 낙원으로 불린다. **2** a place that has everything you need to do a particular activity ‖ 특정한 활동을 하는 데 필요한 모든 것을 갖춘 장소: *This mall is a shopper's paradise.* 이 쇼핑센터는 쇼핑객들의 낙원이다. **3** ⇨ HEAVEN

par·a·dox /ˈpærəˌdɑks/ *n* a statement or situation that seems strange or impossible because it contains two opposing ideas ‖ 두 개의 상반되는 생각을 내포하고 있기 때문에 이상하거나 있을 수 없어 보이는 진술 또는 상황. 역설. 패러독스: *It's a paradox that a rich country has so many poor people.* 부유한 국가에 그렇게 많은 빈민이 있다는 것은 역설적이다. **– paradoxical** /ˌpærəˈdɑksɪkəl/ *adj* **– paradoxically** *adv*

par·af·fin /ˈpærəfɪn/ *n* [U] a soft white substance used as a FUEL or for making CANDLES ‖ 연료로 쓰이거나 양초를 만드는 데 사용되는 연질(軟質)의 하얀 물질. 파라

핀. 석랍(石蠟)

par·a·gon /ˈpærəˌgɑn/ *n* someone who is a perfect example of something ‖ 어떤 것의 완벽한 사례인 사람. 전형. 귀감: *Mrs. Ives considered herself to be a paragon of virtue.* 이브스 여사는 자신을 정숙의 귀감으로 생각했다.

par·a·graph /ˈpærəˌgræf/ *n* a group of several sentences that deal with one idea in a piece of writing ‖ 한 편의 글에서 하나의 생각을 다루는 일단의 여러 문장들. 절. 단락

par·a·keet /ˈpærəˌkit/ *n* a small brightly colored bird with a long tail, that is often kept as a pet ‖ 종종 애완용으로 기르는, 긴 꼬리를 가진 밝은 색깔의 작은 새. 소형 앵무새

par·a·le·gal /ˌpærəˈligəl/ *n* someone whose job is to help a lawyer do his/her work ‖ 변호사의 업무를 돕는 직업인. 변호사 보조원

par·a·llel¹ /ˈpærəˌlɛl/ *n* a connection or SIMILARITY between two things that happen or exist in different places or at different times ‖ 다른 장소 또는 시간에 발생하거나 존재하는 두 가지 사이의 연관 관계나 유사성. 유사물. 유사점: *The article draws a parallel between the political situation now and the situation in the 1930s.* (=it shows how they are similar) 그 기사는 현재의 정치 상황과 1930년대의 상황에 비유하고 있다.

parallel² *adj* two lines that are parallel to each other are the same distance apart along their whole length ‖ 두 개의 선이 처음부터 끝까지 모두 같은 거리로 서로 떨어져 있는. 평행인: *a street running parallel to* (=that is parallel to) *the railroad* 철로와 평행으로 뻗어 있는 거리

parallel³ *v* [T] FORMAL to be very similar to something else ‖ 다른 것과 매우 유사하다. …에 필적[상당, 대응, 일치, 부합]하다: *The Greek stories about Dionysus parallel the Roman ones about Bacchus.* 디오니소스에 대한 그리스 이야기는 바쿠스에 대한 로마의 이야기와 유사하다.

pa·ral·y·sis /pəˈræləsɪs/ *n* [U] **1** the loss of the ability to move or feel part of your body ‖ 신체의 일부를[가] 움직이거나 느끼는 능력의 상실. 마비(증): *Such injuries can cause permanent paralysis.* 그러한 부상은 영구적인 마비를 초래할 수 있다. **2** a lack of ability to operate correctly or to do anything ‖ 정상적으로 움직이거나 무엇이든 할 수 있는 능력의 결여. 정체. 활동 불능. 무력: *So what's* *causing the tax bill paralysis in Congress?* 그래 조세 법안이 의회에서 정체되고 있는 것은 무슨 까닭입니까?

par·a·lyt·ic /ˌpærəˈlɪtɪk/ *n* someone who is completely PARALYZEd ‖ 완전히 마비가 된 사람. 마비[중풍] 환자 –
paralytic *adj*

par·a·lyze /ˈpærəˌlaɪz/ *v* [T] **1** to make someone lose the ability to move part of his/her body, or to feel anything in it ‖ 사람이 신체의 일부를 움직이거나 신체 내에서 어떤 것을 느끼는 능력을 상실하게 하다. 마비시키다 **2** to make something stop being able to operate, or to make someone unable to do anything ‖ 어떤 것이 작동할 수 없게 하거나 사람이 어떤 일을 할 수 없게 하다. (남을) 무기력하게 하다. 정체[마비]시키다: *Heavy snow has paralyzed several cities in the eastern States.* 폭설로 동부주(州)의 여러 도시들이 마비되었다. – **paralyzed** *adj*: *The stroke left him paralyzed and unable to feed himself.* 그는 뇌졸중으로 마비되어 스스로 식사도 할 수 없게 됐다.

par·a·med·ic /ˌpærəˈmɛdɪk/ *n* someone who usually works in an AMBULANCE and is trained to help sick or injured people, but is not a doctor or nurse ‖ 의사나 간호사는 아니지만 보통 구급차에서 근무하면서 환자나 부상자를 돕도록 훈련받은 사람. 구급 의료 대원

pa·ram·et·er /pəˈræmətɚ/ *n* a limit that controls the way that something should be done ‖ 어떤 일이 행해져야 하는 방식을 통제하는 한계. 한정 요소. 제한(범위): *Congress will decide on parameters for the investigation.* 의회는 그 조사의 한계에 관해 결정할 것이다.

par·a·mil·i·tar·y /ˌpærəˈmɪləˌtɛri/ *adj* organized like an army, but not part of the legal military forces of a country ‖ 국가의 정규 군사력의 일부는 아니지만 군대같이 조직된. 비정규군의. 준(準)군사적인: *a paramilitary force* 비정규군 –
paramilitary *n*

par·a·mount /ˈpærəˌmaʊnt/ *adj* more important than anything else ‖ 다른 어떤 것보다 더 중요한. 최고의. 지상의: *The needs of the customer should be paramount.* 고객이 필요로 하는 것이 최우선이 되어야 한다.

par·a·noid /ˈpærəˌnɔɪd/ *adj* **1** DISAPPROVING extremely worried because you believe that you cannot trust other people ‖ 다른 사람을 신뢰할 수 없다고 믿어서 극도로 걱정하는. 편집증적인. 피해망상의: *Ever since her keys were stolen she's been paranoid about going into*

the house alone. 그녀는 열쇠를 도난당한 이후 줄곧 집에 혼자 들어가는 것에 대해 두려워해 왔다. **2** suffering from a mental illness that makes you believe that other people are trying to harm you ‖ 다른 사람이 자신을 해치려 한다고 믿는 정신 질환으로 시달리는. 피해망상증에 걸린 – **paranoia** /ˌpærəˈnɔɪə/ *n* [U]

par·a·pher·na·lia /ˌpærəfɚˈneɪlyə, -fəˈneɪl-/ *n* [U] a lot of small things that belong to someone or that are used for a particular activity ‖ 어떤 사람의 소유이거나 특정한 활동에 사용되는 여러 작은 물건들. 신변 소지품. 필요한 용품[비품]: *photographic paraphernalia* 촬영 장비

par·a·phrase /ˈpærəˌfreɪz/ *v* [T] to express what someone has written or said in a way that is shorter or easier to understand ‖ 어떤 사람의 글이나 말을 이해할 수 있도록 더 짧거나 쉽게 표현하다. 바꾸어 말하다: *Write a paragraph that paraphrases the story.* 그 이야기를 줄여서 한 단락으로 써라. – **paraphrase** *n*

par·a·ple·gic /ˌpærəˈplidʒɪk/ *n* someone who is unable to move the lower part of his/her body ‖ 하체를 움직일 수 없는 사람. 양측 하지(下肢) 마비 환자

par·a·site /ˈpærəˌsaɪt/ *n* **1** a plant or animal that lives on or in another plant or animal and gets food from it ‖ 다른 식물이나 동물에 붙어살면서 거기서 영양분을 얻는 식물이나 동물. 기생 동[식]물. 기생충 **2** a lazy person who does not work but depends on other people ‖ 일하지 않고 남에게 의지하는 게으른 사람. 식객. 기식자 – **parasitic** /ˌpærəˈsɪtɪk/ *adj*

par·a·sol /ˈpærəˌsɔl, -ˌsɑl/ *n* a type of UMBRELLA used for protection from the sun ‖ 햇빛 보호용으로 쓰이는 우산의 일종. 여성용 양산. 파라솔

par·a·troop·er /ˈpærəˌtrupɚ/ *n* a soldier who is trained to jump out of a plane using a PARACHUTE ‖ 낙하산을 이용하여 비행기에서 뛰어내리는 훈련을 받은 군인. 낙하산병

par·cel¹ /ˈpɑrsəl/ *n* **1** ⇨ PACKAGE¹ **2** an area of land that is part of a larger area that has been divided ‖ 더 큰 토지의 일부로서 분할된 토지. 한 구획[필지]

parcel² *v*

parcel sth ↔ **out** *phr v* [T] to divide or share something among several people or groups ‖ 어떤 것을 여러 사람들 또는 집단 사이에 나누거나 공유하다. 구분[배분]하다: *The foundation receives the money, then parcels it out to various* *projects*. 그 재단은 돈을 받아서 여러 사업 계획에 배정한다.

parcel post /ˌ.. ˈ./ *n* [U] the cheapest way of sending packages by mail, because it uses trains and trucks rather than planes ‖ 비행기보다는 기차와 트럭을 이용하기 때문에 가장 저렴하게 우편으로 소포를 보내는 방법. 소포 우편

parched /pɑrtʃt/ *adj* **1 be parched** INFORMAL to be very THIRSTY ‖ 매우 갈증이 나다. (목·입이) 바싹 마르다: *I'm parched!* 목이 탄다! **2** LITERARY extremely dry ‖ (토지 등이) 바싹 마른: *parched land* 바싹 마른 땅

parch·ment /ˈpɑrtʃmənt/ *n* [U] thick yellow-white writing paper that in past times was made of sheep or goat skin ‖ 과거에 양이나 염소 가죽으로 만들었던 두꺼운 황백색의 필기 용지. 양피지

par·don[1] /ˈpɑrdn/ *v* [T] **1 pardon (me)** SPOKEN **a)** used in order to politely say you are sorry when you have done something that is embarrassing or rude ‖ 남을 당혹하게 하거나 무례한 일을 했을 때 미안하다고 정중하게 말하려는 데에 쓰여. 죄송합니다: *Pardon me – I hope I didn't hurt you.* 죄송합니다. 다치시지 않았기를 바랍니다. **b)** used in order to ask someone politely to move so you can go past him/her ‖ 남에게 지나갈 수 있도록 비켜달라고 공손하게 요청하는 데에 쓰여. 실례합니다: *Pardon me, can I just get to my seat?* 죄송합니다, 제 자리로 좀 가도 될까요? **c)** said when you want to politely get someone's attention in order to ask a question ‖ 질문을 하기 위해 정중하게 남의 주목을 끌기 원할 때 말해. 실례지만: *Pardon me, is this the way to City Hall?* 실례지만 이것이 시청으로 가는 길입니까? **d)** used in order to politely ask someone to repeat what s/he has just said ‖ 남이 방금 말한 것을 반복해 달라고 공손하게 요청하는 데에 쓰여. 죄송합니다만: *Pardon me, could you repeat that last number again?* 죄송합니다만, 마지막 번호를 다시 한번 말해 주시겠어요? **e)** used before politely disagreeing with something that someone has said ‖ 남이 말한 것에 대해 정중하게 반대하는 말 앞에 쓰여: *Pardon me, but I don't think that's true.* 죄송합니다만, 그것은 진실이 아니라고 생각합니다. **2** to officially allow someone not to be punished, although a court has proved that s/he is guilty of a crime ‖ 법원이 어떤 사람을 유죄로 판정했음에도 공식적으로 벌은 받지 않게 해주다. (죄를) 면제[사면]하다: *His only chance now is*

for the governor to pardon him. 지금 그에게 남은 유일한 기회는 주지사가 그의 죄를 사면하는 것이다.

pardon[2] *n* an official order allowing someone to be free and stopping his/her punishment ‖ 어떤 사람을 석방하고 형 집행을 중지할 것을 허가하는 공식 명령. 사면. 특사: *Tyler was later granted a pardon.* 타일러는 나중에 사면을 받았다. —see also **I beg your pardon** (BEG)

par·don·a·ble /ˈpɑrdn-əbəl/ *adj* FORMAL possible to forgive or excuse ‖ 용서하거나 눈감아줄 수 있는: *a pardonable error* 너그럽게 봐줄 수 있는 실수

pare /pɛr/ *v* [T] to cut off the thin outer part of something, especially a fruit or vegetable ‖ 특히 과일이나 야채의 얇은 바깥 부분을 잘라내다. 껍질을 벗기다[깎아내다]: *Pare the apples and slice them into chunks.* 사과의 껍질을 깎은 다음 여러 조각으로 잘라라.

pare sth **down** *phr v* [T] to gradually reduce an amount or number ‖ 분량이나 수를 점차 감소시키다. 차차 줄이다: *Production costs were to be pared down.* 생산비는 점차 줄여야 한다.

par·ent /ˈpɛrənt, ˈpær-/ *n* the father or mother of a person or animal ‖ 사람의 아버지나 어머니, 또는 동물의 어미: *My parents are coming to visit next week.* 나의 부모님이 다음 주에 방문하러 오신다. **– parental** /pəˈrɛntl/ *adj*: *parental love* 부모[어버이]의 사랑 —see picture at FAMILY

par·ent·age /ˈpɛrəntɪdʒ, ˈpær-/ *n* [U] someone's parents and the country they are from ‖ 어떤 사람의 부모·모국. 출신. 혈통: *children of French-Canadian parentage* 프랑스계 캐나다인 혈통의 아이들

pa·ren·the·sis /pəˈrɛnθəsɪs/ *n, plural* **parentheses** /-siz/ one of the marks ( ), used in writing to separate additional information from the main information ‖ 주요 정보를 추가 정보와 구분하기 위해 문장에서 쓰이는 부호. 괄호: *The numbers in parentheses refer to page numbers.* 괄호 안의 숫자는 페이지 수를 말한다.

par·ent·hood /ˈpɛrənt,hʊd, ˈpær-/ *n* [U] the state of being a parent ‖ 부모인 상태. 어버이임

par·ish /ˈpærɪʃ/ *n* **1** the area served by a particular church ‖ 특정한 교회가 담당하는 지역. 소교구(小敎區). 지역 교회 **2** the members of a particular church ‖ 특정 교회의 구성원. (소)교구민 –

parishioner /pə'rɪʃənəʳ/ n

par·i·ty /'pærəti/ n [U] the state of being equal, especially having equal pay, rights, or power ‖ 특히 동등한 급여·권리·권력을 가지는 동등한 상태. 동격. 등위: *Our employees are demanding parity with other workers in the industry.* 우리 종업원들은 같은 산업에 종사하는 다른 근로자들과의 동등한 대우를 요구하고 있다.

park¹ /pɑrk/ n a large open area with grass and trees in a town, where people can walk, play games etc. ‖ 사람들이 산책이나 놀이 등을 할 수 있는, 도시 내의 풀과 나무가 있는 널따랗게 탁 트인 구역. 공원 —see also BALL PARK

park² v [I, T] to put a car in a particular place for a period of time ‖ 잠시 특정한 장소에 차를 넣어두다. 주차하다: *Is it okay if I park here?* 여기에 주차해도 괜찮습니까? / *Park your car in the back lot.* 후면 주차장에 차를 주차하시오.

par·ka /'pɑrkə/ n a thick warm coat with a HOOD ‖ 모자가 달린 두꺼운 보온 코트. 파카

park and ride /ˌ. . './ n [U] a system in which you leave your car in a special place in one part of a city and then take a bus or train from there to the center of town ‖ 도시 한 부분의 특별한 장소에 차를 주차시켜 두고 도심부까지 버스나 지하철을 타고 가는 방식. 터미널(역) 주차 통근 방식

park·ing /'pɑrkɪŋ/ n [U] **1** the act of parking a car ‖ 차를 주차하는 행위: *Seth parked right under a "No Parking" sign.* 세스는 "주차금지" 표지판 바로 아래에 차를 주차시켰다. **2** spaces in which you can leave a car ‖ 차를 세워둘 수 있는 공간. 주차 장소: *Parking is available on Lemay Street.* 르메이 거리는 주차가 가능하다. / *We got a parking space near the door.* 우리는 현관 근처에 주차 공간을 확보했다.

parking ga·rage /'.. .ˌ./ n an enclosed building for cars to be parked in ‖ 차를 주차시키기 위한, 벽으로 둘러싸인 건물. 주차 전용 빌딩

parking lot /'.. ./ n an open area for cars to be parked in ‖ 안에 차가 주차되는 개방 구역. 주차장

parking me·ter /'.. ˌ./ n a machine that you must put money into so that you can park your car in the space next to it ‖ 옆에 있는 공간에 주차시키기 위해서 돈을 투입해야 하는 기계. 주차 요금 징수기

park·way /'pɑrkweɪ/ n a wide road in or around a city, usually with grass and trees in the middle or along the sides ‖ 보통 길 중간 또는 양측을 따라 풀과 나무가 있는, 도시 내 또는 도시 근처의 넓은 도로. 공원 도로

par·lia·ment /'pɑrləmənt/ n the group of people who are elected in some countries to make laws and discuss important national affairs ‖ 몇몇 나라에서 법을 제정하고 중요한 국사를 논의하도록 선출된 일단의 사람들. 의회. 국회 – **parliamentary** /ˌpɑrlə'mɛntri, -'mɛntəri/ adj

par·lor /'pɑrləʳ/ n **1** a store or type of business that provides a particular service ‖ 특정한 서비스를 제공하는 가게 또는 사업 유형. …원[점]: *a beauty parlor* 미장원 / *a funeral parlor* 장의사 **2** OLD-FASHIONED a formal room in a house used especially for entertaining visitors in ‖ 특히 방문객을 접대하는 데에 쓰이는 집안의 격식을 갖춘 방. 응접실. 거실

pa·ro·chi·al /pə'roukiəl/ adj **1** only interested in the things that affect you and your local area ‖ 자신과 자신의 지역에 영향을 미치는 일에만 관심을 가지는. (관심사·시야가) 편협한. 지방 근성[지역주의]의: *My cousin's views are fairly parochial.* 나의 사촌의 시각은 너무나 편협하다. **2** relating to a particular church ‖ 특정 교회의. 소교구(小敎區)의: *a parochial school* 교구학교

par·o·dy¹ /'pærədi/ n [C, U] a performance or a piece of writing or music that copies a particular style in a funny way ‖ 특정한 스타일을 우스꽝스럽게 흉내 내는 연기[글, 음악]. (진지한 작품을)익살스럽게 고쳐 놓은 것. 패러디: *a parody of Walt Whitman's poetry* 월트 휘트먼의 시의 패러디

parody² v [T] to copy someone's style or attitude in a funny way ‖ 사람의 스타일이나 태도를 익살스럽게 흉내 내다. 풍자적으로 희화화하다: *a comedian who parodies politicians* 정치인을 희화화하는 코미디언

pa·role /pə'roul/ n [U] permission for someone to leave prison, on the condition that s/he continues to behave well ‖ 계속 바르게 행동한다는 조건으로 어떤 사람을 교도소를 떠나게 하는 것. 가석방: *He was released on parole after serving 5 years.* 그는 5년간 복역한 후에 가석방됐다. – **parole** v [T]

par·quet /pɑr'keɪ, 'pɑrkeɪ/ n [U] small flat blocks of wood laid in a pattern that covers the floor of a room ‖ 방바닥에 무

니가 생기게 까는 작고 편평한 나뭇조각
들. 조각 나무 세공의 마루

par·rot /ˈpærət/ *n* a brightly colored
tropical bird with a curved beak that
can be taught to copy human speech ‖
인간의 말을 흉내 내도록 길들일 수 있는
부리가 굽은 밝은 색깔의 열대 조류. 앵무
새

pars·ley /ˈpɑrsli/ *n* [U] a plant with
groups of curled leaves, used in cooking
or as a decoration on food ‖ 조리용 또는
음식 위의 장식용으로 쓰이는 곱슬곱슬한
잎들이 무성한 식물. 파슬리

pars·nip /ˈpɑrsnɪp/ *n* [C, U] a large
thick white or pale yellow root that is
eaten as a vegetable ‖ 야채로 먹는 크고
굵으며 희거나 연노란 뿌리. 사탕당근

part¹ /pɑrt/ *n*

1 ▶OF A WHOLE 전체 가운데◀ [C, U] a
piece of something or some of
something, such as an object, area,
event, or period of time ‖ 물체·구역·사
건·시간 등의 한 단편 또는 일부. 부분:
Which part of town do you live in? 도시
의 어디쯤에 살고 있니? / *The best part
of the movie was when she hit him.* 그
영화의 압권은 그녀가 그를 때렸을 때였
다. / *The front part of the car was
badly damaged.* 그 차의 앞부분은 심하게
파손되었다. / *A large part of* (=a lot of)
my time is spent reading. 나는 대부분의
시간을 독서로 보낸다. / *We waited for
the better part of* (=most of) *an hour.*
우리는 거의 한 시간 동안을 기다렸다.

2 ▶SEPARATE PIECE 부분품◀ one of the
separate pieces that something is made
of ‖ 사물을 만드는 부분품의 하나. 부품:
Do you sell parts for Ford cars? 포드차
의 부품을 팔고 있습니까?

3 play/have a part in to be one of
several things that make something
happen or be successful ‖ 어떤 일을 일어
나게 하거나 성공하게 하는 여러 가지 일
가운데 하나가 되다. 역할을 하다: *Our
planes played a big part in the attack.*
우리 비행기들이 공격에 큰 몫을 했다.

4 take part to be involved in an
activity, event etc. together with other
people ‖ 다른 사람들과 함께 활동·사건
등에 관여하다. 가담하다. 조력하다: *Ten
runners took part in the race.* 열 명의
주자(走者)가 그 경주에 참가했다.

5 ▶WHAT SB DID 사람이 한 일◀ what
someone did in an activity, especially
one that was shared by several people ‖
특히 여러 사람에게 분담된 활동에서 어떤
사람이 맡아서 한 일. 분담. 역할. 책임:
We'd like to thank Walter for his part in

organizing the concert. 연주회 준비 과정
에서 월터가 한 역할에 대해 감사드리고
싶습니다. / *It was a huge mistake on
her part.* (=that she made) 그것은 그녀
가 저지른 커다란 실수였다.

6 ▶IN A PLAY/MOVIE 연극/영화에서◀
the words and actions of a particular
character in a play, movie etc.,
performed by an actor ‖ 연극·영화 등에
서 배우가 연기하는 특정 등장인물의 말·
동작. (배)역. 대사: *Kessler played/had
the part of Hamlet.* 케슬러는 햄릿 역을
맡았다.

7 ▶QUANTITY 수량◀ a particular
quantity used when measuring different
substances together into a mixture ‖ 서
로 다른 물질들의 양을 재어 혼합물로 섞
을 때 쓰이는 특정한 분량. 비율. 부분:
Mix two parts sand to one part cement.
모래와 시멘트를 2대 1의 비율로 섞어라.

8 ▶HAIR 머리털◀ the line on your head
made by dividing your hair with a comb
‖ 빗으로 머리털을 갈라서 만든 머리 위의
선. 가르마

9 for the most part mostly, in most
places, or most of the time ‖ 거의 모두
[대부분의 장소에서, 시간의 대부분]. 대
개는. 대체로: *She is, for the most part, a
fair person.* 그녀는 대체로 공정한 사람이
다.

10 in part to some degree, but not
completely ‖ 어느 정도이나 완전하게는
아닌. 얼마간: *The accident was due in
part to the bad weather.* 그 사고의 어느
정도는 악천후에 기인했다.

part² *v* **1** [T] to pull the two sides of
something apart, making a space in the
middle ‖ 사물의 양쪽을 잡아당겨 중간에
공간을 만들어 분리시키다. 떼어 놓다. 갈
라[벌려] 놓다: *He parted the curtains
and looked out into the street.* 그는 커
튼을 양쪽으로 제치고 거리를 내다보았
다. **2** [I] FORMAL to separate from
someone, or end a relationship with
him/her ‖ 사람과 헤어지다, 또는 관계를
끝내다. 헤어지다: *The time came for
them to part.* 그들에게 이별의 시간이 왔
다. **3** [T] to divide the hair on your head
into two parts with a comb so that it
makes a line ‖ 머리 위에 선이 생기게 빗
으로 머리카락을 두 부분으로 가르다.
가르마를 타다 **4 part company a)** to
separate from someone, or end a
friendship or business relationship with
someone ‖ 다른 사람과 갈라지다, 또는 우
정이나 사업관계를 끝내다. 헤어지다 **b)**
to no longer agree with someone ‖ 어떤
사람에게 더 이상 동의하지 않다. 결별하

다

part with sth *phr v* [T] to get rid of something although you do not want to ‖ 원하지는 않지만 어떤 것을 없애다. 버리다: *I hated to part with those boots, but they were too old.* 나는 그 부츠를 버리기가 싫었지만 그것들은 너무 낡았다.

part³ *adv* if something is part one thing, part another, it consists of both those things ‖ 사물이 두 개의 다른 것들로 이루어져. 얼마만큼. 어느 정도. 반쯤: *The English test is part written, part spoken.* 그 영어 시험은 쓰기와 회화로 구성되어 있다.

par·tial /'pɑrʃəl/ *adj* **1** not complete ‖ 완전한 것이 아닌. 일부의. 부분적인: *The party was only a partial success.* 파티는 부분적으로 성공했을 뿐이었다. **2 be partial to** sth FORMAL to like something very much ‖ 어떤 것을 아주 많이 좋아한다. 편애하다. 편파적이다: *I'm very partial to chocolate.* 나는 초콜릿이라면 사족을 못 쓴다. **3** ⇨ BIASED

par·ti·al·i·ty /ˌpɑrʃi'æləti/ *n* [U] the fact of unfairly supporting one person or group more than another ‖ 한 사람이나 집단을 다른 쪽보다 불공평하게 더 지원함. 편파적임. 편애. 불공평함: *The city council was accused of partiality in awarding contracts.* 시의회는 공사 계약의 도급 과정에서 불공정하다는 비난을 받았다.

par·tial·ly /'pɑrʃəli/ *adv* not completely ‖ 완전하지 않게. 부분적으로. 어느 정도. 조금: *He's only partially to blame.* 그는 일부만 책임지면 된다.

par·tic·i·pant /par'tɪsəpənt, pɚ-/ *n* someone who is taking part in an activity or event ‖ 활동이나 행사에 참여하는 사람. 참가자. 관계자

par·tic·i·pate /par'tɪsə,peɪt, pɚ-/ *v* [I] to take part in an activity or event ‖ 활동·행사에 참여하다. 참가[관여]하다. 가담하다: *I'd like to thank everyone who participated in tonight's show.* 오늘 밤 쇼에 참가해 주신 여러분께 감사드립니다.

par·tic·i·pa·tion /pɑrˌtɪsə'peɪʃən, pɚ-/ *n* [U] the act of taking part in something ‖ 어떤 일에 참가하는 행위. 참여. 관여. 가입: *The participation of the public in the recycling program has been really great.* 일반 대중의 재활용 프로그램에의 참여는 정말 대단했다.

par·ti·ci·ple /'pɑrtə,sɪpəl/ *n* TECHNICAL in grammar, the form of a verb, usually ending in "-ing" or "-ed," that is used in compounds to make verb tenses, or as an adjective or GERUND ‖ 문법에서, 동

사 시제를 만드는 복합어에 쓰이거나 또는 형용사나 동명사로 쓰이는, 보통 -ing나 -ed로 끝나는 동사 형태. 분사 —see also PAST PARTICIPLE, PRESENT PARTICIPLE

par·ti·cle /'pɑrtɪkəl/ *n* a very small piece of something ‖ 사물의 아주 작은 조각. 미량. 극소: *dust particles* 티끌

par·tic·u·lar¹ /pə'tɪkyələ/ *adj* **1** a particular thing or person is the one that you are talking about, and not any other ‖ 사물이나 사람이 다른 어떤 것도 아닌 지금 언급하고 있는 것인. 다름 아닌 바로 그[저]. 특정의. 특유의: *I'm looking for a particular book; can you help me?* 나는 어떤 책을 찾고 있는데 도와주겠니? ✗DON'T SAY "a book that is particular."✗ "a book that is particular" 라고는 하지 않는다. **2** special or important enough to mention separately ‖ 별도로 언급할 만큼 특별하거나 중요한. 각별한. 현저한: *There was nothing in the letter of particular importance.* 그 편지에는 특별하게 중요한 사항은 아무것도 없었다. **3** very careful about choosing exactly what you like, and not easily satisfied; FUSSY ‖ 좋아하는 것을 매우 세심하게 정확히 선택하고 쉽게 만족하지 않는. 까다로운. 꼼꼼한; ⑨ fussy: *He's very particular about what he eats.* 그는 먹는 것에 대해 매우 까다롭다.

particular² *n* **in particular** special or specific ‖ 특별하거나 특유한. 특히. 특별히: *Is there anything in particular I can help you with?* 특별히 내가 도울 수 있는 어떤 일이 있습니까?

par·tic·u·lar·ly /pə'tɪkyələli, -'tɪkyəli/ *adv* especially ‖ 특별하게. 현저하게. 각별히: *She isn't particularly attractive.* 그녀는 특별나게 매력적이지는 않다.

par·ting¹ /'pɑrtɪŋ/ *n* [C, U] FORMAL an occasion when two people leave each other ‖ 두 사람이 서로 헤어지는 때. 이별

parting² *adj* a **parting kiss/gift/ glance etc.** something that you give someone as you leave ‖ 헤어지면서 어떤 사람에게 해주는 것. 이별의 키스/선물/돌아보기

par·ti·san /'pɑrtəzən, -sən/ *adj* **1** showing support for a particular political party, plan, or leader, and criticizing all others ‖ 특정 정당·계획·지도자에 대한 지지를 나타내고 여타 모든 것을 비판하는. 당파심이 강한. 당파에 치우친: *a partisan speech* 당파적인 연설 **2** a **partisan struggle/conflict** the continuing fight of a group of people against an enemy that has defeated its country ‖ 자국(自國)을 패배시킨 적에 대

항하는 일단의 사람들의 계속적인 투쟁. 빨치산[게릴라] 투쟁/분쟁 – **partisan** n

par·ti·tion¹ /parˈtɪʃən, pə-/ n 1 a thin wall that separates one part of a room from another ‖ 방의 일부분을 다른 부분과 구분하는 얇은 벽. 칸막이(벽). 경계. 구획 2 [U] the separation of a country into two or more independent countries ‖ 한 나라를 둘 이상의 독립 국가로 분리하기. (국가의) 정치적 분할

partition² v [T] to divide a country, room, building etc. into two or more parts ‖ 국가·방·빌딩 등을 둘 이상의 부분으로 나누다. 분할하다. 칸막이로 나누다

partition sth ↔ **off** phr v [T] to divide a room into two parts using a PARTITION ‖ 칸막이를 써서 방을 두 부분으로 나누다. (방·건물을) …으로 칸막이하다

part·ly /ˈpartli/ adv to some degree, but not completely ‖ 어느 정도는 그러나 완전히는 아닌. 부분적으로. 얼마간은: The accident was partly my fault. 그 사고의 어느 정도는 내 잘못이었다.

part·ner /ˈpartnɚ/ n 1 someone with whom you do a particular activity, for example dancing, or playing a game against two other people ‖ 댄스[다른 두 사람에 대항한 시합] 등의 특정 활동을 같이 하는 사람. 동료. 짝패. 파트너: my tennis partner 나의 테니스 파트너 2 one of the owners of a business ‖ 사업 소유자 중의 한 명. 공동 경영[사업]자 3 one of two people who are married, or who live together and have a sexual relationship ‖ 결혼한[함께 사는, 성관계를 갖는] 두 사람 중의 한 명. 배우자. 동거[성교] 상대

part·ner·ship /ˈpartnɚˌʃɪp/ n 1 a relationship in which two or more people, organizations etc. work together to achieve something ‖ 둘 이상의 사람·조직 등이 어떤 것을 성취하려고 함께 일하는 관계. 협력[제휴, 협동, 연합] 관계: We're trying to build a partnership between the business community and colleges. 우리는 기업 사회와 대학간의 협력 관계를 구축하려고 있다. 2 [U] the state of being a partner, especially in business ‖ 특히 사업상의 파트너가 된 상태. 공동 경영[사업](자): We've been in partnership for five years. 우리는 5년간 공동으로 사업을 운영해 왔다. 3 a business owned by two or more partners ‖ 둘 이상의 파트너가 소유한 사업. 조합. 회사

part of speech /ˌ. . ˈ./ n TECHNICAL in grammar, any of the types into which words are divided according to their use, such as noun, verb, or adjective ‖ 문법에서 단어들이 명사, 동사 또는 형용사 등의 쓰임에 따라서 분류되는 한 형태. 품사

par·tridge /ˈpartrɪdʒ/ n [C, U] a fat bird with a short tail that is hunted for food and sport, or the meat from this bird ‖ 식용·스포츠용으로 사냥되는, 짧은 꼬리를 가진 통통한 새, 또는 이 새의 고기. 자고(가기)

part-time /ˌ. ˈ./ adj, adv working or studying for fewer than the number of hours that work is usually done ‖ 정상의 업무 시간보다 더 적은 시간 동안 일하거나 공부하는. 비상근인. 시간제[파트타임]인: Brenda works part-time in our office. 브렌다는 우리 사무실에서 비상근으로 근무한다. / a part-time job 부업 —compare FULL-TIME

part·way /ˌpartˈweɪ/ adv some of the distance into or along a place, or after some of a period of time has passed ‖ 한 장소로 가거나 쭉 따라서 어느 정도의 거리까지, 또는 어느 정도 시간이 흐른 후에. 도중에서[까지]. 중간에: The house sat partway up a canyon. 그 집은 계곡의 다소 위쪽에 위치하고 있다. / Dave arrived partway through the lecture. 데이브는 강의 도중에 도착했다.

par·ty¹ /ˈparti/ n 1 an occasion when people meet together to enjoy themselves by eating, drinking, dancing etc. ‖ 먹고 마시고 춤추는 등 모여서 즐기기 위해 사람들이 만나는 때. 사교적인 모임. 파티: We're having/giving/throwing a party on Saturday. 우리는 토요일에 파티를 연다. / a birthday party 생일 축하 파티 2 an organization of people with the same political aims, that you can vote for in elections ‖ 선거에서 찬성 투표를 할 수 있는, 같은 정치적 목적을 가진 사람들의 조직. 정당: the Democratic Party 민주당 3 a group of people that has been organized in order to do something ‖ 어떤 것을 하기 위해 조직된 일단의 사람들. 단체. 일행. 한패: A search party was formed to find the missing girl. 실종된 소녀를 찾기 위해 수색대가 구성되었다. / Foster, party of six, your table is ready. 포스터, 일행 6명(예약), 당신의 자리가 마련되어 있습니다. 4 one of the people or groups involved in an argument, agreement etc., especially a legal one ‖ 특히 법적인 논쟁·협정 등에 관련된 한 사람 또는 집단. (소송)당사자. 관계[관련]자 5 **party animal** INFORMAL someone who enjoys parties a lot ‖ 파티를 아주 좋아하는 사람.

파티광

party² *v* [I] INFORMAL to enjoy yourself, especially by drinking alcohol, eating, dancing etc. ‖ 특히 술 마시고 식사하고 춤추는 등으로 즐겁게 지내다. 흥청망청 놀다: *We were out partying until 4 a.m.* 우리는 새벽 4시까지 밖에서 흥청망청 놀았다.

pass¹ /pæs/ *v*

1 ▶GO PAST 지나감◀ [I, T] also **pass by** to move to a particular point, object, person etc. and go past him, her, or it ‖ 특정한 지점·물체·사람 등에게로 이동하여 그 옆을 지나가다. 지나치다. 앞지르다. 추월하다: *Angie waved at me as she passed.* 앤지는 지나치면서 나에게 손을 흔들었다. / *A car passed us doing at least 90 miles an hour.* 어떤 차가 최소한 시속 90마일 속도를 내면서 우리를 추월했다.

2 ▶MOVE IN A DIRECTION 어떤 방향으로 움직임◀ [I] to move from one place to another, following a particular direction ‖ 특정한 방향을 따라 한 장소에서 다른 장소로 움직이다. 통과하다. 지나가다: *We passed through Texas on our way to Mexico.* 우리는 멕시코로 가는 도중에 텍사스를 통과했다. / *Pass over the bridge and turn left.* 다리를 건너서 좌회전해라.

3 ▶GO THROUGH/ACROSS ETC. 통과하다/건너 가다◀ [I, T] to go across, through, around etc. something else, or to make something do this ‖ 어떤 것을 건너거나 통과하거나 돌아서 가다, 또는 어떤 것을 그렇게 하게 하다. 행진[전진, 통과]시키다: *The new road passes behind our house.* 새 도로는 우리 집 뒤를 통과한다. / *Pass the rope around the tree.* 로프를 나무에 감아라.

4 ▶GIVE 주다◀ [T] to take something and put it in someone's hand ‖ 어떤 것을 가져다 어떤 사람의 손에 놓아 주다. 건네주다: *Please pass the salt.* 소금 좀 건네 주세요.

5 ▶SPORTS 스포츠◀ [I, T] to kick, throw, or hit a ball or other object to another member of your team ‖ 자기 팀의 다른 동료에게 공이나 다른 물체를 차다[던지다, 쳐주다]. 패스하다: *Dad taught me to pass a football when I was seven.* 아버지는 내가 7살이었을 때 미식축구 공 던지기를 가르쳐 주셨다.

6 ▶TIME ◀ a) [I] if time passes, it goes by ‖ 시간이 지나다. 경과하다: *A year passed before I learned the truth.* 1년이 지나고 나서야 비로소 나는 그 진실을 알았다. **b)** [T] to spend time in a particular way ‖ 특정하게 시간을 보내다. 지내다. 경험하다: *She passed the time by reading.* 그녀는 독서로 시간을 보냈다. / *birds that pass the winter in Canada* 캐나다에서 겨울을 나는 철새들 —see usage note at TIME¹

7 ▶TEST/CLASS 시험/학과목◀ **a)** [I, T] to succeed in a test or class ‖ 시험이나 학과목에서 성공하다. 합격하다: *Do you think you'll pass?* 너는 합격할 거라고 생각하니? / *He's worried he won't pass history.* 그는 역사 과목에서 낙제할까봐 걱정했다. **b)** [T] to officially decide that someone has passed a test ‖ 다른 사람이 시험에서 합격했다고 공식 결정하다. 합격시키다: *The driving tester passed me even though I failed parallel parking.* 내가 평행 주차에 실수를 했는데도 운전면허 시험관은 나를 합격시켰다.

8 ▶LAW/DECISION 법률/결정◀ [T] to officially accept a law or proposal, especially by voting ‖ 특히 투표로 법률·제안을 공식 수용하다: *The motion was passed, 15 votes to 3.* 그 동의는 15대 3의 투표로 가결되었다.

9 ▶END 끝◀ [I] to stop existing or happening; end ‖ 존재 또는 발생이 중단되다. 사라지다. 소멸하다; 끝나다: *The storm soon passed.* 그 폭풍은 곧 소멸됐다. / *Deirdre will be upset for a while, but it'll pass.* 디어드르는 잠시 화가 나겠지만 괜찮아질 것이다.

10 ▶CHANGE 변화◀ [I] FORMAL to change ‖ 바뀌다. (차차 …으로) 변화하다: *When ice melts, it passes from a solid to a liquid state.* 얼음은 녹을 때 고체에서 액체 상태로 변한다.

11 pass judgment to say whether you think someone or something is right or wrong ‖ 사람이나 사물이 옳은지 그른지

에 대한 생각을 말하다. …에 판단을 내리다. 의견을 말하다: *I'm only here to listen, not to pass judgment.* 나는 들으려고 여기 있을 뿐이지 시비를 가리려는 것이 아니다.

12 ▶DON'T KNOW ANSWER 답을 모르다◀ [I] SPOKEN said when you cannot answer a question because you do not know the answer ∥ 답을 몰라서 질문에 답변할 수 없을 때에 쓰여. 통과: *"What year was Einstein born?" "Pass."* "아인슈타인의 출생 연도는?" "통과" —see also **pass the buck** (BUCK¹)

pass away *phr v* [I] a phrase meaning to die, used in order to avoid saying this directly ∥ 죽다를 뜻하는 어구로 이를 직접 언급하는 것을 피하는 데에 쓰여. 사망하다. 서거[영면]하다

pass sb ↔ **by** *phr v* [T] if something passes you by, it exists or happens but you do not have the chance to be involved in it or get any advantage from it ∥ 어떤 것이 존재하거나 일어났지만 관여할 기회를 못 가지고[어떤 이득도 얻지 못하고] 지나쳐 버리다. 부지중에 지나쳐 버리다[놓치다]. 허무하게 흘려보내다: *Robin felt that life was passing her by.* 로빈은 인생이 덧없이 흘러가고 있다고 느꼈다.

pass sth ↔ **down** *phr v* [T] to give or teach something to people who are younger than you or who live after you ∥ 자신보다 젊거나 후세에 사는 사람들에게 어떤 것을 주거나 가르치다. 대대로 전하다: *These traditions have been passed down from one generation to the next.* 이 전통은 한 세대에서 다음 세대로 전해졌다.

pass for sb/sth *phr v* [T] to be very similar to someone or something, so that people think you are that person, or that something is that thing ∥ 어떤 사람 또는 사물과 매우 유사하여 사람들이 바로 그 사람 또는 그 물건으로 생각하다. 종종(가짜) …으로서 통하다. …으로 받아들여지다: *With her hair cut like that, she could pass for a boy.* 그렇게 머리를 잘라서 그녀는 소년으로 생각 될 수 있다.

pass sb/sth **off as** sth *phr v* [T] to try to make people think that someone or something is something that he, she, or it isn't ∥ 사람이나 사물이 실제로 어떤 것이 아닌데도 사람들로 하여금 그것으로 생각하게 하려고 하다. …으로 속여 넘기다. …으로 행세하다: *He managed to pass himself off as a doctor for three years!* 그는 3년이나 용케도 의사 행세를 했어!

pass on *phr v* **1** [T **pass** sth ↔ **on**] to tell someone a piece of information that someone else has told you ∥ 다른 사람한테 들은 정보를 남에게 말하다. 전(달)하다: *She said she'd pass the message on to Ms. Chen.* 그녀는 자신이 첸 여사에게 메시지를 전했다고 말했다. **2** [T **pass** sth ↔ **on**] to give something to someone else ∥ 어떤 것을 다른 사람에게 주다. 넘겨주다: *Take one and pass the rest on to the next person.* 한 개를 갖고 나머지는 다음 사람에게 넘겨주시오.

pass out *phr v* **1** [I] to suddenly become unconscious ∥ 갑자기 의식을 잃다. 기절하다 **2** [T **pass** sth ↔ **out**] to give something to each one of a group of people ∥ 한 집단의 각각의 사람들에게 어떤 것을 주다. 분배[배포]하다: *Please pass out the dictionaries.* 그 사전들을 나누어 주세요.

pass over *phr v* [I,T **pass** sb ↔ **over**] to ignore someone's ability and not give him/her a job s/he wants or deserves ∥ 사람의 능력을 무시하고 그가 원하거나 그에 합당한 업무를 주지 않다. 따돌림[소외]시키다. 일부러 …에서 빠뜨리다

pass up *phr v* [T] **pass up a chance/opportunity/offer** to not use a chance to do something ∥ 어떤 것을 할 수 있는 기회를 이용하지 않다. 가능성/기회/제안을 포기하다. 거절하다

USAGE NOTE pass, passed, and past

Passed is the PAST PARTICIPLE of the verb **pass** : *I think we've just passed the store.* **Past** is an adjective: *I've been busy the past week.*
passed는 동사 **pass**의 과거 분사이다: 우리는 방금 그 가게를 지나친 것 같다. **past**는 형용사이다: 나는 지난주에 바빴다.

---

pass² *n* **1** the act of kicking, throwing, or hitting a ball or other object to another member of your team ∥ 공이나 다른 물체를 팀의 다른 멤버에게 차기[던지기, 쳐주기]. 패스. 송구: *a 30-yard pass* 30야드 패스 **2** an official document that proves you are allowed to enter a building or that you have already paid to do something ∥ 건물에 들어가는 것을 허가받았다는 공식적인 증명서 또는 어떤 것을 할 수 있는 돈을 이미 지불했다는 공식적인 증명서. 통행[출입]증. 입장[승차, 탑승]권: *a bus pass* 버스 승차권 / *a zoo pass* 동물원 입장권 **3** a way through a place that is difficult to cross ∥ 가로지르기 힘든 장소를 통과하는 길. 협로. 통로. 외길: *a narrow mountain pass* 좁은 산길

4 make a pass at sb INFORMAL to try to kiss or touch another person with the intention of having sex with him/her ‖ 성 관계를 맺으려는 의도에서 다른 사람에게 키스를 하거나 만지려고 하다. 이성을 유혹하다. 성관계를 맺으려 꾀다 **5** the act of moving past something ‖ 어떤 것을 지나치며 움직이는 행위. 훑어보기. 대충 점검하기: *Can you make a pass through the room and see if there are any dirty glasses left?* 그 방을 대충 훑어보고 사용한 유리잔들이 남아 있는지를 확인해 볼래?

pass·a·ble /ˈpæsəbəl/ *adj* **1** a road or river that is passable is not blocked, so you can travel along or across it ‖ 길이나 강이 막혀 있지 않아서 그를 따라서 또는 건너서 여행할 수 있는. 통행[통과]할 수 있는 —opposite IMPASSABLE **2** just good enough to be acceptable, but not very good ‖ 아주 좋지는 않지만 받아들일 만큼은 좋은. 그런 대로의. 무난한. 웬만한: *a passable piece of work* 그런대로 괜찮은 한 편의 작품

pas·sage /ˈpæsɪdʒ/ *n* **1** also **pas·sage·way** /ˈpæsɪdʒˌweɪ/ a narrow area with walls on each side, that connects one room or place to another ‖ 한 개의 방이나 장소를 다른 곳과 연결해 주는, 양쪽에 벽이 있는 좁은 구역. 통로. 복도: *a dark passage at the back of the building* 건물 뒤편에 있는 어두운 통로 **2** a short part of a book, poem, speech, piece of music etc. ‖ 책·시·연설·음악의 짧은 일부. 절. 단락. 악구(樂句): *an interesting passage on page 32* 32쪽의 재미난 단락 **3** [U] the action of going across, over, or along something ‖ 어떤 것을 가로질러[넘어서, 쭉 따라] 가는 행위. 통행. 통과: *The bridge isn't strong enough to allow the passage of heavy vehicles.* 그 다리는 무거운 차량이 통과할 만큼 튼튼하지 못하다. **4** a tube in your body that air or liquid can pass through ‖ 공기나 액체가 통과할 수 있는 신체의 도관: *nasal passages* 비강(鼻腔) **5 the passage of time** LITERARY the passing of time ‖ 시간의 흐름: *Her condition improved with the passage of time.* 그녀의 증세는 시간이 경과함에 따라 호전되었다. **6** [singular] a trip on a ship, or the cost of this ‖ 선박 여행, 또는 뱃삯. 승선(권): *She paid for his passage to Bermuda.* 그녀는 버뮤다까지의 그의 뱃삯을 지불했다.

pass·book /ˈpæsbʊk/ *n* a book for keeping a record of the money you put into and take out of your bank account ‖ 은행 계좌의 입출금을 기록하는 장부. 보통 예금 통장

pas·sé /pæˈseɪ/ *adj* no longer modern or fashionable ‖ 더이상 현대적이거나 유행하지 않는. 시대에 뒤진. 구식인: *a writing style that has become passé* 시대에 뒤떨어진 문장 스타일

pas·sen·ger /ˈpæsəndʒɚ/ *n* someone who is traveling in a car, plane, boat etc., but is not driving it ‖ 운전하지는 않고 차·비행기·배 등으로 여행하는 사람. 승객. 여객

pass·er·by /ˌpæsɚˈbaɪ/ *n, plural* **passersby** someone who is walking past a place by chance ‖ 우연히 어떤 장소를 걸어서 지나가는 사람. 통행인: *Several passersby saw the accident.* 여러 명의 통행인이 그 사고를 목격했다.

pass·ing¹ /ˈpæsɪŋ/ *adj* **1** going past ‖ 지나가는. 통과하는: *Our cat likes to watch the passing traffic.* 우리 고양이는 지나가는 자동차들을 보는 것을 좋아한다. **2** done quickly while you are doing something else ‖ 다른 일을 하는 동안에 신속하게 끝난. 순식간에[모르는 새에] 끝난. 얼핏[슬쩍] 이루어진: *He gave the report only a passing glance.* 그는 그 보고서를 얼핏 쳐다봤을 뿐이다. **3** continuing for only a short time ‖ 잠시 동안만 계속하는. 일시적인: *Eating organic food is more than just a passing fad.* 유기농 식품을 먹는 것은 단지 일시적인 유행은 아니다.

passing² *n* **1 in passing** if you say something in passing, you mention it while you are mainly talking about something else ‖ 주로 다른 것에 대해 말하면서 어떤 것을 언급하다. 지나가는 말로: *The actress mentioned in passing that she had once worked in a factory.* 그 여배우는 지나가는 말로 자신이 한때 공장에서 일했다고 말했다. **2** a word meaning someone's death, used in order to avoid saying this directly ‖ 어떤 사람의 죽음을 의미하는 단어로 직접적으로 언급하는 것을 피하는 데에 쓰여. 운명. 영결. 영면

pas·sion /ˈpæʃən/ *n* **1** [C, U] a very strongly felt emotion, especially of love, hatred, or anger ‖ 특히 애정[증오, 분노]을 매우 강하게 느끼는 감정. 열정. 격정: *He spoke with passion about the situation in his country.* 그는 자국(自國)의 상황에 대하여 열정적으로 말했다. / *the passions that influence politics* 정치에 영향을 미치는 열정 / *sexual passion* 정욕 **2** a strong liking for something ‖ 어떤 일에 대한 강렬한 선호. 열광. 열중.

애착: *a passion for fast cars* 빠른 차에 대한 열광

pas·sion·ate /ˈpæʃənɪt/ *adj* showing PASSION, or full of passion ‖ 열정을 보이는 또는 열정으로 가득한. 정열적인: *a passionate kiss* 정열적인 키스 / *a passionate speech* 열정적인 연설 – **passionately** *adv*

pas·sive¹ /ˈpæsɪv/ *adj* **1** tending to accept situations or things that other people do, without attempting to change or fight against them; SUBMISSIVE ‖ 다른 사람이 조성하는 상황이나 일을 변경하거나 대항하려 하지 않고 받아들이는 경향이 있는. 수동적[소극적]인. 무저항인. 순종하는; ⓢ submissive: *"I'm a very passive person," she admitted.* "나는 매우 소극적인 사람이다."라고 그녀는 시인했다. **2** not having a lot of involvement in something that is happening ‖ 발생하고 있는 일에 크게 관여하지 않는. 적극적으로 참가하지 않는. 활동적이 아닌: *Traditional classroom learning is usually very passive.* 전통적인 교실 수업은 대개 매우 수동적이다. – **passively** *adv* – **passivity** /pæˈsɪvəti/ *n* [U]

passive² *n* **the passive (voice)** TECHNICAL in grammar, in the passive voice, the action of the verb has an effect on the subject of the sentence. It is shown in English by the verb "be" followed by a PAST PARTICIPLE. In the sentence, "Oranges are grown in California," the verb is in the passive voice ‖ 문법의 수동태에서 동사의 작용이 문장의 주어에 영향을 주는 것. 수동(형)구문. 영어에서는 과거 분사 앞에 "be"동사를 수반하여 표현된다. "오렌지는 캘리포니아에서 자란다"는 문장에서 동사(are grown)는 수동태를 취하고 있다. — compare ACTIVE²

passive smo·king /ˌ.. ˈ../ *n* the act of breathing in smoke from someone else's cigarette, pipe etc., although you do not want to ‖ 자신이 원하지 않는데도 남의 담배·파이프 등에서 나오는 담배 연기를 들이마시는 것. 간접 흡연

Pass·o·ver /ˈpæsˌoʊvɚ/ *n* [singular] a Jewish holiday in the spring to remember when the Jews in ancient Egypt became free ‖ 고대 이집트에서 유대인들이 해방된 때를 기념하기 위한 봄철의 휴일. 유월절(逾月節)

pass·port /ˈpæspɔrt/ *n* a small official book that proves who you are and what country you are a citizen of, which you must have in order to leave your country and enter other ones ‖ 사람의 신원과 어느 국가의 국민인지를 증명하며 자기 나라를 떠나 다른 나라에 입국하기 위해 반드시 소지해야 하는 작은 책. 여권

pass·word /ˈpæswɚd/ *n* a secret word or phrase that you must use before being allowed to enter a place that is guarded, or use a computer system ‖ 보호되는 장소에 들어가거나 컴퓨터 시스템을 사용하는 것이 허락되기 전에 반드시 사용해야 하는 비밀 단어 또는 어구. 암호(말)

past¹ /pæst/ *adj* **1** having happened, existed, or been experienced before now ‖ 현재보다 앞서서 발생한[존재한, 경험된]. 과거의. 지나간: *He knew from past experience not to argue.* 그는 과거의 경험에서 논쟁해서는 안 된다는 것을 알았다. / *She was obviously trying to make up for past mistakes.* 그녀는 명백하게 과거의 실수를 만회하려 하고 있었다. **2** a little earlier than the present, or up until now ‖ 현재보다 조금 일찍 또는 지금에 이르기까지. 방금 지나간. 최근인. 지금으로부터 …전에: *Tim's been out of town for the past week.* 팀은 지난주에 도시를 떠나 있었다. **3** finished or having come to an end ‖ 끝난 또는 끝에 도달한. 종료된: *The time for discussion is past.* 토론 시간이 끝났다. **4** achieving something in the past, or holding an important position in the past ‖ 과거에 어떤 것을 성취한 또는 요직을 차지한. 전(前)…의. 전직의: *She's a past president of the club.* 그녀는 그 클럽의 전 회장이다. —see usage note at PASS¹

past² *prep* **1** farther than ‖ 보다 더 멀리. 지나간 곳에. 지나가서: *My house is a mile past the bridge.* 우리 집은 그 다리를 지나 1마일쯤에 있다. **2** up to and beyond ‖ 도달해서 그 너머로. 지나쳐서. 추월해서: *Tanya walked right past me!* 타냐는 바로 나를 스쳐서 지나갔다! **3** after a particular time, or older than a particular age ‖ 특정한 시간 뒤에, 특정한 연령보다 많은. 넘어서. 지난. …이상[이후]의: *It's ten past nine.* (=ten minutes after nine o'clock) 지금은 9시 10분이다. / *She must be past eighty.* 그는 80세를 넘은 것이 틀림없다. **4 I wouldn't put it past sb (to do sth)** SPOKEN used in order to say that you would not be surprised if someone did something because it is typical of him/her ‖ 남이 어떤 것을 했다 해도 그 사람에게는 전형적인 일이기 때문에 놀라지 않을 것이라고 말하는 데에 쓰여. 남이 …하고도 남을 것으로[…하지 못할 것도 없다고] 생각하다: *I don't know if he stole*

the car, but I wouldn't put it past him!
나는 그가 그 차를 훔쳤는지 아닌지는 잘
모르지만 그러면 자동차를 훔치고도 남을
것이다!

past³ *n* [singular] **1** the time that
existed before now ‖ 지금 이전에 존재했
던 시간. 과거. 옛날: *People travel more
now than they did in the past.* 사람들은
이제 전에 비해 여행을 더 많이 한다. **2**
all the things that have happened to
someone or that s/he has done before
now ‖ 사람에게 일어났던 또는 지금 이전
에 사람이 했던 모든 일. 과거지사: *She'd
like to forget her past and start all over.*
그녀는 예전의 일은 잊고 처음부터 다시
시작하고 싶어한다.

past⁴ *adv* **1** up to and beyond a
particular place ‖ 특정한 장소에 이르러
서 그 너머로. 지나(쳐)서: *Hal and his
friends drove past at top speed.* 할과 그
의 친구들은 차를 최고 속도로 몰고 지나
갔다. **2 go past** if a period of time goes
past, it passes ‖ 일정 시간이 경과하다.
지나다: *Several weeks went past without
any news from home.* 집으로부터 아무런
소식도 없이 수 주일이 지나갔다.

pas·ta /ˈpɑstə/ *n* [U] an Italian food
made from flour, eggs, and water and
cut into various shapes, usually eaten
with a SAUCE ‖ 밀가루·달걀·물로 만들어
여러 가지 모양으로 잘라서 보통 소스를
곁들여 먹는 이탈리아 음식. 파스타

paste¹ /peɪst/ *n* [C, U] **1** a type of thick
glue that is used for sticking paper
together or onto another surface ‖ 종이
를 서로 붙이거나 다른 표면 위에 붙이는
데에 쓰이는 걸쭉한 접착제의 일종. 풀 **2**
a soft thick mixture that can be easily
shaped or spread ‖ 쉽게 모양을 내거나
늘려 펼 수 있는 말랑말랑하고 된 혼합물.
(가루) 반죽: *Mix the water and the
powder into a smooth paste.* 물과 가루를
반죽이 잘되게 섞어라. **3** a food made by
crushing solid foods into a smooth soft
mixture ‖ 단단한 식품을 으깨어 무르고
부드러운 혼합물로 만든 음식. 페이스트:
tomato paste 토마토 페이스트

paste² *v* [T] to stick paper together or
onto another surface with PASTE ‖ 풀로
종이를 함께 붙이거나 다른 표면에 붙이
다. 풀칠하다. 풀칠하여 붙이다

pas·tel /pæˈstɛl/ *n* **1** a soft pale color,
such as pale blue or pink ‖ 연한 청색이
나 분홍색 등 연하고 옅은 색채. 파스텔색
2 [C, U] a small colored stick for
drawing pictures with, made of a
substance like oily CHALK ‖ 유성(油性) 초
크 같은 물질로 만들어져 그림을 그리는

데에 쓰는 색이 든 작은 막대. 파스텔 –
pastel *adj*

pas·teur·ize /ˈpæstʃəˌraɪz, -stəˌraɪz/ *v*
[T] to heat a liquid, especially milk, in a
special way that kills any BACTERIA in it
‖ 어떤 박테리아라도 죽이는 특별한 방식
으로 액체 특히 우유를 가열하다. 저온 살
균하다 – **pasteurization** /ˌpæs-
tʃərəˈzeɪʃən/ *n* [U]

pas·time /ˈpæs-taɪm/ *n* something
enjoyable that you do when you are not
working ‖ 일하지 않을 때에 즐길 수 있는
것. 오락. 놀이. 기분 전환. 레크리에이
션: *His pastimes include watching TV
and reading.* 텔레비전 시청과 독서는 그
가 기분 전환하는 한 방법이다.

pas·tor /ˈpæstə/ *n* a minister in some
PROTESTANT churches ‖ 일부 개신교의 목
사

pas·tor·al /ˈpæstərəl/ *adj* **1** relating to
the duties of a priest, minister etc.
toward the members of his/her religious
group ‖ 종교 집단의 구성원에 대한 신부·
목사 등의 의무에 관련된. 목사(직)의:
Pastoral visits are made on Fridays. 목
사님은 금요일에 방문한다. **2** LITERARY
typical of the simple peaceful life in the
country ‖ 단조롭고 평화로운 전형적인 시
골 생활의. 전원[목가]적인: *a pastoral
scene* 목가적인 풍경

past par·ti·ci·ple /ˌ. ˈ..../ *n* TECHNICAL
in grammar, a PARTICIPLE that is usually
formed by adding "-ed" to a verb, but
that can be IRREGULAR. It can be used in
compounds to make PERFECT tenses, or
as an adjective. In the sentence "Look
what you have done," "done" is a past
participle ‖ 문법에서, 대개는 동사에
"-ed"를 붙여 만들지만 불규칙적일 수 있
는 분사형. 완료 시제를 만들기 위해 복합
어에 사용되거나 또는 형용사로 사용될 수
있다. 과거 분사(형). 문장 "Look what
you have done(네가 한 것을 봐라)"에서
"done"은 과거 분사이다.

past per·fect /ˌ. ˈ../ *n* **the past
perfect** TECHNICAL in grammar, the
tense of a verb that shows that an
action was completed before another
event or time in the past. In the
sentence "I had finished my breakfast
before Rick called," "had finished" is in
the past perfect ‖ 문법에서, 어떤 행위가
과거의 다른 사건 또는 시간 이전에 완료
되었음을 나타내는 동사의 시제. 과거 완
료. 문장 "I had finished my breakfast
before Rick called. (나는 릭이 전화하기
전에 아침식사를 마쳤다)"에서 "had
finished"는 과거 완료 시제이다.

pas·try /'peɪstri/ n 1 [U] a mixture of flour, fat, and milk or water, used for making the outer part of baked foods such as PIES ‖ 파이 등 구운 식품의 겉 부분을 만드는 데에 쓰이는 밀가루[기름, 우유, 물]의 혼합물. 가루반죽 2 a small sweet cake ‖ 작고 달콤한 케이크

past tense /ˌ. './ n the past tense TECHNICAL in grammar, the tense of a verb that shows that an action or state began and ended in the past. In the sentence, "We walked to school yesterday," "walked" is in the past tense ‖ 문법에서, 행위·상태가 과거에 시작하여 끝난 것을 나타내는 동사의 시제. 과거 시제. "We walked to school yesterday. (우리는 어제 학교에 걸어갔다.)"라는 문장에서 "walked"는 과거 시제이다

pas·ture /'pæstʃɚ/ n [C, U] land that is covered with grass and is used for cattle, sheep etc. to feed on ‖ 소·양 등을 사육하는 데에 쓰이는 풀로 덮인 땅. 방목장. 목초지 – **pasture** v [I, T]

past·y /'peɪsti/ adj looking very pale and unhealthy ‖ 매우 창백하고 건강해 보이지 않는. 창백한. 핏기 없는: a pasty face 핏기 없는 얼굴

pat¹ /pæt/ v -tted, -tting 1 [T] to touch someone or something lightly again and again, with your hand flat ‖ 손바닥으로 가볍게 반복해서 사람이나 사물을 만지다. 가볍게 두드리다[치다]. 쓰다듬다: Giles patted her hand sympathetically. 가일즈는 동정하듯이 그녀의 손을 살짝 두드렸다. 2 **pat sb/yourself on the back** INFORMAL to praise someone or yourself for doing something well ‖ 다른 사람이나 자신이 어떤 것을 잘 했다고 칭찬하다. (등을 두드려) 격려[축하]하다

pat² n 1 an act of touching someone or something with your hand flat, especially in a friendly way ‖ 특히 친밀하게 손바닥으로 사람이나 사물을 만지는 행위. 가볍게 두드리기[쓰다듬기]: He gave the dog a pat on the head. 그는 그 개의 머리를 쓰다듬어 주었다. 2 **a pat of butter** a small amount of butter, often in a flat square shape ‖ 종종 납작하고 네모진 형태를 가진 작은 버터 덩어리 3 **a pat on the back** INFORMAL praise for something that has been done well ‖ 매우 잘한 일에 대한 칭찬: Alex deserves a pat on the back for all his hard work. 알렉스는 열심히 한 모든 일에 대해 칭찬 받을 만하다.

pat³ adv **have sth down pat** to know something thoroughly so that you can say it, perform it etc. without thinking about it ‖ 어떤 일에 대해 철저히 알고 있어서 그것에 대해 생각하지 않고도 말하고 수행할 수 있다. …을 (막힘없이)완전히 알고 있다. 숙지하고 있다

patch¹ /pætʃ/ n 1 a small piece of material used for covering a hole in something, especially clothes ‖ 물건, 특히 옷에 난 구멍을 막는 데에 쓰는 작은 천 조각. (해진 곳에 대는) 헝겊[가죽] 조각 2 a part of an area that is different or looks different from the parts that surround it ‖ 주변의 부분과 다르거나 달라 보이는 지역의 일부분. (다른 것과 달라 보이는) 부분: There may be a few patches of rain near the coast. 해안 근처의 몇몇 지역에서 비가 내릴 가능성이 있습니다. 3 a small area of ground for growing fruit or vegetables ‖ 과일이나 야채를 재배하기 위한 조그만 구획의 땅. 뙈기밭. 텃밭: a cabbage patch 배추밭

patch², **patch up** v [T] to put a small piece of material over a hole, especially in a piece of clothing ‖ 특히 옷에 난 구멍에 작은 천을 대다. (해진 데 등에) 헝겊 조각을 대다[깁다]: patched pants 기워진 바지

patch sth ↔ up phr v [T] to end an argument and become friendly with someone ‖ 남과 다툼을 끝내고 친하게 되다. 조정[해결]하다. 수습하다: I've patched it up with my girlfriend. 나는 여자 친구와 사이가 다시 좋아졌다.

patch·work /'pætʃwɚk/ n [U] a type of sewing in which many different colored pieces of cloth are sewn together to make one large piece ‖ 색깔이 다양한 많은 헝겊 조각으로 큰 조각을 만들기 위해 함께 꿰매 맞춘 재봉 형태. 패치워크: a patchwork quilt 쪽매붙임 퀼트

patch·y /'pætʃi/ adj 1 happening or existing in a number of small separate areas ‖ 상당수의 개별적인 소구역에서 발생하거나 존재하는. 작은 것을 그러모은. 여기저기 있는: patchy fog 드문드문 낀 안개 2 not complete enough to be useful ‖ 쓸모가 있을 만큼 충분히 완전하지 않은. 불완전한. 엉성한: My knowledge of biology is pretty patchy. 생물학에 대한 나의 지식은 아주 단편적이다.

pâ·té /pɑ'teɪ, pæ-/ n [U] a thick smooth food made from meat or fish, that you spread on bread ‖ 빵 위에 펴 바르는 고기나 생선으로 만든 걸쭉하고 부드러운 음식물. 고기파이

pa·tent¹ /'pæt'nt/ n a special document that says that you have the right to make or sell a new invention or product and that no one else is allowed to do so ‖ 새로운 발명품이나 제품을 제조 또는 판매할 권리를 가지고 있으며 그 외의 어느 누구에게도 그런 행위는 허용되지 않는다고 정하는 특별한 문서. 특허(권리)증

patent² *v* [T] to obtain a PATENT ‖ 특허권을 얻다

patent³ *adj* FORMAL clear and easy to notice; OBVIOUS ‖ 분명하고 알아차리기 쉬운. 명백한; ⊞ obvious: *a patent lie* 새빨간 거짓말

pat·ent leath·er /ˌ.. ˈ../ *n* [U] thin shiny leather, usually black ‖ 보통 검정색의 얇고 광택이 나는 가죽. 에나멜 가죽: *patent leather shoes* 에나멜 가죽 구두

pa·tent·ly /ˈpætⁿntli/ *adv* **patently obvious/false/unfair etc.** completely clear, untrue, unfair etc., in a way that anyone can notice ‖ 누구나 알아차릴 수 있을 정도로 아주 분명하게·그릇되게·불공평하게: *patently offensive language* 명백하게 상스러운 말

pa·ter·nal /pəˈtɚnl/ *adj* **1** typical of the way a father feels or acts ‖ 아버지가 느끼거나 행동하는 전형적인 방식의. 아버지 같은. 아버지다운 **2 paternal grandmother/uncle etc.** your father's mother, brother etc. ‖ 아버지의 어머니·형제 등. 친할머니/작은[큰]아버지 – **paternally** *adv* —compare MATERNAL

pa·ter·nal·ism /pəˈtɚnlˌɪzəm/ *n* [U] practice of making decisions for people or organizations, so that they are never able to be responsible themselves ‖ 사람이나 기관에 대해 스스로에게는 책임이 돌아가지 않도록 결정을 내리는 관행. 온정주의. 부자[가족]주의 – **paternalistic** /pəˌtɚnəˈlɪstɪk/ *adj*

pa·ter·ni·ty /pəˈtɚnəti/ *n* [U] LAW the state of being a father ‖ 아버지로서의 위상. 부성

path /pæθ/ *n* **1** a track that people walk along over an area of ground ‖ 일정 구역의 땅 위를 따라 사람이 걸어다니는 길. 소로(小路): *a path through the woods* 숲속으로 통하는 오솔길 **2** a way that allows you to move forward through something ‖ 어떤 것을 통하여 앞으로 나아갈 수 있는 길. 통로: *The police cleared a path through the crowd.* 경찰은 군중 사이로 통로를 만들었다. **3** the direction or line along which someone or something moves ‖ 사람이나 사물이 움직이는 방향이나 노선. 진로. 궤도: *The storm destroyed everything in its path.* 그 폭풍우는 진로에 있는 모든 것을 파괴했다.

pa·thet·ic /pəˈθɛtɪk/ *adj* **1** making you

feel pity or sympathy ‖ 연민이나 동정심을 느끼게 하는. 불쌍한. 측은한: *the pathetic sight of starving children* 기아에 굶주린 아이들의 측은한 광경 **2 very bad, useless, or weak** ‖ 매우 나쁜[쓸모없는, 약한]. 쓸데없는: *Vicky made a pathetic attempt to apologize.* 비키는 사과하려고 애썼지만 허사가 되었다. – **pathetically** *adv*

path·o·log·i·cal /ˌpæθəˈlɑdʒɪkəl/ *adj* **1** pathological behavior or feelings are unreasonable, impossible to control, and caused by a mental illness ‖ 행동이나 감정이 이치에 맞지 않는[통제 불능의, 정신병에 의해 야기되는]. 병적인: *a pathological liar* 병적인 거짓말쟁이 **2** TECHNICAL relating to the causes and effects of disease ‖ 병의 원인과 결과에 관련되는. 병리학상의: *a pathological condition* 병리학상의 증세

pa·thol·o·gy /pəˈθɑlədʒi, pæ-/ *n* [U] the study of the causes and effects of diseases ‖ 병의 원인과 결과에 대한 연구. 병리학 – **pathologist** *n*

pa·thos /ˈpeɪθoʊs, -θɑs, ˈpæ-/ *n* [U] LITERARY the quality that a person or a situation has that makes you feel pity and sadness ‖ 연민과 슬픔을 느끼게 하는 사람이나 상황이 가진 성질. 비애감

path·way /ˈpæθweɪ/ *n* [U] ⇨ PATH

pa·tience /ˈpeɪʃəns/ *n* [U] the ability to wait calmly for a long time or deal with difficulties without becoming angry, anxious, or annoyed ‖ 화를 내거나 초조해 하거나 안달하지 않고 오랫동안 조용히 기다리거나 어려움을 대처하는 능력. 참을성. 인내력: *Finally I lost my patience with him and started shouting.* 결국 나는 참지 못하고 그에게 소리지르기 시작했다. / *The kids are beginning to try my patience.* (=make me stop being patient) 아이들이 내 인내심을 시험하기 시작하고 있다. / *I don't have the patience to sew my own clothes.* 나는 내 옷을 스스로 바느질할 정도의 인내심은 없다.

pa·tient¹ /ˈpeɪʃənt/ *n* someone who is getting medical treatment ‖ 의학 치료를 받고 있는 사람. 환자

patient² *adj* able to wait calmly for a long time or to deal with difficulties without becoming angry, anxious, or annoyed ‖ 화를 내거나 초조해하거나 안달나지 않고 오랫동안 조용히 기다리거나 어려움에 대처할 수 있는. 인내심[참을성]이 있는: *Try to be patient with your students.* 학생들에 대한 인내심을 갖도록 해보세요. – **patiently** *adv* —opposite

IMPATIENT

pat·i·o /ˈpæti,oʊ/ *n* an outside area near a house with a stone floor and no roof, where people can sit, eat etc. ‖ 사람들이 앉거나 식사 등을 할 수 있는, 돌로 된 바닥이 있고 지붕은 없는, 집 근처의 옥외 공간. 옥외 테라스. 안뜰

pa·tri·arch /ˈpeɪtri,ɑrk/ *n* an old man who is respected and who is the most important person in a family or tribe ‖ 가족이나 부족 가운데서 존경받고 가장 중요한 노인. 족장. 장로 —compare MATRIARCH

pa·tri·arch·al /ˌpeɪtriˈɑrkəl/ *adj* **1** ruled or controlled only by men ‖ 남성들에 의해서만 지배되거나 통제되는. 남성 지배의. 가부장제의: *a patriarchal society* 가부장제의 사회 **2** relating to being a PATRIARCH, or typical of a patriarch ‖ 가부장에 관한, 또는 가부장의 전형적 특성의. 가부장의. 족장의

pa·tri·arch·y /ˈpeɪtri,ɑrki/ *n* [C, U] a social system in which men hold all the power ‖ 남성들이 모든 권력을 잡는 사회 체제. 가부장제

pat·ri·cide /ˈpætrə,saɪd/ *n* [U] the crime of killing your father ‖ 자신의 아버지를 죽이는 범죄. 부친 살해(죄)

pat·ri·mo·ny /ˈpætrə,moʊni/ *n* [C, U] FORMAL property that is passed on to you after your father dies ‖ 아버지가 사망한 후에 물려받게 되는 재산. 세습 재산

pa·tri·ot /ˈpeɪtriət/ *n* someone who loves and respects his/her country and is willing to defend it ‖ 나라를 사랑하고 귀하게 여기며 기꺼이 국가를 수호하려는 사람. 애국자

pa·tri·ot·ic /ˌpeɪtriˈɑtɪk/ *adj* willing to defend your country because you love and respect it, or showing pride for your country ‖ 나라를 사랑하고 귀하게 여겨서 기꺼이 나라를 지키려고 하거나, 또는 자기 나라에 대한 자부심을 나타내는. 애국적인: *a patriotic citizen* 애국 시민 / *patriotic songs* 애국가 – **patriotism** /ˈpeɪtriə,tɪzəm/ *n* [U]

pa·trol¹ /pəˈtroʊl/ *n* **1** the action of regularly checking different parts of an area to prevent problems or crime ‖ 문제나 범죄를 예방하기 위해 지역의 여러 곳들을 규칙적으로 점검하는 행위. 순찰. 순회: *Guards were on patrol throughout the night.* 수비대는 밤새도록 순찰했다. **2** a group of police, soldiers, planes etc. that PATROL a particular area ‖ 특정한 지역을 순찰하는 경찰·군인·비행기 등의 집단. 순찰대. 경비대: *the California Highway Patrol* 캘리포니아 고속도로 순

찰대

patrol² *v* **-lled, -lling** [I, T] to regularly check an area in order to prevent problems or crime ‖ 문제나 범죄를 예방하기 위해 지역을 규칙적으로 점검하다. 순찰하다: *soldiers patrolling a prisoner-of-war camp* 전쟁 포로수용소를 순찰하는 군인들

pa·trol·man /pəˈtroʊlmən/ *n* a police officer who PATROLs a particular area ‖ 특정한 지역을 순찰하는 경찰관

pa·tron /ˈpeɪtrən/ *n* **1** someone who supports an organization, artist, musical performer etc., especially by giving money ‖ 특히 자금을 제공하여 단체·예술가·음악 연주자 등을 지원하는 사람. 후원자: *a patron of the arts* 예술의 후원자 **2** someone who often uses a particular store, restaurant, company etc. ‖ 특정한 상점·식당·회사 등을 자주 이용하는 사람. 고객. 단골손님: *We offer a 20% discount for all our regular patrons.* 저희는 단골 손님 모두에게 20%를 할인해 드립니다.

pa·tron·age /ˈpeɪtrənɪdʒ, ˈpæ-/ *n* [U] **1** the action of using a particular store, restaurant, company etc. ‖ 특정한 상점·식당·회사 등을 이용하는 행위. 애용: *Thank you for your patronage.* 애용해 주셔서 감사합니다. **2** the support that a PATRON gives to an organization etc. ‖ 후원자가 단체 등에 제공하는 지원. 후원: *her patronage of the Boston Symphony* 보스턴 심포니에 대한 그녀의 후원 **3** a system in which a powerful person gives money or important jobs to people who support him/her ‖ 권력자가 자신을 지지하는 사람에게 돈이나 요직을 제공하는 제도. 관직 임명(권): *political patronage* 정치적 임명권

pa·tron·ize /ˈpeɪtrə,naɪz, ˈpæ-/ *v* [T] **1** to behave or talk in a way that shows you think someone is less important or intelligent than you ‖ 남을 자신보다 별로 중요하거나 똑똑하지 않게 여긴다는 생각을 드러내며 행동하거나 말하다. 얕잡아 보는 태도로 대하다: *Don't patronize me.* 나를 우습게 여기지 마라. / *a manager who patronizes his employees* 자기 종업원을 얕잡아 보는 태도로 대하는 매니저 **2** to regularly use a particular store, restaurant, company etc. ‖ 특정한 상점·식당·회사 등을 정기적으로 이용하다. …을 단골로 삼다. 애용하다

pa·tron·iz·ing /ˈpeɪtrə,naɪzɪŋ, ˈpæ-/ *adj* showing that you think someone is less important or intelligent than you ‖ 남을 자신보다 별로 중요하거나 똑똑하지

않게 여긴다는 것을 드러내는. 얕보는 듯한. 거만한: *a patronizing attitude* 젠체하는 태도

pat·ter /ˈpætɚ/ *n* [singular] **1** the sound of something lightly hitting a hard surface ‖ 딱딱한 표면을 가볍게 때리는 어떤 소리. 후두두 하는 소리: *the patter of raindrops on the ground* 땅에 후두두 떨어지는 빗방울 소리 **2** very fast and continuous talk ‖ 매우 빠르게 계속되는 말. 빠른 말[대사]: *a car salesman's patter* 자동차 영업 사원의 청산유수 같은 말 – **patter** *v* [I]

---

patterns

checked

patterned

polka dot

plaid

plain

striped

---

pat·tern /ˈpætɚn/ *n* **1** the regular way in which something happens, develops, or is done ‖ 어떤 일이 발생하거나 진전되거나 행해지는 규칙적인 방식. 양식. 경향: *Romantic novels tend to follow a similar pattern*. 연애 소설은 대개 비슷한 형식을 따르는 경향이 있다. / *the behavior patterns of young children* 어린아이들의 행동 양식 **2** a design made from shapes, colors, lines etc. that are arranged in a regular way ‖ 형태·색깔·선 등을 규칙적으로 배열해 만든 디자인. 무늬. 도안: *a pattern of small red and white squares* 적백(赤白)의 작은 정사각형 무늬 / *a dress with a rose pattern* 장미 무늬가 있는 옷 —see picture at ELABORATE¹ **3** a shape that you copy onto cloth, paper etc. when making something, especially clothing ‖ 특히 옷을 만들 때 천이나 종이 등에 대고 본을 뜨는 모양. 본. 형지(型紙): *a skirt pattern* 스커트 본

pat·terned /ˈpætɚnd/ *adj* decorated with a pattern ‖ 무늬로 장식한. 무늬의 모양이 들어간: *patterned sheets* 무늬가 있는 시트 —see picture at PATTERN

pat·ty /ˈpæti/ *n* a round flat piece of cooked meat or other food ‖ 둥글고 납작하게 조리한 고기 조각이나 기타 음식. 패티: *beef patties* 쇠고기 패티

pau·ci·ty /ˈpɔsəti/ *n* [U] **a paucity of** FORMAL less than is needed of something ‖ 어떤 것이 필요한 양보다 적은. 소량의. 부족한: *a paucity of information* 정보의 부족

paunch /pɔntʃ, pɑntʃ/ *n* a man's fat stomach ‖ 남자의 뚱뚱한 배. 올챙이배 – **paunchy** *adj*

pau·per /ˈpɔpɚ/ *n* OLD-FASHIONED someone who is very poor ‖ 매우 가난한 사람. 극빈자. 빈민

pause¹ /pɔz/ *v* [I] to stop speaking or doing something for a short time before starting again ‖ 다시 시작하기 전에 잠시 동안 말이나 행동을 멈추다. 잠시 중단하다: *Tom paused for a moment, and then asked, "So what should I do?"* 톰은 잠시 침묵하다가 "그래서 내가 어떻게 해야 하는데?"라고 물었다.

pause² *n* a short time when you stop speaking or doing something ‖ 말이나 행동을 멈추는 짧은 시간. 중지. 휴지: *After a pause Rick said, "You're right."* 릭은 잠시 멈추었다가 "네 말이 맞다."라고 말했다. / *a long pause in the conversation* 대화의 오랜 중단

pave /peɪv/ *v* [T] **1** to cover a path, road etc. with a hard level surface such as CONCRETE ‖ 길·도로 등을 콘크리트 등의 딱딱하고 평평한 표면으로 덮다. 포장하다 **2 pave the way** to do something that will make an event, development etc. possible in the future ‖ 장차 사건·발달 등이 가능하도록 하는 어떤 일을 하다. 길을 열다. …을 용이하게 하다: *Galileo's achievements paved the way for Newton's scientific laws.* 갈릴레오의 업적은 뉴톤의 과학적 법칙에의 길을 열었다.

pave·ment /ˈpeɪvmənt/ *n* [U] the hard surface of a road ‖ 도로의 딱딱한 표면. 포장 도로(면)

pa·vil·ion /pəˈvɪlyən/ *n* **1** a structure built in a park or at a FAIR, and used as a place for public entertainment, EXHIBITIONs etc. ‖ 공원이나 박람회장에 건설되어 대중오락과 전시회 등의 장소로 쓰이는 건축물. 가설[특설] 건축물 **2** a very large tent ‖ 매우 큰 텐트

paw¹ /pɔ/ *n* the foot of an animal, such as a lion or dog, that has CLAWs (=sharp strong nails) ‖ 갈고리 발톱을 가진 사자나 개 등의 동물의 발

paw² *v* [I, T] **1** if an animal paws something, it touches something with its PAW ‖ 동물이 물건을 발로 건드리다. 발로

긁다: *Tyler's cat pawed at the buttons on Hank's coat.* 타일러의 고양이는 행크의 코트에 달린 단추를 발로 긁었다. **2** INFORMAL to touch someone in a way that is too rough or too sexual ‖ 너무 거칠게 또는 성적으로 남을 만지다. (…을) 함부로 다루다: *He kept trying to paw me in the car.* 그는 차 안에서 계속 나에게 집적대려고 했다.

pawn[1] /pɔn/ *n* someone who is used by a more powerful person or group ‖ 더 강력한 사람이나 집단에 이용되는 사람. 남의 앞잡이. 하수인: *"We're pawns in a big political game," said the miners' spokesman.* "우리는 거대한 정치 게임의 하수인이다."라고 광부 대변인이 말했다.

pawn[2] *v* [T] to leave a valuable object with a PAWNBROKER in order to borrow money ‖ 돈을 빌리기 위해 전당포에 귀중품을 맡기다. …을 저당잡히다

pawn·bro·ker /'pɔn,broukə/ *n* someone whose business is to lend people money in exchange for valuable objects ‖ 귀중품과 교환하여 돈을 빌려주는 사업자. 전당포 주인

pay[1] /peɪ/ *v* paid, paid, paying
1 ▶GIVE MONEY 돈을 주다◀ [I, T] to give someone money for something in order to buy it, or for something s/he has done for you ‖ 구매품의 대가로 또는 남이 자신에게 해준 일에 대한 대가로 남에게 돈을 주다. 지불하다: *We get paid monthly.* 우리는 매달 지급받는다. / *Have you paid the babysitter yet?* 베이비 시터에게 벌써 돈을 지불했니? / *I can't afford to pay that much for a pair of shoes.* 신발 한 켤레 값으로 그렇게 많은 돈을 치를 여유가 없어요. / *Plumbers are paid $40 an hour.* 배관공은 시간당 40달러를 받는다. / *The company's paying for my plane tickets.* 그 회사가 내 비행기 삯을 대고 있다. ✗DON'T SAY "The company's paying my plane tickets."✗ "The company's paying my plane tickets."라고는 하지 않는다.
2 ▶BILL/DEBT 청구서/빚◀ [T] to give a person, company etc. the money that you owe him, her, or it ‖ 빚진 돈을 사람·회사 등에 주다. 치르다. 갚다. 청산하다: *We need to pay the electricity bill soon.* 우리는 곧 전기 요금을 내야 한다.
3 pay attention to carefully listen to or watch someone or something, or to be careful about what you are doing ‖ 사람이나 사물을 주의 깊게 듣거나 지켜보다, 또는 자신이 하는 일에 조심하다. 주목[주의]하다: *Sorry, I wasn't paying attention. What did you say?* 미안해, 주

의하지 않고 있었어. 뭐라고 했지?
4 pay a visit to go to see a particular place or person ‖ 특정한 장소나 사람을 보러 가다. 방문[구경]하다 : *It's about time you paid a visit to the dentist.* 치과에 갔을 시간이다.
5 pay sb a compliment to tell someone that you think s/he is nice, attractive, intelligent etc. ‖ 남이 멋있고 매력적이고 똑똑하다는 등의 자기 생각을 남에게 말하다. 칭찬하다
6 pay your way to pay for your bills, food etc. without needing to use anyone else's money ‖ 다른 사람의 돈을 쓸 필요 없이 계산서·음식 등의 값을 지불하다. 빚지지 않고 살아가다. 자활하다: *She paid her own way through law school.* 그녀는 법대를 다니는 동안 스스로 등록금을 마련했다.
7 ▶GOOD RESULT 좋은 결과◀ [I] to be worth doing, and result in an advantage for you ‖ 행동할 가치가 있고 자신에게 이득이 되다: *Crime doesn't pay.* 범죄는 할 만한 게 못된다. / *It pays to be on time.* 시간을 지키는 것은 가치가 있다.
8 ▶PROFIT 이익◀ [I] to be profitable ‖ 이익이 되다. 수지가 맞다: *We worked hard but couldn't make the business pay.* 우리는 열심히 일했으나 사업의 수지를 맞출 수 없었다.
9 pay tribute to sb/sth to show how much you admire or respect someone or something ‖ 사람이나 사물을 얼마나 존중하거나 존경하는지를 나타내다. …에게 찬사를 보내다. 경의를 표하다: *an evening of jazz to pay tribute to Ella Fitzgerald* 엘라 피츠제럴드에게 경의를 표하는 재즈의 밤
10 pay your respects (to sb) FORMAL to greet someone politely or visit a place, especially in order to say or show that you are sorry that someone has died ‖ 특히 사람이 죽어서 유감의 말이나 표시를 하기 위해 남에게 정중하게 인사하거나 어떤 장소를 방문하다. 조의를 표하다. 추모하다: *Sam came over to pay his respects to the family.* 샘은 그 가족에게 조의를 표하러 왔다.
11 pay your dues to work hard for a long time before you get much money or thanks, or before you become famous ‖ 많은 돈을 벌거나 치사를 받기까지, 또는 유명해지기까지 오랫동안 열심히 일하다. 고된 노력 끝에 권리 등을 획득하다: *He deserves a break; he's paid his dues as an actor.* 그는 한숨 돌릴 만해. 배우로 성공하기까지 할 만큼 했으니까.
12 pay through the nose INFORMAL to

pay far too much money for something ‖ 물건 값으로 너무 많은 돈을 지불하다. 터무니없는 값을 치르다. 바가지 쓰다 — see also **pay/give lip service** (LIP)

pay sb/sth ↔ **back** *phr v* [T] to give someone the money that you owe him/her; REPAY ‖ 남에게 빚진 돈을 갚다. 변제하다;㉰ repay: *Can I borrow $10? I'll pay you back tomorrow.* 10달러 빌릴 수 있겠니? 내일 갚을게.

pay for sth *phr v* [T] to suffer or be punished for doing something ‖ 어떤 행동에 대한 고통이나 벌을 받다. 대가를 치르다: *If you drink any more you'll be paying for it in the morning.* 술을 더 마시면 아침에 고생할 거다.

pay sth ↔ **in/into** *phr v* [T] to put money into a bank account ‖ 은행 계좌에 돈을 넣다. 불입하다. 맡기다: *The check was paid into your account on Friday.* 금요일에 당신 계좌에 수표가 입금됐다.

pay off *phr v* **1** [T **pay** sth ↔ **off**] to pay all the money that you owe for something ‖ 어떤 것에 빚진 돈을 모두 갚다. 청산하다: *We've finally paid off the mortgage.* 우리는 마침내 주택 융자금을 모두 갚았다. **2** [I] if something that you try to do pays off, it is successful ‖ 하고자 하는 일이 성공적이다. 기대했던 성과를 올리다: *Their crazy idea actually paid off.* 그들의 터무니없는 생각이 실제로 성공했어. **3** [T **pay** sb ↔ **off**] to give someone money so that s/he will not tell people about something illegal or dishonest ‖ 불법적이거나 부정직한 일에 대해 남에게 말하지 않도록 어떤 사람에게 돈을 주다. 매수하다. 뇌물을 쓰다

pay out *phr v* [I,T **pay** sth ↔ **out**] to pay a lot of money for something ‖ 어떤 것에 대해 많은 돈을 지불하다. 지출하다: *How much do we pay out in salaries?* 봉급으로 얼마를 지출합니까? / *Last year, $123 million was paid out in health benefits.* 작년에 1억 2천 3백만 달러가 건강 보험 급부금으로 지불되었다.

pay up *phr v* [I] INFORMAL to pay all the money that you owe ‖ 빚을 모두 갚다.

pay² *n* [U] money that you are given for working; SALARY ‖ 일한 대가로 지급받는 돈. 임금. 봉급. 급료;㉰ salary: *The pay will be better at my new job.* 새 직장의 급료가 더 나을 것이다.

USAGE NOTE pay, income, salary, and wage

Pay is a general word for money that someone gets for doing work: *The pay in her new job isn't very good.* **Income** is the money that you or your family receive from any place: *an investment income / Their income is fairly high, with both of them working.* A **salary** is the pay that professional people earn every year: *What's the yearly salary for a teacher?* A **wage** is the pay that someone earns every hour or every week: *The minimum wage is $5.25 an hour. / Our wages have been increased to $500 a week.*
pay는 사람이 일한 대가로 받는 돈에 대한 일반적인 말이다: 그녀가 새 직장에서 받는 봉급은 썩 괜찮은 편이 아니다. **income**은 본인이나 자기 가족이 어떤 곳에서 받는 돈이다: 투자 수입 / 그들은 맞벌이를 해서 수입이 꽤 높다. **salary**는 전문적인 일을 하는 사람이 매년 버는 봉급이다: 교사의 연봉이 얼마입니까? **wage**는 매시간이나 매주 버는 봉급이다. 최소 임금은 시간당 5달러 25센트이다. / 우리 임금은 주당 500달러까지 올랐다.

---

pay·a·ble /'peɪəbəl/ *adj* **1** a bill, debt etc. that is payable must be paid ‖ 청구서와 빚 등이 지불되어야 할. 지급[반제]해야 할: *A standard fee of $35 is payable every three months.* 35달러의 기본요금을 3개월마다 지불해야 한다. **2** **payable to** able to be paid to a particular person or organization ‖ 특정인이나 특정 기관에 지불될 수 있는. 지급 가능한: *Please make the check payable to "Al's Service Station."* (=write this name on the check) "알 서비스 스테이션" 명의로 수표를 발행해 주세요.

pay·check /'peɪtʃɛk/ *n* a check used for paying a worker his/her wages ‖ 근로자에게 임금을 지불하는 데 사용하는 수표. 봉급(지급 수표): *a monthly paycheck* 월급

pay·day /'peɪdeɪ/ *n* [C usually singular] the day when you get your PAYCHECK ‖ 봉급을 받는 날. 봉급[급료]일

pay dirt /'. ./ *n* [U] **hit/strike pay dirt** INFORMAL to make a valuable or useful discovery ‖ 가치 있거나 유용한 발견을 하다. 횡재하다: *In finding the 10,000-year-old elephant, scientists had hit pay dirt.* 과학자들은 만년 된 코끼리의 발견이라는 대단한 개가를 올렸다.

pay·ee /peɪ'i/ *n* TECHNICAL the person who should be paid money, especially by check ‖ 특히 수표로 돈을 지급받아야 될 사람. 수취인. 피지급인

pay·load /'peɪloʊd/ n [C, U] the goods or equipment carried by a truck, plane, or SPACECRAFT ‖ 트럭[비행기, 우주선]으로 운반되는 상품이나 장비. 유료 하중. 유료 탑재량

pay·ment /'peɪmənt/ n 1 an amount of money that should be paid or that has been paid ‖ 지불되어야 하거나 지불된 돈의 액수. 지급[납입]액: *How much are your car payments?* 네 자동차 할부금이 얼마지? 2 [U] the act of paying ‖ 지불하는 행위. 지급. 반제: *Late payment will result in a $10 fine.* 지불이 연체되면 벌금 10달러를 물게 된다.

pay·off /'peɪɔf/ n INFORMAL 1 the good result or the advantage that you get because of doing something ‖ 어떤 일을 해서 얻는 좋은 결과나 이익. 보수: *There's a big payoff for companies that keep their employees happy.* 직원들을 행복하게 해주면 회사들에는 이익이 돌아온다. 2 money that is paid to someone so that s/he will not cause problems, for example by telling people about something illegal or dishonest ‖ 예를 들면 불법적이거나 부정직한 일을 사람들에게 말해서 문제를 야기시키지 않도록 남에게 주는 돈. 뇌물

pay phone /'. ./ n a public telephone that you can use when you put a coin or your CREDIT CARD in it ‖ 동전이나 신용 카드를 넣어 사용할 수 있는 공중전화

pay·roll /'peɪroʊl/ n 1 the list of people who are employed by a company and the amount of money they are paid ‖ 회사에서 채용한 사람들의 명단과 그들에게 지급된 돈의 액수. 봉급 지급[종업원] 명부. 급료 지불표: *We have 127 staff on the payroll.* 급료 지불표 상에 있는 우리 직원은 127명이다. 2 the total amount of wages that a particular company pays ‖ 특정한 회사가 지급하는 임금의 총액. 급료 지불 총액

pay-TV /,. .'./ n [U] television CHANNELs or programs that you must pay to watch ‖ 시청하기 위해 돈을 지불해야 하는 텔레비전 채널이나 프로그램

PBS n [U] Public Broadcasting System; a company in the US that broadcasts television programs without advertisements ‖ Public Broadcasting System(미국 공공방송망)의 약어; 광고 없이 텔레비전 프로그램을 방송하는 미국의 회사

PC¹ n personal computer; a small computer that is used by one person at a time, at work or at home ‖ personal computer(개인용 컴퓨터)의 약어; 직장이

나 집에서 한 번에 한 사람이 사용하는 소형 컴퓨터

PC² adj ⇨ POLITICALLY CORRECT

PDA n personal digital assistant; a very small light computer that you can carry with you, and that you use to store information such as telephone numbers, addresses, and APPOINTMENTS ‖ personal digital assistant(개인용 정보 단말기)의 약어; 전화번호·주소·약속 등의 정보 저장에 이용되는 아주 작고 가벼운 휴대용 컴퓨터

PDF n [U] TECHNICAL portable document format; a way of storing computer FILES so that they can be easily read when they are moved form one computer to another ‖ portable document format(휴대용 문서 형식)의 약어; 컴퓨터 파일들이 한 컴퓨터에서 다른 곳으로 이송될 때 판독하기 쉽게 저장하는 방식

PE n [U] physical education; sports and exercises that are taught as a school subject ‖ physical education(체육)의 약어; 학교 과목으로 배우는 스포츠와 운동

pea /pi/ n [C usually plural] a small round green seed that is cooked and eaten as a vegetable ‖ 야채로 요리해서 먹는 작고 둥근 녹색 씨. 완두콩 —see picture on page 944

peace /pis/ n 1 [U] a situation or period of time in which there is no war or fighting ‖ 전쟁이나 싸움이 없는 상황이나 시기. 평화: *working for world peace* 세계 평화를 위해 일하기 / *Germany has been at peace with France since 1945.* 독일은 1945년 이래 프랑스와 평화를 유지해 왔다. 2 [U] a situation that is very calm, quiet, and pleasant ‖ 매우 평온하고·조용하고·즐거운 상황: *All I want is some peace and quiet.* 내가 원하는 것은 약간의 평화와 조용함뿐이다. / *Mary, let your sister read in peace.* (=without being interrupted) 메리야, 언니가 독서하는 데 방해하지 말고 조용히 해라. 3 [U] a feeling of being calm, happy, and not worried ‖ 평온한·행복한·걱정스럽지 않은 감정: *Will you please call if you're going to be late, just for my peace of mind?* 걱정되지 않게 늦을 것 같으면 전화해 주겠어요? 4 **disturbing the peace** LAW the crime of being too noisy or too violent in a public place ‖ 공공장소에서 너무 시끄럽게 하거나 심한 폭력을 휘두르는 범죄. 치안 방해죄 5 **make (your) peace** to agree to stop fighting with a person or group ‖ 사람이나 집단과 싸움을 중단하기로 동의하다. (…과) 화해하다. 강화하다: *He was anxious to make peace with Jill before she left.* 그는 질이

떠나기 전에 그녀와 화해하기를 몹시 바랐
다.

peace·a·ble /ˈpisəbəl/ *adj* not liking to
argue, or not causing any arguments or
fights ‖ 논쟁하기를 좋아하지 않거나, 또는
논쟁이나 싸움을 일으키지 않는. 평화를
좋아하는. 온순한. 온건한: *peaceable
citizens* 평화적인 시민 – **peaceably**
adv

peace·ful /ˈpisfəl/ *adj* **1** calm, quiet,
and without problems or excitement ‖
평온하고 조용하며 곤란한 문제나 흥분됨
이 없는. 평화로운. 편안한: *a peaceful
vacation in the country* 시골에서의 평온
한 휴가 / *a peaceful night's sleep* 편안한
밤잠 **2** not fighting a war, or
deliberately not being violent ‖ 전쟁을 하
지 않거나 의도적으로 폭력적이지 않은.
평화적인: *a peaceful relationship
between countries* 국가간의 평화적 관계
/ *a peaceful protest against nuclear
weapons* 핵무기에 반대하는 평화적인 시
위 – **peacefully** *adv*

peace·keep·ing /ˈpisˌkipɪŋ/ *adj* trying
to prevent fighting or violence ‖ 싸움이
나 폭력을 방지하려는. 평화 유지의: *the
UN's peacekeeping role* 유엔의 평화 유지
역할

peace·mak·er /ˈpisˌmeɪkɚ/ *n* someone
who tries to persuade people or
countries to stop fighting ‖ 싸움을 중단하
기 위해 사람이나 국가를 설득시키려 하는
사람. 중재인. 조정자

peace·time /ˈpis-taɪm/ *n* [U] a period
when a country is not fighting a war ‖ 국
가가 전쟁을 하지 않는 기간. 평화시 —
opposite WARTIME

peach /pitʃ/ *n* **1** a round juicy yellow-
red fruit that has a large rough seed
and skin that feels FUZZY, or the tree on
which it grows ‖ 크고 울퉁불퉁한 씨와 솜
털 같이 느껴지는 껍질이 있는 둥글고 즙
이 많은 연분홍색 과일, 또는 그 과일이 자
라는 나무. 복숭아(나무) —see picture on
page 944 **2** [U] a pale pink-orange color
‖ 옅은 분홍빛 오렌지 색. 복숭앗빛. 연분
홍색

pea·cock /ˈpikɑk/ *n* a large bird, the
male of which has long blue and green
tail feathers that it can spread out ‖ 펼칠
수 있는 푸른색과 녹색의 긴 꼬리 깃을 가
진 큰 수컷 새. 공작의 수컷

peak¹ /pik/ *n* **1** the time when someone
or something is biggest, most
successful, or best ‖ 사람이나 사물이 가
장 크거나 가장 성공적이거나 가장 좋을
때. 절정. 정점: *Trenton is now at the
peak of his career.* 트렌톤은 현재 그의

경력에 있어 절정에 있다./ *The
company's profits reached a peak in
1992.* 그 회사의 이윤은 1992년에 최고에
이르렀다. **2** the pointed top of a
mountain, or a mountain with a pointed
top ‖ 산의 뾰족한 정상, 또는 뾰족한 정상
이 있는 산. 산꼭대기. 봉우리: *the Alps'
snow-covered peaks* 눈 덮인 알프스의 봉
우리들

peak² *v* [I] to become the biggest, most
successful, or best that someone or
something can be ‖ 사람이나 사물이 가장
크게[성공하게, 최고가] 되다. 절정[최대
한도]에 이르다: *In the 1950s, Chicago's
population peaked at around 3.6
million.* 1950년대에 시카고의 인구는 약
360만 명으로 절정에 달했다.

peaked /pikt/ *adj* pale, and looking
sick ‖ 창백하고 아파 보이는. 안색이 나
쁜. 수척한

peal /pil/ *n* a sudden loud repeated
sound, such as laughter, THUNDER, or
bells RINGing ‖ 웃음소리나 천둥, 또는 벨
소리 등의 갑작스럽고 크게 반복되는 소
리: *Peals of laughter came from the
audience.* 관객들로부터 웃음소리가 계속
터져 나왔다. – **peal** *v* [I]

pea·nut /ˈpinʌt/ *n* a small nut you can
eat that has a soft light brown shell ‖ 부
드럽고 옅은 갈색 껍질이 있으며 먹을 수
있는 조그만 견과. 땅콩

peanut but·ter /ˈ.. ˌ../ *n* [U] a soft
food made from crushed PEANUTs,
usually eaten on bread ‖ 보통 빵에 얹어
먹는 짓이긴 땅콩으로 만든 부드러운 음
식. 땅콩버터: *a peanut butter and jelly
sandwich* 땅콩버터와 젤리 샌드위치

pea·nuts /ˈpinʌts/ *n* [U] INFORMAL a
very small amount of money ‖ 아주 적은
금액. 푼돈: *I'm tired of working for
peanuts.* 푼돈을 벌기 위해 일하는 것이
신물이 난다.

pear /pɛr/ *n* a sweet juicy fruit with a
round wide bottom that becomes
thinner on top near the stem, or the
tree on which it grows ‖ 꼭지 부근의 윗
부분이 점점 홀쭉해지며 그 밑동은 둥글고
넓은 달고 즙이 많은 과일, 또는 그 과일이
자라는 나무. 서양배(나무) —see picture
on page 944

pearl /pɚl/ *n* **1** a valuable small white
round object, that forms inside an
OYSTER and is used in jewelry ‖ 굴 속에서
만들어져 보석으로 사용되는 값비싸며 작
고 동그란 흰색의 물체. 진주: *a pearl
necklace* 진주 목걸이 **2** [U] a pale silver-
white color ‖ 옅은 은백색. 진줏빛

peas·ant /ˈpɛzənt/ *n* a word meaning

someone who does farm work on the piece of land where s/he lives, used especially to describe people who did this in past times || 특히 과거에 농사를 짓던 사람을 기술하는 데에 쓰여, 자신이 살고 있는 땅의 일부에서 농사일을 하는 사람을 뜻하는 단어. 농부

peat /pit/ *n* [U] a substance formed under the surface of the ground from decaying plants, used as soil or as FUEL || 거름이나 연료로 사용되는, 지표면 아래에서 썩은 식물이 만들어낸 물질. 이탄(泥炭)

peb·ble /'pɛbəl/ *n* a small smooth stone that is usually in a river or on a beach || 보통 강이나 해변에 있는 작고 매끄러운 돌. 조약돌. 자갈

pe·can /pə'kɑn, -'kæn/ *n* a long thin sweet nut with a dark smooth shell, or the tree on which these nuts grow || 거무튀튀하고 매끄러운 껍질을 가진 길고 얇으며 맛이 단 견과, 또는 이 견과가 자라는 나무. 피칸(의 열매)

peck¹ /pɛk/, **peck at** *v* [I, T] if a bird pecks something, it quickly moves its beak to hit or pick up something, especially food || 새가 부리를 빠르게 움직여서 특히 먹이 따위를 쪼거나 주워 먹다. (…을) 부리로 쪼다

peck² *n* **1** give sb a peck on the cheek to kiss someone quickly and lightly || 남에게 재빨리 가볍게 키스하다. 남의 볼에 가볍게 키스하다 **2** the action of a bird hitting something with its beak || 새가 부리로 무엇을 쪼는 행위

pe·cu·liar /pɪ'kyulyɚ/ *adj* **1** strange and a little surprising || 이상하고 좀 놀랄 만한. 별난: *She has the peculiar habit of blinking a lot when she talks.* 그녀는 말할 때 눈을 많이 깜박이는 기묘한 습관이 있다. **2** be peculiar to to be a quality that only one particular person, place, or thing has || 어떤 특정한 사람[장소, 물체]만이 가지는 성질이 있다. 독특하다: *the strong flavor that is peculiar to garlic* 마늘 특유의 강한 맛 - **peculiarly** *adv*

pe·cu·li·ar·i·ty /pɪˌkyuli'ærəṭi/ *n* [C, U] an unusual or slightly strange habit or quality, especially one that only a particular person, place etc. has || 특히 어떤 특정한 사람·장소 등만이 가지는 유별나거나 다소 이상한 습관이나 성질. 이상한 태도[버릇]. 기묘함: *At least she knew about his peculiarities before she married him!* 적어도 그녀는 그와 결혼하기 전에 그의 이상한 버릇을 알았어!

ped·a·go·gi·cal /ˌpɛdə'gɑdʒɪkəl/ *adj*

FORMAL relating to methods of teaching || 교수법에 관한. 교수법의 - **pedagogy** /'pɛdəˌgɑdʒi/ *n* [U]

ped·al¹ /'pɛdl/ *n* the part of a bicycle, car, or MOTORCYCLE that you push with your foot in order to make it move || 움직이게 하기 위해 발로 밟는 자전거[차, 오토바이]의 한 부분. 페달: *the gas pedal* 자동차의 액셀러레이터[가속 페달]

pedal² *v* [I, T] to ride a bicycle by pushing the PEDALs with your feet || 발로 페달을 밟아서 자전거를 타다

pe·dan·tic /pə'dænṭɪk/ *adj* paying too much attention to small details and rules, especially because you are trying to prove how much you know || 특히 얼마만큼 아는지를 증명하려고 애쓰기 때문에 세세한 사항과 규칙에 너무 많은 관심을 기울이는. 규칙[세부]에 얽매이는: *a pedantic professor* 규칙에 얽매이는 교수

ped·dle /'pɛdl/ *v* [T] to go from place to place trying to sell something, especially something illegal or cheap || 특히 불법적이거나 값싼 물건을 팔려고 여기저기로 돌아다니다. 행상하다: *Eric was caught peddling drugs.* 에릭은 마약을 팔다가 잡혔다. - **peddler** *n* : *a drug peddler* 마약 암거래상

ped·es·tal /'pɛdəstl/ *n* **1** the base that you put a STATUE or a PILLAR on || 상(像)이나 기둥을 놓는 토대. 대좌(臺座). 주각(柱脚) **2** put sb on a pedestal to admire someone too much because you think s/he is perfect || 남을 완벽하다고 생각하기 때문에 지나치게 존경하다. …을 찬양[우상화]하다

pe·des·tri·an¹ /pə'dɛstriən/ *n* someone who is walking instead of driving a car or riding a bicycle || 차를 몰거나 자전거를 타는 대신에 걷고 있는 사람. 보행자

pedestrian² *adj* **1** relating to PEDESTRIANs, or used by pedestrians || 보행자에 관한, 또는 보행자가 사용하는. 도보인. 보행용의: *a pedestrian crossing* (=where cars must stop to allow people to walk across the street) 횡단보도 **2** ordinary, and not very interesting or exciting || 보통인, 그리 흥미있거나 자극적이지 않은. 평범한. 시시한: *It is a piece of real journalism, rather than the usual pedestrian stuff.* 그것은 보통의 시시한 작품이라기보다 일종의 참된 저널리즘이다.

pe·di·a·tri·cian /ˌpidiə'trɪʃən/ *n* a doctor who treats children || 어린아이를 치료하는 의사. 소아과 의사

pe·di·at·rics /ˌpidi'ætrɪks/ *n* [U] the area of medicine that deals with

peel

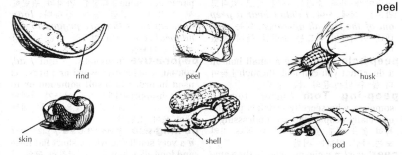

rind   peel   husk

skin   shell   pod

children and their illnesses ‖ 어린아이와 그들의 병을 다루는 의학의 분야. 소아과
ped·i·cure /ˈpɛdɪˌkyʊr/ *n* [C, U] a treatment for the feet that includes cleaning them and cutting the TOENAILs ‖ 발을 깨끗이 하는 일과 발톱을 깎는 일을 포함하는 발의 치료. 발의 전문적 치료
ped·i·gree /ˈpɛdəˌgri/ *n* [C, U] the parents and other past family members of an animal or person, or the written record of them ‖ 동물이나 사람의 어미[부모]와 과거의 다른 가족 구성원들, 또는 이들에 대한 문서 기록. 가계(家系). 혈통. 족보 **– pedigree** *adj* : *a pedigree Great Dane* 혈통이 좋은 그레이트 데인종의 개

pee /pi/ *n* [singular, U] INFORMAL urine, or the act of urinating (URINATE) ‖ 소변, 또는 오줌 누기: *Andy, do you need to go pee before we leave?* 앤디야, 출발하기 전에 소변 봐야 하니? **– pee** *v* [I]

peek¹ /pik/ *v* [I] to quickly look at something, especially something you are not supposed to see ‖ 특히 보지 말아야 할 것을 재빨리 보다. 엿보다. 몰래[살짝] 들여다보다: *The door was open, so I peeked into his office.* 그 문이 열려 있어서 나는 그의 사무실을 엿보았다.

peek² *n* a quick look at something ‖ 어떤 것을 재빨리 보기. 엿보기: *Take a peek in the oven and see if the cake's done.* 케이크가 다 익었는지 오븐을 살짝 들여다 보아라.

peek·a·boo /ˈpikəˌbu/ *interjection, n* [U] a game played with babies and young children, in which you hide your face and then show it again and again, saying "peekaboo!" ‖ "까꿍" 하면서 거듭해서 얼굴을 가렸다가 보여주는, 유아와 어린이들과 함께 하는 놀이. 야웅[까꿍] 놀이

peel¹ /pil/ *v* **1** [T] to remove the skin of a fruit or vegetable ‖ 과일이나 채소의 껍질을 제거하다. 껍질을 벗기다: *Peel the*

potatoes and cut them in half. 감자의 껍질을 벗겨서 반으로 잘라라. **2** [I, T] to remove a thin outside layer from the surface of an object ‖ 물체의 표면에서 얇은 바깥층을 제거하다. 벗기다. 벗다: *Peel the labels off/from the jars before recycling.* 재활용하기 전에 병의 라벨을 벗겨라. **3** [I] if skin, paper, or paint peels, it is loose and coming off in small thin pieces ‖ 피부[종이, 페인트]가 푸석푸석해서 작고 얇은 조각으로 떨어져 나오다. 벗겨지다: *I got sunburned and now my face is peeling.* 햇볕에 타서 지금 내 얼굴의 허물이 벗겨지고 있다.

peel sth ↔ **off** *phr v* [I, T] to take off your clothes, especially if they are wet or tight ‖ 특히 옷이 젖거나 꽉 끼는 경우, 옷을 벗다[벗기다]: *He peeled off his T-shirt and put it in the wash.* 그는 티셔츠를 벗어서 세탁물에 넣었다.

peel² *n* [U] the thick skin of a fruit or vegetable such as an orange, a potato, or a BANANA ‖ 오렌지[감자, 바나나] 등의 과일이나 야채의 두꺼운 껍질

peel·ings /ˈpilɪŋz/ *n* [plural] pieces of skin that are removed from a fruit or vegetable before cooking it ‖ 요리하기 전에 과일이나 야채에서 벗긴 껍질: *carrot peelings* 당근 껍질

peep¹ /pip/ *v* [I] **1** to look at something quickly and secretly ‖ 재빨리 몰래 어떤 것을 보다. 엿보다. 들여다보다: *I saw Joe peeping through the curtains.* 나는 커튼 사이로 엿보고 있는 조를 보았다. **2** to appear ‖ 나타나다. 조금 내밀다. 조금 나타내다: *The sun finally peeped out from behind the clouds.* 태양은 마침내 구름 뒤에서 빼꼼히 고개를 내밀었다.

peep² *n* **1** a quick or secret look at something ‖ 어떤 것을 재빨리, 또는 몰래 보기. 살짝[훔쳐]보기: *Did you get a peep at the audience?* 관객들 좀 내다 봤니? **2** **not (hear) a peep** used in order to say that a child is not making any sounds ‖

어린이가 아무 소리도 내지 않고 있다고 말하는 데에 쓰여: *I didn't hear a peep out of the kids all afternoon.* 나는 오후 내내 아이들이 떠드는 소리를 듣지 못했다.

peep·hole /'piphoʊl/ *n* a small hole in a door that you can look through ‖ 들여다 볼 수 있는 문의 작은 구멍

peep·ing Tom /,pipɪŋ 'tam/ *n* someone who secretly watches people, especially people who are undressing ‖ 특히 옷을 벗고 있는 사람들을 몰래 지켜 보는 사람. 엿보는 사람

peer[1] /pɪr/ *n* someone who is the same age as you, or who has the same type of job, rank etc. ‖ 자신과 나이가 같은 사람, 또는 같은 일·지위 등을 가진 사람. 동료. 또래: *Barton has gained the respect of his peers.* 바튼은 동료들의 존경을 받았다.

peer[2] *v* [I] to look very carefully, especially because you cannot see something well ‖ 물체를 잘 볼 수 없어서 매우 주의 깊게 보다. 응시하다. 눈여겨보다: *Harris peered into the dark closet.* 해리스는 어두운 벽장속을 들여다 봤다.

peer·less /'pɪrlɪs/ *adj* better than any other ‖ 어느 것보다도 더 좋은. 비길 데 없는: *his peerless achievements in science* 과학 분야에서의 비길 데 없는 그의 업적

peer pres·sure /'. ,../ *n* the strong feeling that young people have that they should do the same things that their PEERS are doing ‖ 또래 집단이 행하는 똑같은 행동을 해야만 한다고 젊은이들이 느끼는 강렬한 감정. 또래적 압박감

peeve /piv/ *n* ⇨ **pet peeve** (PET[3])

peg[1] /pɛg/ *n* 1 a short piece of wood or metal that fits into a hole or is fastened to a wall, used for fastening furniture together, for hanging things on etc. ‖ 가구를 서로 고정시키거나 물건을 거는데 쓰이는, 구멍에 끼우거나 벽에 고정시키는 짧은 나무나 금속 조각. 걸이용 못: *a coat peg* 코트 걸이 2 also **tent peg** a pointed piece of wood or metal used for keeping a tent attached to the ground ‖ 텐트를 땅에 고정시키는 데 사용되는 뾰족한 나무나 금속 조각. 천막 말뚝

peg[2] **-gged, -gging** *v* 1 **have sb pegged (as)** to say that someone has a particular type of character ‖ 사람이 특정한 유형의 성격을 지닌다고 말하다. …을 (…으로) 인정하다. 분류하다: *I never had him pegged as a winner.* 나는 절대 그를 승자로 인정하지 않았다. 2 [T] to set prices, wages etc. in relation to a

particular value ‖ 특정한 가치와 관련해서 가격이나 임금 등을 정하다: *loan payment rates that are pegged to the national rates* 국내 이율을 기준으로 정한 대출 지불률

pe·jor·a·tive /pɪ'dʒɔrətɪv, -'dʒɑr-/ *adj* FORMAL a pejorative word or phrase is used in order to insult someone or to show disapproval ‖ 말이나 어구가 남에게 모욕을 주거나 찬성하지 않음을 나타내는 데에 쓰여. 경멸적인. 비난하는

pe·king·ese, pek·in·ese /,pikə'niz/ *n* a very small dog with a short flat nose and long silky hair ‖ 짧고 납작한 코와 기다랗고 부드러운 털을 가진 아주 작은 개. 발바리

pel·i·can /'pɛlɪkən/ *n* a large bird that catches fish for food and holds them in the part of its large beak that is shaped like a bag ‖ 먹이로 물고기를 잡아서 자루 모양의 큰 부리 속에 담는 큰 새. 펠리컨

pel·let /'pɛlɪt/ *n* a small hard ball made from metal, ice, paper, food etc. ‖ 금속·얼음·종이·음식 등으로 만든 작고 딱딱한 알. 알갱이

pelt[1] /pɛlt/ *v* [T] to attack someone by throwing a lot of things at him/her ‖ 많은 물건을 던져서 남을 공격하다: *Two kids were pelting each other with snowballs.* 두 아이가 서로 눈뭉치로 눈싸움을 벌이고 있었다.

pelt[2] *n* the skin of a dead animal with the fur or hair still on it ‖ 털이 아직 붙어 있는 죽은 동물의 가죽. 생가죽. 모피

pel·vis /'pɛlvɪs/ *n* the set of large wide curved bones at the base of your spine, to which your legs are joined ‖ 다리와 연결되어 있고 척추의 기부에 있는 크고 넓게 굽은 뼈. 골반(骨盤) - **pelvic** *adj*

pen[1] /pɛn/ *n* 1 [C, U] an instrument used for writing and drawing in ink ‖ 잉크로 쓰거나 그리는 데 사용되는 도구. 펜: *a ballpoint pen* 볼펜 / *Write your essays in pen* (=using a pen), *not pencil.* 연필을 사용하지 말고 펜으로 수필을 쓰세요. 2 a small area surrounded by a fence, that farm animals are kept in ‖ 가축을 가둬 기르기 위해 울타리로 둘러싼 좁은 지역. 우리 —see also PIGPEN

pen[2] *v* **-nned, -nning** [T] LITERARY 1 to write a letter or note with a pen ‖ 펜으로 편지를 쓰거나 필기를 하다. 펜으로 …을 쓰다 2 [I, T] to prevent a person or animal from leaving an enclosed area ‖ 사람이나 동물이 막힌 공간을 떠나지 못하게 하다. 가두다: *The flu kept him penned in the house for a week.* 독감 때문에 그는 일주일 동안 집에 틀어박혀 있

penetrating

었다.

pe·nal /'pinl/ *adj* 1 relating to the legal punishment of criminals || 범죄자의 법적 처벌에 관한. 형(벌)의. 형사상의: *a penal institution* (=type of prison) 형을 사는 감옥 2 **penal offense** a crime || 형사 범죄

penal code /'.. ,./ *n* a set of laws and the punishments for not obeying these laws || 법률과 이 법률을 준수하지 않은 것에 대한 형벌 체계. 형법전. 형사법전: *the Oregon Penal Code* 오레곤 형법전

pe·nal·ize /'pinl,aɪz, 'pɛn-/ *v* [T] 1 to punish someone or treat him/her unfairly || 남을 처벌하거나 부당하게 대우하다. 처형하다. 불리하게 하다: *If Glenda's been trying her best, she shouldn't be penalized for her low grades.* 글렌다가 최선을 다해왔다면 낮은 점수 때문에 벌 받아서는 안 된다. 2 to punish a player or sports team by giving an advantage to the other team || 상대 팀에 이점을 줌으로써 한 선수나 스포츠 팀을 응징하다. 벌칙[페널티]을 주다[적용하다]: *The Bears were penalized for taking too much time.* 베어스팀은 너무 시간을 끌어서 페널티를 받았다.

pen·al·ty /'pɛnlti/ *n* 1 a punishment for not obeying a law, rule, or legal agreement || 법[규칙, 합법적인 계약] 등을 준수하지 않은 것에 대한 처벌. 형벌. 벌금: *a penalty of $120 for speeding* 속도위반에 대한 벌금 120달러 / *He was given the death penalty.* (=the punishment of being killed) 그는 사형 선고를 받았다. 2 a disadvantage given to a player or sports team for not obeying the rules || 규칙을 따르지 않은 선수나 스포츠 팀에게 주는 불이익. 페널티. 벌

pen·ance /'pɛnəns/ *n* [C, U] a punishment that you accept, especially for religious reasons, to show that you are sorry for doing a bad thing || 특히 종교적 이유로, 악행을 저지른 것에 대해 후회한다는 것을 나타내기 위해 받는 벌. 속죄. 회개

pen·chant /'pɛntʃənt/ *n* a liking for something that you do as a habit || 어떤 일을 습관처럼 하기를 좋아함. 강한 기호. 경향: *Philip has a penchant for smoking French cigarettes.* 필립은 프랑스산 담배 피우기를 무척 좋아한다.

pen·cil /'pɛnsəl/ *n* [C, U] an instrument used for writing and drawing, made of wood with a gray or colored center || 회색, 또는 색깔이 있는 심을 박은 나무로 만들어져, 글을 쓰고 그림을 그리는 데 사용되는 도구. 연필: *Do the math problems in pencil* (=using a pencil), *not pen.* 볼펜 말고 연필로 수학 문제를 풀어라. / *an editor's blue pencil* 편집자의 파란 연필

pencil sharp·en·er /'.. ,../ *n* an object with a small blade inside it, used for making the pointed end of a pencil sharp || 연필의 끝을 뾰족하게 하는 데 쓰이는, 안에 조그만 날이 있는 물체. 연필깎이

pend·ant /'pɛndənt/ *n* a jewel or small decoration that hangs from a chain you wear around your neck || 목에 거는 줄에 매단 보석이나 작은 장식. 펜던트: *a diamond pendant* 다이아몬드 펜던트

pend·ing[1] /'pɛndɪŋ/ *prep* FORMAL until something happens, or while something happens || 어떤 것이 발생할 때까지, 또는 어떤 것이 발생하는 동안. …까지. …동안: *The decision has been delayed pending further research.* 그 결정은 추가 조사를 할 때까지 연기되었다.

pending[2] *adj* FORMAL not yet decided, agreed on, or finished || 아직 결정되지 않은[합의되지 않은, 끝나지 않은]. 미정의. 현안의: *Their divorce is still pending.* 그들의 이혼은 아직 결정되지 않은 상태이다.

pen·du·lum /'pɛndʒələm/ *n* a long stick with a weight on the end of it, that hangs down and swings from side to side, especially in a large clock || 특히 큰 괘종시계에서 아래로 매달려 양 측면으로 흔들리는, 끝에 추가 달린 긴 막대. 진자(振子). 흔들이

pen·e·trate /'pɛnə,treɪt/ *v* 1 [I, T] to enter something or pass through it, especially when this is difficult || 특히 그러기 힘든 경우에, 어떤 것에 들어가거나 관통하다. (…을) 꿰뚫다. (…을) 파고들다: *bullets that can penetrate metal* 금속을 관통할 수 있는 총알 / *Dampness had penetrated into the walls.* 습기가 벽에 스며들었다. 2 [T] to join and be accepted by an organization, business etc. in order to find out secret information || 비밀 정보를 알아내기 위해 조직이나 기업 등에 침투해 들어가다. 잠입하다: *CIA agents had penetrated several left-wing groups.* 미국 중앙 정보국 요원들이 몇 개의 좌익 집단에 잠입했다. 3 [T] to understand something difficult || 어려운 것을 이해하다. 간파하다. 깨닫다: *scientists trying to penetrate the mysteries of nature* 자연의 신비를 캐내려는 과학자들

pen·e·trat·ing /'pɛnə,treɪtɪŋ/ *adj* 1 **penetrating eyes/look/gaze** someone who has penetrating eyes etc. seems able to see what another person is thinking ‖ 다른 사람이 무슨 생각을 하고 있는지 파악이 가능해 보이는. 통찰력 있는. 잘 간파하는. 예리한 눈빛/표정/응시 **2** a penetrating noise or voice is so loud that you hear it very clearly ‖ 소음이나 음성이 너무 커서 아주 분명하게 들리는. 날카로운 **3** showing an ability to understand things quickly and completely ‖ 사물을 빠르고 완전하게 이해하는 능력을 보이는. 이해가 빠른. 총명한: *a penetrating mind* 통찰력 있는 사람 – **penetration** /ˌpɛnəˈtreɪʃən/ *n* [U]

pen·guin /ˈpɛŋgwɪn/ *n* a large black and white Antarctic sea bird, that cannot fly but uses its wings for swimming ‖ 날 수 없지만 수영하는 데 날개를 사용하는 검고 흰 남극의 큰 바닷새. 펭귄

pen·i·cil·lin /ˌpɛnəˈsɪlən/ *n* [U] a substance used as a medicine to destroy BACTERIA ‖ 세균을 박멸하는 약으로 사용되는 물질. 페니실린

pe·nin·su·la /pəˈnɪnsələ/ *n* a piece of land that is almost completely surrounded by water ‖ 거의 완전하게 바다로 둘러싸인 땅. 반도: *the Italian peninsula* 이탈리아 반도 – **peninsular** *adj*

pe·nis /ˈpinɪs/ *n* the outer sex organ of males ‖ 남성의 외부 생식기. 남근. 음경

pen·i·tent /ˈpɛnətənt/ *adj* FORMAL feeling sorry about doing something bad, and showing you do not intend to do it again ‖ 잘못한 일을 죄스러워하고 그 일을 다시는 하지 않겠다는 의도를 보이는. 참회[후회]하는 – **penitence** *n* [U]

pen·i·ten·tia·ry /ˌpɛnəˈtɛnʃəri/ *n* a prison ‖ 교도소: *the state penitentiary* 주(州)교도소

pen·knife /ˈpɛn-naɪf/ *n* ⇨ POCKET KNIFE

pen name /ˈ. ./ *n* a name used by a writer instead of his/her real name; PSEUDONYM ‖ 작가가 실제 이름 대신에 쓰는 이름. 필명. 아호; 㿟 pseudonym

pen·nant /ˈpɛnənt/ *n* a long pointed flag used by schools, sports teams etc., or on ships as a sign ‖ 학교나 스포츠 팀 등이 사용하거나 선박에서 신호로 사용되는 길고 뾰족한 깃발. 기다란 삼각기

pen·ni·less /ˈpɛnɪlɪs/ *adj* having no money ‖ 돈이 없는. 빈털터리의

pen·ny /ˈpɛni/ *n, plural* **pennies 1** a coin used in the US and Canada worth 1 cent (=1/100 of a dollar) ‖ 미국과 캐나다에서 사용되는 1센트짜리 동전. 페니 **2**

a penny/every penny any of your money or all of your money ‖ 자신이 가진 돈의 일부나 전부. 잔돈[푼돈]/모든 돈: *I don't owe her a penny!* 나는 그녀에게 한 푼도 빚을 지지 않았어! / *He spent every penny on his car.* 그는 차에 돈을 몽땅 썼다.

pen pal /ˈ. ./ *n* someone in another country to whom you write letters in order to become his/her friend ‖ 친구가 되기 위해 편지를 쓰는 다른 나라의 사람. 펜팔. 편지 친구

pen·sion /ˈpɛnʃən/ *n* **1** the money that a company pays regularly to someone after s/he RETIRES (=stops working) ‖ 퇴직한 사람에게 회사에서 정기적으로 지불하는 돈. 연금 **2** a small cheap hotel in France and some other European countries ‖ 프랑스나 몇몇 다른 유럽 국가들에서의 작고 저렴한 호텔. 펜션

pension fund /ˈ.. ˌ./ *n* the large amount of money that a company, organization etc. INVESTs and uses for paying PENSIONs ‖ 회사나 기관 등이 투자해서 연금을 지불하는 데 사용하는 큰 액수의 돈. 연금 기금

pension plan /ˈ.. ˌ./ *n* a system for organizing the type of PENSION that a company will give you ‖ 회사가 개인에게 제공할 연금 유형을 조직화하는 체계. 연금 계획

pen·sive /ˈpɛnsɪv/ *adj* thinking about something a lot and seeming slightly sad ‖ 많은 것에 대해 생각하고 약간 슬퍼 보이는. 골똘히 생각에 잠긴. 수심에 잠긴: *He sat by the river, looking pensive.* 그는 수심에 잠긴 모습으로 강가에 앉았다.

Pen·ta·gon /ˈpɛntəˌgɑn/ *n* **the Pentagon** the US government building from which the army, navy etc. are controlled, or the military officers who work in this building ‖ 육군이나 해군 등을 통제하는 미국 정부 건물, 또는 이 건물에서 일하는 군 장교들. 펜타곤

pentagon *n* a flat shape with five sides and five angles ‖ 5변과 5각이 있는 평평한 모양. 오각형 – **pentagonal** /pɛnˈtægənl/ *adj*

Pen·te·cos·tal /ˌpɛntɪˈkɑstl/ *adj* relating to the Christian church whose members believe that the spirit of God can help them to heal diseases and pray in special languages ‖ 성령이 질병을 치료하고 특수 언어[방언]로 기도할 수 있도록 도와준다고 신도들이 믿고 있는 그리스도 교회의. 펜터코스트파의 – **Pentecostal** *n*

pent·house /ˈpɛnthaʊs/ *n* a very

expensive and comfortable apartment on the top floor of a tall building ‖ 높은 건물 최상층의 매우 값비싸고 안락한 아파트. 고급 옥상 주택.

pent-up /ˌ.ˈ.ˌ/ adj pent-up emotions are not expressed for a long time ‖ 감정이 오랫동안 표현되지 않은. 억눌린: *All the pent-up anger she was feeling came out as she cried.* 그녀가 느끼고 있었던 모든 울화가 울면서 분출되었다.

peon /ˈpiɑn/ n OFTEN HUMOROUS someone who works at a boring or physically hard job for low pay ‖ 저임금을 받고 따분한 일, 또는 육체적으로 힘든 일을 하는 사람. 잡역부: *I don't know anything – I'm just one of the peons.* 저는 아무것도 모릅니다. 저는 일개 잡역부일 뿐입니다.

peo·ple¹ /ˈpipəl/ n 1 [plural] men, women, and children ‖ 남자·여자·아이들. 사람들: *I like the people I work with.* 나는 함께 일하는 사람들을 좋아합니다. / *How many people were at the wedding?* 결혼식에 얼마나 많은 사람들이 왔었니? **2 the people** [plural] all the ordinary people in a country or a state ‖ 한 나라나 한 주(州)의 모든 일반 사람들. 국민. 주민: *The US is meant to have "a government of the people, by the people, and for the people."* 미국은 국민의, 국민에 의한, 국민을 위한 정부를 구성하려 한다. **3** FORMAL a race or nation ‖ 인종. 국민: *the peoples of Asia* 아시아의 여러 민족 **4 of all people** SPOKEN used in order to say that someone is the only person who you would not have expected to do something ‖ 누군가가 무엇을 하리라고 기대하지 않았던 유일한 사람임을 말하는 데에 쓰여. 하필이면: *It was Michael Jordan, of all people, who missed the shot that made the Bulls lose.* 불스팀을 패하게 만든 슛을 놓친 사람이 하필이면 마이클 조던이었다. —see usage notes at MAN¹, PERSON

people² v **be peopled with** LITERARY to be filled with people or things of a particular type ‖ 특정한 형태의 사람들이나 사물들로 가득 차다: *Her books are peopled with imaginary creatures.* 그녀의 책들은 상상의 산물들로 가득 차 있다.

pep¹ /pɛp/ v **-pped, -pping**

pep sb/sth ↔ **up** phr v [T] INFORMAL to make something or someone more active, interesting, or full of energy ‖ 사물이나 사람을 보다 활기차게[흥미있게, 활력이 넘치게] 만들다. …을 활기 띠게 하다: *I've added some chilies to pep up the chicken a little.* 나는 닭고기를 조금 더 맛있게 하기 위해 약간의 칠레고추를 첨가했다.

pep² n [U] OLD-FASHIONED physical energy ‖ 신체의 기력. 활기. 원기. 활력: *Ed's always full of pep.* 에드는 항상 기운이 넘친다. – **peppy** adj

pep·per¹ /ˈpɛpɚ/ n **1** [U] a black, pale yellow, or red hot-tasting powder, used in cooking ‖ 요리에 쓰이는 검은색[연노란색, 빨간색]의 매운 맛이 나는 가루. 후추 [고추] 가루 **2** a hollow red, green, or yellow fruit with a sweet or hot taste that is eaten as a vegetable, or added to other foods ‖ 야채로 먹거나 다른 음식에 첨가하는, 달거나 매운 맛이 나는 속이 빈 빨간색[녹색], 노란색] 열매. 피망 —see picture on page 944

pepper² v [T] **1** to scatter things all over or all through something ‖ 사물을 곳곳에 또는 무엇인가에 온통 흩뿌리다: *The article is peppered with quotations.* 그 기사는 인용문 투성이이다. **2** to put pepper in food ‖ 음식에 후추[고추]가루를 넣다

pep·per·mint /ˈpɛpɚˌmɪnt/ n [U] **1** a MINT plant with sweet-smelling hot-tasting leaves used in making candy, tea, and medicine ‖ 사탕·차·약의 제조에 쓰이는, 달콤한 향과 매운 맛을 내는 잎이 달린 박하과 식물. 서양박하 **2** a candy with this taste ‖ 박하 맛 사탕

pep·per·o·ni /ˌpɛpəˈrouni/ n [C, U] a hot-tasting dry Italian SAUSAGE ‖ 매운 맛이 나는, 말린 이탈리아 소시지. 페퍼로니

pep ral·ly /ˈ. ˌ../ n a meeting when people give speeches or shout to encourage and support a team ‖ 사람들이 팀을 격려하고 지지하기 위해 연설을 하거나 소리지르는 모임. 궐기 대회: *The pep rally will be in the gym a half hour before the game starts.* 응원전은 경기가 시작되기 30분 전에 체육관에서 있을 것입니다.

pep talk /ˈ. ./ n INFORMAL a speech that is intended to encourage people to work harder, win a game etc. ‖ 사람들이 더욱 열심히 일하거나 경기 등에서 승리하도록 격려할 목적으로 하는 연설. 격려 연설: *a pre-game pep talk from the football coach* 미식축구 감독의 경기 전 격려의 말

per /pɚ/ prep for each ‖ 각각에 대하여. …당. …마다: *Bananas are 60¢ per pound.* 바나나는 파운드당 60센트이다. / *You need at least half a bottle of wine per person for the party.* 너는 그 파티용으로 적어도 1인당 와인 반병은 필요하다.

per ca·pi·ta /pɚ ˈkæpətə/ adj, adv FORMAL calculated by dividing the total amount of something by the number of people in a particular place ‖ 사물의 총 량을 특정 장소에 있는 사람수로 나누어 계산된. **1인당의**: *The average per capita income in the area is $40,000 a year.* 그 지역의 1인당 평균 수입은 연간 40,000달러이다.

per·ceive /pɚˈsiv/ *v* [T] FORMAL **1** to understand or think about something in a particular way ‖ 특정한 방식으로 무엇을 이해하거나 생각하다. 파악하다: *It is a difficult situation, but we don't perceive it as anything we can't deal with.* 어려운 상황이기는 하지만 그것을 우리가 다룰 수 없는 것으로 생각하지는 않는다. / *I think the public perceives that our industry has a problem.* 나는 대중들이 우리 산업에 문제가 있다는 것을 인지하고 있다고 생각한다. **2** to notice something that is difficult to notice ‖ 알아차리기 어려운 것을 알아채다. 지각하다 : *The sound is too high to be perceived by humans.* 그 소리는 너무 높아서 인간이 인지하기 어렵다.

percent¹ /pɚˈsɛnt/ *adj, adv* **1** equal to a particular amount in every hundred ‖ 100 중에 특정량에 해당되는. 백분의. 퍼센트의. 백에 대하여: *Leave the waitress a 15% tip.* (=a tip of 15 cents for every dollar you have spent on the meal) 웨이트리스에게 15퍼센트의 팁을 남겨라. **2** **a/one hundred percent** completely ‖ 완전히. 전적으로: *I agree with you a hundred percent.* 나는 당신에게 전적으로 동의합니다.

percent² *n* **five/ten etc. percent** five, ten etc. in every hundred ‖ 100에 대하여 5·10 등. 5/10 퍼센트: *The interest rate at the bank is six percent.* (=6%, or six cents on every dollar) 그 은행의 이율은 6퍼센트이다.

per·cent·age /pɚˈsɛntɪdʒ/ *n* **1** [C, U] a particular amount out of every hundred ‖ 100 중의 특정량. 비율: *A high percentage of Internet users are men.* 인터넷 사용자 중 남자의 비율이 높다. / *The percentage of deaths caused by highway accidents has decreased recently.* 간선도로 사고에 의한 사망률은 최근에 감소했다. **2** a share of profits equal to a particular amount in every dollar ‖ 달러당 특정 양에 해당하는 몫의 이익: *He gets a percentage for every book that is sold.* 그는 책 판매 부수당 1퍼센트의 이익을 얻는다.

per·cep·ti·ble /pɚˈsɛptəbəl/ *adj* FORMAL noticeable ‖ 인지할 수 있는: *The accounts show a barely perceptible*

increase in profits. 그 회계 보고서는 수익 증가가 거의 인지할 수 없는 정도임을 보여 준다. —opposite IMPERCEPTIBLE

per·cep·tion /pɚˈsɛpʃən/ *n* **1** the way you understand something and your beliefs about what it is like ‖ 무엇을 이해하는 방식과 사물의 속성에 대한 생각. 인식: *The local library is trying to change the perception that the library is not a fun place to be.* 그 지역 도서관은 도서관이 재미없는 장소라는 인식을 바꾸려고 노력 중이다. **2** [U] the way you use your senses to notice things ‖ 무엇을 알아채기 위해 감각을 이용하는 방법. 지각: *Drugs can change your perception of sounds and sights.* 마약은 청력과 시력을 변화시킬 수 있다. **3** [U] the natural ability to understand or notice something quickly ‖ 무엇을 빨리 이해하거나 알아채는 천부적 능력. 직관: *I was amazed at the perception of Rachel's five-year-old girl.* 나는 레이첼의 다섯 살짜리 딸의 직관력에 놀랐다.

per·cep·tive /pɚˈsɛptɪv/ *adj* good at noticing and understanding what is happening or what someone is thinking or feeling ‖ 발생하는 일, 또는 사람이 생각하거나 느끼는 것을 인지하고 이해하는 데에 능숙한. 직관이 예리한: *A perceptive teacher can really help a shy child.* 잘 이해하는 선생님은 수줍어하는 아이를 잘 도와줄 수 있다.

perch¹ /pɚtʃ/ *n* **1** a branch, stick etc. where a bird sits ‖ 새가 앉는 가지·막대 등. 횃대 **2** INFORMAL a high place where someone can sit or where a building is placed ‖ 사람이 앉을 수 있는 높은 곳, 또는 건물이 위치한 높은 장소: *He watches from his perch halfway up the mountain.* 그는 산 중턱에서 바라보고 있다. **3** [C, U] a fish with sharp pointed fins that lives in rivers, lakes etc., or the meat from this fish ‖ 강·호수 등에 서식하는 날카롭고 끝이 뾰족한 지느러미가 달린 물고기, 또는 이 물고기의 살. 농엇과의 민물 식용어

perch² *v* **1** **be perched on/over etc.** to be in a position on top of or on the edge of something ‖ 어떤 것의 가장 꼭대기 또는 가장자리에 자리잡다: *a house perched on a hill* 언덕 위에 자리한 집 **2** **perch (yourself) on** to sit on top of or on the edge of something ‖ 어떤 것의 꼭대기 또는 가장자리에 앉다: *Wally perched on the gate and stared at us.* 월리는 문에 올라 앉아서 우리를 응시했다. **3** [I] if a bird perches on something, it sits on it ‖ 새가 어떤 것 위에 앉다

per·co·late /'pɚkə,leɪt/ v [I] if a liquid percolates through something, it passes slowly through a material that has small holes in it ‖ 액체가 작은 구멍이 있는 물체를 천천히 통과하다. 삼투하다

per·co·la·tor /'pɚkə,leɪtɚ/ n a pot in which coffee is made by passing hot water again and again through crushed coffee beans ‖ 으깬 커피콩에 뜨거운 물을 거듭 통과시켜 커피를 만드는 용기. 여과기

per·cus·sion /pɚ'kʌʃən/ n [U] the part of an ORCHESTRA that consists of drums and other related instruments ‖ 오케스트라에서 드럼과 동류의 다른 악기들로 구성된 부분. 타악기부

pe·remp·to·ry /pə'rɛmptəri/ adj FORMAL DISAPPROVING showing an expectation of being obeyed immediately ‖ 즉각적인 복종에 대한 기대를 나타내는. 단호한: a peremptory order 단호한 명령

pe·ren·ni·al¹ /pə'rɛniəl/ adj 1 happening again and again, or existing for a long time ‖ 되풀이하여 발생하거나 오랫동안 존재하는. 지속하는: the perennial problem of poverty 끊임없는 빈곤의 문제 2 a plant that is perennial lives for more than two years ‖ 식물이 2년 이상 사는. 다년생의

perennial² n a plant that lives for more than two years ‖ 2년 이상 사는 식물. 다년초. 다년생 식물

per·fect¹ /'pɚfɪkt/ adj 1 of the best possible type or standard ‖ 가능한 최고의 유형이나 기준의. 완벽한: They seemed to have a perfect marriage. 그들은 완벽한 결혼 생활을 하는 것처럼 보였다. 2 exactly right for a particular purpose ‖ 특정 목적에 정확히 맞는. 안성맞춤의: This rug's perfect for the living room. 이 깔개는 거실에 안성맞춤이다. / We've found the perfect place for a vacation. 우리는 휴가를 보내기에 안성맞춤인 장소를 발견했다. 3 complete and without any mistakes or problems ‖ 완전하고 어떠한 실수나 문제도 없는. 완전한. 순전한: a perfect diamond 순수한 다이아몬드 / a car in perfect condition 완벽한 상태의 자동차 / Your English is perfect. 너의 영어는 완벽하다. —opposite IMPERFECT¹ 4 complete or total ‖ 완전한, 전적인: She has a date with a perfect stranger. 그녀는 생판 모르는 사람과의 데이트가 있다. 5 **nobody's perfect** SPOKEN used when you are answering someone who has criticized you ‖ 자신을 비판하는 사람에게 대꾸할 때에 쓰여. 완

벽한 사람은 없다: Yes, I made a mistake – nobody's perfect. 그래, 내가 실수는 했지만 완벽한 사람은 없잖아.

per·fect² /pɚ'fɛkt/ v [T] to make something perfect or as good as you are able to ‖ 무엇을 완벽하게, 또는 할 수 있는 만큼 충실히 하다: She's spending a year in France to perfect her French. 그녀는 불어를 완벽하게 구사하기 위해 1년을 프랑스에서 보내는 중이다.

per·fect³ /'pɚfɪkt/ n TECHNICAL ⇨ FUTURE PERFECT, PAST PERFECT, PRESENT PERFECT

per·fec·tion /pɚ'fɛkʃən/ n [U] 1 the state of being perfect ‖ 완벽한 상태: Claire's parents demanded perfection from her. 클레어의 부모님은 그녀에게 완벽함을 요구했다. / The steak was cooked to perfection. 그 스테이크는 더할 나위 없이 요리가 잘 되었다. 2 the process of making something perfect ‖ 무엇을 완벽하게 만드는 과정. 숙달. 숙련: The perfection of the technology will take years. 그 기술이 완전한 경지에 이르려면 수년이 걸릴 것이다. 3 a perfect example of something ‖ 무엇의 완벽한 예: His acting is perfection. 그의 연기는 완벽하다.

per·fec·tion·ist /pɚ'fɛkʃənɪst/ n someone who is not satisfied with anything unless it is completely perfect ‖ 절대적으로 완벽하지 않으면 어떤 것에도 만족하지 않는 사람. 완벽주의자: You look fine. Don't be such a perfectionist. 너 좋아 보여. 그렇게 완벽주의자처럼 굴지 마.

per·fect·ly /'pɚfɪktli/ adv 1 in a perfect way ‖ 완벽하게: She's always perfectly dressed. 그녀는 늘 더할 나위 없이 멋지게 옷을 입는다. 2 a word meaning very or completely, used when you are annoyed about something ‖ 무엇에 대해 짜증날 때에 쓰여, 매우 또는 완전히를 뜻하는 단어: You know perfectly well what I'm talking about! 내가 무슨 말 하는지 너는 아주 잘 알고 있잖아!

per·fo·rat·ed /'pɚfə,reɪtɪd/ adj 1 a piece of paper that is perforated has a line of small holes in it so that part of it can be torn off easily ‖ 종이가 쉽게 찢어질 수 있게 작은 구멍들로 선을 낸. 바늘구멍이 송송 난 2 a part of your body that is perforated has had a hole torn in it ‖ 신체 부위가 찢어져 구멍이 생긴. 천공된: a perforated eardrum 천공된 고막 – **perforate** v [T]

per·form /pɚ'fɔrm/ v 1 [I, T] to do something to entertain people ‖ 사람들을

즐겁게 해주기 위해 무엇을 하다. 상연[공연]하다: *We saw "Hamlet" performed last week.* 우리는 지난주에 상연된 "햄릿"을 보았다. / *Karen will be performing with her band on Friday.* 카렌은 금요일에 자기의 밴드와 공연할 것이다. **2** [T] to do something such as a job or piece of work, especially something difficult or complicated ‖ 특히 어렵거나 복잡한 일 또는 작업 등을 하다. 실행하다. 해내다: *Surgeons can perform this operation in less than three hours.* 외과 의사들은 세 시간 이내로 이 수술을 해낼 수 있다. / *a minister performing a wedding ceremony* 결혼식을 집전하는 목사 **3 perform well/badly** if a machine performs well or badly, it works in that way ‖ 기계가 잘 돌아가다/잘 돌아가지 않다: *The bike performs well on mountain trails.* 그 자전거는 산길을 잘 달린다.

per·form·ance /pəˈfɔrməns/ *n* **1** an act of performing a play, piece of music etc., or the occasion when this is performed ‖ 연극·음악 등을 공연하는 행위, 또는 이것이 공연되는 때. 상연. 공연: *a beautiful performance of Swan Lake* 아름다운 공연 '백조의 호수' / *The next performance is at 8 o'clock.* 다음 공연은 8시에 있습니다. **2** [U] how successful someone or something is, and how well he, she, or it works ‖ 사람이나 사물의 성공 및 작동 정도. 성취. 성과. 성능: *The country's economic performance has been poor recently.* 그 국가의 경제적 성과[활동]는 최근에 약화되었다. / *The car's performance on wet roads was good.* 젖은 도로에서 그 자동차의 성능은 훌륭했다. **3** [U] the act of doing something, especially your work ‖ 특히 일을 수행하는 행위. 실행: *The accident occurred during the performance of his duties.* 그 사고는 그가 임무를 수행하는 동안 발생했다.

per·form·er /pəˈfɔrmər/ *n* an actor, musician etc. who performs to entertain people ‖ 사람들을 즐겁게 하기 위해 공연하는 배우·음악가 등. 공연자. 연기자. 연주자: *a circus performer* 서커스 공연자

per·form·ing arts /.ˌ.. ˈ./ *n* [plural] arts such as dance, music, or DRAMA, that are performed to entertain people ‖ 사람들을 즐겁게 하기 위해 공연되는 춤[음악, 드라마] 등의 예술. 무대[공연] 예술

per·fume /ˈpərfyum, pərˈfyum/ *n* [C, U] **1** a liquid with a strong pleasant smell, that you put on your skin ‖ 피부에 바르는, 기분 좋은 향기가 강하게 나는 액체. 향수: *What kind of perfume are you wearing?* 어떤 향수 뿌리고 있니? **2 a** pleasant smell ‖ 좋은 냄새. 향기: *the rose's sweet perfume* 장미의 달콤한 향기 – **perfumed** *adj* : *perfumed soap* 향기가 나는 비누

per·func·to·ry /pərˈfʌŋktəri/ *adj* done quickly, carelessly, and without interest ‖ 서둘러서 건성으로 흥미 없이 한. 형식적인: *The guard made a perfunctory check of the room and then left.* 그 감시인은 방을 형식적인 점검만 하고 나갔다. – **perfunctorily** *adj*

per·haps /pərˈhæps/ *adv* **1** possibly; MAYBE ‖ 아마; 囲 maybe: *"Where's Nancy?" "Perhaps she's caught in traffic."* "낸시 어디 있니?" "아마 교통 체증에 걸려 있을 거야." / *This is perhaps Irving's finest novel.* 이것이 아마도 어빙의 최고의 소설일 것이다. **2** SPOKEN used in order to politely ask or suggest something ‖ 무엇을 공손하게 요청하거나 제안하는 데에 쓰여. …하면 어떨까요: *Perhaps you'd like to join us?* 우리와 함께 하는 게 어떨까요?

USAGE NOTE perhaps, maybe, and **may be**

Use **perhaps** or **maybe** to talk about something that is possible. **Maybe** is usually used at the beginning of a sentence or CLAUSE : *Maybe we can get together this weekend.* **Perhaps** is a little more formal, and can be used in other places in a clause: *We can perhaps meet this weekend.* **May** is a modal verb that is sometimes used with the verb "be": *She may be here later.* **perhaps**와 **maybe**는 가능한 것을 언급하는 데에 쓰인다. **maybe**는 보통 문장이나 절의 처음에 쓰인다: 아마도 이번 주말에 우리는 모일 수 있을 것이다. **perhaps**는 다소 격식이 있는 표현으로 절의 다른 위치에 쓰일 수 있다: 우리는 아마도 이번 주말에 만날 수 있을 것이다. **may**는 조동사이며 때때로 "be" 동사와 함께 쓰인다: 그녀는 나중에 여기에 있을 수도 있다.

---

per·il /ˈpɛrəl/ *n* LITERARY **1** [U] danger of being harmed or killed ‖ 해를 입거나 살해당하는 위험: *Everyone feared that the sailors were in great peril.* 선원들이 큰 위험에 처하여 모두가 노심초사했다. **2 the perils of** the dangers involved in a particular activity ‖ 특정 행위에 관련된 위험: *They weren't aware of the perils of climbing a mountain alone.* 그들은 혼

자 등산하는 것에 대한 위험을 알지 못했다.

per·il·ous /ˈperələs/ *adj* LITERARY very dangerous ‖ 매우 위험한: *a perilous journey* 위험한 여행

pe·rim·e·ter /pəˈrɪmətər/ *n* **1** the border around an area of land ‖ 땅의 한 지역을 둘러싼 경계. 주위. 주변: *the perimeter of the airfield* 비행장 경내 **2** the whole length of the border around an area or shape ‖ 지역이나 윤곽을 둘러싼 경계의 전체 길이. 주위의 길이: *the perimeter of a triangle* 삼각형 둘레의 길이

pe·ri·od /ˈpɪriəd/ *n* **1** a length of time ‖ 시간의 길이. 기간: *the period from Christmas Day until New Year's Day* 크리스마스에서 설날까지의 기간 / *a 3-day waiting period for the purchase of a gun* 총기 구입을 위한 3일의 대기 기간 **2** a particular length of time in history or in a person's life ‖ 역사상, 또는 개인의 삶에서 특정한 때의 길이. 시기: *a short period of calm during the Civil War* 남북 전쟁 중 평온했던 짧은 시기 / *the blue period in Picasso's painting* 피카소 화법에서의 암울한 시기 **3** the monthly flow of blood from a woman's body ‖ 여성의 몸에서 한 달에 한 번 있는 출혈. 월경(기) **4** the mark (.) used in writing that shows the end of a sentence or an abbreviation ‖ 문장의 종결이나 약어를 나타내며 작문에 쓰이는 부호. 마침표. 생략점 **5** one of the equal parts that the school day is divided into ‖ 수업일을 동일하게 나눈 부분 중 하나. 수업 시간: *I have a history test during first/second/third period on Tuesday.* 나는 화요일 첫째[둘째, 셋째] 시간에 역사 시험을 친다. **6** one of the equal parts that a game is divided into in a sport such as hockey ‖ 하키 등의 스포츠에서 경기를 동일하게 나눈 부분 중 하나. (시합의 전반·후반 등의) 한 구분. 피리어드 **7** period! SPOKEN said when you have made a decision and you do not want to discuss the subject any more ‖ 결정을 내려서 그 주제에 대하여 더 이상 토론하고 싶지 않을 때에 쓰여. 더 이상 말하지 마!: *I just won't do it, period!* 나는 그냥 그것을 하지 않을 거야, 더 이상 말하지 마!

pe·ri·od·ic /ˌpɪriˈadɪk/, **periodical** *adj* happening again and again, usually at regular times ‖ 보통 규칙적으로 되풀이하여 발생하는. 정기적인: *Dale gets periodic headaches.* 데일은 주기적으로 머리가 아프다.

pe·ri·od·i·cal /ˌpɪriˈadɪkəl/ *n* a magazine, especially one about a serious or TECHNICAL subject ‖ 특히 진지하거나 전문적인 주제에 관한 잡지. 정기 간행물

pe·ri·od·i·cal·ly /ˌpɪriˈadɪkli/ *adv* happening again and again, usually at regular times ‖ 흔히 정기적으로 거듭 발생하여. 주기적으로: *The river periodically floods the valley.* 그 강은 주기적으로 계곡을 범람한다. / *Athletes are periodically tested for drugs.* 운동선수들은 정기적으로 약물 검사를 받는다.

periodic ta·ble /ˌ...ˌ.. ˈ../ *n* [singular] a specially arranged list of the ELEMENTs (=simple chemical substances) ‖ 원소들이 특수하게 나열된 표. 주기율표

pe·riph·e·ral¹ /pəˈrɪfərəl/ *adj* **1** relating to the main idea, question, activity etc., but less important than it ‖ 주요 생각·질문·활동 등과 관련되지만 그것보다 덜 중요한. 주위의: *The building of jet engines is a peripheral business for BMW.* 제트 엔진의 제조는 BMW사의 부수 사업이다. **2** in the outer area of something, or relating to an outer area ‖ 어떤 것의 외부에서, 또는 외부에 관련된: *the peripheral suburbs of a big city* 대도시 외곽의 교외 / *peripheral vision* (=what you can see to the side of you when you look straight ahead) (똑바로 정면을 볼 때 그 측면을 볼 수 있는) 주변시 **3** peripheral equipment can be connected to a computer and used with it ‖ 장비가 컴퓨터에 연결되어 컴퓨터와 함께 쓸 수 있는. 주변 장치의

peripheral² *n* a piece of equipment that is connected to a computer and used with it ‖ 컴퓨터에 연결되어 컴퓨터와 함께 사용되는 기기. 주변 기기

pe·riph·er·y /pəˈrɪfəri/ *n* the outside area or edge of something ‖ 어떤 것의 외부나 가장자리. 주변: *a new neighborhood on the periphery of the city* 도시 주변의 새로운 근린(近隣) 지역 —compare OUTSKIRTS

per·i·scope /ˈperəˌskoʊp/ *n* a long tube with mirrors fitted in it that is used for looking over the top of something, especially in a SUBMARINE ‖ 특히 잠수함에서 어떤 면 위쪽을 보는 데에 쓰이는, 속에 거울이 장착된 긴 관. 잠망경

periscope

per·ish /ˈpɛrɪʃ/ v [I] LITERARY to die ‖ 죽다: *Hundreds perished when the Titanic sank.* 타이타닉 호가 침몰했을 때 수백 명이 사망했다.

per·ish·a·ble /ˈpɛrɪʃəbəl/ adj food that is perishable can become bad quickly ‖ 음식이 빨리 상할 수 있는. 썩기 쉬운: *milk and other perishable items* 우유와 상하기 쉬운 다른 물품들 – **perishables** n [plural]

per·jure /ˈpɚdʒɚ/ v [I] **perjure yourself** to tell a lie in a court of law ‖ 법정에서 거짓말하다. 위증하다

per·ju·ry /ˈpɚdʒəri/ n [U] the crime of telling a lie in a court of law ‖ 법정에서 거짓말을 하는 죄. 위증죄

perk¹ /pɚk/ n money, goods, or other advantages that you get from your work in addition to your pay ‖ 월급 이외에 추가적으로 직장에서 받는 돈[물건, 다른 이익]. 부수입: *A car and travel expenses are perks of the job.* 자동차와 여행 경비는 그 일의 부수입들이다.

perk² v [I, T] INFORMAL to make coffee using a PERCOLATOR ‖ 퍼컬레이터를 써서 커피를 만들다. 퍼컬레이터로 끓이다

perk up phr v **1** [I, T **perk** sb ↔ **up**] to become more cheerful and interested in what is happening around you, or to make someone feel this way ‖ 더 활기를 띠고 주변에서 일어나는 것에 흥미를 갖게 되다, 또는 어떤 사람을 이렇게 만들다. 생기가 돌다[돌게 하다]: *Meg perked up when the music started.* 메그는 음악이 나오기 시작하자 생기가 돌았다. / *A cup of tea will perk you up.* 차 한 잔이 너를 기운나게 할 거야. **2** [I, T **perk** sth ↔ **up**] to become better, more interesting etc., or to make something do this ‖ 더 좋아지거나 더 재미있어지다, 또는 무엇을 이렇게 되도록 만들다: *Lower interest rates may be needed to perk up the economy.* 경제를 활성화하기 위해서는 이율을 더 낮추는 것이 필요할지도 모른다.

perk·y /ˈpɚki/ adj cheerful and full of interest ‖ 활발하고 흥미로 가득 찬: *a perky little girl* 발랄한 작은 소녀

perm¹ /pɚm/ n a way of putting curls into straight hair by treating it with chemicals ‖ 화학 약품으로 처리하여 곧은 머리카락을 곱슬거리게 하는 법. 파마: *Debbie's getting a perm today.* 데비는 오늘 파마를 할 거다.

perm² v [T] to put curls into straight hair using chemicals ‖ 화학 약품을 써서 곧은 머리카락을 곱슬거리게 만들다. 파마하다: *Did you have your hair permed?* 너 파마했니?

per·ma·nent¹ /ˈpɚmənənt/ adj continuing to exist for a long time or for all time ‖ 오랫동안 또는 지속적으로 계속 존재하는. 영구한: *a permanent job* 종신직 / *The UN Security Council has five permanent members.* UN 안전 보장 이사회에는 5개국의 상임 이사국이 있다. – **permanence** n [U] —compare TEMPORARY

permanent² n ⇨ PERM¹

per·ma·nent·ly /ˈpɚmənəntli/ adv always, or for a very long time ‖ 항상, 아주 오랫동안. 영구히: *Do you plan to live here permanently?* 당신은 영구히 여기에 살 생각입니까? / *The school has been permanently closed.* 그 학교는 영구히 폐교되었다.

per·me·ate /ˈpɚmiˌeɪt/ v [I, T] to spread through every part of something ‖ 어떤 곳의 전 지역에 퍼지다: *The smell of smoke permeated the house.* 담배 냄새가 온 집안에 퍼졌다.

per·mis·si·ble /pɚˈmɪsəbəl/ adj FORMAL allowed by law or by the rules ‖ 법이나 규칙에 의해 허용된: *In some religions, divorce is not permissible.* 어떤 종교에서는 이혼이 허용되지 않는다.

per·mis·sion /pɚˈmɪʃən/ n [U] the act of allowing someone to do something ‖ 누가 무엇을 하도록 허락하는 행위. 허가: *You have to ask permission if you want to leave class early.* 만일 네가 조퇴하길 바란다면 허가를 받아야 한다. / *Did your dad give you permission to use the car?* 너희 아빠가 그 차를 쓰라고 허락하셨니? ✗DON'T SAY "the permission."✗ "the permission"처럼 정관사를 붙여 사용하지는 않는다.

per·mis·sive /pɚˈmɪsɪv/ adj allowing actions or behavior that many people disapprove of ‖ 많은 사람들이 용인하지 않는 행위나 행동을 허용하는. 자유방임의. 관대한: *the permissive society of the 1970s* 1970년대의 자유방임 사회

per·mit¹ /pɚˈmɪt/ v **-tted, -tting** FORMAL **1** [T] to allow something to happen, especially by a rule or law ‖ 특히 규칙이나 법률로 어떤 일이 발생하는 것을 허락하다: *Smoking is not permitted inside the building.* 건물 내의 흡연은 허용되지 않습니다. **2** [I] to make it possible for something to happen ‖ 일이 발생하는 것을 가능하게 하다. 허용하다: *We'll probably go to the beach, weather permitting.* (=if the weather is good enough) 날씨가 좋으면 아마도 우리는 해변에 갈 것이다.

per·mit² /ˈpəʳmɪt/ *n* an official written statement giving you the right to do something ‖ 어떤 것을 할 권리를 주는 공식 서면 증명서. 허가증: *You can't park here without a permit.* 당신은 허가증 없이 여기에 주차할 수 없습니다. / *a travel/work permit* 여행[취로] 허가증

per·mu·ta·tion /ˌpəʳmyʊˈteɪʃən/ *n* one of the different ways in which a set of things can be arranged, or put together to make something else ‖ 일련의 사물들을 정렬하거나 조합하여 다른 것을 만들 수 있는 여러 방법 중 하나. 순열. 변경: *Over the years, I've found several permutations of this recipe.* 수년에 걸쳐 나는 이 조리법의 몇 가지 변형을 알게 되었다.

per·ni·cious /pəʳˈnɪʃəs/ *adj* FORMAL very harmful, especially in a way that is not easily noticeable ‖ 특히 쉽게 알아챌 수 없게 매우 해로운. 파멸적인. 치명적인: *the pernicious effect of racial segregation in schools* 교내 인종 차별의 치명적인 결과

per·ox·ide /pəˈrɑk̩ˌsaɪd/ *n* [U] a chemical liquid used in order to make dark hair lighter, or to kill BACTERIA ‖ 검은 머리카락을 밝게 만들거나 박테리아를 죽이는 데에 쓰이는 화학 용액. 과산화물

per·pen·dic·u·lar /ˌpəʳpənˈdɪkyələʳ/ *adj* **1 be perpendicular to** if one line is perpendicular to another line, they form an angle of 90° ‖ 한 선이 다른 선과 90°의 각도를 형성하다. 직각을 이루다 **2** exactly upright and not leaning to one side or the other ‖ 정확히 똑바로 서서 한 쪽 또는 다른 쪽으로 기울지 않은. 직립한: *a perpendicular pole* 곧추선 장대 — compare HORIZONTAL, VERTICAL

per·pe·trate /ˈpəʳpəˌtreɪt/ *v* [T] FORMAL to do something that is morally or legally wrong ‖ 도덕적으로나 법적으로 잘못된 짓을 하다. (과실을) 범하다. 저지르다: *Goodwin denied he had perpetrated the fraud.* 굳윈은 자기가 사기를 쳤다는 것을 부인했다.

per·pe·tra·tor /ˈpəʳpəˌtreɪtəʳ/ *n* FORMAL someone who does something that is a crime ‖ 범죄를 저지른 사람. 범인

per·pet·u·al /pəʳˈpɛtʃuəl/ *adj* **1** continuing all the time without changing ‖ 변함없이 항상 지속되는. 영구적인: *the perpetual noise of the machinery* 끊임없는 기계의 소음 **2** repeated many times in a way that annoys you ‖ 귀찮게 여러 번 되풀이되는: *I'm tired of her perpetual complaining.* 나는 그녀의 끊임없는 불평에 신물이 난다. **– perpetually** *adv*

per·pet·u·ate /pəʳˈpɛtʃuˌeɪt/ *v* [T] to make something continue ‖ 무엇을 계속하게 하다: *We are trying to get rid of books that perpetuate stereotypes.* 우리는 고정 관념을 영속시키는 책들을 없애려고 하고 있다.

per·plex /pəʳˈplɛks/ *v* [T] a problem that perplexes you, confuses you and worries you because it is difficult to understand ‖ 문제가 이해하기 어렵기 때문에 혼란스럽고 걱정하게 하다. 당황하게 하다: *Shea's symptoms perplexed the doctors.* 쉐아의 증상은 의사들을 당황하게 했다. **– perplexed** *adj* **– perplexity** *n* [U]

per·qui·site /ˈpəʳkwəzɪt/ *n* FORMAL ⇨ PERK¹

per se /ˌpəʳ ˈseɪ/ *adv* LATIN used in order to show that something is being considered alone, apart from anything else ‖ 사물이 다른 것과 별도로 단독적인 것으로 간주되고 있음을 나타내는 데에 쓰여. 스스로. 그것 자체가: *Money, per se, is not usually why people change jobs.* 돈 자체는 사람들이 보통 직업을 바꾸는 이유가 아니다.

per·se·cute /ˈpəʳsɪˌkyut/ *v* [T] **1** to treat someone cruelly and unfairly, especially because of his/her religious or political beliefs ‖ 특히 종교적이거나 정치적인 신념 때문에 남을 잔인하고 불공정하게 대하다. 박해하다: *a writer persecuted for criticizing the government* 정부를 비판하여 박해받는 작가 **2** to deliberately cause trouble for someone ‖ 누군가에게 고의적으로 문제를 일으키다. 귀찮게 하다: *Duke said he was being persecuted by a hostile media.* 듀크는 적대적인 언론 매체에 의해 박해받고 있는 중이라고 말했다. **– persecutor** *n*

per·se·cu·tion /ˌpəʳsɪˈkyuʃən/ *n* [U] the act of persecuting (PERSECUTE) someone ‖ 누군가를 박해하는 행위: *Several religious groups suffered persecution under the old Communist regime.* 몇몇 종교 단체들은 구 공산주의 치하에서 박해로 고통받았다.

per·se·ver·ance /ˌpəʳsəˈvɪrəns/ *n* [U] determination to keep trying to do something difficult ‖ 어려운 일을 하기 위해 계속 노력하려는 결단. 인내. 끈기: *You have to admire the perseverance and skill required to build a road through the pass.* 너는 고개를 관통하는 도로를 건설하는 데에 필요한 인내와 기술을 높이 평가해야 한다.

per·se·vere /ˌpəʳsəˈvɪr/ *v* [I] to continue trying to do something difficult in a determined way ‖ 결단력 있게 어려운 일을 하기 위해 계속해서 노력하다. … 을 버티어 내다: *Jeff persevered in his efforts to learn how to ski*. 제프는 스키 타는 법을 배우기 위해 끊임없이 노력했다.

per·sist /pərˈsɪst/ *v* [I] **1** to continue to do something, even though it is difficult or other people do not like it ‖ 어렵거나 다른 사람들이 좋아하지 않을지라도 어떤 것을 계속해서 하다. …을 고집하다: *Her boss persisted in his efforts to ask her for a date*. 그녀의 상사는 끈덕지게 그녀에게 데이트 요청을 했다. **2** to continue to exist or happen ‖ 계속해서 존재하거나 발생하다. 지속하다: *The pain persisted for months, even though the injury had healed*. 부상이 치료되었는데도 고통은 수개월 동안 지속되었다.

per·sist·ence /pərˈsɪstəns/ *n* [U] the act or state of being PERSISTENT ‖ 끈덕진 행동이나 상태. 끈기. 고집: *Brancusi's persistence was finally rewarded with a small part in a TV show*. 브란쿠시는 끈기로 결국 TV 쇼에서 작은 배역을 따냈다.

per·sist·ent /pərˈsɪstənt/ *adj* **1** continuing to exist or happen, especially for longer than is usual ‖ 특히 평소보다 더 오래 끊임없이 존재하거나 일어나는. 지속하는: *Congress needs to address the problem of persistent unemployment*. 의회는 지속적인 실업 문제를 검토할 필요가 있다. **2** continuing to do something even though it is difficult or other people oppose it ‖ 어렵거나 다른 사람이 반대해도 끊임없이 무엇을 계속하는. 끝까지 해내는. 고집하는: *You may not be able to find them easily, but be persistent*. 너는 그것들을 쉽게 찾을 수는 없을지 모르지만 끝까지 해보아라. – **persistently** *adv*: *He persistently denies doing anything wrong*. 그는 잘못한 것이 없다고 끝까지 부인한다.

per·son /ˈpərsən/ *n, plural* **people 1 a** man, woman, or child ‖ 한 명의 남자나 여자, 또는 아이. 사람: *Bert's kind of a hard person to talk to*. 버트는 같이 대화하기 어려운 사람이다. / *Abby's a computer/cat etc. person*. (=someone who likes computers, cats etc.) 애비는 컴퓨터[고양이] 애호가이다. **2 in person** if you do something in person, you do it when you are in a place, not by using a letter or the telephone ‖ 편지 또는 전화를 사용하지 않고 어떤 장소에 있으면서 직접 하는. 몸소. 직접: *You'll have to apply for your passport in person*. 너는 너의 여권을 직접 신청해야 할 것이다. —

see also FIRST PERSON, SECOND PERSON, THIRD PERSON

USAGE NOTE person, persons, people, and peoples

Person means one man, woman, or child: *She's a really generous person*. The plural of **person** is **persons**, but this is only used in very official language. When talking about more than one person, use **people** as the plural: *There were about 100 people at the wedding*. **People** is also a countable noun that means a particular race or group that lives in a particular country. The plural is **peoples**: *the peoples of the Caribbean*.

person은 한 명의 남자나 여자, 또는 아이를 의미한다: 그녀는 정말 관대한 사람이다. **person**의 복수형은 **persons**이지만 이것은 단지 매우 공식적인 표현으로 쓰인다. 한 명 이상에 대해 말할 때는 복수형으로 **people**을 사용한다: 결혼식에 약 100명의 사람들이 참석했다. **people**은 또한 가산 명사로서 특정 국가에 사는 특정 민족이나 집단을 뜻하기도 한다. 복수형은 **peoples**이다: 카리브 해의 여러 민족들

---

per·so·na /pərˈsoʊnə/ *n, plural* **personas** *or* **personae** /-ni/ the way you behave when you are with other people ‖ 다른 사람들과 함께 있을 때의 행동 방식. 페르소나. 남에 대한 태도. 가면. 외적 인격: *You always wonder how different movie stars are from their public personas*. 사람들은 항상 영화배우들의 겉모습과 실제 모습이 얼마나 다른지 궁금해 한다.

per·son·a·ble /ˈpərsənəbəl/ *adj* having a pleasant way of talking and behaving ‖ 상냥하게 말하고 행동하는. 친밀감이 있는: *Beth is a charming personable young woman*. 베스는 매력적이고 상냥한 젊은 여성이다.

per·son·al /ˈpərsənəl/ *adj* **1 ▶RELATING TO YOU** 자신에 관련한◀ belonging to you, or relating to what you know, have done, have experienced etc. ‖ 자신에 속하거나 자신이 아는 것·행한 것·경험한 것 등에 관한. 일신상의: *Please keep all bags and other personal belongings with you*. 모든 가방과 기타 개인 소지품들을 여러분이 보관하세요. / *These women know from personal experience about the problems facing*

single mothers. 이 여성들은 미혼모가 직면하는 문제에 대해 자신의 경험을 통해 알고 있다.
2 ▶PRIVATE 사적인◀ private and concerning only you ‖ 사적이며 오직 자신에 관한: *That's a personal question.* (=a question about things that are private) 그것은 사적인 질문이다. / *Owen has a lot of personal problems.* 오웬은 사적인 문제를 많이 갖고 있다.
3 ▶ONLY YOU 자신만의◀ used in order to emphasize that no one else did or will do something ‖ 본인 외의 다른 누구도 어떤 일을 했거나 할 사람이 없다는 점을 강조하는 데에 쓰여. 몸소[직접] 하는: *Whoopi Goldberg made a personal appearance at the charity event.* 우피 골드버그는 자선 행사에 자신이 직접 참석했다. / *I will give this my personal attention.* 나는 이것에 직접 관심을 기울일 것이다.
4 ▶CRITICISM 비난◀ involving rude or upsetting criticism of someone ‖ 누군가에 대한 무례하거나 화나게 하는 비난이 담긴. 인신 공격의: *Making personal remarks like that isn't professional.* 그 같은 인신 공격을 하는 것은 전문가답지 않다. / *It's nothing personal* (=I am not criticizing you) – *I just don't agree with you.* 나는 너를 비난하지 않아, 단지 너에게 동의하지 않을 뿐이야.
5 personal friend someone you know well, especially someone famous or important ‖ 특히 유명하거나 중요한 잘 알고 있는 사람. 개인적인 친구: *The editor is a personal friend of his.* 그 편집자는 그의 개인적인 친구이다.
6 ▶NOT WORK 일과 관련 없는◀ not relating to your work or business ‖ 일 또는 업무와 관련이 없는: *We're not allowed to make personal phone calls at work.* 우리는 직장에서 개인적인 전화 통화를 하는 것은 허락되지 않는다.
7 ▶YOUR BODY 신체◀ relating to your body or the way you look ‖ 자신의 신체나 모습과 관련된. 신체의, 외관의: *personal hygiene* 개인 위생
personal com·put·er /,... '../ *n* ⇨ PC

per·son·al·i·ty /ˌpɚsəˈnæləti/ *n* **1** [C, U] someone's character, especially the way s/he behaves toward other people ‖ 사람의 기질, 특히 다른 사람에게 행동하는 방식. 성격: *Alice has an outgoing personality.* 앨리스는 외향적인 성격이다. **2** someone who is well known to the public ‖ 대중에게 잘 알려진 사람. 명사: *a TV personality* TV 명사 **3** [U] INFORMAL

the qualities that make someone or something interesting ‖ 사람이나 사물을 흥미 있게 만드는 특성. 개성. 매력: *We liked the name because we thought it had personality.* 우리는 개성이 있다고 생각하여 그 이름을 좋아했다.
per·son·al·ize /ˈpɚsənəˌlaɪz/ *v* **1** to put your name or INITIALs on something ‖ 어떤 것에 자신의 이름 또는 머리글자를 표시하다: *I hate cars with personalized license plates.* 나는 이름이 들어간 번호판을 가진 자동차를 싫어한다. **2** to decorate something in a way you like ‖ 좋아하는 방식으로 어떤 것을 장식하다. 개인의 기호에 맞추다: *Becky has personalized her office with photos and drawings.* 베키는 자기의 사무실을 사진과 그림으로 취향에 맞게 꾸몄다. **3** to make something suitable for what a particular person needs ‖ 어떤 것을 특정인의 요구에 적합하게 만들다. 개인화하다: *a school that personalizes language courses* 어학 교육 과정을 개인에 맞추는 학교 **4** to talk about and criticize people rather than dealing with facts ‖ 사실을 다루기 보다는 사람들을 거론하며 비난하다. 인신공격하다: *Both candidates began personalizing the campaign.* 양 후보들은 상호 비방전을 시작했다.
per·son·al·ly /ˈpɚsənəli/ *adv* **1** SPOKEN used in order to emphasize that you are only giving your own opinion ‖ 단지 본인의 의견을 제시한다는 것을 강조하는 데에 쓰여. 나로서는: *Personally, I don't like horror movies.* 개인적으로, 나는 공포 영화를 좋아하지 않는다. **2** doing or having done something yourself ‖ 무엇을 자기 스스로 하고 있거나 해오고 있는. 몸소. 직접: *She's personally responsible for all the arrangements.* 그녀가 직접 모든 준비에 책임을 진다. **3** said as a criticism of someone's character or appearance ‖ 남의 성격이나 외모에 대한 비평으로 말하여. 개인을 빗대어 말한 것으로: *Dora's in a bad mood – don't take anything she says personally.* (=don't think that she is criticizing you) 도라는 기분이 나쁘거든. 그녀가 한 말을 너를 빗대어 한 것이라고 생각하지 마라. **4** as a friend, or as someone you have met ‖ 친구로서, 또는 만났던 사람으로서. 사적으로. 개인적으로: *I don't know her personally, but I like her books.* 나는 그녀를 개인적으로는 알지 못하지만 그녀의 책들을 좋아한다.
personal pro·noun /,... '../ *n* TECHNICAL in grammar, a PRONOUN used for the person who is speaking, being

spoken to, or being spoken about, such as "I," "you," and "they" ‖ 문법에서 "I," "you," "they" 등의 말을 하는 사람이나 말을 나누고 있는 상대, 또는 언급되는 대상을 가리키는 대명사. 인칭 대명사

per·so·nals /'pɜsənəlz/ *n* **the personals** a part of a newspaper in which people can have private messages printed ‖ 신문에서 사람들이 사적인 메시지를 실을 수 있는 부분. 신문의 개인 소식란

per·son·i·fi·ca·tion /pɜˌsɑnəfə'keɪʃən/ *n* **1 the personification of** someone who has a lot of a particular quality, so that s/he is used as an example of that quality ‖ 특정한 속성을 많이 지니고 있어서 그 속성의 본보기로 쓰이는 사람. …의 상징 [화신]: *Mrs. Grant is the personification of kindness.* 그랜트 부인은 친절한 사람의 전형이다. **2 [C, U]** the representation of a thing or a quality as a person ‖ 사물이나 속성을 사람에 비겨서 표현함. 의인화: *the personification of Justice as a woman holding scales* 정의를 저울을 들고 있는 여자로 의인화함

per·son·i·fy /pɜ'sɑnəˌfaɪ/ *v* [T] **1** to think of or represent a quality or thing as a person ‖ 속성이나 사물을 사람으로 간주하거나 표현하다. 의인화하다: *Time is usually personified as an old man with a beard.* 시간은 흔히 턱수염이 있는 늙은 남자로 의인화된다. **2** to represent a particular quality or thing by being a typical example of it ‖ 어떤 것의 전형적인 예가 되어 특정한 속성이나 사물을 나타내다. 상징하다: *Nathan personifies truthfulness.* 네이선은 진실의 상징이다.

per·son·nel /ˌpɜsə'nɛl/ *n* **1 [plural]** the people who work in a company or for a particular kind of employer ‖ 한 기업에서 일하는 사람들, 또는 특정한 고용주를 위해 일하는 사람들. 전(全) 직원: *All personnel need to have identification cards.* 전 직원은 신분증을 소지해야 한다. / *military personnel* 군인 **2 [U]** ⇨ HUMAN RESOURCES

per·spec·tive /pɜ'spɛktɪv/ *n* **1** a way of thinking about something that is influenced by the type of person you are or the work you do ‖ 자신 같은 사람이나 자신이 하는 일에 의해 좌우되는 사물에 대한 사고 방식. 관점. 견해: *We'll need to ask Dr. Havani for a scientific perspective on the problem.* 우리는 그 문제에 대한 과학적인 견해를 하바니 박사님께 여쭤볼 필요가 있을 것이다. **2 [U]** the ability to think about something

sensibly, so that it does not seem worse than it is ‖ 사물을 분별 있게 생각하여 실제보다 나쁘게 보지 않는 능력. 전체적으로 올바르게 보는 능력: *She's having trouble keeping her problems in perspective.* 그녀는 계속해서 자신의 문제를 올바로 파악하는 데 어려움을 겪고 있다. **3 [U]** a method of drawing a picture that makes objects look solid and shows distance and depth ‖ 물체를 입체적으로 보이게 하고 거리와 깊이가 나타나도록 그림을 그리는 기법. 원근법: *Children's drawings often have no perspective.* 흔히 아이들의 그림에는 원근 감이 없다.

per·spi·ra·tion /ˌpɜspə'reɪʃən/ *n* [U] FORMAL ⇨ SWEAT[2]

per·spire /pɜ'spaɪɜ/ *v* [I] FORMAL ⇨ SWEAT[1]

per·suade /pɜ'sweɪd/ *v* [T] **1** to make someone decide to do something by giving good reasons ‖ 합당한 근거를 제시하여 누군가에게 무엇을 할 결심을 하게 하다. …을 설득하다: *Ken finally persuaded Jo to apply for the job.* 켄은 마침내 그 일에 지원하도록 조를 설득했다. **2** to make someone believe something or feel sure about something; CONVINCE ‖ 누군가에게 무엇을 믿게 하다, 또는 무엇에 대해 확신을 갖게 하다. 확신시키다; 偧 convince: *She persuaded the jury (that) her client was not guilty.* 그녀는 배심원단에게 자신이 변호하는 피고인이 무죄라는 것을 믿게 하였다. / *Valdez believed he could persuade any reporter of anything.* 발데즈는 그가 어느 기자에게나 어떤 것도 납득시킬 수 있을 것이라고 믿었다.

per·sua·sion /pɜ'sweɪʒən/ *n* **1 [U]** the act or skill of persuading someone to do something ‖ 누군가에게 무엇을 하도록 설득하는 행위나 솜씨. 설득(력): *With a little persuasion, Debbie agreed to come with us.* 약간의 설득으로 데비는 우리와 함께 가는 것에 동의했다. **2** a particular belief, especially a political or religious one ‖ 특히 정치적이거나 종교적인 특정한 신념. 신앙. 신조: *Jake and his brother are of different political persuasions.* 제이크와 그의 형은 정치적 신념이 다르다.

per·sua·sive /pɜ'sweɪsɪv/ *adj* able to influence other people to believe or do something ‖ 다른 사람들이 무엇을 믿거나 하도록 영향을 줄 수 있는. 설득력 있는: *a number of persuasive arguments* 수많은 설득력 있는 논의들 / *Erin can be very persuasive.* 에린은 매우 설득력이 있다.

pert /pɚt/ adj 1 amusing in a way that shows a slight lack of respect ‖ 존중함이 다소 없는 듯이 보이면서 웃기는. 버릇없는. 까부는: a pert answer 버릇없는 대답 2 neat and attractive in a cheerful way ‖ 기분 좋게 세련되고 매력적인. 멋진: a pert red ribbon in her hair 그녀 머리의 멋진 빨간 리본

per·tain /pɚˈteɪn/ v

pertain to sth phr v [T] FORMAL to relate directly to something ‖ 무엇에 직접적으로 관련되다: laws pertaining to welfare benefits 복지 수당에 관련되는 법

per·ti·nent /ˈpɚtn-ənt/ adj FORMAL directly relating to something that is being considered; RELEVANT ‖ 고려 중인 것에 직접적인 관계가 있는. 관련된; 유 relevant: Reporters asked a few pertinent questions. 기자들은 몇 가지 관련 질문을 했다.

per·turbed /pɚˈtɚbd/ adj FORMAL worried and annoyed ‖ 걱정되고 초조한. 불안한. 당황한: Kerry was perturbed that the doctors only allowed her to talk to her father for ten minutes. 케리는 의사들이 자신에게 단지 10분 동안만 아버지와 이야기하도록 허락해서 당황했다. – perturb v [T]

pe·ruse /pəˈruz/ v [T] FORMAL to read something in a careful way ‖ 주의 깊게 무엇을 읽다. …을 정독하다: an evening spent perusing the job advertisements 구인광고를 자세히 들여다보면서 보낸 저녁 시간 – perusal n [U]

per·vade /pɚˈveɪd/ v [T] to be in all parts of something ‖ 사물의 곳곳에 있다. 퍼지다. 배어들다: The smoke from the factory pervaded the city. 공장의 연기가 그 도시에 온통 퍼졌다.

per·va·sive /pɚˈveɪsɪv/ adj existing or spreading everywhere ‖ 모든 장소에 존재하거나 퍼지는: a pervasive fear of crime 범죄에 대한 만연한 공포

per·verse /pɚˈvɚs/ adj behaving in an unreasonable way by doing the opposite of what people want you to do ‖ 사람들이 자신에게 하기 원하는 것과 반대로 하여 비이성적으로 행동하는. 비뚤어진: He takes perverse pleasure in arguing with everyone. 그는 모든 사람과 타투는 데에서 비뚤어진 즐거움을 얻는다.

per·ver·sion /pɚˈvɚʒən/ n [C, U] 1 a type of sexual behavior that is considered unnatural and unacceptable ‖ 부자연스럽고 용납할 수 없는 것으로 간주되는 성적 행동 유형. 성도착 2 the act of changing something so that it is no longer right, reasonable, or true ‖ 더 이상 옳지 않거나 합리적이지 않게, 또는 사실이 아니게 어떤 것을 변화시키는 행동. 왜곡. 곡해: a perversion of the truth 진실의 왜곡

per·vert[1] /pɚˈvɚt/ v [T] to change someone or something in a harmful way ‖ 사람이나 사물을 해롭게 변화시키다. 왜곡[곡해]시키다. 그르치다: These genetic experiments pervert nature. 이 유전자 실험들은 자연을 왜곡시킨다.

per·vert[2] /ˈpɚvɚt/ n someone whose sexual behavior is considered unnatural and unacceptable ‖ 부자연스럽고 용납할 수 없는 것으로 간주되는 성적 행동을 하는 사람. 변태. 성도착자

per·vert·ed /pɚˈvɚtɪd/ adj 1 relating to unacceptable and unnatural sexual thoughts or behavior ‖ 용납할 수 없고 부자연스러운 성적 사고나 행동에 관련된. 변태의: They were the most perverted pictures I had ever seen! 내가 본 것 중에 그것들은 가장 변태적인 그림들이었어! 2 morally wrong or unnatural ‖ 도덕적으로 옳지 않거나 부자연스러운. 왜곡된: perverted logic 왜곡된 논리

pes·ky /ˈpɛski/ adj INFORMAL annoying and causing trouble ‖ 짜증나게 하고 문제를 야기하는. 성가신. 귀찮은: a pesky fly 성가신 파리

pes·si·mism /ˈpɛsəˌmɪzəm/ n [U] the feeling of being PESSIMISTIC ‖ 비관적인 느낌. 비관. 염세(주의): There is a lot of pessimism in the country about the economy. 국내에서는 경제에 대한 비관론이 상당히 있다.

pes·si·mist /ˈpɛsəmɪst/ n someone who always expects that the worst thing will happen ‖ 항상 나쁜 일이 일어나리라고 예상하는 사람. 염세주의자: Don't be such a pessimist – things will work out. 염세주의자처럼 굴지 마. 만사가 잘 풀릴 거야 —opposite OPTIMIST

pes·si·mis·tic /ˌpɛsəˈmɪstɪk/ adj expecting that bad things will happen or that a situation will have a bad result ‖ 나쁜 일이 일어나리라고, 또는 상황이 나쁜 결과를 가져오리라고 예상하는. 비관적인. 염세적인: Jonathan is pessimistic about his chances. 조나단은 자신의 가능성에 대해 비관적이다. —opposite OPTIMISTIC

pest /pɛst/ n 1 a small animal or insect that destroys crops or food ‖ 농작물이나 식품을 못쓰게 만드는 작은 동물이나 곤충. 해충 2 INFORMAL an annoying person ‖ 성가신 사람: The kids next door can be real pests. 옆집 아이들은 정말 골칫거리일지 모른다.

pes·ter /'pɛstə/ v [T] to annoy someone by asking for something again and again ‖ 어떤 것을 거듭 요청하여 남을 괴롭히다. 조르다: *Lisa pestered her mother to let her go swimming.* 리사는 어머니에게 수영하러 가게 해달라고 졸랐다.

pes·ti·cide /'pɛstə,saɪd/ n a chemical substance that kills insects that destroy crops ‖ 농작물을 망치는 곤충들을 죽이는 화학 물질. 살충제

pet¹ /pɛt/ n an animal that you keep at home ‖ 집에서 기르는 동물. 애완동물: *Do you have any pets?* 너 애완동물 있니? —see also TEACHER'S PET

pet² v [T] **1** to move your hand over an animal's fur, in order to show it affection ‖ 애정을 보이려고 동물의 털을 손으로 쓰다듬다. 귀여워하다 **2** to kiss and touch someone in a sexual way ‖ 어떤 사람에게 성적으로 키스하며 만지다. 애무하다

pet³ adj **1** **pet project/subject etc.** a plan, subject etc. that you particularly like or are interested in ‖ 특히 좋아하거나 흥미 있는 계획·주제 등: *Congressmen are always looking for funding for their pet projects.* 국회의원들은 항상 자신들의 마음에 드는 프로젝트에 대한 재정적 지출을 모색하고 있다. **2** a pet animal is one that someone keeps at home ‖ 사람이 동물을 집에서 기르는. 애완의: *a pet hamster* 애완용 햄스터 **3** **pet peeve** something that always annoys you, that may not annoy other people ‖ 다른 사람들을 괴롭히지는 않을지라도, 자신을 항상 괴롭히는 것. 싫어하는 것: *One of my pet peeves is people being late for meetings.* 내가 싫어하는 것 중 하나는 회의에 지각하는 사람들이다.

pet·al /'pɛtl/ n the colored part of a flower that is shaped like a leaf ‖ 잎처럼 생긴, 꽃의 색깔을 띤 부분. 꽃잎: *Sunflowers have large petals.* 해바라기는 꽃잎이 크다.

pe·ter /'pitə/ v [I]

peter out phr v [I] to gradually become smaller, fewer, quieter etc. and then no longer exist or happen ‖ 크기·양·소리 등이 점점 줄어들어 더 이상 존재하거나 일어나지 않다. 점점 쇠하여 없어지다: *The trail became narrower and eventually petered out altogether.* 그 오솔길은 점점 좁아지다가 결국엔 완전히 없어졌다.

pe·tite /pə'tit/ adj a woman who is petite is short and thin in an attractive way ‖ 여성이 매력적으로 작고 마른 way. 꽃잎이 크다.

pe·ti·tion¹ /pə'tɪʃən/ v [I, T] to formally ask someone in authority to do something, especially by sending him/her a PETITION ‖ 특히 청원서를 보내는 방식으로 어떤 일을 하기 위해 권한이 있는 사람에게 공식적으로 요청하다. …을 청원하다: *Residents are petitioning against a new prison in the area.* 주민들은 그 지역 내의 새로운 교도소에 반대하는 청원을 하고 있다.

petition² n a piece of paper that asks someone in authority to do or change something, and is signed by a lot of people ‖ 어떤 일을 하거나 변경시키기 위해 많은 사람들의 서명을 받아 권한이 있는 사람에게 요청하는 문서. 청원서: *Will you sign a petition against nuclear testing?* 핵실험에 반대하는 청원서에 서명하시겠습니까? / *Locals drew up a petition to protest the building of a new highway.* 지역민들은 새로운 간선도로로 건설에 항의하는 탄원서를 작성했다.

pet·ri·fied /'pɛtrə,faɪd/ adj **1** extremely frightened ‖ 매우 겁먹은: *We were so petrified by the noise in the attic that we couldn't move.* 우리는 다락방에서 나는 소리에 너무 놀래서 꼼짝할 수 없었다. **2** **petrified wood** wood that has changed into stone over millions of years ‖ 수백만 년에 걸쳐 돌로 변한 나무. 화석이 된 나무 –**petrify** v [T]

pet·ro·chem·i·cal /,pɛtroʊ'kɛmɪkəl/ n a chemical substance obtained from PETROLEUM or natural gas ‖ 석유나 천연 가스에서 얻는 화학 물질. 석유 화학 제품: *the petrochemical industry* 석유 화학 산업

pe·tro·le·um /pə'troʊliəm/ n [U] oil that is obtained from below the surface of the Earth and is used in order to make GASOLINE and other chemical substances ‖ 가솔린과 다른 화학 물질을 만드는 데에 쓰이며 땅속에서 얻는 기름. 석유: *petroleum-based products* 석유를 원료로 한 제품

pet·ty /'pɛti/ adj **1** something that is petty is not serious or important ‖ 사물이 심각하거나 중요하지 않은. 하찮은: *Don't bother me with petty details.* 하찮은 일로 나를 괴롭히지 마. **2** someone who is petty cares too much about things that are not very important or serious ‖ 사람이 그다지 중요하거나 심각하지 않은 일에 지나치게 신경 쓰는. 옹졸한. 쩨쩨한: *Sometimes he's so petty about money.* (=he thinks too much about exactly how much people owe him) 때때로 그는 돈에 너무 인색하다. **3** **petty crime** a crime that is not serious, for example, stealing things that are not expensive ‖ 예를 들어, 비싸지 않은 것을 훔치는 것처럼 중하지 않은 범죄. 경범죄 – **pettiness** *n* [U]

petty cash /,.. './ *n* [U] money that is kept in an office for making small payments ‖ 소액 지급을 위해 사무실에 놓아두는 돈. 소액 현금

petty of·fi·cer, Petty Officer /,.. '..../ *n* an officer who has the lowest rank in the Navy ‖ 해군에서 가장 하위의 책임자. 부사관

pet·u·lant /'pɛtʃələnt/ *adj* behaving in an impatient and angry way, like a child ‖ 아이처럼 참을성 없이 화를 내며 행동하는. 안달하는. 성마른: *You're acting like a petulant four-year-old.* 너는 네 살배기처럼 안달하고 있다.

pew¹ /pyu/ *n* a long wooden seat in a church ‖ 교회의 긴 나무 의자. 신도석

pew² *interjection* said when something smells very bad ‖ 사물이 매우 악취가 날 때에 쓰여. 피유. 휴: *Pew! There must be a farm near here.* 피유! 이 근처에 농장이 있는 게 틀림 없어.

pew·ter /'pyutɚ/ *n* [U] a gray metal made by mixing LEAD and TIN ‖ 납과 주석을 혼합해서 만든 회색 금속. 백납

PG *adj* the abbreviation of "parental guidance," used in order to show that a movie may include parts that are not suitable for young children to see ‖ "parental guidance(보호자 동반[지도]의)"의 약어, 영화가 어린 아이들이 보기에 적합지 않은 부분이 포함되어 있는지를 나타내는 데에 쓰여

phal·lic /'fælɪk/ *adj* like a PENIS, or relating to the penis ‖ 음경 같은, 또는 남근에 관련된. 남근의: *a phallic symbol* (=something that represents a penis) 남근의 상징(물)

phal·lus /'fæləs/ *n* the male sex organ, or a model of it ‖ 남성 성기, 또는 그 모형. 남근상

phan·tom /'fæntəm/ *n* LITERARY **1** ⇨ GHOST **2** something that exists only in your imagination ‖ 오직 상상 속에서만 존재하는 것. 환상. 환영. 심상

Phar·aoh /'fɛroʊ, 'fær-/ *n* a ruler of ancient Egypt ‖ 고대 이집트의 지배자. 파라오

phar·ma·ceu·ti·cal /,fɑrmə'sutɪkəl/ *adj* relating to the production of drugs and medicine ‖ 약과 의약품 생산에 관련된. 제약의. 약제의: *large pharmaceutical companies* 대형 제약회사

phar·ma·cist /'fɑrməsɪst/ *n* someone whose job is to prepare drugs and

medicine ‖ 약과 의약품을 조제하는 직업인. 약사

phar·ma·col·o·gy /,fɑrmə'kɑlədʒi/ *n* [U] the scientific study of drugs and medicines ‖ 약과 의약품의 과학적 연구. 약리학. 약물학 – **pharmacologist** *n*

phar·ma·cy /'fɑrməsi/ *n* a store or a part of a store where medicines are prepared and sold ‖ 의약품을 조제하고 판매하는 상점이나 상점의 일부. 약국

phase¹ /feɪz/ *n* **1** one part of a process in which something develops or grows ‖ 사물이 발전하거나 성장하는 과정의 한 부분. 단계. 국면. 상(相). 양상: *the last phase of the project* 프로젝트의 최종 단계 / *It's normal for a 2-year-old to have tantrums; your child is just going through a phase.* 두 살배기 아이가 떼를 쓰는 것은 정상입니다. 당신의 아이는 따그 단계를 거치고 있습니다. **2** one of the changes in the appearance of the moon or a PLANET when it is seen from the Earth ‖ 지구에서 바라다보이는 달이나 행성의 외형상 변화의 하나. 위상(位相). 차고 이지러짐(의 한 양상)

phase² *v* [T]

phase sth ↔ **in** *phr v* [T] to introduce something gradually ‖ 어떤 것을 점차 도입하다. 단계적으로 채용·시행·적용하다: *New rules about claiming overtime will be phased in over the next two months.* 시간 외 근무 신청에 대한 새 규정이 다음 2개월에 걸쳐 단계적으로 시행됩니다.

phase sth ↔ **out** *phr v* [T] to gradually stop using or providing something ‖ 어떤 것의 사용이나 공급을 점차 중단하다. 단계적으로 폐지[정지]하다. 점차 없애다: *Leaded gas was phased out in the 1970s.* 납이 첨가된 휘발유는 1970년대에 점차 없어졌다.

Ph.D. /,pi eɪt 'di/ *n* Doctor of Philosophy; the highest university degree that can be earned, or someone who has this degree ‖ Doctor of Philosophy(박사)의 약어; 취득할 수 있는 최고의 대학 학위, 또는 이 학위를 가진 사람

pheas·ant /'fɛzənt/ *n* a large colorful bird with a long tail, that is hunted for food and sport, or the meat from this bird ‖ 식용과 스포츠용으로 사냥되는 꼬리가 길고 여러 가지 색을 지닌 큰 새, 또는 이 새의 고기. 핑(고기)

phe·nom·e·nal /fɪ'nɑmənl/ *adj* very unusual and impressive ‖ 매우 특별하고 감명을 주는. 놀랄[괄목할] 만한. 경이적인: *We have a phenomenal view of the* *harbor at night from here.* 여기에서 우리는 항구의 경이로운 야경을 볼 수 있다. – **phenomenally** *adv*

phe·nom·e·non /fɪˈnɑmənən, -ˌnɑn/ *n* 1 *plural* **phenomena** something that happens or exists in society, science, or nature that is unusual or difficult to understand ‖ 사회[과학, 자연]에서 발생하거나 존재하는 특별하거나 이해하기 힘든 것. 현상. 사상(事象). 사건: *Homelessness is not a new phenomenon.* 노숙자 생활은 새로운 현상이 아니다. 2 *plural* **phenomenons** a person or thing that has a rare ability or quality ‖ 희귀한 능력이나 특성을 가진 사람이나 사물. 불가사의. 기재(奇才). 비범한 사람: *Gillespie called him one of the phenomenons of our century.* 길레스피는 그를 금세기의 기재 중 한 명이라 불렀다.

phew /fyu, hwyu/ *interjection* said when you feel tired, hot, or RELIEVED ‖ 피곤·뜨거움·안도감을 느낄 때 쓰여. 아이고. 에그. 휴: *Phew! I'm glad that's over.* 휴! 그게 끝나서 기쁘다.

phial /ˈfaɪl/ *n* a small bottle for liquid medicine ‖ 물약용 작은 병

phi·lan·der·er /fɪˈlændərɚ/ *n* OLD-FASHIONED a man who has sex with many women and does not want a serious relationship ‖ 많은 여성과 성관계를 갖고 진지한 관계를 원하지 않는 남자. 바람둥이 남자 – **philandering** *n* [U]

phi·lan·thro·pist /fɪˈlænθrəpɪst/ *n* someone who gives a lot of money and help to people who need it ‖ 필요한 사람에게 많은 돈과 도움을 주는 사람. 자선가. 박애주의자

phi·lan·thro·py /fɪˈlænθrəpi/ *n* [U] the practice of giving money and help to people who need it ‖ 필요한 사람에게 돈과 도움을 주는 행위. 박애(주의). 자선 – **philanthropic** /ˌfɪlənˈθrɑpɪk/ *adj*

phil·is·tine /ˈfɪləˌstin/ *n* DISAPPROVING someone who does not like or understand art, music, literature etc. ‖ 미술·음악·문학 등을 좋아하지 않거나 이해하지 못하는 사람. 속물. 문외한

phi·los·o·pher /fɪˈlɑsəfɚ/ *n* 1 someone who studies or teaches PHILOSOPHY ‖ 철학을 연구하거나 가르치는 사람. 철학(연구)자: *ancient Greek philosophers* 고대 그리스 철학자들 2 someone who thinks a lot and asks questions about the world, life, death etc. ‖ 많이 생각하고 세계·인생·죽음 등에 대해 질문을 하는 사람. 철인. 현인

phil·o·soph·i·cal /ˌfɪləˈsɑfɪkəl/ *adj* 1 relating to PHILOSOPHY ‖ 철학에 관련된.

철학을 연구하는. 철학에 통달한: *a philosophical discussion* 철학적 토론 2 accepting difficult or unpleasant things calmly ‖ 힘들거나 불유쾌한 일들을 차분하게 받아들이는. 이성적인. 냉정한. 냉철한: *Anderson remains philosophical about his defeat.* 앤더슨은 그의 패배에 대해 달관한 상태이다. – **philosophically** *adv*

phi·los·o·phize /fɪˈlɑsəˌfaɪz/ *v* [I] to talk or think about important subjects and ideas in a serious way ‖ 중요한 주제와 관념에 대해 진지하게 이야기하거나 생각하다. 철학적으로 사색하다

phi·los·o·phy /fɪˈlɑsəfi/ *n* 1 [U] the study of what it means to exist, what good and evil are, what knowledge is, or how people should live ‖ 존재의 의미·선악·지식·삶에 대한 연구. 철학 2 a set of ideas about these subjects ‖ 이들 주제에 대한 일련의 생각. 철학 체계. 철학설: *the philosophy of Plato* 플라톤의 철학(사상) 3 a set of beliefs about how you should live your life, do your job etc. ‖ 삶의 방식·일하는 방식 등에 대한 일련의 신념. 인생[처세] 철학. …관[주의]: *a new business philosophy* 새로운 사업(운영) 철학

phlegm /flɛm/ *n* [U] a thick sticky substance produced in your nose and throat, especially when you have a cold; MUCUS ‖ 특히 감기에 걸렸을 때 코와 목에서 나오는 짙고 끈적한 물질. 가래. 점액; 흅 mucus

phleg·mat·ic /flɛɡˈmætɪk/ *adj* FORMAL calm and not easily excited or worried ‖ 차분하며 쉽게 흥분하거나 걱정하지 않는. 침착한. 냉정한. 냉담한

pho·bi·a /ˈfoʊbiə/ *n* a strong, usually unreasonable, fear of something ‖ 사물에 대한 강한, 보통 불합리한 공포. 공포증: *Holly has a phobia about snakes.* 홀리는 뱀에 대한 공포증이 있다. – **phobic** *adj*

phoe·nix /ˈfiniks/ *n* a bird in ancient stories that burns itself at the end of its life and is born again from the ASHes ‖ 생명이 끝날 때 자신을 불태워 재에서 다시 태어난다는 고대 신화 속의 새. 불사조. 피닉스

phone¹ /foʊn/ *n* 1 a piece of equipment that you use in order to talk with someone in another place; telephone ‖ 다른 장소에 있는 사람과 말하기 위해 사용하는 장비; 전화(기): *What's your phone number?* 전화번호가 몇 번입니까? / *a car phone* 자동차용 전화 2 **be on the phone** to be talking to someone else using a telephone ‖ 전화로 다른 사람과 이야기 중에 있다. 통화 중이다: *I was on the phone for an hour, talking to Lynn.* 나는 린에게 얘기하면서 한 시간 동안 통화 중이었다. —see usage note at TELEPHONE

phone² *v* [I, T] to talk to someone using a telephone; call ‖ 전화를 이용해서 어떤 사람과 말을 하다; 전화하다: *Several people phoned the radio station to complain.* 여러 사람들이 불만을 토로하기 위해 라디오 방송국에 전화했다.

phone book /'. ./ *n* a book containing an alphabetical list of the names, addresses, and telephone numbers of all the people in the area ‖ 그 지역의 모든 사람들의 이름·주소·전화번호를 알파벳순 명단으로 싣고 있는 책. 전화번호부

phone booth /'. ./ *n* a partly enclosed structure containing a telephone that the public can use ‖ 일반인들이 이용할 수 있는 전화기가 들어 있는 부분적으로 막힌 구조물. (공중) 전화 박스

pho·net·ic /fə'nɛtɪk/ *adj* relating to the sounds of human speech ‖ 인간의 말소리에 관한. 음성[발성]의. 발음에 의거한: *a phonetic alphabet* (=that uses signs to represent the sounds) 음표문자[발음기호] – **phonetically** *adv*

pho·net·ics /fə'nɛtɪks/ *n* [U] TECHNICAL the science and study of speech sounds ‖ 발음에 관한 학문과 연구. 음성학

pho·no·graph /'foʊnə,græf/ *n* OLD-FASHIONED ⇨ RECORD PLAYER

pho·ny /'foʊni/ *adj* INFORMAL false or not real, and intended to deceive someone; FAKE ‖ 거짓이거나 진짜가 아니고, 사람을 속이려는 의도의. 가짜의. 허위의. 사기의; 〔 fake: *Dirk gave the cops a phony address.* 더크는 경찰에게 가짜 주소를 대주었다. – **phony** *n*: *She's such a phony!* 그녀는 정말 허풍쟁이구나!

phoo·ey /'fui/ *interjection* used in order to express strong disbelief or disappointment ‖ 강한 불신이나 실망을 표현하는 데에 쓰여. 허. 체. 원

phos·phate /'fasfeɪt/ *n* [C, U] one of the various forms of a salt of PHOSPHORUS, used in industry ‖ 산업용으로 쓰이는 인을 함유한 염기의 다양한 형태 중의 하나. 인산염[광물]

phos·pho·res·cent /ˌfasfə'rɛsənt/ *adj* a substance that is phosphorescent shines slightly because it contains PHOSPHORUS, but produces little or no heat ‖ 물질이 인을 함유하고 있어서 약하게 빛을 발하지만, 거의 또는 전혀 열을 내

지 않는. 인광을 내는. 인광성의 – **phosphorescence** *n* [U]

phos·pho·rus /'fasfərəs/ *n* [U] a poisonous chemical that starts to burn when it is brought out into the air ‖ 공기 중에 노출될 때 불이 붙기 시작하는 유독성 화학물. 인(燐) – **phosphoric** /fas'fɔrɪk, -'far-/ *adj*

pho·to /'foʊtoʊ/ *n* INFORMAL ⇨ PHOTOGRAPH: *Who's the girl in this photo?* 이 사진 속의 여자는 누구예요?

pho·to·cop·i·er /'foʊtə,kapiɚ/ *n* a machine that quickly copies documents onto paper by photographing them ‖ 문서를 사진 찍어 재빠르게 종이에 복사하는 기계. (사진) 복사기

pho·to·cop·y /'foʊtə,kapi/ *n* a copy of a document made by a PHOTOCOPIER ‖ 복사기로 제작된 서류의 복사본: *Make a photocopy of this article for me.* 제게 이 논문 복사본을 만들어 주세요. – **photocopy** *v* [T]

photo fin·ish /ˌ.. '../ *n* the end of a race in which the leaders finish so close together that a photograph has to be taken to show who won ‖ 경주의 끝에 선두 그룹이 서로 아주 근접하게 골인해서 우승자를 가리는 사진을 찍어야 하는 것. 사진 판정. 대접전

pho·to·gen·ic /ˌfoʊtə'dʒɛnɪk/ *adj* always looking attractive in photographs ‖ 사진 속에서 항상 매력적으로 보이는. 사진이 잘 받는: *Julie is very photogenic.* 줄리는 사진이 매우 잘 받는다.

pho·to·graph /'foʊtə,græf/ *n* a picture that is made using a camera ‖ 카메라를 써서 찍은 사진: *an old photograph of my grandfather* 내 할아버지의 오래된 사진 / *Visitors are not allowed to take photographs.* 방문자들의 사진 촬영이 금지되어 있습니다. —see also PICTURE¹ – **photograph** *v* [T]

pho·tog·ra·pher /fə'tagrəfɚ/ *n* someone who takes photographs, especially as a job ‖ 특히 직업으로서 사진을 찍는 사람. 사진사. 사진작가: *a news photographer* 보도 사진기자

pho·to·graph·ic /ˌfoʊtə'græfɪk/ *adj* **1** relating to photographs ‖ 사진에 관련된. 사진(술)의. 사진용: *a photographic image* 사진 영상 **2 photographic memory** the ability to remember exactly every detail of something you have seen ‖ 보았던 사물의 모든 세세한 내용까지 정확히 기억하는 능력. 사진 같은[사실적인, 선명한] 기억력

pho·tog·ra·phy /fə'tagrəfi/ *n* [U] the

art, profession, or process of taking photographs ‖ 사진을 찍는 기술·직업·과 정. 사 진 촬영(술): *I'm taking a photography class in the evenings.* 나는 저녁 때 사진 촬영반 강의를 듣고 있다.

pho·to·syn·the·sis /ˌfoʊtoʊˈsɪnθəsɪs/ *n* [U] TECHNICAL the way that green plants make their food using the light from the sun ‖ 녹색 식물이 태양 광선을 이용하여 영양분을 만드는 방식. 광합성 (작용)

phras·al verb /ˌfreɪzəl ˈvɜˑb/ *n* TECHNICAL in grammar, a verb that changes its meaning when it is used with an adverb or preposition. In the sentence "The rocket blew up," "blew up" is a phrasal verb ‖ 문법에서, 부사나 전치사와 함께 쓰일 때 그 뜻이 변하는 동사. 구동사. 문장 "The rocket blew up," 에서 "blew up"은 구동사이다. —see study note on page 936

phrase¹ /freɪz/ *n* 1 a group of words that has a special meaning ‖ 특별한 의미를 갖는 단어군. 어구. 문구. 말: *Darwin's famous phrase, "the survival of the fittest"* 다윈의 유명한 문구, "적자 생존" 2 TECHNICAL in grammar, a group of words without a main verb that together make a subject, an object, or a verb tense. In the sentence, "We have a brand new car," "a brand new car" is a noun phrase ‖ 문법에서, 함께 쓰여 주어 [목적어, 동사의 시제]를 이루는 주동사가 없는 단어군. 문장 "We have a brand new car,"에서 "a brand new car"는 명사 구이다. 구. 숙어. 관용구 —compare CLAUSE, SENTENCE¹

phrase² *v* [T] to express something in a particular way ‖ 사물을 특정하게 표현하다. …을 말하다[말로 나타내다]: *He phrased his question politely.* 그는 정중 하게 질문을 했다. – **phrasing** *n* [U]

phys·i·cal¹ /ˈfɪzɪkəl/ *adj* 1 relating to someone's body rather than his/her mind or soul ‖ 사람의 마음이나 정신보다 신체에 관련된. 육체적인. 신체의. 육육 의: *physical exercise/contact* 육체적 운 동[접촉] / *a woman of great physical strength* 신체적으로 대단히 강한 여성 2 relating to real things that can be seen, tasted, felt etc. ‖ 보고 맛보고 느낄 수 있 는 등의 실재하는 것과 관련된. 물질(계) 의. 물질적인. 실제의: *our physical environment* 우리의 물리적 환경 3 someone who is physical touches people a lot ‖ 사람들을 많이 만지는. 사람들을 만 지기 좋아하는 4 involving very forceful body movements ‖ 매우 강한 신체 운동과

관련된. 격렬한. 난폭한. 거친: *a very physical dancing style* 매우 격렬한 춤 스 타일 5 relating to or following the laws of nature ‖ 자연 법칙에 관련되거나 따르 는. 자연적인. 자연의. 자연 과학의: *the physical force of gravity* 자연의 중력 6 a physical science such as PHYSICS studies things that are not living ‖ 물리학 등의 학문이 살아 있지 않은 사물들을 연구하 는. 물리(학)의. 물질(계)의: *physical chemistry* 물리 화학 —compare ORGANIC

physical², **physical examination** /ˌ… …ˈ…/ *n* a medical examination by a doctor, for example, before someone is allowed to start a job ‖ 예를 들어, 근무를 허락하기 전에 실시하는 의사에 의한 의료 검진. 신체검사

physical ed·u·ca·tion /ˌ… …ˈ…/ *n* ⇨ PE

phys·i·cal·ly /ˈfɪzɪkli/ *adv* 1 in relation to the body rather than the mind or soul ‖ 마음이나 정신보다 육체와 관련해서. 육 체[신체]적으로(는). 신체적 견지에서(본 다면): *I try to keep myself physically fit.* (=having strong muscles and not much fat) 나는 내 자신의 체격이 알맞게 유지되게 노력한다 2 **physically impossible** not possible according to the laws of nature or what is known to be true ‖ 자연의 법칙이나 사실로 알려져 있 것에 비추어 봤을 때 가능하지 않은. 자연 과학[물리학]적으로 불가능한. 자연의[물 리적] 법칙에 따라 불가능한: *It's physically impossible for penguins to fly.* 자연 법칙상 펭귄이 난다는 것은 불가 능하다.

physical ther·a·py /ˌ… ˈ…/ *n* [U] a treatment for injuries and muscle problems that uses special exercises, rubbing, heat etc. ‖ 특별한 운동·안마·열 등을 이용하는 부상이나 근육 문제의 치료 (법). 물리요법 – **physical therapist** *n*

phy·si·cian /fɪˈzɪʃən/ *n* FORMAL ⇨ DOCTOR¹ —see usage note at DOCTOR¹

phys·ics /ˈfɪzɪks/ *n* [U] the science that deals with the study of physical objects and substances, and natural forces such as light, heat, movement etc. ‖ 자연적인 대 상 물 과 물 질 그 리 고 빛· 열·움직임 등의 자연력의 연구를 다루는 학 문. 물리학 – **physicist** /ˈfɪzəsɪst/ *n*

phys·i·ol·o·gy /ˌfɪziˈɑlədʒi/ *n* [U] a science that deals with the study of how the bodies of living things work ‖ 생명체 의 신체가 어떻게 작용하는가의 연구를 다 루는 과학. 생리학 – **physiological** /ˌfɪziəˈlɑdʒɪkəl/ *adj* —compare ANATOMY

phys·i·o·ther·a·py /ˌfɪzioʊˈθɛrəpi/ *n*

[U] ⇨ PHYSICAL THERAPY

phy·sique /fɪ'zik/ *n* the shape, size, and appearance of someone's body ‖ 인체의 체형·크기·외양. 체격. 몸매: *a man with a powerful physique* 강인한 체격의 남자

pi·an·ist /pi'ænɪst, 'piənɪst/ *n* a person who plays the piano ‖ 피아노 연주자. 피아니스트

pi·an·o /pi'ænoʊ/ *n* a large musical instrument that you play by pressing a row of narrow black and white BARs with your fingers ‖ 손가락으로 한 줄의 검고 흰 좁은 건반을 눌러서 연주하는 큰 악기. 피아노

pic·co·lo /'pɪkə,loʊ/ *n* a musical instrument like a small FLUTE ‖ 작은 플루트처럼 생긴 악기. 피콜로

pick¹ /pɪk/ *v* [T]

1 ▶CHOOSE◀ to choose something or someone from a group of people or things ‖ 일단의 사람들이나 사물들 중에서 한 사물이나 사람을 뽑다. 고르다. 선택[선발]하다: *Katie picked the blue one.* 케이티는 파란색을 선택했다. / *Have you picked a date for the wedding yet?* 결혼식 날짜를 벌써 잡았습니까? / *He picked the Giants to win the division.* 그는 리그전[구역전]에서 이기기 위해 자이언츠팀을 골랐다. / *Phillips is now so successful that he can pick and choose the projects he wants.* (=he can choose only the ones he likes) 필립스는 이제 아주 성공해서 자신이 원하는 프로젝트만을 선택할 수 있다.

2 ▶FLOWER/FRUIT◀ to pull or break off a flower or fruit from a plant or tree ‖ 식물이나 나무에서 꽃이나 과일을 따거나 꺾다. …을 잡아 떼다: *We're going out to the farm on Saturday to pick apples.* 우리는 토요일에 사과를 따러 농장에 간다.

3 ▶REMOVE/PULL OFF◀ 없애다/떼어내다 to remove small things from something, or to pull off small pieces from something ‖ 어떤 것으로부터 작은 것을 제거하다, 또는 어떤 것으로부터 작은 조각들을 떼어내다. 후비다. 떼어내서[벗겨내서] 깨끗이 하다[청소하다]: *picking meat off the bone* 뼈에서 고기를 발라내기 / *Michael, stop picking your nose.* (=cleaning the inside of it with your finger) 마이클, 코 좀 그만 후벼라.

4 pick your way to move carefully through an area, choosing exactly where to walk or drive ‖ 걷거나 운전할 장소를 정확히 선택하면서 조심스럽게 지역을 통과해 움직이다. (발 밑을) 조심하

며 걷다. 조심스레 선택해 나아가다: *Rescue workers picked their way through the rubble.* 구조자들은 잔해더미 사이로 조심스레 나아갔다.

5 pick a fight (with sb) to deliberately begin an argument or fight with someone ‖ 고의로 다른 사람과 말다툼이나 싸움을 시작하다. 싸움을 걸다: *Adam's always picking fights with the younger kids.* 아담은 항상 나이 어린 아이들에게 싸움을 건다.

6 pick sb's brain(s) to ask someone who knows a lot about a subject for information or advice about it ‖ 어떤 주제에 대해 많이 아는 사람에게 정보나 조언을 요청하다. 남의 지식[지혜]을 빌리다. 남에게서 정보[진실, 비밀]를 캐어내다: *If you have time later, could I pick your brains about some legal issues?* 나중에 시간 있으면 몇 가지 법적인 문제에 대해 자문 좀 얻을 수 있어요?

7 pick a lock to use something that is not a key to unlock a door, window etc. ‖ 문·창 등을 열기 위해 열쇠가 아닌 것을 사용하다. 자물쇠를 비틀어서[몰래] 따다 —see also PICKPOCKET

pick at sth *phr v* [T] to eat only a small amount of your food, as if you are not really hungry ‖ 실제로 배가 고프지 않은 것처럼 소량의 음식만을 먹다. 음식을 뜨다 말다[뜨는 둥 마는 둥하다]: *I was so nervous I could only pick at my lunch.* 나는 아주 긴장되어서 점심을 뜨는 둥 마는 둥했다.

pick sb/sth ↔ **off** *phr v* [T] to shoot people or animals one at a time from a long distance away ‖ 사람이나 동물을 멀리 떨어진 거리에서 한 번에 하나씩 쏘다. 하나하나 겨누어 쏘다: *Snipers were picking off anyone who came outdoors.* 저격수는 문 밖으로 나온 사람이면 누구나 한 명씩 저격하고 있었다.

pick on sb *phr v* [T] to unfairly criticize someone again and again, treat someone in an unkind way, or hurt someone ‖ 어떤 사람을 몇 번이고 부당하게 비난하다[불친절하게 대하다, 마음을 아프게 하다]. …의 흠을 들추다[혹평하다]. 사람을 괴롭히다[골리다]: *Greg, stop picking on your sister!* 그레그, 네 여동생 좀 그만 괴롭혀라!

pick sb/sth ↔ **out** *phr v* [T] **1** to choose something carefully from a group of things ‖ 다수의 물건 중에서 어떤 것을 신중하게 선택하다. …을 고르다. 집어내다. 골라내다: *We had a lot of fun picking out a present for Leslie's baby.* 우리는 레슬리의 아기를 위한 선물을 고르면서 즐

거운 시간을 보냈다. **2** to recognize or notice someone or something in a group of people or things ‖ 일단의 사람들이나 사물 속에서 사람이나 사물을 인식하거나 알아보다. …을 찾아내다. 분간[식별]하다: *The victim was able to pick out her attacker from a police lineup.* 피해자는 경찰의 목격자 확인 절차에서 자신을 공격한 자를 찾아낼 수 있었다.

pick sth ↔ **over** *phr v* [T] to carefully examine a group of things in order to choose only the ones you want ‖ 원하는 것만을 뽑기 위해 다수의 사물을 주의 깊게 검사하다. 신중하게 검토하다. 정선하다[골라내다]: *Wash and pick over the beans.* 콩을 씻고 골라라.

pick up *phr v*

1 ▶LIFT UP 들어 올리다◀ [T **pick** sb/sth ↔ up] to hold someone or something and lift him, her, or it from a surface ‖ 사람이나 사물을 잡고 표면에서 올리다. 안아[들어] 올리다: *Pick me up, Daddy!* 아빠, 나 좀 들어 올려 줘요! / *kids picking up shells at the beach* 해변에서 조개껍질을 줍고 있는 아이들 / *I picked up the phone* (=answered the phone) *just as it stopped ringing.* 내가 전화를 받자마자 전화 벨소리가 끊어졌다.

2 ▶GO GET SB/STH 사람/사물을 데리러[가지러] 가다◀ [T **pick** sb/sth ↔ up] to go somewhere, usually in a vehicle, in order to get someone or something ‖ 사람이나 사물을 데려 오려고 보통 차로 어딘가에 가다. …에 태우러[싣다]. 차로 마중나가다[데려오다, 가져오다]: *I'll pick up my stuff around six, okay?* 6시 경에 내 물건을 가지러 갈게, 괜찮지? / *What time should we pick you up at the airport?* 당신을 태우러 몇 시에 공항에 가야 합니까?

3 ▶BUY 사다◀ [T **pick** sth ↔ up] INFORMAL to buy something ‖ 어떤 것을 사다. 지불하다. 사오다[입수하다]: *Will you pick up something for dinner on your way home?* 집에 오는 길에 저녁거리 좀 사올래요? / *The company is picking up the bill for my computer.* (=it is paying for it) 회사가 내 컴퓨터 대금을 지불하고 있다.

4 ▶CLEAN A PLACE 장소를 치우다◀ [I, T **pick** sth ↔ up] to put things away neatly, or to clean a place by doing this ‖ 물건들을 가지런히 치워 놓다, 또는 이렇게 한 장소를 깨끗이 하다. 치우다. 정돈하다. 가지런히 고르다: *Straighten your room and pick up all those papers.* 방을 정돈하고 저 종이를 모두 치워라. / *Pick up the living room, please.* 거실 좀

정돈해 주세요. / *He never picks up after himself.* (=he does not put away the things he has used) 그는 자신이 사용한 물건을 정돈하는 법이 없다.

5 ▶GET BETTER 좋아지다◀ [I] to improve ‖ 개선되다. 되찾다. 회복하다. 나아지다: *Sales should pick up before Christmas.* 크리스마스 이전에 판매가 호전되어야 한다.

6 ▶INCREASE 증가하다◀ [I, T **pick up** sth] to increase or get faster ‖ 증가하거나 더 빨라지다. 속도를 내다[올리다]. 높아지다. 강해지다: *The car was gradually picking up speed.* (=going faster) 차는 점차 속도를 올리고 있었다. / *The wind had picked up considerably.* 바람이 상당히 강해졌다.

7 ▶LEARN 배우다◀ [T **pick** sth ↔ up] to learn something without deliberately trying to ‖ 일부러 노력하지 않고 어떤 것을 배우다. 터득하다. 쉽게 익히다. 귀동냥으로 배우다: *Craig picked up the guitar from his dad.* 크레이그는 아버지에게서 기타를 귀동냥으로 터득했다.

8 ▶ILLNESS 병◀ [T **pick** sth ↔ up] to get an illness from someone ‖ 다른 사람에게서 병을 얻다. 전염되다. 감염되다. …하는 병이 들다[옮다]: *She's picked up a cold from a child at school.* 그녀는 학교에서 다른 아이로부터 감기를 옮았다.

9 ▶NOTICE 알아채다◀ [T **pick** sth ↔ up] to notice, see, or hear something, or to receive signals from something, especially when this is difficult; DETECT ‖ 특히 그렇게 하기 어려울 때 어떤 것을 알아차리다[보다, 듣다], 또는 신호를 받다. 탐지하다. 포착하다; ㊤ detect: *We didn't pick anything up on radar.* 우리는 레이더로 아무것도 포착하지 못했다. / *The dogs were able to pick up the scent.* 개들은 냄새를 탐지할 수 있었다.

10 ▶START AGAIN 다시 시작하다◀ [T **pick** sth ↔ up] to begin a conversation, meeting etc. again, starting from the point where it stopped earlier; RESUME ‖ 대화·회의 등을 이전에 중단됐던 지점에서 다시 시작하다. 재개하다. 속개하다; ㊤ resume: *We'll pick up where we left off after lunch.* 우리는 점심 후에 중단했던 부분에서 (회의를)재개하겠다.

11 ▶POLICE 경찰◀ [T **pick** sb ↔ up] if the police pick someone up, they find him/her and take him/her to the police station; ARREST ‖ 경찰이 사람을 찾아서 경찰서로 데려가다. 체포하다. 연행[검거]하다; ㊤ arrest: *Carr was picked up and taken in for questioning.* 카는 체포되어 심문을 위해 연행되었다.

12 ▶SEX◀ [T **pick** sb ↔ **up**] to talk
to someone you do not know and try to
start a sexual relationship with him/her
‖ 알지 못하는 사람에게 말을 하고 성관계
를 맺으려 하다. 여자를 낚다[꾀다]. 성관
계를 맺기 위해 유혹하다: *a guy trying to
pick up girls at the bar* 바에서 여자들을
유혹하려 하는 남자
13 pick up the pieces (of sth) to get a
situation back to normal after
something bad has happened ‖ 나쁜 일
이 벌어진 후에 상황을 정상으로 돌리다.
수습하다. 정상화시키다. 만회[회복]하
다: *Ralph's trying to pick up the pieces
of his business.* 랠프는 그의 사업을 정상
화시키려 애쓰고 있다.

pick up on sth *phr v* [T] to notice or
understand something that is not easy
to notice, and react to it ‖ 알아채기 쉽지
않은 것을 알아채거나 이해하고 그에 반응
하다. 눈치 채다. 직감적으로 알다[이해하
다]: *Children quickly pick up on
tensions between their parents.* 아이들은
부모 사이의 긴장을 재빨리 눈치 챈다.

pick² *n* **1** [U] choice ‖ 선택: *There are
four kinds of cake, so you can take your
pick.* (=choose one) 네 가지 케이크가 있
으니 너는 네 마음에 드는 것을 고를 수
있다. / *She'll be able to have her pick of
colleges.* (=choose any one she wants)
그녀는 자신이 원하는 대로 대학을 선택할
수 있을 것이다. **2 the pick of sth**
INFORMAL the best thing or things in a
group ‖ 집단 중에서 최고의 사물이나 사
물들. 최상의 것. 정선된 것: *The Doles
will get the pick of the puppies.* 돌즈가
강아지들 중 최고의 것을 살 것이다. **3** a
sharp pointed tool, such as a PICKAX ‖ 곡
괭이 등의 날카롭고 뾰족한 연장. 픽(정의
일종). 얼음 깨는 송곳 **4** a small flat
object that you use for playing an
instrument such as a GUITAR ‖ 기타 등의
악기를 연주하는 데에 사용하는 작고 납작
한 물체. 잭. 픽

pick·ax /'pɪk·æks/ *n* a large tool that
has a long handle and a curved iron end
with two sharp points, used for
breaking up a road, rocks etc. ‖ 도로·바
위 등을 부수는 데에 쓰이는, 긴 손잡이와
구부러진 쇠 끝에 두 개의 뾰족한 날이 달
린 큰 연장. 곡괭이

pick·er /'pɪkɚ/ *n* a person or machine
that picks things such as fruit, cotton
etc. ‖ 열매·목화 등의 사물을 따는 사람이
나 기계. 채집자[기]

pick·et¹ /'pɪkɪt/, **picket line** /'.. ./
n a group or line of people who PICKET a
factory, store etc. ‖ 공장·상점 등에 피켓

시위 하는 사람들의 집단이나 대열. 노조
감시원. 피켓(대): *Two workers were
hurt today trying to cross the picket
line.* (=trying to work during a STRIKE)
두 명의 노동자가 오늘 노동 쟁의 중에 일
하려다가 다쳤다.

picket² *v* [I, T] to stand or march in
front of a factory, store etc. to protest
something, or to stop people from going
in to work during a STRIKE (=time when
everyone refuses to work) ‖ 어떤 일을 항
의하기 위해 공장·상점 등의 앞에 서 있거
나 행진하다, 또는 파업 중에 다른 사람들
이 일하러 들어가는 것을 막다. 피켓 시위
하다. 피켓을 치고 감시하다

picket fence /,.. '. ./
n a fence made of a
line of strong pointed
sticks fixed in the
ground ‖ 땅에 고정된
단단하고 뾰족한 말뚝
이 한 줄로 이루어진
울타리. 말뚝 울타리

picket fence

pick·le¹ /'pɪkəl/ *n* **1**
[C, U] a CUCUMBER
(=vegetable) preserved in VINEGAR and
salt or sugar, or a thin piece of this ‖ 식
초와 소금 또는 설탕에 재워진 오이, 또는
이것의 얇은 조각. 피클(조각). 절임(된
것): *a dill pickle* 딜 피클 **2 be in a
pickle** OLD-FASHIONED to be in a difficult
situation ‖ 어려운 상황에 처하다. 난처한
입장[곤궁, 궁지]에 몰리다. 당황하고 있
다

pick·le² *v* [T] to preserve food in
VINEGAR with salt or sugar and various
SPICEs ‖ 소금이나 설탕과 여러 가지 향신
료와 함께 식초에 음식·식품을 보존하다. 절
이다. 피클로 만들다 – **pickled** *adj* :
pickled onions/herring 양파[청어] 절임

pick-me-up /'. . ,./ *n* INFORMAL
something that makes you feel cheerful
or gives you more energy, especially a
drink or medicine ‖ 특히 음료수나 의약
품으로서, 사람에게 즐거움을 느끼게 하거
나 더 많은 활력을 주는 것. 각성제

pick·pock·et /'pɪk,pakɪt/ *n* someone
who steals things from people's pockets,
especially in public ‖ 특히 공공연하게 사
람들의 주머니에서 물건을 훔치는 사람.
소매치기 —see usage note at THIEF

pick·up /'pɪkʌp/ *n* **1** also **pickup
truck** /'.. ,./ a vehicle with a large open
part at the back that is used for
carrying goods ‖ 뒤쪽에 짐을 나르는 데
쓰이는 지붕이 없는 큰 공간이 있는 차량.
픽업(트럭). 소형 트럭 —see picture on
page 943 **2** the act of taking something

from a place using a vehicle ‖ 차량을 이
용해서 사물을 한 장소에서 실어가기. (화
물의)수집[집배](하기). 모으기: *There is
a regular garbage pickup on Tuesdays.*
화요일에 정기적으로 쓰레기 수거를 한다.
3 [U] INFORMAL the ability of a car to
reach a high speed in a short time ‖ 짧은
시간 안에 고속에 도달하는 차량의 성능.
급가속 능력: *The new models have a lot
of pickup.* 신형 차종은 급가속 능력이 뛰
어나다. **4** INFORMAL the act or process of
improving ‖ 개선해 가는 것이나 그 과정.
회복. 향상. 상승: *a pickup in sales* 판매
의 상승

pick·y /'pɪki/ *adj* INFORMAL, DIS-
APPROVING someone who is picky is
difficult to make happy, because s/he
only likes a small range of things ‖ 사람
이 좁은 범주의 사물만 좋아해서 즐겁게
해주기 어려운. 까다로운. 좀스러운: *a
picky eater* 편식하는 사람 / *Kelly's so
picky about her clothes!* 켈리는 자신의
옷에 대해 너무 까다로워!

pic·nic¹ /'pɪknɪk/ *n* **1** an occasion when
people take food and eat it outdoors, for
example in a park ‖ 사람들이 음식을 가
지고 가서 공원 등의 야외에서 먹는 행사.
피크닉. 소풍. 야유회: *We used to have
picnics down by the creek.* 우리는 냇가
하류 쪽에 피크닉을 가곤 했다. / *Do you
want to go for a picnic this Saturday?*
이번 토요일에 피크닉 가고 싶어요? **2 be
no picnic** INFORMAL to be difficult or
unpleasant ‖ 어렵거나 불쾌하다. 쉬운 일
이 아니다. 놀러 온 것이 아니다: *Riding
the bus to work every day is no picnic!*
매일 직장에 버스를 타고 가는 것은 쉬운
일이 아니야!

picnic² *v* **picnicked, picnicking** [I] to
have a PICNIC ‖ 피크닉을 가다. 들놀이식
으로 식사하다

pic·to·ri·al /pɪk'tɔriəl/ *adj* relating to or
using pictures ‖ 그림에 관련된 또는 그림
을 이용한. 그림으로 본[나타낸]. 그림이
든: *a pictorial history of Montana* 몬태나
주의 그림으로 본 역사

pic·ture¹ /'pɪktʃɚ/ *n*
1 ▶IMAGE 영상◀ a painting, drawing,
or photograph ‖ 회화. 도화. 사진. 그림.
모습. 영상: *I have a picture of my
family on the wall.* 벽에 내 가족 사진이
붙어 있다. / *Draw/paint a picture of
your house.* 너의 집의 그림을 그려라[채
색해라]. / *a group of tourists taking
pictures* (=taking photographs) 사진을
찍고 있는 일단의 관광객 무리 / *Leo's
picture* (=photograph of him) *is in the
newspaper.* 레오의 사진이 신문에 실려

있다.
2 ▶SITUATION 상황◀ [singular] the
general situation in a place,
organization etc. ‖ 어떤 장소·조직 등의
일반적 상황. 형세. 사태. 양상: *The
political picture has greatly changed
since March.* 정치적 상황이 3월 이후 크
게 변했다.
3 ▶DESCRIPTION 묘사◀ [C usually
singular] a description that gives you an
idea of what something is like ‖ 사물이
어떻게 생겼는가에 대한 아이디어를 주는
묘사. 설명. 상세한 기술: *The report
paints a clear picture of life in the
army.* 그 보도는 군대 생활을 생생하게 보
여 준다.
4 be in/out of the picture INFORMAL to
be involved or not be involved in a
situation ‖ 상황에 관련되거나 관련되지
않다. 형세에(서) 개입되다/빠지다: *With
his main rival out of the picture, the
mayor has a chance of winning the
election.* 그의 주요 경쟁자가 그 상황에서
탈락되어서 시장은 선거에서 승리할 기회
가 있다.
5 ▶ON A SCREEN 화면상◀ the image
that you see on a television or in a
movie ‖ 텔레비전이나 영화에서 보는 영
상. 화면. 화상: *Something's wrong with
the picture.* 화면이 뭔가 잘못됐다.
6 get the picture SPOKEN to understand
something ‖ 어떤 것을 이해하다. 상황[사
정]을 파악하다: *I don't want you around
here any more, get the picture?* 나는 네
가 더 이상 이 근처에 얼쩡거리기를 원하
지 않는다, 알아들었어?
7 ▶MOVIE 영화◀ OLD-FASHIONED ⇨
MOVIE: *Grandma loved going to the
pictures.* 할머니는 영화 보러 가기를 좋아
하셨다.

picture² *v* [T] **1** to imagine something,
especially by making an image of it in
your mind ‖ 특히 그 영상을 마음속에 떠
올려서 어떤 것을 상상하다. …을 마음속에
그리다[떠올리다]. 상상으로 생각하다: *I
can still picture him standing there with
his uniform on.* 나는 아직도 그가 유니폼
을 입고 저기에 서 있는 것을 마음속에 떠
올릴 수 있다. / *I can't picture myself as
a mother.* 나는 어머니로서의 내 모습을
상상할 수 없다. **2** to show something or
someone in a photograph, painting, or
drawing ‖ 사물이나 사람을 사진[회화, 도
화]으로 나타내다. 사진[그림]으로 전하다
[표현하다]: *The girl is pictured sitting
on a horse.* 소녀는 말 위에 앉아 있는 모
습이 사진에 찍혔다.

picture book /'.. ,./ *n* a children's

story book that has a lot of pictures in it ‖ 많은 그림이 들어 있는 아이들의 이야기책. 그림책.

pic·tur·esque /ˌpɪktʃəˈrɛsk/ *adj* attractive and interesting ‖ 매력적이고 흥미로운. 그림같이 아름다운[멋있는]. 눈길을 끄는: *a picturesque sunset/village* 그림 같은 일몰[마을]

pid·dling /ˈpɪdlɪŋ/ *adj* INFORMAL small and unimportant ‖ 작고 중요치 않은. 사소한. 하찮은: *a piddling amount of money* 하찮은 금액

pidg·in /ˈpɪdʒən/ *n* [C, U] a language that is a mixture of two other languages and is used by people who do not speak each other's language very well ‖ 두 개의 서로 다른 언어가 혼합되어 서로의 말을 썩 잘하지 못하는 사람들에 의해 사용되는 언어. 혼성어

pie /paɪ/ *n* [C, U] **1** a food usually made with fruit baked inside a covering of PASTRY ‖ 보통 가루 반죽 껍질 안에 과일을 넣어 구워 만든 음식. 파이: *an apple pie* 사과 파이 **2 as easy as pie** INFORMAL very easy ‖ 매우 쉬운. 누워서 떡먹기의. 식은 죽 먹기의 **3 a piece/share/slice of the pie** INFORMAL a share of something such as money or profit ‖ 돈이나 이익 등의 (분배)몫. (전체 …의) 한 조각/몫/편(片): *Landers wants a bigger slice of the pie.* 랜더스는 더 큰 몫을 원한다. **4 pie in the sky** INFORMAL a good plan or promise that you do not think will ever happen ‖ 전혀 일어날 것으로 생각되지 않는 좋은 계획이나 약속. 헛된 기대. 그림의 떡: *The whole idea is pie in the sky, but it's nice to dream about it.* 전체 구상은 그림의 떡이지만 그것에 대해 꿈꾸는 것은 즐거운 일이다.

piece¹ /pis/ *n*
1 ▶PART OF A WHOLE 전체의 일부◀ a part of something that has been separated, broken, or cut off from the rest of it ‖ 나머지로부터 분리된[쪼개진, 잘라내진] 부분적인 것. (전체의) 한 조각. 단편. 파편: *Do you want a piece of pizza?* 피자 한 조각 먹을래? / *The vase lay in pieces* (=broken into many pieces) *on the floor.* 꽃병이 마룻바닥에 조각나 있었다.
2 ▶PART OF A SET 한 세트의 부분◀ a single thing of a particular type, often part of a set of things or part of a larger thing ‖ 특정 종류의 하나, 종종 한 세트의 여러 사물 중 일부분 또는 더 큰 사물 중 일부. 하나. 한 개. 한 조[세트]: *a piece of paper* 종이 한 조각 / *a chess piece* 체스의 말 하나 / *a five-piece band*

(=one with five members) 5인조 밴드 / *a beautiful piece of land on the river* 강위의 아름다운 육지 부분
3 ▶CONNECTED PART 연결된 부분◀ one of several different parts that can be connected together to make something ‖ 사물을 이루기 위해 함께 결합될 수 있는 몇 가지 서로 다른 부분의 하나. 조각. 부분(품): *the pieces of a jigsaw puzzle* 끼워 맞추기용 조각 그림의 조각들
4 a piece of advice/information/ gossip etc. some advice, information etc. ‖ 어떤 충고·정보 등. 하나의 충고/정보/소문: *Let me give you a piece of advice: don't ask her about her mother.* 네게 충고 하나 하자. 그녀에게 어머니에 대해 묻지 말아라.
5 go to pieces to become so upset or nervous that you cannot think or behave normally ‖ 너무 화가 나거나 긴장되어서 정상적으로 생각하거나 행동할 수 없게 되다. 자제심을 잃다. (육체적·정신적으로) 좌절되다: *When she found out what Joe had done, Liz just went to pieces.* 리즈는 조가 무슨 일을 했는지 알았을 때, 그녀는 바로 자제심을 잃었다.
6 smash/tear/rip etc. sth to pieces to damage something severely ‖ 사물을 심하게 손상하다. 산산조각 내다. 발기발기 찢다. …을 조각조각으로 강타하다/찢다/뜯다: *She tore the letter to pieces and burned it.* 그녀는 편지를 발기발기 찢어서 불태웠다.
7 (all) in one piece not damaged or injured ‖ 손상되거나 부상당하지 않아. 무사히. 상처 없이. 원형 그대로: *I'm glad the china arrived all in one piece.* 나는 도자기가 무사히 도착해서 기쁘다.
8 give sb a piece of your mind INFORMAL to tell someone that you are very angry with him/her ‖ 어떤 사람에게 자신이 매우 화가 났다고 말하다. …이 잘못됐다고 따끔하게 말하다. 한마디 해주다: *If I see her, I'll give her a piece of my mind!* 그녀를 보면 한마디 해줄 거야!
9 be a piece of cake INFORMAL to be very easy to do ‖ 하기에 매우 쉽다. 쉽게 할 수 있다. 누워서 떡먹기[식은 죽 먹기]다: *Raising four children hasn't been a piece of cake.* 네 아이를 키우는 것은 쉬운 일이 아니다.
10 ▶ART/MUSIC ETC. 미술/음악 등◀ something that has been written or made by an artist, musician, or writer ‖ 예술가[음악가, 작가]에 의해 쓰여지거나 만들어진 것. 작품. 예술품: *a beautiful piece of work* 아름다운 작품

pieces

a piece of cake

a slice of bread

a lump of sugar

piece² *v*

piece sth ↔ **together** *phr v* [T] **1** to use all the facts or information that you have in order to understand a situation ‖ 상황을 이해하기 위해 가지고 있는 모든 사실이나 정보를 이용하다. …을 종합하다. 짜맞추어 …하다: *Police are still trying to piece together a motive for the shooting.* 경찰은 아직 총격 사건의 동기를 짜맞추느라 애쓰고 있다. **2** to put all the parts of something back into their correct position or order ‖ 사물의 모든 부분을 각기 올바른 위치나 순서로 돌려놓다. 원상대로 조각을 맞추다

piece·meal /'pismil/ *adj, adv* happening or done slowly in separate stages that are not planned or related ‖ 계획이나 관련성 없이 각기 다른 단계로 서서히 일어나거나 행해진. 조금씩(의). 단편적으로(인): *The house was filled with old furniture they'd bought piecemeal.* 그 집은 그들이 조금씩 사놓은 오래된 가구로 채워졌다.

piece rate /'../ an amount of money that is paid for each thing a worker produces ‖ 노동자가 생산하는 각각의 제품에 지불되는 돈의 액수. 생산고당 단가. (도급) 단가: *The piece rate was $2.00 per item.* 단가는 한 개당 2달러이다.

piece·work /'piswərk/ *n* [U] work that is paid by the amount that you do rather than by the number of hours you work ‖ 일한 시간수보다 일한 양에 의해 지불되는 작업. 성과급(成果給) 작업. 도급일

pie chart /'. ./ *n* a circle divided into several parts that shows how something such as business income is divided ‖ 사업 수입 등이 어떻게 분배되는가를 보여주는 몇 개의 부분으로 나누어진 원. 원그래프. 원형 도표

pier /pɪr/ *n* **1** a structure that is built out into the water so that boats can stop next to it ‖ 배가 그 옆에 정박할 수 있게 물 속으로 내달아 지은 구조물. 부두. 선창: *The troop transport ship docked at Pier 5.* 병력 수송선이 5번 부두에 정박했다. **2** a thick post of stone or metal used for supporting something such as a bridge ‖ 다리 등을 지지하는 데에 사용된 돌이나 금속제의 두꺼운 기둥. 교각

pierce /pɪrs/ *v* [T] **1** to make a hole in or through something using an object with a sharp point ‖ 날카로운 끝을 가진 물체로 사물에 구멍을 내거나 뚫다. 꿰찌르다. 꿰뚫다. 관통하다: *Tiffany's getting her ears pierced.* (=having a hole put in her ears for wearing jewelry) 티파니는 그녀의 귀를 뚫고 있다. / *A bullet pierced his body.* 총알이 그의 몸을 관통했다. **2** LITERARY if a bright light or a loud sound pierces something, it is suddenly seen or heard very clearly ‖ 밝은 불빛이나 큰 소리가 갑자기 매우 선명하게 보이거나 들리다. …을 깨뜨리다. 뚫다. 뚫고 들어가다: *The lights from the boat pierced the fog.* 배의 불빛이 안개를 뚫었다.

pier·cing /'pɪrsɪŋ/ *adj* **1** sounding or feeling very sharp and unpleasant ‖ 아주 날카롭고 불쾌한 소리가 나거나 느낌이 드는. 귀청을 뚫는. (뼈에) 사무치는. 지독한: *a piercing cry/scream* 귀청을 찢는 울음[비명] / *an icy piercing wind* 얼음같이 지독한 바람 **2** piercing eyes or looks show that someone notices or understands something more than other people would ‖ 눈이나 시선이 다른 사람들 이상으로 어떤 것을 알아채거나 이해함을 보여주는. 꿰뚫어 보는 듯한. 통찰력 있는. 날카로운: *He looked away from Mr. Darden's piercing eyes.* 그는 다든 씨의 날카로운 시선을 피해 눈을 돌렸다.

pi·e·ty /'paɪəti/ *n* [U] respect for God and religion, shown in the way you behave ‖ 행동하는 방식에서 나타나는, 신과 종교에 대한 존경. 경건. 경애. 신심. 독실함

pig¹ /pɪg/ *n* **1** a farm animal with short legs, a fat, usually pink body, and a curled tail ‖ 다리가 짧고, 보통 분홍빛의 살찐 몸통과 꼬불꼬불한 꼬리를 가진 가축. 돼지 **2** SPOKEN an impolite word meaning someone who eats too much, is very dirty, or is unpleasant in

pig

some way‖너무 많이 먹는[아주 더러운, 다소 불유쾌한] 사람을 의미하는 무례한 말. 돼지(같은 사람). 욕심쟁이‖ *You ate all the pizza, you pig.* 피자를 다 먹어치웠구나, 돼지 같으니라구. **3** SPOKEN OFFENSIVE a police officer‖경찰관. 순경

pig² *v* **-gged, -gging**

pig out *phr v* [I] INFORMAL to eat too much of something you like‖좋아하는 것을 너무 많이 먹다. 걸신들린 듯 먹다. 과식하다: *We pigged out on ice cream last night.* 우리는 어젯밤 아이스크림을 걸신들린 듯 먹었다.

pi·geon /ˈpɪdʒən/ *n* a gray bird with short legs that is common in cities‖도시에 흔하게 있는 짧은 다리의 회색빛 새. 비둘기

pi·geon·hole¹ /ˈpɪdʒənˌhoʊl/ *n* one of the small open boxes in a frame inside a desk, in which letters or papers can be put‖편지나 서류를 넣어둘 수 있게 책상 속에 틀로 짜여진 작고 덮개없는 칸 중의 하나. 작은 칸막이. 분류용 칸막이

pigeonhole² *v* [T] to decide unfairly that someone or something belongs to a particular group or type‖사람이나 사물이 특정 집단이나 종류에 속한다고 부당하게 결정하다. …을 고정 관념을 가지고 보다. 색안경을 끼고 보다: *People find out you've been a bartender and pigeonhole you, so you can never do anything else.* 사람들이 네가 바텐더였다는 것을 알고 고정관념을 갖게 돼서, 너는 결코 다른 일을 할 수 없다.

pigeon-toed /ˌ.. ./ *adj* having feet that point in rather than straight forward‖발가락이 쭉 뻗지 않고 안쪽을 가리키는. 새발의. 새발톱형의

pig·gy /ˈpɪgi/ *n* SPOKEN a word meaning a pig, used when speaking to children‖아이들에게 말할 때 쓰여서 돼지를 의미하는 말. 작은[새끼] 돼지

pig·gy·back ride /ˈpɪgiˌbæk ˌraɪd/ *n* a way of carrying a child by putting him/her on your back‖아이를 등에 업어서 데리고 다니는 방법. 업고[등에 지고] 나르기. 어부바 **– piggyback** *adv*

pig·gy bank /ˈ.. ./ *n* a small container, sometimes in the shape of a pig, used by children for saving coins‖아이들이 동전을 저금하는 데 쓰는, 간혹 돼지 모양을 한 작은 용기. 돼지[소형] 저금통

pig·head·ed /ˈpɪgˌhɛdɪd/ *adj* DISAPPROVING determined to do things the way you want even if there are good reasons not to; STUBBORN‖안 해도 되는

합당한 이유가 있음에도 하고 싶은 대로 어떤 것을 단호하게 하는. 고집 센. 완고한. 옹고집의; ⓐ stubborn

pig·let /ˈpɪglɪt/ *n* a young pig‖새끼 돼지

pig·ment /ˈpɪgmənt/ *n* [C, U] **1** a colored substance that is mixed with oil, water etc. to make paint‖물감을 만들기 위해 기름·물 등과 혼합되는 채색 물질. 그림물감. 안료 **2** the natural substance in plants and animals that gives color to hair, skin, leaves etc.‖머리카락·피부·잎 등에 색깔을 부여하는 식물과 동물체 내의 자연적 물질. 색소

pig·men·ta·tion /ˌpɪgmənˈteɪʃən/ *n* [U] the color that a living thing has, or the general color of someone's hair and skin‖생물체가 지닌 색상이나 사람의 머리·피부의 일반적인 색. 착색. (피부)색

pig·pen /ˈpɪgpɛn/, **pig·sty** /ˈpɪgstaɪ/ *n* **1** a place on a farm where pigs are kept‖돼지를 가두어 두는 농장 내 장소. 돼지우리. 양돈장 **2** INFORMAL a place that is very dirty or messy‖매우 더럽거나 어질러진 곳. (돼지우리 같이) 불결한 곳: *Your bedroom is a pigpen!* 네 침실은 돼지우리 같구나!

pig·tail /ˈpɪgteɪl/ *n* one of two long lengths of hair that has been pulled together and tied at either side of the head, worn especially by young girls‖함께 잡아당겨 머리 양쪽에서 묶는, 특히 소녀들이 하는 두 갈래의 긴 머리 중 하나. 땋아 늘인 머리(변발). 양 끝에서 묶은 머리: *a girl with her hair in pigtails* 머리를 땋아 내린 소녀 **—compare** BRAID¹, PONYTAIL **—see picture at** HAIRSTYLE

pike /paɪk/ *n* [C, U] **1** a large fish that eats other fish and lives in rivers and lakes‖다른 물고기를 잡아먹으며 강과 호수에 서식하는 큰 물고기. 강꼬치고기. 파이크 **2** INFORMAL ⇨ TURNPIKE

pile¹ /paɪl/ *n* **1** a large group of similar things collected or thrown together‖함께 모아지거나 버려진 유사한 것들의 큰 집단. 더미. 무더기: *Stuart sighed and looked at the pile of bills and letters on his desk.* 스튜어트는 한숨을 내쉬고 그의 책상 위의 청구서와 편지더미를 바라봤다. **2** a neat collection of similar things put one on top of the other; STACK‖다른 것 위에 또 다른 하나를 (차곡차곡) 쌓아올린 유사한 사물의 가지런한 모음. 층층이[겹겹이] 쌓은 것. 더미. …층; ⓐ stack: *a pile of folded clothes* 개어져 차곡차곡 쌓인 옷 **3 piles of/a pile of** INFORMAL a lot of something‖많은 사물. 다수[대량](의 것). 산더미: *I have piles of work* *to do tonight.* 나는 오늘 밤 할 일이 산더미 같다. **4** [C, U] the soft short threads on a CARPET ‖ 카펫 위의 부드러운 짧은 실. 보풀. 털: *a deep pile carpet* 털이 긴 카펫 **5** ⇨ PILING

pile² *v* **1** [I, T] also **pile up** to make a pile by collecting things together; STACK ‖ 사물들을 함께 모아서 더미를 이루다. 층층이[차곡차곡] 쌓아 올리다. 무더기로 쌓다; ㉴ stack: *A lot of dishes had piled up in the sink.* 많은 접시가 개수대에 쌓여 있었다. **2** [T] to fill something or cover a surface with a lot of something ‖ 어떤 것을 채우거나 많은 사물로 표면을 덮다. …을 산더미같이 싣다. 수북이 담다: *a plate piled high with spaghetti* 스파게티가 수북이 쌓인 접시

pile in/into sth *phr v* [T] INFORMAL if a group of people pile into a place or vehicle, they all try to get into it quickly and at the same time ‖ 일단의 사람들이 한 장소나 차량에 재빨리 동시에 들어가려[타려] 하다. 우르르 들어가다. 몰려가다: *We all piled into the car and left.* 우리 모두 우르르 차를 타고 떠났다.

pile out *phr v* [I] INFORMAL if a group of people pile out of a place or vehicle, they all try to get out of it quickly and at the same time ‖ 일단의 사람들이 한 장소나 차량에서 재빨리 동시에 나오거나 내리려 하다. 우르르 나오다. 몰려 나오다: *As soon as we stopped, the kids piled out and ran to the beach.* 우리가 차를 세우자마자 아이들이 우르르 내려서 해변으로 달렸다.

pile up *phr v* [I, T] to become larger in quantity or amount, or to make something do this; ACCUMULATE ‖ 양이나 크기에서 더 커지다[많아지다], 또는 사물을 이렇게 되게 하다. 산더미처럼 쌓다[쌓이다]. 모으다. 축적하다; ㉴ accumulate: *Debts from the business were piling up quickly.* 사업상의 빚이 빠르게 눈덩이처럼 불어나고 있었다.

pile-up /ˈpaɪlʌp/ *n* INFORMAL a traffic accident in which several vehicles have crashed into each other ‖ 여러 대의 차량이 서로 충돌한 교통사고. 다중[연쇄] 충돌: *a 16-car pileup* 16중 연쇄 충돌

pil·fer /ˈpɪlfɚ/ *v* [I, T] to steal small amounts of things, or things that are not worth much ‖ 소량의 물건이나 가치가 크지 않은 것들을 훔치다. 좀도둑질하다. 슬쩍 훔치다: *He's been pilfering envelopes from work.* 그는 직장에서 봉투를 좀도둑질하고 있었다.

pil·grim /ˈpɪlgrəm/ *n* someone who travels a long way to a holy place for a religious reason ‖ 종교적 이유로 성지로의 먼 거리를 여행하는 사람. 성지 순례자 [참배자]

pil·grim·age /ˈpɪlgrəmɪdʒ/ *n* [C, U] a trip to a holy place for a religious reason ‖ 종교적 이유로 성지로 가는 여행. 성지 순례: *a pilgrimage to Mecca* 메카 성지 순례

pil·ing /ˈpaɪlɪŋ/ *n* a heavy post made of wood, CEMENT or metal, used for supporting a building or bridge ‖ 건물이나 다리를 지탱하는 데에 쓰이는 나무[시멘트, 금속]로 만든 무거운 기둥. 지주

pill /pɪl/ *n* **1** a small solid piece of medicine that you swallow ‖ 삼켜먹는 작고 단단한 개의 약. 알약. 환약. 정제(약): *She's taking pills to control her blood pressure.* 그녀는 혈압을 억제하는 알약을 먹고 있다. **2 the Pill** a pill that women can take in order to avoid having babies ‖ 여성이 임신하는 것을 피하기 위해 먹을 수 있는 알약. 경구 피임약: *Mary has been on the pill for years now.* 메리는 지금 수년째 피임약을 복용해 왔다. **3** INFORMAL someone who annoys you, often a child ‖ 귀찮게 하는 사람, 종종 어린아이. 진절머리 나는[불쾌한] 놈속 썩이는 자녀: *Stop being such a pill, Darren.* 귀찮게 좀 하지 마, 대런.

pil·lage /ˈpɪlɪdʒ/ *v* [I, T] to steal things from a place using violence, especially during a war ‖ 특히 전쟁 중에, 폭력을 써서 한 장소에서 물건을 훔치다. 약탈[강탈]하다. 노략질하다

pil·lar /ˈpɪlɚ/ *n* **1** a tall solid post used as a support for part of a building; COLUMN ‖ 건물의 일부를 위한 받침대로 사용되는 크고 단단한 지주. 기둥; ㉴ column **2 a pillar of the community/church etc.** an active and important member of a group, organization etc. ‖ 집단·조직 등의 활동적이고 중요한 구성원. 공동체/교회의 기둥[중심 인물, 대들보]

pil·low /ˈpɪloʊ/ *n* a cloth bag filled with soft material, that you put your head on when you sleep ‖ 부드러운 소재로 채워, 잠잘 때 머리를 받치는 천 자루. 베개

pil·low·case /ˈpɪloʊˌkeɪs/ *n* a cloth bag for a PILLOW ‖ 베개용 천 자루. 베갯잇

pi·lot /ˈpaɪlət/ *n* **1** someone who flies an aircraft or STEERS a ship ‖ 항공기를 날게하거나 배를 조종하는 사람. 파일럿. 조종사. 조타수: *an airline pilot* 여객기 조종사 **2** a single television program that is made in order to test whether people like it and want to watch more programs ‖ 사람들이 마음에 들어하며 프

로를 더 보기 원하는지의 여부를 시험하기
위해 만들어진 단편 텔레비전 프로그램.
견본용 필름[프로그램] **3 pilot
program/study** a test that is done to
see if an idea or product will be
successful ∥ 아이디어나 제품이 성공적일
지 알아보기 위해 행해지는 시험. 시험
(용) 프로그램/연구: *We'll start a pilot
program to find the best way of
collecting bottles for recycling.* 우리는 재
활용을 위해 빈 병을 수집하는 최선의 방
법을 찾기 위한 시험 프로그램을 시작할
것이다. – **pilot** *v* [T]

pilot light /'.. ../ *n* a small gas flame
that burns all the time in a piece of
equipment such as a STOVE, that is used
for lighting the whole piece of
equipment ∥ 난로 등의 장비에서 항상 불
이 붙어서 장비 전체에 불을 당기는 데 쓰
이는 작은 가스 불꽃. 점화용 보조 버너
[불꽃]

pimp /pɪmp/ *n* a man who controls
PROSTITUTEs and makes money from
them ∥ 창녀들을 관리하고 그들에게서 돈
을 버는 사람. 포주. 뚜쟁이. 매춘 알선자

pim·ple /'pɪmpəl/ *n* a small raised red
spot on your skin, especially on your
face ∥ 피부, 특히 얼굴에 돋은 작고 붉은
점. 여드름. 뾰루지 – **pimply** *adj*

PIN /pɪn/ *n* Personal Identification
Number; a number that only you know,
that you must give in order to use a
service such as getting money from a
bank machine ∥ Personal Identification
Number(개인 식별 번호)의 약어; 현금 지
급기에서 돈을 인출하는 등 서비스를 이용
하기 위해 제시해야 하는, 본인만 아는 번
호. 비밀번호

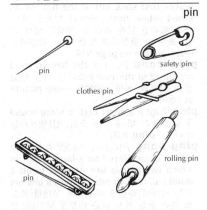

pin

safety pin

clothes pin

rolling pin

pin

pin¹ /pɪn/ *n* **1** a short thin piece of metal
with a sharp point at one end, used

especially for fastening pieces of cloth
together ∥ 특히 천 조각을 함께 고정하는
데 쓰이는, 한 끝이 날카로운 짧고 가느다
란 금속 조각. 핀. 가는 핀 **2** a piece of
jewelry fastened to your clothes by a pin
∥ 핀으로 옷에 부착하는 장신구류. 장식
핀. 브로치. 핀 달린 기장(배지): *What a
pretty pin!* 정말 예쁜 핀이구나! **3** a thin
piece of metal used as a support for
something ∥ 사물의 지지대로서 사용되는
가느다란 금속 조각. 지지[고정] 핀[못]:
He has to have pins put in his ankle. 그
는 발목에 고정 핀들을 박아야 한다. —
see also CLOTHESPIN, PINS AND NEEDLES,
ROLLING PIN, SAFETY PIN

pin² *v* **-nned, -nning 1** [T] to fasten
something or join things together with a
pin or pins ∥ 핀이나 핀들로 어떤 것을 고
정시키거나 사물들을 함께 결합시키다. …
을 핀으로 꽂아 놓다: *Can you pin this
announcement on the bulletin board for
me?* 이 공고문을 나 대신 게시판에 붙여
줄래? / *He wore campaign buttons
pinned to his lapels.* 그는 캠페인 배지를
양복 깃에 핀으로 달았다. **2 pin your
hopes on** to hope that something will
happen, because all your plans depend
on it ∥ 모든 계획이 그것에 달려 있어서 어
떤 일이 일어날 것을 바라다. …에 희망을
걸다. …에만 의존하다: *I hope she's not
pinning all her hopes on winning.* 나는
그녀가 승리에만 모든 희망을 걸지 않기를
바란다. **3 pin the blame on sb** to
blame someone for something, often
unfairly ∥ 종종 어떤 일에 대해 부당하게
남을 비난하다. …에게 비난을 뒤집어씌우
다: *Don't try to pin the blame on me!* 나
에게 엉뚱한 비난의 화살을 돌릴 생각하지
마! **4** [T] to trap someone so that s/he is
unable to move ∥ 사람을 가두어서 움직일
수 없게 하다. 꼼짝 못하게 하다: *He was
pinned under the car.* 그는 차 아래에 깔
려 꼼짝 못했다.

pin sb/sth down *phr v* [T] **1** to make
someone decide something, or tell you
what the decision is ∥ 남에게 어떤 일을
결정하게 하다, 또는 결정의 결과를 밝히
게 하다. …을 분명히 하게 하다: *I
couldn't pin him down to a definite
date for the meeting.* 나는 그에게 그 회
의의 정확한 날짜를 못박게 할 수 없었다.
2 to understand something clearly or be
able to describe exactly what it is ∥ 어떤
것을 분명히 이해하거나 그것이 무엇인지
정확히 설명할 수 있다. …을 명확히 알아
내다[파악하다]: *I can't pin down his
accent.* 그의 억양을 (어느 지방 것인지)
꼭 집어 낼 수 없다.

pin·ball /'pɪnbɔl/ *n* [U] a game played on a machine with lights and bells and a sloping board in which you push buttons to try to keep a ball from rolling off the board ‖ 전등·종·경사진 널빤지가 있는 기계 위에서 공이 널빤지에서 굴러 떨어지는 것을 막기 위해 단추를 누르며 하는 놀이. 핀볼(게임): a *pinball machine* (게임) 기계

pin·cer /'pɪnsɚ, 'pɪntʃɚ/ *n* one of the pair of CLAWs (=sharp curved nails) that some insects and SHELLFISH have ‖ 일부 곤충과 갑각류가 가지고 있는 한 쌍의 발톱 중의 하나. 집게발

pinch¹ /pɪntʃ/ *v* **1** [T] to press a part of someone's flesh very tightly, either between two hard surfaces or between your finger and thumb ‖ 두 개의 단단한 표면 사이 또는 검지와 엄지 사이로 남의 살 일부분을 꽉 쥐다. …을 끼워서 조이다. …을 꼬집다: *Ow! Dad, Carlo pinched me!* 아야! 아빠, 카를로가 저를 꼬집었어요! **2** [I, T] if your clothes, shoes etc. pinch you, they are too tight and hurt you ‖ 옷·신발 등이 너무 조여서 아프다. 꽉 끼어 아프다[다치다] **3 pinch pennies** to be careful to spend as little money as possible ‖ 가능한 한 돈을 거의 안 쓰려고 주의하다. 극도로 절약하다 **4** INFORMAL to steal something that is small or not worth much ‖ 작거나 가치가 별로 없는 것을 훔치다: *I pinched a newspaper from the doctor's office.* 나는 그 의사의 진료실에서 신문을 훔쳤다.

pinch² *n* **1 pinch of salt/pepper etc.** a small amount of salt, pepper etc. that you can hold between your finger and thumb ‖ 검지와 엄지손가락 사이로 집을 수 있는 적은 양의 소금·후추 등. 소량의 소금/후추: *Sprinkle each bun with a pinch of sugar.* 각각의 둥근 빵에 소량의 설탕을 뿌리시오. **2** an act of pinching someone ‖ 남을 꼬집는 행위. 꼬집기: *She gave him a pinch on the cheek.* 그녀는 그의 볼을 꼬집었다. **3 in a pinch** if necessary in a difficult or urgent situation ‖ 어렵거나 위급한 상황에 필요하다면. 만일의 경우[유사시]에는: *I could get $300, maybe $400 dollars in a pinch.* 나는 300달러, 유사시에는 400달러일지라도 살 수 있었다.

pinched /pɪntʃt/ *adj* **1** not having enough money to do what you want ‖ 원하는 것을 하기에 충분한 돈을 가지고 있지 않은. 궁한. 쪼들리는: *financially pinched schools* 재정적으로 쪼들리는 학교들 **2** a pinched face looks thin and unhealthy because someone may be ill, too cold, very old, or tired ‖ 아마도 아파서[너무 추워서, 매우 늙어서, 피곤해서] 얼굴이 야위고 병약해 보이는. 수척해진

pinch-hit /ˌ. './ *v* [I] **1** to BAT for someone else in a game of baseball ‖ 야구 시합에서 다른 사람 대신 공을 치다. 대타자가 되다. 대타하다 **2** to do something for someone else because s/he is suddenly not able to do it ‖ 다른 사람이 갑자기 어떤 일을 할 수 없어서 대신 해주다. 긴급 대역을 맡다: *Could you pinch-hit for Larry in the meeting today?* 오늘 회의에 래리 대신 참석해 줄 수 있어요? **– pinch-hitter** *n*

pin·cush·ion /'pɪn,kuʃən/ *n* a small PILLOW into which you stick pins until you need to use them ‖ 사용할 필요가 있을 때까지 핀들을 꽂아 두는 작은 베개. 바늘겨레. 바늘방석

pine¹ /paɪn/, **pine tree** /'. ./ *n* [C, U] a tree with long leaves shaped like needles, or the wood of this tree ‖ 바늘처럼 생긴 긴 잎을 가진 나무, 또는 이 나무의 목재. 소나무[솔](재목)

pine², **pine away** *v* [I] to gradually become weaker and less healthy because you are very sad and lonely ‖ 매우 슬프고 외로워서 점차적으로 더 약해지고 건강이 상하게 되다. 초췌[수척]해지다

pine for *sb/sth phr v* [T] to become unhappy or ill because you cannot be with someone you love or in a place you love ‖ 사랑하는 사람과 함께 있거나 좋아하는 장소에 있지 못해서 불행해지거나 아프게 되다. …을 애타게 그리워하다[갈망하다]

pine·ap·ple /'paɪn,æpəl/ *n* [C, U] a large brown tropical fruit with pointed leaves that stick out of the top, or its sweet yellow flesh ‖ 꼭대기 밖으로 튀어나온 뾰족한 잎을 가진 큰 갈색의 열대 과일, 또는 그 달콤하고 노란 과육. 파인애플 —see picture on page 944

pine cone /'. ./ *n* the brown seed container of the PINE ‖ 소나무 씨를 담고 있는 갈색의 씨방. 솔방울 —see picture at CONE

ping /pɪŋ/ *n* a short high RINGing sound ‖ 짧고 높은 벨 울리는 소리. 핑[땡](하는 소리) **– ping** *v* [I]

ping-pong /'pɪŋpɑŋ, -pɔŋ/ *n* [U] an indoor game played on a large table, in which two people use PADDLEs to hit a small ball to each other across a low net ‖ 두 사람이 라켓을 사용하여 상대방 쪽으로 작은 공을 쳐서 낮은 네트를 넘기는, 큰 탁자 위에서 하는 실내경기. 탁구

pin·ion /'pɪnyən/ *v* [T] FORMAL to hold

or tie up someone's arms or legs very tightly so s/he cannot move ‖ 움직이지 못하도록 남의 팔이나 다리를 꽉 잡거나 묶다. 포박[결박]하다

pink /pɪŋk/ *adj* **1** pale red ‖ 분홍색의: *a pink dress* 분홍색 드레스 **2** used when talking about things relating to HOMOSEXUAL people ‖ 동성애자와 관련된 것들에 대해서 이야기할 때 쓰여. 동성애자의: *the pink vote in the local election* 지방 선거에서의 동성애자 표 – **pink** *n* [C, U]

pink·ie, pinky /'pɪŋki/ *n* the smallest finger on your hand ‖ 손의 가장 작은 손가락. 새끼손가락

pink slip /'. ./ *n* a written warning you get when your job is going to end because there is not enough work ‖ 충분한 일거리가 없어서 직무가 곧 종료될 때 받는 서면 통지서. 해고 통지서

pin·na·cle /'pɪnəkəl/ *n* **1** [singular] the most successful, powerful, or exciting part of something ‖ 사물의 가장 성공적인 [강력한, 흥분시키는] 부분. 정점. 절정: *She reached the pinnacle of success as a writer at the age of 45.* 그녀는 45세에 작가로서 성공의 정점에 이르렀다. **2** a high mountain top ‖ 높은[뾰족한] 산봉우리 **3** a pointed stone decoration like a small tower on top of a church or castle ‖ 교회나 성의 꼭대기의 작은 탑 같은 뾰족한 돌 장식. 작은 뾰족탑

pin·point¹ /'pɪnpɔɪnt/ *v* [T] **1** to say exactly what the facts about something really are ‖ 어떤 것에 대한 사실이 실제로 어떤 것인지 정확히 말하다. 정확히 지적하다[설명하다]: *It was impossible to pinpoint the cause of the crash.* 그 추락의 원인을 정확히 설명하기는 불가능했다 **2** to find or show the exact position of something ‖ 사물의 정확한 위치를 찾거나 나타내다: *First, we have to pinpoint the location of the leak.* 우선, 우리는 새는 위치를 정확히 찾아내야 한다.

pinpoint² *adj* **with pinpoint accuracy** without even the smallest mistake ‖ 가장 작은 실수조차도 없이. 정확[정밀]하게: *the plane's ability to drop bombs with pinpoint accuracy* 정밀하게 폭탄을 투하하는 항공기의 성능

pinpoint³ *n* a very small area or amount of something ‖ 사물의 매우 작은 구역이나 크기. 아주 작은[사소한] 것[일]: *a tiny pinpoint of light* 아주 작고 희미한 불빛

pin·prick /'pɪn,prɪk/ *n* a very small hole or mark in something, like one made by a pin ‖ 핀으로 만든 것처럼 사물에 난 매우 작은 구멍이나 자국. 작은 핀구멍

pins and nee·dles /ˌ. . '../ *n* **1** the uncomfortable feeling of being PRICKed that you get when your blood returns to a part of your body after it was blocked ‖ 신체 일부분에 피가 막혔다가 되돌아올 때 느끼는 콕콕 쑤시는 불편한 느낌 **2 be on pins and needles** to be very nervous ‖ 매우 불안해하다. 바늘방석에 앉은 것 같다. 좌불안석이다: *Mom's been on pins and needles waiting to hear from you.* 엄마는 네 소식을 기다리며 좌불안석이다.

pin·stripe /'pɪnstraɪp/ *n* dark-colored cloth with a pattern of thin light-colored lines on it ‖ 겉에 가늘고 밝은 색깔의 선 문양이 있는 짙은 색깔의 천. 가는 세로줄 무늬 천: *a blue pinstripe suit* 가는 세로줄 무늬의 파란 양복 – **pinstriped** *adj*

pint /paɪnt/ *n* a unit for measuring liquid, equal to 16 FLUID OUNCEs or 0.4732 liters ‖ 16액량 온스나 0.4732리터와 동등한 액체를 재는 단위. 액량 단위. 파인트

pin·up /'pɪnʌp/ *n* a picture of an attractive person, especially someone famous or someone with few clothes on, that is put up on a wall ‖ 특히 벽에 붙이는 유명하거나 옷을 거의 입지 않은 매력적인 사람의 사진. 유명인[미인] 사진. 핀업

pi·o·neer¹ /ˌpaɪə'nɪr/ *n* **1** one of the first people to travel to a new or unknown place and begin living there, farming etc. ‖ 새롭거나 미지의 장소로 이동해서 그곳에서 거주·농사 등을 시작한 최초의 사람들 중의 한 명. 개척자: *Grandpa's family were pioneers in the Oregon Territory.* 할아버지 가족은 오리건 지역에서 개척자였다. **2** one of the first people to do something that other people will later develop or continue to do ‖ 다른 사람들이 나중에 발전시키거나 계속할 어떤 일을 하는 최초의 사람들 중의 한 명. 선구자: *the pioneers of modern space travel* 현대 우주 여행의 선구자들

pioneer² *v* [T] to be the first one to do, invent, or use something new ‖ 새로운 것을 하는[발명하는, 이용하는] 최초의 사람이 되다. …의 개척[선구]자가 되다: *a hospital pioneering a new type of surgery* 새로운 유형의 수술법을 선도하는 병원

pi·ous /'paɪəs/ *adj* having strong religious beliefs, and showing this in the way you behave ‖ 강한 종교적 신념을 갖고, 행동으로 이것을 나타내는. 신앙심이

깊은. 독실한 —opposite IMPIOUS

pipe¹ /paɪp/ n **1** a tube through which a liquid or gas flows ‖ 액체나 기체가 흐르는 관. (도)관: *a sewer pipe* 하수도관 **2** a thing used for smoking tobacco, consisting of a small tube with a container shaped like a bowl at one end ‖ 한쪽 끝에 사발 모양의 용기가 달린 작은 관으로 만들어져 담배를 피우는 데 사용되는 물건. 담뱃대: *Harry smiled and lit his pipe.* 해리는 웃으면서 파이프에 불을 붙였다. **3** one of the metal tubes that air is forced through in an ORGAN ‖ 풍금에서 공기를 강제로 통하게 하는 금속관 중의 하나. 음관. 파이프 **4** a simple musical instrument like a tube that you blow through ‖ 불어서 소리 내는 관 같은 단순한 악기. 피리

pipe² v [T] to send a liquid or gas through a pipe to another place ‖ 관을 통해서 액체나 기체를 다른 장소로 보내다. …을 관으로 보내다: *oil piped from Alaska* 알래스카에서 송유관으로 보내진 기름

pipe down phr v [I] SPOKEN used in order to tell someone rudely to stop talking or making a noise ‖ 이야기하거나 시끄럽게 하는 것을 멈추라고 남에게 무례하게 말하는 데 쓰여. 입을 다물다: *Pipe down! I'm trying to listen to this!* 입 다물어! 이것을 들을 수가 없잖아!

pipe up phr v [I] INFORMAL to start speaking, or speak more loudly ‖ 말하기 시작하거나, 더 큰 소리로 말하다. 입을 열다. 소리를 높이다: *Dennis piped up, saying he didn't agree.* 데니스는 동의하지 않는다고 말하면서, 목소리를 높였다.

pipe dream /'. ./ n a hope, idea, plan etc. that will probably never work or happen ‖ 어쩌면 결코 이루어지거나 일어날 것 같지 않은 희망·생각·계획 등. 공상. 몽상: *Money and fame – isn't that all a pipe dream?* 부와 명성. 그게 다 허황된 꿈이 아니냐?

pipe·line /'paɪp-laɪn/ n **1** a long line of connecting pipes, used for carrying gas, oil etc. over long distances ‖ 장거리에 걸쳐 가스·기름 등을 운송하는 데 쓰이는 길게 늘어선 연결관들. 수송관. 송유관 **2 be in the pipeline** if a plan, idea or event is in the pipeline, it is still being prepared, but it will happen or be completed soon ‖ 계획[생각, 행사]이 아직 준비 중에 있지만 곧 일어나거나 완성되다. 진행 중이다. 구체화 단계에 있다

pip·ing¹ /'paɪpɪŋ/ n [U] **1** several pipes, or a system of pipes, used for carrying a liquid or gas ‖ 액체나 기체를 나르기 위해 사용되는 몇 개의 관들이나 관들의 체계. 배관 (시설): *Something's wrong with the piping in the building.* 건물의 배관 시설에 뭔가 이상이 있다. **2** thin cloth CORDs used as decorations on clothes and furniture ‖ 옷과 가구의 장식으로 사용되는 얇은 천 끈. 가두리 장식

piping² adj **piping hot** very hot ‖ 몹시 뜨거운: *piping hot soup* 매우 뜨거운 수프

pip·squeak /'pɪpskwik/ n SPOKEN someone whom you think is not worth attention or respect, especially because s/he is small or young ‖ 특히 작거나 어리기 때문에 주목하거나 존중할 만한 가치가 없다고 생각하는 사람. 보잘것없는 사람. 좀팽이: *Shut up, you little pipsqueak!* 닥쳐, 이 좀팽이야!

pi·quant /pi'kant, 'pikənt/ adj FORMAL **1** having a pleasantly hot taste ‖ 시원하게 매운 맛을 지닌. 짜릿한. 얼얼한. 톡 쏘는: *a piquant chili sauce* 얼얼한 칠리 소스 **2** interesting and exciting ‖ 재미있고 흥분시키는. 흥미를 자극하는: *piquant photos of life in Paris* 파리에서의 생활을 담은 흥미진진한 사진들 – **piquancy** /'pikənsi/ n [U]

pique¹ /pik/ v [T] **1 pique sb's interest/curiosity** to make someone very interested in something ‖ 남을 어떤 것에 대해 매우 관심 있게 만들다. 남의 관심/호기심을 불러일으키다: *Go on, you've piqued my interest.* 계속해 봐, 관심이 좀 가는데. **2** FORMAL to make someone feel annoyed or upset ‖ 남을 짜증나게 하거나 화나게 하다. 약을 올리다. 화나게 하다

pique² n [U] FORMAL a feeling of being annoyed or upset ‖ 짜증나거나 화가 난 감정. 화. 분개. 짜증: *Greta left in a fit of pique.* 그레타는 홧김에 떠났다.

pi·ra·cy /'paɪrəsi/ n [U] **1** the act of illegally copying and selling other people's work ‖ 다른 사람들의 작품을 불법적으로 복제해서 판매하는 행위. 저작권 침해: *software piracy* 소프트웨어 저작권 침해 **2** the crime of attacking and stealing from ships ‖ 배를 공격해서 탈취하는 범죄. 해적 행위

pi·ra·nha /pə'ranə, -'ræn-/ n a South American fish with sharp teeth that lives in rivers and eats flesh ‖ 강에 서식하면서 육식하는 날카로운 이가 있는 남미의 물고기. 피라냐

pi·rate¹ /'paɪrɪt/ n **1** someone who illegally copies and sells another person's work ‖ 다른 사람의 작품을 불법적으로 복제해서 판매하는 사람. 저작권 침해자: *We're losing thousands of* *dollars to video pirates.* 우리는 비디오 무단 복제자들 때문에 수천 달러의 손실을 보고 있다. **2** someone who sails on the oceans, attacking other boats and stealing things from them ‖ 바다 위를 항해하며 다른 배들을 공격해서 물건을 도둑질하는 사람. 해적

pirate² *v* [T] to illegally copy and sell other people's work ‖ 다른 사람들의 작품을 불법적으로 복제해서 판매하다. 저작권을 침해하다: *pirated CDs* 불법 복제된 CD들

pir·ou·ette /ˌpɪruˈɛt/ *n* a very fast turn made on one toe or the front part of one foot, especially by a BALLET dancer ‖ 특히 발레 무용수가 한 발가락 또는 한 발의 앞부분으로 하는 매우 빠른 회전. 피루엣. 발끝으로 돌기 – **pirouette** *v* [I]

Pis·ces /ˈpaɪsiz/ *n* **1** [singular] the twelfth sign of the ZODIAC, represented by two fish ‖ 두 마리로 상징되는 황도 12궁의 열두 번째 별자리. 물고기자리 **2** someone born between February 19 and March 20 ‖ 2월 19일과 3월 20일 사이에 태어난 사람. 물고기좌 태생자

piss¹ /pɪs/ *v* SPOKEN an impolite word meaning to URINATE ‖ 소변보기를 의미하는 무례한 단어. 오줌을 누다

piss sb ↔ **off** *phr v* [T] SPOKEN an impolite expression meaning to annoy someone very much ‖ 남을 아주 많이 화나게 하는 것을 의미하는 무례한 표현. …을 열 받게 하다: *It really pisses me off when you treat me like a child.* 네가 나를 어린애 취급할 때면 난 정말로 열 받아.

piss² *n* SPOKEN **1** [singular] an impolite word meaning an act of urinating (URINATE) ‖ 소변을 보는 행위를 의미하는 무례한 단어. 오줌 누기: *I need to take a piss.* 나는 오줌을 누어야겠어. **2** [U] an impolite word meaning URINE ‖ 소변을 의미하는 무례한 단어. 오줌

pissed /pɪst/, **pissed off** /ˌ. ˈ./ *adj* SPOKEN an impolite expression meaning very annoyed ‖ 매우 화가 난 것을 의미하는 무례한 표현. 열 받은: *Frank's really pissed off.* 프랭크는 정말로 열 받았다.

pis·ta·chi·o /pɪˈstæʃiˌoʊ/ *n* a small green nut that you can eat ‖ 먹을 수 있는 작은 녹색 견과. 피스타치오 열매

pis·tol /ˈpɪstl/ *n* a small gun that you can use with one hand ‖ 한 손으로 사용할 수 있는 작은 총. 권총

pis·ton /ˈpɪstən/ *n* a part of an engine consisting of a short solid piece of metal inside a tube, that moves up and down to make the other parts of the engine move ‖ 관 안쪽에 짧고 단단한 금속 조각으로 만들어져 엔진의 다른 부분을 움직이도록 위아래로 움직이는 엔진의 일부분. 피스톤

pit¹ /pɪt/ *n*

1 ▶HOLE 구멍◀ a hole or a low area in the ground, especially one made by digging ‖ 특히 땅을 파서 만든 땅 속의 구멍이나 지면에서 낮은 지역. 구멍. 우묵한 곳: *a barbecue pit* 바비큐 구덩이 / *an open pit mine* (=where minerals are dug out from the surface of the earth) 노천 채굴 갱

2 ▶MARK 표시◀ a small hollow mark in the surface of something ‖ 사물의 표면에 난 작고 우묵한 자국. 표면의 팬 곳: *There are tiny scratches and pits on the windshield.* 자동차 앞유리에 작은 긁힌 자국과 팬 곳들이 있다.

3 ▶MESSY PLACE 엉망인 장소◀ SPOKEN a house or room that is messy or in bad condition ‖ 엉망이거나 상태가 안 좋은 집이나 방. 지저분한[형편없는] 장소: *Erica's house is a total pit!* 에리카의 집은 정말 형편없어!

4 be the pits SPOKEN used in order to say that a thing or situation is very bad ‖ 일이나 상황이 매우 안 좋다는 것을 말하는 데에 쓰여. 최악이다: *That would be the pits if you got sick.* 만약 네가 아프게 되면 그건 최악이야.

5 in the pit of your stomach if you feel bad emotions in the pit of your stomach, they are so strong that you almost feel sick ‖ 나쁜 감정이 너무나 강해서 거의 아플 지경이 되어. 명치에서 속이 메슥거리는: *The strange noises gave her a funny feeling in the pit of her stomach.* 그녀는 이상한 소음 때문에 속이 메슥거리는 기분 나쁜 느낌을 받았다.

6 ▶IN FRUIT 과일 속에◀ the single large hard seed in some fruits ‖ 일부 과일 속에 있는 한 개의 크고 단단한 씨. 핵. 씨: *a peach pit* 복숭아 씨

7 ▶FOR CARS 자동차용◀ a place beside a race track where a race car can quickly get more gas or be repaired ‖ 경주 자동차가 빠르게 휘발유를 더 주입받거나 수리 받을 수 있는 경주 트랙 옆의 장소. 피트

8 ⇨ ORCHESTRA PIT

9 ⇨ MINE²

pit² *v* **-tted, -tting** [T] **1** to take out the single large hard seed inside some fruits ‖ 일부 과일 안에 있는 한 개의 크고 단단한 씨를 꺼내다. 씨를 빼다 **2** to put small marks or holes in the surface of something ‖ 사물의 표면에 작은 자국을 내거나 구멍을 뚫다. …에 구멍을 파다.

우묵하게 하다: *The disease had pitted and scarred his skin.* 그 병은 그의 피부에 곰보 자국과 흉터를 남겼다.

pit sb/sth **against** sb/sth *phr v* [T] to test your strength, ability, power etc. against someone else ‖ 다른 사람에 맞서서 힘·능력·세력 등을 시험하다. …과 싸우게[겨루게] 하다: *This week's big game pits Houston against Miami.* 이번 주의 큰 경기로서 휴스턴과 마이애미가 서로 붙는다.

pit bull ter·ri·er /ˌ. . ˈ.../ *n* a short, extremely strong, and often violent dog ‖ 작으면서 대단히 힘이 세고 종종 사나운 개. 핏불테리어

pitch[1] /pɪtʃ/ *v*

1 ▶THROW 던지다◀ [T] to throw something, especially with a lot of force ‖ 특히 많은 힘을 들여서 사물을 던지다. 던지다. 집어[내]던지다: *Carl tore up Amy's letter and pitched it into the fire.* 칼은 에이미의 편지를 찢어서 불 속에 던졌다. / *a group of men pitching horseshoes in the park* 공원에서 편자 던지기를 하는 한 무리의 남자들

2 ▶BASEBALL 야구◀ [I, T] to throw the ball in a game of baseball ‖ 야구 경기에서 공을 던지다. (…에게) 투구하다: *Who's pitching for the Red Sox today?* 오늘 레드 삭스 투수는 누구냐?

3 ▶FALL 떨어지다◀ [I, T] to fall suddenly and heavily in a particular direction, or to make someone or something fall in this way ‖ 특정한 방향으로 갑자기 묵직하게 떨어지다, 또는 사람이나 사물을 이런 식으로 떨어지게 하다. 곤두박질로 떨어지다[떨어지게 하다]. 고꾸라지다: *A sudden stop pitched her into the windshield.* 차가 갑자기 멈추어서 그녀는 자동차 앞유리로 곤두박질쳤다. / *He tripped and pitched forward into the bushes.* 그는 발이 걸려 덤불 속으로 고꾸라졌다.

4 ▶VOICE/MUSIC 목소리/음악◀ [T] to make a sound be produced at a particular level ‖ 특정한 높이로 소리가 나게 하다. …의 음의 높이를 조절하다: *The song is pitched too high for me.* 그 노래는 내게 너무 고음이었다.

5 pitch a tent to set up a tent ‖ 천막을 치다

6 ▶SELL/PERSUADE 팔다/설득하다◀ [I, T] INFORMAL to try to persuade someone to buy or do something ‖ 남에게 어떤 것을 사거나 하도록 설득하려고 애쓰다. 끈질기게 권유하다: *The meeting is your chance to pitch your ideas to the boss.* 그 회의는 사장에게 당신의 생각을 잘 전

달할 수 있는 기회입니다.

7 ▶SAY/WRITE 말하다/쓰다◀ [T] to say or write something in a way that you know will be understood by particular people; aim ‖ 특정한 사람들이 이해하리라는 것을 인식하고서 어떤 것을 말하거나 쓰다. …을 대상으로 말하다[쓰다]; 목표로 하다: *a TV show pitched at children* 아이들을 대상으로 하는 TV 쇼

8 ▶SHIP/PLANE 배/비행기◀ [I] to move roughly with the back and front going up and down ‖ 뒤와 앞이 위아래로 거칠게 움직이다. 앞뒤로 흔들리다

pitch in *phr v* [I] INFORMAL to start to work eagerly as a member of a group ‖ 한 집단의 일원으로서 열심히 일하기 시작하다. 협력[조력]하다: *If we all pitch in, it won't take very long to finish.* 우리 모두가 협력한다면 곧 끝낼 수 있을 겁니다.

pitch[2] *n* **1** how high or low a musical note or someone's voice is ‖ 음표나 사람 목소리의 높고 낮음의 정도. 소리(음성)의 높낮이. 음높이 **2** a throw of the ball in a game of baseball, or a way in which it can be thrown ‖ 야구 경기에서 볼을 던지기, 또는 볼을 던지는 방법. 투구(법) **3** [singular, U] the strength of your feelings or opinions about something ‖ 어떤 것에 대한 감정이나 의견의 세기. 강도. 정도: *Their excitement rose to fever pitch.* (=a very excited level) 그들의 흥분은 최고조에 달했다. **4** INFORMAL the things someone says in order to persuade people to buy or do something ‖ 사람들이 어떤 것을 사거나 하도록 설득하려고 말하는 것들. 끈질긴 권유. 선전. 광고: *a sales pitch* 판매 광고 **5** [U] a dark sticky substance that is used on roofs, the bottoms of ships etc. to stop water coming through ‖ 물이 들어오는 것을 막기 위해 지붕·배의 바닥 등에 사용되는 끈적거리는 검은 물질. 피치. 역청

pitch black /ˌ. ˈ./ *adj* completely black or dark ‖ 완전히 깜깜하거나 어두운. 새까만. 칠흑 같은: *It was pitch black in the basement and really scary.* 지하실은 칠흑같이 어두웠고 정말 무서웠다.

pitch·er /ˈpɪtʃɚ/ *n* **1** a container used for holding and pouring liquids ‖ 액체를 담고 붓는 데에 사용하는 용기. (물)주전자. 피처: *a pitcher of beer* 맥주 한 피처 —see picture at CONTAINER **2** the baseball player who throws the balls for the BATTER to hit ‖ 타자에게 치라고 공을 던지는 야구 선수. 투수 —see picture on page 946

pitch·fork /ˈpɪtʃfork/ *n* a tool with a long handle and two or three long curved metal points at one end, used especially for lifting HAY (=dried cut grass) ∥ 특히 건초를 들어올리는 데에 쓰이는 긴 손잡이와 한쪽 끝에 두세 개의 길고 굽은 금속 꼬챙이가 달려 있는 도구. 쇠스랑

pit·e·ous /'pɪtiəs/ *adj* LITERARY making you feel pity ∥ 연민을 느끼게 하는. 연민의 정을 자아내는. 애처로운: *a piteous cry* 애처로운 울음(소리)

pit·fall /'pɪtfɔl/ *n* a problem or difficulty that is likely to happen, or a mistake that is likely to be made ∥ 발생할 것 같은 문제나 어려움, 또는 할 것 같은 실수. 숨겨진 위험. 함정: *Following the instructions now can help you avoid a number of pitfalls later on.* 지금 지시 사항을 따르면 나중에 많은 문제들을 피하는 데에 도움이 된다.

pith·y /'pɪθi/ *adj* spoken or written in strong clear language without wasting any words ∥ 말을 조금도 낭비하지 않고 강하고 분명한 언어로 말하거나 쓴. 날카로운. 명쾌한. 힘찬: *pithy comments* 명쾌한 논평

pit·i·ful /'pɪtɪfəl/ *adj* **1** making you feel pity or sympathy ∥ 연민이나 동정을 느끼게 하는. 가여운. 불쌍한: *a pitiful sight* 불쌍한 광경 **2** not good enough to deserve respect ∥ 존경을 받을 만큼 충분히 좋지 않은. 한심한. 형편없는: *His performance last night was pitiful.* 어젯밤 그의 공연은 형편없었다. **– pitifully** *adv*

pit·i·less /'pɪtɪlɪs/ *adj* showing no pity ∥ 아무런 동정도 나타내지 않는. 인정사정 없는. 매정한: *a pitiless dictator* 무자비한 독재자

pit stop /'. ./ *n* **1** a time when a race car stops beside the track in order to get more gas or be quickly repaired ∥ 경주 자동차가 휘발유를 더 얻거나 빨리 수리받기 위해 트랙 옆에 멈추는 시간. 정차 시간 **2 make a pit stop** SPOKEN **a)** to stop when driving on a long trip in order to get food, gas etc. ∥ 운전을 하며 장거리 여행을 할 때 음식·휘발유 등을 얻기 위해 멈추다. 도중에 정차하다 **b)** to go to the toilet ∥ 화장실에 가다.

pit·tance /'pɪt‾ns/ *n* [singular] a very small amount of money ∥ 아주 작은 액수. 약간의 수입[수당]

pit·y¹ /'pɪti/ *n* **1** [U] sympathy for someone who is suffering or unhappy ∥ 고통을 받고 있거나 불행한 사람에 대한 동정. 불쌍히 여김. 동정. 연민: *I don't need your pity!* 나는 네 동정 따위는 필요 없어! **2** [singular] a sad or unfortunate

situation ∥ 슬프거나 유감스러운 상황. 안타까운[애석한] 일: *It's a pity (that) so much time was wasted.* 그렇게 많은 시간이 낭비됐다니 안타까운 일이다. **3 take/have pity on sb** to feel sympathy for someone and do something to help him/her ∥ 남을 동정해서 도와 주려고 어떤 일을 하다. …을 불쌍히[가엾게] 여기다

pity² *v* [T] to feel sympathy for someone because s/he is in a bad situation ∥ 남이 나쁜 상황에 있기 때문에 동정하다. …을 불쌍히 여기다: *I pity anyone who has to live with Sherry.* 나는 셰리와 함께 살아야 하는 사람이라면 누구라도 불쌍히 여긴다.

piv·ot¹ /'pɪvət/ *n* a fixed central point or pin on which something balances or turns ∥ 사물이 균형을 잡거나 회전을 하는 고정된 중앙의 접점이나 축. 회전축

pivot² *v* [I, T] to turn or balance on a central point, or to make something do this ∥ 중앙의 접점 위에서 회전을 하거나 균형을 잡다, 또는 사물을 이렇게 하게 하다. …을 회전시키다. 회전축으로 회전하다: *McGee pivots, and throws the ball to second base.* 맥기는 몸을 홱 돌려 2루로 공을 던진다.

piv·ot·al /'pɪvətəl/ *adj* **a pivotal event/moment/role etc.** an event, moment etc. that has a very important effect on the way something develops ∥ 어떤 일이 발전하는 과정에서 매우 중요한 영향을 미치는 사건·순간 등. 결정적인[중추적인] 사건[순간, 역할]: *Parker played a pivotal role in getting the deal.* 파커는 거래를 성사시키는 데에 중추적인 역할을 했다.

pix·el /'pɪksəl/ *n* TECHNICAL the smallest unit of an image on a computer screen ∥ 컴퓨터 화면상의 영상의 가장 작은 단위. 화소(畫素). 픽셀

pix·ie /'pɪksi/ *n* a very small imaginary creature with magic powers, that looks like a person ∥ 사람처럼 생겨서 마법의 힘을 가진 아주 작은 상상의 창조물. 요정

piz·za /'pitsə/ *n* [C, U] a thin flat round bread, baked with TOMATO, cheese, and usually vegetables or meat on top ∥ 토마토와 치즈 그리고 대체로 맨 위에 야채나 고기를 넣어 구운 얇고 평평하며 둥근 빵. 피자

piz·zazz /pə'zæz/ *n* [U] an exciting quality or style ∥ 흥분시키는 특성이나 양식. 활기. 생기: *a theater show that needs more pizzazz* 활기가 더 필요한 극장 쇼

pj', **PJ's** /'pidʒeɪz/ *n* [plural] SPOKEN ⇨

PAJAMAS

plac·ard /'plækəd, -kɑrd/ *n* a large sign or advertisement that you carry or put on a wall ‖ 들고 다니거나 벽에 붙이는 커다란 전단이나 광고물. 벽보. 게시물

pla·cate /'pleɪkeɪt, 'plæ-/ *v* [T] FORMAL to make someone stop feeling angry by doing special things for him/her ‖ 남에게 특별한 것을 해 주어서 더 이상 화나지 않게 하다. 달래다. 위로[회유]하다 – **placatory** /'pleɪkə,tɔri/ *adj*

place¹ /pleɪs/ *n*

1 ▶POINT/POSITION 지점/위치◀ **a)** any area, point, or position in space; LOCATION ‖ 공간에서의 어떤 지역[지점, 위치]. 장소. 곳; ⓕ location: *Make sure you keep your passport in a safe place.* 반드시 안전한 장소에 여권을 보관해라. / *a beautiful place surrounded by mountains* 산들로 둘러싸인 아름다운 곳 **b)** a particular point on a larger area or thing ‖ 더 큰 지역이나 사물 위의 특정한 지점. 장소. 곳: *a sore place on my knee* 내 무릎의 따끔따끔한 아픈 곳 / *Paint is coming off the wall in places.* (=in some areas, but not others) 그림이 벽의 곳곳에서 떨어져 나가고 있다.

2 ▶WHERE YOU DO STH 어떤 것을 하는 곳◀ a building or area that is used for, or is suitable for, a particular purpose or activity ‖ 특정한 목적이나 활동에 사용되거나 적합한 건물이나 지역. 공간. 장소: *What this town needs is a really good place to eat/drink/dance.* 이 읍이 필요한 것은 먹을[술 마실, 춤출] 수 있는 정말로 좋은 장소이다. / *Mexico's a great place for a vacation.* 멕시코는 휴가를 보내기에 멋진 곳이다. / *A library is no place for a party.* 도서관은 파티를 열 만한 장소가 아니다.

3 ▶BUILDING/TOWN ETC. 건물/도시 등◀ a particular building, town, country etc. ‖ 특정한 건물·도시·국가 등. 거처. 지역. 지방: *She was born in a place called Black River Falls.* 그녀는 "검은 강 폭포"라고 불리우는 지역에서 태어났다. / *I'm going over to Jeff's place* (=his house) *for dinner.* 난 저녁을 먹으러 제프 집에 잠깐 들를 거야.

4 ▶RIGHT POSITION/ORDER 똑바른 위치/순서◀ the right or usual position or order ‖ 똑바른 또는 평소의 위치나 순서. 있어야 할[적당한] 장소: *Put the CDs back in their place.* CD들을 제자리에 되돌려 놓아라. / *By six o'clock, everything was in place for the party.* 6시까지 파티를 위해 모든 것이 제자리에 있었다.

5 take place to happen ‖ 발생하다. 일어

나다: *When did the robbery take place?* 강도 사건은 언제 일어났습니까? —see usage note at HAPPEN

6 ▶IMPORTANCE 중요성◀ the importance or position that someone or something has, compared to other people or things ‖ 사람이나 사물이 다른 사람들이나 사물들에 비해 가지고 있는 중요성이나 위치. 위치. 입장. 처지: *No one could ever take her place.* (=be as important or loved as she is) 누구도 결코 그녀의 자리를 대신할 수는 없을 것이다. / *Carla has friends in high places.* (=with important ranks in society) 칼라는 고위층에 친구들이 있다. / *By the 1950s, cars had taken the place of trains.* (=were used instead of them) 1950년대쯤 자동차는 기차를 대신하기 시작했다. / *There will always be a place for you here.* (=a position for you to have) 이곳에는 너를 위한 자리가 항상 있을 것이다.

7 in place of instead of ‖ …대신에: *Try using mixed herbs in place of salt on vegetables.* 야채에 소금 대신에 혼합 허브를 사용해 봐라.

8 ▶RIGHT OCCASION 옳은 경우◀ the right occasion or situation ‖ 옳은 경우나 상황. 적당한 기회. 호기: *This isn't the place to discuss that, Alanna.* 앨래나, 지금은 그것을 토론할 때가 아니야.

9 sb's place someone's duty or right because of the position s/he has ‖ 그 사람이 가진 지위 때문에 생기는 의무나 권리. 직분: *It's not your place to tell me what to do.* 당신은 나보고 이래라 저래라 말할 입장이 아니다.

10 first/second/third etc. place first, second etc. position in a race or competition ‖ 경주나 경기에서의 첫 번째·두 번째 등의 위치. 1[2,3]위: *Jerry finished in third place.* 제리는 3위로 골인했다.

11 in the first/second/third place SPOKEN used in order to introduce a series of points in an argument or discussion ‖ 논쟁이나 토론에서 일련의 논점을 소개하는 데에 쓰여. 첫[두, 세] 번째로: *Well, in the first place, I can't afford it, and in the second place I'm not really interested.* 우선 첫째로, 그럴 만한 여유가 없고 둘째로 정말로 관심이 없어.

12 ▶SEAT/SPACE 좌석/자리◀ a seat on a bus, train etc., or a position in a line ‖ 버스·기차 등의 좌석이나 줄을 선 위치. 자리. 좌석: *Is this place taken?* (=being used) 이 자리 사람 있습니까? / *Can you*

save my place? (=not let anyone else use it) 내 자리 좀 봐 줄래?
13 all over the place INFORMAL everywhere ‖ 모든 곳에. 도처에: *There were policemen all over the place!* 도처에 경찰이 배치돼 있었어!
14 put sb in his/her place to show someone that s/he is not as important, intelligent etc. as s/he thinks s/he is ‖ 남에게 그 자신이 생각하는 것만큼 중요하며 총명하지 않다는 것을 보여 주다. 남의 콧대를 꺾다. 자기 분수를 알게 하다: *I'd like to put her in her place – the little snob!* 난 그녀가 분수를 좀 알았으면 좋겠어. 속물 같은 것!
15 out of place not suitable for or comfortable in a particular situation ‖ 특정한 상황이 알맞거나 편안하지 않은. 어울리지 않는. 부적당한: *I felt really out of place at Cindy's wedding.* 나는 신디의 결혼식에서 정말 그 자리에 어울리지 않는다는 느낌을 받았다.
16 go places INFORMAL to become successful ‖ 성공하다. 출세하다: *Nick's the kind of guy who could really go places.* 닉은 정말 성공할 수 있는 부류의 남자다.
17 also **Place** used in the names of short streets ‖ 짧은 거리 이름에 쓰여. 거리: *I live at 114 Seaview Place.* 나는 씨뷰 플레이스 114번지에 산다.

USAGE NOTE place, space, and **room**

Use **place** to talk about an area or a particular part of an area: *The best place to sit is right in front of the stage.* Use both **space** and **room** to talk about empty areas. **Space** can mean the size of an area, or it can mean the area itself: *There's a lot of space in the back of these cars. / I had trouble finding a parking space.* **Room** means that there is enough space for a particular purpose: *There's room in the back seat for all three of you.* ✗DON'T SAY "There's enough place."✗
place는 한 지역이나 한 지역의 특정한 부분에 대해서 말할 때 쓴다: 가장 좋은 좌석이 있는 장소는 무대 바로 앞이다. **space**와 **room**은 둘 다 빈 공간에 대해서 말하는 데에 쓴다. **space**는 장소의 크기를 의미하거나 그 장소 자체를 의미할 수도 있다: 이 차들의 뒤에는 많은 공간이 있다./ 나는 주차 공간을 찾는 데에 애를 먹었다. **room**은 특정한 목적을 위한 충분한 공간이 있다는 것을

의미한다: 뒷좌석에는 너희 세 명 모두를 위한 자리가 있다. "There's enough place."라고는 하지 않는다.

place² *v* **1** [T] to put something carefully in an exact place ‖ 사물을 조심스럽게 정확한 장소에 놓다. …을 두다[놓다]: *Seth placed his trophy on the top shelf.* 세스는 맨 위 선반에 트로피를 놓았다. **2** [T] to put someone or something in a particular situation ‖ 사람이나 사물을 특정한 상황에 두다. 배치[배열]하다. …에 놓이게 하다: *You'll be placed with the advanced students.* 너는 상급생 반에 배치될 것이다. **3** [T] to decide that someone or something is important or valuable ‖ 사람이나 사물이 중요하거나 가치가 있는지 결정하다. 판정[평가]하다. …의 위치[등급, 지위]를 정하다: *Your father has placed great trust in you.* 너의 아버지는 너를 대단히 신뢰하고 계신다. / *a teacher who places an emphasis on good grammar* 좋은 문법을 강조하시는 선생님 **4 can't place sb/sth** to be unable to remember exactly why you recognize someone or something ‖ 사람이나 사물을 알게 된 연유를 정확히 기억할 수 없다. 누구인지/무엇인지 알 수 없다: *I recognize her name, but I can't place her.* 나는 그녀의 이름은 알겠는데 그녀가 누구인지는 생각해 낼 수가 없다. **5** [T] to find a job for someone ‖ 남에게 일자리를 찾아주다. …에 앉히다[취직시키다]: *The agency had placed her in/with a local firm.* 그 회사는 그녀를 지사로 발령냈다. **6 place an order** to ask a store or business to get something for you so you can buy it ‖ 상점이나 사업체에 물건을 살 수 있도록 구해 달라고 요구하다. 주문하다

pla·ce·bo /pləˈsiboʊ/ *n* a substance given to someone instead of medicine, without telling him/her it is not real, either because the person is not really sick or because this is part of a test ‖ 그 사람이 정말로 아프지 않아서이든 그것이 실험의 일부분이어서이든 그것이 진짜가 아니란 걸 말하지 않고 약 대신 주는 물질. 가짜 약

place·ment /ˈpleɪsmənt/ *n* [C, U] **1** the act of finding a place for someone to live or work, or the place itself ‖ 남이 살거나 일하는 장소를 찾아주는 행위, 또는 그 자리 자체. 직업 소개. 취직 알선. 일자리: *a job placement* 직업 소개 / *the college placement office* (=where they help you find work) 대학 취업 정보 사무실 **2** the act of putting something or someone in a position, or the position itself ‖ 사물이나 사람을 어떤 위치에 두는 행위, 또는 그 위치 자체. 놓기. 배치. 놓인 자리: *He wasn't satisfied with the furniture placement.* 그는 가구 배치가 마음에 들지 않았다. / *You'll need to take a placement test.* (=test that decides which level of class you can take) 너는 반 배치 고사를 봐야 할 것이다.

pla·cen·ta /pləˈsentə/ *n* a body organ like thick flesh inside the UTERUS that feeds an unborn baby ‖ 태아에 영양분을 공급하는 자궁 안쪽의 두꺼운 살 같은 신체 기관. 태반

plac·id /ˈplæsɪd/ *adj* calm and peaceful ‖ 고요하고 평온한. 차분한. 잔잔한: *a placid expression* 차분한 표현 / *the placid surface of the lake* 호수의 잔잔한 수면 – **placidly** *adv*

pla·gia·rism /ˈpleɪdʒəˌrɪzəm/ *n* [C, U] the act of plagiarizing (PLAGIARIZE), or the idea, phrase, story etc. that has been plagiarized ‖ 표절하는 행위, 또는 표절된 생각[구절, 이야기] 등. 표절(물): *an article full of plagiarisms* 표절로 가득찬 논문 / *She was accused of plagiarism in writing her thesis.* 그녀는 논문을 쓰면서 표절했다고 비난받았다. – **plagiarist** *n*

pla·gia·rize /ˈpleɪdʒəˌraɪz/ *v* [I, T] to take someone else's words, ideas, etc. and copy them, pretending that they are your own ‖ 어떤 사람의 말·생각 등을 취해서 모방하고 나서 그것들이 자기 것인 양 행동하다. 표절하다

plague[1] /pleɪg/ *n* 1 [C, U] an attack of a disease that spreads easily, and kills a large number of people ‖ 쉽게 퍼져서 대량의 사람들을 죽이는 질병의 발병. 역병. 전염병 2 **a plague of rats/locusts etc.** a very large and dangerous number of rats etc. ‖ 매우 많고 위험한 수의 쥐 등. 성가신 쥐[메뚜기]의 떼

plague[2] *v* [T] to make someone suffer over a long period of time, or to cause trouble again and again ‖ 남을 오랜 기간에 걸쳐 고통스럽게 하다, 또는 반복해서 말썽을 일으키다. …을 괴롭히다[성가시게 하다]: *Gloria had always been plagued by ill health.* 글로리아는 항상 건강이 좋지 않아서 고생했다.

plaid /plæd/ *n* [C, U] a pattern of squares and lines, originally from Scotland and used especially on material for clothing ‖ 원래 스코틀랜드에서 유래해서 특히 옷감에 쓰이는 정사각형과 선으로 이루어진 무늬. 체크[격자] 무늬 – **plaid** *adj*: *a plaid work shirt* 체크

무늬 작업 셔츠 —see picture at PATTERN

plain[1] /pleɪn/ *adj* 1 very clear, and easy to understand or recognize ‖ 매우 명확하고 이해하거나 인식하기 쉬운. 명백[분명]한. 평이한: *It's quite plain that you don't agree.* 네가 동의하지 않는다는 것이 매우 분명하다. / *Why don't you tell me in plain English?* (=clearly, without TECHNICAL language) 쉽게 좀 설명해 줄래? 2 without anything added or without decoration; simple ‖ 어떤 것도 덧붙인 것 없거나 장식 없는. 수수한. 꾸밈이 없는. 담백한; 단순한: *plain food* 담백한 음식 / *a plain blue suit* 무늬가 없는 파란 정장 —see picture at PATTERN 3 a word meaning ugly or unattractive, used in order to be polite ‖ 공손하기 위해 사용되는 못생기거나 매력이 없음을 의미하는 단어. 평범한. 보통의: *She's kind of plain, but she has a great personality.* 그녀는 좀 예쁘지 않지만 성격은 아주 좋다.

plain[2] *n* a large area of flat land ‖ 평평한 땅의 넓은 지역. 평원. 평야: *a grassy plain* 초원 / *countless miles of plains* 끝없이 펼쳐진 평원

plain[3] *adv* **plain stupid/wrong/rude etc.** SPOKEN clearly and simply stupid, wrong etc. ‖ 명백하고 분명하게 멍청하고 잘못된. 전적으로 멍청한/잘못된/무례한: *They're just plain lazy.* 그들은 정말 게으르다.

plain·clothes /ˈ. ./ *adj* plainclothes police wear ordinary clothes so that they can work without being recognized ‖ 경찰이 눈에 띄지 않으면서 일할 수 있도록 평상복을 입은. 사복 차림의

plain·ly /ˈpleɪnli/ *adv* 1 in a way that is easy to see, hear, or understand ‖ 보기[듣기, 이해하기] 쉽게. 명백히. 분명하게: *The price is plainly marked on the tag.* 가격은 꼬리표에 분명하게 표시되어 있다. / *Let me speak plainly.* 내가 분명하게 말하지. 2 simply or without decoration ‖ 단순하거나 장식 없이. 소박[수수]하게: *a plainly dressed young girl* 수수하게 옷을 입은 어린 소녀

plain·tiff /ˈpleɪntɪf/ *n* LAW the person in a court of law who ACCUSEs someone else of doing something illegal ‖ 어떤 사람을 불법적인 일을 했다고 고소해 법정에서는 사람. 원고. 고소인 —compare DEFENDANT

plain·tive /ˈpleɪntɪv/ *adj* a plaintive sound is high, like someone crying, and sounds sad ‖ 소리가 사람이 우는 것처럼 높고 슬프게 들리는. 구슬픈. 애처로운: *the plaintive cry of the wolf* 늑대의 구슬

픈 울음소리

plan' /plæn/ *n* **1** something that you have decided to do or achieve ‖ 하거나 성취하기로 결정한 것. 계획: *Her plan is to finish school and then travel for a year.* 그녀의 계획은 학교를 마치고 나서 일년 동안 여행을 하는 것이다. / *We haven't made any fixed plans yet.* 우리 는 아직 별 특별한 계획을 세우지 못했다. / *Sorry, I have plans for tonight.* 미안 해, 오늘 밤은 다른 계획이 있어. / *There's been a change of plan.* (=we have decided to do something else) 계획에 변 경이 생겼다. **2** a set of actions for achieving something in the future ‖ 미래 에 일을 성취하기 위한 일련의 행동들. 계 획. 예정: *NASA has announced plans for a new space station.* 나사는 새 우주 정거장 계획을 발표했다. / *We'll finish in April if everything goes according to plan.* (=if things happen in the way that we arranged or expected) 모든 것이 예 정대로 진행되면 우리는 4월에 끝마칠 것 이다. **3** a drawing of something such as a building, room, or machine, as it would be seen from above, showing the shape, measurements, parts etc. ‖ 위에 서 보는 대로의 모양[치수, 비율] 등을 보 여 주는 건물[방, 기계] 등의 것의 도면. 평면도. 설계도: *Have you seen the plans for the new library?* 신축 도서관의 평면 도를 본 적 있니?

plan' *v* **-nned, -nning 1** [I, T] also **plan out** to think about something you want to do, and how you will do it ‖ 하고 싶은 것·그것을 어떻게 할 것인지에 대해 서 생각하다. (…을) 계획하다. (…의) 계 획을 세우다: *We've been planning our vacation for months.* 우리는 몇 달 동안 휴가 계획을 세우고 있다. **2** [T] to intend to do something ‖ 어떤 것을 하기로 의도 하다. …할 작정이다: *How long do you plan on staying?* 얼마나 머무르실 생각 이십니까? / *Where do you plan to go next year?* 내년에는 어디를 갈 생각이냐? **3** [T] to think about something you are going to make or build, and decide what it will look like ‖ 만들거나 건설하려는 것 에 대해 생각해서 어떤 모습이 될지 결정 하다. …을 설계하다

plane /pleɪn/ *n* **1** a vehicle that flies by using wings and one or more engines; AIRPLANE ‖ 날개와 한 개 이상의 엔진을 이 용해서 나는 탈것. 비행기; 閉 airplane — see picture at AIRPLANE **2** a particular level ‖ 특정한 수준. 정도. 단계. 차원: *Let's try to keep the conversation on a friendly plane.* 화기애애한 분위기에서 대

화를 유지하도록 하자. **3** a tool that has a flat bottom with a sharp blade in it, used for making wooden surfaces smooth ‖ 목재의 표면을 부드럽게 만드는 데에 쓰이는 내부에 날카로운 날이 있는 평평한 바닥을 가진 연장. 대패 **4** TECHNICAL a completely flat surface in GEOMETRY ‖ 기하학에서 완전히 평평한 표 면. 평면

plan·et /'plænɪt/ *n* **1** a very large round object in space that moves around a star, such as the sun ‖ 태양 등의 항성 주 위를 도는 우주의 아주 거대한 구형 물체. 행성: *Mercury is the smallest planet.* 수 성은 가장 작은 행성이다. / *Planet Earth* 지구 행성 **2 what planet is sb on?** SPOKEN HUMOROUS used in order to say that someone's ideas are not sensible ‖ 남의 생각이 지각 없다고 말하는 데에 쓰 여. …는 별나라에서 왔나? – **planetary** /'plænə,tɛri/ *adj*

plan·e·tar·i·um /ˌplænə'tɛriəm/ *n* a building where lights on a curved ceiling show the movements of PLANETS and stars ‖ 둥근 천장의 등들이 행성과 별 들의 움직임을 보여주는 건물. 천체 학습 관. 플라네타륨

plank /plæŋk/ *n* **1** a long flat piece of wood used for building ‖ 건축에 쓰이는 길고 납작한 목재 조각. 두꺼운 판자: *a bridge/floor/dock made out of planks* 두 꺼운 판자로 만든 다리[바닥, 부두] **2** one of the main principles of a political party's statement of its aims ‖ 정당의 목 표를 선언하는 주요 원칙들 중의 하나. 정 당 강령의 한 항목: *Low taxation is the main plank in the party platform.* 낮은 과세가 그 정당 강령의 주요 항목이다.

plank·ton /'plæŋktən/ *n* [U] very small plants and animals that live in the ocean and are eaten by fish ‖ 바다에 서 식하면서 고기에게 먹히는 매우 작은 식물 과 동물. 부유 생물. 플랑크톤

plan·ner /'plænɚ/ *n* someone who plans something, especially someone who plans the way towns grow and develop ‖ 어떤 것을 특히 도시가 성장하 고 발전하는 모습을 계획하는 사람. 계획 [입안]자

plant' /plænt/ *n* **1** a living thing that has leaves and roots and usually grows in the ground, especially one that is smaller than a tree ‖ 특히 나무보다 더 작은 것으로서 잎과 뿌리가 있으며 보통 땅 위에서 자라는 생물. 식물. 풀: *Don't forget to water the plants.* 그 식물들에 물 주는 것을 잊지 마라. / *a tomato plant* 토마토 식물 **2** a factory and all its equipment ‖ 공장과 그곳의 모든 장비. 공장. 설비. 시설: *They've just built a new chemical plant.* 그들은 새 화학 공장을 이제 막 건설했다. **3** INFORMAL someone who has been sent to work for a company or organization in order to find out secret information for the police or another company ‖ 경찰이나 다른 회사를 위해 비밀 정보를 알아내도록 어떤 회사나 조직에서 일하도록 파견된 사람. 첩자

plant² *v* [T] **1** to put plants or seeds in the ground to grow ‖ 식물이나 씨를 자라도록 땅속에 놓다. 심다. 뿌리다: *planting carrots* 당근을 심기 / *a hillside planted with pine trees* 소나무가 심어진 비탈 언덕 **2** INFORMAL to hide stolen or illegal goods in someone's clothes, bags, room etc. in order to make him/her seem guilty ‖ 죄가 있어 보이도록 남의 옷[가방, 방] 등에 훔치거나 불법인 물건을 숨기다. 몰래 두다: *Someone must have planted the drugs on her.* 분명히 누군가가 몰래 그녀에게 마약을 숨겨 놓았을 것이다. **3** to put something firmly somewhere, or to move somewhere and stay there ‖ 사물을 단단하게 어딘가에 두거나 어딘가로 움직여서 그곳에 머무르다. 놓다. 설치하다. 세우다: *Tony planted himself in a chair by the fire.* 토니는 불 옆의 의자에 몸을 파묻었다. **4 plant an idea/ doubt/suspicion** to mention something that makes someone begin to have an idea, doubt etc. ‖ 남에게 생각·의심 등을 시작하게 하는 것을 언급하다. 생각[의심]을 불러일으키다: *Their conversation had planted doubts in Yuri's mind.* 그들의 대화는 유리의 마음에 의심을 불러일으켰다. – **planting** *n* [C, U]: *seasonal planting* 계절에 따른 초목 식재

plan·ta·tion /plæn'teɪʃən/ *n* a large farm, especially in a hot country, where a single crop such as tea, cotton, or sugar is grown ‖ 특히 더운 나라에서 차[목화, 설탕]와 같은 단일 작물을 재배하는 거대한 농장. (대규모) 농장: *a rubber plantation* 고무 농장

plant·er /'plæntɚ/ *n* **1** a container for growing plants in ‖ 속에 식물을 기르는 용기. 화분 **2** someone who owns or is in charge of a PLANTATION ‖ 농장을 소유하거나 책임지고 있는 사람. 농장주. 농장 경영자

plaque /plæk/ *n* **1** a piece of flat metal or stone with writing on it that reminds people of a particular event or person ‖ 사람들에게 특정한 사건이나 사람을 생각

나게 하는 그 위에 글이 쓰여진 납작한 금속이나 돌 조각. 장식판. 패(牌): *A bronze plaque tells of the building's historic past.* 청동판은 건물의 역사적 과거를 말해준다. **2** [U] a harmful substance that forms on your teeth, that BACTERIA can live and breed in ‖ 박테리아가 서식하면서 번식할 수 있는 이빨에 생기는 해로운 물질. 치석

plas·ma /'plæzmə/ *n* [U] the yellowish liquid part of the blood that carries the blood cells ‖ 혈구(血球)들을 나르는 피속의 노란색이 감도는 액체 부분. 혈장

plas·ter¹ /'plæstɚ/ *n* [U] a substance used for covering walls and ceilings to give them a smooth surface ‖ 벽과 천장의 표면을 매끄럽게 하려고 바를 때 사용되는 물질. 회반죽

plaster² *v* [T] **1** to spread or stick something all over a surface so that it is thickly covered ‖ 어떤 표면 전체에 어떤 것을 펼치거나 붙여 놓아서 그 표면을 빽빽이 뒤덮다. …을 덕지덕지 바르다[온통 붙이다]: *a wall plastered with signs* 간판들로 도배된 벽 **2** to cover a surface with PLASTER ‖ 표면을 회반죽으로 덮다. 회반죽을 바르다

plas·tered /'plæstɚd/ *adj* INFORMAL very drunk ‖ 술에 매우 취한: *I got plastered with Sharon last night.* 나는 어젯밤 샤론과 술에 취했다.

plaster of Par·is /ˌplæstɚ əv 'pærɪs/ *n* [U] a mixture of a white powder and water that dries quickly, used especially for making STATUEs ‖ 특히 조상(彫像)을 만드는 데에 사용되는, 빠르게 마르는 하얀 분말과 물의 혼합물. 소석고. 깁스

plas·tic¹ /'plæstɪk/ *adj* **1** made of plastic ‖ 플라스틱으로 만든. 플라스틱(제)의. 비닐(제)의: *a plastic bag* 비닐 봉지 / *plastic spoons/cups/bowls* 플라스틱 숟가락[잔, 사발] **2** seeming artificial or unnatural ‖ 인공적이거나 부자연스럽게 보이는. 합성의: *a plastic smile* 부자연스러운 미소 / *plastic-tasting food* 인공적인 맛이 나는 음식 **3** TECHNICAL a plastic substance such as clay can be formed into many different shapes and then keep the shape ‖ 점토 등의 물질이 다른 많은 형태로 만들어져서 그 모양을 유지할 수 있는. 소조(塑造)할 수 있는. 성형(造型)력의

plastic² *n* [C, U] a light strong material that is chemically produced, that can be made into different shapes when soft and keeps its shape when hard ‖ 녹아 있을 때는 다른 모양으로 만들 수 있고 굳어 있을 때는 그 모양을 유지할 수 있는 화학

적으로 생산되는 가볍고 강한 물질. 플라스틱: *toys made of plastic* 플라스틱으로 만든 장난감들

plas·tic·i·ty /plæˈstɪsəti/ *n* [U] TECHNICAL the quality of being easily made into any shape ‖ 쉽게 어떤 모양으로든 만들어지는 특성. 가소성(可塑性)

plastic sur·ger·y /ˌ.. ˈ.../ *n* [U] the medical practice of changing the appearance of people's faces or bodies, either to improve their appearance or to repair injuries ‖ 외모를 향상시키거나 부상을 치료하기 위해 사람들의 얼굴이나 신체의 모습을 바꾸는 의학적인 시술. 성형술

plate /pleɪt/ *n* **1** a flat, usually round, dish that you eat from or serve food from ‖ 음식을 먹거나 음식을 내놓는 납작하며 보통 동그란 접시. 접시: *a china plate* 사기 접시 **2** also **plateful** /ˈpleɪtfʊl/ the amount that a plate will hold ‖ 접시 하나가 담을 수 있는 양. 한 접시분: *a plate of chicken* 한 접시분의 닭고기 **3** a flat piece of metal, glass, bone etc. ‖ 납작한 금속[유리, 뼈] 등의 조각. 판(금): *An iron plate covered the hole in the sidewalk.* 인도에 난 구멍을 한 철판으로 덮었다. **4 gold/silver etc. plate** ordinary metal with a thin covering of gold, silver etc. ‖ 금·은 등을 얇게 입힌 보통의 금속. 금[은] 도금판 **5** ➪ LICENSE PLATE: *New Jersey plates* 뉴저지 번호판 **6** a thin piece of plastic with false teeth set into it ‖ 의치를 그 안에 박은 얇은 플라스틱 조각. 의치가상(假床). 틀니 한 벌

pla·teau /plæˈtoʊ/ *n* **1** a large area of flat land that is higher than the land around it ‖ 주위의 땅보다 더 높은 평평한 땅의 넓은 지역. 고원 (지대) **2** a period during which the level or amount of something does not change ‖ 사물의 수준이나 양이 변하지 않는 기간. 안정기. 정체 상태: *Inflation rates have reached a plateau.* 물가 상승률이 안정기에 접어들었다. – **plateau** *v* [I]

plat·ed /ˈpleɪtɪd/ *adj* covered with a thin layer of metal, especially gold or silver ‖ 특히 금이나 은 등의 얇은 금속 층으로 덮인. 도금한: *a silver-plated spoon* 은도금한 숟가락

plate glass /ˌ. ˈ./ *n* [U] clear glass made in large thick sheets for use especially in store windows ‖ 특히 상점 유리용으로 커다랗고 두꺼운 판으로 만들어진 투명한 유리. 판유리 – **plate-glass** /ˌ. ˈ./ *adj*

plat·form /ˈplætfɔrm/ *n* **1** a raised structure for people to stand or work on ‖ 사람들이 그 위에 서거나 일할 수 있도록 높인 구조물. (연)단. 대: *He climbed on to the platform and began to address the crowd.* 그는 연단에 올라 군중에게 연설을 하기 시작했다. / *an oil platform off the California coast* 캘리포니아 연안 앞바다의 유정 시설 **2** the main ideas and aims of a political party, especially the ones that they state just before an election ‖ 특히 선거 직전에 공표하는 것으로서 정당의 주요 사상과 목표. 강령. 정강: *Republicans continued to argue about the party platform.* 공화당 의원들은 그 정당의 강령에 대해서 계속 논쟁을 벌였다. **3** the type of computer OPERATING SYSTEM or HARDWARE you are using ‖ 컴퓨터 운영 체제의 유형이나 사용하고 있는 하드웨어. 플랫폼: *an IBM platform* IBM플랫폼 **4** a chance for someone to express his/her opinions ‖ 사람이 자신의 의견을 표현할 수 있는 기회. 연설: *He used the TV interview as a platform for his views on education.* 그는 TV 인터뷰를 자신의 교육관에 대해 말할 수 있는 기회로 삼았다. **5** the raised place in a railroad station where you get on and off a train ‖ 기차를 타고 내리는 기차역의 높인 장소. 플랫폼

plat·ing /ˈpleɪtɪŋ/ *n* [U] a thin layer of metal that covers another metal surface ‖ 다른 금속 표면을 덮는 얇은 금속층. 도금: *silver plating* 은도금

plat·i·num /ˈplætˈnəm, ˈplætˈn-əm/ *n* [U] an expensive heavy silver-white metal that is an ELEMENT and is used in making jewelry ‖ 원소이며 보석을 만들 때 사용하는 비싸고 무거운 은백색의 금속. 백금

plat·i·tude /ˈplætəˌtud/ *n* a boring statement that has been made many times before ‖ 이전에 여러 번 한 지루한 말. 진부한 말. 상투적인 문구: *a speech full of platitudes* 상투적인 문구로 가득 찬 연설

pla·ton·ic /pləˈtɑnɪk/ *adj* a relationship that is platonic is friendly but not sexual ‖ 관계가 성적이지 않고 친한. 정신적인 (사랑의)

pla·toon /pləˈtun/ *n* a small group of soldiers that is part of a COMPANY ‖ 한 중대의 일부인 병사들의 작은 집단. 소대

plat·ter /ˈplætɚ/ *n* **1** a large plate, used for serving food ‖ 음식을 내놓기 위해 사용하는 큰 접시. 대형 접시 **2 chicken/seafood etc. platter** chicken etc. arranged on a plate with other foods and served in a restaurant ‖ 식당

에서 다른 음식들과 함께 한 접시에 놓여
나오는 닭고기 등. 닭고기/해산물 요리

plat·y·pus /'plætəpəs/ *n* a small
Australian animal that lays eggs and
has a beak, but also has fur and feeds
milk to its babies ‖ 알을 낳고 부리가 있
지만 또한 털이 있고 새끼에게 젖을 먹이
는 작은 호주 동물. 오리너구리

plau·dit /'plɔdɪt/ *n* [C usually plural]
FORMAL things you say in order to show
praise and admiration ‖ 칭찬과 감탄을
보여 주기 위해서 말하는 것들. 찬사: *The
magazine has **won plaudits** from media
critics.* 그 잡지는 미디어 비평가들로부터
찬사를 받았다.

plau·si·ble /'plɔzəbəl/ *adj* easy to
believe and likely to be true ‖ 믿기 쉽고
사실일 듯한. 그럴듯한. 정말 같은: *a
plausible story* 그럴듯한 이야기 —
opposite IMPLAUSIBLE

play[1] /pleɪ/ *v*

1 ▶SPORT/GAME 운동 경기/놀이◀ a) [I,
T] to take part or compete in a sport ‖
운동 경기에 참여하거나 경쟁하다. (…을)
하다. (…과) 대전하다: *The guys are out
playing basketball.* 남자들은 밖에서 농구
를 하고 있다. / *Garcia plays for the
Hornets.* 가르시아는 호넷 팀에서 뛴다. /
*The 49ers are playing the Vikings on
Saturday.* (=they are competing against
the Vikings) 포티나이너스는 토요일에 바
이킹과 경기를 갖는다. **b)** [T] to use a
particular piece, card, person etc. in a
game or sport 놀이나 운동경기에서 특정
한 말[카드, 사람] 등을 사용하다. …을 쓰
다[기용하다]: *Play the ace of clubs.* 클럽
짝패 중에서 에이스패를 써라. / *Coach
plans to play Williams at quarterback.*
코치는 쿼터백에 윌리엄스를 기용할 계획
이다.

2 ▶CHILDREN/TOYS 어린이/장난감◀ [I,
T] to do things that you enjoy,
especially to pretend things or to use
toys ‖ 특히 사물을 흉내 내거나 장난감을
사용하여 자신이 즐기는 것을 하다. …놀
이를 하다. 놀다: *He has a lot of toys to
play with.* 그는 가지고 놀 장난감이 아주
많다. / *Andy spends too much time
playing computer games.* 앤디는 컴퓨터
게임에 너무 많은 시간을 보낸다. / *Mom,
can I go over and play with Zachary?*
엄마, 자카리 집에 잠깐 들러 같이 놀아도
돼요?

3 ▶MUSIC 음악◀ a) [I, T] to perform a
piece of music on an instrument ‖ 악기로
음악을 연주하다. 연주하다: *There's a
good band playing on Saturday night.*
토요일 밤에 연주하는 좋은 밴드가 있다.

/ *Matt plays drums.* 매트는 북을 친다.
b) [I, T] to make a radio, STEREO etc.
produce sounds, especially music ‖ 소리
를 특히 음악을 라디오·오디오 등이 소리,
특히 음악 소리를 내게 하다. 틀(어 주)다:
I brought a few CDs to play tonight. 나는
오늘 밤 틀기 위해 CD 몇 개를 가져왔다.

4 play a part/role to have an effect or
influence on something ‖ 어떤 것에 효과
나 영향을 미치다. 역할을 하다: *Political
concerns played no part in my decision.*
정치적 이해 관계는 내 결정에 아무런 역
할도 하지 못했다.

5 ▶THEATER/MOVIE 극장/영화◀ a) [T]
to act one of the characters in a movie,
TV, or theater performance ‖ 영화[TV,
극장 공연]에서 등장인물의 한 역을 연기
하다. …의 배역을 맡(아하)다. 출연하다:
*Polly is playing Celia in "As You Like
It."* 폴리는 "좋으실 대로"에서 셀리아 역
을 맡아한다. **b)** [I] to be performed or
shown at a theater etc. ‖ 극장 등에서 공
연하거나 상영하다: *Have you checked to
see where the movie's playing?* 그 영화
가 어디에서 상영되는지 확인해 봤니?

6 ▶BEHAVE 행동하다◀ [I, T] INFORMAL
to behave in a particular way, or
pretend to have a particular quality, in
order to achieve something ‖ 어떤 일을
달성하기 위해 특정하게 행동하다 또는 특
정한 특성을 가진 것처럼 가장하다. …인
체하다. …처럼 굴다: *If he asks, just
play dumb.* (=pretend you do not know
the answer) 그가 물으면 그냥 모른 척해
라. / *Doctors warned parents to play it
safe* (=do the safest thing) *by
immunizing their children.* 의사들은 부
모들에게 자녀들을 예방 접종시켜서 위험
을 미연에 방지하라고 경고했다. / *Tracy
forced herself to play it cool* (=stay
calm and not be too eager) *with Brad.*
트레이시는 브래드에게 너무 열을 올리지
말자고 자신의 마음을 다잡았다.

7 play ball a) to play by throwing,
kicking, hitting, or catching a ball ‖ 공을
던지고[차고, 치고, 잡고] 놀다. 공놀이를
하다: *Just don't play ball in the house.*
집 안에서는 공놀이 좀 하지 마라. **b)**
INFORMAL to agree to do something that
someone wants you to do ‖ 남이 해 주기
를 바라는 대로 어떤 것을 하는 데에 동의
하다. …하는 대로 협력해 주다: *If you
guys play ball with us, we'll all avoid
problems.* 너희들이 우리에게 협력해 준다
면 우리 모두 문제들을 피할 수 있어.

8 play a trick/joke on sb to do
something to surprise or deceive
someone, and make other people laugh

∥ 남을 놀라게 하거나 속이는 짓을 해서 다른 사람들을 웃게 하다. 남에게 장난을 치다: *It was only some boys playing jokes on each other.* 서로 장난치며 노는 아이들은 일부에 불과했다.

9 play it by ear INFORMAL to decide what to do as things happen, instead of planning anything ∥ 모든 것을 계획하는 대신에 일이 발생했을 때 무엇을 할지를 결정하다. 임기응변으로 대처하다: *"Are you having a barbecue Saturday?" "We'll have to play it by ear; it depends on the weather."* "토요일에 바비큐 파티를 할 거야?" "그때 가 봐야 알 거야. 날씨에 달렸어."

10 play with fire to do something that could have a very bad result ∥ 매우 나쁜 결과를 가져올 수도 있는 일을 하다. 위험한 짓을 하다: *If you invest in high-risk stocks, you're playing with fire.* 위험이 높은 주식에 투자하면 위험한 짓이다.

11 play games DISAPPROVING to use a person or situation in order to get what you want, without caring about what is best for other people ∥ 다른 사람들에게 최선인 것에 대해서는 상관하지 않고 자신이 원하는 것을 얻기 위해 사람이나 상황을 이용하다. 남에게 무책임한 짓을 하다. 좌지우지하다: *We're sick of politicians playing games with the budget.* 우리는 예산을 가지고 자기 마음대로 하는 정치인들에게 신물이 난다.

12 play sth by ear to be able to play music after you have heard it instead of by reading the notes ∥ 악보를 보는 대신에 들어보고서 그 음악을 연주할 수 있다. …을 한 번 듣고 연주하다

13 play your cards right to behave in an effective way in a situation, in order to get what you want ∥ 원하는 것을 얻기 위해 어떤 상황에서 효과적인 방식으로 행동하다. 일을 능숙하게 처리하다: *If you play your cards right, he'll probably pay for your dinner.* 네가 일을 잘 처리하면 그가 아마 저녁 식사를 낼 것이다.

14 play second fiddle to sb/sth to be involved in an activity, but not be as important as the main person or group that is involved in it ∥ 어떤 활동에 관계는 하지만 거기서 중요한 사람이나 집단만큼 중요하게 되지 않다. …의 아래에 서다. …보다 못한 역을 맡다

15 play possum to pretend to be asleep or dead ∥ 자거나 죽은 체하다. 속이다. 시치미떼다

play around *phr v* [I] **1** to spend time having fun, but without having a particular purpose ∥ 재미있지만 특정한

목적 없이 시간을 보내다. 재미삼아 …하다[놀다]: *The kids are playing around outside.* 아이들은 밖에서 놀고 있다. **2** INFORMAL to have a sexual relationship with someone who is not your husband or wife ∥ 남편이나 아내가 아닌 어떤 사람과 성적인 관계를 갖다. 혼외 성관계를 갖다. 밀통하다

play sth ↔ **back** *phr v* [T] to let someone hear or see again something that has been recorded on a TAPE, VIDEO etc. ∥ 테이프·비디오 등에 녹화[녹음]된 것을 남이 다시 듣거나 보게 하다. 재생하다: *Can you play back the trumpet solo to me?* 나에게 트럼펫 솔로 연주를 다시 틀어 줄래요?

play sth ↔ **down** *phr v* [T] to make something seem less important or bad than it really is ∥ 어떤 것을 실제보다 덜 중요하거나 나쁘게 보이게 하다. …을 축소[경시]하다: *The White House tried to play down the latest economic figures.* 백악관은 최근의 경제 수치를 대수롭지 않게 보려고 했다.

play on sth *phr v* [T] to use a feeling or idea in order to gain an advantage ∥ 유리한 입장을 차지하기 위해서 어떤 감정이나 생각을 이용하다. …을 이용하다[틈타다]: *His campaign plays on people's fear of losing their jobs.* 그의 선거 운동은 직장을 잃을지도 모른다는 사람들의 공포심을 이용하고 있다.

play sth ↔ **up** *phr v* [T] to make something seem better or more important than it really is ∥ 어떤 것을 실제보다 더 좋거나 더 중요하게 보이게 하다. …을 중시[강조]하다. 선전하다: *The town has played up its location to attract tourists.* 그 도시는 관광객을 유치하기 위해 그 위치를 선전했다.

play with sth *phr v* [T] **1** to keep touching or moving something ∥ 사물을 계속 만지거나 움직이다. …을 가지고 놀다: *Stop playing with the remote control!* 리모컨을 만지지 마라! **2** to organize or think about something in different ways, to see what works ∥ 어떻게 되는지 보려고 어떤 것을 다른 방식으로 조직하거나 생각해 보다. …을 다양하게 시도해 보다: *I've been playing with the design of the newsletter.* 나는 회보의 디자인을 놓고 여러 가지로 해보고 있어.

play² *n* **1** a story that is written to be performed by actors, especially in a theater ∥ 특히 극장에서 배우들이 공연하기 위해 쓰여진 이야기. 연극. 희곡: *a play about two men on trial for murder* 살인죄로 재판받는 두 남자에 관한 희곡 /

The theater arts class is putting on a play (=performing one) *in the spring.* 극 예술 반은 봄에 연극을 무대에 올릴 것이 다. **2** [C, U] the actions of the people who are playing a game or sport ‖ 놀이 나 운동 경기를 하고 있는 사람들의 행위 들. 경기[시합](동작). 플레이: *Rain stopped play at 5:30 p.m.* 경기는 비 때 문에 오후 5시 30분에 중단되었다. / *Jackson scores with a three-point play!* (=he makes three points by doing one action) 잭슨은 3점 플레이로 득점했어! **3** [U] the things that people, especially children, do for fun, such as using toys ‖ 사람들, 특히 어린이들이 장난감을 이용 하는 등의 재미를 위해 하는 것들. 놀이: *children at play in the sandbox* 모래 상 자에서 노는 어린이들 / *a play area with slides and swings* 미끄럼틀과 그네가 있 는 놀이터 **4 come into play** to be used or have an effect ‖ 적용되거나 효과를 발 휘하다. 작용[활동, 일]하기 시작하다: *Laws on immigration come into play in this case.* 이 사건에는 이민법이 적용된 다. **5 bring/put sth into play** to use something or make it have an effect ‖ 어 떤 것을 적용하거나 효과를 미치게 하다. 발휘[활용]되게 하다: *This is where you should bring your experience into play.* 이곳이 바로 네 경험을 살려서 해야 하는 곳이다. **6 play on words** a use of a word or phrase that is interesting or funny because it has more than one meaning ‖ 하나 이상의 의미를 가지고 있 어서 흥미롭거나 재미있는 단어나 구절을 사용하는 것. 말장난[놀이] —see also PUN

play-act-ing /ˈ. ,../ *n* behavior in which someone pretends to be serious or sincere, but is not ‖ 사람이 진지하거 나 성실한 척 가장하지만 실은 그렇지 않 은 행동. 가장. 꾸밈

play-boy /ˈpleɪbɔɪ/ *n* a rich man who does not work and who spends time enjoying himself with beautiful women, fast cars etc. ‖ 일은 하지 않고 아름다운 여자들·스포츠카 등과 즐기면서 시간을 보 내는 부유한 남자. 한량. 플레이보이

play-by-play /,. . '.·/ *adj* **play-by-play commentary/description** a description of the action in a sports game as it happens, given on television or the radio ‖ 텔레비전이나 라디오에서 중계되 면, 운동 경기의 동작을 그것이 일어날 때 실시간으로 묘사하는 것. 실황 해설[설명]

Play-Doh /ˈpleɪdoʊ/ *n* [U] TRADEMARK a soft substance like colored clay, used by children for making shapes ‖ 어린이들이

모양을 만들 때 사용하는 색깔이 있는 점 토 같은 부드러운 물질. 공작용 점토

play-er /ˈpleɪə/ *n* **1** someone who plays a game, sport, or musical instrument ‖ 놀이[운동 경기, 악기]를 하거나 연주하는 사람. 노는 사람. 경기자. 선수. 연주자: *a piano player* 피아노 연주자 / *a basketball player* 농구 선수 **2** one of the people, companies, or organizations that is involved in a situation ‖ 어떤 상황 에 관련된 사람들[회사들, 조직들] 중의 하나. 중요한 역할[활동]을 하는 사람 [것]: *a major player in the UN peace talks* UN평화 회담의 중요한 역할자

play-ful /ˈpleɪfəl/ *adj* **1** intended to be fun rather than serious, or showing that you are having fun ‖ 진지하기보다는 오 히려 재미있도록 의도된, 또는 재미있게 놀고 있음을 나타내는. 우스운. 재미있는. 장난기 넘치는: *a playful discussion* 재미 있는 토론 / *Michael Gibb's playful music and performances* 마이클 깁스의 즐거운 음악과 공연 / *a playful grin* 장난기 넘치 는 웃음 **2** very active and happy ‖ 매우 활동적이고 즐거워하는. 장난치는. 놀기 좋아하는: *a playful little kitten* 장난치기 좋아하는 작은 고양이 새끼 **– playfully** *adv* **– playfulness** *n* [U]

play-ground /ˈpleɪɡraʊnd/ *n* a small area of land, usually next to a school or in a park, where children can play ‖ 보 통 학교 옆이나 공원 안에 있는, 어린이들 이 놀 수 있는 작은 부지. 운동장. 놀이터

play-house /ˈpleɪhaʊs/ *n* **1** a word meaning "theater," often used as part of a theater's name ‖ 종종 극장 이름의 일부분으로 사용되는 "극장"을 의미하는 단어. (공연) 극장: *the Pasadena Playhouse* 패서디나 극장 **2** a small structure like a house that children can play in ‖ 어린이들이 그 안에서 놀 수 있 는 집 같은 작은 구조물. 어린이 놀이집

play-ing card /ˈ.. ,./ *n* ⇨ CARD¹

play-ing field /ˈ.. ,./ *n* **1** a large piece of ground with particular areas marked off for playing football, baseball etc. ‖ 축 구·야구 등을 하기 위해 표시된 특정한 장 소를 가진 커다란 운동장. 경기장. 구장 **2 level playing field** a situation in which different people, companies, countries etc. can all compete fairly with each other because no one has special advantages ‖ 다른 사람들·회사들·국가들 등이 아무도 특별한 이점을 가지고 있지 않아서 모두가 서로 공정하게 경쟁할 수 있는 상황. 공정한 환경: *"We would like to do business on a more level playing field," said Kokado.* "우리는 좀 더 공정

한 상황에서 사업을 하고 싶다"라고 코카 도는 말했다.

play·mate /ˈpleɪmeɪt/ *n* OLD-FASHIONED a friend you play with when you are a child ‖ 어렸을 때 함께 노는 친구. 소꿉 친구

play·off /ˈpleɪɔf/ *n* a game or series of games played by the best teams or players in a sports competition, in order to decide the final winner ‖ 최종 승자를 결정하기 위해 운동 경기에서 최고의 팀들이나 선수들이 경기하는 경기나 일련의 경기들. 결승 경기. 우승 결정권 시리즈

play·pen /ˈpleɪpɛn/ *n* a piece of equipment with a net or wooden BARS *around it, which young children can play in safely* ‖ 어린 아이들이 안에서 안전하게 놀 수 있게 주위에 망이나 나무 막대를 댄 기구. 유아용 놀이틀

play·room /ˈpleɪrum/ *n* a room for children to play in ‖ 어린이들이 안에서 노는 방. 놀이방

play·thing /ˈpleɪˌθɪŋ/ *n* **1** someone whom you use only for your own amusement, without considering his/her feelings or needs ‖ 자신의 즐거움만을 위해 남의 감정이나 욕구는 고려하지 않고 이용하는 사람. 노리개: *I'm not just your plaything, you know.* 난 말이야, 너의 노리개가 아니야. **2** ⇨ TOY¹

play·wright /ˈpleɪraɪt/ *n* someone who writes plays ‖ 희곡을 쓰는 사람. 극작가

pla·za /ˈplɑzə, ˈplæzə/ *n* an outdoor public place, usually with a lot of stores and small businesses ‖ 보통 많은 상점들과 작은 사업체들이 있는 옥외의 공공장소. 광장: *South Shore Plaza* 사우스 쇼 광장

plea /pli/ *n* **1** a request that is urgent and full of emotion ‖ 긴급하고 매우 감정적인 요청. 탄원. 청원: *a mother's plea for help* 도움을 바라는 어머니의 간절한 요청 **2** LAW a statement by someone in a court of law saying whether s/he is guilty or not ‖ 법정에 선 사람이 자신이 유죄인지 아닌지 말하는 진술. 답변(서). 항변(서): *The defendant entered a plea of "not guilty."* 피고는 "무죄"를 주장했다[탄원했다].

plea-bar·gain /ˈ. ˌ../ *v* [I] to avoid punishment for a serious crime by agreeing to say you are guilty of a less serious one ‖ 덜 중대한 범죄에 대해 유죄 인정에 동의해서 중대한 범죄에 대한 처벌을 면하다. 유죄 답변 거래를 하다

plead /plid/ *v* **pleaded** *or* **pled**, **pleaded** *or* **pled**, **pleading 1** [I] to ask for something you want very much,

in an urgent and anxious way; BEG ‖ 긴급하고 초조해 하면서 아주 많이 원하는 것을 요구하다. 간청[애원]하다; 卿 beg: *Amy pleaded with the stranger to help her.* 에이미는 그 낯선 사람에게 도와달라고 애원했다. **2** [I, T] LAW to officially say in a court of law whether or not you are guilty of a crime ‖ 자신이 어떤 범죄에 대해 유죄인지 아닌지 법정에서 공식적으로 말하다. (…이라고) 답변하다: *"How do you plead?" "Not guilty."* "어떻게 답변하시겠습니까?" "무죄를 주장합니다." / *Parker pled guilty to four charges of theft.* 파커는 네 가지 절도 혐의에 대해 유죄를 인정했다.

pleas·ant /ˈplɛzənt/ *adj* **1** enjoyable, nice, or good ‖ 즐거운, 멋진, 좋은. 유쾌한. 기분 좋은: *He had a pleasant laugh.* 그는 유쾌하게 웃었다. / *a pleasant surprise* 뜻밖의 기쁨 **2** polite, friendly, or kind ‖ 정중한, 친근한, 친절한. 상냥한. 호감이 가는: *a really nice, pleasant man* 정말 멋지고 호감이 가는 남자 — **pleasantly** *adv* —opposite UNPLEASANT

pleas·ant·ry /ˈplɛzəntri/ *n* FORMAL a slightly funny or not very serious remark that you say in order to be polite ‖ 공손하기 위해 말하는 약간은 재미있는 또는 아주 심각하지는 않은 말. 의례적인 말

please¹ /pliz/ *interjection* **1** used in order to be polite when asking for something ‖ 어떤 것을 요구할 때 공손하는 데에 쓰여. 미안하지만: *May I please have a glass of water?* 물 한 잔 좀 주시겠어요? / *Could you answer the door for me, please?* 제 대신 문 쪽에 나가봐 주시겠어요? **2** used in order to be polite when asking someone to do something ‖ 남에게 어떤 것을 해 달라고 정중하게 부탁할 때 쓰여. 제발. 아무쪼록. 부디: *Please put the dirty plates here.* 더러운 접시들은 이곳에 놓아 주세요. / *Patty, sit down, please.* 패티, 좀 앉으세요. **3** SPOKEN said in order to politely accept something that someone offers you ‖ 남이 제공하는 것을 공손하게 받는 데에 쓰여. 좋아요. 그러세요: *"Want some cake, Heather?" "Please."* "헤더, 케이크 좀 먹을래?" "좋아요."

USAGE NOTE please and thank you

Use **please** when asking for something or asking someone to do something: *Could I please borrow your pen? / Will you put the milk in the fridge, please? / Hello. May I* *speak with Alice, please?* Use **please** when saying "yes" in order to be polite: *"Would you like more coffee?" "Yes, please."* Use **thank you** when someone gives you something, does what you have asked, or does or says something that is polite or kind: *"Here's your coat." "Thank you." / Thank you for watering my plants. / "You look nice today." "Thank you!"* Use **thank you** with "no" in order to be polite: *"Would you like more coffee?" "No, thank you."* If someone gives you a present or does something special for you, it is polite to thank him/her in a stronger way: *Thank you very much. That's very kind of you.* In informal situations you can say: *Thanks a lot. That's really nice of you.* When someone thanks you, the most common answer is **you're welcome**: *"Thank you for the card, Uncle Chet." "You're welcome."* In informal speech, we can also say "that's okay," "no problem," or "sure": *"Thanks for the lift." "No problem."*

please는 남에게 어떤 것을 요구하거나 무엇을 해 달라고 부탁할 때 쓴다: 펜 좀 빌려주시겠습니까? / 우유를 냉장고에 넣어 주시겠어요? / 여보세요. 앨리스와 통화를 할 수 있을까요? **please**는 공손함을 말할 때 쓴다: "커피 더 드시겠어요?" "네, 좋아요." **thank you**는 남이 어떤 것을 주었을 때[요구한 것을 해주었을 때, 공손하거나 친절한 일을 하거나 말할 때] 쓴다: "외투 여기 있습니다." "고맙습니다." / 내 화초에 물을 주어서 고마워. / "너 오늘 멋있어 보인다." "고마워!" **thank you**는 공손함을 위해서 "no"와 함께 쓴다: "커피 더 드시겠어요?" "고맙지만 됐습니다." 만약 남이 선물을 주거나 특별한 것을 해 주면 그 사람에게 강도 있게 감사하는 것이 예의이다: 대단히 감사합니다. 매우 친절하시군요. 격식을 차리지 않는 상황에서는 줄여서 쓸 수 있다: 고마워요. 정말로 수고했어요. 남이 감사를 할 때 가장 흔한 대답은 **you're welcome**이다: "쳇 삼촌, 카드를 보내줘서 고마워요." "천만에요." 격식을 차리지 않는 대화에서는 또한 "괜찮습니다"나 "천만에요"나 "천만의 말씀"도 쓸 수 있다: "태워줘서 고마워요." "천만에요."

please² *v* **1** [I, T] to make someone feel happy or satisfied ‖ 남을 기쁘게 하

거나 만족스럽게 하다. (…을) 즐겁게[흐뭇하게] 하다: *Mark has always been hard to please.* 마크는 항상 비위 맞추기 어려운 사람이다. / *We always aim to please.* (=try to make people satisfied) 우리의 목표는 언제나 사람들을 만족시키는 것이다. **2 whatever/however etc. sb pleases** whatever, however etc. someone wants ‖ 어떤 사람이 원하는 것이 무엇이든지·어떻게 원하든지 등. 좋아하는 게 뭐든/어떻게 좋아하든지: *You can do whatever you please, but I'm going out.* 너는 네 하고 싶은 대로 하면 되고 나는 어쨌든 외출할 거야. **3 if you please** SPOKEN FORMAL used in order to politely emphasize a demand ‖ 요구하는 바를 공손하게 강조하는 데에 쓰여. 미안하지만, 괜찮다면: *Close the door, if you please.* 미안하지만 문 좀 닫아 주시겠어요? **– pleasing** *adj* : *a pleasing flavor* 감칠 맛

pleased /plizd/ *adj* **1** happy or satisfied ‖ 기뻐하거나 만족해 하는. 마음에 들어 하는: *Our lawyers are pleased with the judge's decision.* 우리의 변호사들은 판사의 판결에 만족해 한다. **2 (I'm) pleased to meet you** SPOKEN said in order to be polite when you meet someone for the first time ‖ 사람을 처음으로 만났을 때 공손하게 대하는 데에 쓰여. 만나뵙게 돼서 반갑습니다

pleas·ur·a·ble /ˈplɛʒərəbəl/ *adj* FORMAL enjoyable ‖ 즐거운. 유쾌한. 기분 좋은: *We want to make this a pleasurable experience for everyone.* 우리는 이것을 모두에게 유쾌한 경험이 되게 하고 싶다.

pleas·ure /ˈplɛʒɚ/ *n* **1** [U] a feeling of happiness, satisfaction, or enjoyment ‖ 행복[만족, 쾌락]감. 기쁨. 즐거움. 만족: *I often read for pleasure.* 나는 종종 재미삼아 책을 읽는다. / *Marie takes great pleasure in working at the school.* (=she enjoys it a lot) 마리는 학교에서 근무하는 것에 대단히 만족해 한다. **2** an activity or experience that you enjoy very much ‖ 대단히 즐기는 활동이나 경험. 기쁨[즐거움]을 주는 것: *It's a pleasure to finally meet you.* 드디어 만나뵙게 되어 반갑습니다. **3 (it is) my pleasure** SPOKEN a polite phrase used in order to say that you are glad you can do something nice for someone ‖ 남에게 기분 좋은 일을 해줄 수 있어서 기쁘다고 말하는 데에 쓰이는 공손한 어구. 천만에요. 별말씀을: *"Thanks for walking me home." "It was my pleasure."* "집까지 바래다 줘서 고마워요." "별 말씀을."

pleat /plit/ *n* a flat fold in a skirt, pair

of pants, dress etc. ‖ 치마[바지, 드레스] 등의 납작한 주름 – **pleat** v

pleat·ed /'plitɪd/ adj a pleated skirt, pair of pants, dress etc. has a lot of flat narrow folds ‖ 치마[바지, 드레스] 등이 납작하고 좁은 주름이 많은. 주름진

pleb·i·scite /'plɛbə,saɪt/ n [C, U] a system by which everyone in a country votes on an important national decision ‖ 한 국가의 모든 사람이 국가의 중요한 결정에 대해 투표하는 제도. 국민 투표

pled /plɛd/ v a past tense and PAST PARTICIPLE of PLEAD ‖ plead의 과거·과거 분사형

pledge[1] /plɛdʒ/ n **1** a serious promise or agreement to do something or to give money to help a CHARITY ‖ 어떤 것을 하거나 자선 활동을 돕기 위해 돈을 주겠다는 진지한 약속이나 협정. 서약. 맹세: *Several countries made pledges totalling $6 million in aid.* 몇몇 국가들이 총 6백만 달러의 원조금을 약속했다. / *a pledge of $15,000* 만오천 달러의 기부 약속 **2** someone who promises to become a member of a college FRATERNITY or SORORITY ‖ 대학의 남자 사교 단체나 여자 사교 단체의 일원이 되겠다고 서약한 사람. 입회 서약자

pledge[2] v [T] **1** to make a formal, usually public, promise ‖ 격식을 갖춘 보통 공적인 약속을 하다. …을 서약[맹세]하다: *Several companies have pledged to cut pollution by 50% or more.* 몇몇의 회사들은 오염률을 50% 이상 줄이기로 공약했다. **2** to make someone formally promise something ‖ 남에게 공식적으로 어떤 것을 약속하게 하다. …에게 …을 서약[맹세]시키다: *We were all pledged to secrecy.* 우리는 모두 비밀 엄수를 서약했다. **3** to promise to become a member of a college FRATERNITY or SORORITY ‖ 대학의 남자 사교 단체나 여자 사교 단체의 일원이 되기로 약속하다. 입회 서약을 하다

Pledge of Al·le·giance /,. . .'../ n **the Pledge of Allegiance** an official statement said by Americans in which they promise to be loyal to the United States. It is usually said by children every morning at school ‖ 미국인들이 미국에 충성하겠다고 약속할 때 말하는 공식적인 말. 보통 어린이들이 학교에서 매일 아침 말한다. 충성의 맹세

ple·na·ry /'plinəri, 'plɛ-/ adj FORMAL involving all of the members of a committee, organization etc. ‖ 위원회·조직 등의 모든 구성원을 포함하는. 전원 출석의: *a plenary meeting* 전체 회의[총회] / *a plenary speech* (=to all the members) 총회의 연설

plen·ti·ful /'plɛntɪfəl/ adj more than enough in amount or number ‖ 양이나 수에서 충분한 것 이상의. 풍부한. 넉넉한: *a plentiful supply of fish in the bay* 만(灣)에 있는 풍부한 어자원(魚資源) – **plentifully** adv

plen·ty[1] /'plɛnti/ quantifier, n [U] a large amount that is enough or more than enough ‖ 충분하거나 충분한 것 이상의 많은 양. 많음. 다수. 다량: *We have plenty of time to get to the airport.* 우리는 공항에 도착할 충분한 시간이 있다. / *There should be plenty to eat at the picnic.* 소풍을 가서 먹을 것은 풍부할 것이다.

plen·ty[2] adv SPOKEN more than enough; a lot ‖ 충분한 것 이상으로. 충분하게. 넉넉히; 많이: *There's plenty more room in the car.* 그 차에는 훨씬 넉넉한 공간이 있다.

pleth·o·ra /'plɛθərə/ n **a plethora of** FORMAL a very large number ‖ 매우 많은 수. 대량. 다량. 과다: *a plethora of complaints* 과다한 불평들

Plex·i·glass /'plɛksi,glæs/ n [U] TRADEMARK a strong clear type of plastic that can be used instead of glass ‖ 유리 대신에 사용할 수 있는 강하고 투명한 종류의 플라스틱. 플렉시글라스

pli·a·ble /'plaɪəbəl/, **pliant** /'plaɪənt/ adj **1** able to bend without breaking or cracking ‖ 부러뜨리거나 금이 가게 하지 않고 구부릴 수 있는. 휘기 쉬운. 유연한: *Roll the clay until it is soft and pliable.* 부드럽고 유연해질 때까지 점토를 굴려라. **2** easily influenced by others, or willing to accept new ideas ‖ 다른 사람들에게 쉽게 영향을 받는, 또는 새로운 생각을 기꺼이 받아들이는. 유순한. 고분고분한. 적응성이 있는: *Craig had always been too pliant.* 크레이그는 언제나 너무 고분고분했다.

pli·ers /'plaɪɚz/ n [plural] a small metal tool used for bending wire or cutting it ‖ 철사를 구부리거나 자를 때 사용하는 작은 금속 연장. 펜치: *a pair of pliers* 펜치 하나

plight /plaɪt/ n a bad, serious, or sad situation that someone is in ‖ 사람이 처해 있는 나쁜[심각한, 슬픈] 상황. 곤경. 궁지. 역경: *The Governor has done nothing to help the plight of the homeless.* 그 주지사는 노숙자들의 곤궁한 처지를 도우려는 노력을 전혀 하지 않았다. / *the university's financial plight* 그 대학의 재정적 곤경

plod /plɑd/ v **-dded, -dding** [I] to

move or do something too slowly,
because you are tired or bored ‖ 피곤하
거나 지루해서 어떤 것을 아주 천천히 움
직이거나 하다. 터벅터벅 걷다. 천천히 나
아가다: *The movie just plods along
without enough action.* 그 영화는 충분한
액션 장면 없이 천천히 진행된다. / *cattle
plodding through mud* 진흙 위를 터벅
터벅 걸어가는 소떼들

plod·ding /'plɑdɪŋ/ *adj* without any
variety or excitement; boring ‖ 어떠한
다양성이나 흥분도 없는; 지루한. 단조로
운: *a plodding writing style* 단조로운 문
체

plop¹ /plɑp/ *v* -**pped**, -**pping** [T] to sit
down, fall down, or drop something
somewhere in a careless way ‖ 어떤 것
을 부주의하게 어딘가에 앉히다[넘어뜨리
다, 떨어뜨리다]. 털썩 앉다. 벌렁 눕다.
쿵 떨어지다. 풍덩 소리를 내다: *Jaime
plopped down on a sofa.* 제임은 소파에
털썩 주저앉았다. / *His golf ball drifted
and plopped into a pond.* 그의 골프 공
은 한참을 날다 연못 속으로 풍당 빠졌다.
/ *She plopped the book on the table and
stood up.* 그녀는 책을 탁자 위에 털썩 내
려놓고 일어났다.

plop² *n* the sound made by something
when it falls or is dropped into liquid ‖
사물이 넘어지거나 액체 속으로 떨어질 때
나는 소리. 쿵[풍당, 풍덩] 소리

plot¹ /plɑt/ *n* **1** the events that form the
main story of a book, movie, or play ‖
책[영화, 연극]의 주요 이야기를 형성하는
사건들. 줄거리. 플롯: *The plot was
boring, but the special effects were
good.* 줄거리는 지루했지만 특수 효과는
좋았다. **2** a secret plan you make with
other people to do something illegal or
harmful ‖ 불법적이거나 해로운 짓을 하기
위해 다른 사람들과 짜는 비밀 계획. 음
모. 책략: *a plot to kill the President* 대통
령을 살해하려는 음모 **3** a small piece of
land for building or growing things on ‖
그 위에 어떤 것들을 짓거나 기르기 위한
작은 부지. 작은 지면[땅]. 작게 구획된
터

plot² *v* -**tted**, -**tting** **1** [I, T] to make a
secret plan to harm a particular person
or organization ‖ 특정한 사람이나 조직을
해치기 위한 비밀 계획을 짜다. 음모를 꾸
미다. 획책하다: *Brown had plotted to
kill his first wife.* 브라운은 첫 번째 아내
를 죽일 음모를 꾸몄다. **2** [T] also **plot
out** to make lines and marks on a
CHART or map that represent facts,
numbers etc. ‖ 사실·숫자 등을 나타내는
선과 표시를 도표나 지도 위에 하다. 표시

[기입]하다: *plotting earthquakes on a
map* 지도 위에 지진을 표시하기 / *graphs
that plot the company's progress* 회사의
발전 상황을 나타내는 그래프들

plow¹, plough /plaʊ/ *n* a large piece
of equipment used on farms, that cuts
up the surface of the ground so that
seeds can be planted ‖ 씨앗을 심을 수 있
게 땅 표면을 가는 농사 일에 사용하는 큰
장비. 쟁기 —see also SNOWPLOW

plow², plough *v* **1** [I, T] to use a
PLOW in order to cut earth, push snow
off streets etc. ‖ 땅을 갈고 길에서 눈을
치우는 데에 쟁기를 사용하다. 쟁기로 갈
다[일구다]: *We drove through miles of
newly plowed fields.* 우리는 수마일이나
되는 새로 일군 들판을 차로 운전해 갔다.
2 [I] to move with a lot of effort or force
through something ‖ 많은 노력이나 힘을
사용하여 어떤 것을 관통해 이동하다. 전
진하다. 밀어제치고 나아가다: *a ship
plowing through large waves* 큰 파도를
헤치고 나아가는 배

plow sth ↔ **back** *phr v* to use profits to
INVEST in the same company that made
them ‖ 수익을 올렸던 동일한 회사에 투자
하기 위해 수익을 사용하다. 재투자하다:
*Much of their funds are plowed back
into equipment and training.* 그들 자본
의 대부분을 장비와 훈련에 재투자했다.

plow into sth *phr v* [T] to hit something
hard with a car, truck etc. ‖ 자동차·트럭
등으로 어떤 것을 세게 치다. 공격하다: *A
train derailed and plowed into two
houses.* 기차가 탈선하여 두 채의 가옥을
덮쳤다.

plow through sth *phr v* [T] to read all
of something even though it is difficult,
long, or boring ‖ 어떤 것이 어렵거나 분
량이 길거나, 또는 지루하더라도 전부 읽
다. 힘들여 읽다[끝내다]

ploy /plɔɪ/ *n* a way of tricking someone
in order to gain an advantage ‖ 유리한
입장을 차지하기 위해 남을 속이는 방법.
상대의 콧대를 꺾는 책략. 계략: *He
thought the boy's screams were just a
ploy to get attention.* 그는 그 소년의 비
명이 주의를 끌기 위한 계략에 불과하다고
생각했다.

pluck¹ /plʌk/ *v* **1** [T] to pull something
quickly in order to remove it ‖ 사물을 제
거하기 위해 재빨리 잡아당기다. 잡아뜯
다. 뜯어내다: *She plucks her eyebrows.*
(=pulls out hairs from the edges of
them) 그녀는 자기 눈썹을 뽑는다. **2**
pluck up the courage to make yourself
be brave or confident enough to do
something ‖ 어떤 일을 하는 데에 충분한

용기나 자신감을 가지다. 용기를 내다: *I finally plucked up the courage to ask for a raise.* 나는 마침내 용기를 내어 봉급 인 상을 요구했다. **3** to pull the feathers off a chicken or other bird before cooking it ‖ 요리하기 전에 닭이나 다른 새의 깃털을 뽑아내다. 잡아뽑다 **4** to quickly pull the strings of a musical instrument ‖ 재빨리 악기의 현을 잡아당기다. 타다. 켜다

pluck² *n* [U] courage and determination to do something that is difficult ‖ 어려운 일을 하기 위한 용기와 결단 **– plucky** *adj*

plug¹ /plʌg/ *n* **1** the small object at the end of a wire that is used for connecting a piece of electrical equipment to a SOCKET (=supply of electricity) ‖ 전기 장치 를 소켓에 연결시키는 데에 쓰는 전선의 끝에 있는 작은 물체. 플러그

2 a round flat piece of rubber used for blocking the hole in a bathtub or SINK ‖ 욕조나 싱크대의 구멍을 막는 데에 사용하 는 둥글고 납작한 고무 조각. 마개 **3** INFORMAL a way of advertising a book, movie etc. by talking about it on a radio or television program ‖ 라디오나 텔레비 전 프로그램에 책이나 영화 등에 대해 말 함으로써 광고하는 방식. (라디오 · 텔레비 전의) 광고. 선전

plug² *v* **-gged, -gging** [T] **1** also **plug up** to fill a hole or block it ‖ 구멍을 메우 거나 막다: *Firefighters plugged a leak from an explosion at a chemical plant.* 소방수들은 화학 공장의 폭발로 인한 누출 을 막았다. **2** to advertise a book, movie etc. by talking about it on a radio or television program ‖ 라디오나 텔레비전 프로그램에 책이나 영화 등에 대해 말함으 로써 광고하다. 선전[추천]하다

plug away *phr v* [I] to continue working hard at something ‖ 어떤 것을 계속해서 열심히 일[공부]하다. 악착같이[꾸준히] …을 계속하다: *He's been plugging away at his essay all week.* 그는 일주일 내내 자기의 논문을 열심히 작성하고 있었 다.

plug sth ↔ **in** *phr v* [T] to connect a piece of electrical equipment to a SOCKET (=supply of electricity) ‖ 전기 장 치를 소켓에 연결하다. 플러그를 꽂다: *Is the TV plugged in?* 텔레비전 플러그가 꽂혀져 있니? **–opposite** UNPLUG

plug sth **into** *phr v* [T] to connect one

piece of electrical equipment to another ‖ 전기 장치의 하나를 다른 곳에 연결하 다. 장치를 꽂다[끼우다]: *Can you plug the speakers into the stereo for me?* 스 피커를 스테레오 장치에 연결해 주시겠어 요?

plug-in, plug·in /plʌgɪn/ *n* TECHNICAL a piece of computer software that can be used in addition to existing software in order to make particular programs work properly ‖ 특정 프로그램이 정상 작 동하도록 기존의 소프트웨어에 추가해서 사용할 수 있는 컴퓨터 소프트웨어. 플러 그 접속 제품

plum /plʌm/ *n* a soft round, usually purple fruit with a single large seed, or the tree on which it grows ‖ 하나의 큰 씨앗을 가지고 있는 부드럽고 둥근, 일반 적으로 자주색의 과일, 또는 그 과일이 자 라는 나무. 서양자두(나무) **—see picture on page 944**

plum·age /ˈpluːmɪdʒ/ *n* [U] the feathers covering a bird's body ‖ 새의 몸통을 덮 고 있는 깃털. 우모(羽毛)

plumb·er /ˈplʌmər/ *n* someone whose job is to repair water pipes, SINKs, toilets etc. ‖ 수도관·싱크대·변기 등을 수 리하는 직업인. 연관공. 배관공

plumb·ing /ˈplʌmɪŋ/ *n* [U] the system of water pipes in a house or building ‖ 집이나 건물 안의 수도관 체계. 배관 (계 통). (상하) 수도 설비: *Isaac's apartment has a lot of plumbing problems.* 아이삭의 아파트에는 배관에 많 은 문제가 있다.

plume /pluːm/ *n* **1** a small cloud of smoke, dust, gas etc. ‖ 작은 연기·먼지· 가스 등의 구름: *Neighbors noticed plumes of smoke coming from the garage.* 이웃들은 차고에서 피어오르는 연 기 구름을 보았다. **2** a large feather ‖ 큰 깃털

plum·met /ˈplʌmɪt/ *v* [I] **1** to suddenly and quickly decrease in value ‖ 가치가 갑작스럽고 빠르게 감소하다. (가격 등이) 폭락[급락]하다: *House prices have plummeted over the past year.* 집 가격 이 지난해에 급격하게 떨어졌다. **2** to fall suddenly and very quickly from a very high place ‖ 매우 높은 장소에서 갑작스럽 게 아주 빨리 떨어지다. 수직으로 떨어지 다. 곤두박질치다: *Two small planes collided and plummeted to the ground.* 두 대의 소형 비행기가 충돌해서 지면에 곤두박질쳤다.

plump¹ /plʌmp/ *adj* **1** attractively round and slightly fat ‖ 매력적으로 둥그 스름하고 약간 통통한. 포동포동한: *plump* *juicy strawberries* 즙이 많은 딸기 / *plump cushions* 푹신푹신한 쿠션 **2 a** word meaning fat, used in order to be polite ‖ 뚱뚱한의 의미를 예의바르게 사용하는 말. 통통한: *He was 67, short, and a little plump.* 그는 67세로 키가 작고 약간 통통했다. —see usage note at FAT¹

plump² *v*

plump for sth *phr v* [T] INFORMAL to choose something after thinking about all your choices ‖ 선택 가능한 모든 것에 대해 생각한 후에 어떤 것을 선택하다. … 을 강력히 지지하다: *I think I'll plump for the Spanish class.* 나는 스페인어 강의를 선택할 것 같아.

plump sth ↔ **up** *phr v* [T] to make a PILLOW bigger and softer by shaking and hitting it ‖ 베개를 흔들고 (툭툭) 쳐서 보다 크고 부드럽게 만들다. 베개를 불룩하게 하다

plun·der¹ /ˈplʌndɚ/ *v* [I, T] to steal money or property from a place while fighting in a war ‖ 전쟁에서 싸우는 동안 한 곳에서 돈이나 재산을 훔치다. …을 약탈[강탈]하다: *Every building was plundered, even the church.* 심지어 교회를 포함한 모든 건물이 약탈당했다.

plunder² *n* [U] things that are stolen by the fighters during an attack or war ‖ 공격이나 전쟁 기간 동안 전투원들이 훔친 물건. 약탈품

plunge¹ /plʌndʒ/ *v* **1** [I, T] to fall down, especially into water, or to push something down with a lot of force ‖ 특히 물 속으로 떨어지다, 또는 많은 힘을 가해 어떤 것을 밀어내리다. 뛰어들다. 빠지다. (…에) 밀어넣다[쑤셔박다]: *A van ran off a curve and plunged into the river early today.* 오늘 새벽 밴 한 대가 커브 길을 벗어나 강 속으로 빠졌다. / *Barton plunged his hands into his pockets and strode away.* 바턴은 양손을 주머니에 찔러 넣고 성큼성큼 걸어갔다. **2** [I] to suddenly decrease in amount or value ‖ 양이나 가치가 갑자기 감소하다. 급락하다: *The price of gas plunged to 99 cents a gallon.* 휘발유 값이 1갤런에 99센트로 급락했다.

plunge into *phr v* [T] **plunge sb/sth into sth** to put someone or something into a bad or difficult situation ‖ 사람이나 사물을 나쁘거나 어려운 상황에 빠뜨리다. …에 빠지게 하다[몰아넣다]: *The US was suddenly plunged into war.* 미국은 갑자기 전쟁 상태에 돌입했다.

plunge² *n* **1 take the plunge** to decide to do something risky, usually after delaying or worrying about it ‖ 대개 위험성이 있는 일에 대해 미루거나 걱정한 후에 하기로 결정하다. 과감히 일을 단행하다: *I finally took the plunge and moved to Washington.* 나는 마침내 궁리 끝에 큰 결심을 하고 워싱턴으로 이사 갔다. **2 a** sudden decrease in amount, or a sudden fall ‖ 갑작스러운 양의 감소, 또는 급락

plung·er /ˈplʌndʒɚ/ *n* a tool used for unblocking a pipe in a toilet or SINK, consisting of a straight handle with a large rubber cup on its end ‖ 일직선의 손잡이가 있고 그 끝에 큰 고무로 된 컵 모양의 것이 달린, 화장실이나 싱크대의 파이프를 뚫는 데 사용하는 도구. 배수관용 청소 막대

plunk¹ /plʌŋk/ *v* [T] INFORMAL

plunk down sth *phr v* [T] to spend a lot of money for something, or to put something down quickly and loudly ‖ 어떤 것에 많은 돈을 쓰다, 또는 어떤 것을 재빠르고 큰 소리가 나게 내려놓다. 턱 하고 지불하다. …을 털썩 놓다[던지다]: *Plunk down $300,000 and you could have a new house in Sun City.* 30만 달러를 턱 하고 지불하면 선 시티에 새 집을 구입할 수 있다.

plunk² *n* the sound made by something when it is dropped ‖ 사물이 떨어질 때 나는 소리. 쿵 하는 소리

plu·per·fect /ˌpluˈpɚfɪkt/ *n* **the pluperfect** TECHNICAL ⇨ PAST PERFECT

plu·ral /ˈplʊrəl/ *n* **the plural** TECHNICAL in grammar, the form of a word that represents more than one person or thing. For example, "dogs" is the plural of "dog" ‖ 문법에서, 사람이나 사물이 한 명 또는 한 개 이상임을 나타내는 단어의 형태. 복수형. 예를 들면, "dogs"는 "dog"의 복수형이다. — **plural** *adj* : *a plural noun/verb* 복수 명사[동사] —compare SINGULAR¹ —see study note on page 940

plu·ral·i·ty /plʊˈrælətɪ/ *n* [C, U] the largest number of votes in an election, especially when this is less than the total number of votes that all the other people or parties have received ‖ 선거에서 특히, 모든 다른 후보자나 정당이 득표한 총투표수보다 적을 때의 최대 득표수. (당선자와 차점자 간의) 득표차. 초과 득표수

plus¹ /plʌs/ *prep* used when one number or amount is added to another ‖ 하나의 수나 양을 다른 수나 양에 추가할 때 쓰여. …을 더하여: *Three plus six equals nine. (3+6=9)* 3 더하기 6은 9이다. / *The jacket costs $49.95 plus tax.* 그 재킷은 세금을 포함해서 49달러 95센트이

다.

plus² *conjunction* and also ‖ 또한. 게다가: *He's going to college, plus he's working 20 hours a week.* 그는 대학에 갈 것이고 게다가 일주일에 20시간 일할 것이다.

plus³ *adj* **1 A plus/B plus/C plus etc.** a grade used in a system of marking students' work; a C plus is higher than a C, but lower than a B MINUS ‖ 학생의 성적을 매기는 체계에 사용하는 점수; C 플러스는 C보다 높지만 B 마이너스보다는 낮음 **2** greater than zero or than a particular amount ‖ 0보다 크거나 특정한 양 이상의. 더하기 부호의. 양(陽)의. 이상의: *a temperature of plus 12°* 영상 12도가 넘는 온도 / *She makes $50,000 a year plus.* 그녀는 1년에 5만달러 이상을 번다. **3 plus or minus** used in order to give the amount by which another amount can vary ‖ 주어진 양만큼 다른 양에 변화를 가져오는 데에 쓰여. 오차 범위: *The results are accurate within plus or minus 3 percentage points.* 결과는 정확히 플러스 마이너스 3% 범위 내에 있다. —compare minus³

plus⁴ *n* **1** ⇨ PLUS SIGN **2** something that is an advantage or a quality that you think is good ‖ 이점이 되는 것이나 좋다고 생각하는 특성. 이익. 유리한 요소[특질]: *The restaurant's convenient location is a plus.* 그 식당의 지리적 편리함은 유리한 요소이다.

plush /plʌʃ/ *adj* comfortable, expensive, and of good quality ‖ 안락하고 비싸며 좋은 품질의. 호사[사치]스러운: *a large plush office* 크고 호화로운 사무실

plus sign /'. ./ *n* the sign (+) ‖ (+)기호

Plu·to /'plutoʊ/ *n* [singular] a small PLANET, ninth from the sun ‖ 태양으로부터 아홉 번째의 소행성. 명왕성

plu·toc·ra·cy /plu'tɑkrəsi/ *n* a country that is ruled by rich people, or a government that is controlled by them ‖ 부자들에 의해 지배되는 나라, 또는 부자들에 의해 통제되는 정부. 금권 국가[정치]

plu·to·ni·um /plu'toʊniəm/ *n* [U] a metal that is an ELEMENT and is used for producing NUCLEAR power ‖ 원소이자 원자력을 생산하는 데 쓰이는 금속. 플루토늄

ply¹ /plaɪ/ *n* [U] a unit for measuring the thickness of thread, rope, PLYWOOD etc. based on the number of threads or layers that it has ‖ 포함되어 있는 실이나 층의 수에 기초한 실·밧줄·합판 등의 두께

를 재는 단위. 층. 겹. 두께. 가닥

ply² *v* **plied, plied, plying 1 ply your trade** to work at your business or special skill ‖ 자신의 사업이나 특별한 기술을 가지고 일하다. …에 힘쓰다[열중하다]: *Blues bands were plying their trade in bars around town.* 블루스 밴드는 시내 곳곳의 술집에서 활동하고 있었다. **2** [I, T] LITERARY a boat or vehicle that plies between two places travels to those two places regularly ‖ 배나 탈것이 두 장소 사이를 정기적으로 다니다. 왕복하다

ply sb **with** sth *phr v* [T] to continue giving someone large amounts of something, especially food and drinks ‖ 특히 다량의 음식과 음료 등을 남에게 계속해서 주다. …을 귀찮게 권하다

ply·wood /'plaɪwʊd/ *n* [U] a material made of thin sheets of wood stuck together to form a hard board ‖ 딱딱한 판자를 만들기 위해 얇은 나무판을 함께 붙여 만든 재료. 합판. 베니어판

p.m. the abbreviation of "post meridiem"; used after numbers to show times from NOON until just before MIDNIGHT ‖ "post meridiem(오후)"의 약어; 정오부터 자정 직전까지의 시간을 나타내기 위해 숫자 뒤에 쓰여: *I get off work at 5:30 p.m.* 나는 오후 5시 30분에 일을 마친다.

PMS *n* [U] Premenstrual Syndrome; the anger or sadness and physical pain that many women experience before each PERIOD ‖ Premenstrual Syndrome(월경전 증후군)의 약어; 많은 여성들이 매달 생리하기 전에 경험하는 분노나 슬픔과 육체적인 고통

pneu·mat·ic /nʊ'mætɪk/ *adj* **1** TECHNICAL filled with air ‖ 공기가 채워진: *a pneumatic tire* 바람이 가득 들어 있는 타이어 **2** able to work using air pressure ‖ 공기 압력에 의해 작동할 수 있는. 공기 작용에 의한: *a pneumatic drill* 공기 압력 드릴 – **pneumatically** *adv*

pneu·mo·nia /nʊ'moʊnyə/ *n* [U] a serious disease of the lungs, which makes people have difficulty breathing ‖ 사람들을 호흡하기 어렵게 하는 위독한 폐병. 폐렴

P.O. *n* the written abbreviation of POST OFFICE ‖ post office의 약어

poach /poʊtʃ/ *v* **1** [T] to cook food such as eggs or fish in slightly boiling liquid ‖ 계란이나 생선 등의 음식을 살짝 끓는 액체에 요리하다. 데치다[삶다] **2** [I, T] to illegally catch or shoot animals, birds, or fish, especially from private land ‖ 특히 사유지에서 동물[새, 물고기]을 불법적

으로 잡거나 사냥하다. 밀렵[밀어]하다

poach·er /'poʊtʃɚ/ n someone who illegally catches or shoots animals, birds, or fish, especially on private land ‖ 특히 사유지에서 동물[새, 물고기]를 불법적으로 잡거나 사냥하는 사람. 밀렵[밀어]꾼

P.O. Box /,pi 'oʊ ,bɑks/ n Post Office Box; a box in a POST OFFICE that has a special number, to which you can have mail sent instead of to your home ‖ Post Office Box(사서함)의 약어; 우편물을 자택 대신 받아둘 수 있는 특별한 번호가 있는 우체국에 있는 우편함

pock·et¹ /'pɑkɪt/ n **1** a small bag sewn onto shirts, coats, pants, or skirts, often used for putting keys or money in ‖ 종종 열쇠나 돈을 넣는 데 쓰는 셔츠[외투, 바지, 치마]에 꿰매어 만든 작은 주머니. 호주머니: *Julie stuck her hands in her pockets.* 줄리는 호주머니에 양 손을 찔러 넣었다. / *Dad always keeps pens in his shirt pocket.* 아버지는 항상 셔츠 주머니에 펜을 넣고 다니신다. **2** the amount of money you have that you can spend ‖ 가지고 있어 쓸 수 있는 금액. 소지금: *Over $20 million was taken out of the pockets of American taxpayers.* 미국 납세자들의 수중에서 2천만 달러 이상의 세금을 징수했다. **3** a small bag, net, or piece of material that is attached to something such as a car seat, used for holding maps, magazines etc. ‖ 지도·잡지 등을 넣어 두는 데 쓰는, 자동차 좌석 등에 부착된 작은 주머니[그물망, 물체] **4** a small area or amount that is different from what surrounds it ‖ 주위를 둘러싸고 있는 것과 상이한 작은 지역이나 양. 에워싸인 곳. 고립 지대: *Pockets of the Midwest will have thunderstorms tonight.* 중서부 지역에 오늘 밤 심한 뇌우가 예상됩니다.

pocket
pocket

pocket² v [T] to get money in a slightly dishonest way, or by stealing it ‖ 약간 부정한 방법으로, 또는 훔쳐서 돈을 얻다. 착복하다. 횡령하다: *He admitted pocketing $5300 of his own campaign money.* 그는 자신의 선거 자금을 5,300달러 횡령했다고 시인했다.

pocket³, pocket-sized /'.. ,./ adj small enough to fit into a pocket ‖ 주머니 속에 넣기에 알맞을 정도로 작은. 소형의. 포켓형의. 휴대용의: *a pocket calendar* 포켓형 달력 / *a pocket-sized notebook* 주머니 크기의 공책

pock·et·book /'pɑkɪt,bʊk/ n **1** ⇨ WALLET **2** OLD-FASHIONED ⇨ PURSE¹

pock·et·ful /'pɑkɪt,fʊl/ n the amount that will fill a pocket, or a large amount ‖ 주머니를 가득 채울 정도의 양, 또는 다량. 한 주머니 가득. 많은 양. 다수: *a pocketful of small change* 꽤 많은 잔돈

pock·et knife /'pɑkɪt,naɪf/ n, plural **pocket knives** a small knife with a blade that you can fold into its handle ‖ 손잡이 안에 접어 넣을 수 있는 날을 가진 작은 칼. 접칼. 주머니칼

pock·mark /'pɑkmɑrk/ n a small hollow mark on someone's skin, made by a skin disease ‖ 피부병으로 생긴 사람 피부에 난 작고 움푹한 자국. 마맛자국 – **pockmarked** adj

pod /pɑd/ n the long green part of plants such as BEANs and peas, that the seeds grow in ‖ 콩이나 완두콩 등의 식물의 그 안에서 열매가 자라는 긴 초록색 부분. 꼬투리. 깍지: *a pea pod* 완두콩 꼬투리 —see picture at PEEL²

po·di·a·trist /pə'daɪətrɪst/ n a doctor who takes care of people's feet and treats foot diseases ‖ 사람의 발을 보살피고 발의 병을 치료하는 의사. 족병 치료 의사 – **podiatry** n [U]

po·di·um /'poʊdiəm/ n **1** a tall thin desk you stand behind when giving a speech to a lot of people ‖ 많은 사람들에게 연설할 때 그 뒤에 서서 하는 높고 길쭉한 책상. 연단 **2** a small raised area for a performer, speaker, or musical CONDUCTOR to stand on ‖ 공연자[연설자, 음악 지휘자]가 그 위에 서는 높인 작은 곳. 단(壇). 지휘대

po·em /'poʊəm/ n a piece of writing that expresses emotions, experiences, and ideas, especially in short lines using words that RHYME (=have a particular pattern of sounds) ‖ 특히 운율이 있는 단어를 사용해 짧은 행으로 감정·경험·생각을 표현하는 글. 시

po·et /'poʊɪt/ n someone who writes poems ‖ 시를 쓰는 사람. 시인

po·et·ic /poʊ'ɛtɪk/ adj **1** relating to poetry or typical of poetry ‖ 시와 관련되거나 시의 전형적인 특성의. 시의. 시적인 [시와 같은]: *poetic language* 시어 **2** graceful and expressing deep emotions ‖ 우아하며 깊은 감정을 표현하는. 시적 능력[감성]이 풍부한: *a poetic and powerful ballet* 우아하고 힘이 넘치는 발레 – **poetically** adv

poetic jus·tice /,.. '../ n [U] a

situation in which someone who has done something bad suffers in a way that you think s/he deserves ‖ 나쁜 행동을 한 사람은 그만한 고통을 받는다는 상황. 시적 정의. 인과응보. 권선징악

poetic li·cense /ˌ.ˌ.. '../ *n* [U] the freedom to change facts, not obey grammar rules etc. because you are writing poetry ‖ 시를 쓰고 있기 때문에 사실을 바꾸거나 문법 규칙을 따르지 않아도 되는 등의 자유. 시적 허용

po·et·ry /'poʊətri/ *n* [U] **1** poems ‖ 시. 운문: *a book of Emily Dickenson's poetry* 에밀리 디킨슨의 시집 –compare PROSE **2** the art of writing poems ‖ 시를 쓰는 기술. 작시법: *a poetry class* 시작법 강의

pog·rom /'poʊɡrəm/ *n* a planned killing of large numbers of people, especially Jews, done for reasons of race or religion ‖ 인종이나 종교적인 이유로 행해진, 특히 유대인에 대한 계획된 대량 학살

poign·ant /'pɔɪnyənt/ *adj* making you have strong feelings of sadness or pity ‖ 격한 슬픔이나 동정심을 가지게 하는. 감동적인. 통한의[가슴을 에이는]: *poignant childhood memories* 가슴에 이는 듯한 어린 시절의 추억 –**poignancy** *n* [U] –**poignantly** *adv*

poin·set·ti·a /pɔɪn'sɛtiə/ *n* a plant with groups of large bright red or white leaves that look like flowers ‖ 꽃처럼 생긴 크고 밝은 붉은색이나 하얀색의 잎이 많은 식물. 포인세티아. 홍성초

point¹ /pɔɪnt/ *n*
1 ▶**ONE IDEA** 하나의 생각◀ a single fact, idea, or opinion in an argument or discussion ‖ 논쟁이나 토론에서의 하나의 사실[생각, 의견]: *That's a very interesting point.* 그것 참 흥미로운 점이군. / *Jackie pounded the table to make her point.* 재키는 주장을 부각시키기 위해 테이블을 여러 번 세게 두들겼다.
2 ▶**MAIN IDEA** 주된 생각◀ the main meaning or idea in something that is said or done ‖ 말이나 행동에서의 주된 의미나 생각. 요점. 주안점: *Get to the point!* (=say your idea directly) 요점을 말해봐! / *The point is that I don't trust him anymore.* 중요한 것은 내가 더 이상 그를 믿지 않는다는 것이야. / *What's your point?* 요점이 뭐야? / *That's beside the point.* (=it does not relate to the subject) 그것은 주제를 벗어난 것이다.
3 ▶**IN TIME/DEVELOPMENT** 장차/발달◀ a specific moment or time, or a stage in something's development ‖ 특정한 순간이나 시간, 또는 어떤 것의 발달 단계. 시점: *At some point we'll need to get* *some more gas.* 어느 단계에 이르면 우리는 더 많은 휘발유가 필요할 것이다. / *They reached the point where they thought they should get married.* 그들은 자신들이 결혼해야 한다고 생각하는 시점에 도달했다.
4 ▶**PLACE** 장소◀ an exact position or place ‖ 정확한 위치나 장소. 지점: *the point where two lines cross each other* 두 개의 선이 서로 교차하는 점
5 ▶**PURPOSE** 목적◀ [U] the purpose or aim of doing something ‖ 어떤 일을 하는 목적이나 목표: *The whole point of traveling is to experience new things.* 여행의 전적인 목적은 새로운 것을 경험하기 위한 것이다. / *There's no point in going now – we're already too late.* 지금 가봤자 헛수고야. 우린 이미 너무 늦었어. ✗DON'T SAY "There's no point to go now."✗ "There's no point to go now." 라고 하지는 않는다.
6 ▶**QUALITY** 질◀ a particular quality that someone or something has ‖ 사람 또는 사물이 가지는 특정한 자질. 특징. 특질: *Public speaking is one of the Mayor's strong points.* (=best qualities) 대중 연설은 그 시장의 장점 중 하나이다.
7 ▶**GAME/SPORT** 게임/스포츠◀ a unit used for showing the SCORE in a game or sport ‖ 게임이나 운동 경기에서 점수를 나타내는 데 사용하는 단위. 득점. 포인트: *The Rams beat the Giants by six points.* 램즈팀은 자이언츠팀을 6점 차로 이겼다.
8 ▶**IN NUMBERS** 숫자상에서◀ the sign (.) used for separating a whole number from the DECIMALs that follow it ‖ 뒤따르는 소수로부터 정수를 분리하는 데 사용하는 부호(.). 소수점: *four point seven five percent* (=4.75%) 4.75퍼센트
9 ▶**MEASURE** 측정치◀ a measure on a scale ‖ 규모의 측정치: *Stocks were down 12 points today at 5098.* 오늘 주가지수는 5098포인트로 12포인트 하락했다.
10 the high/low point of the best or worst part of something, or the best or worst moment ‖ 어떤 것의 가장 좋거나 나쁜 부분, 또는 가장 좋거나 나쁜 순간: *The high point in my life was having my son.* 내 인생에서 최고의 부분은 내 아들을 둔 것이었다.
11 ▶**SHARP END** 날카로운 끝◀ the sharp end of something ‖ 사물의 날카로운 끝: *the point of a needle* 바늘의 뾰족한 끝
12 up to a point partly, but not completely ‖ 전적으로가 아닌 부분적으로. 어느 정도까지는: *He believed her story, up to a point.* 그는 어느 정도까지

는 그녀의 이야기를 믿었다.

13 make a point of doing something
to deliberately do something ‖ 어떤 것을
의도적으로 하다. 반드시 …하다. …하도
록 노력하다: *Make a point of going to
the French Quarter when you visit New
Orleans.* 뉴올리언스를 방문할 경우에는
프렌치 쿼터에 반드시 들러라.

14 ▶SMALL SPOT 작은 점◀ a very small
spot ‖ 매우 작은 점: *a tiny point of light*
매우 희미한 불빛

15▶ LAND 땅◀ a long thin piece of
land that stretches out into the ocean ‖
바다 쪽으로 쭉 뻗어 있는 길고 좁은 땅.
곶. 갑(岬)

16 to the point only talking about the
most important facts or ideas ‖ 가장 중
요한 사실이나 생각에 대해서만 말하는.
적절하게[한]. 요령 있게[있는]: *Your
business letters should be short and to
the point.* 무역 서신은 간략하고 요점만
말해야 한다.

17 on the point of doing sth going to
do something very soon ‖ 어떤 일을 막
하려고 하는. …의 찰나에: *I was just on
the point of leaving for work when the
phone rang.* 전화가 왔을 때 나는 막 일하
러 가려던 중이었다.

18 the point of no return the moment
when you become so involved in an
activity, situation etc. that it is
impossible for you to stop doing it ‖ 활동
이나 상황 등에 너무 깊이 개입되어 그 행
동을 멈추기 불가능한 순간. 뒤로 물러설
수 없는 단계

SPOKEN PHRASES

19 you/they have a point said when
you think someone's idea or opinion
is right ‖ 남의 생각이나 의견이 옳다고
생각할 때 쓰여. 당신/그들 말에 일리가
있 다: *"The tickets might be too
expensive." "You have a point."* "그
표는 너무 비쌀 것 같아." "네 말이 맞
아." **20 that's not the point** said
when facts or explanations do not
relate to the main facts or ideas ‖ 사실
이나 설명이 주요한 사실이나 생각과 관
련이 없을 때 쓰여. 그건 중요한 게 아
니다: *"But I gave you the money
back." "That's not the point; you
shouldn't have stolen it."* "근데 내가
너한테 그 돈을 다시 돌려 줬잖아." "그
건 중요한 게 아냐. 너는 그 돈을 훔치
지 말았어야 했어." **21 I see your
point** used in order to say that you
accept what someone has said ‖ 남이
말한 것을 받아들인다고 말하는 데에 쓰

여 : *Grandma refuses to go to a
nursing home, and I see her point.* 할
머니는 양로원에 가기를 거부하는데 나
는 할머니를 충분히 이해한다.

—see also GUNPOINT —see usage note at
VIEW¹

point² *v* **1** [I] to show someone
something by holding your finger out
toward it ‖ 자신의 손가락을 사물 쪽으로
뻗어 남에게 그것을 보여 주다. 가리키다:
*John pointed to a chair. "Please, sit
down."* 존은 의자 쪽을 가리키며 "앉으세
요."라고 말했다. / *"That's my car," she
said, pointing at a white Ford.* 그녀는
흰색 포드차를 가리키며 "저것이 내 차
야."라 고 말 했 다. **2** [I, T] to aim
something or to be aimed in a particular
direction ‖ 특정한 방향에 어떤 것을 겨누
거나 겨눠지다: *He pointed a gun at the
old man's head.* 그는 총을 노인의 머리에
겨눴다. / *Hold the bat so that your
fingers point toward its end.* 손가락을
끝 쪽으로 향하게 배트를 잡아라. **3** [T] to
show someone which direction to go ‖ 가
야 할 방향을 남에게 보여 주다. 가리키
다. 알려주다: *There should be signs
pointing the way to her house.* 그녀의
집까지 가는 길을 알려주는 표지판이 있을
것이다. **4 point the finger at sb**
INFORMAL to blame someone; ACCUSE ‖ 남
을 비난하다; ㊞ accuse

point out *phr v* **1** [T **point** sth ↔ **out**]
to tell someone something that s/he does
not already know or has not yet noticed
‖ 남이 아직 알지 못하거나 깨닫지 못하는
것을 남에게 말하다. 지적하다: *Hobart
pointed out that Washington hadn't
won a game in L.A. since 1980.* 호바트는
1980년 이후로 워싱턴팀이 L.A.에서 한
경기도 이기지 못했다고 지적했다. **2** [T
point sb/sth ↔ **out**] to show a person or
thing to someone by pointing at him,
her, or it ‖ 남에게 사람이나 사물을 가리
켜 보여 주다: *Mrs. Lucas pointed out
her new students to us.* 루카스 부인은 우
리에게 자신의 새로운 학생들을 지적해 알
려 주었다.

point to/toward sb/sth *phr v* [T] to
show that something is probably true ‖
어떤 것이 사실일 거라고 나타내다. …을
지적하다: *The report points to stress as
a cause of heart disease.* 그 보고서는 심
장병의 원인으로서 스트레스를 지적했다.

point-blank /ˌ. ˈ./ *adv* **1** if you say
something point-blank, you say it in a
very direct way ‖ 어떤 것을 매우 직접적
으로 말하여. 단도직입적으로: *They*

refused my offer point-blank. 그들은 내 제의를 일언지하에 거절했다. **2 if you shoot a gun point-blank, the person or thing you are shooting is directly in front of you** ‖ 사람이나 사물을 바로 앞에 서 직접적으로 겨누어: *Ralston was shot at point-blank range.* 랄스톤은 바로 눈 앞에서 총에 맞았다.

point·ed /'pɔɪntɪd/ *adj* **1** having a point at the end ‖ 끝이 뾰족한: *cowboy boots with pointed toes* 앞부리가 뾰족한 카우보이 부츠 **2 a pointed question/look/ remark etc.** a direct question, look etc. that deliberately shows that you are bored, annoyed, or do not approve of something ‖ 지루하거나 짜증나거나 어떤 것을 인정하지 않음을 의도적으로 보여 주는 직접적인 질문·표정 등. 날카로운[빈정대는] 질문/표정/말

point·ed·ly /'pɔɪntɪdli/ *adv* deliberately, so that people notice ‖ 사람들이 알아차리게 의도적으로. 드러내놓고: *Wilton pointedly avoided asking Reiter for advice.* 윌턴은 라이터에게 조언을 구하는 것을 드러내놓고 기피했다.

point·er /'pɔɪntɚ/ *n* **1** a helpful piece of advice; TIP ‖ 도움이 되는 조언; 㕬 tip: *I can give you some pointers on how to cook a turkey.* 내가 너한테 칠면조 요리를 어떻게 하는지 몇 가지 조언을 해 줄 수 있다. **2** the thin ARROW that points to a particular place, number, or direction on a piece of equipment such as a computer, watch, or scale ‖ 컴퓨터[시계, 저울] 등의 장치에 있는 특정한 장소[수, 방향]를 가리키는 얇은 화살 모양의 것. (시계·저울의) 바늘. 컴퓨터 화면의 포인터 **3** a long stick used for pointing at things on a map, board etc. ‖ 지도나 칠판 등에 있는 내용을 가리키는 데 사용되는 긴 막대. 지시봉 **4** a hunting dog that points its nose at animals and birds that are hiding ‖ 숨어 있는 동물과 새들이 있는 방향을 코로 (냄새를 맡아) 가리키는 사냥개. 포인터

point·less /'pɔɪntlɪs/ *adj* **1** without any purpose or meaning ‖ 어떤 목적이나 의미 없는. 무의미한: *pointless violence on TV* 텔레비전에 나타난 적절치 못한 폭력성 **2** not likely to have any effect ‖ 어떠한 영향력도 없을 것 같은. 소용없는: *It's pointless trying to talk to him – he won't listen.* 그에게 말하려고 해봤자 소용없어. 그는 들으려고 하지 않아.

point man /'. ./ *n* someone, especially a soldier, who goes ahead of a group to see what a situation is like or if there is any danger ‖ 상황이 어떠한지 또는 어떤

위험성이 있는지 확인하기 위해 무리에서 앞서 가는 사람, 특히 군인. 정찰대의 선두에 서는 척후병[첨병]

point of view /ˌ. . './ *n* **1** a particular way of thinking about or judging a situation ‖ 어떤 상황에 대해 생각하거나 판단하는 특정한 방식. 관점. 견지. 의견. 태도: *From a purely practical point of view, this is not a good decision.* 순전히 실제적인 관점에서 보면 이것은 좋은 결정이 아니다. **2** someone's own personal opinion or attitude about something ‖ 어떤 것에 대한 자신의 개인적인 의견이나 태도: *My parents never seem to be able to see my point of view.* 부모님은 내 생각을 결코 이해하지 못할 것 같다.

poin·ty /'pɔɪnti/ *adj* INFORMAL ⇨ POINTED

poise¹ /pɔɪz/ *n* [U] **1** behavior that shows you are calm, confident, and able to control how you feel ‖ 침착하고 자신감 있고 감정을 조절할 수 있음을 보여주는 행동. 냉정. 태연자약: *Throughout the discussion he never lost his poise.* 토의하는 내내 그는 결코 냉정함을 잃지 않았다. **2** a graceful way of moving or standing ‖ 우아하게 움직이거나 서 있는 태도. 우아한 자세. 몸가짐: *Miss Gaines was tall, thin, and lacking in poise.* 게인즈 양은 키가 크고 말랐으며 자태가 우아하지는 못하다.

poise² *v* [T] to put something in a carefully balanced position, or to hold it there ‖ 사물을 조심스럽게 균형 잡힌 위치에 놓거나 두다. 균형을 유지하다. 균형잡히게 하다: *The reporter sat with his pen poised over a notebook.* 그 기자는 펜을 메모지 위에 적절히 올려놓고 자리에 앉았다.

poised /pɔɪzd/ *adj* **1** completely prepared for something to happen, because it is likely to happen very soon ‖ 어떤 일이 곧 일어날 것 같아서, 그 일에 준비가 완전히 된. …할 태세를 갖춘. 금방이라도 …할 수 있는: *The army was poised to attack.* 군은 공격할 준비가 다 되어 있었다. / *property that is poised for development* 금방이라도 개발할 준비가 되어 있는 땅 **2** not moving, but completely ready to move ‖ 움직이고 있지는 않지만 움직일 준비가 완전히 된: *runners poised at the start of a race* 경주 출발선에서 출발할 자세를 취하고 있는 주자들 **3** behaving in a calm confident way that shows you are able to control how you feel ‖ 자신의 감정을 통제할 수 있음을 나타내는 침착하고 자신감 있는 태도로 행동하는. 태연한: *an attractive* *poised college graduate* 매력있고 침착한 대학 졸업생

poi·son¹ /'pɔɪzən/ *n* [C, U] **1** a substance that can kill you or make you sick if you eat it, breathe it etc. ‖ 먹거나 흡입하면 죽거나 아프게 하는 물질. 독: *A child was rushed to the hospital after eating rat poison.* 한 아이가 쥐약을 먹은 후 급히 병원에 실려갔다. **2** INFORMAL a person, feeling, idea etc. that persuades you to do bad things or makes you feel very unhappy ‖ 설득시켜서 나쁜 짓을 하게 하거나 매우 불행하게 느끼게 하는 사람·감정·생각 등. 해로운 사람[것]: *She's poison, Dale! Don't listen to her!* 그녀는 해를 주는 사람이야, 데일! 그녀 말을 듣지 마!

poison² *v* [T] **1** to kill or harm someone by giving him/her poison ‖ 독을 줘서 남을 죽이거나 해를 끼치다. 독살하다. 독을 쓰다: *Two of the victims had been poisoned with arsenic.* 희생자 중 두 명은 비소에 의해 독살되었다. **2** to make the land, lakes, rivers, air etc. dangerous by adding harmful chemicals to it ‖ 땅·호수·강·대기 등에 해로운 화학 물질을 첨가해 위험하게 하다. 오염시키다: *Chemical waste has poisoned the city's water supply.* 화학 폐기물은 그 도시의 상수도원을 오염시켰다. **3** to influence someone in a bad way or make him/her feel very unhappy ‖ 남에게 나쁜 식으로 영향을 미치거나 불행하게 느끼게 하다. 망치다. 해치다. 더럽히다: *Sex on TV is poisoning our children's minds!* 텔레비전 상의 성적 표현이 우리 아이들의 정신 건강을 해치고 있어!

poi·son·ing /'pɔɪzənɪŋ/ *n* [C, U] an illness that is caused by swallowing, touching, or breathing a poisonous substance ‖ 독성 있는 물질을 삼키거나 만지거나 들이마셔서 생기는 병. 중독: *lead poisoning* 납중독

poison i·vy /ˌ.. '../ *n* [U] a bush or VINE with an oily substance on its leaves that makes your skin hurt if you touch it ‖ 잎 위에 기름기 있는 물질이 있고 접촉하면 사람의 피부를 상하게 하는 관목이나 덩굴 식물. 덩굴옻나무

poi·son·ous /'pɔɪzənəs/ *adj* containing poison or producing poison ‖ 독을 함유하거나 독을 생산하는. 유독한. 독성의. 독을 가진: *a poisonous chemical* 유독한 화학 물질 / *poisonous snakes* 독사 – **poisonously** *adv*

poke /poʊk/ *v* **1** [I, T] to press something quickly and with a lot of force using a pointed object, such as your finger or a stick ‖ 손가락이나 막대기 등의 뾰족한 물체를 사용해 재빠르고 많은 힘을 들여 사물을 누르다. 찌르다. 쑤시다: *Stop poking me!* 나 좀 꾹꾹 찌르지 마! / *He poked at the campfire with a stick.* 그는 막대기로 모닥불을 쑤석거렸다. **2** [I, T] to push something through a space or out of an opening, so that you can see part of it ‖ 어떤 것이 빈 공간으로 밀어져 나왔거나 열린 곳 밖으로 나와서 그것의 일부를 볼 수 있다. 밀다. 쑥 내밀다: *David poked his head around the door and smiled at us.* 데이비드는 문 옆으로 머리를 쑥 내밀더니 우리를 보고 웃었다. / *The roots of the trees are poking up through the sidewalk.* 그 나무뿌리는 보도로 튀어나왔다. **3 poke a hole** to make a hole in something by pushing a pointed object through it ‖ 뾰족한 물체를 사물에 관통시켜 구멍을 내다 **4 poke fun at** to joke about someone in an unkind way ‖ 남에 대해 매정하게 농담하다. 조소하다. 놀리다: *Stop poking fun at your sister!* 네 누이를 그만 놀려라! – **poke** *n*

pok·er /'poʊkɚ/ *n* **1** [U] a card game that people usually play for money ‖ 사람들이 보통 돈을 걸고 하는 카드 게임. 포커 **2** a metal stick used for moving coal or wood in a fire to make it burn better ‖ 더 잘 태우기 위해 불 속의 석탄이나 나무를 움직이는 데 사용하는 금속 막대기. 부지깽이

poker-faced /ˈ.. ˌ./ *adj* showing no expression on your face ‖ 얼굴에 표정을 나타내지 않는. 무표정한: *His poker-faced secretary led us into the office.* 그의 무표정한 비서가 우리를 사무실 안으로 안내했다. – **poker face** *n* [singular]

pok·ey, poky /'poʊki/ *adj* **1** doing things very slowly, especially in a way that you find annoying ‖ 특히 신경질을 날 정도로 아주 천천히 일을 하는. 질질 끄는. 굼뜬: *a pokey driver* 느릿느릿한 운전자 **2** too small and not very pleasant or comfortable ‖ 너무 작아서 그다지 유쾌하거나 편안하지 않은. 비좁은. 초라한: *pokey apartment* 비좁은 아파트

po·lar /'poʊlɚ/ *adj* **1** relating to the North Pole and the South Pole ‖ 북극과 남극과 관련된. 북극[남극]의. 극지의: *polar ice caps* 극지방의 빙관(氷冠) **2 polar opposite** someone or something that is completely opposite to another person or thing in character or style ‖ 특징이나 스타일에서 다른 사람이나 사물과 완전히 정반대의 사람이나 사물: *Louise and her sister are polar opposites.* 루이

스와 그녀의 언니는 완전히 정반대이다.

polar bear /ˌ.. ˌ./ *n* a large white bear that lives near the North Pole ‖ 북극 근처에 사는 크고 흰 곰. 북극곰

po·lar·i·ty /poʊˈlærəti, pə-/ *n* [C, U] FORMAL a state in which two ideas or sides in an argument are completely opposite ‖ 논쟁에서 두 생각이나 양측이 완전히 정반대에 있는 상태. 정반대. 대립: *the growing polarity between workers and management* 노동자와 경영진 사이의 커지는 대립

po·lar·ize /ˈpoʊləˌraɪz/ *v* [I, T] FORMAL to divide into two opposing groups, or to make people do this ‖ 반대되는 두 집단으로 나누다, 또는 사람들을 이렇게 나누어지게 하다. 대립[분열]하다. 대립[양극화]시키다: *The election polarized the city.* 선거로 그 도시는 양극화되었다. – **polarization** /ˌpoʊlərəˈzeɪʃən/ *n* [U]

Po·lar·oid /ˈpoʊləˌrɔɪd/ *n* TRADEMARK a camera that uses a special film to produce a photograph very quickly, or a picture taken with this kind of camera ‖ 사진을 매우 빨리 인화하기 위해 특별한 필름을 사용하는 사진기, 또는 이러한 사진기로 찍은 사진. 폴라로이드 카메라[사진]

Pole /poʊl/ *n* someone from Poland ‖ 폴란드인

pole *n* **1** a long stick or post ‖ 긴 막대기나 기둥: *a telephone pole* (=holding up telephone wires outside) 전신주 / *a fishing pole* 낚싯대 **2** the most northern and southern point on a PLANET ‖ 행성의 가장 북쪽과 남쪽 지점. (천체·지구의) 극: *an expedition to the North Pole* 북극 탐험 **3 be poles apart** to be very different from someone else ‖ 다른 사람과 완전히 다르다. 완전히 상반되다[동떨어지다]: *Dad's and Mark's political views are poles apart.* 아버지와 마크의 정치적 견해는 완전히 상반된다. **4** one of two points at the end of a MAGNET where its power is strongest ‖ 자력이 가장 강한 자석의 양 끝 지점 중의 한 지점. 극 **5** one of the two points at which wires can be fixed onto a BATTERY in order to use its electricity ‖ 전기를 사용하기 위해 전지에 전선을 고정시키는 두 지점 중 하나. 전지의 양극이나 음극

po·lem·ic /pəˈlɛmɪk/ *n* strong arguments that criticize or defend a particular idea, opinion, or person ‖ 특정한 생각[의견, 사람]을 비평하거나 옹호하는 격한 논쟁. 갑론을박 – **polemical** *adj*

pole vault /ˈ. ./ *n* [U] a sport in which

you jump over a high BAR using a special long pole ‖ 특수한 긴 장대를 사용해 높이 있는 막대기를 뛰어넘는 스포츠. 장대높이뛰기

po·lice¹ /pəˈlis/ *n* **1 the police** an official organization that protects people and property and makes sure that everyone obeys the law ‖ 국민과 재산을 보호하고 모든 이들이 법을 잘 준수하도록 하는 공적인 조직. 경찰: *We'll have to tell the police.* 우리는 경찰에 신고해야겠다. **2** [plural] the people who work for this organization ‖ 이러한 조직, 즉 경찰에서 근무하는 사람들. 경찰관: *Police arrived soon after the alarm went off.* 경보가 울리고 난 후 곧 경찰관이 도착했다.

police² *v* [T] **1** to keep order in a place using police ‖ 경찰을 이용해 한 지역의 질서를 유지하다. 치안을 유지하다. …을 단속하다: *new ways of policing the neighborhood* 그 지역의 치안을 지키는 새로운 방법 **2** to control a particular activity or industry by making sure people obey the rules ‖ 사람들이 반드시 규칙을 준수하도록 해서 특정한 활동이나 산업을 통제하다. …을 관리[규제]하다: *an agency that polices the nuclear power industry* 원자력 산업을 규제하는 기구

police de·part·ment /ˈ. .ˌ./ *n* the official police organization in a particular area or city ‖ 특정한 지역이나 도시에 있는 공적인 경찰 조직. 경찰청

police force /ˈ. .ˌ./ *n* all the police officers that work for a particular police organization ‖ 특정한 경찰 조직을 위해 일하는 모든 경찰관. 경찰력. 경찰대

po·lice·man /pəˈlismən/ *n* a male police officer ‖ 남자 경찰관

police of·fi·cer /ˈ. .ˌ./ *n* a member of the police ‖ 경찰관

police state /ˈ. ˌ./ *n* a country where the government strictly controls most of the activities of its citizens ‖ 정부가 시민의 대부분의 활동을 엄격히 통제하는 국가. 경찰 국가

police sta·tion /ˈ. .ˌ./ *n* the local office of the police in a town or city ‖ 한 소도시나 대도시의 지역 경찰서

po·lice·wom·an /pəˈlisˌwʊmən/ *n* a female police officer ‖ 여성 경찰관

pol·i·cy /ˈpɑləsi/ *n* **1** [C, U] a way of doing things that has been officially agreed and chosen by a political party or organization ‖ 정당이나 정치 조직에 의해 공식적으로 승인되고 선택된 것을 하는 방식. 정책. 방침: *the government's foreign policy* 정부의 외교 정책 / *the* *company's policy on maternity leave* 그 회사의 출산 휴가에 대한 방침 **2 a** written agreement with an insurance company‖ 보험 회사와의 서면 계약서. 보험 증권[증서]: *a homeowner's policy* 주택 소유자 보험 증권 **3 [C, U]** a particular principle that you believe in‖ 자신이 믿고 있는 특정한 원칙: *I make it my policy not to gossip.* 남의 말을 하지 않는 것이 내 원칙이다.

po·li·o /ˈpouliˌou/ *n* [U] a serious infectious disease of the nerves in your BACKBONE, often resulting in PARALYSIS (=the inability to move your muscles)‖ 종종 마비 증세가 일어나는 척추뼈 속의 신경의 심각한 전염병. 폴리오. 척수성 소아마비

Po·lish¹ /ˈpouliʃ/ *adj* relating to or coming from Poland‖ 폴란드와 관련된 또는 폴란드에서 온. 폴란드의. 폴란드인의

Polish² *n* **1** [U] the language used in Poland‖ 폴란드에서 사용하는 언어 **2 the Polish** [plural] the people of Poland‖ 폴란드인

pol·ish¹ /ˈpɑliʃ/ *v* [T] to make something smooth, bright, and shiny by rubbing it‖ 사물을 문질러서 매끄럽고 밝고 빛나게 하다. 닦다. 광[윤]을 낸다: *Davy spent all morning polishing his car.* 데이비는 자기 차를 닦는 데 아침 나절을 보냈다. – **polisher** *n*

polish

polish sth ↔ **off** *phr v* [T] INFORMAL to finish food, work etc. quickly or easily‖ 음식·일 등을 재빨리 또는 쉽게 끝내다. 음식을 말끔히 먹어치우다. 일을 재빨리 마무리짓다: *The kids polished off the rest of the cake.* 그 아이들은 남아 있는 케이크를 말끔히 먹어치웠다.

polish sth ↔ **up** *phr v* [T] to improve a skill or an ability‖ 기술이나 능력을 향상시키다. 연마하다: *Barney's taking a class to polish up his writing skills.* 바니는 작문 실력을 향상시키기 위해 강의를 듣고 있다.

polish² *n* **1** a liquid, powder, or other substance used for rubbing into a surface to make it shiny‖ 반짝거리게 만들기 위해 표면을 문지르는 데에 사용하는 액체나 가루 또는 기타 물질. 광택제. 닦는 재료: *furniture polish* 가구 광택제 / *shoe polish* 구두 광택제 **2** [U] great skill and style in the way someone performs,

writes, or behaves‖ 사람이 실행하거나 글을 쓰거나 행동하는 방식에 있어서의 대단한 기술과 양식. 세련. 품위: *Your paper is okay, but it needs a little polish.* 네 리포트는 괜찮지만, 약간의 세련미가 필요하다. **3** an act of polishing a surface to make it smooth and shiny‖ 매끄럽고 반짝이게 하기 위해 표면을 닦는 행위. 광내기: *An occasional polish will keep the table looking new.* 이따금씩 광내기를 하면 그 테이블은 계속 새것처럼 보일 것이다. —see also NAIL POLISH

pol·ished /ˈpɑliʃt/ *adj* **1** shiny because of being rubbed with polish‖ 광택제로 문질러서 빛이 나는. 광택이 나는: *polished furniture* 광택이 나는 기구 **2** done with great skill and style‖ 대단한 기술과 양식으로 된. 세련된. 탁월한. 우수한: *a polished performance* 완벽한 공연 **3** polite and confident‖ 예의 바르고 자신감 있는. 교양 있는. 다듬어진: *polished manners* 교양 있는 예절

po·lite /pəˈlaɪt/ *adj* **1** behaving or speaking in a way that is correct for the social situation you are in‖ 자신이 처해 있는 사회적 상황에 맞게 행동하거나 말하는. 공손한. 예절 바른. 정중한: *It's not polite to talk with food in your mouth.* 입 속에 음식이 든 채로 말하는 것은 예절 바르지 못한 것이다. / *a polite smile* 품위 있는 미소 **2 just being polite** SPOKEN saying something you may not really believe, in order to avoid offending someone‖ 어떤 사람을 기분 나쁘지 않게 하기 위해, 자신이 실제로 믿지 않을 수도 있는 것을 말하는. 겉치레로. 그저 예의상: *Did she really like the gift, or was she just being polite?* 그녀가 그 선물을 정말 좋아했니, 아니면 그냥 겉으로만 좋아했니? – **politely** *adv* – **politeness** *n* [U]

po·lit·i·cal /pəˈlɪtɪkəl/ *adj* **1** relating to the government, politics, and the public affairs of a country‖ 정부·정치·한 나라의 공무와 관련된. 정치의. 국가의. 국정상의: *The US has two main political parties.* 미국에는 두 개의 주요 정당이 있다. / *political campaigns* 정치 운동 / *political activists* 정치 활동가 **2** relating to the way that people, groups, companies etc. try to get advantages for themselves‖ 사람·단체·회사 등이 그들 자신을 위해서 이득을 보려는 방식과 관련된. 정치적인: *Each side had a political reason for being there.* 각 진영은 현존하는 정치적 이유가 있었다. / *It gets too political in the office sometimes.* (=too many people try to get advantages for themselves) 때때로 회사에는 자신들의 이익을 챙기려는 사람들이 너무 많다. **3** interested in or active in politics ‖ 정치에 관심 있거나 적극적인: *Mike's never been political.* 마이크는 절대 정치에 관여하지 않았다. – **politically** *adv*

po·lit·i·cally cor·rect /.,... .'./, **PC** *adj* politically correct language, behavior, and attitudes are considered acceptable because they do not offend women, people of a particular race, DISABLED people etc. ‖ 언어·행동·태도가 여성·특정 인종의 사람들·장애인에게 불쾌감을 주지 않기 때문에 받아들일 만하다고 생각되는 정치적으로 정당한. 편견[차별]이 없는: *It's not politically correct to say "handicapped" anymore.* "handicapped"라고 말하는 것은 이제는 차별적인 표현이다. – **political cor·rectness** *n* [U]

political pris·on·er /.,... '.../ *n* someone who is put in prison because s/he criticizes the government ‖ 정부를 비판해서 투옥된 사람. 정치범

political sci·ence /.,... '../ *n* [U] the study of politics and government ‖ 정치와 정부에 대한 연구. 정치학

pol·i·ti·cian /,pɑlə'tɪʃən/ *n* someone who works in politics ‖ 정계에서 일하는 사람. 정치인: *Unfortunately politicians are not highly trusted these days.* 불행하게도 정치인은 요즘 크게 신뢰를 받지 못하고 있다.

po·lit·i·cize /pə'lɪtəsaɪz/ *v* [T] to make a situation, position, or organization more political or more involved in politics ‖ 상황·입장·조직이 보다 정치적이 되게 하거나 정치에 관련되게 하다. 정치화하다. 정치적으로 다루다: *The issue has recently been politicized.* 그 문제는 최근에 정치화되었다. – **politicized** *adj*

pol·i·tics /'pɑlə,tɪks/ *n* **1** [U] ideas and activities that are concerned with gaining and using power in a country, city etc. ‖ 한 나라나 도시 등에서 권력을 획득하고 이용하는 일에 관련된 생각과 활동. 정치: *She's involved in city politics.* 그녀는 시 정치에 관여했다. / *Politics doesn't interest me.* 나는 정치에 흥미가 없다. **2** [U] the profession of being a politician ‖ 정치인이라는 직업: *He'll retire from politics before the next election.* 그는 다음 선거 전에 정계에서 은퇴할 것이다. **3** [plural] the activities of people who are concerned with gaining personal advantage within a group ‖ 집단 내에서 개인적인 이득을 얻는 일에 관계하고 있는 사람들의 활동.

(당파적·개인적) 이해: *Colin tries not to get involved in office politics.* 콜린 씨는 사무실 내 이해 관계에 관여하지 않으려 한다. **4** [plural] someone's political beliefs and opinions ‖ 남의 정치적 신념과 견해. 정견(政見): *I'm not sure what Ellen's politics are.* 엘렌의 정치적 견해가 무엇인지 모르겠어.

pol·ka /'poʊlkə, 'poʊkə/ *n* a very quick simple dance for people dancing in pairs, or the music for this dance ‖ 사람이 쌍쌍이 추는 매우 빠르고 간단한 춤, 또는 이 춤의 곡. 폴카 – **polka** *v* [I]

polka dot /'.. ,./ *n* one of a number of spots that form a pattern, especially on material for clothing ‖ 특히 옷감에 무늬를 이루는 많은 반점의 하나. 물방울 무늬: *a white dress with red polka dots* 빨간 물방울 무늬가 있는 하얀 드레스 – **polka-dot** *adj* : *a polka-dot scarf* 물방울 무늬 스카프

poll¹ /poʊl/ *n* the process of finding out what people think about something by asking many people the same question, or the record of the result ‖ 많은 사람에게 같은 질문을 해서 일반 사람들이 어떤 일에 대해 어떻게 생각하는가를 알아내는 과정, 또는 그 결과의 기록. 여론 조사: *Recent polls show that support for the President is strong.* 최근의 여론 조사는 대통령에 대한 지지가 강하다는 것을 보여 준다. —see also POLLS

poll² *v* [T] to try to find out what people think about a subject by asking many people the same question ‖ 많은 사람에게 같은 질문을 해서 사람들이 어떤 주제에 대해 생각하는 바를 알아내려고 하다. 여론 조사를 하다: *We polled 600 teachers, asking their opinion on the new education policy.* 우리는 600명의 교사를 대상으로 새 교육 정책에 대한 의견을 묻는 여론 조사를 했다.

pol·len /'pɑlən/ *n* [U] a powder produced by flowers that is carried by the wind or insects to make other flowers produce seeds ‖ 다른 꽃이 씨를 맺도록 바람이나 곤충에 의해 운반되는, 꽃에서 만들어지는 가루. 꽃가루. 화분(花粉)

pollen count /'.. ,./ *n* a measurement of the amount of POLLEN in the air ‖ 공기 중의 꽃가루 양의 측정치. 꽃가루수

pol·li·nate /'pɑlə,neɪt/ *v* [T] to make a flower or plant produce seeds by giving it POLLEN ‖ 꽃이나 식물에 꽃가루를 수분해서 씨를 자라게 하다. …에 수분(授粉)하다 – **pollination** /,pɑlə'neɪʃən/ *n* [U]

polling place /'.. ,./, **polling**

sta·tion /'.. ,../ *n* the place where you can go to vote in an election ‖ 선거 때 투표하러 가는 곳. 투표소

polls /poʊlz/ *n* [plural] **the polls** the voting in an election ‖ 선거에서의 투표 (하기): *Voters go to the polls* (=vote) *on Tuesday.* 유권자는 화요일에 투표한다.

poll·ster /'poʊlstɚ/ *n* someone who prepares and asks questions to find out what people think about a particular subject ‖ 일반 사람들이 특정한 주제에 대해 어떻게 생각하는지 알아보기 위해 질문을 준비하고 물어보는 사람. 여론 조사원

pol·lut·ant /pə'luːt'nt/ *n* a substance that makes air, water, soil etc. dangerously dirty ‖ 공기·물·흙 등을 위험할 정도로 더럽히는 물질. 오염 물질

pol·lute /pə'luːt/ *v* [I, T] to make air, water, soil etc. dangerously dirty ‖ 공기·물·흙 등을 위험할 정도로 더럽히다. 오염시키다: *Gold miners entered the territory, polluting rivers with mercury.* 채금자들은 그 지역에 들어와서, 강을 수은으로 오염시켰다. – **polluter** *n*

pol·lut·ed /pə'luːtɪd/ *adj* full of POLLUTION ‖ 오염 물질로 가득 찬. 오염된: *heavily polluted air/rivers* 몹시 오염된 공기[강]

pol·lu·tion /pə'luːʃən/ *n* [U] **1** the process of polluting (POLLUTE) a place ‖ 어떤 장소를 오염시키는 과정. 오염. 공해: *Toxic waste is a major cause of pollution.* 독성 폐기물이 오염의 주요 원인이다. **2** substances that POLLUTE a place ‖ 어떤 장소를 오염시키는 물질. 오염 물질: *Pollution levels are dangerously high in some cities.* 몇몇 도시는 위험할 정도로 오염 정도가 심하다. —see also NOISE POLLUTION

po·lo /'poʊloʊ/ *n* [U] an outdoor game played between two teams riding horses, who use long wooden hammers to hit a small ball ‖ 작은 공을 치려고 긴 나무 타구봉을 사용하는 말을 탄 두 팀 사이에 치러지는 야외 경기. 폴로

polo shirt /'.. ,../ *n* a shirt with short SLEEVEs and a collar, usually made of cotton ‖ 보통 면으로 만든, 짧은 소매와 칼라가 있는 셔츠. 폴로 셔츠

pol·y·es·ter /'pali,ɛstɚ, ,pali'ɛstɚ/ *n* [U] an artificial material used especially to make cloth ‖ 특히 천을 만드는 데 사용되는 인공 물질. 폴리에스테르

po·lyg·a·my /pə'lɪgəmi/ *n* [U] TECHNICAL the practice of having more than one wife at the same time ‖ 한 명 이상의 아내와 동시에 동거하는 관행. 일부다처제 – **polygamous** *adj* –

polygamist *n*

pol·y·gon /'pali,gan/ *n* TECHNICAL a flat shape with three or more sides ‖ 변이 세 개 이상 있는 평평한 도형. 다각형

pol·y·graph /'pali,græf/ *n* TECHNICAL ⇨ LIE DETECTOR

pol·y·mer /'paləmɚ/ *n* a chemical compound that has a simple structure of large MOLECULEs ‖ 많은 분자의 단순한 구조를 가진 화학 혼합물. 폴리머. 중합체

pol·yp /'paləp/ *n* a small LUMP that grows inside a passage in the body, that is usually not harmful but that can block the passage ‖ 보통 해롭지 않으나 몸의 관(管) 안에서 자라나 관을 막을 수 있는 작은 혹. 종양 돌기. 폴립

pol·y·tech·nic /,pali'tɛknɪk/ *n* a college where you can study technical or scientific subjects ‖ 기술적이거나 과학적인 주제를 연구할 수 있는 대학. 공예 학교. 기술 전문학교

pol·y·un·sat·u·rat·ed fat /,pali-ʌn,sætʃəreɪtɪd 'fæt/ *adj* a kind of fat that comes from vegetables and plants and is healthier than SATURATED FAT from animals ‖ 야채나 식물에서 얻고 동물성 포화 지방보다 더 건강에 좋은 지방의 일종. 다가(多價) 불포화 지방

pom·e·gran·ate /'pamə,grænɪt/ *n* a round fruit with thick red skin and many juicy red seeds that you can eat ‖ 두꺼운 빨간 껍질과 먹을 수 있는 즙이 많은 붉은 씨앗이 있는 둥근 과일. 석류

pomp /pamp/ *n* [U] FORMAL all the impressive clothes, decorations, music etc. that are traditional for an important public ceremony ‖ 중요한 공공 의식용으로 전통적인 모든 인상적인 의상·장식·음악 등. 장관(壯觀). 화려

pom·pom /'pampam/, **pom·pon** /'pampan/ *n* **1** a ball of wool, feathers etc. used as a decoration on clothing ‖ 옷의 장식으로 사용되는 공 모양의 털·깃털 등. 방울술 **2** a large round ball of loose paper or plastic strings connected to a handle, used by CHEERLEADERs ‖ 치어리더가 사용하는, 풀어 헤친 종이나 비닐 끈을 손잡이에 큰 공 모양으로 연결시킨 것. 응원용 큰 방울술

pomp·ous /'pampəs/ *adj* trying to make people think you are important, especially by using a lot of formal words ‖ 특히 격식 차린 말을 많이 써서 남이 당신을 중요하다고 생각하게 하려고 하는. 뽐내는. 젠 체하는: *a pompous speech* 허풍떠는 연설 – **pomposity** /pam'pasəti/ *n* [U]

pon·cho /'pantʃoʊ/ *n* **1** a kind of coat

that is made from a single piece of thick cloth, with a hole in the middle for your head to go through ‖ 머리가 빠져 나오도록 가운데에 구멍이 있는 두꺼운 천 하나로 만든 코트의 일종. 판초 **2** a coat like this that keeps out the rain and has a HOOD (=cover for your head) ‖ 모자가 달려 있고 비를 막는 이런 모양의 코트

pond /pand/ *n* a small area of fresh water that is smaller than a lake ‖ 호수보다 더 작은 민물이 있는 작은 지역. 못. 연못

pon·der /'pandɚ/ *v* [I, T] LITERARY to spend time thinking carefully and seriously about something ‖ 어떤 것에 대해 신중하고 진지하게 생각하면서 시간을 보내다. 깊이 생각하다. 숙고하다: *She pondered her answer for a long time.* 그녀는 오랫동안 자신의 대답을 숙고했다.

pon·der·ous /'pandərəs/ *adj* **1** moving slowly or awkwardly because of being very big ‖ 매우 커서 천천히 또는 어색하게 움직이는. 느릿느릿한: *an elephant's ponderous walk* 코끼리의 느릿느릿한 걸음 **2** boring and too serious ‖ 지루하고 너무 진지한. 답답한: *a ponderous voice* 답답한 목소리

pon·tiff /'pantɪf/ *n* FORMAL the POPE ‖ 교황

pon·tif·i·cate /pan'tɪfə,keɪt/ *v* [I] to give your opinion about something in a way that shows you think you are always right ‖ 자신이 항상 옳다는 생각을 나타내면서 어떤 일에 대해 의견을 말하다. 젠 체하며[거드름을 피우며] 이야기하다: *Anthony likes to pontificate about how wonderful capitalism is.* 앤터니는 자본주의가 얼마나 대단한 것인지에 대해 거드름을 피우며 이야기하기를 좋아한다.

pon·toon /pan'tun/ *n* one of the floating metal containers that are attached to bridges, SEA PLANES etc. in order to make them float ‖ 다리나 수상 비행기 등이 뜨도록 하기 위해 부착하는 부력이 있는 금속통들 중의 하나. 부양함. 폰툰

po·ny¹ /'poʊni/ *n* a small horse ‖ 작은 말. 조랑말

pony² *v*

pony up *phr v* [I, T] INFORMAL to pay for something ‖ 어떤 것에 대해 지불하다. 정산하다: *Opera fans who pony up $34.95 will see a four-hour opera special.* 34달러 95센트를 지불한 오페라 팬은 4시간짜리 특별 오페라를 볼 것이다.

Pony Ex·press /ˌ.. .'./ *n* [singular] a mail service in the 1860s that used horses and riders to carry the mail ‖ 우편물을 운반하기 위해 말과 기수를 사용했던 1960년대의 우편물 서비스. 포니 속달 우편

po·ny·tail /'poʊni,teɪl/ *n* hair tied together at the back of your head ‖ 머리 뒤로 모아 묶은 머리. 포니테일 —see picture at HAIRSTYLE

pooch /putʃ/ *n* INFORMAL HUMOROUS a dog ‖ 개

poo·dle /'pudl/ *n* a dog with thick curly hair that is often cut in a special shape ‖ 종종 특별한 모양으로 털을 깎은, 털이 많고 곱슬곱슬한 개. 푸들 개

pooh-pooh /'pupu, pu'pu/ *v* [T] INFORMAL to say that you think that an idea, suggestion etc. is not very good ‖ 생각이나 제안 등을 그다지 좋지 않게 생각한다고 말하다. 깔보다. 업신여기다: *At first they pooh-poohed the idea.* 처음에 그들은 그 생각에 콧방귀를 뀌었다.

pool¹ /pul/ *n* **1** a structure that has been specially built and filled with water so that people can swim or WADE in it ‖ 사람이 수영하거나 얕은 물에서 놀 수 있도록 특별히 건설되어 물을 채운 구조물. 풀. 수영장 **2** [U] an indoor game played on a cloth-covered table, in which you hit balls with a long stick into pockets at the corners and sides of the table ‖ 긴 막대로 공을 쳐서 테이블 귀퉁이와 측면에 있는 구멍 안으로 넣는, 천으로 덮여진 테이블 위에서 하는 실내 경기. 풀. 당구. 포켓볼 **3 a pool of oil/light etc.** a small area of liquid or light on a surface ‖ 표면에 액체나 빛이 차 있는 작은 영역. 기름탕/양지: *Creighton lay there in a pool of blood.* 크레이튼은 피바다가 된 그곳에 누워 있었다. **4** a small area of still water in the ground ‖ 땅에 물이 괴어 있는 작은 영역. 물웅덩이: *A shallow pool had formed among the rocks.* 얕은 물웅덩이가 바위 사이에 생겼다. **5** a group of people who are available to work or to do an activity when they are needed ‖ 필요할 때 부릴 수 있거나 활동하게 할 수 있는 일단의 사람들. 인재 풀. 공동 이용 노동력: *a secretarial pool* 비서 업무 대행소 / *a talent pool of great student athletes* 우수한 학생 육상 선수의 인재 풀 **6** a number of things or an amount of money that is shared by a group of people ‖ 일단의 사람들이 공유하는 많은 물건이나 금액. …의 총액. 공동 물자[시설, 기금]: *Each ticket won $63 from a prize pool of $376,141.* 각자의 표는 376,141달러의 상금 총액에서 63달러씩을 땄다.

pool² *v* [T] to combine your money, ideas, skills etc. with those of other people so that you can all use them ‖ 다른 사람의 돈·생각·기술 등을 자신의 것과 결합하여 모두 이용할 수 있게 하다. 공유하다. 함께 하다: *If we pool our resources, we can start our own business.* 우리가 자금을 공동 출자하면 우리들만의 사업을 시작할 수 있다.

pool hall /'. ./ *n* a building where people go to play POOL ‖ 사람이 포켓 당구를 하러 가는 건물. 포켓 당구장

pool ta·ble /'. ,./ *n* a cloth-covered table with pockets at the corners and sides, used for playing POOL ‖ 포켓 당구를 하는 데 사용되는 귀퉁이와 측면에 포켓이 구비된 천으로 덮인 테이블. 포켓 당구대

poop¹ /pup/ *n* **1** [U] SPOKEN a word meaning solid waste from your BOWELs, or the act of passing waste, used especially by children ‖ 특히 아이들이 사용하는, 장에서 내보내는 고형 배설물을 의미하는 단어, 또는 배설물을 내보내는 행위. 응가(하는 것) **2 the poop** SPOKEN the latest news about someone or something ‖ 사람이나 사물에 대한 최근 소식. 최신 정보: *So what's the poop on the new guy?* 그래 새로 온 사람에 관한 최신 정보가 무엇이지?

poop² *v* [I, T] INFORMAL a word meaning to pass solid waste from your BOWELs, used especially by children ‖ 특히 아이들이 쓰는, 장에서 고형 배설물을 내보내는 것을 뜻하는 단어. 응가하다

poop out *phr v* [I] SPOKEN to stop trying to do something because you are tired ‖ 피로해서 어떤 일을 포기하다. 지쳐서 그만두다: *She pooped out halfway through the race.* 그녀는 경주 도중에 그만두었다.

pooped /pupt/, **pooped out** *adj* SPOKEN very tired ‖ 몹시 지친. 녹초가 된: *I'm pooped!* 나는 녹초가 되었어!

poop·er scoop·er /'. ,./ *n* INFORMAL a small SHOVEL and a container, used by dog owners for removing their dogs' solid waste from the streets ‖ 개 주인이 거리에서 개의 고형 배설물을 치우는 데 사용하는 작은 삽과 용기

poor /pur, pɔr/ *adj* **1** having very little money and not many possessions ‖ 돈이 거의 없고 소유물이 많지 않은. 가난한. 빈곤한: *She comes from a poor family.* 그녀는 가난한 집안 출신이다. / *a poor country* 가난한 나라 **2 the poor** people who are poor ‖ 가난한 사람들: *a charity that distributes food to the poor* 가난한 사람에게 음식을 나눠주는 자선(행위) **3** not as good as it could be or should be ‖ 가능한 한만큼 또는 당연히 그래야 할 만큼 좋지 않은. 빈약한. 부족한. 모자란: *The soil in this part of the country is poor.* 나라의 이 지역의 땅은 메마르다. / *poor health* 허약한 건강 **4 poor girl/ Mom/man etc.** SPOKEN said in order to show pity for someone because s/he is unlucky, unhappy etc. ‖ 불운하거나 불행한 사람에게 동정을 나타내는 데에 쓰여. 가엾은. 불쌍한: *Poor Dad – everything's going wrong today.* 불쌍한 아빠, 오늘은 만사가 잘못되고 있어요. **5** not good at doing something ‖ 어떤 일을 하는 데에 서투른. 능하지 못한: *a poor reader* 서투른 독자

poor·ly /'pʊrli/ *adv* badly ‖ 나쁘게: *a poorly lit room* 조명이 좋지 않은 방

pop¹ /pɑp/ *v* **-pped, -pping 1** [I, T] to do something that suddenly lets the air out of a container or BALLOON so that a sound like a small explosion is made, or to make a sound like this ‖ 작은 폭발 소리가 나도록 또는 이와 같은 소리를 내기 위해 용기나 풍선 등에서 갑자기 공기를 내보내는 일을 하다. 펑하는 소리를 내다. 펑하고 터뜨리다: *Oh, Jodie, did your balloon pop?* 오, 조디야, 네 풍선이 (펑하고)터졌니? / *popping a champagne cork* 샴페인의 코르크 마개 따기 **2** [I] if your ears pop, you feel the pressure in them suddenly change, for example, when you go up in a plane ‖ 비행기가 올라갈 때 등에 귀에서 압력이 급변하는 것을 느끼다. 귀가 멍해[먹먹해]지다 **3** [I, T] to cook POPCORN until it bursts open ‖ 팝콘이 펑 터질 때까지 열을 가하다. 팝콘을 튈 때까지 볶다: *Why don't we pop some popcorn?* 팝콘 좀 튀겨 먹는 게 어때? **4 pop the question** INFORMAL to ask someone to marry you ‖ 남에게 결혼해 달라고 청하다. 청혼하다. 구혼하다: *Has Dan popped the question yet?* 단이 벌써 청혼했니? **5** [I] SPOKEN to go somewhere or do something quickly, suddenly, or without planning ‖ 빨리·갑자기·계획 없이 어디로 가거나 어떤 일을 하다. 얼른[불쑥, 느닷없이] …하다: *Maybe I'll just pop in on Terry.* (=visit him for a short time) 아마 테리 집을 잠깐 들릴 거야. / *I didn't mean to say that – it just popped out!* 나는 그 말을 할 의도는 아니었어. 그냥 입에서 (불쑥)나와 버린 거야! **6** SPOKEN to hit someone ‖ 남을 때리다: *If you say that again, I'll pop you.* 다시 그 말을 하면 너를 때릴 거야. **7 pop a pill** INFORMAL to take a PILL

‖ (마)약을 상용하다

pop up *phr v* [I] INFORMAL to happen or appear suddenly or without warning ‖ 갑자기 또는 예고 없이 일어나거나 나타나다. 별안간[불쑥] 나타나다. 갑자기 생기다: *Every once in a while a good new band pops up.* 종종 연주 잘 하는 새로운 밴드가 출현하곤 한다.

pop² *n* 1 [U] modern music that is popular with young people ‖ 젊은 사람에게 인기 있는 현대 음악. 팝: *a pop record* 팝 레코드 2 OLD-FASHIONED ⇨ FATHER¹ 3 [U] INFORMAL ⇨ SOFT DRINK, —see culture note at SODA 4 a sudden short sound like a small explosion ‖ 작은 폭발음 같은 갑작스런 짧은 소리. 펑[뻥] 하는 소리: *the pop of an air rifle* 공기총의 (뻥 하는) 소리

pop·corn /ˈpɑpkɔrn/ *n* [U] a type of corn that swells and bursts open when heated, usually eaten warm with butter and salt ‖ 가열할 때 부풀고 터져 보통 버터와 소금을 쳐서 따뜻하게 해서 먹는 옥수수의 일종. 팝콘

Pope /poʊp/ *n* **the Pope** the leader of the Roman Catholic Church ‖ 로마 가톨릭 교회의 지도자. 교황

pop·lar /ˈpɑplə/ *n* [C] a tall thin tree with light green BARK ‖ 나무 껍질이 연녹색인 키가 크고 가느다란 나무. 포플러. 백양나무

pop psy·chol·o·gy /ˌ. .ˈ.../ *n* [U] ways of dealing with problems in life that are made popular on television or in books, but that are not considered scientific ‖ 텔레비전이나 책에서 인기 있으나 과학적이라고 생각되지 않는 인생의 문제들을 다루는 방법. 통속 심리학

pop·py /ˈpɑpi/ *n* a brightly colored flower, usually red, with small black seeds ‖ 작고 검은 씨가 있으며 보통 빨간색인 밝은 색깔의 꽃. 양귀비

pop quiz /ˌ. ˈ./ *n* a short test that is given without any warning in order to check that students have been studying ‖ 학생들이 공부를 하고 있는지를 확인하기 위해 어떤 통고 없이 치는 간단한 시험. 예고 없는[족지] 시험. 즉석 테스트

pops /pɑps/ *adj* **pops concert/ orchestra** a concert or ORCHESTRA that performs popular CLASSICAL MUSIC ‖ 인기 있는 클래식 음악을 연주하는 콘서트나 오케스트라. 팝스 콘서트/오케스트라

Pop·si·cle /ˈpɑpsɪkəl/ *n* TRADEMARK a food made of ice that tastes like fruit, that is frozen onto sticks ‖ 과일 맛이 나고 막대기에 얼려진 얼음으로 만든 음식. 막대기를 꽂은 아이스캔디

pop·u·lace /ˈpɑpyələs/ *n* [singular] FORMAL the ordinary people who live in a country ‖ 한 나라에 사는 보통 사람. 대중. 민중. 서민

pop·u·lar /ˈpɑpyələ/ *adj* 1 liked by a lot of people, or by most of the people in a group ‖ 많은 사람이나 한 집단의 대부분의 사람이 좋아하는. 인기 있는. 평판이 좋은: *a song that's really popular right now* 현재 매우 인기 있는 노래 / *the most popular kid in school* 학교에서 가장 인기 있는 어린이 2 shared, accepted, or done by a lot of people ‖ 많은 사람이 공감하는[받아들이는, 행하는]. 대중적인. 통속적인: *The party had managed to gain massive popular support.* 그 당은 용케도 대규모적인 대중적 지지를 얻어냈다. / *Popular opinion* (=what most people think) *in Peru seems to support the new president.* 페루의 여론은 새 대통령을 지지하는 것 같다.

pop·u·lar·i·ty /ˌpɑpyəˈlærəti/ *n* [U] the quality of being liked or supported by a large number of people ‖ 아주 많은 사람이 좋아하거나 지지하는 특성. 인기. 평판: *The band's popularity has grown steadily in the last five years.* 그 밴드의 인기는 지난 5년 동안 꾸준히 증가했다.

pop·u·lar·ize /ˈpɑpyələˌraɪz/ *v* [T] to make an unknown or difficult subject or idea become well known, accepted, or understood ‖ 알려지지 않거나 어려운 주제나 생각이 잘 알려지게[받아들여지게, 이해되게] 하다. 대중화하다. 보급하다: *Jane Fonda popularized aerobic exercise.* 제인 폰다는 에어로빅 운동을 대중화했다. / *popularizing science* 대중화하는 과학

pop·u·lar·ly /ˈpɑpyələli/ *adv* by most people ‖ 대부분의 사람에 의해. 일반적으로. 널리: *It's popularly believed that people need eight hours of sleep every night.* 사람은 매일 밤 8시간의 잠이 필요하다고 널리 믿어지고 있다.

pop·u·late /ˈpɑpyəˌleɪt/ *v* [T] to fill an area with people or animals who move or live there ‖ 거기서 이동하거나 사는 사람 또는 동물로 한 지역을 채우다. 살다. 거주하다: *a suburb that is densely/ heavily populated by students* 학생들이 밀집해서 [빽빽하게] 사는 교외(지역) / *a sparsely populated area* (=with few people) 인구가 희박한 지역

pop·u·la·tion /ˌpɑpyəˈleɪʃən/ *n* [C, U] 1 the number of people or animals living in a particular area, country etc. ‖ 특정한 지역·나라 등에 살고 있는 사람이나 동

물의 수. 인구. 주민 수. 총수. 개체 수:
What's the population of New York? 뉴
욕 시의 인구는 얼마이냐? / *There was a*
population explosion (=a sudden large
increase in population) *between 1944*
and 1964 in the US. 미국에서 1944년과
1964년 사이에 폭발적 인구 증가가 있었
다. **2** all of the people who live in a
particular area or share a particular
condition ‖ 특정한 지역에 살거나 특정한
환경을 공유하는 모든 사람. 전체 주민.
시민: *Most of the population of Canada*
lives near the US border. 캐나다 인구의
대부분은 미국 국경 근처에 산다. / *an*
increasingly elderly population 점점 고
령화되는 인구

pop·u·lous /ˈpɑpyələs/ *adj* FORMAL
having a large population ‖ 인구가 많은.
인구 밀도가 높은: *the most populous*
country in Africa 아프리카에서 가장 인구
가 많은 나라

pop-up¹ /ˈ. ./ *adj* **1 pop-up book/card**
etc. a book, card etc with a picture that
stands up when you open the pages ‖ 책
장을 열면 그림판이 일어서는 책·카드 등.
돌출 책/카드 **2 pop-up menu/window**
a MENU or WINDOW that can appear
suddenly on a computer screen while
you are using it ‖ 이용하고 있는 동안 컴
퓨터 화면에 갑자기 나타나는 메뉴나 창.
팝업 메뉴/창

pop-up² /ˈ. ./ *n* a WINDOW, often
containing an advertisement, that
suddenly appears on a computer
screen, especially when you are looking
at a website ‖ 특히 웹사이트를 볼 때 컴
퓨터 화면에 갑자기 나타나는, 종종 광고
를 포함한 창. 팝업(광고)창

por·ce·lain /ˈpɔrsəlɪn/ *n* [U] a hard
shiny white substance that is used for
making expensive plates, cups etc., or
objects made of this ‖ 값비싼 접시나 컵
등을 만드는 데 사용되는 단단하고 빛나는
하얀 물질, 또는 이것으로 만든 물건. 자기
(磁器). 자기 제품

porch /pɔrtʃ/ *n* a structure built onto a
house at its front or back entrance, with
a floor and roof but no walls ‖ 마루와 지
붕은 있고 벽이 없이 앞이나 뒤 출입구에
집을 잇대 지은 구조물. 포치. 지붕 달린
현관 —see picture on page 945

por·cu·pine /ˈpɔrkyə,paɪn/ *n* a small
animal with thick QUILLS (=needle-
shaped parts) on its back and sides ‖ 등
과 측면에 밀집한 가시털이 있는 작은 동
물. 호저(豪豬)

pore¹ /pɔr/ *n* one of the small holes in
the skin or in a leaf that liquid can pass

through ‖ 액체가 투과할 수 있는 피부 또
는 잎에 있는 작은 구멍의 하나. (피부·
잎의) 작은 구멍

pore² *v*

pore over sth *phr v* [T] to read or look
at something very carefully for a long
time ‖ 오랫동안 매우 주의 깊게 어떤 것을
읽거나 보다. 숙독하다: *We spent all day*
poring over wedding magazines. 우리는
하루 종일 결혼 잡지를 숙독하며 보냈다.

pork /pɔrk/ *n* **1** the meat from pigs ‖ 돼
지고기: *pork chops* 돼지고기 토막 —see
usage note at MEAT **2** SLANG government
money spent in a particular area in
order to get political advantages ‖ 정치
적 이득을 얻기 위해 특정한 지역에 쓰는
정부 돈. (정부의) 보조금

por·nog·ra·phy /pɔrˈnɑgrəfi/, **porn**
/pɔrn/ *n* [U] magazines, movies etc.
that show sexual acts and images in a
way that is intended to make people feel
sexually excited ‖ 사람을 성적으로 흥분
시키려는 의도로 성행위와 영상을 보여주
는 잡지나 영화 등. 포르노. 춘화 **—**
pornographic /ˌpɔrnəˈgræfɪk/ *adj* **—**
pornographer /pɔrˈnɑgrəfə/ *n*

po·rous /ˈpɔrəs/ *adj* allowing liquid,
air etc. to pass through slowly ‖ 액체나
공기 등이 서서히 통과하게 하는. 물·공
기가 스며드는. 침투성의: *porous rock* 구
멍이 많은 바위

por·poise /ˈpɔrpəs/ *n* a large sea
animal similar to a DOLPHIN, that
breathes air ‖ 공기 호흡을 하는 돌고래
비슷한 몸통이 큰 바다 동물. 쥐돌고래

por·ridge /ˈpɔrɪdʒ, ˈpɑr-/ *n* [U] cooked
OATMEAL ‖ 조리된 오트밀

port /pɔrt/ *n* **1** [C, U] a place where
ships can load and unload people or
things; HARBOR ‖ 배가 사람이나 물건을 싣
고 내리는 장소. 항구; 圈 harbor: *The*
ship was back in port after a week at
sea. 그 배는 해상에 일주일 있은 후에 항
구로 돌아왔다. **2** a town or city with a
HARBOR ‖ 항구가 있는 소도시나 대도시.
항구 도시. 항도: *the port of Wilmington,*
North Carolina 노스캐롤라이나 주 윌밍턴
의 항구 도시 **3** a place on the outside of
a computer where you can connect
another piece of equipment such as a
PRINTER ‖ 프린터 등의 다른 기구를 접속할
수 있는 컴퓨터 외부에 있는 단자. 포트 **4**
[C, U] a strong sweet Portuguese wine ‖
강한 단맛이 도는 포르투갈의 포도주 **5**
[U] the left side of a ship or aircraft
when you are looking toward the front
‖ 앞을 향해 볼 때 선박이나 항공기의 좌
측. 선박의 좌현(左舷). 항공기의 좌측

port·a·ble /'pɔrtəbəl/ *adj* light and easily carried or moved ‖ 가볍고 쉽게 운반되거나 이동되는. 휴대용의: *a portable phone/computer* 휴대용 전화[컴퓨터] — **portable** *n*

por·tal /'pɔrtl/ *n* **1** LITERARY a large gate or entrance to a building ‖ 건물의 큰 정문이나 출입구. 대문 **2** a WEBSITE that helps you find other websites ‖ 다른 웹 사이트들을 찾게 도와주는 웹사이트. 포털 사이트

por·tend /pɔr'tɛnd/ *v* [T] LITERARY to be a sign that something is going to happen, especially something bad ‖ 특히 나쁜 일이 일어날 것이라는 징조이다. 전조가 되다. 예고하다: *strange events that portend some great disaster* 어떤 대재난의 전조가 되는 이상한 사건들 — **portent** /'pɔrtɛnt/ *n*

por·ter /'pɔrtɚ/ *n* **1** someone whose job is to carry travelers' bags at airports, hotels etc. ‖ 공항이나 호텔 등에서 여행객의 가방을 운반하는 직업인. 운반인. 짐꾼 **2** someone whose job is to take care of the part of a train where people sleep ‖ 열차의 침대칸을 담당하는 직업인. 침대차의 보이

port·fo·li·o /pɔrt'fouli,ou/ *n* **1** a large flat case used for carrying drawings, documents etc. ‖ 그림이나 문서 등을 운반하는 데 사용되는 크고 평평한 가방 **2** a collection of drawings or other pieces of work by an artist, photographer etc. ‖ 예술가나 사진작가 등의 그림이나 다른 작품의 컬렉션. 대표 작품을 모은 선집(選集) **3** a collection of SHARES owned by a particular person or company ‖ 특정한 사람이나 회사가 소유하는 주식의 집합. 포트폴리오. 유가증권. 일람표: *an investment portfolio* 투자 구성비(構成比)

port·hole /'pɔrthoul/ *n* a small window on the side of a ship or plane ‖ 배나 비행기의 측면에 있는 작은 창문. 현창(舷窓)

por·ti·co /'pɔrti,kou/ *n* a covered entrance to a building, consisting of a roof supported by PILLARs ‖ 기둥으로 받쳐진 지붕이 있는 현관. 포르티코

por·tion¹ /'pɔrʃən/ *n* **1** a part of something larger ‖ 큰 것의 일부. 부분. 조각: *The news showed only a portion of the interview.* 그 뉴스는 인터뷰의 일부만 보여주었다. / *We put a portion of our pay into a savings account.* 우리는 봉급의 일부를 보통 예금 계좌에 넣었다. **2** an amount of food for one person, especially when served in a restaurant ‖ 특히 식당에서 제공할 때 한 사람의 음식 양. 1인분: *Do you have children's*

portions? 어린이들의 몫이 있니? **3** a share of something such as blame or a duty ‖ 책임이나 의무 등의 분담. 몫. 할당: *Both drivers must bear a portion of the blame.* 두 운전사는 책임을 분담해야 한다.

portion² *v*

portion sth ↔ **out** *phr v* [T] to divide something into parts and give them to several people ‖ 물건을 여러 부분으로 나누어 몇 사람에게 주다. 분배하다. 나눠주다

port·ly /'pɔrtli/ *adj* used in order to describe an older man who is fat in a fairly attractive way ‖ 꽤 매력적으로 살찐 노인을 표현하는 데에 쓰여. 뚱뚱한: *a portly gentleman* 뚱뚱한 신사

por·trait /'pɔrtrɪt/ *n* **1** a painting, drawing, or photograph of a person ‖ 사람의 그림[스케치, 사진]. 초상화. 얼굴 사진: *a family portrait* 가족의 초상화 **2** the story or a description of someone or something, often in the form of a movie ‖ 종종 영화 형태로 된, 사람이나 사물에 대한 이야기나 묘사. 서술: *The movie is a portrait of life in Harlem in the 1940s.* 그 영화는 1940년대 할렘 생활을 묘사하고 있다.

por·trai·ture /'pɔrtrɪtʃɚ/ *n* [U] the art of painting or drawing pictures of people ‖ 사람을 그리거나 스케치 하는 기술. 초상화법. 인물 묘사

por·tray /pɔr'treɪ, pɚ-/ *v* [T] **1** to describe something or someone in the form of a story or film ‖ 이야기나 영화 형태로 사람이나 사물을 묘사하다. 표현하다: *a movie that portrays the life of Charlie Chaplin* 찰리 채플린의 생애를 그린 영화 **2 portray sb/sth as sth** to describe or show someone or something in a particular way, according to your opinion of him/her ‖ 남에 대한 자신의 견해에 따라 사람이나 사물을 묘사하거나 나타내다. 그리다: *In the novel, Elaine's father is portrayed as a cruel tyrant.* 그 소설에서 일레인의 아버지는 잔인한 폭군으로 그려지고 있다. **3** to act the part of a character in a play ‖ 연극에서 등장인물의 역할을 하다. …을 연기하다: *Robin Williams portrayed Peter Pan in the movie.* 로빈 윌리엄스는 그 영화에서 피터팬을 연기했다.

por·tray·al /pɔr'treɪəl, pɚ-/ *n* [C, U] the action of PORTRAYing someone or something, or the book, film, play etc. that results from this ‖ 사람이나 사물을 묘사하기, 또는 이 결과로서 생기는 책·영화·연극 등. 묘사(된 것[작품]): *an* *accurate portrayal of pioneer life* 개척자 생활에 대한 정확한 묘사

Por·tu·guese¹ /ˌpɔrtʃəˈgiz/ *adj* relating to or coming from Portugal ‖ 포르투갈에 관한, 또는 포르투갈 출신의. 포르투갈 (산)의

Portuguese² *n* **1** [U] the language used in Portugal ‖ 포르투갈에서 사용되는 언어. 포르투갈어 **2 the Portuguese** [plural] the people of Portugal ‖ 포르투 갈인

pose¹ /poʊz/ *v* **1 pose a problem/ threat/danger** to cause a problem or danger ‖ 문제나 위험을 초래하다. 문제/ 위협/위험을 가하다: *Nuclear waste poses a threat to the environment.* 핵폐 기물은 환경에 위험이 되고 있다. **2** [I, T] to sit or stand in a particular position in order to be photographed or painted, or to make someone do this ‖ 사진이 찍히거 나 그려지도록 특정한 위치에 앉거나 서 다, 또는 다른 사람에게 이렇게 하도록 하 다. 포즈를 취하다[취하게 하다]: *The astronauts posed for pictures near the shuttle.* 우주 비행사는 우주 왕복선 근처 에서 사진을 찍기 위해 포즈를 취했다. **3 pose a question** to ask a question that needs to be carefully thought about ‖ 신 중하게 고려할 필요가 있는 질문을 하다. 제기하다: *His speech poses an interesting question.* 그의 연설은 흥미있 는 문제를 제기한다. **4 pose as sb** to pretend to be someone else in order to deceive people ‖ 사람을 속이기 위해 다른 사람인 체하다. …이라고 사칭하다: *The thief got in by posing as a repairman.* 그 도둑은 수리공으로 가장하고 들어갔다.

pose² *n* a position in which someone deliberately stands or sits ‖ 사람이 일부 러 서거나 앉는 자세. 자태. 포즈: *She struck a pose* (=stood or sat in a particular position) *with her head to one side.* 그녀는 머리를 한쪽으로 기대며 포즈 를 취했다.

pos·er /ˈpoʊzɚ/ *n* INFORMAL someone who pretends to have a quality or social position s/he does not have, in order to seem impressive to other people ‖ 다른 사람에게 인상적으로 보이기 위해 갖고 있 지 않은 특성이나 사회적 지위가 있는 체 하는 사람. 젠 체하는 사람

posh /pɑʃ/ *adj* expensive and used by rich people ‖ 비싸고 부자가 사용하는. 호 화로운: *a posh restaurant* 호화로운 음식 점

po·si·tion¹ /pəˈzɪʃən/ *n*
1 ▶STANDING/SITTING 서 있는/앉아 있 는◀ the way someone stands or sits, or

the direction in which an object is pointing ‖ 사람이 서 있거나 앉는 방식 또 는 물체가 가리키는 방향. 자세. 위치: *Keep your arms in this position as you dance.* 춤출 때 너의 팔을 이 자세로 유지 하라. / *This exercise is done in a sitting position.* 이 운동은 앉은 자세로 한다.
2 ▶SITUATION 상황◀ [C usually singular] the situation that someone is in, or the situation concerning a particular subject ‖ 사람이 처해 있는 상 황, 또는 특별한 주제에 관한 상황. 상태. 입장: *The company is in a dangerous financial position right now.* 그 회사는 지금 재정적으로 위험한 상태이다. / *I'm afraid I'm not in a position to help you.* (=do not have the power or money to help you) 미안하지만, 나는 너를 도와줄 입장이 아니야.
3 ▶RANK 지위◀ the level or rank someone has in a society or organization ‖ 사람이 사회나 조직에서 갖 는 수준이나 지위. 신분: *Ask someone in a position of authority.* 권한 있는 지위 의 사람에게 물어보라. / *a study on the position of minorities in our society* 우 리 사회의 소수 민족의 지위에 대한 연구
4 ▶OPINION 견해◀ an opinion about a particular subject ‖ 특정한 주제에 대한 견해: *What's the party's position on foreign aid?* 외국 원조에 대한 당의 입장 은 무엇이냐?
5 ▶PLACE 장소◀ [U] the place where someone or something is, in relation to other things ‖ 사람이나 물체가 다른 것들 과 관련하여 있는 장소. (정상) 위치. 적 소: *Help me put the furniture back in position.* 가구를 제자리에 다시 갖다 두는 데 나를 도와 달라.
6 ▶JOB 일◀ a job ‖ 일. 일자리. 직장: *He's applied for a position at the bank.* 그는 그 은행에 취업을 지원했다. —see usage note at JOB
7 ▶SPORTS 스포츠◀ the area where someone plays in a sport, or the type of actions s/he is responsible for doing in a game ‖ 사람이 스포츠에서 경기를 하는 영역 또는 경기에서 책임지고 하는 활동의 유형. 수비 위치. 포지션: *"What position do you play?" "Second base."* "너는 어떤 포지션이냐?" "2루야."
8 ▶RACE/COMPETITION 경주/시합◀ the place that someone has during a race or competition ‖ 사람이 경주나 시합 중에 얻 게 되는 위치: *Paldi has moved into second position.* 팔디는 2루로 이동했다.
position² *v* [T] to put something or someone in a particular place ‖ 물체나

사람을 특정한 장소에 두다: *Police positioned themselves around the bank.* 경찰은 은행 주변에 배치되었다.

pos·i·tive¹ /'pazətɪv/ *adj* **1** very sure that something is right ‖ 어떤 일이 옳다고 매우 확신하는. 확신[자신] 있는: *"Are you sure you don't want a drink?" "Positive."* "너 정말 술은 안 먹을래?" "그렇다니까." **2** considering the good qualities of a situation, person etc., and expecting success ‖ 상황이나 사람 등의 좋은 특성을 고려하고 성공을 예상하는. 적극[긍정]적인: *Sharon has a positive attitude to work.* 샤론은 일하는 태도가 적극적이다. / *So far, we've had mostly positive reactions to the new show.* 지금까지 우리는 새 쇼에 대해 대개 긍정적인 반응을 얻었다. **3** a medical or scientific test that is positive shows signs of what is being looked for ‖ 의료 검사나 과학 실험에서 찾고 있는 것의 징후를 보이는. 양성(반응)의: *Her pregnancy test came out/up positive.* 그녀의 임신 테스트는 양성 반응으로 나왔다. **4** having a good or useful effect, especially on someone's character ‖ 특히 남의 성격에 좋거나 유익한 영향을 끼치는. 긍정적[건설적]인: *Living abroad has been a positive experience for Jim.* 해외에 사는 일은 짐에게 좋은 경험이었다. **5** TECHNICAL a positive number or quantity is higher than zero. (+) is the positive sign ‖ 수나 양이 0보다 큰. 양(陽)의. 플러스의. (+)는 양의 기호이다. **6** TECHNICAL having the type of electrical charge that is carried by PROTONs, shown by a (+) sign on a BATTERY ‖ 전지에 플러스(+) 기호로 나타나고 양성자에 의해 운반되는 종류의 전하를 띤. 양전기의 —opposite NEGATIVE¹

positive² *n* a number that is higher than zero ‖ 0보다 큰 수. 양수

pos·i·tive·ly /'pazətɪvli, ˌpazə'tɪvli·/ *adv* **1** SPOKEN used in order to emphasize what you mean what you are saying ‖ 말하고 있는 것이 진심이라는 것을 강조하는 데에 쓰여. 정말. 확실히. 명백히: *This is positively the last time I'm going to say this.* 이번이 정말 내가 이 말을 하는 마지막이다. **2** INFORMAL used in order to emphasize a strong opinion or a surprising statement ‖ 강한 의견이나 놀라게 하는 말을 강조하는 데에 쓰여. 절대로. 분명히: *Some patients positively enjoy being in the hospital.* 몇몇 환자는 분명히 입원해 있는 것을 즐긴다. **3** in a way that shows you agree with something and want it to succeed ‖ 어떤

일에 동의하고 그 일이 성공하기 원한다는 것을 나타내어. 적극적[긍정적]으로: *News of the changes was received positively.* 변화의 소식은 긍정적으로 받아들여졌다. —see also **think positively** (THINK)

pos·se /'pasi/ *n* a group of men gathered together in past times by a SHERIFF (=local law officer) to help catch criminals ‖ 과거에 범죄자 잡는 것을 돕기 위해 보안관이 모은 일단의 사람들. 범인 추적대

pos·sess /pə'zɛs/ *v* [T] **1** FORMAL to own or have something ‖ 사물을 소유하거나 가지다: *The country possesses nuclear arms.* 그 나라는 핵무기를 보유하고 있다. / *She possesses a great talent for poetry.* 그녀는 시에 대한 훌륭한 재능을 지니고 있다. **2 what possessed sb to...?** SPOKEN said when you cannot understand why someone did something ‖ 남이 어떤 일을 한 이유를 이해할 수 없을 때 쓰여. 무엇에 홀려서 …했느냐?: *What possessed you to buy such an expensive gift?* 도대체 무슨 생각으로 그렇게 비싼 선물을 샀냐? – **possessor** *n*

pos·sessed /pə'zɛst/ *adj* controlled by an evil spirit ‖ 악령에 지배받는. 악령에 홀린. 귀신 들린

pos·ses·sion /pə'zɛʃən/ *n* **1** [C usually plural] something that you own ‖ 소유한 물건. 소유물. 재산: *When they left, they had to sell most of their possessions.* 그들은 떠날 때 대부분의 재산을 팔아야 했다. **2** [U] FORMAL the state of having or owning something ‖ 물건을 가지거나 소유한 상태. 소유(권). 소지. 점유: *He was found in possession of illegal drugs.* 그는 불법 마약을 소지한 것으로 확인되었다. / *When can we take possession of the house?* (=begin to use the house after buying it) 우리는 언제 그 집에 실제 들어가 살 수 있죠?

pos·ses·sive¹ /pə'zɛsɪv/ *adj* **1** wanting someone to have feelings of love or friendship only for you ‖ 남이 오직 당신에 대해서만 사랑이나 우정의 감정을 가지기 원하는. 독점욕이 강한: *I love Dave, but he's very possessive.* 나는 데이브를 사랑하나 그는 매우 독점욕이 강해. **2** unwilling to let other people use something you own ‖ 소유한 물건을 다른 사람이 사용하도록 하지 않는. 소유욕이 강한: *As a child, she was very possessive of her toys.* 어렸을 때 그녀는 자신의 장난감에 대해 소유욕이 매우 강했다.

possessive² *n* **the possessive**

TECHNICAL in grammar, a word such as "my," "its," "their" etc., used in order to show that one thing or person belongs to another person, or is related to that thing or person ‖ 문법에서 사물이나 사람이 다른 사물이나 사람에 속해 있거나 그 사물이나 사람에 관련되어 있는 것을 나타내기 위해 쓰이는 "my" "its" "their" 등의 단어. 소유격 –

possessive *adj : a possessive adjective/pronoun* 소유 형용사[대명사]

pos·si·bil·i·ty /ˌpɑsə'bɪləti/ *n* **1** something that may happen or may be true ‖ 일어나거나 사실일지도 모르는 일. 가능성: *There's a possibility (that) they'll come this weekend.* 그들이 이번 주말에 올 가능성이 있다. / *a possibility of getting a scholarship* 장학금을 탈 가능성 **2** something that gives you an opportunity to do what you want ‖ 원하는 것을 할 수 있는 기회를 주는 것. 실행 가능한[가능성 있는] 것[사항, 수단]: *Fuel cells are another possibility for powering electric cars.* 연료 전지는 전기 차의 동력으로 대체 가능한 수단이다.

pos·si·ble /ˈpɑsəbəl/ *adj* **1 as long/much/soon as possible** as long, soon etc. as you can ‖ 가능한 한 오래나 빨리. 최대한 오래/많이/빨리 등: *They need the tapes as quickly as possible.* 그들은 가능한 한 빨리 그 테이프가 필요하다. / *We kept going for as long as possible.* 우리는 가능한 한 오랫동안 계속했다. **2** able to be done, to happen, or to exist ‖ 행해질 [일어날, 있을] 수 있는. 할 수 있는. 가능한: *Is it possible to give the report to you tomorrow?* 내일 당신에게 보고서를 제출해도 될까요? / *Computer technology makes it possible for people to work at home now.* 컴퓨터 기술은 이제 사람이 집에서 일하는 것을 가능하게 해준다. / *This is the best/worst possible result.* (=it can be no better or worse) 이것은 가능한 최상[최악]의 결과이다. **3 would it be possible to…?** SPOKEN said when asking politely if you can do or have something ‖ 어떤 것을 하거나 가질 수 있는지 정중하게 물어볼 때에 쓰여. …하는 것이 가능할까요? …해 주실 수 있겠습니까?: *Would it be possible to exchange these gloves?* 이 장갑을 교환해 주실 수 있겠습니까? **4** likely to be done, to happen, or to exist ‖ 행해질 [일어날, 있을] 수 있는. 가능성이 있는: *Icy conditions are possible along the coast.* 해안 지역에서는 결빙 현상이 있을 수 있습니다. / *I'm looking for possible research topics.* 저는 연구 주제로 가능성

이 있는 것들을 찾고 있습니다. **5 whenever/wherever possible** every time or place that you have an opportunity to do something ‖ 무엇을 할 수 있는 기회가 있는 어떤 시간이나 장소에서. 가능하면 언제든/어느 곳에서든: *She visits her grandmother whenever possible.* 그녀는 가능한 때는 언제든 할머니를 방문한다. —compare IMPOSSIBLE

pos·si·bly /ˈpɑsəbli/ *adv* **1** used when saying that something may be true or likely ‖ 어떤 것이 사실이거나 일어날지도 모른다고 말할 때에 쓰여. 아마도, …인지도 모르는: *The trial will take place soon, possibly next week.* 재판이 곧, 아마 내주에 열릴 것이다. / *Picasso is quite possibly* (=very likely) *the best painter of this century.* 피카소는 아마도 이 세기의 가장 훌륭한 화가일 것이다. **2** used with MODAL VERBs, especially "can" and "could," to emphasize that something is or is not possible ‖ 어떤 것이 가능하거나 가능하지 않다는 것을 강조하기 위해 조동사 특히 "can"이나 "could"와 함께 쓰여. 어떻게 해서든지. 도저히: *I couldn't possibly eat all that!* 나는 도저히 그 모든 것을 먹을 수가 없었다! / *We did everything we possibly could to help them.* 우리는 힘 닿는 데까지 그들을 도울 수 있는 모든 일을 했다. / *Tracey might possibly have forgotten.* 트레이시는 어쩌면 잊어버렸을 수도 있었다. **3 could/can you possibly…?** SPOKEN said when politely asking someone to do something ‖ 남에게 어떤 것을 해달라고 정중하게 부탁할 때에 쓰여. …해 주시지 않겠습니까?: *Could you possibly turn the radio down?* 라디오 소리를 좀 줄여 주시겠습니까?

pos·sum /ˈpɑsəm/ *n* INFORMAL ⇨ OPOSSUM —see also **play possum** (PLAY[1])

post[1] /poʊst/ *n* **1** a strong upright piece of wood, metal etc. that is fixed into the ground ‖ 땅 속에 고정시킨 똑바로 세운 튼튼한 나무나 금속 등. 말뚝. 기둥. 가주: *a fence post* 울타리(용) 기둥 **2** an important job, especially in the government or military ‖ 특히 정부나 군대의 중요한 일자리. 지위. 직(책): *Biddle was given a new post in the Middle East.* 비들은 중동 지역에 새 직책을 부여받았다. **3** the place where someone has to be in order to do his/her job ‖ 사람이 일을 하기 위해 있어야 하는 장소. 부서. (맡은) 초소[구역]: *The guards cannot leave their posts.* 수비대는 담당 구역을 떠날 수 없다. **4** a military BASE ‖ 군대 주둔지 **5** a message sent to an Internet discussion group so that all members of these groups can read it ‖ 인터넷 토론 그룹에 전송되어 모든 회원이 읽을 수 있는 메시지. 게시물

post² v [T] **1** to put a public notice about something on a wall or BULLETIN BOARD ‖ 벽이나 게시판에 어떤 것에 대한 공공 게시문을 붙이다. …을 공표[공시]하다. …을 발표[게시]하다: *They've posted warning signs on the gate.* 그들은 정문에 경고 표지를 게시했다. **2** to give someone a government job in a foreign country ‖ 누군가에게 해외에 있는 정부 직책을 주다. 배속[배치]하다. 부임시키다: *Officials posted in the area were told to leave.* 그 지역에 배속되었던 관리들은 떠나라는 명령을 받았다. **3** if a company posts its profits, sales, losses etc., it records the money gained or lost in its accounts ‖ 회사가 수익·판매액·손실액 등 그 계정에서 이득을 보거나 손실을 본 금액을 기록하다: *In the final quarter, the company posted $12.4 million in earnings.* 마지막 분기에 그 회사는 1천 2백 40만 달러의 수익을 기록했다.

post·age /ˈpoʊstɪdʒ/ n [U] the money charged for sending a letter, package etc. by mail ‖ 편지나 소포 등을 우편으로 보내는 데 드는 돈. 우편 요금

post·al /ˈpoʊstl/ adj relating to the official mail system that takes letters from one place to another ‖ 한 지역에서 다른 지역으로 편지를 가져다주는 공식적인 우편 제도에 관련된. 우편의. 우체국의: *postal workers* 우체국 직원

postal serv·ice /ˈ.. ˌ../ n the public service for carrying letters, packages etc. from one part of the country to another ‖ 편지·소포 등을 나라의 한 지역에서 다른 지역으로 운반하는 공공 서비스. 우편 업무

post·card /ˈpoʊstkɑrd/ n a card, often with a picture on the front, that can be sent in the mail without an envelope ‖ 종종 앞면에 그림이 있으며 봉투 없이 우편물로 보내는 카드. 우편 엽서: *a postcard of Niagara Falls* 나이아가라 폭포의 그림 우편 엽서 —see picture at CARD¹

post·date /ˌpoʊstˈdeɪt/ v [T] to write a check with a date that is later than the actual date, so that it cannot be used until that time ‖ 수표에 실제 날짜보다 늦은 날짜를 기재하여 그 날짜까지는 통용될 수 없게 하다. 후일 날짜로 매기다

post·doc·tor·al /ˌpoʊstˈdɑktərəl/ adj relating to study done after a PH.D. ‖ 박사 학위 취득 후의 연구에 관련된

post·er /ˈpoʊstɚ/ n a large printed notice, picture etc. used in order to advertise something or as a decoration ‖ 어떤 것을 광고하기 위한 것이나 장식용으로 사용되는 커다랗게 인쇄한 벽보나 그림 등. 포스터. 광고 전단: *We designed the posters for the concert.* 우리는 그 콘서트 포스터를 디자인했다.

pos·te·ri·or /pɑˈstɪriɚ, poʊ-/ n HUMOROUS the part of the body you sit on ‖ 신체의 앉는 부위. 엉덩이. 둔부

pos·te·ri·ty /pɑˈstɛrəti/ n [U] the people who will live after you are dead ‖ 자신이 죽은 후에 살아갈 사람들. 자손. 후예: *I'm saving these pictures for posterity.* 나는 후세를 위해 이 그림을 간직해 두고 있다.

post·grad·u·ate¹ /ˌpoʊstˈgrædʒuɪt/ n someone who is studying to obtain a higher degree after high school or college ‖ 고등학교나 대학을 졸업한 후에 더 높은 학위를 받기 위해 공부하고 있는 사람. 대학(원)생

postgraduate² adj relating to studies done by a POSTGRADUATE ‖ 대학원생이 하는 연구와 관련된. 대학원생의: *a postgraduate scholarship* 대학원 장학금

post·hu·mous /ˈpɑstʃəməs/ adj happening after someone's death ‖ 사람의 죽음 후에 일어나는. 사후의: *a posthumous award* 사후의 상 – **posthumously** adv

Post-it /ˈpoʊstˌɪt/ n TRADEMARK a small piece of paper that sticks to things, used for leaving notes for people ‖ 사람에게 메모를 남기는 데 쓰이는, 물건에 붙이는 작은 종이조각. 포스트잇. 부전지. 붙이는 메모지

post·man /ˈpoʊstmən/ n ⇨ MAILMAN

post·mark /ˈpoʊstmɑrk/ n an official mark made on a letter, package etc. that shows the place and time it was sent ‖ 편지·소포 등을 보낸 장소와 시간을 나타내는 그 위에 찍힌 공식적인 표시. 소인 – **postmark** v [T]: *The card is postmarked Dec. 2.* 그 카드는 12월 2일자 소인이 찍혀 있다.

post·mas·ter /ˈpoʊstˌmæstɚ/ n the person in charge of a POST OFFICE ‖ 우체국을 책임지고 있는 사람. 우체국장

post·mod·ern /ˌ. ˈ../ adj used to describe styles and attitudes that are IRONIC and that are not serious in the way they treat the ideas and beliefs that a lot of people have ‖ 많은 사람이 지닌 사상과 믿음을 다루는 방식에서 풍자적이고 진지하지 않은 스타일과 태도를 말하는 데에 쓰여. 포스트 모던의

post·mor·tem /ˌpoʊstˈmɔrtəm/ *n* **1** an examination of a dead body to discover why the person died ∥ 사람의 사인을 밝히기 위한 시체의 검사. 검시(檢屍). 부검 **2** an examination of why something has failed ∥ 일의 실패 원인에 대한 조사. 사후 검토[분석]

post·na·tal /ˌpoʊstˈneɪtl·/ *adj* TECHNICAL relating to the time after a baby is born ∥ 아기가 태어난 후의 시간과 관련된. 출생 후의: *postnatal care* 출생 후의 보살핌 —compare PRENATAL

post of·fice /ˈ. ˌ../ *n* a place where you can buy stamps, and send letters, packages etc. ∥ 우표를 사고 편지·소포 등을 부치는 곳. 우체국

post of·fice box /ˈ. .. ˌ./ ⇨ P.O. BOX

post·pone /poʊstˈpoʊn/ *v* [T] to change an event to a later time or date ∥ 행사를 나중의 시간이나 날짜로 변경하다. 연기하다. 미루다: *The game was postponed because of rain.* 그 경기는 비 때문에 연기되었다. **- postponement** *n* [C, U]

post·script /ˈpoʊstˌskrɪpt/ *n* ⇨ P.S.

pos·tu·late /ˈpɑstʃəˌleɪt/ *v* [T] FORMAL to suggest that something might have happened or might be true ∥ 어떤 것이 일어났거나 사실일지도 모른다고 시사하다. 가정하다 **- postulate** /ˈpɑstʃəlɪt, -ˌleɪt/ *n*

pos·ture /ˈpɑstʃɚ/ *n* [C, U] the position you hold your body in when you sit or stand ∥ 앉거나 설 때 몸을 유지하는 자세: *Poor posture can lead to back trouble.* 나쁜 자세는 등에 문제를 일으킬 수 있다.

po·sy /ˈpoʊzi/ *n* LITERARY a small BUNCH of flowers ∥ 작은 꽃다발

pot¹ /pɑt/ *n* **1** a container used for cooking, that is round, deep, and usually made of metal ∥ 둥글고 깊으며 보통 금속으로 만들어 요리에 쓰이는 용기. 냄비: *pots and pans* 냄비류 **2** a container with a handle and a small tube for pouring, used for making coffee or tea ∥ 손잡이와 따르기 위한 작은 관이 있어 커피나 차를 만드는 데 사용되는 용기. 포트: *a coffee pot* 커피 포트 — see picture at CONTAINER **3** a container for a plant ∥ 식물용 용기. 화분: *The plant needs a new pot.* 그 화초는 새 화분이 필요하다. —see picture at CONTAINER **4 go to pot** INFORMAL if an organization or a place goes to pot, its condition becomes worse because no one takes care of it ∥ 조직이나 장소가 아무도 돌보지 않아서 상태가 더 악화되다. 영락[황폐]하다. 망하다: *The university has gone to pot since we were there.* 그 대학은 우리가 그곳에 다닌 이후로 영락해 갔다. **5 the pot** INFORMAL all the money that people have risked in a game of cards ∥ 카드 놀이에서 사람들이 건 모든 돈. 판돈. 한번에 건 돈 전부 **6** ⇨ MARIJUANA

pot² *v* [T] to put a plant in a pot filled with soil ∥ 식물을 흙이 가득찬 화분에 넣다. 화분에 식물을 심다

po·tas·si·um /pəˈtæsiəm/ *n* [U] a silver-white soft metal that is used in making soaps and FERTILIZERS ∥ 비누와 비료를 만드는 데 쓰이는 은백색의 연한 금속. 칼륨

po·ta·to /pəˈteɪṭoʊ, -ṭə/ *n, plural* **potatoes** [C, U] a hard round white root with a brown or pale yellow skin, cooked and eaten as a vegetable ∥ 야채로 요리해서 먹으며 갈색이나 엷은 노란색 껍질이 있는 딱딱하고 둥근 하얀 뿌리. 감자 —see also HOT POTATO —see picture on page 944

potato chip /ˈ.. ˌ./ *n* one of many thin hard pieces of potato that have been cooked in oil, and that are sold in packages ∥ 기름에 튀겨 포장해서 파는 얇고 굳어서 바삭바삭한 많은 감자 조각의 하나. 감자 튀김 —see picture at CHIP¹

pot·bel·ly /ˈpɑt̚ˌbɛli/ *n* a large round stomach that sticks out ∥ 튀어나온 크고 둥근 배. 똥배. 올챙이배 **- potbellied** *adj*

po·ten·cy /ˈpoʊt̚nsi/ *n* [U] **1** the strength of the effect of a drug, medicine, alcohol etc. on your mind or body ∥ 마약·약·알코올 등이 마음이나 신체에 미치는 영향력. 효력. 효능: *high-potency vitamins* 효능이 좋은 비타민 **2** a man's ability to have sex ∥ 성교를 할 수 있는 남자의 능력. 성교 능력

po·tent /ˈpoʊt̚nt/ *adj* powerful and effective ∥ 강력한. 효력 있는: *a potent weapons system* 강력한 무기 체계 / *potent drugs* 효능 있는 약

po·ten·tial¹ /pəˈtɛnʃəl/ *adj* possible ∥ 가능한. 일어날[나게 될] 가능성이 있는. 잠재적인: *It's a new system with many potential problems.* 그것은 많은 잠재적인 문제들을 내포한 새 시스템이다. / *He's having lunch with some potential clients.* (=people who may use his services) 그는 고객이 될 만한 몇몇 사람들과 점심 식사를 하고 있다.

potential² *n* [U] **1** [singular] the possibility that something will develop or happen in a particular way ∥ 어떤 이 특정하게 전개되거나 일어날 가능성.

잠재성: *There's a potential for conflict in the area.* 그 지역에는 분쟁이 일어날 가능성이 있다. **2** [U] a natural ability that could develop to make you very good at something ‖ 어떤 일을 매우 잘하도록 발전할 수 있는 타고난 능력. 잠재력. 소질: *She was told she had great potential as a singer.* 그녀는 가수로서의 큰 잠재 능력이 있다는 말을 들었다.

po·ten·tial·ly /pəˈtɛnʃəli/ *adv* if something is potentially dangerous, useful, embarrassing etc., it does not have that quality now, but it may develop it later ‖ 지금은 위험하거나 유용하거나 난처하게 하지 않지만 나중에 발현할 수 있는. 잠재적으로. 가능성으로서: *potentially dangerous fireworks* 잠재적으로 위험한 불꽃놀이 / *a potentially fatal disease* (=one that could kill you) 잠재적으로 치명적인 질병

pot·hold·er /ˈpɑtˌhoʊldɚ/ *n* a piece of thick material used for holding hot cooking pans ‖ 뜨거운 요리 냄비를 드는 데 쓰이는 두꺼운 직물. 냄비용 장갑

pot·hole /ˈpɑthoʊl/ *n* a hole in the surface of a road that makes driving difficult ‖ 운전을 어렵게 하는 도로 표면의 구멍. 팬 구멍

po·tion /ˈpoʊʃən/ *n* LITERARY a drink intended to have a special or magic effect on the person who drinks it ‖ 마시는 사람에게 특별하거나 마법적인 효과를 미치도록 한 음료. 약. 독약. (마법에서 사용하는 것의) 1회 복용량: *a love potion* 사랑의 묘약, 미약(媚藥)

pot luck /ˌ. ˈ./ *n* **take pot luck** INFORMAL to choose something without knowing very much about it ‖ 어떤 것에 관해 충분히 알지 않고 선택하다. 되는 대로 고르다: *Nobody knew about any good restaurants, so we took pot luck.* 좋은 식당을 아는 사람이 없어서 우리는 되는 대로 골랐다.

pot·luck /ˌpɑtˈlʌk/ *adj* **a potluck dinner/lunch etc.** a meal in which everyone who is invited brings something to eat ‖ 초대받은 각자가 먹을 것을 가져오는 식사. 각자 음식을 가져와서 나누어 먹는 저녁/점심

pot pie /ˌ. ˈ./ *n* meat and vegetables covered with PASTRY and baked in a deep dish ‖ 속이 깊은 접시에 고기와 야채를 넣고 위에 가루 반죽을 덮어 구운 것. 고기나 야채를 넣어 구운 파이

pot·pour·ri /ˌpoʊpʊˈri/ *n* [U] a mixture of dried flowers and leaves kept in a bowl to make a room smell nice ‖ 방에서 좋은 냄새가 나도록 단지에 보관한 마른 잎과 꽃의 혼합물. 향단지

pot shot /ˌ. ˈ./ *n* **take a pot shot at** INFORMAL to shoot at someone or something without aiming carefully ‖ 주의깊게 겨누지 않고 사람이나 사물을 쏘다. 난사하다

pot·ter·y /ˈpɑtɚi/ *n* [U] **1** objects made out of baked clay ‖ 구운 찰흙으로 만든 물체. 도기(류): *a pottery bowl* 도기 사발 **2** the activity of making objects out of baked clay ‖ 구운 찰흙으로 물체를 만드는 활동. 도기 제조술[업]: *a pottery class* 도기 수업 – **potter** *n*

pot·ty /ˈpɑti/ *n* SPOKEN a word meaning a toilet, used when speaking to children ‖ 아이들에게 말할 때에 쓰이는 변기를 의미하는 단어

pouch /paʊtʃ/ *n* **1** a small leather or cloth bag used for keeping and carrying things in, especially in past times ‖ 특히 과거에 물건의 보관 및 운반에 쓰이던 가죽이나 천으로 만든 작은 가방 **2** a pocket of skin that MARSUPIALs keep their babies in ‖ 유대 동물이 새끼를 기르는 가죽 주머니. 육아낭

poul·try /ˈpoʊltri/ *n* [U] birds that are kept on farms for supplying eggs and meat, or the meat from these birds ‖ 달걀·고기 공급용으로 농장에서 사육하는 조류, 또는 이 새들의 고기. 가금(家禽)(의 고기)

pounce /paʊns/ *v* [I] to suddenly jump on a person or animal after waiting to catch him, her, or it ‖ 사람이나 동물을 잡기 위해 기다리다가 갑자기 덤벼들다. 갑자기 덮치다: *The cat likes to pounce on people when they come through the door.* 그 고양이는 사람들이 문을 열고 들어갈 때 갑자기 덤벼들기를 좋아한다.

pound' /paʊnd/ *n* **1** written abbreviation **lb.** a unit for measuring weight, equal to 16 OUNCEs or 453.6 grams ‖ 16온스나 453.6그램에 상당하는 중량 측정 단위. 파운드: *a pound of apples* 사과 1파운드 / *She's lost/gained 10 pounds this year.* (=her weight has gone down or up by 10 pounds) 그녀는 금년에 체중이 10파운드 빠졌다[늘었다]. **2 the pound** a place where lost dogs and cats are kept until the owner claims them ‖ 잃어버린 개·고양이 등을 주인이 나타나 찾아갈 때까지 수용하는 장소. 공설 우리 **3 5-pounder/2-pounder etc.** INFORMAL an animal or fish that weighs a particular number of pounds ‖ 특정 파운드의 무게가 나가는 동물이나 물고기. 5/2파운드짜리: *Ben caught a 5-pounder in the Kootenai River.* 벤은 쿠테나이 강

에서 5파운드짜리 물고기를 잡았다.

pound² *v* **1** [I, T] to hit something hard many times, in order to make a loud sound or to damage something ‖ 큰 소리를 내거나 사물을 파손시키려고 어떤 것을 여러 차례 세게 치다: *Someone was pounding on their door late last night.* 누군가가 어젯밤 늦게 그들의 문을 쾅쾅 두드리고 있었다. / *The boys pounded the bottles with their sticks until they had all broken.* 그 소년들은 병이 모두 깨질 때까지 막대기로 쳤다. **2** [I] if your heart pounds, it beats very quickly ‖ 심장이 매우 빨리 뛰다. 세차게 고동치다 **3** [I] to walk or run quickly with heavy steps ‖ 무거운 걸음으로 걷거나 빨리 달리다. 쿵쾅거리며 걷다[달리다]: *I heard the sound of heavy boots pounding on the floor.* 나는 마루 위를 쿵쾅거리며 걷고 있는 육중한 부츠 소리를 들었다. **4** [T] to attack a person or place for a long time ‖ 오랫동안 사람이나 장소를 공격하다: *Enemy guns pounded the city until morning.* 적의 포화는 아침까지 그 도시에 계속되었다.

pound cake /ˈ. ./ *n* a heavy cake made from flour, sugar, eggs, and butter ‖ 밀가루·설탕·달걀·버터로 만든 중량감이 있는 케이크. 파운드 케이크

pour /pɔr/ *v* **1** [T] to make a liquid or a substance such as salt or sand flow out of or into something ‖ 액체 또는 소금·모래 등의 물질을 어떤 것에서 또는 어떤 것에 흐르게 하다. 따르다. 붓다. 쏟다: *Shall I pour more champagne?* 샴페인을 좀 더 따를까요? / *Pour yourself more coffee if you'd like some.* 좀 더 마시고 싶으면 커피를 더 따라라. **2 it pours (down)** if it pours, a lot of rain comes out of the sky ‖ 하늘에서 많은 비가 내리다. 비가 억수같이 쏟아지다: *It's been pouring all afternoon.* 오후 내내 비가 억수같이 쏟아지고 있다. — see usage note at WEATHER **3** [I] to flow quickly and in large amounts ‖ 대량으로 빠르게 흐르다. 쏟아져 나온다: *Fuel poured out of the plane.* 연료가 비행기에서 쏟아져 나왔다. **4** [I] if people or things pour into or out of a place, a lot of them arrive or leave at the same time ‖ 많은 사람이나 물건이 동시에 도착하거나 떠나다. 대량으로 이동하다. 쇄도하다: *Letters are pouring in from people all over the state.* 주(州)의 각지로부터 편지

pour

가 쇄도하고 있다. / *People poured out of their houses into the streets.* 사람들이 집에서 거리로 쏟아져 나왔다. **5 pour money/aid etc. into** to provide a lot of money over time to pay for something ‖ 어떤 값을 지불하기 위해 오랜 기간 많은 돈을 제공하다. …에 돈/원조를 쏟아붓다: *Thomas has poured thousands of dollars into his shop.* 토머스는 그의 가게에 수천 달러를 쏟아부었다.

pour sth ↔ **out** *phr v* [T] to tell someone everything about your thoughts, feelings etc. ‖ 자기의 생각·감정 등에 대한 모든 것을 남에게 말하다. 토로하다. 털어놓다: *Sonia poured out all her frustrations to Val.* 소니아는 그녀의 모든 좌절감을 밸에게 털어놓았다.

pout /paʊt/ *v* [I, T] to push out your lips because you are annoyed, or in order to look sexually attractive ‖ 화가 나서 또는 성적으로 매력 있게 보이려고 입술을 내밀다. 삐죽거리다: *Stop pouting and eat your dinner.* 그만 삐죽거리고 저녁을 먹어라. – **pout** *n*

pov·er·ty /ˈpɑvəti/ *n* **1** the situation or experience of being poor ‖ 가난한 상황이나 경험. 빈곤: *He worked all his life to avoid the poverty he knew as a child.* 그는 어려서 경험한 가난을 벗어나려고 평생을 일했다. / *families living in extreme poverty* 극도의 가난속에서 살고 있는 가족들 **2 the poverty line** the income below which a person or a family is officially considered to be very poor and in need of help ‖ 일정 소득 이하의 사람이나 가족은 공식적으로 극빈으로 간주되어 구호 대상이 되는 소득 수준. 빈곤선: *Her salary keeps the family just above the poverty line.* 그녀는 빈곤선을 겨우 초과하는 급여로 가족을 부양한다.

poverty-strick·en /ˈ... ,../ *adj* extremely poor ‖ 매우 가난한. 가난에 시달리는: *a poverty-stricken neighborhood* 매우 가난한 이웃

P.O.W. *n* the abbreviation of PRISONER OF WAR ‖ prisoner of war의 약어: *a P.O.W. camp* 포로수용소

pow·der¹ /ˈpaʊdə/ *n* **1** [C, U] a dry substance in the form of very small grains ‖ 아주 작은 입자 형태로 된 마른 물질. 가루. 분말: *talcum powder* 활석 가루 / *baking powder* 베이킹 파우더 **2 powder keg** a dangerous situation or place where violence or trouble could suddenly start ‖ 폭력이나 분쟁이 갑자기 일어날 수도 있는 위험한 상황이나 장소. 화약고: *The city has become a powder keg since the demonstration.* 그 도시는

시위가 시작된 이래 화약고가 되었다.

powder² *v* [T] **1** to put powder on your skin ‖ 피부에 분을 바르다 **2 powder your nose** a phrase meaning to go to the toilet, used by women in order to be polite ‖ 화장실에 가는 것을 뜻하는, 여성들이 완곡하게 사용하는 어구

pow·dered /'paʊdəd/ *adj* produced or sold in the form of powder ‖ 가루 형태로 생산되거나 판매되는. 분말의: *powdered milk* 분유

powder room /'.. ,./ *n* a polite phrase meaning a women's public toilet ‖ 여성용 공중 화장실을 의미하는 완곡한 어구

pow·der·y /'paʊdəri/ *adj* like powder or easily broken into powder ‖ 가루 모양의, 가루가 되기 쉬운: *powdery snow* 가루눈

pow·er¹ /'paʊɚ/ *n*

1 ▶CONTROL SB/STH 사람/사물의 통제◀ [U] the ability or right to control people or events ‖ 사람이나 사건을 통제하는 능력이나 권한. 권력. 지배력: *The factory has too much power over its employees.* 그 공장은 직원들에 대해 지나치게 많은 권한을 가지고 있다. / *People go into politics because of power, not money.* 사람들은 돈 때문이 아니라 권력 때문에 정치에 입문한다.

2 ▶POLITICAL 정치적인◀ [U] political control of a country or government ‖ 국가나 정부의 정치적인 지배. 통치권. 정권: *The current leader has been in power for ten years.* 현재의 지도자는 10년 동안 정권을 잡고 있다. / *He came to power* (=began to control the country) *after the revolution.* 그는 혁명 후에 정권을 장악했다.

3 ▶ENERGY 힘◀ [U] energy such as electricity that can be used to make a machine, car etc. work ‖ 기계·자동차 등을 작동시키는 데에 쓰일 수 있는 전기 등의 에너지. 힘. 전력: *The storm caused a power failure/cut* (=a time when there is no electricity) *in our area.* 그 폭풍으로 인해 우리 지역은 정전이 되었다. / *electricity produced by nuclear/solar power* 핵[태양] 에너지에 의해 발전된 전기

4 ▶AUTHORITY 권한◀ [C, U] the legal right or authority to do something ‖ 어떤 것을 하기 위한 법적 권한이나 권위: *Congress has the power to declare war.* 의회는 선전 포고의 권한을 가지고 있다. / *Only the police have the power of arrest.* 경찰만이 체포 권한이 있다.

5 ▶COUNTRY 국가◀ a country that is very strong and important ‖ 매우 강력하

고 영향력 있는 국가. 강대국: *Germany is a major industrial power in Europe.* 독일은 유럽의 주요 공업 대국이다. / *a meeting of world powers* (=the strongest countries in the world) 세계 강대국 회의

6 ▶PHYSICAL 물리적인◀ [U] the physical strength of something such as an explosion, natural force, or animal ‖ 폭발물[자연력, 동물] 등의 물리적인 힘: *The power of the eruption blew away the whole mountainside.* 화산 폭발의 위력은 산허리를 온통 날려 버렸다.

7 ▶NATURAL ABILITY 타고난 능력◀ [C, U] a natural or special ability to do something ‖ 어떤 것을 할 수 있는 타고나거나 특별한 능력: *the power of sight/speech* 시력[발표력] / *She has the power to make an audience laugh or cry.* 그녀는 청중을 웃고 울리는 능력이 있다.

8 be in sb's power to be in a situation in which someone has control over you ‖ 남이 자신을 지배하는 상황에 있다. …의 지배하에 있다

9 do everything in your power to do everything that you are able or allowed to do ‖ 할 수 있거나 하도록 허용된 모든 일을 하다: *I did everything in my power to save her.* 나는 그녀를 구하기 위해 할 수 있는 한 모든 일을 다했다.

10 earning/purchasing etc. power the ability to earn money, buy things etc. ‖ 돈을 벌거나 물건을 구입할 수 있는 능력. 수익(능)력/구매력: *the purchasing power of middle-class teenagers* 중산층 10대들의 구매력

11 the powers that be INFORMAL the people who have positions of authority, and whose decisions affect your life ‖ 권한 있는 자리에 있어서 그들의 결정이 타인의 삶에 영향을 미치는 사람들. 당국자. 관리: *The hardest part will be persuading the powers that be at City Hall to agree.* 가장 어려운 부분은 시 당국자를 설득하여 동의를 얻어내는 일일 것이다.

12 to the power of 3/4/5 etc. TECHNICAL if a number is increased to the power of 3, 4, 5 etc., it is multiplied by itself 3, 4, 5 etc. times ‖ 어떤 수를 자신의 수로 세 번·네 번·다섯 번 곱함. 3/4/5제곱 —see usage note at FORCE¹

power² *v* **1 solar-powered/nuclear-powered etc.** working or moving by means of a BATTERY etc. ‖ 전지 등의 수단으로 작동하거나 움직이는. 태양 에너지를 이용한/핵에너지를 이용한: *a battery-*

powered flashlight 전지로 작동하는 손전 등 **2** [T] to supply power to a vehicle or machine ‖ 차량이나 기계에 동력을 공급 하다: *a car powered by solar energy* 태 양 에너지로 움직이는 자동차 **3** [I, T] to do something quickly and with a lot of strength ‖ 신속하고 힘껏 어떤 것을 하다. 힘차게 …하다: *Ms. Graf has powered her way through the first three rounds at Wimbledon.* 그라프 양은 윔블던 대회 의 첫 3라운드를 힘찬 모습으로 통과했다.

power sth ↔ **up** *phr v* [T] to make a machine, especially a computer, start working ‖ 기계, 특히 컴퓨터를 작동시키 다: *Never move a computer while it is powered up.* 컴퓨터가 켜져 있는 동안에 는 컴퓨터를 절대 움직이지 마라.

power base /'.. ,./ *n* the group of people in a particular area that supports a politician or leader ‖ 어떤 정 치가나 지도자를 지지하는 특정 지역 내의 일단의 사람들. 세력 기반. 거점

pow·er·boat /'.. ,./ *n* a boat with a powerful engine that is used for racing ‖ 경주용으로 쓰이는 강력한 엔진을 부착 한 배. 동력선. 모터보트

pow·er·ful /'pauəfəl/ *adj* **1** able to control and influence events and other people's actions ‖ 사건과 타인의 행위를 통제하고 영향을 미칠 수 있는. 강력한. 강한 힘을 가진: *a meeting of the world's most powerful leaders* 세계 최강국 지도 자들의 회의 **2** having a lot of power, strength, or force ‖ 막대한 힘이나 체력, 또는 세력을 지닌: *a powerful engine* 강 력한 엔진 / *a powerful man* 건강한 남자 / *a powerful explosion* 강력한 폭발 **3** having a strong effect on someone's feelings or ideas ‖ 사람의 감정이나 생각 에 강력한 영향을 미치는. 효과적인. 설득 력 있는: *Hate is a dangerously powerful emotion, Krista.* 증오는 위험스러울 정도 로 강한 감정이야, 크리스타. / *a powerful argument against eating meat* 육식을 반 대하는 설득력 있는 주장 **4** having a strong effect on your body ‖ 신체에 강한 영향을 미치는. 효능이 뛰어난: *a powerful drug/medicine* 잘 듣는 약 – **powerfully** *adv*

pow·er·house /'pauə,haus/ *n* **INFORMAL 1** a country, company, organization etc. that has a lot of power or influence ‖ 강력하거나 큰 영향력이 있 는 국가·회사·조직 등 **2** someone who has a lot of energy ‖ 기운이 넘치는 사람. 정력가

pow·er·less /'pauəlɪs/ *adj* unable to stop or control something because you do not have the power, strength, or right to do so ‖ 그렇게 할 능력[체력, 권 한]을 갖고 있지 않아서 어떤 것을 중단하 거나 통제할 수 없는. 무능한. 무력한: *The small group of soldiers was powerless to stop the attack.* 소규모의 군인들로 그 공격을 막아내기에는 무력했 다. – **powerlessness** *n* [U]

power line /'.. ,./ *n* a large wire above or under the ground that takes electricity from one place to another ‖ 전기를 한 장소에서 다른 장소로 전달하는 지상이나 지하의 굵은 전선. 송전선

power of at·tor·ney /,.. '../ *n* [C, U] LAW the legal right to do things for someone else in his/her business or personal life, or the document that gives this right ‖ 다른 사람의 사업이나 사 생활을 위해서 일을 하는 법적 권한, 또는 이 권한을 수여하는 문서. 위임(장)

power plant /'.. ,./, **power station** /'.. ,./ *n* a building where electricity is made ‖ 전기를 생산하는 건물. 발전소

power steer·ing /,.. '../ *n* [U] a special system that makes it easier for the driver of a vehicle to STEER (=change the direction of the vehicle) ‖ 차량의 운전자가 핸들을 쉽게 조작하게 하 는 특수한 장치. 파워 핸들

power tool /'.. ,./ *n* a tool that works by using electricity ‖ 전기로 작동하는 도 구. 전기 기구

pow·wow /'pau wau/ *n* a meeting or discussion, especially a meeting of a Native American tribe ‖ 특히 아메리카 원주민 부족의 회의나 토론

pp. the written abbreviation of "pages" ‖ pages의 약어: *Read pp. 20-35.* 20페이 지에서 35페이지까지 읽어라.

PR *n* **1** [U] ⇨ PUBLIC RELATIONS **2** the written abbreviation for Puerto Rico ‖ Puerto Rico(푸에르토리코)의 약어

prac·ti·ca·ble /'præktɪkəbəl/ *adj* FORMAL able to be used successfully in a particular situation ‖ 특정한 상황에서 유 효하게 사용할 수 있는. 실용적인. 실제로 사용할 수 있는: *a practicable idea* 현실 적인 생각

prac·ti·cal /'præktɪkəl/ *adj* **1** relating to real situations and events rather than ideas ‖ 관념보다는 실제 상황이나 사건에 관 련된. 실제의: *Do you have a lot of practical experience as a mechanic?* 기 계공으로서 실지 경험이 많습니까? / *I deal with practical matters, like finding people places to stay.* 나는 사람들에게 체류할 곳을 찾아주는 일 같은 실제적인 일을 취급한다. **2** sensible and likely to succeed or be effective ‖ 분별 있고 성공 적이거나 효과적일 것 같은. 실용적인: *We have to be practical and not spend so much money.* 우리는 실리적이어야 하며 돈을 많이 써서는 안 된다. / *Is that a practical solution to the problem?* 그것 이 그 문제에 대한 실용적인 해결책입니 까? **3** designed to be useful, or to be suitable for a particular purpose ‖ 유용 하거나 특정 목적에 알맞도록 고안된. 유 용한: *She gives practical gifts, such as clothes.* 그녀는 옷 같은 유용한 선물을 준 다. / *a practical car for a family* 가족용 의 실용적인 차 **4 for all practical purposes** used in order to describe what the real situation is, although it might seem to be different ‖ 보는 것과는 다른 듯한 실제 상황을 설명하는 데에 쓰 여. 실제로는: *For all practical purposes, the election is over.* (=we already know who the winner is) 사실 그 선거는 당선 자가 결정된 것이나 다름없다.

prac·ti·cal·i·ty /ˌpræktɪˈkæləti/ *n* **1 practicalities** [plural] the real facts of a situation, rather than ideas about how it might be ‖ 어떤 것에 대한 관념적인 생 각이 아니라 상황에 관한 실제적 사실. 실 제적인 것: *We have to think about practicalities, like how long it will take, and how much it will cost.* 우리는 기간은 얼마나 걸리고 비용은 얼마나 소요될 것인 지 등의 실제적인 사항들을 생각해야 한 다. **2** [U] how sensible and suitable an idea is ‖ 생각의 분별 있고 적합한 정도. 실용[실제]성: *It's a nice idea, but I'm not sure about the practicality of it.* 그것 은 좋은 생각이지만 나는 그것의 실용성에 대해서는 확신이 서지 않는다.

practical joke /ˌ… ˈ·/ *n* a trick that is intended to surprise someone and make other people laugh ‖ 사람을 놀라게 해서 다른 사람들을 웃기려는 술수. (실제 행동 이 따르는) 못된 장난

prac·ti·cally /ˈpræktɪkli/ *adv* **1** SPOKEN almost ‖ 거의: *Practically everyone was there.* 거의 모든 사람들이 거기 있었다. / *She practically jumped out of her chair.* 그녀는 의자에서 거의 튀어나오다시피 했 다. **2** in a sensible way ‖ 분별 있게. 실제 적 견지에서: *Vasko just doesn't think practically.* 바스코는 정말이지 실질적으 로 생각하지를 않는다.

prac·tice¹ /ˈpræktɪs/ *n*

1 ▶SKILL 기술◀ [U] **a)** regular activity that you do in order to improve a skill or ability ‖ 기술이나 능력을 향상시키려고 하는 규칙적인 활동. 연습. 훈련: *It takes a lot of practice to be a good piano*

player. 훌륭한 피아노 연주자가 되기 위 해서는 많은 연습이 필요하다. **b)** the period of time in which you do this ‖ 연 습을 하는 일정 기간: *We have football practice tonight.* 우리는 오늘 밤 축구 연 습 시간이 있다.

2 ▶STH THAT IS USUALLY DONE 일상적 으로 하는 것◀ [C, U] **a)** something that people do often and in a particular way ‖ 사람들이 종종 특정하게 하는 일. 관행. 습관: *unsafe sexual practices* 위험한 성 행위 **b)** something that people do in a particular way because it is usually done that way in their religion, society, organization etc.; CUSTOM ‖ 종교·사회·조 직 등에서 보통 특정한 방식으로 행해졌기 때문에 사람들이 그 방식으로 하는 일. 관 례. 관행. 관습; ⓟ custom: *the practice of kissing someone as a greeting* 인사로 남에게 키스를 하는 관습 / *It's standard/normal practice to do the payroll in this way.* 이런 식으로 봉급을 지급하는 것이 보통의[정상적인] 관행이 다.

3 in practice used in order to describe what the real situation is rather than what seems to be true ‖ 사실처럼 보이는 것이 아닌 실제 상황을 설명하는 데에 쓰 여. 실제는: *Annette is the head of the company, but in practice Sue runs everything.* 아네트가 그 회사의 사장이지 만 수가 모든 것을 운영한다.

4 ▶DOCTOR/LAWYER 의사/변호사◀ the work of a doctor or lawyer, or the place where s/he works ‖ 의사나 변호사의 업 무, 또는 그들이 일하는 장소. 개업[업 무](장소): *She has a successful medical/legal practice.* 그녀는 의사업[변 호사업]을 성공적으로 하고 있다.

5 be out of practice to be unable to do something well because you have not done it for a long time ‖ 오랫동안 하지 않아서 어떤 것을 잘 할 수 없다. 서투르 다. 숙련되어 있지 않다: *I'd like to sing with you, but I'm really out of practice.* 나는 너와 노래하고 싶지만 정말이지 지금 은 연습 부족으로 솜씨가 없어.

6 put sth into practice to start using an idea, plan, method etc. instead of just thinking about it or studying it ‖ 생 각이나 연구만 하기보다 상상·계획·방법 등을 활용하기 시작하다. 실행하다: *Now's your chance to put the skills you've learned into practice.* 지금이야말로 네가 배운 기술을 발휘할 기회이다.

practice² *v* **1** [I, T] to do an activity regularly to improve your skill or ability ‖ 기술이나 능력을 향상시키기 위해 규칙

적으로 활동을 하다. 연습[훈련]하다: *Gail practices the piano more than an hour every day.* 게일은 매일 한 시간 이상씩 피아노 연습을 한다. **2** [I, T] to work as a doctor or lawyer ‖ 의사나 변호사로서 일하다. 개업[영업]하다: *Bill is practicing law/medicine in Ohio now.* 빌은 지금 오하이오에서 변호사[의사]로 일하고 있다. **3** [T] to do an activity as a habit, or to live according to the rules of a religion ‖ 습관으로서 어떤 활동을 하거나, 또는 종교의 계율에 따라 살다. …을 실천하다. 준수하다: *The posters encourage young people to practice safe sex.* 그 포스터는 젊은이들이 안전한 성행위를 실천하도록 장려한다.

prac·ticed /'præktɪst/ *adj* good at doing something because you have done it many times before ‖ 전에 많이 했기 때문에 어떤 것을 하는 데에 능숙한. 숙련된: *a practiced pilot* 숙련된 조종사

prac·tic·ing /'præktɪsɪŋ/ *adj* **1 a practicing doctor/lawyer/architect etc.** someone who has trained as a doctor, lawyer etc., and who still works as one ‖ 의사·변호사 등으로 교육을 받고 지금도 일하고 있는 직업인. 현역 의사/변호사/건축가 **2 a practicing Catholic/Jew/Muslim etc.** someone who obeys the rules of a particular religion ‖ 특정 종교의 계율을 지키는 사람. 현 가톨릭/유대교/이슬람교 신자

prac·ti·tion·er /præk'tɪʃənɚ/ *n* FORMAL someone who is trained to do a particular type of work that involves a lot of skill ‖ 많은 기술이 필요한 특정한 형태의 업무를 하도록 교육받은 사람. 개업자: *a tax practitioner* 개업 세무사 / *Dr. Reynolds is a family/general practitioner.* (=a doctor who treats general medical problems) 레이놀즈 박사는 가정의[일반 개업 의사]이다.

prag·mat·ic /præg'mætɪk/ *adj* dealing with problems in a sensible and practical way rather than following a set of ideas that are considered correct ‖ 틀림없다고 여겨지는 일련의 관념을 따르기보다는 오히려 분별 있고 실용적인 방법으로 문제를 처리하는. 실리[실용, 실제]적인: *The diet gives you pragmatic suggestions for eating healthily.* 그 식이 요법은 건강한 식사를 위한 실제적인 제안을 한다.

prag·ma·tism /'prægmə,tɪzəm/ *n* [U] a tendency to deal with problems in a PRAGMATIC way ‖ 문제를 실리적으로 처리하는 경향. 실용주의. 프래그머티즘 – **pragmatist** *n*

prai·rie /'prɛri/ *n* a large area of flat land in North America that is covered in grass ‖ 풀로 덮여 있는 북미의 넓고 평평한 지대. 북미 대초원 지대

prairie dog /'.. ,./ *n* a North American animal with a short tail that is related to a SQUIRREL, that lives in holes on a PRAIRIE ‖ 북미 대초원의 굴속에 사는 다람쥣과의 짧은 꼬리를 가진 북미산(産) 동물. 프레리도그

praise[1] /preɪz/ *v* [T] **1** to say publicly that someone has done something well or that you admire him/her ‖ 남이 어떤 일을 잘했다고, 또는 그 사람을 훌륭하게 생각한다고 공공연히 말하다. 칭찬하다: *Mr. Bonner praised Jill for the quality of her work.* 보너 씨는 질의 업무에 대해서 우수하다고 그녀를 칭찬했다. **2** to give thanks or honor to God ‖ 신에게 감사를 드리거나 경의를 표하다. 찬양하다

praise[2] *n* [U] **1** words that you say or write to praise someone or something ‖ 사람이나 사물을 칭찬하려고 말이나 글로 하는 말. 칭찬. 찬사: *The papers were full of praise for the quick actions of the fire department.* 신문마다 소방서의 신속한 조치에 대한 찬사로 가득했다. **2** an expression of respect or thanks to God ‖ 신에 대한 존경이나 감사의 표현. 찬미. 찬양

praise·wor·thy /'preɪz,wɚði/ *adj* FORMAL deserving praise ‖ 칭찬을 받을 만한. 칭찬할 만한. 기특한

prance /præns/ *v* [I] to walk, moving your body in a confident way so people will notice you ‖ 사람들이 알아차리게 자신 있게 몸을 놀리며 걷다. 의기양양하게 활보하다: *He started prancing around in front of the video camera.* 그는 비디오 카메라 앞에서 뽐내며 걷기 시작했다.

prank /præŋk/ *n* a trick that is intended to make someone look silly ‖ 사람을 바보처럼 보이게 하려는 술수. (못된) 장난. 농담: *Ms. Jong pulled the prank* (=tricked someone) *with the help of her college roommate.* 종 양은 대학 룸메이트의 도움을 받아 장난을 쳤다.

prank·ster /'præŋkstɚ/ *n* someone who plays PRANKs on people ‖ 사람들에게 장난치는 사람. 장난꾸러기

prat·tle /'prætl/ *n* silly or unimportant things that someone talks about continuously ‖ 사람이 계속해서 말하는 우습거나 중요하지 않은 말. 수다. 실없는 소리 – **prattle** *v* [I]

prawn /prɔn/ *n* a sea animal like a large SHRIMP, that is often eaten in restaurants ‖ 레스토랑에서 종종 먹는 큰

새우 같은 바다 동물. 참새우

pray /preɪ/ v [I, T] **1** to speak to a god or gods in order to ask for help or give thanks ‖ 도움을 청하거나 감사를 드리려고 신이나 신들에게 말하다. 기도하다. 빌다: *You don't have to go to church to pray.* 기도하기 위해 교회에 가야 하는 것은 아니다. / *people praying for peace at the Wailing Wall* 통곡의 벽에서 평화를 기원하는 사람들 **2** to wish or hope for something very strongly ‖ 어떤 것을 아주 열렬히 원하거나 바라다. 간청하다: *We're praying for good weather tomorrow.* 우리는 내일 날씨가 좋기를 간절히 바라고 있다.

prayer /prɛr/ n **1** words that you say when praying to a god or gods ‖ 신이나 신들에게 기도할 때 하는 말. 기도문: *Have you said your prayers yet?* 벌써 기도를 드렸니? **2** [U] the act or regular habit of praying ‖ 기도하는 행위나 기도하는 규칙적인 습관. 기도: *a time of prayer* 기도 시간 **3 not have a prayer** INFORMAL to have no chance of succeeding ‖ 성공할 가망이 없다: *The Seahawks don't have a prayer of winning.* 시혹스 팀은 우승할 가망이 전혀 없다.

preach /pritʃ/ v **1** [I, T] to give a speech, usually in a church, about a religious subject ‖ 보통 교회에서 종교적인 주제에 대해 연설을 하다. 설교[설법]하다: *Pastor Young preached a sermon on forgiveness.* 영 목사는 용서에 관해서 설교를 했다. **2** [T] to talk about how good or important something is and to try to persuade other people to do or accept it ‖ 어떤 것이 얼마나 훌륭하거나 중요한 것인지 언급하면서 다른 사람에게 그것을 하거나 받아들이도록 설득하려 하다. 역설하다. 권면하다: *You're the one who's always preaching honesty, and then you lie to me!* 항상 정직을 권면하는 네가 나에게 거짓말을 하다니! **3** [I] to give advice in a way that annoys people ‖ 사람들에게 짜증나게 충고를 하다. 훈계하다: *My dad's been preaching at me about not studying enough.* 아빠는 내게 공부를 열심히 하지 않는다고 계속 훈계하신다.

preach·er /ˈpritʃɚ/ n someone who talks about religious subjects, usually in a church ‖ 보통 교회에서 종교적인 주제에 관해 말하는 사람. 설교자. 목사

preach·y /ˈpritʃi/ adj INFORMAL trying very hard to persuade people to accept a particular opinion, in a way that annoys them ‖ 사람들을 짜증나게 특정한

의견을 받아들이도록 아주 열심히 설득하려 하는. 설교조의

pre·am·ble /ˈpri,æmbəl/ n FORMAL a statement at the beginning of a book, speech etc. ‖ 책·연설 등에서 처음에 하는 말. 서문. 전문. 서두: *the preamble to the Constitution* 헌법 전문(前文)

pre·ar·ranged /ˌpriəˈreɪnʒd/ adj planned before ‖ 사전에 계획된. 예정된: *We can have a driver pick you up at a prearranged time.* 우리는 예정된 시간에 너를 태우러 갈 운전사를 확보할 수 있다.

pre·car·i·ous /prɪˈkɛriəs, -ˈkær-/ adj **1** likely to become dangerous ‖ 위험하게 될 것 같은. 불안정한: *The newspaper is in a precarious financial position/situation.* 그 신문사의 재정 상태는 불안정하다. **2** likely to fall, or likely to cause something to fall ‖ 떨어질 듯한, 또는 어떤 것을 떨어뜨릴 듯한. 위태로운: *The cup was in a precarious position at the edge of the table.* 그 컵은 테이블 모서리의 위태로운 자리에 놓여 있었다. — **precariously** adv

pre·cau·tion /prɪˈkɔʃən/ n something that you do to prevent something bad or dangerous from happening ‖ 나쁘거나 위험스러운 일이 일어나는 것을 막기 위해 하는 일. 예방 조치. 사전 대책. 조심: *Always take precautions when riding your bicycle at night.* 야간에 자전거를 탈 때는 항상 조심해라. / *The nuclear power station was shut down as a precaution against any other accidents.* 또 다른 사고에 대한 예방책으로 핵발전소는 폐쇄되었다.

pre·cau·tion·a·ry /prɪˈkɔʃəˌnɛri/ adj done as a PRECAUTION ‖ 예방 조치로서 행해지는. 경계의. 예방의: *The doctors have put him in the hospital as a precautionary measure.* 의사들은 예방책으로 그를 입원시켰다.

pre·cede /prɪˈsid/ v [T] FORMAL to happen or exist before something else ‖ 다른 것보다 앞서 일어나거나 존재하다. 앞서다. 선행하다: *The fire was preceded by a loud explosion.* 큰 폭발음이 화재에 앞서 있었다.

prec·e·dence /ˈprɛsədəns/ n [U] **take/have precedence** to be more important or urgent than someone or something else ‖ 다른 사람이나 사물보다 더 중요하거나 긴박하다. …에 우선하다: *This project takes precedence over everything else, until it is finished.* 이 프로젝트는 완료될 때까지 다른 모든 것에 우선한다.

prec·e·dent /ˈprɛsədənt/ n FORMAL an

action or official decision that is used as an example for a similar action or decision at a later time ‖ 후일의 유사한 행위나 결정에 대한 사례로 쓰이는 행위나 공식적 결정. 전례. 선례. 판례: *The trial set a precedent for civil rights legislation.* 그 재판은 민권법 입법에 선례를 만들었다.

pre·ced·ing /prɪˈsidɪŋ, ˈprisidɪŋ/ *adj* FORMAL happening or coming before something else ‖ 다른 것보다 앞서서 발생하거나 나온. 선행하는. 전의: *The events of the preceding week worried him.* 지난주의 사건으로 그는 걱정했다.

pre·cept /ˈprisɛpt/ *n* FORMAL a rule that helps you decide how to think or behave in a situation ‖ 어떤 상황에서 생각하거나 행동하는 방법을 결정하는 데 도움을 주는 규칙. (규범으로서의) 가르침. 교훈. 계율: *the moral precepts of Judaism* 유대교의 도덕상의 계율

pre·cinct /ˈprisɪŋkt/ *n* **1** a part of a city that has its own police force, government officials etc. ‖ 자체적인 경찰력·공무원 등을 갖춘 시의 한 구역. 지구. 관구: *the 12th precinct* 제12지구 **2 precincts** FORMAL the area around an important building ‖ 중요 건물 주변의 지역. 주변. 부근

pre·cious¹ /ˈprɛʃəs/ *adj* **1** extremely important to you ‖ 자신에게 매우 중요한. 소중한. 귀중한: *Those memories of my wife are the most precious to me.* 내 아내에 관한 그 기억들은 나에게 가장 소중하다. **2** valuable because of being rare or expensive ‖ 희귀하거나 비싸서 가치 있는. 귀한. 값진: *a precious jewel/stone/metal* 값진 보석[보석, 귀금속] **3** SPOKEN used in order to describe someone or something that is small and pretty ‖ 작고 귀여운 사람이나 사물을 묘사하는 데에 쓰여. 귀여운. 사랑스러운: *What a precious little girl!* 정말 귀여운 작은 소녀구나!

precious² *adv* **precious little/few** INFORMAL very little or very few ‖ 아주 적은: *We had precious little time to prepare for the trip.* 우리는 여행을 준비할 시간이 거의 없었다.

prec·i·pice /ˈprɛsəpɪs/ *n* a very steep side of a mountain or cliff ‖ 산이나 절벽의 매우 가파른 쪽. 벼랑

pre·cip·i·tate¹ /prɪˈsɪpəˌteɪt/ *v* FORMAL to make something happen suddenly ‖ 어떤 것을 갑자기 일어나게 하다. 재촉하다. 촉진하다: *Massive selling precipitated the stock market crash of 1929.* 대량 매도는 1929년의 주식 시장의

붕괴를 촉진했다.

pre·cip·i·tate² /prɪˈsɪpətɪt/ *adj* FORMAL done too quickly, especially without thinking carefully enough ‖ 충분히 주의 깊게 생각하지 않고 너무 급히 한. 허둥대는. 경솔한: *Be careful of taking precipitate action.* 경솔한 행동을 주의해라.

pre·cip·i·ta·tion /prɪˌsɪpəˈteɪʃən/ *n* [C, U] TECHNICAL rain or snow that falls on the ground, or the amount that falls ‖ 지상에 내리는 비나 눈, 또는 내리는 양. 강우[강설, 강수](량)

pre·cip·i·tous /prɪˈsɪpətəs/ *adj* FORMAL **1** a precipitous change is sudden and unpleasant ‖ 변화가 갑작스럽고 불쾌한: *a precipitous drop in property values* 재산 가치의 급락(急落) **2** a precipitous action or event happens too quickly and is not well planned ‖ 행위나 사건이 너무 급속히 일어나고 잘 계획되지 않는. 황급한. 허둥대는 **3** dangerously high or steep ‖ 위험스럽게 높거나 가파른. 깎아지른 듯한. 급경사의: *precipitous cliffs* 깎아지른 듯한 벼랑

pré·cis /ˈpreɪsi/ *n, plural* **précis** /-siz/ FORMAL a statement that gives the main ideas of a piece of writing, speech etc. ‖ 글·연설 등의 요지를 나타내는 진술. 대요. 요약

pre·cise /prɪˈsaɪs/ *adj* **1** exact and correct in every detail ‖ 모든 세부 사항이 정확하고 틀림없는. 명확한. 정밀한: *I can't tell you the precise amount I paid.* 나는 내가 지불한 정확한 액수를 네게 말할 수 없다. / *We need a more precise method of measurement.* 우리는 더 정밀한 측정 방법이 필요하다. **2 to be precise** used when you add exact details about something ‖ 어떤 것에 대하여 정확한 세부 사항을 추가할 때에 쓰여. 엄밀하게 말하면: *He was born in April, on the 4th to be precise.* 그는 4월에 태어났는데 정확히 말하면 4월 4일이다.

pre·cise·ly /prɪˈsaɪsli/ *adv* **1** exactly ‖ 정확히: *I do not remember precisely what happened.* 나는 무슨 일이 일어났는지 정확하게 기억하지 못한다. / *The numbers were not precisely accurate.* 그 숫자들은 엄밀하게 정확하지는 않았다. **2** SPOKEN used in order to agree with what someone has just said ‖ 어떤 사람이 방금 말한 내용에 동의하는 데에 쓰여. 그렇고 말고요: *"So Clark is responsible for the mistake." "Precisely."* "그러니까 클라크가 그 실수에 대해 책임이 있어요." "그렇고 말고요."

pre·ci·sion /prɪˈsɪʒən/ *n* [U] the quality

of being very exact ‖ 아주 정확한 성질. 정확(성): *The weight of an atom can be measured with great precision.* 원자의 무게는 아주 정확하게 측정할 수 있다. – **precision** *adj* : *precision bombing* 정밀 조준 폭격

pre·clude /prɪˈklud/ *v* [T] FORMAL to prevent something or make it impossible to happen ‖ 어떤 것을 막거나 일어나지 않도록 하다. …을 방해하다: *Poor eyesight may preclude you from driving at night.* 약시(弱視)는 너의 야간 운전을 불가능하게 할지 모른다.

pre·co·cious /prɪˈkoʊʃəs/ *adj* a precocious child behaves like an adult in some ways, especially by asking intelligent questions ‖ 어린이가 특히 총 명한 질문을 하여 어떤 면에서 어른같이 행동하는. 조숙한. 어른스러운

pre·con·ceived /ˌprikənˈsivd/ *adj* preconceived ideas are formed about something before you know what it is really like ‖ 어떤 것에 대한 실상을 알기 전에 미리 개념이 형성된. 미리 생각한. 선 입관을 가진: *He has a lot of preconceived ideas/notions about what living in America is like.* 그는 미국 생활 에 대해 많은 선입관을 갖고 있다.

pre·con·cep·tion /ˌprikənˈsɛpʃən/ *n* an idea that is formed about something before you know what it is really like ‖ 어떤 것에 대한 실상을 알기 전에 미리 형 성되어 있는 생각. 편견. 선입관

pre·con·di·tion /ˌprikənˈdɪʃən/ *n* something that must happen before something else can happen ‖ 다른 일이 일어나기 전에 일어나야 하는 일. 전제 조 건: *An end to the fighting is a precondition for peace negotiations.* 전 투를 끝내는 것이 평화 협상을 위한 전제 조건이다.

pre·cur·sor /ˈpriˌkɚsɚ, prɪˈkɚsɚ/ *n* FORMAL something that happened or existed before something else and influenced its development ‖ 다른 것보다 앞서 일어나거나 존재하여 그 발전에 영향 을 미치는 것. 전신: *This machine is a precursor of the computer.* 이 기계는 컴 퓨터의 전신이다.

pre·date /priˈdeɪt/ *v* [T] to happen or exist earlier than something else ‖ 다른 것보다 일찍 발생하거나 존재하다. …에 선행하다: *These animals predate humans.* 이 동물들은 인류 이전부터 존재 한다.

pred·a·tor /ˈprɛdətɚ/ *n* an animal that kills and eats other animals ‖ 다른 동물 들을 죽여서 먹는 동물. 육식 동물

pred·a·to·ry /ˈprɛdəˌtɔri/ *adj* **1** predatory animals kill and eat other animals ‖ 동물이 다른 동물을 죽여서 먹 는. 포식성의 **2** eager to use someone's weakness to get an advantage ‖ 이득을 얻으려고 열심히 남의 약점을 이용하는: *The danger is from predatory foreign companies who buy other businesses and shut them down.* 위험은 다른 기업을 매입해서 폐쇄하는 약탈적인 외국 기업으 로부터 야기된다.

pred·e·ces·sor /ˈprɛdəˌsɛsɚ/ *n* **1** someone who had a job before someone else began to do it ‖ 다른 사람이 일을 시 작하기 전에 그 일을 했던 사람. 전임자. 선배: *My predecessor worked here for ten years.* 나의 전임자는 여기서 10년 동 안 근무했다. **2** something such as a machine or system that existed before another one ‖ 다른 것 이전에 존재했던 기계나 시스템 등의 것. 이전의 것. 전신 (前身): *a computer that is much faster than its predecessors* 그 이전의 것들보다 훨씬 더 빠른 컴퓨터

pre·des·ti·na·tion /ˌpridɛstəˈneɪʃən/ *n* [U] the belief that God or FATE has decided everything that will happen and that no one can change this ‖ 앞으로 발 생할 모든 일은 신이나 운명이 결정했으며 아무도 이것을 변경할 수 없다는 믿음. 숙 명. 천명. 예정설

pre·des·tined /priˈdɛstɪnd/ *adj* something that is predestined is certain to happen and cannot be changed ‖ 어떤 것이 확실히 일어나며 변경할 수 없는. 운 명 지워진

pre·de·ter·mined /ˌpridɪˈtɚmɪnd/ *adj* FORMAL decided or arranged before ‖ 이 전에 결정되거나 준비된. 예정된: *The doors unlock at a predetermined time.* 그 문들은 정해진 시간에 열린다.

pre·dic·a·ment /prɪˈdɪkəmənt/ *n* a difficult or unpleasant situation in which you must decide what to do ‖ 할 일을 결정해야 하는 곤란하거나 불쾌한 상 황. 곤경. 궁지: *It was Raoul who got us in this predicament in the first place.* 맨 처음 우리를 이런 곤경에 빠뜨린 사람은 라울이었다.

pred·i·cate /ˈprɛdɪkɪt/ *n* TECHNICAL in grammar, the part of a sentence that has the main verb, and that tells what the subject is doing or describes the subject. In the sentence, "He ran out of the house," "ran out of the house" is the predicate ‖ 문법에서 주어가 하고 있 는 동작을 나타내거나 주어를 설명하는 주 동사가 들어 있는 문장의 일부분. 술부.

"He ran out of the house(그는 집에서 뛰어 나왔다)."라는 문장에서 "ran out of the house"는 술부이다. —compare SUBJECT

pred·i·ca·tive /'prɛdɪ,kətɪv, -,keɪtɪv/ *adj* TECHNICAL in grammar, a predicative adjective or phrase comes after a verb and describes the subject, such as "sad" in "She is sad" ‖ 문법에서 "She is sad(그녀는 슬프다)."에서 "sad" 등의 형용사나 구가 동사 뒤에 놓여 주어를 설명하는. 서술적인. 술어의

pre·dict /prɪ'dɪkt/ *v* [T] to say that something will happen before it happens ‖ 어떤 일이 발생하기 이전에 그 발생할 일을 말하다. 예측[예상]하다: *The newspapers are predicting a close election.* 신문마다 막상막하의 선거가 될 것으로 내다보고 있다. / *My grandmother predicted (that) Sal and I would be married within a year.* 할머니는 샐과 내가 1년 안에 결혼할 것이라고 예상했다.

pre·dict·a·ble /prɪ'dɪktəbəl/ *adj* behaving or happening in a way that you expect ‖ 예상한 대로 행동하거나 일이 일어나는. 예측할 수 있는: *You're so predictable!* 네가 하는 짓이 뻔하지 뭐! / *The snow had a predictable effect on traffic.* 그 눈은 교통에 예상했던 영향을 끼쳤다. – **predictably** *adv* : *Predictably, the new TV series was as bad as the old one.* 예상대로 새로운 텔레비전 시리즈는 예전 것과 마찬가지로 형편없었다. – **predictability** /prɪˌdɪktə'bɪləti/ *n* [U]

pre·dic·tion /prɪ'dɪkʃən/ *n* [C, U] a statement saying that something is going to happen, or the act of making statements of this kind ‖ 어떤 일이 발생할 것이라는 진술, 또는 이런 유의 진술을 하는 행위. 예상. 예측: *I don't want to make a prediction about how popular the book will be.* 나는 그 책이 얼마나 인기가 있을지에 대한 예측을 하고 싶지 않다. – **predictive** *adj*

pred·i·lec·tion /ˌprɛdl'ɛkʃən, ˌprid-/ *n* FORMAL the tendency to like a particular kind of person or thing ‖ 특정한 유의 사람이나 사물을 좋아하는 경향. 편애: *a predilection for chocolate* 초콜릿을 특히 좋아함

pre·dis·posed /ˌpridɪ'spoʊzd/ *adj* **predisposed to/toward** likely to behave or think in a particular way, or to have a particular health problem ‖ 특정한 방식으로 행동하거나 생각하기 쉬운, 또는 특정한 건강 문제가 있기 쉬운. …의 경향이 있는. 병에 걸리기 쉬운: *The judge said that Stein was "predisposed to violence."* 그 판사는 스타인이 폭행을 하는 경향이 있다고 말했다.

pre·dis·po·si·tion /ˌpridɪspə'zɪʃən/ *n* a tendency to behave in a particular way or suffer from a particular health problem ‖ 특정한 방식으로 행동하거나 특정의 건강 문제로 고통을 받는 경향. 병에 대한 소인(素因): *a predisposition to/toward skin cancer* 피부암에 걸리기 쉬운 소인(素因)

pre·dom·i·nance /prɪ'dɑmənəns/ *n* FORMAL **1** [singular] a larger number or amount of one type of thing or person in a group than of any other type ‖ 한 집단 내에서 한 종류의 사물이나 사람의 수나 양이 다른 종류보다 더 많음. 우위. 우세: *the predominance of auto workers in our city* 우리 도시의 자동차 근로자의 수적 우세 **2** [U] the most power or importance in a particular group or area ‖ 특정 집단이나 지역에서 가장 강하거나 중요함: *American predominance in world economics* 세계 경제에서의 미국의 지배력

pre·dom·i·nant /prɪ'dɑmənənt/ *adj* more powerful, common, or noticeable than others ‖ 다른 것보다 더 강력하거나 일반적이거나 눈에 띄는. 우세한. 현저한: *The environment is the predominant social issue in the nineties.* 90년대에는 환경이 주요한 사회 이슈이다.

pre·dom·i·nant·ly /prɪ'dɑmənəntli/ *adv* mostly or mainly ‖ 대부분, 주로: *a college in a predominantly middle class neighborhood* 주로 중산층 인근에 있는 대학

pre·dom·i·nate /prɪ'dɑməˌneɪt/ *v* [I] to have the most importance, or to be the most in number ‖ 최고의 중요성을 띠거나 수가 가장 많다. 우위를 차지하다. 우세하다: *a district where Democrats predominate* 민주당원이 우세한 지구

pre·em·i·nent /pri'ɛmənənt/ *adj* much more important or powerful than all others in a particular group ‖ 특정 집단 내의 다른 모든 사람들보다 훨씬 더 중요하거나 역량 있는. 출중한. 우위의: *a preeminent political figure* 정계의 뛰어난 인물 – **preeminence** *n* [U]

pre·empt /pri'ɛmpt/ *v* [T] to make what someone is about to do unnecessary or not effective, by doing something else first ‖ 다른 일을 먼저 해서 남이 하려는 일을 불필요하거나 효과 없게 하다. 선수를 쳐서 회피하다: *Approval of the plan would preempt a strike by 110,000 city employees.* 그 계

획의 승인으로 선수를 쳐서 11만 시 공무원들의 파업을 피할 수 있을 것이다. -

preemptive *adj* : *a preemptive attack on an enemy naval base* 적 해군 기지에 대한 선제 공격

preen /prin/ *v* **1 preen yourself** DISAPPROVING to spend a lot of time making yourself look good ‖ 멋지게 보이는 일에 많은 시간을 보내다. 멋을 부리다. 치장하다: *He's always preening himself in the mirror.* 그는 항상 거울 앞에서 모양을 내고 있다. **2** [I, T] if a bird preens or preens itself, it cleans itself and makes its feathers smooth ‖ 새가 몸을 깨끗이 하고 깃털을 매끈하게 하다. 새가 몸과 깃털을 다듬다

pre·ex·ist·ing /ˌpriɪgˈzɪstɪŋ/ *adj* existing already, or before something else ‖ 이미 또는 다른 것에 앞서서 존재하는. 기존의: *Most insurance policies exclude all pre-existing medical conditions.* 대부분의 보험 증권들이 모든 기존의 병력은 제외하고 있다.

pre·fab·ri·cat·ed /priˈfæbrəˌkeɪtɪd/, **prefab** /priˈfæb, ˈprifæb/ *adj* built from parts made in a factory and put together somewhere else ‖ 공장에서 만든 부분품을 다른 곳에서 조립하여 지은. 조립식인: *prefabricated homes* 조립식 주택

pref·ace[1] /ˈprɛfɪs/ *n* an introduction at the beginning of a book or speech ‖ 책이나 연설의 처음의 도입부. 서문. 서두

preface[2] *v* [T] FORMAL to say or do something first before saying or doing something else ‖ 다른 것을 말하거나 하기 전에 먼저 어떤 것을 말하거나 하다: *He prefaced his remarks with an expression of thanks to the audience.* 그는 청중들에게 감사의 표현으로 말문을 열기 시작했다.

pre·fer /prɪˈfə/ *v* **-rred, -rring** [T] **1** to like someone or something more than someone or something else ‖ 다른 사람이나 사물보다 어떤 사람이나 사물을 더 좋아하다. …보다 …을 더 좋아하[선호]하다: *She prefers walking to driving.* 그녀는 운전보다 걷기를 더 좋아한다. / *Which color do you prefer?* 어떤 색깔을 더 좋아하니? / *I would prefer not to come on Tuesday.* 나는 화요일에 오지 않았으면 좋겠다. / *I prefer to watch movies with other people.* 나는 다른 사람들과 함께 영화를 보는 것을 좋아한다. ✗DON'T SAY "I prefer to watching."✗ "I prefer to watching."이라고는 하지 않는다. **2 I would prefer it if** used in order to tell someone politely not to do something ‖

정중하게 남에게 어떤 것을 하지 말라고 말하는 데에 쓰여: *I'd prefer it if you didn't smoke in the house.* 나는 네가 집 안에서는 담배를 안 피웠으면 좋겠다.

pref·er·a·ble /ˈprɛfərəbəl/ *adj* better or more suitable ‖ 더 나은. 더 적합한: *Anything is preferable to war.* 어떤 것이든 전쟁보다는 낫다.

pref·er·a·bly /ˈprɛfərəbli/ *adv* used in order to show which person, thing, place, or idea you think would be the best choice ‖ 자신이 생각하기에 어떤 사람[사물, 장소, 생각]이 최선의 선택인지를 나타내는 데에 쓰여. 차라리. 되도록이면: *You should see a doctor, preferably a specialist.* 너는 의사의 진찰을 받아야 한다. 가급적이면 전문의를 만나라.

pref·er·ence /ˈprɛfrəns, -fərəns/ *n* **1** if someone has a preference for something, s/he likes it more than another thing ‖ 사람이 다른 것보다 더 좋아하는 것. 더 좋아함. 선호: *We have always had a preference for small cars.* 우리는 항상 소형차를 더 선호했었다. / *Many travelers carry US dollars in preference to their own currency.* 많은 여행객들이 자국 화폐보다 미국 달러를 선호하여 소지한다. **2 give/show preference to** to treat someone better than you treat other people ‖ 다른 사람들보다 어떤 사람을 더 잘 대하다. 편애하다: *Teachers sometimes show preference to smarter students.* 교사들은 때로 더 똑똑한 학생을 편애한다.

pref·er·en·tial /ˌprɛfəˈrɛnʃəl/ *adj* treating one person or group better than others ‖ 한 사람이나 집단을 다른 사람이나 집단보다 더 잘 대우하는. 우대하는: *Bank officials denied that the senator was getting preferential treatment.* 은행 임원들은 그 상원 의원이 특별 대우를 받고 있다는 사실을 부인했다.

pre·fix /ˈpriˌfɪks/ *n* TECHNICAL in grammar, a group of letters that is added to the beginning of a word in order to make a new word, such as "mis-" in "misunderstand" —compare SUFFIX ‖ 문법에서 "misunderstand"의 "mis-"와 같이 새 단어를 만들기 위해 단어의 앞부분에 추가하는 일련의 문자. 접두사

preg·nan·cy /ˈprɛgnənsi/ *n* [C, U] the condition of being PREGNANT, or the period of time when a woman is pregnant ‖ 임신한 상태, 또는 여성이 임신했을 때의 기간. 임신. 임신 기간: *You should not drink alcohol during your* *pregnancy.* 임신 기간 중에 술을 마셔서 는 안 된다.

preg·nant /ˈprɛgnənt/ *adj* **1** having an unborn baby growing in your body ‖ 몸 에서 태아가 자라고 있는. 임신 중의: *She's three months pregnant.* 그녀는 임 신 3개월이다. / *I didn't intend to get pregnant.* 나는 임신할 마음이 없었다. **2** LITERARY full of meaning or importance that is not expressed ‖ 표현되지 않은 의 미 또는 중요성으로 가득한. 의미심장한. 시사적인. 내포하고 있는: *a pregnant silence* 의미심장한 침묵

pre·heat /priˈhit/ *v* [T] to heat an OVEN to a particular temperature before cooking food in it ‖ 음식을 요리하기 전에 오븐 등을 일정한 온도까지 가열하다. 예 열하다

pre·his·tor·ic /ˌprihɪˈstɔrɪk/ *adj* relating to the time in history before anything was written down ‖ 어떤 것이 기록되기 이전의 역사상 시기와 관련된. 유사(有史) 이전의. 선사(先史) 시대의: *prehistoric cave drawings* 선사 시대의 동굴 벽화 – **prehistorically** *adv* – **prehistory** /priˈhɪstəri/ *n* [U]

pre·judge /ˌpriˈdʒʌdʒ/ *v* [T] to form an opinion about someone or something before knowing all the facts ‖ 모든 사실 을 알기 전에 사람 또는 사물에 대한 의견 을 형성하다. …을 미리 판단하다

prej·u·dice¹ /ˈprɛdʒədɪs/ *n* [C, U] an unfair feeling of dislike against someone who is of a different race, sex, religion etc. ‖ 다른 인종·성·종교 등을 가진 사람 을 싫어하는 불공평한 감정. …에 대한 편 견. 혐오감: *There are laws that discourage racial/sexual prejudice in society.* 사회에는 인종적[성적] 편견을 버 리도록 하는 법률들이 있다. / *public prejudice against single mothers* 미혼 모에 대한 대중의 편견

prejudice² *v* [T] to influence someone so that s/he has an unfair opinion about someone or something before s/he knows all the facts ‖ 누군가가 모든 사실 을 알기도 전에 어떤 사람 또는 사물에 대 한 불공정한 견해를 갖게 영향을 미치다. (남에게) 편견을 갖게 하다. (남에게) … 을 공연히 싫어하게 하다: *Watson's wild appearance may prejudice the jury against him.* 왓손의 험상궂은 외모는 배 심원들에게 그에 대한 편견을 갖게 할지도 모른다.

prej·u·diced /ˈprɛdʒədɪst/ *adj* having an unfair feeling of dislike for someone who is of a different race, sex, religion etc. ‖ 다른 인종·성·종교 등을 가진 사람

을 불공평하게 싫어하는 감정을 가진. 편 견을 가진. 불공평한: *Kurt is so prejudiced against gay people!* 커트는 동성애자들에 대한 심한 편견이 있어!

prej·u·di·cial /ˌprɛdʒəˈdɪʃəl/ *adj* FORMAL influencing people to think in a particular way about someone or something, especially so that they have a bad opinion of him, her, or it ‖ 사람들 로 하여금 어떤 사람 또는 사물에 대해 특 별하게 생각하게끔 영향을 주어 그것들에 대한 좋지 않은 견해를 갖게 하는. 편견을 갖게 하는. 편파적인: *prejudicial remarks* 편파적인 말

pre·lim·i·nar·y¹ /prɪˈlɪməˌnɛri/ *adj* happening before something that is more important, often in order to prepare for it ‖ 흔히 어떤 일에 대한 준비 를 하기 위해서, 더 중요한 일에 앞서 일어 나는. 예비의. 준비의. 서두의: *a preliminary investigation* 예비 조사

preliminary² *n* [C usually plural] something that is done at the beginning of an activity, event etc., often in order to prepare for it ‖ 흔히 어떤 일에 대한 준 비를 위해 활동·사건 등의 처음에 이루어 지는 일. 예비[준비] 단계. 사전 준비: *the preliminaries of the competition* 경기의 사전 준비

prel·ude /ˈprɛlud, ˈprɛlyud/ *n* **1** **be a prelude to** to happen just before something else, often as an introduction to it ‖ 흔히 어떤 일에 대한 도입으로써 다 른 일 바로 이전에 일어나다. …의 전조가 되다: *The attack may be a prelude to full-scale war.* 그 공격이 전면전에 대한 전조가 될 수도 있다. **2** a short piece of music that comes before a large musical piece ‖ 긴 곡(曲)에 앞서 나오는 짧은 곡. 전주곡. 서곡

pre·mar·i·tal /ˌpriˈmærətl/ *adj* happening or existing before marriage ‖ 결혼 이전에 발생하거나 존재하는. 혼전 의: *premarital sex* 혼전 성관계

pre·ma·ture /ˌpriməˈtʃʊr, -ˈtʊr/ *adj* **1** happening too early or before the right time ‖ 너무 일찍 또는 적정한 시기 이전에 발생하는. 너무 이른. 때 아닌. 시기상조 의: *He suffered a premature death at the age of 35.* 그는 35세에 요절했다. **2** a premature baby is born before the usual time ‖ 아기가 보통보다 빨리 태어난. 조산 의

pre·ma·ture·ly /ˌpriməˈtʃʊrli/ *adv* before the time that something usually happens or is supposed to happen ‖ 어떤 일이 일반적으로 발생하거나 발생 예정인 시기보다 앞서. 너무 이르게. 조산으로:

The sun causes your skin to age prematurely. 햇빛이 네 피부의 노화를 촉진시킨다. / *a baby born prematurely* 조산아

pre·med·i·tat·ed /priˈmɛdə,teɪtɪd/ *adj* a premeditated action has been planned and done deliberately ‖ 행동 등을 신중하게 계획하고 실행한. 미리 계획된. 의도적인: *a premeditated murder* 계획적인 살인 – **premeditation** /pri,mɛdəˈteɪʃən/ *n* [U]

pre·men·stru·al /priˈmɛnstrəl/ *adj* TECHNICAL happening just before a woman's PERIOD (=monthly flow of blood) ‖ 여성의 월경기 직전에 일어나는. 월경 전의

premenstrual syn·drome /.,.. '../ *n* [U] ⇨ PMS

pre·mier¹, Premier /prɪˈmɪr, -ˈmyɪr, ˈprimɪr/ *n* the head of a government ‖ 정부의 수장(首長). 수상. 국무총리

premier² *adj* FORMAL best or most important ‖ 가장 좋거나 가장 중요한. 제1위의. 최고의: *a premier wine from Bordeaux* 보르도산(産) 최고 와인

pre·miere /prɪˈmɪr, -ˈmyɪr, -ˈmyɛr/, **première** *n* the first public performance of a movie or play ‖ 영화나 연극의 첫 번째 공개 공연. (연극의) 첫날. 초연(初演): *the 1955 premiere of "Cat on a Hot Tin Roof"* 1955년에 초연된 "뜨거운 양철 지붕 위의 고양이" – **premiere** *v* [I, T]

prem·ise /ˈprɛmɪs/ *n* FORMAL a statement or idea that you think is true and use as a base for developing other ideas ‖ 다른 아이디어를 개발하기 위한 기초로 쓰이는, 자신이 사실이라고 생각하는 진술이나 생각. …이라는 전제: *The proposal is based on the premise that the budget will be balanced in three years.* 그 제안은 3년내에 예산 균형이 이루어 질 것이라는 전제에 근거하고 있다.

prem·is·es /ˈprɛmɪsɪz/ *n* [plural] the buildings and land that a store, company etc. uses ‖ 상점·회사 등이 사용하는 건물과 대지. 구내. 부지 내: *He was ordered off the premises.* (=out of the building) 그는 건물에서 퇴거하라는 명령을 받았다. / *Do not smoke on the premises.* (=in the building) 건물 내에서는 담배를 피우지 마라.

pre·mi·um /ˈprimiəm/ *n* **1** an amount of money that you pay for something such as insurance ‖ 보험 등에 지불하는 금액. 보험료: *annual premiums* 연간 보험료 **2 be at a premium** difficult to get because a lot of people want it ‖ 많은 사

람들이 원하기 때문에 얻기가 힘든. 프리미엄이 붙어 있는. 크게 수요가 있는: *Hotel rooms are at a premium around major holidays.* 주요 휴일이 다가오면 호텔 객실의 수요는 크게 증가한다. **3 put/place a premium on sth** to think that one quality or activity is much more important than others ‖ 하나의 성질 또는 활동이 다른 것보다 훨씬 더 중요하다고 생각하다. 중요시하다: *The club puts a premium on loyalty.* 그 클럽에서는 성실을 중요시한다.

pre·mo·ni·tion /,priməˈnɪʃən, ,prɛ-/ *n* a feeling that something bad is about to happen ‖ 나쁜 일이 발생할 것이라는 느낌. 예감. 징후: *She had a horrible premonition that something would happen to the children.* 그녀는 아이들에게 무슨 일이 일어날 것이라는 끔찍한 예감이 들었다.

pre·mon·i·to·ry /prɪˈmɑnə,tɔri/ *adj* FORMAL giving a warning that something bad is going to happen ‖ 어떤 나쁜 일이 일어날 것이라는 것을 경고하는. 예고하는. 미리 경고하는

pre·na·tal /,priˈneɪtəl/ *adj* TECHNICAL relating to unborn babies and the care of women who are PREGNANT ‖ 태아와 임신한 여성의 보호에 관한. 출생[출산] 전의 —compare POSTNATAL

pre·oc·cu·pa·tion /pri,ɑkyəˈpeɪʃən/ *n* **1** [singular, U] the state of being PREOCCUPIED ‖ 몰두한 상태. 몰두. 열중: *His growing preoccupation with his health began to affect his work.* 그는 자신의 건강에 대한 관심이 증가 하면서 업무에 영향을 미치기 시작했다. **2** something that you think about a lot ‖ 많이 생각하는 일. 최대의 관심사: *I have the usual preoccupations of job, money, and family.* 나는 보통 직업·금전·가족에 대해 관심이 있다.

pre·oc·cu·pied /priˈɑkyə,paɪd/ *adj* thinking or worrying about something a lot, so that you do not pay attention to other things ‖ 어떤 사물에 대해 많이 생각하거나 걱정해서 다른 것에는 관심이 없는. 열중한. …에 몰두한: *What's wrong? You seem preoccupied with something today.* 무슨 일 있어? 너 뭔가에 정신이 팔린 것 같아 보여.

pre·oc·cu·py /priˈɑkyə,paɪ/ *v* [T] if something preoccupies you, you think or worry about it a lot ‖ 뭔가에 대해 많이 생각하거나 걱정하게 하다. 남을 …으로 열중하게 하다. 몰두시키다: *Rowan had let the deal preoccupy him completely.* 로완은 그가 전적으로 그 거

래에 집중할 수 있게 했다.

pre·or·dained /ˌpriɔrˈdeɪnd/ *adj* FORMAL certain to happen because God or FATE has already decided it || 신 또는 운명이 그것을 이미 결정했기 때문에 확실히 발생하는. 예정한. 운명 지워진

prep /prɛp/ *v* **-pped, -pping** [T] INFORMAL to prepare someone for an operation in a hospital || 어떤 사람을 병원에서 수술 준비를 시키다

pre·paid /ˌpriˈpeɪd/ *adj* a prepaid envelope does not need a stamp because the person receiving it has already paid the cost || 우편물을 수령하는 사람이 우편요금을 이미 지불해서 편지 봉투에 우표가 필요 없는. …을 선납한

prep·a·ra·tion /ˌprɛpəˈreɪʃən/ *n* **1** [U] the act or process of preparing something || 어떤 일을 준비하는 행위 또는 과정. 채비. 대비: *The church was cleaned in preparation for the wedding.* 결혼식을 대비하여 교회가 청소되었다. / *Fresh fish needs very little preparation.* 싱싱한 물고기는 거의 손질이 필요 없다. **2 preparations** [plural] arrangements for something that is going to happen || 발생할 일에 대한 준비: *They are making preparations for the President's visit.* 그들은 대통령의 방문에 대비해서 준비를 하고 있다.

pre·par·a·to·ry /prɪˈpærəˌtɔri, -ˈpɛr-, ˈprɛprə-/ *adj* done in order to get ready for something || 뭔가를 준비하기 위해서 한. (…의) 예비[준비]인: *preparatory work* 준비 작업

pre·pare /prɪˈpɛr/ *v* **1** [T] to make something ready to be used || 사용하기 위해 어떤 것을 준비하다: *The rooms still need to be prepared for the guests.* 그 방은 아직 손님을 맞을 준비가 필요하다. / *I haven't prepared my report for the meeting yet.* 나는 아직 그 회의를 위한 보고서를 준비하지 않았다. **2** [I, T] to make plans or arrangements soon || 곧 발생할 일에 대비한 계획 또는 준비를 하다: *I hope you've begun to prepare for the test.* 나는 네가 시험 준비를 시작했길 바란다. / *The Bears are preparing to play the Redskins next week.* 베어스 팀은 다음 주 레드스킨스 팀과 대전을 하기 위해 준비 중에 있다. **3** [T] to make yourself or someone else ready to deal with something that will happen soon || 자신이나 다른 사람에게 곧 발생할 일을 처리할 준비를 하게 하다: *You should probably prepare yourself for some bad news.* 아마 너는 조금 나쁜 소식을 들

을 마음의 준비를 해야 할 것이다. **4** [T] to give someone the training, skill etc. that s/he needs to do something || 어떤 일을 하는 데 필요한 훈련·기술 등을 남에게 제공하다: *My job is to prepare these soldiers for war.* 나의 직무는 이 군인들이 전쟁에 대비하게 하는 것이다. **5** [T] to make food or a meal ready to eat || 음식을 만들거나 식사할 준비를 하다: *This dish can be prepared the day before.* 이 요리는 전날 준비할 수 있다.

USAGE NOTE prepare and get ready

Use **prepare** to talk about making or producing something that is ready to be used: *Edwards only had two days to prepare the report. / This dish can be prepared ahead of time.* Use **get ready** to talk about doing the things that you need to do so you are ready for an activity: *You guys still have to get your stuff ready for school. / Natalie's upstairs getting ready for her date.* ✗DON'T SAY "preparing for her date."✗ In informal speech, you can usually use **get ready** *instead of* **prepare**: *I have to get supper ready now.*
사용하기 위해 준비하는 어떤 것을 만드는 것에 대해 말할 때는 **prepare**를 쓴다: 에드워드는 그 리포트를 준비하는 데에 단 이틀만이 걸렸다. / 이 요리는 미리 준비될 수 있다. 어떤 활동을 준비할 수 있도록 필요한 일을 하는 것에 대해 말할 때는 **get ready**를 쓴다: 아직 너희들은 학교에 가져갈 준비물을 챙겨야 해. / 나탈리는 위층에서 데이트 준비를 하고 있다. "preparing for her date."라고는 하지 않는다. 비격식 회화에서는 **prepare** 대신에 보통 **get ready**를 쓸 수 있다: 나는 지금 저녁 준비를 해야 해.

---

pre·pared /prɪˈpɛrd/ *adj* **1** ready to do something or to deal with a particular situation || 어떤 일을 할 준비가 된 또는 특정 상황을 처리할 준비가 되어 있는: *She was not mentally prepared for the shock of losing her job.* 그녀는 직장을 잃은 충격에 대한 마음의 준비가 되어 있지 않았다. **2 be prepared to do sth** to be willing to do something if it is necessary || 필요한 어떤 일을 기꺼이 하려고 하다. …할 준비[각오]가 되어 있다: *Is he prepared to accept the offer?* 그는 그 제안을 받아들일 준비가 되어 있니? / *I am not prepared to discuss this any further with you now.* 나는 지금 너와 이것에 대

해 더 이상 토론할 준비가 되어 있지 않다.
3 arranged and ready to be used, before
it is needed ‖ 필요로 하기 이전에 사용할
준비가 되어 있는. 미리 준비된: *The
police read out a prepared statement to
the press and refused to make any other
comment.* 경찰은 언론에 준비된 성명문을
낭독하고 다른 어떠한 논평을 하는 것도
거부했다.

pre·par·ed·ness /prɪ'pɛrɪdnɪs/ *n* [U]
the state of being ready for something ‖
어떤 일에 대한 준비가 되어 있는 상태. 대
비. 준비: *military preparedness* 군사 대
비

pre·pon·der·ance /prɪ'pandərəns/ *n*
FORMAL a larger number or amount of
one type of thing or person in a group
than any other type ‖ 한 집단 내에서
한 유형의 사물 또는 사람의 수나 양이 어
떤 다른 것보다 더 큰 것. 우월. 우세. 능
가하기: *There's a preponderance of
women in the orchestra.* 그 오케스트라에
는 여성의 수가 더 많다.

prep·o·si·tion /ˌprɛpə'zɪʃən/ *n*
TECHNICAL in grammar, a word or
phrase that is used before a noun,
pronoun, or GERUND to show place,
time, direction etc. ‖ 문법에서 장소·시
간·방향 등을 나타내기 위해 명사·대명
사·동명사 앞에 쓰는 단어 또는 어구. 전치
사 In the phrase "at the bank," "at" is a
preposition "at the bank"라는 어구에서
"at"는 전치사이다. – **prepositional**
adj —see study note on page 938

pre·pos·ter·ous /prɪ'pastərəs/ *adj*
completely unreasonable or silly;
ABSURD ‖ 완전히 비합리적이거나 바보 같
은. 상식을 벗어난. 터무니없는; ⑳
absurd: *That's a preposterous story!* 그
것은 터무니없는 이야기다!

prep·py /'prɛpi/ *adj* INFORMAL preppy
styles or clothes are very neat and
CONSERVATIVE in a way that is typical of
people who go to expensive private
schools ‖ 비싼 사립학교에 다니는 사람 특
유의 방식으로 스타일이나 옷이 아주 단정
하고 보수적인. 사립학교 학생[출신]의

prep school /'. ./ *n* INFORMAL a
private school that prepares students
for college ‖ 대학생이 되는 준비를 하는
사립학교. (진학을 위한) 사립 중등학교

pre·reg·is·ter /pri'rɛdʒɪstə/ *v* [I] to put
your name on a list for a particular
course of study, school etc. before the
official time to do so ‖ 공식적인 등록 시
기 이전에 특정 교과 과정·학교 등을 위한
명부에 이름을 올리다. 사전에[미리] 등
록하다 – **preregistration** /ˌprireɗʒɪ's-

treɪʃən/ *n* [U]

pre·req·ui·site /pri'rɛkwəzɪt/ *n*
FORMAL something that is necessary
before something else can happen or be
done ‖ 다른 일이 발생할 수 있거나 발생
하기 전에 필요한 어떤 일. 사전에[우선]
필요한 것. …의 필요[전제] 조건: *A
degree in French is a prerequisite for
the job.* 프랑스어 학위가 그 직무의 전제
조건이다.

pre·rog·a·tive /prɪ'ragətɪv/ *n* a special
right that someone has because of
his/her importance or position ‖ 사람의
중요성이나 직위로 인해 그 사람이 가진
특권. 특전. 대권적 권능: *It's my
prerogative as his mother to take him
out of school.* 엄마로서 내가 학교에서 그
를 데리고 나가는 것은 나의 자유이다.

pres·age /'prɛsɪdʒ, prɪ'seɪdʒ/ *v* [T]
LITERARY to be a warning or sign that
something is going to happen, especially
something bad ‖ 특히 나쁜 일이 발생할
것이라는 경고 또는 표시가 되다. (사건
등의) 전조가 되다. …을 예언하다

Pres·by·te·ri·an /ˌprɛzbə'tɪriən, prɛs-/
adj relating to the Protestant church
that follows the teachings of John Knox,
which includes strict rules for behavior
‖ 엄격한 행동 계율이 있는 존 녹스의 가
르침을 따르는 프로테스탄트 교회에 관련
된. 장로 교회의 – **Presbyterian** *n*

pre·school /'priskul/ *n* a school for
young children between two and five
years of age ‖ 2세에서 5세 사이의 어린
이 학교. 유치원. 보육원 – **preschool**
adj – **preschooler** *n*

pre·scribe /prɪ'skraɪb/ *v* [T] **1** to say
what medicine or treatment a sick
person should have ‖ 환자가 복용해야 하
는 약품 또는 치료에 대해 말하다. 처방하
다: *Dr. Dawson prescribed some
sleeping pills for me.* 도슨 박사는 나에게
약간의 수면제를 처방해 주었다. **2**
FORMAL to state officially what should be
done in a particular situation ‖ 특정한
상황에서 해야 할 일을 공식적으로 말하
다. 지시하다. …이라는 것을 규정하다[명
령하다]: *a punishment prescribed by the
law* 법률로 규정한 처벌

pre·scrip·tion /prɪ'skrɪpʃən/ *n* **1** a
piece of paper on which a doctor writes
what medicine a sick person should
have, or the medicine itself ‖ 환자가 복
용해야 하는 약품에 관해 의사가 기재한
한 장의 종이, 또는 그 약. 처방전. 처방
약: *a prescription for his chest pains* 흉
부 통증 처방전 **2** an idea or suggestion
about how to solve a problem or

improve a situation ‖ 문제를 해결하는 방법이나 상황을 개선시키는 방법에 대한 아이디어 또는 제안. 규정: *What's your prescription for a happy marriage?* 너는 행복한 결혼 생활이 무엇이라 규정하느냐?

pre·scrip·tive /prɪˈskrɪptɪv/ *adj* FORMAL saying how something should be done or what someone should do ‖ 일이 어떻게 행해져야 하는지 또는 사람이 무엇을 해야 하는지를 말하는. 규정[지시]하는. 규범적인

pres·ence /ˈprɛzəns/ *n* **1** [U] the state of being present in a particular place ‖ 특정 장소에 나타나 있는 상태. 존재, 출석: *The UN is concerned about the presence of nuclear weapons in Asia.* 국제 연합은 아시아에 핵무기가 있다는 것에 대해 우려하고 있다. / *The jury's presence is not needed for this part of the trial.* 재판 중 이 부분에 있어서는 배심원의 출석을 필요로 하지 않는다. **2 in sb's presence** with someone or in the same place as him/her ‖ 남과 함께, 또는 그 사람과 동일한 장소에서. 면전에서: *Everyone was afraid to voice an opinion in his presence.* 모두들 그의 면전에서 의견을 말하는 것을 두려워했다. **3** [U] the ability to impress people with your appearance or manner ‖ 외모 또는 태도로 사람들에게 인상을 심어주는 능력. 풍채, 관록: *The best actors always have great presence on stage.* 그 최고의 배우는 무대 위에서 항상 풍채가 당당했다. **4** [singular] a group of people from another country who are in a place to watch or influence what is happening ‖ 발생하고 있는 일을 감시하거나 영향을 미치기 위해 다른 나라에서 특정 장소로 온 일단의 사람들. (타국 군대의) 주둔. 주둔군: *the end of the American military presence in Vietnam* 미군의 베트남 주둔 종식 **5 have the presence of mind to do sth** to have the ability to deal with a dangerous situation calmly and quickly ‖ 위험한 상황을 침착하고 신속하게 처리할 능력을 가지다. …할 만큼 침착하다: *Bill had the presence of mind to call 911 after the fire started.* 빌은 화재가 발생한 후에도 911 긴급 전화를 할 만큼 침착했다. **6 make your presence felt** to have a strong effect on other people or situations ‖ 다른 사람 또는 상황에 강한 영향을 미치다. 자신의 존재를 부각시키다: *Hanley has made his presence felt since joining the company.* 핸리는 입사이래 자신의 존재를 부각시켜 왔다.

pres·ent¹ /ˈprɛzənt/ *adj* **1 be present** FORMAL to be in a particular place ‖ 특정한 장소에 있다. 출석하고 있다. 존재하고 있다: *How many people were present at the board meeting?* 이사회에 몇 명이 참석했습니까? **2** happening or existing now ‖ 현재 발생하거나 존재하는. 현재의. 현존하는: *We are unable to answer your questions at the present time.* 우리는 네 질문에 지금 답변할 수 없다.

pre·sent² /prɪˈzɛnt/ *v* [T] **1** to give something to someone, especially at an official or public occasion ‖ 특히 공식적 또는 공개 행사에서 남에게 어떤 것을 주다. 증정[기증, 선물]하다: *Mr. Davis presented the winning team with a gold cup.* 데이비스 씨는 우승 팀에게 골드 컵을 수여했다. **2** to give or show information about something or someone in a particular way ‖ 특별하게 사물이나 사람에 관한 정보를 주거나 나타내다. 제공하다: *Her book is presented as an answer to the problems of modern marriage.* 그녀의 책은 현대 결혼 생활의 문제점에 대한 해답을 제공한다. / *The way you present yourself is very important.* 네가 네 자신을 표현하는 방법은 매우 중요하다. **3** to cause something such as a problem or difficulty to happen or exist ‖ 문제점이나 난관 등이 발생하거나 존재하게 하다. (곤란 등을)생기게 하다: *The heavy rains presented a new difficulty for the rescue workers.* 폭우로 근로자들을 구조하는 데 새로운 문제가 생겼다. **4** to give a performance in a theater etc., or broadcast it on television or radio ‖ 극장 등에서 상연하다, 또는 텔레비전이나 라디오에서 방송하다: *The Roxy is presenting a production of "Waiting for Godot" this week.* 록시 극장은 이번 주에 "고도를 기다리며"라는 작품을 상연하고 있다. **5** to introduce someone formally to someone else ‖ 남을 다른 사람에게 정식으로 소개하다. 인사시키다: *May I present my parents, Mr. and Mrs. Benning.* 제 부모님인 베닝 부부를 소개해 드리겠습니다.

pre·sent³ /ˈprɛzənt/ *n* **1** something that you give to someone on a special occasion; GIFT ‖ 특별한 때에 남에게 주는 것. 선물; ㉔ gift: *a birthday/Christmas/ anniversary present* 생일[크리스마스, 기념일] 선물 **2 the present a)** the time that is happening now ‖ 지금 일어나고 있는 시간. 현재: *The ensemble will play works from the Renaissance up to the present.* 그 합주단은 르네상스 시대부터 현재까지의 작품을 연주할 것이다. **b)** TECHNICAL in grammar, the form of a verb that shows what exists or is happening now ‖ 문법에서 현재 존재하거 나 벌어지고 있는 일을 나타내는 동사의 형태. 현재 시제 **3 at present** at this time; now ‖ 현재; 지금: *We have no plans at present for closing the factory.* 우리는 현재 공장을 폐쇄할 계획이 없다.

pre·sent·a·ble /prɪˈzɛntəbəl/ *adj* attractive and neat enough to be seen or shown in public ‖ 대중에게 보이거나 나타내기에 충분히 매력적이고 단정한. 남 앞에 내놓을 만한. 보기 흉하지 않은: *Do I look presentable?* 내 모습이 남 앞에 내놓을 만합니까?

pres·en·ta·tion /ˌprizənˈteɪʃən, ˌprɛ-/ *n* **1** the act of giving someone a prize or present at a formal ceremony ‖ 공식적인 의식에서 남에게 상이나 선물을 주는 행위. 증정. 수여: *the presentation of the Oscars* 오스카상의 수여 **2** a formal talk about a particular subject ‖ 특정 주제에 관한 공식적인 말. 발표. 설명: *She gave a short presentation on/about the new product.* 그녀는 신제품에 관한 간단한 발표를 했다. **3** the way in which something is shown, said etc. to others ‖ 다른 사람들에게 어떤 것을 보여 주거나 말하는 등의 방식. 공개. 상연. 상영: *As a chef I care about the presentation of food as well as its taste.* 나는 주방장으로서 그 맛뿐 아니라 음식을 전시하는 것에도 신경을 쓴다. **4** FORMAL the act of giving something to someone ‖ 어떤 것을 남에게 주는 행위. 제출. 제시: *Most airlines will refund your money on presentation of* (=when you give them) *a letter from a doctor.* 대부분의 항공사들은 의사의 소견서를 제출하면 요금을 환불해 준다.

pres·ent-day /ˌ.. ˈ./ *adj* modern or existing now ‖ 현대의. 지금 존재하는. 오늘날의: *The colonists settled near present-day Charleston.* 식민지 개척자들은 오늘날의 찰스톤 근처에 정착했다.

pres·ent·ly /ˈprɛzəntli/ *adv* FORMAL **1** at this time; now ‖ 현재; 지금: *Presently I am unemployed.* 현재 나는 실업자이다. **2** OLD-FASHIONED in a short time; soon ‖ 짧은 시간 내에; 곧. 이내

present par·ti·ci·ple /ˌ.. ˈ..../ *n* TECHNICAL in grammar, a PARTICIPLE that is formed by adding "-ing" to a verb. It can be used in compounds to make CONTINUOUS tenses, as in "she's sleeping," as an adjective, as in "the sleeping child," or as a GERUND, as in "I like cooking" ‖ 문법에서 동사에 "-ing"를 붙여서 만드는 분사. 현재 분사. "She's

sleeping"에서처럼 진행형 시제를 만드는 복합어로, 또는 "the sleeping child"에서 처럼 형용사로, 또는 "I like cooking"에서 처럼 동명사로 사용될 수 있다

present per·fect /ˌ.. ˈ../ *n* **the present perfect** TECHNICAL in grammar, the tense of a verb that shows a time up to and including the present, and is formed with "have" and the PAST PARTICIPLE. In the sentence "Ken has traveled all over the world," "has traveled" is in the present perfect ‖ 문법에서 현재를 포함한 현재까지의 시간을 나타내는 동사의 시제로, "have"와 과거 분사로 형성된다. 현재 완료. "Ken has traveled all over the world."라는 문장에서 "has traveled"는 현재 완료이다

present tense /ˌ.. ˈ./ *n* **the present tense** TECHNICAL in grammar, the form of a verb that shows what is true, what exists, or what is happening now. In the sentence "I always leave for work at 8:00," "leave" is in the present tense ‖ 문법에서 현재 진리이거나 존재하는, 또는 현재 벌어지고 있는 일을 나타내는 동사의 형태. 현재 시제. "I always leave for work at 8:00."이라는 문장에서 "leave"는 현재 시제이다

pres·er·va·tion /ˌprɛzərˈveɪʃən/ *n* [U] the act of keeping something unharmed or unchanged, or the degree to which it is unharmed or unchanged ‖ 어떤 것이 손상되거나 변경되지 않게 보존하는 행위, 또는 손상되거나 변경되지 않은 정도. 보존[보관](상태): *the preservation of the rainforest* 열대 우림의 보존 / *The painting was in a good/bad state of preservation.* 그 그림은 보존 상태가 양호했다[불량했다].

pre·serv·a·tive /prɪˈzɚvətɪv/ *n* [C, U] a chemical substance that prevents food or wood from decaying ‖ 음식이나 나무의 부패를 막는 화학 물질. 방부제

pre·serve¹ /prɪˈzɚv/ *v* [T] **1** to keep something or someone from being harmed, destroyed, or changed too much ‖ 사물이나 사람이 크게 해를 입거나 파괴되거나 변경되는 것을 막다. 보존[보호, 보관]하다: *The house is part of local history, and should be preserved.* 그 집은 향토 역사의 일부이기에, 보존되어야 한다. / *It is important to preserve the achievements of the last few years.* 지난 몇 년간의 위업을 보존하는 일은 중요하다. **2** to keep food for a long time by treating it so that it will not decay ‖ 부패하지 않게 처리하여 장기간 음식물을 보관하다. 보존 가공하다: *cucumbers* *preserved in vinegar* 식초에 절인 오이

preserve² *n* **1 be the preserve of** if an activity or place is the preserve of a particular group of people, only that group is able or allowed to do it or use it ‖ 특정한 일단의 사람들만이 활동을 하거나 장소를 이용할 수 있다, 또는 그것이 허용되다. …의 영역[분야]이다: *Politics is no longer the preserve of wealthy white males.* 정치는 더 이상 부유한 백인 남성들만의 영역이 아니다. **2** [C] an area of land or water in which animals, fish, or trees are protected ‖ 동물[물고기, 나무]이 보호되는 지역 또는 수역. 보호구: *the Denali National Park and Preserve* 드날리 국립공원과 보호구 **3** a sweet food such as JAM made from large pieces of fruit boiled with sugar ‖ 큰 과일 조각들에 설탕을 넣어 끓여 만든 잼 등의 달콤한 음식물. 설탕절임. 보존 식품

pre·shrunk /ˌpriːˈʃrʌŋk/ *adj* preshrunk clothes are sold after they have been made smaller by being washed ‖ 옷을 세탁해서 더 작게 만든 뒤에 판매하는. 방축 가공한: *preshrunk jeans* 방축 가공한 진바지

pre·side /prɪˈzaɪd/ *v* [I] to be in charge of a formal meeting, ceremony, important situation etc. ‖ 공식 회의·의식·중요 상황 등을 책임지다. 사회를 맡다. 주재하다: *Judge Baxter presided over the trial.* 백스터 판사는 그 재판을 주재했다.

pres·i·den·cy /ˈprɛzədənsi/ *n* **1** the job or office of president ‖ 대통령의 직무 또는 지위: *Robinson has again been elected to the presidency.* 로빈슨은 대통령직에 재선출되었다. **2** the period of time that someone is president ‖ 대통령으로서의 기간. 대통령의 임기: *the early days of her presidency* 그녀의 대통령 임기의 초반

pres·i·dent, President /ˈprɛzədənt/ *n* **1** the official leader of a country that does not have a king or queen ‖ 왕 또는 여왕이 없는 국가의 공식적인 지도자. 대통령: *the President of Mexico* 멕시코 대통령 / *President Lincoln* 링컨 대통령 **2** someone who is in charge of a business, bank, club, college etc. ‖ 사업·은행·클럽·대학 등의 책임을 맡고 있는 사람. 회장. 총재. 총장: *the President of Brown University* 브라운 대학의 총장

pres·i·den·tial /ˌprɛzəˈdɛnʃəl/ *adj* relating to the job or office of president ‖ 대통령의 직무 또는 지위에 관련한. 대통령(직)의: *the presidential candidate/election* 대통령 후보자[선거]

President's Day /ˈ... ˌ./ *n* a US holiday on the third Monday in February to remember the BIRTHDAYs of George Washington and Abraham Lincoln ‖ 조지 워싱턴과 에이브러햄 링컨의 생일을 기념하기 위한 2월의 셋째 월요일인 미국의 공휴일. 대통령의 날

press¹ /prɛs/ *v*

press

1 ▶WITH FINGER 손가락으로◀ [T] to push something with your finger to make a machine do something, make a bell ring etc. ‖ 기계가 무엇인가를 하도록 또는 초인종이 울리도록 하기 위해 손가락으로 어떤 것을 누르다. (…에) …을 누르다. …을 눌러 움직이다: *Mrs. Mott pressed the doorbell again.* 모트 여사는 초인종을 다시 눌렀다. / *Press F8 to copy a file.* 파일을 복사하려면 F8을 눌러라.

2 ▶PUSH AGAINST 대고 누르다◀ [T] to push something firmly against something else and keep it there for a period of time ‖ 다른 사물에 대고 세게 어떤 것을 누른 상태로 한동안 멈추어 있다: *He pressed his hand down over the wound.* 그는 그 상처를 손으로 내리눌렀다. / *Their faces were pressed against the window.* 그들의 얼굴은 창문에 눌려졌다.

3 ▶IRON 다림질하다◀ [T] to make clothes smooth using heat; IRON ‖ 열을 이용해서 옷을 구김살이 없게 하다. 다리다; ㊉ iron: *I need to have this suit cleaned and pressed.* 나는 이 양복 한 벌을 세탁하고 다림질을 해야 한다.

4 ▶PERSUADE 설득하다◀ [T] to try very hard to persuade someone to do something or tell you something ‖ 남에게 어떤 일을 하라고 하거나 자신에게 무언가를 말하라고 설득하기 위해 대단히 노력하다. 강요하다: *Detectives had been pressing him for details.* 형사들은 그에게 상세한 진술을 강요했었다.

5 ▶MOVE 움직이다◀ [I] to move in a particular direction by pushing ‖ 밀어서 특정한 방향으로 움직이다: *The crowd pressed forward to see what was happening.* 군중은 무슨 일이 일어나고 있는지 보려고 앞으로 밀고 나아갔다.

6 ▶HEAVY WEIGHT 과중◀ [T] to put pressure or weight on something to make it flat, crush it etc. ‖ 물체를 평평하게 하고 분쇄하기 위해 그것에 압력 또는 무게를 가하다. …을 …으로 압축, 압착:

a machine for pressing olives/grapes 올리브[포도] 압축기

7 press charges to say officially that someone has done something illegal so that a court must decide if s/he is guilty ‖ 어떤 사람이 불법적인 일을 했기 때문에 법원이 유죄인지 아닌지를 판결해야 한다고 공식적으로 말하다.

press on/ahead *phr v* [I] to continue doing something without stopping ‖ 중지하지 않고 어떤 일을 계속하다. 매진하다. 밀고 나아가다: *The army crossed the river and pressed on/ahead to the border.* 군대는 강을 건너 국경으로 밀고 나아갔다.

press² *n* **1 the press** the people who write news reports for newspapers, radio, or television, or the reports that are written ‖ 신문[라디오, 텔레비전]을 위한 뉴스 보도문을 쓰는 사람, 또는 그 쓰여진 보도문. 기자. 출판물: *Members of the press were waiting outside.* 보도진은 밖에서 대기하고 있었다. / *Of course, the incident was in the national press the next day.* 물론 그 사고는 다음날 전국에 보도되었다. **2** a business that prints and sometimes sells books ‖ 인쇄 및 때때로 책을 파는 사업. 출판부: *the University Press* 대학 출판부 **3** ⇨ PRINTING PRESS **4 good/bad press** the good or bad opinion of something given by newspapers, radio, or television ‖ 신문[라디오, 텔레비전]이 제공하는, 어떤 것에 대한 좋거나 나쁜 의견. 매스컴의 호평/악평 **5** a piece of equipment that makes something flat or forces liquid out of something ‖ 물체를 납작하게 만들거나 어떤 것에서 액체를 짜내는 장비. 압축 기계: *a flower press* 꽃 압착기 / *a wine press* 포도 짜는 기계 **6 go to press** if a newspaper, magazine, or book goes to press, it begins to be printed ‖ 신문[잡지, 책]이 인쇄되기 시작하다. 인쇄소에 보내어지다

press a·gent /'. ,../ *n* someone whose job is to give photographs or information about a famous person to newspapers, radio, or television ‖ 유명 인사에 관한 사진이나 정보를 신문[라디오, 텔레비전]에 제공하는 직업인. 신문[홍보, 선전] 담당자

press con·ference /'. ,../ *n* a meeting at which someone makes official statements to people who write news reports ‖ 뉴스 기사를 작성하는 사람들에게 어떤 사람이 공식 진술을 하는 모임. (공동) 기자 회견: *The Governor held a press conference last night.* 그

주지사는 어젯밤에 기자 회견을 열었다.

press corps /'. ./ *n* a group of people who usually write the news reports that come from a particular place ‖ 보통 뉴스 기사 작성을 하는 특정 장소에서 온 일단의 사람들. 기자단: *the White House press corps* 백악관 출입 기자단

pressed /prɛst/ *adj* **be pressed for time/money etc.** to not have enough time, money etc. ‖ 시간·금전 등을 충분히 갖고 있지 않다. 시간/돈에 쪼들리다: *I can't stop now – I'm pressed for time.* 나는 시간이 충분치 않기 때문에 지금 중단할 수 없다.

press·ing /'prɛsɪŋ/ *adj* needing to be dealt with very soon; URGENT ‖ 아주 조만간 처리할 필요가 있는. 긴급한; 윤 urgent: *Environmental pollution is our most pressing concern.* (=what we are most worried about) 환경오염은 가장 시급한 우리의 관심사이다.

press re·lease /'. .,./ *n* an official statement that gives information to the newspapers, radio, or television ‖ 신문[라디오, 텔레비전]에 정보를 제공하는 공식적인 진술. 공식 발표: *The movie studio issued a press release announcing that the contract had been signed.* 그 영화사는 그 계약이 성사되었음을 공식 발표 했다.

pres·sure¹ /'prɛʃə/ *n* **1** [U] an attempt to make someone do something by using influence, arguments, threats etc. ‖ 영향력·주장·협박 등을 이용하여 사람이 어떤 일을 하게 하려는 시도. 압박. 압력. 강제력: *The group is putting pressure on the state to change the smoking laws.* 그 단체는 흡연법을 개정하라고 주(州) 당국에 압력을 가하고 있다. / *NASA is under political pressure to start a new space program.* 미국 항공 우주국은 새로운 우주 계획에 착수하라는 정치적 압력을 받고 있다. **2** [C, U] the conditions of your work, family, or way of living that make you anxious and cause problems ‖ 자신을 불안하게 하고 문제를 야기하는 업무[가족, 생활 방식]의 상태. (사태·일 등의) 절박. 긴급: *Their team always plays best under pressure.* 그들의 팀은 긴장 속에서 항상 최선을 다해 경기를 한다. / *the pressures of modern life* 현대 생활의 중압감 **3** [C, U] the force or weight that is being put on something, or the strength of this force or weight ‖ 어떤 것에 가해지는 힘이나 무게, 또는 이러한 힘이나 무게의 세기. 압력: *The pressure of the water turns the wheel.* 물의 압력으로 인해 바퀴가 돈다. / *The* *gas is stored at high/low pressure*. 그 가스는 고압[저압]으로 저장된다.

pressure² *v* [T] to try to make someone do something by using influence, arguments, threats etc. ‖ 영향력·주장·협박 등을 이용하여 사람에게 어떤 일을 시키려고 노력하다. 강요하다. 압박하다: *Some parents pressure their kids too much.* 일부 부모들은 자녀들에게 지나치게 많은 압력을 가한다.

pressure cook·er /'.. ,../ *n* a tightly covered cooking pot that cooks food very quickly using hot steam ‖ 뜨거운 증기를 이용해서 매우 신속히 음식을 요리하는 꽉 덮이는 요리 솥. 압력솥[냄비]

pres·sured /'prɛʃəd/ *adj* feeling a lot of worry because of the number of things that you have to do ‖ 사람이 해야 할 일의 양 때문에 걱정을 하는. (심리적으로) 억압된. 압박된: *Her job makes her feel pressured all the time.* 그녀는 일 때문에 항상 압박감을 느낀다.

pressure group /'.. ,./ *n* a group of people or an organization that tries to influence what the public thinks about things, and what the government does about things ‖ 어떤 것에 대한 일반 대중의 생각과 정부가 하는 일에 대해 영향을 미치려고 하는 일단의 사람들이나 조직. 압력 단체

pres·sur·ized /'prɛʃə,raɪzd/ *adj* in an aircraft that is pressurized, the air pressure inside is similar to the pressure on the ground ‖ 항공기 내의 기압이 지상의 기압과 비슷한. 기압을 정상으로 유지하는

pres·tige /prɛ'stiʒ, -'stidʒ/ *n* [U] the respect or admiration that someone or something receives, usually as a result of success, high quality etc. ‖ 보통 성공의 결과 또는 고급 품질 등으로 사람이나 사물이 받는 존경이나 칭송. 명성. 위신. 인기: *Being a doctor has a certain amount of prestige.* 의사라는 직업은 어느 정도의 명성을 갖고 있다. **– prestige** *adj* : *a prestige automobile* (=one that a rich person drives) 고급차

pres·tig·ious /prɛ'stidʒəs, -'sti-/ *adj* admired or respected as one of the best and most important ‖ 가장 좋고 최고로 중요한 것 중의 하나로 칭송받거나 존경받는. 유명한. 일류의. 신망 있는: *a prestigious award for writers* 작가에게 주는 권위가 있는 상

pre·sum·a·bly /prɪ'zuməbli/ *adv* used in order to say that something is likely to be true, although you are not certain ‖ 확신하지는 못하지만 어떤 것이 사실일 것 같다고 말하는 데에 쓰여. 가정상. 추측상. 생각건대. 아마: *Presumably, your suitcase was put on the wrong flight.* 아무래도 네 여행 가방은 다른 비행기에 잘못 실린 것 같다.

pre·sume /prɪ'zum/ *v* **1** [T] to think that something is likely to be true, although you are not certain ‖ 확신하지는 못하지만 어떤 것이 사실일 거라 생각하다. 추정[가정]하다. …이라고 생각하다: *I presume (that) this price includes all transportation and hotels.* 이 가격은 교통비와 호텔료 일체가 포함되었다고 생각한다. **2** [T] to accept that something is true until it is proved untrue, especially in law ‖ 특히 법에서 사실이 아님이 밝혀질 때까지는 사실로 인정하다. 간주하다: *She is missing and is presumed dead.* 그녀는 실종되어 사망한 것으로 간주되었다. **3** [I] FORMAL to behave rudely by doing something that you do not have the right to do ‖ 그렇게 할 권한이 없는 일을 하며 무례하게 행동하다. 뻔뻔스럽게[건방지게] 굴다. 주제넘게 나서다: *Don't presume to tell me how to raise my children!* 내 아이들을 어떻게 길러야 하는지에 대해 나에게 주제넘게 말하지 마라!

presume on/upon sb/sth *phr v* [T] FORMAL to use someone's kindness, trust etc. in a way that is wrong, usually by asking him/her for more than you should ‖ 어떤 사람의 친절·신뢰 등을 이용해서 보통 부당하게 정도 이상으로 어떤 것을 요구하다: *She has no right to presume on us by asking us to invite her friends.* 그녀는 우리에게 자신의 친구들을 초청해 달라는 뻔뻔한 요청을 할 권리가 없다.

pre·sump·tion /prɪ'zʌmpʃən/ *n* **1** an act of thinking that something must be true ‖ 어떤 것이 틀림없는 사실이라고 생각하는 행위. 추정. 확신: *There should always be a presumption of innocence until someone is proven guilty.* 유죄로 확정되기 전까지는 항상 무죄로 추정되어야 한다. **2** [U] FORMAL behavior that is not respectful or polite, and that shows you are too confident ‖ 정중하거나 예의 바르지 못하고 지나친 자신감을 나타내는 행위. 뻔뻔스러움. 주제넘음. 건방짐

pre·sump·tu·ous /prɪ'zʌmptʃuəs/ *adj* showing disrespect as a result of being too confident ‖ 너무 자신만만해서 존경심을 보이지 않는. 주제넘은. 건방진. 뻔뻔스러운: *It was a little presumptuous of him to assume he spoke for me as well.* 게다가 그가 나를 변호한 것을 생각해 보

면 그는 좀 주제넘었다.

pre·sup·pose /ˌprisəˈpouz/ v [T]
FORMAL to depend on something that is
thought to be true; ASSUME ‖ 사실이라 생
각되는 어떤 것에 의지하다. …을 전제로
하 다 ; ㊂ assume: *All your plans
presuppose that the bank will be
willing to lend us the money.* 네 모든 계
획은 그 은행이 우리에게 자금을 기꺼이
대출해 줄 것이라는 것을 전제로 한다. –
presupposition /ˌprisʌpəˈzɪʃən/ n [C,
U]

pre·tend[1] /prɪˈtɛnd/ v [I, T] **1** to
behave as if something is true when you
know it is not ‖ 어떤 것이 사실이 아님을
알고 있으면서도 그것이 사실인 듯 행동하
다. …임을 가장하다. …인 체하다: *Terry
pretended to be asleep.* 테리는 자는 척
했다. / *She pretended (that) she didn't
remember me.* 그녀는 나를 기억하지 못
하 는 척 했 다 . **2** to imagine that
something is true or real, as a game ‖ 놀
이로, 어떤 것을 사실이거나 진짜라고 상
상하다. (어린이가) 흉내내기 놀이를 하
다: *Let's pretend we're on the moon!* 우
리가 달나라에 있다고 가정을 하자!

pretend[2] adj a word meaning
IMAGINARY, used especially by or when
talking to children ‖ "상상의"를 뜻하는
단어로, 특히 어린이가 하는 말이나 어린
이에게 하는 말에 쓰여: *We sang songs
around a pretend campfire.* 우리는 모형
모닥불 근처에서 노래를 불렀다.

pre·tense /ˈpritɛns, prɪˈtɛns/ n **1**
[singular, U] an attempt to pretend that
something is true ‖ 어떤 것을 사실이라고
속이려는 시도. 속임수: *Kevin made a
pretense of enjoying his dinner, but I
know he didn't like it.* 케빈은 저녁 식사
를 즐기고 있는 척 했지만 나는 그가 좋아
하지 않았다는 것을 안다 **2 under false
pretenses** if you do something under
false pretenses, you do it by pretending
that something is true when it is not ‖ 실
제로는 아니지만 어떤 것을 사실이라 가장
하여 하는. 거짓 핑계로: *He would get
women to come into his home under
false pretenses, and then attack them.*
그는 거짓 핑계로 여자들을 집에 불러들이
곤 해서 성폭행을 했다.

pre·ten·sion /prɪˈtɛnʃən/ n [C usually
plural] an attempt to seem more
important, wealthy etc. than you really
are ‖ 실제보다 더 중요하거나 부유해 보
이려는 등의 시도. 잘난 체함. …을 뽐냄:
a nice young man without pretensions
젠체하지 않는 멋진 젊은이

pre·ten·tious /prɪˈtɛnʃəs/ adj trying to

seem more important, wealthy etc. than
you really are ‖ 실제보다 더 중요하거나
부유해 보이려고 노력하는. 우쭐해하는.
젠 체 하 는 : *There were a bunch of
pretentious people at the gallery
opening.* 미술관 개관식에 한 무리의 거들
먹거리는 사람들이 있었다. —opposite
UNPRETENTIOUS

pre·text /ˈpritɛkst/ n a reason that is
given for doing something, in order to
hide the real reason ‖ 실제 이유를 숨기
려고, 어떤 행동을 하기 위해 대는 이유.
핑계. 구실: *He got into the building on
the pretext of checking the heating.* 그
는 난방 장치 점검을 핑계로 건물에 들어
갔다.

pret·ty[1] /ˈprɪti/ adv INFORMAL **1** fairly,
but not completely ‖ 상당하지만 완전히는
아닌. 비교적. 꽤: *My parents were
pretty strict.* 우리 부모님은 비교적 엄격
하셨다. / *"How are you feeling?" "Oh,
pretty good."* "기분이 어때?" "어, 상당히
좋아." **2** very ‖ 매우: *Dad was pretty
angry about it.* 아버지는 그것에 대해 매
우 화가 나셨다. **3 pretty much** almost
completely ‖ 거의 완전하게: *I'm pretty
much done with my homework.* 나는 숙
제를 거의 다했다.

pretty[2] adj **1** a woman or child who is
pretty is attractive ‖ 여성이나 아이가 매
력적인. 귀여운: *a very pretty little girl*
아주 귀여운 여자 아이 **2** attractive or
pleasant to look at or listen to ‖ 보거나
듣기에 매력적이거나 유쾌한. 멋부린. 고
운: *a pretty pink dress* 아름다운 분홍 드
레스 / *a song with a pretty tune* 선율이
아 름 다 운 노 래 **3 not a pretty
picture/sight** very ugly, upsetting, or
worrying ‖ 매우 추한[심란하게 하는, 걱
정스러운]: *With the fire still burning at
2 a.m., the area wasn't a pretty sight.*
새벽 2시에도 여전히 불길이 일고 있어서
그 일대는 엉망진창이었다. —see usage
note at BEAUTIFUL

pret·zel /ˈprɛtsəl/ n a salty type of
bread, baked in the shape of a loose
knot ‖ 느슨한 매듭 모양으로 구운 짭짤한
유형의 빵. 프레첼 —see picture at BREAD

pre·vail /prɪˈveɪl/ v [I] FORMAL **1** to
manage to win or to remain in control
after a struggle or argument ‖ 싸우거나
논쟁한 뒤에 가까스로 이기거나 통제하에
두다. 우세하다. 능가하다. 유력하다: *The
Celtics have prevailed all season.* 셀틱스
팀은 시즌 내내 우세했다 **2** if a belief,
attitude etc. prevails, it exists among a
group of people ‖ 믿음·태도 등이 일단의
사람들 가운데에 존재하다. …사이에 보급

[유행]되고 있다: *A belief in magic still prevails in some societies.* 주술적인 믿음이 아직 일부 사회에서 유행되고 있다.

prevail on/upon sb *phr v* [T] FORMAL to persuade someone ‖ 남을 설득시키다: *I might be willing to prevail upon the committee to reconsider its decision.* 내가 그 결정을 재고하도록 위원회를 기꺼이 설득할 수도 있다.

pre·vail·ing /prɪˈveɪlɪŋ/ *adj* **1** very common in a particular place at a particular time; CURRENT ‖ 특정한 시기에 특정한 장소에서 매우 보편적인. 널리 퍼진[보급된]. 일반적인; ㊤ current: *Williams' books challenged prevailing views of US history.* 윌리암의 저서는 미국 역사에 대한 보편적인 견해에 문제를 제기했다. **2 prevailing wind** a wind that blows over a particular area for most of a period of time ‖ 거의 일정 기간 내내 특정 지역에 불어오는 바람. 우세풍(優勢風)

prev·a·lent /ˈprɛvələnt/ *adj* common at a particular time or in a particular place ‖ 특정 시기나 특정 장소에서 보편적인. 널리 퍼진. 유행하는: *The disease is more prevalent among young people.* 그 병은 젊은이들 사이에 더 유행하고 있다. – **prevalence** *n* [U]

pre·vent /prɪˈvɛnt/ *v* [T] to stop something from happening, or stop someone from doing something ‖ 어떤 일이 일어나는 것을 막다, 또는 남이 어떤 일을 하는 것을 막다. 방해하다. 예방하다: *I'm trying to prevent a fight.* 나는 싸움을 막기 위해 노력하고 있다. / *A knee injury has prevented Larry from playing tennis.* 무릎 부상으로 래리는 테니스를 치지 못했다. – **preventable** *adj*

pre·ven·ta·tive /prɪˈvɛntətɪv/ *adj* ⇨ PREVENTIVE

pre·ven·tion /prɪˈvɛnʃən/ *n* [U] the act of preventing something, or the actions that you take in order to prevent something ‖ 어떤 것을 막는 행위나 어떤 것을 막기 위해 취하는 행동. 저지. 방해. 예방. 방지: *crime prevention* 범죄 예방 / *the prevention of war* 전쟁의 방지

pre·ven·tive /prɪˈvɛntɪv/ *adj* intended to prevent something you do not want to happen ‖ 일어나기 원하지 않는 것을 막으려는 의도를 가진. 예방의. 방해의. 방지에 쓰이는: *preventive medicine* (=that prevents people from becoming sick) 예방 의학

pre·view /ˈprivyu/ *n* **1** an occasion when you see a movie, play etc. before it is shown to the public ‖ 대중에게 보이기 이전에 영화나 연극 등을 보는 경우. 시사(회). 시연 **2** an advertisement for a movie or television program that often consists of short parts of it ‖ 종종 짧막한 부분들로 구성된, 영화나 텔레비전 프로그램에 대한 광고. 예고편. 프로의 예고 – **preview** *v* [T]

pre·vi·ous /ˈpriviəs/ *adj* **1** happening or existing before a particular event, time, or thing ‖ 특정한 사건[시간, 사물] 이전에 발생하거나 존재하는. 이전의. 앞의. 먼저의. 사전의: *She has two children from a previous marriage.* 그녀는 이전의 결혼 생활에서 태어난 두 아이가 있다. **2 previous to sth** FORMAL before a particular time or event ‖ 특정한 시간이나 사건 이전에. …에 앞서서. …보다 전에: *Previous to becoming a writer, Cathy taught history.* 캐시는 작가가 되기 전에는 역사를 가르쳤다.

pre·vi·ous·ly /ˈpriviəsli/ *adv* before now, or before a particular time ‖ 지금보다 이전에, 또는 특정한 시간 전에. 미리. 전에: *They offered Bill a position that had not existed previously.* 그들은 전에는 없었던 직위를 빌에게 제의했다.

pre·war /ˌpriˈwɔr/ *adj, adv* happening or existing before a war, especially World War I or World War II ‖ 특히 세계 1차 대전이나 제2차 세계 대전 전에 발생하거나 존재한. 전쟁 전의[에]: *the country's prewar population* 그 나라의 전쟁 전의 인구

prey¹ /preɪ/ *n* **1** [U] an animal that is hunted and eaten by another animal ‖ 다른 동물이 사냥해서 먹는 동물. 먹이. 밥: *a tiger stalking its prey* 먹잇감에 살금살금 접근하고 있는 호랑이 **2 bird/beast of prey** a bird or animal that lives by killing and eating other animals ‖ 다른 동물을 죽여서 먹으며 살아가는 새나 동물. 맹금류/육식수 **3 fall prey to sth** to be affected by something unpleasant ‖ 불쾌한 것에 의해 영향을 받다. …의 포로가 되다: *More teenagers are falling prey to gang violence.* 더 많은 십대들이 갱단의 폭력에 희생물이 되고 있다.

prey² *v*

prey on sb/sth *phr v* [T] **1** if an animal or bird preys on another animal or bird, it hunts and eats it ‖ 동물이나 새가 또 다른 동물이나 새를 사냥해서 먹다. 잡아먹다 **2** to try to influence or deceive weaker people ‖ 약자에게 영향을 끼치거나 속이려 들다. 등쳐먹다. 속이다: *dishonest salesmen who prey on old people* 노인들을 등쳐먹는 정직하지 못한 영업사원들

price¹ /praɪs/ *n* **1** [C, U] the amount of money that must be paid in order to buy something ‖ 물건을 사기 위해 지불해야 하는 돈의 액수. 값. 가격: *House prices have gone up again.* 집값이 또다시 올랐다. / *The price is $49.95.* 가격은 49달러 95센트이다. / *I can't believe how high/low their prices are.* 그들의 가격이 얼마나 높은지[낮은지] 믿을 수가 없다. / *Fish is lower in price in the coastal towns.* 생선 가격은 해안 도시에서는 더 싸다. —compare COST¹ **2** [C, U] something bad that you must deal with in order to have or do something else ‖ 다른 것을 가지거나 하기 위해서 치러야 하는 나쁜 것. 희생의 대가: *Bad health is the price you pay for smoking.* 흡연을 함으로써 치러야 할 대가는 건강의 악화이다. **3 at a price a)** used in order to say that you can buy something, but only if you pay a lot of money ‖ 많은 돈을 지불해야만 물건을 살 수 있다고 말하는 데에 쓰여. 상당한 가격으로: *You can buy excellent wine here – at a price.* 여기에서 상당히 비싼 가격으로 고급 와인을 살 수 있다. **b)** used in order to say that something can be achieved, but that it involves something unpleasant ‖ 불쾌한 일을 겪어야지만 어떤 일을 성취할 수 있다고 말하는 데에 쓰여. 상당한 대가[희생]를 치르고: *She was finally made department manager, but at what price!* 그녀는 상당한 대가를 치르고서야 마침내 부장이 되었다. **4 at any price** even if something is extremely difficult ‖ 무엇이 매우 어렵다고 해도. 어떠한 희생을 치르더라도. 무슨 일이 있어도: *They were determined to have a child at any price.* 그들은 무슨 일이 있어도 아기를 가지기로 결정했다. **5 asking price** the price that someone who is selling something says s/he wants for it ‖ 물건을 파는 사람이 물건 값으로 원하는 가격. (파는 쪽의) 부르는 값. 제시 가격: *The asking price was $500, but we paid $350 for it.* 제시 가격이 500달러였지만 우리는 그것을 사는 데 350달러를 지불했다.

price² *v* [T] **1** to give a price to something that is for sale ‖ 판매용 물건에 가격을 제시하다. 값을 정하다[매기다]: *a reasonably priced pair of shoes* 합리적인 가격의 구두 한 켤레 **2** to put a sign on goods that shows how much they cost ‖ 값이 얼마나 하는지 나타내려고 상품에 표시를 하다. 가격표를 붙이다 **3** to compare the prices of similar things ‖ 비슷한 물건의 가격을 비교하다: *I've been pricing VCRs.* 나는 VCR의 가격을

비교하고 있었다.

price·less /ˈpraɪslɪs/ *adj* **1** so valuable that you cannot calculate a financial value ‖ 너무 가치있어 금전상의 가치를 계산할 수 없는. 아주 귀중한. 돈으로는 살 수 없는: *priceless antiques* 아주 귀중한 골동품 **2** extremely important or useful ‖ 매우 중요하거나 유용한: *priceless skills/information* 아주 유용한 기술[정보] **3** INFORMAL very funny or silly ‖ 매우 재미있거나 어리석은. 아주 즐거운. 믿을 수 없도록 어처구니 없는: *The look on his face when I walked in the room was priceless.* 내가 방으로 걸어 들어갔을 때 그의 얼굴 표정은 정말 가관이었다.

pric·ey, pricy /ˈpraɪsi/ *adj* INFORMAL expensive ‖ 비싼: *a pricey restaurant* 값 비싼 식당

prick¹ /prɪk/ *v* **1** [T] to make a small hole in the surface of something, using a sharp point ‖ 끝이 날카로운 물건을 사용해 어떤 것의 표면에 작은 구멍을 내다. 찌르다. 찔러 상처나게 하다: *Prick the pie dough all over with a fork.* 포크로 파이 반죽에다 두루 구멍을 내라. **2 prick up its ears** if an animal pricks up its ears, it raises them and points them toward a sound ‖ 동물이 귀를 세워 소리 나는 쪽으로 향하다. 귀를 쫑긋 세우다

prick² *n* **1** a slight pain you get when something sharp goes into your skin ‖ 날카로운 것으로 피부를 찔렀을 때 느끼는 가벼운 통증. 따끔거림: *She felt a sharp prick when the needle went into her finger.* 그녀는 바늘에 손가락을 찔렸을 때 매우 따끔거렸다. **2** a small hole in the surface of something, made by a sharp point ‖ 끝이 날카로운 것으로 만든 어떤 것의 표면에 난 작은 구멍. 점. 자그마한 상처 자국

prick·le¹ /ˈprɪkəl/ *n* **1** a long thin sharp point on the skin of some plants and animals ‖ 일부 식물과 동물의 껍질이나 피부에 난 길고 가늘며 끝이 날카로운 것. 가시 **2** a stinging feeling on your skin ‖ 피부에 느껴지는 따끔한 느낌. 찌르는 듯한 아픔

prickle² *v* [I, T] to have an unpleasant stinging feeling on your skin, or to make someone feel this ‖ 피부에 불쾌한 따끔거리는 느낌이 나다. 또는 남에게 이러한 느낌을 느끼게 하다. 따끔거리다. 따끔거리게 하다: *That sweater always prickles me.* 그 스웨터를 입으면 항상 따끔거려.

prick·ly /ˈprɪkli/ *adj* **1** covered with PRICKLES ‖ 가시로 뒤덮인. 가시가 많은: *prickly bushes* 가시투성이 덤불 **2** making you have a stinging feeling on your skin ‖ 피부에 따끔거리는 느낌을 갖게 만드는. 따끔따끔 아픈: *a prickly wool jacket* 따끔거리는 양털 재킷

pride¹ /praɪd/ *n* [U] **1** a feeling of satisfaction and pleasure in what you have done, or in what someone connected with you has done ‖ 자신이 한 것, 또는 자신과 관련된 사람이 한 것에 대한 만족감과 즐거움. 자부심: *Everyone on our team takes great pride in the quality of their work.* 우리 팀의 모든 사람들은 작업의 질에 대단한 자부심을 가지고 있다. / *They always talk about their son with pride.* 그들은 항상 아들에 대해 자랑스럽게 얘기한다. **2** a feeling that you like and respect yourself and that you deserve to be respected by other people ‖ 자기 자신을 좋아하고 존중하는 느낌, 또한 다른 사람에게서 존경을 받을 만하다고 생각되는 감정. 자존심: *I think you hurt his pride by laughing at the way he speaks English.* 네가 그의 영어 말투를 비웃어서 그의 자존심을 상하게 한 것 같아. **3** a feeling that you are better than other people ‖ 자신이 다른 사람보다 더 낫다고 느끼는 감정. 자만심. 교만. 우월감: *Beattie's pride kept him from asking for a loan.* 비티는 자존심 때문에 돈을 꾸어 달라는 말을 하지 못했다. **4 sb's pride and joy** someone or something that is very important to someone ‖ 누군가에게 아주 중요한 사람이나 사물. 자랑거리: *Ken's new car is his pride and joy.* 켄의 새 자동차는 그의 자랑거리이다. **5 swallow your pride** to ignore your feelings of pride and do something that seems necessary, even though you do not want to do it ‖ 비록 하고 싶지는 않지만 자존심을 무시하고 필요하다고 생각되는 것을 하다. 자존심을 억누르다. 모욕을 참다: *You're just going to have to swallow your pride and apologize.* 당신은 그냥 자존심을 억누르고 사과를 해야 할 것이다.

pride² *v* **pride yourself on sth** to be very proud of something that you do well, or of a quality that you have ‖ 자신이 잘 하는 것이나 자신이 가지고 있는 자질을 매우 자랑스러워하다: *Sandy prides herself on her ability to speak four languages.* 샌디는 4개 국어를 구사하는 능력을 자랑스러워한다.

priest /prist/ *n* someone who is specially trained to perform religious duties and ceremonies, for example, in the Roman Catholic Church ‖ 로마 가톨릭 교회 등에서, 종교적 임무와 의식을 수행하기 위해 특별히 훈련받은 사람. 신부.

사제. 목사. 성직자

priest·ess /ˈpristɪs/ *n* a woman with religious authority and duties in some non-Christian religions ‖ 일부 기독교 이외의 종교에서 종교적 권한과 임무를 가진 여성. 여승. 여성 성직자

priest·hood /ˈpristhʊd/ *n* **the priesthood** the position of being a priest ‖ 성직자로서의 지위. 사제직. 성직: *Angelo has decided to enter the priesthood.* (=become a priest) 안젤로는 사제가 되기로 결심했다.

prim /prɪm/ *adj* very formal in the way you behave, and easily shocked by anything rude ‖ 매우 격식을 차려 행동하며 무례한 것이라면 쉽게 충격을 받는. 깐깐한. 꼼꼼한. 까다로운: *Janet's much too prim and proper to laugh at a joke like that.* 자넷은 그런 농담을 그냥 웃어넘기기에는 너무 깐깐하다. – **primly** *adv*

pri·ma·cy /ˈpraɪməsi/ *n* [U] the state of being the thing or person with the most importance or authority ‖ 사물이나 사람이 가장 중요하거나 가장 권위를 가진 상태. 탁월함. 걸출함. 제1위. 수위: *No one ever questioned the primacy of the church in their lives.* 그들 중 누구도 자신들의 삶에서 교회가 가장 중요함을 의심하지 않았다.

prima don·na /ˌprimə ˈdɑnə, ˌprɪmə-/ *n* someone who thinks that s/he is very good at what s/he does, and demands a lot of attention and admiration from other people ‖ 자신이 하는 일에 매우 뛰어나다고 생각하며 다른 사람으로부터의 많은 관심과 칭송을 바라는 사람. 허영심이 강한 사람

pri·mal /ˈpraɪməl/ *adj* primal emotions or attitudes are very strong, and seem to come from a part of someone's character that is ancient or like an animal ‖ 감정이나 태도가 매우 강렬하며 고대 사람의 특성이나 동물성의 일부에서 유래한 듯한. 원시의

pri·mar·i·ly /praɪˈmɛrəli/ *adv* mainly ‖ 주로: *We do sell paintings, but this is primarily a furniture store.* 우리는 그림도 팔지만, 원래 이곳은 가구점이다.

pri·mar·y¹ /ˈpraɪˌmɛri, -məri/ *adj* most important; main ‖ 가장 중요한; 주요한: *I used his book as my primary source of information.* 나는 그의 책을 나의 주요한 정보의 원천으로 사용했다.

primary² *n* an election in the US in which people vote to decide who will be their political party's CANDIDATE for a political position ‖ 정치적 지위를 놓고 당원들이 누가 자기 정당의 후보자가 될 것

인가를 결정하려고 투표하는 미국 내 선거. 예비선거

primary care /ˌ... ˈ./ *n* [U] the main medical help that you get, unless your doctor decides that you need to see a SPECIALIST (=doctor with special skills) ‖ 자신의 담당 의사가 전문의의 진찰을 받아야 한다고 결정하지 않는 한 받게 되는 주요한 의학적 도움. 초기 치료[진찰]

primary col·or /ˌ... ˈ../ *n* one of the three colors – red, yellow, and blue – that you can mix together to make any other color ‖ 여타의 색을 만들기 위해 함께 섞을 수 있는 빨강·노랑·파랑의 3색 중의 하나. 원색

primary school /ˈ... ˌ./ *n* ⇨ ELEMENTARY SCHOOL

pri·mate /ˈpraɪmeɪt/ *n* a member of the group of MAMMALs that includes humans and monkeys ‖ 인간과 원숭이를 포함한 포유동물 집단의 하나. 영장류

prime¹ /praɪm/ *adj* **1** most important ‖ 가장 중요한: *Smoking is the prime cause of heart disease.* 흡연은 심장병을 일으키는 가장 중요한 원인이다. **2** of the very best quality or kind ‖ 최고의 질이나 종류의. 탁월한. 출중한. 최상의: *The house is in a prime location.* 그 집은 가장 좋은 곳에 위치해 있다. **3 prime example** a very good example of something ‖ 어떤 것의 아주 좋은 예. 최적의 예: *There are excellent children's facilities – a prime example is the Children's Science Museum.* 훌륭한 아동용 시설물들이 있는데 최적의 예는 어린이 과학 박물관이다.

prime² *n* **be in your prime/be in the prime of life** to be at the time in your life when you are strongest and most active ‖ 자신의 삶에서 가장 강하고 활동적인 시기이다. 인생의 전성기이다

prime³ *v* [T] **1** to prepare someone for a situation so that s/he knows what to do ‖ 무엇을 할지 알도록 남에게 특정 상황에 대비하게 하다. 미리 알려 주다: *The senators were primed to ask some tough questions.* 그 상원의원들은 몇 가지 곤란한 질문을 할 준비가 되어 있었다. **2** to put a special layer of paint on a surface, to prepare it for the main layer ‖ 주칠을 할 준비를 하기 위해 표면에 페인트의 특별한 칠을 하다. …을 밑칠하다. 애벌칠하다 **3** to prepare a PUMP to work by filling it with a liquid ‖ 물을 채워서 펌프를 작동시킬 준비를 하다. 펌프에 마중물을 붓다

prime min·is·ter /ˌ. ˈ.../ *n* the leader of the government in countries that have a PARLIAMENT ‖ 의회가 있는 나라에

서 내각의 지도자. 수상. 국무총리

prime num·ber /ˌ. ˈ../ *n* a number that can only be divided by itself and the number one ‖ 그 자신과 1로만 나뉘는 수. 소수

prim·er /ˈpraɪmɚ/ *n* [C, U] a special paint that is spread over the bare surface of wood, metal etc. before the main layer of paint is put on ‖ 주칠을 칠하기 이전에 나무나 금속 등의 맨 표면에 고루 칠하는 특별한 칠. 밑칠. 애벌칠

prime time /ˌ. ˈ./ *n* [U] the time in the evening when the largest number of people are watching television ‖ 가장 많은 수의 사람들이 텔레비전을 시청하는 저녁 시간. 황금 시간대

pri·me·val /praɪˈmivəl/ *adj* belonging to the earliest period of the Earth's existence ‖ 지구가 존재한 시기 중 가장 초기에 속하는. 원시시대의. 고대의: *primeval forests* 원시림

prim·i·tive /ˈprɪməṭɪv/ *adj* **1** belonging to an early stage of the development of humans or animals ‖ 인간이나 동물의 발달 단계 중 초기에 속하는. 원시(시대)의. 태고의: *primitive societies* 원시 사회 **2** very simple, uncomfortable, or without modern features ‖ 매우 단순한[불편한, 현대적인 특징이 없는]. 미개의. 미발달의. 문명화가 되지 않은: *primitive living conditions* 문명화가 되지 않은 생활 여건

pri·mor·di·al /praɪˈmɔrdiəl/ *adj* existing at the beginning of time or the beginning of the Earth ‖ 시간이나 지구의 시작[생성] 시기에 존재하는. 원시의. 원시 시대부터 있는. 최초의. 초생의: *the primordial seas* 원시의 바다

primp /prɪmp/ *v* [I, T] DISAPPROVING to try to make yourself look attractive by arranging your hair, putting on MAKEUP etc. ‖ 머리를 다듬거나 화장 등을 해서 자신을 매력적으로 보이게 하려고 하다. 단정히 꾸미다. 맵시내다

prim·rose /ˈprɪmroʊz/ *n* a very brightly colored spring flower ‖ 매우 밝은 색깔의 봄꽃. 앵초. 달맞이꽃

prince /prɪns/ *n* **1** the son of a king or queen, or one of his or her close male relatives ‖ 왕이나 여왕의 아들, 또는 왕이나 여왕의 가까운 남자 친척 중의 사람. 왕자. 왕자의 남자 **2** a male ruler of some small countries ‖ 몇몇 작은 나라의 남자 지도자. 군주. 대공: *Prince Rainier of Monaco* 모나코의 레이니에 대공

prince·ly /ˈprɪnsli/ *adj* good enough for a prince, or typical of a prince ‖ 왕자에게 걸맞게 좋은, 또는 왕자의 전형적인 특징을 지닌. 왕자다운. 훌륭한. 장대한: *a* *princely gift* 기품 있는 선물

prin·cess /'prɪnsɪs, -sɛs/ *n* **1** the daughter of a king or queen, or one of his or her close female relatives ‖ 왕이나 여왕의 딸, 또는 왕이나 여왕의 가까운 여자 친척 중 한 사람. 공주. 왕족인 여자 **2** the wife of a prince ‖ 왕자의 아내

prin·ci·pal¹ /'prɪnsəpəl/ *adj* most important; main ‖ 가장 중요한; 주요한: *Her principal reason for taking the job is to travel.* 그녀가 그 일자리를 잡은 주요한 이유는 여행을 가기 위한 것이다.

principal² *n* **1** someone who is in charge of a school ‖ 학교를 책임지고 있는 사람. 교장 **2** [singular] **a)** an amount of money lent to someone, on which INTEREST is paid ‖ 이자를 받는, 남에게 빌려준 금액. 원금 **b)** an amount of money that you have saved or INVESTed, and that earns interest ‖ 이자 수익을 올리는 저축하거나 투자한 금액. 저축[투자]액 **3** the main person in a business or organization, who can make business decisions ‖ 업무상의 결정을 할 수 있는, 사업체나 조직에서의 주요한 인물. 장. 사장. 업주

prin·ci·pal·i·ty /ˌprɪnsəˈpæləti/ *n* a country ruled by a prince ‖ 왕자에 의해 지배되는 나라. 공국

prin·ci·pally /'prɪnsəpli/ *adv* mainly ‖ 주로: *Bus drivers are on strike, principally over wages.* 버스 기사들은 주로 임금 인상에 관한 문제로 파업 중이다.

prin·ci·ple /'prɪnsəpəl/ *n* **1** [C, U] a moral rule or set of ideas that makes you behave in a particular way ‖ 특정한 방식으로 행동하게 만드는 도덕 규칙이나 사고 체계. 주의. 행동 지침. 신조. 신념: *Our beliefs are based on the principle that everyone is equal.* 우리의 믿음은 모든 사람은 평등하다는 신념에 기초하고 있다. / *She doesn't eat meat on principle.* (=because of a moral idea) 그녀는 자기 신념에 따라 고기를 먹지 않는다. **2** a rule that explains the way something works ‖ 사물이 작동하는 방식을 설명하는 규칙. 원리. 법칙: *the principle of the steam engine* 증기 기관의 원리 **3 in principle a)** if something is possible in principle, there is no good reason why it should not happen ‖ 어떤 일이 왜 발생해서는 안 되는가에 대한 적절한 이유가 없는. 원칙적으로: *In principle, you can leave work early on Friday, but it's not always possible.* 원칙적으로 당신은 금요일에 일찍 퇴근할 수 있지만 항상 그런 것은 아니다. **b)** if you agree in principle, you agree about a general plan or idea

without the details ‖ 세부 사항이 없는 대략적인 계획이나 생각에 동의하는. 대체로: *We're hoping the contract will be approved in principle.* 우리는 그 계약이 대체로 승인되리라 기대하고 있다.

prin·ci·pled /'prɪnsəpəld/ *adj* having strong beliefs about what is morally right and wrong ‖ 무엇이 도덕적으로 옳고 그른지에 대해 강한 믿음을 가진. 도덕 관념으로 꽉 찬. …의 신조를 가진: *Most of them were highly principled and able people.* 그들 중 대부분은 신조가 결고하고 능력 있는 사람들이었다.

prin·ci·ples /'prɪnsəpəlz/ *n* [plural] **1** strong ideas about what is morally right or wrong, that you try to follow in everything you do ‖ 자신이 하는 모든 것에서 따르고자 하는, 도덕적으로 옳거나 그른 것에 대한 굳건한 생각. 신조. 신념. 도의: *That guy has no principles – he'd cheat his own mother.* 그는 도의를 모르는 녀석이야. 아마 자기 엄마도 속일 걸. **2** the general rules on which a skill, science etc. is based ‖ 기술이나 과학 등이 기초로 삼는 일반적인 법칙: *the principles of geometry* 기하학의 법칙

print¹ /prɪnt/ *v* **1** [I, T] to produce words, numbers, or pictures on paper, using a machine that puts ink onto the surface ‖ 표면 위에 잉크를 바르는 기계를 이용해 종이에 글[수, 그림]을 찍어내다. …을 인쇄하다: *The books are printed in Canada.* 그 책들은 캐나다에서 인쇄된다. / *a machine that can print 60 pages a minute* 1분에 60페이지를 인쇄할 수 있는 기계 **2** [T] to produce many copies of a book, newspaper etc. ‖ 많은 부수의 책·신문 등을 생산하다. 간행[발행]하다: *We're printing 10,000 copies to start with.* 우리는 초판으로 1만부를 발행할 것이다. **3** [T] to print a letter, speech etc. in a newspaper, book, or magazine ‖ 신문[책, 잡지]에 글·말 등을 인쇄하다. …을 싣다: *Newspapers no longer print the kind of news most people want to read.* 신문에는 대부분의 사람들이 읽기 원하는 종류의 뉴스가 더 이상 실리지 않는다. **4** [I, T] to write words by hand without joining the letters ‖ 필기체를 쓰지 않고 손으로 글을 쓰다. 인쇄체로[또박또박] 쓰다: *Please print your name in capital letters.* 당신의 이름을 대문자로 또박또박 쓰세요. **5** [T] to produce a photograph on special paper ‖ 특수한 종이에 사진을 제작하다. 인화하다

print sth ↔ **off/out** *phr v* [T] to produce a printed copy of a computer document ‖ 컴퓨터 문서의 인쇄본을 만들

다. 인쇄 출력하다. 프린트아웃하다

print² *n* **1** [U] writing that has been printed in books, newspapers etc. ‖ 책·신문 등에 인쇄된 글: *I can't read small print without my glasses.* 나는 안경 없이는 작은 글씨를 읽을 수 없다. / *Just because you see something in print, it doesn't mean it's true.* 단지 어떤 것을 인쇄된 글로 본다고 해서 그것이 사실임을 의미하는 것은 아니다. **2 be in print/be out of print** if a book is in print or out of print, it is or is not available to buy ‖ 책을 살 수 있거나 살 수 없다. 책이 출판되다/절판되다 **3 the fine/small print** the details of a legal document, often in very small writing ‖ 종종 매우 작은 글씨로 씌어져 있는 법적인 서류의 세부사항: *The small print said we couldn't sublet the apartment.* 그 계약서의 세목에 따르면 우리는 그 아파트를 전대할 수 없다. **4** a picture that has been printed from a small sheet of metal or block of wood, or a copy of a painting ‖ 작은 금속 조각이나 나무판으로 인쇄한 그림, 또는 그림의 복사본. 판화. 복제 그림 **5** a photograph printed on paper ‖ 종이에 인화한 사진: *You can pick up your prints on Friday.* 당신 사진은 금요일에 찾을 수 있습니다. **6** a mark made on a surface or in a soft substance by something that has been pressed onto it ‖ 무엇이 위에서 눌러 표면이나 부드러운 물질에 생긴 자국: *a cat's paw print in the yard* 마당에 찍힌 고양이 발자국 —see also FOOTPRINT **7** [C, U] cloth that has a colored pattern on it ‖ 채색 무늬가 있는 천. 날염 천. 프린트 천: *She was wearing a print dress and white shoes.* 그녀는 프린트 천으로 된 드레스를 입고 흰 구두를 신고 있었다.

print·er /'prɪntɚ/ *n* **1** a machine connected to a computer that can copy documents from a computer onto paper ‖ 종이 위에 컴퓨터 문서를 출력할 수 있는, 컴퓨터와 연결된 기계. 프린터 **2** someone who owns or works in a printing business ‖ 인쇄업을 소유하거나 인쇄업에 종사하는 사람. 인쇄업자

print·ing /'prɪntɪŋ/ *n* [U] **1** the act or process of making a book, magazine etc. using a machine ‖ 기계를 사용해 책·잡지 등을 만드는 행위나 과정. 인쇄: *a printing error* 인쇄상의 오류 **2** all the copies of a book that are printed at one time ‖ 한 번에 인쇄되는 책의 모든 부수. 1회분의 인쇄 부수. …쇄(刷): *a novel in its third printing* 3쇄를 찍어낸 소설

printing press /'.. ../ *n* a machine

that prints newspapers, books etc. ‖ 신문·책 등을 인쇄하는 기계. 인쇄기

print·out /'prɪntaʊt/ *n* [C, U] paper with printed information on it, produced by a PRINTER ‖ 그 위에 정보를 인쇄한, 프린터로 출력한 종이. 인쇄물

pri·or /'praɪɚ/ *adj* FORMAL **1 prior to** before ‖ 전의: *We didn't know what had been discussed prior to the meeting.* 우리는 그 회의 전에 무엇이 토의되었는지 알지 못했다. **2** done, planned, or existing earlier than something else; PREVIOUS ‖ 다른 것보다 더 일찍 행해진[계획된, 존재하는]. 먼저의. 앞선; 冊 previous: *I couldn't attend because of a prior commitment.* 나는 사전 약속 때문에 참석할 수가 없었다.

pri·or·i·tize /praɪ'ɔrəˌtaɪz/ *v* [T] to put the things you must deal with in order of importance, so that you can deal with the most important ones first ‖ 가장 중요한 것을 먼저 다룰 수 있도록, 처리해야 할 것을 중요한 순서에 따라 두다. …에 우선순위를 매기다. 중요한 것부터 들다: *The mayor promises to prioritize neighborhood improvement projects.* 시장은 지역 환경 개선 계획을 먼저 이행하겠다고 약속한다. **- prioritization** /praɪˌɔrətəˈzeɪʃən/ *n* [U]

pri·or·i·ty /praɪ'ɔrəti/ *n* **1** the thing that you think is most important and that needs attention before anything else ‖ 가장 중요하게 여기며 다른 것에 앞서 주의를 기울일 필요가 있는 것. 우선하는 것. 더 중요한 것: *Let's decide what our priorities are.* 우리에게 우선적으로 중요한 것을 결정하자. **2 have priority (over)** to be considered most important and dealt with before anything or anyone else ‖ 가장 중요하게 여겨 다른 어떤 것이나 사람보다 앞서 다루다. …에 우선하다: *Help the children first – they have priority over everyone else.* 먼저 아이들을 도와주세요. 아이들은 다른 모든 사람들보다 우선합니다.

prism /'prɪzəm/ *n* a transparent block of glass that breaks up white light into different colors ‖ 흰 빛이 분열되면서 여러 다른 색깔로 나타나는 투명한 유리 덩어리. 프리즘. 분광기

pris·on /'prɪzən/ *n* [C, U] a large building where people are kept as a punishment for a crime, or while waiting to go to court for their TRIAL ‖ 사람들이 범죄에 대한 처벌로서 갇혀 있거나 재판을 받기 위해 법정 출두를 기다리는 동안 갇혀 있는 큰 건물. 교도소. 구치소: *Williams was sent to prison for six* *years for rape*. 윌리엄스는 강간죄로 6년 동안 감옥에 수감되었다.

pris·on·er /'prɪzənə/ *n* **1** someone who is kept in a prison as a punishment for a crime ‖ 범죄에 대한 처벌로서 감옥에 갇혀 있는 사람. 죄수 **2** someone who is taken by force and kept somewhere, for example during a war ‖ 전쟁 기간 등에 강제로 잡혀서 어딘가에 갇혀 있는 사람. 포로: *The captain was taken prisoner by enemy soldiers*. 그 지휘관은 적군에게 포로로 잡혔다. / *They kept/held her prisoner for three months*. 그들은 그녀를 3개월 동안 포로로 잡아 두었다.

prisoner of war /ˌ... . '../, **P.O.W.** *n* a member of the military who is caught by the enemy during a war and kept as a prisoner ‖ 전쟁 동안에 적군에게 잡혀 감옥에 갇혀 있는 군인. 전쟁 포로

pris·sy /'prɪsi/ *adj* INFORMAL too worried about behaving correctly, and easily shocked by anything rude ‖ 올바르게 행동하는 것에 대해 몹시 염려하며 무례한 것이라면 쉽게 충격을 받는. 점잔빼는. 까다로운

pris·tine /'prɪˌstin, prɪ'stin/ *adj* extremely clean, and not spoiled at all by use ‖ 지극히 깨끗하며 전혀 사용하지 않아 망쳐지지 않은. 초기 상태의. 손대지 않은 상태의: *a 1973 Volkswagen Beetle in pristine condition* 초기의 상태를 유지하고 있는 1973년식 폭스바겐 비틀 자동차 / *pristine wilderness areas* 전인미답의 야생(생태)지역

pri·va·cy /'praɪvəsi/ *n* [U] **1** the state of being able to be alone, and not seen or heard by other people ‖ 다른 사람이 보거나 들을 수 없이 혼자 있을 수 있는 상태. 비밀. 은밀: *Joan read the letter in the privacy of her own room*. 조안은 자기 방에서 남몰래 그 편지를 읽었다. **2** the state of being able to keep your own affairs secret ‖ 자기 자신의 일을 비밀로 해둘 수 있는 상태. 사생활. 프라이버시. 사적 자유: *our legal right to privacy* 법적인 사생활 보장권

CULTURE NOTE privacy

In the US and Canada, privacy is important. This does not just mean having time or a place to be alone. It also means that there are particular subjects that are considered private, that you should not usually talk about with other people. For example, you should not ask how old someone is, how much money s/he makes, or how

much s/he paid for something. You should only talk about religion or politics with friends, and it is not polite to ask someone whom s/he voted for.

미국과 캐나다에서 프라이버시는 중요하다. 이것은 단지 혼자 있는 시간이나 장소를 가진다는 것만을 뜻하지는 않는다. 프라이버시는 또한 일반적으로 다른 사람에게 얘기하지 말아야 하는, 사적인 영역으로 간주되는 특정한 문제가 있다는 것을 의미한다. 예를 들어, 남의 나이가 얼마나 되는지, 남이 얼마나 돈을 버는지, 어떤 것에 얼마만큼의 돈을 지불했는지는 묻지 말아야 하는 것이다. 친구들과 종교나 정치에 대해서만 얘기를 나누어야 하며, 누구에게 투표를 했는지 묻는 것은 실례가 된다.

pri·vate¹ /'praɪvɪt/ *adj* **1** only for use by one particular person or group, not for everyone ‖ 모든 사람이 아니라 특정한 한 사람이나 한 단체만이 사용하기 위한. 개인에 속하는. 개인 전용의: *The family has a private plane*. 그 가족은 그들의 전용 비행기가 있다. / *Rooms are available for private parties*. 방들은 사적인 파티에 이용할 수 있다. **2** secret or personal and not for sharing with others ‖ 비밀이거나 사적이어서 다른 사람과 공유하지 않는: *her private thoughts* 그녀의 개인적인 생각 / *You had no right to look at my private papers*. 당신은 내 개인적인 서류를 볼 권한이 없었다. **3** not relating to, owned by, or paid for by the government ‖ 정부와 관련되지 않은[정부가 소유하지 않은, 정부가 지불하지 않은]. 민간의. 사설의. 사립의. 사유의: *a private school* 사립학교 **4** separate from your work or your official position, and not related to it ‖ 자신의 직장이나 자신의 공적인 지위와 별개인, 또한 그것과 관련이 없는. 사적인: *The president will be making a private visit to Mexico*. 대통령은 멕시코에 사적인 일로 방문할 예정이다. **5** quiet and without lots of people ‖ 조용하고 사람들이 많지 않은: *Is there a private corner where we can talk?* 우리끼리 얘기할 조용한 곳이 있느냐? – **privately** *adv* : *Is there someplace we can talk privately?* 우리가 은밀히 얘기할 수 있는 곳이 있느냐?

private² *n* **1 in private** without other people listening or watching ‖ 다른 사람이 듣거나 보지 않고. 은밀히. 남몰래: *Miss Schultz, I need to speak to you in private*. 슐츠 양, 당신에게 은밀히 얘기할 게 있어요. **2** also **Private** someone who has the lowest rank in the Army or Marines ‖ 육군이나 해병대에서 가장 낮은 계급을 가진 사람. 사병. 이[일]등병

private en·ter·prise /,.. '...'/ *n* [U] the economic system in which private businesses can compete, and the government does not control industry ‖ 민간 기업들이 서로 경쟁하고 정부가 산업을 통제하지 않는 경제 제도. 민간 기업

private in·ves·ti·gat·or /,.. .'....'/, **private detec·tive** /,.. .'../ *n* someone whom you pay to do things such as look for information or missing people, or follow someone and report on what s/he does ‖ 정보나 실종된 사람을 찾거나 남을 미행하여 그 사람이 하는 일을 보고하는 등의 일을 돈을 받고 하는 사람. 사립탐정

private parts /,.. './, **pri·vates** /'praɪvɪts/ *n* [plural] INFORMAL an expression meaning "sex organs," used in order to avoid naming them directly ‖ 성기를 직접 호칭하는 것을 피하는 데에 사용하는 "성기"를 의미하는 표현. 음부

pri·va·tion /praɪ'veɪʃən/ *n* [C, U] FORMAL a lack of the things that everyone needs, such as food, warmth, and shelter ‖ 음식·따뜻함·안식처 등의 모든 사람들이 필요로 하는 것의 부족. 결핍. 궁핍

pri·vat·ize /'praɪvə,taɪz/ *v* [T] if a government privatizes an industry, service etc. that it controls or owns, it sells it to private owners —compare NATIONALIZE, SOCIALIZE ‖ 정부가 관리하거나 소유하는 산업·서비스 등을 민간 소유자들에게 팔다. …을 민영화하다

priv·i·lege /'prɪvlɪdʒ, -vəlɪdʒ/ *n* **1** a special advantage that is given only to one person or group of people ‖ 한 사람이나 한 무리의 사람들에만 주어지는 특별한 혜택. 특권. 특전: *In some poorer countries, education is a privilege, not a right.* 몇몇 가난한 나라에서 교육은 당연한 권리가 아니라 특권이다. **2** [U] the state of having more advantages or rights than other people, for example because you are rich or powerful ‖ 예를 들어 부자이거나 권력이 있어서 다른 사람보다 더 많은 혜택과 권리를 가지고 있는 상태. 특권: *a position of privilege* 특권 신분 **3** [singular] something that you are lucky to have the chance to do, and that you enjoy very much ‖ 운 좋게 어떤 것을 할 기회를 가지게 되어 매우 많이 즐기는 것. 영광: *It's been a privilege to meet you, sir.* 당신을 만나 뵙게 되어 영광입니다. – **privileged** *adj*

priv·y¹ /'prɪvi/ *adj* FORMAL **privy to sth** sharing secret knowledge of something ‖ 어떤 일에 대한 비밀 정보를 나누는. 내밀히 관여하는. 내통하는: *Only three people were privy to our plans.* 단지 세 명만이 우리의 계획에 내밀히 관여하고 있었다.

priv·y² *n* ⇨ OUTHOUSE

prize¹ /praɪz/ *n* something that is given to someone who is successful in a competition, race, game of chance etc. ‖ 시합·경주·운에 맡기고 하는 게임 등에서 승리한 사람에게 주어지는 것. 상. 상품. 상금: *Her roses won first/second/third prize at the flower show.* 그녀의 장미는 꽃 전시회에서 1등[2등, 3등] 상을 수상했다.

prize² *adj* **1** good enough to win a prize or to have won a prize ‖ 상을 탈 만큼 또는 상을 탄 만큼 충분히 좋은. 상을 받을 만한: *prize cattle* 입상한 소 **2 prize money** money that is given to the person who wins a competition, race etc. ‖ 시합·경주 등에서 승리한 사람에게 주어지는 돈. 상금

prize³ *v* [T] to think that someone or something is very important or valuable ‖ 사람이나 사물이 매우 중요하거나 가치 있다고 생각하다. …을 소중히 하다. 귀중히 여기다: *a necklace that his mother had prized* 그의 어머니가 소중하게 여겼던 목걸이

prized /praɪzd/ *adj* very important or valuable to someone ‖ 누구에게 매우 중요하거나 가치 있는: *Nick's motorbike is his most prized possession.* 닉의 오토바이는 그의 보물 1호이다.

prize·fight /'praɪzfaɪt/ *n* a BOXING match in which the competitors are paid ‖ 경쟁자들이 돈을 받고 하는 권투 시합. 현상[프로] 권투 시합

pro /proʊ/ *n* **1** INFORMAL ⇨ PROFESSIONAL²: *It's a pleasure to watch a real pro like Browning skate.* 브라우닝 같은 진짜 프로 선수가 스케이트를 타는 것을 보는 일은 즐겁다. **2** something that is an advantage ‖ 이득이 되는 것. 유리한 점: *We discussed the pros and cons* (=the advantages and disadvantages) *of starting our own business.* 우리는 우리 자신의 사업을 시작하는 것에 대한 유리한 점과 불리한 점에 대해 토의했다.

prob·a·bil·i·ty /,prɑbə'bɪləti/ *n* **1** [singular, U] how likely it is that something will happen, exist, or be true ‖ 어떤 일이 일어날[존재할, 사실일] 법한 정도. 개연성. 있을 법한 가망: *There is little probability of the hostages being* *released soon.* 인질이 곧 풀려날 가능성은 회박하다. **2 in all probability** very probably ‖ 매우 가망이 있는. 아마. 십중팔구: *There will, in all probability, be parts that you do not understand.* 아마도 네가 이해하지 못하는 부분이 있을 것이다. **3** something that is likely to happen or exist ‖ 일어나거나 존재할 것 같은 일. (실제로) 일어남직함[한 사태]: *War is a real probability unless the talks succeed.* 그 회담이 성공하지 못한다면 전쟁이 진짜 일어날지도 모른다.

prob·a·ble /'prɑbəbəl/ *adj* likely to happen, exist, or be true ‖ 일어날[존재할, 사실일] 것 같은. 있음직한. 가망이 있는: *It is highly probable that the mayor will be reelected.* 그 시장은 재선 출마될 가능성이 아주 높다. / *The probable cause of the plane crash was ice on the wings.* 그 비행기 추락의 유력한 원인은 날개에 덮인 얼음이다.

prob·a·bly /'prɑbəbli/ *adv* likely to happen, exist, or be true ‖ 일어날[존재할, 사실일] 것 같이. 아마. 대개는. 십중팔구는: *We'll probably go to Florida next year.* 우리는 아마도 내년에 플로리다로 갈 것이다.

pro·ba·tion /prou'beɪʃən/ *n* [U] **1** a system that allows some criminals to leave prison early or not to go to prison at all, if they promise to behave well for a specific period of time ‖ 일부 범죄인들이 특정 기간 동안 (죄를 다시 짓지 않고) 바르게 처신할 것을 약속하면, (형기보다) 빨리 출옥을 허용하거나 교도소에 가지 않도록 허용하는 제도. 가석방. 집행유예: *Preston's been on probation for three years.* 프레스톤은 3년간의 집행유예 기간에 있다. **2** a period of time during which someone who has just started a job is tested to see whether s/he is suitable for what s/he is doing ‖ 일을 막 시작한 사람이 하고 있는 일에 적합한지 알아보기 위해 검증 받는 동안의 기간. 견습 기간 – **probationary** /prou'beɪʃə,nɛri/ *adj*

probation of·fi·cer /.'.. ,.../ *n* someone whose job is to watch, advise, and help people who have broken the law and are on PROBATION ‖ 법을 어겨 가석방[집행유예] 중인 사람을 감시하고 충고하며 도와주는 직업인. 보호 감찰관

probe¹ /proub/ *v* [I, T] **1** to ask questions in order to find things out ‖ 실체를 알아내기 위해 질문을 하다. 철저히 조사하다: *Reporters are already probing into the affair.* 기자들은 이미 그 사건에 대해 철저히 조사하고 있다. **2** to look for something or examine something, using

a long thin instrument ‖ 가늘고 긴 기구를 사용해 어떤 것을 찾거나 조사하다. 탐침으로 살피다. 정밀 조사하다 – **probing** *adj*

probe² *n* **1** a long thin instrument that doctors and scientists use to examine parts of the body ‖ 의사와 과학자들이 신체 부위를 조사하기 위해 사용하는 가늘고 긴 도구. 탐침 **2** a SPACECRAFT without people in it, that is sent into space to collect information ‖ 정보를 수집하기 해 우주로 보내는, 사람이 타지 않은 우주선. 우주 탐사기 **3** a word meaning a very thorough process of asking questions in order to find things out, used especially by newspapers; INQUIRY ‖ 특히 신문에서 쓰여, 실체를 발견하기 위해 매우 철저히 질문하는 과정을 의미하는 말. 적발 조사; ⑩ inquiry

prob·lem /'prɑbləm/ *n* **1** a difficult situation or person that has to be dealt with or thought about ‖ 처리하거나 고려해야 할 어려운 상황이나 사람. 문제점. 곤란한 일. 다루기 어려운 사람: *I've been having a few problems with my car.* 내 차에 약간의 문제점이 있었다. / *Wilson insists there isn't a drug problem in the school.* 윌슨은 교내에 마약 문제가 없다고 주장한다. / *When did the problem first arise/occur?* 그 문제가 처음으로 일어난 때가 언제였니? ✗DON'T SAY "When did the problem happen?"✗ "When did the problem happen?"이라고는 하지 않는다. / *Unemployment remains a serious problem here.* 이곳에는 실업이라는 심각한 문제점이 남아 있다. ✗DON'T SAY "an important problem."✗ "an important problem"이라고는 하지 않는다. **2** a question that must be answered, especially one relating to numbers or facts ‖ 대답해야 하는, 특히 숫자나 사실과 관련된 질문. 문제. 과제: *The test will have 20 algebra problems.* 그 시험에는 대수학 20문제가 나올 것이다.

SPOKEN PHRASES

3 no problem a) used in order to say that you are very willing to do something ‖ 어떤 일을 아주 기꺼이 하겠다고 말하는 데에 쓰여. 문제 없어. 좋습니다: *"Could you go to the store for me?" "Sure, no problem."* "시장 좀 봐다 줄 수 있어요?" "물론, 그럴게요." **b)** used after someone has thanked you or said s/he is sorry ‖ 남이 자신에게 감사함이나 미안함을 표현한 후에 쓰여. 천만에요. 괜찮습니다: *"Thanks so* *much for all your help." "Oh, no problem." "도와 주셔서 정말 감사합니다." "천만에요."* **4 that's your/his/ their etc. problem** used in order to say that someone else is responsible for dealing with a situation, not you ‖ 상황을 해결하는 데에 책임이 있는 사람은 자신이 아니라 다른 사람이라고 말하는 데에 쓰여. 네가/그가/그들이 알아서 할 문제이다: *If you can't get yourself there on time, that's your problem.* 만일 네가 정시에 그곳에 도착하지 못하더라도 그건 내가 알 바 아니다. **5 What's your problem?** used in order to ask someone what is wrong, in a way that shows you think s/he is not being reasonable ‖ 남이 이치에 맞지 않는 상태라는 자신의 생각을 나타내어, 무엇이 잘못된 건지 남에게 묻는 데에 쓰여. 문제가 뭔데? 왜 그래?: *Look, what's your problem? It's my decision!* 이봐, 뭐가 문제야? 그건 내 결정이란 말야!

prob·lem·at·ic /ˌprɑbləˈmætɪk/ *adj* full of problems and difficult to deal with ‖ 문제로 가득하며 다루기 어려운. 문제의. 문제가 되는. 해결이 어려운: *The situation has become somewhat problematic.* 그 상황은 다소 해결하기 어려워졌다. **– problematically** *adv*

pro·ce·dure /prəˈsidʒɚ/ *n* [C, U] the correct or normal way of doing something ‖ 어떤 것을 하는 옳거나 정상적인 방식. 절차. 과정: *the procedure for shutting down a computer* 컴퓨터를 끄는 절차 / *a common medical procedure* (=treatment that follows a set of rules) 통상적인 의료 절차 **– procedural** *adj*

pro·ceed /prəˈsid, prou-/ *v* [I] **1** to continue to do something that has already been started, especially after a short pause ‖ 특히 잠시 쉰 후에 이미 시작한 것을 계속해서 하다. 속행하다. 진행하다: *Talks are proceeding smoothly.* 회담은 원만하게 속행되고 있다. **2 proceed to do sth** to do something next ‖ 다음으로 어떤 것을 하다. 그 다음[이어서] …하다: *Larry joined us, and proceeded to take over the whole conversation.* 래리는 우리들 사이에 낀 다음 전체 대화를 주도해 나갔다. **3** FORMAL to move in a particular direction ‖ 특정한 방향으로 움직이다. 나아가다. 전진하다: *Please proceed to the nearest exit.* 가장 가까운 출구로 가세요.

pro·ceed·ings /prəˈsidɪŋz, prou-/ *n* [plural] **1** an event or series of actions ‖ 사건이나 일련의 행동. 진행. 절차. 처리: *We watched the proceedings from a third floor window.* 우리는 3층 창문에서 그 진행 과정을 지켜보았다. **2** actions taken in a law court or in a legal case ‖ 법정이나 법적인 사건에서 행해지는 행위. 소송: *legal proceedings* 법적인 소송 절차

pro·ceeds /ˈprousidz/ *n* [plural] the money that has been gained from doing something or selling something ‖ 어떤 것을 하거나 팔아서 얻은 돈. 매상고. 수익. 수입: *All the proceeds from the bake sale will go toward buying new uniforms.* 빵을 판 모든 수익금은 새 유니폼을 사는 데 쓰일 것이다.

pro·cess¹ /ˈprɑsɛs, ˈprou-/ *n* **1** a series of actions, developments, or changes that happen naturally ‖ 자연스럽게 일어나는 일련의 행위[발달, 변화]. 일련의 작용: *the aging process* 노화 작용 / *the digestive process* 소화 작용 **2** a series of actions that someone does in order to achieve a particular result ‖ 사람이 특정한 결과를 이루기 위해 하는 일련의 행동. 과정: *She's learning to read, but it's a slow process.* 그녀는 읽기를 배우고 있지만 그 진행 과정이 더디다. **3 be in the process of doing sth** to have started doing something and not yet be finished ‖ 어떤 일을 하기 시작해서 아직 끝내지 못하다. …이 진행 중에 있다: *We're in the process of moving to a new office building.* 우리는 새 사무실 건물로 이전하는 중이다. **4** a system or a treatment of materials that is used for producing goods ‖ 제품을 생산하는 데에 사용되는 시스템이나 원료의 처리 과정. 제조법. 제조 공정: *an industrial process* 산업 공정

process² *v* [T] **1** to treat food or some other substance by adding other substances to it, for example to give it color or keep it fresh ‖ 색깔을 내거나 신선도를 유지시키는 등의 목적으로, 음식이나 다른 어떤 물질에 또 다른 물질을 추가해서 처리하다. 가공하다: *processed cheese* 가공된 치즈 **2** to deal with information in an official way ‖ 공식적으로 정보를 다루다. 처리[정리]하다: *Your membership application is still being processed.* 당신의 회원 신청서는 아직 처리 중에 있습니다. **3** to put information into a computer to be examined ‖ 검사될 수 있게 자료를 컴퓨터에 입력하다. 처리하다 **– processing** *n* [U]

pro·ces·sion /prəˈsɛʃən/ *n* **1** a line of people or vehicles moving slowly as part of a ceremony ‖ 의식의 한 부분으로서 사

람들이나 차량 등이 천천히 움직이는 줄. 행렬: *a funeral procession* 장례 행렬 — compare PARADE¹ **2** several people or things of the same kind, appearing or happening one after the other ‖ 잇따라 나타나거나 일어나는 같은 종류의 여러 사람이나 사물. 출현: *an endless procession of people giving speeches* 연설하는 사람들의 끊임없는 출현

pro·ces·sion·al /prəˈsɛʃənl/ *adj* relating to or used during a PROCESSION ‖ 행렬과 관련되거나 행진 중에 사용되는. 행렬(용)의: *processional music* 행진곡

pro·ces·sor /ˈprɑsɛsɚ/ *n* ⇨ CPU —see also FOOD PROCESSOR

pro·claim /proʊˈkleɪm, prə-/ *v* [T] FORMAL to say officially and publicly that something is true or exists ‖ 어떤 것이 사실이거나 존재한다고 공식적·공개적으로 말하다. 공표[발표]하다. 선언하다: *A national holiday was proclaimed.* 국경일이 공표되었다.

proc·la·ma·tion /ˌprɑkləˈmeɪʃən/ *n* an official public statement that tells citizens what will be done about something important ‖ 중요한 것이 행해질 것이라고 시민들에게 공식적·공개적으로 알리는 발표. 선언. 공표. 공포: *the Emancipation Proclamation* (=that freed the US SLAVES) 미국의 노예 해방 선언

pro·cras·ti·nate /prəˈkræstəˌneɪt/ *v* [I] to delay doing something that you ought to do ‖ 해야 할 일을 하지 않고 미루다. 지연되다. 질질 끌다. 꾸물대다: *If you keep on procrastinating, you won't have time to do it right.* 계속 꾸물댄다면 그것을 시간 내에 제대로 할 수 없을 것이다. – **procrastination** /prəˌkræstəˈneɪʃən/ *n* [U] – **procrastinator** /prəˈkræstəˌneɪtɚ/ *n*

pro·cre·ate /ˈproʊkriˌeɪt/ *v* [I, T] FORMAL to produce children or baby animals ‖ 아기 또는 동물의 새끼를 낳다 – **procreation** /ˌproʊkriˈeɪʃən/ *n* [U]

pro·cure /proʊˈkyʊr, prə-/ *v* [T] FORMAL to obtain something, especially something that is difficult to get ‖ 특히 얻기 힘든 것을 획득하다. 손에 넣다. 입수하다: *Clark was accused of procuring guns for the rebels.* 클라크는 반군에게 총기를 대준 혐의로 기소되었다. – **procurement** *n* [U]

prod¹ /prɑd/ *v* **-dded, -dding** [I, T] **1** to strongly encourage someone to do something ‖ 남이 어떤 것을 하도록 강하게 자극을 주다. 불러일으키다. …하도록 재촉하다: *We had to prod Randall into applying for the job.* 우린 랜달이 그 일자

리에 지원하게 재촉해야 했다. **2** ⇨ POKE

prod² *n* something you POKE animals with in order to make them move in a particular direction ‖ 동물들을 특정한 방향으로 움직이게 하기 위해 쿡쿡 찌르는 것. 가축몰이용 막대

prod·i·gal /ˈprɑdɪgəl/ *adj* FORMAL tending to waste what you have, especially money ‖ 자신이 소유한 것, 특히 돈을 낭비하는 경향이 있는. 낭비하는. 방탕한

pro·di·gious /prəˈdɪdʒəs/ *adj* FORMAL impressively large or skillful in a way that surprises people; AMAZING ‖ 사람들이 깜짝 놀랄 정도로 엄청나게 크거나 솜씨가 좋은. 거대한. 막대한. 비상한. 보통이 아닌; 㕵 amazing: *He eats a prodigious amount of food.* 그는 음식을 엄청나게 먹는다. / *a prodigious feat* (=impressive achievement) 대단한 위업 – **prodigiously** *adv*

prod·i·gy /ˈprɑdədʒi/ *n* a young person who is extremely good at doing something ‖ 어떤 것을 하는 데 대단히 능란한 어린 사람. 천재. 신동: *Mozart was a child prodigy.* 모짜르트는 신동이었다. —compare GENIUS

pro·duce¹ /prəˈdus/ *v* **1** [T] to grow something or make it naturally ‖ 어떤 것을 기르거나 자연적으로 만들어내다. 재배하다. …을 산출하다: *This region produces most of the state's corn.* 이 지역은 주의 옥수수의 대부분을 생산한다. / *Trees produce carbon dioxide.* 나무는 이산화탄소를 만들어낸다. **2** [T] to make something happen or develop, or have a particular result or effect ‖ 어떤 것을 발생시키거나 발달시키다, 또는 특정한 결과나 영향력을 가지다. …을 불러 일으키다. 결과를 내다: *The announcement produced shouts of anger.* 그 발표로 분노의 아우성이 터져 나왔다. / *The drug can produce side effects in some people.* 그 약은 일부 사람들에게는 부작용을 일으킬 수 있다. **3** [T] to show something so it can be seen or considered ‖ 보거나 고려할 수 있게 사물을 보이다. …을 제시하다. 보여주다: *Officer Ryan asked the suspect to produce his driver's license.* 라이언 경관은 용의자에게 운전 면허증을 보여 달라고 요청했다. **4** [I, T] to make something using an industrial process ‖ 산업 공정을 이용해 물건을 만들다. 제조하다: *The challenge is to produce cheap electricity.* 그 시도는 값싼 전력을 만들어 내기 위한 것이다. **5** [T] to control the preparation of a play, movie etc. and then show it to the public ‖ 연극·영화 등

의 준비를 총괄해서 대중에게 보이다. 제작[연출]하다 **6** [T] to make something using skill and imagination ‖ 기술과 상상력을 사용해서 어떤 것을 만들다: *Diane produced a fantastic meal.* 다이앤은 환상적인 음식을 만들었다.

prod·uce² /ˈprɑdus, ˈprou-/ *n* [U] food that has been grown or farmed, especially fresh fruits and vegetables ‖ 재배되거나 경작된 먹을거리, 특히 신선한 과일과 야채. 농산물. 청과물. 수확물: *the produce section of the supermarket* 슈퍼마켓의 청과물 코너

pro·duc·er /prəˈdusɚ/ *n* **1** a person, company, or country that makes or grows goods, foods, or materials ‖ 제품[식료품, 원료] 등을 만들거나 산출하는 사람[회사, 나라]. 생산[제조]자: *Scotland is a producer of high quality wool.* 스코틀랜드는 고품질의 양모 생산국이다. **2** someone who controls the preparation of a play, movie etc., but who does not direct the actors ‖ 직접 배우들을 감독하지는 않고 연극·영화 등의 준비를 총괄하는 사람. 제작자

prod·uct /ˈprɑdʌkt/ *n* **1** [C, U] something useful that is grown, made in a factory, or taken from nature ‖ 재배하거나 공장에서 제조하거나, 또는 자연에서 얻은 유용한 것. 생산물. 제품: *None of our products are tested on animals.* 우리 제품 중 어느 것도 동물에 대한 시험을 한 것은 없다. / *dairy products* 유제품 **2 be the product of sth** to be the result of experiences or of good or bad conditions ‖ 경험, 또는 좋거나 나쁜 조건의 결과이다: *Criminals are often the product of bad homes.* 범죄자들은 종종 불우한 가정환경의 산물이다. **3** the number you get by multiplying two or more numbers ‖ 두 개나 그 이상의 숫자를 곱해서 얻은 수. 곱. 적

pro·duc·tion /prəˈdʌkʃən/ *n* **1** [U] the process of making or growing things, or the amount that is produced ‖ 물건을 만들거나 산출해 내는 과정, 또는 생산된 양. 생산. 산출. 생산고. 산출액: *Steel production has decreased by 35%.* 강철 생산이 35% 감소했다. **2** something produced by skill or imagination, such as a play or movie ‖ 기술이나 상상력에 의해 만들어진 영화나 연극 등의 것: *a new Broadway production of "Follies"* 브로드웨이의 새 연극 "Follies"

pro·duc·tive /prəˈdʌktɪv/ *adj* producing or achieving a lot ‖ 많이 생산하거나 얻는. 결실이 많은. 산출력이 있는: *productive land* 비옥한 땅 / *a very*

productive conference 매우 생산적인 회의 **– productively** *adv* —opposite UNPRODUCTIVE

pro·duc·tiv·i·ty /ˌproudəkˈtɪvəti, ˌprɑ-/ *n* [U] the rate at which goods are produced, and the amount produced ‖ 제품이 생산되는 비율, 또한 생산된 양. 생산성. 생산력: *Factory managers want to increase the workers' productivity.* 공장장은 노동자들의 생산성 향상을 원한다.

prof /prɑf/ *n* **1** SPOKEN ⇨ PROFESSOR **2 Prof.** the written abbreviation of PROFESSOR ‖ professor의 약어

pro·fane /prouˈfeɪn, prə-/ *adj* showing disrespect for God or for holy things, by using rude words or religious words wrongly ‖ 무례한 말이나 종교적으로 그릇된 말을 사용해서 신이나 신성한 것에 대해 불경함을 표시하는. 신성을 더럽히는. 모독적인: *profane language* 신성을 모독하는 말

pro·fan·i·ty /prouˈfænəti, prə-/ *n* [C, U] a rude word, or a religious word used wrongly, that shows disrespect for God or for holy things ‖ 신이나 신성한 것에 대한 불경함을 나타내는 무례한 말이나 종교적으로 잘못 사용된 말. 신성 모독적 발언. 모독적인 말

pro·fess /prəˈfɛs, prou-/ *v* [T] FORMAL **1** to make a claim about something, especially a false one ‖ 특히 거짓된 것에 대해 주장하다. 단언하다. 잘라 말하다: *Although he professes to be a vegetarian, he eats fish.* 비록 그는 채식주의자라고 공언하지만 생선은 먹는다. **2** to express a personal feeling or belief freely, and not try to hide it ‖ 개인적인 감정이나 믿음을 숨기려고 하지 않고 자유롭게 표현하다: *Fabian longed to profess his love for her.* 파비안은 그녀에 대한 자기의 사랑을 솔직히 표현하고 싶었다. **– professed** *adj*

pro·fes·sion /prəˈfɛʃən/ *n* **1** a job that needs special education and training ‖ 특별한 교육과 훈련이 필요한 일. 전문직: *He's a lawyer by profession.* (=as his job) 그의 직업은 변호사이다. —see usage note at JOB **2** [singular] all the people in a particular profession ‖ 특정한 직업에 종사하는 모든 사람: *the teaching profession* 교직자 **3** FORMAL a statement of your belief, opinion, or feeling ‖ 자신의 믿음[의견, 감정]을 말함. 공언. 고백

pro·fes·sion·al' /prəˈfɛʃənl/ *adj* **1** doing a job, sport, or activity for money ‖ 돈을 벌기 위해 일[스포츠, 활동]을 하는. 직업의. 직업적인: *a professional* *baseball player* 프로 야구 선수 **2** professional sports are played by people who are paid ‖ 사람들이 돈을 받고 스포츠에서 경기를 하는. 프로의 **3** relating to a job that needs special education and training ‖ 특별한 교육과 훈련이 필요한 직업과 관련된. 전문적인. 전문의: *You should speak to a lawyer for professional advice.* 변호사에게 전문적인 상담을 받아 보세요. **4** showing that someone has been well trained and is good at his/her work ‖ 어떤 사람이 제대로 훈련받고 자신의 일에 능숙하다는 것을 나타내는. 전문직의: *This report looks very professional.* 이 보고서는 매우 전문가적인 솜씨가 느껴진다. – **professionally** *adv*

professional² *n* **1** someone who earns money by doing a job, sport, or activity that other people do just for enjoyment ‖ 다른 사람들은 재미로만 하는 일[스포츠, 활동]을 해서 돈을 버는 사람. 직업[프로] 선수 —compare AMATEUR² **2** someone who works in a job that needs special education and training ‖ 특별한 교육과 훈련이 필요한 일을 하는 사람. 전문직 종사자. 전문가: *a health care professional* 건강 관리 전문가 **3** someone who has a lot of experience and does something very well ‖ 경험이 많고 어떤 일을 매우 잘 하는 사람. 숙련자. 능숙한 사람: *Holt thinks his co-workers don't see him as a true professional.* 홀트는 동료들이 자기를 진정한 전문가로 보지 않는다고 생각한다.

pro·fes·sion·al·ism /prə'fɛʃənəl,ɪzəm, -ʃənl-/ *n* [U] the skill and high standards of behavior expected of a PROFESSIONAL person ‖ 전문가에게 기대되는 기술과 높은 수준의 품행. 전문적 기술. 전문가 기질. 프로 근성

pro·fes·sor /prə'fɛsɚ/ *n* a teacher at a university or college, especially one who has a high rank ‖ 특히 높은 지위를 가진 종합 대학이나 단과대학의 교수: *Thank you, Professor Drexler.* 감사합니다, 드렉슬러 교수님. / *my history professor* 내 역사학 교수

prof·fer /'prɑfɚ/ *v* [T] FORMAL to offer something to someone ‖ 무엇을 누군가에게 제의하다. …을 내놓다 – **proffer** *n*

pro·fi·cien·cy /prə'fɪʃənsi/ *n* [U] the ability to do something with a high level of skill ‖ 높은 수준의 기술을 가지고 어떤 것을 하는 능력. 능숙. 숙달. 숙련: *a math proficiency test* 수학 능력 시험

pro·fi·cient /prə'fɪʃənt/ *adj* able to do something with a high level of skill ‖ 높

은 기술 수준으로 어떤 일을 할 수 있는. 능숙한. 숙달한. 숙련된: *Gwen's proficient in three languages.* 그웬은 3개 국어에 능통하다. – **proficiently** *adv*

pro·file¹ /'proʊfaɪl/ *n* **1** a side view of someone's head ‖ 사람 머리의 옆모습. 옆얼굴: *a drawing of her in profile* 그녀의 옆얼굴 그림 **2** a short description that gives important details about someone or something ‖ 사람이나 사물에 대한 중요한 상세 정보를 주는 짧은 설명. 프로필: *a profile of her career* 그녀의 경력 프로필 **3 keep a low profile** to behave quietly and avoid doing things that will make people notice you ‖ 조용하게 행동하고 사람들의 눈에 띄게 될 행동을 피하다. 눈에 띄지 않다. 저자세를 유지하다

profile² *v* [T] to write or give a short description of someone or something ‖ 사람이나 사물에 대한 간단한 설명을 쓰거나 제공하다. …의 개략을 쓰다[말하다]: *His new play was profiled in last Sunday's newspaper.* 그의 새 연극은 지난 일요일 신문에 간략하게 소개되었다.

prof·it¹ /'prɑfɪt/ *n* **1** [C, U] money that you gain by selling things or doing business ‖ 물건을 팔거나 사업을 해서 버는 돈. 수익. 이윤. 이득: *Eric made a profit of $23,000 when he sold his house.* 에릭은 자기 집을 팔아서 2만 3천 달러의 수익을 올렸다. / *They sold the company at a huge profit.* 그들은 거대한 이윤을 남기고 그 회사를 매각했다. **2** [U] an advantage that you gain from doing something ‖ 어떤 것을 해서 얻는 혜택. 이득. 이익: *reading for profit and pleasure* 이로움과 즐거움을 위한 독서

profit² *v* [T] FORMAL to be useful or helpful to someone ‖ 사람에게 유용하거나 도움이 되다. 이익을 얻다. 득을 보다: *It might profit you to meet her in person.* 그녀를 네가 직접 만나는 것이 도움이 될 것이다.

profit by/from sth *phr v* [T] to learn from something that happens, or get something good from a situation ‖ 일어난 일에서 무엇인가를 얻거나 어떤 상황을 통해 좋은 것을 얻다. …에서 이득을 얻다. 덕을 입다[보다]: *The rebels will profit from the army's mistakes.* 반군들은 그 군대의 실수로 덕을 볼 것이다.

prof·it·a·bil·i·ty /,prɑfɪtə'bɪləti/ *n* [U] the state of producing a profit, or the degree to which a business or activity is PROFITABLE ‖ 수익을 내는 상태, 또는 사업이나 활동이 이익을 내는 정도. 수익성

prof·it·a·ble /'prɑfɪtəbəl/ *adj* producing a profit or a useful result ‖ 수익이나 유

용한 결과를 내는. 이익이 되는. 이로운.
유익한: *The company has had a profitable year.* 그 회사는 올해 흑자를 내었다. - **profitably** *adv*

prof·it·eer /ˌprɑfəˈtɪr/ *n* a person or company that makes unfairly large profits, especially by selling things at very high prices when they are difficult to get ‖ 특히, 사람들이 물건을 구하기 어려울 때 매우 높은 가격으로 팔아서 불공정하게 큰 수익을 올리는 사람이나 회사. 부당 이득자. 악덕 업자 - **profiteering** *n* [U]

profit mar·gin /ˈ.. ˌ../ *n* the difference between the cost of producing something and the price you sell it at ‖ 물건을 생산하는 비용과 그것을 파는 가격과의 차이. 이윤폭. 이익률

profit shar·ing /ˈ.. ˌ../ *n* [U] a system in which workers are allowed to share some of their company's profits ‖ 노동자들이 회사 수익의 일부를 분배받게 허용된 제도. 이익 분배제

prof·li·gate /ˈprɑfləgɪt/ *adj* FORMAL **1** wasting money in a careless way ‖ 부주의하게 돈을 낭비하는 **2** behaving in an immoral way ‖ 부도덕하게 행동하는. 품행이 나쁜. 방탕한. 부도덕한

pro·found /prəˈfaʊnd/ *adj* **1** having a strong influence or effect ‖ 강한 영향력이나 효과를 가진. (충격 등이) 심한: *Her death was a profound shock to all of us.* 그녀의 죽음은 우리 모두에게 대단한 충격이었다. **2** showing strong serious feelings ‖ 강하고 진지한 감정을 나타내는. (슬픔·욕망 등이) 깊은: *a profound apology* 심심한 사과 **3** showing great knowledge and understanding ‖ 대단한 지식과 이해를 나타내는. 학식이 깊은. 해박한: *a profound book* 심오한 책 - **profoundly** *adv* - **profundity** /prəˈfʌndəti/ *n* [C, U]

pro·fuse·ly /prəˈfyusli/ *adv* many times, or in large numbers or amounts ‖ 여러 번, 또는 많은 수나 양으로. 풍부하게. 실컷. 지나치게: *Keiko thanked them profusely.* 케이코는 그들에게 지나치게 감사를 표시했다. - **profuse** *adj*

pro·fu·sion /prəˈfyuʒən/ *n* [singular, U] a very large amount ‖ 매우 많은 양. …의 대량. 다수: *Poppies grew in profusion over the hillsides.* 양귀비가 산비탈에 걸쳐 빽빽하게 자랐다.

prog·e·ny /ˈprɑdʒəni/ *n* [U] LITERARY the babies of a person or animal ‖ 사람의 아기나 동물의 새끼. 자손. 후계자

prog·no·sis /prɑgˈnoʊsɪs/ *n, plural* **prognoses** /-siz/ TECHNICAL **1** a

doctor's opinion of how an illness or disease will develop ‖ 질병이 어떻게 진행되어 갈지에 대한 의사의 의견. 예후. 치료 후의 병의 경과의 예상 **2** a judgment about what will happen in the future, based on information or experience ‖ 정보나 경험에 근거한, 장차 무슨 일이 발생할지에 대한 판단. …에 대한 예상[예측]

pro·gram' /ˈproʊgræm, -grəm/ *n* **1** a show on television or radio ‖ 텔레비전이나 라디오의 프로: *There's a program about whales on channel 9.* 9번 채널에서 고래에 대한 프로를 한다. **2** a set of instructions given to a computer to make it do a particular job ‖ 특정한 작업을 하도록 컴퓨터에 내리는 일련의 지시. 컴퓨터의 프로그램: *a software program that helps you with household finances* 가정의 재정 관리를 도와주는 소프트웨어 프로그램 **3** a set of planned activities with a specific purpose ‖ 특정한 목적을 가진 일련의 계획된 활동. 행동 계획. 과정. 일정: *Stanford's MBA program* 스탠포드 대학 경영학 석사과정 / *a government program to house the homeless* 노숙자들에게 거처할 곳을 주기 위한 정부의 계획 / *Lucy's exercise program includes weight lifting and swimming.* 루시는 웨이트 트레이닝과 수영을 포함한 운동 계획을 가지고 있다. **4** a printed description of what will happen at a play, concert etc. and of the people who will be performing ‖ 연극·콘서트 등에서 무엇이 있을지 그리고 공연을 할 사람이 누구인지에 대한 인쇄된 설명서. 진행표 **5 get with the program** SPOKEN used in order to tell someone to pay attention to what needs to be done, and do it ‖ 남에게 앞으로 무엇을 끝내고 무엇을 할 필요가 있는지에 주의하도록 말하는 데에 쓰여

program² *v* **-mmed, -mming** [T] **1** to set a machine to operate in a particular way ‖ 특정한 방식으로 작동되도록 기계를 맞추다: *I've programmed the VCR to record that movie you wanted.* 나는 네가 보기를 원했던 그 영화를 VCR로 예약 녹화해 놓았다. **2** to give a set of instructions to a computer to make it do a particular job ‖ 특정한 작업을 하도록 컴퓨터에 일련의 지시를 내리다. 프로그램을 작성하다

pro·gram·mer /ˈproʊˌgræmə, -grəmə/ *n* someone whose job is to write programs for computers ‖ 컴퓨터 프로그램을 짜는 직업인. 프로그래머 - **programming** *n* [U]

prog·ress' /ˈprɑgrəs, -grɛs/ *n* [U] **1** the

process of getting better at doing something, or getting closer to finishing or achieving something ‖ 일을 하는 데 있어서 보다 잘 되어가거나 일을 마치거나 이루는 데 보다 가까워지는 과정. 진행. 진전. 진척: *Nick has made a lot of progress since coming to our school.* 닉은 우리 학교에 온 이후로 많이 좋아졌다. / *We've been watching the progress of the trial with interest.* 우리는 흥미 있게 그 재판의 진행 과정을 지켜보고 있다. **2** all of the improvements, developments, and achievements that happen in science, society, work etc. ‖ 과학·사회·노동 등의 분야에서 일어나는 모든 향상·발달·성취. 진보: *technological progress* 기술 발달 **3 in progress** happening now, and not yet finished ‖ 아직 끝나지 않고 지금 발생하고 있는. 진행 중인. 행해지고 있는: *Please do not enter while there is a class in progress.* 수업이 진행되는 동안에는 교실에 들어가지 마세요. **4** movement toward a place ‖ 한 장소를 향해 움직임. 전진: *The ship made slow progress through the rough sea.* 그 배는 거친 바다를 헤치며 천천히 나아갔다.

pro·gress[2] /prəˈgrɛs/ *v* [I] **1** to develop, improve, or become more complete over a period of time ‖ 일정한 기간에 걸쳐 발전되거나 향상되거나 더욱 완전하게 되다. 숙달되다. 진보하다: *Work on the new building progressed quickly.* 새 건물 작업이 신속히 진척되었다. **2** to move forward ‖ 앞쪽으로 이동하다. 전진하다. 나아가다: *We progressed slowly toward the front of the arena.* 우리는 경기장 앞쪽으로 천천히 나아갔다.

pro·gres·sion /prəˈgrɛʃən/ *n* [singular, U] **1** a process of change or development ‖ 변화나 발달 과정. 진전. 진보: *Doctors are worried by the rapid progression of her illness.* 의사들은 그녀의 병이 급속히 진행되어 걱정스러워 한다. **2** movement toward a particular place ‖ 특정한 장소 쪽으로의 움직임. 전진. 진행

pro·gres·sive[1] /prəˈgrɛsɪv/ *adj* **1** supporting new or modern ideas and methods ‖ 새롭거나 현대적인 생각과 방법을 지지하는. 진보적인. 진취적 기상을 가진: *a progressive attitude* 진취적인 태도 **2** becoming better, worse, or more complete over a period of time ‖ 일정한 기간에 걸쳐 보다 좋아지거나 나빠지거나 완전해지는. 점진적인: *a progressive disease* 진행되고 있는 병 –
progressively *adv*

pro·gres·sive[2] *n* TECHNICAL **the progressive** ⇨ CONTINUOUS[2]

pro·hib·it /proʊˈhɪbɪt, prə-/ *v* [T] **1** to officially make an activity illegal, or to officially not allow it ‖ 공식적으로 어떤 활동을 불법화하거나 허용하지 않다. 금지하다. 금하다: *Smoking in this building is prohibited.* 이 건물내에서 흡연은 금지되어 있다. / *Stores are prohibited from selling alcohol to people under 21.* 상점에서는 21살 미만의 미성년자에게 술을 파는 것이 금지되어 있다. **2** to make something impossible or prevent it from happening ‖ 어떤 일을 불가능하게 하거나 일어나는 것을 방해하다: *His bad eyesight prohibited him from becoming a pilot.* 시력이 나빠서 그는 비행기 조종사가 되지 못했다.

pro·hi·bi·tion /ˌproʊəˈbɪʃən/ *n* [C, U] FORMAL the act of officially making something illegal or officially not allowing it, or an order that does this ‖ 공식적으로 어떤 것을 불법화시키는 행위, 또는 이러한 불법적인 것을 공식적으로 허용하지 않는 행위, 또는 이러한 불법적인 행위를 못하게 하는 명령. 금지. 금지령: *a prohibition on cigarette advertising* 담배 광고의 금지 **2 Prohibition** the period from 1919 to 1933 in the US when the production and sale of alcoholic drinks was illegal ‖ 주류의 생산과 판매가 불법이었던 미국에서의 1919년에서 1933년까지의 기간. 미국의 금주법 시행 시대

pro·hib·i·tive /proʊˈhɪbətɪv, prə-/ *adj* preventing people from doing or buying something ‖ 사람들이 어떤 것을 하거나 사는 것을 막는. 금지의. 금지하는. (값이)터무니없는: *The cost of property in some large cities is prohibitive.* 몇몇 대도시에서의 부동산 값은 터무니없다. –
prohibitively *adv*

pro·ject[1] /ˈprɑdʒɛkt, -dʒɪkt/ *n* **1** a carefully planned piece of work ‖ 주의 깊게 계획된 일. 계획[기획]안(案): *the new highway project* 새로운 간선도로 계획안 / *My school project is on Virginia State history.* 나의 학교 과제물은 버지니아 주의 역사에 관한 것이다. **2 the projects** ⇨ HOUSING PROJECT

pro·ject[2] /prəˈdʒɛkt/ *v* **1** [T] to use the information you have now to calculate or plan what will happen in the future ‖ 현재 가지고 있는 정보를 이용해서 미래에 일어날 것을 계산하거나 계획하다. …을 어림잡다[산출하다]. …을 계획[기획]하다: *projected sales for next year* 내년도 추정 매출 / *A visit by the president is projected for March.* 대통령의 방문은 3

월로 잡혀 있다. **2** [T] to make other people have a particular idea about you ‖ 다른 사람들에게 자신에 대한 특정한 생각을 가지게 만들다. …의 이미지를 주다: *Jim always projects an image of self-confidence.* 짐은 항상 자신감 있는 이미지를 심어준다. **3** [I, T] to speak or sing loudly enough to be heard by everyone in a big room or theater ‖ 큰 실내나 극장에서 모든 사람들이 들을 수 있을 정도로 크게 말하거나 노래하다. 소리를 내지르다 **4** [T] to use light to make an image appear on a screen or surface ‖ 스크린이나 표면에 영상이 나타나게 하기 위해 불빛을 사용하다. …에 영사하다. 투영하다 **5** [I, T] to stick out beyond an edge or surface ‖ 가장자리나 표면 바깥으로 튀어나오다. 돌출하다. 돌출시키다: *The garage roof projects over the driveway.* 차고의 지붕이 진입로 위로 튀어나와 있다. **6** [T] FORMAL to throw something through the air with great force ‖ 어떤 것을 힘껏 공중으로 던지다. 내던지다. 발사하다

pro·jec·tile /prəˈdʒɛktl, -ˌtaɪl/ *n* FORMAL an object that is thrown or fired from a weapon ‖ 무기로 쏘아 내거나 발사한 물체. 발사체

pro·jec·tion /prəˈdʒɛkʃən/ *n* **1** a statement about something you think will happen ‖ 일어날 것이라 생각되는 것에 대한 진술. 예측. 추정. 산출: *this year's sales projections* 올해의 매출 예상 **2** something that sticks out beyond an edge or surface ‖ 가장자리나 표면 밖으로 튀어나온 것. 돌출(부). 융기 **3** [C, U] the act of using light to make an image appear on a screen or surface, or the image itself ‖ 스크린이나 표면에 영상이 나타나도록 불빛을 사용하는 행위, 또는 영상 그 자체. 투영. 영사. 영상: *film projection* 필름의 영사

pro·jec·tion·ist /prəˈdʒɛkʃənɪst/ *n* someone whose job is to operate a PROJECTOR ‖ 영사기를 작동시키는 직업인. 영사 기사

pro·jec·tor /prəˈdʒɛktə/ *n* a piece of equipment that uses light to make a movie or pictures appear on a screen ‖ 스크린 위에 영화나 그림을 나타나게 하기 위해 불빛을 사용하는 장비. 프로젝터. 투영기. 영사기. 환등기

pro·le·tar·i·at /ˌproʊləˈtɛriət/ *n* **the proletariat** the people in a society who are poor, own no property etc. ‖ 가난하고 자신의 재산 등을 소유하고 있지 않은 사회 계층. 프롤레타리아 계급. 무산자 계급 – **proletarian** *adj*

pro·lif·er·ate /prəˈlɪfəˌreɪt/ *v* [I] FORMAL to rapidly increase in number and spread to many different places ‖ 수가 급속히 증가하여 여러 다른 장소에 퍼지다. 급증하다. 만연하다: *Projects to clean up the environment are proliferating.* 환경을 정화하자는 계획이 급속히 확산되고 있다. – **proliferation** /prəˌlɪfəˈreɪʃən/ *n* [singular, U]

pro·lif·ic /prəˈlɪfɪk/ *adj* producing a lot of something ‖ 어떤 것을 많이 생산하는. 다산의. 열매를 많이 맺는. 다작의: *Agatha Christie was a prolific writer.* 아가사 크리스티는 다작 작가였다. – **prolifically** *adv*

pro·logue /ˈproʊlɑg, -lɔg/ *n* the introduction to a book, movie, or play ‖ 책·영화·연극에 대한 도입부. 서문. 서언. 프롤로그

pro·long /prəˈlɔŋ/ *v* [T] to make something such as a feeling, activity, or state continue longer ‖ 감정·활동·상태 등을 더 오래 지속시키다. …을 연장하다. …을 늘리다: *high-tech machinery that prolongs people's lives* 사람의 생명을 연장시키는 최첨단의 기계 장치

pro·longed /prəˈlɔŋd/ *adj* continuing for a long time ‖ 오랫동안 계속되는. 연장되는. 장기의: *a prolonged illness* 장기간 계속되는 병

prom /prɑm/ *n* a FORMAL dance party for HIGH SCHOOL students, that usually happens at the end of a school year ‖ 보통 학년 말에 있는, 고등학생을 위한 공식적인 댄스 파티: *the senior prom* (=dance for students in their last year of school) 고교 졸업생의 댄스 파티

prom·e·nade /ˌprɑməˈneɪd, -ˈnɑd/ *n* OLD-FASHIONED a walk for pleasure in a public place, or a wide path where you can do this ‖ 공공장소에서 즐기기 위해 걷는 것, 또는 이것을 할 수 있는 넓은 길. 산책. 산보. 산책길[로] – **promenade** *v* [I]

prom·i·nence /ˈprɑmənəns/ *n* [U] the fact of being important and famous ‖ 중요하고 유명하다는 사실. 현저. 탁월. 저명: *Stallone rose to prominence* (=became famous) *with the movie "Rocky."* 스탤론은 "록키"라는 영화로 유명해졌다.

prom·i·nent /ˈprɑmənənt/ *adj* **1** famous or important ‖ 유명하거나 중요한. 저명한. 탁월한: *prominent politicians* 저명한 정치인들 **2** large and sticking out ‖ 크고 튀어나와 있는. 돌출한. 두드러진: *a prominent nose* 아주 큰 코 **3 a prominent place/position**

somewhere that is easily seen ‖ 쉽게 볼
수 있는 곳. 눈에 띄는 장소/위치: *The
family portrait was hung in a prominent
place on the wall.* 그 가족의 초상화는 벽
위의 눈에 확 띄는 곳에 걸려 있었다. –
prominently *adv*

pro·mis·cu·ous /prə'mɪskyuəs/ *adj*
having sex with a lot of people ‖ 많은 사
람들과 성교를 가지는. 난교의: *In the
study, single men under 30 were the
most promiscuous group.* 연구로는, 30세
미만의 미혼 남성들이 성적으로 가장 문란
한 집단이었다. – **promiscuity**
/ˌprɑmɪ'skyuəti/ *n* [U]

prom·ise¹ /'prɑmɪs/ *v* **1** [I, T] to make
a statement that you will definitely do
something or that something will
definitely happen ‖ 어떤 일을 확실히 하
겠다고 말을 하다, 또는 어떤 일이 확실히
일어날 거라고 말을 하다. 약속하다: *You
promised me (that) you wouldn't be
late!* 너는 나한테 지각하지 않겠다고 약속
했잖아! / *She's promised to clean her
room.* 그녀는 자기 방을 청소하겠다고 약
속했다. / *I've already promised them a
ride to the dance.* 나는 춤추러 갈 때
그들을 태워 주겠다고 이미 약속했다. **2**
[T] to make people expect that
something will happen ‖ 사람들에게 무엇
이 일어날 거라고 기대하게 하다. …의 가
망이 있다. …할 듯하다: *The game
promises to be exciting.* 그 게임은 흥미
진진할 것 같다. **3 I can't promise
anything** SPOKEN used in order to tell
someone that you will try to do what
s/he wants, but you may not be able to
‖ 남이 원하는 것을 자신이 해보겠지만 할
수 없을 지도 모른다고 남에게 말하는 데
에 쓰여. …을[아무것도] 장담할 수는 없
다

promise² *n* **1** a statement that you will
definitely do something or that
something will definitely happen ‖ 어떤
것을 확실히 하겠다는 언급 또는 어떤 일
이 반드시 일어날 거라는 언급. 약속. 맹
세: *You made me a promise, and I
expect you to keep it.* (=do what you
said you would do) 당신은 나에게 약속을
했고 나는 당신이 약속을 지킬 거라 기대
한다. / *Christy broke her promise to
practice the flute every day.* (=she failed
to practice) 크리스티는 매일 플루트를 연
습할 거라는 자신의 약속을 깨뜨렸다. / *a
promise of help* 도움을 주겠다는 약속 **2**
[U] signs that something or someone
will be good or successful ‖ 사물이나 사
람이 좋아지거나 성공할 것이라는 징조.
밝은 전망. 유망함: *He shows a lot of*

promise as a writer. 그는 작가로서 대단
히 장래성이 있다.

prom·is·ing /'prɑmɪsɪŋ/ *adj* showing
that someone or something is likely to
be successful in the future ‖ 사람이나 사
물이 장래에 성공하게 될 것 같아 보이는.
전도유망한. 가망 있는. 기대할 수 있는:
a promising young singer 장래가 촉망되
는 젊은 가수 – **promisingly** *adv*

pro·mo /'proumou/ *n, adj* INFORMAL ⇨
PROMOTIONAL

prom·on·to·ry /'prɑmən,tɔri/ *n* a high
piece of land that goes out into the
ocean ‖ 바다 쪽으로 튀어나온 높은 지역.
곶. 갑(岬)

pro·mote /prə'mout/ *v* [T] **1** to help
something develop and be successful ‖
어떤 것이 발전하고 성공하는 것을 돕다.
…을 조장[조성]하다. 촉진[장려]하다:
*Davis works to promote understanding
between cultures.* 데이비스는 문화들간
의 이해를 증진시키기 위해 일한다. **2**
to advertise a product or event ‖ 제품이
나 행사를 광고하다. …의 판매[보급]를
촉진하다: *The company is spending
millions promoting its new software.* 그
회사는 자사의 새 소프트웨어를 광고하는
데 수백 만 달러를 지출하고 있다. **3** to
give someone a better, more
responsible position at work ‖ 사람에게
직장에서 더 낫고 더 책임이 따르는 지위
를 주다. 승진시키다: *Ted was promoted
to senior sales manager.* 테드는 수석 영
업 부장으로 승진했다. **4** to be
responsible for arranging a large public
event such as a concert or a sports
game ‖ 콘서트나 스포츠 경기 등의 대규
모 공공 행사 준비를 책임 맡다. …을 주
최하다

pro·mot·er /prə'mouta/ *n* someone
whose job is to arrange large public
events such as concerts or sports games
‖ 콘서트나 스포츠 경기 등의 대규모 공공
행사를 준비하는 직업인. 프로모터. 주최
자

pro·mo·tion /prə'mouʃən/ *n* **1** [C, U] a
move to a better, more responsible
position at work ‖ 직장에서 더 낫고 더
책임이 따르는 지위로 이동함. 승진. 진
급: *She received a promotion to
Lieutenant.* 그녀는 중위로 진급했다. **2**
[C, U] an activity intended to advertise a
product or event, or the thing that is
being advertised ‖ 제품이나 행사를 광고
하려는 활동, 또는 광고하고 있는 물건. 선
전. 판매 촉진의 상품: *a sales promotion*
판매 촉진 (활동)

pro·mo·tion·al /prə'mouʃənl/ *adj*

promotional products and activities are made or organized in order to advertise something ‖ 제품·활동 등이 물건을 광고하기 위해 이루어지거나 조직된. 판매 촉진 장려용의. 선전용의

prompt¹ /prɑmpt/ v 1 [T] to make someone do something, or to help him/her remember to do it ‖ 남에게 어떤 일을 하게 하다, 남에게 그 일을 하는 것을 기억하도록 하다. 남을 촉구하여 …시키다. 재촉하다: *News of the scandal prompted a Senate investigation.* 그 추문 관련 뉴스는 상원의 조사를 촉발했다. / *Alex does practice his drums, but he needs prompting.* 알렉스는 드럼 연습을 하는데 그에게는 격려가 필요하다. 2 [I, T] to remind someone, especially an actor, of the next words in a speech ‖ 특히 배우에게 다음 대사를 생각나게 하다. 무대 뒤에서 대사를 일러주다

prompt² *adj* 1 done quickly, immediately after something else, or at the right time ‖ 다른 것 뒤에 재빨리 곧바로 하는, 또는 바로 그때에 행하는. 즉석의. 즉각적인. 신속한: *We request prompt payment of bills.* 우리는 즉각적인 요금 지불을 요청합니다. 2 someone who is prompt arrives at the right time or does something on time ‖ 사람이 정각에 도착하는, 또는 어떤 것을 정각에 하는. 시간을 지키는. 지체 없는. 재빠른 –
promptly *adv* : *The disease is not fatal if treated promptly.* 그 병은 즉시 치료한다면 치명적이지는 않다. / *He gave the roses to Joanna, who promptly burst into tears.* 그가 조안나에게 장미꽃을 주자 그녀는 곧바로 울음을 터뜨렸다.

prompt³ *n* a sign on a computer screen that shows that the computer has finished one operation and is ready to begin the next ‖ 컴퓨터가 한 작업을 마치고 다음 작업을 시작할 준비가 되어 있다는 것을 나타내는 컴퓨터 스크린상의 신호. 프롬프트. 지시 메시지

prone /proun/ *adj* 1 likely to do something or suffer from something ‖ 어떤 일을 하거나 당하기 쉬운. …의 경향이 있는. …하기 쉬운: *a narrow river that is prone to flooding* 범람하기 쉬운 좁은 강 / *As a child she was accident prone.* (=often had accidents) 어린 시절에 그녀는 자주 사고를 일으켰다. 2 FORMAL lying down flat, especially with the front of your body facing down ‖ 특히 신체의 앞부분을 지면을 향하고 납작 엎드린. 포복한

prong /prɔŋ, prɑŋ/ *n* 1 one of the thick sharp pointed parts on the end of some

tools, such as a PITCHFORK ‖ 쇠스랑 등 일부 연장의 끝에 있는 두껍고 날카로우며 뾰족한 부분의 하나. 뾰족한 끝[기구]. 갈래 —compare TINE 2 **two-pronged, three-pronged etc.** a two-pronged or three-pronged attack, approach, plan etc. comes from two or three directions or uses two or three methods at the same time ‖ 공격·접근·계획 등이 두세 방면으로부터 오는, 또는 동시에 두세 가지 방법을 사용하는. 두[세] 방면에서의

pro·noun /ˈprounaun/ *n* TECHNICAL in grammar, a word that is used instead of a noun or noun phrase. In the sentence "He brought me a chair and I sat on it," the words "he," "me," "I," and "it" are pronouns ‖ 문법에서, 명사나 명사구 대신에 사용되는 단어. 대명사. "He brought me a chair and I sat on it."의 문장에서 "he," "me," "I,"와 "it"은 대명사이다.

USAGE NOTE pronoun agreement

Pronouns such as **everyone**, **anyone**, and **someone** are singular, and should be used with singular verbs and pronouns: *Has everyone finished his or her drink?* However, in speech and informal writing, we usually use plural pronouns instead: *Anyone can use the library, can't they? / Someone has left their backpack behind.*

everyone, anyone, someone 등의 대명사는 단수이며, 단수 동사와 단수 대명사와 함께 사용되어야 한다: 모두 다 마셨느냐? 그러나 구어와 비격식체 문장에서 단수 대명사 대신에 복수 대명사를 보통 사용한다: 누구든지 그 도서관을 이용할 수 있죠, 그렇죠? / 어떤 사람이 자기 배낭을 깜박 잊고 두고 갔다.

---

pro·nounce /prəˈnauns/ *v* [T] 1 to make the sound of a letter, word etc. in the correct way ‖ 올바르게 글자·단어 등의 소리를 내다. 발음하다: *How do you pronounce your name?* 당신 이름을 어떻게 발음합니까? 2 to state something officially and formally ‖ 어떤 것을 공식적이고 격식을 차려 말하다. 선언[선고, 표명]하다: *He was pronounced dead at 11:00 p.m.* 그는 오후 11시에 사망했다고 발표되었다.

pro·nounced /prəˈnaunst/ *adj* very strong or noticeable ‖ 매우 강하거나 뚜렷한. 명백한. 현저한: *Harold walks with a pronounced limp.* 해롤드는 눈에 띄게 절뚝거리며 걷는다.

pro·nounce·ment /prəˈnaunsmənt/ *n*

FORMAL an official public statement ‖ 공식적인 공공 성명. 공고. 선언. 발포

pron·to /ˈprɑntoʊ/ *adv* SPOKEN a word meaning quickly or immediately, used especially when you are annoyed ‖ 특히 화났을 때 쓰여, 빨리 또는 즉시를 뜻하는 말. 재빨리. 곧: *Get in the house, pronto!* 집에 들어가, 어서!

pro·nun·ci·a·tion /prəˌnʌnsiˈeɪʃən/ *n* **1** [C, U] the way in which a language or a particular word is pronounced ‖ 한 언어나 특정 단어가 발음되는 방식. 발음 (법): *There are two different pronunciations of "read."* "read"를 발음하는 두 가지 다른 방법이다. **2** [singular, U] a particular person's way of pronouncing a word or words ‖ 특정한 개인이 한 단어나 단어들을 발음하는 방식. 개인의 발음법[벽]

proof /pruf/ *n* **1** [U] facts, information, documents etc. that prove something is true ‖ 어떤 것이 사실임을 증명하는 사실·정보·서류 등. 증거. 증명: *Do you have any proof that this is your bag?* 이 가방이 네 것이라는 어떤 증거가 있느냐? / *Returns will be accepted with proof of purchase.* (=something that proves that you bought the thing) 물품을 구입한 증거가 있기만 하다면 반품은 인정 된다. **2** TECHNICAL a printed copy of a piece of writing, used in order to find and remove mistakes before the final printing is done ‖ 최종적으로 인쇄하기 전에 오류를 발견하고 제거하기 위해 사용하는 원고의 인쇄부본. 교정쇄 **3** [U] a measurement of how much alcohol is in a drink. For example, 40 proof is 20% alcohol ‖ 술에 얼마만큼의 알코올이 있는지를 알아보는 측정치. 도수. 예를 들어 40도라는 것은 20퍼센트의 알코올을 함유하고 있다는 것이다

proof·read /ˈpruf-rid/ *v* [I, T] to read something in order to correct any mistakes in it ‖ 오류를 바로잡기 위해 어떤 것을 읽다. 교정쇄를 보다 – **proofreader** *n*

prop¹ /prɑp/ *v* **-pped, -pping** [T] to support something or keep it in a particular position ‖ 어떤 것을 받치다 또는 특정 위치로 유지시키다. 기대어 세우다: *He propped his bike against the fence.* 그는 자전거를 담에 기대 놓았다. / *The gate had been propped open with a brick.* 문은 벽돌로 받쳐 열어 놓았다.

prop sth ↔ **up** *phr v* [T] **1** to prevent something from falling by putting something against it or under it ‖ 다른 것을 어떤 것에 기대 놓거나 받쳐 놓아서

넘어지지[떨어지지] 않게 하다. 받쳐 세우다. 지탱하다: *Steel poles prop up the crumbling walls.* 강철 기둥이 허물어져 가고 있는 벽을 지탱한다. **2** to help something to continue to exist ‖ 어떤 것이 계속 존재하는 것을 돕다: *Willis sold stocks to prop up his failing company.* 윌리스는 자기의 쓰러져 가고 있는 회사를 지탱하기 위해 주식을 팔았다.

prop² *n* **1** an object placed under or against something to hold it in a position ‖ 어떤 것을 어떤 위치에 지탱시키기 위해 괴거나 기대서 받쳐 놓은 것. 받침대 **2** an object such as a book, weapon etc. used by actors in a play or movie ‖ 연극이나 영화에서 배우들이 사용하는 책·무기 등의 물체. 소품

prop·a·gan·da /ˌprɑpəˈgændə/ *n* [U] false or partly false information that is given to the public by a government or political party in order to make people agree with them ‖ 사람들이 자신들에게 찬동하도록 하기 위해 정부나 정당에 의해 대중에게 전달되는 거짓되거나 부분적으로 거짓된 정보. 유언비어. 거짓 정보. 허위 보도 – **propagandist** *n* – **propagandize** *v* [I, T]

prop·a·gate /ˈprɑpəˌgeɪt/ *v* FORMAL **1** [T] to share ideas, information, or beliefs with many people ‖ 많은 사람들과 생각·정보·믿음을 나누다. 전하다. 보급시키다. 선전하다: *a journal that propagates scientific developments* 과학적 발전을 전하는 잡지 **2** [I, T] to grow or produce new plants, or to make a plant do this ‖ 새로운 식물을 기르거나 재배하다, 또는 식물을 이렇게 하게 하다. 식물을 번식하다[시키다] – **propagation** /ˌprɑpəˈgeɪʃən/ *n* [U]

pro·pel /prəˈpɛl/ *v* **-lled, -lling** [T] **1** to make someone achieve something, or to make something happen or develop ‖ 남이 어떤 것을 이루게 하다, 또는 어떤 것이 일어나거나 발전되게 하다. 남을 몰아대다. 재촉하다. 촉진시키다: *The actress's striking good looks helped propel her to stardom.* 그 여배우는 뛰어난 미모 덕분에 스타덤에 올랐다. **2** to move, drive, or push something forward ‖ 어떤 것을 앞으로 움직이게[운전해 나가게, 밀고 나가게] 하다. …을 나아가게 하다. 추진시키다: *old ships propelled by steam* 증기로 추진되는 낡은 배

pro·pel·ler /prəˈpɛlər/ *n* a piece of equipment that consists of two or more blades that spin around to make a ship or aircraft move ‖ 배나 항공기를 움직이

도록 회전하는 두 개 이상의 날개로 구성된 장비. 프로펠러

pro·pen·si·ty /prə'pɛnsəti/ *n* FORMAL a natural tendency to behave or develop in a particular way ‖ 특정하게 행동하거나 발전하는 타고난 경향. 성향. 버릇: *Bubba had a propensity to gain weight.* 버바는 살이 찌는 체질이었다.

prop·er /'prɑpɚ/ *adj* **1** correct, or right for a particular situation ‖ 특정한 상황에 옳거나 적절한. 적합한. 알맞은. 바람직한: *Put that back in its proper place.* 그것을 제자리에 갖다 놓아라. / *You have to go through the proper procedures.* 너는 적절한 절차를 거쳐야 한다. **2** socially correct and acceptable ‖ 사회적으로 옳고 받아들여질 수 있는. 예의 바른. 고상한: *I didn't think it was proper to ask for her phone number so soon.* 나는 그렇게 빨리 그녀의 전화번호를 물어보는 것은 예의 바르지 않다고 생각했다. **3** inside the limits of an area or subject ‖ 한 지역이나 주제의 범위 안의. 진정한. 그 자체의: *We no longer live in Dallas proper; we moved to Mesquite.* 우리는 이제 댈러스에 살지 않고 메스키트로 이사했다.

prop·er·ly /'prɑpɚli/ *adv* correctly, in a way that is right or suitable ‖ 올바르게, 적당하고 적합하게. 적절히. 알맞게: *She can read German but has trouble speaking it properly.* 그녀는 독일어를 읽을 수는 있지만 말은 제대로 하지 못한다.

proper noun /ˌ.. './, **proper name** *n* TECHNICAL in grammar, a noun such as "Mike," "Paris," or "Easter" that is the name of a particular person, place, or thing and is spelled with a capital letter ‖ 문법에서 특정한 사람·장소·물건의 이름이고 대문자로 철자하는 "Mike," "Paris," "Easter" 등의 명사. 고유명사

prop·er·ty /'prɑpɚti/ *n* **1** [U] something that someone owns ‖ 사람이 소유한 것. 소유물. 재산: *Police recovered some of the stolen property.* 경찰은 도둑맞은 물건의 일부를 되찾았다. **2** [C, U] land, buildings, or both together ‖ 토지, 건물, 또는 두 가지 다. 부동산. 사유지: *We have several lovely properties for sale in that area.* 우리는 그 지역에서 팔려고 내놓은 멋진 부동산을 여럿 가지고 있다. / *Get off! This is private property!* 나가시오! 이곳은 개인 사유지입니다! **3** a natural quality of something ‖ 사물의 자연적 성질. 특성. 속성: *an herb with healing properties* 치료하는 성질이 있는 약초

proph·e·cy /'prɑfəsi/ *n* a statement that tells what will happen in the future,

often made by someone with religious or magical power ‖ 종종 종교상의 능력이나 마력을 가진 사람이 미래에 일어날 일에 대해 하는 말. 예언. 계시

proph·e·sy /'prɑfə,saɪ/ *v* [I, T] to use religious or magical knowledge to say what will happen in the future ‖ 장래에 무슨 일이 일어날지 말하기 위해 종교적이거나 마법적인 지식을 사용하다. …을 예언하다. 계시하다

proph·et /'prɑfɪt/ *n* someone who says what will happen in the future and teaches people more about a religion ‖ 장래에 무슨 일이 일어날지를 말하고 사람들에게 종교에 대해 더욱 많이 가르치는 사람. 예언자. 계시자

pro·phet·ic /prə'fɛtɪk/ *adj* relating to correctly saying what will happen in the future ‖ 장래에 무슨 일이 일어날지 정확하게 말하는 것과 관련된. 예언(자)의. 예언하는[력을 가진]: *The Ambassador's warnings proved prophetic.* (=what he warned about actually happened) 그 대사의 경고는 실제 일어날 일을 예언한 셈이 되었다. – **prophetically** *adv*

pro·pi·tious /prə'pɪʃəs/ *adj* FORMAL likely to bring good results; FAVORABLE ‖ 좋은 결과를 낼 것 같은. 형편이 좋은. 상서로운. 길조의; ⑩ favorable: *Circumstances were propitious for investment.* 환경은 투자하기에 딱 맞았다.

pro·po·nent /prə'poʊnənt/ *n* someone who supports something or persuades people to do something ‖ 어떤 것을 지지하거나 사람들에게 어떤 것을 하도록 설득하는 사람. 지지자. 찬성자. 제안자. 발의자: *a proponent of gay rights* 동성애자의 권리 지지자 —compare OPPONENT

pro·por·tion /prə'pɔrʃən/ *n* **1** a part or share of a larger amount or number of something ‖ 어떤 것의 상위 크기의 양이나 수 중 일부분이나 지분. 부분: *The proportion of adults who smoke is lower than before.* 담배를 피우는 성인의 숫자가 전보다 줄어들었다. **2** [C, U] the relationship between the amounts, numbers, or sizes of related things ‖ 관련된 사물들의 양[수, 크기] 사이의 관계. 비. 비율: *Girls outnumber boys at the school by a proportion of three to one.* 그 학교에서 여학생 수는 남학생을 3대 1의 비율로 초과한다. / *Taxes rise in proportion to the amount you earn.* 세금은 당신이 버는 돈의 액수에 비례하여 오른다. **3** [U] the correct relationship between the size or shape of the different parts of something ‖ 사물의 각기 다른 부분의 크기나 모양 사이의 적절

한 관계. 균형. 조화. 걸맞음: *The porch is out of proportion with the rest of the house.* 그 포치[돌출 현관]는 그 집의 나머지 부분과 어울리지 않는다. **4 sense of proportion** the ability to judge what is most important and what is not important in a situation ‖ 한 상황에서 무엇이 가장 중요하고 무엇이 중요하지 않은지 판단하는 능력. (일의 경중을 판단하는) 균형 감각 **5 get/blow things out of proportion** to react to a situation as if it is worse or more serious than it really is ‖ 상황이 실제보다 더 나쁘거나 더 심각한 것처럼 반응하다. …을 실제보다 더 심각하게 받아들이다

pro·por·tion·al /prəˈpɔrʃnəl, -ˈpɔrʃənl/, **pro·por·tion·ate** /-ʃənɪt/ *adj* staying in a particular relationship with another thing in size, amount, or importance ‖ 크기[양, 중요성]에서 또 다른 것과 특정한 관계를 유지하는. …에 비례하는. 상대적인. 균형 잡힌: *The number of Representatives each state has is proportional to its population.* 각 주의 하원 의원 수는 그 주의 인구에 비례한다. **– proportionally** *adv*

pro·pos·al /prəˈpoʊzəl/ *n* **1** [C, U] a plan or idea that is officially suggested for someone to consider, or the act of suggesting this ‖ 남에게 검토하도록 공식적으로 제안한 계획이나 생각, 또는 이렇게 제안하는 행위. 제의. 계획. 기획. 안(案): *a proposal to build a new hospital* 새 병원을 지으려는 계획 **2** the act of asking someone to marry you ‖ 남에게 결혼해 달라고 요청하는 행위. 프러포즈. 구혼: *Did you accept his proposal?* 그의 청혼을 승낙했니?

pro·pose /prəˈpoʊz/ *v* **1** [T] to officially suggest that something be done ‖ 어떤 것을 하기를 공식적으로 제의하다: *I propose that we close the meeting.* 나는 회의를 마칠 것을 제의합니다. **2** [I] to ask someone to marry you ‖ 남에게 결혼하자고 요청하다. 청혼하다: *Has he proposed yet?* 그가 벌써 청혼했니? **3** [T] FORMAL to intend to do something ‖ 어떤 것을 하려고 하다. …을 꾀하다. 기도[계획]하다: *What do you propose to do about it?* 당신은 그것에 대해 무엇을 하려고 하느냐?

prop·o·si·tion¹ /ˌprɑpəˈzɪʃən/ *n* **1** a statement in which you express a judgment or opinion ‖ 판단이나 의견을 표현하는 말. 제안. 제의. 건의: *a nation dedicated to the proposition that all people are created equal under the law* 모든 사람이 법 앞에 평등하다는 정신에

충실한 나라 **2** an offer, plan, or idea, especially in business or politics ‖ 특히 사업이나 정치에서의 제의[계획, 생각]. 기획. 안(案): *Her latest proposition seemed to be a good investment.* 그녀의 가장 최근의 기획안은 좋은 투자가 될 것처럼 보였다. / *Proposition 13 on the ballot* 투표에 부쳐진 제안 13호

proposition² *v* [T] to suggest to someone that s/he have sex with you, especially in exchange for money ‖ 특히 돈을 주고, 남에게 성교를 갖자고 제의하다. 성적 유혹

pro·pri·e·tar·y /prəˈpraɪəˌtɛri/ *adj* information or products that are proprietary can only be known about or sold by a particular company ‖ 정보나 제품이 특정 회사만이 알 수 있거나 판매할 수 있는. 독점권[전매특허]의

pro·pri·e·tor /prəˈpraɪət̬ər/ *n* FORMAL an owner of a business ‖ 사업의 소유자. 경영주[자]

pro·pri·e·ty /prəˈpraɪət̬i/ *n* [singular, U] FORMAL correct social or moral behavior ‖ 사회적 또는 도덕적으로 올바른 행동. 올바름. 예의바름. 예의범절: *We doubt the propriety of her going there alone.* 우리는 그녀가 그곳에 혼자 가는 것이 올바른 행동인지 의문스럽다.

pro·pul·sion /prəˈpʌlʃən/ *n* [U] TECHNICAL the force that moves a vehicle forward, or the system used in order to make this happen ‖ 차량을 앞으로 가게 하는 힘, 또는 이렇게 하는 데 쓰이는 시스템. 추진(력). 추진체: *jet propulsion* 제트 추진(체)

pro ra·ta /ˌproʊ ˈreɪt̬ə, -ˈrɑt̬ə/ *adj* TECHNICAL calculated or paid according to exactly how much of something is used or how much work is done ‖ 정확히 어떤 것이 얼마나 많이 사용되었거나 얼마나 많은 작업량이 끝났는지에 따라 계산되거나 지불된. 비례한

pro·sa·ic /proʊˈzeɪ-ɪk/ *adj* FORMAL boring, ordinary, or lacking in imagination ‖ 지루한. 평범한. 상상력이 부족한: *a prosaic style of writing* 단조로운 문체 **– prosaically** *adv*

pro·scribe /proʊˈskraɪb/ *v* [T] FORMAL to officially stop the existence or use of something ‖ 어떤 것의 존재나 사용을 공식적으로 중단시키다. 금지하다: *laws to proscribe child labor* 아동 노동을 금지하는 법 **– proscription** /proʊˈskrɪpʃən/ *n* [C, U]

prose /proʊz/ *n* [U] written language in its usual form, not as poetry ‖ 운문의 형식이 아닌 보통의 형식으로 된 문어. 산문

pros·e·cute /'prɑsə,kyut/ v [I, T] to say officially that you think someone is guilty of a crime and must be judged by a court of law ‖ 남이 유죄라고 생각하여 법정에서 재판을 받아야 된다고 생각하는 것을 공식적으로 말하다. 기소[고소]하다: *He was prosecuted for theft.* 그는 절도 혐의로 기소되었다.

pros·e·cu·tion /,prɑsə'kyuʃən/ n **1 the prosecution** the people in a court of law who are trying to prove that someone is guilty of a crime ‖ 법정에서 어떤 사람이 범죄에 대해 유죄임을 증명하려고 하는 사람들. 기소[소추]측. 검찰(측): *a witness for the prosecution* 검찰측 증인 —compare DEFENSE¹ **2** [C, U] the process or act of prosecuting (PROSECUTE) someone ‖ 남을 기소하는 과정이나 행위. 기소[고발](절차)

pros·e·cu·tor /'prɑsə,kyuɚ/ n a lawyer who is trying to prove in a court of law that someone is guilty of a crime ‖ 법정에서 어떤 사람이 범죄에 대해 유죄임을 증명하려고 하는 법률가. 검찰관. 검사

pros·e·lyt·ize /'prɑsələ,taɪz/ v [I, T] FORMAL to try to persuade someone to join a religious group, political party etc. ‖ 남을 종교 단체·정당 등에 가입하도록 설득하려고 하다. 전향[개종]시키다. 가담[입회]시키다

pros·pect¹ /'prɑspɛkt/ n **1** [C, U] something that is possible or likely to happen in the future, or the possibility itself ‖ 장래에 가능하거나 일어날 것 같은 것, 또는 그 가능성. 가망[공산](성). 예상[기대](되는 것): *There's every prospect of ending the war soon.* 전쟁이 곧 끝날 가능성이 충분히 있다. / *a company with good prospects for growth* 성장 가능성이 큰 회사 / *Valerie couldn't bear the prospect of returning to Miami.* 발레리는 마이애미로 되돌아가야 할지도 모른다는 생각에 견딜 수 없었다. **2 (sb's) prospects** someone's chances of success in the future ‖ 사람이 장래에 성공할 가능성. 장래성: *His job prospects are not very good.* 그의 직업의 장래성은 그다지 좋지 않다.

prospect² v [I, T] to look for things such as gold, silver, and oil in the ground or under the ocean ‖ 지하나 해저에서 금·은·석유 등을 찾다. 시굴하다. 채광하다: *men prospecting for gold* 금을 시굴하고 있는 사람들 – **prospector** n

pro·spec·tive /prə'spɛktɪv/ adj **1** likely to do a particular thing ‖ 특정한 일을 할 것 같은. 예상되는. 가망 있는: *a prospective buyer for the house* 집을 살 가망이 있는 고객 **2** likely to happen ‖ 발생할 것 같은: *the prospective costs of the deal* 거래의 기대 비용

pro·spec·tus /prə'spɛktəs/ n **1** a small book that gives details about a university, or that advertises a new business ‖ 대학교에 관한 상세한 설명을 하거나 신규 사업을 선전하는 소책자. 학교 안내서. 사업의 소개서 **2** an official statement that describes a business opportunity ‖ 사업의 가망성을 설명하는 공식 문서

pros·per /'prɑspɚ/ v [I] to be successful and become rich ‖ 성공해서 부자가 되다. 번창하다: *an environment in which small businesses can prosper* 소규모 사업이 번창할 수 있는 환경

pros·per·i·ty /prɑ'spɛrəti/ n [U] the condition of having money and being successful ‖ 돈이 있고 성공한 상태. 번영. 성공: *a time of economic prosperity* 경제적 번영기

pros·per·ous /'prɑspərəs/ adj successful and rich ‖ 성공하고 부유한. 번영하는: *a prosperous community* 번영하는 사회

pros·the·sis /prɑs'θɪsɪs/ n, plural **prostheses** /prɑs'θisiz/ TECHNICAL an artificial leg, tooth, arm or other part of the body ‖ 인공적인 다리나 치아, 팔, 또는 기타 신체 기관. 보철물(補綴物) – **prosthetic** /prɑs'θɛtɪk/ adj

pros·ti·tute¹ /'prɑstə,tut/ n someone who has sex with people to earn money ‖ 돈 때문에 사람들과 성관계를 갖는 사람. 매춘부. 남창

prostitute² v **1 prostitute yourself** to have sex with someone for money ‖ 돈을 위해 남과 성관계를 갖다. 매춘하다 **2** [T] to use your skills and abilities to do something people do not think is valuable, usually in order to earn money ‖ 보통 돈을 벌려고 사람들이 가치가 없다고 생각하는 것을 하는 데에 자신의 기술과 능력을 사용하다: *He's prostituting his acting talent doing TV commercials.* 그는 TV 상업 광고를 찍으면서 그의 연기적 재능을 써먹고 있다.

pros·ti·tu·tion /,prɑstə'tuʃən/ n [U] the work of PROSTITUTEs ‖ 매춘부의 일. 매춘

pros·trate¹ /'prɑstreɪt/ adj **1** FORMAL so shocked or upset that you can no longer do anything ‖ 더 이상 어떤 것도 할 수 없도록 매우 충격을 받거나 당황한: *Mrs. Klinkman was prostrate with grief.* 클린크만 여사는 슬픔으로 기진맥진했다. **2**

lying flat on the ground with your face down ‖ 얼굴을 아래로 향한채 바닥에 납작하게 엎드린. 부복한: *His body was found prostrate on the floor.* 그의 시신은 바닥에 엎드린 채로 발견되었다.

prostrate² *v* [T] **prostrate yourself** to lie flat on the ground with your face down, in order to show praise or respect ‖ 찬양이나 존경을 표시하려고 얼굴을 아래로 향하고 바닥에 납작하게 엎드리다

pro·tag·o·nist /proʊˈtæɡənɪst/ *n* FORMAL the main character in a play, movie, or story ‖ 연극이나 영화, 또는 소설에서의 주요 인물. 주인공.

pro·tect /prəˈtɛkt/ *v* [T] to prevent someone or something from being harmed or damaged ‖ 사람이나 사물이 해를 입거나 손상을 당하는 것을 막다. …을 보호하다: *a lotion to protect you from sunburn* 햇볕에 타는 것을 막아주는 로션 / *a plan to protect the town against another attack* 그 도시를 또 다른 공격에서 방어하려는 계획 – **protected** *adj*: *a protected species* 보호종 (種) – **protector** *n*: *a chest protector* 가슴 보호구[가슴받이]

pro·tec·tion /prəˈtɛkʃən/ *n* **1** [U] the act of protecting, or the state of being protected ‖ 보호하는 행위, 또는 보호되는 상태. 보호: *Heidi's thin coat gave little protection against the cold.* 헤이디의 얇은 코트는 추위를 거의 막아주지 못했다. **2** [singular] something that protects someone or something ‖ 사람, 또는 사물을 보호하는 것. 방호물: *A car alarm provides/gives some protection against theft.* 자동차 도난 경보장치는 도난을 다소 방지해 준다.

pro·tec·tive /prəˈtɛktɪv/ *adj* **1** used or intended for protection ‖ 보호에 쓰이는, 보호를 꾀한. 보호용의: *a protective covering for the computer* 컴퓨터 보호덮개 **2** wanting to protect someone from danger or harm ‖ 남을 위험이나 위해로부터 보호하려는: *She's overly protective of her children.* 그녀는 자신의 아이들을 과잉 보호한다.

pro·té·gé /ˈproʊtəˌʒeɪ, ˌproʊtəˈʒeɪ/ *n* a young person who is guided and helped by someone who has power, wealth, or more experience ‖ 권력자나 부자, 또는 경험이 많은 사람에게 지도와 원조를 받는 젊은 사람. 피보호자. 부하. 제자

pro·tein /ˈproʊtin/ *n* [C, U] one of the many substances in foods such as meat and eggs that helps your body to grow and be healthy ‖ 신체를 성장하게 하고

건강을 유지하도록 도와주는, 고기와 계란 등의 음식에 들어 있는 많은 물질 중의 하나. 단백질

pro·test¹ /ˈproʊtɛst/ *n* **1** a strong public complaint about something that you disagree with or think is unfair ‖ 동의하지 않거나 불공정하다고 생각하는 것에 대한 공공연한 강한 불만. 항의: *Almirez led a protest against the construction of a new shopping mall.* 알미레즈는 새로운 쇼핑몰의 설립에 대한 항의를 주도했다. **2 do sth under protest** to do something in a way that shows you do not want to do it, because you think it is wrong or unfair ‖ 그릇되거나 불공평하다고 여겨서 하고 싶지 않다는 것을 나타내며 무엇을 하다. 마지못해 …을 하다

pro·test² /ˈproʊtɛst, prəˈtɛst/ *v* **1** [I, T] to say or do something publicly to show that you disagree with something or think that it is unfair ‖ 동의하지 않거나 불공평하다고 생각한다는 것을 보여주기 위해 공공연하게 무엇을 말하거나 하다. …에 항의하다: *a group protesting against human rights abuses* 인권 남용에 대해 항의하는 단체 / *Students carried signs protesting the war.* 학생들은 전쟁을 반대하는 몸짓을 하였다. —compare COMPLAIN **2** [T] to state very strongly that something is true, especially when other people do not believe you ‖ 특히 다른 사람들이 믿지 않을 경우, 사실임을 아주 강력히 언급하다. 확언하다. 주장하다: *Throughout the trial, he kept protesting his innocence.* 재판 내내 그는 자신의 결백을 주장하고 있었다. – **protestation** /ˌprɑtəˈsteɪʃən, ˌproʊ-/ *n*

Prot·es·tant /ˈprɑtəstənt/ *adj* relating to a part of the Christian church that separated from the Roman Catholic Church in the 16th century ‖ 16세기 로마 가톨릭 교회에서 분리된 기독교 일파에 관련된. 개신교의 – **Protestant** *n* – **Protestantism** *n* [U]

pro·to·col /ˈproʊtəˌkɔl, -ˌkɑl/ *n* **1** [singular, U] the system of rules for the correct way to behave on official occasions ‖ 공식적인 의식에서 바르게 행동하기 위한 규칙 체제. 의례: *Even touching the Queen is a breach of protocol.* (=it is not allowed) 여왕의 (몸에) 닿는 것조차 의례에 어긋난다. **2** an official statement of the rules that a group of countries have agreed to follow in dealing with a particular problem ‖ 일단의 국가들이 특정 문제를 다루는 데 따르기로 동의한 공식적인 규칙에 관한 성명서. 의정서. 조약안: *the Montreal*

Protocol on greenhouse gases 온실 가스에 대한 몬트리올 의정서

pro·ton /ˈprovtɑn/ *n* TECHNICAL a part of an atom that has a positive electrical CHARGE ‖ 원자의 양성 전하를 띠는 부분. 양성자

pro·to·type /ˈprovtə،taɪp/ *n* a model of a new car, machine etc., used in order to test the design before it is produced ‖ 생산되기 전 설계도를 시험하기 위해 쓰이는 새로운 자동차·기계 등의 모델. 견본

pro·tract·ed /prov'træktɪd, prə-/ *adj* continuing for a long time, usually longer than necessary ‖ 보통 필요 이상으로 오랫동안 지속되는. 오래 끈. 연장된: *a messy protracted divorce* 지저분하게 오래 끈 이혼 – **protraction** /prov'-trækʃən, prə-/ *n* [U]

pro·trac·tor /prov'træktɚ, prə-/ *n* a flat tool shaped like a half circle, used for measuring and drawing angles ‖ 각을 재고 그리는 데에 쓰는 반원 모양의 납작한 도구. 각도기

pro·trude /prov'trud/ *v* [I] FORMAL to stick out from somewhere ‖ 어딘가에서 튀어나오다. 돌출하다: *a rock protruding from the water* 문 밖으로 돌출한 암석 – **protruding** *adj* – **protrusion** /prov'truʒən/ *n* [C, U]

proud /pravd/ *adj* **1** feeling pleased with your achievements, family, country etc. because you think they are very good ‖ 매우 훌륭하다고 여겨 업적·가족·국가 등에 만족해하는. 자랑스러운: *We're really proud of you for getting straight A's.* 우리는 네가 올 A를 받아서 정말 자랑스럽다 / *We're proud to announce the birth of our son.* 우리 아들 생일을 알리게 되어 기쁩니다. / *I'm proud (that) the team's done so well.* 나는 그 팀이 아주 잘 해낸 것에 대해 자랑스럽게 생각한다. **2** thinking that you are more important, skillful etc. than you really are ‖ 자신을 실제보다 더 중요하고 능숙하게 생각하는. 거만한: *Raffery had always been a proud man.* 래프리는 항상 거만한 사람이었다. **3 do sb proud** to make someone feel proud of you by doing something well ‖ 자신이 무엇을 아주 잘 하여 남이 자랑스럽게 여기게 하다: *Congratulations, Natalie – you've sure done us proud.* 나탈리, 축하해. 네가 우리 체면을 확실히 살려 줬구나. **4** too embarrassed or ashamed to allow other people to help you when you need it ‖ 너무 난처하거나 창피하여 도움이 필요할 때 다른 사람들이 도와주는 것을 허락하지 않는. 자존심이 있는: *Terry was too proud*

to ask his family for money. 테리는 자존심이 너무 강하여 자신의 가족에게 돈을 부탁하지 않았다. – **proudly** *adv* —see also PRIDE¹

prove /pruv/ *v* **proved, proved** or **proven, proving** [T] **1** to show that something is definitely true ‖ 무엇이 명확하게 사실이라는 것을 보여주다. …을 입증하다: *They have enough evidence to prove that she is guilty.* 그들은 그녀가 유죄임을 입증할 충분한 증거를 갖고 있다. **2** to show over time that someone or something has a particular quality ‖ 사람이나 사물이 특정한 속성을 가졌다는 것이 오랜 시간에 걸쳐서 나타내다. …임이 판명되다: *The answering machine has proven to be very useful.* 자동 응답기는 매우 유용한 것으로 입증되었다. **3 prove yourself** to show how good you are at doing something ‖ 무엇을 하는 데에 얼마나 유능한지를 나타내다. 역량을 나타내다: *At seventeen years old, she had yet to prove herself on the pro golf tour.* 17살 때 그녀는 프로 골프 시합에서 자신의 역량을 채 나타내지 못했다. – **provable** *adj*

prov·en¹ /ˈpruvən/ *adj* shown to be real or true ‖ 실제나 진실로 나타난. 증명된: *a proven method of learning* 증명된 학습 방법

proven² *v* a PAST PARTICIPLE of PROVE ‖ prove의 과거 분사형

prov·erb /ˈprɑvɚb/ *n* a short statement that most people know, that contains advice about life ‖ 대부분의 사람들이 알고 있는, 삶에 관한 조언이 담긴 짧은 문구. 속담. 격언

pro·ver·bi·al /prə'vɚbiəl/ *adj* known by most people, and usually relating to a PROVERB ‖ 보통 속담과 관련되어 대부분의 사람들에게 알려진. 속담의: *I was running around like the proverbial headless chicken!* 나는 속담의 머리 없는 닭처럼 바쁘게 뛰어다니고 있었지! – **proverbially** *adv*

pro·vide /prə'vaɪd/ *v* [T] **1** to give or supply something to someone ‖ 누군가에게 무엇을 주거나 공급하다. 제공하다: *I work with a service that provides shelter for the homeless.* 나는 집 없는 사람들에게 보호 시설을 제공하는 부문에서 일한다. / *This should provide you with all the details you need.* 이것은 네가 필요로 하는 모든 세목을 제공해 줄 것이다. **2 provide that** FORMAL if a law or rule provides that something must happen, it states that something must happen ‖ 법이나 규정이 어떤 일이 발생해

야 한다고 말하다. …을 규정하다

provide for sb/sth *phr v* [T] **1** to give someone the things s/he needs, such as money, food, or clothing ‖ 누군가에게 돈이나 음식, 또는 옷 등의 필요로 하는 것을 주다. 필요한 것을 대주다: *Dad always thought a man should provide for his family.* 아빠는 항상 남자는 자신의 가족을 부양해야 한다고 생각했다. **2** to make plans in order to deal with something that might happen in the future ‖ 앞으로 발생할지 모르는 일을 다룰 계획을 세우다. …에 대비하다: *The hotel is examining ways to provide for the disabled.* 그 호텔은 장애인을 대비한 통로를 검토 중이다.

pro·vid·ed /prəˈvaɪdɪd/, **provided that** *conjunction* used in order to say that something will only happen if another thing happens first ‖ 다른 일이 먼저 일어나야만 어떤 일이 발생할 것이라고 말하는 데에 쓰여. 만약 …이면: *Talks will take place in July, provided that enough progress has been made.* 충분히 진전된다면, 7월에 회담이 열릴 것이다.

prov·i·dence /ˈprɑvədəns/ *n* [singular, U] a force that some people believe controls our lives in the way God wants ‖ 신이 뜻대로 우리의 삶을 통제한다고 일부 사람들이 믿고 있는 힘. 신의(神意). 섭리: *an act of divine providence* 신의 섭리에 따르는 행동

prov·i·den·tial /ˌprɑvəˈdɛnʃəl/ *adj* FORMAL happening just when you need it; LUCKY ‖ 필요로 할 때 바로 발생하는. 시기 적절한; 汉 lucky: *a providential opportunity* 천우신조의 기회

pro·vid·er /prəˈvaɪdɚ/ *n* **1** a person or company that provides something such as a service ‖ 서비스 등을 제공하는 사람이나 기업. 공급자: *a health-care provider* 건강관리 담당자 **2** someone who gives his/her family the money, food, clothes etc. that they need ‖ 가족들이 필요로 하는 돈·음식·옷 등을 제공하는 사람. 부양자

pro·vid·ing /prəˈvaɪdɪŋ/, **providing that** *conjunction* ⇨ PROVIDED

prov·ince /ˈprɑvɪns/ *n* **1** one of the large areas into which some countries are divided ‖ 몇몇 지역으로 나눠지는 큰 지역들 중 하나. 도. 주(州). 지방: *the provinces of Canada* 캐나다의 주(州)들 **2 sb's province** FORMAL a subject that someone is responsible for or knows a lot about ‖ 누군가가 책임을 맡고 있거나 많이 알고 있는 주제. 부문. 분야: *Sales forecasts are not within my province.* 판

매액 예측은 내 소관이 아니다.

pro·vin·cial /prəˈvɪnʃəl/ *adj* **1** unwilling to accept new ideas or to think about things in a new way ‖ 새로운 생각을 받아들이려 하지 않거나 무엇에 대해 새로운 방식으로 생각하려 하지 않는. 편협한: *They were narrowly provincial in their outlook.* 그들의 시야는 좁고 편협했다. **2** relating to a PROVINCE ‖ 지방에 관한. 지방의: *the provincial government of Quebec* 퀘백 주 정부

pro·vi·sion /prəˈvɪʒən/ *n* **1** [C, U] the act of providing something that someone needs now or will need in the future ‖ 누군가가 당장이나 앞으로 필요로 하는 것을 제공하는 행위. 공급: *the provision of services for the elderly* 노인을 위한 서비스 제공 / *He has made provisions for his wife in his will.* 그는 유언에서 자신의 아내몫을 마련해 놓았다. **2** a condition in an agreement or law ‖ 협정이나 법의 조건. 조항: *the provisions of the treaty* 그 조약의 조항들 —see also PROVISIONS

pro·vi·sion·al /prəˈvɪʒənl/ *adj* existing for only a short time and likely to be changed in the future ‖ 단지 잠시 있다가 장차 변화될 것 같은. 일시적인. 임시의: *A provisional government was set up after the revolution.* 혁명 후 임시 정부가 수립되었다.

pro·vi·sions /prəˈvɪʒənz/ *n* [plural] food supplies, especially for a trip ‖ 특히 여행을 위한, 비축 식량: *We had enough provisions for two weeks.* 우리는 2주분의 충분한 식량을 갖고 있었다.

pro·vi·so /prəˈvaɪzoʊ/ *n* FORMAL a condition that you ask for before you will agree to something ‖ 무엇에 동의하기 전 요구하는 조건. 단서: *Tom's grandson inherited his money with the proviso that he go to college.* 톰의 손자는 자신이 대학에 간다는 조건부로 톰의 돈을 물려받았다.

prov·o·ca·tion /ˌprɑvəˈkeɪʃən/ *n* [C, U] an action or event that makes someone angry, or that is intended to do this ‖ 사람을 화나게 하거나 화나게 할 작정으로 하는 행위나 사건. 자극. 유인(誘因): *My client was attacked without provocation!* 나의 고객이 이유도 없이 공격 받았지 뭐야!

pro·voc·a·tive /prəˈvɑkətɪv/ *adj* **1** intending to make someone angry or cause a lot of discussion ‖ 사람을 화나게 하거나 많은 논쟁을 야기하려는. 자극적인. 도발적인: *a provocative new book on the meanings of dreams* 꿈의 의미에 관

한 자극적인 새 도서 **2 intending to make someone sexually excited** ‖ 남을 성적으로 흥분시키려는. 자극적인: *a provocative dress* 자극적인 옷

pro·voke /prə'vouk/ *v* [T] **1 to make someone very angry, especially by annoying him/her** ‖ 특히 사람을 괴롭혀서 매우 화나게 하다: *She did hit him, but he provoked her into doing it.* 그녀가 그를 때렸으나, 그가 그녀의 화를 돋구었다. **2 to cause a sudden reaction or feeling** ‖ 갑작스런 반응이나 감정을 일으키다. 유발하다: *Miller scored a touchdown, provoking cheers from the crowd.* 밀러는 관중들의 환호를 일으키는 터치다운을 했다.

pro·vost /'prouvoust/ *n* **an important official at a university, one rank below its president** ‖ 대학교에서 총장의 한 계급 밑에 있는 중요한 임원. 학장

prow /prau/ *n* **the front part of a ship or boat** ‖ 선박이나 소형 범선의 앞부분. 뱃머리

prow·ess /'prauɪs/ *n* [U] FORMAL **strength and skill at doing something** ‖ 무엇을 하는 데에 있어서의 힘과 기술. 역량: *a man of great athletic prowess* 운동 능력이 대단한 사람

prowl¹ /praul/ *v* [I, T] **to move around an area quietly, trying not to be seen or heard** ‖ 보이거나 들리지 않도록, 한 지역을 조용히 돌아다니다. 배회하다: *a tiger prowling through the jungle* 밀림을 어슬렁거리는 호랑이

prowl² *n* **be on the prowl to be moving quietly, hunting for an animal or person to attack** ‖ 공격할 동물이나 사람을 찾아서 조용히 움직이다. 헤매다

prowl·er /'praulə/ *n* **someone who moves around quietly at night, especially near your house, in order to steal something or harm you** ‖ 특히 물건을 훔치거나 사람을 해치기 위해 집 주위를 밤에 조용히 돌아다니는 사람. 좀도둑

prox·im·i·ty /prak'sɪməti/ *n* [U] FORMAL **nearness in distance or time** ‖ 거리나 시간상으로 가까움. 근접함: *We chose this house because of its proximity to the school.* 우리는 이 집이 학교에 가깝기 때문에 선택했다.

prox·y /'praksi/ *n* **1 someone whom you choose to represent you, especially to vote instead of you at an election** ‖ 특히 선거에서 자신을 대신해 투표하도록 선택한 사람. 대표자 **2 (do sth) by proxy to do something by arranging for someone else to do it for you** ‖ 자신을 위해 다른 사람이 하도록 조처하여 어떤 것

을 하다. 대리로 (…을 하다)

prude /prud/ *n* DISAPPROVING **someone who is very easily shocked by anything relating to sex** ‖ 성에 관련한 어떤 것에도 매우 쉽게 놀라는 사람. 고상한 체하는 사람 – **prudish** *adj*

pru·dent /'prudnt/ *adj* **sensible and careful, especially by avoiding risks that are not necessary** ‖ 특히 필연적이지 않은 위험을 피해서 분별 있고 조심성 있는. 신중한: *It would not be prudent to spend so much money now.* 지금 너무 많은 돈을 쓰는 것은 현명하지 않을 것이다. – **prudence** *n* [U]

prune¹ /prun/, **prune back** *v* [T] **to cut off some of the branches of a tree or bush to make it grow better** ‖ 더 잘 자라게 하려고 나무나 덤불의 가지들을 약간 잘라내다. 가지를 치다

prune² *n* **a dried PLUM** ‖ 말린 자두

pru·ri·ent /'prʊriənt/ *adj* **showing too much interest in sex** ‖ 성(性)에 지나친 관심을 보이는. 음란한 – **prurience** *n* [U]

pry /praɪ/ *v* **pried, pried, prying 1** [T] **to force something open, or to force it away from something else** ‖ 무엇을 억지로 열거나 다른 것으로부터 억지로 떼어 놓다: *They finally pried the window open.* 그들은 결국 창문을 억지로 열었다. / *I had to use a screwdriver to pry the lid off the paint can.* 나는 페인트 통 뚜껑을 열려고 나사 드라이버를 사용해야 했다. **2** [I] **to try to find out details about someone's private life in an impolite way** ‖ 예의 없게 남의 사생활에 대해 세세히 알아내려고 하다. 캐다. 들춰내다: *I didn't mean to pry into your personal life.* 내가 너의 사생활을 꼬치꼬치 캐려고 했던 건 아니야.

P.S. *n* **the abbreviation of** POSTSCRIPT; **a note that you add to the end of a letter, that gives more information** ‖ postscript(추신)의 약어; 정보를 더 제공하기 위해 편지 마지막에 덧붙이는 메모

psalm /sɑm/ *n* **a song or poem praising God** ‖ 신을 찬양하는 노래나 시. 성가

pseu·do·nym /'sudn,ɪm, 'sudə,nɪm/ *n* **a false name used by someone, especially a writer, instead of his/her real name** ‖ 특히 작가가 본명 대신에 사용하는 가짜 이름. 가명. 필명

psych /saɪk/ *v*

psych sb ↔ **out** *phr v* [T] INFORMAL **to do or say things that will make your opponent feel nervous or confused** ‖ 상대방을 초조하거나 난처하게 만들 짓을 하거나 말하다. …을 겁먹게 하다: *Ignore* *him – he's just trying to psych you out.* 그에게 신경 쓰지 마. 그는 단지 너를 겁주려고 그러는 거야.

psych sb/yourself up *phr v* [T] INFORMAL to prepare someone mentally before doing something so s/he feels confident ‖ 누군가에게 무엇을 하기 전에 마음의 준비를 해서 자신감을 갖도록 하다. 자신감을 고양하다: *soldiers trying to psych themselves up for combat* 전투에 대한 사기를 높이려고 애쓰는 군인들

psy·che /'saɪki/ *n* TECHNICAL someone's mind or basic nature that controls how s/he thinks or behaves ‖ 사고 방식이나 행동 방식을 조정하는 사람의 마음이나 본성. 정신. 마음

psyched /saɪkt/, **psyched up** *adj* SPOKEN **be psyched (up)** to be mentally prepared for and excited about an event, activity etc. ‖ 사건·행위 등에 마음의 준비가 되어 흥분한: *Bryony's totally psyched about/for her date.* 브라이오니는 그녀의 데이트에 완전히 들떠 있었다.

psy·che·del·ic /ˌsaɪkə'dɛlɪk/ *adj* **1** psychedelic drugs such as LSD make you see things that do not really exist ‖ LSD 등의 마약이 실제하지 않는 것을 보게 하는. 환각적인 **2** psychedelic art, clothing etc. has a lot of bright colors and patterns ‖ 예술이나 옷 등이 다채로운 밝은 색깔과 무늬들을 하고 있는. 화려한

psy·chi·a·trist /saɪ'kaɪətrɪst, sə-/ *n* a doctor who studies and treats mental illness ‖ 정신 질환을 연구하고 치료하는 의사. 정신과 의사 —compare PSYCHOLOGIST

psy·chi·a·try /saɪ'kaɪətri, sə-/ *n* [U] the study and treatment of mental illness ‖ 정신 질환의 연구와 치료. 정신 의학 –**psychiatric** /ˌsaɪki'ætrɪk/ *adj* : *a psychiatric hospital* 정신 병원

psy·chic¹ /'saɪkɪk/ *adj* **1** relating to strange events involving the power of the human mind ‖ 인간의 정신력에 대한 기이한 일과 관련된. 심령적인: *a mysterious psychic phenomenon* 신비한 심령 현상 **2** affecting the mind rather than the body ‖ 육체보다 정신에 영향을 미치는. 정신의: *a psychic disorder* 정신 분열

psychic² *n* someone who has strange powers such as the ability to know what will happen in the future ‖ 미래에 발생할 것을 아는 능력 등의 기이한 재능을 가진 사람. 무당

psy·cho /'saɪkoʊ/ *n* SLANG someone who is likely to behave in a violent or crazy way ‖ 난폭하거나 미친 듯이 행동하

려는 사람. 정신 병자

psy·cho·a·nal·y·sis /ˌsaɪkoʊə'næləsɪs/ *n* [U] a way of treating someone who is mentally ill by talking to him/her about his/her past life, feelings etc. to find out the cause of the illness ‖ 병의 원인을 찾아내기 위해 과거의 생활·감정 등에 관하여 대화를 하여 정신 질환자를 치료하는 방법. 정신 분석법 –**psychoanalyze** /ˌsaɪkoʊ'ænlˌaɪz/ *v* [T]

psy·cho·an·a·lyst /ˌsaɪkoʊ'ænl-ɪst/ *n* someone who treats people using PSYCHOANALYSIS ‖ 정신 분석법을 이용하여 사람들을 치료하는 사람. 정신 분석 학자

psy·cho·log·i·cal /ˌsaɪkə'lɑdʒɪkəl/ *adj* **1** relating to the way people's minds work and the way this affects their behavior ‖ 사람들의 정신 작용법과 이것이 그들의 행동에 미치는 면에 관련한. 정신적인: *Loss of memory is often a psychological problem that can be treated.* 기억 상실은 종종 치료될 수 있는 정신적인 문제이다. **2** relating to PSYCHOLOGY ‖ 심리학에 관한. 심리학적: *a psychological test* 심리학적인 실험 –**psychologically** *adv*

psy·chol·o·gist /saɪ'kɑlədʒɪst/ *n* someone who is trained in PSYCHOLOGY ‖ 심리학 교육을 받은 사람. 심리학자 —compare PSYCHOLOGIST

psy·chol·o·gy /saɪ'kɑlədʒi/ *n* **1** [U] the scientific study of the mind and how it works, and how mental problems can be treated ‖ 정신·정신 작용 방법·정신병 치료법에 관한 과학적 연구. 심리학: *a professor of psychology* 심리학 교수 **2** [C, U] the usual way that a particular person or group thinks and reacts ‖ 특정의 사람이나 단체가 일상적으로 생각하고 반응하는 방식. 심리(상태): *a study into the psychology of soldiers in the field* 전장에서의 군인 심리 상태에 관한 연구

psy·cho·path /'saɪkə,pæθ/ *n* someone who has a mental illness that makes him/her behave in a violent or criminal way ‖ 난폭하거나 범죄적 성향으로 행동하게 하는 정신 질환이 있는 사람. 정신병 질환자 –**psychopathic** /ˌsaɪkə'pæθɪk/ *adj*

psy·cho·sis /saɪ'koʊsɪs/ *n, plural* **psychoses** /saɪ'koʊsiz/ [C, U] TECHNICAL a serious mental illness that may cause changes in someone's behavior ‖ 사람의 행동에 변화를 가져올 수 있는 심각한 정신 질환. 정신 이상

psy·cho·so·mat·ic /ˌsaɪkoʊsə'mætɪk/ *adj* TECHNICAL a psychosomatic illness is caused by fear or anxiety rather than by any physical problem ‖ 질병이 어떤 신체적인 문제에 의해서라기보다는 두려움이나 불안으로 야기되는. 심신(心神)의

psy·cho·ther·a·py /ˌsaɪkoʊˈθɛrəpi/ *n* [U] the treatment of mental illness by using PSYCHOLOGY rather than drugs or medicine ‖ 약이나 의술보다는 심리학을 이용하는 정신 질환 치료법. 정신 요법 – **psychotherapist** *n*

psy·chot·ic /saɪˈkɑtɪk/ *adj* TECHNICAL relating to mental illness, or resulting from it ‖ 정신병에 관한 또는 정신병으로 인한. 정신병의: *psychotic behavior* 정신병적 행위 – **psychotic** *n*

pt. the written abbreviation of PART and PINT ‖ part 및 pint의 약어

PTA *n* Parent-Teacher Association; an organization of teachers and parents that works to improve a particular school ‖ Parent-Teacher Association(학부모회)의 약어; 특정 학교를 발전시키기 위해 일하는 교사와 학부모의 모임

pub /pʌb/ *n* a comfortable BAR that often serves food ‖ 종종 음식을 제공하는 편안한 주점. 선술집

pu·ber·ty /ˈpyubəti/ *n* [U] the stage of physical development when you change from a child to an adult who is able to have children ‖ 아이에서 아이를 가질 수 있는 성인으로 변화할 때의 신체 발달 단계. 사춘기: *Our daughter is just reaching puberty.* (=starting to develop physically) 우리 딸은 이제 막 사춘기가 되었습니다.

pu·bes·cent /pyuˈbɛsənt/ *adj* a pubescent boy or girl is going through PUBERTY ‖ 소년이나 소녀가 사춘기를 지나고 있는. 사춘기의

pu·bic /ˈpyubɪk/ *adj* relating to or near the sex organs ‖ 성기와 관련된, 또는 성기 근처의. 치부의: *pubic hair* 음모

pub·lic¹ /ˈpʌblɪk/ *adj* **1** relating to all the ordinary people in a country or city ‖ 국가나 도시의 일반인 모두에 관계된. 공공의: *We acted out of concern for public welfare.* 우리는 공공복지에 대한 관심 때문에 행동했다. **2** available for anyone to use ‖ 누구든지 사용 가능한. 공중의. 대중의: *a public swimming pool* 대중 수영장 / *public transportation* 대중 교통 **3** relating to the government and the services that it provides ‖ 정부 및 정부가 제공하는 서비스의. 공립의: *It has been eight years since she was elected to public office.* (=a job in the government) 그녀가 공무직에 선임된 지 8년이 되었다. / *the public library system*

공립 도서관 체계 **4** known about by most people ‖ 대부분의 사람들에게 알려진: *Last night the name of the killer was made public.* 간밤에 살인자의 이름이 공개되었다. / *a public figure* (=well-known person) 유명인 **5** intended for anyone to know, see, or hear ‖ 누구나 알거나 보거나 듣게 하려는. 공공연한: *I think public displays of emotion are embarrassing!* 감정을 공공연히 드러내는 일은 당혹스러운 것 같아! **6 go public a)** to tell everyone about something that was secret ‖ 비밀을 모든 사람에게 말하다. 공개하다: *They finally went public with news of their engagement.* 그들은 자신들의 약혼 소식을 마침내 공개했다. **b)** to begin to sell SHAREs in your company ‖ 기업의 주식을 팔기 시작하다. 주식을 공개하다 —opposite PRIVATE¹, — see also PUBLICLY

public² *n* **1 the public** all the ordinary people in a country or city ‖ 시골이나 도시의 모든 일반인들. 대중: *The museum is open to the public five days a week.* 그 박물관은 일주일에 5일 일반에게 공개한다. / *This product is not for sale to the general public.* 이 제품은 일반인에게는 판매하지 않는다. **2 in public** in a place where anyone can know, see, or hear ‖ 누구나 알거나 보거나, 또는 들을 수 있는 곳에서. 공개석상에서: *He was always very nice to her in public.* 그는 공개석상에서 그녀에게 늘 대단히 친절했다. **3** [singular, U] the people who like to listen to a particular singer, read a particular writer etc. ‖ 특정 가수의 노래를 듣거나 특정 작가의 책을 읽는 것을 좋아하는 사람. 팬: *A star has to try to please her public.* 스타인 그녀는 자신의 팬을 즐겁게 해주기 위해 노력해야 한다.

public ac·cess /ˌ.. ˈ../ *n* [U] a situation in which anyone can enter a place or use a service ‖ 누구든지 장소에 들어갈 수 있거나 서비스를 이용할 수 있는 상황. 공적(公的) 이용권: *a public access TV channel* (=one that will allow anyone to make a program) 시청자 제작 프로그램 TV 채널

public ad·dress sys·tem /ˌ.. .ˈ. ˌ../ *n* ⇨ PA²

public as·sist·ance /ˌ.. .ˈ../ *n* [U] the government programs that help poor people get food, homes, and medical care ‖ 정부가 빈민들을 도와 음식·주거·의료를 제공하는 프로그램. 공적 부조. 생활 보호 —compare WELFARE

pub·li·ca·tion /ˌpʌbləˈkeɪʃən/ *n* **1** [U] the process of printing a book, magazine etc. and offering it for sale to the public ‖ 대중에게 판매하기 위해 책·잡지 등을 인쇄하여 공급하는 과정. 출판: *There may be a delay of up to eight weeks before publication.* 출판되기까지 8주가 지연될지도 모른다. **2** a book, magazine etc. ‖ 책·잡지 등. 출판물: *a monthly publication for stamp collectors* 우표 수집가를 위한 월간 출판물 **3** [U] the act of making something known to the public ‖ 무엇을 대중에게 알리는 일. 발표: *The authorities tried to stop the publication of the test results.* 당국은 시험 결과에 대한 발표를 막으려 했다.

public de·fen·der /ˌ.. .'../ *n* a lawyer who is paid by the government to defend people who cannot pay for a lawyer themselves ‖ 스스로 변호사 선임 비용을 낼 수 없는 사람들을 변호하기 위해 정부가 비용을 지불하는 변호사. 관선 변호인

public hous·ing /ˌ.. '../ *n* [U] houses or apartments built by the government for poor people ‖ 빈민들을 위해 정부가 지은 주택이나 아파트. 공영 주택

pub·li·cist /'pʌbləsɪst/ *n* someone whose job is to make sure that famous people or new products, movies, books etc. get a lot of PUBLICITY ‖ 유명인이나 신상품·영화·책 등이 많은 평판을 확실히 얻게 하는 직업인. 홍보 담당원

pub·lic·i·ty /pəˈblɪsəti/ *n* [U] **1** attention that someone or something gets from newspapers, television etc. ‖ 사람이나 사물이 신문·TV 등에서 받는 관심. 주지. 평판: *a murder trial that received a lot of publicity* 많은 평판을 얻은 살인사건 재판 **2** the business of making sure that people know about what a famous person is doing, or about a new product, movie, book etc. ‖ 유명인이 하고 있는 일이나 신제품·영화·책 등에 대해 사람들이 확실히 알도록 하는 일. 홍보 – **publicize** /'pʌbləˌsaɪz/ *v* [T]

pub·lic·ly /'pʌblɪkli/ *adv* **1** in way that is intended for anyone to know, see, or hear ‖ 누구든지 알거나 보거나, 또는 듣게 할 의도로. 공개적으로: *I don't like to talk publicly about what I say to players privately.* 나는 내가 선수들에게 사적으로 하는 말에 대해 공개적으로 말하고 싶지 않다. / *Lozansky was jailed for publicly criticizing the government.* 로잔스키는 정부를 공개적으로 비판하여 투옥되었다. **2** by the government, as part of its services ‖ 정부의 서비스 일환으로. 공적으로 : *The hospitals are publicly operated in cities, suburbs, and rural areas.* 도시·교외·시골의 병원들은 공적으로 운영된다. **3** a company that is publicly owned has sold SHAREs in it to the public ‖ 기업이 일반인에게 주식을 팔아. 공개되어 **4** among the ordinary people in a country or city ‖ 시골이나 도시의 일반 대중들 사이에서. 여론으로: *the publicly unpopular Vietnam war* 여론상 평판이 좋지 않은 베트남 전쟁

public re·la·tions /ˌ.. '../, **PR** *n* **1** [plural] the relationship between an organization and the public ‖ 조직과 일반인들 사이의 관계. 대(對)사회적 관계: *Organizing events for charity is always good for public relations.* 자선 행사를 마련하는 것은 대(對)사회적 관계에 항상 유용하다. **2** [U] the work of explaining what a company does so the public will approve of it ‖ 대중이 수긍할 수 있도록 기업이 하는 일을 설명하는 일. 홍보: *the public relations department* 홍보부

public school /'.. ,./ *n* a free local school that is controlled and paid for by the government ‖ 정부가 관리하고 비용을 지급하는 무료 지역 학교. 공립학교

public tel·e·vi·sion /ˌ.. '..../ *n* [U] a television program or service that is paid for by the government, large companies, and the public ‖ 정부·대기업·일반 대중이 돈을 지불하는 텔레비전 프로그램이나 서비스. 공공 텔레비전 방송

pub·lish /'pʌblɪʃ/ *v* **1** [I, T] to arrange for a book, magazine etc. to be written, printed, and sold ‖ 책·잡지 등이 집필·인쇄·판매되도록 조처하다. 출판하다: *a book that was first published in 1851* 1851년에 초판된 책 **2** [T] if a newspaper, magazine etc. publishes something such as a letter, it prints it for people to read ‖ 신문·잡지 등이 편지 등을 사람들이 읽을 수 있게 인쇄하다: *The article was published in the Los Angeles Times.* 그 기사는 로스앤젤레스 타임지에 실렸다. **3** [T] to make official information available for everyone to use ‖ 모든 사람이 사용할 수 있도록 공공 정보화하다. 공표하다: *New guidelines for social studies education were published this year.* 사회과 교육에 대한 새 지침이 올해 공표되었다. – **publishing** *n* [U]

pub·lish·er /'pʌblɪʃɚ/ *n* a person or company that arranges the writing, printing, and sale of books, newspapers etc. ‖ 책·신문 등의 집필·인쇄·판매를 조처하는 사람이나 회사. 출판업자. 출판사 – **publishing** *n* [U]: *I work in publishing.* 나는 출판업에 종사한다.

puck /pʌk/ *n* a hard flat circular piece

of rubber that you hit with a stick in the game of HOCKEY ‖ 하키 경기에서 스틱으로 치는 딱딱하고 둥그렇고 납작한 고무 조각. 퍽

puck·er /'pʌkə/, **pucker up** v **1** [I, T] INFORMAL if your mouth puckers or you pucker it, your lips are pulled together tightly ‖ 양 입술이 서로 세게 당겨지다. 입술을 오므리다. 입술이 오므라들다: *She puckered up, ready for his kiss.* 그녀는 그의 키스에 대비하여 입술을 오므렸다. **2** [I] if cloth puckers, it gets folds in it so that it is no longer flat ‖ 천이 더 이상 납작 하지 않게 주름이 잡히다. – **puckered** adj – **pucker** n

pud·ding /'pʊdɪŋ/ n [C, U] a thick sweet creamy food made with milk, eggs, sugar, and flour, that is eaten cold ‖ 우유·계란·설탕·밀가루로 만들어 차갑게 해서 먹는 걸쭉하고 달콤하며 크림이 많은 음식. 푸딩: *chocolate pudding* 초콜릿 푸딩

pud·dle /'pʌdl/ n a small pool of water on a road, path etc., often caused by rain ‖ 종종 비로 인해 생긴, 도로·오솔길 등의 작은 물웅덩이: *children splashing in the puddles* 물웅덩이에서 물을 튀기는 아이들

pudg·y /'pʌdʒi/ adj fatter than usual ‖ 보통보다 살찐. 포동포동한: *short pudgy fingers* 짧고 통통한 손가락 – **pudginess** n [U]

pu·er·ile /'pyʊrəl, -raɪl/ adj FORMAL silly and stupid; CHILDISH ‖ 바보 같고 어리석은. 유치한; ㈜ childish: *puerile humor* 유치한 유머

puff¹ /pʌf/ v **1** [I] to breathe quickly and with difficulty as the result of a physical effort ‖ 육체적으로 애쓴 결과로 급하고 힘들게 숨쉬다. 숨을 헐떡이다: *Max was puffing heavily after climbing the stairs.* 맥스는 계단을 올라간 뒤에 심하게 숨을 헐떡이고 있었다. **2** [I, T] to breathe smoke from a cigarette, pipe etc. in and out ‖ 궐련·파이프에서 나오는 연기를 마셨다가 내뿜다. 담배를 뻐끔뻐끔 피우다: *William sat there puffing on his pipe.* 윌리엄은 파이프 담배를 뻐끔뻐끔 피우면서 거기에 앉았다. **3** [I, T] to blow steam or smoke out of something ‖ 물체에서 증기나 연기를 내뿜다: *an old car puffing fumes* 매연을 뿜는 낡은 자동차

puff sth ↔ **out** phr v [T] to make something bigger by filling it with air ‖ 무엇에 공기를 가득 채워 더 크게 만들다. …을 부풀리다: *a frog with its throat puffed out* 목을 부풀린 개구리

puff up phr v **1** [I,T also **puff** sth ↔ **up**]

to become bigger by filling with air, or to make something do this ‖ 공기가 가득 차서 더 크게 되다, 또는 커지게 하다. 부풀다. 부풀리다: *Birds puff up their feathers to stay warm.* 새들은 몸을 따뜻하게 하려고 깃털을 불룩하게 부풀린다. **2** [I] if your eye, face etc. puffs up, it swells ‖ 눈·얼굴 등이 붓다: *My eye puffed up where he hit me.* 그가 때린 내 눈 부위가 부어 올랐다.

puff² n **1** the action of breathing smoke into your mouth and blowing it out again ‖ 입 속으로 연기를 마셨다가 다시 내뱉는 행동. (담배의) 한 모금: *He took a puff on his cigar.* 그는 엽궐련을 한 대 피웠다. **2** a sudden short movement of air, smoke, or wind ‖ 공기나 연기, 또는 바람 등의 갑작스런 짧은 움직임. 한 차례 불기[일기]: *puffs of smoke coming from the chimney* 굴뚝에서 푹푹 나오는 연기 **3** a word used for various things that are light or seem full of air ‖ 가볍거나 공기로 가득 찬 것 같은 다양한 사물들에 쓰이는 단어: *a cream puff* (=light PASTRY) 슈크림 / *a powder puff* (=for putting powder on your body) 분첩

puf·fin /'pʌfɪn/ n a North Atlantic bird with a black and white body and a large, brightly colored beak ‖ 검고 흰 몸통과 밝은 색의 큰 부리가 있는 북대서양의 새. 바다오리

puff·y /'pʌfi/ adj puffy eyes, cheeks, faces etc. are swollen ‖ 눈·볼·얼굴 등이 부어오른: *Her eyes were red and puffy from crying.* 그녀의 눈은 울어서 빨갛게 부어올랐다. – **puffiness** n [U]

pug·na·cious /pʌg'neɪʃəs/ adj FORMAL very eager to quarrel or fight with people ‖ 사람들과 말다툼이나 싸움을 몹시 하고 싶어하는. 호전적인

puke /pyuk/ v [I, T] SLANG ⇨ VOMIT¹ – **puke** n [U]

pull¹ /pʊl/ v

1 ▶**MOVE TOWARD YOU** 자기 쪽으로 이동시키다◀ [I, T] to use your hands to move something toward you ‖ 무엇을 손을 써서 자기 쪽으로 이동시키다. 당기다. 끌다: *Mom, Sara's pulling my hair!* 엄마, 새라가 내 머리카락을 잡아당겨요! / *Wilson quickly pulled the door open.* 윌슨은 재빨리 문을 잡아당겨 열었다. / *Help me pull the trunk into the corner.* 트렁크를 구석으로 끌게 도와 줘. —opposite PUSH¹ —see picture on page 947

2 ▶**REMOVE** 제거하다◀ [T] to remove something from its place, especially by using force ‖ 특히 힘을 써서 어떤 것을 원래 있던 자리에서 제거하다. 뽑다. 빼

다: *She has to have her wisdom teeth pulled.* 그녀는 사랑니를 뽑아야만 한다. / *The baby's pulled everything out of the cupboards.* 그 아기는 찬장에서 모든 것을 끄집어 냈다. / *Some guy pulled a gun on one of the bank tellers.* (=he took out a gun and pointed it at someone) 어떤 사람이 은행 창구 직원 한 명에게 총을 빼 들었다.

3 ▶MAKE STH FOLLOW YOU 무엇을 끌려오게 하다◀ [I, T] to use a rope, chain etc. to make something move behind you in the direction you are moving ∥ 밧줄·쇠사슬 등을 이용하여 움직이는 방향으로 무엇이 뒤에서 움직이게 하다: *a car pulling a camper behind it* 뒤에 캠핑용 자동차를 끄는 차 —opposite PUSH[1]

4 ▶MUSCLE 근육◀ [T] to injure a muscle by stretching it too much while exercising ∥ 운동 중에 근육을 지나치게 긴장시켜 다치다: *I pulled a muscle in my thigh playing volleyball.* 나는 배구 경기 하다가 대퇴부 근육을 다쳤다.

5 pull sb's leg INFORMAL to tell someone something that is not true, as a joke ∥ 남에게 사실이 아닌 것을 농담으로 말하다. 남을 놀리다: *He never said that! You're pulling my leg!* 그는 절대 그렇게 말하지 않았어! 너 나 놀리는 거지!

6 pull strings to use a special position or relationship that you have in order to get something ∥ 무엇을 얻으려고 가지고 있는 특별한 지위나 관계를 이용하다. 백을 쓰다: *Samuels pulled strings to get her daughter a job in Mitchell's office.* 사무엘스는 그녀의 딸을 미첼의 회사에 취업시키려고 줄을 댔다.

7 ▶MOVE YOUR BODY 몸을 움직이다◀ [I, T] to use force to move your body somewhere ∥ 몸을 어딘가로 움직이기 위해 힘을 쓰다: *She pulled away from him in horror.* 그녀는 무서워 그에게서 도망쳤다. / *The kids pulled themselves up onto the platform.* 아이들은 플랫폼에 스스로 올라갔다.

8 pull the strings to control something, especially when you are not the person who is supposed to be controlling it ∥ 특히 조종하기로 되어 있지 않은 사람이 무엇을 조종하다. 막후에서 조종하다: *Who is really pulling the strings in the White House?* 백악관의 막후 조종자는 누구냐?

9 pull your weight to do your share of the work ∥ 자기 몫의 일을 하다: *If you don't start pulling your weight around here, you'll be fired!* 만약 여기에서 네 몫을 하지 않으면 너는 해고당해!

10 pull a stunt/trick/joke/prank

INFORMAL to do something that annoys or harms other people ∥ 다른 사람들을 성가시게 하거나 해치는 일을 하다. 책략을 쓰다/속이다/농담하다/장난치다: *kids pulling practical jokes* 못된 장난을 치는 아이들

11 ▶CLOTHING 옷◀ [I, T] if you pull a piece of clothing on or off, you put it on or take it off quickly ∥ 옷을 재빠르게 입거나 벗다

12 pull the rug out from under sb to suddenly take away something that someone was depending on to achieve what s/he wanted ∥ 어떤 사람이 원하는 것을 이루기 위해 믿고 있었던 것을 갑자기 빼앗다. 남의 신뢰를 앗아가다

13 pull a fast one SPOKEN to deceive someone ∥ 사람을 속이다: *Are you trying to pull a fast one on me?* 너 나 속이려고 하니?

pull sth ↔ **apart** *phr v* [T] to separate something into two or more pieces or groups ∥ 무엇을 둘 이상의 조각이나 그룹으로 나누다. …을 떼어놓다: *Loosen the roots and gently pull the plants apart.* 뿌리를 느슨하게 하고 부드럽게 묘목들을 떼어놓으세요. / *the ethnic problems that pulled Yugoslavia apart* 유고슬라비아를 분리시키는 인종 문제

pull away *phr v* [I] **1** to move ahead of a competitor by going faster or being more successful ∥ 더 빨리 가거나 보다 성공하여 경쟁자를 앞서다: *Chicago pulled away in the third quarter to win, 107-76.* 시카고 팀은 3쿼터에서 107대 76으로 앞서갔다. **2** to start to drive away from the place your car was stopped ∥ 정차한 장소에서 차를 몰고 가다. 발차하여 떠나다: *Grant pulled away from the curb.* 그랜트는 연석에서 차를 발차시켰다.

pull sth ↔ **down** *phr v* [T] to destroy something or make it no longer exist ∥ 무엇을 파괴하거나 더 이상 존재하지 않게 만들다. 헐다: *Citizens of Berlin pulled down the wall dividing their city.* 베를린 시민들은 그들의 도시를 가르는 벽을 헐어 버렸다.

pull for sb *phr v* [T] INFORMAL to encourage a person or team to succeed ∥ 성공하도록 사람이나 팀을 격려하다. 성원하다: *Good luck, Joey, we're pulling for you.* 행운을 빌어, 조이. 우리가 너를 성원하고 있어.

pull in *phr v* **1** [I,T **pull** sth ↔ **in**] to move a car into a particular space and stop it ∥ 차가 특정 장소에 들어와 멈추다: *Kevin pulled in behind me and parked.* 케빈은 내 뒤에 들어와서 주차했다. **2** [T

pull in sth] INFORMAL to get money, business etc., by doing something to attract people's attention ‖ 사람의 관심을 끌기 위해 무엇을 하여 돈·일 등을 얻다: *Hall pulled in 58% of the vote.* 홀은 총 투표수의 58%를 얻었다.

pull off *phr v* **1** [T **pull** sth ↔ **off**] INFORMAL to succeed in doing something difficult ‖ 어려운 것을 하는 데에 성공하다. …을 잘 해내다: *The Huskies pulled off a win in Saturday's game against WSU.* 허스키는 WSU를 상대로 한 토요일 경기에서 용케 이겼다. **2** [T **pull off** sth] to leave a road in order to stop or to turn into another road ‖ 멈추거나 다른 길로 들어가기 위해 길을 벗어나다: *I had to pull off the road, I was laughing so hard.* 나는 너무 웃겨서, 도로에 차를 대야 했다.

pull out *phr v* **1** [I] to drive a car onto a road from where you have stopped ‖ 멈췄던 장소에서 도로로 발차하다 **2** [I,T **pull** sb/sth ↔ **out**] to get yourself or someone else out of a bad or dangerous situation ‖ 나쁘거나 위험한 상황에서 자신이나 남을 빠져나오게 하다. 빠져나오다. 빠져나오게 하다: *Investors can pull out at any time by selling their shares.* 투자자들은 언제든지 자기들의 주식을 팔고 빠져나올 수 있다. **3 pull out all the stops** to do everything you can in order to make something succeed ‖ 무엇을 성공시키기 위해서 할 수 있는 모든 것을 하다. 모든 수단을 다 동원하다: *Fred's pulling out all the stops for his daughter's wedding.* 프레드는 그의 딸 결혼식을 위해 모든 수단을 동원하고 있다.

pull over *phr v* [I,T **pull** sb/sth ↔ **over**] to drive to the side of a road and stop your car, or to make someone do this ‖ 도로 한쪽으로 차를 세우거나 한쪽에 차를 대게 만들다. 차를 길가에 세우다: *We didn't realize we were speeding until the highway patrol pulled us over.* 우리는 고속도로 순찰대가 차를 길 옆에 세우라고 할때에야 비로소 우리가 과속하고 있다는 것을 깨달았다.

pull through *phr v* [I,T **pull** sb **through**] INFORMAL **1** to stay alive after a serious injury or illness, or to help someone do this ‖ 심각한 부상이나 질병 후에 살아나거나, 또는 남을 도와 살아나게 하다: *We all prayed that he would pull through.* 우리 모두는 그가 살아나기를 기도했다. **2** to continue to live or exist after being in a difficult or upsetting situation ‖ 어렵거나 당황스러운 상황이 있고 나서 계속해서 살거나 존

재하다. 난국을 극복하다: *The city managed to pull through its financial crisis.* 그 도시는 재정난을 겨우 극복했다.

pull together *phr v* **1** [I] to work hard with other people to achieve something ‖ 무엇을 성취하기 위해 다른 사람들과 열심히 일하다. 협력하여 일하다: *After the hurricane, neighbors pulled together to help each other.* 허리케인이 지나간 후 이웃들은 서로 도와 협력하여 일했다. **2 pull yourself together** INFORMAL to force yourself to stop being nervous, afraid, or disorganized ‖ 초조하거나 무섭거나, 또는 혼란스러운 상태를 스스로 멈추게 하다. 마음을 가라앉히다. 정신차리다: *Stop crying and pull yourself together!* 울지 말고 진정해!

pull up *phr v* **1** [I] to stop the car you are driving ‖ 운전하던 차가 멈추다. (차가) 서다: *A red Buick pulled up at the stop lights.* 빨간색의 뷰익 자동차가 정지 신호에서 멈춰섰다. **2 pull up a chair** to get a chair and sit down near someone ‖ 의자를 다른 사람 옆에 대어 앉다 **3** [T **pull** sth ↔ **up**] to use force to take plants out of the ground ‖ 힘을 써서 땅에서 풀을 뽑다. 잡아 뽑다. 뿌리째 뽑다

pull² *n* **1** an act of using force to move something toward you or in the same direction as you are going ‖ 자기 쪽으로 무엇을 움직이기 위해, 또는 자신이 가려는 방향과 같은 방향으로 이동시키기 위해 힘을 쓰는 행위. 끌어당기기: *Give the rope a strong pull.* 밧줄을 강하게 잡아당겨라. **2** [C usually singular] a strong force such as GRAVITY that makes things move in a particular direction ‖ 무엇을 특정 방향으로 움직이게 하는 중력 등의 강한 힘. 끄는 힘. 견인력: *the gravitational pull of the moon* 달의 중력 **3** [singular, U] INFORMAL power that gives you an unfair advantage ‖ 자신에게 불공정한 이익을 주는 힘. 영향력. 연줄: *a family with a lot of political pull* 정치적 연줄이 많은 가족

pul·ley /ˈpʊli/ *n* a piece of equipment consisting of a wheel over which you pull a chain or rope to lift heavy things ‖ 무거운 것을 들어올리기 위해 쇠사슬 또는 밧줄을 잡아당기는 바퀴가 달린 기구. 도르래

pull·out /ˈpʊlaʊt/ *n* **1** the act of an army, business etc. leaving a particular place ‖ 군대·기업체 등이 특정 장소를 떠나는 행위. 철수: *the pullout of NATO troops from the region* 그 지역에서의 NATO군의 철수 **2** part of a book or magazine that can be removed ‖ 책이나

잡지의 떼어낼 수 있는 부분. (책이나 잡지안에) 접어 넣은 페이지

pull·o·ver /'pʊl,oʊvə/ *n* a SWEATER without buttons ‖ 단추가 없는 스웨터. 풀오버

pull-up /'. ./ *n* an exercise in which you use your arms to pull yourself up to a metal BAR that is above your head ‖ 머리 위에 있는 철봉 위로 팔을 이용하여 자신을 끌어올리는 운동. 턱걸이

pul·mo·nar·y /'pʊlmə,nɛri, 'pʌl-/ *adj* TECHNICAL relating to or affecting the lungs ‖ 폐에 관련된, 또는 폐에 영향을 미치는. 폐의: *pulmonary disease* 폐병

pulp[1] /pʌlp/ *n* [U] **1** the soft inside part of a fruit or vegetable ‖ 과일 또는 채소 내부의 부드러운 부분. 과육(果肉) **2** a very soft substance that is almost liquid ‖ 거의 액체 상태의 매우 부드러운 물질. 펄프: *wood pulp* 목재 펄프 **3 beat sb to a pulp** INFORMAL to hit someone again and again until s/he is seriously injured ‖ 중상을 입을 때까지 누군가를 거듭하여 때리다. 늘씬하게 패주다

pulp[2] *adj* pulp books, magazines etc. are usually of poor quality and tell stories about sex and violence ‖ 책·잡지 등이 보통 질이 낮고 성(性)과 폭력에 관한 이야기를 하는. 저속한: *pulp novels* 저속한 소설

pulp[3] *v* [T] to beat or crush something until it becomes soft and like a liquid ‖ 부드럽고 액체처럼 될 때까지 무엇을 두드리거나 으깨다. …을 걸죽하게 만들다

pul·pit /'pʊlpɪt, 'pʌl-/ *n* a structure like a tall box at the front of a church, from which someone speaks ‖ 누군가가 연설할 수 있도록 교회 정면에 놓여 있는 높은 상자 모양의 구조물. 설교단

pul·sate /'pʌlseɪt/ *v* [I] to make sounds or movements that are strong and regular like a heart beating ‖ 심장 박동처럼 강하고 규칙적으로 소리를 내거나 움직이다. 진동하다: *loud pulsating music* 크게 진동하는 음악 – **pulsation** /pʌl'seɪʃən/ *n* [C, U]

pulse[1] /pʌls/ *n* **1** [C usually singular] the regular beat that can be felt as your heart pumps blood around your body ‖ 심장에서 몸 전체로 피를 뿜어낼 수 있는 규칙적인 박동. 맥박: *When I found him he didn't have a pulse.* 내가 그를 발견했을 때 그는 맥박이 없었다. **2** [C usually singular] also **pulse rate** the number of regular beats per minute as your heart pumps blood around your body ‖ 심장이 몸 전체로 피를 뿜어낼 때의 1분당 규칙적인 박동수. 맥박수: *A*

nurse came in and took my pulse. (=counted the number of beats) 한 간호사가 들어와서 나의 맥박수를 쟀다. **3** [C usually plural] a seed such as beans and PEAs that can be eaten ‖ 먹을 수 있는 콩·완두 등의 씨. 콩류 **4** an amount of light, sound, or energy that continues for a very short time ‖ 매우 짧은 시간 동안 지속되는 빛[소리, 에너지]의 양. 펄스: *an electric pulse* 전기 펄스

pulse[2] *v* [I] to move or flow with a steady rapid beat or sound ‖ 일정하며 빠른 박자나 소리를 내며 움직이거나 흐르다. 고동치다: *blood pulsing through the veins* 고동쳐 혈관을 흐르는 혈액

pul·ver·ize /'pʌlvə,raɪz/ *v* [T] **1** to crush something into powder ‖ 무엇을 부수어 가루로 만들다: *a machine that pulverizes rocks* 암석을 부수는 기계 **2** INFORMAL to defeat someone completely, especially in a sport or game ‖ 특히 스포츠나 게임에서 남을 완전히 패배시키다. 타도하다 – **pulverization** /,pʌlvərə'zeɪʃən/ *n* [U]

pu·ma /'pumə, 'pyumə/ *n* ⇨ COUGAR

pum·ice /'pʌmɪs/ *n* [C, U] very light rock from a VOLCANO, or a piece of this that you rub on your skin to make it soft ‖ 화산에서 나온 매우 가벼운 암석이나 피부를 부드럽게 하려고 문지르는 이 암석 조각. 부석(浮石). 속돌

pum·mel /'pʌməl/ *v* [T] to hit someone or something many times with your FISTs ‖ 사람이나 사물을 수차례 주먹으로 때리다

pump[1] /pʌmp/ *n* **1** a machine that forces liquid or gas into or out of something ‖ 힘을 들여 액체나 가스를 무엇의 안으로 집어넣거나 밖으로 빼내는 기계. 펌프. 양수기: *a water/air/gas pump* 양수기[공기 펌프, 가스 펌프] **2** a woman's shoe that is plain and does not fasten ‖ 장식이 없고 신발 끈을 매지 않는 여자 구두. 펌프스: *a pair of black pumps* 검정 펌프스 한 켤레

pump[2] *v* **1** [T] to make liquid or gas move in a particular direction using a pump ‖ 펌프를 이용하여 특정 방향으로 액체나 가스를 이동시키다. 펌프로 퍼올리다[퍼내다]: *a machine that pumps water into the fields* 들판으로 물을 퍼올리는 기계 **2** [I] to move liquid very quickly in and out or up and down ‖ 액체를 안팎이나 상하로 매우 빠르게 움직이다. (펌프처럼) 상하로 움직이다: *His heart was pumping fast.* 그의 심장은 빨리 뛰고 있었다. **3 pump sb (about sth)** INFORMAL to ask someone a lot of questions about something in order to find out information ‖ 정보를 알아내려고 남에게 무엇에 관해 많은 질문을 하다 **4 pump money into sth** INFORMAL to spend a lot of money on something such as a project ‖ 프로젝트 등에 많은 돈을 쓰다 **5 pump iron** INFORMAL to lift heavy weights regularly in order to get bigger and stronger muscles ‖ 근육을 더 크고 강하게 하기 위해 규칙적으로 무거운 역기를 들다. (아령 등으로) 몸을 단련하다

pump out *phr v* **1** [I,T **pump** sth ↔ **out**] to produce or supply something in large amounts ‖ 물체를 대량으로 생산하거나 공급하다. 계속 생산[공급]하다: *Loud music was pumping out of the speakers.* 요란한 음악이 스피커에서 계속해서 흘러 나오고 있었다. **2** [T **pump** sth ↔ **out**] to remove liquid from something using a pump ‖ 펌프를 이용해 무엇에서 액체를 제거하다. …에서 물을 퍼내다: *We had to pump the basement out after the pipes burst.* 우리는 파이프가 터진 후에 지하실에서 물을 퍼내야 했다.

pump up *phr v* [T] **1** [**pump** sb ↔ **up**] to increase someone's interest or excitement about something ‖ 무엇에 관한 남의 관심이나 흥분을 증가시키다. 흥을 북돋우다: *cheerleaders pumping up a crowd* 관중의 흥을 돋우는 치어리더들 **2** [**pump** sth ↔ **up**] to fill something such as a tire with air; INFLATE ‖ 타이어 등에 공기를 채우다; ㉣ inflate

pum·per·nick·el /ˈpʌmpɚˌnɪkəl/ *n* [U] a heavy dark brown bread ‖ 흑갈색의 막빵. 조제한 호밀빵

pump·kin /ˈpʌmpkɪn, ˈpʌŋkɪn/ *n* [C, U] a very large orange fruit that grows on the ground, or the inside of this eaten as food ‖ 땅 위에서 자라는 매우 큰 오렌지색의 열매나 음식으로 먹는 그것의 속. 호박: *pumpkin pie* 호박 파이 —see picture on page 944

pun /pʌn/ *n* an amusing use of a word or phrase that has two meanings, or of words with the same sound but different meanings. For example, Seven days without water makes one weak. (=1 week) ‖ 두 가지 뜻을 가진 단어나 구, 또는 동음이의어를 재미있게 사용함. 말장난. 약해진다고 물을 들면 물 없이 7일을 보내면 사람이 약해진다(one weak)[1주일이 된다(1 week)]. – **pun** *v* [I]

punch¹ /pʌntʃ/ *v* [T] **1** to hit someone or something hard with your FIST (=closed hand) ‖ 주먹으로 사람이나 사물을 세게 치다. 주먹으로 …을 쥐어박다: *Zach punched his brother right in the*

face. 재크는 동생의 오른쪽 얼굴을 주먹으로 때렸다. **2** to make a hole in something using a metal tool or other sharp object ‖ 금속 도구나 다른 예리한 물체를 사용하여 무엇에 구멍을 뚫다: *The conductor came along and punched our tickets.* 차장이 다가와서 우리 표에 구멍을 뚫었다. **3 punch a clock** to record the time that you start or finish work by putting a card into a special machine ‖ 특수 기계 안에 카드를 넣어 일을 시작하거나 마친 시간을 기록하다. 출퇴근 카드에 시간을 찍다

punch in *phr v* [I] to record the time that you arrive at work by putting a card into a special machine ‖ 특수 기계에 카드를 넣어 직장에 도착한 시간을 기록하다. 타임리코더를 찍고 출근하다

punch out *phr v* [I] to record the time that you leave work by putting a card into a special machine ‖ 특수 기계에 카드를 넣어 직장에서 떠나는 시간을 기록하다. 타임리코더로 시간을 찍고 퇴근하다

punch² *n* **1** a quick strong hit made with your FIST (=closed hand) ‖ 주먹으로 빠르고 강하게 한 대 침. 펀치: *a punch in the stomach* 복부의 일격(一擊) **2** [U] a drink made from fruit juice, sugar, water, and sometimes alcohol ‖ 과즙·설탕·물에 때때로 술을 섞어 만든 음료. 펀치 **3** a metal tool for cutting holes or for pushing something into a small hole ‖ 잘라내어 구멍을 내거나 무엇을 밀어 구멍을 내는 금속 도구. 펀치. 천공기: *a three-hole punch* 구멍 세 개짜리 펀치 **4** [U] a strong effective quality that makes people interested ‖ 사람들을 흥미롭게 하는 매우 효과적인 특성. 큰 효과: *We need something to give the ad campaign some punch.* 우리는 광고 캠페인에 효력을 높일 무엇인가가 필요하다.

punch·ing bag /ˈ.. ˌ./ *n* **1** a heavy leather bag that hangs from a rope, that is hit for exercise ‖ 밧줄로 매달아 운동을 하기 위해 치는 무거운 가죽 가방. 샌드백 **2 use sb as a punching bag** INFORMAL to hit someone hard, or to criticize someone a lot ‖ 누군가를 세게 치거나 몹시 비난하다

punch line /ˈ. ./ *n* the last few words of a joke or story, that make it funny or surprising ‖ 농담이나 이야기를 재미있거나 놀랍게 만드는 결정적인 글귀. 급소가 되는 글귀

punc·tu·al /ˈpʌŋktʃuəl/ *adj* arriving, happening etc. at exactly the time that has been arranged ‖ 정해진 시간에 정확히 도착하거나 발생하는. 시간을 엄수하

는 : *They're always punctual for appointments.* 그들은 항상 약속 시간을 잘 지킨다. – **punctuality** /ˌpˌʌŋktʃuˈæləti/ *n* [U]

punc·tu·ate /ˈpʌŋktʃuˌeɪt/ *v* [T] **1** to divide written work into sentences, phrases etc. using COMMAS, PERIODS etc. ‖ 글을 쉼표·마침표 등을 이용하여 문장·구 등으로 구분하다. 구두점을 찍다 **2 be punctuated by/with sth** to be interrupted many times by a noise ‖ 소음으로 수차례 방해받다: *A conversation with the Morgans is punctuated with brotherly insults and jokes.* 모건과의 대화는 격의 없는 욕설과 농담으로 중단되었다.

punc·tu·a·tion /ˌpʌŋktʃuˈeɪʃən/ *n* [U] the way that PUNCTUATION MARKS are used in a piece of writing ‖ 글에서 구두점을 사용하는 방법. 구두법

punctuation mark /ˌ...ˈ.. ˌ./ *n* a sign, such as a COMMA or QUESTION MARK, that is used in dividing a piece of writing into sentences, phrases etc. ‖ 글을 문장·구 등으로 구분하는 데에 쓰이는 쉼표나 물음표 등의 부호. 구두점

punc·ture¹ /ˈpʌŋktʃɚ/ *n* a small hole made when something is PUNCTUREd ‖ 무엇이 찔려서 생긴 작은 구멍. 펑크

puncture² *v* [I, T] to make or get a small hole in something, so that air or liquid can get out ‖ 공기나 액체가 빠져나갈 수 있게 무엇에 작은 구멍을 내거나 구멍이 나다. 구멍이 뚫리다. 구멍을 뚫다 : *Jay's in the hospital with a punctured lung.* 제이는 폐에 구멍이 나서 입원해 있다.

pun·dit /ˈpʌndɪt/ *n* someone who knows a lot about a particular subject, and is often asked for his/her opinion ‖ 특정 주제에 대해 많이 알고 있어서 종종 견해에 대한 청탁을 받는 사람. 전문가: *political pundits* 정치 전문가

pun·gent /ˈpʌndʒənt/ *adj* having a strong smell or taste ‖ 강한 냄새나 맛이 나는. 자극적인. 얼얼한: *the pungent smell of onions* 자극적인 양파 냄새

pun·ish /ˈpʌnɪʃ/ *v* [T] to make someone suffer because s/he has done something wrong or broken the law ‖ 남이 나쁜 짓을 하거나 법을 어겨서 고통을 주다. 처벌하다: *Danny was punished for breaking a window.* 대니는 창문을 깨서 벌을 받았다.

pun·ish·a·ble /ˈpʌnɪʃəbəl/ *adj* deserving legal punishment ‖ 법적 처벌을 받을 만한. 벌을 받아 마땅한: *Murder is punishable by life imprisonment.* 살

인죄는 종신형에 처해야 마땅하다.

pun·ish·ing /ˈpʌnɪʃɪŋ/ *adj* making you feel very tired and weak ‖ 매우 피곤하고 약하게 하는. 지쳐 빠지게 하는: *a punishing walk* 몹시 지치게 하는 보행

pun·ish·ment /ˈpʌnɪʃmənt/ *n* **1** a way in which a person or an action is punished ‖ 사람이나 행위가 처벌받는 상태. 처벌받기: *There are harsh/severe punishments for drug dealing.* 마약 거래는 엄한[가혹한] 처벌을 받는다. ✗DON'T SAY "strict/strong punishments."✗ "strict/strong punishments"라고는 하지 않는다. **2** [U] the act of punishing someone, or the process of being punished ‖ 남을 처벌하는 행위, 또는 처벌받는 과정: *We are determined that the terrorists will not escape punishment.* 우리는 테러리스트들이 처벌을 피할 수 없을 것이라고 판단했다. / *As punishment, Marshall had to stay after school.* 벌로 마샬은 방과 후 학교에 남아야 했다. — see also CAPITAL PUNISHMENT

pu·ni·tive /ˈpyunətɪv/ *adj* intended as punishment ‖ 처벌을 위한. 징벌적인. 처벌의: *The government's first punitive action/measure was to take away the organization's federal funding.* 정부의 첫 번째 제재 조치는 그 조직의 연방 재원을 박탈하는 것이었다. / *punitive damages* (=money that is paid as a punishment) 징벌적 손해 배상금

punk /pʌŋk/ *n* [U] **1** also **punk rock** /ˌ. ˈ./ a type of loud violent music popular in the late 1970s and 1980s, played by people with brightly colored hair, who wore chains, pins, and torn clothing ‖ 밝게 머리카락을 염색하고 쇠사슬·핀·찢어진 옷을 착용한 사람들이 연주한, 1970년대 후반과 1980년대에 유행한 요란하고 격렬한 양식의 음악. 펑크(록) **2** INFORMAL a boy or young man who likes to start fights, do things that are illegal, etc. ‖ 싸움 걸기를 좋아하며 불법적인 일 등을 하는 소년이나 젊은이. 불량배

punt /pʌnt/ *n* in football, a long kick that you make after dropping the ball from your hands ‖ 미식축구에서, 손에서 공을 떨어뜨린 후 멀리 발로 차기. 펀트 – **punt** *v* [I, T]

pu·ny /ˈpyuni/ *adj* small, thin, and weak ‖ 작고 호리호리하고 연약한. 가냘픈. 왜소한: *a puny little kid* 가냘프고 작은 아이

pup /pʌp/ *n* **1** ⇨ PUPPY **2** a young SEAL or OTTER ‖ 어린 물개나 수달

pu·pil /ˈpyupəl/ *n* **1** a child or young person in school ‖ 학교를 다니는 어린이

나 젊은이. 학생 **2** the small black round area in the middle of your eye ‖ 눈 중앙의 조그맣고 둥글며 까만 부분. 동공

pup·pet /ˈpʌpɪt/ n **1** a model of a person or animal that you can move by pulling strings that are attached to parts of its body, or by putting your hand inside it ‖ 몸의 곳곳에 부착된 줄을 당기거나 그 안에 손을 넣어서 움직일 수 있는 사람이나 동물의 모형. 꼭두각시. 손가락 인형: *a puppet show* 인형극 **2** a person or organization that is no longer independent, and is controlled by someone else ‖ 더 이상 독립적이지 않고 남에게 통제받는 사람이나 조직. 괴뢰. 꼭두각시: *a puppet government* 괴뢰 정부

pup·pet·eer /ˌpʌpɪˈtɪr/ n someone who performs with PUPPETS ‖ 꼭두각시로 공연하는 사람. 꼭두각시 부리는 사람

pup·py /ˈpʌpi/ n a young dog ‖ 어린 개. 강아지

puppy love /ˈ.. ./ n [U] a young boy's or girl's love for someone, that people do not think of as serious ‖ 사람들이 심각하게 생각하지 않는 어떤 사람에 대한 어린 소년이나 소녀의 사랑. 풋사랑

pur·chase¹ /ˈpɚtʃəs/ v [T] to buy something ‖ 무엇을 사다. 구입하다: *The insurance company will try to convince customers to purchase the full range of insurance.* 그 보험회사는 고객들을 전 범위 보상보험에 가입하도록 납득시키기 위해 노력할 것이다. / *Maybe the best gift is one that has not been purchased.* 아마도 최고의 선물은 구입하지 않은 것일지도 모른다.

purchase² n **1** [C, U] the act of buying something ‖ 무엇을 구입하는 행위. 구입: *The two women had just made several large purchases.* 두 여자는 단지 몇 개의 큰 물건만 샀다. **2** something that has been bought ‖ 구입된 것. 구매품: *The store will deliver your purchases.* 그 가게는 너의 구매품을 배달해 줄 것이다.

pure /pyʊr/ adj **1** not mixed with anything else ‖ 다른 어떤 것과도 섞이지 않은. 순수한: *pure gold* 순금 **2** complete ‖ 완전한: *It was pure chance that we were there at the same time.* 우리가 동시에 그곳에 있었다는 것은 완전히 우연이었다. ✗DON'T SAY "the chance was pure."✗ "the chance was pure."라고는 하지 않는다. **3** clean, without anything harmful or unhealthy ‖ 해롭거나 유해한 것이 없이 깨끗한: *pure drinking water* 깨끗한 식수 **4 pure science/math etc.** work done in order to increase our knowledge of something rather than to

make practical use of it ‖ 무엇을 실제 사용하기보다는 지식을 증대시키기 위해 행해진 일. 순수 과학/순수 수학: *pure research* 순수 연구 —compare APPLIED **5** LITERARY having the quality of being completely good or moral ‖ 완전히 선하거나 도덕적인 특성을 지닌. 순결한

pu·ree /pyʊˈreɪ/ n [C, U] food that is boiled or crushed until it is almost a liquid ‖ 거의 액체가 될 때까지 끓이거나 으깬 음식. 퓌레: *tomato puree* 토마토 퓌레 – **puree** v [T]

pure·ly /ˈpyʊrli/ adv completely and only ‖ 완전하면서도 오로지. 전적으로. 단지: *He did it for purely selfish reasons.* 그는 단지 이기적인 이유로 그것을 했다. / *We met purely by chance.* 우리는 참으로 우연히 만났다.

pur·ga·to·ry /ˈpɚgəˌtɔri/ n [U] a place where, according to Roman Catholic beliefs, the souls of dead people must suffer for the bad things they have done, until they are good enough to enter heaven ‖ 로마 가톨릭 교리에 따르면 죽은 사람들의 영혼이 천당에 들어갈 만큼 충분히 선해질 때까지 저질렀던 나쁜 일에 대한 고통을 받는 장소. 연옥(煉獄)

purge /pɚdʒ/ v [T] **1** to force your opponents to leave an organization or place, often by using violence ‖ 종종 폭력을 써서 조직이나 장소에서 상대를 강제로 떠나게 하다. 추방하다. 숙청하다: *The army was purged of anyone the government considered dangerous.* 군대는 정부가 위험하다고 생각하는 인사를 숙청했다. **2** TECHNICAL to get rid of something bad that is in your body, or of bad feelings ‖ 몸 안의 나쁜 것이나 좋지 않은 감정을 없애다. 깨끗이 하다. 정화하다 – **purge** n

pu·ri·fy /ˈpyʊrəˌfaɪ/ v [T] to remove the dirty or unwanted parts from something ‖ 사물의 더럽거나 필요없는 부분들을 제거하다. 정화[정제]하다: *The water should be purified before drinking.* 물은 마시기 전에 정화되어야 한다. – **purification** /ˌpyʊrəfəˈkeɪʃən/ n [U]

pur·ist /ˈpyʊrɪst/ n someone who has very strict ideas about what is right or correct in a particular subject ‖ 특정 주제의 옳거나 정확한 것에 대하여 매우 엄격한 관념을 지닌 사람. 순수주의자

Pur·it·an /ˈpyʊrətən, -rətⁿ/ n a member of a Protestant religious group in the 16th and 17th centuries, who wanted to make religion simpler ‖ 16·17세기에 종교를 보다 단순화하고 싶어 했던 개신교 종교 단체의 일원. 청교도

pu·ri·tan·i·cal /ˌpyʊrəˈtænɪkəl/ *adj*
having strict attitudes about religion
and moral behavior ‖ 종교와 도덕적 행위
에 대해 엄격한 태도를 취하는. 엄격한.
금욕적인: *puritanical parents who won't
let their children go to dances* 자녀들이
춤추러 가는 것을 허락하지 않는 엄격한
부모

pu·ri·ty /ˈpyʊrəti/ *n* [U] the quality or
state of being pure ‖ 순수한 특성이나 상
태. 깨끗함. 청결: *The purity of the
sound/colors was incredible.* 소리[색]의
순도는 믿을 수 없을 정도였다. / *religious
purity* 종교적 순수성

pur·ple /ˈpəpəl/ *n* [U] a dark color
made from red mixed with blue ‖ 빨강에
파랑이 혼합된 어두운 색. 자줏빛 –
purple *adj*

pur·port /pəˈpɔrt/ *v* **1 purport to be**
FORMAL to claim to be someone or to do
something, especially when it is possible
that the claim is not true ‖ 특히 주장이
사실이 아닐 가능성이 있을 때, 아무개라
는 사람이라고 하거나 무엇을 한다고 주장
하다. …이라고 칭하다[주장하다]: *He
purports to be the son of the wealthy
Italian banker.* 그는 부유한 이탈리아 은
행가의 아들이라고 자칭한다. **2 be
purported to be** to claim that
something is true, especially when it is
possible that it is not true ‖ 특히 사실이
아닐 가능성이 있을 때, 무엇이 사실이라
고 주장하다: *The painting is purported
to be the work of Monet.* 그 그림은 모네
의 작품으로 주장되고 있다. – **purport**
/ˈpəpɔrt/ *n*

pur·pose /ˈpəpəs/ *n* **1** the aim that an
event, process, or activity is supposed
to achieve ‖ 행사[과정, 행위]가 달성하기
로 되어 있는 목적. 목표. 의도: *The
purpose of this exercise is to increase
your strength.* 당신의 체력을 증강시키는
것이 이 운동의 목적이다. / *The Red
Cross sent supplies for medical
purposes.* 적십자는 의료용 물자를 보냈
다. / *For the purposes of the report, low
income was defined as $30,000 a year
for a family of four.* 보고의 목적으로 저
소득은 4인 가족당 연간 30,000달러로 정
의되었다. **2 on purpose** deliberately ‖
고의로: *Firefighters believe the fire was
started on purpose.* 소방수들은 그 화재
를 고의로 일으킨 것으로 여긴다. **3** [U]
determination to succeed in what you
want to do ‖ 하고 싶은 것을 성취하려는
결심. 의지력. 결의: *She came back from
vacation with a new sense of purpose.*
그녀는 새로운 결의를 하고 휴가에서 돌아

왔다.

pur·pose·ful /ˈpəpəsfəl/ *adj* having a
clear aim or purpose; determined ‖ 분명
한 목표나 의도를 지닌; 결연한: *a
purposeful ambitious young woman* 목
적이 있고 야심에 찬 젊은 여자

pur·pose·ly /ˈpəpəsli/ *adv* deliberately
‖ 고의로: *They purposely left him out of
the discussion.* 그들은 고의로 토론에서
그를 제외시켰다.

purr /pə/ *v* [I] **1** if a cat purrs, it makes
a soft low sound in its throat ‖ 고양이가
목구멍에서 부드럽고 낮은 소리를 내다.
가르랑거리다 **2** if an engine purrs, it
works perfectly and makes a quiet
smooth sound ‖ 엔진이 잘 작동하고 조용
하고 듣기 좋은 소리를 내다. 경쾌한 소리
를 내다 – **purr** *n*

purse¹ /pəs/ *n* **1** a bag used by women
to carry money and personal things ‖ 돈
과 개인 용품들을 갖고 다니는 여성용 가
방. 핸드백: *I think my glasses are still in
my purse.* 내 생각엔 안경이 아직 내 핸드
백 속에 있는 것 같아. **2 control/hold
the purse strings** to control the money
in a family, company etc. ‖ 가족·회사 등
의 돈을 관리하다

purse² *v* [T] **purse your lips** to bring
your lips together tightly in a circle,
especially to show disapproval ‖ 특히 불
만을 나타내기 위해 양 입술을 동그랗게
오므리다. 입술을 꽉 다물다

purs·er /ˈpəsə/ *n* an officer who is
responsible for the money on a ship and
is in charge of the passengers' rooms,
comfort etc. ‖ 배의 돈을 책임지고 승객의
방·편안함을 관리하는 고급 선원. 사무장

pur·sue /pəˈsu/ *v* [T] FORMAL **1** to
continue doing an activity or trying to
achieve something over a long time ‖ 활
동을 계속하거나 오랜 시간에 걸쳐 무엇을
성취하기 위해 계속해서 노력하다. 착실하
게 밀고 나가다: *Thomas is pursuing a
doctorate in biology.* 토마스는 생물학 박
사 학위 과정을 밟고 있는 중이다. **2** to
chase or follow someone or something
in order to catch him, her, or it ‖ 사람이
나 사물을 잡으려고 뒤쫓거나 따라가다.
…을 추적하다: *The police are pursuing
the suspect along Nordhoff Blvd.* 경찰은
노드호프 대로를 따라 피의자를 쫓고 있
다. **3 pursue the matter/question** to
continue trying to persuade someone,
ask, or find out about a particular
subject ‖ 계속해서 남을 설득하거나 특정
주제에 대해 묻거나, 또는 알아내려고 애
쓰다: *The company plans to pursue the
matter in court.* 그 기업은 법정에서 그

문제를 추궁할 계획이다.

pur·suit /pəˈsuːt/ n 1 [U] the act of chasing or following someone ‖ 누군가를 뒤쫓거나 따라가는 행위. 추적: *police cars in hot pursuit of the robbers* (=following close behind them) 강도를 맹렬히 추적하는 경찰차 2 FORMAL the act of trying to achieve something in a determined way ‖ 단호하게 무엇을 이루려고 노력하는 행위. 추구: *the right to life, liberty, and the pursuit of happiness* 삶·자유·행복 추구의 권리 3 FORMAL an activity that you spend a lot of time doing ‖ 자기가 많은 시간을 들여 하는 행위. 일: *Nancy enjoys outdoor pursuits.* 낸시는 옥외에서 하는 일을 즐긴다.

pur·vey·or /pəˈveɪə/ n FORMAL someone who supplies information, goods, or services to people as a business ‖ 사업상 사람들에게 정보나 물건, 또는 서비스를 제공하는 사람. 조달자: *purveyors of fine cheeses* 좋은 치즈의 조달자 **- purvey** v [T]

pus /pʌs/ n [U] a thick yellowish liquid produced in an infected part of your body ‖ 신체의 감염된 부분에 생기는 탁하고 노르스름한 액체. 고름

push¹ /pʊʃ/ v

1 ▶MOVE 움직이다◀ [I, T] to move a person or thing away from you by pressing with your hands ‖ 손으로 밀어서 사람이나 물건을 자신에게서 떨어뜨려 놓다. 밀다: *A couple of guys were pushing an old Volkswagen down the street.* 두 사람이 낡은 폭스바겐을 길 아래쪽으로 밀고 있었다. / *Lisa pushed Amy into the pool.* 리자는 에이미를 수영장 속으로 밀었다. / *Can you push harder?* 좀 더 세게 밀어 줄래? 움직이지 않아. —opposite PULL¹ — see picture on page 947

2 ▶MAKE STH START/STOP 무엇을 가동시키다/정지시키다◀ [I, T] to press a button, SWITCH etc. to make a machine start or stop working ‖ 기계를 작동시키거나 정지시키려고 버튼·스위치 등을 누르다: *Just push the off button.* 꼭 정지 버튼을 눌러라.

3 ▶TRY TO GET PAST SB 누군가를 제치려 애쓰다◀ [I, T] to move somewhere by pushing people away from you ‖ 자신에게서 사람들을 밀어내며 어딘가로 가다. 밀어제치고 나아가다: *Heather pushed past us without speaking.* 헤더는 말없이 우리를 밀어제치고 지나갔다. / *people trying to push their way to the front* 앞쪽으로 밀어제치고 나아가려는 사람들

4 ▶PERSUADE 설득하다◀ [I, T] to try to persuade someone to accept or do something ‖ 무엇을 받아들이거나 하도록 누군가를 설득하려고 하다. 강행[강요]하다. 추진하다: *The agency is pushing to increase US exports.* 그 대행사는 미국 수출 증대를 추진하고 있다. / *citizens pushing for stricter gun controls* 보다 엄격한 총기 규제를 요구하는 시민들 / *My parents pushed me into going to college.* 부모님은 나에게 대학에 갈 것을 강요했다.

5 ▶WORK HARD 열심히 일하다◀ [T] to make someone work very hard ‖ 남을 아주 열심히 일하게 하다. 몰아대다: *Royce has been pushing himself too much lately.* 로이스는 너무 지나치게 늦게까지 자신을 혹사시켜 오고 있다.

6 ▶INCREASE/DECREASE 증가하다/감소하다◀ [I, T] to increase or decrease an amount, number, or value ‖ 양이나 수, 또는 가치를 증가시키거나 감소시키다. 늘리다. 늘다: *New medical technology has pushed the cost of health care up/higher.* 새로운 의학 기술이 의료비를 상승시켰다. / *The recession has pushed stock market prices down/lower.* 경기 침체로 주가(株價)가 하락했다.

7 ▶DRUGS 마약◀ [T] INFORMAL to sell illegal drugs ‖ 불법적인 마약을 팔다. 마약을 밀매하다

8 push your luck/push it INFORMAL to do something or ask for something again, when this is likely to annoy someone or be risky ‖ 남을 귀찮게 하거나 위험의 소지가 있는 경우에 자꾸 무엇을 하거나 요청하다. 독촉하다: *Don't push it! I'll tell you when I'm ready.* 재촉하지 마! 준비되면 너한테 말할 테니까.

push ahead phr v [I] to continue with a plan or activity in a determined way ‖ 단호하게 계획이나 활동을 계속하다. 추진하다. 밀고 나아가다: *The airport is pushing ahead with its program to expand.* 그 공항은 확장 계획을 계속 추진 중이다.

push around phr v [T **push sb ↔ around**] INFORMAL to tell someone who is less important or weaker than you what to do in a rude or threatening way ‖ 자신보다 덜 중요하고 보다 약한 사람에게, 해야 할 것을 무례하거나 위협적으로 말하다. (자꾸 지시하여)못살게 굴다: *Don't let your boss push you around.* 네 상사가 네게 이래라 저래라 하게 놔두지 마. / *A bunch of boys were pushing one of the younger kids around.* 한 무리의 소년들이 자신들보다 어린 아이들 중 한

명을 못살게 굴고 있었다.

push on *phr v* [I] to continue traveling somewhere or trying to achieve something ‖ 어딘가로 여행을 계속하거나 무엇을 이루려고 계속해서 애쓰다. 여행이나 업무를 계속하다: *The others stopped for a rest, but I pushed on to the top.* 다른 사람들은 쉬기 위해 멈췄으나 나는 정상으로 계속해서 올라갔다.

push sth ↔ **through** *phr v* [T] to persuade someone to accept a law, policy, plan etc., even though there is opposition to it ‖ 법·정책·계획 등을 반대가 있더라도 받아들이도록 남을 설득하다. 억지로 통과시키다: *Wilson pushed through a measure to increase the state sales tax.* 윌슨은 주(州) 판매세를 증가시키기 위한 법안을 억지로 통과시켰다.

push² *n* [C usually singular] **1** the act of pushing someone or something ‖ 사람이나 물체를 미는 행위. 밀기: *Just give the door a push if it's stuck.* 문이 움직이지 않는다면 한 번 밀어봐라. **2** an attempt to get or achieve something ‖ 무엇을 얻거나 성취하기 위한 시도. 노력: *Eastern Europe's push to modernize their economies* 동유럽의 경제를 현대화하려는 노력 **3 if/when push comes to shove** when or if a situation becomes extremely difficult ‖ 상황이 매우 어려워질 때나 어려워지면. 위급한 때에: *If push comes to shove, I can always rent out the house.* 상황이 어려워지면, 나는 언제든지 집을 세놓을 수 있다. **4** an attack in which an army goes into a particular area ‖ 군대가 특정 지역에 진입하는 공격. 대공격. 돌격: *the army's push into enemy territory* 적군 영토로의 군의 돌격

push·er /'pʊʃɚ/ *n* INFORMAL someone who sells illegal drugs ‖ 마약을 파는 사람. 마약 밀매자

push·o·ver /'pʌʃ,oʊvɚ/ *n* INFORMAL **be a pushover** to be easy to persuade, influence, or defeat ‖ 설득하거나 영향을 미치거나, 또는 패배시키기 쉽다

push-up /'. ./ *n* an exercise in which you lie on the floor on your front and push yourself up with your arms ‖ 엎드려 뻗쳐서 양팔로 자신을 들어올리는 운동. 엎드려 팔굽혀펴기

push·y /'pʊʃi/ *adj* so determined to succeed and get what you want that you behave in a rude way ‖ 성공하여 자신이 원하는 것을 얻기 위해 지나치게 단호하여 무례하게 구는. 뻔뻔한. 밀어붙이는: *pushy salespeople* 뻔뻔한 판매원들

puss·y·cat /'pʊsi,kæt/ *n* INFORMAL **1**

also **puss** a word meaning a cat, used when talking to children ‖ 아이들에게 말할 때 쓰이는 고양이를 뜻하는 단어. 야옹이 **2** someone who is kind and gentle ‖ 친절하고 다정한 사람. 호감을 주는 사람

puss·y·foot /'pʊsi,fʊt/ *v* [I] INFORMAL to be too careful and afraid to do something ‖ 일을 하는 데에 너무 조심스럽고 두려워하다. 망설이다. 주저하다: *Stop pussyfooting around and decide!* 망설이지 말고 결정해!

puss·y wil·low /,pʊsi 'wɪloʊ/ *n* a tree with long thin branches and soft round flowers that look like fur ‖ 길고 가는 가지들과 부드럽고 둥근 모양의 털처럼 생긴 꽃이 있는 나무. 갯버들의 일종

put /pʊt/ *v* **put, put, putting** [T]
1 ▶MOVE TO PLACE/POSITION◀ 장소/위치로 움직이다 to move someone or something into a particular place or position ‖ 특정 장소나 위치로 사람이나 사물을 이동시키다. 놓다. 두다: *Where did you put the newspaper?* 너 신문을 어디에 두었니? / *Put everything in the dishwasher and start it, okay?* 식기 세척기 안에 모두 넣은 다음 작동시켜라, 알겠어? / *I put some money into our account.* 나는 우리 예금 계좌에 약간의 돈을 넣었다. / *It's time to put the kids to bed.* (=make them go into their beds) 지금은 아이들을 재울 시간이다.

Bill put on his jacket.

2 ▶CHANGE◀ 바꾸다 to change someone's situation or the way s/he feels ‖ 누군가의 상황이나 느낌을 바꾸다: *The recent layoffs put 250 people out of work.* 최근의 임시 해고로 인해 250명이 직장을 잃었다. / *Ohio State's win put them in the playoffs.* 오하이오 주의 승리는 그들을 플레이오프에 진출하게 했다. / *music to put you in a relaxed mood* 너를 편안하게 해 주는 음악

3 ▶WRITE◀ 쓰다 to write or print something in a particular place ‖ 특정 장소에 무엇을 쓰거나 인쇄하다: *Put your name at the top of your answer sheet.* 답안지 맨 위에 네 이름을 적어라. / *We put an ad in the paper.* 우리는 신문에 광고를 냈다.

4 put emphasis/pressure/blame etc. on to emphasize something, make someone feel pressure, blame someone etc. ‖ 무엇을 강조하다, 남에게 압박감을

주다, 남을 비난하다: *People are starting to put pressure on Congress to pass gun control laws.* 사람들은 총기 규제법을 통과시키기 위해 의회에 압력을 가하기 시작하고 있다.

5 put an end/stop to sth to stop something such as an activity that is harmful or not acceptable ‖ 해롭거나 인정되지 않는 행동 등을 멈추다. …을 그만두다: *The pollution is caused by too many people driving to work; the city wants to put a stop to this practice.* 너무 많은 사람들이 직장에 차를 몰고 가서 대기 오염이 발생한다. 시민들은 이러한 관행이 중단되기를 희망한다.

6 ▶EXPRESS 표현하다◀ to say or express something in a particular way ‖ 특정하게 무엇을 말하거나 표현하다: *To put it bluntly, a lot of people just don't like her.* 솔직하게 말해서, 많은 사람들이 그녀를 좋아하지 않는다. / *Well, let me put it this way: he's lied to us before.* 좋아, 이렇게 말할게. 그가 전에 우리에게 거짓말을 했어.

7 ▶HAVE IMPORTANCE/QUALITY 중요성/특성이 있다◀ to consider something to have a particular level of importance or quality ‖ 무엇이 특정 수준의 중요성이나 특성이 있다고 생각하다. …이라고 평가하다: *Almeida says he "puts his family first."* 알메이다는 "그의 가족을 우선으로 여긴다"고 말한다. / *The new study puts UCLA among the top five research universities in the US.* 그 새로운 연구는 UCLA를 미국 내 상위 5개 연구 대학들 속에 들게 한다.

8 put sth behind you to try to forget about a bad experience or a mistake so that it does not affect you now ‖ 나쁜 경험이나 실수에 대해 현재 영향을 미치지 않도록 잊으려고 애쓰다: *Vietnam veterans talked of the need to put the war behind them.* 베트남전 참전 용사들은 그 전쟁을 잊어야 할 필요성에 대해 말했다.

9 put faith/confidence/trust etc. in to trust or believe in someone or something ‖ 사람이나 사물을 신뢰하거나 믿다: *These people put little trust in doctors.* 이 사람들은 의사들을 거의 신뢰하지 않는다. —see also **put your mind to** (MIND¹)

put sth ↔ **aside** *phr v* [T] **1** to ignore a problem or disagreement in order to achieve something ‖ 무엇을 달성하려고 문제나 불일치를 무시하다. …을 제쳐놓다: *Try to put your feelings aside and look at the facts.* 너의 감정을 떠나서 사실을 보려고 노력해라. **2** to save something to be used or dealt with later ‖ 나중에 사용되거나 처리되도록 무엇을 저축하다: *I have money put aside for emergencies.* 나는 긴급한 경우를 대비해서 돈을 저축했다.

put sth ↔ **away** *phr v* [T] to put something in the place where it is usually kept ‖ 무엇을 일상적으로 두는 장소에 놓다. 치우다: *Those kids never put anything away!* 저 아이들은 어떤 것도 절대 치우지 않아!

put sth ↔ **back** *phr v* [T] to put things or people in the place or situation they were before ‖ 사물이나 사람들을 전에 있던 장소나 상황에 놓다. 되돌려 놓다: *Put the milk back in the fridge, please.* 우유를 냉장고에 도로 넣어 주세요. / *a program to put people back to work* 사람들을 직장으로 되돌려 보내는 프로그램

put down *phr v* [T] **1** [**put** sb **down**] INFORMAL to criticize someone and make him/her feel silly or stupid ‖ 누군가를 비난하여 어리석거나 멍청한 기분이 들게 하다. 창피하게 만들다: *The teachers here never put you down.* 여기에 계신 선생님들은 너를 절대 창피하게 만들지 않는다. **2** [**put** sth ↔ **down**] INFORMAL to write something on a piece of paper ‖ 무엇을 종이에 적다. 기입하다: *I put down that I'd be available to work on Saturdays.* 나는 토요일에 일할 수 있다고 적었다. **3** [**put** sb/sth ↔ **down**] to use force to stop people who are fighting against a government ‖ 정부를 상대로 투쟁하고 있는 사람들을 무력으로 저지하다. 진압하다: *Soldiers were sent to put down the rebellion.* 그 반란을 진압하기 위해 군인들이 파견되었다.

put sth ↔ **forward** *phr v* [T] to suggest a plan, idea etc. ‖ 계획·생각 등을 제안하다: *a treaty put forward by the Dutch* 네덜란드인이 제안한 협정

put sth ↔ **in** *phr v* [T] **1** to add or replace equipment ‖ 장비를 설치하거나 교체하다: *We had to have a new furnace put in.* 우리는 새 난로를 설치해야만 했다. **2** to ask for something in an official way ‖ 공식적으로 무엇을 요청하다. (요구 등을) 제기하다: *Sawyer put in his expenses claim last week.* 소이어는 지난주에 그의 비용을 청구했다. **3** to spend time doing something ‖ 무엇을 하는 데에 시간을 쓰다: *Doug is putting in a lot of hours at work.* (=he is working a lot) 더그는 일에 많은 시간을 보내고 있다.

put sth **into** sth *phr v* [T] **1 put energy/effort/enthusiasm etc. into**

sth to use energy etc. when you are doing something ‖ 무엇을 하는 데에 힘을 쓰다. …의 힘/노력/열정을 쏟다: *Koskoff put a lot of time and effort into this project.* 코스코프는 이 프로젝트에 많은 시간과 노력을 쏟았다. **2 put sth into action/effect/practice** to start using something such as an idea or plan ‖ 생각이나 계획 등을 행사하거나 시행하다. …을 실행에 옮기다/시행하다/실행하다: *The college hopes to put the changes into effect by August 1.* 그 대학은 변화들이 8월 1일까지는 시행되기를 희망한다.

put off *phr v* [T] **1 [put sth ↔ off]** to delay something, or to delay doing something ‖ 무엇을 늦추거나 무엇을 하는 것을 미루다: *Many Americans put off filling out their tax forms as long as possible.* 많은 미국인들은 그들의 세무 서류 작성을 가능한 한 오랫동안 미룬다. **2 [put sb ↔ off]** to make someone dislike something or someone, or to make him/her not want to do something ‖ 어떤 사람이 사물이나 남을 싫어하거나 무엇을 하고 싶지 않게 만들다. 불쾌하게 하다. …할 마음이 없게 만들다: *Don't be put off by the restaurant's decor; the food is excellent.* 식당 장식 때문에 기분 나빠하지 마라. 음식은 훌륭하거든.

put on *phr v* [T]
1 ▶CLOTHES 옷◀ [put sth ↔ on] to dress yourself in a piece of clothing ‖ 옷을 입다: *Put your coat on – it's cold.* 코트를 입어라. 날씨가 춥다. —see usage note at DRESS¹

2 ▶AFFECT/INFLUENCE 작용하다/영향을 미치다◀ [put sth ↔ on sth] to do something that affects or influences something else ‖ 다른 것에 작용하거나 영향을 미치는 무엇을 하다: *The government put a freeze on the construction of new nuclear power plants.* (=they stopped it) 정부는 새 핵발전소 건설을 동결시켰다[중단시켰다].

3 put on weight/5 pounds etc. to become fatter ‖ 살이 찌다. 살찌다/5파운드가 늘다

4 ▶ON SKIN 피부에◀ [put sth ↔ on] to use MAKEUP etc. on your skin ‖ 피부에 화장을 하다. 화장품을 바르다: *I hardly ever put on lipstick.* 나는 립스틱을 발라 본 적이 거의 없어.

5 ▶MUSIC 음악◀ [put sth ↔ on] to begin to play a record, TAPE, VIDEO etc. ‖ 음반·테이프·비디오 등을 틀다: *Let's put on some music.* 음악 좀 틀자.

6 ▶EVENT/PLAY 행사/연극◀ [put sth ↔ on] to arrange an event, concert, play

etc., or to perform in one ‖ 행사·콘서트·연극 등을 준비하거나 공연하다: *The West Valley Symphony is putting on a concert for charity.* 웨스트 밸리 교향악단은 자선 콘서트 공연을 하고 있다.

7 ▶START EQUIPMENT 장치를 작동시키다◀ [put sth ↔ on] to make something such as a piece of equipment begin working ‖ 장치 등을 작동하게 하다. 가동시키다: *It's cold in here. Why don't you put on the heat?* 여기는 춥다. 난방 장치를 가동시키지 그래?

8 ▶FOOD 음식◀ [put sth ↔ on] to begin to cook something on a STOVE ‖ 무엇을 레인지 위에 올려 놓고 요리하기 시작하다. 음식을 만들기 시작하다: *Let me just put the potatoes on.* 나는 감자 요리만 할게.

put out *phr v* [T] **1 [put sth ↔ out]** to stop a fire, cigarette etc. from burning ‖ 불·담배 등이 타는 것을 끄다: *The fire caused $500,000 in damage before they put it out.* 그들이 진화하기 전에 그 화재는 500,000 달러의 손해를 입혔다. **2 [put sth ↔ out]** to produce something, especially something such as a book, record, movie etc. ‖ 특히 책·음반·영화 등을 제작하다: *They've put out three books now on vegetarian cooking.* 그들은 현재 채식주의자 요리법에 관한 세 권의 책을 출판했다. **3 [put sth ↔ out]** to place things where people can find and use them ‖ 물건을 사람들이 찾아서 쓸 수 있는 장소에 두다: *I'm just going to put out cold cuts, bread, and stuff for lunch.* 나는 점심 식사로 얇게 저민 냉육(冷肉)하고 빵이랑 음료만 내놓을 작정이야. **4 [put sth ↔ out]** to put something outside the house ‖ 무엇을 집 밖에 두다. 내쫓다: *Has anybody put the cat out yet?* 아직 아무도 고양이를 내쫓지 않았니? **5 [put sb ↔ out]** to make more work or cause problems for someone ‖ 남에게 일을 더 시키거나 문제가 발생하게 하다. 폐를 끼치다: *Will it put you out if I bring another guest?* 제가 또 다른 손님을 데려오면 폐가 될까요? **6 put out your hand/foot etc.** to move your hand etc. away from your body ‖ 손 등을 몸으로부터 멀리 뻗다. 내밀다: *Jack put out his foot and tripped her.* 잭은 발을 뻗어 그녀가 걸려 넘어지게 했다.

put through *phr v* [T] **1 [put sb through sth]** to make someone do something that is very unpleasant or difficult ‖ 남에게 매우 불쾌하거나 어려운 일을 하게 하다. 남에게 시련을 당하게 하다: *My father's drinking problem put* *my mother through hell.* 나의 아버지의 음주 문제는 어머니를 힘들게 했다. **2 put sb through school/university etc.** to pay for someone to go to school etc. ‖ 남이 학교 등을 갈 수 있도록 돈을 지불하다. 남을 원조하여 학교를 졸업시키다 **3 [put sb through]** to connect someone to someone else on the telephone ‖ 누군가를 전화로 다른 사람에게 연결하다. 전화를 연결하다

put sth to sb *phr v* [T] to suggest something such as a plan to a person or group ‖ 계획 등을 개인 또는 그룹에게 제안하다: *The proposal was put to the committee on January 9.* 그 제안은 1월 9일에 위원회에 상정되었다.

put sth ↔ together *phr v* [T] **1** to build or fix something by joining its different parts together ‖ 각종 부품 등을 결합시켜 무엇을 만들거나 수리하다: *The store will put together bicycles and other large toys for you.* 그 상점은 너를 위해 자전거와 대형 장난감을 갖춰 놓을 것이다. **2** to organize, collect, or prepare the different parts of something such as a plan ‖ 계획의 여러 부분들을 체계화하거나 모으거나, 또는 준비하다. 종합하다. 한데 모으다: *Franklin has put together a program to help families in need.* 프랭클린은 빈곤 가정을 돕기 위한 프로그램을 구성했다. **3 put together** combined ‖ 결합한: *He earns more than the rest of us put together.* 그는 우리들 중 나머지 사람들이 번 돈을 합친 것보다 많이 번다.

put up *phr v* [T] **1 [put sth ↔ up]** to build something such as a wall or building, or to raise something so that it is upright ‖ 벽이나 건물 등을 세우거나 무엇을 수직이 되도록 들어올리다: *The developers plan to put up a 15-story office building.* 개발업자들은 15층짜리 사무용 빌딩을 지을 계획이다. **2 [put sth ↔ up]** to attach a picture etc. to a wall or decorate things, so people can see them ‖ 사람들이 볼 수 있도록 벽에 그림을 붙이거나 물건들을 장식하다: *putting up Christmas decorations* 크리스마스 장식 달기 **3 put sth up for sale/discussion/review etc.** to make something available to be sold, discussed etc. ‖ 무엇이 팔리거나 논의될 수 있게 하다. …을 팔려고 내놓다/논의에 부치다/검열에 부치다 **4 [put sb up]** INFORMAL to let someone stay in your house ‖ 누군가를 자신의 집에 머물게 하다. 숙박시키다: *I can put Jared up for the night.* 나는 재러드를 하룻밤 재워줄

수 있다. **5 put up money/$500/$3 million etc.** to give money to be used for a particular purpose ‖ 특정 목적에 쓰이도록 돈을 내주다. 돈을/500달러/삼백만 달러를 걸다: *Furth put up $42,000 in prize money for the contest.* 퍼스는 그 경기에 상금 42,000달러를 걸었다. **6 put up resistance/a fight/a struggle** to argue against or oppose something in a determined way, or to fight against someone who is attacking you ‖ 단호하게 무엇에 반대하거나 자신을 공격하는 사람과 싸우다. 저항하다 /싸우다: *Opponents of the bill are putting up a good fight in the Assembly.* 그 법안의 반대자들은 국회에서 선전(善戰)하고 있다.

put sb up to sth *phr v* [T] to suggest or encourage someone to do something wrong, silly, or dangerous ‖ 누군가에게 나쁘거나 어리석거나, 또는 위험한 일을 하도록 제의하거나 부추기다. 남을 부추겨 …하게 하다: *Jim wouldn't usually play such a stupid trick; someone must have put him up to it.* 짐은 평소에 그런 바보 같은 속임수는 쓰지 않았다. 누군가가 부추겨서 하도록 한 것이 틀림없다.

put up with sth *phr v* [T] to accept a bad situation without complaining ‖ 불평 없이 나쁜 상황을 받아들이다. 참다. 인내하다: *I'm not going to put up with being treated like that.* 나는 그렇게 취급받는 것을 참지 못할 것이다. —see usage note at BEAR¹

put-down /ˈ. ./ *n* INFORMAL something you say that is intended to make someone feel stupid and unimportant ‖ 남에게 어리석고 하찮다는 느낌이 들게 하려고 하는 말. 몰아세우는 말. 모욕의 말

put out /ˌ. ˈ./ *adj* be/feel put out to feel upset or offended ‖ 당황하다, 기분이 상하다: *I was put out because it was obvious that she didn't like my cooking.* 나는 그녀가 내 요리를 좋아하지 않은 것이 분명했기 때문에 기분이 나빴다.

pu·tre·fy /ˈpyutrə,faɪ/ *v* [I, T] FORMAL to decay and smell very bad ‖ 썩어서 악취가 나다. 부패하다. 부패시키다

pu·trid /ˈpyutrɪd/ *adj* very decayed and bad-smelling ‖ 심하게 썩어 악취가 나는

putt /pʌt/ *v* [I, T] to hit a GOLF ball gently along the ground toward the hole ‖ 골프 공을 지면을 따라 구멍 쪽으로 가볍게 치다. 퍼트하다. 가볍게 치다 – **putt** *n*

put·ter /ˈpʌtɚ/ *v* [I] to spend time doing things that are not very important, in a relaxed way ‖ 느긋하게 시시한 일을 하면서 시간을 보내다. 빈둥

거리다: *He's been puttering around the yard all morning.* 그는 아침 내내 정원을 어슬렁거렸다.

put·ty /'pʌti/ *n* [U] a soft substance that becomes hard when it dries, used for example for fixing glass into window frames ‖ 예를 들어 창틀에 유리를 고정시키는 데에 쓰이는, 건조되면 단단해지는 부드러운 물질. 퍼티

put up·on /'. .,./ *adj* **be/feel put upon** to think that other people are treating you unfairly by expecting too much of you ‖ 다른 사람들이 자신에게 지나치게 기대하여 부당한 대우를 하고 있다고 여기다. 혹사[학대]당하다: *She makes me feel that she is being put upon if I ask her to help.* 내가 그녀에게 도움을 청하면, 그녀는 그녀를 혹사시키는 느낌이 들게 한다.

puz·zle¹ /'pʌzəl/ *n* **1** a game or toy that has a lot of pieces that you have to fit together ‖ 많은 조각들을 모아 맞춰야 하는 게임이나 장난감: *a 500-piece jigsaw puzzle* 500쪽의 조각 그림 퍼즐 **2** a game in which you have to think hard to solve a difficult question or problem ‖ 어려운 질문이나 문제를 해결하기 위해 열심히 생각해야 하는 게임: *a book of crossword puzzles* 크로스워드 퍼즐 책 **3** something that is difficult to understand or explain ‖ 이해하거나 설명하기 어려운 것. 골칫거리: *The way the stock market works has always been a puzzle to me.* 주식 시장이 운영되는 원리는 항상 나에게 골칫거리였다.

puzzle² *v* **1** [T] to make someone confused or unable to understand something ‖ 남을 당황하게 하거나 무엇을 알 수 없게 하다: *At first, doctors were puzzled by the infection.* 처음에, 의사들은 감염으로 애를 먹었다. **2** [I, T] to think for a long time about something because you cannot understand it ‖ 이해할 수 없기 때문에 사물에 대해 오랫동안 생각하다. 골똘히[깊이] 생각하다: *Jill puzzled over the first question on the exam for ten minutes.* 질은 시험의 첫 문제를 10분 동안 골똘히 생각했다.

puz·zled /'pʌzəld/ *adj* confused and unable to understand something, or showing this ‖ 당황스럽고 어떤 것을 이해할 수 없는, 또는 이런 것을 드러내는. 곤혹스러운: *a puzzled expression* 곤혹스러운 표정

pyg·my /'pɪgmi/ *n* **1** also **Pygmy** someone who belongs to a race of very small people from parts of Asia and Africa ‖ 아시아와 아프리카 지역 출신의 소인족(小人族). 피그미 **2** a very small type of animal ‖ 매우 작은 유형의 동물. 왜소한 동물: *a pygmy rabbit* 소형 토끼

py·lon /'paɪlɑn/ *n* one of the tall metal structures that supports wires carrying electricity across the country ‖ 전 국토에 전기를 보내는 전선을 지탱하는 높은 금속 구조물 중의 하나. (고압선용의) 철탑

pyr·a·mid /'pɪrəmɪd/ *n* **1** a large stone building with a flat base and sides shaped like TRIANGLEs that form a point at the top ‖ 꼭대기에서 한 점이 되는, 밑면은 평평하고 측면은 삼각형 모양을 한 거석(巨石) 건축물. 피라미드 **2** something that has this shape ‖ 이러한 형태의 물건

pyre /paɪr/ *n* a high pile of wood on which a dead body is placed to be burned in a funeral ceremony ‖ 장례식에서 시체가 타도록 안치되는 높은 장작 더미. 화장용 장작 더미

Py·rex /'paɪrɛks/ *n* [U] TRADEMARK a special type of strong glass that does not break at high temperatures and is used for making cooking dishes ‖ 고온에서 깨지지 않아 요리용 그릇을 만드는 데에 쓰이는 특수 형태의 강화 유리. 파이렉스. 내열성이 강한 유리

py·thon /'paɪθɑn, -θən/ *n* a large tropical snake that kills animals for food by crushing them ‖ 먹기 위해 동물들을 짜부라뜨려서 죽이는 열대산의 큰 뱀. 비단뱀

Qq

Q, q /kyu/ *n* the seventeenth letter of the English alphabet ‖ 영어 알파벳의 열일곱째 자

Q-tip /'kyu tɪp/ *n* TRADEMARK a small thin stick with cotton at each end, used for cleaning places that are difficult to reach, such as your ears ‖ 귓속 등 닿기 힘든 곳을 깨끗이 하는 데에 쓰이는, 양쪽 끝에 솜이 달린 작고 가는 막대. 면봉

quack¹ /kwæk/ *v* [I] to make the sound that ducks make ‖ 오리가 내는 소리를 내다. 꽥꽥거리다[꽥꽥 소리를 내다]

quack² *n* **1** INFORMAL someone who pretends to be a doctor ‖ 의사인 체하는 사람. 돌팔이[사이비] 의사 **2** the sound a duck makes ‖ 오리가 내는 소리. 꽥꽥(소리)

quad /kwɑd/ *n* INFORMAL a square open area with buildings all around it, especially in a school or college ‖ 특히 학교나 대학에서 사방 주변에 건물로 싸인 사각형의 개방된 공간. 사각형 안뜰

quad·ran·gle /'kwɑdræŋgəl/ *n* **1** ⇨ QUAD **2** TECHNICAL a flat shape that has four straight sides ‖ 네 개의 곧은 변이 있는 평면 모양. 사각형. 사변형

quad·rant /'kwɑdrənt/ *n* **1** a quarter of a circle ‖ 사분원(四分圓)(호) **2** a quarter of an area, especially of land ‖ 한 지역 특히 땅의 사분면: *the town's southwest quadrant* 도시의 남서 사분면 **3** a tool for measuring angles ‖ 각도를 재는 도구. 상한의(象限儀)

quad·ra·phon·ic /,kwɑdrə'fɑnɪk/ *adj* using a system of sound recording, broadcasting etc. in which sound comes from four different SPEAKERs at the same time ‖ 동시에 네 개의 서로 다른 스피커에서 소리가 나오는 소리 녹음·방송 등의 시스템을 이용하는. 4채널(방식)의

quad·ri·lat·er·al /,kwɑdrə'læṭərəl/ *n* a flat shape with four straight sides ‖ 네 개의 곧은 변이 있는 평면 형태. 사변형 – **quadrilateral** *adj*

quad·ri·ple·gic /,kwɑdrə'plidʒɪk/ *n* someone who has PARALYSIS of both arms and both legs ‖ 양 팔과 양 다리가 마비된 사람. 사지 마비 환자 – **quadriplegic** *adj*

quad·ru·ped /'kwɑdrə,pɛd/ *n* TECHNICAL an animal that has four feet ‖ 발이 네 개인 동물. 네발짐승

quad·ru·ple¹ /kwɑ'drupəl/ *v* [I, T] to increase and become four times as big or as high, or to make something do this ‖ 네 배만큼 증가하거나 커지다, 또는 어떤 것을 이렇게 하게 하다. 네 배가 되다. 네 배로 하다[만들다]: *The number of car owners quadrupled in just five years.* 차량 소유자 수가 꼭 5년 만에 네 배가 되었다.

quad·ru·ple² *adj, quantifier* four times as big, as many, or as much ‖ 네 배 크기[숫자, 수량]의. 네 배의: *Patients were given quadruple the normal dose of the drug.* 환자들은 정상 복용량의 네 배의 약을 받았다.

quad·ru·plet /kwɑ'druplɪt/ *n* one of four babies born at the same time to the same mother ‖ 같은 어머니에게서 동시에 태어난 네 아이 중의 하나. 네 쌍둥이 중의 하나

quag·mire /'kwægmaɪɚ, 'kwɑg-/ *n* **1** a difficult or complicated situation ‖ 어렵거나 복잡한 상황. 곤경. 궁지. 빠져 나오기 곤란한 상태: *Income tax regulations are sometimes a quagmire.* 소득세 규정은 때때로 골칫거리이다. **2** an area of soft wet muddy ground ‖ 부드럽고 질척한 진흙 땅. 수렁. 늪. 습지

quail /kweɪl/ *n* [C, U] a small fat bird with a short tail, that is hunted and shot for food and sport, or the meat from this bird ‖ 식용과 스포츠용으로 사냥해서 잡는 짧은 꼬리에 작고 똥똥한 새, 또는 이 새의 고기. 메추라기

quaint /kweɪnt/ *adj* unusual and attractive, especially in an old-fashioned way ‖ 특히 고풍스럽게, 특이하고 매력적인. 예스럽고 아취[매력] 있는. 별나고 아름다운: *a quaint restaurant* 예스럽고 아취 있는 레스토랑

quake¹ /kweɪk/ *v* [I] **1** to shake in an uncontrolled way, usually because you are afraid ‖ 보통 두려워서, 억제할 수 없이 떨다. 두려워서 전율하다. 사시나무 떨듯하다 **2** if the earth, a building etc. quakes, it shakes violently ‖ 땅·건물 등이 심하게 흔들리다. 흔들흔들 움직이다. 진동하다

quake² *n* INFORMAL ⇨ EARTHQUAKE

Quak·er /'kweɪkɚ/ *adj* relating to the Society of Friends, a Christian religious group that opposes violence, has no religious leaders or ceremonies, and holds its religious meetings in silence ‖

폭력을 반대하며, 종교적 지도자나 의식이 없고, 침묵으로 예배를 드리는 기독교 종교 단체인 프렌드 교회와 관련된. 퀘이커 (교도)의 - **Quaker** *n*

qual·i·fi·ca·tion /ˌkwɑləfəˈkeɪʃən/ *n* **1** [C usually plural] a skill, personal quality, or type of experience that makes you suitable for a particular job or position ‖ 특정 직업이나 직위에 적합하게 하는 기술[개인의 자질, 경험의 종류]. 소질. 적성. 능력: *Her qualifications include teaching math and science.* 그녀는 수학과 과학을 교습할 능력이 있다. **2** [C, U] the achievement of an official standard in order to do a job, enter a sports competition etc. ‖ 어떤 일을 하거나 스포츠 경기에 참여하기 위한 공식적 기준의 달성. 자격. 필요 조건. 요건: *her qualification for the Olympic swimming team* 그녀의 올림픽 수영팀 입단 자격 **3** [C, U] something that you add to a statement to limit its effect or meaning ‖ 발언의 효과나 의미를 제한하기 위해 덧붙이는 것. 조건. 단서 (조항): *You have the right to refuse without qualification.* 당신은 조건 없이 거절할 권리를 갖고 있습니다.

qual·i·fied /ˈkwɑləˌfaɪd/ *adj* **1** having the right knowledge, experience, skills etc. for a particular job ‖ 특정 업무에 적합한 지식·경험·기술 등을 가진. 자질[능력]이 있는. 적격[적임]인: *a qualified teacher* 자격을 갖춘 교사 **2** qualified agreement, approval etc. is limited in some way because you do not completely agree ‖ 협정·승인 등이 완전히 동의되지 않아서 일부는 제한된[한정된]. 조건부의. 손질[수정]된

qual·i·fi·er /ˈkwɑləˌfaɪɚ/ *n* **1** someone who has reached the necessary standard for entering a competition ‖ 경기 참가에 필요한 기준에 도달한 사람. 유자격자. 자격 취득자. 예선 통과자 **2** TECHNICAL in grammar, a word or phrase that acts as an adjective or adverb, that limits or adds to the meaning of another word or phrase. In the sentence "She rode off happily on her new red bike," "happily," "new," and "red" are qualifiers ‖ 문법에서, 다른 단어나 구의 뜻을 제한하거나 추가하는, 형용사나 부사의 역할을 하는 단어나 구. 한정사. "She rode off happily on her new red bike.(그녀는 자신의 빨간 새 자전거를 신나게 탔다.)."라는 문장에서 "happily" "new" "red"는 한정사이다

qual·i·fy /ˈkwɑləˌfaɪ/ *v* **1** [I] to pass an examination or reach the standard of knowledge or skill that you need in order to do something ‖ 특정 일을 하는 데에 필요한 시험에 통과하거나 지식이나 기술 수준에 도달하다. 인가[면허]를 얻다. 자격을 취득하다: *Those who qualify as stock brokers must work for the company for five years.* 주식 중개인 자격을 취득한 사람들은 회사에서 5년 동안 일해야 한다. / *He's hoping to qualify for the US Open.* 그는 US Open 대회에 나갈 자격을 얻기를 희망하고 있다. **2** [I] to have the right to claim something ‖ 어떤 것을 요구할 권리를 갖다. …할 자격[권한]을 갖추다. 기준에 부합하다: *Only members of the credit union can qualify for loans.* 오직 신용조합의 회원만이 대출 신청을 할 수 있다. **3** [T] to mean that someone is suitable to do or be something ‖ 사람이 무엇인가를 하거나 어떤 것이 되기에 적합함을 의미하다. …에 알맞게[적합하게] 하다. 자격[권한]을 주다[갖다]: *The fact that you've been to France doesn't qualify you as an expert on the French.* 네가 프랑스에 가봤다는 사실이 네게 프랑스어 전문가라는 자격이 주어지지는 않는다. **4** [T] to add something to what has already been said in order to limit its effect or meaning ‖ 그 효과나 의미를 제한하기 위해 이미 말한 내용에 어떤 것을 덧붙이다. …으로 한정[제한]하다. 수정[손질]해서 …하다: *Let me qualify that statement.* 내가 그 진술서를 수정하게 해주세요.

qual·i·ta·tive /ˈkwɑləˌteɪtɪv/ *adj* relating to the quality or standard of something, rather than amount or number ‖ 사물의 크기나 숫자보다 질이나 수준에 관련되는. 질적인: *a qualitative study of the health care program* 의료 보호 제도의 질적인 연구 —compare QUANTITATIVE

qual·i·ty¹ /ˈkwɑləti/ *n* **1** the good parts of someone's character ‖ 어떤 사람의 개성 중 좋은 부분. 소질. 소양. 품성. 재능: *The boys follow Lucas because he has qualities they admire.* 소년들은 루카스가 그들이 존경할 만한 성품을 가졌기 때문에 따른다. / *the qualities of honesty and independence* 정직하고 독립적인 품성 **2** [C, U] the degree to which something is good or bad ‖ 사물의 좋거나 나쁨의 정도. 품질. 질: *high/low quality recording equipment* 고급[저급] 녹음 장비 / *a sewing machine of poor/good quality* 나쁜[좋은] 품질의 재봉틀 / *We're trying to improve the quality of life for the people in this area.* 우리는 이 지역 사람들의 삶의 질을

높이려고 애쓰고 있다. **3** [U] a high standard‖ 높은 표준. 고급. 상등. 양질. 우수성: *a company that guarantees quality in its service* 그 서비스의 우수성을 보증하는 회사 **4** something that is typical of something and makes it different from other things‖ 사물의 특색을 나타내고 다른 것들과 구별되게 하는 것. 본래의 성질[본질]. 특성. 속성: *There is a wild quality in his books that keeps you reading.* 그의 책은 눈을 뗄 수 없게 만드는 흥미진진한 특성이 있다.

quality² *adj* of a high standard‖ 높은 표준의. 양질의. 고급의. 상품의: *quality products* 고급 제품

quality con·trol /'... ,../ *n* [U] the practice of checking goods as they are produced, to make sure their quality is good enough‖ 상품의 품질이 아주 좋은 가를 확인하기 위해, 생산될 때 상품을 검사하는 일. 품질 관리

quality time /'... ,./ *n* [U] the time that you spend giving someone, especially a family member, your full attention‖ 어떤 사람, 특히 가족의 구성원에게 모든 관심을 기울이면서 보내는 시간. 귀중한[소중한] 시간

qualm /kwam, kwɔm/ *n* [C usually plural] a feeling of slight worry because you are not sure that what you are doing is right‖ 현재 하고 있는 것이 옳은지 확신하지 못해서 약간 걱정하는 감정. 마음의 꺼림칙함. 양심의 가책. 불안. 염려: *He has no qualms about saying "no" to his children.* 그는 자신의 아이들에게 "안 돼"라고 전혀 거리낌이 없이 말한다.

quan·da·ry /'kwandri, -dəri/ *n* **be in a quandary about/over sth** to be unable to decide what to do about a difficult problem or situation‖ 어려운 문제나 상황에 대해 무엇을 할 것인지 결정할 수 없다. …에 대해/…을 두고 곤혹스러워[난처해]하다. 어찌할 바를 모르다: *The college is in a quandary as to whether it should build more student housing or give more financial aid.* 대학은 더 많은 학생 주거 시설을 지어야 할지 또는 더 많은 재정 지원을 해주어야 할지 결정을 못하고 있다.

quan·ti·fi·er /'kwantə,faɪɚ/ *n* TECHNICAL in grammar, a word or phrase that is used with a noun to show quantity. In the sentence "There were only a few people at the party," "few" is a quantifier‖ 문법에서, 수량을 나타내기 위해 명사와 함께 쓰이는 단어나 구. 수량사. 수량 형용사. "There were only a

few people at the party."라는 문장에서 "few"는 수량사[수량 형용사]이다

quan·ti·fy /'kwantə,faɪ/ *v* [T] to measure something and express it as a number‖ 사물을 측정해서 숫자로 표시하다. …의 분량을 정하다[나타내다]. …을 정량화[수치화]하다: *People's attitudes have changed, but it is difficult to quantify this change.* 사람들의 태도는 변했지만 그 변화를 수치화하기는 어렵다. – **quantifiable** /,kwantə'faɪəbəl/ *adj*

quan·ti·ta·tive /'kwantə,teɪtɪv/ *adj* relating to amounts rather than to the quality or standard of something‖ 사물의 품질이나 기준보다 양에 관련된. 분량의. 양적인. 수량화한: *a quantitative difference* 양적인 차이 / *quantitative studies/data* 계량적 연구[데이터] — compare QUALITATIVE

quan·ti·ty /'kwantəti/ *n* [C, U] an amount of something that can be counted or measured‖ 셀 수 있거나 측정될 수 있는 것의 양. 수량. 분량. 정량: *a small quantity of ice cream* 적은 분량의 아이스크림 / *large quantities of water* 많은 양의 물 / *an increase in the quantity of new business* 새로운 사업체 수의 증가

quan·tum leap /,kwantəm 'lip/ *n* a very large and important improvement‖ 매우 크고 중요한 개선. 비약적 발전. 획기적 발전: *a quantum leap in medical science* 의학에서의 획기적 발전

quar·an·tine /'kwɔrən,tin, 'kwar-/ *n* [U] a time when a person or animal is kept apart from others in case she, he, or it has a disease‖ 사람이나 동물이 병이 걸린 경우에 다른 사람이나 동물들로부터 떼어 놓는 기간. (강제) 격리[억류]: *The dogs were kept in quarantine for three months.* 개들은 석 달 동안 격리되어 있었다. – **quarantine** *v* [T]

quark /kwark/ *n* TECHNICAL a very small piece of matter that forms part of an atom‖ 원자의 일부를 이루는 물질의 매우 작은 입자. 쿼크

quar·rel¹ /'kwɔrəl, 'kwarəl/ *n* **1** an angry argument‖ 화가 나서 하는 말다툼. 싸움. 반목. 불화: *The shooting was a result of a quarrel between neighbors.* 총격 사건은 이웃간 불화의 결과였다. **2 have no quarrel with** FORMAL to have no reason to dislike someone or disagree with an idea, decision etc.‖ 어떤 사람을 싫어하거나 생각·결정 등에 반대할 아무 이유를 갖지 않다. …에 아무 불만이 없다: *We have no quarrel with* *the court's decision.* 우리는 법원의 판결에 이의가 없다.

quarrel² *v* [I] to have an angry argument ‖ 화가 나서 다툼을 벌이다. 말다툼[언쟁]하다. 싸우다. 티격태격하다: *We can hear the people who live next door quarreling with each other.* 우리는 이웃에 사는 사람들이 서로 싸우는 소리를 들을 수 있다.

quar·rel·some /ˈkwɔrəlsəm, ˈkwɑr-/ *adj* too ready to argue about things ‖ 어떤 일에 대해 언쟁할 태세인. 싸우기[말다툼하기] 좋아하는. 토론[언쟁]을 자주 하는

quar·ry¹ /ˈkwɔri, ˈkwɑri/ *n* **1** a place where large amounts of stone, sand etc. are dug out of the ground ‖ 대량의 돌·모래 등이 땅에서 채굴되는 곳. 채석장 **2** an animal or person that you are hunting or chasing ‖ 사냥하거나 뒤쫓는 동물이나 사람. 노리갯감. 노리는[공격의] 대상

quar·ry² *v* [T] to dig out stone, sand etc. from a QUARRY ‖ 채석장에서 돌·모래 등을 파내다. 채석하다. 채취하다

quart /kwɔrt/, *written abbreviation* **qt.** *n* a unit for measuring liquid, equal to 2 PINTs or 0.9463 liters ‖ 액체를 재는 단위로 2파인트나 0.9463리터에 상당함. 쿼트

quar·ter /ˈkwɔrtɚ/ *n*
1 one of four equal parts into which something can be divided ‖ 사물을 4등분으로 똑같이 나눈 것들 중 하나. 4분의 1. 4등분(중 하나): *Cut the sandwiches into quarters.* 샌드위치를 4등분하시오. / *A quarter of Canada's population is French speaking.* 캐나다 인구의 4분의 1은 프랑스어를 한다. **2** one of the four periods of 15 minutes into which each hour can be divided ‖ 한 시간을 15분씩 4개로 나눈 것 중 하나. 15분: *Can you be ready in a quarter (of an) hour?* 15분 내에 준비할 수 있어요? / *It's a quarter to/after five.* (=15 minutes before or after 5 o'clock) 5시 15분 전[후]이다. **3** a coin used in the US and Canada worth 25 cents (=¼ of a dollar) ‖ 미국과 캐나다에서 쓰이는 25센트짜리 동전. 쿼터 (동전). 25센트 **4** a word meaning a period of three months, used when discussing bills, wages, and income ‖ 3개월의 주기를 의미하는 말로 청구서·임금·소득을 논할 때 쓰여. 4분기 중 1분기: *Profits were down in the fourth quarter.* 4분기에는 수익이 감소했다. **5**

quarter

quarter

one of the four periods into which a year at school or college is divided ‖ 학교나 대학에서 1년을 4개로 나눈 주기 중의 하나. |학기 —compare SEMESTER **6** one of the four equal times into which games of some sports are divided ‖ 몇몇 스포츠 경기에서 경기 시간을 똑같이 4등분한 것 중의 하나. |쿼터 —see also QUARTERS

quar·ter·back /ˈkwɔrtɚˌbæk/ *n* the player in football who directs the OFFENSE and throws the ball ‖ 미식축구에서 공격을 지시하고 공을 던지는 선수. 쿼터백 —see picture on page 946

quar·ter·fi·nal /ˌkwɔrtɚˈfaɪnl/ *n* one of the set of four games near the end of a competition, whose winners play in the two SEMIFINALs ‖ 경기 대회 결선 무렵 네 개 조 시합 중 하나로 그 승자가 두 개 조의 준결승전에서 경기를 치르게 됨. 준준결승(전)

quar·ter·ly¹ /ˈkwɔrtɚli/ *adj, adv* produced or happening four times a year ‖ 1년에 네 번씩 발행되거나 일어나는. 계절[분기]마다의. 연 4회씩: *a quarterly report* 분기 보고서

quarterly² *n* a magazine that is produced four times a year ‖ 1년에 네 번 발행되는 잡지. 계간지

quar·ters /ˈkwɔrtɚz/ *n* [plural] the house or rooms where you live, especially if you are in the army ‖ 특히 군대에서 거주하는 집과 방들. 막사. 병사(兵舍). 숙소

quar·tet /kwɔrˈtɛt/ *n* **1** a piece of music written for four performers ‖ 네 명의 연주자를 위해 작곡된 음악 작품. 사중창[주]단. 콰르텟 **2** a group of four things or people ‖ 네 개의 사물들이나 사람들 집단. 4인조. 4개 한 조[벌]

quartz /kwɔrts/ *n* [U] a hard mineral substance that is used in making electronic watches and clocks ‖ 전자 손목시계나 벽시계를 만드는 데에 쓰이는 단단한 광물질. 석영

qua·sar /ˈkweɪzɑr/ *n* TECHNICAL a very bright, very distant object similar to a star ‖ 별과 유사한 매우 밝고 멀리 떨어진 물체. 준항성체. 준성(準星)

quash /kwɑʃ/ *v* [T] FORMAL **1** to officially state that a judgment or decision is no longer legal or correct ‖ 판단이나 결정이 더 이상 법적 효력이 없거나 올바르지 않다고 공식 선언하다. 무효로 하다. 취소[폐기·각하]하다: *The judge quashed the decision of a lower court.* 판사는 하급법원의 판결을 파기했다. **2** to use force to end protests or to stop people who are not obeying the law ‖ 항의를 종식시키거나 법을 따르지 않는 사람들을 막기 위해 무력을 사용하다. 진압하다. 억누르다.

qua·ver /'kweɪvɚ/ *v* [I, T] if your voice quavers, it shakes as you speak, especially because you are nervous ‖ 특히 긴장해서 말할 때 목소리가 떨리다. 떨리는 목소리로 말하다[노래하다]

quay /kei, ki/ *n* a place where boats can be tied up or loaded ‖ 배를 정박시키거나 짐을 적재할 수 있는 장소. 부두. 선창. 안벽(岸壁)

quea·sy /'kwizi/ *adj* feeling sick; NAUSEOUS ‖ 구토증이 나는. 욕지기나는[메스꺼운, 구역질 나는]; ㉤ nauseous – **queasiness** *n* [U]

queen /kwin/ *n* **1** also **Queen** the female ruler of a country who is from a royal family, or the wife of a king ‖ 왕가 출신의 여성 국가 통치자, 또는 왕의 부인. 여왕. 왕후. 왕비. 후비 **2** a large female BEE, ANT etc. that lays the eggs for a whole group ‖ 전체 집단을 위해 알을 낳는 벌·개미 등의 몸집 큰 암컷. 여왕개미[벌] **3** the woman who wins a beauty competition ‖ 미인 선발 대회에서 우승한 여성. (미의) 여왕

queen-size /'. ./ *adj* larger than the standard size ‖ 표준 크기보다 큰. 퀸사이즈의: *a queen-size bed* 퀸사이즈 침대

queer /kwɪr/ *adj* OLD-FASHIONED strange ‖ 이상한. 별난. 괴상한. 이상야릇한: *a queer expression* 이상한 표현

quell /kwɛl/ *v* [T] **1** to make a violent situation end ‖ 난폭한 상황을 종식시키다. 평정[진압]하다: *The military were sent out to quell the rioting.* 군대가 폭동을 진압하기 위해 파견되었다. **2** to stop feelings of doubt, worry, and anxiety from getting stronger ‖ 의심·걱정·두려움의 감정이 더 강해지는 것을 막다. 누그러지게 하다[가라앉히다]. 억누르다 : *City officials were trying to quell public fears about the spread of the disease.* 시 당국자들은 질병 확산에 대한 일반 국민의 공포를 진정시키려고 애쓰고 있었다.

quench /kwɛntʃ/ *v* [T] **quench your thirst** if a drink quenches your thirst, it makes you stop feeling thirsty ‖ 음료가 목마름을 없애 주다. 갈증을 해소시키다[풀다]

que·ry /'kwɪri/ *n* FORMAL a question ‖ 질문. 의문. 의혹 – **query** *v* [T]

que·sa·dil·la /ˌkwesəˈdilə/ *n* [C] a Mexican dish made of TORTILLAs filled with cheese and sometimes meat ‖ 치즈와 때때로 고기를 채운 토르티야로 만든 멕시코 음식. 케사디아

quest /kwɛst/ *n* LITERARY a long search for something ‖ 사물에 대한 오랜 탐색. 탐구. 추구 – **quest** *v* [I]

ques·tion¹ /'kwɛstʃən, 'kwɛʃtʃən/ *n* **1** a type of phrase used in order to ask for information ‖ 정보를 묻는 데에 쓰는 어구의 일종. 의문문. 질문. 물음: *I have a question about the math homework.* 수학 숙제에 대한 질문이 있습니다. / *Do you mind if I ask you a personal question?* 사적인 질문 하나 해도 괜찮습니까? **2** a subject that needs to be discussed or a problem that needs to be solved; ISSUE ‖ 토론이 필요한 주제나 해결되어야 할 문제. 현안[과제]. 문제(점). ㉤ issue: *The question is whether more troops should be sent.* 문제는 더 많은 군대가 파견되어야 하는가이다. / *a debate on the question of tax cuts* 세금 삭감 현안에 대한 논쟁 **3** a feeling of doubt about something ‖ 어떤 것에 대한 의심의 감정. 의문(의 여지): *The recent fighting has called into question* (=made people have doubts about) *the government's power to keep the peace.* 최근의 전쟁은 정부의 평화 유지력에 대해 의심을 품게 했다. **4 without question a)** definitely ‖ 확실히. 틀림없이. 문제없이. 분명히: *Their weapons technology is without question a threat to us.* 그들의 무기 기술은 분명히 우리에게 위협적이다. **b)** without complaining or asking why ‖ 불평 없이 또는 이유를 물어보지 않고. 여러 말 없이. 의심할 여지없이: *They accepted our demands without question.* 그들은 군말 없이 우리의 요구를 받아들였다. **5 in question** the person or thing that is in question is the one that is being discussed ‖ 사람이나 사물이 현재 논의되고 있는. 문제시되고 있는. 당해의: *The document in question is a report dated June 18, 1948.* 논란이 되고 있는 문서는 1948년 6월 18일자 보고서이다. **6 be out of the question** used in order to emphasize that what someone wants to do is not possible or not allowed ‖ 사람이 하고 싶어하는 것이 가능하지 않거나 허용되지 않는다는 것을 강조하는 데에 쓰여. 생각할 수 없는. 문제 밖의[불가능한]: *A career in basketball is out of the question, unless he works harder at it.* 그가 더 열심히 하지 않는 한 야구에서의 경력은 생각조차 할 수 없다. **7 (that's a) good question!** SPOKEN said when you are admitting you do not know the answer to a question ‖ 의문에 대한 대답을 모른다고 인정할 때에 쓰여.

Q

(그거) 좋은 질문이군요. 잘 지적해 주었습니다!: *"If we don't have enough people to help, how can we finish the job?" "Good question!"* "도와 줄 사람이 충분치 않다면, 어떻게 우리가 일을 끝낼 수 있어요?" "좋은 질문입니다!"

question² *v* [T] **1** to ask someone questions, especially about a crime ‖ 어떤 사람에게 특히 범죄에 대한 의문을 묻다. …에 대해 질문하다. 캐묻다. 심문하다: *Police are questioning three men about the murder.* 경찰은 살인 사건에 대해 세 명의 남자를 심문하고 있다. **2** to stop trusting someone or start to have doubts about something ‖ 사람을 신뢰하지 않다, 또는 사물에 대해 의심을 갖기 시작하다. …을 의심하다[문제 삼다]. …에 이의를 제기하다: *Are you questioning my honesty?* 당신은 제 정직성을 의심하십니까? —see usage note at ASK

ques·tion·a·ble /ˈkwɛstʃənəbəl/ *adj* **1** questionable actions or behavior are likely to be dishonest or morally wrong ‖ 활동이나 행위가 부정직하거나 도덕적으로 잘못된 것 같은. 미심쩍은. 수상한. 문제가 있는 **2** uncertain or possibly not correct ‖ 불확실한 또는 틀릴 수 있는. 모호[애매]한. 의문의 여지가 있는: *It is questionable what the law would accomplish.* 그 법이 어떤 성과를 이루게 될지는 의문스럽다. **3** used in order to describe someone or something that you think is not legal or not morally correct ‖ 불법적이거나 도덕적으로 옳지 않다고 생각하는 사람이나 사물을 묘사하는 데에 쓰여. 의심스러운. 문제의 소지가 있는: *Barton has been involved in some questionable financial deals.* 바튼은 다소 문제가 있는 금융 거래에 관련되어 있다.

ques·tion·ing /ˈkwɛstʃənɪŋ/ *adj* a questioning look or expression shows that you need more information or that you doubt something ‖ 표정이나 표현이 무엇을 더 알고 싶다거나 어떤 것이 의심스럽다는 것을 보여 주는. 의문을 나타내는. 의아스러운

question mark /ˈ.. ,./ *n* the mark (?), used in writing at the end of a question ‖ 작문에서 의문문 끝에 쓰이는 기호(?). 의문 부호. 물음표

ques·tion·naire /ˌkwɛstʃəˈnɛr/ *n* a written set of questions about a particular subject given to a large number of people, in order to collect information ‖ 정보를 수집하기 위해 다수의 사람들에게 특정 주제에 대하여 주어진 일련의 질문. 질문서[표]. 앙케트. 설문조사

quib·ble /ˈkwɪbəl/ *v* [I] to argue about something that is not very important ‖ 그다지 중요하지 않은 사물에 대해 논쟁하다. 쓸데없는 언쟁을 벌이다. 트집을 잡다: *They're just quibbling over the details now.* 그들은 지금 세부 사항에 대해 트집을 잡고 있을 뿐이다.

quiche /kiʃ/ *n* a type of food that consists of PASTRY filled with a mixture of eggs, cheese, vegetables etc. ‖ 계란·치즈·채소 등의 혼합물을 채운 반죽으로 만들어진 음식 종류. 키시(파이의 일종)

quick¹ /kwɪk/ *adj* **1** quick actions or events are done or happen in a very short time ‖ 행동이나 사건이 아주 짧은 시간 안에 행해지거나 발생하는. 재빠른. 순식간에. 금방[곧] 끝나는: *I'll just take a quick shower first.* 나는 우선 재빨리 샤워를 하겠다. / *Snyder is quick to reward her employees for good work.* 스나이더는 그녀의 종업원들이 일을 잘 하면 곧바로 보상을 한다. / *Don't make any quick movements, or you'll scare the rabbit.* 절대 급하게 움직이지 마라, 그렇지 않으면 토끼가 겁먹고 달아난다. / *I promise I'll be quick – just give me a minute to talk to her.* 빨리 끝내겠다고 약속할 테니, 그녀에게 말할 시간을 조금만 줘. **2** able to learn and understand things in a short time; intelligent ‖ 짧은 시간 안에 어떤 것을 배우고 이해할 수 있는. 영리한. 기민한. 이해가 빠른. 똑똑한: *Carolyn's a quick learner.* 캐롤린은 빨리 배운다[이해한다].

quick² *adv* SPOKEN NONSTANDARD ⇨ QUICKLY: *Come quick! Larry's on TV!* 빨리 와 봐! 래리가 TV에 나와! / *It was all over pretty quick.* 그것은 순식간에 모두 끝났다.

quick·en /ˈkwɪkən/ *v* [I, T] to become quicker, or to make something do this ‖ 더 빨라지다, 또는 무엇인가를 더 빠르게 하다. 서두르(게 하)다: *Realizing they were late, they quickened their pace.* (=walked faster) 그들은 늦었다는 것을 깨닫고 더 빠르게 걸었다.

quick·ie /ˈkwɪki/ *adj* happening or done quickly ‖ 빨리 일어나거나 행해지는. 속성의. 급성의. 몹시 급한: *a quickie divorce* (=one that is done cheaply and quickly) 속성 이혼 – **quickie** *n*

quick·ly /ˈkwɪkli/ *adv* **1** fast, or done in a short amount of time ‖ 빠르게, 또는 짧은 시간 안에 행해져. 서둘러. 신속히: *Don't eat too quickly.* 너무 빨리 먹지 마라. / *It's amazing how quickly she's grown.* 그녀가 이렇게 빨리 자라다니 놀랍

다. **2** for a short amount of time ‖ 짧은 시간 동안. 금방. 곧. 얼른: *I'll just run to the store quickly, and then we can eat.* 금방 가게에 달려갈게, 그런 다음에 같이 먹자.

quick·sand /'kwɪksænd/ *n* [C, U] wet sand that is dangerous because it pulls you down into it if you walk on it ‖ 사람이 그 위를 걸으면 밑으로 끌어당기기 때문에 위험한 젖은 모래. 유사(流砂)

quid pro quo /ˌkwɪd proʊ 'kwoʊ/ *n* FORMAL something that you give or do in exchange for something else, especially when this arrangement is not official ‖ 특히 공적인 협정이 아닐 경우, 다른 것에 대한 대가로 주거나 해주는 것. …의 답례(품). 보수

qui·et¹ /'kwaɪət/ *adj* **1** not making a lot of noise ‖ 많은 소음을 내지 않는. 조용한. 고요한. 소음이 없는: *Be quiet! Daddy has a headache.* 조용히 해라! 아빠가 머리가 아프시단다. **2** not busy, or not full of people or activity ‖ 바쁘지 않은, 또는 사람이나 활동으로 가득 차 있지 않은. 한적한. 평온한. 한산한: *We live in a quiet neighborhood.* 우리는 한적한 동네에 산다. / *Business has been really quiet recently.* 최근 사업이 정말 한산해졌다. **3** not speaking or not likely to say much ‖ 말하지 않는 또는 말을 많이 할 것 같지 않은. 말 없는. 말수가 적은. 얌전한: *She was described as quiet and hard-working.* 그녀는 조용하고 열심히 일하는 것으로 묘사되었다. —see also **keep (sth) quiet** (KEEP)

quiet², **quiet down** *v* [I, T] to become calmer and less active or noisy, or to make someone do this ‖ 더 조용해지거나 덜 활동적이거나 덜 소란스러워지다, 또는 어떤 사람을 이렇게 하게 하다. …을 가라앉히다[가라앉게 하다]. 진정하다[진정시키다]: *Quiet down and get ready for bed!* 조용히 하고 잠잘 준비 해라!

quiet³ *n* the state of being quiet and not active ‖ 조용하고 활동적이지 않은 상태. 고요. 정적. 평온. 안정: *Can't we have some peace and quiet around here!* 여기서 좀 평화롭고 조용하게 있을 수 없을까!

qui·et·ly /'kwaɪətli/ *adv* **1** without making much or any noise ‖ 소음을 많이 또는 전혀 내지 않고. 조용히. 가만히. 평온하게: *Ron shut the door quietly.* 론은 조용히 문을 닫았다. / *"I'm sorry," he said quietly.* "미안해요." 그는 조용히 말했다. **2** in a way that does not attract attention ‖ 주의를 끌지 않게. 차분히. 수

수하게. 티나지 않게: *The meeting was quietly arranged to keep the reporters away.* 보도진을 따돌리기 위해 회의는 드러나지 않게 준비되었다.

quill /kwɪl/ *n* **1** a large feather, or a pen made from a large feather, used in past times ‖ 큰 깃털, 또는 과거에 사용된 큰 깃털로 만든 펜. (꽁지)깃. 깃털 펜 **2** one of the sharp needles on the backs of some animals, such as the PORCUPINE ‖ 고슴도치 등의 일부 동물의 등에 있는 날카로운 가시의 하나. 뻣뻣한 털

quilt /kwɪlt/ *n* a warm thick cover for a bed, made by sewing two layers of cloth together with a filling of cloth or feathers ‖ 두 겹의 천을 함께 꿰맨 후 천이나 깃털로 속을 채워 만든 따뜻하고 두꺼운 침대 덮개. 누비이불[퀼트]. 두꺼운 침대 커버: *a patchwork quilt* 조각보 누비이불

quilt

quilt·ed /'kwɪltɪd/ *adj* quilted cloth has a thick layer of material sewn to it in a pattern of stitches ‖ 속에 두툼한 소재를 채운 천을 바늘땀으로 무늬를 넣어 누빈. 누비이불 모양의

quint·es·sen·tial /ˌkwɪntə'sɛnʃəl/ *adj* being a perfect example of a particular type of person or thing ‖ 특정한 유형의 사람이나 사물의 완벽한 실례인. 본질적인. 전형적인: *New York is the quintessential big city.* 뉴욕은 전형적인 대도시이다. – **quintessentially** *adv* – **quintessence** /kwɪn'tɛsəns/ *n* [U]

quin·tet /kwɪn'tɛt/ *n* five singers or musicians who perform together ‖ 함께 공연하는 5명의 가수나 연주자들. 5인조. 5중주[창]단

quin·tu·plet /kwɪn'tʌplɪt, -'tu-/ *n* one of five babies who are born at the same time to the same mother ‖ 같은 어머니에게서 동시에 태어난 5명의 아기 중 하나. 5쌍둥이(의 하나)

quip /kwɪp/ *v* **-pped**, **-pping** [I] to make an amusing remark ‖ 우스운 말을 하다. 빈정대다. 놀리다. 야유하다 – **quip** *n*

quirk /kwək/ *n* **1** a strange habit or feature that someone or something has ‖ 사람이나 사물이 가진 이상한 습관이나 특성. 기발함. (기묘한) 버릇. 기벽(奇癖): *The fact that we don't say the "g" in the word "gnat" is just a quirk of language.* 우리가 단어 "gnat"에서 "g"를 발음하지 않는 사실은 언어상의 이상한 습

관일 뿐이다. **2** something strange that happens by chance ‖ 우연히 일어나는 이상한 것. 뜻밖의 사건[사고]: *By a quirk of timing, her granddaughter was born on her birthday.* 우연한 시간적 일치로 그녀의 손녀딸이 그녀의 생일날 태어났다.

quirk·y /'kwɚki/ *adj* slightly strange or unusual ‖ 약간 이상하거나 특별한. 기발한. 기묘한: *a quirky sense of humor* 기발한 유머 감각

quit /kwɪt/ *v* **quit, quit, quitting 1** [I, T] INFORMAL to leave a job, school etc., especially because it makes you annoyed or unhappy ‖ 직장·학교 등이 특히 자신을 괴롭히거나 불행하게 해서 떠나다. 사직[퇴직]하다. 그만두다: *They gave the position to someone else, so I quit.* 그들이 그 직위를 다른 사람에게 주어서 나는 사직했다. / *When did you quit your job?* 언제 직장을 그만두었지? **2** [T] INFORMAL to stop doing something that is bad ‖ 나쁜 것을 하는 것을 중단하다. 끊다. …을 단념[체념, 포기]하다: *I quit smoking three years ago.* 나는 3년 전에 담배를 끊었다.

quite /kwaɪt/ *adv*, quantifier **1** very, but not extremely ‖ 극단적이진 않지만 매우. 완전히. 아주: *His hair is quite thin on top now.* 그의 머리는 이제 윗부분이 상당히 빠진 상태이다. / *I thought the instructions were quite clear.* 나는 그 지시 사항들이 아주 분명했다고 생각했다. **2 not quite** not completely or not exactly ‖ 완전하거나 정확하지 않게. 완전히[아주, 꼭] …하지는 않은[…은 아닌]: *I'm not quite sure how the system works.* 그 시스템이 어떻게 작동하는지 확실히 아는 것은 아니다. / *It happened not quite thirty years ago.* 그것은 꼭 30년 전에 일어났던 것은 아니다. / *Lewis isn't quite as fast as he used to be.* 루이스는 예전처럼 그렇게 빠르지는 않다. **3** used when an amount or number is large, but not extremely large ‖ 양이나 수가 크지만 극히 크지는 않을 때에 쓰여. 꽤. 상당히: *They've had quite a bit of snow this year.* (=a lot of snow) 올해 상당량의 눈이 내렸다. / *There were quite a few people at the party.* (=a lot of people) 파티에는 많은 사람들이 있었다. / *We haven't seen each other in quite a while.* (=a long time) 우리는 상당히 오랫동안 서로 보지 못했다. **4** used in order to emphasize the fact that something is unusually good, bad etc. ‖ 사물이 특별하게 좋거나 나쁘다는 등의 사실을 강조하는 데에 쓰여. 사실. 정말. 실제로: *That's quite a coat, where did you buy it?* 그거

정말 좋은 코트인데, 어디서 샀어? / *Roby made quite an impression on the kids.* 로비는 아이들에게 꽤 좋은 인상을 주었다.

quits /kwɪts/ *adj* INFORMAL **call it quits a)** to agree that an argument or debt is settled ‖ 논쟁이나 빚이 해결된 것으로 합의하다. 일단락 짓다. 그만하기로 하다: *If you give me $20, we'll call it quits.* 네가 20달러를 내게 주면 모두 끝난다. **b)** to stop doing something ‖ 어떤 일 하는 것을 중단하다. 사직하다. 그만두다. 끝내다: *Baird will call it quits after two terms as mayor.* 베어드는 시장으로서 두 번의 임기를 마친 후 그만둘 것이다.

quit·ter /'kwɪtɚ/ *n* INFORMAL DIS-APPROVING someone who stops doing a job, activity, or duty because it becomes difficult ‖ 일[활동, 의무]이 어려워져서 그만두는 사람. 쉽게 체념[포기]해 버리는 사람. 겁쟁이. 비겁자

quiv·er¹ /'kwɪvɚ/ *v* [I] to shake slightly because you are angry, upset, or anxious ‖ 화가 나서[흥분해서, 걱정해서] 약간 떨리다. 흔들리다. 진동하다: *The girl quivered with fear.* 소녀는 두려움으로 떨었다.

quiver² *n* **1** a slight shaking movement ‖ 약간 떨리는 움직임. 떨림. 진동 **2** a long case used for carrying ARROWS ‖ 화살을 운반하는 데 쓰는 긴 통. 화살통. 전동(箭筒)

quix·ot·ic /kwɪk'sɑtɪk/ *adj* having ideas and plans that are based on hopes and are not practical ‖ 희망에 근거하여 현실적이지 않은 생각이나 계획을 가진. 돈키호테식인[같은, 다운]. 비현실[공상]적인

quiz¹ /kwɪz/ *n* **1** a small test ‖ 간단한 시험. 간단한[약식] 시험[테스트]: *We have a math quiz on Friday.* 우리는 금요일에 수학 쪽지 시험이 있다. **2** a competition in which you have to answer questions ‖ 질문에 답해야 하는 시험. 퀴즈 대회[프로]: *a quiz show on TV* 텔레비전 퀴즈 쇼

quiz² *v* **-zzed, -zzing** [T] to ask someone a lot of questions ‖ 사람에게 많은 질문을 하다. 이것저것 질문하다. 심문하다: *His parents quizzed him about who he was out with the night before.* 그의 부모는 전날 밤 그가 누구와 외출했는지에 대해 그에게 이것저것 물었다.

quiz·zi·cal /'kwɪzɪkəl/ *adj* **a quizzical look/smile/expression** a look etc. that shows you have a question ‖ 의문을 가지고 있음을 나타내는 표정 등. 미심쩍어하는 표정/웃음/표현

quo·rum /'kwɔrəm/ *n* the smallest number of people that must be at a meeting in order for official decisions to be made ∥ 공식적 결정을 내리기 위해 회의에 참석해야 하는 최소 인원수. 정족수

quo·ta /ˈkwoʊtə/ *n* a particular amount that you are expected to have, or the limit on the amount of something you are allowed to have ∥ 가질 것으로 예상되는 특정 양, 또는 갖는 것이 허용되는 사물의 양에 대한 한계. 몫. 할당[분담]액[량]: *a salesman trying to fill his quota* (=sell the amount he is expected to sell) 자신의 할당량을 채우려 애쓰는 판매원

quot·a·ble /ˈkwoʊtəbəl/ *adj* a quotable remark is interesting and worth repeating ∥ 어떤 말이 흥미롭고 남에게 전할 가치가 있는. 인용할 가치가 있는

quo·ta·tion /kwoʊˈteɪʃən/ *n* **1** words from a book, poem etc. that you repeat in your own speech or piece of writing ∥ 책·시 등에서 발췌하여 자신의 말이나 글 속에 다시 쓰는 말. 인용문[어구]: *a quotation from Shakespeare* 셰익스피어 작품의 인용 **2** a written statement of the exact amount of money that a service will cost ∥ 서비스 가격의 정확한 액수를 기록한 표. 시가[시세](표). 시가 견적: *The insurance company sent us a quotation.* 보험회사는 우리에게 시세표를 보냈다. **3** [U] the act of quoting (QUOTE) something ∥ 어떤 것을 인용하는 행위

quotation mark /.ˈ.. ˌ./ *n* [C usually plural] a mark (" or ") used in writing before and after any words that are being QUOTEd ∥ 글에 인용된 모든 말의 앞과 뒤에 쓰이는 부호 (" "). 인용 부호. 따옴표

quote¹ /kwoʊt/ *v* **1** [I, T] to repeat exactly what someone else has said or written ∥ 다른 사람이 말하거나 쓴 것을 그대로 반복하다. …을 인용하다. 인용해 쓰다[말하다]: *The papers quoted Hanson as saying, "I'm guilty, but I'm not going to jail!"* "나는 죄가 있지만 감옥에는 가지 않을 것이다!"라는 핸슨의 말이 신문에 인용되었다. / *a line quoted from her famous poem* 그녀의 유명한 시에서 인용된 구절 **2** [T] to give proof for what you are saying by mentioning a particular example of something ∥ 다른 사물의 특정 예를 거론함으로써 자신이 말하고 있는 것에 대한 증거를 제시하다. 증거로 …을 들다. 예를 들다[(끌어)대다]: *Dr. Morse quoted three successful cases in which patients used the new drug.* 모스 박사는 환자들이 신약을 사용해 성공한 세 가지 사례를 들었다. **3** [T] to tell a customer the price you will charge him/her for a particular service ∥ 특정 서비스에 대해 고객에게 부과할 가격을 말해 주다. 시세를 매기다[제시하다]. 값을 어림잡다: *The first insurance company quoted me the lowest price.* 첫 번째 보험회사가 가장 낮은 보험료를 제시했다. **4** **quote ... unquote** SPOKEN used when you are repeating the exact words someone else used ∥ 다른 사람이 사용했던 말을 그대로 반복할 때에 쓰여. (인용의 시작과 끝을 알리며) 말하기를 …이라고 했다: *... and Mr. Wigan said, quote, "Go to hell," unquote.* 그리고 위건 씨가 말하길, "지옥에나 가라,"고 했다.

quote² *n* INFORMAL ⇨ QUOTATION

quo·tient /ˈkwoʊʃənt/ *n* TECHNICAL a number that is the result of one number being divided by another ∥ 한 수가 다른 수에 의해 나누어진 결과로서의 수. 몫

R¹, r /ɑr/ the eighteenth letter of the English alphabet ‖ 영어 알파벳의 열여덟째 자

R² *adj* the abbreviation of "restricted," used in order to show that no one under the age of 17 can go to a particular movie unless a parent comes with him/her ‖ 17세 미만은 누구나 부모 동반 없이는 특정한 영화를 보러 갈 수 없다는 것을 나타내는 데에 쓰이는 "보호자 동반"의 약어

R & B *n* [U] rhythm and blues; a type of popular music that is a mixture of BLUES and JAZZ, usually played on electric instruments ‖ rhythm and blues(리듬 앤 드 블루스)의 약어; 보통 전기 악기로 연주되는, 블루스와 재즈가 혼합된 대중 음악의 한 유형

R & D *n* [U] research and development; the part of a business concerned with studying new ideas and planning new products ‖ research and development(연구 개발)의 약어; 새 아이디어의 연구와 새 제품의 기획에 관련된 사업 부문

R & R *n* [U] rest and relaxation; a vacation given to people in the army, navy etc. after a long time of hard work or during a war ‖ rest and relaxation(휴식과 긴장 완화)의 약어; 오랫동안 열심히 일한 후나 전쟁 중에 육군이나 해군 등의 근무자들에게 주는 휴가

rab·bi /ˈræbaɪ/ *n, plural* **rabbis** a Jewish religious leader ‖ 유대인의 종교 지도자. 유대인 율법학자. 라비

rab·bit /ˈræbɪt/ *n* a common small animal with long ears and soft fur, that lives in the ground ‖ 긴 귀와 부드러운 털이 있고 육지에 사는 흔한 작은 동물. 토끼

rab·ble /ˈræbəl/ *n* a noisy crowd of people who are likely to cause trouble ‖ 문제를 일으킬 것 같은 소란스러운 사람들의 무리. 무질서한 군중. 오합지졸

rab·id /ˈræbɪd/ *adj* suffering from RABIES ‖ 광견병에 걸린: *a rabid dog* 광견병에 걸린 개

ra·bies /ˈreɪbiz/ *n* [U] a disease that kills animals and people that are bitten by an infected animal ‖ 감염된 동물에 물린 동물과 사람을 죽이는 병. 공수병. 광견병

rac·coon /ræˈkun/ *n* an animal with black fur around its eyes and black and white bands on its tail ‖ 눈 주위에 검은 털과 꼬리에 검고 하얀 줄무늬가 있는 동물. 미국 너구리

race¹ /reɪs/ *n* **1 a** competition to find out who can run, drive, swim etc. the fastest ‖ 누가 가장 빨리 달릴 수·운전할 수·수영할 수 있는가를 가리기 위한 시합. 경주. 레이스: *Greg finished third in the race.* 그레그는 그 경주에서 3등 했다. **2** [C, U] one of the groups that humans are divided into, based on their skin color, the shape of their face or body, their type of hair etc. ‖ 피부색·얼굴이나 몸의 모양·모발 종류 등을 근거로 인간을 분류한 집단의 하나. 인종: *Our company employs people from all races and religions.* 우리 회사는 모든 인종과 종교 출신의 사람을 채용한다. **3 a** group of people with the same customs, language, history etc. ‖ 동일한 관습·언어·역사 등을 가진 사람들의 집단. 민족 **4** a competition for power or a political position ‖ 권력이나 정치적 지위를 얻기 위한 경쟁. 선거전: *Chirac lost the 1988 presidential race.* 시라크는 1988년 대통령 선거전에서 패했다. **5 a race against time** a situation in which something difficult must be done before a particular time ‖ 특정한 시간 전에 어려운 일을 끝마쳐야 하는 상황. 시간 싸움
—see also ARMS RACE, HUMAN RACE

race

USAGE NOTE race, nation, state, and tribe

Use these words to talk about groups of people. The largest group is a **race**, which means people who have the same skin color, type of hair, and physical features: *The survey was given to people of different races and ages.* A **nation** is a country and its social and political structure, or a group of people with the same history and language: *Leaders of several Western nations are meeting in Paris this week.* Use **state** when talking about politics or the government of a country: *The state still owns much of the country's media.* A **tribe** is a

group of families within a country who are the same **race**, and have the same traditions and the same leader: *The Navajo tribe is the second largest in the US.*
사람들의 집단에 대해 말하기 위해 이들 단어를 쓴다. **race**는 같은 피부색·모발 종류·신체 특징을 가진 사람들을 뜻하는 가장 큰 집단이다: 그 조사는 각기 다른 인종과 연령대의 사람들에게 시행되었다. **nation**은 한 나라와 그 사회적·정치적 구조, 또는 같은 역사와 언어를 가진 사람들의 집단이다: 몇몇 서구 국가의 지도자들이 이번 주 파리에서 만난다. 한 나라의 정치나 정부를 이야기할 때 **state**를 쓴다: 그 국가는 아직도 자국 매스 미디어를 많이 소유하고 있다. **tribe**는 같은 인종(race)이며 같은 전통과 지도자를 가진 한 나라 안의 가족 집단이다: 나바호 종족은 미국에서 두 번째로 큰 종족이다.

race² *v* **1** [I, T] to compete in a race, or to ride a horse, car etc. in a race ‖ 경주에서 경쟁하다, 또는 경주에서 말이나 차 등을 타다. 경주에 참여하다. …을 타고 경주하다: *Schumacher will be racing in the Monaco Grand Prix.* 슈마허는 모나코 그랑프리에서 경주할 것이다. / *Which boat will you be racing?* 당신은 어떤 배로 경주할 것인가? **2** [I, T] to go very quickly, or to make someone or something do this ‖ 매우 빨리 가다, 또는 사람이나 사물을 이렇게 하게 하다. 질주하다. 전 속력으로 달리다[달리게 하다]: *I raced down the stairs to answer the phone.* 나는 전화를 받으려고 계단을 달려서 내려왔다. / *The crash victims were raced to Pacific Hospital.* 자동차 충돌 사고의 희생자들이 퍼시픽 병원으로 급히 이송되었다. **3** if your heart or mind races, it is working harder and faster than usual ‖ 가슴이나 마음이 보통보다 더 심하고 빠르게 움직이다. 두근거리다. 고동치다 **4** if an engine races, its parts are moving too fast ‖ 엔진의 부품이 너무 빨리 움직이다. 헛돌다. 공전하다

race·course /ˈreɪs-kɔrs/ *n* a track that runners, cars, horses etc. use in a race ‖ 경주자·자동차·말 등이 시합에서 사용하는 트랙. 경주 트랙. 경주로

race re·la·tions /ˈ. .ˌ../ *n* [plural] the relationship between two groups of people who are from different RACES but who live in the same city, country, or area ‖ 다른 인종 출신이지만 같은 도시[나라, 지역]에 사는 두 집단의 사람들 사이의 관계. 인종간의 관계

rac·es /ˈreɪsɪz/ *n* **the races** an event at which horses are raced against each other, especially for money ‖ 특히 돈을 목적으로 말을 서로 경주시키는 일. 경마

race·track /ˈreɪs-træk/ *n* a track around which runners, cars, horses etc. race ‖ 경주자·차·말 등이 경주하는 트랙. 경주 트랙. 경주로

ra·cial /ˈreɪʃəl/ *adj* **1** relating to the relationships between different races of people ‖ 서로 다른 인종의 사람들 간의 관계와 관련된. 인종[민족]간의: *a fight against racial discrimination* (=unfair treatment of people because of their race) 인종 차별 철폐 투쟁 **2** relating to people's race ‖ 사람들의 인종에 관한. 인종[민족]의: *racial groups* 인종 집단 – **racially** *adv*

rac·ing /ˈreɪsɪŋ/ *n* [U] **horse/car/ bicycle/dog etc. racing** the sport of racing horses, cars etc. ‖ 말·차 등을 경주시키는 스포츠. 경마/자동차 경주/경륜/경견

rac·ism /ˈreɪsɪzəm/ *n* [U] **1** unfair treatment of people, or violence against them, because they belong to a different race from yours ‖ 자신과 다른 인종에 속한다는 이유로 다른 사람들에 대한 부당한 대우나 폭력 행사. 인종 차별 (주의): *claims of police brutality and racism* 경찰의 잔혹 행위와 인종 차별에 대한 주장 **2** the belief that some races of people are better than others ‖ 일부 인종의 사람들이 다른 사람들보다 우수하다는 신념. 인종적 우월감[편견] – **racist** *adj, n*

rack¹ /ræk/ *n* a frame or shelf for holding things, usually with BARs or hooks ‖ 보통 막대나 갈고리가 있어 물건을 걸어두는 데 사용하는 틀이나 선반. … 걸이. 시렁: *a spice rack* 양념 선반 / *towel racks* 수건걸이

rack² *v* [T] **1 rack your brain(s)** to think very hard or for a long time ‖ 매우 열심히 또는 오랫동안 생각하다. 머리를 쥐어짜다: *I had to rack my brains to remember his name.* 나는 그의 이름을 기억해 내려고 머리를 쥐어짜야만 했다. **2 be racked with pain/guilt** feeling great physical pain, or feeling very guilty ‖ 심한 육체적 고통이나 느끼는. 고통/죄책감으로 시달리다

rack sth ↔ **up** *phr v* [T] INFORMAL to make the value, amount, or level of something increase; ACCUMULATE ‖ 사물의 가치[양, 수준]를 증가하게 하다. 획득해서 쌓아가다. 축적하다; ㉮ accumulate: *The Seahawks have racked up enough wins to get into the playoffs.* 시

호크스 팀은 승리를 충분히 거두어서 플레이오프전에 진출할 수 있게 됐다.

rack·et /ˈrækɪt/ *n* **1** INFORMAL a loud noise ‖ 큰 소음. 소동. 소란: *What's all the racket?* 이 소동은 다 뭐야? **2** INFORMAL a dishonest way of obtaining illegal goods ‖ 불법적인 물건을 획득하는 부정한 방법. 부정 수단. 밀매매: *He runs a drugs racket.* 그는 마약 밀매를 한다. **3** a thing used for hitting the ball in games such as tennis, consisting of a light stick with a round firm net at the top ‖ 위쪽에 둥글고 탄탄한 그물이 달린 가벼운 막대로 이루어져 테니스 등 경기에서 공을 치는 데 사용되는 것. 라켓

rack·et·ball /ˈrækɪtˌbɔl/ *n* [U] an indoor game in which two players use RACKETs to hit a small rubber ball against the four walls of a square court ‖ 두 선수가 정사각형 코트의 네 벽에 대고 작은 고무공을 치기 위해 라켓을 사용하는 실내 경기. 라켓볼

rack·et·eer·ing /ˌrækəˈtɪrɪŋ/ *n* [U] a crime that consists of getting money dishonestly, using a carefully planned system ‖ 주의깊게 계획한 방법을 이용하여 부정하게 돈을 얻는 범죄. 갈취. 협잡 – **racketeer** *n*

rac·quet /ˈrækɪt/ *n* ⇨ RACKET

rac·y /ˈreɪsi/ *adj* exciting in a sexual way ‖ 성적으로 흥분시키는. 선정적인

ra·dar /ˈreɪdɑr/ *n* [C, U] a method of finding the position of things such as planes by sending out radio waves, or the piece of equipment that does this ‖ 전파를 발사하여 비행기 등의 물체의 위치를 찾아내는 방법, 또는 이 일을 하는 장비. 레이더: *The aircraft is designed to be difficult to spot on radar.* 그 비행기는 레이더로 발견하기 어렵게 고안되었다.

ra·di·al tire /ˌreɪdiəl ˈtaɪr/, **radial** *n* a car tire with wires inside the rubber to make it stronger and safer ‖ 더 튼튼하고 안전하게 하기 위해 고무 안에 철사를 넣은 자동차 타이어. 레이디얼 타이어

ra·di·ance /ˈreɪdiəns/ *n* [U] **1** great happiness or love that shows in the way someone looks ‖ 사람의 외모로 나타나는 큰 행복이나 사랑. 밝음. 밝게 빛남: *the radiance of youth* 젊음의 발산 **2** soft light that shines from or onto something ‖ 물체에서 또는 물체로 비치는 부드러운 빛. 밝은 빛. 광휘

ra·di·ant /ˈreɪdiənt/ *adj* **1** full of happiness and love, in a way that shows in your face ‖ 얼굴에 나타나도록 행복과 사랑이 가득 찬. 밝은. 환한: *a radiant smile* 환한 웃음 **2** TECHNICAL sending out

light or heat ‖ 빛이나 열을 발하는. 빛나는. 복사(輻射)의 – **radiantly** *adv*

ra·di·ate /ˈreɪdiˌeɪt/ *v* **1** [I, T] if someone radiates a feeling or quality, or if it radiates from him/her, s/he shows it in a way that is easy to see ‖ 사람의 감정이나 특성이 알아보기 쉽게 나타나다. 발(산)하다[내키다]: *Janine radiates confidence.* 재닌은 자신감이 넘친다. **2** [I, T] if something radiates light or heat, or if light or heat radiates, it is sent out in all directions ‖ 어떤 것이 빛이나 열을 모든 방향으로 내보내다. 방출하다. 발하다: *warmth radiating from the heater* 히터에서 방출하는 온기 **3** [I] to spread out from a central point ‖ 중심점에서 퍼져 나가다. 방사상으로 퍼지다: *pain radiating down his leg* 다리를 따라 밑으로 퍼져 나가는 고통

ra·di·a·tion /ˌreɪdiˈeɪʃən/ *n* [U] **1** a form of energy that comes from NUCLEAR reactions, that is harmful to living things in large amounts ‖ 많은 양으로는 생물에게 해로운, 핵반응에서 나오는 에너지 형태. 방사능: *radiation exposure* 방사능 피폭 **2** energy in the form of heat or light sent out as beams that you cannot see ‖ 볼 수 없는 광선으로 발산되는 열이나 빛 형태의 에너지. 복사(輻射) 에너지: *ultraviolet radiation from the sun* 태양에서 나오는 자외선

ra·di·a·tor /ˈreɪdiˌeɪtər/ *n* **1** a piece of equipment used for heating a room, consisting of a hollow metal container fixed to a wall and connected to hot water pipes ‖ 벽에 고정되어 온수관에 연결된 속이 빈 금속 용기로 이루어져 방을 덥히는 데 쓰이는 장비. 라디에이터. 방열기 **2** the part of a car or plane that stops the engine from getting too hot ‖ 엔진이 너무 뜨거워지는 것을 막는 자동차나 비행기의 부품. 냉각기

rad·i·cal¹ /ˈrædɪkəl/ *adj* **1** thorough and complete, so that something is very different ‖ 어떤 것이 전혀 달라지게 철저하고 완전한. 철두철미한. 극단적인: *radical changes to the tax system* 조세 제도의 철저한 개혁 / *a radical new idea for treating the disease* 질병을 치료하는 완전히 다른 새 개념 **2** supporting complete political or social change ‖ 완전한 정치적 또는 사회적 변화를 지지하는. 과격한. 급진적인: *radical demands for reform* 개혁에 대한 급진적인 요구 – **radically** *adv*

radical² *n* someone who wants thorough and complete social and political change ‖ 철저하고 완전한 사회

적·정치적 변화를 바라는 사람. 과격론자.
급진주의자 **– radicalism** *n* [U]

ra·di·o¹ /ˈreɪdiˌoʊ/ *n* **1** a piece of
electronic equipment that you use to
listen to music or programs that are
broadcast, or the programs themselves
‖ 방송되는 음악이나 프로그램을 듣기 위
해 사용하는 전자 장비, 또는 프로그램 그
자체. 라디오 (프로그램): *Have you
heard Sting's new song on the radio?*
라디오에서 스팅의 새 노래를 들어 봤어?
/ *I listen to the radio in the car on the
way home from work.* 나는 퇴근길에 차
에서 라디오를 듣는다. **2** [U] the activity
of making and broadcasting programs
that can be heard on a radio ‖ 라디오로
들을 수 있는 프로그램을 만들고 방송하는
활동. 라디오 방송(업): *He'd like a job in
radio.* 그는 라디오 방송 일을 하고 싶어
한다. **3** [C, U] a piece of electronic
equipment that can send and receive
spoken messages, or the sending or
receiving of these messages ‖ 구두 메시
지를 보내고 받을 수 있는 전자 장비, 또는
이 메시지를 보내거나 받기. 무전(기): *the
ship's radio* 배의 무전기 / *We've lost
radio contact.* 우리는 무전 교신이 끊겼
다.

radio² *v* [I, T] to send a message using
a radio ‖ 무전을 사용하여 메시지를 보내
다. …을 무선 호출하다. …에 무전 연락
하다: *We'll have to radio Chicago for
permission to land.* 우리는 착륙 허가를
위해 시카고(공항)에 무선 호출해야겠다.

ra·di·o·ac·tive /ˌreɪdioʊˈæktɪv/ *adj*
containing RADIATION ‖ 방사능을 함유하
는: *radioactive waste* 방사성 폐기물

ra·di·o·ac·tiv·i·ty /ˌreɪdioʊækˈtɪvəti/ *n*
[U] **1** a quality that some substances
have that makes them send out
RADIATION ‖ 방사선을 방출하게 하는 일부
물질이 가진 성질. 방사능 **2** the energy
produced in this way ‖ 이렇게 방출된 에
너지. 방사능 에너지: *High levels of
radioactivity remained in the area after
the explosion.* 고준위(高準位)의 방사능
에너지가 폭발 후 그 일대에 남아 있었다.

ra·di·ol·o·gist /ˌreɪdiˈɑlədʒɪst/ *n* a
hospital doctor who is trained in the use
of RADIATION to treat people ‖ 사람들을
치료하기 위한 방사선 사용을 훈련받은 병
원 의사. 방사선과 의사

ra·di·ol·o·gy /ˌreɪdiˈɑlədʒi/ *n* [U] the
study of the use of RADIATION and X-RAYs
in medical treatment ‖ 의학적 치료에서
의 방사선과 X선의 사용 연구. 방사선학

ra·di·o·ther·a·py /ˌreɪdioʊˈθɛrəpi/ *n* [U]
the treatment of illnesses using

RADIATION ‖ 방사선을 사용한 병의 치료.
방사선 요법

rad·ish /ˈrædɪʃ/ *n* a small red or white
root that has a slightly hot taste and is
eaten raw as a vegetable ‖ 약간 매운맛이
나며 야채로서 날로 먹는 작고 빨갛거나
하얀 뿌리. 무

ra·di·um /ˈreɪdiəm/ *n* [U] a very
RADIOACTIVE metal that is an ELEMENT ‖
원소이면서 방사능이 높은 금속. 라듐

ra·di·us /ˈreɪdiəs/ *n, plural* **radii**
/ˈreɪdiaɪ/ **1** the distance from the center
to the edge of a circle ‖ 원의 중심에서부
터 가장자리까지의 거리. 반지름. 반경 —
see picture at DIAMETER **2 within a 10
mile/100 meter etc. radius** within a
distance of 10 miles etc. in all directions
from a particular place ‖ 특정한 장소에
서 모든 방향으로 10마일 등의 거리 안에.
반경 10마일/100미터 이내

ra·don /ˈreɪdɑn/ *n* [U] a RADIOACTIVE
gas that is an ELEMENT ‖ 원소인 방사성
기체. 라돈

raf·fle¹ /ˈræfəl/ *n* a type of competition
or game in which people buy tickets
with numbers on them in order to try to
win prizes ‖ 사람들이 상을 타기 위해 숫
자가 적혀 있는 표를 사는 시합이나 게임
의 일종. 복권식 판매

raffle², **raffle off** *v* [T] to offer
something as a prize in a RAFFLE ‖ 복권
식 판매에서 상품으로 어떤 것을 제공하
다. …을 복권식 판매로 팔다

raft /ræft/ *n* **1** a flat floating structure
used as a boat or to sit on, jump from
etc. when you are swimming ‖ 수영할 때
배로서[앉기 위해, 뛰어드는 데] 등에 사
용되는 물 위에 떠 있는 평평한 구조물. 뗏
목 **2** a small flat rubber boat filled with
air ‖ 공기로 채운 작고 평평한 고무보트.
구명 고무보트 **3 a raft of** a large
number of things or a large amount of
something ‖ 많은 수나 양의 것. 다수[다
량](의): *There are plenty of restaurants
and a raft of motels.* 많은 음식점과 다수
의 모텔이 있다.

raf·ter /ˈræftɚ/ *n* one of the large
sloping pieces of wood that form the
structure of a roof ‖ 지붕의 구조를 형성
하는 크고 경사진 목재의 하나. 서까래

raft·ing /ˈræftɪŋ/ *n* [U] the sport of
traveling down a fast-flowing river in a
rubber RAFT ‖ 고무보트로 강의 급류를 내
려가는 스포츠. 래프팅

rag¹ /ræg/ *n* **1** a small piece of old cloth
‖ 낡은 천의 작은 조각. 헝겊 조각. 넝마
조각: *a rag for washing the car* 자동차
닦기용 헝겊 조각 **2 in rags** wearing old

torn clothes ∥ 낡고 찢어진 옷을 입고 있는. 누더기를 걸친: *beggars dressed in rags* 누더기를 걸친 거지들 **3 go from rags to riches** to become very rich after starting your life very poor ∥ 아주 가난하게 인생을 시작한 후에 매우 부유하게 되다. 무일푼에서 부자가 되다

rag² *v* **-gged, -gging**

rag on sb *phr v* [T] SPOKEN **1** to make jokes and laugh at someone in order to embarrass him/her ∥ 남을 난처하게 하기 위해 농담을 하고 비웃다. …을 괴롭히다. 놀려대다: *Everybody's ragging on Steve about his new haircut.* 누구나 스티브의 새 머리 모양에 대해 놀려대다 **2** to criticize someone in an angry way ∥ 남에게 화를 내며 비난하다. …을 꾸짖다. 나무라다: *Stop ragging on me - I'll apologize to her later.* 내게 야단 좀 그만 쳐라. 내가 나중에 그녀에게 사과할게.

rag·a·muf·fin /ˈræɡəˌmʌfɪn/ *n* LITERARY a dirty young child wearing torn clothes ∥ 해어진 옷을 입은 지저분한 어린 아이. 부랑아

rag·bag /ˈræɡbæɡ/ *n* **a ragbag of** a confused mixture of things that do not seem to go together or make sense ∥ 어울리거나 이치에 맞아 보이지 않은 혼란스런 것들의 뒤섞임. 뒤범벅: *a ragbag of ideas* 이것저것 그러모은 아이디어들

rag doll /'. ./ *n* a soft DOLL made of cloth ∥ 헝겊으로 만든 부드러운 인형. 봉제 인형

rage¹ /reɪdʒ/ *n* [C, U] a strong feeling of anger that you cannot control ∥ 억제할 수 없는 격한 분노의 감정. 격노. 노발대발: *When he refused to help, she flew into a rage.* (=suddenly became very angry) 그가 도움을 거절했을 때 그녀는 발끈 화를 냈다.

rage² *v* [I] **1** to continue happening with great force or violence ∥ 아주 맹렬하거나 격렬하게 계속 일어나다. 맹위를 떨치다: *The battle raged for several days.* 전투가 며칠 동안 격심했다. / *Outside a storm was raging.* 밖에는 폭풍우가 맹위를 떨쳤다. **2** to feel extremely angry about something and to show this ∥ 어떤 것에 대해 매우 화를 내고 분노를 드러내 보이다. 몹시 화내다: *Tom raged at himself for having been so stupid.* 톰은 너무나 어리석게 행동한 자기 자신에게 몹시 화가 났다.

rag·ged /ˈræɡɪd/, **raggedy** /ˈræɡɪdi/ *adj* **1** torn and in bad condition ∥ 찢어지고 나쁜 상태인. 해진. 너덜너덜[누덕누덕]한: *raggedy blankets* 다 해진 담요 **2** not straight or neat, but with rough

uneven edges ∥ 가장자리가 똑바르거나 말끔하지 않으며 거칠고 고르지 않은. 울퉁불퉁[들쭉날쭉]한. 손질되지 않은: *a ragged beard* 텁수룩한 수염 **3** wearing clothes that are old, torn, and dirty ∥ 낡고 찢어지고 더러운 옷을 입은. 누더기를 걸친: *ragged children* 누더기를 걸친 아이들

rag·tag /ˈræɡtæɡ/ *adj* looking messy and wearing dirty torn clothes ∥ 지저분하게 보이고 더럽고 찢어진 옷을 입은. 불결한: *a ragtag army* 오합지졸의 군대

rag·time /ˈræɡtaɪm/ *n* [U] a type of JAZZ music with a quick strong beat, popular in the US in the early 1900s ∥ 1900년도 초에 미국에서 유행한 빠르고 강한 박자의 재즈 음악의 일종. 래그타임

rah-rah /ˈrɑrɑ/ *interjection, adj* an expression meaning HOORAY, often used in order to describe someone who supports something without thinking about it enough ∥ "만세"를 뜻하는 표현. 종종 충분하게 생각하지 않고 어떤 것을 지지하는 사람을 묘사하는 데에 쓰여. 만세. 열광적인: *I'm just not a rah-rah American.* 나는 무조건 열광하는 미국인은 아니야.

raid¹ /reɪd/ *n* **1** a short attack on a place by soldiers, planes, or ships, intended to cause damage but not to take control ∥ 장악할 의도가 아니라 피해를 줄 목적으로 군인[비행기, 배]가 가하는 한 장소에 대한 짧은 공격. 급습. 습격: *an air raid* 공습 **2** a sudden visit by the police when they are searching for something ∥ 물건을 수색하고 있는 경찰의 갑작스런 방문. 현장 급습. 불시 단속[수색]: *Drug dealers were arrested after a police raid.* 마약 거래자들이 경찰의 현장 급습 후에 체포되었다.

raid² *v* [T] **1** if the police raid a place, they enter it suddenly to search for something illegal ∥ 경찰이 불법적인 것을 찾아 갑자기 한 장소에 들이닥치다. …을 불시에 단속[수색]하다 **2** to make a sudden attack on a place ∥ 한 장소에 갑작스런 공격을 가하다. …을 급습[습격]하다: *A group of soldiers raided enemy headquarters.* 일단의 군인들이 적의 본부를 급습했다. **3** INFORMAL to take or steal a lot of things from a place ∥ 어떤 곳에서 많은 것들을 취하거나 훔치다. 탈탈 털다[비우다]. 텅텅 비게 하다: *The kids raided the refrigerator after school.* (=ate a lot of food) 그 아이들은 방과 후에 냉장고를 텅 비워 버렸다. – **raider** *n*

rail¹ /reɪl/ *n* **1** a long piece of wood or

metal that is fixed along or around something, especially to keep you from falling‖ 특히 사람이 떨어지지 않도록 어떤 것을 따라 또는 그 주위에 박아 놓은 긴 나무나 금속. 난간. 울타리: *Tourists stood at the rail taking pictures of the falls.* 관광객들은 그 폭포를 사진 찍으면서 난간에 서 있었다. / *a bath rail* 욕조 난간 **2** one of the two long metal tracks fixed to the ground that trains move along‖ 기차가 따라 움직이는 지면에 고정시킨 두 개의 긴 금속제 궤도의 하나. 철도의 레일[선로]

rail² *v* [I] LITERARY to complain angrily about something that you think is unfair‖ 부당하다고 생각하는 것에 화를 내며 불평하다. 욕하다. 악담하다

rail·ing /'reɪlɪŋ/ *n* a fence consisting of a piece of wood or metal supported by upright posts, which keeps people from falling over an edge or helps support them going up stairs‖ 사람이 가장자리 너머로 떨어지지 않게 막아 주거나 계단을 올라가는 것을 지탱하도록 도와주는, 수직 기둥이 떠받치는 나무나 금속으로 이루어진 울타리. 난간: *kids climbing over the railings* 난간 위로 올라서는 아이들

rail·road¹ /'reɪlroʊd/ *n* **1** a method of traveling or moving things around by train‖ 기차로 여행하거나 사물을 수송하는 방법. 철도 (수송) **2** **the railroad** all the work, equipment etc. relating to a train system‖ 철도 체계와 관련된 모든 일이나 시설 등. 철도 선로[시설, 회사]: *My grandfather works on/for the railroad.* 나의 할아버지는 철도 회사에서 일하신다.

rail·road² *v* [T] to force or persuade someone to do something without giving him/her enough time to think about it‖ 남에게 어떤 것에 대해 생각할 충분한 시간도 주지 않고 억지로 시키거나 설득하다. 몰아대다. 서두르다: *This complex bill should not be railroaded through the House.* 이 복잡한 입법안은 의회를 급히 통과시켜서는 안 된다.

rain¹ /reɪn/ *n* [U] water that falls in small drops from clouds in the sky‖ 하늘의 구름에서 작은 방울로 떨어지는 물. 비. 빗물: *We'd better hurry; it looks like rain.* (=it is probably going to rain) 서두르는 게 좋겠어. 비가 올 것 같다. — see usage note at WEATHER

rain² *v* **it rains** if it rains, drops of water fall from clouds in the sky‖ 물방울들이 하늘의 구름에서 떨어지다. 비가 오다: *Is it still raining?* 아직 비가 오니?

rain down *phr v* [I,T **rain down** sth] if

something rains down or is rained down, it falls in large quantities‖ 사물이 대량으로 떨어지다. 비처럼 내리다. 쏟아져 내리다: *Falling rocks rained down on cars and houses.* 낙석들이 자동차와 집 위에 비처럼 쏟아졌다.

rain sth ↔ **out** *phr v* [T] if an event is rained out, it has to stop because there is too much rain‖ 비가 너무 많이 내려 행사를 중단해야 하다. 우천으로 중지[연기]하다: *We had tickets to the Blue Jays game, but it was rained out.* 우리는 블루 제이스 경기 표가 있었지만 비 때문에 연기되었다.

rain·bow /'reɪnboʊ/ *n* a large curve of different colors that can appear in the sky when there is both sun and rain‖ 햇빛과 비가 둘 다 있을 때 하늘에 나타나는 큰 곡선 모양의 서로 다른 색깔들. 무지개

rain check /'. ./ *n* **1** **take a rain check** SPOKEN used in order to say that you would like to accept an invitation or offer later, but you cannot right now‖ 당장은 할 수 없지만 나중에 초대나 제안을 받아들이고 싶다고 말하는 데에 쓰여. 다음 기회로 미루다: *I'm sorry, but I'm busy on Saturday - can I take a rain check?* 미안하지만 토요일에 바빠서 다음 기회에 약속할 수 있을까? **2** a ticket for an outdoor event, game etc. that you can use another day, given to people if the event has to stop because of rain‖ 비 때문에 행사가 중단되면 사람들에게 주어지는, 다른 날에 사용할 수 있는 야외 행사나 경기 등의 표. 우천 교환권

rain·coat /'reɪnkoʊt/ *n* a coat that you wear to protect yourself from the rain‖ 비로부터 자신을 가리기 위해 입는 외투. 비옷

rain·drop /'reɪndrɑp/ *n* a single drop of rain‖ 하나의 빗방울

rain·fall /'reɪnfɔl/ *n* [C, U] the amount of rain that falls on an area in a particular time‖ 특정한 시간에 한 지역에 내리는 비의 양. 강우량: *The rainfall this winter has been unusually low.* 이번 겨울에는 강우량이 유난히 낮았다.

rain for·est /'. ,../ *n* an area of thick forest with tall trees that are very close together, growing in a place where it rains a lot‖ 비가 많이 오는 곳에서 자라며, 키 큰 나무가 매우 빽빽하게 들어선 무성한 숲지대. 열대 우림 (지역)

rains /reɪnz/ *n* **the rains** a time in the year when there is a lot of rain in tropical countries; MONSOON‖ 열대 국가에서 비가 많이 내리는 연중의 시기. 우기; ㉌ monsoon

rain·storm /'reɪnstɔrm/ *n* a storm with a lot of rain and strong winds ‖ 많은 비와 강한 바람을 동반한 폭풍. 폭풍우

rain·water /'reɪnˌwɔtɚ, -ˌwɑ-/ *n* [U] water that has fallen as rain ‖ 비로 떨어진 물. 빗물

rain·y /'reɪni/ *adj* **1** having a lot of rain ‖ 많은 비가 내리는: *a rainy weekend* 비가 많이 오는 주말 **2 rainy day** a difficult time when you will need money that you do not need now ‖ 현재는 필요하지 않은 돈이 필요할 수 있는 어려운 시기. 곤궁할 때. 만일의 경우: *"You'd better save that money for a rainy day."* (=for a time when you need it) "너는 만일의 경우에 대비하여 그 돈을 저축하는 것이 낫다."

raise¹ /reɪz/ *v* [T]

1 ▶MOVE◀ 이동시키다 to move or lift something to a higher position or to an upright position ‖ 어떤 것을 더 높은 위치나 똑바로 세운 위치까지 이동시키거나 들어올리다. …을 높이[올리다, 달다]. …을 일으키다[세우다]: *The flag is raised at school every morning.* 국기가 매일 아침 학교에 게양된다. / *Raise your hand if you know the answer.* 답을 알고 있으면 손을 드세요.

raise

2 ▶INCREASE◀ 증가하다 to increase an amount, number, or level ‖ 양[수, 수준]을 증가시키다. 올리다. 높이다. 증대시키다: *a plan to raise taxes* 세금 인상 계획 / *Don't raise your voice at me, young man.* (=speak loudly and angrily) 내게 언성 높이지 말게, 젊은 친구.

3 ▶IMPROVE◀ 개선하다 to improve the quality or standard of something ‖ 어떤 것의 질이나 수준을 개선하다. 높이다. 올리다. 향상시키다: *This bill is all about raising standards in our schools.* 이 법안은 순전히 학교들의 수준을 향상시키기 위한 것이다.

4 ▶CHILDREN/ANIMALS/CROPS◀ 아이들/동물들/농작물◀ to take care of children, animals, or crops until they are fully grown ‖ 아이들[동물, 농작물]이 완전히 자랄 때까지 돌보다. 기르다. 양육하다. 재배하다. 사육하다: *They've raised seven children.* 그들은 일곱 명의 아이들을 길렀다. / *He wants to try raising corn.* 그는 옥수수를 재배해 보고 싶어한다.

5 ▶GET MONEY/SUPPORT◀ 돈/지원을 얻다◀ to collect money, support etc. so that you can use it to help people ‖ 사람을 돕는 데 사용할 수 있도록 돈이나 지원 등을 모으다. 모금하다: *We've raised $10,000 for cancer research.* 우리는 암 연구를 위해 만 달러를 모금했다.

6 ▶FARMING◀ 농사◀ to grow plants or keep animals to sell ‖ 팔기 위해 식물을 기르거나 동물을 키우다. 재배하다. 사육하다: *Most of their income is from raising pigs.* 그들 수입의 대부분은 돼지를 키우는 데서 나온다.

7 raise a question/objection etc. to begin to talk or write about a something that you want someone to consider ‖ 남에게 고려해 주길 원하는 것에 대해 말하거나 쓰기 시작하다. 의문/반대를 제기하다: *Maryann raised the issue of marriage again.* 매리언은 결혼 문제를 다시 제기했다.

8 raise hell/Cain etc. INFORMAL **a)** to behave in a wild noisy way that upsets other people ‖ 다른 사람들의 기분을 상하도록 거칠고 소란스럽게 행동하다. 소란을 피우다: *The guys were out raising hell in the bars last night.* 그 녀석들은 어젯밤 외출해서 술집에서 소란을 피웠다. **b)** to protest something in an angry and threatening way ‖ 화를 내며 위협적으로 어떤 것을 항의하다. 난리를 치다: *Jenny raised a fuss when the nurse tried to give her a shot.* 제니는 간호사가 주사를 놓으려고 하자 난리를 쳤다. —see usage note at RISE¹

raise² *n* an increase in the money you earn ‖ 버는 돈의 증가. 인상[상승](액): *a raise of $100 a month* 매달 100달러의 인상액

rai·sin /'reɪzən/ *n* a dried GRAPE ‖ 건포도

rake¹ /reɪk/ *n* a gardening tool used for gathering dead leaves etc. ‖ 낙엽 등을 모으는 데 쓰이는 원예 도구. 갈퀴. 고무레

rake² *v* **1** [I, T] also **rake up** to move a RAKE across a surface in order to make the soil level, gather dead leaves etc. ‖ 땅을 평평하게 하거나 낙엽 등을 긁어모으기 위해 지표면에 갈퀴질을 하다. 갈퀴로 긁어모으다: *raking up the leaves in the fall* 가을에 갈퀴로 낙엽을 긁어모으기 **2** [T] to separate or tear apart things that are part of a group by moving something through it with force ‖ 힘으로 사물을 통과시켜 집단의 일부를 분리하거나 잡아떼다. 가르다. 뜯어 발기다: *She raked her fingers through her hair and screamed.* 그녀는 손가락으로 머리를 억지로 쓸어내다 비명을 질렀다. **3 rake sb over the coals** to speak angrily to someone who has done something wrong ‖ 나쁜 짓을 한 사람에게 화를 내며 말하다. 잘못을 들추어내며 질타하다

rake sth ↔ **in** *phr v* [T] INFORMAL to earn a lot of money without trying very hard ‖ 매우 열심히 노력하지 않고 많은 돈을 벌다. 돈을 긁어모으다[왕창 벌다]: *The toy stores rake it in during Christmas.* 장난감 가게는 크리스마스에 한몫 단단히 잡는다.

rake sth ↔ **up** *phr v* [T] to talk about something from the past that people would rather not mention ‖ 사람이 언급하지 않으려 하는 과거의 일을 이야기하다. …을 폭로하다. 들추어내다: *Why do you have to rake up that old argument again?* 왜 그 오래된 논쟁을 네가 다시 들춰내야 하니?

ral·ly[1] /ˈræli/ *n* **1** a large public meeting to support a political idea, sports event etc. ‖ 정치적 사상·스포츠 행사 등을 지지하는 대규모 대중 모임. 집회. 대회: *a campaign rally* 선거 운동 집회 **2** a car race on public roads ‖ 일반 도로에서 행하는 자동차 경주. 랠리: *the Monte Carlo Rally* 몬테카를로 랠리

rally[2] *v* **1** [I, T] to come together or bring people together to support an idea, a political party etc. ‖ 사상·정당 등을 지지하기 위해 모이거나 사람을 불러모으다. 결집[집결]하다[시키다]: *The President's speech rallied more supporters.* 대통령의 연설은 더 많은 지지자를 불러모았다. **2** [I] to become stronger again after a time of weakness or defeat ‖ 약해지거나 패배한 다음에 다시 더 강해지다. 회복되다. 다시 기운[원기, 힘]을 얻다: *The price of gold rallied after a slight drop.* 금값이 약간 떨어진 후에 다시 올랐다.

rally around *phr v* [I,T **rally around** sb/sth] if a group of people rally around, they all try to help you in a difficult situation ‖ 일단의 사람들이 모두 어려운 처지에 있는 사람을 도우려 하다. 도우러 모이다[몰려들다]: *Her friends all rallied around when her father died.* 그녀의 친구들은 그녀의 아버지가 돌아가셨을 때 도우러 모두 모였다.

RAM /ræm/ *n* [U] TECHNICAL random access memory; the part of a computer that keeps information for a short time so that it can be used immediately ‖ random access memory(램)의 약어; 정보가 즉시 사용될 수 있도록 짧은 시간 동안 보관되는 컴퓨터의 부품 —compare ROM

ram[1] /ræm/ **-mmed, -mming** *v* [T] **1** to

run or drive into something, or to push something using a lot of force ‖ 어떤 것 속으로 부딪치거나 돌진하다, 또는 많은 힘을 써서 어떤 것을 밀어 넣다. 들이받다. 박아[쑤셔] 넣다: *The bus had rammed into the truck.* 그 버스는 트럭을 들이받았다. / *He rammed the key into the lock.* 그는 열쇠를 자물쇠에 쑤셔 넣었다. **2 ram** sth **down** sb's **throat** to try to force someone to accept an idea or opinion by repeating it again and again ‖ 남에게 거듭 반복하여 말함으로써 생각이나 의견을 억지로 받아들이도록 하려 하다. 밀어붙이다. 강요하다: *I don't like people who try to ram their religious beliefs down my throat.* 나는 자기들의 종교적 신앙을 나에게 강요하는 사람을 좋아하지 않는다.

ram[2] *n* a fully grown male sheep ‖ 완전히 성장한 숫양

Ram·a·dan /ˈrɑməˌdɑn/ *n* [singular] the ninth month of the Muslim year, during which no food may be eaten during the hours of the day when it is light ‖ 햇빛이 있는 낮 시간 동안에는 어떤 음식도 먹지 않는 회교력(曆)의 제9월. 라마단

ram·ble[1] /ˈræmbəl/ *v* [I] **1** to talk in a very confused way, not staying with one subject ‖ 한 주제에만 고정시키지 않고 매우 혼란스럽게 말하다. 장황하게[요점 없이] 이야기하다[늘어놓다]: *His speeches tend to ramble.* 그의 연설은 장황하게 늘어지는 경향이 있다. **2** to go on a walk for pleasure ‖ 즐기기 위해 산책하다. 거닐다. 소요하다: *We rambled through the woods all afternoon.* 우리는 오후 내내 숲 속을 거닐었다.

ramble on *phr v* [I] to talk or write for a long time in a way that other people think is boring ‖ 다른 사람이 지루하다고 생각하도록 오랫동안 말하거나 쓰다. 장광설을 늘어놓다: *Sara rambled on about her trip to New York.* 사라는 자신의 뉴욕 여행에 대해 장황하게 늘어놓았다.

ramble[2] *n* a long walk for pleasure ‖ 즐기기 위한 긴 산책. 소요. 만보(漫步)

ram·bling /ˈræmblɪŋ/ *adj* **1** speech or writing that is rambling is very long and does not seem to have any clear organization or purpose ‖ 말이나 글이 매우 길고 어떤 분명한 짜임새나 목적도 없는 것 같은. 산만한. 두서없는: *a long rambling letter* 길고 두서없는 편지 **2** a building that is rambling has an irregular shape and covers a large area ‖ 건축물이 불규칙한 모양으로 넓은 지역을 덮고 있는. 사방팔방으로 뻗은. 무

R

질서하게 뻗어 있는: *a rambling old house* 무질서하게 자리를 차지하고 있는 낡은 집

ram·bunc·tious /ræm'bʌŋkʃəs/ *adj* noisy, full of energy, and behaving in a way that cannot be controlled ‖ 시끄럽고 활기가 넘치며 통제할 수 없게 행동하는. 떠들썩하게 날뛰는. 다루기 힘든: *rambunctious children* 다루기 힘든 아이들

ram·i·fi·ca·tion /ˌræməfə'keɪʃən/ *n* FORMAL a result of something that happens or that you do, that has an effect on other things ‖ 다른 일들에 영향을 미치는, 발생하거나 자신이 한 일의 결과. 영향. 파급 (효과): *the economic ramifications of rising oil prices* 유가 상승의 경제적 파급 (효과)

ramp /ræmp/ *n* **1** a road for driving onto or off a large main road ‖ 큰 간선 도로를 진입하거나 나가기 위한 도로. 램프 **2** a slope that has been built to connect two places that are at different levels ‖ 높이가 다른 두 장소를 연결하여 지은 비탈길. 경사로: *ramps for wheelchair users* 휠체어 사용자용 경사로

ram·page¹ /'ræmpeɪdʒ, ræm'peɪdʒ/ *v* [I] to rush around in groups and behave wildly or violently ‖ 떼를 지어 몰려다니며 거칠거나 격렬하게 행동하다. 사납게[난폭하게] 돌아다니다: *drunken college students rampaging through the streets* 거리를 미친 듯이 날뛰며 돌아다니는 술 취한 대학생들

ram·page² /'ræmpeɪdʒ/ *n* **on the rampage** rushing around in a wild and violent way ‖ 거칠고 격렬하게 몰려다니는. 미친 듯이 날뛰는: *gangs on the rampage* 미친 듯이 날뛰는 깡패들

ramp·ant /'ræmpənt/ *adj* spread across or affecting a large area and difficult to control ‖ 넓은 지역에 퍼지거나 영향을 미치며 통제하기 어려운. 걷잡을 수 없는. 만연하는: *rampant inflation* 걷잡을 수 없는 인플레이션 **– rampantly** *adv*

ram·rod /'ræmrɑd/ *n* **ramrod stiff/straight** sitting or standing with your back straight and your body stiff ‖ 등을 반듯이 하고 몸을 뻣뻣하게 해서 앉거나 서 있는. 부동 자세의

ram·shack·le /'ræm,ʃækəl/ *adj* badly built and needing to be repaired ‖ 부실하게 지어져서 수리를 요하는. 금시라도 무너질 듯한: *a ramshackle farm house* 금시라도 무너질 듯한 농가

ran /ræn/ *v* the past tense of RUN ‖ run의 과거형

ranch /ræntʃ/ *n* a very large farm where cattle, horses, or sheep are raised ‖ 소[말, 양]를 기르는 아주 큰 농장. 대규모의 목(축)장

ranch·er /'ræntʃə/ *n* someone who owns or works on a RANCH ‖ 대목장을 소유하거나 거기서 일하는 사람. 목장주. 목장 일군: *a cattle rancher* 소 목장주 **– ranch** *v* [I] **– ranching** *n* [U]

ranch house /'. ./ *n* a house built on one level, with a roof that does not slope much ‖ 물매가 가파르지 않은 지붕이 있는 단층으로 지은 집. 랜치 하우스 **—see picture on page 945**

ran·cid /'rænsɪd/ *adj* food such as milk or butter that is rancid smells or tastes unpleasant because it is no longer fresh ‖ 우유나 버터 등 음식이 더 이상 신선하지 않아서 고약한 냄새나 맛이 나는. 상하여 악취가 나는: *rancid butter* 상한 버터

ran·cor /'ræŋkə/ *n* [U] FORMAL a feeling of hatred, especially when you cannot forgive someone ‖ 특히 남을 용서할 수 없을 때의 증오의 감정. 원한. 앙심: *The discussion proceeded honestly and without rancor.* 그 토론은 진지하고 적의 없이 진행되었다. **– rancorous** /'ræŋkərəs/ *adj*

ran·dom /'rændəm/ *adj* **1** happening or chosen without any definite plan, aim, or pattern ‖ 어떤 명확한 계획[목적, 규칙적 양상] 없이 일어나거나 선택된. 되는 대로[닥치는 대로]의. 임의의. 무작위의: *a random survey* 무작위 조사 **2 at random** in a completely unplanned way ‖ 완전히 무계획적으로. 되는 대로. 무작위로: *The winning numbers will be chosen at random.* 당첨 번호는 무작위로 추첨됩니다. **– randomly** *adv*

random ac·cess mem·o·ry /ˌ... ...'.../ *n* [C, U] RAM

rang /ræŋ/ *v* the past tense of RING ‖ ring의 과거형

range¹ /reɪndʒ/ *n*
1 ▶GROUP 집단◀ a group of things that are different, but belong to the same general type ‖ 서로 다르지만 동일한 일반적인 유형에 속하는 사물의 집단. 범위. 영역: *books on a wide range of subjects* 광범위한 주제에 관한 책들
2 ▶NUMBER LIMITS 수의 제한◀ the limits within which amounts, levels, ages etc. can vary ‖ 양·수준·연령 등이 변할 수 있는 한도. 변동의 범위[한계, 폭]. 대(帶): *The house is beyond/out of our price range.* (=more than our limit) 그 집은 우리의 (예상) 가격대를 넘어선다[벗어난다]. / *games for the 8-12 age range* 8-12세 연령대용의 게임

3 ▶LIMITS TO POWER/ACTIVITY 힘/활동
의 한계◀ the limits to the amount of
power or responsibility that a person or
organization has, or the types of activity
they are allowed to do ‖ 사람이나 기관이
갖는 권한이나 책임의 크기의 한계, 또는
할 수 있게 허용되는 활동 종류들의 한계.
범위. 영역: *The issue falls outside the
range of the investigation.* 그 문제는 조
사의 범위 밖에 있다.
4 ▶PRODUCTS 상품들◀ a set of similar
products made by a particular company
or available in a particular store ‖ 특정
한 회사가 만들거나 특정한 상점에서 구입
할 수 있는 일련의 유사한 상품들. 상품의
종류[범위]. 기종: *a new range of
mountain bikes* 신기종의 산악자전거
5 ▶DISTANCE 거리◀ **a)** [U] the
distance within which something can be
seen or heard or at which a particular
weapon can hit things ‖ 어떤 것이 보이
거나 들릴 수 있는 또는 특정한 무기가 사
물을 맞힐 수 있는 거리. 가시[가청] 거
리. 유효[사정] 거리: *He was shot at
point-blank range.* (=from very close)
그는 바로 눈앞에서 총에 맞았다. / *I was
out of her range of vision.* 나는 그녀의
시계 밖에 있었다. **b)** the distance at
which a vehicle such as an aircraft can
travel before it needs more FUEL ‖ 비행
기 등 탈것이 추가적인 연료 공급 없이 이
동할 수 있는 거리. 항속 거리: *missiles
with a range of more than 300 miles*
300마일 이상 사정거리의 미사일들
6 ▶MOUNTAINS 산맥◀ a line of
mountains or hills ‖ 한 줄로 늘어선 산들
이나 언덕들. 산맥: *the Cascade Range* 캐
스케이드 산맥
7 ▶FOR PRACTICE 연습용◀ an area of
land where you can practice using
weapons ‖ 무기 사용을 연습하는 부지. 사
격 연습장: *a rifle range* 소총 사격 연습장
8 ▶LAND 부지◀ [C, U] a large area of
grassy land used by cattle ‖ 소를 키우는
데 사용하는 넓은 지역의 목초지. 방목 지
대
9 ▶COOKING ◀ ⇨ STOVE
range² v [I] **1** to vary between
particular limits ‖ 특정한 범위 사이에서
변동하다. 걸치다. 오르내리다. 움직이다:
toys ranging in price from $5 to $25 가
격대가 5달러에서 25달러선인 인형들 **2**
to deal with a large number of subjects
‖ 수많은 주제를 다루다. 미치다. 이르다:
Her speech ranged over several topics.
그녀의 연설은 여러 가지 주제에 미쳤다.
3 if animals range somewhere, they
move over a wide area of land ‖ 동물이

광범위한 지역에서 이동하다. 분포[서식]
하다
rang·er /ˈreɪndʒɚ/ *n* someone whose
job is to watch and take care of a forest
or area of public land and the people
and animals that use it ‖ 삼림이나 공공
부지와 이를 이용하는 사람과 동물을 감시
하고 돌보는 직업인. 삼림 감시원: *a
forest ranger* 산림 감시대원
rank¹ /ræŋk/ *n* [C, U] the position or
level that someone has in an
organization ‖ 사람이 조직에서 가지는 지
위나 등급. 계급. 신분: *He's just been
promoted to the rank of Sergeant.* 그는
이제 막 하사[경사]로 승진했다.
rank² *v* **1** [I] to have a particular
position in a list of people or things that
are put in order of quality or
importance ‖ 질이나 중요성의 순서대로
배열된 사람이나 사물의 목록에서 특정 순
위를 갖다. …에 오르다. …순위[지위]를
차지하다: *Gail ranks third in her class
at school.* 게일은 자기 학교의 학급에서 3
등이다. **2** [T] to decide the position
someone or something should have on a
list, based on quality or importance ‖ 질
이나 중요성을 근거로, 한 목록에서 사람
이나 사물이 차지해야 할 위치를 정하다.
분류하다. 등급을 매기다: *a list of wines
ranked by quality and price* 품질과 가격
으로 등급이 매겨진 포도주 목록
rank³ *adj* having a very strong and
unpleasant smell or taste ‖ 아주 독하고
역한 맛이나 냄새가 나는. 악취가 나는:
rank meat 상한 고기
rank and file /ˌ. . ˈ./ *n* **the rank and
file** the ordinary members of an
organization rather than the leaders ‖
지도자가 아닌 조직의 일반 구성원들. 일
반 사원[회원]. 사병
rank·ing¹ /ˈræŋkɪŋ/ *n* the position or
level that someone has on a list of
people who have a particular skill ‖ 어떤
사람이 특정한 기술을 가진 사람들 목록에
서 차지하는 지위나 등급. 랭킹. 서열. 순
위: *the skater's national ranking* 그 스케
이트 선수의 국내 랭킹
ranking² *adj* a ranking person has a
high position in an organization or is
one of the best at an activity ‖ 사람이 조
직 내에서 고위직을 가지거나 활동 분야에
서 최고 중의 한 명인. 상위[상급]의. 탁
월한. 일류의: *the ranking officer* (현장에
서) 계급이 제일 높은 장교
ran·kle /ˈræŋkəl/ *v* [I, T] if something
rankles or rankles you, it still annoys
you a long time after it happened ‖ 어떤
일이 일어난 오랜 후에도 아직도 사람을

괴롭히다. 마음에 사무치다[맺히다]

ran·sack /'rænsæk/ v [T] **1** to go
through a place stealing things and
causing damage. ‖ 물건을 훔치고 손해를
끼치며 어떤 장소를 지나가다. 약탈하다:
The victim's house had been ransacked.
피해자의 집은 철저히 약탈되었다. **2** to
search a place very thoroughly ‖ 장소를
아주 철저히 수색하다. 샅샅이 뒤지다[찾
다]: *He ransacked his drawers but
couldn't find his birth certificate.* 그는
모든 서랍을 샅샅이 뒤졌으나 자신의 출생
증명서를 찾을 수가 없었다.

ran·som /'rænsəm/ n [C, U] an
amount of money paid to free someone
who is held as a prisoner ‖ 포로로 잡혀
있는 사람을 풀어 주도록 지불하는 금
액. 몸값: *The kidnappers demanded
$50,000 in ransom.* 그 유괴범들은 몸값
으로 5만 달러를 요구했다. **– ransom** v
[T]

rant /rænt/ v [I] to talk or complain in a
loud, excited, and confused way ‖ 큰 소
리로 흥분해서 혼란스럽게 말하거나 불평
하다. 고함치다. 부르짖다. 호언장담하다:
*She ranted about how unfairly her boss
treated her.* 그녀는 자신의 사장이 자신을
얼마나 부당하게 대우했는가에 대해 큰 소
리로 불평했다. / *You can rant and rave*
(=rant continuously), *but I won't change
my mind.* 네가 아무리 고래고래 소리쳐도
나는 마음을 바꾸지 않는다.

rap¹ /ræp/ n **1** [C, U] a type of popular
music in which the words are not sung,
but spoken in time to music with a
steady beat ‖ 가사가 노래로 불려지는 것
이 아니라 일정한 박자를 갖춘 음악에 따
라 말해지는 대중 음악의 한 유형. 랩음악
2 a quick light hit or knock ‖ 빠르고 가볍
게 치거나 때리기. 가볍게[톡톡] 두드리
기: *a rap at the door* 문을 가볍게 두드리
는 소리 **3** [singular] blame or
punishment for a mistake or crime ‖ 잘못
이나 범죄에 대한 비난이나 처벌. 책망.
징벌. 범죄 용의[혐의]: *a murder rap* 살
인 용의 / *He got himself a good lawyer
to beat the rap.* (=avoid punishment) 그
는 처벌을 모면하기 위해 좋은 변호사를
고용했다. / *I'd rather drive, so I don't
have to take the rap* (=be blamed) *for
getting lost.* 나는 길을 잃어버리는 데 대
한 비난을 받을 필요가 없도록 차라리 직
접 운전하겠다. **4 get a bad/bum rap** to
be unfairly criticized, or to be treated
badly ‖ 부당하게 비난받거나 형편없이 대
우받다. 홀대받다. 오명을 뒤집어쓰다:
*The city got a bum rap in the 1980s as
being a center of crime and drug*

trafficking. 그 시는 1980년대에 범죄와
마약 밀거래의 중심지라는 오명을 뒤집어
썼다.

rap² v **-pped, -pping 1** [I, T] to hit or
knock something quickly and lightly ‖ 빠
르고 가볍게 사물을 치거나 때리다. 가볍
게[톡톡] 두드리다: *It sounded like
someone was rapping on the window.* 누
군가가 창문을 두드리는 것 같은 소리가
들렸다. **2** [T] to criticize or blame
someone ‖ 남을 비난하거나 나무라다. 꾸
짖다. 책망하다: *a movie rapped by
critics for its violence* 그 폭력성 때문에
비평가들에 의해 혹평 받은 영화 **3** [I] to
say the words of a RAP song ‖ 랩송의 가
사를 말하다. 랩하다

rape¹ /reɪp/ v [T] to force someone to
have sex by using violence ‖ 폭력을 써서
남에게 성교를 강요하다. 강간하다

rape² n **1** [C, U] the crime of forcing
someone to have sex by using violence ‖
폭력을 써서 남에게 성교를 강요하는 범
죄. 강간: *a rape victim* 강간 피해자 **2**
sudden unnecessary destruction,
especially of the environment ‖ 특히 환
경의 갑작스럽고 불필요한 파괴(행위). 자
연 환경 파괴 행위: *the rape of our rain
forests* 세계의 열대 우림 지대 파괴

rap·id /'ræpɪd/ adj done very quickly,
or happening in a short time ‖ 매우 빨리
끝나거나 짧은 시간 안에 벌어지는. 빠른.
신속한: *the tree's rapid growth* 나무의
빠른 성장 / *rapid political changes* 급속
한 정치적 변화 **– rapidly** adv **–
rapidity** /rə'pɪdəti/ n [U]

rap·ids /'ræpɪdz/ n [plural] part of a
river where the water looks white
because it is moving very fast over rocks
‖ 물이 바위 위로 매우 빠르게 흘러서 하
얗게 보이는 강의 부분. 여울. 급류

rap·ist /'reɪpɪst/ n someone who has
forced someone else to have sex by
using violence ‖ 남에게 폭력을 써서 성교
를 강요한 사람. 강간자[범]

rap·port /ræ'pɔr, rə-/ n [C, U] friendly
agreement and understanding between
people ‖ 사람들 사이의 친밀한 일치와 이
해. 친밀한 (인간) 관계: *She can create
an immediate rapport with her
audience.* 그녀는 청중들과 즉각적으로 친
밀한 관계를 형성할 수 있다.

rap·proche·ment /ˌræprouʃ'mɑn/ n
[singular, U] FORMAL increasing good
relations between two countries or
groups of people, after a time of
unfriendly relations ‖ 비우호적인 시기를
거친 후에 두 나라나 두 집단의 사람들 사
이의 확대되고 있는 선린 관계. 국교 회

복. 화해. 친선: *Both sides are hoping for a swift rapprochement.* 양측은 빠른 국교 회복을 희망하고 있다.

rapt /ræpt/ *adj* so interested in something that you do not notice anything else ‖ 어떤 것에 너무 흥미를 가져서 다른 것은 눈에 들어오지 않는. 몰두해 있는. 넋을 잃은: *The children were listening, rapt, to the story teller.* 아이들은 넋을 잃고 구연동화가에게 귀 기울이고 있었다.

rap·ture /'ræptʃɚ/ *n* [U] great excitement, pleasure, and happiness ‖ 대단한 흥분·즐거움·행복감. 환희. 황홀: *a look of rapture on her face* 그녀의 얼굴의 환희의 표정 – **rapturous** *adj*

rare /rɛr/ *adj* 1 not seen or found very often, or not happening very often ‖ 아주 자주 보이거나 발견되지 않는, 또는 그리 자주 발생하지 않는. 드문. 진귀한: *Thunderstorms are rare here.* 심한 뇌우는 이곳에서 드물다. / *a rare form of cancer* 드문 형태의 암 **2** meat that is rare has only been cooked for a short time and is still red ‖ 고기가 짧은 시간 동안만 요리되어서 여전히 붉은. 설구운. 덜 익은: *Antonio likes his steaks rare.* 안토니오는 설구운 스테이크를 좋아한다.

USAGE NOTE rare and scarce

Use **rare** to talk about something that is valuable and that there is not much of: *Rare coins are usually worth a lot of money.* Use **scarce** to talk about something that is difficult to get at a particular time: *During the war, food and clothing were scarce.* **rare**는 가치가 있으며 그렇게 많지 않은 것에 대해서 말할 때 쓴다: 진귀한 동전은 대체로 값어치가 많이 나간다. **scarce**는 특정한 때에 구하기 힘든 것에 대해서 말할 때 쓴다: 전시에는 식량과 의복이 귀했다.

---

rare·ly /'rɛrli/ *adv* not often ‖ 자주 …않다. 드물게: *She's rarely home these days.* 그녀는 요즘 좀처럼 집에 있지 않다. / *Secretaries are rarely given the thanks they deserve.* 비서들은 마땅히 받아야 할 감사 인사를 받는 일이 드물다.

rar·ing /'rɛrɪŋ/ *adj* **raring to go** INFORMAL very eager to start an activity ‖ 어떠한 활동을 매우 간절히 시작하고 싶어 하는. 몹시 …하고 싶어하는. …하고 싶어 근질근질한: *We got up early, raring to go.* 우리는 몹시 가고 싶어서 일찍 일어났다.

rar·i·ty /'rɛrəṭi/ *n* **be a rarity** to not

happen or exist very often ‖ 매우 자주 발생하거나 존재하지 않다. 좀처럼 없는[드문] 일이다: *Old cars in good condition are a rarity.* 오래된 차의 상태가 좋은 것은 드문 일이다.

ras·cal /'ræskəl/ *n* HUMOROUS a child who behaves badly but whom you still like ‖ 버릇없이 행동하지만 여전히 좋아하는 어린이. 장난꾸러기. 개구쟁이. 악동

rash¹ /ræʃ/ *adj* done too quickly without thinking carefully first, or behaving in this way ‖ 먼저 신중히 생각하지 않고 너무 급히 행해진, 또는 이런 식으로 행동하는. 무모한. 경솔한. 무분별한: *rash decisions* 경솔한 결정 / *a rash and reckless young man* 경솔하고 무모한 젊은이

rash² *n* **1** a lot of red spots on someone's skin, caused by an illness or a reaction to a substance such as food, plants, or medicine ‖ 질병이나 음식[식물, 약] 등의 물질에 대한 반응으로 인해 사람의 피부에 난 많은 붉은 반점. 발진. 뾰루지. 두드러기 **2 a rash of** INFORMAL a large number of unpleasant events, changes etc. within a short time ‖ 짧은 시간 내에 일어난 아주 많은 불쾌한 사건들이나 변화들 등. 다발. 빈발: *a rash of drive-by shootings* 빈발하는 주행 중인 차에서의 총격

rasp·ber·ry /'ræz,bɛri/ *n* a soft sweet red BERRY ‖ 부드럽고 달콤하며 빨간 장과 (漿果). 나무딸기 —see picture on page 944

rasp·y /'ræspi/ *adj* making a rough unpleasant sound ‖ 거칠고 불쾌한 소리를 내는. 귀에 거슬리는. 삐걱거리는: *Marlon Brando's raspy voice in "The Godfather"* "대부"에서의 말론 브란도의 거친 목소리 – **rasp** *v* [I] – **rasp** *n*

rat¹ /ræt/ *n* **1** an animal that looks like a large mouse with a long tail ‖ 긴 꼬리를 가진 큰 생쥐처럼 생긴 동물. 쥐 **2** INFORMAL someone who has been disloyal to you or has deceived you ‖ 자신에게 충직하지 못했거나 자신을 속였던 사람. 변절[배신, 밀고]자: *That rat Bruce just did it for the money.* 그 배신자 브루스는 단지 돈 때문에 그 짓을 했다.

rat² *v* **-tted, -tting** [I] OLD-FASHIONED to be disloyal to someone by telling someone in authority about something wrong that s/he has done ‖ 남이 저지른 잘못에 대해서 권한 있는 사람에게 말해서 그 사람을 배반하다. 변절[배신, 밀고]하다: *You'd better not rat on me!* 나를 배신 하기만 해봐라!

rate¹ /reɪt/ *n* **1** the number of times

something happens over a period of time ‖ 일정한 기간에 걸쳐서 어떤 것이 발생하는 횟수. (비)율: *a country with a low birth rate* 출산율이 낮은 국가 / *a high crime rate* 높은 범죄율 **2** a charge or payment set according to a standard scale ‖ 기준 등급표에 따라서 매긴 요금이나 지불금. 요금. 가격. 시세: *What's the going rate* (=the usual amount paid for work) *for a piano teacher?* 피아노 선생님의 교습비가 보통 얼마죠? / *The Federal Reserve lowered interest rates today.* 연방 준비 제도 이사회는 오늘 이 자율을 낮추었다. **3** the speed at which something happens over a period of time ‖ 일정 기간 동안 어떤 일이 발생하는 속도. 속도. 진도: *Our money was running out at an alarming rate.* 우리의 돈은 놀라운 속도로 바닥나고 있었다. **4 at this rate** SPOKEN used in order to say what will happen if things continue to happen in the same way ‖ 어떤 일이 똑같이 계속 발생한다면 어떻게 될 것인지 말하는 데에 쓰여. 이런 상태[속도]로: *At this rate, we'll never finish on time.* 이런 속도로는 결코 제때에 끝마치지 못할 것이다. **5 at any rate** SPOKEN used when you are giving one definite fact in a situation that is not sure or not satisfactory ‖ 불확실하거나 만족스럽지 못한 상황에서 하나의 확실한 사실을 제시할 때 쓰여. 어쨌든. 하여튼: *He's planning to come. At any rate, I think that's what he said.* 그는 올 생각을 하고 있어. 어쨌든 그는 그렇게 말했던 것 같아. **6 first-rate/second-rate/third-rate** of good, bad, or very bad quality ‖ 좋은[나쁜, 매우 나쁜] 품질의. 일등급/이등급/삼등급의: *a third-rate movie* 3류 영화 **7** the speed a vehicle is traveling ‖ 탈것이 이동하는 속도: *Jet fighters sped past at an amazing rate.* 제트 전투기는 놀라운 속도로 지나갔다.

rate² v 1 [T] to have a particular opinion about the value or worth of something ‖ 사물의 가치나 값어치에 대해 특정한 의견을 가지다. …을 평가하다: *Johnson is rated one of the best basketball players.* 존슨은 최고의 농구 선수 중의 한 명으로 평가된다. **2 X-rated/R-rated etc.** used in order to show that a movie has been officially approved for people of a particular age to see ‖ 영화가 특정한 연령의 사람들이 볼 수 있게 공식적으로 승인되었음을 나타내는 데에 쓰여. X 등급의/R 등급의 **3** [T] INFORMAL to deserve something ‖ 어떤 것을 받을 만한 자격이 있다. …의 가치가

있다: *You all rate a big thank-you for your work.* 여러분 모두 자신들이 한 일에 대해 큰 감사를 받을 만 합니다.

rath·er /ˈræðɚ/ *adv, quantifier* **1 rather than** a phrase meaning instead of, used when you are comparing two things or situations ‖ '…대신에'를 의미하는 어구로, 두 가지 것이나 상황을 비교할 때. …보다는 오히려: *We decided to have the wedding in the summer rather than in the spring.* 우리는 봄보다는 오히려 여름에 결혼식을 올리기로 결정했다. / *Religious instruction belongs in church rather than in the public schools.* 종교적 가르침은 공립학교에서보다는 오히려 교회에 알맞다. **2 would rather** used when you would prefer to do or have one thing more than another ‖ 한 가지 것을 다른 것보다 더 하거나 가지기를 선호할 때 쓰여. 오히려[차라리] …하고 싶다: *I hate sitting doing nothing; I'd rather be busy.* 나는 아무것도 하지 않고 앉아 있는 게 싫다. 난 차라리 바쁜 게 낫다. / *Dave would rather have a dog than a cat, but I like cats.* 데이브는 고양이보다는 개를 가지고 싶어하지만 나는 고양이를 좋아한다. / *He said he would rather not risk it.* 그는 차라리 그것을 위험하게 하지 않겠다고 말했다. **3** FORMAL used in order to give more correct or specific information about what you have said ‖ 이미 한 말에 대해서 더 올바르거나 구체적인 정보를 제시하는 데에 쓰여. 더 정확히[적절하게] 말하자면: *Lucy, or Susie rather, asked me to come tonight.* 루시가, 아니 수지가 오늘 밤 오라고 나에게 말했다. **4** fairly or to some degree ‖ 상당히 또는 어느 정도로. 꽤. 다소. 얼마간: *Some of the photographs are rather grainy and blurred.* 그 사진들의 일부는 다소 선명하지 못하고 흐릿하다.

rat·i·fy /ˈrætəˌfaɪ/ *v* [T] to make a written agreement official by signing it ‖ 서면 협정에 조인함으로써 공식화하다. 비준하다: *Both nations ratified the treaty.* 양국은 그 조약에 비준했다. – **ratification** /ˌrætəfəˈkeɪʃən/ *n* [U]

rat·ing /ˈreɪtɪŋ/ *n* a level on a scale that shows how popular, good, important etc. someone or something is ‖ 사람이나 사물이 얼마나 인기 있는지·좋은지·중요한지 등을 나타내는 등급표상의 수준. 등급. …율: *The governor's approval rating is high.* 그 주지사의 지지율은 높다.

ra·tings /ˈreɪtɪŋz/ *n* **the ratings** [plural] a list that shows which movies, television programs etc. are the most popular ‖ 어떤 영화나 텔레비전 프로그램

등이 가장 인기 있는지를 나타내는 목록. 순위(표): *Her show is at the top of the ratings.* 그녀의 쇼는 시청률 순위에서 1 위를 차지하고 있다.

ra·ti·o /ˈreɪʃi̱ˌoʊ, ˈreɪʃoʊ/ *n* a relationship between two amounts, represented by two numbers that show how much bigger one amount is than the other ‖ 하나의 수량이 다른 수량보다 얼마나 더 큰 지를 나타내는 두 개의 수로 표현되는 두 수량 사이의 관계. 비(율): *The ratio of boys to girls in the class is 2:1.* (=two boys for each girl) 그 학급의 남녀 비율은 2:1이다.

ra·tion[1] /ˈræʃən, ˈreɪ-/ *n* a limited amount of something such as food or gas that you are allowed to have when there is not much available ‖ 사용할 수 있는 양이 그렇게 많지 않을 때 갖도록 허용되는 음식이나 휘발유 등의 제한된 양. 할당[배급]량: *a ration of sugar* 설탕 배급량

ration[2] *v* [T] to control the supply of something by allowing people to have only a limited amount of it ‖ 사람들에게 제한된 수량만 갖도록 허락함으로써 어떤 것의 공급을 통제하다. …을 할당[배급]하다: *Coffee was rationed during the war.* 커피는 전시에 배급제로 나눠졌다. — **rationing** *n* [U]

ra·tion·al /ˈræʃənəl/ *adj* **1** based on reason rather than on emotion ‖ 감정보다는 오히려 이성에 기초한. 합리적인: *a rational decision* 합리적인 결정 / *There must be a rational explanation for their disappearance.* 그들이 사라진 것에 대해서 논리적인 설명이 필요하다. **2** able to think clearly and make good decisions; SENSIBLE ‖ 명확하게 생각해서 좋은 결정을 내릴 수 있는. 이성을 갖춘 이성적인. 분별 있는; 〔유〕 sensible: *a rational person* 합리적인 사람 — **rationally** *adv* — **rationality** /ˌræʃəˈnæləti/ *n* [U] —opposite IRRATIONAL

ra·tion·ale /ˌræʃəˈnæl/ *n* [C, U] FORMAL the reasons and principles on which a decision, plan etc. is based ‖ 결정·계획 등의 근거가 되는 이유와 원칙들. 논리적 근거: *I can't see the rationale behind his plan.* 나는 그의 계획에서 논리적인 근거를 찾을 수가 없다.

ra·tion·al·ize /ˈræʃnəˌlaɪz, -nlˌaɪz/ *v* [I, T] to think of reasons, especially reasons that are not good or sensible, to explain your behavior or attitudes ‖ 자신의 행동이나 태도를 설명하기 위해 특히 좋지 않거나 올바르지 않은 이유들을 생각하다. …을 합리화하다: *He rationalized*

that his parents would have given him the money anyway, so why not just take it? 그는 어차피 그 돈을 부모님이 주었을 텐데 그냥 가져가지 못할 이유가 없다고 합리화했다. — **rationalization** /ˌræʃnələˈzeɪʃən/ *n* [C, U]

ra·tions /ˈræʃənz, ˈreɪ-/ *n* [plural] the food that is given to a soldier each day during a war ‖ 전시에 매일 군인에게 주는 음식. 1일분의 양식

rat race /ˈ. ./ *n* [U] **the rat race** INFORMAL the unpleasant situation in business, politics etc. in which people are always competing against each other ‖ 사람들이 항상 서로간에 경쟁하는 사업·정치 등에서의 불쾌한 상황. 무익한 경쟁[노력]. 격심한 생존 경쟁

rat·tle[1] /ˈrætl/ *v* **1** [I, T] to shake with quick repeated knocking sounds, or to make something do this ‖ 빠르고 반복적인 두드리는 소리를 내며 흔들리다, 또는 어떤 것이 이렇게 하게 하다. 덜거덕덜거덕 소리나다. …을 덜거덕거리게 하다: *There was something rattling around in the trunk.* 차 트렁크 속에서 뭔가가 이리 저리 덜컹거렸다. **2** [T] INFORMAL to make someone lose his/her confidence and become nervous ‖ 어떤 사람을 자신감을 잃고 불안하게 하다. 당황하게 하다: *Don't get rattled – just stay calm.* 당황하지 말고 그냥 침착해.

rattle sth ↔ **off** *phr v* [T] to say something very quickly and easily without effort ‖ 애쓰지 않고 어떤 것을 매우 빠르게 말하다. 줄줄 늘어놓다. 재잘거리다: *She rattled off the names of all the states.* 그녀는 모든 주들의 이름을 줄줄 말해 나갔다.

rat·tle[2] *n* **1** a baby's toy that makes a noise when it is shaken ‖ 흔들 때 소리가 나는 아기의 장난감. 딸랑이 **2** [singular] the noise that you hear when the parts of something knock against each other ‖ 사물의 부분들이 서로 부딪힐 때 들리는 소음. 덜거덕 소리

rat·tler /ˈrætlɚ, ˈrætl-ɚ/ *n* INFORMAL ⇨ RATTLESNAKE

rat·tle·snake /ˈrætlˌsneɪk/ *n* a poisonous American snake that makes a noise with its tail ‖ 꼬리로 소리를 내는 미국산 독사. 방울뱀

rau·cous /ˈrɔkəs/ *adj* a raucous voice or noise is very loud and unpleasant ‖ 목소리나 소음이 매우 크고 불쾌한. 쉰 목소리의. 귀에 거슬리는: *a raucous laugh* 귀에 거슬리는 웃음소리 — **raucously** *adv*

raun·chy /ˈrɔntʃi, ˈrɑn-/ *adj* INFORMAL intended to make you think about sex ‖

자신에게 섹스에 대해 생각을 하게끔 의도
된. 외설스런. 야한: *a raunchy movie* 야
한 영화

rav·age /'rævɪdʒ/ *v* [T] to destroy,
ruin, or damage something badly;
DEVASTATE ‖ 어떤 것을 심하게 파괴하다
[망치다, 손상을 입히다]. …을 약탈하다.
황폐케 하다; 圓 devastate: *a forest
ravaged by fire* 화재로 황폐화된 산림

rav·ag·es /'rævɪdʒɪz/ *n* **the ravages of
sth** LITERARY damage or destruction
caused by something such as war,
disease, time etc. ‖ 전쟁·질병·세월 등으
로 인한 손상이나 파괴. …의 파괴(된 자
취). 참화

rave[1] /reɪv/ *v* [I] **1** to talk in an excited
way about something because you think
it is very good ‖ 어떤 것이 매우 좋다고
생각해서 그것에 대해 흥분해서 말하다.
열변을 토하다. 극찬하다: *Everybody
raved about the movie, but I hated it.*
모든 사람들이 그 영화를 극찬했지만 나는
매우 싫어했다. **2** to talk in a wild angry
way ‖ 거칠게 화를 내며 말하다. 소리[고
함]치다

rave[2] *adj* **rave reviews** strong praise
for a new movie, book, restaurant, or
product ‖ 새로운 영화[책, 식당, 제품]에
대한 열렬한 칭찬. 격찬. 호평: *The book
had/got rave reviews.* 그 책은 호평을
받았다.

rave[3] *n* an event at which young people
dance all night to loud music with a
strong beat ‖ 젊은이들이 강렬한 박자의
시끄러운 음악에 맞춰 밤새 춤을 추는 행
사. 떠들썩한 파티

ra·ven /'reɪvən/ *n* a large black bird ‖
커다란 검은 새. 큰[갈]까마귀

rav·en·ous /'rævənəs/ *adj* extremely
hungry ‖ 몹시 배고픈

ra·vine /rə'vin/ *n* a deep narrow valley
with steep sides ‖ 양 옆이 가파른 깊고 좁
은 계곡. 협곡. 골짜기

rav·ing /'reɪvɪŋ/ *adj* INFORMAL talking or
behaving in a crazy way ‖ 미친 듯이 말
하거나 행동하는. 헛소리를 하는. 미쳐 날
뛰는: *a raving lunatic* 광란하는 미치광이
- **raving** *adv*: *raving mad/drunk* 완전
히 미친[취한]

rav·ings /'reɪvɪŋz/ *n* [plural] things
that someone says that are crazy ‖ 남이
말도 안 된다고 말하는 것들. 헛소리. 허
튼소리. 허풍

rav·ish·ing /'rævɪʃɪŋ/ *adj* a word
meaning "very beautiful," used
especially to describe people ‖ "매우 아
름다운"을 의미하는 단어, 특히 사람들을
묘사하기 위해 쓰여. 황홀하게 하는. 매혹

적인

raw /rɔ/ *adj* **1** not cooked ‖ 요리되지 않
은. 날것의: *raw onions* 생양파 **2** raw
cotton, sugar, and other materials are
still in their natural state, and have not
been prepared for people to use ‖ 목
화·설탕·다른 원료들이 아직 자연 상태 그
대로이고 사람들이 사용하도록 준비되지
않은. 가공하지 않은. 원료 그대로의:
natural gas and other raw materials 천
연 가스와 다른 원자재들 **3** skin that is
raw is red and sore ‖ 피부가 빨갛고 쓰라
린. 피부가 벗겨진. 찰과상의 **4** not
experienced, fully trained, or
completely developed ‖ 경험이 없는 [충
분히 숙련되지 않은, 완전히 발달되지 못
한]. 미숙한. 미완의: *raw recruits in the
army* (=people who have just joined the
army) 군대의 새 입영자들 / *This idea
was the raw material* (=an idea that is
not developed) *for his new play.* 이 생각
은 그의 새 희곡을 위한 구상일 뿐이었다.
5 a raw emotion or quality is strong,
natural, and easy to notice ‖ 감정이나 특
성이 강렬하고 꾸밈없으며 알아채기 쉬운.
세련되지 않은. 조야한의: *raw courage* 만
용 **6 a raw deal** unfair treatment ‖ 불공
평한 대우: *She deserved a raise; I think
she's getting a raw deal.* 그녀는 봉급이
인상됐어야 했어. 나는 그녀가 불공평한
대우를 받고 있는 것 같아.

ray /reɪ/ *n* **1** a narrow beam of light
from the sun, a lamp etc. ‖ 태양·등불 등
에서 나오는 가는 광선: *the sun's rays* 태
양 광선 —see picture at GREENHOUSE
EFFECT **2 ray of hope/comfort etc.**
something that provides a small amount
of hope, comfort etc. ‖ 조그만 희망·위안
등을 제공하는 것. 한 가닥의 희망/위안

ray·on /'reɪɑn/ *n* [U] a smooth material
like silk used for making clothes ‖ 옷을
만드는 데 사용하는 비단 같은 부드러운
섬유. 인조견사. 레이온

raze /reɪz/ *v* [T] to destroy a city,
building etc. completely ‖ 도시·건물 등
을 완전히 파괴하다. …을 부수다[쓰러뜨
리다]: *Three buildings had been razed
to make way for a new mall.* 새로운 쇼
핑몰을 짓기 위해 세 개의 건물이 철거되
었다.

ra·zor /'reɪzɚ/ *n* a sharp instrument for
removing hair from the body ‖ 몸에서 털
을 제거하기 위한 날카로운 도구. 면도칼.
면도기: *an electric razor* 전기면도기

razor blade /'.. ,./ *n* a small flat blade
with a very sharp cutting edge, used
in some RAZORs ‖ 일부 면도기에서 사용되
는, 매우 날카로운 절단면을 가진 작고 납

작한 칼날. 면도날

razz /ræz/ v [T] INFORMAL to try to embarrass or annoy someone by making jokes about him/her; TEASE ‖ 남에 대해서 농담을 함으로써 그 사람을 당황하게 하거나 괴롭히려고 하다. …을 조소[조롱]하다; ⓨ tease: *The kids were razzing Tom about Jenny.* 아이들은 톰에게 제니에 대해서 놀려대고 있었다.

Rd. *n* the written abbreviation of ROAD ‖ road의 약어

-'re /ə/ v the short form of "are" ‖ "are"의 단축형: *We're (=we are) ready to go.* 우린 갈 준비가 되어 있다.

re /ri/ *prep* a word meaning "about" or "regarding," used in business letters to introduce the **main subject** ‖ 주요 화제를 꺼내기 위해 업무 서신에서 사용되는 "…에 대하여"나 "…에 관하여"를 의미하는 단어: *Re your letter of June 10...* 귀하의 6월 10일자 서신에 관하여…

reach¹ /ritʃ/ v 1 [T] to arrive at a particular place ‖ 특정한 장소에 도착하다. 도달하다: *It took four days for the letter to reach me.* 그 편지가 내게 도착하는 데 4일이 걸렸다. **2** [I, T] to move your hand or arm in order to touch, hold, or pick up something ‖ 어떤 것을 만지기[잡기, 줍기] 위해 손이나 팔을 움직이다. 뻗치다: *He threatened me and reached for his knife.* 그는 나를 협박하더니 칼을 잡으려고 손을 뻗었다. / *Mike reached out and took her hand.* 마이크는 손을 내밀어 그녀의 손을 잡았다. / *Jean can't reach the cans on the top shelf.* 선반 꼭대기에 있는 통들에 진은 손이 닿지 않는다. **3** [I, T] to be big enough, long enough etc. to get to a particular level or point ‖ 특정한 수준이나 지점에 이를 정도로 크기·길이 등이 충분하다. (…에) 닿다[이르다]: *Will the ladder reach the roof?* 사다리가 지붕에 닿을까? / *The rope won't reach.* 그 밧줄은 닿지 않을 거야. **4** [T] to increase, decrease, or develop to a particular level or standard over time ‖ 시간이 걸려 특정한 수준이나 기준까지 증가[감소, 발전]하다. …에 (도)달하다. 이르다: *The temperature will reach 95° today.* 온도는 오늘 화씨 95°까지 오릅니다. / *The land has reached the point* (=reached a situation) *at which no crops can be grown on it.* 그 땅은 어떤 농작물

reach

She can't reach the top of the tree.

도 자랄 수 없는 지경에 이르렀다. **5 reach a decision/agreement etc.** to succeed in deciding something, agreeing on something etc. ‖ 어떤 것의 결정·동의 등에서 성공하다. 결론/합의에 이르다 **6** [T] to speak to someone, especially by telephone ‖ 특히 전화상으로 남과 이야기하다. …과 연락하다[접촉하다]: *I wasn't able to reach him yesterday.* 나는 어제 그와 연락이 되지 않았다. **7** [T] if something such as a message reaches a lot of people, it is seen or heard by them ‖ 메시지 등이 많은 사람들에게 도달하여 보거나 듣다. 시청[청취]하다. 영향을 미치다: *a TV program that reaches millions of homes* 수백만 가정이 시청하는 텔레비전 프로그램

reach² *n* **1** [singular, U] the distance that you can stretch out your arm to touch something ‖ 팔을 뻗어서 어떤 것을 만질 수 있는 거리. 손이 닿는 범위: *The box on top of the table was just out of her reach.* 그녀의 손은 그 탁자 위의 상자에 닿을락 말락했다. **2 within reach (of sth) a)** within a distance that you can easily travel ‖ 쉽게 이동할 수 있는 거리 내에. (…과) 가까운 거리에: *We live within easy reach of the city.* 우리는 그 도시와 정말 가까운 거리에 살고 있다. **b)** also **in reach** easy to achieve or get with the skills, power, money etc. that you have ‖ 가지고 있는 기술·힘·자금 등으로 이루거나 얻기 쉬운. …이 가능한 범위[영역] 내의: *This house is within reach of the first-time home buyer.* 이 집은 처음 집을 구매하는 사람도 살 수 있는 정도의 집이다. **3 beyond the reach/out of reach** difficult to achieve or get because you do not have enough skill, power, or money ‖ 충분한 기술[힘, 자금]이 없어서 성취하거나 얻기 어려운. …의 손이 미치지 않는 범위에: *Computer crime is beyond the reach of the regular police force.* 컴퓨터 범죄는 정규 경찰 인력으로 막기에는 무리이다.

re·act /ri'ækt/ v [I] **1** to behave in a particular way because of what someone has done or said to you ‖ 남이 자기에게 했거나 말한 것 때문에 특정하게 행동하다. 반응하다: *How did she react to the news?* 그녀는 그 소식에 어떻게 반응했니? / *The audience reacted by shouting and booing.* 관객은 소리를 지르고 야유를 하는 반응을 보였다. **2 react against sth** to show that you do not like or agree with something by deliberately doing the opposite ‖ 고의로

반대의 것을 함으로써 어떤 것을 좋아하지 않거나 동의하지 않는다는 것을 보이다. …에 반항[반발]하다: *He reacted against his parents' strictness by running away.* 그는 부모님의 엄격함에 대한 반발로 가출했다. **3** TECHNICAL to change when mixed with another substance ‖ 다른 물질과 섞일 때 변하다. 반응하다 —compare OVERREACT

re·ac·tion /riˈækʃən/ n **1** [C, U] something that you feel or do because of what has happened to you or been said to you ‖ 자기에게 발생했거나 자신이 들었던 것 때문에 느끼거나 하는 것. 반응: *What was his reaction to the question?* 그 질문에 대한 그의 반응은 어땠어? — see also **gut reaction/feeling etc.** (GUT¹) **2** a bad effect, such as an illness from food that you have eaten or from a drug that you have taken ‖ 먹은 음식이나 복용한 약으로 인한 병 등의 나쁜 효과. 부작용: *Grant had a reaction to the medicine.* 그랜트는 그 약에 부작용을 보였다. **3** [singular] a change in someone's attitudes, behavior etc. because s/he does not agree with something that was done in the past ‖ 과거에 행해졌던 어떤 것에 동의하지 않아 생긴 사람의 태도·행동 등의 변화. 반발: *strong public reaction against nuclear tests* 핵 실험에 대한 대중의 강한 반발 **4** [C, U] a change that happens when two or more chemical substances are mixed together ‖ 둘 이상의 화학 물질이 함께 섞일 때 발생하는 변화. 화학 반응 —see also REACTIONS

re·ac·tion·ar·y /riˈækʃə,nɛri/ adj DISAPPROVING strongly opposed to social or political change ‖ 사회적 또는 정치적 변화에 강하게 반대하는. 반동적인. 보수적인 – **reactionary** n

reactions /riˈækʃənz/ n [plural] your ability to move quickly when something dangerous happens ‖ 위험한 일이 발생했을 때 빠르게 움직이는 능력. 순발력: *an athlete with quick reactions* 순발력이 빠른 운동 선수

re·ac·tor /riˈæktɚ/ n ⇨ NUCLEAR REACTOR

read /rid/ v **read** /rɛd/, **read** /rɛd/, **reading 1** [I, T] to look at written words, numbers, or signs and understand what they mean ‖ 쓰여진 글[숫자, 기호]을 보고 의미하는 바를 이해하다. (…을) 읽다[판독하다]: *Can Billy read yet?* 빌리가 벌써 글을 읽을 수 있니? / *She sat reading a magazine.* 그녀는 앉아서 잡지를 읽었다. / *I can't*

actually read music, but I can play the guitar. 나는 사실 악보는 볼 줄 모르지만 기타는 칠 수 있다. **2** [I, T] to find out information from books, newspapers etc. ‖ 책·신문 등에서 정보를 알아내다. (…에서) 읽어서 알다[보다]: *I read about the accident in the paper.* 나는 신문에서 그 사고에 대해 읽었다. / *I read that you can buy that new pain killer now.* 이제 그 새로운 진통제를 살 수 있다는 글을 봤다. **3** [I, T] to say written or printed words to other people ‖ 쓰여지거나 인쇄된 글을 다른 사람에 말하다. (…을) 낭독하다. 읽어주다: *Each student had to read his or her report.* 학생들은 각자 자신의 리포트를 낭독해야 했다. / *Read to me, Mommy.* 엄마, 저에게 읽어주세요. **4 read between the lines** to guess what someone really feels or means, even when his/her words do not show it ‖ 남이 정말로 느끼거나 의미하는 것을 그 사람이 말로 나타내지 않더라도 추측하다. 행간의 뜻을 읽어내다. 말 이외의 진짜 의미를 알아채다: *You have to read between the lines to understand what the writer is saying.* 그 작가가 무슨 말을 하고 있는지 이해하려면 작가가 쓴 글에서 진짜 의미하는 것을 알아내야 한다. **5 read sb's mind/thoughts** to guess what someone is thinking ‖ 남이 생각하고 있는 것을 추측하다. 남의 마음/생각을 읽어내다: *"Hey," said Sarah, reading Kate's thoughts, "I'm scared too."* 사라가 케이트의 생각을 읽어내고선 말했다. "이봐, 나도 무서워." **6** [T] if a measuring instrument reads a particular number, it shows that number ‖ 측정 기구가 특정한 수를 나타내다. 가리키다. 표시하다: *What does your gas meter read?* 가스 미터기 눈금이 얼마로 나왔어? **7** [T] to understand a remark, situation etc. in a particular way ‖ 발언·상황 등을 특정하게 이해하다. …로 해석하다: *The movie could be read as a protest against the Church.* 그 영화는 기독교 전체에 대한 항의로 해석될 수도 있다. **8 well-read** having read a lot of books ‖ 많은 책을 읽은. 박식한

read sth **into** sth *phr v* [T] to think that a situation, action etc. means more than it really does ‖ 어떤 상황·행동 등이 실제 이상의 의미를 가진다고 생각하다. …을 …으로 해석하다[읽어내다]: *You shouldn't read so much into what she says.* 너는 그녀가 하는 말에 너무 많은 의미를 두어서는 안 돼.

read up on sth *phr v* [T] to read a lot about something so that you know a lot about it ‖ 어떤 것에 대해서 많이 읽어서 그것에 대해서 많이 알고 있다. 철저하게 공부하다: *We need to read up on the new tax laws.* 새로운 세법을 확실히 익혀 둘 필요가 있다.

read·a·ble /'ridəbəl/ *adj* **1** interesting, enjoyable, or easy to read ‖ 흥미로운, 즐거운, 읽기 쉬운. 재미있게 읽을 수 있는: *The magazine is now more readable and stylish.* 그 잡지는 이제 더 읽을 만하고 멋있어졌다. **2** clear and able to be read; LEGIBLE ‖ 명확하게 읽을 수 있는. 판독할 수 있는; 유 legible —see also MACHINE-READABLE

read·er /'ridɚ/ *n* **1** someone who reads a lot, or reads in a particular way ‖ 책을 많이 읽거나 특정한 방식으로 읽는 사람. 독서가: *an avid reader* (=someone who likes to read a lot) 탐독가 / *a fast/slow reader* 빠르게[느리게] 읽는 사람 **2** someone who reads a particular book, newspaper etc. ‖ 특정한 책·신문 등을 읽는 사람. 독자: *Many of our readers wrote in to complain.* 우리의 많은 독자들이 불평하는 편지를 보내왔다.

read·er·ship /'ridɚˌʃɪp/ *n* [C, U] the people who read a particular newspaper, magazine etc. ‖ 특정한 신문·잡지 등을 읽는 사람들. 구독[독자]층

read·i·ly /'rɛdl-i/ *adv* **1** quickly and easily ‖ 빠르고 쉽게. 곧. 즉시. 쉽사리: *The information is readily available on computer.* 그 정보는 컴퓨터로 쉽사리 이용할 수 있다. **2** quickly, willingly, and without complaining ‖ 빠르게, 기꺼이, 불평 없이. 자진해서. 이의 없이: *Chip readily agreed to help.* 칩은 기꺼이 돕겠다고 했다.

read·i·ness /'rɛdɪnɪs/ *n* [singular, U] willingness to do something ‖ 어떤 것을 기꺼이 하려 함. 기꺼이[자진해서] 함: *I admire his readiness to help people.* 나는 그가 자진해서 사람들을 도우려 하는 것을 높게 평가한다. **2** [U] the state of being prepared and ready for something that might happen ‖ 발생할지도 모를 것에 대비해 준비하고 있는 상태. 준비. 채비: *The army was standing by in readiness for an attack.* 군은 공격에 대비해 대기하고 있었다.

read·ing /'ridɪŋ/ *n* **1** [C, U] the activity of looking at and understanding written words ‖ 쓰여진 글을 보고서 이해하는 행위. 독서: *I enjoy reading and swimming.* 나는 독서와 수영을 즐긴다. / *a careful reading of the contract* 계약서를 주의 깊게 읽음 **2** the way that you understand something, or your opinion about what

a statement, event, article, piece of music etc. means; INTERPRETATION ‖ 사물을 이해하는 방식 또는 진술·사건·기사·음악 등이 의미하는 바에 대한 의견. 읽는 법. 해석. 견해; 유 interpretation: *What's your reading of the situation, Herb?* (=what do you think has caused the situation, or what might happen?) 허브, 너는 이 상황을 어떻게 해석하니? **3** the books, articles etc. that you read ‖ 읽는 책이나 기사들 등. 읽을거리: *I have a lot of reading to do for class.* 나는 수업 준비로 읽어야 할 게 아주 많다. **4** a number or amount shown on a measuring instrument ‖ 측정 기구에 나타나는 수나 양. 표시 도수. 눈금: *The man came to take a reading from the electric meter.* 그 남자가 전기 계량기의 눈금을 보러 왔다.

re·ad·just /ˌriə'dʒʌst/ *v* **1** [I] to change the way you do things because of a new job, situation, or way of life ‖ 새로운 직업[상황, 생활 방식] 때문에 기존의 하던 방식을 바꾸다. 다시 적응하다: *After the war, I needed time to readjust to life at home.* 전쟁 후에, 나는 집에서의 일상생활에 다시 적응하는 데 시간이 걸렸다. **2** [T] to make a small change to something, or move something to a new position ‖ 사물에 작은 변화를 가하다, 또는 사물을 새로운 위치로 옮기다. 재조정하다: *Remember to readjust the mirrors in the car.* 잊지 말고 차의 거울들을 맞게 재조정하시오. – **readjustment** *n* [C, U]

read-on·ly mem·o·ry /ˌ. ˌ.. '.../ *n* [C, U] ⇨ ROM

read·out /'rid-aʊt/ *n* a record of information produced by a computer that is shown on a screen or in print ‖ 컴퓨터가 만드는, 화면상이나 지면상에 나타나는 정보의 기록. (정보) 읽어내기. 그 정보

read·y /'rɛdi/ *adj* **1** someone that is ready is prepared or able to do something ‖ 사람이 어떤 것을 할 준비가 되어 있거나 할 수 있는. 준비[채비]가 된: *Aren't you ready yet?* 아직 준비 안 됐어? / *We're just about ready to eat.* 우리 이제 막 먹으려던 참이다. / *Go get ready* (=do the things you need to do) *for bed.* 가서 잠잘 준비를 해라. / *I don't think Joey is ready for school yet.* 조이는 아직 등교할 준비가 안 된 것 같다. **2** something that is ready has been prepared and can be used, eaten etc. immediately ‖ 어떤 것이 준비되어서 즉시 사용할 수 있거나 먹을 수 있는. 준비가 된: *Is supper ready?* 저녁이 준비되었니?

/ *The dry cleaning will be ready to be picked up on Monday.* 드라이 클리닝은 월요일에 찾을 수 있게 준비됩니다. / *Are you getting ready for* (=preparing things for) *the camping trip?* 야영을 갈 준비가 되어 가고 있니? / *The bus only takes exact change, so have your money ready.* 그 버스는 (잔돈을 거슬러 주지 않고) 정확한 잔돈만을 받으니까 돈을 미리 준비해야 돼. **3** willing or likely to do something ‖ 어떤 것을 기꺼이 하거나 할 것 같은. 기꺼이 …하는. 바야흐로 …하려는: *She looked really upset and ready to cry.* 그녀는 정말로 속상해서 곧 울 듯이 보였다. **4 ready cash/money** money that is available to be used immediately ‖ 즉시 사용 가능한 돈. 현금 **5 (get) ready, (get) set, go!** used in order to tell people to start a race ‖ 사람들에게 경주를 시작하라고 말하는 데에 쓰여. 제자리에, 준비, 땅! —see usage note at PREPARE

ready-made /ˌ.. '.·/ adj ready to be used immediately ‖ 즉시 사용할 수 있게 준비된. 기성품의: *ready-made clothing* 기성복

real¹ /ril/ adj **1** not imaginary but actually existing ‖ 상상이 아닌 실제로 존재하는. 현실의. 실재하는: *The new system has real advantages.* 새로운 시스템은 실제로 이점이 있다. / *There is a very real danger/possibility/risk of an explosion.* 폭발의 위험[가능성, 우려]이 매우 현존한다. **2** true and not pretended ‖ 진실되고 가장하지 않은. 진짜의. 진정한: *What's the real reason you were late?* 네가 늦은 진짜 이유가 뭐냐? **3** not false; GENUINE ‖ 가짜가 아닌. 진짜의; 矯 genuine: *real gold* 진짜 금 / *"Jack" isn't his real name.* "잭"은 그의 진짜 이름이 아니다. **4** used in order to emphasize what you are saying ‖ 말하고 있는 것을 강조하는 데에 쓰여. 정말의: *Matt's a real jerk.* 매트는 정말 바보다. / *It's a real pleasure to meet you.* 당신을 만나 뵙게 돼서 정말 기쁩니다. **5 the real world** also **real life** the world that people actually live in, as opposed to an imaginary one ‖ 상상의 세계와 반대되는 것으로서 사람들이 실제 살고 있는 세계. 현실 세계: *Things don't happen like that in the real world.* 현실 세계에서는 그런 일은 일어나지 않아. **6 the real thing/McCoy** INFORMAL a thing or person that is the actual one and not a copy ‖ 복사본이 아닌 실제의 사물이나 사람. 진짜. 본인: *This isn't Mexican food from a box. This is the real thing!* 이건

간이음식점에서 산 멕시코 음식이 아니야. 이건 진짜 정통 멕시코 음식이야!

SPOKEN PHRASES
---

7 said when something is the way you think it should be ‖ 어떤 것이 마땅히 그래야 한다고 생각하는 식일 때에 쓰여. 진짜의. 정말의: *Now that's real coffee!* 그래 이게 진짜 커피지! **8 real live** used in order to emphasize how rare or unusual something is ‖ 어떤 것이 얼마나 희귀하거나 별난 것인지를 강조하는 데에 쓰여. 진짜의: *Wow! A real live movie star!* 우아! 진짜 영화 스타야! **9 be for real** used in order to say that someone or something is actually what s/he seems to be, or actually means what s/he says ‖ 사람이나 사물이 실제로 그 겉모습과 같은지, 또는 실제로 말하고 있는 바를 의미하는지를 말하는 데에 쓰여. 정말[진심]이다: *Are you for real?* (=do you really mean what you are saying?) 너 정말이야? **10 get real** used in order to tell someone that what s/he is suggesting is not sensible or possible ‖ 남에게 그 사람이 제안하는 것이 엉뚱하거나 불가능하다고 말하는 데에 쓰여. 정신 차려라. 꿈 깨: *You may just have to get real and get a job like everybody else!* 너도 이제 정신 차려서 다른 사람처럼 직장을 구해라!

real² adv SPOKEN NONSTANDARD very ‖ 매우. 정말로. 참으로: *I'm real sorry!* 정말 미안해!

real es·tate /'. .ˌ.·/ n [U] **1** property such as houses or land ‖ 주택이나 토지 등의 자산. 부동산: *Real estate prices fell again last year.* 부동산 시세는 작년에 다시 떨어졌다. / *Japanese investment in US real estate* 미국 부동산에 대한 일본인의 투자 **2** the business of selling houses or land ‖ 주택이나 토지를 파는 사업. 부동산 중개업

real estate a·gent /'. .. ˌ..·/ n someone whose job is to sell houses or land ‖ 주택이나 토지를 파는 직업인. 부동산 중개업자. 공인 중개사

re·al·ism /'riəˌlɪzəm/ n [U] the ability to deal with situations in a practical or sensible way ‖ 상황을 실제적이거나 분별 있게 처리하는 능력. 현실주의

re·al·ist /'riəˌlɪst/ n someone who thinks in a REALISTIC way ‖ 현실적으로 생각하는 사람. 현실주의자

re·al·is·tic /ˌriə'lɪstɪk/ adj practical and sensible, or dealing with situations in this way ‖ 실제적이며 분별 있는 또는 이런 식으로 상황을 처리하는. 현실주의의. 현실적인: *You have to be realistic about your chances of winning.* (=realize that you may not win) 너는 이길 수 있는 가능성을 현실적으로 생각해야 돼. / *realistic sales targets* (=sensible ones, that can be achieved) 현실적인 판매 목표 — opposite UNREALISTIC

re·al·is·tic·ally /ˌriə'lɪstɪkli/ *adv* **1** in a REALISTIC way ‖ 현실적인 방법으로. 실제적으로: *We can't realistically hire new people without any money.* 우리는 현실적으로 돈도 없이 새로운 사람들을 고용할 수는 없다. **2** described or shown in a way that is very similar to real life ‖ 실물과 매우 유사하게 묘사하거나 나타내어. 사실적으로: *a realistically drawn picture* 사실적으로 그려진 그림

re·al·i·ty /ri'æləti/ *n* **1** [C, U] what is true or what actually happens, not what is imagined or not real ‖ 상상적인 것이거나 가공적인 것이 아니라 진짜거나 실제로 발생한 것. 현실. 실체. 본질: *Being aware of dangers on the street at night is one of the realities of living in the city.* 밤거리의 위험성을 알고 있다는 것이 도시 생활의 실체들 중의 하나이다. / *It's best to accept the reality of the situation.* 지금 상황의 현실을 인정하는 것이 가장 낫다. **2 in reality** used in order to say that something is different from what seems to be true ‖ 사물이 사실적인 것과는 동떨어졌다고 말하는 데에 쓰여. 실은. 실제로는: *He said he'd retired, but in reality, he was fired.* 그는 퇴직했다고 말했지만 실은 해고를 당했다. **3 become a reality/make sth a reality** to begin to exist or happen, or to make something do this ‖ 존재하거나 발생하기 시작하다, 또는 사물을 이렇게 하게 하다. 실제가 되다. …을 실제가 되게 하다: *Money from two major companies helped to make the Children's Center a reality.* 두 대기업의 기부금이 어린이 센터를 현실화할 수 있게 도왔다. **4 reality check** INFORMAL an occasion when you consider the facts of a situation, as opposed to what you would like or what you have imagined ‖ 하고 싶은 것이나 상상해 왔던 것과는 반대되게 어떤 상황의 실상들을 고려할 때의 경우. 현실 직시: *It's time for a reality check: the team isn't as good as people think.* 이제 현실을 직시할 때다. 우리 팀은 사람들이 생각하는 만큼 잘 하지 못해.

re·al·i·za·tion /ˌriələ'zeɪʃən/ *n* [singular, U] **1** the act of understanding or realizing something that you did not know before ‖ 전에는 알지 못했던 것들을 이해하거나 깨닫는 행동. 인식. 깨달음: *We finally came to the realization that the business wasn't going to work.* 우리는 마침내 사업이 안 될 것이라고 깨닫게 되었다. **2** the act of achieving what you had planned or hoped to do ‖ 계획했거나 하기를 희망했던 것을 성취하는 행동. 실현: *Harry sacrificed everything for the realization of his dream.* 해리는 자기 꿈을 실현하기 위해 모든 것을 희생했다.

re·al·ize /'riəˌlaɪz/ *v* [T] **1** to know or understand the importance of something that you did not know before ‖ 전에는 알지 못했던 것의 중요성을 알거나 이해하다. …을 깨닫다[실감하다]: *I'm sorry, I didn't realize (that) it was so late.* 미안해, 나는 이렇게 늦은 줄 미처 몰랐어. / *He obviously didn't realize the dangers involved.* 그는 분명히 내포된 그 위험을 깨닫지 못했다. **2 realize a hope/goal/dream etc.** to achieve something you have been hoping for, working for etc. ‖ 계속 바라고 일해 오던 것을 성취하다. 희망/목표/꿈을 달성[실현]하다 **3 sb's (worst) fears were realized** used in order to say that the thing that someone was afraid of actually happened ‖ 사람이 두려워했던 것이 실제로 발생했다고 말하는 데에 쓰여. …이 (가장) 두려워하던 것이 현실로 나타났다: *Morris's worst fears were realized when the police came to his door.* 모리스가 가장 두려워하던 일은 경찰이 그의 집 앞에 왔을 때 현실로 나타났다.

real·ly /'rili/ *adv* **1** a word meaning "very" or "very much," used in order to emphasize something ‖ "매우" 또는 "대단히"를 뜻하는 단어로 어떤 것을 강조하는 데 쓰여. 아주. 정말로: *Yeah, he's a really nice guy.* 그래, 그는 정말로 멋진 남자야. / *I don't really trust him.* 나는 그를 전적으로 신뢰하지 않는다. **2** used in order to emphasize that something is true, especially when people might think something else is true ‖ 특히 사람들이 다른 것이 사실이라고 생각할 수도 있을 때에 어떤 것이 사실이라고 강조하는 데 쓰여. 실제로(는). 참으로: *This doll might really be valuable.* 이 인형은 실제로는 값비쌀지도 모른다. / *No, really, I'm fine.* 아니, 정말로 난 괜찮아.

SPOKEN PHRASES

3 really? used when you are surprised about or interested in what someone has said ‖ 남이 한 말에 대해

서 놀라거나 관심이 있을 때에 쓰여. 정말(로)? 설마: *"Jay got promoted." "Really? When?"* "제이가 승진했어요." "정말로요? 언제요?" **4 not really** used in order to say "no," especially when something is not completely true‖특히 어떤 것이 완전히 사실이 아닐 때 "아니"라고 말하는 데에 쓰여. 꼭[반드시] 그런 것은 아니야. (별로) 그렇지는 않다: *"Is that salsa hot?" "Not really."* (=not too hot) "그 살사 소스 맵니?" "그렇게 맵지는 않아." **5 (yeah) really** used in order to agree with someone‖남에게 동의하는 데에 쓰여. 그러게 말이야. 정말이야: *"I just want to meet a nice guy." "Yeah, really."* "나는 정말 멋진 남자를 만나고 싶어." "그러게 말이야."

realm /rɛlm/ *n* **1** an area of knowledge, interest, or thought‖지식[관심, 생각]의 영역. 범위. 분야: *new discoveries in the realm of science* 과학 분야에서의 새로운 발견들 **2** LITERARY a country ruled over by a king or queen‖왕이나 여왕이 통치하는 나라. 왕국

R **real-time** /'. ./ *adj* TECHNICAL a real-time computer system deals with information as fast as it receives it‖컴퓨터 시스템이 정보를 받아들이자마자 바로 처리하는. 실시간의 -**real time** *n* [U]

real·tor /'riltɚ/ *n* ⇨ REAL ESTATE AGENT

real·ty /'rilti/ *n* [U] ⇨ REAL ESTATE

ream /rim/ *n* **1 reams of sth** INFORMAL a lot of something‖어떤 것이 많음. 대량: *He took reams of notes in the class.* 그는 그 수업 시간에 노트 필기를 많이 했다. **2** TECHNICAL 500 sheets of paper‖종이 5백장. 연(連)

reap /rip/ *v* [I, T] to get something good because of the hard work that you have done‖일을 열심히 해서 좋은 것을 얻다. (…을) 거두다. 획득하다: *The company has reaped the benefits of their advertising campaign.* 그 회사는 광고의 덕을 봤다.

rear¹ /rɪr/ *n* **1 the rear** the back part of an object, vehicle, building etc.‖물체·탈것·건물 등의 뒷부분. 뒤. 후방. 배후: *There are more seats at the rear of the theater.* 극장 뒤쪽에는 좌석이 더 있다. **2** ⇨ REAR END **3 bring up the rear** to be at the back of a line or group of people that is moving forward‖앞으로 움직이는 행렬이나 일단의 사람들의 뒤쪽에 있다. 후위를 맡아보다. 맨 뒤에 오다: *The kids came around the corner with*

Donny bringing up the rear. 아이들은 도니를 맨 뒤에 따라오게 하고선 모퉁이를 돌아서서 왔다.

rear² *v* **1** [T] to care for a person, animal, or plant until s/he or it is fully grown‖사람[동물, 식물]이 완전히 자랄 때까지 돌보다. 기르다. 부양하다. 사육하다: *She reared seven children by herself.* 그녀는 혼자서 일곱 명의 아이들을 길렀다. **2** [I] also **rear up** if an animal rears, it rises up on its back legs‖동물이 뒷다리로 일어서다. 뒷다리로 곧추서다 **3 rear its ugly head** if a problem rears its ugly head, it appears or happens‖어떤 문제의 추악한 면모가 나타나거나 발생하다. 고개를 쳐들다: *We must attack racism whenever it rears its ugly head.* 우리는 인종주의가 고개를 쳐들 때마다 비판해야만 한다.

rear³ *adj* relating to the back of something‖사물의 뒤와 관련 있는. 뒤쪽의. 후방의. 배후의: *the rear wheels of the car* 자동차의 뒷바퀴 / *the rear entrance of the hospital* 병원의 후문

rear end /ˌ. './ *n* SPOKEN the part of your body that you sit on‖앉는 신체의 일부. 궁둥이. 둔부: *He fell right on his rear end!* 그는 넘어지며 엉덩방아를 찧었어!

rear-end /ˌ. './ *v* [T] INFORMAL to hit the back of someone's car with another car‖남의 차 뒤쪽을 다른 차로 치다. …을 들이받다: *Someone rear-ended us on the freeway.* 누군가가 고속도로에서 우리 차의 뒷부분을 들이받았다.

re·ar·range /ˌriə'reɪndʒ/ *v* [T] to change the position or order of things‖사물의 위치나 순서를 바꾸다. …을 재정리[재배열]하다: *We rearranged the furniture in the living room.* 우리는 거실의 가구를 재배치했다. -**rearrangement** *n* [C, U]

rear·view mir·ror /ˌ.. '../ *n* the mirror in a car that you use to see what is behind you when you are driving‖운전할 때 자기 뒤쪽에 있는 것을 보기 위해 사용하는 차의 거울. 백미러

rear·ward /'rɪrwɚd/ *adv* in, toward, or at the back of something‖사물의 뒤쪽으로[을 향해, 에]. 뒤로[에]. 배후로[에]: *a rearward facing seat* 뒤로 향해진 좌석

rea·son¹ /'rizən/ *n* **1** [C, U] the cause or fact that explains why something happens or exists‖어떤 것이 왜 발생하거나 존재하는지 설명하는 원인이나 사실. 이유. 까닭: *Did he give any reason for quitting?* 그가 왜 그만두는지 이유라도 말했어? / *There is no reason to believe* *that he is guilty.* 그가 유죄라고 믿을 만한 아무런 이유도 없다. —see usage note at EXCUSE² **2** [U] sensible judgment and understanding ‖ 분별 있는 판단과 이해. 지각. 분별. 사리: *Randy is not the kind of man who listens to reason.* (=is persuaded by reason) 랜디는 사리에 귀기울이는 부류의 사람이 아니다. / *You can choose the car you want, within reason.* (=within sensible limits) 너는 적절한 한도 내에서 원하는 차를 고를 수 있다. **3** [U] the ability to think, understand, and form judgments that are based on facts ‖ 사실에 근거해서 생각하고 이해하고 판단을 내리는 능력. 이성. 판단력: *a conflict between reason and emotion* 이성과 감정 사이의 갈등 **4** **all the more reason to do sth** used in order to say that what has just been mentioned is another reason for doing what you have suggested ‖ 방금 언급된 말이 이미 자신이 제안했던 것을 할 다른 이유가 된다고 말하는 데에 쓰여. …을 할 이유가 하나 더 생겼다: *"I have no money." "All the more reason to stay home with me tonight."* "나는 돈이 없어." "오늘 밤 나하고 함께 집에서 머무를 이유가 하나 더 생겼군."

reason² v **1** [T] to form a particular judgment about something after thinking about the facts ‖ 사실들에 대해서 생각한 연후에 어떤 것에 대한 특정한 판단을 내리다. 추론하다. 결론을 내리다: *The jury reasoned that he could not have committed the crimes.* 배심원단은 그가 그 범죄들을 저지를 수 없었을 거라고 결론을 내렸다. **2** [I] to think about facts clearly and make judgments ‖ 사실들에 대해서 명확히 생각해서 판단하다: *Small children do not have the ability to reason.* 아주 어린 아이들은 판단 능력이 없다.

reason with sb *phr v* [T] to talk to someone in order to persuade him/her to be more sensible ‖ 더 분별 있도록 설득하려고 남에게 이야기하다. 깨우쳐 주다. (논리적으로) 설득하다: *I tried to reason with her, but she wouldn't listen.* 나는 그녀를 설득해 보려고 애썼지만 들으려 하지 않았다.

rea·son·a·ble /ˈriznəbəl, -zən-/ *adj* **1** fair and sensible ‖ 공정하고 합당한. 이치[도리, 사리]에 맞는. 공평한: *a reasonable suggestion* 이치에 맞는 제안 / *He seemed like a reasonable guy.* 그는 분별 있는 남자처럼 보였다. **2** a reasonable amount, number, or price is not too much or too big ‖ 양[수, 가격]이

너무 많거나 크지 않은. 적당한. 알맞은: *The store sells good furniture at reasonable prices* 그 상점은 적당한 가격에 좋은 가구를 판매한다. – **rea·son·a·ble·ness** *n* [U] —opposite UN-REASONABLE

rea·son·a·bly /ˈriznəbli/ *adv* **1** fairly but not completely ‖ 완전히는 아니지만 상당히. 무리 없이. 꽤: *I did reasonably well on the test.* 나는 그 시험을 꽤 잘 봤다. **2** in a way that is fair or sensible ‖ 공정하거나 분별력 있게. 이치에 맞게. 이성적으로: *"I'm sure we can find an answer," Steve said reasonably.* "난 우리가 해답을 구할 수 있다고 믿는다."라고 스티브는 분별있게 말했다.

rea·soned /ˈrizənd/ *adj* based on careful thought; SENSIBLE ‖ 주의 깊은 사고에 근거한. 사리에 맞는. 심사숙고한; ㊌ sensible: *a reasoned argument* 사리에 맞는 주장

rea·son·ing /ˈrizənɪŋ/ *n* [U] the process of thinking carefully about something in order to make a judgment ‖ 판단을 내리기 위해 사물에 대해 주의 깊게 생각하는 과정. 추리. 추론: *a decision based on sound reasoning* (=good reasoning) 합리적인 추론에 근거한 결정 / *I don't understand your line of reasoning.* (=the way you are thinking) 나는 네 사고 방식을 이해하지 못하겠어.

re·as·sur·ance /ˌriəˈʃʊrəns/ *n* [C, U] something that you say or do to make someone feel less worried about a problem ‖ 남이 어떤 문제에 대해서 덜 걱정하도록 말하거나 하는 것. 안심시키는 말[것]: *I need some reassurance that I won't be fired.* 저는 제가 해고되지 않을 거라는 확실한 보장이 필요합니다. / *He didn't give me any reassurances.* 그는 내게 어떤 확신도 주지 않았다.

re·as·sure /ˌriəˈʃʊr/ *v* [T] to make someone feel calm and less worried about a problem ‖ 남이 어떤 문제에 대해서 침착하고 덜 걱정하게 하다. 안심시키다: *Kids need to be reassured that their parents love them no matter what.* 아이들에게는 부모들이 무슨 일이 있어도 자기들을 사랑한다고 안심시킬 필요가 있다.

re·as·sur·ing /ˌriəˈʃʊrɪŋ/ *adj* making someone feel calm and less worried ‖ 남을 진정시키고 걱정을 덜 하게 하는. 안심시키는: *a quiet reassuring voice* 안심시키는 조용한 목소리 – **reassuringly** *adv*

re·bate /ˈribeɪt/ *n* an amount of money that is paid back to you when you have paid too much rent, taxes etc. ‖ 너무 많

은 임대료·세금 등을 지불했을 때 돌려받는 액수. 환불금: *a tax rebate* 환불 세금

reb·el¹ /'rɛbəl/ *n* **1** someone who REBELs against people in authority ‖ 권력을 잡고 있는 사람들에게 반역하는 사람. 반역[반란]자: *Rebels have overthrown the government.* 반란군은 정부를 전복했다. **2** someone who does not do things in the way that other people want him/her to do them ‖ 다른 사람들이 해주기를 원하는 대로 행동하지 않는 사람. 반항자: *She was a rebel at school.* 그녀는 학교에서 반항아였다.

rebel² *v* **-lled, -lling** [I] to oppose or fight against someone who is in authority ‖ 권력을 잡고 있는 사람에 대해 반대하거나 싸우다. 반역[반항]하다: *Brando played a character who rebels against small-town attitudes.* 브란도는 소읍의 텃세에 대항해서 싸우는 역할을 연기했다.

re·bel·lion /rɪ'bɛlyən/ *n* [C, U] **1** an organized attempt to change the government using violence ‖ 폭력을 사용해서 정부를 바꾸려는 조직적인 시도. 반역. 반란: *He led an armed rebellion against the government.* 그는 정부에 대항하는 무장 반란군을 이끌었다. **2** opposition to someone in authority ‖ 권위를 행사하는 사람에게 반대함. 반항: *teenage rebellion* 십대의 반항 — compare REVOLUTION

re·bel·lious /rɪ'bɛlyəs/ *adj* **1** deliberately disobeying someone in authority ‖ 권위를 행사하는 사람에게 고의적으로 불복종하는. 반항하는: *I was a rebellious child.* 나는 반항아였다. **2** fighting against the government by using violence ‖ 폭력을 사용해서 정부에 대항해 싸우는. 반역[반란]의: *rebellious troops* 반란군

re·birth /ri'bɚθ, 'ribɚθ/ *n* [singular] a change that results in an old idea, method etc. becoming popular again ‖ 옛 사상·방법 등이 다시 인기를 얻게 되는 변화. 재생. 부활

re·bound¹ /'ribaʊnd, rɪ'baʊnd/ *v* **1** [I] if a ball rebounds, it moves quickly back after hitting something solid ‖ 볼이 단단한 것을 치고 나서 거꾸로 빠르게 움직이다. 되튀다: *The ball rebounded off the hoop.* 공은 농구 골대를 맞고 되튀었다. **2** to increase again after decreasing; IMPROVE ‖ 감소한 이후에 다시 증가하다. 회복[반등]하다; ⑩ improve: *Oil prices rebounded this week.* 유가가 이번 주 들어 반등했다.

re·bound² /'ribaʊnd/ *n* **on the**

rebound someone who is on the rebound is upset or confused because a romantic relationship has ended ‖ 사람이 연애 관계가 끝나서 속상하거나 혼란스러운. (실연 등의) 반발로

re·buff /rɪ'bʌf/ *v* [T] FORMAL to be unkind to someone who is trying to be friendly or helpful ‖ 친해지려고 하거나 도움이 되고자 애쓰는 사람에게 불친절하게 …을 거절함[퇴짜 놓다]: *His offer of help was rebuffed.* 그의 돕겠다는 제안은 거절당했다. **– rebuff** *n*

re·build /ri'bɪld/ *v* [T] **1** to build something again, after it has been damaged or destroyed ‖ 사물이 손상되거나 파괴된 이후에 다시 짓다. 개축하다: *The freeway system was quickly rebuilt after the earthquake.* 고속도로는 지진이 있은 후에 빠르게 다시 지어졌다. **2** to make something strong and successful again ‖ 사물을 다시 강하고 성공적이게 하다. 재건하다: *attempts to rebuild the area's economy* 그 지역의 경제를 재건하려는 시도

re·buke /rɪ'byuk/ *v* [T] FORMAL to criticize someone because s/he has done something wrong ‖ 남이 잘못된 짓을 해서 그 사람을 비난하다. 몹시 비난하다. 질책하다: *The band has been rebuked by the critics for writing racist songs.* 그 밴드는 인종 차별적인 노래를 작곡해 부른다고 평론가들로부터 호된 비난을 받았다. **– rebuke** *n* [C, U]

re·but /rɪ'bʌt/ *v* **-tted, -tting** [T] FORMAL to give reasons to show that a statement or a legal charge that has been made against you is false ‖ 자신에게 불리한 진술이나 법적인 혐의가 잘못됐다는 것을 나타내기 위해 이유들을 대다. …을 반박[반론]하다. 반증을 들다 **– rebuttal** /rɪ'bʌtl/ *n*

re·cal·ci·trant /rɪ'kælsətrənt/ *adj* FORMAL refusing to obey or be controlled, even after being punished ‖ 처벌을 받은 이후에도 복종하거나 통제되기를 거부하는. 반항[저항]하는. 말을 듣지 안 듣는 **– recalcitrance** *n* [U]

re·call¹ /rɪ'kɔl/ *v* [T] **1** to remember something ‖ 어떤 것을 상기[기억]해 내다. 회상하다: *I don't recall meeting him.* 나는 그를 만난 기억이 없다. / *He couldn't recall who he had spoken to.* 그는 누구에게 얘기했었는지 생각해 낼 수 없었다. **2** to ask people to return a product they bought from your company because something may be wrong with it ‖ 자기 회사에서 구매한 제품에 이상이 있을 수도 있어서 사람들에게 반품을 요청

하다. …을 회수[리콜]하다

re·call² /rɪˈkɔːl, ˈriːkɔːl/ *n* **1** [U] the ability to remember something you have learned or experienced ‖ 배우거나 경험한 것을 기억하는 능력. 기억력: *She has total recall* (=ability to remember everything) *of what she has read.* 그녀는 읽은 것은 모두 기억한다. **2** a situation in which a company RECALLs a product ‖ 회사가 제품을 회수하는 상황. 불량 제품의 회수. 리콜

re·cant /rɪˈkænt/ *v* [I, T] FORMAL to say publicly that you no longer have a particular religious or political belief ‖ 이제는 특정한 종교적 또는 정치적 신념을 가지고 있지 않다고 공개적으로 말하다. (…을) 부인[철회]하다

re·cap /ˈriːkæp, rɪˈkæp/ *n* [C usually singular] INFORMAL the act of repeating the main points of something that has just been said ‖ 방금 말한 것의 주요 논점을 반복하는 행위. 요약. 개괄: *And now for a recap of tonight's news.* 그러면 이제 오늘 밤 주요 뉴스를 살펴보겠습니다. – **recap** *v* [I, T]

re·cap·ture /riˈkæptʃɚ/ *v* [T] **1** to make someone experience or feel something again ‖ 남에게 어떤 것을 다시 경험하거나 느끼게 하다. …을 상기시키다 [생각나게 하다]: *a movie that recaptures the innocence of childhood* 어린 시절의 천진난만함을 상기시키는 영화 **2** to win a piece of land back that you have lost in a war, or to win a political position again after losing it ‖ 전쟁에서 잃은 땅을 되찾다, 또는 정치적 지위를 잃은 후에 다시 얻다. 되찾다. 탈환하다: *Christians recaptured Budapest from the Ottoman Empire in 1686.* 기독교인들은 1686년에 부다페스트를 오토만 제국으로부터 되찾았다. **3** to catch a prisoner or animal that has escaped ‖ 도망친 죄수나 동물을 잡다. 다시 붙잡다[체포하다]: *Both men were recaptured by the police.* 두 남자 모두 경찰에게 다시 체포되었다.

re·cede /rɪˈsiːd/ *v* [I] **1** if something you see, feel, or hear recedes, it gets further and further away until it disappears ‖ 사물이 완전히 없어질 때까지 점점 더 멀어져 가서 볼 수[느낄 수, 들을 수] 없게 되다. 사라져 가다. 약해지다: *The sound receded into the distance.* 그 소리는 멀리 사라져 갔다. / *Tensions between the two countries have receded for the moment.* 양국간의 긴장 관계는 당장은 사라졌다. **2** if your hair recedes, you gradually lose the hair at the front

of your head ‖ 머리의 앞쪽에 있는 머리카락을 점차 잃게 되다. 이마가 벗겨지다 **3** if water recedes it moves back from an area that it was covering ‖ 물이 차있던 지역에서 빠지다. 썰물이 되다

re·ceipt /rɪˈsiːt/ *n* **1** a piece of paper that shows that you have received money or goods ‖ 돈이나 물품을 받았다는 것을 나타내는 종잇조각. 영수증: *Be sure and keep your receipts for tax purposes.* 세금 처리용으로 영수증을 잘 보관하시오. **2** [U] FORMAL the act of receiving something ‖ 어떤 것을 받는 행위. 수령. 인수: *The contract becomes valid on/upon receipt of* (=when we receive) *your letter.* 계약은 귀하의 서신을 받는 즉시 법적으로 유효하게 됩니다.

re·ceive /rɪˈsiːv/ *v* [T] **1** to be given something officially ‖ 어떤 것을 공식적으로 받다. …을 (수여)받다: *He received an award from the college.* 그는 대학에서 상을 수여받았다. **2** FORMAL to get a letter, telephone call etc. ‖ 편지·전화 등을 받다. 수신하다: *Have you received my letter?* 내 편지 받아 봤니? **3** FORMAL if you receive medical treatment, an injury etc., it happens or is done to you ‖ 의학적 치료·부상 등이 발생하거나 행해지다. …을 받다[입다]: *My father is receiving chemotherapy.* 나의 아버지는 화학 치료를 받고 계신다. **4** FORMAL to accept or welcome someone officially as a guest or member of a group ‖ 남을 손님이나 어떤 단체의 일원으로서 공식적으로 받아들이거나 환영하다. 맞이하다. …으로 인정하다: *Perez was received at the White House and given the award.* 페레즈는 백악관에 영접되어서 상을 받았다.

re·ceiv·er /rɪˈsiːvɚ/ *n* **1** the part of a telephone that you hold next to your mouth and ear ‖ 입과 귀 옆에 대는 전화기의 일부분. 수화기 —see usage note at TELEPHONE **2** a piece of electronic equipment in a STEREO that changes electrical signals into sound, then makes them loud enough to hear ‖ 전기 신호를 소리로 바꾼 다음 들을 수 있을 정도로 크게 만드는 스테레오의 전자 장비. 수신기 **3** someone who is officially in control of a company or business that is BANKRUPT (=has no money) ‖ 파산한 회사나 사업체를 공식적으로 관리하는 사람. 파산 (재산) 관리인 **4** in football, the player who is allowed to catch the ball ‖ 미식축구에서 공을 받을 수 있는 선수. 리시버 —see picture on page 946

re·ceiv·er·ship /rɪˈsiːvɚˌʃɪp/ *n* [U] **go into receivership** if a company or business goes into receivership, it starts to be controlled by an official RECEIVER ∥ 회사나 사업체가 파산 재산 관리인에의해 공식적으로 관리되기 시작하다. 법정 관리 상태에 들어가다

re·cent /'risənt/ *adj* having happened or begun to exist only a short time ago ∥ 불과 얼마 전에 일어났거나 존재하기 시작한. 최근의. 근간의. 새로운. 근래의: *In a recent interview, she said she wanted to try a singing career.* 최근 인터뷰에서 그녀는 가수로서 활동해 보고 싶다고 말했다. / *The most recent edition of the magazine has Roseanne's picture on it.* 그 잡지의 최신호는 로지앤의 사진을 표지에 싣고 있다. / *Their businesses have had troubles in recent years/months.* 그들의 사업은 최근 몇 년[몇 달]간 어려움을 겪었다. —see usage note at NEW

re·cent·ly /'risəntli/ *adv* **1** not long ago ∥ (그리) 오래지 않아. 최근에. 얼마 전. 새로이: *We recently moved from Ohio.* 우리는 최근에 오하이오에서 이사 왔다. **2** during the recent period of days or weeks; lately ∥ 최근 며칠간 또는 몇 주간 동안. 요근래에. 요즈음; 최근에: *I haven't seen him recently.* 나는 요근래에 그를 보지 못했다. —see usage note at LATELY

re·cep·ta·cle /rɪ'sɛptəkəl/ *n* FORMAL a container ∥ 용기. 그릇

re·cep·tion /rɪ'sɛpʃən/ *n* **1** a large formal party to celebrate something or to welcome someone ∥ 어떤 일을 축하하거나 어떤 사람을 환영하기 위한 대규모의 공식 파티. 환영회: *a wedding reception* 결혼 피로연 / *a reception for the visiting professors* 방문 (교환) 교수에 대한 환영연 **2** a way of reacting to a person or idea that shows what you think of him, her, or it ∥ 어떤 사람이나 생각에 대해 어떻게 생각하는가를 보여주는 반응. 받아들이기. 수용(방법). 접대: *He got a warm reception* (=a friendly greeting) *from the crowd.* 그는 군중들로부터 따뜻한 환대를 받았다. **3** [U] the quality of the sound of your radio or the picture of your television ∥ 라디오의 소리나 텔레비전 화상의 질. 수신 (상태). 감도: *My TV gets good reception.* 내 텔레비전 수신 상태는 양호하다.

re·cep·tion·ist /rɪ'sɛpʃənɪst/ *n* someone whose job is to welcome and help people at a hotel, business office etc. ∥ 호텔·사업장 등에서 사람들을 맞아들이고 도와주는 직업인. (프런트) 안내인. 접수[응접]계원

re·cep·tive /rɪ'sɛptɪv/ *adj* willing to listen to new ideas or new opinions ∥ 새로운 생각이나 견해를 기꺼이 듣는. 잘 받아들이는[수용하는]. 수용력이 있는: *Ron isn't very receptive to other people's suggestions.* 론은 다른 사람들의 제안을 잘 받아들이지 않는다.

re·cess /'risɛs, rɪ'sɛs/ *n* **1** [U] a time when children are allowed to go outside to play during the school day ∥ 학생들의 학교생활 동안 밖에 나가서 놀도록 허용된 시간. 휴식 시간: *Charlie got into a fight during/at recess.* 찰리는 휴식 시간 동안/에 싸움을 했다. **2** [C, U] a time of rest during the working day or year at a law court, government etc. ∥ 법원·정부 등의 근무일이나 근무년도 중의 휴지 기간. 휴회[휴관] 기간: *Congress is in recess until January.* 의회는 1월까지 휴회 중이다. **3** a space in the wall of a room for shelves, cupboards etc. ∥ 방의 벽에 선반·찬장 등을 위해 낸 공간. 벽장. 오목한 [쑥 들어간] 부분

re·ces·sion /rɪ'sɛʃən/ *n* a period of time when there is less business activity, trade etc. than usual ∥ 평상시보다 사업 활동·거래 등이 뜸해지는 기간. 경기 후퇴[침체]. 일시적인 불경기

re·charge /ri'tʃɑrdʒ/ *v* [T] to put a new supply of electricity into a BATTERY ∥ 배터리에 전기를 새로 공급해 넣다. 전지를 재충전하다 – **rechargeable** *adj*

rec·i·pe /'rɛsəpi/ *n* **1** a set of instructions that tells you how to cook something ∥ 어떤 것의 요리법을 알려 주는 일련의 지시 (사항). 조리[요리]법: *a recipe for chocolate cake* 초콜릿 케이크 만드는 법 **2** INFORMAL **be a recipe for sth** to be likely to cause a particular result ∥ 거의 확실하게 특정 결과를 일으키다. …의 비결[비법, 원인]이 되다. …하기 십상이다: *Inviting Paul and his ex-wife to the party was a recipe for disaster.* 폴과 그의 전(前) 부인을 파티에 초대한 것은 파티를 망치는 길이었다.

re·cip·i·ent /rɪ'sɪpiənt/ *n* FORMAL someone who receives something ∥ 어떤 것을 받는 사람. 수령인. 수취인. 수혜자: *Bauer has been the recipient of many honors.* 바우어는 많은 훈장을 받아온 장본인이었다.

re·cip·ro·cal /rɪ'sɪprəkəl/ *adj* FORMAL a reciprocal agreement, relationship etc. is one where two groups of people do or give the same things to each other ∥ 협정·관계 등에서 두 집단의 사람들이 서로에게 똑같은 것을 하거나 주는. 상호간의. 호혜의

re·cip·ro·cate /rɪ'sɪprə,keɪt/ v [I, T] FORMAL to do or give something because something similar has been done or given to you ‖ 자신에게 비슷한 것을 하거나 줬기 때문에 어떤 것을 하거나 주다. 대가로[답례로] …을 해주다[하다]. 보답하다

re·cit·al /rɪ'saɪtl/ n a public performance of a piece of music or poetry, usually by one person ‖ 보통 한 사람에 의한 음악이나 시의 대중 공연. 독주[독창]회. 암송[낭독]회: a piano recital 피아노 독주회

re·cite /rɪ'saɪt/ v [I, T] to say something such as a poem, story etc. that you know by memory ‖ 시·이야기 등을 기억해서 말하다. 암송하다. …을 낭송[낭독]하다: Everyone had to recite a poem today at school. 오늘 학교에서 모든 학생들이 시 하나를 암송해야 했다. – **recitation** /ˌrɛsə'teɪʃən/ n [C, U]

reck·less /'rɛklɪs/ adj not caring about danger or the bad results of your behavior, or showing this quality ‖ 자신의 행위로 인한 위험성이나 나쁜 결과를 개의치 않는, 또는 이러한 성질을 보이는. 앞뒤를 가리지 않는. 무모한. 함부로 하는: As a boy he was wild and reckless. 소년 시절 그는 난폭하고 앞뒤 가리지 않았다. / reckless driving 난폭한 운전 / reckless decisions 무모한 결정 – **recklessly** adv – **recklessness** n [U]

reck·on /'rɛkən/ v [T] **1** to guess a number, amount etc. without calculating it exactly ‖ 정확히 계산하지 않고 숫자·양 등을 추정하다. 추산하다: The software company reckons it will sell 2.5 million units this year. 그 소프트웨어 회사는 올해 2백5십만 개를 팔 것으로 추산한다. **2** SPOKEN to think or suppose ‖ 생각하거나 가정하다. …으로 판단[간주]하다: I reckon they'll be late. 나는 그들이 늦을 것이라 생각한다.

reckon with sb/sth phr v [T] to consider a possible problem when you think about the future ‖ 미래에 대해 생각할 때 가능성이 있는 문제를 고려하다. 미리 생각해 두다. …에 대처하다: The new team is a force to be reckoned with. (=something to consider seriously) 그 새 팀은 만만하게 봐서는 안 될 강팀이다.

reck·on·ing /'rɛkənɪŋ/ n [U] calculation that is not exact ‖ 정확하지는 않은 계산. 추산: By my reckoning, we should be there by now. 내 추산대로라면, 우리는 지금쯤 거기 있어야 한다.

re·claim /rɪ'kleɪm/ v [T] **1** to ask for something to be given back to you ‖ 자신이 되돌려받아야 할 것을 요구하다. …의 반환을 요구하다. 되돌려 받다: reclaiming lost luggage 분실된 짐을 되찾기[반환 요구] **2** to make something able to be used, when it has never been used or has not been used for a while ‖ 한 번도 이용하지 않았거나 한동안 이용하지 않은 사물을 이용할 수 있게 하다. …을 재생 이용하다. (토지를) 간척[개간]하여 이용하다: The organization is trying to reclaim desert land for farming. 그 단체는 황무지를 농지로 개간하려 하고 있다. – **reclamation** /ˌrɛklə'meɪʃən/ n [U]

re·cline /rɪ'klaɪn/ v **1** [I, T] to push the back of a seat or chair so that it slopes backward, so that you can lean back in it ‖ 좌석이나 의자의 뒤를 밀쳐서 경사지게 해 기댈 수 있게 하다. 뒤로 젖히다[기울이다, 눕히다]: The front seats of the car recline. 차의 앞좌석은 뒤로 눕혀진다. **2** [I] to lie or sit back in a relaxed way ‖ 편안하게 눕거나 뒤로 기대 앉다. 기대다. 기대어 쉬다: people reclining on the grass in the sunshine 햇살이 비치는 잔디에 누워서 쉬는 사람들

rec·luse /'rɛklus/ n someone who likes to live alone and avoids other people ‖ 혼자서 살며 다른 사람들을 피하고 싶어하는 사람. 세상을 등진[속세를 떠난] 사람. 은둔자 – **reclusive** /rɪ'klusɪv/ adj

rec·og·ni·tion /ˌrɛkəg'nɪʃən/ n **1** [singular, U] public admiration and thanks for someone's work or achievements ‖ 누군가의 작품이나 업적에 대한 대중의 칭송과 감사. 인정. 평가. 표창. 포상: She was given an award in recognition of 25 years of service. 그녀에게 25년간의 근무에 대한 공로로 상이 주어졌다. / His music didn't receive recognition in his lifetime. 그의 음악은 그의 생전에는 인정을 받지 못했다. **2** [U] the act of recognizing someone or something ‖ 사람이나 사물을 인식하기. 알아보기. 들은 적이 있음

rec·og·niz·a·ble /ˌrɛkəg'naɪzəbəl/ adj able to be easily recognized ‖ 쉽게 인식될 수 있는. 분간이 가는. 분별[구별]할 수 있는: The car was barely recognizable when they pulled it out of the river. 그 차는 그들이 강에서 인양했을 때 거의 형체를 알아볼 수 없었다.

rec·og·nize /'rɛkəg,naɪz/ v [T] **1** to know someone or something that you have seen before ‖ 전에 보았던 사람이나 사물을 알아보다. 분간[식별]하다. …을 인식하다: I recognized him from an old

R

photograph. 나는 옛날 사진에서 그를 알아보았다. **2** to accept officially that an organization, government etc. is legal ‖ 조직·정부 등이 합법적임을 공식 인정하다. 승인[용인]하다: *The UN has refused to recognize the new government.* UN은 그 새 정부의 승인을 거부했다. **3** to accept and admit that something is true or real ‖ 어떤 것이 사실이거나 실재한다고 받아들이고 시인하다. 인정하다. 인지하다: *Dr. Campbell recognizes that the treatment may cause problems for some patients.* 캠벨 박사는 그 치료법이 일부 환자들에게는 문제를 일으킬 수 있다고 인정한다. **4** to thank someone officially for something that s/he has done ‖ 다른 사람이 했던 일에 대해 공식적으로 감사하다. 표창하다. 사의를 표하다: *Tonight we'd like to recognize some people who have worked very hard for us.* 오늘밤 우리는 우리를 위해서 아주 열심히 일해 오신 몇 분에게 사의를 표하고 싶습니다.

re·coil /'rɪkɔɪl, rɪ'kɔɪl/ *v* [I] to move back suddenly from something that you do not like or are afraid of ‖ 좋아하지 않거나 두려워하는 것에서 갑자기 뒤로 물러서다. …게 움찔하다. 뒷걸음치다: *Emily recoiled at the sight of the snake.* 에밀리는 뱀을 보고 뒷걸음쳤다.

rec·ol·lect /ˌrɛkə'lɛkt/ *v* [T] OLD-FASHIONED to remember something ‖ 무언가를 기억하다. 생각해 내다. 회상하다: *I don't recollect her name.* 나는 그녀의 이름이 기억나지 않는다.

rec·ol·lec·tion /ˌrɛkə'lɛkʃən/ *n* [C, U] FORMAL something from the past that you remember, or the act of remembering it ‖ 기억하고 있는 과거의 것, 또는 기억하기. 회상. 기억(력). 기억되는 일. 추억: *He has no recollection of the crash.* 그는 충돌 사고에 대한 기억이 하나도 나지 않는다.

rec·om·mend /ˌrɛkə'mɛnd/ *v* [T] **1** to advise someone to do something ‖ 남에게 어떤 것을 하라고 충고하다. …을 장려하다. …할 것을 권(고)하다: *She recommended that I try the soup.* 그녀는 내게 수프를 맛보라고 권했다. / *We recommend hiring a professional designer.* 우리는 전문 디자이너를 고용할 것을 권고합니다. **2** to praise someone or something as being good for a particular purpose ‖ 다른 사람이나 사물이 특정 목적에 적합하다고 칭찬하다. …을 추천[천거]하다: *Can you recommend a local restaurant?* 이 지역 식당을 하나 추천해 주실 수 있어요? **3 sth has little/nothing etc. to recommend it** used in order to say that something has few or no good qualities ‖ 사물이 좋은 특성을 거의 또는 전혀 갖고 있지 않다고 말하는 데에 쓰여. 쓸 만한[권할 만한] 것이 거의/전혀 없다: *The hotel has little to recommend it, except that it's cheap.* 그 호텔은 싸다는 것 외에 권할 만한 것이 거의 없다.

USAGE NOTE recommend, suggest, ask, insist, request, demand

When you use these verbs with "that," use only the INFINITIVE form of the verb without "to," even if the subject is singular: *I recommend that this plan be accepted. / May I suggest that he meet us later? / We ask that the committee review the facts.* 이들 동사들은 "that"과 함께 사용할 때는 주어가 단수일지라도 동사에 "to"가 없는 부정사형 만을 쓴다: 이 계획은 승인되어야 한다고 권고합니다. / 그가 우리와 나중에 만나는 것이 어떨까요? / 우리는 위원회가 그 사실을 재검토해 볼 것을 요청합니다.

---

rec·om·men·da·tion /ˌrɛkəmən'deɪʃən/ *n* **1** advice given to someone, especially about what to do ‖ 다른 사람에게, 특히 무엇을 할 것인지에 대해 말해 주는 충고. 권고. 추천[권장]하는 말: *The committee was able to make detailed recommendations to the school.* 위원회는 그 학교에 세부적인 권고를 할 수 있었다. / *the department's recommendation that he be fired* 그를 해고시켜야 한다는 그 부서의 권고 **2** [U] the action of saying that someone or something is good for a particular purpose ‖ 사람이나 사물이 특정 목적에 적합하다고 말하는 것. 추천. 천거. 권장: *We took the tour on a friend's recommendation.* 우리는 한 친구의 권유에 따라 여행을 갔다. **3** a letter or statement that someone is suitable for a particular job, course of study etc. ‖ 어떤 사람이 특정 직업·연구 과정 등에 적합하다는 편지나 진술(서). 추천장[서]: *Can you write a recommendation for me?* 저에게 추천서를 하나 써 주시겠습니까?

rec·om·pense /'rɛkəm,pɛns/ *v* [T] FORMAL to give someone a payment for trouble or losses that you have caused ‖ 어떤 사람에게 자신이 초래한 문제나 손실에 대해 지불하다. (손해, 상해 등에) 배상[보상]을 하다 **– recompense** *n* [singular, U]

rec·on·cile /'rɛkən,saɪl/ *v* **1** be

reconciled (with) to have a good relationship with someone again after arguing with him/her ‖ 다른 사람과 다툰 후에 다시 좋은 관계가 되다. 화해하다. 화목해지다: *His parents are now reconciled with each other.* 그의 부모는 지금은 서로 화해해서 사이가 좋다. **2** [T] to show that two different ideas, situations etc. can exist together and are not opposed to each other ‖ 두 가지 서로 다른 생각·상황 등이 공존할 수 있고 서로 상반되지 않음을 보여주다. …을 조화[일치]시키다. 서로 어울리게 하다: *How can he reconcile his religious beliefs with all this gambling?* 그는 어떻게 이 모든 도박 행위들을 그의 종교적 신앙과 양립시킬 수 있을까?

reconcile sb/yourself to sth *phr v* [T] to make someone able to accept an unpleasant situation ‖ 어떤 사람에게 불쾌한 상황을 받아들일 수 있게 하다. 용인[납득]하게 하다. 감수[체념]하게 하다: *She never reconciled herself to her son's drug problem.* 그녀는 결코 아들의 마약 문제를 용인할 수 없었다.

rec·on·cil·i·a·tion /ˌrɛkən‚sɪliˈeɪʃən/ *n* [C, U] a situation in which two people, countries etc. become friendly again after arguing or fighting with each other ‖ 두 사람·국가 등이 서로 간에 분쟁이나 싸움 후에 다시 친하게 되는 상황. 화해: *There is still hope of a reconciliation between the two groups.* 그 두 집단간에는 아직 화해할 가망성이 있다.

re·con·di·tion /ˌrikənˈdɪʃən/ *v* [T] to repair something so that it works well or looks good again ‖ 사물이 다시 잘 작동하거나 좋아 보이게 고치다. …을 수리[수선]하다. 재조정하다: *a reconditioned vacuum cleaner* 중고 진공청소기

re·con·nais·sance /rɪˈkɑnəsəns, -zəns/ *n* [C, U] the activity of sending out aircraft or soldiers in order to get information about the enemy ‖ 적에 대한 정보를 얻으려고 항공기나 군인들을 파견하는 활동. 정찰. 척후(활동) − **reconnoiter** /ˌrikəˈnɔɪtə/ *v* [I, T]

re·con·sid·er /ˌrikənˈsɪdə/ *v* [I, T] to think again about something in order to decide if you should change your opinion ‖ 자신의 의견을 바꿔야 할지를 결정하기 위해 사물에 대해 다시 생각하다. …을 재고하다. 고쳐 생각하다: *Won't you reconsider our offer?* 우리 제안을 다시 생각해 보지 않을래? − **reconsideration** /ˌrikən‚sɪdəˈreɪʃən/ *n* [U]

re·con·sti·tute /riˈkɑnstə‚tut/ *v* [T] **1** to make a group, organization etc. exist in a different form ‖ 집단·조직 등을 다른 형태로 존재하게 만들다. …을 다시 구성[편성, 재정]하다: *The four political groups will be reconstituted as a new party.* 네 개의 정치 집단이 하나의 새 정당으로 재편될 것이다. **2** to change dried food into its original form by adding water to it ‖ 건조식품에 물을 추가하여 원래의 형태로 변화시키다. 원상태로 돌리다

re·con·struct /ˌrikənˈstrʌkt/ *v* [T] **1** to produce a complete description of something that happened by collecting pieces of information ‖ 정보의 단편들을 모아서 일어났던 일을 완벽하게 묘사해 내다. 재현[재구성]하다: *Police have reconstructed the events leading up to the crime.* 경찰은 범죄의 실마리가 되는 사건들을 재구성했다. **2** to build something again after it has been destroyed or damaged ‖ 사물이 파괴되거나 손상된 후에 다시 만들다. 재건[개축, 복구]하다. 재축조하다

re·con·struc·tion /ˌrikənˈstrʌkʃən/ *n* **1** [U] work that is done to repair damage to a city, industry etc. especially after a war ‖ 특히 전쟁 후에 도시·산업 등에 대한 피해를 회복하려고 행하는 일. 재건. 복구: *the reconstruction of the former East Germany* 이전 동독의 재건 **2** a medical operation to replace a bone or part of the body that has been damaged ‖ 손상된 뼈나 신체 부위를 대체하는 의료 시술. 복원[개조] 수술: *hip reconstruction* 엉덩이 복원(수술)

re·cord¹ /ˈrɛkəd/ *n* **1** [C, U] information about something that is written down so that it can be looked at in the future ‖ 기록되어서 미래에 볼 수 있게 된 사물에 대한 정보. 기록(문서). 공식 문서. 보존되어 있는 정보·지식: *Keep a record of how much you spend on this trip.* 이번 여행에 얼마를 지출하는지 기록하세요. / *the highest water levels on record.* (=that have been written in records) 기록상 최고의 수위 **2** the fastest speed, longest distance, highest or lowest level etc. ever ‖ 지금까지 최고 속도·최장 거리·최고나 최저 수준 등. …한 최고[최저, 최신] 기록. 보유 기록: *She broke the record for the 1500 meter run.* 그녀는 1500m 경주의 기록을 깼다. / *a record high/low temperature* 기록적인 최고[최저] 기온 **3** the known facts about someone's past behavior and how good or bad it has been ‖ 사람의 과거 행위와 그 선악의 정도에 대해 알려진 사실. 경력. 이력. 내력. 전력(前

歷): *Our company has a good/bad record for giving money to charity.* 우리 회사는 자선금을 많이[조금] 기부한다. **4** a round flat piece of plastic on which music is stored ‖ 음악이 저장되는 둥글고 평평한 플라스틱 조각. 음반. 레코드: *a record collection* 음반 수집(품) **5 off/on the record** not official and not meant to be repeated, or official and able to be repeated ‖ 비공식적이고 말을 전하면 안 되는, 또는 공식적이고 말을 전할 수 있는. 비공식[비공개]의[로]/공식[공개]의[로]: *Canelli told us off the record that he had new evidence.* 카넬리는 그가 새 증거를 가지고 있다고 비공개를 전제로 우리에게 말했다. **6 for the record** used in order to tell someone that what you are saying should be remembered ‖ 현재 말하고 있는 것을 기억해야 한다고 다른 사람에게 말하는 데에 쓰여. 기록으로 남기기 위해[위한]. 분명히 말해서: *For the record, my salary has never been close to $1 million!* 정확하게 말해서, 내 봉급은 한 번도 백만 달러에 근접해 본 적이 없다.

re·cord² /rɪˈkɔrd/ *v* **1** [T] to write information down so that it can be looked at in the future ‖ 미래에 볼 수 있도록 정보를 기록해 놓다. 기록[기재]하다. 적어 두다: *All the data is recorded on computer.* 모든 데이터가 컴퓨터에 기록된다. **2** [I, T] to store pictures, a television show etc. on VIDEO ‖ 사진·TV쇼 등을 비디오에 저장하다. 녹화하다. 비디오로 찍다: *Will you record "The X-Files" for me?* "X파일" 프로를 녹화해 주시겠습니까? / *A friend who owns a camcorder recorded their wedding for them.* 비디오 카메라를 가진 친구가 그들의 결혼식을 녹화했다. —compare FILM² **3** [I, T] to store music, sound etc. on something so that it can be listened to again ‖ 음악·소리 등을 사물에 저장해서 다시 들을 수 있게 하다. 녹음하다: *Recently the group finished recording their third album.* 최근에 그 그룹은 3집 앨범 녹음 작업을 끝냈다. **4** [T] to measure the size, speed, temperature etc. of something so that it can be seen ‖ 볼 수 있게 사물의 크기·속도·기온 등을 재다. …을 표시[기록]하다. 가리키다

record-break·ing /ˈ.. ˌ../ *adj* better, higher, faster etc. than anything done before ‖ 전에 행해진 어떤 것보다 나은·높은·빠른 등의. 기록을 깨는. 기록적인: *a record-breaking speed/flight etc.* 전례 없는 속도[비행]

re·cord·er /rɪˈkɔrdɚ/ *n* **1** ⇨ TAPE RECORDER **2** a small wooden musical

instrument shaped like a tube, that you play by blowing into it ‖ 불어서 연주하는 관 모양의 작은 나무 악기. 리코더

re·cord·ing /rɪˈkɔrdɪŋ/ *n* a piece of music, speech etc. that has been recorded ‖ 녹음된 음악·연설 등. 녹음. 기록: *a recording of Vivaldi's "Gloria"* 비발디의 (녹음) 음악 "글로리아"

record play·er /ˈ.. ˌ../ *n* a piece of equipment for playing records ‖ 음반을 재생하기 위한 장비. 전축. 레코드플레이어

re·count¹ /rɪˈkaʊnt/ *v* [T] **1** FORMAL to tell a story or describe a series of events ‖ 이야기를 하거나 일련의 사건을 묘사하다. 상술하다. 자세히 말하다: *a TV movie recounting the war years* 그 전쟁 시대를 자세히 조명한 TV 영화 **2** to count something again ‖ 사물을 다시 세다. 다시 헤아리다

re·count² /ˈrikaʊnt/ *n* a process of counting votes again ‖ 득표수를 다시 계산하는 과정. 투표의 재검표

re·coup /rɪˈkup/ *v* [T] to get back money you have lost or spent ‖ 잃어버렸거나 써버린 돈을 되찾다. 벌충하다. 매우다. 보상을 받다. 회복시키다: *The agency should recoup its investment in a year.* 그 중개 회사는 1년 안에 투자금을 회수해야 한다.

re·course /ˈrikɔrs, rɪˈkɔrs/ *n* [U] FORMAL something you can do to help yourself in a difficult situation, or the act of doing this ‖ 어려운 상황에서 스스로를 돕기 위해 할 수 있는 것, 또는 이렇게 하기. 방도. (자조)수단. 의지(하기): *The police had no recourse but to shoot.* (=shooting was their only choice) 경찰은 총을 쏠 수밖에 없었다.

re·cov·er /rɪˈkʌvɚ/ *v* **1** [I] to get better after an illness, injury, shock etc. ‖ 병·부상·충격 등의 이후 (상태가) 좋아지다. 회복하다. 낫다: *My uncle is recovering from a heart attack.* 내 삼촌은 심장 마비에서 회복 중이시다. **2** [I] to return to a normal condition after a period of trouble or difficulty ‖ 곤란하거나 어려운 시기 후에 정상 상태로 돌아가다. 원상대로 되다. 회복[복구]되다: *The economy will take at least three years to recover.* 경제가 회복되기 위해서는 최소한 3년이 걸릴 것이다. **3** [T] to get back something that was taken from you, lost, or almost destroyed ‖ 빼앗긴[잃어버린, 거의 파괴된] 것을 되찾다. 벌충하다. 회수하다. 보상을 받다: *The police managed to recover the stolen goods.* 경찰은 도난품들을 겨우 회수했다. **4** [T] to get back your ability to control your feelings or your body ‖ 감정이나 신체에 대한 통제 능력을 되찾다. 회복하다. 건강 [능력]을 되찾다: *He never recovered the use of his arm.* 그는 팔을 다시는 쓸 수 없게 되었다.

re·cov·er·y /rɪˈkʌvəri/ *n* **1** [C, U] the process of getting better after an illness, injury etc. ‖ 병·부상 등 후에 좋아지는 과정. 회복. 재활: *a quick recovery from the flu* 감기에서의 빠른 회복 **2** [C, U] the process of returning to a normal condition after a period of trouble or difficulty ‖ 곤란하거나 어려운 시기 후에 정상적인 상태로 돌아가는 과정. 회복. 복구. 복귀: *Oklahoma's economic recovery* 오클라호마의 경제 회복 **3** [U] the act of getting something back ‖ 사물을 되돌려 받기. 되찾기. 회수: *the recovery of the stolen jewels* 도난당한 보석을 되찾음

re·cre·ate /ˌrikriˈeɪt/ *v* [T] to make something exist again or be experienced again ‖ 사물을 다시 존재하게 하거나 다시 경험하게 하다. 재구성하다. 재현[복원] 하다: *a museum that recreates a Native American settlement* 아메리칸 인디언 촌락을 복원한 박물관

rec·re·a·tion /ˌrɛkriˈeɪʃən/ *n* [C, U] an activity that you do for pleasure or fun ‖ 즐거움이나 재미를 위해 하는 활동. 휴양. 휴식. 레크리에이션. 여가 활동: *The new park is being built to provide recreation especially for kids.* 새 공원은 특히 아이들에게 놀이터를 제공하기 위해 만들어지고 있다. / *the city's Parks and Recreation department* 시립공원 및 휴양 시설 담당 부서 – **recreational** *adj* — see usage note at SPORT

re·crim·i·na·tion /rɪˌkrɪməˈneɪʃən/ *n* [C usually plural, U] a situation in which people blame each other, or the things they say when they are blaming each other ‖ 사람들이 서로 비난하는 상황, 또는 서로 비난할 때 말하는 것들. 비난에 비난으로 맞서기. 상호 비방. 비난(하는 말)

re·cruit¹ /rɪˈkrut/ *v* [I, T] to find new people to work in a company, join an organization, do a job etc. ‖ 회사에 근무할[조직에 가입할, 일을 할] 새 사람을 찾다. 새로 모집하다[보충하다]. 신입 사원 [회원]을 맞추다이다: *The coaches are visiting colleges in order to recruit new players.* 감독들은 새로운 선수들을 모집하기 위해 대학을 방문하고 있다. – **recruitment** *n* [U] – **recruiter** *n*

recruit² *n* someone who has recently joined a company or an organization ‖ 회사나 조직에 최근에 합류한 사람. 신입. 신참자. 신병. 신입 회원. 신입 사원

rec·tan·gle /ˈrɛkˌtæŋgəl/ *n* a shape with four straight sides, two of which are usually longer than the other two, and four RIGHT ANGLEs ‖ 네 개의 직선 중 보통 두 개의 직선이 다른 두 개보다 길며 네 각이 직각인 형태. 직사각형 – **rectangular** /rɛkˈtæŋgyələ/ *adj* —see picture at SHAPE

rec·ti·fy /ˈrɛktəˌfaɪ/ *v* [T] FORMAL to correct something that is wrong ‖ 잘못된 것을 바로잡다. …을 시정[수정]하다. 조정[정정]하다: *All efforts to rectify the problem have failed.* 문제점을 시정하려는 모든 노력이 실패했다.

rec·tor /ˈrɛktə/ *n* **1** a priest who is in charge of a local Episcopal church ‖ 지역 성공회 교회를 책임지고 있는 성직자. 교구(주임) 목사 **2** the person in charge of some colleges or schools ‖ 일부 대학이나 학교의 책임자. 교[학, 총]장

rec·tum /ˈrɛktəm/ *n* TECHNICAL the lowest part of your BOWELs ‖ 창자의 가장 하부. 직장(直腸) – **rectal** /ˈrɛktl/ *adj*

re·cu·per·ate /rɪˈkupəˌreɪt/ *v* [I] to get better after an illness, injury etc. ‖ 병·부상 등 후에 좋아지다. 회복하다. 재기하다: *Jan is still recuperating from her operation.* 잰은 아직 수술에서 회복 중이다. – **recuperation** /rɪˌkupəˈreɪʃən/ *n* [U]

re·cur /rɪˈkə/ *v* **-rred, -rring** [I] to happen again, or to happen several times ‖ 다시 발생하다, 또는 여러 번 발생하다. 되풀이되다. 반복[재발]하다: *a recurring dream* 되풀이되는 꿈 – **recurrence** *n* [C, U] – **recurrent** *adj*

re·cy·cla·ble /riˈsaɪkləbəl/ *adj* able to be RECYCLEd ‖ 재사용[재생]될 수 있는. 재생 이용할 수 있는: *recyclable bottles* 재활용 병 – **recyclable** *n* [C usually plural]

re·cy·cle /riˈsaɪkəl/ *v* [I, T] to put used objects or materials through a special process, so that they can be used again ‖ 사용된 물체나 소재를 특수 처리 과정을 거쳐 다시 사용할 수 있다. 재활용[재생] 하다. 재생 이용하다: *bottles that can be recycled* 재활용될 수 있는 병들 – **recycled** /ˌriˈsaɪkəld/ *adj*: *recycled paper* 재활용지 – **recycling** *n* [U]

red¹ /rɛd/ **-dder, -ddest** *adj* **1** having the color of blood ‖ 핏빛 색을 가진. 붉은. 빨간: *a red dress* 빨간 드레스 **2** hair that is red is an orange-brown color ‖ 머리가 적갈색인. 주홍색의 **3** skin that is red is a bright pink color ‖ 피부가 선홍색

R

인. 진분홍색의 **4** a wording meaning COMMUNIST that is considered to be offensive ‖ 무례한 표현으로 간주되는 공산주의자를 의미하는 말. 빨갱이 – **redness** *n* [U]

red² *n* **1** [C, U] a red color ‖ 붉은 색깔. 적색 **2 be in the red** to owe more money than you have ‖ 소유한 것보다 더 많은 돈을 빚지다. 적자를 내다 – opposite **be in the black** (BLACK²) **3 see red** to become very angry ‖ 매우 화나게 되다. 분노[격분]하다: *The way he treated his dog just made me see red.* 그가 개를 다루는 모습에 그냥 나는 화가 치밀어 올랐다.

red-blood·ed /ˌ. '../ *adj* **red-blooded male/American/capitalist etc.** HUMOROUS used in order to emphasize that someone has all of the qualities that a typical man, American etc. is supposed to have ‖ 전형적인 남자·미국인 등이 가지고 있을 거라 기대되는 모든 특성을 누군가가 가지고 있음을 강조하는 데에 쓰여. 남성적인 남자/전형적인 미국인/열렬한 자본주의자: *As any red-blooded male will tell you, football is one of America's major religions.* 남성적인 미국 남자라면 누구나 말하듯이, 미식축구는 미국의 주요 종교 중의 하나라고 볼 수 있다.

red car·pet /ˌ. '../ *n* [singular] special treatment that you give someone important who is visiting you ‖ 방문하는 중요한 사람에게 제공하는 특별대우. (빨간 카펫을 말아 주는) 성대한 환영. 정중한 환대. 융숭한 접대: *Hollywood stars who visit the restaurant are given the red carpet treatment.* 그 음식점에 들르는 할리우드 스타들은 융숭한 대접을 받는다.

Red Cres·cent /ˌ. '../ *n* [singular] a part of the Red Cross that works in Muslim countries ‖ 이슬람교 국가들에서 일하는 적십자사의 지부. 회교 국가들의 적십자사

Red Cross /ˌ. './ *n* [singular] an international organization that helps people who are suffering as a result of war, floods, disease etc. ‖ 전쟁·홍수·질병 등으로 고통 받는 사람들을 돕는 국제 조직. 적십자사

red·den /'rɛdn/ *v* [I, T] to become red, or to make something do this ‖ 빨갛게 되다, 또는 사물을 이렇게 되게 하다. …을 [이] 붉게 만들다[물들다]: *Tina's face reddened with embarrassment.* 티나의 얼굴은 당황해서 빨개졌다.

re·deem /rɪ'dim/ *v* [T] FORMAL **1**

redeeming quality/value etc. a good quality etc. that keeps something from being completely bad or wrong ‖ 사물을 완전히 나쁘거나 잘못되지 않게 막아주는 좋은 특질 등. 순화[정화]시키는 특성/가치: *The TV programs he watches have no redeeming social value.* 그가 보는 TV 프로그램은 사회를 순화시켜주는 가치가 전혀 담겨 있지 않다. **2** to exchange a piece of paper representing an amount of money for the money that it is worth ‖ 일정 액수의 돈을 표시하는 종이 조각을 그만한 가치의 돈과 교환하다. 태환(兌換)하다. 액면가 = 증서[상품권]를 현금화하다: *Redeem this coupon for 20¢ off a jar of coffee.* 커피 한 병 가격에서 이 쿠폰으로 20센트만큼 제해서 계산하세요. **3 redeem yourself** to do something to improve other people's opinion of you, after you have behaved badly or failed ‖ 나쁜 행동을 했거나 실패한 후에 다른 사람들의 견해를 개선하기 위해 어떤 일을 하다. 잘못[결점]을 메우다[벌충하다]. 불명예를 회복[만회]하다 **4** a word meaning to free someone from the power of evil, used especially in the Christian religion ‖ 특히 기독교에서 쓰여 악의 힘에서 다른 사람을 자유롭게 하는 것을 의미하는 말. 죄[악]으로부터 구하다. 속죄[구원]하다 – **redeemable** *adj*

re·demp·tion /rɪ'dɛmpʃən/ *n* [U] **1 past/beyond redemption** too bad to be saved, improved, or fixed ‖ 너무 나빠서 구조되거나 개선되거나 고쳐지거나 할 수 없는. 회복할 가망이 없는. 구제할 수 없는 **2** the state of being freed from the power of evil, believed by Christians to be made possible by Jesus Christ ‖ 기독교도들이 믿는, 예수 그리스도에 의해 악의 힘으로부터 구원될 수 있는 상태. 죄갚음. 속죄. 구원

re·de·vel·op /ˌridə'vɛləp/ *v* [T] to make an area more modern by putting in new buildings or changing old ones ‖ 새로운 건물을 짓거나 옛 건물을 바꿔서 한 지역을 더 현대화하다. …을 재건[재개발]하다 – **redevelopment** *n* [C, U]

red-eye /'. ./ *n* [U] INFORMAL a plane with PASSENGERs on it that makes a trip that starts late at night and arrives early in the morning ‖ 승객을 싣고 심야에 출발해서 새벽에 도착하는 여객기. 야간 비행편[항공편]. 심야 항공(편): *the red-eye from Chicago to Seattle* 시카고에서 시애틀로 가는 야간 항공편

red-hand·ed /ˌ. '../ *adj* **catch sb red-handed** INFORMAL to catch someone at the moment when s/he is doing something wrong ‖ 나쁜 짓을 하고 있는 순간에 사람을 잡다. 현장에서 체포하다. 현행범으로 붙잡다: *She was caught red-handed taking money from the register.* 그녀는 계산대에서 돈을 훔치다가 현장에서 잡혔다.

red·head /'rɛdhɛd/ *n* someone who has red hair ‖ 머리털이 붉은 사람

red her·ring /ˌ. '../ *n* a fact or idea that is not important but is introduced in order to take your attention away from something that is important ‖ 중요한 어떤 것으로부터 주의[관심]를 돌리기 위해 도입되는 중요하지 않은 사실이나 생각. 주의를 유인하는 것. 남을 속이는[현혹시키는] 것

red-hot /ˌ. '../ *adj* extremely hot ‖ 매우 뜨거운. 시뻘겋게 단. 적열(赤熱)의. 작열하는: *red-hot metal* 시뻘겋게 단 금속

re·di·rect /ˌridi'rɛkt, -dai-/ *v* [T] to send something in a different direction, or use something for a different purpose ‖ 사물을 다른 방향으로 보내다, 또는 사물을 다른 목적으로 쓰다. 다시 향하게 하다. 새로운 방향으로 돌리다[돌려쓰다]: *Our mail has been redirected to the new house.* 우리 우편물이 새 집으로 전송되었다. / *She needs to redirect her energy into something more useful.* 그녀는 자신의 역량을 좀더 유용한 곳에 쓸 필요가 있다.

red-light dis·trict /ˌ. '. ˌ../ *n* the area of a city where there are many PROSTITUTE*s* ‖ 많은 창녀들이 있는 도시의 구역. 홍등가

red meat /ˌ. './ *n* [U] dark colored meat such as BEEF ‖ 쇠고기 등의 짙은 색을 띤 고기. 붉은 고기. 생고기

red·neck /'rɛdnɛk/ *n* INFORMAL DISAPPROVING someone who lives in a country area, is not educated, and has strong unreasonable opinions ‖ 시골 지역에 살며 교육받지 않고 강한 불합리한 견해를 가진 사람. 무식한 백인 노동자. 편협한 반동주의자

re·do /ri'du/ *v* [T] to do something again ‖ 어떤 일을 다시 하다. …을 고쳐[재차] 하다: *You'll have to redo this essay.* 너는 이 작문 숙제를 다시 해야 하겠다.

re·dou·ble /ri'dʌbəl/ *v* [T] **redouble your efforts** to greatly increase your efforts to do something ‖ 어떤 일을 하는 노력을 크게 늘리다. 노력을 배가하다

re·dress /rɪ'drɛs/ *v* [T] FORMAL to correct something that is wrong, not equal, or unfair ‖ 잘못되거나 불평등하거나 불공정한 것을 바로잡다. 고치다. 교정

하다: *Tax laws help the rich, not the poor; Congress should redress the balance.* 세법(稅法)은 부자에게 유리하고 가난한 사람에게는 그렇지 않다. 의회는 이 불균형을 바로잡아야 한다 – **redress** /'ridrɛs, rɪ'drɛs/ *n* [U]

red tape /ˌ. './ *n* [U] official rules that seem unnecessary and that delay action ‖ 불필요해 보이고 행동을 지연시키는 관청식의 규정들. 관료적 형식주의. 형식주의적 절차[관례]

re·duce /rɪ'dus/ *v* [I, T] to become smaller or less in size, amount, price etc., or to make something do this ‖ 크기·양·가격 등에서 더 작아지거나 줄어들다, 또는 사물을 이렇게 만들다. 감소하다[시키다]. 축소되다[하다]: *a jacket reduced from $75 to $35* 75달러에서 35달러로 (가격이)낮아진 재킷 / *Reduce the heat and simmer the rice for another 10 minutes.* 불을 약하게 해서 10분 더 쌀을 끓이세요.

reduce sb/sth **to** sth *phr v* [T] **1 reduce sb to tears/silence/poverty etc.** to make someone cry, be silent, become poor etc. ‖ 다른 사람을 울게·침묵하게·가난하게 만들다. 울음/침묵/가난 상태로 빠뜨리다[가 되게 하다]: *They were reduced to begging on the streets.* 그들은 길거리에서 구걸하는 신세로 전락되었다. **2 reduce sth to rubble/ashes/ruins** to destroy something completely, especially a building or city ‖ 사물 특히 건물이나 도시를 철저히 파괴하다. 파편더미/잿더미/폐허로 부수어 버리다

re·duc·tion /rɪ'dʌkʃən/ *n* [C, U] a decrease in size, amount, price etc. ‖ 크기·양·가격 등에서의 감소. 축소. 절감: *a reduction in the price of gasoline* 휘발유 가격의 인하

re·dun·dant /rɪ'dʌndənt/ *adj* not necessary because something else means or does the same thing. For example, "female sister" is a redundant phrase ‖ 다른 것이 똑같은 것을 의미하거나 똑같은 기능을 해서 필요치 않은. 예를 들어, "female sister"는 반복적인 구문임. 장황한. 과잉의. 여분의. 과외의 – **redundancy** *n* [U]

red·wood /'rɛdwʊd/ *n* [C, U] a very tall tree that grows near the coast in Oregon and California ‖ 오리건과 캘리포니아 해안 근처에서 자라는 매우 키가 큰 나무. 미국삼나무

reed /rid/ *n* **1** a tall plant like grass that grows near water ‖ 물가에서 자라는 풀 같은 키가 큰 식물. 갈대(줄기) **2** a thin piece of wood in some musical instruments that produces a sound when you blow over it ‖ 몇몇 악기에서 입으로 불어 소리를 내는 얇은 나뭇조각. 리드(악기)

re·ed·u·ca·tion /ˌ. ..'../ n [U] the process of teaching someone to think or behave differently, especially about politics ‖ 다른 사람에게 특히 정치에 대해 다르게 생각하거나 행동하도록 가르치는 과정. 재교육. (개조) 특별 교육 - **re·educate** /. '../ v [T]

reef /rif/ n a line of sharp rocks or a raised area of sand near the surface of the sea ‖ 해수 표면 근처의 날카로운 바위들의 열이나 해수 표면까지 모래가 솟은 지역. 암초. 초(礁). 모래톱

reek /rik/ v [I] to smell strongly of something unpleasant ‖ 불쾌한 것에서 강한 냄새가 풍기다. 지독한 악취를 내뿜다. 냄새가 나다: *His breath reeked of garlic.* 그의 입에서 마늘 냄새가 강하게 났다. - **reek** n [singular]

reel¹ /ril/ n 1 a round object onto which things such as special string for FISHING or film can be wound ‖ 특수한 낚싯줄이나 필름 등이 감길 수 있는 둥근 물체. 릴. 감는 틀. 실패. 얼레 2 the amount that one of these objects will hold ‖ 이들 물체 중 하나가 보유할 수 있는 양. 한 릴[롤] 분량. 한 타래(의 양): *a reel of film* 한 통의 필름

reel² v 1 [I] to walk in an unsteady way and almost fall over, as if you are drunk ‖ 취한 것처럼 불안정하게 거의 넘어질 것처럼 걷다. 비틀거리다. 휘청거리다. 흔들흔들 걷다: *A guy came reeling down the hallway.* 한 남자가 복도를 비틀거리며 다가왔다. 2 **be reeling** to be so badly affected or shocked by a situation that you do not know what to do next ‖ 어떤 상황에 의해 심하게 영향 받거나 충격 받아서 다음에 무엇을 할지 알 수 없게 되다. 흔들리다. 휘청대다. 타격을 받아 정신을 차리지 못하다: *The hotel chain is still reeling from the effects of their financial and legal problems.* 그 호텔 체인점은 재정적·법적 문제의 영향으로 아직 휘청대고 있다. 3 [T] to wind or unwind string for FISHING on a REEL ‖ 릴의 낚싯줄을 감았다 풀었다 하다

reel sth ↔ **off** phr v [T] INFORMAL to repeat a lot of information quickly and easily ‖ 많은 정보를 재빠르고 쉽게 반복하다. 줄줄 풀어내다[외워내다]. 술술 계속하다[말하다]: *Andy can reel off the names of all the state capitals.* 앤디는 모든 주의 주도 이름을 줄줄 외워낼 수 있다.

re·e·lect /ˌriə'lɛkt/ v [T] to elect someone again ‖ 사람을 다시 뽑다. 재선출하다 - **reelection** /riə'lɛkʃən/ n [C, U]

re·en·act /ˌ. .'./ v [T] to perform the actions of a story, crime etc. that happened in the past ‖ 과거에 일어났던 이야기·범죄 등의 행동을 연기하다. …을 재연(再演)하다. 재구성해 보여주다: *children re-enacting the Christmas story* 크리스마스 이야기를 재연하는 아이들 - **re-enactment** n

re·en·try /ri'ɛntri/ n [C, U] an act of entering a place or situation again ‖ 어떤 장소나 상황에 다시 들어가기. 재진입(하기): *a spacecraft's reentry into the Earth's atmosphere.* 우주선의 지구 대기권으로의 재진입

ref /rɛf/ n SPOKEN ⇨ REFEREE¹

re·fer /rɪ'fɚ/ v -**rred**, -**rring**
refer to phr v [T] 1 [**refer to** sb/sth] to mention or speak about someone or something ‖ 사람이나 사물에 대해 언급하거나 말하다. …이라고 부르다. 인용하다: *He referred to her simply as "my friend."* 그는 그녀를 단순히 "내 친구"라고만 언급했다. 2 [**refer to** sth] to look at a book, map, piece of paper etc. for information ‖ 정보를 (찾기)위해 책·지도·서류 등을 보다. 참조[조사]하다. 문의[조회]하다: *Refer to page 14 for instructions.* 지시 사항은 14페이지를 참조하시오. 3 [**refer to** sb/sth] if a statement, number, report etc. refers to someone or something, it is about that person or thing ‖ 진술·숫자·보고 등이 어떤 사람이나 사물에 대한 것이다. …을 표현[표시]하다. …과 관련을 가지다: *The blue line on the graph refers to sales.* 그래프상의 청색 선은 판매(량)을 나타낸다. 4 [**refer** sb/sth **to** sb/sth] to send someone or something to another place or person for information, advice, or a decision ‖ 사람이나 사물을 ·정보[충고, 결정]를 위해 다른 장소나 사람에게 보내다. 조회[조사]시키다. 참조[유의]시키다: *Professor Harris referred me to an article she had written.* 해리스 교수는 내게 그녀가 썼던 논문을 참조하라고 했다.

ref·er·ee¹ /ˌrɛfə'ri/ n someone who makes sure that the rules are followed during a game in sports such as football, basketball, or BOXING ‖ 미식축구[농구, 권투] 등의 스포츠 시합 중에 규정이 지켜지는지 확인하는 사람. 심판. 주심

USAGE NOTE referee and umpire

Both of these words mean the person who makes sure that the rules are followed in a sports game. Use **referee** with basketball, boxing, football, hockey, soccer, and wrestling. Use **umpire** with baseball, tennis, and volleyball.

이들 두 단어 모두 스포츠 경기에서 규정이 지켜지는지 확인하는 사람을 의미한다. **referee**는 농구·권투·미식축구·하키·축구·레슬링에서 쓴다. **umpire**는 야구·테니스·배구에서 쓴다.

referee² *v* [I, T] to be the REFEREE for a game ‖ 시합의 심판이 되다. 심판을 보다 [맡다]

ref·er·ence /'rɛfrəns/ *n* **1** [C, U] something you say or write that mentions another person or thing ‖ 다른 사람이나 사물을 언급하는 말이나 글. 언급. 논급(한 것[말]): *In his letter, Sam made no reference to his illness.* 그의 편지에서 샘은 자신의 병에 대해 아무런 언급도 하지 않았다. **2** [C, U] the act of looking at something for information, or the book, magazine etc. you get the information from ‖ 정보를 (얻기)위해 사물을 찾아보기, 또는 정보를 얻어내는 책·잡지 등. 참고[참조](사항). 참고[인용] 문헌: *Keep a dictionary on your desk for easy reference.* 참고하기 쉽게 사전을 책상 위에 놓아두세요. / *the reference section of the library* 도서관의 참고 문헌 서가 **3 a)** a letter containing information about you that is written by someone who knows you well, usually to a new employer ‖ 자신을 잘 아는 다른 사람이 보통 새 고용주에게 써 보내는, 자신에 대한 정보가 들어 있는 서한. 추천서[장]. 보증서. 소개장 **b)** the person who writes this letter ‖ 이 서한을 써 주는 사람. 추천인. (신원) 보증인 **4** a note that tells you where the information that is used in a book, article etc. comes from ‖ 책·논문 등에서 사용된 정보의 출전을 알리는 표지. 참조(문헌). 주(註). 참조 부호[표]

reference book /'.. ,./ *n* a book, such as a dictionary, that you look at to find information ‖ 정보를 알아내기 위해 찾아보는 사전 등의 책. 참고 서적

reference li·brar·y /'.. ,.../, **reference room** /'.. ,./ *n* a public library or a room in a library, that contains REFERENCE BOOKS that you can use but not take away ‖ 이용할 수는 있

지만 가지고 나갈 수는 없는 참고 서적들을 비치하고 있는 공공도서관이나 도서관의 열람실. 참고 열람실. 자료실

ref·er·en·dum /,rɛfə'rɛndəm/ *n, plural* **referenda** /-də/ *or* **referendums** [C, U] an occasion when you vote in order to make a decision about a particular subject, rather than voting for a person ‖ 사람에게 투표하는 것이 아니라 특정 주제에 대해 의사 결정하기 위해 투표하는 경우. 국민투표(제도)

re·fill¹ /ri'fɪl/ *v* [T] to fill something again ‖ 물건을 다시 채우다. 리필하다: *Could you refill the glasses, please?* 잔을 다시 채워 주시겠습니까? – **refillable** *adj*

re·fill² /'rɪfɪl/ *n* **1** a container filled with a particular substance that you use to REFILL something ‖ 물건을 다시 채우기 위해 사용하는 특정 물질로 채워진 용기. 리필. 보충용 물품(통): *refills for an ink pen* 펜에 갈아넣을 잉크 **2** SPOKEN another drink to REFILL your glass ‖ 잔을 다시 채우는 또 한 잔의 음료. 한 잔 더. 추가 잔: *Would you like a refill?* 한 잔 더 하시겠습니까?

re·fi·nance /ri'faɪnæns, ,rifə'næns/ *v* [T] to borrow or lend money in order to change the way someone pays back a debt ‖ 빚을 상환하는 방식을 바꾸기 위해 돈을 빌리거나 빌려주다. …에 재융자하다. 상환금을 빌려주다: *We'd like to refinance the house to make the payments smaller.* 지불금을 더 줄이기 위해 집을 (담보로)재융자 받고 싶습니다.

re·fine /rɪ'faɪn/ *v* [T] **1** to make a substance more pure using an industrial process ‖ 산업 공정을 거쳐 물질을 더 순수하게 만들다. 정제[제련]하다. 불순물을 제거하다: *Gasoline is refined from crude oil.* 휘발유는 원유에서 정제된다. **2** to improve a method, plan, system etc. by making some changes to it ‖ 방법·계획·체계 등에 어떤 변화를 줘서 개선하다. …을 세련되게[고상하게] 하다. …을 한층 우아[정교]하게 하다: *Ideas from Lopez's short stories are further refined in his novels.* 로페즈의 단편 소설에서 나오는 아이디어는 그의 장편 소설에서 더욱 정교하게 펼쳐진다.

re·fined /rɪ'faɪnd/ *adj* **1** made more pure using an industrial process ‖ 산업 공정을 거쳐 더 순수하게 만들어진. 정제[제련]된. 순화된: *refined flour* 정백분(精麥粉) **2** improved and made more effective ‖ 개선되고 더 효과적으로 된. 치밀한. 정확한. 엄밀한: *a refined method of measurement* 정교한 측정 방법 **3**

polite, educated, and interested in art, music, and literature ‖ 정중하고 교양 있으며 예술·음악·문학에 관심 있는. 세련된. 우아한. 고상한

re·fine·ment /rɪˈfaɪnmənt/ n 1 [U] the process of improving something or making a substance more pure ‖ 사물을 개선하거나 물질을 더 순수하게 만드는 과정. 정제. 제련. 정화. 순화: *the refinement of sugar* 설탕의 정제(과정) / *the refinement of their economic theories* 그들 경제 이론의 정교화 2 a change to an existing product, plan, system etc. that improves it ‖ 기존의 제품·계획·체계 등을 개선시켜 주는 변화. 개량. 개선. 정교화(사항): *We've added a number of refinements to the design.* 우리는 그 디자인을 많이 개선했다. 3 [U] the quality of being REFINED ‖ 품위 있는 특성. 세련. 우아[고상]함

re·fin·er·y /rɪˈfaɪnəri/ n a factory where something such as oil, sugar, or metal is REFINED ‖ 기름[설탕, 금속] 등이 정제[제련]되는 공장. 정제[제련]소. 정유소

re·fin·ish /riˈfɪnɪʃ/ v [T] to give the surface of something, especially wood, a new appearance by painting or polishing it ‖ 특히 나무 등 사물의 표면에 칠이나 광택으로 새로운 외양을 주다. 표면을 새로 끝손질하다: *Dad refinished Grandma's old desk.* 아버지는 할머니의 낡은 책상을 깨끗이 손질했다.

re·flect /rɪˈflɛkt/ v 1 [T] to show or be a sign of a particular situation, idea, or feeling ‖ 특정 상황[생각, 감정]을 나타내거나 그것의 표시가 되다. …을 반영[발현]하다. 재현[표출]하다: *Children's behavior reflects their environment.* 아이들의 행동은 그들의 환경을 반영한다. / *People's opinions about Congress have been reflected in the election results.* 의회에 대한 사람들의 의견은 선거 결과에 반영됐다. 2 [I] to think carefully ‖ 신중하게 생각하다. 심사숙고하다. 곰곰이 생각하다. 회고[상기]하다: *Please take some time to reflect on our offer.* 우리 제안을 시간을 두고 심사숙고해 보세요. 3 [I, T] if a surface reflects light, heat, or an image, it throws back the light etc. that hits it ‖ 표면에 부딪치는 빛[열, 상(像)]을 되돌려 보내다. 반사[반향]하다. 비추다[비치다]: *mountains reflected in the lake* 호수에 비친 산들 / *sunlight reflecting off*

reflect
reflection

the whitewashed houses 하얗게 칠해진 집에서 반사되어 나오는 햇빛

reflect on sb/sth *phr v* [T] to influence people's opinion of someone or something, especially in a bad way ‖ 사람이나 사물에 대한 일반의 여론에 특히 나쁘게 영향을 끼치다. …을 반영하다. 나쁜 인상[이미지]을 주다: *behavior that reflects badly on the school* 학교의 이름을 욕되게 하는 행위

re·flec·tion /rɪˈflɛkʃən/ n 1 [C, U] careful thought, or an idea or opinion based on this ‖ 이에 기초한 주의 깊은 생각[사상, 견해]: *a writer's reflections on America in the 1920s* 1920년대 미국에 대한 어느 작가의 고찰 / *taking time for reflection* 시간을 갖고 심사숙고하기 2 something that shows, or is a sign of, a particular situation, fact, or feeling ‖ 특정 상황[사실, 감정]을 나타내거나 그것의 표시가 되는 것. 반영. 표출. 발현. 발로: *The rise in crime is a reflection of a violent society.* 범죄의 증가는 폭력 사회의 반영이다. / *If your kids are bad, it's a reflection on you.* (=a sign that you are a bad parent) 당신의 아이가 불량하다면 그것은 당신의 모습이 반영된 것입니다. 3 an image REFLECTed in a mirror or a similar surface ‖ 거울이나 유사한 표면에 반사된 모습. 반사상. 이미지. 비친 그림자[것, 상(像)]: *We looked at our reflections in the pool.* 우리는 풀장에 비친 우리의 모습을 바라봤다. —see picture at REFLECT 4 [U] the light or heat that is REFLECTed from something ‖ 사물로부터 반사된 빛이나 열. 반사광[열]

re·flec·tive /rɪˈflɛktɪv/ adj 1 a reflective surface REFLECTs light ‖ 표면이 빛을 반사하는. 반영하는. 반사에 의한 2 thinking quietly, or showing that you are doing this ‖ 조용히 생각하는, 또는 이렇게 하는 것을 보여 주는. 사색에 잠기는. 깊이 생각하는: *He was in a reflective mood.* 그는 사색에 잠겨 있었다.

re·flec·tor /rɪˈflɛktə/ n a small piece of plastic that REFLECTs light ‖ 빛을 반사하는 작은 플라스틱 조각. 반사물[면, 장치]. 반사기. 반사경

re·flex /ˈriflɛks/ n [C usually plural] a sudden physical reaction that you have without thinking about it ‖ 그것에 대한 생각 없이 행해진 갑작스런 신체적 반응. 반사 작용[행동]. 반사 운동(신경): *basketball players with good reflexes* (=the ability to react quickly) 뛰어난 반사 신경을 가진 야구선수

re·flex·ive /rɪˈflɛksɪv/ n TECHNICAL in

grammar, a verb or a pronoun that shows that an action affects the person or thing that does the action. In the sentence "I enjoyed myself," "myself" is reflexive ‖ 문법에서 행동이 그 행동을 하는 사람이나 사물에 영향을 미침을 보여주는 동사나 대명사. 재귀동사[대명사]. 문장 "I enjoyed myself"에서 "myself"는 재귀대명사이다 - **reflexive** *adj*

re·form¹ /rɪ'fɔrm/ *v* **1** [T] to improve an organization or system by making a lot of changes to it ‖ 많은 변화를 가해서 조직이나 체제를 개선하다. …을 개혁[쇄신]하다. 보다 좋게 바꾸다: *plans to reform the tax laws* 세법(稅法) 개혁안 **2** [I, T] to improve your behavior by making a lot of changes to it, or to make someone do this ‖ 많은 변화를 가해서 행동거지를 개선하다, 또는 다른 사람을 이렇게 하게 하다. 개심시키다. 교정(矯正)하다. 교화시키다: *a reformed criminal/alcoholic etc.* (=someone who is no longer a criminal etc.) 교화된 범죄인[알콜 중독자] / *No one believes that Uncle Max has reformed.* 아무도 맥스 삼촌이 개과천선했다고 믿지 않는다.

reform² *n* [C, U] a change made to an organization or system in order to improve it ‖ 조직이나 체제를 개선하기 위해 가해진 변화. 개량. 개혁. 쇄신: *educational reforms* 교육 개혁

ref·or·ma·tion /ˌrɛfɚ'meɪʃən/ *n* [C, U] an improvement made by changing something a lot ‖ 사물을 크게 바꾸어서 만들어진 개선(사항). 개량. 개혁. 쇄신: *the reformation of the welfare system* 복지 제도의 개혁

re·form·er /rɪ'fɔrmɚ/ *n* someone who works hard to make a lot of changes in order to improve a government or society ‖ 정부나 사회를 개선하기 위한 많은 변화를 이루도록 열심히 일하는 사람. 개량[혁신]자. 개혁가

reform school /.'. ,./ *n* a special school where young people who have broken the law are sent ‖ 법을 위반한 청소년들이 보내지는 특수학교. 소년원. 감화원

re·frain¹ /rɪ'freɪn/ *v* [I] FORMAL to stop yourself from doing something ‖ 자신이 어떤 일을 하는 것을 막다. 삼가다. 자제하다. 억제하다. 참다: *Please refrain from smoking.* 담배 피우는 것을 삼가 주세요.

refrain² *n* part of a song that is repeated, especially at the end of each VERSE ‖ 특히 시가(詩歌)의 각 (구절의)끝에 반복되는 노래 부분. 반복구. 후렴

re·fresh /rɪ'frɛʃ/ *v* **1** [T] to make someone feel less tired or less hot ‖ 사람을 덜 피곤하거나 덜 덥게 하다. 기분이 나게[활기 띠게] 하다. 기분을 전환시키다: *A shower will refresh you.* 샤워를 하면 기분이 상쾌해질 것입니다. **2 refresh sb's memory** to say something that makes someone remember something ‖ 남에게 어떤 일을 기억하게 하는 것을 말하다. 기억을 되살려주다[새롭게 하다]: *Please refresh my memory – what was your last job?* 기억이 안 나서 그러는데요. 당신의 전 직업이 무엇이었지요? - **refreshed** *adj*

re·fresh·er course /.'.. ,./ *n* a training class that teaches you about new developments in a subject or skill you have already studied or learned ‖ 이미 공부하거나 배운 주제나 기술에서 새로 발전된 사항을 가르치는 훈련반. 재교육 강습[연수]. 재교육 코스

re·fresh·ing /rɪ'frɛʃɪŋ/ *adj* **1** making you feel less tired or less hot ‖ 덜 피곤하거나 덜 덥게 하는. 심신을 상쾌하게 하는. 기운이 나게[활기를 띠게] 하는: *a refreshing drink* 청량 음료 **2** pleasantly different from what is familiar and boring ‖ 익숙하거나 지루한 것과는 다르게 유쾌한. 재미있는. 참신한. 괄목할 만한: *Their music makes a refreshing change from typical radio songs.* 그들의 음악은 전형적인 라디오 음악과는 다른 참신한 변화를 준다. - **refreshingly** *adv*

re·fresh·ment /rɪ'frɛʃmənt/ *n* **1** [C usually plural] food and drinks that are provided at a meeting, party, sports event etc. ‖ 회의·파티·운동 경기 등에서 제공되는 음식과 음료. 간단한 식사. 다과: *Refreshments will be served after the concert.* 콘서트 후에 다과가 제공됩니다. **2** [U] food and drinks in general ‖ 일반적인 음식과 음료. (기운을 차리게 하는) 음식물

re·frig·er·ate /rɪ'frɪdʒə,reɪt/ *v* [T] to make something such as food and drinks cold in order to preserve them ‖ 음식과 음료 등을 보존하기 위해 차게 하다. 냉각시키다. 냉장[냉동](보존)하다: *Refrigerate the sauce overnight.* 소스를 밤새 냉장 보존하시오. - **refrigeration** /rɪˌfrɪdʒə'reɪʃən/ *n*

re·frig·er·a·tor /rɪ'frɪdʒə,reɪtɚ/ *n* a large piece of kitchen equipment used for keeping food and drinks cold, shaped like a metal cupboard and kept cold by electricity ‖ 금속제 찬장 모양을 하고 전기로 차게 유지되며 음식과 음료를

차갑게 보존하는 데 쓰이는 대형 주방 기구. 냉장고. 냉동 장치 —see picture at KITCHEN

re·fuel /ri'fyul/ v [I, T] to fill a vehicle or plane with FUEL again before continuing on a trip ‖ 차량이나 비행기가 운행을 계속하기 전에 연료를 다시 채우다. 재급유하다. 연료를 보급하다

ref·uge /'rɛfyudʒ/ n a place that provides protection or shelter from bad weather or danger ‖ 악천후나 위험으로부터 보호 또는 피난할 수 있는 장소. 피난[대피]처. 숨는 곳. 긴급 보호 시설: *About 50 families have taken refuge* (=found protection) *in a Red Cross shelter.* 약 50가구가 적십자사가 제공하는 피난처에 피난했다.

ref·u·gee /ˌrɛfyu'dʒi·/ n someone who has been forced to leave his/her country, especially during a war ‖ 특히 전쟁 중에 자신의 나라를 강제로 떠나게 된 사람. 피난민. 망명자

re·fund¹ /'rifʌnd/ n an amount of money that is given back to you if you are not satisfied with the goods or services you have paid for ‖ 돈을 지불한 재화나 용역이 만족스럽지 않으면 되돌려 받게 되는 돈의 액수. 환불금: *Two cups were broken, so they gave me a refund.* 컵 두 개가 깨져서 그들은 내게 환불을 해 주었다.

re·fund² /rɪ'fʌnd/ v [T] to give someone his/her money back because something is wrong with the goods or services s/he paid for ‖ 누군가가 돈을 지불하고 산 재화나 용역이 잘못 되어서 돈을 되돌려 주다. 환불하다

re·fur·bish /rɪ'fɚbɪʃ/ v [T] to thoroughly repair and improve a building by painting it, cleaning it etc. ‖ 건물을 페인트칠하고 청소해서 완전히 수리하고 개선하다. …을 일신하다. 개장하다 – **refurbishment** n [C, U]

re·fus·al /rɪ'fyuzəl/ n [C, U] an act of saying or showing that you will not do, accept, or allow something ‖ 어떤 것을 하지[인정하지, 허용하지] 않겠다고 말하거나 보여주는 행위. 거절. 거부: *His refusal to take the drug test caused him to lose his job.* 그는 약물 검사 받는 것을 거부해서 일자리를 잃었다.

re·fuse¹ /rɪ'fyuz/ v **1** [I, T] to say or show that you will not do or accept something ‖ 어떤 것을 하지 않거나 인정하지 않겠다고 말하거나 보여주다. 거절하다. 사절[사퇴]하다: *I asked her to marry me, but she refused.* 나는 그녀에게 결혼해 달라고 청했지만 그녀는 거절했

다. / *Cindy refuses to go to school.* 신디는 학교에 가기를 거부하고 있다. / *an offer that's too good to refuse* (=so good that you cannot say no) 거절하기엔 너무나 좋은 제안 **2** [T] to not give or allow someone to have something that s/he wants ‖ 다른 사람에게 원하는 것을 주지 않거나 갖게 허용하지 않다. …을 (주기를)거절[거부]하다. 퇴짜 놓다: *We were refused permission to enter the country.* 우리는 그 나라의 입국 허가를 거부당했다.

USAGE NOTE reject, turn down, refuse, and **decline**

Use all of these words in order to show that you do not accept something. If you **reject** something or someone, you say firmly that you will not accept an offer, a suggestion, someone's friendship etc.: *They have until December 19 to accept or reject the proposal. / Kieran's book got rejected by every publisher.* **Turn down** is an informal way to say **reject:** *You'd be stupid to turn down such a good job offer.* If you **refuse** something, you say no, although someone very much wants you to accept it: *Peggy refused all offers of help.* If you **decline** an offer, you say politely that you cannot or will not accept it: *I'm sorry, but I'll have to decline the invitation.*

이들 모든 단어들은 어떤 것을 받아들이지 않는다는 것을 나타내는 데에 쓴다. 사물이나 사람을 **reject**하면 제안·제의·다른 사람의 우정 등을 받아들이지 않겠다고 확고히 말하는 것이다: 그들은 12월 19일까지 그 제안을 수용하든지 거절하든지 해야 한다. / 키란의 책은 모든 출판사에서 거부당했다. **turn down**은 **reject**함을 말하는 비격식적 방법이다: 네가 그렇게 좋은 직장 제의를 거절하는 것은 바보 같은 짓일 것이다. 어떤 것을 **refuse**하면 비록 다른 사람이 자신이 받아들이기를 대단히 바라지만 안된다고 말하는 것이다: 페기는 돕겠다는 모든 제의를 거부했다. 제안을 **decline**하는 것은 받아들일 수 없거나 받아들이지 않겠다고 정중하게 말하는 것이다: 미안합니다만 초청을 사양해야만 하겠습니다.

---

ref·use² /'rɛfjus/ n [U] FORMAL waste material; TRASH ‖ 폐기물. 쓰레기; ㉴ trash

re·fute /rɪ'fyut/ v [T] FORMAL to prove

that a statement or idea is not correct or fair ‖ 말이나 생각이 옳지 않거나 공정하지 않다는 것을 증명하다. …을 논박하다. 반박하다: *Jamieson refuted the charges in court.* 재미슨은 법정에서 그 혐의를 반박했다.

re·gain /rɪˈgeɪn/ *v* [T] to get something back ‖ 어떤 것을 되찾다. …을 회복하다. …을 되찾다: *Valerie's slowly regaining her health after her operation.* 발레리는 수술 후에 서서히 건강을 회복하고 있다.

re·gal /ˈriɡəl/ *adj* typical of a king or queen or suitable for a king or queen ‖ 왕이나 여왕의 특색을 잘 나타내는, 또는 왕이나 여왕에 어울리는. 왕의. 왕다운

re·ga·lia /rɪˈɡeɪlyə/ *n* [U] traditional clothes and decorations, used at official ceremonies ‖ 공식적인 의식에 사용되는 전통적인 옷과 장식. 정식 의복. 정장: *academic regalia* 학교 (졸업) 예복

re·gard¹ /rɪˈɡɑrd/ *n* FORMAL **1** [U] respect for someone or something, or careful attention that shows this ‖ 사람이나 사물에 대한 존경, 또는 이것을 나타내는 주의깊은 관심. 배려: *He's always been held in high regard* (=respected very much) *by the entire department.* 그는 항상 전체 부서원들에게 대단히 존경받는다. / *You have no regard for my feelings!* 너는 나의 감정을 조금도 배려하지 않아! **2 with/in regard to** FORMAL used in order to say what you are talking or writing about ‖ 어떤 것에 대해 이야기하거나 쓰는지를 말하는 데에 쓰여. …에 관해서: *Several changes have been made with regard to security.* 안전과 관련해서 몇 가지 변화가 있었다.

regard² *v* [T] **1** to think about someone or something in a particular way ‖ 특정하게 사람이나 사물을 생각하다. 간주하다. 여기다: *I've always regarded you as my friend.* 나는 항상 당신을 나의 친구로 여겼다. **2** FORMAL to look at someone or something, especially in a particular way ‖ 특히 특정하게 사람이나 사물을 보다. …을 유심히 보다. 지켜보다: *She regarded him thoughtfully.* 그녀는 그를 골똘히 바라보았다.

re·gard·ing /rɪˈɡɑrdɪŋ/ *prep* FORMAL a word used especially in business letters to introduce the particular subject you are writing about ‖ 글을 쓰고 있는 특정 주제를 도입하기 위해 특히 상용 서신에서 쓰이는 단어. …에 관하여: *Regarding your recent inquiry, I've enclosed a copy of our new brochure.* 귀하의 최근 문의에 관하여, 저희 회사의 새 팸플릿 한 부를 동봉합니다.

re·gard·less /rɪˈɡɑrdlɪs/ *adv* **1 regardless of** in spite of difficulties or opposition ‖ 어려움이나 반대에도 불구하고. …에 관계없이. 개의치 않고: *He'll sign that contract regardless of what anyone says!* 그는 남이 어떻게 말하든 상관없이 그 계약서에 서명할 거야! **2** without being affected by different situations, problems etc. ‖ 다른 상황이나 문제 등에 영향 받지 않은. 그것과는 관계없이: *You get a lot of criticism but you just have to continue, regardless.* 너는 많은 비판을 받고 있지만 개의치 말고 계속해야 한다.

re·gards /rɪˈɡɑrdz/ *n* [plural] good wishes ‖ 좋은 소망의 말. 안부. 인사의 말: *My cousin sends his regards.* 나의 사촌이 안부를 전한다.

re·gat·ta /rɪˈɡɑtə, -ˈɡæ-/ *n* a race for rowing or sailing boats ‖ 배를 젓거나 항해하는 경주. 보트[요트] 경기 대회

re·gen·er·ate /rɪˈdʒɛnəˌreɪt/ *v* [I, T] FORMAL to develop and grow strong again, or to make something do this ‖ 다시 발달하여 강해지거나 어떤 것을 이렇게 만들다. 재생하다[시키다]: *Given time, the forest will regenerate.* 시간이 지나면 삼림은 되살아날 것이다. – **regeneration** /rɪˌdʒɛnəˈreɪʃən/ *n* [U]

re·gent /ˈridʒənt/ *n* a member of a small group of people that makes decisions about education in a US state, or that governs a university ‖ 미국 주에서 교육에 관해 결정하거나 대학을 운영하는 소규모 집단의 일원. 주립대학·교육기관의 이사. 평의원: *the Iowa Board of Regents* 아이오와 평의회

reg·gae /ˈrɛɡeɪ/ *n* [U] a type of popular music from Jamaica ‖ 자메이카에서 유래한 대중음악의 한 유형. 레게

re·gime /reɪˈʒim, rɪ-/ *n* **1** a government that has not been elected in fair elections ‖ 공정한 선거로 선출되지 않은 정부. 비민주적 수단에 의한 정권 **2** a particular system of government or management, especially one you disapprove of ‖ 특히 인정할 수 없는 특정 체제의 정부나 관리. 정치 제도[체제]. 관리 방식: *the Communist regime* 공산주의 체제 **3** ⇨ REGIMEN

reg·i·men /ˈrɛdʒəmən/, **regime** *n* a special plan for eating, exercising etc. that is intended to improve your health ‖ 건강을 증진시키려는 의도로 먹거나 운동하는 것 등에 대한 특별한 계획. 양생[섭생]법. 식이요법

reg·i·ment /ˈrɛdʒəmənt/ *n* a large group of soldiers consisting of several

BATTALIONs ‖ 몇 개의 대대로 구성되어 있는 대규모 군인 집단. 연대 – **regimental** /ˌrɛdʒəˈmɛntl/ adj

reg·i·ment·ed /ˈrɛdʒəˌmɛntɪd/ adj controlled very strictly ‖ 매우 엄격하게 통제 받는. 엄격한 규제를 받는: *Prisoners follow a highly regimented schedule.* 죄수들은 매우 엄격히 통제된 일정을 따른다. – **regimentation** /ˌrɛdʒəmənˈteɪʃən/ n [U]

re·gion /ˈridʒən/ n 1 a fairly large area of a state, country etc., usually without exact limits ‖ 보통 정확한 경계가 없는 주나 나라 등의 상당히 넓은 지역. 지방: *Snow is expected in mountain regions.* 산악 지역에서 눈이 내릴 것으로 예상됩니다. 2 the area around a particular part of your body ‖ 신체의 특정 부위 주변의 부분: *pain in the lower back region* 허리 부위의 통증 3 **(somewhere) in the region of** about; APPROXIMATELY ‖ 약…. …근처에. 가량; ⓟ approximately: *It will cost in the region of $750.* 약 750달러의 비용이 들 것이다.

re·gion·al /ˈridʒənl/ adj relating to a particular REGION ‖ 특정한 지역의. 지방의: *regional customs* 지방 풍습 – **regionally** adv

reg·is·ter¹ /ˈrɛdʒəstɚ/ n 1 a book containing an official list or record of something ‖ 사물의 공식적인 목록이나 기록을 포함하는 책. 기록[등록, 등기]부. 명부: *the National Register of Historic Places* 전미 사적지 명부 2 the place where the warm or cool air of a heating system comes into a room, with a metal cover you can open or close ‖ 난방 장치에서 덥거나 찬 공기가 방으로 들어오는, 개폐가 가능한 금속 덮개가 달린 곳. 냉난방의 통풍 조절 장치 3 ⇨ CASH REGISTER

register² v 1 [I, T] to record a name, details about something etc. on an official list ‖ 공식 목록에 이름·세부 사항 등을 기록하다. 등록하다. 기재하다: *The car is registered in my sister's name.* 그 차는 내 여동생의 명의로 등록되어 있다. 2 [I, T] to officially arrange to attend a particular school, university, or course; ENROLL ‖ 특정한 학교나 대학, 또는 강좌에 출석하는 것을 공식적으로 준비하다. 입학 수속을 하다. 수강 신청을 하다; ⓟ enroll: *How many students have registered for the European History class?* 유럽사 강의에 몇 명이 수강 신청을 했습니까? 3 [T] to express a feeling or opinion about something ‖ 사물에 대한 감정이나 의견을 나타내다: *Her face registered surprise and shock.* 그녀의 얼

굴에는 놀람과 충격이 나타났다. 4 [I, T] if an instrument registers an amount or if an amount registers on it, the instrument shows or records that amount ‖ 기기가 양을 나타내거나 기록하다. …을 기록하여 보여주다. 표시하다: *The thermometer registered 74°F.* 온도계가 화씨 74도를 기록했다. 5 to send a package or letter by REGISTERED MAIL ‖ 등기 우편으로 소포나 편지를 보내다

registered mail /ˌ... ˈ./ n [U] a service in which the post office records the time when your mail is sent and delivered ‖ 우체국에서 우편물이 발송되고 배달될 때의 시간을 기록하는 우편. 등기 우편

registered nurse /ˌ... ˈ./, **RN** n someone who has been trained and is officially allowed to work as a nurse ‖ 교육을 받고 간호사로서 일하도록 공식적으로 허가받은 사람. 공인 간호사

reg·is·trar /ˈrɛdʒəˌstrɑr/ n someone who is in charge of official records, especially in a college ‖ 특히 대학에서 공식적인 기록을 담당하는 사람. 학적 담당 직원. 학적계

reg·is·tra·tion /ˌrɛdʒəˈstreɪʃən/ n 1 [U] the process of officially arranging to attend a particular school, university, or class; ENROLLMENT ‖ 특정한 학교나 대학, 또는 강좌에 출석하는 것을 공식적으로 준비하는 과정. 등록. 수강신청; ⓟ enrollment: *fall quarter registration* 가을 학기 등록 2 [U] the act of recording names and details on an official list ‖ 공식 목록에 이름과 세부 사항을 기록함. 기재. 등록. 등기 3 an official piece of paper containing details about a vehicle and the name of its owner ‖ 차량과 차량 소유자명에 관한 세부 사항을 포함하는 공식 문서. 자동차 등록증

reg·is·try /ˈrɛdʒəstri/ n a place where official records are kept ‖ 공식 기록이 보관된 곳. 등기소. 등록소

re·gress /rɪˈgrɛs/ v [I] FORMAL to go back to an earlier, less developed state ‖ 이전의 덜 발달된 상태로 돌아가다. 예전 상태로 돌아가다. 역행[퇴보]하다 – **regression** /rɪˈgrɛʃən/ n [U] —compare PROGRESS²

re·gret¹ /rɪˈgrɛt/ v **-tted, -tting** [T] 1 to feel sorry about something you have done and wish you had not done it ‖ 자신이 한 일에 대해 유감스러워하고 그런 일을 하지 않았으면 좋았다고 생각하다. 후회하다. 뉘우치다: *I've always regretted selling my dad's old fishing rod.* 나는 항상 아빠의 낡은 낚싯대를 판

것을 후회했다. / *He regrets that he never went to college.* 그는 대학에 가지 않은 것을 후회한다. **2** FORMAL to be sorry and sad about a situation ‖ 특정 상황에 대해 미안해하고 슬퍼하다. 유감으로 여기다: *I regret that I will be unable to attend.* 유감스럽지만 참석할 수 없습니다.

regret² *n* [C, U] sadness that you feel about something because you wish it had not happened or that you had not done it ‖ 일이 일어나지 않았거나 자신이 그 일을 하지 않았으면 좋았다고 생각하기 때문에 느끼는 슬픔. 후회. 유감: *The company expressed deep regret at the accident.* 그 회사는 그 사건에 깊은 유감을 표명했다. / *Carl said he had no regrets about his decision.* 칼은 자신의 결정에 대해 후회는 없다고 말했다. − **regretfully** *adv* − **regretful** *adj*

re·gret·ta·ble /rɪˈɡrɛtəbəl/ *adj* something that is regrettable makes you feel sorry or sad because it has unpleasant results ‖ 어떤 일이 불쾌한 결과를 가져오기 때문에 미안함이나 슬픔을 느끼게 하는. 유감스러운. 애석한: *a regrettable mistake* 유감스러운 실수 − **regrettably** *adv*

re·group /ˌriˈɡrup/ *v* [I, T] to form a group again in order to be more effective, or to make people do this ‖ 더 효과적으로 되기 위해 집단을 다시 형성하다, 또는 사람에게 이렇게 하게 하다. 재편성[재결성]하다: *The party needs time to regroup politically.* 그 당은 정치적으로 재정비하기 위한 시간이 필요하다.

reg·u·lar¹ /ˈrɛɡyələ/ *adj* **1** ▶REPEATED 반복되는◀ repeated, with the same amount of time or space between each thing and the next ‖ 각각의 일과 그 다음의 일 사이에 동일한 시간이나 공간을 두고 반복되는. 규칙적인: *His heartbeat is strong and regular.* 그의 심장 박동은 강하고 규칙적이다. / *Planes were taking off at regular intervals.* 비행기가 규칙적인 간격으로 이륙하고 있었다.

2 ▶NORMAL SIZE 보통 크기◀ of standard size ‖ 표준 크기의. 보통의: *fries and a regular coke* 감자 튀김과 보통 크기의 콜라

3 ▶SAME TIME 같은 시간◀ happening or planned for the same time every day, month, year etc. ‖ 매일·매달·매년 등 같은 시간에 일어나거나 계획된. 정기적인. 정례의: *regular meetings* 정례 모임 / *Once I start working regular hours, things should get better.* 일단 내가 규칙

적으로 일을 하기 시작하면 상황은 더 좋아질 거야.

4 ▶HAPPENING OFTEN 자주 일어나는◀ happening or doing something very often ‖ 매우 자주 일어나거나 어떤 것을 하는. 통상의. 습관적인: *He's one of our regular customers.* 그는 단골 고객 중의 한 명이다.

5 ▶USUAL 평소의◀ normal or usual ‖ 정상적이거나 평소의. 정식[정규]의: *She's not our regular babysitter.* 그녀는 평소의 아기 봐주는 사람이 아니다.

6 ▶ORDINARY 일반적인◀ ordinary ‖ 일반적인: *I'm just a regular doctor, not a specialist.* 나는 전문의가 아니고 일반 의사다.

7 ▶EVENLY SHAPED 고른 형태의◀ evenly shaped with parts or sides of equal size ‖ 부분이나 측면이 같은 크기의 고른 형태인. 정연한. 균형 잡힌: *regular features* (=an evenly shaped face) 단정한 용모

8 ▶GRAMMAR 문법◀ TECHNICAL a regular verb or noun changes its forms in the same way as most verbs or nouns. The verb "walk" is regular, but "be" is not ‖ 동사나 명사가 대부분의 동사나 명사와 같은 방식으로 형태를 변화시키는. 규칙적인. 규칙 변화의. 동사 "walk"는 규칙 동사이지만 "be"동사는 아니다 − **regularity** /ˌrɛɡyəˈlærəti/ *n* [U]

regular² *n* **1** INFORMAL a customer who goes to the same store, restaurant etc. very often ‖ 매우 자주 같은 상점이나 식당 등을 가는 고객. 단골손님 **2** [U] gas that contains LEAD ‖ 납을 함유하는 휘발유. 표준 휘발유 —compare UNLEADED

reg·u·lar·ly /ˈrɛɡyələli, ˈrɛɡyəli/ *adv* **1** at regular times, for example every day, week, or month ‖ 매일이나 매주, 또는 매달 등의 규칙적인 시간에. 정규적으로. 규칙적으로: *Brush your teeth and see your dentist regularly.* 규칙적으로 이를 닦고 치과 의사의 진찰을 받아라. **2** often ‖ 자주: *Janet comes to visit regularly.* 재닛이 자주 방문한다.

reg·u·late /ˈrɛɡyəˌleɪt/ *v* [T] **1** to control an activity or process, usually by having rules ‖ 보통 규칙이 있어 활동이나 과정을 관리[통제]하다. 규제하다: *The use of these drugs is strictly regulated.* 이 약의 사용은 엄격히 규제된다. **2** FORMAL to make a machine work at a particular speed, temperature etc. ‖ 기계를 특정한 속도·온도 등으로 작동시키다. 기계를 조절[조정]하다: *Use this dial to regulate the sound.* 소리를 조절하려면 이 다이얼을 사용해라.

reg·u·la·tion /ˌrɛɡyəˈleɪʃən/ *n* **1** an official rule or order ‖ 공식적인 규칙이나 명령. 규정. 법규: *safety regulations* 안전 법규 **2** [U] control over something, especially by rules ‖ 특히 규칙에 의한 사물에 대한 통제. 규제: *the regulation of public spending* 공공 지출의 규제

reg·u·la·to·ry /ˈrɛɡyələˌtɔri/ *adj* FORMAL having the purpose of controlling an activity or process, especially by rules ‖ 특히 규칙에 의해 활동이나 과정을 통제하는데 목적을 둔. 규제의. 조정력을 가진: *the Nuclear Regulatory Commission* 핵무기 규제 위원회

re·gur·gi·tate /rɪˈɡɚdʒəˌteɪt/ *v* FORMAL **1** [I, T] VOMIT **2** [T] to repeat facts, ideas etc. without understanding them clearly ‖ 명확히 이해하지 않고 사실·생각 등을 반복하다. 그대로 되뇌다: *I want my students to think for themselves – not to regurgitate what they've read.* 나는 학생들이 읽은 것을 그대로 반복하지 말고 그들 스스로 생각하길 바란다. – **regurgitation** /rɪˌɡɚdʒəˈteɪʃən/ *n* [U]

re·hab /ˈrihæb/ *n* [U] INFORMAL ⇨ REHABILITATION: *Frank's been in rehab for six weeks.* 프랭크는 6주 동안 사회 복귀 훈련을 받았다.

re·ha·bil·i·tate /ˌriəˈbɪləˌteɪt, ˌrihə-/ *v* [T] **1** to help someone to live a healthy or useful life again after s/he has been sick or in prison ‖ 병을 앓거나 수감 생활후 다시 건강하거나 유익한 삶을 살도록 도와주다. 기능 회복 훈련을 하다. 갱생시키다: *rehabilitating young criminals* 젊은 범죄자들을 갱생시키기 **2** to improve a building or area so that it is in a good condition again ‖ 다시 좋은 환경이 되도록 건물이나 지역을 개선하다. 재정비하다

re·ha·bil·i·ta·tion /ˌriəˌbɪləˈteɪʃən, ˌrihə-/ *n* [U] the process of curing someone who has an alcohol or drug problem ‖ 술이나 마약 문제가 있는 사람을 치료하는 과정. 사회 복귀 훈련[치료]

re·hash /riˈhæʃ/ *v* [T] INFORMAL to use the same ideas again in a new form that is not really different or better ‖ 실제로 다르지도 더 좋지도 않은 새로운 형식으로 동일한 아이디어를 다시 사용하다. …을 재탕하다. 고쳐 말하다: *He keeps rehashing the same old speech.* 그는 똑같은 오래된 연설을 계속하여 다시 써 먹는다. – **rehash** /ˈrihæʃ/ *n*

re·hears·al /rɪˈhɚsəl/ *n* [C, U] a period of time or a particular occasion when all the people in a play, concert etc. practice it before giving a public performance ‖ 연극·콘서트 등에서 모든 사람들이 공개 공연을 하기 전에 연습하는 시간이나 특별한 경우. 리허설. 예행 연습: *We only have one more rehearsal before the concert.* 우리는 콘서트 전에 단 한 번 더 리허설을 가진다.

re·hearse /rɪˈhɚs/ *v* [I, T] to practice something such as a play or concert before giving a public performance ‖ 공개 공연하기 전에 연극이나 콘서트 등을 연습하다. 리허설하다

re·house /ˌriˈhaʊz/ *v* [T] to put someone in a new or better home ‖ 사람을 새집이나 더 좋은 집에 두다. (남에게) 새 주택을 주다: *Many people had to be rehoused after the war.* 많은 사람들이 전후(戰後)에 새로운 집에서 살아야 했다.

reign¹ /reɪn/ *n* **1** the period of time during which someone rules a country ‖ 어떤 사람이 나라를 통치하는 기간. 치세(治世). 시대: *the reign of Queen Anne* 앤 여왕 치세 **2** the period of time during which a particular situation or state exists ‖ 특정한 상황이나 상태가 존재하는 기간. 통치. 지배. 군림: *a reign of terror* (=when a government kills many of its opponents) 공포 통치 기간

reign² *v* [I] **1** **the reigning champion** the most recent winner of a competition ‖ 시합의 가장 최근 우승자. 타이틀을 보유하고 있는 현 챔피언 **2** LITERARY to exist for a period of time as a very important or noticeable feature ‖ 아주 중요하거나 눈에 띄는 특징으로서 일정 기간 동안 존재한다. 우세[군림]하다. 만연하다: *Confusion reigned this week over the budget proposals.* 예산안으로 이번 주에는 혼란스러웠다. **3** to be the ruler of a country ‖ 한 국가의 지배자가 되다. 지배하다. 통치하다

re·im·burse /ˌriɪmˈbɚs/ *v* [T] FORMAL to pay money back to someone ‖ 남에게 돈을 갚아 주다. 변상하다. 배상하다: *The company will reimburse you for your travel expenses.* 회사가 당신에게 여행 경비를 환급해 줄 것이다. – **reimbursement** *n* [U]

rein /reɪn/ *n* **1** [C usually plural] a long narrow band of leather that is fastened around a horse's head in order to control it ‖ 말을 통제하기 위해 말의 머리 둘레에 고정시킨 길고 좁은 가죽 띠. 고삐 **2** **free rein** complete freedom to say or do things the way you want to ‖ 자신이 원하는 방식으로 말을 하거나 일을 하는 완전한 자유: *The magazine gives free rein to its writers in matters of style.* 그잡지는 문체 문제에 있어 작가들에게 자율

권을 준다. **3 keep a tight rein on** to control someone or something strictly ‖ 사람이나 사물을 엄격하게 통제하다. …의 고삐를 죄다: *The government is trying to keep a tight rein on public spending.* 정부는 공공 지출을 엄격하게 통제하려고 애쓰고 있다.

re·in·car·nate /ˌriːinˈkɑːrneɪt/ *v* **be reincarnated** to be born again in another body after you have died ‖ 죽은 후 다른 육체로 다시 태어나다. 환생하다

re·in·car·na·tion /ˌriːinkɑːrˈneɪʃən/ *n* **1** [U] the act of being born again in another body after you have died ‖ 죽은 후에 다른 육체로 다시 태어남. 환생. 윤회 **2** the person or animal that REINCARNATED person has become ‖ 사람이 환생해서 되는 사람이나 동물. 화신(化身): *Many Hindus view him as the reincarnation of the god Vishnu.* 많은 힌두교 신자들은 그를 비슈누 신의 화신으로 여긴다.

rein·deer /ˈreɪndɪr/ *n* a type of DEER with long horns that lives in very cold places ‖ 매우 추운 곳에서 사는 긴 뿔이 달린 사슴의 일종. 순록

re·in·force /ˌriːinˈfɔːrs/ *v* [T] **1** to do something to make an opinion, statement, feeling etc. stronger or to support it ‖ 의견·진술·감정 등을 더 강하게 하거나 지지하기 위해 어떤 일을 하다. 강화[증강]하다. 보강하다: *The fire safety rules will be reinforced by regular drills.* 화재 안전 규칙은 규칙적인 훈련으로 보강될 것이다. **2** to make something such as a part of a building, a piece of clothing etc. stronger ‖ 건물의 일부·옷 등을 더 강하게 하다: *a wall reinforced with concrete* 콘크리트 강화 벽

re·in·force·ment /ˌriːinˈfɔːrsmənt/ *n* [U] **1** the act of doing something to make an opinion, statement, feeling etc. stronger ‖ 의견·진술·감정 등을 더 강하게 하는 일을 함. 강화. 보강: *Positive reinforcement helps kids behave better.* 아이들에게 격려를 더해줄수록 아이들은 말을 더 잘 듣게 된다. **2** the act of reinforcing (REINFORCE) a wall, building etc. ‖ 벽·건물 등을 강화함

re·in·force·ments /ˌriːinˈfɔːrsmənts/ *n* [plural] more soldiers who are sent to an army to make it stronger ‖ 군대를 더 강화하기 위해 파견되는 더 많은 군인들. 증원 부대. 지원 병력

re·in·state /ˌriːinˈsteɪt/ *v* [T] **1** to put someone back into a job that s/he had before ‖ 사람을 전에 가졌던 일자리로 되

돌리다. 복직시키다: *Two employees who were wrongfully fired will be reinstated.* 부당하게 해고된 두 근로자는 복직될 것이다. **2** if a law, system, or practice is reinstated, it begins to be used after not being used ‖ 법[제도, 관습]이 사용되지 않던 상태였다가 쓰이기 시작하다. 부활시키다 **– reinstatement** *n* [C, U]

re·in·vent /ˌriːinˈvɛnt/ *v* [T] **1** to produce an idea, method etc. that is based on something that existed in the past, but is slightly different ‖ 과거에 존재했던 것을 바탕으로 하지만 약간 다른 생각·방법 등을 만들다. 재발명[고안]하다: *plans to reinvent the American educational system* 미국 교육 제도를 개혁하려는 계획 **2 reinvent the wheel** INFORMAL to waste time trying to find a way of doing something, when someone else has already discovered the best way to do it ‖ 다른 사람이 이미 어떤 일을 하는 최선의 방법을 발견했는데도 그 일을 하기 위한 방법을 발견하느라 시간을 낭비하다. 불필요한 일을 하다. 헛수고 하다

re·is·sue /riˈɪʃu/ *v* [T] to produce a record, book etc. again, after it has not been available for some time ‖ 한동안 구입이 불가능했던 레코드·서적 등을 다시 생산하다. 재발매하다 **– reissue** *n*

re·it·er·ate /riˈɪtəˌreɪt/ *v* [T] FORMAL to say something more than once ‖ 어떤 것을 한 번 이상 말하다. 반복하여 말하다. 되풀이하다 **– reiteration** /riˌɪtəˈreɪʃən/ *n* [C, U]

re·ject[1] /rɪˈdʒɛkt/ *v* [T] **1** to refuse to accept, believe in, or agree with something ‖ 어떤 일을 받아들이기[믿기, 동의하기]를 거부하다. 거절[사절]하다: *I rejected the company's offer.* 나는 그 회사의 제안을 거절했다. **2** to refuse to accept someone for a job, school etc. ‖ 일자리·학교 등에서 어떤 사람을 받아들이기를 거부하다. 불합격시키다: *Yale rejected his application.* 예일 대학은 그의 입학지원을 거절했다. **3** to stop giving someone love or attention ‖ 남에게 사랑이나 관심을 주지 않다. 애정을 거부하다: *She feels rejected by her parents.* 그녀는 부모님한테 버림받았다고 생각한다. **—see usage note at REFUSE**

re·ject[2] /ˈriːdʒɛkt/ *n* a product that is thrown away because it is damaged or imperfect ‖ 손상되거나 불완전하기 때문에 버려진 제품. 불량품. 불합격품

re·jec·tion /rɪˈdʒɛkʃən/ *n* **1** [C, U] the act of not accepting, believing in, or agreeing with something ‖ 어떤 일을 받아들이지[믿지, 동의하지] 않음. 거절. 각

하: *The council's rejection of the proposal was unexpected.* 그 제안에 대한 위원회의 거절은 뜻밖이었다. **2** the act of not accepting someone for a job, school etc. ‖ 일자리·학교 등에서 사람을 받아들이지 않음. 거절. 거부: *She got a lot of rejections before the book was finally published.* 그녀의 책은 결국 출판되기까지 수없이 퇴짜 맞았다. **3** [U] a situation in which someone stops giving you love or attention ‖ 누군가 자신에게 사랑이나 관심을 더 이상 주지 않는 상태: *I couldn't deal with any more rejection.* 나는 더 이상 퇴짜 맞는 것을 참을 수 없었다.

re·joice /rɪˈdʒɔɪs/ *v* [I] LITERARY to feel or show that you are very happy ‖ 자신이 매우 행복하다는 것을 느끼거나 나타내다. 기뻐하다

re·joic·ing /rɪˈdʒɔɪsɪŋ/ *n* [U] FORMAL extreme happiness that is shown by a lot of people ‖ 많은 사람이 보여주는 극도의 행복. 기쁨. 환희

re·join /rɪˈdʒɔɪn/ *v* [T] to go back to a group of people, organization etc. that you were with before ‖ 전에 자신이 있었던 사람들의 집단·조직 등으로 돌아가다. 복귀[재합류]하다. 재회하다: *Hiroko rejoined her family in Japan.* 히로코는 일본에 있는 가족과 재회했다.

re·join·der /rɪˈdʒɔɪndɚ/ *n* FORMAL a reply, especially a rude one ‖ 대답, 특히 거친 대답. 말대꾸. 반론

re·ju·ve·nate /rɪˈdʒuvəˌneɪt/ *v* [T] **1** to make someone feel or look young and strong again ‖ 누구를 다시 젊고 강하게 느끼게 또는 보이게 하다. 젊어지게 하다. 활력을 되찾게 하다: *Exercise rejuvenates the body.* 운동은 신체에 활력을 되찾게 한다. **2** to make a system or place better again ‖ 체제나 장소를 다시 더 좋게 만들다. 회생시키다: *the rejuvenated downtown area* 활력을 되찾은 번화가 –
rejuvenation /rɪˌdʒuvəˈneɪʃən/ *n* [singular, U]

re·kin·dle /riˈkɪndl/ *v* [T] **1** to make someone have a particular feeling, thought etc. again ‖ 남에게 다시 특별한 감정·사상 등을 갖게 하다. 되살아나게 하다: *a chance to rekindle an old romance* 옛 사랑을 되살릴 기회 **2** to start a fire again ‖ 다시 불붙이다. 점화하다

re·lapse /rɪˈlæps/ *n* [C, U] **1** a situation in which someone feels sick again after feeling better ‖ 사람이 병이 나은 듯하다가 다시 아픈 상태. 재발: *He's had/suffered a relapse.* 그는 병이 재발했다. **2** a situation in which someone or

something gets worse after being good for a while ‖ 사람이나 사물이 잠시 동안 좋은 상태였다가 더 나빠지는 상태. 되돌아가기. 타락. 퇴보: *a relapse into drug abuse* 마약 남용으로의 타락[퇴보] –
relapse *v* [I]

re·late /rɪˈleɪt/ *v* **1** [I, T] to make or show a connection between two or more ideas or subjects ‖ 둘 이상의 생각이나 주제 사이를 연관짓다, 또는 연관성을 보이다. …을 관련[결부]시키다: *I don't understand how the two ideas relate.* 나는 그 두 생각이 어떻게 결부되는지 이해가 안 간다. **2 war-related/drug-related** etc. caused by or relating to war, drugs etc. ‖ 전쟁·마약 등에 의해 야기되거나 관련된. 전쟁과 관련된/마약과 관련된: *There were very few alcohol-related deaths on the roads this month.* 이번 달 도로에서의 알코올 관련 사망은 거의 없었다. **3** [T] FORMAL to tell a story to someone ‖ 남에게 이야기하다. 말하다. 설명하다

relate to sb/sth *phr v* [T] **1** to be concerned with or connected to a particular subject ‖ 특별한 주제와 관련되거나 연결되다. 관계가 있다: *Mr. Harrison's point relates to the first question he was asked.* 해리슨의 요점은 그가 받은 첫 번째 질문과 연관된다. **2** to be able to understand someone's problems, feelings etc. ‖ 남의 문제·감정 등을 이해할 수 있다. 이해하다. 받아들이다: *I find it hard to relate to kids.* 나는 어린이를 이해하는 것이 어렵다.

re·lat·ed /rɪˈleɪtɪd/ *adj* **1** connected by similar ideas or dealing with similar subjects ‖ 비슷한 생각과 연결된 또는 비슷한 주제를 다루는. 관련[관계]된: *lung cancer and related medical problems* 폐암과 관련된 의료 문제 / *The study compares Czech, Polish, and other related Slavic languages.* 그 연구는 체코어와 폴란드어 그리고 다른 관련 슬라브어를 비교한다. —opposite UNRELATED **2** connected by a family relationship ‖ 가족 관계로 연결된. 친척의: *Are you related to Paula?* 너는 폴라의 친척이니?

re·la·tion /rɪˈleɪʃən/ *n* **1 in relation to** used when comparing two things or showing the relationship between them ‖ 두 사물을 비교하거나 그들 사이의 관계를 보여줄 때 쓰여. …에 관하여. …과 비교하여: *The area of land is tiny in relation to the population.* 땅 면적은 인구와 비교하면 작다. **2** [C, U] a connection between two things ‖ 두 사물 사이의 연관. 관련. 관계: *Doctors say* *there was no **relation** between the drugs he was taking and his death.* 의사들은 그가 복용 중인 약과 그의 죽음 사이에는 아무런 관련이 없다고 말한다. / *This case bears no **relation** to* (=is not connected with or similar to) *the Goldman trial.* 이 사건은 골드만 재판과 아무 관련이 없다. **3** a member of your family; RELATIVE ‖ 가족의 일원. 친척. 친척 관계; ⊞ relative: *Joan Bartell, the author, is no **relation** to Governor Bartell.* 작가인 조안 바텔은 바텔 주지사와 친척 관계가 아니다.

re·la·tions /rɪˈleɪʃənz/ *n* [plural] **1** official connections between companies, countries etc. ‖ 회사·국가 등 사이의 공식적인 관계: *Nixon's visit to China strengthened East-West **relations**.* 닉슨의 중국 방문은 동서 관계를 강화했다. / *The US has maintained diplomatic **relations** with Laos.* 미국은 라오스와의 외교 관계를 유지하였다. **2** the way people or groups of people behave toward each other ‖ 사람이나 집단이 서로에 대해 행동하는 방식. 관계. 사이: *Relations between the two families were never good.* 두 가족 사이의 관계는 결코 좋지 않았다. —see also PUBLIC RELATIONS

re·la·tion·ship /rɪˈleɪʃənˌʃɪp/ *n* **1** the way in which two people or groups behave toward each other ‖ 두 사람이나 집단이 서로에 대하여 행동하는 방식. 관계. 사이: *The police have a good **relationship** with the community.* 경찰은 지역 사회와 좋은 관계를 유지한다. **2** a situation in which two people have sexual or romantic feelings for each other ‖ 두 사람이 서로에 대해 성적이거나 낭만적인 감정이 있는 상황. 성적[연애] 관계: *My parents had a strong **relationship**.* 나의 부모님은 금실이 무척 좋으셨다. / *He's much happier now that he's in a **relationship**.* 그는 연애 관계를 맺고 있는 지금 훨씬 더 행복하다. **3** [C, U] the way in which two or more things are related to each other ‖ 두 가지 이상의 사물이 서로 관련되어 있는 방식. 관계. 연관성: *the **relationship** between pay and performance at work* 봉급과 업무 수행 능력 사이의 관계

rel·a·tive¹ /ˈrɛlətɪv/ *n* a member of your family ‖ 자기 가족의 일원. 친척: *I have **relatives** in Minnesota.* 나는 미네소타에 친척들이 있다.

relative² *adj* **1** having a particular quality when compared with something else ‖ 다른 것과 비교할 때 특별한 성질이

있는. 상대적인: *The 1950s were a time of **relative** peace/calm/prosperity for the country.* 1950년대는 그 나라가 상대적으로 화평한[평온한, 번영한] 시기였다. **2 relative to sth** relating to or compared with a particular subject ‖ 특별한 주제와 관련되거나 비교되는. …과 비교하면: *Demand for corn is low **relative** to the supply.* 옥수수에 대한 수요는 공급에 비해 낮다.

relative clause /ˌ… ˈ./ *n* TECHNICAL in grammar, a part of a sentence that has a verb in it and is joined to the rest of the sentence by a RELATIVE PRONOUN. In the sentence "The dress that I bought is too small," "that I bought" is the relative clause ‖ 문법에서, 문장 내에 동사가 있고 나머지 문장과 관계 대명사로 연결되는 문장의 일부. 관계사절 "The dress that I bought is too small,"의 문장에서 "that I bought"는 관계사절이다

rel·a·tive·ly /ˈrɛlətɪvli/ *adv* to a particular degree, especially when compared to something similar ‖ 특히 비슷한 것과 비교할 때, 특정한 정도로. 비교적: *I woke up **relatively** early this morning.* 나는 오늘 아침 비교적 일찍 일어났다.

relative pro·noun /ˌ… ˈ../ *n* TECHNICAL in grammar, a PRONOUN such as "who," "which," or "that," which connects a RELATIVE CLAUSE to the rest of the sentence. In the sentence "The dress that I bought is too small," "that" is the relative pronoun ‖ 문법에서 관계사절을 나머지 문장에 연결하는 "who"나 "which" 또는 "that" 등의 대명사. 관계 대명사 "The dress that I bought is too small,"의 문장에서 "that"은 관계 대명사이다

rel·a·tiv·i·ty /ˌrɛləˈtɪvəti/ *n* [U] **1** TECHNICAL the relationship between time, space, and movement, which changes with increased speed ‖ 속도가 증가하여 변하는 시간·공간·운동 사이의 관계. 관련성. 상관성. 상대성: *Einstein's theory of **relativity*** 아인슈타인의 상대성 이론 **2** the state of being RELATIVE ‖ 상대적인 상태. 상대성

re·lax /rɪˈlæks/ *v* **1** [I, T] to become more calm and less worried, or to make someone do this ‖ 더 조용해지고 덜 걱정하다, 또는 사람에게 이렇게 하게 하다. 편히 쉬(게 하)다. 편하게 하다: *It's hard to **relax** after work.* 근무 후 쉬기란 어렵다. / *The whiskey **relaxed** me.* 그 위스키가 나를 편안하게 했다. **2** [I, T] if a part of your body relaxes or you relax it, it becomes less stiff and tight ‖ 신체 부위의 뻣뻣함과 당김이 덜해지다. 긴장이 풀리다. 긴장을 풀다. 근육을 이완하다: *Try to relax your neck.* 목의 긴장을 풀도록 해 봐. / *Let your muscles relax.* 근육의 긴장을 풀어라. **3** [T] to make rules, controls etc. less strict ‖ 규칙·통제 등을 덜 엄격하게 하다. 완화하다: *relaxing the immigration laws* 이민법을 완화하기

re·lax·a·tion /ˌrilæk'seɪʃən/ *n* **1** [C, U] the state of being relaxed in your mind and body, or the process of becoming this way ‖ 마음과 몸이 편안한 상태, 또는 이렇게 되는 과정. 휴식. 이완: *Make time for exercise and relaxation.* 운동과 휴식에 시간을 할애해라. / *relaxation of the back muscles* 등 근육의 이완 **2** [U] the process of making rules, controls etc. less strict ‖ 규칙·통제 등을 덜 엄격하게 하는 과정. 완화: *the relaxation of travel restrictions* 여행 제한의 완화

re·lay¹ /'rileɪ, rɪ'leɪ/ *v* [T] **1** to pass a message from one person or place to another ‖ 한 사람이나 장소에서 다른 사람이나 장소로 메시지를 전하다: *Could you relay the message to Mary for me?* 나 대신 메리에게 메시지를 전해 주시겠습니까? **2** to send out a radio or television signal ‖ 라디오나 텔레비전의 신호를 보내다. 중계하다. 중계로 보내다

relay² /'rileɪ/ also **relay race** /'.. ../ *n* a race in which each member of a team runs or swims part of the distance ‖ 팀의 각 구성원이 일정한 거리의 일부를 달리거나 수영하는 경주. 릴레이 경주

re·lease¹ /rɪ'lis/ *v* [T] **1** to let someone be free after keeping him/her as a prisoner ‖ 누구를 죄수로 가두었다가 자유롭게 하다. 석방하다: *Three hostages were released this morning.* 3명의 인질이 오늘 아침 석방되었다. **2** to stop holding something ‖ 무엇을 더 이상 잡지 않다. 풀어 주다: *He released her arm when she screamed.* 그는 그녀가 소리치자 그녀의 팔을 풀어 주었다. **3** to let news or information be known publicly ‖ 소식이나 정보를 공개적으로 알려지게 하다. 공표[공개]하다: *Details of the crime have not been released.* 그 범죄의 상세한 내용은 알려지지 않았다. **4** to make a movie or record available for people to buy or see ‖ 영화나 레코드를 사람들이 사거나 볼 수 있게 하다. 개봉하다. 발매하다: *Simon has released a new album.* 사이먼은 새 앨범을 발매했다. **5** to allow a patient to leave a hospital ‖ 환자에게 병원을 떠나도록 허용하다. 퇴원을 허락하다

release² *n* **1** [singular] the act of releasing (RELEASE) someone ‖ 남을 석방함. 석방. 방면: *After his release from prison, he worked as a carpenter.* 감옥에서 석방된 후에 그는 목수로 일했다. **2** a new movie or record that is available for people to see or buy ‖ 사람들이 보거나 살 수 있는 새 영화나 레코드[음반]. 개봉 영화. 신발매 음반: *the singer's latest release* 그 가수의 최신 음반 **3** [U] a feeling that you are free from worry or pain ‖ 걱정이나 고통에서 자유로운 감정. 감정의 해방: *a sense of emotional release* 정서적 해방감 —see also PRESS RELEASE

rel·e·gate /'rɛləˌgeɪt/ *v* [T] FORMAL to make someone or something less important than before ‖ 이전보다 사람이나 사물을 덜 중요하게 만들다. 좌천시키다. 강등시키다: *He's been relegated to the role of assistant.* 그는 보좌역으로 좌천되었다.

re·lent /rɪ'lɛnt/ *v* [I] to let someone do something that you refused to let him/her do before ‖ 전에는 남에게 허용하지 않던 것을 허용하다. 마음이 누그러지다[풀어지다]. 관대해지다: *Park officials relented, and allowed campers to stay.* 공원 관리들은 관대해져서 야영객들이 머무는 것을 허용했다.

re·lent·less /rɪ'lɛntlɪs/ *adj* **1** continuous and strong ‖ 계속적이고 강한. 심한. 혹독한: *the relentless heat of the desert* 사막의 혹독한 더위 **2** continuing to do something in a determined way ‖ 단호하게 어떤 것을 계속하는. 무자비한. 가혹한: *the lawyer's relentless questioning* 변호사의 가차없는 질문 공세 **– relentlessly** *adv*

rel·e·vance /'rɛləvəns/ also **relevancy** /'rɛləvənsi/ *n* [U] the degree to which something relates to a particular subject or problem ‖ 어떤 것이 특정한 주제나 문제와 관련되는 정도. 관련성: *a statement with no relevance to the issue* 그 문제와 전혀 관련성이 없는 진술 —opposite IRRELEVANCE

rel·e·vant /'rɛləvənt/ *adj* directly relating to the subject or problem being discussed ‖ 논의되고 있는 주제나 문제와 직접적으로 관계가 있는. 관련된. 적절한: *The question is not relevant to my point.* 그 질문은 내 요점과는 관계가 없다. —opposite IRRELEVANT

re·li·a·ble /rɪ'laɪəbəl/ *adj* able to be trusted; DEPENDABLE ‖ 믿을 수 있는. 신뢰[의지]할 수 있는; ⑪ dependable: *a reliable car* 신뢰할 수 있는 차 / *reliable* *financial information* 확실한 금융 정보 – **reliably** *adv* – **reliability** /rɪˌlaɪəˈbɪləti/ *n* [U] —opposite UNRELIABLE

re·li·ance /rɪˈlaɪəns/ *n* [singular, U] the state of being dependent on something ‖ 어떤 것에 의지하고 있는 상태. 의존: *the country's reliance on imported oil* 수입 석유에 대한 그 나라의 의존 상태

re·li·ant /rɪˈlaɪənt/ *adj* **be reliant on/upon** to depend on something or someone ‖ 사물이나 사람에 의존하다: *The country is reliant on foreign aid.* 그 나라는 외국 원조에 의지하고 있다.

rel·ic /ˈrɛlɪk/ *n* an old object or habit that reminds people of the past ‖ 사람들에게 과거를 상기시키는 오래된 물건이나 습관. 유물. 유적. 자취. 잔재: *ancient Roman relics* 고대 로마 유적

re·lief /rɪˈlif/ *n* **1** [singular, U] a feeling of comfort and happiness because something bad did not happen or is finished ‖ 나쁜 일이 일어나지 않았거나 끝난 상태이기 때문에 안심하고 행복한 감정. 안도(감): *It was a relief to know that the children were safe.* 아이들이 안전하다는 것을 알고 안심했다. / *Exams are finally over. What a relief!* 시험이 마침내 끝났어. 이젠 안심이야! **2** [U] the reduction of pain ‖ 고통의 경감. 완화: *a medicine for pain relief* 진통제 **3** [U] money, food, clothing etc. given to people who need them ‖ 필요한 사람들에게 제공하는 돈·음식·옷 등. 구호품. 구호금: *federal relief* (=money from the government) *for farmers* 농민을 위한 정부 구호금 **4** TECHNICAL a raised shape or decoration on a surface ‖ 표면에 도드라진 모양이나 장식. 돋을새김. 양각. 부조(浮彫): *a marble relief* 대리석 부조

relief map /ˌ. ˈ. ˌ/ *n* a map on which mountains, hills etc. are raised ‖ 산·언덕 등이 솟아 있는 지도. 등고선으로 나타낸 기복 지도

re·lieve /rɪˈliv/ *v* [T] **1** to make a pain, problem, bad feeling etc. less severe ‖ 고통·문제·나쁜 감정 등을 덜 심하게 하다. 경감[완화]시키다: *The county is building a new school to relieve overcrowding.* 그 군은 과밀 학급을 완화시키기 위해 새 교사(校舍)를 짓고 있다. / *We tried to relieve the boredom/tension by singing.* 우리는 노래를 불러서 지루함[긴장감]을 완화시키려 했다. **2** to replace someone else at a job or duty when s/he is finished for the day ‖ 하루의 근무시간이 끝난 경우에 임무 문

에 다른 사람을 교체하다. 교대하다: *The guards are relieved at six o'clock.* 보초는 6시에 교대된다. **3 relieve yourself** a polite expression meaning to URINATE ‖ 오줌을 누다를 뜻하는 완곡한 표현

relieve sb of sth *phr v* [T] FORMAL to help someone by carrying something heavy or by doing something difficult for him/her ‖ 무거운 물건을 옮기거나 어려운 일을 해서 남을 돕다. …에게서 (괴로움·고통 등을) 덜어 주다[제거하다]

re·lieved /rɪˈlivd/ *adj* feeling happy because something bad did not happen or is finished ‖ 나쁜 일이 일어나지 않거나 끝나서 기뻐하는. 안심하는. 안도하는: *I was relieved to be out of the hospital.* 나는 병원을 퇴원해서 안심했다. / *We were relieved that Brian was home safe.* 우리는 브라이언이 집에 무사히 돌아와서 안심했다.

re·li·gion /rɪˈlɪdʒən/ *n* [C, U] a belief in one or more gods and the activities relating to this belief, or a particular system of belief ‖ 유일신이나 또는 다신에 대한 믿음과 이 믿음에 관련된 활동, 또는 특정한 믿음 체계. 종교: *the study of religion* 종교 연구 / *the Muslim religion* 이슬람교

re·li·gious /rɪˈlɪdʒəs/ *adj* **1** relating to religion ‖ 종교와 관련된. 종교의. 종교적인: *religious beliefs* 종교적 믿음 **2** believing strongly in your religion and obeying its rules ‖ 종교를 열렬하게 믿고 그 종교 규칙을 따르는. 신앙심이 깊은. 독실한: *a very religious woman* 독실한 여성

re·li·gious·ly /rɪˈlɪdʒəsli/ *adv* **1** regularly and thoroughly or completely ‖ 규칙적이고 철저하거나 완전하게. 어김 없이: *He exercises religiously.* 그는 규칙적으로 운동한다. **2** in a way that is related to religion ‖ 종교와 관련된 방식으로. 종교적으로

re·lin·quish /rɪˈlɪŋkwɪʃ/ *v* [T] FORMAL to give up your position, power, rights etc. ‖ 지위·권력·권리 등을 포기하다. 단념하다: *The party refused to relinquish power.* 그 당은 권력을 포기하지 않았다.

rel·ish¹ /ˈrɛlɪʃ/ *v* [T] to enjoy something or like it ‖ 어떤 것을 즐기거나 좋아하다. 음미하다: *Jamie didn't relish the idea of getting up early.* 제이미는 일찍 일어난다는 점이 마음에 들지 않았다.

rel·ish² *n* **1** [C, U] a cold SAUCE eaten especially with meat to add taste ‖ 맛을 더하기 위해 특히 고기와 함께 먹는 차가운 소스. 렐리시: *pickle relish* 피클 렐리시 **2** [U] great enjoyment of something ‖ 어

떤 것을 대단히 즐김. 음미: *Barry ate with great relish.* 배리는 아주 맛있게 먹었다.

re·live /ˌriˈlɪv/ *v* [T] to experience something again that happened in past times, or to remember it clearly ‖ 과거에 일어난 일을 다시 체험하다, 또는 그것을 명확하게 기억하다: *Tarrant was forced to relive the experience by watching it on film.* 태런트는 영화로 그것을 봄으로써 어쩔 수 없이 그 경험을 다시 떠올리게 되었다.

re·lo·cate /riˈloʊˌkeɪt/ *v* [I, T] to move to a new place ‖ 새 장소로 옮기다. 이전하다[시키다]: *Our company relocated to the West Coast.* 우리 회사는 서부 해안으로 이전했다. **– relocation** /ˌrilouˈkeɪʃən/ *n* [U]

re·luc·tant /rɪˈlʌktənt/ *adj* unwilling and slow to do something ‖ 어떤 일 하는 것에 마음이 내키지 않거나 느리게 하는. 꺼리는. 마지못해 하는: *She was very reluctant to ask for help.* 그녀는 도움 청하는 것을 매우 꺼려했다. **– reluctance** *n* [singular, U] **– reluctantly** *adv*

re·ly /rɪˈlaɪ/ *v*

rely on/upon sb/sth *phr v* [T] to trust or depend on someone or something ‖ 사람이나 사물을 신뢰하거나 의지하다: *We're relying on him to help.* 우리는 그가 도와줄 것으로 믿고 있어요.

re·main /rɪˈmeɪn/ *v* [I] **1** to continue to be in the same state or condition ‖ 같은 상태나 조건에 계속 처해 있다. 계속 …이다. 여전히 …의 상태로 있다: *The communist party remains in power.* 공산당이 여전히 정권을 쥐고 있다. / *Veltman remained silent.* 벨트만은 여전히 침묵하고 있었다. **2** to continue to exist after others have gone or been destroyed ‖ 다른 것들이 사라지거나 파괴된 후에 계속 존재하다. 남아 있다: *Only half the statue remains.* 그 동상은 절반만 남아 있다. **3 it remains to be seen** used when it is still uncertain whether something will happen ‖ 어떤 일이 일어날지 아직 확실하지 않을 때에 쓰여. 두고 보아야 하다. 확신할 수 없다: *It remains to be seen whether the operation was successful.* 그 수술이 성공할지는 두고 보아야 한다. **4** FORMAL to stay in the same place or position without moving or leaving ‖ 움직이거나 떠나지 않고 같은 장소나 위치에 머물다: *He remained in his office, unwilling to speak to anyone.* 그는 누구에게도 말하려고 하지 않은 채 자기 사무실에 머물렀다. **—see also** REMAINS

re·main·der /rɪˈmeɪndɚ/ *n* **the remainder (of sth)** the rest of something after everything else has gone or been dealt with ‖ 다른 모든 것이 사라지거나 처리된 후의 나머지. 잔여물. 남아 있는 것: *the remainder of the semester* 그 학기의 나머지 기간

re·main·ing /rɪˈmeɪnɪŋ/ *adj* having been left when other similar things or people have gone or been dealt with ‖ 다른 비슷한 사물이나 사람이 사라지거나 처리된 후에 남겨진. 남아 있는. 남은: *The remaining puppies were given away.* 남아 있는 강아지들은 나눠 주었다.

re·mains /rɪˈmeɪnz/ *n* [plural] **1** the parts of something that are left after the rest has been destroyed ‖ 어떤 것이 파괴되고 남아 있는 부분. 유물. 유적: *We visited the remains of the temple.* 우리는 그 절의 유적을 구경하러 갔다. **2** FORMAL a person's body after s/he has died ‖ 사후의 시체. 유해

re·make /ˈrimeɪk/ *n* a movie or song that has the same story as one that was made before ‖ 과거에 제작된 것과 같은 줄거리로 된 영화나 노래. 영화·곡의 개작판. 리메이크: *a remake of "The Wizard of Oz"* "오즈의 마법사"의 개작판 **– remake** /riˈmeɪk/ *v* [T]

re·mark¹ /rɪˈmɑrk/ *n* something that you say ‖ 말하는 것. 의견. 견해: *Carl made a sarcastic remark.* 칼은 비꼬는 말을 했다.

remark² *v* [T] to say something ‖ 어떤 것을 말하다. 언급하다: *One woman remarked that Galen was handsome.* 한 여자가 갈렌이 잘 생겼다고 말했다.

remark on/upon sth *phr v* [T] to notice that something has happened and to say something about it ‖ 일이 일어난 것을 알아차리고 그것에 대해 말하다. …에 대해 한 마디 하다. 촌평하다: *Everyone remarked on the new carpet.* 저마다 그 새 카펫에 관해 한 마디씩 했다.

re·mar·ka·ble /rɪˈmɑrkəbəl/ *adj* very unusual or noticeable in a way that deserves attention or praise ‖ 관심이나 칭찬을 받을 정도로 매우 유별나거나 눈에 띄는. 주목할 만한: *He called Gorbachev "one of the most remarkable men in history."* 그는 고르바초프를 "역사상 가장 뛰어난 위인 중의 한 사람"이라고 말했다.

re·mar·ka·bly /rɪˈmɑrkəbli/ *adv* in an amount or to a degree that is surprising ‖ 놀랄만한 크기나 정도로. 대단히: *Charlotte and her cousin look remarkably similar.* 샬럿과 그녀의 사촌은 대단히 비슷해 보인다.

re·marry /ri'mæri/ *v* [I, T] to marry again || 다시 결혼하다. 재혼하다[시키다]: *He's been divorced and remarried several times.* 그는 여러 번 이혼하고 재혼했다. – **remarriage** *n* [C, U]

re·me·di·al /rɪ'midiəl/ *adj* **1 remedial class/education etc.** a special class etc. for students who are having difficulty learning something || 무엇을 배우는 데에 어려움을 겪는 학생들을 위한 특별 반. 보충[강화] 학습반/교육 **2** FORMAL intended to provide a cure or improvement in something || 무엇을 치료하거나 개선시키려는. 치료[교정]해 주는: *remedial exercises for a weak back* 허약한 허리교정 운동

rem·e·dy¹ /'rɛmədi/ *n* **1** a successful way of dealing with a problem || 문제를 다루는 성공적인 방법. 구제(책). 개선 방법: *an economic remedy for unemployment* 실업의 경제적인 해결책 **2** a medicine that cures pain or illness || 고통이나 병을 고치는 약. 치료약: *an excellent remedy for teething pain* 이가 나올 때의 통증에 대한 탁월한 치료약

remedy² *v* [T] to deal successfully with a problem or improve a bad situation || 문제를 성공적으로 해결하거나 나쁜 상황을 개선하다. 바로잡다. 고치다: *The hospital is trying to remedy the problem.* 병원은 그 문제를 개선하려고 노력 중이다.

re·mem·ber /rɪ'mɛmbɚ/ *v* **1** [I, T] to have a picture or idea in your mind of people, events etc. from the past || 과거의 사람·사건 등에 대해 마음속에 이미지나 생각을 가지다. 기억하다: *Do you remember the first job you ever had?* 전에 네가 처음으로 가졌던 직업을 기억하니? / *Mr. Daniels has lived there for as long as I can remember.* 내 기억으로는 다니엘 씨 가족들이 그곳에 살았다. **2** [I, T] to bring information or facts that you know back into your mind || 아는 정보나 사실을 되생각해 내다. 상기하다: *She suddenly remembered (that) she had to go to the dentist.* 그녀는 치과에 가야 한다는 사실이 갑자기 떠올랐다. / *Can you remember her name?* 그녀의 이름이 기억나니? **3** [I, T] to not forget to do something || 무엇을 하는 것을 잊지 않다. 염두에 두다. 기억하고 있다: *Remember to get some milk at the store today!* 오늘 잊지 말고 가게에서 우유를 좀 사라! — compare REMIND **4** [T] to think about someone who has died, with special respect and honor || 특별한 존경과 경의를 가지고 죽은 사람을 생각하다. 기리다:

remembering those who fought in Korea 한국 참전 용사를 기리며 **5 be remembered for/as sth** to be famous for something important that you did || 자신이 한 중요한 일로 유명하다: *She'll be remembered as one of the best female athletes of the decade.* 그녀는 10년간의 가장 훌륭한 여자 선수 중 한 명으로 이름을 얻을 것이다. / *He is remembered for his achievements in the world of quantum physics.* 그는 양자 물리학계에서 이룩한 업적으로 유명하다.

USAGE NOTE remember and remind

Use **remember** to say that you are the one who is remembering something: *Do you remember that guy we met at the party? / I can't remember how much I paid for it. / He suddenly remembered he had to go to the bank.* Use **remind** to say that it is someone or something else that is making you remember something: *Doesn't she remind you of Nicole? / Please remind me to call him later today.* ✗DON'T SAY "remember me to call him."✗ 자신이 어떤 것을 기억하고 있는 사람임을 말하는 데에 **remember**를 쓴다: 우리가 파티에서 만난 그 남자 기억하니? / 그것에 얼마를 지불했는지 기억이 안 나요. / 그는 은행에 가야 한다는 사실이 문득 떠올랐다. 다른 사람이나 사물이 자신에게 어떤 것을 기억나게 한다고 말하는 데에 **remind**를 쓴다: 그녀를 보면 너는 니콜이 생각나지 않니? / 오늘 늦게 그에게 전화하라고 저에게 일러 주세요. "remember me to call him." 이라고 하지 않는다.

---

re·mem·brance /rɪ'mɛmbrəns/ *n* the act of remembering and giving honor to someone who has died || 죽은 사람을 기억하거나 경의를 표함. 기억. 회상. 추도: *She planted a tree in remembrance of her husband.* 그녀는 남편을 추도하여 나무 한 그루를 심었다.

re·mind /rɪ'maɪnd/ *v* [T] **1** to make someone remember something that s/he must do || 남에게 해야 할 일을 기억나게 하다. 생각나게 하다. 일깨워 주다. 상기시키다: *Remind me to stop by the post office.* 잊지 말고 우체국에 들르라고 저에게 일러 주세요. **2 remind sb of** to make someone remember someone or something from past times || 남에게 과거의 사람이나 일을 기억나게 하다. …에게 …을 상기시키다: *Wendy reminds me of*

(=looks or acts like) *her mother*. 웬디를 보면 나는 그녀의 어머니가 생각난다. — see usage note at REMEMBER

re·mind·er /rɪ'maɪndə/ *n* something that makes you notice or remember something else ‖ 다른 것을 알아차리거나 기억나게 하는 것. 생각나게 하는 사람[것]. 추억: *The photos were a painful reminder of his first wife.* 그 사진들은 그의 첫 부인을 생각나게 하는 가슴 아픈 추억이었다.

rem·i·nisce /ˌrɛmə'nɪs/ *v* [I] to talk or think about pleasant events in your past ‖ 과거의 즐거운 일들을 이야기하거나 생각하다. 즐겁게 회상하다: *Petty sat reminiscing about the old days of rock 'n' roll.* 페티는 앉아서 옛날의 로큰롤 시대를 즐겁게 회상하고 있었다. – **reminiscence** *n* [C, U]

rem·i·nis·cent /ˌrɛmə'nɪsənt/ *adj* **reminiscent of sth** reminding you of something ‖ 어떤 것을 생각나게 하는. …을 회상하게 하는. 연상시키는: *His voice is reminiscent of Frank Sinatra's.* 그의 목소리는 프랭크 시내트라의 목소리를 생각나게 한다.

re·miss /rɪ'mɪs/ *adj* FORMAL careless about doing something that you ought to do ‖ 해야 하는 일을 하는 데에 부주의한. 태만한. 성의 없는: *The nurses were accused of being remiss in their duties.* 그 간호사들은 업무 태만죄로 고발당했다.

re·mis·sion /rɪ'mɪʃən/ *n* [C, U] a period of time when an illness improves ‖ 병이 나아지는 시기. 회복. 진정: *Her cancer is in remission.* 그녀의 암은 회복 상태에 있다.

re·mit /rɪ'mɪt/ *v* **-tted, -tting** [I, T] FORMAL to send a payment by mail ‖ 우편으로 지불 금액을 보내다. 송금하다

re·mit·tance /rɪ'mɪtˌns/ *n* [C, U] FORMAL the act of sending money by mail, or the amount of money that is sent ‖ 우편으로 돈을 보냄, 또는 보낸 돈의 액수. 송금. 송금액

rem·nant /'rɛmnənt/ *n* a small part of something that remains after the rest has been used or destroyed ‖ 어떤 것이 사용되거나 파괴된 후에 남는 작은 부분. 잔여. 유물. 자취: *the remnants of a 14th century castle* 14세기 성의 자취

re·mod·el /ˌri'madl/ *v* [T] to change the shape or appearance of something ‖ 어떤 것의 모양이나 모습을 바꾸다. …의 형을 바꾸다. 개조하다: *We've had the kitchen remodeled.* 우리는 부엌을 개조했다.

rem·on·strate /'rɛmənˌstreɪt,

rɪ'man,streɪt/ *v* [I] FORMAL to tell someone that you strongly disapprove of what s/he has done ‖ 남이 한 일에 강력하게 반대한다고 말하다. 항의하다. 이의를 제기하다

re·morse /rɪ'mɔrs/ *n* [U] a strong feeling of being sorry for doing something very bad ‖ 매우 나쁜 일을 한 것에 대해 미안해하는 격한 감정. 깊은 후회. 양심의 가책: *Keating showed no remorse for his crime.* 키팅은 자신의 범죄에 전혀 뉘우침을 보이지 않았다. – **remorseful** *adj* – **remorseless** *adj*

re·mote /rɪ'moʊt/ *adj* **1** far away in distance or time ‖ 거리나 시간이 멀리 떨어진. 먼: *a remote planet* 멀리 떨어진 행성 / *the remote past* 먼 과거 **2** very slight or small ‖ 아주 적거나 작은. 희박한. 미약한: *There's a remote possibility/chance that the operation will not work.* 그 작동이 안 될 가능성[기회]은 거의 없다. **3** very different from something else, or not closely related to it ‖ 다른 것과 아주 다른, 또는 그것과 긴밀히 관련되지 않은. 동떨어진: *subjects that are remote from everyday life* 일상 생활과 동떨어진 주제들 – **remoteness** *n*

remote ac·cess /.ˌ. '../ *n* [U] a system that allows you to use information on a computer that is far away from your computer ‖ 자신의 컴퓨터에서 멀리 떨어typed 컴퓨터 상의 정보를 이용할 수 있게 해주는 시스템. 원격 접속 (기능)

remote con·trol /.ˌ. .'./, also **remote** *n* a piece of equipment that you use to control a radio, television, toy etc. from a distance ‖ 멀리서 라디오·텔레비전·장난감 등을 조종하기 위해 사용하는 기구. 리모트 컨트롤 – **remote-controlled** *adj*: *a remote-controlled airplane* 원격 조종 비행기

re·mote·ly /rɪ'moʊtli/ *adv* used in order to emphasize a negative statement ‖ 부정어를 강조하는 데에 쓰여. 아주 조금. 관계가 별로 없어: *The two situations are not even remotely similar.* 그 두 상황은 아주 조금도 비슷하지 않다.

remote work·ing /.ˌ. '../ *n* [U] a situation in which people do their work at home, using a computer that is connected to the computer system in an office ‖ 사람들이 사무실의 컴퓨터와 연결된 컴퓨터를 이용해 집에서 일을 하는 상황. 원격[재택] 근무

re·mov·a·ble /rɪ'muvəbəl/ *adj* able to

be removed ‖ 제거할 수 있는. 떼어낼 수 있는: *a table with a removable middle* 중앙을 떼어낼 수 있는 테이블

re·mov·al /rɪ'muvəl/ n [C, U] the act of removing something ‖ 어떤 것을 제거함. 제거. 철수: *the removal of foreign troops from the country* 그 나라에서 외국 군대의 철수

re·move /rɪ'muv/ v [T] **1** to take something away from, out of, or off the place where it is ‖ 물건을 그 물건이 있는 장소에서 치우다[꺼내다, 없애다]. …을 옮기다[이동시키다]. 제거하다: *Remove the pan from the oven to cool.* 오븐에서 냄비를 꺼내 식혀라. / *The old paint will have to be removed first.* 오래된 페인트를 먼저 제거해야 하겠다. **2** to end something such as a problem, law, system etc. ‖ 문제·법률·제도 등을 끝내다. 제거하다: *The threat of a world war had been removed.* 세계 전쟁의 위협이 제거되었다. **3 be (far) removed from sth** to be very different from something else ‖ 다른 일과 매우 다르다. …과 동떨어지다: *This job is far removed from anything that I've done before.* 이 일은 내가 전에 했던 일과는 동떨어진 것이다. **4** to make someone leave a job ‖ 어떤 사람을 일자리에서 떠나게 하다. (지위·공직에서) 면직[해임, 해고]하다: *The Mayor has been removed from office.* 그 시장은 공직에서 해임되었다.

re·mov·er /rɪ'muvɚ/ n [C, U] **paint/stain etc. remover** a substance that removes paint etc. from something else ‖ 다른 물체에서 페인트 등을 제거하는 물질. 페인트/얼룩 제거제

re·mu·ner·ate /rɪ'myunəˌreɪt/ v [T] FORMAL to pay someone for something s/he has done ‖ 남이 한 일에 대해 대가를 지불하다. 보수를 지불하다. 사례하다 – **remuneration** /rɪˌmyunə'reɪʃən/ n [C, U]

Ren·ais·sance /'rɛnəˌzɑns, -ˌsɑns, ˌrɛnə'sɑns/ n **1 the Renaissance** the time in Europe between the 14th and 17th centuries when a lot of new art and literature was produced ‖ 많은 신예술과 문학이 만들어진 14세기와 17세기 사이의 유럽 역사 시기. 르네상스. 문예 부흥(기) **2** [singular] a new interest or development in something that has not been popular ‖ 인기가 없는 것의 새로운 관심이나 발달. 부흥. 부활: *a jazz renaissance* 재즈의 부흥

re·name /ri'neɪm/ v [T] to change the name of something ‖ 어떤 것의 이름을 바꾸다. …을 개명(改名)하다: *They*

renamed the airport in honor of President Kennedy. 그들은 케네디 대통령을 기리기 위해 공항에 새 이름을 붙였다.

rend /rɛnd/ v **rent, rent, rending** [T] LITERARY to tear or break something into pieces ‖ 어떤 것을 찢거나 깨뜨려 조각을 내다. …을 박살내다. 분쇄하다

ren·der /'rɛndɚ/ v [T] FORMAL **1** to give someone something ‖ 남에게 어떤 것을 주다. (사물을) 주다. 하다: *The management discussed the issue before rendering a decision.* 경영층은 결정을 내리기 전에 그 쟁점을 논의했다. / *payment for services rendered* (=for work someone has done) 능률급 **2** to cause someone or something to be in a particular state ‖ 사람이나 사물을 특수한 상태로 되게 하다. …을 …으로 만들다: *The accident rendered her left leg useless.* 그 사고는 그녀의 왼쪽 다리를 못 쓰게 만들었다. **3** to express or present something in a particular way ‖ 어떤 것을 특정하게 표현하거나 제시하다. 나타내다. 보이다: *In her paintings she renders feelings by using specific colors.* 그녀는 자신의 그림에 독특한 색깔을 사용하여 감정을 나타낸다.

ren·der·ing /'rɛndərɪŋ/ n the particular way a painting, story etc. is expressed ‖ 그림·이야기 등이 표현되는 특별한 방식. 묘사. 표현. 연출. 연주: *Coppola's rendering of the Dracula story* 코폴라의 드라큘라 이야기 연출

ren·dez·vous¹ /'rɑndeɪˌvu, -dɪ-/ n, plural **rendezvous** an arrangement to meet someone at a particular time and place, or the place where you meet ‖ 특정한 시간·장소에서 어떤 사람을 만날 예정, 또는 그 만나는 장소. 만나기. 만나는 장소: *The rendezvous is set for Central Park.* 만나는 장소는 센트럴 파크로 정해져 있다.

rendezvous² v [I] to meet someone at a particular place and time ‖ 특정한 장소·시간에서 어떤 사람을 만나다. 회동하다: *The boat rendezvoused with two others near Cuba.* 그 배는 쿠바 근해에서 다른 배 두 척과 만났다.

ren·di·tion /rɛn'dɪʃən/ n [U] the way that a play, piece of music, art etc. is performed or made ‖ 연극·음악·미술 등이 공연되거나 제작되는 방식. 연출[연주]. 표현: *a wonderful rendition of "Turandot"* 훌륭한 "Turandot"의 연출

ren·e·gade /'rɛnəˌgeɪd/ n someone who joins an opposing side in a war, political or religious organization etc. ‖

전쟁이나 정치 단체 또는 종교 단체 등에서 반대편에 합류하는 사람. 변절자. 배반자. 배교자(背敎者). 반역자 **– renegade** *adj* : *renegade soldiers* 반역 군인들

re·nege /rɪˈnɛg, -ˈnɪg/ *v* [I] to not do something that you promised to do ‖ 하기로 약속했던 어떤 것을 하지 않다. (약속을)어기다: *The company claims that the city reneged on the deal/promise.* 그 회사는 시 당국이 거래[약속]를 어겼다고 주장했다.

re·new /rɪˈnu/ *v* [T] **1** to arrange for a contract, official document etc. to continue ‖ 계약·공적 문서 등이 계속되도록 준비하다. 기한을 연장하다. 갱신하다: *It's time to renew our insurance.* 우리의 보험을 갱신해야 할 시기이다. **2** to begin to do something again ‖ 다시 어떤 것을 하기 시작하다. …을 재개하다: *Congress renewed its demand for tax cuts.* 의회는 세금 삭감에 대한 요구를 재개했다. **3** to give someone new strength ‖ 어떤 사람에게 새로운 힘을 주다. 부활시키다. 회복하다 **– renewal** *n* [C, U]

re·new·a·ble /rɪˈnuəbəl/ *adj* **1** able to be replaced by natural processes so that it is never used up ‖ 결코 고갈되지 않도록 자연적인 과정에 의해 보전될 수 있는. (자원 등이) 재생 가능한: *a renewable energy source* 재생 가능한 에너지원(源) **2** a renewable contract, ticket etc. can be made to continue after the date that it is supposed to end ‖ 계약·티켓 등이 만료 예정 기간 뒤에 다시 기한을 연장할 수 있는. 갱신 가능한 **—opposite** NONRENEWABLE

re·newed /rɪˈnud/ *adj* increasing again after not being very strong ‖ 그렇게 강하지 않은 상태 뒤에 다시 증가하는[강해지는]. 새롭게 된. 회복[부흥]된: *Kathleen began her paper again with renewed energy/interest.* 캐슬린은 기운을 회복하여[흥미를 일으켜] 그녀의 과제물을 다시 시작했다.

re·nounce /rɪˈnaʊns/ *v* [T] **1** to say publicly that you will no longer try to keep something, or will not stay in an important position ‖ 어떤 것을 더 이상 지키려고 하지 않겠다거나 중요한 직위에 남아 있지 않겠다는 것을 공개적으로 말하다. 단념[포기]하다. 사퇴[사임]하다: *Grayson renounced his claim to the family fortune.* 그레이슨은 가족의 재산에 대한 그의 권리를 포기했다. **2** to say publicly that you no longer believe in or support an idea, religion etc. ‖ 어떤 사상·종교 등을 더 이상 믿거나 지지하지 않음을 공개적으로 말하다. 버리다. 거부[부

인]하다: *He renounced his faith in Judaism.* 그는 유대교의 신앙을 버렸다.

ren·o·vate /ˈrɛnəˌveɪt/ *v* [T] to repair something such as building so that it is in good condition again ‖ 다시 양호한 상태가 되도록 건물 등을 수리하다. …을 다시 새롭게 하다. 쇄신[혁신]하다. …을 수선하다 **– renovation** /ˌrɛnəˈveɪʃən/ *n* [C, U]

re·nowned /rɪˈnaʊnd/ *adj* famous for a special skill or for something that you have done ‖ 특별한 기술이나 자기가 성취한 일로 유명한. 명성 있는: *a renowned singer of the late 19th century* 19세기 후반의 유명한 가수 **– renown** *n* [U]

rent¹ /rɛnt/ *v* **1** [I, T] to pay money regularly to live in a place that belongs to someone else ‖ 다른 사람이 소유한 장소에서 살기 위해 정기적으로 돈을 지불하다. 임차하다. 세를 얻다: *They're renting an apartment near the beach.* 그들은 해변 가에 있는 아파트에 세 들어 있다. / *We'll rent for six months.* 우리는 6개월간 세를 얻을 것이다. **2** [T] to pay money for the use of something for a short period of time ‖ 단기간 동안 어떤 것의 사용에 대한 대가로 돈을 지불하다. 사용료[임차료]를 내고 쓰다: *rent a movie/car* 영화[자동차]를 임차하다 **3** [T] also **rent sth ↔ out** to let someone live in a place that you own in return for money ‖ 돈을 대가로 받고 자기 소유의 장소에 사람이 살게 허락하다. 임대하다. 세를 놓다: *They've rented out their house for the summer.* 그들은 여름 동안 집을 세 놓았다. **– renter** *n*

rent² *n* [C, U] **1** the amount of money you pay for the use of a house, room, car etc. that belongs to someone else ‖ 다른 사람 소유의 집·방·차 등의 사용 대가로 지불하는 금액. 임차료. 집세. 방세: *Office rents are very high here.* 이곳의 사무실 임차료는 매우 높다. **2 for rent** available to be rented ‖ 빌릴 수 있는. 임대용의

rental¹ /ˈrɛntl/ *n* **1** [C, U] an arrangement by which you rent something ‖ 어떤 것을 빌릴 수 있는 제도. 임대[임차]: *a video rental store* 비디오 임대 가게 **2** [U] the money that you pay to rent something ‖ 어떤 것을 빌리려고 지불하는 돈. 임대료. 사용료: *Ski rental is $14.* 스키 임대료는 14달러이다.

rental² *adj* available to be rented or being rented ‖ 빌릴 수 있는 또는 빌린. 임대의: *a rental car* 임대차 / *rental properties* 임대용 재산

rent con·trol /ˈ. ˌ./ *n* [U] a situation

in which a city or state uses laws to limit the price of renting apartments ‖ 시 당국 또는 주 정부가 법률을 행사하여 임대 아파트의 가격을 제한하는 상태. (정부의) 집세 통제

re·nun·ci·a·tion /rɪˌnʌnsiˈeɪʃən/ n [C, U] FORMAL the act of renouncing (RENOUNCE) something ‖ 어떤 것을 포기하는 행위. 부인[거부]

re·or·ga·nize /riˈɔrgəˌnaɪz/ v [I, T] to arrange or organize something in a new and better way ‖ 어떤 것을 새롭고 더 낫게 배열하거나 조직하다. 재조직하다. 재편[재건]하다: *The filing system needs to be reorganized.* 서류 분류 체계는 재정비되어야 한다. – **reorganization** /riˌɔrgənəˈzeɪʃən/ n [U]

rep /rɛp/ n **1** INFORMAL someone who represents an organization or a company and its products; representative ‖ 단체나 회사와 그 제품을 대표하는 사람. 대리인. 대표. 외판원; 대표자: *a sales rep* 세일즈맨[판매 대리인, 외판원] **2** SLANG ⇨ REPUTATION

re·pair¹ /rɪˈpɛr/ n **1** [C usually plural, U] something that you do to fix something that is broken or damaged ‖ 고장 나거나 파손된 것을 고치기 위해 하는 일. 수리. 수선: *They're doing repairs on the bridge.* 그들은 다리를 수리하고 있다. / *The car's in the shop for repair.* 그 차는 수리를 위해 공장에 들어가 있다. **2 in good/bad repair** in good or bad condition ‖ (정비·보수·유지·손질이)잘된[나쁜] 상태에 있는. 정비가 양호한/불량한: *The roads are in good repair.* 그 도로는 보수가 잘되어 있다.

repair² v [T] to fix something that is broken or damaged ‖ 고장 나거나 파손된 어떤 것을 고치다. 수리[수선]하다: *I have to get the TV repaired.* 나는 텔레비전을 수리해야 한다.

re·pair·man /rɪˈpɛrmən/ n someone whose job is to fix a particular type of thing ‖ 특정한 유형의 물건을 수리하는 직업인. 수리공: *a TV repairman* 텔레비전 수리공

rep·a·ra·tion /ˌrɛpəˈreɪʃən/ n [C, U] FORMAL payment made to someone for damage, injury etc. that you have caused ‖ 어떤 사람에게 자신이 일으킨 파손·상해에 대해 지불하는 것. 보상. 배상

re·pa·tri·ate /riˈpeɪtriˌeɪt/ v [T] to send someone or something back to the country he, she, or it comes from ‖ 사람이나 물건을 본국으로 돌려보내다. (포로 등을) 본국으로 송환하다[귀환시키다] – **repatriation** /riˌpeɪtriˈeɪʃən/ n [U]

re·pay /rɪˈpeɪ/ v [T] **1** to pay back money that you have borrowed ‖ 꾼 돈을 갚다. 상환하다. 반제하다: *How long will it take to repay the loan?* 그 대출금을 상환하는 데는 얼마나 오래 걸릴까? **2** to show someone that you are grateful for his/her help ‖ 남에게 그 도움에 대해 감사함을 나타내다. 보답하다. 은혜를 갚다: *How can I ever repay you?* 제가 어떻게 보답을 하지요? – **repayment** n [C, U]

re·peal /rɪˈpil/ v [T] to officially end a law ‖ 공식적으로 법률을 폐지하다: *In 1933, Prohibition was finally repealed.* 1933년에 금주법(禁酒法)이 마침내 폐지되었다. – **repeal** n [U]

re·peat¹ /rɪˈpit/ v [T] **1** to say or do something again ‖ 어떤 것을 다시 말하거나 어떤 일을 다시 하다. 반복하다: *Sally kept repeating, "It wasn't me, it wasn't me."* 샐리는 계속 반복해서 "그것은 내가 아니었어요. 그것은 내가 아니었어요."라고 했다. / *You'll have to repeat the class.* 너는 수업을 다시 받아야 할 것이다. **2** to say something that you have heard someone else say ‖ 어떤 사람에게서 들은 내용을 (남에게) 말하다: *Please don't repeat any of this to Bill.* 빌에게는 이것을 조금도 말하지 마세요.

repeat² n **1** an event that is just like something that happened before ‖ 전에 일어났던 일과 똑같은 사건. 되풀이. 반복: *I don't want to see a repeat performance of last year.* (=I do not want something bad to happen again) 나는 지난해의 나쁜 일이 재발되는 것을 보고 싶지 않다. **2** ⇨ RERUN

re·peat·ed /rɪˈpitɪd/ adj done or happening again and again ‖ 반복적으로 하거나 발생한. 되풀이된. 자주 있는: *Repeated attempts to fix the satellite have failed.* 위성을 고치려는 반복된 시도들이 실패로 끝났다. – **repeatedly** adv

re·pel /rɪˈpɛl/ v **-lled, -lling 1** [T] if something repels you, it forces you to go away in order to avoid it ‖ 어떤 것이 자신으로 하여금 그것을 피해 멀리 떨어지게 하다. 쫓아버리다. 격퇴하다. 물리치다: *Tear gas was used to repel the rioters.* 최루 가스가 폭도들을 물리치는 데에 사용되었다. **2** [I, T] TECHNICAL if two things repel each other, they push each other away with a MAGNETIC force ‖ 두 개의 물체가 자석의 힘으로 서로를 밀어내다. 반발하다. …을 서로 밀어내다

re·pel·lent¹ /rɪˈpɛlənt/ n [C, U] a substance that keeps insects away from you ‖ 곤충을 가까이 오지 못하게 하는 물질. 방충제: *mosquito repellent* 모기 방충

제

repellent² *adj* extremely unpleasant or nasty ‖ 극도로 불쾌하거나 더러운. 혐오감을 주는. 기분 나쁜: *repellent behavior* 혐오감을 주는 행동

re·pent /rɪˈpɛnt/ *v* [I, T] FORMAL a word meaning to be sorry for something that you have done, used especially by religious people ‖ 특히 교인이 사용하는, 자신이 한 일에 대한 후회스러움을 뜻하는 말. 후회하다. 뉘우치다. 참회하다 –

repentance *n* [U] – **repentant** *adj*

re·per·cus·sion /ˌripəˈkʌʃən/ *n* [C usually plural] the effect that an action or event has, even a long time after it has happened ‖ 어떤 행동이나 사건이 일어난 지 한참 후에도 가지는 영향. 반향. 파문: *Their civil war had international repercussions.* 그들의 내전은 국제적인 반향을 불러일으켰다.

rep·er·toire /ˈrɛpəˌtwɑr/ *n* [C usually singular] all the plays, pieces of music etc. that a performer or group can perform ‖ 연기자나 단체가 공연할 수 있는 모든 연극·음악 등. 공연[연주] 종목 일람. 레퍼토리

rep·e·ti·tion /ˌrɛpəˈtɪʃən/ *n* [C, U] the act of saying or doing the same thing again, or many times ‖ 같은 말이나 행동을 다시, 또는 여러 차례 하는 행위. 되풀이. 반복: *the repetition of old stories* 옛 이야기들의 반복 / *kids learning the times tables by repetition* 암송으로 구구단을 배우고 있는 아이들

rep·e·ti·tious /ˌrɛpəˈtɪʃəs/ *adj* saying or doing the same thing many times, so that people become bored ‖ 사람들이 싫증을 낼 정도로 똑같은 말이나 행동을 여러차례 하는. 자꾸 반복되는. 장황한. 지루한: *a repetitious speech* 지루한 연설

re·pet·i·tive /rɪˈpɛtətɪv/ *adj* done many times in the same way ‖ 같은 방식으로 여러 차례 하는. 되풀이되는. 반복적인: *repetitive exercises* 반복 운동

re·phrase /riˈfreɪz/ *v* [T] to express something in different words so that its meaning is clearer or more acceptable ‖ 어떤 것을 의미가 더 명료하거나 더 쉽게 받아들일 수 있도록 다른 말로 표현하다. …을 고쳐[바꾸어] 말하다: *OK, let me rephrase the question.* 좋아, 그 질문을 다른 말로 물어볼게.

re·place /rɪˈpleɪs/ *v* [T] **1** to start doing something or being used instead of another person or thing ‖ 다른 사람 또는 사물을 대신하여 어떤 것을 하거나 쓰이기 시작하다. …을 대신하다. 후임이 되다: *Val will be replacing Brian as editor.* 밸은 브라이언의 후임으로 편집장이 될 것이다. **2** to buy something that is newer or better in order to use it instead of something that is old or broken ‖ 낡거나 고장 난 사물을 대신하여 사용하기 위해 더 새롭거나 더 좋은 것을 사다. 바꾸다. 새것으로[더 좋은 것으로] 대체하다: *Our VCR isn't working, but we can't afford to replace it.* 우리 VCR은 작동하지 않는다. 그렇지만 우리는 새 것을 살 여유가 없다. **3** to put something back in its correct place ‖ 사물을 제자리에 돌려 놓다. …을 되돌려[원래대로] 놓다: *Please replace the books when you are finished.* 다 읽고 나서 그 책들을 제자리에 돌려놓으세요.

re·place·ment /rɪˈpleɪsmənt/ *n* **1** someone or something that replaces another person or thing ‖ 다른 사람이나 사물을 대신하는 사람 또는 사물. 후계[후임]자. 대리인. 교체[교대]자: *We're waiting for Mr. Dunley's replacement.* 우리는 던리 씨의 후임자를 기다리고 있다. **2** [U] the act of replacing something ‖ 어떤 것을 대체하기. 교체

re·play /ˈripleɪ/ *n* [C, U] an action in a sport that you see on television, that is immediately shown again ‖ 텔레비전으로 곧바로 다시 비쳐 주어 즉시 다시 볼 수 있는 스포츠에서의 경기장면. 즉시 재생 (장면): *On the replay you can see the foul.* 즉시 재생 장면에서는 파울을 확인할 수 있다.

re·plen·ish /rɪˈplɛnɪʃ/ *v* [T] FORMAL to fill something again or make something complete again ‖ 사물을 다시 채우다 또는 다시 완전하게 하다. 보충[보급]하다. 원래대로 가득 채우다: *The charity urgently needs to replenish food supplies.* 그 자선 단체는 긴급하게 식량 부족분을 보충 공급해야 한다. –

replenishment *n* [U]

re·plete /rɪˈplit/ *adj* FORMAL full ‖ 가득 찬. 꽉 찬: *He said the report was "replete with errors."* 그 리포트는 "오류 투성이"였다고 그는 말했다.

rep·li·ca /ˈrɛplɪkə/ *n* a very good copy of a piece of art, a building etc. ‖ 미술품·건물 등을 아주 똑같이 만든 복제품. 모사화. 모조품: *an exact replica of the White House* 백악관의 정교한 모형

rep·li·cate /ˈrɛpləˌkeɪt/ *v* [T] FORMAL to do or make something again, so that you get the same result or make an exact copy ‖ 같은 결과를 얻거나 정확한 복제품을 만들도록 어떤 것을 다시 하거나 만들다. …을 모사[복제]하다: *Scientists are trying to replicate Hudson's*

experiment. 과학자들은 허드슨의 실험을 복원하려고 노력하고 있다. —
replication /ˌrɛplə'keɪʃən/ *n* [C, U]
re·ply¹ /rɪ'plaɪ/ *v* [I, T] to answer someone by saying or writing something ‖ 어떤 것을 말하거나 써서 사람에게 답변하다. …에 대답하다: *"Of course," she replied.* "물론입니다."라고 그녀는 대답했다. / *I haven't replied to his letter yet.* 나는 아직 그의 편지에 답장을 쓰지 못했다. —see usage note at ANSWER¹
reply² *n* [C, U] something that is said, written, or done in order to reply to someone ‖ 다른 사람에게 응답하기 위해 말해진[쓰여진, 행해진] 것. 대답. 회답. 응수. 반응: *There have been no replies to our ad.* 우리 광고에 대한 반응이 없었다. / *Marcy said nothing in reply.* (=as a reply) 마시는 아무런 응답의 말도 하지 않았다.
re·port¹ /rɪ'pɔrt/ *n* **1** a written or spoken description of a situation or event that gives people information ‖ 사람들에게 어떤 상황이나 사건에 대한 정보를 주기 위해 글로 쓰거나 말로 하는 설명. 보고(서): *a police report on the accident* 그 사건에 관한 경찰의 보고(서) / *a weather report* 기상 통보[일기 예보] **2** a piece of writing in which someone carefully examines a particular subject ‖ 어떤 사람이 특정 주제를 주의 깊게 조사하여 쓴 글. 조사[연구] 보고(서). 리포트: *the company's annual report* 회사의 연차 보고서 / *a book report* 독후감 리포트 **3** FORMAL the noise of an explosion or shot ‖ 폭발이나 총격의 큰 소음. 폭발음. 총성
report² *v* **1** [I, T] to tell someone about something, especially in newspapers and on television ‖ 특히 신문·텔레비전에서 어떤 것에 대해 다른 사람에게 말하다. …을 보도하다[전하다]. 기사는 …에 쓰다: *The Daily Gazette reported the story.* 데일리 가제트는 그 이야기를 보도했다. / *Here's Kathy Levy, reporting on the latest developments.* 캐시 레비입니다. 최신 속보를 말씀드리겠습니다. **2** [T] to tell someone in authority that a crime or accident has happened ‖ 범죄나 사고가 발생했다고 당국자에게 말하다. 신고하다: *Who reported the fire?* 누가 그 화재를 신고했지? **3** [T] to complain officially about someone to people in authority ‖ 당국자에게 공식적으로 어떤 사람에 대해 불평하다. …을 …에 일러바치다. 고자질하다: *Somebody reported Kyle for smoking in school.* 카일이 교내에서 흡연했다고 누군가가 고자질했다. **4** [I] to

state officially to someone in authority that you have arrived in a place ‖ 사람이 어떤 장소에 도착했다고 책임자에게 공식적으로 말하다. (도착 등을) 신고[보고]하다: *Visitors must report to the main reception desk.* 방문자는 중앙 접수대에 방문 신청을 해야 합니다. / *One of the soldiers had not reported for duty.* 군인 중 한 명이 임무 복귀 신고를 하지 않았다.
report back *phr v* [I] to bring someone information that s/he asked you to find ‖ 어떤 사람이 알아보라고 요청한 정보를 그 사람에게 가져다 주다. (의뢰자에게) 결과를 보고하다: *The committee reported back to Congress.* 위원회는 의회에 결과를 보고했다.
report card /.'. ,./ *n* a written statement giving a student's grades ‖ 학생의 성적을 알려주는 문서로 된 진술. 성적표. 통지표
re·port·ed·ly /rɪ'pɔrtɪdli/ *adv* according to what people say ‖ 사람들이 말한 것에 따라. 전하는 바에 의하면. 소문에 의하면: *She's reportedly one of the richest women in Europe.* 전하는 말에 의하면 그녀는 유럽에서 가장 부유한 여인 중의 한 명이다.
re·port·ed speech /.,.. '.'./ *n* [U] TECHNICAL in grammar, the style of speech or writing that is used for reporting what someone says, without repeating the actual words. The sentence "She said she didn't feel well" is an example of reported speech ‖ 문법에서 실제로 한 말을 그대로 되풀이하여 말하지 않고 남이 말한 내용을 전하는 데에 사용하는 발언법이나 문장 작성법. 간접 화법. 문장 "She said she didn't feel well."은 간접 화법의 예이다
re·port·er /rɪ'pɔrtɚ/ *n* someone whose job is to write or tell about events in a newspaper or on radio or television ‖ 신문[라디오, 텔레비전]에서 사건들에 대해 기사를 게재하거나 보도하는 직업인. (보도) 기자. 리포터
re·pos·i·to·ry /rɪ'pazəˌtɔri/ *n* a place where things are kept safely ‖ 물건들을 안전하게 보관하는 장소. 저장실. 수납 창고. 보고(寶庫): *a repository for nuclear waste* 핵 폐기물 저장소
re·pos·sess /ˌripə'zɛs/ *v* [T] to take back something that someone has paid part of the money for, because s/he cannot pay the rest of the money ‖ 구입자가 나머지 돈을 지불할 수 없어서 일부의 대금을 받고 판 물건을 회수하다. (채권자가 상품을 특히 대금의 지불 불능으

로)회수[인수]하다: *I have to pay them $450 or they'll repossess the car.* 나는 그들에게 450달러를 지불해야 한다. 그렇지 않으면 그들이 차를 회수해 갈 것이다.

rep·re·hen·si·ble /ˌrɛprɪ'hensəbəl/ *adj* FORMAL reprehensible behavior is very bad and deserves criticism ‖ 행동이 아주 나쁘고 비난받을 만한. 야단맞아 싼. 괘씸한

rep·re·sent /ˌrɛprɪ'zɛnt/ *v* [T] **1** to do things or speak officially for someone else ‖ 공식적으로 다른 사람을 위해 일을 하거나 말을 하다. …의 대리를 하다. 대표하다: *Craig hired a lawyer to represent him.* 크레이그는 그를 대리할 변호사를 고용했다. / *She represents the 5th congressional district of Texas.* 그녀는 텍사스의 제5 하원 의원 선거구를 대표한다. **2** to be a sign or mark for something else ‖ 다른 사물을 표시나 부호로 나타내다. …을 표현[표시]하다. 상징하다: *The green triangles on the map represent campgrounds.* 지도상의 녹색 삼각형들은 야영지를 나타낸다. **3** if art represents something, it shows or means a thing or idea ‖ 미술 작품 등이 물건 또는 생각을 나타내거나 의미하다. 그리다. 서술[묘사]하다: *a painting representing heaven and hell* 천당과 지옥을 묘사한 그림 **4 represent yourself as sth** to say that you are something that you are not ‖ 자신이 실제로는 그렇지 않은 어떤 사람이라고 말하다. …이라고 자칭하다: *He represents himself as an expert in prison law.* 그는 자신이 행형법(行刑法)의 전문가라고 자칭한다.

rep·re·sen·ta·tion /ˌrɛprɪzɛn'teɪʃən, -zən-/ *n* **1** [U] the state of having someone to speak, vote, or make good decisions for you ‖ 자신을 위해 발언하는[투표하는, 좋은 결정을 하는] 사람을 가지고 있는 상태. 대표(제). 대의제: *There is no representation on the council for the Hispanic community.* 시의회에는 히스패닉계(系)를 위한 대표가 없다. **2** something, for example, a painting or sign, that shows or describes something else ‖ 예를 들면 그림이나 기호 같은 다른 어떤 사물을 나타내거나 설명하는 것. 표시. 표현. 묘사. 서술: *The model is a representation of how the atom is split.* 그 모형은 원자가 분열하는 방법을 표현하고 있다.

rep·re·sent·a·tive¹ /ˌrɛprɪ'zɛntətɪv/ *n* **1** someone who is chosen to act, speak, vote etc. for someone else ‖ 다른 사람을 위해 활동·발언·투표 등을 하도록 선출된 사람. 대표(자). 대리인 **2 Repre-**

sentative a member of the House of Representatives in the US Congress ‖ 미국 의회의 하원 의원

rep·re·sent·a·tive² *adj* **1** like other members of the same group; typical ‖ 같은 집단의 다른 구성원들과 같은; 대표적인. 전형적인: *The sample is representative of the total population.* 그 표본은 전체 인구를 대표하고 있다. **2** relating to a system of government in which people elect other people to represent them ‖ 사람들이 자신들을 대표할 다른 사람들을 선출하는 정부 시스템에 관한. 대의제[대표제]의: *representative democracy* 의회 민주주의

re·press /rɪ'prɛs/ *v* [T] **1** to stop yourself from expressing a feeling ‖ 감정의 표현을 스스로 중단하다. 억제하다. 억누르다: *It's not healthy to repress your emotions.* 네 감정을 억제하는 것은 건강에 좋지 않다. **2** to control people by using force ‖ 힘을 사용하여 사람들을 통제하다. 진압하다. 억압[탄압]하다

re·pressed /rɪ'prɛst/ *adj* DISAPPROVING having feelings or desires that you do not express ‖ 감정이나 욕망을 겉으로 드러내지 않고 있는. (심리적으로) 억제된. 억압된: *a sexually repressed man* 성적으로 억압된 남자

re·pres·sion /rɪ'prɛʃən/ *n* [U] **1** the use of force to control people ‖ 사람들을 통제하기 위한 힘의 사용. 진압. 탄압. 억제: *Stalin's repression of religious groups* 스탈린의 종교 단체 탄압 **2** the action of stopping yourself from feeling an emotion, or the state of having done this ‖ 감정을 느끼는 것을 스스로 중단하는 행위, 또는 이렇게 된 상태. 억압. 억제

re·pres·sive /rɪ'prɛsɪv/ *adj* cruel and severe ‖ 잔인하고 가혹한. 탄압적인. 억압적인: *a repressive political system* 탄압적인 정치 제도

re·prieve /rɪ'priv/ *n* **1** a delay before something unpleasant continues ‖ 불쾌한 일이 계속되기 전의 연기. (걱정 등의) 일시적 경감. 일시적 모면: *a reprieve from the pain* 통증의 일시적 경감 **2** an official order that prevents a prisoner from being killed as a punishment ‖ 형벌로서 죄수를 죽이는 것을 막는 공식적인 명령. (특히 사형수의) 형 집행의 유예[취소]. 처형 연기 —compare PARDON² – **reprieve** *v* [T]

rep·ri·mand /'rɛprəˌmænd/ *v* [T] to tell someone officially that s/he has done something wrong ‖ 어떤 사람이 나쁜 일을 했다고 공식적으로 말하다. …을 질책[비난]하다. (공식적으로) 견책[징계, 게

고]하 다 : *Several managers were reprimanded for their treatment of women.* 여러 명의 지배인들이 여성 처우에 대해 비난을 받았다. **- reprimand** n [C, U]

re·pris·al /rɪˈpraɪzəl/ n [C, U] a violent action that punishes your enemy for something bad that s/he has done ‖ 나쁜 짓을 한 적을 처벌하는 폭력적인 조치. 보복 행위(공격, 조치): *He's afraid to help the police for fear of reprisals against his family.* 그는 가족에 대한 보복이 두려워서 경찰을 돕는 것을 망설이고 있다.

re·prise /rɪˈpriːz/ v [I, T] to perform a particular character from a play, movie etc. again, or to sing a particular song again ‖ 연극·영화 등에서 특정한 등장인물역을 다시 연기하다, 또는 특정한 노래를 다시 부르다. 반복 (연주)하다. 재활동 [재연]하다: *Hamilton refused to reprise her role as the Wicked Witch.* 해밀턴은 사악한 마녀의 역(役)을 다시 맡는 것을 거절했다.

re·proach¹ /rɪˈproʊtʃ/ n **1** [C, U] criticism or disapproval, or a remark that expresses this ‖ 비판이나 불찬성, 또는 이런 것을 표현한 말. 질책. 잔소리. 비난(하는 말): *His mother gave him a look full of reproach.* 그의 어머니는 그에게 잔뜩 질책하는 표정을 지었다. **2 above/beyond reproach** impossible to criticize; perfect ‖ 비난하는 것이 불가능한. 비난의 여지가 없는; 완벽한: *The actions of the police should be above reproach.* 경찰의 조치는 비난의 여지가 없어야 한다.

reproach² v [T] to criticize someone and try to make him/her sorry for doing something ‖ 어떤 일을 한 것에 대해 사람을 비판하고 후회하게 만들어 하다. 꾸짖다. 책망하다. 비난하다: *Mrs. Winters reproached her son for his rude behavior.* 윈터스 여사는 무례한 행동을 한 아들을 꾸짖었다.

re·pro·duce /ˌriːprəˈduːs/ v **1** [I, T] to produce young plants or animals ‖ 어린 식물이나 동물을 생산하다. 번식하다[시키다]: *Most birds and fish reproduce by laying eggs.* 대부분의 새들과 물고기들은 알을 낳아 번식한다. **2** [T] to make a copy of something ‖ 어떤 것을 복사[복제]하다: *The colors were difficult to reproduce.* 그 색깔은 재현하기가 어려웠다.

re·pro·duc·tion /ˌriːprəˈdʌkʃən/ n **1** [U] the act or process of producing young plants or animals ‖ 어린 식물이나 동물을 생산하는 행위 또는 과정. 생식 (작용).

번식: *Cold weather affects the insect's reproduction.* 추운 날씨는 곤충의 번식에 영향을 미친다. **2** [C, U] the act of copying something such as a book or painting, or the copy itself ‖ 책이나 그림 같은 것을 복사하는 행위, 또는 그 복사본. 모조 [모사] (본). 복제품 [화]: *a reproduction of Homer's painting* 호머 그림의 복제화

re·pro·duc·tive /ˌriːprəˈdʌktɪv/ adj relating to the process of producing young plants and animals ‖ 어린 식물이나 동물을 생산하는 과정에 관한. 번식의. 생식의: *the reproductive system of mammals* 포유동물의 번식 체계

re·prove /rɪˈpruːv/ v [T] FORMAL to criticize someone for doing something bad ‖ 나쁜 짓을 했다고 사람을 비난하다. 야단치다. 질책하다

rep·tile /ˈrɛptaɪl, ˈrɛptl/ n an animal such as a snake or LIZARD that lays eggs, and whose blood changes temperature with the environment around it ‖ 알을 낳으며 혈액이 주변 환경에 따라 체온을 변화시키는 뱀이나 도마뱀 등의 동물. 파충류의 동물 **- reptilian** /rɛpˈtɪliən/ adj

re·pub·lic /rɪˈpʌblɪk/ n a country governed by elected representatives and led by a president ‖ 선출된 대표들이 다스리고 대통령이 영도하는 국가. 공화국 —compare MONARCHY

re·pub·li·can¹ /rɪˈpʌblɪkən/ adj **1 Republican** relating to or supporting the Republican Party ‖ 공화당과 관련되거나 또는 공화당을 지지하는. 공화당의: *a Republican candidate for the Senate* 공화당의 상원 의원 후보 **2** relating to a REPUBLIC ‖ 공화국에 관련된. 공화국의. 공화 정체의: *a republican system of government* 공화제 정부 **- Republicanism** n [U]

republican² n **1 Republican** someone who supports the Republican Party or is a member of it ‖ 공화당 지지자나 공화당원 —see culture note at PARTY¹ **2** someone who believes in REPUBLICs, or works to make his/her country become one ‖ 공화 정체를 신봉하는 사람, 또는 나라를 공화제로 만들려고 일하는 사람. 공화주의자 —compare DEMOCRAT

Republican Par·ty /ˌ... ˈ../ n [singular] one of the two main political parties of the US ‖ 미국의 주요한 두 정당 중의 하나. 공화당

re·pu·di·ate /rɪˈpyuːdiˌeɪt/ v [T] FORMAL to disagree strongly with someone or something and refuse to have any association with him, her, or it; REJECT

‖ 사람이나 사물에 강하게 반대하고 그와는 어떠한 유대관계도 갖기를 거부하다. 부인[거절]하다. 인연을 끊다; ㉺ reject: *Angelides publicly repudiated his friend's statements.* 앤젤리데스는 공공연하게 그의 친구의 말을 부인했다. – **repudiation** /rɪˌpyudiˈeɪʃən/ n [U]

re·pug·nance /rɪˈpʌgnəns/ n [U] FORMAL a feeling of strong dislike; DISGUST ‖ 강하게 싫어하는 감정. 혐오. 증오. 반감; ㉺ disgust

re·pug·nant /rɪˈpʌgnənt/ adj FORMAL very unpleasant and offensive ‖ 매우 불쾌하고 무례한. 용납되지 않는. 반대[적대]하는: *behavior that is morally repugnant* 도덕적으로 용납되지 않는 행동

re·pulse /rɪˈpʌls/ v [T] **1** if something repulses you, it makes you feel sick even to think about it ‖ 사물이 생각하는 것조차도 역겹게 느끼게 하다. 혐오감이 들게[싫증나게] 하다: *The nation was repulsed by the crime.* 그 국민은 범죄에 신물이 났다. **2** to defeat a military attack ‖ 군사적 공격을 물리치다. 격퇴하다: *The enemy forces were repulsed with the help of French troops.* 적군은 프랑스 군대의 지원으로 격퇴되었다.

re·pul·sion /rɪˈpʌlʃən/ n **1** [singular, U] a sick feeling that you get from seeing or thinking about something unpleasant ‖ 불쾌한 일을 보거나 생각하여서 갖게 되는 역겨운 감정. 반감. 혐오감 **2** [U] TECHNICAL the electric or MAGNETIC force by which one object pushes another one away from it ‖ 한 물체가 다른 것을 멀리 밀쳐내는 전기나 자기(磁氣)의 힘. 반발력[작용]. 척력

re·pul·sive /rɪˈpʌlsɪv/ adj so unpleasant that you almost feel sick ‖ 아주 불쾌해서 거의 혐오감을 느끼는. 역겨운. 역겹게 느끼게 하는. 메스꺼워지는: *morally repulsive behavior* 도덕적으로 혐오감을 일으키는 행동

rep·u·ta·ble /ˈrɛpyətəbəl/ adj respected for being honest and doing good work ‖ 정직하고 좋은 일을 하는 것으로 평판있는. 존경할 만한. 평판이 좋은: *a reputable construction company* 명성이 높은 건설 회사

rep·u·ta·tion /ˌrɛpyəˈteɪʃən/ n the opinion that people have of someone or something because of what has happened in the past ‖ 과거에 발생한 일로 인해 사람이나 사물에 대해 사람들이 갖고 있는 견해. 평판. 세평. 명성: *a man with a reputation for honesty* 정직한 것으로 평판을 받는 남자

re·pute /rɪˈpyut/ n [U] FORMAL ⇨ REPUTATION: *a pianist of great repute* 대단한 명성이 있는 피아니스트

re·put·ed /rɪˈpyutɪd/ adj FORMAL according to what most people think or say ‖ 대부분의 사람들이 생각하거나 말하는 것에 의하면. …이라는 평판인. …으로 통하고 있는: *He is reputed to be a millionaire.* 그는 백만장자로 통하고 있다. – **reputedly** adv

re·quest¹ /rɪˈkwɛst/ n the act of asking for something politely or formally ‖ 어떤 것을 공손히 또는 격식을 갖춰 요청하는 행위. 부탁. 요구. 의뢰. 간청. 탄원: *We've made a request for new equipment.* 우리는 새로운 장비를 요청했다. / *Drinks are available on request.* (=if you ask for them) 음료는 요구하시는 대로 제공합니다. / *I called the police at her request.* (=because she asked me to) 나는 그녀의 부탁으로 경찰에 전화를 했다.

request² v [T] to ask for something politely or formally ‖ 어떤 것을 공손하게 또는 격식을 갖춰 요청하다. (간)청하다: *We request that everyone be quiet.* 우리는 모두 조용히 해 주기를 부탁합니다. — see usage notes at ask, RECOMMEND

req·ui·em /ˈrɛkwiəm/ n [C, U] a Christian ceremony of prayers for someone who has died, or a piece of music written for this ceremony ‖ 죽은 사람을 위한 기독교의 기도 의식, 또는 이 의식을 위해 작곡한 음악. 추도 미사. 진혼곡

re·quire /rɪˈkwaɪɚ/ v [T] **1** to need something ‖ 어떤 것을 필요로 하다: *Roses require a lot of sunshine.* 장미는 많은 햇빛을 필요로 한다. **2** FORMAL to demand officially that someone do something because of a law or rule ‖ 법률이나 규칙에 의해 사람이 어떤 것을 하도록 공식적으로 요구하다. (법률·규칙 등에 의해) …을 남에게 요구하다[명하다]: *Everyone is required by law to wear seat belts.* 누구나 법에 의해 안전벨트를 착용해야 한다.

re·quire·ment /rɪˈkwaɪɚmənt/ n **1** a quality or skill that is needed or asked for in a particular situation ‖ 특정한 상황에서 필요하거나 요청되는 특성 또는 기능. (필요) 요건. 자격: *Each state has different requirements for its government workers.* 주(州)마다 주 정부 공무원의 자격은 상이하다. **2 meet sb's requirements** to provide or do everything that someone needs ‖ 어떤 사람이 필요로 하는 모든 것을 제공하거나 해주다. 남의 요구에 응하다: *The*

contract meets all our requirements.
그 계약은 우리의 모든 요건을 충족한다.

req·ui·site /ˈrɛkwəzɪt/ *adj* FORMAL needed for a particular purpose ‖ 특정 목적에 필요한. 필수의. 불가결한

req·ui·si·tion /ˌrɛkwəˈzɪʃən/ *n* [C, U] FORMAL an official demand to have something, usually made by the army ‖ 보통 군대에서, 어떤 것을 취득하기 위해 공식적으로 요구하는 것. 징발. 징용 – **requisition** *v* [T]

re·route /riˈraʊt, riˈrut/ *v* [T] to make vehicles, aircraft etc. go a different way from the way they usually go ‖ 차·비행기 등을 평소 가는 길에서 다른 길로 가게 하다. …의 여정[코스]을 변경하다: *Traffic has been rerouted across the bridge.* 차량들은 다리를 건너서 코스를 바꾸었다.

re·run /ˈrirʌn/ *n* a television program or a movie that is being shown again ‖ 다시 방영하는 텔레비전 프로그램 또는 영화. 재방송. 재상영: *a rerun of "Cheers"* "Cheers"의 재방영 – **rerun** /riˈrʌn/ *v* [T]

re·sale /ˈriseɪl/ *n* the state of being sold again ‖ 다시 판매되는 상태. 재판매. 전매 (轉賣): *the resale value of the house* 그 집의 전매 가치

re·scind /rɪˈsɪnd/ *v* [T] to officially end a law, agreement, or decision ‖ 법률[협정, 결정]을 공식적으로 폐지[철회]하다. 폐기하다

res·cue¹ /ˈrɛskyu/ *v* [T] to save someone or something from harm or danger ‖ 사람이나 사물을 위해나 위험에서 구하다. 구조[구출]하다: *He rescued two people from the fire.* 그는 화재에서 두 사람을 구조 했다. – **rescuer** *n*

rescue² *n* an act of saving someone or something from harm or danger ‖ 사람이나 사물을 위해나 위험에서 구조하는 행위. 구출. 구조: *They are trained for air rescues.* 그들은 공중 구조에 대비해 훈련을 받고 있다. / *A nearby boat came to the rescue.* (=saved or helped someone) 근처의 배가 구조하러 왔다.

re·search¹ /ˈrisərtʃ, rɪˈsərtʃ/ *n* [U] serious study of a subject that is intended to discover new facts about it ‖ 주제에 대한 새로운 사실을 발견하려는 진지한 연구. 조사. 탐구: *scientific research on/into heart disease* 심장병에 대한 과학적인 연구 / *Holmes is doing research* (=finding information) *for a book on the Middle Ages.* 홈스는 중세에 관한 서적을 조사하고 있다.

research² *v* [I, T] to study a subject in

detail so you can discover new facts about it ‖ 주제에 대한 새로운 사실을 발견할 수 있도록 상세하게 연구하다. 조사 [탐구]하다: *Conner spent eight years researching the history of the region.* 코너는 그 지역의 역사를 연구하면서 8년을 보냈다. – **researcher** *n*

re·sem·blance /rɪˈzɛmbləns/ *n* [C, U] if there is a resemblance between two things or people, they are similar to each other ‖ 두 물건이나 두 사람 간의 비슷한 점. 유사(성). 닮은 것[사람]: *There's a slight resemblance between Mike and his cousin.* (=they look like each other) 마이크와 그의 사촌은 약간 닮은 데가 있다.

re·sem·ble /rɪˈzɛmbəl/ *v* [T] to look like, or be similar to, someone or something ‖ 어떤 사람이나 사물과 같아 보이거나 유사하다. …을 닮다. …과 비슷하다: *She resembles her mother in many ways.* 그녀는 많은 점에서 어머니를 닮았다.

re·sent /rɪˈzɛnt/ *v* [T] to feel angry and upset about something that someone has done to you ‖ 남이 자신에게 한 일에 대해 화가 나고 상심하다. 분개하다. 노하다. 원망하다: *I've always resented my father for leaving the family.* 나는 항상 가족을 떠난 아버지를 원망했다.

re·sent·ful /rɪˈzɛntful/ *adj* feeling angry and upset about something that someone has done, or showing this ‖ 남이 한 일에 대해 화를 내고 기분이 상한, 또는 이를 나타내는. 분개하고[화가 나 원망하고] 있는. 몹시 싫어하는: *a resentful look* 원망스런 표정

re·sent·ment /rɪˈzɛntˈmənt/ *n* [U] a feeling of anger about something that someone has done to you ‖ 남이 자신에게 한 일에 대한 분노의 감정. 분개. 분노. 적의. 원한

res·er·va·tion /ˌrɛzəˈveɪʃən/ *n* 1 an arrangement that you make so that a place in a hotel, on a plane etc. is kept for you to use ‖ 호텔·비행기 등의 자리를 자신이 이용할 수 있게 해두는 약속. 예약: *Have you made reservations at the restaurant yet?* 벌써 식당 예약을 했니? 2 [C, U] a feeling of doubt because you do not agree completely with a plan, idea etc. ‖ 계획·생각 등에 완전히 동의하지 않기 때문에 의심하는 감정. 삼가기. 거리낌. 감추기: *I still have reservations about promoting O'Neil.* 나는 오닐을 승진시키는 데 대해 아직 주저하고 있다. 3 an area of land in the US on which some Native Americans live ‖ 아메리카 원주민

이 사는 지역. (인디언) 보호 구역

re·serve¹ /rɪ'zɜːrv/ v [T] **1** to arrange for a place in a hotel, on a plane etc. to be kept for you to use ‖ 호텔·비행기의 자리를 이용하기 위해 보존하도록 준비하다. 예약하다: *I'd like to reserve a table for 8:00.* 저는 8시에 테이블 하나를 예약하고 싶습니다. **2** to keep something separate so that it can be used for a particular purpose ‖ 특정 목적으로 사용할 수 있게 어떤 것을 따로 떼어 놓다. 따로 두다. 남겨 두다: *a parking space reserved for the disabled* 장애인을 위해 따로 남겨 둔 주차 공간

reserve² n **1** an amount of something that is kept to be used in the future when it may be needed ‖ 장래 필요할 때에 이용하도록 보존된 일정량의 물건. 비축. 축적. 예비품: *Water reserves are dangerously low.* 물의 저수량이 위험할 정도로 적다. / *We keep some money in reserve for emergencies.* 우리는 긴급 시에 대비하여 약간의 예비 돈을 보관해 두고 있다. **2** [U] the quality of being unwilling to express your emotions or talk about your problems ‖ 감정을 잘 표현하려 하지 않거나 문제점을 잘 말하지 않으려는 성질. 감정을 표현하지 않음. 삼가기. 자제: *His natural reserve stopped him from saying anything.* 그는 타고난 신중함으로 어떤 말도 하지 못했다. **3** an area of land where wild animals, plants etc. are protected ‖ 야생 동물·식물 등이 보호되는 지역. 야생 보호 지역: *a nature reserve* 자연 보호 구역 **4** [U] also **reserves** a military force that a country has in addition to its usual army ‖ 국가가 상비군 외에 보유하는 병력. 예비군

re·served /rɪ'zɜːrvd/ adj unwilling to express your emotions or talk about your problems ‖ 감정을 나타내거나 자신의 문제에 대해 말하기를 꺼리는. 마음을 털어놓지 않는. 주저하는. 말이 없는: *a cool reserved young man* 똑똑하고 신중한 젊은이

res·er·voir /'rɛzə‚vwɑr, -zə-, -‚vwɔr/ n **1** a special lake where water is stored to be used by people in a city ‖ 도시 사람들이 사용하도록 물이 저장된 특별한 호수. 저수지. 수원지 **2** a large amount of something that has not been used yet ‖ 아직 사용되지 않은 다량의 물건. 축적[저장](소): *a reservoir of oil beneath the desert* 사막의 지하 유류 저장소

re·set /'riset/ adj **reset button/switch** a control that is used to make a machine or instrument ready to work again ‖ 기계나 기구의 재가동 준비를 하

는 데에 쓰이는 제어 기능. 리셋 버튼/스위치

re·shuf·fle /ri'ʃʌfəl/ v [T] to change the jobs of people who work in an organization ‖ 조직에서 근무하는 사람들의 직무를 바꾸다. (내각 등을) 개편하다: *The company is expected to reshuffle its top managers.* 그 회사는 최고 경영진을 개편할 것으로 예상된다. – **reshuffle** n

re·side /rɪ'zaɪd/ v [I] FORMAL to live in a particular place ‖ 특정한 장소에 살다. 거주하다: *Mexican citizens who legally reside in the US* 미국에서 합법적으로 거주하고 있는 멕시코 시민들

res·i·dence /'rɛzədəns/ n FORMAL **1** the place where you live ‖ 사람이 사는 장소. 거처. 저택: *a private residence* 사택(私宅) **2** [U] the state of living in a place ‖ 어떤 장소에 살고 있는 상태. 거주 **3 in residence** living or working in a place ‖ 어떤 장소에서 살거나 일하는. (예술가·작가 등이)전속으로 되어. 주재[재학, 거주]하여: *Mr. Moreau is our artist in residence.* 모로우 씨는 우리의 전속 미술가이다.

res·i·den·cy /'rɛzədənsi/ n a period of time during which a doctor receives special training in a particular type of medicine ‖ 의사가 의학의 특정 분야에 관해 특별한 교육을 받는 기간. 레지던트 과정

res·i·dent /'rɛzədənt/ n **1** someone who lives in a place such as a house or apartment ‖ 집이나 아파트 등의 장소에 사는 사람. 거주자: *a park for local residents* 지역 주민을 위한 공원 **2** a doctor working at a hospital where s/he is being trained ‖ 수련을 받고 있는 병원에서 근무하고 있는 의사. 레지던트 – **resident** adj

res·i·den·tial /‚rɛzə'dɛnʃəl/ adj a residential area consists of private houses, with no offices or businesses ‖ 지역이 사무실이나 사업체는 없고 개인 주택들로 이루어진. 거주의. 주거용의[에 알맞은]

re·sid·u·al /rɪ'zɪdʒuəl/ adj FORMAL remaining after a process, event etc. is finished ‖ 과정·사건 등이 끝난 뒤에 남아 있는. 잔여[잔류]의: *the residual effects of radiation exposure* 방사선 노출[피폭]의 후유증

res·i·due /'rɛzə‚du/ n a substance that remains after something else has disappeared or been removed ‖ 다른 사물이 없어지거나 제거된 뒤에 남는 물질. 잔류물. 찌꺼기: *an oily residue* 기름 찌꺼기

re·sign /rɪ'zaɪn/ *v* [I, T] **1** to leave your job or position officially because you want to ‖ 자신이 원해서 공식적으로 직무나 직위를 떠나다. (공식) 사임하다. 사직하다 : *Burton resigned from the company yesterday.* 버튼은 어제 회사를 사직했다. **2 resign yourself to sth/to doing sth** to accept something that is unpleasant but cannot be changed ‖ 불쾌하지만 변경될 수 없는 일을 받아들이다. (운명 등에)기꺼이 따르다[복종하다]. 감수(甘受)하다: *I've resigned myself to living in the city for a while.* 나는 어쩔 수 없이 한동안 도시 생활을 했다.

res·ig·na·tion /ˌrɛzɪg'neɪʃən/ *n* [C, U] the act of RESIGN*ing*, or a written statement to say you are doing this ‖ 사임하는 행위, 또는 사임한다는 것이 적힌 글로 쓴 진술서. 사임. 사직(서): *Did Johnson hand in his resignation?* (=give his resignation to the manager) 존슨은 사직서를 제출했니? **2** [U] the feeling of accepting an unpleasant situation that you cannot change ‖ 자신이 바꿀 수 없는 불쾌한 상황을 받아들이는 감정. 단념[감수]의 심정. 유감: *I could hear the resignation in his voice.* 나는 체념 섞인 그의 목소리를 들을 수 있었다.

re·signed /rɪ'zaɪnd/ *adj* accepting an unpleasant situation that you cannot change, or showing that you feel this ‖ 바꿀 수 없는 불쾌한 상황을 받아들이는, 또는 이러한 느낌을 나타내는. (불쾌한 일을) 묵묵히 따르는. 단념[체념]하고 있는: *He's resigned to the fact that she's leaving.* 그는 그녀가 떠난다는 사실에 체념했다. / *a resigned voice/look* 체념의 목소리[표정]

re·sil·ience /rɪ'zɪlyəns/ *n* [U] **1** the ability to quickly become strong, healthy, or happy, after a difficult situation, illness etc. ‖ 어려운 상황·병 등의 사후에 빠르게 강해지는[건강해지는, 행복해지는] 능력. 회복력. 복원력: *Experts say this is a sign of the economy's resilience.* 전문가들은 이것이 경기 회복의 신호라고 말한다. **2** the ability of a substance such as rubber to return to its usual shape when pressure is removed ‖ 압력이 제거되면 평상의 모습으로 되돌아가는 고무 등 물질의 능력. 탄력. 탄성 **– resilient** *adj*

res·in /'rɛzən/ *n* **1** [U] a thick sticky liquid that comes from some trees ‖ 몇몇 나무들에서 나오는 걸쭉하고 끈적끈적한 액체. 송진 **2** a chemical substance used for making plastics ‖ 플라스틱을 제조하는 데에 쓰이는 화학 물질. 수지

re·sist /rɪ'zɪst/ *v* **1** [I, T] to not accept changes, or to try to prevent changes from happening ‖ 변화를 받아들이지 않다, 또는 변화가 발생하는 것을 막으려 하다. 거부하다. 방해[저지]하다. 거스르다: *People generally resist change.* 사람들은 일반적으로 변화에 저항한다. / *Residents were ordered to evacuate, but they resisted.* 주민들은 피난 명령을 받았으나 따르지 않았다. **2** [I, T] to oppose or fight against someone or something ‖ 사람이나 사물에 대항하여 반대하거나 싸우다. 저항[반항]하다. 반대하다: *resisting enemy attacks against the city* 도시에 대한 저항군의 공격 / *When the girls resisted, the man let go of them.* 소녀들이 저항하자 그 남자는 그녀들을 보내줬다. **3** [I, T] to try hard not to do something that you want to do ‖ 하고 싶은 일을 하지 않으려고 무척 애쓰다. 견디다. 참다. 삼가다: *I couldn't resist laughing at him.* 나는 그를 보고 웃음을 참을 수 없었다. / *Carter found their offer hard to resist.* 카터는 그들의 제안을 거절하는 것이 힘들다는 것을 알았다. **4** [T] to not be changed or harmed by something ‖ 어떤 것에 의해 변경되거나 해를 받지 않다. 견디다. 침범당하지 않다: *They say vitamin C helps you resist colds.* 그들은 비타민 C가 감기 예방에 도움이 된다고 말한다.

re·sist·ance /rɪ'zɪstəns/ *n* **1** [singular, U] a refusal to accept new ideas or changes ‖ 새로운 생각이나 변화를 받아들이는 것에 대한 거절. 반대: *There is strong public resistance to the new taxes.* 새로운 조세에 대한 일반 대중의 심한 반대가 있다. **2** [singular, U] fighting against someone or something ‖ 사람이나 사물에 대항한 싸움. 저항. 반항: *The rebels put up fierce resistance against the army.* 반군들은 군대에 대항하여 격렬하게 저항했다. **3** [singular, U] the ability to avoid the effects of a disease or drug ‖ 질병이나 약의 효과를 피하려는 능력. 내성 : *Your body has built up a resistance to the penicillin.* 너의 신체는 페니실린에 대한 내성이 길러졌다. **4** [U] TECHNICAL the degree to which a substance can stop electricity from going through it ‖ 물질이 전기를 통과하지 못하도록 막을 수 있는 정도. 저항

re·sis·tant /rɪ'zɪstənt/ *adj* **1** not easily harmed or damaged by something ‖ 어떤 것에 의해 쉽게 해를 받거나 파손되지 않는. 저항력 있는. 저항하는: *a heat-resistant/fire-resistant cover* 내열[내화

(耐火)〕덮개 **2 unwilling to accept something** ‖ 어떤 것을 받아들이기를 주저하는. 꺼리는: *people who are resistant to change* 변화를 꺼리는 사람들

res·o·lute /ˈrɛzəˌlut/ *adj* doing something because you feel very strongly that you are right ‖ 자신이 옳다고 아주 굳게 생각하기 때문에 어떤 것을 하는. 굳게 결심하고 있는. 의지가 굳은 **- resolutely** *adv*

res·o·lu·tion /ˌrɛzəˈluʃən/ *n* **1** a formal or official decision agreed on by a group, especially after a vote ‖ 특히 투표 후에 집단적으로 합의가 이루어진 공식적이거나 직무상의 결정. 결의: *a budget resolution in Congress* 의회의 예산 결의안 **2** [singular, U] the final solution to a problem or difficulty ‖ 문제나 난점에 대한 최종적인 해결책. 해답. 해법: *a peaceful resolution to the crisis* 위기에 대한 평화적인 해결책 **3** a promise that you make to yourself to do something ‖ 어떤 것을 하기로 자신에게 한 약속. 결심: *Have you made any New Year's resolutions?* 어떤 새해 결심을 했니? **4** [U] the quality of having strong beliefs and determination ‖ 강한 신념과 결단력을 가진 특성. 단호함. 불굴. 견인불발

re·solve¹ /rɪˈzɑlv/ *v* **1** [T] to find an answer to a problem or a way of dealing with it ‖ 문제에 대한 해답 또는 그것을 처리하는 방법을 찾다. 해결하다. 풀다: *The president is trying to resolve the situation quickly.* 대통령은 그 상황을 신속하게 해결하려고 노력하고 있다. **2** [I] to make a definite decision to do something ‖ 어떤 것을 하기로 분명히 결정을 하다. 작정하다. 결심하다: *Joan resolved to continue working after she had children.* 조앤은 아이들이 생긴 뒤에도 계속 근무하기로 결심했다 **3** [I, T] to make a formal decision to do something, especially by voting ‖ 특히 투표로, 어떤 것을 하기로 공식적인 결정을 내리다. 의결[결의]하다

resolve² *n* [U] FORMAL strong determination to succeed in doing something ‖ 어떤 일을 하는 데에 있어서 성공하려는 강한 결단. 결심. 결의

res·o·nant /ˈrɛzənənt/ *adj* having a deep clear loud sound that continues for a long time ‖ 오랫동안 계속되는 깊고 맑은 큰 소리가 나는. 울려 퍼지는. 잘 울리는: *a resonant voice* 낭랑한 목소리 **- resonance** *n* [U]

res·o·nate /ˈrɛzəˌneɪt/ *v* [I] to make a deep clear loud sound that continues for a long time ‖ 오랫동안 계속되는 깊고 맑

은 큰 소리를 내다. 울려퍼지다. 반향하다

re·sort¹ /rɪˈzɔrt/ *n* **1** a place where many people can go for a vacation, with hotels, swimming pools etc. ‖ 많은 사람들이 휴가를 갈 수 있는 호텔·수영장 등이 있는 곳. 행락지. 휴양지: *a beach resort* 해변 휴양지 **2 as a last resort** if everything else that you have tried fails ‖ 시도해 본 다른 모든 것이 실패한다면. 최후의 수단으로: *You could, as a last resort, sleep in the car.* 너는 최후의 수단으로 차에서 잘 수 있었다.

resort² *v*

resort to sth *phr v* [T] to do something or use something in order to succeed, even if it is bad ‖ 어떤 것이 나쁘더라도, 성공하기 위해서 그것을 하거나 사용하다. 의지하다. 호소하다: *She finally resorted to threats to get him to stop smoking.* 결국 그녀는 그가 담배를 끊도록 하는 데 협박을 사용했다.

re·sound /rɪˈzaʊnd/ *v* [I] **1** to be full of sound; ECHO ‖ 소리가 가득 차다. 울리다. 반향하다; ⑨ echo: *a room resounding with laughter* 큰 웃음소리가 울려 퍼지는 방 **2** if a sound resounds, it continues loudly and clearly for a long time ‖ 소리가 오랫동안 크고 맑게 계속되다. 울려 퍼지다. 반향하다

re·sound·ing /rɪˈzaʊndɪŋ/ *adj* **1** a resounding noise is loud and clear ‖ 소음이 크고 맑은. 울려 퍼지는. 반향하는: *a resounding crash* 메아리치는 요란한 소리 **2** a resounding success/victory etc. a very great and complete success, victory etc. ‖ 아주 훌륭하고 완전한 성공·승리 등. 완전한 성공/승리 **- resoundingly** *adv*

re·source /ˈrisɔrs, rɪˈsɔrs/ *n* **1** [C usually plural] something such as land, minerals, or natural energy that exists in a country and can be used in order to increase its wealth ‖ 한 국가에 존재하여 국부(國富)를 증대시키기 위해 사용될 수 있는 토지·광물질·천연자원 등의 것. (나라의) 자원. 부(富): *a country rich in natural resources* 천연자원이 풍부한 나라 **2** something that can be used in order to make a job or activity easier ‖ 어떤 일이나 활동을 보다 쉽게 하는 데에 쓰일 수 있는 것. 수단. 방책. 방편: *resource materials for teachers* 교육 자료 **—see also** RESOURCES

re·source·ful /rɪˈsɔrsfəl/ *adj* good at finding ways to deal with problems effectively ‖ 문제를 효과적으로 처리하는 방법을 찾는 데 능숙한. 재치 있는. 꾀바른. 머리 회전이 빠른 **- resourceful-**

ness *n* [U]
re·sour·ces /'ri,sɔrsɪz/ *n* [plural] all the money, property, skills etc. that you have available to use ‖ 사용할 수 있는 모든 돈·재산·기능 등. 자원(력). 재원: *Our financial resources are limited.* 우리의 재원은 한정되어 있다. —see also HUMAN RESOURCES
re·spect¹ /rɪ'spɛkt/ *n* **1** [U] admiration for someone because of his/her knowledge, skill etc. ‖ 지식·기술 등을 보유한 사람에 대한 감탄. 존경. 경의: *I have great respect for her work as a writer.* 나는 작가로서 그녀의 작품에 대해 깊은 존경심을 갖고 있다. **2** [U] the attitude of not being rude to someone or not damaging something because you think he, she, or it is important or impressive ‖ 사람이나 사물이 중요하거나 인상적이라고 생각해서 무례하지 않거나 사물을 훼손하지 않으려는 태도. 존중. 중시. 배려: *You ought to show more respect to your grandfather.* 너는 할아버지께 더 많은 존경심을 표해야 한다. / *These kids have no respect for other people's property.* 이 아이들은 다른 사람들의 재산을 중시하지 않는다. —opposite DISRESPECT **3 in one respect/in some respects/in every respect** used in order to say that something is true in one way, some ways, or in every way ‖ 어떤 것이 한 가지 면에서나 여러 가지 면에서, 또는 모든 면에서 사실이다라는 것을 말하려는 데에 쓰여. 한 가지/몇 가지/모든 점에서: *In some respects, Leon is right.* 몇 가지 점에서는 레온이 옳다. **4 with (all due) respect** FORMAL used before disagreeing with someone, in order to be polite ‖ 정중하게 상대방에 대한 이의를 제기하기 전에 쓰이는. …은 대단히 지당[죄송]하지만: *With all due respect to you sir, that is not the point.* 선생님 대단히 죄송합니다만 그것은 요점이 아닙니다. **5 with respect to** FORMAL concerning a particular thing, or concerning something that has just been mentioned; REGARDING ‖ 특정한 일에 관해서는, 방금 언급한 것에 대해. …에 관해서는[대해서는]; ㉾ regarding: *With respect to your question about jobs, all our positions are filled.* 일자리에 관한 당신의 질문에 관해서라면, 우리는 모두 충원이 되었습니다. —see also RESPECTS
respect² *v* [T] **1** to admire someone because of his/her knowledge, skill etc. ‖ 지식·기능 등을 이유로 남을 칭송하다. …을 존경하다: *The students like and respect him.* 학생들은 그를 좋아하고 존

경한다. **2 respect sb's wishes/rights etc.** to be careful not to do anything against someone's wishes, rights etc. ‖ 남의 희망·권리 등에 반대되는 어떤 것도 하지 않으려고 주의하다. 남의 희망/권리 등을 존중하다 **3 respect the law/Constitution etc.** to be careful not to disobey the law, Constitution etc. ‖ 법률·헌법 등을 위반하지 않으려고 주의하다. 법률/헌법을 존중하다
re·spect·a·ble /rɪ'spɛktəbəl/ *adj* **1** having standards of behavior or appearance that people approve of and admire ‖ 사람들이 인정을 하고 칭송을 하는 행동이나 외모의 기준을 갖고 있는. 단정한. 고상한: *a respectable family* 훌륭한 가문 / *Go wash up and make yourself look respectable.* 가서 깨끗이 씻고 단장해라. **2** showing skills, knowledge etc. that people admire ‖ 사람들이 칭찬하는 기능·지식 등을 보여주는. 존경할 만한. 훌륭한: *Kemp has done a respectable job.* 켐프는 훌륭한 일을 했다. – **respectably** *adv* – **respectability** /rɪ,spɛktə'bɪləṭi/ *n* [U]
re·spect·ed /rɪ'spɛktɪd/ *adj* admired by many people because of your work, skills etc. ‖ 자신의 일·기능 등의 이유로 많은 사람들로부터 칭찬받는. 훌륭한, 평판 있는: *a respected leader* 훌륭한 지도자
re·spect·ful /rɪ'spɛktfəl/ *adj* feeling or showing respect ‖ 존경을 느끼거나 나타내는. 존경하는. 정중한. …에 경의를 표하는 – **respectfully** *adv* —opposite DISRESPECTFUL
re·spec·tive /rɪ'spɛktɪv/ *adj* people's respective jobs, houses etc. are the separate ones that each of them has ‖ 직업·집 등을 별도로 가지는. 각각의. 개개의: *the two sisters and their respective husbands* 두 자매와 그들 각자의 남편들
re·spec·tive·ly /rɪ'spɛktɪvli/ *adv* each separately in the order mentioned ‖ 언급된 순서에 따라 각각 별개로. 차례대로. 각각. 저마다: *The dollar and yen rose 2% and 3% respectively.* 달러와 엔화는 각각 2%와 3% 상승했다.
re·spects /rɪ'spɛkts/ *n* [plural] **1** polite greetings ‖ 예의바른 인사. 문안: *Give my respects to your parents.* 부모님께 안부 전해 주십시오. **2 pay your (last/final) respects** to go to a funeral to show that you liked and respected someone ‖ 장례식에 가서 자신이 어떤 사람을 좋아하고 존경했다는 것을 나타내다. 장례식에 참석하다. 최후의 경의를 표하다
res·pi·ra·tion /,rɛspə'reɪʃən/ *n* [U] TECHNICAL the process of breathing ‖ 숨

쉬는 과정. 호흡 (작용) —see also
ARTIFICIAL RESPIRATION

res·pi·ra·tor /'rɛspə,reɪtəʳ/ *n* a piece of equipment that covers the nose and mouth and helps someone to breathe ‖ 코와 입을 덮어서 사람이 숨쉬는 것을 돕는 기구. 인공호흡 장치

res·pi·ra·to·ry /'rɛsprə,tɔri/ *adj* TECHNICAL relating to breathing ‖ 호흡에 관련된. 호흡(용)의. 호흡 기관의: *the respiratory system* 호흡계

res·pite /'rɛspɪt/ *n* [singular, U] a short time of rest from something unpleasant such as pain, effort, or trouble ‖ 고통[노력, 고민] 등 불쾌한 일에서 벗어난 잠깐의 휴식. 일시적 중단. 연기. 유예: *The Northwest should have a brief respite from the rain today.* 노스웨스트 항공은 오늘 우천으로 인해 잠시 운항을 중지해야 하겠습니다.

re·splend·ent /rɪ'splɛndənt/ *adj* FORMAL very beautiful in appearance, in a way that looks expensive ‖ 외형이 매우 아름다워 비싸 보이는. 화려한. 눈부신

re·spond /rɪ'spand/ *v* **1** [I] to react to something that has been said or done ‖ 말하거나 행해진 것에 대해 반응하다. 대답[응답]하다: *Voters responded to the tax increases by voting against the Democrats.* 유권자들은 민주당에 투표하지 않음으로써 세금 인상에 대응했다. **2** [I] to say or write something as a reply ‖ 대답으로서 어떤 것을 말하거나 기재하다. 응답하다: *How did he respond to your question?* 네 질문에 그가 어떻게 대답했니? **3** [I] to improve as a result of a particular medical treatment ‖ 특정한 의학 치료의 결과로 나아지다. (자극 등에) 반응하다: *Her cancer is responding well to the drugs.* 그녀의 암은 약물에 좋은 반응을 보이고 있다. —see usage note at ANSWER¹

re·sponse /rɪ'spans/ *n* [C, U] something that is said, written, or done as a reaction or reply to something else ‖ 다른 어떤 것에 대한 반응 또는 대답으로서 말하는[쓰는, 행하는] 것. 응답: *I am writing in response to your advertisement.* 귀사의 광고를 보고 이 글을 씁니다. / *We've had a good response to our appeal for help.* 우리는 도움을 호소해서 좋은 반향을 일으켰다.

re·spon·si·bil·i·ty /rɪ,spansə'bɪləti/ *n* **1** [U] a duty to be in charge of or take care of something ‖ 무엇을 담당하거나 보살피는 의무. 책임. 책무: *Do you think he's ready for more responsibility?* 그가 더 많은 책임을 질 준비가 되어 있다고 생

각하니 ? / *Terry said he'd take responsibility for* (=agree to be in charge of) *organizing the trip.* 그가 책임지고 여행을 준비하기로 했다고 테리가 말했다. **2** something that you have a duty to do, be in charge of, or take care of ‖ 할 의무가 있거나 책임이 있거나 돌보아야 하는 일. 책임져야 할 대상: *The president has many responsibilities.* 대통령은 책무가 많다. **3** [U] blame for something bad ‖ 나쁜 일에 대한 비난: *No one has accepted/taken responsibility for the bombing.* 아무도 그 폭격에 대해 책임을 지지 않았다.

re·spon·si·ble /rɪ'spansəbəl/ *adj* **1** if you are responsible for something bad, it is your fault ‖ 나쁜 일이 자기의 과실인. 책임이 있는. 책임을 져야 하는: *a gang responsible for several robberies* 몇 개의 강도 사건에 대한 책임이 있는 폭력단 **2** in charge of or taking care of something ‖ 어떤 일을 책임지고 있거나 그것을 돌봐야 하는. 책임을 맡고 있는: *She's responsible for our foreign sales.* 그녀는 해외 영업을 담당하고 있다. **3** **responsible job/position/post** a job in which the ability to make good judgments and decisions is needed ‖ 훌륭한 판단과 결정을 하는 능력이 필요한 업무. 책임이 무거운 일/책임을 수반하는 지위 **4** sensible and able to be trusted ‖ 분별 있고 믿을 수 있는. 믿을 만한. 신뢰할 수 있는: *a responsible young man* 믿을 만한 젊은이 **5** **be responsible to** if you are responsible to someone, that person is in charge of your work and you must explain your actions to him/her ‖ 어떤 사람이 자신의 일에 대한 책임을 맡고 있어서 그 사람에게 자신의 행동에 대해 설명해야 하는. 사람이 남에게 …할 책임이 있는

re·spon·si·bly /rɪ'spansəbli/ *adv* in a sensible way that makes people trust you ‖ 사람들이 자신을 믿도록 분별있게. 책임을 가지고. 확실히: *Can I trust you to behave responsibly while I'm gone?* 내가 출타 중에 네가 책임감 있게 행동하리라는 것을 믿어도 되겠니?

re·spon·sive /rɪ'spansɪv/ *adj* **1** ready to react in a useful or helpful way ‖ 유용하거나 도움이 되는 방식으로 반응할 준비가 되어 있는. 응답하는. 반응을 보이는: *a company that is responsive to your business needs* 귀사의 요구에 반응을 보이는 회사 **2** able or willing to give answers or show your feelings about something ‖ 어떤 것에 대해 대답할 수 있거나 기꺼이 대답하려 하는, 또는 감정을

나타낼 수 있거나 나타내려고 하는. 반응에 민감한: *Utley was awake and responsive after the surgery.* 어틀리는 수술 후에 깨어나서 반응을 보였다. − **responsiveness** *n* [U] —opposite UNRESPONSIVE

rest¹ /rɛst/ *n* **1 the rest a)** what is left after everything else has been used, dealt with etc. ‖ 다른 모든 것이 사용되거나 처리되고 난 후 남아 있는 것. 나머지: *What should I do with the rest of the pizza?* 남은 피자를 어떻게 해야 하지? **b)** the others in a group, or the other part of something ‖ 어떤 집단 내의 다른 사람들, 또는 사물의 다른 부분. 나머지 사람[부분]: *Sam's here today, but he'll be away for the rest of the week.* 샘은 오늘 여기 있지만 나머지 주일에는 여기 없을 것이다. / *I'll read you the rest tomorrow night.* 나머지 부분은 내가 내일 밤에 읽어 주마. **2** [C, U] a period of time when you can relax or sleep ‖ 편히 쉬거나 잘 수 있는 일정한 시간. 휴식. 수면: *I need to get some rest.* 나는 좀 쉬어야겠어. **3 put/set sb's mind at rest** to make someone feel less anxious or worried ‖ 남을 덜 불안하거나 걱정하게 하다. 남을 안심시키다 **4 come to rest** to stop moving ‖ 움직임을 멈추다. 정지하다: *The truck went off the road and came to rest at the bottom of the hill.* 그 트럭은 도로에서 벗어나서 언덕 아래에서 멈춰 섰다. **5 lay/put sth to rest** to get rid of a false idea or belief by showing that it is not true ‖ 사실이 아님을 나타냄으로써 잘못된 생각이나 신념을 제거하다. (소문 등을) 가라앉히다: *I'm glad those rumors have been put to rest.* 나는 그 소문들이 잠잠해져서 기쁘다. **6 at rest** TECHNICAL not moving ‖ 움직이지 않고. 정지하여. 휴식하여

rest² *v* **1** [I] to stop doing something and relax or sleep for a period of time ‖ 무엇을 하는 것을 멈추고 일정 시간 동안 쉬거나 잠자다. 휴식하다: *Do you want to rest before we go on?* 계속하기 전에 쉬고 싶니? **2 rest your feet/legs/eyes etc.** to stop using a part of your body for a period of time because it is feeling sore or tired ‖ 통증을 느끼거나 피곤해서 일정 시간 동안 신체 부위의 사용을 멈추다. 발/다리/눈을 쉬다: *We stopped at a cafe for a while to rest our legs.* 우리는 다리를 쉬려고 잠시 카페에 들렀다. **3** [T] to support an object or part of your body by putting it on or against something ‖ 어떤 것에 놓거나 기대어 물건이나 신체 일부를 지탱하다. 기대다: *The baby*

rested his head on my shoulder. 그 아기는 머리를 내 어깨 위에 올려 놓았다. / *Rest your bike against the wall.* 네 자전거를 벽에 기대어 놓아라. **4 rest assured (that)** FORMAL used in order to tell someone that what you say is true ‖ 말한 내용이 사실이라고 남에게 말하는 데에 쓰여. …에 안심하다: *You can rest assured that we'll do all we can.* 우리가 할 수 있는 모든 것을 다 할 테니 너는 안심해도 좋다. **5 sb will not rest until** LITERARY if someone will not rest until something happens, s/he will not be satisfied until it happens ‖ 어떤 일이 발생할 때까지는 만족하지 않을 것이다 **6 rest in peace** a phrase written on a grave stone ‖ 묘비에 쓰여진 말. 편히 잠드소서 **7 rest on your laurels** to be satisfied with what you have done, and not do anything more ‖ 사람이 한 일에 만족하여 더 이상 어떤 일을 하지 않다. 이미 성취한 성공·명예 등에 만족하다: *We can't rest on our laurels; the market is too competitive.* 우리는 우리가 이룬 성공에 만족할 수 없다. 시장은 너무나 경쟁이 심하다.

rest on/upon sth *phr v* [T] FORMAL to depend on or be based on something ‖ 어떤 것에 의지하거나 근거하다. …에 좌우되다. 기초를 두다: *His future in sports rests on this meeting with the coaches.* 스포츠에서의 그의 장래는 이번 코치들과의 미팅에 달려 있다.

rest with sb *phr v* [T] if a decision rests with someone, s/he is responsible for it ‖ 결정에 대한 책임을 지고 있다. …에 달려 있다. …나름이다: *The final decision rests with you.* 최후의 결정은 너에게 달려 있다.

re·state /riˈsteɪt/ *v* [T] to say something again in a different way, so that it is clearer or more strongly expressed ‖ 어떤 것을 보다 명쾌하게 또는 강하게 표현하기 위해 다르게 다시 말하다. …을 다시[고쳐] 말하다: *Hersh restated his confidence in Glidden's abilities.* 허쉬는 글리든의 능력에 대한 그의 확신을 재차 이야기했다. − **restatement** *n* [C, U]

res·tau·rant /ˈrɛs.trɑnt, ˈrɛstə.rɑnt, ˈrɛstərənt/ *n* a place where you can buy and eat a meal ‖ 식사를 사서 먹을 수 있는 장소. 식당

CULTURE NOTE getting attention in a restaurant

In the US and Canada, when you are in a restaurant and want to get the

attention of a waiter or waitress, you can look at him or her and raise your hand slightly. This shows that you are ready to order, would like the check etc.
미국과 캐나다에서, 식당에서 웨이터나 웨이트리스를 부르고 싶을 때 그들을 쳐다보며 손을 살짝 든다. 이것은 음식을 주문할 준비가 되어 있거나, 계산을 하고 싶다는 것 등을 나타낸다.

rest·ful /ˈrɛstfəl/ adj peaceful and quiet ‖ 평화롭고 조용한. 차분한: *a restful weekend* 평온한 주말

rest home /ˈ. ./ n ⇨ NURSING HOME

res·ti·tu·tion /ˌrɛstəˈtuʃən/ n [U] FORMAL the act of giving back to the owner something that was lost or stolen, or of paying for damage ‖ 분실되거나 도난당한 물건을 주인에게 되돌려주는 행위, 또는 파손에 대한 지불 행위. 반환. 손해 배상[보상, 변상]

res·tive /ˈrɛstɪv/ adj FORMAL ⇨ RESTLESS

rest·less /ˈrɛstlɪs/ adj 1 unable to keep still, especially because you are impatient, anxious, or bored ‖ 특히 참을성이 없어서[걱정해서, 지루해서] 가만히 있지 못하는. 침착하지 못한. 안절부절못하는: *The children are getting restless.* 아이들이 가만히 있지 못하고 있다. 2 not satisfied and wanting new experiences ‖ 만족하지 못하고 새로운 경험을 원하는. 활동적인. 정체되지 않은: *I could see she was restless and thinking about a new job.* 나는 그녀가 안주하지 않고 새 직업을 생각하고 있다는 것을 알 수 있었다. – **restlessness** n [U] – **restlessly** adv

re·store /rɪˈstɔr/ v [T] 1 to make something as good as it was before ‖ 예전처럼 좋은 것을 만들다. 수복[복원]하다. 되살리다: *restoring antique furniture* 고가구의 복원 2 to make something exist again ‖ 사물을 다시 존재하게 하다. 회복[복귀]시키다: *The army was called in to restore order.* 질서 회복을 위해 군대가 소집되었다. 3 FORMAL to give back to someone something that was lost or stolen ‖ 분실되거나 도난당한 것을 사람에게 되돌려 주다. 반환하다: *The stolen horses were restored to their rightful owner.* 도난당한 말들은 정당한 소유자에게 반환되었다. – **restoration** /ˌrɛstəˈreɪʃən/ n [C, U]

re·strain /rɪˈstreɪn/ v [T] 1 to physically prevent someone from doing something ‖ 사람이 어떤 일을 하는 것을 물리적으로 막다. 억제하다. 제지하다: *He*

had to be *restrained* by his teammates *from* attacking the referee. 그가 심판을 공격하는 것을 그의 팀 동료들이 저지해야 했다. 2 to control something ‖ 어떤 것을 규제하다. 제한하다: *new taxes to restrain the demand for foreign goods* 외국 상품에 대한 수요를 제한하기 위한 새로운 조세

re·strained /rɪˈstreɪnd/ adj behavior that is restrained is calm and controlled ‖ 행동이 차분하고 절제된. 삼가는

re·straint /rɪˈstreɪnt/ n 1 [U] calm and controlled behavior ‖ 차분하고 절제된 행동. 자제. 인내력: *I think you showed great restraint, considering what she said.* 그녀가 한 말을 생각하면 나는 네가 대단한 인내심을 보였다고 생각한다. 2 [C, U] something that controls what you can say or do ‖ 말하거나 행동할 수 있는 것을 통제하는 것. 억제. 제지. 규제: *Budget cuts have put restraints on public spending.* 예산 삭감은 공공 지출을 제한했다.

re·strict /rɪˈstrɪkt/ v [T] to control something or keep it within limits ‖ 한도 내에서 어떤 것을 통제하거나 유지하다. …을 제한[한정]하다: *new laws to restrict the sale of guns* 총기 판매를 제한하는 새로운 법

re·strict·ed /rɪˈstrɪktɪd/ adj 1 controlled or limited ‖ 통제되거나 제한된. 한정된: *The sale of alcohol is restricted to people over the age of 21.* 술 판매는 21세 이상의 사람들로 제한되어 있다. 2 only allowed to be seen or used by a particular group of people ‖ 특정한 일단의 사람들에게만 관람되거나 이용되는 것이 허용되는. 특정 계급[집단]에 한정된: *a restricted area used by the army* 부대용 제한 구역

re·stric·tion /rɪˈstrɪkʃən/ n [C, U] a rule or set of laws that limits what you can do or what is allowed to happen ‖ 사람이 해도 되는 것 또는 발생이 허용되는 것을 제한하는 규칙이나 일련의 법률. 제한. 한정: *There's a restriction on how many tickets you can buy.* 네가 구입할 수 있는 입장권의 수는 제한되어 있다. / *freedom to travel without restriction* 무제한으로 여행하는 자유

re·stric·tive /rɪˈstrɪktɪv/ adj tending to restrict you too much ‖ 사람을 지나치게 제한하는 경향의. 제한[한정]적인: *complaints about restrictive trade policies* 제한적인 무역 정책에 대한 불만

rest·room /ˈrɛstrum/ n a room with a toilet, in a public place such as a restaurant or theater ‖ 식당이나 극장 등

의 공공장소에서 변기가 있는 방. 화장실. 휴게실 —see usage note at TOILET

re·struc·ture /ˌriˈstrʌktʃə/ *v* [T] to change the way in which something such as a business or system is organized ‖ 기업이나 체제 등이 조직화되는 방식을 바꾸다. …의 구조를 개혁하다 **– restructuring** *n* [U]

re·sult¹ /rɪˈzʌlt/ *n* **1** [C, U] something that happens or exists because of something else ‖ 다른 어떤 것 때문에 발생하거나 존재하는 일. 결과. 성과. 효과: *As a result of* (=because of) *the snow storm, there is no school today in most of the tri-city area.* 눈보라 때문에 오늘 세 도시 대부분의 지역에서 휴교한다. / *Ann missed several tests, with the result that she failed the class.* 앤은 시험에 여러 번 빠져서 결국 낙제를 하게 됐다. **2** the answers that are produced by a scientific or medical study or test ‖ 과학적 또는 의학적 연구나 테스트로 산출된 해답. 결과: *When will you have the results of my blood test?* 제 혈액검사 결과가 언제 나옵니까?

result² *v* [I] to happen or exist because of something ‖ 어떤 것 때문에 발생하거나 존재하다. …의 결과로 생기다. 일어나다: *an illness resulting from eating bad food* 나쁜 음식을 먹어서 생기는 질병

result in sth *phr v* [T] to make something happen ‖ 어떤 것을 발생하게 하다. …으로 끝나다. 귀착하다: *The fire resulted in the death of two children.* 화재로 인하여 두 명의 아이들이 사망했다.

re·sult·ant /rɪˈzʌltənt, -tⁿt/ *adj* FORMAL happening or existing because of something else ‖ 어떤 다른 일 때문에 발생하거나 존재하는. 결과로서 생기는

re·sume /rɪˈzum/ *v* [I, T] FORMAL to start doing something again after a pause ‖ 멈추었다가 어떤 것을 다시 시작하다. 재개하다: *Thielen hopes to resume his duties soon.* 틸렌은 곧 자신의 직무를 다시 시작하기를 바란다. **– resumption** /rɪˈzʌmpʃən/ *n* [singular, U]

ré·su·mé /ˈrɛzəˌmeɪ, ˌrɛzəˈmeɪ/ *n* a written list and description of your education and your previous jobs, that you use when you are looking for a job ‖ 직업을 구할 때 사용하는 자신이 받은 교육 및 이전 직장을 적은 목록과 설명. 이력서

re·sur·face /ˌriˈsɚfɪs/ *v* **1** [I] to appear again ‖ 다시 나타나다: *Old arguments began to resurface at last week's meeting.* 오랜 논쟁이 지난주 회의에서 다시 표면화되기 시작했다. **2** [I] to come

back up to the surface of the water ‖ 수면 위로 다시 돌아오다. (잠수함이) 다시 부상하다 **3** [T] to put a new surface on a road ‖ 도로 위에 새로운 표면을 입히다. 도로를 재포장하다

re·sur·gence /rɪˈsɚdʒəns/ *n* [singular, U] if there is a resurgence of a harmful belief or activity, it reappears and becomes stronger ‖ 해로운 신념이나 활동 등이 다시 나타나고 더 강해짐. 재기. 부활: *a resurgence of racial violence* 인종 폭동의 재현 **– resurgent** *adj*

res·ur·rect /ˌrɛzəˈrɛkt/ *v* [T] to bring an old practice, belief etc. back into use or fashion ‖ 옛 관행·신념 등을 다시 사용하거나 유행하게 하다. 되살리다. 부활시키다: *Designers in the 1990s resurrected the styles of the 1960s.* 1990년대의 디자이너들은 1960년대의 스타일을 다시 유행하게 했다.

res·ur·rec·tion /ˌrɛzəˈrɛkʃən/ *n* [U] the act of bringing an old practice, belief etc. back into use or fashion ‖ 옛 관행·신념 등을 다시 사용하거나 유행하게 하는 행위. 부활. 회복. 재생. 재유행

re·sus·ci·tate /rɪˈsʌsəˌteɪt/ *v* [T] to make someone breathe again after s/he has almost died ‖ 사람이 거의 죽을 뻔한 이후에 다시 호흡을 하게 하다. (인공호흡 등으로) 소생시키다. …을 되살리다 **– resuscitation** /rɪˌsʌsəˈteɪʃən/ *n* [U]

re·tail¹ /ˈriteɪl/ *n* [U] the sale of goods in stores to people for their own use ‖ 자신이 사용하려는 사람들에게 가게의 상품을 판매하는 것. 소매 —compare WHOLESALE²

retail² *v* **retail for/at** to be sold at a particular price in stores ‖ 가게에서 특정 가격으로 판매되다. 상품이 …값으로 소매되다: *This item retails for $469.* 이 상품은 소매 값으로 469달러입니다.

retail³ *adv* from a RETAILER ‖ 소매상인으로부터. 소매 값으로: *We bought it retail.* 우리는 그것을 소매로 구입했다.

re·tail·er /ˈriˌteɪlɚ/ *n* someone who sells goods to the public, using a store ‖ 가게를 이용하여, 일반인에게 상품을 파는 사람. 소매상인 —compare WHOLESALER

re·tain /rɪˈteɪn/ *v* [T] **1** to keep something or to continue to have something ‖ 어떤 것을 유지하다, 또는 계속 지니다. 보유하다: *Steamed vegetables retain more of their flavor and color.* 찐 야채는 그 향과 색깔이 보다 선명하게 유지된다. / *a town that has retained its colonial charm* 식민지풍의 매력을 계속 지니고 있는 도시 **2** to keep facts in your memory ‖ 사람의 기억 속에 어떤 사실을

간직하다. 잊지 않고 있다: *She retains most of what she reads.* 그녀는 자신이 읽은 대부분의 내용을 기억하고 있다. – **retention** /rɪˈtɛnʃən/ *n* [U]

re·tain·er /rɪˈteɪnər/ *n* **1** an amount of money that you pay regularly to someone such as a lawyer, so that s/he will continue to work for you ‖ 자신을 위해 일을 계속해 주도록 변호사 등에게 정기적으로 지급하는 금액. 변호사 의뢰료 **2** a small plastic and wire object that you wear in your mouth to make your teeth stay straight ‖ 사람의 치아를 곧게 유지시키려고 입에 끼우는 작은 플라스틱과 철사로 만든 물체. 치아 (교정용) 고정 장치

re·take /ˌriˈteɪk/ *v* [T] to get control of something again ‖ 사물에 대한 통제력을 다시 가지다. …을 다시 취하다[차지하다]: *Rebels have retaken the city.* 반란군들은 그 도시를 다시 점령했다.

re·tal·i·ate /rɪˈtælieɪt/ *v* [I] to do something bad to someone because s/he has done something bad to you ‖ 남이 자신에게 나쁜 짓을 했기 때문에 그 사람에게 나쁜 짓을 하다. (남에게) 복수하다. (어떤 수단으로) 보복하다. (어떤 행위에) 앙갚음하다: *When the police moved in, the angry crowd retaliated by throwing rocks.* 경찰이 진입하자 성난 군중들은 돌을 던지며 응수했다.

re·tal·i·a·tion /rɪˌtæliˈeɪʃən/ *n* [U] the act of retaliating (RETALIATE) ‖ 보복 행위. 복수. 앙갚음: *The teenager was killed in retaliation for a similar killing in a nearby neighborhood.* 인근에서 유사한 살해에 대한 보복으로 그 10대가 피살되었다.

re·tard¹ /rɪˈtɑrd/ *v* [T] FORMAL to delay the development of something, or to make something happen more slowly ‖ 사물의 발전을 지연시키다, 또는 어떤 일의 발생을 더욱 느리게 하다. (성장 · 진보 등을) 더디게 하다. …을 늦추다 – **retardation** /ˌritɑrˈdeɪʃən/ *n* [U]

retard² /ˈritɑrd/ *n* SLANG OFFENSIVE a stupid person ‖ 바보 같은 사람. 지능 발달이 늦은 사람. 지진아

re·tard·ed /rɪˈtɑrdɪd/ *adj* less mentally developed than other people ‖ 다른 사람들보다 정신적으로 덜 발달된. 지능 발달이 늦은: *training programs for retarded adults* 지능이 낮은 성인을 위한 교육 프로그램

USAGE NOTE retarded

Using the word **retarded** to talk about someone who has difficulty

---

learning things is offensive. It is more polite to say that a person is "mentally challenged" or has "special needs."

어떤 것을 배우는 데 어려움이 있는 사람을 말할 때 **retarded**란 단어를 쓰는 것은 모욕적인 표현이다. "mentally challenged" 또는 "special weeds"가 있는 사람이라고 말하는 것이 보다 예의 바른 표현이다.

---

retch /rɛtʃ/ *v* [I] if you retch, you feel like you are VOMITing but nothing comes out of your stomach ‖ 토할 것 같은 느낌이 들지만 위에서 아무것도 나오지 않다. 구역질나다. 헛구역질하다

re·think /ˌriˈθɪŋk/ *v* [I, T] to think about a plan or idea again in order to decide if any changes should be made ‖ 어떤 변화가 발생해야 할지 결정하기 위해 계획이나 생각에 대하여 다시 생각하다. 재고하다

ret·i·cent /ˈrɛtəsənt/ *adj* unwilling to talk about what you know or how you feel ‖ 자신이 알고 있는 내용이나 자신의 느낌에 대해 말하기를 꺼리는. 입이 무거운. 말이 적은[삼가는]: *She was very reticent about her reasons for leaving.* 그녀는 떠난 이유에 대해서 말을 하는 것을 아주 꺼려했다. – **reticence** *n* [U]

ret·i·na /ˈrɛtn̩ə/ *n* the area at the back of your eye that sends an image of what you see to your brain ‖ 사람이 본 상(像)을 뇌에 보내는 눈 뒤쪽에 있는 부위. (눈의) 망막

ret·i·nue /ˈrɛtn̩ˌu/ *n* a group of helpers or supporters who are traveling with an important person ‖ 중요한 사람과 동행하는 일단의 조력자들이나 지지자들. 수행원[단]: *the president's retinue* 대통령의 수행원

re·tire /rɪˈtaɪr/ *v* **1** [I, T] to stop working, usually because of old age, or to make someone do this ‖ 보통 고령 때문에 일하는 것을 그만두다, 또는 어떤 사람을 이렇게 하게 하다. 퇴직[은퇴]하다[시키다]: *Barney wants to retire next year.* 바니는 내년에 은퇴하고 싶어한다. **2** [I] FORMAL to go away to a quiet place ‖ 조용한 곳으로 떠나다. …으로 물러가다: *He retired to his room.* 그는 자기 방으로 물러갔다. **3** [I] FORMAL to go to bed ‖ 자다. 잠자리에 들다

re·tired /rɪˈtaɪrd/ *adj* retired people have stopped working, usually because they are old ‖ 보통 연로해서, 일을 중단한. 퇴직한: *a retired teacher* 퇴직 교사

re·tire·ment /rɪˈtaɪrmənt/ *n* **1** [C, U]

the act of retiring (RETIRE) from your job ‖ 직장에서 퇴직하는 행위. 은퇴. 퇴역: *a party for Bill's retirement* 빌의 퇴직 파티 **2** [singular, U] the period of time after you have retired ‖ 퇴직한 후의 시기. 한거: *a long and happy retirement* 길고 행복한 퇴직 생활

re·tir·ing /rɪ'taɪərɪŋ/ *adj* **1** not wanting to be with other people ‖ 다른 사람과 어울리기를 원하지 않는. 수줍은. 소극적인: *a shy and retiring woman* 수줍고 소극적인 여인 **2 the retiring president/ manager etc.** a president etc. who is soon going to RETIRE ‖ 대통령 등이 곧 퇴직할 예정인. 퇴직할 대통령/관리자

re·tort /rɪ'tɔrt/ *v* [T] to reply quickly, in an angry or humorous way ‖ 화내거나 유머러스한 방식으로 재빨리 대답하다. …에 …으로 응수하다. …으로 말대꾸하다 [반박하다]: *"It's all your fault!" he retorted.* "그건 모두 네 잘못이야!"라고 그는 되받아쳤다. – **retort** *n*

re·trace /ri'treɪs/ *v* [T] **1** to go back the way you have come ‖ 사람이 온 길을 되돌아가다: *She retraced her steps to try to find her ring.* 그녀는 반지를 찾으려고 온 길을 되돌아갔다. **2** to repeat exactly the same trip that someone else has made ‖ 다른 사람이 했던 여행을 똑같이 정확하게 반복하다. …을 거슬러 올라가 자취를 살펴보다[조사하다]: *The ships are retracing Columbus's route across the Atlantic to North America.* 그 선박은 대서양을 횡단해서 북미에 이르기까지 콜럼버스의 항로를 거슬러 올라가며 자취를 살펴보고 있다.

re·tract /rɪ'trækt/ *v* **1** [T] to make an official statement saying that something you said earlier is not true ‖ 사람이 전에 말한 것이 사실이 아니라고 공식적인 진술을 하다. 철회하다: *He confessed to the crime but later retracted his statement.* 그는 죄를 자백했으나 나중에 그의 말을 철회했다. **2** [I, T] if a part of something retracts or is retracted, it moves back into the main part ‖ 사물의 일부가 주요 부분으로 다시 돌아가다 또는 되돌리다. 원 위치하다[시키다] – **retraction** /rɪ'trækʃən/ *n* [C, U]

re·tract·a·ble /rɪ'træktəbəl/ *adj* a retractable part of something can be pulled back into the main part ‖ 사물의 일부를 주요 부분으로 도로 당겨 넣을 수 있는. 접어 넣을 수 있는: *a knife with a retractable blade* 접어 넣을 수 있는 날이 달린 칼

re·tread /'ritrɛd/ *n* an old tire with a new rubber surface put onto it ‖ 헌 타이

어에 다시 새 고무 표면을 붙인 것. 재생 타이어

re·treat¹ /rɪ'trit/ *v* [I] **1** to decide not to do what you have promised or planned because it seems too difficult or extreme ‖ 너무 어렵거나 극단적으로 보이기 때문에 사람이 약속하거나 계획한 것을 하지 않기로 결정하다. 물러서다. 그만두다: *The president seems to be retreating from his pledge to cut taxes.* 대통령은 조세를 삭감하겠다는 자신의 공약에서 손을 떼고 있는 것 같다. **2** to move away from a place or person ‖ 장소나 사람으로부터 멀어지다. 물러서다. 도망가다: *"We need another lamp," she called after the retreating servant.* "우리는 또 다른 등이 필요해." 그녀는 물러나고 있는 하인 뒤에서 소리쳤다. **3** to stop being involved with society or other people at all ‖ 사회나 다른 사람들과 관계하는 것을 전적으로 중단하다. 칩거하다: *After her death, he retreated into himself and stopped working altogether.* 그녀가 죽은 뒤에 그는 자신의 세계에 몰두하면서 함께 일하는 것을 중단했다. **4** if an army retreats it stops fighting and moves away from the enemy ‖ 군대가 전투를 중지하고 적으로부터 멀리 떨어지다. 후퇴[철수, 퇴각]하다

retreat² *n* **1** the act of deciding to do or believe something that is less extreme or difficult than what you had planned, promised, or believed before ‖ 사람이 전에 계획했던[약속했던, 믿었던] 것보다 덜 극단적이거나 덜 어려운 일을 하거나 믿기로 결정하는 행위. 물러섬. 후퇴: *a retreat from his original position on welfare spending* 복지비 지출에 대한 그의 본래 입장의 철회 **2** a place you can go to that is quiet or safe ‖ 사람이 갈 수 있는 조용하거나 안전한 곳. 피난처. 은신처: *a mountain retreat* 산의 피난처 **3** [C, U] a decision to no longer be involved with society or other people at all ‖ 사회나 남들과 더 이상 전혀 관계하지 않으려는 결정. 은둔. 칩거: *The philosopher's retreat from society produced some of his greatest works.* 그 철학자는 사회에서 떨어져 은거 생활을 하며 그의 위대한 몇몇 작품을 창작했다. **4** [C, U] an army's movement away from the enemy ‖ 적으로부터 멀어지는 군대의 이동. 철수. 후퇴: *Napoleon's retreat from Moscow* 모스크바에서 나폴레옹의 후퇴 **5** [C, U] a movement away from a place or person ‖ 장소나 사람에게서 멀리 떨어짐

re·tri·al /ˌri'traɪl, 'ritraɪl/ *n* the process of judging a law case in court again ‖ 법

원에서 다시 법률 사건을 심판하는 과정. 재심: *My lawyer demanded a retrial.* 나의 변호사는 재심을 청구했다.

ret·ri·bu·tion /ˌrɛtrəˈbyuʃən/ *n* [singular, U] punishment that is deserved ‖ 받아 마땅한 처벌. 보복. 응보: *Employees need to feel they can express their views without fear of retribution.* 고용자들은 보복의 두려움 없이 자신들의 견해를 밝힐 수 있다는 생각이 필요하다.

re·trieve /rɪˈtriv/ *v* [T] to find something and bring it back ‖ 사물을 찾아서 되가져오다. 되찾다. 회수하다: *You can retrieve the document by clicking on the icon.* 너는 아이콘을 클릭하여 그 문서를 검색할 수 있다. / *He retrieved the book from the shelf and handed it to me.* 그는 선반에서 그 책을 꺼내서 나에게 건네주었다. – **retrieval** *n* [U]

re·triev·er /rɪˈtrivɚ/ *n* a type of dog that can be trained to find and bring back birds that its owner has shot ‖ 주인이 사격해서 맞춘 새를 찾아서 되가져올 수 있도록 훈련받은 개의 종류. 사냥감을 찾아 가져오는 사냥개

ret·ro·ac·tive /ˌrɛtroʊˈæktɪv/ *adj* a law or decision that is retroactive is effective from a particular date in the past ‖ 법률이나 결정들이 과거의 특정한 일자(日字)부터 유효한. …까지 소급하는: *a retroactive pay increase* 소급 유효한 봉급 인상 – **retroactively** *adv*

ret·ro·spect /ˈrɛtrəˌspɛkt/ *n* **in retrospect** when you think about the past, and know more now than you did then ‖ 사람이 과거에 대해 생각해 볼 때 그 당시에 했던 것보다 지금 더 많이 알다. 회상해 보면. 돌이켜 생각하면: *In retrospect, it was the wrong time to leave my job.* 회상해 보면, 그때는 내 일을 사직하기에는 좋지 않은 시기였다.

re·tro·spec·tive /ˌrɛtrəˈspɛktɪv/ *adj* concerned with the past ‖ 과거에 관련된. 회고적인. 되돌아보는: *a retrospective look at Capra's movies* 카프라 감독 영화 다시 보기

re·try /riˈtraɪ/ *v* [I] to judge a law case in court again ‖ 법원에서 법률 사건을 다시 재판하다. 재심하다

re·turn[1] /rɪˈtɚn/ *v*
1 ▸**GO BACK** 되돌아가다◂ [I] to go back to a place where you were before, or to come back from a place ‖ 사람이 전에 있었던 장소로 돌아가다, 또는 어떤 장소로 되돌아오다. 되돌아가다[오다]: *Kevin has just returned from Texas.* 케빈은 텍사스에서 방금 돌아왔다. / *She didn't return until after 8 o'clock.* 그녀는 8시가 지나서까지 돌아오지 않았다. ✗DON'T SAY "return back."✗ "return back"이라고는 하지 않는다.

2 ▸**PREVIOUS STATE** 이전의 상태◂ [I] to be in a previous state or condition again ‖ 다시 이전의 상태나 상황으로 되다. 되돌아가다: *Things will soon return to normal.* 상황은 곧 정상으로 되돌아갈 것이다.

3 ▸**GIVE BACK** 되돌려주다◂ [T] to give something back, or put something back in its place ‖ 사물을 되돌려주다, 또는 원래 자리에 도로 갖다 놓다. 반환[반송]하다: *Will you return these books to the library for me?* 내 대신 이 책들을 도서관에 반납해 주겠니? / *It didn't fit, so I returned it.* (=took it back to the store) 그것이 맞지 않아서 반품했다.

4 ▸**HAPPEN AGAIN** 재발하다◂ [I] to start to happen or exist again ‖ 다시 발생하거나 존재하기 시작하다. 재발하다. 되살아나다: *Take two of these pills if the pain returns.* 만일 통증이 재발하면 이 알약 2개를 먹어라.

5 ▸**START AGAIN** 재개하다◂ [I] to go back to an activity, discussion etc. that was stopped or interrupted ‖ 중단되거나 방해 받았던 활동·토론 등으로 되돌아가다: *Let's return to the subject of your previous employment.* 저번 네 일자리에 대한 애기로 돌아가자. / *Does she plan to return to work after the baby is born?* 아기가 태어난 뒤에 그녀는 직장에 되돌아갈 계획이니?

6 ▸**DO STH SIMILAR** 유사한 일을 하다◂ [T] to react to something someone has done, by doing something similar ‖ 비슷한 일을 함으로써 남이 한 일에 대해 반응하다. …과 비슷한 것으로 반환하다: *Why didn't you return my call?* 왜 내 전화에 답신을 하지 않았니? / *She's really helped me recently, and I wanted to return the favor.* 최근에 그녀가 정말로 나를 도와주어서 나는 그녀의 호의에 보답하고 싶었다.

7 return a verdict if a JURY returns their VERDICT, they say whether someone is guilty or not ‖ 배심원이 유죄 여부에 대해 말하다. 배심원이 피고를 …이라고 평결하다

8 ▸**MONEY** 금전◂ [T] if an INVESTMENT returns a particular amount of money, that is how much profit it produces ‖ 투자 등이 특정 액수의 수익을 낳다. (이익·소득 등을) 생기게 하다. 가져오다

return[2] *n*
1 ▸**GOING BACK** 돌아감◂ [singular, U] the act of going back to a place where

you were before, or of coming back from a place ‖ 사람이 전에 있었던 장소로 돌아가는 행위, 또는 어떤 장소에서 돌아오는 행위. 귀환. 귀성: *We're all looking forward to your return!* 우리 모두는 너의 귀환을 기대하고 있다! / *I expect to meet her on/upon her return*. (=when she returns) 나는 그녀가 돌아와서 그녀를 만나기를 기대한다.
2 ▶GIVING STH BACK 사물의 반환◀ [U] the act of giving something back, or of putting something back in its place ‖ 사물을 되돌려 놓거나 사물을 그 본래 자리에 되돌려 놓는 행위. 반환. 반송: *a reward for the return of the stolen necklace* 도난당한 목걸이의 반환에 대한 사례금
3 ▶STH HAPPENING AGAIN 재발◀ the fact of something starting to happen or to exist again ‖ 어떤 것이 다시 발생하거나 존재하기 시작함. 되살아남: *the return of spring* 다시 돌아온 봄
4 ▶STH STARTING AGAIN 다시 시작함◀ [singular] the act of going back to an activity, discussion, way of doing something etc. that was stopped or interrupted ‖ 중단되거나 방해받았던 활동・토론・행동 방식으로 되돌아가는 행위. 복귀: *her return to full-time work* 그녀의 상근직으로의 복귀 / *There cannot be a return to the old way of life*. 옛날 생활 방식으로 되돌아갈 수는 없다.
5 ▶MONEY 금전◀ [C, U] the amount of profit an INVESTMENT produces ‖ 투자가 낳는 일정량의 수익. 수입: *He expects a big return on his shares*. 그는 그의 몫으로 큰 수입을 기대한다.
6 in return (for) in exchange for, or as payment for something ‖ 어떤 것에 대한 교환으로서, 또는 어떤 것에 대한 보수로서. (…에 대한) 대답[답례]으로서: *I'd like to buy you a drink in return for all you've done*. 당신이 해주신 모든 일에 대한 답례로 제가 술을 사고 싶습니다.
7 ▶STATEMENT 진술◀ a statement or set of figures given as a reply to an official demand ‖ 공식적인 요청에 대한 응답으로서 제시한 진술이나 수치. 신고(서). 보고(서): *a tax return* 조세 신고
re·turn·a·ble /rɪ'tənəbəl/ *adj* returnable bottles, containers etc. can be given back to the store ‖ 병・용기 등을 가게에 되돌려 줄 수 있는. (빈 병 등) 반환할 수 있는
re·un·ion /ri'yunyən/ *n* **1** a meeting of people who have not met for a long time ‖ 오랫동안 만나지 못했던 사람들과의 만남. 재회. 재회의 모임: *a college reunion* 대학 동창회 **2** [U] the state of being brought together again after a period of being separated ‖ 일정 기간 헤어져 있다가 다시 모인 상태. 재결합: *an emotional reunion after a long separation* 오랜 이별 뒤의 감동적인 재결합
re·u·nite /ˌriyu'naɪt/ *v* [I, T] to come together again, or to be brought together again after a period of being separated ‖ 일정 기간 헤어져 있다가 다시 모이거나 다시 화해하다. 재결합하다[시키다]. 재회하다[시키다]: *That spring, he was at last reunited with his children*. 그해 봄에 그는 마침내 그의 자녀들과 재결합되었다.
Rev. the written abbreviation of REVEREND ‖ Reverend의 약어
rev¹ /rɛv/ *n* [C usually plural] INFORMAL one REVOLUTION of an engine ‖ 엔진의 1회전
rev², rev up *v* **-vved, -vving** [I, T] if you rev an engine, or if it revs, it works faster ‖ 엔진이 더 빨리 작동하다. 엔진 등의 속도가[를] 급히 올라가다[올리다]
re·val·ue /ri'vælyu/ *v* [T] to examine something again in order to calculate its present value ‖ 그 현재 가치를 계산하기 위해 사물을 다시 조사하다. …을 재평가하다 **- revaluation** /ri,vælyu'eɪʃən/ *n* [C, U] —compare DEVALUE
re·vamp /ri'væmp/ *v* [T] INFORMAL to change something in order to improve it ‖ 어떤 것을 개선하기 위해 바꾸다. …을 개조[수리, 쇄신]하다. 개정[수정]하다: *a bill that would revamp federal banking laws* 연방 은행법을 개정하는 법안
re·veal /rɪ'vil/ *v* [T] **1** to show something that was previously hidden ‖ 전에는 숨겨졌던 사물을 보여주다. 드러내다: *The curtains opened to reveal a darkened stage*. 어두워진 무대를 드러내기 위해 커튼이 열렸다. **2** to make something known that was previously secret ‖ 전에 비밀이었던 것을 알려지게 하다. 알리다. 밝히다. 폭로하다: *The newspaper story revealed a huge cover-up*. 그 신문 기사는 엄청난 은폐를 폭로했다. / *She suddenly revealed that she had once been married*. 그녀는 갑자기 자신이 한때 결혼했었다는 사실을 밝혔다.
re·veal·ing /rɪ'vilɪŋ/ *adj* **1** showing someone's character or feelings ‖ 사람의 성격이나 감정을 나타내는. (숨겨진 것을) 드러나게 하는. 계발적인: *Some of her comments were very revealing*. 그녀의 논평 중 어떤 부분에는 매우 깊은 뜻이 있었다. **2** revealing clothes show parts of your body that are usually kept covered

‖ 옷이 보통 가려져 있는 신체의 일부가 보이는. 노출이 심한. 속이 들여다보이는

rev·el /ˈrɛvəl/ *v*

revel in sth *phr v* [T] to enjoy something very much ‖ 어떤 것을 매우 많이 즐기다. …에 골몰하다: *Bobby seemed to revel in my undivided attention.* 보비는 내가 전념하는 것에 매우 기뻐하는 듯했다.

rev·e·la·tion /ˌrɛvəˈleɪʃən/ *n* [C, U] a surprising and previously secret fact that suddenly becomes known, or the act of making this fact known ‖ 갑자기 알려진 놀랍고 전에는 비밀이었던 사실, 또는 이 사실을 알리는 행위. 뜻밖의 새 사실[놀랄 만한 것]. 폭로: *strange revelations about her past* 그녀의 과거에 대한 이상한 뜻밖의 사실

rev·el·er /ˈrɛvələ/ *n* someone who is enjoying drinking, dancing, and eating, especially at a party ‖ 특히 파티에서 (술) 마시고 춤추고 먹기를 좋아하는 사람. 술잔치를 벌이기 좋아하는 사람. 난봉꾼. 도락자

rev·el·ry /ˈrɛvəlri/ *n* [C, U] wild noisy dancing, eating, drinking etc. ‖ 광란의 시끄러운 춤·음식·음주 등. 흥청대는 술잔치. 야단법석

re·venge¹ /rɪˈvɛndʒ/ *n* [U] something you do in order to punish someone who has harmed or offended you ‖ 남에게 해를 끼치거나 감정을 상하게 한 사람을 복수하기 위해서 행하는 일. 복수. 원한. 보복(행위): *I think that Brennan lied in order to get/take revenge on the company for firing him.* 나는 브레넌이 회사에서 해고당한 것에 보복하기 위해 거짓말을 했다고 생각한다. / *a bomb attack in revenge for the killing of ten prisoners* 10명의 죄수를 살해한 데 대한 앙갚음으로 행해진 폭탄 공격

revenge² *v* [T] to punish someone who has harmed or offended you ‖ 사람을 해치거나 감정을 상하게 한 사람을 처벌하다. (남에게) 복수하다. 원한을 풀다 — see also AVENGE

rev·e·nue /ˈrɛvəˌnu/ *n* [U] **1** money that is earned by a company ‖ 회사에서 벌어들인 돈. 총수입 **2** money that the government receives from tax ‖ 정부가 세금으로 받아들인 돈. 세입

re·ver·ber·ate /rɪˈvɜbəˌreɪt/ *v* [I] **1** if a loud sound reverberates, it is heard many times as it is sent back from different surfaces ‖ 큰 소리가 다른 표면으로부터 되돌아오면서 여러 번 들리다. 울려 퍼지다. 진동하다: *Their voices reverberated around the empty church.* 그들의 목소리는 텅빈 교회 근방에 울려 퍼졌다. **2** to have a strong effect that continues for a long time ‖ 오랫동안 계속되는 강한 영향을 가지다. 영향을 주다. 반향을 불러일으키다: *The fall of stock prices continues to reverberate in the market.* 주가의 하락은 시장에 계속적인 반향을 불러일으킨다. — **reverberation** /rɪˌvɜbəˈreɪʃən/ *n* [C, U]

re·vere /rɪˈvɪr/ *v* [T] FORMAL to greatly respect and admire someone ‖ 사람을 대단히 존경하고 칭송하다. 우러러 공경하다: *He was revered as a leader.* 그는 지도자로서 대단한 공경을 받았다.

rev·er·ence /ˈrɛvrəns/ *adj* FORMAL respect and admiration ‖ 존경과 칭송. 숭상. 경의: *a reverence for tradition* 전통에 대한 숭배 — **reverent** *adj* — **reverently** *adv* —opposite IRREVERENT

Rev·er·end /ˈrɛvrənd, -ərənd/ *n* a minister in the Christian church ‖ 크리스트교회의 목사. 신부. 성직자: *Reverend Larson* 라슨 목사님

rev·er·ie /ˈrɛvəri/ *n* [C, U] a state of imagining or thinking about pleasant things ‖ 즐거운 것들에 대해 상상하거나 생각하는 상태. 환상. 몽상

re·ver·sal /rɪˈvɜsəl/ *n* [C, U] the act of changing an arrangement, process, or action in order to do the opposite ‖ 반대로 하기 위해 배열[과정, 행동]을 바꾸는 행위. 역전. 반전: *a reversal of the usual policy* 평소 방침의 반전 / *a reversal of the court's decision* 법정 판결의 파기

re·verse¹ /rɪˈvɜs/ *v* **1** [T] to change something, such as a decision, judgment, or process, so that it is the opposite of what it was before ‖ 결정[판단, 절차] 등을 이전과 반대가 되도록 바꾸다. …을 역으로[거꾸로] 하다: *The judge reversed his original decision and set her free.* 판사는 자신의 원판결(原判決)을 뒤집고 그녀를 석방했다. **2** [I, T] to move backward, especially in a vehicle ‖ 특히 자동차에서 후진하다. 반대 방향으로 움직이다: *Reverse the car through the gate.* 그 차를 후진하여 정문을 통과해라. / *reversing out of a driveway* 진입로에서의 후진 **3** [T] to change around the usual order of the parts of something ‖ 어떤 것의 일부의 통상 순서를 완전히 바꾸다. (정)반대가 되게 하다: *Let's reverse the order of the songs and sing "Freedom" first.* 노래의 순서를 바꾸어 "자유"를 제일 먼저 부르자. — **reversible** *adj* : *a reversible coat* 양면 겸용 코트

reverse² *n* **1** [U] the control in a vehicle that makes it go backward ‖ 차량을 뒤로 가게 하는 운전. 후진(기어[운전]): *Put the car in reverse.* 차를 후진시키시오. **2 the reverse** the opposite ‖ 반대: *He did the reverse of what we expected and bought us all a drink.* 그는 우리가 예상했던 것과 반대로 우리 모두에게 술을 샀다. **3 in reverse** done in the opposite way or with the opposite effect ‖ 반대로 되거나 역효과를 갖게 된: *Welfare is taxation in reverse.* 복지는 돌려받는 세금이다.

reverse³ *adj* opposite of what is usual or to what has just been stated ‖ 보통의 것과 반대이거나 방금 언급된 것에 반대되는. 거꾸로 된. 반대의: *Put the letters of the words in reverse order and see what it spells.* 그 단어들의 알파벳을 거꾸로 놓고 어떤 글자가 되는지 보세요.

reverse dis·crim·i·na·tion /ˌ.. ...ˈ../ *n* [U] a phrase meaning a situation in which a woman or a MINORITY such as an African-American is chosen for a job even though s/he is not the best person for the job, used by people who do not approve of this ‖ 여성이나 아프리카계 미국인 등 소수 인종이 직업을 구할 때 최적의 인재가 아니더라도 선택받는 상황을 뜻하는 어구로 이러한 상황을 찬성하지 않는 사람들이 쓰는 표현. 역차별 —compare AFFIRMATIVE ACTION

re·vert /rɪˈvɚt/ *v* **revert to sth** to go back to a previous situation, condition, use, or habit ‖ 원래의 상황[상태, 쓰임, 습관]으로 돌아가다. 되돌아가다. 복귀하다: *Leningrad reverted to its former name of St. Petersburg.* 레닌그라드는 전의 명칭이었던 상트 페테르부르크로 되었다. — **reversion** /rɪˈvɚʒən/ *n* [singular, U]

re·view¹ /rɪˈvyu/ *n* **1** [C, U] an act of carefully examining, considering, and judging a situation or process ‖ 상황이나 절차를 주의 깊게 검사·고려·판단하는 행위. (재)검토. 재고: *an urgent review of safety procedures* 안전 조치의 긴급 점검 / *Our salaries are currently under review.* (=being examined and considered) 우리의 봉급은 현재 검토되고 있다. **2** an article that gives an opinion about a new book, play, movie etc. ‖ 새로운 책·연극·영화 등에 대한 의견을 실은 기사. 평론. 비평 기사: *His book got very good reviews.* 그의 책은 호평을 받았다.

review² *v* **1** [T] to examine, consider, and judge a situation or process carefully ‖ 상황이나 절차를 신중하게 검

사·생각·판단하다. (재)검토[재고]하다: *The state is reviewing its education policy.* 주 당국은 교육 정책을 재검토 중이다. **2** [I, T] to write an article that gives your opinion about a new book, play, movie etc. ‖ 새로운 책·연극·영화 등에 대한 자신의 의견을 실은 기사를 쓰다. 비평을 쓰다. 비평하다: *He reviews movies for our local newspaper.* 그는 우리 지역 신문에 영화 비평을 쓴다. **3** [I, T] to prepare for a test by studying books, notes, reports etc. ‖ 시험을 준비하기 위해 책·필기장·보고서 등을 공부하다. …을 복습하다

re·view·er /rɪˈvyuɚ/ *n* someone who writes articles that give his/her opinion about new books, plays, movies etc. ‖ 새로운 책·연극·영화 등에 대한 의견을 실은 기사를 쓰는 사람. 비평가

re·vile /rɪˈvaɪl/ *v* [T] FORMAL to express hatred of someone or something ‖ 사람이나 사물에 대한 증오를 표현하다. …을 욕하다. 욕설을 퍼붓다

re·vise /rɪˈvaɪz/ *v* [T] **1** to change your opinions, plans etc. because of new information or ideas ‖ 새로운 정보나 생각 때문에 자신의 의견을 바꾸다. …을 고치다[변경하다]: *The hotel operator said it will revise plans for the new building.* 호텔 운영자는 신축 건물에 대한 계획을 수정할 것이라고 말했다. **2** to improve a piece of writing ‖ 원고를 수정하다. 개정[교정]하다

re·vi·sion /rɪˈvɪʒən/ *n* **1** [C, U] the process of improving something, especially a piece of writing ‖ 특히 원고를 수정하는 과정. 개정. 교정 **2** a piece of writing that has been improved ‖ 수정된 원고. 개정[교정]본

re·vi·tal·ize /riˈvaɪṭlˌaɪz/ *v* [T] to make something become strong, active, or powerful again ‖ 어떤 것을 다시 강하게[활기 있게, 힘있게] 만들다. 새로운 활력을 주다: *The city has begun to revitalize the downtown area.* (=make businesses stronger, rebuild buildings etc.) 그 도시는 상업지구에 새로운 활력을 불어넣기 시작했다. — **revitalization** /riˌvaɪṭləˈzeɪʃən/ *n* [U]

re·viv·al /rɪˈvaɪvəl/ *n* **1** [C, U] a process in which something becomes active, strong, or popular again ‖ 사물이 다시 활기 있게[강하게, 인기 있게] 되는 과정. 재생. 회복. 소생: *the revival of the fishing industry* 수산업의 부흥 **2** a new performance of a play that has not been performed for a long time ‖ 오랫동안 공연되지 않았던 연극의 새 공연. (옛

연극·영화 등의) 재상연. 재공연: *a revival of "Oklahoma!"* 영화 "오클라호마!"의 재상영 **3** a public religious meeting that is intended to make people interested in Christianity ‖ 사람들이 기독교에 관심을 갖게 할 의도의 대중 종교 집회. 신앙 부흥 특별 전도 집회

re·vive /rɪ'vaɪv/ *v* [I, T] **1** to become conscious or healthy, or make someone do this ‖ 의식이나 건강을 회복하다, 또는 남을 이렇게 하게 하다. 소생하다[시키다]: *We revived her with cold water.* 우리는 냉수로 그녀를 정신차리게 했다. **2** to come back into use or existence, or bring something back into use or existence ‖ 재사용이나 부활하다, 또는 어떤 것을 재사용하게 하거나 부활시키다. 재가동시키다. 재개하다: *The television station decided to revive some old TV shows from the 1950s and 60s.* 텔레비전 방송국은 1950년대와 60년대의 몇몇 예전 텔레비전 쇼를 재방영하기로 결정했다.

re·voke /rɪ'voʊk/ *v* [T] to officially state that a law, decision etc. is no longer effective ‖ 법·결정 등이 이제는 효력이 없다는 것을 공식적으로 언급하다. …을 무효로 하다. 파기[취소]하다: *Her driver's license has been revoked.* 그녀의 운전 면허증은 취소되었다.

re·volt¹ /rɪ'voʊlt/ *v* **1** [I] to refuse to obey a government, law etc., often using violence against it ‖ 정부·법 등에 반대하기 위해 종종 폭력을 쓰며 따르기를 거부하다. 반항하다. 반란을 일으키다: *The people revolted against the military government.* 국민은 군사 정권에 반기를 들었다. **2** [T] to make you feel sick and shocked ‖ 토할 것 같게 하고 충격 받게 하다. …에 혐오감[반감]을 느끼게 하다: *I was revolted by what I saw.* 나는 내가 본 것에 비위가 상했다.

revolt² *n* [C, U] strong and often violent action against a government, law etc. ‖ 정부·법 등에 반대하는 강력하면서 때로는 폭력적인 행동. 반란. 폭동: *The entire nation is in revolt.* 전국이 반란 상태에 놓여 있다. / *The revolt is over.* 폭동은 끝났다.

re·volt·ing /rɪ'voʊltɪŋ/ *adj* extremely unpleasant ‖ 매우 불쾌한. 혐오감을 가지게 하는: *What a revolting meal!* 정말 역겨운 음식이군!

rev·o·lu·tion /ˌrɛvə'luʃən/ *n* **1** [C, U] a time of great, usually sudden, social and political change, especially when force is used in order to change a ruler or political system ‖ 특히 지배자나 정치 체제를 바꾸기 위해 무력이 쓰이는 보통

갑작스런 사회·정치적 대변혁의 시기. 혁명. 대변혁: *the Russian Revolution* 러시아 혁명 **2** a complete change in ways of thinking, methods of working etc. ‖ 사고 방식·작업 방법 등의 완전한 변화. 혁신: *Computer technology has caused a revolution in business practices.* 컴퓨터 기술은 사업 운영 형태에 대변혁을 가져왔다. **3** [C, U] one complete circular movement or spin around a central point ‖ 1회의 순환 운동 또는 축을 중심으로 한 1회전. 회전. 선회: *The earth makes one revolution around the sun each year.* 지구는 1년마다 태양의 주위를 한 바퀴씩 돈다. / *a wheel turning at a speed of 100 revolutions per minute* 1분당 100회전의 속도로 도는 바퀴

rev·o·lu·tion·ar·y¹ /ˌrɛvə'luʃəˌnɛri/ *adj* **1** completely new and different ‖ 완전히 새롭고 다른. 혁신의[적인]: *a revolutionary new treatment for cancer* 혁신적인 새로운 암 치료법 **2** relating to a political or social REVOLUTION ‖ 정치적 또는 사회적 혁명과 관련한. 혁명의[적인]: *a revolutionary army* 혁명군

revolutionary² *n* someone who joins in or supports a political or social REVOLUTION ‖ 정치적 또는 사회적 혁명에 가담하거나 지지하는 사람. 혁명당원. 혁명론자[가]

rev·o·lu·tion·ize /ˌrɛvə'luʃəˌnaɪz/ *v* [T] to completely change the way people think or do things ‖ 사람들의 사고방식이나 행동 방식을 완전히 변화시키다. 대변혁을 일으키다: *new machines that revolutionized the entire industry* 전체 산업을 대변혁시킨 신기계들

re·volve /rɪ'valv/ *v* [I, T] to spin around a central point, or to make something do this ‖ 중심점 주위를 빙빙 돌다, 또는 사물을 이렇게 하게 하다. 회전하다. 순환하다: *The wheels began to revolve slowly.* 바퀴가 천천히 돌기 시작했다. – **revolving** *adj* : *a revolving door* 회전문

revolve around sb/sth *phr v* [T] **1** to have something as a main subject or purpose ‖ 어떤 것을 주요 대상이나 목적으로 갖다. …을 중심으로 맴돌다[되풀이되다]: *Her life seems to revolve around her job.* 그녀의 생활은 일을 중심으로 돌아가는 것 같다. **2** to move in circles around something ‖ 사물 주위로 원을 그리며 움직이다. 원을 그리며 돌다: *The moon revolves around the earth.* 달은 지구의 주위를 운행한다.

re·volv·er /rɪ'valvə/ *n* a type of small gun that you hold in one hand ‖ 한 손으

로 잡는 소총의 한 종류. 권총

re·vue /rɪˈvyu/ n a show in a theater that includes singing, dancing, and telling jokes || 노래·춤·농담을 포함하는 극장 쇼. 시사 풍자극. 레뷰

re·vul·sion /rɪˈvʌlʃən/ n [U] a strong feeling of being sick and shocked || 역해지고 충격 받은 강한 느낌. 혐오. 증오

re·ward¹ /rɪˈwɔrd/ n [C, U] something, especially an amount of money, that is given to someone for doing something good, providing information etc. || 좋은 일·정보 제공을 한 데 대해 사람에게 주어지는 것, 특히 돈. 보수. 보상(금): *The police are offering a reward for information.* 경찰은 정보 제공에 대해 사례금을 주고 있다. —compare AWARD²

reward² v [T] to give something to someone, especially an amount of money, for doing something good, providing information etc. || 선행·정보 제공 등에 대해 다른 사람에게 특히 돈을 주다. 보수[상]를 주다. 보상[답례]하다: *To train a dog, reward him with food and praise.* 개를 훈련하기 위해서, 상으로 먹을 것과 칭찬을 해 주어라. / *She was generously rewarded for her work.* 그녀는 자기가 한 일에 대해 후한 보수를 받았다.

re·ward·ing /rɪˈwɔrdɪŋ/ adj making you feel happy and satisfied || 행복하고 만족하게 하는. 가치[보람] 있는: *a rewarding job* 보람 있는 일

re·wind /ˌriˈwaɪnd/ v [I, T] to make a TAPE go back to the beginning || 테이프를 처음으로 돌려놓다. …을 다시 감다. 반대로 감다

re·work /ˌriˈwɔrk/ v [T] to change or improve a plan, piece of music, story etc. so that you can use it || 계획·음악·이야기 등을 쓸 수 있게 바꾸거나 개선하다. 개정하다

re·write /ˌriˈraɪt/ v [T] to write something again using different words in order to make it clearer or more effective || 보다 분명하거나 효과적으로 만들기 위해, 다른 단어들을 사용하여 어떤 것을 다시 쓰다. 바꿔 쓰다. 고쳐 쓰다 – **rewrite** /ˈriraɪt/ n

rhap·so·dy /ˈræpsədi/ n a piece of music that is written to express emotion, and does not have a regular form || 규칙적인 형태 없이 감정을 표현하기 위해 쓰여진 곡. 광시곡. 랩소디

rhet·o·ric /ˈrɛtərɪk/ n [U] **1** speech or writing that sounds impressive, but is not actually sincere or very useful || 사실은 진실하거나 그렇게 유용하지 않지만,

인상적으로 들리는 말이나 글. 수사적인 말[글]. 미사여구: *There's a lot of rhetoric about supporting education, but very little is actually done.* 교육 지원에 대한 미사여구들이 많지만 실제로 행해지는 것은 거의 없다. **2** the art of speaking or writing in order to persuade or influence people || 사람들을 설득하거나 영향을 미치기 위한 화술이나 수사법(修辭法) – **rhetorical** /rɪˈtɔrɪkəl/ adj – **rhetorically** adv

rhe·tor·i·cal ques·tion /ˌ... ˈ.../ n a question that you ask as a way of making a statement, without expecting an answer || 대답을 기대하지 않고 말을 하는 방법으로서 묻는 질문. 수사 의문문

rheu·ma·tism /ˈrumə.tɪzəm/ n [U] a disease that makes your joints or muscles painful and stiff || 관절이나 근육을 아프고 굳어지게 하는 질병. 류머티즘

rhine·stone /ˈraɪnstoʊn/ n [C, U] a jewel made from glass or a rock that is intended to look like a DIAMOND || 의도적으로 다이아몬드처럼 보이도록 유리나 돌로 만든 보석. 모조 다이아몬드

rhi·noc·er·os /raɪˈnɑsərəs/, **rhino** /ˈraɪnoʊ/ n a large heavy animal with thick rough skin and one or two horns on its nose || 두껍고 거친 피부를 갖고 코 위에 한 개나 두 개의 뿔이 있는 몸집이 크고 육중한 동물. 코뿔소

rho·do·den·dron /ˌroʊdəˈdɛndrən/ n a large bush with groups of red, purple, pink, or white flowers || 빨간색[자주색, 분홍색, 흰색]의 많은 꽃이 있는 큰 관목(灌木). 진달래속의 식물

rhu·barb /ˈrubɑrb/ n [U] a plant with long thick red stems that are cooked and eaten as a fruit || 길고 두꺼운 빨간 줄기를 과일처럼 요리해 먹는 식물. 장군풀. 대황(大黃)

rhyme¹ /raɪm/ n **1** a word that ends with the same sound as another word || 다른 단어와 똑같은 음으로 끝나는 단어. 동운어(同韻語): *I can't find a rhyme for "donkey."* 나는 "donkey"의 동운어를 못 찾겠어. **2** a short poem or song, especially for children, using words that rhyme || 특히 아이들을 위해 압운으로 쓴 짧은 시나 노래 —see also NURSERY RHYME **3** [U] the use of words that rhyme in poetry, especially at the ends of lines || 특히 시행의 끝에서 압운의 사용. 압운: *Parts of Shakespeare's plays are written in rhyme.* 셰익스피어 희곡 중 일부는 압운으로 쓰여 있다. **4 without rhyme or reason** in a way that cannot be reasonably explained || 합리적으로 설

명될 수 없게. (아무런) 이유 없이: *Joe's moods change without rhyme or reason.* 조의 기분은 아무런 이유 없이 변한다.

rhyme² *v* **1** [I] if two words or lines of poetry rhyme, they end with the same sound ‖ 두 단어나 두 시행의 끝소리가 일치하다. 운이 맞다: *"House" rhymes with "mouse."* "house"는 "mouse"와 운이 맞는다. **2** [T] to put two or more words together to make them rhyme ‖ 2개 이상의 단어들을 서로 압운시키다. 운을 맞추다[맞춰 달다]: *You can't rhyme "box" with "backs."* 너는 "box"와 "backs"를 압운시킬 수 없다.

rhythm /ˈrɪðəm/ *n* [C, U] a regular repeated pattern of sounds in music, speech etc. ‖ 음악·말 등에서 소리가 규칙적으로 반복되는 형태. 리듬. 율동. 음조. 억양

rhythm and blues /ˌ... ˈ./ *n* [U] ⇨ R & B

rhyth·mic /ˈrɪðmɪk/ *adj* having RHYTHM ‖ 리듬을 갖는. 리드미컬한. 율동적인: *fast rhythmic music* 빠른 리듬의 음악

RI the written abbreviation of Rhode Island ‖ Rhode Island(로드아일랜드 주)의 약어

rib¹ /rɪb/ *n* **1** one of the 12 pairs of curved bones that surround your lungs, or one of the similar bones in an animal ‖ 폐를 감싸는 12쌍의 만곡형 뼈 중 하나, 또는 동물의 비슷한 뼈 중 하나. 늑골. 갈빗대 **2** a piece of meat that includes an animal's rib ‖ 동물의 갈비뼈를 포함한 고깃덩이. 고기가 붙은 갈비: *beef ribs* 소갈비

rib² *v* **-bbed, -bbing** [T] INFORMAL to make jokes about someone and laugh at him/her, but in a friendly way ‖ 친근하게 남을 놀리며 비웃다. …으로 놀리다: *John always gets ribbed about being bald.* 존은 항상 대머리로 놀림받는다.

rib·ald /ˈraɪbɔld, ˈrɪbəld/ *adj* ribald jokes, remarks, songs etc. are humorous, rude and usually about sex ‖ 농담·말·노래 등이 우습고 무례하며 보통 외설적인. 상스러운. 점잖지 못한

ribbed /rɪbd/ *adj* having a pattern of raised lines ‖ 돋아진 선 무늬가 있는. 골이 진[있는]: *a ribbed sweater* 골이 지게 짠 스웨터

rib·bon /ˈrɪbən/ *n* **1** [C, U] a long narrow piece of cloth, used for tying things or as a decoration ‖ 사물을 묶거나 장식으로 쓰이는 길고 폭이 좁은 천 조각. 리본. 띠: *a red ribbon in her hair* 그녀 머리에 달린 빨간 리본 **2** a colored ribbon that is given as a prize in a

competition ‖ 경기에서 상으로 수여되는 색깔 리본. (훈장) 리본 —see also BLUE RIBBON **3** a long narrow piece of cloth with ink on it that is used in a TYPEWRITER ‖ 위에 잉크가 묻어 있어 타자기에 쓰이는 길고 폭이 좁은 천 조각. 타자기 리본

rib cage /ˈ. ./ *n* the structure of RIBS around your lungs and heart ‖ 폐와 심장을 둘러싼 늑골 구조. 흉곽(胸廓)

rice /raɪs/ *n* [U] a white or brown grain grown in wet fields, that is eaten after it has been boiled ‖ 논에서 자라고 끓인 후 먹을 수 있는 흰색이나 갈색의 낟알. 쌀

rice paddy /ˈ. ˌ../ *n* ⇨ PADDY

rich /rɪtʃ/ *adj* **1** having a lot of money or valuable possessions ‖ 돈이나 값비싼 소유물을 많이 가진. 부유한: *a very rich man* 매우 재산이 많은 남자 / *a rich and powerful nation* 부유하고 힘 있는 국가 **2** rich foods contain a lot of butter, cream, sugar, or eggs, and make you feel full very quickly ‖ 음식이 버터[크림, 설탕, 계란]을 많이 함유하고 있어 아주 빨리 포만감을 느끼게 하는. 기름진: *a rich chocolate cake* 초콜릿이 듬뿍 든 케이크 **3** containing a lot of something good ‖ 좋은 것을 많이 포함한. 풍부한: *foods that are rich in vitamins* 비타민이 풍부한 음식 / *a rich cultural heritage* 풍부한 문화 유산 **4 the rich** people who have a lot of money or valuable possessions ‖ 돈이나 값비싼 소유물을 많이 가진 사람. 부자 **5** very deep and strong ‖ 매우 진하고 강한. 색이 짙은[선명한]. 강렬한: *a rich dark blue* 짙은 청색 / *the rich tone of a cello* 첼로의 굵직한 소리 **6** good for growing plants in ‖ 식물이 자라기에 좋은. 비옥한: *rich soil* 비옥한 토양 **7** expensive and beautiful ‖ 값비싸고 아름다운. 호화로운: *rich silk* 화사한 비단 **– richness** *n* [U]

rich·es /ˈrɪtʃɪz/ *n* [plural] LITERARY a lot of money or valuable possessions ‖ 많은 돈이나 값비싼 소유물. 부(富)

rich·ly /ˈrɪtʃli/ *adv* **1** in a beautiful or expensive way ‖ 아름답거나 값비싸게. 화려하게: *a richly decorated fabric* 화려하게 장식된 천 **2 richly deserve** to completely deserve something ‖ 어떤 것을 마땅하게 받을 만하다. 당연히 …하다: *They got the punishment they so richly deserved.* 그들은 아주 마땅하게 받을 만한 벌을 받았다. **3** in large amounts ‖ 양이 많게. 풍부하게. 충분히: *He was richly rewarded for his work.* 그는 자기의 일에 대해 충분한 보상을 받았다.

rick·et·y /ˈrɪkəti/ *adj* a rickety piece of

furniture, stair etc. is in bad condition and is likely to break if you use it ‖ 가구·계단 등이 상태가 나쁘고 사용하면 부서질 것 같은. 삐걱삐걱거리는. 부서질 것 같은

rick·shaw /'rɪkʃɔ/ n a small vehicle used in Asia for carrying one or two passengers, that is pulled by someone walking or riding a bicycle ‖ 아시아에서 사람이 걷거나 자전거를 타고 끌어 한 두 명의 승객을 실어 나르는 데에 사용하는 소형의 탈것. 인력거

ric·o·chet /'rɪkəˌʃeɪ/ v [I] if something such as a bullet or a thrown rock ricochets, it changes direction when it hits a surface ‖ 탄환이나 던진 돌 등이 표면에 부딪쳐 방향이 바뀌다. 튀다. 스쳐날다 – **ricochet** n

rid[1] /rɪd/ adj **1 get rid of a)** to throw away something that you do not want or use ‖ 원하지 않거나 쓰지 않는 것을 내버리다. 없애다. 제거하다: *Do you want to get rid of these old shirts?* 이 헌 셔츠들을 모두 내버릴 거니? **b)** to make something that is unpleasant go away, stop happening, or stop existing ‖ 불쾌한 것을 떨쳐 버리다[발생하지 못하게 하다, 존재하지 않게 하다]. …에서 벗어나다: *I can't get rid of this cold.* 이 감기가 떨어지지가 않아. **c)** to make someone who annoys you leave ‖ 귀찮게 괴롭히는 사람을 떠나게 하다. 떨쳐버리다: *I couldn't get rid of her – she just sat there talking about herself all night.* 그녀가 밤새 거기에 앉아서 자신에 대해 말해서 나는 그녀를 떨쳐버릴 수 없었어. **2 be rid of** to have gotten rid of someone who annoys you or something that is unpleasant ‖ 괴롭히는 사람이나 불쾌한 것에서 벗어나다. …에서 해방되다. 자유로워지다: *He's gone, and I'm glad to be rid of him.* 그가 가버렸고, 나는 그에게서 벗어나서 기쁘다.

rid[2] v **rid, rid, ridding**
rid sb/sth **of** sth phr v [T] **1** to remove something or someone that is bad or harmful from a place, organization etc. ‖ 장소·조직 등에서 나쁘거나 해로운 사물이나 사람을 없애다. 제거하다. 쫓아내다: *efforts to rid the government of corrupt officials* 정부에서 부패 공무원들을 추방하려는 노력 **2 rid yourself of** sth to stop having a feeling, thought, or problem that was causing you trouble ‖ 골치 아프게 하는 느낌[생각, 문제]을 떨쳐 버리다. 헤어나다. 벗어나다

rid·dance /'rɪdns/ n **good riddance** SPOKEN said when you are glad that

someone or something has gone away ‖ 사람이나 사물이 없어져서 기쁠 때 쓰여. 앓던 이 빠진 것 같다

rid·dle /'rɪdl/ n **1** a difficult and amusing question that you must guess the answer to ‖ 답을 추측해야 하는 어려우면서도 재미있는 문제. 수수께끼 **2** a mysterious action, event, or situation that you do not understand and cannot explain ‖ 이해가 안 되고 설명할 수 없는 신비한 행위[사건, 상황]. 이해할 수 없는 일[것, 사람]: *His disappearance is a riddle.* 그의 실종은 수수께끼 같은 일이다.

rid·dled /'rɪdld/ adj **riddled with** very full of something, especially something bad or unpleasant ‖ 특히 나쁘거나 불쾌한 것으로 매우 가득 찬. …으로 가득 찬: *Your paper is good, but it is riddled with spelling mistakes.* 너의 과제물은 좋으나 틀린 철자들로 가득 차 있다.

ride[1] /raɪd/ v **rode, ridden** /'rɪdn/, **riding 1** [I, T] to sit on an animal, especially a horse, or on a bicycle, and make it move along ‖ 특히 말 등 동물, 또는 자전거 위에 앉아서 움직이게 하다. 말을 타다. 타고 가다: *We went riding (=horses) in the mountains.* 우리는 산에서 말을 탔다. / *Can you ride a bike?* 자전거 탈 수 있어? **2** [I, T] to travel in a car, train, or other vehicle ‖ 차[기차, 다른 탈것]으로 이동하다. 차를 타다[타고 다니다]: *She feels sick when she rides in the car for too long.* 그녀는 너무 오랫동안 차를 타면 멀미를 한다. / *Fred rides the subway to work everyday.* 프레드는 매일 지하철로 통근한다. **3 let** sth **ride** SPOKEN to take no action about something that is wrong or unpleasant ‖ 잘못되거나 불쾌한 것에 대해 아무런 조치를 취하지 않다. 그냥 놔두다. 그 상태로 내버려 두다[방치하다]: *I didn't like what he was saying, but I let it ride.* 나는 그가 하는 말이 싫었지만 그냥 놔뒀어. **4** [T] SPOKEN to annoy someone by repeatedly criticizing him/her again and again, or asking him/her to do things again and again ‖ 반복하여 계속 남을 비난하거나 계속 일을 하라고 구하며 괴롭히다. (…을 의도적이고 계속적으로) 놀리다. 비웃다: *Stop riding her – she's doing her best!* 그녀를 놀리지 마라. 그녀는 최선을 다하고 있는 거야!

ride on sth phr v [T] if something is riding on something else, it depends on it ‖ 어떤 것이 다른 것에 의존하고 있다. …에 달려[걸려] 있다: *He knew he had*

ride²

to win - his reputation was riding on it.
자기의 평판이 달려 있었기 때문에 그는
이겨야 한다는 것을 알고 있었다.

ride sth ↔ **out** *phr v* [T] to come out of
a difficult situation, bad experience etc.
without being harmed by it ‖ 피해 받지
않고 어려운 상황·나쁜 경험 등에서 벗어
나다. …을 잘 넘기다. 극복하다: *The
company managed to ride out the
scandal.* 그 기업은 추문을 용케 잘 넘겼
다.

ride² *n* **1** a trip in a car, train, or other
vehicle ‖ 차[기차, 다른 탈것]를 타고 가
기. 승차. 탑승: *Have you gone for a
ride in Peggy's new car yet?* 너 페기의
새 자동차를 벌써 타 봤니? / *Mick gave
me a ride to work.* 미이 나를 직장까지
차로 태워줬다. **2** a large machine that
people ride on for pleasure at a FAIR or
AMUSEMENT PARK ‖ 박람회나 놀이공원에서
재미로 타는 대형 기계. 놀이 기구: *Have
you been on the new ride at
Disneyland?* 디즈니랜드에서 새로운 놀이
기구 타 봤니? **3** a trip on an animal,
especially a horse, or on a bicycle ‖ 특히
말, 또는 자전거를 타고 가기. 타고 놀러가
기. 승마: *It's a beautiful day - do you
want to go for a ride.* 날씨 좋다. 말[자
전거] 타러 갈래?

rid·er /'raɪdɚ/ *n* someone who rides a
horse, bicycle etc. ‖ 말·자전거 등을 타는
사람. 타는[모는] 사람

ridge /rɪdʒ/ *n* **1** a long area of high
land, especially at the top of a mountain
‖ 특히 산꼭대기의 높고 길게 뻗은 지역.
산등성이. 능선: *the ridge along the
Virginia-Kentucky border* 버지니아-켄터
키 경계에 걸쳐 있는 능선 **2** a long
narrow raised part of a surface ‖ 표면에
서 좁고 길게 융기한 부분. 등(마루):
ridges on the soles of her shoes 그녀의
구두 밑창에서 솟은 부분

rid·i·cule¹ /'rɪdə,kyul/ *n* [U] unkind
laughter, or remarks intended to make
someone or something seem stupid ‖ 비
웃음, 또는 사람이나 사물을 의도적으로
바보처럼 보이게 만드는 말. 조소. 조롱:
Tracy has become an object of ridicule.
(=a person that everyone laughs at) 트
레이시는 조롱거리가 되었다.

ridicule² *v* [T] to laugh at a person,
idea etc., or to make unkind remarks
about him, her, or it ‖ 사람·생각 등을 비
웃다, 또는 사람이나 사물에 대해 비웃는
말을 하다. 조롱[조소]하다. 놀리다: *They
all ridiculed my plan.* 그들은 모두 나의
계획을 비웃었다.

ri·dic·u·lous /rɪ'dɪkyələs/ *adj* silly or

unreasonable ‖ 어리석거나 터무니없는.
웃기는. 어처구니없는: *What a ridiculous
idea!* 정말 터무니없는 생각이구나! –
ridiculously *adv*

rid·ing /'raɪdɪŋ/ *n* [U] the sport of riding
horses ‖ 말을 타는 스포츠. 승마

rife /raɪf/ *adj* **1** if something bad is rife,
it is very common ‖ 나쁜 것이 아주 흔한.
보편화된. 유행하는: *Disease is rife in
the region.* 그 지역에는 질병이 유행하고
있다. **2 rife with** full of something bad
‖ 나쁜 것으로 가득 찬. 퍼져 있는. 난무
하는: *The office is rife with rumors
about his resignation.* 사무실에 그의 사
직에 대한 소문들이 무성하다.

riff /rɪf/ *n* a repeated series of notes in
popular music ‖ 대중음악에서 일련의 반
복되는 음조. 리프. 반복 악절

ri·fle¹ /'raɪfəl/ *n* a gun with a long
BARREL (=tube-shaped part) that you
hold up to your shoulder to shoot ‖ 사격
하기 위해 어깨에 견착시키는 총열이 긴
총. 라이플 총. 소총

rifle² *v* [T] to search through a place
and steal things from it ‖ 한 장소를 샅샅
이 뒤져 물건을 훔치다. …을 털어가다[훔
쳐가다]: *It looked like someone had been
rifling through my desk.* 누군가가 내 책
상을 뒤진 것 같았다.

rift /rɪft/ *n* **1** a serious disagreement ‖
심각한 의견 차이. 불화. 반목: *a growing
rift between the two countries* 커져가는
양국간 불화의 골 **2** a crack or narrow
opening in a large piece of rock, group
of clouds etc. ‖ 큰 암석 덩어리·일단의 구
름떼 등의 갈라진 금이나 좁은 틈. (암석
의) 균열. (구름 등의) 사이

rig¹ /rɪg/ *v* **-gged, -gging** [T] **1** to
arrange or influence an election,
competition etc. in a dishonest way so
that you get the result that you want ‖
선거·경기 등에서 원하는 결과를 얻기 위
해 부정직하게 조처하거나 영향을 주다.
부정 수단으로 조작하다: *The
newspapers claimed that the election
had been rigged.* 신문에서는 선거가 조작
되었다고 주장했다. **2** to provide a ship
with ropes, sails etc. ‖ 배에 밧줄·돛 등을
장비하다. 배에 돛 등을 갖추다

rig sth ↔ **up** *phr v* [T] INFORMAL to
make simple equipment, furniture etc.
out of materials that you can find
quickly and easily ‖ 빠르고 쉽게 찾을 수
있는 재료로 간단한 장비·가구 등을 만들
다. 급조하다. 임시변통으로 만들다: *We
rigged up a shelter using a big piece of
plastic we found.* 우리는 발견한 큰 플라
스틱 조각을 이용해 대피소를 만들었다.

rig² *n* **1** a large structure used for digging to find oil ∥ 석유 시추에 쓰이는 대형 구조물. 유정(油井)의 굴착 장치 **2** INFORMAL a large TRUCK ∥ 대형 트럭

rig·a·ma·role /ˈrɪɡəməˌroʊl/ *n* [singular, U] ⇨ RIGMAROLE

rig·ging /ˈrɪɡɪŋ/ *n* [U] all the ropes, sails etc. on a ship ∥ 배의 밧줄·돛 등 모든 것. 배의 삭구(索具) 장치

right¹ /raɪt/ *adj* **1** correct or true ∥ 옳은. 사실의. 바른. 정확한: *Did you get the right answer?* 정답을 맞췄습니까? / *Their predictions were right.* 그들의 예측은 정확했다. **2** on the right, which is the side of the body that has the hand most people write with ∥ 대부분의 사람들이 글을 쓰는 손이 있는 몸의 우측면의. 오른쪽의. 우측의: *Make a right turn after the gas station.* 주유소 다음에서 우회전하시오. / *Raise your right hand.* 오른손을 드시오. **3** best or most suitable for a particular situation or purpose ∥ 특정 상황이나 목적에 가장 또는 최대로 적합한. 최적의. 꼭 맞는: *You need to have the right people running it to make it work.* 그 일을 해내도록 운영할 최적의 관리자를 둘 필요가 있다. **4** morally correct, or done according to the law ∥ 도덕적으로 옳은, 또는 법에 따라 행해진. 올바른. 적법한: *What he did wasn't right, but he was angry.* 그가 한 것은 정당하지 않았으나 그는 화를 내고 있었다. **5 be in the right place at the right time** to be in a place or position that allows you to gain an advantage for yourself ∥ 스스로 이익을 얻을 수 있는 장소나 위치에 있다. 기회를 잘 타다

SPOKEN PHRASES
---

6 that's right said when something that is said or done is correct, or when you remember something or are reminded of it ∥ 듣거나 행해진 것이 옳은 때, 또는 어떤 것을 기억해 낼 때나 상기될 때 쓰여. 맞아. 그렇지: *"Dave just turned 60?" "That's right."* "데이브 나이가 이제 막 60이 됐어?" "맞아." / *"No, you taped over Star Trek." "Oh, that's right."* "아니, 너 스타트랙 테이프에 녹음했지." "아, 맞다." **7** said in order to ask if what you have said was correct ∥ 말한 것이 맞았는지 묻는 데 쓰여. 그렇지?: *You wanted to go to the mall, right?* 너 쇼핑센터에 가고 싶었구나, 맞지? **8 yeah, right** said when you do not believe what has just been said ∥ 방금 들은 것을 믿지 않을 때 쓰여: *He says,*

"I'll call you," and I'm like, "yeah, right." 그가 "내가 전화할게."라고 말해서 나는 "뭐, 그러던가."라고 말했다. **9** said in order to agree with what someone has said, to show that you are listening, or to show that what s/he has said is correct ∥ 남이 한 말에 동의하는 데에, 듣고 있다는 것을 보이는 데에, 남이 말한 것이 맞다는 것을 보이는 데에 쓰여. 맞아. 그래: *"I got so bored…" "Right." "…and I quit."* "난 너무 지겨웠어…" "그래." "…그래서 그만뒀어!" **10** used in order to check that someone understands and agrees with what you have said ∥ 자신이 말한 것을 어떤 사람이 이해하고 동의하는지 확인하는 데 쓰여. 맞지. 그렇지: *If people are comfortable, they're more likely to talk, right?* 사람들이 편안하면 더 얘기하려고 하겠지. 맞지?

– **rightness** *n* [U] —see also ALL RIGHT

right² *adv* **1** exactly in a particular position or place ∥ 특정 위치나 장소에 정확하게. 바로[꼭] …에: *Shut up, he's right behind you!* 조용히 해, 그가 바로 네 뒤에 있어! / *His phone number's right there on the desk.* 그의 전화번호는 책상 위 바로 거기에 있다. **2** immediately ∥ 즉시. 당장(에): *Send back your copy of the contract right away.* 계약서 사본을 당장 돌려보내라. / *I need it right now!* 나는 지금 당장 그것이 필요해! / *I'll be right there.* (=I am coming now) 내가 바로 거기로 갈게. / *She went to the grocery store, but she'll be right back.* (=come back soon) 그녀는 식품점에 갔으나 바로 돌아올 것이다. **3** correctly ∥ 정확히. 바르게: *They didn't spell my name right.* 그들은 내 이름을 바르게 철자하지[쓰지] 않았다. **4** toward the direction or side that is on the right ∥ 우측 (방향)으로: *Turn right at the lights.* 신호등에서 우회전해라 **5** all the way to something, through something etc. ∥ 어떤 것에 이르거나 지날 때까지 줄곧. 똑바로. 계속: *Go right to the end of the road.* 도로의 끝까지 가라. / *You can see right through her bathing suit!* 너는 그녀의 수영복을 꿰뚫어 볼 수 있어! **6 sb will be right with you** used in order to say that someone will come soon to help or talk to you ∥ 돕거나 얘기해줄 어떤 사람이 곧 올 거라고 말하는 데 쓰여: *Your waitress will be right with you.* 담당 웨이트리스가 곧 올 겁니다.

right³ *n* **1** something that you are

allowed to do or have according to the law or according to moral ideas ∥ 법이나 도덕 관념에 따라 행동이나 소유가 허가되는 것. 권리: *Women didn't have the right to vote until 1920.* 여성들은 1920년도까지 투표권을 갖지 못했다. / *the right to free speech* 언론의 자유에 대한 권리 / *a country in which every citizen enjoys equal rights* (=rights that are the same for everyone) 모든 시민들이 동등한 권리를 누리는 국가 —see also CIVIL RIGHTS, HUMAN RIGHTS **2** [singular] the side of your body that has the hand that most people write with, or the direction toward this side ∥ 대부분의 사람들이 글을 쓰는 손이 있는 몸의 측면, 또는 이 측면으로 향하는 방향. 오른쪽. 우측: *Our house is on the right.* 우리 집은 우측에 있다. / *The matches are in the top drawer to your right.* 너의 오른 맨 윗 서랍 안에 성냥이 있다. **3** [U] behavior that is morally correct ∥ 도덕적으로 올바른 행동: *The lawyers said that Snyder did not know right from wrong* (=know what is morally correct and what is not) *at the time of the crime.* 변호사는 스나이더가 범죄 당시 옳고 그름을 알지 못했다고 말했다. **4 in his/her/its own right** considered alone, without depending on anyone or anything else ∥ 어떤 사람이나 사물에 의지함이 없이 혼자라고 생각되는. 자기만으로. 혼자서. 남을 의지하지 않고: *San Jose is a city in its own right, not just a suburb of San Francisco.* 산호세는 단지 샌프란시스코의 교외가 아니라 독자적인 도시이다. **5 have a right to be/do sth** to have a good reason to do something, feel something, expect something etc. ∥ 어떤 것을 행할·느낄·기대할 정당한 이유가 있다. 당연히 …할 만하다: *Weil has every right to be suspicious of him.* 웨일은 그를 당연히 의심할 만하다. / *We didn't promise them anything; they have no right to be angry.* 우리는 그들에게 아무 것도 약속하지 않았기 때문에 그들은 화를 낼 이유가 없다. **6 the right** in politics, the right are people who believe that the government should not try to change or control social problems or businesses by making too many rules or limits; CONSERVATIVE ∥ 정치에서, 정부는 지나치게 많은 규칙이나 제한을 만들어 사회적 문제나 사업을 변화시키거나 통제하려 하지 않아야 한다고 믿는 사람들. 우파; 卽 conservative —see also RIGHTS

right⁴ *v* [T] **1** to put something back in an upright position ∥ 사물을 똑바로 선

위치로 돌려놓다. 똑바로 세우다: *We finally managed to right the canoe.* 우리는 마침내 가까스로 카누를 바로 세울 수 있었다. **2 to correct something** ∥ 어떤 것을 교정하다. 고치다: *an attempt to right the wrong* (=correct something bad that was done) *of discrimination* 차별의 부당함을 고치려는 시도

right an·gle /ˌ. '../ *n* an angle of 90°, like the angles at the corners of a square ∥ 정사각형 모서리의 각과 같은 90도(각). 직각(直角) **– right-angled** /ˌ. '../ *adj*

right·eous /ˈraɪtʃəs/ *adj* **1 righteous indignation/anger etc.** strong feelings of anger when you think a situation is not morally right or fair ∥ 상황이 도덕적으로 올바르거나 공정하지 않다고 생각할 때의 강한 분노감. 분개. 의분(義憤) **2** LITERARY morally good and fair ∥ 도덕적으로 바르고 공정한: *a righteous man* 덕망 있는 사람 **3** SLANG extremely good ∥ 매우 좋은: *a righteous dude* 굉장한 녀석 **– righteousness** *n* [U] **– righteously** *adv*

right field /ˌ. '../ *n* [singular] the area in baseball in the right side of the OUTFIELD ∥ 야구에서 외야의 우측 지역. (외야의) 우익

right·ful /ˈraɪtfəl/ *adj* according to what is legally and morally correct ∥ 적법하고 도덕적으로 바른 것을 따르는. 합법적인. 정당한: *the property's rightful owner* 재산의 적법한 소유자 **– rightfully** *adv*

right-hand /ˈ. ./ *adj* **1** on your right side ∥ 오른편의: *Make a right-hand turn.* 우회전하세요. **2 sb's right-hand man** the person who supports and helps someone the most, especially in his/her job ∥ 어떤 사람을 특히 업무에서, 가장 잘 지지하고 도와주는 사람. 심복. 믿을 만한 사람

right-hand·ed /ˌ. '../ *adj* **1** someone who is right-handed uses his/her right hand for most things ∥ 사람이 대부분의 일에 오른손을 사용하는. 오른손잡이의 **2** done with the right hand ∥ 오른손으로 한: *a right-handed punch* 오른손 펀치 **– right-handed** /ˌ. '../ *adv*

right-handed

right·ly /ˈraɪtli/ *adv* **1** correctly, or for a good reason ∥ 올바르게 또는 타당한 이유로. 정확하게. 당연하게: *She rightly* *pointed out that this won't solve the problem.* 그녀는 이것이 문제를 해결할 수 없을 것이라고 정확히 지적했다. / *The book has rightly been called "an American Classic."* 그 책은 "미국의 고전"으로 당연히 일컬어져 왔다. **2 I can't rightly say/I don't rightly know** SPOKEN said when you are not sure whether something is correct ‖ 어떤 것이 정확한지 확신할 수 없을 때에 쓰여. …을 단언할 수는 없다/…을 반드시 아는 것은 아니다

right of way /ˌ. . ˈ./ *n* [U] the right to drive into or across a road before other vehicles ‖ 다른 차량보다 먼저 도로에 진입하거나 가로지를 수 있는 권리. 통행 우선권

rights /raɪts/ *n* [plural] legal permission to print or use a story, movie etc. in another form ‖ 소설·영화 등을 또 다른 형태로 발행 또는 사용할 수 있는 법적 인가. 저작권. 소유권: *Several movie studios are bidding for the rights to Crichton's last book.* 몇 개의 영화사들은 크리츠튼의 마지막 저서에 대한 판권을 얻기 위해 노력 중이다.

right-wing /ˌ. ˈ./ *adj* supporting the political aims of the RIGHT ‖ 우파의 정치적 목적을 지지하는. 우익의: *a right-wing newspaper* 우익 신문 **– right-winger** *n* **– right wing** *n* [singular]

rig·id /ˈrɪdʒɪd/ *adj* **1** rigid methods, systems etc. are very strict and difficult to change ‖ 방법·체계 등이 매우 엄격하여 바꾸기 어려운. 엄격한: *a rigid belief in the Bible* 성경에 대한 굳은 신념 **2** someone who is rigid is very unwilling to change his/her ideas ‖ 사람이 생각을 바꾸려 하지 않는. 완고한. 융통성이 없는 **3** stiff and not moving or bending ‖ 뻣뻣하고 움직이거나 구부러지지 않는. 굳은. 딱딱한. 휘지 [굽지] 않는: *a tent supported on a rigid frame* 단단한 틀로 지탱되는 텐트 **– rigidly** *adv* **– rigidity** /rɪˈdʒɪdəti/ *n* [U]

rig·ma·role /ˈrɪɡməˌroʊl/ *n* [singular, U] a set of actions that seems silly ‖ 어리석게 여겨지는 일련의 행동. 복잡한 과정. 형식적인 까다로운 절차: *the rigmarole of filling out all these forms* 이 모든 서식에 기입하는 번거로운 과정

rig·or /ˈrɪɡɚ/ *n* **1** [U] great care and thoroughness in making sure that something is correct ‖ 어떤 것의 정확함을 담보하기 위한 깊은 주의와 철저함. 엄밀. 정확: *the rigor of scientific proof* 과학적 증거의 정확성 **2 the rigors of** the unpleasant conditions of a difficult situation ‖ 어려운 상황의 불쾌한 상태. 호

됨. 혹독: *the rigors of a Canadian winter* 캐나다 겨울의 혹독함 **3** [U] FORMAL the state of being strict or severe ‖ 엄중하거나 엄격한 상태. 엄함. 엄격함: *the full rigor of the law* 법의 준엄함

rig·or mor·tis /ˌrɪɡɚ ˈmɔrtɪs/ *n* [U] the condition in which someone's body becomes stiff after s/he dies ‖ 죽은 후 사람의 몸이 뻣뻣해지는 상태. 사후(死後) 경직

rig·or·ous /ˈrɪɡərəs/ *adj* **1** careful and thorough ‖ 주의 깊고 철저한. 아주 엄밀한. 면밀한: *rigorous safety checks* 철저한 안전 검사 **2** very strict or severe ‖ 매우 엄격하거나 가혹한. 엄중한. 혹독한: *a school with a rigorous curriculum* 교과 과정이 엄격한 학교 **– rigorously** *adv*

rile /raɪl/, **rile** sb **up** *v* [T] INFORMAL to make someone very angry ‖ 남을 매우 화나게 하다

rim /rɪm/ *n* **1** the outside edge of something circular, such as a glass or a wheel ‖ 유리컵이나 바퀴 등의 바깥쪽의 둥근 가장자리. 외륜(外輪). 테두리 **2 -rimmed** with a particular type of rim ‖ 특별한 형태의 테를 가진: *gold-rimmed glasses* 금테 안경

rind /raɪnd/ *n* [C, U] the thick outer skin of some foods or fruits, such as BACON, cheese, and LEMONs ‖ 베이컨·치즈·레몬 등의 일부 음식이나 과일의 두꺼운 외피(外皮). 껍질 —see picture at PEEL²

ring¹ /rɪŋ/ *n* **1** a piece of jewelry that you wear on your finger ‖ 손가락에 끼는 보석류. 반지 —see picture at JEWELRY **2** a circular line or mark ‖ 둥근 선이나 표시: *counting the rings in a tree trunk* 나무 줄기의 나이테 세기 **3** an object in the shape of a circle ‖ 동그란 형태의 물체. 고리: *a key ring* 열쇠 고리 **4** a group of people or things arranged in a circle ‖ 둥글게 배열된 일단의 사람이나 사물. 원형. 진: *surrounded by a ring of enemy tanks* 적의 탱크들에 의해 둥글게 포위되다 **5** a group of people who illegally control a business or criminal activity ‖ 불법적으로 사업 또는 범죄 활동을 조종하는 일단의 사람. 도당. 일당: *a drug ring* 마약 밀매단 **6** the sound made by a bell or the act of making this sound ‖ 종이 내는 소리, 또는 이 소리를 내기. 초인종 (울리기). 벨: *a ring at the door* 현관의 벨소리 **7** a small square area where people BOX or WRESTLE, or the large circular area surrounded by seats at a CIRCUS ‖ 사람들이 권투나 레슬링을 하는 조그만 사각의

장소 또는 서커스에서 객석으로 둘러싸인 큰 원형 장소. 링. 공연장

ring² *v* **rang, rung, ringing 1** [I, T] to make a bell make a sound, especially to call someone's attention to you ‖ 특히 다른 사람의 주의를 끌기 위해 벨을 울리다: *I rang the bell but there was no answer.* 내가 벨을 울렸으나 아무런 대답도 없었다. / *Please ring for assistance.* 도움을 청하려면 벨을 울리시오. **2** [I] if a bell rings, it makes a noise ‖ 벨이 소리를 내다. 울리다: *The telephone's ringing.* 전화벨이 울리고 있다. —see usage note at TELEPHONE **3** [I] if your ears ring, they are filled with a continuous sound ‖ 귀에 계속 소리가 울리다. 윙윙 울리다 **4 ring a bell** INFORMAL if something rings a bell, you think you have heard it before ‖ 전에 들어본 것 같다. …을 생각나게 하다: *Her name rings a bell, but I can't remember her face.* 그녀의 이름은 생각났지만 얼굴은 기억해 낼 수가 없다. **5 not ring true** if something does not ring true, you do not believe it ‖ 어떤 것을 믿지 않다. 진실로 들리지 않다: *His excuse didn't really ring true.* 그의 변명은 실로 진실처럼 들리질 않았다.

ring out *phr v* [I] if a voice, bell etc. rings out, it makes a loud and clear sound ‖ 목소리·벨 등이 요란하고 뚜렷하게 울리다. 울려 퍼지다: *The sound of a shot rang out.* 총소리가 요란히 울렸다.

ring sth ↔ **up** *phr v* [T] to press buttons on a CASH REGISTER to record how much money is being put inside ‖ 금전 등록기 안에 넣는 돈의 액수를 기록하기 위해 버튼을 누르다: *She rang up our purchases.* 그녀는 우리의 구매품을 금전 등록기에 입력했다.

ring³ *v* **ringed, ringed, ringing** [T] **1** to surround something ‖ 어떤 것을 에워싸다. 둥글게 포위하다: *The police ringed the building.* 경찰은 그 빌딩을 포위했다. **2** to draw a circular mark around something ‖ 어떤 것 주위에 둥근 표시를 그리다. 둥글게 두르다

ring·lead·er /ˈrɪŋˌlidə/ *n* someone who leads a group that is doing something illegal or wrong ‖ 불법적이거나 잘못된 일을 하는 단체를 이끄는 사람. 주모자. 우두머리: *Police arrested the two ringleaders last night.* 경찰은 지난밤 두 명의 주모자를 체포했다.

ring·let /ˈrɪŋlɪt/ *n* a long curl of hair that hangs down ‖ 아래로 늘어진 긴 곱슬머리

ring·side /ˈrɪŋsaɪd/ *n* [singular] the area nearest to the performance in a

CIRCUS, BOXING match etc. ‖ 서커스·권투 경기 등에서 공연이나 경기하는 곳과 가장 가까운 자리. 링 근처의 맨 앞줄 자리: *a ringside seat* 링 옆의 맨 앞줄 좌석

ring·tone /ˈrɪŋtoʊn/ *n* the sound made by a telephone, especially a MOBILE PHONE, when someone is calling it ‖ 누군가가 전화를 할 때 전화, 특히 휴대 전화가 내는 소리. 전화벨 소리

ring·worm /ˈrɪŋwəm/ [U] a common disease that gives you red rough circles on your skin ‖ 피부에 거칠거칠한 붉은 반점이 생기는 흔한 질병. 도장 부스럼. 백선(白癬)

rink /rɪŋk/ *n* a building with a specially prepared area with a smooth surface where you can SKATE ‖ 스케이트를 탈 수 있도록 표면을 매끄럽게 특별히 설치한 구역이 있는 건물. 스케이트장

rink·y-dink /ˈrɪŋki ˌdɪŋk/ *adj* INFORMAL cheap and of bad quality ‖ 싸고 질이 낮은. 싸구려의. 하찮은

rinse¹ /rɪns/ *v* [T] to use clean water in order to remove dirt, soap, etc. from something ‖ 어떤 것으로부터 먼지·비누 등을 제거하기 위해 깨끗한 물을 사용하다. …을 물로 씻어내다: *Rinse the lettuce in cold water.* 찬물로 상추를 씻으시오. / *Let me just rinse the sand off my feet.* 내 발의 모래만 씻어 낼게요.

rinse sth ↔ **out** *phr v* [T] to wash something with clean water but not soap ‖ 비누를 사용하지 않고 깨끗한 물로 물건을 씻다. 헹구다: *Please rinse out your bottles before recycling them.* 재활용하기 전에 병을 헹궈 주세요.

rinse² *n* **1** an act of rinsing (RINSE) something ‖ 어떤 것을 헹구는 행위. 헹구기: *a dishwasher's rinse cycle* 식기 세척기의 헹군 단계 **2** [C, U] a product used for slightly changing the color of hair ‖ 머리색을 약간 바꾸는 데 쓰는 제품. 린스제: *a brown rinse* 갈색 린스

ri·ot¹ /ˈraɪət/ *n* **1** a situation in which a crowd of people behaves in a violent and uncontrolled way ‖ 다수의 사람들이 난폭하고 통제할 수 없도록 행동하는 상황. 폭동. 소요: *Rises in food prices caused riots and strikes.* 식품 가격의 상승이 폭동과 파업을 야기했다. **2** [singular] someone or something that is very funny or enjoyable ‖ 아주 재미있거나 유쾌한 사람 또는 사물: *Jack's a real riot at a party.* 잭은 파티에서 아주 재미있는 사람이다. **3 read sb the riot act** INFORMAL to warn someone angrily that s/he must stop doing something wrong ‖ 남에게 잘못된 행동을 그만두라고 화내

며 경고하다

riot² *v* [I] if a crowd of people riots, they all behave violently in a public place ‖ 다수의 사람들이 모두 공공장소에서 난폭하게 행동하다. 폭동[소동]을 일으키다 – **rioter** *n*

ri·ot·ing /ˈraɪətɪŋ/ *n* [U] violent and uncontrolled behavior from a crowd that is out of control ‖ 통제에서 벗어난 군중들의 난폭하고 제멋대로인 행동. 폭동. 소요: *Rioting broke out in the city late last night.* 지난밤 늦게 그 도시에서 폭동이 일어났다.

ri·ot·ous /ˈraɪətəs/ *adj* **1** wild, exciting, and not controlled ‖ 몹시 흥분되며 자극적이고 통제되지 않는. 소란을 피우는: *riotous celebrations* 요란스러운 축하 행사 **2** noisy, possibly dangerous, and not controlled ‖ 시끄럽고 위험 가능성이 있으며 통제가 불가능한. 폭동의[을 일으키는]: *riotous crowds* 폭동을 일으키는 군중들

RIP the abbreviation of "Rest in Peace," written on the stone over a grave ‖ 묘석에 쓰인 "Rest in Peace(고이 잠드소서)"의 약어

rip

rip   rip up

rip¹ /rɪp/ *v* **-pped, -pping** **1** [I, T] to tear something or be torn quickly and violently ‖ 어떤 것을 찢다, 또는 빠르고 거칠게 찢겨지다. 짝 잡아찢다[뜯다]: *Oh, no! I've just ripped my sleeve.* 어머, 안돼! 내 소매가 찢어졌어. / *Don't pull the curtain; it'll rip.* 커튼을 잡아당기지 마시오. 찢어집니다. / *Impatiently, Sue ripped the letter open.* 조바심이 난 듯, 수는 편지를 짝 찢어서 개봉했다. **2** [I] to move quickly and violently ‖ 빠르고 거칠게 움직이다. 돌진하다. 세차게 관통하다: *a tornado ripping through an area* 지역을 휩쓸고 지나간 토네이도 **3** **Let 'er rip!** SPOKEN used in order to tell someone to make a car, boat etc. go as fast as it can ‖ 남에게 차·배 등을 가능한 한 빨리 움직이게 하라고 말하는 데 쓰여. 최고(속도)로 몰아라[운전해라]!

rip off *phr v* [T] SPOKEN **1** [**rip** sb ↔ **off**] to charge someone too much money for

something ‖ 어떤 사람에게 어떤 것에 대해 너무 많은 돈을 청구하다. …에게 바가지 씌우다: *The taxi driver tried to rip me off!* 그 택시 기사는 나한테 바가지를 씌우려고 했어! **2** [**rip off** sth] to steal something ‖ 어떤 것을 훔치다: *Someone ripped off Dan's car stereo.* 누군가가 댄의 자동차 스테레오를 훔쳐 갔어.

rip sth ↔ **up** *phr v* [T] to tear something into several pieces ‖ 어떤 것을 몇 개의 조각들로 찢다. 갈기갈기[발기발기] 찢다: *Fran ripped up her contract.* 프랜은 자신의 계약서를 갈기갈기 찢었다.

rip² *n* a long tear or cut ‖ 길게 찢어지거나 잘라짐. 째진[터진] 곳[틈]

rip·cord /ˈrɪpkɔrd/ *n* the string that you pull to open a PARACHUTE ‖ 낙하산을 펼치려고 당기는 줄

ripe /raɪp/ *adj* **1** ripe food or crops are ready to eat ‖ 음식이나 곡물이 먹을 만큼 숙성한. 익은. 여문: *Those peaches don't look ripe yet.* 그 복숭아들은 아직 안 익은 것 같아. **2** **be ripe for** to be in the right condition for something ‖ 어떤 것을 위한 알맞은 상태에 있다: *The area is ripe for a major earthquake.* 그 지역은 대규모 지진이 발생하기에 적합한 장소이다. **3** **the time is ripe (for)** used in order to say it is the right time for something to happen ‖ 어떤 것이 발생하기 위한 적시라고 말하는 데에 쓰여. 기회가 무르익다. 절호의 기회이다: *The time is ripe for trade talks.* 지금이야말로 무역회담을 할 절호의 시기다. **4** **ripe old age** if you live to a ripe old age, you are very old when you die ‖ 죽게 될 정도로 매우 늙은. 노령의 – **ripeness** *n* [U]

rip·en /ˈraɪpən/ *v* [I, T] to become RIPE, or to make something do this ‖ 익다, 또는 사물을 익게 만들다. 여물다[게 하다]. 숙성하다[시키다]: *Corn ripens quickly in hot weather.* 옥수수는 더운 날씨에 빨리 여문다.

rip-off /ˈrɪpɔf/ *n* SPOKEN something that is unreasonably expensive, and makes you feel cheated ‖ 어떤 것이 터무니없이 비싸고, 속았다고 느끼게 하는 것. 바가지. 폭리. 착취: *The drinks in the hotel bar are a ripoff!* 호텔 바의 술값은 바가지다!

rip·ple /ˈrɪpəl/ *v* **1** [I, T] to move in small waves, or to make something do this ‖ 잔물결로 움직이다, 또는 잔물결이 일게 하다. 파문을 만들다. 물결치다: *a flag rippling in the wind* 바람에 나부끼는 깃발 **2** [I] to make a noise like water that is flowing gently ‖ 잔잔하게 흐르는 물소리를 내다. 물결치는[흐르는] 소리를

내다: *water rippling over rocks* 바위 위를 졸졸 흐르는 물 **3** [I] to pass from one person to the next like a wave ∥ 물결처럼 한 사람에게서 다음 사람으로 전해지다. 번지다. 파급되다: *Laughter rippled through/ around the crowd.* 웃음이 군중들 사이로 번졌다.

ripple

ripple² *n* **1** a small low wave on the surface of a liquid ∥ 액체 표면 위의 작고 낮은 물결. 잔물결. 파문: *a breeze making ripples on the lake* 호수에 잔물결을 일으키는 산들바람 **2** a feeling or sound that spreads through a person or group because of something that happens ∥ 발생한 어떤 것 때문에 사람 또는 집단 사이로 전파되는 느낌이나 소리. 파문: *A ripple of laughter/nervousness ran through the audience.* 파문처럼 인 웃음[긴장감]이 청중 사이로 퍼져갔다.

rip·roar·ing /ˌ. '..·/ *adj, adv* INFORMAL noisy, exciting, and not controlled ∥ 소란스럽고 떠들썩 하며 통제되지 않는. 야단법석인: *We were having a rip-roaring time!* 우리는 실컷 떠들고 즐기는 중이었어! / *rip-roaring drunk* 만취

rise¹ /raɪz/ *v* **rose, risen** /ˈrɪzən/, **rising** [I]

1 ▶INCREASE 증가하다◀ to increase in number, amount, quality, or value ∥ 수[양, 질, 가치]가 증가하다. 늘다. 오르다. 상승하다: *World oil prices are rising.* 세계 유가(油價)가 상승하고 있다. / *Tourism rose by 4% last year.* 관광 여행이 지난해 4% 증가했다. / *The population has risen steadily/sharply since the 1950s.* 1950년대 이래로 인구는 꾸준히[급속하게] 늘어나고 있다.

2 ▶GO UP 올라가다◀ to go up ∥ 올라가다. 솟아오르다: *Smoke rose from the chimney.* 굴뚝에서 연기가 솟아올랐다. / *Flood waters are still rising in parts of Missouri.* 미주리 일부 지역에는 홍수가 아직도 불어나고 있다. —opposite FALL¹

3 ▶STAND 서다◀ to stand up ∥ 일어서다: *Thornton rose to his feet and turned to speak to them.* 손튼은 일어서서 그들에게 연설하기 위해 돌아섰다.

4 to become important, powerful, successful, or rich ∥ 중요해지다[강해지다, 성공하다, 부유해지다]: *the story of how Marilyn Monroe rose to stardom* 마릴린 몬로가 스타덤에 오른 과정에 관한

이야기

5 ▶VOICE/SOUND 음성/소리◀ to be heard, especially by getting louder or stronger ∥ 특히, 점점 더 크거나 세게 들리다. 높아지다: *Traffic noise rose from the street below.* 교통 소음이 아래쪽 거리에서 점점 크게 들려왔다.

6 ▶SUN/MOON/STAR 해/달/별◀ to appear in the sky ∥ 하늘에 나타나다. 뜨다. 떠오르다: *We'd been traveling for over an hour before the sun rose.* 우리는 해뜨기 전 약 한 시간 이상 이동하고 있었다. —opposite SET¹

7 ▶EMOTION 감정◀ to get stronger ∥ 보다 강해지다. 세지다. 치솟다: *You could feel the excitement rising as we waited.* 우리가 기다리는 동안 당신은 더욱 흥분되는 느낌을 받았을 것이다.

8 ▶MOUNTAIN/BUILDING 산/건물◀ to be or seem taller than anything else around ∥ 주변의 다른 어떤 것보다 더 높거나 높은 것처럼 보이다: *Then they could see Mount Shasta rising in the distance.* 그때 그들은 멀리 우뚝 솟은 샤스타 산을 볼 수 있었다.

9 ▶BREAD/CAKES 빵/케이크◀ if bread, cakes etc. rise, they become bigger as they bake, or because they contain YEAST ∥ 빵·케이크 등이 구워지면서, 또는 이스트를 함유하고 있기 때문에 더 커지다. 부풀어 오르다

10 rise to the occasion/challenge to deal with a difficult situation or problem successfully by doing things better than you have done them before ∥ 전에 했던 것보다 일들을 더 잘 해서 어려운 상황이나 문제를 성공적으로 처리하다. 상황/도전에 잘 대처하다[극복하다]

11 all rise SPOKEN FORMAL used in order to tell people to stand up when a judge enters a court of law ∥ 판사가 법정에 들어설 때 사람들에게 일어서라고 말하기 위해 쓰여. 일동 기립

12 ▶BED 잠자리◀ LITERARY to get out of bed in the morning ∥ 아침에 잠자리에서 나오다. 일어나다. 기상하다

13 ▶AGAINST A GOVERNMENT 정부에 반대해서◀ LITERARY also **rise up** to try to defeat the government or army that is in control of your country; REBEL ∥ 국가를 통제하고 있는 정부나 군대를 타도하려 하다. …에 반항[반대]하여 들고 일어나다. 봉기하다; ㉮ rebel

rise above sth *phr v* [T] to be good or wise enough to deal with an insult or unpleasant situation without becoming upset by it ∥ 화내지 않고 모욕 또는 불쾌한 상황을 이겨낼 만큼 충분히 착하거나

현명하다. 극복하다. 초연[초월]하다: *You ought to be able to **rise** above all that silly fighting.* 너는 그 모든 어리석은 싸움에 대해 초연할 수 있어야 한다.

USAGE NOTE rise and raise

Rise means "to move to a higher position" and does not have an object: *The curtain rose and the play began.* **Raise** means "to move someone or something to a higher position" and always has an object: *They raised the curtain and the play began.*
rise는 목적어 없이 "더 높은 위치로 이동하는 것"을 뜻한다: 막이 오르고 연극이 시작됐다. **raise**는 항상 목적어를 취하며, "사람 또는 사물을 더 높은 위치로 이동시키는 것"을 뜻한다: 막이 오르자 연극이 시작됐다.

---

rise² *n* **1** an increase in number, amount, or value ‖ 수[양, 가치]의 증가. 상승. 증대: *a 10% **rise** in car sales* 자동차 판매의 10퍼센트 증가 / *a tax **rise*** 세금 인상 **2** [singular] the achievement of importance, success, or power ‖ 중요성[성공, 힘]의 획득. 출세: *a book about his **rise** to fame/power* 그가 얻은 명성[권력]에 관한 책 **3 give rise to sth** to be the reason something happens or begins to exist ‖ 어떤 것이 발생하거나 또는 생겨나기 시작한 원인이 되다. …을 일으키다. 낳다. 초래하다: *a new industry that gave **rise** to scores of new companies* 수십 개의 새로운 기업을 탄생시킨 신(新)산업(분야) **4** an upward slope ‖ 오르막: *a slight **rise** in the road* 도로의 완만한 오르막 **5 get a rise out of sb** to make someone annoyed or embarrassed by making a joke about him/her ‖ 남에 대한 농담을 해서 화나거나 당황하게 만들다. …을 약올리다: *Ask about his car – that always gets a **rise** out of him.* 그의 차에 대해 물어봐. 그건 항상 그를 약 오르게 만들거든.

ris·er /ˈraɪzɚ/ *n* **early/late riser** someone who usually wakes up very early or very late ‖ 보통 매우 일찍 또는 매우 늦게 일어나는 사람. 조기 기상자/늦잠 자는 사람

ris·ers /ˈraɪzɚz/ *n* [plural] a set of wooden or metal steps for a group of people to stand on ‖ 일단의 사람들이 그 위에 올라가 서기, 세트로 된 일련의 나무 또는 금속제의 계단. (관람·사진 촬영용의) 계단 모양의 발판

risk¹ /rɪsk/ *n* **1** [C, U] the chance that something bad may happen ‖ 나쁜 일이 발생할 수 있는 가능성. 위험. 우려: *Think about the **risks** in starting a new business.* 새로운 사업을 시작할 때의 위험에 대해 생각해 봐라. / *the **risk** of cancer from smoking* 흡연으로 인한 암의 위험 / *There was a **risk** (that) he would say no.* 그가 아니라고 말할 우려가 있었다. **2 take a risk/run the risk** to do something even though there is a chance that something bad will happen ‖ 나쁜 일이 발생할 가능성이 있을지라도 어떤 것을 하다. 감히 위험을 무릅쓰다: *You'll be running the **risk** of getting caught.* 너는 붙잡힐 위험을 무릅써야 할 것이다. **3 at risk** likely to be harmed or put in a bad situation ‖ 해를 입거나 나쁜 상황에 처할 가능성이 있는. 위험에 처할: *I'm not going to put my officers at **risk**.* (=make them do something dangerous) 나는 내 부하 경찰관들을 위험에 빠뜨리지 않을 것이다. / *people at **risk** from radiation poisoning* 방사능 중독의 위험에 처한 사람들 / *He's at **risk** of losing his job.* 그는 직업을 잃을 위험에 처해 있다. **4 at your own risk** if you do something at your own risk, no one else is responsible if something bad happens ‖ 나쁜 일이 발생할 경우, 자신 혼자서 책임을 지는 일을 하다. 자신의 책임으로[에서]: *Customers may park here at their own **risk**.* 이곳의 주차에 따른 위험은 고객의 책임입니다. **5** something that is likely to hurt you or be dangerous ‖ 해를 끼칠 수 있거나 위험할 수 있는 것. 위험물[요인]. 위협: *health **risks** from air pollution* 대기 오염으로 인한 건강을 해칠 위험 / *the **risk** factors for heart disease* (=things that you likely to get sick) 심장병에 걸릴 위험 요인 **6 insurance/credit risk** a person or business to whom it is a good or bad idea to give insurance or lend money ‖ 사람이나 기업이 보험을 들거나 돈을 대출하기에 위험도가 낮은 또는 높은. 보험/신용 위험도: *Drivers under 21 are considered poor insurance **risks**.* 21세 이하 운전자들은 위험도가 높은 피보험자로 간주된다.

risk² *v* [T] **1** to put something in a situation in which it could be lost, destroyed, or harmed ‖ 어떤 것을 상실될 수[파괴될 수, 해로울 수] 있는 상황에 처하게 하다. 위험에 내맡기다. …을 위태롭게 하다: *I'm not going to **risk** my life/neck to save a cat!* 나는 고양이를 살리기 위해 내 목숨[목]을 걸진 않을 거야! / *She risked her career by running for* *governor.* 그녀는 자신의 경력을 내걸고 주지사 선거에 출마했다. **2 to do something that you know may have bad results** ‖ 나쁜 결과를 초래할 수도 있다는 것을 알면서 어떤 것을 하다. 위험을 무릅쓰다. …을 각오하다: *Some people have risked returning home, although the war is not over.* 몇몇 사람들은 전쟁이 끝나지 않았음에도 불구하고 위험을 무릅쓰고 고향으로 돌아갔다.

risk·y /'rɪski/ *adj* involving a risk that something bad will happen ‖ 나쁜 일이 발생할 위험이 있는. 위험한. 모험적인: *a risky financial investment* 위험한 금융 투자 / *Buying a used car is a risky business.* (=a situation or action that may be bad) 중고차 구입은 위험한 일이다. **– riskiness** *n* [U]

ris·qué /rɪs'keɪ/ *adj* a joke, remark etc. that is risqué is slightly shocking because it is about sex ‖ 농담·발언 등이 성에 관한 것이어서 약간 충격적인. 음란한. 외설적인

rite /raɪt/ *n* **1** a ceremony that is always performed in the same way, often for a religious purpose ‖ 흔히 종교적 목적으로, 항상 같은 방식으로 거행되는 의례. (종교) 의식: *funeral rites* 장례식 **2 rite of passage** a special ceremony or action that is a sign of a new time in someone's life ‖ 사람의 일생에서 새로운 시기의 상징이 되는 특별한 의식 또는 행위. 통과의례

rit·u·al¹ /'rɪtʃuəl/ *n* [C, U] a ceremony or set of actions that is always done in the same way ‖ 항상 같은 방식으로 행해지는 의식 또는 일련의 행위. 의식 절차. 의식의 일정한 형식: *I love all the rituals of making food at Thanksgiving.* 나는 추수 감사절에 음식을 만드는 모든 의식(집행) 절차들을 좋아한다.

ritual² *adj* **1** done as part of a RITE or RITUAL ‖ 의식 또는 관례의 일부로서 행해진. 의식의: *ritual prayers* 기도 의식(儀式) **2** done in a fixed and expected way, but without really meaning anything ‖ 사실 아무 의미도 없이, 고정적이고 예상된 방식으로 행해진. 관습[관례]적인: *ritual campaign promises* 의례적인 선거 공약

ritz·y /'rɪtsi/ *adj* INFORMAL fashionable and expensive ‖ 멋이 있고 값비싼. 호화로운. 우아한: *a ritzy neighborhood* 상류층 동네

ri·val¹ /'raɪvəl/ *n* a person, group, or organization that you compete with ‖ 경쟁하는 사람[집단, 조직]. 경쟁 상대. 라이벌: *a business/football rival* 사업[미식

축구] 경쟁자

rival² *adj* **rival company/team/player etc.** a person, group, or organization that competes against you ‖ 사람[집단, 조직]이 자신과 맞서 겨루는. 경쟁사/팀/선수: *rival airlines* 경쟁 항공사

rival³ *v* [T] to be as good or important as someone or something else ‖ 남 또는 다른 사물만큼 좋거나 중요하다. …에 필적하다: *As a writer, Laurier could not rival Blake.* 작가로서, 로리어는 블레이크와 대적할 수 없었다.

ri·val·ry /'raɪvəlri/ *n* [C, U] continuous competition ‖ 지속적인 경쟁. 경쟁[대립] 관계: *rivalry in the auto industry* 자동차 산업에서의 경쟁(관계)

riv·er /'rɪvɚ/ *n* **1** a natural and continuous flow of water in a long line that goes into an ocean, lake etc. ‖ 대양·호수 등으로 길게 흘러 들어가는 자연적이고 끊임없이 흐르는 물. 강. 하천: *the Colorado River* 콜로라도 강 / *up river* (=in the opposite direction that a river is flowing) 강 상류에 / *down river* (=in the same direction that a river is flowing) 강 하류에 **2** a large amount of moving liquid ‖ 다량의 액체의 움직임. 다량의 흐름: *a river of lava from the volcano* 화산에서 분출한 용암의 흐름

riv·er·bed /'rɪvɚˌbɛd/ *n* the ground over which a river flows ‖ 위로 강이 흐르는 땅바닥. 강바닥

riv·er·side /'rɪvɚˌsaɪd/ *n* [singular] the land on the sides of a river ‖ 강 옆의 땅. 강가. 강변: *a cottage on the riverside* 강변의 작은 별장

riv·et¹ /'rɪvɪt/ *n* a metal pin for fastening flat pieces of metal together ‖ 철판 조각들을 서로 고정시키는 금속 못. 대갈못. 리벳

rivet² *v* [T] **1** to attract and hold someone's attention ‖ 남의 주의를 끌어 붙잡아 두다. …의 주의를 집중시키다: *People sat riveted to their TVs during the trial.* 사람들은 재판이 진행되는 동안에 TV에서 눈을 떼지 못하고 앉아 있었다. **2** to fasten something with RIVETs ‖ 물체를 대갈못으로 고정하다. 리벳으로 죄다

riv·et·ing /'rɪvɪtɪŋ/ *adj* extremely interesting ‖ 매우 흥미로운. 흥미진진한: *a riveting movie* 흥미진진한 영화

R.N. *n* the abbreviation of REGISTERED NURSE ‖ registered nurse의 약어

roach /roʊtʃ/ *n* ⇨ COCKROACH

road /roʊd/ *n* **1** [C, U] also **Road** a specially prepared hard surface for vehicles to travel on ‖ 차량이 통행할 수 있게 특별히 시설된 단단한 지표면. 도로.

The gas station's just up/down the road. (=farther along the road) 주유소는 길 바로 위쪽[아래쪽]에 있다. / *the main road out of town* 도시를 빠져나가는 주요 도로 / *a side/back road* (=a small one that is not used very much) 샛길[뒷길] / *She lives out on Park Road.* 그녀는 파크 로드의 외곽 지역에 산다. / *Watch out for ice on the roads.* (=all the streets and roads in an area) 모든 도로상의 결빙 주의 —see usage note at STREET **2 on the road (to)** traveling for a long distance, especially in a car ‖ 특히 자동차로 장거리를 여행하는. 여행 도중의. 여행에 나선: *We've been on the road since 7:00 a.m.* 우리는 아침 7시부터 계속 여행 중이다. **3 on the road to success/recovery etc.** developing in a way that will result in success, health etc. ‖ 성공·건강 등의 결실을 얻는 과정으로 발전하는. 성공/회복의 과정에 있어

road·block /'roʊdblɑk/ *n* **1** something that stops the progress of something you want to achieve ‖ 달성하고 싶어하는 것의 진전을 막는 것. 장애[방해]가 되는 것: *The greatest roadblock to success is the men's lack of skill.* 성공으로 가는 데 가장 큰 장애물은 남자들의 수완 부족이다. **2** something that is put across a road to stop traffic ‖ 통행을 막기 위해 도로를 가로질러 세워 놓는 물건. 노상 장애물: *Police put up roadblocks to catch drunk drivers.* 경찰은 음주 운전자들을 적발하기 위해 노상장애물을 설치했다.

road·house /'roʊdhaʊs/ *n* a restaurant or BAR on a road outside a city ‖ 도시 교외의 도로상의 식당이나 주점. 가로변의 여관[술집]

road·kill /'roʊdkɪl/ *n* [U] INFORMAL animals that are killed by cars on a road or HIGHWAY ‖ 도로 또는 간선도로 상에서 차에 치어 죽은 동물

road·run·ner /'roʊd,rʌnɚ/ *n* a small bird that runs very fast and lives in the southwest US ‖ 미국의 남서 지역에 살며 매우 빠르게 달리는 작은 새. (미국산) 뻐꾸깃과의 일종

road·side /'roʊdsaɪd/ *n* [singular] the edge of a road ‖ 길 가: *a roadside restaurant* 노변 식당

road test /'. ./ *n* an occasion when a company tests the quality of a car it has made by driving it in bad conditions ‖ 기업이 만든 자동차의 품질을 시험하기 위해 나쁜 상태에서 주행하는 일. (차의) 노상 테스트 —compare TEST DRIVE

road trip /'. ./ *n* SLANG a long trip in a car, taken for pleasure ‖ 즐기기 위해 가

는 장거리 자동차 여행

road·way /'roʊdweɪ/ *n* [singular] the part of the road that is used by vehicles ‖ 차량이 사용하는 도로의 일부. 차도

road·wor·thy /'roʊd,wɚði/ *adj* if a vehicle is roadworthy it is in good enough condition to be driven ‖ 자동차가 주행하기에 충분히 좋은 상태에 있는. 노상 주행에 알맞은

roam /roʊm/ *v* [I, T] to walk or travel for a long time with no clear purpose ‖ 분명한 목적 없이 오랫동안 걷거나 여행하다. 배회하다: *gangs roaming the city* 도시를 배회하는 폭력배들 / *bears roaming through the forest* 숲을 돌아다니는 곰들

roar¹ /rɔr/ *v* **1** [I] to make a deep, very loud noise ‖ 아주 깊고 큰 소리를 내다. 울부짖다. 으르렁거리다: *lions roaring* 포효하는 사자들 **2** [I] to travel very fast, making a loud noise ‖ 크게 울리는 소리를 내며 매우 빠르게 움직이다. 굉음을 내며 돌진하다: *planes roaring overhead* 머리 위에서 굉음을 내고 있는 비행기 **3** [I, T] to say something with a deep loud voice ‖ 깊고 큰 소리로 어떤 것을 말하다. …을 큰 소리로 고함치다: *"Get out of here now!" he roared.* "여기서 당장 나가!"라고 그는 고함쳤다.

roar² *n* a deep loud continuous sound ‖ 끊임없이 깊고 아주 큰 소리. 울부짖음. 고함. 으르렁거림: *a roar of laughter* 폭소 / *the roar of the engine* 엔진의 굉음

roar·ing /'rɔrɪŋ/ *adj* **1** making a deep, very loud continuous noise ‖ 끊임없이 깊고 아주 큰 소리를 내는. 으르렁거리는. 노호[포효]하는. 떠들썩한: *roaring floodwaters* 노호하는 홍수 **2 roaring fire** a fire that burns with a lot of flames and heat ‖ 많은 화염과 열을 내며 타는 불꽃. 이글거리는 불꽃

roast¹ /roʊst/ *v* [I, T] to cook something in an OVEN or over a fire ‖ 오븐 또는 불 위에서 어떤 것을 요리하다. 굽다

roast² *n* **1** a large piece of ROASTed meat ‖ 구운 고기의 큰 덩어리. 불고기 **2** an outdoor party at which food is cooked on an open fire ‖ 음식을 화톳불로 요리하는 야외 파티. 로스트 (피크닉): *a hot dog roast* 핫도그 로스트

roast³ *adj* ROASTed ‖ 구운: *roast beef* 구운 쇠고기

rob /rɑb/ *v* **-bbed, -bbing** [T] to steal money or things from a person, bank etc. ‖ 사람·은행 등으로부터 돈 또는 물건을 훔치다. …을 강탈하다. 빼앗다: *Two men were arrested for robbing a supermarket.* 두 남자는 슈퍼마켓 강도 혐의로 체포되었다.

Use these words to talk about taking something that belongs to someone else. **Rob** is used to describe the act of taking money or property from a person or place: *Someone robbed the bank last night. / We don't carry cash because we're afraid we'll get robbed.* ✗DON'T SAY "someone stole a bank" or "we're afraid we'll get stolen."✗ **Steal** is used to talk about the actual things that are taken: *Matt's bike was stolen while he was on vacation. / They caught him trying to steal some cigarettes.* ✗DON'T SAY "Matt's bike was robbed" or "rob some cigarettes."✗ rob과 steal은 남의 소유물을 빼앗는 것에 대해 말할 때 쓴다. **rob**은 사람 또는 장소에서 돈이나 재산을 탈취하는 행위를 나타내기 위해 쓰인다: 누군가가 지난밤에 은행을 털었다. / 우리는 강도당할 것이 걱정되어 현금을 가지고 다니지 않는다. "someone stole a bank" 또는 "we're afraid we'll get stolen." 이라고는 하지 않는다. **steal**은 도난당한 실제 물건에 대해 말하기 위해 쓰인다: 매트의 자전거는 방학 동안 도둑맞았다. / 그들은 담배를 약간 훔치려고 하는 그를 붙잡았다. "Matt's bike was robbed." 또는 "rob some cigarettes"라고는 하지 않는다.

rob·ber /ˈrɑbɚ/ *n* someone who steals things, especially from stores or banks ‖ 특히 가게 또는 은행에서 물건을 훔치는 사람. 도둑. 강도: *an armed robber* (=one that carries a gun) 무장 강도 — see usage note at THIEF

rob·ber·y /ˈrɑbəri/ *n* [C, U] the crime of stealing money or things from a person or place ‖ 사람 또는 장소에서 돈이나 물건을 훔치는 범죄. 약탈. 강탈. 강도질: *Several robberies took place over the weekend.* 주말 동안 몇 건의 강도 사건이 발생했다. / *They're in prison for armed robbery.* (=robbery using a gun) 그들은 무장 강도죄로 수감되어 있다.

robe /roʊb/ *n* a long loose piece of clothing ‖ 길고 낙낙한 옷. 예복. 관복: *pajamas and a matching robe* 파자마와 그에 어울리는 옷 / *a judge's robe* 판사의 법복

rob·in /ˈrɑbɪn/ *n* a common wild bird with a red chest and brown back ‖ 가슴이 붉고 등은 갈색인 흔한 야생 새. 유럽울새

ro·bot /ˈroʊbɑt, -bʌt/ *n* a machine that can move and do some of the work of a person, and is controlled by a computer ‖ 움직일 수 있어 사람이 하는 일의 일부를 하며 컴퓨터에 의해 제어되는 기계. 로봇: *industrial robots* 산업용 로봇 – **robotic** /roʊˈbɑtɪk, rə-/ *adj*

ro·bot·ics /roʊˈbɑtɪks/ *n* [U] the study of how ROBOTs are made and used ‖ 로봇을 제작하고 사용하는 방법에 대한 연구. 로봇 공학

ro·bust /roʊˈbʌst, ˈroʊbʌst/ *adj* strong and healthy or not likely to have problems ‖ 힘세고 건강하거나 문제가 없을 것 같은. 튼튼한. 강건한: *a surprisingly robust 70-year-old* 놀랍게 강건한 70세 노인 / *a more robust economy* 더욱 탄탄한 경제

rock¹ /rɑk/ *n* **1** [U] a type of stone that forms part of the Earth's surface ‖ 지표면의 일부를 형성하는 돌의 형태. 암반: *a tunnel cut through solid rock* 암반을 뚫어서 낸 터널 **2** a large piece of stone ‖ 돌의 큰 조각. 바위: *Let's sit down on that rock and rest.* 저 바위에 앉아서 쉬자. **3** a type of popular modern music with a strong loud beat, played on GUITARS and drums ‖ 기타와 드럼으로 연주되는 강하고 시끄러운 박자를 가진 현대 대중음악의 한 형태. 록음악 **4** INFORMAL a DIAMOND or other jewel ‖ 다이아몬드나 다른 보석 **5 be between a rock and a hard place** to have a choice between two things, both of which are unpleasant ‖ 내키지 않는 두 가지 중 하나를 선택하다. (선택을 강요당해) 진퇴양난에 빠지다 —see also ROCKS

rock² *v* **1** [I, T] to move gently, leaning from one side to the other, or to make something do this ‖ 한쪽에서 다른 쪽으로 기울면서 부드럽게 움직이다, 또는 사물이 이렇게 되게 하다. …을 부드럽게 흔들다 [흔들리다]: *Jane sat rocking the baby.* 제인은 앉아서 아기를 살살 흔들었다. / *Waves were making the boat rock.* 파도로 배가 흔들리고 있었다. **2** [T] to make the people in a place feel very shocked or surprised ‖ 한 장소의 사람들을 큰 충격에 빠지거나 놀라게 하다. …을 넋빠지게 하다. 동요시키다: *a city rocked by violence* 폭력으로 충격에 빠진 도시 **3** to play or dance to ROCK'N'ROLL music ‖ 록큰롤을 연주하거나 그것에 맞춰 춤추다 **4 rock the boat** INFORMAL to cause problems for other members of a group by criticizing something or trying to change the way something is done ‖ 어떤 것을 비판하거나 행해지는 방식을 바꾸

rock and roll /ˌ. . '../ *n* [U] ⇨
ROCK'N'ROLL

rock bot·tom /ˌ. '../ *n* [U] **hit/reach
rock bottom** INFORMAL to become as
bad as something can possibly be ‖ 어떤
것이 가능한 한도까지 나빠지다. 최악으로
떨어지다: *By June, their marriage had
hit rock bottom.* 6월쯤에, 그들의 결혼 생
활은 최악으로 떨어졌다.

rock-bottom /ˌ. '../ *adj* rock-bottom
prices are as low as they can possibly be
‖ 가격이 가능한 한 가장 낮은. 최저가인

rock·er /'rɑkɚ/ *n* **1** ⇨ ROCKING CHAIR **2
be off your rocker** SPOKEN to be crazy
‖ 미치다. 제정신이 나가다

rock·et¹ /'rɑkɪt/ *n* **1** a machine that is
shaped like a tube, used for traveling or
carrying things into space, or to carry
bombs ‖ 우주로 여행하거나 사물을 운반
해 갈 때, 또는 폭탄을 나르기 위해 쓰이는
관처럼 생긴 기계. 로켓 **2** an explosive
that goes high in the air and explodes
with many bright colors ‖ 고공으로 올라
가 다양한 밝은 색의 빛을 내며 터지는 폭
발물. (불꽃놀이용) 폭죽

rocket² *v* [I] **1** to move somewhere
very fast ‖ 매우 빠르게 어떤 곳으로 이동
하다. 돌진하다: *a train rocketing
through a tunnel* 터널을 빠르게 통과하
는 기차 **2** to achieve a successful
position very quickly ‖ 매우 빨리 성공적
위치에 오르다. 급상승하다: *a song that
has rocketed to number one in the
charts* 인기 가요 순위 표에서 1위로 급상
승한 노래

rock·ing chair /'..
ˌ./ *n* a chair that has
two curved pieces of
wood fixed under it,
so that it ROCKs ‖ 흔들
거릴 수 있게 바닥에
고정된 두 개의 구부러
진 나뭇조각을 댄 의자.
흔들의자

rocking chair

rocking horse /'.. ˌ./ *n* a wooden
horse for children that ROCKs when you
sit on it ‖ 그 위에 앉으면 흔들리는 어린이
용 목마. 흔들목마

rock'n'roll /ˌrɑkən'roʊl/ *n* [U] a type of
music with a strong loud beat and
played on GUITARs and drums, that
became popular in the 1950s ‖ 기타와 드
럼으로 연주하는, 강하고 시끄러운 박자를
띠고 있는 1950년대에 유행하게 된 음악
의 유형. 로큰롤

rocks /rɑks/ *n* [plural] INFORMAL **on the**
rocks a) alcoholic drinks that are
served on the rocks have ice in them ‖
술에 얼음을 넣어 제공하는. 물을 타지 않
고 얼음을 넣는 **b)** a relationship or
marriage that is on the rocks is failing ‖
관계나 결혼 생활이 실패한 상태에 있는.
파경[파탄]을 맞은

rock·y /'rɑki/ *adj* **1** covered with rocks
or made of rock ‖ 바위로 덮여 있거나 바
위로 이루어진. 암석이 많은. 바위로 된:
the rocky coast of Maine 메인 주의 암석
해안 **2** INFORMAL a relationship or
situation that is rocky is difficult and
may not continue ‖ 관계나 상황이 어렵고
계속되지 않을 듯한. 힘겨운. 험난한: *He
had a rocky start as chairman.* 그는 회
장으로서 힘겹게 출발했다.

rod /rɑd/ *n* a long thin pole or stick,
made of wood, metal, or plastic ‖ 나무
[금속, 플라스틱]로 만들어진 길고 가는
장대나 막대: *a fishing rod* 낚싯대

rode /roʊd/ *v* the past tense of RIDE ‖
ride의 과거형

ro·dent /'roʊdnt/ *n* one of a group of
small animals with long sharp front
teeth, such as rats or rabbits ‖ 쥐나 토끼
등 길고 날카로운 앞니를 가진 작은 동물
군 중의 하나. 설치류(동물)

ro·de·o /'roʊdiˌoʊ, roʊ'deɪoʊ/ *n* a
competition in which COWBOYs ride wild
horses, and catch cattle with ropes ‖ 카
우보이들이 야생마를 타고 밧줄로 소를 잡
는 시합. 로데오 경기

roe /roʊ/ *n* [C, U] fish eggs ‖ 물고기 알.
곤이. 어란(魚卵)

rogue¹ /roʊg/ *adj* **1** a rogue person or
organization does not follow the usual
rules or methods and often causes
trouble ‖ 사람 또는 조직이 일반적인 규칙
이나 방법을 따르지 않으며 종종 말썽을
일으키는. 통제에서 벗어난. 이탈한 **2** a
rogue animal leaves its group and starts
causing damage ‖ 동물이 무리를 떠나 해
를 끼치기 시작하는

rogue² *n* a man who often behaves in a
slightly bad or dishonest way, but
whom people still like ‖ 종종 약간 나쁘거
나 정직하지 못하게 행동하지만 사람들이
여전히 좋아하는 남자. 건달

rogu·ish /'roʊgɪʃ/ *adj* typical of a
ROGUE, or behaving like a rogue ‖ 건달의
전형적인, 또는 건달처럼 행동하는. 건달
의. 못된: *a roguish smile* 짓궂은 미소

role /roʊl/ *n* **1** the position, job, or
function someone or something has in a
particular situation or activity ‖ 사람 또
는 사물이 특정한 상황이나 활동에서 가지
는 지위[업무, 기능]. 역할. 임무. 구실:

We're looking seriously at the role of education in our society. 우리는 사회에서의 교육의 역할을 진지하게 고찰하고 있다. / *companies that play a major/key role in the world's economy* 세계 경제에서 주요한 역할을 하는 회사들 **2** the character played by an actor ‖ 배우가 연기하는 등장인물의 역할. (배)역: *Brendan will play the role of Romeo.* 브렌단은 로미오 역을 할 것이다. **3** the position someone has or the way s/he is expected to behave in an organization, relationship etc. ‖ 어떤 조직·관계 등에서 그 사람에게 기대되는 행동 방식 또는 그 사람이 가지고 있는 지위. 역할. 임무: *women's role in society* 여성의 사회적 역할

role mod·el /'. ,../ *n* someone whom people try to copy because they admire him/her ‖ 사람들이 존경하기 때문에 모방하려고 애쓰는 사람. 역할 모델

role-play /'. ./ *n* [C, U] an exercise in which you behave in the way that someone else would behave in a particular situation ‖ 다른 사람이 특정한 상황에서 행동할 법한 방식으로 자신이 행동하는 연습. 역할극: *ideas for classroom role-plays* 교실 역할극을 위한 다양한 생각들 **– role-play** *v* [I, T]

roll¹ /roʊl/ *v*

1 ▶BALL/BODY 공/몸◀ [I, T] to move by turning over and over, or from side to side, or to make something do this ‖ 반복해서 또는 좌우로 돌면서 움직이다, 또는 이렇게 되도록 하다. 굴리다. 구르다. 돌리다. 돌다: *Don't let the ball roll into the street.* 공이 거리로 굴러가게 하지 마라. / *Roll the wine barrels into the corner.* 구석으로 포도주 통을 굴려라. / *a ship rolling on the waves* 파도에 흔들리는 배 / *The dog's been rolling in something stinky.* 그 개는 냄새나는 물건에서 계속 뒹굴고 있다.

2 ▶LIQUID/VEHICLE 액체/탈것◀ [I] to move steadily and smoothly ‖ 꾸준하게 그리고 부드럽게 움직이다. 흐르다. 구르다: *Tears rolled down his cheeks.* 눈물이 그의 볼을 타고 흘러내렸다. / *The van was starting to roll backward.* 그 승합차는 뒤쪽으로 움직이기 시작하고 있었다.

3 ▶PAPER/STRING 종이/끈◀ [T] to curl or wind something into the shape of a tube or ball ‖ 물건을 관이나 공 모양으로 말거나 감다: *Roll the string into a ball.* 이 끈을 공 모양으로 감아라. / *Bob rolled another cigarette.* 보브는 담배 한 개비를 더 말았다.

4 ▶SUBSTANCE 물질◀ [T] also **roll out**

to make something flat by moving something round and heavy over it ‖ 물건 위로 둥글고 무거운 것을 움직여서 납작하게 만들다. 밀어 펴다: *Roll the pie crust thin.* 파이 껍질을 얇게 밀어라.

5 ▶SOUND 소리◀ [I] if a drum or THUNDER rolls, it makes a long deep sound ‖ 북이나 천둥이 길고 깊은 소리를 내다. 울리다. 울려 퍼지다

6 roll your eyes to move your eyes around and up to show that you think someone or something is stupid ‖ 어떤 사람이나 사물이 어리석다는 자신의 생각을 나타내려고 눈을 옆과 위로 움직이다. 한심하다는 듯이 눈을 굴리다

7 ▶MACHINE 기계◀ [I] if a machine rolls, it operates ‖ 기계가 작동하다. 돌다: *Keep the camera rolling!* 카메라를 계속 돌려!

8 be rolling in the aisles INFORMAL if people in a theater are rolling in the aisles, they are laughing a lot ‖ 극장에 있는 사람들이 많이 웃다. 포복절도하다

9 (all) rolled into one including several things in one thing ‖ 한 가지 것에 여러 가지 것을 포함하는. 합쳐서 하나로 된: *The class was a history, art, and language course all rolled into one.* 그 반은 역사, 미술, 그리고 어학 과정 모두를 하나로 합한 반이었다.

SPOKEN PHRASES
---

10 ▶ACTION 행동◀ [I] to begin doing something ‖ 무언가를 하기 시작하다. 착수하다: *Are we ready to roll here?* 지금 시작할 준비가 됐니?

11 ▶LEAVE 떠나다◀ to leave a place ‖ 한 장소를 떠나다. 출발하다: *Okay, let's roll.* 좋아, 출발하자

12 be rolling in it to be extremely rich ‖ 굉장히 부유하다

---

roll around *phr v* [I] INFORMAL if a regular time or event rolls around, it arrives or happens again ‖ 규칙적인 시간이나 행사가 다시 도래하거나 발생하다. 다시 돌아오다: *By the time Friday night rolled around, we were too tired to go out.* 금요일 밤이 다시 돌아올 때쯤에는 우리는 너무나 피곤해서 외출하지 못했다.

roll sth ↔ **back** *phr v* [T] to reduce the price of something ‖ 물건의 가격을 줄이다. 낮추다. 끌어내리다: *a promise to roll back taxes* 세금을 원래 수준으로 낮추겠다는 약속

roll sth ↔ **down** *phr v* [T] **roll a window down** to open a car window ‖ 차 창문을 열다. 차 창문을 내리다

roll in *phr v* [I] **1** INFORMAL to arrive in large numbers or quantities ‖ 많은 수나 양이 도착하다. 쇄도하다: *Money started rolling in after the first calls for help.* 첫 번째 원조 요청 이후에 돈이 쏟아져 들어오기 시작했다. **2** INFORMAL to arrive later than expected ‖ 예상보다 더 늦게 도착하다. 뒤늦게 나타나다: *They finally rolled in at 4:00.* 그들은 마침내 4시나 되어 모습을 나타냈다. **3** if mist, clouds etc. roll in, they begin to cover an area of the sky or land ‖ 안개·구름 등이 하늘이나 땅의 일정한 지역을 뒤덮기 시작하다. 끼기 시작하다

roll sth ↔ **out** *phr v* [T] to make something flat and straight after it has been curled into a tube shape ‖ 관 모양으로 말아져 있던 것을 납작하고 곧게 만들다. 펴다: *Roll out your sleeping bag.* 침낭을 펴라.

roll over *phr v* [I] to turn your body around once so that you are lying in a different position ‖ 몸을 한 번 뒤집어서 다른 자세로 눕다. 뒤집다: *Ralph rolled over onto his stomach.* 랄프는 몸을 뒤집어 배를 깔고 누웠다.

roll up *phr v* **1** [T **roll** sth ↔ **up**] to curl something such as cloth or paper into a tube shape ‖ 천이나 종이 등의 것을 관 모양으로 말다. …을 둥글게 말다 **2 roll a window up** to close a car window ‖ 차 창문을 닫다. 차 창문을 올리다

roll[2] *n* **1** a piece of paper, film, money etc. that has been curled into the shape of a tube ‖ 관 모양으로 말린 종이·필름·돈 등의 조각. …뭉치. 두루마리: *a roll of dollar bills* 달러 지폐 한 뭉치 —see picture at FOLD[2] **2** a small round LOAF of bread for one person ‖ 1인분의 작고 둥근 빵 덩어리. 롤빵 —see picture at BREAD **3** an official list of the names of people at a meeting, in a class etc. ‖ 모임·수업 등에 참석하는 사람들의 공식적인 이름 목록. 명부. 출석[출근]부: *the union membership roll* 노동조합 회원 명부 — see also ROLL CALL **4 be on a roll** INFORMAL to be having a lot of success with what you are trying to do ‖ 하고자 노력하는 것에 대단히 성공하고 있는 상태이다. 계속 성공하다[이기다]: *I don't want to stop playing – I'm on a roll!* 나는 게임을 그만두고 싶지 않아. 오늘 승승장구야! **5** [singular] the movement of a ship or plane when it leans from side to side ‖ 배나 비행기가 좌우로 기울 때의 움직임. 좌우로 흔들림 **6** a long deep sound ‖ 길고 깊은 소리. 울림. 울려 퍼짐: *the roll of drums/thunder* 북[천둥]의 둥둥거림[우르르거림]

roll call /ˈ. ./ *n* [C, U] the act of reading out an official list of names to check who is present at a meeting or in a class ‖ 모임이나 수업에 누가 참석했는지 확인하려고 공식적인 명단을 소리 내어 읽는 행위. 출석 확인

roll·er /ˈroʊlɚ/ *n* **1** a tube-shaped piece of wood, metal etc. that can be rolled over and over ‖ 나무·금속 등의 관 모양으로 되어, 계속해서 굴릴 수 있는 물건. 굴림대. 밀대. 롤러: *paint rollers* 페인트 롤러 **2** one of several tubes that women wind their hair around to make it curl ‖ 여자들이 머리를 곱슬거리게 하려고 머리털을 마는 여러 개의 관들 중의 하나. 머리 마는 기구

Roll·er·blade /ˈroʊlɚˌbleɪd/ *n* TRADEMARK a special boot with a single row of wheels fixed under it ‖ 신발 밑에 바퀴가 한 줄로 부착된 특수 신발. 롤러브레이드 —compare ROLLER SKATE

roller coast·er /ˈ.. ˌ../ *n* **1** a track with sudden steep slopes and curves, that people ride on in special cars at FAIRs and AMUSEMENT PARKs ‖ 박람회와 놀이공원에서 사람들이 특수한 차를 타는, 갑작스럽고 가파른 경사와 굴곡이 있는 선로. 롤러 코스터 **2** a situation that is impossible to control because it keeps changing very quickly ‖ 계속해서 매우 빠르게 변하기 때문에 통제하기가 불가능한 상황. 기복이 심함: *I feel like I'm on an emotional roller coaster.* 나는 지금 감정의 기복이 심한 상태인 것 같다.

roller skate /ˈ.. ˌ../ *n* a special boot with four wheels fixed under it ‖ 신발 밑에 바퀴 네 개가 부착된 특수 신발. 롤러스케이트 − **rollerskate** *v* [I] − **rollerskating** *n* [U]

rol·lick·ing /ˈrɑlɪkɪŋ/ *adj* noisy and cheerful ‖ 시끄럽고 쾌활한. 신나게 떠들어대는: *a rollicking good time* 왁자지껄 흥겨운 한때

roll·ing /ˈroʊlɪŋ/ *adj* rolling hills have many long gentle slopes ‖ 언덕이 길고 완만한 경사가 많은. 완만한 기복이 있는

rolling pin /ˈ.. ˌ./ *n* a long tube-shaped piece of wood used for making PASTRY flat and thin before you cook it ‖ 요리하기 전에 반죽을 납작하고 얇게 만들 때 사용하는 긴 관 모양의 나무. 밀방망이 —see picture at PIN[1]

ro·ly-po·ly /ˌ.. ˈ../ *adj* a roly-poly person or animal is short and fat ‖ 사람이나 동물이 작고 뚱뚱한. 땅딸막한. 오동통한

ROM /rɑm/ *n* [U] TECHNICAL Read-Only

Memory; the part of a computer where permanent instructions and information are stored —compare RAM ‖ Road-Only Memory(읽기 전용 기억 장치)의 약어; 영구적인 지시 사항과 정보가 저장되어 있는 컴퓨터의 일부분

Ro·man Cath·o·lic /ˌroʊmən ˈkæθlɪk/ *adj* relating to the part of the Christian religion whose leader is the Pope ‖ 지도자가 교황인 크리스트교의 한 파와 관련되는. 로마 가톨릭 교회의: *the Roman Catholic Church* 로마 가톨릭 교회 – **Roman Catholic** *n*

ro·mance /ˈroʊmæns, roʊˈmæns/ *n* **1** a relationship between two people who love each other ‖ 서로 사랑하는 두 사람 사이의 관계. 연애. 로맨스: *a summer romance* 여름날의 로맨스 **2** a story about love between two people ‖ 두 사람 사이의 사랑에 관한 이야기. 연애 소설 **3** [U] the feeling of excitement and adventure that is connected with a particular place, activity etc. ‖ 특정한 장소·활동 등과 연관되는 흥분과 모험의 감정. 낭만적인 기분: *the romance of the theater* 극장의 로맨틱한 분위기

Roman nu·mer·al /ˌ.. ˈ.../ *n* a number in a system that was used in ancient Rome, that uses letters instead of numbers ‖ 숫자 대신 글자를 사용하는 고대 로마에서 쓰이던 체계에서의 수. 로마 숫자: *XXVII is the Roman numeral for 27.* XXVII는 27의 로마 숫자이다.

ro·man·tic¹ /roʊˈmæntɪk/ *adj* **1** showing strong feelings of love ‖ 사랑의 격한 감정을 나타내는. 낭만적인. 로맨틱한 : *"Paul gave me roses for our anniversary." "How romantic!"* 풀은 기념일에 나에게 장미를 줬어." "정말 낭만적이다!" **2** involving feelings of love ‖ 사랑의 감정을 내포하는. 연애의: *a romantic relationship* 연애 관계 **3** a romantic story or movie is about love ‖ 이야기나 영화가 사랑에 관한. 연애의: *a new romantic comedy* 새로운 로맨틱 코미디 **4** not practical, and basing your actions too much on an imagined idea of the world ‖ 실제적이지 않으며 지나치게 공상의 세계에 기초해 행동하는. 공상적인. 비현실적인: *romantic ideas about becoming famous* 스타가 되는 상상 – **romantically** *adv*

romantic² *n* **1** someone who shows strong feelings of love and likes doing things relating to love ‖ 사랑의 격한 감정을 나타내며 사랑과 관련된 것을 하기 좋아하는 사람. 낭만적인 사람: *Oh Jim, you're so romantic!* 짐, 당신은 정말 낭만

적인 사람이에요! **2** someone who is not practical and bases his/her actions too much on an imagined idea of the world ‖ 실제적이지 않으며 지나치게 공상의 세계에 기초해 행동하는 사람. 공상[몽상]가: *You're a hopeless romantic.* 너는 못 말리는 공상가야.

ro·man·ti·cize /roʊˈmæntəˌsaɪz/ *v* [T] to talk or think about things in a way that makes them seem more attractive ‖ 사물을 더 매력적으로 보이게 말하거나 생각하다. 낭만적으로 묘사[생각]하다: *a romanticized idea of country life* 시골 생활을 낭만적으로 그리는 생각

romp /rɑmp/ *v* [I] to play in a noisy way by running, jumping etc. ‖ 달리거나 높이 뛰면서 시끄럽게 놀다. 뛰놀며 떠들다: *puppies romping in the yard* 뜰에서 뛰어노는 강아지들 – **romp** *n*

roof¹ /ruf, rʊf/ *n* **1** the outside surface on top of a building or vehicle ‖ 건물이나 탈것의 꼭대기에 있는 외부 표면. 지붕. 옥상: *The storm ripped the roof off our house.* 그 폭풍은 우리 집 지붕을 날려버렸다. / *a ski rack for the car roof* 차 지붕용 스키대 선반 —see picture on page 945 **2** the top of a passage under the ground ‖ 지하 통로의 꼭대기. 천장: *The roof of the tunnel suddenly collapsed.* 터널 천장이 갑자기 붕괴되었다. **3 a roof over your head** a place to live ‖ 살 곳. (거주할) 집. 가정: *They're worried about keeping a roof over their heads.* 그들은 계속 거주할 집에 대해서 걱정한다. **4** the hard upper part of the inside of your mouth ‖ 입 안의 단단한 윗부분. 입천장 **5 the roof caves/falls in** INFORMAL if the roof caves or falls in, something bad suddenly happens to you ‖ 안 좋은 일이 갑자기 발생하다 **6 under one roof** in one building ‖ 한 건물 안에: *It's a restaurant and three bars all under one roof.* 한 건물 안에 식당 하나와 술집 세 개가 모두 있다.

roof² *v* [T] to put a roof on a building ‖ 건물 위에 지붕을 얹다. 지붕을 (…으로) 이다: *a house roofed with tiles* 지붕에 기와를 얹은 집

roof·ing /ˈrufɪŋ/ *n* [U] material for making or covering roofs ‖ 지붕을 만들거나 덮는 재료. 지붕 재료

roof·top /ˈruftɑp/ *n* the top surface of a building ‖ 건물의 꼭대기 표면. 지붕. 옥상: *Beyond the rooftops she could see the bay.* 그녀는 지붕 너머로 만(灣)을 볼 수 있었다.

rook·ie /ˈrʊki/ *n* someone who has just started doing a job or playing a professional sport, and has little experience ‖ 어떤 일이나 프로 경기 출전을 막 시작해서 경험이 별로 없는 사람. 초보자. 신참. 신인(선수): *a rookie policeman* 신참 경찰관

room¹ /rum, rʊm/ *n* **1** a part of the inside of a building that has its own walls, floor, and ceiling ‖ 자체의 벽·바닥·천장이 있는 건물 내의 일부분. 방: *the living room* 거실 / *Is Sally still in the computer room?* 샐리는 아직도 컴퓨터실에 있니? **2** [U] enough space for a particular purpose ‖ 특정한 목적을 위한 충분한 공간. 자리. 여지: *Save room for dessert!* 후식은 먹을 수 있게 먹어라! / *There isn't enough room in my closet for my coats.* 내 옷장에는 외투를 넣을 충분한 공간이 없다. —see usage note at PLACE¹ **3** **there's room for improvement** used in order to say that someone's work needs to be improved ‖ 남의 일이 개선될 필요가 있다고 말하는 데에 쓰여. 개선의 여지가 있다

room² *v* [I] **room with sb** to share the room that you live in with someone, for example at college ‖ 예컨대 대학에서 남과 거주하는 방을 공유하다. …과 한 방을 쓰다

room and board /ˌ. . ˈ./ *n* [U] a room to sleep in, and meals ‖ 잠을 자는 방과 식사. 식사를 제공하는 하숙: *How much do you pay for room and board?* 너는 하숙비로 얼마를 내니?

room·mate /ˈrum-meɪt/ *n* someone with whom you share a room, apartment, or house ‖ 방[아파트, 집]을 공유하는 사람. 동거인

room serv·ice /ˈ. ˌ../ *n* [U] a service provided by a hotel, by which food, drinks etc. can be brought to a guest's room ‖ 음식·음료 등을 객실까지 가져다 주는 호텔이 제공하는 서비스. 룸서비스

room·y /ˈrumi, ˈrʊmi/ *adj* with plenty of space inside ‖ 안의 공간이 많은. 널찍한: *a roomy car* 실내 공간이 넓은 자동차

roost /rust/ *n* a place where birds rest and sleep ‖ 새들이 쉬고 잠자는 장소. 보금자리. 새집 –**roost** *v* [I]

roost·er /ˈrustɚ/ *n* a male chicken ‖ 수탉

root¹ /rut, rʊt/ *n* **1** the part of a plant or tree that grows under the ground ‖ 식물이나 나무의 땅 밑에서 자라는 부분. 뿌리: *Be careful of the roots when you plant the roses.* 장미를 심을 때 뿌리를 조심해라. **2** the basic or main part of a problem or idea ‖ 어떤 문제나 생각의 기본적이거나 주요한 부분. 근본. 본질. 근

원: *Allergies are often the root of* (=are the cause of) *health problems.* 알레르기는 종종 건강 문제의 근본적인 원인이다. / *We need to try to deal with the root causes of drug abuse.* 약물 남용의 근본적인 원인을 해결하려는 노력이 필요하다. / *the roots of Marxism* 마르크스주의의 본질 **3** the part of a tooth, hair etc. that is fixed to the rest of the body ‖ 치아나 머리카락이 신체에 고정되어 있는 부분. …뿌리. …근 **4** **take root a)** if an idea takes root, people begin to accept or believe it ‖ 사람들이 어떤 사상을 받아들이거나 믿기 시작하다. 정착하다. 뿌리를 내리다: *helping democracy take root* 민주주의가 정착하는 데 힘씀. **b)** if a plant takes root, it grows into the ground ‖ 식물이 땅 속으로 자라다. 뿌리를 내리다 **5** TECHNICAL in grammar, the basic part of a word that shows its main meaning. For example, the root of "disagree" is "agree" ‖ 문법에서 주요 의미를 나타내는 한 단어의 근본이 되는 부분. 어근. 예를 들면, "disagree"의 어근은 "agree"이다 —see also ROOTS, SQUARE ROOT

root² *v* **1** **be rooted in** to have developed from something and be strongly influenced by it ‖ 어떤 것에서 발전하여 그것의 영향을 강하게 받다. …에 근원[연원]을 두다: *a holiday that is rooted in old customs* 옛날 풍습에서 기인한 휴일 **2** [I] to search for something by moving things around ‖ 물건을 주위로 옮기면서 무엇인가를 찾다. 헤집다. 뒤지다: *"Now where are my gloves?" she said, rooting around in the closet.* "지금 내 장갑이 어디 있지?" 그녀는 옷장을 뒤지며 말했다. **3** [I, T] to grow roots or to fix a plant firmly by its roots ‖ 뿌리가 자라게 하거나 식물을 그 뿌리로 튼튼하게 고정하다. 뿌리내리게 하다. 뿌리를 내리다: *The bulbs will root in spring.* 구근 식물은 봄에 뿌리를 내린다.

root for sb *phr v* [T] INFORMAL **1** to support a sports team or player by shouting and cheering ‖ 스포츠 팀이나 선수에게 소리치고 환호하여 지지하다. 응원하다. 성원하다: *We always root for the Yankees.* 우리는 항상 뉴욕 양키즈를 응원한다. **2** to support and encourage someone in a competition, test, or difficult situation ‖ 시합[시험, 어려운 상황]에 있는 사람을 지지하고 격려하다: *Good luck – I'll be rooting for you!* 행운을 빈다. 내가 너를 응원할게!

root sth ↔ **out** *phr v* [T] to find out where a particular problem exists and get rid of it ‖ 특정한 문제가 있는 곳을 찾

아내어 제거하다. …을 근절하다[뿌리 뽑다]: *We are doing all we can to root out violence in the schools.* 우리는 학교에서 폭력을 뿌리 뽑기 위해서 할 수 있는 모든 것을 다하고 있다.

root beer /'. ./ *n* [C, U] a sweet non-alcoholic drink made from the roots of some plants ‖ 일부 식물의 뿌리로 만든 알코올이 없는 달콤한 음료. 루트 비어

root·less /'rutlɪs/ *adj* having nowhere that you feel is really your home ‖ 정말로 자기 집이라고 느낄 만한 곳이 어디에도 없는. 정처 없는. 노숙자의

roots /ruts, rʊts/ *n* [plural] 1 the origins of a custom or TRADITION that has continued for a long time ‖ 오랜 시간 동안 계속되어 온 관습이나 전통의 기원. 뿌리. 연원: *Jazz has its roots in African music.* 재즈는 아프리카 음악에 그 기원을 두고 있다. 2 **sb's roots** someone's connection with a place because s/he was born there or his/her family lived there ‖ 어떤 사람이 그곳에서 태어났거나 가족이 그곳에서 살았기 때문에 갖는 그 장소와의 연관. 연고. 고향: *her rural roots in southern Illinois* 남부 일리노이에 있는 그녀의 시골 고향 3 **put down roots** to start to feel that a place is your home ‖ 어떤 장소를 자기 고향으로 느끼기 시작하다. 정착하다

rope¹ /roʊp/ *n* [C, U] very strong thick string, made by twisting together many threads ‖ 많은 실을 서로 꼬아서 만든 매우 튼튼하고 두꺼운 끈. 밧줄: *The rope was there to keep the climbers from falling.* 그 밧줄은 등산객들의 추락을 방지하기 위한 것이었다. —see also ROPES

rope² *v* 1 [T] to tie things together using rope ‖ 밧줄을 이용해서 사물을 한데 묶다. 밧줄로 묶다: *Harvey roped his horse to a nearby tree.* 하비는 말을 근처의 나무에 묶었다. 2 [T] to catch an animal using a circle of rope ‖ 올가미 줄을 이용해서 동물을 잡다. 올가미 줄을 던져 잡다

rope sb ↔ in/into *phr v* [T] INFORMAL to persuade someone to help you in a job or activity ‖ 어떤 일이나 활동에서 자신을 돕도록 남을 설득하다. 남을 끌어들이다[유인하다]: *Who roped you into doing the dishes?* 누가 너를 부추겨서 설거지를 시켰니?

rope sth ↔ off *phr v* [T] to surround an area with ropes in order to separate it from another area ‖ 한 지역을 다른 지역으로부터 분리하기 위해서 밧줄로 한 지역을 둘러싸다. 밧줄을 둘러치다: *Police roped off the area of the robbery.* 경찰

은 강도사건 지역을 밧줄로 둘러쳤다.

ropes /roʊps/ *n* [plural] 1 **know the ropes** to know how to do all the parts of a job because you have a lot of experience of it ‖ 어떤 일에 관해 많은 경험을 가지고 있어서 그 일을 모두 할 수 있다. 요령을 알고 있다 2 **show sb the ropes** to show someone the things s/he needs to know in order to do a job ‖ 어떤 일을 하기 위해서 알아야 하는 것들을 남에게 보여주다. 남에게 요령을 알려주다

ro·sa·ry /'roʊzəri/ *n* a string of BEADS used by Roman Catholics for counting prayers ‖ 로마 가톨릭에서 기도 수를 세기 위해서 사용되는 한 줄의 구슬. (로자리오) 묵주

ro·sé /roʊˈzeɪ/ *n* [U] pink wine ‖ 분홍색 포도주. 로제

rose¹ /roʊz/ *n* 1 a common sweet-smelling flower that grows on a bush that has THORNS (=sharp points on a stem) ‖ 덤불에 자라며 가시가 있는 향긋한 냄새가 나는 흔한 꽃. 장미 2 [U] a pink color ‖ 분홍색. 장밋빛

rose² *v* the past tense of RISE ‖ rise의 과거형

Rosh Ha·sha·nah /ˌrɑʃ həˈʃɑnə/ *n* Jewish New Year, in late September or early October ‖ 9월 말이나 10월 초의 유대인 신년. 유대 신년제

ros·ter /'rɑstɚ/ *n* a list of people's names showing the jobs they must do and when they must do them ‖ 해야 하는 일과 그 일을 해야 하는 시간을 나타내는 사람들의 명단. 근무 당번표

ros·trum /'rɑstrəm/ *n* a small PLATFORM (=raised area) that you stand on in front of an AUDIENCE ‖ 청중 앞에서 위에 올라서는 작은 단. 연단. 강단

ros·y /'roʊzi/ *adj* 1 pink ‖ 분홍색의. 장밋빛의: *rosy cheeks* 장밋빛 볼 2 seeming to offer hope of success or happiness ‖ 성공이나 행복의 희망을 제시하는 듯한. 유망한. 낙관적인: *a rosier future* 보다 낙관적인 미래

rot¹ /rɑt/ *v* **-tted, -tting** [I, T] to decay by a gradual natural process, or to make something do this ‖ 자연적으로 점차 썩다, 또는 사물을 썩히다. 부패하다[시키다]. 상하다[상하게 하다]: *Sugar rots your teeth.* 설탕은 이를 썩게 한다. / *old buildings that were left to rot* 방치되어 부식된 낡은 건물들

rot² *n* [U] the natural process of decaying, or the part of something that has decayed ‖ 자연적으로 썩는 과정, 또는 사물의 썩은 부분. 부패(물): *a tree full of rot* 온통 썩은 나무

ro·ta·ry /'routəri/ *adj* **1** turning in a circle around a fixed point, like a wheel ‖ 바퀴처럼, 고정된 지점 주위를 원을 그리며 도는. 회전하는: *the rotary movement of helicopter blades* 헬리콥터 날개의 회전 운동 **2** having a main part that does this ‖ 회전하는 주요 부품을 가진. 회전식의: *a rotary engine* 회전 엔진

ro·tate /'routeit/ *v* **1** [I, T] to turn around a fixed point, or to make something do this ‖ 고정된 지점 주위를 돌다, 또는 사물을 이런 식으로 돌리다. 회전하다[시키다]: *The Earth rotates every 24 hours.* 지구는 24시간마다 자전한다. / *Rotate the handle to the right.* 손잡이를 오른쪽으로 돌려라. **2** [I, T] if a job rotates or people rotate jobs, they each do the job for a fixed period of time ‖ 사람들이 정해진 시간 동안 각자 똑같은 일을 하다. 교대로 근무하다[시키다]: *We try to rotate the boring jobs.* 우리는 지루한 일을 교대로 하려고 노력한다. **3** [T] to regularly change the crops grown on a piece of land ‖ 토지에서 재배되는 농작물을 정기적으로 바꾸다. 윤작하다

ro·ta·tion /rou'teiʃən/ *n* **1** [C, U] the action of turning around a fixed point, or one complete turn ‖ 고정된 지점 주위를 도는 동작이나 한 번의 완전한 회전. 순환: *the rotation of the Earth on its axis* 자신을 축으로 하는 지구의 자전 / *The wheel makes 10 rotations a minute.* 그 바퀴는 분당 10회 회전한다. **2** [U] the practice of changing regularly from one thing to another or changing the person who does a particular job ‖ 한 가지 것에서 다른 것으로 규칙적으로 바꾸는 행위나 특정한 일을 하는 사람을 바꾸는 행위. 교대. 윤번: *We work in rotation.* 우리는 교대로 작업한다. / *crop rotation* 농작물의 윤작 **3** a complete turn around a fixed point ‖ 고정된 지점 주위를 완전하게 한 번 돎. 회전

ROTC /'rɑtsi, ˌɑr ou ti 'si/ *n* Reserve Officer's Training Corp; an organization that trains students to be US army officers ‖ Reserve Officer's Training Corp(학생 군사 훈련단. 학군단)의 약어; 미육군 장교가 될 학생들을 훈련시키는 조직

rote /rout/ *n* [U] **learn sth by rote** to learn something by repeating it until you remember it, without understanding it ‖ 어떤 것을 이해하지 않고 기억할 때까지 반복해서 배우다. …을 기계적으로 외우다

ro·tis·ser·ie /rou'tisəri/ *n* a piece of equipment for cooking meat by turning it around and around on a metal ROD ‖ 금속 막대에 달린 고기를 계속해서 돌려 요리하는 장비. 불고기 굽는 회전식 기구

ro·tor /'routər/ *n* the part of a machine that turns around on a fixed point ‖ 고정된 지점 주위를 도는 기계의 부분. 회전자

rot·ten /'rɑt̚n/ *adj* **1** badly decayed ‖ 심하게 부패한. 썩은. 악취를 풍기는: *rotten apples* 썩은 사과 **2** INFORMAL very nasty or unpleasant ‖ 매우 고약하거나 불쾌한. 역겨운: *What a rotten thing to do!* 이거 정말 하기가 고약하군! **3** INFORMAL very bad at doing something, or badly done ‖ 어떤 일을 아주 못하거나 형편없이 한. 젬병인. 형편없는: *I'm a rotten cook.* 나는 요리에는 젬병이다. **4 feel rotten** to feel ill or unhappy about something ‖ 어떤 일에 대해서 속상하거나 기쁘지 않은. 기분이 좋지 않은. 마음이 무거운: *She felt rotten about having to fire him.* 그녀는 그를 해고해야 하는 것 때문에 마음이 무거웠다.

ro·tund /rou'tʌnd/ *adj* having a fat round body ‖ 살찌고 둥근 몸을 가지고 있는. 통통하게 살찐

ro·tun·da /rou'tʌndə/ *n* a round building or hall, especially one with a DOME ‖ 특히 둥근 지붕이 있는 둥근 건물이나 홀. 원형 건축물[홀]

rouge /ruʒ/ *n* [U] ⇨ BLUSH[2]

rough[1] /rʌf/ *adj* **1** having an uneven surface ‖ 고르지 못한 표면을 가지는. 거친. 울퉁불퉁한: *Our jeep's good for traveling over rough ground.* 우리 지프차는 울퉁불퉁한 지면을 달리기에 그만이다. **2** not exact or not containing many details ‖ 정밀하지 않거나 세부 사항을 많이 포함하지 않는. 대강의. 개략적인: *Can you give us a rough idea of the cost?* 대략적인 비용을 제시해 주시겠어요? / *a rough draft of the speech* 연설의 대강의 초안 **3** using force or violence; not gentle ‖ 완력이나 폭력을 사용하는. 거친. 난폭한; 부드럽지 않은: *Ice hockey is a rough sport.* 아이스하키는 거친 스포츠이다. **4** a rough area has a lot of violence and crime ‖ 폭력과 범죄가 많은 지역인. 우범 지역의: *a rough part of the city* 도시의 우범 지대 **5** a rough period of time is one when you have a lot of problems and difficulties ‖ 어느 기간에 많은 문제와 어려움을 가지고 있는. 고된. 힘든: *She's had a rough couple of weeks.* 그녀는 힘든 몇 주를 보냈다. / *I had a rough night.* (=I did not sleep well) 나는 밤에 잠을 잘 자지 못했다. **6** with strong winds or storms ‖ 강풍이나 폭풍을 동반한. 사나운. 험악한: *A sailboat sank in* *rough seas.* 범선 한 척이 사나운 파도속에 침몰했다. **7 not fair or kind** ‖ 공정하거나 친절하지 않은. 매정한: *Don't be so rough on her.* (=be kinder) 그녀에게 너무 매정하게 굴지 마라. — **roughness** *n* [U]

rough² *v* **rough it** INFORMAL to live in conditions that are not very comfortable ‖ 매우 편안하지 못한 상황에서 살다. 불편한[원시적인] 생활을 하다: *We're going to rough it in the mountains for a few days.* 우리는 며칠 동안 산에서 원시적인 생활을 할 거야.

rough *sb* ↔ **up** *phr v* [T] INFORMAL to attack someone by hitting him/her ‖ 남을 때리면서 공격하다. 거칠게 다루다. 혼내주다

rough³ *adv* **play rough** to play in a fairly violent way ‖ 상당히 난폭하게 경기를 하다. 거칠게 경기하다

rough·age /ˈrʌfɪdʒ/ *n* [U] a substance in some foods that helps your BOWELs to work ‖ 장의 활동을 돕는 몇몇 음식물 속의 물질. 섬유질

rough-and-tum·ble /ˌ. . '../ *adj* full of people competing, often in a nasty way ‖ 종종 험악하게 경쟁하는 사람들로 가득 찬. 난폭한. 무법의. 마구잡이의: *the rough-and-tumble world of politics* 험악한 정치계

rough·house /ˈrʌfhaʊs/ *v* [I] to play in a noisy physical way ‖ 시끄럽게 몸을 움직이며 놀다. 야단법석을 떨다

rough·ly /ˈrʌfli/ *adv* **1** not exactly; about ‖ 정확하지 않게. 어림잡아; 대략: *Roughly 100 people came.* 대강 100명의 사람들이 왔다. **2** not gently or carefully ‖ 부드럽거나 주의 깊지 않게. 거칠게. 아무렇게나: *Don't pet the cat so roughly!* 그 고양이를 너무 거칠게 다루지 마라!

rough·neck /ˈrʌfnɛk/ *n* INFORMAL a large strong rude man who enjoys fighting ‖ 싸우는 것을 좋아하는 (몸집이) 크고 강하며 무례한 남자. 난폭한 남자

rough·shod /ˈrʌfʃɑd/ *adv* **ride roughshod over sb/sth** to behave in a way that ignores other people's feelings or opinions ‖ 다른 사람들의 감정이나 의견을 무시하는 식으로 행동하다. …을 거칠게 다루다. 끽소리 못하게 하다

rou·lette /ruˈlɛt/ *n* [U] a game played for money in which you try to guess which hole a small ball on a spinning wheel will fall into ‖ 회전하는 바퀴 모양의 것 위의 작은 공이 어느 구멍 속으로 떨어질지를 맞추는 데에 돈을 걸고 하는 게임. 룰렛

round¹ /raʊnd/ *adj* **1** shaped like a circle, a ball, or the letter "o" ‖ 원[공, 문자 "O"]처럼 생긴. 둥근. 원형의: *a round table* 둥근 탁자 / *a tree with round berries* 둥근 과실이 열리는 나무 / *the baby's round cheeks* 아기의 둥근 볼 **2 in round figures/numbers** not expressed as an exact number but as the nearest 10, 100, 1000 etc. ‖ 정확한 수가 아닌 가장 근접한 10·100·1000 등으로 표현되는. 대략적인 수치/숫자로: *What's the annual profit, in round figures?* 연간 수익이 대략적인 수치로 얼마나 됩니까? — **roundness** *n* [U]

round² *n*

1 ▶CONNECTED EVENTS 연관된 행사들◀ a number of events that are related ‖ 관련이 있는 많은 행사들: *the latest round of peace talks* 가장 최근의 연속적인 평화 회담

2 round of applause a time when people are clapping (clap) to show that they enjoyed a performance ‖ 공연이 즐거웠다는 것을 나타내려고 사람들이 박수를 치는 순간. 일제히 터지는 박수갈채

3 ▶DRINKS 술◀ alcoholic drinks bought for all the people in a group, usually by one person ‖ 대체로 한 사람이 한 무리의 사람들 모두에게 사는 술. (술을 좌중의 모두에게 살 때) 그 한 잔씩의 술

4 ▶SPORTS 스포츠◀ **a)** a complete game of GOLF ‖ 골프의 완전한 한 경기. 한 라운드 **b)** one of the periods of fighting in BOXING or WRESTLING ‖ 권투나 레슬링에서 싸우는 시간 중의 하나. 라운드. 회 **c)** one of the parts of a competition that you have to finish before you can go to the next part ‖ 다음 경기로 진출하기 전에 끝마쳐야 하는 한 시합을 이루는 경기들 중의 한 경기. 회전: *Graf has made it to the third round.* 그라프는 3회전에 진출했다.

5 ▶SHOT 발사◀ a single shot from a gun ‖ 총으로 쏘는 한 발. 한 방: *The soldier fired several rounds before escaping.* 그 병사는 도주하기 전에 총을 여러 발 발사했다.

6 ▶SONG 노래◀ a song for three or four singers who each start the same tune at different times, until all of them are singing ‖ 서너 명의 노래 부르는 사람들이 모두 함께 노래할 때까지 같은 곡을 시차를 두고 시작하는 노래. 윤창 —see also ROUNDS

round³ *v* [T] **1** to go around something such as a bend or the corner of a building ‖ 굽이나 건물의 모퉁이 등을 돌아서가다. 돌다. 돌아가다: *The Porsche* *rounded the bend at 120 mph.* 그 포르쉐는 시속 120마일로 커브를 돌았다. **2** also **round off** to make something round ‖ 사물을 둥글게 하다: *Round the corners of the table with a jigsaw.* 실톱으로 탁자의 모서리를 둥글게 만들어라.

round sth ↔ **off** *phr v* [I, T] to change an exact figure to the nearest whole number ‖ 정확한 수치를 가장 근접한 정수로 바꾸다. 반올림하다

round sth ↔ **out/off** *phr v* to make something complete by adding something to it, or by doing one final thing ‖ 무엇인가를 추가하거나, 하나의 최종적인 것을 함으로써 어떤 것을 완전하게 하다. …을 완성하다[마무리하다]: *Jeff rounded out his degree by studying in Spain for a year.* 제프는 일년 동안 스페인에서 공부해서 학위를 마쳤다.

round sth ↔ **up** *phr v* [T] to find and gather together a group of people or things ‖ 일단의 사람들이나 사물들을 찾아서 한데 모으다. 그러모으다: *Police rounded up 20 people for questioning.* 경찰은 심문하기 위해 20명의 사람들을 경찰서로 불러 모았다.

round⁴ *adv* ⇨ **all year round** (YEAR) — see also AROUND

round·a·bout /ˈraʊndəˌbaʊt/ *adj* not done in the shortest most direct way ‖ 가장 짧고 가장 직접적으로 이루어지지 않은. 우회의[적인]: *a roundabout route to avoid heavy traffic* 교통 정체를 피하기 위한 우회로

rounds /raʊndz/ *n* [plural] the usual visits or checks that someone makes as a part of his/her job, especially a doctor ‖ 특히 의사가 업무의 일부로서 하는 일상적인 방문이나 검사. 회진

round-the-clock /ˌ. .ˈ./ *adj* all the time, both day and night ‖ 밤낮 가리지 않고 항상. 24시간 계속의. 불철주야의: *round-the-clock hospital care* 24시간 병원의 (환자) 진료[간호]

round-trip /ˌ. ˈ./ *adj* a round-trip ticket is for taking a trip from one place to another and back again ‖ 표가 한 장소에서 다른 장소로 여행을 갔다가 다시 돌아올 수 있는. 왕복의 —see also ONE-WAY

round·up /ˈraʊndʌp/ *n* an occasion when a lot of people or animals are brought together, often by force ‖ 많은 사람들이나 동물들을 종종 강제로 불러 모으는 경우. 몰아들이기. 일제 검거: *a roundup of criminal suspects* 범죄 피의자들의 일제 검거

rouse /raʊz/ *v* [I, T] **1** to wake up, or

wake someone up ‖ 깨어나거나 남을 깨우다: *We were roused from a deep sleep.* 우리는 깊은 잠에서 깨어났다. **2** to make someone become excited enough to start doing something ‖ 남이 어떤 것을 시작하도록 충분히 자극을 하다. 분발케 하다: *King's speech roused his supporters toward greater efforts.* 킹의 연설은 지지자들이 더 많은 노력을 하도록 각성시켰다.

rous·ing /ˈraʊzɪŋ/ *adj* making people feel excited and eager to do something ‖ 사람들을 흥분시켜서 어떤 것을 열렬히 하고 싶게 하는. 분발[각성]시키는: *a rousing speech/song* 고무하는 연설[기운을 돋우는 노래]

rout /raʊt/ *v* [T] to defeat someone completely in a battle, competition, election etc. ‖ 전투·시합·선거 등에서 남을 완전히 패배시키다. 완패[궤멸]시키다 – **rout** *n* [singular]

route¹ /rut, raʊt/ *n* the way from one place to another, especially one that is shown on a map ‖ 특히 지도에 나타난, 한 장소에서 다른 장소로 가는 길. 도로. 노선: *What is the shortest route from Memphis to Atlanta?* 멤피스에서 애틀랜타까지 가는 가장 가까운 지름길은 어떤 것입니까? / *We had to take a longer route because of the snow.* 우리는 눈 때문에 우회도로를 택해야 했다.

route² *v* [T] to send something or someone by a particular ROUTE ‖ 사물이나 사람을 특정 경로로 보내다. …으로 보내다[발송하다]: *All the military supplies were routed through Turkey.* 모든 군수품은 터키를 경유해 수송되었다.

rou·tine¹ /ruˈtin/ *n* [C, U] the usual or normal way in which you do things ‖ 어떤 일을 하는 평소의 또는 정상적인 방법. 일상적인 일. 일과: *Harry doesn't like any change in his daily routine.* 해리는 하루의 일과에서 변화가 생기는 것을 좋아하지 않는다. / *We shouldn't accept TV violence as routine.* 텔레비전 속의 폭력을 일상적인 일로 받아들여서는 안 된다.

routine² *adj* **1** regular and usual ‖ 규칙적이며 일상적인: *a routine medical test* 정기 건강 검진 / *a few routine questions* 일상적인 몇 가지 질문들 **2** ordinary and boring ‖ 평범하고 지루한. 판에 박힌. 타성적인: *a routine job* 판에 박힌 일 – **routinely** *adv*

rov·ing /ˈroʊvɪŋ/ *adj* traveling or moving from one place to another ‖ 한 장소에서 다른 장소로 이동하거나 움직이는. 이동하는: *a roving reporter* 현장 이동 취재 기자

row

There are two seats in the front row.

row¹ /roʊ/ n **1** a line of things or people next to each other ‖ 사람들이나 물체들이 서로 나란히 늘어선 줄. 열. 줄: *a row of houses* 한 줄로 늘어선 주택 **2 three/four etc. in a row** three times, four times etc. together and in the same way ‖ 계속하여 같은 식으로 세 번·네 번 등. 잇따라 세 번/네 번: *We've lost four games in a row.* 우리는 네 경기를 잇따라 졌다. **3** a line of seats in a theater, large room etc. ‖ 극장·거대한 실내 등의 한 줄의 좌석. 가로 줄: *I sat in the front row.* 나는 앞줄에 앉았다.

row² v [I, T] to make a boat move by using OARs ‖ 노를 사용해서 배를 움직이게 하다. (배를) 젓다. 저어가다: *Slowly, she rowed across the lake.* 그녀는 천천히 배를 저어 호수를 건넜다.

row·boat /ˈroʊboʊt/ n a small boat that you move by using OARs ‖ 노를 사용해서 움직이는 작은 배. 노젓는 배

row·dy /ˈraʊdi/ adj behaving in a noisy way that is not controlled ‖ 통제되지 않고 떠들썩대며 행동하는. 난폭한. 소란스러운: *a group of rowdy children* 한 무리의 소란스러운 어린이들 – **rowdiness** n [U]

row·ing /ˈroʊɪŋ/ n [U] the sport or activity of making a boat move by using OARs ‖ 노를 사용해서 배를 움직이게 하는 경기나 활동. 배젓기. 조정

roy·al /ˈrɔɪəl/ adj relating to or belonging to a king or queen ‖ 왕이나 여왕에 관련되거나 속하는. 왕[여왕]의. 왕족의: *the royal family* 왕실 / *the royal palace* 왕궁

roy·al·ties /ˈrɔɪəltiz/ [plural] payments made to the writer of a book or piece of music ‖ 책이나 곡의 작자에게 주는 지불금. 인세. 저작권 사용료

roy·al·ty /ˈrɔɪəlti/ n [U] members of a royal family ‖ 왕실의 구성원들. 왕족

rpm n revolutions per minute; a unit for measuring the speed of an engine ‖ revolutions per minute(분당 회전수)의 약어; 엔진의 속도를 측정하는 단위

RSVP an abbreviation that is written on invitations in order to ask someone to reply ‖ 남에게 회신을 요청하기 위해 초대장에 쓰는 약어. 회답 요망

rub¹ /rʌb/ v **-bbed, -bbing 1** [I, T] to move your hand, a cloth etc. over a surface while pressing against it ‖ 손·천 등을 어떤 표면에 대고 누르면서 움직이다. 문지르다. 비비다: *The stain should come out if you rub harder.* 더 세게 문지르면 그 얼룩은 빠질 거야. / *Can you rub some lotion on my back please?* 내 등에 로션 좀 발라 줄래? **2** [I] to move around while pressing against another surface ‖ 다른 표면에 대고 누르면서 이리저리 움직이다. 스치다. 닿다: *My shoes are rubbing against my heels.* 신발에 뒤꿈치가 쓸린다. **3 rub it in** INFORMAL to remind someone of something that s/he wants to forget, especially because s/he is embarrassed about it or ashamed of it ‖ 특히 난처하게 생각하거나 부끄럽게 여겨 잊고 싶어 하는 것을 남에게 상기시키다. 아픈 데를 또 건드리다. 듣기 싫게 되뇌다: *"You went out with Wanda in sixth grade, didn't you?" "Yeah, don't rub it in!"* "너 6학년 때 완다랑 사귀었지? 안 그래?" "그래, 아픈 데 또 건드리지 마!" **4 rub sb the wrong way** INFORMAL to annoy someone by the way you talk or behave toward him/her ‖ 남에게 말하거나 행동하는 태도로 그 사람을 짜증나게 하다. 남을 화나게 하다. 남의 비위를 거스르다: *I think Marilyn rubs him the wrong way.* 마릴린이 그의 비위를 거스른 것 같아. **5 rub shoulders with sb** INFORMAL to spend time with rich famous people ‖ 부유하고 유명한 사람들과 시간을 보내다. …과 교제하다. …와 잘 지내다 **6 rub off on sb** if a feeling, quality, or habit rubs off on you, you start to have it because you are with another person who has it ‖ 어떤 감정[자질, 습관]을 가진 사람과 함께 있어 자신도 그것을 가지기 시작하다. 남에게 영향을 미치다: *Her positive attitude seemed to rub off on everyone.* 그녀의 긍정적인 태도는 모두에게 영향을 미치는 듯했다.

rub down phr v [T] **1** [rub sth ↔ down] to make a surface dry or smooth by pressing against it with a cloth ‖ 천으로 표면에 대고 눌러대면서 건조시키거나 매끄럽게 하다. …을 닦다[윤내다] **2** [rub sb down] to press someone's muscles to make him/her relax, especially after exercise ‖ 특히 운동 후에 긴장을 풀게 하려고 남의 근육을 누르다. 남을 마사지해 주다

rub² *n* an act of rubbing something or someone ‖ 물체나 사람을 문지르는 동작. 문지름: *Could you give me a back rub?* 등 좀 문질러 줄래요?

rub·ber /ˈrʌbə/ *n* **1** [U] a substance used for making tires, boots etc., that is made from chemicals or the liquid that comes out of tropical trees ‖ 화학 물질이나 열대 나무에서 나오는 액체로 만드는, 타이어·장화 등을 만들 때 사용하는 물질. 고무: *rubber gloves* 고무장갑 **2** INFORMAL ⇨ CONDOM

rubber band /ˌ.. ˈ., ˈ.. ˌ./ *n* a thin circular piece of rubber used for keeping things together ‖ 어떤 것들을 합쳐 둘 때 사용하는 가는 원형의 고무 조각. 고무 밴드

rub·ber·neck /ˈrʌbəˌnɛk/ *v* [I] INFORMAL to look around at something such as an accident while you are driving or walking past ‖ 운전을 하거나 걸어 지나가면서 사고 등을 둘러보다. 목을 빼고 살피다. 구경하다

rubber-stamp /ˌ.. ˈ./ *v* [T] to give official approval to something without really thinking about it ‖ 어떤 것에 대해서 실제로 생각하지 않고 공식적인 승인을 내리다. 충분히 검토하지 않고 인가하다

rub·ber·y /ˈrʌbəri/ *adj* **1** looking or feeling like rubber ‖ 고무처럼 생겼거나 느껴지는. 고무 같은: *a rubbery steak* 질긴 스테이크 **2** if your legs or knees are rubbery, they are weak and unsteady ‖ 다리나 무릎이 약하고 불안정한. 약한. 흔들거리는

rub·bish /ˈrʌbɪʃ/ *n* [U] ⇨ GARBAGE

rub·ble /ˈrʌbəl/ *n* [U] broken stones or bricks from a building, wall etc. that has been destroyed ‖ 파괴된 건물·벽 등의 부서진 돌이나 벽돌들. 잔해. 돌부스러기: *a pile of rubble* 잔해 더미

rub·down /ˈrʌbdaʊn/ *n* **give sb a rubdown** to rub someone's body in order to make him/her relax, especially after exercise ‖ 특히 운동 후에 긴장을 풀어 주기 위해 남의 몸을 문지르다. 남에게 마사지를 해주다

ru·bel·la /ruˈbɛlə/ *n* [U] TECHNICAL ⇨ MEASLES

ru·by /ˈrubi/ *n* [C, U] a dark red jewel, or the color of this jewel ‖ 암적색의 보석이나 이 보석의 색깔. 루비. 홍옥. 심홍색 – **ruby** *adj*

ruck·us /ˈrʌkəs/ *n* [singular] INFORMAL a noisy argument or confused situation ‖ 시끄러운 논쟁이나 혼란한 상황. 격렬한 논쟁. 야단법석. 소동: *What's all the ruckus about?* 이게 다 무슨 야단법석들

이냐?

rud·der /ˈrʌdə/ *n* a flat part at the back of a boat or aircraft that is turned in order to change the direction in which the vehicle moves ‖ 이동하는 방향을 바꾸기 위해 돌리는 배나 항공기의 뒷부분에 있는 납작한 부분. 키. 방향타 — see picture at AIRPLANE

rud·dy /ˈrʌdi/ *adj* a ruddy face looks pink and healthy ‖ 얼굴이 분홍빛으로 건강해 보이는. 불그스름한. 혈색이 좋은

rude /rud/ *adj* **1** speaking or behaving in a way that is not polite ‖ 공손하지 않게 말하거나 행동하는. 버릇없는. 무례한: *a rude remark* 무례한 말 / *Don't be rude to your grandmother!* 할머니께 버릇없이 굴지 마라! ✗DON'T SAY "rude with."✗ "rude with"라고는 하지 않는다. **2** relating to sex in an offensive way ‖ 불쾌감을 주는 식으로 섹스와 관련되는. 상스러운. 저질의: *a rude gesture* 상스러운 몸짓 **3 a rude awakening** a situation in which someone suddenly realizes something unpleasant ‖ 사람이 갑자기 불쾌한 것을 깨닫는 상황. 불현듯한 자각 [환멸] – **rudely** *adv* – **rudeness** *n* [U]

ru·di·men·ta·ry /ˌrudəˈmɛntri, -ˈmɛntəri/ *adj* FORMAL **1** rudimentary knowledge or understanding is very simple and basic ‖ 지식이나 이해가 매우 단순하고 기초적인. 기본[초보]의: *a rudimentary knowledge of geometry* 기하학에 대한 기초 지식 **2** not very advanced or developed ‖ 매우 앞서 있거나 발전되지 않은. 갓 시작한. 미발달한. 미숙한: *rudimentary equipment* 원시적인 장비

ru·di·ments /ˈrudəmənts/ *n* [plural] FORMAL the most basic parts of a subject ‖ 한 주제의 가장 기본적인 부분. 근본. 기초: *They know the rudiments of grammar.* 그들은 문법의 기초는 안다.

rue /ru/ *v* [T] LITERARY to wish that you had not done something; REGRET ‖ 어떤 것을 하지 않았으면 좋았다고 생각하다. 뉘우치다. 후회하다; ㉠ regret: *She'll rue the day that she met him.* 그녀는 그를 만났던 날을 후회하게 될 거야.

rue·ful /ˈrufəl/ *adj* showing that you wish you had not done something ‖ 어떤 것을 하지 않았으면 좋았다는 것을 나타내는. 후회하는. 침울한: *a rueful smile* 후회의 미소 – **ruefully** *adv*

ruf·fle¹ /ˈrʌfəl/ *v* [T] **1** to make a smooth surface uneven or messy ‖ 매끄러운 표면을 고르지 못하거나 엉망으로 만들다. 주름지게 하다. 물결을 일으키다.

어지럽히다: *Brian's dad reached over and ruffled his hair.* 브라이언의 아빠는 손을 뻗어 브라이언의 머리를 헝클어뜨렸다. **2** also **ruffle sb's feathers** to offend, annoy, or upset someone ‖ 남을 기분 상하게[짜증나게, 화나게] 하다: *Don't let yourself get ruffled over what he said.* 그가 한 말 때문에 기분 상해 하지 마라.

ruffle² *n* a band of cloth sewn in folds as a decoration around the edges of a shirt, skirt, etc. ‖ 셔츠·치마 등의 가장자리 주위에 장식으로서 주름을 잡아 꿰맨 천의 띠. 주름 장식[깃] **– ruffled** *adj*

rug /rʌg/ *n* **1** a piece of thick cloth, wool etc. that is put on the floor as a decoration ‖ 장식물로 바닥 위에 까는 두꺼운 천·양모 등. 깔개. 융단. 양탄자 — compare CARPET¹ **2** HUMOROUS ⇨ TOUPEE **—see also pull the rug out from under sb** (PULL¹)

rug·by /ˈrʌgbi/ *n* [U] an outdoor game played by two teams with an OVAL ball that you kick or carry ‖ 두 팀이 타원형의 공을 차거나 들고 뛰며 경기하는 실외 경기. 럭비

rug·ged /ˈrʌgɪd/ *adj* **1** land that is rugged is rough, rocky, and uneven ‖ 땅이 거칠고 바위가 많으며 고르지 못한. 울퉁불퉁한. 바위투성이의 **2** attractively strong ‖ 매력적으로 강한. 튼튼한. 늠름한. 억센: *a rugged face* 늠름한 얼굴 / *She's really a rugged character in this play.* 그녀는 이 연극에서 정말로 억센 배역이다.

ru·in¹ /ˈruɪn/ *v* [T] **1** to spoil or destroy something completely ‖ 어떤 것을 완전히 망치거나 파괴하다: *He ruined our evening by getting drunk.* 그는 술에 취해서 우리의 저녁 시간을 망쳐 놓았다. / *Our credit will be ruined if we don't pay the bills right now.* 지금 당장 청구서 요금을 내지 않으면 우리의 신용은 무너질 것이다. **2** to make someone lose all his/her money ‖ 남에게 모든 돈을 잃게 하다. 파산[파멸]시키다. 영락하게 하다

ru·in² *n* **1** [U] a situation in which something is damaged, spoiled, or destroyed ‖ 사물이 손상을 입거나 망쳐지거나 파괴되는 상황. 파괴. 붕괴: *The old barn has fallen into ruin.* 그 낡은 헛간은 무너졌다. / *financial ruin* 재정적인 파탄 **2 be in ruins** to be badly damaged or destroyed ‖ 심하게 손상을 입거나 파괴되다. 황폐해 있다: *The country's economy is in ruins.* 그 국가 경제는 황폐해 있다. **3** [U] a situation in which someone has lost his/her social position,

or all his/her money ‖ 사람이 사회적 지위나 모든 돈을 잃은 상황. 파멸. 파산: *Jack's gambling eventually led to his ruin.* 잭은 도박을 하다가 결국 파멸에 이르렀다. **4** also **ruins** [plural] the part of a building that is left after the rest has been destroyed ‖ 건물의 나머지가 부서진 이후에 남은 건물의 부분. 폐허. 유적: *the ruins of the Artemis temple* 아르테미스 신전의 폐허

ru·in·ous /ˈruɪnəs/ *adj* causing great destruction or loss of money ‖ 엄청난 파괴나 금전의 상실을 초래하는. 파괴적인. 파산[영락]시키는: *a ruinous decision* 파멸을 가져오는 결정

rule¹ /rul/ *n* **1** an instruction that says how something is to be done or what is allowed ‖ 무엇을 어떻게 해야 하는지 또는 허락되는 것이 무엇인지를 나타내는 지시 사항. 규칙. 규정: *Erin knows the rules of the game.* 에린은 그 경기의 규칙을 안다. / *Well, that's what happens if you break the rules.* (=disobey them) 규칙을 어기면 그렇게 되는 거야. / *It's against the rules to have alcohol in your room.* 방에 술을 놔두는 것은 규정 위반이다. **2** [U] the government of a country by a particular group of people or by using a particular system ‖ 특정한 집단의 사람들에 의해 또는 특정한 제도를 이용해서 한 국가를 다스림. 지배. 통치: *a country under foreign rule* 외세의 지배 하에 있는 국가 / *majority rule* (=government by the political party that most people voted for) 다수당의 통치 **3 as a (general) rule** usually ‖ 일반적으로. 대체로: *As a rule, I try to drink a pint of water a day.* 나는 대체로 하루에 0.5ℓ 정도의 물을 마시려고 노력한다. **4 bend/stretch the rules** to allow something to happen even if it is against the rules ‖ 설령 규정에 어긋나더라도 어떤 일이 발생하도록 허용하다. 규칙[규정]을 어기다. 악용하다: *Can't we bend the rules just this once?* 딱 이번 한 번만 규정에 예외를 두면 안 될까요? **5 rule of thumb** a principle that is based on practical experience, and that works most of the time ‖ 실제 경험에 근거하며 대부분의 경우에 적용되는 원칙. 경험 법칙: *As a rule of thumb, chicken should be cooked 15 minutes for each pound.* 경험상으로 보면, 닭고기는 각 파운드당 15분간 요리해야 한다. **6 rule the roost** INFORMAL to be the most powerful person in a group ‖ 한 집단 내에서 가장 힘 있는 사람이 되다. 지배하다. 좌지우지하다: *She likes to think she rules the* *roost around here.* 그녀는 자기가 이곳을 좌지우지한다고 생각하는 경향이 있다. **7 sb/sth rules** INFORMAL used in order to say that the team, school etc. mentioned is better than anyone else ‖ 언급한 팀·학교 등이 다른 팀·학교보다 더 낫다고 말하는 데에 쓰여. …이 최고다: *Midland High rules!* 미들랜드 고교가 최고야!

rule² *v* **1** [I, T] to have the official power to control a country and its people, especially as a MONARCH ‖ 특히 군주로서 한 국가와 그 국민들을 통치하는 공식적인 권력을 가지다. 지배[통치]하다: *The story is set during the time when the Pharaohs ruled (over) Egypt.* 그 이 야기의 배경은 파라오가 이집트를 통치하 던 시기이다. **2** [I, T] to make an official decision about something such as a legal problem ‖ 법적인 문제 등에 대해 공 식적인 결정을 내리다. 판결하다: *The judge ruled that the baby belonged with his real father.* 판사는 그 아기가 친부의 아기라고 판결했다. / *The board rules on matters between unions and city government.* 이사회는 노조와 시 정부 사 이의 문제에 대해서 결정한다. **3** [T] if a feeling or desire rules someone, it controls his/her life, so that s/he does not have time for other things ‖ 어떤 감 정이나 욕망이 사람의 인생을 지배해서 다 른 것을 할 시간이 없다. …을 좌지우지하 다: *Don't let your job rule your life.* (=control you) 일이 네 인생을 지배하지 않게 해라.

rule sth/sb out *phr v* [T] to decide that something is not possible or suitable ‖ 어떤 것이 가능하거나 알맞지 않다고 결정 하다. …을 배제하다: *We can't rule out the possibility that he has left the country.* 그가 그 나라를 떠났을 가능성도 배제할 수는 없다.

ruled /ruld/ *adj* ruled paper has parallel lines printed across it ‖ 종이에 가로로 인쇄된 평행선들이 있는. 괘선을 넣은

rul·er /'rulɚ/ *n* **1** someone such as a king who has official power over a country and its people ‖ 한 국가와 그 국 민들에게 공식적인 권력을 행사하는 왕 등 의 사람. 통치자. 지배자 **2** a flat narrow piece of plastic, metal etc. with straight edges that you use for measuring things and drawing straight lines ‖ 물체를 측정 하며 직선을 그릴 때 사용하는 테두리가 곧은 납작하고 가는 플라스틱·금속 등의 물건. 자: *a 12-inch ruler* 12인치 자

rul·ing¹ /'rulɪŋ/ *n* an official decision, especially one made by a law court ‖ 특 히 법원에서 내리는 공식적인 결정. 판결: *the Supreme Court's ruling on the case* 그 사건에 대한 대법원의 판결

ruling² *adj* **the ruling class/party** the group that controls a country or organization ‖ 한 국가나 조직을 지배하는 집단. 지배 계급/집권당[여당]

rum /rʌm/ *n* [C, U] a strong alcoholic drink made from sugar ‖ 설탕으로 만든 독한 술. 럼주

rum·ble /'rʌmbəl/ *v* **1** [I] to make a lot of long low sounds ‖ 길고 낮은 소리를 많 이 내다. 우르르 울리다. 덜거덕거리다: *Thunder rumbled in the distance.* 멀리서 우르르 천둥소리가 났다. **2** [I, T] OLD-FASHIONED to fight with someone ‖ 남과 싸우다 – **rumble** *n* [singular]

ru·mi·nate /'rumə,neɪt/ *v* [I] FORMAL to think about something for a long time ‖ 오랫동안 어떤 것에 대해서 생각하다. 심 사숙고하다: *He sat ruminating on the meaning of life.* 그는 앉아서 인생의 의미 에 대해 곰곰이 생각했다.

rum·mage /'rʌmɪdʒ/ *v* [I] to search for something by moving things around ‖ 물 체를 이리저리 옮기면서 무엇을 찾다. 샅 샅이 뒤지다: *Kerry was rummaging through a drawer looking for a pen.* 케 리는 펜을 찾으려고 서랍을 샅샅이 뒤지고 있었다.

rummage sale /'.. ,./ *n* an event at which old clothes, furniture, toys etc. are sold ‖ 헌 옷·가구·장난감 등을 파는 행사. 자선 바자

rum·my /'rʌmi/ *n* [U] any of several simple card games for two or more players ‖ 두 명 이상이 하는 여러 간단한 카드 게임 중의 하나. 러미

ru·mor /'rumɚ/ *n* [C, U] information that is passed from one person to another and which may not be true ‖ 한 사람에게서 다른 사람에게로 전해지며 사 실이 아닐지도 모르는 정보. 소문. 풍문: *Have you heard the rumor about Sam and Kelly?* 샘과 켈리에 관한 소문 들었 니? / *Rumor has it (that)* (=there is a rumor that) *Jean's getting married again.* 진이 재혼할 거라는 소문이 있다.

ru·mored /'rumɚd/ *adj* if something is rumored to be true, people are saying that it may be true but no one knows for certain ‖ 어떤 것이 사실일지 모른다고 사 람들이 말하지만 아무도 확실히는 알지 못 하는. 소문이 난: *It was rumored that a magazine had offered a lot of money for her story.* 한 잡지사가 그녀의 이야기에 많은 돈을 제의했다는 소문이 있었다.

rump /rʌmp/ *n* **1** [C, U] the part of an animal's back that is just above its legs, or the meat from this part ‖ 동물의 다리 바로 위쪽에 있는 뒤쪽 부위나 이 부위의 고기. 둔부. 엉덩잇살 **2** INFORMAL the part of your body on which you sit; BOTTOM ‖ 앉을 때 닿는 신체 부위. 엉덩이; 卽 bottom

rum·ple /ˈrʌmpəl/ *v* [T] to make hair, clothes etc. messy or WRINKLEd ‖ 머리카락·옷 등을 엉망으로 만들거나 주름지게 하다. 헝클어 놓다. 구기다 **-rumpled** *adj* : *a rumpled shirt* 구겨진 셔츠

run¹ /rʌn/ *v* **ran, run, running**

1 ▶MOVE 움직이다◀ **a)** [I] to move very quickly, moving your legs faster than when you walk ‖ 걸을 때보다 더 빠르게 다리를 움직여서 매우 빠르게 움직이다. 달리다. 뛰다: *Some kids were running down the street.* 몇 명의 아이들 그 거리를 내달리고 있었다. / *If we run, we can still catch the bus.* 뛰어가면 우리는 그 버스를 아직 잡아 탈 수 있어. —see picture on page 947 **b)** [I, T] to move quickly or make something do this ‖ 빠르게 움직이거나 무엇을 빠르게 움직이게 하다: *A car ran off the road right here.* 자동차 한 대가 바로 이 도로를 내달렸다. / *Let me just run the vacuum cleaner over the carpet.* 카펫에 진공청소기 돌리는 것은 내가 할게.

2 ▶BE IN CHARGE OF 책임을 맡고 있다◀ [T] to control, organize, or operate a business, organization etc. ‖ 사업체·조직 등을 관리[조직, 운영]하다: *The company runs cross-country skiing tours in Vermont.* 그 회사는 버몬트에서 크로스컨트리 스키 관광업을 한다. / *He simply ran that business into the ground.* (=made it fail) 그는 그 사업을 완전히 말아먹었다.

3 ▶MACHINES 기계◀ [I, T] to operate or be operated ‖ 작동시키거나 작동되다. 돌리다. 돌다: *The radio runs on/off batteries.* (=uses batteries to work) 그 라디오는 건전지로 작동된다. / *I forgot to run the dishwasher.* 식기 세척기 돌리는 것을 깜빡했다. / *Nate left the engine running.* 네이트는 엔진을 계속 돌아가게 놔두었다. / *The ad says the computer can be up and running* (=working) *in less than an hour.* 그 광고에 따르면 그 컴퓨터는 한 시간 이내에 작동 가능하다.

4 ▶MONEY/NUMBERS 돈/숫자◀ [I, T] to be at a particular level, length, amount, price etc. ‖ 특정한 수준·길이·양·가격 등에 이르다. (…에) 이르다. …이다: *Unemployment is running at 5%.* 실업

률이 5%에 이르고 있다. / *The report runs to 700 pages.* 그 보고서는 700쪽에 이른다. / *debts running into millions of dollars* 수백만 달러에 이르는 부채

5 ▶GO SOMEWHERE 어딘가로 가다◀ [I, T] SPOKEN to go somewhere quickly, either walking or in a car ‖ 걸어서 또는 차로 빠르게 어딘가에 가다. 달려가다: *I need to run out to my car; I left my books in it.* 내 차에 달려가 봐야 해. 그 안에 책을 놓고 왔거든. / *Jean's downtown, running a few errands.* (=going places to buy or do things) 진은 몇 가지 심부름을 하러 시내에 갔다.

6 ▶NEWS/STORIES/ADVERTISEMENTS 뉴스/이야기/광고◀ [I, T] to print or broadcast a story etc. ‖ 이야기 등을 인쇄하거나 방송하다. 싣다. 내보내다: *What does it cost to run an ad in the local paper?* 지역 신문에 광고를 내는 데 비용이 얼마입니까? / *They ran the item on the 6 o'clock news.* 그들은 6시 뉴스에 그 기사를 내보냈다.

7 run smoothly/run according to plan to happen in the way that you want or expect ‖ 원하거나 기대한 대로 발생하다. 순조롭게/계획대로 진행되다: *The tour guide helps to keep things running smoothly.* 그 관광 가이드는 모든 것이 순조롭게 진행되도록 했다.

8 ▶ELECTION 선거◀ [I] to try to be elected ‖ 당선되려고 노력하다. 입후보하다: *Barbara Boxer ran for the Senate in 1992.* 바바라 복서는 1992년에 상원 의원에 입후보했다. / *Dole ran against Clinton.* 돌은 클린턴의 맞상대로 입후보했다.

9 ▶TEST/PROCESS 검사/과정◀ [T] to do something such as a medical test or an EXPERIMENT, in which you do things in a particular order ‖ 특정한 순서대로 어떤 것을 하는 의학적 검사나 실험 등을 하다. …을 행하다[실시하다]: *The doctors say they need to run a few tests first.* 의사들은 먼저 몇 가지 검사를 실시해야 한다고 말한다.

10 run late/run on time/run early to arrive, go somewhere, or do something late, at the right time, or early ‖ 늦게[정시에, 일찍] 도착하거나 어딘가에 가거나 무엇을 하다: *Sorry you had to wait; I've been running late all day.* 기다리게 해서 미안해. 내가 하루 종일 늦는구나.

11 ▶WATER/LIQUIDS 물/액체◀ [I] to flow ‖ 흐르다: *The sweat was just running down my face.* 얼굴에서 땀이 마구 흘러내리고 있었다. / *Who left the water running?* (=still flowing from a

pipe) 누가 물이 흐르게 그냥 놔두었니? /
I need a Kleenex; my nose is running.
(=producing liquid) 휴지가 있어야겠어.
콧물이 흐른다.

12 ▶**CONTINUE** 계속하다◀ [I] to
continue to be used, performed etc. for
a particular length of time ‖ 특정한 기간
동안 계속해서 사용되거나 실행되다. 계속
[지속]되다: *The contract runs through to
2002.* 그 계약은 2002년까지 유효하다. /
*"WKRP" ran for five seasons, from
1978-1982.* "WKRP"는 1978년부터
1982년까지 5년 동안 지속되었다.

13 ▶**ROADS/PIPES/FENCES** 길/파이프/울
타리◀ [I, T] to exist in a particular
place or continue in a particular
direction, or to make something do this
‖ 특정한 장소에 존재하거나 특정한 방향
으로 이어지다, 또는 어떤 것을 이렇게 하
게 하다. 뻗다[뻗게 하다]. 관통하다[시키
다]: *They want to run a pipeline
through protected parts of Alaska.* 그들
은 알래스카의 보호 구역을 관통하는 파이
프라인을 놓고 싶어한다. / *A small path
runs between the two beaches.* 두 해변
사이로 작은 길이 뻗어 있다.

14 ▶**BUSES/TRAINS** 버스/기차◀ [I] to
take people from one place to another ‖
사람들을 한 장소에서 다른 장소로 나르
다. 다니다. 운행하다: *Subway trains run
every 7 minutes.* 지하철은 7분마다 운행
된다.

15 be running short/low to have very
little of something left ‖ 어떤 것이 매우
적게 남겨져 있다. 모자라다. 부족하다:
*Hospitals in the war-torn nation are
running low on medical supplies.* 전쟁
으로 피폐된 그 국가의 병원들은 의료품들
이 바닥나 가고 있다. / *Lend me $20, will
you? I'm running short of cash.* 20달러
만 빌려 줄래? 현금이 부족해서 그래.

16 ▶**TOUCH** 만지다◀ [T] to touch
something by moving your hand along
its surface ‖ 표면을 따라 손을 움직여서
사물을 만지다. …에 쓱 스치다: *Doug ran
his fingers through her silky black hair.*
더그는 그녀의 부드러운 검은 머리를 손가
락으로 어루만졌다.

17 run deep if a feeling runs deep,
people feel it very strongly ‖ 사람들이 어
떤 감정을 매우 강하게 느끼다. 아주 깊다:
*Resentment against the military runs
deep around here.* 이곳에서는 군부에 대
한 원한이 아주 깊다.

18 run in the family if something such
as a quality, disease, or skill runs in the
family, many people in that family have
it ‖ 특정 가족의 많은 사람들이 어떤 특성

[질병, 솜씨] 등을 가지고 있다. 집안 내력
이다

19 run drugs/guns etc. to bring drugs
etc. into a country illegally ‖ 한 국가에
마약 등을 불법적으로 가져오다. 마약/총
기 등을 밀수입하다

20 ▶**COLOR** 색깔◀ [I] if color or
MAKEUP runs, it spreads from one area
of cloth or skin to another when it gets
wet ‖ 천이나 피부가 젖었을 때 색깔이나
화장이 한 곳에서 다른 곳으로 퍼지다. 번
지다

21 ▶**CLOTHING** 의복◀ [I] if a woman's
PANTY HOSE run, they get a long thin
hole in them ‖ 여자의 팬티스타킹에 길고
가는 구멍이 나다. (줄이) 나가다

22 run a temperature/fever to have a
body temperature that is higher than
normal, because you are sick ‖ 몸이 아
파서 정상보다 더 높은 체온을 가지다. 열
이 나다

23 ▶**FEELING** 느낌◀ [I] to move from
one part of your body to another ‖ 몸의
한 부분으로부터 다른 부분으로 이동하다.
따끔하게 지나다: *a pain running down
her leg* 그녀의 다리 쪽으로 내려오는 통증

24 run the show to be in charge of an
event or situation ‖ 어떤 행사나 상황을
책임지고 있다. 주관하다. 주도권을 쥐고
있다: *Who's running this show anyway?*
그런데 이 행사는 누가 주관하고 있니?

25 run aground/ashore if a ship runs
aground or ashore, it cannot move
because the water is not deep enough ‖
수심이 충분히 깊지 않아서 배가 움직일
수 없다. 좌초하다

run across sb/sth *phr v* [T] to meet or
find someone or something by chance ‖
사람이나 사물을 우연히 만나거나 발견하
다: *I ran across some old love letters
the other day.* 나는 요전 날 오래된 연애
편지 몇 통을 우연히 발견했다.

run after sb/sth *phr v* [T] to chase
someone or something ‖ 사람이나 사물을
쫓다. …을 쫓다[추적하다]: *She started
to leave, but Smith ran after her.* 그녀가
떠나기 시작하자 스미스는 그녀를 뒤쫓았
다.

run around *phr v* [I, T] to go to
different places and do different things,
especially in a disorganized way ‖ 특히
무질서하게 여러 장소에 다니며 여러가지
일들을 하다. 바쁘게 움직이며 다니다:
*Everyone was running around trying
to help us get ready for the party, and
causing more problems in the process.*
모두가 우리를 도와 파티를 준비하려고 분
주히 움직였지만 그러는 가운데 문제만 더

일으키고 있었다.

run away *phr v* [I] **1** to leave a place in order to escape from someone or something ‖ 사람이나 어떤 것으로부터 도 망치려고 어떤 장소를 떠나다. 달아나다. 도망가다: *Kathy ran away from home at the age of 16.* 케시는 16살 때 집에서 가 출했다. **2** to try to avoid an unpleasant situation ‖ 불쾌한 상황을 피하려고 애쓰 다. 도피하다: *He used drugs as a way of running away from his problems.* 그는 자신의 문제로부터 도피하는 수단으로써 약물을 사용했다.

run sth by sb *phr v* [T] to ask someone about something in order to get his/her opinion or permission ‖ 의견이나 허락을 얻기 위해서 남에게 어떤 것에 대해서 묻 다. …에게 …에 관해서 의견을 듣다: *You'd better run that contract by a lawyer.* 그 계약은 변호사와 상담하는 것 이 좋을 거야.

run down *phr v* **1** [T **run sb ↔ down**] to hit a person or animal with a car while you are driving, and kill or injure him, her, or it ‖ 운전 중에 차로 사람이나 동물을 치어서 죽이거나 부상을 입히다. …을 치다. …을 받아 넘어뜨리다: *A drunk driver ran down a 14-year-old girl in Landsdowne Road yesterday.* 음 주 운전자가 어제 랜즈다운 로드에서 14 세 소녀를 치었다. **2** [I,T **run sth ↔ down**] to gradually lose power, or to make something do this ‖ 점차 힘을 잃거 나 잃게 하다. 약해지다. 약해지게 하다: *Don't leave it switched on – you'll run down the batteries.* 전원을 켜놓지 마라. 건전지가 닳는다.

run into *phr v* [T] **1** [**run into sb**] INFORMAL to meet someone by chance ‖ 어떤 사람을 우연히 만나다: *I run into her sometimes on campus.* 나는 학내에 서 가끔 그녀를 우연히 만난다. **2 run into trouble/debt/problems etc.** to begin to have difficulties ‖ 어려움에 처하 기 시작하다. 곤란/부채/문제에 부딪히다: *Bond's company ran into trouble when it couldn't repay its debts.* 본드의 회사는 부채를 상환할 수 없게 되자 곤경에 처하 게 되었다. **3** [**run into sb/sth**] to hit someone or something with a car or other vehicle ‖ 차나 다른 탈것으로 사람 이나 사물을 치다. …에 충돌하다[부딪히 다]: *He lost control of the car and ran into a guardrail.* 그는 차를 제어하지 못 하고 난간을 들이받았다.

run off *phr v* **1** [I] to leave a place or person when you are not supposed to ‖ 떠나지 말아야 할 때 어떤 장소나 사람을

떠나다. 도망치다: *Our dog keeps running off.* 우리 개는 내 곁에 붙어있 지 않는다. **2** [T **run sth ↔ off**] to quickly print copies of something ‖ 어떤 것의 복사본을 빠르게 인쇄하다. …을 복 사하다: *Please run off 100 photocopies.* 100장 복사해 주시겠어요.

run off with *phr v* [T] **1** [**run off with sb**] to go away with someone because you are having a sexual relationship with him/her and other people do not approve ‖ 누군가와 성적인 관계를 갖고 있는데 다른 사람들이 인정하지 않아서 그 사람과 함께 멀리 달아나다. …과 눈맞아 달아나다: *Her husband ran off with an old girlfriend.* 그녀의 남편은 옛 애인과 눈 맞아 달아나 버렸다. **2** [**run off with sth**] to steal something and go away ‖ 물 건을 훔쳐 도망치다. …을 가지고 달아나 다: *Looters smashed windows and ran off with TVs and VCRs.* 약탈자들은 창문 을 부수고 들어와 TV와 VCR을 가지고 달 아났다.

run out *phr v* [I] **1** to use all of something, so that there is none left ‖ 사 물을 모두 다 사용해서 아무 것도 남아 있 지 않다. 다 하다. 없어지다: *My pen's running out of ink.* 내 펜은 잉크가 다 떨어져 간다. / *I'm running out of ideas.* (=I do not have any more) 내 아이디어가 바닥나고 있다. **2** to be used or finished ‖ 사용되거나 끝나다. 다 되다: *They need to make a deal, but time is running out.* 그들은 거래를 성사시켜야 하지만 시간이 얼마 없다. **3** to come to the end of a period of time when something is allowed to be done or used ‖ 무엇을 하거 나 사용하도록 허용된 기간이 종료되다. ‖ 만기가 되다: *My contract runs out in September.* 내 계약은 9월에 만료된다.

run sb/sth ↔ over *phr v* [T] to hit someone or something with a car or other vehicle, and drive over him, her, or it ‖ 차나 다른 탈것으로 사람이나 사물 을 치고 그 위로 지나가다: *I think you just ran over some broken glass.* 네 차가 부서진 유리 조각 위로 지 나간 것 같아.

run through sth *phr v* [T] **1** to read, check, or explain something quickly, especially a list ‖ 특히 목록을 빠르게 읽 다[확인하다, 설명하다]. …을 훑어보다. 간추리다: *I'd like to run through the agenda with you before the meeting.* 저 는 회의 전에 당신과 이 의제를 한 번 훑 어보고 싶습니다. **2** to repeat something, so that you will remember it ‖ 어떤 것을 반복해서 기억하게 하다. 연습하다: *Let's* *run through that scene again.* 그 장면을 다시 연습합시다. **3** to be present in many parts of something ‖ 어떤 것의 많은 부분들에 존재하다. 널리 퍼져 있다: *Unfortunately, there's a racist streak that runs through this community.* 불행히도, 이 지역 사회에 인종 차별적인 경향이 널리 퍼져 있다.

run up sth *phr v* [T] to make a debt, cost, price etc. greater ‖ 빚·비용·가격 등을 더 많게 하다. 늘리다. 올리다: *We ran up a huge phone bill.* 우리는 전화 요금이 엄청나게 나왔다.

run up against sth *phr v* [T] to suddenly have to deal a problem when you are trying to do something ‖ 어떤 일을 하려고 애쓰고 있을 때 갑자기 어떤 문제를 처리해야 하다. …에 부딪히다: *The campaign ran up against stiff opposition.* 그 캠페인은 완강한 반대에 부딪혔다.

run² *n*

1 ▶RUNNING 달리기◀ an act of running ‖ 달리는 행위. 뛰기. 달리기: *He usually goes for a run before breakfast.* 그는 대체로 아침 식사 전에 조깅을 한다. / *a 10K fun run* 10km의 즐거운 달리기

2 in the short/long run from now until a period of time that will come soon, or from now until far in the future ‖ 지금부터 곧 다가올 기간까지나 지금부터 먼 미래까지. 단기/장기적으로 보면: *In the long run, the rain forest itself is worth more than the timber in it.* 장기적으로 보면, 우림 그 자체는 그 안에 있는 목재 이상의 가치가 있다.

3 ▶BASEBALL 야구◀ a point in a baseball game ‖ 야구 경기에서의 점수. …점: *The Cubs had 3 runs in the sixth inning.* 컵스 팀은 6회에 3점을 획득했다.

4 ▶PLAY/MOVIE ETC. 연극/영화 등◀ a period of time during which a play, movie, or television show is shown or performed regularly ‖ 연극[영화, 텔레비전 쇼] 등이 규칙적으로 상영되거나 공연되는 기간. 상영[공연] 기간: *The play starts an 8-week run on Friday.* 그 연극은 금요일에 8주 공연을 시작한다.

5 be on the run to be trying to escape from someone, especially the police ‖ 특히 경찰로부터 도망치려고 애쓰다. 달아나다. 도피하다: *In his book, he describes what it's like to live on the run.* 그는 자신의 책에서 도피하며 산다는 것이 어떤 것인지 묘사하고 있다.

6 ▶CLOTHES 옷◀ a long hole in a pair of nylons ‖ 나일론 스타킹에 난 긴 구멍. 줄이 나간 곳

7 ▶REGULAR TRIP 규칙적인 이동◀ a regular trip made by a person or a vehicle that carries a lot of people ‖ 사람이나 많은 사람들을 실어 나르는 탈것이 하는 규칙적인 이동. 운행. 주행: *I'm doing the school run this week.* (=taking my children to school) 나는 이번 주에 아이들을 학교에 데려다 주고 있다. / *the daily ferry run* 하루 한 번 운행하는 나룻배

8 ▶MONEY 돈◀ [singular] an occasion when a lot of people take their money out of a bank or buy a lot of one particular thing at the same time ‖ 많은 사람들이 동시에 은행에서 돈을 인출하거나 하나의 특정한 사물을 많이 사는 경우. 대규모 인출. 큰 수요: *Managers were trying to prevent a run on the bank.* 지점장들은 그 은행에 대한 대규모 예금 인출 사태를 막아 보려고 애쓰고 있었다.

9 ▶ELECTION 선거◀ [singular] an attempt to be elected ‖ 당선되려는 시도. 입후보. 출마: *Turner is making his first run for public office.* 터너는 처음으로 공직에 출마하고 있다.

10 make a run for it to try to get away from a place quickly ‖ 빨리 어떤 장소에서 도망치려고 애쓰다. 서둘러 도망가다: *The soldiers made a run for it, trying to get across the border without getting caught.* 병사들은 잡히지 않고 국경을 넘으려고 급히 도망갔다.

11 a run of a series of events that happen one right after another ‖ 하나의 사건 직후에 다른 사건이 발생하는 일련의 사건들. 연속: *Sondheim's run of successful musicals* 손드하임 뮤지컬의 계속된 성공

12 have the run of sth to be allowed to go anywhere or do anything in a place ‖ 어떤 장소에서 어디든 가거나 무엇이든 할 수 있도록 허락되다. …에서 맘대로 할 수 있다: *Their dog has free run of the house.* 그들의 개는 그 집에서 맘대로 뛰어다닌다.

13 give sb a run for his/her money to make an opponent or competitor work very hard to beat you ‖ 적수나 경쟁자로 하여금 자신을 물리치기 위해 더욱 열심히 하게 하다. …과 막상막하로 경쟁하다: *The White Sox gave the A's a run for their money, but lost in the ninth inning.* 화이트삭스 팀은 에이스 팀과 9회까지 접전을 벌였으나 결국 패했다.

14 ▶SPORTS 스포츠◀ a special area for people to ski down, or a track for people to slide down in a BOBSLED etc. ‖ 사람들이 스키를 타고 내려오는 특별한 구

역이나 봅슬레이 등으로 미끄러져 내려오는 트랙. 비탈 코스. 슬로프

run·a·round /'rʌnə,raʊnd/ n **give/get the runaround** INFORMAL to not give someone the information or help s/he has asked for, and send him/her to another place to get it‖ 남에게 그 사람이 요구한 정보나 도움을 주지 않고 다른 데서 구하라고 보내다. 남을 허탕치게 하다/허탕치다: *I keep calling to find out about my car, but I just get the runaround—nobody will tell me what's wrong with it.* 나는 내 차의 소재를 파악하려고 계속 전화하고 있지만 허탕만 치고 있다. 내 차가 어떻게 됐는지 아무도 말을 안 해주려 한다.

run·a·way¹ /'rʌnə,weɪ/ n someone, especially a child, who has left home or the place where s/he is supposed to be‖ 당연히 있어야 할 집이나 장소를 떠난 사람, 특히 아이. 가출 청소년. 도망자

runaway² adj moving fast and out of control‖ 빠르게 움직이며 통제를 벗어난. 달아난. 탈주한: *a runaway train* 탈주한 기차

run-down /'rʌndaʊn/ n a quick report or explanation of a situation, event etc.‖ 어떤 상황·사건 등에 대한 빠른 보고나 설명. 요약: *Can you give me a rundown on what happened while I was gone?* 내가 없는 사이에 무슨 일이 있었는지 나에게 간단히 말해 줄래요?

run-down /,. '../ adj **1** a building or area that is run-down is in very bad condition‖ 건물이나 지역의 상태가 매우 안 좋은. 황폐한: *a run-down motel* 다 쓰러져 가는 모텔 **2** someone who is run-down is very tired and not very healthy‖ 사람이 매우 지치고 아주 건강하지 않은. 피로한. 건강이 안 좋은: *He's been feeling run-down lately.* 그는 최근에 몸의 컨디션이 안 좋다.

rung¹ /rʌŋ/ v the PAST PARTICIPLE of RING‖ ring의 과거 분사형

rung² n **1** one of the steps of a LADDER‖ 사다리의 여러 단(段) 중의 하나. 가로장 —see picture at LADDER **2** INFORMAL a particular level or position in an organization‖ 한 조직 내의 특정한 수준이나 지위. 단계: *The changes didn't affect people on the lower rungs of the company.* 그 변화는 회사의 하층부에 있는 사람들에게는 영향을 미치지 않았다.

run-in /'. ./ n an argument or disagreement with someone in authority‖ 직권 있는 사람과의 논쟁이나 의견 차이. 싸움. 언쟁: *Barry had a run-in with the police.* 배리는 경찰들과 언쟁을 벌였다.

run·ner /'rʌnɚ/ n **1** someone who runs as a sport‖ 운동 경기로서 달리는 사람. (경)주자: *a long-distance runner* 장거리 주자 **2** one of the long thin blades of metal on the bottom of a SLED‖ 썰매 밑의 길고 가는 금속 날 중의 하나. 날

runner-up /,.. '../ n, plural **runners-up** the person or team that finishes second in a race or competition‖ 경주나 시합에서 2위로 끝마친 사람이나 팀. 2위 선수[팀]. 차점자

run·ning¹ /'rʌnɪŋ/ n [U] **1** the activity of running‖ 달리는 행위. 달리기. 경주: *Do you want to go running?* 달리기 하고 싶니? **2** be in the running/be out of the running** to have some chance of winning or being successful, or to have no chance‖ 이기거나 성공할 수 있는 가망이 상당히 있거나 전혀 없다. 승산이 있다/없다: *Is MERC still in the running for the contract?* MERC가 아직도 그 계약을 성사시킬 승산이 있나요? **3** the running of sth** the way that a business, organization etc. is managed or organized‖ 사업체·조직 등이 관리되거나 조직되는 방법. …의 경영[운영, 관리]: *He is not involved in the day-to-day running of the business.* 그는 매일의 회사 운영에는 관여하지 않고 있다.

running² adj **1 running water** water that comes from a FAUCET‖ 수도꼭지에서 나오는 물. 수돗물: *a house with no running water* 수돗물이 나오지 않는 집 **2 running battle/argument** an argument that continues over a long period of time‖ 오랜 기간에 걸쳐 계속되는 논쟁. 오래된[질질 끄는] 전투/논쟁: *They're in a running battle with the neighbors about the fence between their yards.* 그들은 양쪽 마당 사이에 있는 울타리를 놓고 이웃과 지리한 싸움을 벌이고 있다. **3 running commentary** a spoken description of an event while it is happening, especially a sports event‖ 특히 스포츠 경기가 진행되고 있는 동안 그 경기에 대해 말로 기술함. 생중계. 실황 방송 **4** done while you are running‖ 달리면서 하는: *a running jump* 멀리뛰기 **5 running total** a total that is always being increased as new costs, amounts etc. are added to it‖ 새로운 비용·양 등이 추가되어서 시종 증가하고 있는 합계. 현재 금액[수량]. 누계

running³ adv **three years/five times etc. running** for three years, five times etc. without change or interruption‖ 변화나 중단 없이 3년 동안·다섯 번 등. 삼

년/다섯 번 연속하여[잇달아]: *This is the fourth day running that it has rained.* 오늘로서 나흘 연속 비가 내리고 있다.

running back /'.. ,./ *n* [C, U] in football, a player whose main job is to run with the ball ‖ 미식축구에서 주요 임무가 공을 가지고 달리는 선수. 러닝백 — see picture on page 946

running mate /'.. ,./ *n* the person who is chosen by someone who wants to become the US President to be the Vice President if they win the election ‖ 미국의 대통령이 되고자 하는 사람이 선택한, 선거에서 이길 경우 부통령이 되는 사람. 부통령 후보

run·ny /'rʌni/ *adj* INFORMAL **1** a runny nose has liquid coming out of it because you are sick ‖ 아파서 코에서 액체가 나오는. 콧물이 나는 **2** not solid or thick enough ‖ 충분히 단단하거나 두껍지 않은. 물컹한. 너무 무른: *runny eggs* 물컹한 알들

run-of-the-mill /,. . . '.·/ *adj* not special or interesting; ORDINARY ‖ 특별하거나 흥미롭지 않은. 흔해 빠진. 평범한; ㊎ ordinary: *It's not the usual run-of-the-mill job.* 그것은 그저 그런 흔해 빠진 일이 아니야.

runs /rʌnz/ *n* INFORMAL **the runs** ⇨ DIARRHEA

run-up /'. ./ *n* **the run-up to sth** the period of time just before an important event ‖ 중요한 행사 직전의 기간. …의 준비 기간: *Most stores are hiring more staff in the run-up to Christmas.* 대부분의 상점들이 성탄절 대목을 맞아 직원을 더 고용하고 있다.

run·way /'rʌnweɪ/ *n* a very long surface like a wide road that aircraft leave from and come down on ‖ 항공기가 이·착륙하는 넓은 도로 같이 매우 긴 표면. 활주로

rup·ture¹ /'rʌptʃɚ/ *n* **1** [C, U] an occasion when something suddenly breaks apart or bursts ‖ 사물이 갑자기 산산조각 나거나 터지는 경우. 파열: *the rupture of a blood vessel* 혈관 파열 **2** a situation in which two people, groups, countries etc. disagree and end their relationship ‖ 두 사람·집단·국가 등이 의견이 맞지 않아 관계를 끝내는 상황. 단절. 불화

rupture² *v* [I, T] to break or burst, or to make something do this ‖ 깨지거나 터지다, 또는 사물을 이렇게 하게 만들다. 파열하다[시키다]: *An oil pipeline ruptured early this morning.* 송유관이 오늘 새벽에 파열되었다.

ru·ral /'rʊrəl/ *adj* relating to country areas rather than the city ‖ 도시보다는 오히려 시골 지역과 관련되는. 시골의: *a peaceful rural setting* 평화로운 시골 배경 —compare URBAN

ruse /ruz/ *n* FORMAL something you do in order to deceive someone; trick ‖ 남을 속이기 위해 하는 짓. 계략. 책략. 음모; 술책

rush¹ /rʌʃ/ *v* **1** [I, T] to move or do something very quickly ‖ 어떤 것을 매우 빠르게 움직이거나 하다. 돌진하다[시키다]. (…을) 서두르다: *It's an important decision; don't rush it.* 이건 중요한 결정이야. 서두르지 마라. / *There's no need to rush – we have plenty of time.* 서두를 필요 없어. 시간은 많아. / *Everyone was rushing to catch the last bus.* 마지막 버스를 타기 위해 모든 사람들이 서두르고 있었다. **2** [T] to take or send something somewhere very quickly ‖ 어떤 것을 어딘가로 매우 빠르게 가지고 가거나 보내다. 서둘러 나르다[보내다]: *We had to rush Helen to the hospital.* 우리는 헬렌을 병원으로 급히 데려가야 했다. **3** [T] to try to make someone do something quickly ‖ 남이 어떤 것을 빨리 하게 하려고 애쓰다. 재촉[채근]하다: *Don't rush me – let me think.* 재촉하지 마. 생각 좀 하자.

rush around *phr v* [I] to try to do a lot of things quickly in a short period of time ‖ 짧은 기간 안에 많은 것을 빨리 하려고 애쓰다. 분주하게 돌아다니다

rush into sth *phr v* [T] to get involved in something quickly without thinking carefully about it ‖ 어떤 것에 대해서 주의 깊게 생각하지 않고 빠르게 관여하다. 성급하게[무턱대고] 행동하다: *My mother's worried that I'm rushing into getting married.* 나의 어머니는 내가 서둘러 결혼하는 것에 대해서 걱정하신다.

rush sth ↔ **through** *phr v* [T] to get something such as a new law approved more quickly than usual ‖ 새로운 법 등이 보통 때보다 더 빨리 승인되게 하다. 급히 통과시키다

rush² *n* **1** [singular] a sudden fast movement of things or people ‖ 사물이나 사람의 갑작스럽고 빠른 움직임. 돌진: *They all made a rush for the door.* 그들 모두는 문을 향해 돌진했다. **2** [singular, U] a situation in which you need to hurry, especially because a lot of people want to do or get something ‖ 특히 많은 사람들이 어떤 것을 하거나 얻고 싶어 하기 때문에 서두를 필요가 있는 상황. 쇄도. 급박. 대단한 수요: *There's a big* *rush to get tickets.* 표를 구하려는 수요가 엄청나다. **3 the rush** the time when a place or group of people are very busy ‖ 어떤 장소나 일단의 사람들이 매우 바쁜 시간. 분주. 붐빔: *the Christmas rush for shoppers* 쇼핑객들로 붐비는 성탄절 시즌 **4** INFORMAL a strong, usually pleasant feeling that you get from taking a drug or from doing something exciting ‖ 약물을 복용하거나 흥분되는 일을 해서 얻는, 강하고 대체로 유쾌한 느낌. 쾌감. 황홀감

rush hour /ˈ. ./ *n* [C, U] the time of day when there are a lot of vehicles on the road because people are going to and from work ‖ 사람들이 출퇴근을 해서 도로에 차량이 많은 낮 시간. 혼잡한 시간. 러시아워

Rus·sian¹ /ˈrʌʃən/ *adj* **1** relating to or coming from Russia ‖ 러시아와 관련되거나 러시아 출신의. 러시아의. 러시아인[산]의 **2** relating to the Russian language ‖ 러시아어와 관련된. 러시아어의

Russian² *n* **1** [U] the language used in Russia ‖ 러시아에서 사용되는 언어. 러시아어 **2** someone from Russia ‖ 러시아 출신의 사람. 러시아인

rust¹ /rʌst/ *n* [U] the reddish-brown substance that forms on iron, steel etc. when it gets wet ‖ 철·강철 등에 습기가 찰 때 형성되는 적갈색의 물질. 녹: *spots of rust on the fender* 펜더에 슨 녹

rust² *v* [I, T] to become covered with RUST, or to make something do this ‖ 녹으로 뒤덮이다, 또는 사물을 녹으로 뒤덮다. 녹슬다. …을 녹슬게 하다: *a lock that has rusted shut* 녹이 슬어 닫혀 있는 자물쇠

rus·tic /ˈrʌstɪk/ *adj* APPROVING simple and old-fashioned in a way that is typical of the country ‖ 시골의 전형적인 모습으로 수수하고 구식인. 소박한. 꾸밈없는: *a rustic mountain cabin* 소박한 산골 오두막

rus·tle¹ /ˈrʌsəl/ *v* **1** [I, T] if leaves, papers etc. rustle, or you rustle them, they make a soft noise as they rub against each other ‖ 잎·종이 등이 서로 스칠 때 부드러운 소리를 내다. 바스락거리다 **2** [T] to steal farm animals such as cattle or horses ‖ 소나 말 등의 가축을 훔치다

rustle sth ↔ **up** *phr v* [T] INFORMAL to find or make something quickly, especially food for a meal ‖ 특히 식사할 음식 등을 빠르게 찾거나 만들다. …을 급히 만들다

rustle² *n* [singular] the noise made when something RUSTLEs ‖ 사물이 바스락거릴 때 나는 소리. 바스락거리는 소리: *the rustle of dry leaves* 바스락거리는 마른 나뭇잎

rus·tler /ˈrʌslə/ *n* someone who steals farm animals such as cattle or horses ‖ 소나 말 등의 가축을 훔치는 사람. 가축 도둑

rust·proof /ˈrʌstpruf/ *adj* metal that is rustproof will not RUST ‖ 금속이 녹슬지 않는. 방수(防銹)성의

rust·y /ˈrʌsti/ *adj* **1** covered with RUST ‖ 녹으로 뒤덮인: *rusty nails* 녹슨 못 **2** if someone's skill is rusty, it is not as good as it once was because s/he has not practiced ‖ 계속 연습을 하지 않아서 어떤 사람의 기술이 예전만큼 좋지 못한. 무디어진. 서툴게 된: *My tennis is a little rusty.* 내 테니스 실력은 조금 녹이 슬었다.

rut /rʌt/ *n* **1 in a rut** INFORMAL living or working in a situation that does not change, and so is boring ‖ 변하지 않아서 지루한 상황에서 살거나 일하는. 판에 박힌 생활의: *Meredith felt she was stuck in a rut in her job at the library.* 메러디스는 도서관에서 일하며 판에 박힌 생활에 매어 있다고 느꼈다. **2** a deep narrow track left in the ground by a wheel ‖ 바퀴가 지면에 남긴 깊고 좁은 자국. 바퀴자국

ru·ta·ba·ga /ˈrutə,beɪɡə/ *n* a large round yellow vegetable ‖ 크고 둥글며 노란 채소. 순무의 일종

ruth·less /ˈruθlɪs/ *adj* **1** cruel and without pity ‖ 잔인하고 동정심 없는. 무자비한. 냉혹한: *a ruthless killer* 무자비한 살인자 **2** very determined to do whatever is necessary to succeed, or showing this quality ‖ 성공하기 위해 필요한 것은 무엇이든지 한다고 단단히 마음 먹은, 또는 이러한 특성을 나타내는. 인정사정없는: *a ruthless businessman* 인정사정없는 사업가 / *ruthless determination* 단호한 결심 — **ruthlessly** *adv* — **ruthlessness** *n* [U]

RV *n* recreational vehicle; a large vehicle with cooking equipment, beds etc. that a family uses for traveling or camping ‖ recreational vehicle(레저용 차량)의 약어; 가족이 여행하거나 캠핑할 때 사용하는 요리 기구·침대 등을 갖춘 큰 차량

rye /raɪ/ *n* [U] a type of grain that is used for making bread and WHISKEY (=alcohol) ‖ 빵과 위스키를 만들 때 사용하는 곡물의 일종. 호밀 —see picture at BREAD

Ss

S, s /ɛs/ *n* the nineteenth letter of the English alphabet ‖ 영어 알파벳의 열아홉 째 자

S the written abbreviation of SOUTH or SOUTHERN ‖ south, 또는 southern의 약어

-'s /z, s, ɪz/ **1** the short form of "is" ‖ "is"의 단축형: *What's that?* 그게 뭐냐? **2** the short form of "has" ‖ "has"의 단축형: *He's gone out.* 그는 나가 버렸다. **3** used in order to show the POSSESSIVE form of nouns ‖ 명사의 소유격을 나타내는 데에 쓰여: *Bill is one of Jason's friends.* 빌은 제이슨의 친구 중 한 사람이다. / *the company's plans* 그 회사의 계획 **4** the short form of "let," used only with "let" to form "let's" ‖ "us"의 단축형으로 "let"와 함께 할때만 "let's"의 형태로 쓰여: *Let's go, or we'll be late.* 가자, 그렇지 않으면 늦을 거야.

USAGE NOTE 's and s'

Use **'s** at the end of a word to show that something belongs to a particular person: *Mary's book / my mom's car.* Use **'s** after plural nouns that do not end in "s": *women's rights / the children's toys.* However, use **s'** when the plural noun does end in "s": *our parents' house / the dogs' food.* Use **'s** after a person's name, even if it ends in "s": *Ms. Collins's office / Kris's new boyfriend.*

's는 사물이 특정인에게 속한다는 것을 나타내기 위해 단어의 끝에 쓴다: 메리의 책 / 내 엄마의 차. "s"로 끝나지 않는 복수 명사 뒤에 **'s**를 사용한다: 여성의 권리 / 아이들의 장난감. 그러나 복수 명사가 "s"로 끝날 때에는 **s'**를 쓴다: 우리 부모님의 집 / 개들의 먹이. 사람의 이름이 "s"로 끝나더라도 인명 뒤에서는 **'s**를 쓴다: 콜린스 씨의 사무실 / 크리스의 새 남자 친구

Sab·bath /'sæbəθ/ *n* [singular] **the Sabbath** the day of the week that Jews or Christians consider to be a day for resting and praying, either Saturday or Sunday ‖ 유대인이나 크리스트교인들이 쉬고 기도하기 위한 날로 생각하는 주(週) 중의 토요일이나 일요일. 안식일

sab·bat·i·cal /sə'bætɪkəl/ *n* [C, U] a period when someone who teaches stops doing his/her usual work to travel and study ‖ 선생이 여행하고 연구하기 위해 일상의 업무 수행을 중단 하는 기간. 휴가 연도. 안식년: *Prof. Morris is away on sabbatical this semester.* 모리스 교수는 이번 학기가 안식 휴가 연도로 부재 중이다.

sa·ber /'seɪbɚ/ *n* a military sword ‖ 군용(軍用) 칼. 군도

sa·ble /'seɪbəl/ *n* [C, U] an expensive fur used for making coats, or the small animal this fur comes from ‖ 코트 제조에 쓰이는 값비싼 모피, 또는 이러한 모피를 얻을 수 있는 작은 동물. 담비(의 모피)

sab·o·tage¹ /'sæbə,tɑʒ/ *v* [T] to secretly damage or destroy something so that an enemy cannot use it, or so that a situation has the result you want ‖ 어떤 것을 적이 사용하지 못하게 하거나, 또는 상황이 자신이 원하는 결과가 되도록 은밀히 손상을 가하거나 파괴하다. …을 파괴[방해]하다: *Four sailors threatened to sabotage the boat's nuclear reactor.* 네 명의 선원들은 그 배의 원자로를 파괴하겠다고 협박했다. / *Rebels tried to sabotage the elections by killing candidates.* 반란군은 후보들을 죽여서 그 선거를 방해하려고 했다. – **saboteur** /,sæbə'tɚ/ *n*

sabotage² *n* [U] damage that has been done deliberately to something in order to harm an enemy ‖ 적에게 해를 입히려고 고의로 사물에 입힌 피해. 방해 행위[공작]. 사보타주: *The company claimed the crash was caused by sabotage.* 회사 측은 태업으로 도산되었다고 주장했다.

sac /sæk/ *n* TECHNICAL a part shaped like a small bag inside a plant or animal, that contains air or liquid ‖ 식물이나 동물의 내부의 공기나 액체가 담긴, 작은 주머니같이 생긴 부분. 낭(囊). 액낭

sac·cha·rin /'sækərɪn/ *n* [U] a chemical substance that tastes very sweet and is used instead of sugar ‖ 매우 단맛이 나며 설탕 대신에 쓰이는 화학 물질. 사카린

sac·cha·rine /'sækərɪn/ *adj* too romantic in a way that seems silly and not sincere ‖ 어리석고 진실돼 보이지 않을 정도로 지나치게 낭만적인. 달콤한: *a saccharine love story* 달콤한 사랑 이야기

sa·chet /sæ'ʃeɪ/ *n* a very small plastic, paper, or cloth bag containing a liquid

or powder ∥ 액체나 가루가 담긴 플라스틱
이나 종이, 또는 헝겊으로 된 아주 작은 주
머니. 향주머니: *a sachet of dried
lavender* 말린 라벤더를 넣은 향주머니

sack¹ /sæk/ n **1** a large bag made of
strong cloth, plastic, or paper in which
you carry or keep things ∥ 물건을 운반하
거나 보관하는 데에 사용하는 질긴 천이나
플라스틱, 또는 종이로 만든 큰 가방. 부
대. 마대. 봉지: *a sack of potatoes* 감자
한 부대 **2** also **sackful** the amount that
a sack can contain ∥ 한 부대에 담을 수
있는 양. 한 부대분의 양 —see also **hit
the sack** (HIT)

sack² v [T] to steal and destroy things
in a city that has been defeated by an
army ∥ 군대에게 함락당한 도시에서 물건
을 훔치고 파괴하다. 약탈하다: *The
Vandals sacked Rome in 455 A.D.* 반달
족은 서기 455년에 로마를 약탈했다.

sack out *phr v* [I] INFORMAL to go to
sleep ∥ 잠들다: *The party went on so late
that everyone just sacked out on the
floor.* 그 파티는 너무 늦게까지 계속되어
서 모든 사람들이 바닥에서 잠이 들고 말
았다.

sac·ra·ment /'sækrəmənt/ n an
important Christian ceremony such as
marriage or COMMUNION ∥ 결혼이나 성찬
등의 크리스트교의 중요한 의식. 성례. 성
사

sa·cred /'seɪkrɪd/ adj **1** relating to a
god or religion, and believed to be holy
∥ 신이나 종교에 관련되어 신성하다고 믿
는. 종교적인. 거룩한: *sacred writings/
music/rituals* 성전[성가, 종교적인 의식]
2 extremely important to someone ∥ 사
람에게 극히 중요한: *The Big Sur
coastline is seen as a sacred resource.*
빅 서 해안 지대는 긴요한 자원으로 간주
된다.

sacred cow /ˌ.. './ n DISAPPROVING a
belief, object etc. that is so important to
someone that s/he will not let anyone
criticize or change it ∥ 아무에게도 비난하
거나 변경하는 것을 허용치 않을 정도로
누군가에게 중대한 신념·물체 등. 신성불
가침의 것

sac·ri·fice¹ /'sækrəˌfaɪs/ n [C, U] **1**
something that you decide not to have
or not to do in order to get something
that is more important ∥ 더 중요한 것을
얻기 위해 가지거나 하지 않기로 마음먹는
것. 희생(되는 것): *Her parents made a
lot of sacrifices to put her through
college.* 그녀의 부모님들은 그녀를 대학
졸업 시키기 위해 많은 희생을 했다. **2** an
object or animal that is SACRIFICEd 희생

되는 물건이나 동물. 제물 –**sacrificial**
/ˌsækrəˈfɪʃəl/ adj

sac·ri·fice² v **1** [T] to not have or do
something that is valuable or important
in order to get something that is more
important ∥ 더 중요한 것을 얻으려고 값
지거나 중요한 것을 가지거나 하지 않다.
희생하다: *It's not worth sacrificing your
health for your job.* 일은 건강을 희생할
만큼의 가치가 있는 것이 아니다. **2** [I, T]
to offer something to a god as part of a
ceremony, often by killing it ∥ 의식의 일
환으로 종종 어떤 것을 죽여 신에게 바치
다. 제물을 바치다: *Priests sacrificed two
bulls on the altar.* 제사장은 제단 위의 황
소 두 마리를 제물로 바쳤다.

sac·ri·leg·ious /ˌsækrəˈlɪdʒəs/ adj
treating something holy or important in
a bad way that does not show respect
for it ∥ 신성하거나 중요한 것에 대해 경의
를 표하지 않고 무례하게 대하는. 신성을
더럽히는. 모독적인: *It would be
sacrilegious to tear down the old city
library.* 그 유서 깊은 시립 도서관을 부수
는 것은 모독적인 일이 될 것이다. –
sacrilege /'sækrəlɪdʒ/ n [C, U]

sac·ro·sanct /'sækroʊˌsæŋkt/ adj too
important to be changed or criticized in
any way ∥ 너무 중요하여 어떤 방식으로든
바뀌거나 비난 받을 수 없는. 더할 나위
없이 신성한: *Our time spent together as
a family is sacrosanct.* 가족이 함께 보내
는 우리의 시간은 신성한 것이다.

sad /sæd/ adj -**dder**, -**ddest** **1**
unhappy, especially because something
unpleasant has happened to you ∥ 특히
불쾌한 일이 자신에게 일어나서 행복하지
않은. 슬픈: *Linda looks very sad today.*
린다는 오늘 매우 슬퍼 보인다. / *I liked
living in Vancouver, and I was sad to
leave it.* 나는 밴쿠버에 사는 것이 좋았고
그래서 그곳을 떠나는 것이 슬펐다. —
opposite HAPPY **2** a sad event, story etc.
makes you feel unhappy ∥ 사건·이야기
등이 불행한 느낌을 주는. 슬픔을 자아내
는: *Have you heard the sad news about
Mrs. Winters?* 너 윈터 부인에 대한 슬픈
소식 들었어? / *It's sad that two city
parks had to close down.* 두 시립공원이
폐쇄될 수밖에 없었다는 점이 슬프다. **3**
very bad or unacceptable ∥ 매우 나쁜, 받
아들일 수 없는: *It's a sad state of
affairs* (=bad situation) *when a person
isn't safe at home anymore.* 더 이상 사
람들이 집에서 안전하지 않다면 그것은 비
참한 상황이다. –**sadness** n [singular,
U]

sad·den /'sædn/ v [T] FORMAL to make

someone feel sad or disappointed‖ 누군 가를 슬프거나 실망스럽게 만들다: *It saddened me to hear of your father's death.* 네 아버지 사망 소식을 들으니 슬 퍼졌다.

sad·dle¹ /ˈsædl/ *n* **1** a seat made of leather that is put on a horse's back so that you can ride it‖ 말을 탈 수 있도록 말 등에 올려놓는 가죽으로 만든 좌석. 안 장 **2** a seat on a bicycle or a MOTORCYCLE ‖ 자전거나 오토바이의 안장

saddle² *v* [T] to put a SADDLE on a horse‖ 말 위에 안장을 놓다

saddle up *phr v* [I, T] to put a SADDLE on a horse, or to sit on the saddle that is on a horse‖ 말 위에 안장을 놓다, 또는 말 위에 놓인 안장에 앉다

saddle sb **with** sth *phr v* [T] to give someone a job, problem etc. that is difficult or boring‖ 누군가에게 어렵거 나 지루한 일이나 문제 등을 주다. …을 부과하다[지우다]: *Wesley managed to saddle Harris with all the photocopying.* 웨슬리는 해리스에게 온갖 복사하는 일을 용케 떠맡겼다.

sad·dle·bag /ˈsædl͵bæg/ *n* a bag that you carry things in that is attached to a SADDLE on a horse or a bicycle‖ 말이나 자전거의 안장에 부착되어 물건을 나르는 데에 쓰는 주머니. 안낭(鞍囊)

sa·dism /ˈseɪdɪzəm/ *n* [U] the practice of getting pleasure, especially sexual pleasure, from being cruel to someone ‖ 남에게 잔인하게 굴어서 특히 성적인 쾌 락을 얻는 습관. 사디즘. 가학성 음란증 – **sadistic** /səˈdɪstɪk/ *adj* : *a sadistic ruler* 잔혹한 통치자 – **sadist** /ˈseɪdɪst/ *n* –compare MASOCHISM

sad·ly /ˈsædli/ *adv* **1** in a sad way‖ 슬 프게. 슬픈 듯이: *Jimmy nodded sadly.* 지미는 슬픈 듯이 머리를 끄덕였다. **2 sadly (enough)** unfortunately‖ 불행하 게도: *Sadly, most small businesses fail in the first year.* 불행하게도 대부분의 영 세 기업들이 첫 해에 도산한다.

sa·fa·ri /səˈfɑri/ *n* a trip through the country areas of Africa in order to watch wild animals‖ 야생 동물을 보려고 아프리카의 외곽 지역을 지나는 여행: *The Bakers are on safari in Zaire.* 베이커 씨 가족은 자이레에서 사파리 여행 중이다.

safe¹ /seɪf/ *adj* **1** not in danger of being harmed or stolen‖ 위해를 입거나 도난당 할 위험이 없는. 안전한. 위험이 없는: *I'd feel safer driving with someone else.* 다 른 사람과 함께 타고 가면 보다 안심할 텐 데. / *Nothing can keep a city safe from terrorist attacks.* 아무 것도 테러리스트의

공격으로부터 도시를 안전하게 지킬 수는 없다. / *Both children were found, safe and sound.* (=unharmed) 두 어린이들은 무사히 발견되었다. **2** not likely to cause or allow any physical injury or harm‖ 육체적인 부상이나 위해를 일으키거나 허 용할 것 같지 않은. 위험할 것 같지 않은: *a safe water supply* 안전한 물 공급 / *Is it safe to swim here?* 여기서 수영해도 안 전합니까? / *Have a safe trip/drive!* 안전 한 여행[운전]이 되기를! / *The kids watched from a safe distance.* 아이들은 안전 거리를 확보하고 지켜보았다. **3** a safe place is one where something is not likely to be stolen or lost‖ 장소가 어떤 것을 도난당하거나 잃어버리지 않을 것 같 은: *Keep your passport in a safe place.* 당신의 여권을 안전한 곳에 보관해라. **4** not involving any risk and very likely to succeed‖ 어떠한 위험도 없고 성공할 가 능성이 높은: *Gold is a safe investment.* 금은 안전한 투자 대상이다. / *I think it's a safe bet that he'll remember your birthday.* 그가 네 생일을 기억하리라는 것은 틀림없다고 생각한다. **5 to be on the safe side** used when you are being very careful in order to avoid an unpleasant situation‖ 불쾌한 상황을 피 하기 위해 매우 조심할 때에 쓰여. 신중을 기하다: *We'll each keep a copy of the lease to be on the safe side.* 우리는 신중 을 기하기 위해 각자 임대차 계약서 사본 을 보관할 것이다. **6** not likely to cause disagreement‖ 이의 제기를 할 것 같지 않은: *It is safe to say that most Internet users are men.* 대부분의 인터넷 사용자가 남성이라고 해도 이의가 없을 것이다. – **safely** *adv*: *Drive safely!* 안전하게 운전 해라!

safe² *n* a strong metal box or cupboard with a lock on it, where you keep money and valuable things‖ 돈과 귀중품 을 보관하는 자물쇠를 채운 강한 금속제 상자나 벽장. 금고

safe-de·pos·it box /ˈ. .͵.. ͵./ *n* a small box used for keeping valuable objects, usually in a special room in a bank‖ 보통 은행 안의 특별실에 있는 귀 중품을 보관하는 데에 쓰이는 작은 상자. 은행의 대여 금고

safe·guard /ˈseɪfgɑrd/ *n* a law, agreement etc. that is intended to protect someone or something from possible dangers or problems‖ 일어날 가능성이 있는 위험이나 문제들로부터 사 람이나 사물을 보호하기 위한 법·계약 등. 보호책: *safeguards against misuse of medications* 약물 오용에 대한 보호책 –

safeguard *v* [T]: *laws to safeguard wildlife in the area* 그 지역의 야생 생물을 보호하기 위한 법

safe ha·ven /ˌ. '../ *n* a place where someone can go in order to escape from possible danger or attack ‖ 발생 가능성이 있는 위험이나 공격을 피하기 위해 사람이 갈 수 있는 곳. 안전한 장소. 대피소

safe·keep·ing /ˌseɪf'kipɪŋ/ *n* [U] **for safekeeping** if you put something somewhere for safekeeping, you put it in a place where it will not get damaged, lost, or stolen ‖ 손상이나 분실, 또는 도난당하지 않도록. 보관하려고

safe sex /ˌ. '../ *n* [U] ways of having sex that reduce the risk of getting a sexual disease, especially by the use of a CONDOM ‖ 특히 콘돔을 이용한, 성병에 걸리는 위험을 줄이는 성교법

safe·ty /'seɪfti/ *n* [U] **1** the state of being safe from danger or harm ‖ 위험이나 위해로부터 안전한 상태. 안전. 무사: *Some students are concerned about safety on campus.* 교내에서의 안전을 염려하는 학생들도 있다. **2** how safe someone or something is ‖ 사람이나 사물의 안전성: *There are fears for the safety of the hostages.* 인질들의 안전이 염려된다. / *Parents are worried about the safety of the toy.* 부모들은 장난감의 안전성에 대해 걱정한다.

safety belt /'.. ˌ./ *n* ⇨ SEAT BELT

safety net /'.. ˌ./ *n* **1** a system or arrangement that helps people who have serious problems ‖ 중대한 문제가 있는 사람을 돕는 시스템이나 해결책. 안전책. 사회 보장 (제도): *Too many people do not have the safety net of insurance.* 아주 많은 사람들이 보험이라는 안전책을 가지고 있지 못하다. **2 a** large net used for catching someone who is performing high above the ground if s/he falls ‖ 지상의 높은 곳에서 공연하는 사람이 만일에 떨어질 경우 받치기 위해 쓰이는 대형 그물. 안전망

safety pin /'.. ˌ./ *n* a wire pin with a cover that its point fits into so that it cannot hurt you ‖ 사람이 다치지 않게 하려고 끝을 안으로 넣고 덮개를 한 철사로 만든 핀. 안전핀 —see picture at PIN¹

safety ra·zor /'.. ˌ../ *n* a RAZOR that has a cover over part of the blade to protect your skin ‖ 피부를 보호하기 위해 칼날부분 위에 덮개가 있는 면도기. 안전면도기

safety valve /'.. ˌ./ *n* **1** something you do that allows you to express strong feelings such as anger, without doing any harm ‖ 아무런 해도 입히지 않으면서 노여움 등의 강렬한 감정을 표현할 수 있게 하는 것. 감정의 무난한 배출구: *Exercise is a good safety valve for stress.* 운동은 스트레스를 푸는 좋은 배출구이다. **2 a** part of a machine that allows gas, steam etc. to be let out when the pressure is too high ‖ 압력이 너무 높을 때 가스나 증기 등이 배출되도록 한 기계의 일부분. 안전 밸브

sag /sæg/ *v* **-gged, -gging** [I] **1** to sink or bend down and away from the usual position ‖ 가라앉거나 구부러져 평소의 위치에서 벗어나 있다. 내려앉다. 늘어지다: *The branches sagged under the weight of the snow.* 나뭇가지들은 눈의 무게로 축 늘어졌다. **2** to become weaker or less valuable ‖ 약해지거나 가치가 덜해지다. 약해지다. 가치가 떨어지다: *efforts to boost the sagging economy* 침체된 경제를 활성화시키기 위한 노력

sa·ga /'sɑgə/ *n* a long story or description of events ‖ 사건에 대한 긴 이야기나 묘사. 무용담. 대하소설

sage /seɪdʒ/ *adj* LITERARY very wise, especially as a result of being old ‖ 특히 나이가 들어 아주 현명한. 슬기로운

sage·brush /'seɪdʒbrʌʃ/ *n* [U] a small bush with a strong smell, that grows on dry land in western North America ‖ 북아메리카의 서부의 건조지에서 자라는 향이 강한 작은 관목. 산쑥

Sag·it·tar·i·us /ˌsædʒə'tɛriəs/ *n* **1** [singular] the ninth sign of the ZODIAC, represented by a man with a BOW and ARROWs ‖ 활과 화살을 지닌 남성으로 상징되는 황도 12궁도의 아홉째 별자리. 궁수자리 **2** [C] someone born between November 22 and December 21 ‖ 11월 22일에서 12월 21일 사이에 태어난 사람. 궁수좌 태생의 사람

said¹ /sɛd/ *v* the past tense and PAST PARTICIPLE of SAY ‖ say의 과거·과거 분사형

said² *adj* LAW used when giving more information about someone or something that has just been mentioned ‖ 방금 언급된 사람이나 사물에 대한 더 많은 정보를 줄 때에 쓰여. 앞서 말한: *The said robbery happened about 5:00.* 앞서 말한 강도 사건은 5시경에 발생했다.

sail¹ /seɪl/ *v* **1** [I] to travel across an area of water in a boat or ship ‖ 보트나 배를 타고 수역(水域)을 여행하다. 항행[범주, 항해]하다: *We sailed along the coast of Alaska.* 우리는 알래스카의 해안을 따라 항해했다. **2** [I, T] to direct or control the movement of a boat or ship

‖ 보트나 배의 이동을 지시하거나 통제하다. 배를 조종하다: *The captain sailed the ship safely past the rocks.* 선장은 배를 안전하게 조종하여 암초를 지나가게 했다. / *I'd like to learn how to sail.* 배를 조종하는 법을 배우고 싶다. **3** [I] to start a trip by boat or ship ‖ 보트나 배로 여행을 시작하다. 출범[출항]하다: *What time do we sail?* 우리 몇 시에 출항하지?

sail² *n* **1** a large piece of strong cloth fixed onto a boat, so that the wind will push the boat along ‖ 바람이 배를 밀어 나아갈 수 있도록 배 위에 설치한 질긴 대형 천 조각. 돛: *a yacht with white sails* 흰 돛을 단 요트 **2 set sail** to begin a trip by boat or ship ‖ 보트나 배로 여행을 시작하다. 출항하다: *The ship will set sail at dawn.* 그 배는 새벽에 출항할 것이다.

sail·boat /ˈseɪlboʊt/ *n* a small boat with one or more sails ‖ 한 개 또는 그 이상의 돛을 가진 작은 배. 범선.

sail·ing /ˈseɪlɪŋ/ *n* [U] the sport of traveling through water in a SAILBOAT ‖ 요트를 타고 물을 가로질러 가는 스포츠. 요트 경기

sail·or /ˈseɪlɚ/ *n* **1** someone who works on a ship ‖ 배 위에서 일하는 사람. 선원. 뱃사람 **2** someone who is in the Navy ‖ 해군에서 복무하는 사람. 수병. 해군 군인

saint /seɪnt/ *n* **1** also **Saint** someone who is honored by the Catholic Church after death because s/he has suffered for his/her religious beliefs ‖ 종교적 믿음으로 고통을 받아서 사후에 가톨릭교회에서 추앙받는 사람. 성인(聖人). 성자 **2** SPOKEN someone who is very good, kind, or patient ‖ 매우 착하거나 친절하거나, 또는 인내심이 강한 사람. 성인군자: *You're a real saint to help us like this.* 이렇게 우리를 도와주니 당신은 정말 훌륭한 분입니다. – **sainthood** /ˈseɪnthʊd/ *n* [U]

Saint Ber·nard /ˌseɪnt bɚˈnɑrd/ *n* a very large strong dog with long hair ‖ 털이 긴 매우 크고 힘센 개. 세인트 버너드

sake /seɪk/ *n* [U] **1 for the sake of/for sb's sake** in order to help, improve, or please someone or something ‖ 사람이나 사물을 돕거나 향상시키거나, 또는 기쁘게 하기 위한. …을 위한/누군가를 위한: *Both sides are willing to take risks for the sake of peace.* 양 진영은 평화를 위해 기꺼이 위험을 감수하고 있다. / *I have to be nice to her, for Kathy's sake.* 캐시를 위해 그녀에게 잘해 주어야 한다. **2 for goodness'/Pete's/heaven's etc. sake** SPOKEN said when you are annoyed, surprised, impatient etc. ‖ 화나거나 놀랐을 때 또는 참지 못할

때에 쓰여. 제발. 아무쪼록. 부디. 도대체: *Why didn't you tell me, for heaven's sake?* 도대체 너는 왜 안 말한 거야?

sal·a·ble, saleable /ˈseɪləbəl/ *adj* something that is salable can be sold, or is easy to sell ‖ 물건이 팔릴 수 있는, 또는 팔기 쉬운. 시장성이 있는. 잘 팔리는: *salable merchandise* 잘 팔리는 제품

sal·ad /ˈsæləd/ *n* [C, U] **1** a mixture of raw vegetables, for example LETTUCE, CUCUMBER, and TOMATO ‖ 상추·오이·토마토 등의 생야채의 혼합물. 샐러드 **2** raw or cooked food cut into small pieces and served cold ‖ 작은 조각으로 잘라 차게 내놓는 날음식이나 조리된 음식. 샐러드 요리: *potato salad* 감자 샐러드

salad bar /ˈ.. ˌ./ *n* a place in a restaurant where you can make your own SALAD ‖ 본인이 자신의 샐러드를 만들 수 있는 식당 내의 장소. 샐러드 바

salad dress·ing /ˈ.. ˌ./ *n* [C, U] a liquid mixture for putting on SALADs to give them a special taste ‖ 특별한 맛을 내기 위해 샐러드 위에 뿌리는 액체 혼합물. 샐러드 드레싱

sal·a·man·der /ˈsæləˌmændɚ/ *n* a small animal similar to a LIZARD, that can live in water and on land ‖ 수중과 육지에서 살 수 있는 도마뱀과 비슷하게 생긴 작은 동물. 도롱뇽

sa·la·mi /səˈlɑmi/ *n* [C, U] a large SAUSAGE with a strong taste, that is eaten cold ‖ 차게 해서 먹는 강한 맛이 나는 큰 소시지. 살라미 소시지

sal·a·ried /ˈsælərid/ *adj* receiving a SALARY ‖ 봉급을 받는: *salaried workers* 월급쟁이

sal·a·ry /ˈsæləri/ *n* [C, U] money that you receive every month as payment from the organization you work for ‖ 근무하는 조직에서 보수로써 매달 받는 돈. 봉급. 월급: *She earns a good salary.* 그녀는 월급을 많이 받는다. —compare WAGES, —see usage note at PAY²

sal·a·ry·man /ˈsælərimən/ *n plural* **salarymen** a man who works in an office, often for many hours each day, and receives a salary as payment, especially in Japan ‖ 특히 일본에서 보통 매일 장시간 동안 일하고 대가로 월급을 받는 사람. 샐러리맨

sale /seɪl/ *n* **1** [C, U] the act of giving property, food, or other goods to someone in exchange for money ‖ 돈을 받고 남에게 부동산이나 식품, 또는 다른 상품을 주는 행위. 판매. 매각: *The sale of alcohol is strictly controlled by state laws.* 알코올 판매는 주(州)법으로 엄격히

통제되고 있다. / *Business is slow; I haven't made a sale* (=sold something) *all day.* 경기가 좋지 않아서 나는 하루 종일 팔지를 못했다. **2 for sale** available to be bought ‖ 팔 수 있는. 팔려고 내놓은: *They had to put their home up for sale.* 그들은 자기들의 집을 팔려고 내놓아야 했다: *Is this table for sale?* 이 테이블 파는 것입니까? **3 a** time when stores sell their goods at lower prices than usal ‖ 가게들이 평소보다 저렴한 가격으로 물건을 파는 시간. 염가 판매. 특매: *There's a great sale on at Macy's now.* 지금 메이시 백화점에서 대염가 판매를 하고 있다. **4 on sale** available to be bought in a store, or available for a lower price than usual ‖ 가게에서 구입할 수 있거나 평소보다 저렴한 값에 살 수 있는. 팔려고 내놓은. 특매[특가]로: *Don found a really good CD player on sale.* 돈은 정말 좋은 CD 플레이어를 염가로 구입했다.

sales /seɪlz/ *n* [plural] **1** the total number of products that a company sells during a particular time, measured in the amount of money they bring to the company ‖ 제품이 회사에 벌어들이는 금액으로 측정된, 회사가 특정 기간 동안에 판매한 제품의 총 수. 매상. 판매액: *a company with sales of $60 million per year* 연매출 6천만 달러의 회사 **2** [U] the part of a company that deals with selling products ‖ 제품 판매를 취급하는 회사의 한 부서. 판매부: *Sally got a job as sales manager.* 샐리는 영업 부장으로서 일자리를 얻었다.

sales clerk /'. ./ *n* someone who sells things in a store ‖ 가게에서 물건을 파는 사람. 점원.

sales·man /'seɪlzmən/ *n* a man whose job is to sell things ‖ 물건 판매를 하는 남성. 판매원. 세일즈맨: *a used car salesman* 중고차 판매원 / *a traveling salesman* 외판원

sales·per·son /'seɪlz,pɚsən/ *n* someone whose job is to sell things ‖ 물건 판매를 하는 직업인. 판매원

sales rep·re·sent·a·tive /'. ..,..../ also **sales rep** /'. ./ someone who travels around selling his/her company's products ‖ 자사 제품을 팔면서 돌아다니는 사람. 외판원

sales slip /'. ./ *n* a small piece of paper that you are given in a store when you buy something; RECEIPT ‖ 가게에서 물건을 사면 받는 작은 종이 조각. 판매 전표. 영수증. ㉿ receipt

sales tax /'. ./ *n* [C, U] a tax that you

pay in addition to the cost of something you are buying ‖ 구입하는 물건 가격에 추가로 지불하는 세금. 판매세.

sales·wom·an /'seɪlz,wʊmən/ *n* a woman whose job is selling things ‖ 물건 판매를 하는 여성. 여성 판매원

sa·li·ent /'seɪliənt/ *adj* FORMAL most noticeable or important ‖ 가장 두드러지거나 중요한. 현저한: *the salient points of the plan* 그 계획서에서 가장 중요한 점 **– salience** *n* [U]

sa·line /'seɪlin, -laɪn/ *adj* containing or consisting of salt ‖ 소금을 포함하거나 소금으로 구성된. 염분의: *a saline solution* (=liquid with salt in it) 식염수 **– saline** *n* [U]

sa·li·va /sə'laɪvə/ *n* [U] the liquid that is produced naturally in your mouth ‖ 입 안에서 자연적으로 생겨나는 액체. 침. 타액

sal·i·vate /'sælə,veɪt/ *v* [I] TECHNICAL to produce more SALIVA in your mouth than usual because you see or smell food ‖ 음식을 보거나 냄새를 맡아서 평소보다 입에 침이 많이 생기다. 침을 많이 흘리다. 군침을 흘리다

sal·low /'sæloʊ/ *adj* sallow skin looks slightly yellow and unhealthy ‖ 피부가 약간 노랗고 건강해 보이지 않는. 누르스름한. 혈색이 나쁜

salm·on /'sæmən/ *n* [C, U] a large ocean fish with silver skin and pink flesh, or the meat from this fish ‖ 은빛 몸통에 분홍색 살을 지닌 큰 바닷물고기, 또는 이 물고기의 살코기. 연어(의 살)

sa·lon /sə'lɑn/ *n* a place where you can get your hair cut, have a MANICURE etc. ‖ 머리카락을 자르고 손톱 손질을 할 수 있는 곳. 미용실: *a beauty salon* 미용실

sa·loon /sə'lun/ *n* a place where alcoholic drinks were sold and drunk in the western US in the 19th century ‖ 19 세기에 미국 서부에서 알코올 음료를 팔고 마시던 곳. 술집. 바

sal·sa /'sælsə, 'sɔl-/ *n* [U] **1** a SAUCE made from onions, TOMATOes, and hot-tasting PEPPERs that you put on Mexican food ‖ 멕시코 요리에 넣는, 양파와 토마토, 그리고 매운 맛이 나는 후추로 만든 소스. 살사 소스 **2** a type of Latin American dance music ‖ 라틴 아메리카 댄스 음악의 일종. 살사

salt¹ /sɔlt/ *n* **1** [U] a natural white mineral that is added to food to make it taste better ‖ 음식을 더 맛있게 하기 위해 첨가하는 천연의 흰 무기질. 소금 **2** TECHNICAL a type of chemical, formed by combining an acid with another substance ‖ 산에 다른 물질을 조합하여 만든 일종의 화학 물질. 염

salt[2] v [T] to add salt to food to make it taste better ‖ 음식을 더 맛있게 하기 위해 소금을 치다

salt sth ↔ **away** phr v [T] to save money for future use, especially dishonestly ‖ 장차 사용하려고 특히 부정하게 돈을 저축하다

salt[3] adj **1** preserved by salt ‖ 소금에 의해 보존된. 소금에 절인: *salt pork* 소금에 절인 돼지고기 **2** containing salt or salt water ‖ 소금이나 소금물을 함유하는: *a salt lake* 함수호

salts /sɔlts/ n [plural] a mineral substance like salt that is used as a medicine or to make your bath smell good ‖ 약으로, 또는 목욕물에 좋은 냄새를 내기 위해 쓰이는 소금 같은 광물질. 방향염(芳香鹽)

salt shak·er /'. ,../ n a small container for salt ‖ 소금을 담는 작은 용기. 소금 뿌리개

salt·wa·ter /'sɔlt˺,wɔtɚ, -,wɑ-/ adj living in SALTY water ‖ 소금물에 사는. 바다의: *saltwater fish* 바닷물고기

salt·y /'sɔlti/ adj tasting of or containing salt ‖ 소금 맛이 나는, 소금을 함유한 – **saltiness** n [U]

sal·u·ta·tion /,sælyə'teɪʃən/ n [C, U] FORMAL a greeting, especially one at the beginning of a letter, such as "Dear Mr. Roberts" ‖ 특히 "Dear Mr. Roberts" 등의 편지 서두의 인사말

sa·lute[1] /sə'lut/ v [I, T] to move your right hand to your head in order to show respect to an officer in the Army, Navy etc. ‖ 육군이나 해군 등에서 장교에게 존경심을 표하려고 오른쪽 손을 머리에 올리다. 경례하다

salute[2] n **1** an act of saluting (SALUTE) ‖ 경례하는 행위. 경례 **2** an occasion when guns are fired into the air in order to show respect for someone ‖ 어떤 사람에게 존경심을 나타내기 위해 공중에 총을 발사하는 의식. 예포: *a 21-gun salute* 21발의 예포

sal·vage[1] /'sælvɪdʒ/ v [T] to save something from a situation in which other things have already been damaged, destroyed, or lost ‖ 다른 것들이 이미 손상된[파괴된, 상실된] 상황에서 어떤 것을 구하다. 구출하다: *Farmers are trying to salvage their wheat from the heavy rains.* 농민들은 폭우로부터 그들의 밀을 지키려고 안간힘을 쓰고 있다.

salvage[2] n [U] the act of salvaging (SALVAGE) something, or the things that

are salvaged ‖ 무엇을 구하는 행위, 또는 구한 물건. 구조 활동. 구출 물품: *salvage crews (=people who are salvaging things)* 구조대

sal·va·tion /sæl'veɪʃən/ n [U] **1** the state of being saved from evil by God, according to the Christian religion ‖ 크리스트교에 따르면 신에 의해 악으로부터 구출되는 상태. 구원 **2** something that prevents danger, loss, or failure ‖ 위험이나 손실, 또는 실패를 방지하는 것. 구제. 구출. 보호: *Donations of food and clothing have been the salvation of the refugees.* 음식과 의류의 기증품으로 난민들을 구제해왔다.

Salvation Ar·my /.,.. '../ n **the Salvation Army** a Christian organization that tries to help poor people ‖ 빈민들을 애써 돕는 기독교 단체. 구세군

salve /sæv/ n [C, U] **1** a substance that you put on sore skin to make it less painful ‖ 통증을 덜 느끼게 하기 위해 염증을 일으킨 피부에 바르는 물질. 연고 **2** something you do to make a situation better ‖ 상황을 더 좋게 만들기 위해 하는 것. 위로. 위안 – **salve** v [T]

sal·vo /'sælvoʊ/ n FORMAL **1** the first of a series of actions or statements, especially in a situation in which people are arguing ‖ 사람들이 논쟁하고 있는 상황에서 일련의 행동이나 말 중의 첫 번째 것: *His opening salvo was an angry criticism of his former employer.* 토론에서 그의 첫마디는 그의 전(前) 고용주에 대한 격렬한 비판이었다. **2** the firing of several guns in a battle or as part of a ceremony ‖ 전투에서 또는 의식의 일부로서 여러 개의 총을 발사하는 것. 예포의 일제 사격. 폭탄의 일제 투하

Sa·mar·i·tan /sə'mærət˺n/ also **good Samaritan** n someone who helps you when you have problems ‖ 문제가 있을 때에 도와주는 사람. 곤경에 처한 사람을 돕는 사람

same[1] /seɪm/ adj **1 the same person/place etc. a)** one particular person, place etc. and not a different one ‖ 다른 것이 아닌 특정의 한 사람 또는 한 장소 등. 동일인/동일 장소: *They go to the same place for their vacation every summer.* 그들은 매년 여름휴가를 같은 곳으로 간다. / *Kim's birthday and Roger's are on the same day.* 김의 생일과 로저의 생일은 같은 날이다. **b)** used in order to say that two or more people, things etc. are exactly like each other; IDENTICAL ‖ 둘이나 그 이상의 사람·사물 등이 서로 아

주 똑같다고 말하는 데에 쓰여; ㊨ identical: *She does the same job as I do, but in a bigger company.* 그녀는 내가 하는 일과 똑같은 일을 하지만 그녀는 나보다 더 큰 회사에 다닌다. ✗DON'T SAY "She does the same job like I do."✗ "She does the same job like I do."라고는 하지 않는다. **2** used in order to say that a particular person or thing does not change ‖ 특정한 사람이나 물건이 변하지 않는다고 말하는 데에 쓰여. 같은. 변함없는: *She keeps playing the same songs.* 그녀가 계속하여 같은 곡을 연주하고 있다. **3 at the same time** if two things happen at the same time they happen together ‖ 동시에: *How can you type and talk at the same time?* 어떻게 당신은 동시에 타자를 치면서 얘기도 할 수 있느냐? **4 the same old story/excuse etc.** INFORMAL something that you have heard many times before ‖ 여러 번 들었던 것. 여러 번 들은 이야기[변명]: *It's the same old story – his wife doesn't understand him.* 그의 아내가 그를 이해하지 못한다는 얘기는 전에 여러 번 들었어. **5 same difference** SPOKEN used in order to say that different actions, behavior etc. have the same result ‖ 다른 조치나 행동 등이 동일한 결과를 낸다고 말하는 데에 쓰여. 결국 똑같은 것. 아무 차이가 없음: *"Should I e-mail them or fax a letter?" "Same difference."* "편지를 이메일로 보내야 하나, 아니면 팩스로 보내야 하나?" "어떻게 하든 마찬가지야." **6 by the same token** in the same way or for the same reasons ‖ 같은 방식으로, 같은 이유로. 마찬가지로: *You need to try to understand Dave's work, but by the same token, Dave should try to come home earlier.* 당신은 데이브가 하는 일을 이해하려고 노력해야 하겠지만 마찬가지로 데이브는 보다 일찍 귀가하려 노력해야 한다. **7 be in the same boat** to be in the same difficult situation that someone else is in ‖ 다른 사람이 처해 있는 것과 같이 어려운 상황에 처해 있다. 같은 입장[운명]에 있다: *Everyone has to work overtime – we're all in the same boat.* 우리는 모두 같은 입장에 있기 때문에 모두 시간외 근무를 해야한다.

same² *pron* **1 the same a)** used in order to say that two or more people, actions, or things are exactly like each other ‖ 둘 또는 그 이상의 사람이나 행위, 또는 사물이 서로 정확히 같다고 말하는 데에 쓰여. 같은 사람[것, 일]: *Thanks – I'll do the same for you one day.* 고마워. 언젠가 나도 네게 너처럼 해줄게. / *The* houses may look the same, but one's slightly larger.* 그 집들은 똑같아 보일지 모르지만 한 집은 조금 더 크다. **b)** used in order to say that a particular person or thing does not change ‖ 특정한 사람이나 물건이 변하지 않는다고 말하는 데에 쓰여: *She keeps playing the same songs.* 그녀는 계속 같은 곡을 연주하고 있다. / *"How's Danny?" "Oh, he's the same as ever."* "대니 어때?" "응, 그는 항상 그렇지 뭐." ✗DON'T SAY "He's same as ever."✗ "He's same as ever."라고는 하지 않는다. **2 (and the) same to you!** SPOKEN used as a reply to a greeting or as an angry reply to a rude remark ‖ 인사에 대한 응답이나 무례한 말에 대하여 화가 나서 하는 대꾸로 쓰여. 당신도: *"Have a good weekend!" "Thanks, same to you!"* "주말 잘 보내!" "고마워. 너도!" **3 same here** SPOKEN said in order to tell someone that you feel the same way as him/her ‖ 자신도 상대가 느끼는 것과 같이 느낀다고 상대에게 말하는 데에 쓰여. 동감이다: *"I hate shopping malls." "Same here."* "나는 쇼핑몰이 정말 싫어." "나도 그래."

same·ness /'seimnis/ *n* [U] a boring lack of variety, or the quality of being very similar to something else ‖ 지루하게 다양성이 부족하거나, 또는 다른 것과 매우 유사한 성질. 단조로움. 비슷비슷함: *There's a sameness to all these highrise buildings.* 이 고층 건물들은 모두 비슷비슷하다.

sam·ple¹ /'sæmpəl/ *n* **1** a small part or amount of something that is examined or used in order to find out what the rest is like ‖ 나머지 상태를 알아보려고 검사하거나 써보는 일부 또는 소량의 물건. 견본. 샘플: *Do you have a sample of your work?* 당신 작품의 견본이 있습니까? / *free samples of a new shampoo* 새로운 샴푸의 무료 견본 **2** a group of people who have been chosen to give information by answering questions ‖ 질문에 답을 하여 정보를 제시하도록 선택된 일단의 사람들: *a random sample of 500 college students* (=one in which you choose people without knowing anything about them) 무작위로 표본된 추출 대학생 500명

sample² *v* [T] **1** to taste a food or drink in order to see what it is like ‖ 상태를 알아보기 위해 음식이나 음료를 맛보다. 시식[시음]하다: *We sampled several kinds of cheese.* 우리는 여러 종류의 치즈를 시식했다. **2** to choose some people from a larger group in order to ask them questions ‖ 질문을 하려고 보다 큰 그룹에서 몇몇 사람들을 선택하다: *Over 25% of the people sampled said TV is their favorite form of entertainment.* 표본 추출된 사람들 중 25퍼센트 이상이 텔레비전은 자신들이 가장 좋아하는 오락거리라고 말했다.

san·a·to·ri·um /ˌsænəˈtɔriəm/ *n* a hospital for sick people who are getting better but still need rest and care ‖ 아직 휴식과 치료가 더 필요하지만 회복 중인 병자를 위한 병원. 요양소

sanc·ti·fy /ˈsæŋktəˌfaɪ/ *v* [T] to make something holy ‖ 어떤 것을 신성하게 하다. 신성시하다

sanc·ti·mo·ni·ous /ˌsæŋktəˈmoʊniəs/ *adj* behaving as if you are morally better than other people ‖ 도덕적으로 타인들보다 더 나은 듯이 행동하는. 성자인 체 하는: *Don't talk to me in that sanctimonious way!* 내게 그렇게 성자처럼 말하지 마라!

sanc·tion¹ /ˈsæŋkʃən/ *n* **1** [U] official permission, approval, or acceptance ‖ 공식적인 허락이나 승인, 또는 수용. 허가. 인가: *The protest march was held without government sanction.* 그 데모 행진은 정부의 승인 없이 열렸다. **2** something, such as a punishment, that makes people obey a rule or law ‖ 사람들이 규칙이나 법을 준수하도록 만드는 처벌 등의 것. 벌칙. 처벌: *Cranley's behavior deserves the severest sanction the committee can give.* 크랜리의 행동은 위원회가 내릴 수 있는 가장 엄한 처벌을 받을 만한 것이다. —see also SANCTIONS

sanction² *v* [T] FORMAL to officially accept or allow something ‖ 어떤 것을 공식적으로 받아들이거나 허용하다. …을 공인[용인]하다: *The UN refused to sanction the use of force.* 유엔은 무력 사용을 허용하지 않았다.

sanc·tions /ˈsæŋkʃənz/ *n* [plural] official orders or laws stopping trade, communication etc. with another country, as a way of forcing its leaders to make political changes ‖ 다른 나라의 지도자들에게 정치적 변화를 이루도록 압력을 가하는 수단으로써 그 나라와의 무역·통신 등을 금지하는 공식적인 명령이나 법률. 제재(조치): *Several governments imposed trade sanctions on (=started using sanctions against) countries that use chemical weapons.* 몇몇 정부들이 화학 무기를 사용하는 국가들에게 무역 제재 조치를 취했다.

sanc·ti·ty /ˈsæŋktəti/ *n* [U] **the sanctity of sth** the quality that makes

something so important that it must be respected and preserved ‖ 마땅히 존경과 보호를 받아야 할 정도로 어떤 것을 긴요하게 만드는 특성. 거룩함. 신성함. 존엄성: *the sanctity of marriage* 결혼의 신성함

sanc·tu·ar·y /ˈsæŋktʃuˌɛri/ *n* **1** [C, U] a peaceful place that is safe and provides protection, especially for people who are in danger ‖ 특히 위험에 처한 사람들을 보호해 주는 안전하고 평화로운 장소. 안식처. 피난처: *The rebel leader took sanctuary in an embassy.* 그 반란 지도자는 대사관으로 피했다. **2** an area for birds or animals where they are protected and cannot be hunted ‖ 새나 동물들이 보호를 받고 사냥이 금지된 지역. 조수 보호 구역. 금렵구 **3** the room where Christian religious services take place ‖ 크리스천이 예배를 올리는 장소. 예배를 올리는 곳. 교회

sanc·tum /ˈsæŋktəm/ *n* **1 the inner sanctum** HUMOROUS a place that only a few important people are allowed to enter ‖ 소수의 요인만 들어가도록 허용된 곳. 사실(私室): *We were only allowed into the director's inner sanctum for a few minutes.* 우리는 단지 몇분간만 그 이사의 내실에 있도록 허락 받았다. **2** a holy place inside a TEMPLE ‖ 사원 내의 신성한 장소. 성소

sand¹ /sænd/ *n* [U] the substance that forms deserts and BEACHes, and consists of many small grains ‖ 사막과 해변을 형성하는 매우 작은 알갱이로 구성된 물질. 모래

sand² *v* [T] **1** to make a surface smooth by rubbing it with SANDPAPER or a special piece of equipment ‖ 사포나 특수 장비로 문질러 표면을 매끄럽게 하다 **2** to put sand on a frozen road to make it safer ‖ 안전하게 하려고 언 도로 위에 모래를 뿌리다

san·dal /ˈsændl/ *n* a light open shoe that you wear in warm weather ‖ 따뜻한 날씨에 신는 터진 가벼운 신발. 샌들 — see picture at SHOE¹

sand·bag¹ /ˈsændbæg/ *n* a bag filled with sand, used for protection from floods, explosions etc. ‖ 홍수·폭발 등으로부터 보호하는 데에 쓰이는 모래로 채워진 주머니. 모래 주머니

sandbag² *v* **-gged, -gging** [I, T] **1** to build small walls with SANDBAGs in order to protect a place from a flood, explosion etc. ‖ 홍수·폭발 등으로부터 장소를 보호하려고 모래주머니로 작은 벽을 쌓다. …에 모래주머니를 쌓다 **2** to deliberately do something to prevent a process from happening or being successful ‖ 절차가 진행되거나 성공하지 못하게 고의로 어떤 일을 하다.: *Senator Murphy has been accused of sandbagging the investigation.* 머피 상원의원은 수사 방해 혐의로 기소되었다.

sand·bank /ˈsændbæŋk/ *n* a raised area of sand in a river, ocean etc. ‖ 강이나 바다 등의 모래가 높이 솟아 있는 지역. 모래톱. 모래 언덕

sand·blast /ˈsændblæst/ *v* [T] to clean or polish metal, stone, glass etc. with a machine that sends out a powerful stream of sand ‖ 강력한 모래 줄기를 내보내는 기계로 금속이나 돌 또는 유리 등을 청소하거나 윤이 나게 하다. 모래 분사로 청소하다[윤내다]

sand·box /ˈsændbɑks/ *n* a special area of sand for children to play in ‖ 그 안에서 아이들이 놀도록 모래가 깔린 특별한 장소. 모래 상자

sand·cas·tle /ˈsænd,kæsəl/ *n* a small model of a castle made out of sand, usually by children on a BEACH ‖ 보통 아이들이 해변에서 모래로 만드는 작은 성 모양의 것. 모래성

sand dune /ˈ. ./ *n* ⇨ DUNE

sand·man /ˈsændmæn/ *n* [singular] a man in children's stories who makes children sleep by putting sand in their eyes ‖ 아이들의 눈 속에 모래를 넣어 잠들게 만드는 동화 속의 남자. 잠귀신

sand·pa·per /ˈsænd,peɪpɚ/ *n* [U] strong paper covered with a rough substance, used for rubbing wood in order to make it smooth ‖ 나무를 매끄럽게 하기 위해 문지르는 데에 쓰이는, 표면이 거칠거칠한 물질로 덮여있는 질긴 종이. 사포 **– sandpaper** *v* [T]

sand·pip·er /ˈsænd,paɪpɚ/ *n* a small bird with long legs and a long beak, that lives by the ocean ‖ 긴 다리와 긴 부리를 가지고 해안가에 사는 작은 새. 도요의 일종

sand·stone /ˈsændstoʊn/ *n* [U] a type of soft yellow or red rock ‖ 연노란색 또는 빨간색 암석의 일종. 사암(砂巖)

sand·storm /ˈsændstɔrm/ *n* a storm in the desert in which sand is blown around by strong winds ‖ 강한 바람에 의해 주변에 모래가 날리는 사막의 폭풍. (사막의) 모래 폭풍

sand·wich¹ /ˈsændwɪtʃ/ *n* two pieces of bread with cheese, meat, egg etc. between them, usually eaten for LUNCH ‖ 두 개의 빵 조각 사이에 치즈·고기·계란 등을 넣어 보통 점심으로 먹는 것. 샌드위

치: *tuna fish sandwiches* 참치 샌드위치

sandwich² *v* [T] **be sandwiched between** to be in a very small space between two other things ‖ 두 개의 다른 사물들 사이의 아주 좁은 공간에 놓이다. … 사이에 끼이다: *a motorcycle sandwiched between two vans* 두 대의 밴 차량 사이에 끼인 오토바이

sand·y /ˈsændi/ *adj* **1** covered with sand ‖ 모래로 덮인. 모래를 포함하는[가득 찬]. 모래투성이의: *My towel's so sandy!* 내 수건이 온통 모래투성이네! **2** sandy hair is dark BLOND ‖ 머리털이 황갈색인. 모래 빛의

sane /seɪn/ *adj* **1** able to think in a normal and reasonable way ‖ 정상적이고 이성적으로 생각할 수 있는. 제정신의. 미치지 않은 **—opposite** INSANE **2** reasonable and based on sensible thinking ‖ 합리적이고 분별 있는 사고에 기초한. 사고방식이 건전한[양식 있는]. 사리분별이 있는: *a sane solution to a difficult problem* 어려운 문제에 대한 분별 있는 해결책

sang /sæŋ/ *v* the past tense of SING ‖ sing의 과거형

san·guine /ˈsæŋgwɪn/ *adj* FORMAL cheerful and hopeful about the future ‖ 미래에 대해 기운차고 희망적인. 자신감이 넘치는. 낙천적인. 쾌활한: *Smith's lawyers aren't very sanguine about the outcome of the trial.* 스미스의 변호사는 재판의 결과에 대해 그다지 낙관적이지 않다.

san·i·tar·i·um /ˌsænəˈtɛriəm/ *n* ⇨ SANATORIUM

san·i·tar·y /ˈsænə,tɛri/ *adj* **1** relating to health, especially to the removal of dirt, infection, or human waste ‖ 건강과 관련된, 특히 먼지[감염 매체, 쓰레기] 제거와 관련된. 위생상의: *Workers complained about sanitary arrangements at the factory.* 근로자들은 공장에서의 위생 처리 방법에 대해 불평했다. **2** clean and not involving any danger to your health ‖ 깨끗하고 건강에 아무런 해를 끼치지 않는. 청결한. 위생적인: *All food is stored under sanitary conditions.* 모든 식품이 위생적인 상태로 저장되어 있다.

sanitary nap·kin /ˌ.... ˈ../ *n* a piece of soft material that a woman wears in her underwear when she has her PERIOD ‖ 여성이 월경 기간 동안 속옷 속에 착용하는 부드러운 물질. 생리대

san·i·ta·tion /ˌsænəˈteɪʃən/ *n* [U] the protection of public health by removing and treating waste, dirty water etc. ‖ 오

물·오수 등을 없애고 처리해서 대중의 건강을 보호하기. 공중위생(수단)[설비]

san·i·tize /ˈsænə,taɪz/ v [T] **1** to make news, literature etc. less offensive by taking out anything unpleasant ‖ 뉴스·문학 등에서 불유쾌한 것들을 모두 제거해서 덜 유해하게 만들다. 순화시키다. 건전하게 고치다. 순화하다: *The coach's actual remarks have been sanitized so they can be printed.* 코치의 실제 발언은 순화되었기 때문에 인쇄될 수 있다. **2** to clean something thoroughly, removing dirt and BACTERIA ‖ 먼지와 박테리아를 제거해서 사물을 철저하게 청소하다. 위생적으로 만들다. 청결하게 하다

san·i·ty /ˈsænəti/ n [U] **1** the ability to think in a normal and reasonable way ‖ 정상적이고 합리적으로 생각하는 능력. 온건한[건전한] 마음. 평상심: *I went away for the weekend to try and keep my sanity.* 나는 평상심을 찾고 유지하기 위해 주말에는 멀리 떠난다. **2** the condition of being mentally healthy ‖ 정신적으로 건강한 상태. 제정신. 온전한 정신: *He lost his sanity after his children were killed.* 그는 아이들이 살해된 후에 정신이 나가 버렸다.

sank /sæŋk/ v the past tense of SINK ‖ sink의 과거형

San·ta Claus /ˈsæntə ˌklɔz/, **Santa** n an old man with red clothes and a long white BEARD, who children believe brings them presents at Christmas ‖ 아이들이 크리스 마스에 자신들에게 선물을 가져다 준다고 믿는, 빨간 옷을 입고 길고 하얀 턱 수염이 있는 노인. 산타클로스

sap¹ /sæp/ n **1** [U] the watery substance that carries food through a plant ‖ 식물의 내부를 통해 양분을 운반하는 물로 된 물질. 수액(樹液) **2** INFORMAL a stupid person who is easy to deceive or treat badly ‖ 속이거나 함부로 다루기 쉬운 멍청한 사람. 바보

sap² v **-pped, -pping** [T] to gradually make something weak or destroy it ‖ 사물을 점차로 약하게 만들거나 파괴하다. 약화시키다. 무너뜨리다: *The illness sapped her strength.* 병으로 그녀의 체력이 약해졌다.

sap·phire /ˈsæfaɪɚ/ n [C, U] a transparent bright blue jewel ‖ 투명한 밝은 청색의 보석. 사파이어

sap·ling /ˈsæplɪŋ/ n a young tree ‖ 어린 나무. 묘목

sap·py /ˈsæpi/ adj expressing love and emotions in a way that seems silly ‖ 바보처럼 보이게 사랑과 감정을 표현하는. 얼간이 같은. 지나치게 감상적인: *a sappy*

love song 얼간이 같은 사랑 노래

Sa·ran Wrap /səˈræn ˌræp/ n [U] TRADEMARK thin transparent plastic used for wrapping food ‖ 식품을 포장하는 데에 쓰이는 얇고 투명한 플라스틱. 미국제 합성수지 포장지

sar·casm /ˈsɑr,kæzəm/ n [U] a way of speaking or writing in which you say the opposite of what you mean in order to make an unkind joke or to show that you are annoyed ‖ 고약한 농담을 하거나 화가 났음을 보여주기 위해 뜻하는 것과 반대로 말을 하거나 글을 쓰는 수법. 풍자. 야유. 빈정댐: *"I'm glad you came early," said Jim, with heavy sarcasm.* "일찍 와 줘서 기쁘군." 심하게 빈정대며 짐이 말했다.

sar·cas·tic /sɑrˈkæstɪk/ adj using SARCASM ‖ 풍자를 사용하는. 비꼬아 말하는. 빈정대는. 야유하는: *Do you have to be so sarcastic?* 너 꼭 그렇게 빈정대며 말해야 하니? **– sarcastically** adv

sar·dine /sɑrˈdin/ n [C, U] **1** a young HERRING (=a type of fish), or the meat from this fish, usually sold in cans ‖ 새끼 청어, 또는 보통 통조림에 넣어 파는 이 생선의 고기. 새끼 청어(통조림) **2 be packed like sardines** to be crowded tightly together in a small space ‖ 좁은 공간에 서로 빽빽하게 밀집되어 있다. 꽉 들어차다. 꼭꼭 채워 넣어지다

sar·don·ic /sɑrˈdɑnɪk/ adj speaking or smiling in an unpleasant way that shows you do not have a good opinion of someone or something ‖ 사람이나 사물에 대해 좋은 생각을 갖고 있지 않다는 것을 보여주기 위해 불쾌하게 말하거나 미소 짓는. 조소[냉소]적인. 비웃는

sa·ri /ˈsɑri/ n a type of loose clothing worn by many Indian and Bangladeshi women, and some Pakistani women ‖ 다수의 인도와 방글라데시 여성과 일부 파키스탄 여성이 입는 헐렁한 옷의 일종. 사리

SASE n self addressed stamped envelope; an envelope that you put your name, address, and a stamp on, so that someone else can send you something ‖ self addressed stamped envelope(회신용 우표 부착 봉투)의 약어; 자신의 이름·주소를 쓰고 우표를 붙여서 다른 사람이 자신에게 어떤 것을 보낼 수 있게 한 봉투

sash /sæʃ/ n **1** a long piece of cloth that you wear around your waist like a belt ‖ 벨트처럼 허리 주위에 두르는 긴 천 조각. 장식 허리띠: *a white dress with a blue sash* 청색 장식 허리띠가 달린 하얀 드레스 **2** a long piece of cloth that you wear over one shoulder and across your

chest as a sign of a special honor ‖ 특별
한 명예의 표시로 한쪽 어깨에 걸쳐 가슴
을 사선으로 두르는 긴 천 조각. 어깨 장
식띠. 현장(懸章) **3** a frame that has a
sheet of glass fixed into it to form part
of a window ‖ 한 장의 유리가 부착되어
창문의 부분을 이루는 틀. 새시. 창틀

sass /sæs/ v [T] SPOKEN to talk in a
rude way to someone you should
respect ‖ 존경해야 하는 사람에게 무례하
게 말하다. 건방지게 말대꾸하다: *Don't
sass me, young lady!* 말대꾸하지 말아요,
어린 아가씨!

sass·y /'sæsi/ adj INFORMAL rude to
someone you should respect ‖ 존경해야
하는 사람에게 무례한. 건방진. 뻔뻔스러
운: *a sassy child* 건방진 아이

sat /sæt/ v the past tense and PAST
PARTICIPLE of SIT ‖ sit의 과거·과거 분사형

Sa·tan /'seɪtn/ n [singular] the Devil,
considered to be the main evil power
and God's opponent ‖ 주된 악의 세력이
며 신의 적대자로 간주되는 악마. 사탄

sa·tan·ic /sə'tænɪk, seɪ-/ adj **1** relating
to practices that treat the Devil like a
god ‖ 악마를 신처럼 섬기는 관행의. 악마
의[같은]: *satanic rites* 악
마 숭배 의식 **2** extremely cruel or evil ‖
극도로 잔인하거나 사악한. 극악무도한.
악마 같은: *satanic laughter* 사악한 웃음

sa·tan·is·m /'seɪtn,ɪzəm/ n [U] the
practice of treating the Devil like a god
‖ 악마를 신처럼 섬기는 관행. 악마 숭배.
악마주의 **– satanist** n

sat·el·lite /'sætl,aɪt/ n **1** a machine
that has been sent into space and goes
around the Earth, moon etc., used for
electronic communication ‖ 우주로 발사
되어 지구·달 등 주변을 돌며 전자 통신에
이용되는 기계. (인공) 위성: *a broadcast
coming in by satellite* 위성에 의해 수신
되는 방송[위성 방송] **2** a moon that
moves around a PLANET ‖ 행성 주위를 도
는 달. 위성 **3** a country, town, or
organization that is controlled by or is
dependent on another larger one ‖ 다른
더 큰 것에 의해 지배받거나 의존하는 나
라[도시, 조직]. 위성 국가[도시]. 다른
것에 의존[종속]하는 것

satellite dish /'... ,./ n a large
circular piece of metal that receives the
signals for SATELLITE TELEVISION ‖ 위성 텔
레비전의 신호를 수신하는 금속제의 큰 원
형 물체. 파라볼라 안테나. 위성 (접시)
안테나

satellite tel·e·vi·sion /,... '..../,
satellite TV n [U] television
programs that are broadcast using

SATELLITEs in space ‖ 우주의 위성을 이용
해 방송하는 TV 프로그램. 위성 방송. 위
성 TV

sat·in /'sætn/ n [U] a type of cloth that
is very smooth and shiny ‖ 매우 매끄럽고
빛나는 천의 종류. 공단. 수자직(繻子織)

sat·in·y /'sætn-i/ adj smooth, shiny,
and soft like SATIN ‖ 공단처럼 매끄럽고
빛나고 부드러운. 공단의[같은]: *satiny
material* 공단 재질

sat·ire /'sætaɪɚ/ n **1** [U] a way of
talking or writing about something that
is funny and also makes people see its
faults ‖ 사물에 대해 우스꽝스럽고 또한
사람들이 그 결점을 보게 하는 식의 화법
이나 작법. 풍자(법) **2** a play, story etc.
written in this way ‖ 이런 수법으로 쓰여
진 희곡·소설 등. 풍자 문학 (작품): *a
social satire* 사회 풍자극[작품] **–
satirical** /sə'tɪrɪkəl/ adj **– satirically**
adv

sat·i·rist /'sætərɪst/ n someone who
writes SATIRE ‖ 풍자 문학 작품을 쓰는 사
람. 풍자가. 풍자 작가

sat·i·rize /'sætə,raɪz/ v [T] to use
SATIRE to make people see someone or
something's faults ‖ 사람이나 사물의 결
점을 사람들이 보도록 풍자를 이용하다.
…을 풍자하다. …을 비꼬다[비아냥거리
다]: *a movie satirizing the fashion
industry* 패션 산업을 풍자하는 영화

sat·is·fac·tion /,sætɪs'fækʃən/ n **1** [C,
U] a feeling of happiness or pleasure
because you have achieved something
or got what you wanted ‖ 무엇을 달성하
거나 원하는 것을 얻어서 행복하거나 기쁜
감정. 만족[충족](감): *He looked around
the room with satisfaction.* 그는 만족감
을 느끼며 그 방을 둘러보았다. / *Both
leaders expressed satisfaction with the
talks.* 양측 지도자들은 회담에 만족감을
표명했다. **2** [U] the act of filling a need,
demand, claim etc. ‖ 필요·요구·주장 등
을 채워 주기. 만족하기[시키기]. 실현.
달성: *the satisfaction of our spiritual
needs* 우리의 정신적 욕구의 충족 **3 to
sb's satisfaction** as well or completely
as someone wants ‖ 다른 사람이 원하는
만큼 충분하거나 완벽하게. 만족하게. 확
실하게: *I'm not sure I can answer that
question to your satisfaction.* 나는 네가
만족할 만큼 그 질문에 답을 할 수 있을
지 확실하지 않다.

sat·is·fac·to·ry /,sætɪs'fæktəri, -tri/
adj **1** good enough for a particular
situation or purpose ‖ 특정 상황이나 목
적에 충분히 좋은. 만족할 만한. 훌륭한:
The students are not making

satisfactory progress. 학생들은 만족할 만한 진척을 보이지 않고 있다. **2** making you feel pleased and happy ‖ 기쁘고 행복하게 만드는. 만족한. 흡족한: *a satisfactory result* 흡족한 결과 – **satisfactorily** *adv* —opposite UNSATISFACTORY, —compare SATISFYING

sat·is·fied /'sætɪsˌfaɪd/ *adj* **1** pleased because something has happened in the way that you want, or because you have achieved something ‖ 어떤 일이 원하는 대로 일어나서, 또는 어떤 일을 달성해서 기쁜. 만족한: *Most of our customers are satisfied with the food we provide.* 우리 고객들의 대다수는 우리가 제공하는 음식에 만족해 한다. **2** feeling sure that something is right or true ‖ 어떤 일이 옳거나 사실이라고 확신하는. 납득하는. 이해하는: *I'm satisfied (that) he's telling the truth.* 나는 그가 사실대로 말하고 있다고 확신한다. **3 satisfied?** SPOKEN said in order to ask if someone is pleased with what has happened, especially when you are not ‖ 특히 자신은 만족하지 않을 때 다른 사람에게 일어난 일에 대해 흡족한지를 묻는 데에 쓰여. 충분해[만족해]? (이제) 됐지?: *Okay, okay, I was wrong - satisfied?* 그래, 그래, 내가 잘못 됐다. (이제) 됐지? —opposite DISSATISFIED

sat·is·fy /'sætɪsˌfaɪ/ *v* [T] **1** to make someone happy by providing what s/he wants or needs ‖ 다른 사람이 원하거나 필요한 것을 제공해서 행복하게 해주다. …을 만족시키다. 충족시키다: *She doesn't feel she works hard enough to satisfy her boss.* 그녀는 사장을 만족시킬 만큼 열심히 일한다고 생각하지 않는다. **2** to provide someone with enough information to show that something is true or has been done correctly ‖ 어떤 일이 사실이거나 올바르게 실행됐다는 것을 보여주기 위해 다른 사람에게 충분한 정보를 제공하다. …을 이해[납득]시키다: *The evidence isn't enough to satisfy us that he's innocent.* 그 증거는 그가 결백하다는 것을 우리가 납득할 만큼 충분하지 않다. **3** FORMAL to be good enough for a particular purpose, standard etc. ‖ 특정 목적·기준 등에 충분할 만큼 좋다. …의 조건[요건]을 채우다[충족시키다]. …에 부응하다: *I'm afraid you haven't satisfied the college entrance requirements.* 너는 대학 입학 요건을 충족시키지 못하는 것 같다.

sat·is·fy·ing /'sætɪsˌfaɪ·ɪŋ/ *adj* **1** making you feel pleased and happy, especially because you have got what

you wanted ‖ 특히 원했던 것을 얻었기 때문에 기쁘고 행복하게 느끼게 하는. 만족[충족]시키는: *a satisfying career* 만족할 만한 경력 **2** food that is satisfying makes you feel that you have eaten enough ‖ 음식을 충분히 먹었다고 느끼게 하는. 만족스러운. 충분한: *a satisfying meal* 만족스러운[충분한] 음식 —opposite UNSATISFYING, —compare SATISFACTORY

sat·u·rate /'sætʃəˌreɪt/ *v* [T] **1** to make something completely wet ‖ 사물을 완전히 젖게 만들다. 물에 흠뻑 적시다. 물이 흠뻑 스며들게 하다: *The rain saturated the soil.* 비가 땅을 흠뻑 적셨다. **2** to make something very full of a particular type of thing ‖ 사물을 특정 종류의 것으로 가득 차게 하다. …으로 채우다. 넘치게 하다: *The market was saturated with too many exercise videos.* (비디오테이프) 시장은 너무 많은 운동 비디오테이프로 넘쳐났다. – **saturation** /ˌsætʃəˈreɪʃən/ *n* [U]

sat·u·rat·ed fat /ˌ.... '../ *n* [C, U] a type of fat from meat and milk products ‖ 고기와 유제품에서 나오는 지방 종류. 포화지방

Sat·ur·day /'sætɚdi, -ˌdeɪ/, *written abbreviation* **Sat.** *n* the seventh day of the week ‖ 주중의 일곱째 날. 토요일. —see usage note at SUNDAY

Sat·urn /'sætɚn/ *n* [singular] the second largest planet, sixth from the sun ‖ 태양에서 여섯째 자리의 두 번째로 큰 행성. 토성

sauce /sɔs/ *n* [C, U] a thick cooked liquid that is served with food to give it a particular taste ‖ 음식에 특별한 맛을 주기 위해 같이 제공되는 진한 조리된 액체. 소스: *spaghetti with tomato sauce* 토마토 소스를 곁들인 스파게티 (요리)

sauce·pan /'sɔsˌpæn/ *n* a deep round metal container with a handle, used for cooking ‖ 손잡이가 달리고 조리에 이용되는 깊고 둥근 금속제 용기. 스튜냄비 —see picture at PAN¹

sau·cer /'sɔsɚ/ *n* a small round plate that you put a cup on ‖ 컵을 올려놓는 작고 둥근 접시. 찻잔 받침 접시

sau·cy /'sɔsi/ *adj* slightly rude, in a way that is amusing ‖ 즐기는 식으로 약간 무례한. 건방진. 뻔뻔스러운: *a saucy look* 건방진 표정

sau·er·kraut /'saʊɚˌkraʊt/ *n* [U] a salty German food made of CABBAGE ‖ 양배추로 만들어진 짭짤한 독일식 식품. 양배추 절임

sau·na /'sɔnə/ *n* **1** a room that is filled

with steam to make it very hot, in which people sit because it is considered healthy ‖ 사람들이 건강에 좋다고 여겨 들어가 앉는 실내를 아주 뜨겁게 하는 증기로 채워진 방. 사우나 목욕탕[실] **2** a time when you sit or lie in a room like this ‖ 이러한 방에 앉거나 누워 있는 시간. 사우나 목욕: *It's nice to have a sauna after swimming.* 수영 후 사우나 목욕을 하는 것은 좋다.

saun·ter /'sɔntɚ, 'sɑn-/ *v* [I] to walk in a slow and confident way ‖ 천천히 자신 있게 걷다. 어슬렁어슬렁 돌아다니다. 어슬렁거리며 지나가다: *He sauntered up to her and grinned.* 그는 어슬렁거리며 그녀에게 다가가 씩 웃었다.

sau·sage /'sɔsɪdʒ/ *n* [C, U] a mixture of meat and SPICEs eaten hot or cold, often for breakfast ‖ 종종 아침 식사로 뜨겁거나 차게 해서 먹는 고기와 양념의 혼합물. 소시지. 순대

sau·té /sɔ'teɪ/ *v* [T] to cook something quickly in a little hot oil or fat ‖ 소량의 뜨거운 기름이나 지방질에 사물을 재빨리 조리하다. …을 살짝 데치다. 소테로 만들다(튀기다)

sav·age¹ /'sævɪdʒ/ *adj* **1** very cruel and violent ‖ 매우 사납고 난폭한. 포악[흉악]한. 잔인한: *savage fighting* 난폭한 싸움 **2** criticizing someone or something very severely ‖ 사람이나 사물을 매우 심하게 비난하는. 맹렬히 공격하는. 맹비난하는: *a savage attack on the newspaper industry* 신문 산업에 대한 맹렬한 비난 **3** very severe and harmful ‖ 매우 심하고 해로운. 가혹한. 난폭한: *savage measures to control the budget* 예산을 통제하기 위한 가혹한 수단 **4** OLD-FASHIONED ⇨ PRIMITIVE **– savagely** *adv*

sav·age² *n* OLD-FASHIONED an insulting word for someone from a country where the way of living seems simple and undeveloped ‖ 생활 방식이 단순하고 미개발된 것 같은 나라에서 온 사람에 대한 모욕적인 말. 야만[미개]인

savage³ *v* [T] **1** to attack someone violently, causing serious injuries ‖ 심한 부상을 입히면서 사람을 난폭하게 공격하다. 맹렬히[흉포하게] 공격하다. …을 짓밟다[유린하다]: *The boy was savaged by dogs.* 소년은 개에게 심하게 물렸다. **2** to criticize someone or something very severely ‖ 사람이나 사물을 극심하게 비난하다. 무차별하게[맹렬하게] 비난하다: *a movie savaged by the critics* 비평가들에게 맹비난 당한 영화

sav·age·ry /'sævɪdʒri/ *n* [C, U] extremely cruel and violent behavior ‖

극도로 잔인하고 난폭한 행위. 만행. 포악한 행위

save¹ /seɪv/ *v*

1 ▸FROM HARM/DANGER◂ 위해/위험으로부터 ◂ [T] to make someone or something safe from danger, harm, or destruction ‖ 사람이나 사물을 위험[위해, 파괴]으로부터 안전하게 하다. 구하다. 구조[구출]하다: *We are working to save the rain forest from destruction.* 우리는 열대 우림지가 파괴되지 않도록 지키기 위해 노력하고 있다. / *The new speed limit should save more lives.* 새로운 속도 제한 (규정)은 분명 더 많은 생명을 구할 것이다.

2 ▸MONEY◂ 돈 ◂ [I, T] also **save up** to keep money so that you can use it later ‖ 나중에 사용할 수 있게 돈을 보관하다. 저축하다. 모으다: *I'm saving up to buy a car.* 나는 차를 사기 위해 저축하고 있다. / *Brian's saved $6000 to put toward a new house.* 브라이언은 새 집에 돈을 쏟아 넣기 위해 6천 달러를 모았다.

3 ▸NOT WASTE◂ 낭비하지 않다 ◂ [T] to use less time, money, energy etc. so that you do not waste any ‖ 시간·돈·에너지 등을 적게 사용해서 조금도 낭비하지 않다. 아껴 쓰다. 절약하다: *We'll save time if we take a cab.* 우리가 택시를 타면 시간을 아낄 것이다.

4 ▸TO USE LATER◂ 나중에 사용하다 ◂ [T] to keep something so that you can use or enjoy it in the future ‖ 장래에 쓰거나 즐길 수 있게 어떤 것을 보존하다. 아껴두다. 보관하다. …을 챙겨[확보해] 두다. 간직해 두다: *Let's save the rest of the pie for later.* 나중을 위해 나머지 파이는 보관해 두자.

5 ▸HELP TO AVOID◂ 회피하도록 돕다 ◂ [T] to help someone by making it unnecessary for him/her to do something unpleasant or difficult ‖ 다른 사람을 도와 불유쾌하거나 어려운 일을 할 필요가 없게 하다. …하는 수고[절차]를 덜어주다. …을 면하게[생략하게] 해주다: *If you could pick up the medicine, it would save me a trip to the pharmacy.* 네가 약을 사 줄 수 있다면 내가 약국에 가는 수고를 덜 텐데.

6 ▸COLLECT◂ 수집하다 ◂ [T] also **save sth ▸ up** to keep all the objects of a particular kind that you can find, so that they can be used for a special purpose ‖ 찾아낼 수 있는 특정 종류의 모든 대상물들을 보관해서 특별한 목적에 쓰일 수 있게 하다. …을 모아 두다. …을 수집하다: *She's saving foreign coins for her son's collection.* 그녀는 아들의 수집

을 (돕기)위해 외국 동전들을 모아두고 있다.

7 ▶**KEEP FOR SB** …대신 지켜주다◀ [T] to stop people from using something so that it is available for someone else ‖ 다른 사람이 이용할 수 있도록 사람들이 그것을 쓰지 못하게 막다. …을 지켜주다[확보해 주다]. 대신 보관[보유]해 주다: *We'll save you a seat in the theater.* 우리가 극장에서 네 자리를 맡아 줄게.

8 ▶**COMPUTER** 컴퓨터◀ [I, T] to make a computer keep the work that you have done on it ‖ 컴퓨터상에서 한 일을 컴퓨터에 보관하게 하다. (데이터를) 저장하다 [시 키 다] —see also **save your breath/don't waste your breath** (BREATH), **lose/save face** (FACE¹)

save on sth *phr v* [T] to avoid wasting something by using as little as possible of it ‖ 가능한 한 적은 양을 사용해서 사물이 낭비되는 것을 피하다. 절약하다. 아껴 쓰다: *We turn the heat off at night to save on electricity.* 우리는 전기를 절약하기 위해 밤에는 난방 장치를 끈다.

save² *n* an action by the GOALKEEPER in SOCCER, HOCKEY etc. that prevents the other team from getting a point ‖ 축구·하키 등에서 다른 팀이 점수를 내는 것을 막는 골키퍼의 활동. 득점 저지 (활동)

sav·er /'seɪvɚ/ *n* **1** -**saver** something that prevents loss or waste ‖ 손실이나 낭비를 막는 것. 절약하는 것[장치]: *time-savers like instant food and microwave cooking* 인스턴트 식품이나 전자렌지 요리 같은 시간을 절약해 주는 것 **2** someone who saves money in a bank ‖ 은행에 돈을 저축하는 사람. 저축가. 절약가

sav·ing grace /ˌ.. './ *n* a good or acceptable quality that makes something not completely bad ‖ 어떤 것을 철저히 나쁘게 만들지 않는 좋거나 인정할 만한 특성. 장점. 벌충하는 특성[특징]: *The movie's only saving grace is its beautiful scenery.* 그 영화의 유일한 장점은 아름다운 배경 화면이다.

sav·ings /'seɪvɪŋz/ *n* **1** [plural] all the money that you have saved, especially in a bank ‖ 특히 은행에 저축한 모든 돈. 저축(금). 저금 **2** [singular] an amount of something that you have not used or do not have to spend ‖ 사용하지 않았거나 소비할 필요가 없는 사물의 양. 절약 [절감]된 것: *Enjoy 25% savings on our regular prices.* 정상 가격의 25% 절약 혜택을 누리세요.

savings ac·count /'.. ˌ./ *n* a bank account that pays INTEREST on the money you have in it ‖ 예치한 돈에 이자

를 지불해 주는 은행 계좌. 보통 예금 계좌

savings and loan /ˌ.. . './ *n* a business similar to a bank where you can save money, and that also lends money for things such as houses ‖ 예금이 가능하고 주택 등을 위해 돈을 대출할 수도 있는 은행과 유사한 사업. 저축 대출 (사)업

savings bank /'.. ./ *n* a bank whose business is mostly from SAVINGS ACCOUNTS and from LOANS for houses ‖ 영업의 대부분이 보통 예금 계좌와 주택 자금 대출로 이뤄지는 은행. 저축은행

sav·ior /'seɪvjɚ/ *n* **1** someone or something that saves you from a difficult or dangerous situation ‖ 어렵거나 위험한 상황에서 자신을 구해주는 사람이나 사물. 구제자. 구원자 **2 the/our Savior** another name for Jesus Christ, used in the Christian religion ‖ 기독교에서 쓰이는 예수 그리스도의 또 다른 이름. 구세주. 하느님

sa·vor /'seɪvɚ/ *v* [T] to make an activity or experience last as long as you can, because you are enjoying every moment of it ‖ 매순간을 즐기고 있기 때문에 활동이나 경험을 할 수 있는 만큼 오랫동안 지속시키다. 천천히 맛보며 즐기다. 음미하다: *Drink it slowly and savor every drop.* 천천히 마시고 한 방울 한 방울 음미하세요.

sa·vor·y /'seɪvəri/ *adj* having a pleasant smell or taste, especially one that is related to salty foods ‖ 특히 소금기 있는 음식이, 기분 좋은 향과 맛을 가진. 맛있는. 풍미 있는. 맛이 당기는: *a savory aroma* 식욕을 돋우는 맛있는 냄새 —see also UNSAVORY

sav·vy /'sævi/ *n* [U] INFORMAL practical knowledge and ability ‖ 실제적인 지식과 능력. 실용 지식. 경험상의 지식: *marketing savvy* 마케팅 지식 – **savvy** *adj*: *a savvy businesswoman* 경험 많은 여성 사업가

saw¹ /sɔ/ *v* the past tense of SEE ‖ see의 과거형

saw² *n* a tool that has a flat blade with a row of sharp points, used for cutting wood ‖ 한 줄로 된 날카로운 끝이 달린 납작한 날이 있어 나무를 자르는 데 쓰이는 연장. 톱(이 부착된 연장)

saw³ *v* **sawed, sawn** *or* **sawed, sawing** [I, T] to cut something using a SAW ‖ 톱을 이용해서 사물을 자르다. …을 톱으로 켜다[자르다]: *We decided to saw off the lower branches of the apple tree.* 우리는 사과나무의 아래쪽 가지를 잘라내

기로 결정했다.

saw·dust /'sɔːdʌst/ n [U] very small pieces of wood that are left when you cut wood with a SAW ‖ 톱으로 나무를 자를 때 남게 되는 나무의 매우 작은 조각들. 톱밥

saw·mill /'sɔːmɪl/ n [U] a factory where trees are cut into boards ‖ 통나무를 잘라서 널빤지를 만드는 공장. 제재소

sawn /sɔːn/ v the PAST PARTICIPLE of SAW ‖ saw의 과거 분사형

sax /sæks/ n INFORMAL ⇨ SAXOPHONE

sax·o·phone /'sæksəˌfoʊn/ n a metal musical instrument that you play by blowing into it and pressing special buttons, used especially in JAZZ and dance music ‖ 바람을 불어 넣으며 특수 버튼[키]을 누르면서 연주하는, 특히 재즈나 댄스 음악에서 쓰이는 금관악기. 색소폰

say¹ /seɪ/ v **said, said, saying,** *third person singular, present tense* **says** ‖ 3인칭 단수 현재형은 says

1 ▶SPEAK 말하다◀ [T] to speak words ‖ 말을 하다. …이라고[…을] 말하다. 소리를 입 밖에 내다: *He said he'd call back.* 그는 다시 전화하겠다고 말했다. / *Tell her I said hi.* 내가 안부 전하더라고 그녀에게 전해줘. / *Say bye-bye, Melissa.* 멜리사, 안녕하고 인사해라.

2 ▶EXPRESS STH …을 표현하다◀ [I, T] to express a thought, feeling, opinion etc. in words ‖ 생각·감정·의견 등을 말로 표현하다. 표명하다. 나타내어 말하다: *He didn't seem to understand what I said.* 그는 내가 말한 것을 이해하지 못했던 것 같다. / *Did she say what time to come?* 그녀는 몇 시에 오겠다고 말했니? / *The doctor says (that) I can't go home yet.* 의사는 내가 아직 집에 갈 수 없다고 말한다. / *That's a pretty mean thing to say.* 그런 말을 하는 것은 아주 못된 짓이다. / *Every time I want to cook, Mom says no.* (=refuses to let me) 내가 요리하고 싶을 때마다 어머니가 안 된다고 하신다.

3 ▶WITHOUT WORDS 말없이◀ [I, T] to express something without using words ‖ 말을 하지 않고 무엇을 나타내다. 표현[표시]하다. …이라고 전달하다: *Her smile says it all.* (=her smile expresses her happiness) 그녀의 웃음이 모든 것을 말해준다. / *What is Hopper trying to say in this painting?* 호퍼가 이 그림에서 표현하고자 하는 것이 무엇입니까?

4 ▶GIVE INFORMATION 정보를 주다◀ [T] to give information in writing, pictures, or numbers ‖ 문장[그림, 숫자]으로 정보를 주다. 가리키다. …뜻을 나타

내다[지시하다]: *The clock said quarter after six.* 시계가 6시 15분을 가리켰다. / *What do the instructions say?* 설명서에 뭐라고 써 있지?

5 to say the least used when what you have said could have been stated much more strongly ‖ 말한 것이 훨씬 더 강하게 언급된 것일 수도 있을 때 쓰여. 최소한도로 말해서. 줄잡아 말해도: *The house needs work, to say the least.* 최소한도로 말해도 이 집은 공사가 필요하다.

6 go without saying used when what you have said or written is so clear that it really did not need to be stated ‖ 말하거나 글로 썼던 것이 너무 명백해서 실제 언급될 필요가 없을 때 쓰여. …은 말할 나위[필요]도 없다: *It goes without saying that the taxpayers will be outraged.* 납세자들이 격분하리라는 것은 말할 나위도 없다.

7 that is to say used before describing what you mean in more detail or more clearly ‖ 의미하는 바를 더욱 자세하게 또는 더 명백하게 기술하기 전에 쓰여. 바꾸어 말하면. 즉. 말하자면: *Things still aren't equal. That is to say, women still are not paid as much as men.* 세상살이가 아직도 공평치 않다. 즉 말하자면 여성들이 여전히 남자만큼 많은 보수를 받지 못하고 있다.

8 having said that used before saying something that makes the opinion you have given seem less strong ‖ 제시한 의견이 덜 강하게 보이게 하는 어떤 말 앞에 쓰여. …임에도 불구하고. …이라고 말했지만: *The movie is sloppily made, but having said that, it's still a cute picture to take the kids to.* 그 영화는 적당히 만들어졌지만 그럼에도 불구하고 여전히 아이들을 데려가서 볼 만한 재미있는 영화이다.

SPOKEN PHRASES

9 be saying used in phrases to emphasize that you are trying to explain what you mean in a way that someone will understand better ‖ 자신이 의미하는 바를 다른 사람이 더 잘 이해할 수 있게 설명하고자 함을 강조하는 데에 쓰여. 그저 …을 말하려고 한다[말하고 있다]: *All I'm saying is that he should have been more careful.* (=used when you do not want someone to be angry about what you have said) 내가 말하려 하는 것은 그저 그가 좀 더 조심했어야 했다는 것이다. / *I'm not saying this is more important, I'm just saying that I'm* *more interested in it.* 내 말은 이것이 더 중요하다는 것이 아니라, 다만 그것 에 더 관심이 있다는 말이다. / *Well, you're not really being fair, (do you) see what I'm saying?* (=do you understand me?) 저기, 사실 당신은 공 평하지 않군요. 제 말뜻 아시겠어요?

10 say to yourself to think something ‖ 무엇을 생각하다. 마음속으 로 생각하다: *I was worried about it, but I said to myself, "You can do this."* 나는 그것이 걱정됐지만 "너는 이 것을 할 수 있어"라고 마음속으로 생각 했다.

11 [T] to suggest or suppose something ‖ 무엇을 제시하거나 가정하 다. 말해 보다. 말하자면: *Meet me at, let's say, 7 o'clock.* 글쎄, 나와 7시에 만나기로 하자. / *Say you were going to an interview. What would you wear?* 네가 면접시험에 간다고 가정해 보자. 너는 무엇을 입을 거니?

12 say when used when you want someone to tell you when you have given him/her the correct amount of something, especially a drink ‖ 특히 마실 것을 남에게 따를 때, 적당한 양을 받았을 때의 순간을 말해 주기를 원할 때 쓰여. 됐으면 얘기해요

13 Say what? said when you have not heard something that someone said, or when you cannot believe that something is true ‖ 다른 사람이 말한 것을 듣지 못했을 때, 또는 어떤 일이 사실이라는 것을 믿을 수 없을 때 쓰여. 뭐라고 (했지)? 정말로 (그렇게 말했 어)?

USAGE NOTE say, tell, speak, and **talk**

Say and **tell** are always followed by objects. **Tell** can be followed by a DIRECT OBJECT or an INDIRECT OBJECT: *Keith is good at telling stories. / Could you tell me how to get to the library?* **Say** is never used with an indirect object: *She won't say anything. / Dad said "no."* ✗DON'T SAY "Dad said me 'no.'"✗ **Say** can be followed by CLAUSES beginning with "that": *He said that he saw Marcia yesterday.* **Tell** can also be used in this way, but only with an indirect object: *He told me that he saw Marcia yesterday.* You can also use **tell** to give orders or to talk about giving orders: *Tell Jan to come home right*

now! / She told us to sit down. Both **speak** and **talk** are used in situations in which one person is talking, but **speak** is more formal: *He spoke for an hour about the economy. / He talked for hours about his girlfriend.* You can also use **talk** to show that two people are having a conversation: *Ron was talking to Helen in the corner.* Use **speak** to ask politely for someone on the telephone: *Hello, may I speak to Sandra Wright, please?*

say와 **tell**은 언제나 목적어를 수반한 다. tell은 직접 또는 간접 목적어를 수 반할 수 있다: 키이쓰는 이야기를 재미 있게 한다. / 도서관에 가는 길을 가르 쳐 주시겠습니까? **say**는 절대 간접 목 적어와 같이 쓰이지 않는다: 그녀는 아 무것도 말하지 않을 것이다. / 아빠는 "안돼"라고 말했다. "Dad said me 'no'." 라고는 하지 않는다. **say**는 "that"으로 시작하는 절을 수반할 수 있다: 그는 어제 마샤를 보았다고 말했 다. **tell**도 역시 이렇게 쓸 수 있지만, 오직 간접 목적어와 함께 쓴다: 그는 내 게 어제 마샤를 봤다고 말했다. **tell**은 또 명령을 내릴 때 또는 명령을 내리는 것에 대해 말할 때 쓸 수 있다: 잰에게 지금 당장 집에 오라고 말해라! / 그녀는 우리에게 앉으라고 말했다. **speak**와 **talk**는 둘 다 한 사람이 말하는 상황에 서 쓰이지만 **speak**는 보다 격식적이 다: 그는 경제에 대해 한 시간 동안 연 설했다. / 그는 여러 시간 동안 자기 여 자 친구에 대해 말했다. **talk**는 또한 두 사람이 대화를 하고 있음을 나타내는 데 쓴다: 론은 구석에서 헬렌에게 이야기하 고 있었다. **speak**는 전화상으로 다른 사람을 바꿔주기를 정중히 요청할 때 쓴 다: 여보세요, 산드라 라이트 씨 좀 바꿔 주시겠어요?

say² n [singular, U] **1** the right to help decide something ‖ 어떤 것을 결정하는 것을 돕는 권리. 결정권: *Members felt that they had had no say in the proposed changes.* 회원들은 제안된 변경 과정에서 결정권이 없었다고 생각했다. / *Who has the final say?* 누가 최종 결정권 을 가지고 있습니까? **2 have your/their say** to give your opinion on something ‖ 무엇에 대한 의견[견해]을 제시하다. 너의 /그들의 발언권을 갖다[하고 싶은 말을 하다]: *You'll all have the chance to have your say.* 너희들 모두 하고 싶은 말을 할 기회를 가질 것이다.

say·ing /ˈseɪ-ɪŋ/ *n* a well-known

statement that expresses an idea most people believe is true and wise; PROVERB ‖ 대다수 사람들이 진실이며 현명하다고 믿는 생각을 표현하는 유명한 말. 속담. 격언. 경구. 명언; ㋐ proverb

SC the written abbreviation of South Carolina ‖ South Carolina(사우스캐롤라이나 주)의 약자

scab /skæb/ *n* **1** a hard layer of dried blood that forms over a cut or wound ‖ 베인 데나 상처난 데 위에 생긴 말라붙은 피의 굳은 층. (피)딱지 **2** INFORMAL an insulting word for someone who works in a place where other people refuse to work because they are on STRIKE ‖ 다른 사람들이 파업 중이어서 작업하기를 거부한 곳에서 작업하는 사람들에게 하는 모욕적인 말. 파업 방해자. 파업 비참가자

scads /skædz/ *n* [plural] INFORMAL large numbers or quantities of something ‖ 사물의 많은 숫자나 양. 다수. 다량: *scads of money* 떼돈

scaf·fold /'skæfəld, -foʊld/ *n* **1** a structure built next to a building or high wall, for people to stand on while they work on the building or wall ‖ 건물이나 높은 담장에 붙여 지어져 사람들이 건물이나 담에서 일을 하는 동안 서 있을 수 있게 한 구조물. 비계 **2** a structure used in past times for killing criminals by hanging them from it ‖ 과거에 죄수들을 목매달아 처형하는 데 쓰였던 구조물. 처형대. 교수대

scaf·fold·ing /'skæfəldɪŋ/ *n* [U] poles and boards that are built into a structure for people to stand on when they are working on a high wall or the outside of a building ‖ 사람들이 높은 담이나 건물 외부에서 일할 때 서 있을 수 있는 구조물로 지어진 기둥과 판자. 비계. 발판

scald /skɔld/ *v* [T] to burn yourself with hot liquid or steam ‖ 뜨거운 액체나 증기로 화상을 입다. 데게 하다. 열상을 입히다: *Ow! That coffee scalded my tongue.* 억! 저 커피에 혀가 데었어. –**scald** *n*

scald·ing /'skɔldɪŋ/ *adj, adv* extremely hot ‖ 극히 뜨거운. 델 정도로 뜨거운. 펄펄 끓는: *scalding hot water* 펄펄 끓는 물

scale¹ /skeɪl/ *n*
1 ▶SIZE 크기◀ [singular, U] the size or level of something, when compared to what is normal ‖ 통상적인 것에 비했을 때의 사물의 크기나 수준. 규모. 정도. 스케일: *a large/small scale project* 대/소규모 프로젝트 / *They built their new house on a grand scale.* (=it is very big) 그들

은 새 집을 대규모로 지었다.
2 ▶MEASURING SYSTEM 측정 체계◀ [C usually singular] a system for measuring the force, speed, amount etc. of something, or for comparing it with something else ‖ 사물의 힘·속도·크기 등을 측정하거나 그것을 다른 것과 비교하는 체계. 척도. 기준. 등급: *a company's pay scale* 회사의 급여 체계 / *On a scale from 1 to 10, I'd give it an 8.* 1부터 10까지의 기준으로, 나는 그것에 8(점)을 주겠어.
3 ▶FOR WEIGHING 중량 측정용◀ [C usually plural] a machine or piece of equipment for weighing people or objects ‖ 사람이나 사물의 중량을 재는 기계나 장비류. 저울. 천칭[저울](의 접시): *Here, put the bag of apples on the scales.* 여기 사과가 든 자루를 저울에 올려 놓으세요.
4 ▶MEASURING MARKS 측정 눈금◀ a set of marks with regular spaces between them on an instrument that is used for measuring ‖ 측정용 기구 위에 서로 일정한 간격으로 된 일련의 표시. 저울눈. 자: *a ruler with a metric scale* 미터법 눈금이 새겨진 자
5 ▶MAP/DRAWING 지도/제도◀ [C, U] the relationship between the size of a map, drawing, or model and the actual size of the place or thing that it represents ‖ 지도[제도, 모형]의 크기와 그것이 나타내는 장소나 사물의 실제 크기 사이의 관계. (축소) 비율. 축척. 비례 (척): *a scale of 1 inch to the mile* 마일당 1인치의 비율
6 ▶MUSIC 음악◀ a series of musical notes that have a fixed order and become gradually higher or lower in PITCH ‖ 고정된 순서를 가지고 음높이가 점차 높아지거나 낮아지는 일련의 음표들. 음계(音階)
7 ▶ON FISH 물고기에◀ [C usually plural] one of the small flat pieces of hard skin that cover the bodies of fish, snakes etc. ‖ 물고기·뱀 등의 신체를 덮는 작고 납작하며 단단한 피부 조각들의 하나. 비늘

scale² *v* [T] **1** to climb to the top of something that is high ‖ 높은 사물의 꼭대기에 올라가다. 기어오르다. …에 이르다: *scaling a 40-foot wall* 40피트짜리 벽을 오르기 **2** to remove the SCALES from a fish ‖ 물고기에서 비늘을 제거하다. 벗기다

scale sth ↔ **back/down** *phr v* [T] to reduce the size of something such as an organization or plan ‖ 조직이나 계획 등

어떤 것의 크기를 줄이다. …의 규모를 축소하다: *The factory managers have made a decision to scale back production*. 공장 관리자들은 생산 규모를 축소하기로 결정했다.

scal·lop /'skæləp, 'skɑləp/ *n* [C, U] a small sea animal that has a hard flat shell, or the meat from this animal ‖ 단단하고 납작한 껍질을 가진 작은 바다 동물, 또는 이 동물의 고기. 큰가리비 (조개의 일종)

scal·loped /'skæləpt, 'skɑ-/ *adj* cloth or objects that have scalloped edges are cut in a series of small curves as a decoration ‖ 천이나 물체의 가장자리가 일련의 작은 곡선 모양으로 잘려 장식된. 물결 모양의 테를 두른[장식한]

scalp¹ /skælp/ *n* the skin on the top of your head, where your hair grows ‖ 머리카락이 자라는 머리 상부의 피부. 머리 가죽

scalp² *v* [T] **1** INFORMAL to buy tickets for an event and sell them again at a much higher price ‖ 행사용 표를 사서 훨씬 더 높은 가격에 다시 되팔다. 전매하다. 프리미엄을 붙여 팔다. 암표를 판매하다 **2** to cut off a dead enemy's SCALP as a sign of victory ‖ 승리의 표시로 죽은 적의 머리 가죽을 잘라내다. …의 머리가죽을 벗기다

scal·pel /'skælpəl/ *n* a small and very sharp knife used by doctors during operations ‖ 수술 중에 의사가 사용하는 작고 매우 날카로운 칼. 외과[해부]용 메스

scal·y /'skeɪli/ *adj* **1** an animal that is scaly is covered with small flat pieces of hard skin ‖ 동물이 단단하고 작고 납작한 피부 조각으로 덮인. 비늘에 덮인. 비늘 모양의 **2** scaly skin is dry and rough ‖ 피부가 건조하고 거친. 비늘처럼 거친[벗겨지는]

scam /skæm/ *n* SLANG a dishonest plan, usually to get money ‖ 보통 돈을 빼앗기 위한 부정직한 계획. (신용) 사기. 편취

scam·per /'skæmpɚ/ *v* [I] to run with short quick steps, like a child or small animal ‖ 어린아이나 작은 동물처럼 짧고 빠른 걸음으로 달리다. 허둥지둥 도망치다. 종종걸음으로 달려가다: *A mouse scampered into its hole.* 생쥐가 쥐구멍으로 허둥지둥 도망쳐 들어갔다.

scan /skæn/ *v* **-nned, -nning 1** [I, T] also **scan through** to read something quickly in order to understand its main meaning or to find a particular piece of information ‖ 주요 의미를 이해하거나 특정한 정보를 찾기 위해 빠르게 어떤 것을 읽다. …을 대충 보다. 훑어보다: *I had a chance to scan through the report on the plane.* 나는 비행기 안에서 보고서를 훑어볼 기회가 있었다. **2** [T] to examine an area carefully, because you are looking for a particular person or thing ‖ 특정 사람이나 사물을 찾고 있기 때문에 한 구역을 주의 깊게 조사[검사]하다. …을 자세히[꼼꼼히] 살피다. …을 눈여겨보다: *Lookouts were scanning the sky for enemy planes.* 감시원들이 적기를 찾아 하늘을 샅샅이 살피고 있었다. **3** [T] if a machine scans an object or a part of your body, it produces a picture of what is inside ‖ 물체나 인체 부위의 내부 그림을 기계가 출력해 내다. 정밀 조사하다[해서 내부를 비추다]: *All luggage has to be scanned at the airport.* 모든 수하물들은 공항에서 검색되어야 한다. **4** if a piece of computer equipment scans an image, it copies it from paper onto the computer ‖ 컴퓨터 장비류가 종이에 있는 영상을 컴퓨터에 복사하다. 스캔하다. 주사(走査)하다 – **scan** *n* —see also SCANNER

scan·dal /'skændl/ *n* [C, U] something that has happened that people think is immoral or shocking ‖ 사람들이 비도덕적이거나 충격적으로 생각하는 일어난 일. 추문. 스캔들. 의혹[수치] 사건: *a scandal involving several important politicians* 몇몇 중요 정치인들이 관련된 추문 / *Reporters are always looking for scandal and gossip.* 기자들은 항상 스캔들과 가십거리를 찾고 있다.

scan·dal·ize /'skændl,aɪz/ *v* [T] to do something that shocks people very much ‖ 사람들에게 크게 충격적인 어떤 일을 하다. 남을 분개시키다. 아연실색케 하다: *a crime that has scandalized the entire city* 시 전체를 충격으로 몰아넣은 범죄

scan·dal·ous /'skændl-əs/ *adj* completely immoral and shocking ‖ 철저히 비도덕적이고 충격적인. 수치스러운. 창피한. 지독한: *scandalous behavior* 수치스러운 행동

scan·ner /'skænɚ/ *n* TECHNICAL **1** a machine that passes a BEAM of ELECTRONs over an object or a part of your body in order to produce a picture of what is inside ‖ 물체 내부의 영상을 생성하기 위해 대상 물체나 신체 부위 위로 전자 광선을 통과시키는 기계. 스캐너. 주사기 **2** a piece of computer equipment that copies an image from paper onto the computer ‖ 종이에 있는 영상을 컴퓨터에 복사하는 컴퓨터 장비류. 스캐너

scant /skænt/ *adj* not enough ‖ 충분치

않은. 빠듯한. 빈약한. 한정된. 얼마 안 되는: *After two weeks, they had made scant progress.* 2주일이 지났지만 그들은 거의 진척을 보지 못했다.

scant·y /'skænti/ *adj* not big enough for a particular purpose ‖ 특정 목적에 충분할 만큼 크지 않은. 불충분한. 변변치 않은. 거의 없는. 적은: *a scanty bikini* 겨우 가리는 비키니 - **scantily** *adv*: *scantily dressed* 아슬아슬하게 옷을 입은

scape·goat /'skeɪpgoʊt/ *n* someone who is blamed for something bad that happens, even if it is not his/her fault ‖ 발생한 나쁜 일이 자신의 잘못이 아님에도 비난당하는 사람. 희생양. 속죄양 - **scapegoat** *v* [T]

scar¹ /skɑr/ *n* 1 a permanent mark on your skin from a cut or wound ‖ 베이거나 다쳐서 피부에 남은 영구적 자국. 상처. 흉터 2 a permanent emotional or mental problem caused by a bad experience ‖ 나쁜 경험에서 초래된 영구적인 감정이나 정신상의 문제. 마음의 상처

scar² *v* **-rred, -rring** [T] 1 to have or be given a permanent mark on your skin from a cut or wound ‖ 베이거나 다쳐서 피부에 영구적 흔적을 가진 또는 주어진. …에 자국[흉터]을 남기다[얻다]: *The fire had left him scarred for life.* 그는 화재로 인해 일생 동안 남을 흉터를 입었다. 2 to have or be given permanent emotional or mental problems because of a bad experience ‖ 나쁜 경험으로 감정적 또는 정신적으로 영구적인 문제를 갖거나 문제가 주어지다. 평생 가는 마음의 상처가 생기다[를 받다]: *Rob's parents' divorce left him emotionally scarred.* 로브의 부모의 이혼은 그에게 정서적으로 평생 남는 상처를 냈다.

scarce /skɛrs/ *adj* if food, clothing, water etc. is scarce, there is not enough of it available ‖ 음식·옷·물 등이 쓸 수 있을 만큼 충분치 않은. 모자라는. 불충분한 —see usage note at RARE

scarce·ly /'skɛrsli/ *adv* 1 almost not at all, or almost none at all ‖ 거의 무엇하지 않는, 또는 거의 아무도 없는. 겨우. 가까스로: *Their teaching methods have scarcely changed in the last 10 years.* 그들의 교수법은 지난 10년간 거의 변하지 않았다. 2 definitely not, or almost certainly not ‖ 명확히 아닌, 또는 거의 확실히 아닌. 아마[절대] …아닌: *Owen is really angry, and you can scarcely blame him.* 오웬이 진짜 화가 나 있어서 너는 아마 그를 비난할 수 없을 것이다.

scar·ci·ty /'skɛrsəti/ *n* [C, U] a situation in which there is not enough of something ‖ 사물이 충분치 않은 상황. 부족. 결핍: *a scarcity of quality child care* 빈약한 아동 보호 (프로그램)

scare¹ /skɛr/ *v* INFORMAL 1 [I, T] to become frightened, or to make someone feel frightened ‖ 겁이 나다, 또는 다른 사람을 겁먹게 하다. 겁주다. 겁을 (집어) 먹다[두려워하다]: *Walter scares easily.* 월터는 쉽게 겁을 먹는다. / *Don't do that! You scared me to death/scared the hell out of me!* (=scared me very much) 그렇게 하지 마! 놀라서 죽을 뻔 했어! 2 **scare sb into doing sth** to make someone do something by frightening or threatening him/her ‖ 사람에게 겁을 주거나 위협해서 어떤 일을 하게 하다. 겁을 주어 …한 상태로[하게] 만들다: *Maybe we can scare the kids into behaving till their mom comes back.* 아이들 어머니가 돌아올 때까지 아이들에게 겁을 주어 얌전히 행동하게 만들 수도 있겠다.

scare sb/sth ↔ off/away *phr v* [T] 1 to make someone or something go away by frightening him, her, or it ‖ 사람 또는 사물을 겁을 주어 가버리게 하다. 위협해서 쫓아 버리다: *We lit fires to scare away the wild animals.* 우리는 야생 동물들을 위협해서 쫓아내기 위해 불을 피웠다. 2 to make someone uncertain or nervous so that s/he does not do something s/he was going to do ‖ 다른 사람이 하려고 하는 것을 하지 못하도록 불확실하게 또는 긴장하게 만들다. 겁이 나서 …하지 못하게 하다[멀리하게 하다]: *I'd like to call him, but I don't want to scare him off.* 나는 그를 부르고 싶지만 그를 겁먹게 해서 가버리게 만들고 싶지 않다.

scare sth ↔ up *phr v* [T] SPOKEN to make something although you have very few things to make it from ‖ 비록 만들어 낼 자원이 거의 없지만 무엇을 만들다. 만들어내다[얻다]. 마련하다: *I'll try to scare up some breakfast.* 내가 아침 식사를 약간 마련해 보겠다.

scare² *n* 1 [singular] a sudden feeling of fear ‖ 갑작스런 두려운 느낌. 공포. 불안: *What a scare you gave me!* 네가 얼마나 날 놀래켰는지! 2 a situation in which a group of people become frightened about something ‖ 일단의 사람들이 어떤 것에 대해 겁을 내게 된 상태. 공황 (상태). 공포 시기: *a bomb scare* 폭탄의 위협(에 대한 공포심)

scare·crow /'skɛrkroʊ/ *n* an object made to look like a person, that a farmer puts in a field to frighten birds ‖ 농부가 새를 쫓기 위해 들판에 세워 두는,

사람처럼 보이게 만든 물체. 허수아비

scared /skɛrd/ adj INFORMAL frightened by something or nervous about something; afraid ‖ 어떤 것에 의해 겁이 난, 또는 어떤 것에 대해 겁을 먹은; 두려워하는. 무서워하는: *We were scared (that) something terrible might happen.* 우리는 끔찍한 일이 일어날까봐 두려웠다. / *I'm scared of flying.* 나는 비행기 타는 것이 무섭다. / *Steve heard some noise, and he was scared stiff/scared to death.* (=extremely frightened) 스티브는 뭔가 소리를 들었고 겁이 나서 몸이 굳어졌다[죽을 정도로 무서워졌다].

scarf¹ /skɑrf/ n, plural **scarves** or **scarfs** a piece of material that you wear around your neck, head, or shoulders to keep warm or to look attractive ‖ 보온하기 위해 또는 매력적으로 보이기 위해 목[머리, 어깨] 주변에 두르는 섬유 조각. 스카프. 목도리

scarf² v [I, T] SLANG

scarf sth ↔ **down/up** phr v [T] to eat something very quickly ‖ 무엇을 매우 빨리 먹다. 게걸스럽게[요란하게] 먹다

scar·let /ˈskɑrlɪt/ n [U] a very bright red color ‖ 매우 밝은 빨간색. 주홍[진홍]색 – **scarlet** adj

scarves /skɑrvz/ n the plural of SCARF ‖ scarf의 복수형

scar·y /ˈskɛri/ adj INFORMAL frightening ‖ 겁나게 하는. 무서운. 무시무시한: *a scary movie* 공포 영화

scat /skæt/ interjection said in order to tell a small animal to go away ‖ 작은 동물에게 사라지라고 말하는 데에 쓰여. 저리가: *Go on, cat! Scat!* 어서, 고양이야! 저리가!

scath·ing /ˈskeɪðɪŋ/ adj scathing remarks, COMMENTs etc. criticize someone or something very severely ‖ 발언·언급 등이 사람이나 사물을 매우 심하게 비난하는. 용서 없는. 통렬한

scat·ter /ˈskætɚ/ v 1 [I, T] to move or be made to move in many different directions ‖ 여러 다른 방향으로 움직이거나 움직이게 하다. …이 사방으로 흩어지다[흩어지게 하다]. 분산하다[시키다]: *He pulled out a gun and the crowd scattered.* 그가 총을 빼들었고 군중들은 사방으로 흩어졌다. 2 [T] to throw or drop a lot of things over a wide area ‖ 넓은 지역 위로 많은 것들을 내던지거나 또는 떨어뜨리다. …을 뿌리다. 흩뜨리다: *Clothes had been scattered across the floor.* 옷들이 바닥 여기저기에 흩어져 있었다.

scat·ter·brained /ˈskætɚˌbreɪnd/ adj

INFORMAL tending to forget or lose things because you do not think in an organized way ‖ 체계적으로 생각하지 않기 때문에 사물을 잊거나 잃어버리는 경향이 있는. 주의가 산만한. 침착하지 못한

scav·enge /ˈskævɪndʒ/ v [I, T] to search for things to eat or use among unwanted food or objects ‖ 버려진 음식이나 물건 속에서 먹거나 사용할 만한 것들을 찾아내다. 쓰레기더미를 뒤지다: *wild dogs scavenging for food* 음식을 찾아 쓰레기를 뒤지는 들개들 – **scavenger** n

sce·nar·i·o /sɪˈnɛriˌoʊ, -ˈnær-/ n 1 a situation that could possibly happen but has not happened yet ‖ 필시 일어날 수도 있지만 아직 일어나지 않은 상황. 예상된 전개. 예정된 계획. 시나리오: *Even in the worst-case scenario* (=if the worst possible thing happens), *we'll still get the money back.* 최악의 상황이 일어난다고 해도 우리는 여전히 돈을 돌려받을 것이다. 2 a description of the story in a movie, play etc. ‖ 영화·연극 등의 줄거리 묘사. 시나리오. 각본. 대본

scene /sin/ n
1 ▶PLAY/MOVIE 연극/영화◀ a part of a play or movie during which the action all happens in one place over a short period of time ‖ 짧은 시간에 걸쳐 모든 동작이 한 장소에서 일어나는 연극 또는 영화의 한 부분. 장면. 신. 무대. 장: *She comes on in Act 2, Scene 3.* 그녀는 2막 3장에서 등장한다. / *a love scene* 애정 표현 장면
2 ▶VIEW/PICTURE 경치/풍경◀ a view of a place as you see it, or as it appears in a picture ‖ 바라보거나 또는 사진에 나타나는 한 장소의 풍경. 경치. 경관. 풍경: *a peaceful country scene* 평화로운 시골 풍경 ✗DON'T SAY "There's a nice scene from my window."✗ SAY "There's a nice view." "There's a nice scene from my window."라고는 하지 않고 "There's a nice view."라고 한다.
3 ▶ACCIDENT/CRIME 사고/범죄◀ [singular] the place where something bad happened ‖ 나쁜 일이 발생한 곳. 장소. 현장: *Firefighters arrived on/at the scene within minutes.* 소방수들이 수분 내에 (화재) 현장에 도착했다. / *the scene of the crime* 범죄 현장
4 **the music/fashion/political etc. scene** a particular set of activities and the people who are involved in them ‖ 특정한 분야의 활동들과 거기에 관련된 사람들. 활동 분야. …계(界). 음악/패션/정치계: *Lisa always knows what's*

happening on the fashion scene. 리사는 패션계의 동향을 항상 알고 있다.

5 ▶ARGUMENT 언쟁◀ a loud angry argument, especially in a public place ‖ 특히 공공장소에서 큰 소리로 화를 내며 하는 말다툼. 소동[추태]. 구겅거리: *Sit down and stop making a scene!* 추태 좀 그만 부리고 앉아라!

6 not sb's scene INFORMAL not the type of thing someone likes ‖ 어떤 사람이 좋아하는 종류가 아닌. 취미[관심의 대상, 기호]가 아닌: *Loud parties aren't really my scene.* 시끌벅적한 파티는 정말 내 취향이 아니다.

7 behind the scenes secretly ‖ 비밀리에. 뒤에서. 남몰래: *You have no idea what goes on behind the scenes.* 너는 뒷전에서 무슨 일이 일어나는지 모른다.

8 set the scene a) to provide the conditions in which an event can happen ‖ 사건이 일어날 수 있는 조건을 제공하다. …을 준비[마련]하다. …하는 여건을 조성하다: *Interest in fitness set the scene for the success of sport shoes.* 체형 관리에 대한 관심은 스포츠 신발업의 성공을 위한 여건을 조성한다. **b)** to describe the situation before you begin to tell a story ‖ 이야기를 시작하기 전에 상황을 묘사[설명]하다. 상황 설명을 하다. 배경을 설명하다 —see usage note at VIEW²

sce·ner·y /'sinəri/ *n* [U] **1** the natural features of a place, such as mountains, forests etc. ‖ 산·숲 등의 한 장소의 자연적 특성. 풍경. 경치. 경관: *What beautiful scenery!* 얼마나 멋진 광경인가! **2** the painted background, furniture etc. used on a theater stage ‖ 극장의 무대에서 사용되는, 채색된 배경·가구 등. 무대 배경[장치]

sce·nic /'sinɪk/ *adj* with beautiful views of nature ‖ 아름다운 자연 경관을 가진. 풍경의. 경치의. 경치가 좋은: *Let's take the scenic route home.* 경치 좋은 길을 택해 집에 가자.

scent /sɛnt/ *n* **1** a particular smell, especially a pleasant one ‖ 특히 기분 좋은 특정의 냄새. 향기. 향. 달콤한 냄새: *the scent of roses* 장미 향기 **2** the smell left behind by an animal or person ‖ 동물이나 사람이 뒤에 남긴 냄새. 냄새 흔적. 풍기는 냄새: *The dog ran for the door when he picked up his owner's scent.* 개는 주인의 냄새를 맡자 문 쪽으로 달려갔다. **3** [C, U] ⇨ PERFUME —see usage note at SMELL²

scent·ed /'sɛntɪd/ *adj* having a particular smell, especially a pleasant

one ‖ 특정의, 특히 기분 좋은 냄새를 가진. 향기로운: *a room scented with spring flowers* 봄꽃 향이 풍기는 방

scep·ter /'sɛptɚ/ *n* a short decorated stick carried by kings and queens at special ceremonies ‖ 왕과 왕비가 특별 의식에 지참하는 장식된 짧은 봉. 홀(笏)

sched·ule¹ /'skɛdʒəl, -dʒul/ *n* **1** [C, U] a plan of what someone is going to do and when s/he is going to do it ‖ 어떤 사람이 하려는 일과 하려는 때에 대한 계획. 일정[예정](표). 스케줄: *I have a very full schedule this week.* (=I am very busy) 나는 이번 주 일정이 아주 꽉 차 있다. / *We're on schedule to finish in May.* (=we will finish by the planned date) 우리는 5월에 끝낼 예정이다. **2** a list that shows the times that buses, trains etc. leave or arrive at a particular place ‖ 버스·기차 등이 특정 장소를 출발하거나 도착하는 시간을 나타내는 목록(표). 시간표

schedule² *v* [T] to plan that something will happen at a particular time ‖ 어떤 일이 특정 시간에 일어나도록 계획하다. …하도록[…시간·기일로] 예정하다. …하는 스케줄을 잡다: *The meeting has been scheduled for Friday.* 회의는 금요일 날로 계획되어 있었다. / *Another new store is scheduled to open in three weeks.* 또 다른 새 점포가 3주 후에 개점할 예정이다.

scheme¹ /skim/ *n* **1** a plan, especially to do something bad or illegal ‖ 특히 나쁘거나 불법적인 것을 하기 위한 계획. 음모. 모의. …(하는) 안(案): *a scheme to avoid paying taxes* 세금을 면탈하려는 음모 **2** a system that you use to organize something ‖ 어떤 것을 조직화하는 데 이용하는 체계. 구성. 조직: *a bright color scheme for decorating the kitchen* 부엌을 장식하기 위한 밝은 색 배열

scheme² *v* [I] to secretly make dishonest plans to get or achieve something; PLOT ‖ 무엇을 얻거나 달성하기 위해 비밀리에 부정직한 계획을 세우다. 꾀하다[꾸미다, 획책하다]; ⑤ plot: *politicians scheming to win votes* 투표에서의 승리를 획책하는 정치인들 — **schemer** *n*

schism /'sɪzəm, 'skɪzəm/ *n* [C, U] FORMAL the separation of a group of people into two groups as the result of a disagreement ‖ 불화의 결과로 일단의 사람들이 두 집단으로 분리되는 것. 분열. 분파

schiz·o·phre·ni·a /ˌskɪtsə'friniə/ *n* [U] a mental illness in which someone's thoughts and feelings become separated from what is really happening around him/her ‖ 사람의 생각과 감정이 주위에서 실제로 일어나고 있는 일과 분리되는 정신 질환. 정신 분열증 **– schizophrenic** /ˌskɪtsəˈfrɛnɪk/ *adj, n*

schlep¹, schlepp /ʃlɛp/ *v* **-pped, -pping** [T] INFORMAL to carry something heavy, or to go somewhere in a tired way ‖ 무거운 것을 운반하다, 또는 지친 듯이 어디로 가다. 무겁게 움직이다. 질질 끌다: *I don't want to schlep this all the way across town.* 나는 이것을 계속 질질 끌고 읍내를 돌아다니고 싶지 않다.

schlep², schlepp *n* INFORMAL **1** a lazy stupid person ‖ 게으르고 바보 같은 사람. 멍청이. 얼간이 **2** a long trip that makes you tired ‖ 사람을 피곤하게 만드는 긴 여행. 긴 여정. 원거리 여행

schlock /ʃlɑk/ *n* [U] INFORMAL things that are cheap, bad, or useless ‖ 싼[질 나쁜, 쓸모없는] 것. 싸구려 (물건). 하찮은 것

schmaltz·y /ˈʃmɔltsi, ˈʃmɑl-/ *adj* INFORMAL dealing with strong emotions such as love and sadness in a way that seems silly and insincere ‖ 사랑·슬픔 등의 강렬한 감정에 분별 없고 거짓되어 보일 정도로 대처하는. 지나치게 감상적인. 과장된 감정으로 표현하는: *schmaltzy music* 감상적인 음악 **– schmaltz** *n* [U] —compare SENTIMENTAL

schmooze /ʃmuz/ *v* [I] INFORMAL to talk about things that are not important ‖ 중요치 않은 것들을 이야기하다. 시시한 이야기를 늘어놓다: *drinking and schmoozing at a party* 파티에서 술 마시고 시시덕거리는 것

schmuck /ʃmʌk/ *n* INFORMAL an insulting word meaning someone who is stupid or does things you do not like ‖ 멍청하거나 자신이 좋아하지 않는 일을 하는 사람을 의미하는 모욕적인 말. 멍청이. 반편. 얼간이

schnapps /ʃnæps/ *n* [U] a strong alcoholic drink ‖ 알코올 성분이 강한 술. 슈냅스

schol·ar /ˈskɑlɚ/ *n* **1** someone who knows a lot about a particular subject ‖ 특정 분야에 대해 많이 아는 사람. 학자 **2** someone who has been given a SCHOLARSHIP to study at a college or university ‖ 단과 대학이나 종합 대학교에서 장학금을 받고 공부하는 사람. 장학생. 장학금 수령자

schol·ar·ly /ˈskɑlɚli/ *adj* **1** concerned with serious study of a particular subject ‖ 특정 분야의 진지한 연구에 관련된. 학술적인. 전문적인: *a scholarly journal* 학술(전문)지 **2** someone who is scholarly spends a lot of time studying, and knows a lot about a particular subject ‖ 사람이 연구에 많은 시간을 쏟고 특정 분야에 대해 많이 알고 있는. 학자의. 학술 연구가의

schol·ar·ship /ˈskɑlɚˌʃɪp/ *n* **1** an amount of money that is given to someone by an organization to help pay for his/her education ‖ 어떤 사람의 교육비 지불을 돕기 위해 단체에서 주는 일정 액의 돈. 장학금 **2** [U] the methods that are used in serious studying, or the knowledge that comes from this ‖ 중요한 연구에 이용되는 방법, 또는 여기에서 나온 지식. 학문. 학식

scho·las·tic /skəˈlæstɪk/ *adj* relating to schools or teaching ‖ 학교 또는 교육에 관련된. 학교[대학]의. 교육의. 연구의: *an excellent scholastic record* 뛰어난 연구 기록

school¹ /skul/ *n*

1 ▶BUILDING 건물◀ [C, U] a place where children are taught ‖ 아이들이 교육 받는 곳. 학교. 교사(校舎): *Which school did you go to?* 어느 학교 다녔지요? / *I can get some work done while the kids are at school.* (=studying in the school building) 아이들이 학교에 있는 동안 나는 일을 좀 끝낼 수 있다.

2 ▶TIME AT SCHOOL 학교에서의 시간◀ [U] the time spent at school ‖ 학교에서 보내는 시간. 수업(시간). 공부(시간): *What are you doing after school?* 방과 후에 뭘 할 거니?

3 ▶TEACHERS/STUDENTS 교사/학생들◀ the students and teachers at a school ‖ 학교에 있는 학생들과 교사들: *The whole school was sorry when she left.* 그녀가 떠날 때 교사와 학생 전체가 슬퍼했다.

4 in school attending a school ‖ 학교에 출석하고 있는. 수학 중의. 재학 중의: *Are your boys still in school?* 댁의 자제들은 아직 재학 중입니까?

5 ▶FOR ONE SUBJECT 한 분야에 대해◀ [C, U] a place where a particular subject or skill is taught ‖ 특정 분야나 기술을 가르치는 곳. 각종 (전문) 학교. 교습소. 훈련소. 양성소: *an art school* 예술 학교

6 ▶ UNIVERSITY 대학◀ **a)** a department that teaches a particular subject at a university ‖ 대학에서 특정 분야를 가르치는 학부. 전문학부. 대학원: *the Harvard School of Law* 하버드 법대 [법학부] **b)** INFORMAL a college or university ‖ 단과 대학 또는 종합 대학교:

S

"Where did you go to school?" "UC San Diego." "어느 학교 출신입니까?" "UC 샌디에이고입니다."

7 ▶ART/IDEAS 예술/사상◀ a number of people who are considered as a group because of their style of work, or their ideas ‖ 그들의 작품 스타일이나 사상 때문에 한 집단으로 생각되는 일군의 사람들. 유파.: *the Dutch school of painting* 네덜란드 회화 학파

8 school of thought an opinion or way of thinking about something that is shared by a group of people ‖ 일단의 사람들이 공유하는 사물에 대한 견해나 사고 방식. 양식. 주의: *One school of thought says that red wine is good for you.* 어느 학설은 적포도주가 사람에게 좋다고 한다.

9 ▶FISH 물고기◀ a large group of fish or other sea creatures that are swimming together ‖ 함께 헤엄쳐 다니는 큰 집단의 물고기나 다른 해양 생명체들. 한 떼. 무리: *a school of dolphins* 돌고래 떼

school² *v* [T] FORMAL to train or teach someone ‖ 사람을 훈련시키거나 가르치다. 교육하다. 훈육하다. 훈련하다: *The children are schooled in music and art from a very early age.* 그 아이들은 아주 어린 나이 때부터 음악과 미술 교육을 받는다.

school·ing /'skulɪŋ/ *n* [U] education at school ‖ 학교 교육. (교실) 수업[가르치기]. 교수[교습]

schoo·ner /'skunɚ/ *n* a fast sailing ship with two sails ‖ 돛이 두 개 달린 쾌속선. 쌍돛대 이상의 중형선. 스쿠너

sci·ence /'saɪəns/ *n* **1** [U] knowledge that is based on testing and proving facts, or the study that produces this knowledge ‖ 사실을 시험하고 증명하는 데에 기초를 둔 지식, 또는 이 지식을 산출하는 연구. 과학. 과학적[체계적] 지식: *the application of science and technology to everyday life* 과학과 기술의 일상생활에의 적용 **2** [C, U] a particular area of science, such as BIOLOGY or chemistry, or a subject that is studied like a science ‖ 생물학이나 화학 등 과학의 특정 영역, 또는 과학처럼 연구되는 분야. 학문(의 한 분야). …학: *the social sciences* 사회 과학

science fic·tion /ˌ.. '../ *n* [U] books and stories about imaginary worlds or imaginary developments in science, such as travel in space ‖ 우주여행 등 상상의 세계나 과학에서의 발전에 대한 책과 이야기. (공상) 과학 소설. SF 소설

sci·en·tif·ic /ˌsaɪən'tɪfɪk/ *adj* **1** relating to science, or using its methods ‖ 과학에 관한, 또는 과학적 방법을 사용하는. 과학(상)의. 과학적인: *scientific discoveries* 과학적 발견 / *a scientific experiment* 과학 실험 **2** done very carefully, using an organized system ‖ 조직화된 체계를 써서 매우 주의 깊게 행해진. 과학적 방법을 쓰는. 과학적인. 정밀한: *We do keep records, but we're not very scientific about it.* 우리는 계속 기록하고 있지만 그에 대해 그다지 과학적이지 못하다. —opposite UNSCIENTIFIC

sci·en·tist /'saɪəntɪst/ *n* someone who works in science ‖ 과학 분야에서 연구하는 사람. 과학자

sci-fi /ˌsaɪ'faɪ/ *n* [U] INFORMAL ⇨ SCIENCE FICTION

scin·til·lat·ing /'sɪntl̩ˌeɪtɪŋ/ *adj* interesting, amusing, and intelligent ‖ 재미있는·즐거운·지적인. 호기심을 끄는. 재치가 번뜩이는[넘치는]: *a scintillating speech* 재치가 넘치는 연설

scis·sors /'sɪzɚz/ *n* [plural] a tool for cutting paper, made of two sharp blades that are joined in the middle and that have handles on one end ‖ 두 개의 예리한 날이 중간에서 접합되어 있으며 한쪽 끝에 손잡이가 달린, 종이를 자르는 데 쓰이는 연장. 가위: *Hand me that pair of scissors, please.* 그 가위 좀 내게 건네줘.

scoff /skɔf, skaf/ *v* [I] to laugh at a person or idea, or to make unkind remarks, in a way that shows you think he, she, or it is stupid ‖ 다른 사람이나 생각을 멍청하다고 생각하는 듯이 비웃거나 무례한 발언을 하다. 조소하다. 놀리다: *Other lawyers scoffed at his methods.* 다른 변호사들은 그의 방법을 비웃었다.

scold /skould/ *v* [T] to tell someone in an angry way that s/he has done something wrong ‖ 다른 사람에게 잘못된 짓을 했다고 화내는 투로 말하다. 꾸짖다. 야단치다: *Mom scolded me for wasting electricity.* 어머니는 내가 전기를 낭비한다고 야단치셨다. **- scolding** *n* [C, U]

scoop¹ /skup/ *n* **1** a deep spoon for picking up or serving food such as flour or ICE CREAM ‖ 밀가루나 아이스크림 등 식품을 뜨거나 제공하는 깊은 스푼. 작은 삽. 숟가락 **2** also **scoopful** the amount that a scoop will hold ‖ 큰 숟가락이 담을 수 있는 양. 한 번 푸는 양. 한 숟가락 분량: *two scoops of sugar* 설탕 두 스푼 (분량) **3** an important or exciting news story that is printed in one newspaper before any of the others know about it ‖ 다른 신문사들이 알기 전

에 한 신문에 인쇄된 중요하거나 흥미진진한 기사 내용. 특종

scoop² *v* [T] to pick something up with a SCOOP, a spoon, or with your curved hand ‖ 어떤 것을 작은 삽[숟가락, 오므린 손]으로 떠내다. 퍼내다. 푸다: *She scooped up a handful of sand.* 그녀는 모래를 한 움큼 퍼올렸다.

scoot /skut/ *v* [I] INFORMAL to leave a place quickly ‖ 한 장소를 재빨리 떠나다. 빨리[급히] 가다. 달려가다: *Go to bed, Andrew – scoot!* 잠자러 가라, 앤드류. 빨리!

scoot·er /'skutɚ/ *n* **1** a small two-wheeled vehicle like a bicycle with an engine ‖ 자전거와 유사한 엔진이 달린 작은 이륜차(二輪車). 스쿠터 —see picture on page 943 **2** a child's vehicle with two small wheels, an upright handle, and a narrow board that you stand on with one foot, while the other foot pushes the vehicle along the ground ‖ 두 개의 작은 바퀴와 수직으로 된 손잡이 그리고 좁은 보드가 달려 있고, 한 발로 그 보드에 올라서서 다른 발로 땅을 차서 미는 아동용 탈 것. 킥보드

scope¹ /skoup/ *n* [U] **1** the range of things that a subject, activity, book etc. deals with ‖ 주제·활동·책 등이 다루는 사물의 영역. 범위. 범주. 한계: *A thorough discussion of this subject is beyond the scope of this paper.* 이 주제에 대한 철저한 토론은 이 논문의 범주를 넘어선다. **2** the opportunity to do or develop something ‖ 무엇을 하거나 개발하는 기회. 여지. 자유. 배출구: *I want a job with scope for promotion.* 나는 진급의 기회가 있는 직업을 원한다.

scope² *v*

scope sb/sth ↔ **out** *phr v* [T] SPOKEN to look at someone or something to see what he, she, or it is like ‖ 다른 사람이나 사물이 어떻게 생겼는지 알아보기 위해 바라보다. …을 잘 보다[조사하다]. 둘러보다. 살펴보다: *Let's scope out that new bar tonight.* 오늘 밤 그 새 술집이 어떤지 둘러보자.

scorch¹ /skɔrtʃ/ *v* [I, T] if you scorch something, or if it scorches, its surface burns slightly and changes color ‖ 어떤 것의 표면이 약간 타거나 색깔이 변하다[변하게 하다]. …의 겉이 타다[태우다]. 그을다 [그을리다]: *Turn down the iron or you'll*

scorch

scorch your shirt. 다리미 온도를 줄여라, 그렇지 않으면 셔츠가 눋게 된다.

scorch² *n* a mark made on something where its surface has been burned ‖ 불에 탄 물건의 표면에 만들어진 자국. 눋은 [그을린] 자국

scorch·er /'skɔrtʃɚ/ *n* INFORMAL an extremely hot day ‖ 몹시 무더운 날. (타는 듯) 뜨거운 날: *It's going to be a real scorcher.* 정말 무더운 날이 될 것 같다.

scorch·ing /'skɔrtʃɪŋ/ *adj* INFORMAL extremely hot ‖ 몹시 무더운. 타는 듯한. 지독하게 더운: *It's scorching outside!* 바깥 날씨가 타는 듯하다!

score¹ /skɔr/ *n* **1** the number of points that a person or team wins or earns in a game, competition, or test ‖ 사람이나 팀이 시합[경연, 시험]에서 따거나 얻은 득점의 수. 점수. 성적. 스코어: *The final score was 35 to 17.* 최종 스코어는 35대 17이었다. / *I got a **higher/lower** score than Tracy on the geometry test.* 나는 기하학 시험에서 트레이시보다 더 높은[낮은] 점수를 받았다. / *Who's going to **keep** score?* (=record the scores as a game is played) 누가 점수를 기록할래? **2** a paper copy of a piece of music for a group of performers, or the music itself ‖ 일단의 연주자들을 위한 악보, 또는 음악 그 자체: *a movie score* 영화 음악 **3** **know the score** INFORMAL to know the real facts of a situation, including any unpleasant ones ‖ 어떤 불쾌한 것들도 포함해서 상황의 실상을 알다. 진상을 알다 [파악하다]. 실태를 바로 보다: *He knew the score when he decided to get involved.* 그는 개입하기로 결정했을 때 실태를 잘 알고 있었다. **4 on that score** SPOKEN concerning the subject you have just mentioned ‖ 방금 언급했던 주제에 관련한. 그 점에서. 이[그] 이유로: *We've got plenty of money, so don't worry on that score.* 우리는 자금이 많으니까 그 점에 대해서는 걱정 마라. **5** OLD-FASHIONED twenty ‖ 숫자 20. 20의 집단[단위]: *four-score years ago* (=80 years ago) 80년 전 —see also **settle the score** (SETTLE)

score² *v* **1** [I, T] to win or earn points in a game, competition, or test ‖ 시합[경연, 시험]에서 점수를 따거나 얻다. …을 득점하다. 성적[점수]을 기록하다: *Dallas scored right before the end of the game.* 달라스는 게임 종료 직전에 점수를 냈다. / *Mr. Burke's class scored about six points higher than the others.* 버크 선생의 반은 다른 반들보다 6점 정도 더 높은 성적을 기록했다. **2** [T] to give a particular number of points in a game, competition, or test ‖ 시합[경연, 시험]에서 특정 숫자의 점수를 주다. 득점시키다. 채점하다[해서 점수를 주다]: *The exams will be scored by computer.* 시험은 컴퓨터로 채점될 것이다. **3 score points** INFORMAL to do or say something to please someone or to make him/her feel respect for you ‖ 어떤 사람을 기쁘게 하거나 상대방에게 존경심을 느끼게 하는 행동이나 말을 하다. 점수를 얻다. 호평을 받다. 환심을 사다: *Does she think she can score points with me by making me cookies?* 그녀는 내게 과자를 구워 주어서 내 환심을 살 수 있다고 생각할까? **4** [I, T] INFORMAL to be very successful in something you do ‖ 하는 일에서 매우 성공적이다. 성공하다. 호평을 받다: *Barnes has scored again with another popular book.* 반즈는 또 다른 인기 있는 책으로 다시 호평을 받았다. **5** [I, T] SLANG to manage to get something you want, especially sex or illegal drugs ‖ 원하는 것 특히 섹스나 불법적 마약 등을 어렵게 얻어내다. …을 입수하다. 훔치다 —see also SCORES

score·board /'skɔrbɔrd/ *n* a sign on which the SCORE of a game is shown as it is played ‖ 게임이 진행되는 동안 점수가 표시되는 표지(판). 득점(게시)판

score·card /'skɔrkɑrd/ *n* a printed card used for writing the SCORE of a game as it is played ‖ 게임이 진행되는 동안 게임의 점수를 기록하는 데 쓰이는 인쇄된 카드. 점수[득점]표

scor·er /'skɔrɚ/ *n* **1** someone who earns a point in a game ‖ 게임에서 점수를 얻는 사람. 득점자 **2** also **score-keeper** someone who records the number of points won in a game or competition as it is played ‖ 진행되고 있는 시합이나 경기에서 획득한 점수를 기록하는 사람. (득점) 기록원

scores /skɔrz/ *n* [plural] a large number, but usually less than a hundred ‖ 큰 숫자이지만 보통 1백보다 작은 수. 다수. 많은 수: *On the playground, scores of children ran and screamed.* 운동장에서 많은 수의 아이들이 뛰면서 소리쳤다.

scorn¹ /skɔrn/ *n* [U] strong criticisms of someone or something that you think is not worth any respect at all ‖ 존경할 가치가 전혀 없다고 생각하는 사람이나 사물에 대한 강한 비판. 경멸. 업신여기기. 말보기. 냉소: *The media has heaped/poured scorn on the President's speech.* 언론은 대통령의 연설에 냉소를

퍼부었다. **– scornful** *adj*

scorn² *v* [T] FORMAL to show in an unkind way that you think that a person, idea, or suggestion is stupid or not worth accepting ‖ 사람[사상, 제안]이 바보 같고 받아들일 가치가 없다고 생각한다는 것을 무례하게 나타내다. 경멸하다. 업신여기다. 깔보다. 무시하다: *He scorned the opinions of anyone who disagreed with him.* 그는 자신과 생각이 일치하지 않는 사람들의 의견을 무시했다.

Scor·pi·o /'skɔrpi‚ou/ *n* **1** [singular] the eighth sign of the ZODIAC, represented by a SCORPION ‖ 전갈로 상징되는 황도 12궁의 여덟째 별자리. 전갈자리 **2** someone born between October 24 and November 21 ‖ 10월 24일부터 11월 21일 사이에 태어난 사람. 전갈좌 태생자

scor·pi·on /'skɔrpiən/ *n* a creature like a large insect, that has a poisonous tail ‖ 독이 있는 꼬리가 달린 큰 벌레 같이 생긴 생물. 전갈

Scotch /skɑtʃ/ *n* [C, U] a type of WHISKEY (=a strong alcoholic drink) made in Scotland, or a glass of this drink ‖ 스코틀랜드에서 만들어진 위스키 종류, 또는 이 술의 한 잔. 스카치 위스키 (한 잔)

scotch *v* **scotch a rumor** stop a RUMOR (=story about someone) from spreading ‖ 소문이 퍼지는 것을 막다. 소문을 없애다[제거하다]

Scotch tape /‚. '. / *n* [U] TRADEMARK sticky thin clear plastic in a long narrow band, used for sticking paper and other light things together ‖ 좁고 긴 띠 모양으로 되어 종이와 다른 가벼운 사물들을 함께 붙이는 데 사용되는 끈끈하고 얇고 투명한 비닐 수지. (반)투명 접착 테이프. 스카치 테이프

scot-free /‚skɑt 'fri/ *adv* **get off scot-free** INFORMAL to avoid being punished although you deserve to be ‖ 처벌되어야 마땅함에도 처벌되는 것을 모면하다

Scot·tish /'skɑtɪʃ/ *adj* relating to or coming from Scotland ‖ 스코틀랜드와 관련되거나 스코틀랜드에서 온. 스코틀랜드 (산)의

scoun·drel /'skaundrəl/ *n* OLD-FASHIONED a bad or dishonest man ‖ 불량하거나 부정직한 남자. 무뢰한. 건달. 깡패. 악한. 악당

scour /skauɚ/ *v* [T] **1** to search very carefully and thoroughly through an area or a document ‖ 한 지역이나 서류를 아주 세심하고 철저히 조사하다. 수색하다. 찾아다니다: *Detectives scoured her letters for clues.* 형사들은 단서를 찾으려

고 그녀의 편지를 철저히 조사했다. **2**
also **scour out** to clean something
very thoroughly by rubbing it with a
rough material ‖ 거친 소재로 어떤 것을
아주 철저히 문질러 깨끗이 하다. 문질러
[닦아] 없애다

scourge /skɔ˞dʒ/ n FORMAL something
that causes a lot of harm or suffering ‖
많은 피해나 고통을 초래하는 것. 재앙.
괴로움[고통]을 주는 것: *the scourge of
war* 전쟁의 참화 **– scourge** v [T]

scout¹ /skaʊt/ n **1** a soldier who is sent
to search an area in front of an army
and get information ‖ 부대의 전면에서
지역을 수색하고 정보를 수집하기 위해 파
견되는 병사. 정찰[척후]병 **2** someone
whose job is to look for good sports
players, musicians etc. in order to
employ them ‖ 고용하기 위해 훌륭한 운
동선수·음악가 등을 찾아내는 직업인. 스
카우트. 발굴자: *a talent scout* 연기자 발
굴자

scout² v **1** [I] also **scout around** to
look for something in a particular area
‖ 특정 지역에서 무엇을 찾다. 조사[탐색]
하다. 찾아내다: *I'm going to scout
around for a place to buy some beer.* 내
가 맥주를 좀 살 수 있는 곳을 찾으러 돌
아보겠다. **2** [T] also **scout out** to
examine a place or area in order to get
information about it, especially for
military reasons ‖ 특히 군사적 이유로 한
장소나 지역에 대한 정보를 얻기 위해 조
사하다. 수색[정찰]하다. 척후 활동을 하
다: *Two men went off to scout out the
woods ahead.* 두 병사가 앞쪽 숲을 정찰
하러 갔다. **3** [T] also **scout for** to look
for good sports players, musicians etc.
in order to employ them ‖ 우수한 운동선
수나 음악가 등을 채용하기 위해 찾아내
다. …을 발굴하다. 찾아내다

scowl /skaʊl/ v [I] to look at someone
or something in an angry or
disapproving way ‖ 화난 투로 또는 불만
스럽게 사람이나 사물을 보다. 얼굴을[인
상을] 찌푸리다[찌푸리며 보다]: *Tom just
scowls at me when we meet.* 우리가 만
날 때 톰은 나를 보고 그저 얼굴을 찌푸리
기만 한다. **– scowl** n

Scrab·ble /ˈskræbəl/ n [U] TRADEMARK
a game using a special board and small
objects with letters on them, in which
you try to make words out of the letters
‖ 특수한 (게임)판과 글자가 쓰여진 작은
물체를 이용해 그 글자로 단어를 만들어
보는 게임. 단어 맞추기 게임. 스크래블

scrab·ble v [I] to quickly feel around
with your fingers, especially in order to

look for something ‖ 특히 어떤 것을 찾기
위해 손가락으로 여기저기 재빨리 더듬다.
손으로 수석거리다. 이리저리 찔러보다:
*Police scrabbled through garbage cans
looking for the wallet.* 경찰은 지갑을 찾
으려고 쓰레기통을 수석거렸다.

scrag·gly /ˈskrægli/ adj growing in a
way that looks uneven and messy ‖ 고르
지 않고 지저분하게 보이도록 자란. 불규
칙적인. 울퉁불퉁한. 덥수룩한: *a
scraggly beard* 덥수룩하게 난 턱수염

scram /skræm/ v **-mmed, -mming** [I]
INFORMAL to leave a place very quickly,
especially because you are not wanted
‖ 특히 환영받지 않기 때문에 어떤 장소에
서 급히 떠나다. 나가다. 달아나다: *Get
out of here! Scram!* 여기서 나가! 꺼져 버
려!

scram·ble¹ /ˈskræmbəl/ v **1** [I] to
climb up or over something quickly,
using your hands to help you ‖ 의지하기
위해 손을 사용해서 어떤 것 위로 또는 어
떤 것을 타고 재빨리 올라가다. 기어오르
다: *Andy scrambled easily over the
wall.* 앤디는 그 벽을 타고 쉽게 기어 올라
갔다. **2** [I] to rush and struggle with
other people in order to get or do
something ‖ 어떤 것을 얻거나 하기 위해
다른 사람들과 함께 덤벼들어 몸싸움을 벌
이다. 서로 가지려[빼앗으려] 하다. 앞을
다투다. 밀치며 나아가다: *people
scrambling for safety* 안전한 곳을 찾아
앞 다투며 서로 밀치는 사람들 **3** [T] to
mix electronic signals so that they
cannot be understood without a special
piece of equipment ‖ 특별한 장비 없이
해독할 수 없도록 전자적인 신호를 섞다.
암호 신호를 섞어 넣다. 신호를 변조하
다: *All messages are scrambled for
security reasons.* 모든 메시지는 보안상
의 이유로 신호가 변조되었다. —opposite
UNSCRAMBLE **4** [T] to mix up the order of
letters, words etc., so that the meaning
is not clear ‖ 뜻이 불분명해지도록 글자·
단어 등의 순서를 섞다. …을 마구 뒤섞다
5 scramble an egg to cook an egg by
mixing the white and yellow parts
together and heating it ‖ 계란의 흰자와
노른자를 서로 섞어 열을 가해 요리하다.
계란을 스크램블로 요리하다

scramble² n [singular] **1** a quick and
difficult climb in which you have to use
your hands to help you ‖ 의지하기 위해
손을 사용해서 잽싸고 힘들게 기어오르기.
손발을 다 써서 타고 오르기: *a rough
scramble over loose rocks* 불안한 암벽을
힘들게 기어오름 **2** a situation in which
people rush and struggle with each

other in order to get or do something ‖ 어떤 것을 얻거나 하기 위해 서로 덤벼들어 다투는 상황. …의 쟁탈(전). 아귀다툼: *a scramble for the best seats* 가장 좋은 자리를 차지하기 위한 아귀다툼 / *a scramble for federal funding* 연방 기금을 얻기 위한 쟁탈전

scrap¹ /skræp/ *n* **1** a small piece of paper, cloth etc. ‖ 종이·천 등의 작은 조각. 동강. 단편: *a scrap of paper* 종잇조각 **2** [U] materials or objects that are no longer suitable for the purpose they were made for, but can be used again in another way ‖ 다른 방식으로는 다시 사용할 수 있지만 더 이상 만든 본래의 목적으로 사용하기에는 적당하지 않은 재료나 물체. 쓸모없는 것. 부스러기: *scrap metal* 부스러기 금속 **3** a small piece of information ‖ 단편적인 정보: *There isn't a scrap of evidence to support her story.* 그녀의 이야기를 뒷받침해 줄 증거는 조금도 없다. **4** INFORMAL a short fight or argument that is not very serious ‖ 그리 심하지 않은 짧은 싸움이나 논쟁: *Katie got into a little scrap at school.* 캐티는 학교에서 사소한 다툼에 휘말렸다.

scrap² *v* **-pped, -pping 1** [T] INFORMAL to decide not to do or use something because it is not practical ‖ 실제적이지 못해서 어떤 것을 하거나 사용하지 않기로 결정하다. 버리다. 폐지하다: *We've decided to scrap the whole idea of renting a car.* 우리는 차를 빌리겠다는 모든 계획을 포기하기로 결정했다. **2** [T] to take apart an old machine, vehicle etc., and use its parts in some other way ‖ 낡은 기계·탈 것 등을 분해하고 그 부품들을 다른 용도로 사용하다. 해체하다. 고물로 분류하다: *equipment to be sold or scrapped* 팔리거나 해체될 장비

scrap·book /'skræpbʊk/ *n* a book with empty pages in which you can stick pictures, newspaper articles, or other things you want to keep ‖ 자신이 보관하기 원하는 그림[신문 기사, 기타의 것]을 붙일 수 있는 빈 페이지로 된 책. 스크랩북

scrape¹ /skreɪp/ *v* **1** [T] to remove something from a surface, using the edge of a knife, stick etc. ‖ 칼날·꼬챙이 등을 써서 표면으로부터 어떤 것을 제거하다. 긁어내다. 닦아내다: *Jerry bent to scrape the mud off his boots.* 제리는 장화에 묻은 진흙을 떼내기 위해 허리를 구부렸다. **2** [I, T] to rub against a rough surface in a way that causes slight damage or injury, or to make something do this ‖ 약간의 손상이나 상처가 날 정도로 거친 표면에 대고 비비다, 또는 어떤 것

을 이렇게 하게 하다. 문지르다. 문대다. 까지게[상처 나게] 하다: *I scraped my knee on the sidewalk.* 나는 인도에 (넘어져) 무릎이 까졌다. **3** [I, T] to make a noise by rubbing roughly against a surface ‖ 표면에다 대고 거칠게 비벼서 소리를 내다. 박박 긁다. 문질러서 요란한 소리를 내다: *Metal scraped when he turned the key.* 그가 열쇠를 돌리자 쇠가 긁히는 소리가 났다.

scrape by *phr v* [I] to have just enough money to live ‖ 간신히 살아갈 돈을 가지고 있다. 근근이 살아가다: *They just manage to scrape by on her salary.* 그들은 그녀의 봉급으로 근근이 살아간다.

scrape sth ↔ **together/up** *phr v* [T] to get enough money for a particular purpose, when this is difficult ‖ 어려운 상황에서 특정한 목적을 위해 충분한 돈을 모으다. 애써 모으다. 그러모으다: *We're trying to scrape together enough money for a vacation.* 우리는 휴가에 쓸 충분한 돈을 모으려고 애쓰고 있다.

scrape² *n* **1** a mark or slight injury caused by rubbing against a rough surface ‖ 거친 표면에다 대고 문질러 생긴 자국이나 가벼운 상처. 스친[긁힌] 상처[자국]. 생채기: *Steve only got a few cuts and scrapes.* 스티브는 약간 베이고 긁힌 상처가 났다. **2** INFORMAL a situation in which you get into trouble or have difficulties ‖ 곤란에 처하거나 어려운 상황. 곤경. 곤란. 궁지: *Harper has had previous scrapes with the law.* 하퍼는 이전에 법을 어겨 궁지에 빠진 적이 있다.

scrap·py /'skræpi/ *adj* INFORMAL always wanting to argue or fight ‖ 항상 다투거나 싸우기 원하는. 공격적인. 싸움[다툼]을 좋아하는

scraps /skræps/ *n* [plural] pieces of food that are left after you have finished eating ‖ 식사를 하고 난 후 남은 음식 찌꺼기. 잔반: *Save the scraps for the dog.* 개에게 줄 음식 찌꺼기를 남겨라.

scratch¹ /skrætʃ/ *v* **1** [I, T] to rub a part of your body with your FINGERNAILs ‖ 손톱으로 몸의 한 부분을 긁다: *Will you scratch my back?* 내 등 좀 긁어 줄래? / *a dog scratching itself* 몸을 긁적대고 있는 개 **2** [T] to make a small cut in a surface, or to remove something from a surface, using something sharp ‖ 날카로운 것을 사용해 표면에 작은 긁힌 자국을 내거나 표면에서 어떤 것을 제거하다. 긁어서 새기다. 긁어 없애다. 깎아내다: *Did the cat scratch you?* 그 고양이가 너를 할퀴었니? / *The paint's been scratched off the wall here.* 벽의 이곳이

페인트가 벗겨졌다. **3** [I] to make a noise by rubbing something sharp or rough on a hard surface ‖ 딱딱한 표면에 날카롭거나 거친 것을 문질러 소리를 내다. 긁다. 긁는 소리를 내다: *Didn't you hear the dog scratching at the door?* 그 개가 문을 긁는 소리를 듣지 못했니? **4 scratch the surface** to deal with only a very small part of a subject ‖ 단지 주제의 매우 작은 일부만을 다루다. 피상적으로 다루다: *We've been studying the stars for years, but we've only scratched the surface.* 우리는 오랫동안 별에 대해서 연구하고 있지만 그것은 단지 수박 겉핥기식이었다. **5** [T] INFORMAL to stop planning to do something because it is no longer possible or practical ‖ 더 이상 가능하지 않거나 실제적이지 않아서 어떤 것을 할 계획을 중단하다. 취소하다. 포기하다: *I guess we can scratch that idea.* 나는 우리가 그 계획을 취소할 수 있다고 생각한다. **6** [T] to remove a person or thing from a list ‖ 사람이나 물건을 명단에서 빼다. 지우다. 삭제하다: *Her name had been scratched from/off the list of competitors.* 그녀의 이름은 참가자의 명단에서 삭제되었다.

scratch² *n* **1** a small cut or mark on the surface of something or on someone's skin ‖ 사물의 표면이나 사람 피부 위의 작은 상처나 자국. 긁힌 상처 [자국]. 생채기: *Where did this scratch on the car come from?* 이 차의 긁힌 자국은 어디에서 생긴 것이냐? **2 from scratch** without using anything that was prepared before ‖ 전에 준비되었던 것은 아무것도 사용하지 않고. 처음부터. 무에서부터: *I made the cake from scratch.* 내가 완전히 처음부터 이 케이크를 만들었다. **3 not come/be up to scratch** INFORMAL to not be good enough for a particular standard ‖ 특정한 수준에 맞을 만큼 충분히 좋지 않은. 일정 수준에 미치지 못하는: *Your work hasn't really been up to scratch lately.* 당신의 일은 요즘 정말 기대에 미치지 못해 왔다. **4** a sound made by something sharp or rough being rubbed on a hard surface ‖ 날카롭거나 거친 것이 딱딱한 표면에 문질러서 나는 소리. 찍찍 긁는 소리: *You could hear the dry scratch of his pen as he wrote.* 그가 글씨를 쓸 때 펜이 찍찍 긁히는, 귀에 거슬리는 소리를 들을 수 있을 것이다. **5** [singular] the act of rubbing a part of your body with your FINGERNAILs ‖ 손톱으로 몸의 일부를 긁는 행동. (가려운 데를)긁기: *My back needs a good scratch.* 나는 등이 가려워 박박 긁

고 싶다. **6 without a scratch** INFORMAL without being injured at all ‖ 전혀 상처를 입지 않고. 생채기 하나 없이: *Stuart was hurt in the accident, but Max escaped without a scratch.* 스튜어트는 그 사고로 다쳤지만 맥스는 생채기 하나 없었다.

scratch pa·per /'. ,../ *n* [U] cheap paper, or paper that has already been used on one side, that you can write notes or lists on ‖ 메모나 목록을 쓸 수 있는 값싼 종이나 이미 한쪽 면을 사용한 종이. 메모 용지. 이면지

scratch·y /'skrætʃi/ *adj* **1** scratchy clothes or materials have a rough surface and are uncomfortable to wear or touch ‖ 옷이나 섬유의 표면이 거칠고 입거나 닿기가 불편한. 옷이 따끔거리는. 가려운: *a scratchy pair of wool socks* 털실로 만든 따끔거리는 양말 한 켤레 **2** a voice that is scratchy sounds deep and rough ‖ 목소리가 깊고 거친. 처음의 갈라진 소리의. 새된 소리의 **3** a scratchy throat is sore ‖ 목구멍이 아픈

scrawl /skrɔl/ *v* to write something in a fast, careless, or messy way ‖ 어떤 것을 빠르게[경솔하게, 지저분하게] 쓰다. 아무렇게나 휘갈겨 쓰다. 낙서하다: *a telephone number scrawled on a piece of paper* 종잇조각에 휘갈겨 쓴 전화 번호 **– scrawl** *n*

scraw·ny /'skrɔni/ *adj* looking thin and weak in an unattractive way ‖ 보기 싫을 정도로 마르고 약하게 보이는. 말라빠진. 야윈: *a scrawny little kid* 야위고 키가 작은 아이

scream¹ /skrim/ *v* [I, T] to make a loud high noise with your voice, or shout something loudly because you are hurt, frightened, excited etc. ‖ 다쳐서[겁에 질려서, 흥분해서] 크고 높은 목소리를 내거나 크게 소리 지르다. 비명을 지르다. 외치다. 고함치다: *Suddenly she screamed, "Look out!"* 갑자기 그녀는 "조심해!"라고 고함쳤다. / *The baby was screaming for her bottle.* 그 아기는 젖병을 달라고 소리쳐 울고 있었다.

scream² *n* **1** a loud high noise that you make when you are hurt, frightened, excited etc. ‖ 다칠[겁에 질릴, 흥분할] 때 내는 크고 높은 소음. 비명(소리): *I thought I heard a child's scream.* 나는 한 아이의 비명을 들은 것 같았다. **2** a very loud high sound ‖ 매우 크고 높은 소리. 날카로운 소리. 귀청을 찢는 소리: *the scream of the jet engines* 제트 엔진의 쏴 하는 날카로운 소리 **3 be a scream** INFORMAL to be very funny ‖ 매

우 웃기다. 재미있다: *"How was the show?" "It was a scream."* "그 쇼 어땠니?" "매우 재미있었어."

screech /skri:tʃ/ v **1** [I, T] to make a very high loud unpleasant sound ‖ 매우 높고 큰 불쾌한 소리를 내다. 새된 소리[비명]를 지르다. 날카로운 (목)소리를 내다: *The motor screeched when we turned it on.* 그 모터는 전원을 켰을 때 끽끽 하는 소리를 냈다. / *"Get out of my way!" she screeched.* "비켜!"라고 그녀는 날카롭게 외쳤다. **2 screech to a halt/stop/standstill** if a vehicle screeches to a halt, it stops very suddenly, so that its BRAKES make an unpleasant high sound ‖ 브레이크가 불쾌한 높은 소리를 낼 정도로 차량을 급격하게 멈추다. (차 등이)끽 소리를 내며 멈추다. 급정거하다 **– screech** n

screen¹ /skri:n/ n **1** the flat glass part of a television or a computer ‖ 텔레비전이나 컴퓨터의 편평한 유리 부분. 화면: *It's easier to correct your work on screen than on paper.* 네 작업은 지면에서보다 화면에서

screen

수정하는 것이 더 쉽다. **2** a large flat white surface that movies are shown on in a movie theater ‖ 영화관에서 영화가 투사되는 넓고 편평한 흰 색의 표면. 스크린. 영사막. 은막 **3** a wire net that covers an open door or window so that air can get inside a house but insects cannot ‖ 집 안으로 공기는 들어올 수 있지만 벌레들은 들어올 수 없도록 열려진 문이나 창문에 덧대는 철망. 방충용 철망: *screens on the windows* 창의 방충망 / *a screen door* 방충 덧문 **4** a piece of material on a frame that can be moved, used for dividing one part of a room from another ‖ 방의 한 부분을 다른 부분과 나누는 데 사용되는, 움직일 수 있는 틀에 부착된 소재. 칸막이. 병풍 **5** [singular, U] movies, or the business of making movies ‖ 영화나 영화 제작 사업. 영화(업)계: *a chance to appear on the big screen* (=in a movie) *with Robert DeNiro* 로버트 드니로와 함께 영화에 출연할 기회

screen² v [T] **1** to do medical tests on people in order to discover whether they have a particular illness ‖ 특정한 질병이 있는지 알아보기 위해 사람들에게 의학적 검사를 하다. 검진하다: *Women over the age of 50 are screened for breast*

cancer. 50세가 넘는 여성들은 유방암에 대한 검사를 받는다. **2** to test people in order to find out whether they are suitable for a particular job or organization ‖ 사람을 특정한 일이나 조직에 적합한지 알아보기 위해 검사하다. 심사하다. 선별하다. 걸러내다: *Every job applicant is screened before the interview.* 모든 구직자들은 면접 전에 전형을 거친다. **3** also **screen off** to hide or protect something by putting something in front of it ‖ 어떤 것 앞에 다른 것을 놓아서 숨기거나 보호하다. 가리다. 차단[차폐]하다: *Part of the murder victim's house was screened off by the police.* 피살자의 집의 일부가 경찰에 의해 차단되었다. **4 screen calls** to find out who is calling you on the telephone, especially by using an ANSWERING MACHINE, so that you do not have to speak to someone you do not want to ‖ 원하지 않는 사람과 통화하지 않도록 자동 응답기를 사용해서 자신에게 전화하고 있는 사람을 알아내다. 전화를 선별하여 받다

screen·play /'skri:nplei/ n a story written for a movie or a television show ‖ 영화나 텔레비전 쇼를 위해 씌어진 이야기. 시나리오. 대본. 각본

screen saver /'., ,../ a computer program that makes a moving image appear on a computer screen when no work has been done on the computer for a period of time so that the screen does not become damaged ‖ 화면이 손상되지 않도록 일정 시간 컴퓨터로 작업을 하지 않으면 컴퓨터 화면에 움직이는 영상을 나타나게 하는 컴퓨터 프로그램. 화면 보호기

screen·writ·er /'skri:n,raitə/ n someone who writes SCREENPLAYS ‖ 시나리오를 쓰는 사람. 시나리오[대본] 작가

screw¹ /skru:/ n **1** a thin pointed piece of metal that you push and turn in order to fasten pieces of wood or metal together ‖ 나무나 금속 조각을 함께 고정시키기 위해 눌러 돌리는 가늘고 끝이 뾰족한 금속 조각. 나사(못) **2 have a screw loose** INFORMAL OFTEN HUMOROUS to be slightly crazy ‖ 약간 미치다. 머리가 이상하다[돌다]

screw² v **1** [T] to fasten two objects together using a screw ‖ 나사를 사용해 두 물체를 서로 단단히 고정시키다. 나사로 죄다: *Screw the boards together using the half-inch screws.* 반 인치 나사못을 사용해 그 판자들을 함께 단단히 고정시켜라. **2** [T] to fasten or close something by turning it until it cannot be turned any more ‖ 더 이상 돌아가지 않을 때까지 돌려서 어떤 것을 단단히 조이거나 꼭 닫다. …을 비틀어서 죄다[밀착하다]: Don't forget to screw the top back on. 뚜껑을 되돌려 닫는 것을 잊지 마라. **3** [T] SPOKEN an impolite word meaning to treat someone dishonestly or unfairly ‖ 남을 부정직하게 또는 불공정하게 다루는 것을 의미하는 무례한 말. 남을 속이다[사기치다]: We really got screwed on that deal. 우리는 그 거래에서 완전히 사기 당했다.

screw around phr v [I] SPOKEN to waste time or behave in a silly way ‖ 시간을 낭비하거나 어리석게 행동하다. 시시한 짓으로 시간을 보내다. 빈둥거리다: Stop screwing around and get back to work! 빈들빈들 시간 낭비하지 말고 일이나 해!

screw up phr v **1** [I, T **screw sth up**] INFORMAL to make a bad mistake that ruins what you intended to do ‖ 자신이 하고자 했던 것을 망치는 큰 실수를 하다. 엉망[뒤죽박죽]으로 만들다. 못쓰게 만들다: I can't believe they screwed up our plane tickets. 그들이 우리의 비행기 표를 못쓰게 만들다니 믿을 수 없다. **2** [T **screw sb ↔ up**] INFORMAL to make someone feel extremely unhappy, confused, or anxious, especially for a long time ‖ 특히 오랫동안 남을 아주 불행하게[혼란스럽게, 걱정스럽게] 느끼게 하다. 고달프게 만들다. 괴롭히다: Carole's family really screwed her up. 캐롤의 가족들은 그녀를 정말 괴롭게 만들었다. **3 screw up your face/lips/eyes etc.** to tighten the muscles in your face etc. ‖ 얼굴 등의 근육을 조이다. 얼굴을 찌푸리다/입술을 꽉 다물다/눈을 꼭 감다

screw·ball /'skrubɔl/ n INFORMAL someone who seems very strange, silly, or crazy ‖ 매우 이상해[어리석어, 미쳐] 보이는 사람. 괴짜. 기인 - **screwball** adj

screw·driv·er /'skru,draɪvɚ/ n a tool with a long thin metal end, used for turning screws ‖ 나사를 돌리는 데 사용되는 길고 가는 금속제 끝을 가진 도구. 드라이버

screwed up /ˌ. '../ adj INFORMAL **1** very unhappy, confused, or anxious because you have had bad experiences in the past ‖ 과거에 나쁜 경험을 가졌기 때문에 매우 불행한[혼란스러운, 괴로워하는]. 정신적으로 혼돈된. 당황한: These poor kids, they're so screwed up from their parents' divorce. 이 가련한 아이들은 부모들의 이혼으로 매우 혼란에 빠져

있다. **2** not working, or in a bad condition ‖ 작동하지 않는, 또는 나쁜 상태의. 고장 난. 망가진: My left leg got screwed up playing football. 내 왼쪽 다리는 미식축구를 하다가 다쳤다.

screw·y /'skrui/ adj INFORMAL slightly strange or crazy ‖ 약간 이상하거나 미친. 별난. 터무니없는: a screwy plan 터무니없는 계획

scrib·ble /'skrɪbəl/ v **1** also **scribble down** [T] to write something quickly in a messy way ‖ 어떤 것을 지저분하게 재빨리 쓰다. 휘갈겨 쓰다. 끼적거리다: He scribbled down his phone number on a business card. 그는 명함에다 자기의 전화번호를 휘갈겨 썼다. **2** [I] to draw marks that do not mean anything ‖ 아무 의미도 없는 표시들을 그리다. 낙서하다: Stop scribbling on the desk! 책상에 낙서하지 마라! - **scribble** n - **scribbles** n [plural]

scribe /skraɪb/ n someone in past times whose job was to copy or record things by writing them ‖ 어떤 것을 글씨로 써서 필사하거나 기록하는 일을 했던 예전의 직업인. 필경사(筆耕士). 사본 필사자. 서기

scrimp /skrɪmp/ v **scrimp and save** to try to save as much money as you can, even though you have very little ‖ 비록 돈은 적게 가지고 있지만 가능한 한 많은 돈을 모으려고 노력하다. 몹시 절약[긴축]하다. 인색하게 굴다: We had to scrimp and save the first few years we were married. 우리는 결혼하고 첫 몇 해 동안은 허리띠를 졸라매고 절약해야 했다.

script /skrɪpt/ n **1** the written form of a speech, play, television or radio show, or movie ‖ 연설[연극, 텔레비전이나 라디오 쇼, 영화]의 대본. 각본: Bring your script to rehearsal. 리허설에 당신의 대본을 가지고 오시오. **2** [C, U] the set of letters used in writing a language; ALPHABET ‖ 언어를 쓰는 데 사용되는 일련의 글자들. 문자; 웝 alphabet: Arabic script 아라비아 문자 **3** [singular, U] writing done by hand, especially so that the letters of the words are joined ‖ 단어의 글자들이 연결되도록 손으로 쓴 글씨. 서체: cursive script 필기체

script·ed /'skrɪptɪd/ adj a scripted speech or broadcast has been planned and written down so that it can be read ‖ 연설이나 방송이 읽을 수 있도록 사전에 원고가 마련된. 대본이 있는

scrip·ture /'skrɪptʃɚ/ n **1** [U] also **the (Holy) Scripture** the Bible ‖ 성서 **2** [C, U] the holy books of a particular

religion ‖ 특정 종교의 성스러운 책. 경전
- **scriptural** adj

script·writ·er /ˈskrɪptˌraɪtɚ/ n
someone who writes SCRIPTs for movies,
television programs etc. ‖ 영화·텔레비전
프로그램 등의 대본을 쓰는 사람. 극작가.
시나리오 작가

scroll¹ /skroʊl/ n a long piece of paper
that is rolled up and has official writing
on it ‖ 공식적인 기록이 들어 있는 둘둘 말
린 긴 종잇조각. 두루마리(문서)

scroll² v [I, T] to move information up
or down a computer screen so that you
can read it ‖ 읽을 수 있도록 컴퓨터 화면
상의 정보를 올리거나 내리거나 하다. (…
을) 스크롤하다

scrooge /skrudʒ/ n INFORMAL someone
who hates to spend money ‖ 돈 쓰는 것
을 싫어하는 사람. 수전노. 구두쇠

scro·tum /ˈskroʊtəm/ n the bag of flesh
on a man or male animal that contains
the TESTICLEs ‖ 남성이나 수컷의 고환을
감싸고 있는 살주머니. 음낭

scrounge /skraʊndʒ/ v INFORMAL **1** [T]
to get money or something you want by
asking other people to give it to you
instead of earning it or paying for it
yourself ‖ 자신이 직접 벌거나 돈을 지불
하지 않고 다른 사람에게 달라고 해서 돈
이나 자신이 원하는 것을 얻다. 거저 얻
다. 슬쩍 가지다. 등쳐서 얻다: *Sarah
was scrounging cigarettes off the guys
all night.* 사라는 저녁 내내 남자들에게서
담배를 얻어 피우고 있었다. **2** [I] to
search for something such as food or
supplies ‖ 음식이나 물품 등을 찾다. 찾아
다니다. 뒤지고 다니다: *a sculpture built
from materials scrounged from
junkyards* 폐품 처리장에서 찾아낸 재료
로 만든 조각품

scrub¹ /skrʌb/ v **-bbed, -bbing** [I, T]
to clean something by rubbing it very
hard with a stiff brush or rough cloth ‖
뻣뻣한 솔이나 거친 천으로 매우 세게 문
질러 어떤 것을 깨끗이 하다. 박박 문질러
깨끗이 하다: *Don't forget to scrub
behind your ears.* 귀 뒤쪽을 문질러 깨끗
하게 씻는 것을 잊지 마라. / *scrub the
floor* 마루를 박박 문질러 깨끗이 하다.

scrub² n [U] low bushes and trees that
grow in very dry soil ‖ 매우 마른 땅에서
자라는 키 작은 덤불이나 나무. 관목(숲)

scruff /skrʌf/ n **by the scruff of the
neck** if you hold an animal or person by
the scruff of the neck, you hold the fur,
flesh, or clothes at the back of his, her,
or its neck ‖ 사람이나 동물의 목덜미의 털
[살, 옷]을 잡는. 목덜미를 움켜잡는: *The*

cat had a kitten by the scruff of its neck.
그 고양이는 새끼 고양이의 목덜미를 물었
다.

scruff·y /ˈskrʌfi/ adj dirty and messy ‖
더럽고 지저분한. 지저분하게 어질러진.
칠칠치 못한: *a scruffy kid* 더럽고 지저분
한 아이

scrump·tious /ˈskrʌmpʃəs/ adj
INFORMAL food that is scrumptious tastes
very good ‖ 음식이 아주 맛있는

scrunch /skrʌntʃ/ v

scrunch sth ↔ up phr v [T] to twist or
crush something into a small shape ‖ 어
떤 것을 작은 모양으로 비틀거나 찌부러뜨
리다. 납작하게 구기다. 꾸깃꾸깃하게 뭉
치다: *He scrunched up his napkin.* 그는
냅킨을 꾸깃꾸깃하게 뭉쳤다.

scru·ple /ˈskrupəl/ n [C usually plural]
an idea of what is right and wrong, that
prevents you from doing something that
is considered bad ‖ 나쁘게 생각되는 것을
못하게 막는 옳고 그름에 대한 생각. 양심
의 가책. 도덕관념: *He wondered if Gwen
had any religious scruples about sex.* 그
는 그웬에게 섹스에 대한 무슨 종교적 거
리낌이 있는 것은 아닌지 의아해했다.

scru·pu·lous /ˈskrupyələs/ adj **1** done
very carefully so that every detail is
correct ‖ 매사가 올바르도록 매우 조심스
럽게 행해지는. 세심한. 꼼꼼한. 빈틈없
는: *his scrupulous attention to detail* 사
소한 것에까지 신경 쓰는 그의 세심한 주
의력 **2** careful to be honest, fair, and
morally correct ‖ 정직하고 공정하며 도덕
적으로 올바르도록 주의하는. 양심적인.
신중한. 결백한: *He carried out his task
with great care and scrupulous
fairness.* 그는 자신의 직무를 대단히 주의
를 기울여 양심적이고 공평하게 처리했다.
- **scrupulously** adv —opposite
UNSCRUPULOUS

scru·ti·nize /ˈskrutˑnˌaɪz/ v [T] to
examine someone or something very
carefully and completely ‖ 사람이나 사물
을 매우 주의 깊고 완벽하게 조사하다. …
을 정밀하게 조사하다. 속속들이 알아보
다: *Sherman got out and scrutinized the
fender.* 셔먼은 밖으로 나와서 자동차의
펜더를 자세히 살펴보았다.

scru·ti·ny /ˈskrutˑn-i/ n [U] the process
of examining something carefully and
completely ‖ 어떤 것을 주의 깊고 완벽하
게 조사하는 과정. 정밀한 조사. 속속들이
알아보기. 꼬치꼬치 따지기: *Closer
scrutiny shows that the numbers don't
add up.* 보다 정밀한 조사로 숫자가 맞지
않는다는 것을 밝혀냈다.

scu·ba div·ing /ˈskubə ˌdaɪvɪŋ/ n [U]

the sport of swimming under water while breathing from a container of air on your back ‖ 등에 있는 산소통으로 숨을 쉬면서 물 밑에서 수영하는 스포츠. 스쿠버 다이빙

scuff /skʌf/ v [T] to make a mark on a smooth surface by rubbing something rough against it ‖ 거친 것을 대고 문질러 부드러운 표면에 자국을 내다. …에 문질러서 흠을 내다: *I've already scuffed my new shoes.* 벌써 내 새 구두가 흠집이 났다.

scuf·fle /ˈskʌfəl/ n a short fight that involves only a few people and is not very serious ‖ 단지 몇 사람만이 관련되고 그리 심각하지 않은 짧은 싸움. 가벼운 싸움. 드잡이: *A policeman was injured in a scuffle with demonstrators yesterday.* 경찰관 한 명이 어제 시위자들과의 한바탕 드잡이에서 부상을 당했다. **– scuffle** v [I, T]

sculp·tor /ˈskʌlptɚ/ n an artists who makes SCULPTUREs ‖ 조각품을 만드는 예술가. 조각가

sculp·ture /ˈskʌlptʃɚ/ n 1 [C, U] objects made from clay, wood, metal etc. as a form of art and often shaped like people or animals ‖ 예술의 한 형태로, 점토·나무·금속 등으로 만든 흔히 사람이나 동물 같은 모습의 물체. 조각품: *a bronze sculpture by Peter Helzer* 피터 헬저 작(作) 청동 조각품 **2** [U] the art of making these objects ‖ 이들 조각품을 만드는 예술. 조각술: *a sculpture class* 조각술 강의

sculp·tured /ˈskʌlptʃɚd/ adj **1** decorated with SCULPTUREs ‖ 조각으로 장식한: *the sculptured entrance of the church* 조각으로 장식한 교회의 출입구 **2 sculptured muscles/features etc.** muscles etc. that look like an artist shaped them because they are so smooth and perfect ‖ 너무 매끄럽고 완벽해서 마치 예술가가 만든 것처럼 보이는 근육 등. 조각같이 잘 발달된 근육/단정한 용모

scum /skʌm/ n **1** [singular, U] the thick messy substance that forms on the surface or at the bottom of a liquid ‖ 액체의 표면이나 바닥에 형성되는 질척거리고 지저분한 물질. 찌꺼기. 버캐. 더껑이: *Green scum covered the old pond.* 녹조류 부유물이 오래된 연못을 뒤덮었다. **2** SPOKEN ⇨ SCUMBAG

scum·bag /ˈskʌmbæg/ n SPOKEN an unpleasant person that you do not like, trust, or respect ‖ 좋아하지[믿지, 존경하지] 않는 불쾌한 사람. 징그러운 놈. 쓰레기 같은 인간: *What a scumbag!* 인간 쓰레기 같으니라구!

scur·ri·lous /ˈskɚələs, ˈskʌr-/ adj a scurrilous remark, article etc. contains untrue statements that are intended to make someone or something seem bad ‖ 발언·기사 등이 다른 사람이나 사물을 나쁘게 보이게 하려는 거짓 진술을 포함하고 있는. 업신여기는. 중상[비방]하는

scur·ry /ˈskɚi, ˈskʌri/ v [I] to move very quickly with small steps ‖ 종종걸음으로 매우 빨리 움직이다. 급히 가다. 후다닥 뛰어가다: *squirrels scurrying around* 날쌔게 뛰어 돌아다니는 다람쥐

scut·tle /ˈskʌtl/ v **1** INFORMAL to ruin someone's plans or chance of being successful ‖ 성공할 수 있는 남의 계획이나 기회를 망치다. 단념[철회]시키다. 무산시키다: *Plans for the freeway have been scuttled due to lack of money.* 그 고속도로를 건설하려는 계획은 자금 부족으로 무산되었다. **2** [I] to run quickly with small steps ‖ 종종걸음으로 빨리 달리다. 허둥지둥 달리다. 서두르다: *crabs scuttling along the beach* 해변을 따라 종종걸음으로 빨리 달아나고 있는 게 **3** [T] to sink a ship, especially in order to prevent it from being used by an enemy ‖ 특히 적에게 이용되는 것을 막기 위해 배를 가라앉히다

scythe /saɪð/ n a farming tool with a long curved blade, used for cutting grain or long grass ‖ 곡초나 긴 풀을 자르는 데 사용하는 길게 휜 날을 가진 농기구. 풀 베는 큰 낫

SD the written abbreviation of South Dakota ‖ South Dakota(사우스다코타 주)의 약어

SE the written abbreviation of SOUTHEAST ‖ southeast의 약어

sea /si/ n **1** a large area of salty water that is smaller than an ocean, or that is enclosed by land ‖ 대양보다는 좀 작거나 육지에 의해 둘러싸인 넓은 염수 지역. 바다. …해: *the North Sea* 북해 / *the Mediterranean Sea* 지중해 **2** a word meaning the ocean that is used when talking about traveling in a ship or boat ‖ 배나 보트로 여행하는 것에 대해 이야기할 때 쓰이는 바다를 의미하는 말. 바다. 해양: *The boat was heading out to sea.* (=traveling away from land) 그 보트는 바다를 향해 나가고 있었다. **3 a sea of** a large number or amount of something ‖ 어떤 것의 많은 수나 양: *a sea of people* 엄청난 사람들 **4 the seas** LITERARY the ocean ‖ 바다

sea·bed /ˈsibɛd/ n the land at the

bottom of the sea ‖ 바다 밑바닥의 땅. 해저

sea·far·ing /ˈsiˌfɛrɪŋ/ adj LITERARY relating to ships that travel in the ocean, and the people who work on them ‖ 바다에서 항행하는 배와 그 배에서 일하는 사람들과 관련된. 해상 여행의. 선원 직업의

sea·food /ˈsifud/ n [U] ocean animals such as fish and SHELLFISH that can be eaten ‖ 먹을 수 있는 물고기와 조개 등 바다 동물. 해산물

sea·gull /ˈsigʌl/ n a common gray and white bird that lives near the sea and has a loud cry ‖ 바닷가에 살며 큰 울음소리를 내는, 희고 잿빛이 나는 흔한 새. 갈매기

sea·horse /ˈsihɔrs/ n a small sea fish that has a head and neck that look like those of a horse ‖ 머리와 목이 말처럼 생긴 작은 바닷물고기. 해마

seal¹ /sil/ n **1** a large sea animal that has smooth fur, eats fish, and lives by the ocean in cold areas ‖ 매끄러운 털을 가지고 있고 물고기를 먹으며 추운 지역의 바닷가에 사는 몸집이 큰 바다 동물. 바다표범. 물개 **2** an official mark that is put on documents, objects etc. in order to prove that they are legal or real ‖ 서류나 물건 등이 합법적이거나 진짜라는 것을 증명하기 위해 그 위에 찍는 공식적인 표식. 봉인. 도장. 인장: *The letter had the seal of the Department of Justice at the top.* 그 편지는 맨 위에 법무부의 인장이 찍혀 있었다. **3** a piece of rubber or plastic used on a pipe, machine, container etc. in order to prevent something such as water or air from going into or out of it ‖ 물이나 공기 등의 것이 드나드는 것을 막기 위해 파이프·기계·용기 등에 사용되는 고무나 플라스틱 조각. 패킹(packing) **4** a piece of WAX, plastic etc. that you break in order to open a new container ‖ 새 용기를 열기 위해 깨뜨리는 밀랍·플라스틱 등의 조각. 밀봉재. 봉인(물). 봉인지: *Do not use this product if the seal on the bottle is broken.* 병의 봉인이 터진 경우에는 이 제품을 사용하지 마십시오. **5 seal of approval** if you give something your seal of approval, you say that you accept or approve of it, especially officially ‖ 어떤 것을 특히 공식적으로 받아들이거나 승인한다는 말. 정식 인가: *The board denied the film its seal of approval.* 위원회는 그 영화의 정식 인가를 거부했다.

seal² v [T] **1** also **seal up** to close an entrance, container, or hole so tightly that no air, water etc. can go into or out of it ‖ 출입구[용기, 구멍]를 꼭 닫아서 공기·물 등이 전혀 드나들 수 없게 하다. 밀봉하다. 밀폐하다: *Many of the tombs have remained sealed since the 16th century.* 많은 무덤들이 16세기 이후로 밀봉된 채 그대로 있다. **2** to close an envelope, package etc. using something sticky, such as TAPE or glue ‖ 테이프나 풀 등 점착성이 있는 것을 사용해서 봉투·꾸러미 등을 밀봉하다 **3 seal a deal/agreement etc.** to do something that makes a promise, agreement etc. seem more definite or official ‖ 약속·협정 등을 보다 명확하거나 공식적으로 보이게 하는 것을 하다. 거래/협정에 (도장을 찍어)보증[조인]하다 : *Everything is finished – we just have to seal the deal with our signatures.* 모든 것이 끝났다. 이제 우리는 서명으로 그 거래를 보증만 하면 된다.

seal sth ↔ **in** phr v [T] to stop something from going out of the thing it is contained in ‖ 용기에 들어 있는 것이 바깥으로 빠져 나가는 것을 막다. 봉하다. 밀봉[밀폐]하다: *Our hamburgers are flame-grilled to seal in freshness and flavor.* 우리의 햄버거는 신선함과 맛을 유지하기 위해 불에다 굽는다.

seal sth ↔ **off** phr v [T] to stop people entering a particular area or building, especially because it is dangerous ‖ 특히 위험하기 때문에 특정한 지역이나 건물에 사람들이 들어가는 것을 막다. 봉쇄하다. 출입 금지시키다: *Soldiers sealed off the area after the recent bombing.* 군인들은 최근에 폭탄이 터지고 난 후 그 지역을 봉쇄했다.

sealed /sild/ adj something that is sealed is completely closed and cannot be opened unless it is broken, cut, or torn ‖ 완전히 밀폐되어 깨지[자르지, 찢지] 않으면 열 수 없는. 밀봉된: *a sealed envelope* 봉인된 봉투 / *a sealed window* 밀폐된 창문

sea lev·el /ˈ. ˌ../ n [U] the average level of the sea, used as a standard for measuring the height of an area of land, such as a mountain ‖ 산 등 육지의 한 지역의 높이를 재기 위한 기준으로 사용되는 바다의 평균 수면. 평균 해면. 해발: *200 feet above sea level* 해발 200피트

sea li·on /ˈ. ˌ../ n a large type of SEAL that lives on the coasts of the Pacific Ocean ‖ 태평양 연안에 사는 큰 물개의 일종. 강치

seam /sim/ n **1** the line where two

pieces of cloth have been sewn together ‖ 두 조각의 천이 서로 기워진 선. 솔기: *His jacket was ripped at the shoulder seams.* 그의 재킷의 어깨솔기가 터졌다. **2** a layer of a mineral, such as coal, that is under the ground ‖ 지하에 묻힌 석탄 등 광물의 층 **3** the line where two pieces of metal, wood etc. have been joined together ‖ 금속·나무 등의 두 조각이 함께 결합된 선. 이음매

sea·man, Seaman /'siːmən/ *n* someone who has the lowest rank in the Navy ‖ 해군에서 가장 낮은 계급을 가진 사람. 수병

seam·less /'siːmlɪs/ *adj* **1** done or made so well, that you do not notice where one part ends and another part begins ‖ 한 부분의 끝과 또 다른 부분의 시작 부분을 알아챌 수 없을 정도로 매우 잘 하거나 만든. 매끄러운. 감쪽같은. 끊긴 데 없는: *The show is a seamless blend of song, dance, and storytelling.* 그 쇼는 노래와 춤과 이야기가 매끄럽게 조화되어 있다. **2** not having any SEAMs ‖ 이음매가 없는: *seamless stockings* (이음매 없이)통으로 짠 스타킹

seams·tress /'siːmstrɪs/ *n* a woman whose job is to make and sew clothes ‖ 옷을 만들고 재봉질하는 여성 직업인. 여자 재봉사. 침모(針母)

seam·y /'siːmi/ *adj* unpleasant and involving crime, violence, POVERTY, or immoral behavior ‖ 불쾌하고 범죄[폭력, 가난, 부도덕 행위]를 포함하는. 추악한. 더러운. 어두운 이면의: *the seamy streets of the city* 도시의 어두운 뒷골목

sé·ance /'seɪɑːns/ *n* a meeting where people try to talk to the spirits of dead people, or to receive messages from them ‖ 사람들이 죽은 사람의 영혼에게 말하거나 그들로부터 메시지를 받으려고 하는 모임. 교령회(交靈會)

sea plane /'. ./ *n* a plane that can land on water ‖ 물 위에 착륙할 수 있는 비행기. 수상 비행기

sear /sɪr/ *v* [T] **1** to burn something with a sudden very strong heat ‖ 매우 강한 열로 순간적으로 어떤 것을 태우다. 표면을 태우다. 그슬리다. …을 불에 데다: *The heat from the fire seared her skin.* 그녀의 피부는 그 불의 열기에 데었다. **2** to cook the outside of a piece of meat quickly at a very high temperature ‖ 고기의 바깥 부분을 매우 높은 온도로 재빨리 굽다. (고기 등을)강한 불에서 단시간 굽다 **– searing** *adj*

search¹ /sɜːtʃ/ *n* **1** [C] an attempt to find someone or something that is

difficult to find ‖ 찾기 어려운 사람이나 사물을 찾으려는 시도. 수사. 수색. 탐색: *Police called off the search for* (=officially stopped looking for) *the missing girl.* 경찰은 실종된 소녀 수색을 중단했다. / *Denise went off in search of a hammer.* 데니스는 망치를 찾으러 가버렸다. **2** [singular] an attempt to find the answer to or explanation of a difficult problem ‖ 어려운 문제의 답이나 설명을 찾기 위한 시도. 추구. 조사: *He traveled around the world in search of the truth.* 그는 진리를 찾아서 전세계를 여행했다.

search² *v* **1** [I, T] to look carefully for someone or something that is difficult to find ‖ 찾기 힘든 사람이나 사물을 주의 깊게 찾다. 뒤지다: *I searched all over the house, but I couldn't find them anywhere.* 나는 온 집안을 샅샅이 뒤졌지만 어디에서도 그것들을 찾을 수 없었다. / *animals searching for food* 먹을 것을 찾고 있는 동물 **2** [T] if the police etc. search someone, they look in his/her pockets, clothes, or bags for guns, drugs etc. ‖ 경찰 등이 사람의 주머니[옷, 가방]에서 총·마약 등을 찾다. 조사하다. 수색하다: *We were all searched at the airport.* 우리 모두는 공항에서 수색당했다. **3** [I] to try to find an answer or explanation for a difficult problem ‖ 어려운 문제에 대한 답이나 설명을 찾으려고 하다. 추구하다. 탐색하다: *Scientists have spent years searching for a solution.* 과학자들은 해결책을 모색하느라 수년간을 보냈다.

search en·gine /'. ,../ *n* a computer PROGRAM that helps you find information on the Internet ‖ 인터넷 상에서 정보를 찾게 도와 주는 컴퓨터 프로그램. 검색 엔진

search·ing /'sɜːtʃɪŋ/ *adj* trying hard to find out details, facts, or someone's feelings and thoughts ‖ 세부 사항[사실, 다른 사람의 감정이나 생각]을 발견하러 위해 열심히 노력하는. 수사하는. 면밀한. 예리한: *He gave me a searching look.* 그는 날카로운 시선을 나에게 보냈다. / *searching questions* 예리한 질문들

search·light /'sɜːtʃlaɪt/ *n* a large bright light used for finding people, vehicles etc. at night ‖ 밤에 사람·탈것 등을 찾기 위해 사용되는 아주 크고 밝은 등. 탐조등

search par·ty /'. ,../ *n* a group of people organized to look for someone who is lost ‖ 실종된 사람을 찾기 위해 조직된 일단의 사람들. 수색대

search war·rant /'. ,../ *n* a legal

document that officially allows the police to search a building ‖ 경찰에게 건물을 수색하도록 허용하는 공식적인 법률 문서. (가택) 수색 영장

sea·shell /'siʃɛl/ *n* the shell that covers some types of ocean animals ‖ 일부 종류의 바다 동물을 싸고 있는 껍데기. 바닷조개의 조가비

sea·shore /'siʃɔr/ *n* [U] **the seashore** the land along the edge of the ocean ‖ 바닷가를 따라서 나 있는 땅. 해변 —compare BEACH —see usage note at SHORE

sea·sick /'si,sɪk/ *adj* feeling sick because of the movement of a boat or ship ‖ 보트나 배의 움직임으로 인해 토할 것 같은 느낌이 드는. 뱃멀미의 – **seasickness** *n* [U]

sea·side /'sisaɪd/ *adj* relating to the land next to the sea or the ocean ‖ 바다나 대양에 인접한 땅과 관련된. 해변의. 해안의: *a seaside inn* 해변가의 여관

sea·son¹ /'sizən/ *n* **1** one of the four main periods in the year; winter, spring, summer, or fall ‖ 한 해의 네 개의 주요한 기간 중 하나. 철. 계절. 사철 중의 하나; 겨울, 봄, 여름, 또는 가을 **2** a period of time in a year when something happens most often or when something is usually done ‖ 어떤 것이 가장 자주 일어나거나 일상적으로 이뤄지는 1년 중의 한 시기. 철. 활동기. 시즌: *The rainy/wet season usually starts in May.* 장마철은 보통 5월에 시작한다. / *It's football/baseball/basketball season.* (=the period when football etc. is played regularly) 미식축구[야구, 농구] 시즌이다. / *Everything gets so busy during the holiday season.* (=the period from Thanksgiving to New Year's) 연말 기간에는 모든 것이 매우 바빠진다. **3 be in season** if particular vegetables or fruit are in season, it is the time of year when they are ready to be eaten ‖ 특정 야채나 과일이 한창 먹을 수 있게 준비된 연중의 시기이다. 제철[한창 때]이다 **4 out of season** if someone hunts or catches fish out of season, s/he is doing it when it is not legal ‖ 사람이 시즌을 벗어난 시기에 불법적으로 사냥하거나 고기를 잡는. 철이 지난. 금렵[금어]기의

season² *v* [T] to add salt, pepper etc. to food in order to make it taste better ‖ 맛을 더 좋게 하기 위해서 음식에다 소금·후추 등을 치다. 양념하다. 맛을 들이다: *The salad was seasoned with fresh herbs.* 그 샐러드는 신선한 허브로 조미되었다.

sea·son·a·ble /'siznəbəl/ *adj* **seasonable weather/temperatures** weather that seems typical for a particular season ‖ 특정한 계절에 전형적인 것으로 여겨지는 날씨. 계절에 알맞은 날씨/온도 —opposite UNSEASONABLE

sea·son·al /'sizənəl/ *adj* only happening, available, or needed during a particular season ‖ 특정한 계절에만 일어나는[이용 가능한, 필요한]. 계절에 한정된[따른]: *Jim hires high school kids for seasonal help at the farm.* 짐은 농장에서 한 철 동안 도움을 받기 위해서 고등학생들을 고용한다.

sea·soned /'sizənd/ *adj* **seasoned soldier/lawyer/dancer etc.** someone who has had a lot of experience as a soldier etc. ‖ 군인 등으로서 많은 경험을 가진 사람. 숙련된[베테랑] 군인/변호사/무용수: *Even the seasoned professionals were impressed by her speech.* 숙련된 전문가들조차도 그녀의 연설에 감동을 받았다.

sea·son·ing /'sizənɪŋ/ *n* [C, U] salt, pepper, SPICEs etc. that you add to food to make it taste better ‖ 맛을 더 좋게 하기 위해 음식에다 넣는 소금·후추·향신료 등. 조미료

season tick·et /,.. '../ *n* a ticket that allows you to go on a trip, go to a theater, watch a sports team etc. as often as you want during a certain period of time ‖ 일정한 기간 동안 원하는 만큼 자주 여행을 갈[극장을 갈, 스포츠 경기 등을 볼 수 있는] 수 있는 표. 정기권. 정기 승차권[입장권]

seat¹ /sit/ *n* **1** something such as a BENCH or chair that you can sit on, especially one in a restaurant, plane, or theater ‖ 특히 식당[비행기, 극장]에서 앉을 수 있는 벤치나 의자 등의 것. 좌석. 자리: *I think I left my sweater in the front/back seat of Mom's car.* 내 스웨터를 엄마 차 앞[뒤]좌석에다 놔두고 온 것 같아. / *We had great seats at the Giants game.* 우리는 자이언츠 팀 경기에서 좋은 자리에 앉았다. —see picture at ROW¹ **2 take/have a seat** to sit down ‖ 앉다: *Please take a seat, Ms. Carson.* 카슨 씨, 자 앉으세요. **3** the part of a chair, bicycle etc. that you sit on ‖ 의자나 자전거 등의 앉는 부분 **4** a position as a member of the government or a group that makes official decisions ‖ 공식적인 결정을 내리는 정부나 집단의 일원으로서의 지위. 의석. 의장[위원]직: *The Republican Party won two more seats in the Senate.* 공화당은 상원에서 의석을 두

개 더 확보했다. **5 seat of learning/ government etc.** FORMAL a place, usually a city, where a university or government is based ‖ 대학이나 정부가 근거지로 삼은 곳, 보통 도시. 배움의 터전/정부 소재지 —see also **take a back seat** (BACK SEAT)

seat[2] *v* [T] **1 be seated a)** to be sitting down ‖ 앉아 있다. 자리하다[잡다]: *Schultz was seated next to the President throughout the speech.* 슐츠는 연설 내내 대통령 바로 옆에 자리했다. **b)** SPOKEN FORMAL used in order to politely ask someone to sit down ‖ 남에게 앉으라고 정중하게 요청하는 데에 쓰여. 착석하십시오: *Would everyone please be seated.* 모두 앉아 주세요. **2 seat yourself** to sit down somewhere ‖ 어딘가에 앉다: *Seating himself on a nearby chair, he asked, "So how can I help?"* 옆에 있는 의자에 앉으며 그는 "그래 뭘 도와 줄까?"라고 말했다. **3** to make someone sit in a particular place ‖ 남에게 특정한 장소에 앉게 하다. …을 좌석에 안내하다. …에게 자리를 찾아 주다: *The hostess will seat you soon.* 안내원이 곧 자리로 안내할 겁니다. **4** if a room, vehicle, theater etc. seats a particular number of people, it has enough seats for that number ‖ 방·탈것·극장 등이 특정한 수의 사람들이 앉을 수 있는 충분한 좌석을 가지고 있다. …명의 좌석을 가지다: *The new Olympic stadium seats over 70,000.* 새 올림픽 경기장은 7만명 이상을 수용한다.

seat belt /'. ./ *n* a strong belt attached to the seat of a car or plane, that you fasten around yourself for protection in an accident ‖ 사고시 보호를 위해 사람이 매는, 자동차나 비행기 좌석에 부착된 강한 벨트. 좌석[안전]벨트[띠]: *Please fasten your seat belts.* 안전벨트를 매 주십시오. —see picture on page 943

seat·ing /'sitɪŋ/ *n* [U] seats that are available or arranged in a particular way ‖ 특정한 방식으로 이용할 수 있거나 배열된 좌석. 좌석 배치. 좌석수: *Have you made the **seating arrangements/ plans** for your wedding reception yet?* (=planned where people will sit) 벌써 너의 결혼 피로연을 위한 자리 배치를 다 했느냐?

sea ur·chin /'. ,../ *n* a small round sea animal that is covered with sharp points ‖ 뾰족한 가시로 뒤덮인 작고 둥근 바다 동물. 성게

sea·weed /'siwid/ *n* [U] a common plant that grows in the ocean ‖ 바다에서

자라는 흔한 식물. 해초. 바닷말. 해조

sec /sɛk/ *n* SPOKEN a short form of "second" ‖ "second"의 단축형: *Wait a sec – I'm coming too!* 잠깐만 기다려. 나도 갈게!

se·cede /sɪ'sid/ *v* [I] FORMAL to formally stop being part of a country, especially because of a disagreement ‖ 특히 불화 때문에 어떤 나라의 일부분이 되는 것을 공식적으로 그만두다. 탈퇴하다. 분리하다: *The southern states wanted to secede from the US in the 1850s.* 1850년대 남부의 주들은 미국에서 분리되기를 원했다. – **secession** /sɪ'sɛʃən/ *n* [singular, U]

se·clud·ed /sɪ'kludɪd/ *adj* very private and quiet ‖ 매우 은밀하고 조용한. 외딴. 격리된: *a relaxing vacation on a secluded island* 외딴 섬에서의 느긋한 휴가

se·clu·sion /sɪ'kluʒən/ *n* [U] the state of being private and away from other people ‖ 다른 사람들과 교제하지 않고 떨어져 있는 상태. 은둔. 독거(獨居): *He lives in seclusion inside the old castle.* 그는 오래된 성 안에서 은둔 생활을 한다.

sec·ond[1] /'sɛkənd/ *number, pron* **1** 2nd; someone or something that is after the first one ‖ 첫 번째 다음의 사람이나 사물. 제2의[두 번째인] 사람[것]: *Debbie came in second in the women's marathon.* (=was the one after the winner in a race) 데비는 여성 마라톤 대회에서 2등으로 들어왔다. / *September 2nd* (=second day of September) 9월 2일 **2 be second to none** to be better than anyone or anything else ‖ 다른 어떤 사람이나 어떤 것보다 좋다. 아무에게도 뒤지지 않다. 매우 뛰어나다: *The service in that hotel is second to none.* 그 호텔의 서비스는 최상이다.

second[2] *n* **1** a period of time equal to 1/60 of a minute ‖ 1분의 60분의 1과 같은 시간. 초: *It takes about 30 seconds for the computer to start up.* 그 컴퓨터를 부팅[시동]하는 데에 약 30초가 걸린다. **2** SPOKEN a very short period of time ‖ 매우 짧은 시간. 잠시. 순간: *I'll be off the phone **in a second**!* 금방 전화를 끊을게(기다려)! / *Wait **just a second.*** 잠깐만 기다려라.

sec·ond·ar·y /'sɛkən,dɛri/ *adj* **1** not as important or valuable as something else ‖ 다른 것만큼 중요하거나 가치가 있지 않은. 부수적인. 보조적인: *For many students, academic life is secondary.* 많은 학생들에게 학업은 부수적인 것이다. **2** developing from something of the same

type, or coming from it ‖ 같은 종류의 것
에서 발달된, 또는 그것으로부터 나온. 파
생적인. 이차적인: *a
secondary infection* 2차 감염
secondary school /'.... ,./ *n* a
school in the US or Canada that children
go to after ELEMENTARY SCHOOL and
before college ‖ 미국이나 캐나다에서 초
등학교를 졸업하고 대학에 가기 전에 학생
들이 가는 학교. 중등학교
second base /,.. './ *n* [singular] in
baseball, the second place that a player
must touch before s/he can gain a point
‖ 야구에서 점수를 내기 위해 반드시 밟아
야 하는 두 번째의 누(壘). 2루 —see
picture on page 946
second class /,.. './ *n* [U] a way of
traveling, especially on trains, that is
cheaper but not as comfortable as FIRST
CLASS ‖ 1등 칸만큼 안락하지는 않지만 보
다 저렴하게, 특히 기차로, 여행하는 방식.
2등 칸[석]
second-class /,.. '.'/ *adj* **1**
considered to be less important than
other people or things ‖ 다른 사람들이나
사물들보다 덜 중요하게 생각되는. 2등의.
2류의. 뒤떨어진: *They treated us like
second-class citizens.* (=people who
are not as important as other people in
society) 그들은 우리를 열등한 시민처럼
취급했다. **2** relating to cheaper and less
comfortable seats on a train, bus etc. ‖
기차·버스 등에서 보다 값싸고 덜 편안한
좌석과 관련된. 2등 칸[석]의: *second-
class tickets* 2등 칸[석] 표
second-guess /,.. '.'/ *v* [T] **1** to
criticize something after it has already
happened ‖ 어떤 일이 이미 일어난 뒤에
비판하다. 사후 비판[충고]하다: *There's
no point in second-guessing what
should have been done.* 했어야 했는 데
하고 뒤늦게 비판해 봐야 아무 소용없다.
2 to try to guess what will happen, or to
say what someone will do before s/he
does it ‖ 무엇이 일어날지 추측하려고 애
쓰다, 또는 남이 행동을 하기 전에 무엇을
할지에 대해 말하다. …을 예언[예견, 예
보], 예측]하다: *You have to try to
second-guess the other team's moves.* 너
는 상대 팀의 전략을 예측하려고 노력해야
한다.
second·hand /,.. '.'/ *adj* **1**
secondhand clothes, furniture, books
etc. have already been owned or used
by someone else ‖ 옷·가구·책 등이 이미
다른 사람에 의해 소유되었거나 사용된.
중고품의. 헌: *We bought a cheap
secondhand car.* 우리는 값싼 중고차를

한 대 샀다. **2** a secondhand report,
information etc. is something that you
are told by someone different than the
person who originally said it ‖ 보고나 정
보 등이 처음에 말한 사람과는 다른 사람
에 의해 말하여진. 얻어들어서 아는. 전해
들은 – **secondhand** /,.. '.'/ *adv*
sec·ond·ly /'sɛkəndli/ *adv* used in
order to introduce the second fact,
reason etc. that you want to talk about
‖ 자신이 말하고 싶은 두 번째의 사실·이
유 등을 도입하는 데에 쓰여. 둘째로. 다
음으로: *And secondly, a large number of
her poems deal with love.* 그리고 두 번
째는, 그녀의 상당히 많은 시가 사랑을 다
루고 있다.
second na·ture /,.. '../ *n* [U]
something you have done so often that
you now do it without thinking a lot
about it ‖ 너무 자주 해서 지금은 그것에
대해 많이 생각하지 않고도 하는 것. 제2
의 천성. 습관. 습벽: *After you get used
to driving a car, it becomes second
nature.* 차를 운전하는 것에 익숙해진 뒤
에는 모든 것이 습관적이 된다.
second per·son /,.. '../ *n* [singular]
TECHNICAL in grammar, a form of a verb
or PRONOUN that you use to show the
person you are speaking to. "You" is a
second person pronoun, "you are" is
the second person singular of the verb
"to be" ‖ 문법에서 자신이 말하고 있는 상
대를 나타내기 위해 사용하는 동사나 대명
사의 한 형태. 2인칭. "you"는 2인칭 대명
사이다. "you are"에서 "are"는 "be"동사
의 2인칭 단수형이다
second-rate /,.. '.'/ *adj* not very good
‖ 그리 좋지는 않은. 2류의. 보통의. 평범
한: *second-rate hospitals* 2류 병원들
sec·onds /'sɛkəndz/ *n* [plural] **1**
another serving of the same food after
you have eaten your first serving ‖ 음식
1인분을 먹고 난 후 같은 음식의 추가 1인
분. 또 한 그릇: *Would anyone like
seconds?* 누구 한 그릇 더 드실 분 없어
요? **2** goods sold cheaply because they
are not perfect ‖ 완벽하지 않기 때문에
값싸게 팔리는 물건. 2급품. 등외[하자]
품: *factory seconds* 공장의 2급품
second wind /,.sɛkənd 'wɪnd/ *n*
[singular] the return of strength during
hard physical activity, when it seemed
one had become too tired to continue ‖
심한 육체 활동 중에 사람이 너무 피곤해
서 더 이상 계속할 수 없을 듯할 경우 힘
이 회복되는 것. 원기 회복: *Susan got her
second wind in the last lap of the race.*
수잔은 그 경주의 마지막 한 바퀴에서 기

운을 회복했다.

se·cre·cy /'sikrəsi/ n [U] the act of keeping something such as information secret, or the state of being secret ‖ 정보 등을 비밀로 지키기, 또는 비밀인 상태. 내 밀(內密): *They had to meet in secrecy because of the war.* 그들은 전쟁 때문에 은밀히 만나야 했다.

se·cret¹ /'sikrɪt/ adj known about by only a few people ‖ 극소수 사람들만이 알 고 있는. 비밀의[인]. 기밀의: *I can't believe you've kept your wedding secret from your parents.* (=did not tell them about it) 너희 결혼식을 부모님에게 비밀로 했다니 믿을 수가 없구나. / *secret government files* 정부의 비밀 문서 – **secretly** adv

secret² n an idea, plan, fact etc. that you try to hide because you do not want everyone to know about it ‖ 모든 사람들 이 그것에 대해 아는 것을 원하지 않아서 숨기려고 하는 생각·계획·사실 등. 비밀 [기밀](사항): *Can you keep a secret?* (=not tell a secret) 비밀 지킬 수 있지?

secret a·gent /,.. '../ n someone who secretly collects information or watches people for a government ‖ 정부를 위해서 은밀하게 정보를 수집하거나 사람들을 감 시하는 사람. 비밀 요원. 첩보원

sec·re·tar·y /'sɛkrə,tɛri/ n 1 someone whose job is to TYPE letters, keep records, arrange meetings, answer telephones etc. in an office ‖ 사무실에서 편지 타이핑·기록 보관·회의 준비·전화 수신 등을 하는 직업인. 비서 2 an official who is in charge of a large government department in the US ‖ 미국의 큰 정부 부서를 책임지고 있는 고관. 장관: *the Secretary of Defense* 국방 장관 3 an official in an organization whose job is to write down notes from meetings, write letters etc. ‖ 업무가 회의의 내용을 기록하거나 편지를 쓰는 일 등인 단체 내 의 직원. 서기: *Julie was elected secretary of the poetry club.* 줄리는 시 동 호 회 의 서 기 로 선 출 되 었 다 . – **secretarial** /,sɛkrə'tɛriəl/ adj

se·crete /sɪ'krit/ v [T] 1 if part of a plant or animal secretes a substance, it produces that substance ‖ 식물이나 동물 의 기관이 어떤 물질을 생산해 내다. …을 분비하다: *The animal secretes a scent to keep attackers away.* 그 동물은 공격자 들을 방어하기 위해 악취를 분비한다. 2 FORMAL to hide something ‖ 어떤 것을 숨 기다 – **secretion** /sɪ'kriʃən/ n [C, U]

se·cre·tive /'sikrətɪv/ adj behaving in a way that shows you do not want to tell

people your thoughts, plans etc. ‖ 자신 의 생각이나 계획 등을 남에게 말하고 싶 지 않다는듯이 행동하는. 숨기는. 터놓지 않는

secret serv·ice /,.. '../ n **the Secret Service** a US government department whose main purpose is to protect the President ‖ 대통령을 보호하는 것이 주요 목적인 미국의 정부 부서. 미국의 재무부 검찰국

sect /sɛkt/ n a group of people with its own set of beliefs or religious habits, especially one that has separated from a larger group ‖ 특히 보다 큰 단체로부터 떨어져 나온, 자신들만의 믿음 체계나 종 교적 관습을 가지고 있는 사람들의 집단. 교파. 종파. 분파

sec·tar·i·an /sɛk'tɛriən/ adj supporting a particular religious group and its beliefs, or relating to the differences between religious groups ‖ 특정한 종교 단체와 믿음을 지지하는, 또는 종교 단체 들 간의 차이와 관련된. 분파의. 종파의. 교파의: *sectarian violence* 종파 간의 폭 력 행위 —opposite NON-SECTARIAN

sec·tion¹ /'sɛkʃən/ n 1 one of the parts that an object, group, place etc. is divided into ‖ 나뉘어져 있는 물체·집단 ·장소 등의 부분들 중 하나. 잘라낸 부분 [조각]. 구역. 과. 파: *the poorer sections of Brooklyn* 브루클린의 빈민 지 역 / *Does this restaurant have a smoking section?* 이 식당에는 흡연 구역 이 있습니까? / *The rocket is built in sections.* (=in parts that are then fitted together) 그 로켓은 조립식으로 만들어진 다. 2 one of the parts of a book or newspaper ‖ 책이나 신문의 부분들 중 한 부분. 난(欄): *Are you still reading the sports section?* 아직까지 스포츠란을 읽 고 있니? – **sectional** adj

section² v [T] TECHNICAL to cut or draw a SECTION of something such as a part of the body or a building ‖ 신체나 건물의 한 부분 등의 단면을 자르거나 그리다. … 의 단면도를 그리다. 단면이 나오도록 절 단하다

section sth off phr v [T] to divide an area into SECTIONs ‖ 한 지역을 여러 구역 으로 나누다. 구획하다. 구분하다: *The old part of the graveyard had been sectioned off by trees.* 그 묘지의 오래된 구역은 나무들로 구분되어 있었다.

sec·tor /'sɛktə/ n 1 a part of a particular economic system, such as a business, industry, or trade ‖ 기업[산업, 무역] 등 특정한 경제 체제의 한 부분. (경 제) 부문 . 활동 분야[영역]: *the* *public/private sector of the health industry* (=the part controlled by the government or by private companies) 건강 산업의 공공[민간] 부문 **2** one of the parts that an area is divided into for military purposes ‖ 군사적 목적으로 나누어진 지역 중의 한 부분: *the former eastern sector of Berlin* 베를린의 구동독 군사 지역

sec·u·lar /'sɛkyələ/ *adj* not religious or not controlled by a religious authority ‖ 종교적이지 않거나 종교적 권위로 통제되지 않는. 세속적인. 비종교적인: *secular universities* 비종교적인 대학

se·cure¹ /sɪ'kyʊr/ *adj* **1** not likely to change or be at risk ‖ 변하거나 위험에 처할 것 같지 않은. 안정된: *a secure job* 안정된 직업 **2** safe and protected from danger ‖ 위험으로부터 안전하고 보호된. 안전한. 위험이 없는: *The garage isn't a very secure place.* 그 차고는 그리 안전한 곳이 못 된다. **3** fastened, locked, or guarded ‖ 단단히 묶인[잠긴, 지켜진]. 안전하게 보관된: *He made sure the knife was secure on his belt.* 그는 자기의 벨트에 꽂혀져 있는 칼을 확인했다. **4** confident and having no doubts or worries ‖ 확신하며 의심이나 걱정을 하지 않은. 확고한. 굳건한: *financially secure* (=not needing to worry about having enough money) 재정적으로 튼튼한

se·cure² *v* [T] **1** to get or achieve something important, especially after a lot of effort ‖ 특히 많은 노력을 한 후에 중요한 것을 얻거나 이루다. 확보하다: *a treaty designed to secure peace* 평화를 확보하기 위해 입안된 조약 **2** to make something safe from being attacked or harmed ‖ 공격이나 위해로부터 어떤 것을 안전하게 하다. 지키다: *Armed forces were called out to secure the border.* 군대가 국경을 지키기 위해 소집되었다. **3** to fasten or tie something tightly in a particular position ‖ 어떤 것을 특정한 위치에 꽉 고정시키거나 묶다. 단단히 고정하다[잡아매다]: *We secured the boat and jumped onto the rocks.* 우리는 배를 정박시키고 바위 위로 뛰어올랐다.

se·cu·ri·ty /sɪ'kyʊrəti/ *n* [U] **1** the state of being safe, or the things you do to keep someone or something safe ‖ 안전한 상태, 또는 사람이나 사물을 안전하게 지키기 위해 하는 것. 안전. 무사: *national security* 국가의 안전 / *Allow plenty of time for airport security checks.* 공항의 안전 점검을 위해 충분한 시간을 허용해 주십시오. **2** protection from change, risks, or bad situations ‖

변화[위험, 나쁜 상황]로부터의 보호. 방위. 방어. 안전성: *the security of working for a large, powerful corporation* 유력한 대기업에서 일하는 데서 오는 안전성 / *economic security* 경제적 안정(성) **3** the guards who protect a business's buildings, equipment, and workers ‖ 사무용 빌딩·장비·일하는 사람들을 보호하는 경비원. 보안 요원: *Security is coming over to check the area.* 경비원이 그 구역의 (안전을) 점검하기 위해 오고 있다. **4** a feeling of being safe and protected ‖ 안전하고 보호받고 있는 느낌. 안심. 안도(감): *Rules and order can give a child a sense of security.* 규칙과 질서는 아이에게 안도감을 줄 수 있다.

security de·pos·it /.'… .,./ *n* an amount of money you give to a LANDLORD before you move into a place, that will be returned to you later if you do not damage his/her property ‖ 한 장소로 이사오기 전에 집주인에게 주어서 그 사람의 재산에 손해를 입히지 않으면 나중에 다시 돌려받게 되는 돈. 보증금

se·dan /sɪ'dæn/ *n* a large car that has seats for at least four people and has a TRUNK ‖ 최소한 네 사람이 앉을 수 있는 좌석과 트렁크를 가지고 있는 큰 차. 세단형 자동차 —see picture on page 943

se·date /sɪ'deɪt/ *adj* slow, formal, or not very exciting ‖ 느릿한[격식 차린, 그리 흥분하지 않은]. 온화한. 침착한. 조용한. 수수한. 활기 없는: *his calm sedate manner* 그의 조용하고 침착한 태도

se·dat·ed /sɪ'deɪtɪd/ *adj* made sleepy or calm by being given a special drug ‖ 특별한 약을 먹어서 잠이 들거나 진정되게 하는. 진정시키는

sed·a·tive /'sɛdətɪv/ *n* a drug used in order to make someone sleepy or calm ‖ 사람을 잠이 들거나 차분해지게 하기 위해 사용되는 약. 진정제

sed·en·tar·y /'sɛdn,tɛri/ *adj* a sedentary job involves sitting down or not moving very much ‖ 일이 앉아서 하거나 그리 많이 움직이지 않아도 되는. (일 등이) 앉아서 일하는

sed·i·ment /'sɛdəmənt/ *n* [singular, U] the solid material, such as dirt, that settles at the bottom of a liquid ‖ 액체의 밑바닥에 침전되는 진흙 같은 단단한 물질. 침전물. 앙금. 퇴적물

sed·i·men·ta·ry /,sɛdə'mɛntri, -'mɛntəri/ *adj* made of the SEDIMENT at the bottom of lakes, oceans etc. ‖ 호수·바다 등의 밑바닥의 침전물로 만들어진. 침전으로 생기는. 퇴적성의: *sedimentary* *rock* 퇴적암

se·di·tion /sɪˈdɪʃən/ *n* [U] FORMAL
speech, writing, or actions that try to
encourage people to disobey a
government ‖ 사람들에게 정부에 불복종
할 것을 조장하는 말[글, 행동]. 반정부적
선동. 반란. 폭동 – **seditious** *adj*

se·duce /sɪˈdus/ *v* [T] to persuade
someone to do something, especially to
have sex, by making it seem extremely
attractive ‖ 어떤 것을 대단히 매력적으로
보이게 해서 그것을, 특히 성교를 하자고
남을 꼬드기다. 유혹하다. 꼬드겨 …에 끌
어들이다: *It's the story of a teenage girl
who seduces an older man.* 그것은 나이
든 남성을 유혹한 십대 소녀의 이야기이
다. – **seduction** /sɪˈdʌkʃən/ *n* [C, U]

se·duc·tive /sɪˈdʌktɪv/ *adj* **1** sexually
attractive ‖ 성적으로 매력 있는. 유혹[매
혹]적인: *a woman with a seductive voice*
매혹적인 목소리를 가진 여성 **2** very
attractive to you ‖ 매우 유혹적인. 거절할
수 없는. 혹하게 하는: *a seductive job
offer* 혹하게 하는 일자리 제의

see /si/ *v* saw, seen, seeing
1 ▶USE EYES 눈을 사용하다◀ [I, T] to
use your eyes to notice people or things
‖ 사람이나 사물을 보기 위해 눈을 사용하
다. 보이다. 보다: *I can't see without my
glasses.* 나는 안경 없이는 볼 수 없다. / *I
saw a necklace I really liked at the
mall.* 나는 쇼핑몰에서 내가 정말 좋아하
는 목걸이를 보았다. / *He's seen "Star
Wars" about eight times.* 그는 "스타 워
즈"란 영화를 약 여덟 번 보았다.
2 ▶UNDERSTAND 이해하다◀ [I, T] to
understand or realize something ‖ 어떤
것을 이해하거나 깨닫다. 알다: *Do you
see how it works?* 어떻게 작동하는지 알
겠지? / *I can see (that) Yolanda might
not like it.* 내가 보기에는 욜란다가 그것
을 좋아할 것 같지 않다. / *(You) see,
she's not really old enough for this book
yet.* (=used when you are explaining
something to someone) 자, 그녀가 이 책
을 보기에는 아직 어리다는 것을 알겠지.
/ *"It goes in the red box." "Oh, I see."*
(=I understand) "그것은 붉은색 상자 안
에 넣어야 돼." "응, 알겠어." / *At 14, he
couldn't see the point of* (=understand
the reason) *staying in school.* 열네 살 때
그는 왜 학교에 다녀야하는지를 이해할 수
없었다. / *Do you see what I mean about
the camera being broken?* 너는 카메라가
부숴진 데 대해 내가 말하는 것을 이해하
겠니?
3 ▶VISIT/MEET 방문하다/만나다◀ [T] to
visit, meet, or have a meeting with

someone ‖ 방문하다, 만나다, 남과 모임을
가지다: *I saw BJ the other day.* 나는 며
칠 전 비제이를 만났다. / *You ought to
see a doctor.* 당신은 진찰 받으러 가야 한
다.
4 ▶FIND OUT 찾다◀ [T] to find out
information or a fact ‖ 정보나 사실을 찾
다. 검색하다. 알아보다: *Plug it in and
see if it's working.* 플러그를 꽂고 그것이
작동되는지 알아봐. / *I'll see what's
playing at the movie theater.* 그 극장에
서 무엇이 상영되는지 알아봐야겠다. / *I
guess we'll have to wait and see what
happens.* 나는 우리가 무슨 일이 일어날
지 기다려 봐야 한다고 생각해.
5 ▶CONSIDER 여기다◀ [T] to consider
someone or something in a particular
way ‖ 다른 사람이나 사물을 특정하게 생
각하다. 여기다: *Fights on TV can make
children see violence as normal.* 텔레비
전에서의 폭력 장면은 아이들이 폭력을 대
수롭지 않은 거라고 생각하게 만들 수 있
다. / *He sees himself as the next John
Wayne.* 그는 자기 자신을 제2의 존 웨인
이라고 여긴다. / *Well, the way I see it,
that school is no worse than any other.*
글쎄, 내가 생각하기에 그 학교는 다른 학
교 못지 않다.
6 ▶EXPERIENCE 경험◀ [T] to have
experience of something ‖ 어떤 것을 경
험하다. 겪다. 체험하다: *The attorney
said he had never seen a case like this
before.* 그 변호사는 전에 이와 같은 사건
은 한 번도 겪어 보지 못했다고 말했다.
7 ▶HAPPEN 일어나다◀ [T] to be the
time when or place where something
happens ‖ 어떤 일이 일어난 시간이나 장
소가 되다: *This year has seen a 5%
increase in burglaries.* 올해 강도 사건이
5퍼센트 증가했다.
8 ▶THINK 생각하다◀ [I, T] to think
something, especially about what is
going to happen in the future ‖ 특히 장
래에 무엇이 일어날지에 대해 생각하다.
예상[예측]하다. 내다보다: *We were
supposed to have a vacation in May,
but I don't see that happening.* 우리는 5
월에 휴가를 가질 예정이었지만 그렇게 될
것 같지 않다.
9 ▶MAKE SURE 확실히 하다◀ [T] to
make sure or check that something is
done correctly ‖ 사물이 옳게 되었는지 확
인하거나 검사하다. 알아보다: *Please see
that everything is put back where it
belongs.* 모든 것이 제자리에 되돌려놓아
졌는지 확인하세요.
10 be seeing sb to be having a
romantic relationship with someone ‖ 누

군가와 사랑하는 사이가 되다. …을 사귀다. …과 연인 관계가 되다
11 see eye to eye to agree with someone ‖ 남에게 동의하다: *My mother and I have never seen eye to eye about things.* 내 어머니와 나는 일에 대해 의견의 일치를 본 적이 전혀 없었다.

SPOKEN PHRASES

12 see you used in order to say goodbye to someone you will meet again ‖ 다시 만날 사람에게 작별 인사하는 데에 쓰여. 또 봐. 나중에 봐: *Okay, I'll see you.* (=later) 알았어. 안녕. / *See you, Ben.* 나중에 또 봐, 벤.

13 let's see/let me see said when you are trying to remember something or think about something ‖ 어떤 것을 기억해 내거나 생각하려고 할 때 쓰여. 으응, 가만 있자. 좀 생각해 보자: *Let's see. Was it a week ago I talked to you?* 가만 있자. 내가 너와 얘기한 때가 일주일 전이었던가?

14 I don't see why not said when you mean yes ‖ 긍정을 뜻할 때 쓰여. 안 될 이유가 없다. 물론이다. 그렇다: *"Would that be legal?" "I don't see why not."* "그거 합법적일까요?" "그렇고 말고요."

15 I'll/we'll see said when you do not want to make a decision immediately, especially when you are talking to a child ‖ 의사 결정을 바로 하고 싶지 않을 때, 특히 아이들에게 얘기할 때 쓰여. 곧 알게 될 것이다. 좀 더 상황을 지켜 보자. 생각해 보자: *"Can we go to Disney World this year?" "We'll see."* "우리 올해 디즈니 월드에 갈 수 있죠?" "응. 좀 더 생각해 보고 결정하자."

16 you should have seen sb/sth said when you think someone or something you have seen was very funny, surprising etc. ‖ 자신이 본 사람이나 사물이 매우 우스꽝스럽거나 놀랍다고 생각할 때 쓰여. (그 꼴을) 봤어야 했는데: *You should've seen the look on her face!* 아, 정말 그녀의 얼굴 표정을 봤어야 했는데!

—see also **see clear to sth** (CLEAR³)
see about sth *phr v* [T] **1** to make arrangements or deal with something ‖ 어떤 것을 준비하거나 다루다. 처리하다: *Tran went to see about a job.* 트란은 일자리를 알아보러 갔다. **2 we'll see about that** SPOKEN said when you intend to stop someone doing something s/he has planned ‖ 남이 계획했던 것을 못 하게 하

려고 할 때 쓰여. 나중에 해. 지금은 안 돼: *"I'm going to Tim's." "We'll see about that. I need help with dinner."* "저는 팀의 집에 가려고 해요." "나중에 가, 저녁 식사 준비를 도와 줘야지."

see sb ↔ **off** *phr v* [T] to go to an airport, station etc. to say goodbye to someone who is leaving ‖ 떠나는 사람을 환송하기 위해 공항이나 역 등에 가다. 배웅하다. 전송하다: *The soldiers were seen off by friends and relatives.* 그 군인들은 친구들과 친척들의 배웅을 받았다.

see sb **out** *phr v* [T] to go with someone to the door when s/he leaves ‖ 남이 떠날 때 문까지 그 사람과 같이 가다. 문까지 배웅하다: *No, that's okay, I'll see myself out.* (=go by myself to the door) 아니, 괜찮아요. 일부러 배웅해 주지 않아도 돼요.

see through *phr v* [T] **1** [**see through sb/sth**] to be able to recognize the truth when someone is trying to persuade or deceive you ‖ 남이 자신을 설득하거나 속이려고 할 때 진실을 분별해 낼 수 있다. 진상을 알아채다[간파하다]: *I can see right through his lies.* 나는 그가 거짓말을 하면 대번에 알 수 있다. **2** [**see sb/sth through**] to continue doing something difficult until it is finished, or to continue helping someone during a difficult time ‖ 힘든 것이 끝날 때까지 계속해서 하다, 또는 어려울 때 남을 계속해서 돕다: *Miller is determined to see the project through.* 밀러는 그 계획이 끝날 때까지 계속하기로 결심했다. / *Mom was always there to help see me through.* 어머니는 내가 어려울 때 나를 돕기 위해 항상 거기에 있었다.

see to sth *phr v* [T] to deal with something or make sure that it happens ‖ 어떤 것을 다루거나 어떤 일이 확실히 일어나도록 하다: *"We'll see to it that he does well," said Coach Green.* "우리는 그가 잘하도록 조처하겠습니다."라고 그린 감독은 말했다.

USAGE NOTE see, look, and watch

See is a general word that means "to notice something with your eyes": *I can't see any signs for the highway.* Use **look** when someone deliberately turns his/her eyes toward someone or something and pays attention to him, her, or it: *Look at all the balloons!* Use **watch** for activities or programs that you pay attention to for a period of time: *Jeff's watching the game on*

TV.

see는 "눈으로 어떤 것을 보다"를 의미하는 일반적인 말이다: 간선도로로 안내하는 어떤 표지도 보이지 않는다. **look**은 사람이 일부러 시선을 다른 사람이나 사물 쪽으로 돌리고 주의를 기울일 때 쓴다: 저 풍선들 좀 봐. **watch**는 얼마동안 주의를 기울이는 활동이나 프로그램에 대해 쓰인다: 제프는 텔레비전에서 그 경기를 보고 있다.

seed¹ /sid/ *n, plural* **seed** *or* **seeds** **1** [C, U] a small hard object produced by plants, from which a new plant will grow‖새 식물이 자랄, 식물에 의해 생산되는 작고 딱딱한 물체. 씨. 씨앗: *an apple seed* 사과 씨 **2 (the) seeds of sth** the beginning of something that will grow and develop‖자라고 발전될 것의 시작. 근원. 원인. 기원: *He was able to sow the seeds of doubt in the minds of the jury.* 그는 배심원단의 마음속에 의문의 씨앗을 품게 할 수 있었다.

seed² *v* [T] to plant seeds in the ground‖땅에다 씨를 심다. 파종하다

seed·ling /ˈsidlɪŋ/ *n* a young plant grown from seed‖씨에서 자란 어린 식물. 묘목

seed mon·ey /ˈ. ˌ../ *n* the money needed to start a new business idea or project‖새로운 사업 구상이나 프로젝트를 시작하는 데 필요한 돈. 종자돈

seed·y /ˈsidi/ *adj* INFORMAL looking dirty or poor, and often being related to illegal or immoral activity‖더럽거나 가난해 보이며 종종 불법적이거나 비도덕적인 활동과 관련되어 있는. 보기 흉한. 허름한. 수상쩍은: *the seedy side of town* 도시의 슬럼가 지역

see·ing /ˈsiɪŋ/ *conjunction* because a particular fact or situation is true‖특정한 사실이나 상황이 사실이기 때문에. …이므로. …인 이상: *You can stay out later tonight, seeing that/as it's the weekend.* 주말이니까 너는 오늘 밤 늦게까지 외출해도 된다.

seeing eye dog /ˌ.. ˈ. ˌ./ *n* a dog that is trained to guide blind people‖맹인들을 안내하기 위해 훈련된 개. 맹도견(盲導犬)

seek /sik/ *v* **sought**, **sought**, **seeking** **1** [I, T] to try to find or get something‖어떤 것을 찾거나 얻어내려하다. 찾다. 모색하다. 추구하다: *The UN is seeking a political solution to the crisis.* 유엔은 위기에 대한 정치적인 해결책을 찾고 있다. **2** [T] FORMAL to try to achieve or do something‖어떤 것을 성

취하거나 하려고 하다. …하려 하다[고 노력하다]: *The Governor will not say whether he will seek reelection next year.* 주지사는 내년에 재선을 노릴 것인지 말하지 않을 것이다. **3 seek advice/help etc.** FORMAL to ask someone for advice, help etc.‖남에게 충고·도움 등을 요청하다. 충고/도움을 구하다

seem /sim/ *v* [linking verb] **1** to appear to be a particular thing or to have a particular quality or feeling‖특정한 것으로 보이다. 또는 특정한 자질이나 감정을 가진 것으로 드러나다. …처럼 보이다[생각되다]. 여겨지다: *Henry seems very confused.* 헨리는 매우 당황한 것처럼 보인다. / *There seems to be a problem with the brakes.* 브레이크에 문제가 있는 것처럼 보인다. / *The dream seemed very real to me.* 그 꿈은 나에게 매우 현실적인 것처럼 여겨졌다. **2** to appear to exist or be true‖존재하거나 사실인 것으로 보이다. …인 것 같다: *We seem to have turned onto the wrong road.* 우리는 길을 잘못 들어선 것 같다.

seem·ing /ˈsimɪŋ/ *adj* FORMAL appearing to be true even though it may not be‖비록 사실이 아닐지 몰라도 사실인 것처럼 보이는. 외관상의. 표면의. 겉치레의. 겉보기만의: *her seeming calm* 그녀의 외관상의 차분함 —compare APPARENT

seem·ing·ly /ˈsimɪŋli/ *adv* in a way that appears to be true but may not be‖사실이 아닐지 몰라도 사실인 것처럼 보이게. 겉보기로는. 겉으로 판단하기에는. 외양은: *a seemingly endless stretch of land* 겉보기에 끝없이 펼쳐진 땅 —compare APPARENTLY

seen /sin/ *v* the PAST PARTICIPLE of SEE‖see의 과거 분사형

seep /sip/ *v* [I] to flow slowly through small holes or cracks‖작은 구멍이나 갈라진 틈을 통해 천천히 흐르다. 새어나오다. 스며들다: *Water was seeping through the ceiling.* 물이 천장에서 새고 있었다. — **seepage** *n* [singular, U]

see·saw¹ /ˈsisɔ/ *n* a long board on which children play, that is balanced in the middle so that when one end goes up the other end goes down‖한쪽 끝이 올라가면 다른 한쪽 끝이 내려갈 수 있게 중간 부분에 균형이 잡힌, 아이들이 노는 긴 판. 시소(판). 시소놀이

seesaw² *v* [I] to move suddenly up and down or from one condition to another and back again‖갑자기 위아래로 움직이거나 한 상황에서 또 다른 상황으로 움직

이다가 다시 원래대로 가다. 널뛰기하다. 등락을 반복하다: *Stock prices seesawed throughout the morning.* 주가는 오전 내내 널뛰기 장세를 보였다.

seethe /siθ/ v [I] to be so angry that you are almost shaking ‖ 너무 화가 나서 거의 부들부들 떨다. (노여움·불만·흥분 등으로) 끓어오르다: *Holly was seething with rage.* 홀리는 분노로 몸을 부들부들 떨고 있었다. **- seething** *adj*

seg·ment /'sɛgmənt/ n a part of something that is divided from the whole ‖ 전체에서 나뉘어진 것의 한 부분. 단편. 구분: *a large segment of the population* 인구의 대다수 / *an orange segment* 오렌지 한 조각

seg·ment·ed /'sɛgmɛntɪd/ *adj* divided into separate parts ‖ 각 부분으로 나뉘어진. 분절된: *the segmented body of an insect* 곤충의 분절된 몸

seg·re·gate /'sɛgrə,geɪt/ v [T] to separate one group of people from others because of race, sex, religion etc. ‖ 인종·성·종교 등 때문에 다른 사람들로부터 한 집단의 사람들을 분리하다. 격리하다. 차별하여 분리[격리]하다: *The Group Areas Act segregated housing along racial lines.* 집단 지역법은 인종별로 주택을 분리했다. **- segregation** /,sɛgrə'geɪʃən/ n [U] —compare INTEGRATE

seg·re·gat·ed /'sɛgrə,geɪtɪd/ *adj* segregated buildings or areas can only be used by members of a particular race, sex, religion etc. ‖ 건물이나 지역이 특정 인종·성·종교 등의 사람들만이 사용할 수 있는. 특정 인종[집단]에 한정된: *racially segregated schools* 특정 인종 전용 학교

seis·mic /'saɪzmɪk/ *adj* TECHNICAL relating to or caused by EARTHQUAKEs ‖ 지진과 관련되거나 지진으로 야기된. 지진의[에 의한]: *a period of seismic activity* 지진 활동 주기

seis·mol·o·gy /,saɪz'mɑlədʒi/ n [U] the scientific study of EARTHQUAKEs ‖ 지진의 과학적 연구. 지진학 **- seismologist** n

seize /siz/ v 1 [T] to take hold of something quickly and forcefully; GRAB ‖ 어떤 것을 재빨리 그리고 힘차게 붙잡다. 꽉 잡다. 움켜쥐다; 〔동〕 grab: *Ron seized the child's arm and lifted her into the boat.* 론은 아이의 팔을 꽉 잡고 보트로 끌어올렸다. 2 **seize control/power** to take control of a place suddenly using military force ‖ 군사력을 이용해 갑자기 한 장소를 지배하다. 점거

하다: *Rebels seized control of the embassy.* 반란군들은 대사관을 점거했다. 3 [T] to take away something such as illegal guns, drugs etc. ‖ 불법적인 총이나 마약 등의 것을 빼앗다. 압류[압수]하다: *Police seized 10 kilos of cocaine.* 경찰은 코카인 10킬로를 압수했다.

sei·zure /'siʒɚ/ n 1 [U] the act of taking control or possession of something suddenly ‖ 사물을 갑자기 지배하거나 소유하는 행위. 압수. 압류. 강탈. 탈취: *the seizure of illegal firearms* 불법 무기의 압수 2 a short time when someone is unconscious and cannot control the movements of his/her body ‖ 사람이 의식이 없고 자기의 몸을 마음대로 움직일 수 없는 잠깐 동안. 발작(의 기간): *an epileptic seizure* 간질의 발작

sel·dom /'sɛldəm/ *adv* very rarely ‖ 매우 드물게. 좀처럼 …않다: *Glenn seldom eats breakfast.* 글렌은 좀처럼 아침을 먹지 않는다.

se·lect¹ /sɪ'lɛkt/ v [T] to choose something or someone ‖ 사물이나 사람을 선택하다. 골라내다. 선출하다. 뽑다: *Regina was selected to read her story first.* 레지나가 제일 먼저 자신의 이야기를 읽도록 선택되었다.

select² *adj* FORMAL consisting of or used by a small group of specially chosen people ‖ 특별히 선택된 소집단의 사람들로 구성되거나 그들이 이용하는. 선택된. 선발된: *a select club* 정선된 회원제 클럽

se·lec·tion /sɪ'lɛkʃən/ n 1 [C, U] the act of choosing something or someone, or the thing or person that is chosen ‖ 사물이나 사람을 선택하는 행위, 또는 선택된 사물이나 사람. 선발[선택]자[물]: *Would you care to make a selection from our dessert tray?* 우리의 디저트 접시에서 (뭐 좀) 골라 드시겠습니까? 2 a collection of things, especially things for sale ‖ 특히 팔려고 내놓은 물건의 수집물. 정선품: *a store with a wide selection of jewelry* 각종 보석류를 갖춘 가게

se·lec·tive /sɪ'lɛktɪv/ *adj* careful about what you choose to do, buy etc. ‖ 자신이 하거나 사기 위해 선택하는 것에 대해 신중한. 안목이 높은. 선택 능력이 있는: *She's very selective about what kind of clothes she wears.* 그녀는 자신이 입는 옷을 고르는 안목이 매우 높다.

self /sɛlf/ n, plural **selves** [C, U] the type of person you are, including your character, abilities etc. ‖ 자신의 성격이나 능력 등을 포함한 자신의 타입. 자기(자신). 개성. 본성: *He's starting to feel like his old self again.* (=feel normal again, after feeling bad or sick) 그는 이전의 자기 자신처럼 다시 느끼기 시작하고 있다. / *trying to develop a child's sense of self* 아이의 자아 의식을 개발시키기 위한 노력

self·ab·sorbed /ˌ. .ˈ./ *adj* so concerned about yourself or your own problems that you forget about other people ‖ 다른 사람들에 대해서는 잊을 정도로 자기 자신이나 자기 자신의 문제들에 지나치게 신경 쓰는. 자기 일에 몰두[전념]하고 있는. 자아도취인

self·ap·point·ed /ˌ. .ˈ./ *adj* thinking that you are the best person to do something when you are not ‖ 어떤 것을 하는 데에 자신이 가장 적임자가 아닌 데도 적임자라고 생각하는. 자처하는. 자천(自薦)의: *a self-appointed guardian of morality* 도덕성의 수호자라 자천하는 사람

self·as·sured /ˌ. .ˈ./ *adj* confident about what you are doing ‖ 자신이 하고 있는 것에 대해 자신이 있는. 자기 과신의. 자신이 있는 – **self-assurance** *n* [U]

self·cen·tered /ˌ. .ˈ./ *adj* interested only in yourself and never caring about other people; SELFISH ‖ 다른 사람들을 전혀 신경 쓰지 않고 자기 자신에만 관심을 기울이는. 자기 중심적인. 이기적인; ⑩ selfish: *You're acting like a self-centered child.* 너는 이기적인 아이처럼 행동하고 있구나.

self·con·fi·dent /ˌ. .ˈ./ *adj* being confident in your abilities, appearance etc., and not shy or nervous with people ‖ 자신의 능력·모습 등에 자신이 있고 사람들에게 부끄러움을 타지 않거나 소심하지 않은. 자신 있는 – **self-confidence** *n* [U]

self·con·scious /ˌ. .ˈ./ *adj* worried and embarrassed about what you look like or what other people think of you ‖ 자신이 어떻게 보일지 또는 다른 사람들이 자신을 어떻게 생각할지 걱정하고 난처해 하는. 이목을 꺼리는[의식하는]: *She feels self-conscious about wearing glasses.* 그녀는 안경을 쓰는 것에 대해 꺼리는 마음을 가지고 있다.

self·con·tained /ˌ. .ˈ./ *adj* complete in itself and not needing other things to make it work ‖ 작동하는 데에 그것 자체로 완벽하고 다른 것이 필요하지 않은. 자급자족의. 자기 충족적인: *a self-contained economy* 자급자족적인 경제

self·con·trol /ˌ. .ˈ./ *n* [U] the ability to control your feelings and behavior even when you are angry, excited, or upset ‖ 화난[흥분된, 마음이 상한] 때조차도 자신의 감정과 행동을 통제하는 능력. 자제(심). 극기: *His lack of self-control caused problems in the classroom.* 그는 자제심 부족으로 학급 내에서 문제를 일으켰다.

self·de·feat·ing /ˌ. .ˈ./ *adj* making a situation have a bad result for you ‖ 상황이 자신에게 나쁜 결과를 가져오게 하는. 자멸적인. 스스로를 망치는: *He made several self-defeating statements during the interview.* 그는 인터뷰하는 동안에 자기에게 불리한 여러 말을 했다.

self·de·fense /ˌ. .ˈ./ *n* [U] the use of force to protect yourself from attack ‖ 공격으로부터 자신을 보호하기 위해 힘을 사용하는 것. 자위. 자기 방어. 정당방위: *She shot the man in self-defense.* 그녀는 정당방위로 그 남자를 쏘았다.

self·de·ni·al /ˌ. .ˈ./ *n* [U] the practice of not having or doing the things that you enjoy, either because you cannot afford it or for moral or religious reasons ‖ 어떤 것을 할 여유가 없기 때문에 또는 도덕적이거나 종교적 이유 때문에 자신이 즐기는 것을 가지지 않거나 하지 않는 행위. 자제. 극기. 금욕

self·de·struc·tive /ˌ. .ˈ./ *adj* self-destructive actions are likely to harm or kill the person who is doing them ‖ 자신이 하는 행동이 스스로에게 해를 입히거나 죽일 것 같은. 자멸적인. 자기 파괴적인

self·dis·ci·pline /ˌ. .ˈ./ *n* [U] the ability to make yourself do the things that you ought to do without someone else making you do them ‖ 남이 하라고 강요하지 않아도 자기가 해야 하는 것을 스스로 하는 능력. 자기 단련[수양] – **self-disciplined** *adj*

self·em·ployed /ˌ. .ˈ./ *adj* working for yourself rather than for a company ‖ 회사를 위해서가 아니라 자기 자신을 위해 일하는. 자영(업)의. 자기 사업을 하는

self·es·teem /ˌ. .ˈ./ *n* [U] the feeling that you are someone who deserves to be liked, respected, and admired ‖ 자신이 호감·존경·찬사를 받을 만한 사람이라고 느끼는 감정. 자부심. 자긍심

self·ev·i·dent /ˌ. .ˈ./ *adj* clearly true and needing no proof; OBVIOUS ‖ 명백하게 사실이고 증명할 필요 없는. 자명한. 뻔한; ⑩ obvious

self·ex·plan·a·to·ry /ˌ. .ˈ..../ *adj* clear and easy to understand, with no need for explanation ‖ 설명할 필요 없이 분명하고 쉽게 이해할 수 있는. 자명한. 설명을 요하지 않는: *The instructions are self-explanatory.* 그 제품의 사용 설명서

는 설명할 필요가 없이 자명하다.

self·ful·fil·ling proph·e·cy /ˌ. ..ˌ..
'.../ *n* a statement about what will
happen in the future, that becomes true
because you changed your behavior to
make it happen ‖ 어떤 일을 일으키기 위
해 자신의 태도를 바꾸었기 때문에 사실이
되어 버리는, 장차 일어날 일에 대한 말.
자기 충족적인 예언

self-help /ˌ. './ *n* the use of your own
efforts to deal with your problems
instead of depending on other people ‖
문제를 다른 사람들에게 의존하는 것 대신
에 스스로 처리하려고 노력함. 자조. 자립

self-i·mage /ˌ. './ *n* the idea that you
have of your own abilities, appearance,
and character ‖ 자신의 능력·모습·성격에
대해 자신이 가지고 있는 생각. 자아상(自
我像): *a man with a poor self-image* 변
변치 못한 자아상을 가진 남자

self-im·por·tant /ˌ. .'../ *adj* thinking
you are more important than other
people ‖ 자신이 다른 사람들보다 더 중요
하다고 생각하는. 잘난 체하는. 거만한.
자만심이 강한

self-im·prove·ment /ˌ. .'../ *n* [U] the
activity of trying to learn more skills or
to deal with your problems better ‖ 더
많은 기술을 배우려고 하거나 자신의 문제
를 더 잘 처리하려는 활동. 자기 개선

self-in·dul·gent /ˌ. .'../ *adj* allowing
yourself to have or enjoy something that
you do not need ‖ 자신에게 필요하지 않
은 것을 가지거나 즐기도록 허용하는. 방
종한. 멋대로 하는: *spoiled self-
indulgent teenagers* 버릇없이 자라 멋대
로 하는 십대들 – **self-indulgence** *n*
[singular, U]

self-in·flict·ed /ˌ. .'../ *adj* a self-
inflicted injury, problem etc. is one that
you have caused yourself ‖ 상처·문제 등
이 자기 자신에게 일으킨. 자초한. 자해의:
a self-inflicted gunshot wound 자해 총상

self-in·terest /ˌ. './ *n* [U] concern for
what is best for you rather than for
other people ‖ 다른 사람들보다 자신에게
최고인 것에 대해 관심을 가지는 것. 자기
이익[본위]. 이기심[주의]: *It's in the
employer's self-interest to help
employees stay with health care.* 고용자의 건
강 관리를 돕는 것은 고용주 자기 자신을
위한 것이다.

self·ish /'sɛlfɪʃ/ *adj* caring only about
yourself rather than about other people
‖ 다른 사람들보다는 자기 자신에 대해서
만 신경을 쓰는. 이기적인: *a selfish and
ambitious man* 이기적이고 야망이 큰 사
내 – **selfishness** *n* [U] – **selfishly**

adv —opposite UNSELFISH

self·less /'sɛlflɪs/ *adj* caring about
other people more than about yourself
‖ 자기 자신보다는 다른 사람들에 대해 신
경을 쓰는. 이기심[욕심]이 없는

self-made /ˌ. '. ./ *adj* successful and
wealthy because of your own efforts ‖ 자
기 자신의 노력 덕분에 성공하여 부자가
된. 자수성가한: *a self-made millionaire*
자수성가한 백만장자

self-pit·y /ˌ. '../ *n* [U] the feeling of
being too sorry for yourself ‖ 자기 자신
에게 너무 미안하게 생각하는 느낌. 자신
을 동정하는 태도. 자기 연민: *Ryan was
always patient and never gave in to
self-pity.* 라이언은 항상 참을성이 있었고
결코 자기 연민에 빠지지 않았다.

self-por·trait /ˌ. '../ *n* a picture that
you make of yourself ‖ 자신이 자기 자신
을 그린 그림. 자화상

self-pos·sessed /ˌ. '../ *adj* calm and
confident because you are in control of
your feelings ‖ 자신이 자기 감정을 지배
하고 있기 때문에 냉정하고 자신감이 있
는. 냉정[침착, 차분]한

self-pres·er·va·tion /ˌ. ..'../ *n* [U]
keeping yourself from being harmed or
killed ‖ 부상을 당하거나 죽임을 당하는
것으로부터 자기 자신을 지킴. 자위(自衛)
(본능). 자기 보존: *White had a strong
instinct for self-preservation.* 화이트는
강한 자위 본능을 느꼈다.

self-re·li·ance /ˌ. .'../ *n* [U] the ability
to act and make decisions by yourself
without depending on other people ‖ 다
른 사람들에게 의존하지 않고 혼자서 행동
하고 결정하는 능력. 자립. 독립. 자기 의
존[신뢰] – **self-reliant** *adj*

self-re·spect /ˌ. .'../ *n* [U] a feeling of
confidence and pride in your abilities,
ideas, and character ‖ 자신의 능력·생각
·성격에 대해 느끼는 자신감·자긍심. 자존
(심). 자중(自重) – **self-respecting**
adj : *No self-respecting union would
give up its right to strike.* 자중하는 노동
조합은 파업할 권리를 포기하지 않을 것이
다.

self-re·straint /ˌ. .'./ *n* [U] the ability
to control what you do or say in
situations that upset you ‖ 자기를 당황하
게 하는 상황에서 행동하는 것이나 말하는
것을 제어하는 능력. 자제. 극기

self-right·eous /ˌ. '../ *adj* too proud
and sure that your beliefs, attitudes etc.
are right, in a way that annoys other
people ‖ 다른 사람들을 짜증나게 할 정도
로 자신의 신념·태도 등이 옳다고 지나치
게 자만하며 확신하는. 독선적인

self-sac·ri·fice /. '.../ n [U] the act of giving up what you need or want in order to help someone else ‖ 타인을 돕기 위해 자신이 필요로 하는 것이나 원하는 것을 포기하는 행위. 자기 희생. 헌신 – **self-sacrificing** adj

self-sat·is·fied /. '.../ adj ⇨ SMUG

self-seek·ing /. '...'/ adj doing things only to get an advantage for yourself ‖ 오로지 자신을 위한 이익을 얻기 위해 어떤 것을 하는. 이기주의의. 자기 본위의: *a dishonest and self-seeking politician* 불성실하고 자기 본위인 정치가

self-serv·ice /. '...'/, **self serve** /. './ adj used in order to describe places where you get things for yourself, rather than being served ‖ 접대를 받는 것이 아니라 스스로 물건을 취하는 장소를 표현하는 데에 쓰여. 셀프서비스의: *a self-service gas station* 셀프서비스 주유소

self-start·er /. '...'/ n someone who is able to work without needing other people's help or a lot of instructions ‖ 타인의 도움이나 많은 가르침의 필요 없이 일할 수 있는 사람. 일을 자발적으로 하는 사람

self-styled /. '../ adj having given yourself a title, position etc. without having a right to it ‖ 아무 권한이 없으면서 자신에게 칭호나 직위를 주는. 자칭의. 자처하는: *a self-styled computer expert* 자칭 컴퓨터 전문가

self-suf·fi·cient /. .'...'/ adj able to provide for all your needs without help from other people ‖ 다른 사람들의 도움 없이 필요한 것을 모두 제공할 수 있는. 자급자족할 수 있는: *a country that is self-sufficient in food production* 식량 생산의 자급자족국 – **self-sufficiency** n [U]

self-sup·port·ing /. .'...'/ adj able to earn enough money to support yourself ‖ 자립하기에 충분한 돈을 벌 수 있는. 자립한: *a self-supporting museum* 자영 박물관

sell /sɛl/ v **sold, sold, selling 1** [I, T] to give something to someone in exchange for money ‖ 돈과 교환하여 남에게 물건을 주다. 팔다: *We sold the car for $5000.* 우리는 그 차를 5천 달러에 팔았다. / *Scott wants to sell his stereo to me.* 스콧은 내게 자기 스테레오를 팔고 싶어한다. —compare BUY **2** [T] to offer something for people to buy ‖ 사려는 사람들에게 물건을 제공하다. 팔다: *Do you sell oriental rugs?* 동양 양탄자가 있습니까? **3** [T] to make someone want to buy something ‖ 남에게 물건을 사고 싶게 하다. 판매를 촉진하다. 판촉하다:

Sensational headlines are what sell newspapers. 세상을 떠들썩하게 하는 헤드라인은 신문의 판매를 촉진하는 것이다. **4** [I] to be bought by people in large numbers or amounts ‖ 많은 수나 양이 사람들에게 팔리다: *Toys based on the movie are really selling.* 영화에 나오는 것을 장난감으로 만든 것이 정말 잘 팔리고 있다. **5** [I, T] to try to make someone accept a new plan, idea etc., or to become accepted ‖ 사람이 새로운 계획이나 생각을 받아들이게 하다, 또는 받아들여지다. 납득시키다. 인정받다: *Now we have to try to sell Monica on the idea.* 자, 우리는 그 생각을 모니카에게 납득시켜야 해. **6 sell yourself short** INFORMAL to not have the confidence in your abilities that you should have, so that you do not take advantage of opportunities ‖ 기회를 이용할 수 없을 정도로 스스로가 가진 능력에 자신감이 없다. 자신을 과소평가하다

sell sth ↔ **off** phr v [T] to sell a large number of things because you need the money ‖ 돈이 필요하여 물건을 대량으로 팔다. 대량 방출하다: *They're selling off her paintings in an auction today.* 그들은 오늘 경매로 그림을 대방출하고 있다.

sell out phr v [I] **1** to sell all of what was for sale so that there is none left ‖ 남는 것이 없도록 팔려고 내놓은 물건을 몽땅 팔다. 매진되다: *I'm sorry, but the tickets are all sold out.* 미안합니다만 그 티켓은 모두 매진입니다. **2** INFORMAL to do something that is against your beliefs or principles, in order to get power or money ‖ 권력이나 돈을 얻으려고 신념이나 원칙에 반하는 일을 하다. 팔다. 배반하다: *Neil accused him of selling out to big business.* 닐은 대기업에 팔아 버린 일에 대해 그를 책망했다.

sell up phr v [I] to sell everything you have because you want the money ‖ 돈을 원하기 때문에 소유한 것을 모두 팔다. 팔아 치우다. 처분하다: *The Martins eventually sold up and moved to Florida.* 마틴 가족들은 결국은 재산을 팔아 치우고 플로리다로 이사갔다.

sell·er /'sɛlɚ/ n **1** a person or company that sells something ‖ 물건을 파는 사람이나 회사. 판매인. 세일즈맨: *the largest seller of microwave ovens* 전자레인지를 가장 많이 파는 판매인 —compare BUYER **2 good/best/biggest etc. seller** a product that a company sells a lot of ‖ 한 회사가 많이 파는 상품. 잘 팔리는 상품: *The multi-CD player is our biggest seller.* 멀티시디 플레이어는 우리 회사의

가장 잘 팔리는 상품이다.

sell·ing point /.. ,./ *n* a special
feature of a product that will make
people want to buy it ‖ 사람들이 물건을
사고 싶게 하는 상품의 특징. 제품의 장점

sell·out /'sɛlaʊt/ *n* [singular] **1** a
performance, sports event etc. for
which all the tickets have been sold ‖ 표
가 모두 팔린 공연이나 스포츠 행사. 입장
권이 매진된 흥행. 만원: *a sellout crowd
of 45,769* 4만 5천 769명 만원을 이룬 관
중 **2** INFORMAL a situation in which
someone does something that is against
his/her beliefs or principles, especially
in order to get power or money ‖ 사람이
특히 권력이나 돈을 얻기 위해 신념이나
원칙에 반하는 일을 하는 상황. 배반. 배
신. 변절: *Some people may call the deal
a sellout.* 어떤 사람들은 그 거래를 배신
이라고 부를지도 모른다.

selves /sɛlvz/ *n* the plural of SELF ‖ self
의 복수

se·man·tics /sə'mæntɪks/ *n* [U] the
study of the meaning of words ‖ 말의 의
미에 대한 연구. 의미론 – **semantic** *adj*

sem·blance /'sɛmbləns/ *n* a condition
or quality that is at least slightly like
another one ‖ 다른 사람과 다소라도 닮은
조건이나 성질. 유사. 비슷한 것: *I'm just
trying to create some semblance of
order here.* 나는 지금 이곳에서 훈련 같은
것을 좀 만들려는 중이다.

se·men /'simən/ *n* [U] the liquid that is
produced by the male sex organs and
contains SPERM ‖ 남성 성기에서 생성되고
정자가 들어 있는 액체. 정액

se·mes·ter /sə'mɛstɚ/ *n* one of two
periods into which a year at school or
college is divided ‖ 학교나 대학의 1년을
나눈 두 기간의 하나. 학기 —compare
QUARTER

sem·i·cir·cle /'sɛmi,sɚkəl/ *n* **1** half a
circle ‖ 반원(半圓) **2** a group arranged
in a curved line ‖ 곡선으로 배열된 집단.
반원형의 것: *Could everyone please sit
in a semicircle?* (=sit in a curved line)
모두 반원형으로 앉아 주시겠습니까?

sem·i·co·lon /'sɛmi,koʊlən/ *n* the
mark (;) used in writing to separate
independent parts of a sentence or list ‖
문장이나 목록의 독립적인 부분을 구별하
기 위해 글에 쓰이는 부호(;). 세미콜론

sem·i·con·duct·or /.. ,../ *n* a
substance such as SILICON that is used in
electronic equipment to allow electricity
to pass through it ‖ 전기를 통하게 하는
전기 기구에 사용되는 실리콘 등의 물질.
반도체

sem·i·fi·nal /'sɛmi,faɪnl, 'sɛmaɪ-,
,sɛmi'faɪnl/ *n* one of two sports games
whose winners then compete against
each other to decide who wins the
whole competition ‖ 전(全) 경기의 승자를
가리기 위해 우승자끼리 서로 겨루는 두
스포츠 경기 중 하나. 준결승 —compare
QUARTERFINAL

sem·i·nal /'sɛmənəl/ *adj* new and
important, and influencing the way
something develops in the future ‖ 새롭
고 중요하며 어떤 것이 앞으로 전개될 방
식에 영향을 끼치는. 매우 독창적인. 영향
력이 큰: *a seminal book* 영향력 있는 책
/ *seminal research* 매우 독창적인 연구

sem·i·nar /'sɛmə,nɑr/ *n* a short course
or a special meeting that people attend
in order to study a particular subject ‖
사람들이 특정한 주제를 연구하기 위해 참
석하는 단기 강좌나 특별한 회의. 세미나:
a seminar on teaching English in China
중국에서의 영어 교습에 관한 세미나 / *a
series of management seminars* 일련의
경영 세미나

sem·i·nary /'sɛmə,nɛri/ *n* a college at
which people study religion and can
train to be priests or ministers ‖ 사람들
이 종교를 연구하고 사제나 목사가 되기
위해 훈련받는 대학. 신학교

sem·i·pre·cious /,sɛmi'prɛʃəs/ *adj* a
semiprecious jewel or stone is valuable,
but not as valuable as a DIAMOND or
RUBY ‖ 보석이 다이아몬드나 루비만큼은
아니지만 값진. 준보석의

Se·mit·ic /sə'mɪtɪk/ *adj* relating to the
race of people that includes Jews,
Arabs, and other ancient peoples from
the Middle East ‖ 유대인·아랍인·중동 출
신의 다른 고대인을 포함하는 인종에 관련
된. 셈족의

sen·ate /'sɛnɪt/ *n* **the Senate** the
smaller of the two groups of people who
make the laws in countries such as the
US and Australia ‖ 미국·호주 등의 국가
에서 법을 제정하는 사람들의 두 집단 중
에서 작은 것. 상원 —compare HOUSE OF
REPRESENTATIVES

sen·a·tor, Senator /'sɛnətɚ/ *n* a
member of the Senate ‖ 상원 의원:
Senator Feinstein 파인스타인 상원 의원
– **senatorial** /,sɛnə'tɔriəl/ *adj*

send /sɛnd/ *v* **sent, sent, sending**
[T] **1** to arrange for something to go or
be taken to another place, especially by
mail ‖ 무엇을 특히 우편으로 다른 장소로
가거나 운반되도록 조치하다. 보내다. 부
치다: *Have you sent the bank a letter
yet?* 너 벌써 은행에 편지를 부쳤니? /

Valerie's asking us to send her more money. 발레리는 자기에게 돈을 더 부칠 것을 우리에게 부탁하고 있어요. **2 to make someone go somewhere** ‖ 누군가를 어디로 보내다. 파견하다: *The UN is sending troops to the region.* 유엔은 그 지역에 군대를 파견하고 있다. / *We all got sent home from school at noon.* 우리는 모두 정오에 학교에서 집으로 돌아왔다. / *If anyone knocks, please send them away.* 누군가 문을 두드리면 그들을 쫓아 보내시오. **3 to arrange for someone to go somewhere and stay there** ‖ 누군가를 어딘가로 보내서 그곳에 머물도록 조처하다: *Morrison was sent to jail for five years.* 모리슨은 5년 동안 투옥되었다. **4 send your love/best wishes etc.** to ask someone to give your greetings, good wishes etc. to someone else ‖ 인사·소망 등을 다른 사람에게 전해 달라고 누군가에게 부탁하다: *Mark sends his love.* 마크가 사랑한다고 전해 달래. **5 to make someone or something do something** ‖ 사람이나 사물이 무엇을 하게 하다: *A shortage of oil sent prices up this week.* (=made them increase) 석유 부족으로 이번 주에 가격이 올랐다. / *The blast sent people running for safety.* 돌풍이 불어 사람들은 안전을 위해 계속해서 달렸다. **6** INFORMAL to make someone feel happy ‖ 남을 행복하게 하다: *Oh, doesn't his music just send you?* 오, 그의 음악에 방금 황홀해지지 않았니?

send away for sth *phr v* [T] to order something through the mail ‖ 우편으로 물건을 주문하다: *I sent away for a pair of sandals.* 나는 우편으로 샌들 한 켤레를 주문했다.

send sth ↔ **down** *phr v* [T] to make something lose value ‖ 어떤 것의 가치를 떨어뜨리다. 내리다: *The news sent the price of gold down.* 그 소식으로 인해 금값이 하락했다.

send for sb/sth *phr v* [T] to ask or order someone to come to you, or that something be brought or mailed to you ‖ 남이 자신에게 오도록 요구 또는 명령하다, 또는 물건이 오거나 부쳐지게 하다. 부르다. 주문하다: *An ambulance was sent for, but it was too late.* 앰뷸런스 한 대를 불렀으나 너무 늦게 왔다. / *Send now for your free catalog.* 지금 무료 카탈로그를 신청하십시오.

send in *phr v* [T] **1** [**send** sth ↔ **in**] to send something, usually by mail, to a place where it can be dealt with ‖ 관련처에 보통 우편으로 어떤 것을 보내다. 제출

하다: *Did you send in your application?* 신청서를 제출했습니까? **2** [**send** sb ↔ **in**] to send soldiers, police etc. somewhere to deal with a dangerous situation ‖ 군인이나 경찰 등을 위험한 상황을 조처할 곳으로 보내다. 파견하다: *Finally, the mayor had to send in the police.* 결국 시장은 경찰을 파견했다.

send off *phr v* [T] **1** [**send** sth ↔ **off**] to mail something somewhere ‖ 물건을 어떤 곳으로 부치다. 발송하다: *Riley sent off copies to everyone in the family.* 릴리는 가족 모두에게 사본을 보냈다. **2** [**send** sb ↔ **off**] to make someone go somewhere ‖ 남을 어디로 가게 하다. 보내다: *We got sent off to camp every summer.* 우리는 여름마다 야영[캠프]하며 보냈다.

send sb/sth ↔ **out** *phr v* [T] to make something or someone go from one place to various other places ‖ 사물이나 사람을 한 장소에서 여러 다른 장소로 가게 하다. 보내다. 배부하다: *The wedding invitations were sent out weeks ago.* 결혼 청첩장이 몇 주 전에 배부되었다.

send-off /'. ./ *n* INFORMAL an occasion when people gather together to say goodbye to someone who is leaving ‖ 사람들이 떠나는 사람과 작별하느라고 함께 모이는 의식. 송별회: *We wanted to give you a big send-off.* 우리는 네게 성대한 송별회를 열어 주고 싶었다.

se·nile /'sinaɪl/ *adj* mentally confused or behaving strangely, because of old age ‖ 노령으로 인해 정신적으로 혼란하거나 이상하게 행동하는. 노망한 – **senility** /sɪ'nɪləti/ *n* [U]

Se·nior /'sinyɚ/, *written abbreviation* **Sr.** *adj* used after the name of a man who has the same name as his son ‖ 아들과 같은 이름을 가진 남성의 이름 뒤에 쓰여. 아버지의. 1세의: *Robert Burrelli, Sr.* 로버트 부렐리 1세 —compare JUNIOR

senior[1] *n* **1** a student in the last year of HIGH SCHOOL or college ‖ 고등학교나 대학의 최종 학년의 학생. 최상급생 **2 be two/five/ten etc. years sb's senior** to be two, five, ten etc. years older than someone ‖ 남보다 2살·5살·10살 등이 많다. …보다 두/다섯/열 살 위이다 —compare JUNIOR[1]

senior[2] *adj* older, or of higher rank ‖ 나이가 많거나 계급이 높은. 연장의. 상급의: *a senior officer in the Navy* 해군의 상급 장교 —compare JUNIOR[2]

senior cit·i·zen /,.. '.../ *n* an old person, especially someone over the age of 65 ‖ 노령자, 특히 65세 이상의 노인

senior high school /ˌ.. '. ˌ./ *n* ⇨
HIGH SCHOOL

se·nior·i·ty /ˌsinˈyɔrəti, -ˈyar-/ *n* [U]
the state of being older or higher in
rank than someone else, which often
gives you an advantage ‖ 종종 이점이 되
는, 다른 사람보다 나이가 많거나 지위가
높은 상태. 연상[손위, 선배]임: *a worker
with ten years' seniority at the plant* 그
공장에서 10년 고참인 근로자

sen·sa·tion /sɛnˈseɪʃən/ *n* **1** [C, U] the
ability to feel, or a feeling that you get
from your senses or an experience ‖ 오
감이나 경험에서 얻는 감지력이나 느낌.
감각. 지각. 기분: *Matt had a burning
sensation in his arm.* 매트는 팔이 타는
듯한 느낌이 들었다. / *I had the
strangest sensation that I was being
watched.* 감시받고 있는 듯한 아주 이상
한 기분이 들었다. **2** extreme excitement
or interest, or someone or something
that causes this ‖ 극단적인 흥분이나 흥
미, 또는 이것의 원인이 되는 사람이나 사
물. 센세이션. 대소동(거리): *News of the
discovery caused a great sensation in
the art world.* 그 발견에 대한 소식은 예
술계에 큰 센세이션을 일으켰다.

sen·sa·tion·al /sɛnˈseɪʃənl/ *adj* **1**
DISAPPROVING intended to shock or excite
people ‖ 사람에게 충격을 주거나 흥분하
게 하려는. 선풍적인. 떠들썩하게 하는: *a
sensational news report of the murder*
세상을 떠들썩하게 한 살인 사건에 대한
뉴스 보도 **2** very interesting or exciting
‖ 매우 흥미있고 흥분되는: *a sensational
finish to the race* 경주의 아슬아슬한 골
인

sen·sa·tion·al·ism /sɛnˈseɪʃənlˌɪzəm/
n [U] DISAPPROVING a way of reporting
events or stories that is intended to
shock or excite people ‖ 사람들에게 충격
을 주거나 흥분시키려는 의도로 사건이나
이야기를 보도하는 방식. 선정주의

sense¹ /sɛns/ *n*
1 ▶JUDGMENT 판단력◀ [U] good
understanding and judgment, especially
about practical things ‖ 특히 실제적인 일
에 대한 뛰어난 이해와 판단력. 사려. 분
별: *Earl had the sense not to move the
injured man much.* 얼은 사려 깊게도 부
상자를 심하게 움직이지 않았다. —
compare COMMON SENSE
2 ▶FEELING 느낌◀ [singular] a feeling
about something ‖ 어떤 것에 대한 느낌.
기분: *She felt a strong sense of
accomplishment.* 그녀는 강한 성취감을
느꼈다. / *At the end you have that sense
of a shared experience.* 종국에는 너는 경

험을 공유하는 그런 느낌을 맛보게 된다.
/ *a child's sense of self-esteem*
(=his/her feelings about himself/herself)
어린이의 자부심
3 make sense a) to have a clear
meaning that is easy to understand ‖ 이
해하기 쉬운 명백한 뜻이 있다. 이해할 수
있다. 뜻이 통하다: *Do these instructions
make any sense to you?* 너는 이 지시들
을 알겠니? / *I can't make sense of the
report.* 나는 그 보고서를 이해할 수 없어.
b) to have a good reason or explanation
‖ 좋은 이유나 해명이 되다. 이치에 맞다:
*Why would she wander off alone? It
doesn't make sense.* 그녀는 왜 혼자 배회
하지? 납득이 되지 않네. **c)** to be a
sensible thing to do ‖ …하는 것은 현명한
일이다: *It makes sense to take care of
your health while you're young.* 젊었을
때 건강을 돌보는 것은 현명한 일이다.
4 in a sense/in some senses in only
one way or only some ways, when there
are more things to be considered ‖ 고려
할 사항이 더 있음에도 단 한 가지나 몇몇
방법으로. 어떤 의미로는/어느 정도는: *In
one sense he's right, but things are
more complicated than that.* 어떤 의미에
서는 그의 말이 맞지만 일은 그것보다 더
복잡해.
5 ▶SEE/SMELL ETC. 보다/냄새를 맡다◀
one of the five natural powers of sight,
hearing, touch, taste, and smell ‖ 시각·
청각·촉각·미각·후각의 5가지 타고난 능
력 중의 하나. 감각. 오감(五感)의 하나:
a dog with a strong sense of smell 후각
이 예민한 개
6 in the sense that used in order to
say that something you have just said is
true in a particular way ‖ 방금 말한 것이
어떤 특정한 면에서는 사실이라고 말하
는 데에 쓰여. …의 의미에서: *The
experiment was a success in the sense
that we got the results we were looking
for.* 그 실험은 우리가 찾는 결과를 얻었다
는 의미에서 성공이었다.
7 sb's senses someone's ability to
know and do what is sensible in a
situation ‖ 어떤 상황에서 무엇이 현명한
것인가 알고 행동하는 능력. 의식. 제정
신: *I'm glad that Lisa finally came to
her senses* (=realized what was
sensible) *and sold that car.* 리사가 마침
내 정신을 차려 그 차를 팔았다니 기쁘다.
/ *Have you lost your senses?* (=are you
crazy?) 너 미쳤니?
8 ▶ABILITY 능력◀ [singular] a natural
ability to judge something ‖ 사물을 판단
하는 타고난 능력. 의식. 감각: *When we*

were in the woods, I lost all sense of direction. (=ability to know where I was) 우리가 숲 속에 있을 때 나는 모든 방향 감각을 잃었다.
9 sense of humor the ability to understand and enjoy things that are funny, or to make people laugh ‖ 재미있는 일을 이해하고 즐기거나 사람을 웃기는 능력. 유머 감각: *Larry has a great sense of humor.* 래리는 유머 감각이 뛰어나다.
10 ▶MEANING 의미◀ the meaning of a word, phrase, sentence etc. ‖ 단어나 어구나 문장 등의 의미. 뜻: *Many words have more than one sense.* 많은 단어들이 한 가지 이상의 뜻을 갖고 있다. / *In what sense is the term used?* 그 용어는 어떤 의미로 쓰이나?
11 there's no sense in (doing) sth SPOKEN used in order to say that it is not sensible to do something ‖ 어떤 것을 하는 것은 현명하지 않다는 것을 말하는 데에 쓰여. …해봐야 소용없다[헛일이다]: *There's no sense in getting upset about it now.* 지금 그 일에 기분 나빠해봐야 소용없다.
sense² v [T] to feel that something exists or is true without being told or having proof ‖ 들은 것이나 증거 없이 어떤 것이 있거나 사실인 것을 느끼다. 깨닫다. 알아채다: *Sonya sensed that David wanted to be alone.* 소냐는 데이비드가 혼자 있고 싶어하는 것을 알아챘다.
sense·less /'sɛnslɪs/ *adj* **1** happening or done for no good reason or with no purpose ‖ 정당한 이유나 목적 없이 일어나거나 행한. 무의미한. 어리석은: *the senseless killing of innocent people* 죄 없는 사람들에 대한 무분별한 살인 **2** INFORMAL not conscious ‖ 의식이 없는. 인사불성의: *The pitcher missed, hit him in the head, and knocked him senseless.* 투수가 볼을 잘못 던져 볼이 그의 머리를 강타하자 그는 의식을 잃고 쓰러졌다.
sen·si·bil·i·ty /ˌsɛnsə'bɪləti/ *n* [C, U] the way that someone reacts to particular subjects or types of behavior ‖ 사람이 특정한 주제나 행동의 유형 등에 반응하는 방식. 감수성. 감성: *We apologize if we have offended the sensibilities of our viewers.* 저희가 시청자 여러분의 기분을 상하게 해드렸다면 사과드립니다. / *our moral sensibility* 우리의 도덕적 감수성
sen·si·ble /'sɛnsəbəl/ *adj* **1** showing good judgment; reasonable ‖ 뛰어난 판단을 보이는. 분별 있는; 합리적인: *Come on, be sensible.* 자, 분별 있게 굴어라. /

The question is how to manage profits in a sensible way. 그 질문은 현명하게 이익을 관리하는 법이다. **2** suitable for a particular purpose; practical ‖ 특정한 목적에 알맞은; 실용적인: *sensible clothes for camping in* 야영하기에 알맞은 옷 – **sensibly** *adv*

USAGE NOTE sensible and sensitive

Use **sensible** to talk about someone who makes good, reasonable decisions and who does not behave in a stupid or dangerous way: *She's sensible enough not to drive when she's drunk.* Use **sensitive** to talk about someone who is easily upset or offended: *He's sensitive about his height, so don't mention it.*
sensible은 정당하고 합리적인 결정을 내리고 어리석거나 위험하게 행동하지 않는 사람을 언급하는 데에 쓰인다: 그녀는 술에 취했을 때 운전을 하지 않을 정도로 분별이 있다. 쉽게 당황하거나 기분이 상하는 사람을 언급하는 데에는 **sensitive**가 쓰인다: 그는 자기의 키에 민감하니까 키 이야기는 하지 마라.

---

sen·si·tive /'sɛnsətɪv/ *adj* **1** able to understand the feelings, problems etc. of other people ‖ 다른 사람의 감정이나 문제 등을 이해할 수 있는. 이해심이 있는: *a husband who is sensitive to his wife's needs* 아내의 요구를 잘 헤아리는 남편 — opposite INSENSITIVE **2** easily offended or hurt by the things that other people do or say ‖ 다른 사람이 하는 행동이나 하는 말에 쉽게 기분이 상하거나 상처를 받는. 신경질적인. 상처받기 쉬운: *Chrissy is very sensitive about her weight.* 크리시는 자기 몸무게에 아주 민감하다. **3** having a greater ability than usual to feel or measure a physical effect ‖ 물리적인 영향을 느끼거나 측정하는 데에 보통 이상의 큰 능력이 있는. 민감한: *My teeth are really sensitive to cold.* 나의 이는 추위에 아주 민감해. / *a highly sensitive thermometer* 고감도의 온도계 **4** a sensitive situation or subject needs to be dealt with very carefully because it may offend people ‖ 상황이나 주제가 사람들을 기분 나쁘게 할지도 모르기 때문에 매우 조심스럽게 다뤄져야 하는. 미묘한: *The interviewer avoided asking questions on sensitive issues.* 그 탐방기자는 미묘한 문제에 대해 질문하는 것을 피했다. – **sensitivity** /ˌsɛnsə'tɪvəti/ *n* [U] – **sensitively** /'sɛnsətɪvli/ *adv* — see usage note at SENSIBLE

sens·or /'sɛnsɚ, -sɔr/ *n* TECHNICAL a piece of equipment that finds heat, light, sound etc., even in very small amounts ‖ 열·빛·소리 등을 극소량일지라도 탐지해 내는 기구. 센서. 감지 장치

sen·so·ry /'sɛnsəri/ *adj* relating to your senses of sight, hearing, smell, taste, or touch ‖ 시각[청각, 후각, 미각, 촉각]에 관련한. 감각(상)의: *sensory perception* 지각

sen·su·al /'sɛnʃuəl/ *adj* relating to or enjoying physical pleasure, especially sexual pleasure ‖ 육체적인 쾌락, 특히 성적 쾌락에 관련되거나 즐기는. 육감적인: *a sensual massage* 관능적인 마사지 / *Tina's very sensual.* 티나는 매우 육감적이다. – **sensuality** /,sɛnʃu'æləti/ *n* [U]

sen·su·ous /'sɛnʃuəs/ *adj* pleasing to your senses ‖ 감각을 즐겁게 하는. 감각적인: *the sensuous feel of a silk scarf* 비단 스카프의 감각적인 감촉

sent /sɛnt/ *v* the past tense and PAST PARTICIPLE of SEND ‖ send의 과거·과거 분사형

sen·tence¹ /'sɛntˈns, -təns/ *n* **1** TECHNICAL in grammar, a group of written or spoken words that has a subject and a verb, and expresses a complete thought or asks a question ‖ 문법에서 주어와 동사를 갖추어 완전한 생각을 표현하거나 질문을 하는, 글로 쓰거나 입으로 말한 단어들의 집합체. 문장 **2** a punishment that a judge gives to someone who is guilty of a crime ‖ 판사가 죄를 범한 사람에게 내리는 처벌. 판결. 형: *a 10-year sentence for arson* 방화죄에 대한 10년형

sentence² *v* [T] to give a legal punishment to someone who is guilty of a crime ‖ 죄를 범한 사람에게 법적 처벌을 내리다. …에게 형을 선고하다. 판결을 내리다: *He was sentenced to life in prison for the murder.* 그는 살인죄로 종신형을 선고받았다.

sen·ti·ment /'sɛntəmənt/ *n* **1** [C, U] FORMAL an opinion or feeling that you have about something ‖ 어떤 것에 대해 가지는 의견이나 느낌: *Pacifist sentiment was strong among the demonstrators.* 데모대 사이에서 평화주의자의 의견이 강했다. / *"Anderson ought to be fired." "My sentiments exactly."* (=I completely agree) "앤더슨은 해고되어야 해." "전적으로 동감해." **2** [U] feelings such as pity, love, or sadness that are considered to be too strong ‖ 너무 격하다고 생각되는 연민이나 사랑, 또는 슬픔 등의 감정. 감상: *There's no room for sentiment in business!* 사업에는 감상이 개입할 여지란 없지!

sen·ti·men·tal /,sɛntə'mɛntl·/ *adj* **1** showing emotions such as love, pity, and sadness too strongly ‖ 사랑·연민·슬픔 등의 감정을 너무 강하게 드러내 보이는. 지나치게 감상적인: *a sentimental movie* 감상적인 영화 / *Laurie still gets sentimental about our old house.* 로리는 아직도 우리의 옛집에 대해서는 감상적이 된다. **2** based on or relating to feelings rather than being practical ‖ 실제적이기보다는 감정에 기초를 두거나 관련된. 감정적인. 감정에 따른: *a sentimental view of the past* 과거에 대한 감상적인 시각 / *The watch wasn't worth much, but it had great sentimental value.* 그 시계는 값어치가 큰 것은 아니었지만 매우 애착이 가는 물건이었다. – **sentimentality** /,sɛntəmɛn'tæləti/ *n* [U]

sen·try /'sɛntri/ *n* OLD-FASHIONED a soldier standing outside a building as a guard ‖ 파수병으로 건물 밖에 서 있는 병사. 보초(병)

sep·a·ra·ble /'sɛpərəbəl/ *adj* able to be separated from something else ‖ 다른 것에서 분리할 수 있는 —opposite INSEPARABLE

sep·a·rate¹ /'sɛprɪt/ *adj* **1** not relating to each other or affecting each other in any way ‖ 서로 관련이 없거나 어떤 식으로든 서로 영향을 주지 않는. 독립된. 별개의: *He keeps his professional life separate from his private life.* 그는 직장생활과 사생활을 구분지어 해나간다. / *It's a completely separate issue.* 그것은 완전히 별개의 문제이다. **2** not joined to each other or touching each other ‖ 서로 연결되지 않거나 서로 접촉하지 않는. 갈라진. 분리된: *There is a small smoking area separate from the main dining room.* 본식당과는 분리된 좁은 흡연 구역이 있다. **3** different ‖ 다른: *a word with four separate meanings* 4개의 각기 다른 뜻을 갖고 있는 단어 – **separately** *adv*

sep·a·rate² /'sɛpə,reɪt/ *v* **1** [I, T] to divide or split something into two or more parts, or to make something do this ‖ 사물을 둘 이상의 부분으로 나누거나 쪼개다, 또는 사물을 이렇게 되게 하다. 가르다. 분리하다: *Ms. Barker separated the class into four groups.* 바커 여사는 그 학급을 네 그룹으로 나눴다. / *At this point the satellite separates from the launcher.* 이 지점에서 인공위성은 발사대에서 분리된다. **2** [T] to be between two things so that they cannot touch each other or connect to each other ‖ 두사물 사이에서 서로 접촉할 수 없게 하거나 연결되지 않도록 하다. 떼어놓다: *A curtain separated one patient's area from another.* 커튼이 한 환자와 다른 환자와의 구역을 분리했다. **3** [I, T] to move apart, or to make people do this ‖ 갈라지다, 또는 사람들을 떼어놓다. 헤어지게 하다: *Police moved in to separate the crowd.* 경찰이 군중을 해산시키기 위해 진입했다. **4** [I] to start to live apart from your husband, wife, or sexual partner ‖ 남편이나 아내, 또는 성적인 파트너와 떨어져 살기 시작하다. 별거하다: *When did Lyle and Jan separate?* 라일과 잰은 언제 별거했니?

sep·a·rat·ed /'sɛpə,reɪṭɪd/ *adj* no longer living with your husband, wife, or sexual partner ‖ 남편이나 아내, 또는 성적인 파트너와 더 이상 함께 살지 않는. 별거 중인: *Her parents are separated.* 그녀의 부모님은 별거 중이시다.

sep·a·ra·tion /,sɛpə'reɪʃən/ *n* **1** [U] FORMAL the act of separating or the state of being separate ‖ 떼어놓는 행위나 떨어져 있는 상태. 분리: *the separation of powers between Congress and the President* 의회와 대통령 사이의 권력의 분리 **2** [C, U] a period of time when two or more people live apart from each other ‖ 두 사람 이상이 서로 떨어져 사는 시기. 이별[별거](기): *Kim asked Bob for a legal separation.* 김은 보브에게 법적인 별거를 요청했다. / *Separation from the family is hard on children.* 가족과의 이별은 아이들에게 힘들다.

Sep·tem·ber /sɛp'tɛmbɚ/, *written abbreviation* **Sept.** *n* the ninth month of the year ‖ 그 해의 9번째 달. 9월 — see usage note at JANUARY

sep·ul·cher /'sɛpəlkɚ/ *n* LITERARY a large TOMB ‖ 큰 무덤. 매장소

se·quel /'sikwəl/ *n* **1** a movie, book etc. that continues the story of an earlier one ‖ 전편의 이야기가 이어지는 영화나 책 등. 속편. 후편 **2** an event that is related to an earlier event ‖ 이전의 사건에 관련된 사건. 후속 사건

se·quence /'sikwəns/ *n* [C, U] **1** a series of related events or actions that have a particular result ‖ 특정한 결과를 낳는 일련의 관련된 사건이나 행동: *This quarter we'll study the sequence of events that led to World War I.* 이번 학기에 우리는 1차 세계 대전을 유발한 일련의 사건들을 공부 할 것이다. **2** the order that things are supposed to have, or in

which actions are supposed to be done ‖ 사물이 갖춰야 하는 순서, 또는 행동이 이뤄져야 하는 순서: *Two of the pages were out of sequence.* (=not in order) 페이지 중에 두 페이지는 순서대로 되어 있지 않았다. / *Try to place the following pictures in sequence.* 다음 그림들을 차례대로 놓아 보거라. **–sequential** /sɪ'kwɛnʃəl/ *adj*

se·quin /'sikwɪn/ *n* a small round piece of flat metal that is shiny and is sewn on clothes for decoration ‖ 반짝이며 장식용으로 옷에 꿰매어 다는 작고 둥글고 납작한 금속 조각. 시퀸

se·quoi·a /sɪ'kwɔɪə/ *n* ⇨ REDWOOD

ser·e·nade¹ /,sɛrə'neɪd/ *n* a song or piece of music that someone performs outside at night for the person s/he loves ‖ 사랑하는 사람을 위해 밤에 집 밖에서 부르거나 연주하는 노래나 곡. 세레나데. 소야곡 **–serenade** *v* [T]

se·rene /sə'rin/ *adj* **1** someone who is serene is very calm and not at all worried ‖ 사람이 매우 차분하고 전혀 근심이 없는. 안정된 **2** a place that is serene is peaceful and quiet ‖ 장소가 평화롭고 조용한. 평온한 **–serenity** /sɪ'rɛnəṭi/ *n* [U]

ser·geant, Sergeant /'sɑrdʒənt/ *n* a middle rank in the army, police etc., or someone who has this rank ‖ 군대나 경찰 등에서의 중간 계급, 이런 계급을 가진 사람. 부사관. 경사

se·ri·al¹ /'sɪriəl/ *adj* arranged or happening one after the other in the correct order ‖ 올바른 순서로 잇달아 배열되거나 일어나는. 연속하는. 일련의 순차적인: *serial processing on a computer* 컴퓨터의 직렬 처리

serial² *n* a story that is broadcast or printed in several separate parts ‖ 여러 독립된 부분으로 방송되거나 인쇄된 이야기. 연속[연재]물. 연속극

serial kill·er /'... '../ *n* someone who has killed several people in the same way, one after the other ‖ 잇달아 같은 방식으로 여러 사람들을 죽이는 사람. 연쇄 살인범

serial num·ber /'... ,../ *n* one of a series of numbers printed on a large number of similar things such as televisions, so that you can tell them apart ‖ 텔레비전 등의 대량의 비슷한 물건에 구별할 수 있도록 인쇄된 일련 번호 중의 하나. 일련[제조] 번호

se·ries /'sɪriz/ *n, plural* **series** **1** a group of events or actions of the same kind that happen one after the other ‖

잇달아 발생하는 동종의 일단의 사건이나 행동. 시리즈. 연속: *There has been a series of accidents along this road.* 이 도로를 따라 사고들이 잇따라 발생했다. **2** a set of television or radio programs with the same characters or on the same subject ‖ 등장인물이나 주제가 같은 텔레비전이나 라디오의 연속된 프로그램. 시리즈. 연속물: *a new comedy series* 새 코미디 시리즈

se·ri·ous /'sɪriəs/ *adj* **1** a serious problem, situation etc. is bad or dangerous and makes people worry ‖ 문제나 상황 등이 나쁘거나 위험하여 사람들을 걱정시키는. 중대한. 심각한: *Her mother's been in a serious accident.* 그녀의 어머니는 심각한 사고를 당했다. **2 be serious** to be sincere about what you say or do ‖ 말하거나 행동하는 것에 진지하다: *John is serious about finding a new career.* 존은 진지하게 새 직업을 찾고 있다. / *You can't be serious!* (=I do not believe you) 농담이겠지! **3** important and deserving a lot of attention ‖ 중요하여 많은 주의를 요하는: *Raising children is a serious business.* 아이를 양육하는 것은 중요한 일이다. **4** a serious romantic relationship is intended to continue for a long time ‖ 연인 사이를 오래 지속할 작정인. 진지한: *So, are you two serious?* 그래, 너희 둘은 진지한 사이니? - **seriousness** *n* [U]

se·ri·ous·ly /'sɪriəsli/ *adv* **1** in a serious way ‖ 진지하게. 심각하게: *I'm seriously worried about Ben.* 나는 벤이 몹시 염려된다. **2 take sb/sth seriously** to believe that someone or something is important and worth paying attention to ‖ 사람이나 사물이 중요하여 주의를 기울일 만한 가치가 있다고 여기다. 진지하게 대하다[취급하다]: *You can't take everything he says so seriously.* 너는 그가 말하는 것을 모두 그렇게 진지하게 받아들이면 안 된다.

ser·mon /'sɚmən/ *n* **1** a talk about a religious subject, usually given at a church and based on the Bible ‖ 보통 교회에서 하는, 성경에 근거를 둔 종교적 주제에 대한 강연. 설교 **2** INFORMAL a talk in which someone gives you unwanted moral advice ‖ 누군가가 하는 원치 않는 도덕적 충고. 훈계 —see also PREACH

ser·pent /'sɚpənt/ *n* LITERARY a snake ‖ 뱀

ser·rat·ed /sə'reɪtɪd, 'sɛˌreɪtɪd/ *adj* **serrated knife/edge** with a sharp edge made of a row of connected V shapes like teeth ‖ V자 모양들이 이(齒)처럼 일렬

로 연결되어 만들어진 날카로운 날을 갖고 있는. 톱니식 칼/가장자리

se·rum /'sɪrəm/ *n* [C, U] TECHNICAL a liquid taken from animal's blood that is put into someone's blood in order to fight an infection ‖ 병의 감염에 맞서도록 사람의 피에 넣는 동물의 피에서 채취한 액체. 혈청 —compare VACCINE

serv·ant /'sɚvənt/ *n* someone who is paid to clean someone's house, cook food for him/her etc. ‖ 돈을 받고 남의 집을 청소하고 남을 위해 요리 등을 해 주는 사람. 하인. 종

serve¹ /sɚv/ *v*

1 ▶FOOD/DRINKS 음식/음료수◀ [I, T] to give someone food or drinks as part of a meal ‖ 남에게 식사의 일부로 음식이나 음료수를 제공하다. 식사 시중을 들다: *Dinner will be served at 8:00.* 식사는 8시에 제공된다. / *pie served with ice cream* 아이스크림과 함께 내놓은 파이 / *Why aren't you out there serving the guests?* 왜 거기 나가서 손님 시중을 들지 않는 거죠?

2 ▶BE USED 사용되다◀ [I, T] to be for a particular purpose ‖ 특정한 목적용이다. …에 쓸모 있다: *The couch can also serve as a bed.* 그 소파는 침대로도 쓸 수 있다.

3 ▶DO A JOB 일을 하다◀ [I, T] to spend time doing a particular job, especially one that is helpful ‖ 특정한 일, 특히 유익한 일을 하면서 시간을 보내다. 근무하다: *Kelly served a three-year term in the Army.* 켈리는 군대에서 3년간 복무했다.

4 ▶PROVIDE STH …을 공급하다◀ [T] to provide someone with something that is useful or necessary ‖ 남에게 유용하거나 필요한 것을 공급하다. 제공하다: *We're your local Ford dealers, serving Sioux Falls for over 25 years.* 우리는 25년 이상을 수폴스 시(市)에서 영업하고 있는 여러분 지역의 포드차 딜러입니다.

5 ▶IN PRISON 교도소에서◀ [T] to spend a particular amount of time in prison ‖ 교도소에서 특정한 기간을 보내다. 복역하다: *Baxter served a five-year sentence for theft.* 백스터는 절도죄로 5년을 복역했다.

6 ▶LEGALLY 법적으로◀ [T] to officially give or send someone a legal document ‖ 공식적으로 남에게 법률 문서를 주거나 보내다. 송달[교부]하다: *Jones was served a summons to appear in court.* 존스는 법정에 출두하라는 소환장을 받았다.

7 ▶SPORTS 스포츠◀ [I, T] to start

playing a game such as tennis by throwing the ball into the air and hitting it to your opponent ‖ 볼을 공중으로 던져 상대편에게 쳐서 테니스 등의 경기를 시작 하다. 서브하다

8 it serves sb right SPOKEN used in order to say that someone deserves something unpleasant, because s/he has done something stupid or unkind ‖ 누군 가가 어리석거나 불친절한 일을 했기 때문 에 불쾌한 일을 당할 만하다고 말하는 데 에 쓰여. 그래 싸다. 꼴 좋다: *I'm sorry Eddie had an accident, but it serves him right for driving so fast!* 에디가 사고를 당해서 안됐지만 그렇게 빨리 차를 모니 그래도 싸!

serve² *n* the action in a game such as tennis in which you throw the ball into the air and hit it to your opponent ‖ 볼을 공중에 던져 상대편에게 치는 테니스 등의 경기에서의 행동. 서브

serv·er /ˈsɚvɚ/ *n* **1** a special spoon, fork etc. used for putting a particular type of food on a plate ‖ 특정한 종류의 음식을 접시에 담기 위해 쓰이는 특별한 숟가락이나 포크 등. 서버: *a pair of wooden salad servers* 나무로 만든 한 벌 의 샐러드 서버 **2** the main computer on a NETWORK that controls all the others ‖ 다른 모든 컴퓨터를 통제하는 네트워크상 의 주 컴퓨터 **3** someone who brings you food in a restaurant ‖ 음식점에서 음식을 날라 오는 사람. 시중드는 사람 **4** a player who hits the ball to begin a game such as tennis ‖ 테니스 등의 경기에서 공 을 쳐서 게임을 시작하는 선수. 서버. 서 브하는 사람

serv·ice¹ /ˈsɚvɪs/ *n*
1 ▶IN A STORE ETC. 가게 등에서◀ [U] the help that people who work in a restaurant, hotel, store etc. give you ‖ 음식점·호텔·가게 등에서 일하는 사람이 고객에게 주는 도움. 손님 시중[접대]. 서 비스: *The food is terrific but the service is lousy.* 음식은 훌륭하지만 서비스는 형 편 없 다 . / *the customer service department* 고객 서비스부

2 public services things such as hospitals, schools etc. that are provided for the public to use ‖ 대중이 이용하도록 제공되는 병원·학교 등의 것들. 공익사업

3 ▶WORK DONE 행한 일◀ [C, U] the work that you do for someone or an organization ‖ 어떤 사람이나 기관을 위해 하는 일. 근무. 봉사. 도움: *He retired after 20 years of service.* 그는 20년을 근 무하고 은퇴했다. / *You may need the services of a lawyer.* 너는 변호사의 도움

이 필요할지 모른다.

4 ▶CEREMONY 의 식◀ a formal religious ceremony, especially in a church ‖ 특히 교회에서의 공식적인 종교 의식. 예배: *Father Palmer will be conducting the funeral service.* (=be in charge of the ceremony) 팔머 신부는 장 례 미사를 주재할 예정이다.

5 ▶BUSINESS 사업◀ a business that provides help or does jobs for people rather than producing things ‖ 물건을 생 산하기보다 사람들을 위해 도움을 주거나 일을 하는 사업. 공공사업: *She operates a cleaning service.* 그녀는 청소업을 한다.

6 ▶HELP 도움◀ [singular, U] help that you give to someone ‖ 남에게 주는 도움: *"Thank you so much." "I'm glad to be of service."* (=to help) "대단히 감사합니 다." "도움이 되어 기쁩니다."

7 the service a country's military forces, especially considered as a job ‖ 특히 직업의 하나로 본, 한 국가의 군대: *Stan joined the service after high school.* 스탠은 고등학교 졸업 후에 군대에 입대했다.

8 ▶GOVERNMENT 정 부◀ an organization that works for government ‖ 정부를 위해 일하는 기관. 정부 기관[부 처]: *the diplomatic service* 외무부

9 be at your service FORMAL to be available to help you if you need something ‖ 무엇이 필요하다면 도울 수 있다: *We're at your service, Ma'am.* 부 인, 언제든 도와드리겠습니다.

10 ▶SPORTS 스포츠◀ an act of hitting the ball to your opponent to start a game such as tennis ‖ 테니스 등의 경기 를 시작하기 위해 상대편에게 공을 쳐 넣 는 행위. 서비스. 서브

11 in service/out of service to be available or not available for people to use ‖ 사람이 사용할 수 있는, 또는 사용할 수 없는. 작동하는/작동하지 않는: *an elevator/bus/telephone that is out of service* 작동하지 않는 엘리베이터[버스, 전화]

service² *v* [T] **1** to examine a machine or vehicle and fix it if necessary ‖ 기계나 탈것을 검사하며 필요한 수리를 하다. 정 비하다: *When's the last time you had the car serviced?* 그 차를 마지막으로 정 비한 것이 언제지? **2** to provide people with something that they need ‖ 사람들에 게 필요한 것을 제공하다: *buses that service the local community* 지역 사회에 서비스를 제공하는 버스들

serv·ice·a·ble /ˈsɚvɪsəbəl/ *adj* ready or suitable to be used for a particular purpose ‖ 특정 목적에 쓰이도록 준비되거나 특정 목적으로 쓰기에 적합한. 유용한

service charge /'.. ,./ *n* an amount of money that is added to the price of something in order to pay for extra services that you use when buying it ‖ 물건을 살 때 이용하는 특별 서비스에 대하여 지불하도록 물건 값에 추가되는 금액. 서비스 요금: *For phone orders, there's a $1 service charge.* 전화 주문에는 서비스 요금이 1달러 붙는다.

serv·ice·man /'sɚvɪs,mæn, -mən/ *n* a man who is a member of the military ‖ 군인

service sta·tion /'.. ,../ *n* ⇨ GAS STATION

serv·ice·wom·an /'sɚvɪs,wʊmən/ *n* a woman who is a member of the military ‖ 여자 군인

ser·vile /'sɚvəl, -vaɪl/ *adj* willing to obey someone completely ‖ 남에게 완전히 복종하려 하는. 비굴한

serv·ing /'sɚvɪŋ/ *n* an amount of food that is enough for one person; HELPING ‖ 한 사람에게 충분한 음식의 양. 1인분; 倒 helping

ser·vi·tude /'sɚvə,tud/ *n* [U] the condition of being a SLAVE or being forced to obey someone ‖ 노예이거나 남에게 복종하도록 강요당한 상태. 예속

ses·sion /'sɛʃən/ *n* **1** a period of time used for a particular purpose, especially by a group of people ‖ 특히 일단의 사람들이 특정한 목적을 위해 쓰는 시간. 활동 기간: *a question-and-answer session after the meeting* 회의 후의 질의응답 시간 **2** a formal meeting, especially of a law court or government organization ‖ 특히 법정이나 정부 기관의 공식 모임. 개정. 개회: *The State Court is now in session.* 주(州) 법정은 지금 개정 중이다. **3** a part of the year when classes are given at a university ‖ 대학에서 수업을 받는 그 해의 한 부분. 학기

set[1] /sɛt/ *v* **set, set, setting**

1 ▶RECORD/STANDARD ETC. 기록/표준◀ [T] to do or decide something that other things are compared to or measured against ‖ 다른 일과 비교되거나 비교 평가되는 일을 하거나 결정하다: *Carl Lewis set a world record.* 칼 루이스는 세계 기록을 수립했다. / *The government has set standards for water cleanliness.* 정부는 물의 청결 기준을 세웠다. / *Parents should set an example for their children.* (=behave in the way they want their children to behave) 부모님은 아이들에게 본을 보여야 한다.

2 ▶PRICE/TIME ETC. 가격/시간◀ [T] to decide that something will happen at a particular time, cost a particular amount etc. ‖ 어떤 것이 특정한 시간에 발생하고 특정액의 값이 나가도록 결정하다: *The price was set too high.* 그 가격이 너무 높게 책정되었다. / *The satellite launch date was set for May.* 위성 발사 날짜가 5월로 정해졌다.

3 ▶PUT STH SOMEWHERE 물건을 어디에 놓다◀ [T] to put something somewhere carefully ‖ 조심스럽게 물건을 어디에 놓다: *Just set that bag down on the floor.* 그 가방을 그냥 마루에 내려놓으시오.

4 ▶MAKE STH READY 사물을 준비하다◀ [T] to arrange something or put it in a particular position, so that it is ready to be used or done ‖ 바로 사용하거나 수행되도록 특정한 위치에 사물을 배열하거나 놓다: *I set my alarm for 6:30.* 나는 자명종을 6시 30분에 맞췄다. / *How many people should I set the table for?* (=put knives, plates etc. on it) 몇 사람용의 식사를 준비해야 하죠?

5 ▶FIRE 불◀ to make something start burning ‖ 물건에 불을 붙이다: *Angry mobs set the building on fire.* 성난 폭도가 그 건물에 방화했다. / *Careless campers set fire to the dry brush.* 부주의한 야영객들이 마른 덤불에 불을 냈다.

6 ▶MOVIE/STORY ETC. 영화/소설◀ [T] if a play, movie, story etc. is set in a place or at a particular time, the events in it happen there or at that time ‖ 연극·영화·소설 속의 사건을 특정한 장소나 시간에 일어나도록 잡다. 무대를 특정 장소[시간]로 설정하다: *Clavell's epic novel is set in 17th century Japan.* 클라벨의 서사시적인 소설은 17세기 일본을 무대로 하고 있다.

7 set sb/sth straight to correct something or someone ‖ 사람이나 사물을 바로잡다: *The company wants to set the record straight* (=explain the true situation) *about its safety procedures.* 그 회사는 안전 조치에 대한 실상을 설명하기를 원한다.

8 set the stage/scene to make it possible for something to happen ‖ 어떤 것의 발생을 가능하게 하다: *Recent pay cuts set the stage for a strike.* 최근의 임금 삭감은 파업을 야기시켰다.

9 set sth in motion to make something start happening ‖ 일이 발생하게 하다. 일을 시작하다: *Once the process is set in motion, we cannot stop it.* 일단 그 과정이 시작되면 우리는 그것을 멈출 수 없다.

10 ▶SUN/MOON 태양/달◀ [I] when the

sun or moon sets, it moves lower in the sky until it can no longer be seen ‖ 해나 달이 보이지 않게 될 때까지 하늘에서 아래쪽으로 움직이다. 지다

11 set your sights on sth to decide that something is your aim ‖ 무엇인가에 목표를 정하다. 노리다. 겨냥하다: *Annie set her sights on the most popular boy in school.* 애니는 학교에서 가장 인기 있는 소년에게 눈독을 들였다.

12 set your mind to sth to decide that you are willing to work hard for something ‖ 기꺼이 무엇을 열심히 하기로 결정하다: *You can do anything that you set your mind to.* 너는 하기로 마음먹은 일은 무엇이든 할 수 있어.

13 set foot in/on to go into or onto a place ‖ 장소에 들어가다. …에 발을 들여 놓다: *The event is attracting people who have never before set foot in a museum.* 그 행사는 전에 박물관에 가 본적 없는 사람들의 마음을 끌고 있다.

14 set sb free/loose to allow a person or animal to leave a prison or CAGE, or to untie him, her, or it ‖ 사람이나 동물이 교도소나 새장을 떠나가게 하거나 풀어주다. 놓아주다. 해방시키다: *Do you mean he set all the lab animals loose?* 그가 실험실의 동물을 모두 놔주었다는 말입니까?

15 set sail to start sailing somewhere ‖ 어딘가로 항해를 시작하다. 항해를 떠나다

16 set to work to start doing something, or to make someone start doing something ‖ 어떤 것을 하기 시작하다, 또는 누군가가 어떤 일을 시작하게 만들다: *Volunteers set to work clearing trash from the field.* 자원 봉사자들이 현장에 있는 쓰레기를 청소하기 시작했다.

17 ▶BECOME SOLID 굳어지다◀ [I] if a liquid mixture sets, it becomes hard and solid ‖ 액체 혼합물이 딱딱하게 굳다. 응고하다: *The concrete will set within two hours.* 콘크리트는 두 시간 내에 굳을 것이다.

18 set sth to music a) to write music for a story or poem ‖ 이야기나 시에 곡을 붙이다. 작곡하다: *poems set to music by Lloyd Webber* 로이드 웨버가 곡을 붙인 시들 **b)** to arrange something so that it can be done while music plays ‖ 음악이 연주되는 동안 무엇을 끝마치도록 조정하다: *exercise routines set to music* 음악에 맞춘 운동 순서

19 set a trap a) to invent a plan that will catch someone doing something wrong ‖ 나쁜 일을 한 사람을 잡을 계획을 세우다: *Police set a trap for the thieves.* 경찰은 도둑을 잡을 계획을 세웠다. **b)** to

make a trap ready to catch an animal ‖ 동물을 잡기 위해 덫을 놓다.

20 ▶BONE 뼈◀ [T] to put the ends of a broken bone back together so that it will heal ‖ 치유될 수 있도록 부러진 뼈의 끝을 제자리에 맞추다. 정골하다. 접골하다

21 ▶ATTACH 부착하다◀ [T] to attach or glue something into a surface ‖ 물건을 표면에 부착하거나 붙이다. 박다: *a diamond set in a gold ring* 금반지에 박은 다이아몬드

22 ▶HAIR 머리털◀ [T] to arrange someone's hair while it is wet, so that it will have a particular style when it is dry ‖ 마르면 특정한 모양이 되도록 젖어 있을 때 누군가의 머리털을 정돈하다. 세트하다. 손질하다

23 set great store by to consider something to be very important 무엇을 매우 중요하게 생각하다. 중시[존중]하다: *Greg sets great store by his friends' trust.* 그레그는 그의 친구들의 신뢰를 중시한다. —see also **(get) ready, (get) set, go!** (READY)

set about sth *phr v* [T] **set about doing sth** to begin doing something ‖ 무엇을 하기 시작하다. 착수[개시]하다: *Johnny set about improving his Spanish before his trip.* 조니는 여행하기 전에 스페인어 실력을 쌓기 시작했다.

set sb **against** sb *phr v* [T] to make someone start to argue or fight with someone else ‖ 누군가를 다른 사람과 논쟁하거나 싸우게 하다. 적대시키다. 반대하게 하다: *The issue sets Republicans against one another.* 그 문제는 공화당원들끼리 서로 논쟁하게 만든다.

set sth ↔ **apart** *phr v* [T] to make someone or something different from other similar people or things ‖ 사람이나 사물을 다른 비슷한 사람이나 사물과 구별되게 하다. 눈에 띄게 하다: *The movie's realistic characters set it apart from other gangster pictures.* 실감나는 등장인물들로 그 영화는 다른 갱 영화와는 차별화되었다.

set sth ↔ **aside** *phr v* [T] **1** to save something for a special purpose ‖ 특별한 목적으로 무엇을 확보해 두다. 떼어놓다: *Hotels must set aside 50% of their rooms for non-smokers.* 호텔은 방의 50%를 비흡연자용으로 따로 확보해야 한다. **2** to decide not to be affected or influenced by a particular belief, idea etc. ‖ 특정한 신념이나 생각 등에 영향이나 지배를 받지 않도록 정하다. 무시하다. 제쳐놓다: *They should set politics aside and do what is best for the country.* 그들

은 정치는 제쳐두고 나라를 위해 최선을 다해야 한다.

set back *phr v* [T] **1** [**set** sb/sth ↔ **back**] to delay the progress or development of someone or something ‖ 사람이나 사물의 진보나 발달을 지연시키다: *Officials fear that the incident will set back race relations.* 관리들은 그 사건이 인종 간의 관계를 퇴보시킬 것을 염려한다. **2** [**set** sb **back**] to cost someone a lot of money ‖ 남에게 많은 비용을 쓰게 하다: *Dinner set us back $300.* 우리는 정찬에 300달러가 들었다.

set sth ↔ **down** *phr v* [T] to make a rule or write something in an official document ‖ 규칙을 정하거나 어떤 것을 공식 문서화하다: *The rules of the game were clearly set down.* 게임 규칙이 확실히 정해졌다.

set forth sth *phr v* [T] FORMAL **1** to establish rules, principles etc. ‖ 규칙·원칙 등을 세우다: *a document setting forth guidelines for behavior* 행동 지침을 규정하는 문서 **2** to write or talk about an idea, rule etc., in order to explain it ‖ 설명하기 위해 생각·규칙 등을 쓰거나 이야기하다: *Rousseau set forth his educational theories in the book "Emile."* 루소는 "에밀"이라는 책에서 자신의 교육 이론을 설명했다.

set in *phr v* [I] if something sets in, especially something unpleasant, it begins and is likely to continue ‖ 특히 불쾌한 일이 시작되어 계속될 조짐이다: *As warm weather set in, the ice began to melt.* 따뜻한 날씨가 계속됨에 따라 얼음이 녹기 시작했다.

set off *phr v* **1** [T **set** sth ↔ **off**] to make something start happening or make people suddenly start doing something ‖ 일이 일어나게 하거나 사람들이 갑자기 어떤 일을 시작하게 하다. …을 일으키다: *The attack set off another round of fighting.* 그 공격은 또 한 차례의 싸움을 유발했다. / *The rains set off a mudslide that killed 15 people.* 그 비는 15명의 인명을 앗아간 진흙 사태를 일으켰다. **2** [T **set** sth ↔ **off**] to make something explode ‖ 무엇을 폭발시키다: *The bomb was set off by a remote control device.* 그 폭탄은 원격 조종 장치로 폭발되었다. **3** [T **set** sth ↔ **off**] to make machinery or electronic equipment, especially an ALARM, start working ‖ 기계나 전자 기구 특히 경보기를 작동시키다: *A fire in the kitchen set off the smoke alarms.* 부엌의 화재로 화재 경보기가 작동되었다. **4** [I] to leave a

place in order to go somewhere, especially somewhere far away ‖ 어디로인가 특히 멀리 가기 위해 어떤 장소를 떠나다. 출발하다. 여행 가다: *Thousands of people set off for the West during the 1800s.* 수천 명이 1800년대에 서부로 떠났다.

set out *phr v* **1 set out to do sth** to deliberately start doing something ‖ 신중히 일을 시작하다. 착수[기도, 시도]하다: *He set out to make a movie about his experiences in Vietnam.* 그는 베트남에서의 자신의 경험에 대한 영화 제작에 착수했다. **2** [I] to leave a place, especially to begin a trip ‖ 특히 여행을 시작하려고 장소를 떠나다. 여행을 떠나다. 출발하다: *The couple set out for Fresno at about 9:30.* 그 부부는 9시 30분경에 프레스노로 여행을 떠났다. **3** [T **set out** sth] to write or talk about ideas, rules etc. in a clear and organized way ‖ 생각·규칙 등을 명백하고 체계적으로 쓰거나 이야기하다. 정연하게 설명하다: *He is the first candidate to set out his foreign policy proposals.* 그는 자신의 외교 정책안을 정연하게 설명할 첫 후보자이다.

set up *phr v* **1** [I,T **set** sth ↔ **up**] to start a company, organization, business etc. ‖ 회사·단체·사업 등을 시작하다. 개업하다: *The county has set up a special education program for teenage mothers.* 그 국가는 십대 어머니를 위한 특별 교육 프로그램을 시작했다. **2** [T **set** sth ↔ **up**] to prepare something or make arrangements for something ‖ 무엇을 준비하거나 무엇을 위한 조치를 취하다: *Chris, could you help me set up the computer?* 크리스, 컴퓨터 가동 준비를 도와주시겠습니까? / *I called the doctor's to set up an appointment.* 나는 약속을 정하기 위해 의사에게 전화했다. **3** [T **set** sth ↔ **up**] to build something or put it somewhere ‖ 무엇을 건설하거나 어딘가에 놓다: *The police set up a roadblock to try to catch the criminals.* 경찰은 범죄자를 잡기 위해 바리케이드를 설치했다. **4** [T **set** sb ↔ **up**] to deliberately make people think that someone has done something wrong ‖ 고의로 사람들로 하여금 누군가가 잘못을 저질렀다고 생각하게 하다. 죄를 덮어씌우다: *Hudson accused his partners of setting him up.* 허드슨은 자기의 동업자들이 자기에게 죄를 덮어씌운다고 고소했다. **5 set up shop** to start a business ‖ 사업을 시작하다: *They set up shop in 1993 in Mason's basement.* 그들은 메이슨의 지하실에서 1933년에 창

업을 했다.

set² n 1 a group of things that belong together ‖ 소속을 함께 하는 일단의 물건들. 한 세트[벌, 조]: *a set of dishes* 접시 한 세트 / *a chess set* 체스 세트 **2** a television or radio ‖ 텔레비전이나 라디오: *a color TV set* 컬러 텔레비전 세트 **3** a place where a movie or television program is acted and filmed ‖ 영화나 텔레비전 프로그램을 연기하고 촬영하는 장소. 촬영 현장: *OK, everybody, quiet on the set!* 좋아, 모두 촬영장에서는 정숙히! **4** one part of a game such as tennis or VOLLEYBALL ‖ 테니스나 배구 등의 경기의 한 부분. 세트: *Sampras leads two sets to one.* 샘프라스는 세트스코어 2대 1로 앞서고 있다. **5** the things that are put on a stage to make the background for a play ‖ 연극의 배경을 만들기 위해 무대에 놓는 물건들. 무대 장치. 세트

set³ adj 1 a set time, amount, price etc. is fixed and cannot be changed ‖ 시간·양·가격 등이 고정되어 바꿀 수 없는. 정해진. 규정된: *We meet at a set time each week.* 우리는 매주 정해진 시간에 만난다. **2** INFORMAL ready to do something ‖ 무엇을 할 준비가 되어 있는: *If everyone is all set, we'll start the meeting.* 우리는 모든 사람들이 준비되면, 회의를 시작할 것입니다. **3 be set on/upon/against sth** INFORMAL to be very determined about something ‖ 무엇에 대해 몹시 단호하다: *Jerry's dead set against paying the extra money for the trip.* 제리는 그 여행에 추가 경비를 지불하는 일에 결사반대하고 있다. **4** being in a particular place or position ‖ 특정한 장소나 위치에 있는: *a castle set on a hill* 언덕 위에 있는 성

set·back /ˈsɛtˌbæk/ *n* something that delays your progress or makes things worse than they were ‖ 진보를 지연시키는 것, 또는 과거보다 일을 악화시키는 것. 진보의 방해. 후퇴: *The peace talks suffered a setback when fighting resumed this week.* 평화 회담은 이번 주에 전투가 재개되면서 결렬되었다.

set·ter /ˈsɛtɚ/ *n* a dog with long hair, often used in hunting to find birds and animals ‖ 새와 동물을 찾아내도록 종종 사냥에 이용되는 털이 긴 개. 세터

set·ting /ˈsɛtɪŋ/ *n* [C usually singular] **1** all the things that surround someone or something ‖ 사람이나 사물을 둘러싼 모든 것. 주위 환경: *a cabin in a mountain setting* 산 속에 있는 오두막 **2** a position of the controls on a machine, piece of electronic equipment etc. ‖ 기

계·전자 기구 등의 조절 위치: *Turn the microwave to its highest setting.* 전자레인지를 최고 수준까지 돌려라. **3** the place or time in which the events in a book or movie happen ‖ 책이나 영화에서 사건이 발생한 장소나 시간. 배경. 무대: *London is the setting for his most recent novel.* 런던은 그의 가장 최근 소설의 배경이다.

set·tle /ˈsɛtl/ *v*
1 ▶END ARGUMENT 논쟁을 매듭짓다◀ [I, T] to end an argument or a bad situation by agreeing to do something ‖ 무엇을 하기로 동의함으로 논쟁이나 나쁜 상황을 매듭짓다. 해결하다: *They can't seem to settle their arguments without fighting.* 그들은 싸우지 않고는 논쟁을 해결할 수 없을 것 같다. / *The company agreed to settle with them out of court.* (=without arguing in a court of law) 그 회사는 소송을 하지 않고 그것들을 매듭짓는 것에 동의했다.
2 ▶COMFORTABLE POSITION 안락한 장소◀ [I, T] to put yourself or someone else in a comfortable position ‖ 자신이나 다른 사람을 편안한 자세로 두다. 쉬다. 안치하다: *Dave settled back and turned on the TV.* 데이브는 의자에 편히 기대고 텔레비전을 틀었다. / *Grandpa settled himself in the car.* 할아버지는 차 안에서 느긋하게 쉬었다.
3 ▶DECIDE STH 무엇을 결정하다◀ [T] to decide on something, or organize the details of something that will happen in the future ‖ 무엇을 정하거나 장차 일어날 일의 세부 사항을 정리하다. 확정하다: *We have to get the details of the trip settled soon.* 우리는 여행의 세부 일정을 곧 정해야 한다.
4 ▶IN A NEW PLACE 새 장소에서◀ a) [I, T] to start a new town or city in a place where no one has lived before ‖ 전에 아무도 살지 않은 장소에 새로운 읍이나 도시를 건설하다. 새 정착촌을 세우다: *They came from England to settle in America.* 그들은 미국에 정착하기 위해 영국에서 왔다. / *the men and women who settled Alaska* 알래스카를 개척한 남성들과 여성들 **b)** [I] to begin to live in a place where you intend to live for a long time ‖ 오랫동안 살기로 작정한 곳에서 살기 시작하다. 정착하다: *My family moved around a lot before settling in Los Angeles.* 나의 가족은 로스앤젤레스에 정착하기 전에 이사를 많이 했다.
5 ▶SNOW/DUST 눈/먼지◀ [I] if snow, dust etc. settles, it falls to the ground and stays there ‖ 눈이나 먼지 등이 땅에

떨어져 있다. 가라앉다. 쌓이다: *When the dust settled, we could see the damage done by the tornado.* 우리는 먼지가 가라앉자 토네이도가 남긴 피해를 알 수 있었다.

6 ▶BILL/DEBT 계산/빚◀ [T] if you settle a bill, account, debt etc. you pay the money that you owe ‖ 청구서·외상·빚 등 자신이 빚진 돈을 지불하다. 청산하다

7 settle a score to do something bad to someone because s/he has done something bad to you ‖ 상대방이 자신에게 나쁜 짓을 했기 때문에 상대방에게 나쁜 짓을 하다. 담판을 짓다. 복수하다

8 settle your stomach/nerves to do something that makes you stop feeling sick or nervous ‖ 메스꺼움이나 불안을 없애는 무엇인가를 하다. 위를 가라앉히다/신경을 안정시키다: *Drink some mint tea. It'll settle your stomach.* 박하 차를 좀 마셔라. 그것이 위를 가라앉힐 것이다.

settle down *phr v* [I] **1** to become calmer and less active or noisy ‖ 더 조용해지거나 활력이나 시끄러움이 덜해지다. 가라앉다. 진정되다: *Kids, settle down and eat your dinner.* 애들아, 조용히 하고 저녁을 먹어라. **2** to start living in one place, working, and behaving in a responsible way ‖ 한 곳에서 생활을 시작하면서 책임 있게 일하고 행동하다. 정착하다. 안정하다: *My parents want me to marry Jim and settle down.* 나의 부모님은 내가 짐과 결혼해서 정착하기를 원한다. **3** to begin to do something and to give it all your attention ‖ 무엇을 하기 시작하여 모든 관심을 그것에 쏟다. 본격적으로 착수하다. 전념하다: *When he finally settled down to work, it was 10:30.* 그가 마침내 본격적으로 일에 착수했을 때는 10시 30분이었다.

settle for *phr v* [T] to accept something that is less than what you wanted ‖ 원했던 것에 미달되는 것을 받아들이다. …으로 만족하다: *We looked at some nice apartments, but we had to settle for the cheapest one.* 우리는 몇 개의 좋은 아파트를 보았으나 가장 싼 아파트에 만족해야만 했다.

settle in, settle into *phr v* [I] to become happier and more comfortable in a new situation or place ‖ 새 상황이나 새 장소에서 점차 행복하고 편안해지다. 익숙해지다. 적응하다: *Adam seems to have settled in at his new school.* 아담은 그의 새 학교에 적응한 것처럼 보인다.

settle on/upon *phr v* [T] to decide to do or have something after thinking about many possibilities ‖ 많은 가능성을

생각한 후에 무엇을 하거나 가지기로 결정하다: *They haven't settled on a name for the baby yet.* 그들은 아기의 이름을 아직 정하지 않았다.

settle up *phr v* [I] INFORMAL to pay money that you owe for something ‖ 무엇인가에 진 빚을 갚다. 청산하다

set·tled /'sɛtld/ *adj* **1** unlikely to change ‖ 쉽게 변하지 않는. 고정된. 정해진: *the settled life of a farmer* 농부의 정해진 생활 **2 feel/be settled** to feel comfortable about living or working in a particular place ‖ 특정한 장소에서의 생활이나 일에 대해 안락함을 느끼다. 편안하다: *We don't feel settled in our new house yet.* 우리는 아직 새집이 편치를 않다. —compare UNSETTLED

set·tle·ment /'sɛtlmənt/ *n* **1** an official agreement or decision that ends an argument ‖ 논쟁을 끝내는 공식적인 협정이나 결정. 합의. 타결: *The two sides have reached a settlement* (=made an agreement) *in the land dispute.* 양측이 땅 분쟁에 타결을 보았다. **2** [C, U] a payment of money that you owe someone or that someone owes to you ‖ 자신이 남에게 또는 남이 자신에게 지고 있는 빚을 갚음. 청산. 결산: *He accepted a financial settlement of $500.* 그는 빚 500달러를 돌려받았다. **3** [U] the movement of a large number of people into a new place in order to live there ‖ 새로운 곳에서 살려고 많은 사람들이 이동하는 것. 이주. 이민: *the settlement of the Oklahoma territory* 오클라호마 지역으로의 이주 **4** a place where people live, especially where no one lived before ‖ 특히 전에는 아무도 살지 않았던, 사람들이 사는 장소. 개척지: *a Stone Age settlement* 석기 시대의 주거지

set·tler /'sɛtlə, 'sɛtl-ə/ *n* someone who goes to live in a new place, usually where there were few people before ‖ 보통 전에는 사람이 거의 없던 새로운 곳에서 살기 위해 가는 사람. 이주자. 개척자: *early settlers of the American West* 미국 서부의 초기 개척자들

set·up /'. ./ *n* [C usually singular] **1** a way of organizing or arranging something ‖ 사물을 조직화하거나 배열하는 방법. 배치. 조직. 구성: *Do you like the new setup at work?* 직장의 새로운 배치가 마음에 듭니까? **2** INFORMAL a dishonest plan that is intended to trick someone ‖ 남을 속이려는 부정직한 계획. 함정. 음모. 속임수: *I knew immediately that the whole thing was a setup.* 나는 그 모든 일이 음모라는 것을 즉시 알았다.

sev·en /'sɛvən/ *number* **1** 7 ‖ 7 **2** seven o'clock ‖ 7시: *The movie starts at seven.* 그 영화는 7시에 시작한다.

sev·en·teen /ˌsɛvən'tin-/ *number* 17 ‖ 17 – **seventeenth** *number*

sev·enth /'sɛvənθ/ *number* **1** 7th ‖ 일곱 번째 **2** 1/7 ‖ 7분의 1 **3 be in seventh heaven** INFORMAL to be extremely happy ‖ 매우 행복하다: *The kids were in seventh heaven when we were staying on the farm.* 아이들은 우리가 농장에 묵고 있었을 때 매우 행복해 했다.

Seventh Day Ad·vent·ist /ˌ.. ˌ. .'../ *adj* relating to a Christian group that believes that Christ will soon come again to Earth ‖ 예수가 곧 지구에 다시 온다고 믿는 기독교 단체에 관한. 제7일 안식일 재림파의 – **Seventh Day Adventist** *n*

sev·en·ty /'sɛvənti/ *number* **1** 70 ‖ 70 **2 the seventies a)** the years between 1970 and 1979 ‖ 1970년과 1979년 사이의 해들. 70년대 **b)** the numbers between 70 and 79, especially when used for measuring temperature ‖ 특히 온도를 측정하는 데에 쓰이는 70과 79 사이의 숫자들. 70도대 – **seventieth** /'sɛvəntiɪθ/ *number* : *her seventieth birthday* 그녀의 일흔 번째의 생일

sev·er /'sɛvɚ/ *v* [T] FORMAL **1** to cut through something completely ‖ 무엇을 완전히 자르다. 절단하다: *His finger was severed in the accident.* 그의 손가락은 그 사고로 절단되었다. **2** to end a relationship or agreement with someone ‖ 남과의 관계나 계약을 끝내다. 단절하다: *The deal severs all ties between the two organizations.* 그 거래는 두 기관 사이의 모든 유대 관계를 단절시킨다. – **severance** *n* [U]

sev·er·al /'sɛvrəl/ *quantifier* a number of people or things that is more than a few, but not a lot ‖ 많지는 않고 조금보다는 많은 사람 또는 물건의 수. 몇몇의: *I called her several times on the phone.* 나는 그녀에게 몇 차례 전화를 했다. / *I've talked to several of my students about this.* 나는 이것에 관해서 나의 몇몇 학생에게 말했다. —compare FEW —see study note on page 940

sev·er·ance pay /'sɛvrəns ˌpeɪ/ *n* [U] money you get from a company that you worked for because you no longer have a job ‖ 더 이상 직장에 없기 때문에 근무했던 회사에서 받는 금전. 퇴직금

se·vere /sə'vɪr/ *adj* **1** very bad or serious ‖ 매우 나쁘거나 심한. 중한: *severe head injuries* 심각한 머리 부상 /

severe problems 심각한 문제들 **2** not kind or friendly ‖ 친절하거나 우호적이지 않은. 엄한. 가혹한: *severe criticism* 가혹한 비평 / *a severe look on her face* 그녀의 무서운 얼굴 표정 —compare STRICT – **severity** /sɪ'vɛrəti/ *n* [C, U]

se·vere·ly /sə'vɪrli/ *adv* very badly or to a great degree ‖ 매우 나쁘게 또는 대단한 정도로. 엄하게. 심하게: *a country severely affected by drought* 가뭄의 영향을 심하게 받은 국가 / *She was punished severely for her actions.* 그녀는 자신의 행동에 대해 가혹하게 처벌받았다.

sew /soʊ/ *v* **sewed, sewn** or **sewed, sewing** [I, T] to join pieces of cloth together or attach something to a piece of cloth using a needle and thread ‖ 바늘과 실을 사용하여 헝겊 조각을 함께 붙이거나 어떤 것을 헝겊 조각에 덧붙이다. 꿰매다. 꿰매어 붙이다. 바느질[재봉]하다: *Can you sew a button on this shirt for me?* 이 셔츠에 단추 하나 꿰매어 달아 주시겠어요? – **sewing** *n* [U]

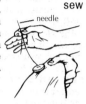

sew / needle

sew sth ↔ up *phr v* [T] **1** to close or repair something by sewing it ‖ 바느질을 해서 어떤 것을 막거나 수리하다. (구멍 등을) 꿰매다. 봉합하다: *I need to sew up this hole in my jeans.* 나는 내 진바지에 있는 이 구멍을 기워서 막아야 한다. **2** INFORMAL to gain control over a situation so that you are sure to win or get an advantage ‖ 확실히 이기거나 이점을 얻도록 상황에 대한 지배권을 얻다. …을 획득[확보]하다: *The Republicans think they have the election sewn up.* 공화당원들은 자신들이 그 선거에서 승리를 확보했다고 생각한다.

sew·age /'suɪdʒ/ *n* [U] the waste material and used water that is carried away from houses by SEWERs ‖ 집의 하수관에 의해서 배출되는 폐기물과 폐수. 오수. 하수

sew·er /'suɚ/ *n* a pipe or passage under the ground that carries away waste material and used water from houses, factories etc. ‖ 집·공장 등에서 폐기물·폐수를 배출하는 지하의 도관 또는 통로. 하수관. 하수구

sewn /soʊn/ *v* a PAST PARTICIPLE of SEW ‖ sew의 과거 분사형

sex /sɛks/ *n* **1** [U] the activity that a male and a female do together in order to produce children or for pleasure;

SEXUAL INTERCOURSE ‖ 아기를 낳거나 쾌락을 위해 남녀가 함께 하는 행위. 성교; ㊤ sexual intercourse: *She said she wouldn't have sex with him until she knew him better.* 그녀는 그를 더 잘 알 때까지는 그와 성행위를 하지 않겠다고 말했다. / *There are some sex scenes in the movie.* 그 영화에는 성행위 장면이 약간 있다. **2** [U] the condition of being male or female ‖ 남성 또는 여성됨의 조건. 성(性): *I don't care what sex the baby is, as long as it's healthy.* 나는 아기가 건강하기만 하면 남아이건 여아이건 개의치 않는다. **3** one of the two groups of people or animals, male and female ‖ 사람이나 동물의 암·수 두 개 집단 중의 하나. 남성. 여성: *He isn't comfortable with members of the opposite sex.* (=people that are not his own sex) 그는 이성들하고 같이 있으면 편안하지가 않다.

sex ed·u·ca·tion /ˈ. ...,/ *n* [U] education in schools about sexual activity and sexual relationships ‖ 성행위와 성관계에 대한 학교에서의 교육. 성교육

sex·ism /ˈsɛk,sɪzəm/ *n* [U] the belief that one sex, especially the female sex, is weaker, less intelligent, or less important than the other ‖ 하나의 성(性) 특히 여성이 다른 성, 즉 남성보다 더 약하다는[덜 지적이라는, 덜 중요하다는] 신념. (직업·정치 등에서의) 성차별(주의). 성에 따른 편견

sex·ist /ˈsɛksɪst/ *adj* relating to or showing SEXISM ‖ 성차별에 관련된, 또는 성차별을 나타내는. 성차별주의자의: *a book about sexist attitudes in the military* 군(軍) 내부에서의 성 차별적인 태도에 관한 책 **– sexist** *n*

sex sym·bol /ˈ. ,../ *n* someone famous who many people think is very sexually attractive ‖ 많은 사람들이 매우 성적인 매력이 있다고 생각하는 유명인사. 성적 매력이 넘치는 사람

sex tour·is·m /ˈ. ,../ *n* [U] the activity of travelling to other countries in order to have sex, especially sexual activities that are illegal in your own country ‖ 특히 자국에서는 불법인 성행위를 갖기 위해 다른 나라로 여행하는 행위. 섹스 관광

sex·u·al /ˈsɛkʃuəl/ *adj* **1** relating to sex ‖ 성에 관련된. 성(性)의. 성적인: *sexual contact* 성적 접촉 / *sexual passion* 정욕 **2** involving a male and a female ‖ 남녀에 관계되는. 남녀의: *children learning their sexual roles* 자신들의 성적 역할을 배우는 아이들 **– sexually** *adv*

sexual ha·rass·ment /,... .'..., ,...

SEXUAL INTERCOURSE ‖ sexual remarks, looks, or touching that you do not want, especially from someone that you work with ‖ 특히 직장에 같이 근무하는 사람으로부터의 원하지 않는 성적인 말[표정, 접촉]. 성적으로 괴롭히기. 성희롱

sexual in·ter·course /,... '.../ *n* [U] FORMAL the physical act of sex between two people ‖ 두 사람 간의 육체적인 성행위. 성교. 섹스

sex·u·al·i·ty /,sɛkʃuˈæləti/ *n* [U] all the things that someone does or feels that are related to sexual activity ‖ 성행위에 관련되어 사람이 하거나 느끼는 모든 것. 성. 성적 특질[능력]

sex·y /ˈsɛksi/ *adj* sexually exciting or attractive ‖ 성적으로 흥분시키거나 매력이 있는. 섹시한: *a sexy woman* 섹시한 여자

Sgt. *n* the written abbreviation of SERGEANT ‖ sergeant의 약어

sh /ʃ/ *interjection* ⇨ SHH

shab·by /ˈʃæbi/ *adj* **1** old and in bad condition because of being used a lot ‖ 많이 사용해서 낡고 상태가 나쁜. 낡아빠진. 닳은: *shabby hotel rooms* 낡아 빠진 호텔 방들 **2** unfair or wrong ‖ 정당하지 않거나 잘못된. 비천한. 비루한: *I don't deserve this kind of shabby treatment.* 나는 이와 같은 비천한 대우를 받을 만한 사람이 아니다. **– shabbily** *adv*

shack¹ /ʃæk/ *n* a small building that has not been built very well ‖ 그다지 잘 지어지지 않은 작은 건물. 판잣집. 오두막집

shack² *v*

shack up *phr v* [I] INFORMAL to start living with someone and having sex with him/her ‖ 남과 함께 살며 성교를 갖기 시작하다. (남과) 동거하다: *I found out that she was shacked up with some guy from Florida.* 나는 그녀가 플로리다에서 온 어떤 녀석과 동거했다는 것을 알아냈다.

shack·le¹ /ˈʃækəl/ *n* one of a pair of metal rings joined by a chain, that is used for keeping a prisoner's hands or feet together ‖ 죄수의 손 또는 발을 함께 속박하는 데에 쓰이는, 쇠사슬에 의해 연결된 한 쌍의 금속 고리 중의 하나. 수갑. 족쇄

shack·le² *v* [T] **1 be shackled by sth** to be prevented from doing what you want to do by something ‖ 어떤 것에 의해 사람이 하고 싶은 일을 저지당하다. …을 구속[속박]하다. 방해하다: *a company shackled by debts* 채무로 꼼짝 못하는 회사 **2** to put SHACKLES on someone ‖ 어떤 사람에게 수갑을 채우다

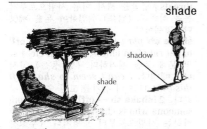

shade

shadow

shade

shade¹ /ʃeɪd/ n 1 [singular, U] an area that is cooler and darker because the light of the sun cannot reach it ‖ 햇빛이 닿을 수 없어서 더 서늘하고 어두운 지역. 그늘(진 곳): *boys sitting in the shade of a tree* 나무 그늘에 앉아 있는 소년들 —compare SHADOW¹ 2 something that reduces or blocks light, especially a cover that you pull across a window ‖ 빛을 감소시키거나 차단하는 것, 특히 창문을 가로질러 치는 덮개. 블라인드. 커튼: *Can you close/open the shades in the living room?* 거실의 블라인드를 닫아[열어] 주겠니? 3 a particular degree of a color ‖ 색깔의 특정한 정도. 색조: *a darker shade of red/green/blue* 빨간색[녹색, 파란색]의 더 어두운 색조 4 **shade of meaning/opinion etc.** a slight difference in things such as a meaning etc. ‖ 의미 등에서의 사소한 차이. 의미/의견 등의 미묘한 차이: *a word with many shades of meaning* 의미의 미묘한 차이가 많이 있는 단어 5 **a shade** very slightly, a little bit ‖ 극소, 아주 조금: *The room is a shade too hot for me.* 그 방은 나에게는 약간 좀 덥다.

USAGE NOTE shade and shadow

Shade is an area where there is no sunlight: *It's too hot here – let's find some shade.* A **shadow** is a dark shape you see on a surface that is caused by something blocking the light: *Mommy, my shadow is longer than yours!*
shade는 햇빛이 없는 지역이다: 이곳은 너무 덥구나. 그늘을 찾아보자. **shadow**는 빛을 차단하는 물체에 의해서 생긴 면에서 볼 수 있는 어두운 형상을 말한다: 엄마, 내 그림자가 엄마 그림자보다 더 길어요!

---

shade² v [T] to protect something from direct light or heat ‖ 직접적인 광선 또는 열로부터 사물을 보호하다. (광선 등으로부터) 차단하다: *She used her hand to shade her eyes from the sun.* 그녀는 햇

빛이 닿지 않게 그녀의 눈을 손으로 가렸다.

shades /ʃeɪdz/ n [plural] INFORMAL ⇨ SUNGLASSES

shad·ow¹ /ˈʃædoʊ/ n 1 a dark shape that an object or a person makes on a surface when it is between that surface and the light ‖ 물체 또는 사람이 지표와 빛 사이에 있을 때 지표면에 생기는 어두운 형상. 그림자. 영상: *The bright lights behind us cast strange shadows on the wall.* 우리 뒤쪽의 밝은 빛이 벽에 이상한 그림자를 드리웠다. —compare SHADE¹ — see picture at SHADE¹ 2 [C, U] darkness caused when light is prevented from coming into a place ‖ 빛이 어떤 장소에 들어오는 것을 차단할 때 생기는 어두움. 그늘. 어둠. 응달: *Most of the room was in shadow.* 대부분의 방은 그늘이 졌다. */ He waited in the shadows.* 그는 그늘 속에서 기다렸다. 3 **without/beyond a shadow of a doubt** without any doubt at all ‖ 어떤 의심도 전혀 없이. 아무런 의심할 여지없이: *I think he's guilty beyond any shadow of a doubt.* 나는 전혀 의심할 여지없이 그가 유죄라고 생각한다. —see usage note at SHADE¹

shadow² v [T] to follow someone closely in order to watch what s/he is doing ‖ 남이 하는 일을 감시하기 위해 근접하여 뒤따르다. …을 미행하다. …의 뒤를 좇다

shadow e·con·o·my /ˌ.. ˈ...../ n TECHNICAL business activities that are difficult for the authorities to find out about, for example because they are illegal ‖ 불법이기 때문에 당국이 알아내기 어려운 사업 활동. 지하 경제

shad·ow·y /ˈʃædoʊi/ adj 1 mysterious and difficult to know anything about ‖ 관련된 어떤 것도 알아내기가 불가사의하고 어려운. 그림자 같은[처럼 희미한]. 실체가 없는: *a shadowy figure from his past* 그 과거를 알 수 없는 수상쩍은 사람 2 full of shadows and difficult to see ‖ 그늘이 가득하고 보기 어려운. 그늘이 많은. 그늘에 싸인[덮인]: *a shadowy corner* 그늘진 구석

shad·y /ˈʃeɪdi/ adj 1 protected from the sun or producing shade ‖ 햇빛이 차단되거나 그늘을 만드는. 그늘진[지게 하는]: *a shady spot for a picnic* 피크닉을 위한 그늘진 장소 / *a shady tree* 그늘지게 하는 나무 2 INFORMAL not honest or legal ‖ 정직하거나 합법적이지 않은. 떳떳하지 못한. 수상한: *a shady business deal* 수상한 사업 거래

shaft /ʃæft/ n 1 a passage that goes up

through a building or down into the ground ‖ 건물을 위로 관통하거나 땅속으로 내려가는 통로. 위아래로 관통한 수직 공간: *an elevator shaft* 엘리베이터 통로 **2** a long handle on a tool, SPEAR etc. ‖ 연장·창 등에 있는 긴 손잡이. 자루 **3 shaft of light/sunlight** a narrow beam of light ‖ 가는 빛줄기. 한 줄기의 빛/햇빛

shag·gy /'ʃægi/ *adj* **1** shaggy hair or fur is long and messy ‖ (머리털·부드러운 털 등이) 길고 뒤얽힌 털투성이의. 복슬복슬한. 텁수룩한: *a shaggy red beard* 텁수룩한 빨간 턱수염 **2** having shaggy hair ‖ 텁수룩한 머리털을 가지고 있는

shake¹ /ʃeɪk/ *v* **shook, shaken, shaking 1** [I, T] to move up and down or from side to side with quick movements, or to make something do this ‖ 빠른 동작으로 위아래나 양옆으로 움직이다, 또는 사물이 이렇게 움직이게 하다. 흔들리다[흔들다]. 떨리다[떨다]. 진동하다: *His hands were shaking.* 그는 손은 부들부들 떨리고 있었다. / *Shake the bottle to mix the oil and vinegar.* 기름과 식초가 섞이도록 병을 흔들어라. **2 shake your head** to move your head from side to side as a way of saying no ‖ "아니오."라고 말하는 표시로써 머리를 양옆으로 움직이다. 고개를 가로젓다 —compare NOD **3 shake hands (with sb)** to hold someone's hand in your hand and move it up and down, as a greeting or a sign that you have agreed on something ‖ 인사 또는 어떤 것에 동의하는 표시로 남의 손을 잡고서 위아래로 움직이다. (남과) 악수하다 **4** [T] to hold someone by his/her shoulders and quickly push and pull him/her backward and forward ‖ 어떤 사람의 어깨를 잡고 앞뒤로 빠르게 밀고 당기다. 잡아 흔들다: *He shook Gus and threw him to the floor.* 그는 구스를 잡아 흔들어서 마루에 내동댕이쳤다. **5** [I] if your voice shakes, it sounds nervous and unsteady ‖ 목소리가 긴장되고 불안정하다. 떨리다 **6 be/look/feel shaken** to be frightened, shocked, or upset ‖ 놀라다[충격 받다, 심란해지다]. 동요되다/충격을 받은 것처럼 보이다/혼란을 느끼다: *Mark looked shaken as he put down the phone.* 마크는 전화를 끊었을 때 충격을 받은 것처럼 보였다.

shake sb **down** *phr v* [T] INFORMAL to get money from someone by using

shake hands

threats ‖ 협박을 해서 어떤 사람으로부터 돈을 취하다. (남을) 위협하여 돈을 빼앗다. 갈취하다

shake off *phr v* [T] **1** [**shake** sth ↔ **off**] to get rid of an illness, problem etc. ‖ 질병·문제 등을 제거하다. (병 등을) 고치다. 떼내다: *I can't seem to shake off this cold.* 나는 이 감기를 고칠 수 없을 것 같다. **2** [**shake** sb ↔ **off**] to escape from someone who is chasing you ‖ 자신을 추적하는 사람으로부터 도망치다. (추적자 등을) 따돌리다. 떨쳐버리다

shake sth ↔ **out** *phr v* [T] to shake something such as a cloth so that small pieces of dirt, dust etc. come off ‖ 천 등을 흔들어서 작은 먼지·오물 등을 털어 버리다

shake sb/sth ↔ **up** *phr v* [T] **1** if an unpleasant experience shakes someone up, s/he is shocked or upset by it ‖ 사람이 불쾌한 경험 등으로 충격 받거나 심란해지다. 남의 감정을 어지럽히다. 동요시키다: *The accident really shook her up.* 그 사고는 정말로 그녀를 불안에 떨게 했다. **2** to make changes to an organization, country etc. to make it more effective ‖ 조직·국가 등을 더욱 효율적으로 바꾸다. (대규모로) 재편성하다. 개편하다 —see also SHAKEUP

shake² *n* **1** an act of shaking ‖ 흔드는 행위. 흔들기: *Give the ketchup bottle a good shake.* 케첩 병을 잘 흔들어라. **2** ⇨ MILKSHAKE

shake·down /'ʃeɪkdaʊn/ *n* **1** INFORMAL the act of getting money from someone by using threats ‖ 협박을 하여 어떤 사람에게서 돈을 취하는 행위. 갈취 **2** a final test of a vehicle or system for problems before it is put into general use ‖ 탈것이나 시스템이 널리 쓰이기 전에 하는 문제점에 대한 최종 검사. 시운전. 성능 시험: *a shakedown process* 시운전 과정

shak·en /'ʃeɪkən/ *v* the PAST PARTICIPLE of shake ‖ shake의 과거 분사형

shake·up /'ʃeɪk-ʌp/ *n* a process in which an organization, company etc. makes a lot of changes in order to be more effective ‖ 조직·회사 등이 더 능률적으로 되기 위해 큰 개편을 하는 과정. (인사·회사의) 대정리[개조]. 대이동. 대개편. 쇄신

shak·y /'ʃeɪki/ *adj* **1** weak and unsteady because of illness, old age, or shock ‖ 질병[고령, 충격]으로 인해 약하고 불안정한. 무너질 것 같은. 비틀거리는: *a shaky voice* 떨리는 목소리 **2** not likely to last a long time or be successful ‖ 오래 가거나 성공적일 것 같지 않은. 위

태위태한: *a shaky marriage* 위태로운 결혼 생활 않은. **3** not solid or firm‖ 단단하거나 굳지 않은. 불안정한: *a shaky ladder* 부서질 것 같은 사다리

shall /ʃəl; *strong* ʃæl/ *modal verb* **1** FORMAL used in order to say what will happen or what must happen‖ 일어날 또는 반드시 일어나야 하는 일을 말하려는 데에 쓰여. …일것이다: *The right to a trial by jury shall be preserved.* 배심 재판을 받을 권리는 보호될 것이다. **2** used in order to ask a question, especially as a way of suggesting something‖ 특히 어떤 것을 제안하는 방식으로 질문을 하는데에쓰여. … 할까요: *Shall I turn on the air conditioner?* 에어컨을 켤까요? **3** FORMAL used in order to say what you are going to do in the future‖ 장차 하려는 일을 말하는 데에 쓰여. …할 작정이다: *I shall keep her picture always.* 나는 항상 그녀의 사진을 간직할 것이다. —see study note on page 932

USAGE NOTE shall, will, and should

Use both **shall** and **will** to talk about future time. Use **will** to talk about what you are planning to do: *I'll* (=I will) *call the travel agency tomorrow.* Use **shall** to mean "do you want me to?": *Shall I call the travel agency for you?* In informal speech, we often use **should** instead of **shall**: *Should I call the travel agency for you?*

shall과 **will**은 모두 장래에 대해 말할 때 쓴다. **will**은 하기로 계획한 것에 대해 말할 때에 쓴다: 나는 내일 여행사에 전화할 것이다. "내가 해 주기를 원하십니까?"를 뜻하는 데는 **shall**을 쓴다: 제가 대신 여행사에 전화해 드릴까요? 비격식 회화에서 우리는 **shall** 대신에 **should**를 자주 쓴다: 제가 대신 여행사에 전화해 드릴까요?

shal·lot /ˈʃælət, ʃəˈlɑt/ *n* a vegetable like a small onion‖ 작은 양파 같은 야채. 설롯

shal·low /ˈʃæloʊ/ *adj* **1** not deep, measuring only a short distance from the top to the bottom‖ 수면에서 바닥까지의 깊이가 아주 짧아 깊지 않은. 얕은: *a shallow baking dish* 얕은 빵 굽는 그릇 / *a shallow pool* 얕은 수영장 **2** not showing any serious or careful thought‖ 조금도 진지하거나 신중한 생각을 보이지 않는. 깊이가 없는. 천박한: *a shallow argument* 깊이 없는 논쟁 —see picture at DEEP¹

sham¹ /ʃæm/ *n* [singular] something that deceives people by seeming good or true when it is not‖ 사실은 그렇지 않지만 좋거나 진짜 같이 보여서 사람을 기만하는 물건. 모조품: *We found out later that the insurance company was a sham.* 그 보험회사는 엉터리였다는 것을 우리는 나중에 알아냈다.

sham² *adj* not real; FAKE‖ 진짜가 아닌. 가짜의; ⓊFfake: *sham jewelry* 가짜 보석

sham·bles /ˈʃæmbəlz/ *n* [singular] INFORMAL **be (in) a shambles a)** to be very badly organized, and fail completely‖ 아주 엉망으로 구성되어 완전히 실패하다. 수라장이 되다. 파멸하다: *The whole evening was a shambles – the food never even arrived.* 그날 저녁은 모든 게 엉망이었어. 주문한 음식은 도착하지도 않았고. **b)** to be very messy or damaged‖ 매우 어질러져 있거나 망가지다: *The apartment was a shambles.* 그 아파트는 난장판이었다.

shame¹ /ʃeɪm/ *n* **1** the feeling of being guilty or embarrassed that you have after doing something that is wrong‖ 잘못된 일을 한 뒤에 자신이 가지는 죄의식 또는 난처함. 부끄러움. 수치심: *a deep sense of shame* 깊은 수치심 —compare EMBARRASSED, ASHAMED **2 it's/what a shame** SPOKEN used in order to say that a situation is disappointing, and you wish things had happened differently‖ 상황이 실망스럽고 일이 다른 양상으로 발생했기를 원한다고 말하는 데에 쓰여. 유감이다. 너무하다: *It's such a shame (that) Margaret couldn't come.* 마가렛이 오지 못한다니 유감이다. **3 Shame on you!** SPOKEN used in order to tell someone that s/he should feel ashamed of something that s/he has done‖ 남에게 한 일에 대해 부끄럽게 여기라고 말하는 데에 쓰여. 창피하지도 않으니!: *Shame on you for not telling me about that sooner.* 그것에 대해 내게 좀 더 빨리 말하지 않은 것을 부끄러운 줄 알아라. **4 put sth/sb to shame** to be much better than something or someone else and make the other seem bad when you compare the two‖ 다른 사물이나 사람보다 훨씬 좋아서 두 개를 비교할 경우 반대쪽을 나쁘게 보이게 하다. 부끄럽게[무안하게, 무색하게] 하다. …을 압도하다: *This party puts my little dinner to shame.* 이 파티는 나의 작은 저녁 모임을 무색하게 한다. **5** [U] loss of honor; DISGRACE‖ 명예의 상실. 불명예. 치욕; ⓊF disgrace: *His behavior brought shame on the whole family.* 그의 행동은 가족

전체를 치욕스럽게 했다.

shame² v [T] to make someone feel ashamed ‖ 어떤 사람에게 부끄러움을 느끼게 하다. 창피주다. 수모를 주다: *He was shamed into admitting he'd stolen the money.* 그는 창피를 당하며 돈을 훔친 사실을 시인했다.

shame·faced /ˈʃeɪmfeɪst/ adj looking ashamed or embarrassed ‖ 창피해 하거나 당혹해 하는. 부끄러워하는. 숫기 없는

shame·ful /ˈʃeɪmfəl/ adj so bad that someone should be ashamed ‖ 아주 나빠서 사람이 창피해 해야 하는. 부끄러워해야 할. 부끄러운: *a shameful and cowardly action* 부끄럽고 비겁한 행동 – **shamefully** adv

shame·less /ˈʃeɪmlɪs/ adj feeling no shame ‖ 부끄러움을 느끼지 않는. 뻔뻔스러운. 파렴치한: *a shameless liar* 파렴치한 거짓말쟁이 – **shamelessly** adv

sham·poo¹ /ʃæmˈpu/ n [C, U] a liquid soap used for washing your hair, a CARPET etc. ‖ 머리를 감거나 카펫을 빠는 데에 쓰이는 액체 비누. 샴푸

shampoo² v [T] to wash something with SHAMPOO ‖ 어떤 것을 샴푸로 씻다

sham·rock /ˈʃæmrɑk/ n a small green plant with three leaves on each stem, that is the national sign of Ireland ‖ 아일랜드의 국장(國章)으로 각 줄기에 잎이 세 개 달린 작은 녹색 식물. 클로버의 일종

shan·ty /ˈʃænti/ n a small building that has not been built very well; SHACK ‖ 그렇게 잘 지어지지 않은 작은 건물. 오두막집. 판잣집; 유 shack

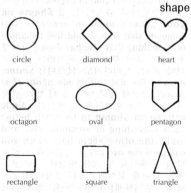

shape

circle   diamond   heart

octagon   oval   pentagon

rectangle   square   triangle

shape¹ /ʃeɪp/ n 1 [C, U] the outer form of something that you can see or feel ‖ 사람이 보거나 느낄 수 있는 사물의 겉모양. 형상. 외형. 윤곽: *a cake in the shape of a heart* 하트형(型)의 케이크 2 **in good/bad/poor shape** in good, bad

etc. condition or health ‖ 상태 또는 건강이 좋은/나쁜/좋지 않은: *The old car's still in good shape.* 그 낡은 차는 아직도 상태가 좋다. 3 **in shape/out of shape** in a good or bad state of health or physical FITNESS ‖ 건강이나 몸매 상태가 좋거나 나쁜 상태에 있는. 본래의[정상적인] 상태에 있는/몸의 상태가 나쁜: *What do you do to keep in shape?* 좋은 몸매를 유지하기 위해 무엇을 합니까? 4 [singular] a particular combination of qualities and features that something has ‖ 사물이 가지고 있는 특질과 형상의 특정한 조합. 구체화된 형태. 형세: *These trade laws are responsible for the shape of Japanese industry today.* 이 무역법에 따라 오늘날 일본의 산업 구조가 그 형태를 갖추고 있다. 5 a particular form such as a circle, square, TRIANGLE etc. ‖ 원·사각형·삼각형 등 같은 특정 모양 6 **take shape** to develop into a clear and definite form ‖ 명확하고 일정한 형태로 발전하다. …에서 형태를 이루다. 명확하게 되다. 구체화되다: *His plan was beginning to take shape.* 그의 계획은 구체화되기 시작하고 있었다. 7 something or someone that you cannot see clearly enough to recognize ‖ 인식할 만큼 분명하게 볼 수 없는 사물 또는 사람. 실루엣. 환영. 환상: *He was just a shape in the mist.* 그는 마치 안개 속의 환영 같았다.

shape² v [T] 1 to influence something such as a belief or opinion and make it develop in a particular way ‖ 신념·견해 등에 영향을 주어 특정하게 발전하게 하다. …을 구체화[실현]하다. …을 형성하다: *an event that shaped public opinion* 여론을 불러일으킨 사건 2 to make something have a particular shape ‖ 어떤 것을 특정한 형상을 갖게 하다. …이 되도록[…모양으로] 만들다: *Shape the clay into small balls.* 찰흙을 작은 공 모양으로 만들어라.

shape up phr v [I] INFORMAL to develop and improve ‖ 진전되고 개선되다. 더 좋게 만들다. 더 나아지다: *Our plans to visit Germany are shaping up.* 우리의 독일 방문 계획은 진전되고 있다. / *You better shape up John, or you're off the team.* 존, 너는 분발해야 한다, 아니면 팀에서 빼겠다.

shaped /ʃeɪpt/ adj having a particular shape ‖ 특정한 형상을 가지는. …형(形)의: *The box is egg-shaped.* 그 상자는 달걀 모양이다.

shape·ly /ˈʃeɪpli/ adj having an attractive shape ‖ 매력적인 모양을 가진.

보기 좋은. 잘생긴. 균형 잡힌: *her long shapely legs* 그녀의 보기 좋게 긴 다리

share¹ /ʃɛr/ v 1 [I, T] to have or use something that other people have or use at the same time ‖ 다른 사람이 동시에 갖거나 사용하는 사물을 가지거나 사용하다. 공동으로 쓰다[갖다]. 나눠 쓰다: *All the kids had to share the same bathroom.* 모든 아이들이 욕실 하나를 공동으로 써야 했다. / *There's only one book – we'll have to share.* 책이 오직 한 권밖에 없어서 우리는 같이 봐야 한다. **2** [T] to let someone have or use something that belongs to you ‖ 남에게 자신의 소유물을 갖게 하거나 사용하게 하다. …을 남과 공유하다. 일부를 타인이 사용하게 하다: *Will you share your toys with Ronnie?* 네 장난감을 로니와 같이 갖고 놀겠니? **3** [I, T] to divide something between two or more people ‖ 둘 이상의 사람 사이에 어떤 것을 분할하다. …을 나누다. 분배[할당]하다: *I took the cookies to work to share with everybody.* 나는 모두 같이 나눠먹으려고 쿠키를 직장에 갖고 갔다. / *We share the expenses for the house.* 우리는 생활비를 분담한다. **4** [T] to have the same interest, opinion etc. as someone else ‖ 다른 사람과 똑같은 흥미·견해 등을 가지다. 공유하다. 같이하다: *Does Molly share your interest in stamp collecting?* 몰리는 너와 같이 우표 수집에 흥미를 갖고 있니? **5** [I, T] to tell someone else about an idea, secret, problem etc. ‖ 생각·비밀·문제 등에 대해 다른 사람에게 말하다. …에 대하여 남과 이야기하다. 남에게 알리다: *Thank you for sharing your feelings with me.* 네 감정을 나에게 말해준 데 대해 고맙다.

share² n **1** [singular] the part of something that is owned, done, or used by you ‖ 자신에 의해 소유되는[실현되는, 사용되는] 사물의 일부. 몫. 부담. 분담: *I paid my share of the bill and left.* 나는 계산서의 내 몫을 지불하고 떠났다. **2 have/get your share** as much of something as you could reasonably expect to have ‖ 어떤 것을 당연히 그러리라 기대하는 만큼 많이 갖다. 자기 몫을 확보하다: *Rob's certainly getting his share of attention from the women.* 로브는 확실히 다른 남자들 못지않게 여자들로부터 사랑을 받고 있다. **3** one of the equal parts into which the ownership of a company is divided ‖ 회사의 소유권이 분할되어 있는 동등한 부분의 하나. (자본 등의) 분담 소유(권). 주. 주식: *He wants to buy/sell 500 shares in CNN.* 그는 CNN의 500주를 사기를[팔기를] 원

한다. —compare STOCK¹

shark /ʃɑrk/ n a large sea fish with very sharp teeth ‖ 매우 날카로운 이빨을 가진 몸집이 큰 바다 물고기. 상어

sharp¹ /ʃɑrp/ adj

sharp

1 ▶ABLE TO CUT 자를 수 있는◀ having a very thin edge or point that can cut things easily ‖ 물건을 쉽게 자를 수 있는 매우 가는 날이나 끝을 가진. 날카로운. 뾰족한. 잘 드는: *a sharp knife* 잘 드는 칼 —compare DULL¹, BLUNT¹

a sharp pencil

a blunt pencil

2 ▶DIRECTION 방향◀ making a sudden change in direction ‖ 방향을 갑자기 바꾸는. 가파른. 급격한. 급한: *a sharp turn in the road* 도로의 급커브

3 ▶INTELLIGENT 지능◀ able to think and understand things very quickly ‖ 일을 아주 빠르게 생각하고 이해할 수 있는. 머리가 예민한. 총명한. 눈치 빠른: *She's a very sharp lawyer.* 그녀는 매우 총명한 변호사이다.

4 ▶REMARK 말◀ criticizing in a severe and angry way ‖ 엄격하고 성난 방식으로 비평하는. 통렬한. 모진

5 ▶PAIN 통증◀ sudden and very bad ‖ 갑작스럽고 매우 심한. 격렬한: *a sharp pain in my chest* 가슴의 격통

6 ▶CHANGE 변화◀ a sharp increase or decrease is big and very sudden ‖ 증감(폭[률])이 매우 크고 갑작스런. 급격한. 급등[급락]의: *a sharp increase in prices* 가격 급등 —see picture at INCREASE²

7 ▶EYES 눈◀ able to see or notice things very easily ‖ 물건을 아주 쉽게 볼 수 있거나 알아차릴 수 있는: *Lenny has a sharp eye for detail.* 렌니는 세세한 것까지 알아보는 예리한 눈을 가지고 있다.

8 ▶CLOTHES 옷◀ attractive and stylish ‖ 매력적이고 멋진: *My grandfather was a sharp dresser.* (=wore stylish clothes) 나의 할아버지는 맵시 있게 차려입는 사람이었다.

9 ▶SOUNDS 소리◀ loud, short, and sudden ‖ 소리가 크며 짧고 갑작스런. 날카로운. 새된: *a sharp cry* 날카로운 울음소리

10 ▶PICTURE 그림◀ having a shape that is clear and detailed ‖ 분명하고 상세한 모양을 가진. 윤곽이 뚜렷한. 선명한: *a sharp picture on the TV* 텔레비전 상의 윤곽이 또렷한 화상 —see picture at GRAINY

11 a sharp tongue the ability to

express anger or unkind thoughts well ‖ 분노나 심술궂은 생각을 잘 나타내는 능력. 독설

12 ▶MUSIC 음악◀ a musical note that is sharp is played or sung slightly higher than it should be ‖ 음표가 본래 연주하거나 노래하는 것보다 약간 더 높은. 반음 높은 -compare FLAT

13 ▶TASTE 맛◀ having a strong taste ‖ 독한 맛을 가진. 자극적인. 신. 매운: *sharp Cheddar cheese* 자극적인 체더치즈 - **sharply** *adv* - **sharpness** *n* [U]

sharp² *adv* **at 8 o'clock/two-thirty etc. sharp** at exactly 8:00, 2:30 etc. ‖ 정확히 8시, 2시 30분 등에. 8시/2시 30분 정각에: *I expect you to be here at 10:30 sharp.* 여기서 10시 30분 정각에 너를 만나기를 기대한다.

sharp·en /ˈʃɑrpən/ *v* [I, T] to make something sharper, or become sharper ‖ 어떤 것을 더 날카롭게 하다, 또는 더 날카롭게 되다. 갈다. 깎다: *sharpening a pencil* 연필 깎기

sharp·en·er /ˈʃɑrpənɚ/ *n* a tool or machine that SHARPENs pencils, knives etc. ‖ 연필·칼 등을 깎거나 가는 연장 또는 기계

shat·ter /ˈʃætɚ/ *v* **1** [I, T] to break suddenly into very small pieces, or to make something do this ‖ 갑자기 매우 작은 조각들로 부서지다, 또는 사물을 이렇게 되게 하다. 산산이 부서지다[부수다]. 분쇄되다[하다]: *My cup fell to the floor and shattered.* 내 컵이 마루에 떨어져 산산이 부서졌다. **2 shatter sb's hopes/ dreams etc.** to completely destroy someone's hopes or beliefs ‖ 사람의 희망·신념을 완전히 파괴하다. 꺾다. 좌절시키다: *A knee injury shattered his hopes of becoming a baseball player.* 무릎 부상으로 야구 선수가 되려는 그의 희망이 좌절되었다.

shave¹ /ʃeɪv/ *v* **1** [I, T] to cut off hair very close to the skin, especially from your face, legs etc. ‖ 특히 얼굴·다리 등에서 피부의 털을 바짝 깎다. 면도하다. 털을 밀다 **2** to remove very thin pieces from the surface of something using a sharp tool ‖ 날카로운 연장을 사용하여 물체의 표면으로부터 아주 가는 조각들을 제거하다. 깎다[깎아내다]. 대패질하다

shave² *n* **1** [C usually singular] an act of shaving (SHAVE) ‖ 털을 깎는 행위. 면도: *I need a shave.* 나는 면도를 해야 해. **2 a close shave** a situation in which you only just avoid an accident or something bad ‖ 사람이 사고나 나쁜 일을 겨우 피한 상황. 위기일발: *We had a close shave on the highway yesterday – a huge truck almost pushed us off the road.* 우리는 어제 고속도로에서 간신히 위기를 모면했다. 대형 트럭이 우리 차를 도로 밖으로 거의 밀어 버렸다.

shav·er /ˈʃeɪvɚ/ *n* a tool used for shaving (SHAVE) ‖ 면도하는 데 쓰이는 연장. (전기) 면도기

shav·ings /ˈʃeɪvɪŋz/ *n* [plural] very thin pieces of something such as wood that are cut from a surface ‖ 표면으로부터 깎아낸 나무 등의 매우 얇은 조각들. 깎아낸 부스러기. 대패밥

shawl /ʃɔl/ *n* a piece of cloth that is worn around the shoulders or head for warmth ‖ 보온을 위해 어깨나 머리에 두르는 천 조각. 어깨걸이. 숄

s/he /ˌʃi ɚ ˈhi/ *pron* used in writing when the subject of the sentence can be either male or female ‖ 문장의 주어가 남성 또는 여성 어느 쪽으로나 될 수 있을 때 문장에서 쓰여. 그 남자/여자는[가]

she¹ /ʃi/ *pron* **1** a female person or animal who has been mentioned or is known about ‖ 언급되거나 알려진 여성 또는 암컷. 그녀: *"Where's Kate?" "She went out to the car."* "케이트는 어디 갔니?" "그녀는 자동차에 갔어." / *"I saw Suzy today." "Oh really, how is she?"* "나는 오늘 수지를 봤어." "아, 정말, 그녀는 잘 지내?" / *She's (=she is) my sister.* 그녀는 내 누이동생이다. **2** used when talking about a car or ship that has been mentioned ‖ 언급된 자동차 또는 선박에 대해 말할 때 쓰여

she² *n* [singular] a female ‖ 여성, 암컷: *What a cute dog! Is it a she or a he?* 정말 귀여운 개구나! 암컷이니 수컷이니?

sheaf /ʃif/ *n, plural* **sheaves 1** wheat, corn etc. that is tied together after it has been cut ‖ 자른 뒤에 함께 묶어 놓은 밀·옥수수 등. (곡식의) 단 **2** several pieces of paper held or tied together ‖ 함께 매거나 묶은 여러 장의 종이. 다발. 뭉치. 묶음

shear /ʃɪr/ *v* **sheared, sheared** *or* **shorn, shearing** [T] to cut the wool off a sheep ‖ 양에서 털을 깎다. 털을 자르다

shears /ʃɪrz/ *n* [plural] a tool like a large pair of scissors ‖ 한 짝의 큰 가위 같은 연장. 전단기(剪斷機)

sheath /ʃiθ/ *n* a cover for the blade of a knife or sword ‖ 칼이나 검의 날을 넣어두는 덮개. 칼집

sheathe /ʃið/ *v* [T] to put a knife or sword into a SHEATH ‖ 작은 칼이나 검을 칼집에 넣다

sheaves /ʃivz/ *n* the plural of SHEAF ‖ sheaf의 복수형

she'd /ʃid/ **1** the short form of "she had" ‖ "she had"의 단축형: *She'd forgotten to close the door.* 그녀는 문을 닫는 것을 잊어버렸다. **2** the short form of "she would" ‖ "she would"의 단축형: *She said she'd love to come.* 그녀는 오고 싶다고 말했다.

shed¹ /ʃɛd/ *n* a small building used especially for storing things ‖ 특히 물건을 보관해 두는 데 사용되는 작은 건물. 헛간. 광: *a tool shed in the back yard* 뒷마당의 연장 헛간

shed² *v* **shed, shed, shedding** [T] **1** to drop something or allow it to fall off, especially as part of a natural process ‖ 특히 자연적인 과정의 일부로서 사물이 떨어지거나 떨어지게 허용하다. (눈물을) 흘리다. (잎·털 등을) 자연히 떨어뜨리다. 벗다: *Snakes regularly shed their skin.* 뱀들은 정기적으로 자신들의 허물을 벗는다. **2** to get rid of something that you do not want ‖ 원하지 않는 것을 제거하다. 줄이다. 버리다: *I'd like to shed a few pounds before summer.* (=lose some weight) 나는 여름 이전에 몇 파운드는 감량하고 싶다.

sheen /ʃin/ *n* [singular, U] a smooth shiny appearance ‖ 부드럽고 번쩍이는 모습. 번쩍임. 광채. 광휘: *the beautiful sheen of her hair* 그녀의 머리의 아름다운 광택

sheep /ʃip/ *n, plural* **sheep** a farm animal that eats grass and is kept for its wool and its meat ‖ 풀을 먹으며 양털과 그 고기를 위해 사육하는 농장의 동물. 양

sheep·ish /ˈʃipɪʃ/ *adj* uncomfortable or embarrassed because you have done something silly or wrong ‖ 어리석거나 나쁜 일을 해서 불편하거나 당황하는. 부끄러워[수줍어]하는. 주저주저하는: *Renny apologized, looking sheepish.* 레니는 부끄러워하는 표정으로 사과했다. – **sheepishly** *adv*

sheer /ʃɪr/ *adj* **1 sheer joy/luck/bliss etc.** joy, luck etc. with no other feeling or quality mixed with it ‖ 그것과 혼합된 다른 감정 또는 특질이 없는 기쁨/행운 등. 순전한 기쁨/행운/축복: *people dancing and singing with sheer joy* 정말로 기뻐서 춤추고 노래하는 사람들 **2 the sheer size/weight/numbers etc.** used in order to emphasize how big, heavy etc. something is ‖ 사물이 크거나 무거운 등의 정도를 강조하는 데 쓰여. 엄청난 크기/무게/숫자: *The most impressive thing about Alaska is its sheer size.* 알래스카

에 대해 가장 인상적인 것은 정말 엄청난 그 크기이다. **3** a sheer drop, cliff etc. is extremely steep ‖ 낭떠러지·절벽 등이 극심하게 가파른. 깎아지른 듯한

sheet /ʃit/ *n* **1** a large piece of thin cloth that you put on a bed to lie on or under ‖ 침대에 깔아 그 위 또는 아래에서 잠자기 위한 커다란 얇은 천. (침대의) 시트: *Have you changed the sheets?* (=put clean sheets on the bed) 시트를 바꿨니? **2** a thin flat piece of something such as paper, metal, or glass ‖ 종이[금속, 유리] 등의 얇고 평평한 조각. 폭넓고 얇은 면[판]. 한 장의 종이: *a sheet of paper* 종이 한 장 **3** a large flat area of something such as ice or water that is spread over a surface ‖ 지표에 퍼져 있는 얼음이나 물 등의 평평하고 넓은 지역: *The road was covered with a sheet of ice.* 도로는 빙판으로 덮여 있었다

sheik, sheikh /ʃik, ʃeɪk/ *n* **1** an Arab chief or prince ‖ 아랍의 족장이나 왕자. 수장(首長) **2** a Muslim religious teacher or leader ‖ 이슬람교도의 종교 교사 또는 지도자. 교주(敎主)

shelf /ʃɛlf/ *n, plural* **shelves** a long flat board fixed on a wall, in a frame etc. on which you put or store things ‖ 벽·장 등에 고정되어 그 위에 물건을 올려 놓거나 보관하는 길고 평평한 판자. 선반: *two shelves for books* 서적용 선반 두 개 / *a jar on the top shelf* 꼭대기 선반 위에 있는 항아리

she'll /ʃɪl, ʃil/ the short form of "she will" ‖ "she will"의 단축형: *She'll be here around 8:00.* 그녀는 8시경에 여기 올 것이다.

shell¹ /ʃɛl/ *n* **1** the hard outer covering of a nut, egg, seed, and some types of animal ‖ 견과·달걀·씨앗·일부 종류의 동물의 딱딱한 외피. 껍질. 깍지. 조가비: *looking for sea shells on the beach* 해변에서 바다 조개[조가비] 찾기 / *The turtle pulled its head into its shell.* 거북이는 그 귀갑 속으로 머리를 당겨 넣었다. **2** an explosive that is fired from a large gun, or the metal container that this is in ‖ 대포에서 발사되는 폭발물, 또는 이것이 들어 있는 금속 용기. 포탄 (탄피). 탄약통

shell² *v* [T] to fire SHELLs at something ‖ 어떤 것에 포탄을 발사하다. …을 포격하다

shell out *phr v* [T] INFORMAL to pay money for something, often when you do not want to ‖ 종종 원하지 않는 경우에 어떤 것을 위해 돈을 내다. 기부하다. (전액)지불하다: *We had to shell out over $400 to get the car fixed.* 우리는 차를 수

리하는 데 400달러 이상을 지불해야 했
다.

shell·fish /ˈʃɛlˌfɪʃ/ *n, plural* **shellfish**
[C, U] a small sea or water animal that
has a shell, or this animal eaten as a
food ‖ 껍질이 있는 작은 바다 또는 민물
동물, 또는 음식으로 먹는 이 동물. 갑각류
동물(새우·게 등). 조개

shel·ter¹ /ˈʃɛltɚ/ *n* **1** [C, U] a place
with a roof over it that protects you
from danger or the weather, or the
protection that it gives ‖ 위험·기후로부터
사람을 보호해 주는 지붕이 있는 장소, 또
는 그것이 제공하는 보호. 대피[보
호](소). 피난(처): *a shelter for battered
women* (가정 내 폭력으로)매 맞는 여자를
위한 보호 시설 / *The family took shelter
in the cellar when the tornado hit.* 그 가
족은 토네이도가 불어 닥쳤을 때 지하실에
대피했다. **2** [U] a place to live,
considered as one of the basic needs of
life ‖ 삶의 기본적인 필요조건 중의 하나로
간주되는 거주지. 주거. 거처. 집:
*providing food and shelter for the
homeless* 집 없는 사람들을 위한 음식과
거처의 제공

shelter² *v* [I, T] to provide a place
where someone or something is
protected, especially from danger or
from the weather, or to stay in such a
place ‖ 특히 위험이나 기후로부터 사람이
나 사물이 보호받는 장소를 제공하다, 또
는 그러한 장소에서 머물다. …에게 피난
처[숙소]를 제공하다. …으로부터 피난하
다. …을 숨겨주다: *People were
sheltering in doorways, under bridges,
anywhere.* 사람들은 대문간에, 다리 아래
등 어디든지 피난하고 있었다. / *families
who sheltered Jews from the Nazis* 나치
로부터 유대인을 숨겨주었던 가족들

shel·tered /ˈʃɛltɚd/ *adj* **1** protected
from anything that might hurt, upset,
or shock you ‖ 사람을 다치게 할 수·심란
하게 할 수·충격을 줄 수 있는 것으로부터
보호된. 지켜진. 격리된: *Gina had a
sheltered childhood.* 지나는 어린 시절 사
회 시설의 보호를 받았다. **2** protected
from the weather ‖ 날씨로부터 보호된.
지켜진. 가리워져 있는: *a sunny
sheltered beach* 일광을 차단한 해변

shelve /ʃɛlv/ *v* [T] **1** to decide not to
continue with a plan, although you
might continue with it later ‖ 비록 나중
에 계속할지라도 어떤 계획을 계속하지 않
기로 결정하다. …을 보류하다. 뒤로 미루
다: *The project has been shelved due to
lack of funding.* 그 사업 계획은 자금 부
족으로 보류되었다. **2** to put something,

usually a book, on a shelf ‖ 보통 책을 서
가에 넣다. 선반에 얹다[놓다]

shelves /ʃɛlvz/ *n* the plural of SHELF ‖
shelf의 복수형

shelv·ing /ˈʃɛlvɪŋ/ *n* [U] a set of
shelves, or the material used for them ‖
한 조(組)의 선반이나 선반용 재료

she·nan·i·gans /ʃəˈnænɪgənz/ *n*
[plural] INFORMAL tricks or slightly
dishonest behavior; MISCHIEF ‖ 속임수나
약간 비정직한 행동. 사기. 협잡; ☞
mischief

shep·herd /ˈʃɛpɚd/ *n* someone whose
job is to take care of sheep ‖ 양을 돌보는
직업인. 양치기

sher·bet /ˈʃɚbɪt/ *n* [U] a frozen sweet
food made from water, fruit, sugar, and
sometimes milk and eggs ‖ 물·과일·설탕
그리고 때로는 우유·달걀로 만드는 달콤한
냉동식품. 셔벗(빙과)

sher·iff /ˈʃɛrɪf/ *n* a chief police officer
in a COUNTY who is elected ‖ 선출되는 군
(郡)지역의 경찰 책임자. 보안관

sher·ry /ˈʃɛri/ *n* [C, U] a pale or dark
brown strong wine, or a glass of this
drink ‖ 엷은 또는 진한 갈색의 독한 와인,
또는 이 술의 한 잔. 셰리주

she's /ʃiz/ **1** the short form of "she is"
‖ "she is"의 단축형: *She's my little
sister.* 그녀는 내 어린 누이동생이다. **2**
the short form of "she has" ‖ "she has"
의 단축형: *She's invited us to a party.* 그
녀는 우리를 파티에 초대했다.

shh /ʃ/ *interjection* used in order to tell
someone to be quiet ‖ 조용히 하라고 남
에게 말하는 데 쓰여. 쉿. 조용히: *Shh! I
can't hear what he's saying.* 쉿! 그가 무
어라고 말하는지 들을 수 없잖아.

shield¹ /ʃild/ *n* **1**
something that
protects someone or
something from being
hurt or damaged ‖ 다
치거나 파손되는 것으
로부터 사람·사물을 보
호하는 것. 보호[차폐]
물: *police carrying
riot shields* 폭동 진압
방패를 들고 있는 경찰
/ *the heat shield on a
rocket* 로켓 표면의 열 차폐물 **2** a broad
piece of metal used in past times by
soldiers to protect themselves in battle,
or something that has this shape ‖ 전투
에서 자신을 보호하기 위해 군인들이 예전
에 사용했던 넓은 금속판, 또는 이런 형태
를 가진 물건. 방패(모양의 물건)

shield² *v* [T] to protect someone or

shield

shield

riot shield

something from being hurt, damaged, or upset ‖ 사람이나 사물이 다치는[손상되는, 마음 상하는] 것으로부터 보호하다. 막아주다. 지켜주다: *Of course, you try to shield your children from bad influences.* 물론 너는 아이들을 나쁜 영향으로부터 보호하려고 애쓰고 있다. / *a hat to shield your face from the sun* 햇빛으로부터 얼굴을 가려주는 모자

shift¹ /ʃɪft/ *n* **1** a change in the way most people think about something, or in the way something is done ‖ 대부분의 사람들이 어떤 것에 대해 생각하는 방식 또는 어떤 것이 행해지는 방식에서의 변화. 이동. 이전. 전화. 추이: *Polls show a shift in public opinion.* 여론 조사는 대중 여론의 추이를 보여주고 있다. **2** one of the three 8-hour periods in a day during which a particular group of workers are at work ‖ 근로자의 특정 집단이 근무하고 있는 하루 세 번의 8시간 중의 하나. 3교대제의 근무(시간). 교대([근무]조): *Lou's on the night/day shift this week.* 루는 이번 주에 야간/주간 교대[근무]조이다. —see also GEAR SHIFT

shift² *v* **1** [I] to change your opinion or attitude ‖ 사람의 견해 또는 태도를 바꾸다. 전환하다: *Washington's policy toward Taiwan appears to have shifted.* 대만에 대한 워싱턴의 정책은 바뀐 것처럼 보인다. **2** [I, T] to move something from one place to another, or to change your body's position ‖ 한 장소에서 다른 장소로 사물을 움직이다, 또는 신체의 자세를 바꾸다. 옮기다. 장소[주소(등)]를 이동시키다: *We have to shift the couch that way.* 우리는 소파를 저렇게 옮기지 않으면 안 된다. / *Jan shifted uncomfortably in her seat.* 잰은 자기 자리에서 불편하게 뒤척였다. **3** [I, T] to change the GEARs when you are driving ‖ 운전할 때 변속기를 바꾸어 넣다: *Shift into second gear.* 2단 기어를 바꿔 넣어라.

shift·less /ˈʃɪftlɪs/ *adj* not at all interested in working; lazy ‖ 일하는 데에 전혀 관심이 없는. 무능한. 수단이 없는. 게으른

shift·y /ˈʃɪfti/ *adj* someone who is shifty or has shifty eyes looks like s/he cannot be trusted ‖ 사람이나 눈이 믿을 수 없는 것처럼 보이는. 간사해 보이는. 속임수가 많은

shim·mer /ˈʃɪmɚ/ *v* [I] to shine with a soft light that seems to shake slightly ‖ 약간 흔들리는 듯이 보이는 부드러운 불빛으로 반짝이다. 희미하게[어른어른] 빛나다: *a lake shimmering in the moonlight* 달빛에 어른어른 빛나는 호수 —**shimmer** *n* [singular]

shin /ʃɪn/ *n* the front part of your leg between your knee and your foot ‖ 무릎과 발 사이에 있는 다리의 앞부분. 정강이(뼈) —see picture at BODY

shine¹ /ʃaɪn/ *v* **shone, shone, shining** **1** [I] to produce light ‖ 빛나다. 비치다. 번쩍이다: *The sun was shining brightly all day.* 태양은 하루 종일 밝게 빛나고 있었다. **2** [I] to look bright and smooth ‖ 밝고 부드럽게 보이다. 밝게 빛나다. 반짝이다: *Dan polished the car until it shone.* 댄은 그 차를 윤이 날 때까지 닦았다. **3** [T] to point a light toward a particular place or in a particular direction ‖ 특정한 장소 또는 방향으로 빛을 가리키다. (불빛 등을) 어느 방향으로 돌리다. 비추다: *Shine the flashlight over here.* 회중전등으로 여기를 비춰라. **4** [I] if your eyes or face shine, they show you are happy ‖ 눈·얼굴 등이 행복한 것을 나타내다. 생기를 띠다: *Jenny's eyes shone with excitement.* 제니의 눈은 흥분으로 환하게 빛났다. **5** [I] to be extremely good at doing something so that other people notice you ‖ 어떤 것을 하는 데 있어서 너무나 훌륭하여서 다른 사람들이 알아차리다. 출중하다. 탁월하다. 뛰어나다. 빼어나다: *How can you expect to shine in a job that doesn't interest you?* 네가 흥미를 갖지 못하는 일에서 어떻게 두각을 나타내기를 기대할 수 있느냐?

shine² *v* **shined, shined, shining** [T] to make the surface of something such as a shoe smooth and bright by rubbing it ‖ 구두 등 사물의 표면을 문질러서 매끄럽고 광택이 나게 하다. 윤[광]내다. …을 닦다

shine³ *n* [singular, U] the brightness that something has ‖ 사물이 지니고 있는 빛남. 광휘. 광채: *hair with lots of shine* 매우 윤기 있는 머리(털)

shin·gle /ˈʃɪŋɡəl/ *n* [C, U] one of many thin pieces of wood or other material used for covering a roof or a wall ‖ 지붕 또는 벽을 덮는 데 사용되는 많은 얇은 나뭇조각, 또는 다른 재료의 하나. 널. 지붕널

shin·ny /ˈʃɪni/ *v* [I] **shinny up/down** INFORMAL to climb quickly up or down a tree or a pole ‖ 나무 또는 장대를 빠르게 기어오르거나 내려오다

shin splints /ˈ../ *n* [plural] INFORMAL a condition in which you have pain and swelling in your shins, caused by running on hard surfaces ‖ 단단한 바닥

면을 달려서 생긴 정강이뼈의 통증과 부기가 있는 상태. 정강이뼈의 염증

shin·y /'ʃaɪni/ *adj* bright and smooth looking‖밝고 부드럽게 보이는. 빛나는. 윤이 나는. 반짝이는: *shiny hair* 윤이 나는 머리 / *shiny leather boots* 반들거리는 가죽 부츠

ship¹ /ʃɪp/ *n* **1** a large boat used for carrying people and things on the ocean‖바다에서 사람과 물건을 나르는 데 사용되는 큰 배. 선박: *a cruise ship* (장기 여행용) 순항선. 유람선 **2** a space vehicle‖우주선: *a rocket ship* 로켓 우주선

ship² *v* **-pped, -pping** [T] **1** to deliver goods‖상품을 배송하다. 부치다. …을 보내다: *They ship food all over the country.* 그들은 전국에 식량을 보낸다. **2** to send or carry something by sea‖사물을 해로로 보내거나 나르다. 배로 보내다

ship·load /'ʃɪploʊd/ *n* the number of people or things a ship can carry‖선박이 운송할 수 있는 사람 또는 물건의 수량. 배 한 척분의 적하량[승선 인원]

ship·ment /'ʃɪpmənt/ *n* [C, U] a load of goods being delivered, or the act of sending them‖운송되는 상품의 적재량, 또는 그것을 보내기. 선적[선하](량). 발송. 출하: *a shipment of TVs* 텔레비전의 선적 / *the shipment of goods by rail* 철도에 의한 상품의 발송

ship·ping /'ʃɪpɪŋ/ *n* [U] **1 shipping and handling** the price charged for delivering goods‖상품을 발송하는 데 매겨지는 가격. 발송 제(諸)경비: *Please add $2.95 to cover shipping and handling.* 발송 제경비 2달러 95센트를 추가해 주세요. **2** ships considered as a group, or anything that is related to business done by ships‖집단으로 간주되는 선박들, 또는 선박들을 이용하여 하는 사업에 관련된 모든 것. 해운(업). 상선[선박](수, 톤수): *The canal has been closed to shipping.* 그 운하는 상선들에게 폐쇄되어 있다.

ship·wreck¹ /'ʃɪp-rɛk/ *n* [C, U] the destruction of a ship by a storm or an accident, or the damaged ship itself‖폭풍 또는 사고로 인한 선박의 파괴, 또는 파손된 선박 자체. 난파(선): *survivors of a shipwreck* 난파선의 생존자들

ship·wreck² *v* **be shipwrecked** to have been in a ship that has been destroyed by a storm or an accident‖폭풍 또는 사고로 인해 파괴된 선박 안에 있었다. 난파하다: *a TV show about a group of people who had been shipwrecked on a desert island* 무인도에 난파된 일단의 사람들에 대한 텔레비전 쇼

ship·yard /'ʃɪp-yard/ *n* a place where ships are built or repaired‖선박이 건조되거나 수리되는 장소. 조선소

shirk /ʃɚk/ *v* [I, T] to avoid doing something you should do‖사람이 당연히 해야 할 일을 하는 것을 피하다. …을 게을리 하다. 회피하다: *We cannot simply shirk our duty/responsibility to the UN.* 우리는 단지 우리의 의무[책임]을 UN에 미뤄버릴 수는 없다.

shirt /ʃɚt/ *n* **1** a piece of clothing that covers the upper part of your body and your arms, and has a collar and usually buttons down the front‖몸의 상체와 팔을 덮으며 깃이 달렸고 보통 전면 아래쪽까지 단추를 채우는 옷. 와이셔츠. 셔츠. 속옷 —compare BLOUSE —see picture at CLOTHES —see also T-SHIRT **2 keep your shirt on** SPOKEN used in order to tell someone who is angry or upset to stay calm‖화나 있거나 마음이 상한 사람에게 진정하라고 말하는 데에 쓰여. 침착하다. 냉정을 유지하다

shirt·sleeves /'ʃɚtslivz/ *n* **in your shirt sleeves** wearing a shirt but no JACKET‖재킷 없이 셔츠를 입은. 셔츠 바람으로

shish kebab /'ʃɪʃ kɪbab/ *n* [C] small pieces of meat and vegetables that are put on a long thin metal stick and cooked‖기다랗고 가는 금속 막대에 끼워서 구워진 고기와 야채의 작은 조각들. 고기와 야치를 꼬챙이에 끼워 구운 요리

shiv·er¹ /'ʃɪvɚ/ *v* [I] to shake slightly because you are cold or frightened‖사람이 춥거나 놀라서 약간 떨다. 와들와들[덜덜] 떨다. 전율하다: *a dog shivering with cold/fear* 추위/공포로 덜덜 떨고 있는 개

shiver² *n* a shaking movement of your body that happens when you are cold or afraid‖사람이 춥거나 두려운 경우에 발생하는 신체를 떠는 동작. 떪. 몸의 떨림. 전율. 오한: *a shiver of cold* 추위로 떪 / *A shiver ran down my spine.* (=I felt afraid) 등골이 오싹했다. **– shivery** *adj*

shoal /ʃoʊl/ *n* **1** a small hill of sand just below the surface of water, that is dangerous for boats‖선박에 위험한, 바로 수면 아래에 있는 작은 모래 언덕. 모래톱. 사주(沙洲) **2** a large group of fish that swim together‖함께 헤엄을 치는 커다란 물고기 떼

shock¹ /ʃak/ *n* **1** [C usually singular] an unexpected and unpleasant event or piece of news that makes you extremely upset‖사람을 극도로 심란하게 하는 예상 밖의 불쾌한 사건 또는 뉴스. 충격. 돌발

shoes

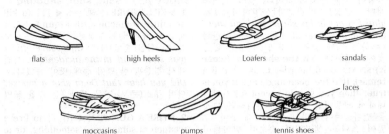

flats　　　high heels　　　Loafers　　　sandals

laces

moccasins　　　pumps　　　tennis shoes

적인 대사건: *Rob's death came as a complete shock to us.* 로브의 죽음은 우리에게는 완전한 충격이었다. **2** [singular, U] the feeling of surprise and DISBELIEF you have when something unexpected and unpleasant happens ‖ 예상 밖의 불쾌한 일이 일어난 경우 사람이 가지는 놀랍고 불신하는 감정. 정신적 타격. 분개. 놀람: *He'll get a shock when he sees the phone bill.* 그가 전화 요금 청구서를 보면 충격을 받을 것이다. / *Everyone was in shock at the news of the bombing.* 모든 사람이 폭격 소식에 충격을 받았다. **3** a sudden painful feeling caused by a flow of electricity passing through your body ‖ 사람의 신체를 통과하는 전기의 흐름에 의한 갑작스런 통증. 전기 쇼크: *Ow! The toaster gave me a shock.* 아얏! 토스터에 감전됐어. **4** [U] TECHNICAL a medical condition in which someone is very weak, often after an unpleasant experience ‖ 종종 불쾌한 경험 뒤에 사람이 매우 약해져 있는 의학적 증세. 쇼크 (상태). 진탕증(震盪症): *The crash victims are being treated for shock.* 그 추락 사고의 조난자들은 쇼크에 대한 치료를 받고 있다 **5** ⇨ SHOCK WAVE **6** ⇨ SHOCK ABSORBER

shock² *v* [I, T] **1** to make someone feel very surprised, and usually upset or offended ‖ 사람을 매우 놀라게 하고, 보통 심란하게 하거나 불쾌하게 하다. …을 움찔 놀라게 하다. 쇼크를 받다. (남에게) 충격을 주다: *The shooting has shocked the entire community.* 그 총격 사건은 전체 지역 사회에 충격을 주었다. / *It shocked us to learn what the real price was.* 실제 가격이 얼마였는지를 알고는 우리는 충격을 받았다. **2** [T] to give someone an electric shock ‖ 사람에게 전기 쇼크를 주다. 감전시키다 – **shocked** *adj*

shock ab·sorb·er /'. .,../ *n* a piece of equipment connected to each wheel of a

vehicle to make traveling more comfortable and less BUMPY ‖ 차량의 운행을 더욱 편안하고 덜 덜컹거리게 하기 위해 차량의 바퀴 각각에 접속된 장치. 완충기

shock·ing /'ʃɑkɪŋ/ *adj* very offensive or upsetting ‖ 매우 불쾌하거나 심한한. 충격[쇼크]을 주는. 깜짝 놀라게 하는. 소름 끼치는: *a shocking crime* 충격적인 범죄

shock wave /'. ./ *n* **1** [C usually plural] a strong feeling of shock that people have when something bad happens unexpectedly ‖ 나쁜 일이 예상 밖에 발생할 때 사람들이 받는 강한 충격의 느낌. 충격파: *The stock market crash sent shock waves through Wall Street.* 주식 시장의 붕괴로 월 스트리트에 충격을 가하였다. **2** [C, U] a strong movement of air, heat, or the earth from an explosion, EARTHQUAKE etc. ‖ 폭발·지진 등으로부터 오는 대기·열·지표의 강한 움직임. 충격파. 여파

shod¹ /ʃɑd/ *adj* LITERARY wearing shoes ‖ 신발을 신은

shod² *v* the past tense and PAST PARTICIPLE of SHOE ‖ shoe의 과거·과거 분사형

shod·dy /'ʃɑdi/ *adj* **1** done or made cheaply or carelessly ‖ 값싸게 또는 공들이지 않고 행해지거나 만들어진. 형편없는. 조잡한. 싸구려의: *Whoever fixed the roof did a shoddy job.* 누가 지붕을 수리했는지 모르지만 형편없이 일을 했다. **2** unfair and dishonest ‖ 공정하지 않고 정직하지 않은. 비열한. 허울만의: *a shoddy trick* 비열한 책략

shoe¹ /ʃu/ *n* **1** something that you wear to cover your feet, that is made of leather or some other strong material ‖ 가죽이나 몇몇 다른 튼튼한 소재로 만들어서 발을 덮기 위해 신는 것. 구두. 신(발). 단화: *a pair of high-heeled shoes* 굽이 높은 한 켤레의 구두 / *tennis shoes* 테니스화 **2 be in sb's shoes** to be in the situation that someone else is in ‖ 다른 사람이 처한 상황에 놓이다. 남의 입장에 서다. 입장을 바꿔보다[생각하다]: *I'm glad I'm not in his shoes, with all those debts to pay.* 나는 그 모든 채무를 상환해야 하는 그와 같은 입장에 서 있지 않은 것이 다행이다. **3 if the shoe fits, (wear it)** SPOKEN used in order to say that if a remark that has been made about you is true, then you should accept it ‖ 사람에 대해서 만들어진 발언이 진실이라면 그것을 받아들여야 한다고 말하는 데 쓰여. 그 말이 옳다고 생각되면 순순히 받아들이게: *"Are you saying I'm a liar?" "If the shoe fits, ..."* "너 내가 거짓말쟁이라고 말하는 거야?" "내가 충고하는 말이 옳다고 생각되면……"

shoe² *v* **shod, shod, shoeing** [T] to put a strong metal cover on the bottom of a horse's foot ‖ 말의 발바닥에 강한 금속 덮개를 붙이다. 말에 편자를 박다

shoe·horn /'ʃuhɔrn/ *n* a curved piece of plastic or metal that you use to help you put a shoe on easily ‖ 사람이 구두를 쉽게 신는 것을 돕는 데 사용하는 굽은 플라스틱 또는 금속 조각. 구둣주걱

shoe·lace /'ʃuleɪs/ *n* a thin piece of string or leather that you use to tie your shoes ‖ 구두를 매는 데 사용하는 가느다란 줄 또는 가죽. 구두끈

shoe·string /'ʃu,strɪŋ/ *n* **on a shoestring** done or made without spending very much money ‖ 아주 많은 돈을 소비하지 않고 행해지거나 만들어진. 약간의 돈으로. 근근이: *a movie made on a shoestring* 소액으로 제작한 영화

shone /ʃoʊn/ *v* the past tense and PAST PARTICIPLE of SHINE ‖ shine의 과거·과거분사형

shoo /ʃu/ *interjection* said in order to tell an annoying child or animal to go away ‖ 귀찮게 하는 아이 또는 동물을 가버리라고 말하는 데 쓰여. 쉬(이) 하고 소리쳐서 쫓다. 억지로 떠나게 하다 ‐ **shoo** *v* [T]: *Aunt Betty shooed us out of the kitchen.* 베티 외숙모는 우리에게 식당에서 나가라고 소리쳤다.

shoo-in /'. ./ *n* INFORMAL someone who is expected to win easily in an election or race ‖ 선거·경주에서 쉽게 승리가 예상되는 사람. 승리가 확실시되는 후보자[경쟁자]: *Senator Perry is a shoo-in for reelection.* 페리 상원의원은 재선에서 승리가 확실시되는 후보자이다.

shook /ʃʊk/ *v* the past tense of SHAKE ‖ shake의 과거형

shook-up /,. '. ./ *adj* SPOKEN NONSTANDARD ⇨ **be/look/feel shaken**

(SHAKE¹)

shoot¹ /ʃut/ *v* **shot, shot, shooting**
1 ▶KILL/INJURE◀ 살해/부상 [T] to kill or injure someone with a gun ‖ 총으로 사람을 죽이거나 부상을 입히다. 총으로 쏘다. 사살[총살]하다: *One police officer was shot dead in the incident.* 그 사건에서 경찰관 한 명이 총에 맞아 죽었다. / *Did you hear that Dean shot a moose?* 딘이 무스(큰 사슴)를 쏘았다는 것을 들었니?

2 ▶FIRE A GUN◀ 발사 [I, T] to fire a weapon at someone or something, or to make a weapon fire ‖ 사람 또는 사물에 대해 무기를 발사하다, 또는 무기가 발사되게 하다. 발포하다[쏘다]. 사격하다: *They drove up and just started shooting at people.* 그들은 차를 타고 가서 사람들에게 바로 총을 쏘기 시작했다. / *learning to shoot a gun* 사격 연습

3 ▶MOVE◀ 움직임 [I, T] to move quickly in a particular direction, or to make something move in this way ‖ 특정한 방향으로 재빨리 움직이다, 또는 사물을 이렇게 움직이게 하다. (물건을) 갑자기 움직이다. 내달리다. 분사[분출]시키다: *The fountain shot a stream of water 10 feet high.* 그 분수는 10피트 높이의 물줄기를 분출했다. / *A severe pain shot through his chest.* 격통이 가슴 전체에 퍼졌다.

4 ▶PHOTO/MOVIE◀ 사진/영화 [I, T] to take photographs or make a movie ‖ 사진을 찍거나 영화를 제작하다. 촬영(을 개시)하다: *Spielberg is shooting on location.* 스필버그는 야외 촬영 중이다.

5 ▶SPORTS◀ 스포츠 [I, T] to throw, kick, or hit a ball toward the place where you can make points ‖ 득점할 수 있는 곳으로 공을 던지다[차다, 치다]. 슛하다. 슛으로 득점을 올리다: *Let's go shoot some hoops/baskets.* 농구하러 가자.

6 ▶GO AHEAD◀ 어서(말 해) SPOKEN said in order to tell someone you are ready to listen ‖ 들을 준비가 되어 있다고 남에게 말하는 데 쓰여. 어서(해): *"I've got a question." "Okay, shoot."* "질문이 하나 있는데." "좋아, 어서 해."

7 shoot the breeze INFORMAL to have a friendly conversation about unimportant things ‖ 사소한 일에 관해 친밀한 대화를 나누다. 수다를 떨다. 잡담하다

8 shoot your mouth off INFORMAL to talk too much, especially about your opinions or a secret ‖ 특히 자신의 견해·비밀에 관해서 너무 많이 말하다. 마구 지

멀이다. 지나치게 말을 많이 하다: *Don't go shooting your mouth off about this.* 이것에 대해서 네 이야기를 너무 많이 하지 말아라.

shoot ↔ sb/sth **down** *phr v* [T] **1** to destroy an enemy plane while it is flying ‖ 비행 중인 적의 항공기를 파괴하다. 격추하다. 쏘아 떨어뜨리다: *The plane was shot down over the ocean.* 그 비행기는 바다 위에 격추되었다. **2** to say that what someone suggests is wrong or stupid ‖ 남이 제안한 내용이 잘못되거나 어리석다고 말하다. (남을) 비방하다. (사람·논의를) 논파하다: *Terry's boss shot down all her ideas.* 테리의 사장은 그녀의 모든 아이디어들을 깎아 내렸다.

shoot for sth *phr v* [T] INFORMAL to try to achieve something ‖ 어떤 것을 성취하려고 노력하다. 노리다. …을 목표로 노력하다: *Okay, we'll shoot for 1:30.* (=try to do something by then) 좋아 우리는 1시 30분까지 해 보겠다.

shoot up *phr v* **1** [I] to quickly increase in number, size, or amount ‖ 수[크기, 분량]가 급격하게 늘어나다. 앙등[급등]하다. 급증[급성장]하다: *Oil prices have shot up again.* 유류 가격은 다시 급등했다. / *Your son's really shot up* (=grown very tall) *lately.* 네 아들이 최근에 정말 많이 컸다. **2** [I, T] INFORMAL to put illegal drugs into your body using a needle ‖ 주사기로 신체에 불법 마약류를 주입하다. (마약을) 정맥에 주사하다

shoot² *n* **1** an occasion when someone takes photographs or makes a movie ‖ 사람이 사진을 찍거나 영화를 촬영하는 때. 촬영: *a photo/fashion shoot* 사진[패션] 촬영 **2** a new part of a plant ‖ 식물의 새싹. 새순

shoot³ *interjection* said when you are annoyed, disappointed, or surprised ‖ 사람이 귀찮을[실망할, 놀랐을] 때 말해. 쳇. 제기랄: *Oh shoot, I forgot to get Dan's stuff from the dry cleaners.* 아 제기랄, 세탁소에서 댄의 옷가지를 찾는 것을 잊었네.

shoot·ing /ˈʃutɪŋ/ *n* **1** a situation in which someone is killed or injured by a gun ‖ 사람이 총에 맞아 죽거나 부상당하는 상황. 총격 사건: *Two teenagers were killed in a drive-by shooting.* 10대 두 명이 주행 중 총격 사건으로 사망했다. **2** [U] the sport of killing animals and birds with guns; HUNTING ‖ 총으로 동물·새를 쏘아 죽이는 스포츠. 총사냥; 徊 hunting

shooting star /ˌ.. ˈ./ *n* a piece of rock or metal from space that burns brightly as it falls toward the earth; METEOR ‖ 지구를 향해 떨어지면서 밝게 불타는, 우주로부터 날아오는 바위나 금속 조각. 유성. 별똥별; 徊 meteor

shop¹ /ʃɑp/ *n* **1** a small store that sells only a particular type of goods ‖ 특정한 종류의 상품만을 판매하는 작은 가게. 상점. 소매점: *a card shop* 카드 가게 **2** a place where things are made or repaired ‖ 물건이 만들어지거나 수리되는 장소. 작업장. 제작소. 공장: *a bicycle repair shop* 자전거 수리 공장 **3** [U] a subject taught in school, in which students use tools and machinery to make things out of wood and metal, or learn to fix things such as cars and electrical objects ‖ 학생들이 도구와 기계를 사용하여 나무·금속으로 물품을 제작하거나 자동차·전기 제품 등의 용품을 수리하는 것을 가르치는 학교의 교과목. 직업 훈련(과정[교실]). 공작(실) —see also **set up shop** (SET)

shop² *v* **-pped, -pping** [I] to go to one or more stores to buy things ‖ 물건을 사러 한 가게 이상을 가다. 쇼핑하다: *I've been out shopping for some things I need for the house.* 나는 집에서 필요한 물건을 몇 가지 구입하러 외출했다. – **shopper** *n* —see also SHOPPING

shop around *phr v* [I] to compare the price and quality of different things before you decide which to buy ‖ 어떤 것을 구입할 것을 결정하기 전에 서로 다른 물건들의 가격과 품질을 비교하다. 상품을 보러[조사하러] 다니다: *It's a good idea to shop around before buying a laptop.* 노트북 컴퓨터를 구입하기 전에 다른 물건들의 가격과 품질을 조사해 보러 다니는 것은 현명한 생각이다.

shop·lift /ˈʃɑpˌlɪft/ *v* [I, T] to take something from a store without paying for it ‖ 물건 값을 지불하지 않고 가게에서 어떤 것을 가져 가다. (가게에서 물건을) 슬쩍하다 – **shoplifter** *n* —see usage note at THIEF

shop·lift·ing /ˈʃɑpˌlɪftɪŋ/ *n* [U] the crime of taking things from stores without paying for them ‖ 물건 값을 지불하지 않고 가게에서 물건들을 가져가는 범죄. 가게 물건을 슬쩍하기

shop·ping /ˈʃɑpɪŋ/ *n* [U] **1** the activity of going to stores to buy things ‖ 물건을 구입하기 위해 가게에 가는 행위. 쇼핑. 물건 사기: *We'd better start our Christmas shopping early.* 우리는 크리스마스 쇼핑을 일찍 시작하는 것이 좋겠다. **2 go shopping** to go to stores to buy things, especially clothes ‖ 특히 옷을 사

기 위해 가게에 가다 **3** [singular] the things you have bought, usually food ‖ 보통 식품인 산 물건들. 구입 물품: *The boys helped me bring the shopping in from the car.* 아이들이 차에서 내가 식품들을 들여오는 것을 도와주었다.

shopping cen·ter /'.. ,./ *n* a group of stores built together in one area ‖ 한 지역에 같이 세워진 일군의 상점들. 쇼핑센터

shopping mall /'.. ,./ *n* ⇨ MALL

shore¹ /ʃɔr/ *n* [C, U] the land along the edge of a large area of water ‖ 넓은 수역의 가장자리를 쭉 따라 있는 땅. 바닷가. 호숫가. 해안: *a house on the eastern shore of the bay* 그 만의 동쪽 바닷가에 있는 집 한 채

> **USAGE NOTE shore, bank, coast, and seashore**
>
> Use **shore** to talk about the land along the edge of the ocean or a lake: *We watched as the boat came closer to shore.* Use **bank** to talk about the land along the edge of a river: *The river overflowed its banks during the storm.* Use **coast** to talk about the total area of land near the ocean: *They live in a little town on the southeast coast.* **Seashore** is similar in meaning to **coast**, and is used especially in the names of places: *The state has set up a research center at the Cape Hatteras National Seashore.* A **beach** is a part of the **shore**, usually covered by sand or smooth stones, where you go for pleasure: *Let's take a walk on the beach.*
> 바다 또는 호수의 가장자리를 따라 있는 육지에 대해 말할 때는 **shore**를 쓴다: 우리는 배가 해안으로 접근하고 있는 것을 지켜 봤다. 강의 가장자리를 따라서 있는 땅에 대해 말할 때는 **bank**를 쓴다: 폭풍우로 강의 제방이 범람했다. **coast**는 바다에 접한 육지 전체를 말하는데 쓴다: 그들은 남동 연안에 있는 작은 도시에서 산다. **seashore**는 **coast**와 유사한 의미이고 특히 장소의 이름에 쓰인다: 주(州)당국은 Cape Hatteras National Seashore에 연구소를 설립했다. **beach**는 보통 모래나 매끈한 자갈로 덮여서 사람들이 즐기기 위해 찾아가는, **shore**의 일부분이다.

shore² *v*

shore sth **up** *phr v* [T] **1** to support a wall with large pieces of wood, metal etc. to stop it from falling down ‖ 붕괴되

지 않게 나무·금속 등의 큰 조각들로 벽을 받치다. …에 버팀목을 괴다. …을 지주로 받치다 **2** to help or support something that is likely to fail or is not working well ‖ 실패할 것 같거나 제대로 운영되지 않는 것을 돕거나 지원하다. 구제하다: *The money is needed to shore up the failing bank.* 파산 은행을 지원하기 위한 자금이 필요하다.

shorn /ʃɔrn/ *v* a PAST PARTICIPLE of SHEAR ‖ shear의 과거 분사형

short¹ /ʃɔrt/ *adj*

1 ▶LENGTH/DISTANCE 길이/거리◀ not long ‖ 길지 않은. (거리가) 짧은: *Sophie has got short blond hair.* 소피는 짧은 금발의 머리를 했다. / *It's only a short distance from here to the river.* 여기서 강까지는 짧은 거리일 뿐이다.

2 ▶TIME 시간◀ happening for only a little time or for less time than usual ‖ 짧은 시간 동안 또는 보통보다 적은 시간 동안 발생하는. (시간이) 짧은: *Last week's meeting was really short.* 지난주의 모임은 정말 짧았다.

3 ▶PERSON 사람◀ not as tall as average height ‖ 평균 키만큼 크지 않은. 키가 작은. 높이가 낮은: *I'm too short to reach the shelf.* 나는 키가 너무 작아서 선반에 닿지 못한다.

4 ▶NOT ENOUGH 불충분한◀ not having enough of something you need ‖ 자신이 필요한 것을 충분히 갖지 못한. 부족한. 적은: *I'm short of cash right now.* 나는 지금 현금이 부족하다. / *I'm five dollars short.* 나는 5달러가 부족하다. / *We're two players short of a team.* (=we need two more players) 우리는 한 팀을 이루는 데 두 선수가 부족하다.

5 be in short supply to not be available in large quantities ‖ 다량으로 사용할 수 없는. 공급 부족의[이 딸리는]: *Fruit and sugar were in short supply then.* 과일과 설탕은 그 당시에 공급이 부족했다.

6 on short notice with very little warning that something is going to happen ‖ 어떤 것이 발생하려고 한다는 경고가 거의 없이. 짧은[불충분한] 경고로: *Sorry, we can't come on such short notice.* 미안합니다. 우리는 그렇게 짧은 (기간의) 예고로는 올 수가 없습니다.

7 in short order very quickly ‖ 매우 빨리. 곧: *His demands were met in short order.* 그의 요구는 곧 충족되었다.

8 be short for to be a shorter way of saying a name ‖ 더 짧게 이름을 말하다. 단축형으로 이름을 말하다: *Her name is Becky, short for Rebecca.* 그녀의 이름은 레베카를 짧게 줄인 베키다.

9 for short as a shorter way of saying a name ‖ 이름을 더 짧게 말해. 줄여서[단축 형으로] (불러서): *It's called the Message Handling System – MHS for short.* 그것은 메시지 처리 체계라고 한다. 줄여서 MHS이다.

10 in the short run/term during a short period of time after the present ‖ 현재 이후의 다시간 동안. 단기적으로/단 기간 내에: *These policies will only help us in the short term – in 10 years things will change.* 이 정책은 단기적으로 우리 에게 도움이 될 수 있을 뿐이다. 10년 후 에는 상황이 바뀔 것이다

11 get the short end of the stick INFORMAL to be the one in a group who has to do a job that no one wants to do ‖ 집단 내에서 아무도 하고 싶어 하지 않 는 일을 해야 하는 사람이 되다. …을 (떠)맡게 되다

12 be short with to speak to someone in a rude or unfriendly way ‖ 무례하고 불친절하게 남에게 말하다. 무뚝뚝하게[함 부로] 말하다: *Sorry I was so short with you on the phone.* 미안해. 전화로 너무 무뚝뚝하게 말했어. **– shortness** *n* [U]

short² *adv* **short of (doing) sth** without actually doing something ‖ 실제 로는 어떤 것을 하지 않고. 거의 …인[할 만큼]: *They've cut the budget and the workforce – everything short of canceling the project altogether.* 그들은 예산과 인력 등 그 사업 계획을 몽땅 취 소하지 않을 뿐 거의 모든 것을 삭감했다. **—see also cut sth short** (CUT¹), **fall short (of)** (FALL¹), **be running short/low** (RUN¹), **stop short of sth** (STOP¹)

short³ *n* **1 in short** used when you want to say the most important point in a few words ‖ 아주 중요한 사항을 몇 마 디로 말하고 싶을 때 쓰여. 간단히 말해 서. 요약하면. 결국: *In short, I don't think we can do it.* 요컨대 우리는 그것을 할 수 없다고 생각한다. **2** INFORMAL a short movie that is shown before the main movie in a theater ‖ 극장에서 본 영 화 이전에 보여주는 짧은 영화. 단편 영화 **3** INFORMAL ⇨ SHORT CIRCUIT

short⁴ *v* [I, T] INFORMAL to have a bad electrical connection that makes a machine stop working correctly, or to make something do this ‖ 불량한 전기 접 속으로 기계가 제대로 작동하는 것을 막 다, 또는 사물을 이렇게 만들다. 단락[쇼 트]하다. …을 단락[쇼트·누전]시키다

short·age /ˈʃɔrtɪdʒ/ *n* [C, U] a situation in which there is not enough of something that people need ‖ 사람들이 필요한만큼 사물이 충분하지 않은 상황. 결핍. 부족: *food shortages* 식량 부족 / *a shortage of medicine* 의약품 부족

short·bread /ˈʃɔrtˌbrɛd/ *n* [U] a hard sweet cookie made with a lot of butter ‖ 버터를 많이 넣고 만든 파삭파삭하고 달콤 한 쿠키. 쇼트브레드

short-change /ˌ.ˈ./ *v* [T] **1** to treat someone unfairly by not giving him/her what s/he deserves ‖ 사람이 마땅히 받아 야 할 것을 주지 않아서 불공정하게 대우 하다. 남과 부정하게 거래하다. (특히) 남을 속이다: *The miners felt short-changed by the new contract.* 광부들은 새 계약으로 기만당했다고 생각했다. **2** to give back too little money to someone who has paid you for something ‖ 어떤 것에 대하여 지불한 사람에게 돈을 너무 적게 돌려주다. (남에게) 잔돈을 모자라게 주다

short circuit /ˌ.ˈ./ *n* a bad electrical connection that makes a machine stop working correctly ‖ 기계가 제대로 작동하 지 못하게 만드는 불량한 전기 접속. 단락 (短絡). 쇼트. 누전 **– short circuit** *v* [I, T]

short·com·ing /ˈʃɔrtˌkʌmɪŋ/ *n* [C usually plural] a fault in someone's character, or in a product, system etc. ‖ 사람의 성품의 결점, 또는 제품·시스템 등에서의 잘못. 단점: *shortcomings in the public health system* 공중 보건 시스템의 단점

short cut /ˈ. ./ *n* **1** a quicker more direct way of going somewhere ‖ 어딘가 로 가는 더 빠르고 곧장 가는 길. 지름길: *Let's take a short cut across the park.* 공원을 가로질러 지름길로 가자. **2** a quicker way of doing something ‖ 어떤 것을 하는 더 빠른 방법. 지름길. 첩경: *There are no short cuts to finding a job.* 일자리를 구하는 데 첩경은 없다.

short·en /ˈʃɔrtn/ *v* [I, T] to become shorter, or to make something shorter ‖ 더 짧아지거나 어떤 것을 더 짧게 하다. 줄다. 줄이다: *Can you help me shorten this skirt?* 이 치마 줄이는 것 좀 도와줄 래?

short·en·ing /ˈʃɔrtn-ɪŋ, -nɪŋ/ *n* [U] fat made from vegetable oil that you mix with flour when making PASTRY ‖ 반죽을 만들 때 밀가루와 함께 섞는 야채 기름으 로 만든 지방. 쇼트닝

short·fall /ˈʃɔrtfɔl/ *n* the difference between the amount you have and the amount you need or expect ‖ 가지고 있 는 총계와 필요하거나 기대하는 총계 사이

의 차이. 부족액(량): *shortfalls in the city's budget* 시 예산의 부족(액)

short·hand /ˈʃɔrthænd/ *n* [U] a fast method of writing using special signs or shorter forms to represent letters, words, and phrases ‖ 문자·단어·어구를 나타내는 특수한 기호나 단축형을 사용해서 글을 빠르게 쓰는 방법. 속기(법): *taking notes in shorthand* 속기로 받아 적기

short-lived /ˌʃɔrtˈlɪvd/ *adj* existing only a short time ‖ 짧은 시간 동안만 존재하는. 단명한. 일시적인: *a short-lived fashion* 일시적인 유행

short·ly /ˈʃɔrtli/ *adv* **1** very soon ‖ 곧, 바로: *I expect him home shortly.* 그 사람은 곧 집에 들어올 거야. / *The President left for Washington shortly before noon.* 대통령은 정오 바로 직전에 워싱턴으로 떠났다. **2** speaking in a way that is not patient ‖ 진득하지 않게 말하는. 간략[간결]하게. 짧게: *"Yes, yes, I understand," he said shortly.* "그래, 그래, 이해해."라고 그는 짧게 말했다.

short-or·der cook /ˌ. ˌ.. ˈ./ *n* someone in a restaurant kitchen who makes the food that can be prepared easily or quickly ‖ 쉽게 또는 빠르게 준비될 수 있는 음식을 만드는 식당 주방에 있는 사람. 즉석 요리사

short-range /ˌ. ˈ./ *adj* designed to travel or operate only within a short distance ‖ 짧은 거리 이내에서만 이동하거나 작동하도록 고안된. 사정거리가 짧은. 단거리의: *short-range nuclear weapons* 단거리 핵무기

shorts /ʃɔrts/ *n* [plural] **1** pants that end at or above the knees ‖ 무릎이나 그 위까지 닿는 바지. 반바지: *a pair of tennis shorts* 테니스용 반바지 **2** men's UNDERPANTS ‖ 남자용 팬티

short·sight·ed, short-sighted /ˌʃɔrtˈsaɪtɪd/ *adj* **1** not considering the future effects of something ‖ 어떤 것의 미래의 영향을 고려하지 않는. 근시안적인: *short-sighted planning* 근시안적인 계획 **2** unable to see very far without GLASSES ‖ 안경 없이는 아주 멀리 볼 수 없는. 근시의

short·stop /ˈʃɔrtstɑp/ *n* [C, U] the position in baseball between SECOND BASE and THIRD BASE or the person who plays this position ‖ 야구에서 2루와 3루 사이의 수비 위치나 이 위치를 맡은 사람. 유격수 (위치) —see picture on page 946

short sto·ry /ˌ. ˈ../ *n* a short written story, usually about imaginary events ‖

대체로 가공의 사건들에 대해 짧게 씌어진 이야기. 단편 소설

short-term /ˌ. ˈ./ *adj* continuing for only a short time into the future ‖ 장래 짧은 기간 동안만 지속되는. 단기간의. 단기적인: *short-term loans* 단기 만기 대출 —compare LONG-TERM, —see also **in the short/long term** (TERM)

short wave /ˌ. ˈ./ *n* [U] radio broadcasting that can be sent around the world ‖ 전 세계로 보낼 수 있는 라디오 방송. 단파 방송

shot¹ /ʃɑt/ *n*

1 ▶GUNS 총◀ an act of firing a gun ‖ 총을 쏘는 행위. 발포. 발사. 사격: *Troops fired a warning shot.* 군인들은 경고 사격을 했다.

2 ▶DRUG 약◀ the act of putting medicine or legal drugs into your body using a needle ‖ 주사 바늘을 사용해서 몸 속으로 약이나 합법적인 약물을 넣는 행위. 주사: *Have you had your flu shot?* 독감 예방 주사 맞았니?

3 ▶MOVIES/PHOTOGRAPHS 영화/사진◀ **a)** a photograph ‖ 사진. 사진 한 컷: *a beautiful shot of the countryside around Prague* 프라하 주변 시골을 찍은 아름다운 사진 **b)** the view of something in a movie, television program, or photograph ‖ 영화[텔레비전 프로그램, 사진] 속의 어떤 것의 광경. 한 장면[컷]: *close-up shots of the actress* 그 여배우를 클로즈업한 장면

4 ▶ATTEMPT 시도◀ INFORMAL an attempt to do something or achieve something ‖ 어떤 것을 하거나 성취하려는 시도. 기도: *Marty always wanted to take a shot at acting.* 마티는 언제나 연기에 도전해 보고 싶어했다.

5 ▶DRINK 술◀ a small amount of a strong alcoholic drink ‖ 소량의 도수 높은 술. (샷잔으로) 한 잔

6 ▶SPORT 스포츠◀ an attempt to throw, kick, or hit the ball toward the place where you can get a point ‖ 점수를 얻을 수 있는 곳을 향해 공을 던지는[차는, 치는] 시도. 일타. 한 번 던지기[찌르기]: *Nice shot!* 나이스 샷!

7 a shot in the arm something that makes you more confident or successful ‖ 더 자신 있거나 성공적이게 하는 것. 활력소. 자극물[제]: *Winning the scholarship was a real shot in the arm for Mike.* 장학금을 받은 것은 마이크에게 큰 힘이 되었다.

8 like a shot very quickly ‖ 매우 신속히. 급히. 즉시: *He jumped up like a shot and ran to the door.* 그는 즉시 벌떡 일어

나더니 문 쪽으로 내달렸다. —see also BIG SHOT, LONG SHOT ‖

shot² *adj* **be shot** INFORMAL to be in bad condition or useless ‖ 나쁜 상태거나 쓸모 없게 되다. 못쓰게 되다: *This battery is shot – do we have another one?* 이 건전 지는 수명이 다 됐는데 다른 건전지 없니?

shot³ *v* the past tense and PAST PARTICIPLE of SHOOT ‖ shoot의 과거·과거 분사형

shot·gun /ˈʃɑtˌɡʌn/ *n* a long gun, used for shooting animals and birds ‖ 동물과 새를 쏠 때 사용하는 긴 총. 엽총. 산탄총

shotgun wed·ding /ˌ. ˈ../ *n* a wedding that has to take place immediately because the woman is going to have a baby ‖ 여자가 곧 출산하 기 때문에 즉시 치러야 하는 결혼. 마지못 해 하는 결혼

shot put /ˈ. ./ *n* [singular] a sport in which you throw a heavy metal ball as far as you can ‖ 할 수 있는 한 멀리 무거 운 쇠공을 던지는 운동. 포환던지기 – **shot putter** *n*

should /ʃəd/ strong /ʃʊd/ *modal v* **1** used when giving or asking for advice or an opinion ‖ 충고 또는 의견을 주거나 요청 할 때 쓰여. …해야 하다: *You shouldn't* (=should not) *get mad so easily.* 너무 쉽게 화를 내서는 안 된다. / *The county should purchase the land to make a park.* 군(郡)당국은 공원을 조성하 기 위해 그 땅을 매입해야 한다. / *They should have called the police.* 그들은 경 찰을 불렀어야 했다. / *Should I wear my gray dress?* 회색 드레스를 입어야 하나 요? **2** used in order to say that you expect something to happen or be true ‖ 어떤 것이 일어나거나 사실이 될 것으로 기대한다고 말하는 데에 쓰여. 아마[틀림 없이] …일 것이다: *Yvonne should be back by 8:00.* 이본은 8시까지는 돌아올 것이다. / *He's a good cook, so there should be good food.* 그는 훌륭한 요리사 이니까 음식도 훌륭할 것이다. **3** FORMAL used like "if" in formal CONDITIONAL sentences that use the present TENSE ‖ 현 재 시제를 사용하는 격식을 차린 조건절에 서 "if" 처럼 쓰여. 만약에[가령] …(한다 면): *Should you decide to accept the offer, please return the enclosed form.* 그 제안을 받아들이기로 결정하신다면 동 봉한 양식을 반송해 주십시오. —see usage note at SHALL —see study note on page 932

shoul·der¹ /ˈʃoʊldɚ/ *n* **1** one of the two parts of the body at each side of the neck where the arm is connected ‖ 팔이

연결된 목의 양쪽 각각에 있는 몸의 두 개 인 부분 중의 하나. 어깨: *Andy put his arm around his wife's shoulder.* 앤디는 아내의 어깨에 자신의 팔을 둘렀다. / *When we asked him what was wrong, he just shrugged his shoulders.* (=raised them to show that he did not know or care) 우리가 그에게 무엇이 잘 못되었는지 물었을 때 그는 그저 어깨를 으쓱하여 보일 뿐이었다 **2** the part of a shirt, coat etc. that covers your shoulders ‖ 어깨를 덮고 있는 셔츠[코트] 등의 부분. 어깨를 덮는 부분 **3 a shoulder to cry on** someone who gives you sympathy ‖ 동정해 주는 사람. 어려울 때 의지가 되는 사람: *Diane's always there when I need a shoulder to cry on.* 다이앤은 내가 어려울 때 항상 의지가 되 어 주었다. **4** an area of ground beside a road where drivers can stop their cars if they are having trouble ‖ 운전자들이 문 제가 있을 때 차를 멈출 수 있는 길 옆의 일정한 지면. 갓길. 노견

shoulder² *v* **1** [T] **shoulder the responsibility/burden/costs etc.** to accept a difficult or unpleasant responsibility, duty etc. ‖ 어렵거나 불쾌 한 책임·의무 등을 받아들이다. 책임/짐/ 비용을 떠맡다: *Carrie shouldered the burden of taking care of three young kids alone.* 캐리는 혼자서 어린 세 아이를 돌보는 짐을 졌다. **2** to push through a crowd of people using your shoulders ‖ 어깨를 써서 붐비는 군중 속을 뚫고 나가 다. …을 어깨로 밀다[밀치다]: *He shouldered his way to the front of the room.* 그는 그 방 앞쪽까지 어깨로 밀치고 나아갔다.

shoulder bag /ˈ.. ./ *n* a woman's PURSE that hangs from the shoulder by a long piece of material ‖ 긴 소재 조각으로 어깨로부터 내려뜨린 여자의 지갑. 여성용 숄더백

shoulder blade /ˈ.. ./ *n* one of the two flat bones on each side of your back ‖ 등 양쪽에 있는 두 개의 납작한 뼈 중의 하나. 어깨뼈. 견갑골

should·n't /ˈʃʊdnt/ *modal v* the short form of "should not" ‖ "should not"의 단 축형: *You shouldn't work so hard.* 너무 심하게 일해선 안 된다.

shout¹ /ʃaʊt/ *v* [I, T] to say something very loudly ‖ 아주 크게 어떤 것을 말하다. 큰 소리 치다. 외치다: *Someone shouted, "She's over here!"* "그녀는 이쪽에 있어!" 라고 누군가가 외쳤다. / *"Welcome everyone!" he shouted to the crowd.* "여 러분 반갑습니다!"라고 그는 군중을 향해

외쳤다.

shout at sb *phr v* [T] to say something loudly to someone because you are angry ‖ 화가 나서 남에게 어떤 것을 큰 소리로 말하다. …에게 고함치다: *The two women were shouting at each other outside the supermarket.* 두 여자가 슈퍼마켓 밖에서 서로에게 고함을 지르고 있었다.

shout sb ↔ **down** *phr v* [T] to shout in order to prevent someone from being heard ‖ 남이 계속 말하는 것을 막기 위해서 소리치다. 고함쳐서 침묵시키다: *The mayor was shouted down at the meeting.* 사람들은 그 모임에서 소리를 질러 시장의 입을 막았다.

shout² *n* **1** a loud call that expresses anger, excitement etc. ‖ 화·흥분 등을 표현하는 큰 소리의 외침. 함성. 고함: *suddenly there was a shout from upstairs* 갑자기 위층에서 고함 소리가 들렸다. **2 give sb a shout** SPOKEN to go and find someone and tell him/her something ‖ 가서 사람을 찾아서 어떤 것을 말해주다. …에게 알리다: *If you can find out any more information, give me a shout.* 정보를 무어라도 더 찾을 수 있으면 내게 알려줘.

shove /ʃʌv/ *v* **1** [I, T] to push someone or something in a rough or careless way, using your hands or shoulders ‖ 손이나 어깨를 사용해서 거칠거나 부주의하게 사람이나 사물을 밀다. 떼밀다. 밀치다: *Some reporters were pushed and shoved* (=pushed in a crowd) *as they tried to get near the President.* 일부 기자들은 대통령 근처로 다가가려다가 밀쳐지고 떼밀렸다. **2** INFORMAL to put something somewhere carelessly or without thinking much ‖ 부주의하게 또는 별 생각 없이 어떤 것을 어딘가에 놓다. 처넣다. 던져놓다: *Just shove those papers into the drawer for now.* 우선은 그 서류들을 서랍 속에 밀어 넣어 둬라. **3 shove it** SPOKEN an impolite phrase said when you are very annoyed or angry and you do not want to talk to someone any longer ‖ 매우 짜증나거나 화가 나서 더 이상 남과 말하고 싶지 않을 때 말하는 무례한 어구. 집어쳐: *"Just shove it, Tony,"* *she said as she walked out.* "토니, 집어쳐."라고 그녀는 걸어 나가면서 말했다. **– shove** *n*

shove off *phr v* [I] to push a boat away from the land, usually with a pole ‖ 보통 장대로 배를 육지에서 밀어내다. 배를 물가에서 떼밀어 내다

shov·el¹ /ʃʌvəl/ *n* **1** a tool with a long handle, used for digging or moving earth, stones etc. ‖ 흙·돌 등을 파거나 옮길 때 사용하는 긴 손잡이가 달린 연장. 삽 —see picture at DIG¹ **2** a part of a large vehicle or machine used for digging or moving earth ‖ 흙을 파거나 옮기는 데 쓰이는 대형 차량이나 기계의 일부. (동력) 삽. (포크레인 등의) 버킷

shovel² *v* **1** [I, T] to dig or move earth, stones etc. with a SHOVEL ‖ 삽으로 흙·돌 등을 파거나 옮기다. 삽으로 뜨다[퍼내다]: *When are you going to shovel the driveway?* (=shovel snow from the driveway) 언제 진입로에서 눈을 치울래? **2 shovel** sth **into/onto** sth to put large amounts of something into a place quickly ‖ 어떤 것의 많은 양을 한 곳에 빠르게 (퍼)담다. …을 퍼 넣다[밀어 넣다]: *He sat at the table shoveling his dinner into his mouth.* 그는 식탁에 앉아 저녁을 게걸스럽게 먹었다.

show¹ /ʃoʊ/ *v* **showed, shown, showing**
1 ▶MAKE SOMETHING CLEAR 어떤 것을 명확하게 하다◀ [T] to make it clear that something is true or exists by providing facts or information ‖ 사실이나 정보를 제공해서 어떤 것이 사실이거나 존재한다는 것을 명확하게 하다. …을 증명하다[가리키다]: *The report shows a rise in employment.* 그 보고서는 고용률의 상승을 보여 준다. / *a receipt showing that they had already paid* 그들이 이미 지불했다는 것을 증명하는 영수증 / *The article shows how attitudes have changed in the South.* 그 기사는 남부에서 태도가 얼마나 변했는지를 잘 보여 준다.
2 ▶HOW YOU FEEL 감정 상태◀ [T] to show how you feel by the way that you behave ‖ 행동하는 방식으로 기분이 어떤지를 나타내다. …을 드러내다[나타내다]: *Even after a long hike, he showed no signs of being tired.* 그는 오래 걸은 이후에도 지친 기색을 전혀 보이지 않았다. / *Her face showed her disappointment.* 그녀는 얼굴에 실망의 빛을 드러냈다.
3 ▶INFORMATION 정보◀ [T] if a picture, map etc. shows something, you can see it on the picture, map etc. ‖ 그림·지도 등에서 어떤 것을 볼 수 있다. …을 보여주다: *a figure showing the digestive system* 소화 기관을 보여주는 그림
4 ▶LET SB SEE 남이 보게 하다◀ [T] to let someone see something ‖ 남에게 어떤 것을 보게 하다. …을 보여주다[전시하다]: *Karen showed us her wedding pictures.* 카렌은 우리에게 자기 결혼사진

을 보여줬다 / *He's showing his paintings at the art gallery.* 그는 미술관에 자기 그림을 전시하고 있다.

5 ▶EXPLAIN STH 어떤 것을 설명하다◀ [T] to tell someone how to do something or where something is ‖ 남에게 어떤 일을 하는 방법이나 소재를 말해주다. …을 알려주다[설명하다]: *Show Beth where to put the cake for the party.* 파티용 케이크를 어디에 두어야 할지 베스에게 알려줘라. / *Can you show me how to play the game?* 그 놀이를 어떻게 하는지 나에게 알려줄래?

6 ▶GUIDE SB 남을 안내하다◀ [T] to go with someone and guide him/her to a place ‖ 남과 함께 가서 어떤 장소로 안내하다. …을 구경[견학]시켜 주다: *Thanks for showing us around the new building.* 새로운 건물을 구경시켜 주어서 고맙습니다.

7 ▶CAN BE SEEN 볼 수 있다◀ [I, T] if something shows, it can be seen ‖ 어떤 것을 볼 수 있다. 보이다. 드러내다: *His muscles showed beneath his shirt.* 그의 셔츠 밑으로 근육이 드러나 보였다.

8 have something/nothing to show for to have achieved something or nothing after working towards an aim ‖ 목표를 향해 노력한 이후에 어떤 것을 성취하거나 아무것도 성취하지 못하다. 많은 것을 이루다/아무것도 이루지 못하다: *I've been practicing so hard, and I still have nothing to show for it.* 나는 아주 열심히 연습을 해왔는데 그에 대해 여전히 보여줄 만한 게 아무것도 없다.

9 ▶MOVIE 영화◀ [I, T] if a movie is showing at a theater, or if a theater is showing a movie, you can see it there ‖ 영화를 영화관에서 볼 수 있다. 상영하다[되다]: *What's showing at the Carlton?* 칼튼 극장에서는 무슨 영화를 하고 있나?

10 show a profit/loss if a business shows a profit or loss, its accounts show that it made a profit or a loss ‖ 사업체가 수익을 냈는지 손실을 봤는지를 장부가 보여주다. 수익/손실로 나타나다 —see usage note at LEARN

show sb ↔ **around** (sth) *phr v* [T] to go with someone around a place when s/he first arrives in order to show what is important, interesting etc. ‖ 남이 처음으로 어떤 곳에 왔을 때 중요한·흥미로운 것 등이 무엇인지 보여주기 위해 그 사람과 함께 돌아다니다. …에게 (…을) 구경시켜 주다: *Mrs. Doney will show you around the museum.* 도니 부인이 박물관을 구경시켜 드릴 겁니다.

show off *phr v* **1** [I] to try to do things that will make people admire you or what you have ‖ 사람들로 하여금 자신 또는 자기가 가진 것을 감탄하게 만들 일을 하려 하다. 보란 듯이 내보이다. 뽐내다: *Jason's showing off in front of the girls.* 제이슨은 여자들 앞에서 허세부리고 있다. **2** [T **show** sth ↔ **off**] to show something to many people because you are very proud of it ‖ 어떤 것을 매우 자랑스럽게 여겨서 많은 사람들에게 보여주다. …을 자랑[과시]하다: *The Wilsons are having a party to show off their new house.* 윌슨 가족은 새 집을 자랑하려고 파티를 열고 있다. **3** [T **show** sth ↔ **off**] if one thing shows off another thing, it makes the other thing look especially attractive ‖ 하나의 것이 다른 것을 특히 매력적으로 보이게 하다. …을 돋보이게 하다: *Your blue tablecloth really shows off the white dishes.* 파란 식탁보가 정말로 하얀 접시들을 돋보이게 한다.

show up *phr v* **1** [I] INFORMAL to arrive at the place where someone is waiting for you ‖ 남이 기다리고 있는 장소에 도착하다. 나타나다. 출석하다: *The coach was mad because Bill showed up late for the game.* 감독은 빌이 경기에 늦게 나타나서 화가 났다. **2** [I] to be easy to see or notice ‖ 보거나 알아채기 쉽다. 눈에 띄다: *The doctor said that the bacteria didn't show up at first under the microscope.* 의사는 처음에는 박테리아가 현미경으로 봐도 눈에 띄지 않았다고 말했다. **3** [T **show** sb ↔ **up**] to do something in order to embarrass someone or make him/her seem stupid when other people are there ‖ 다른 사람들이 그곳에 있을 때 남을 당황하게 하거나 멍청해 보이게 하려고 어떤 것을 하다. 남을 창피 당하게 하다[바보로 만들다]: *I don't like the way you try to show me up.* 나는 네가 다른 사람들 앞에서 나를 바보로 만드는 게 마음에 안 들어.

show² *n* **1** a performance in a theater or on radio or television ‖ 극장[라디오, 텔레비전]에서의 공연. 쇼. 프로. 상연 작품: *a new show opening on Broadway* 브로드웨이에서 개막하는 새로운 쇼 / *a popular TV show* 인기 있는 TV 쇼 **2** a collection of things for the public to look at ‖ 일반 대중이 볼 수 있도록 한 사물의 수집 전시. 전시[전람]회. 품평[박람]회: *the spring flower show* 봄맞이 꽃박람회 **3 be on show** to be shown to the public ‖ 일반 대중에게 보여지다. 전시되다[중이다]: *The photographs will be on show until the end of the month.* 그 사진들은 이달 말까지 전시될 것이다. **4 a show of**

a) something that shows what something is like, how someone feels etc. ‖ 사물이 어떤 모습인지·사람이 어떻게 느끼는지 등을 나타내는 것. 표시. 기미. 시위: *The army marched through the town in a show of force.* 군대는 무력을 시위할 목적으로 시내를 행진했다. **b)** something that you do to make people think that something is true ‖ 사람들이 어떤 것을 사실로 생각하도록 하기 위해 하는 것. 가장. 시늉. 꾸밈: *She made a show of interest.* 그녀는 관심 있는 척했다. **5 let's get this show on the road** SPOKEN said when you want to tell people it is time to start working or start a trip ‖ 일이나 여행을 시작할 때가 됐다고 사람들에게 말하고 싶을 때 쓰여. 이제 이 계획[사업, 일]을 시작합시다

show and tell /ˌ. . ˈ./ *n* [U] a time during the school day when young children tell the other children in their class about a favorite object they have brought with them ‖ 수업 시간에 어린이들이 자기가 가져온 좋아하는 물건에 대해서 다른 어린이들에게 말하는 학교 생활 중의 시간. 발표회

show biz /ˈʃoʊ bɪz/ *n* [U] INFORMAL ⇨ SHOW BUSINESS

show busi·ness /ˈ. ˌ../ *n* [U] the entertainment industry ‖ 연예업[계]: *She started in show business as a child.* 그녀는 어려서부터 연예계에서 시작했다.

show·case /ˈʃoʊkeɪs/ *n* **1** an event or situation that is designed to show the good qualities of a person, organization etc. ‖ 사람·조직 등의 장점들을 보여주려고 마련된 행사나 상황. 시연장. 전시[시범](장): *Bryan Adams's new album is a showcase for his talents.* 브라이언 아담스의 새 앨범은 그의 재능을 잘 보여주고 있다. **2** a glass box showing objects for people to look at in a store, an art show etc. ‖ 상점이나 미술 전시회 등에서 사람들이 볼 수 있도록 물건들을 보여주는 유리 상자. 유리 진열장

show·down /ˈʃoʊdaʊn/ *n* a meeting, argument, fight etc. that will settle a disagreement or competition that has continued for a long time ‖ 오랫동안 계속된 불화나 경쟁을 해결할 모임·논쟁·싸움 등. 최종 대결: *a showdown between the top two teams in the league* 리그의 최상위 두 팀 간의 최종 대결

show·er¹ /ˈʃaʊɚ/ *n* **1** a thing that you stand under to wash your whole body ‖ 아래에 서서 몸 전체를 씻는 것. 샤워기: *The phone always rings when I'm in the shower.* 내가 샤워할 때면 항상 전화가

울린다. **2** an act of washing your body while standing under the shower ‖ 샤워기 아래에 서서 몸을 씻는 행위. 샤워: *Hurry up! I want to take a shower too.* 서둘러! 나도 샤워하고 싶단 말이야. **3** a short period of rain ‖ 짧은 동안의 비. 소나기: *Showers are expected later today.* 오늘 늦게 소나기가 예상됩니다. —see usage note at WEATHER **4** a party at which presents are given to a woman who is going to get married or have a baby ‖ 곧 결혼하거나 출산할 여자에게 선물을 주는 파티. 축하 선물 증정 파티: *We're having a baby shower for Paula on Friday.* 우리는 금요일에 폴라에게 출산 축하 선물 증정 파티를 열어줄 거야.

show·er² *v* **1** [I] to wash your whole body while standing under a SHOWER ‖ 샤워기 아래에 서서 몸 전체를 씻다. 샤워하다: *Is there time to shower before we leave?* 떠나기 전에 샤워할 시간이 있니? **2** [T] to generously give someone a lot of things ‖ 남에게 많은 것을 풍족히 주다. …에게 아낌없이 주다: *The children are showering the new puppy with attention.* 아이들은 새 강아지에게 애정을 쏟아 붓고 있다.

show·er·y /ˈʃaʊəri/ *adj* raining frequently for short periods ‖ 짧은 동안 비가 자주 내리는: *a showery day* 소나기가 자주 내리는 날

show·ing /ˈʃoʊɪŋ/ *n* **1** an occasion when a movie, art show etc. can be seen or looked at ‖ 영화·미술 전시회 등을 보거나 구경할 수 있는 때. 상영. 전시회: *a special showing of Georgia O'Keeffe's paintings* 조지아 오키프 그림의 특별 전시회 **2** something that shows how well or badly you are doing ‖ 얼마나 잘 하는지 또는 못하는지를 보여주는 것. (가시적) 지표[성과]. 외형: *The senator made a strong showing at the polls.* 그 상원 의원은 여론 조사에서 좋은 지표를 나타냈다.

show·man /ˈʃoʊmən/ *n* someone who is good at entertaining people and getting a lot of public attention ‖ 사람들을 즐겁게 하고 대중의 주목을 많이 받는 데 재주가 있는 사람. 연예인 **– showmanship** *n* [U]

shown /ʃoʊn/ *v* the PAST PARTICIPLE of SHOW ‖ show의 과거 분사형

show-off /ˈ. ./ *n* INFORMAL someone who always tries to show how smart or how much skill s/he has so that other people will admire him/her ‖ 다른 사람들이 우러러보도록 자기가 얼마나 똑똑한지 또는 얼마나 많은 능력을 가지고 있는

지를 보여주려고 항상 애쓰는 사람. 자기 자랑꾼: *Don't be such a show-off!* 자기 자랑 좀 작작 해라!

show·piece /'ʃoupis/ *n* something that an organization, government etc. wants people to see because it is a successful example of what they are doing ‖ 조직·정부 등이 자신들이 하는 일의 성공적인 실례로서 사람들에게 보여주고 싶어하는 것. 전시용 우수 견본[사례]

show·room /'ʃourum/ *n* a large room where you can look at things that are for sale ‖ 판매 중인 물건을 볼 수 있는 커다란 실내. 진열[전시]실: *a car show-room* 자동차 전시장

show·y /'ʃoui/ *adj* very colorful, big, expensive etc. in a way that attracts people's attention ‖ 사람들의 주목을 끌게 매우 색이 다채로운·큰·비싼. 화사한. 화려한. 현란한: *showy clothes* 화려한 옷

shrank /ʃræŋk/ *v* the past tense of SHRINK ‖ shrink의 과거형

shrap·nel /'ʃræpnəl/ *n* [U] small pieces of metal from a bomb, bullet etc. that are scattered when it explodes ‖ 폭탄·탄환 등이 폭발할 때 흩어지는 작은 금속 조각. 파편

shred[1] /ʃrɛd/ *n* **1** a small thin piece that is torn or cut roughly from something ‖ 어떤 것에서 거칠게 찢어지거나 잘린 작고 얇은 것. 끄트러기. 조각: *The kitten had torn/ripped the toy to shreds.* 새끼 고양이가 장난감을 갈기갈기 찢어 놓았다. **2** a very small amount ‖ 매우 작은 양. 아주 조금. 소량: *There's not a shred of evidence to prove he's guilty.* (=none at all) 그의 유죄를 입증할 증거는 눈곱만치도 없다.

shred[2] *v* **-dded, -dding** [T] **1** to cut or tear something into SHREDs ‖ 어떤 것을 갈기갈기 자르거나 찢다. 잘게 자르다[썰다] **2** to put a document into a SHREDDER ‖ 서류를 서류 절단기에 넣다. 서류를 파쇄하다

shred·der /'ʃrɛdə/ *n* a machine that cuts documents into small pieces so that no one can read them ‖ 아무도 읽지 못하게 서류를 작은 조각으로 자르는 기계. 서류 파쇄기

shrewd /ʃrud/ *adj* good at judging what people or situations are really like, especially in a way that makes you successful ‖ 특히 사람을 성공하게 만드는 방식으로 다른 사람들이나 상황의 실제 상태를 판단하는 데 능력이 있는. 통찰력이 있는. 명민한: *a shrewd businesswoman* 명민한 여성 사업가

shriek /ʃrik/ *n* **1** a very high loud

sound ‖ 매우 높은 고음. 날카로운 소리. 부르짖음: *the shriek of an owl* 올빼미의 날카로운 울음소리 **2** a high loud sound that you make with your voice because you are frightened, excited, angry etc. ‖ 겁을 먹은·흥분한·화가 나는 등으로 목소리를 크고 높게 내는 소리. 비명. 외침: *She gave a shriek of delight and hugged him.* 그녀는 기쁨의 비명을 지르며 그를 껴안았다. **– shriek** *v* [I]

shrill /ʃrɪl/ *adj* very high and unpleasant ‖ 매우 높고 불쾌한. 날카로운 [새된](소리의): *shrill voices* 크고 날카로운 목소리

shrimp /ʃrɪmp/ *n* [C, U] **1** a small curved sea animal that has ten legs and a soft shell, or the meat from this animal ‖ 열 개의 다리와 부드러운 껍질을 가진 작고 등이 휜 바다 동물이나 이 동물의 고기. 작은 새우 **2** INFORMAL an unkind word for someone who is very small ‖ 매우 작은 사람을 이르는 무례한 단어. 땅꼬마

shrine /ʃraɪn/ *n* **1** a place that is related to a holy event or holy person, and that people visit to pray ‖ 성스러운 사건이나 사람과 관련되어서 사람들이 참배하기 위해 방문하는 장소. 사당. 제단 **2** a place that people visit and respect because it is related to a famous person ‖ 유명한 사람과 관련되어서 사람들이 방문하여 경의를 표하는 장소. 성지. 전당: *Elvis Presley's home has become a shrine.* 엘비스 프레슬리 집은 성지가 되었다.

shrink[1] /ʃrɪŋk/ *v* **shrank, shrunk, shrinking 1** [I, T] to become smaller or to make something smaller ‖ 더 작아지거나 어떤 것을 더 작게 하다. 오그라들다. …을 줄어들게 하다: *My sweater shrank in the wash.* 내 스웨터는 세탁 과정에서 쭈그러들었다. **2** [I] to become smaller in amount, size, or value ‖ 양·크기·가치에서 더 작아지다. 감소하다. 줄어들다: *The economy has shrunk by 20% in the last two years.* 경제는 지난 2년간 20% 감소했다.

shrink from sth *phr v* [T] to avoid doing something difficult or unpleasant ‖ 어렵거나 불쾌한 것을 하기를 피하다. 뒷걸음치다. …에서 꽁무니 빼다: *She shrank from telling us the news.* 그녀는 우리에게 그 소식을 말하기를 꺼렸다.

shrink[2] *n* INFORMAL humorous a PSYCHIATRIST

shrink·age /'ʃrɪŋkɪdʒ/ *n* [U] the act of shrinking, or the amount that something shrinks ‖ 줄어드는 행위, 또는

어떤 것이 줄어드는 양. 수축(량). 감소 (량): *Make the pants longer to allow for shrinkage.* 수축되는 것을 감안해서 바지를 더 길게 만들어라.

shrink-wrapped /'. ,./ *adj* goods that are shrink-wrapped are wrapped tightly in plastic ‖ 물품이 비닐로 꽉 조이게 포장된. 수축 포장된 – **shrink-wrap** *n* [U]

shriv·el /'ʃrɪvəl/ **shrivel up** *v* [I, T] if something shrivels or is shriveled, it becomes smaller and its surface is covered in lines because it is dry or old ‖ 어떤 것이 마르거나 낡아서 더 작아지고 그 표면이 주름들로 덮이게 되다. 주름지다[잡히다]. 시들다. 쭈그러들다 – **shriveled** *adj* : *a shriveled old man* 주름이 진 노인

shroud¹ /ʃraʊd/ *n* **1** a cloth that is wrapped around a dead person's body before it is buried ‖ 묻기 전에 시신을 감싸는 천. 수의 **2** something that hides or covers something ‖ 어떤 것을 숨기거나 덮는 것. 가리개. 덮개

shroud² *v* **be shrouded in mist/smoke etc.** to be covered and hidden by mist, smoke etc. ‖ 안개·연기 등으로 뒤덮이거나 감추어지다. 안개[연기] 등에 휩싸이다: *mountains shrouded in clouds* 구름에 휩싸인 산들

shrub /ʃrʌb/ *n* a small bush ‖ 작은 덤불. 관목

shrub·ber·y /'ʃrʌbəri/ *n* [U] SHRUBS planted close together in a group ‖ 집단적으로 함께 촘촘히 심어진 관목들. 관목 숲 —see picture on page 945

shrug /ʃrʌg/ *v* **-gged, -gging** [I, T] to raise and then lower your shoulders in order to show that you do not know something or do not care about something ‖ 어떤 것을 모르거나 상관하지 않는다는 것을 나타내려고 양 어깨를 올렸다가 내리다. 양 어깨를 추이다[으쓱하다]: *Dan shrugged and went back to what he was doing.* 단은 어깨를 한 번 추어 보이고는 하던 일을 계속했다. – **shrug** *n*

shrug sth ↔ **off** *phr v* [T] to treat something as unimportant and not worry about it ‖ 어떤 것을 중요하지 않으며 걱정할 것이 없는 듯이 취급하다. 대수롭지 않게 여기다: *Marge tried to shrug off the boss's criticism.* 마지는 사장의 비판을 대수롭지 않게 여기려고 했다.

shrunk /ʃrʌŋk/ *v* the PAST PARTICIPLE of SHRINK ‖ shrink의 과거 분사형

shrunk·en /'ʃrʌŋkən/ *adj* having become smaller or been made smaller ‖ 더 작아졌거나 더 작아지게 된. 줄어든.

쭈그러든: *a shrunken old woman* 왜소해진 노부인

shuck /ʃʌk/ *v* [T] to remove the outer cover of a vegetable such as corn or peas, or the shell of OYSTERS or CLAMS ‖ 옥수수나 완두콩 등의 야채의 외피나 굴이나 조개의 껍데기를 제거하다. …의 껍질을 벗기다

shucks /ʃʌks/ *interjection* OLD-FASHIONED said in order to show you are a little disappointed about something ‖ 어떤 것에 대해 약간 실망한 것을 나타내는 데 쓰여. 쳇. 빌어먹을. 아뿔사

shud·der /'ʃʌdəʳ/ *v* [I] to shake because you are frightened or cold, or because you think something is very unpleasant ‖ 겁을 먹거나 추워서 또는 어떤 것이 매우 불쾌하다고 생각하여서 떨다. 몸서리치다. 치를 떨다: *Gwen shuddered as she described the man who had attacked her.* 그웬은 자신을 공격한 남자를 묘사하면서 몸서리쳤다. – **shudder** *n*

shuf·fle¹ /'ʃʌfəl/ *v* **1** [I] to walk slowly and noisily, without lifting your feet off the ground ‖ 지면에서 발을 들지 않고 천천히 소리를 내며 걷다. 발을 질질 끌며 걷다: *an old man shuffling across the room* 실내를 가로질러 발을 질질 끌며 걷는 노인 **2** [T] to move something such as papers or cards into a different position ‖ 종이나 카드 등을 다른 위치로 이동시키다. 뒤섞다. 뒤죽박죽으로 하다: *Ginny shuffled the papers on her desk.* 지니는 책상 위에 있는 서류들을 서로 뒤섞었다. **3 shuffle your feet** to move your feet slightly because you are bored or embarrassed ‖ 지루하거나 당황해서 발을 약간 움직이다. 다리를 떨다[흔들다]: *Ernie looked nervous and shuffled his feet.* 어니는 긴장해 보였는데 발을 가만두지 않았다.

shuffle² *n* **1** the act of shuffling (SHUFFLE) your feet ‖ 발을 질질 끄는 행동. 발을 질질 끌기 **2** the act of shuffling (SHUFFLE) papers or cards ‖ 서류나 카드를 뒤섞는 행동. 뒤섞기 **3** the act of officially changing the members of an organization ‖ 조직의 구성원을 공식적으로 바꾸는 행위. 재편성. 개편: *a management shuffle* 경영진 개편

shuf·fle·board /'ʃʌfəl,bɔrd/ *n* [U] a game in which you use a long stick to push a flat round object along a smooth surface toward an area with numbers on it ‖ 긴 막대를 써서 납작하고 둥근 물체를 부드러운 표면을 따라 숫자가 적힌 지역을 향해 밀어내는 놀이. 원반 밀어치기

shun /ʃʌn/ v -nned, -nning [T] to avoid someone or something deliberately ‖ 사람이나 사물을 의도적으로 피하다. …을 꺼리다

shunt /ʃʌnt/ v [T] to give someone or something a less important position than he, she, or it deserves ‖ 사람이나 사물에게 마땅히 받아야 하는 것보다 덜 중요한 자리를 주다. 제쳐놓다. 따돌리다: *Too often the needs and problems of education are shunted aside.* 교육의 필요성과 문제들은 너무나 자주 묵살되어진다.

shush /ʃʌʃ, ʃuʃ/ v **1 shush!** SPOKEN said in order to tell someone, especially a child, to be quiet ‖ 특히 어린애에게 조용히 하라고 말하는 데에 쓰여. 쉿: *"Shush!" said Tim. "Don't talk so loud."* "쉿! 너무 크게 말하지 마."라고 팀이 말했다. **2** [T] to tell someone to be quiet ‖ 남에게 조용히 하라고 말하다. …을 침묵시키다: *She started to complain, but Betty shushed her.* 그녀는 불평을 하기 시작했지만 베티가 그녀의 입을 막았다.

shut¹ /ʃʌt/ v **shut, shut, shutting 1** [I, T] to close something, or to become closed ‖ 어떤 것을 닫거나 닫히다: *Do you want me to shut the window?* 창문을 닫을까? / *I heard the back door shut.* 나는 뒷문이 닫히는 소리를 들었다. / *She leaned back and shut her eyes.* 그녀는 뒤로 기대고서는 눈을 감았다. **2 shut your mouth/trap/face!** SPOKEN used in order to rudely and angrily tell someone to stop talking ‖ 남에게 이야기하지 말라고 무례하게 화를 내며 말하는 데에 쓰여. 입 닥쳐!

shut down phr v [I,T **shut** sth ↔ **down**] if a company, factory, large machine etc. shuts down or is shut down, it stops operating ‖ 회사·공장·큰 기계 등이 작동을 멈추다. 폐쇄하다. 가동을 중단하다: *Three nuclear generators were shut down for safety reasons.* 세 기(基)의 핵 발전기가 안전상의 이유로 폐쇄되었다. / *The factory will shut down for two weeks this month.* 그 공장은 이 달에 2주 동안 가동을 중단할 것이다.

shut off phr v **1** [I,T **shut** sth ↔ **off**] if a machine, tool etc. shuts off or if you shut it off, it stops operating ‖ 기계·도구 등이 작동을 멈추다. …을 끄다[꺼지다·중단[정지]하다: *We shut the engine off when it overheated.* 우리는 엔진이 과열되자 껐다. / *The heat shuts off automatically.* 난방 장치는 자동적으로 꺼진다. **2** [T **shut** sth ↔ **off**] to prevent goods or supplies from being available or being delivered ‖ 상품이나 물품을 이용할 수 있거나 배달되는 것을 막다. 끊다. 차단하다: *Food, oil, and gas supplies were shut off during the fighting.* 음식, 기름, 그리고 가스 공급이 교전 중에 끊겼다.

shut sb/sth **out** phr v [T] **1** [**shut** sb ↔ **out**] to deliberately not let someone join in an activity, process etc. ‖ 남을 어떤 활동·과정 등에 의도적으로 참여시키지 않다. …을 따돌리다[배제하다]: *Some people are being shut out of the health care system.* 일부 사람들은 건강 보험에서 배제되고 있다. **2** [**shut** sth ↔ **out**] to stop yourself from seeing, hearing, or thinking about something ‖ 어떤 것에 대해서 보는[듣는, 생각하는] 것을 막다. …을 차단[단절]시키다: *He can shut out the rest of the world when he's working.* 그는 일을 할 때는 세상모르게 몰두한다. **3** [**shut out** sb] to defeat an opposing team and prevent them from getting any points ‖ 상대 팀을 패배시키고 점수를 한 점도 얻지 못하게 막다. 완봉승하다: *The Blue Jays shut out the Phillies 3-0.* 블루 제이즈는 필리즈를 3대 0으로 완봉했다.

shut sb/sth **up** phr v **1 shut up!** SPOKEN said in order to tell someone rudely to stop talking ‖ 남에게 말하지 말라고 무례하게 말하는 데에 쓰여. 입 닥쳐: *Just shut up; I'm trying to think.* 입 좀 다물어, 생각 중이잖아. **2** [T **shut** sb **up**] to make someone stop talking or be quiet ‖ 남이 말하는 것을 막거나 조용하도록 하다. 남을 입 다물게 하다: *The only way to shut her up is to feed her.* 그녀의 입을 다물게 하는 유일한 방법은 음식을 먹이는 것이다.

shut² adj not open; closed ‖ 열리지 않은; 닫힌: *Is the door shut tight?* 문이 꽉 잠겼니?

shut·down /ˈʃʌtdaʊn/ n the closing of a factory, business, or piece of machinery ‖ 공장[사업체, 기계]의 폐쇄. 조업 중단, 운전 중지: *the shutdown of a paper mill* 제지 공장의 폐쇄

shut-eye /ˈ. ./ n [U] INFORMAL sleep ‖ 잠: *I really need some shut-eye.* 나는 정말 눈 좀 붙여야겠다.

shut-in /ˈ. ./ n someone who is sick or DISABLED and cannot leave the house easily ‖ 아프거나 신체 장애가 있어서 집을 쉽게 떠날 수 없는 사람. (거동할 수 없어) 집[병원]에 틀어박힌 사람

shut·ter /ˈʃʌtər/ n **1** one of a pair of wooden or metal covers on the outside of a window, that can be closed ‖ 창문의

바깥쪽에서 닫을 수 있게 한 두 짝의 나무
나 금속 덮개 중의 하나. 덧문. 셔터 —
see picture on page 945 **2** a part of a
camera that opens to let light onto the
film ‖ 빛이 필름에 비치도록 열리는 사진
기의 일부분. 셔터

shut·tle¹ /'ʃʌtl/ n **1** a plane, bus, or
train that makes regular short trips
between two places ‖ 두 장소 사이를 정
기적으로 짧게 왕복하는 비행기[버스, 기
차]. 정기 왕복 교통 기관: *the Wash-
ington-New York shuttle* 워싱턴-뉴욕 간
정기 왕복 교통 기관 **2** a space vehicle
that can fly into space and return to
Earth and be used more than once ‖
우주 공간으로 비행한 다음 지구로 귀환하
고 한 번 이상 사용할 수 있는 우주선. 우
주 왕복선: *the launch of the Atlantis
space shuttle* 아틀란티스 우주 왕복선의
발사

shuttle² v **1** [T] to move people from
one place to another place that is close
‖ 사람들을 한 곳에서 가까운 다른 곳으로
이동시키다. 실어 나르다: *Passengers are
shuttled to the hotel by bus.* 승객들은 버
스로 호텔까지 이동했다. **2** [I] to travel
frequently between two places ‖ 두 장소
사이를 자주 이동하다. 빈번하게 왕복하
다: *The visitors were shuttled between
the hotel and the conference center
twice a day.* 방문객들은 하루에 두 번씩
호텔과 회의장을 왕복했다.

shut·tle·cock /'ʃʌtl,kɑk/ n a small
light object that you hit over the net in
the game of BADMINTON ‖ 배드민턴 경기
에서 네트 위로 치는 작고 가벼운 물체. 깃
털공. 셔틀콕

shy¹ /ʃaɪ/ adj **1** too nervous and
embarrassed to talk to people in a
confident way ‖ 너무 불안하고 당황해서
자신 있게 사람들에게 말할 수 없는. 부끄
럼타는. 수줍어하는: *Cal's painfully shy.*
(=extremely shy) 칼은 매우 수줍어한다.
2 unwilling to do something or get
involved in something ‖ 어떤 것을 하거나
관여하려고 하지 않는. …에 마음이 내키
지 않는. …을 꺼리는: *He's not shy
about showing off his wealth.* 그는 자신
의 부유함을 뽐내는 데에 주저하지 않는
다. **-shyly** adv **-shyness** n [U]

shy² v [I] if a horse shies, it makes a
sudden movement away from something
because it is frightened ‖ 말이 겁을 먹어
서 어떤 것에서 갑작스럽게 물러서다. 뒷
걸음을 치다

shy away from sth phr v [T] to avoid
doing something because you are not
confident enough about it ‖ 어떤 것에 대

해서 충분히 자신감이 없기 때문에 어떤
일을 하는 것을 피하다. …을 (회)피하다:
*Erik had always shied away from
speaking in public.* 에릭은 언제나 청중
앞에서 연설하는 것을 피해 왔었다.

shy·ster /'ʃaɪstɚ/ n INFORMAL a
dishonest person, especially a lawyer or
politician ‖ 부정직한 사람, 특히 변호사나
정치인. 악덕 변호사. 부정한 정치인

sib·ling /'sɪblɪŋ/ n **1** FORMAL your
brother or sister ‖ 자신의 형제나 자매.
동기 **2 sibling rivalry** competition
between brothers and sisters for the
attention of their parents ‖ 부모의 관심
을 받기 위한 형제·자매들 사이의 경쟁.
동기간의 경쟁

sic¹ /sɪk/ adv LATIN used after a word
that you have copied into a piece of
writing in order to show that you know
it was not spelled or used correctly ‖ 철
자나 용법이 바르지 않다는 것을 알고 있
다는 것을 나타내기 위해 문장에 인용한
말 뒤에 쓰여. 원문대로

sic² v **-cced, -ccing** [T] INFORMAL to
tell a dog to attack someone ‖ 개에게 남
을 공격하라고 말하다. …에게 덤벼들게
하다

sick¹ /sɪk/ adj **1** suffering from a
disease or illness ‖ 질병이나 병으로 고통
받는. 병든. 아픈: *Nina's not coming in
today; she's sick.* 니나는 오늘 못 올 거
야. 아프거든. / *Everyone ate the same
thing, but I was the only one who got
sick.* 모두가 같은 것을 먹었지만 나만 유
일하게 아팠다. **2 be sick** to bring food
up from your stomach through your
mouth; VOMIT ‖ 음식을 위에서 입으로 토
해내다. 구역질[욕지기]나다[하다]; 逾
vomit: *Uh oh, the dog's going to be sick!*
아이구 저런, 개가 토하려고 해! **3 feel
sick (to your stomach)** to feel as if you
are going to VOMIT ‖ 곧 토할 것처럼 느끼
다. 욕지기 나다: *I felt so sick after
eating all that popcorn.* 나는 그 모든 팝
콘을 먹고 나니 완전히 토할 것 같았다. **4
be sick (and tired) of/be sick to
death of** to be angry and bored with
something that has been happening for
a long time ‖ 오랫동안 벌어지고 있는 것
에 화가 나고 지루해지다. …에 질리다[넌
더리가 나다]: *I'm sick to death of all
this arguing.* 나는 이제 이 모든 말다툼에
넌더리가 난다. **5 make me sick** SPOKEN
to make you feel strong anger and
disapproval ‖ 분노와 불만을 격하게 느끼
게 하다. 화나게[구역질나게] 하다:
*People who treat animals like that make
me sick.* 동물을 저렇게 취급하는 사람을

보면 정말로 참을 수가 없어. **6** someone who is sick does things that are strange and cruel ‖ 사람이 괴상하고 잔인한 짓을 하는. 정상이 아닌: *The murders are obviously the work of a sick mind.* 그 살인들은 분명히 정신 이상자의 소행이다. **7** sick stories, jokes etc. deal with death and suffering in a cruel or unpleasant way ‖ 이야기·농담 등이 잔인하거나 불쾌하게 죽음과 고통을 다루는. 병적인. 불건전한. 기분 나쁜

sick² *n* [plural] **the sick** people who are sick ‖ 아픈 사람들. 환자: *nurses taking care of the sick and wounded* 환자와 부상자들을 돌보는 간호사들

sick·en /ˈsɪkən/ *v* **1** [T] to make you feel strong anger and disapproval ‖ 분노와 불만을 격하게 느끼게 하다. 울화가 치밀게 하다: *We were sickened by newspaper reports of child abuse.* 우리는 아동 학대에 대한 신문 기사에 울화가 치밀었다. **2** [I] to become sick ‖ 아프게 되다. 병들다

sick·en·ing /ˈsɪkənɪŋ/ *adj* **1** making you feel sick ‖ 토할 것 같게 하는. 속이 울렁이게[메스껍게] 하는: *The plane dropped with sickening speed.* 비행기는 구토할 정도로 빠른 속도로 하강했다. **2** making you feel strong anger and disapproval ‖ 분노와 불만을 격하게 느끼게 하는. 울화가 치미는. 넌더리[구역질] 나는: *It's sickening to see so many poor people in such a wealthy country.* 그렇게 부유한 나라에서 그토록 많은 가난한 사람들을 보는 것은 울화가 치미는 일이다.

sick·le /ˈsɪkəl/ *n* a tool with a blade in the shape of a hook, used for cutting wheat ‖ 밀을 자르는 데에 사용하는 갈고리 모양의 날이 있는 도구. 작은 낫

sick leave /ˈ. ./ *n* [U] the time you are allowed to be away from work because of sickness ‖ 병 때문에 직장에 결근해도 되는 기간. 병가

sick·ly /ˈsɪkli/ *adj* **1** weak, unhealthy, and often sick ‖ 약하고, 건강하지 않고, 종종 아픈. 병약한: *a sickly child* 병약한 아이 **2** unpleasant and making you feel sick ‖ 불쾌하고 토할 것 같게 하는. 구역질 나는. 메스꺼운: *the sickly smell of rotten eggs* 썩은 계란의 메스꺼운 냄새

sick·ness /ˈsɪknɪs/ *n* **1** [U] the state or feeling of being sick; ILLNESS ‖ 아픈 상태나 느낌. 병. 건강치 못함; 몐 illness: *soldiers suffering from hunger and sickness* 굶주림과 질병으로 고통 받는 병사들 **2** an illness ‖ 병: *common sicknesses such as colds and ear*

infections 감기와 중이염 등의 흔한 병 **3 air/travel/car etc. sickness** a feeling that you are going to VOMIT, that you get when you travel in a plane, car etc. ‖ 비행기·차 등으로 여행할 때 갖게 되는 곧 토할 것 같은 느낌. 비행기[여행, 차] 등의 멀미 —see also MORNING SICKNESS —see usage note at DISEASE

sick pay /ˈ. ./ *n* [U] wages paid by an employer to a worker who cannot work because of illness ‖ 병 때문에 일할 수 없는 근로자에게 고용주가 지불하는 임금. 병가 수당

side¹ /saɪd/ *n*

1 ▶PART OF AN AREA 영역의 부분◀ one of the two areas that something is divided into ‖ 어떤 것이 나뉘어진 두 영역 중의 하나. 쪽. 편: *Jim grew up on Detroit's east side.* 짐은 디트로이트 동부에서 자랐다. / *They own a house on the other side of the lake.* 그들은 호수의 반대편에 집 한 채를 소유하고 있다. / *A computer sits to one side of the desk.* 컴퓨터는 책상의 한쪽에 놓여 있다.

2 ▶NEXT TO …의 옆◀ the place or area directly next to someone or something ‖ 사람이나 사물의 바로 옆에 있는 장소나 지역. 옆. 곁: *They walked side by side.* (=next to each other) 그들은 나란히 걸었다. / *Her mother was always at her side in the hospital.* 그녀의 어머니는 병원에서 항상 그녀의 곁을 지켰다.

3 ▶EDGE 가장자리◀ the part of an object or area that is farthest from the middle ‖ 한 물체나 지역의 중앙에서 가장 먼 부분. 가장자리: *He was standing at the side of the field.* 그는 경기장 가장자리에 서 있었다.

4 ▶OF A BUILDING/VEHICLE ETC. 건물/탈것 등의◀ a surface of something that is not its front, back, top, or bottom ‖ 앞[뒤, 꼭대기, 바닥]이 아닌 사물의 표면. 옆면. 측면: *A truck ran into the left side of the bus.* 트럭은 버스의 좌측을 들이받았다.

5 ▶FLAT SURFACE 납작한 표면◀ one of the flat surfaces of something ‖ 사물의 납작한 표면들 중의 하나. 면: *A cube has six sides.* 정육면체는 면이 6개이다.

6 ▶OF A THIN OBJECT 얇은 물체의◀ one of the two surfaces of a thin flat object ‖ 얇고 납작한 물체의 양 면 중의 한 면. 면. 쪽: *You can write on both sides of the paper.* 그 종이의 양 면을 쓸 수 있다.

7 -sided having a particular number of sides ‖ 특정한 수의 면을 가진. …의 면 [변]을 가진: *a set of eight-sided dishes*

8각 접시 한 세트

8 from side to side moving continuously from right to left ‖ 오른쪽에서 왼쪽으로 끊임없이 움직이는. 좌우로: *They sang and danced, swaying from side to side.* 그들은 몸을 좌우로 흔들면서 노래하고 춤을 추었다.

9 from all sides from every direction ‖ 모든 방향으로부터. 사방에서: *enemy gunfire coming from all sides* 사방에서 날아오는 적의 총격

10 ▶SUBJECT/SITUATION 주제/상황◀ one part of a subject, problem, or situation ‖ 주제[문제, 상황]의 한 부분. (측)면. 국면: *I'd like to hear her side of the story.* 나는 그녀 쪽 이야기를 들어보고 싶다. / *We need to look at the issue from all sides.* 우리는 그 문제를 모든 측면에서 바라볼 필요가 있다.

11 ▶ IN AN ARGUMENT/WAR/COMPETITION 논쟁/전쟁/시합에서◀ one of the people, groups, teams, or countries opposing each other in a quarrel, war, competition etc. ‖ 싸움[전쟁, 시합] 등에서 서로 대항하는 사람[집단, 팀, 국가]의 한쪽. 편[쪽]: *Nancy's on our side.* (=agrees with us) 낸시는 우리 편이다. / *The two team captains chose sides.* (=chose who would be on his/her team) 두 팀의 주장은 편을 갈랐다.

12 ▶FOOD 음식◀ a dish that you eat in addition to the main dish of a meal in a restaurant ‖ 식당에서 식사의 주요리에 추가하여 먹는 음식. 부식: *I'll have the roast beef sandwich with a side of fries.* 구운 쇠고기 샌드위치에 감자칩을 곁들여 주세요.

13 on the side a) in addition to your regular job, sometimes illegally ‖ 때때로 불법적으로 정규 직업에 추가하여. 부업으로: *He runs a little business on the side.* 그는 부업으로 작은 사업체를 운영한다. **b)** in addition to the main dish that you order in a restaurant ‖ 식당에서 주문한 주요리에 추가하여. 부식으로: *Could I have a salad on the side?* 샐러드를 곁들여 주시겠어요?

14 ▶PART OF YOUR BODY 몸의 일부◀ the part of your body from your shoulder to the top of your leg ‖ 어깨에서 다리의 맨 위까지의 몸의 일부. 옆구리: *She was wounded in her right side.* 그녀는 오른쪽 옆구리에 부상을 입었다.

15 ▶OF A FAMILY 가족의◀ the parents, grandparents etc. of your mother or father ‖ 어머니나 아버지의 부모·조부모 등. …쪽. 친가[외가]의: *Her father's side of the family is German.* 그녀의 아버지는

독일계다.

16 ▶MOUNTAIN/VALLEY 산/계곡◀ one of the sloping areas of a hill, valley etc. ‖ 언덕·계곡 등의 비탈진 지역 중의 하나. 산중턱. (경)사면

side² adj 1 in or on the side of something ‖ 사물의 옆의[에]. 측부[측면]의: *You can leave by the side door.* 옆문으로 나가도 된다. **2 side street/road etc.** a street, road etc. that is smaller than a main street ‖ 큰길보다 더 작은 길·도로 등. 옆길[샛길]/이면로: *They live on a side street off Reseda Blvd.* 그들은 리세다 대로의 이면로에 산다. **3** from the side of something ‖ 사물의 옆에서. 측면에서의: *a side view of the statue* 동상의 옆 모습

side³ v [I] **side with/against** to support or argue against a person or group in a quarrel, fight etc. ‖ 다툼·싸움 등에서 사람이나 집단에 지지하거나 반대해 논쟁하다. …에 편들다[반대하다]: *Democrats sided with the President on the issue of gun control.* 민주당 의원들은 총기 규제 문제에 있어서 대통령을 지지했다.

side·board /'saɪdbɔrd/ **n** a long low piece of furniture in a DINING ROOM that you store dishes and glasses in ‖ 접시와 유리 컵들을 넣는 식당의 길고 낮은 가구. 찬장

side·burns /'saɪdbɜnz/ **n** [plural] hair that grows down the sides of a man's face in front of his ears ‖ 남자의 귀 앞쪽 얼굴 옆 아래로 나는 털. 구레나룻

side·car /'saɪdkɑr/ **n** an enclosed seat that is joined to the side of a MOTORCYCLE and has a separate wheel ‖ 오토바이 옆에 붙어 있으며 바퀴가 따로 있는 차체로 둘러싸서 만든 좌석. 사이드카

side dish /'. ./ **n** a dish that is served along with the main food at a meal ‖ 식사할 때 주요리와 함께 제공되는 음식. 부식. 곁들인 음식: *grilled chicken with a side dish of roasted peppers* 볶은 후추를 곁들인 석쇠에 구운 닭고기

side ef·fect /'. .,./ **n 1** an effect that a drug has on your body in addition to the intended effect ‖ 약이 의도된 효과에 추가하여 몸에 미치는 영향. 부작용: *The most common side effect is a slight fever.* 가장 흔한 부작용은 미열이다. **2** an unexpected result of an activity, situation, or event ‖ 활동[상황, 행사]의 예기치 못한 결과. 부작용: *A side effect of tuna fishing was the death of thousands of dolphins.* 참치 잡이의 부작용은 수 천

마리 돌고래의 죽음이었다.

side·kick /'saɪd,kɪk/ *n* INFORMAL a friend or helper of someone who is more important ‖ 더 중요한 사람의 친구나 조력자. (단짝) 친구[동료]. 조수: *Batman's sidekick, Robin* 배트맨의 조수, 로빈

side·line¹ /'saɪdlaɪn/ *n* **1** one of the two lines that form the edges of a field where sports are played, and the area just outside these lines ‖ 운동 경기가 진행되는 경기장 가장자리를 형성하는 두 개의 선 중의 하나와 이 선들 바로 밖의 지역. 옆줄(밖). 장외 —see picture on page 946 **2** something that you do to earn money in addition to your regular job ‖ 정식 직업에 더하여 돈을 벌려고 하는 일. 부업: *Mark does translation work as a sideline.* 마크는 부업으로 번역 일을 한다. **3 on the sidelines** not taking part in an activity even though you want to ‖ 비록 하고 싶지만 활동에 참여하지 않는. 지켜보기만 하는. 방관하는: *There are still buyers on the sidelines waiting to get stocks.* 아직도 재고가 쌓이기를 기다리며 팔짱만 끼고 있는 구매자들이 있다.

sideline² *v* [I, T] **be sidelined** to not be included in a game or event because you are injured or because you are not as good as someone else ‖ 부상을 당했거나 다른 사람만큼 잘하지 못해서 경기나 행사에 포함되지 못하다. 출전하지 못하다. 결장하다: *Their quarterback was sidelined with a knee injury.* 그들의 쿼터백은 무릎 부상으로 출장하지 못했다.

side·long /'saɪdlɔŋ/ *adj* **sidelong look/glance** a way of looking at someone by moving your eyes to the side, done secretly or when you are nervous ‖ 몰래 또는 긴장할 때 하는 것으로, 눈을 옆으로 움직여서 남을 바라보는 방법. 곁눈질

side or·der /'. ,../ *n* ⇨ SIDE¹

side·show /'saɪdʃoʊ/ *n* a separate small part of a CIRCUS or a FAIR, that often has very unusual performers ‖ 종종 아주 별난 공연자가 출연하는 서커스나 박람회의 별개의 작은 부분. 작은 쇼. 여흥

side·step /'saɪdstɛp/ *v* **1** [T] to avoid talking about or dealing with something that is unpleasant or difficult ‖ 불쾌하거나 어려운 것에 대해서 말하거나 처리하기를 피하다. (비켜서) 회피하다. 빠져나가다: *Congressman Howell sidestepped the reporters' questions.* 하원 의원 호웰은 기자들의 질문을 회피했다. **2** [I, T] to step quickly to one side to avoid an

accident ‖ 사고를 피하려고 빠르게 한쪽으로 발을 내딛다. (…을) 옆으로 한 발짝 비켜 피하다

side·swipe /'saɪdswaɪp/ *v* [T] to hit the side of a car or other vehicle with the side of your car ‖ 자신의 차의 측면으로 어떤 차나 다른 탈것의 옆면을 치다. …을 차의 옆으로 들이받다. 스치다

side·track /'saɪdtræk/ *v* [T] to make someone stop doing or saying something by making him/her interested in something else ‖ 남이 다른 것에 관심을 가지게 해서 어떤 것을 하거나 말하는 것을 막다. (주의를) 딴 데로 돌리다[빗나가게 하다]: *I think we're getting side-tracked from the main issue here.* 우리는 지금 주요 쟁점에서 옆길로 벗어나고 있는 것 같아.

side·walk /'saɪdwɔk/ *n* a hard surface or path for people to walk on along the side of a street ‖ 사람들이 거리의 옆을 따라 걸을 수 있는 단단한 지표면이나 길. 인도. 보도 —see picture on page 945

side·ways /'saɪdweɪz/ *adv* toward one side, or with the side facing forward ‖ 한쪽을 향하거나 측면이 앞을 향하여. 옆으로[을 향해]. 비스듬히: *Mel's car slid sideways as it hit the ice.* 멜의 차는 빙판길을 통과하면서 옆으로 미끄러졌다. / *They had to turn the couch sideways to get it through the door.* 그들은 문을 통과하기 위해 소파를 비스듬히 돌려야 했다.

sid·ing /'saɪdɪŋ/ *n* [U] wood, metal, or plastic in long narrow pieces, used for covering the sides of houses ‖ 주택의 측면을 덮는 데 쓰이는 길고 좁은 목재[금속, 플라스틱]. (외벽용) 널빤지. 판자

si·dle /'saɪdl/ *v* [I] to walk toward someone or something slowly, as if you do not want to be noticed ‖ 마치 눈에 띄고 싶지 않은 것처럼 사람이나 사물을 향해 천천히 걷다. 가만가만 다가가다: *Theo sidled up to me with an embarrassed look.* 시오는 난처한 표정을 지으며 내게 살며시 다가왔다.

siege /sidʒ/ *n* a situation in which an army surrounds a place and stops supplies of food, weapons etc. from getting to it ‖ 군대가 한 장소를 둘러싸고 음식·무기 등의 보급품이 도달하는 것을 차단하는 상황. 포위 공격: *a city under siege* (=surrounded by an army) 포위 공격을 받고 있는 도시

si·es·ta /si'ɛstə/ *n* a NAP (=short period of sleep) taken in the afternoon by people who live in hot countries ‖ 더운 국가에 사는 사람들이 오후에 자는 선잠. 낮잠. 오수

sieve /sɪv/ *n* a kitchen tool that looks like a wire net, used for separating solids from liquids or small pieces from large pieces ‖ 액체에서 고체를 또는 큰 조각에서 작은 조각을 분리하는 데에 쓰이는 철망처럼 생긴 주방 기구. 체 — **sieve** *v* [T]

sift /sɪft/ *v* [T] **1** to put flour, sugar etc. through a SIEVE in order to remove large pieces ‖ 큰 덩어리를 제거하려고 밀가루·설탕 등을 체로 거르다. 체로 치다. 체질하다 **2** also **sift through** to examine information, documents etc. very carefully in order to find something ‖ 어떤 것을 찾으려고 정보·서류 등을 매우 주의 깊게 조사하다. 면밀히 조사하다: *It will take a while to sift through all these files.* 이 모든 파일들을 면밀히 조사하려면 꽤 시간이 걸릴 것이다.

sigh¹ /saɪ/ *v* [I] to breathe out loudly and slowly, especially when you are tired or in order to express a strong emotion ‖ 특히 지쳤을 때 또는 격한 감정을 표현하기 위해 큰 소리로 천천히 숨을 내쉬다. 한숨 쉬다: *She sighed with satisfaction.* 그녀는 만족하며 한숨을 내쉬었다.

sigh² *n* an act of SIGHing, or the sound of sighing ‖ 한숨 쉬는 동작이나 한숨 쉬는 소리. 한숨(소리): *Judy sat down with a sigh of relief.* 주디는 안도의 한숨을 쉬며 앉았다.

sight¹ /saɪt/ *n*
1 ▶ABILITY TO SEE 볼 수 있는 능력◀ [U] the physical ability to see ‖ 볼 수 있는 신체적 능력. 시력. 시각: *My grandmother is losing her sight.* 나의 할머니는 시력이 약해지신다.
2 ▶ACT OF SEEING 보는 행위◀ [singular, U] the act of seeing something ‖ 사물을 보는 행위. 봄. 보기. 일견: *I always faint at the sight of blood.* 나는 피를 보면 언제나 기절한다. / *We caught sight of* (=suddenly saw) *Henry as we turned the corner.* 우리는 모퉁이를 돌다가 헨리의 모습을 봤다.
3 ▶STH YOU SEE 보는 것◀ something you can see, especially if it is something beautiful, unusual etc. ‖ 특히 아름답거나 유별나거나 등 한 경우 볼 수 있을 만한 것. 광경. 장관. 명소. 관광지: *The Wrigley Building is one of the most famous sights in Chicago.* 리글리 빌딩은 시카고에서 가장 유명한 명소 중의 하나다.
4 in/within sight a) inside the area that you can see ‖ 볼 수 있는 범위 안에. 시야[시계] 내에. 보이는 거리에: *There was nobody in sight.* 아무도 눈에 띄지 않았다[없었다]. / *We camped within sight of the beach.* 우리는 해변이 보이는 곳에서 캠핑을 했다. **b)** likely to happen soon ‖ 곧 일어날 것 같은. 가까워진. 근접한: *Peace is in sight.* 평화가 바로 눈앞에 있다.
5 out of sight outside the area that you can see ‖ 볼 수 있는 범위 밖에. 시야[시계] 밖의. 안 보이는 거리에: *The police parked down the road, out of sight of the house.* 경찰은 그 집이 안 보이는 도로에 주차를 했다.
6 lose sight of to be so concerned with unimportant details that you forget to think about the thing you are supposed to be doing or aiming for ‖ 중요하지 않은 세부 사항에 너무 관심을 기울여서 마땅히 해야 하거나 목표로 삼은 것에 대해서 생각할 것을 잊다. …을 못 보고 놓치다[잊어버리다]: *I think the party has lost sight of its ideals.* 그 정당은 (정작 중요한) 자신의 이상은 잊어버린 것 같아.
7 out of sight, out of mind used in order to say that you will soon forget someone or something if you do not see him, her, or it for a period of time ‖ 한 동안 사람이나 사물을 보지 않으면 곧 잊어버릴 거라고 말하는 데에 쓰여. 눈에서 멀어지면 마음에서도 멀어진다
8 ▶ON A WEAPON 무기에서◀ [C usually plural] the part of a gun or weapon that helps you aim at something ‖ 사물을 겨누게 해주는 총이나 무기의 부분. 가늠쇠[자] —see usage note at VIEW²

sight² *v* [T] to see something from a long distance away, especially something you have been looking for ‖ 특히 찾고 있는 것을 멀리 떨어져서 보다. …을 발견[목격]하다: *Two bears have been sighted in the area.* 곰 두 마리가 그 지역에서 목격돼 왔다.

sight·ed /ˈsaɪtɪd/ *adj* able to see; not blind ‖ 볼 수 있는. 눈이 보이는. 시력이 있는; 눈멀지 않은

sight·ing /ˈsaɪtɪŋ/ *n* an occasion when something is seen, especially when it is something unusual or rare ‖ 특히 별나거나 희귀한 것이 보이는 때. 목격. 발견: *Many UFO sightings have been reported in the area.* 그 지역에서 많은 UFO 목격 사실이 보고되었다.

sight·less /ˈsaɪtlɪs/ *adj* LITERARY blind ‖ 눈먼. 눈이 안 보이는

sight·read /ˈsaɪtˌrid/ *v* [I, T] to play or sing written music that you have never looked at or practiced before ‖ 전에 한 번도 보거나 연습한 적이 없는 악보상의

음악을 연주하거나 노래부르다. (…을) 한 번 보고 연주[노래]하다

sight·see·ing /'saɪt‚siːŋ/ *n* [U] the activity of visiting famous or interesting places, especially as a tourist ‖ 특히 관광객으로서 유명하거나 흥미 있는 장소를 방문하는 활동. 관광. 구경: *After the conference was over, we went sightseeing.* 우리는 회의가 끝나고 나서 관광을 했다. **– sightseer** *n*

sign¹ /saɪn/ *n* **1** a piece of paper, metal etc. in a public place that gives information such as directions or prices, or tells people what to do ‖ 방향이나 가격 등의 정보를 제공하거나 사람들에게 무엇을 할지를 알리는 공공 장소에 있는 종이·금속 등의 조각. 표지. 간판: *Just follow the signs that say "Montlake Bridge."* "몬트레이크 다리"라고 씌어진 표지판만 그대로 따라가라. / *a no smoking sign* 금연 표지판 **2** an event, fact etc. that shows that something exists or is happening, or that it will happen in the future ‖ 어떤 일이 존재하거나 일어나고 있다는 또는 장차 일어날 것이라는 것을 나타내는 사건·사실 등. 징조. 징후: *The train showed no signs of slowing down.* 기차의 속도는 줄어들 조짐을 전혀 보이지 않았다. / *Extreme tiredness is an early sign of the disease.* 극도의 피곤함은 질병의 초기 징후이다. **3** a picture or shape that has a particular meaning; SYMBOL ‖ 특정한 의미를 가지는 그림이나 모양. 기호. 부호; 冏 symbol: *A dollar sign looks like "$."* 달러 기호는 "$"처럼 생겼다. **4** a movement or sound that you make without speaking, in order to tell someone something ‖ 남에게 어떤 것을 말하려고 말없이 하는 동작이나 소리. 신호. 몸짓. 손짓: *a sign of greeting* 인사의 표시 **5** one of the SYMBOLs of the ZODIAC ‖ 황도 12궁의 상징들 중의 하나. 궁: *I'm a Cancer. What's your sign?* 나는 게자리야. 너는 무슨 자리니?

sign² *v* **1** [I, T] to write your name on a letter or document to show that you wrote it or agree with it ‖ 편지나 서류에 그것을 썼거나 그것에 동의한다는 것을 나타내기 위해 이름을 쓰다. 서명하다: *Please sign on the dotted line.* 점선에 서명해 주십시오. / *Sign your name here.* 이곳에 서명해 주십시오. / *Did you sign the check?* 수표에

sign

signature

서명했니? **2** [T] to officially agree to employ someone ‖ 사람을 고용하기로 공식적으로 동의하다. (고용) 계약에 서명하다. …과 계약하다: *Columbia Records signed her to a three-year contract.* 컬럼비아 음반 회사는 그녀와 3년 계약에 서명했다. **3** [I] to tell someone something by using movements ‖ 동작을 사용해서 남에게 어떤 것을 말하다. 신호하다. 몸짓[손짓]으로 알리다: *She signed to us to get out of the way.* 그녀는 우리에게 비키라고 손짓을 했다.

sign sth ↔ **away** *phr v* [T] to sign a document that gives something you own to someone else ‖ 소유하고 있는 것을 다른 사람에게 넘기는 서류에 서명하다. …을 서명하여 양도하다: *The Puyallup Tribe signed away much of their land rights.* 푸얄럽족은 토지 소유권의 많은 부분을 양도해 버렸다.

sign for sth *phr v* [T] to sign a document to prove that you have received something ‖ 어떤 것을 받았다는 것을 증명하려고 서류에 서명하다. …을 접수 확인하다[서명하다]: *Can you please sign for the package?* 소포인수에 서명해 주시겠습니까?

sign in *phr v* [I] to write your name in a book when you enter a hotel, an office building etc. ‖ 호텔·사무실 건물 등에 들어갈 때 명부에 이름을 쓰다. 서명하고 들어가다

sign off *phr v* **1** [I] to say goodbye at the end of a radio or television broadcast, or at the end of a letter ‖ 라디오나 텔레비전 방송의 끝에, 또는 편지의 끝에 작별 인사를 하다. 끝 인사를 하다 **2** [I, T **sign** sth ↔ **off**] to officially say or show that you approve of a document, plan, or idea ‖ 서류[계획, 아이디어]를 찬성한다고 공식적으로 말하거나 나타내다. (…을) 인정[승인]하다: *Garcia claimed he had never signed off on the deal.* 가르시아는 그 거래를 승인한 적이 결코 없다고 주장했다.

sign out *phr v* **1** [I] to write your name in a book when you leave a hotel, an office building etc. ‖ 호텔·사무실 건물 등을 떠날 때 명부에 이름을 쓰다. 서명하고 나가다 **2** [T **sign** sth **out**] to write your name on a form or in a book to show that you have taken or borrowed something ‖ 어떤 것을 가져갔거나 빌렸다는 것을 나타내려고 서식이나 명부에 이름을 쓰다. 서명 반출하다: *Who do I see about signing out a company car?* 회사차를 빌리려면 누구에게 찾아가 봐야죠?

sign sth ↔ **over** *phr v* [T] to sign an

official document that gives something you own to someone else ‖ 소유하고 있는 것을 다른 사람에게 넘기는 서류에 서명하다. 서명하여 양도하다: *Dad signed his truck over to me when he got his new car.* 아빠는 새 차를 샀을 때 나에게 트럭을 양도하셨다.

sign up *phr v* **1** [T **sign** sb ↔ **up**] to officially allow someone to work for a company or organization ‖ 사람이 회사나 조직에서 일하는 것을 공식적으로 허가하다. …을 (계약하여) 고용하다: *The Yankees signed him up when he finished college.* 양키즈 팀은 그가 대학을 끝마쳤을 때 그와 선수 입단 계약을 했다. **2** [I] to put your name on a list because you want to take a class, belong to a group etc ‖ 수업을 듣거나 집단에 소속되고 싶어서 (가입) 명부에 이름을 올리다. 등록하다: *About 20 people signed up for the workshop.* 약 20명 정도의 사람들이 그 워크숍에 등록했다.

sig·nal' /'sɪgnəl/ *n* **1** a sound, action, or event that gives information or tells someone to do something ‖ 정보를 주거나 어떤 사람에게 어떤 것을 하라고 알리는 소리[동작, 사건]. 신호: *The runners waited for the signal to go.* 주자들은 출발 신호를 기다렸다. / *a traffic signal* (=a light telling drivers when to stop or go) 교통 신호 **2** a series of light waves, sound waves etc. that carry an image, sound, or message to something such as a radio or television ‖ 영상[소리, 메시지]을 라디오나 텔레비전 등에 보내는 일련의 빛이나 소리의 파동 등. 신호(파): *broadcasting signals* 방송 신호

signal² *v* **1** [I, T] to make a movement or sound, without speaking, that gives information or tells someone to do something ‖ 말을 하지 않고 정보를 주거나 어떤 사람에게 어떤 것을 하라고 알리는 동작이나 소리를 하다. …을 신호로 알리다. 신호를 보내다: *Marshall pushed his plate away and signaled for coffee.* 마셜은 접시를 옆으로 치우고는 커피를 달라는 신호를 했다. **2** [T] to be a sign or proof of something ‖ 어떤 것의 징조나 증거가 되다. …의 전조가 되다: *The March elections signaled the end of a nine-year civil war.* 3월 선거는 9년간의 내전을 종식하는 신호탄이 됐다. **3** [T] to make something clear by what you say or do ‖ 말이나 행동으로 어떤 것을 분명하게 하다. …임을 알리다: *Carter has signaled his intention to run for mayor.* 카터는 시장에 입후보하겠다는 의도를 표시했다.

signal³ *adj* FORMAL important ‖ 중요한. 현저한. 주목할 만한: *a signal achievement/failure* 탁월한 위업[심각한 실패]

sig·na·to·ry /'sɪgnə,tɔri/ *n* FORMAL one of the people or countries that sign an agreement ‖ 협정에 서명한 사람들이나 국가들 중의 하나. 서명[조인]자[국]

sig·na·ture /'sɪgnətʃɚ/ *n* your name written the way you usually write it, for example at the end of a letter, on a check etc. ‖ 예를 들면 편지의 끝·수표 등에 항상 쓰는 방식으로 쓰는 이름. 서명 —see picture at SIGN²

sig·nif·i·cance /sɪg'nɪfəkəns/ *n* [U] the importance or meaning of something, especially something that might affect you in the future ‖ 특히 장차 영향을 미칠지도 모를 것의 중요성이나 의미. 중대성. 의의: *I hope you all understand the significance of this contract.* 여러분 모두가 이 계약의 중대성을 잘 이해하시길 바랍니다.

sig·nif·i·cant /sɪg'nɪfəkənt/ *adj* **1** noticeable or important ‖ 주목할 만하거나 중요한. 중대한. 의의 있는: *Picasso is one of the most significant artists of the 20th century.* 피카소는 20세기의 가장 중요한 예술가들 중의 한 명이다. **2** having a special meaning that is not known to everyone ‖ 모든 사람들이 다 알지는 못하는 특별한 의미를 가지다. 의미심장한. 뜻이 있는 듯한: *Ginger and Tom exchanged significant looks.* 진저와 톰은 의미심장한 표정을 교환했다. — **significantly** *adv* —opposite INSIGNIFICANT

significant oth·er /.,... '../ *n* HUMOROUS someone you have a serious sexual relationship with ‖ 깊은 성관계를 맺고 있는 사람. 연인. 애인

sig·ni·fy /'sɪgnə,faɪ/ *v* [T] **1** to represent, mean, or be a sign of something ‖ 어떤 것을 상징하다[의미하다, 어떤 것의 징조가 되다]. …을 알리다. …의 전조가 되다: *Changes in the weather may signify that pollution is affecting our climate.* 날씨의 변화는 오염이 기후에 영향을 미치고 있다는 의미가 될 수도 있다. **2** to express a wish, feeling, or opinion by doing something ‖ 어떤 것을 함으로써 소망[감정, 의견]을 표현하다. …을 나타내다. 표명하다: *Everyone nodded to signify their agreement.* 모두가 고개를 끄덕여 동의의 뜻을 표명했다.

sign·ing /'saɪnɪŋ/ *n* [U] the act of signing something such as an agreement or a contract ‖ 협정이나 계약 등에 서명하는 행위. 서명: *Twelve representatives were present for the signing of the agreement.* 12명의 대표들이 협정 조인(식)에 참석했다.

sign lan·guage /'. ˌ../ *n* [C, U] a language that uses hand movements instead of spoken words, used by people who cannot hear ‖ 말 대신에 손동작을 사용하는, 청각 장애자들에 의해 사용되는 언어. 수화

sign·post /'saɪnpoʊst/ *n* **1** something that is used for holding a street sign up ‖ 도로 표지를 높이 고정하는 데에 사용하는 것. 도로 표지 기둥 **2** something that shows you what is happening or what you should do ‖ 일어나고 있는 일이나 해야 하는 일을 보여 주는 것. 단서. 지표. 지침: *The employment figures are a key signpost of the economy's performance.* 고용 수치는 경제 성과에 대한 주요 지표이다.

si·lence¹ /'saɪləns/ *n* **1** [U] complete absence of sound or noise ‖ 소리나 소음이 전혀 없음. 고요. 정적: *Nothing disturbed the silence of the night.* 아무 것도 밤의 정적을 깨뜨리지 않았다. **2** [C, U] complete quiet because no one is talking, or a period of complete quiet ‖ 아무도 말하지 않아서 완전히 조용함, 또는 이 완전히 조용한 시간. 침묵. 무언: *There was a long silence before he spoke again.* 그는 긴 침묵 후에 다시 말했다. / *The judge called for silence in the courtroom.* 판사는 법정에서 정숙하라고 요구했다.

silence² *v* [T] **1** to make someone stop criticizing or giving his/her opinions ‖ 남이 비판하거나 의견을 말하는 것을 못 하게 하다. …을 침묵시키다: *Independent media reports have been silenced by the state.* 주당국은 독자적인 언론 보도에 재갈을 물렸다. **2** to stop someone from talking, or to stop something from making noise ‖ 남이 말하는 것을 막거나 어떤 것이 시끄럽게 하지 못하게 하다. …을 조용하게 만들다: *Kim tried to silence the shrieking baby by giving her a bottle.* 킴은 빽빽 울어대는 아기에게 젖병을 물려 조용하게 하려고 애썼다.

si·lenc·er /'saɪlənsɚ/ *n* a thing that is put on the end of a gun so that it makes less noise when it is fired ‖ 총구에 끼워서 발사할 때 소리를 덜 나게 하는 것. 소음기

si·lent /'saɪlənt/ *adj* **1** not saying anything or making any noise; quiet ‖ 아무 말도 하지 않거나 아무 소리도 내지 않

는. 말없는. 고요한; 조용한: *The crowd fell silent* (=became quiet) *when the President appeared.* 대통령이 나타나자 청중은 조용해졌다. **2** failing or refusing to talk about something ‖ 어떤 것에 대해 말하지 못하거나 말하지 않는. 말이 안 나오는. 무언의: *John remained silent when asked about the money.* 존은 돈에 대해 질문 받았을 때 아무 말이 없었다. **3** **give sb the silent treatment** to not talk to someone to show that you are angry or upset about something s/he did ‖ 남이 한 짓에 대해서 화가 나거나 기분이 상한 것을 나타내려고 그 사람과 말을 하지 않다. 남을 침묵으로 대하다[무시하다] **– silently** *adv*

silent part·ner /ˌ.. '../ *n* someone who owns part of a business but does not make decisions about how it operates ‖ 사업체의 일부분을 소유하지만 운영 방식에 대해서는 결정을 하지 않는 사람. 익명 사원

sil·hou·ette¹ /ˌsɪluˈɛt, 'sɪluˌɛt/ *n* a dark shape or shadow, seen against a light background ‖ 빛을 배경으로 해서 보이는 어두운 형태나 그림자. 실루엣

silhouette² *v* [T] to appear as a SILHOUETTE ‖ 실루엣으로 나타나다. …을 실루엣으로 나타내다: *skyscrapers silhouetted against the sky* 하늘을 배경으로 음영을 드리운 초고층 빌딩들

sil·i·con /'sɪlɪˌkɑn, -kən/ *n* [U] an ELEMENT that is often used for making glass, bricks, parts for computers etc. ‖ 종종 유리·벽돌·컴퓨터 부품 등을 만드는 데에 쓰이는 원소. 실리콘. 규소

silk /sɪlk/ *n* [C, U] a thin thread produced by a SILKWORM, or the soft, usually shiny cloth made from this thread ‖ 누에가 뽑아내는 가는 실, 또는 이 실로 만든 부드럽고 보통 빛나는 천. 비단. 명주실: *a silk shirt* 비단 셔츠

silk·en /'sɪlkən/ *adj* LITERARY soft and smooth like silk, or made of silk ‖ 비단처럼 부드럽고 매끄러운, 또는 비단으로 만든. 비단 같은. 비단의: *her silken hair* 그녀의 비단결 같은 머리

silk·worm /'sɪlk-wɚm/ *n* a type of CATERPILLAR (=insect) that produces silk ‖ 비단을 뽑아내는 애벌레의 일종. 누에

silk·y /'sɪlki/ *adj* soft and smooth like silk ‖ 비단처럼 부드럽고 매끄러운. 비단결 같은. 비단의: *silky fur* 비단 같은 모피

sill /sɪl/ *n* the narrow flat piece of wood at the base of a window frame ‖ 창틀 바닥의 좁고 납작한 목재 조각. 창턱

sil·ly /'sɪli/ *adj* not sensible or serious; stupid ‖ 지각이 없거나 진지하지 않은. 어

리석은. 우스운; 멍청한: *I felt very silly
wearing that huge hat.* 나는 저 커다란
모자를 쓰고 있으면서 바보처럼 느껴졌다.
/ *a silly joke* 말도 안 되는 농담 –
silliness *n* [U]

si·lo /ˈsaɪloʊ/ *n* **1** a tall round building
used for storing grain, animal food etc.
‖ 곡물·동물 사료 등을 저장하는 데에 사
용하는 높고 둥근 건축물. 사일로 **2** a
large structure under the ground from
which a MISSILE can be fired ‖ 미사일을
발사할 수 있는 지하의 커다란 구조물. 지
하 격납 발사 설비

silt /sɪlt/ *n* [U] sand or mud that is
carried by the water in a river, and
settles in a bend of the river or in the
entrance to a port ‖ 강물에 운반되어 강
의 굽이나 항구의 입구에 가라앉은 모래나
진흙. 침니(沈泥)

sil·ver[1] /ˈsɪlvə/ *n* [U] **1** a valuable shiny
white metal that is an ELEMENT and is
used for making jewelry, spoons etc. ‖
원소로서 보석·숟가락 등을 만드는 데에
사용하는 가치 있고 빛나는 하얀 금속. 은
2 the color of this metal ‖ 이 금속의 색
깔. 은색

silver[2] *adj* **1** made of silver ‖ 은으로 만
든. 은의: *a silver spoon* 은수저 **2** colored
silver ‖ 은색의: *a silver dress* 은색 드레
스 **3 be born with a silver spoon in
your mouth** to be born into a rich
family ‖ 부유한 가정에 태어나다. 행운을
타고 태어나다

silver an·ni·ver·sa·ry /ˌ..ˈ.../ *n* the
date that is exactly 25 years after an
important event, especially a wedding ‖
특히 결혼 등의 중요한 행사 후 정확히 25
년이 되는 날짜. 은혼식

silver med·al /ˌ.. ˈ../ *n* a prize that is
given to someone who finishes second in
a race, competition etc., and that is
usually made of silver ‖ 경주·시합 등에
서 두 번째로 골인한 사람에 수여되는,
보통 은으로 만든 상. 은메달

silver plate /ˌ.. ˈ./ *n* [U] metal with a
thin covering of silver ‖ 은으로 얇게 덮은
금속. 은도금 – **silver-plated** /ˌ.. ˈ../
adj: a silver-plated bowl 은도금한 사발

sil·ver·smith /ˈsɪlvəˌsmɪθ/ *n* someone
who makes things out of silver ‖ 은으로
물건들을 만드는 사람. 은세공사

sil·ver·ware /ˈsɪlvəˌwɛr/ *n* [U] objects
such as knives, spoons, and forks that
are made of silver or any other metal ‖
은이나 다른 금속으로 만든 칼·숟가락·포
크 등의 물건. 은식기류

sim·i·lar /ˈsɪmələ/ *adj* almost the same
but not exactly the same ‖ 거의 똑같지만

정확히 똑같지는 않은. 유사한. 비슷한:
His interests are similar to mine. 그의
관심사는 나와 유사하다. / *The two
paintings are very similar in style.* 그
두 그림은 양식 면에서 매우 흡사하다. /
kids with similar backgrounds 가정 환경
이 비슷한 아이들 —opposite DISSIMILAR

sim·i·lar·i·ty /ˌsɪmə'lærəti/ *n* **1** [U] the
quality of being similar to something
else; RESEMBLANCE ‖ 다른 것과 유사한 특
성. 비슷함. 유사성; 㐀 resemblance:
*There's a similarity between the two
men.* 그 두 남자 사이에는 유사성이 있다.
2 a particular way in which things or
people are similar ‖ 사물이나 사람이 특
정하게 유사함. 유사점. 상사점: *Discuss
the similarities and differences
between the two writers.* 그 두 작가 사
이의 유사점과 상이점에 대해 논하라.

sim·i·lar·ly /ˈsɪmələli/ *adv* in a similar
way ‖ 비슷하거나. 유사하게. 같게: *two
men who were dressed similarly* 비슷하
게 입은 두 사람 / *Men must wear suits;
similarly, women must wear a skirt or
dress and not pants.* 남자는 반드시 양복
을 입어야 하고, 똑같이 여자는 바지가 아
니라 치마나 드레스를 입어야 한다.

sim·i·le /ˈsɪməli/ *n* an expression in
which you compare two things using the
words "like" or "as," for example "as
red as blood" ‖ 예를 들어 "as red as
blood"처럼 "like"나 "as" 등의 단어를 써
서 두 가지 것을 비교하는 표현(법). 직유
(법) —compare METAPHOR

sim·mer /ˈsɪmə/ *v* **1** [I, T] to cook food
slowly and not allow it to boil ‖ 음식을
천천히 익히고 끓지 않게 하다. 서서히 끓
이다. 조리다: *Let the soup simmer for 5
minutes.* 수프를 5분간 서서히 끓게 하세
요. **2 simmer down!** SPOKEN said in
order to tell someone to be less excited
or angry and more calm ‖ 어떤 사람에게
흥분이나 화를 가라앉히고 더 차분해지라
고 말하는 데에 쓰여. 진정해. 그렇게 흥
분하지 마 – **simmer** *n* [singular]

sim·per /ˈsɪmpə/ *v* [I] to smile in a way
that is silly and annoying ‖ 바보 같고 짜
증나게 웃다. 실실 (바보처럼) 웃다. 선웃
음[억지웃음]을 웃다

sim·ple /ˈsɪmpəl/ *adj* **1** not difficult or
complicated; easy ‖ 어렵거나 복잡하지
않은. 간단한; 쉬운: *a simple math
problem* 간단한 수학 문제 **2** without a
lot of decoration or things that are not
necessary; plain ‖ 불필요한 많은 장식이
나 사물들이 없는. 수수한. 장식 없는; 간
결한: *a simple white dress* 수수한 흰 옷
/ *a simple meal* 간단한 식사 —see

picture at ELABORATE¹ **3** not involving anything else ‖ 다른 어떤 것도 포함하지 않은. 순전한. 완전한: *The simple fact/truth is she was hired because she can do the job.* 그녀는 순전히 그 일을 할 수 있어서 고용됐을 뿐이다. ✗DON'T SAY "The fact is simple."✗ "The fact is simple."이라고는 하지 않는다. **4** consisting of only one or a few necessary parts ‖ 단 하나나 몇 가지 필요한 부분들로만 이루어진. 간소한: *simple tools like a hammer and saw* 망치와 톱 같은 간단한 연장들 **5** ordinary and not special in any way ‖ 평범하고 어떤 면으로도 특별하지 않은. 단순한. 평범한: *the simple life of a farmer* 농부의 평범한 생활 **6** OLD-FASHIONED not very intelligent ‖ 그다지 총명하지 않은. 잘 속는. 어수룩한 **7 simple past/present/future** TECHNICAL a tense of a verb that is formed without using a PARTICIPLE ‖ 분사(형)를 사용하지 않고 만들어진 동사의 시제. 단순 과거/현재/미래

simple in·terest /ˌ.. '../ *n* [U] INTEREST that you pay on an amount of money that you INVEST, which does not include the interest that it has earned ‖ 투자금이 벌어들인 이자는 포함되지 않고 투자한 금액에 지불되는 이자. 단리(單利) —compare COMPOUND INTEREST

simple-mind·ed /ˈ.. ˌ.., ˌ.. '../ *adj* not able to understand complicated things; FOOLISH ‖ 복잡한 것들을 이해할 수 없는. 단순한. 모자라는. ⊕ foolish

sim·plic·i·ty /sɪmˈplɪsəti/ *n* [U] **1** the quality of being easy to do or understand, and not complicated ‖ 행하거나 이해하기 쉽고 복잡하지 않은 특성. 간단. 평이. 단순(성): *For the sake of simplicity* (=to make things easier) *the questions can only be answered "True" or "False."* 단순화하기 위해 질문은 오직 "참"이나 "거짓"으로 대답할 수 있다. **2** the quality of being plain rather than having a lot of decoration ‖ 장식이 많기보다 평범한 특성. 검소. 수수

sim·pli·fy /ˈsɪmpləˌfaɪ/ *v* [T] to make something clearer and easier to do or understand ‖ 어떤 것을 더 분명하고 쉽게 행하거나 이해하게 만들다. …을 단순[간단, 평이]하게 하다. 간략[간소]화하다: *How can we simplify these instructions?* 이들 지시문들은 어떻게 간략화할 수 있을까요? – **simplification** /ˌsɪmpləfəˈkeɪʃən/ *n* [U] —see also OVERSIMPLIFY —compare COMPLICATE

sim·plis·tic /sɪmˈplɪstɪk/ *adj* DIS-APPROVING treating difficult subjects

in a way that is too SIMPLE ‖ 어려운 과제를 너무 단순하게 취급하는. 지나치게 단순화한

sim·ply /ˈsɪmpli/ *adv* **1** only; just ‖ 오직. 단지. 그저; 다만: *You can't hit someone simply because you want to.* 단지 네가 그러고 싶다고 해서 어떤 사람을 때릴 수는 없다. **2** used in order to emphasize what you are saying; really ‖ 말하고 있는 것을 강조하는 데에 쓰여. 아주. 완전히; 정말로: *What he said simply isn't true!* 그가 한 말은 완전히 사실이 아니다! **3** in a way that is easy to understand ‖ 이해하기 쉽게. 간단[평이, 명료]하게: *To put it simply* (=explain it in a simple way), *the bank decided not to lend us the money.* 간단히 말해서 은행에서 우리에게 돈을 빌려주지 않기로 결정했다. **4** in a plain and ordinary way ‖ 간소하고 평범하게. 수수[검소]하게: *Alanna was dressed quite simply.* 알라나는 아주 검소하게 차려 입었다.

sim·u·late /ˈsɪmyəˌleɪt/ *v* [T] to make or do something that is not real but looks, sounds, or feels as though it is real ‖ 어떤 것이 실재가 아니지만 실재하는 것처럼 보이게[소리 나게, 느끼게] 만들어나다. 가상[모의] 상황을 조성하다. 실제를 가정하다: *an experiment to simulate the effects of being weightless* 무중력 (상태) 효과의 가상 실험 – **simulator** *n* : *a flight simulator* 모의 비행 실습기 – **simulated** *adj*

sim·u·la·tion /ˌsɪmyəˈleɪʃən/ *n* [C, U] something you do or make in order to practice what you would do in a real situation ‖ 실제 상황에서 하게 될 것을 연습하기 위해 하거나 만드는 것. 모의실험. 시뮬레이션: *Students have had to learn about the planes by computer simulation and from textbooks.* 학생들은 컴퓨터 모의 실험과 교재로 항공기에 대해 배워야 했다.

si·mul·ta·ne·ous /ˌsaɪməlˈteɪniəs/ *adj* happening or done at exactly the same time ‖ 정확히 같은 시간에 일어나거나 행해지는. 동시에 존재하는[작용하는]: *a simultaneous broadcast on TV and radio* TV와 라디오로의 동시 방송 – **simultaneously** *adv*

sin¹ /sɪn/ *n* **1** something you do that is against religious laws ‖ 종교 율법에 반해서 행한 것. 죄. 죄악. 죄업: *the sin of greed* 탐욕의 죄 **2** [singular] INFORMAL something that you do not approve of ‖ 용인하지 않는 것. 위배. 위반. 반칙 (행위): *It's a sin to waste food – eat what's on your plate!* 음식을 낭비하는 것은 죄악

이다. 접시에 있는 것을 다 먹어라!

sin² *v* **-nned, -nning** [I] to do something wrong that is against religious laws ‖ 종교적인 율법에 어긋난 잘못을 저지르다. 죄를 짓다[범하다]

since¹ /sɪns/ *conj* **1** at or from a particular time in the past ‖ 과거의 특정 시간에 또는 특정 시간으로부터. 그 이후 [이래]: *I haven't seen him since we graduated from high school.* 나는 고등학교를 졸업한 이래 그를 보지 못했다. **2** during the period of time after another time or event in the past ‖ 과거의 또 다른 시점 또는 사건 이후의 시간 동안. 그때부터 지금까지 사이에. 그 이후로 현재까지: *Jim's been working at Citibank ever since he finished college.* 짐은 대학을 마친 이래 죽 시티뱅크에서 근무해 왔다. **3** because ‖ … 때문에. …이므로: *You'll have to get up early, since the bus leaves at 7 a.m.* 버스가 아침 7시에 떠나기 때문에 너는 일찍 일어나야 할 것이다. —see usage note at AGO

since² *prep* **1** at or from a time or event in the past ‖ 과거의 시점이나 사건에서 또는 그로부터. …이후 계속. …부터 지금[이때]까지 계속: *I've been here since 8 o'clock.* 나는 8시부터 여기 있었다. / *Trade has improved since the end of the war.* 종전 이래로 무역 거래가 개선되어 왔다. **2 since when?** SPOKEN used in questions to show anger or surprise ‖ 분노나 놀람을 나타내기 위해 의문문에 쓰여. 언제부터 …되었니?: *Since when does having a fast car mean you're a success?* 언제부터 빠른 차를 갖는 것이 성공을 의미하게 됐느냐?

USAGE NOTE since and for

When you use **since** and **for** with the PRESENT PERFECT tense, they both mean "from a time in the past until now." Use **since** with specific dates: *I've lived here since 1996.* Use **for** with periods of time: *I've lived here for two years.* ✗DON'T SAY "I've lived here since two years."✗
since와 **for**는 현재 완료 시제와 함께 쓸 때 둘 다 "과거 한 시점에서 지금까지"를 의미한다. **since**는 구체적인 날짜와 함께 쓴다: 나는 1996년 이래 여기서 살아왔다. **for**는 시간의 기간과 함께 쓴다: 나는 여기서 2년 동안 살아왔다. "I've lived here since two years."라고는 하지 않는다.

---

since³ *adv* **1** at a time in the past after another time or event in the past ‖ 과거

의 또 다른 시간이나 사건 후 과거의 한 시점에. (현재보다) …전에. 그 후[이래]: *His ex-wife has since remarried, but he's still single.* 그의 전 부인은 그 후 결혼했지만 그는 아직도 독신이다. **2** for the whole of a period of time after an event or time in the past ‖ 과거의 사건이나 시점 이후 그 모든 시간 동안. 그 이후 계속해서. 그때부터 지금까지 죽: *He graduated in 1983 and has lived in San Diego ever since.* ‖ 그는 1983년에 졸업했고 그 이래 죽 샌디에이고에 살았다.

sin·cere /sɪnˈsɪr/ *adj* honest and true, or based on what you really feel or believe ‖ 정직하고 진실한. 또는 진정으로 느끼거나 믿는 것에 기초한. 성실한. 솔직한. 거짓[꾸밈] 없는: *As a friend, he is both sincere and loyal.* 친구로서 그는 성실하면서도 충직하다. / *a sincere apology* 솔직한 사과 —opposite INSINCERE

sin·cere·ly /sɪnˈsɪrli/ *adv* **1** in a sincere way ‖ 진실하게. 충심[진심]으로. 성실하게: *I sincerely hope we meet again.* 나는 진심으로 우리가 다시 만나게 되기를 바랍니다. **2 Sincerely/Sincerely yours** an expression you write at the end of a formal letter before you sign your name ‖ 격식체의 편지 끝에 서명하기 전에 쓰는 표현. 경구(敬具)

sin·cer·i·ty /sɪnˈsɛrəti/ *n* [U] the quality of being honest, and really meaning or believing what you say ‖ 정직하고 말하는 바를 실제로 의미하거나 믿는 특성. 성실. 진실. 솔직. 진심

sin·ew /ˈsɪnju/ *n* [C, U] TECHNICAL a strong CORD in the body that connects a muscle to a bone ‖ 근육을 뼈에 연결하는 몸 속의 강한 인대. 힘줄

sin·ew·y /ˈsɪnjui/ *adj* having strong muscles ‖ 강한 근육을 가진. 건강한. 근육이 불거진: *sinewy arms* 근육질의 팔 (뚝)

sin·ful /ˈsɪnfəl/ *adj* **1** morally wrong; WICKED ‖ 도덕적으로 잘못된. 사악한. 죄 많은; ⓟ wicked: *a sinful man* 사악한 사람 **2** INFORMAL very bad or wrong ‖ 매우 나쁘거나 잘못된. 그릇된. 치욕[수치]스런: *a sinful waste of money/time* 돈[시간]의 부끄러운 낭비

sing /sɪŋ/ *v* **sang, sung, singing 1** [I, T] to make musical sounds, songs etc. with your voice ‖ 목소리로 음악적인 소리·노래 등을 하다. 노래하다: *Do you like singing folk songs?* 포크송[민요] 부르기를 좋아하십니까? / *Jana sings in the church choir.* 제이나는 교회 성가대에서 노래한다. **2** [I] if birds sing, they produce high musical sounds ‖ 새가 날카

로운 음악 소리를 내다. 새가 울다. 지저 귀다 **3 sing sb to sleep** to sing to a child until s/he goes to sleep ‖ 아이가 잠 들 때까지 노래를 불러주다. 자장가를 불 러주다 **- singing** n [U]: *a career in singing* 성악[가수] 경력

sing along *phr v* [I] to sing with someone else who is already singing or playing music ‖ 이미 노래하고 있거나 음 악을 연주하고 있는 어떤 사람과 같이 노 래하다. 맞춰서 노래하다. 합창하다

sing out *phr v* [I, T] to sing or shout loudly and clearly ‖ 크고 분명하게 노래 하거나 외치다. 큰 소리로 외치다[노래하 다]. 고함치다

sing. the written abbreviation of SINGULAR ‖ singular의 약어

singe /sɪndʒ/ v [I, T] to burn something slightly on the surface or edge, or to be burned in this way ‖ 사물의 표면이나 가 장자리를 약간 태우다, 또는 이렇게 태워 지다. 눋다. 눌리다. 그슬다. 그슬리다: *Fortunately, the fire only singed his hair.* 다행히 그 화재로 그는 머리카락만 그슬렸을 뿐이다. **- singe** n

sing·er /ˈsɪŋɚ/ n someone who sings, especially as a job ‖ 특히 직업으로서 노 래하는 사람. 가수. 성악가: *an opera singer* 오페라 가수

sin·gle[1] /ˈsɪŋɡəl/ adj **1** only one ‖ 단 하 나의. 유일한. 하나뿐인: *We lost the game by a single point.* 우리는 단 한 점 차로 시합에서 졌다. / *a single sheet of paper* 단 한 장의 종이 **2** not married ‖ 결혼하지 않은. 독신의. 미혼의: *Terry is 34 years old and he's still single.* 테리는 34세이고 아직도 독신이다. / *a club for single men/women* 독신 남성용[여성용] 클럽 **3** intended to be used by only one person ‖ 단 한 사람이 사용하도록 의도된. 혼자만의. 일인용의: *a single room/bed* ‖ 독실[1인용 침대] **—compare** DOUBLE[1] **4** used in order to emphasize a separate thing ‖ 분리된 것을 강조하는 데에 쓰여. 개개의. 각기의: *The single biggest/ greatest problem we have is money.* 우리가 가진 각자의 최대 문제는 돈이다. / *She visits her mother every single day.* 그녀는 매일매일 어머니를 방문한 다.

single[2] n **1** a musical recording of only one song ‖ 단 한 곡의 음악 녹음. 싱글판: *Have you heard his new single?* 그의 새 싱글판 들어봤어? **2** a one-dollar bill ‖ 1 달러짜리 지폐 **—see also** SINGLES

single[3] v

single sb/sth ↔ **out** *phr v* [T] to choose someone or something from among a group, especially in order to praise or criticize him, her, or it ‖ 특히 칭찬하기 나 비난하기 위해 집단 중에서 사람이나 사물을 뽑다. 선발[선출]하다. …에서 선 택하다: *The medical center has been singled out for criticism because of its high death rates.* 그 의료 센터는 높은 사 망률 때문에 비난의 대상이 되었다.

sin·gle-breast·ed /ˌ.. ˈ.../ adj a single-breasted jacket (=coat) has one row of buttons on the front ‖ 재킷[상의] 이 앞쪽에 단추가 한 줄인. 싱글형의

single file /ˌ.. ˈ./ n [U] **in single file** in a line with one person behind the other ‖ 차례로 다른 사람 뒤에 줄을 지어. 일렬 (종대)로: *Soldiers marched in single file along the quay.* 군인들은 부두를 따라서 일렬종대로 행진했다.

single-hand·ed·ly /ˌ.. ˈ.../, **single-handed** /ˌ.. ˈ../ adv done by one person with no help from anyone else ‖ 전혀 다른 사람의 도움 없이 한 사람에 의 해 행해져. 단독으로. 독력으로

single-mind·ed /ˌ.. ˈ.../ adj having one clear purpose and working hard to achieve it ‖ 하나의 분명한 목적을 가지고 그것을 달성하기 위해 열심히 일하는. 외 곬의. 일편단심의. 한결같은: *a single-minded determination to succeed* 성공 하려는 한결같은 결의

sin·gles /ˈsɪŋɡlz/ n [plural] people who are not married ‖ 결혼하지 않은 사 람들. 독신자들: *a singles bar* (=where single people can go to drink and meet people) 독신 남녀 전용 바

sin·gly /ˈsɪŋgli/ adv one at a time ‖ 한 번에 하나씩. 따로따로. 각각: *We sell doughnuts singly or by the dozen.* 우리 는 도넛을 하나씩 또는 12개들이 한 상자 씩 판다.

sing·song /ˈsɪŋsɔŋ/ n [singular] a way of speaking in which your voice rises and falls repeatedly in a boring way ‖ 목 소리가 지루하게 반복적으로 오르내리며 말하는 방식. 단조로운 억양[말투] **- singsong** adj: *a singsong voice* 단조로 운 목소리

sin·gu·lar /ˈsɪŋgyələ/ n **the singular** TECHNICAL in grammar, the form of a word that represents only one person or thing. For example, "child" is in the singular ‖ 문법에서 단 한 사람이나 사물 을 나타내는 단어 형태. 단수(형). 예를 들어 "child"는 단수형이다 **- singular** adj: *a singular noun/verb* 단수 명사 [동 사] **—compare** PLURAL **—see study note on page 940**

sin·gu·lar·ly /ˈsɪŋgyələli/ adv FORMAL

very noticeably; PARTICULARLY ‖ 매우 눈에 띄게. 두드러지게; ㉤ particularly: *She wore a singularly inappropriate dress to the ceremony.* 그녀는 그 의식에는 유난히 어울리지 않는 옷을 입었다.

sin·is·ter /'sɪnɪstə/ *adj* seeming to be bad or evil ‖ 나쁘거나 악해 보이는. 불길한. 사악한: *There was something sinister about the way he looked.* 그가 바라보는 눈길이 왠지 불길해 보였다.

sink¹ /sɪŋk/ *v* **sank** or **sunk, sunk, sinking**

1 ▶IN WATER 물 속에◀ [I, T] to go down or make something go down below the surface of water ‖ 수면 아래로 내려가다, 또는 사물을 내려가게 하다. 가라앉다[앉히다]. 침몰하다[시키다]: *Bill dove for his wallet, but it sank to the bottom of the lake.* 빌은 지갑을 찾으러 잠수했지만 그것은 호수 바닥까지 가라앉았다. / *The submarine sank four ships before it was destroyed.* 그 잠수함은 격침되기 전에 4척의 배를 침몰시켰다. — compare DROWN

2 ▶MOVE DOWNWARD 내려가다◀ a) [I] to fall down heavily, especially because you are weak or tired ‖ 특히 약하거나 피곤해서 무겁게 떨어지다. 주저앉다. 무너지듯 쓰러지다: *Lee sank into a chair and went to sleep.* 리는 의자에 주저앉아 잠들어 버렸다. **b)** [I] to move down slowly to a lower level ‖ 더 낮은 수준[위치]으로 천천히 내려가다. 하강하다. 떨어지다. 점차 낮아지다: *The sun sank behind the horizon.* 해가 지평선 너머로 졌다.

3 ▶GET WORSE 나빠지다◀ [I] to gradually get into a worse state ‖ 점차 나쁜 상태로 들어가다. …에 빠지다. 쇠약해지다. 악화되다: *Krista could see Ari sinking into depression.* 크리스타는 아리가 우울증에 빠져드는 것을 알 수 있었다.

4 ▶DECREASE 감소하다◀ [I] to decrease in amount, number, value etc. ‖ 양·수·가치 등에서 감소하다. 줄어들다. 낮아지다: *House prices in the area are sinking fast.* 그 지역의 주택 가격이 급속히 떨어지고 있다.

5 be sunk INFORMAL to be in a situation in which you are certain to fail or have a lot of problems ‖ 확실히 실패하거나 많은 문제점을 가진 상태로 되다. 영락[파멸]하다. 끝장나다: *If he doesn't lend us the money, we're sunk!* 그가 우리에게 그 돈을 빌려주지 않으면 우리는 끝장이다!

6 your heart sinks/your spirits sink if your heart or spirits sink, you lose your

hope or confidence ‖ 희망이나 자신감을 잃다. 의기소침하다. 낙심하다

7 ▶MONEY 돈◀ [T] to spend a lot of money on something; INVEST ‖ 어떤 일에 많은 돈을 쓰다. …에 투자하다; ㉤ invest: *They had sunk thousands into that house.* 그들은 그 집에 수천 달러의 돈을 들였다.

8 ▶SPORTS 스포츠◀ [T] to get a basketball or GOLF ball into a basket or hole ‖ 농구공이나 골프공을 바스켓이나 홀에 넣다

sink in *phr v* [I] if information, facts etc. sink in, you begin to understand them or realize their full meaning ‖ 정보·사실 등을 이해하거나 그것들의 완전한 의미를 깨닫기 시작하다. 마음에 스며들다[새겨지다]: *At first, what she said didn't really sink in.* 처음에는 그녀가 한 말이 정말로 이해되지 않았다.

sink² *n* an open container in a kitchen or BATHROOM that you fill with water to wash dishes, your hands etc. ‖ 접시·손 등을 씻기 위해 물을 채우는, 부엌이나 욕실의 뚜껑 없는 용기. 세면대. 개수[싱크]대 —see picture at KITCHEN

sink·hole /'sɪŋkhoʊl/ *n* a hole in the ground that is made when the roof of a CAVE falls in ‖ 동굴의 천장이 무너져 내려 생긴 땅에 난 구덩이. 함몰지(陷沒地)

sink·ing /'sɪŋkɪŋ/ *adj* **a sinking feeling** a feeling that you get when you realize that something very bad is beginning to happen ‖ 아주 나쁜 일이 일어나려 한다는 것을 인식할 때 드는 느낌. 불길한 예감

sin·ner /'sɪnə/ *n* someone who does something wrong that is against religious laws ‖ 종교 율법에 어긋나는 잘못을 한 사람. 종교[도덕]상의 죄인

si·nus /'saɪnəs/ *n* TECHNICAL one of the pair of hollow spaces in the bones of your face behind your nose ‖ 코 뒤쪽 얼굴뼈 속에 있는 한 쌍의 빈 공간 중의 하나. 부비강(副鼻腔)

sip¹ /sɪp/ *v* [I, T] to drink something slowly, swallowing only small amounts ‖ 물과 소량만을 삼키면서 어떤 것을 천천히 마시다. …을 홀짝홀짝[조금씩] 마시다: *Mrs. Hong sat sipping her tea.* 홍 여사는 차를 홀짝거리며 앉아 있었다.

sip² *n* a very small amount of a drink ‖ 매우 소량의 음료. 한 모금: *He took a sip of coffee.* 그는 커피 한 모금을 마셨다.

si·phon¹ /'saɪfən/ *n* a bent tube that you use to get liquid out of a container by holding one end of the tube at a lower level than the container ‖ 관의 한쪽 끝을 용기보다 낮은 위치에 두어서 용

기에서 액체를 빼내는 데 쓰는 구부러진
관. 사이펀. 흡입관

siphon² *v* [T] **1** to remove liquid from a
container using a SIPHON ‖ 사이펀을 써서
용기에서 액체를 옮기다. …을 사이펀으로
빨아들이다 **2** to take money from an
organization's account over a period of
time, especially secretly ‖ 특히 비밀리에
일정 기간에 걸쳐 조직의 계좌로부터
돈을 취하다. 몰래 빼돌리다. (부정하게)
유용하다: *The cash was stolen,
siphoned off to the black market.* 그 현
금은 도난당해 암시장으로 빼돌려졌다.

sir /sə/ *n* **1** SPOKEN used in order to
speak politely to a man when you do not
know his name ‖ 이름을 모르는 남자를
정중하게 부르는 데에 쓰여. 님. 귀하. 선
생님: *Can I help you, sir?* 도와드릴까요,
선생님? / *Dear Sir* (=used at the
beginning of a business letter to a man
when you do not know his name) 친애하
는 님께 **2 Sir** a title used before the
name of a KNIGHT ‖ 기사(작위자)의 이름
앞에 쓰는 칭호. …경(卿): *Sir Lancelot* 랜
슬롯 경

sire /saɪə/ *v* [T] to be the father of an
animal, especially a horse ‖ 짐승, 특히
말의 아비가 되다. 종마가 되다 **– sire** *n*

si·ren /'saɪrən/ *n* a piece of equipment
that makes very loud warning sounds,
used on police cars, fire engines etc. ‖
경찰차·소방차 등에 쓰여 매우 큰 경고음
을 내는 장비. 사이렌

sir·loin /'sələɪn/, **sirloin steak** /ˌ..
'./ *n* [C, U] a good piece of meat cut
from the back of a cow ‖ 암소의 등 쪽에
서 잘라낸 맛좋은 고기 부위. 등심

sis·sy /'sɪsi/ *n* INFORMAL a boy that
other boys do not approve of because he
likes doing things that girls do ‖ 여자 아
이들이 하는 행동을 하기 좋아해서 다른
남자 아이들이 용납하지 않는 소년. 계집
애 같은 소년 **– sissy** *adj*

sis·ter /'sɪstə/ *n* **1** a girl or woman
who has the same parents as you ‖ 자신
과 같은 부모를 가진 소녀나 여자. 누이.
자매: *Isn't that your big/little* (=older or
younger) *sister?* 저기 네 언니[여동생]
아니냐? —see picture at FAMILY **2** a
woman who belongs to the same race,
religion, organization etc. as you ‖ 자신
과 같은 인종·종교·조직 등에 소속된 여
자. 여자 동료. 자매 **3** also **Sister** ⇨
NUN: *Sister Frances* 프란시스 자매 **–
sisterly** *adv* —compare BROTHER¹

sis·ter·hood /'sɪstəˌhʊd/ *n* [U] a
strong loyalty among women who share
the same ideas and aims ‖ 같은 생각이나

목표를 공유한 여자들 사이의 강한 충실
성. 자매적 유대감 —compare BROTH-
ERHOOD

sister-in-law /ˈ.. .ˌ./ *n, plural*
sisters-in-law 1 the sister of your
husband or wife ‖ 남편이나 부인의 누이
나 자매. 시누이. 처형. 처제 **2** the wife
of your brother, or the wife of your
husband or wife's brother ‖ 형제의 아내,
또는 남편이나 아내의 형제의 아내. 형수.
제수. 올케(언니). 동서. 처남댁 —see
picture at FAMILY

sitting on a chair　　　　　sitting at a desk

sit /sɪt/ *v* **sat, sat, sitting**
1 ▶ON A SEAT 좌석에◀ [I] **a)** to be in a
chair, on a seat etc. with the top half of
your body upright and your weight
resting on your BUTTOCKs ‖ 상반신을 곧
게 펴서 체중은 엉덩이에 실어서 의자·좌
석 등에 있다. 앉아 있다: *The children
sat around her on the floor.* 아이들은 그
녀를 둘러싸고 바닥에 앉아 있었다. / *I
was sitting at my desk writing a letter.*
나는 편지를 쓰면서 책상에 앉아 있었다.
b) to move to a sitting position after you
have been standing ‖ 서 있다가 앉은 자
세로 옮기다. 앉다. 착석하다: *He came
and sat beside/next to her.* 그는 다가와
서 그녀의 옆 자리에 앉았다.
2 ▶IN A POSITION 어떤 위치에◀ [I] to
lie or be in a particular position ‖ 특정
위치에 놓여 있다. 위치[존재]하다: *A
number of old books sat on the shelf.* 상
당수의 고서적들이 선반에 놓여 있었다.
**3 ▶NOT DO ANYTHING 아무것도 하지
않다◀** [I] to stay in one place for a long
time, especially doing nothing useful ‖
특히 쓸모 있는 일을 아무것도 하지 않고
한 자리에 오랫동안 머무르다. 가만히 (앉
아) 있다: *I can't sit here all day, I have
work to do.* 나는 해야 할 일이 있어 온종
일 여기 머무를 수 없다. / *Don't just sit
there – help me!* 그저 거기에 가만히 있지
말고 나를 도와 줘!
4 ▶MAKE SB SIT 사람을 앉히다◀ [T] to
make someone sit somewhere ‖ 어떤 사
람을 어떤 곳에 앉게 하다. 앉히다. 착석
시키다: *She sat the boy in a corner.* 그

녀는 소년을 구석(자리)에 앉혔다.

5 sit tight to stay where you are and not move, or to stay in the same situation and not do anything, while you are waiting for something ‖ 어떤 것을 기다리는 동안 현재 있는 곳에 머물러 움직이지 않거나 같은 상태로 머무르며 아무 것도 하지 않다. 딱 버티고[꼼짝 않고] 있다: *Investors should sit tight and see what happens in a few days.* 투자자들은 꼼짝 않고 있으면서 며칠 후에 무슨 일이 벌어질지 지켜볼 것이다.

6 sit still to sit somewhere without moving around in your seat ‖ 자기 좌석에서 움직이지 않고 어떤 곳에 앉아 있다. 가만히[잠자코] 앉아 있다: *Sit still and let me fix your hair.* 네 머리를 손질하도록 가만히 앉아 있어라.

7 not sit well with sb if a situation, plan etc. does not sit well with someone, it makes him/her feel anxious and unhappy ‖ 상황·계획 등이 사람을 불안하고 즐겁지 않게 느끼게 하다. 어울리지[마음에 들지] 않다

8 ▶MEET 만나다◀ [I] to have an official meeting ‖ 공식적 모임[회의]을 갖다. 개회[개정]하다: *The court sits once a month.* 법정은 한 달에 한 번씩 개정한다.

sit around *phr v* [I] to spend time resting or not doing anything useful ‖ 쉬거나 쓸모 있는 일을 아무 것도 하지 않으면서 시간을 보내다. 하는 일 없이 지내다. 빈둥빈둥 보내다: *Dan just sits around and watches TV all the time.* 댄은 항상 그저 빈둥거리면서 TV만 본다.

sit back *phr v* [I] to get into a comfortable position, or not get involved in something ‖ 편안한 자세를 취하거나 다른 일에 개입하지 않다. (의자에) 깊숙이 앉아 쉬다. 수수방관하다. 손을 떼다: *Just sit back and relax – I'll make dinner.* 그냥 편안히 앉아서 쉬어라. 내가 저녁을 준비할게.

sit down *phr v* [I] to move into a sitting position after you have been standing ‖ 서 있다가 앉은 자세로 옮기다. 앉다: *Bobby, get over here and sit down.* 바비, 이리 와서 앉아라.

sit in *phr v* [I] **1 sit in for sb** to do a job, go to a meeting etc. instead of the person who usually does it ‖ 보통 그 일을 하던 사람 대신에 업무를 수행하거나 회의 등에 참석하다. 남을 대신하다. 대신해서 …하다: *He's only sitting in for Sally while she's gone.* 그는 단지 샐리가 부재 중이어서 그녀를 대신할 뿐이다. **2 sit in on sth** to be present somewhere but not get involved in the activity ‖ 어떤

가에 참석하지만 활동에는 관여하지 않는. 참가하다. 참관하다: *Do you mind if I sit in on your class?* 당신 반(수업)에 참관해도 괜찮아요?

sit on sth *phr v* [T] [I] to be a member of an organization or other official group ‖ 조직이나 다른 공식 단체의 일원이 되다. 참여[관계]하다: *Hawkins sits on several government committees.* 호킨스는 몇몇 정부 위원회의 일원이다.

sit sth ↔ **out** *phr v* [T] to stay where you are until something finishes and not get involved in it ‖ 어떤 일이 끝날 때까지 현재 있는 곳에 남아서 개입하지 않다. 참여하지 않다. 빠져서 구경만 하다: *I think I'll sit this dance out.* 이번 춤에서 빠질 생각이다.

sit through sth *phr v* [T] to go to a meeting, performance etc. and stay until it finishes, even if it is very long or boring ‖ 회의·공연 등에 가서 아주 길거나 지루해도 끝날 때까지 머물다. 끝까지 머물다. 참고 앉아서 보다[듣다]: *We had to sit through a three-hour meeting this morning.* 우리는 오늘 아침 3시간짜리 회의에 끝까지 앉아 있어야 했다.

sit up *phr v* **1** [I] to move to a sitting position after you have been lying down ‖ 누워 있다가 앉은 자세로 옮기다. 일어나 앉다: *He finally was able to sit up in bed and eat something.* 그는 마침내 침대에 일어나 앉아서 뭔가를 먹을 수 있게 되었다. **2** [I] to stay awake and not got to bed ‖ 깨어 있으면서 잠자리에 들지 않다. 자지 않고 일어나 있다: *We sat up all night waiting for her to come home.* 우리는 밤새워 그녀가 집에 오기를 기다렸다. **3 sit up and take notice** to suddenly start paying attention to someone or something ‖ 갑자기 사람이나 사물에 주의를 기울이기 시작하다. 관심을 나타내다[보이다]: *The success of writers like Paretsky has made publishers sit up and take notice.* 파레츠키 같은 작가의 성공은 출판업자들의 관심을 불러일으키기 시작했다.

sit·com /ˈsɪtˌkɑm/ *n* [C, U] a funny television program in which the same characters appear in different situations each week ‖ 똑같은 등장인물들이 매주 다른 상황에 출연하는, 사람들을 웃기는 텔레비전 프로그램. 시트콤

sit-down /ˌ. ˈ./ *adj* **1** a sit-down meal or restaurant is one in which you sit at a table and eat a formal meal ‖ 식사나 식당이 테이블에 앉아서 격식을 갖추고 식사를 하는. 앉아서 하는. 착석 전용의 **2 sit-down protest/strike etc.** an occasion when a large group of people protest something by not moving from a particular area until the problem is solved ‖ 대규모 집단의 사람들이 문제가 해결될 때까지 특정 구역에서 움직이지 않고 어떤 일을 항의하는 경우. 연좌[농성] 시위/파업

site¹ /saɪt/ *n* **1** a place where something important or interesting happened ‖ 중요하거나 재미있는 일이 일어났던 곳. 유적. 자취. 현장: *the site where the Pilgrims landed* 최초의 청교도 이주자들의 정착지 **2** an area where something is being built or will be built ‖ 어떤 것이 지어지고 있거나 지어질 지역. 부지. 용지: *a construction site* 건축 부지

site² *v* **be sited** to be put or built in a particular place ‖ 특정 장소에 놓이거나 지어지다. 위치하다. 위치에 놓이다

sit-in /'. ./ *n* a protest in which people sit down and refuse to leave a place until their demands are dealt with ‖ 사람들이 앉아서 자신들의 요구가 해결될 때까지 자리를 떠나기를 거부하는 항의. 연좌[농성] 시위

sit·ter /'sɪtɚ/ *n* SPOKEN a word meaning BABYSITTER, used especially when the person is taking care of older children ‖ '애 봐주는 사람'을 의미하는 단어로 특히 나이든 아이들을 돌보는 사람에게 쓰여. 애[어린이] 봐주는 사람

sit·ting /'sɪtɪŋ/ *n* **at/in one sitting** during one continuous period of time when you are sitting in a chair ‖ 한 번 의자에 앉아서 계속되는 시간 동안. 한 자리에서. 한 번 앉아서: *Morris read the whole book in one sitting.* 모리스는 한 자리에서 그 책을 다 읽었다.

sit·u·at·ed /'sɪtʃu,eɪtɪd/ *adj* **be situated** to be in a particular place or position ‖ 특정 장소나 위치에 놓이다. 위치하다. 자리잡다: *The hotel is situated in the old market district.* 그 호텔은 예전 시장 지역에 위치해 있다.

sit·u·a·tion /,sɪtʃu'eɪʃən/ *n* a combination of all that is happening and all the conditions that exist at a particular time and place ‖ 일어나고 있는 모든 것들과 특정 시간과 장소에 존재하는 모든 조건들의 조합. 상황. 형세. 입장. 처지: *The present economic/ political situation in the country is very unstable.* 그 나라의 현 경제[정치] 상황은 아주 불안정하다. / *What would you do if you were in my situation?* 네가 내 처지라면 어떻게 하겠니?

situation comedy /,.... '../ *n* ⇨ SITCOM

sit-up /'. ./ *n* [C usually plural] exercises for your stomach, in which you sit up from a lying position while keeping your feet on the floor ‖ 발을 바닥에 계속 붙이고 누운 자세에서 상체를 일으키는 복부 운동. 윗몸 일으키기

six /sɪks/ *number* **1** 6 ‖ (기수의) 6 **2** six o'clock ‖ 6시: *I get out of class at six.* 나는 6시에 수업이 끝난다.

six-pack /'. ./ *n* six bottles or CANs of a drink sold together as a set ‖ 한 세트로서 함께 팔리는 여섯 병이나 캔들이 음료. 6개들이 묶음: *a six-pack of beer* 맥주 여섯 병[캔]들이 묶음

six·teen /,sɪk'stin/ *number* 16 ‖ (기수의) 16 – **sixteenth** *number*

sixth /sɪksθ/ *number* **1** 6th ‖ (서수의)여섯 번째 **2** 1/6 ‖ 6분의 1

sixth sense /,. './ *n* [singular] a special ability to feel or know something without using any of your five usual senses such as hearing or sight; INTUITION ‖ 청각이나 시각 등 보통의 오감을 전혀 사용하지 않고 어떤 일을 느끼거나 알 수 있는 특별한 능력. 제6감. 직감; ㉨ intuition

sixty /'sɪksti/ *number* **1** 60 ‖ (서수의)60 **2 the sixties a)** the years between 1960 and 1969 ‖ 1960년과 1969년 사이의 해. 60년대 **b)** the numbers between 60 and 69, especially when used for measuring temperature ‖ 특히 온도를 잴 때 숫자 60과 69 사이의 수. 60도대 – **sixtieth** /'sɪkstiɪθ/ *number*

siz·a·ble, sizeable /'saɪzəbəl/ *adj* fairly large ‖ 상당히 큰. 꽤 큰. 상당한 크기의: *a sizable crowd of people* 상당히 많은 군중들

size¹ /saɪz/ *n* **1** [C, U] how big or small something is ‖ 사물의 크거나 작은 정도. 크기. 대소: *A diamond's value depends on its size and color.* 다이아몬드의 가치는 그 크기와 색에 달려 있다. / *They wanted so much money for houses half the size of ours!* 그들이 우리 집 크기의 절반밖에 안 되는 집을 놓고 그렇게 많은 돈을 원했다니! **2** [U] the fact of being very big ‖ 매우 큼. 상당한 크기. (양적인) 크기: *I couldn't believe the sheer size of the ship.* 나는 그 배의 엄청난 크기를 믿을 수가 없었다. **3** one of the standard measures in which clothes, goods etc. are made and sold ‖ 옷·상품 등이 제작되고 판매되는 표준 치수들 중의 하나. 크기. 사이즈: *This shirt is the wrong size.* 이 셔츠는 크기가 맞지 않다. ✗DON'T SAY "have a size."✗ "have a size"라고는 하지 않는다. / *They didn't have anything in* *my size*: *a size 10 shoe* 10호짜리 내 신발 치수에 맞는 것이 그곳에는 전혀 없었다. **4 large-sized/medium-sized etc.** large, average etc. in size ‖ 크기가 대형·평균 등인. 대짜/중짜 크기의: *a pocket-sized calculator* 주머니(에 들어가는) 크기의 계산기

size² *v*

size sb/sth ↔ **up** *phr v* [T] INFORMAL to think carefully about a situation or person so that you can decide how to react ‖ 상황이나 사람에 대해 대응 방법을 결정할 수 있도록 주의 깊게 생각하다. …을 평가[판단]하다: *Julie is able to size up people quickly.* 줄리는 사람들을 재빨리 파악할 수 있다.

siz·zle /ˈsɪzəl/ *v* [I] to make a sound like water falling on hot metal ‖ 물이 뜨거운 금속 위로 떨어지는 것과 같은 소리를 내다. 지글지글[칙칙] 소리 나다: *bacon sizzling in the pan* 냄비에서 지글거리는 베이컨

skate¹ /skeɪt/ *n* **1** ⇨ ICE SKATE² **2** ⇨ ROLLER SKATE **3** [C, U] a large flat sea fish ‖ 크고 납작한 바닷물고기. 홍어

skate² *v* [I] to move on SKATEs ‖ 스케이트로 움직이다. 스케이트를 타다[지치다]: *I never learned how to skate.* 나는 스케이트 타는 법을 전혀 배우지 못했다. **- skating** *n* [U]: *Let's go skating.* 스케이트 타러 가자. **- skater** *n*

skate·board /ˈskeɪtˌbɔrd/ *n* a short board with two wheels at each end, on which you stand and ride, pushing your foot along the ground in order to move ‖ 양 끝에 두 개씩 바퀴가 달려 그 위에 서서 움직이기 위해 한 발로 땅을 박차면서 타는 짧은 판. 스케이트 보드 **- skateboarding** *n* [U]

skel·e·ton /ˈskɛlətʰn/ *n* **1** the structure consisting of all the bones in a human or animal body ‖ 인간이나 동물의 몸체에서 모든 뼈로 이루어져 있는 구조. 해골. 골격: *the human skeleton* 인간의 해골 **2 have a skeleton in the closet** to have a secret about something embarrassing or unpleasant that happened to you in the past ‖ 과거에 일어났던 창피하거나 불쾌한 일에 대한 비밀을 가지고 있다. 집안의 비밀을 숨기다. 남모르는 비밀이 있다 **3 skeleton staff/crew/service** only enough people to keep an operation or organization working ‖ 활동이나 조직의 가동을 겨우 유지할 정도의 인원수. 최소한의 직원/승무원/서비스 **- skeletal** *adj*

skep·tic /ˈskɛptɪk/ *n* someone who does not believe something unless s/he

has definite proof ‖ 명백한 증거를 갖지 않는 한 어떤 것도 믿지 않는 사람. 회의론자. 의심 많은 사람

skep·ti·cal /ˈskɛptɪkəl/ *adj* doubting or not believing something ‖ 어떤 것을 의심하거나 믿지 않는. 회의적인. 의심 많은: *He's very skeptical about astrology.* 그는 점성술에 대해 아주 회의적이다. **- skepticism** /ˈskɛptəˌsɪzəm/ *n* [U]

sketch¹ /skɛtʃ/ *n* **1** a drawing that you do quickly and without a lot of details ‖ 많은 세부적인 부분을 담지 않고 재빨리 그린 그림. 스케치. 밑그림. 소묘: *a pencil sketch of a bird* 새의 연필 소묘화 **2** a short written or spoken description without a lot of details ‖ 많은 세부 사항 없이 기술한 짧은 글이나 말. 개요. 줄거리. 골자. 윤곽: *The New Yorker had an interesting sketch of E.B. White's life.* 뉴욕 시민은 E. B. 화이트의 삶에 대한 재미있는 이야기를 알고 있었다. **3** a short humorous scene that is part of a longer performance ‖ 긴 공연의 한 부분인 짧고 익살스러운 장면. 촌극: *a comic sketch* 희극적 촌극

sketch² *v* [I, T] to draw a SKETCH of something ‖ 사물의 밑그림을 그리다. (…을) 스케치[사생]하다

sketch in sth *phr v* [T] to add more information without giving too many details ‖ 지나친 세부 사항은 주지 않고 정보를 더 추가하다. …의 개요를 말하다[쓰다]. 덧붙여 말하다[설명하다]: *I'll try to sketch in the historical background.* 제가 역사적 배경을 개괄해 보도록 하겠습니다.

sketch sth ↔ **out** *phr v* [T] to describe something in a few words, giving only the basic details ‖ 어떤 것에 대해 오직 기초적 사항들만 주면서 몇 마디로 묘사하다. 약술[약기]하다: *Rob sketched out a plan for next year's advertising campaign.* 로브는 내년 광고 활동 계획을 약술했다.

sketch·y /ˈskɛtʃi/ *adj* not thorough or complete, and not having enough details to be useful ‖ 철저하거나 완전하지 않고 쓸모 있는 충분한 세부 사항이 없는. 개략[요점]만의. 대략적인: *We only have sketchy information as to the cause of the fire.* 우리는 화재의 원인에 대해 대략적인 정보만 가지고 있을 뿐이다.

skew /skyu/ *v* [T] to affect a test, election, RESEARCH etc. so that the results are not balanced, and therefore not correct ‖ 시험·선거·연구 등에 영향을 미쳐 결과가 균형을 이루지 못해서 정확하

지 않게 하다. 빗나가게 하다. 왜곡하다
- skewed *adj* : *Sometimes the data can be badly skewed.* 때때로 데이터는 심하게 왜곡될 수 있다.

skew·er /'skyuəʳ/ *n* a long metal or wooden stick that you put through a piece of raw food that you want to cook ‖ 조리하고자 하는 식품의 원재료에 찔러 넣는 긴 금속이나 나무 막대기. (요리용) 꼬치[꼬챙이] **- skewer** *v* [T]

ski¹ /ski/ *n, plural* **skis** one of a pair of long narrow pieces of wood or plastic that you fasten to boots so you can move easily on snow ‖ 부츠에 부착해서 눈 위에서 쉽게 이동할 수 있게 한, 한 쌍의 길고 좁은 나무 또는 플라스틱으로 된 기구 중 하나. 스키

ski² *v* **skied, skied, skiing** [I] to move over snow on skis ‖ 스키로 눈 위를 이동하다. 스키를 타다: *Do you know how to ski?* 너 스키 탈 줄 아니? **- skiing** /'skiɪŋ/ *n* [U]: *We're going skiing this weekend.* 우리는 이번 주말에 스키를 타러 가려고 한다. **- skier** *n*

skid¹ /skɪd/ *v* **-dded, -dding** [I] if a vehicle skids, it slides sideways suddenly and you cannot control it ‖ 차량이 갑자기 옆으로 미끄러져서 제어할 수 없게 되다. 차가 옆으로 미끄러지다: *A car skidded on the ice and went in a ditch.* 차 한 대가 빙판 위에서 미끄러져 도랑에 빠졌다.

skid² *n* a sudden sliding movement of a vehicle that you cannot control ‖ 차량의 통제할 수 없는 갑작스럽게 미끄러지는 움직임. 미끄러지기

skids /skɪdz/ *n* [plural] **be on the skids/hit the skids** INFORMAL to begin to fail ‖ 실패하기 시작하다. 내리막길에 접어들다[사태가 악화되다]/쇠퇴[파멸, 타락]하다: *That was when his career hit the skids.* 그때가 바로 그의 경력이 내리 막길을 걷기 시작한 순간이었다.

skies /skaɪz/ *n* **the skies** a word meaning the sky, used especially when describing the weather ‖ 하늘을 의미하는 말로서 특히 날씨를 묘사할 때에 쓰여. 하늘. 날씨

skill /skɪl/ *n* [C, U] an ability to do something very well, especially because you have learned and practiced it ‖ 특히 배우고 익혀서 어떤 일을 아주 잘 할 수 있는 능력. 기능. 기술. 재능. 솜씨: *All you need are some basic computer skills.* 당신은 약간의 기본적인 컴퓨터 기술만 갖추면 된다. / *a painter of great skill* 솜씨가 대단한 화가 —see usage note at ABILITY

skilled /skɪld/ *adj* having the training and experience needed to do something well ‖ 어떤 것을 잘 하는 데 필요한 훈련과 경험을 가진. 숙련된. 능숙한. 기술이 좋은: *a highly skilled mechanic* 고도로 숙련된 정비공[기술자] **—opposite** UNSKILLED

skil·let /'skɪlɪt/ *n* a heavy FRYING PAN, usually made of iron ‖ 보통 쇠로 만든 대용량 냄비. 스튜 냄비

skill·ful /'skɪlfəl/ *adj* good at doing something that you have learned and practiced ‖ 배우고 익힌 것을 하는 데 뛰어난. 숙련된. 솜씨 있는: *a skillful doctor* 실력 있는 의사 **- skillfully** *adv*

skim /skɪm/ *v* **-mmed, -mming 1** [T] to remove something that is floating on the surface of a liquid ‖ 액체의 표면에 떠 있는 것을 제거하다. …을 걷어내다: *Skim the fat off the soup.* 수프에서 기름기를 걷어내라. **2** [I, T] also **skim through** to read something quickly to find the main facts or ideas in it ‖ 주요 사실이나 요지를 찾기 위해 어떤 것을 재빨리 읽다. 대충[죽] 훑어보다[조사하다]: *Jim skimmed the contract until he found the section on money.* 짐은 금액에 관한 부분을 찾을 때까지 계약서를 대충 훑어 내려갔다. **3** [T] to move along quickly, nearly touching the surface of something ‖ 거의 접촉하듯이 빠르게 사물의 표면을 따라 움직이다. 표면을 스쳐 지나가다[미끄러져 가다]: *birds skimming the tops of the trees* 나무 위를 스치듯이 날아가는 새들

skim milk /ˌ. './ *n* [U] milk that has had most of its fat removed from it ‖ 대부분의 지방분이 제거된 우유. 탈지유(脫脂乳)

skimp /skɪmp/ *v* [I, T] to not use enough money, time, effort etc. on something, so it is unsuccessful or of bad quality ‖ 어떤 것에 충분한 돈·시간·노력 등을 쓰지 않아서 성공적이지 못하거나 질이 나빠지게 하다. 인색하게 굴다. 아까워하다. …의 수고를 아끼다: *You shouldn't skimp on buying good shoes for the children.* 너는 아이들에게 좋은 신발을 사주는 것을 아까워해서는 안 된다.

skimp·y /'skɪmpi/ *adj* too small in size or quantity ‖ 크기나 양이 너무 작은. 불충분한. 빈약한: *a skimpy little dress* (몸에) 꼭 끼게 작은 드레스 / *a skimpy meal* 빈약한 식사

skin¹ /skɪn/ *n*

1 ▶ON A BODY 신체상의◀ [C, U] the natural outer covering of a human's or animal's body ‖ 인간이나 동물 신체의 타

고난 외피. 피부. 살갗: *I can't wear wool; it makes my skin itch.* 나는 모직물 옷을 입지 못한다. 그것을 입으면 피부가 가렵다. / *a skin disease* 피부병
2 ▶ANIMAL SKIN 동물의 피부◀ [C, U] the skin of an animal used as leather, clothes etc. ‖ 가죽·옷 등으로 쓰이는 동물의 피부. 가죽: *a tiger skin rug* 호랑이 가죽[호피] 깔개
3 ▶FOOD 음식◀ [C, U] the natural outer layer of some fruits and vegetables ‖ 일부 과일과 채소들의 천연적인 바깥 층. 껍질: *banana skins* 바나나 껍질 / *the skin of an onion* 양파 껍질 — see picture at PEEL²
4 -skinned having a particular type or color of skin ‖ 특정한 형태나 색깔의 피부를 가진. …한 피부[가죽]의: *a dark-skinned woman* 까무잡잡한 피부의 여성
5 ▶LAYER 층◀ [C, U] a thin solid layer that forms on the top of a liquid such as paint or milk when it gets cool or is left uncovered ‖ 페인트나 우유 등 액체가 냉각되거나 뚜껑이 열려 있을 때 맨 위에 형성되는 얇고 단단한 층. 피막
6 make sb's skin crawl to make someone feel uncomfortable, nervous, or slightly afraid ‖ 사람을 불편하게[불안하게, 약간 겁이 나게] 하다. 피부가 스멀거리게[소름이 끼치게] 하다: *He also had a way of making your skin crawl.* 그 또한 너를 불안하게 하는 구석이 있었다.
7 (do sth) by the skin of your teeth INFORMAL to only just succeed in doing something ‖ 어떤 것을 하는 데 간신히 성공하다. 가까스로 …하다: *We made it there by the skin of our teeth.* 우리는 가까스로 거기에 당도했다.
8 get under sb's skin INFORMAL to annoy someone, especially by the way you behave ‖ 특히 행동하는 방식에 의해 사람을 화나게 하다. 남을 초조하게[짜증나게] 하다: *Her silly voice really gets under my skin.* 그녀의 바보 같은 어투는 정말 나를 짜증나게 한다.
9 have thin/thick skin to be easily upset or not easily upset by criticism ‖ 비판으로 쉽게 흥분되거나 쉽게 흥분되지 않다. …에 민감/둔감하다
skin² *v* **-nned, -nning** [T] to remove the skin from an animal, fruit, or vegetable ‖ 동물[과일, 채소]의 가죽[껍질, 외피]을 벗기다
skin-deep /ˌ.ˈ./ *adj* **beauty is only skin deep** a phrase meaning that being a good person is better than being beautiful ‖ 착한 사람이 아름다운 것보다 더 낫다는 것을 의미하는 어구. 미모는 가

죽 한 꺼풀 차이일 뿐이다. 심성이 외모보다 중요하다
skin·flint /ˈskɪnˌflɪnt/ *n* INFORMAL someone who does not want to spend or give away money; MISER ‖ 돈을 쓰거나 나눠 주기를 원하지 않는 사람. 지독한 구두쇠; ㊲ miser
skin·head /ˈskɪnhɛd/ *n* a young person who SHAVES off his/her hair and often behaves violently against people who are not white ‖ 머리를 박박 밀고 종종 백인이 아닌 사람들에게 난폭하게 행동하는 젊은 사람. 스킨헤드족
skin·ny /ˈskɪni/ *adj* extremely thin, or too thin ‖ 극도로 홀쭉한, 또는 지나치게 마른. 피골이 상접한. 말라빠진: *I was a really skinny kid.* 나는 정말로 말라깽이 아이였다. —see usage note at THIN¹
skinny dip·ping /ˈ.. ˌ../ *n* [U] INFORMAL swimming without any clothes on ‖ 옷을 전혀 입지 않고 하는 수영. 알몸[나체] 수영
skin-tight /ˌ. ˈ./ *adj* clothes that are skin-tight fit tightly against your body ‖ 옷이 몸에 꼭 맞는. 꽉 끼는: *skin-tight jeans* 꽉 끼는 청바지
skip /skɪp/ *v* **-pped, -pping 1** [T] to not do something that you would usually do or that you should do ‖ 보통 (규칙적으로) 하던 일이나 당연히 해야 하는 일을 하지 않다. …을 거르다. 빠뜨리다. 빼먹다: *I tend to skip breakfast.* 나는 아침(밥)을 거르는 편이다. / *Butch got in trouble for skipping school.* 부치는 학교를 빼먹은 것이 들통이 났다. **2** [I] to move forward with quick jumps from one foot to the other ‖ 한 발에서 다른 발로 빨리 뛰어서 앞으로 나아가다. 깡충 뛰다. 뛰어 넘다: *children skipping down the street* 거리를 깡충깡충 뛰며 가는 아이들 **3** [I] to go from one subject, place etc. to another in no particular order ‖ 한 주제·장소 등에서 특정한 순서 없이 다른 곳으로 넘어가다. 건너뛰다. 갑자기 …으로 바뀌다: *The speaker skipped around from one topic to another.* 연설자는 한 주제에서 다른 주제로 이리저리 화제를 바꾸었다. **4** [I, T] to not notice or do something, either deliberately or by accident, even though it is the next thing you would usually do ‖ 보통은 다음 순서로 하게 될 일이지만 고의든 우연이든 그것을 인식하지 못하거나 하지 않다. …을 빠뜨리다. 빼먹다: *Oh, I skipped over that question.* 아차, 그 문제를 빼먹었구나. **5** [I] also **skip rope** to play with a JUMP ROPE ‖ 줄넘기 줄로 놀다. 줄넘기하다
skip·per /ˈskɪpɚ/ *n* INFORMAL someone

who is in charge of a ship; CAPTAIN ‖ 배를 책임지고 있는 사람. 선장; ㊋ captain

skir·mish /'skɚmɪʃ/ *n* a military fight between small groups of people or soldiers ‖ 소규모의 사람들이나 군인들간의 군사적 전투. 소전투. 작은 충돌: *a border skirmish* 국경에서의 접전

skirt¹ /skɚt/ *n* a piece of women's clothing that fits around the waist and hangs down like a dress ‖ 허리둘레에 맞추어 드레스처럼 내려뜨려 입는 여성복. 치마 —see picture at CLOTHES

skirt², skirt around *v* [T] **1** to go around the outside edge of a place ‖ 한 장소의 외곽을 돌아가다. …의 주변[가장자리]을 따라 지나다. …을 따라 우회하다: *The soldiers skirted around the town and crossed the river.* 군인들은 도시를 우회해서 강을 건넜다. **2** to avoid an important problem, subject etc. ‖ 중요한 문제·주제 등을 피하다. …을 회피하다. 피해 가다: *Would you just stop skirting the issue?* 말 좀 돌리지 말아주시겠어요?

skit /skɪt/ *n* a short funny performance ‖ 짧고 웃기는 공연. 촌극. 소희극: *a skit about buying a car* 자동차 구매에 관한 촌극

skit·tish /'skɪtɪʃ/ *adj* nervous, frightened, or not sure about something ‖ 어떤 것에 대해 불안한[겁먹은, 자신 없는]. 잘 놀라는. 소심한: *He was skittish about lending her money.* 그는 그녀에게 돈을 빌려 주는 데 대해 소심하게 굴었다.

skulk /skʌlk/ *v* [I] to hide or move around quietly because you do not want to be seen ‖ 눈에 띄기를 원치 않아서 조용히 숨거나 돌아가다. 살금살금 숨다[행동하다]. 잠행하다: *Two men were skulking in the shadows.* 두 남자가 어둠 속에 가만히 숨어 있었다.

skull /skʌl/ *n* the bones of a person's or animal's head ‖ 사람이나 동물의 머리뼈. 두개골

skull·cap /'skʌlkæp/ *n* a small cap worn sometimes by priests or Jewish men ‖ 사제나 유대인들이 때때로 쓰는 작은 모자. 챙 없는 사발 모양 모자

skunk /skʌŋk/ *n* a small black and white animal that produces an unpleasant smell if it is attacked ‖ 공격을 당하면 불쾌한 냄새를 뿜어내는 검은색과 흰색이 섞인 작은 동물. 스컹크

sky /skaɪ/ *n* [singular, U] **1** the space above the earth where the sun, clouds, and stars are ‖ 태양·구름·별들이 있는 지구 상공의 공간. 하늘. 창공: *a clear blue sky* 청명한 푸른 하늘 / *a patch of sky between the clouds* 구름 사이로 비치는

한 조각의 하늘 **2 the sky's the limit** SPOKEN used in order to say that there is no limit to what someone can achieve, spend, win etc. ‖ 사람이 달성·소비·승리 등을 할 수 있는 데에 한계가 없다고 말하는 데에 쓰여. 무제한이다[으로 가능하다] —see also SKIES

sky·div·ing /'skaɪˌdaɪvɪŋ/ *n* [U] the sport of jumping from an aircraft and falling through the sky before opening a PARACHUTE ‖ 비행기에서 뛰어내려 낙하산을 펼치기 전까지 하늘에서 하강하는 스포츠. 스카이다이빙. 고공점프 – **skydiver** *n* [U]

sky-high /ˌ. '. / *adj* INFORMAL extremely high or expensive ‖ 매우 높거나 비싼. 하늘에 닿을 듯한. 하늘 높이(치솟는): *Prices at the auction were sky-high.* 경매 가격들이 (천정부지로) 치솟았다. – **sky-high** *adv*

sky·light /'skaɪlaɪt/ *n* a window in the roof of a building ‖ 건물 지붕의 창문. 천창(天窓)

skyscraper   skyline

sky·line /'skaɪlaɪn/ *n* the shape made by tall buildings or hills against the sky ‖ 하늘을 배경으로 높은 건물이나 언덕에 의해 만들어진 윤곽. 스카이라인

sky·rock·et /'skaɪˌrakɪt/ *v* [I] to increase suddenly and by large amounts ‖ 갑작스럽게 큰 규모[액수]로 증가하다. 급상승하다. 치솟다[아 오르다]: *Property values have skyrocketed in the past year.* 부동산 가치가 지난 한 해 동안 급등했다.

sky·scrap·er /'skaɪˌskreɪpɚ/ *n* a very tall building in a city ‖ 도시의 매우 높은 건물. 마천루

slab /slæb/ *n* a thick flat piece of a hard material such as stone ‖ 돌 등 단단한 재질의 두껍고 평평한 조각. (바닥)판(板): *a concrete slab* 콘크리트 판

slack¹ /slæk/ *adj* **1** hanging loosely, or not pulled tight ‖ 헐렁하게 늘어지거나 꽉 당겨지지 않은. 느슨한: *a slack rope* 느슨한 밧줄 **2** with less business activity than usual ‖ 평소보다 사업 활동이 줄어든. 부진한. 불황[불경기]의: *a slack* *period in the travel business* 여행업의 불황기 **3** not taking enough care to do things correctly ‖ 일을 똑바로 하기 위한 충분한 주의를 기울이지 않는. 태만히[게을리] 하는: *Rich is starting to get slack in his work.* 리치는 자기 업무에 태만해지기 시작하고 있다.

slack² *n* **1 take/pick up the slack a)** to do additional work that needs to be done because the person who usually does it is not there ‖ 통상적으로 그 일을 하는 사람이 자리에 없어서 마쳐야 될 필요가 있는 추가 작업을 하다. 빈 자리[부족분]를 메우다[보충하다]: *With McGill gone, I expect the rest of you to take up the slack.* 맥길이 가고 없으므로, 남아 있는 여러분이 그의 자리를 보충해 주기를 바랍니다. **b)** to make a rope tighter ‖ 밧줄을 더 팽팽하게 만들다. 졸라매다. 느슨함을 죄다 **2 cut/give sb some slack** INFORMAL to allow someone to make mistakes without getting angry at him/her ‖ 어떤 사람이 실수하는 것을 화를 내지 않고 용인하다. 남의 숨통을 틔워 주다. 여유를 주다: *Cut her some slack – she's only been working here two weeks!* 그녀의 숨통 좀 틔워 줘라. 그녀는 여기서 겨우 2주째 일하고 있잖아! **3** [U] looseness in the way something such as a rope hangs or is fastened ‖ 밧줄 등의 물건이 달려 있거나 매인 상태의 느슨함. 늘어짐. 헐렁함

slack³, slack off *v* [I] **1** to not work as quickly as you should on your job ‖ 업무에서 해야 하는 만큼 빠르게 일하지 않다. 굼뜨다. 느려터지다: *She's always slacking off near the end of the day.* 그녀는 하루 일이 끝날 무렵에는 언제나 굼떠진다. **2** ⇨ SLACKEN **– slacker** *n*

slack·en /'slækən/, **slack off** *v* [I, T] to gradually become slower, weaker, or less active, or to make something do this ‖ 점차로 더 느려지다[약해지다, 덜 활발해지다], 또는 사물을 이렇게 하게 하다. 굼떠지다. 부진해지다. 꿈뜨게 하다: *We left the cabin once the rain slackened off.* 우리는 일단 빗줄기가 약해지자 오두막집을 떠났다.

slacks /slæks/ *n* [plural] ⇨ PANTS

slag /slæg/ *n* [U] waste material that is left when metal is obtained from rock ‖ 암석에서 금속을 얻어낸 후 남는 폐기물. 슬래그. 광재(鑛滓)

slain /sleɪn/ *v* the PAST PARTICIPLE of SLAY ‖ slay의 과거 분사형

slake /sleɪk/ *v* [T] LITERARY **slake your thirst** to drink so that you are not THIRSTY ‖ 목마르지 않게 (음료를) 마시다.

갈증을 풀다[해소하다]

slam¹ /slæm/ *v* **-mmed, -mming 1** [I, T] if a door, gate etc. slams, or someone slams it, it shuts loudly with a lot of force ‖ 문·대문 등이 강한 힘으로 큰 소리를 내며 닫히다, 또는 누군가가 닫다. 쿵[꽝] 하고 닫다[닫히다]: *Baxter left the room, slamming the door.* 백스터는 꽝 하고 문을 닫으며 방을 떠났다. **2** [T] to hit something or someone against a surface, quickly and violently ‖ 사물이나 사람을 표면에다 빠르고 난폭하게 치다. 내던지다. 내동댕이치다: *Manya slammed the phone down.* 마냐는 전화기를 탁 하고 내려놓았다. / *Muggers had slammed him up against a wall.* 노상강도들은 그를 세게 벽에 대고 밀쳤다. **3** INFORMAL to criticize someone strongly, especially in a newspaper report ‖ 특히 신문 보도에서 어떤 사람을 강하게 비판하다. …을 혹평하다. 형편없이 깎아내리다: *Mayor Watson was slammed in the press for not acting sooner.* 왓슨 시장은 신속한 조치를 취하지 않았다고 언론으로부터 맹비난당했다.

slam² *n* [C usually singular] the noise or action of hitting or closing something hard ‖ 사물을 세게 치거나 닫는 소음이나 동작. 쿵[꽝](하는 소리). 난폭하게 닫기

slan·der /'slændɚ/ *n* [C, U] a spoken statement about someone that is not true and is intended to damage the good opinion that people have of him/her ‖ 누군가에 대해서 사람들이 가진 좋은 여론을 해치려는 뜻이 담긴, 사실이 아닌 발언. 중상. 비방 **– slander** *v* [T] **– slanderous** *adj* —compare LIBEL¹

slang /slæŋ/ *n* [U] very informal language that uses new or rude words instead of the usual word for something, often used only by people who belong to a particular group ‖ 어떤 것에 대해 일상적 용어 대신 새롭거나 무례한 단어를 쓰고, 종종 특정 집단에 속한 사람들에 의해서만 쓰이는 매우 비격식적 언어. 속어. 은어. 비어 **– slangy** *adj*

slant¹ /slænt/ *v* [I] to slope or move in a sloping line ‖ 경사진 선으로 기울거나 움직이다. 비스듬해지다[히 가다]. 기울다. 경사지다: *a two-door car with a slanted rear window* 비스듬한 뒷창문이 달린 투도어 차

slant² *n* **1** a sloping position or angle ‖ 기울어진 위치나 각도. 경사. 비탈. 사면: *The house sits on a slant.* 그 집은 비탈에 자리잡고 있다. **2** a way of writing or thinking about a subject that shows support for a particular set of ideas or beliefs‖ 특정 사상이나 신념 체계에 대한 지지를 나타내는 한 주제에 대한 문장 작법이나 사고 방식. 경향. 편향(偏向). 관점: *a feminist slant on Dickens's novels* 디킨스 소설에 대한 여성 편향적 시각

slap¹ /slæp/ *v* **-pped, -pping** [T] to hit someone quickly with the flat part of your hand‖ 사람을 손바닥으로 빠르게 때리다. …을 찰싹 때리다: *She spun around and slapped his face.* 그녀는 빙글 돌아서서 그의 뺨을 찰싹 때렸다.

slap sth ↔ **on** *phr v* [T] to put or spread something quickly on a surface in a careless way‖ 사물을 아무렇게나 재빨리 표면 위에 붙이거나 바르다. …에 묻히다. 칠하다: *Just slap a coat of paint on, and it'll be as good as new.* 그냥 페인트를 한 겹 덧칠하면 새것처럼 좋아질 것이다.

slap² *n* **1** a quick hit with the flat part of your hand‖ 손바닥으로 빠르게 때리기. 찰싹 때리기 **2 a slap in the face** something that someone does that shocks and upsets you, because it makes you realize s/he does not support you‖ 충격을 주고 화가 나게해서 자신을 지지하지 않는다는 것을 깨닫게 하는 어떤 사람이 하는 짓. 모욕. 거절. 비난: *This decision is a slap in the face to the Florida Legislature.* 이 결정은 플로리다 주 의회에 대한 모욕이다. **3 a slap on the wrist** INFORMAL a punishment that is not very severe‖ 매우 심하지는 않은 벌. 가벼운 질책[꾸지람]

slap·dash /'slæpdæʃ/ *adj* careless and done too quickly‖ 부주의하고 너무 빨리 행해진. 겉날리는. 아무렇게나 한: *a slapdash job of painting the house* 아무렇게나 한 주택 도색

slap·stick /'slæp،stɪk/ *n* [U] humorous acting in which the actors fall over, throw things at each other etc.‖ 배우가 넘어지거나 서로 물건을 집어던지는 등의 우스꽝스런 연기. 야단법석을 떠는 희극

slash¹ /slæʃ/ *v* **1** [I, T] to cut or try to cut something in a violent way with a sharp weapon, making a long deep cut‖ 날카로운 무기로 난폭하게 길고 깊은 상처를 내며 사물을 베려고 하거나 자르다. 깊이 베다[베어 버리다]. 난도질하다: *Police said the victim had her throat slashed with a razor.* 경찰은 희생자의 목이 면도칼에 깊이 베였다고 말했다. **2** [T] INFORMAL to greatly reduce an amount or price‖ 양이나 가격을 크게 줄이다. 대폭 삭감하다. 크게 깎다: *Many companies are slashing jobs to reduce*

spending. 많은 회사들이 지출을 줄이기 위해 일자리를 대폭 줄이고 있다.

slash² *n* **1** a quick movement that you make with a sharp weapon in order to cut someone or something‖ 사람이나 사물을 베기 위해 날카로운 무기로 하는 빠른 동작. 휙 휘두르기[베기]. 일격 **2** also **slash mark** a line (/) used in writing to separate words, numbers etc.‖ 단어나 숫자 등을 분리하기 위해 작문에서 쓰는 선(/). 사선 **3** a long narrow wound on your body, or a long narrow cut in a piece of material‖ 신체상의 좁고 길게 난 상처, 또는 물체의 좁고 길게 잘린 자국. 깊은 상처. 베어진 곳

slat /slæt/ *n* a thin flat piece of wood, plastic, or metal‖ 나무[플라스틱, 금속]의 얇은 판 조각. 살. 미늘창살

slate¹ /sleɪt/ *n* **1** [U] a dark gray rock that can be easily split into thin flat pieces‖ 얇은 판 조각으로 쉽게 쪼개지는 암회색 바위. 점판암. 슬레이트 **2** a list of people that voters can choose in an election‖ 유권자가 선거에서 선택할 수 있는 사람의 명단. 후보자 명단

slate² *v* **1 be slated to be/do** sth to be expected to get a particular position or job‖ 특정 지위나 직무를 맡기로 예정되다. …(후보자)로 내세우다[예정되다]/…할[될] 예정[계획]이다: *Manley is slated to become the next principal.* 맨리는 차기 교장이 될 것으로 예정되어 있다. **2 be slated for** to be expected to happen at a time in the future‖ 미래의 한 시점에서 일어날 것으로 기대되다. …을 예정하다[계획하다]: *The corner office buildings are slated for demolition.* 귀퉁이의 사무실 빌딩은 철거될 예정이다.

slath·er /'slæðɚ/ *v* [T] to put a thick layer of a soft substance onto something‖ 어떤 것 위에 부드러운 물질을 두꺼운 층으로 바르다. 칠하다: *fresh bread slathered with butter* 버터가 많이 발린 신선한 빵

slaugh·ter /'slɔt̬ɚ/ *v* [T] **1** to kill a lot of people in a cruel or violent way‖ 잔인하거나 난폭하게 많은 사람을 죽이다. 대량 학살[참살]하다 **2** to kill an animal for food‖ 식용으로 동물을 죽이다. 도살하다 **3** INFORMAL to defeat an opponent by a large number of points‖ 큰 점수(차)로 적을 패배시키다. 대파하다. 완패시키다 – **slaughter** *n* [U]

slaugh·ter·house /'slɔt̬ɚ،haʊs/ *n* a building where animals are killed‖ 동물을 도살하는 건물. 도살장

slave¹ /sleɪv/ *n* **1** someone who is owned by another person and works without pay for him/her ‖ 다른 사람에 의해 소유되어 대가 없이 일하는 사람. 노예. 종 **2 be a slave to/of** to be completely influenced by something so that you cannot make decisions based on your own opinions ‖ 어떤 것에 의해 완전히 영향 받아서 자신의 의견에 기초한 어떤 결정도 하지 못하다. …에 종속되다 /…의 노예가 되다: *a slave to fashion* 유행의 노예[유행을 너무 따르는 사람]

slave[2] *v* [I] to work very hard ‖ 매우 열심히 일하다. 노예같이 뼈 빠지게 일하다. 혹사당하다: *Michael's been slaving in the kitchen all day.* 마이클은 온종일 부엌에서 혹사 당하고 있다.

slave driv·er /'. ,../ *n* INFORMAL someone who makes people work extremely hard ‖ 사람들을 극심하게 일하게 하는 사람. 엄한[심하게 부려먹는] 고용주[상사, 감독]

slave la·bor /,. '../ *n* [U] **1** INFORMAL work for which you are paid a very small amount of money ‖ 매우 적은 액수의 돈을 지급받고 하는 일. 저임금[노예적] 노동: *$2.00 an hour? That's slave labor!* 한 시간에 2달러라고? 그건 저임금 노동이다[노예력 착취야]! **2** work done by SLAVEs, or the slaves that do this work ‖ 노예에 의해 행해지는 일, 또는 이 일을 하는 노예들. 노예의 노동[직무]. 노예 노동력

slav·er·y /'sleɪvəri/ *n* [U] the system of having SLAVEs, or the condition of being a slave ‖ 노예를 소유하는 체제, 또는 노예라는 상태. 노예 제도. 노예의 처지[신분]: *Slavery was abolished after the Civil War.* 노예 제도는 미국 남북전쟁 후 폐지되었다.

slav·ish /'sleɪvɪʃ/ *adj* DISAPPROVING showing that someone is too willing to behave like or obey someone else ‖ 사람이 지나치게 거리낌없이 남을 따라 행동하거나 남에게 복종함을 보이는. 노예적인. 굴종적인. 흉내만 내는: *a slavish imitation of Scorsese's style* 스코르시스 감독 스타일을 흉내낸 모방작 / *slavish devotion to duty* 임무에 대한 노예적 헌신

slay /sleɪ/ *v* **slew, slain, slaying** [T] LITERARY to kill someone violently ‖ 어떤 사람을 난폭하게 죽이다. 살해하다: *Kennedy was slain in Dallas.* 케네디는 댈러스에서 살해당했다. **– slaying** *n*

slea·zy /'slizi/ *adj* low in quality, immoral, and unpleasant ‖ 질이 낮고 부도덕하며 불쾌한. 저속한. 천박한. 추잡한: *sleazy bars* 추잡스런 술집 / *a sleazy lawyer* 천박한 변호사

sled /slɛd/ *n* a vehicle that slides over snow, often used by children ‖ 종종 아이들에 의해 사용되는 눈 위로 미끄러져 가는 탈것. 썰매. **– sled** *v* [I]

sledge ham·mer /'slɛdʒ ,hæmə/ *n* a large heavy hammer ‖ 크고 무거운 망치. 대형 쇠망치. 모루채

sleek /slik/ *adj* **1** smooth and shiny ‖ 매끈(매끈)하고 빛나는. 반들반들한. 윤기나는: *a cat's sleek fur* 고양이의 반드르르한 털 **2** attractive and expensive ‖ 매력적이고 값비싼. 고급(형)의. 세련된: *a sleek car* 잘 빠진 고급 차

sleep[1] /slip/ *v* **slept, slept, sleeping** **1** [I] to be asleep ‖ 잠들다. 자다. 잠자다: *I slept well last night.* 나는 지난밤에 잘 잤다. / *If you're tired, why don't you sleep late tomorrow? (=sleep until late in the morning)* 피곤하면 내일 늦잠을 주무시지요? ✗DON'T SAY "I slept early." SAY "I went to sleep / bed early."✗ "I went early."라고 하지 않고 "I went to sleep / bed early."라고 한다. **2 sleep on it** SPOKEN to think about something carefully before you make a decision ‖ 결정을 내리기 전에 주의 깊게 무엇에 대해 생각하다. …을 하룻밤 자며 생각하다. 결정을 다음날까지 미루다: *Sleep on it, and we'll discuss it tomorrow.* 잘 생각해봐, 내일 의논하게. **3 sleep tight** said in order to tell someone, especially a child, that you hope s/he sleeps well ‖ 어떤 사람 특히 아이에게 잘 자기를 바란다고 말하는 데에 쓰여. 잘 자[푹 자](라) **4** [T] to have enough beds for a particular number of people ‖ 특정수의 사람들을 위한 충분한 침상을 구비하다. …분의 숙박 시설이 있다. …이 숙박할 수 있다: *The tent sleeps six.* 그 텐트는 6명이 잘 수 있다[6인용이다]. **5 sleep like a log** SPOKEN to sleep very well without waking up ‖ (중간에) 깨지 않고 매우 잘 자다. 숙면하다. 깊이 잠들다

sleep around *phr v* [I] DISAPPROVING to have sex with many people ‖ 많은 사람과 성관계를 갖다. 여러 남자[여자]와 관계하다

sleep in *phr v* [I] to sleep later than usual in the morning ‖ 아침에 평소보다 늦게까지 자다. 늦잠자다: *I slept in till 10:00 on Saturday.* 나는 토요일에 아침 10시까지 늦잠을 잤다.

sleep sth ↔ **off** *phr v* [T] to sleep until you no longer feel sick, especially after being drunk ‖ 특히 술 취한 다음에 더 이상 메슥거리지 않을 때까지 자다. 잠을 자서 숙취를 해소하다: *drunks sleeping it off in the jail cells* 유치장에서 곯아떨어

진 주정꾼들

sleep over *phr v* [I] to sleep at someone's house for a night ‖ 다른 사람의 집에서 하룻밤 동안 자다. 남의 집에 묵다: *Mom, can I sleep over at Ann's tonight?* 엄마, 오늘밤 앤네 집에서 자도 돼요?

sleep through sth *phr v* [T] to sleep while something noisy is happening ‖ 소란스러운 일이 일어나고 있는 동안 잠자다. 잠을 깨지 않고[모른 채] 그대로 자다: *How could you have slept through the earthquake?* 도대체 어떻게 지진 속에서 그대로 잘 수 있었니?

sleep together *phr v* [I] INFORMAL to have sex with someone you are not married to ‖ 결혼하지 않은 상대와 성관계를 갖다. 동침하다. 같이 자다: *Are you sure they're sleeping together?* 그들이 동침하고 있는 게 확실해?

sleep with *phr v* [T] INFORMAL to have sex with someone you are not married to ‖ 결혼하지 않은 상대와 성관계를 갖다. 배우자가 아닌 남과 자다. 불륜을 저지르다: *Everyone knows he's sleeping with Diana.* 그가 다이아나와 불륜 관계를 맺고 있는 것을 모두가 안다.

sleep² *n* **1** [U] the natural state of being asleep ‖ 잠이 든 자연적 상태. 수면. 잠: *I had trouble getting to sleep last night.* (=succeeding in sleeping) 나는 지난밤 잠드는 데 애를 먹었다. / *Ed sometimes talks in his sleep.* (=while he is sleeping) 에드는 때로 잠꼬대를 한다. **2** [singular] a period of sleeping ‖ 잠자는 시간. 수면 시간. 한숨 자기: *You'll feel better after a good night's sleep.* (=a night when you sleep well) 너는 하룻밤 푹 자고 나면 좋아질 것이다. **3 go to sleep** to start sleeping ‖ 잠자기 시작하다. 잠자러 가다. 잠들다: *Katherine went to sleep about 7:00 last night.* 캐서린은 지난밤 7시쯤에 잠들었다. — compare **fall asleep** (ASLEEP) **4 don't lose sleep over it** SPOKEN said in order to tell someone not to worry about something ‖ 무엇에 대해 걱정하지 말라고 다른 사람에게 말하는 데에 쓰여. (잠을 이루지 못할 정도로) …을 조바심내지[애태우지] 마라 **5 put** sth **to sleep** to give an animal drugs so that it dies without pain ‖ 동물에게 약을 먹여서 고통 없이 죽게 하다. 안락사시키다

sleep·er /'slipɚ/ *n* **1** someone who is asleep ‖ 잠자(고 있)는 사람: *Sam's a heavy/light sleeper.* (=he sleeps well or wakes up easily) 샘은 깊은 잠[선잠]을 자는 사람이다. **2** a movie, book etc. that

is suddenly and unexpectedly successful ‖ 갑자기 예상 밖으로 성공적인 영화·책 등

sleeping bag /'.. ,./ *n* a large warm bag for sleeping in ‖ 그 안에서 잠자기 위한 큰 보온용 포대. 침낭

sleeping pill /'.. ,./ *n* a PILL that helps you to sleep ‖ 잠자게 도와주는 알약. 수면제

sleep·less /'sliplɪs/ *adj* unable to sleep ‖ 잠을 잘 수 없는. 잠 못 이루는. 불면(증)의: *We spent a sleepless night waiting for her to call.* 우리는 그녀의 전화를 기다리며 밤새 잠들지 못했다. – **sleeplessness** *n* [U]

sleep·walk·er /'slip,wɔkɚ/ *n* someone who walks while s/he is sleeping ‖ 잠자면서 걸어다니는 사람. 몽유병자 – **sleepwalk** *v* [I] – **sleepwalking** *n* [U]

sleep·y /'slipi/ *adj* **1** tired and ready for sleep ‖ 피곤해서 잠들 준비가 된. 졸리는. 졸음이 오는: *I don't know why I'm so sleepy.* 왜 이렇게 졸리는지 모르겠다. **2** quiet and without much activity ‖ 조용하고 많은 활동이 없는. 활기 없는. 나른한: *a sleepy little town* 활기 없는 소읍 – **sleepily** *adv* – **sleepiness** *n* [U]

sleep·y·head /'slipi,hɛd/ *n* SPOKEN someone, especially a child, who looks as if s/he wants to go to sleep ‖ 자고 싶은 듯해 보이는 사람, 특히 그러한 아이. 잠꾸러기: *It's time for bed, sleepyhead.* 자러 갈 시간이다. 잠꾸러기야.

sleet /slit/ *n* [U] freezing rain ‖ 얼어붙어 내리는 비. 싸라기눈. 진눈깨비 – **sleet** *v* [I] —see usage note at WEATHER

sleeve /sliv/ *n* **1** the part of a piece of clothing that covers your arm or part of your arm ‖ 팔 전체나 일부분을 덮는 옷의 부분. 소매. 소맷자락: *a blouse with short sleeves* 짧은 소매의 블라우스 **2 -sleeved** having a particular type of sleeve ‖ 특정한 형태의 소매가 달린. 소매가 …인: *long-sleeved shirts* 소매가 긴 셔츠 **3 have** sth **up your sleeve** INFORMAL to have a secret plan that you are going to use later ‖ 나중에 사용할 비밀 계획을 가지다. …이라는 최후의 수단[비장의 무기]이 있다. …을 비밀로 해두다: *Janssen usually has a few surprises up his sleeve.* 잰슨은 보통 몇 가지 깜짝 놀랄 계획을 비밀리에 가지고 있다.

sleeve·less /'slivlɪs/ *adj* without SLEEVES ‖ 소매가 없는. 민소매의: *a sleeveless dress* 민소매 드레스

sleigh /sleɪ/ *n* a large vehicle pulled by animals, used for traveling on snow ‖ 눈

위를 지나가는 데 쓰이는, 동물이 끄는 큰
탈것. 썰매

sleight of hand /ˌslaɪt əv ˈhænd/ *n*
[U] quick skillful movements with your
hands when performing magic tricks ‖
마술 공연할 때의 빠르고 능숙한 손놀림.
날랜 솜씨. 요술. 술책

slen·der /ˈslɛndɚ/ *adj* thin and
graceful ‖ 가느다랗고 우아한. 호리호리
한. 날씬한: *long slender fingers* 길고 가
느다란 손가락 —see usage note at THIN¹

slept /slɛpt/ *v* the past tense and PAST
PARTICIPLE of SLEEP ‖ sleep의 과거·과거
분사형

sleuth /sluθ/ *n* OLD-FASHIONED someone
who tries to find out information about
a crime ‖ 범죄에 대한 정보를 알아내려고
하는 사람. 탐정. 형사

slew¹ /slu/ *n* **a slew of** INFORMAL a
large number ‖ 많은 수. 다량[다수]의: *a
slew of new TV programs* 많은 새 TV 프
로그램

slew² *v* the past tense of SLAY ‖ slay의
과거형

slice¹ /slaɪs/ *n* **1** a flat piece of bread,
meat etc. cut from a larger piece ‖ 큰 덩
어리에서 잘라낸 빵·고기 등의 납작한 조
각. 얇은 조각. 한 조각: *Cut the tomato
into thin slices.* 토마토를 얇은 조각으로
자르세요. —see picture at PIECE¹ **2** a
part or a piece of something ‖ 사물의 일
부나 한 조각. 부분. (나눈) 몫: *The
German company wants a slice of the
US market.* 독일 회사들은 미국 시장의
일부를 원한다. **3 a slice of life/history
etc.** something that seems typical of
life, the history of a place etc. ‖ 인생·어
떤 곳의 역사 등의 전형으로 보이는 것. 인
생/역사의 한 단면: *The old theater is a
real slice of history.* 그 오래된 영화관은
역사의 한 단면이다.

slice² *v* [T] **1** also **slice up** to cut
meat, bread etc. into thin flat pieces ‖
고기·빵 등을 얇고 납작한 조각으로 자르
다. 저미다. 얇게 베다[잘라내다]: *Could
you slice the bread?* 빵 좀 잘라 주시겠어
요? **2** to reduce the size or amount of
something ‖ 사물의 크기나 양을 줄이다.
깎아내다. 삭감하다: *The budget for
schools was sliced by $100 million.* 학교
예산이 1억 달러가 삭감됐다. **3 no
matter how you slice it** INFORMAL used
in order to say that even if you consider
a situation in many different ways, it is
always the same ‖ 상황을 아무리 여러 다
양한 방식으로 고려해도 여전히 똑같다고
말하는 데에 쓰여. 백방으로 생각해 봐도.
아무리 감안해도: *No matter how you*

slice it, we have a big problem. 네가 아
무리 그 상황을 감안한다 해도 우리는 여
전히 큰 문제를 안고 있다.

slick¹ /slɪk/ *adj* **1** good at persuading
people, often in a way that is slightly
dishonest ‖ 종종 약간 부정직하게 사람을
설득하는 데에 능한. 말솜씨가 좋은. 언변
이 능란한. 교묘한: *a slick sales man* 언
변이 좋은 판매원 / *slick commercials* 교
묘한 선전 광고 **2** smooth and slippery ‖
반들반들하고 미끄러운. 미끌미끌한: *The
roads are slick with ice.* 도로가 얼음으
로 미끄럽다

slick² *n* ⇨ OIL SLICK

slick³ *v*

slick *sth* ↔ **down/back** *phr v* [T] to
make hair smooth and shiny by using
oil, water etc. ‖ 기름·물 등을 써서 머리
를 매끄럽고 윤이 나게 하다. 반드르르하
게 하다

slide¹ /slaɪd/ *v* **slid** /slɪd/, **slid**,
sliding 1 [I, T] to move smoothly on or
along a surface, or to make something
move in this way ‖ 표면 위나 표면을 따라
매끄럽게 움직이다, 또는 다른 사물을 이
렇게 움직이게 하다. 미끄러지다[지게 하
다]. 미끄럼을 타다[활주시키다]:
children sliding on the ice 얼음 위에서
미끄럼을 타는 아이들 / *She slid the box
across the floor.* 그녀는 바닥을 가로질러
상자를 미끄러뜨렸다. **2** [I] to become
lower in value, number, or amount etc.
‖ 가치[수, 양] 등에서 낮아지다. 내리다.
(미끄러지듯) 떨어지다: *Car sales slid
0.5 % in July.* 자동차 판매량이 7월에
0.5% 떨어졌다. **3** [T] to gradually start
to have a particular problem, attitude
etc. ‖ 특정한 문제·태도 등을 점차 갖기
시작하다. …에 모르는 사이에 빠져 들다:
*Morrison gradually slid into alcohol
and drug abuse.* 모리슨은 점차 술과 마
약의 남용에 빠져 들었다. **4 let** *sth* **slide**
INFORMAL to ignore something ‖ 무엇을
무시하다. 등한시하다. 내버려 두다: *I
didn't agree, but I let it slide.* 나는 동의
하지 않았지만 돼 가는 대로 내버려 두었
다.

slide² *n* **1** a large structure for children
to slide down while playing ‖ 아이들이
놀면서 미끄러져 내리는 큰 구조물. 미끄
럼틀[대] **2** a small piece of film in a
frame that shows a picture on a screen,
when you shine light through it ‖ 빛을
통과시켜 비추면 영사막에 그림이 나타나
는, 틀 속에 넣은 작은 필름 조각. 슬라이
드 (필름): *slides of our vacation* 우리 휴
가 때에 찍은 슬라이드 필름 **3** a decrease
in the price, value, etc. of something ‖

어떤 것의 가격·가치 등의 감소. 하락: *a slide in the President's popularity* 대통령의 인기도의 하락 **4** a situation in which someone gradually begins to have a particular problem, attitude etc. ‖ 사람이 점차 특정 문제·태도 등을 갖기 시작하는 상황: *School officials are worried about the slide in student performance.* 학교 관계자들은 학생들의 성적이 하락하는 것을 우려하고 있다. **5** a sudden fall of earth, stones, snow etc. down a slope ‖ 흙·돌·눈 등이 갑자기 경사면을 (굴러) 떨어짐. 낙석. 붕괴. 사태(沙汰): *a rock slide* 산사태 **6** a small piece of thin glass used for holding something when you look at it under a MICROSCOPE ‖ 현미경 아래 물체를 고정해 놓고 관찰할 때 쓰이는 작고 얇은 유리 조각. 슬라이드

slide pro·jec·tor /'. .,../ *n* a piece of equipment that makes SLIDEs appear on a screen ‖ 슬라이드 영상이 영사막 위에 나타나게 하는 장비. 환등기. 슬라이드 필름 영사기

sliding scale /,.. './ *n* a system for paying taxes, wages etc. in which the amount that you pay changes when there are different conditions ‖ 조건이 달라질 때 지불하는 액수가 달라지는 세금·임금 등의 지불 체계. 슬라이딩 스케일(방식)

sli·er /'slaɪə/ *adj* the COMPARATIVE of SLY ‖ sly의 비교급

sli·est /'slaɪ-ɪst/ *adj* the SUPERLATIVE of SLY ‖ sly의 최상급

slight¹ /slaɪt/ *adj* **1** not serious or important ‖ 심하거나 중요하지 않은. 얼마 안 되는. 약간의: *I'm afraid there will be a slight delay.* (=short delay) 약간의 지체가 있을까 걱정됩니다. **2** thin and delicate ‖ 마르고 연약한. 홀쭉한. 허약한: *a slight old lady* 연약한 노부인

slight² *v* [T] to offend someone by treating him/her rudely ‖ 어떤 사람을 무례하게 대해서 기분 나쁘게 하다. 모욕[무시, 냉대]하다. 얕보다: *Meg felt slighted at not being invited to the party.* 메그는 파티에 초대받지 못한 것에 대해 무시당했다고 느꼈다. – **slighting** *adj*

slight³ *n* FORMAL a remark or action that offends someone ‖ 어떤 사람을 기분 상하게 하는 발언이나 행동. 모욕: *I consider the comment a slight on the quality of our work!* 나는 그 발언을 우리 작품의 질에 대한 모욕이라고 생각해!

slight·ly /'slaɪtli/ *adv* **1** a little ‖ 약간. 조금: *She raised her eyebrow slightly.* 그

녀는 눈썹을 약간 치켜 올렸다. **2 slightly built** having a thin and delicate body ‖ 마르고 연약한 신체를 가진. 섬세한[가냘픈] 몸매의

slim¹ /slɪm/ *adj* **1** attractively thin ‖ 매력적으로 마른. 호리호리한. 날씬한. 가느다란: *tall and slim* 키가 크고 날씬한 — see usage note at THIN¹ **2** very small in amount ‖ 양이 매우 적은. 얼마 안 되는. 불충분한. 근소한: *a slim lead in the polls* 여론 조사에서 근소한 우세 **3 slim chance/hopes etc.** very little chance etc. of getting what you want ‖ 원하는 것을 얻기가 매우 어려운 기회. 희박한 기회/희망: *We have a slim chance of winning.* 우리는 승리할 가능성이 희박하다.

slim² *v* **-mmed, -mming**
slim down *phr v* [I, T] **1** to become thinner by eating less, exercising etc. ‖ 덜 먹거나 운동 등으로 마르게 되다. 날씬해지다. 살이 빠지다: *I've been trying to slim down since Christmas.* 나는 크리스마스 이후로 살을 빼려고 노력하고 있는 중이다. **2** to reduce the size or number of something ‖ 사물의 크기나 수를 줄이다. 감소[축소]하다: *Apex Co. is slimming down its workforce to cut costs.* 아펙스 기업은 비용을 줄이기 위해 인력을 감축하고 있다. – **slimming** *n* [U]

slime /slaɪm/ *n* [U] a thick slippery substance that looks or smells unpleasant ‖ 불쾌한 모양이나 냄새를 지닌 끈끈하고 미끈거리는 물질. 점액(물)

slim·y /'slaɪmi/ *adj* **1** covered with SLIME ‖ 점액물로 덮여 있는. 곤죽 같은. 끈적끈적한: *slimy rocks* (이끼 등으로) 미끈거리는 바위들 **2** INFORMAL friendly in a way that is not pleasant or sincere, because you want to get something for yourself ‖ 자신을 위한 어떤 것을 얻길 바라기 때문에 즐겁거나 진실되지 않게 친근한. 아첨하는. 착 달라붙는: *He's so slimy!* 그는 진짜 아첨이 심해!

sling¹ /slɪŋ/ *v* **slung, slung, slinging** [T] to throw something somewhere with a wide uncontrolled movement ‖ 물건을 어딘가로 크게 내저어 아무렇게나 던지다. 홱 내던지다: *She slung her purse over her shoulder.* 그녀는 핸드백을 어깨에 홱 멨다.

sling² *n* **1** a piece of cloth tied around your neck to support your injured arm or hand ‖ 부상당한 팔이나 손을 지탱하려고 목에 둘러서 묶는 천 조각. 삼각건: *Emily's arm has been in a sling for six weeks.* 에밀리는 6주 동안 팔을 삼각건으로 목에 걸고 있었다. **2** ropes or strong pieces of cloth for holding heavy objects that need to be lifted or carried ‖ 들어올리거나 운반해야 하는 무거운 물체를 묶는 밧줄 또는 튼튼한 천 조각

sling·shot /'slɪŋʃɑt/ *n* a stick in the shape of a Y with a thin band of rubber attached, used by children to throw stones ‖ 아이들이 돌멩이를 쏘기 위해 쓰는 얇은 고무 띠가 달린 Y자 형태의 막대기. 새총

slink /slɪŋk/ *v* **slunk, slunk, slinking** [I] to move somewhere quietly and secretly ‖ 조용히 그리고 몰래 어딘가로 움직이다. 살금살금 움직이다[걷다]: *The cat slunk behind the chair.* 고양이는 의자 뒤로 살금살금 걸어갔다.

slip[1] /slɪp/ *v* **-pped, -pping 1** [I] to accidentally slide a short distance quickly, or to fall by sliding in this way ‖ 사고로 짧은 거리를 빠르게 미끄러지다 또는 이런 식으로 미끄러지며 넘어지다. 미끄러지다. 미끄러져 넘어지다: *Joan slipped and fell.* 조안은 미끄러져 넘어졌다. / *The knife slipped and cut her finger.* 칼이 빗나가 그녀는 손가락을 베었다. **2** [I] to move quietly or secretly ‖ 조용히 또는 몰래 움직이다. 살짝 가다[나가다, 들어가다]: *After dinner, Al slipped outside.* 저녁 식사 후 앨은 슬그머니 밖으로 나갔다. **3** [T] to put something somewhere or give someone something quietly or secretly ‖ 조용히 또는 몰래 어떤 것을 어딘가에 넣거나 남에게 주다. 슬쩍 넣다[건네다]: *She slipped his wallet out of his pocket.* 그녀는 그의 지갑을 슬그머니 주머니에서 꺼냈다. / *Dad slipped me $50 when Mom wasn't looking.* 아빠는 엄마가 보지 않을 때 50달러를 나에게 슬쩍 주셨다. **4** [I] to become worse or lower than before ‖ 전보다 더 악화 또는 저하되다. 쇠퇴하다: *Standards have slipped in the restaurant since the head chef left.* 수석 요리사가 떠난 후 그 식당은 수준이 떨어졌다. **5 slip your mind** if something slips your mind, you forget to do it ‖ 어떤 것을 하는 것을 잊어버리다: *I'm so sorry – it completely slipped my mind.* 정말 미안해. 완전히 깜빡 했어.

slip into sth *phr v* [T] to put clothes on quickly ‖ 옷을 잽싸게 입다. 훌렁 입다: *I'll just slip into something more comfortable.* 나는 그냥 좀 더 편한 것으로 얼른 갈아 입을 거야.

slip sth ↔ **off** *phr v* [T] to take clothes off quickly ‖ 옷을 잽싸게 벗다. 훌렁 벗다: *He slipped off his coat and went upstairs.* 그는 코트를 훌렁 벗고 윗층으로 올라갔다.

slip sth ↔ **on** *phr v* [T] to put clothes on quickly ‖ 옷을 잽싸게 입다: *She slipped the dress on over her head.* 그녀는 옷을 머리 위로 잽싸게 입었다.

slip out *phr v* [I] if something slips out, you say it without intending to ‖ 그럴 의도 없이 어떤 것을 말하다. 무심코 말하다: *I'm sorry I spoiled the surprise; it just slipped out.* 미안해 내가 깜짝 파티를 망쳤어. 그냥 무심코 말이 나와 버렸어.

slip out of sth *phr v* [T] to take clothes off quickly ‖ 옷을 잽싸게 벗다: *Ken slipped out of his shoes.* 켄은 신발을 잽싸게 벗었다.

slip up *phr v* [I] to make a mistake ‖ 실수하다. 잘못하다: *They slipped up and sent me the wrong form.* 그들은 실수로 나에게 잘못된 서식(書式)을 보냈다.

slip[2] *n* **1** a small or narrow piece of paper ‖ 작거나 좁은 종잇조각. 좁고 긴 쪽지: *a slip of paper with her phone number on it* 그녀의 전화번호가 적힌 종이 쪽지 **2** a piece of clothing worn under a dress or skirt, that hangs from the shoulders or waist ‖ 드레스나 치마 속에 입는 어깨 또는 허리에서부터 내려오는 옷. 슬립 **3 a slip of the tongue** something that you say when you meant to say something else ‖ 어떤 말을 하려고 하면서 다른 말을 한 것. 말실수 **4 give sb the slip** INFORMAL to succeed in escaping from someone who is chasing you ‖ 쫓고 있는 사람으로부터 도망치는 데 성공하다. 남을 따돌리다: *He gave the police the slip.* 그는 경찰을 따돌렸다.

slip·knot /'slɪpnɑt/ *n* a knot that you can make tighter or looser by pulling one of its ends ‖ 한쪽 끝을 잡고 당겨 더 단단하게 또는 느슨하게 할 수 있는 매듭. 풀매듭

slipped disc, slipped disk /ˌ. ˈ./ *n* a painful injury caused when a part between the bones in your back moves out of place ‖ 척추 뼈 사이 부분이 자리를 이탈해서 생기는 고통스런 부상. 디스크. 추간판 헤르니아

slip·per /'slɪpɚ/ *n* a light soft shoe that you wear in your house ‖ 집에서 신는 가볍고 편한 신발. 슬리퍼

slip·per·y /'slɪpəri/ *adj* **1** smooth and difficult to hold, walk on etc., especially because of being wet ‖ 특히 젖어 있어서 매끈하고 쥐거나 걷기 등이 힘든. 미끄러운. 반들반들한: *Careful, the sidewalk's slippery.* 조심, 보도가 미끄러움. **2** INFORMAL not to be trusted ‖ 믿을 수 없는. 종잡을 수[파악할 수] 없는: *a* *slippery character* 믿지 못할 성격

slip·shod /'slɪpʃɑd/ *adj* done too quickly and carelessly ‖ 너무 빠르고 부주의하게 된. 단정치 못한. 되는 대로의: *slipshod work* 되는 대로 해치운 일

slip-up /'. ./ *n* a careless mistake that spoils a process or plan ‖ 과정이나 계획을 망치는 부주의한 실수. 실책. 간과: *One slip-up cost us $100,000.* 한 번의 실수가 우리에게 10만달러를 치르게 했다.

slit /slɪt/ *v* **slit, slit, slitting** [T] to make a straight narrow cut in cloth, paper etc. ‖ 천·종이 등을 일직선으로 가늘게 자르다. 가늘고 길게 베다: *Slit the pie crust before baking.* 굽기 전 파이 껍질에 칼집을 가늘게 내어라. – **slit** *n*

slith·er /'slɪðɚ/ *v* [I] to slide across a surface, twisting and moving like a snake ‖ 뱀처럼 구불구불 움직이면서 표면을 미끄러져 나아가다. 주르르 미끄러지다

sliv·er /'slɪvɚ/ *n* a very small thin pointed piece of something that has been cut or broken off something else ‖ 다른 것으로 잘리거나 깨어진 매우 작고 가늘고 뾰족한 물체의 조각. 쪼개진 조각: *a small sliver in his finger* (=a sliver of wood) 그의 손가락에 박힌 작은 나무 조각 / *a sliver of pie* 파이 조각 – **sliver** *v* [T] —compare SPLINTER¹

slob /slɑb/ *n* INFORMAL someone who is lazy, dirty, messy, or rude ‖ 게으른[더러운, 지저분한, 무례한] 사람. 게으름뱅이. 얼간이: *The guy is a total slob.* 그 남자는 정말 게으름뱅이이다.

slob·ber /'slɑbɚ/ *v* [I] to let SALIVA (=liquid produced in your mouth) come out of your mouth and run down ‖ 입에서 침이 나와 흘러내리게 하다. 군침을 흘리다: *The dog's slobbered all over the rug!* 개가 양탄자 위에 온통 침을 흘려 놨어!

slog /slɑg/ *v* **-gged, -gging** [I] **1** to walk somewhere with difficulty ‖ 힘들게 어딘가로 걸어가다. 고생하며 나아가다: *soldiers slogging through the mud* 진흙 속을 고생하며 나아가는 군인들 **2** to work very hard at something without stopping ‖ 멈추지 않고 어떤 일을 매우 열심히 하다: *I've been slogging through a boring 400 page novel.* 나는 지루한 400 페이지 분량의 소설을 열심히 읽어 오고 있다.

slo·gan /'sloʊgən/ *n* a short phrase that is easy to remember, used by politicians, companies that are advertising etc. ‖ 정치가·기업들 홍보하는 등에 쓰는 기억하기 쉬운 짧은 문구. 슬로건. 선전 문구: *The crowd shouted*

anti-racist slogans. 군중은 인종 차별에 반대하는 슬로건을 외쳤다.

slop¹ /slɑp/ *v* **-pped, -pping 1** [I, T] to make liquid move around or over the edge of something, or to move in this way ‖ 액체를 어떤 것의 가장자리 주변이나 위로 움직이게 하다, 또는 이렇게 움직이다. 흘리다. 엎지르다: *The coffee slopped out of the cup and all over me.* 컵에서 커피가 엎질러져 온통 나에게 흘렀다. **2** [T] to feed SLOP to pigs ‖ 돼지에게 먹이를 주다. 꿀꿀이죽을 먹이다

slop² *n* [U] **1** food waste that is used for feeding animals ‖ 동물 사료로 쓰이는 음식 찌꺼기. 잔반 **2** food that is too soft and tastes bad ‖ 너무 멀겋고 맛없는 음식. 돼지죽 같은 음식: *I'm not eating that slop!* 나는 그 꿀꿀이죽 같은 음식을 먹지 않을 거야!

slope¹ /sloʊp/ *n* **1** a piece of ground or a surface that is higher at one end than the other ‖ 한쪽 끝이 다른 쪽 끝보다 더 높은 대지나 지표면. 경사면: *a ski slope* 스키 슬로프 **2** the angle at which something slopes ‖ 어떤 것의 경사진 각도. 경사도: *a slope of 30°* 30도의 경사도

slope² *v* [I] if the ground or a surface slopes, it is higher at one end than the other ‖ 대지나 지표면의 한쪽 끝이 다른 쪽 끝보다 더 높다. 경사지다: *fields sloping to the road* 도로로 경사져 뻗은 들판

slop·py /'slɑpi/ *adj* **1** not neat, careful, or thorough ‖ 꼼꼼하지[주의 깊지, 철저하지] 않은. 부주의한: *sloppy work* 얼렁뚱땅 해치운 일 **2** loose-fitting and not looking neat ‖ 헐렁하고 단정해 보이지 는. 헐렁헐렁한: *big sloppy sweatshirts* 크고 헐렁한 땀복 **3** wet and dirty ‖ 질고 더러운. 질척질척한: *a sloppy lick from the dog* 개가 침이 뒤범벅이 되어 핥음 – **sloppily** *adv* – **sloppiness** *n* [U] —compare MESSY

slosh /slɑʃ/ *v* [I] **1** to walk through water or mud noisily ‖ 물이나 진흙 속을 소리를 내며 걷다. 흙탕을 튀기며[철벅거리며] 걷다: *kids sloshing through puddles* 물웅덩이 속을 철벅거리며 걷는 아이들 **2** if a liquid in a container sloshes, it moves against the sides of the container ‖ 용기 속의 액체가 가장자리에 철렁철렁 부딪치다: *water sloshing around in the bottom of the boat* 배의 바닥에 철렁대는 물

sloshed /slɑʃt/ *adj* INFORMAL drunk ‖ 술취한: *Gus was sloshed even before the party started.* 거스는 파티가 시작되기도 전에 술에 취했다.

slot¹ /slɑt/ n **1** a long narrow hole made in a surface ‖ 표면에 난 길고 가는 홈[자국, 틈]. 동전 투입구: *Which slot do the coins go in?* 어떤 투입구에 동전을 넣어야 합니까? **2** a time, position, or opportunity for something ‖ 어떤 것의 시간[지위, 기회]: *the top-rated TV show in its time slot* 그 시간대의 가장 인기 있는 TV 쇼

slot² v **-tted, -tting** [I, T] to put something into a SLOT, or to go in a slot ‖ 가는 홈에 어떤 것을 넣다, 또는 가는 홈에 들어가다. …을 (사이에) 끼워 넣다[꽂다]: *The cassette slots in here.* 카세트는 여기에 꽂는다. / *The instructions tell you how to slot the shelf together.* 그 사용 지시문은 선반을 서로 어떻게 끼워 맞추는지 알려준다.

slot in phr v [I, T **slot** sb/sth **in**] INFORMAL to find a time or a place for someone or something in a plan, organization etc. ‖ 계획·조직 등에서 어떤 사람이나 사물을 위한 시간 또는 장소를 찾아보다. (스케줄 사이에) 끼워 넣다: *Can you slot me in today?* 오늘 나에게 시간 좀 내어 줄 수 있니?

sloth /slɔθ, sloʊθ/ n **1** a slow-moving animal from Central and South America ‖ 느리게 움직이는 중앙·남아메리카산 동물. 나무늘보 **2** [U] LITERARY laziness ‖ 게으름 **– slothful** adj

slot ma·chine /ˈ. ./ n a machine in which you put a coin, and which gives you more money back if three of the same pictures appear ‖ 3개의 그림이 똑같이 나타나면 넣은 동전보다 더 많이 되돌려 주는 기계. 슬롯 머신. 자동 도박기

slouch¹ /slaʊtʃ/ v [I] to stand, sit, or walk with your shoulders bent forward ‖ 어깨를 앞으로 구부리고 서다[앉다, 걷다]. 구부정하게 서다[앉다, 걷다]: *Don't slouch like that; you'll hurt your back.* 그렇게 구부정하게 있지 마. 허리 아플 거야.

slouch² n **1** the position of your body when you SLOUCH ‖ 구부정하게 몸을 앞으로 구부린 자세. 앞으로 수그린 축 처진 태도 **2 be no slouch (at)** INFORMAL to be very good or skillful at something ‖ 어떤 것에 매우 능숙하거나 솜씨 있다. 곧잘[패] 하다: *He's no slouch at football.* 그는 미식축구를 곧잘 한다.

slough¹ /slaʊ, sluː/ n a wet area that is full of mud and dirty water that does not flow ‖ 진흙과 흐르지 않는 더러운 물로 가득 찬 진창. 진구렁

slough² /slʌf/ v

slough sth ↔ **off** phr v [T] **1** TECHNICAL to get rid of a dead outer layer of skin ‖ 죽은 외피를 제거하다. 탈피하다 **2** LITERARY to get rid of a feeling, belief etc. ‖ 감정·생각 등을 없애다. 버리다

slov·en·ly /ˈslʌvənli, ˈslɑ-/ adj dirty, messy, and careless ‖ 더러운, 지저분한, 부주의한. 추접스러운: *slovenly housekeeping* 지저분한 살림살이

slow¹ /sloʊ/ adj **1** not moving, being done, or happening quickly ‖ 빠르게 움직이지[이뤄지지, 발생하지] 않는. 느린, 천천히 하는: *They've been slow in answering our letters.* 그들은 우리의 편지에 대해 늦게 답장을 해 왔다. / *The slowest runners started at the back.* 가장 느린 주자들이 뒷편에서 출발했다. / *businesses that are slow to react to market trends* 시장 동향에 대한 반응이 느린 기업들 **2** a clock that is slow shows a time earlier than the true time ‖ 시계가 실제 시간보다 이전의 숫자를 가리켜. 느린, 늦은: *My watch is a few minutes slow.* 내 시계는 몇 분 정도가 느리다. **3** if business is slow, there are not many customers ‖ 사업에 고객이 많지 않은. 부진한. 활기 없는: *It's been a slow day.* 장사가 안 되는 날이었다. **4** not quick at understanding things ‖ 이해력이 빠르지 않은. 이해력이 더딘. 둔한: *The school gives extra help for slower students.* 학교는 이해가 더딘 학생들을 위해 과외 지도를 해주고 있다.

slow² v [I, T] also **slow up** to become slower or make something slower ‖ 더디어지다, 또는 어떤 것을 더디게 하다. 늦추다. 지체시키다: *Road work slowed up traffic this morning.* 도로공사가 오늘 아침 교통을 정체시켰다.

slow down phr v [I,T **slow** sth ↔ **down**] to become slower or make something slower ‖ 더 느려지다 또는 어떤 것을 느리게 하다. (속도가[를]) 떨어지다[늦추다]: *Dave's back trouble is slowing him down.* 허리가 아파서 데이브는 천천히 움직인다. / *Slow down – no running by the pool.* 천천히, 풀장 주변에서 뛰지 말 것.

slow³ adv NONSTANDARD ⇨ SLOWLY

slow·down /ˈsloʊdaʊn/ n a time when an activity takes place slowly, especially when workers are protesting about something ‖ 특히 근로자들이 어떤 것에 대해 항의하고 있을 때 작업이 더디게 이뤄지는 시기. 태업: *Sales have fallen since workers began their slowdown.* 노동자들이 태업을 시작한 후로 판매가 감소되었다.

slow·ly /ˈsloʊli/ adv at a slow speed or

rate ‖ 느린 속도나 정도로. 천천히: *The car was moving slowly down the street.* 그 자동차는 거리 아래쪽으로 느리게 움직이고 있었다. / *The medicine is slowly decreased until the patient is better.* 환자가 더 나을 때까지 약은 서서히 줄어든다.

slow mo·tion /ˌ. '../ *n* [U] movement in a movie or television program that is shown at a much slower speed than the speed at which it happened ‖ 영화나 텔레비전 프로그램에서 실제 속도보다 훨씬 느린 속도로 보여지는 동작. 슬로모션: *a replay of the goal shown in slow motion* 슬로모션으로 보여준 득점 장면의 재생

slow·poke /'sloupouk/ *n* SPOKEN someone who moves or does things too slowly ‖ 매우 느리게 움직이거나 일하는 사람. 둔한 사람. 멍청이: *Hurry up, slowpoke, or we'll be late.* 서둘러, 굼벵아, 그렇지 않으면 우린 늦을 거야.

slow-wit·ted /ˌ. '../ *adj* not quick to understand things ‖ 사물을 이해하는 것이 빠르지 않은. 우둔한

sludge /slʌdʒ/ *n* [U] a soft thick substance made of mud, waste, oil etc. ‖ 진흙·쓰레기·기름 등으로 생긴 연질의 걸쭉한 물질. 진창. 침전물. 찌꺼기

slug[1] /slʌg/ *n* 1 INFORMAL a bullet ‖ 총알. 총탄. 산탄 2 a small creature with a soft body and no legs, like a SNAIL without a shell ‖ 부드러운 몸에 다리가 없고 껍데기가 없는 달팽이 같은 작은 동물. 민달팽이 3 INFORMAL a small amount of a drink, especially alcohol ‖ 적은 양의 음료수, 특히 술. (술 등의) 한 잔: *a slug of whiskey* 위스키 한 잔 4 INFORMAL a piece of metal used illegally instead of a coin in machines that sell things ‖ 자동판매기에 동전 대신 넣는 불법적인 금속 조각. 가짜 주화 5 a hard hit ‖ 강타: *a slug on the jaw* 턱에 가한 강타

slug[2] *v* **-gged, -gging** [T] 1 INFORMAL to hit someone hard with your closed hand ‖ 주먹으로 남을 세게 때리다. 구타하다: *I stood up and he slugged me again.* 내가 일어서자 그는 나를 다시 구타했다. 2 to hit a ball hard ‖ 공을 세게 치다. 강타하다 3 **slug it out** to argue or fight until someone wins or something has been decided ‖ 누군가가 이기거나 어떤 것이 결정날 때까지 다투거나 싸우다. 끝까지 맹렬히 싸우다: *The two sides are slugging it out in court.* 양측은 법정에서 끝까지 맹렬히 싸우고 있다.

slug·gish /'slʌgɪʃ/ *adj* moving, working, or reacting more slowly than normal ‖ 보통보다 더 느리게 움직이는[일

하는, 반응하는]. 느릿한: *The traffic was sluggish downtown.* 교통은 번화가에서 지체되었다.

sluice[1] /slus/ *n* a passage for water to flow through, with a gate that can stop the water if necessary ‖ 필요하면 물을 차단할 수 있는 수문이 달린, 물이 흐르는 통로. 배수로

sluice[2] *v* [T] to wash something with a lot of water ‖ 많은 물로 어떤 것을 씻다. 물을 퍼부어 씻다

slum[1] /slʌm/ *n* an area of a city with old buildings in very bad condition, where many poor people live ‖ 낡아서 상태가 매우 나쁜 건물들이 많고, 거기서 가난한 사람들이 많이 살고 있는 도시 지역. (도시의) 빈민가: *She grew up in the slums of L.A.* 그녀는 로스앤젤레스 빈민가에서 성장했다.

slum[2] *v* **-mmed, -mming** [I, T] to spend time in conditions that are much worse than those you are used to ‖ 예전보다 훨씬 나쁜 생활 여건 속에서 시간을 보내다: *We traveled around the country, slumming it.* 우리는 최대한 절약하며 국내를 여행했다.

slum·ber /'slʌmbɚ/ *n* [singular] LITERARY sleep ‖ 잠 – **slumber** *v* [I]

slumber par·ty /'.. ˌ../ *n* a party in which a group of children, especially girls, sleep at one child's house ‖ 특히, 소녀들이 한 아이의 집에서 자면서 노는 파티. 파자마 파티

slump[1] /slʌmp/ *v* [I] 1 to suddenly go down in price, value, or number ‖ 가격[가치, 수]이 갑자기 내려가다. 폭락하다. 뚝 떨어지다: *Car sales have slumped recently.* 최근에 자동차 매출이 뚝 떨어졌다. 2 **be slumped** to be sitting with your body leaning forward ‖ 몸을 앞쪽으로 기대고 앉아 있다. 앞쪽으로 구부리다[엎어지다]: *He was found slumped over the steering wheel of his car.* 그는 그의 차의 핸들 위에 엎어져 있는 채 발견되었다.

slump[2] *n* 1 a sudden fall in prices, sales, profits etc. ‖ 가격·매출·이윤 등의 급락. 폭락: *a slump in the housing market* 주택 시장의 침체 2 a time when companies or sports teams are not successful ‖ 기업이나 스포츠 팀이 성공적이지 못한 시기. 불황. 슬럼프: *The Yankees needed this win to pull them out of a slump.* 양키즈 팀은 슬럼프에서 빠져 나오기 위해서 이번 승리가 필요했다.

slung /slʌŋ/ *v* the past tense and PAST PARTICIPLE of SLING ‖ sing의 과거·과거 분

사형

slunk /slʌŋk/ v the past tense and PAST
PARTICIPLE of SLINK ‖ slink의 과거·과거
분사형

slur¹ /slɚ/ v -rred, -rring 1 [I, T] to
speak unclearly without separating
words or sounds ‖ 단어나 소리들을 구분
없이 불분명하게 말하다. 분명치 않게 발
음하다. 흘려 말하다: *After a few drinks,
he started to slur his words.* 술을 몇 잔
마신 후, 그는 혀가 꼬이기 시작했다. **2**
[T] to criticize someone or something
unfairly ‖ 사람이나 사물을 부당하게 비난
하다. …을 중상[비방]하다

slur² n 1 an unfair criticism ‖ 부당한 비
난. 중상. 비방: *racial slurs* 인종적 비방
2 an unclear way of speaking in which
the words are not separated ‖ 단어들을
구분 없이 불분명하게 하는 말. 분명치 않
은 발음: *an injury that caused a slur in
her speech* 그녀의 발음을 분명치 않게 만
든 부상

slurp /slɚp/ v [I, T] to drink a liquid
while making a noisy sucking sound ‖ 음
료를 시끄럽게 들이켜는 소리를 내며 마시
다. 시끄럽게 소리내며 마시다: *Stop
slurping your soup!* 수프를 후루룩거리며
먹지 마라! – **slurp** n

slush /slʌʃ/ n 1 [U] partly melted snow
‖ 부분적으로 녹은 눈. 진창눈 **2** a drink
made by partly freezing a sweet liquid ‖
달콤한 액체를 부분적으로 얼려 만든 음
료. 슬러시: *orange slush* 오렌지 슬러시
– **slushy** adj

slush fund /'. ./ n money that is
available to be used but is not kept for
one particular purpose ‖ 하나의 특정 목
적을 위해 보관되지 않고 언제든지 사용할
수 있는 돈. 비자금

slut /slʌt/ n OFFENSIVE a woman who
has sex with many different people ‖ 다
른 많은 사람들과 성관계를 갖는 여자. 매
춘부

sly /slaɪ/ adj **slyer** or **slier, slyest** or
sliest 1 using tricks and dishonesty to
get what you want ‖ 원하는 것을 얻기 위
해 속임수를 쓰며 정직하지 못한. 교활한.
간교한: *He's sly and greedy.* 그는 교활하
고 탐욕스럽다. **2** showing that you know
something that others do not know ‖ 남
들이 모르는 것을 안다고 재는. 능청맞은.
음흉한: *a sly smile* 능청맞은 미소 **3 on
the sly** INFORMAL secretly doing
something you are not supposed to be
doing ‖ 하게 되어 있지 않은 어떤 것을 몰
래 하는. 남모르게. 슬그머니: *He's been
smoking on the sly.* 그는 몰래 담배를 피
워 오고 있다. – **slyly** adv

smack¹ /smæk/ v [T] **1** to hit someone
or something, especially with your open
hand ‖ 특히 손바닥으로 사람이나 사물을
때리다. …을 철썩 때리다: *She smacked
him hard across the face.* 그녀는 그의 얼
굴을 세게 때렸다. **2 smack your lips** to
make a short loud noise with your lips,
especially because something looks
good to eat ‖ 특히 어떤 것이 맛있어 보여
서 입술로 짧고 큰 소리를 내다. (입술을)
쩝쩝거리다

smack of sth phr v [T] to seem to have
a particular quality ‖ 특정한 성질을 가진
것처럼 보이다. …의 기미[기색]가 있다:
*a policy that smacks of age
discrimination* 연령 차별적 경향이 있는
정책

smack² n **1** a hit with your open hand,
or a noise like the sound of this ‖ 손바닥
으로 때리기, 또는 이 소리 같은 소음. 찰
싹 때리기[때리는 소리]: *a smack on the
head* 머리의 가격 **2** [U] SLANG ⇨ HEROIN

smack³ adv INFORMAL **1** exactly or
directly in, on, or through something ‖
정확히 또는 바로 어떤 것 안에 있거나 위
에 있거나, 또는 통해 있어. 정면에. 한가
운데: *an old building smack (dab) in
the middle of campus* 교내 한복판에 있
는 오래된 건물 **2** to hit something
directly with a lot of force ‖ 세게 정통으
로 어떤 것을 치다. 정통[정면]으로: *The
van ran smack into the wall.* 그 승합차
는 벽을 정통으로 들이받았다.

small /smɔl/ adj **1** not large in size or
amount ‖ 크기나 양이 많지 않은. 작은.
적은: *Rhode Island is the smallest state.*
로드아일랜드는 가장 작은 주이다. / *a
store selling small appliances* 작은 기구
들을 판매하는 가게 **2** unimportant or
easy to deal with ‖ 중요치 않거나 다루기
쉬운. 하찮은. 사소한: *a small problem*
사소한 문제 **3** a small child is young ‖ 아
이들이 어린. 나이어린: *She has two
small children.* 그녀에겐 두 명의 어린 자
녀가 있다. **4 small business/farm** a
business etc. that does not produce or
use large amounts of money ‖ 많은 돈을
벌거나 쓰지 않는 기업 등. 소기업/소규모
농장: *Magill started a small business
publishing reference works.* 매길은 참고
서적을 출판하는 소규모 사업을 시작했다.
5 small fortune a lot of money ‖ 많은
돈. 큰돈. 목돈: *That house must have
cost him a small fortune.* 그는 그 집을
큰돈을 들여 산 것이 틀림없다. **6 the
small of your back** the part of your
back just above your BUTTOCKs ‖ 엉덩이
바로 위의 등 쪽 부분. 허리의 잘록한 등

쪽 부분 – **small** *adv* : *He writes so small I can't read it.* 그는 글씨를 너무 작게 써서 읽을 수가 없다.

small change /ˌ. './ *n* [U] money in coins of low value ‖ 액면가가 낮은 동전으로 된 돈. 잔돈

small claims court /ˌ. '. ˌ./ *n* a court that deals with cases that involve small amounts of money ‖ 소액 관련 사건을 다루는 법정. (미국의) 소액 재판소

small fry /'. ./ *n* [U] INFORMAL **1** children ‖ 아이들 **2** unimportant people or things ‖ 중요하지 않은 사람이나 사물. 피라미

small-mind·ed /ˌ.'../ *adj* DISAPPROVING only interested in things that affect you, and too willing to judge people according to your own opinions ‖ 오직 자신에게 영향을 미치는 것들에만 관심을 가지며 지나치게 자신의 생각에 따라 사람들을 판단하려고 하는. 도량[속]이 좁은. 이기적인: *greedy small-minded people* 탐욕스럽고 이기적인 사람들

small po·ta·toes /ˌ. .'../ *adj* INFORMAL not very big or important ‖ 매우 크지 않거나 중요하지 않은. 하찮은. 시시한: *Compared to his salary, mine is small potatoes.* 그의 봉급에 비교하면, 내 봉급은 푼돈이다.

small·pox /'smɔlpɑks/ *n* [U] a serious disease that causes spots that leave marks on your skin ‖ 피부에 자국을 남기는 반점이 생기는 심각한 질병. 천연두

small-scale /ˌ. '../ *adj* not very big, or not involving a lot of people ‖ 매우 크지 않거나 많은 사람들과 관련되지 않은. 소규모의: *small-scale map* 축척이 작은 지도 / *small-scale development* 소규모의 개발

small talk /'. ./ *n* [U] polite friendly conversation about unimportant subjects ‖ 시시한 주제에 관한 예의 바르고 사교적인 대화. 잡담: *He's not very good at making small talk.* 그는 사교적인 대화를 나누는데 서투르다.

small-time /ˌ. '../ *adj* unimportant or not successful ‖ 중요하지 않거나 성공적이지 않은. 삼류의. 하찮은: *a small-time gangster* 삼류 건달

smart¹ /smɑrt/ *adj* **1** intelligent ‖ 총명한. 똑똑한. 영리한: *Jill's a smart kid.* 질은 총명한 아이이다. **2** making good judgments or decisions ‖ 판단이나 결정이 뛰어난. 현명한: *I don't think that would be a very smart move.* (=good decision or plan) 나는 그것이 가장 현명한 조치일 거라고 생각하지 않는다. **3** smart machines, weapons etc. use

computers or advanced TECHNOLOGY to work ‖ 기계·무기 등이 컴퓨터나 최신 기술을 사용하여 작동시키는. 컴퓨터화된. 고성능의 **4** saying funny or intelligent things in a way that is rude and not respectful ‖ 무례하고 정중하지 않게, 우습거나 재치 있는 것을 말하는. 건방진. 똑똑한 체하는: *Don't get smart with me, young lady!* 아가씨, 내 앞에서 똑똑한 체하지 마! **5** OLD-FASHIONED neat and fashionable ‖ 단정하고 멋이 있는. 말쑥한. 세련된 – **smartly** *adv* : *smartly dressed men* 말쑥하게 차려입은 남자

smart² *v* [I] **1** to be upset because someone has offended you ‖ 남이 불쾌하게 해서 기분이 상하다. 감정을 해치다: *He's still smarting from the insult.* 그는 그 모욕으로 여전히 분개하고 있다. **2** if a part of your body smarts, it hurts with a stinging pain ‖ 신체의 일부분이 쑤시며 아프다. 욱신거리다

smart al·eck /'smɑrt ˌælɪk/, **smart ass** *n* INFORMAL someone who says funny or intelligent things in a rude way ‖ 재미있거나 재치 있는 것들을 무례하게 이야기하는 사람. 시건방진[잘난 체하는] 놈

smart card /'. ./ *n* a small plastic card that can be used in many ways, for example as a key, as a bank card, as IDENTIFICATION etc. ‖ 열쇠·신용 카드·신분증 등처럼 많은 용도로 쓰일 수 있는 작은 플라스틱 카드. 스마트 카드

smarty pants /'smɑrti ˌpænts/ *n* HUMOROUS ⇨ SMART ALECK

smash¹ /smæʃ/ *v* **1** [I, T] to break into many small pieces violently, or to make something do this ‖ 많은 작은 조각들로 심하게 부서지다, 또는 어떤 것을 이렇게 되게 하다. 산산조각이 나다[을 내다]. 분쇄하다: *The plates smashed on the floor.* 접시들이 바닥에 떨어져 산산이 부서졌다. / *Rioters smashed store windows and set fire to cars.* 폭도들은 상점의 유리창을 박살내고 차에 불을 질렀다. **2** [I, T] to hit an object or surface violently, or to make something do this ‖ 강하게 물체나 표면을 치다, 또는 어떤 것을 이렇게 하게 하다. 세게 부딪치다. 강타하다: *Murray smashed his fist against the wall.* 머레이는 주먹으로 벽을 세게 쳤다. **3** [T] to destroy something such as a political system or criminal organization ‖ 정치 체제나 범죄 조직 등을 파괴하다. 타파하다. 없애다: *Police have smashed a drug smuggling ring.* 경찰은 마약 밀수단을 일망타진했다.

smash sth ↔ **in** *phr v* [T] to hit

something so violently that you damage it || 어떤 것을 매우 세차게 쳐서 손상을 가하다. 때려부수다. 깨뜨리다: *Pete's window was smashed in by the driver of the other car.* 다른 차의 운전자가 피트의 차창을 때려 부셨다.

smash sth ↔ **up** *phr v* [T] to damage or destroy something || 어떤 것을 손상시키거나 파괴하다. 찌부러뜨리다. 박살내다: *She smashed up the truck in an accident.* 그녀의 트럭은 사고로 박살이 났다.

smash² *n* also **smash hit** a very successful new play, movie, song etc. || 매우 성공적인 새 연극·영화·노래 등. 대성공. 대히트: *the band's latest smash-hit single* 그 그룹의 가장 최근에 대히트한 싱글판

smashed /smæʃt/ *adj* INFORMAL drunk || 취한. 곤드레만드레 취한

smat·ter·ing /'smætərɪŋ/ *n* a small number or amount of something || 어떤 것의 작은 수나 양. 소수. 조금: *a smattering of applause* 빈약한 박수갈채 / *He has a smattering of French.* (=he knows a little French) 그는 불어를 조금밖에 모른다.

smear¹ /smɪr/ *v* **1** [I, T] to spread a liquid or soft substance on a surface, or to become spread on a surface || 표면에 액체나 매끈한 물질을 바르다, 또는 표면에 퍼지다. …에 칠하다[번지다]: *Jill smeared lotion on Rick's back.* 질은 릭의 등에 로션을 발랐다. / *The note was damp and the ink had smeared.* 노트가 축축해서 잉크가 번졌다. **2** [T] to spread an untrue story about someone in order to harm him/her || 남을 해치기 위해 있지도 않은 이야기를 퍼뜨리다. 명예 훼손을 하다

smear² *n* **1** a mark that is left when a substance is spread on a surface || 물질이 표면에 번져 남은 자국. 얼룩: *a dirty smear* 더러운 얼룩 **2** an untrue story about someone that is meant to harm him/her || 남을 해치려는 거짓된 이야기. 명예 훼손. 중상

smell¹ /smɛl/ *v* **1** [I] to have a particular smell || 특정 냄새를 갖다. 냄새가 나다: *The room smelled of fresh flowers.* 방에서 상쾌한 꽃향기가 났다. / *This wine smells like berries.* 이 포도주는 딸기 향이 난다. **2** [I] to have an unpleasant smell; STINK || 불쾌한 냄새가 나다. 악취가 나다; ㈜ stink: *Something in the refrigerator smells.* 냉장고 안의 뭔가에서 악취가 난다. **3** [I, T] to notice or recognize a particular smell, or to be

able to do this || 특정 냄새를 알아채거나 분간하다, 또는 이렇게 할 수 있다. 냄새를 맡다[맡을 수 있다]. 후각이 있다: *I smell something burning!* 타는 냄새가 나! / *I've got a cold and I can't smell at all.* 나는 감기에 걸려서 전혀 냄새를 맡을 수 없어. **4** [T] to put your nose near something and breathe in, to discover what type of smell it has || 무슨 냄새가 나는지 알기 위해 어떤 것 근처에 코를 대고 숨을 들이쉬다. 코로 냄새를 맡다[맡아 보다]: *Come and smell these roses.* 와서 이 장미 향 좀 맡아 봐.

smell² *n* **1** the quality that you recognize by using your nose || 코로 감지하는 특성. 냄새: *the smell of fresh bread* 신선한 빵 냄새 **2** an unpleasant smell; STINK || 불쾌한 냄새. 악취; ㈜ stink: *What's that smell in the basement?* 지하실에서 나는 저 악취는 뭐지? **3** [U] the ability to notice or recognize smells || 냄새를 알아채거나 분간할 수 있는 능력. 후각: *an excellent sense of smell* 뛰어난 후각

USAGE NOTE smell, odor, scent, fragrance, and **aroma**

Use **smell** in a general way to talk about something that you notice or recognize using your nose: *the smell of rotten eggs* / *There are some wonderful smells coming from the kitchen.* An **odor** is an unpleasant smell: *The odor of stale smoke was in the air.* A **scent** is what something smells like, especially something that smells pleasant: *a cleaning liquid with a pine scent.* A **fragrance** is an extremely pleasant **scent**: *the deliciously sweet fragrance of the flowers.* An **aroma** is a pleasant smell from food or drinks: *The aroma of fresh coffee filled the house.*

smell은 일반적으로 코를 사용해서 알아채거나 분간하는 것에 대해 말하는 데 쓴다: 썩은 계란 냄새 / 부엌에서 뭔가 맛있는 냄새가 난다. **odor**는 악취이다: 공기 중에 퀴퀴한 연기 냄새가 났다. **scent**는 냄새가 나는 것이 어떤 냄새, 특히 어떤 좋은 냄새가 나는지 말할 때 쓴다: 솔향기가 나는 세제액. **fragrance**는 아주 좋은 향기이다: 향기롭고 달콤한 꽃향기. **aroma**는 음식이나 음료에서 나는 좋은 냄새이다: 갓 만든 커피 향이 집안 가득 퍼졌다.

---

smell·y /'smɛli/ *adj* having an unpleasant smell || 불쾌한 냄새가 나는.

악취가 나는: *smelly socks* 고약한 냄새가 나는 양말

smelt /smɛlt/ *v* [T] to melt a rock that contains metal in order to remove the metal ‖ 금속을 추출하기 위해 광석을 녹이다. 광석을 용해하다. 제련하다

smidg·en /'smɪdʒən/, **smidge** /smɪdʒ/ *n* [singular] INFORMAL a small amount of something ‖ 소량의 것. 조금: *"Want some more wine?" "Just a smidgen."* "포도주 더 마실래?" "조금만 더."

smile /smaɪl/ *v* **1** [I] to have a happy expression on your face in which your mouth curves up ‖ 입 꼬리가 올라가며 얼굴에 행복한 표정을 짓다. 미소 짓다. 방긋 웃다: *Keith smiled at me.* 키스는 나를 보고 미소 지었다. / *a smiling baby* 미소 짓는 아기 **2** [T] to say or express something with a smile ‖ 미소를 지으며 어떤 것을 말하거나 표현하다: *She smiled her thanks.* 그녀는 감사의 미소를 지었다. – **smile** *n* : *a wide smile* 함박웃음

smirk /smɚk/ *v* [I] to smile in an unpleasant or unkind way ‖ 불쾌하거나 심술궂게 웃다. 능글맞게 웃다. 히죽히죽 웃다: *Both officers smirked and laughed at him.* 두 명의 경찰관이 히죽히죽 그를 비웃었다. – **smirk** *n*

smith /smɪθ/ *n* **1** **goldsmith/ silversmith etc.** someone who makes things from gold, silver etc. ‖ 금·은 등으로 물건을 만드는 사람. 금/은 세공인 **2** ⇨ BLACKSMITH

smith·er·eens /ˌsmɪðə'rinz/ *n* **blown/ smashed etc. to smithereens** INFORMAL broken into very small pieces ‖ 매우 잘게 부숴진. 산산조각으로 터진/박살난

smit·ten /'smɪt̬n/ *adj* **be smitten** to suddenly feel that you love someone or like something very much ‖ 갑자기 남을 사랑하거나 어떤 것을 대단히 좋아하는 감정을 느끼다. 매료되다: *He's absolutely smitten with that new girl.* 그는 저 새로운 소녀에게 완전히 반했다.

smock /smak/ *n* a loose piece of clothing like a long shirt, worn to protect your clothes ‖ 옷을 보호하기 위해 입는, 긴 셔츠같이 생긴 헐렁한 옷. 겉옷

smog /smag, smɔg/ *n* [U] unhealthy air in cities that is a mixture of smoke, gases, chemicals etc. ‖ 연기·가스·화학 성분 등이 섞인, 건강에 해로운 도시의 공기. 스모그. 연무 – **smoggy** *adj*

smoke¹ /smoʊk/ *n* **1** [U] the white, gray, or black gas that is produced by something burning ‖ 타고 있는 물체에서 나오는 하얀색[회색, 검정색]의 가스. 연기. **2** INFORMAL a cigarette or drugs that are smoked ‖ 피우는 담배나 마약: *Do you have a smoke?* 담배 있어요? **3 go up in smoke** INFORMAL if your plans go up in smoke, you cannot do what you intended to do ‖ 계획했던 것을 할 수 없게 되다. 수포로 돌아가다

smoke² *v* **1** [I, T] to suck or breathe in smoke from your cigarette, PIPE etc. ‖ 담배·담뱃대 등에서 연기를 빨아들이거나 들이마시다. 흡연하다: *Do you mind if I smoke?* 제가 담배 피워도 괜찮겠습니까? / *Ed smokes Cuban cigars.* 에드는 쿠바산 시가를 피운다. **2** [I] to send out smoke ‖ 연기를 내뿜다. 연기가 나다: *a smoking chimney* 연기가 나는 굴뚝 **3** [T] to give fish or meat a special taste by hanging it in smoke ‖ 생선이나 고기를 연기 속에 걸어두어 특별한 맛을 내다. …을 훈제하다 – **smoking** *n* [U]

smok·er /'smoʊkɚ/ *n* someone who smokes ‖ 흡연하는 사람. 흡연자 — opposite NONSMOKER

smoke screen /'. ./ *n* something that you say or do to hide your real plans or actions ‖ 실제의 계획이나 행위를 감추기 위해 말하거나 행하는 것. 연막. 위장. 변장

smoke·stack /'smoʊkstæk/ *n* a tall CHIMNEY at a factory or on a ship ‖ 공장이나 선박 위의 높은 굴뚝

smok·ing gun /ˌ.. './ *n* INFORMAL definite proof of who is responsible for something or how something really happened ‖ 어떤 일에 대해 누가 책임이 있는지 또는 실제로 어떻게 일어났는지에 대한 명백한 증거. 확증. 물증. 유죄 증거: *It was strong evidence, but certainly no smoking gun.* 그것은 강력한 증거였지만 확실한 결정적 증거는 아니었다.

smok·y /'smoʊki/ *adj* **1** filled with smoke ‖ 연기로 가득 찬. 연기가 자욱한: *a smoky room* 연기로 자욱한 방 **2** producing a lot of smoke ‖ 많은 연기를 내는. 연기가 뭉게뭉게 솟는: *a smoky fire* 연기를 내뿜는 화재 **3** having the taste, smell, or appearance of smoke ‖ 연기의 맛[냄새, 모양]이 나는. 연기 같은: *smoky cheese* 훈제 치즈

smol·der /'smoʊldɚ/ *v* [I] **1** to burn slowly without a flame ‖ 불꽃을 내지 않고 서서히 타다: *The factory is still smoldering after last night's blaze.* 공장은 어젯밤에 불이 난 후 여전히 불씨가 남아 있다. **2** to have strong feelings that are not expressed ‖ 드러내지 않는 강한

감정을 갖다. (감정 등이) 속에서 맺히다:
Nick left Judy smoldering with anger.
닉은 속으로 분노에 차 있는 주디를 내버
려 두었다.

smooch /smutʃ/ v [I] INFORMAL to kiss
someone in a romantic way ‖ 낭만적으로
키스하다 - **smooch** n

smooth¹ /smuð/ adj **1** having an even
surface ‖ 표면이 평평한. 평탄한. 반반한.
매끄러운: *a smooth road* 평탄한 도로 /
smooth skin 매 끄 러 운 피 부 **2** a
substance that is smooth is thick but has
no big pieces in it ‖ 물질이 걸쭉하지만 큰
덩어리가 지지 않은. 잘 개어진. 잘 섞인:
smooth peanut butter 잘 개어진 땅콩버
터 **3** a way of doing something that is
smooth is graceful and has no sudden
changes ‖ 어떤 것을 하는 방식이 우아하
면서 갑작스런 변화가 없는. 부드러운. 자
연스러운: *Swing the tennis racket in one
smooth motion.* 유연하게 테니스 라켓
을 단번에 휘둘러라. **4** operating or
happening without problems ‖ 문제없이
작동하거나 발생하는. 원활히 움직이는.
순조로운: *No one said marriage would
always be smooth.* 결혼 생활이 항상 순
조로울 거라고 아무도 말하지 않았다. **5**
polite and confident in a way that
people do not trust ‖ 사람들이 신뢰할 수
없을 정도로 예의 바르고 자신 있어 하는.
세련된. 유창한: *a smooth talker* 달변
가 - **smoothly** adv - **smoothness** n
[U]

smooth² v [T] **1** also **smooth
out/down** to make something flat by
moving your hands across it ‖ 손으로 쓰
다듬어서 어떤 것을 반반하게 만들다. 구
김을 펴다. 매만지다: *Tanya sat down,
smoothing her skirt.* 타냐는 치마의 주름
을 반듯하게 매만지며 앉았다. **2** also
smooth away to take away the
roughness from a surface ‖ 표면의 거친
면을 없애다. 매끄럽게 하다. 고르다: *a
face cream that smoothes away lines* 주
름살을 펴주는 얼굴 크림

smooth sth ↔ **over** phr v [T] to make
problems or difficulties seem less
important ‖ 문제나 어려움을 덜 중요한
것처럼 보이게 만들다. 일을 무리 없게 만
들다. 수월하게 만들다: *He depended on
Nancy to smooth over any troubles.* 그
는 어떤 문제라도 매끄럽게 처리해 내는
낸시에게 의지했다.

smor·gas·bord /ˈsmɔrɡəsˌbɔrd/ n [C,
U] a meal in which people serve
themselves from a large number of
different foods ‖ 다양한 종류의 음식에서
스스로 가져다 먹는 식사. 스모가스보드.
뷔페(식사)

smoth·er /ˈsmʌðɚ/ v [T] **1** to kill
someone by putting something over
his/her face so that s/he cannot breathe
‖ 얼굴 위에 어떤 것을 놓아서 숨을 쉴 수
없게 만들어 죽이다. …을 질식(사)시키다
2 to put a large amount of a substance
on or into something ‖ 많은 양의 물질을
어떤 것 위나 안에 넣다. …을 듬뿍 치다
[바르다]: *a cake smothered with/in
chocolate* 초콜릿이 잔뜩 발린 케이크 **3**
to express your feelings for someone so
strongly that your relationship cannot
develop normally ‖ 남에 대한 자신의 감
정을 너무 강하게 표현하여 관계가 정상적
으로 발전할 수 없게 되다. 숨막히게 하다
4 to make a fire stop burning by
preventing air from reaching it ‖ 공기가
닿는 것을 차단해서 불이 타는 것을 막다.
불을 …으로 덮어 끄다

smudge¹ /smʌdʒ/ n a dirty mark ‖ 더러
운 자국. 얼룩 - **smudgy** adj

smudge² v [I, T] if a substance such as
ink or paint smudges or is smudged, it
becomes messy or unclear because
someone has touched or rubbed it ‖ 잉크
나 페인트 등을 누가 만지거나 문질러서
엉망이 되거나 지저분해지다[하게 하다].
…에 얼룩을 내다[얼룩지다]. 더럽히다:
Now look, you've smudged my drawing!
자 봐, 네가 내 그림에 얼룩을 냈잖아! /
Your lipstick is smudged. 네 립스틱이 번
졌다.

smug /smʌɡ/ adj -**gger**, -**ggest**
DISAPPROVING showing that you are very
satisfied with how smart, lucky, or good
you are ‖ 자신의 똑똑함[운좋음, 능숙함]
에 대단한 만족감을 나타내는. 잘난 체하
는. 자부심이 강한: *a smug smile* 우쭐대
는 미소 - **smugly** adv

smug·gle /ˈsmʌɡəl/ v [T] to take
something illegally from one place to
another ‖ 한 장소에서 다른 곳으로 어떤
것을 불법적으로 가져가다. …을 밀수입
[수출]하다: *cocaine smuggled from
South America into the United States* 남
미에서 미국으로 밀수입된 코카인 -
smuggler n - **smuggling** n [U]

smut /smʌt/ n [U] DISAPPROVING books,
stories, pictures etc. that are about sex
‖ 성(性)에 관한 책·소설·그림 등. 외설물
- **smutty** adj

snack /snæk/ n a small amount of food
that you eat between meals or instead
of a meal ‖ 식사 사이에 또는 식사 대신
먹는 소량의 음식. 간식

snack bar /ˈ. ./ n a place where you
can buy SNACKs ‖ 간식을 살 수 있는 장

소. 간이 식당. 스낵바

sna·fu /'snæfu, snæ'fu/ *n* [singular] INFORMAL a situation in which something does not happen the way it should ‖ 어떤 일이 예상대로 일어나지 않는 상황. 엉망 진창인 상태. 대혼란

snag¹ /snæg/ *n* **1** INFORMAL a sudden difficulty or problem ‖ 갑작스런 어려움이 나 문제. 뜻하지 않은 장애[방해]: *The project hit a snag when costs got out of hand.* 그 프로젝트는 비용이 과도하게 초과되자 어려움에 봉착했다. **2** a thread that has been accidentally pulled out of a piece of cloth because it has gotten stuck on something sharp or pointed ‖ 날카롭거나 뾰족한 것에 걸려서 뜻하지 않게 천 조각에서 풀려나온 실. 풀어진 올. (올이 풀려) 찢긴 곳

snag² *v* **-gged, -gging 1** [I, T] to become stuck on something sharp or pointed, or to make something do this ‖ 날카롭거나 뾰족한 것에 걸리다, 또는 어떤 것을 걸리게 만들다. 걸려 찢어지다[찢어지게 하다]: *Marty's fishing line snagged on a tree branch.* 마티의 낚싯줄이 나뭇가지에 걸렸다. **2** [T] INFORMAL to get someone to notice you, or to manage to get something ‖ 어떤 사람의 주의를 끌다, 또는 용케 어떤 것을 얻다. …을 재빨리 잡다: *Can you snag that waiter for me?* 저 웨이터 좀 불러 주실래요? / *"That's mine!" she yelled, snagging the necklace.* "그건 내 거야!" 그녀는 목걸이를 잡아채며 소리질렀다.

snail /sneɪl/ *n* **1** a small creature with a soft body and no legs that has a round shell on its back ‖ 부드러운 몸에 다리가 없으며 등에 동그란 껍데기가 있는 작은 동물. 달팽이 **2 at a snail's pace** extremely slowly ‖ 매우 느리게

snake¹ /sneɪk/ *n* a REPTILE (=type of animal) with a long thin body and no legs ‖ 길고 가는 몸에 다리가 없는 파충류. 뱀

snake² *v* [I] LITERARY to move in long twisting curves ‖ 길게 꼬인 곡선으로 움직이다. 굽이치며 나아가다: *The train snaked its way through the hills.* 그 기차는 구불거리며 오르막길을 통과했다.

snap¹ /snæp/ *v* **-pped, -pping 1** [I, T] if something long and thin snaps, or if you snap it, it breaks with a short loud noise ‖ 가늘고 긴 물체가 짧고 큰 소리를 내며 부러지다. 딱 부러지다[부러뜨리다]: *He snapped the chalk in two.* (=into two pieces) 그는 딱 소리를 내며 분필을 두 동강 냈다. / *Dry branches snapped under their feet.* 마른 가지들이 그들의 발

밑에서 탁 소리를 내며 부러졌다. **2** [I, T] to move into a particular position with a short loud noise, or to make something move like this ‖ 짧고 큰 소리를 내며 특정 위치로 움직이다. 또는 어떤 것을 이렇게 움직이게 만들다. 날쌔게 행동하다. 재빨리 움직이다: *The pieces just snap together like this.* 그 조각들은 이렇게 딱 맞물린다. / *She snapped her briefcase open/shut.* 그녀는 그녀의 가방을 탁 하고 열었다[닫았다]. **3** [I] to speak quickly in an angry way ‖ 화가 나서 재빨리 말하다. 호되게 말하다[쏘아붙이다]: *I'm sorry I snapped at you.* 너에게 쏘아붙여서 미안해. **4** [I] if an animal such as a dog snaps, it tries to bite you ‖ 개 등 동물이 사람을 물려고 하다. 덥석 물다 **5 snap your fingers** to make a short loud noise by moving a finger quickly across the thumb on the same hand ‖ 같은 손의 엄지에 다른 한 손가락을 빠르게 교차시켜 짧고 큰 소리를 내다. 손가락으로 딱 소리를 내다 **6** [T] to stop a series of events ‖ 일련의 사건들을 중단시키다: *Tampa snapped an eight-game losing streak on Saturday.* 탬파 팀은 토요일에 여덟 경기 연패 행진의 고리를 끊었다. **7** [I] to suddenly become unable to control a strong feeling such as anger or worry ‖ 갑자기 분노나 걱정 등의 강한 감정을 억제할 수 없게 되다. 갑자기 못 견디게 되다. 터져 나오다: *I don't know what happened—I guess I just snapped.* 나도 왜 그랬는지 모르겠어. 나도 모르게 그냥 폭발해 버린 것 같아.

snap out of sth *phr v* [T] INFORMAL to suddenly stop being sad, tired, upset, etc. ‖ 갑자기 슬프고 피곤하고 화가 난 상태에서 벗어나다. …으로부터 회복하다. 기운을 내다: *Come on, Gary, snap out of it.* 어서, 게리, 기운 내.

snap up *phr v* [T] **1** [**snap** sth ↔ **up**] to buy something immediately, especially because it is very cheap ‖ 특히 어떤 것이 매우 싸서 즉시 사다. 서둘러[앞 다투어] 사다: *snapping up bargains at a sale* 염가 판매에서 싼 물건들을 사들이기 **2** [**snap** sb ↔ **up**] to eagerly take an opportunity to have someone as part of your company, team etc. ‖ 기업·팀 등의 일원으로 어떤 사람을 영입할 기회를 얼른 잡다. 나꿔채다. 스카우트하다

snap² *n* **1** [singular] a sudden short loud noise, especially of something breaking or closing ‖ 특히 물체가 부러지거나 닫힐 때 나는 갑작스러운 짧고 큰 소리. 탁 소리: *I heard a snap, and then the tree just fell over.* 뚝 하는 소리가 나

더니 그 나무는 바로 쓰러졌다. **2 a small metal object that fastens clothes by pressing two parts together** ‖ 두 짝을 서로 눌러 옷을 여미는 작은 금속 물체. 똑딱단추 **3 be a snap** INFORMAL to be very easy to do ‖ 하기가 아주 쉽다. 식은 죽 먹기다: *Making pie crust is a snap.* 파이 껍질 만들기는 식은 죽 먹기다. **4** ⇨ SNAPSHOT —see also **cold snap** (COLD¹)

snap³ *adj* **snap judgment/decision** a judgment or decision made too quickly ‖ 너무 서둘러 내린 판단이나 결정. 즉석의[느닷없는] 판단/결정

snap·drag·on /'. ,../ *n* a white, yellow, or red garden flower ‖ 정원에 가꾸는 하얀[노란, 빨간] 색 꽃. 금어초

snap·per /'snæpɚ/ *n* [C, U] a common fish that lives in warm seas, or the meat from this fish ‖ 따뜻한 바다에서 사는 흔한 물고기, 또는 이 물고기의 살. 물퉁돔

snap·py /'snæpi/ *adj* **1 make it snappy** SPOKEN said in order to tell someone to hurry ‖ 어떤 사람에게 서두르라고 말하는 데에 쓰여. 서둘러. 빨리 **2** spoken or written in a short, clear, and often funny way ‖ 간결하고 분명하며 종종 재미있게 말하거나 쓰는. 간단명료한. 똑 떨어지는: *a snappy answer* 간단명료한 대답 **3** quick to react in an angry or annoyed way ‖ 화를 내거나 신경질적으로 성급하게 반응하다. 팔팔한. 성급한: *You don't have to be so snappy!* 그렇게 흥분할 필요 없어! **4** INFORMAL snappy clothes are attractive and fashionable ‖ 옷이 매력적이고 세련된. 멋진: *a snappy blue blazer* 멋진 파란색 스포츠 상의

snap·shot /'snæpʃɑt/ *n* an informal photograph ‖ 격식이 없는 사진. 스냅 사진

snare¹ /snɛr/ *n* a trap for catching an animal ‖ 동물을 잡기 위한 함정. 덫

snare² *v* [T] **1** to catch an animal using a SNARE ‖ 덫을 놓아 동물을 잡다 **2** to catch someone, especially by tricking him/her ‖ 특히 남을 속여서 잡다: *Ships patrol the coast to snare drug dealers.* 배들이 마약 밀매자들을 잡기 위해 해안을 순찰한다.

snarl /snɑrl/ *v* **1** [I, T] to speak or say something in an angry way ‖ 화를 내며 어떤 것을 이야기하거나 말하다. 고함치다: *"Shut up!" he snarled.* "입 닥쳐!"라고 그는 고함쳤다. **2** [I] if an animal snarls it makes a low angry sound and shows its teeth ‖ 동물이 낮고 사나운 소리를 내면서 이빨을 드러내다. 으르렁거리다 **3** [I, T] also **snarl up** if traffic snarls or is snarled, it cannot move ‖ 교

통이 마비되다. 혼잡해지다. 정체되다 **4** [I] if hair, thread, wires etc. snarl, they become twisted and messy ‖ 머리카락·실·전선 등이 얽혀서 엉망이 되다. 헝클어지다 – **snarl** *n*

snarl-up /'. ./ *n* INFORMAL a situation that prevents work from continuing or traffic from moving ‖ 작업을 계속하지 못하는 상황이나 교통이 소통되지 않는 상황. 혼란. 분규. 교통 체증

snatch¹ /snætʃ/ *v* [T] **1** to take something away from someone, especially by force ‖ 특히 힘을 써서, 남에게서 어떤 것을 빼앗다. 낚아채다: *Huong saw two youths snatch a woman's purse.* 후옹은 두 명의 젊은이가 여자의 지갑을 낚아채는 것을 보았다. **2** to quickly take the opportunity to do something ‖ 잽싸게 어떤 것을 할 기회를 잡다. (기회를 엿보아) 획득하다: *I managed to snatch an hour's sleep on the bus.* 나는 용케도 버스에서 한 시간의 잠을 잤다.

snatch² *n* **a snatch of conversation/song etc.** a short and incomplete part of something that you hear ‖ 짧고 불완전하게 들은 것의 일부. 한두 마디의 대화/노래

snaz·zy /'snæzi/ *adj* INFORMAL very bright, attractive, and fashionable ‖ 매우 눈부시며 매력적이고 세련된. 멋진: *a snazzy new car* 멋진 새 차

sneak¹ /snik/ *v* **sneaked** or **snuck**, **sneaked** or **snuck**, **sneaking 1** [I] to go somewhere quietly and secretly ‖ 조용히 몰래 어딘가로 가다. 살금살금[살짝] 걷다[숨다, 도망치다]: *Three boys tried to sneak past the guard.* 세 명의 소년들은 경비원을 몰래 지나치려 했다. **2** [T] to take something somewhere secretly ‖ 어떤 것을 어딘가에 슬쩍 가져가다. 몰래 가지고 들어가다[나가다]: *students sneaking beer up to their dorm rooms* 기숙사 방에 맥주를 몰래 가지고 들어온 학생들 **3 sneak a look/glance at** to look at something quickly and secretly ‖ 어떤 것을 슬쩍 잽싸게 보다. 훔쳐보다: *I sneaked a look at her diary.* 나는 그녀의 일기장을 슬쩍 훔쳐보았다.

sneak up *phr v* [I] to come near someone very quietly, so s/he does not see or hear you ‖ 남이 보거나 듣지 못하게 아주 조용히 가까이 가다. 살그머니 다가서다: *Don't sneak up on me like that!* 그렇게 살그머니 나한테 다가오지 마! / *Erickson snuck up behind him and grabbed the gun.* 에릭슨은 그의 뒤로 몰래 다가가서 총을 잡았다.

sneak² *n* INFORMAL someone who does things secretly and cannot be trusted ‖ 무엇을 몰래 해서 신뢰가 가지 않는 사람. 음흉한 사람

sneak·er /'snikər/ *n* ⇨ TENNIS SHOE

sneak·ing /'snikɪŋ/ *adj* **have a sneaking suspicion/feeling** to think you know something without being sure ‖ 확신 없이 어떤 것을 알고 있다고 생각하다. 은근한 의심/느낌을 가지다: *I have a sneaking suspicion that he's dating someone else.* 나는 그가 다른 사람과 데이트하고 있다고 내심 의심하고 있다.

sneak·y /'sniki/ *adj* doing things in a secret and often dishonest way ‖ 무엇을 남몰래, 종종 정직하지 않게 하는. 엉큼한. 음흉한

sneer /snɪr/ *v* [I] to show you have no respect for a person or idea by the expression on your face, or by the way you talk about him, her, or it ‖ 어떤 사람이나 생각을 존중하지 않는다는 뜻을 얼굴 표정이나 말하는 태도로 나타내다. 비웃다. 냉소[조소]하다: *Ned always sneered at the type of people who went to the opera.* 네드는 항상 오페라를 보러 가는 부류의 사람들을 비웃었다. **– sneer** *n*

sneeze /sniz/ *v* [I] **1** to suddenly have air burst out of your nose in an uncontrolled way, for example when you are sick ‖ 예를 들어 아플 때, 억제할 수 없이 갑자기 코에서 공기가 터져 나오게 하다. 재채기하다: *I've been sneezing all night!* 나는 밤새 재채기했어! **2 sth is nothing to sneeze at** INFORMAL used in order to say that something is impressive enough to be considered important ‖ 어떤 것이 중요하게 여겨질 만큼 충분히 인상적이라고 말하는 데에 쓰여. 만만치 않다. 무시 못하다: *With 35 nations involved, the competition is nothing to be sneezed at.* 35개국이 참가한 이 시합은 만만히 볼 게 아니다. **– sneeze** *n*

snick·er /'snɪkər/ *v* [I] to laugh quietly at something that is not supposed to be funny ‖ 웃어서는 안 되는 것에 대해 조용히 웃다. 킬킬 웃다 **– snicker** *n*

snide /snaɪd/ *adj* funny but unkind ‖ 웃기지만 호의적이지 않은. 비꼬는. 가시 돋친: *a snide remark about her clothes* 그녀의 옷에 대해 비꼬는 말

sniff /snɪf/ *v* **1** [I] to breathe air into your nose with a loud sound, especially in short breaths ‖ 특히 짧은 호흡으로, 큰 소리를 내며 코로 공기를 들이마시다. 코를 킁킁거리다: *Stop sniffing and blow your nose!* 그만 훌쩍이고 코를 풀어라! **2**

[I, T] to breathe in through your nose in order to smell something ‖ 어떤 것의 냄새를 맡기 위해 코로 숨을 들이마시다. …의 냄새를 맡다: *cats sniffing at their food* 음식 냄새를 맡고 있는 고양이들 **– sniff** *n*

sniff at sth *phr v* [T] to refuse something in a proud way ‖ 거만하게 어떤 것을 거절하다. 경멸적으로[하찮게] 대하다: *A job with them is nothing to sniff at.* (=something you should not refuse) 그들과의 일은 쉽게 거절할 게 아니다.

sniff sth ↔ **out** *phr v* [T] to discover or find something by its smell ‖ 냄새로 어떤 것을 발견하거나 찾아내다. …을 냄새로 알아내다[탐지하다]: *dogs that sniff out drugs* 마약 탐지견들[마약을 냄새로 알아내는 개들]

snif·fle /'snɪfəl/ *v* [I] to SNIFF again and again, especially when you are crying or are sick ‖ 특히 울거나 아플 때, 계속 코를 훌쩍거리다

snif·fles /'snɪfəlz/ *n* **the sniffles** a slight cold ‖ 가벼운 감기: *Max has had the sniffles all week.* 맥스는 일주일 내내 감기 기운이 있었다.

snig·ger /'snɪɡər/ *v* [I] ⇨ SNICKER

snip /snɪp/ *v* **-pped, -pping** [I, T] to cut something with scissors using quick small cuts ‖ 가위로 빠르고 잘게 가위질해서 어떤 것을 자르다. 싹둑싹둑 자르다 **– snip** *n*

snipe /snaɪp/ *v* [I] **1** to criticize someone in an unkind way ‖ 냉정하게 남을 비난하다. 혹평하다. 비방하다: *I wish you two would stop sniping at each other.* 너희 둘이 서로 비난하는 것을 그만 두었으면 좋겠다. **2** to shoot at unprotected people from a hidden position ‖ 숨어서 무방비 상태의 사람들을 쏘다. 저격하다

snip·er /'snaɪpər/ *n* someone who shoots at unprotected people from a hidden position ‖ 숨어서 무방비 상태의 사람을 쏘는 사람. 저격수

snip·pet /'snɪpɪt/ *n* **snippet of information/news etc.** a small piece of information etc. ‖ 단편적인 정보 등. 토막 정보/뉴스

snit /snɪt/ *n* **be in a snit** INFORMAL to be unreasonably annoyed about something ‖ 어떤 것에 대해 공연히 화가 나 있다. 신경이 곤두서 있다: *Dan's in a snit because I used his flashlight.* 댄은 내가 그의 손전등을 사용했다고 골이 나 있다.

snitch /snɪtʃ/ *v* INFORMAL **1** [I] DISAPPROVING to tell someone that someone else has done something wrong because you want him/her to be punished ‖ 어떤 사람이 처벌 받기를 원해서 그의 잘못을 다른 사람에게 말하다. … 을 고자질하다 **2** [T] to steal something, especially something that is small and not valuable ‖ 특히 작고 하찮은 것을 훔치다. 좀도둑질하다: *I snitched a couple of cookies.* 나는 과자 두어 개를 슬쩍했다. **– snitch** *n*

sniv·el·ing /'snɪvəlɪŋ/ *adj* behaving or speaking in a weak complaining way, especially while crying ‖ 특히 울면서 나약하게 투정을 부리며 행동하거나 말하는. 우는 소리를 하는: *a sniveling little brat* 찡찡대는 버릇없는 꼬마

snob /snɑb/ *n* **1** someone who thinks s/he is better than people from a lower social class ‖ 자신이 낮은 사회 계층의 사람들보다 더 낫다고 생각하는 사람. 속물. 잘난 체하는 [콧대 높은] 사람 **2** **music/wine etc. snob** someone who knows a lot about music etc. and thinks his/her opinions are better than other people's ‖ 자신이 음악 등에 대해 많이 알고 있으며 자신의 의견이 다른 사람들의 의견보다 더 낫다고 생각하는 사람. 음악/포도주에 정통한 척하는 사람

snob·ber·y /'snɑbəri/ *n* [U] the attitudes and behavior of SNOBs ‖ 속물 같은 태도와 행동. 속물 근성

snob·bish /'snɑbɪʃ/, **snobby** /'snɑbi/ *adj* having attitudes and behavior that are typical of a SNOB ‖ 속물 같은 태도와 행동을 하는. 속물의

snoop /snup/ *v* [I] to try to find out about someone's private affairs by secretly looking at his/her things ‖ 남의 일들을 몰래 엿보아서 사생활을 캐내려고 하다. 기웃거리며 다니다: *I caught her snooping in/around my office.* 그녀는 내 사무실을 기웃거리다가 나에게 들켰다. **– snoop** *n*

snoot·y /'snuti/ *adj* typical of people who think they are better than other people, or full of people like this ‖ 다른 사람들보다 더 낫다고 생각하는 사람들의 전형인, 또는 이런 사람들로 가득 찬. 건방진. 자부심이 강한: *snooty restaurant service* 뻣뻣한 식당 서비스 / *a snooty East Coast private college* 콧대 높은 이스트 코스트 사립대학

snooze /snuz/ *v* [I] INFORMAL to sleep for a short time ‖ 짧은 시간 동안 자다. 선잠 자다. 졸다: *Dad was snoozing on the sofa.* 아빠는 소파에서 졸고 있었다. **– snooze** *n*

snore /snɔr/ *v* [I] to make a loud noise each time you breathe while you are

asleep ‖ 자는 동안 숨을 쉴 때마다 큰 소리를 내다. 코를 골다 **– snore** *n*

snor·kel¹ /'snɔrkəl/ *n* a tube that allows a swimmer to breathe air when s/he is under water ‖ 수중에서 수영하는 사람이 공기를 호흡하게 해주는 튜브. 잠수자의 호흡 기구. 스노클

snorkel² *v* [I] to swim using a SNORKEL ‖ 스노클을 사용하여 수영하다. 스노클링하다 **– snorkeling** *n* [U]

snort /snɔrt/ *v* **1** [I, T] to make a noise by forcing air out through your nose, in order to express anger or annoyance, or while laughing ‖ 노여움이나 귀찮음을 나타내기 위해, 또는 웃는 동안에 코를 통하여 공기를 세차게 뿜어내서 소리를 내다. 콧방귀를 뀌다. 콧바람을 불다: *Olsen snorted at the suggestion.* 올슨은 그 제안에 콧방귀를 뀌었다. **2** [T] SLANG to take illegal drugs by breathing them in through your nose ‖ 코로 마약을 흡입하여 불법적인 마약을 복용하다. 마약을 코로 흡입하다 **– snort** *n*

snot /snɑt/ *n* INFORMAL **1** [U] an impolite word meaning the thick liquid that is produced in your nose ‖ 코에서 나오는 진한 액체를 의미하는 점잖지 못한 단어. 콧물 **2** someone who is SNOTTY ‖ 건방진 사람, 코흘리개

snot·ty /'snɑti/ *adj* INFORMAL **1** showing that you think you are better than other people; SNOBBISH ‖ 자신이 다른 사람들보다 더 낫다고 생각하는 것을 나타내는. 건방진; ⑪ snobbish: *a snotty rich woman* 콧대 높은 부유한 여성 **2** an impolite word meaning wet and dirty with the thick liquid that is produced in your nose ‖ 코에서 나오는 진한 액체로 축축하고 더러워진 것을 뜻하는 점잖지 못한 단어. 콧물로 더러워진: *a snotty handkerchief* 콧물로 지저분한 손수건

snout /snaʊt/ *n* the long nose of some kinds of animals, such as pigs ‖ 돼지 등의 일부 동물의 긴 코. 주둥이

snow¹ /snoʊ/ *n* **1** [U] water frozen into soft white pieces that fall like rain in cold weather ‖ 추운 날씨에 부드럽고 하얀 조각으로 얼어서 비같이 내리는 물. 눈 **2** a period of time during which snow falls ‖ 눈이 내리는 기간: *the first snow of the winter* 겨울의 첫눈 —see usage note at WEATHER

snow² *v* **1 it snows** if it snows, snow falls from the sky ‖ 하늘에서 눈이 내리다. 눈이 오다: *Look, it's snowing!* 봐봐, 눈이 오고 있어! **2 be snowed in** to be unable to leave a place because so much snow has fallen there ‖ 너무 많은

눈이 내려서 어떤 장소를 떠날 수 없게 되다. 눈에 갇혀 꼼짝 못하다: *We were snowed in for a week.* 우리는 일주일 동안 눈에 갇혀 꼼짝 못했다. **3 be snowed under (with sth)** to have more work than you can deal with ‖ 다룰 수 있는 것보다 더 많은 일이 있다. 할 일이 산더미 같다: *I'd love to go, but I'm totally snowed under right now.* 가고 싶지만 지금 나는 할 일이 산더미 같아. **4** [T] INFORMAL to make someone believe or support something that is not true ‖ 남에게 사실이 아닌 것을 믿거나 지지하게 하다. …을 감언으로 믿게 하여[속여서] …시키다: *Even the banks were snowed by this charming conman.* 심지어 은행들까지도 이 멋진 사기꾼에게 속아 넘어갔다.

snow·ball¹ /'snoʊbɔl/ *n* **1** a ball made out of snow ‖ 눈으로 만든 공. 눈뭉치. 눈덩이: *kids throwing snowballs* 눈 뭉치를 던지는 아이들 **2 not have a snowball's chance (in hell)** INFORMAL to have no possibility of success ‖ 성공 가능성이 전혀 없다. 전혀 가망이 없다

snowball² *v* [I] if a problem or situation snowballs, it gets bigger or harder to control at a faster and faster rate ‖ 문제나 상황이 점점 더 빠른 속도로 더 커지거나 통제하기 어렵게 되다. 눈덩이처럼 불어나다[심해지다]

snow·bound /'snoʊbaʊnd/ *adj* unable to leave a place because there is too much snow ‖ 너무 많은 눈이 와서 어떤 장소를 떠날 수 없는. 눈에 갇힌

snow·drift /'snoʊˌdrɪft/ *n* a large amount of snow piled up by the wind ‖ 바람에 의해 쌓인 많은 양의 눈. 바람에 날려 쌓인 눈더미

snow·fall /'snoʊfɔl/ *n* [C, U] an occasion when snow falls from the sky, or the amount that falls in a particular period of time ‖ 하늘에서 눈이 내리는 때, 또는 특정한 기간에 내리는 눈의 양. 강설(량): *Their average annual snowfall is 24 inches.* 그들의 연간 평균 강설량은 24인치이다. */ a light snowfall* 적은 강설량

snow·flake /'snoʊfleɪk/ *n* a small soft white piece of frozen water that falls as snow ‖ 눈으로 내리는 작고 부드러운 하얀 조각의 언 물. 눈송이

snow job /'. ./ *n* INFORMAL an act of making someone believe something that is not true ‖ 남에게 사실이 아닌 것을 믿게 하기. 감언이설로 상대방을 속이기[설득하기]

snow·man /'snoʊmæn/ *n* a figure of a person made out of snow ‖ 눈으로 만든 사람의 형상. 눈사람

snow·plow /'snoʊplaʊ/ *n* a vehicle or piece of equipment for pushing snow off roads ‖ 눈을 도로에서 밀어내는 차량이나 장비. 제설차[기]

snow·shoe /'snoʊʃu/ *n* one of a pair of wide flat frames used for walking on snow without sinking ‖ 눈 위를 빠지지 않고 걸어다니는 데 사용되는 한 쌍의 넓고 편평한 틀 중의 하나. 눈덧신

snow·storm /'snoʊstɔrm/ *n* a storm with strong winds and a lot of snow ‖ 강한 바람과 많은 눈을 동반한 폭풍. 눈보라

snow-white /ˌ. './ *adj* pure white ‖ 순백의. 눈같이 흰. 새하얀

snow·y /'snoʊi/ *adj* **1** snowing, or full of snow ‖ 눈이 내리는, 또는 눈이 많은: *snowy weather* 눈이 오는 날씨 **2** LITERARY pure white ‖ 순백의. 눈같이 흰: *snowy white hair* 눈같이 흰 머리(털)

snub /snʌb/ *v* **-bbed, -bbing** [T] to be rude to someone, especially by ignoring him/her ‖ 특히 남을 무시하여 무례하게 대하다. 냉대하다. 거들떠보지도 않다: *Despite her success, the critics snubbed her.* 그녀의 성공에도 불구하고 비평가들은 그녀를 거들떠보지도 않았다. – **snub** *n*

snuck /snʌk/ *v* a past tense and PAST PARTICIPLE of SNEAK ‖ SNEAK 의 과거·과거분사형

snuff¹ /snʌf/, **snuff out** *v* **1** [T] to put out a CANDLE flame by covering it or pressing the burning part with your fingers ‖ 불꽃을 덮거나 손가락으로 심지를 눌러서 촛불을 끄다 **2** INFORMAL to stop something completely ‖ 철저히 어떤 것을 중단시키다. 근절시키다. 멸절시키다: *laws intended to snuff out smoking in public places* 공공장소에서 흡연을 근절시킬 목적의 법률 **3** SLANG to kill someone ‖ 남을 죽이다

snuff² *n* [U] tobacco made into a powder, which people SNIFF through their noses ‖ 사람이 코로 흡입하는 가루로 만든 담배. 코담배

snug /snʌg/ *adj* **-gger, -ggest 1** warm and comfortable ‖ 따뜻하고 편안한. 아늑한. 안락한: *a snug little room* 아늑하고 조그만 방 **2** clothes that are snug fit fairly tightly ‖ 옷이 꼭 맞는 – **snugly** *adv*

snug·gle /'snʌgəl/, **snuggle up** *v* [I] INFORMAL to get into a warm comfortable position ‖ 따뜻하고 안락한 자세가 되다. 바싹 달라붙다. 글어[껴]안다: *couples snuggling up on cold winter nights* 추운 겨울밤에 꼭 끌어안고 있는

연인들

so¹ /sou/ *adv* **1 so...that** used in order to describe or emphasize a quality ‖ 특성을 표현하거나 강조하는 데에 쓰여. 너무 …해서 …할 수 없다: *Jack is so fat that he can't get through the door.* 잭은 너무 뚱뚱해서 그 문을 통과할 수 없다. **2** SPOKEN NONSTANDARD said in order to emphasize an adjective ‖ 형용사를 강조하는 데에 쓰여. 너무. 매우: *That party was so boring!* 그 파티는 너무 지루했디! **3** used in order to talk about an idea, situation etc. that has already been mentioned ‖ 이미 언급된 생각이나 상황 등을 이야기하는 데에 쓰여. 그렇게. 그와 같이: *"Will I need my coat?" "I don't think so."* "외투가 필요할까?" "그렇지 않을걸." **4** a word meaning "also," used at the beginning or in the middle of sentences ‖ 문장의 시작이나 중간에 쓰여, "역시"를 뜻하는 단어. …도. 마찬가지로: *Vince is an idiot and so is his wife.* 빈스는 천치이고 그의 아내도 역시 마찬가지야. **5** a word meaning "very," used in order to emphasize feelings ‖ 감정을 강조하는 데에 쓰여, "매우"를 뜻하는 단어. 아주. 몹시: *I'm so glad you could come.* 네가 올 수 있게 돼서 매우 기뻐. **6 or so** used when you cannot be exact about a number, amount, or period of time ‖ 수[양, 기간]에 대해 정확하지 않을 때 쓰여. 그 정도 즘: *He left a week or so ago.* 그는 일주일 전쯤에 떠났다. / *Dena had five drinks or so.* 데나는 다섯 잔 정도 마셨다. **7 and so on/forth** used after a list to show that there are other similar things that could also be mentioned ‖ 동시에 언급될 수 있는 다른 비슷한 것들이 계속 있다는 것을 나타내기 위해 목록 뒤에 쓰여. 기타 등등: *a room full of old furniture, paintings, rugs, and so forth* 오래된 가구, 그림, 깔개와 기타 등등으로 가득 찬 방 **8 so as (not) to do sth** in order to do or not do something ‖ 어떤 것을 하기나 하지 않도록: *Try to remain calm so as not to alarm anyone.* 아무도 놀라지 않게 침착하도록 하세요.

SPOKEN PHRASES

9 said in order to get someone's attention, especially in order to ask him/her a question ‖ 특히 질문을 하려고 남의 주의를 얻는 데에 쓰여. 그래: *So, what do you think of the school?* 그래서, 학교를 어떻게 생각하니? **10** said when you are making sure that you have understood something 어떤 것을 이해했다는 것을 확실히 할 때 쓰

여. 그러니까: *So you aren't actually leaving until Friday?* 그러니까 너는 금요일까지는 실제로 떠나지 않는다는 거지? **11** used with a movement of your hand when you are describing how big, tall etc. something or someone is, or how to do something ‖ 사물이나 사람이 얼마나 크거나 키가 큰지, 또는 일을 하는 방법을 설명할 때 손의 동작과 함께 쓰여. 이만큼의. 이렇게: *It was about so big.* 그것은 대강 이 정도 크기였어. / *Then you fold the paper like so.* 그리고 나서 종이를 이렇게 접으세요. **12** also **so what?** used in order to say impolitely that you do not think that something is important ‖ 어떤 것을 중요하게 생각하지 않는다고 무례하게 말하는 데에 쓰여. 그래서: *"I'm going to tell Mom what you said." "So?"* "나는 네가 한 말을 엄마에게 말할 거야." "그래서?" / *Yes, I'm late. So what?* 그래, 지각했어. 그래서 어쨌다는 거야? **13 so long!** used in order to say goodbye ‖ 작별 인사하는 데에 쓰여. 잘 가. 또 봐! **14 so help me** said in order to threaten someone, although you will probably not do what you say ‖ 어쩌면 말한 것을 하지는 않을지라도 남을 위협하는 데 쓰여. 맹세코. 진정으로: *Shut up or so help me I'll kill you!* 입 닥쳐, 그렇지 않으면 정말 너를 죽일 거야! **15 so much for** used in order to say that something you tried to do did not work, or something that was promised did not happen ‖ 하려고 한 것이 되지 않았거나 약속된 일이 일어나지 않았다고 말하는 데에 쓰여. (너무해서) 말할 수도 없다. …도 안 되다니: *Well, so much for getting out of here at five o'clock.* 허 참, 5시에 여기서 나가는 것도 안 되다니.

—see usage notes at AS¹, SUCH

so² *conjunction* **1** used in order to show why something happens; therefore ‖ 어떤 일이 왜 일어났는지 보여 주는 데에 쓰여. 그래서. 그 결과로. 따라서: *I got hungry, so I made a sandwich.* 나는 배가 고파서 샌드위치를 만들었어. ✗DON'T SAY "Since I got hungry, so I made a sandwich."✗ "Since I got hungry, so I made a sandwich."라고는 하지 않는다. **2 so (that)** in order to make something happen, or make something possible ‖ 어떤 일이 일어나거나 가능하도록 하기 위해. …하도록. …하기 위하여. …할 수 있게: *I put your keys in the drawer so they* *wouldn't get lost.* 내가 네 열쇠를 분실되지 않도록 서랍에 넣었다.

so³ *adj* **sth is so** used in order to say that something is true ‖ 어떤 것이 사실이라고 말하는 데 쓰여. 정말인. 사실인: *Please, say it isn't so!* 제발, 그렇지 않다고 말하세요! / *Is that so?* 그것이 사실입니까?

soak /souk/ *v* [I, T] **1** if you soak something or let it soak, you cover it with liquid for a period of time ‖ 어떤 것을 한동안 액체로 덮이게 하다[젖게 하다]. 적시다. 잠기다. 담그다: *Just put that dish in the sink to soak.* 그 접시를 싱크대 물에 담가 두어라. / *Soak the beans overnight.* 콩을 밤새 물에 담가 두어라. **2** if water soaks somewhere or soaks something, it makes something completely wet ‖ 물이 어떤 곳이나 사물에 스며들어 완전히 적시다. (깊이) 스며들다[배다]. 흠뻑 젖게 하다: *The rain had soaked through her jacket.* 그녀는 비 때문에 재킷이 흠뻑 젖었다. **3** [T] INFORMAL to make someone pay a very large amount of money for something ‖ 남에게 어떤 것에 매우 많은 돈을 지불하게 하다. 터무니없는 값[세금]을 부르다[매기다]. 바가지 씌우다: *a tax designed to soak the rich* 부자에게 중과세하도록 계획된 세금

soak sth ↔ **up** *phr v* [T] **1** if something soaks up a liquid, it takes the liquid into itself; ABSORB ‖ 어떤 것이 액체를 내부로 받아들이다. 흡수하다. 빨아들이다; ㈜ absorb: *Serve grilled bread for soaking up the broth.* 수프에 적셔 먹을 구운 빵을 제공합니다. **2** to enjoy everything about an experience ‖ 어떤 경험에 대한 모든 것을 즐기다: *I'm going to spend a week just soaking up the sunshine.* 나는 그저 일광욕을 즐기면서 일주일을 보낼 예정이다. **3** INFORMAL to learn a lot quickly ‖ 많은 것을 빨리 배우다. 지식·정보를 (빨리) 흡수하다

soaked /soukt/ *adj* very wet ‖ 심하게 젖은. 흠뻑 젖은: *I'm absolutely soaked.* 나는 온몸이 흠뻑 젖었다.

soak·ing /'soukɪŋ/, **soaking wet** /,..'./ *adj* completely wet ‖ 완전히 젖은. (물이 흐를 정도로) 흠뻑 젖은: *Your shoes are soaking wet!* 너의 신발이 흠뻑 젖었구나!

so-and-so /'. . ,./ *n* SPOKEN used in order to talk about someone, without saying his/her name ‖ 이름을 말하지 않고 어떤 사람을 말하는 데에 쓰여. 아무개. 모모

soap¹ /soup/ *n* **1** [U] the substance that you use with water to wash things, especially your body ‖ 물체, 특히 몸을 씻기 위해 물과 함께 쓰는 물질. 비누: *a bar of soap* 비누 한 개 **2** INFORMAL ⇨ SOAP OPERA

soap² *v* [T] to rub soap on someone or something ‖ 사람이나 물건을 비누로 문지르다. 비누질하다

soap·box /'soupbɑks/ *n* **get on your soapbox** INFORMAL to tell people your opinions about something in a loud and forceful way ‖ 사람들에게 어떤 것에 대해 크고 힘차게 의견을 말하다. 자기 주장을 내세우다

soap ope·ra /'. ,../ *n* a television or radio story about the daily lives of the same group of people, which is broadcast regularly ‖ 텔레비전이나 라디오에 규칙적으로 방송되는, 일단의 동일 인물들의 일상생활에 대한 이야기. 연속극

soap·y /'soupi/ *adj* containing soap ‖ 비누를 함유한. 비누투성이의: *soapy water* 비눗물

soar /sɔr/ *v* [I] **1** to increase quickly to a high level ‖ 높은 수준까지 빠르게 증가하다. 급등하다. 치솟다: *The temperature soared to 97°.* 기온이 97도까지 치솟았다. **2** to fly, especially very fast or very high up in the air ‖ 특히 공중으로 매우 빠르게 또는 매우 높이 날다. 하늘 높이 날아오르다: *birds soaring overhead* 머리 위로 날아오르는 새들 **3** to look very tall and impressive ‖ 매우 커서 인상적으로 보이다. 높이 솟다: *The cliffs soar 500 feet above the sea.* 그 절벽은 해발 5백 피트 위로 치솟아 있다. – **soaring** *adj*

S.O.B. *n* SLANG ⇨ **son of a bitch** (SON)

sob /sɑb/ *v* **-bbed, -bbing** [I] to cry while breathing in short sudden bursts ‖ 짧고 갑작스럽게 숨을 내뿜으며 울다. 흐느끼다 – **sob** *n*

so·ber¹ /'soubɚ/ *adj* **1** not drunk ‖ 술 취하지 않은. 술 마시지 않은 **2** extremely serious ‖ 매우 진지한. 냉정한. 근엄한. 사려 깊은: *Much sober thought is required to make the right choice.* 올바른 선택을 하는 데 보다 냉정한 사고가 요구된다. **3** plain and not at all brightly colored ‖ 평범하고 전혀 현란하지 않은. 수수한. 차분한: *a sober gray suit* 수수한 회색 양복 – **soberly** *adv* – **sobriety** /sou'braiɹti, sə-/ *n* [U]

sober² *v* [I, T] to become more serious, or to make someone do this ‖ 더 진지해지다, 또는 남을 이렇게 하게 하다. 진지해지게 하다 – **sobering** *adj* : *a sobering thought* 진지한 생각

sober (sb) ↔ **up** *phr v* [I, T] to gradually become less drunk, or to make someone do this ‖ 점차 술이 덜 취하게 되다, 또는 남을 이렇게 하게 하다. 술이 깨다[깨게 하다]: *Some black coffee might sober you up.* 블랙커피를 좀 마시면 술이 좀 깰거야.

sob sto·ry /'. ,../ *n* INFORMAL a story that someone tells you in order to make you feel sorry for him/her ‖ 남의 동정을 사기 위해서 하는 이야기. 눈물을 자아내는[감상적인] 이야기

so-called /, '../ *adj* **1** used in order to show that you think the name that someone or something is called is wrong ‖ 사람이나 사물의 불리우는 이름이 잘못됐다고 생각하고 있음을 보여주는 데에 쓰여. 이른바. 소위: *the so-called freedom fighters* 소위 자유의 투사들 **2** used in order to show that something or someone is usually called a particular name ‖ 사물이나 사람이 보통 특정한 이름으로 불려진다는 것을 나타내는 데에 쓰여. 이른바. 소위: *Only so-called "safe and sane" fireworks are allowed.* 이른바 "안전하고 정상적인" 불꽃놀이 종류만 허용된다.

soc·cer /'sakɚ/ *n* [U] an outdoor game in which two teams of 11 players try to kick a ball into their opponents' GOAL ‖ 11명의 선수로 된 두 팀이 공을 차서 서로 상대 팀의 골대 안에 넣으려 하는 야외 경기. 축구

so·cia·ble /'souʃəbəl/ *adj* friendly and liking to be with other people ‖ 우호적이며 다른 사람들과 함께 있는 것을 좋아하는. 사교적인. 붙임성 있는 —opposite UNSOCIABLE

so·cial /'souʃəl/ *adj* **1** relating to human society and its organization, or the quality of people's lives ‖ 인간 사회와 그 조직, 또는 사람들의 생활의 특성에 관한. 사회의. 사회적인: *We ought to be dealing with the real social issues such as unemployment.* 우리는 실업 등과 같은 실제 사회 문제들을 해결해야 한다. **2** relating to the position in society that you have ‖ 사회 내에서의 지위와 관련된. 사회적인: *friends from different social backgrounds* 사회적 배경이 다른 친구들 **3** relating to the things that you do with other people, especially for enjoyment ‖ 특히 즐기기 위해 다른 사람들과 함께 하는 일과 관련된. 친목(활동)의: *Ellis always had an active social life.* 엘리스는 항상 활동적인 사회생활을 했다. **4** social animals live together in groups, rather than alone ‖ 동물이 혼자보다 집단

으로 함께 사는. 군거(群居)성의. 사회생활을 영위하는 – **socially** *adv*

social climb·er /'. ,../ *n* DISAPPROVING someone who does anything s/he can to move into a higher social class ‖ 보다 높은 사회 계층으로 옮겨 가기 위해 어떤 일이든지 하는 사람. 입신 출세주의자

so·cial·is·m /'souʃə,lɪzəm/ *n* [U] an economic and political system that tries to give equal opportunities to all people, and in which most businesses belong to the government ‖ 모든 사람에게 동등한 기회를 주려 하고 대부분의 기업이 정부에 속하는 경제적·정치적 제도. 사회주의 – **socialist** *n, adj*

so·cia·lite /'souʃə,laɪt/ *n* someone who is well known for going to many fashionable parties ‖ 사교 파티에 많이 가는 것으로 유명한 사람. 사교계의 명사

so·cial·ize /'souʃə,laɪz/ *v* **1** [I] to spend time with other people in a friendly way ‖ 친밀하게 다른 사람들과 시간을 보내다. 남과 격의 없이 교제하다: *I hate having to socialize with strangers.* 나는 낯선 사람과 사귀어야 하는 것을 싫어한다. **2** [T] if a government socializes an industry, service etc., it takes it away from private owners in order to control it ‖ 정부가 산업·서비스 등을 통제하기 위해 개인 소유주로부터 빼앗다. 국유[국영]화하다: *socialized medicine* 의료 국영화 제도[국가 의료 제도] —opposite PRIVATIZE

social sci·ence /,.. '../ *n* **a)** [U] the study of people in society, that includes history, politics, ECONOMICS, SOCIOLOGY, and ANTHROPOLOGY ‖ 역사·정치학·경제학·사회학·인류학과 같이 사회 안의 사람들을 연구하는 학문. 사회 과학 **b)** any one of these subjects ‖ 이들 과목 중의 하나

Social Se·cu·ri·ty /,.. .'.../ *n* [U] a US government program into which workers must pay money, that gives money to old people and others who cannot work ‖ 근로자는 돈을 내야 하고, 그 돈을 노인과 일할 수 없는 다른 사람에게 나누어 주는 미국 정부 프로그램. 사회 보장 제도

social stud·ies /'.. ,../ *n* [plural] ⇨ SOCIAL SCIENCE

social work·er /'.. ,../ *n* someone who is trained to help people with particular social problems, such as being unable to work ‖ 일할 수 없는 등의 특정한 사회 문제를 가진 사람들을 돕기 위해 교육을 받은 사람. 사회 복지사 – **social work** *n* [U]

so·ci·e·ty /sə'saɪəti/ *n* **1** [C, U] a large group of people who share the same laws, ways of doing things, religions, etc. ‖ 같은 법률·일하는 방식·종교 등을 공유하는 사람들의 대규모 집단. 사회: *a study of 19th century Western society* 19세기 서구 사회의 연구 / *a democratic society* 민주 사회 **2** [U] people in general ‖ 일반적인 사람들. 세상 사람들. 인간[인류] 사회: *Society's attitude toward smoking has changed a lot in recent years.* 흡연에 대한 사회의 태도는 최근에 많이 변했다. **3** an organization with members who share similar interests, aims etc. ‖ 비슷한 관심·목표 등을 공유하는 회원들의 조직. 협회. 단체: *the American Cancer Society* 미국 암협회 **4** [U] the fashionable group of people who are rich ‖ 부유한 상류 집단 사람들. 상류 사회(사람들). 사교계: *a society wedding* 상류층의 결혼

so·ci·o·ec·o·nom·ic /,soʊsioʊ,ɛkə'-namɪk, -,ikə-/ *adj* relating to both social and economic conditions ‖ 사회적이고 경제적 상황에 관련된. 사회 경제적인: *people with a low socioeconomic status* 사회 경제적인 지위가 낮은 사람들

so·ci·ol·o·gy /,soʊsi'ɑlədʒi/ *n* [U] the scientific study of societies and the behavior of people in groups ‖ 사회와 집단 내의 사람들의 행태에 대한 과학적인 학문. 사회학 - **sociologist** *n*

so·ci·o·path /'soʊsiə,pæθ, -ʃiə-/ *n* TECHNICAL someone whose behavior toward other people is strange and possibly dangerous ‖ 다른 사람들에 대한 행동이 이상하고 위험할 수 있는 사람. 반사회적인 인물

sock¹ /sɑk/ *n* a piece of clothing that you wear on your foot inside your shoe ‖ 신을 신을 때 발에 신는 의류의 하나. 짧은 양말: *a pair of socks* 양말 한 켤레

sock² *v* INFORMAL **1** [I, T] to affect something or someone very badly ‖ 다른 사물이나 사람에게 매우 심하게 영향을 미치다. …에게 충격을 주다: *They were socked with a $5000 tax bill.* 그들은 5천 달러짜리 세금 고지서에 충격을 받았다. **2** [T] to hit someone very hard ‖ 남을 아주 세게 때리다. 강타하다: *Somebody socked him in the mouth.* 누군가가 그의 입을 강타했다. **3** be socked in to be completely covered by FOG ‖ 안개로 완전히 뒤덮이다: *The airport was socked in for six hours.* 그 공항은 6시간 동안 안개로 뒤덮였다.

sock·et /'sɑkɪt/ *n* **1** the place in a wall where you can connect electrical

equipment to the supply of electricity ‖ 전기 기구를 전원에 연결할 수 있는 벽에 있는 부분. 소켓 —see picture at PLUG¹ **2** the hollow part of something such as a joint, into which another round part fits ‖ 다른 둥근 부분이 그 속에 들어가게 된 관절 등의 우묵한 부분. 와(窩): *the shoulder/elbow socket* 어깨[팔꿈치]와

sod /sɑd/ *n* [U] a piece of dirt with grass growing on top of it ‖ 위에 풀이 자라고 있는 흙덩어리. 사각형의 뗏장. 잔디

so·da /'soʊdə/ *n* [C, U] **1** also **soda pop** ⇨ SOFT DRINK **2** also **soda water** water that contains BUBBLES, often added to alcoholic drinks ‖ 종종 주류에 첨가되는, 거품을 함유하는 물. 소다수. 탄산수

sod·den /'sɑdn/ *adj* very wet and heavy ‖ 매우 젖어 있고 무거운. 흠뻑 젖은: *sodden clothing* 흠뻑 젖은 옷

so·di·um /'soʊdiəm/ *n* [U] a silver-white metal that is an ELEMENT that produces salt when mixed with CHLORINE ‖ 염소와 혼합할 때 소금을 생성하는 원소인 은백색의 금속. 나트륨

so·fa /'soʊfə/ *n* a comfortable seat that is wide enough for two or three people to sit on ‖ 두 사람이나 세 사람이 앉을 만큼 넓은 안락한 의자. 소파

soft /sɔft/ *adj* **1** not hard, firm, or stiff, but easy to press ‖ 단단하지[견고하지, 딱딱하지] 않아 쉽게 눌리는. 푹신한: *a soft pillow* 푹신한 베개 **2** smooth and pleasant to touch ‖ 만지기에 부드럽고 기분 좋은. 매끈한: *soft skin* 부드러운 피부 **3** soft sounds are quiet ‖ 소리가 조용한. 듣기 좋은 **4** soft colors or lights are not too bright ‖ 색이나 빛이 너무 밝지 않은. 차분한 **5** not of the strongest or most harmful kind ‖ 가장 독하지 않거나 가장 해롭지 않은 종류의. 순한. 약한: *soft* *drugs* 독하지 않은 약 **6** INFORMAL a soft job, life etc. does not involve hard work or difficulties ‖ 직업·생활 등이 힘들거나 어렵지 않은. 수월한. 편안한 **7** INFORMAL not strict enough ‖ 엄하지 않은. 관대한: *The Governor does not want to seem soft on crime.* 주지사는 범죄에 관대한 것처럼 보이기를 원하지 않는다. **8** soft water does not contain a lot of minerals ‖ 물이 광물질을 함유하지 않은. 연수(軟水)의 **9 have a soft spot for sb** to like someone ‖ 다른 사람을 좋아하다: *She's always had a soft spot for Grant.* 그녀는 항상 그랜트를 좋아했다. **– softly** *adv* **– softness** *n* [U]

soft·ball /'sɔftbɔl/ *n* **a)** [U] an outdoor game similar to baseball but played with a slightly larger and softer ball ‖ 야구와 비슷하나 약간 더 크고 부드러운 공을 가지고 경기하는 옥외 경기. 소프트볼 **b)** [C] the ball used in this game ‖ 이 경기에서 사용되는 공

soft-boiled /ˌ. '../ *adj* an egg that is soft-boiled has been boiled until the white part is solid, but the yellow part is still liquid ‖ 계란을 흰자는 단단하지만 노른자는 아직 액체 상태일 때까지 삶는. 반숙의[으로 삶는]

soft drink /'. ./ *n* a sweet drink that contains BUBBLES and has no alcohol in it ‖ 거품을 함유하고 알코올이 들어 있지 않은 달콤한 음료수. 청량음료: *cola and other soft drinks* 콜라와 다른 청량음료 —see culture note at SODA

soft·en /'sɔfən/ *v* [I, T] **1** to become softer, or to make something do this ‖ 부드러워지다, 또는 사물을 이렇게 되게 만들다. 부드럽게 하다: *a lotion that helps to soften your skin* 피부를 부드럽게 해주는 로션 **2** to become less strict or severe, or to make something do this ‖ 덜 엄격하거나 덜 심각하게 하다, 또는 사물을 이렇게 만들다. 누그러지게 하다: *Goldberg tried to soften the blow (=make bad news less upsetting) with a joke.* 골드버그는 농담으로 충격을 완화시키려고 했다. / *Pale flowered wallpaper softens the look of the room.* 엷은 꽃 무늬 벽지는 방을 온화하게 보이게 한다. — opposite HARDEN

soften sb ↔ **up** *phr v* [T] INFORMAL to be nice to someone so that s/he will do something for you ‖ 남이 당신을 위해 어떤 일을 할 수 있도록 남에게 친절히 하다. 남의 태도를 부드럽게 하다

soft·heart·ed /ˌsɔft'hɑrtɪd/ *adj* kind and sympathetic ‖ 친절하고 동정적인. 상냥한

soft-ped·al /ˌsɔftˌpɛdl/ *v* [T] INFORMAL to make something seem less extreme than it really is ‖ 사물을 실제보다 덜 극단적으로 보이게 하다. 어조를 누그러뜨리다: *While meeting the voters, he soft-pedaled his racist views.* 유권자를 만나는 동안 그는 자기의 인종 차별적 견해를 누그러뜨렸다.

soft sell /ˌ. './ *n* [singular] a way of selling something in which you are gently persuaded to buy it ‖ 물건을 사도록 부드럽게 권유하여 물건을 파는 방법. 상냥한[은근한] 상술

soft-spok·en /ˌ. '../ *adj* having a quiet gentle voice ‖ 조용하고 상냥한 목소리를 가진. 부드럽게 말하는

soft touch /ˌ. './ *n* INFORMAL someone who is easy to deceive or persuade to do something ‖ 속이거나 어떤 일을 하도록 설득하기 쉬운 사람. 잘 속는 사람

soft·ware /'sɔft-wɛr/ *n* [U] a set of PROGRAMs (=instructions) that you put into a computer when you want it to do a particular job ‖ 컴퓨터로 어떤 특정한 일을 하기 원할 때 컴퓨터에 넣는 일련의 프로그램. 소프트웨어: *word processing software* 워드 프로세싱 소프트웨어 — compare HARDWARE

soft·y /'sɔfti/ *n* INFORMAL someone who is very kind and sympathetic, or is easily persuaded ‖ 매우 친절하고 여린, 또는 쉽게 설득되는 사람. 유약한 사람: *He seems aggressive, but really he's just a big softy.* 그는 적극적인 것처럼 보이나 실제로 그는 덩치가 큰 나약한 남자에 불과해.

sog·gy /'sɑgi/ *adj* very wet and soft ‖ 매우 축축하고 물렁물렁한. 함빡 젖은. 진득진득한: *She thought the pie crust was kind of soggy.* 그녀는 파이 껍질이 좀 진득진득하다고 생각했다.

SOHO /'souhou/ small office/home office; a room in someone's home with electronic equipment such as a computer and a FAX MACHINE, that is used as a place in which to work ‖ small office/home office(소규모 재택 사업장)의 약어; 컴퓨터·팩시밀리 등을 갖추고 사무실로 사용되는 가정 내의 방

soil¹ /sɔɪl/ *n* [C, U] the top layer of the earth in which plants grow ‖ 식물이 자라는 땅의 맨 위층. 토양. 흙: *sandy soil* 사질(沙質)토. 모래땅

soil² *v* [T] FORMAL to make something dirty ‖ 사물을 더럽히다. 얼룩지게 하다 **– soiled** *adj*

so·journ /'soudʒən/ *n* FORMAL a period of time that you stay in a place that is not your home ‖ 집이 아닌 곳에서 머무는 기간. 체류. - **sojourn** v [I]

sol·ace /'salıs/ n [U] a feeling of happiness after having been very sad or upset ‖ 매우 슬프거나 기분 나쁜 후의 행복감. 위로. 위안: *Since Mom's death we've found solace in our family.* 우리는 엄마가 돌아가신 후 가족 안에서 위안을 찾으려 했다.

so·lar /'soulɚ/ adj relating to the sun or the sun's power ‖ 태양이나 태양의 힘에 관한. 태양의: *a solar eclipse* 일식 / *solar energy* 태양 에너지

solar pan·el /,.. '../ n a piece of equipment that changes the sun's light into electricity ‖ 태양의 빛을 전기로 변환시키는 장치의 하나. 태양 전지판

solar sys·tem /'.. ,../ n **1 the solar system** the earth and all the PLANETs, moons etc. that move around the sun ‖ 태양의 주위를 도는 지구·모든 행성들·달 등. 태양계 **2** a similar type of system that moves around another star ‖ 다른 항성의 주위를 도는 비슷한 유형의 행성계. 태양계 이외의 행성계

sold /sould/ v the past tense and PAST PARTICIPLE of SELL ‖ sell의 과거·과거 분사형

sol·der¹ /'sadɚ, 'sɔ-/ v [T] to join metal surfaces together or to repair them using melted metal ‖ 녹은 금속을 사용해서 금속 표면을 접합하거나 수리하다. 납땜질하다

sol·der² n [U] the metal that is used in order to SOLDER something ‖ 물건을 납땜질하는 데에 쓰이는 금속. 땜납

sol·dier /'souldʒɚ/ n a member of the army, especially someone who is not an officer ‖ 군대의 일원, 특히 장교가 아닌 사람. 군인. 병사

sold-out /,. './ adj if a concert, movie etc. is sold out, all the tickets for it have been sold ‖ 콘서트나 영화 등의 표가 모두 팔린. 매진된

sole¹ /soul/ adj **1** the sole person, thing etc. is the only one of its type ‖ 사람이나 물건이 그 종류 중에서 오직 하나인. 단 한 사람[개]의. 유일한: *the sole survivor of the plane crash* 비행기 추락의 유일한 생존자 **2** only concerning or belonging to one group or person ‖ 단지 한 집단이나 사람에만 관계하거나 속하는. 독점적인. 단독의: *sole ownership of the company* 그 회사의 단독 소유권

sole² n **1** the bottom of your foot ‖ 발바닥 **2** the bottom part of a shoe, not including the heel ‖ 뒤꿈치를 포함하지 않는 구두의 바닥 부분. 신발 바닥. 구두

창 **3** [C, U] a common flat sea fish, or the meat from this fish ‖ 흔한 납작한 바닷고기, 또는 이 물고기의 살. 서대(고기)

sole·ly /'souli/ adv only, or not involving anyone or anything else ‖ 유일하게, 또는 다른 어떤 사람이나 사물도 포함하지 않게. 오직. 오로지. 단지. 다만: *We were solely responsible for the mistakes.* 우리는 그 실수에 대해 전적으로 책임이 있었다.

sol·emn /'saləm/ adj very serious ‖ 매우 진지한. 엄숙한. 장엄한: *a solemn humorless man* 엄숙하고 유머 없는 사람 / *a solemn ceremony* 엄숙한 의식 / *a solemn promise* (=one that you will definitely keep) 진지한 약속 - **solemnly** adv - **solemnity** /sə'lɛmnəti/ n [U]

so·lic·it /sə'lısıt/ v **1** [T] to ask someone for something such as money, help, or information ‖ 돈[도움, 정보] 등을 남에게 부탁하다. 간청하다. 탄원하다: *We were unable to solicit any support from the government.* 우리는 정부의 어떤 지원도 요청할 수 없었다. **2** [I] to offer to have sex with someone for money ‖ 돈을 벌기 위해 다른 사람과의 성교를 제의하다. 창녀가 손님을 유인하다. 매춘하다: *Twelve women were arrested for soliciting.* 열 두 명의 여성이 매춘 혐의로 체포되었다. - **solicitation** /sə,lısə'teıʃən/ n [C, U]

so·lic·i·tor /sə'lısıtɚ/ n **1** someone who goes from place to place trying to sell goods ‖ 물건을 팔려고 여기저기로 돌아다니는 사람. 외판원. 방문 판매원: *The sign said "No Solicitors."* 게시판에는 "방문 판매원 금지"라고 쓰여져 있었다. **2** the main law officer of a city, town, or government department ‖ 시[읍, 정부] 부서의 주요한 법률 관리. 법무관

so·lic·it·ous /sə'lısətəs/ adj very eager to make someone feel safe or comfortable ‖ 남을 안심하게 또는 편안하게 해주려고 매우 열심인. 세심한. 꼼꼼한: *Our tour guide was extremely solicitous.* 우리의 여행 가이드는 매우 꼼꼼했다.

sol·id¹ /'salıd/ adj **1** firm and usually hard, without spaces or holes ‖ 보통 틈이나 구멍이 없이 단단하고 보통 딱딱한. 속이 비지 않은. 충실한: *solid rock* 단단한 바위 / *The lake in the park is frozen solid.* 그 공원의 호수는 단단하게 얼어 있다. **2 solid gold/silver/oak etc.** completely made of gold etc. ‖ 완전히 순금 등으로 만든. 순금/순은/순수 오크재로 된: *a solid gold necklace* 순금 목걸이 **3**

strong and well made ‖ 강하고 잘 만든. 튼튼한. 견고한: *a good solid chair* 좋고 튼튼한 의자 **4** continuously, without any pauses ‖ 중단 없이 계속(해서). 연속. 꼬박: *She didn't talk to me for three solid weeks.* 그녀는 꼬박 3주 동안 나에게 말하지 않았다. **5** based on definite facts or a definite principle ‖ 분명한 사실이나 원칙에 근거한. 확실한: *solid information* 확실한 정보 **6** loyal and able to be trusted or depended on ‖ 충성스럽고 신뢰하거나 믿을 수 있는. 충실한. 견실한: *a solid citizen* 건실한 시민 **– solidly** *adv* **– solidity** /sə'lɪdəti/ *n* [U]

sol·id² *n* TECHNICAL an object or substance that has a firm shape and is not a gas or liquid ‖ 단단한 모양을 갖고 기체나 액체가 아닌 물체나 물질. 고체 — see also SOLIDS

sol·i·dar·i·ty /ˌsɑlə'dærəti/ *n* [U] the loyalty and support of a group of people that share the same aim or opinions ‖ 같은 목적이나 의견을 공유하는 일단의 사람들 사이의 충성과 지지. 단결. 결속: *Hundreds of workers went to the meeting to show their solidarity.* 수백 명의 근로자들이 단결을 과시하기 위해 그 모임에 갔다.

so·lid·i·fy /sə'lɪdəˌfaɪ/ *v* **1** [I, T] to become solid, or to make something solid ‖ 굳어지다, 또는 사물을 단단하게 하다. 응고[응결]시키다: *Crystals form when the liquid solidifies.* 수정이 액체가 응고될 때 형성된다. **2** [T] to make a plan, agreement, or feeling more definite ‖ 계획[합의, 감정]을 더 명확하게 하다. 공고히 하다. 결속시키다: *Working together has solidified our friendship.* 함께 일하는 것이 우리의 우정을 돈독하게 만들었다.

solids /'sɑlɪdz/ *n* [plural] food that is not liquid ‖ 액체가 아닌 음식. 고형식(固形食): *The doctor says I can't eat solids for another week.* 의사는 한 주일 더 고형식을 먹어서는 안 된다고 한다.

solid-state /ˌ.. '../ *adj* a solid-state electrical system uses TRANSISTORs ‖ 트랜지스터를 이용하는 전기 시스템의. 솔리드 스테이트의. 고체 상태의

so·lil·o·quy /sə'lɪləkwi/ *n* a speech in a play that a character says to himself/herself so that the people watching know his/her thoughts ‖ 관객이 자신의 생각을 알도록 극 중 등장인물이 자기 자신에게 말하는 대사(臺詞). 독백. 혼잣말

sol·i·taire /'sɑləˌtɛr/ *n* [U] **1** a card game for one player ‖ 혼자서 하는 카드

놀이 **2** a piece of jewelry that has only one jewel in it ‖ 보석을 하나만 박은 귀금속류: *a diamond solitaire ring* 다이아몬드 한 알 박힌 반지

sol·i·tar·y /'sɑləˌtɛri/ *adj* **1** a solitary person or thing is the only one in a place ‖ 사람이나 물체가 한 장소에 홀로 있는. 외로운. 고독한. 외딴: *A solitary figure waited by the door.* 어떤 사람이 혼자 문 옆에서 기다렸다. **2** done alone or spending time alone ‖ 단독으로 행해지거나 혼자서 시간을 보내는: *a solitary game* 혼자서 하는 게임 / *a solitary life* 고독한 삶

solitary con·fine·ment /ˌ..... '../ *n* [U] a punishment in which a prisoner is kept alone and is not allowed to talk to or see anyone else ‖ 죄수를 혼자 감금하여 다른 누구와도 이야기하거나 면회하는 것을 허락하지 않는 형벌. 독방 감금

sol·i·tude /'sɑləˌtud/ *n* [U] the state of being alone and away from other people ‖ 혼자 다른 사람들과 떨어져 있는 상태. 고독. 독거(獨居): *She spent the last years of her life living in solitude.* 그녀는 자신의 마지막 생애를 쓸쓸히 보냈다.

so·lo¹ /'soʊloʊ/ *adj* alone, without anyone else helping you ‖ 다른 누구의 도움 없이 혼자서 하는. 독연[독창, 독주]의. 단독의: *his first solo flight* 그의 첫 단독 비행 **– solo** *adv*

solo² *n* **1** a piece of music written for one performer ‖ 한 연주자를 위해 작곡된 곡. 독창곡. 솔로 **2** a job or performance that is done alone, such as flying a plane, dancing, singing etc. ‖ 비행·춤·노래 등 혼자서 하는 일이나 연기

so·lo·ist /'soʊloʊɪst/ *n* a musician who performs a SOLO ‖ 솔로로 공연하는 음악가. 독창자. 독주자

sol·stice /'sɑlstɪs, 'sɔl-/ *n* the day on which there is either the most or the least hours of light from the sun ‖ 태양의 일조 시간이 가장 많거나 가장 적은 날. 지(至). 하지·동지의 지점(支點): *the summer/winter solstice* 하지[동지]

sol·u·ble /'sɑlyəbəl/ *adj* a soluble substance can be DISSOLVEd in a liquid ‖ 물질이 액체에 용해되는. 녹는. 가용성(可溶性)의 **—opposite** INSOLUBLE

so·lu·tion /sə'luʃən/ *n* **1** a way of solving a problem or dealing with a difficult situation ‖ 문제를 풀어내거나 어려운 상황을 해결하는 방법. 해결(책). 해답: *Has anyone found a solution to question 7?* 누가 7번 문제에 대한 해답을 찾았니? / *The only solution was to move into a quieter apartment.* 유일한 해결책

은 더 조용한 아파트로 이사 가는 것뿐이었다. **2** a liquid mixed with a solid or a gas, usually without a chemical change ‖ 보통 화학 변화 없이 고체나 기체와 혼합된 액체. 용액.

solve /salv/ v [T] to find an answer to a problem or a way of dealing with a difficult situation ‖ 문제의 해답이나 어려운 상황을 해결하는 방법을 알아내다. 풀다. 해결[해명]하다: *The tax may be the only way to solve the city's budget crisis.* 세금이 그 시의 예산 위기를 해결하는 유일한 방법일지 모른다. **– solvable** *adj*

sol·vent¹ /'salvənt/ *adj* having enough money to pay your debts ‖ 빚을 갚을 수 있을 만큼의 돈이 있는. 지급 능력이 있는 **– solvency** *n* [U]

solvent² *n* a substance, usually a liquid, that can change a solid substance into a liquid ‖ 고형 물질을 액체로 바꿀 수 있는 물질, 보통 액체. 용매. 용제

som·ber /'sambɚ/ *adj* **1** sad and serious; GRAVE ‖ 슬프고 심각한. 엄숙한. 침울한; 〔유〕 grave: *a somber mood* 우울한 기분 / *a somber funeral service for 10 Marines* 10명의 해병 대원을 위한 엄숙한 장례식 **2** dark, or not having any bright colors ‖ 어두운, 또는 밝은 색깔이 전혀 없는. 칙칙한: *a somber room* 칙칙한 방

some¹ /səm; *strong* sʌm/ *quantifier* **1** an amount or number of something that is not specific ‖ 구체적이지 않은 사물의 양이나 수. 얼마간의. 다소의. 조금의: *Do you want some coffee?* 커피 좀 마실래? / *I need to buy some new socks.* 나는 새 양말을 몇 개 사야 한다. **2** a few of the people or things in a group, or part of an amount of something ‖ 집단 내의 몇몇 사람이나 사물, 또는 사물의 총량 중 일부. 몇몇의. 약간의: *Some guys at work have extra tickets to the Superbowl.* 직장의 몇몇 사람은 전미 프로 미식축구 선수권 대회의 여분의 표가 있다. / *I've lost some weight.* 나는 몸무게가 좀 줄었다. **3** a fairly large amount of something ‖ 사물의 상당히 많은 양. 상당한. 꽤: *It was some time before the police finally arrived.* 상당한 시간이 지난 후에 경찰이 마침내 도착했다. —see study note on page 941

some² *pron* **1** an amount or number of something that is not specific ‖ 구체적이지 않은 물건의 양이나 수. 얼마간. 다소. 조금: *Can I use some of your lotion?* 네 로션 좀 써도 괜찮겠니? / *She likes flowers, so I bought her some for her birthday.* 그녀가 꽃을 좋아해서 그녀의 생일 때 내가 꽃을 좀 사주었다. **2** a few of the people or things in a group, or part of an amount of something ‖ 집단 내의 몇몇 사람이나 사물, 또는 사물의 총량 일부. 몇몇. 약간: *Some of the roads were closed because of the snow.* 몇 개의 도로는 눈 때문에 폐쇄되었다. **3 and then some** INFORMAL and more ‖ 더욱 더. 그 위에 (더 많이): *He has enough money to buy the house and then some!* 그는 그 집을 사고도 남을 만큼의 돈이 있어!

some³ *determiner* **1** INFORMAL used when you are talking about a person or thing that you do not know, remember, or understand ‖ 알지[기억하지, 이해하지] 못하는 사람이나 사물에 대해 이야기할 때에 쓰여. 어떤. 누군가[무엇인가]의: *I read about it in some magazine.* 나는 어떤 잡지에서 그것에 관해 읽었다. / *For some reason or other they decided to move to Detroit.* 어떤 이유에서든 아니면 다른 이유에서든 그들은 디트로이트로 이사 가기로 결정했다. **2 some friend/help! etc.** SPOKEN said when you are annoyed because someone or something has disappointed you ‖ 다른 사람이나 어떤 일이 자신을 실망시켜서 화가 났을 때에 쓰여. 대단한 친구/도움이구나!: *I can't believe you told Mom. Some brother you are!* 네가 엄마한테 고자질했다니 믿을 수가 없구나. 내 동생 정말 잘났구나!

some⁴ *adv* **1** a little more or a little less than a particular number or amount ‖ 특정한 수나 양보다 다소 많거나 작은. 대

략. 약 ··· : *Some 700 homes were damaged by the storm.* 약 700가구가 그 폭풍우로 피해를 입었다. **2 some more** an additional number or amount of something ‖ 추가적인 사물의 수나 양. 조금 더: *Would you like some more cake?* 케이크 좀 더 드시겠어요?

some·bod·y /'sʌm,bɑdi, -,bʌdi/ *pron* ⇨ SOMEONE —see usage notes at ANYONE, SOME¹

some·day /'sʌmdeɪ/ *adv* at an unknown time in the future ‖ 미래의 불확실한 시간에. 언젠가: *Someday I'm going to Spain.* 언젠가 나는 스페인에 갈 것이다.

some·how /'sʌmhaʊ/ *adv* **1** in some way, although you do not know how ‖ 방법을 알지 못하지만 어떤 방법으로든. 어떻게든지 하여. 여하튼: *We'll find your bag somehow.* 우리는 어떻게 하든 너의 가방을 찾을 것이다. **2** for some reason that you cannot understand ‖ 이해할 수 없는 어떤 이유로. 어쩐지. 웬일인지: *Somehow I don't trust him.* 나는 아무래도 그를 믿을 수 없어.

some·one /'sʌmwʌn/ *pron* a word meaning a particular person, used when you do not know or do not say who that person is ‖ 그 사람이 누구인지 알 수 없거나 말할 수 없을 때 쓰여 특정한 사람을 뜻하는 단어. 누군가. 어떤 사람: *Be careful! Someone could get hurt.* 조심해라! 누군가 다칠 수도 있어. / *"Does Mike still live here?" "No, someone else* (=a different person) *is renting it now."* "마이크가 아직 이곳에 살고 있니?" "아니, 지금은 다른 사람이 세 들어 살고 있어." —see usage notes at ANYONE, PRONOUN

some·place /'sʌmpleɪs/ *adv* SPOKEN ⇨ SOMEWHERE, —see usage note at ANYONE

som·er·sault /'sʌmɚ,sɔlt/ *n* the action of rolling forward until your feet go over your head and touch the ground again ‖ 양 발이 머리를 넘어가서 다시 땅에 닿을 때까지 앞으로 회전하는 행위. 공중제비. 재주넘기 – **somersault** *v* [I]

some·thing /'sʌmθɪŋ/ *pron* **1** a word meaning a particular thing, used when you do not know its name, exactly what it is etc. ‖ 사물의 이름이나 정확한 정체 등을 모를 때에 쓰여 그 특정한 사물을 뜻하는 단어. 무언가. 어떤 것[일]: *He said something about a Halloween party.* 그는 할로윈 파티에 대해 어떤 말을 했다. / *There's something in my eye.* 내 눈 속에 무언가가 있다. / *I don't eat eggs. Could I have something else?* (=something

different) 나는 계란을 먹지 않는데 다른 것이 있니? **2 something like** used when you cannot be exact about a number or amount ‖ 숫자나 양에 대해 정확히 말할 수 없을 때에 쓰여. 대략. ···가량: *There are something like 3000 homeless people in this city.* 이 시에는 대략 3천 명의 노숙자들이 있다. **3 have something to do with** to be connected or related to a person, thing, or activity in a way that you are not sure about ‖ 확실히 알 수 없는 방식으로 사람[사물, 활동]에 연결되거나 관련되다. ···에 연관[관련]되어 있다: *High-fat diets may have something to do with the disease.* 고지방 음식 섭취가 그 질병과 관련 있을지 모른다. **4 something to eat/drink** some food or a drink ‖ 어떤 음식이나 음료수. 먹을[마실] 것: *We went out for something to eat after the movie.* 우리는 영화를 보고 나서 뭔가 먹으러 나갔다. **5 something to do** an activity or job ‖ 활동이나 일. 할 일[거리]: *I'll go to the store; it'll give me something to do.* 나는 상점에 가겠다. 그러면 일거리가 생길 것이다. **6 twenty-something/thirty-something** INFORMAL used when someone is between the ages of 20 to 29, 30 to 39 etc. ‖ 사람이 20세에서 29세이거나 30세에서 39세 등 사이에 있을 때. 20 몇 살/30 몇 살

┌─────── SPOKEN PHRASES ───────

7 or something... said when you cannot remember or cannot be exact ‖ 기억할 수 없거나 정확하지 않을 때에 쓰여. ···이든가 뭔가: *Maybe I cooked it too long or something.* 아마 나는 너무 오랫동안 그것을 요리했거나 어떻게 했던 것 같아. / *I saw him on "The Tonight Show" or something like that.* 나는 "투나잇 쇼"인가 뭔가에서 그를 보았다. **8 be (really) something** used when something is impressive or unusual ‖ 사물이 인상적이거나 유별날 때에 쓰여. 별거다. 대단하다. 유다르다: *It's really something to see all the hot air balloons taking off together.* 열기구가 한꺼번에 날아오는 것을 보는 것은 정말 인상적이다.

some·time /'sʌmtaɪm/ *adv* at an unknown time in the past or future ‖ 과거나 미래의 불확실한 시간에. 어떤 때. 언젠가: *I'll call you sometime next week.* 내가 다음 주 중에 너에게 전화할게.

some·times /'sʌmtaɪmz/ *adv* on some occasions, but not always ‖ 항상은 아니

고 어떤 때에. 때때로. 이따금: *Sometimes I don't get home until 9:00 at night.* 이따금 나는 밤 9시까지 귀가하지 않는다.

some·way /'sʌmweɪ/ *adv* INFORMAL ⇨ SOMEHOW

some·what /'sʌmwʌt/ *adv* a little; slightly ‖ 얼마간. 조금. 어느 정도; 약간: *I feel somewhat responsible for the accident.* 나는 그 사고에 어느 정도 책임을 느낀다.

some·where /'sʌmwɛr/ *adv* **1** in a place or to a place that is not specific ‖ 구체적이지 않은 장소에서 또는 장소로. 어딘가에[로, 에서]: *I think he wants you to drive him somewhere.* 내가 생각하기에 그는 당신이 자신을 어딘가까지 차로 태워다 주기를 바라는 것 같다. / *Do you want to eat lunch here or somewhere else?* (=somewhere different) 점심 식사를 여기에서 할까요 아니면 다른 곳에서 할까요? — see usage note at ANYONE **2 somewhere around/between etc.** a little more or a little less than a particular number or amount ‖ 특정한 수나 양보다 조금 많거나 조금 적은. 대략 … 정도: *A good CD player costs somewhere around $500.* 좋은 CD 플레이어는 대략 500달러 정도 한다. **3 somewhere along the line/way** used in order to say that you are not sure when something happened ‖ 어떤 일이 언제 발생했는지 확실하지 않다는 것을 말하는 데에 쓰여. 선상/도상의 어딘가에서: *Somewhere along the line I made a mistake.* 어딘가에서 내가 실수를 했다.

son /sʌn/ *n* **1** your male child ‖ 자신의 사내 아이. 아들: *My son is 12.* 내 아들은 12살이다. —see picture at FAMILY

SPOKEN PHRASES

2 [singular] used by an older person as a friendly way to talk to a boy or young man ‖ 나이 든 사람이 소년이나 젊은이에게 친근하게 말하는 데에 쓰여. 얘. 이봐. 여보게: *What's your name, son?* 여보게, 이름이 뭔가? **3 son of a bitch** a rude expression that shows you are angry or surprised ‖ 화가 나거나 놀랐다는 것을 나타내는 무례한 표현. 개자식. 후레자식 **4 son of a gun** used in order to talk to a man you know and like ‖ 잘 알고 좋아하는 사람에게 말하는 데에 쓰여. 여 자네. 야 임마: *John, you old son of a gun, how are you?* 존, 야 임마, 잘 지내냐?
---

so·na·ta /sə'nɑtə/ *n* a piece of CLASSICAL MUSIC usually for two instruments, one of which is a piano ‖ 보통 두 개의 악기로 연주되며 그 중 하나는 피아노인 클래식 곡. 소나타

song /sɔŋ/ *n* **1** a short piece of music with words ‖ 가사가 있는 짧은 악곡. 노래. 가곡: *Turn up the radio; this is my favorite song.* 라디오 소리를 키워 봐. 이건 내가 좋아하는 노래야. **2** [C, U] the musical sounds made by birds ‖ 새가 부르는 음악적인 소리. 새의 울음소리. 지저귐 **3** [U] the act of singing, or the art of singing ‖ 노래 부르는 행위, 또는 가창법 **4 for a song** very cheaply ‖ 매우 싸게. 헐값[싸구려]으로: *We bought it for a song at the flea market.* 우리는 벼룩시장에서 그것을 헐값에 샀다.

son·ic /'sɑnɪk/ *adj* TECHNICAL relating to sound ‖ 소리에 관한. 음향의

sonic boom /ˌ.. './ *n* the loud sound that an aircraft makes when it reaches the SOUND BARRIER ‖ 비행기가 음속 장벽에 도달할 때에 내는 큰 소리. 음속 폭음. 충격 파음

son-in-law /'. . .ˌ./ *n* the husband of your daughter ‖ 딸의 남편. 사위 —see picture at FAMILY

son·net /'sɑnɪt/ *n* a poem that has 14 lines that RHYME with each other in a particular pattern ‖ 일정한 형태에 따라 서로 운이 맞는 14행이 있는 시. 소네트

so·no·rous /'sɑnərəs/ *adj* having a deep pleasantly loud sound ‖ 깊고 듣기 좋은 큰 소리를 가진. 소리가 울리는[울려 퍼지는]. 낭랑한: *a sonorous voice* 낭랑한 목소리

soon /sun/ *adv* **1** in a short time from now, or a short time after something has happened ‖ 지금부터 짧은 시간 안에, 또는 어떤 일이 일어난 후 짧은 시간안에. 곧. 이내. 머지않아: *"How soon* (=how quickly) *can you leave for New York?"* 얼마나 빨리 뉴욕으로 떠날 수 있니? / *Soon another fire truck arrived.* 곧 다른 소방차가 도착했다. **2 as soon as** immediately after something has happened ‖ 어떤 일이 일어난 후 곧. …하자마자. …하자 곧: *I tried to call you as soon as I heard the news.* 그 소식을 듣자마자 너에게 전화하려고 했다. **3 sooner or later** used when you think something will definitely happen ‖ 어떤 일이 틀림없이 일어난다고 생각할 때에 쓰여. 머지않아. 조만간: *Sooner or later Joe's going to get hurt.* 조만간 조는 다칠 거야. **4 the sooner…the better** used in order to say that it is important that something happen soon ‖ 어떤 일이

soot 1576

빨리 일어나는 것이 중요하다고 말하는 데에 쓰여. 이르면 이를수록[빠르면 빠를수록] 좋다: *The sooner you finish this report, the better.* 이 리포트를 빨리 끝내면 끝낼수록 좋다. **5 no sooner had...than** used when something has happened almost immediately after something else ∥ 어떤 일이 다른 일이 있고 나서 그 즉시 일어날 때에 쓰여. …하자마자: *No sooner had I stepped in the shower than the phone rang.* 내가 막 샤워하려고 들어가자마자 전화가 울렸다. —see also **would (just) as soon** (WOULD)

soot /sʊt/ n [U] black powder that is produced when something burns ∥ 어떤 것이 탔을 때 생기는 검은 가루. 검댕

soothe /suð/ v [T] **1** to make someone feel less worried, angry, or upset ∥ 사람을 덜 걱정하게[화나게, 기분 상하게] 하다. 달래다. 진정시키다: *School officials were trying to soothe anxious parents.* 학교 관계자들은 걱정하는 부모들을 진정시키려고 했다. **2** to make a pain stop hurting as much ∥ 통증이 지금만큼 아픈 것을 중단시키다. 누그러뜨리다. 덜다: *a gel that soothes aching muscles* 근육 통증을 진정시키는 젤

sooth·ing /ˈsuðɪŋ/ adj making someone feel less worry, anger, sadness, or pain ∥ 남을 덜 걱정하게[분노하게, 슬프게, 고통스럽게] 하는. 달래는. 위로하는: *She spoke in a soothing voice.* 그녀는 위로하는 목소리로 말했다. / *a soothing oil* 통증 완화 기름

sop /sɑp/ v **-pped, -pping**
sop sth ↔ up phr v [T] INFORMAL to remove a liquid from a surface using something that will ABSORB the liquid ∥ 액체를 흡수하는 것을 사용하여 표면의 액체를 제거하다. 빨아들이다. 훔치다: *I took a piece of bread to sop up the gravy.* 나는 빵 한 조각을 사용하여 육즙을 빨아들였다.

so·phis·ti·cat·ed /səˈfɪstəˌkeɪtɪd/ adj **1** confident and having knowledge about subjects that are considered socially important such as art, literature, music etc. ∥ 자신 있고 예술·문학·음악 등 사회적으로 중요하다고 여겨지는 주제에 관해 지식이 있는. 세련된. 세상 물정에 밝은: *a sophisticated young man* 세련된 젊은이 **2** made or designed well, and often complicated ∥ 잘 만들어지거나 설계되어 종종 복잡한. 정교한. 정밀한: *highly sophisticated nuclear missiles* 고도로 정밀한 핵 미사일 / *a sophisticated technique* 정교한 기술 —opposite UNSOPHISTICATED

so·phis·ti·ca·tion /səˌfɪstəˈkeɪʃən/ n [U] the quality of being SOPHISTICATED ∥ 세련된 특성. 세련. 정교: *He has a reputation for wealth and sophistication.* 그는 부와 세련으로 평판이 나 있다. / *the sophistication of new technology* 신기술의 정교함

soph·o·more /ˈsɑfmɔr/ n a student in the second year of HIGH SCHOOL or college ∥ 고등학교나 대학교의 2학년생

soph·o·mor·ic /ˌsɑfˈmɔrɪk/ adj very silly and unreasonable ∥ 매우 어리석고 불합리한. 미숙한: *sophomoric humor* 어리석은 유머

sop·o·rif·ic /ˌsɑpəˈrɪfɪk/ adj FORMAL making you feel ready to sleep ∥ 졸리게 만드는. 최면성의. 졸리운. 졸린 듯한

sop·ping /ˈsɑpɪŋ/, **sopping wet** /ˌ.. ˈ./ adj very wet ∥ 매우 젖은. 흠뻑 젖은: *By the time I got home, I was sopping wet.* 집에 돌아왔을 때, 나는 흠뻑 젖었다.

so·pra·no /səˈprænoʊ/ n [C, U] a woman, girl, or young boy singer with a very high voice ∥ 매우 높은 목소리를 가진 여성[소녀, 나이 어린 소년] 가수. 소프라노 가수

sor·bet /sɔrˈbeɪ, ˈsɔrbət/ n [C, U] a sweet frozen food made from fruit juice, sugar, and water ∥ 과일 주스·설탕·물로 만든 달콤하게 얼린 음식. 셔벗

sor·cer·er /ˈsɔrsərə/, **sor·ce·ress** /ˈsɔrsərəs/ n a man or woman who uses magic and gets help from evil spirits ∥ 마법을 써서 악령의 도움을 받는 남자 또는 여자. 마법사. 마술사

sor·cer·y /ˈsɔrsəri/ n [U] magic that uses the power of evil spirits ∥ 악령의 힘을 이용하는 마법

sor·did /ˈsɔrdɪd/ adj involving immoral or dishonest behavior ∥ 부도덕하거나 부정직한 행동에 관련된. 야비한. 비천한: *all the sordid details of the Watergate scandal* 워터게이트 스캔들에 대한 온갖 추잡한 세부 사항

sore¹ /sɔr/ adj **1** painful as a result of a wound, infection, or too much exercise ∥ 상처나 감염으로 인해서, 또는 운동을 너무 많이 하여 아픈. 몸이 아픈: *My knee's a little sore from running yesterday.* 나는 어제 달리기를 해서 무릎이 조금 아프다. / *a sore throat* 아픈 목 **2 sore point/spot** something that is likely to make someone upset or angry if you talk about it ∥ 언급하면 남의 기분을 망치거나 화나게 만들 것 같은 것. 아픈 곳. 약점: *Don't mention marriage – it's a sore point with him.* 결혼에 대해서는

언급하지 마라. 그것은 그에게 아픈 상처이다. **3** OLD-FASHIONED upset, angry, or annoyed ‖ 기분이 상한, 화난, 짜증이 난 – **soreness** n [U]

sore² n an infected place on the body ‖ 신체의 감염 부위. 상처. 헌 데. 아픈 데

sore·ly /'sɔrli/ adv very much ‖ 아주 상당히. 몹시. 심하게: He will be sorely missed by everyone. 모든 이들이 그를 몹시 그리워할 것이다.

so·ror·i·ty /sə'rɔrəti, -'rɑr-/ n a club for women at a college or university ‖ 단과 대학이나 종합 대학의 여성용 클럽. 여학생 클럽 —compare FRATERNITY

sor·row /'sɑroʊ, 'sɔ-/ n [C, U] a feeling of great sadness, or an event that makes you feel great sadness ‖ 매우 슬픈 느낌, 매우 슬프게 느끼게 만드는 사건. 슬픔. 비통. 비탄. 슬픔의 원인: Our prayers are with you in your time of sorrow. 우리의 기도는 슬픔에 빠져 있는 당신과 함께 할 것입니다. / the joys and sorrows of family life 가정생활의 기쁨과 슬픔 – **sorrowful** adj

sor·ry /'sɑri, 'sɔri/ adj **1 sorry/I'm sorry** SPOKEN **a)** said when you feel ashamed or unhappy about something bad that you have done ‖ 자신이 저지른 나쁜 행동에 부끄럽거나 불만스러울 때에 쓰여. 유감이다: I'm sorry, I didn't mean to scare you. 유감이지만, 당신을 겁주려고 한 것은 아니었습니다. **b)** said as a polite way to excuse or correct yourself ‖ 자신을 정중하게 변명하거나 바로잡는 데에 쓰여. 미안한: Sorry for calling so late. 너무 늦게 전화해서 미안해. / I'm sorry about that! (=used as an apology) 그것에 대해서 죄송합니다! ✗DON'T SAY "I'm sorry for that."✗ "I'm sorry for that."이라고는 하지 않는다. **2** feeling ashamed, embarrassed, or unhappy about something you have done ‖ 자신이 한 행동에 대해 부끄럽게 여기거나 당황해 하는, 또는 불만스러워 하는: Keith looked really sorry after he yelled at you. 키스는 너에게 고함을 치고 나서 정말 미안해 하는 것 같았다. **3** to feel pity or sympathy for someone because s/he is in a bad situation ‖ 남이 좋지 않은 상황에 처해 있어서 연민이나 동정심을 느끼는. 딱한. 가엾게 생각하는: Stop feeling sorry for yourself! 자신에 대한 연민일랑 그만둬! / I'm sorry to hear that your mother died 어머니께서 돌아가셨다는 소식을 들으니 참 안됐습니다. —see usage note at SYMPATHY **4** feeling disappointed about a situation ‖ 상황에 대해 실망감을 느끼는. 후회하는: Dad's still sorry that

he never joined the army. 아빠는 군에 입대하지 않은 것에 대해 아직까지도 후회하고 있다. **5** INFORMAL very bad ‖ 매우 나쁜: That's the sorriest excuse I've ever heard. 그것은 내가 들어본 것 중 가장 구차한 변명이다. —see usage note at APOLOGIZING

sort¹ /sɔrt/ n **1 sort of** SPOKEN **a)** slightly; a little ‖ 약간; 조금: I still feel sort of tired. 나는 아직 조금 피곤하다. **b)** used when you cannot be exact or do not want to give details ‖ 정확하지 않거나 상세하게 말하고 싶지 않을 때에 쓰여: He got a sort of special degree from the university. 그는 그 대학에서 일종의 특수 학위를 취득했어. **2 a type of person, thing, action etc.** ‖ 사람·물건·행동 등의 유형. 종류. 성격. 성질: What sort of damage do these insects do? 이 곤충들은 어떤 유형의 위해를 끼치느냐? **3** an action done by a computer in order to organize information in a particular way ‖ 컴퓨터가 특정한 방식으로 정보를 조직화하기 위해 수행하는 행위. 정렬(整列) —compare **kind of** (KIND¹)

sort² v [T] to put things in a particular order, or to arrange them in groups according to size, type etc. ‖ 사물을 특정한 순서에 따라 배치하거나 크기·종류 등에 따라 집단별로 배열하다. 분류[구분]하다. 정렬하다: All the letters have to be sorted and delivered by Friday. 모든 편지들은 금요일까지 분류되어 배달되어야 한다.

sort sth ↔ **out** phr v [T] **a)** to organize something that is messy, complicated, or in the wrong order ‖ 혼란스럽거나 복잡하거나 순서가 잘못되어 있는 것을 분류하다: It took us three hours to sort out our tax receipts. 우리는 세금 영수증을 분류하는 데에 3시간이 걸렸다. **b)** to separate something from a group ‖ 한 집단에서 무엇을 골라내다. 가려내다: I need to sort out which clothes I should pack. 나는 어떤 옷을 꾸려야할지 골라야만 한다.

sort through sth phr v [T] to look at many similar things in order to find the one you want ‖ 자신이 원하는 것을 찾기 위해 여러 유사물들을 조사하다. 구분[정리]하다: Greg sorted through the mail, looking for the letter. 그레그는 그 편지를 찾기 위해 우편물을 정리했다.

sort·a /'sɔrtə/ SPOKEN NONSTANDARD a short form of "sort of" ‖ "soft of"의 단축형: Don't you think he's sorta cute? 그가 약간 귀엽다고 생각하지 않니?

SOS n [singular] used as a signal by a

ship or plane that needs help ‖ 도움이 필요한 배나 비행기의 신호로 쓰여. 조난 신호

so·so /'. ./ *adj, adv* SPOKEN neither very good nor very bad ‖ 매우 좋지도 매우 나쁘지도 않은. 그저 그런: *"How was the movie?" "So-so."* "그 영화 어땠어?" "그저 그랬어."

souf·flé /su'fleɪ/ *n* [C, U] a baked dish that is light and made from eggs, flour, milk, and sometimes cheese ‖ 계란·밀가루·우유 및 때때로 치즈를 넣어 구운 가벼운 요리. 수플레 요리

sought /sɔt/ *v* the past tense and PAST PARTICIPLE of SEEK ‖ seek의 과거·과거 분사형

sought-af·ter /'. ,../ *adj* wanted by a lot of people, but difficult to get ‖ 많은 사람들이 원하지만 얻기 힘든. 인기 있는. 수요가 많은: *one of the world's most sought-after chefs* 세계에서 가장 인기 있는 요리사 중의 한 사람

soul /soʊl/ *n* **1** the part of a person that is not physical and contains his/her thoughts, feelings, character etc., which many people believe exists after death ‖ 많은 사람들이 죽은 후에 존재한다고 믿는, 육체가 아닌 사람의 생각·감정·성격 등을 포함한 부분. 영혼. 혼. 넋 **2** a person ‖ 사람: *Don't you dare tell a soul!* 절대로 아무에게도 말하지 마라! **3** [U] a type of popular modern music that often expresses deep emotions, usually performed by Black singers and musicians ‖ 보통 흑인 가수와 음악가에 의해 연주되는, 종종 강렬한 감정을 표현하는 현대 대중음악의 한 형태. 솔 음악 **4** [U] a special quality that makes you feel strong emotions ‖ 강렬한 감정을 느끼게 만드는 특별한 자질. 정열. 기백: *His poetry lacks soul.* 그의 시는 기백이 부족하다.

soul·ful /'soʊlfəl/ *adj* expressing deep sad emotions ‖ 깊고 슬픈 감정을 표현하는: *a soulful cry* 북받치는 울음

soul·less /'soʊl-lɪs/ *adj* lacking the qualities that make people feel interest, emotions, or excitement ‖ 사람들을 흥미나 감동, 또는 흥분을 느끼게 만드는 자질이 부족한. 혼이 깃들지 않은. 시시한: *a soulless town* 생기 없는 도시

soul-search·ing /'. ,../ *n* [U] the act of carefully examining your thoughts and feelings in order to make a decision ‖ 의사 결정을 하기 위해 자신의 생각과 감정을 주의 깊게 살펴보는 행동. 자기 분석[반성]: *After much soul-searching, she decided that she could never marry*

him. 그녀는 심사숙고한 후에 자기는 그와 결코 결혼할 수 없을 거라는 결론을 내렸다.

sound¹ /saʊnd/ *n* **1** [C, U] something that you hear, or something that can be heard ‖ 듣거나 들리는 것. 소리: *the sound of breaking glass* 유리를 깨는 소리 / *There's no sound coming from the TV.* 텔레비전에서 아무 소리도 나지 않는다. —see usage note at NOISE **2 by the sound of it/things** SPOKEN according to what you have heard or read about something ‖ 무엇에 대해 듣거나 읽은 것에 따르면. 듣기로는: *By the sound of it, he's being forced out of his job.* 듣기로는, 그는 직장을 나가라는 압력을 받고 있다고 한다. **3** a long wide area of water that connects two larger areas of water ‖ 보다 큰 두 해역을 연결하는 길고 넓은 해역. 해협

sound² *v* **1** [linking verb] someone or something that sounds good, strange etc. seems that way when you hear or read about him, her, or it ‖ 사람이나 사물이 자신이 듣거나 읽은 것처럼 보이다. …처럼 들리다[보이다]: *Your friend sounds like a nice guy.* 당신의 친구는 좋은 사람 같다. **2** [linking verb] to seem to show a particular quality or emotion with your voice ‖ 목소리로 특정한 자질이나 감정을 나타내는 것 같다: *You sound upset. Are you OK?* 기분이 안 좋아 보이는데, 괜찮니? **3 sounds good** SPOKEN said in order to accept something that someone has suggested ‖ 누군가가 제안한 것을 받아들이는 데에 쓰여. 좋아: *"Do you want Thai food tonight?" "Sounds good."* "오늘 저녁에 태국 음식 먹을래?" "좋아." **4** [I, T] to produce a noise, or to make something do this ‖ 소음을 내다, 또는 소음을 내게 하다: *The church bells sounded.* 교회 종소리가 울렸다.

sound off *phr v* [I] to express a strong opinion or complaint, often in a loud or annoying way ‖ 종종 큰 소리나 신경질적으로 강력하게 의견을 표현하거나 불평을 하다: *We were told not to sound off about our problems to the press.* 우리는 언론에 우리의 문제들을 노골적으로 말하지 말라는 얘기를 들었다.

sound out *phr v* [T] [**sound** sb/sth ↔ **out**] to talk to someone in order to find out what s/he thinks about a plan or idea ‖ 계획이나 개념에 대한 생각을 알아내려고 남에게 말하다. 의향을 타진하다: *We've found a way of sounding out public opinion on the issue.* 우리는 그 문제에 대한 여론을 알아보는 방법을 찾아내

었다.

sound³ *adj* **1** practical, based on good judgment, and likely to produce good results ‖ 실제적인, 좋은 판단에 근거한, 좋은 결과를 낼 것 같은: *Our helpline offers sound advice to new parents.* 우리 전화 상담은 갓 부모가 된 사람에게 적절한 조언을 제공한다. / *a sound investment* 안전한 투자 **2** in good condition and not damaged in any way ‖ 어떤 식으로든 위해를 받지 않은 좋은 상태의. 온전한: *The roof leaks, but the floors are sound.* 지붕은 새지만 마루는 상태가 양호하다. **3 of sound mind** LAW not mentally ill ‖ 정신적으로 병들지 않은. 건전한 —opposite UNSOUND

sound⁴ *adv* **sound asleep** completely asleep ‖ 완전히 잠들어: *Bonita was sound asleep.* 보니타는 깊이 잠들어 있었다.

sound bar·ri·er /'. ‚.../ *n* **the sound barrier** the point when an aircraft reaches the speed of sound ‖ 비행기가 음속에 도달할 때의 지점. 음속 장벽

sound bite /'. ./ *n* a short phrase used by politicians or companies that are advertising, that is supposed to represent the most important part of what they are saying ‖ 정치인이나 기업이 주장하는 것 중의 가장 중요한 부분을 나타내고 있는 것으로 여겨지는, 광고할 때 사용하는 짧은 말. 짧게 발췌한 방송용 어구. 정치인의 어록

sound·card,   sound   card /'saʊnd,kɑrd/ *n* a CIRCUIT BOARD that can be added to a computer so that it is able to produce sound ‖ 소리를 낼 수 있도록 컴퓨터에 추가될 수 있는 회로판. 사운드 카드

sound ef·fects /'. ‚./ *n* [plural] special sounds used in order to make a movie, television show etc. seem more real ‖ 영화나 텔레비전 쇼 등을 보다 사실적으로 보이게 하기 위해 사용되는 특수한 소리. 음향 효과

sound·ing board /'.. ‚./ *n* someone you discuss your ideas with before using them ‖ 자신의 생각을 활용하기 전에 그것에 대한 논의를 벌이는 상대방. 반응을 보기 위해 이용되는 사람

sound·ly /'saʊndli/ *adv* **1 sleep soundly** to sleep well, without waking up or dreaming ‖ 중간에 깨거나 꿈도 꾸지 않고 잘 자다. 푹 자다: *I always sleep soundly at my parents' house.* 나는 부모님 댁에서는 항상 푹 잘 잔다. **2** completely or severely ‖ 완전히, 맹렬히: *Washington was soundly defeated in*

the final match. 워싱턴 팀은 마지막 경기에서 완전히 대파 당했다. **3** in a way that is strong and unlikely to break ‖ 강하고 쉽게 부숴지지 않게. 견고하게: *The building is soundly designed.* 그 건물은 견고하게 설계되었다.

sound·proof¹ /'saʊndpruf/ *adj* a soundproof wall, room etc. is one that sound cannot go through or go out of ‖ 벽이나 방 등이 소리가 밖에서 들리거나 밖으로 새어나가지 못하는. 방음의

soundproof² *v* [T] to make something SOUNDPROOF ‖ 무엇을 방음이 되게 하다. 방음 장치를 하다

sound·track /'saʊndtræk/ *n* the recorded music from a movie ‖ 영화에서 녹음이 된 음악. 사운드 트랙

soup¹ /sup/ *n* [C, U] a hot liquid food that usually has pieces of meat or vegetables in it ‖ 보통 고기 조각이나 야채가 들어 있는 뜨거운 유동식. 수프: *chicken noodle soup* 닭 누들 수프

soup² *v*

soup sth ↔ **up** *phr v* [T] to improve something such as a car by making it more powerful or more exciting ‖ 차 등을 더욱 강력하거나 더욱 자극적으로 만들어 향상시키다. 마력을 증대시키다 — **souped-up** /ˌ '. ./ *adj*

soup kitch·en /'. ‚../ *n* a place where free food is given to people who have no home ‖ 집이 없는 사람들에게 음식을 무료로 주는 곳. 무료 급식소

sour¹ /saʊɚ/ *adj* **1** having an acid taste, like the taste of a LEMON ‖ 레몬 맛처럼 신맛이 나는. 신. 시큼한: *sour green apples* 시큼한 풋사과 **2** milk or other food that is sour is not fresh and has an unpleasant taste and smell ‖ 우유나 다른 음식이 신선하지 못하고 불쾌한 맛과 냄새가 나는. 상한: *The milk has gone sour.* 그 우유는 상했다. **3** unfriendly or unhappy ‖ 불쾌한, 불행한: *a sour expression* 불쾌한 표현 **4 go/turn sour** INFORMAL to stop being enjoyable or satisfactory ‖ 재미있거나 만족스럽지 못하게 되다. 못쓰게 되다. 악화되다: *By that time, their relationship had turned sour.* 그 때쯤 그들의 관계는 악화되었다.

sour² *v* **1** [I] to stop being enjoyable or satisfactory ‖ 재미있거나 만족스럽지 못하게 되다. 악화되다: *Relations between the two countries had soured.* 두 나라 사이의 관계가 악화되었다. **2** [I, T] to become sour, or make a food do this ‖ 시어지다, 또는 음식을 시게 하다

source /sɔrs/ *n* **1** the thing, place, person etc. that you obtain something from ‖ 무엇인가를 얻어내는 사물·장소·사람. 근원. 근본. 원천: *Tourism is the city's greatest source of income.* 관광 사업은 그 도시의 가장 큰 수입원이다. / *gasoline and other sources of energy* 휘발유와 다른 에너지원 **2** the cause of a problem, or the place where it starts ‖ 문제의 원인이나 문제가 시작된 곳. 원인: *Grant has always been a source of trouble in the classroom.* 그랜트는 언제나 그 학급에서 말썽의 원인이 되었다. **3** a person, book, or document that you get information from ‖ 정보를 얻는 사람이나 책 또는 서류. 출처. 정보원. 출전: *Reliable sources say the company is going bankrupt.* 믿을 만한 소식통에 의하면 그 회사는 도산이 임박해 있다. **4** the place where a stream or river starts ‖ 시내나 강이 시작되는 곳. 수원지

sour cream /ˌ. ˈ./ *n* [U] a thick white cream with a sour taste, used in cooking ‖ 요리할 때 사용하는 신맛이 나는 걸쭉한 흰 크림. 산패유(酸敗乳)

sour·dough /ˈsaʊɚdoʊ/, **sour·dough bread** /ˈ.. ˌ./ *n* [U] a type of bread with a slightly sour taste ‖ 약간 신맛이 나는 빵 종류 —see picture at BREAD

south[1], **South** /saʊθ/ *n* [singular, U] **1** the direction toward the bottom of the world, or to the right of someone facing the rising sun ‖ 지구의 밑쪽을 향한 방향, 또는 떠오르는 태양을 마주해서 오른쪽의 방향. 남(쪽): *Which way is south?* 어느 쪽이 남쪽이지? **2 the south** the southern part of a country, state etc. ‖ 국가·주(州) 등의 남쪽 부분. 남부 지방: *Rain will spread to the south later today.* 오늘 늦게 남부 지방으로 비는 확산됩니다. **3 the South** the southeastern states of the US ‖ 미국 남동부의 주들 **4 down South** in or to the South of the US ‖ 미국의 남부 지방에서, 또는 남부 지방으로: *We moved down South in 1996.* 우리는 1996년에 남부 지방으로 이사했다. —see usage note at NORTH[3]

south[2] *adj* **1** in, to, or facing south ‖ 남쪽의, 남향의: *The hotel's about two miles south of Monterey.* 그 호텔은 몬테레이에서 남쪽으로 약 2마일 거리에 있다. / *the south wall of the building* 그 건물의 남쪽 벽 **2 south wind** a wind coming from the south ‖ 남쪽에서 불어오는 바람. 남풍

south[3] *adv* toward the south ‖ 남쪽을 향해서: *Go south on I-35 to Des Moines.* 데모인까지 I-35번 도로를 따라 남쪽으로 가라. / *The window faces south.* 그 창문은 남쪽으로 나 있다.

South A·mer·i·ca /ˌsaʊθ əˈmɛrəkə/ *n* one of the seven CONTINENTs, that includes land south of the Caribbean Sea and north of Antarctica ‖ 카리브 해의 남쪽 땅과 남극 대륙의 북쪽 땅을 포함한, 일곱 대륙 중 하나. 남아메리카 대륙 –**South American** *adj*

south·bound /ˈsaʊθbaʊnd/ *adj* traveling or leading toward the south ‖ 남쪽으로 여행하거나 이끄는. 남쪽으로 향하는. 남하하는: *southbound traffic* 남행하는 차량 / *the southbound lanes of the freeway* 고속도로의 남행 차선

south·east[1] /ˌsaʊθˈist◂/ *n* [U] **1** the direction that is exactly between south and east ‖ 정확히 남쪽과 동쪽 중간의 방향. 남동: *southeast Utah* 유타 주의 남동부 **2 the Southeast** the southeast part of a country, state etc. ‖ 국가·주(州) 등의 남동부 –**southeastern** *adj*

southeast[2] *adj, adv* in or toward the southeast ‖ 남동에 있는, 남동쪽으로 향하는: *flying southeast* 남동향 비행 / *a southeast wind* 남동풍

south·er·ly /ˈsʌðɚli/ *adj* **1** in or toward the south ‖ 남쪽에 있는, 남쪽을 향하는: *sailing in a southerly direction* 남쪽 방향으로의 항해 **2** a southerly wind comes from the south ‖ 바람이 남쪽에서 불어오는

south·ern /ˈsʌðɚn/ *adj* in or from the south part of an area, state, country etc. ‖ 한 지역이나 주(州) 또는 국가 등의 남쪽(지방)의, 또는 남쪽으로부터의: *southern New Mexico* 뉴멕시코 주 남부 —see usage note at NORTH[3]

south·ern·er /ˈsʌðɚnɚ/ *n* someone who comes from the SOUTHERN part of a country or the southern HEMISPHERE ‖ 한 국가의 남쪽 지방이나 남반구 출신의 사람. 남부[남국]인

south·ern·most /ˈsʌðɚnˌmoʊst/ *adj* farthest south ‖ 최남단의: *the southernmost tip of the island* 그 섬의 최남단

South Pa·cif·ic /ˌ. .ˈ../ *n* **the South Pacific** the southern part of the Pacific Ocean where there are groups of islands, such as New Zealand and Polynesia ‖ 뉴질랜드와 폴리네시아 등의 섬들이 무리지어 있는 태평양의 남쪽 부분. 남태평양

South Pole /ˌ. ˈ./ *n* **the South Pole** the most southern point on the surface of the earth, or the area around it ‖ 지구 표면에서 가장 남쪽 지점, 또는 그 주변 지역. 남극 (지역)

south·ward /'sauθwəd/ *adj, adv* toward the south ‖ 남쪽을 향한. 남쪽을 향하여

south·west¹ /ˌsauθ'wɛst·/ *n* **1** the direction that is exactly between south and west ‖ 정확히 남쪽과 서쪽의 중간 방향. 남서(쪽) **2 the Southwest** the southwest part of a country, state etc. ‖ 국가·주 등의 남서쪽 부분. 남서 지방 – **southwestern** *adj*

southwest² *adj, adv* in, from, or toward the southwest ‖ 남서쪽에(있는), 남서쪽에서(의), 남서쪽을 향한[향해서]: *driving southwest* 남서행 운행 / *a southwest wind* 남서풍

sou·ve·nir /ˌsuvə'nır, 'suvə,nır/ *n* an object that you keep to remind yourself of a special occasion or a place that you have visited ‖ 자신이 탐방한 특별한 행사나 장소를 회상하기 위해 보관하는 물건. 기념품

sov·er·eign¹ /'savərın/ *adj* **1** having the highest power or authority in a country ‖ 한 나라에서 가장 높은 힘이나 권력을 가진. 통치권을 가진 **2** a sovereign country is independent and governs itself ‖ 나라가 독립해서 스스로 통치하는. 자치의. 독립의 – **sovereignty** *n* [U]

sovereign² *n* FORMAL a king or queen ‖ 왕이나 여왕. 주권자. 통치자

So·vi·et /'souviːt, -vi,ɛt/ *adj* relating to or coming from the former Soviet Union ‖ 구 소비에트 연방과 관련되거나 소비에트 연방에서 나온. 소비에트의

sow¹ /sou/ *v* **sowed, sown** *or* **sowed, sowing** [I, T] to plant or scatter seeds on a large piece of ground ‖ 땅에 씨를 심거나 뿌리다: *We sow the corn in the early spring.* 우리는 초봄에 옥수수 씨를 뿌린다.

sow² /sau/ *n* a female pig ‖ 암퇘지

soy·bean /'sɔıbin/ *n* a bean used especially for making foods that can be eaten instead of meat ‖ 특히 고기 대신에 먹을 수 있는 음식을 만들기 위해 사용하는 콩

spa /spa/ *n* a place that people go to in order to improve their health, especially a place where the water has special minerals in it ‖ 특히 특수 무기질을 함유한 물이 있는 곳으로서 사람들이 건강 증진을 위해 가는 곳. 온천(장)

space¹ /speıs/ *n* **1** [U] the amount of an area, room, container etc. that is empty or available to be used ‖ 한 지역이나 방 또는 용기 등의 비어 있거나 사용할 수 있는 크기. 장소. 공간: *Is there any more space in the basement?* 지하실에 공간이 좀 더 있느냐? / *There's not enough space in the computer's memory.* 컴퓨터의 기억 장치에는 충분한 공간이 없다. **2** [C, U] an empty area that is used for a particular purpose ‖ 특정한 목적에 사용되는 텅 빈 지역. 공간: *There were no parking spaces.* 주차할 공간이 없었다. / *6900 square feet of office space for sale* 팔려고 내놓은 6900평방피트의 사무실 공간 **3** the empty area between two things; GAP ‖ 두 물체 사이의 텅 빈 지역. 틈; 阁 gap: *There's a space for it there-between the books.* 두 책 사이에 그것을 넣을 틈이 있다. **4** [U] the area outside the Earth's air where the stars and PLANETs are ‖ 별들이나 행성들이 있는 지구의 대기권 밖에 있는 지역. 우주: *a satellite traveling through space* 우주를 항행하는 인공위성 **5 in/during the space of** within a particular period of time ‖ 특정한 기한 안에: *In the space of a few seconds it was done.* 그것은 몇 초 안에 이루어졌다. **6** [C, U] empty land that does not have anything built on it ‖ 건조물이 없는 빈 땅: *a fight to save the city's open spaces* 도시의 빈터를 확보하려는 싸움 **7** [U] opportunities to do what you want or to be alone ‖ 원하는 것을 할 기회, 또는 혼자 있을 기회: *I need more space, Joe.* 나는 좀 더 혼자 있고 싶어, 조. —see usage note at PLACE¹

space² *v* [T] **1** to arrange objects, events etc. so that they have an equal amount of space or time between them ‖ 사물들이나 사건들 등을 공간적이나 시간적으로 동일한 간격을 두도록 조정하다. 일정한 간격을 두다: *Space the plants four inches apart.* 그 식물들은 4인치의 간격을 두어라. **2** *also* **space out** [I] SLANG to stop paying attention and begin to look in front of you without thinking ‖ 주의를 기울이지 않고 아무 생각 없이 앞쪽을 바라보다. 멍하게 바라보다 – **spacing** *n* [U]

space-age /'. ./ *adj* INFORMAL very modern ‖ 매우 현대적인. 최신식의: *space-age design* 매우 현대적인 디자인

space ca·det /'. ,./, **space case** /'. ,./ *n* SLANG someone who is SPACEY ‖ 멍해 있는 사람

space·craft /'speıs-kræft/ *n* a vehicle that can travel in space ‖ 우주를 항행할 수 있는 비행체. 우주선

spaced /speıst/, **spaced out** /ˌ. '. ./ *adj* SLANG ⇨ SPACEY

space·ship /'speıs,ʃıp/ *n* a word meaning SPACECRAFT, used especially in

stories ‖ 특히 소설에서 쓰이는 우주선을
의미하는 단어

space shut·tle /'. ,../ *n* a SPACECRAFT
for carrying people into space, that can
be used more than once ‖ 한 번 이상 사
용 가능한, 우주로 사람들을 수송하기 위
한 우주선. 우주 왕복선

space·y /'speɪsi/ *adj* SPOKEN behaving
as if you do not know what is happening
‖ 마치 무슨 일이 일어나고 있는지 모르는
것처럼 행동하는: *Is she on drugs or just
really spacey?* 그녀는 마약을 한 거니 아
니면 정말 멍청한 거니?

spa·cious /'speɪʃəs/ *adj* having a lot of
space in which you can move around ‖
돌아다닐 수 있는 많은 공간이 있는. 널찍
한. 넓은: *a spacious car/room/house* 널
찍한 차[방, 집]

spade /speɪd/ *n* **1** ⇨ SHOVEL¹ **2** a
playing card with one or more black
shapes like pointed leaves on it ‖ 뾰족한
나뭇잎 같은 하나 또는 그 이상의 검은 색
무늬가 있는 카드. 스페이드(패)

spa·ghet·ti /spə'gɛti/ *n* [U] long thin
pieces of PASTA that look like strings ‖ 끈
처럼 생긴 길고 가느다란 모양의 파스타.
스파게티

Spam /spæm/ *n* [U] TRADEMARK a type
of inexpensive CANNED meat made
mainly of PORK ‖ 주로 돼지고기로 만든
비싸지 않은 통조림 고기의 일종

spam /spæm/ *n* [U] E-MAIL messages
that a computer user has not asked for
and does not want to read, for example
from someone who is advertising
something ‖ 컴퓨터 사용자가 요청하지도
않고 읽고 싶지도 않은, 일례로 어떤 것을
광고하는 사람에게서 온, 이메일 메시지.
스팸(메일)

span¹ /spæn/ *n* **1** the amount of time
during which something continues to
exist or happen ‖ 무엇이 계속 존재하거나
일어나는 기간: *Most children have a
short attention span.* 대부분의 아이들은
집중 시간이 짧다. / *The mayfly has a
two-day life span.* (=lives for two days)
하루살이는 수명이 이틀이다. **2** a period
of time between two dates or events ‖ 두
날짜나 두 사건 사이의 기간: *Over a span
of five years, they planted 10,000 new
trees.* 5년에 걸쳐서 그들은 만 그루의 나
무를 새로 심었다. **3** the distance from
one side of something to the other ‖ 무엇
의 한쪽에서 다른 쪽까지의 거리. 전장: *a
wing span of three feet* 3피트의 날개 길
이

span² *v* **-nned, -nning** [T] **1** to include
all of a period of time ‖ 전(全)기간을 포

함하다. 시간적으로 …에 이르다[걸치다]:
*Mariani's career spanned 45 years of
change in Hollywood.* 마리아니의 경력은
할리우드 변천사에서 45년에 이른다. **2** to
go from one side of something to the
other ‖ 무엇의 한 쪽에서 다른 쪽까지 가
다. 공간적으로 …에 이르다[걸치다]: *a
bridge spanning the river* 그 강 위에 놓
여져 있는 다리

span·gle /'spæŋgəl/ *n* ⇨ SEQUIN –
spangled *adj*

span·iel /'spænyəl/ *n* a dog with long
hair and long ears ‖ 긴 털과 긴 귀를 가
진 개. 스패니얼

Span·ish¹ /'spænɪʃ/ *adj* **1** relating to or
coming from Spain ‖ 스페인과 관련된, 스
페인 출신의. 스페인의 **2** relating to the
Spanish language ‖ 스페인어와 관련된.
스페인어의

Spanish² *n* **1** [U] the language used in
places such as Mexico, Spain, and
South America ‖ 멕시코·스페인·남미 등
에서 사용되는 언어. 스페인어 **2 the
Spanish** [plural] the people of Spain,
considered as a single group ‖ 단일 민
족으로 간주되는 스페인 사람들. 스페인
인

spank /spæŋk/ *v* [T] to hit a child on
the BUTTOCKs with your open hand ‖ 손
바닥으로 아이의 볼기를 때리다 –
spanking *n* [C, U]

spar /spar/ *v* **-rred, -rring** [I] to
practice BOXING or MARTIAL ARTS with
someone ‖ 남과 권투나 무술 연습을 하다.
스파링하다. 연습 시합을 하다

spare¹ /spɛr/ *adj* **1 spare key/battery
etc.** a key etc. that you have in addition
to the one you usually use, so that it is
available if it is needed ‖ 필요할 때 사용
할 수 있도록 평상시 사용하는 것에 추가
하여 가지고 있는 열쇠 등. 예비 열쇠/전
지 **2** not being used by anyone and
therefore available for use ‖ 아무도 사용
하지 않아 사용이 가능한. 여분의: *a spare
bedroom* 여분의 침대 **3 spare time** time
when you are not working ‖ 일하지 않는
때. 여가. 한가한 시간: *I play tennis in
my spare time.* 나는 여가에 테니스를 친
다. **4 spare change** coins that you can
afford to give to someone ‖ 남에게 그냥
줄 수 있는 동전. 잔돈

spare² *v* [T] **1** to prevent someone from
having to do something difficult or
unpleasant ‖ 남이 해야만 하는 어렵거나
불쾌한 일을 하지 않게 하다: *I was trying
to spare you unnecessary work.* 나는 네
가 불필요한 일을 하지 않아도 되도록 노
력하고 있었다. **2 $20/an hour etc. to**

spare $20, one hour etc. that is left in addition to what you use or need to do something ‖ 무엇을 하는 데에 사용하거나 필요한 것 외에 추가로 남겨 둔 20달러·한 시간 등. 여분의 20달러/한 시간: *We made it to the airport with 10 minutes to spare.* 우리는 공항에 10분 여유 있게 도착했다. **3 Could you spare (me)...?** SPOKEN used in order to ask someone if s/he could lend or give you something, or if s/he has time to talk to you ‖ 남에게 무엇을 빌려 주거나 줄 수 있는지, 또는 얘기할 시간이 있는지를 묻는 데에 쓰여: *Could you spare me 20 minutes of your time?* 20분만 시간 좀 내어 주시겠습니까? **4 spare no expense/effort etc.** to use as much money, effort etc. as necessary to do something ‖ 무엇을 하는 데에 필요한 만큼 많은 돈과 노력을 들이다. 비용/노력을 아끼지 않다: *We will spare no expense in buying new equipment.* 우리는 새로운 장비 구입에 비용을 아끼지 않을 것이다. **5** to not damage or harm someone or something, when other people or things are being killed or damaged ‖ 사람이나 사물이 살해되거나 손상을 입을 때에 다른 사람이나 사물을 해치거나 피해를 주지 않다: *Only the children's lives were spared.* 단지 아이들의 목숨만은 살렸다.

spare³ *n* an additional key, BATTERY etc. that you keep so that it is available if it is needed ‖ 필요한 때에 사용할 수 있도록 보관하는 보조 열쇠·전지 등. 예비품: *The back left tire is flat – is there a spare in the trunk?* 왼쪽 뒷타이어가 펑크가 났다. 트렁크에 예비 타이어가 있니?

spar·ing·ly /ˈspɛrɪŋli/ *adv* using or giving only a little of something ‖ 무엇을 조금만 쓰거나 조금만 줘서. 절약하여. 검 Plan하여: *People are being asked to use water sparingly this summer.* 사람들은 올여름에 물을 아껴 쓰라는 요청을 받고 있다. **– sparing** *adj*

spark¹ /spark/ *n* **1** a very small flash of fire coming from a larger fire or from hitting two hard objects together ‖ 보다 큰 불에서, 또는 두 개의 단단한 물체를 서로 부딪쳐서 생기는 아주 작은 불꽃. 불똥 **2** a flash of light caused by electricity passing across a small space ‖ 작은 공간을 통과하는 전기에서 일어나는 불꽃. 스파크 **3 spark of interest/intelligence etc.** a small amount of interest, etc. that you see in someone's expression or behavior ‖ 남의 표정이나 행동에서 드러나는 적은 흥미 등. 약간의 흥미/지성: *As*

she spoke, she saw a spark of hope in Tony's eyes. 그녀는 말하면서 토니의 눈에서 번득이는 작은 희망의 불꽃을 보았다.

spark² *v* **1** [T] also **spark off** to make something start happening ‖ 무엇을 일어나게 하다: *The speech sparked off riots in the city.* 그 연설은 그 도시에 폭동을 일으켰다 **2** [I] to produce SPARKs ‖ 불꽃을 내다

spar·kle /ˈsparkəl/ *v* [I] **1** to shine in small bright flashes ‖ 작고 밝은 섬광을 발하다. 반짝거리다. 빛나다: *diamonds sparkling in the light* 불빛에 반짝거리는 다이아몬드 **2** if someone's eyes sparkle, they shine because s/he is happy or excited ‖ 눈이 행복하거나 흥분해서 반짝거리다 **– sparkle** *n* [C, U]

spark·ler /ˈsparklɚ/ *n* a thin stick that you hold, which makes SPARKs when you burn it ‖ 태우면 불꽃을 내는 손에 쥐는 가는 막대기

spark plug /ˈ. ./ *n* a part in a car engine that produces the SPARK to make the gas burn ‖ 가스가 타도록 불꽃을 내는 자동차 엔진의 한 부분. 점화 플러그

spar·row /ˈspæroʊ/ *n* a common small brown or gray bird ‖ 보통 갈색이나 회색의 작은 새. 참새

sparse /spars/ *adj* small in number or amount, and usually scattered over a large area ‖ 수나 양적으로 적으면서 넓은 지역에 흩어져 있는. 드문. 희박한. 산재하는: *sparse vegetation* 드문드문 있는 초목 **– sparsely** *adv* : *sparsely populated* 인구가 희박한

spar·tan /ˈspartᵊn/ *adj* very simple and without comfort ‖ 매우 간소하고 편안하지 않은: *spartan living conditions* 검소하고 엄격한 생활 여건

spasm /ˈspæzəm/ *n* **1** a sudden movement in which your muscles become tight in an uncontrolled way ‖ 근육이 억제 불가능하게 굳어지는 돌연한 변화. 경련. 쥐: *back spasms* 등의 경련 **2** a short period during which a strong feeling or reaction to something happens ‖ 일순간의 강한 감정이나 무엇에 대해 일어나는 반응. 발작: *spasms of laughter* 터져 나오는 웃음

spas·mod·ic /spæzˈmɑdɪk/ *adj* **1** happening for short periods of time but not regularly or continuously ‖ 규칙적이거나 계속적이 아니라 잠시 일어나는. 돌발적인. 단속적인: *my spasmodic efforts to stop smoking* 금연을 위한 나의 단속적인 노력 **2** relating to a muscle SPASM ‖ 근육의 경련에 관련된. 경련성의 **–**

spasmodically *adv*

spas·tic /'spæstɪk/ *adj* OLD-FASHIONED having uncontrolled SPASMs as a result of a disease ‖ 질병의 결과로 억제할 수 없는 경련을 일으키는. 뇌성 마비의

spat[1] /spæt/ *n* INFORMAL an argument or disagreement that is not important; quarrel ‖ 중요하지 않은 논쟁이나 불화. 승강이; 언쟁

spat[2] *v* a past tense and the PAST PARTICIPLE of SPIT ‖ spit의 과거·과거 분사형

spate /speɪt/ *n* **a spate of sth** a large number of similar events that happen in a short period of time ‖ 짧은 기간에 일어나는 많은 유사한 사건. 대량[다수]의…: *a spate of burglaries in the area* 그 지역에서의 수많은 강도사건

spa·tial /'speɪʃəl/ *adj* TECHNICAL relating to the position, size, or shape of things ‖ 사물의 위치·규모·모양과 관련된. 공간의[에 관한]

spat·ter /'spætɚ/ *v* [I, T] if a liquid spatters or you spatter it, drops of it fall onto a surface ‖ 액체가 표면에 떨어지다. 튀다. 튀기다: *Rain began to spatter on the steps.* 비가 계단 위에 흩뿌리기 시작했다.

spat·u·la /'spætʃələ/ *n* a kitchen tool with a wide flat part, used for lifting and spreading food ‖ 음식을 들어올리고 펴는 데에 사용되는 넓고 평평한 부분이 있는 주방 기구. 뒤집개

spawn[1] /spɔn/ *v* **1** [T] to make something happen or start to exist ‖ 무엇을 일어나게 또는 존재하기 시작하게 하다. …을 야기시키다: *The book "Dracula" has spawned a number of movies.* "드라큘라"란 책은 수많은 영화를 만들어냈다. **2** [I, T] if a fish or FROG spawns, it lays a lot of eggs together ‖ 물고기나 개구리가 많은 알을 한꺼번에 낳다

spawn[2] *n* [U] the eggs of a fish or FROG laid together in a soft group ‖ 무더기로 낳아 놓은 말랑한 물고기나 개구리의 알

spay /speɪ/ *v* [T] to remove part of a female animal's sex organs so that she cannot produce babies ‖ 새끼를 낳지 못하도록 동물 암컷의 성기의 일부를 제거하다. 난소를 제거[절제]하다

speak /spik/ *v* **spoke**, **spoken**, **speaking**
1 ▶TALK TO SB 누구에게 이야기하다◀ [I] to talk to someone about something or have a conversation ‖ 무엇에 관해 이야기하거나 대화를 나누다: *Hello, can I speak to Mr. Sherwood please?* 여보세요, 셔우드 씨 좀 바꿔주시겠습니까? / *We need to speak with/to you before you leave.* 우리는 네가 떠나기 전에 너와 이야기를 해야 한다.
2 ▶SAY WORDS 말하다◀ [I] to use your voice to say words ‖ 목소리를 이용하여 말을 하다: *Most children don't begin to speak until they are over a year old.* 대부분의 아이들은 한 살이 넘어서야 비로소 말을 하기 시작한다.
3 ▶LANGUAGE 언어◀ [T] to be able to talk in a particular language ‖ 특정한 언어로 대화할 수 있다: *My brother speaks English/French.* 내 형[동생]은 영어를 [프랑스어를] 구사한다. ✗DON'T SAY "My brother speaks in English/French."✗ "My brother speaks in English/French." 라고는 하지 않는다.
4 generally/technically etc. speaking used in order to say that you are expressing a general, technical etc. opinion ‖ 일반적인·전문적인 의견을 표현하고 있다는 것을 나타내는 데에 쓰여. 일반적으로/전문적으로 말하면: *Generally speaking, I agree with you, but this case is different.* 일반적으로 말하면 나는 너에게 동의하지만 이번 경우는 다르다.
5 so to speak SPOKEN used in order to say that the expression you have used does not have its usual meaning ‖ 자신이 사용한 표현이 일반적인 뜻으로 한 것이 아니라는 것을 말하는 데에 쓰여. 말하자면: *He found the problem in his own back yard, so to speak.* (=affecting him or his family, or the area he lives in) 그는 (그나 그의 가족, 또는 그가 살고 있는 곳에 영향을 미치는) 말하자면 그 자신과 관련된 주변 문제를 발견했다.
6 speaking of... SPOKEN used when you want to say more about someone or something that has just been mentioned ‖ 방금 막 언급된 사람이나 사물에 대해 더 언급하고 싶을 때에 쓰여. …에 대해서 말인데: *Speaking of Jody, how is she?* 조디 말인데, 그녀는 어때?
7 ▶ABOUT SB/STH 사람/사물에 대해◀ [I] to tell someone about a particular subject or person ‖ 특정한 주제나 사람에 대해 남에게 말하다: *He spoke of/about his love of the theater.* 그는 연극에 대한 자신의 사랑에 대해 말했다.
8 speak your mind to say exactly what you think ‖ 생각하는 것을 정확히 말하다. 털어놓고 말하다: *Dana always speaks her mind.* 다나는 항상 툭 털어놓고 말한다.
9 none/nothing to speak of nothing large or important enough to mention ‖ 언급할 정도로 충분히 크거나 중요하지 않

다: *"Did you get any snow last week?"* *"None to speak of."* "네가 살고 있는 곳에 지난 주 눈이 좀 왔느냐?" "특별히 말할 정도로 그리 많이 오지는 않았어." **10 ▶GIVE A SPEECH◀** 연설을 하다◀ [I] to make a formal speech ‖ 공식적인 연설을 하다: *I get so nervous if I have to speak in public.* 내가 대중 앞에서 연설해야 하는지 매우 걱정된다. —see usage note at SAY

speak for sb/sth *phr v* [T] **1** to express the feelings, thoughts etc. of another person or group of people ‖ 다른 사람 또는 일단의 사람들의 감정이나 생각 등을 표현하다: *I'm speaking for the whole family when I say "thank you" to all of you.* 내가 여러분 모두에게 "감사합니다" 라고 할 때는 전 가족의 뜻을 표현하고 있는 것입니다. **2 sth speaks for itself** to show something so clearly that no explanation is necessary ‖ 무엇이 설명할 필요 없이 너무 명백하다는 것을 나타내다. …은 자명하다: *Our profits speak for themselves.* (=our profits show how good or bad our business is) 우리의 수익이 모든 것을 말해준다[사업이 호황인지 불황인지를 보여 준다]. **3 be spoken for** to be promised to someone else ‖ 다른 사람에게 예약되어 있다: *This puppy is already spoken for.* 이 강아지는 이미 예약되어 있다.

speak out *phr v* [I] to say publicly what you think about something, especially as a protest ‖ 특히 항의로서 무엇에 대해 생각하고 있는 것을 공공연히 말하다. 털어놓고[솔직하게] 의견을 말하다: *people speaking out against human rights abuses* 인권 남용에 대해 소리 높여 말하고 있는 사람들

speak up *phr v* [I] **1** SPOKEN used in order to ask someone to speak more loudly ‖ 남에게 말을 더 크게 하라고 요구하는 데에 쓰여. 큰 소리로 말하다: *Could you speak up please, I can't hear you.* 좀더 크게 말해 주시겠어요. 안 들려요. **2** to say publicly what you think about something ‖ 무엇에 대해 생각하고 있는 것을 공공연히 말하다. 털어놓고 이야기하다: *If we don't speak up nobody will help us.* 우리가 만일 솔직하게 말하지 않으면 아무도 우리를 도와주지 않을 것이다.

speak·er /'spikɚ/ *n* **1** someone who makes a speech ‖ 연설하는 사람. 연설가. 강연자: *Our speaker this evening is Professor Gill.* 오늘 밤 연사는 질 교수입니다. **2 English/French etc. speaker** someone who speaks English, French

etc. ‖ 영어·프랑스어 등을 구사하는 사람 **3** the part of a radio, CD PLAYER etc. where the sound comes out ‖ 라디오나 CD 플레이어 등의 소리가 나오는 부분. 스피커

spear¹ /spɪr/ *n* a pole with a sharp pointed blade at one end, used as a weapon ‖ 무기로 쓰이는 한쪽 끝에 뾰족한 날이 달린 장대. 창

spear² *v* [T] **1** INFORMAL to push a pointed object such as a fork into something so you can pick it up ‖ 집어 올릴 수 있도록 어떤 것에 포크 등의 뾰족한 물체를 찔러 넣다 **2** to push or throw a SPEAR into something to kill it ‖ 죽이기 위하여 어떤 것에 창을 찔러 넣거나 던지다

spear·head /'spɪrhɛd/ *v* [T] to lead an attack or an organized action ‖ 공격이나 조직화된 행동을 이끌다. …의 선두에 서다: *a labor strike spearheaded by the workers* 노동자들이 주도한 노동 파업

spe·cial¹ /'spɛʃəl/ *adj* **1** better, more important, or deserving more love and attention than ordinary things, events, or people ‖ 더 좋은, 더 중요한, 또는 평범한 물건이나 사건 또는 사람들보다 더 사랑스럽고 주목할 만한: *I want to go somewhere special for our anniversary.* 나는 우리 기념일을 위해 특별한 곳에 가고 싶다. / *This is a special occasion.* 이 것은 특별히 중요한 경우이다. / *Gordon's a special friend of ours.* 고든은 우리의 각별한 친구이다. **2** different from what is usual ‖ 보통의 것과는 다른. 특별한: *special facilities for language learners* 어학 학습자용 특수 시설 **3 special care/attention etc.** more care, attention etc. than is usual ‖ 평소 이상의 보살핌이나 주목. 각별한 배려/관심: *We try to give special care to the youngest patients.* 우리는 가장 어린 환자들에게 각별한 주의를 쏟으려 한다.

special² *n* **1** something that is not ordinary or usual, but is made or done for a particular purpose ‖ 평범하거나 일상적인 것이 아니고 특정한 목적을 위해 만들어지거나 행하여진 것. 특별한 것[사람]: *a two-hour TV special on the election* 텔레비전의 두 시간짜리 선거 특별 프로그램 **2** a meal, dish, or cheaper price that a restaurant, supermarket etc. offers for a short time only ‖ 식당·슈퍼마켓 등이 잠시 동안만 제공하는 식사나 요리, 또는 보다 값싼 가격. 특매품. 서비스 요리: *What are today's lunch specials?* 오늘 점심 특별식은 뭐냐? / *Chickens are on special this week.* 닭은

금주의 특매품이다.

special ed·u·ca·tion /ˌ... ...ˈ.../ *n* [U]
education for children who have
physical or mental problems ‖ 신체적으
로나 정신적으로 문제가 있는 아이들을 위
한 교육. 특수 교육

special ef·fects /ˌ... ˈ./ *n* [plural]
images or sounds of something that
does not really exist or did not really
happen, made especially for a movie or
television program ‖ 특히 영화나 텔레비
전 프로그램용으로 만들어진 실재하지 않
거나 실제로 일어나지 않은 것의 영상이나
소리. 특수 효과[촬영]

spe·cial·ist /ˈspɛʃəlɪst/ *n* someone who
knows a lot about a particular subject
or has a lot of skill in it ‖ 특정한 주제에
대해 많이 알거나 많은 기술을 가진 사람.
전문가: *a heart specialist* 심장 전문의

spe·cial·ize /ˈspɛʃəˌlaɪz/ *v* [I] to limit
most of your study, business etc. to a
particular subject or activity ‖ 연구·사업
등의 대부분을 특정한 학과나 활동에 한정
시키다. 전공하다. 전문으로 하다: *a law-
yer who specializes in divorce cases* 이
혼 소송을 전문으로 하는 변호사 –
specialization /ˌspɛʃələˈzeɪʃən/ *n* [C, U]

spe·cial·ized /ˈspɛʃəˌlaɪzd/ *adj*
developed for a particular purpose ‖ 특
정한 목적을 위해 개발된. 전문의. 전문화
된: *a job that requires specialized
knowledge* 전문 지식이 필요한 직업

spe·cial·ly /ˈspɛʃəli/ *adv* 1 for one
particular purpose ‖ 특정한 목적을 위해:
*The plane is specially designed for
spying.* 그 비행기는 첩보수집을 목적으로
특별히 설계된 것이다. 2 SPOKEN
especially ‖ 특별히: *I had it made
specially for you.* 나는 특별히 당신을 위
해서 그것을 만들었다

spe·cial·ty /ˈspɛʃəlti/ *n* 1 a subject that
you know a lot about, or a skill that you
have ‖ 많이 아는 학과, 또는 자신이 가지
고 있는 기술. 전공. 전문. 장기. 특기:
*His specialty is mid-19th century
literature.* 그의 전공은 19세기 중엽 문학
이다. 2 a food or product that is very
good, produced in a particular
restaurant, area etc. ‖ 특정한 식당이나
지역 등에서 생산되는 매우 좋은 음식이나
생산품. 특제품. 특산품: *The grilled fish
is their specialty.* 구운 생선 요리는 그들
의 특제 요리이다.

spe·cies /ˈspiʃiz, -siz/ *n, plural*
species a group of animals or plants
of the same kind that can breed with
each other ‖ 서로 번식시킬 수 있는 같은
종류의 동물이나 식물의 무리. 종(種)

spe·cif·ic /spɪˈsɪfɪk/ *adj* 1 used when
talking about a particular thing, person,
time etc. ‖ 특정한 사물·사람·시간 등에
대해 말할 때에 쓰여. 일정한. 특정한:
*There are three specific types of
treatment for this disease.* 이 병에는 세
가지 특정한 치료법이 있다. / *specific
issues to discuss* 토의할 특정한 문제 2
detailed and exact ‖ 자세하고 정확한. 구
체적인: *Can you be more specific?* 더 구
체적으로 말씀해 주시겠습니까?

spe·cif·i·cal·ly /spɪˈsɪfɪkli/ *adv* 1 for a
particular type of person or thing ‖ 특정
한 사람이나 사물에 대하여. 특히: *a book
written specifically for young teenagers*
특히 어린 십대들을 위해 씌여진 책 2 in
a detailed or exact way ‖ 구체적으로, 정
확히: *I was told specifically to arrive 10
minutes early.* 나는 확실히 10분 전에 도
착하라는 이야기를 들었다.

spec·i·fi·ca·tion /ˌspɛsəfəˈkeɪʃən/ *n* [C
usually plural] a detailed instruction
about how something should be done,
made etc. ‖ 무엇이 마땅히 수행·제조되어
야 하는 방법에 대한 상세한 지시. 내역.
명세서. 시방서: *a rocket built to exact
specifications* 정확히 시방서에 따라 만들
어진 로켓

spe·cif·ics /spɪˈsɪfɪks/ *n* [plural]
particular and exact details ‖ 특정하고
정확한 상술. 세목: *We can discuss the
specifics of the deal later.* 우리는 차후
에 그 거래의 세목을 토의할 수 있다.

spe·ci·fy /ˈspɛsəˌfaɪ/ *v* [T] to state
something in an exact and detailed way
‖ 무엇을 정확하고 상세하게 말하다. …을
일일이 열거하다. 구체적으로 말하다:
*The original plan didn't specify how the
money should be spent.* 최초의 계획에는
그 자금이 어떻게 지출되어야 하는지가 명
기되어 있지 않았다.

spec·i·men /ˈspɛsəmən/ *n* 1 blood,
skin, etc. that is taken from your body
to be tested or examined ‖ 시험하거나 검
사하기 위해 신체에서 채취된 피나 피부
등. 표본. 시료: *We need a urine
specimen for drug testing.* 우리는 마약
복용 여부 검사를 위해 샘플로 사용될 소
변이 필요하다. 2 a single example of
something from a larger group of
similar things ‖ 일단의 큰 유사한 것들 중
의 본보기. 견본. 실례: *This specimen
was found in northwestern China.* 이 표
본은 중국 북서부 지방에서 발견되었다.

spe·cious /ˈspiʃəs/ *adj* FORMAL seeming
to be true or correct, but really false ‖
사실이거나 옳게 보이지만 실제로는 거짓
인. 겉만 번드르르한. 남의 눈을 속이는:

a specious argument 겉만 번지르르한 주장

speck /spɛk/ *n* a very small mark, spot, or piece of something ‖ 매우 작은 점이나 반점, 또는 어떤 작은 조각. 얼룩. 흠 . 미진 (微塵): *a speck of dirt/dust/blood* 작은 얼룩[미세한 먼지, 혈흔]

speck·led /'spɛkəld/ *adj* covered with a lot of small spots or marks ‖ 많은 반점과 얼룩으로 뒤덮인. 얼룩덜룩한. 반점이 있는: *speckled eggs* 반점이 있는 계란

spec·ta·cle /'spɛktəkəl/ *n* **1** an unusual or strange thing or situation that you see ‖ 눈에 보이는 평범하지 않거나 이상한 사물이나 상황. 구경거리: *Watching my parents dance was quite a spectacle.* 내 부모님이 춤추는 것을 보는 것은 대단한 구경거리였다. **2** a public scene or show that is very impressive ‖ 매우 인상적인 공공연한 장면이나 쇼. 장관: *the spectacle of the Thanksgiving parade* 추수 감사절 행렬의 장관(壯觀)

spec·ta·cles /'spɛktəkəlz/ *n* [plural] FORMAL ⇨GLASSES

spec·tac·u·lar¹ /spɛk'tækyələ/ *adj* very impressive or exciting ‖ 매우 인상적이거나 흥미로운. 구경거리의. 장대한. 극적인: *a spectacular view of the Grand Canyon* 그랜드 캐니언의 장관 – **spectacularly** *adv*

spectacular² *n* an event or performance that is very big and impressive ‖ 매우 크고 인상적인 행사나 공연. 초대작. 특별 흥행물

spec·ta·tor /'spɛkteɪtə/ *n* someone who watches an event, game etc. ‖ 행사나 경기 등을 관람하는 사람. 구경꾼. 관객: *Over 50,000 spectators saw the final game.* 5만 명이 넘는 관중들이 결승전을 관람했다.

spec·ter /'spɛktə/ *n* **1 the specter of sth** something that frightens you because it will cause problems for you if it happens ‖ 만일 발생하면 문제가 생기기 때문에 두렵게 만드는 것. …에 대한 공포: *The specter of war lingered over the talks.* 전쟁에 대한 공포가 회담을 할 때마다 맴돌았다. **2** LITERARY ⇨ GHOST

spec·trum /'spɛktrəm/ *n* **1** a complete or very wide range of opinions, ideas, situations etc. ‖ 의견·생각·상황 등의 완전하거나 매우 넓은 범위: *The officials represent a wide spectrum of political opinion.* 관료들은 폭넓은 정견을 나타낸다. **2** the set of different colors that is produced when light passes through a PRISM ‖ 빛이 프리즘을 통과할 때에 생기는

일련의 다양한 색깔들. 스펙트럼

spec·u·late /'spɛkyə,leɪt/ *v* **1** [I, T] to guess why something happened or what will happen next without knowing all the facts ‖ 사실을 모두 알지 못한 채 일이 일어난 까닭이나 다음에 일어날 일을 추측하다. 억측하다: *Police refuse to speculate on the murderer's motives at this time.* 경찰은 이번에는 살인의 동기에 대해 추측하는 것을 거부했다. **2** [I] to buy goods, property etc., hoping to make a large profit when you sell them ‖ 팔 때 큰 수익을 올릴 거라 기대하며 물건이나 부동산 등을 사다. 투기하다. 시세를 예측하고 사다 – **speculator** *n*

spec·u·la·tion /,spɛkyə'leɪʃən/ *n* [C, U] the act of speculating (SPECULATE) ‖ 추측하는 행위. 추측. 억측: *There is continued speculation about the future of the company.* 그 회사의 장래에 대한 추측이 계속 나돈다.

spec·u·la·tive /'spɛkyələtɪv, -,leɪtɪv/ *adj* **1** based on SPECULATION ‖ 추측에 근거한: *a speculative story in the newspapers* 신문의 추측 기사 **2** bought or done in order to make a profit later ‖ 나중에 수익을 올리기 위해 사거나 행한. 투기적인: *a speculative investment in real estate* 부동산의 투기성 투자

sped /spɛd/ *v* the past tense and PAST PARTICIPLE of SPEED ‖ speed의 과거·과거 분사형

speech /spitʃ/ *n* **1** a talk, especially a formal one about a particular subject, given to a group of people ‖ 일단의 사람들에게 하는, 특정한 주제에 대한 공식적인 발언. 연설. 담화: *The President gave a speech in Congress on the state of the nation.* 대통령은 의회에서 국정(國情)에 관한 연설을 했다. / *My dad will make a short speech at the wedding.* 아빠는 결혼식에서 짧게 연설을 할 것이다. **2** [U] the ability to speak, or the way someone speaks ‖ 말하는 능력이나 방식. 언어 능력. 말투. 말씨: *Her speech was slow and distinct.* 그녀의 말투는 느리고 뚜렷했다. **3** [U] spoken language rather than written language ‖ 문어가 아닌 구어

speech·less /'spitʃlɪs/ *adj* unable to speak because you are angry, shocked, upset etc. ‖ 화나거나 충격을 받거나, 또는 심란하여 말할 수 없는: *Boyd's answer left her speechless.* 그녀는 보이드의 대답에 말문이 막혔다.

speed¹ /spid/ *n* **1** [C, U] how fast something moves or travels ‖ 무엇이 빠르게 움직이거나 이동하는 정도. 속력. 속도: *The cyclists were riding at a speed* *of 35 mph.* 사이클 선수들은 시속 35마일의 속도로 달리고 있었다. / *a car traveling at high speed* 고속으로 달리고 있는 자동차 ✗DON'T SAY "in high speed"✗ "in high speed"라고는 하지 않는다. **2** [U] the rate at which something happens or is done ‖ 무엇이 일어나거나 행해지는 속도: *I'm amazed by the speed at which computers have changed modern life.* 나는 컴퓨터가 현대 생활을 변화시킨 속도에 놀랐다. **3 -speed** having a particular number of GEARS ‖ 특정한 수의 기어를 가진: *a 10-speed bicycle* 10단 기어 자전거 **4** [U] SLANG an illegal drug that makes you very active ‖ 사람을 매우 활력적으로 만드는 마약. 각성제

speed² *v* **sped** *or* **speeded, sped** *or* **speeded, speeding 1** [I] to move or happen quickly ‖ 빨리 움직이거나 일어나다: *The train sped along at over 80 miles an hour.* 그 기차는 시속 80마일이 넘는 속도로 질주했다. **2 be speeding** to be driving faster than the legal limit ‖ 법적인 제한 속도 이상으로 빨리 달리고 있다. 과속하다

speed up *phr v* [I, T] to move or happen faster, or to make something do this ‖ 더 빨리 움직이거나 일어나다, 또는 무엇을 더 빨리 움직이거나 일어나게 하다: *an attempt to speed up production at the factory* 그 공장에서의 생산 속도를 높이려는 시도 / *We sped up to pass the car in front of us.* 우리는 앞차를 추월하기 위해 속도를 높였다.

speed·boat /'spidbout/ *n* a small boat with a powerful engine that can go very fast ‖ 매우 빨리 갈 수 있는 강력한 엔진이 달린 작은 보트. 고속 모터보트

speed·ing /'spidɪŋ/ *n* [U] the action of traveling too fast in a vehicle ‖ 탈것으로 너무 빨리 달리는 행위. 속도위반: *I got a ticket for speeding.* 나는 속도위반으로 딱지를 떼었다.

speed lim·it /'. ,../ *n* the fastest speed that you are allowed to drive on a particular road ‖ 특정한 도로에서 운전하도록 허용된 최고의 속도. 제한 속도: *a 40 mph speed limit* 시속 40마일의 제한 속도

speed·om·e·ter /spɪ'dɑmətə/ *n* an instrument in a vehicle that shows how fast it is going ‖ 얼마나 빨리 가고 있는지를 나타내는 차량에 있는 계기. 속도계 — see picture on page 943

speed·y /'spidi/ *adj* happening or done quickly, or working quickly ‖ 빨리 일어나거나 행해진, 또는 빨리 일하는. 빠른. 신속한: *We're hoping for a speedy end*

to the troubles. 우리는 그 분쟁에 대한 신속한 종결을 바라고 있다. / *a speedy computer chip* 속도가 빠른 컴퓨터 칩 - **speedily** *adv*

spell¹ /spɛl/ *v* **1** [I, T] to form a word by writing or saying the letters in the correct order ‖ 글자를 옳은 순서로 쓰거나 말해서 단어를 만들다. 철자하다: *My last name is Haines, spelled H-A-I-N-E-S.* 내 성은 하인즈이며 H-A-I-N-E-S로 철자한다. / *Our three-year-old is already learning to spell.* 우리의 세 살 된 아이는 벌써 철자법을 배우고 있다. **2 spell trouble/defeat/danger etc.** if a situation spells trouble etc., it makes you expect trouble ‖ 곤란 등을 예상하게 하다. 곤란/패배/위험을 초래하다: *The latest setback may spell defeat for the Democrats in the election.* 최근의 어려움이 민주당에 선거의 패배를 가져올지도 모른다. **3** [T] if letters spell a word, they form it ‖ 글자가 단어를 형성하다

spell sth ↔ **out** *phr v* [T] to explain something clearly and in detail ‖ 무엇을 분명하고 상세하게 설명하다: *Do I have to spell it out for you? John's seeing another woman.* 그것을 당신에게 상세히 설명해야 합니까? 존은 다른 여자와 사귀고 있어요.

spell² *n* **1** magic, or the special words or ceremonies used in making it happen ‖ 마술, 또는 무슨 일이 일어나게 하는 데에 쓰이는 특수한 말이나 의식. 주문(呪文). 마법. 마력: *The witches cast a spell on the young prince.* 마녀들은 젊은 왕자에게 마법을 걸었다. **2** a period of a particular type of weather, activity etc. ‖ 특정한 날씨나 행동 등이 계속되는 기간: *We've had a cold/warm/wet/dry spell for most of January.* 거의 1월 내내 추운[따스한, 습한, 건조한] 날씨였다.

spell·bound /'spɛlbaʊnd/ *adj* extremely interested in something you are listening to ‖ 자신이 듣고 있는 것에 매우 흥미를 느끼는. 넋을 잃은: *We were spellbound by his stories.* 우리는 그의 이야기에 넋이 나가 있었다.

spell·ing /'spɛlɪŋ/ *n* **1** [U] the ability to spell words in the correct way ‖ 단어를 올바르게 철자하는 능력: *His spelling has improved.* 그의 철자 능력이 향상되었다. **2** the way that a word is spelled ‖ 단어를 철자하는 방식. 철자법: *There are two different spellings for this word.* 이 단어에는 두 가지 다른 철자법이 있다.

spelling bee /'.. ,./ *n* a spelling competition done by students ‖ 학생들이 하는 철자 경기

spend /spɛnd/ *v* **spent, spent, spending 1** [I, T] to use your money to buy or pay for something ‖ 무엇을 사거나 지불하는 데에 돈을 쓰다. 들이다: *I spent $ 40 on these shoes.* 나는 이 신발에 40달러를 지불했다. / *How much do you want to spend?* 얼마까지 쓸 생각이세요? **2** [T] to use time doing a particular activity ‖ 특정한 활동을 하는 데에 시간을 쓰다. 보내다. 지내다: *I need to spend more time with my family.* 나는 가족과 더 많은 시간을 함께 보낼 필요가 있다. / *We spent the whole morning by the pool.* 우리는 아침 내내 수영장에서 시간을 보냈다. —see usage note at TIME¹

spend·ing /ˈspɛndɪŋ/ *n* [U] the amount of money spent on something, especially by the government ‖ 특히 정부에 의한, 무엇에 지불하는 액수. 지출: *a cut in defense/public spending* 방위비[공공 지출]의 삭감

spend·thrift /ˈspɛndˌθrɪft/ *n* someone who spends a lot of money in a careless way ‖ 부주의하게 많은 돈을 쓰는 사람. 낭비자

spent¹ /spɛnt/ *v* the past tense and PAST PARTICIPLE of SPEND ‖ spend의 과거·과거 분사형

spent² *adj* **1** already used and now empty or useless ‖ 이미 사용하여 지금은 비어 있거나 쓸모없는. 다 써버린: *spent cartridges* 다 쓴 카트리지 **2** LITERARY extremely tired ‖ 매우 피곤한. 지쳐버린

sperm /spɚm/ *n* **1** *n, plural* **sperm** a cell produced by the male sex organ that joins with an egg to produce new life ‖ 남성의 성기에서 생성되어 난자와 결합하여 새로운 생명을 낳는 세포. 정자 **2** [U] ⇨ SEMEN

spew /spyu/, **spew out** *v* [I, T] to flow out of something in large quantities, or to make something do this ‖ 다량으로 무엇이 흘러나오다, 또는 다량으로 흘러나오게 하다. 분출되다. 분출시키다: *Smoke and gas were spewing out of the volcano.* 연기와 가스가 화산에서 분출되고 있었다.

sphere /sfɪr/ *n* **1** something in the shape of a ball ‖ 공 모양으로 생긴 것. 구: *The earth is a sphere.* 지구는 둥근 모양이다. **2** a particular area of work, interest, knowledge etc. ‖ 일·흥미·지식 등의 특정 분야. 범위. 영역: *He works mainly in the sphere of international banking.* 그는 주로 국제 은행 업무 분야에서 일한다.

spher·i·cal /ˈsfɪrɪkəl, ˈsfɛr-/ *adj* having a round shape like a ball ‖ 공처럼 둥근 형태를 띤. 구형의

sphinx /sfɪŋks/ *n* an ancient Egyptian image of a lion with a human head ‖ 사람의 머리를 가진 고대 이집트의 사자 상(像). 스핑크스

spice¹ /spaɪs/ *n* **1** [C, U] a powder or seed taken from plants that is put into food to give it a special taste ‖ 특별한 맛을 내기 위해 음식에 넣는, 식물에서 추출한 가루나 씨. 양념. 향신료: *herbs and spices* 허브와 향료 **2** [singular, U] interest or excitement that is added to something ‖ 무엇에 첨가된 흥미나 자극. 맛. 묘미: *Variety is the spice of life!* 다양성이 바로 인생의 묘미지[맛이지]! – **spiced** *adj*

spice², **spice up** *v* [T] **1** to add interest or excitement to something ‖ 무엇에 흥미와 자극을 더하다. …에 묘미를 곁들이다: *I need a few jokes to spice up my speech.* 나는 내 연설에 묘미를 더할 농담 몇 마디가 필요하다. **2** to add SPICE to food ‖ 음식에 향신료를 넣다

spick-and-span /ˌspɪk ən ˈspæn/ *adj* very clean and neat ‖ 아주 깔끔하고 단정한. 산뜻한

spic·y /ˈspaɪsi/ *adj* food that is spicy contains a lot of SPICEs ‖ 음식이 양념을 많이 한. 양념이 된: *spicy meatballs* 양념이 된 미트볼

spi·der /ˈspaɪdɚ/ *n* a small creature with eight legs that makes WEBS (=sticky nets) to catch insects ‖ 끈끈한 줄을 쳐서 곤충을 잡는, 여덟 개의 다리를 가진 작은 생물. 거미

spi·der·y /ˈspaɪdəri/ *adj* writing that is spidery has long thin lines and is normally not very neat ‖ 필적이 가늘고 길어서 보통 그다지 깔끔하지 않은. 필적이 구불구불한. 지렁이체의

spiel /ʃpil, spil/ *n* INFORMAL a long explanation of something, often used in order to try to persuade someone that something is good or true ‖ 종종 어떤 것이 좋거나 사실이라는 것을 어떤 사람에게 설득하기 위해 하는 장황한 설명: *I gave her the spiel about how good the product was, but she didn't buy any.* 나는 그녀에게 그 상품이 얼마나 좋은지 장황하게 설명을 늘어놓았지만 그녀는 아무것도 사지 않았다.

spif·fy /ˈspɪfi/ *adj* INFORMAL fashionable or attractive ‖ 최신식의, 또는 매력적인. 멋있는: *a spiffy little car* 멋진 소형차

spike¹ /spaɪk/ *n* something that is long and thin with a sharp point, especially a piece of metal ‖ 특히 금속 조각으로 된 길고 가늘며 끝이 뾰족한 것. 대못. 스파이크 - **spiky** *adj*

spike² *v* [T] **spike sb's drink** to add alcohol or a drug to what someone is drinking ‖ 남이 마시는 것에 알코올이나 마약을 넣다

spill¹ /spɪl/ *v* 1 [I, T] if a liquid spills or you spill it, it flows over the edge of a container by accident ‖ 액체가 우연히 용기 가장자리를 넘쳐 흐르거나 액체를 흘리다. 엎질러지다. 엎지르다: *I spilled coffee on my shirt.* 나는 셔츠에 커피를 엎질렀다. 2 [I] if people spill out of a place, they move out in large groups ‖ 사람들이 어떤 장소에서 대규모로 나오다. 쏟아져 나오다 3 **spill your guts** INFORMAL to tell someone a lot of personal things, especially because you are upset ‖ 특히 심란하여 남에게 사적인 이야기를 많이 하다. 속마음을 털어놓다: *The guy next to me at the bar tried to spill his guts to me.* 술집에서 내 옆 남자는 자신의 이야기를 나에게 털어놓으려 했다.

spill over *phr v* [I] if a problem or bad situation spills over, it begins to affect other places, people etc. ‖ 문제나 나쁜 상황이 다른 장소·사람들 등에 영향을 미치기 시작하다. 번지다: *There's a danger that the war will spill over into other countries.* 전쟁이 다른 국가들로 번질 위험이 있다.

spill² *n* an act of SPILLing something or the amount that is spilled ‖ 무엇을 엎지르는 행위나 엎지른 양: *a huge oil spill in the Atlantic* 대서양에서의 막대한 양의 기름 누출

spin¹ /spɪn/ *v* **spun, spun, spinning** 1 [I, T] to turn around and around very quickly, or to make something do this ‖ 빠르게 회전하다, 또는 무엇을 빠르게 회전시키다. 빙빙 돌다[돌리다]: *skaters spinning on the ice* 얼음 위에서 빙빙 돌며 스케이트 타는 사람들 / *He grabbed Lisa by the arm and spun her around.* (=turned her around) 그는 리사의 팔을 잡고 빙빙 돌렸다. 2 [I, T] to make cotton, wool etc. into thread by twisting it together ‖ 면화·양모 등을 서로 꼬아 실을 잣다. 방적하다 3 [T] if an insect spins a WEB or a COCOON, it produces thread and makes it ‖ 곤충이 실을 내어 거미줄이나 고치를 치다 4 **spin a tale/**

yarn/story to tell a story that you have invented ‖ 만들어낸 이야기를 말하다. 장황하게 꾸며낸 이야기를 하다

spin² *n* 1 an act of turning around quickly ‖ 빠르게 회전하는 행위. 회전: *The truck went into a spin.* 그 트럭은 급회전을 했다. 2 a way of saying or showing something that makes it seem to have particular qualities, used especially in politics and advertising ‖ 특히 정치와 광고에 쓰여, 무엇에 특정한 속성이 있는 듯이 말하거나 보여주는 방법: *a news report with a pro-abortion spin* 낙태를 지지하는 쪽으로 몰아가려는 뉴스 보도 —see also SPIN DOCTOR 3 **spin control** the act or skill of describing a bad situation in a way that makes it seem better than it is, used especially in politics and advertising ‖ 특히 정치와 광고에 쓰여, 나쁜 상황을 실제보다 좋아 보이게 설명하는 행위나 기술. 정보 조작(술) 4 INFORMAL a short trip in a car for pleasure ‖ 재미로 차를 타고 한바탕 달리기: *Would you like to go for a spin?* 차로 드라이브 갈래?

spin·ach /ˈspɪnɪtʃ/ *n* [U] a vegetable with large dark green leaves ‖ 진초록색의 잎이 큰 야채. 시금치

spi·nal /ˈspaɪnl/ *adj* relating to or affecting the SPINE ‖ 척추에 관련되거나 영향을 미치는. 척추의: *a spinal injury* 척추 부상

spinal cord /ˈ.. ./ *n* the long string of nerves that go from your brain down your back, through your SPINE ‖ 척추를 통해 머리에서 등으로 내려오는 기다란 신경 줄기. 척수

spin·dly /ˈspɪndli/ *adj* long and thin and not strong ‖ 길고 가늘며 강하지 못한. 가냘픈: *spindly legs* 가냘픈 다리

spin doc·tor /ˈ. ,../ *n* INFORMAL someone who describes a situation in a way that makes it seem better than it is ‖ 상황을 실제보다 좋아 보이는 것처럼 설명하는 사람. 언론 담당 조언자: *a White House spin doctor* 백악관의 언론 담당 조언자

spine /spaɪn/ *n* 1 also **spinal column** the long row of bones down the center of your back ‖ 길게 열을 이루어 내려오는 등 중앙의 뼈. 척추 2 a stiff sharp point on an animal or plant ‖ 동물이나 식물의 끝이 뻣뻣하고 뾰족한 부분. 가시: *cactus spines* 선인장 가시 3 the part of a book that the pages are attached to ‖ 책의 페이지들이 부착되어 있는 부분. 책의 등

spine·less /ˈspaɪnlɪs/ *adj* lacking courage and determination ‖ 용기와 결

단이 부족한. 나약한: *He's too spineless to speak for himself.* 그는 너무나 용기가 없어서 자기 생각을 말하지 못한다.

spinning wheel /'.. ,./ *n* a small machine used in past times to make thread ‖ 실을 잣기 위해 예전에 썼던 작은 기계. 물레

spin-off /'. ./ *n* **1** a useful product that developed unexpectedly from something else ‖ 어떤 다른 것에서 예기치 않게 생긴 유용한 산물. 예기치 않은 부산물 **2** a television program using characters that were originally on a different program ‖ 원래 다른 프로그램에 나왔던 등장인물을 이용하는 텔레비전 프로그램. 속편

spin-ster /'spɪnstɚ/ *n* OLD-FASHIONED an older unmarried woman who is not likely to marry ‖ 결혼할 것 같지 않는 나이든 처녀. 노처녀

spi-ral¹ /'spaɪrəl/ *n* a curve in the form of a continuous line that winds around a central point ‖ 중심을 감아 돌며 계속적인 선을 이루는 곡선. 나사선 **– spiral** *adj*: *a spiral staircase* 나선형 계단

spiral² *v* [I] to move up or down in the shape of a spiral ‖ 나사선 모양으로 위나 아래로 움직이다. 나선형으로 움직이다: *a leaf spiraling to the ground* 땅으로 나선형을 그리며 떨어지는 잎

spire /spaɪɚ/ *n* a tower that rises steeply to a point, especially on a church ‖ 특히 교회의 꼭대기가 가파르게 솟은 탑. 뾰족탑

spir-it¹ /'spɪrɪt/ *n* **1** [C, U] the qualities that make someone live the way s/he does, and make him/her different from other people, and that are often believed to continue to exist after death ‖ 다른 사람과 구별되게 만들며 종종 사후에도 계속해서 존재한다고 믿어지는, 삶의 방식을 결정하는 특성. 정신. 마음: *I'm 85, but I still feel young in spirit.* 나는 85세이지만 여전히 마음은 젊다. / *I can still feel her spirit in this house.* 나는 여전히 이 집에서 그녀의 영혼을 느낄 수 있다. **2** a living thing without a physical body such as an ANGEL or GHOST ‖ 천사나 혼령 등의 육신이 없이 살아 있는 것. 유령. 정령 **3** [U] courage and determination ‖ 용기와 결단력. 기백: *I admired the spirit with which she fought for her rights.* 나는 그녀가 자기의 권리를 위해 투쟁하는 그 기백에 감탄했다. **4** [singular] the attitude that you have toward something ‖ 무엇에 대하여 지니고 있는 태도: *There's a real spirit of cooperation between the two clubs.* 두

클럽 간에는 진실한 협동심이 존재한다. **5 team/community/public etc. spirit** the strong feeling that you belong to a particular group and you want to help it ‖ 특정 집단에 속하여 그 집단을 돕고 싶어 하는 강한 마음. 팀/공동체/공공 의식 **6** [C usually plural] a strong alcoholic drink such as WHISKEY ‖ 위스키 등의 도수 높은 술. 증류주 **—see also** SPIRITS

spirit² *v* [T] **spirit sb/sth away** to remove someone or something from a place in a secret or mysterious way ‖ 장소에서 사람이나 사물을 몰래 또는 불가사의하게 없애다. 유괴하다. 행방불명되게 하다: *After the concert the band was spirited away in a cab.* 콘서트가 끝난 후 그 밴드는 택시를 타고 홀연히 사라졌다.

spir-it-ed /'spɪrɪtɪd/ *adj* having a lot of courage and determination ‖ 용기와 결단력이 넘치는: *She made a spirited defense of the plan.* 그녀는 그 계획에 대해 맹렬한 방어를 했다. **—opposite** DISPIRITED

spir-its /'spɪrɪts/ *n* [plural] how happy or sad someone feels at a particular time ‖ 특정 시점에 느끼는 행복이나 슬픔의 정도. 기분: *The children were in high spirits* (=happy and excited) 아이들은 기분이 매우 좋았다. / *Her spirits rose* (=she became happy) *when she heard the news.* 그녀는 그 소식을 듣자 기분이 좋아졌다.

spir-i-tu-al¹ /'spɪrɪtʃuəl, -tʃəl/ *adj* **1** relating to the spirit rather than the body or mind ‖ 육체나 마음이 아니라 정신에 관련된. 정신의: *spiritual health and well-being* 정신 건강과 행복 **2** relating to religion ‖ 종교에 관한. 종교적인: *spiritual songs* 찬송가 / *a very spiritual woman* 매우 종교적인 여성 **– spiritually** *adv*

spiritual² *n* a religious song first sung by the black people of the US when they were SLAVES ‖ 미국의 흑인들이 노예였을 때 처음 부른 종교적 노래. 영가

spit¹ /spɪt/ *v* **spit** or **spat, spat, spitting 1** [I, T] to force a small amount of liquid, blood, food etc. from your mouth ‖ 입으로 소량의 침·피·음식 등을 뱉다: *He spat on the ground.* 그는 바닥에 침을 뱉었다. **2 spit it out** SPOKEN used in order to tell someone to say something s/he does not want to say, or is having trouble saying ‖ 남이 말하고 싶지 않거나 말하기 곤란한 것을 이야기하라고 말하는 데에 쓰여. 실토하다: *Tell me what you did – come on, spit it out.* 무슨 일을 했는지 말해봐. 자, 숨김없이 털어놔.

spit² *n* **1** [U] INFORMAL ⇨ SALIVA **2** a long thin stick that you put through meat to cook it over a fire ‖ 불 위에다 요리하기 위해 고기에 꽂는 길고 가는 막대기. 꼬치. 꼬챙이

spite¹ /spaɪt/ *n* **1 in spite of** although; DESPITE ‖ 무엇에도 불구하고; 斑 despite: *She loved him in spite of the fact that he drank too much.* 그녀는 그가 지나치게 술을 많이 마심에도 불구하고 그를 사랑했다. **2** a feeling of wanting to hurt, annoy, or upset someone ‖ 누군가를 마음 아프게[짜증나게, 화나게] 하고 싶은 감정. 악의: *Lola refused to let her ex-husband see the children out of spite.* (=because of spite) 롤라는 악의로 전 남편이 아이들을 만나는 것을 허락하지 않았다.

spite² *v* [T] to annoy or upset someone deliberately ‖ 남을 고의로 괴롭히거나 당황하게 하다: *He's doing this just to spite me!* 그는 순전히 나를 괴롭히려고 이 짓을 한다니까!

spite·ful /ˈspaɪtfəl/ *adj* intending to annoy or upset someone ‖ 남을 괴롭히거나 당황하게 하려는. 심술궂은. 악의적인

splash¹ /splæʃ/ *v* **1** [I, T] if a liquid splashes or you make it splash, it falls on something or hits against it ‖ 어떤 것 위에 액체가 떨어지거나 액체를 떨어뜨리다: *He splashed some cold water on his face.* 그는 찬물을 얼굴에 끼얹었다. / *water splashed down onto the rocks* 바위 위에 떨어지는 물 **2** [I, T] to make water go up into the air by hitting it or moving around in it ‖ 물을 치거나 물 속에서 이리저리 움직여 공중으로 물이 솟게 하다. 튀기다: *We were splashing each other in the pool.* 우리는 수영장에서 서로에게 물을 튀기고 있었다. / *children splashing around in puddles* 물웅덩이에서 물장구치는 아이들

splash² *n* **1** the sound of SPLASHing ‖ 물을 튀기는 소리. 텀벙. 철벅: *Jerry jumped into the water with a loud splash.* 제리는 첨벙 소리를 내며 물속으로 뛰어들었다. **2** a small amount of a liquid that has SPLASHed onto something, or a mark made by this ‖ 무엇에 튄 소량의 액체나 그 액체가 튀겨서 생긴 자국: *splashes of paint on my pants* 내 바지에 튀긴 페인트 얼룩 **3 a splash of color** color that you add to something to make it brighter ‖ 좀 더 밝게 하려고 무엇에 추가하는 색

splash·y /ˈsplæʃi/ *adj* big, bright, and very easy to notice ‖ 크고 산뜻하여 알아채기 매우 쉬운. 두드러진: *a splashy tie* 화려한 넥타이

splat /splæt/ *n* [singular] the sound made when something wet hits a hard surface ‖ 젖은 것이 딱딱한 표면에 부딪힐 때 나는 소리. 철썩

splat·ter /ˈsplætɚ/ *v* [I, T] if a liquid splatters, it hits against a surface ‖ 액체가 표면에 부딪히다. 튀다. 튀기다: *rain splattering against the window* 창문에 튀기는 빗방울

splay /spleɪ/, **splay out** *v* [I, T] to spread something apart such as your fingers or legs ‖ 손가락이나 다리 등을 좍 벌리다. …을 펼치다

splen·did /ˈsplɛndɪd/ *adj* **1** excellent ‖ 훌륭한: *a splendid vacation* 환상적인 휴가 **2** beautiful or impressive ‖ 아름답거나 인상적인. 멋진: *a splendid view from the balcony* 발코니에서 보는 멋진 경관 – **splendidly** *adv*

splen·dor /ˈsplɛndɚ/ *n* [U] impressive beauty ‖ 인상적인 아름다움. 화려함. 웅장함: *the splendor of Yosemite Valley* 요세미티 협곡의 웅장함

splice /splaɪs/ *v* [T] to join the ends of two pieces of film, wire etc. so they form one piece ‖ 두 개의 필름·철사 등의 끝을 연결하여 하나로 만들다. 잇다

splint /splɪnt/ *n* a flat piece of wood, metal etc. that is attached to someone's arm or leg to prevent a broken bone from moving ‖ 부러진 뼈가 움직이지 못하도록 팔이나 다리에 부착하는 나무·금속 등의 납작한 조각. (접골용) 부목

splinter¹ /ˈsplɪntɚ/ *n* **1** a small sharp piece of wood, glass, or metal that has broken off of a larger piece ‖ 보다 큰 조각에서 깨진, 작고 날카로운 나무[유리, 금속] 조각. 파편: *I have a splinter in my finger.* 손가락을 가시에 찔렸다. — compare SLIVER **2 splinter group/organization** a group of people that separate from a larger organization because they have different ideas ‖ 사상이 달라서 더 큰 조직에서 분리된 일단의 사람들. 분파

splinter² *v* [I, T] to break into thin sharp pieces, or to cause something to do this ‖ 얇고 날카로운 조각이 되다, 또는 조각을 내다

split¹ /splɪt/ *v* **split, split, splitting 1** [I, T] also **split up** to divide or make something divide into two or more groups, parts etc. ‖ 갈라지다, 또는 무엇이 두 개 이상의 집단·부분 등으로 갈라지게 하다. 쪼개지다. 쪼개다: *We'll split up into three work groups.* 우리는 3개의 작업조로 나눌 것이다. / *Try splitting this section into two.* 이 부분을 둘로 나눠 봐

라. **2** [I, T] to tear or break something along a straight line, or to be torn or broken in this way ‖ 직선으로 무엇을 찢거나 깨뜨리다, 또는 직선으로 찢어지거나 깨지다: *He split his pants when he bent over.* 그가 몸을 굽혔을 때 바지가 터졌다. / *The board had split in two.* 판자가 두 동강이 났다. **3** [T] to divide something among two or more people in equal parts ‖ 두 명 이상의 사람끼리 동일하게 무엇을 나누다. 분배하다: *We decided to split the money between us.* 우리는 그 돈을 우리끼리 나누기로 결정했다. **4** [I] SLANG to leave quickly ‖ 빨리 떠나다

split up *phr v* [I] to end a marriage or a relationship ‖ 결혼 생활이나 어떤 관계를 끝내다. 이혼하다. 갈라서다: *Eve's parents split up when she was three.* 이브의 부모님은 이브가 세 살 때 이혼했다.

split² *n* **1** a long straight hole caused when something breaks or tears ‖ 무엇이 깨지거나 째져서 생기는 길고 곧은 구멍. 조개진 금. 균열: *a split in the seam of my skirt* 내 치마 솔기의 터진 곳 **2** a serious disagreement that divides an organization or group of people ‖ 조직이나 일단의 사람들을 분열시키는 심각한 의견 불일치. 분화. 분열: *a split in the Republican Party* 공화당의 분열

split-lev·el /ˌ. ˈ.../ *adj* a split-level house has a ground floor that is on two different levels ‖ 집의 두 마루가 높이가 다른

split sec·ond /ˌ. ˈ../ *n* a split second an extremely short period of time ‖ 극히 짧은 시간. 순식간: *I only had a split second to decide.* 나는 순식간에 결정했다. – **split-second** /ˌ. ˈ../ *adj*

split·ting /ˈsplɪtɪŋ/ *adj* **splitting headache** a very painful HEADACHE ‖ 매우 고통스러운 두통. 지독한 두통

splurge /splɝdʒ/ *v* [I] INFORMAL to spend more money than you can usually afford ‖ 보통 쓸 수 있는 돈보다 더 많은 돈을 쓰다. 돈을 물 쓰듯 쓰다: *We went shopping and splurged on clothes.* 우리는 쇼핑가서 옷을 사는 데 돈을 물 쓰듯 썼다.

spoil /spɔɪl/ *v* **spoiled** *or* **spoilt** /spɔɪlt/ **spoiled** *or* **spoilt, spoiling 1** [T] to ruin something by making it less attractive, enjoyable, useful etc. ‖ 무엇을 매력·재미·유용성 등을 덜하게 하여 망가뜨리다. 망쳐놓다: *Don't let his bad mood spoil your evening.* 그가 기분이 안 좋다고 너의 저녁을 망치게 하지 마라. **2** [I] to start to decay ‖ 썩기 시작하다: *The meat has spoiled.* 고기가 상했다. **3** [T] to

treat someone in a way that is very kind or too generous ‖ 매우 친절하거나 지나치게 관대하게 남을 대하다. 지나친 대접을 하다: *a hotel that spoils its guests* 손님에게 지나치게 서비스하는 호텔

spoiled /spɔɪld/ *adj* a child who is spoiled is rude and behaves badly because s/he is always given what s/he wants ‖ 아이가 항상 자신이 원하는 것을 얻기 때문에 무례하고 못되게 행동하는. 버릇없이 자란: *a spoiled brat* 버릇없는 꼬마

spoils /spɔɪlz/ *n* [plural] things taken by an army from a defeated enemy, or things taken by thieves ‖ 군대가 패배한 적군에게서 강탈한 물건이나 도둑이 훔친 물건. 전리품. 약탈물. 장물

spoil·sport /ˈspɔɪlspɔrt/ *n* INFORMAL someone who spoils other people's fun ‖ 사람들의 흥을 깨는 사람: *Come on and play, don't be a spoilsport.* 어서 와서 놀아라. 분위기 깨지 말고.

spoke¹ /spoʊk/ *v* the past tense of SPEAK ‖ speak의 과거형

spoke² *n* one of the thin metal BARs that connect the outer ring of a wheel to the center, especially on a bicycle ‖ 특히 자전거 바퀴의 바깥 테를 중앙부에 연결시키는 가는 금속 철사들 중의 하나. 바퀴의 살

spok·en¹ /ˈspoʊkən/ *v* the PAST PARTICIPLE of SPEAK ‖ speak의 과거 분사형

spoken² *adj* **1 spoken English/language** the form of language that you speak rather than write ‖ 글로 쓰는 것이 아니라 말하는 언어의 형태. 구어 영어/구어(口語) **2 -spoken** speaking in a particular way ‖ 특정한 방식으로 말하는. 어조가 …한: *a soft-spoken man* (=he speaks quietly) 부드러운 어조의 남자

spokes·man /ˈspoʊksmən/ *n* a male SPOKESPERSON ‖ 남성 대변인

spokes·per·son /ˈspoʊksˌpɝsən/ *n* someone who has been chosen to speak officially for a group, organization, government etc. ‖ 집단·조직·정부 등을 위해 공식적으로 말하도록 뽑힌 사람. 대변인

spokes·wom·an /ˈspoʊksˌwʊmən/ *n* a female SPOKESPERSON ‖ 여성 대변인

sponge¹ /spʌndʒ/ *n* **1** [C, U] a piece of a very light substance that is full of small holes and is used for washing or cleaning something ‖ 작은 구멍이 많이 나 있고 무엇을 씻거나 깨끗이 하는 데에 쓰이는 매우 가벼운 물체. 스펀지 **2** a sea animal with a soft body, from which sponges are made ‖ 스펀지를 만드는, 몸

이 부드러운 해면동물

sponge² *v* 1 [T] also **sponge down** to wash something with a wet SPONGE ‖ 젖은 스펀지로 무엇을 씻다 2 [T] to remove liquid from a surface using a sponge ‖ 스펀지를 써서 표면의 물기를 제거하다. 스펀지로 훔치다 3 [I] to get money, food etc. from someone without working for it ‖ 일하지 않고 남에게서 돈·음식 등을 얻어내다. 우려내다: *He's been sponging off his friends for years.* 그는 수년간을 친구들에게 기식(寄食)하고 있다.

sponge cake /'. ./ *n* [C, U] a light cake made with eggs, sugar, and flour but usually no fat ‖ 계란·설탕·밀가루로 만들지만 일반적으로 지방이 없는 말랑말랑한 케이크. 스펀지 케이크

spong·y /'spʌndʒi/ *adj* soft and full of holes like a SPONGE ‖ 스펀지처럼 말랑말랑하고 구멍이 많은. 해면질의: *spongy wet earth* 스펀지 같이 젖은 땅

spon·sor¹ /'spɑnsəˈ/ *n* 1 a person or company that SPONSORs a television show, sports event etc. ‖ 텔레비전 쇼·스포츠 경기 등을 후원하는 사람이나 기업. 후원자: *the sponsor of the French Open* (테니스의) 프랑스 오픈의 후원업체 2 someone who SPONSORs a person for CHARITY ‖ 자선으로 남을 후원하는 사람. 독지가. 자선 기금 기부자

sponsor² *v* [T] 1 to give money to a television show, sports event etc. in exchange for the right to advertise your products at the event ‖ 텔레비전 쇼·스포츠 경기 등에 자신의 상품을 광고할 수 있는 권리에 대한 대가로 돈을 지불하다. 스폰서가 되다 2 to officially support a proposal for a new law ‖ 새로운 법률안을 공식적으로 지지하다 3 to give someone money for a CHARITY if s/he walks, runs, swims etc. a particular distance ‖ 일정 거리를 걷거나 달리거나, 또는 수영 등을 하면 남에게 자선기금을 주다. 목표를 달성하는 조건으로 기부하다

spon·ta·ne·i·ty /ˌspɑntəˈneɪəti, ˌspɑntˈnˈeɪ-/ *n* [U] the quality or state of being SPONTANEOUS ‖ 자연스러운 성질이나 상태. 자연스러움

spon·ta·ne·ous /spɑnˈteɪniəs/ *adj* happening or done without being planned or organized, because you suddenly want to do it ‖ 갑자기 하고 싶어져서 계획이나 준비 없이 발생하거나 이뤄진. 자연적인. 즉흥적인: *a spontaneous decision* 즉흥적인 결정 **– spontaneously** *adv*

spoof /spuf/ *n* a funny performance that copies a serious book, play, movie etc. and makes it seem silly ‖ 진지한 책·연극·영화 등을 우스꽝스럽게 모사한 책이 있는 공연. 패러디: *a spoof on/of one of Shakespeare's tragedy plays* 셰익스피어 비극 중의 한 작품에 대한 패러디 **– spoof** *v* [T]

spook¹ /spuk/ *n* INFORMAL ⇨ GHOST

spook² *v* [T] INFORMAL to frighten someone ‖ 남을 놀라게 하다: *Being alone all night really spooked me.* 밤새 혼자 있다는 것이 정말 나를 섬뜩하게 했다.

spook·y /'spuki/ *adj* INFORMAL strange or frightening; EERIE ‖ 괴상하거나 섬뜩한. 무시무시한; ⑩ eerie: *a spooky old house* 으스스한 오래된 집

spool /spul/ *n* an object shaped like a small wheel that you wind wire, thread, camera film etc. around ‖ 철사·실·카메라 필름 등을 감는, 작은 바퀴처럼 생긴 물체. 실패. 감는 틀. 릴

spoon¹ /spun/ *n* a tool used for eating, cooking, and serving food, shaped like a small bowl with a long handle ‖ 긴 손잡이가 달린 작은 사발 모양의, 식사·조리·음식 접대에 쓰이는 도구. 숟가락

spoon² *v* [T] to pick up or move food with a spoon ‖ 숟가락으로 음식을 뜨거나 옮기다: *Spoon the sauce over the fish.* 생선 위에 소스를 숟가락으로 떠 부어라.

spoon-feed /'. ./ *v* [T] 1 to give too much help to someone ‖ 남을 지나치게 많이 도와주다. 과보호하다. 주입식으로 가르치다: *Spoon-feeding students does not help them remember things.* 주입식 교육을 받은 학생들은 스스로 뭔가를 기억하게 하지 못한다. 2 to feed a baby with a spoon ‖ 아기에게 숟가락으로 먹이다

spoon·ful /'spunfʊl/ *n* the amount that a spoon can hold ‖ 숟가락으로 뜰 수 있는 양. 한 숟가락 가득: *a spoonful of sugar* 설탕 한 숟가락

spo·rad·ic /spəˈrædɪk/ *adj* not happening regularly, or happening only in a few places ‖ 규칙적으로 발생하지 않거나 단지 몇몇 장소에서만 발생하는. 산발적인: *sporadic bombing* 산발적인 폭격 **– sporadically** *adv*

sport¹ /spɔrt/ *n* 1 a physical activity in which people compete against each other, and that has rules ‖ 사람들이 규칙을 갖추어 서로 경쟁하는 육체적 활동. 스포츠. 운동(경기): *Baseball's my favorite sport.* 야구는 내가 가장 좋아하는 스포츠이다. / *Do you play any sports?* 어떤 운동이든 하고 있습니까? 2 **good/bad sport** someone who can or cannot deal with defeat or being joked

about without becoming angry or upset
‖ 화내거나 당황하지 않고 패배를 인정할
줄 알거나 모르는 사람, 또는 농담을 받아
넘길 줄 알거나 모르는 사람

USAGE NOTE sport, recreation, game, and hobby

Use **sport** to talk about an activity that uses physical effort and skill, has rules, and is done in competition: *Her favorite sport is basketball.* / *I'm no good at sports.* Use **recreation** to talk about all the activities that people do in order to relax: *the city's Parks and Recreation Department.* Use **game** to talk about a particular competition in a sport: *We went to my brother's football game last night.* You can also use **game** to talk about a competition that involves using mental skill, knowledge, or luck: *How about a game of cards?* Use **hobby** to talk about an activity that you do in your free time, usually alone: *Her hobbies are reading and music.*

sport는 규칙을 갖추어 경쟁을 벌이며 육체적 노력과 기술을 발휘하는 행위를 언급하는 데에 쓰인다: 그녀가 좋아하는 스포츠는 농구이다. / 나는 운동을 잘 못한다. **recreation**은 사람들이 휴식을 취하기 위해 하는 모든 행동을 언급하는 데에 쓰인다: 시 공원 휴양부. **game**은 스포츠의 특정한 경기를 언급하는 데에 쓰인다: 우리는 간밤에 오빠의 미식축구 경기를 보러 갔다. 또한 **game**은 정신적 능력[지식, 운]이 관련된 경기를 언급하는 데에도 쓰인다: 카드 게임을 하면 어떨까? **hobby**는 자유 시간에 보통 혼자서 하는 행위를 말한다: 그녀의 취미는 독서와 음악이다.

---

sport² *v* to wear or show something in a proud way ‖ 자랑스럽게 무엇을 착용하거나 내보이다. …를 과시하다: *He walked in today sporting a new suit.* 그는 오늘 새 양복을 입고 뽐내며 걸어 들어왔다.

sport·ing /ˈspɔrtɪŋ/ *adj* **1** relating to sports ‖ 스포츠에 관한. 스포츠의: *a new sporting goods* (=sports equipment) *store* 새로운 스포츠 용품점 **2 a sporting chance** a good chance of succeeding or winning ‖ 성공하거나 승리할 수 있는 상당한 가능성

sports /spɔrts/ *adj* **1** relating to sports or used for sports ‖ 스포츠에 관한, 또는 스포츠에 쓰이는. 스포츠(용)의: *a sports club* 스포츠클럽 **2 on the subject of sports** ‖ 스포츠 분야의: *I like reading the*

sports pages. (=in a newspaper) 나는 스포츠면 읽는 것을 좋아한다.

sports car /ˈ. ./ *n* a low fast car, often with a roof that can be folded back ‖ 차체가 낮으며 종종 뒤로 접을 수 있는 지붕 달린 쾌속 자동차. 스포츠카

sports·cast /ˈspɔrts-kæst/ *n* a television program of a sports game ‖ 스포츠 경기 텔레비전 프로그램

sports jack·et /ˈ. ,../, **sports coat** /ˈ. ./ *n* a man's comfortable JACKET worn on informal occasions ‖ 격식을 차리지 않는 경우에 입는 편안한 남성용 재킷. 스포츠 재킷. 캐주얼한 상의

sports·man·ship /ˈspɔrtsmən,ʃɪp/ *n* [U] behavior that is fair, honest, and polite in a game or sports competition ‖ 게임이나 스포츠 경기에서의 공정하고 정직하며 예의바른 행동. 정정당당한 태도: *I was very impressed with the team's spirit and sportsmanship.* 나는 그 팀의 기백과 정정당당한 태도에 매우 감동 받았다.

sports·wear /ˈspɔrtswɛr/ *n* [U] clothes that are suitable for informal occasions ‖ 격식을 갖추지 않는 경우에 알맞은 옷. 평상시[캐주얼]복

sport·y /ˈspɔrti/ *adj* designed to look attractive in a bright informal way ‖ 화려하고 격식이 없어 매력적으로 보이게 디자인된. 화려한. 발랄한: *a sporty red car* 멋진 빨간 차

spot¹ /spɑt/ *n*
1 ▶PLACE 장소◀ a particular place ‖ 특정 장소: *Oh, sorry, I'm sitting in your spot.* 아, 미안해, 내가 네 자리에 앉았구나. / *a popular vacation spot* 인기 있는 휴양지
2 ▶COLORED AREA 채색된 부분◀ a small round area on a surface, that is a different color from the rest ‖ 나머지 부분과 색이 다른 표면 위의 작고 둥근 부분. 반점: *a white dog with black spots* 검은 반점이 있는 흰 개
3 ▶MARK 자국◀ a dirty mark on something ‖ 무엇에 묻은 더러운 자국. 얼룩: *paint spots on the floor* 마루 위의 페인트 얼룩
4 on the spot INFORMAL **a)** immediately ‖ 즉시: *Cathy was offered the job on the spot.* 캐시는 즉각적으로 그 일자리를 제안 받았다. **b)** at the place where something is happening ‖ 무엇이 발생한 장소에서. 그 자리에서: *He had a heart attack and died on the spot.* 그는 심장마비로 그 자리에서 숨졌다.
5 ▶APPEARANCE 출현◀ a short appearance on TV, radio etc. ‖ 텔레비

전·라디오 등에의 짧은 출현: *an advertising spot* 광고 시간

6 ▶POSITION 위치◀ a position in a competition ‖ 경쟁에서의 위치: *a movie in the number one spot* 1위에 있는 영화

7 put sb on the spot to make someone do something or answer a question that s/he does not want to, by making him/her feel embarrassed not to do it ‖ 하지 않으면 난처하게 만들어, 남에게 하고 싶지 않은 일이나 대답을 하게 하다. 곤란에 처하게 하다: *Don't put me on the spot like that in front of your parents.* 네 부모님 앞에서 그렇게 나를 곤란하게 만들지 마라.

8 bright spot something that is good in a bad situation ‖ 나쁜 상황 가운데 좋은 것: *Foreign trade is the one bright spot in the economy.* 경제의 유일한 희망은 대외 무역 부분이다. —see also **hit the spot** (HIT¹)

spot² *v* **-tted, -tting** [T] **1** to notice or recognize something that is difficult to see, or that you are looking for ‖ 보기 어렵거나 찾고 있던 것을 알아채거나 인지하다. 발견[탐지]하다: *A helicopter pilot spotted the wreckage of the plane.* 헬기 조종사는 비행기 잔해를 발견했다. / *She has a good eye for spotting talent.* 그녀는 재능을 발견하는 데에 뛰어난 눈을 가졌다. **2** to give the other player in a game an advantage ‖ 경기에서 다른 선수에게 이점을 주다. 경기 상대에게 핸디캡으로 점수를 주다: *Come on, I'll spot you 10 points if you play.* 자 어때, 경기를 하겠다면 내가 10점을 줄게.

spot check /'. ./ *n* a quick examination of a few things or people in a group, to see whether everything is correct or satisfactory ‖ 모든 것이 정확하거나 만족스러운지 알아보기 위한 물건이나 집단 내의 사람들 중 몇몇에 대한 즉각적인 검사. 무작위 추출 검사: *Health inspectors will make spot checks throughout the state.* 위생 검사관이 전 지역에 걸쳐 무작위 추출 검사를 할 것이다.

spot·less /'spɑtlɪs/ *adj* **1** completely clean ‖ 아주 깨끗한. 티끌 한 점 없는: *Donna keeps her car spotless.* 도나는 차를 티끌 한 점 없이 깨끗이 유지한다. **2** completely honest and good ‖ 아주 정직하고 착한. 결점이 없는: *a spotless reputation* 흠잡을 데 없는 명성

spot·light¹ /'spɑtlaɪt/ *n* **1** a very powerful light that can be directed at someone or something, or the light made by this ‖ 사람이나 사물에 비출 수 있는 매우 강한 조명, 또는 이렇게 비춘 빛. 스포트라이트: *theater spotlights* 극장의 스포트라이트 **2 the spotlight** something that makes people pay attention to someone or something ‖ 사람들에게 다른 사람이나 사물에 관심을 갖게 만드는 것. 세상의 주시[주목]. 각광: *Russia is back in the media spotlight again.* 러시아는 다시 언론의 주목을 받고 있다.

spotlight² *v* [T] to make people pay attention to someone or something ‖ 사람들에게 다른 사람이나 사물에 관심을 갖게 하다. …에 주의를 돌리게 하다: *a music festival that spotlights modern composers* 현대 작곡가들에게 초점을 맞춘 음악제

spot·ty /'spɑti/ *adj* **1** good in some parts but not in others ‖ 일부는 좋지만 일부는 그렇지 않은. 불규칙한: *The stock market showed spotty gains.* 주식 시장이 부분적인 호황세를 띄었다. **2** covered with spots ‖ 얼룩으로 덮여 있는. 얼룩덜룩한. 얼룩투성이의: *a spotty camera lens* 뿌연 카메라 렌즈

spouse /spaʊs/ *n* FORMAL a husband or wife ‖ 남편이나 아내. 배우자

spout¹ /spaʊt/ *n* an opening through which liquid comes out ‖ 액체가 나오는 구멍. 분출구. 주둥이: *a teapot with a wide spout* 주둥이가 넓은 찻주전자 —see picture at TEAPOT

spout² *v* **1** [I, T] if a liquid spouts or is spouted, it comes out of a narrow place with a lot of force ‖ 액체가 힘차게 좁은 장소에서 나오다. 내뿜다. 분출하다: *A leak spouted from the garden hose.* 정원 호스에 생긴 구멍에서 물이 뿜어져 나왔다. / *a whale spouting water* 물을 내뿜는 고래 **2** [I] INFORMAL also **spout off** to talk a lot in a boring way ‖ 지겹게 말을 많이 하다. 장광설을 늘어놓다: *He's always spouting off about politics.* 그는 항상 정치에 대해 장광설을 늘어놓는다.

sprain /spreɪn/ *v* [T] to injure a joint in your body by suddenly twisting it ‖ 몸의 관절이 갑자기 뒤틀려 부상당하다. 염좌하다. 삐다: *Amy sprained her ankle when she fell.* 에이미는 넘어지면서 발목을 삐었다. **— sprain** *n*

sprang /spræŋ/ *v* the past tense of SPRING ‖ spring의 과거형

sprawl /sprɔl/ *v* [I] **1** also **sprawl out** to lie or sit with your arms or legs stretched out ‖ 팔이나 다리를 쫙 펴고 눕거나 앉다. 대자로 눕다. 널브러지다: *When we got home, Carey was sprawled* *on the sofa.* 우리가 집에 도착했을 때, 캐리는 소파에 널브러져 있었다. **2 if a building or town sprawls, it spreads out over a wide area** ‖ 건물이나 도시가 넓은 지역에 뻗어 있다. 불규칙하게 퍼지다 – **sprawl** *n* [singular, U]: *urban sprawl* 도시의 팽창

spray¹ /spreɪ/ *v* [T] **1 to make a liquid come out of a container, in order to make a stream of very small drops** ‖ 액체를 미세한 방울 줄기를 이루어 용기·호스 등에서 나오게 하다. 분무기로 뿌리다: *Spray a little perfume on the backs of your knees too.* 무릎 뒤쪽에도 향수를 조금 뿌려라. **2 [I] to be scattered in small drops or pieces through the air** ‖ 공중으로 작은 방울이나 조각들이 흩어지다. 물보라가 날리다[치다]: *He started to fire, bullets spraying everywhere.* 그가 총을 발사하기 시작하자 사방으로 총알이 비산했다.

spray² *n* **1** [C, U] liquid that is forced out of a container to spread out in very small drops ‖ 아주 작은 방울이 비산하도록 용기 밖으로 내뿜어지는 액체. 분무액: *hair spray* 헤어스프레이 **2** a special container that makes liquid SPRAY ‖ 액체를 분무하는 특수 용기. 분무기: *a non-aerosol spray* 비연무질 분사기 **3** [U] water that is thrown up in very small drops from the ocean ‖ 대양에서 미세한 방울이 되어 치솟는 바닷물. 물보라. 비말(飛沫) **4** leaves and flowers arranged as a decoration ‖ 장식으로 놓인 잎과 꽃. 장식용 꽃가지: *a spray of violets* 제비꽃가지

spray

spread¹ /spred/ *v* **spread, spread, spreading**
1 ▶OPEN/ARRANGE 펼치다/배열하다◀ [T] also **spread out to open something so that it covers a big area, or to arrange a number of things over a big area** ‖ 넓은 지역을 덮도록 무엇을 벌리다, 또는 넓은 지역에 걸쳐 수많은 것을 배열하다. 펼치다. 퍼다: *Tracy had a map spread out over the floor.* 트레이시는 바닥에 지도를 펼쳐 놓았다. / *The population is evenly spread across the state.* 인구가 주 전체에 고르게 분포되어 있다. / *He sat with books and papers spread over the table.* 그는 책과 서류를 탁자 위에 펼쳐 놓은 채 앉았다.
2 ▶GET BIGGER/WORSE 확대되다/악화되다◀ [I, T] **to get bigger or worse by**

having an effect on more people or places, or on a larger area ‖ 더 많은 사람들이나 장소, 또는 더 넓은 지역에 영향을 미쳐 커지거나 악화되다. 만연하다: *Rain will spread throughout the area by tonight.* 비는 오늘밤까지 전역으로 확산될 것입니다. / *Cancer has spread to her lungs.* 암이 그녀의 폐까지 전이됐다.
3 ▶INFORMATION/IDEAS 정보/생각◀ [I, T] **to make something widely known, or to become widely known** ‖ 무엇을 널리 알리다, 또는 널리 알려지다. 퍼뜨리다. 퍼지다: *News of her arrest quickly spread.* 그녀의 체포 소식은 빠르게 퍼졌다. / *Don't listen to him; he's always spreading rumors.* 그의 말을 듣지 마라. 그는 항상 유언비어를 퍼뜨린다.
4 ▶SOFT SUBSTANCE 부드러운 물질◀ [T] **to put a soft substance onto a surface in order to cover it** ‖ 표면을 덮으려고 부드러운 물질을 바르다: *toast spread with butter and jam* 버터와 잼이 발라진 토스트
5 ▶PUSH APART 벌리다◀ [I, T] also **spread apart to push your arms, legs, or fingers wide apart** ‖ 팔[다리, 손가락]을 좍 넓게 펼치다. 벌리다: *"Spread your legs!" one cop shouted.* "다리 벌려!"라고 한 경찰관이 소리쳤다.
6 ▶DO STH GRADUALLY 차차 무엇을 하다◀ [T] also **spread out to do something gradually over time** ‖ (장)기간에 걸쳐서 점진적으로 무엇을 하다. 끌다. …동안 계속되다: *You can spread the payments over a year.* 당신은 지불을 1년에 걸쳐 낼 수 있다.
7 spread yourself thin to accept too many duties so you are always too busy ‖ 너무 많은 일을 받아들여 항상 바쁘다. 한꺼번에 많은 일을 하려고 하다: *You've been spreading yourself too thin lately.* 너는 최근에 너무 많은 일을 해오고 있어.
8 ▶WINGS 날개◀ [T] also **spread open if a bird or insect spreads it's wings, it stretches them wide** ‖ 새나 곤충이 날개를 넓게 펴다

spread out *phr v* [I] **if a group of people spread out, they move apart from each other in order to cover a wide area** ‖ 넓은 지역을 감당하려고 일단의 사람들이 서로 떨어져 움직이다. 흩어지다. 분산하다: *If we spread out, it should be easier to find her.* 만약 우리가 흩어지면 틀림없이 그녀를 찾기가 훨씬 수월해진다.

spread² *n* **1** [singular] the increase in the area or number of people that something has an effect on ‖ 영향을 미치는 지역이나 사람 수의 증가. 확대. 확산: *More education is needed to control the spread of TB.* 결핵의 확산을 막기 위해 더 많은 교육이 필요하다. **2** [C, U] a soft food that you put on bread ‖ 빵 위에 바르는 연질의 음식. 스프레드: *cheese spread* 치즈 스프레드 / *a low-fat spread* 저지방 스프레드 **3** INFORMAL a large meal for several people on a special occasion ‖ 특별한 경우에 몇몇 사람들을 위해 준비된 많은 음식: *Kay always puts on a great spread.* 케이는 항상 진수성찬을 준비한다. **4** a special article or advertisement in a newspaper or magazine ‖ 신문이나 잡지의 특별한 기사나 광고: *a two-page spread* 좌우 양면에 걸친 기사 **5** a large farm or RANCH ‖ 큰 농장이나 목장 **6** TECHNICAL the difference between two amounts, such as the buying and selling price of a SHARE on the STOCK MARKET ‖ 주식 시장의 주식 매수가와 매도가 등의 두 수량간의 차이. 시세폭. 마진

spread·sheet /'sprɛdʃit/ *n* TECHNICAL a type of computer program that can show and calculate information about sales, taxes, payments etc. ‖ 매출액·세금·지출 등에 대한 정보들을 나타내며 계산해내는 컴퓨터 프로그램. 스프레드시트

spree /spri/ *n* a short period in which you do something that you enjoy, especially spending money or drinking ‖ 특히 돈을 쓰거나 술을 마시는 등의 자신이 즐기는 것을 하는 짧은 시간: *I see you went on a shopping spree!* 나는 네가 흥청망청 쇼핑한 것을 알아!

sprig /sprɪg/ *n* a small stem or part of a branch with leaves or flowers on it ‖ 잎이나 꽃이 달린 작은 줄기나 가지 부분: *a sprig of parsley* 파슬리 줄기

spring¹ /sprɪŋ/ *v* **sprang, sprung, springing 1** [I] to jump suddenly and quickly in a particular direction ‖ 특정한 방향으로 갑자기 그리고 빠르게 뛰다. 홱 뛰다: *He turned off the alarm and sprang out of bed.* 그는 자명종을 끄고 침대에서 벌떡 일어났다. / *a cat springing at a mouse* 쥐에게 홱 달려드는 고양이 **2** [I] to appear suddenly on someone's face or in his/her eyes ‖ 얼굴이나 눈에 갑자기 나타나다: *Tears sprang to her eyes as she spoke.* 그녀는 말하면서 갑자기 눈물이 눈에서 솟았다. **3 spring to mind** to immediately be thought of ‖ 금방 마음에 떠오르다: *Pam's name springs to mind as someone who*

could do the job. 그 일을 할 수 있는 사람으로 즉각 팸의 이름이 떠올랐다. **4 spring into action/spring to life** to suddenly become active or start doing things ‖ 갑자기 활기를 띠거나 무엇을 하기 시작하다. 활기/생기를 띠다: *The whole school springs into action at Homecoming.* 전 학교가 동창회로 활기를 띤다. **5 spring open/shut** to open or close suddenly and quickly ‖ 돌연히 빨리 열리거나 닫히다: *The lid of the box sprang open.* 상자 뚜껑이 확 열렸다. **6 spring to sb's defense** to immediately help someone who is being attacked or criticized ‖ 공격이나 비난을 받는 사람을 즉시 돕다. 옹호[비호]하다: *Molly sprang to her daughter's defense.* 몰리는 즉각 딸을 비호했다. **7 spring a leak** if a boat or a container springs a leak, it begins to let liquid in or out through a crack or hole ‖ 배나 용기의 깨진 틈이나 구멍으로 물이 드나들기 시작하다. 새는 곳이 생기다. 새기 시작하다

spring for sth *phr v* [T] INFORMAL to pay for something ‖ 무엇에 대한 값을 지불하다: *I might spring for a pizza.* 내가 피자 값을 내야 할지도 모른다.

spring sth **on** sb *phr v* [T] INFORMAL to tell someone news that surprises or shocks him/her ‖ 남에게 놀랍거나 충격적인 소식을 전하다. 불쑥[느닷없이] 말을 꺼내다: *I'm sorry to have to spring this on you.* 불쑥 너에게 이런 이야기를 하게 되어 유감이야.

spring up *phr v* [I] to suddenly appear or start to exist ‖ 갑자기 나타나거나 생기기 시작하다: *All along the railroad, new towns sprang up.* 철로를 따라 죽 신도시가 생겨났다.

spring² *n* **1** the season between winter and summer, when leaves and flowers appear ‖ 잎과 꽃이 피는 겨울과 여름 사이의 계절. 봄: *The park opens in (the) spring.* 그 공원은 봄에 개장한다. / *I'm going to Cancun this spring.* 나는 올 봄에 칸쿤에 갈 거야. / *last/next spring* (=the spring before or after this one) 작년[내년] 봄 **2** a place where water comes up naturally from the ground ‖ 물이 자연적으로 땅에서 솟아나는 장소. 샘. 수원지 **3** a twisted piece of metal that will return to its original shape after it has been pressed or pulled ‖ 눌리거나 당겨진 후에 원래의 형태로 되돌아오는 나선형의 금속 조각. 용수철 **4** [U] the ability of a chair, bed etc. to return to its normal shape after being pressed down ‖ 내리눌려진 후에 정상적인 형태로 되돌

아오는 의자·침대 등의 성능. 탄력. 탄성 **5** a sudden quick movement or jump in a particular direction ‖ 특정한 방향으로 의 빠르고 갑작스런 움직임이나 도약. 뛰기.

spring·board /'sprɪŋbɔrd/ *n* **1** something that helps you to become involved in an activity ‖ 어떤 활동에 참가할 수 있게 도와주는 것. 계기를 주는 것. 발판: *His computer knowledge provided a springboard for his career.* 그의 컴퓨터 지식은 그의 성공을 위한 발판이 되었다. **2** a strong board that bends, used in order to jump high ‖ 높이 뛰기 위해 쓰이는 휘어지는 튼튼한 판(板). 구름판. 도약판

spring break /,. './ *n* a vacation from school in the spring, that is usually two weeks long ‖ 보통 2주간의 학교 봄방학

spring chick·en /,. './ *n* **be no spring chicken** HUMOROUS to no longer be young ‖ 더 이상 어리지 않다

spring fe·ver /,. '../ *n* [U] a sudden feeling of energy and wanting to do something new and exciting, that you get in the spring ‖ 봄에 생기는, 새롭고 흥미 있는 일을 하려는 갑작스런 활력과 욕구의 느낌. 봄바람

spring·time /'sprɪŋtaɪm/ *n* [U] the time of year when it is spring ‖ 봄철

spring·y /'sprɪŋi/ *adj* returning quickly to its original shape after being pressed ‖ 눌린 후 원상태로 빠르게 돌아오는. 탄력[복원력] 있는: *springy grass* 복원력이 좋은 풀[잔디]

sprin·kle¹ /'sprɪŋkəl/ *v* **1** [T] to scatter small drops of liquid or small pieces of something onto something else ‖ 무엇에 작은 방울이나 조각들을 흩뿌리다: *spaghetti sprinkled with parmesan* 파르마산(産) 치즈를 뿌린 스파게티 **2** [I] to rain lightly ‖ 비가 조금씩 오다. 가랑비를 뿌리다: *It was sprinkling when we left.* 우리가 떠날 때 가랑비가 오고 있었다.

sprinkle² *n* **1** small pieces of food, or a light layer of these ‖ 음식의 작은 조각이나 그 조각의 얇은 층. 소량: *chocolate sprinkles* 잘게 뿌려진 초콜릿 / *a sprinkle of grated cheese* 소량의 치즈 가루 **2** a light rain ‖ 가랑비: *There will be sprinkles of rain over Oregon.* 오리건 주에 가랑비가 내릴 것입니다

sprin·kler /'sprɪŋklɚ/ *n* a piece of equipment used for scattering drops of water on grass to make it grow ‖ 잔디가 자라도록 물방울을 뿌리는 데에 쓰는 장비. 스프링클러. 살수기

sprint /sprɪnt/ *v* [I] to run very fast for

a short distance, usually in a race ‖ 보통 경주에서, 단거리를 매우 빠르게 달리다. 전력질주하다 **– sprinter** *n* **– sprint** *n*

sprout¹ /spraʊt/ *v* **1** [I, T] to start to grow or send up new growth ‖ 새싹이 자라기 시작하거나 싹트게 하다. 싹트다. 발아하다: *a plant sprouting new flowers* 새로운 꽃을 피우는 식물 / *seeds beginning to sprout* 싹트기 시작하는 씨앗 **2** also **sprout up** to appear suddenly in large numbers ‖ 갑자기 많이 생기다: *new homes sprouting up in the suburbs* 교외에 갑자기 들어선 새로운 집들

sprout² *n* **1** a new growth on a plant ‖ 식물의 새싹 **2** a BEAN or other plant that is not fully grown and is eaten in SALADS ‖ 샐러드로 먹는 다 자라지 않은 콩이나 다른 식물. 싹: *alfalfa sprouts* 자주개자리의 싹 **3** ⇨ BRUSSELS SPROUT

spruce¹ /sprus/ *n* [C, U] a tree with short leaves shaped like needles, or the wood of this tree ‖ 바늘 모양의 짧은 잎이 있는 나무, 또는 이 나무의 목재. 가문비나무 (목재)

spruce² *v*

spruce up *phr v* [I, T] INFORMAL to make yourself or a place look better or neater ‖ 자신이나 장소를 더 낫거나 말쑥해 보이게 만들다. 멋부리다: *I want to spruce up a little before dinner.* 나는 저녁 먹기 전에 약간 치장을 하고 싶다.

sprung /sprʌŋ/ *v* the past tense and PAST PARTICIPLE of SPRING ‖ spring의 과거·과거 분사형

spry /spraɪ/ *adj* a spry old person is active and cheerful ‖ 사람이 활기차고 유쾌한. 활발한

spud /spʌd/ *n* INFORMAL ⇨ POTATO

spun /spʌn/ *v* the past tense and PAST PARTICIPLE of SPIN ‖ spin의 과거·과거 분사형

spunk·y /'spʌŋki/ *adj* INFORMAL brave and full of energy ‖ 용감하고 힘이 넘치는. 원기 왕성한: *The movie is about a spunky girl who wants to play basketball.* 그 영화는 농구를 하고 싶어 하는 패기와 원기가 넘치는 소녀에 대한 이야기이다. **– spunk** *n* [U]

spur¹ /spɚ/ *n* **1** a sharp pointed object on the heel of a rider's boot ‖ 승마자의 장화 뒷굽에 달린 날카롭고 뾰족한 물체. 박차 **2 on the spur of the moment** without planning ahead of time ‖ 미리 계획하지 않고. 갑자기. 충동적으로: *You can't just get married like that, on the spur of the moment.* 너는 그렇게 앞뒤 분간도 없이 결혼해서는 안 돼.

spur² *v* **-rred, -rring** [T] **1** to make an

improvement or change happen faster ‖ 개선이나 변화가 빠르게 일어나게 하다. 박차를 가하다: *Growth in the city was spurred by cheap housing.* 저렴한 집값은 그 도시의 성장에 박차를 가했다. **2** also **spur on** to encourage someone to do or continue doing something ‖ 무엇을 하거나 계속하게 하라고 남을 격려하다. …을 자극하다: *Her sister's success spurred her on to practice harder.* 그녀는 여동생이 성공한 데에 자극되어 더욱 열심히 연습하게 되었다.

spu·ri·ous /'spyʊriəs/ *adj* FORMAL **1** based on incorrect reasoning ‖ 부정확한 추론에 근거한. 비논리적인: *spurious arguments* 그릇된 주장 **2** not sincere ‖ 진실되지 않은. 거짓된: *spurious sympathy* 가장된 동정

spurn /spɚn/ *v* [T] LITERARY to refuse to accept something or to have a relationship with someone, in an unkind way ‖ 무엇을 받아들이거나 남과 관계를 맺기를 냉정히 거절하다. 쌀쌀맞게 퇴짜놓다: *a spurned lover* 퇴짜 맞은 애인

spurt¹ /spɚt/ *v* [I] **1** to flow out suddenly with a lot of force ‖ 갑자기 세차게 뿜어 내다. 분출하다: *Blood spurted from his arm.* 그의 팔에서 피가 뿜어 나왔다. **2** to suddenly move forward very quickly ‖ 돌연히 매우 빠르게 앞으로 움직이다. 전력으로 돌진하다. 스퍼트하다: *Liz spurted past the other runners.* 리즈는 다른 주자들을 제치고 전속력으로 달렸다.

spurt² *n* **1** a stream of liquid that comes out suddenly ‖ 갑자기 뿜어 나오는 물줄기. 분출: *Water was coming out of the faucet in spurts.* (=quickly for short periods) 수도꼭지에서 물이 뿜어 나오고 있었다. **2** a short sudden increase in activity, effort, or speed ‖ 활동[노력, 속도]의 일순간의 증가. 분발: *a growth spurt* 급성장

sput·ter /'spʌtɚ/ *v* **1** [I] to make several quick soft sounds ‖ 몇 차례 급속히 낮은 소리를 내다. 탁탁 소리를 내다: *The engine sputtered and died.* 엔진이 탁탁 소리를 내다가 꺼져버렸다. **2** [I, T] to talk quickly in short confused phrases, especially because you are angry ‖ 특히 화가 나서, 짤막하게 횡설수설 급히 말하다. 다급히 말하다

spy /spaɪ/ *v* [I] to secretly collect information or watch people, usually for a government or company ‖ 보통 정부나 기업을 위해 몰래 정보를 수집하거나 사람들을 감시하다. 염탐하다: *He's in prison for spying.* 그는 간첩죄로 수감되어 있다.

/ *Stop spying on the neighbors!* 이웃사람들을 몰래 감시하지 마라! – **spy** *n* : *a government spy* 정부 스파이

squab·ble /'skwɑbəl/ *v* [I] to argue continuously about something unimportant ‖ 시시한 것에 대하여 계속 말다툼하다. 승강이하다: *What are those kids squabbling about now?* 지금 저 아이들은 무슨 일로 말다툼을 하고 있죠? – **squabble** *n*

squad /skwɑd/ *n* an organized group of people who do a job that needs special skills ‖ 특별한 기술이 필요한 일을 하는 조직화된 일단의 사람들. 단(團). 팀: *a cheerleading squad* 응원단 / *soldiers in the bomb squad* 폭발물 반의 병사들

squad car /'. ./ *n* a car used by police on duty ‖ 경찰이 근무시간에 사용하는 자동차. 경찰 순찰차. 패트롤 카

squad·ron /'skwɑdrən/ *n* a military force consisting of a group of aircraft or ships ‖ 일단의 항공기나 선박들로 구성된 군대. 비행편대. 소함대: *a bomber squadron* 폭격기 편대

squal·id /'skwɑlɪd/ *adj* **1** extremely dirty, unhealthy, and unsafe ‖ 매우 더러운·비위생적인·위험한. 누추한: *squalid living conditions* 누추한 주거 환경 **2** ⇨ IMMORAL

squall /skwɔl/ *n* a sudden strong wind that brings rain or snow ‖ 비나 눈을 동반하는 갑작스런 강풍. 돌풍

squal·or /'skwɑlɚ/ *n* [U] extremely dirty, unhealthy, and unsafe conditions ‖ 매우 더러운·비위생적인·위험한 상태. 누추함: *people living in squalor* 누추하게 사는 사람들

squan·der /'skwɑndɚ/ *v* [T] to waste your time, or spend money carelessly on useless things ‖ 쓸데없는 데에 생각없이 시간을 허비하거나 돈을 소모하다. 낭비하다 : *They've squandered thousands on that old house.* 그들은 저 낡은 집에 수천 만원을 낭비했다.

square¹ /skwɛr/ *adj* **1** having four equal sides and four right angles ‖ 네 변이 똑같고 네 각이 직각인. 정사각형의: *a square window* 정사각형의 창문 **2** **square inch/meter etc.** a measurement of an area whose length is equal to its width ‖ 길이와 너비가 같은 구역의 측정 단위. 제곱 인치/미터: *two square acres of land* 2평방 에이커의 땅 **3** like a square in shape ‖ 사각 모양의. 네모난: *a square jaw* 각진 턱 **4 a square deal** honest and fair treatment from someone ‖ 남에게서 받는 정직하고

공평한 대우: *a car dealer that gives customers a square deal* 고객에게 공정한 거래를 하는 자동차 매매인 **5 a square meal** a complete satisfying meal ‖ 완전하고 만족스러운 식사. 알찬 식사 **6 be square** if two people are square, they do not owe each other any money ‖ 두 사람이 서로 빚지지 않다. 대차 관계가 없다: *Here's your $20, so now we're square.* 여기 20달러 줄게, 그러면 이제 우리는 계산 끝난 거다. **7** INFORMAL someone who is square is boring and unfashionable ‖ 사람이 따분하고 유행에 뒤떨어진. 구식의 **8** OLD-FASHIONED honest ‖ 정직한: *I'm being square with you.* 나는 너에게 솔직하다.

square² *n* **1** a shape with four straight equal sides forming four right angles ‖ 네 각이 직각을 이루고 네 변이 동일한 직선인 형태. 정사각형 —see picture at SHAPE **2** a broad open area with buildings around it in the middle of a town ‖ 주변에 건물이 있는, 시가지 중앙의 개방된 널찍한 장소. 광장: *Times Square* 타임스 광장 **3 be back to square one** to be back in exactly the same situation that you started from ‖ 정확히 처음 시작했던 동일한 상황으로 되돌아가다. 원점으로 되돌아가다: *If things go wrong, we're back to square one.* 일이 어그러지면 우리는 원점으로 되돌아간다. **4** TECHNICAL the result of multiplying a number by itself. For example, the square of 5 is 25 ‖ 자체 수를 다시 곱한 결과. 제곱(수). 예를 들면 5의 제곱은 25이다 **5** OLD-FASHIONED DISAPPROVING someone who always obeys the rules and never seems to have fun ‖ 항상 규칙에 따르고 재미있을 것 같지 않은 사람. 융통성 없는 사람

square³ *v* [T] technical to multiply a number by itself ‖ 자체 수를 다시 곱하다. 제곱하다

square sth ↔ **away** *phr v* [T] to finish dealing with something ‖ 무엇의 처리를 마치다. …의 정리[준비]를 하다: *Peter needs another day to get things squared away at home.* 피터는 집에서 일을 마무리하려면 하루가 더 필요하다.

square off *phr v* [I] to get ready to fight someone by facing him/her ‖ 남과 마주하여 싸울 준비를 하다. 싸울 태세를 취하다

square up *phr v* [I] to pay money that you owe ‖ 빌린 돈을 갚다. 청산하다: *I'll get the drinks, and we can square up later.* 나 술을 먹어야겠어. 그리고 우리가 나중에 갚으면 돼.

square⁴ *adv* SPOKEN NONSTANDARD ⊳

SQUARELY

square dance /'. ./ *n* a type of dance in which four pairs of dancers face each other in a square ‖ 사각으로 네 쌍이 서로 마주보며 추는 춤의 일종. 스퀘어 댄스

square·ly /'skwɛrli/ *adv* **1** exactly or completely ‖ 정확히, 완전히: *The report puts the blame squarely on the senior managers.* 그 보고서는 상임 이사에게 전적으로 책임을 묻고 있다. / *Clark was hit squarely on the right elbow by a fast ball.* 클라크는 오른쪽 팔꿈치에 빠른 공을 정확히 맞았다. **2** directly and with confidence ‖ 직접적으로 자신감에 차서. 거리낌 없이: *I promise I will squarely face the challenges of leadership.* 약속하건대 나는 지도력에 대한 도전에 맞서겠다.

square root /, '. / *n* TECHNICAL the number that, when multiplied by itself, equals a particular number. For example, the square root of 9 is 3 ‖ 자체 수를 다시 곱하면 특정의 숫자가 되는 수. 제곱근. 예를 들면 9의 제곱근은 3이다

squash¹ /skwɑʃ, skwɔʃ/ *v* INFORMAL **1** [T] to press something into a flat shape, often damaging it; CRUSH ‖ 종종 망가뜨리기도 하며 무엇을 눌러 납작하게 만들다. 짓눌러 찌그러뜨리다; ㊦ crush: *My hat got squashed on the flight.* 도망하면서 내 모자가 찌그러졌다. **2** [I, T] to push yourself or someone else into a space that is too small ‖ 자신 또는 남을 아주 협소한 장소로 밀어넣다: *Seven of us squashed into the car.* 우리들 일곱 명은 그 차를 비집고 탔다.

squash² *n* **1** [C, U] one of several types of heavy hard fruits, such as a PUMPKIN, that is cooked and eaten as a vegetable ‖ 호박 등의 요리해서 야채로 먹는 딱딱하고 묵직한 몇 가지 열매 중의 하나. 호박속 과실 —see picture on page 944 **2** [U] an indoor game similar to RACKETBALL ‖ 라켓볼과 비슷한 실내 게임

squat¹ /skwɑt/ *v* [I] **1** also **squat down** to sit with your knees bent under you and balancing on your feet ‖ 무릎을 구부리고 앉아서 발로 균형을 유지하다. 웅크리고 앉다 **2** to live in a building or on a piece of land without permission and without paying rent ‖ 건물이나 땅에 허가 없이 임대료도 내지 않고 살다. 무단 거주하다

squat² *adj* short and thick, or low and wide ‖ 짧고 두꺼운, 또는 낮고 넓은. 땅딸막한: *small squat houses* 작달막한 집들 / *a squat cartoon figure* 땅딸막한 만화 속의 인물

squawk /skwɔk/ v [I] if a bird squawks, it makes a loud angry cry ‖ 새가 신경질적으로 크게 울다. 꽥꽥 울다 –
squawk n

squeak¹ /skwik/ v [I] 1 to make a very short high noise or cry ‖ 매우 짧고 높게 시끄러운 소리나 울음소리를 내다. 찍찍[삐걱삐걱] 소리 내다: Is that your chair squeaking? 네 의자가 삐걱거리니? 2 **squeak by/through** INFORMAL to manage to succeed, but not by very much ‖ 대단히가 아니라 가까스로 성공하다: The Bulls have squeaked through into the playoffs. 불스 팀은 간신히 결승전에 진출했다.

squeak² n a very short high noise or cry ‖ 매우 짧고 높게 나는 시끄러운 소리나 울음소리. 찍찍[삐삐] 하는 소리: the squeak of a mouse 쥐가 찍찍 우는 소리

squeak·y /ˈskwiki/ adj 1 making very high noises that are not loud ‖ 크진 않지만 아주 높은 시끄러운 소리를 내는: a squeaky voice 앙앙거리는 소리 / squeaky bed springs 삐걱거리는 침대 스프링 2 **squeaky clean** INFORMAL **a)** never having done anything morally wrong ‖ 도덕적으로 잘못한 것이 하나도 없는. 청렴결백한 **b)** completely clean ‖ 매우 깨끗한: squeaky clean hair 청결한 머리카락

squeal¹ /skwil/ v [I] 1 to make a long loud high sound or cry ‖ 길고 크면서도 높은 소리나 울음소리를 내다. 비명을 지르다: squealing tires 끼익하고 소리를 내는 타이어 / children squealing with excitement 흥분해서 소리 지르는 아이들 2 **squeal (on sb)** INFORMAL to tell the police about someone you know who has done something wrong ‖ 자신이 아는 잘못을 저지른 사람을 경찰에 알리다. 밀고하다

squeal² n a long loud high sound or cry ‖ 길게 내지르는 크고 높은 소리나 울음. 다소 긴 비명. 꽥 소리: squeals of delight 기쁨의 외침

squeam·ish /ˈskwimɪʃ/ adj easily upset by the sight of unpleasant things ‖ 불쾌한 것을 보면 금세 속이 거북한: I couldn't be a doctor – I'm too squeamish. 나는 의사가 될 수 없었어. 나는 툭하면 속이 거북해지거든.

squeeze¹ /skwiz/ v 1 [T] to press something firmly inwards, especially with your hand ‖ 특히 손으로 무엇을 안쪽으로 세게 누르다. 꽉 쥐다. 꼭 껴안다: She squeezed Jim's shoulder gently. 그녀는 짐의 어깨를 부드럽게 꼭 껴안았다. 2 [T] to twist or press something in

order to get liquid out of it ‖ 액체를 얻기 위해 무엇을 비틀거나 누르다. 짜다. 짜내다: Squeeze some lemon juice onto the salad. 샐러드 위에 레몬즙을 조금 짜 넣어라. 3 [I, T] to try to make a person or thing fit into a small space ‖ 협소한 공간 안에 사람이나 사물을 끼워 넣기 위해 애쓰다. 쑤셔 넣다: Can you squeeze in next to Rick? 릭 옆으로 비집고 들어갈 수 있겠니? 4 **squeeze sb out (of sth)** to not let someone take part in something ‖ 남을 무엇에 참여하지 못하게 하다. …에서 쫓아내다: Some small businesses are being squeezed out of the market. 몇 개의 소기업들이 시장에서 퇴출당하고 있다 5 **squeeze sb/sth in** INFORMAL to manage to do something although you are very busy ‖ 매우 바쁜데도 용케 무엇을 하다. 간신히 …을 하다: Professor Lang can squeeze you in (=have time to see you) at 2:00. 랭 교수님은 2시에야 당신을 간신히 만날 수 있습니다. 6 [T] to strictly limit the amount of money that is available to an organization ‖ 조직이 사용할 수 있는 돈의 양을 엄격히 규제하다. …을 경제적으로 압박하다: a school squeezed by budget cuts 예산 삭감으로 압박 받는 학교

squeeze² n 1 **a (tight) squeeze** a situation in which there is only just enough room for things or people to fit somewhere ‖ 사물이나 사람들이 어떤 장소에 겨우 들어가기에 맞는 공간이 있는 상황. 혼잡: It'll be a tight squeeze with six of us in the car. 차 안에 우리 6명이 타면 아주 꽉 끼게 될 것이다. 2 an act of pressing something firmly inwards with your hand ‖ 손으로 무엇을 안쪽으로 세게 누르는 행위. 꽉 쥐기: Laurie gave his hand a little squeeze. 로리는 그의 손을 조금 세게 쥐었다. 3 a small amount of something you get by squeezing ‖ 짜내어 얻은 소량의 것: a squeeze of lime juice 짜낸 소량의 라임즙 4 **a/the squeeze** a situation in which wages, prices, borrowing money etc. are strictly controlled ‖ 임금·가격·돈 빌리기 등이 엄격하게 규제받는 상황. 경제적인 곤경[긴축]: Congress is likely to put the squeeze on farm programs. 의회가 농업 프로그램을 축소할 것 같다.

squelch /skwɛltʃ/ v 1 [T] INFORMAL to stop something such as an idea or action from spreading or continuing ‖ 생각이나 행동 등의 확산이나 지속을 막다. 진압[억압]하다: Store owners said the law would squelch competition. 상점 주인은 그 법이 경쟁을 억제할 것이라고 말

했다. **2** [I] ⇨ SQUISH

squid /skwɪd/ n a sea creature with a long soft body and 10 TENTACLEs (=arms) ‖ 다리가 열 개에 몸체가 길고 유연한 해양 생물. 오징어

squig·gle /'skwɪgəl/ n a short line in writing or drawing that curls and twists ‖ 꼬불꼬불하고 이리저리 비틀리게 쓰거나 그린 짧은 선. 아무렇게나 휘갈긴 것 - **squiggly** adj

squint /skwɪnt/ v [I] to look at something with your eyes partly closed in order to see better or because of bright light ‖ 무엇을 더욱 잘 보려고 또는 빛이 밝아서 눈을 부분적으로 감고 보다. 눈을 가늘게 뜨고 보다: *He looked at me, squinting in the sun.* 그는 햇빛 때문에 눈을 가늘게 뜨고 나를 봤다. - **squint** n

squire /skwaɪɚ/ n a man who owned most of the land around a country village in past times ‖ 과거에 부락 주변의 대부분의 땅을 소유한 사람. 지방의 대지주[유지]

squirm /skwɚm/ v [I] to twist your body from side to side because you are uncomfortable or nervous ‖ 불편하거나 초조해서 이리저리 몸을 뒤틀다. 꿈틀거리다. 몸부림치다: *Stop squirming so I can comb your hair!* 내가 네 머리를 빗을 수 있게 꿈틀거리지 좀 마라!

squir·rel /'skwɚəl/ n a small animal with a FURRY tail that lives in trees and eats nuts ‖ 나무에 살며 견과를 먹는 털이 많은 긴 꼬리가 달린 동물. 다람쥐

squirt¹ /skwɚt/ v **1** [I, T] if you squirt liquid or it squirts, it is forced out of a narrow hole in a thin fast stream ‖ 좁은 구멍으로 가늘고 빠르게 물줄기가 뿜어나오다. 분출하다[시키다]: *Orange juice squirted onto her dress.* 오렌지 주스가 그녀의 옷에 튀었다. / *You need to squirt some oil onto the lock.* 너는 자물쇠에 약간의 기름을 칠 필요가 있다. **2** [T] to hit or cover someone or something with a stream of liquid ‖ 사람이나 사물에 물줄기를 쏘거나 뒤집어씌우다. 뿌리다. 적시다: *Mom! Tom's squirting me with the hose!* 엄마! 톰이 호스로 나한테 물을 뿌린대요!

squirt² n **1** a fast thin stream of liquid ‖ 한 줄기의 빠르고 가늘게 내뿜는 유체. 분출: *a squirt of ketchup* 케첩 한 번 뿌리기 **2** SPOKEN an insulting word for someone who is young, short, or not important ‖ 어린[부족한, 시시한] 사람을 일컫는 모욕적인 말. 애송이, 풋내기: *Get out of my way, squirt.* 저리 비켜라, 애송이야.

squish /skwɪʃ/ v **1** [I, T] INFORMAL ⇨ SQUASH¹ **2** [I] to make a sucking sound by moving through something soft and wet, such as mud ‖ 진흙 등의 물컹거리며 질척한 것을 지나가며 빠는 소리를 내다. 철떡철떡 소리를 내다

squish·y /'skwɪʃi/ adj soft and wet, or easy to SQUEEZE ‖ 말랑말랑하며 질척한, 또는 짜내기 쉬운. 질퍽한: *squishy mud* 질퍽한 진흙

Sr. n the written abbreviation of SENIOR ‖ senior의 약어

St. n **1** the written abbreviation of STREET ‖ street의 약어 **2** the written abbreviation of SAINT ‖ saint의 약어

stab¹ /stæb/ v **-bbed**, **-bbing 1** [T] to push a sharp object into someone or something, using a lot of force ‖ 세게 힘을 주어 사람이나 사물에 날카로운 것을 들이밀다. 찌르다: *She says he stabbed her with the bread knife.* 그녀는 그가 빵칼로 그녀를 찔렀다고 말했다. **2 stab sb in the back** INFORMAL to do something bad to someone who likes and trusts you; BETRAY ‖ 자신을 좋아하고 믿는 사람에게 못된 짓을 하다. …을 배반하다; ㉴ betray

stab² n **1** an act of STABbing or trying to stab someone ‖ 남을 찌르는 행위나 찌르려는 시도: *The victim had four stab wounds.* 그 피해자는 네 군데의 자상(刺傷)을 입었다. **2 take a stab at (doing) sth** INFORMAL to try to do something that is difficult or that you have never done ‖ 어렵거나 전혀 해보지 않았던 것을 해보다. 시도해 보다: *Carla decided to take a stab at learning to sail.* 칼라는 항해하는 것을 배워 보기로 결심했다.

stab·bing /'stæbɪŋ/ n a crime in which someone is STABbed ‖ 사람이 자상을 입은 범죄. 자상 사건

sta·bil·i·ty /stə'bɪləti/ n [U] the condition of being strong, steady, and not changing ‖ 견고하고 지속적이며 변하지 않는 상태. 안정(성): *a long period of political stability* 장기적인 정치적 안정기 —opposite INSTABILITY

sta·bi·lize /'steɪbə,laɪz/ v [I, T] to become firm and steady or not change any more, or make something do this ‖ 고정·안정되거나 더 이상 변하지 않다, 또는 어떤 것을 이렇게 되게 하다. 안정되다[시키다]: *The financial markets are finally stabilizing.* 금융 시장이 마침내 안정되고 있다. / *A rod is put in to stabilize the broken bone.* 부러진 뼈를 고정시키기 위해 부목을 댔다. - **stabilization** /,steɪbələ'zeɪʃən/ n [U] —opposite

DESTABILIZE

sta·ble¹ /'steɪbəl/ *adj* **1** steady and not likely to move or change ‖ 꾸준하여 움직이거나 변하지 않을 듯한. 안정된: *Be careful - the ladder doesn't look stable.* 조심해라. 사다리가 불안정해 보인다. / *a stable marriage* 안정된 결혼 생활 **2** calm, reasonable, and not easy to upset ‖ 침착한·합리적인·쉽게 마음이 상하지 않는. 안정된: *mentally stable* 정신적으로 안정된 —opposite UNSTABLE

stable² *n* a building where horses are kept ‖ 말이 사육되는 건물. 마구간

stack¹ /stæk/ *n* a neat pile of things ‖ 물건을 반듯하게 쌓아 놓은 것. 더미: *a stack of magazines on the table* 탁자 위의 잡지 더미

stack² *v* **1** [I, T] also **stack up** to form a neat pile, or put things into a neat pile ‖ 반듯한 더미를 이루거나 사물들을 반듯한 더미로 쌓다. 산더미처럼 쌓이다[쌓다]: *Just stack the dishes in the sink for now.* 우선은 싱크대에 그릇들을 쌓아 놓아라. / *chairs that are designed to stack easily* 쌓기 쉽게 고안된 의자 **2** [T] to put piles of things on or in a place ‖ 어떤 곳이나 안에 물건들을 겹겹이 쌓다. 쌓아 올리다: *Al has a job stacking shelves in the supermarket.* 앨은 슈퍼마켓에서 진열대에 상품을 쌓아 올리는 일을 한다.

stack up *phr v* [I] INFORMAL to compare with something else of the same kind ‖ 동종의 다른 것에 견주다. …에 필적하다: *a new PC that stacks up well against the others on the market* 시장에서 다른 PC들과 충분히 겨룰 수 있는 새로운 개인용 컴퓨터

stacks /stæks/ *n* [plural] **the stacks** the part of a library where most of the books are kept ‖ 도서관에서 대부분의 책을 보관하는 장소. 서고(書庫)

sta·di·um /'steɪdiəm/ *n, plural* **stadiums** *or* **stadia** /'steɪdiə/ a large field for playing sports, surrounded by a building that has many rows of seats ‖ 열을 이룬 수많은 좌석들을 가진 건축물로 둘러싸인 스포츠 경기용의 널찍한 터. 경기장: *a football stadium* 미식축구 경기장

staff¹ /stæf/ *n* the group of people who work for an organization ‖ 조직에 근무하는 일단의 사람들. 직원: *Lisa's on the city planning staff.* 리사는 도시 계획 직원이다. / *a meeting of library staff members* 도서관 직원들의 모임

staff² *v* [T] to provide the workers for an organization ‖ 조직에 직원을 대주다. …에 직원을 배치하다: *a hospital staffed by experienced nurses* 경험 많은 간호사가 배치된 병원 - **staffing** *n* [U]: *staffing costs* 인건비

staff·er /'stæfɚ/ *n* one of the people who works for an organization ‖ 조직에 근무하는 사람들 중의 한 명. 직원: *a Mercury News staffer since 1967* 1967년 이래의 Mercury News의 기자

stag /stæg/ *n* a fully grown male DEER ‖ 완전히 성장한 수사슴 —see also STAG NIGHT

stage¹ /steɪdʒ/ *n* **1** a particular state or level that someone or something reaches in a process ‖ 과정 중에 사람이나 사물이 도달한 특정한 상태나 수준. 단계: *The disease is still in its early stages.* 그 질병은 여전히 초기 단계에 있다. / *At this stage no one is sure what to do next.* 현 단계에서는 어느 누구도 다음에 해야 할 일을 확신할 수 없다. / *Children go through various stages of development.* 아이들은 다양한 성장 단계를 거친다. / *the planning stage of the project* 프로젝트의 기획 단계 **2** the raised floor in a theater where plays are performed ‖ 극장에서 연극이 상연되는 높게 만든 단. 무대 **3** [singular, U] the profession of acting ‖ 연기하는 직업. 배우(업): *Lina's always wanted to be on stage.* 리나는 항상 배우가 되고 싶어 했다. **4** a place where something important happens ‖ 중요한 일이 벌어지는 장소. 무대: *the world political stage* 세계의 정치 무대 **5** **s/he's going through a stage** INFORMAL used in order to say that someone young will soon stop behaving in a particular way ‖ 젊은이가 특정하게 행동하는 것을 곧 그만둘 것이라고 말하는 데에 쓰여. 사람이 성장 과정에 있다 —see also **set the stage/scene (for sth)** (SET¹)

stage² *v* [T] **1** to organize an event that people will notice or come to see ‖ 사람들이 주목하거나 보러 올 행사를 준비하다. …을 기획하다: *They're staging five plays this summer.* 그들은 올여름에 5편의 연극을 무대에 올릴 계획이다. / *factory workers staging a strike* 파업을 꾀하고 있는 공장 노동자들 **2** to start doing something again after you have stopped for a while ‖ 잠시 동안 중단한 후 다시 무엇을 하기 시작하다. …무대에 복귀하다: *After five years, Johnson is staging a comeback in basketball.* 5년이 지난 후, 존슨은 다시 농구에 복귀할 예정이다.

stage·coach /'steɪdʒkoʊtʃ/ *n* a closed vehicle pulled by horses, that carried passengers in past times ‖ 예전에 말이 끌어 승객을 실어 나르던, 지붕을 씌운 차량. 역마차

stage fright /'. ./ *n* [U] nervousness that some people feel before they perform in front of a lot of people ‖ 많은 사람들 앞에서 공연하기에 앞서 일부 사람들이 느끼는 초조함. 무대 공포증

stage man·ag·er /'. ,...,...,/ *n* someone who is responsible for a theater stage during a performance ‖ 공연하는 동안 극장 무대를 책임지는 사람. 무대 감독

stag·ger¹ /'stægɚ/ *v* **1** [I] to walk or move in an unsteady way ‖ 불안정하게 걷거나 움직이다. 비틀거리다: *A man came staggering down the stairs.* 한 남자가 계단을 비틀거리며 내려왔다. **2** [T] to arrange for things to be done at different times, so that they do not all happen at the same time ‖ 모든 일들이 동시에 발생하지 않고 서로 다른 시간에 이뤄지도록 배치하다. 어긋나게 배치하다. …에 시차를 두다: *Student registration will be staggered to avoid delays.* 학생들의 등록은 지체되는 것을 막기 위해 시차 조정이 될 것이다.

stagger² *n* an unsteady movement of someone who has difficulty walking ‖ 걷는 데에 어려움이 있는 사람의 불안정한 움직임. 비틀거리기

stag·ger·ing /'stægərɪŋ/ *adj* very surprising or shocking, and almost unbelievable ‖ 너무 놀랍거나 충격적이어서 거의 믿을 수 없는. 혼이 나갈 만한: *She spends a staggering amount of money on clothes.* 그녀는 옷에 엄청난 돈을 쓴다.

stag·ing /'steɪdʒɪŋ/ *n* [C, U] the art of performing a play, or the way this is done ‖ 연극을 상연하는 기술, 또는 상연되는 방법. 연극 연출: *a modern staging of "Romeo and Juliet"* "로미오와 줄리엣"의 현대적 연출

stag·nant /'stægnənt/ *adj* **1** stagnant water or air does not move or flow and often smells bad ‖ 물이나 공기가 움직이거나 흐르지 않아 종종 악취가 나는. 괴어 있는. 괴어서 썩은 **2** not changing or improving ‖ 변화나 진전이 없는. 침체한: *Steel production has stayed stagnant.* 강철 생산이 침체되어 있다.

stag·nate /'stægneɪt/ *v* [I] to stop developing or improving ‖ 발전하기 또는 나아지기가 중단되다. 침체되다. 발달[진보, 향상]이 멎다: *a stagnating economy* 침체되어 있는 경제 – **stagnation** /stæg'neɪʃən/ *n* [U]: *political stagnation* 정치적인 부진

stag night /'. ./ *n* a night before a man's wedding that he spends with his male friends, drinking and having noisy fun ‖ 술 마시고 떠들썩하게 놀면서 남자 친구들과 보내는 남성의 결혼식 전날 밤(의 모임). 스태그 (파티)

staid /steɪd/ *adj* serious, old-fashioned, and boring in the way you live, work, or dress ‖ 사람의 생활하는[일하는, 옷 입는] 방식이 진지하고 구식이며 지루한. 침착한. 근엄한. 착실한: *a staid old bachelor* 근엄한 늙은 독신자

stain¹ /steɪn/ *v* **1** [I, T] to accidentally make a colored mark on something, especially one that is difficult to remove, or to be marked in this way ‖ 물건에 색이 있는 자국, 특히 제거하기 곤란한 것을 우연히 만들다, 또는 이렇게 자국이 남겨지다. …을 얼룩지게 하다. 더럽히다[더러워지다]: *This carpet stains easily.* 이 카펫은 쉽게 얼룩진다. / *a tablecloth stained with wine* 포도주로 얼룩진 식탁보 **2** [T] to paint wood with a STAIN ‖ 목재에 (보호용) 스테인을 칠하다. 착색[염색]하다

stain² *n* **1** a mark that is difficult to remove ‖ 제거하기 힘든 자국. 얼룩. 더러움. 오점: *I got coffee stains on my shirt.* 내 셔츠에 커피 얼룩이 졌다. **2** [C, U] thin paint used for protecting wood and making it darker ‖ 나무를 보호하고 색을 진하게 하는 데 쓰이는 묽은 페인트. 스테인 (목재의 염료)

stain·less steel /,.. './ *n* [U] a type of steel that does not RUST ‖ 녹슬지 않는 철의 일종. 스테인리스 (강철)

stair /stɛr/ *n* one of the steps in a set of stairs ‖ 일련의 계단에서 층계들 중의 하나. 계단(의 단): *Jane sat on the bottom stair.* 제인은 맨 아랫계단(의 단)에 앉았다.

stair·case /'stɛrkeɪs/ *n* a set of stairs inside a building, and the structure that supports it ‖ 건물 내의 계단과 그것을 지지하는 구조물

stairs /stɛrz/ *n* [plural] a set of steps built for going from one level of a building to another ‖ 건물의 한 층에서 다른 층으로 가기 위해 만든 연속된 단. 계단: *Bev ran up/down the stairs.* 베브는 계단을 뛰어올라[내려] 갔다. / *The office is up one flight of stairs.* (=the stairs between two floors of a building) 그 사무실은 (층 사이의) 한 층계 위에 있다. — see also DOWNSTAIRS, UPSTAIRS¹, — compare STEP¹

stair·way /'stɛrweɪ/ *n* a set of stairs and the structure that supports it, either inside or outside a building ‖ 건물의 안 또는 밖에 있는 연속된 계단과 이를 지지하는 구조물. 계단

stake¹ /steɪk/ n 1 a pointed piece of wood, metal etc. that is pushed into the ground to hold a rope, mark a particular place etc. ‖ 로프를 고정하고 특정 장소를 표시하는 등을 위해 땅에 박아 넣는 뾰족한 나무·금속 등의 조각. 말뚝. 막대기 2 **be at stake** if something is at stake, you will lose it if a plan or action is not successful ‖ 계획이나 조치가 성공하지 못하면 어떤 것을 상실하는. 돈[상금]이 걸려 있는. (생명·명예·안전 등이) 위기에 처한 3 **have a stake in** to have an important part or share in a business, plan etc. ‖ 사업·계획 등에서 중요한 부분 또는 몫을 가지다. …에 (지분) 참여하다[관계가 있다]. …에 이해관계를 갖다: *a 5% stake in the company* 회사에서 5%의 지분 참여 4 [C usually plural] money risked on the result of a game, race etc.; BET ‖ 게임·경주 등의 결과에 따라 잃을 위험이 있는 돈. 내기(에 건) 돈; ⓊⓈ bet

stake² v [T] 1 to risk something on the result of a game, race etc., or on the result of a plan or action ‖ 게임·경주 등의 결과, 또는 계획이나 활동의 결과에 어떤 것을 걸다. (생명·돈 등을) …에 걸다: *The President is staking his reputation on the peace plan.* 대통령은 그의 명성을 평화안에 걸고 있다. 2 **stake (out) a claim** to say publicly that you think you have a right to have or own something ‖ 어떤 것을 갖거나 소유할 권리가 있다고 생각함을 공개적으로 말하다. 권리를 주장하다[내세우다]: *The two tribes have both staked a claim to the territory.* 두 부족은 모두 그 영토에 대한 권리를 주장했다.

stake sth ↔ **out** phr v [T] INFORMAL to watch a place secretly and continuously ‖ 어떤 장소를 비밀리에 계속적으로 감시하다: *The police have been staking out the club for weeks.* 경찰은 수 주일 동안 그 클럽을 감시해 오고 있다.

stake·out /ˈsteɪkaʊt/ n the act of watching a place secretly and continuously ‖ 어떤 장소를 비밀리에 계속적으로 감시하는 행위. 경찰의 잠복

stale /steɪl/ adj 1 no longer fresh ‖ 더 이상 신선하지 않은. 김빠진. 딱딱한. 퀴퀴한: *stale bread* 딱딱해진 빵 2 no longer interesting ‖ 더 이상 흥미 없는. 진부한. 재미없는: *a stale old joke* 진부한 상투적인 농담

stale·mate /ˈsteɪlmeɪt/ n [C, U] a situation in which neither side in an argument, battle etc. can gain an advantage ‖ 논쟁·전투 등에서 쌍방 어느 쪽도 이득을 얻을 수 없는 상황. 쌍방의 수가 모두 막힌 판국

stalk¹ /stɔk/ n the main stem of a plant ‖ 식물의 줄기. 대

stalk² v 1 [T] to follow a person or animal quietly in order to catch or kill him, her, or it ‖ 사람이나 동물을 잡거나 죽이기 위해 조용히 추적하다. 몰래 다가가다 2 [I] to walk in a proud or angry way ‖ 자랑스럽게 또는 화난 태도로 걷다. 화난 발 걸음으로[거드름 피우며] 걷다: *Sheryl turned and stalked out of the room.* 쉐릴은 돌아서서 화난 발걸음으로 방을 나갔다.

stalk·er /ˈstɔkɚ/ n someone who often follows someone else, often in order to annoy or harm him/her ‖ 괴롭히거나 해치려고 자주 다른 사람을 따라다니는 사람. 스토커 – **stalking** n [U]

stall¹ /stɔl/ n 1 a small enclosed area for washing or using the toilet ‖ 목욕 또는 화장실 이용을 위한 칸막이된 좁은 구역. (화장실·샤워장의) 칸막이. 한 칸: *a shower stall* 샤워실 2 an enclosed area in a building for an animal, especially a horse ‖ 동물 특히 말을 위한 건물 내 칸막이 구역. 마구간. 외양간 3 an occasion when an engine suddenly stops working ‖ 엔진이 갑자기 작동을 멈추는 일. (엔진·자동차의) 실속(失速). 추력 상실: *Then the plane went into a stall.* 그 때 그 비행기는 추력을 잃었다.

stall² v [I, T] 1 if an engine stalls or you stall it, it suddenly stops working ‖ (엔진이) 갑자기 작동을 멈추다. 실속이 일어나다[으키다]: *My car always stalls when it's cold.* 내 차는 추울 때면 항상 멎어 버린다. 2 INFORMAL to deliberately delay doing something, or to make someone else do this ‖ 어떤 것을 하는 것을 고의로 지연시키다, 또는 다른 사람에게 이렇게 하게 하다. (일을) 늦추다[방해하다]. 오도가도 못하게 하다: *Quit stalling and answer my question!* 말 돌리지 말고 내 질문에 대답해! / *I'll try to stall him for a few minutes.* 내가 몇 분 동안 그를 속여서 잡아 놓도록 해볼게.

stal·lion /ˈstælyən/ n a fully grown male horse ‖ 충분히 성장한 수컷 말. 종마

stal·wart /ˈstɔlwɚt/ n someone who strongly supports a particular organization or set of ideas ‖ 특정한 조직 또는 신념 체계를 강력하게 지지하는 사람. 열렬한 지지자 – **stalwart** adj : *a stalwart supporter* 열렬한 지지자

stam·i·na /ˈstæmənə/ *n* [U] physical or mental strength that lets you continue doing something for a long time ‖ 사람에게 장시간 어떤 것을 계속해서 하게 하는 육체적 또는 정신적인 힘. 체력. 정력. 지구력. 스태미너

stam·mer /ˈstæmə/ *v* [I, T] to repeat the first sound of a word because you have a speech problem, or because you are nervous ‖ 사람이 언어 장애가 있거나 긴장되어서 단어의 첫 소리를 반복하다. 더듬더듬 말하다. 말을 더듬다 — **stammer** *n* [singular] —see also STUTTER

stamp¹ /stæmp/ *n* **1** a small piece of paper that you stick onto an envelope or package that shows you have paid to mail it ‖ 우편물 발송을 위한 요금을 납부했다는 것을 나타내기 위해 봉투 또는 소포에 붙이는 작은 종이 조각. 우표 **2** a tool for printing a mark onto a surface, or the mark made by this tool ‖ 표면에 표시를 찍는 데 쓰이는 도구, 또는 이런 도구에 의해 찍힌 마크. 스탬프. (검인)도장. 소인(消印): *a passport stamp* 여권의 공인(公印) **3 have/bear the stamp of sth** to clearly have a particular quality ‖ 특정한 특성을 분명히 가지다. …한 특징이 있다. …임을 나타내다: *a speech that bears the stamp of authority* 권위있는 연설

stamp² *v* **1** [I] to lift up your foot and put it down hard, or to walk in this way ‖ 발을 들어서 세게 내려놓다, 또는 이런 방식으로 걷다. (힘껏)짓밟다. 쿵쿵 걷다[구르다]: *Tony stamped upstairs.* 토니는 이층으로 쿵쿵 걸어 올라갔다. **2** [T] to put a pattern, sign, or letters on something using a special tool ‖ 특별한 도구를 사용하여 사물에 무늬[부호, 문자]를 넣다. 각인하다. 새기다. 찍다: *Please stamp the date on all incoming mail.* 모든 도착 우편물에 날짜를 찍어 주세요. **3** [T] to stick a stamp onto an envelope or package ‖ 봉투 또는 소포 위에 우표를 붙이다

stamp sth ↔ **out** *phr v* [T] to get rid of something ‖ 어떤 것을 제거하다. …을 분쇄[근절]하다. 밟아서 (짓)뭉개다: *efforts to stamp out drug abuse* 약물 남용을 근절시키기 위한 노력

stam·pede /stæmˈpid/ *n* **1** an occasion when a large number of animals suddenly start running together ‖ 많은 수의 동물이 갑자기 함께 뛰기 시작하는 경우. 놀라서 우르르 도망치기. 궤주(潰走) **2** a sudden rush by a lot of people who all want to do the same thing or go to the same place ‖ 같은 일을 하거나 같은 장소에 가고 싶어 하는 많은 사람들의 갑작스런 돌진. 쇄도. 우르르 몰려오기[들기]: *a stampede to buy gold before the price goes up* 가격 등귀 전 금 구입의 쇄도 — **stampede** *v* [I, T]

stance /stæns/ *n* **1** an opinion that is stated publicly ‖ 공개적으로 언명된 견해. 입장. 자세. 태도: *Senator, what is your stance on nuclear tests?* 상원 의원님, 핵실험에 대한 입장은 무엇입니까? **2** the way in which you stand during a particular activity ‖ 특정한 활동 중에 사람이 취하는 태도. 스탠스. 자세. 태세

stanch /stæntʃ/ *v* [T] ⇨ STAUNCH²

stand¹ /stænd/ *v* **stood, stood, standing**

1 ▶STAND 서다◀ [I] to be on your feet in an upright position ‖ 똑바른 자세로 (발로) 서다. 서 있다: *Jeff and I were standing there and saw it all.* 제프와 나는 거기 서서 그것을 모두 보았다. / *Hundreds of people stood watching.* 수백 명의 사람들이 서서 구경했다. / *Stand still* (=stand without moving) *and let me comb your hair.* 꼼짝 말고 서 있어, 네 머리 빗질하게. / *A policeman told everyone to stand back/aside.* (=stand farther away from something) 경찰관은 모든 사람들에게 뒤로 물러서라고[옆으로 비켜서라고] 말했다.

2 ▶START STANDING 서기 시작하다◀ [I] also **stand up** to move so that you are standing ‖ 일어선 상태가 되도록 움직이다. 일어서다[나다]. 기립하다: *Please stand for the singing of the National Anthem.* 애국가 제창을 위해 기립해 주세요. / *Everybody stood up to applaud.* 모든 사람이 기립하여 박수를 쳤다.

3 ▶UPRIGHT POSITION 똑바로 선 자세◀ [I, T] to be in an upright position somewhere, or to put something in an upright position ‖ 어떤 장소에 똑바로 선 자세로 있다, 또는 어떤 것을 똑바로 선 자세로 놓다. 세우다. 바로 서 있다: *We'll stand the Christmas tree in the corner.* 우리는 구석에 크리스마스트리를 세울 거다. / *There's now a parking lot where the theater once stood.* 한때 극장이 서 있었던 곳에 지금은 주차장이 있다. / *The house has stood empty* (=not been lived in) *for 20 years.* 그 집은 20년간 빈 채로 서 있었다.

4 ▶LEVEL/AMOUNT 수준/크기◀ [I] to be at a particular level or amount ‖ 특정한 수준 또는 양이다. …이다. …을 가리키다[기록하다]: *The unemployment rate stood at 8% in January.* 실업률은 1월에

8%를 기록했다.

5 can't stand SPOKEN to dislike something or someone very much ‖ 다른 사물이나 사람을 매우 싫어하다. …을 참을 수[견딜 수] 없다: *Dave can't stand dogs.* 데이브는 개들을 아주 싫어한다. / *I can't stand to waste anything.* 나는 무엇이든 낭비하는 것을 참을 수 없다. — see usage note at BEAR¹

6 stand to do sth to be likely to do or have something ‖ 어떤 것을 하거나 가질 것 같다. …할 형세에 있다. …상태이다: *The company stands to make more than $12 million on the deal.* 그 회사는 그 거래에서 1200만 달러 이상을 벌 것 같다.

7 ▶NOT CHANGE 변하지 않다◀ [I] to continue to exist or be correct, and not change ‖ 계속해서 존속하거나 옳으며 변하지 않다. 먼저[본래]대로이다. 효과를 유지하다: *The Supreme Court let stand the ruling of the lower court.* 대법원은 하급 법원의 결정을 그대로 유지하게 했다 [인정했다] / *Horowitz has stood firm on his refusal.* (=refused to change it) 호로윗츠는 그의 거부 입장에 단호했다.

8 ▶HEIGHT 높이◀ [I] to have a particular height ‖ 특정한 높이를 가지다. …높이에 이르다. …이다: *The Eiffel Tower stands 300 meters high.* 에펠탑은 높이가 300미터이다.

9 stand a chance (of doing sth) to be likely to succeed in doing something ‖ 어떤 것을 하는 데 성공할 것 같다. …할 가망이 있다: *You don't stand a chance of going out with her.* 너는 그녀와 데이트하러 갈 가망성이 없다.

10 ▶BE GOOD ENOUGH 충분히 좋다◀ [T] to be good enough or strong enough to remain unharmed or unchanged by something ‖ 어떤 것에 의해서 피해를 받지 않거나 변경당하지 않을 만큼 충분히 좋거나 강하다. 고수하다. 견디다. 끄떡도 않다: *jeans that can stand the rough wear kids give them* 아이들이 험하게 입어도 견디어낼 수 있을 만큼 질긴 진 바지 / *Their marriage has certainly stood the test of time.* 그들의 결혼은 분명 세월의 시련을 견디어냈다.

11 ▶IN STATE/SITUATION 상태/상황에서 ◀ [I, linking verb] to be in or remain in a particular state or situation ‖ 특정한 상태 또는 상황에 처해 있거나 그대로 남아 있다. …한 상태이다. 상태·태도를 취하다: *US warships stood ready to block all trade in the area.* 미국 전함들은 그 지역 내 모든 교역을 봉쇄할 준비 태세를 취했다. / *The offer, as it stands, is not acceptable.* 현상태로는 그 제안은 받아들일 만하지 않다.

12 stand in the way/in sb's way to prevent someone from doing something, or prevent something from happening or developing ‖ 사람이 어떤 것을 하는 것을 막다, 또는 발생하거나 발전하지 못하게 막다. 남의 방해를 하다. 앞을 가로막다: *Some important objections still stand in the way of an agreement.* 몇몇 영향력 있는 반대가 여전히 협정 타결을 가로막고 있다.

13 ▶BEAR/ACCEPT 참다/수용하다◀ [T] to be able to accept or deal with something unpleasant or difficult ‖ 불쾌하거나 곤란한 일을 받아들이거나 처리할 수 있다. 참아내다. 용인하다: *He could hardly stand the pain any longer.* 그는 더 이상 통증을 거의 참을 수 없었다.

14 where/how you stand what your opinion about something is ‖ 어떤 것에 대한 사람의 견해는. …에 대한 입장은: *Voters are not sure where she stands on the issue of immigration.* 투표자들은 이민 문제에 관한 그녀의 입장이 어떤지를 모르고 있다.

15 know where you stand to know what someone's opinion of you is, or to know what s/he wants you to do ‖ 자신에 대한 남의 의견이 무엇인지를 알다, 또는 남이 자신에게 하기 원하는 것을 알다. 자신의 입장[처지]을 알다: *You just never know where you stand with Walter.* 너는 월터와의 관계에서 네 입장을 전혀 알지 못한다.

16 stand on your own two feet to be independent and not need help from other people ‖ 독립하여 타인의 도움이 필요 없다. 혼자 힘으로 해나가다

17 it stands to reason used in order to say that something is clearly true ‖ 어떤 것이 분명히 진실이라는 것을 말하려는 데 쓰여. 어김 없이[분명히] …이다. …하는 것이 이치[사리]에 맞다: *It stands to reason that children will imitate their parents.* 아이들이 그들의 부모를 닮는다는 것은 당연하다.

18 could stand used in order to say that someone should do something or that something should be different ‖ 사람이 어떤 것을 해야 한다거나 어떤 것이 달라야 한다는 것을 말하려는 데 쓰여. …했어야 했다. …할 수 있었다: *I could stand to lose a little weight.* 나는 체중을 약간 줄였어야 했다. / *That skirt could stand to be longer.* 그 스커트는 더 길었어야 했다.

19 stand pat to refuse to change a decision, plan etc. ‖ 결정·계획 등의 변경

을 거부하다. (결심을) 고수하다. 굽히지[바꾸지] 않다: *Lurie has been standing pat, waiting for the best offer.* 루리는 최선의 제의를 기다리면서 결심을 굽히지 않았다.
20 stand on your head/hands to support yourself on your head or hands in an upright position, with your feet in the air ‖ 발을 공중으로 똑바로 선 자세로 머리 또는 손으로 자신을 지탱하다. 물구나무서다 —see also **be on guard/ stand guard** (GUARD¹)
stand around *phr v* [I] to stand somewhere and not do anything ‖ 어떤 곳에 서서 아무 일도 하지 않다. 우두커니 서 있다: *Everybody was just standing around talking.* 모두들 우두커니 서서 잡담만 하고 있을 뿐이었다.
stand by *phr v* **1** [T **stand by** sth] to decide what to do, say, or believe, and not change this ‖ 무엇을 할지[말할지, 믿을지] 결정하고 이것을 변경하지 않다. 지키다．고수하다: *The doctors are standing by their original statements.* 의사들은 그들의 애초의 발언을 고수하고 있다. / *If you don't stand by your principles, they won't respect you.* 만일 네가 네 원칙을 지키지 않는다면 그들은 너를 존경하지 않을 것이다. **2** [T **stand by** sb] to stay loyal to someone and support him/her in a difficult situation ‖ 어려운 상황에 있는 사람을 충실하게 남아서 지지하다. (곁에 남아) 지켜주다: *Matt's parents have stood by him through his drug problem.* 매트의 부모님은 그가 마약 문제를 겪는 동안 내내 그를 지켜주었다. **3** [I] to be ready to do something ‖ 어떤 것을 할 준비가 되어 있다. 대기[대비]하다: *Fire crews are now standing by.* 소방대원들은 지금 대기 중이다. **4** [I] to not do anything to help someone, or to not prevent something from happening ‖ 누군가를 돕는 어떤 일도 하지 않다, 또는 어떤 것이 발생하는 것을 막지 않다. 수수방관하다: *Muldrow said that while one officer stood by, another hit the boy.* 멀드로는 한 경찰관이 방관하는 동안 다른 경찰관이 그 소년을 때렸다고 말했다.
stand for sth *phr v* [T] **1** to represent a word, phrase, or idea ‖ 어휘[구절, 생각]를 나타내다. 의미하다. 상징이다: *VA stands for Veterans Administration.* VA는 재향 군인 회를 의미한다. **2** to support an idea, principle etc. ‖ 생각·원칙 등을 지지하다. …을 인정하다. …의 편을 들다: *Martin Luther King stood for fairness and racial equality.* 마틴 루터

킹은 공평과 인종 평등을 주창했다.
stand out *phr v* [I] **1** to be clearly better than other things or people ‖ 다른 물건 또는 사람들보다 더 낫다. 뛰어나다. 걸출하다: *Morrison stands out as the most experienced candidate.* 모리슨은 가장 노련한 후보로 단연 뛰어나다. **2** to be very easy to see or notice ‖ 보거나 인식하기 매우 쉽다. 사람 눈에 띄다. 두드러지다: *In her red dress, she really stood out in the crowd.* 그녀의 빨간 드레스로 그녀는 정말로 군중 가운데서 눈에 띄었다.
stand up *phr v* **1** [I] to be proven to be true or correct ‖ 진실 또는 정확한 것으로 증명되다. 여전히 유효하다. 통하다. 인정되다: *The accusations will never stand up in court.* 그 기소는 법정에서 결코 인정되지 못할 것이다. / *Lo's studies stood up to close scrutiny from experts.* 로의 연구는 전문가들의 면밀한 조사에 부합되었다[부합되어 인정받았다]. **2** [T **stand** sb **up**] to not meet someone when you have promised to meet him/her ‖ 사람을 만나기로 약속을 했을 때 사람을 만나지 않다. 이성을 기다리게 만들다. 바람맞히다: *My date stood me up last night.* 지난밤 내 데이트 상대가 나를 바람맞혔어. **3** [I] to remain in good condition after being used a lot or in a bad situation ‖ 많이 사용된 후 또는 악조건 속에서도 좋은 상태를 유지하다. 견디어 내다. 끄떡없다: *The equipment did not stand up under battlefield conditions.* 그 장비는 실전(實戰) 상황 하에서 견뎌내지 못했다.
stand up for sb/sth *phr v* [T] to support or defend someone or something when s/he or it is being attacked or criticized ‖ 다른 사람·사물이 공격 또는 비판을 당하는 경우에 지지하거나 지켜주다. (남·주의·주장을) 옹호하다[…편을 들다]. …을 위해 일어서다: *Don't be afraid to fight by standing up for your rights.* 너의 권리를 위해 싸우는 것을 두려워 마라.
stand up to sb *phr v* [T] to be brave and refuse to do or say what someone is trying to make you do or say ‖ 다른 사람이 하거나 말하라고 시키는 것을 용감하게 거부하다. …에 과감히 맞서다: *He became a kind of hero for standing up to the local gangs.* 그는 그 지역 갱단에 과감히 맞서서 영웅 같이 되었다.
stand² *n* **1** a piece of furniture or equipment for supporting something ‖ 어떤 것을 떠받치는 가구 또는 장비. 받침대. 연단. 연주대: *a music stand* 악보대

2 a table or small structure, usually outside or in a large building, where you can buy something ‖ 물건을 구입할 수 있는 보통 야외나 큰 건물 내부에 있는 테이블 또는 작은 구조물. 판매대. 매점: *a hotgog stand* 핫도그 매점 **3** an opinion that you state publicly ‖ 공개적으로 말하는 견해. 입장. 태도: *Bradley was unwilling to take a stand* (=say what his opinion was) *on the issue.* 브래들리는 그 쟁점에 관한 입장을 밝히는 것을 꺼렸다 **4** the place in a court of law where someone sits when the lawyers ask him/her questions ‖ 법정에서 변호사의 질문을 받는 사람이 앉는 장소. 증인석: *Shaw had lied on the stand.* (=when he was answering questions) 쇼는 증인심문에서 위증했다. / *Epstein will take the stand* (=begin answering questions) *Friday.* 엡스테인은 금요일에 증언대에 선다. **5** an effort to defend yourself or to oppose something ‖ 자신을 방어하거나 어떤 것에 반대하는 노력. 저항. 방어. 옹호: *Lassiter feels he has to make a stand to protect the Alaska wilderness.* 라시터는 자신이 알래스카의 대자연을 보호하기 위해 맞서서 싸워야 한다고 느낀다. —see also STANDS

stand-a-lone /ˌ.. ˈ../ *adj* working on its own without being controlled by anything else ‖ 다른 무엇에 의해 통제되지 않고 스스로 작동하는. (주변 장치가) 독립하여 조작이 가능한: *a stand-alone computer* 독립 운용 컴퓨터

stan-dard¹ /ˈstændəd/ *n* **1** a level of quality, skill, or ability that is considered to be acceptable ‖ 받아들일 만한 것으로 간주되는 품질[기술, 능력]의 수준. 표준. 규격: *They have to meet/reach a certain standard or they won't pass.* 그들은 어떤 기준에 부합[도달]해야 한다. 그렇지 않으면 그들은 합격할 수 없다. / *Mr. Williams sets very high standards for all his students.* 윌리엄스 씨는 그의 모든 학생들에게 아주 높은 평가 기준을 설정하고 있다. **2** the ideas of what is good or normal that someone uses to compare one thing with another ‖ 사람이 한 물건을 다른 것과 비교하는 데 사용하는 무엇이 좋거나 정상인지에 대한 생각. 규범. 척도. 기준: *By American standards, Rafael's salary is pretty low.* 미국인의 기준에 의하면 라파엘의 급여는 아주 낮은 것이다.

standard² *adj* normal or usual ‖ 표준의 또는 보통의. 모범적인. 통례의: *Security checks are now standard practice/procedure.* 안전 점검은 이제 통례적인

관행[절차]이 되어 있다. —compare NONSTANDARD, SUBSTANDARD

stan-dard-ize /ˈstændəˌdaɪz/ *v* [T] to make all the things of one particular type the same as each other ‖ 특정한 한 종류의 모든 것들을 서로 동일하게 하다. …을 규격화[표준화]하다: *national standardized tests* 전국적으로 표준화된 시험 – **standardization** /ˌstændədəˈzeɪʃən/ *n* [U]

standard of liv·ing /ˌ.. ˈ../ *n* the amount of wealth and comfort that a person, group, or country has ‖ 사람[집단, 국가]이 가진 부(富)와 안락함의 크기. 생활수준

stand·by /ˈstændbaɪ/ *n* **1** someone or something that is ready to be used when needed ‖ 필요한 때 이용할 준비가 되어 있는 사람 또는 사물. 대체물. 대체요원: *a standby power generator* 예비[대체] 발전기 **2 on standby a)** ready to be used when needed ‖ 필요시 이용될 준비가 되어 있는. 대기하여[상태인]: *The police have been kept on standby in case of trouble.* 경찰은 혼란시에 대비하여 대기 상태로 있다. **b)** ready to travel on a plane if there are any seats left when it is ready to leave ‖ 출발 준비가 되어 있는 항공편의 좌석이 남아 있을 때 그 비행기로 여행할 준비가 되어 있는. 공석탑승[대기](자) 명단의: *The flight is full, but we can put you on standby.* 그 항공편은 만원입니다만 저희는 선생님을 공석 탑승 대기자로 올려 놓겠습니다.

stand-in /ˈ. ./ *n* someone who does the job or takes the place of someone else for a short time ‖ 잠시 타인의 업무를 보거나 타인을 대신하는 사람. 대역. 대리(인)

stand·ing¹ /ˈstændɪŋ/ *adj* **1** continuing to exist; permanent ‖ 계속해서 존재하는. 항상 가능한; 영속적인: *We have a standing offer to use their beach cabin.* 우리는 해변에 있는 그들의 작은 집을 언제라도 이용할 수 있게 허락을 받아 놓고 있다. **2** done from a standing position ‖ 서 있는 자세에서 이뤄진. 선 채로의[하는]: *a standing ovation* (=when people stand to CLAP after a performance) (공연 후의) 기립 박수

standing² *n* [U] someone's rank or position in a system, organization, etc., based on what other people think of him/her ‖ 타인이 어떤 사람에 대해 어떻게 생각하는지에 근거한 어떤 사람의 체제·조직 등에서의 계급이나 지위. 명성. 평판. 자리매김: *the President's standing in the opinion polls* 여론 조사에서의 대통

령의 평판

stand·off /'stændɔf/ *n* a situation in which neither side in a fight or battle can gain an advantage ‖ 싸움·전투에서 그 어느 쪽도 이득을 얻을 수 없는 상황. 무승부. 호각. 교착 상태

stand·out /'stændaut/ *n* someone who is better at doing something than other people in a group ‖ 집단내의 다른 사람들보다 어떤 것을 더 잘하는 사람. 뛰어난 [걸출한] 사람 – **standout** *adj*

stand·point /'stændpɔint/ *n* a particular person's or group's way of thinking about a problem or subject; POINT OF VIEW ‖ 문제 또는 주제에 관하여 특정한 사람 또는 집단이 생각하는 방식. 견지. 관점; ㊀ point of view

stands /stændz/ *n* [plural] the place where people sit to watch a sports game ‖ 스포츠 게임을 관람하기 위해 사람들이 앉아 있는 자리. (경기장의) 관람석. 스탠드

stand·still /'stænd,stɪl/ *n* [singular] a situation in which there is no movement or activity at all ‖ 동작 또는 활동이 전혀 없는 상황. 정지. 휴지. 정체: *Strikes brought production to a standstill.* 파업으로 생산이 중단되었다.

stand·up /'stændʌp/ *adj* INFORMAL standup COMEDY involves one person telling jokes as a performance ‖ 코미디쇼에서 한 사람이 연기로서 농담을 하는. 독백하는. 홀로 연기하는 – **standup** *n* [C, U]

stank /stæŋk/ *v* the past tense of STINK ‖ stink의 과거형

stan·za /'stænzə/ *n* a group of lines that forms part of a poem ‖ 시의 일부를 구성하는 일단의 행. 연(聯). 절. 스탠자

sta·ple¹ /'steɪpəl/ *n* **1** a small thin piece of metal with ends that bend, used in order to hold pieces of paper together or to hold something in place ‖ 종이를 함께 매어 묶거나 사물을 한곳에 고정시키는 데 쓰이는 양 끝이 굽은 작고 가는 금속 조각. 꺾쇠. 스테이플러용 철침 **2** a food that is needed and used all the time ‖ 항시 필요하여 쓰이는 식품. 기본[필수] 식품: *staples like flour and rice* 밀가루나 쌀 같은 기본 식품 – **staple** *adj*

staple² *v* [T] to fasten things together with a STAPLE ‖ 스테이플로 물건을 서로 고정시키다. 철하다

sta·pler /'steɪplɚ/ *n* a tool used for putting STAPLEs through paper, wood etc. ‖ 종이·나무 등에 철침을 박아 넣는 데 쓰이는 도구. 스테이플러

star¹ /star/ *n* **1** a very large amount of burning gases in space, that looks like a point of light in the sky at night ‖ 밤하늘에서 빛의 점같이 보이는 우주 공간의 매우 큰 불타고 있는 가스 덩어리. 별. 항성 **2** a shape with five or six points sticking out of it, that is sometimes used as a sign of quality or rank ‖ 때로는 품질 또는 계급의 표시로 사용되는 5개 또는 6개의 꼭지점이 돌출해 있는 형상. 별 모양(의 것). 별표 **3** a famous performer in entertainment or sports ‖ 연예계 또는 스포츠계의 유명한 공연자·경기자. 유명인. 인기연예인[선수]: *a movie star* 인기 영화 배우 **4** INFORMAL someone who is particularly good at something ‖ 어떤 것에 특별히 능숙한 사람. 대가. 거장. 거물: *Jim is definitely our star player.* 짐은 확실히 우리의 주전 선수이다. **5 the stars/sb's stars** the power of the stars to affect what happens, that some people believe in ‖ 일부 사람들이 믿는, 장래 일어나는 일에 영향을 미치는 별의 힘. (운수에 영향을 미친다고 생각되는) 타고난 별/사람의 운수

star² *v* -**rred, -rring** **1** [T] if a movie, play etc. stars someone, that person acts the part of the main character ‖ 영화·연극 등에서 어떤 사람이 주인공역을 연기하다. 주연 출연하다: *a movie starring Bruce Willis* 브루스 윌리스 주연의 영화 **2** [I] to act the part of the main character in a movie, play etc. ‖ 영화·연극 등에서의 주인공의 역할을 맡다. (배우 등이) …에 주인공 역을 맡다: *This is her first time starring in a TV comedy.* TV 코미디에서 그녀가 주연을 한 것은 이번이 처음이다.

star·board /'starbɚd/ *n* [U] the right side of a ship or aircraft when you are looking toward the front ‖ 전면을 향해 보았을 때 선박 또는 항공기의 오른쪽. 우측(진행) 방향. 우현(右舷)

starch¹ /startʃ/ *n* **1** [C, U] a substance in such foods as bread, rice, and potatoes ‖ 빵·쌀·감자 등의 식품에 들어 있는 물질. 녹말. 전분 **2** [U] a substance used for making cloth stiff ‖ 옷을 빳빳하게 하는 데 쓰이는 물질. 풀

starch² *v* [T] to make cloth stiff using STARCH ‖ 풀을 사용하여 옷을 빳빳하게 하다. …에 풀을 먹이다

starch·y /'startʃi/ *adj* containing a lot of STARCH ‖ 녹말을 많이 함유한: *starchy foods* 녹말이 많이 들어 있는 식품

star·dom /'stardəm/ *n* [U] the situation of being a famous performer ‖ 유명 연기자가 되어 있는 상황. 스타의 지위[신분]

stare¹ /stɛr/ *v* [I] **1** to look at someone

or something for a long time without moving your eyes ‖ 눈을 움직이지 않고 장시간 동안 사람 또는 물체를 바라보다. 응시하다. 노려보다. 말똥말똥 쳐다보다: *Stop staring at me!* 나를 빤히 쳐다보지 마세요! **2 be staring sb in the face** INFORMAL to be very clear and easy to see or understand; OBVIOUS ‖ 보거나 이해하기에 매우 분명하고 쉽다. (사실 등이) …에게 명백해지다. 바로 눈앞에 있다; ⓢ obvious

stare² *n* the expression on your face when you STARE ‖ 사람이 응시할 때 얼굴의 표정

star·fish /'star,fɪʃ/ *n* a flat sea animal that is shaped like a star ‖ 별 같은 모양으로 되어 있는 납작한 바다 동물. 불가사리

stark¹ /stark/ *adj* **1** very simple and severe in appearance ‖ 외양이 매우 단순하고 모진. 불모의. 황량한: *the stark beauty of the desert* 사막의 황량한 아름다움 **2** unpleasantly clear and impossible to avoid ‖ 불쾌하게 분명하고 피하기가 불가능한. 엄연한. 적나라한: *the stark realities of drug addiction* 마약 중독의 엄연한 현실 **– starkly** *adv*

stark² *adv* **stark naked** INFORMAL not wearing any clothes ‖ 아무 옷도 입지 않은. 벌거벗은

star·let /'starlɪt/ *n* a young actress who plays small parts in movies and is hoping to become famous ‖ 영화에서 작은 배역의 연기를 하면서 유명하게 되기를 바라고 있는 젊은 여배우. 장래가 촉망되는 젊은 여배우

star·light /'starlaɪt/ *n* [U] the light that comes from the stars ‖ 별에서 오는 빛. 별빛

star·ling /'starlɪŋ/ *n* a common European bird that is black and slightly green ‖ 검고 약간 녹색인 흔한 유럽의 새. 찌르레기

star·lit /'star,lɪt/ *adj* made brighter by the light of the stars ‖ 별빛으로 더욱 밝아진. 별빛의. 별이 총총한: *a starlit night* 별이 총총한 밤

star·ry /'stari/ *adj* having many stars ‖ 별이 많은: *a starry sky* 별이 총총한 하늘

starry-eyed /'.. ,./ *adj* INFORMAL hopeful about things in a way that is silly or unreasonable ‖ 바보 같고 비합리적으로 사물에 대해 희망에 찬. 몽상적인. 비현실적인: *a starry-eyed teenager* 공상적인 눈초리를 한 10대

Stars and Stripes /,. . './ *n* [singular] the flag of the US ‖ 미국 국기. 성조기

Star-Span·gled Ban·ner /,. .. '../ *n* [singular] the national ANTHEM (=song) of the US ‖ 미국 국가(國歌)

star-stud·ded /'. ,../ *adj* including many famous performers ‖ 많은 유명 연기자를 포함하는. 기라성 같은 저명인사들이 죽 늘어선. (쇼 등이) 유명 스타들이 참석한: *a star-studded cast* 유명 배우들이 기라성처럼 줄이은 배역

start¹ /start/ *v*

1 ▶BEGIN DOING STH …하기를 시작하다◀ [I, T] to begin doing something ‖ 어떤 것을 하기 시작하다. 시작되다: *Have you started making dinner?* 저녁 식사를 만들기 시작했니? / *I didn't start work until 9:30.* 나는 9시 30분까지는 일을 시작하지 않았다. / *It's starting to rain.* 비가 오기 시작했다.

2 ▶BEGIN HAPPENING 일어나기 시작하다◀ [I, T] to begin happening, or to make something do this ‖ 일어나기 시작하다, 또는 어떤 것을 이렇게 하게 하다. 나타나다. 생기다. 발생하다: *The race starts in 10 minutes.* 경주는 10분 후에 시작된다. / *The fire was started by a loose wire.* 화재는 낡은 전선이 발단이 되어 일어났다.

3 to start with SPOKEN **a)** said in order to emphasize the first of a list of facts or opinions ‖ 사실 또는 의견의 나열 중 첫번째를 강조하는 데 쓰여. 우선. 첫째로. 맨 먼저: *There's a lot wrong with those kids; to start with, they're rude.* 그 아이들은 나쁜 점이 많아요. 무엇보다도 무례하지요. **b)** said when talking about the beginning of a situation that later changes ‖ 나중에는 바뀌는 상황의 시작 단계에 대해 말할 때 쓰여. 처음에는: *I was nervous to start with, but then I was fine.* 처음에 나는 긴장했었지만 그리고 나서는 적응이 되었다.

4 ▶JOB/SCHOOL 직장/학교◀ [I, T] to begin a new job, or to begin going to school, college etc. ‖ 새로운 직무를 시작하다, 또는 학교·대학 등에 다니기 시작하다: *How soon can you start?* 얼마나 일찍 (일을)시작할 수 있지요? / *Mark's starting school/college in the fall.* 마크는 가을에 학교[대학교]를 가려고 한다.

5 ▶TRIP 여행◀ [I] also **start off/out** to begin a trip ‖ 여행을 시작하다. 출발하다/떠나다: *You'll have to start early if you want to get there by noon.* 정오까지 거기 도착하고 싶으면 일찍 출발해야 할 것이다. / *We didn't get started until after dark.* 우리는 날이 어두워질 때까지 출발하지 않았다.

6 ▶CAR 자동차◀ [I, T] also **start up** if

you start a car or engine, or if it starts, it begins to work ‖ 자동차나 엔진이 작동하기 시작하다. …을 시동하다: *Can't you get that engine started?* 그 엔진을 시동걸 수 없니?

7 ▶ROAD/RIVER 도로/강◀ [I] if a road, river etc. starts somewhere, it begins in that place ‖ 도로·강 등이 어떤 곳에서 시작하다. 기점하다. 발원하다: *The Red River starts in New Mexico.* 레드 강은 뉴멕시코에서 발원한다.

8 ▶PRICES 가격◀ [I] if prices start at or from a particular figure, that is the lowest figure at which you can buy something ‖ 가격이 어떤 것을 살 수 있는 가장 낮은 액수에 있다. 최저가에서 시작하다[출발하다]

9 ▶BUSINESS/CLUB 사업/클럽◀ [T] also **start up** to make something begin to exist ‖ 어떤 것을 존재하기 시작하게 하다. 설립하다. (사업 등을) 일으키다: *Sally decided to start up a club for single mothers.* 샐리는 미혼모를 위한 클럽을 설립하기로 결정했다.

10 ▶MOVE SUDDENLY 갑자기 움직이다◀ [I] to move suddenly because you are surprised or afraid ‖ 사람이 놀라거나 두려워서 갑자기 움직이다. 펄쩍 뛰어[날아]오르다. 움찔[흠칫]하다

start sb/sth ↔ **off** *phr v* [I, T] to begin an activity, or to help someone do this ‖ 활동을 시작하다, 또는 사람이 이렇게 하는 것을 돕다: *Let's start off by reviewing what we did last week.* 우리가 지난주에 한 것을 검토하는 것으로 시작합시다.

start on *phr v* [T] **1** [**start on** sth] to begin working on something ‖ 어떤 것에 대한 일을 시작하다. 개시하다. 착수하다: *You'd better get started on your homework.* 네 숙제를 시작하는 것이 좋겠다. **2** [**start** sb **on** sth] to make someone start doing or using something ‖ 사람으로 하여금 어떤 것을 하거나 사용하기 시작하게 하다. …을 시작하게[쓰게] 하다: *How old was she when you started her on solid food?* 네가 그녀에게 고형식을 먹이기 시작했을 때 그녀는 몇 살이었니?

start over *phr v* [I] to start doing something again from the beginning so that you can correct what was wrong the first time ‖ 첫 번째 할 때의 잘못이었던 것을 고칠 수 있도록 어떤 것을 처음부터 다시 시작하다. 원점에서 다시 시작하다. 새출발하다: *Coming back home was like a chance to start over.* 집에 돌아오는 것은 새출발할 기회 같았다.

USAGE NOTE start and begin

Usually, these words mean the same thing. However **start** has some special meanings for which **begin** cannot be used. Use **start** to talk about making a machine work: *Bob couldn't start the car. You should also use* **start** to talk about making something begin to exist: *Starting a new business is hard work.* 보통 이 두 말은 같은 의미이다. 그렇지만 **start**는 **begin**이 사용될 수 없는 몇몇 특별한 의미를 갖고 있다. 기계를 작동시키는 데 대해 말을 할 때는 **start**를 사용한다: 보브는 차를 시동할 수 없었다. 사물이 존재하기 시작하게 하는 데 대해 말할 때 또한 **start**를 사용해야 한다: 신규 사업을 개시한다는 것은 어려운 일이다.

---

start² *n* **1** the beginning of an activity, event, or situation ‖ 활동[사건, 상황]의 시작. 시초. 개시: *Hurry, or we'll miss the start of the show.* 서둘러라, 그렇지 않으면 우리는 쇼의 시작을 놓치게 될 것이다. / *They've had problems (right) from the start.* 그것은 (바로)시작부터 문제가 있었다. / *It was a close race from start to finish.* 그것은 처음부터 끝까지 우열을 가리기 힘든 경주였다. **2 it's a start** used in order to say that something you have achieved may not be impressive, but it will help with a bigger achievement ‖ 사람이 성취한 일이 대단하지는 않을지라도 그것이 보다 큰 성취를 이루는 데 도움이 될 것이란 것을 말하는 데 쓰여. (지금은) 단지 시작일 뿐이야: *We only have $92 million of the $600 million needed, but it's a start.* 우리는 필요한 6억 달러 중에서 9천 2백만 달러만 있을 뿐이지만 그것은 단지 시작일 뿐이야. **3 for a start** INFORMAL said in order to emphasize the first of a list of facts or opinions ‖ 사실 또는 의견의 목록 중에서 첫 번째를 강조하는 데 쓰여. 우선. 첫 번째로. 맨 먼저: *I don't think she'll get the job. She's too young, for a start.* 나는 그녀가 직장을 얻을 것이라고는 생각하지 않는다. 우선 첫 번째로 그녀는 너무 어려. **4** [singular] a sudden movement caused by fear or surprise ‖ 공포 또는 경악에 의해 발생된 갑작스런 동작. 움찔[흠칫]하기. 놀라기: *Ed woke up with a start.* 에드는 깜짝 놀라 잠을 깨었다.

start·er /'stɑrtɚ/ *n* **1** a person, horse etc. that is in a race when it starts ‖ 경

주가 시작될 때 참가해 있는 사람·말 등.
출전자[마(馬)]: *Of the eight starters,
only three finished the race.* 8명의 출전
자 중에서 오로지 3명만이 경주를 마쳤다.
2 someone who gives the signal for a
race to begin ‖ 경주의 시작 신호를 하는
사람. (경주 등의) 스타트 담당자 **3** also
starter motor a piece of equipment
for starting an engine ‖ 엔진을 시동하는
장치. 시동기. 스타터

start·ing line·up /,.. '../ *n* the best
players on a sports team, who play
when the game begins ‖ 경기 시작시에
경기를 하는 스포츠 팀의 최고 선수들. 선
발 출장 선수

star·tle /'stɑrtl/ *v* [T] to make someone
suddenly surprised or slightly shocked ‖
사람을 갑자기 놀라게 하거나 약간 충격
받게 하다. …을 깜짝 놀라게 하다: *The
sudden noise behind her startled her.* 그
녀의 뒤에서 들려온 갑작스런 소음이 그녀
를 놀라게 했다. - **startling** *adj* :
startling news 놀랄 만한 뉴스

start-up /'. ./ *adj* start-up costs are
related to beginning and developing a
new business ‖ 비용이 새로운 기업을 설
립하여 발전시키는 데 관련된. 조업 개시
를 위한. 이제 막 활동을 시작한

star·va·tion /stɑr'veɪʃən/ *n* [U]
suffering or death caused by not having
enough to eat ‖ 충분히 먹지 못해서 생긴
고통 또는 죽음. 기아[아사](상태). 굶주
림

starve /stɑrv/ *v* **1** [I, T] to suffer or die
because you do not have enough to eat,
or to make someone do this ‖ 음식을 충
분히 먹지 못하여 고통 받거나 죽다, 또는
사람을 이렇게 되게 하다. 굶어죽다. …을
굶겨 죽이다: *animals that have been
starved to death* 굶어서 죽은 동물들 /
starving refugees 배고픈 피난민들 **2 be
starving/starved** SPOKEN to be very
hungry ‖ 매우 굶주리다: *When do we
eat? I'm starving!* 우리 언제 밥을 먹지?
배고파단 말이야! **3 be starved for/of
sth** to not be given something very
important ‖ 아주 중요한 것이 주어지지
않다. 결핍되다. 굶주리다: *That poor
kid's just starved for attention.* 저 불행
한 아이는 애정에 굶주려 있다.

stash¹ /stæʃ/ *v* [T] INFORMAL to keep
something in a safe, often secret, place
‖ 물건을 안전한 종종 아무도 모르는 장소
에 보관하다. …을 간수해 두다. 숨겨 두
다: *He has money stashed away in a
Swiss bank.* 그는 스위스 은행에 돈을 숨
겨두었다.

stash² *n* INFORMAL an amount of

something, especially an illegal drug,
that is kept in a secret place ‖ 비밀 장소
에 보관 중인, 특히 불법 마약의 분량. 숨
겨진 것[마약]

state¹ /steɪt/ *n* **1** the condition that
someone or something is in at a
particular time ‖ 사람 또는 사물이 특정
한 시간에 처해 있는 상태. 사정. 형세:
Your car's in a bad state. 네 차는 상태가
나쁘다. / *The driver was in a state of
shock.* 그 운전자는 쇼크 상태에 있었다.
/ *You can't take a test in this state of
mind.* 너는 이러한 마음 상태로는 시험을
칠 수 없다. **2** also **State** one of the
areas with limited law-making powers
that some countries, such as the US,
are divided into ‖ 미국 등 몇몇 국가에서
분할되어 제한된 입법권을 가진 영역
의 하나. 주(州). 주정부. 주당국: *the
state of Oklahoma* 오클라호마 주 **3** [C,
U] also **State** a country or its
government ‖ 국가 또는 그 정부. 중앙 정
부: *a meeting between heads of state* 주
지사 회의 **4** [U] the official ceremonies
and events relating to governments and
rulers ‖ 정부와 통치자에 관련된 공식적
인 의식과 행사. 국가적 행사: *the
President's state visit to Moscow* 대통령
의 모스크바 공식 방문 **5 be in a
state/get into a state** SPOKEN to be or
become very nervous or anxious ‖ 매우
초조하거나 걱정스러운 상태에 있다[되
다]. …한 상태다/상태에 빠지다 ─see
usage note at RACE¹

state² *v* [T] FORMAL **1** to give a piece of
information or your opinion about
something by saying or writing it clearly
‖ 어떤 것에 대하여 분명히 말하거나 글을
써서 정보나 자신의 의견을 주다. …을 분
명히[정식으로, 정확히] 말하다. 공표하
다: *The witness stated that he had
never seen the woman before.* 그 증인은
그 여자를 전에 본 적이 없다고 말했다. **2**
if a document, ticket etc. states
information, it contains the information
written clearly ‖ 문서·입장권 등이 분명
하게 문자화된 정보를 포함하다. (날짜·
가격 등을) 지정하다. 정하다

state·ly /'steɪtli/ *adj* impressive in style
or size ‖ 양식 또는 크기에서 인상적인. 당
당한. 장중한. 장엄한: *a stately mansion*
대저택

state·ment /'steɪtmənt/ *n* **1** an
opinion or a piece of information that is
spoken or written officially and publicly
‖ 공식적이며 공개적으로 언명된 또는 문
서화된 의견 또는 정보. 성명(서). 발표:
The company will make a statement

about the accident later today. 회사는 오늘 늦게 그 사고에 관하여 성명을 발표할 것이다. **2** a list showing amounts of money paid, received etc. and their total ‖ 지출·수입의 금액과 그 총액을 나타내는 목록. 계산서[표]. 계좌 수지 보고서: *a bank statement* 은행의 계좌 수지 보고서 **3 make a statement** to do something that shows your beliefs or political opinions ‖ 자신의 신념 또는 정치적 견해를 나타내는 것을 하다. 성명[주장]을 발표하다. (의견을) 표현하다: *Why get your nose pierced? Are you trying to make a statement?* 너는 어째서 코를 뚫었니? 자기 표현[주장]을 하려는 거니?

state-of-the-art /ˌ. . ˈ./ *adj* using the newest methods, materials, or knowledge ‖ 최신의 방법[재료, 지식]을 사용하는. 최첨단 기술을 사용한. 최신식의: *state-of-the-art technology* 최첨단 기술

States /steɪts/ *n* INFORMAL **the States** the US ‖ 미국

states·man /ˈsteɪtsmən/, **stateswom·an** /ˈsteɪts,wʊmən/ *n* a political or government leader, especially one who is known as being wise and fair ‖ 정계나 정부의 지도자, 특히 지혜롭고 공정한 것으로 알려진 사람. 정치가 – **statesmanlike** *adj* – **statesmanship** *n* [U]

stat·ic[1] /ˈstætɪk/ *adj* **1** not moving, changing, or developing ‖ 움직이지 않는 [변화하지 않는, 발전하지 않는]. 정적인. 정지된: *static prices* 변화가 없는 가격 **2** static electricity collects on the surface of objects and can give you a small electric shock ‖ 전기가 물체의 표면에 모여서 사람에게 작은 전기 쇼크를 줄 수 있는. 정전기의

static[2] *n* [U] noise caused by electricity in the air that spoils the sound on a radio or TV ‖ 라디오 또는 텔레비전의 소리를 망쳐놓는 대기 중의 전기에 의해 일어나는 잡음. 공전(空電)에 의한 전파 방해

sta·tion[1] /ˈsteɪʃən/ *n* **1** a place where public vehicles stop so that passengers can get on and off, goods can be loaded etc. ‖ 대중교통편이 승객들이 타거나 내리도록 정차하며 화물 등을 실을 수 있는 장소. 정거장: *a bus/train station* 버스[기차] 정류장[역] **2** a building or place that is a center for a particular type of service or activity ‖ 특정한 유형의 서비스 또는 활동을 위한 중심지가 되는 건물 또는 장소. 서(署). 국(局). 사업소: *a*

police station 경찰서 / *a gas station* 주유소 **3** a company that broadcasts on radio or television, or its programs that you receive ‖ 라디오 또는 텔레비전으로 방송하는 회사, 또는 그의 수신 프로그램. 방송(국): *a country music station* 컨트리 뮤직 방송국

sta·tion[2] *v* [T] to put someone in a particular place in order to do a particular job or military duty ‖ 특정한 직무 또는 군사적 임무를 수행하기 위해 특정한 장소에 사람을 두다. 배치하다. 주둔시키다: *My uncle's stationed in Germany right now.* 나의 삼촌은 지금 독일에 배치되어 있다.

sta·tion·a·ry /ˈsteɪʃəˌnɛri/ *adj* not moving ‖ 움직이지 않는. 정지한: *a stationary vehicle* 정지한 차량

sta·tion·er·y /ˈsteɪʃəˌnɛri/ *n* [U] materials that you use for writing, such as paper, pens, pencils etc. ‖ 종이·펜·연필 등 글 쓰는 데에 사용하는 재료들. 문방구. 필기 용구

station wag·on /ˈ.. ˌ../ *n* a car with a door at the back, and a lot of space for boxes, cases etc. ‖ 뒤쪽에 문이 있고 상자·용기 등을 넣는 공간이 큰 차. 스테이션 왜건 —see picture on page 943

sta·tis·tic /stəˈtɪstɪk/ *n* [singular] a single number that represents a fact or measurement ‖ 어떤 진상 또는 측정치를 나타내는 하나의 수. 통계량. 통계치: *Is he aware of the statistic that two out of three marriages fail?* 3쌍 중 2쌍은 결혼에 실패한다는 통계를 그는 알고 있습니까? – **statistical** *adj* : *statistical analysis* 통계적인 분석 – **statistically** *adv*

stat·is·ti·cian /ˌstætəsˈtɪʃən/ *n* someone who works with STATISTICS ‖ 통계로 업무를 보는 사람. 통계가. 통계학자

sta·tis·tics /stəˈtɪstɪks/ *n* **1** [plural] a collection of numbers that represent facts or measurements ‖ 사실 또는 측정한 양을 나타내는 수의 모음. 통계: *Statistics show that 35% of new businesses fail in their first year.* 통계는 신생 기업의 35%가 그 첫 해에 망한다는 것을 보여 준다. **2** [U] the science of dealing with and explaining such numbers ‖ 그러한 수들을 처리하고 설명하는 학문. 통계학

stat·ue /ˈstætʃu/ *n* something that looks like a person or animal, and is made of stone, metal etc. ‖ 돌·금속 등으로 만들어진 사람이나 동물 모양의 물체. 상(像). 조상. 입상. 소상

stat·u·ette /ˌstætʃuˈɛt/ *n* a very small

STATUE ‖ 아주 작은 조상(彫像)

stat·ure /'stætʃər/ n [U] FORMAL **1** the degree to which someone is admired or regarded as important ‖ 사람이 칭송되거나 중요하게 여겨지는 정도. 명성. 평판: *a musician of great stature* 위대한 음악가 **2** someone's height ‖ 사람의 키. 신장

sta·tus /'steɪtəs, 'stæ-/ n **1** [C, U] the legal or official position or condition of a person, group, country etc. ‖ 사람·집단· 국가 등의 법적 또는 공식적인 지위나 상태. 신분. 상황: *Please state your name, age and marital status.* (=whether you are married or not) 이름·나이·결혼 여부를 말하세요. **2** [U] a high social position that makes people recognize and respect you ‖ 사람들이 인식하고 존경하게 하는 높은 사회적 지위. 높은 지위: *a status symbol* (=something that shows your high social position) 지위[신분]의 상징 **3 the status of sth** what is happening at a particular time in a situation ‖ 어떤 상황의 특정한 시간에 일어나고 있는 일. (사물의) 상태: *No one would comment on the status of her application.* 그녀의 지원 상황에 대해서 아무도 언급하려고 하지 않았다.

status quo /ˌsteɪtəs 'kwoʊ, ˌstæ-/ n the state of a situation at a particular time ‖ 특정한 시간에서의 상황의 상태. 현재의 상황. 현상(現狀)

stat·ute /'stætʃut/ n FORMAL a law or rule that has been formally written down ‖ 정식으로 기록된 법률 또는 규칙. 법령. 법규

stat·u·to·ry /'stætʃəˌtɔri/ adj FORMAL fixed or controlled by law ‖ 법에 의해 정해지거나 통제된. 법정(法定)의: *statutory rights* 법으로 정한 권리

statutory rape /ˌ.... './ n the crime of having sex with someone who is below a particular age ‖ 특정 연령 이하의 사람과 성교하는 범죄. 법정(法定) 강간. 미성년자에 대한 강간

staunch¹ /stɔntʃ, stantʃ/ adj very loyal ‖ 매우 충실한. 견실한. 확고한. 충직한: *a staunch supporter* 확고한 지지자 – **staunchly** adv

staunch² v [T] to stop the flow of a liquid, especially of blood from a wound ‖ 액체 특히 상처에서 피가 흐르는 것을 막다. 지혈하다. 유출을 멎게 하다

stave /steɪv/ v

stave sth ↔ **off** phr v [T] to stop someone or something from reaching you or affecting you for a period of time ‖ 사람 또는 사물이 일정 기간 동안 자신에게 도달하거나 영향을 미치는 것을 막다. 가까이 하지 않다. (재해·위험 등을) 저지하다: *White blood cells stave off infection and disease.* 백혈구는 감염과 질병을 저지한다.

stay¹ /steɪ/ v **1** [I] to continue to be in a particular position, place, or state ‖ 특정한 위치[장소, 상태]에 계속 있다. 머무르다. 남아 있다: *How long is it going to stay this cold?* 이 추위가 얼마나 오래 계속될까? / *Stay right there! I'll be back in a minute.* 바로 저기에 있어! 곧 돌아올게. / *Stay away from my wife!* 내 마누라에게서 떨어져! / *I had to stay late at work.* 나는 밤늦게까지 일해야 했다. / *I stayed up* (=stayed awake) *all night.* 나는 밤새 자지 않고 깨어 있었다. / *Are you going to stay in* (=not leave your home) *tonight?* 너 오늘 밤에 집에 있을 거니? / *Someone has to stay behind* (=stay after others have left) *and clean up this mess.* 누군가는 남아서 이 쓰레기를 청소해야 한다. **2** [I] to live in a place for a short time as a visitor or guest ‖ 방문객 또는 손님으로 잠시 어떤 장소에서 산다. 묵다. 체재하다: *She's staying with us for a week.* 그녀는 우리와 함께 일주일 동안 묵고 있다. / *Where are you staying while you're here?* 이곳에 있는 동안 어디에 묵을 거니? ✗DON'T SAY "Where do you stay?"✗ "Where do you stay?"라고는 하지 않는다 **3 stay put** INFORMAL to remain in one place and not move ‖ 한 장소에 남아 있고 움직이지 않다. 그대로 있다. 제자리에 있다.

stay on phr v [I] to continue to do a job or to study after the usual or expected time for leaving ‖ 평상시 또는 떠나기로 예정된 시간 이후에도 직무 또는 공부를 계속하다. 계속 남아 있다. 유임하다: *Rachelle is staying on for a fifth year in college.* 레이첼은 대학에 5년째 계속 남아 있다.

stay² n **1** a limited time of living in a place ‖ 어떤 장소에서 사는 한정된 시간. 체재 기간: *a stay in the hospital* 병원 입원 **2** [C, U] LAW the stopping or delay of an action because a judge has ordered it ‖ 판사가 명령했기 때문에 행위[활동]가 중단되거나 연기되는 것. (집행의) 일시 정지. 소송의 중단

stead·fast /'stɛdfæst/ adj LITERARY faithful and very loyal ‖ 충실하고 매우 성실한. 견실한. 확고한: *Carlos remained steadfast in his beliefs.* 칼로스는 자신의 신념에 변함이 없었다.

stead·y¹ /'stɛdi/ adj **1** firmly in one place without moving, shaking, or falling ‖ 움직이지[흔들리지, 떨어지지] 않

고 한 장소에 굳건히 있는. 확고한. 고정된: *Keep the ladder steady.* 사다리를 흔들리지 않게 하라. **2** moving, happening, or developing in a continuous gradual way ‖ 끊임없이 점진적으로 움직이는[발생하는, 발전하는]. 끊임없는. 한결 같은. 규칙적인: *steady progress* 꾸준한 전진 **3** a steady level, speed etc. stays about the same ‖ 수준·속도 등이 대체로 동일하게 유지되는. 일정한. 불변의 **4 steady job/work/income** a job etc. that will continue over a long period of time ‖ 장시간 동안 계속될 직장 등. 안정된[정해진] 직업/일/수입 **– steadily** *adv* **– steadiness** *n* [U] —opposite UNSTEADY

steady² *v* [I, T] to become more calm or controlled, or to make someone or something do this ‖ 더욱 진정되거나 더 통제되다, 또는 사람이나 사물을 이렇게 하게 하다. …을 고정[안정]되다[시키다]. (남을) 침착하게 하다: *"Watch the steps," he said, steadying her with his hand.* "발밑을 조심해."라고 그는 자신의 손으로 그녀를 진정시키면서 말했다.

steady³ *adv* **go steady (with sb)** to have a long romantic relationship with someone ‖ 남과 장기간 연애 관계를 가지다. (정해진 한 사람의 이성과만) 데이트하다 **– steady** *n*

steak /steɪk/ *n* [C, U] a thick flat piece of meat or fish ‖ 두껍고 편평한 고기 또는 생선 조각. 스테이크

steal¹ /stil/ *v* **stole, stolen, stealing** **1** [I, T] to take something that belongs to someone else without his/her permission, and not give it back ‖ 허락 없이 다른 사람이 소유한 물건을 가져가고 돌려주지 않다. …을 훔치다. 도둑질하다: *Two local men were arrested for stealing a car.* 두 명의 지방 남자가 차량 절도 혐의로 체포되었다. / *When did you find out your partner was stealing from you?* 파트너가 당신 것을 훔치고 있다는 것을 언제 알았습니까? —see usage note at ROB ‖ **2** [I] LITERARY to move quietly without anyone noticing you ‖ 아무도 모르게 조용히 움직이다. …을 몰래 움직이다

steal² *n* INFORMAL something that costs much less than it is worth ‖ 그 가치보다 훨씬 적은 비용이 든 사물. 거저나 다름없이 입수한 물건. 횡재: *At $15 a bottle, their Merlot is a real steal.* 1병에 15달러이니까 그들의 멀롯 포도주는 정말 횡재야.

stealth /stɛlθ/ *n* [U] the action of doing something quietly and secretly ‖ 조용히 비밀리에 어떤 것을 하는 행위. 은밀히[몰래] 하기 **– stealthily** *adv* : *moving stealthily* 몰래 움직이기 **– stealthy** *adj*

steam¹ /stim/ *n* **1** [U] the gas that water produces when it is boiled ‖ 물이 끓을 때 발생하는 가스. (수)증기. 김: *a steam engine* (=that uses steam to operate) 증기 기관(차) **2 let/work/ blow off steam** to get rid of your anger, excitement, or energy by shouting or doing something active ‖ 소리를 지르거나 적극적인 일을 하여 분노[흥분, 힘]를 제거하다. 울분을 발산시키다 **3 run out of steam** to no longer have the energy or the support you need to continue doing something ‖ 어떤 것을 계속하는 데에 필요한 에너지나 지원이 더 이상 없다. 힘이 다하다

steam² *v* [U] **1** [I] to send out steam ‖ 증기를 내보내다. 발산[증발]하다: *steaming coffee* 김이 나는 커피 **2** [T] to cook something using steam ‖ 증기를 이용하여 어떤 것을 요리하다. …을 찌다: *Steam the vegetables for five minutes.* 5분 동안 채소를 쪄라.

steam sth ↔ **up** *phr v* [I, T] to cover or be covered with steam ‖ 증기로 덮거나 덮이다. 증기로 흐리다. 김이 서리다: *My glasses are steamed up.* 내 안경은 김이 서려 있다.

steam·roll /'stimroul/ *v* [T] INFORMAL to defeat an opponent or force someone to do something by using all your power or influence ‖ 자신의 모든 힘이나 영향력을 써서 반대자를 패배시키거나 어떤 사람에게 강제로 어떤 것을 하게 하다. 반대를 물리치다. …을 제압하다. …을 강제하다

steam·roll·er /'stim,roulɚ/ *n* a heavy vehicle with very wide wheels for making road surfaces flat ‖ 도로 표면을 편평하게 하는 매우 큰 바퀴가 있는 무거운 차량. (도로 공사용의) 스팀롤러

steam·y /'stimi/ *adj* **1** full of steam, or covered with steam ‖ 수증기로 가득 찬, 또는 수증기로 덮인. 김이 자욱한: *steamy windows* 김으로 흐린 창문들 **2** sexually exciting ‖ 성적으로 흥분시키는. 에로틱한. 관능적인: *a steamy love scene* 에로틱한 러브 신

steel¹ /stil/ *n* [U] **1** a strong hard metal that can be shaped easily, made of iron and CARBON ‖ 철과 탄소로 만들어져 쉽게 모양을 만들 수 있는 강하고 단단한 금속. 강철 **2 nerves of steel** the ability to be brave and calm in a dangerous or difficult situation ‖ 위험하거나 힘든 상황에서 용감하고 침착할 수 있는 능력. 강인한 신경

steel² *v* [T] **steel yourself** to prepare

yourself to do something that you know will be unpleasant ‖ 불쾌하리라고 알고 있는 일을 하기 위해 스스로 준비하다. … 하려고 결심하다. 마음을 굳게 먹다

steel wool /ˌ. ˈ./ n [U] a rough material made of steel wires, used in order to make surfaces smooth, remove paint etc. ‖ 표면을 부드럽게 하고 칠을 제거하는 등에 쓰이는 강철 선으로 만든 거친 물질. (연마용) 강철 솜. 강면(鋼綿)

steel·y /ˈstili/ adj extremely strong and determined ‖ 매우 강하고 단호한. 강철 같은 . 견고한 . 무정한: a steely expression 냉혹한 표정

steep¹ /stip/ adj 1 a road, hill etc. that is steep slopes at a high angle ‖ 도로·언덕 등이 급한 각도로 경사져 있는. 가파른. 경사가 급한 2 a steep increase or rise in something is large and happens quickly ‖ 어떤 것의 증가나 상승이 크고 순식간에 일어난. 급증[급상승]한. 엄청나게 오른 3 INFORMAL steep prices, charges etc. are very expensive ‖ 가격·요금 등이 매우 비싼. 터무니[어처구니]없이 비싼 **– steeply** adv **– steepen** v [I, T]

steep² v [I, T] to put something in a liquid and leave it there, or to be left in a liquid ‖ 어떤 것을 액체에 넣어 놓고 그대로 두다, 또는 액체에 들어 있다. 담겨 있다. 담그다

stee·ple /ˈstipəl/ n a tall pointed tower on a church ‖ 교회의 높고 뾰족한 탑. 첨탑

steer¹ /stɪr/ v 1 [I, T] to control the direction that a vehicle goes in ‖ 차가 나아가는 방향을 제어하다. …을 조종하다: The bumps in the road were making it hard to steer. 도로의 옹기가 방향 조종하는 것을 힘들게 하고 있었다. 2 [T] to influence someone's behavior or the way a situation develops ‖ 어떤 사람의 행동이나 상황이 진전되는 방식에 영향을 미치다. …으로 향하게 하다. 방향을 잡아 주다: Helen tried to steer the conversation away from school. 헬렌은 화제를 학교(이야기)에서 돌리려고 했다. 3 [T] to guide someone to a place ‖ 사람을 어떤 장소로 안내하다. 이끌다: Bobby took my arm and steered me into the next room. 보비는 나의 팔을 잡고 옆방으로 이끌었다. 4 **steer clear (of)** INFORMAL to try to avoid someone or something that is unpleasant ‖ 불쾌한 사람이나 사물을 피하려고 하다. 가까이 가지 않다. …을 피하다

steer² n a young male cow that has had part of its sex organs removed ‖ 생식기

일부를 제거한 어린 수송아지

steer·ing /ˈstɪrɪŋ/ n [U] the parts of a vehicle that allow you to control the direction it goes in ‖ 탈것의 진행 방향을 제어하게 해 주는 부분. (차의) 방향 전환 장치. (배의) 조타 장치

steering wheel /ˈ.. ˌ./ n a wheel that you turn to control the direction a vehicle goes in ‖ 탈것의 진행 방향을 제어하기 위해 돌리는 손잡이. (자동차의) 핸들. (배의) 타륜 **—see picture on page 943**

stel·lar /ˈstɛlɚ/ adj 1 done extremely well ‖ 매우 잘 끝난. 훌륭한. 일류의: a stellar performance 일류의 연기[연주] 2 TECHNICAL relating to the stars ‖ 별에 관련된. 별 같은. 별 모양의

stem¹ /stɛm/ n 1 a long thin part of a plant, from which leaves or flowers grow ‖ 잎이나 꽃이 자라는, 식물의 길고 가는 부분. 줄기. 대 2 the thin part of a wine glass, between the base and the wide top ‖ 기저부와 넓게 벌어진 상부 사이에 있는 포도주 잔의 가는 부분. (술잔 등의) 굽

stem² v -mmed, -mming [T] **stem the tide/flow of** to stop something from spreading or growing ‖ 어떤 것이 퍼지거나 자라는 것을 막다. …을 저지[억지]하다: Even the Great Fire could not stem the tide of immigrants to Chicago. (시카고의) 대 화재조차도 시카고로의 이민 행렬을 막을 수 없었다.

stem from sth phr v [T] to develop as a result of something else ‖ 다른 것의 결과로서 발전하다. …에서 일어나다[생기다]: Her back problems stem from holding her baby on one hip. 그녀의 허리 문제는 아기를 한쪽 엉덩이로 업어서 생긴 것이다.

stem cell /ˈ. ˌ./ n TECHNICAL a special type of cell in the body that can divide in order to form other types of cells that have particular qualities or purposes ‖ 특정한 성질이나 목적을 가진 다른 종류의 세포를 만들기 위해 분리해 낼 수 있는 인체 내의 특수한 종류의 세포. 줄기 세포

stench /stɛntʃ/ n a strong unpleasant smell ‖ 강렬하고 불쾌한 냄새. 악취

sten·cil¹ /ˈstɛnsəl/ n a piece of plastic, paper etc. in which patterns or letters have been cut ‖ 무늬나 문자가 새겨진 플라스틱이나 종이 등. 스텐실. 형판(型板)

stencil² v [T] to put a pattern or letter on a surface by painting or drawing through the holes in a STENCIL ‖ 스텐실의 구멍을 통해 칠하거나 그려서 표면에 무늬나 문자를 넣다. …에 스텐실을 대고

찍다

ste·nog·ra·pher /stə'nɑgrəfɚ/ *n*
someone whose job is to write down
what someone else is saying by
SHORTHAND ∥ 속기를 사용해서 다른 사람
이 말하는 것을 받아 적는 직업인. 속기사
– stenography *n* [U]

step¹ /stɛp/ *n*

1 ▶MOVEMENT 움직임◀ the act of
putting one foot down in front of the
other one in order to move along ∥ 이동
하기 위해 한 발을 다른 발 앞에 내려놓는
동작. (발)걸음. 걸음걸이: *Take two
steps forward and one step back.* 두 걸
음 앞으로 나갔다가 한 걸음 뒤로 가라.

2 ▶ACTION 행동◀ one of a series of
things that you do in order to deal with
a problem or to produce a particular
result ∥ 문제를 처리하거나 특정한 결과를
만들기 위해 하는 일련의 일들 중의 하나.
조치. 단계: *We must take steps* (=take
action) *to make sure it never happens
again.* 다시는 그런 일이 발생하지 않도록
확실한 조치를 취해야 한다. / *an
important first step toward peace* 평화
를 향한 중요한 첫 단계

3 ▶STAIR 계단◀ a flat narrow surface,
especially one in a series, that you put
your foot on when you are going up or
down, especially outside a building ∥ 특
히 건물 밖에 있는 것으로서 올라가거나
내려갈 때 발을 딛는, 특히 연속된 편평하
고 좁은 면. 단(段). 층계. 계단: *Jenny
waited on the church steps.* 제니는 교회
계단에서 기다렸다. **—compare** STAIRs

4 ▶IN A PROCESS 과정 속에서◀ a stage
in a process or a position on a scale ∥ 절
차 속에서의 한 국면 또는 저울 상의 한
위치. 단계. 눈금: *That promotion was
quite a step up for her.* 그 승진은 그녀에
게 대단한 상승이다. **—see also** STEP-BY-
STEP

5 ▶DANCING 춤◀ a movement of your
feet in dancing ∥ 춤출 때 발의 움직임. 스
텝: *I'm always getting the steps wrong.*
난 항상 스텝을 잘못 밟는다.

6 watch your step SPOKEN **a)** to be
careful about what you say or how you
behave ∥ 자신의 말이나 행동거지를 조심
하다. 신중히 행동하다[말하다] **b)** to be
careful when you are walking ∥ 걸을 때
조심하다. 발 밑을 조심하다

7 in step/out of step a) having ideas
that are the same as, or different from,
other people's ∥ 다른 사람들과 똑같이,
또는 전혀 다르게 생각하는. …과 일치하
여/동떨어져: *"Perhaps I haven't kept in
step with the voters,"* Hannigan

admitted. "아마 나는 유권자들과 호흡을
같이 해 오지 못했던 것 같아."라고 해니
건은 인정했다. **b)** moving your feet in
the same way as, or a different way
from, people you are walking or
marching with ∥ 함께 걷거나 행진하는 사
람들과 같게 또는 다르게 발을 움직이는.
…과 보조를 맞추어/맞추지 않고

8 ▶SOUND 소리◀ the sound you make
when you take a step ∥ 한 걸음을 걸을
때 나는 소리. 발소리 **—see also**
FOOTSTEP

step² *v* **-pped, -pping** [I] **1** to put one
foot down in front of the other one in
order to move along ∥ 이동하기 위해 한
발을 다른 발 앞에 내려놓다. 걸음을 옮기
다. 발을 내딛다: *Step aside/back and
let the doctor through.* 옆으로 비켜서서
[뒤로 물러나서] 의사가 지나가게 해라. **2**
to bring your foot down on something ∥
어떤 것에 발을 내려놓다. 밟다: *Yuck!
What did you step in?* 으악! 너 뭘 밟았
냐? **3 step out of line** to behave badly
by doing something that you are not
expected to or told not to do ∥ 할 것으
로 기대되지 않거나 하지 말라고 지시받은
것을 함으로써 나쁘게 행동하다. 벗어난
행동을 하다. 독자적인 행동을 취하다 **4
step on it** SPOKEN said when you want
someone to go somewhere faster,
especially in a car ∥ 특히 차 속에서, 남이
어딘가를 더 빠르게 가기 원할 때 쓰여. 액
셀러레이터를 더 밟다. 급히 서두르다: *If
you don't step on it we'll miss the plane.*
네가 급히 서두르지 않으면 우리는 비행기
를 놓칠 거야. **5 step on sb's toes** to
offend or upset someone, especially by
trying to do his/her work ∥ 특히 남의 일
을 하려고 해서, 그 사람의 기분을 상하게
하거나 화나게 하다. 남의 감정을 해치다

step down/aside *phr v* [I] to leave
your job or official position because you
want to or think you should ∥ 자기가 원
하거나 그렇게 해야 한다고 생각해서 직책
이나 공식적인 지위를 떠나다. 사임[사직]
하다. 물러나다: *He's decided to step
down at the end of the year.* 그는 연말
에 물러나기로 결심했다.

step forward *phr v* [I] to come and
offer help ∥ 와서 도움을 주다. 앞으로 나
서다. 출두하다: *Several volunteers have
kindly stepped forward.* 몇 명의 자원
봉사자들이 고맙게도 나서 주었다.

step in *phr v* [I] to become involved in a
discussion or disagreement, especially
in order to stop the trouble ∥ 특히 말썽
을 막기 위해서 토론이나 불화에 관여하게
되다. 개입하다. 끼어들다: *The referee*

stepped in to separate the players. 심판이 선수들을 떼어놓기 위해 개입했다.

step out *phr v* [I] to go out for a short time || 짧은 시간 동안 밖에 나가다. 잠깐 나가다[외출하다]: *Molly just stepped out but she'll be back soon.* 몰리는 방금 외출했지만 곧 돌아올 겁니다.

step sth ↔ **up** *phr v* [T] to increase the amount of an activity or the speed of a process || 활동량이나 진행 속도를 증가시키다. 늘리다. 증대시키다: *The industry has stepped up efforts to clean up its pollution.* 그 산업은 오염을 정화하려는 노력을 증대시켜 왔다.

step·broth·er /'stɛp₁brʌðɚ/ *n* a boy or man whose father or mother has married your mother or father || 자신의 어머니나 아버지와 결혼한 아버지나 어머니의 어리거나 장성한 아들. 이복[의붓] 형제

step-by-step /₁․․ ․ ʹ․․/ *adj* a step-by-step plan, method etc. deals with things carefully and in a particular order || 계획·방법 등이 일을 주의 깊고 특정한 순서로 다루는. 단계적인

step·child /'stɛp-tʃaɪld/ *n* a child that your husband or wife has from a relationship before your marriage || 남편이나 아내가 자신과의 결혼 전 관계에서 가진 아이. 의붓자식

step·daugh·ter /'stɛp₁dɔtɚ/ *n* a daughter that your husband or wife has from a relationship before your marriage || 남편이나 아내가 자신과의 결혼 전 관계에서 가진 딸. 의붓딸

step·fa·ther /'stɛp₁faðɚ/ *n* a man who is married to your mother but who is not your father || 어머니와 결혼했지만 친아버지는 아닌 남자. 의붓아버지. 계부

step·lad·der /'stɛp₁lædɚ/ *n* a LADDER with two sloping parts that are attached at the top so that it can stand without support || 두 개의 경사진 부분이 꼭대기에서 서로 붙어 있어 받치지 않아도 설 수 있는 사다리. 발판 사다리. 접사다리

step·moth·er /'stɛp₁mʌðɚ/ *n* a woman who is married to your father but who is not your mother || 아버지와 결혼했지만 (친)어머니는 아닌 여자. 의붓어머니. 계모

stepped-up /₁․ ʹ․/ *adj* done more quickly or with more effort than before || 이전보다 더 서둘러서 또는 더 노력을 해서 된. 증가된. 확대된. 강화된: *stepped-up factory production* 증가된 공장 생산량

stepping-stone /'․․ ₁․/ *n* 1 something that helps you to improve or become more successful || 향상하거나 더 성공적으로 될 수 있도록 돕는 것. 디딤돌. 발판: *a stepping-stone to a better job* 더 좋은 직업으로의 디딤돌 2 one of a row of stones that you walk on to get across a stream || 개울을 건너려고 밟는 일렬로 된 돌들 중의 하나. 디딤돌. 징검다리돌

step·sis·ter /'stɛp₁sɪstɚ/ *n* a girl or woman whose father or mother has married your mother or father || 자신의 어머니나 아버지와 결혼한 아버지나 어머니의 어리거나 장성한 딸. 이복[의붓] 자매

step·son /'stɛpsʌn/ *n* a son that your husband or wife has from a relationship before your marriage || 남편이나 아내가 자신과의 결혼 전 관계에서 가진 아들. 의붓아들

ster·e·o /'stɛri₁oʊ, 'stɪr-/ *n* 1 a machine for playing records, CDs etc. that produces sound from two SPEAKERs || 두 개의 스피커에서 소리를 내는, 음반·CD 등을 틀기 위한 기계. 입체 음향 재생 장치. 스테레오 2 **in stereo** if music or a broadcast is in stereo, the sound it makes is directed through two SPEAKERs || 음악이나 방송 소리가 두 개의 스피커를 통해 나와. 입체 음향으로

ster·e·o·type¹ /'stɛriə₁taɪp, 'stɪr-/ *n* an idea of what a particular type of person or thing is like that many people have, and that is wrong or unfair || 특정한 유형의 사람이나 사물은 어떠어떠하다고, 많은 사람들이 가지고 있는 틀리거나 공정하지 못한 생각. 고정 관념 – **stereotypical** /₁stɛrioʊʹtɪpɪkəl/ *adj*

stereotype² *v* [T] DISAPPROVING to decide that some people have particular qualities or abilities because they belong to a particular race, sex etc. || 어떤 사람들이 특정한 인종·성별 등에 속해 있어서 특정한 특성이나 능력을 지니고 있다고 단정하다. …을 고정 관념으로 보다. 정형화하다: *Homeless people are often stereotyped as a bunch of alcoholics.* 종종 노숙자들을 알코올 중독자들의 무리로 보는 고정 관념이다.

ster·ile /'stɛrəl/ *adj* 1 sterile people or animals are not able to produce babies || 사람이나 동물이 아기[새끼]를 낳을 수 없는. 불임의 2 completely clean and not containing any BACTERIA || 완전히 깨끗하며 어떠한 세균도 가지고 있지 않은. 무균의. 살균한: *a sterile bandage* 무균 붕대 3 lacking new ideas or imagination || 새로운 생각이나 상상력이 부족한. 상상력 [독창성]이 결핍된: *sterile concepts* 독창성이 없는 개념 – **sterility** /stəʹrɪləti/ *n* [U]

ster·il·ize /'stɛrə,laɪz/ v [T] **1** to make something completely clean and kill any BACTERIA in it ‖ 어떤 것을 완전히 깨끗하게 하고 그 안의 세균을 모두 죽이다. …을 살균[소독]하다: *sterilized surgery equipment* 소독한 수술 장비 **2** to make a person or animal unable to have children ‖ 사람이나 동물이 아이[새끼]를 가질 수 없게 하다. …을 불임시키다[단종하다] – **sterilization** /ˌstɛrələ'zeɪʃən/ n [C, U]

ster·ling /'stɜrlɪŋ/ adj **sterling quality/effort/character etc.** the best quality, effort etc. ‖ 최고의 자질·노력 등. 훌륭한[진정한] 자질/노력/인품

sterling sil·ver /ˌ.. '../, **sterling** n [U] a metal that is over 92% pure silver ‖ 순은이 92%를 넘는 금속. (법정) 순은

stern¹ /stɜrn/ adj very strict and severe ‖ 매우 엄격하고 심한. 엄정한. 단호한: *stern discipline* 엄한 훈련 / *a stern expression* 단호한 표정 – **sternly** adv

stern² n the back part of a ship ‖ 배의 뒷부분. 고물. 선미

ste·roid /'stɛrɔɪd, 'stɪrɔɪd/ n a drug used especially for treating injuries, that people sometimes use illegally to improve their sports performance ‖ 특히 부상을 치료하는 데에 사용하며 사람들이 불법적으로 운동 능력을 향상시키려고 가끔 사용하는 약물. 스테로이드

steth·o·scope /'stɛθə,skoup/ n an instrument used by doctors to listen to someone's heart or breathing ‖ 의사들이 어떤 사람의 심장이나 호흡 소리를 듣기 위해 사용하는 기구. 청진기

stew¹ /stu/ n a food made of meat and vegetables, cooked in liquid ‖ 고기와 야채를 재료로 하여 액체 상태로 요리된 음식. 스튜 (요리)

stew² v **1** [T] to cook something slowly in liquid ‖ 어떤 것을 천천히 액체 상태로 요리하다. …을 스튜 요리하다: *stewed tomatoes* 토마토 스튜 **2** INFORMAL [I] to worry because of something that has happened or that you have done ‖ 일어났거나 한 일 때문에 걱정하다. 속을 태우다. 조바심하다

stew·ard /'stuəd/ n **1** OLD-FASHIONED a man who is a FLIGHT ATTENDANT ‖ 항공 승무원인 남자. 남자 항공 승무원 **2** also **shop steward** a worker who represents the members of a UNION ‖ 노동조합의 조합원들을 대표하는 근로자. 직장 대표 위원 **3** a man who is responsible for the comfort of the passengers on a ship ‖ 배의 승객들을 편안하게 할 책임을 지는 사람. 승객 담당자

stew·ard·ess /'stuədɪs/ n OLD-FASHIONED a woman who is a FLIGHT ATTENDANT ‖ 항공 승무원인 여자. 여자 항공 승무원

stick¹ /stɪk/ v **stuck, stuck, sticking** **1** [I, T] to attach something to something else using a sticky substance, or to become attached to a surface ‖ 끈적거리는 물질을 사용해서 물체를 다른 물체에 부착하다, 또는 표면에 부착되게 되다. …을 붙이다. (달라)붙다: *Did you remember to stick a stamp on the envelope?* 봉투에 잊지 않고 우표를 붙였니? / *leaves sticking to the windshield* 차 앞유리에 달라붙은 나뭇잎들 **2** [T] INFORMAL to put something somewhere ‖ 물체를 어딘가에 놓다. …을 놓다: *Just stick your coat on that chair.* 그냥 저 의자 위에 네 외투를 놓아라. **3** [I, T] to push a pointed object into something, or to be pushed into something in this way ‖ 뾰족한 물건을 어떤 것에 밀어넣거나, 또는 이렇게 어떤 것에 밀어넣어지다. 찌르다[찔리다]. 꽂다[꽂히다]: *Ow! That pin stuck me!* 아야! 저 핀에 찔렸어! / *There's a nail sticking through the board here.* 이곳에 판자를 뚫고 나온 못이 있다. **4** [I, T] if something sticks or is stuck, it is fixed and difficult to move ‖ 어떤 것이 고정되어 움직이기 어렵다. 옴짝달싹 못하다[못하게 하다]: *Hey, this door is stuck.* 이봐, 이 문은 옴짝달싹 안해.

stick around phr v [I] INFORMAL to stay or wait in a particular place ‖ 특정한 장소에서 머물거나 기다리다. 근처를 떠나지 않다

stick by sb/sth phr v [T] INFORMAL **1** to continue to give your support to someone ‖ 남을 계속 지지하다. 계속 도와주다: *Laura has always stuck by me.* 로라는 항상 나를 계속 도와 주었다. **2** to decide what to do, say, or believe, and not change this ‖ 행할[말할, 믿을] 것을 결정해 놓고 이것을 바꾸지 않다. …을 고수하다: *Barnes is sticking by his decision to testify.* 반즈는 증언하겠다는 결심을 고수하고 있다.

stick out phr v **1** [I] if a part of something sticks out, it comes out further than the rest of a surface or comes out through a hole ‖ 물건의 일부분이 표면의 다른 부분보다 많이 나오거나 구멍을 통해 나오다. 튀어나오다 **2** [T **stick** sth ↔ **out**] to deliberately make something come forward or out ‖ 의도적으로 어떤 것을 앞이나 밖으로 나오게 하다. …을 내밀다: *Jamie stuck out his* *foot to trip his brother.* 제이미는 동생을 넘어뜨리려고 발을 내밀었다. **3 stick out (like a sore thumb)** INFORMAL to look very unsuitable and different from everyone or everything else ‖ 매우 부적절하며 다른 모든 사람이나 사물과 다르게 보이다. (이상한 것으로 인해) 눈에 잘 띄다 **4 stick your neck out** INFORMAL to take the risk of saying or doing something that may be wrong, or that other people may disagree with ‖ 틀리거나 다른 사람들이 동의하지 않을 수도 있는 것을 말하거나 행하는 위험을 감수하다. 위험·잘못을 무릅쓰다[무릅쓰고 … 하다] **5 stick your tongue out (at sb)** to quickly put your tongue outside your mouth and back in again, in order to be rude ‖ 예의 없이 보이게 입 밖으로 혀를 재빨리 내밀었다가 다시 넣다. 조롱하다 **6 stick it out** INFORMAL to continue doing something that is difficult, boring etc. ‖ 어렵고 지루한 일을 계속 하다. 끝까지 견디어 내다

stick to sth *phr v* [T] **1** to decide what to do, say, or believe, and not change this ‖ 행할[말할, 믿을] 것을 결정하고 이것을 바꾸지 않다. …을 고수하다: *That's my story and I'm sticking to it.* 그게 나의 주장이고 나는 그것을 고집하고 있다. / *If you're driving, stick to soft drinks.* 운전을 할 거면 비(非)알코올성 음료수만 마셔. **2 stick to your guns** to continue to say or do something, although people disagree with you ‖ 비록 사람들이 동의하지 않지만 어떤 것을 계속 말하거나 하다. 자기 의견을 고수하다

stick together *phr v* [I] INFORMAL if people stick together, they continue to support each other ‖ 사람들이 계속 서로를 지지하다. 서로 협력하다. 일치단결하다

stick up *phr v* [I] if a part of something sticks up, it is raised up or points upward above a surface ‖ 물체의 일부분이 표면 위로 솟아 있거나 위쪽을 향해 있다. 위로 튀어나오다

stick up for sb *phr v* [T] INFORMAL to defend someone who is being criticized ‖ 비판받고 있는 사람을 옹호하다. …을 변호[지지]하다

stick with *phr v* [T] INFORMAL **1** [**stick with** sb] to stay close to someone when there is a risk you could be separated ‖ 헤어질 수 있는 위험이 있을 때 어떤 사람 곁에 가까이 머무르다. …에 붙어 있다 **2** [**stick with** sb/sth] to continue doing something or supporting someone ‖ 계속 어떤 것을 하거나 남을 지지하다. …을 계

속하다. …에 충실하다: *Let's just stick with the original plan.* 원래 계획대로 계속 밀고 나가자. **3** [**stick** sb **with** sth] to give someone a difficult or unpleasant responsibility ‖ 남에게 어렵거나 불쾌한 책무를 지우다. 남에게 …을 떠맡기다: *I'll go as long as I don't get stuck with paying the bill again!* 다시 요금 계산을 하게 하지 않는다면 난 갈 거야! **4 stick with it** to continue doing something that is difficult, boring etc. ‖ 어렵고 지루한 일을 계속 하다. 끝까지 견디어 내다 **5** [**stick with** sb] to remain in your memory ‖ 기억 속에 남아 있다: *One thing he said has stuck with me ever since.* 그가 말한 한 가지가 그 이후로 내 머리 속에서 떠나질 않았다.

stick² *n* **1** a long thin piece of wood that has fallen or been cut from a tree ‖ 나무에서 떨어졌거나 잘려진 길고 가는 나무토막. 막대기. 나뭇가지 **2 stick of celery/gum etc.** a long thin piece of something ‖ 물건의 길고 가는 조각. 셀러리 줄기/껌 한 개 **3** a long thin piece of wood or metal that you use for a particular purpose ‖ 특정한 목적을 위해 사용하는 길고 가는 나무나 금속. 지팡이. 스틱: *a walking stick* 지팡이 / *a hockey stick* 하키 스틱 —see also **get the short end of the stick** (SHORT¹), STICKS

stick·er /ˈstɪkɚ/ *n* a small piece of paper or plastic with a picture or writing on it, that you can stick onto something ‖ 그림이나 글이 있고 어떤 것에 붙일 수 있는, 작은 종이나 비닐 조각. 스티커

stick-in-the-mud /ˈ. . . ˌ./ *n* someone who is not willing to try anything new, or does not want to go out and have fun ‖ 새로운 것을 전혀 시도하려 하지 않거나 외출해서 즐기는 것을 원하지 않는 사람. 고루한[구태의연한] 사람

stick·ler /ˈstɪklɚ/ *n* **be a stickler for rules/punctuality etc.** to think that rules etc. are extremely important, and expect people to follow them ‖ 규칙 등이 매우 중요하다고 생각하고 사람들이 그것들을 따를 것으로 기대하다. 규칙/시간 엄수에 까다로운 사람이다

sticks /stɪks/ *n* SPOKEN **the sticks** an area that is very far from a town or city ‖ 소도시나 대도시에서 매우 먼 지역. 오지. 벽지

stick shift /ˈ. ./ *n* **1** a piece of equipment in a car that you move with your hand to control its GEARS ‖ 차의 기어를 제어하려고 손으로 움직이는 차의 장

치. 수동 변속기 **2 a car that uses this
system** ‖ 이 방식을 사용하는 차. 수동 변
속 차 —compare AUTOMATIC²

stick·y /'stɪki/ *adj* **1** made of or
covered with a substance that sticks to
surfaces ‖ 표면에 들러붙는 물질로 만들어
졌거나 뒤덮인. 달라붙는. 끈적끈적한:
sticky candy 끈적거리는 사탕 / *Your
hands are sticky.* 네 손은 끈적끈적해. **2**
weather that is sticky is very hot and
the air feels wet ‖ 날씨가 매우 덥고 대기
가 축축하게 느껴지는. 무더운. 후텁지근
한 **3** INFORMAL a sticky situation,
question, or problem is difficult or
dangerous to deal with ‖ 상황[질문, 문
제]이 다루기 어렵거나 위험한. 곤란한.
난처한 – **stickiness** *n* [U]

stiff¹ /stɪf/ *adj* **1** difficult to bend or
move ‖ 구부리거나 움직이기 어려운. 뻣뻣
한. 딱딱한: *stiff cardboard* 뻣뻣한 마분
지 **2** if a part of your body is stiff, your
muscles hurt and it is difficult to move ‖
근육이 아프고 움직이기 어려운. 뻐근한.
경직된 **3** more difficult, strict, or severe
than usual ‖ 보통보다 더 어려운[엄격한,
심한]. 엄한: *a stiff fine* 엄격한 벌금 **4**
thick and almost solid ‖ 진하고 거의 굳
은. 된. 응고한: *Beat the egg whites until
stiff.* 계란 흰자가 응고 할 때까지 저어라.
5 unfriendly or very formal ‖ 친절하지
않거나 매우 형식적인. 단호한. 딱딱한.
어색한: *a stiff smile* 어색한 미소 **6 a
stiff wind/breeze** a fairly strong wind
or BREEZE ‖ 꽤 강한 바람이나 산들바람.
강풍/산들바람 **7 a stiff drink** a very
strong alcoholic drink ‖ 매우 독한 술 –
stiffly *adv* – **stiffness** *n* [U]

stiff² *adv* INFORMAL **bored/scared/
worried stiff** extremely bored etc. ‖ 몹
시 따분한, 겁먹은, 걱정하는

stiff³ *n* **1** SLANG the body of a dead
person ‖ 죽은 사람의 몸. 시체 **2 working
stiff** INFORMAL an ordinary person who
works ‖ 일하는 평범한 사람. 노동자

stiff⁴ *v* [T] INFORMAL to not pay someone
money that you owe him/her or that
s/he expects to be given ‖ 빚지거나 남이
받을 것으로 기대하는 돈을 지불하지 않
다. 빚을 갚지 않다. 팁을 주지 않다

stiff·en /'stɪfən/ *v* **1** [I] to suddenly
become unfriendly or anxious ‖ 갑자기
쌀쌀맞아지거나 초조해지다. 강경해지다.
긴장하다: *Harold stiffened, sensing
danger.* 해럴드는 위험을 감지하자 긴장했
다. **2** [I, T] also **stiffen up** to become
difficult to bend or move, or to make
something do this ‖ 구부리거나 움직이기
어렵게 되거나, 또는 어떤 것을 이렇게 되

게 하다. 경직되다[경직시키다]. 뻣뻣해지
다 [뻣뻣하게 하다]: *My knee has
stiffened up.* 내 무릎이 경직되었다.

sti·fle /'staɪfəl/ *v* **1** [T] to stop
something from happening, developing,
or being expressed ‖ 어떤 일이 발생하는
[발달하는, 표현되는] 것을 막다. 억압[억
제, 탄압]하다. 억누르다: *Annette felt
college was stifling her creativity.* 어네
트는 대학이 자신의 창의력을 억누르고 있
다고 느꼈다. **2** [I, T] to make someone
feel unable to breathe comfortably, or
to feel this way ‖ 사람이 편안하게 숨을
쉴 수 없다고 느끼게 하다, 또는 이런 식으
로 느끼다. 숨이 막히다[막히게 하다]. 질
식하다[질식시키다] – **stifling** *adj* :
stifling heat 숨 막히는 열기

stig·ma /'stɪgmə/ *n* [singular, U] shame
or difficulty caused by a strong feeling
in society that a type of behavior is
wrong or bad ‖ 어떤 종류의 행동이 잘못
되고 나쁘다는 사회 내의 강한 감정에서
생긴 치욕이나 어려움. 오명. 낙인: *the
stigma attached to AIDS* 에이즈에 붙은
오명 – **stigmatize** /'stɪgmə,taɪz/ *v* [T]

still¹ /stɪl/ *adv* **1** up to a particular
point in time and continuing at that
moment ‖ 특정한 시점까지 그리고 그 순
간에도 계속되어. 아직(도). 여전히: *Do
you still play tennis?* 너 아직도 테니스를
치니? **2** even later or for even longer
than expected ‖ 예상보다 훨씬 더 늦게
또는 훨씬 더 오랫동안. 아직도. 여태:
Why are you still here? 너 왜 아직도 여
기 있냐? **3** in spite of what has just been
said or done ‖ 방금 말하거나 한 것임에도
불구하고. 그래도. 그럼에도 불구하고:
Well, I still think Eric's weird. 나는 그래
도 에릭이 이상하다고 생각해. **4 still
colder/harder/better etc.** also
colder/harder/better etc. still even
colder, harder etc. than something else
‖ 다른 것보다 훨씬 더 춥고 단단한 등. 더
욱 더 추운[단단한, 좋은]: *Could we do
still better? Of course.* 우리가 더욱 더 잘
할 수 있을까? 물론이지. **5 be still going
strong** to continue to be active or
successful, even after a long time ‖ 장시
간 경과 후에도 계속 활동적이거나 성공적
이다. 계속 번창하고 있다. 잘 되어 가고
있다: *We've been partners for 25 years,
and we're still going strong.* 우리는 25
년간 동업자였고 여전히 유대가 돈독하다.

USAGE NOTE still and yet

Use **still** to talk about a situation that
continues to exist at the present time.

Still is usually used before the verb: *I still see Jeannie from time to time. / The club still sends him the newsletter.* However, if the verb is "be", still is used after it: *I hope these potatoes are still good. / She's still on the phone.* If the sentence has a group of verbs in it, still is used after the first verb: *You can still catch up with them if you hurry. / We're still waiting to hear from Tim.* If a sentence has a negative word in it, still is used before it: *I still don't understand today's assignment. / We bought more food, but there's still not enough for everyone.* Use yet in negative sentences and questions to talk about something that you expect to happen, but which has not happened. Usually, yet is used at the end of a sentence: *I haven't finished the book yet. / Is Mark back from lunch yet?*

still은 현재 계속 존재하는 상황에 대해서 말하는 데에 쓴다. still은 대체로 동사 앞에 쓰인다: 나는 여전히 지니를 가끔 본다. / 그 클럽은 아직도 그에게 회보를 보낸다. 하지만 동사가 "be"이면 still은 그 뒤에 쓰인다; 이 감자들이 아직도 좋기를 바란다. / 그녀는 아직도 전화 중이다. 만약 문장이 몇 개의 동사들을 가지고 있다면 still은 첫 번째 동사 뒤에 쓰인다: 서두르면 너는 아직 그들을 따라잡을 수 있어. / 우리는 아직도 팀의 소식을 기다리고 있다. 만약 문장이 부정어를 가지고 있다면 still은 그 앞에 쓰인다: 나는 아직도 오늘의 임무를 이해하지 못하겠어. / 우리는 음식을 더 샀지만 모든 사람에게는 충분하지 않아. yet은 발생할 것으로 기대하지만 발생하지 않은 일에 대해서 말할 때 부정문과 의문문에서, 보통 문장의 끝에 쓴다: 나는 그 책을 아직 다 읽지 못했다. / 마크가 점심을 먹고 이미 돌아왔나요?

still² *adj* **1** not moving || 움직이지 않는. 정지하여[가만히] 있는: *Just keep/stand/ stay still while I tie your shoes.* 내가 네 신발 끈을 묶는 동안 그저 가만히 있어. **2** quiet and without any activity || 조용하고 어떠한 활동도 없는. 고요한. 잠잠한: *At that time of day, the forest was still.* 하루 중 그 시간에는 숲이 고요했다. **– stillness** *n* [U]

still³ *n* **1** a piece of equipment for making alcoholic drinks out of grain or potatoes || 곡물이나 감자로 술을 만들기

위한 설비. 증류기 **2** a photograph of a scene from a movie || 영화의 한 장면의 사진. 스틸 사진 **3 the still of the night/evening etc.** LITERARY the calm and quiet time of the night etc. || 밤 등의 고요하고 조용한 시간. 밤/저녁의 정적

still·born /ˌstɪlˈbɔrn-/ *adj* born dead || 죽은 채 태어난. 사산의 **– stillbirth** /ˈstɪlbɚθ/ *n* [C, U]

still life /ˈ. ./ *n, plural* **still lifes** [C, U] a picture of an arrangement of objects, especially flowers and fruit || 특히 꽃과 과일 등이 배열된 모습을 그린 그림. 정물화

stilt·ed /ˈstɪltɪd/ *adj* stilted writing or speaking is formal and unnatural || 글이나 말이 형식적이고 부자연스러운. 딱딱한. 과장된

stilts /stɪlts/ *n* [plural] a pair of poles you can stand on, used for walking high above the ground || 지면 위로 높이 걸을 때 사용하는 그 위에 설 수 있는 한 쌍의 장대. 죽마(竹馬)

stim·u·lant /ˈstɪmyələnt/ *n* **1** a drug or substance that makes you feel more active || 더욱 활기 차게 하는 약이나 물질. 흥분[자극, 각성]제 **2** something that encourages more of an activity or helps a process to develop faster || 활동을 더욱 고무시키거나 과정이 더 빠르게 전개되도록 돕는 것. 자극(제). 격려

stim·u·late /ˈstɪmyəˌleɪt/ *v* [T] **1** to encourage more of an activity, or to help a process develop faster || 활동을 더욱 고무시키거나 과정이 더 빠르게 전개되도록 돕다. …을 자극[격려]하다: *efforts to stimulate the economy* 경기를 부양하려는 노력 / *Light stimulates plant growth.* 빛은 식물의 생장을 촉진한다. **2** to make someone excited about and interested in something || 남에게 어떤 것에 대해 흥분하고 흥미를 갖게 하다. …을 자극시키다. 흥미를 돋우다: *projects designed to stimulate children's curiosity* 어린이들의 호기심을 자극하도록 고안된 프로젝트 **3** to increase the energy of someone or something || 사람이나 사물의 활력을 증가시키다. 기운[활기]을 북돋우다 **– stimulating** *adj* : *a stimulating conversation* 격려의 대화 **– stimulation** /ˌstɪmyəˈleɪʃən/ *n* [U]

stim·u·lus /ˈstɪmyələs/ *n, plural* **stimuli** /-laɪ/ **1** [singular, U] something that encourages more of an activity or helps a process to develop faster || 활동을 더욱 고무시키거나 과정이 더 빠르게 전개되도록 돕는 것. 격려. 자극(제) **2** something that makes someone or something move or react ‖ 사람이나 사물을 움직이거나 반응하게 하는 것. 자극물. 흥분제

sting¹ /stɪŋ/ v **stung, stung, stinging**
1 [T] if an insect or plant stings you, it hurts you with its sharp point or points ‖ 곤충이나 식물이 날카로운 바늘이나 침으로 아프게 하다. …을 찌르다[쏘다]: *Jamie was stung by a bee.* 제이미는 벌에 쏘였다. **2** [I, T] to feel a sharp pain in your eyes, throat, or skin, or to make someone feel this ‖ 눈[목구멍, 피부]에 심한 통증을 느끼다, 또는 남에게 이것을 느끼게 하다. 찌르듯 아프다. 얼얼[따끔따끔]하다[하게 하다]: *My eyes sting.* 내 눈이 따끔거린다. / *The smoke stung my throat.* 연기 때문에 목이 따끔따끔했다. **3 be stung by sth** to be upset or badly affected by something ‖ 어떤 것에 의해 마음이 상하거나 기분 나쁘게 영향을 받다. …에 화가 나다. 괴로움을 당하다: *Pearson was stung by her criticisms.* 피어슨은 그녀의 비판 때문에 속이 무척 상했다.

sting² n **1** a wound made when an insect or plant stings you ‖ 곤충이나 식물이 찌를 때 생기는 상처. 쏘인[찔린] 상처: *a bee sting* 벌에 쏘인 상처 **2** [singular] a sharp pain that you feel in your eyes, throat, or skin ‖ 눈[목구멍, 피부]에 느끼는 심한 통증. 얼얼함. 따끔따끔함 **3** a trick used for catching someone while s/he is doing something illegal ‖ 불법적인 일을 하고 있는 사람을 붙잡는 데에 쓰이는 술책. 함정 수사

sting·er /ˈstɪŋɚ/ n the point on a creature's body that contains poison, for example on a bee ‖ 예를 들면 벌과 같은 생물의 몸에 있는 독이 든 날카로운 바늘. 침. 가시

sting·ray /ˈstɪŋreɪ/ n a large flat fish that has a long tail like a whip with stingers on it ‖ 침이 있는 채찍 같은 긴 꼬리가 달린 넓적한 물고기. 노랑가오리

stin·gy /ˈstɪndʒi/ adj not willing to spend money or share something even though you have enough ‖ 비록 충분히 가지고 있지만 돈을 쓰거나 어떤 것을 나누기를 꺼리는. 인색한. 구두쇠의: *She's so stingy.* 그녀는 아주 인색하다. – **stinginess** n [U]

stink¹ /stɪŋk/ v **stank, stunk, stinking 1** [I] to have a very strong and unpleasant smell ‖ 매우 독하고 불쾌한 냄새가 나다. 악취가 나다: *The dog's breath stinks!* 그 개의 입 냄새는 지독해! **2 sth stinks!** SPOKEN said when you think something is bad or unfair ‖ 어떤

것이 나쁘거나 부당하다고 생각할 때 쓰여. …이 형편없어[고약해]!: *Don't eat there – the food stinks.* 거기서 먹지 마. 음식이 형편없어. – **stinky** adj

stink sth ↔ **up** phr v [T] INFORMAL to fill a place with a very strong and unpleasant smell ‖ 어떤 장소를 매우 독하고 불쾌한 냄새로 채우다. 악취로 가득 차게 하다: *He's stinking up the house with cigar smoke!* 그는 집안을 온통 시가 연기로 가득 채우고 있어!

stink² n **1 make/cause/raise a stink** to complain about something so that people pay attention to you ‖ 사람들이 주목하도록 어떤 것에 대해서 불평하다. 소동[말썽]을 일으키다: *I'm going to raise a stink if they don't change our tickets.* 그들이 우리의 표를 바꿔주지 않으면 난 소란을 피울 거야. **2** a strong unpleasant smell ‖ 독하고 불쾌한 냄새. 악취

stink·er /ˈstɪŋkɚ/ n INFORMAL someone who behaves badly, or something that is of bad quality ‖ 못되게 행동하는 사람이나 질이 나쁜 것. 비열한[고약한] 녀석. 저질의 것

stink·ing /ˈstɪŋkɪŋ/ adj **1** having a strong unpleasant smell ‖ 독하고 불쾌한 냄새가 나는. 악취를 풍기는: *stinking socks* 냄새가 고약한 양말 **2** SPOKEN said when you think something is bad, unfair, or untrue ‖ 어떤 것이 나쁘다[부당하다, 사실이 아니다]라고 생각할 때 쓰여. 지독한. 말도 안 되는: *I won't work for a stinking $2.50 an hour!* 나는 시간당 말도 안 되는 2달러 50센트를 받고는 일 안 해!

stint¹ /stɪnt/ n a job or position that you have for a limited period ‖ 제한된 기간 동안 가지고 있는 일자리나 지위. 할당된 기간(의 일): *a five-year stint teaching English in Korea* 한국에서 영어를 가르치는 5년의 기간

stint² v [I] ⇨ SKIMP

sti·pend /ˈstaɪpɛnd, -pənd/ n an amount of money paid regularly to someone such as a priest or student so that s/he can live ‖ 성직자나 학생 등에게 생활할 수 있도록 정기적으로 지불되는 금액. 봉급. 장학금: *a monthly stipend* 월 지불금

stip·u·late /ˈstɪpyəˌleɪt/ v [T] to say that something must be done because of an agreement ‖ 협정 때문에 반드시 어떤 것을 해야 한다고 말하다. 조건으로서 …을 요구[약정]하다: *The contract stipulates that we receive 25% of the profits.* 우리는 수익금의 25%를 받는다고

계약서에 규정되어 있다.

stip·u·la·tion /ˌstɪpyəˈleɪʃən/ *n* something specific that must be done as part of an agreement ǁ 협정의 일부분으로서 반드시 해야 하는 특정한 것. 조건. 조항: *Mr. Gleason agreed, with the stipulation that his name was not used.* 글리슨 씨는 자기 이름이 사용되지 않는다는 조건으로 동의했다.

stir¹ /stɚ/ *v* **-rred, -rring 1** [T] to mix a liquid or food by moving a spoon around in it ǁ 액체나 음식을 숟가락으로 휘저어서 섞다. 휘젓다. 뒤섞다: *Stir the mixture until smooth.* 잘 섞일 때까지 혼합물을 휘저어라.

stir

2 [I, T] to move slightly, or to make someone or something do this ǁ 약간 움직이다, 또는 사람이나 사물이 이렇게 하게 하다. (…을) 살짝 움직이다: *Rachel stirred in her sleep.* 레이첼은 자면서 몸을 뒤척였다. **3** [T] to make someone feel a strong emotion ǁ 남에게 강한 감정을 느끼게 하다. …을 각성시키다[불러일으키다]: *The killings stirred citizens to protest.* 그 살육은 시민들의 항의를 불러일으켰다.

stir sth ↔ **up** *phr v* [T] to deliberately try to cause problems or make people argue ǁ 고의로 문제를 일으키거나 사람들이 분쟁을 일으키게 하려고 하다. …을 선동하다[부추기다]: *If you let him stay, he'll just stir up more trouble.* 만약 네가 그를 머물러 있게 한다면 그는 문제만 더 일으킬 거야.

stir² *n* **1** a strong feeling such as excitement or anger, felt by many people ǁ 많은 사람들이 느끼는 흥분이나 분노 등의 강한 감정. 동요. 소동: *The movie caused such a stir that it was finally banned.* 그 영화는 큰 소동을 일으켜 마침내 상영이 금지되었다. **2** [singular] an act of STIRring something ǁ 물건을 휘젓는 행위. 휘젓기. 뒤섞기

stir-fry /ˈ. ./ *v* [T] to quickly cook meat, vegetables etc. in a little oil over very high heat ǁ 고열로 끓는 약간의 기름 속에서 고기·야채 등을 빨리 요리하다. 프라이팬에 재빨리 볶다 – **stir-fry** *n*

stir·rup /ˈstɚəp, ˈstɪrəp/ *n* one of the two metal parts on a horse's SADDLE that you put your foot in ǁ 발을 끼워 넣는 말 안장의 두 개의 금속 부분 중의 하나. 등자(鐙子)

stitch¹ /stɪtʃ/ *n* **1** one of the small lines of thread where a piece of cloth has been sewn ǁ 천 조각을 꿰매는 실의 작은 선들 중의 하나. 한 바늘[땀]: *tiny stitches in the sleeves* 소매의 작은 바늘땀들 **2** [C usually plural] a piece of thread, plastic etc. used for fastening together the edges of a wound ǁ 상처의 가장자리를 함께 봉합할 때 사용하는 실·플라스틱 등의 한 조각. 한 바늘: *Nancy had 14 stitches in her leg.* 낸시는 다리에 14바늘을 꿰맸다. **3** one of the small circles that you KNIT when you are making a SWEATER ǁ 스웨터를 만들 때 짜는 작은 원들 중의 하나. 한 코 **4** [singular] a sharp pain in a muscle near your waist, that you get from exercising too much ǁ 너무 많이 운동을 해서 얻는 허리 근처 근육의 심한 통증. 쑤심. 격통 **5 not a stitch (of clothing)** INFORMAL no clothes at all ǁ 전혀 옷을 입지 않고. 실오라기 하나 걸치지 않고: *He stood there without a stitch on.* 그는 실오라기 하나 걸치지 않고 거기에 서 있었다. — see also STITCHES

stitch² *v* [T] to sew two pieces of cloth together, or to sew something onto a piece of cloth ǁ 두 개의 천 조각을 함께 꿰매거나 어떤 것을 하나의 천 조각에 붙여 꿰매다. …을 깁다. …에 꿰매어 붙이다: *a shirt stitched with gold thread* 금실로 바느질을 한 셔츠 – **stitching** *n* [U]

stitch sth ↔ **up** *phr v* [T] to sew together the edges of a wound or two pieces of cloth ǁ 상처의 가장자리나 두 개의 천을 함께 꿰매다. …을 꿰매다. 봉합하다

stitch·es /ˈstɪtʃɪz/ *n* [plural] **in stitches** INFORMAL unable to stop laughing ǁ 웃는 것을 멈출 수 없는. 배꼽을 쥐고 웃어. 포복절도하여: *Tony kept us in stitches all night.* 토니는 밤새도록 우리들을 계속 배꼽을 쥐고 웃게 했다.

stock¹ /stak/ *n* **1** [C, U] a supply of something that is kept to be sold or used later ǁ 나중에 팔거나 사용하려고 보관하는 사물의 공급품. 재고(품). 저장(품): *"Do you sell batteries?" "Sorry, they're out of stock."* (=we do not have any more) "건전지 있나요?" "죄송합니다. 다 떨어졌습니다." / *stocks of canned food in the cupboard* 찬장에 쌓인 통조림 음식 **2** [C] a SHARE in a company ǁ 회사의 주식. 주(株). 증권 **3** [U] the number of SHAREs that a person owns, or the total value of a company's shares ǁ 사람이 소유하고 있는 주식의 수나 회사 주식의 총가치. 주식 수. 회사의 총자산 **4** [U] a liquid made from boiling meat, bones, or vegetables, used especially for making soups ‖ 특히 수프를 만들 때 사용하는 고기[뼈, 채소]를 끓여서 만든 액체. 국물: *chicken stock* 닭고기 국물 **5 take stock (of sth)** to think carefully about everything that has happened so that you can decide what to do next ‖ 다음에 무엇을 할지를 결정할 수 있도록 발생한 모든 것에 대해서 주의 깊게 생각하다. 자세히 조사[검토]하다: *We need to take stock of the situation.* 우리는 현 상황을 자세히 검토할 필요가 있다. **6** someone's family, especially those that lived in a particular place in past times ‖ 특히 과거 시대에 특정한 장소에 살았던 어떤 사람의 가족. 가계. 혈통. 가문: *She comes from old New England stock.* 그녀는 옛 뉴잉글랜드 혈통 출신이다. **7** ⇨ LIVE-STOCK

stock² *v* [T] to have a supply of something available to be sold or used ‖ 어떤 것의 공급품을 팔거나 사용할 수 있게 하다. 상품을 갖추다[취급하다]: *Do you stock camping equipment?* 캠핑 장비가 있습니까?

stock up *phr v* [I] to buy a lot of something that you intend to use later ‖ 나중에 사용할 의도로 물건을 많이 사다. 사재기하다: *stocking up on groceries* 식료품 사재기

stock·ade /stɑˈkeɪd/ *n* a wall built to defend a place, made from large upright pieces of wood, or the area inside this ‖ 어떤 장소를 방어하려고 크고 곧은 목재로 만들어 세운 방벽이나 이것의 안쪽 지역. 방책 (지역)

stock·brok·er /ˈstɑkˌbroʊkɚ/ *n* someone whose job is to buy and sell STOCKs, BONDs, and SHAREs for other people ‖ 다른 사람들을 위해 주식·채권·증권을 사고파는 직업인. 증권 중개인 – **stockbroking** *n* [U]

stock cer·tif·i·cate /ˈ. ...,.../ *n* an official document that proves you own SHAREs of a company ‖ 한 회사의 주식을 소유하고 있다는 것을 증명하는 공식적인 서류. 증권. 주권(株券)

stock ex·change /ˈ. ...,./ *n* the business of buying and selling STOCKs and SHAREs, or the place where this happens ‖ 주식과 증권을 사고파는 업무, 또는 이것이 발생하는 장소. 증권 거래소

stock·hold·er /ˈstɑkˌhoʊldɚ/ *n* someone who owns STOCK ‖ 주식을 소유한 사람. 주주

stock·ing /ˈstɑkɪŋ/ *n* **1** a very thin piece of clothing that fits closely over a woman's foot and most of her leg ‖ 여자의 발과 다리에 꽉 끼게 신는 매우 얇은 의류. 스타킹: *silk stockings* 비단 스타킹 **2** a thing like a large sock that is hung by the FIREPLACE before Christmas to be filled with presents ‖ 성탄절 전에 벽난로 옆에 걸어 두어 선물들로 채우는 커다란 양말 같은 것. 긴 양말

stock mar·ket /ˈ. ...,./ *n* **1** ⇨ STOCK EXCHANGE **2** the average value of STOCKs sold in the STOCK EXCHANGE ‖ 증권 거래소에서 팔리는 주식의 평균 가격. 주가. 주식 시세

stock option *n* STOCK that a company offers to sell to an EMPLOYEE at a price that is lower than the usual price ‖ 일반 가격보다 낮은 가격에 회사가 종업원에게 매도하겠다고 제시한 주식. 스톡 옵션

stock·pile /ˈstɑkpaɪl/ *n* a large supply of something that you collect in order to use it in the future ‖ 장차 사용하려고 모은 사물의 많은 물량. 비축(분): *a stockpile of weapons* 비축 무기 – **stockpile** *v* [T]

stock-still /ˌ. ˈ./ *adv* not moving at all ‖ 전혀 움직이지 않고. 꼼짝 않고. 부동으로: *The deer stood stock-still, listening.* 그 사슴은 꼼짝 않고 서서 귀를 기울이고 있었다.

stock·y /ˈstɑki/ *adj* having a short, heavy, strong-looking body ‖ 키가 작고 중량이 나가며 강건해 보이는 몸을 지닌. 땅딸막한. 작고 단단한: *a stocky man* 땅딸막한 남자

stock·yard /ˈstɑkyɑrd/ *n* a place where cattle are kept before being sold or killed for their meat ‖ 식용으로 팔리거나 도살하기 전에 소를 보관하는 장소. 임시 가축 수용장

stodg·y /ˈstɑdʒi/ *adj* a stodgy person is boring and formal ‖ 사람이 따분하고 격식을 차리는. 고루한. 구식의: *a stodgy old professor* 고루한 노교수

sto·ic /ˈstoʊɪk/, **sto·i·cal** /ˈstoʊɪkəl/ *adj* not showing your emotions or not complaining when something bad happens to you ‖ 안 좋은 일이 발생했을 때 감정을 보이거나 불평하지 않는. 태연한. 냉철한. 극기의 – **stoicism** /ˈstoʊɪˌsɪzəm/ *n* [U]

stoke /stoʊk/ *v* [I, T] to add more wood or FUEL to a fire ‖ 불에 장작이나 연료를 더 넣다. 불을 돋우다[때다]

stoked /stoʊkt/ *adj* SLANG very happy and excited about something ‖ 어떤 것에 대해서 매우 기뻐하고 흥분하는. 열광하는. 기뻐 날뛰는

stole¹ /stoʊl/ *v* the past tense of STEAL ‖

steal의 과거형

stole² *n* a long straight piece of cloth or fur that a woman wears over her shoulders ‖ 여성이 어깨에 걸쳐 입는 길고 곧은 천이나 모피 조각. 여성용 어깨걸이

sto·len /'stəʊlən/ *v* the PAST PARTICIPLE of STEAL ‖ steal의 과거 분사형

stol·id /'stɑlɪd/ *adj* not showing a lot of emotion ‖ 감정을 많이 보이지 않는. 둔감한. 신경이 무딘 - **stolidly** *adv*

stom·ach¹ /'stʌmək/ *n* **1** the organ in your body that DIGESTs the food you eat ‖ 먹은 음식을 소화시키는 몸의 기관. 위: *My stomach hurts.* 내 위가 아프다. **2** the front part of your body, below your chest ‖ 가슴 아래의 몸의 앞부분. 배. 복부: *I always sleep on my stomach.* 나는 항상 배를 깔고 잔다. **3** the ability and willingness to do something unpleasant ‖ 불쾌한 것을 하는 능력과 자발성. 하고 싶은 기분[욕망, 용기]: *I didn't have the stomach to watch him fight.* 나는 그가 싸우는 것을 보고 싶은 마음이 없었다.

stomach² *v* [T] to be able to deal with something that is unpleasant ‖ 불쾌한 것을 해결할 수 있다. …을 참다. …에 견디다: *I just can't stomach moving to another place.* 나는 다른 곳으로 이사하는 것을 참을 수 없을 뿐이다.

stom·ach·ache /'stʌmək,eɪk/ *n* a pain in your stomach ‖ 위의 통증. 복통. 위통

stomp /stɑmp, stɔmp/ *v* [I] to step very hard on the ground or to walk this way, usually because you are angry ‖ 보통 화가 나서 지면을 세게 밟거나 이런 식으로 걷다. 발을 세게 구르다. 쿵쿵거리며 걷다: *"Shut up!" Peter yelled, and stomped off.* "입 닥쳐!"라고 피터는 소리치고 발을 쿵쾅거리며 나갔다.

stone¹ /stəʊn/ *n* **1** a small rock or a piece of rock ‖ 작은 돌이나 돌의 한 조각. 돌. 돌멩이 **2** [U] rock, or a hard mineral substance ‖ 암석, 또는 단단한 광물질. 바위. 석재. 돌: *stone benches* 돌 벤치 / *a wall made of stone* 돌로 만든 담 **3** a jewel ‖ 보석: *a gold-plated necklace with fake stones* 가짜 보석을 박은 금도금한 목걸이 **4** a ball of hard material that can form in an organ such as the KIDNEY or BLADDER ‖ 콩팥이나 방광 등의 기관에 형성될 수 있는 단단한 물질의 덩어리. 결석(結石)

stone² *adv* **stone cold/deaf/dead** completely cold, DEAF, or dead ‖ 완전히 차가운[귀먹은, 죽은]: *The pasta was stone cold when it was served.* 그 파스타는 나왔을 때 완전히 식어 있었다.

stone³ *v* [T] to kill or hurt someone by throwing stones at him/her ‖ 돌을 던져서 남을 죽이거나 다치게 하다. 돌로 때리다[죽이다]

stoned /stəʊnd/ *adj* SLANG feeling very calm, or unable to control your behavior, because you have taken an illegal drug ‖ 불법적인 약물을 복용해서 매우 평온함을 느끼거나, 또는 행동을 통제할 수 없는

stone·wall /'stəʊnwɔl/ *v* [I, T] to deliberately delay doing something or refuse to give information about it ‖ 의도적으로 어떤 것을 하기를 지연하거나 어떤 것에 대한 정보 주는 것을 거절하다. (…을) 의도적으로 방해[방해]하다: *The union is stonewalling on the contract.* 노동조합은 그 계약을 의도적으로 지연시키고 있다.

stone·work /'stəʊnwɜk/ *n* [U] the parts of a building made of or decorated with stone ‖ 석재로 만들었거나 장식한 건물의 부분. (건축물의) 석조 부분

ston·y /'stəʊni/ *adj* **1** covered with stones or containing stones ‖ 돌로 뒤덮였거나 돌이 들어 있는. 돌이 많은. 돌투성이의: *a stony path* 자갈길 **2** showing no emotion or pity ‖ 감정이나 연민을 보이지 않는. 냉혹한. 무자비한: *a stony silence* 싸늘한 침묵

stony-faced /'.. ,./ *adj* showing no emotion, pity, or friendliness ‖ 감정[연민, 친근감]을 보이지 않는. 무표정한. 차가운

stood /stʊd/ *v* the past tense and PAST PARTICIPLE of STAND ‖ stand의 과거·과거 분사형

stool /stul/ *n* **1** a chair without a support for your back ‖ 등받이가 없는 의자: *a bar stool* (등받이 없는) 술집 의자 / *a piano stool* 피아노 의자 **2** TECHNICAL a piece of solid waste from the body ‖ 몸에서 나온 고형 배설물. 대변

stoop¹ /stup/ *v* [I] **1** to bend your body forward and down, especially your head and shoulders ‖ 특히 머리와 어깨 등의 몸을 앞으로 구부려 숙이다. 몸을 굽히다[구부리다]. 웅크리다: *Troy stooped to pick up his pencil.* 트로이는 연필을 줍기 위해 몸을 숙였다. **2** to do something that other people consider to be bad or morally wrong ‖ 다른 사람들이 나쁘거나 도덕적으로 잘못됐다고 생각하는 일을 하다. 치사한 나쁜 짓을 하다: *No one believed he would stoop to lying.* 아무도 그가 거짓말할 정도까지 치사해질 것이라고 믿지 않았다.

stoop² *n* **1** the position you hold your

body in when you STOOP ‖ 몸을 숙여서 계속 그대로 유지하는 자세. 구부정한[웅크린] 자세 **2** a set of stairs leading up to a city house, or the flat area at the top of them ‖ 도시 주택으로 통하는 일련의 계단이나 그 꼭대기의 평평한 지역. 현관 입구의 계단

stop[1] /stap/ v **-pped, -pping 1** [I, T] to end an action, activity, movement, or event, or to make something end ‖ 동작[활동, 움직임, 사건]을 끝내다, 또는 어떤 것이 끝나게 하다. …을 그만두다[멈추다]. 중단[중지]하다[시키다]: *Stop! I can't run that fast.* 멈춰! 나는 그렇게 빨리 달리지 못해. / *We couldn't stop laughing.* 우리는 웃지 않을 수가 없었다. / *I hope the rain stops soon.* 비가 곧 그치기를 바란다. / *How did they stop the fight?* 그들은 어떻게 해서 싸움을 그쳤지? **2** [T] to prevent someone from doing something ‖ 남을 무엇을 하지 못하게 막다. …을 막다. 그만두게 하다: *She can't stop me from leaving!* 그녀는 내가 떠나는 것을 막을 수 없어! **3** [I] to pause during an activity, trip etc. in order to do something ‖ 어떤 것을 하려고 활동·여행 등 도중에 정지하다. 멈추다. 정지하다: *Let's stop at a cafe and get some lunch.* 카페에 들러 점심 좀 먹자. / *We stopped for gas in Louisville.* 우리는 루이빌에서 기름을 넣으려고 정차했다. **4** **stop it/that!** SPOKEN said when you want someone to stop annoying or upsetting you ‖ 어떤 사람에게 괴롭히거나 화나게 하는 것을 멈추기를 원할 때 쓰여. 그만해! 그만둬!: *Stop it! That hurts!* 그만해! 아파! **5** [T] to make someone stop walking or traveling, especially to talk to him/her ‖ 특히 말을 걸려고, 남이 걷거나 이동하는 것을 멈추게 하다. …을 (멈춰) 세우다: *He's been stopped twice by the police for speeding.* 그는 과속으로 두 번이나 경찰에 의해 정지당했다. **6 stop short of sth** to stop before you do one more thing that would be too dangerous, risky etc. ‖ 너무 위험하거나 무모하게 될 한 가지 것을 하기 직전에 중단하다. …까지는 이르지 않다. 거의 …할 뻔하다: *Tom stopped short of calling her a liar.* 톰은 자칫 그녀를 거짓말쟁이라고 부를 뻔했다. **7 stop (dead) in your tracks** to stop suddenly, especially because something has surprised or frightened you ‖ 특히 어떤 것이 놀라게 하거나 겁을 먹게 해서 갑자기 멈추다. 그 자리에 딱 멈춰 서다

stop by *phr v* [I] to quickly visit a person or place, especially before going somewhere else ‖ 특히 다른 곳에 가기 전에 사람이나 장소를 잠시 방문하다. 들르다: *It was nice of Judy to stop by.* 주디가 잠깐 들러 주어서 고마웠다.

stop in *phr v* [I] INFORMAL to make a short visit to a place or person, especially when you are going somewhere else ‖ 특히 다른 곳에 가면서 어떤 장소나 사람을 잠시 방문하다. 잠깐 들르다[방문하다]: *Let's stop in at Gary's on the way.* 가는 도중에 게리 집에 잠깐 들르자.

stop off *phr v* [I] to quickly visit a place that is near to where you are going ‖ 어떤 곳에 가고 있는 도중에 그곳에 가까운 장소를 급히 방문하다. 들러 가다. 경유하다: *I need to stop off at the post office.* 나는 우체국에 잠깐 들러야 해.

stop sth ↔ up *phr v* [T] **1** to block a hole in something, especially a pipe ‖ 특히 관 등의 구멍을 막다. 틀어막다. 폐쇄하다: *The sink's stopped up again.* 싱크대가 또 막혔다. **2 be stopped up** if your nose or head is stopped up, it is blocked with thick liquid because you have a cold ‖ 감기가 걸려서 진한 액체로 코나 머리가 막히다. 막히다 —see also PLUG[2]

stop[2] *n* **1** the action of stopping or of being stopped ‖ 멈추거나 멈춰진 동작. 멈춤. 정지. 중단: *The taxi came to a stop outside his hotel.* 택시는 그의 호텔 밖에서 정차했다. / *Mrs. Drayton put a stop to the gossip.* (=stopped it from continuing) 드레이튼 부인은 잡담을 중단했다. **2** a place where you stop during a trip, or the short period you spend at that place ‖ 여행 도중에 멈추는 장소 또는 그 장소에서 보내는 짧은 기간. 체류지[기간]: *Our first stop is Brussels, and then we're going to Paris.* 우리의 첫 체류지는 브뤼셀이고 다음에 파리에 간다. **3** a place where a bus or train regularly stops for its passengers ‖ 버스나 기차가 승객을 (태우거나 내리게 하기) 위해 규칙적으로 멈추는 장소. 정류장. 역: *I get off at the next stop.* 나는 다음 정류장[역]에서 내린다. —see also **pull out all the stops** (PULL[1])

stop·gap /'stapgæp/ *n* a solution, plan, person etc. that you use until you have a better one ‖ 더 나은 것이나 사람이 있을 때까지 사용하는 해결책·계획·사람 등. 임시변통. 미봉책. 대리. 임시: *a stopgap measure to deal with the parking problem* 주차 문제를 처리하기 위한 임시 조치

stop·light /'staplaɪt/ *n* a set of red, yellow, and green lights used for controlling traffic ‖ 교통을 통제하는 데 사용하는 빨간·노란·파란 불의 한 세트. 교통 신호등

stop·o·ver /'stɑpˌoʊvɚ/ *n* a short time between parts of a trip, especially a long plane trip ‖ 특히 장거리 비행 여행 사이의 짧게 멈춘 시간. 중간 기착 (시간): *a three-hour stop over in Atlanta* 애틀랜타에서의 3시간의 중간 기착

stop·page /'stɑpɪdʒ/ *n* **1** an occasion when workers stop working as a protest ‖ 근로자들이 항의로서 작업을 중단하는 경우. 파업: *a two-month work stoppage* 두 달간의 파업 **2** something that blocks a tube, pipe, or container ‖ 튜브[파이프, 용기]를 막는 것. 뚜껑. 마개. 막힌 것

stop·per /'stɑpɚ/ *n* a piece of plastic, CORK etc. that you put in the top of a bottle to close it ‖ 막으려고 병의 주둥이에 집어넣는 플라스틱·코르크 등의 조각. 마개. 뚜껑

stop·watch /'stɑpwɑtʃ/ *n* a watch used for measuring the exact time it takes to do something, such as run a race ‖ 경주 등을 하는 데 걸리는 정확한 시간을 재는 데 쓰는 시계. 스톱워치

stor·age /'stɔrɪdʒ/ *n* [U] the act or state of keeping something in a special place when it is not being used ‖ 사용되지 않을 때 특정한 장소에 사물을 보관하는 행위나 상태. 저장. 보관: *the safe storage of chemical weapons* 화학 무기의 안전한 보관 / *There's storage space in the garage.* 차고에 저장 공간이 있다. / *The furniture is in storage until we find a new house.* 우리가 새집을 구할 때까지 가구는 보관 상태에 있다.

store¹ /stɔr/ *n* **1** a large room or building where goods are sold to the public ‖ 일반 사람들에게 상품을 파는 커다란 실내나 건물. 가게. 상점: *a book/shoe/liquor store* 서점[신발 가게, 주류 판매점] / *I'm going to the store to get some milk.* 나는 우유 좀 사러 가게에 갈 거야. —see also DEPARTMENT STORE **2** a supply of something, especially something that you can use later ‖ 특히 나중에 사용할 수 있는 물건의 비축. 비축 [축적](물): *a store of information* 정보의 축적 / *secret stores of weapons* 비밀 저장된 무기 **3 be in store** to be about to happen to someone ‖ 누군가에게 곧 일어나려 하다. …을 위해 대기하다[준비되다]: *There's a surprise in store for you tomorrow!* 내일 너를 깜짝 놀라게 할 일이 준비되어 있어!

store² *v* [T] **1** also **store away** to put things away and keep them there until you need them ‖ 물건들을 치우고 그것들을 필요할 때까지 그곳에 보관하다. …을 저장[보관]하다: *All my old clothes are stored in the basement.* 내 낡은 옷은 모두 지하실에 보관돼 있다. **2** to keep facts or information in a computer ‖ 컴퓨터에 자료나 정보를 보관하다. …을 저장하다: *You can store your files on this disk.* 여러분은 이 디스크에 파일들을 저장할 수 있습니다.

store·house /'stɔrhaʊs/ *n* **1 a storehouse of information/methods etc.** something that can give you a lot of information, methods etc. ‖ 많은 정보·방법 등을 줄 수 있는 것. 지식/방법의 보고: *The craft shop is a storehouse of ideas for gifts and decorations.* 공예품 가게는 선물과 장식품을 다양하게 고를 수 있는 보고다. **2** OLD-FASHIONED ⇨ WAREHOUSE

store·keep·er /'stɔrˌkipɚ/ *n* someone who owns or is in charge of a store ‖ 상점을 소유하거나 맡고 있는 사람. 가게 주인. 점포주

store·room /'stɔr-rum/ *n* a room where goods are stored ‖ 상품이 저장된 실내. 저장실

sto·rey /'stɔri/ *n* ⇨ STORY

stork /stɔrk/ *n* a tall white water bird with long legs and a long beak ‖ 긴 다리와 긴 부리를 지닌 키가 크고 하얀 물새. 황새

storm¹ /stɔrm/ *n* **1** a period of bad weather when there is a lot of wind, rain, snow etc. ‖ 바람·비·눈 등이 많은 악천후의 기간. 폭풍(우): *a snow storm* 눈보라 —see usage note at WEATHER **2** a situation in which people suddenly become angry and excited ‖ 사람들이 갑자기 화가 나거나 흥분되는 상황. (감정 등의) 격발. 폭발: *The mayor's policies caused a storm of opposition.* 시장의 정책들은 거센 반대를 불러일으켰다. **3 dance/talk/work etc. up a storm** INFORMAL to do something with a lot of excitement and effort ‖ 크게 흥분하고 노력하여 어떤 것을 하다. 신나게 춤추다/말하다/일하다: *Jenny and I cooked up a storm.* 제니와 나는 신나게 요리를 했다. **4 take sb/sth by storm** to suddenly become very successful and admired in a particular place ‖ 특정한 장소에서 갑자기 매우 성공적이고 칭송을 받게 되다. …을 매료하다[사로잡다]: *a new show that's taking Broadway by storm* 브로드웨이를 매료시킨 새로운 쇼

storm² *v* **1** [T] to attack a place and enter it with a lot of force ‖ 어떤 장소를

공격하고 강제적으로 진입하다. 돌진해 들어가다. 급습[돌격]하다: *Enemy troops storm ed the city.* 적군이 그 도시를 급습했다. **2** [I] to go somewhere fast because you are very angry ‖ 매우 화가 나서 어딘가에 빠르게 가다. 격한 기세로 돌진하다: *Jack stormed in, demanding an explanation.* 잭이 들이닥쳐서 해명을 요구했다.

storm·y /ˈstɔrmi/ *adj* **1** full of rain, strong winds, snow etc. ‖ 비·강풍·눈 등으로 가득 찬. 폭풍(우)의. 날씨가 험악한: *stormy weather* 악천후 / *a stormy day* 폭풍우 치는 날 **2** a stormy relationship or situation is one in which people are very angry, excited, and unreasonable ‖ 사람들이 매우 화가 나고 흥분하여 비이성적인 관계나 상황이 된. 난폭한. 험악한

sto·ry /ˈstɔri/ *n* **1** a description of an event that is intended to entertain people ‖ 사람들을 즐겁게 할 의도의 어떤 사건에 대한 기술. 이야기: *The movie is based on a true story.* 그 영화는 실화에 바탕하고 있다. / *a ghost/bedtime/love story* 유령[동화, 사랑] 이야기 / *Grandma used to read/tell us stories every night.* 할머니는 우리에게 매일 밤 이야기를 읽어[들려]주시곤 했다. **2** a report in a newspaper or news broadcast about a recent event ‖ 최근 사건에 대한 신문이나 뉴스 방송의 보도. 기사: *a front-page story in "The Chronicle"* "더 크라니클"지에 실린 일면 기사 **3** a floor or level of a building ‖ 건물의 층이나 층수: *There's a balcony on the third story.* 3층에는 발코니가 있다 / *a three-story building* (=with three levels) 3층 건물 **4 it's a long story** SPOKEN said when you think something will take too long to explain ‖ 어떤 것이 설명하려면 너무 오래 걸릴 것으로 생각할 때 쓰여. 말하자면 길다: *It's a long story – I'll tell you later.* 말하자면 길어. 나중에 이야기해 줄게. **5 to make a long story short** SPOKEN said when you want to finish explaining something quickly ‖ 어떤 것을 급하게 설명해서 끝내고 싶을 때 쓰여. 짧게[간략히] 말하다: *To make a long story short, she got mad and left.* 간단히 말해서, 그녀는 화가 나서 떠났다. **6** an excuse, explanation, or lie ‖ 변명[해명, 거짓말]: *Do you believe his story?* 너는 그의 말을 믿냐?

sto·ry·tell·er /ˈstɔri,tɛlɚ/ *n* someone who tells stories ‖ 이야기를 들려주는 사람. 이야기꾼

stout¹ /staʊt/ *adj* **1** fairly fat and heavy ‖ 꽤 살찌고 무게가 나가는. 뚱뚱한. 튼튼한: *a stout middle-aged man* 몸집이 좋은 중년 남성 **2** brave and determined ‖ 용감하고 결단력이 있는. 대담한. 단호한: *a stout defender of human rights* 인권의 든든한 옹호자

stout² *n* [U] a strong dark beer ‖ 독한 흑맥주. 스타우트

stove /stoʊv/ *n* a piece of kitchen equipment on which you cook food in pots and pans, and that contains an OVEN ‖ 냄비와 프라이팬을 올려 놓고 음식을 요리하고 오븐이 들어 있는 주방 기구. 스토브

stow /stoʊ/, **stow away** *v* [T] to put something away neatly in a place until you need it again ‖ 사물을 다시 필요할 때까지 어떤 장소에 깔끔하게 치워 놓다. 집어[채워], 챙겨넣다: *Please stow all carry-on baggage under your seat.* 휴대 수화물은 모두 좌석 밑에 집어넣어 주세요.

stow·a·way /ˈstoʊə,weɪ/ *n* someone who hides on an aircraft, ship etc. in order to travel without paying ‖ 돈을 내지 않고 여행하기 위해 항공기·배 등에 숨어 든 사람. 밀항자

strad·dle /ˈstrædl/ *v* [T] **1** to sit or stand with your legs on either side of something ‖ 어떤 것의 양쪽으로 다리를 벌리고 앉거나 서다. 다리를 벌리고 앉다[서다]: *boys straddling the railings* 난간에 걸터앉아 있는 소년들 **2** to seem to agree with two different opinions about something ‖ 어떤 것에 대한 두 가지 상반된 의견에 동의하는 것처럼 보이다. …의 찬반을 분명히 하지 않다. 양다리를 걸치다: *The government is straddling the issue of lowering taxes.* 정부는 세금 인하 문제에 이중적인 입장을 취하고 있다.

strag·gle /ˈstrægəl/ *v* [I] if people in a large group straggle, they move away from the group one at a time ‖ 대규모 집단 속에 있는 사람들이 한 번에 한 명씩 떨어져 나오다. 빠져나오다. 낙오하다: *Travelers were beginning to straggle out of Customs.* 여행객들은 하나씩 세관을 빠져나오기 시작하고 있었다.

strag·gly /ˈstrægli/ *adj* INFORMAL growing or spreading out in a messy, uneven way ‖ 엉망이고 고르지 못하게 자라거나 산재해 있는. 마구 자란. 헝클어진: *straggly hair* 헝클어진 머리

straight¹ /streɪt/ *adv* **1** in a straight line ‖ 일직선으로. 똑바로: *Stand up straight!* 똑바로 서라! / *The bathroom's straight down the hall.* 화장실은 홀을 곧장 내려가서 있다. / *She kept staring* *straight ahead.* 그녀는 앞쪽을 똑바로 계속 응시하고 있었다. **2** immediately, directly, or without any delay ‖ 즉시, 바로, 지체 없이. 곧바로: *Why didn't you go straight to the police?* 왜 경찰서로 곧장 가지 않았니? / *Come home straight after school.* 학교 끝나면 바로 집으로 와라. **3** happening one after the other in a series ‖ 잇따라 연속적으로 일어나. 계속해서: *He worked 18 hours straight without a break.* 그는 쉬지 않고 18시간을 계속 일했다. **4 not see/think straight** to be unable to see or think clearly ‖ 명확하게 보거나 생각할 수 없다. 제대로[똑똑히] …하지 못하다: *It was so noisy, I could hardly think straight.* 너무나 시끄러워서 생각을 제대로 할 수가 없었다. **5 get/keep sth straight** SPOKEN to correctly understand the facts about a situation without being confused ‖ 혼동되지 않고 어떤 상황에 대한 사실을 올바르게 이해하다. 분명하게 이해하다. 분명히 하다: *Let me get this straight: Don's not coming, but Peggy is?* 분명하게 하자. 돈은 오지 않고, 그럼 페기는? / *I can't keep all their names straight.* 나는 그들 모두의 이름을 제대로 파악할 수가 없어.

straight² *adj* **1** not bent or curved ‖ 구부러지거나 굽지 않은. 곧은. 일직선의: *a straight line* 직선 / *My sister has straight hair.* (=without curls) 내 언니의 머리는 생머리다. **2** level or upright, and not bent or leaning ‖ 수평적이거나 수직적이고 구부러지거나 기울지 않은. 수평의. 수직의. 직립의: *Is this sign straight?* 이 간판은 똑바르냐? / *straight teeth* 고른 이 **3** honest and direct ‖ 정직한. 솔직한. 숨김없는. 성실한: *I wish you'd give me a straight answer.* 나는 네가 솔직한 대답을 해주길 바란다. **4** one after the other ‖ 잇따른. 연속한: *The Australian team won three straight victories.* 호주 팀은 세 번 연속 우승했다. **5 get straight A's** to earn the grade "A" in all of your school subjects ‖ 전 학과목에서 "A"학점을 따다. 전과목 A를 얻다 **6 a straight face** a serious expression on your face even though you want to laugh or smile ‖ 웃거나 미소 짓고 싶은데도 불구하고 얼굴에 짓는 심각한 표정. 정색. 진지한 표정: *How did you manage to keep a straight face?* 너는 어떻게 웃지 않고 정색을 할 수 있었니? **7** INFORMAL ⇨ HETEROSEXUAL **8** alcoholic drinks that are straight do not have any ice, water etc. added to them ‖ 술이 얼음·물 등을 첨가하지 않은. 얼음[물]을 타

지 않은 **9** INFORMAL unwilling to take risks or do exciting things ‖ 위험을 감수하거나 모험적인 것을 하기 좋아하지 않는. 보수적인. 인습적인: *"What's his girlfriend like?" "She's pretty straight."* "그의 여자 친구는 어떤 사람이야?" "그 여자는 꽤 보수적이야."

straight³ *n* **the straight and narrow** a sensible and moral way of living ‖ 지각 있고 도덕적인 생활 방식. 정직한[올바른] 생활: *Without his father to keep him on the straight and narrow, Abe went into debt.* 그를 바르게 살도록 이끌어줄 아버지가 없어서 에이브는 빚을 졌다.

straight·en /'streɪtʔn/ *v* **1** [I, T] to become straight or make something straight ‖ 곧아지다 또는 어떤 것을 곧게 하다. 바르게 하다[펴다]: *Try straightening out your legs.* 다리를 곧게 펴 봐. **2** [T] also **straighten up** to clean a room that is messy ‖ 어질러진 방을 청소하다. …을 정리하다

straighten sb/sth ↔ **out** *phr v* [T] to deal with a difficult situation or solve a problem ‖ 어려운 상황을 처리하거나 문제를 풀다. 바로잡다. …을 해결하다: *I'll talk to him and see if I can straighten things out.* 내가 그 사람과 얘기해서 문제를 해결할 수 있는지 볼게.

straighten up *phr v* [I] to start behaving well ‖ 행동거지를 잘 하기 시작하다. 올바르게 살다: *You straighten up right now, young man!* 젊은이, 지금 당장 똑바로 살게!

straight·for·ward /ˌstreɪt'fɔrwəd/ *adj* **1** simple or easy to understand ‖ 간단하거나 이해하기 쉬운. 수월한: *The exam questions are fairly straightforward.* 그 시험 문제는 상당히 쉬웠다. **2** honest and not hiding what you think ‖ 정직하고 생각하는 바를 숨기지 않는. 진솔한. 솔직한: *a straightforward response* 솔직한 대답

straight·jack·et /'streɪtˌdʒækɪt/ *n* ⇨ STRAITJACKET

strain¹ /streɪn/ *n* **1** [C, U] worry that you feel because you are always busy or always dealing with problems ‖ 항상 바쁘거나 문제들을 처리해야 하기 때문에 느끼는 걱정. 중압[압박]감: *He couldn't cope with the strain of being a lawyer.* 그는 변호사 생활의 중압감을 견딜 수가 없었다. **2** a problem or difficulty caused by using too much of something ‖ 어떤 것을 너무 많이 사용해서 일어나는 문제나 어려움. 부담. 과로: *Paying for our kids' educations put a huge strain on our savings.* 아이들 교육비 지출이 저

축에 큰 부담을 주고 있다. **3** [U] a force that pulls, stretches, or pushes something] 힘. 인장력. 압력: *The rope snapped under the strain.* (=because of the force) 밧줄은 무게를 이기지 못하고 끊어졌다. **4** [C, U] an injury caused by stretching a muscle or using part of your body too much] 근육이 늘어나거나 몸의 일부를 너무 많이 사용해서 일어난 부상. 삠. 접질림. 과로: *eye strain* 눈의 피로 —compare SPRAIN **5** [C, U] a difficult situation, that causes problems in a relationship, so that two people or groups are no longer friendly or no longer trust each other] 상호 관계에서 문제를 일으켜 두 사람이나 집단이 더 이상 친근하거나 서로를 더 이상 믿지 않는 어려운 상황. 소원해짐: *The strain was beginning to show in their marriage.* 그들의 결혼 생활에 금이 가기 시작하고 있었다. **6** one of the particular varieties of a plant, animal, or living thing] 식물[동물, 생물]의 특정한 종류들 중의 하나. 변종: *a new strain of the virus* 그 바이러스의 새로운 변종

strain² *v* **1** [T] to injure part of your body by stretching it too much] 신체의 일부를 너무 무리하게 뻗어서 다치다. 삐다. 접지르다: *Kevin strained a muscle in his neck.* 케빈은 목의 근육이 뻐끗했다. **2** [I, T] to use a lot of effort, supplies, or money to try to do something] 어떤 것을 하려고 많은 노력[물품, 돈]을 사용하다. 무리하게 쓰다. 혹사하다: *She moved closer, straining to hear what they said.* 그녀는 그들이 하는 말을 들으려고 귀를 쫑긋 세우며 더 가까이 다가갔다. / *The lack of federal money is straining the University's finances.* 연방 정부의 기금 부족 때문에 그 대학은 재정적으로 부담을 느끼고 있다. **3** [T] to cause problems in a relationship] 상호 관계에서 문제를 일으키다. 긴장시키다: *It's one of the issues that is straining relations between the countries.* 그것이 양국간의 관계를 긴장시키고 있는 문제들 중의 하나이다. **4** [T] to separate solid things from a liquid by pouring the mixture through a STRAINER or cloth] 체나 천에 혼합물을 부어 통과시켜 액체로부터 고형 물질을 분리시키다. 거르다 **5** [I] to pull hard at something or push hard against something] 어떤 것을 세게 당기거나 밀다. 잡아당기다. 밀어붙이다: *a boat straining against the wind* 바람을 가르고 나가는 배

strained /streɪnd/ *adj* **1** unfriendly, uncomfortable, and showing a lack of trust] 불친절한, 불편한, 신뢰 부족을 나타내는. 부자연한. 어색한. 거북한: *a strained conversation* 부자연스런 대화 **2** worried and tired] 걱정하고 지친. 피곤한. 긴장된: *Alex looks strained.* 알렉스는 피곤해 보인다.

strain·er /'streɪnə/ *n* a kitchen tool used for separating solid food from a liquid] 액체로부터 고형 음식을 분리할 때 사용하는 주방 기구. 체

strait /streɪt/ *n* a narrow passage of water that joins two larger areas of water] 두 개의 더 큰 수역(水域)을 연결하는 좁은 수로. 해협: *the Strait of Gibraltar* 지브롤터 해협

strait·jack·et /'streɪt‚dʒækɪt/ *n* a special coat for violent or mentally ill people that prevents them from moving their arms] 난폭한 사람들이나 정신 질환자들이 팔을 움직이지 못하게 막는 특수한 상의. 구속복

strand /strænd/ *n* a single thin piece of thread, hair, wire etc.] 실·머리카락·철사 등의 가느다란 한 줄. 가닥. 올

strand·ed /'strændɪd/ *adj* needing help because you are unable to move from a particular place] 특정 장소에서 움직일 수 없어서 도움이 필요한. 막다른 골목에 다다른. 막혀 오도가도 못하는: *I was stranded at the airport without any money.* 나는 돈 한 푼도 없이 공항에서 오도 가도 못했다.

strange¹ /streɪndʒ/ *adj* **1** unusual, surprising, or difficult to understand] 보통과 다르거나 놀랍거나, 또는 이해하기 어려운. 이상한. 별난: *I had a strange dream last night.* 나는 간밤에 묘한 꿈을 꾸었다. / *It's strange that Brad isn't here yet.* 브래드가 아직 여기에 없다니 이상하다. / *That's strange – I thought I left my keys on the table.* 그것 참 이상하네. 내 생각에는 탁자 위에 열쇠를 놓아두었는데. / *At first the city seemed strange to me.* 처음에 그 도시는 내게 괴상스러워 보였다. ✗DON'T SAY "the city seemed strange for me."✗ "the city seemed strange for me"라고는 하지 않는다. **2** not familiar] 익숙하지 않은. 잘 모르는. 낯선: *I was all alone in a strange country.* 나는 낯선 나라에서 완전히 혼자였다. – **strangeness** *n* [U]

strange² *adv* SPOKEN NONSTANDARD strangely] 이상하게: *Reed has been acting strange.* 리드는 이상하게 행동하고 있었다.

strange·ly /'streɪndʒli/ *adv* in an unusual or surprising way] 보통과 다르거나 놀랍게. 이상하게 기묘하게: *Cathy* *was strangely silent at dinner.* 캐시는 저녁 식사 때 이상하게 조용했다.

strang·er /'streɪndʒɚ/ *n* **1** someone you do not know ‖ 알지 못하는 사람. 낯선 사람. 남: *Mom told us never to talk to strangers.* 엄마는 우리에게 낯선 사람과 절대 말하지 말라고 하셨다. **2** someone in a new and unfamiliar place or situation ‖ 새롭고 익숙하지 않은 장소나 상황에 있는 사람. 신참자. 문외한: *a stranger to New York* 뉴욕에 새로 온 사람

stran·gle /'stræŋgəl/ *v* [T] to kill someone by tightly pressing his/her throat with your hands, a rope etc. ‖ 손·로프 등으로 누군가의 목을 꼭 졸라서 죽이다. 교살하다. 질식사시키다. —
strangulation /ˌstræŋgyə'leɪʃən/ *n* [U]

stran·gle·hold /'stræŋgəl,hoʊld/ *n* the power to completely control something ‖ 사물을 철저히 통제하는 힘. 속박. 지배: *The government had a stranglehold on the media.* 정부는 매스 미디어[대중 매체]를 완전히 지배했다.

strap¹ /stræp/ *n* a strong band of cloth or leather that is attached to a shoe, bag etc. to make sure it does not fall down or off ‖ 떨어져 내리거나 벗겨지지 않도록 신발·가방 등에 부착된 천이나 가죽으로 된 질긴 끈: *a watch strap* 손목시계 끈 / *bra straps* 브래지어 끈

strap² *v* **-pped, -pping** [T] to fasten someone or something to a place using one or more STRAPs ‖ 하나 이상의 끈을 써서 사람이나 물건을 어떤 장소에 고정시키다. 묶다. 매다: *Make sure your backpack is strapped on tightly.* 네 배낭이 잘 매였는지 확인해라.

strap·less /'stræplɪs/ *adj* a strapless dress, BRA, etc. does not have any STRAPs over the shoulders ‖ 옷·브래지어 등이 어깨에 걸치는 끈이 전혀 없는. 어깨끈이 없는

strapped /stræpt/ *adj* INFORMAL having little or no money to spend ‖ 쓸 돈이 거의 또는 전혀 없는. 돈에 궁한[조들리는]: *I'd offer to pay, but I'm strapped for cash.* 내가 내고 싶은데 현금이 전혀 없다.

stra·ta /'stræṭə, 'streɪṭə/ *n* the plural of STRATUM ‖ stratum의 복수형

strat·a·gem /'stræṭədʒəm/ *n* a trick or plan used for deceiving an enemy or gaining an advantage ‖ 적을 속이거나 이득을 얻기 위해 쓰이는 속임수나 계획. 계략. 책략

stra·te·gic /strə'tidʒɪk/ *adj* **1** done as part of a military, business, or political plan ‖ 군사적이나 사업적인, 또는 정치적인 계획의 일환으로 행한. 전략적인: *the strategic position of US armed forces in Europe* 유럽에서의 미군사력의 전략적 지위 **2** useful for a particular purpose, especially fighting a war ‖ 특정 목적, 특히 전투를 하는 데에 유용한. 전술상 불가결한: *strategic missiles* 전략 미사일

strat·e·gy /'stræṭədʒi/ *n* **1** [C, U] the set of plans and skills used in order to gain success or achieve an aim ‖ 성공을 얻어내거나 목표를 달성하는 데에 쓰이는 일련의 계획과 기술. 방법. 방책: *a strategy for improving adult education programs* 성인 교육 프로그램을 개선하기 위한 방책 **2** [U] a country's plans for how to use its armies, equipment etc. effectively during a war ‖ 전쟁 중 군대·장비 등을 효율적으로 사용하는 방법에 관한 국가의 계획. 전략. 전술

strat·i·fied /'stræṭə,faɪd/ *adj* **1** [U] separated into different social classes ‖ 각각 다른 사회적 계층으로 나뉜. 계층화된: *a stratified society* 계층화된 사회 **2** [C, U] rocks or soil that are stratified have separated into different layers ‖ 바위 또는 토양이 각각 다른 층으로 나누어진. 몇 개의 지층으로 이루어진 —
stratify *v* [T]

strat·o·sphere /'stræṭə,sfɪr/ *n* the stratosphere the outer layer of air surrounding the earth, starting about six miles above the earth ‖ 지상 6마일쯤에서 시작되는, 지구를 둘러싼 대기의 외곽층. 성층권

stra·tum /'stræṭəm, 'streɪ-/ *n, plural* **strata** /-ṭə/ **1** a layer of a particular type of rock or dirt ‖ 특정한 형태의 바위나 흙의 층. 지층 **2** a social class in society ‖ 사회 내의 계급. 계층

straw /strɔ/ *n* **1** [C, U] dried stems of wheat or similar plants, used for making things such as baskets, or a single stem of this ‖ 바구니 등의 물건을 만드는 데에 쓰이는 밀이나 유사한 식물들의 건조된 줄기, 또는 이것의 한 으로서. (밀)짚. 지푸라기: *a straw hat* 밀짚모자 **2** a thin tube of plastic used for sucking a drink from a bottle or cup ‖ 병이나 컵의 음료수를 빨아들이는 데에 쓰는 가는 플라스틱 대롱. 빨대. 스트로 —see picture at GLASS **3** the last/final straw the last problem in a series of problems that makes you finally get angry ‖ 일련의 문제들 중에서 결국 화나게 하는 최종 문제. 견딜 수 없는 마지막 단계[한계에 상황]

straw·ber·ry /'strɔ,bɛri/ *n* a sweet red BERRY with small pale seeds on its surface ‖ 표면에 회백색의 작은 씨들이 박힌 달콤한 빨간 작은 과일. 딸기 —see picture on page 944

stray¹ /streɪ/ v to move away from a safe or familiar area without intending to ‖ 그럴 생각 없이 안전하거나 익숙한 곳에서 벗어나다. 길을 잃다: *The kitten had strayed from its mother.* 그 새끼 고양이는 어미를 잃어버렸다.

stray² adj **1** a stray animal is lost or has no home ‖ 동물이 길을 잃거나 집이 없는. 길 잃은 **2** accidentally separated from a larger group ‖ 우연히 큰 집단에서 떨어져 나온. 외톨이의: *a few stray hairs* 몇 가닥의 빠져버린 머리카락

stray³ n an animal that is lost or has no home ‖ 길을 잃거나 집이 없는 동물

streak¹ /strik/ n **1** a colored line or thin mark ‖ 색깔 있는 선이나 엷은 자국. 줄무늬: *a few gray streaks in her hair* 그녀의 머리카락 중 몇 가닥의 흰 머리카락 **2** a quality you have that seems different from the rest of your character ‖ 본인 성격의 다른 부분과 달라 보이는 어떤 특성. 경향. 성향. 기질: *Richard has a wild streak in him.* 리차드에게는 난폭한 기질이 있다. **3** a period when you are always successful or always failing ‖ 항상 성공적이거나 항상 실패하는 기간. 연속기. 일련: *Our team was on a winning streak.* 우리 팀은 연승 행진 중이었다. **– streaky** adj

streak² v **1** [T] to cover something with STREAKs ‖ 줄로 사물을 덮다. …에 줄(무늬)을 넣다: *Marcia's face was streaked with sweat.* 마시아의 얼굴에는 땀이 줄줄 흘렀다. **2** [I] to move or run very quickly ‖ 매우 빨리 움직이거나 달리다. 번개같이 가다[날래게 이동하다]: *A fighter jet streaked across the sky.* 전투기가 창공을 번개같이 가로질렀다.

stream¹ /strim/ n **1** a natural flow of water that is smaller than a river ‖ 강보다는 작은 자연적인 물의 흐름. 시내. 개울: *We used to go fishing in this stream.* 우리는 이 냇가로 낚시하러 가곤 했다. **2** a long continuous series of people, vehicles, events etc. ‖ 사람·차량·사건 등이 길게 계속 이어짐. 끊임없는 움직임. 연속(됨): *a stream of cars* 끊임없이 이어지는 차량 / *a stream of ideas* 꼬리를 물고 이어지는 생각 **3** a flow of water, gas, smoke etc. ‖ 물·가스·연기 등의 흐름. 수류. 조류. 기류: *a stream of warm air* 난기류

stream² v [I] to move quickly and continuously in one direction, especially in large amounts ‖ 한 방향으로, 특히 대량으로 재빠르게 계속적으로 움직이다. 속속 이어지다. 쇄도하다: *Tears were streaming down his cheeks.* 눈물이 그의 볼을 타고 줄줄 흘러내리고 있었다. / *People streamed out of the movie theater.* 사람들이 영화관에서 줄지어 쏟아져 나왔다.

stream·er /ˈstrimɚ/ n a long narrow flag or piece of colored paper used as a decoration for special events ‖ 특별한 행사의 장식물로 쓰이는 길고 좁은 깃발이나 색종이 조각. 기(旗)드림. 색 테이프

stream·line /ˈstrimlaɪn/ v [T] **1** to make something such as a business or process become simpler and more effective ‖ 일·과정 등을 보다 단순하고 효과적이 되게 하다. 합리화[간소화, 효율화]하다: *The hospital has streamlined the paperwork for nurses.* 그 병원은 간호사들의 서류 정리 작업을 간소화했다. **2** to make something have a smooth shape so that it moves easily through the air or water ‖ 물체를 매끈한 형태를 갖게 해서 대기나 물 속에서 더 쉽게 움직이게 하다. 유선형으로 만들다 **– streamlined** adj: *streamlined cars* 유선형 자동차들

street /strit/ n **1** a road in a town or city with houses, stores etc. on one or both sides ‖ 한쪽 또는 양쪽에 집·점포 등이 들어선 소도시나 대도시의 길. 거리. 가로: *What street do you live on?* 어느 거리에 사시죠? / *the corner of Main Street and 4th Avenue* 메인가와 4번가의 모퉁이 **2 the streets** used when talking about the busy part of a city, where there is a lot of activity, excitement, and crime ‖ 많은 활동·자극·범죄가 있는 도시의 복잡한 구역을 언급하는 데에 쓰여. 시내. 중심가: *homeless people living on the streets* 시내에서 지내고 있는 노숙자들

USAGE NOTE street and road

A **street** is in a town or city. A **road** is usually in the country. Sometimes however, the word **road** is used in the names of **streets**, especially wide ones.
street는 소도시나 대도시에 있다. **road**는 보통 교외에 있다. 그러나 때때로 **road**는 특히 대로인 경우에 **street**를 대신하여 쓰인다.

---

street·car /ˈstritˌkar/ n an electric bus that moves along metal tracks in the road ‖ 도로상의 금속제 궤도를 따라 움직이는 전기 버스. 노면[시가] 전차

street light, street·light /'strit-lait/ *n* a light on a long pole that stands next to a street ‖ 도로변에 서 있는 긴 기둥 위의 등. 가로등 —see picture on page 945

strength /strɛŋkθ, strɛnθ/ *n*

1 ▶PHYSICAL 육체적◀ [U] the physical power and energy that you have ‖ 사람이 가진 육체적 힘과 기력. 체력: *I didn't have the strength to get up.* 나는 일어날 힘이 없었다. / *Bruce is lifting weights to build up his strength.* 브루스는 힘을 기르기 위해 역기를 들고 있다.

2 ▶DETERMINATION 결의◀ [U] the quality of being brave or determined in dealing with difficult situations ‖ 어려운 상황을 처리하는 용감하거나 단호한 특성. 정신력. 용기. 결단력: *It took great strength to raise three children by herself.* 그녀 혼자서 세 아이를 키우는 데는 대단한 용기가 필요했다.

3 ▶COUNTRY/SYSTEM ETC. 나라/제도◀ [U] the power of an organization, country, or system ‖ 조직이나 국가, 또는 체제의 힘. 능력. 세력. 국세(國勢): *The US increased its military strength in the region.* 미국은 그 지역의 군사력을 증강했다.

4 ▶FEELING/BELIEF ETC. 감정/신념◀ [U] how strong a feeling, belief, or relationship is ‖ 감정이나 신념, 또는 관계 등의 강도. 세기: *The strength of their marriage was being tested.* 그들의 결혼 생활의 강도는 시험받고 있었다.

5 ▶QUALITY/ABILITY 특성/능력◀ a particular quality or ability that makes someone or something successful and effective ‖ 사람이나 사물을 성공적이고 효과적으로 만들어 주는 특정한 성질이나 능력. 강점. 장점: *His ambition is both a strength and a weakness.* 그의 야망은 강점이자 약점이다. / *the strengths of the argument* 그 논쟁의 장점

6 ▶ALCOHOL/MEDICINE 술/약◀ [C, U] how strong a liquid such as an alcoholic drink, medicine, or cleaning liquid is ‖ 알코올 음료나 의약품, 또는 세정액 등의 강도. 효능. 효과. 농도: *a full-strength fabric cleaner* 초강력 직물 세제

7 ▶MONEY 화폐◀ the value of a particular type of money when compared to other types ‖ 다른 종류의 화폐들과 비교해 본 특정 종류 화폐의 가치. 강세. 환율의 세기: *The yen gained in strength against the dollar today.* 엔화는 오늘 달러화에 대해 강세를 보였다.

8 on the strength of sth because of something that persuaded or influenced you ‖ 설득했거나 영향을 미쳤던 것 때문에. …의 덕분에. …에 입각[의거]하여: *We chose this car on the strength of his advice.* 우리는 그의 충고에 따라서 이 차를 선택했다. —compare WEAKNESS —see usage note at FORCE¹ ‖

strength·en /'strɛŋkθən, 'strɛnθən/ *v* **1** [I, T] to become stronger, or to make something such as a feeling, belief, or relationship stronger ‖ 더 강하게 되다, 또는 감정이나 신념, 또는 관계 등을 더 강하게 하다. 강해지다. 강화하다: *The problems had strengthened their relationship.* 그 문제는 그들의 관계를 더욱 강화시켰다. **2** [T] to make something such as your body or a building stronger ‖ 사람의 육체나 건물 등을 더욱 튼튼하게 하다. 강화하다. 견고하게 하다: *an exercise to strengthen your arms* 팔(힘)을 강화하는 운동 / *extra supports to strengthen the bridge* 다리를 견고하게 하기 위한 보강 지지대 **3** [I, T] to increase in value or improve, or to make something do this ‖ 가치가 증가하거나 개선되다, 또는 사물을 이렇게 하게 하다. 증강되다. 증강시키다: *new trade agreements to strengthen the economy* 경제를 진작시키기 위한 새로운 무역 협정 —opposite WEAKEN

stren·u·ous /'strɛnyuəs/ *adj* using a lot of effort or strength ‖ 많은 노력이나 힘을 사용하는. 정력적인. 격렬한: *strenuous exercise* 격렬한 운동 / *strenuous objections to the plan* 계획에 대한 격렬한 반대 - **strenuously** *adv*

strep throat /ˌstrɛp 'θroʊt/ *n* [U] INFORMAL a fairly common medical condition in which your throat is very sore ‖ 아주 흔히 볼 수 있는, 목이 매우 아픈 의학적 증상. 급성인후염

stress¹ /strɛs/ *n* **1** [C, U] continuous feelings of worry caused by difficulties in your life that prevent you from relaxing ‖ 긴장을 풀지 못하게 하는 생활의 어려움으로 초래된 지속적인 불안감. 압박감. 긴장감. 스트레스: *Baxter's under a lot of stress at work.* 백스터는 직장에서 많은 스트레스를 받고 있다. / *the stresses and strains of modern life* 현대 생활의 스트레스와 긴장감 **2** [U] special attention or importance given to an idea or activity; EMPHASIS ‖ 어떤 생각이나 활동에 부여된 특별한 주의나 중요성. 강조. 역설. 중점; ㉠ emphasis: *In his report, he laid stress on the need for more teachers.* 그의 보고에서 그는 더 많은 교사가 필요하다고 역설했다. **3** [C, U] the physical force or pressure on an object‖ 대상물에 대한 물리적 힘이나 압력. 압박: *rocks subjected to stress and high temperatures* 압력과 고온 하에 놓인 암석 **4** [C, U] the degree to which you emphasize a word or part of a word when you say it‖ 말할 때 낱말이나 낱말의 일부를 강조하는 정도. 강세. 악센트

stress² *v* [T] **1** to emphasize a statement, fact, or idea‖ 발언이나 사실, 또는 생각을 강조하다. 역설하다: *She stressed the need for more health education for teens.* 그녀는 10대들을 위한 더 많은 건강 교육의 필요성을 역설했다. **2** also **stress out** SPOKEN to become STRESSED‖ 스트레스를 받다. 스트레스가 쌓이다: *Terry's stressing about his midterms .* 테리는 중간고사에 대해 스트레스를 받고 있다. **3** to say a word or part of a word loudly or with more force‖ 단어나 단어의 일부를, 크게 또는 더 힘주어 말하다. 강세[악센트]를 두다

stressed /strɛst/ also **stressed out** *adj* SPOKEN so worried and tired that you cannot relax‖ 너무 걱정되고 피로해서 쉴 수 없는. 스트레스가 쌓인: *She was really stressed out about all the problems at home.* 그녀는 가정의 제반사에 대한 스트레스로 정말 지쳤다.

stress·ful /ˈstrɛsfəl/ *adj* making you worry a lot‖ 많이 걱정하게 하는. 스트레스가 많은: *They're living under very stressful conditions.* 그들은 매우 스트레스가 많은 환경 속에서 살고 있다.

stretch¹ /strɛtʃ/ *v* **1** [I, T] also **stretch out** to become bigger or looser as a result of being pulled, or to make something do this by pulling it‖ 잡아당겨진 결과로 더 커지거나 헐렁해지다, 또는 물건을 잡아당겨 이렇게 하게 하다. 늘어나다. 늘이다: *Dad stretched my T-shirt!* 아빠가 내 티셔츠를 늘여 놨어요! / *My new sweater has stretched.* 새 스웨터가 늘어났다. **2** [I, T] to reach out your arms, legs, or body to full length‖ 팔이나 다리, 또는 몸을 완전히 뻗다. 한껏 펴다[펼치다]. 내밀다: *He stretched his arms out to try to reach the branch.* 그는 가지를 잡으려고 손을 한껏 뻗쳤다. / *Be sure to stretch before you exercise.* 운동하기 전에 준비 운동을 꼭 해라. **3** [I] to spread out over a large area, or continue for a long period‖ 넓은 지역에 걸쳐 뻗어 있다, 또는 장기간 동안 계속되다. …까지 펼쳐지다[달하다, 미치다]: *The desert stretched to the horizon.* 사막이 지평선까지 뻗어 있었다. / *The project will probably stretch into next year.* 그 프로젝트는 아마 내년까지 계속

될 것이다. **4** [I] if cloth stretches, it changes shape when you pull or wear it, and becomes its original shape when you stop‖ 옷이 당기거나 입으면 형태가 바뀌고, 놔두면 원래의 형태가 되다. 탄력적이다. 잘 늘어나다: *The shorts stretch to fit your shape.* 그 반바지는 네 체형에 맞게 잘 늘어난다. **5** [T] to pull something so it is tight‖ 무엇을 잡아당겨서 팽팽하게 하다. 팽팽하게 치다. 세게 당기다: *We can stretch a rope between two trees.* 우리는 두 나무 사이에 로프를 팽팽히 당겨 칠 수 있다. **6 stretch sth to the limit** to use as much of a supply of something as is available, without having enough for anything else‖ 다른 용도에 쓸 만큼 충분히 갖추지 못하고 쓸 수 있는 최대량을 사용하다. 한계에 도달하다: *Our resources are already stretched to the limit.* 우리의 자원은 이미 한계에 달했다. **7 stretch your legs** INFORMAL to go for a walk‖ 산책하러 가다

stretch out *phr v* [I] INFORMAL to lie down so you can rest or sleep‖ 쉬거나 잘 수 있게 눕다. 늘어지게 눕다: *I'll just stretch out on the couch for a while.* 잠깐만 소파에 쭉 뻗고 누워야겠다.

stretch² *n* **1** an area of water or land‖ 수역, 또는 지역. 구간: *a dangerous stretch of road* 위험한 도로 구간 **2** a continuous period of time‖ 연속된 기간. 일련의 기간. 연속: *During the summer we worked 12 hours at a stretch.* (=without stopping) 여름 내내 우리는 12시간씩 연속해서 일했다. **3** the action of stretching part of your body‖ 신체의 일부를 뻗는 동작. 뻗기·펴기. 신장 **4** [U] the ability of a material to become bigger or longer without tearing‖ 소재가 찢어지지 않고 커지거나 길어지는 능력. 신장력. 탄력성 **5 not by any stretch (of the imagination)** SPOKEN used in order to say that something is definitely not true‖ 어떤 것이 분명히 사실이 아니라고 말하는 데에 쓰여. 아무리 생각해 봐도 …아닌: *She's not fat, by any stretch of the imagination.* 아무리 생각해도 그녀는 뚱뚱하지 않다.

stretch·er /ˈstrɛtʃɚ/ *n* a covered frame on which you carry someone who is injured or too sick to walk‖ 부상당하거나 너무 아파 걸을 수 없는 사람을 운반하는 커버를 씌운 틀. 들것. 스트레처

strew /struː/ *v* **strewed, strewn** /struːn/ *or* **strewed, strewing** [T] to throw or drop a number of things over an area in a messy way‖ 많은 것을 어떤 지역에 어수선하게 던지거나 떨어뜨리다.

흩뿌리다: *Papers were strewn all over the floor.* 서류가 온 바닥 위에 흩어져 있었다.

strick·en /ˈstrɪkən/ *adj* FORMAL experiencing the bad effects of trouble, illness, sadness etc. ‖ 고통·아픔·슬픔 등의 나쁜 결과를 경험한. …을 입은[당한, 겪은], 받은: *a woman stricken by grief* 슬픔을 겪은 여성 —see also POVERTY-STRICKEN

strict /strɪkt/ *adj* **1** demanding that rules should be obeyed ‖ 규칙이 지켜져야 함을 요구하는. 엄한. 엄격한: *Her parents are very strict.* 그녀의 부모는 매우 엄격하다. / *Strictly speaking* (=to be exact about what I am saying) the drug has not yet been approved for use. 엄격히 말해서 그 약은 아직 사용이 승인되지 않았다. **2** a strict rule, order etc. must be obeyed ‖ 규정·명령 등이 반드시 준수되어야 하는. 엄중한. 엄수하야 하는: *I have strict instructions not to let you stay up late.* 나는 너를 밤늦게까지 자지 않고 있지 못하게 하라는 엄중한 지시를 받았다. **3** very exact and correct ‖ 매우 정확하고 틀림없는. 엄밀한. 면밀한: *It's not a restaurant in the strictest sense of the word – it's more like a cafe.* 그것은 단어의 엄밀한 의미로는 레스토랑이 아니다. 그것은 오히려 카페에 가깝다.

strict·ly /ˈstrɪktli/ *adv* **1** exactly and correctly ‖ 정확하고 틀림없게. 엄밀히. 엄중히: *That is not strictly true.* 그것은 엄밀하게 사실이 아니다. **2** used in order to emphasize what you are saying ‖ 말하고 있는 것을 강조하는 데 쓰여. 정말로. 꼭: *Our drug treatment program is strictly voluntary.* 우리의 마약 치유 프로그램은 정말 자발적이다. **3** only used for a particular purpose or by a particular person ‖ 오직 특정 목적을 위해서나 특정인에 의해서만 사용되는. 전적으로. 순전히: *These bowls are strictly for decoration; they're too delicate to be used.* 이 그릇들은 순전히 장식용이다. 그것들은 너무 약해서 쓸 수 없다. **4** in a way that must be obeyed ‖ 반드시 준수되어야 한다는 식으로. 절대적으로. 엄격하게: *Smoking is strictly forbidden in the hospital.* 병원 내 흡연은 엄격하게 금지되어 있다.

stride¹ /straɪd/ *v* **strode**, **stridden** /ˈstrɪdn/, **striding** [I] to walk with quick long steps ‖ 빠르고 큰 걸음으로 걷다. 성큼성큼 걷다. 활보하다: *He strode across the room.* 그는 방을 성큼성큼 가로질러 갔다.

stride² *n* **1** a long step that you take when you walk ‖ 걸을 때 취하는 큰 걸음. 활보. 한달음 **2** **make (great) strides** to develop or make progress quickly ‖ 빠르게 발전하거나 진보를 이루다. 장족의 발전을 하다: *The city has made great strides in cleaning up its streets.* 그 도시는 거리 청소 분야에서 장족의 발전을 했다. **3** **take sth in stride** to deal with a problem calmly without becoming annoyed or upset ‖ 짜증나거나 심란해하지 않고 문제를 차분히 처리하다. …을 냉철하게 해내다. 침착하게 받아들이다: *He took it in his stride when I said "no."* 내가 "아니."라고 말했을 때 그는 침착하게 받아들였다.

stri·dent /ˈstraɪdnt/ *adj* **1** showing determination and a strong opinion that may be unpleasant to other people ‖ 다른 사람에게는 불쾌할 수 있는 결단력과 강한 견해를 나타내는. 집요한. 단호한. 귀찮은: *a strident denial of the charges* 사례금에 대한 단호한 거부 **2** a sound that is strident is loud and unpleasant ‖ 소리가 크고 불쾌한. 귀에 거슬리는. 날카로운: *her strident voice* 그녀의 날카로운 목소리

strife /straɪf/ *n* [U] FORMAL trouble or disagreement between two people or groups; CONFLICT ‖ 두 사람이나 집단 사이의 분쟁이나 불화. 투쟁. 반목; ⑲ conflict

strike¹ /straɪk/ *v* **struck**, **struck** *or* **stricken**, **striking**

1 ▶HIT 때리다◀ [T] FORMAL to hit someone or something ‖ 사람이나 물체를 때리다. 치다. 두드리다: *He was struck on the head by a falling rock.* 그는 떨어지는 돌에 머리를 맞았다. / *The car stopped when it struck a tree.* 그 차는 나무를 들이받고 멈췄다.

2 ▶THOUGHT/IDEA 생각/아이디어◀ [T] if a thought or idea strikes you, you suddenly realize it or think of it ‖ 생각이나 아이디어를 갑자기 깨닫거나 생각하다. (문득) 떠오르다. 갑자기 생각나다: *It suddenly struck me that Nora had told the truth.* 노라가 진실을 말했다는 생각이 문득 떠올랐다.

3 **strike sb as sth** to seem to someone to have a particular quality ‖ 누군가에게 특정한 성질을 가진 것으로 보이게 하다. …이라고 느끼게 하다. 인상을 주다: *She strikes me as being a very intelligent woman.* 그녀는 내게 매우 총명한 여성이라는 인상을 준다.

4 ▶WORK 작업◀ [I] to deliberately stop working for a time because of a disagreement about pay, working conditions etc. ‖ 임금·근로 조건 등에 대

한 불화로 일부러 한동안 일을 중단하다. 동맹 파업을 하다: *The dock workers are preparing to strike for shorter work days.* 부두 노동자들은 근로 일수 단축을 위한 파업 중이다.

5 ▶ATTACK 공격◀ [I] to attack quickly and suddenly ‖ 재빠르고 갑작스럽게 공격하다: *The police are waiting for the killer to strike again.* 경찰은 살인자가 다시 습격하기를 기다리고 있다.

6 strike a balance to give the correct amount of attention or importance to two opposing ideas or situations ‖ 두 가지 상반되는 생각 또는 상황에 똑같은 정도의 관심이나 중요성을 부여하다. 균형을 유지하다. 공정을 기하다: *It's never easy to strike a balance between work and family.* 일과 가정 사이에서 균형을 유지하기란 결코 쉽지 않다.

7 ▶STH UNPLEASANT 불쾌한 것◀ [I] if something unpleasant strikes, it happens suddenly ‖ 불쾌한 일이 갑자기 발생하다. 터지다. 내습하다: *The tornado struck in the middle of the night.* 토네이도가 한밤중에 내습했다.

8 strike a deal to agree to do something if someone else does something for you ‖ 다른 사람이 자신에게 어떤 것을 해주면 자신도 어떤 것을 해주기로 동의하다. 협정[협의]하다: *The dispute ended when the company struck a deal with the union.* 그 분규는 회사가 노조와 협정을 맺자 종식되었다.

9 strike a chord to make someone feel that s/he agrees with, likes, or is similar to someone or something ‖ 남에게 다른 사람이나 사물을 찬성하거나 좋아하거나 또는 유사하다는 느낌이 들게 하다. 일치감[동질감]을 자아내다: *The way he writes strikes a chord with me.* 그가 글을 쓰는 방식은 나와 흡사하다.

10 strike a match to make a match burn ‖ 성냥불을 켜다

11 strike oil/gold etc. to discover oil, gold etc. in the ground ‖ 땅 속에서 석유·금 등을 찾아내다. 기름/금을 발견하다

12 ▶CLOCK 시계◀ [I, T] if a clock strikes or strikes one, three, six etc., its bell sounds one, three, six etc. times to show the time ‖ 시계가 시간을 알리기 위해 종이 한 번, 세 번, 여섯 번 울리다. 치다: *The clock struck four.* (=4 o'clock) 시계가 4시를 알렸다. —see usage note at HIT¹

strike down *phr v* to make a law or formal decision stop being legal or officially accepted ‖ 법 또는 공식 결정이 합법적이 되거나 공인되는 것을 중단시키

다. 폐지하다. 파기하다: *An appeals court struck down the decision to set him free.* 항소 법원은 판결을 파기하고 그를 석방했다.

strike out *phr v* **1** [I] INFORMAL to be unsuccessful at something ‖ 어떤 일에 실패하다: *"Did she say she'd go out with you?" "No, I struck out."* "그녀가 너하고 데이트하러 간다고 했니?" "아니, 퇴짜 맞았어." **2** [I,T **strike** sb ↔ **out**] to get three STRIKEs in baseball so that you are not allowed to continue to try to hit, or to make someone do this ‖ 야구에서 스트라이크 3개를 얻어서 계속 치는 것이 허용되지 않다, 또는 남을 이렇게 하게 하다. 삼진 당하다[시키다] **3** [I] to start a difficult trip or experience ‖ 어려운 여행이나 경험을 시작하다. 나아가다: *We struck out for home in the blinding snow.* 우리는 앞이 보이지 않는 눈보라 속에서 집을 향해 나아갔다.

strike up *phr v* [T] **1 strike up a conversation/friendship etc.** to start a conversation, friendship etc. with someone ‖ 누군가와 대화·교제 등을 시작하다. **2** [I, T] to begin to play or sing something ‖ 어떤 것을 연주하거나 노래하기 시작하다: *The band struck up an Irish tune.* 악단은 아일랜드 곡조를 연주하기 시작했다.

strike² n 1 a time when a group of workers STRIKE ‖ 일단의 노동자들이 파업하는 때. 스트라이크. 동맹 파업: *The union decided to go on strike.* 노조는 파업에 들어가기로 결정했다. **2** a military attack ‖ 군사 공격. 공습(攻襲): *threats of an air strike* 공습(空襲)의 위협 **3 two/three etc. strikes against** two, etc. qualities that are considered to be wrong, bad, or a disadvantage ‖ 그릇되거나 나쁘게, 또는 불리하게 여겨지는 속성 두 가지. …에 대한 두/세 가지 단점: *It's expensive and too big - that's two strikes against it.* 그것은 비싸고 너무 크다. 그게 두 가지 단점이야. **4** in baseball, an attempt to hit the ball that fails, or a ball that is thrown toward the hitter within the correct area, but is not hit ‖ 야구에서 공을 치려 했지만 실패한 것, 또는 타자를 향해 정확한 구역 내로 던져졌지만 치지 못한 볼. 스트라이크

strik·er /'straɪkə/ *n* someone who does not work because s/he is on STRIKE ‖ 동맹 파업 중이어서 일하지 않는 사람. 파업 참가자

strik·ing /'straɪkɪŋ/ *adj* **1** unusual or interesting enough to be noticed ‖ 알아채기 충분할 만큼 특별하거나 흥미로운.

이목[주의]을 끄는: *There's a striking similarity between the two girls.* 두 소녀 사이에는 놀랄 만한 유사성이 있다. **2** very attractive, often in an unusual way ∥ 종종 특이하게 아주 매력적인. 인상적인: *a man with a striking face* 인상적인 얼굴의 남자

string¹ /strɪŋ/ *n* **1** [C, U] a strong thread made of several threads twisted together, used for tying things ∥ 몇 가닥의 실을 함께 꼬아 만들어 물건을 묶는 데 쓰는 튼튼한 줄. 줄. 노끈: *We tied a string around the box.* 우리는 박스를 끈으로 동여맸다. **2** a number of similar things or events that happen one after the other ∥ 줄줄이 일어나는 다수의 비슷한 일들이나 사건들. 일련. 한 줄. 연속된 것: *The police asked me a string of questions.* 경찰은 내게 연속적으로 질문했다. **3 no strings attached** having no special conditions or limits on an agreement, relationship etc. ∥ 협정·관계 등에 어떤 특별한 조건이나 제한이 없는. 부대조건이 없는: *a guaranteed interest-free loan – no strings attached* 무이자 보증 대출. 부대조건 없음 **4 first/second/third string** in sports, a player who is judged to have the highest, second highest etc. level of skill in playing a particular position ∥ 스포츠에서 특정 포지션을 맡는 솜씨가 1·2위 등의 수준으로 판단되는 선수. 1군/2군/3군: *the second string quarterback.* 2군 쿼터백 **5 a string of pearls/beads etc.** a lot of PEARLS, BEADS etc. on a string ∥ 줄에 꿰인 많은 진주·구슬 등. 한 줄의 진주/구슬 **6** one of the long thin pieces of wire that is stretched across a musical instrument to produce sound ∥ 소리를 내도록 악기에 팽팽히 맨 길고 가는 철사 줄 중의 하나. 현. 스트링 —see also STRINGS

string² *v* **strung, strung, stringing** [T] to join things together using string, or hang up decorations in this way ∥ 줄을 이용해서 물건을 서로 결합시키다, 또는 장식물을 이렇게 늘어뜨리다. 실에 꿰다. …에 실[줄]을 달다: *Dad was busy stringing up Christmas lights.* 아빠는 크리스마스 전등을 매다느라 바빴다. — see also STRUNG-OUT

string sb **along** *phr v* [T] INFORMAL to continue to promise to do something that you do not intend to do, especially in relationships ∥ 특히 인간 관계에서, 할 의사가 없는 것을 하겠다고 계속해서 약속하다. …한다고 속이다. 거짓 약속을 늘어놓다: *Jerry's been stringing her*

along for years – he'll never marry her. 제리는 수년 동안 그녀에게 거짓말을 늘어놓고 있지만 그는 결코 그녀와 결혼하지 않을 것이다.

string bean /'. ./ *n* ⇨ GREEN BEAN

strin·gent /'strɪndʒənt/ *adj* stringent rules, laws etc. strictly control something ∥ 규칙·법 등이 어떤 것을 엄격히 통제하는. 엄한. 엄격[엄중]한: *stringent laboratory conditions* 실험실의 엄중한 조건들

strings /strɪŋz/ *n* [plural] **the strings** the people in an ORCHESTRA who play instruments such as the VIOLIN, CELLO etc. ∥ 바이올린·첼로 등의 악기를 연주하는 관현악 단원들. 현악부[파트]. 현악주자들

string·y /'strɪŋi/ *adj* food that is stringy has thin hard pieces in it that are difficult to CHEW ∥ 음식이, 씹기 힘든 가늘고 단단한 조각이 속에 들어 있는. 심줄투성이의. 섬유질의

strip¹ /strɪp/ *v* **-pped, -pping 1** [I,T] also **strip off** to take off your clothes, or take someone else's clothes of him/her ∥ 옷을 벗거나 남의 옷을 벗기다. 발가벗다[벗기다]: *He stripped and got into the shower.* 그는 발가벗고 샤워를 시작했다. **2** [T] to remove something that is covering the surface of something else ∥ 어떤 것의 표면을 덮고 있는 것을 제거하다. 껍질을 벗기다: *It took all day to strip the paint off the walls.* 벽에서 페인트를 벗겨내는 데 온종일이 걸렸다. **3 strip sb of sth** to take away something important from someone such as his/her possessions, rank, or property ∥ 누군가로부터 소유물이나 지위, 또는 재산 등의 중요한 것을 빼앗다. 없애다. 박탈하다

strip² *n* **1** a long narrow piece of cloth, paper etc. ∥ 천·종이 등의 길고 좁은 조각: *Tear the paper into one-inch strips.* 종이를 1인치 폭의 긴 가닥으로 찢어라. **2** a long narrow area of land ∥ 대지의 길고 좁은 구역. 뙈기. 작은 조각: *a strip of sand* 길고 좁은 모래밭

stripe /straɪp/ *n* a long narrow line of color ∥ 길고 좁은 색선. 줄(무늬): *a shirt with blue and red stripes* 청색과 적색 줄무늬 셔츠 —see picture at PATTERN

striped /straɪpt, 'straɪpɪd/ *adj* having a pattern of STRIPEs ∥ 줄무늬가 있는. 줄무늬의: *a blue and white striped shirt* 청백색 줄무늬 셔츠 —see picture at PATTERN

strip·per /'strɪpɚ/ *n* someone whose job is to perform by taking off his/her clothes in a sexually exciting way ∥ 성적으로 자극되게 옷을 벗고 공연하는 직업

인. 스트립쇼를 하는 사람. 스트리퍼

strip·tease /'strɪptiz/ *n* [C, U] the dance that a STRIPPER does ‖ 스트리퍼가 하는 댄스. 스트립쇼

strive /straɪv/ *v* **strove** *or* **strived, striven** /'strɪvən/ *or* **strived, striving** [I] FORMAL to try very hard to get or do something ‖ 무엇을 얻거나 하려고 열심히 노력하다. 애쓰다. 분투하다: *Ross is constantly striving for perfection.* 로스는 항상 완벽해지기 위해 애쓰고 있다.

strode /stroʊd/ *v* the past tense of STRIDE ‖ stride의 과거형

stroke[1] /stroʊk/ *n* **1** a sudden illness in which an ARTERY (=tube) in your brain bursts or becomes blocked ‖ 뇌 속의 동맥이 터지거나 막히는 갑작스런 질병. 뇌졸중: *Since Tom had a stroke he's had trouble talking.* 톰은 뇌졸중을 일으킨 후 언어 장애를 겪고 있다. **2** a repeated movement of your arms in a sport such as swimming ‖ 수영 등의 스포츠에서 반복되는 팔 동작. 한 번 움직임. 한 번 젓기: *back stroke* 배영(背泳) **3 stroke of luck** something lucky that happens to you ‖ 일어나는 다행스러운 일: *By some stroke of luck, we got the last hotel room.* 우연한 행운으로 우리는 마지막 남은 호텔 방을 잡았다. **4** a single movement of a pen or brush, or a line made by doing this ‖ 펜이나 붓의 한 차례의 움직임, 또는 이렇게 해서 만들어진 선. 일필. 한 획

stroke[2] *v* [T] to move your hand gently over something ‖ 물건 위로 손을 부드럽게 움직이다. 쓰다듬다. 어루만지다: *She stroked the baby's face.* 그녀는 아기의 얼굴을 어루만졌다.

stroke

stroll /stroʊl/ *v* [I] to walk in a slow relaxed way ‖ 천천히 편안하게 걷다. 한가로이 거닐다. 산책하다: *We strolled along the beach.* 우리는 해변을 따라서 산책했다. – **stroll** *n*

stroll·er /'stroʊlɚ/ *n* a chair on wheels in which a small child sits and is pushed along ‖ 유아를 앉혀서 밀고 가는 바퀴 달린 의자. 유모차

strong /strɒŋ/ *adj*

1 ▶PHYSICAL 육체적인◀ having a lot of physical power ‖ 상당한 체력이 있는. 힘이 센. 강한: *We need a few strong people to help move these boxes.* 우리는 이 상자들을 옮겨 줄 몇 명의 힘센 사람이 필요하다. / *the strongest muscles in your body* 인체에서 가장 강한 근육

2 ▶NOT EASILY BROKEN 쉽게 부서지지 않는◀ not easily broken or damaged ‖ 쉽게 부서지거나 손상되지 않는. 튼튼한. 질긴. 견고한: *a strong rope* 질긴 로프 / *a strong adhesive* 강력한 접착제

3 ▶POWER 힘◀ having a lot of power or influence ‖ 많은 힘이나 영향력을 가진. 강력한. 권력[세력]이 강한: *a strong leader* 강력한 지도자 / *a strong army* 강력한 군대

4 ▶FEELINGS 감정◀ strong feelings, ideas etc. are ones that are very important to you ‖ 감정·생각 등이 아주 중대한. 열렬한. 철저한: *a strong belief in God* 신에 대한 열렬한 믿음 / *As a child she showed a strong interest in art.* 어렸을 때 그녀는 미술에 대단한 흥미를 보였다.

5 ▶ARGUMENT 논쟁◀ a strong reason, opinion, etc. is one that is likely to persuade other people ‖ 이유·의견 등이 다른 사람들을 설득할 수 있는. 설득력 있는. 유력한: *There's strong evidence to suggest that he's innocent.* 그가 결백하다는 것을 시사해 주는 유력한 증거가 있다.

6 ▶NOT TOO UPSET 쉽게 화내지 않는◀ able to deal with problems without becoming too upset or worried by them ‖ 너무 심란해 하거나 걱정하지 않고 문제를 처리할 수 있는. 굳센. 단호한. 대담한: *Do you think she's strong enough to handle this?* 그녀가 이 문제를 다룰 만큼 강인하다고 생각하십니까?

7 ▶TASTE/SMELL 맛/향◀ having a taste, smell, color etc. that is easy to notice ‖ 쉽게 알아챌 수 있는 맛·향·색 등을 띤. 진한. 독한: *strong coffee* 진한 커피

8 ▶RELATIONSHIP 관계◀ a strong relationship or friendship is likely to last a long time ‖ 관계·우정이 오랫동안 지속될 것 같은. 견실한. 끈질긴. 굳건한: *a strong bond between the two brothers* 두 형제 간의 돈독한 우애

9 50/1000/75,000 etc. strong used in order to give the number of people in a group ‖ 한 집단 내의 사람들의 수를 제시하는 데에 쓰여. 총원 50/1,000/75,000명: *Our staff is over a thousand strong.* 우리 직원은 총원 일천 명을 상회한다. —**strong** *adv*

strong·hold /'strɒŋhoʊld/ *n* **1** an area where there is a lot of support for a particular attitude, way of life, political party etc. ‖ 특정 태도·생활 방식·정당 등에 대한 상당한 지지가 있는 지역. 거점. 본거지: *a Republican stronghold* 공화당

의 본거지 **2** an area that is strongly defended ‖ 강력하게 방어되는 지역. 최후의 보루: *a rebel stronghold* 반군의 보루

strong·ly /'strɔŋli/ *adv* **1** if you feel or believe something strongly, you are very sure and serious about it ‖ 어떤 것을 느끼거나 믿는 데 있어서 확신 있고 진지하게. 강하게. 굳세게: *I feel strongly that medical records should be private.* 나는 진료 기록이 비밀로 유지되어야 함을 통감한다. **2** in a way that persuades someone to do something ‖ 누군가에게 무엇을 하라고 설득하는 투로. 강경하게. 단호히 : *I strongly urge/advise/encourage you to get more facts before deciding.* 나는 네게 결정하기 전에 더 많은 사실을 알아보기를 강력히 촉구한다[충고한다, 권유한다]. / *The company strongly believes that it's time for a change.* 회사는 지금이 변화의 시기임을 굳게 믿고 있다. **3** in a way that is easy to notice ‖ 쉽게 알아볼 수 있게. 강하게. 세차게. 지독하게: *The house smelled strongly of gas.* 그 집은 가스 냄새가 지독하게 났다.

strong-willed /ˌ. '../ *adj* having a lot of determination to do what you want; STUBBORN ‖ 원하는 것을 하기 위한 상당한 결단력을 지닌. 의지가 굳은. 단호한; 谿 stubborn: *a strong-willed child* 고집이 센 아이

strove /stroʊv/ *v* the past tense of STRIVE ‖ strive의 과거형

struck /strʌk/ *v* the past tense and PAST PARTICIPLE of STRIKE ‖ strike의 과거·과거 분사형

struc·tur·al /'strʌktʃərəl/ *adj* relating to the structure of something ‖ 사물의 구조에 관한. 구조상의: *structural damage to the aircraft* 그 비행기에 입힌 구조적 손상

struc·ture¹ /'strʌktʃɚ/ *n* **1** [C, U] the way in which the parts of something connect with each other to form a whole ‖ 사물의 부분들이 서로 연결되어 전체를 이루는 방식. 구조. 구성. 조직: *Children need a stable family structure to feel secure.* 아이들은 안심할 수 있는 안정적인 가정 구조가 필요하다. / *chemical structure* 화학적 구조 / *sentence structure* 문장 구조 **2** something that has been built ‖ 축조된 것. 건축. 건조. 구조물: *The bridge was an impressive structure.* 그 다리는 인상적인 축조물이었다. / *a huge steel structure* 거대한 강철 구조물

structure² *v* [T] to arrange something

carefully in an organized way ‖ 사물을 주의 깊게 조직적으로 배열하다. 체계[조직]화하다: *The business should be structured to meet demand.* 사업은 수요에 부응해 조직화돼야 한다.

strug·gle¹ /'strʌgəl/ *v* [I] **1** to try very hard to achieve something, even though it is difficult ‖ 비록 어렵지만 뭔가를 달성하기 위해 매우 열심히 노력하다. 고생하여[힘들여] …하다: *After Hal lost his job we had to struggle to pay the bills.* 핼이 직장을 잃은 후 우리는 납부금을 내느라 고생해야 했다. **2** to fight someone who is attacking you or holding you ‖ 자신을 공격하거나 붙잡고 있는 사람과 싸우다. 맞붙다: *She struggled with the man and screamed for help.* 그녀는 그 남자와 싸우면서 도와달라고 비명을 질렀다. **3** to move somewhere with a lot of difficulty ‖ 힘겹게 어딘가로 가다. 허우적대며 움직이다: *He struggled up the stairs with the luggage.* 그는 짐을 들고 계단을 허덕거리며 올라갔다.

struggle² *n* **1** a long hard fight for freedom, political rights etc. ‖ 자유·정치적 권리 등을 위한 길고 힘든 싸움. 투쟁. 고투: *His death led to a struggle for power within the country.* 그의 죽음은 그 국가 내부의 권력 투쟁을 야기시켰다. **2** a fight between two people for something ‖ 어떤 것을 위한 두 사람 사이의 싸움. 맞붙음. 경쟁. 다툼

strum /strʌm/ *v* **-mmed, -mming** [I, T] to play an instrument such as a GUITAR by moving your fingers across the strings ‖ 손가락을 현 위로 이동시키며 기타 등의 악기를 연주하다. 가볍게 치다. 퉁기다

strung /strʌŋ/ *v* the past tense and PAST PARTICIPLE of STRING ‖ string의 과거·과거 분사형

strung-out /ˌ. '../ *adj* INFORMAL badly affected by a drug so that you cannot react normally, or so tired or worried that you cannot react normally ‖ 마약에 심하게 취해서, 또는 너무 피곤하거나 걱정되어서 정상적으로 반응하지 못하는. 마약 중독의. 녹초가 된

strut¹ /strʌt/ *v* **-tted, -tting** [I] **1** to walk in a proud way with your head up and your chest pushed forward ‖ 머리를 쳐들고 가슴을 앞으로 내밀며 자랑스럽게 걷다. 뽐내며[과시하며] 걷다: *Ray was strutting around telling everyone how he'd won.* 레이는 그가 어떻게 승리했는가를 모두에게 이야기하며 뽐내며 돌아다니고 있었다. **2 strut your stuff** HUMOROUS to show proudly what you can do or

what you have ‖ 할 수 있는 것이나 가진
것을 자랑스럽게 보여주다. 자신의 역량을
과시하다

strut² *n* a long thin piece of metal or
wood used for supporting a part of a
bridge, the wing of an aircraft etc. ‖ 다
리의 한 부분·항공기의 날개 등을 지지하
는 데에 쓰이는 금속 또는 나무로 된 길고
가는 토막. 버팀목. 지주(支柱)

stub¹ /stʌb/ *n* **1** the short part of
something that is left after the rest has
been used ‖ 쓰고 남은 물건의 짧은 부분.
토막. 동강. 부스러기: *a pencil stub* 몽당
연필 **2** the part of a ticket that is
returned to you as proof that you have
paid ‖ 값을 지불한 증명으로 되돌려 받는
표의 일부분. 보관용 부본

stub² *v* **-bbed, -bbing** [T] **stub your
toe** to hurt your toe by hitting it against
something ‖ 물체에 발가락을 부딪쳐서 다
치다. 발부리를 채다

stub sth ↔ **out** *phr v* [T] to stop a
cigarette from burning by pressing the
end of it against something ‖ 담배의 끝
을 물체에 대고 눌러서 담배가 타지 못하
게 하다. 담배를 비벼 끄다

stub·ble /'stʌbəl/ *n* [U] the very short
stiff hairs on a man's face when he has
not SHAVEd ‖ 면도하지 않은 남자 얼굴의
매우 짧고 뻣뻣한 털. 짧게 난[까실까실
한] 수염 **– stubbly** *adj*

stub·born /'stʌbən/ *adj* refusing to
change your opinions, beliefs etc.
because you believe you are right ‖ 자신
이 옳다고 믿기 때문에 의견·신념 등을 바
꾸기 거부하는. 완고한. 고집 센. 완강한:
Pat's a stubborn woman. 팻은 고집 센
여자이다.

stub·by /'stʌbi/ *adj* short and thick or
fat ‖ 짧고 굵거나 통통한. 뭉툭한. 땅딸막
한: *his stubby fingers* 그의 뭉툭한 손가락
들

stuc·co /'stʌkoʊ/ *n* [U] a CEMENT
mixture used especially for covering the
outside walls of houses ‖ 특히 집의 외벽
을 바르는 데에 쓰이는 시멘트 혼합물. 회
반죽

stuck¹ /stʌk/ *v* the past tense and PAST
PARTICIPLE of STICK ‖ stick의 과거·과거 분
사형

stuck² *adj* **1** not able to move ‖ 움직일
수 없는. 고정된. 붙박힌: *Our car got
stuck in the mud.* 우리 차는 진흙에 빠졌
다. **2** not able to continue working on
something because it is too difficult ‖ 너
무 어려워서 어떤 일을 계속 진행할 수 없
는. 곤혹스러운: *Can you help me with
this? I'm stuck.* 이것 좀 도와 줄래? 어찌

할 바를 모르겠어. **3** not able to get away
from a boring or unpleasant situation ‖
지루하거나 불쾌한 상황에서 빠져나갈 수
없는. 꼭 붙잡힌. 꼼짝할 수 없는: *I'm
tired of being stuck at home all day with
the kids.* 하루 종일 아이들과 집에 틀어박
혀 있는 일이 지겹다.

stuck-up /ˌ. '../ *adj* INFORMAL proud
and unfriendly because you think you
are better than other people ‖ 자신을 다
른 사람들보다 낫다고 여겨서 거만하고 불
친절한. 우쭐대는. 건방진

stud /stʌd/ *n* **1** [C, U] an animal such
as a horse that is kept for breeding ‖ 번
식용으로 사육되는 말 등의 동물. 씨짐승.
종축: *a stud farm* 종축 목장 **2** SLANG a
man who is very active sexually ‖ 성적으
로 매우 활력적인 남자. 섹스에 강한 남자
3 a small round piece of metal that is
put on a surface for decoration ‖ 장식으
로 표면에 부착하는 작고 둥근 금속 조각.
장식 못. 장식 단추: *a leather jacket
with silver studs* 은빛 단추가 달린 가죽
재킷 **4** a small round EARRING ‖ 작고 둥
근 귀걸이. 피어싱용 고리

stud·ded /'stʌdɪd/ *adj* decorated with
a lot of STUDs or jewels ‖ 많은 장식용 단
추와 보석으로 장식된: *a bracelet
studded with diamonds* 다이아몬드가
줄줄이 박힌 팔찌 **—see also** STAR-
STUDDED

stu·dent /'studnt/ *n* **1** someone who is
studying at a school, university etc. ‖ 학
교·대학 등에서 공부하고 있는 사람. 학
생. 생도: *a first-year medical student*
의대 1년생 / *She has 30 students in her
class.* 그녀의 반에는 30명의 학생들이 있
다. **2 a student of sth** someone who is
very interested in a particular subject ‖
특정 주제에 매우 관심이 있는 사람. …의
학자. 연구가

student bod·y /ˌ.. '../ *n* all the
students in a school, university etc. ‖ 학
교·대학 등의 모든 학생들. 학생 전체. 전
학생: *Molly is president of the student
body.* 몰리는 전교[총학생] 회장이다.

stud·ied /'stʌdid/ *adj* studied behavior
is deliberate and intended to have a
particular effect on other people ‖ 행위
가 고의적이며 다른 사람들에게 특별한 영
향을 미치기 위해 의도된. 고의의. 계획적
인: *a studied manner of speaking* 가장된
말투

stud·ies /'stʌdiz/ [plural] subjects that
people study ‖ 사람들이 연구하는 주제:
Are you doing well in your studies? 연
구는 잘 되어 가고 있습니까?

stu·di·o /'studiˌoʊ/ *n* **1** a room where

television and radio programs are made and broadcast ∥ 텔레비전·라디오 프로그램이 제작되고 방송되는 방. 방송실. 스튜디오. 녹음실 **2** a movie company or the place where movies are made ∥ 영화사나 영화가 제작되는 장소. 영화 촬영소. 영화사. 스튜디오: *the big Hollywood studios* 거대 할리우드 영화사들 **3** a room where a painter or photographer works ∥ 화가나 사진가가 작업하는 방. 작업실. 스튜디오. 화실: *an art studio* 미술 작업실 **4** also **studio apartment** a small apartment with one main room ∥ 큰 방 하나로 된 작은 아파트. 스튜디오 아파트. 원룸아파트

stu·di·ous /'studiəs/ *adj* spending a lot of time reading and studying ∥ 독서와 연구에 많은 시간을 쓰는. 열심히 공부하는. 학구적인

stud·y[1] /'stʌdi/ *n* **1** a piece of work that is done to find out more about a particular subject or problem , and that is usually written in a report ∥ 특정 주제나 문제에 대해 더 많이 알아내려고 행한, 대개 보고서로 쓰여진 한편의 연구 업적. 연구 논문: *My nephew is doing a study of teenagers' language for his thesis.* 내 조카는 논문을 위해 10대들의 언어에 대한 연구를 하고 있다. **2** [U] the activity of studying a particular subject ∥ 특정 주제에 대한 연구 활동. 연구. 학문: *the study of ancient history* 고대 역사의 연구 **3** a room in a house that is used for work or study ∥ 집에서 업무나 연구용으로 쓰이는 방. 서재. 연구실. 공부방 —see also **STUDIES**

study[2] *v* **1** [I, T] to spend time going to classes, reading etc. to find out more about a particular subject ∥ 특정 주제에 대해 더 많이 알아내려고 수업에 가거나 독서 등을 하며 시간을 보내다. 배우다. 연구하다. 공부하다: *I'm studying medicine at NYU.* 나는 뉴욕대에서 의학을 공부하고 있다. */ Are you studying to be a lawyer?* 변호사가 되려고 공부하십니까? **2** [T] to examine something carefully to find out more about it ∥ 사물에 대해 더 많은 것을 알아내기 위해 면밀히 조사하다. 검토하다. 엄밀히 관찰하다: *Dr. Brock is studying how the disease affects children.* 브록 박사는 그 질병이 아이들에게 어떤 영향을 미치는지 조사하고 있다.

stuff[1] /stʌf/ *n* [U] INFORMAL **1** a substance or material of any sort ∥ 어떤 종류의 물질이나 재료. 소재: *What's this stuff on the floor?* 마루 위에 있는 이건 뭐야? */ Don't drink that stuff!* 그런 것은

마시지 마라! **2** a number of different things ∥ 많은 다양한 것들. 물건. 것: *I need a place to store my stuff for a while.* 나는 내 짐들을 한동안 보관해 둘 장소가 필요하다. **3** all the activities that someone does ∥ 사람이 하는 온갖 활동. 하는 일. 작업: *We have a load of stuff to do before we leave .* 우리는 떠나기 전에 해야 할 일이 많다.

stuff[2] *v* [T] **1** to push things into a small space quickly ∥ 물건을 작은 공간에 재빨리 밀어 넣다. 꾸려 넣다. 채워 넣다: *He stuffed some clothes into a bag and left.* 그는 가방에 몇몇 옷가지들을 챙겨서 떠났다. **2** to fill something with a soft material until it is full ∥ 가득 찰 때까지 부드러운 소재로 어떤 것을 채우다. 채워 넣다. 메우다: *a pillow stuffed with feathers* 깃털로 채워 넣은 베개 **3 be stuffed** INFORMAL to be so full of food that you cannot eat any more ∥ 음식으로 가득 차서 더 이상 먹을 수 없게 되다. 배가 꽉 차다. 배부르다: *The cake looks great, but I'm stuffed!* 케이크가 맛있어 보이기는 한데 배가 너무 불러! **4** to fill a chicken, vegetable etc. with a mixture of food before cooking it ∥ 조리하기 전에 닭·야채 등을 혼합한 음식물로 채우다. 소를 넣다 **5** to fill the skin of a dead animal in order to make the animal look alive ∥ 살아 있는 것처럼 보이게 죽은 동물의 가죽에 채워 넣다. 박제로 만들다

stuffed-up /ˌ. ˈ./ *adj* INFORMAL having a STUFFY nose or head ∥ 코가 꽉 막히거나 머리가 무거운. 코가 막힌. 머리가 답답한

stuff·ing /'stʌfɪŋ/ *n* [U] **1** a mixture of food that you put inside a chicken, vegetable etc. before cooking it ∥ 조리하기 전에 닭·야채 등의 속을 채우는 식품의 혼합물. 소 **2** material that is used for filling something such as a PILLOW ∥ 베개 등의 것을 채우는 데에 쓰이는 소재. 속

stuff·y /'stʌfi/ *adj* **1** not having enough fresh air ∥ 신선한 공기가 충분하지 못한. 통풍이 안 되는. 숨 막히는. 답답한: *a stuffy room* 공기가 탁한 방 **2** boring and old-fashioned ∥ 따분하고 구식인. 시시한. 지루한. 케케묵은: *Rob's family is really stuffy.* 롭의 가족은 정말 구식이다. **3** a stuffy nose is filled with thick liquid because you are sick ∥ 아파서 코가 진득한 액체로 가득 찬. 코가 막힌[답답한]

stum·ble /'stʌmbəl/ *v* [I] **1** to almost fall down while you are walking ∥ 걷다가 거의 넘어질 뻔하다. 발부리가 걸리다. 채어 비틀거리다: *She stumbled coming out* *of the house.* 그녀는 집을 나서며 비틀거렸다. **2** to stop or make a mistake when you are reading or speaking to people ‖ 낭독하거나 사람들에게 말할 때 막히거나 실수하다. 더듬거리다: *He was stumbling over the words of his speech.* 그는 연설 중 말이 막혀 더듬거렸다.

stumble on/across sth *phr v* [T] to discover something or meet someone by chance ‖ 우연히 사물을 발견하거나 누군가를 만나다. …을 우연히 찾아내다[마주치다]: *We thought that we'd stumbled on a cure for the disease.* 우리는 그 질병의 치료법을 우연히 발견했었다고 생각했다.

stumbling block /'.. ,./ *n* a problem that prevents you from achieving something ‖ 어떤 것을 달성하지 못하게 가로막는 문제. 방해물. 장애물: *The question of funding is still our major stumbling block.* 자금 조달 여부가 여전히 우리의 주된 장애물이었다.

stump¹ /stʌmp/ *n* **1** the part of a tree that remains in the ground after the rest has been cut down ‖ 나무의 나머지 부분이 잘려지고 난 다음에 땅에 남아 있는 부분. 그루터기. **2** the part of an arm, leg etc. that remains when the rest has been cut off ‖ 팔·다리 등의 잘려 나가고 남은 나머지 부분

stump² *v* **1 be stumped (by sth)** to be unable to think of an answer to a difficult question ‖ 어려운 질문에 대한 답을 생각할 수 없다. 쩔쩔매다. 답이 막혀 당황하다: *We were completely stumped by her question.* 우리는 그녀의 질문에 (답이 막혀)완전히 쩔쩔맸다. **2** [T] to ask someone a difficult question so that s/he is unable to think of an answer ‖ 누군가에게 어려운 질문을 해서 답을 생각할 수 없게 하다. 어려운 질문으로 당황하게 하다: *The question stumped everyone in the room.* 그 질문은 그 방에 있는 모든 사람들을 난처하게 했다.

stump for sb *v* [T] to try to influence people to vote for a particular person ‖ 특정인에게 찬성 투표하도록 사람들에게 영향을 주려 하다. …의 지원 유세를 하다

stun /stʌn/ *v* **-nned, -nning** [T] **1** to surprise or shock someone so much that s/he does not react ‖ 반응을 나타내지 못할 정도로 누군가를 놀라게 하거나 충격을 주다. 아연실색케 하다: *Everyone was stunned by Betty's answer.* 모두가 베티의 답변에 아연실색했다. **2** to make someone unconscious for a short time by hitting him/her on the head ‖ 누군가의 머리를 때려서 잠시 의식을 잃게 하다.

기절[실신]시키다

stung /stʌŋ/ *v* the past tense and PAST PARTICIPLE of STING ‖ sting의 과거·과거 분사형

stunk /stʌŋk/ *v* the past tense and PAST PARTICIPLE of STINK ‖ stink의 과거·과거 분사형

stun·ning /'stʌnɪŋ/ *adj* **1** extremely attractive or beautiful ‖ 극도로 매력적이거나 아름다운. 기막히게 예쁜: *You look stunning in that dress.* 네가 그 드레스를 입으니 눈이 부신다 **2** very surprising or shocking ‖ 매우 놀랍거나 충격적인. 아연하게 하는: *a stunning answer* 아연실색케 하는 답변

stunt¹ /stʌnt/ *n* **1** a dangerous action that is done to entertain people, usually in a movie ‖ 보통 영화에서 사람들을 즐겁게 해주기 위해 하는 위험한 동작. 스턴트 **2** something silly or dangerous that you do, especially to make someone pay attention to you ‖ 특히 자신에게 주의를 기울이게 하려고 하는 바보 같거나 위험스러운 행동: *Don't ever pull a stunt like that* (=do something like that) *again!* 다시는 절대 그런 바보 같은 짓은 하지 마라!

stunt² *v* [T] to stop someone or something from growing or developing correctly ‖ 사람이나 사물이 똑바로 자라거나 발전하는 것을 막다. 발육을 가로막다. 성장을 저해하다: *Lack of food has stunted their growth.* 식량 부족이 그들의 발육을 저해했다.

stunt man /'. ./, **stunt wom·an** /'. ,../ *n* a man or woman whose job is to take the place of an actor when something dangerous has to be done in a movie ‖ 영화에서 위험스러운 연기를 해야 할 때 배우를 대신하는 남성이나 여성 직업인. 스턴트 맨. 스턴트 우먼

stu·pe·fied /'stupə,faɪd/ *adj* so surprised or bored that you cannot think clearly ‖ 너무 놀라거나 지겨워서 명확히 생각할 수 없는. 멍해진. 흐리멍덩해진 – **stupefy** *v* [T]

stu·pe·fy·ing /'stupə,faɪ-ɪŋ/ *adj* making you feel so surprised or bored that you cannot think clearly ‖ 너무 놀라거나 지겨워져서 분명히 생각할 수 없게 하는. 멍해지게[망연자실케] 하는 – **stupefied** *adj*

stu·pen·dous /stu'pɛndəs/ *adj* extremely large or impressive ‖ 극히 크거나 인상적인. 놀랄 만큼 큰. 엄청난: *a stupendous achievement* 놀랄 만한 업적

stu·pid /'stupɪd/ *adj* **1** showing a lack of good sense or judgment; silly ‖ 분별력

이나 판단력의 부족을 보이는. 우둔한. 멍청한; 어리석은: *How could you be so stupid?* 너는 어쩌면 그렇게 멍청할 수 있느냐? / *He's always saying stupid things and getting into fights.* 그는 항상 어리석은 말만 일삼으며 싸움에 말려들고 있다. **2** an insulting word used in order to describe someone who is not intelligent ‖ 똑똑하지 못한 사람을 묘사하는 데에 쓰이는 모욕적인 말. 바보. 멍청이. 얼간이: *I know that – I'm not stupid!* 그건 나도 알아. 난 바보가 아니란 말이야! **3** SPOKEN used when talking about something that annoys you ‖ 짜증나게 하는 것에 대해 말할 때에 쓰여. 화가 치미는. 지긋지긋한: *I can't get this stupid door open!* 이 빌어먹을 문을 열 수가 없네! **– stupidity** /stu'pɪdəti/ *n* [C, U]

stu·por /'stupɚ/ *n* [C, U] a state in which you cannot think, see etc. clearly ‖ 생각·인식 등을 확실하게 할 수 없는 상태. 무감각 상태. 인사불성(상태): *We found him in a drunken stupor.* 우리는 술 취해 인사불성인 그를 발견했다.

stur·dy /'stɚdi/ *adj* strong and not likely to break or be hurt ‖ 강하고 쉽게 부서지거나 다치지 않을 것 같은. 억센. 튼튼한: *a sturdy table* 튼튼한 탁자

stut·ter /'stʌtɚ/ *v* [I, T] to speak with difficulty because you repeat the first sound of a word ‖ 단어의 첫 소리를 반복하면서 힘들게 말을 하다. 말을 더듬다: *"I w-w-want to g-g-go too,"* he stuttered. "나도 가-가-가고 시-시-싶어"라고 그는 더듬거리며 말했다. **– stutter** *n* [singular] —see also STAMMER

style¹ /staɪl/ *n* **1** [C, U] a way of doing, making, painting etc. something that is typical of a particular period of time or group of people ‖ 특정 시기 또는 특정 집단의 사람들에게 전형적인 것을 하고 만들며 그리는 등의 방식. 양식. 형(型). 형식: *He's trying to copy Van Gogh's style of painting.* 그는 반 고흐의 화법을 모사하려 하고 있다. / *architecture in the Gothic style* 고딕 양식의 건축 **2** the particular way that someone behaves, works, or deals with other people ‖ 사람이 행동하는[일하는, 다른 사람을 대하는] 특정한 방식. 행동 양식. 생활 양식: *Carolyn has an informal style of teaching.* 캐롤린은 격식에 매이지 않는 교수법을 갖고 있다. **3** [C, U] a fashion or design, especially in clothes or hair ‖ 특히 의복이나 머리 모양에서의 유행 또는 양식. 스타일: *His clothes are always in style.* 그의 의상은 항상 유행을 따르고 있

다. **4** [U] the particular way you do things that makes people admire you ‖ 사람들을 감탄하게 만드는 어떤 일을 하는 특정한 방식. 멋. 품위. 기품: *You may not like him, but you have to admit that he has style.* 네가 그를 좋아하지 않을지 모르지만 그가 멋있다는 것은 인정해야 한다.

style² *v* [T] to cut someone's hair in a particular way ‖ 사람의 머리털을 특정하게 자르다. 특정한 형태로 머리를 깎다

styl·ish /'staɪlɪʃ/ *adj* attractive in a fashionable way ‖ 유행에 맞게 매력적인. 유행의. 멋진. 현대식의: *a very stylish woman* 매우 멋있는 여성 / *stylish clothes* 유행에 맞는[멋진] 옷

sty·lis·tic /staɪ'lɪstɪk/ *adj* relating to the style of a piece of writing or art ‖ 문장이나 그림의 형식에 관한. 문체[화풍]의: *I've made a few stylistic changes to your report.* 내가 네 보고서의 문체를 조금 바꿨다.

styl·ized /'staɪə,laɪzd/ *adj* done in an artificial style that is not natural or like real life ‖ 자연스럽지 않거나 실생활과 같지 않고 인위적 형식으로 행한. 인습화한. 틀에 박힌

sty·mie /'staɪmi/ *v* [T] INFORMAL to prevent someone from doing what s/he has planned or wants to do ‖ 어떤 사람이 계획했거나 하고 싶어하는 것을 못하게 하다. 방해하다. 좌절시키다: *All of our efforts to talk with him have been stymied.* 그와 대화를 해보려는 우리의 모든 노력은 좌절되었다.

suave /swɑv/ *adj* attractive, confident, and relaxed, but often in a way that is not sincere ‖ 종종 진실되진 않지만 매력적이고 자신만만하며 느긋한. (표면상으로) 온화한

sub /sʌb/ *n* **1** INFORMAL ⇨ SUBMARINE **2** INFORMAL ⇨ SUBSTITUTE¹ **3** a very large long SANDWICH ‖ 아주 크고 긴 샌드위치

sub·com·mit·tee /'sʌbkə,mɪti/ *n* a small group formed from a committee to deal with a particular problem in more detail ‖ 특정 문제를 보다 상세히 다루기 위해 위원회에서 조직한 작은 집단. 분과위원회

sub·con·scious /ˌsʌb'kɑnʃəs/ *adj* ⇨ UNCONSCIOUS **– subconscious** *adj* **– subconsciously** *adv*

sub·con·ti·nent /ˌsʌb'kɑntʲn-ənt, -tənənt/ *n* a large area of land that forms part of a CONTINENT ‖ 대륙의 일부를 형성하는 큰 땅덩어리. 아(亞)대륙: *the Indian subcontinent* 인도 아대륙

sub·cul·ture /'sʌb,kʌltʃɚ/ *n* the

behavior, beliefs, activities etc. of a particular group of people in a society that are different from the rest of the society ‖ 사회 내의 나머지 사람들과 다른 특정 집단 사람들의 행동·신념·활동 등. 특정 계층 문화: *the drug subculture* 마약 (상용자) 문화

sub·di·vide /ˌsʌbdəˈvaɪd, ˈsʌbdə,vaɪd/ *v* [T] to divide something into smaller parts ‖ 사물을 더 작은 부분으로 나누다. 재분할하다

sub·di·vi·sion /ˈsʌbdə,vɪʒən/ *n* an area of land for building a number of houses on, or these houses once they are built ‖ 많은 수의 집들을 짓기 위한 부지, 또는 건축된 이들 가옥들. 단지

sub·due /səbˈdu/ *v* [T] to control someone, especially by using force ‖ 누군가를 특히 무력을 써서 통제하다. 제압[진압, 억제]하다: *The nurses were trying to subdue a violent patient.* 간호사들이 난폭한 환자를 진정시키려고 애쓰고 있었다.

sub·dued /səbˈdud/ *adj* **1** a person or sound that is subdued is unusually quiet ‖ 사람·소리가 보통과 다르게 조용한. 가라앉은. 나직한: *Jason looked subdued after talking to the principal.* 제이슨은 교장에게 말한 후 가라앉아 있는 것 같았다. **2** subdued colors, lights etc. are less bright than usual ‖ 색·빛 등이 보통보다 덜 밝은. 칙칙한. 튀지 않는

sub·ject¹ /ˈsʌbdʒɪkt/ *n* **1** something that you are talking or writing about ‖ 현재 말하거나 쓰고 있는 대상. 주제. 화제. 논제: *Stop trying to change the subject!* (=talk about something else) 화제를 바꾸려고 하지 마라! / *She's written several books on the subject of ancient Ireland.* 그녀는 고대 아일랜드를 주제로 책을 몇 권 집필했다. **2** an area of knowledge that you study at a school or university ‖ 학교나 대학에서 공부하는 지식의 영역. 학과. 교과. 과목: *"What's your favorite subject?" "Science."* "제일 좋아하는 과목이 뭐야?" "과학이야." **3** TECHNICAL in grammar, a noun, noun phrase, or pronoun that usually comes before the verb in a sentence, and represents the person or thing that does the action of the verb or about which something is stated. In the sentence "Jean loves her cats," "Jean" is the subject ‖ 문법에서 보통 문장의 동사 앞에 위치하여 그 동사의 동작을 하거나 언급되고 있는 사람이나 사물을 나타내는 명사나 명사구, 또는 대명사. 주어. 주부. "Jean loves her cats."라는 문장에서 "Jean"은

주어이다. **4 subject matter** the subject that is being discussed in a book, shown in a movie or play etc. ‖ 책에서 논의되거나 영화나 연극에서 나타내고 있는 주제: *The subject matter of this film may not be suitable for young children.* 이 영화의 주제는 어린아이들에게 맞지 않을 수도 있다. **5** a person or animal that is used in a test or EXPERIMENT ‖ 시험 또는 실험에서 쓰이는 사람이나 동물. 피험자: *All the subjects were men between the ages of 18 and 25.* 피험자는 모두 18세부터 25세 사이의 남자들이었다. **6** the particular person, object etc. that you paint or photograph ‖ 자신이 그리거나 사진에 담는 특정 사람·물체 등. 대상. 피사체 **7** someone who is from a country that has a king or queen ‖ 왕이나 여왕이 있는 국가의 출신자. 국민. 신민(臣民)

subject² *adj* **be subject to sth** to be likely to be affected by something, or to be dependent on something ‖ 어떤 것에 영향을 받거나 의존적이 되기 쉽다. …을 받기[당하기] 쉽다. …에 좌우되다. …을 조건으로 하다: *All prices are subject to change.* 모든 가격들은 변동 가능합니다. / *The pay raise is subject to the management's approval.* 임금 인상은 경영진의 승인을 받아야 한다.

subject³ /səbˈdʒɛkt/ *v* **subject sb/sth to sth** *phr v* [T] to force someone or something to experience something unpleasant ‖ 어떤 사람이나 사물에 불쾌한 일을 겪게 하다. 강제로 …하게[당하게] 하다: *He subjected his victims to extreme torture.* 희생자들은 그에게서 극도의 고문을 당했다.

sub·jec·tive /səbˈdʒɛktɪv/ *adj* a statement, attitude etc. that is subjective is influenced by personal opinion or feelings rather than facts ‖ 발언·태도 등이 사실보다 개인적 의견이나 감정에 영향 받은. 주관의. 주관적인 — compare OBJECTIVE²

sub·ju·gate /ˈsʌbdʒə,geɪt/ *v* [T] FORMAL to force a person or group to obey you ‖ 사람이나 집단을 강제로 복종하게 하다. 예속시키다 **— subjugation** /ˌsʌbdʒəˈgeɪʃən/ *n* [U]

sub·junc·tive /səbˈdʒʌŋktɪv/ *n* TECHNICAL in grammar, a verb form used in order to express doubt, wishes, or possibility. In the sentence "He suggested we leave early," "leave" is in the subjunctive ‖ 문법에서 의심[소망, 가능성]을 표현하는 데에 쓰이는 동사 형태. 가정법 동사. "He suggested we leave early." 문장에서 "leave"는 가정법 형태

로 쓰였다

sub·let /sʌb'lɛt, 'sʌblɛt/ v **-tted, -tting** [I, T] to take rent from someone for a room, house etc. that you rent from someone else ‖ 남에게서 임차한 방·집 등을 누군가에게 (빌려 주고) 임대료를 받다. 전대(轉貸)[재임대]하다: *I'm subletting the room for the summer.* 나는 여름 동안 방을 재임대하고 있다. – **sublet** /'sʌblɛt/ n

sub·lime /sə'blaɪm/ adj excellent in a way that makes you feel very happy ‖ 매우 만족스럽게 느낄 만큼 뛰어난. 최고의. 탁월한. 빼어난

sub·lim·i·nal /ˌsʌb'lɪmənl/ adj subliminal messages, suggestions etc. affect the way you think without you noticing it ‖ 메시지·제안 등이 부지불식간에 생각하는 방식에 영향을 미치는. 잠재의식에 호소하는

sub·ma·rine /'sʌbməˌrin, ˌsʌbmə'rin/ n a ship that can travel under water ‖ 물속에서 이동할 수 있는 배. 잠수함

sub·merged /səb'mɜrdʒd/ adj completely under the surface of the water ‖ 완전히 수면 아래의. 물속의[에 가라앉은]: *cars submerged by the flood* 홍수로 물에 잠긴 차들 – **submersion** /səb'mɜrʒən/ n [U]

sub·mis·sion /səb'mɪʃən/ n **1** [U] the state of accepting that someone else has power over you ‖ 자신에게 남이 힘을 행사하는 것을 받아들이는 상태. 복종. 굴복. 항복: *The prisoners were starved into submission.* 죄수들을 굶겨서 복종시켰다. **2** [C, U] the act of giving a piece of writing to someone so s/he can consider or approve it, or the piece of writing itself ‖ 검토하거나 승인할 수 있게 남에게 문서를 제시하는 행위, 또는 그 문서. 제출(물): *All submissions must be received by the 15th of March.* 모든 제출물들은 3월 15일까지 제출해야 한다.

sub·mis·sive /səb'mɪsɪv/ adj always willing to obey someone ‖ 항상 남에게 기꺼이 복종하려고 하는. 순종적인: *a submissive wife* 순종적인 아내

sub·mit /səb'mɪt/ v **-tted, -tting 1** [T] to give a piece of writing to someone so s/he can consider or approve it ‖ 검토하거나 승인하도록 남에게 문서를 주다. 제출하다: *I submitted my plan to the committee yesterday.* 나는 어제 나의 계획안을 위원회에 제출했다. **2** [I, T] to obey someone who has power over you, especially because you have no choice ‖ 특히 대안이 없기 때문에 권력을 가진 사람에게 복종하다. 굴복하다. 굴복시키다 :

We refused to submit to the kidnapper's demands. 우리는 유괴범의 요구에 응하기를 거부했다.

sub·or·di·nate¹ /sə'bɔrdənɪt/ n FORMAL someone who has a lower position or less authority than someone else ‖ 다른 사람보다 지위가 낮거나 권한이 적은 사람. 부하. 하급[종속]자: *He ignored the suggestions from his subordinates.* 그는 부하들의 제안을 무시했다.

subordinate² adj FORMAL less important than something else, or lower in rank or authority ‖ 다른 사람보다 중요도나 계급, 또는 권위가 더 낮은. 하위[하급]의: *a subordinate position* 하위 지위

sub·or·dinate³ /sə'bɔrdnˌeɪt/ v [T] to put someone or something in a SUBORDINATE position ‖ 사람이나 사물을 하위에 놓다 – **subordination** /sə,bɔrdn'eɪʃən/ n [U]

sub·poe·na /sə'pinə/ n LAW an official document that orders someone to go to and talk in a TRIAL in a court of law ‖ 어떤 사람에게 법정의 재판에 출석하여 진술할 것을 명령하는 공식 문서. 소환장 – **subpoena** v [T]

sub·scribe /səb'skraɪb/ v [I] to pay money regularly to have a newspaper or magazine sent to you ‖ 신문이나 잡지를 받아 보기 위해 정기적으로 돈을 지불하다. 정기[예약] 구독하다: *What magazines do you subscribe to?* 당신은 어떤 잡지를 구독합니까? – **subscriber** n

subscribe to sth phr v [T] to agree with or support an idea, opinion etc. ‖ 생각이나 의견 등을 동의하거나 지지하다. 찬성하다 : *They obviously don't subscribe to his theory.* 그들은 분명히 그의 이론에 동의하지 않는다.

sub·scrip·tion /səb'skrɪpʃən/ n an amount of money that you pay regularly to receive copies of a newspaper or magazine ‖ 신문이나 잡지를 받기 위해 정기적으로 지불하는 금액. (정기) 구독료

sub·se·quent /'sʌbsəkwənt/ adj FORMAL coming after or following something else ‖ 다른 것의 뒤에 오거나 뒤따르는. 후속의: *Her physical condition improved in subsequent years.* 그녀의 건강 상태는 해를 거듭하면서 나아졌다. – **subsequently** adv : *The charges against him were subsequently dropped.* 그에 대한 고소가 뒤이어 취하되었다.

sub·ser·vi·ent /səb'sɜrviənt/ adj too willing to do what other people want you to do ‖ 타인들이 해주기 바라는 일을 기꺼이 하려고 하는. 굴종하는. 빌붙는. 추종하는 - **subservience** *n* [U]

sub·side /səb'saɪd/ *v* [I] to become less strong or loud ‖ 강도나 시끄러움이 덜해지다. 가라앉다. 진정되다: *The storm subsided around dawn.* 폭풍은 새벽쯤에 진정되었다.

sub·sid·i·ar·y¹ /səb'sɪdi,ɛri/ *n* a company that is owned or controlled by another company ‖ 다른 회사가 소유하거나 지배하는 회사. 자(子)회사

subsidiary² *adj* relating to the main situation or business, but less important or smaller than it ‖ 주요한 상황이나 사업과 관련이 있지만 그보다는 중요도가 덜하며 작은. 부수적인. 종속하는: *He played a subsidiary role in the negotiations.* 그는 협상에서 보조적인 역할을 했다.

sub·si·dize /'sʌbsə,daɪz/ *v* [T] to pay a SUBSIDY ‖ 보조금을 지급하다: *housing that is subsidized by the government* 국고 보조를 받은 주택

sub·si·dized /'sʌbsə,daɪzd/ *adj* to be paid for by a SUBSIDY ‖ 보조금이 지급된: *subsidized meals/education* 국고 보조 식사[교육]

sub·si·dy /'sʌbsədi/ *n* money that is paid by the government in order to help with the cost of something ‖ 어떤 것의 비용을 원조하기 위해 정부가 지급하는 돈. 보조금. 장려금

sub·sist /səb'sɪst/ *v* [I] to stay alive using only small amounts of food or money ‖ 오직 약간의 음식이나 돈만을 사용하면서 살아 남다. 생존하다. 살아가다: *The prisoners subsisted on rice and water.* 죄수들은 쌀과 물로 연명했다. – **subsistence** *n* [U]: *subsistence farming* 자급 농업

sub·stance /'sʌbstəns/ *n* **1** a type of solid or liquid that has particular qualities ‖ 특정한 성질이 있는 고체나 액체의 유형. 물질. 물체: *The bag was covered with a sticky substance.* 그 가방은 끈적끈적한 물질로 덮여 있었다. / *poisonous/hazardous/toxic substance* 유독[유해, 독성] 물질 / *illegal substances* (=drugs) 마약 **2** [singular, U] the most important ideas in a document, speech, report etc. ‖ 문서·연설·보고서 등에서 가장 중요한 개념. 골자. 요지: *The news report said little about the substance of the peace talks.* 그 뉴스 보도는 평화 회담의 요지에 대해서는 거의 언급하지 않았다. **3** FORMAL facts that are true and important ‖ 진실되고 중요한 사실. 실질. 내용. 실체: *There's no substance to*

his arguments. 그의 주장에는 알맹이가 없다.

substance a·buse /'.. .,./ *n* [U] TECHNICAL the habit of taking too many illegal drugs so that you are harmed by them ‖ 몸을 해칠 정도로 너무 지나치게 마약을 복용하는 습관. 마약 남용

sub·stand·ard /,sʌb'stændəd/ *adj* not as good as the average, or not as good as usual ‖ 평균보다 좋지 않거나 보통보다 좋지 않은. 표준 이하의. 불충분한: *substandard health care* 불충분한 의료 서비스

sub·stan·tial /səb'stænʃəl/ *adj* **1** large enough in amount or numbers to be noticed ‖ 눈에 뜨일 정도로 양이 많거나 수가 큰. 상당한: *She earns a substantial income.* 그녀는 상당한 소득을 벌어들이고 있다. **2** large and strongly made ‖ 크고 강하게 만든. 견고한. 튼튼한

sub·stan·tial·ly /səb'stænʃəli/ *adv* very much ‖ 상당히. 충분히. 대폭: *Prices have increased substantially.* 가격이 대폭 인상되었다.

sub·stan·ti·ate /səb'stænʃi,eɪt/ *v* [T] FORMAL to prove the truth of something that someone has said ‖ 어떤 사람이 말한 것의 진실성을 입증하다. 실증하다

sub·sti·tute¹ /'sʌbstə,tut/ *n* **1** someone who does someone else's job while s/he is away, sick etc. ‖ 다른 사람이 부재 중이거나 와병(臥病) 중일 때 그 사람의 일을 하는 사람. 대리인: *Rona is working as a substitute teacher.* 로나는 대리 교사로 근무하고 있다. **2** something new or different that you use or do instead of what you used or did before ‖ 전에 사용했거나 행했던 것 대신에 사용하거나 행하는 새롭거나 전혀 다른 것. 대용품: *a sugar substitute* 설탕 대용품 / *There is no substitute for* (=nothing better than) *a good diet.* 적절한 식사를 대신할 것은 아무것도 없다.

substitute² *v* **1** [T] to use something new or different instead of something else ‖ 어떤 것 대신에 새롭거나 다른 물건을 사용하다. 대용하다: *You can substitute margarine for butter in this recipe.* 이 조리법에서는 버터 대신에 마가린을 사용할 수 있습니다. **2** [I, T] to do someone's job for a short time until s/he is able to do it again ‖ 남이 다시 일할 수 있을 때까지 잠시 동안 그 사람의 일을 하다. 대리가 되다. …을 대리하다 – **substitution** /,sʌbstə'tuʃən/ *n* [C, U]

sub·ter·fuge /'sʌbtə,fyudʒ/ *n* [C, U] FORMAL a trick or dishonest way of doing something, or the use of this ‖ 어떤 일을

하는 계교나 부정직한 방법, 또는 이것을 사용하는 것. 구실. 핑계. 속임수

sub·ter·ra·ne·an /ˌsʌbtəˈreɪniən/ adj TECHNICAL beneath the surface of the earth; UNDERGROUND ‖ 지구 표면 밑의. 지하의; ⓟunderground: a subterranean lake 지하 호수

sub·ti·tles /ˈsʌbˌtaɪtlz/ n [plural] words on a movie screen that translate what the actors are saying when the movie is in a foreign language ‖ 영화가 외국어로 상영될 때 배우가 하는 말을 번역한 영화 화면 상의 대사. 대사 자막 – **subtitled** adj

sub·tle /ˈsʌtl/ adj 1 not easily noticed unless you pay careful attention ‖ 세심히 주의하지 않으면 쉽게 눈에 띄지 않는. 미묘한: She noticed some subtle changes in his personality. 그녀는 그의 성격상의 몇 가지 미묘한 변화를 눈치챘다. 2 a subtle taste or smell is pleasant and delicate ‖ 맛이나 냄새가 기분 좋고 은은한: the subtle scent of mint in the air 공기 중의 은은한 박하향 3 a subtle person, plan etc. skillfully hides what he, she, or it intends to do or achieve ‖ 사람 또는 계획 등이 행하거나 이루려는 것을 교묘히 숨기는. 교활한. 음흉한 – **subtly** /ˈsʌtl-i, ˈsʌtli/ adv

sub·tle·ty /ˈsʌtlti/ n [C, U] the quality of being SUBTLE, or something that is subtle ‖ 미묘함, 또는 미묘한 것: the subtlety of the wine's flavor 포도주 맛의 미묘함 / The subtleties of the story do not translate well into other languages. 그 소설의 미묘한 점은 다른 언어로 번역이 잘 되지 않는다.

sub·tract /səbˈtrækt/ v [T] to take a number or amount from something larger ‖ 더 큰 것에서 수나 양을 덜어내다. 빼다. 감하다: If you subtract 15 from 25 you get 10. 25에서 15를 빼면 10이 된다. – **subtraction** /səbˈtrækʃən/ n —compare ADD

sub·urb /ˈsʌbəb/ n an area away from the center of a city, but still part of it, where a lot of people live ‖ 도시의 중심에서 멀리 떨어졌지만 여전히 도시의 일부로서 많은 주민들이 살고 있는 지역. 교외: We moved to the suburbs last year. 우리는 작년에 교외로 이사갔다. / a suburb of Chicago 시카고 교외

sub·ur·ban /səˈbəbən/ adj relating to a SUBURB ‖ 교외에 관련된. 교외의: suburban life 교외 생활 / suburban Cleveland (=the suburban areas around Cleveland) 클리블랜드 교외

sub·ur·bi·a /səˈbəbiə/ n [U] all

SUBURBs in general ‖ 일반적인 교외 전체: life in suburbia 교외의 생활

sub·ver·sive /səbˈvəsɪv/ adj intending to destroy or damage a government, society, religion etc. ‖ 정부·사회·종교 등을 파괴하거나 해치려고 하는. 전복시키는. 파괴적인: a subversive speech 전복을 꾀하는 연설

sub·vert /səbˈvət/ v [T] FORMAL to act in a SUBVERSIVE way ‖ 파괴하는 식으로 행동하다. 전복[타도, 파괴]하다

sub·way /ˈsʌbweɪ/ n a railroad that runs under the ground in cities ‖ 도시의 지하 밑으로 달리는 철도. 지하철

suc·ceed /səkˈsid/ v 1 [I] to do what you have tried to do, or to reach a high position in something such as your job ‖ 하려고 애써온 것을 하거나 직장 등에서 높은 지위에 도달하다. 성공하다: Finally, I succeeded in convincing Anna that I was right. 마침내 내가 옳다는 것을 안나에게 확신시키는 데 성공했다. / She gave herself five years to succeed as a writer. 그녀는 작가로 성공하기 위해 5년을 바쳤다. 2 [I] to have the result or effect that something is intended to have ‖ 취하려는 결과나 효과를 보다. 성과를 거두다: Our advertising campaign succeeded in attracting more customers. 우리의 광고 활동은 더 많은 고객을 끌어들이는 성과를 올렸다. 3 [I, T] to be the next person to take a position or do a job after someone else ‖ 어떤 지위를 맡을 다음 사람이 되거나 다른 사람에 이어서 일을 하다. 후임이 되다. 계승하다: Mr. Harvey will succeed Mrs. Lincoln as chairman. 하비 씨가 링컨 여사의 뒤를 이어 의장이 될 것이다. —compare FAIL¹

suc·ceed·ing /səkˈsidɪŋ/ adj coming after something else ‖ 다른 것 뒤에 오는. 계속되는: Sales improved in succeeding years. 판매는 해마다 나아졌다.

suc·cess /səkˈsɛs/ n 1 [U] the achievement of doing what you have tried to do or want to do ‖ 하려고 애써오거나 하고 싶은 것을 달성함. 성공: We had no/some success in developing a better engine. 우리는 더 나은 엔진의 개발에 전혀 성공하지 못했다[상당히 성공했다]. 2 something that has the result or effect that you intended ‖ 의도한 결과나 효과를 거둔 것. 대성공: Jackie's wedding was a big/huge/great success. 재키의 결혼은 대성공이었다. 3 someone who does very well or reaches a high position in something such as his/her job ‖ 직장 등에서 매우 유능하거나 높은

지위에 오르는 사람. 성공한 사람: *He wants to be a success.* 그는 성공한 사람이 되기를 원한다. **4 success story** someone or something that becomes successful in spite of difficulties ‖ 역경에도 불구하고 성공하게 되는 사람이나 사물. 성공담(의 주인공) —opposite FAILURE

suc·cess·ful /sək'sɛsfəl/ *adj* **1** having the result or effect that you intended ‖ 의도한 결과나 효과가 있는. 성과를 거둔: *The surgery was completely successful.* 수술은 완전히 성공적이었다. **2** well known and respected as a result of earning a lot of money ‖ 상당한 돈을 벌어서 잘 알려지고 존경받는. 성공한: *a successful businessman* 성공한 기업인 - **successfully** *adv* —opposite UNSUCCESSFUL

suc·ces·sion /sək'sɛʃən/ *n* **1 in succession** happening one after the other ‖ 잇따라 일어나는. 연달아: *The team has won four championships in succession.* 그 팀은 4회 연속 우승했다. **2 a succession of sth** a number of people or things that happen or follow one after another ‖ 잇따라 일어나거나 뒤따르는 많은 사람 또는 일. …의 연속: *A succession of bad investments led to the failure of the business.* 계속적인 잘못된 투자가 그 사업의 실패로 이어졌다. **3** [U] the act of taking over an important job, position etc., or the right to be the next to take it ‖ 중요한 일이나 지위 등을 이어받은 행위, 또는 그 일이나 지위 등을 다음에 물려받게 되는 권리. 계승[승계](권)

suc·ces·sive /sək'sɛsɪv/ *adj* happening, existing, or following one after the other ‖ 잇따라 일어나거나 존재하거나 뒤따르는. 연속하는: *Babe Ruth hit three successive home runs in one game.* 베이브 루스는 한 경기에서 연달아 3개의 홈런을 쳤다. - **successively** *adv*

suc·ces·sor /sək'sɛsɚ/ *n* someone who takes a job or position that was held before by someone else ‖ 다른 사람이 전에 보유했던 일이나 지위를 맡는 사람. 후계자. 상속인: *No one was certain who Mao's successor would be.* 누가 모택동의 후계자가 될지 아무도 확신하지 못했다. - **successively** *adv*

suc·cinct /sək'sɪŋkt, sə'sɪŋkt/ *adj* clearly expressed in a few words ‖ 몇 마디 말로 명백하게 표현한. 간결한 - **succinctly** *adv*

suc·cor /'sʌkɚ/ *n* LITERARY help ‖ 원조

suc·cu·lent /'sʌkyələnt/ *adj* juicy and tasting very good ‖ 즙이 많고 맛이 매우 좋은: *a succulent steak* 육즙이 많은 스테이크 - **succulence** *n* [U]

suc·cumb /sə'kʌm/ *v* [I] FORMAL **1** to stop trying to oppose a person or a strong desire, and allow him, her, or it to persuade or influence you; YIELD ‖ 어떤 사람 또는 강한 욕망에 애써 반대하다 말고 그 사람이나 욕망이 자신을 설득하거나 영향을 미치게 하다. 지다. 굴복하다; ㉧ yield: *Eventually, she succumbed to his charms.* 마침내, 그녀는 그의 매력에 넘어갔다. **2** to become very sick or die from an illness ‖ 매우 아프거나 병으로 죽다

such /sʌtʃ/ *determiner, pron* **1** used in order to talk about a person or thing that is like the one that you have just mentioned ‖ 방금 말한 것과 같은 사람이나 사물을 언급하는 데에 쓰여. 그[이]와 같은. 그런. 이런: *Such behavior is not acceptable here.* 그런 행동은 이곳에서 용인되지 않는다. / *What would you do in such a situation?* 너라면 그런 상황에서 어떻게 하겠니? / *"Did you get the job?" "No such luck."* (=I wasn't lucky) "그 일 자리 잡았니?" "운이 안 따랐어." **2 such as** used when giving an example of something ‖ 사물의 예를 들 때에 쓰여. …과 같은. …등: *He likes dangerous sports such as mountain climbing.* 그는 산악 등반과 같은 위험한 스포츠를 좋아한다. / *big cities such as New York, Tokyo, and London* 뉴욕·도쿄·런던 등의 대도시들 **3** used in order to emphasize an amount or degree ‖ 양이나 정도를 강조하는 데에 쓰여. 대단히: *We had such fun at your party!* 우리는 네 파티에서 무척 즐거웠어! / *I was in such a hurry that I left my lunch at home.* 나는 몹시 서두르는 바람에 집에 도시락을 두고 왔다. / *Mandy's such a nice person.* 맨디는 아주 멋진 사람이야. **4 there's no such person/thing as** used in order to say that a particular type of person or thing does not exist ‖ 특정한 유형의 사람이나 사물은 존재하지 않는다고 말하는 데에 쓰여. …과 같은 사람[것]은 없다: *There's no such thing as a perfect job.* 완벽한 직업 같은 것은 없다. **5 as such** exactly what the word used is understood to mean ‖ 사용된 단어가 의미하는 대로 정확히 이해되는 것으로서. 그러한 것으로서. 그런 자격으로: *He doesn't have a degree as such, just a lot of business courses.* 그는 여러 비즈니스 코스를 거쳤을 뿐 그에 상응하는 학위는 없다.

USAGE NOTE such and so

Use **such** and **so** to emphasize a particular quality that a person or thing has. Use **so** just before an adjective: *Your dress is so pretty. / Some people are so rude.* However, if the adjective is used before a noun, use **such**: *She has such pretty eyes. / Mark is such a good swimmer.* You can also use **so** to emphasize an adverb: *He always sings so loudly.* **such**와 **so**는 사람이나 사물이 가진 특정한 성질을 강조하는 데에 쓰인다. **so**는 형용사 바로 전에 쓰인다: 너의 드레스는 매우 아름답구나. / 어떤 사람들은 아주 무례하다. 그러나 형용사가 명사 앞에 사용되면 **such**가 쓰인다: 그녀는 눈이 매우 아름답다. / 마크는 수영을 아주 잘한다. 부사를 강조하기 위해 또한 **so**를 쓸 수 있다: 그는 항상 아주 우렁차게 노래한다.

---

such-and-such /ˈ. . ˌ./ *determiner* SPOKEN used instead of the name of something ‖ 사물의 명칭 대신에 쓰여. 여차여차한: *You can say that when you press such-and-such a key, such-and-such happens.* 이러이러한 키를 누르면 이러이러한 일이 일어난다고 말할 수 있다.

suck /sʌk/ *v* 1 [I, T] to hold something in your mouth and pull on it with your tongue and lips ‖ 입으로 어떤 것을 잡고 혀와 입술로 잡아당기다. 빨다: *Don't suck your thumb, Katie.* 케이티, 엄지손가락을 빨지 마라. / *Ben was sucking on a piece of candy.* 벤은 사탕을 빨아먹고 있었다. 2 [T] to pull someone or something with a lot of force ‖ 사람이나 사물을 세차게 끌다. 집어삼키다: *A man almost got sucked under by the current.* 한 남자가 급류에 휩쓸릴 뻔했다. 3 **get sucked into (doing) sth** to make someone become involved in something unpleasant ‖ 다른 사람을 불쾌한 일에 연루시키다: *I'm not going to get sucked into an argument with you guys.* 나는 너희들과의 논쟁에 말려들지 않을 거야. 4 [I] SPOKEN to be bad or unpleasant ‖ 나쁘거나 불쾌하다. 형편없다. 최악이다: *It sucks having to stay inside all day.* 하루 종일 실내에만 있어야 하다니 죽을 맛이군. / *The band was great, but his singing sucked.* 그 밴드는 훌륭했으나 그의 노래는 형편없었다.

suck up to sb *phr v* [I] SPOKEN to say or do things someone wants in order to make him/her like you or to get what

you want ‖ 남에게 자신을 좋아하게 하거나 자신이 원하는 것을 얻기 위해 남이 원하는 것을 말하거나 하다. …에게 아첨하다: *She's always sucking up to the director.* 그녀는 항상 그 이사에게 아첨한다.

suck·er /ˈsʌkɚ/ *n* 1 INFORMAL someone who is easily tricked ‖ 쉽게 속는 사람. 봉. 호구: *Ellen always was a sucker.* 엘렌은 항상 너무나 잘 속았다. 2 SPOKEN a thing ‖ 것: *Do you know how much this sucker cost me?* 이것이 얼마인지 아니? 3 **be a sucker for sth** to like something so much that you cannot refuse it ‖ 거부할 수 없을 정도로 대단히 어떤 것을 좋아하다. …에 약하다[사족을 못 쓰다]: *I'm a sucker for old movies.* 나는 옛날 영화라면 사족을 못 쓴다. 4 ⇨ LOLLIPOP

suc·tion /ˈsʌkʃən/ *n* [U] the process of removing air or liquid from a container or space so that another substance can be pulled in, or so that two surfaces stick together ‖ 다른 물질을 끌어당기거나 두 표면이 서로 들러붙도록 용기 또는 공간에서 공기나 액체를 제거하는 과정. 흡인. 흡입

sud·den /ˈsʌdn/ *adj* 1 done or happening unexpectedly ‖ 갑자기 하거나 일어나는. 갑작스러운. 돌연한: *We've had a sudden change of plans.* 우리에게 갑작스러운 계획의 변화가 있었다. 2 **all of a sudden** without any warning ‖ 아무런 경고 없이. 느닷없이. 갑자기: *All of a sudden, the lights went out.* 갑자기 불이 나갔다.

sud·den·ly /ˈsʌdnli/ *adv* quickly and unexpectedly ‖ 빠르고 뜻밖에. 갑자기. 느닷없이: *She suddenly realized what she'd done.* 그녀는 갑자기 자신이 무슨 짓을 했는지 깨달았다. / *"Now I remember!" Bill said suddenly.* "이제 생각난다!"라고 빌은 느닷없이 말했다.

suds /sʌdz/ *n* [plural] the BUBBLEs that form on top of water with soap in it ‖ 비눗물 위에 생기는 거품. 비누 거품 – **sudsy** *adj*

sue /su/ *v* [I, T] to make a legal claim against someone, especially for money, because s/he has harmed you in some way ‖ 자신에게 남이 어떤 식으로 해를 끼쳤기 때문에, 특히 돈을 목적으로 남에게 소송을 제기하다. 고소하다: *She plans to sue the company for $1 million.* 그녀는 그 회사를 상대로 일백만 달러의 청구 소송을 제기할 계획이다.

suede /sweɪd/ *n* [U] soft leather with a slightly rough surface ‖ 겉죽이 약간 거친 부드러운 가죽. 스웨이드 가죽

suf·fer /'sʌfə/ v 1 [I, T] to experience something bad, such as pain, sickness, or the effects of a bad situation ‖ 고통이나 질병, 또는 좋지 못한 상황으로 인한 영향 등의 궂은 일을 경험하다. 고통 받다: *Neil suffered a heart attack last year.* 닐은 작년에 심근 경색을 앓았다. / *Marnie suffers from headaches.* 마르니는 두통으로 고생하고 있다. / *Small businesses are suffering financially right now.* 작은 기업은 지금 재정적으로 어려움을 겪고 있다. 2 [T] if someone suffers a bad experience, it happens to him/her ‖ 사람이 나쁜 경험을 겪다: *The mayor has suffered a defeat in the election.* 그 시장은 선거에서 패배했다. 3 [I] to become worse in quality ‖ 질이 더 나빠지다: *Andy's work began to suffer after his divorce.* 앤디의 작업은 이혼 후에 나빠지기 시작했다. – **sufferer** n – **suffering** n [C, U]

suf·fice /sə'faɪs/ v [I] FORMAL to be enough ‖ 충분하다. 족하다: *A few examples will suffice to show this is true.* 몇 가지 예를 들면 이것이 사실이라는 것을 보여주기에 족할 것이다.

suf·fi·cient /sə'fɪʃənt/ adj FORMAL as much as you need for a particular purpose; enough ‖ 특정한 목적에 필요한 만큼의; 충분한: *They had sufficient evidence to send him to prison.* 그들은 그를 감옥에 보낼 만큼 충분한 증거가 있었다. – **sufficiency** n [singular, U] — opposite INSUFFICIENT

suf·fix /'sʌfɪks/ n TECHNICAL in grammar, a letter or letters added to the end of a word in order to make a new word, such as "ness" at the end of "kindness" ‖ 문법에서 "kindness"의 끝의 "ness" 등 처럼 새로운 단어를 만들기 위해 단어 끝에 덧붙인 글자나 글자들. 접미사 —compare PREFIX, AFFIX

suf·fo·cate /'sʌfə,keɪt/ v 1 [I, T] to die or kill someone by preventing him/her from breathing ‖ 남을 숨을 쉬지 못하게 하여 죽게 하거나 죽이다. 질식사하다. 질식사시키다: *One firefighter was suffocated by the smoke.* 한 소방관이 연기에 질식사했다. 2 **be suffocating** INFORMAL to feel uncomfortable because there is not enough fresh air ‖ 신선한 공기가 충분히 없기 때문에 편하지 않다. 숨이 막히다 – **suffocation** /,sʌfə'keɪʃən/ n [U]

suf·frage /'sʌfrɪdʒ/ n [U] FORMAL the right to vote ‖ 투표권. 참정권

sug·ar /'ʃʊgə/ n [U] a sweet white or brown substance that is obtained from plants and used for making food and drinks sweet ‖ 식물에서 채취하여 음식과 음료를 달게 하는 데 사용되는 희거나 누런 달콤한 물질. 설탕: *Do you take sugar in your coffee?* 커피에 설탕을 탑니까? – **sugary** adj : *sugary snacks* 달콤한 간식

sug·ared /'ʃʊgəd/ adj covered in sugar ‖ 설탕으로 덮인. 설탕으로 달게 한: *sugared almonds* 설탕을 입힌 아몬드

sug·gest /səg'dʒɛst, sə'dʒɛst/ v [T] 1 to tell someone your ideas about what should be done ‖ 일을 어떻게 할 것인가에 대해 남에게 생각을 말하다. 제안[제의]하다: *They suggested meeting for drinks first.* 그들은 우선 모여서 술 한잔 하자고 제안했다. / *Don suggested that we go swimming.* 돈은 우리에게 수영 가자고 제의했다. 2 to say that someone or something is good for a particular purpose; RECOMMEND ‖ 사람이나 사물이 특정한 목적에 좋다고 말하다. 추천하다; ⑭ recommend: *Gina Reed's name has been suggested for the job.* 지나 리드의 이름이 그 자리에 추천되었다. 3 to make someone think that a particular thing is true; INDICATE ‖ 누군가에게 특정한 일이 사실이라고 생각하게 하다. 암시하다. 넌지시 나타내다; ⑭ indicate: *The article suggested that Nachez might run for mayor.* 그 기사는 나체즈가 시장에 출마할지 모른다고 암시했다. —see usage note at RECOMMEND

sug·gest·i·ble /səg'dʒɛstəbəl, sə'dʒɛs-/ adj easily influenced by other people or by things you see and hear ‖ 다른 사람이나 보고 듣는 일에 의해 쉽게 영향 받는. 영향 받기 쉬운

sug·ges·tion /səg'dʒɛstʃən, sə'dʒɛs-/ n 1 an idea or plan that someone mentions ‖ 누군가가 말하는 생각이나 계획. 제안: *We've had some suggestions on good plays to see in New York.* 우리는 뉴욕에서 볼 만한 연극에 대한 몇 가지 제언을 받았다. / *Can I make a suggestion?* 제안할까요? / *They accepted the suggestion that Todd go first.* 그들은 토드가 먼저 간다는 제안을 받아들였다. 2 [U] the act of telling someone your idea about what should be done ‖ 일을 어떻게 할 것인가에 대해 남에게 생각을 말하는 행위. 제안함: *I took the class at my adviser's suggestion.* 지도 교사의 제의에 따라 나는 그 수업을 받았다. 3 **suggestion that/of** a slight possibility ‖ 약간의 가능성. 기색. 조짐: *The police said that there was no suggestion of murder.* 경찰은 살인의 기미는 없다고 말했다.

sug·ges·tive /səg'dʒɛstɪv, sə'dʒɛs-/ *adj* **1** making you think of sex‖ 성을 생각나게 하는. 선정적인: *a suggestive remark* 외설적인 말 **2** reminding you of something‖ 무엇을 생각나게 하는. 연상시키는: *a spotted rug, suggestive of leopard skin* 표범 가죽을 연상시키는 얼룩무늬의 양탄자

su·i·ci·dal /,suə'saɪdl/ *adj* **1** wanting to kill yourself‖ 스스로 죽고 싶어 하는. 자살의: *Fay's very unhappy–suicidal, in fact.* 페이는 매우 불행해서 사실 자살하고 싶은 기분이다. **2** behavior that is suicidal is dangerous and likely to result in death‖ 행동이 위험스럽고 죽음에 이를 듯한. 자멸적인. 무모한

su·i·cide /'suə,saɪd/ *n* **1** [C, U] the act of killing yourself‖ 스스로 죽는 행위. 자살: *Her brother committed suicide last year.* 그녀의 남동생은 작년에 자살했다. **2** political/social etc. suicide something you do that ruins your job or position in society‖ 사회에서 자신의 직업이나 지위를 파멸시키는 것. 정치적/사회적 자살 행위

suit¹ /sut/ *n* **1** a set of clothes made of the same material, including a short coat with pants or a skirt‖ 바지나 스커트에 짧은 코트를 포함하는, 같은 옷감으로 만든 한 벌의 옷. 신사복·여성복 정장 한 벌. 슈트: *a dark gray suit* 어두운 회색 슈트 **2** a piece or pieces of clothing used for a special purpose‖ 특별한 목적용으로 사용되는 옷의 하나나 한 벌: *a swimming suit* 수영복 **3** [C, U] ⇨ LAWSUIT : *A homeowner filed suit against the county and lost.* 자택 소유자가 군(郡)을 상대로 소송을 제기해서 패소했다. **4** one of the four types of cards in a set of playing cards‖ 카드놀이에서 한 벌로 된 4가지 유형의 카드 중의 하나. 짝패 한 벌

suit² *v* [T] **1** to be acceptable or right for you‖ 받아들일 수 있거나 적당하다. 만족할 만하다: *"Is tomorrow at 10:00 okay?" "That suits me fine."* (=is acceptable to me) "내일 10시는 괜찮니?" "그 시간이면 딱 좋아." **2** to make someone look attractive‖ 사람을 매력적으로 보이게 하다. 어울리다: *Short hair suits you.* 짧은 머리가 너에게 어울린다. **3** suit yourself SPOKEN said in order to tell someone that s/he can do whatever s/he wants to do, usually in a way that shows you are annoyed or upset‖ 보통 화가 나거나 심란하다는 점을 표시하는 투로 남에게 하고 싶은 일은 무엇이든지 하라고 말하는 데 쓰여. 마음대로[좋도록]

해: *"I'm not sure I want to go tonight." "Suit yourself."* "나는 오늘밤에 가고 싶지 않아." "마음대로 해." **4** to have the right qualities to do something‖ 무엇을 하기에 적합한 속성이 있다. 적합하다: *Lucy's ideally suited for the job.* 루시는 그 일에 정말 안성맞춤이다. —see usage note at APPROPRIATE¹

suit·able /'sutəbəl/ *adj* right or acceptable for a particular purpose or situation‖ 특정한 목적이나 상황에 맞거나 받아들일 수 있는. 적합한. 어울리는: *This book isn't suitable for young children.* 이 책은 어린 아이에게 적합하지 않다. - **suitably** *adv* - **suitability** /,sutə'bɪləti/ *n* [U] —opposite UNSUITABLE —see usage note at APPROPRIATE¹

suit·case /'sut˺keɪs/ *n* a bag or box with a handle, for carrying your clothes when you travel‖ 여행할 때 옷을 넣어 가지고 다니는 데 사용하는 손잡이가 있는 가방이나 상자. 슈트케이스

suite /swit/ *n* **1** a set of expensive rooms in a hotel‖ 호텔의 한 세트의 비싼 방들. 스위트룸: *the honeymoon suite* 신혼여행의 스위트룸 **2** a set of matching furniture for a room‖ 방에 어울리는 한 벌의 가구: *a living room suite* 한 벌의 거실 가구 세트 **3** a piece of music made up of several short parts‖ 몇 개의 짧은 부분으로 이루어진 음악 곡. 모음곡. 조곡(組曲): *the Nutcracker Suite* 호두까기 인형 모음곡

suit·or /'sutə/ *n* OLD-FASHIONED a man who wants to marry a particular woman‖ 특정한 여성과 결혼하기를 원하는 남자. 구혼자

sul·fur /'sʌlfə/ *n* [U] a yellow strong-smelling chemical that is an ELEMENT‖ 화학 원소로 독한 냄새가 나는 노란 화학 약품. 유황

sulk /sʌlk/ *v* [I] to show that you are annoyed about something by being silent and looking unhappy‖ 아무 말도 않고 불만스럽게 보임으로써 무엇에 대해 짜증내고 있다는 것을 나타내다. 부루퉁[실쭉]해지다: *Stop sulking; you can go out and play later.* 부루퉁해 있지 마라. 나중에 밖에 나가서 놀 수 있으니까. - **sulky** *adj*

sul·len /'sʌlən/ *adj* silently showing anger or bad temper‖ 말없이 분노나 나쁜 기분을 보이는. 시무룩한

sul·phur /'sʌlfə/ *n* [U] ⇨ SULFUR

sul·tan /'sʌlt˺n/ *n* a ruler in some Muslim countries‖ 몇몇 회교국의 지배자. 회교국의 군주. 술탄

sul·try /'sʌltri/ *adj* **1** weather that is sultry is hot with no wind ‖ 날씨가 바람이 없이 더운. 무더운 **2** a woman who is sultry is very sexually attractive ‖ 여성이 성적으로 매우 매력적인. 섹시한. 관능적인

sum[1] /sʌm/ *n* **1** an amount of money ‖ 돈의 액수. 금액: *The city has spent a large sum of money on parks.* 그 도시는 공원 건설에 거액을 들였다. **2 the sum of** the total when you add two or more numbers together ‖ 둘 이상의 숫자를 함께 더할 때의 합계. 총계: *The sum of 4 and 5 is 9.* 4와 5의 합계는 9이다.

sum[2] *v* **-mmed, -mming**
sum up *phr v* [I, T] to end a discussion or speech by giving the main information about it in a short statement ‖ 짤막한 말로 주요한 정보를 제시하여 토론이나 연설을 마치다. 요약하다: *So, to sum up, we need to organize our time better.* 그래서, 요컨대 우리는 시간을 보다 만족스럽게 편성해야 해.

sum·ma·rize /'sʌmə,raɪz/ *v* [I, T] to make a short statement that gives only the main information about an event, plan, report etc. ‖ 행사·계획·보고 등에 대한 주요한 정보만을 제공하는 짧은 진술을 하다. 요약하다

sum·ma·ry /'sʌməri/ *n* a short statement that gives the main information about an event, plan, report etc. ‖ 행사나 계획이나 보고서 등에 대한 주요한 정보만을 제시하는 짧은 말. 요약. 개요: *Read the article and write a summary of it.* 그 기사를 읽고 요약하여 써라. / *In summary, more research is needed.* 요약을 하면, 연구가 보다 더 필요하다. — **summary** *adj*: *summary information* 개략적인 정보

sum·mer /'sʌmɚ/ *n* the season between spring and fall, when the weather is hottest ‖ 날씨가 가장 더울 때인 봄과 가을 사이의 계절. 여름. 하계: *The pool is open in (the) summer.* 수영장은 여름에 개장한다. / *We're going to Mt. Whitney this summer.* 우리는 이번 여름에 휘트니 산에 가려고 한다. / *last/next summer* (=the summer before or after this one) 지난[다음] 여름

summer school /'.. ,./ *n* [C, U] classes that you can take in the summer at a school or college ‖ 학교나 대학에서 여름에 받을 수 있는 수업. 하기 학교

sum·mer·time /'sʌmɚ,taɪm/ *n* [U] the time of year when it is summer ‖ 여름의 시기. 여름철. 하계

summer va·ca·tion /,.. '../ *n* [C, U] the time during the summer when schools are closed, or a trip you take during this time ‖ 학교가 휴교하는 여름 동안의 기간, 또는 이 기간 동안에 하는 여행. 여름 방학(동안의 여행)

sum·mit /'sʌmɪt/ *n* **1** a set of meetings among the leaders of several governments ‖ 몇몇 정부의 지도자들 사이의 일련의 회의. 수뇌[정상] 회담: *an economic summit* 경제 정상 회담 **2** the top of a mountain ‖ 산의 정상

sum·mon /'sʌmən/ *v* [T] FORMAL **1** to officially order someone to come to a particular place ‖ 누군가에게 특정한 장소로 올 것을 공식적으로 명령한다. 소환하다. 호출하다: *I was summoned to the principal's office.* 나는 교장실로 호출 받았다. **2** also **summon up** to make a great effort to use your strength, courage, etc. ‖ 힘이나 용기 등을 발휘하려고 대단히 노력하다. 내다. 불러일으키다: *Tim summoned up his courage to ask Kay for a date.* 팀은 용기를 내어 케이에게 데이트 신청을 했다.

sum·mons /'sʌmənz/ *n, plural* **summonses** an official order to appear in a court of law ‖ 법정에 출석하라는 공식적인 명령. 출석 명령. 소환장

sump·tu·ous /'sʌmptʃuəs/ *adj* very impressive and expensive ‖ 매우 멋지며 비싼. 고가의. 호화로운: *a sumptuous meal* 호화로운 식사

sun[1] /sʌn/ *n* **1** the large bright star in the sky that gives us light and heat, and around which the Earth moves ‖ 우리에게 빛과 열을 주며 지구가 그 주위를 도는 크고 밝은 별. 태양 —see picture at GREENHOUSE EFFECT **2** [U] the heat and light that come from the sun ‖ 태양에서 나오는 열과 빛: *Val lay in the sun, listening to the radio.* 발은 양지에 누워서 라디오를 듣고 있었다. **3** any star around which PLANETS move ‖ 행성들이 그 주위를 도는 별. 항성

sun[2] *v* **-nned, -nning** [T] **sun yourself** to sit or lie outside when the sun is shining ‖ 태양이 비칠 때 밖에서 앉거나 눕다. 햇볕을 쬐다. 일광욕을 하다

sun·bathe /'sʌnbeɪð/ *v* [I] to sit or lie outside in the sun in order to become tan (=brown) ‖ 햇볕에 타도록 태양이 쬐는 밖에서 앉거나 눕다. 일광욕을 하다 – **sunbathing** *n* [U]

sun·block /'sʌnblɑk/ *n* [U] a cream that you put on your skin that completely prevents the sun from burning you ‖ 태양으로부터 화상을 충분히 막도록 피부에 바르는 크림. 선블록

sun·burn /'sʌnbɚn/ *n* [U] the

condition of having skin that is red and painful as a result of spending too much time in the sun ‖ 햇볕에서 너무 많은 시간을 보낸 결과로 피부가 빨갛고 고통스러워지는 상태. 피부의 변색. 햇볕에 탐 — **sunburned** *adj*

sun·dae /'sʌndi, -deɪ/ *n* a dish of ICE CREAM, fruit, nuts, and sweet SAUCE ‖ 아이스 크림·과일·견과·달콤한 소스로 만든 음식. 선데이: *a hot fudge sundae* 핫 퍼지 선데이 —see picture at DESSERT

Sun·day /'sʌndi, -deɪ/, *written abbreviation* **Sun.** *n* the first day of the week ‖ 주의 첫째 날. 일요일

USAGE NOTE Sunday

Use the preposition "on" to talk about a particular day in the week that has just passed or the week that is coming: *Let's go to the mall on Friday. / Susan arrived on Saturday.* Use "last" before the name of a day to talk about something that happened the week before this one: *I had lunch with Lucy last Tuesday.* ✗DON'T SAY "on last Tuesday."✗ Use "next" before the name of a day to talk about something that will happen during the week after this one: *We'll see you next Thursday.* ✗DON'T SAY "on next Thursday."✗ Use the name of the day to say that something happens every week on that particular day: *Monday is my day off. / We always go bowling on Wednesdays.* Only use "the" in front of the name of a day if you are talking about a particular day of a particular week: *Can we meet on the Monday before Thanksgiving?*
바로 지나간 주나 다가오는 주(週)의 특정한 날을 언급하는 데에는 전치사 "on"을 쓴다: 금요일에 쇼핑센터에 갑시다. / 수잔은 토요일에 도착했다. 지난주에 일어난 일을 언급하는 데에는 요일 이름 앞에 "last"를 쓴다: 나는 지난주 화요일에 루시와 점심 식사를 했다. "on last Tuesday"라고는 하지 않는다. 다음 주 중에 일어날 일을 언급하는 데에는 요일 이름 앞에 "next"를 쓴다: 우리는 다음 주 목요일에 당신을 만나겠다. "on next Tuesday"라고는 하지 않는다. 일이 특정한 요일에 매주 일어나는 것을 언급하는 데에는 요일 이름을 쓴다: 나는 월요일에 비번이다. / 우리는 항상 수요일마다 볼링을 하러 간다. 특정한 주의

특정한 요일을 언급한다면 요일 이름 앞에 "the"만 쓴다: "우리 추수 감사절 이전 월요일에 만날까요?"

Sunday School /'·· ,·/ *n* [C, U] a class in a church where children go to be taught about their religion ‖ 아이들이 종교에 관해 배우기 위해 가는 교회의 학급. 주일 학교

sun·dial /'sʌndaɪl/ *n* an object that shows the time by the shadow of a POINTER on a flat surface that is marked with the hours ‖ 시간이 표시되어 있는 편평한 표면에 바늘의 그림자로 시간을 나타내는 물체. 해시계

sun·down /'sʌndaʊn/ *n* [U] ⇨ SUNSET

sun·dry /'sʌndri/ *adj* FORMAL ⇨ MISCELLANEOUS

sun·flow·er /'sʌn,flaʊɚ/ *n* a tall plant with large yellow flowers whose seeds can be eaten or used for making oil ‖ 씨는 먹거나 기름을 만드는 데 사용되며 크고 노란 꽃이 열리는 키 큰 식물. 해바라기

sung /sʌŋ/ *v* the PAST PARTICIPLE of SING ‖ sing의 과거 분사형

sun·glass·es /'sʌn,glæsɪz/ *n* [plural] dark glasses that you wear in order to protect your eyes when the sun is bright ‖ 태양이 빛날 때 눈을 보호하기 위해 쓰는 검은 안경. 선글라스. 색안경

sunk¹ /sʌŋk/ *v* the past tense and PAST PARTICIPLE of SINK ‖ sink의 과거·과거 분사형

sunk² *adj* INFORMAL in a lot of trouble, or having failed ‖ 많은 어려움에 처하거나 실패한. 끝장난: *If we can't finish by 5:00, we're sunk.* 5시까지 끝마치지 않으면 우리는 끝장이다.

sunk·en /'sʌŋkən/ *adj* 1 having fallen to the bottom of the sea ‖ 바다의 밑바닥까지 떨어진. 침몰한. 가라앉은: *a sunken ship* 가라앉은 배 2 built or placed at a lower level than the surrounding area ‖ 주변 지역보다 더 낮은 수준에 세워지거나 위치한. 한 단 낮은 곳에 있는: *a sunken garden* 지면보다 한 단 낮은 정원

sun·light /'sʌnlaɪt/ *n* [U] natural light that comes from the sun ‖ 태양에서 비치는 자연적인 빛. 일광. 햇빛: *These plants don't need much sunlight.* 이들 식물은 햇빛이 많이 필요하지 않다.

sun·lit /'sʌn,lɪt/ *adj* made brighter by light from the sun ‖ 햇빛에 의해 더 밝아진. 햇볕이 가득한. 볕이 드는: *a sunlit kitchen* 햇볕이 가득한 부엌

sun·ny /'sʌni/ *adj* 1 full of light from the sun ‖ 햇빛이 가득한. 햇빛이 찬란한: *a sunny day* 햇빛이 가득한 날 2

cheerful and happy ‖ 명랑하고 즐거운. 쾌활한: *a sunny personality* 명랑한 성격

sun·rise /'sʌnraɪz/ *n* [U] the time when the sun first appears in the morning ‖ 태양이 아침에 최초로 떠오르는 시간. 일출. 해돋이

sun·roof /'sʌnruf/ *n* a part of the roof of a car that you can open ‖ 자동차 지붕의 열리는 부분. 차 지붕의 개폐식 채광창

sun·screen /'sʌnskrin/ *n* [C, U] a cream that you put on your skin that will stop the sun from burning you for a period of time ‖ 일정한 시간 동안 햇빛에 타지 않게 피부에 바르는 크림. 햇볕[자외선] 차단제

sun·set /'sʌnsɛt/ *n* [U] the time of day when the sun disappears and night begins ‖ 태양이 사라지고 밤이 시작되는 하루의 시간. 일몰. 해넘이

sun·shine /'sʌnʃaɪn/ *n* [U] the light and heat that comes from the sun ‖ 태양에서 나오는 빛과 열. 햇빛. 일광: *Let's go out and enjoy the sunshine.* 나가서 햇빛을 만끽하자.

sun·tan /'sʌntæn/ *n* ⇨ TAN²

sun·up /'sʌnʌp/ *n* [U] ⇨ SUNRISE

su·per¹ /'supɚ/ *adj* INFORMAL extremely good ‖ 아주 좋은. 우수한: *He's a super soccer player.* 그는 일류 축구 선수이다.

super² *n* SPOKEN a building SUPERINTENDENT ‖ 건물 관리인

super³ *adv* SPOKEN extremely ‖ 매우. 아주. 지극히: *a super expensive restaurant* (음식 값이) 아주 비싼 식당

su·perb /sʊ'pɚb/ *adj* extremely good; excellent ‖ 매우 좋은; 훌륭한: *a superb dinner* 훌륭한 저녁 –**superbly** *adv*

Super Bowl /'.. ,./ *n* a football game played once a year in order to decide which professional team is the best in the US ‖ 어떤 프로 팀이 미국에서 가장 우수한가를 가리기 위해 일년에 한 번 하는 미식축구 경기. 슈퍼볼. 프로 미식축구 챔피언 결정전

su·per·fi·cial /ˌsupɚ'fɪʃəl/ *adj* 1 based only on the first things you notice, not on complete knowledge ‖ 철저한 지식에 기초한 것이 아니라 처음으로 알게 된 사물에만 근거를 둔. 피상적인: *There are superficial similarities between the two novels, but that's all.* 그 두 소설 사이에는 피상적인 유사점은 있지만 그것으로 끝이다. / *He's made only a superficial study of law.* 그는 법률을 피상적으로만 공부했다. 2 affecting only the surface of your skin or the outside part of something ‖ 피부의 표면이나 사물의 바깥 부분에만 영향을 끼치는: *She had some*

superficial cuts on her arm. 그녀는 팔에 몇 군데 살짝 베인 상처가 있었다. 3 someone who is superficial does not think about things that are serious or important; SHALLOW ‖ 사람이 진지하거나 중요한 사물에 대해 심사숙고 하지 않는. 깊이가 없는; ㊒ shallow –**superficially** *adv*

su·per·flu·ous /sʊ'pɚfluəs/ *adj* FORMAL more than is needed or wanted; unnecessary ‖ 필요한 것이나 원하는 것 이상의. 과잉의; 불필요한: *superfluous details* 필요 이상의 상세함

su·per·high·way /ˌsupɚ'haɪweɪ/ *n* a very large road on which you can drive fast for long distances between cities ‖ 도시들간의 장거리를 고속 주행할 수 있는 매우 넓은 도로. 고속도로 —see also INFORMATION SUPERHIGHWAY

su·per·hu·man /ˌsupɚ'hyumən-/ *adj* using powers that are much greater than ordinary ones ‖ 일반인들보다 훨씬 더 센 힘을 사용하는. 초인적인: *a superhuman effort to finish the job* 그 일을 끝내려는 초인적인 노력

su·per·in·tend·ent /ˌsupɚɪn'tɛndənt/ *n* 1 someone who is responsible for a place, job, activity etc. ‖ 장소·일·활동 등을 책임지는 사람. 관리자. 감독자: *Mel's just been hired as superintendent of sales.* 멜은 이제 막 영업 관리자로 채용되었다. 2 someone who takes care of an apartment building ‖ 아파트 건물을 관리하는 사람. 아파트 관리인 3 someone who is responsible for all the schools in a particular area of the US ‖ 미국의 특정한 지역에서 모든 학교를 책임지는 사람. 지방 교육 위원회의 교육감

su·pe·ri·or¹ /sə'pɪriɚ, sʊ-/ *adj* 1 better than other similar people or things ‖ 다른 비슷한 사람이나 사물보다 더 나은. 우월한. 우수한: *I believe Matisse's work is superior to Picasso's.* 나는 마티스의 작품이 피카소의 작품보다 우수하다고 생각한다. ✗DON'T SAY "superior than."✗ "superior than"이라고는 하지 않는다. 2 extremely good in quality ‖ 질이 매우 좋은. 고급의. 상질의: *superior wines* 고급 포도주 3 showing that you think you are better than other people ‖ 남들보다 더 낫다고 생각한다는 것을 보여주는. 교만한. 자만한: *a superior attitude* 교만한 태도 —opposite INFERIOR¹

su·pe·ri·or² *n* someone who has a higher rank or position than you in a job ‖ 직장에서 자신보다 더 높은 계급이나 지위에 있는 사람. 윗사람. 상사: *I'll have to discuss it with my superiors.* 나는 상사

와 그것을 의논해야 할 것이다. —
opposite INFERIOR²

su·pe·ri·o·ri·ty /sə,pɪri'ɔrəṭi, -'ɑr-/ n
[U] **1** the quality of being better than
other things ‖ 다른 것보다 더 나음. 우월.
상위: *the country's military superiority
over its neighbors* 이웃 나라에 대한 그
나라의 군사적인 우위 **2** an attitude that
shows you think you are better than
other people ‖ 남들보다 더 낫다고 생각한
다는 것을 보여주는 태도. 교만: *Janet
always spoke with an air of superiority.*
자넷은 항상 교만한 태도로 말했다.

su·per·la·tive¹ /sə'pɜlətɪv, sʊ-/ adj
excellent ‖ 우수한. 최고의. 더할 나위 없
는: *a superlative actor* 최고의 배우

superlative² n **1 the superlative**
TECHNICAL in grammar, the form of an
adjective or adverb that shows the
highest degree of a particular quality.
For example, "fastest" is the
superlative of "fast" ‖ 문법에서 특정한
성질의 가장 높은 정도를 나타내는 형용사
나 부사의 형태. 최상급. 예를 들면
"fastest"는 "fast"의 최상급이다. **2** a
word in this form, used when
expressing praise or admiration ‖ 칭찬이
나 감탄을 표현할 때 사용되는 이 형태의
단어. 최상급의 단어 —see study note on
page 931

su·per·mar·ket /'supɜ,mɑrkɪt/ n a
very large store that sells many
different kinds of food and things
need for the house ‖ 사람들이 가정에서
필요로 하는 여러 다양한 종류의 음식이나
물건을 파는 매우 큰 상점. 슈퍼마켓

su·per·nat·u·ral /,supɜ'næt∫ərəl,
-t∫rəl-/ n **the supernatural** events,
powers, abilities, or creatures that are
impossible to explain by science or
natural causes ‖ 과학이나 자연 원인으로
설명할 수 없는 사건이나 힘, 또는 능력이
나 존재. 초자연적인 것[현상, 존재] –
supernatural adj : *supernatural
powers* 초자연적인 힘

su·per·pow·er /'supɜ,paʊɜ/ n a
country that has very great military and
political power ‖ 아주 막강한 군사력·정
치력을 가진 나라. 초강대국

su·per·sede /,supɜ'sid/ v [T] to
replace something that is older or less
effective with something new or better
‖ 새롭거나 더 나은 물건으로 보다 낡거나
효과가 덜한 물건을 대신하다. 대체하다: *
TV had superseded radio by the 1960s.*
텔레비전은 1960년대에 라디오를 대신했
다.

su·per·son·ic /,supɜ'sɑnɪk-/ adj faster

than the speed of sound ‖ 소리의 속도보
다 더 빠른. 초음속의: *supersonic jets* 초
음속 제트기들

su·per·star /'supɜ,stɑr/ n an
extremely famous performer, especially
a musician or movie actor ‖ 매우 유명한
연기자, 특히 음악가나 영화배우

su·per·sti·tion /,supɜ'stɪ∫ən/ n [C, U]
DISAPPROVING a belief that some objects
or actions are lucky and some are
unlucky ‖ 어떤 물건 또는 행동은 행운이
있으며 어떤 것은 재수가 없다는 믿음.
미신

su·per·sti·tious /,supɜ'stɪ∫əs/ adj
DISAPPROVING believing that some objects
or actions are lucky or unlucky ‖ 어떤 물
건이나 행동이 행운이 있거나 재수가 없다
고 믿는. 미신적인

su·per·struc·ture /'supɜ,strʌkt∫ɜ/ n
[singular, U] a structure that is built on
top of the main part of something such
as a ship or building ‖ 배나 건물 등의 주
요 부분 위에 세워진 구조. 상부 구조

su·per·vise /'supɜ,vaɪz/ v [I, T] to be
responsible for a group of workers or
students and make sure that they do
their work correctly ‖ 일단의 근로자나
학생을 책임지며 그들이 할 일을 제대로
하는지를 확인하다. 감독[관리, 지휘]하다
– **supervision** /,supɜ'vɪʒən/ n [U]:
working under supervision 감독하의 작
업

su·per·vis·or /'supɜ,vaɪzɜ/ n someone
who SUPERVISEs workers or students ‖ 근
로자들이나 학생들을 감독하는 사람. 감
독. 관리자 – **supervisory** adj: *a
supervisory role* 감독의 역할

sup·per /'sʌpɜ/ n an informal meal
that is eaten in the evening; dinner ‖ 저
녁에 먹는 격식 차리지 않는 식사; 저녁 식
사: *What's for supper?* (=what will we
eat?) 저녁 식사는 뭐지? —see usage
note at MEAL TIMES

sup·plant /sə'plænt/ v [T] FORMAL to
take the place of another person or
thing ‖ 다른 사람이나 물건을 대신하다.
대체하다: *The old factories have all been
supplanted by new high-tech industries.*
오래된 공장들이 새로운 첨단 기술 산업으
로 모두 대체되었다.

sup·ple /'sʌpəl/ adj able to bend and
move easily ‖ 쉽게 구부리고 움직일 수 있
는. 나긋나긋한. 유연한: *a supple dancer*
몸이 유연한 댄서 / *supple leather* 나긋나
긋한 가죽

sup·ple·ment¹ /'sʌpləmənt/ n **1**
something that is added to something
else to improve it ‖ 개선하기 위해 어떤

것에 추가되는 것. 추가물. 보충물:
dietary supplements 식이 요법의 보조
식품 **2** an additional part of something
such as a newspaper, magazine etc. ‖ 신
문·잡지 등의 추가 부분. 부록. 증보. 보
유: *the Sunday supplement* 선데이 부록

sup·ple·ment² /'sʌplə,mɛnt/ *v*
supplement a salary/income/diet to
add something to what you earn or eat
in order to improve it ‖ 향상시키기 위해
자신이 벌거나 먹는 것에 어떤 것을 더하
다. 월급/수입/식단을 보충하다: *He took
a night job to supplement their income.*
그는 수입을 보충하기 위해 밤일을 했다.

sup·ple·men·tal /,sʌplə'mɛntl/,
supple·men·tary /-'mɛntri,
-'mɛntəri/ *adj* additional ‖ 보충의. 추가
의: *The doctor recommended taking
supplementary vitamins.* 의사는 비타민
을 보충하여 복용하라고 권고했다.

sup·pli·er /sə'plaɪɚ/ *n* a company that
provides a particular product ‖ 특정한
상품을 공급하는 회사. 공급자: *medical
suppliers* 의료기[의약품] 공급자

sup·plies /sə'plaɪz/ *n* [plural] food,
clothes, and things that are necessary
for daily life, especially for a particular
period ‖ 특히 특정한 기간 동안 일상생활
에 필요한 음식·옷·물건. 생활 필수품:
supplies for a camping trip 캠핑 여행에
필요한 물품들

sup·ply¹ /sə'plaɪ/ *n* **1** [C, U] an amount
of something that is available to be
used, or the process of providing this ‖
사용될 수 있는 물건의 양이나 이것을 공
급하는 과정. 공급(량): *Supplies of fresh
fruit arrive daily.* 신선한 과일이 매일 입
하된다. / *Oklahoma's large supply of oil*
오클라호마의 기름의 대량 공급 / *the
supply of oxygen to the brain* 뇌에의 산
소 공급 **2** a system that is used in order
to provide gas, water etc. ‖ 가스·물 등을
제공하기 위해 사용되는 시스템: *We've
had problems with the water supply
lately.* 우리는 최근에 상수도 문제가 생겼
다.

sup·ply² *v* [T] to provide people with
something that they need or want,
especially regularly over a long time ‖ 특
히 오랫동안에 걸쳐서 규칙적으로 필요하
거나 원하는 것을 사람들에게 제공하다.
공급하다. 대주다: *Workers are supplied
with masks and special clothing.* 근로자
들은 마스크와 특별한 옷을 지급받는다. /
*He was arrested for supplying drugs to
dealers.* 그는 마약을 거래상에게 공급한
혐의로 체포되었다.

supply and de·mand /.,. . .'./ *n* [U]

the relationship between the amount of
goods for sale and the amount that
people want to buy, especially the way
this relationship influences prices ‖ 팔려
는 물건의 양과 사람들이 사기 원하는 양
사이의 관계로, 특히 이 관계가 가격에 영
향을 미치는 면. 수요와 공급

sup·port¹ /sə'pɔrt/ *v* [T] **1** to say that
you agree with an idea, group, person
etc. and want him, her, or it to succeed
‖ 생각·집단·사람 등에 동의하며 사람이
나 그것이 성공하기를 바란다고 말하다.
지지[지원, 후원]하다: *The union will
support workers' demands for a pay
raise.* 노동조합은 근로자의 임금 인상 요
구를 지지할 것이다. **2** to hold the weight
of something in order to prevent it from
falling ‖ 쓰러지지 않도록 무엇의 무게를
받치다. 지탱하다. 버티다: *an arch
supported by two columns* 두 기둥으로
받친 아치 **3** to help and encourage
someone ‖ 남을 도와 주고 격려하다. …의
기운을 돋우다: *I appreciate your
supporting me during my divorce.* 나의
이혼 기간 동안 당신이 나를 격려해 주셔
서 감사합니다. **4** to provide enough
money for someone to live ‖ 사람이 살기
에 충분한 돈을 제공하다. 부양하다. 먹여
살리다: *How can Brad support a family
on his salary?* 브래드는 어떻게 그의 월
급으로 가족을 부양할 수 있을까? **5** to
get money in order to pay for a bad
habit ‖ 나쁜 습관에 돈을 지불하기 위해
자금을 입수하다. (마약·나쁜 버릇 등을)
계속하다: *He's started stealing to
support his drug habit.* 그는 마약 상용
습관을 계속하기 위해 절도를 시작했다. **6**
to prove that something is true ‖ 무엇이
사실임을 증명하다. 입증하다. 뒷받침하
다: *There is now enough data to support
the theory.* 이제 그 이론을 입증할 자료가
충분히 있다.

support² *n* **1** [U] the things people do
to help an idea, plan, group etc.
succeed, or the act of encouraging it ‖
생각·계획·집단 등이 성공하도록 돕기 위
해 사람들이 하는 일들, 또는 그것을 격려
함. 지원. 지지: *The proposal has won
the support of local businesses.* 그 제안
은 지방 기업의 지지를 얻었다. **2** [U] help
and encouragement that you give
someone ‖ 누군가에게 주는 도움과 격려.
후원. 원조: *My parents have given me
a lot of support.* 나의 부모님은 내게 많
은 후원을 해 주었다. **3** [C, U] an object
that holds up something else ‖ 다른 것을
지지하는 물체. 지지물. 지주: *supports
for the roof* 지붕의 지주들

sup·port·er /sə'pɔrtər/ n someone who supports a particular person, group, or plan || 특정한 사람이나 집단, 또는 계획을 지지하는 사람. 후원자. 지지자: *Supervisor Carter's supporters say he has been treated unfairly.* 감독자 카터의 지지자들은 그가 불공평한 대우를 받았다고 말한다.

sup·port·ive /sə'pɔrtɪv/ adj giving help or encouragement to someone in a particular situation || 특정한 상황에서 남에게 도움이나 격려를 하는. 지지하는: *Larry's always been supportive of my working.* 래리는 항상 내가 하는 일을 지지해 왔다.

sup·pose¹ /sə'pouz/ v [T] **1 be supposed to do sth a)** used in order to say what someone should or should not do , especially because of official rules || 특히 공식적인 규칙 때문에 사람이 해야 한다거나 하지 않아야 한다는 것을 말하는 데에 쓰여. …하기로 되어 있다. …해야만 하다: *You're supposed to wear a seat belt in the car.* 너는 차 안에서 안전벨트를 착용해야만 한다. **b)** used in order to say or ask what should happen || 무슨 일이 일어날지 말하거나 묻는 데에 쓰여: *The checks were supposed to arrive two weeks ago.* 그 수표는 2주 전에 도착하기로 되어 있었다. / *What time is the movie supposed to start?* 그 영화가 몇 시에 시작되느냐? **2 be supposed to be sth** to be believed to be true or real by many people || 많은 사람들에 의해 사실이나 정말이라고 믿겨지다. …으로 간주되다[여겨지다]: *This is supposed to be the oldest theater in New York.* 이 극장은 뉴욕에서 가장 오래된 것으로 간주된다. **3** to think that something is probably true || 어떤 것이 아마도 사실이라고 생각하다: *I suppose it's not very important.* 나는 그것은 그다지 중요하지 않다고 생각한다.

SPOKEN PHRASES
---

4 I suppose (that) used when saying in an angry way that you think something is true || 자신이 사실이라고 여기는 것을 화를 내며 말할 때 쓰여: *I suppose you thought that was funny!* 내 생각에는 네가 그걸 우습게 여긴것 같은데! **5 suppose/supposing** used in order to ask someone to imagine what might happen || 남에게 어떤 일이 일어날지 상상해 보라고 요구하는 데에 쓰여: *Suppose you do get the job. Who'd take care of the kids?* 당신이 그 직장을 구했다고 가정해라. 누가 아

이들을 돌볼 거냐? **6 What's that supposed to mean?** said when you are annoyed by what someone has just said || 남이 방금 말한 것에 화가 날 때 쓰여. (당혹·노여움을 나타내어) 그게 무슨 뜻이야?: *"I'll keep your idea in mind." "Keep it in mind! What's that supposed to mean?"* "나는 당신의 생각을 명심하겠다." "그 생각을 명심한다고! 도대체 그 말이 무슨 뜻이야?"

sup·pose² conjunction SPOKEN **1** used in order to ask what might happen || 어떤 일이 일어날지 묻는 데에 쓰여. 만일 …이라면: *Don't do it. Suppose Mom found out?* 그거 하지 마라. 엄마가 알았다고 생각해 볼래? **2** used in order to suggest something || 어떤 것을 제안하는 데에 쓰여. …하면 어떨까: *Suppose we try to finish this part first.* 이 부분을 먼저 끝마치면 어떨까?

sup·posed /sə'pouzd/ adj used in order to show that you do not think something is true or real, although other people claim it is || 다른 사람들이 사실이라고 주장할지라도 자신은 사실이거나 진짜가 아니라고 생각하는 것을 나타내는 데에 쓰여. 추정된. 가정의: *the supposed link between violent movies and crime* 폭력 영화와 범죄 사이의 추정된 관련성

sup·pos·ed·ly /sə'pouzɪdli/ adv used when saying what other people claim is true or real, especially when you do not think they are right || 특히 자신은 남들이 주장하는 것이 옳지 않다고 여기면서, 다른 사람들이 사실이거나 진짜라고 주장하는 것을 말할 때 쓰여. 필경. 아마: *He had to deliver supposedly important papers.* 그는 필경 중요한 서류를 전달해야 했다. / *Supposedly, he's rich and handsome.* 소문으로는 그는 부유한 미남이다.

sup·pos·ing /sə'pouzɪŋ/ conjunction ⇨ SUPPOSE²

sup·po·si·tion /ˌsʌpə'zɪʃən/ n [C, U] something that you think is true even though you are not certain and cannot prove it || 확실하지 않고 증명할 수 없을 지라도 사실이라고 생각하는 것. 가정

sup·press /sə'prɛs/ v [T] **1** to stop people from opposing the government, especially by using force || 특히 무력을 사용하여 사람들이 정부를 반대하지 못하게 하다. 억압[진압]하다: *The army was called in to suppress the revolt.* 그 반란을 진압하기 위해 군대가 소집되었다. **2**

to stop yourself from showing your feelings ‖ 감정을 드러내지 않다. 억제하다. 참다: *Andy could barely suppress his anger.* 앤디는 간신히 그의 분노를 참았다. **3** to prevent important information or opinions from becoming known ‖ 중요한 정보나 의견이 알려지지 않게 하다. 은폐하다: *His lawyer suppressed some of the evidence.* 그의 변호사는 그 증거의 일부를 은폐했다. **–suppression** /sə'prɛʃən/ *n* [U]

su·prem·a·cy /sə'prɛməsi, su-/ *n* [U] a position in which a group or idea is more powerful or advanced than anything else ‖ 집단이나 생각이 다른 것보다 더 강력하거나 앞서 있는 입장. 우위. 우월. 지배. 패권: *the supremacy of their army* 그들 군대의 우위

su·preme /sə'prim, su-/ *adj* **1** having the highest position of power, importance, or influence ‖ 권력이나 중요성, 또는 영향력이 가장 높은 위치에 있는. 최고의: *the Supreme Commander of the UN forces* 유엔군의 최고 사령관 **2** the greatest possible ‖ 가장 가능한. 최대의. 궁극의: *a supreme honor* 최대의 명예 **–supremely** *adv*

Supreme Court /·,· '·/ *n* [singular] the court of law with the most authority in the US ‖ 미국에서 가장 권위 있는 법원. 연방 대법원

sur·charge /'sɚtʃɑrdʒ/ *n* money that you have to pay in addition to the basic price of something ‖ 물건의 기본 가격에 추가로 지불하는 돈. 추가 요금

sure¹ /ʃʊr, ʃɚ/ *adj* **1** certain about something ‖ 무엇에 대해 확신하는. 의심할 여지 없는: *Are you sure (that) you've met him before?* 너 전에 그를 만난 적이 있는 게 확실해? / *I knew I'd like it, but I wasn't sure about/of the kids.* 내가 그것은 좋아하리라는 것을 알았으나 아이들에 대해서는 확신이 없었다. / *Garvey isn't sure who he can trust.* 가비는 신뢰할 만한 사람이 누구인지 확신이 들지 않는다. **2 make sure a)** to check that something is true or that something has been done ‖ 무엇이 사실이거나 완료되었는지를 조사하다. 확인하다: *He called to make sure (that) we got home okay.* 그는 우리가 집에 무사히 도착했는지 확인차 전화를 했다. **b)** to do something so that you are certain that something will happen ‖ 일어날 일을 확인차 무엇을 하다: *I wanted to make sure (that) I got an appointment.* 나는 약속이 있는지 확인하고 싶었다. **3** certain to happen or succeed ‖ 일어나거나 성공하는 것이 확실

한. 꼭 …하는: *The county fair is sure to appeal to everyone.* 군 박람회는 모든 사람의 마음에 들 것이 확실하다. / *Investing in the stock market is not a sure thing.* (=it is risky) 주식 시장에 투자하는 것은 성공이 확실치 않다. **4 be sure of sth** to be certain to get something or certain that something will happen ‖ 무엇을 획득하거나 무엇이 일어나리라는 것이 확실하다. …을 확신하다: *The Giants are now sure of a place in the playoffs.* 자이언츠 팀은 이제 플레이오프 진출을 확신한다. **5 sure of yourself** confident about your own abilities and opinions ‖ 자신의 능력과 의견에 대해 자신하는. 자신감 있는: *Hirsch appeared very calm and sure of himself.* 허쉬는 매우 침착하고 자신감 있게 나타났다. **6 sure thing** SPOKEN said in order to agree to something ‖ 무엇에 동의하는 데에 쓰여. 물론이죠. 그럼요: *"See you Friday." "Yeah, sure thing."* "금요일에 봐요." "네, 그렇게 하세요."

USAGE NOTE sure, certain, and **certainly**

Sure and **certain** mean the same thing. However, **certain** is more formal than **sure**. **Certain** can be used in the phrase "It is certain that": *It is not certain that the plans will be approved.* ✗DON'T SAY "It is sure that."✗ You can use both **sure** and **certainly** to answer a question with a definite "yes." However, **sure** is much more common: *"Can you help me carry this?" "Sure."* Only use **certainly** in a formal situation. **sure**와 **certain**은 의미가 동일하다. 그러나 **certain**은 **sure**보다 더 격식적이다. **certain**은 "It is certain that" 의 어구로 쓰일 수 있다: 그 계획이 승인될지는 확실하지 않다. "It is sure that"이라고는 하지 않는다. 질문에 명백히 "예"라고 대답하는 데에 **sure**와 **certainly**를 쓸 수 있다. 그러나 **sure**를 더 흔히 쓴다: "이것을 운반하는 데 나를 도와 줄래?" "물론이지." 격식적인 상황에서는 **certainly**만 쓴다.

---

sure² *adv* **1 for sure** INFORMAL **a)** certainly ‖ 확실히. 틀림없이: *I think he's married, but I don't know for sure.* 그가 결혼했다고 생각하지만 확실히는 모르겠어. **b)** used in order to emphasize that something is true ‖ 무엇이 사실이라는 것을 강조하는 데에 쓰여: *It's a lot better than it was, that's for sure.* 그것은 예전

보다 많이 나아진 것 같아, 틀림없어. **2** **sure enough** INFORMAL used in order to say that something happened in the way someone thought it would ‖ 사람이 생각한 대로 무엇이 일어났다고 말하는 데에 쓰여. 예상대로: *Sure enough, by the age of 30, I was bald too.* 예상대로 30살쯤에 나도 대머리가 되었다. **3** INFORMAL used in order to admit that something is true, before you say something very different ‖ 아주 다른 내용을 말하기 전에 무엇이 사실이라는 점을 인정하는 데에 쓰여. 확실히: *Sure, he's cute, but I'm still not interested.* 확실히 그는 귀엽지만 나는 아직 관심이 없어.

SPOKEN PHRASES

4 said in order to say yes to someone ‖ 남에게 긍정의 말을 하는 데에 쓰여. 물론. 좋고말고: *"Can I read your paper?" "Sure."* "네 논문을 읽어봐도 될까?" "그럼." **5** said in order to emphasize a statement; certainly ‖ 진술을 강조하는 데에 쓰여; 확실히: *It's sure nice outside tonight.* 오늘 밤 바깥이 확실히 좋은데. / *Well, it sure doesn't make my job any easier.* 글쎄, 그것이 정말 내 일을 보다 쉽게 할 것 같지는 않아. **6** used as a way of replying when someone thanks you ‖ 누군가가 감사할 때 대답의 형태로 쓰여. 천만에: *"Hey, thanks for your help." "Sure."* "이봐, 도와줘서 고맙네." "천만에."

—see usage note at YES

sure-fire /ˌ. ˈ./ *adj* INFORMAL certain to succeed ‖ 성공할 것이 틀림없는. 확실한: *a sure-fire way to make a million bucks* 백만 달러를 버는 확실한 방법

sure·ly /ˈʃʊrli, ˈʃɜli/ *adv* used in order to show that you think something must be true ‖ 무엇이 사실임에 틀림없다고 생각하는 것을 나타내는 데에 쓰여. 확실히. 틀림없이: *Surely you won't go there alone!* 분명히 너는 혼자서는 그곳에 가지 않을 걸!

surf

surf¹ /sɜf/ *v* [I] **1** to ride on ocean waves standing on a special board ‖ 특수 판자 위에 서서 바다의 파도를 타다. 파도타기를 하다 **2** **surf the net** to look quickly through the information on the INTERNET for information that interests you ‖ 흥미를 주는 정보를 찾기 위해 인터넷에서 신속히 정보를 샅샅이 뒤지다. 인터넷에서 정보 검색하다 **– surfer** *n* **– surfing** *n* [U]: *Didn't you go surfing at Ventura?* 너는 서핑하러 벤투라에 가지 않았니? —see also **channel hop/surf** (CHANNEL)

surf² *n* [U] waves that come onto the beach and have white BUBBLES on top of them ‖ 꼭대기에 흰 거품이 일며 해변쪽으로 밀려오는 파도

sur·face¹ /ˈsɜfəs/ *n* **1** the outside or top layer of something ‖ 무엇의 외부나 제일 위층. 표면. 외면. 수면: *a cleaner for all your kitchen surfaces* 만능 주방 표면용 세제 / *the Earth's surface* 지표면 / *leaves floating on the surface of the lake* 호수의 수면에 떠 있는 나뭇잎들 **2** **the surface** the qualities that someone or something seems to have until you learn more about them ‖ 사람이나 사물에 대하여 많이 알 때까지의 그 사람이나 사물이 띠고 있는 듯한 특성. 외관. 겉보기: *He seems quiet on the surface, but he really likes to talk.* 그는 겉보기에는 과묵해 보이지만 사실상 대화하기를 좋아한다. / *Under the surface, there were problems at the bank.* 속을 들여다 보면 그 은행은 문제가 있었다.

surface² *v* **1** [I] to rise to the surface of water ‖ 수면에 떠오르다: *Whales were surfacing near our boat.* 고래들이 우리 배 근처에서 떠오르고 있었다. **2** [I] to become known about or easy to notice ‖ 무엇에 대해 알려지거나 쉽게 눈에 띄다. 표면화하다: *Old arguments are starting to surface.* 오래된 논쟁이 표면화하기 시작하고 있다. **3** [T] to put a surface on a road ‖ 도로에 포장을 하다

surf·board /ˈsɜfbɔrd/ *n* a long special board that you stand on to ride on ocean waves ‖ 바다의 파도를 타기 위해 서 있는 긴 특수 판자. 파도타기 널. 서프보드

surge¹ /sɜdʒ/ *v* [I] **1** if a crowd of people surges, it suddenly moves forward together very quickly ‖ 군중이 갑자기 아주 빠르게 함께 전진하다. 밀려오다. 쇄도하다 **2** also **surge up** to begin to feel an emotion very strongly ‖ 매우 격한 감정을 느끼기 시작하다. 끓어오르다. 격동하다: *Rage surged up inside* *her.* 그녀의 마음속에 분노가 치밀었다.

surge² *n* **1** a sudden large increase in something ‖ 사물의 갑작스러운 상당한 증가. 급상승. 비등: *a surge of excitement* 흥분의 고조 / *a surge in oil prices* 석유 가격의 급등 **2** a sudden movement of a lot of people ‖ 많은 사람들의 갑작스러운 이동. 쇄도: *a surge of refugees into the country* 그 나라로 밀려오는 피난민들

sur·geon /ˈsɜ˞dʒən/ *n* a doctor who does operations in a hospital ‖ 병원에서 수술을 하는 의사. 외과 의사 —see usage note at DOCTOR¹

sur·ger·y /ˈsɜ˞dʒəri/ *n* [U] medical treatment in which a doctor cuts open your body to fix, change or remove something inside ‖ 의사가 몸을 절개하여 안에 있는 것을 치료하거나 변경하거나, 또는 제거하는 치료. 수술: *heart surgery* 심장 수술 / *plastic surgery* 성형 수술

sur·gi·cal /ˈsɜ˞dʒɪkəl/ *adj* relating to or used for medical operations ‖ 수술에 관련되거나 수술에 쓰이는. 수술의. 외과용의: *surgical gloves* 수술 장갑

sur·ly /ˈsɜ˞li/ *adj* bad-tempered, unfriendly, and often rude ‖ 심술궂고 친절하지 않고 종종 무례한. 무뚝뚝한. 붙임성 없는. 퉁명스러운: *surly behavior* 무뚝뚝한 행동

sur·mise /sə˞ˈmaɪz/ *v* [T] FORMAL to guess that something is true using information you have ‖ 가진 정보를 이용하여 무엇이 사실임을 추측하다. 짐작하다

sur·mount /sə˞ˈmaʊnt/ *v* [T] FORMAL to succeed in dealing with a problem or difficulty ‖ 문제나 어려움을 해결하는 데 성공하다. 극복하다. 이겨내다

sur·pass /sə˞ˈpæs/ *v* [T] to be better or greater than someone or something else ‖ 다른 사람이나 사물보다 더 낫거나 더 좋다. 능가하다. 초월하다: *Japan has surpassed other countries in technology.* 일본은 기술에서 다른 나라들을 능가했다. / *His success had surpassed their hopes/expectations.* 그의 성공은 그들의 희망[기대]을 뛰어 넘었다.

sur·plus¹ /ˈsɜ˞plʌs/ *n* [C, U] **1** more of something than is needed or used ‖ 필요하거나 사용하는 이상의 것. 나머지. 잉여: *a surplus of goods* 남아도는 상품 **2** money that a country or company has after it has paid for the things it needs ‖ 국가나 회사가 필요한 것에 대한 값을 치르고 난 후에 가지고 있는 돈. 잉여금: *a budget surplus* 예산 잉여금 —opposite DEFICIT **3** the state of having sold more goods to another country than you have

bought from it ‖ 다른 나라로부터 사 온 것보다 다른 나라에 물건을 더 많이 판 상태. 흑자: *a trade surplus with China* 중국과의 무역 흑자

surplus² *adj* more than what is needed or used ‖ 필요하거나 사용하는 것 이상의. 여분의. 잉여의: *surplus corn* 남아도는 옥수수

sur·prise¹ /sə˞ˈpraɪz, səˈpraɪz/ *n* **1** [C, U] something that is unexpected or unusual ‖ 예기치 않거나 유별난 일. 뜻밖의 일. 놀라운 사건: *What a surprise to see you here!* 너를 여기서 만나다니 참으로 뜻밖의 걸! / *It came as no surprise when Jeff moved to Chicago.* (=we expected it would happen) 제프가 시카고로 이사갔을 때 그럴거라고 생각했었다. / *Dad, I have a surprise for you!* 아빠, 깜짝 놀랄 일이 있어요! **2** [U] the feeling you have when something unexpected or unusual happens ‖ 예기치 않거나 유별난 일이 일어날 때의 느낌. 놀람. 경악: *Imagine our surprise when we heard the news!* 우리가 그 소식을 들었을 때 얼마나 놀랐을까 상상해 봐! **3 catch/take sb by surprise** to happen in an unexpected way ‖ 예기치 않게 일어나다. …을 불시에 덮치다. 기습하다: *The heavy snowfall had caught everyone by surprise.* 폭설이 모든 사람을 불시에 덮쳤다. **4 Surprise!** SPOKEN said at the same time as you show someone something that s/he did not expect, such as a gift ‖ 선물 등의 기대하지 않은 것을 남에게 보여주면서 쓰여. 짠. 놀랐지: *Close your eyes, Joanne – Surprise!* 조안, 눈을 감아봐. 자 놀랐지!

surprise² *v* [T] **1** to make someone feel surprised ‖ 남을 놀라게 하다. 경악하게 하다. 놀래키다: *"Pam got fired." "It doesn't surprise me."* "팸이 해고됐어." "그리 놀라운 소식도 아닌데." **2** to find, catch, or attack someone when s/he does not expect it ‖ 예상하고 있지 않을 때 남을 발견하거나 체포하거나, 또는 공격하다. 기습하다. 현장을 잡다: *A security guard surprised the robber.* 한 경비원이 그 강도를 현장에서 잡았다.

sur·prised /sə˞ˈpraɪzd, sə-/ *adj* having a feeling of surprise ‖ 놀람의 감정을 가진. 놀란: *We were surprised (that) David got the job.* 우리는 데이비드가 취직했다는 소식에 놀랐었다. / *I'm surprised at how much it costs.* 나는 그것의 가격에 놀랐다. / *Judy seemed surprised by his answer.* 주디는 그의 대답에 놀란 것 같았다. ✗DON'T SAY "surprised for."✗ "surprised for"라고는

하지 않는다.

sur·pris·ing /səˈpraɪzɪŋ, sə-/ *adj*
unusual or unexpected ‖ 이상하거나 예
기치 않은. 놀랄 만한: *surprising news* 놀
랄 만한 소식 / *It's hardly/scarcely
surprising that they lost the game.* 그들
이 그 경기에 졌다는 것은 그리 놀랄 일이
아니다. **- surprisingly** *adv: The test
was surprisingly easy.* 그 시험은 놀라울
정도로 쉬웠다.

sur·real /səˈril/ *adj* very strange, like
something from a dream ‖ 꿈에서나 나오
는 듯이 매우 이상한. 초현실주의의[적
인]: *a surreal movie* 초현실적인 영화

sur·re·al·is·tic /ˌsə,riəˈlɪstɪk/ *adj* using
qualities, images etc. that are SURREAL
‖ 초현실주의적인 성질·이미지 등을 사용
하는. 초현실주의의: *a surrealistic
painter* 초현실주의 화가

sur·ren·der /səˈrɛndə/ *v* **1** [I] to say
officially that you want to stop fighting
because you know that you cannot win
‖ 이길 수 없다는 것을 알기 때문에 싸움
을 그만두고 싶다고 공식적으로 말하다.
항복하다: *The hijackers were given one
hour to surrender.* 공중 납치 범인들에게
한 시간의 항복할 시간이 주어졌다. **2** [T]
FORMAL to give up something such as a
ticket or PASSPORT to an official ‖ 관리에
게 표나 여권 등을 넘겨주다. 당국에 제출
하다[맡기다] **3** [T] FORMAL to give up
something that is important or
necessary, often because you feel forced
to ‖ 종종 어쩔 수 없기 때문에 중요하거나
필요한 것을 포기하다: *She agreed to
surrender her baby for adoption.* 그녀는
입양을 시키려고 자기 아기를 갖는 것을
포기하는 데 동의했다. **- surrender** *n*
[U]

sur·rep·ti·tious·ly /ˌsəəpˈtɪʃəsli,
ˌsʌrəp-/ *adv* done secretly or quietly so
that other people do not notice ‖ 다른 사
람들이 알아차리지 못하도록 은밀하게 또
는 조용히 하여. 남의 눈을 속여. 몰래 -
surreptitious *adj*

sur·ro·gate /ˈsəəgɪt, ˈsʌrə-/ *adj* taking
the place of someone or something else
‖ 다른 사람이나 다른 것을 대신하는. 대
리의. 대용의: *The organization acts as
a surrogate family for runaways.* 그 단
체는 가출인들에게 가족을 대신 한다. -
surrogate *n*

surrogate moth·er /ˌ... ˈ../ *n* a
woman who has a baby for another
woman who cannot have children ‖ 아이
들을 가질 수 없는 다른 여성을 위해 대신
아기를 낳아주는 여성. 대리모

sur·round /səˈraʊnd/ *v* [T] **1** to be all

around someone or something ‖ 사람이
나 사물의 주위 전체에 있다. 둘러[에워]
싸다: *a lake surrounded by trees* 나무로
둘러싸인 호수 **2** to be closely related to
a situation or event ‖ 상황이나 사건에 밀
접하게 관련되어 있다: *Secrecy
surrounded the President's visit to
Geneva.* 대통령의 제네바 방문은 비밀에
부쳐졌다. **- surrounding** *adj: the
surrounding countryside* 근처의 시골

sur·round·ings /səˈraʊndɪŋz/ *n*
[plural] all the things that are around
you, and where they are ‖ 주변에 있는
모든 사물들과 그 사물들이 있는 곳. 환경:
*It took me a few weeks to get used to my
new surroundings.* 내가 새 환경에 익숙
해지는 데 수 주일이 걸렸다.

sur·veil·lance /səˈveɪləns/ *n* [U] the
act of carefully watching a particular
person or place that might be related to
a crime ‖ 범죄와 관련이 되어 있는지 모
르는 특정한 사람이나 장소를 주의 깊게
지켜보는 행위. 감시: *Police have the
suspect under surveillance.* 경찰은 피의
자를 감시하고 있다.

sur·vey¹ /ˈsəveɪ/ *n* **1** a set of questions
that you ask a large number of people,
in order to find out about their opinions
and behavior ‖ 의견과 반응을 알아보려고
많은 사람들에게 물어보는 일련의 질문들.
조사. 검사: *We're taking a survey of
people's eating habits.* 우리는 사람들의
식성을 조사하고 있다. **2** a careful
examination of an area, used for
making a map of that area ‖ 그 지역의
지도 제작에 이용하기 위한 한 지역의 주
의 깊은 조사. 측량. 측지

sur·vey² /səˈveɪ/ *v* [T] **1** to ask a large
number of people a set of questions in
order to find out about their opinions or
behavior ‖ 의견이나 반응을 알아보려고
많은 사람들에게 일련의 질문을 하다. 조
사하다: *More than 50% of the students
surveyed said they exercise regularly.*
조사받은 학생들 중 50 퍼센트 이상이 규
칙적으로 운동을 한다고 말했다. **2** to look
at someone or something carefully so
that you can make a decision, or find
out more information ‖ 의사 결정을 하거
나 더 많은 정보를 찾을 수 있게 사람이나
사물을 주의 깊게 보다. 둘러보다. 점검하
다: *Kramer surveyed the damage to his
car.* 크레이머는 자기 차의 손상된 부분을
살펴보았다. **3** to examine and measure
an area of land in order to make a map
‖ 지도를 만들기 위해 한 지역의 땅을 조
사하고 측정하다. 측량하다

sur·vey·or /səˈveɪə/ *n* someone whose

job is to measure and record the details of an area of land ‖ 한 지역의 땅의 세목을 측량하고 기록하는 직업인. 측량 기사

sur·viv·al /sə'vaɪvəl/ *n* [U] the state of continuing to live or exist, especially after a difficult or dangerous situation ‖ 특히 어렵거나 위험한 상황을 겪고 난 후 계속해서 살아 있거나 존재하는 상태. 생존. 존속: *Doctors say the operation will increase his chances of survival.* 의사들은 수술이 그의 생존 가능성을 높일 거라고 말한다.

sur·vive /sə'vaɪv/ *v* [I, T] **1** to continue to live after an accident, illness, etc. ‖ 사고·질병 등을 겪고 난 후 계속해서 살다. 살아남다: *Only one person survived the crash.* 단 한 사람만이 그 추돌 사고에서 살아남았다. **2** to continue to exist or be involved in an activity in spite of difficulties ‖ 어려움에도 불구하고 계속 존재하거나 어떤 활동에 관계하다: *Few small businesses survived the recession.* 극소수의 영세 기업들이 불황 속에서 살아남았다. / *The surviving teams will play each other on Sunday.* 살아남은 팀들은 일요일에 서로 경기를 벌일 것이다.

sur·vi·vor /sə'vaɪvə/ *n* **1** someone who continues to live after an accident, illness etc ‖ 사고·질병 등을 겪고 난 후 계속 살아남은 사람. 생존자: *Two of the survivors were hospitalized.* 생존자 중 두 명이 병원에 입원했다. **2** someone who continues trying and is unwilling to lose hope in spite of difficulties ‖ 어려움에도 불구하고 계속 노력하고 희망을 잃지 않으려 하는 사람. 곤경을 극복해 나가는 사람

sus·cep·ti·ble /sə'sɛptəbəl/ *adj* **1** likely to be affected by a particular illness or problem ‖ 특정한 질병이나 문제에 쉽게 영향을 받는. 흔들리기[감염되기] 쉬운: *I've always been very susceptible to colds.* 나는 항상 감기에 매우 잘 걸렸다. **2** easily influenced or affected by something ‖ 무엇에 쉽게 영향이나 작용을 받는. 민감한: *Children are particularly susceptible to horror movies.* 아이들은 특히 공포 영화에 곧잘 영향을 받는다.

sus·pect¹ /'sʌspɛkt/ *n* someone who may be guilty of a crime ‖ 범인일지 모르는 사람. 피의자: *the police's main suspect* 경찰의 주요 피의자

sus·pect² /sə'spɛkt/ *v* [T] **1** to think that someone may be guilty of a crime ‖ 어떤 사람이 범죄가 있을지 모른다고 생각하다. 혐의를 두다: *a woman who is suspected of murder* 살인 혐의를 받고 있는 여성 **2** to think that something is likely, especially something bad ‖ 어떤 일이 특히 나쁜 일이기 쉽다고 생각하다: *She suspected (that) Sandra had been lying.* 그녀는 산드라가 거짓말을 해 오고 있는 것은 아닌가 생각했다. **3** to doubt that someone or something is completely honest, sincere, or real ‖ 사람이나 사물이 완전히 정직하거나 성실하거나, 또는 진짜일 수 있는 지를 의심하다. 수상히 여기다: *Do you have reason to suspect his motives?* 그의 동기를 의심할 만한 이유가 있습니까?

sus·pect³ /'sʌspɛkt/ *adj* difficult to believe or trust ‖ 믿거나 신뢰하기 어려운. 의심스러운. 수상한: *Her explanation seems suspect.* 그녀의 설명은 의심스러워 보인다.

sus·pend /sə'spɛnd/ *v* [T] **1** to officially stop something from continuing, usually for a short time ‖ 보통 잠시 동안 무엇을 계속하는 것을 공식적으로 멈추다. 일시 정지[중지]하다: *The bus service has been suspended until further notice.* 그 버스의 운행은 차후의 통고가 있을 때까지 중단되었다. **2** to officially stop someone from working, driving, or going to school for a fixed period, because s/he has broken the rules ‖ 사람이 규칙을 어겨서 일정 기간 동안 일이나 운전, 또는 등교를 공식적으로 못하게 하다. 정직[운전면서 정지, 정학]시키다: *Joey was suspended from school.* 조이는 정학당했다. / *Drunk drivers will have their licenses suspended.* 음주 운전자들은 운전면허가 정지된다. **3** to hang something from something else ‖ 무엇을 다른 것에 매달다. 걸다: *a chandelier suspended from the ceiling* 천장에 매달린 샹들리에

sus·pend·ers /sə'spɛndəz/ *n* [plural] two bands of cloth that go over your shoulders and are attached to your pants to hold them up ‖ 바지에 부착되어 바지를 흘러내리지 않게 유지시키는, 어깨를 넘어가는 두 가닥의 천으로 된 띠. 멜빵

sus·pense /sə'spɛns/ *n* [U] a feeling of not knowing what is going to happen next ‖ 다음에 일어날 일을 알지 못하는 느낌. 긴장감: *Don't keep us in suspense. What happened?* 우리를 긴장시키지 마. 무슨 일이야?

sus·pen·sion /sə'spɛnʃən/ *n* **1** [U] the act of officially stopping something from continuing for a period of time ‖ 일정 기간 동안 공식적으로 무엇을 계속하지 못하게 하는 행위. 보류. 연기: *Bad weather*

led to the suspension of the game. 악천
후로 그 경기는 연기되었다. **2** an act of
removing someone from a school or job
for a short time, in order to punish
him/her ‖ 벌주기 위해 잠시 누군가에게
학교나 직장을 떠나 있도록 하는 행위. 정
학. 정직: *a three-day suspension for
cheating* 커닝에 대한 3일간의 정학 **3** [U]
equipment attached to the wheels of a
vehicle to make it BOUNCE less ‖ 튀어오르
는 것을 줄이려고 탈것의 바퀴에 부착한
장비. 완충 장치

sus·pi·cion /sə'spɪʃən/ *n* **1** [C, U] a
feeling or belief that something is
probably true ‖ 무엇이 아마도 사실일 것
이라고 생각하는 느낌이나 믿음. 혐의. 의
심: *Potter was arrested on suspicion of
robbery.* 포터는 강도 혐의로 체포되었다.
/ *I'm not sure who erased the file, but I
have my suspicions.* 그 파일을 지운 사
람이 누구인지 확신할 수는 없지만 의심
가는 데는 있다. **2** [U] lack of trust ‖ 믿음
의 부족. 의심. 의혹: *She always treated
us with suspicion.* 그녀는 항상 우리를
의혹을 가지고 대했다.

sus·pi·cious /sə'spɪʃəs/ *adj* **1** not
willing to trust someone or something ‖
사람이나 사물을 기꺼이 신뢰하려하지 않
는. 미심쩍은. 수상한: *I'm suspicious of
her intentions.* 그녀의 의도가 미심쩍다.
2 making you think that something bad
or illegal is happening ‖ 나쁘거나 불법적
인 것이 일어나고 있다고 생각하게 하는:
*Passengers should report any bags that
look suspicious.* 승객은 의심스러워 보이
는 어떤 가방도 보고해야 한다. –
suspiciously *adj* : *It looks suspiciously like someone has tampered with
the lock.* 누군가가 그 자물쇠에 손을 댄
것처럼 수상쩍어 보인다.

sus·tain /sə'steɪn/ *v* [T] **1** to make it
possible for someone or something to
continue to exist over a period of time ‖
사람이나 사물이 일정 기간에 걸쳐 계속
존재 할 수 있게 하다. 유지하다. 지속하
다: *The nation's economy was largely
sustained by foreign aid.* 그 나라의 경제
는 주로 외국의 원조에 의해 유지되었다.
**2 sustain injuries/damages/
losses** FORMAL to be injured or
damaged, or to lose a lot of money or
soldiers ‖ 상처나 손상을 입거나, 많은 돈
이나 군인들을 잃다. 상해/손상/손실을 입
다: *Three firefighters sustained minor
injuries from the blaze.* 3명의 소방관들
은 화염에 작은 부상을 입었다.

sus·tained /sə'steɪnd/ *adj* continuing
for a long time ‖ 오랫동안 계속하는. 지속

된. 한결같은: *A sustained effort is
needed to fight drug abuse.* 약물 남용과
싸우기 위해서는 부단한 노력이 필요하다.

SUV *n* sport-utility vehicle; a type of
vehicle that is bigger than a car and is
made for travelling over rough ground
‖ sport-utility vehicle(스포츠형 다목적
자동차)의 약어; 승용차보다 더 크며 험한
지형을 주행하기 위해 제조된 차량의 일종

svelte /svɛlt/ *adj* thin and graceful ‖ 날
씬하고 우아한: *a svelte young woman* 날
씬하고 우아한 젊은 여성

SW the written abbreviation of
southwest ‖ southwest의 약어

swab /swɑb/ *n* a small stick with a
piece of soft material on the end, used
for cleaning wounds or putting on
medicine ‖ 상처를 소독하거나 약을 바르
는 데에 쓰는, 끝에 부드러운 소재가 달린
작은 막대기. 면봉: *a cotton swab* 면봉 –
swab *v* [T]

swag·ger /'swægɚ/ *v* [I] to walk
proudly, swinging your shoulders in a
way that seems too confident ‖ 아주 자신
있는 듯한 투로 어깨를 흔들며 자랑스럽게
걷다. 뽐내며[거드름 피우며] 걷다 –
swagger *n* [singular, U]: *an arrogant
swagger* 거만한 태도

swal·low¹ /'swɑloʊ/ *v* **1** [T] to make
food or drink go down your throat ‖ 음식
이나 음료가 목을 내려가게 하다. 삼키다.
들이켜다 **2** [I] to make this type of a
movement, especially because you are
nervous ‖ 특히 초조하여 (침을) 삼키는
행동을 하게 하다: *He swallowed
anxiously before answering.* 그는 초조하
여 대답하기 전에 침을 꿀꺽 삼켰다. **3** [T]
INFORMAL to believe a story or
explanation that is not actually true ‖ 실
제로 진실이 아닌 이야기나 설명을 믿다.
곧이곧대로 믿다: *You didn't swallow
that story about Harry, did you?* 너 해리
에 대한 그 이야기를 곧이곧대로 믿지는
않았겠지, 그렇지? **4 swallow your
pride** to do something that seems
necessary even though you feel
embarrassed or ashamed ‖ 당혹스럽거나
부끄럽게 느낄지라도 필요해 보이는 것을
하다. 자존심을 억누르다

swallow sb/sth ↔ **up** *phr v* [T] to make
someone or something disappear by
surrounding or taking control of him,
her, or it ‖ 사람이나 사물을 둘러싸거나
통제하여 사라지게 하다: *Most of the
forest was swallowed up by the
growing city.* 대부분의 숲은 도시가 성장
함에 따라 사라졌다.

swallow² *n* **1** an act of making food or

drink go down your throat ǁ 음식이나 음료를 목으로 넘어가게 하는 행위. 삼키기. 들이켜기: *Mike drank his beer in one swallow.* 마이크는 맥주를 단숨에 마셨다. **2** a common small bird with pointed wings and a tail with two points ǁ 뾰족한 날개와 둘로 갈라진 꼬리가 있는 흔한 작은 새. 제비

swam /swæm/ v the past tense of SWIM ǁ swim의 과거형

swamp¹ /swɑmp, swɔmp/ n [C, U] land that is always very wet and sometimes covered with water ǁ 항상 상당히 축축하며 때때로 물로 뒤덮인 땅. 늪. 습지

swamp² v [T] **1** INFORMAL to suddenly give someone more work, problems etc. than s/he can deal with ǁ 갑자기 다룰 수 있는 것보다 더 많은 일·문제점 등을 누군가에게 부여하다. …이 홍수처럼 밀려오다: *We've been swamped with job applications.* 구직 지원서가 우리에게 쇄도했다. **2** to suddenly cover something with a lot of water so that it causes damage ǁ 어떤 것을 갑자기 많은 물로 뒤덮어 손상을 입히다. 물에 잠기게 하다

swan /swɑn/ n a large white bird with a long neck, that lives near lakes and rivers ǁ 호숫가나 강가에 사는 목이 긴, 크고 흰 새. 백조

swank /swæŋk/, **swank·y** /'swæŋki/ adj INFORMAL very fashionable or expensive ǁ 매우 멋있거나 값비싼. 호화로운: *a swank New York hotel* 호화로운 뉴욕 호텔

swap /swɑp/ v -pped, -pping [I, T] to exchange something you have for something that someone else has ǁ 자신이 가지고 있는 것과 다른 사람이 가지고 있는 것을 교환하다. 맞바꾸다. 교역하다: *Can I swap seats with you?* 제가 당신과 자리를 바꿀 수 있을까요? – **swap** n

swarm¹ /swɔrm/ v [I] to move in a large uncontrolled crowd ǁ 통제되지 않는 대규모 무리로 움직이다: *Tourists swarmed around the museum.* 관광객들은 그 박물관 주위에 떼지어 모였다.

swarm with sth phr v [T] to be full of a moving crowd of people, birds, or insects ǁ 움직이는 사람들이나 새들, 또는 곤충들의 무리로 가득하다: *The beaches were swarming with people all summer long.* 해변들은 여름 내내 사람들로 들끓고 있었다.

swarm² n a large group of insects that move together ǁ 함께 움직이는 곤충의 큰 무리. 떼: *a swarm of bees* 벌떼

swarth·y /'swɔrði, -θi/ adj DISAPPROVING having dark skin ǁ 까무잡잡한 피부

를 가진. 거무스름한

swat /swɑt/ v -tted, -tting [T] to hit something with a swinging movement of your hand ǁ 손을 휘둘러 어떤 것을 때리다: *trying to swat a fly* 손을 휘둘러 파리를 잡으려 함 – **swat** n

swatch /swɑtʃ/ n a small piece of cloth that is used as a SAMPLE to show what a material is like ǁ 옷감의 재질이 어떠한지를 보여 주는데 견본으로 쓰이는 작은 천 조각. 재료 견본

swath /swɑθ, swɔθ/ n a long area that is different from the areas on either side of it ǁ 양쪽 어느 쪽과도 상이한 긴 지역: *The hurricane cut a wide swath through South Carolina.* 허리케인이 사우스캐롤라이나 주를 광범위하게 휩쓸었다.

sway¹ /sweɪ/ v **1** [I, T] to move slowly from one side to another ǁ 양쪽으로 천천히 움직이다. 흔들리다. 흔들다: *palm trees swaying in the breeze* 미풍에 흔들리고 있는 야자수 **2** [T] to try to influence someone to make a particular decision ǁ 남이 특정한 결정을 내리도록 영향을 미치려고 하다. 흔들리게 하다: *Nothing you say will sway her.* 네가 말하는 어떤 것도 그녀에게 영향을 주진 못할 것이다.

sway² n [singular, U] **1** a swinging movement from one side to another ǁ 양쪽으로 흔들리는 움직임. 동요. 흔들림: *the sway of her hips* 그녀의 엉덩이의 씰룩임 **2** LITERARY the power to rule or influence people ǁ 사람들을 지배하거나 영향을 미치는 힘. 지배력. 영향력

swear /swɛr/ v **swore**, **sworn**, **swearing** **1** [I] to use offensive language ǁ 모욕적인 언어를 사용하다. 욕하다. 악담하다: *Don't swear in front of the children.* 아이들 앞에서 욕하지 마라. **2** [I, T] to make a very serious promise or threat ǁ 매우 진지한 약속이나 위협을 하다. 맹세하다. 선서하다: *Do you swear to tell the truth?* 당신은 진실을 말할 것을 맹세합니까? / *I swear I'll kill him!* 맹세코 나는 그를 죽여 버리고 말겠어! **3** [T] SPOKEN used in order to emphasize that something is true ǁ 어떤것이 사실이라는 것을 강조하는 데에 쓰여. 장담하다: *I swear (to God) that's the ugliest dog I've ever seen!* 장담하건대 저 개는 내가 여태까지 본 개 중 제일 못생긴 개야! / *I could've sworn* (=I was certain) *I put the receipt in my pocket.* 내가 영수증을 주머니에 넣은 것은 확실했다. —see also **swear/dirty/cuss word** (WORD¹)

swear by sth phr v [T] INFORMAL to strongly believe that something is effective ‖ 어떤 것이 효과가 있다고 확실히 믿다: *Heidi swears by vitamin C for preventing colds.* 헤이디는 비타민 C가 감기 예방에 효과가 있다고 확실히 믿고 있다.

swear sb ↔ **in** *phr v* [T] **1** to make someone publicly promise to be loyal to a country or an important job ‖ 남에게 국가나 중요 업무에 충성할 것을 공식적으로 맹세하게 하다. 선서 취임시키다: *The new governor was sworn in today.* 그 새 주지사는 오늘 취임 선서했다. **2** to make someone give an official promise in a court of law ‖ 남을 법정에서 공식적인 약속을 하게 하다: *The bailiff was swearing in the jury.* 집행관은 배심원단에 선서를 하게 하고 있었다.

swear off sth *phr v* [T] to decide to stop doing something that is bad for you ‖ 자신에게 해로운 것을 하지 않기로 결심하다. 맹세하고 끊다. 그만둔다고 맹세하다: *I'm swearing off alcohol after last night!* 나는 간밤 이후로 금주하고 있어!

sweat¹ /swɛt/ *v* **1** [I] to have liquid coming out through your skin, especially when you are hot or nervous ‖ 특히 덥거나 초조할 때, 피부에서 액체가 흘러나오다. 땀을 흘리다: *Lynn was sweating after the long climb.* 린은 오랫동안 등산을 하고 난 후 땀을 흘리고 있었다. **2** [I] INFORMAL to work hard ‖ 열심히 일하다: *I spent all night sweating over my term paper.* 나는 밤새 기말보고서 작성에 매달렸다. **3 don't sweat it** SPOKEN used in order to tell someone not to worry about something ‖ 남에게 어떤 것에 대하여 걱정하지 말라고 말하는 데에 쓰여: *Mom, don't sweat it. I'll eat later.* 엄마 걱정하지 마. 나중에 먹을게.

sweat sth ↔ **out** *phr v* [T] to continue doing something until it is finished, even though it is difficult ‖ 어렵다 하더라도 끝날 때까지 어떤 것을 계속하다: *Just sweat it out until the end of the month.* 월말까지만 버텨봐.

sweat² *n* **1** [U] liquid that comes out through your skin, especially when you are hot or nervous; PERSPIRATION ‖ 특히 덥거나 초조할 때 피부에서 흘러나오는 액체. 땀; ㊤ perspiration: *By noon, Ian was dripping with sweat.* 정오쯤에 이안은 땀을 흘리고 있었다. **2** [singular] a condition in which you are SWEATing ‖ 땀을 흘리고 있는 상태: *Steve broke into a sweat* (=started to sweat) *as soon as he went on stage.* 스티브는 무대에 나가자마자 곧바로 땀을 흘리기 시작했다. **3 no sweat** SPOKEN used in order to say

that you can do something easily ‖ 어떤 것을 쉽게 할 수 있다고 말하는 데에 쓰여. 걱정 마라. 식은 죽 먹기야: *"Can you give Kara a ride home?" "Yeah, no sweat!"* "카라를 집까지 태워다 줄 수 있겠니?" "그래, 걱정 마라!"

sweat·er /'swɛtɚ/ *n* a piece of warm KNITted clothing for the top half of your body ‖ 상체용으로 털실로 짠 따뜻한 옷. 스웨터 —see picture at CLOTHES

sweats /swɛts/ *n* [plural] INFORMAL **1** a set of clothes made of thick soft cotton, usually worn for playing sports ‖ 보통 운동을 하는 데 입는, 두껍고 부드러운 면으로 만든 옷 한 벌. 스웨트 슈트 **2 pants** of this type ‖ 이러한 종류의 바지. 스웨트 팬츠 —see picture at CLOTHES

sweat·shirt /'swɛt-ʃɚt/ *n* a thick soft cotton shirt, usually worn for playing sports ‖ 보통 운동을 하는 데 입는 두껍고 부드러운 면으로 만든 셔츠 —see picture at CLOTHES

sweat·shop /'swɛt-ʃɑp/ *n* a factory where people work hard in bad conditions for very little money ‖ 노동자들이 소액을 받으며 열악한 작업 환경 속에서 열심히 일하는 공장. 노동 착취 공장

sweat·y /'swɛti/ *adj* covered with SWEAT, or smelling of sweat ‖ 땀으로 흠뻑 젖은, 또는 땀 냄새가 나는: *I've just been working out, so I'm all sweaty.* 나는 금방 운동을 끝내서 온통 땀투성이다.

sweep¹ /swip/ *v* swept, swept, sweeping **1** [T] also **sweep up** to clean the dirt from the floor or ground using a BROOM ‖ 빗자루를 사용하여 마루나 땅의 먼지를 청소하다. 쓸다. 청소하다 **2** [I] to move quickly or with a lot of force ‖ 재빨리 또는 전력으로 움직이다: *Ms. Ellis swept into the meeting demanding an explanation.* 엘리스 양은 해명을 요구하며 회의장으로 획 들어갔다. **3 sweep the country/nation** to quickly affect or become popular with most of the people in a country ‖ 한 나라의 대부분의 국민들에게 빠르게 영향을 미치거나 유명해지다. 전국을 휩쓸다: *a fashion trend that is sweeping the nation* 전국을 휩쓸고 있는 패션 경향

sweep sth ↔ **away** *phr v* [T] to completely destroy something or make something disappear ‖ 어떤 것을 완전히 파괴하거나 사라지게 하다. 쓸어[날려]버리다: *Entire houses were swept away by the floods.* 전(全)가옥이 홍수에 쓸려 내려갔다.

sweep² *n* **1** a long swinging movement of your arm, a weapon etc. ‖ 팔이나 무

기 등을 크게 한 번 휘두르는 동작. 한 번 휘두르기 **2** a long curved line or area of land ‖ 땅의 길게 굽은 경계선이나 지역. 곡선. 만곡부: *the sweep of the bay* 완만한 만 **3** [C usually singular] a search or attack that moves through a particular area ‖ 특정한 지역을 두루 돌아다니는 수색이나 공격: *Soldiers made a sweep of the village.* 군인들은 그 마을을 두루 수색했다.

sweep·ing /'swipɪŋ/ *adj* **1** affecting many things, or affecting one thing very much ‖ 많은 것에 영향을 미치거나 하나에 상당히 많은 영향을 미치는. 광범위한. 결정적인: *sweeping changes* 전면적인 변화 **2 sweeping statement/generalization** a statement that is unfair because it is too general and includes people or things that should not be included ‖ 너무 광범위하고 포함되지 않아야 할 사람이나 사물들이 포함되어 정당하지 않은 말. 총괄적인 진술/개괄

sweep·stakes /'swipsteɪks/ *n* a type of BETting in which the winner gets all the money risked by everyone else ‖ 승자가 다른 모든 사람들이 건 전액을 갖는 내기의 일종

sweet /swit/ *adj* **1** having a taste like sugar ‖ 설탕 같은 맛이 나는. 단: *Is your lemonade too sweet?* 네 레모네이드는 너무 달지? / *a sweet apple* 달콤한 사과 **2** having a pleasant smell or sound ‖ 기분 좋은 냄새나 소리를 가진. 감미로운: *a sweet-smelling rose* 향긋한 향이 나는 장미 / *the sweet sounds of the cello* 첼로의 감미로운 소리 **3** kind, gentle, and friendly ‖ 친절한, 온화한, 다정한: *a sweet smile* 사랑스러운 웃음 / *a sweet little boy* 귀여운 어린 소년 **4 have a sweet tooth** to like to eat sweet foods ‖ 단 음식 먹는 것을 좋아하다 **5** making you feel pleased and satisfied ‖ 기분 좋고 만족스럽게 느끼게 하는. 상쾌한. 유쾌한: *Revenge is sweet!* 복수는 통쾌해! – **sweetly** *adv* – **sweetness** *n* [U]

sweet·en /'switn/ *v* **1** [I, T] to become or make something sweeter ‖ 어떤 것이 달게 되다 또는 어떤 것을 달게 만들다. 달아지다. 달게 하다: *Sweeten the mixture with honey.* 혼합물에다 벌꿀을 섞어 달게 만들어라. **2 sweeten the deal/pot/offer etc.** to make a deal seem more acceptable, usually by offering more money ‖ 보통 더 많은 금액을 제공하여 거래를 보다 만족스러워 보이게 만들다. 거래/상품/제안의 가치를 높이다: *They sweetened the deal with a 10% discount.* 그들은 10퍼센트 할인을 하여 그 거래의 매력을 높였다.

sweet·en·er /'switn-ə, -nə/ *n* **1** [C, U] a substance used instead of sugar to make food or drinks taste sweeter ‖ 음식이나 음료에 단맛을 더 내려고 설탕 대신 쓰이는 물질. 인공 감미료 **2** INFORMAL something that you give to someone to persuade him/her to do something ‖ 어떤 것을 하도록 설득하며 남에게 주는 것. 뇌물 : *Car dealers are offering sweeteners like 15% financing.* 자동차 판매상은 약 15퍼센트 정도의 구입자금 대출을 유인책으로 내놓고 있다.

sweet·heart /'swithɑrt/ *n* **1** someone that you love, or a way of talking to him/her ‖ 사랑하는 사람, 또는 사랑하는 사람에게 말을 거는 방식. 애인. 여보. 당신. 자기: *Good night, sweetheart.* 잘 자, 자기. **2** ⇨ SWEETIE

sweet·ie /'switi/ *n* SPOKEN **1** used in order to speak to someone that you love, especially a child ‖ 사랑하는 사람, 특히 아이에게 말하는 데에 쓰여. 여보. 아가: *Do you want some ice cream, sweetie?* 아이스크림 먹고 싶니, 애야? **2** someone who is kind and generous ‖ 친절하고 관대한 사람: *Pat's such a sweetie!* 패트는 정말 친절해!

sweet po·ta·to /'. .,../ *n* a root that looks like an orange potato, cooked and eaten as a vegetable ‖ 야채로써 요리해서 먹는 오렌지색 감자처럼 생긴 뿌리. 고구마

sweets /swits/ *n* [plural] INFORMAL sweet food or candy ‖ 달콤한 음식이나 사탕. 단것

swell¹ /swɛl/ *v* **swelled, swollen, swelling 1** [I] also **swell up** to gradually increase in size, especially because of an injury ‖ 특히 부상으로 인해 점차 크기가 커지다. 붓다. 부풀다: *My ankle swelled up like a balloon.* 내 발목은 풍선처럼 부어올랐다. **2** [I, T] to gradually increase in amount or number ‖ 양이나 수가 점점 증가하다. 늘다. 붇다. 증대하다: *The city's population has swollen to 2 million.* 그 도시의 인구는 2백만 명으로 증가했다. **3 swell with pride/anger etc.** to feel very proud, angry etc. ‖ 매우 자랑스럽게 느끼다 또는 매우 화가 나다. 의기양양해지다/분노가 치솟다

swell² *n* a long smooth wave in the ocean ‖ 바다의 크고 완만한 파도. 너울

swell³ *adj* OLD-FASHIONED very good ‖ 매우 좋은: *I had a really swell time.* 나는 정말 멋진 시간을 보냈어.

swell·ing /'swɛlɪŋ/ *n* [C, U] an area on your body that becomes larger than

usual because of injury or sickness ‖ 부
상이나 병으로 평소보다 커진 신체 부위.
혹. 부기: *the pain and swelling in her
knee* 그녀의 무릎의 통증과 부기

swel·ter·ing /ˈswɛltərɪŋ/ *adj*
unpleasantly hot ‖ 불쾌할 정도로 더운.
무더운: *a sweltering summer day* 무더운
여름날 —see usage note at TEMPERATURE

swept /swɛpt/ *v* the past tense and
PAST PARTICIPLE of SWEEP ‖ sweep의 과
거·과거 분사형

swerve /swəv/ *v* [I] to turn suddenly
and dangerously while driving or flying
‖ 운전하거나 비행하는 중에 갑작스럽
고 위험스럽게 방향을 바꾸다: *Mark
swerved to avoid hitting a deer.* 마크는
사슴을 치지 않기 위해 갑자기 방향을 홱
틀었다.

swift /swɪft/ *adj* happening or moving
very quickly ‖ 매우 빠르게 일어나거나 움
직이는. 재빠른. 급속의: *a swift response*
즉답 / *a swift river* 물살이 센 강 –
swiftly *adv*

swig /swɪg/ *v* **-gged, -gging** [T]
INFORMAL to drink something quickly
and in large amounts ‖ 무엇을 급하게 많
이 마시다. 죽[벌떡벌떡] 마시다 – **swig**
n : *Zach took a swig of Coke.* 재크는 콜
라를 벌컥벌컥 마셨다.

swill¹ /swɪl/ *n* [U] food for pigs; SLOP ‖
돼지 먹이. 돼지 사료; ⊕ slop

swill² *v* [T] to drink something in large
amounts ‖ 무엇을 많이 마시다: *swilling
beer all day* 하루 종일 맥주를 벌컥거림

swim¹ /swɪm/ *v* **swam, swum,
swimming** **1** [I] to move through the
water by using your arms, legs etc. ‖ 팔
이나 다리 등을 써서 물속을 움직이다. 헤
엄치다. 수영하다: *Can Lucy swim?* 루
시는 수영할 줄 알아? / *fish swimming
up the stream* 시내를 거슬러 헤엄치고
있는 물고기 **2** [T] to cross a pool, lake
etc. or go a particular distance by
swimming ‖ 수영장이나 호수 등을 가로질
러 가다, 또는 수영으로 특정한 거리를 가
다: *He swims 20 laps a day.* 그는 하루에
20바퀴를 수영한다. **3** [I] if your head
swims, you feel confused or DIZZY ‖ 머리
가 혼란스럽거나 어지럽다 **4** [I] if
something you are looking at swims, it
seems to move around, usually because
you are sick ‖ 몸이 아파서 물체가 빙빙
도는 것처럼 보이다 **5 be swimming
in/with sth** to be covered or
surrounded by liquid ‖ 액체에 의해 덮이
거나 둘러싸이다. 액체에 잠기다[젖다]:
meatballs swimming in sauce 소스가 그
득한 미트볼 – **swimming** *n* [U]: *Do you*

want to go swimming? 수영하러 가고
싶니?

swim² *n* a period when you swim ‖ 수영
하는 시간: *Would you like to go for a
swim after work?* 일 끝난 후에 수영하러
가시겠어요?

swimming pool /ˈ.. ˌ./ *n* ⇨ POOL¹

swim·suit /ˈswɪmsut/ *n* ⇨ BATHING SUIT

swin·dle¹ /ˈswɪndl/ *v* [T] to get money
from someone by tricking him/her ‖ 남을
속여서 돈을 빼앗다. 사취하다 –
swindler *n*

swindle² *n* a situation in which
someone gets money from someone else
by tricking him/her ‖ 어떤 사람이 남을
속여서 돈을 빼앗는 상황. 사취

swine /swaɪn/ *n, plural* **swine** OLD-
FASHIONED **1** a pig ‖ 돼지 **2** INFORMAL
someone who is rude or morally bad ‖
무례하거나 부도덕한 사람. 비열한 사람

swing¹ /swɪŋ/ *v* **swung, swung,
swinging** [I, T] **1** to move backward
and forward while hanging from a
particular point, or to make something
move in this way ‖ 특정한 지점에 매달려
서 앞뒤로 움직이다, 또는 어떤 것을 앞뒤
로 움직이게 하다. 흔들리다. 흔들다:
*They walked hand in hand, swinging
their arms.* 그들은 손을 맞잡고 팔을 흔들
면서 걸었다. / *a sign swinging in the
wind* 바람에 흔들리는 간판 **2** to move
smoothly in a curved direction, or to
make something move this way ‖ 방향을
비틀며 매끄럽게 움직이다, 또는 어떤 것
을 이렇게 움직이게 하다. 빙글 돌다. 빙
글 돌리다: *The screen door kept
swinging open/shut.* 그 망으로 된 문은
계속 열렸다[닫혔다] 했다.

swing around *phr v* [I, T] to turn
around quickly, or to make something
do this ‖ 재빨리 회전하다, 또는 어떤 것을
이렇게 회전시키다: *Mitch swung around
to face her.* 미치는 그녀를 마주보도록 홱
돌아섰다.

swing at sb/sth *phr v* [T] to try to hit
someone or something with your hand
or with an object that you are holding ‖
손이나 쥐고 있는 물건으로 사람이나 사물
을 치려고 하다. 치다. 스윙하다: *He
swung at the ball and missed.* 그는 그
공을 치려고 휘둘렀는데 빗맞았다.

swing by *phr v* [I, T] INFORMAL to
quickly visit a person or place before
going somewhere else ‖ 다른 곳에 가기
전에 사람이나 장소를 급히 방문하다. 잠
시 …에 들르다: *Can we swing by the
store on the way home?* 우리 귀가 길에
가게에 잠깐 들를 수 있을까?

swing² *n* **1** a seat hanging from ropes or chains, on which children swing ‖ 아이들이 타고 앞뒤로 흔드는, 밧줄이나 쇠사슬에 매달린 의자. 그네: *a bunch of kids playing on the swings* 그네를 타며 노는 한 무리의 아이들 **2** an attempt to hit someone or something by swinging your arm, an object etc. ‖ 팔이나 물체 등을 휘둘러 사람이나 사물을 치려는 시도. 때리기. 치기. 스윙: *Then he tried to take a swing at me.* 그 때에 그는 나를 때리려고 했다. **3** a change from one feeling, opinion etc. to another ‖ 어떤 감정·의견 등에서 다른 감정·의견 등으로의 변동: *a big swing in public opinion* 여론의 큰 변동 **4 be in full swing** if a party, event etc. is in full swing, it is at its highest level of activity ‖ 파티나 행사 등이 활기가 최고로 오르다. 절정이다

swing·ing /'swɪŋɪŋ/ *adj* HUMOROUS exciting, fun, and enjoyable ‖ 흥분되며 재미있고 즐거운. 활기찬: *a swinging party* 활기찬 파티

swipe¹ /swaɪp/ *v* **1** [I, T] also **swipe at** to hit or try to hit someone or something by swinging your arm very quickly ‖ 팔을 재빨리 휘둘러 사람이나 사물을 치거나 치려고 하다. 강타하다 **2** [T] INFORMAL to steal something ‖ 무엇을 훔치다: *Somebody swiped my wallet.* 누군가가 내 지갑을 훔쳤다.

swipe² *n* the act of hitting someone or something by swinging your arm very quickly ‖ 팔을 재빨리 휘둘러 사람이나 사물을 치는 행위. 강타: *Shelly took a swipe at her brother.* 셸리는 자기의 남동생을 딱 때렸다.

swirl¹ /swɜl/ *v* [I, T] to turn around and around, or to make something do this ‖ 빙빙 돌다, 무엇을 빙빙 돌게 하다: *Swirl the wine around in the glass like this.* 이렇게 잔에 있는 와인을 휘휘 돌려라.

swirl² *n* a SWIRLing movement or pattern ‖ 빙글빙글 도는 움직임이나 무늬: *decorative swirls in the cake frosting* 케이크에 장식크림을 빙빙 돌려 장식한 것

swish /swɪʃ/ *v* [I, T] to move quickly through the air with a soft sound like a whistle, or to make something do this ‖ 휘파람 같은 부드러운 소리를 내며 공중을 재빨리 통과하거나, 또는 무엇을 이렇게 하게 하다. 휙 움직이다. 휙 휘두르다: *a cow swishing its tail* 꼬리를 휙 휘두르고 있는 소 – **swish** *n* [singular]

Swiss¹ /swɪs/ *adj* relating to or coming from Switzerland ‖ 스위스와 관련된, 스위스에서 온. 스위스의. 스위스제의

Swiss² *n* the Swiss [plural] the people of Switzerland, considered as a single group ‖ 하나의 집합체로 본 스위스 사람들. 스위스 국민

switch

switch on   switch off

switch¹ /swɪtʃ/ *v* **1** [I, T] to change from doing or using one thing to doing or using something else ‖ 어떤 것을 하거나 사용하는 것에서 다른 것을 하거나 사용하는 것으로 바꾸다. 전환하다. 돌리다: *He studied biology before switching (over) to law.* 그는 법학으로 전공을 바꾸기 전에 생물학을 공부했다. / *Here, switch hands and see if that works better.* 자, 손을 바꾸고 더 잘되는지 봐라. **2** [T] to replace someone or something with a different person or object ‖ 사람이나 사물을 다른 사람이나 대상물로 대체하다: *We must have accidentally switched umbrellas.* 우연히 우리가 우산을 바꿔 간게 틀림없다.

switch off *phr v* **1** [I, T **switch** sth ↔ **off**] to turn off a machine, radio, light etc. by using a SWITCH ‖ 스위치를 이용해서 기계·라디오·전등 등을 끄다: *Be sure to switch off the lights when you leave.* 나갈 때 반드시 전등을 꺼라. **2** [I] INFORMAL to stop listening or paying attention to someone ‖ 남에게 귀를 기울이거나 주의를 기울이는 것을 그만두다: *He just switches off when he's tired.* 그는 피곤하면 그저 아무 생각도 안 한다.

switch on *phr v* [I, T **switch** sth ↔ **on**] to turn on a machine, radio, light etc. by using a SWITCH ‖ 스위치를 이용해서 기계·라디오·전등 등을 켜다

switch² *n* **1** the part that you move up or down on a machine, radio, light etc. so that it starts or stops operating ‖ 기계·라디오·전등 등을 작동시키거나 작동을 멈추도록 올리거나 내리는 부분. 스위치: *Where's the on/off switch?* 불을 켜는 [끄는] 스위치가 어디 있느냐? / *a light switch* 전등 스위치 **2** a change ‖ 전환. 변경: *Tom's glad he made the switch from his old job.* 톰은 옛 직업을 바꾼 것에 대해 만족스러워한다. **3** a thin stick that bends easily ‖ 잘 휘는 가는 막대기.

회초리

switch·board /ˈswɪtʃbɔrd/ n a piece of equipment that directs all the telephone calls made to or from a particular business, hotel etc. ‖ 특정한 사업소나 호텔 등으로 걸려오거나 이곳에서 거는 모든 전화를 관리하는 장비. 전화 교환대

swiv·el /ˈswɪvəl/, **swivel around** v [I, T] to turn around while remaining in the same place, or to make something do this ‖ 그대로 한 곳에서 돌거나 무엇을 이렇게 돌게 하다. 회전하다 회전시키다: *She wants a chair that swivels.* 그녀는 회전의자를 원한다.

swol·len[1] /ˈswoʊlən/ v the PAST PARTICIPLE of SWELL ‖ swell의 과거 분사형

swollen[2] adj 1 a part of your body that is swollen is bigger than usual because of injury or sickness ‖ 신체 부위가 부상이나 병으로 평소보다 커진. 부어오른 2 a swollen river has more water in it than usual ‖ 강의 물이 평소보다 많은. 불어난

swoon /swun/ v [I] OLD-FASHIONED to feel so much emotion that you almost FAINT (=lose consciousness) ‖ 거의 기절할 정도로 격심한 감정을 느끼다. 정신이 희미해지다. 기절하다. 황홀해지다

swoop /swup/ v [I] to suddenly and quickly move downwards through the air, especially to attack something ‖ 특히 무엇을 공격하기 위해 공중에서 갑작스럽고 재빠르게 하강하다. 급강하다: *An owl swooped down and grabbed a mouse.* 올빼미 한 마리가 급강하해서 쥐 한 마리를 낚아챘다. – **swoop** n

sword /sɔrd/ n a weapon with a long sharp blade and a handle ‖ 길고 날카로운 날과 손잡이가 달린 무기. 검. 칼

sword·fish /ˈsɔrd,fɪʃ/ n a large fish with a long pointed upper jaw shaped like a sword ‖ 칼 모양의 길고 뾰족한 위턱을 가진 큰 물고기. 황새치

swore /swɔr/ v the past tense of SWEAR ‖ swear의 과거형

sworn[1] /swɔrn/ v the PAST PARTICIPLE of SWEAR ‖ swear의 과거 분사형

sworn[2] adj 1 **sworn statement/ testimony** a statement, testimony that someone makes after officially promising to tell the truth ‖ 진실을 말할 것을 공약하고 나서 하는 진술·증언. 선서 진술/증언 2 **sworn enemies** two people or groups who will always hate each other ‖ 항상 서로를 미워할 두 사람이나 그룹. 불구대천의 원수

swum /swʌm/ v the PAST PARTICIPLE of SWIM ‖ swim의 과거 분사형

swung /swʌŋ/ v the past tense and PAST PARTICIPLE of SWING ‖ swing의 과거·과거 분사형

syc·a·more /ˈsɪkə,mɔr/ n [C, U] an eastern North American tree with broad leaves, or the wood from this tree ‖ 북아메리카 동부산의 잎이 넓은 나무, 또는 이 나무의 목재. 플라타너스(목재)

syc·o·phant /ˈsɪkəfənt/ n FORMAL someone who always praises someone else in order to gain an advantage ‖ 이득을 보기 위해 항상 다른 사람을 칭찬하는 사람. 알랑쇠. 아첨꾼

syl·la·ble /ˈsɪləbəl/ n TECHNICAL each part of a word that contains a single vowel sound ‖ 하나의 모음을 포함한 단어의 각 부분. 음절

syl·la·bus /ˈsɪləbəs/ n, plural **syllabuses** or **syllabi** /-baɪ/ a plan that shows a student what s/he will be studying in a particular subject ‖ 특정한 과목에서 공부하게 될 것을 학생들에게 보여주는 계획. 개요. 교수 요목

sym·bol /ˈsɪmbəl/ n 1 a picture, person, object etc. that represents a particular quality, idea, organization etc. ‖ 특정한 자질이나 생각, 또는 조직 등을 상징하는 그림·인물·물체 등. 상징. 표상. 심벌: *the five-ring symbol of the Olympic Games* 올림픽 경기의 상징인 오륜 / *De Gaulle became a symbol of French pride and patriotism.* 드골은 프랑스의 긍지와 애국심의 표상이 되었다. —see also SEX SYMBOL ‖ 2 a letter, number, or sign that represents a sound, amount, chemical substance etc. ‖ 소리·양·화학 물질 등을 나타내는 글자나 숫자 또는 기호. 부호. 기호: *What's the chemical symbol for iron?* 철의 화학 기호가 뭐지?

sym·bol·ic /sɪmˈbɑlɪk/ adj representing a particular event, process, situation etc. ‖ 특정한 행사·과정·상황 등을 대표하는. 상징하는: *a red rose, symbolic of love* 사랑의 상징인 붉은 장미 – **symbolically** adv

sym·bol·ism /ˈsɪmbə,lɪzəm/ n [U] the use of SYMBOLs to represent things ‖ 사물을 대표하는 상징의 사용. 상징. 상징적 표현: *There's a lot of religious symbolism in his paintings.* 그의 그림에는 종교적 상징이 많이 들어 있다.

sym·bol·ize /ˈsɪmbə,laɪz/ v [T] 1 to be a SYMBOL of something ‖ 어떤 것의 상징이다. …을 상징하다: *A wedding ring symbolizes a couple's vows to each other.* 결혼반지는 부부 상호간의 맹세를 상징한다 2 to represent something by using a SYMBOL ‖ 심볼을 이용하여 무엇을 나타내다. 상징화하다: *Death is often symbolized by the color black.* 죽음은 종종 검은 색으로 상징화된다.

sym·met·ri·cal /sə'mɛtrɪkəl/, **sym·met·ric** /sə'mɛtrɪk/ *adj* having two halves that are exactly the same size and shape ‖ 정확히 크기와 모양이 같은 반쪽짜리로 된. 대칭적인 — opposite ASYMMETRICAL

sym·me·try /'sɪmətri/ *n* [U] exact likeness in size and shape between two halves or sides of something ‖ 사물의 두 개의 반쪽짜리나 두 면 사이의 크기와 모양이 정확히 같음. 대칭. 균형

sym·pa·thet·ic /ˌsɪmpə'θɛtɪk/ *adj* 1 showing that you understand how sad, hurt, lonely etc. someone feels ‖ 남이 얼마나 슬퍼하고·아파하고·외로워하는지에 대한 이해를 나타내는. 동정적인. 동정심을 느끼는: *a sympathetic nurse* 동정심이 많은 간호사 2 willing to support someone's plans, actions, ideas etc. ‖ 남의 계획·행동·생각 등을 기꺼이 지지하는. 공감하는. 호의적인: *He's fairly sympathetic to the staff's concerns.* 그는 직원들의 관심사에 꽤 호의적이다 – **sympathetically** *adv* —opposite UNSYMPATHETIC

sym·pa·thize /'sɪmpəˌθaɪz/ *v* [I] 1 to understand how sad, hurt, lonely etc. someone feels ‖ 남이 얼마나 슬퍼하고·아파하고·외로워하는지를 이해하다. 동정하다. 측은히 여기다: *I sympathize with those people who lost their jobs.* 나는 직장을 잃은 사람들을 동정한다. 2 to support a country, plan, action etc. ‖ 국가·계획·행동 등을 지지하다. 동의하다. 동조 [공명]하다: *Very few people sympathize with his views on racial separation.* 극소수의 사람들만이 그의 인종 분리에 대한 견해에 동조한다.

sym·pa·thy /'sɪmpəθi/ *n* [C, U] 1 a feeling of support for someone who is sad, hurt, lonely etc. ‖ 슬프고, 아프며 외로운 사람에 대해 격려하는 감정. 동정심: *I have no sympathy for people like her.* 나는 그녀 같은 사람들에게는 동정심을 느끼지 않는다. / *I'm sorry to hear Bill died; you have my sympathies.* 빌이 죽었다니 참 안 됐습니다. 2 support for someone's plan, actions, ideas etc. ‖ 남의 계획·행동·생각 등에의 지지. 공감. 동의: *Students marched in sympathy with the strikers.* (=to show support for them) 학생들은 그 파업자들을 지지하여 함께 행진을 했다.

There are several ways of showing sympathy. For example, if a friend has just said that s/he has failed a test, you can say **I'm sorry** or **that's too bad.** If someone tells you that a friend or family member has died, you can say **I'm very sorry** or **my sympathies.** You can also offer to help by saying, "**Is there anything I can do?**"
동정심을 나타내는 데는 여러 가지 방법이 있다. 예를 들어, 친구가 시험에 낙제했다고 말한다면, **I'm sorry** 또는 **that's too bad**로 말할 수 있다. 만일 누군가가 당신에게 친구나 가족이 죽었다고 말한다면 **I'm very sorry** 또는 **my sympathies** 라고 말할 수 있다. 또한 "**Is there anything I can do?**"라고 말하여 도와주겠다고 제의할 수도 있다.

sym·pho·ny /'sɪmfəni/ *n* a long piece of music written for an ORCHESTRA ‖ 오케스트라를 위해 쓰여진 규모가 큰 음악 작품. 교향곡. 심포니

symp·tom /'sɪmptəm/ *n* 1 a physical condition that shows you may have a particular disease ‖ 특정한 질병을 가지고 있을지도 모른다는 것을 나타내는 신체적 상태. 증상. 징후: *medicine that helps relieve your cold symptoms* 당신의 감기 증상을 완화하는 데 도움이 되는 약 2 a sign that a serious problem exists ‖ 심각한 문제가 있다는 신호. 징조. 조짐. 전조: *Rising crime rates are another symptom of a society in trouble.* 범죄율 증가는 사회가 문제에 빠졌다는 또다른 징조다. – **symptomatic** /ˌsɪmptə'mætɪk/ *adj*

syn·a·gogue /'sɪnəˌgɑg/ *n* a building where Jewish people go to have religious services ‖ 유대교인들이 예배하기 위해 가는 건물. 유대교의 예배당

sync /sɪŋk/ *n* INFORMAL **in sync/out of sync** **a)** happening or moving at the same time or rate, or not doing this ‖ 동시에 또는 같은 속도로 일어나거나 움직이는, 또는 이런 식으로 일어나거나 움직이지 않는. 동조하여/동조하지 않는: *Unfortunately, the band wasn't in sync with the drummer.* 불행하게도 그 밴드는 그 드럼주자와 음을 맞추지 못했다. **b)** doing or saying things that are suitable or not suitable for a situation ‖ 상황에 맞게 또는 맞지 않게 행동하거나 말하는: *His message was out of sync with the* *mood of the country.* 그의 메시지는 그 나라의 분위기에 맞지 않았다.

syn·chro·nize /ˈsɪŋkrəˌnaɪz/ *v* **1** [T] to make two or more things happen or move at the same time or rate ‖ 둘 또는 그 이상의 것들이 동시에 또는 같은 속도로 일어나거나 움직이게 하다. 동시성을 갖게 하다. 일치시키다: *The attack was synchronized with a bombing in Washington.* 그 공격은 워싱턴에 대한 폭탄 투하와 동시에 이루어졌다. **2** to make two or more watches or clocks show exactly the same time ‖ 두 개 이상의 손목시계나 괘종시계가 정확히 같은 시간을 나타내게 하다. 시간을 맞추다 – **synchronization** /ˌsɪŋkrənəˈzeɪʃən/ *n* [U]

syn·di·cate /ˈsɪndəkɪt/ *n* [C, U] **1** a group of people, companies etc. that join together to achieve a particular aim ‖ 특정한 목적을 이루기 위해 함께 합친 일단의 사람이나 회사 등. 신디케이트. 기업 연합. 조직적 갱단: *the city's largest crime syndicate* 그 도시의 가장 큰 범죄 조직 **2** an organization that sells someone's articles, photographs, television shows etc. to several different newspapers or broadcasting companies ‖ 여러 다른 신문사나 방송사에 남의 기사나 사진·텔레비전 쇼 등을 파는 조직. 통신사

syn·di·cat·ed /ˈsɪndəˌkeɪṭɪd/ *adj* a syndicated newspaper COLUMN, television program etc. is bought and used by several different newspapers or broadcasting companies ‖ 신문의 칼럼이나 텔레비전 프로그램 등을 여러 다른 신문사나 방송사에서 동시에 구입하여 사용하는 – **syndication** /ˌsɪndəˈkeɪʃən/ [U]

syn·drome /ˈsɪndroʊm/ *n* TECHNICAL a set of physical or mental conditions that show you have a particular disease ‖ 특정한 질병이 있음을 나타내는 일련의 신체적 또는 정신적인 증상. 증후군

syn·od /ˈsɪnəd/ *n* an important meeting of church members to make decisions concerning the church ‖ 교회에 관련된 결정을 내리는 교인들의 중요한 회의. 교회 회의

syn·o·nym /ˈsɪnəˌnɪm/ *n* TECHNICAL a word with the same meaning or almost the same meaning as another word. For example, "mad" and "angry" are synonyms ‖ 다른 단어와 같은 의미나 거의 유사한 의미를 가진 단어. 동의어. 예를 들면 "mad" 와 "angry" 는 동의어이다 —opposite ANTONYM

syn·on·y·mous /sɪˈnɑnəməs/ *adj* **1** having a strong association with another quality, idea, situation etc. ‖ 다른 자질·생각·상황 등과 상당한 관련이 있는 : *He thinks that being poor is synonymous with being a criminal.* 그는 가난한 것이 범죄자가 되는 것과 상당한 관련이 있다고 생각한다. **2** having the same or nearly the same meaning ‖ 같거나 거의 같은 의미를 가진. 뜻이 같은. 동의어인

syn·op·sis /sɪˈnɑpsɪs/ *n, plural* **synopses** /-siz/ a short description of the main parts of a story ‖ 이야기의 중심적인 부분들에 대한 간략한 설명. 개략. 요약. 개요

syn·tax /ˈsɪntæks/ *n* [U] TECHNICAL the way words are arranged in order to form sentences or phrases ‖ 단어들이 문장이나 구를 만들기 위해 배열되는 방식. 구문론. 통어론

syn·the·sis /ˈsɪnθəsɪs/ *n* [C, U] the act of combining several things into a single complete unit, or the combination that is produced ‖ 여러 가지 사물들을 하나의 완전한 단일체로 결합시키는 행위, 또는 생겨난 결합체. 통합. 종합. 통합체: *the study of protein synthesis* 단백질 합성에 대한 연구 / *a synthesis of reports from Canada and Sweden* 캐나다와 스웨덴 보고서의 종합판

syn·the·size /ˈsɪnθəˌsaɪz/ *v* [T] to combine several ideas, styles, methods, substances etc. in order to produce something ‖ 무엇을 생산하기 위해 여러 생각·양식·방법·물질 등을 결합하다. 종합하다. 통합하다. 합성해서 만들다: *Scientists can now synthesize the drug.* 과학자들은 현재 그 약을 합성해서 만들 수 있다.

syn·the·siz·er /ˈsɪnθəˌsaɪzɚ/ *n* an electronic musical instrument that can sound like various different musical instruments ‖ 다양한 여러 가지 악기 소리를 낼 수 있는 전자 악기. 신시사이저

syn·thet·ic /sɪnˈθeṭɪk/ *adj* **1** made by combining several different substances ‖ 여러 다른 물질을 결합해서 만든. 합성의: *synthetic fabrics like acrylic and polyester* 아크릴과 폴리에스테르 같은 합성 섬유 **2** not natural; artificial ‖ 천연적이 아닌; 인공적인 – **synthetically** *adv*

syph·i·lis /ˈsɪfəlɪs/ *n* [U] a very serious disease that is passed from one person to another during sex ‖ 성교를 통해서 한 사람에게서 다른 사람에게 전염되는 위험한 병. 매독

sy·ringe /səˈrɪndʒ/ *n* a hollow tube and needle used for removing blood or other liquids from your body, or putting drugs etc. into it ‖ 몸에서 혈액이나 다른 액체를 빼내거나 체내에 약물을 주입하는 데에 쓰이는 속이 빈 관이나 바늘. 세척기. 피하 주사기. 관장기

syr·up /'sɚəp, 'sɪrəp/ n [U] thick sticky liquid made from sugar ‖ 설탕으로 만든 걸쭉하고 끈적거리는 액체. 시럽 – **syrupy** adj —see picture at MEDICINE

sys·tem /'sɪstəm/ n **1** a set of related or connected things that work together as a single unit ‖ 하나의 단일체로 함께 작동하는 일련의 관련되거나 결합된 것들. 체계. 시스템: *Oregon's school system* 오리건의 학교 조직 체계 / *the public transportation system* 대중 교통망 / *a car alarm system* 자동차 경보 장치 / *the company's computer system* 그 회사의 컴퓨터 시스템 **2** an organized set of rules, methods, or plans used by a particular group or for a particular purpose ‖ 특정 집단이 또는 특정 목적을 위해 사용하는 조직화된 일련의 규칙이나 방법, 또는 계획: *a system for electing city officials* 시의 관료를 선출하는 제도 / *the nation's legal system* 그 나라의 법

체제 **3** a set of parts in your body, such as bones or particular organs, considered as a single unit ‖ 하나의 단일 체로 여겨지는 뼈 또는 특정 기관(器官)등의 일련의 신체 부위. 조직. 계통. 기관: *the digestive system* 소화 계통 **4 the system** INFORMAL the rules, TRADITIONs, government, institutions etc. in a society that seem to control how you live ‖ 생활 방식을 통제하는 듯한 사회 내의 규칙·전통·정부·단체 등: *Believe me, you can't beat the system!* (=do things in a different way than the system says) 정말이야, 네가 체제를 흔들어 놓을 수는 없다고! **5 get sth out of your system** INFORMAL to do something that helps you stop feeling angry, annoyed, or upset ‖ 화나거나 짜증나거나 기분이 엉망인 것을 진정시키도록 돕는 일을 하다. …을 떨쳐 버리다. …에서 홀가분해지다

sys·tem·at·ic /ˌsɪstə'mætɪk/ adj as part of an organized plan or process; THOROUGH ‖ 조직화된 계획이나 과정의 일부분인. 체계적인. 철저한; ㉑ thorough: *a systematic search* 철저한 조사 – **systematically** adv

Tt

T, t /ti/ **1** the twentieth letter of the English alphabet ‖ 영어 알파벳의 스무째 자 **2 to a T/to a tee** INFORMAL exactly or perfectly ‖ 정확하게, 완벽하게: *a dress that fit her to a T* 그녀에게 꼭 맞는 드레스

tab /tæb/ *n* **1** the amount you owe for a restaurant meal or a service that many people use ‖ 많은 사람들이 이용하는 식당의 식사나 서비스에 대해 지불해야 할 금액. 계산[청구]서: *Our lunch tab came to $53.* 우리의 점심 값은 53달러가 나왔다. / *The city is picking up the tab for street repairs.* (=is paying for them) 시 당국은 도로 보수 비용을 지불하고 있다. **2 keep tabs on sb/sth** INFORMAL to carefully watch what someone or something is doing ‖ 사람이나 사물이 하고 있는 것을 주의 깊게 관찰하다. …을 감시하다: *The police are keeping close tabs on her.* 경찰은 그녀를 밀착 감시하고 있다. **3** a small piece of metal, plastic, or paper that you pull to open a container ‖ 용기를 열기 위해서 잡아당기는 작은 금속[플라스틱, 종이]조각. 뚜껑 **4** a small piece of paper on plastic you attach to a page, FILE etc. in order to find it easily ‖ 쉽게 찾기 위해 페이지·파일 등에 부착하는 플라스틱 위에 있는 작은 종잇조각. 색인표. 꼬리표

tab·by /'tæbi/ *n* a cat with orange, gray, or brown marks on its fur ‖ 털에 주황색[회색, 갈색] 무늬가 있는 고양이. 얼룩고양이

tab·er·na·cle /'tæbə,nækəl/ *n* a church or other building used by some religious groups ‖ 일부 종교 단체가 사용하는 교회나 그 밖의 건물. 예배당

ta·ble¹ /'teɪbəl/ *n* **1** a piece of furniture with a flat top supported by legs ‖ 다리로 지지되는 윗면이 평평한 가구. 탁자. 식탁: *the kitchen table* 주방 식탁 **2** a list of numbers, facts, or information arranged in rows across and down a page ‖ 페이지 상에서 종횡으로 열을 이루어 배열된 숫자[사실, 정보] 목록. 표. 일람표: *Check the book's table of contents.* 책의 목차를 확인해라. / *The report is full of tables and statistics.* 그 보고서는 일람표와 통계 자료가 가득하다. **3 set the table** to put knives, forks, dishes etc. on a table before a meal ‖ 식사 전에 식탁 위에 나이프·포크·접시 등을 놓다. 식

탁을 차리다 **4 clear the table** to take all the empty dishes off a table after a meal ‖ 식사 후에 식탁에서 빈 그릇을 모두 치우다. 식탁을 치우다 **5 turn the tables on sb** to change a situation completely so that someone loses an advantage and you gain one ‖ 남이 이점을 상실하고 자신이 이점을 얻도록 상황을 완전히 바꾸다. 형세[국면]를 일변시키다 **6 at the table** when sitting at a table having a meal ‖ 식탁에 앉아 식사를 할 때. 식사 중에: *It's not polite to blow your nose at the table.* 식사 중에 코를 푸는 것은 예의가 아니다. **7 under the table** INFORMAL done secretly and usually illegally ‖ 은밀하게 보통 불법적으로 이뤄진. 남몰래: *Payments were made under the table to avoid taxes.* 조세를 회피하기 위해 지불은 비밀리에 이루어졌다. **8** the group of people sitting around a table ‖ 탁자 주변에 앉아 있는 일단의 사람들. 동석자들. 좌중의 사람들: *The whole table got up and left.* 좌중의 모든 사람들은 일어서서 가버렸다.

table² *v* [T] **table a bill/proposal/ offer etc.** to decide to deal with an offer, idea etc. later ‖ 제의·생각 등을 나중에 처리하기로 결정하다. 의안/제안/신청을 보류하다

ta·ble·cloth /'teɪbəl,klɔθ/ *n* a cloth used for covering a table ‖ 식탁이나 탁자를 덮는 데 쓰는 천. 식탁보. 테이블보

ta·ble·spoon /'teɪbəl,spun/ *n* **1** a special large spoon used for measuring food ‖ 음식을 계량하는 데 쓰이는 특수 대형 스푼. 테이블스푼 **2** a large spoon used for eating food ‖ 음식을 먹는 데 사용하는 큰 스푼 **3** also **tablespoonful** the amount this spoon holds ‖ 이 스푼에 담는 분량. 테이블스푼 하나 가득한 양

tab·let /'tæblɪt/ *n* **1** a small round piece of medicine; PILL ‖ 작고 둥그런 약제. 정제; ㈜ pill: *vitamin C tablets* 비타민 C 정제 **2** a set of pieces of paper for writing on that are glued together at the top ‖ 맨 위를 함께 풀로 붙인 필기용의 종이철. 떼어 쓰는 메모첩 **3** a flat piece of hard clay or stone that has words cut into it ‖ 글자를 새겨 넣은 굳은 찰흙이나 돌로 된 편평한 조각. 명판(銘板). 패(牌)

table ten·nis /'.. ,../ *n* [U] ⇨ PING-PONG

tab·loid /'tæblɔɪd/ *n* a newspaper that

has small pages, a lot of photographs, short stories, and not much serious news ‖ 페이지 수는 적으며 사진은 많고 단편적인 이야기에 가치 있는 뉴스는 없는 신문. 타블로이드판 신문

ta·boo /təˈbuː, tæ-/ *n* [C, U] something you must avoid doing or saying because society thinks it is offensive embarrassing, or wrong ‖ 사회가 무례하거나 당혹스럽게, 또는 잘못된 것으로 생각하기 때문에 사람이 피해야 하는 일이나 말. 금기. 터부 **– taboo** *adj* : *a taboo subject* 금기인 주제

tab·u·late /ˈtæbyəˌleɪt/ *v* [T] to arrange facts, numbers, or information together in lists, rows etc. ‖ 목록·열 등에 사실[숫자, 정보]을 함께 배열하다. 일람표로 만들다[나타내다] **– tabulation** /ˌtæbyəˈleɪʃən/ *n* [U]

tac·it /ˈtæsɪt/ *adj* tacit agreement, approval, or support is given without being spoken or officially agreed ‖ 암묵[시인, 지지] 등이 언급이나 공식적 동의 없이 이루어진. 암묵의 **– tacitly** *adv*

tac·i·turn /ˈtæsəˌtɚn/ *adj* not usually talking a lot, so that you seem unfriendly ‖ 보통 말을 많이 하지 않아 다정해 보이지 않는. 과묵한. 입이 무거운

tack¹ /tæk/, **tack up** *v* [T] to attach a notice on a wall, board etc. using a THUMBTACK ‖ 압핀을 사용하여 벽·게시판 등에 공고를 붙이다. …을 압정으로 고정시키다

tack sth ↔ **on** *phr v* [T] INFORMAL to add something to something that already exists or is complete ‖ 이미 존재하거나 완성된 사물에 어떤 것을 추가하거나 덧붙이다. 첨가하다: *Joan tacked a few words on the end of my letter.* 조안은 나의 편지 끝에 몇 자 추가했다.

tack² *n* **1 a different/new/similar etc. tack** to do something that is different, new, or similar to what someone else does ‖ 다른 사람이 하는 것과 다르거나 새로운, 또는 유사한 방식으로 어떤 일을 하다: *If polite requests don't work, you'll have to try a different tack.* 만일 정중한 요청이 효과가 없으면 너는 다른 방식으로 시도해 봐야 한다. **2** ⇨ THUMBTACK **3** a small nail with a sharp point and a flat top ‖ 끝이 뾰족하고 대가리가 납작한 작은 못. 압정: *carpet tacks* 카펫 고정 못

tack·le¹ /ˈtækəl/ *v* [T] **1** to make a determined effort to deal with a difficult problem ‖ 어려운 문제를 처리하기 위해 단호한 노력을 하다: *a new attempt to tackle homelessness* 무주택 문제를 단호

히 척결하려는 새로운 시도 **2** to force someone to the ground to stop him/her from running, especially in football ‖ 특히 미식축구에서 선수가 뛰는 것을 막으려고 선수를 땅바닥으로 처박히게 하다. 태클하다: *Edwards was tackled on the play.* 에드워즈는 그 플레이에서 태클을 당했다.

tackle² *n* **1** the act of tackling (TACKLE) someone ‖ (남을) 태클하는 행위. 태클 **2** [C, U] in football, one of the players who play on the outside of the GUARDS ‖ 미식축구에서 가드들의 바깥쪽에서 경기하는 선수들 중의 한 명. 태클 **3** [U] the equipment used in some sports such as FISHING ‖ 낚시 등의 일부 스포츠에서 사용되는 도구 **4 ropes and** PULLEYS (=wheels) used for moving a ship's sails, heavy weights etc. ‖ 선박의 돛이나 무거운 물건을 움직이는 데 사용하는 밧줄과 도르래

tack·y /ˈtæki/ *adj* **1** INFORMAL not fashionable and of bad quality ‖ 유행이 지나고 품질이 나쁜. 볼품없는. 초라한: *tacky furniture* 촌스러운 가구 **2** slightly sticky ‖ 약간 끈적한 **– tackiness** *n* [U]

ta·co /ˈtɑːkoʊ/ *n* a Mexican-American food made from a fried corn TORTILLA, that is folded and filled with meat, beans etc. ‖ 구운 옥수수로 만든 토르티야를 접어서 고기·콩 등을 채워 넣은 멕시코 본고장의 미국 음식. 타코

tact /tækt/ *n* [U] the ability to say or do things carefully and politely so that you do not embarrass or upset someone ‖ 남을 당황스럽게 만들거나 화나지 않도록 조심스럽고 정중하게 말하거나 무엇을 하는 능력. 재치. 센스

tact·ful /ˈtæktfəl/ *adj* careful not to say or do something that will upset or embarrass someone else ‖ 남을 화나게 하거나 당황하게 할 말이나 행위를 하지 않도록 주의하는. 센스[재치] 있는: *a tactful response* 센스[재치] 있는 대답 **– tactfully** *adv*

tac·tic /ˈtæktɪk/ *n* [C usually plural] **1** a skillfully planned action used for achieving something ‖ 어떤 것을 달성하는 데 쓰이는 잘 구성된 행위. 방책. 책략: *the aggressive tactics of the salesman* 판매원의 공격적인 판매술 **2** the way the military uses its armies, weapons etc. in order to win a battle ‖ 군대가 전투에서 승리하기 위해 병력·무기 등을 사용하는 방법. 전술

tac·ti·cal /ˈtæktɪkəl/ *adj* **1 tactical weapon/missile/aircraft etc.** a weapon etc. that is used over a short distance ‖ 단거리에 사용되는 무기 등. 전술 병기/미사일/항공기 **2** done in order to help you achieve what you want ‖ 원하는 것의 달성을 돕도록 행해진. 전술적인: *a tactical move to avoid criticism* 비판을 피하기 위한 전략적인 조치 — **tactically** *adv*

tad /tæd/ *n* SPOKEN **a tad** a small amount ‖ 소량: *Could you turn up the sound just a tad?* 소리를 약간만 높여 주시겠어요?

tad·pole /'tædpoʊl/ *n* a small creature with a long tail that lives in water and becomes a FROG or TOAD ‖ 물에 살며 개구리나 두꺼비가 되는, 긴 꼬리가 달린 작은 생물. 올챙이

taf·fy /'tæfi/ *n* [U] a soft CHEWY candy, usually made from brown sugar or MOLASSES ‖ 보통 갈색 설탕이나 당밀로 만든 부드럽고 꼭꼭 씹어야 하는 사탕. 태피

tag¹ /tæg/ *n* **1** a small piece of paper, metal, or plastic that is put on something or on someone's clothes and shows information about it ‖ 물건이나 옷에 부착되어 그것에 관한 정보를 나타내는 종이[금속, 플라스틱]로 된 작은 조각. 꼬리표. 물표: *I can't find the price tag on these jeans.* 나는 이 진 바지의 가격표를 못 찾겠다. / *Where's your name tag?* 네 이름표는 어디 있니? **2** [U] a children's game in which one player chases and tries to touch the others ‖ 술래가 뒤쫓아 가서 다른 사람들을 살짝 치려고 애쓰는 아이들의 놀이. 술래잡기

tag² *v* **-gged, -gging** [T] to fasten a TAG onto something ‖ 물건에 꼬리표를 붙이다: *Scientists have now tagged most of the bay's seals.* 과학자들은 이제 만에 있는 대부분의 바다표범들에게 꼬리표를 붙였다.

tag along *phr v* [I] INFORMAL to go somewhere with someone, especially when s/he does not want you to ‖ 특히 남이 원하지 않는데도 그 사람과 어딘가에 가다. 따라[붙어]다니다: *My little brother always tagged along with us.* 내 남동생은 항상 우리를 따라다녔다.

tail¹ /teɪl/ *n* **1** the movable part at the back of an animal's body ‖ 동물의 몸통 뒷부분에 있는 움직일 수 있는 부분. 꼬리: *a dog wagging its tail* 꼬리를 흔들고 있는 개 **2** the back part of an aircraft ‖ 비행기의 뒷부분. 꼬리부분 —see picture at AIRPLANE **3** the end or back part of something, especially something long and thin ‖ 특히 길고 가는 것의 끝이나 뒷부분. 끄트머리. 후부: *the tail of a comet* 혜성의 꼬리 **4 the tail end of sth** the

last part of an event, situation, or period of time ‖ 사건[상황, 기간]의 마지막 부분. 후반부: *the tail end of the century* 세기말 **5** INFORMAL someone whose job is to secretly watch and follow someone such as a criminal ‖ 범죄자 등을 몰래 감시하고 뒤쫓는 직업인. 미행자. 스파이 —see also TAILS

tail² *v* [T] INFORMAL to secretly watch and follow someone such as a criminal ‖ 범죄자 등을 몰래 감시하고 뒤쫓다. 미행하다

tail off *phr v* [I] to gradually become quieter, smaller, weaker etc. ‖ 점차로 더 조용해지고 작아지고 약해지다. 차차 줄어들다: *His voice tailed off as he saw his father approaching.* 아버지가 가까이 오는 것을 보자 그의 목소리는 작아졌다.

tail·coat /'teɪlkoʊt/ *n* ⇨ TAILS

tail·gate¹ /'teɪlgeɪt/ *v* [I, T] to drive too closely behind another vehicle ‖ 다른 차량의 뒤를 바짝 따라가다

tailgate² *n* a door at the back of a vehicle, especially a PICKUP, that opens down ‖ 차량, 특히 소형 트럭의 아래로 여는 뒷문

tail·light /'teɪl-laɪt/ *n* one of the two red lights at the back of a vehicle ‖ 차량의 후부에 있는 두 개의 빨간 등 중의 하나. 미등 —see picture on page 943

tai·lor¹ /'teɪlɚ/ *n* someone whose job is to make clothes, especially men's clothes, that are measured to fit each customer perfectly ‖ 특히 남성복을 각 고객에게 정확하게 맞게 재어서 만드는 직업인. 재단사. 재봉사

tailor² *v* [T] **tailor sth to/for sb** to make something be exactly what someone wants or needs ‖ 남이 원하거나 요구하는 것을 정확하게 만들다. …을 …에게 맞추다: *a special music class tailored to young children* 어린 아이들에게 맞춘 특별 음악반

tai·lor·ing /'teɪlərɪŋ/ *n* [U] the way that clothes are made, or the job of making them ‖ 옷을 만드는 방식, 또는 옷을 만드는 직업. 양복 짓는 기술. 양복[재봉]업

tailor-made /ˌ.. '.../ *adj* **1** exactly right for only one particular person, place, situation, purpose etc. ‖ 특정한 단 하나의 사람·장소·상황·목적 등에 정확히 맞는: *The job seems tailor-made for him.* 그 일은 그에게 안성맞춤으로 보인다. **2** made by a TAILOR ‖ 재단사가 만든. 맞춤의: *a tailor-made suit* 맞춤 양복

tail·pipe /'teɪlpaɪp/ *n* ⇨ EXHAUST²

tails /teɪlz/ *n* **1** [plural] a man's suit coat with two long parts that hang down the back, worn to formal events ‖ 격식 있는 행사에 입으며 뒤쪽에 두 개의 긴 부분이 드리워진 남성 정장. 연미복 **2** the side of a coin that does not have a picture of someone's head on it ‖ 사람의 초상화가 없는 동전의 면. 동전 뒷면 — opposite HEADS

tail·spin /'teɪlspɪn/ *n* **1 go into a tailspin** to begin to have great problems you cannot control ‖ 통제할 수 없는 큰 문제를 갖기 시작하다. 손을 쓸 수 없는 사태[위기]에 봉착하다: *Following the announcement, stock prices went into a tailspin.* 그 발표가 있자 주가는 곤두박질 쳤다. **2** an uncontrolled fall of a plane through the air, in which the back spins in a wider circle than the front ‖ 공중에서 비행기가 앞쪽보다는 꼬리가 더 넓은 원을 그리고 돌아 통제 불능 상태로 강하하기. 비행기의 나선식 급강하

taint /teɪnt/ *v* [T] **1** to make someone or something seem less honest, respectable, or good ‖ 사람이나 사물에게 정직성[존경심, 양호함]을 덜해 보이게 만들다. 타락[손상]시키다. 더럽히다: *Her reputation was tainted by the murder trial.* 그녀의 명성은 살인 재판으로 실추되었다. **2** to ruin something by adding an unwanted substance to it ‖ 바람직하지 못한 물질을 추가하여 어떤 것을 망쳐놓다. 오염시키다: *All the blood supplies were tainted with bacteria.* 공급되는 혈액은 모두 박테리아로 오염되었다. – **taint** *n*

taint·ed /'teɪntɪd/ *adj* **1** food or drink that is tainted is not safe to eat because it is spoiled or contains poison ‖ 음식이나 음료수가 상하거나 독이 들어 있어서 먹기에 안전하지 않은 **2** affected or influenced by something illegal, dishonest, or morally wrong ‖ 불법적이거나 부정직한, 또는 도덕적으로 잘못된 일에 영향을 받거나 좌우되는. 부패한: *tainted witnesses* 타락한 증인들

Tai·wan·ese /,taɪwɑ'niz/ *adj* relating to or coming from Taiwan ‖ 대만에 관련되거나 대만에서 온. 대만(산)의

take after

He takes after his father.

take¹ /teɪk/ *v* **took, taken, taking** [T]

1 ▶MOVE 옮기다◀ to move someone or something from one place to another ‖ 사람이나 사물을 한 장소에서 다른 장소로 이동시키다. 가지고[데리고] 가다: *I was going to take some work home.* 나는 일부 일을 집에 가져가려고 했다. / *Take a piece of cake for your husband.* 남편을 위해 케이크 한 조각 가져가라. / *Merritt was taken by ambulance to the nearest hospital.* 메릿은 가장 가까운 병원에 구급차로 이송되었다.

2 ▶DO STH 무엇을 하다◀ used with a noun to show that something is being done ‖ 어떤 일이 이루어지고 있는 것을 나타내려고 명사와 같이 쓰여. 행하다. 실행하다: *Here, take a look.* 여기 좀 봐봐. / *Let me just take a quick shower first.* 내게 우선 샤워만 얼른 하게 해줘. / *The new rules take effect October 1.* 새 규칙은 10월 1일자로 발효한다.

3 take a picture/photograph/video etc. to photograph, VIDEOTAPE etc. something ‖ 어떤 것의 사진·비디오테이프 등을 찍다: *Here's a picture of me that was taken at camp.* 여기 야영지에서 찍은 내 사진이 있다. / *They took an X-ray of her leg.* 그들은 그녀의 다리에 엑스레이를 찍었다.

4 ▶NEED STH 무엇을 필요로 하다◀ to need something in order to do something or for something to happen ‖ 무엇을 하거나 무엇이 일어나는 데에는 어떤 것을 필요로 하다: *It takes about three days to drive up there.* 자동차로 그곳에 도착하는 데 약 3일이 걸린다. / *It'll take a lot of planning, but I think it can be done.* 그것은 많은 계획이 필요하지만 이루어질 수 있다고 나는 생각한다. / *What kind of gas does your car take?* 너의 차에는 어떤 종류의 기름을 넣느냐?

5 ▶ACCEPT 수락하다◀ to accept or receive something ‖ 무엇을 수락하거나 받다: *Are you going to take the job?* 그 일을 맡을 거냐? / *Do you take Visa?* 비자 카드도 받습니까? / *Take my advice and go see a doctor.* 내 충고를 따라 의사의 진찰을 받아 봐라. / *Why should I take the blame?* 내가 왜 비난을 받아야 되니?

6 ▶STUDY 배우다◀ to study a particular subject ‖ 특정한 과목을 공부하다: *We had to take three years of English.* 우리는 영어를 3년간 공부해야 했다. / *She wants to take ballet.* 그녀는 발레를 배우고 싶어한다.

7 take a test/exam to write or do a test ‖ 필기나 실기 시험을 보다: *I'm taking my driving test next week.* 나는

T

다음 주에 운전 시험을 본다.

8 ▶GET/STEAL 습득하다/훔치다◀ to steal something or borrow it without someone's permission ‖ 사물을 훔치거나 남의 허락 없이 빌리다. 빼앗다: *They took all her jewelry.* 그들은 그녀의 보석을 모두 빼앗았다.

9 ▶REMOVE 제거하다◀ to remove something from a particular place ‖ 특정한 장소에서 무엇을 제거하다. 치우다: *Can you take the turkey out of the oven for me?* 오븐에서 칠면조를 좀 꺼내줄래?

10 ▶HOLD/PUT 잡다/놓다◀ to reach for something and then hold it or put it somewhere ‖ 어떤 것에 손을 내밀어서 (붙)잡거나 어딘가에 두다: *Let me take your coat.* 코트를 저에게 주세요.

11 ▶GET CONTROL 통제하다◀ to get possession or control of something ‖ 무엇을 소유하거나 통제하다. 차지하다. 점유하다: *Rebel forces have taken control of the airport.* 반란군은 공항을 장악했다.

12 ▶BEAR 참다◀ to bear or accept something unpleasant ‖ 불쾌한 일을 참거나 받아들이다: *Jeff can't take the stress.* 제프는 스트레스를 참지 못한다. / *She's taken a lot of abuse from him.* 그녀는 그의 학대를 많이 참고 견뎠다. / *Losing the game by only one point was hard to take.* (=difficult to accept) 단지 1점 차이로 게임에서 패배한다는 것은 받아들이기 힘들었다.

13 not take sth lying down to refuse to accept being treated badly ‖ 부당하게 대우받는 것을 거부하다. …을 감수하지 않다: *I'm not going to take this lying down! You'll be hearing from my lawyer!* 나는 이렇게 당하지 만은 않을 거야! 너 내 변호사가 연락할 거야!

14 ▶MEDICINE/DRUG 의약품/마약◀ to swallow or INJECT a medicine or drug ‖ 의약품이나 마약을 삼키거나 주사하다: *He doesn't smoke, drink, or take drugs.* (=illegal drugs) 그는 담배나 술이나 마약을 하지 않는다. / *Why don't you take an aspirin or something?* 아스피린 같은 거라도 먹지 그러니?

15 ▶TRAVEL 여행하다◀ to use a car, bus, train etc. to go somewhere, or to travel using a particular road ‖ 자동차·버스·기차 등을 이용하여 어딘가를 가거나 특정 도로를 이용하여 여행하다: *I'll take the subway home.* 나는 지하철 타고 집에 가야겠어. / *Take the next turn on the right.* 다음에 우회전을 해라. —see usage note at TRANSPORTATION

16 ▶UNDERSTAND/CONSIDER 이해하다/고려하다◀ to understand or consider

something in a particular way ‖ 무엇을 특정하게 이해하거나 고려하다: *He takes his job very seriously.* 그는 자신의 일을 매우 진지하게 대한다. / *I didn't mean for you to take what I said literally.* 내가 말한 것을 네가 곧이곧대로 받아들이라는 뜻은 아니었어.

17 ▶WRITE 쓰다◀ also **take down** to write down information ‖ 정보를 기록하다. 적다. 적어 두다: *He's not here; can I take a message?* 그는 지금 여기에 없습니다. 제가 전언을 적어 둘까요? / *Let me take down your phone number.* 네 전화번호를 적어둘게.

18 ▶MEASURE/TEST 측정하다/시험하다◀ to test or measure something ‖ 무엇을 시험하거나 측정하다: *Sit here and we'll take your blood pressure.* 여기 앉으세요, 혈압을 측정하겠어요.

19 ▶USE 사용하다◀ a word meaning to use something, used when giving instructions ‖ 지시를 할 때 쓰이는, 무엇을 사용한다는 뜻의 말: *Take some flour and add enough water to make a paste.* 밀가루를 가지고 충분히 물을 부어서 반죽을 만들어라.

20 ▶HAVE SPACE FOR 공간을 확보하다◀ to have enough space to contain a particular number of people or things ‖ 특정한 수의 사람이나 물건을 수용하기 위한 충분한 공간이 있다. …을 수용할 수 있다: *The station wagon takes six people.* 그 스테이션 왜건은 6인승이다.

21 ▶FEELINGS/REACTIONS 느낌/반응◀ to have a particular feeling or reaction when something happens ‖ 어떤 일이 발생할 경우에 특별한 감정이나 반응을 가지다. 느끼다. 품다: *His family took the news pretty hard.* (=were very upset) 그의 가족은 그 뉴스를 듣고 매우 괴로워했다. / *She doesn't seem to take a lot of interest in her kids.* 그녀는 자기 아이들에게 많은 관심을 보이는 것 같지 않다.

22 ▶BUY 구입하다◀ to decide to buy something ‖ 무엇을 사기로 결정하다: *He gave me a discount so I said I'd take it.* 그가 할인을 해줘서 나는 사겠다고 했다.

23 ▶SIZE 크기◀ to wear a particular size of clothing or shoes ‖ 특정 크기의 옷이나 구두를 입거나 신다: *Jim takes an extra large shirt.* 짐은 특대 셔츠를 입는다.

24 take it upon yourself to decide to do something even though no one has asked you to do it ‖ 아무도 그것을 하라고 요구하지 않았는데도 무엇을 하기로 결정하다. 스스로 결정하다[떠맡다]: *Parents have taken it upon themselves to raise* *extra cash for the school.* 부모들은 스스로 학교를 위해 별도의 현금을 모금하기로 결정했다.

25 ▶FOOD/DRINKS 음식/음료◀ [T] to use something such as salt, sugar, milk etc. in your food or drinks ‖ 음식이나 음료수에 소금·설탕·우유 등을 사용하다. 넣다. 타다: *Do you take cream in your coffee?* 커피에 크림을 탈까요? —see also **take care** (CARE²), **take care of** (CARE²), **take part** (PART¹), **take place** (PLACE¹),

take after sb *phr v* [T] to look or behave like another member of your family ‖ 가족의 다른 구성원과 똑같이 보이거나 행동하다. 닮다: *Jenny takes after her dad.* 제니는 자기 아버지를 닮았다.

take sth ↔ **apart** *phr v* [T] to separate something into pieces ‖ 사물을 조각으로 분리하다. 분해하다: *Vic took apart the faucet and put in a new washer.* 빅은 수도꼭지를 떼어내고 새 세탁기를 설치했다.

take away *phr v* [T] **1** [**take** sth ↔ **away**] to remove something from someone or somewhere ‖ 사람이나 어떤 장소에서 무엇을 제거하다. 치우다. 빼앗다: *One more ticket and your license will be taken away.* 한 번 더 딱지를 떼이면 면허 취소입니다. **2** [**take** sb ↔ **away**] to bring someone to a prison or hospital from his/her home ‖ 어떤 사람을 그의 집에서 교도소나 병원으로 데리고 가다: *Hyde was taken away in handcuffs.* 하이드는 수갑을 찬 채 연행되었다.

take sth ↔ **back** *phr v* [T] **1** to return something to the store where you bought it ‖ 물건을 구입한 가게에 돌려주다. 반품하다: *You should take it back if it doesn't fit.* 맞지 않으면 반품해야 한다. **2** to admit that something you said was wrong ‖ 말한 것이 잘못됐다고 시인하다. 취소[철회]하다: *All right, I'm sorry, I take it back.* 알았어요. 미안합니다. 그 말은 취소예요.

take sth ↔ **down** *phr v* [T] to remove something from its place, especially by separating it into pieces ‖ 특히 분해하여 본래 위치에서 무엇을 제거하다. 해체하다: *We take down the Christmas tree on January 6.* 우리는 1월 6일에 크리스마스 트리를 치운다. —opposite **put up** (PUT)

take in *phr v* [T] **1** [**take** sth ↔ **in**] to collect or earn an amount of money ‖ 일정량의 돈을 모으거나 벌다: *We've taken in $100,000 so far for charity.* 우리는 자선기금으로 지금까지 10만 달러를 모금했다. **2** [**take** sth ↔ **in**] to notice, understand, and remember things ‖ 사물을 알아차리고 이해하며 기억하다: *Babies take in an amazing amount of information.* 아기들은 놀라운 양의 정보를 이해한다. **3** [**take** sth ↔ **in**] to bring something to a place in order to be repaired ‖ 수리하려고 사물을 어떤 장소로 가져가다: *I need to take the car in for a tune-up.* 엔진 조정을 위해 자동차를 정비소에 맡겨야겠다. **4** [**take** sb/sth ↔ **in**] to let someone or something stay in your house or a shelter, because she, he, or it has nowhere else to stay ‖ 사람이나 물건이 아무 데도 머물 곳이 없어서 자신의 집이나 피난처에 머물게 하다. 수용하다: *The Humane Society took in almost 38,000 cats and dogs last year.* 동물 애호 협회는 지난해 거의 3만 8천 마리의 고양이와 개를 수용했다. **5** [**take in** sth] to go to see something, such as a movie, play etc. ‖ 영화·연극 등을 보러 가다: *tourists taking in the sights* 관광 중인 여행객들 **6 be taken in** to be deceived by someone or something ‖ 사람이나 사물에 속다: *The bank had been taken in by the forged receipts.* 그 은행은 위조 영수증으로 사기당했다. **7** [**take** sth ↔ **in**] to make part of a piece of clothing smaller ‖ 옷의 일부분을 더 작게 만들다. 치수를 줄이다: *If we take in the waist, Doris's wedding dress will fit you.* 허리 치수를 줄이면 도리스의 웨딩 드레스는 너에게 맞을 거야.

take off *phr v* **1** [T **take** sth ↔ **off**] to remove something ‖ 무엇을 제거하다. 없애다: *Your name has been taken off the list.* 너의 이름은 목록에서 삭제됐다. / *Take your shoes off in the house.* 실내에서는 신발을 벗어라. **2** [I] if an aircraft or space vehicle takes off, it rises into the air ‖ 항공기나 우주선이 허공으로 상승하다. 이륙하다 **3** [I] INFORMAL to leave a place ‖ 어떤 장소를 떠나다: *We packed everything in the car and took off.* 우리는 차에 모든 것을 싣고 출발했다. **4** [T **take** sth ↔ **off**] also **take off work** to not go to work for a period of time ‖ 일정 기간 직장에 나가지 않다. 휴가를 얻다: *I'm taking some time off work to go to the wedding.* 나는 결혼식에 가기 위해 직장에 얼마 동안 휴가를 낼 예정[작정]이다. **5** [I] to suddenly become successful ‖ 갑자기 성공하다. 일이 잘 되다: *Her career took off after she won a prize on TV's "Star Search."* "스타 탐방"이란 텔레비전 프로그램에서 상을 탄 이후로 그녀의 인생은 출세가도를 달렸다

take on *phr v* [T] **1** [**take** sb ↔ **on**] to

compete or fight against someone ‖ 남에게 대항하여 경쟁하거나 싸우다. 도전하다: *The winner of this game will take on Houston in the championships.* 이 경기의 승자는 챔피언 결정전에서 휴스턴과 맞붙는다. **2** [**take on** sth] to begin to have a different quality or appearance ‖ 다른 성질이나 외관을 갖기 시작하다. 취하다. 띠다: *Once we had children, Christmas took on a different sort of importance.* 일단 우리에게 아이들이 생기자 크리스마스는 또 다른 중요성을 띠었다. **3** [**take** sth ↔ **on**] to start doing some work or to start being responsible for something ‖ 어떤 일을 하기 시작하거나 어떤 것에 대해 책임지기 시작하다. 일을 떠맡다. 책임을 지다: *Ethel agreed to take on the treasurer's position.* 에델은 경리부장직을 맡는 것에 동의했다. **4** [**take** sb **on**] to start to employ someone ‖ 사람을 고용하기 시작하다. 고용하다: *The team has taken on a new coach.* 그 팀은 새 코치를 고용했다.

take out *phr v* [T] **1** [**take** sb **out**] to go with someone to a restaurant, movie, party etc., and pay for his/her meal and entertainment ‖ 남과 함께 식당·영화·파티 등에 가서 식사와 유흥비를 지불하다. 데리고 나가다: *We're taking Sabina out for dinner.* 우리는 저녁 식사에 사비나를 데리고 나가려고 한다. **2** [**take** sth ↔ **out**] to arrange to get something from a bank, court, insurance company etc. ‖ 은행·법원·보험 회사 등에서 무엇을 얻으려고 협정을 맺다. 가입하다. 받다: *The couple took out a $220,000 mortgage.* 그 부부는 22만 달러의 주택 융자를 받았다.

take sth ↔ **out on** sb *phr v* [T] to behave angrily toward someone because you are upset or angry about something else ‖ 자신이 어떤 것에 대해 속상하거나 화가 나서 남에게 화를 내면서 행동하다. 분풀이하다 : *Why are you taking it out on me? It's not my fault!* 너 왜 나에게 화풀이를 하니? 내 잘못이 아냐!

take over *phr v* [I,T **take** sth ↔ **over**] to get control of or become responsible for something ‖ 무엇을 관리하거나 책임지게 되다. 인계받다. 남을 대신하여 떠맡다: *Jack is supposed to take over for Carmen while she's on maternity leave.* 출산 휴가 동안 카르멘의 일을 잭이 대신 떠맡기로 되어 있다. / *His son will take over the business.* 그의 아들이 그 사업을 이어받을 것이다.

take to *phr v* [T] **1** [**take to** sb/sth] to quickly start to like someone or something ‖ 사람이나 사물을 곧 좋아하기 시작하다: *The two women took to each other right away.* 그 두 여자는 곧 서로 좋아하게 되었다. **2** [**take to** sth] to go out and walk somewhere, for a particular reason ‖ 특별한 이유로 나가서 어딘가를 걸어가다. 누비다: *Thousands of protesters took to the streets.* 수천 명의 항의자들이 거리를 행진했다. **3** **take to doing sth** to begin doing something regularly ‖ 규칙적으로 무엇을 하기 시작하다. …하게 되다. 습관이 되다: *Sandra has taken to getting up early to go jogging.* 산드라는 조깅을 하려고 일찍 일어나는 것이 습관이 되었다.

take up *phr v* [T] **1** [**take up** sth] to begin doing a job or activity ‖ 어떤 일이나 활동을 하기 시작하다. 착수하다: *I've just taken up tennis.* 나는 막 테니스를 시작했다. **2** [**take up** sth] if something takes up time or space, it fills or uses it ‖ 어떤 것이 시간이나 장소를 메우거나 이용하다. 차지하다: *The program takes up a lot of memory on the hard drive.* 그 프로그램은 하드 드라이브에서 많은 용량을 차지한다. **3** [**take** sth ↔ **up**] to begin discussing or considering something ‖ 무엇을 논의하거나 생각하기 시작하다. 거론하다: *The Senate will take up the bill in the next few weeks.* 상원은 다음 수 주일 안에 그 법안을 처리할 것이다.

take sb **up on** sth *phr v* [T] to accept an offer, invitation etc. ‖ 제의·초청 등을 받아들이다: *A number of students have taken him up on his offer of extra help.* 많은 학생들이 그의 과외 지도 제의를 받아들였다.

take up with *phr v* [T] **1** [**take** sth ↔ **up with** sb] to discuss something with someone, especially a complaint or problem ‖ 특히 불만 사항이나 문제를 남과 의논하다: *You should take it up with the union.* 너는 노동 조합과 그것을 의논해야 한다. **2** [**take up with** sb] to begin a friendship or a romantic relationship, especially with someone you should not have a relationship with ‖ 특히 관계를 맺지 말아야 할 사람과 우정이나 연애 관계를 시작하다. 바람직하지 못한 인물과 친해지다: *Nina has taken up with her boss.* 니나는 자신의 사장과 불륜 관계를 맺어 왔다.

take² *n* **1** the act of filming a scene for a movie or television program ‖ 영화나 텔레비전 프로그램을 위한 장면을 촬영하는 행위. 한 장면[컷]: *We had to shoot five takes for the explosion scene.* 우리는 폭

발 장면을 위해서 다섯 장면을 촬영해야 했다. **2** [singular] INFORMAL ⇨ TAKINGS

tak·en /'teɪkən/ v the PAST PARTICIPLE of TAKE ‖ take의 과거 분사형

take·off /'teɪk-ɔf/ n [C, U] **1** the time when an aircraft rises into the air ‖ 항공기가 하늘로 상승하는 때. 이륙 **2** a funny performance that copies the style of a particular show, movie, or performer ‖ 특정한 쇼[영화, 연기자]의 스타일을 흉내내는 재미있는 연기. 익살스러운[풍자적인] 흉내

take·out /'teɪk-aʊt/ n **1** a meal you buy from a restaurant that you eat somewhere else ‖ 다른 곳에서 먹으려고 식당에서 사는 음식. 음식점에서 사가지고 오는 요리 **2** a restaurant that sells this food ‖ 이러한 음식을 파는 식당 – **takeout** adj

take·o·ver /'teɪk,oʊvɚ/ n the act of getting control of something such as a company, country, or political group ‖ 회사[국가, 정치 집단] 등에 대한 지배권을 취하는 행위. 탈취. 점거. 인수. 접수: a military takeover 군부의 장악

tak·ings /'teɪkɪŋz/ n [plural] the amount of money earned by a small business or from an activity ‖ 영세 사업이나 활동으로부터 얻은 매상고. 수입: the day's takings 일일 매출액

tal·cum pow·der /'tælkəm ,paʊdɚ/ n [U] a fine powder that you put on your skin to keep it dry ‖ 피부를 건조하게 유지하기 위해 바르는 미세한 분말. 탤컴 파우더

tale /teɪl/ n a story about imaginary events ‖ 가공의 사건에 관한 이야기: a book of fairy tales 동화책

tal·ent /'tælənt/ n **1** [C, U] a natural ability to do something well ‖ 무엇을 잘 하는 타고난 능력. 재능. 소질: great musical talent 대단한 음악적 재능 / a talent for painting 그림에 대한 소질 — see usage note at ABILITY **2** [singular] a person or people who have talent ‖ 재능을 가진 사람이나 사람들: She's the best legal talent in the city. 그녀는 그 시의 최고의 법률가이다. / scouts checking out the talent (=people who have talent) 재능을 가진 사람들을 발굴하는 신인 발굴자

tal·ent·ed /'tæləntɪd/ adj very good at something that not everyone can do ‖ 누구나 할 수 있는 것이 아닌 일에 뛰어난. 유능한: a talented actor 재능있는 배우

tal·is·man /'tælɪsmən, -lɪz-/ n an object that some people think can protect them ‖ 일부 사람들이 자신들을 보호할 것이라고 생각하는 물체. 부적

talk¹ /tɔk/ v **1** [I] to say things to someone; speak ‖ 남에게 무엇을 말하다; 이야기하다: Who's he talking to on the phone? 그는 전화로 누구와 얘기하고 있니? / How old was your baby when she started to talk? 네 딸은 몇 살에 말을 시작했니? ✗DON'T SAY "talk English/Chinese etc." say "speak English/Chinese etc."✗ "talk English/Chinese 등"으로 말하지 않고 "speak English/Chinese 등"으로 말한다. **2** [I, T] to discuss something with someone ‖ 남과 무엇을 의논하다: I'd like to talk with you in private. 나는 은밀히 너와 의논하고 싶다. / Grandpa never talks about the war. 할아버지는 그 전쟁에 대해서 전혀 말씀을 하지 않으신다. / Those guys are always talking sports. (=discussing them) 저 사람들은 항상 스포츠에 대해 논한다. **3 talk your way out of sth** INFORMAL to use excuses or explanations to avoid an unpleasant situation ‖ 불쾌한 상황을 피하려고 핑계를 대거나 해명을 하다. …을 교묘한 말로 벗어나다: He always manages to talk his way out of trouble. 그는 항상 곤경을 모면할 핑계를 잘 꾸며내고 있다. **4** [I] to tell someone secret information because you are forced to ‖ 강요당해서 남에게 비밀 정보를 말하다. 비밀을 누설하다. 입을 열다: Prisoners who refused to talk were shot. 비밀 누설을 거부한 죄수들은 총살당했다.

SPOKEN PHRASES

5 talk dirty to talk in a sexual way to someone in order to make them feel sexually excited ‖ 성적으로 흥분시키려고 남에게 성적인 이야기를 하다. 음란한 이야기를 하다 **6 talk tough** to tell people very strongly what you want, or to threaten them ‖ 자신이 원하는 것을 강력히 사람들에게 말하다, 또는 사람들을 협박하다. 강력히 주장하다 **7 what are you talking about?** said when someone has just said something stupid or annoying ‖ 남이 방금 어리석거나 짜증나는 이야기를 했을 때 쓰여. 무슨 말을 하고 있는 거야: Aliens? UFOs? What are you talking about? 외계인? 미확인 비행 물체? 도대체 그게 무슨 소리야? **8 we're/you're talking** used in order to tell someone an amount ‖ 남에게 수량을 말하는 데에 쓰여: We're talking at least ten days to fix the car. 그 자동차를 고치려면 적어도 10일은 걸린다는 말입니다. **9 talk about funny/stupid/rich etc.** said in order to emphasize a quality that someone or something has ‖ 사람이나 사물에게 있는 속성을 강조하는 데에 쓰여. 정말 대단히 재미있다/어리석다/부자이다: *Talk about smart! Kim got straight A's at Harvard.* 정말 굉장히 명석한데! 김군이 하버드 대학에서 올A를 받았어.

—see usage note at SAY

talk back *phr v* [I] to rudely answer someone who is older or has more authority than you ‖ 나이가 많거나 권위가 더 있는 사람에게 무례하게 대답하다. 말대꾸하다: *Don't talk back to your father!* 너 아버지에게 말대꾸하지 마라!

talk down to sb *phr v* [T] to speak to someone as if you think you are smarter or more important than s/he is ‖ 자기가 남보다 더 영리하거나 더 중요한 듯이 남에게 말하다. 남을 경멸하는 투로 말하다: *He always explained things but never talked down to me.* 그는 내게 항상 일들을 설명했지만 결코 나를 무시하는 투로 말하지 않았다.

talk sb **into** sth *phr v* [T] to persuade someone to do something ‖ 남에게 무엇을 하도록 설득하다. 남을 설득하여 …하게 하다: *Maybe I can talk Vicky into driving us to the mall.* 내가 비키에게 우리를 쇼핑센터까지 차로 데려다 달라고 설득할 수 있을 거야.

talk sb **out of** sth *phr v* [T] to persuade someone not to do something ‖ 남을 설득하여 무엇을 하지 않게 하다. 남을 설득하여 …을 중지시키다: *Brenda talked me out of quitting my job.* 브렌다는 나를 설득하여 퇴직을 하지 못하게 했다.

talk sth ↔ **over** *phr v* [T] to discuss all the details of something, usually before making a decision about it ‖ 보통 무엇에 대하여 결정을 내리기 전에 상세한 모든 내용을 의논하다

talk² *n* **1** a conversation ‖ 대화: *Steve and I had a long talk last night.* 스티브와 나는 지난밤에 긴 대화를 나눴다. **2** a speech or LECTURE ‖ 연설, 강의: *Ms. Mason will be giving a talk on the Civil War.* 메이슨 여사는 남북 전쟁에 대해 강연을 할 것이다. **3** [U] news that is not official or not completely true ‖ 공식적인 것이 아니거나 완전히 진실한 것이 아닌 뉴스. 세평. 소문: *There was talk of the factory closing down.* 공장을 폐쇄한다는 풍문이 있었다. **4** [U] a particular type of speech ‖ 말의 독특한 유형. 말투. 어조: *Carrie still uses baby talk.* 캐리는 아직도 어린아이 말투를 쓴다. **5 it's just/only** talk used in order to say that something is likely to be untrue ‖ 무엇이 허위일 것 같다고 말하는 데에 쓰여. 그것은 공론(空論)에 불과하다: *Don't worry about it; it's just talk.* 그것에 대해 걱정하지 마라. 그것은 빈말일 뿐이야. —see also SMALL TALK, TALKS

talk·a·tive /'tɔkətɪv/ *adj* liking to talk a lot ‖ 말을 많이 하는 것을 좋아하는. 말이 많은

talk·er /'tɔkə/ *n* INFORMAL someone who talks a lot ‖ 말을 많이 하는 사람. 수다쟁이

talks /tɔks/ *n* [plural] a series of formal discussions between two governments, organizations etc. ‖ 두 정부·조직 등 사이의 일련의 공식 논의. 회담: *the latest trade talks* 최근의 무역 회담

talk show /'. ./ *n* a television or radio show in which people answer questions about themselves or discuss important subjects ‖ 사람들이 자신에 관한 질문에 답하거나 중요한 주제를 논의하는 텔레비전이나 라디오의 쇼. 토크쇼. 대담 프로

tall /tɔl/ *adj* **1** having a greater than average height ‖ 평균 키나 높이보다 주 큰. 키가 큰. 높은: *the tallest boy in the class* 반에서 가장 키가 큰 소년 / *tall buildings* 높은 건물 —see picture at HEIGHT **2** having a particular height ‖ 특정한 키를 가진: *My brother's almost 6 feet tall.* 내 동생의 키는 거의 6피트이다. —see picture at HEIGHT **3 a tall order** INFORMAL a piece of work or a request that will be extremely difficult to do ‖ 지극히 하기 어려운 일이나 요구. 무리한 주문 **4 a tall tale** a story you tell to make something sound more exciting, dangerous etc. than it really was ‖ 실제보다 더 재미있고 위험하게 들리도록 하는 이야기. 과장된 이야기

tal·low /'tælou/ *n* [U] hard animal fat used for making CANDLEs and soap ‖ 양초와 비누를 만드는 데 사용되는 굳은 동물 지방. 수지(獸脂)

tal·ly¹ /'tæli/ *n* a record of how much you have won, spent, used etc. so far ‖ 현재까지의 득점·소비·사용 등에 대한 기록: *Somebody should be keeping a tally of how much we owe.* 누군가는 우리의 채무가 얼마나 되는지에 대한 계산을 기록하고 있어야 한다.

tally² *v* **1** [T] also **tally up** to calculate the total number of points won, things done etc. ‖ 득점·성과 등에 대한 전체의 수를 계산하다. 합계[집계]하다: *Can you tally up the scores?* 네가 점수를 집계해

줄래? **2** [I] if two numbers, statements, dates etc. tally, they match each other exactly ∥ 두 숫자·진술·날짜 등이 서로 정확히 부합하다. 일치하다: *The signatures should tally with the names on the list.* 서명은 목록상의 이름과 일치해야 한다.

Tal·mud /'tɑlmʊd, 'tælməd/ *n* **the Talmud** the collection of writings that Jewish laws are based on ∥ 유대 율법이 기초를 둔 문서들의 집성본. 탈무드

tal·on /'tælən/ *n* one of the sharp curved nails on the feet of some birds that hunt ∥ 사냥하는 몇몇 새들의 발에 난 날카롭게 굽은 발톱의 하나. 맹금류의 발톱

tam·bou·rine /,tæmbə'rin/ *n* a circular musical instrument with small pieces of metal around the edge, played by hitting or shaking it ∥ 치거나 흔들어서 연주하는 테두리 주변에 작은 금속 조각이 달린 둥그런 악기. 탬버린

tame¹ /teɪm/ *adj* **1** a tame animal has been trained to live with people or work for them ∥ 동물이 사람들과 같이 살거나 사람들을 위해 일하도록 훈련된. 길들여진 **2** INFORMAL not as exciting, violent, or offensive as you had expected ∥ 기대했던 만큼 재미있거나 폭력적이거나, 또는 공격적이지 않은. 활기 없는. 지루한: *"How was the movie?" "Pretty tame."* 영화는 어땠어? "아주 지루했어."

tame² *v* [T] to train a wild animal so that it will not hurt people ∥ 사람들을 해치지 않도록 야생 동물을 훈련시키다. 길들이다

tam·per /'tæmpə/ *v*

tamper with sth *phr v* [T] to change something without permission, usually in order to damage it ∥ 보통 손상시키려고 허락 없이 어떤 것을 변경하다. 함부로 손을 대다: *Several bottles of aspirin had been tampered with.* 몇 개의 아스피린 병에 누군가가 무단으로 손을 댔다.

tam·pon /'tæmpɑn/ *n* a tube-shaped piece of cotton that a woman puts in her VAGINA during her PERIOD ∥ 여자가 월경 기간에 질 속에 삽입하는 튜브 모양의 솜 조각. 탐폰

tan¹ /tæn/ *adj* **1** having a pale yellow-brown color ∥ 연한 황갈색의: *tan leather shoes* 황갈색 가죽 구두 **2** having darker skin after spending a lot of time in the sun ∥ 햇볕에서 오랜 시간을 보낸 뒤에 보다 거무스름해진 피부를 지닌. 햇볕에 탄: *Your face is really tan.* 너의 얼굴은 정말 구릿빛이구나.

tan² *n* **1** the darker skin some people get when they spend a lot of time in the sun; SUNTAN ∥ 햇볕에서 장시간을 보낼 때 일부 사람들에게 생기는 보다 거무스름한 피부. 구릿빛 피부; suntan: *I want to get a tan.* 나는 햇볕에 살갗을 태우고 싶다. **2** [U] a pale yellow-brown color ∥ 연한 황갈색

tan³ *v* **-nned, -nning 1** [I] to get darker skin by spending time in the sun ∥ 햇볕에서 시간을 보내어 보다 거무스름한 피부가 되다. 햇볕에 타다: *I don't tan easily.* 나는 햇볕에 잘 타지 않는다. **2** [T] to change animal skin into leather by putting a special acid on it ∥ 동물의 생가죽에 특수한 산을 발라서 가죽으로 바꾸다. 무두질하다

tan·dem /'tændəm/ *n* **1 in tandem** FORMAL together or at the same time ∥ 함께, 또는 동시에. 협력하여: *Police are working in tandem with local schools to reduce car thefts.* 자동차 절도를 감소시키려고 경찰은 지역의 학교와 협력하고 있다. **2** a bicycle built for two riders sitting one behind the other ∥ 두 사람이 앞뒤로 앉아 타도록 제조된 자전거. 2인승 자전거

tan·gent /'tændʒənt/ *n* **go off on a tangent** to suddenly start talking or thinking about a completely different subject ∥ 갑자기 완전히 다른 주제에 대하여 말하거나 생각하기 시작하다. 말·생각이 주제를 벗어나다: *It was hard to keep Maria from going off on a tangent.* 마리아가 주제를 벗어나 옆길로 새는 것을 막기가 어려웠다. **- tangential** /tæn'dʒɛnʃəl/ *adj* : *tangential comments* 주제를 벗어난 논평

tan·ger·ine /,tændʒə'rin/ *n* a sweet fruit that looks like a small orange ∥ 작은 오렌지처럼 생긴 달콤한 과일. 귤 — see picture on page 944

tan·gi·ble /'tændʒəbəl/ *adj* real, definite, and able to be shown or touched ∥ 실재하고 명확하며 볼 수 있거나 만질 수 있는. 명백한. 실재하는. 유형의: *tangible proof* 명백한 증거 — opposite INTANGIBLE

tan·gle¹ /'tæŋgəl/ *n* hair, threads, knots etc. that have become twisted together ∥ 함께 뒤얽힌 머리카락·실·매듭 등: *tangles in her hair* 뒤엉킨 그녀의 머리카락 / *a tangle of branches* 뒤얽힌 가지들

tan·gle² *v* [I, T] to become twisted together, or to make the parts of something do this ∥ 함께 얽히거나 사물의 일부를 이렇게 되게 만들다. 엉키다. 엉키게 하다: *My hair tangles easily.* 내 머리카락은 쉽게 엉킨다.

tangle with sb *phr v* [T] INFORMAL to

argue or fight with someone ‖ 남과 논쟁하거나 싸우다. 다투다

tan·gled /'tæŋgəld/, **tangled up** adj
1 twisted together ‖ 함께 얽힌. 뒤얽힌:
tangled string/hair/branches 뒤얽힌 줄
[머리카락, 가지] 2 complicated and
confusing ‖ 복잡하고 혼란스러운: *tangled
emotions* 혼란한 감정

tan·go /'tæŋgoʊ/ n **the tango** a slow
dance from South America, or the
music for this dance ‖ 남미의 느린 춤이
나 이 춤을 위한 음악. 탱고(곡)

tang·y /'tæŋi/ adj tasting or smelling
both sweet and sour ‖ 달콤하면서도 시큼
한 맛이나 냄새가 나는. 싸한. 코를 쏘는.
달콤새콤한 – **tang** n [singular]

tank¹ /tæŋk/ n 1 a large container for
holding liquid or gas ‖ 액체나 가스를 담
는 대형 용기. 탱크: *a fish tank* 어항 / *a
car's gas tank* 자동차의 연료 탱크 2 a
heavy military vehicle with a large gun
and metal belts over its wheels ‖ 대포와
그 바퀴 위에 금속제 무한궤도를 두른 무
거운 군용 차량. 전차. 탱크

tank² v

tank sth ↔ **up** phr v [T] to fill a car's
TANK with gas ‖ 차의 연료 탱크를 휘발유
로 가득 채우다

tan·kard /'tæŋkəd/ n a large metal cup
used for drinking beer ‖ 맥주를 마시는
데 사용하는 커다란 금속 컵

tank·er /'tæŋkə/ n a vehicle or ship
used for carrying a large amount of
liquid or gas ‖ 대량의 액체나 가스를 운반
하는 데 사용하는 차량이나 선박. 유조선.
탱크 로리: *an oil tanker* 유류 수송선[차]

tan·ta·lize /'tæntl,aɪz/ v [T] to make
someone feel a very strong desire for
something that is difficult to get ‖ 어떤
사람에게 얻기 어려운 것에 대한 매우 강
한 욕망을 느끼게 하다. 감질나게 하다

tan·ta·liz·ing /'tæntl,aɪzɪŋ/ adj making
you want something very much ‖ 무엇을
몹시 원하게 하는. 감질나게 하는: *tanta-
lizing smells coming from the kitchen* 부
엌에서 나는 군침 흘리게 하는 냄새

tan·ta·mount /'tæntə,maʊnt/ adj **be
tantamount to sth** to be almost the
same thing as something else ‖ 다른 어
떤 것과 거의 같다. …나 다름없다: *His
refusal to speak was tantamount to
admitting he was guilty.* 그의 진술 거부
는 자신의 유죄를 인정하는 것과 다름없었
다.

tan·trum /'tæntrəm/ n **have/throw a
tantrum** to suddenly become very
angry, noisy, and unreasonable ‖ 갑자기
매우 화가 나서 소란스럽고 분별이 없어지

다. 버럭 화를 내다

tap¹ /tæp/ v **-pped, -pping** 1 [I, T] to
gently hit your finger or foot against
something ‖ 손가락이나 발을 무엇에 가볍
게 치다. 가볍게 두드리다: *Someone was
tapping on the window outside.* 누군가
가 밖에서 창문을 가볍게 두드리고 있었
다. / *Caroline tapped her feet in time to
the music.* 캐롤라인은 발로 음악에 박자
를 맞췄다. 2 [I, T] to use something or
become able to use something ‖ 무엇을
이용하거나 이용할 수 있게 되다: *With
the Internet you can tap into
information from around the world.* 인터
넷으로 너는 전 세계의 정보를 활용할 수
있다. / *tapping the country's natural
resources* 국가의 천연 자원의 활용 3 [T]
to put a TAP on someone's telephone ‖
남의 전화를 도청하다

tap² n 1 an act of hitting something
gently, especially to get someone's
attention ‖ 특히 남의 주의를 끌기 위해
무엇을 가볍게 치는 행위: *Suddenly I felt
a tap on my shoulder.* 갑자기 나는 내 어
깨를 가볍게 치는 것을 느꼈다. 2 an
object used for letting liquid out of a
BARREL ‖ 통에서 액체를 나오게 하는 데
쓰이는 물체. (통의) 꼭지 3 a small
electronic object that allows you to
secretly listen to someone's telephone
conversations ‖ 남의 전화 대화를 몰래 들
을 수 있는 작은 전자 기구. 도청기 **4 on
tap a)** beer that is on tap comes from a
BARREL ‖ 맥주가 술통에서 나오는 **b)**
INFORMAL available to be used ‖ 언제든지
쓸 수 있는: *unlimited data on tap* 언제든
지 쓸 수 있는 무한한 데이터 5 [U] ⇨
FAUCET —see also TAPS

tap danc·ing /'. ,../ n [U] a type of
dancing in which you make a noise with
special shoes that have metal pieces on
the bottom ‖ 바닥에 금속 조각을 붙인 특
수 구두로 소리를 내는 춤의 일종. 탭 댄
스 – **tap dance** v [I]

tape¹ /teɪp/ n 1 **a)** [U] a thin narrow
band of plastic material used for
recording sounds, VIDEO pictures, or
computer information ‖ 소리나 비디오
화상, 또는 컴퓨터 정보의 기록에 쓰이는
플라스틱으로 된 얇고 좁은 띠. 테이프:
Did you get the interview on tape?
(=recorded on tape) 그 인터뷰를 테이프
에 녹음했습니까? —see also VIDEOTAPE
b) a flat plastic case that contains this
type of tape ‖ 이런 종류의 테이프가 들어
있는 납작한 플라스틱 케이스: *Can I
borrow your old Beatles tape?* 네 오래된
비틀즈 테이프를 빌려 줄래? / *a blank*

tape (=with nothing recorded on it) 공
테이프 **2** [C, U] a narrow band of sticky
material used for sticking things
together, such as paper or packages ‖
종이·포장 등의 물건을 함께 붙이는 데 쓰
이는 끈적거리는 물질로 된 폭이 좁은 띠.
접착테이프

tape² v **1** [I, T] to record sounds or
pictures onto a TAPE ‖ 테이프에 소리나
화상을 기록하다. 녹음[녹화]하다 —see
also VIDEOTAPE² **2** to stick something
onto something else using TAPE ‖ 테이프
를 사용하여 무엇을 다른 것에 붙이다. 접
착테이프로 붙이다: *He has lots of
postcards taped to his wall.* 그는 많은
그림엽서를 벽에 테이프로 붙였다. **3** [T]
also **tape up** to firmly tie a BANDAGE
around an injury ‖ 상처 부위에 붕대를
단단히 매다. 싸매다. 고정시키다

tape deck /'. ./ *n* the part of a STEREO
used for recording and playing sounds
on a TAPE ‖ 테이프로 소리를 녹음하고 재
생하는 데 쓰이는 입체 음향 장치의 일부.
녹음 재생 장치

tape meas·ure /'. ,../ *n* a long band
of cloth or metal with inches,
CENTIMETERs etc. marked on it, used for
measuring things ‖ 물건을 측정하는 데
쓰이는, 인치·센티미터 등의 표시가 되어
있는 천이나 금속제의 긴 띠. 줄자

ta·per¹ /'teɪpɚ/ *v* [I, T] to become
gradually narrower towards one end ‖
한쪽 끝으로 가면서 점점 가늘어지다 –
tapered *adj*: *pants with tapered legs*
다리 아래로 갈수록 좁아지는 바지
taper off *phr v* [I] to decrease
gradually ‖ 점차로 감소하다 / *The rain
finally tapered off in the afternoon.* 빗
발이 마침내 오후 들어 차차 약해졌다.

ta·per² *n* a long thin CANDLE ‖ 길고 가는
양초

tape re·cord·er /'. .,../ *n* a piece of
electronic equipment used for recording
and playing sounds on a TAPE ‖ 테이프로
녹음하고 재생하는 데 쓰이는 전자 장치.
녹음기 – **tape record** *v* [T]

tap·es·try /'tæpɪstri/ *n* [C, U] heavy
cloth with colored threads woven into it
to make a picture, or a large piece of
this cloth ‖ 색실로 그림을 넣어 짠 무거운
천이나 이 천으로 된 큰 직물

tape·worm /'teɪpwɚm/ *n* a long flat
PARASITE that can live inside the
INTESTINEs of people and animals ‖ 사람·
동물의 장 내부에 살 수 있는 길고 납작한
기생충. 촌충

taps /tæps/ *n* [singular] a tune played
on the BUGLE at night in an army camp

or at a military funeral ‖ 군인 막사나 군
장례식에서 야간에 나팔로 연주하는 곡.
소등[장송] 나팔

tap wa·ter /'. ,../ *n* [U] water that
comes out of a FAUCET ‖ 수도꼭지에서 나
오는 물. 수돗물

tar¹ /tɑr/ *n* [U] a black substance that is
thick and sticky, and is used on road
surfaces, roofs etc. to protect them
from water ‖ 방수하려고 도로 표면·지붕
등에 사용하는 걸쭉하고 끈적끈적한 검은
물질. 콜타르. 피치. 타르

tar² *v* **-rred, -rring** [T] to cover
something with TAR ‖ 무엇을 타르로 덮
다. 타르를 칠하다

ta·ran·tu·la /tə'ræntʃələ/ *n* a large
hairy poisonous SPIDER ‖ 크고 털이 많은
독거미. 타란툴라

tar·dy /'tɑrdi/ *adj* late, or done too
slowly ‖ 늦은, 너무 더디 행한: *If you are
tardy once more you'll have to stay
after school.* 한 번 더 지각하면 방과 후에
남아야 한다. – **tardiness** *n* [U]

tar·get /'tɑrgɪt/ *n* **1** an object, person,
or place that is deliberately chosen to be
attacked ‖ 공격할 수 있게 용의주도하게
선택한 물건이나 사람 또는 장소. 표적.
목표물: *a military target* 군사 목표물 **2**
an aim or result that you try to achieve
‖ 성취하려는 목표나 결과. 달성[도달] 목
표: *We're trying to reach a target of $2
million in sales.* 우리는 2백만 달러의 매
출 목표를 달성하려고 노력하고 있다. **3**
something that you practice shooting at
‖ 사격 훈련을 하면서 겨냥하는 것. 과녁:
Pete missed the target by two inches. 피
트는 과녁에서 2인치 빗맞췄다.

target² *v* [T] **1** to aim something at
someone or something ‖ 무엇을 사람이나
사물에 겨냥하다: *missiles targeted on/at
European cities* 유럽의 도시들을 겨냥한
유도탄 **2** to try to make something have
an effect on a limited group or area ‖ 무
엇을 제한된 집단이나 지역에 효과를 미치
도록 노력하다. 목표로 삼다: *welfare
programs targeted at the unemployed*
실업자를 대상으로 하는 복지 계획 **3** to
deliberately attack someone or
something ‖ 사람이나 물건을 용의주도하
게 공격하다. 표적으로 삼다: *Smaller
banks with less security have been
targeted.* 보안이 취약한 소규모 은행들이
표적이 되어 왔다.

tar·iff /'tærɪf/ *n* a tax on goods that are
brought into a country or taken out of it
‖ 국내로 들여오거나 국외로 나가는 물품
에 대한 조세. 관세

tar·mac /'tɑrmæk/ *n* ⇨ ASPHALT

tar·nish /ˈtɑrnɪʃ/ v **1** [T] to make someone or something less impressive or respectable ‖ 사람이나 사물을 덜 인상적이거나 덜 존경스럽게 만들다. 더럽히다. 손상하다: *More violence will tarnish the school's reputation.* 더 이상의 폭력은 학교의 명성을 손상시킬 것이다. **2** [I] if a metal tarnishes, it becomes darker and less shiny ‖ 금속이 더욱 거무스름해지고 반짝임이 덜해지다. 변색하다

tar·ot /ˈtærou/ n [singular, U] a set of cards used for telling what might happen to someone in the future ‖ 사람에게 미래에 일어날 일을 말하는 데 쓰이는 한 벌의 카드. 타로 카드

tarp /tɑrp/, **tar·pau·lin** /tɑrˈpɔlən/ n [C, U] a cloth that water cannot go through, used for protecting things from the rain ‖ 물건들을 비로부터 보호하는 데 쓰이는, 물이 통과할 수 없는 천. 방수천

tar·ry /ˈtæri/ v [I] LITERARY to stay in a place too long, or delay going somewhere ‖ 한 장소에 너무 오래 머무르거나 어딘가로 가는 데 지체하다

tart¹ /tɑrt/ adj pleasantly sour ‖ 적당히 신: *tart green apples* 새콤한 풋사과

tart² n a small PIE without a top, usually containing fruit ‖ 보통 속에 과일이 든, 위에 다른 재료를 올리지 않은 작은 파이

tar·tan /ˈtɑrtʰn/ n [C, U] a traditional Scottish PLAID pattern, or cloth with this pattern ‖ 전통적인 스코틀랜드의 체크무늬나 이 무늬가 있는 천

tar·tar /ˈtɑrtə/ n [U] a hard substance that forms on teeth and can damage them ‖ 치아에 형성되어 치아를 손상시킬 수 있는 굳은 물질. 치석

tartar sauce /ˌ.. ˌ./ n [U] a cold white thick SAUCE often eaten with fish ‖ 흔히 생선과 함께 먹는 차고 흰 걸쭉한 소스. 타르타르소스

task /tæsk/ n **1** a job or particular thing that you have to do, especially a difficult or annoying one ‖ 해야만 하는, 특히 힘들거나 곤혹스러운 직무나 특정의 일: *the dangerous task of rescuing crash victims* 충돌 사고의 희생자를 구조하는 위험스러운 작업 **2 take sb to task** to angrily criticize someone for doing something wrong ‖ 일을 잘못 하는 데 대해 격분하여 남을 비평하다. 남을 비난[질책]하다

task force /ˈ. ./ n a group that is formed in order to do a particular job, especially a military or political one ‖ 특히 군사적 또는 정치적인 특정 직무를 수행하려고 구성된 집단. 기동부대. 대책본부

tas·sel /ˈtæsəl/ n a group of threads tied together at one end and hung as a decoration on curtains, clothes etc. ‖ 한쪽 끝을 함께 묶어 커튼·옷 등에 장식으로 매달아 놓는 실 뭉치. (장식) 술 – **tasseled** adj

taste¹ /teɪst/ n **1** the feeling that is produced when your tongue touches a particular food or drink ‖ 혀가 특정한 음식이나 음료수에 닿을 때 생기는 느낌. 미각: *I don't like the taste of garlic.* 나는 마늘 맛을 좋아하지 않는다. / *a bitter taste* 쓴맛 **2** [C, U] the particular type of music, clothes, art etc. that someone prefers ‖ 누군가가 좋아하는 특정 형태의 음악·의상·예술 등. 취향: *Sheila has strange taste in clothes.* 쉴라는 옷에 별난 취향이 있다. **3** [U] the enjoyment of something ‖ 무엇을 즐김. 취미. 기호: *She never lost her taste for travel.* 그녀는 결코 여행에 대한 취미를 잃지 않았다. **4** a small amount of a food or drink, eaten to find out what it is like ‖ 맛이 어떤지 알기 위해 먹어 보는 소량의 음식이나 음료: *Here, have a taste and tell me what you think.* 이봐, 시식해 보고 어떻게 생각하는지 나에게 말해 줘. **5 be in good/bad/poor taste** to be suitable or unsuitable for a particular occasion ‖ 특정한 경우에 맞거나 맞지 않다. 취향이 뛰어나다/나쁘다/떨어지다: *a joke in very bad taste* 아주 품위 없는 농담

taste² v **1** [I] to have a particular type of taste ‖ 특정한 유형의 맛이 있다. 맛이 나다: *What does the soup taste like?* 그 수프는 어떤 맛이 나니? / *This milk tastes a little sour.* 이 우유는 약간 상한 맛이 난다. XDON'T SAY "is tasting."X "is tasting"이라고는 하지 않는다. **2** [T] to put a small amount of food or drink in your mouth in order to find out what it is like ‖ 맛이 어떤지 알려고 음식이나 음료를 입에 조금 넣다. 시식[시음]하다: *Taste this and see if it needs more salt.* 이것을 맛보고 소금을 더 넣어야 하는지를 알아봐라. **3** [T] to experience the particular taste of a food or drink ‖ 음식이나 음료의 특정한 맛을 경험하다. …의 맛을 느끼다: *My cold's so bad I can't taste a thing.* 나는 감기가 너무 심해서 아무 맛도 느낄 수 없다. XDON'T SAY "I am not tasting."X "I am not tasting."이라고는 하지 않는다.

taste·ful /ˈteɪstfəl/ adj chosen, decorated, or made in a way that is attractive and of good quality ‖ 매력적이며 품질이 뛰어나게 선택하거나 장식하거나 또는 제조한. 품위 있는. 고상한: *Frank was dressed in casual but* *tasteful clothes.* 프랭크는 평상복이지만 품위 있는 옷을 입었다. **-tastefully** *adv* : *a tastefully furnished apartment* 품위 있는 가구가 갖추어진 아파트

taste·less /ˈteɪstlɪs/ *adj* 1 OFFENSIVE, unsuitable, or of bad quality ‖ 공격적이거나 부적절하거나, 또는 저질인. 천박한: *tasteless jokes* 천박한 농담 2 not having any taste ‖ 아무 맛도 없는: *tasteless food* 맛없는 음식

tast·er /ˈteɪstɚ/ *n* someone whose job is to test the quality of a food or drink by tasting it ‖ 맛을 보고 음식이나 음료의 품질을 시험하는 직업인. 맛 감정인: *wine tasters* 와인 감정인

tast·ing /ˈteɪstɪŋ/ *n* an event where you can try different kinds of food and drinks ‖ 다양한 종류의 음식물을 맛볼 수 있는 행사. 시음[시식, 감정]회: *a cheese tasting* 치즈 시식회

tast·y /ˈteɪsti/ *adj* having a very good taste ‖ 매우 맛이 좋은: *tasty fish* 맛 좋은 생선

tat·tered /ˈtætɚd/ *adj* old and torn ‖ 낡고 찢어진. 넝마의. 누덕누덕한: *tattered curtains* 너덜너덜한 커튼

tat·ters /ˈtætɚz/ *n* [plural] **in tatters a)** clothes that are in tatters are old and torn ‖ 옷이 낡고 찢어진. 넝마가 된. 다 해진 **b)** completely ruined ‖ 완전히 못 쓰게 된: *All his great plans lay in tatters.* 모든 그의 훌륭한 계획은 무용지물이 되었다

tat·tle /ˈtætl/ *v* [I] if a child tattles, s/he tells a parent or teacher that another child has done something bad ‖ 어떤 아이가 부모나 교사에게 다른 아이가 한 나쁜 짓을 말하다. 고자질하다

tat·tle·tale /ˈtætl̩teɪl/ *n* SPOKEN a word meaning someone who TATTLEs, used especially by children ‖ 특히 어린이가 사용하는 고자질쟁이를 뜻하는 말

tat·too /tæˈtu/ *n* a picture, word etc. that is put permanently onto your skin using a needle and ink ‖ 바늘과 잉크를 사용하여 피부에 영구적으로 새긴 그림·문자 등. 문신의 무늬 **-tattooed** *adj* **-tattoo** *v* [T]

taught /tɔt/ *v* the past tense and PAST PARTICIPLE of TEACH ‖ teach의 과거·과거분사형

taunt /tɔnt, tɑnt/ *v* [T] to try to make someone upset or angry by saying something unkind ‖ 심술궂게 말해서 남을 심란하게 하거나 분노하게 만들려고 하다. (남을) 비웃다: *The other kids taunted him about his weight.* 다른 아이들이 그의 체중에 관해서 그를 비웃었다.

-taunt *n*

Tau·rus /ˈtɔrəs/ *n* 1 [singular] the second sign of the ZODIAC, represented by a BULL ‖ 황소로 상징되는 황도 십이궁의 둘째 별자리. 황소자리 2 someone born between April 20 and May 20 ‖ 4월 20일과 5월 20일 사이에 태어난 사람. 황소좌 태생자

taut /tɔt/ *adj* 1 stretched tight ‖ 팽팽히 뻗은. 팽팽한: *a taut rope* 팽팽히 친 밧줄 2 seeming worried ‖ 불안해 보이는: *a taut look on his face* 그의 얼굴의 불안해 하는 표정 **-tautly** *adv*

tav·ern /ˈtævɚn/ *n* a BAR that usually only serves beer and wine ‖ 보통 맥주와 와인만을 파는 술집. 선술집

taw·dry /ˈtɔdri/ *adj* cheap and of bad quality ‖ 값싸고 나쁜 질의. 싸구려의: *tawdry jewelry* 값싸고 번지르르한 보석 **-tawdriness** *n* [U]

taw·ny /ˈtɔni/ *adj* having a light gold-brown color ‖ 밝은 황갈색을 띤: *tawny fur* 황갈색의 모피

tax¹ /tæks/ *n* [C, U] the money you must pay the government, based on how much you earn, what you buy, where you live etc. ‖ 소득·구매·주거 등에 근거해서 국가에 납부해야 하는 돈. 세금. 조세: *a 13% tax on cigarettes* 담배에 붙은 13퍼센트의 세금 / *I only earn $25,000 a year after taxes.* (=after paying tax) 나는 세금을 제하고 1년에 겨우 25,000달러만 번다.

tax² *v* [T] 1 to charge a tax on something ‖ 어떤 것에 세금을 부과하다. 과세하다: *Incomes of under $30,000 are taxed at 15%.* 3만 달러 이하의 소득에는 15퍼센트의 세금이 부과된다. 2 **tax sb's patience/strength etc.** to use almost all of someone's PATIENCE, strength etc. ‖ 사람의 인내심·힘 등의 거의 모두를 사용하다. …을 소진하다. 바닥내다: *His constant questions had begun to tax her patience.* 그의 계속되는 질문으로 그녀의 인내심은 한계에 다다르기 시작했다.

tax·a·tion /tækˈseɪʃən/ *n* [U] the system of charging taxes, or the money collected from taxes ‖ 세금을 부과하는 제도, 또는 세금으로 징수된 돈. 과세[징세](액). 세수

tax ex·empt /ˈ. .,./ *adj* not TAXed, or not having to pay tax ‖ 세금이 부과되지 않는, 또는 세금을 안 내도 되는. 면세의: *tax-exempt savings* 비과세 저축 / *a tax-exempt charity* 비과세 자선 기금

tax·i¹ /ˈtæksi/, **tax·i·cab** /ˈtæksiˌkæb/ *n* a car with a driver whom you pay to drive you somewhere ‖ 자신을 어떤 곳에

운전해서 데려다 주도록 운전사에게 돈을 지불하는 차. 택시: *We'll just take a taxi home.* 우리는 그냥 택시를 타고 집에 가겠다.

taxi² *v* [I] if a plane taxis, it moves slowly on the ground ‖ 비행기가 지상에서 천천히 움직이다. (유도로를) 이동하다

tax·i·der·my /'tæksə,dɜrmi/ *n* [U] the process of specially treating and filling the body of a dead animal, bird, or fish so that it still looks alive ‖ 동물[새, 물고기]이 여전히 살아 있는 것처럼 보이도록 사체를 특수하게 처리해서 안을 채워 넣는 과정. 박제(술)

tax·ing /'tæksɪŋ/ *adj* making you feel very tired, weak, or annoyed ‖ 매우 피곤하게[약하게, 귀찮게] 느끼게 하는. 부담이 무거운. 고생이 많은: *a taxing job* 힘들고 성가신 일

taxi stand /'.. ,./ *n* a place where TAXIS wait in order to get passengers ‖ 승객을 태우기 위해 택시가 기다리는 장소. 택시 승차장

tax·pay·er /'tæks,peɪɚ/ *n* someone who pays taxes ‖ 세금을 내는 사람. 납세자

tax shel·ter /'. ,../ *n* a plan or method that allows you to legally avoid paying tax ‖ 합법적으로 세금 내는 것을 피하게 해주는 계획이나 방법. 세금을 모면하기 위한 (회계) 수단

TB *n* the abbreviation of TUBERCULOSIS ‖ tuberculosis의 약어

tbsp. *n* the written abbreviation of TABLESPOON ‖ tablespoon의 약어

T cell, T-cell /'ti sel/ *n* a type of WHITE BLOOD CELL that helps the body fight disease ‖ 인체가 질병과 싸우도록 돕는 백혈구의 일종. 티세포

tea /ti/ *n* **1** [U] a drink made by pouring boiling water onto dried leaves ‖ 말린 잎에다 끓는 물을 부어 만든 음료수. 차: *a cup of tea* 차 한 잔 **2** [C, U] dried leaves, flowers etc., used for making a hot drink ‖ 뜨거운 음료수를 만드는 데 사용되는 말린 잎이나 꽃 등. 차잎: *mint tea* 박하차잎 / *herbal teas* 허브차잎

tea bag /'. ./ *n* a small paper bag with dried leaves in it, used for making tea ‖ 차를 만드는 데 사용되는, 안에 말린 잎을 넣은 작은 종이 봉지. 티백

teach /titʃ/ *v* **taught, taught, teaching 1** [I, T] to give lessons in a school or college ‖ 학교나 대학에서 수업을 하다. 가르치다. 교육하다: *Mr. Rochet has been teaching for 17 years.* 로쳇 씨는 17년 동안 가르치는 일을 해오고 있다. / *She teaches math at Jackson High*

School. 그녀는 잭슨 고등학교에서 수학을 가르친다. **2** [T] to show someone how to do something ‖ 남에게 어떤 것을 하는 법을 보여주다. …을 가르치다. 훈련시키다: *My dad taught me how to swim.* 아버지는 나에게 수영하는 법을 가르쳐 주셨다. **3 teach sb a lesson** INFORMAL to make someone avoid doing something bad or unwise again ‖ 남이 나쁘거나 어리석은 일을 다시 하는 것을 피하게 하다. 남에게 교훈을 주다[가르치다]: *Well, I hope that being locked out teaches him a lesson.* 글쎄, 집밖으로 쫓아내 문을 잠궈버린 벌에서 그가 교훈을 얻기를 바래. —see usage note at LEARN

teach·er /'titʃɚ/ *n* someone whose job is to teach ‖ 가르치는 일을 하는 직업인. 교사. 선생: *Mr. Paulin is my history teacher.* 폴린 씨는 내 역사 선생님이다.

teacher's pet /,.. '. / *n* a teacher's favorite student, especially one that the other students dislike ‖ 교사가 가장 좋아하는, 특히 다른 학생들이 싫어하는 학생. 교사의 총애를 받는 학생

teach·ing /'titʃɪŋ/ *n* [U] the work that a teacher does, or the profession of being a teacher ‖ 교사가 하는 일, 또는 교사로서의 직업. 가르치기. 교수. 수업. 교직: *I'd like to go into teaching when I finish college.* 나는 대학을 졸업하면 교편을 잡고 싶다.

tea co·sy /'. ,../ *n* a thick cover that you put over a TEAPOT to keep the tea hot ‖ 차를 따뜻하게 유지하기 위해 찻주전자에 덮어씌우는 두꺼운 덮개. 보온 커버

tea·cup /'tikʌp/ *n* a cup that you serve tea in ‖ 차를 담아 내놓는 잔. 찻잔

teak /tik/ *n* [C, U] a tall Southern Asian tree, or the very hard wood of this tree used for making ships and furniture ‖ 키가 큰 남부 아시아산 나무, 또는 배와 가구를 만드는 데 쓰이는 이 나무의 아주 단단한 목재. 티크나무 (목재)

team¹ /tim/ *n* **1** a group of people who compete against another group in a sport, game etc. ‖ 스포츠나 게임 등에서 다른 집단과 맞서 겨루는 일단의 사람들. 팀: *Which team is winning?* 어느 팀이 이기고 있냐? / *Manuel is on the swimming team.* 마뉴엘은 수영 팀에 들어 있다. **2** a group of people who are chosen to work together to do a particular job ‖ 특정한 일을 함께 하도록 선택된 일단의 사람들. 동료. 단: *a team of doctors* 의료진 **3** two or more animals that are used for pulling a vehicle ‖ 탈것을 끄는 데 쓰이는 둘 이상의 동물들

team² *v*

team up *phr v* [I] to form a team with another person, company etc. in order to work together ‖ 함께 일하기 위해 다른 사람·회사 등과 팀을 이루다. 협력[협동] 하다: *We're teaming up with another publisher to do the book.* 우리는 그 책을 내기 위하여 다른 출판업자와 협력하고 있다.

team·mate /'tim-meɪt/ *n* someone who plays or works on the same team as you ‖ 같은 팀에서 경기하거나 일하는 사람. 팀의 한 사람[일원]

team play·er /ˌ. '../ *n* INFORMAL someone who works well with other people so that the whole group is successful ‖ 전체 집단을 성공시키기 위해 다른 사람과 잘 어울려 일하는 사람. 조직 내에서 협력하여 조직의 성공에 기여하는 사람

team·ster /'timstɚ/ *n* someone whose job is to drive a TRUCK ‖ 트럭을 운전하는 직업인. 수송 트럭 운전사

team·work /'timwɚk/ *n* [U] the ability of a group to work well together, or the effort the group makes ‖ 집단이 함께 어울려 일을 잘해내는 능력, 또는 그 집단이 하는 노력. 팀워크. 공동 작업. 협력

tea·pot /'tipɑt/ *n* a container used for serving tea, that has a handle and a SPOUT ‖ 손잡이와 주둥이가 달려 있으며 차를 따르는 데 사용하는 용기. 찻주전자

teapot

spout

tear¹ /tɛr/ *v* **tore, torn, tearing** *v* **1** **a)** [T] to put a hole in a piece of paper, cloth etc. by pulling it very hard or by accidentally letting it touch something sharp ‖ 매우 세게 당기거나 우연히 날카로운 것에 걸려 종이·옷 등에 구멍을 내다. 찢다. 째다: *You've torn your sleeve.* 네 옷소매가 찢어졌다. / *He tore the envelope open.* 그는 봉투를 찢어서 열었다. / *Oh no, I tore a hole in my jeans!* 이런, 내 청바지에 구멍이 났어! **b)** [I] to become damaged in this way ‖ 이렇게 손상이 되다. 째지다. 찢어지다: *Be careful, you don't want your dress to tear!* 조심해, 네 드레스를 찢어 먹지 않으려면! **2** [I] INFORMAL to move very quickly, often in a careless or violent way ‖ 종종 부주의하거나 격하게 매우 빨리 움직이다. 황급히 [심하게] 움직이다: *Two kids came tearing around the corner.* 두 명의 아이들이 모퉁이를 황급히 돌아 달려 왔다. **3**

[T] to remove something by tearing it ‖ 어떤 것을 떼어내서 없애다. 잡아떼다. 쥐어뜯다. 뜯어내다: *The storm actually tore the door off its hinges.* 폭풍으로 그 문짝은 경첩에서 거의 떨어져 나갔다.

tear apart *phr v* [T] **1** [**tear** sb **apart**] to make someone feel extremely unhappy or upset ‖ 남을 아주 불행하게 또는 속상하게 느끼게 하다. 마음을 (갈가리) 찢어 놓다: *It tears me apart to see Lisa cry.* 리사가 우는 것을 보니 내 마음이 찢어지듯 아프다. **2** [**tear** sth ↔ **apart**] to make a group, organization etc. start having problems ‖ 단체·조직 등이 문제를 갖기 시작하게 하다. 분란을 일으키다. (화목을) 깨뜨리다: *Your drinking is tearing this family apart!* 당신이 술을 마셔서 이 가정을 산산이 깨뜨리고 있어!

tear sth ↔ **down** *phr v* [T] to deliberately destroy a building ‖ 건물을 일부러 파괴시키다. …을 부수다: *My old school was torn down last year.* 나의 모교는 작년에 철거되었다.

tear into sb/sth *phr v* [T] INFORMAL to strongly criticize someone or something ‖ 어떤 사람이나 사물을 강하게 비판하다. …을 욕하다. 공격하다: *Then he started tearing into her for spending money.* 그 때 그는 그녀가 돈을 쓴 것에 대해 강하게 비난하기 시작했다.

tear sth ↔ **up** *phr v* [T] to destroy something, especially paper, by tearing it into a lot of little pieces ‖ 특히 종이를 많은 작은 조각으로 찢어서 파기하다. 갈기갈기 찢어 버리다[없애다]: *He tore up all of Linda's old letters.* 그는 린다의 옛 편지들을 모두 찢어 없애버렸다.

tear² /tɪr/ *n* a drop of liquid that flows from your eyes when you cry ‖ 울 때 눈에서 흘러나오는 액체 방울. 눈물: *She ran away with tears in her eyes.* 그녀는 눈물을 흘리며 뛰쳐 나갔다. / *Suddenly Brian burst into tears.* (=started crying) 갑자기 브라이언은 울음을 터뜨렸다.

tear³ /tɛr/ *n* a hole in a piece of paper, cloth etc. where it has been torn ‖ 종이·천 조각 등의 찢어진 구멍. 째진 틈. 찢어진 곳. 해진 데

tear·drop /'tɪrdrɑp/ *n* a single tear ‖ 한 방울의 눈물

tease¹ /tiz/ *v* **1** [I, T] to try to embarrass or annoy someone by making jokes about him/her ‖ 남에 대해서 농담을 해 당황하게 하거나 괴롭히려 하다. 놀려 화나게 하다: *Don't cry. I was just teasing.* 울지 마. 그저 놀렸을 뿐이었

어. / *Johnny, stop teasing your sister!* 쟈니, 네 누이를 그만 놀려! **2** [T] to comb your hair in the wrong direction so that it looks thicker ‖ 머리카락이 보다 숱이 많게 보이도록 (머리가 자라는) 역(逆)방향으로 머리를 빗다. 머리칼을 곤두세우다

tease² *n* someone who enjoys teasing (TEASE) people ‖ 남을 놀리는 것을 즐기는 사람

tea·spoon /'tispun/ *n* **1** a small spoon used for STIRing a cup of tea or coffee ‖ 한 잔의 차나 커피를 휘젓는 데 사용되는 작은 숟가락. 찻숟가락 **2** a special spoon used for measuring food ‖ 음식의 양을 재는 데 사용되는 특별한 스푼. 숟가락 **3** also **teaspoonful** the amount this spoon can hold ‖ 이 숟가락이 담을 수 있는 양. 한 스푼 분량

teat /tit/ *n* a NIPPLE on a female animal ‖ 암컷 동물의 젖꼭지

tech·ni·cal /'tɛknɪkəl/ *adj* **1** relating to the practical skills, knowledge, and methods used in science or industry ‖ 과학이나 산업에서 사용되는 실용적인 기술·지식·방법과 관련된. 기술상의. 공업 기술의. 응용과학의: *technical experts* 기술 전문가 / *technical training* 기술 훈련 **2** relating to a particular subject or profession ‖ 특정한 주제나 직업과 관련된. 전문적인: *a legal document full of technical terms* 전문 용어로 가득한 법률 문서

tech·ni·cal·i·ties /,tɛknɪ'kæləṭiz/ *n* [plural] the details of a system or process that you need special knowledge to understand ‖ 이해하기 위해 특별한 지식이 필요한 상세한 체계나 과정. 전문적인 문제[사항, 표현]

tech·ni·cal·i·ty /,tɛknɪ'kæləṭi/ *n* a small detail in a law or rule ‖ 법률이나 규칙에 있어서의 세세한 사항. 전문적 성질. 전문적 용어의 사용

tech·ni·cal·ly /'tɛknɪkli/ *adv* according to the exact details of a rule or law ‖ 아주 상세한 규칙이나 법률에 따라. 기술적[전문적]으로(는). 엄밀히 말하면: *Technically, he's responsible for fixing all the damage.* 엄밀히 말하면 그가 모든 피해를 해결할 책임이 있다.

tech·ni·cian /tɛk'nɪʃən/ *n* a trained worker who does a job relating to science or industry ‖ 과학이나 산업에 관련된 일을 하는 숙련된 인력. 기술자. 전문가: *a lab technician* 실험실 기술자

tech·nique /tɛk'nik/ *n* [C, U] a special method of doing something ‖ 어떤 것을 하는 특별한 방법. 기법. 수법. 테크닉: *new techniques for teaching English* 영

어를 가르치는 새로운 기법 / *the artist's talent and technique* 그 예술가의 재능과 기량

tech·nol·o·gy /tɛk'nɑlədʒi/ *n* [C, U] a combination of all the knowledge, equipment, methods etc. that is used in scientific or industrial work ‖ 과학적이거나 산업적인 일에 쓰이는 모든 지식·장비·방법 등의 조합(된 것). 과학[공업] 기술. 테크놀러지: *medical technology* 의학 기술 / *developing new technologies* 새로운 과학 기술을 개발하기 **–technological** /,tɛknə'lɑdʒɪkəl/ *adj*

ted·dy bear /'tɛdi ,bɛr/ *n* a soft toy shaped like a bear ‖ 곰 같은 모양의 폭신폭신한 장난감. 테디 베어

te·di·ous /'tidiəs/ *adj* boring, and continuing for a long time ‖ 지루하고 장기간 계속되는. 싫증나는. 장황한: *a tedious discussion* 지루한 토론

te·di·um /'tidiəm/ *n* [U] the quality of being TEDIOUS ‖ 지루한 특성. 권태. 단조로움

tee /ti/ *n* a small object used for holding a GOLF ball, or the raised area from which you hit the ball ‖ 골프공을 올려놓는 데 사용되는 작은 물체, 또는 골프공을 치는 높게 돋아진 구역. 공을 올려놓는 대. 첫 타구 때 공을 티업하는 마운드

teem /tim/ *v*

teem with sth *phr v* [T] to be full of people or animals that are all moving around ‖ 이리저리 움직이고 있는 사람들이나 동물들로 가득 차다. 많이 있다. 풍부하다: *lakes teeming with fish* 물고기로 가득한 호수 **–teeming** *adj*: *the teeming streets of Cairo* 카이로의 북적북적대는 거리

teen /tin/ *n* INFORMAL ⇨ TEENAGER **–teen** *adj*

teen·age /'tineɪdʒ/ *adj* aged between 13 and 19, or relating to someone who is ‖ 13세에서 19세 사이의 나이의, 또는 이러한 사람과 관련된. 틴에이저[십대]의: *our teenage son* 십대인 우리 아들 ✗DON'T SAY "our son is teenage."✗ "our son is teenage"라고는 하지 않는다.

teen·ag·er /'ti,neɪdʒɚ/ *n* someone who is between 13 and 19 years old ‖ 13세에서 19세 사이의 사람. 틴에이저. 십대

teens /tinz/ *n* [plural] the period in your life when you are aged between 13 and 19 ‖ 일생중의 13세에서 19세 사이의 기간: *She got married when she was still in her teens.* 그녀는 아직 10대였을 때 결혼했다.

tee·ny /'tini/, **teeny-weeny** /,tini 'wini/ *adj* SPOKEN very small; TINY ‖ 매

우 작은. 조그마한; 㽞 tiny

tee shirt /'. . ./ *n* ⇨ T-SHIRT

tee·ter /'tiṭə/ *v* [I] **1** to move or stand in an unsteady way ‖ 불안정하게 움직이거나 서다. 비틀비틀 움직이다[서있다]. 기우뚱거리다: *teetering in high-heeled shoes* 하이힐을 신고 비틀비틀 걷기 **2 be teetering on the brink/edge of** to be very likely to become involved in a dangerous situation ‖ 위험한 상황에 빠질 가능성이 아주 농후하다. 거의 …이 일어나려 하고 있다. 위험한 지경에 달해 있다: *a country teetering on the brink of revolution* 혁명 발발 직전의 나라

teeth /tiθ/ *n* the plural of TOOTH ‖ tooth 의 복수형

teethe /tið/ *v* [I] if a baby is teething, his/her first teeth are growing ‖ 어린아이의 이빨이 나기 시작하다. 젖니가 나다

tee·to·tal·er /ˌti'toʊṭlə/ *n* someone who never drinks alcohol ‖ 절대 술을 마시지 않는 사람. 절대 금주주의자

Tef·lon /'tɛflɑn/ *n* [U] TRADEMARK a special material that stops things from sticking to it, often used in making pans ‖ 종종 냄비를 만드는 데 사용되는, 음식이 눌러 붙는 것을 막는 특별한 물질. 테플론

tel·e·com·mu·ni·ca·tions /ˌtɛləkəˌmyunə'keɪʃənz/ *n* [U] the process or business of sending and receiving messages by telephone, radio, SATELLITE etc. ‖ 전화·라디오·인공위성 등으로 메시지를 보내고 받는 과정이나 사업. 원격 통신(업)

tel·e·com·mut·er /'tɛləkəˌmyuṭə/ *n* someone who works at home instead of in an office, but uses the telephone and a computer to communicate with the people s/he works with ‖ 사무실 대신에 집에서 일하지만 같이 일하는 사람들과 의사소통을 하기 위해 전화나 컴퓨터를 사용하는 사람. 재택 근무자

tel·e·con·fer·ence¹ /'tɛləˌkɑnfrəns/ *n* a business meeting in which people in different places communicate by telephone, television etc. ‖ 서로 다른 지역의 사람들이 전화·텔레비전 등으로 통신하는 업무상 회의. 원격(전화[화상])회의

tel·e·gram /'tɛləˌgræm/ *n* a message sent by TELEGRAPH ‖ 전신 장치에 의해 보내진 메시지. 전보

tel·e·graph /'tɛləˌgræf/ *n* [C, U] a method of sending messages using electrical signals, or the equipment used for sending these messages ‖ 전기적인 신호를 사용하여 메시지를 보내는 방법, 또는 이러한 메시지를 보내는 데 쓰이

는 장비. 전신. 전보. 전신기

te·lep·a·thy /tə'lɛpəθi/ *n* [U] the ability to communicate thoughts directly to someone else's mind without speaking, writing, or using signs ‖ 말[글, 신호]을 사용하지 않고 다른 사람의 마음에 직접적으로 생각을 전달하는 능력. 텔레파시. 정신 감응 능력

tel·e·phone¹ /'tɛləˌfoʊn/ *n* ⇨ PHONE¹

telephone² *v* [I, T] ⇨ PHONE²

USAGE NOTE telephone, phone, call, and other words used for telephoning

Use each of these words as a verb. **Call** is the most common, and **telephone** is not very common: *I think I'll call Pedro. / Chris phoned to say he'd be late.* A **call**, **phone call**, or **telephone call** is the action of telephoning: *Give me a call later in the week. / Kerry, there's a phone call for you.* To make a telephone call, you find the **phone number** in the **telephone/phone book.** Then you **dial** the number. If you need help with a call, you dial the **operator.** The phone will **ring**, and if the person is there, s/he will **answer** by **picking up the receiver.** If s/he is not there, you can leave a message on the **answering machine.** If s/he is already talking on the phone, the **line** will be **busy.** When you finish talking, you **hang up.** To make a telephone call in a public place, you can go to a **telephone/phone booth.**

이 단어들은 각기 동사로 쓰인다. **call** 이 가장 흔하게 쓰이고 **telephone**은 그리 자주 쓰이지 않는다: 나는 페드로에게 전화할 생각이다. / 크리스는 늦겠다고 전화했다. **call, phone call, telephone call**은 전화를 하는 행동을 가리킨다: 주중 나중에 전화해라. / 케리, 전화 받아. 전화를 걸기 위해 전화번호부에서 전화번호를 찾고 그 다음 전화번호를 누른다. 만일 전화 거는 데 도움이 필요하면 전화 교환원을 호출한다. 전화벨이 울리고 그곳에 사람이 있으면 수화기를 들어 대답할 것이다. 만일 그곳에 사람이 없으면 전화 자동 응답기에다 메시지를 남길 수 있다. 만일 통화하고 싶은 사람이 이미 통화를 하고 있으면 통화 중이 된다. 통화가 끝났을 때는 전화를 끊는다. 공공장소에서 전화를 걸기 위해서는 공중 전화 박스에 갈 수 있다.

telephone bank·ing /'... ,../ *n* a service provided by banks so that people can find out information about their bank account, pay bills etc by telephone rather than by going to a bank ‖ 사람들이 은행에 가는 대신에 전화로 은행 계좌·요금 결제 등에 대한 정보를 알 수 있게 은행이 제공하는 서비스. 텔레뱅킹

tel·e·pho·to lens /,tɛlə,foʊtoʊ 'lɛnz/ *n* a camera LENS that makes things that are far away seem closer and larger ‖ 멀리 있는 것을 더 가깝고 더 크게 보이게 하는 카메라 렌즈. 망원 렌즈

tel·e·scope¹ /'tɛlə,skoʊp/ *n* a piece of equipment shaped like a tube, used for making things that are far away seem closer and larger so you can look at them ‖ 보다 더 가깝고 보다 더 크게 보이게 하여 멀리 있는 것을 볼 수 있게 사용되는 관처럼 생긴 기기. 망원경

telescope² *v* to make a series of events seem to happen in a shorter amount of time ‖ 일련의 사건들이 보다 짧은 시간 안에 일어난 것처럼 보이게 하다. …을 단축하다. 집약해서 보여주다

tel·e·scop·ic /,tɛlə'skɑpɪk/ *adj* relating to a TELESCOPE, or using a telescope ‖ 망원경과 관련된, 망원경을 사용한: *a telescopic lens* 망원 렌즈 / *telescopic observation* 망원경에 의한 관측

tel·e·thon /'tɛlə,θɑn/ *n* a special television program that continues for several hours and is intended to persuade people to give money to a CHARITY ‖ 몇 시간 동안 계속해서 자선 기금에 돈을 기부해 달라고 사람들을 설득할 의도의 특별 텔레비전 프로그램. 장시간 자선 기금 모금 방송

tel·e·vise /'tɛlə,vaɪz/ *v* [T] to broadcast something on television ‖ 어떤 것을 텔레비전에 방송하다: *Is the game going to be televised?* 그 경기는 텔레비전에서 방송될 예정이냐?

tel·e·vi·sion /'tɛlə,vɪʒən/ *n* **1** also **television set** /'.... ,./ a thing shaped like a box with a screen, on which you can see programs that are broadcast ‖ 방송되는 프로그램을 볼 수 있는, 화면을 가진 상자처럼 생긴 것. 텔레비전 수상기: *a big-screen television* 대형 화면 텔레비전 **2** [U] the programs that you can watch and listen to on a television ‖ 텔레비전에서 보고 들을 수 있는 프로그램: *He's been watching television all day.* 그는 하루 종일 텔레비전을 보고 있다. / *Guess who's being interviewed on television tonight?* 오늘밤 텔레비전에서

인터뷰하는 사람이 누군지 맞춰봐? **3** [U] the activity of making and broadcasting programs that can be seen and heard on a television ‖ 텔레비전에서 보고 들을 수 있는 프로그램을 만들고 방송하는 활동. 방송 분야[산업]: *a job in television* 텔레비전 방송 분야 일[직업]

tell /tɛl/ *v* **told, told, telling**

tell off

1 ▶INFORMATION 정보◀ [T] to give someone facts or information in speech or writing ‖ 남에게 사실이나 글로 정보를 주다. 말하다. 말해 주다. 이야기하다: *Tell Mark I said hi.* 마크에게 인사[안부] 전해줘. / *Did you tell Jennifer about the party?* 그 파티에 대해 제니퍼에게 말했니? / *Could you tell me how to make that cheesecake?* 저 치즈케이크를 만드는 방법을 내게 알려줄 수 있습니까? / *Dad used to tell us bedtime stories.* 아버지는 잠자기 전에 우리에게 옛날 이야기를 들려주곤 했다.

2 ▶RECOGNIZE 인식하다◀ [I, T] to be able to recognize or judge something correctly ‖ 어떤 것을 정확하게 알아보거나 판단할 수 있다. 분간하다. 식별하다: *I could tell it was a serious discussion.* 나는 그것이 심각한 토론이라는 것을 알 수 있었다. / *Carol puts the twins in different color booties so you can tell them apart.* 캐롤은 쌍둥이에게 서로 다른 색깔로 짠 유아용 털신발을 신겨서 너는 분간할 수 있을 것이다. / *Use plain yogurt instead of sour cream - you can't tell the difference.* 산패유(酸敗乳) 대신에 (향료가 들어가지 않은) 보통의 요구르트를 사용하십시오. 차이가 거의 없습니다. / *"How long will it take?" "It's hard to tell."* "얼마나 걸릴까?" "대답하기 어려워." ▶

3 ▶WHAT SB SHOULD DO 누군가가 해야 할 것◀ [T] to say that someone should or must do something ‖ 남이 어떤 것을 해야만 한다고 말하다. 명하다. 지시하다: *Tell her to put on her coat - it's cold.* 그녀에게 코트를 입어야 한다고 말해라. 날씨가 추워. / *Stop telling me what to do all the time!* 항상 내게 지시하는 것 좀 그만 둬!

4 tell yourself to encourage yourself to do something, or remind yourself of the facts of a situation that upsets or worries you ‖ 어떤 것을 하도록 스스로 용기를 북돋우다, 또는 자신의 감정을 상

하게 하거나 걱정스럽게 하는 상황에 대한 사실을 스스로에게 주지시킨다. 스스로 다 짐하다[상기시키다]: *I kept telling myself to relax.* 나는 계속해서 내 자신에게 긴장할 것 없다고 말했다.

5 ▶**SIGN** 신호◀ [T] to give information in a way other than using speech or writing ‖ 말이나 글 이외의 다른 방식으로 정보를 주다. …을 나타내다[표현하다]: *This red light tells you it's recording.* 이 빨간 불빛은 녹음되고 있다는 것을 알려 준다.

6 there's no telling what/how/ whether etc. used in order to say that it is impossible to know what will happen next ‖ 앞으로 무엇이 일어날지 알 수가 없다고 말하는 데에 쓰여. 무엇/어떻게/어느 쪽이 될지 모른다[알 수 없다]: *There's just no telling what kids will say next.* 아이들이 다음에 무엇을 말할지 전혀 알 수가 없다.

7 all told in total ‖ 합계해서. 통틀어: *All told, 40,000 airline workers have lost their jobs this year.* 올해 전부 4만 명의 항공사 노동자들이 일자리를 잃었다.

8 ▶**STH WRONG** 잘못한 것◀ [I, T] SPOKEN to tell someone in authority about something wrong that someone else has done ‖ 다른 사람이 한 잘못에 대해 책임자에게 말하다. 고자질하다: *Don't, Connie! I'm going to tell on you!* 하지 마, 코니! 내가 다 이를 거야!

SPOKEN PHRASES
---

9 (I'll) tell you what said in order to suggest something ‖ 어떤 것을 제안하는 데에 쓰여. 이봐 내 말 좀 들어보게. 내가 말해볼게: *Tell you what, call me on Friday, and we'll make plans then.* 이봐 내 말 좀 들어봐, 금요일에 나에게 전화해. 그런 다음 계획을 짜 보자고.

10 I tell you/I'm telling you/let me tell you said in order to emphasize something ‖ 어떤 것을 강조하는 데에 쓰여. 참으로. 정말이야. 말해 두건대: *I'm telling you, the gossip in this place is unbelievable!* 정말이야, 이 지역의 소문은 엄청 심해!

11 tell me about it said in order to say that you already know how bad something is ‖ 어떤 것이 얼마나 나쁜지 이미 알고 있다고 말하는 데에 쓰여. 그러게 말이야. 누가 아니래: *"She's so arrogant!" "Yeah, tell me about it."* "그녀는 너무 오만해!" "그래, 누가 아니라니."

12 (I) told you (so) said when someone does something you have

warned him/her about, and it has a bad result ‖ 자신이 경고한 것을 남이 하고, 그것이 나쁜 결과를 낼 때에 쓰여. 그것 봐. 내가 뭐랬니. 내가 (이미) 말했지: *Told you. I knew that car was a bad buy.* 그것 봐. 내가 뭐랬니. 나는 그 차를 잘못 산 것을 알았어.

13 to tell (you) the truth said in order to emphasize that what you are saying is true ‖ 자신이 사실을 말하고 있다고 강조하거나 인정하는 데에 쓰여. 사실은. 사실대로 말하면: *I don't know how you cope, to tell you the truth.* 사실대로 말하면 나는 네가 어떻게 대처하는지 모르겠다.

14 you never can tell/you can never tell used in order to say that you can never be certain about what will happen in the future ‖ 장래에 무엇이 일어날지에 대해 결코 확신할 수 없다고 말하는 데에 쓰여. 글쎄 어떻게 될지 모른다. (외관만으로는) 알 수 없다: *They're not likely to win, but you never can tell.* 그들이 이길 것 같지는 않지만 글쎄 어떻게 될지는 모르는 일이지.

15 to hear sb tell it used in order to say that someone is giving his/her opinion of an event, and it may not be the exact truth ‖ 다른 사람이 어떤 사건에 대해 의견을 제시하면서 그것이 정확하게 사실일지는 모른다고 말하는 데에 쓰여. …의 말대로라면. …의 말을 빌리자면: *Well, to hear her tell it, it was all Monica's fault.* 글쎄, 그녀의 말을 빌리자면 그것은 모두 모니카의 실수라고 하던데.

—see usage note at SAY

tell sb ↔ **off** *phr v* [T] to talk angrily to someone when s/he has done something wrong ‖ 남이 나쁜 행동을 했을 때 그 사람에게 화를 내며 말하다. (남을) …의 일로 꾸짖다. 야단치다: *I'm going to get told off for being late.* 나는 지각한 것에 대해 꾸지람을 들을 것이다.

tell·er /'tɛlɚ/ *n* someone whose job is to receive money from, and pay out money to, the customers in a bank ‖ 은행에서 고객들로부터 돈을 받고 지불해 주는 일을 하는 사람. 금전 출납 계원. 은행원

tell·ing /'tɛlɪŋ/ *adj* **1** a remark that is telling shows what you really think, although you may not intend it to ‖ 비록 자신이 의도하지는 않았을지 모르지만 실제로 자신의 생각을 나타내는 말을 하는. (비밀·정체 등을) 밝히는. 나타내는 **2** having a great or important effect;

SIGNIFICANT ‖ 대단하고 중요한 영향력을 가진. 효험 있는. 효과적인. 감동시키는; ⑩ significant: *a telling argument* 설득력 있는 주장

tell·tale /ˈtɛlteɪl/ *adj* clearly showing something that is unpleasant or supposed to be secret ‖ 불쾌하거나 비밀로 지켜지기로 한 것을 명확하게 나타내는. 속사정[비밀]을 폭로하는[털어놓는]. …의 표시[증거]가 되는: *the telltale signs of drug addiction* 마약 중독의 명백한 표시

temp¹ /tɛmp/ *n* an office worker who is only employed for a limited period of time ‖ 단지 제한된 기간 동안만 고용된 사무직 근로자. 임시 고용인

temp² *v* [I] to work as a TEMP ‖ 임시 고용인으로 일하다: *Anne's temping until she can find another job.* 앤은 또 다른 일자리를 얻을 수 있을 때까지 임시직으로 일하고 있다.

tem·per¹ /ˈtɛmpɚ/ *n* **1** [C, U] a tendency to become suddenly angry ‖ 갑자기 화를 내는 경향. 기분. 기질. 성미: *John needs to learn to control his temper.* 존은 자기 성질을 억제할 줄 알아야 한다. **2** [singular, U] an uncontrolled feeling of anger that continues for a short time ‖ 짧은 시간 동안 지속되는 억누를 수 없는 화나는 감정. 화. 짜증. 노기: *You're certainly in a foul temper* (=angry) *this morning.* 너는 오늘 아침에 확실히 화가 난 모양이구나. **3 lose/keep your temper** to suddenly become very angry, or to stay calm ‖ 갑자기 매우 화를 내다, 또는 침착함을 유지하다. 화를 내다/침착성을 잃지 않다 **4 have a quick/hot/slow temper** to get angry very easily, or not very easily ‖ 매우 쉽게 화를 내다, 또는 그리 쉽게 화를 내지 않다. 성질이 급하다/불같다/원만하다 **5 -tempered** having a particular type of temper ‖ 특정한 유형의 기질을 가진. 기질[성미]이 …인: *a bad-tempered old man* 성미가 고약한 노인 / *a good-tempered child* (=a happy one) 성품이 좋은 아이

temper² *v* [T] **1** to make metal harder by heating it and then making it cold ‖ 열을 가하고 나서 냉각시켜 금속을 더 단단하게 만들다. 금속을 강화하다. 담금질하다: *tempered steel* 담금질한 강철 **2** FORMAL to make something less difficult or severe ‖ 어떤 것을 덜 어렵거나 덜 심하게 하다. …을 부드럽게 하다. 누그러뜨리다. 진정시키다. 억누르다: *criticism tempered with humor* 유머로 부드럽게 한 비평

tem·per·a·ment /ˈtɛmprəmənt/ *n* [C, U] the part of your character that makes you likely to be happy, angry, sad etc. ‖ 행복하게·화나게·슬프게 할 수도 있는 사람의 특성 부분. 기질. 성질. 성미. 성품: *a baby with a calm temperament* 조용한 성미를 가진 아기

tem·per·a·men·tal /ˌtɛmprəˈmɛntl/ *adj* **1** tending to get upset, excited, or angry very easily ‖ 매우 쉽게 기분이 상하는[흥분하는, 화내는] 경향이 있는. 신경질적인. 까다로운. 변덕스러운 **2** a temperamental machine does not always work correctly ‖ 기계가 항상 제대로 작동하지는 않는. 고장이 잘 나는. 민감한

tem·per·ance /ˈtɛmprəns/ *n* [U] the practice of never drinking alcohol ‖ 절대로 술을 마시지 않음. 금주

tem·per·ate /ˈtɛmprɪt/ *adj* weather or a part of the world that is temperate is never very hot or very cold ‖ 날씨나 지역이 결코 매우 덥거나 춥지 않은. 온화한 기후의. 온대의: *a temperate climate* 온대 기후

tem·per·a·ture /ˈtɛmprətʃɚ/ *n* **1** [C, U] how hot or cold something is ‖ 어떤 것이 얼마나 뜨거운지 또는 차가운지를 나타내는 것. 온도. 기온: *Water freezes at a temperature of 32°F.* 물은 화씨 32도의 온도에서 언다. / *a gradual rise/fall in temperature* 온도의 점진적인 상승[하강] / *Store this product at room temperature.* (=the normal temperature in a room) 이 제품은 실온에서 보관하시오. **2 sb's temperature** the temperature of your body, used as a measure of whether you are sick or not ‖ 사람이 아픈지 아프지 않은지의 측정치로 사용되는 신체의 온도. 체온. 발열(상태): *It's time to take your temperature.* (=measure it) 체온 잴 시간입니다. / *I think I have a temperature.* (=have one that is higher than normal) 나는 몸에 열이 좀 있는 것 같아.

USAGE NOTE temperature

Many words are used in order to describe the temperature of the air or of a substance. Air or a substance that is **cold** has a low temperature: *a nice cold drink* / *It's too cold to go swimming.* Air or a substance that is **cool** has a low temperature but is not **cold**: *cool breezes* / *Serve the Beaujolais cool.* Air or a substance that is **warm** is pleasant: *It's warm enough outside to go to the beach.* / *The water in the pool is nice and warm.* Air or a substance that is **hot** has a high temperature: *The coffee's still too hot to drink.* / *It's too hot to sit in the sun.* Some words are used only to describe the temperature of air. **Bitter** and **freezing** mean "extremely cold and unpleasant": *a bitter wind* / *It's freezing in here!* Air that is **chilly** is cold enough to make you feel uncomfortable. A day that is **humid** or **muggy** makes you feel uncomfortable because the air feels wet, heavy, and warm. Weather that is **sweltering** is very hot and makes you feel wet and uncomfortable. A room that is **stifling** is very hot and is difficult to breathe in. Some words are used only to describe substances. Water or a drink that is **tepid** is only slightly warm in a way that is unpleasant. Water or food that is **lukewarm** is slightly warm and not as warm or cold as it should be. Water or a substance that is **boiling** is so hot that it BUBBLES.

많은 단어들이 대기나 물질의 온도를 설명하는 데 사용된다. 차가운(**cold**) 대기나 물질은 온도가 낮다: 알맞게 차가운 음료수 / 수영하기에는 너무 춥다. 시원한(**cool**) 대기나 물질은 낮은 온도를 가지고 있지만 차갑지는 않다: 시원한 바람. / 보졸레 포도주는 차게 해서 내놓으세요. 따뜻한(**warm**) 대기나 물질은 기분이 좋다: 바깥 기온이 해변에 나가기에 충분할 만큼 따뜻하다. / 수영장의 물이 알맞게 따뜻하다. 뜨거운(**hot**) 대기나 물질은 높은 온도를 가지고 있다: 커피는 아직도 마시기에 너무 뜨겁다. / 너무 뜨거워서 햇볕 속에 앉아 있을 수가 없다. 어떤 단어들은 단지 대기의 온도만을 설명하는 데 사용된다. **bitter**와 **freezing**은 "몹시 춥고 싫음"을 의미한다: 살을 에는 바람 / 이곳은 추워 죽겠어! 싸늘한(**chilly**) 대기는 불편하게 느낄 정도로 추운 것을 나타낸다. **humid** 또는 **muggy**한 날은 대기가 습하고 후텁지근하며 더워서 불편하게 느끼게 한다. **sweltering**한 날씨는 매우 덥고 습해서 기분 나쁘게 느끼게 한다. **stifling**한 방은 매우 덥고 숨쉬기 어렵다. 어떤 단어들은 단지 물질을 설명하기 위해 사용된다. **tepid**한 물이나 마실 것은 불쾌할 정도로 단지 약간 미지근하다. **lukewarm**한 물이나 음식은 약간 미

지근하고 (맛을 제대로 내기 위해) 마땅 할 만큼 충분히 따뜻하거나 차갑지 않다. **boiling**한 물이나 물질은 아주 뜨거워 펄펄 끓는 것을 의미한다.

tem·pest /ˈtɛmpɪst/ *n* LITERARY a violent storm ‖ 격심한 폭풍

tem·pes·tu·ous /tɛmˈpɛstʃuəs/ *adj* always full of strong emotions ‖ 항상 격한 감정으로 차 있는. 격렬한. 난폭한: *a tempestuous relationship* 극히 사이가 안 좋은 관계

tem·plate /ˈtɛmpleɪt/ *n* **1** a sheet of paper, plastic, or metal in a special shape, used in order to help you cut other materials in the same shape ‖ 다른 소재를 같은 모양으로 자르도록 도와주는 데 쓰이는 특별한 형태의 종이[플라스틱, 금속]의 얇은 판. 형판(型板) **2** a system for arranging information on a computer screen ‖ 컴퓨터 화면상에서 정보를 배열하기 위한 시스템. 템플리트. 보기판

tem·ple /ˈtɛmpəl/ *n* **1** a building where people go to WORSHIP in some religions ‖ 일부 종교에서 신자들이 예배를 보러 가는 건물. 신전. 사원 **2** the fairly flat area on the side of your head, between your eye and your ear ‖ 눈과 귀 사이의, 머리 옆면의 아주 평평한 곳. 관자놀이

tem·po /ˈtɛmpoʊ/ *n* **1** the speed at which music is played ‖ 음악이 연주되는 속도. 템포. 리듬. 박자 **2** the speed at which something happens; PACE ‖ 어떤 일이 일어나는 속도. 템포; ㈜ pace: *the tempo of city life* 도시 생활의 템포

tem·po·rar·y /ˈtɛmpəˌrɛri/ *adj* existing or happening for only a limited period of time ‖ 단지 제한된 시기 동안 존재하거나 일어나는. 일시적인. 임시의: *Linda is here on a temporary basis while Jane is away.* 린다는 제인이 떠나 있는 동안 임시로 여기에 와 있다. — **temporarily** /ˌtɛmpəˈrɛrəli/ *adv* : *The library is temporarily closed.* 그 도서관은 일시적으로 폐쇄된다. —compare PERMANENT[1]

tempt /tɛmpt/ *v* **1** [T] to make someone want to have or do something although it is wrong, bad, silly etc., by making it seem attractive ‖ 어떤 것이 잘못된·나쁜·어리석은 것이라 하더라도 매력적으로 보이게 해서 다른 사람이 가지거나 하고 싶어 하게 만들다. 유혹하다. 꾀어내다: *They're offering free gifts to tempt people to join.* 사람들이 가입할 마음이 들도록 그들은 공짜 선물을 제공하고 있다. / *Can I tempt you with another* *piece of cake?* 당신에게 케이크 한 조각 더 드려 볼까요[드시겠습니까]? **2 be tempted to do sth** to consider doing something that may not be a good idea ‖ 좋은 생각이 아닐지도 모르는 어떤 것을 하려고 생각하다. …할 기분이 나게 되다. 마음이 일다: *I'm tempted to just go out and buy a new car.* 나는 당장 밖에 나가 새 차를 사고 싶은 마음이 든다. **3 tempt fate** to do or say something that might end the good luck you have had ‖ 자신이 가진 행운을 끝장낼지 모르는 것을 하거나 말하다. 운명을 시험하다. 감히[외람되게] …하다 **- tempting** *adj*

temp·ta·tion /tɛmpˈteɪʃən/ *n* [C, U] **1** a strong desire to have or do something although it is wrong, bad, silly etc., because it seems attractive ‖ 비록 어떤 것이 잘못된·나쁜·어리석은 등의 것일지라도 매력적으로 보이기 때문에 가지거나 하려 하는 강한 욕구. 충동. 유혹: *I really had to resist the temptation to slap her.* 나는 정말 그녀의 뺨을 때리고 싶은 유혹을 참아야 했다. **2** something that makes you have this desire ‖ 이러한 욕구를 가지게 하는 것. 유혹하는 것: *Having candy in the house is a great temptation!* 집안에 사탕이 있다는 것은 큰 유혹이야!

ten[1] /tɛn/ *number* **1** 10 ‖ 10 **2** ten o'clock ‖ 10시: *I have a meeting at ten.* 나는 10시에 모임이 있다.

ten[2] *n* a piece of paper money worth $10 ‖ 10달러짜리 지폐

te·na·cious /təˈneɪʃəs/ *adj* very determined to do something, and unwilling to stop trying ‖ 어떤 것을 하는 데 매우 결연하고 그 시도를 멈추려고 하지 않는. 몹시 집착하는. 고집 센. 끈질긴 **- tenacity** /təˈnæsəti/ *n* [U]

ten·an·cy /ˈtɛnənsi/ *n* [C, U] the right to use a house, room etc. that is rented, or the period of time during which you have this right ‖ 빌린 집·방 등을 사용할 권리, 또는 이러한 권리를 가지는 동안의 기간. 차용[임차](기간)

ten·ant /ˈtɛnənt/ *n* someone who lives in a house, room etc. and pays rent to the person who owns it ‖ 소유주에게 임대료를 지불하고 어떤 집이나 방에 사는 사람. 임차인

tend /tɛnd/ *v* **1 tend to do sth** to be likely to do a particular thing ‖ 특정한 것을 할 것 같다. …하는 경향이 있다: *It tends to be very wet at this time of year.* 매년 이맘때 쯤에는 매우 습기가 많은[비가 많이 오는] 경향이 있다. **2 tend bar** to work as a BARTENDER ‖ 바텐더로서

일하다 **3** [T] also **tend to** to take care of someone or something ‖ 사람이나 사물을 돌보다. …에 신경을 쓰다: *Rescue teams were tending to the survivors.* 구조대는 생존자들을 돌보고 있었다.

tend·en·cy /ˈtɛndənsi/ *n* **1** a part of your character that makes you likely to develop, think, or behave in a particular way ‖ 사람을 특정하게 발현할 [생각할, 행동할] 것 같게 하는 성격. 성향. 버릇. 소질: *He has a tendency to talk too much.* 그는 말을 너무 많이 하는 경향이 있다. **2** a change or development that is happening, or an action that usually happens ‖ 현재 일어나고 있는 변화나 발전, 또는 일상적으로 일어나는 활동. 경향. 추세. 기미: *There's a tendency for men to marry younger women.* 남자들은 보통 자기보다 젊은 여성과 결혼하려는 경향이 있다.

ten·der[1] /ˈtɛndɚ/ *adj* **1** tender food is easy to cut and eat ‖ 음식이 자르고 먹기 쉬운. (음식이) 부드러운 **—opposite** TOUGH[1] **2** a tender part of your body is painful if someone touches it ‖ 신체 부위가 다른 사람이 만지면 아픈. (연)약한 민감한 **3** gentle in a way that shows love ‖ 사랑을 표현하듯이 정다운. 다정한: *a tender look* 다정한 표정 **4** LITERARY young and inexperienced ‖ 젊고 미숙한. 어린(나이의): *He lost his father at the tender age of seven.* 그는 일곱 살의 어린 나이에 아버지를 잃었다. **- tenderly** *adv* **- tenderness** *n* [U]

tend·er[2] *v* **1** [I] to make a formal offer to buy all or part of a company ‖ 한 회사 전체나 일부분을 사기 위해 공식적인 신청을 하다. 입찰하다 **2** [T] to make a formal offer to do something ‖ 어떤 것을 한다는 공식적인 의사 표시를 하다. 표명하다: *The senator has offered to tender his resignation.* (=officially say that he is going to leave his job) 그 상원의원은 사직서를 제출하겠다는 공식적인 의사 표시를 했다.

tend·er[3] *n* a formal offer to buy all or part of a company ‖ 한 회사의 전부나 일부를 사기 위한 공식적인 신청. 입찰 (신청)

ten·der·heart·ed /ˌtɛndɚˈhɑrtɪd/ *adj* very kind and gentle ‖ 매우 친절하고 온화한. 다정한

ten·der·ize /ˈtɛndəˌraɪz/ *v* [T] to make meat softer by preparing it in a special way ‖ 고기를 특별한 방식으로 준비해서 더 부드럽게 만들다. 연하게 하다

ten·don /ˈtɛndən/ *n* a thick strong

string-like part of your body that connects a muscle to a bone ‖ 뼈에다 근육을 접합시키는 두껍고 질긴 끈 같은 신체의 일부분. 힘줄

ten·dril /ˈtɛndrəl/ *n* a thin curling piece of something such as hair or the stem of a plant ‖ 머리털이나 식물 줄기 등의 가느다랗고 둥글게 말린 것. 덩굴 모양의 것

ten·e·ment /ˈtɛnəmənt/ *n* a large building divided into apartments, especially in a poor area of a city ‖ 특히 도시 빈민가의 여러 개의 집으로 나뉘어진 큰 건물. 싸구려 아파트. 공동 주택

ten·et /ˈtɛnɪt/ *n* a principle or belief ‖ 주의나 신조. 교리: *the tenets of Buddhism* 불교의 교리

ten·nis /ˈtɛnɪs/ *n* [U] a game in which two or four people use RACKETs to hit a ball to each other across a net ‖ 두 명 또는 4명의 사람들이 라켓을 사용해 서로 공을 쳐서 네트를 넘기는 경기. 테니스

tennis shoe /ˈ.. ˌ./ *n* a light shoe used for sports ‖ 운동하는 데 신는 가벼운 신발. 테니스화 —see picture at SHOE

ten·or /ˈtɛnɚ/ *n* [C, U] 1 a male singer with a high voice ‖ 높은 성부를 가진 남성 가수. 테너 2 **the tenor of** FORMAL the general meaning or quality of something ‖ 어떤 것의 일반적인 의미나 성질. 취지. 대의. 대요: *the tenor of the president's speech* 대통령 연설의 대요

tense[1] /tɛns/ *adj* 1 nervous and anxious ‖ 신경질적이고 걱정하는. 긴장한. 정신을 바싹 차린: *You seem really tense – what's wrong?* 너 정말 긴장하고 있는 것 같은데 무슨 일이야? / *a tense situation* 긴박한 상황 2 unable to relax because your muscles feel tight and stiff ‖ 근육이 팽팽하고 뻣뻣하게 느껴져 이완시킬 수 없는. 긴장된

tense[2], **tense up** *v* [I, T] to become tight and stiff, or to make your muscles do this ‖ 팽팽하고 뻣뻣하게 되다, 또는 근육이 이런 식으로 되게 하다. 근육 등이 [을] 긴장하다[시키다]

tense[3] *n* [C, U] TECHNICAL in grammar, one of the forms of a verb that shows actions or states in the past, now, or in the future. For example, "he studied" is in the past tense, "he studies" is in the present tense, and "he will study" is in the future tense ‖ 문법에서 과거[현재, 미래]의 행동이나 상태를 나타내는 동사의 한 형태. 시제. 예를 들어 "he studied"는 과거 시제이고, "he studies"는 현재 시제, "he will study"는 미래 시제이다

ten·sion /ˈtɛnʃən/ *n* 1 [C, U] the feeling that exists when people do not trust each other and may suddenly attack each other ‖ 사람들이 서로 믿지 않고 서로 갑자기 공격할지도 모를 때 존재하는 느낌. 긴장(관계[상태]): *efforts to calm racial tensions* 인종간의 긴장을 완화하려는 노력 2 [U] a nervous and anxious feeling ‖ 긴장되고 걱정되는 느낌. 불안: *The tension became unbearable and I wanted to scream.* 참을 수 없을 정도로 긴장되어 나는 비명을 지르고 싶었다. 3 [U] tightness or stiffness in a wire, rope, muscle etc. ‖ 전선·줄·근육 등의 팽팽하고 뻣뻣함. (인)장력: *You can increase the tension by turning this screw.* 이 나사를 돌려서 장력을 증가시킬 수 있습니다.

tent /tɛnt/ *n* a shelter that you can easily move, made of cloth or plastic and supported by poles and ropes ‖ 천이나 플라스틱으로 만들고 지주나 밧줄로 지탱되는, 쉽게 이동할 수 있는 주거. 텐트. 천막: *Where should we pitch the tent?* (=put up the tent) 어디에다 텐트를 쳐야 하죠?

ten·ta·cle /ˈtɛntəkəl/ *n* one of the long thin parts like arms of a creature such as an OCTOPUS ‖ 문어 등 생물의 팔 같은 길고 가는 부위의 하나. 촉수. 촉각 —see picture at OCTOPUS

ten·ta·tive /ˈtɛntətɪv/ *adj* 1 not definite or certain ‖ 명확하거나 확실하지 않은. 확정되지 않은. 시험[임시]적인: *tentative plans* 임시적인 계획 2 done without confidence ‖ 자신감없이 하는. 머뭇거리는. 결단을 못 내리는: *a tentative smile* 조심스러운 미소 – **tentatively** *adv*

tenth /tɛnθ/ *number* 10th ‖ 열 번째. 제 10

ten·u·ous /ˈtɛnyuəs/ *adj* **tenuous link/relationship etc.** a connection, relationship etc. that seems weak or not real ‖ 약하거나 실재하지 않는 것처럼 보이는 연관성·관계 등. 희박한[빈약한] 관련성/관계 – **tenuously** *adv*

ten·ure /ˈtɛnyɚ/ *n* [U] 1 the right to stay permanently in a teaching job at a university ‖ 대학에서 영구히 교직에 남을 수 있는 권리. (대학 교수의 정년까지의) 장기[종신] 재직권 2 FORMAL the period of time when someone has an important job ‖ 어떤 사람이 중요한 직무를 보유하고 있는 기간. 재직 기간: *the Mayor's tenure in office* 시장의 재직 기간

tepee, teepee /ˈtipi/ *n* a round tent used by some Native Americans ‖ 일부 북미 인디언에 의해 사용된 둥근 천막. 티피

tep·id /'tɛpɪd/ *adj* tepid liquid is slightly warm ‖ 액체가 약간 따뜻한. 미지근한

te·qui·la /tə'kilə/ *n* [U] a strong alcoholic drink made in Mexico ‖ 멕시코에서 제조된 도수가 센 술. 테킬라

ter·a·byte /'tɛrə,baɪt/ *n* a unit for measuring the amount of information a computer can store or use, equal to a TRILLION BYTE*s* ‖ 1조 바이트와 동일한, 컴퓨터가 저장하거나 사용 가능한 정보량을 측정하는 단위. 테라바이트

term¹ /tɘm/ *n* **1** a word or expression that has a particular meaning, especially in a technical or scientific subject ‖ 특히 기술적이거나 과학적인 분야에서 특정한 의미를 가진 단어나 표현. (학술) 용어. 전문어: *I don't understand these legal terms.* 나는 이들 법률적 용어들을 이해할 수가 없어. **2** a fixed or limited period of time, especially in politics or education ‖ 특히 정치나 교육에 있어서의 정해지거나 제한된 기간. 학기. 임기: *a four-year term of office* 4년의 임기 **3 in the long/short term** during a long or short period from now ‖ 지금으로부터 길거나 짧은 기간 동안에. 장기/단기간에: *The company's prospects look better in the long term.* 그 회사의 전망은 장기적으로는 더 나아 보인다. — see also TERMS

term² *v* [T] FORMAL to name or describe something in a particular way ‖ 어떤 것을 특정하게 명명하거나 설명하다. …으로 부르다. …이라고 (지)칭하다: *The meeting could hardly be termed a success.* 그 모임은 성공적이라고 도저히 말할 수 없었다.

ter·mi·nal¹ /'tɘmənəl/ *adj* **1** a terminal disease cannot be cured, and causes death ‖ 병이 치료될 수 없고 사망에 이르게 하는. (병이) 말기적인. 불치의. 죽음에 이르는: *terminal cancer* 말기 암 **2** **terminal decline/decay** the state of becoming worse and worse and never getting better ‖ 점점 더 나빠지고 결코 더 나아지지 않는 상태. 치명적인 쇠퇴[쇠망] –**terminally** *adv* : *terminally ill* 말기의 병인

terminal² *n* **1** a big building where you go to get onto planes, buses, or ships, or where goods are loaded on them ‖ 비행기[버스, 배]를 타러 가거나 그것들에 짐이 실리는 큰 건물. 터미널 **2** a computer KEYBOARD and screen connected to a computer that is somewhere else ‖ 다른 곳에 있는 컴퓨터에 연결된 키보드와 화면. 단말기[장치] **3** one of the points at which you can connect wires to an electrical CIRCUIT ‖ 전기 회로에 전선을 연결시킬 수 있는 한 지점. 단자(端子)

ter·mi·nate /'tɘmə,neɪt/ *v* [I, T] FORMAL **1** ⇨ END² **2** FORMAL to FIRE someone from his/her job ‖ 남을 그 직에서 해고하다 –**termination** /,tɘmə'neɪ-ʃən/ *n* [C, U]

ter·mi·nol·o·gy /,tɘmə'nɑlədʒi/ *n* [C, U] the technical words or expressions that are used in a particular subject ‖ 특정한 분야에서 사용되는 전문적인 단어나 표현. 술어. (전문) 용어: *scientific terminology* 과학 용어

ter·mi·nus /'tɘmənəs/ *n* the place at the end of a railroad or bus line ‖ 철도나 버스 노선의 끝에 있는 곳. 종점. 종착역

ter·mite /'tɘmaɪt/ *n* an insect that eats wood from trees and buildings ‖ 나무와 건물의 목재를 먹는 곤충. 흰개미

terms /tɘmz/ *n* [plural] **1** the parts of an agreement, contract etc. ‖ 협정이나 계약 등의 일부분. 조건. 조항: *Sign here to say you agree to the terms and conditions.* 당신이 그 조항과 조건에 동의하는 것을 표시하기 위해 여기에 서명하시오. **2 in terms of** used when explaining or discussing how a particular fact or event is related to something ‖ 특정한 사실이나 사건이 어떤 것과 어떻게 관련되어 있는지 설명하거나 논할 때에 쓰여. …의 점[관점, 각도, 기준]에서. …에 관하여. …에 기초하여: *In terms of sales, the book hasn't been very successful.* 매출이라는 점에서 보면 그 책은 그리 성공적이지 못했다. **3 in financial/artistic etc. terms** if you describe or consider something in financial etc. terms, you are thinking of it in a financial etc. way ‖ 어떤 것을 금전적인 방식 등으로 생각하거나 고려하여. 재정적/예술적 관점에서: *A million years isn't a very long time in geological terms.* 백만 년은 지질학적인 관점에서 보면 그리 긴 시간은 아니다. **4 in no uncertain terms** in a clear and usually angry way ‖ 분명하고 보통 화내는 식으로. 직설적[노골적]으로. 대놓고. 분명하게: *He told me in no uncertain terms not to come back.* 그는 나에게 다시 오지 말라고 단호하게 말했다. **5 be on good/bad/friendly etc. terms** to have a particular type of relationship with someone ‖ 남과 특정한 형태의 관계를 가지다. 사이가 좋다/사이가 나쁘다/우호적이다: *He hasn't been on good terms with his father for years.* 그는 오랫동안 자기 아버지와 사이가 좋지 않았다. **6 be on speaking terms** to be friendly with someone and able to talk to him/her ‖ 남과 친하고 말을 나눌 수 있는 사이이다. 대화 관계를 유지하다: *We're barely on speaking terms now.* 우리는 지금 거의 말도 나누지 않는 사이이다. **7 come to terms with** to understand and deal with a difficult problem or situation ‖ 어려운 문제나 상황을 이해하고 해결하다. …을 인정하다[받아들이다]. …을 체념하다: *It was hard to come to terms with Marie's death.* 마리의 죽음을 받아들이기는 어려웠다.

ter·race /'tɛrɪs/ *n* **1** a flat outdoor area next to a building or on a roof, where you can eat, relax etc. ‖ 음식을 먹거나 휴식을 취하는, 건물이나 지붕에 이어져 있는 평평한 옥외 공간. 테라스 **2** a flat area cut out of the side of a hill, often used for growing crops on ‖ 종종 곡물을 재배하는 데 사용되는 언덕의 측면을 잘라낸 평평한 지역. 단지(段地). 계단식 대지

ter·ra·cot·ta /,tɛrə'katə/ *n* [U] hard red-brown baked clay ‖ 딱딱한 적갈색의 구운 점토. 테라코타: *a terracotta pot* 질그릇 단지

ter·rain /tə'reɪn/ *n* [C, U] land of a particular type ‖ 특정한 형태의 땅. 지형. 지세: *rocky/hilly/rough terrain* 암벽[언덕이 많은, 울퉁불퉁한] 지대

ter·res·tri·al /tə'rɛstriəl/ *adj* TECHNICAL **1** relating to the earth rather than to the moon, stars, or other PLANETs ‖ 달[항성, 다른 행성]보다는 지구에 관련된. 지구의 **2** living on or relating to land rather than water ‖ 물보다는 뭍에 살거나 뭍과 관련된. 육지의. 육생[육서]의

ter·ri·ble /'tɛrəbəl/ *adj* **1** extremely severe and causing harm or damage ‖ 매우 극심하고 상해나 손상을 일으키는. 가혹한. 혹독한: *a terrible accident* 끔찍한 사고 **2** INFORMAL very bad or unpleasant ‖ 매우 나쁘거나 불쾌한. 형편없는. 지독한: *a terrible movie* 형편없는 영화 **3** making you feel afraid or shocked ‖ 두려움이나 충격을 느끼게 하는. 무서운. 무시무시한: *a terrible noise* 무시무시한 소리

ter·ri·bly /'tɛrəbli/ *adv* **1** very badly ‖ 매우 나쁘게. 형편없게: *We played terribly, and that's why we lost.* 우리는 형편없이 경기를 했고 그것이 패배한 이유이다. **2** extremely ‖ 지독하게. 몹시. 매우: *I'm terribly sorry, but the answer is no.* 대단히 죄송하지만 대답은 노이다.

ter·ri·er /'tɛriə/ *n* a small active type of dog ‖ 작고 활동적인 종의 개. 테리어

ter·rif·ic /tə'rɪfɪk/ *adj* INFORMAL **1** very good or enjoyable ‖ 매우 좋거나 즐거운.

훌륭한. 굉장한: *a terrific party* 훌륭한 파티 **2** very large in size or degree ‖ 크기나 정도에서 매우 큰. 대단한. 엄청난: *It's a terrific honor to win this award.* 이 상을 수상하는 것은 대단한 영광입니다. **– terrifically** *adv*

ter·ri·fy /'tɛrə,faɪ/ *v* [T] to make someone extremely afraid ‖ 남을 매우 두려워하게 하다. 겁나게 하다. 위협하다: *The thought of giving a speech terrified her.* 그녀는 연설한다는 생각에 겁이 났다. **– terrifying** *adj*

ter·ri·to·ri·al /,tɛrə'tɔriəl/ *adj* **1** relating to land that is owned or controlled by a particular country, ruler etc. ‖ 특정한 나라·통치자 등에 의해 소유되거나 지배되는 땅과 관련된. 영토[영역]의[에 관한]: *US territorial waters* 미국 영해 **2** territorial animals or people closely guard the place they consider to be their own ‖ 동물이나 사람이 자기들의 소유라고 생각되는 곳을 엄격히 지키는. 영역성을 가진

ter·ri·to·ry /'tɛrə,tɔri/ *n* **1** [C, U] land that is owned or controlled by a particular country, ruler etc. ‖ 특정한 나라·지배자 등에 의해 소유되거나 지배되는 땅. 영토: *Canadian territory* 캐나다령 **2** [U] land of a particular type ‖ 특정한 형태의 땅. 지역. 지방: *unexplored territory* 미 탐사지 **3** [C, U] the area that an animal, person, or group considers to be its own ‖ 동물·사람·집단이 자기의 소유라고 생각하는 땅. 영역. 세력권 **4** [C, U] an area of business for which someone is responsible ‖ 사람이 책임을 져야 할 사업상의 지역. 담당[영업] 구역: *the Chicago sales territory* 시카고의 판매 구역 **5 come/go with the territory** to be a natural and accepted part of a particular job, situation, place etc. ‖ 특정한 직업·상황·장소 등의 자연스럽고 인정되는 부분이다. …이 속성이다. …하는 것이 당연하다: *You'd better get used to criticism from the press – it comes with the territory.* 당신은 언론의 비판에 익숙해지는 게 좋아. 비판하는 것이 언론의 직무야.

ter·ror /'tɛrə/ *n* **1** [C, U] a feeling of extreme fear, or something that causes this ‖ 극도의 공포감, 또는 이것을 일으키는 것. 두려움. 공포의 대상: *She ran away in terror.* 그녀는 두려워서 도망쳤다. / *the terrors of war* 전쟁의 공포 **2** INFORMAL a very annoying person, especially a child ‖ 매우 귀찮게 괴롭히는 사람, 특히 아이. 골치 아픈 사람[아이]. 장난꾸러기

ter·ror·ism /'tɛrə,rɪzəm/ n [U] the use of violence to obtain political demands ‖ 정치적인 요구를 얻어내기 위한 폭력 사용. 테러 행위. 테러리즘 **– terrorist** n **– terrorist** adj : terrorist bombings 테러범의 폭탄 폭파

ter·ror·ize /'tɛrə,raɪz/ v [T] to deliberately frighten people by threatening to harm them, especially so they will do what you want ‖ 특히 자신이 원하는 것을 사람들이 하도록, 위해를 입히겠다고 위협해서 일부러 사람들을 두려움에 떨게 하다. …을 무서워하게 하다. 위협하다[해서 …하게 하다]

ter·ry·cloth /'tɛri,klɔθ/ n [U] thick cotton cloth used for making TOWELs ‖ 수건을 만드는 데 사용되는 두꺼운 무명천. 테리 직물

terse /tɜs/ adj a terse reply, message etc. uses very few words and often shows that you are annoyed ‖ 답변·메시지 등이 매우 적은 단어만 사용하며 종종 짜증나 있음을 보여 주는. 간단명료한. 간결한. 쌀쌀맞은 **– tersely** adv

test¹ /tɛst/ n **1** a set of questions or exercises to measure someone's skill, ability, or knowledge ‖ 사람의 기술[능력, 지식]을 가늠하기 위한 일련의 질문이나 연습 문제. 테스트. 시험: I have a history test tomorrow. 나는 내일 역사 시험을 친다. / Paul passed/failed his driver's test the first time. 폴은 첫 번째에 운전면허 시험을 통과했다[떨어졌다]. / All students must take a placement test. 모든 학생들은 배치고사를 봐야 한다. ✗DON'T SAY "make a test." SAY "take a test."✗ "make a test"라고 하지 않고 "take a test"라고 한다. **2** the process of examining something carefully in order to see what it is like or to find out something ‖ 어떤 것의 상태를 알아내거나 어떤 것을 찾아내기 위해 사물을 주의 깊게 검사하는 과정. 테스트. 시험. 검사: They're going to run/do some tests on my blood. 그들은 내 혈액에 몇 가지 검사를 실시할 예정이다. **3** a situation in which the qualities of something are clearly shown ‖ 사물의 특성이 명백히 나타나는 상황. 시금석. 척도: Living together will really put their relationship to the test. (=find out how good it is) 함께 사는 것이 서로의 관계가 얼마나 좋은지 알아보는 실제적 시금석이 된다. / Today's race is a real test of skill. 오늘의 경주가 기술의 실제적인 시험 무대이다.

test² v [T] **1** to measure someone's skill, ability, or knowledge, using a test ‖ 시험

을 이용해 사람의 기술[능력, 지식]을 측정하다. …을 시험[검사, 테스트]하다: We're being tested on grammar tomorrow. 우리는 내일 문법 시험을 치르게 된다. **2** to examine or use something in order to find out what it is like or to find out something ‖ 어떤 것의 상태를 알아보거나 어떤 것을 찾아내기 위해 사물을 검사하거나 사용하다. 시험[실험]하다: testing nuclear weapons 핵무기를 실험하기 **3** to show how good or strong something is ‖ 무엇이 얼마나 좋은지 또는 강한지 나타내다. …을 시험하다. …의 시금석이 되다: The next six months will test your powers of leadership. 앞으로의 6개월 동안이 당신의 지도력을 시험하는 기간이 될 것이다.

tes·ta·ment /'tɛstəmənt/ n FORMAL **1** a **testament to sth** something that shows or proves something else very clearly ‖ 다른 것을 매우 명확하게 보이거나 증명하는 것. 증거. 입증: His latest record is a testament to his growing musical abilities. 그의 최근의 음반은 그의 음악적 재능이 성장하고 있음을 입증하는 것이다. **2** ⇨ WILL² —see also NEW TESTAMENT, OLD TESTAMENT

test ban /'. ./ n an agreement between countries to stop testing NUCLEAR WEAPONs ‖ 핵무기 실험을 막기 위한 나라들간의 협정. 핵실험 금지 협정

test case /'. ./ n a legal case that makes a particular principle clear and is used as a standard for similar cases ‖ 특정한 원칙을 명확하게 만들며 유사한 사건들의 기준으로 사용되는 법률 사건. 선례적 사건

test drive /'. ./ n an occasion when you drive a car and decide if you want to buy it ‖ 차를 한 번 타보고 그것을 살지 안 살지 결정할 때의 경우. 시승. 시운전 **– test-drive** v [T]

tes·ti·cle /'tɛstɪkəl/ n, plural **testicles** or **testes** /'tɛstiz/ one of the two round organs below a man's PENIS that produce SPERM ‖ 정자를 생산하며 내는 남성의 성기 아래에 있는 두 개의 둥근 기관 중 하나. 고환

tes·ti·fy /'tɛstə,faɪ/ v [I, T] to make a formal statement of what is true, especially in a court of law ‖ 특히 법정에서 무엇이 사실인지 공식적인 진술을 하다. 증언하다: Two men testified that they saw you there. 2명의 남자가 거기서 당신을 보았다고 증언했어요. / You can't make me testify against my husband. 당신은 내게 내 남편에게 불리한 증언을 하게 할 수 없어요.

tes·ti·mo·ni·al /ˌtɛstəˈmoʊniəl/ *n* something that is given or said to someone to show thanks or admiration ‖ 감사나 존경을 표시하기 위해 남에게 주거나 말하는 것. 표창장. 감사장

tes·ti·mo·ny /ˈtɛstəˌmoʊni/ *n* [C, U] **1** a formal statement of what is true, especially one made in a court of law ‖ 특히 법정에서 이루어지는, 무엇이 사실인지에 대한 공식적인 진술. 증언 **2** something that shows or proves something else very clearly ‖ 다른 어떤 것을 매우 명확하게 나타내거나 입증하는 것. 증거. 증명: *an achievement that's a testimony to his hard work* 그가 열심히 일했다는 것을 입증하는 업적[실적]

test pi·lot /ˈ. ˌ../ *n* a pilot who flies new aircraft in order to test them ‖ 새로운 비행기를 시험하기 위해 비행해 보는 조종사. 테스트 파일럿

test tube /ˈ. ./ *n* a small glass container shaped like a tube that is used in scientific tests ‖ 과학 실험에서 사용되는 관처럼 생긴 작은 유리 용기. 시험관

tes·ty /ˈtɛsti/ *adj* impatient and easily annoyed ‖ 참을성 없고 쉽게 화를 내는. 성미가 급한. 성말 있는: *a testy old man* 화를 잘 내는 노인 – **testily** *adv*

tet·a·nus /ˈtɛtˀn-əs, -nəs/ *n* [U] a serious disease caused by infection in a cut or wound, that makes your muscles become stiff ‖ 근육을 굳어지게 하며 베인 곳이나 상처에 감염되어 일어나는 중병. 파상풍

teth·er /ˈtɛðɚ/ *n* a rope or chain to which something is tied ‖ 어떤 것을 잡아매는 밧줄이나 사슬

text /tɛkst/ *n* **1** [U] the writing in a book, magazine etc. rather than the pictures, or any written material ‖ 책이나 잡지 등에서의 그림보다는 글, 또는 글로 쓰어진 모든 자료. 본문. 텍스트 **2 the text of sth** the exact words of something ‖ 어떤 것의 정확한 말. 원문. 원고: *The entire text of the speech was printed in the newspaper.* 그 연설의 전체 원문이 신문에 실렸다.

text·book[1] /ˈtɛkstˌbʊk/, **text** *n* a book that contains information about a subject ‖ 한 주제에 관한 정보를 담고 있는 책. 교과서. 교본: *a history textbook* 역사 교과서

textbook[2] *adj* **a textbook example/case** a very clear and typical example of how something should happen or be done ‖ 어떤 것이 어떻게 발생되어야 하는지 또는 이루어져야 하는지에 대한 매우 분명하고 전형적인 예. 교과서적인[모범적

인] 예(例)/사례

tex·tile /ˈtɛkstaɪl/ *n* any material that is made by weaving ‖ 짜서 만든 모든 섬유. 직물

textiles /ˈtɛkstaɪlz/ *n* [plural] the industry that makes cloth ‖ 옷감을 만드는 산업. 섬유 산업

tex·ture /ˈtɛkstʃɚ/ *n* [C, U] the way that a surface, material etc. feels when you touch it, and how smooth or rough it looks ‖ 표면이나 물체 등을 만졌을 때의 촉감, 또는 부드럽거나 거칠게 보이는 정도. 감촉. 질감. 결: *fabric with a coarse texture* 거친 질감의 천

tex·tured /ˈtɛkstʃɚd/ *adj* having a surface that is not smooth ‖ 부드럽지 않은 표면을 가진. …결[질감]을 가진. 거친 질감의: *a wall with a textured surface* 표면이 거친 벽

than /ðən, ðɛn; *strong* ðæn/ *conjunction, prep* used when comparing two things, amounts etc. that are different ‖ 두 개의 서로 다른 사물이나 수량 등을 비교할 때에 쓰여. …보다는. …에 비하여: *He's been unemployed for more than a year.* 그는 1년 이상 실직해 있었다. / *Jean's taller than Stella.* 진은 스텔라보다 키가 더 크다. / *I can swim better than you.* 나는 너보다 수영을 더 잘 할 수 있다.

thank /θæŋk/ *v* [T] **1** to tell someone that you are pleased and grateful for a gift or for something that s/he has done ‖ 남에게 받은 선물이나 남이 해준 것에 대해 기쁘고 고맙다고 말하다. 감사하다. 고마워하다: *We would like to thank everyone for helping.* 우리는 모두에게 도와준 데 대해 감사를 표하고 싶다. **2 thank God/goodness/heavens** SPOKEN said when you are very glad about something ‖ 어떤 것에 대해 매우 기뻐할 때에 쓰여. (…이라니) 고맙다. 잘 되었다: *Thank God no one was hurt!* 아무도 다치지 않아 천만 다행이야! **3 have sb to thank (for sth)** SPOKEN used in order to say who is responsible for something happening ‖ 일어나고 있는 일이 누구 때문인지 말하는 데에 쓰여. …의 덕택[탓]이다: *The team has Jones to thank for keeping them in the game.* 그 팀은 존스의 덕택으로 경기를 잘해나가고 있다.

thank·ful /ˈθæŋkfəl/ *adj* glad and grateful that something good has happened ‖ 어떤 좋은 일이 일어난 것에 대해 기쁘고 감사하는. 고맙게 생각하는. 감사를 나타내는: *Our family does have a lot to be thankful for.* 우리 가족은 정말

감사 해야 할 일 이 많습니다. / *I'm thankful (that) I didn't have to go to the dentist.* 나는 치과에 가지 않아도 된 것에 감사하고 있다. **– thankfully** *adv : Thankfully, everything turned out all right.* 고맙게도, 모든 것이 이상 없는 것 으로 판명됐다.

thank·less /'θæŋklɪs/ *adj* a thankless job is difficult and you do not get much praise for doing it ‖ 일이 어렵고 그 일로 칭찬을 많이 받지 못하는. 일이 생색나지 않은. 보람 없는

thanks¹ /θæŋks/ *interjection* INFORMAL **1** ⇨ THANK YOU¹: *Can I borrow your pen? Thanks a lot.* 펜 좀 빌릴 수 있을까? 정 말 고마워. / *Thanks for giving me a ride to school.* 학교까지 태워다 줘서 고마워 요. **2 thanks/no thanks** said in order to accept or refuse something that someone is offering you ‖ 남이 제안하고 있는 것을 받아들이거나 거절하는 데에 쓰 여. 고마워요/괜찮아요: *"Can I give you a hand?"* (=help you) *"Oh, thanks."* "좀 도 와 드릴까요?" "예, 고마워요."

thanks² *n* [plural] **1** the things that you say or do to show that you are grateful to someone ‖ 어떤 사람에게 고맙다는 것 을 나타내기 위해 말하거나 행하는 것. 사 의. 감사(의 말[표시]): *He left without saying a word of thanks.* 그는 고맙다는 말 한 마디 없이 떠났다. **2 thanks to** because of ‖ …때문에. …덕택에: *We're late, thanks to you.* 우리는 너 때문에 늦 었다.

Thanks·giv·ing /ˌθæŋks'ɡɪvɪŋ/ *n* [C, U] **1** a holiday in the US and Canada in the fall when families have a large meal together to celebrate and be thankful for food, health, families etc. ‖ 가족들이 다 함께 풍성한 식사를 하며 음식·건강·가 족 등을 축하하고 감사해 하는 미국과 캐 나다에서의 가을철 축제일. 추수 감사절 **2** the period of time just before and after this day ‖ 이 날의 바로 전후의 기간. 추수 감사절(축제[휴가]) 기간: *Where are you going for Thanksgiving?* 추수 감사절(휴 가)에 어디로 갈 거야?

thank you¹ /'. ./ *interjection* **1** said in order to tell someone that you are grateful for something that s/he has done ‖ 남이 해준 것에 대해 감사하다고 말하는 데에 쓰여. 고마워: *"Here's the book you wanted, Katy." "Oh, thank you."* "케이티, 네가 원했던 책 여기 있 어." "그래, 고마워." / *Thank you for coming to my birthday party.* 내 생일 파 티에 와주어서 고마워. ✗DON'T SAY "I thank you for coming."✗ "I thank you

for coming."이라고는 하지 않는다. **2 thank you/no thank you** said in order to accept or refuse something that someone is offering you ‖ 남이 자신에게 제안하고 있는 것을 받아들이거나 거절하 는 데에 쓰여. 고마워요/괜찮아요[고맙지 만 …않겠어요]: *"Would you like another cookie?" "No thank you."* "과자를 더 드 시겠어요?" "아니요, 괜찮습니다." —see usage note at PLEASE¹

thank you² *adj* **thank you letter/gift/note etc.** a letter, gift etc. that is given to someone to thank him/her for something ‖ 어떤 것에 대해 남에게 고마움을 표현하기 위해 주는 편 지·선물 등. 감사 편지/선물/쪽지

thank you³ *n* something that you say or do to thank someone for something ‖ 남에게 무엇에 대하여 감사하기 위해 말하 거나 하는 것. 사례: *Please accept this gift as a thank you for your support.* 당 신의 지지에 대한 사례로 이 선물을 받아 주세요.

that¹ /ðæt/ *determiner, pron, plural* **those 1** used when talking about someone or something that is farther away in time, distance, etc. than someone or something else ‖ 어떤 사람 이나 사물보다 시간·거리 등에 있어 더 멀 리 떨어진 사람이나 사물을 언급할 때에 쓰여. 저(것): *Her mother gave her that necklace.* (=the one she is wearing) 그녀 의 어머니가 저 목걸이를 그녀에게 주셨 다. / *What should I do with that?* (=something you are pointing to) 저걸로 내가 뭘 해야 되지? —compare THIS¹ **2** used when talking about someone or something that has already been mentioned or is already known about ‖ 이미 언급되거나 이미 알고 있는 사람이나 사물에 대해 언급할 때에 쓰여: *"Here's a picture of Kelly and me." "Oh, that's cute."* "켈리와 내 사진이야." "아, 귀엽 다." / *I had to park in that lot by the library.* 나는 도서관 옆에 있는 저 주차장 에 주차해야 했다. / *We met for coffee later that day.* 우리는 그날 늦게 커피를 마시기 위해 만났다. **3 that's it a)** used when what you have mentioned is all of something or the end of something ‖ 자 신이 말한 것이 무엇의 전부이거나 끝일 때에 쓰여. 이게 전부[끝]이다: *It rains in February and that's it for the year.* 2월 에 비가 오는데 그것이 그 해의 전부다. **b)** SPOKEN used in order to tell someone that s/he has done something correctly ‖ 남이 무엇을 정확히 했다고 말하는 데에 쓰여. 바로 그거야: *Wave bye-bye, Ian.*

That's it! 이안, 안녕하고 손 흔들어. 그렇지! **4 that is** used in order to correct a statement or give more exact information about something ‖ 진술을 정정하거나 무엇에 대한 보다 정확한 정보를 제공하는 데에 쓰여. 즉. 다시 말하면: *It's a seven day trip. That is, it's five days there plus two days driving.* 7일이 걸리는 여행이다. 다시 말하면 그곳에서 5일 있고 이틀간의 드라이브가 추가된다.

SPOKEN PHRASES

5 at that said in order to give more information ‖ 더 많은 정보를 제공하는 데에 쓰여. 게다가. 더구나: *She's pregnant, and having twins at that!* 그녀가 임신했는데 그것도 쌍둥이야! **6 that's that** said when something is completely finished or when a decision will not be changed ‖ 무엇이 완전히 끝나거나 결정이 변동이 없을 때에 쓰여. 그것으로 끝이다. 그것으로 결정났다: *You're not going and that's that!* 네가 가지 않겠다면 그럼 그걸로 결정난 거다! **7 that's all there is to it** said in order to emphasize that something is simple to do, explain etc. ‖ 무엇을 하거나 설명하는 것이 간단하다는 것을 강조하는 데에 쓰여. 그것에 대해서는 그게 전부다: *We lost because we didn't play well. That's all there is to it.* 우리가 경기를 잘 하지 못했기 때문에 졌다. 그뿐이야.

USAGE NOTE that, who, whom, and which

Use **that** to talk about people and things, but **whom** only for people: *There's the car that I saw yesterday. / There's the girl that I saw yesterday. / There's the girl whom I saw yesterday.* If you add more information to a sentence that is about an idea or thing, use **which:** *He broke his leg, which meant he couldn't come with us.* If you add information about a person, use **who:** *I'm going to visit my parents, who live in San Diego.* In formal speech and writing, if a noun phrase is used after **that** or **whom**, we often leave out these words: *The question (that) she asked was impolite. / The man (whom) the police arrested is my neighbor.*

that은 사람과 사물을 언급하는 데에 쓰이나 **whom**은 단지 사람에게만 쓴

다: 내가 어제 봤던 차가 있다. / 내가 어제 봤던 소녀가 있다. / 내가 어제 봤던 소녀가 있다. 만일 문장에 견해나 정황에 대한 더 많은 정보를 추가할 경우에는 **which**를 쓴다: 그는 다리가 부러져서 우리와 함께 올 수 없었다. 만일 사람에 대한 정보를 추가할 경우에는 **who**를 쓴다: 나는 부모님을 찾아뵐 예정인데 그분들은 샌디에이고에 사신다. 비격식적인 말과 글에서 명사구 앞에 **that**이나 **whom**을 쓰는 경우에 종종 이 단어들을 생략하기도 한다: 그녀가 한 질문은 무례했다. / 경찰이 체포한 그 남자는 내 이웃사람이다.

that² /ðət; *strong* ðæt/ *conjunction* used in order to introduce a CLAUSE that is the object of a sentence, shows a result, or gives information about a person, thing, time etc. that has already been mentioned ‖ 문장의 목적절을 도입하거나 결과를 나타내거나 이미 언급된 사람·사물·시간 등에 대한 정보를 제공하는 데에 쓰여: *The rules state that if the ball hits the line, it's in.* 규칙은 만일 공이 선에 맞으면 공은 선 안에 있다는 것을 명시한다. / *Is it true that the Nelsons are moving?* 넬슨네가 이사간다는 게 사실이니? / *I was so hungry that I ate the whole pizza.* 나는 너무 배가 고파서 피자 한 판을 다 먹었다. / *They're showing the movie that you wanted to see.* 그들은 네가 보고 싶어하던 영화를 상영하고 있다. / *Have you gotten the letter that I sent you?* 내가 보낸 편지 받았니? —see also **so...that** (SO¹)

that³ /ðæt/ *adv* **1 that long/much/big etc.** SPOKEN used when talking about the size, number, or amount of something ‖ 무엇의 크기[수, 양]를 언급할 때에 쓰여. 그 길이만큼/그 양만큼/그 크기만큼: *I hadn't been waiting that long.* 나는 그렇게 오래 기다리진 않았어. **2 not that much/long/big etc.** SPOKEN not very much, long etc. ‖ 매우 많거나 길지 않은. 그다지 많지/길지/크지 않은: *His parents are big people, but he's not that tall.* 그의 부모님은 키가 크지만, 그는 그다지 크지 않다.

thatch /θætʃ/ *n* dried STRAW used for making roofs ‖ 지붕을 만드는 데 쓰이는 말린 짚. 이엉 —**thatched** *adj*

thaw¹ /θɔ/ *v* **1** [I, T] also **thaw out** if ice or snow thaws or is thawed, it becomes warmer and turns into water ‖ 얼음이나 눈이 따뜻해져서 물이 되다. 녹다. 녹이다 **2** [I, T] also **thaw out** if frozen food thaws or is thawed, it becomes soft so it is ready to be cooked ‖ 냉동식품이 녹아 요리할 수 있게 되다. 해동되다[시키다] **3** [I] to become more friendly and less FORMAL ‖ 보다 우호적이 고 덜 서먹서먹하게 되다. 누그러지다. 풀 리 다 : *Relations between the two countries are beginning to thaw.* 두 나라 의 관계가 해빙되기 시작하고 있다. — compare MELT

thaw² *n* **1** [singular] a period of warm weather during which snow and ice melt ‖ 눈과 얼음이 녹고 날씨가 따뜻한 시 기. 해빙기: *the spring thaw* 봄의 해빙기 **2** a time when a relationship becomes more friendly ‖ 관계가 보다 우호적이 되 는 시기. 긴장 완화기

the¹ /ðə, *before a vowel* ði; *strong* ði/ *definite article, determiner* **1** used before nouns to show that you are talking about a particular person or thing, especially when it has already been mentioned or when there is only one ‖ 특히 이미 언급된 것이거나 하나밖 에 없는 특정한 사람이나 사물에 대해 언 급하고 있음을 나타내려고 명사 앞에 쓰 여. 그: *I need to go to the grocery store.* 나는 그 식료품점에 가야 한다. / *That's the dress I want.* 저게 내가 바라는 그 옷 이야. / *Hand me the red book.* 거기 빨간 색 책을 내게 건네줘라. —compare A **2** used as part of some names ‖ 고유명사의 일부분으로 쓰여: *the United States* 미합 중국 / *The Morrisons are planning to buy a new house.* (=used when you are talking about the whole family) 모리슨 집안의 사람들은 새 집을 구매할 계획을 짜고 있다. **3** used before an adjective to make it into a noun ‖ 형용사를 명사로 만 들기 위해 그 앞에 쓰여: *They provide services for the blind.* 그들은 맹인을 위 한 서비스를 제공한다. **4** used before a singular noun to show that you are talking about that thing in general ‖ 단 수 명사 앞에서 그 사물에 대해 총체적으 로 말하고 있음을 보여주는 데 쓰여: *The computer has changed the way people work.* 컴퓨터는 사람들의 작업 방식을 변 화시켰다. **5** used instead of "each" or "every" ‖ "each"나 "every"대신에 쓰여. 각. 당: *Our car gets about 35 miles to the gallon.* 우리 차는 갤런당 약 35마일 을 간다. **6** used before the names of musical instruments ‖ 악기명 앞에 쓰여: *Kira's learning to play the piano.* 키라는 피아노 연주를 배우고 있다. **7** used in order to mention a part of the body or something that belongs to someone ‖ 신 체의 일부나 누군가의 소유물을 언급하는

데에 쓰여: *The ball hit him right in the eye!* 공이 그의 눈을 정통으로 맞췄어! / *The car* (=our car) *broke down again.* 우 리 차가 또 고장났다. **8** used when talking about a particular period of time, especially a DECADE or date, or the time when a particular event happened ‖ 특히 특정한 사건이 발생한 연대나 날 짜, 또는 시간대 등 특정한 시기에 대해 언 급하는 데에 쓰여: *music of the fifties* (=the 1950s) 1950년대의 음악 / *Immigrants poured into America in the late 1800s.* 1800년대 후반에는 이주자가 미국으로 쇄도했다. / *the Depression years* 세계 대공황기 **9** used in order to emphasize that someone or something is important or famous ‖ 사람이나 사물 이 중요하거나 유명하다는 것을 강조하기 위해 쓰여: *It's definitely the movie to see.* 정말 볼 만한 최고의 영화이다.

USAGE NOTE using **the**

Do not use **the** with uncountable nouns when you are using the general sense of the noun: *My favorite food is ice cream.* ✗DON'T SAY "My favorite food is the ice cream."✗ Use **the** with uncountable nouns when you mean a particular thing: *The ice cream we bought yesterday is already gone!* Do not use **the** with plural uncountable nouns when you are using the general sense of the noun: *Beth likes cats.* ✗DON'T SAY "Beth likes the cats."✗ Use **the** with plural uncountable nouns when you mean a particular group of things: *The cats we saw in the pet store were cute.* Use **the** to talk about something that is the only one of its type: *The sun is really hot today.*
총칭하는 의미로 명사를 쓰는 경우 불가 산 명사는 **the**와 함께 쓰지 못한다: 내 가 가장 좋아하는 음식은 아이스크림이 다. "My favorite food is the ice cream."이라고는 하지 않는다. 특정한 것을 뜻할 때는 불가산 명사는 **the**와 함께 쓴다: 우리가 어제 사온 아이스크 림은 벌써 다 먹었어! 총칭하는 의미로 쓰인 복수형 불가산 명사는 **the**와 함께 쓰지 못한다: 베스는 고양이를 좋아한 다. "Beth likes the cats."라고는 하지 않는다. 일단의 특정한 것들을 뜻하는 복수 불가산 명사는 **the**와 더불어 쓰인 다: 우리가 애완동물 가게에서 본 고양 이들은 귀여웠다. 그 종류 중에서 유일 무이한 것을 언급하는 데에는 **the**를 쓴 다: 오늘은 햇빛이 정말 뜨겁다.

the² *adv* used in comparisons ‖ 비교에 쓰여: *She's the smartest kid in her class.* 그녀는 자기 반에서 가장 똑똑한 아이이다. / *The more you practice, the better you'll play.* 더 많이 연습하면 할수록 더 잘 할 수 있을 거야.

the·a·ter /'θiətɚ/ *n* **1** a building with a stage where plays are performed ‖ 연극이 상연되는 무대가 있는 건물. 극장: *the Apollo Theater* 아폴로 극장 **2** [U] the work of acting in, writing, or organizing plays ‖ 연극을 연기하거나 집필하거나, 또는 연출하는 행위. 연극업(계): *She's been working in theater for many years.* 그녀는 수년 동안 연극계에서 종사해 오고 있다. **3** a building where movies are shown ‖ 영화가 상영되는 건물. 영화관. 극장

the·at·ri·cal /θi'ætrɪkəl/ *adj* **1** relating to the theater ‖ 연극에 관련된. 연극의: *an expensive theatrical production* 고비용의 연극 제작 **2** behaving in a way that is intended to make people notice you ‖ 사람들이 주목하게 만들 의도로 행동하는. 과장된. 일부러 꾸민: *a theatrical gesture* 과장된 몸짓 **– theatrics** *n* [plural]

theft /θɛft/ *n* [C, U] the act or crime of stealing something ‖ 무엇을 훔치는 행위나 범죄. 도둑질. 절도: *car theft* 차량 절도 / *the theft of their luggage* 그들의 여행 가방 절도죄

their /ðɚ; *strong* ðɛr/ *possessive adj* **1** belonging or relating to the people, animals, or things that have been mentioned, or are known about ‖ 언급되었거나 알고 있는 사람들이나 동물, 또는 사물에 속하거나 관계되는. 그들의: *The guests left their coats on the bed.* 손님들은 침대 위에 자신들의 코트를 남겨두었다. / *Their little boy plays with Morgan sometimes.* 그들의 어린 사내아이는 가끔 모건과 함께 논다. **2** NONSTANDARD used instead of "his" or "her" after words such as someone, anyone, everyone etc. ‖ someone·anyone·everyone 등의 단어 뒤에서 "his" 또는 "her" 대신 쓰여: *Everybody has their own ideas about it.* 모두가 그것에 대해 그들 나름의 생각을 갖고 있다.

theirs /ðɛrz/ *possessive pron* **1** the thing or things belonging to or relating to the people or things that have been mentioned, or are known about ‖ 언급되었거나 알고 있는 사람들 또는 사물들에 속하거나 관계되는 것(들). 그들의 것: *Some friends of theirs are staying with them.* 그들의 몇몇 친구들은 그들과 함께 살고 있다. / *When our washing machine broke the neighbors let us use theirs.* 우리 세탁기가 고장 났을 때 이웃사람들이 자기네 것을 사용하게 해 줬다. **2** NONSTANDARD used instead of "his" or "hers" after words such as someone, anyone, everyone etc. ‖ someone·anyone·everyone 등의 단어 뒤에서 "his" 또는 "hers" 대신 쓰여: *Okay, get your coats. Does everyone have theirs?* 좋아, 코트 입어라. 다들 자기 코트 입었지?

them /ðəm, əm; *strong* ðɛm/ *pron* **1** the object form of "they" ‖ "they"의 목적격. 그들을. 그들에게: *Has anybody seen my keys? I can't find them.* 누구 내 열쇠 본 사람 있어요? 열쇠를 못 찾겠어. / *My folks wanted me to tell them all about my trip.* 내 가족들은 그들에게 내 여행에 대한 모든 것을 들려주길 바랐다. **2** NONSTANDARD used instead of "him" or "her" after words such as someone, anyone, everyone etc. ‖ someone·anyone·everyone등의 단어 뒤에서 "him" 또는 "her" 대신에 쓰여: *Somebody phoned for you, so I told them to call back later.* 어떤 사람이 너한테 전화했었어, 그래서 내가 나중에 다시 하라고 말했어. —see usage note at ME

theme /θim/ *n* **1** the main subject or idea in a book, movie, speech etc. ‖ 책·영화·연설 등의 주요 문제나 관념. 주제. 제목: *The theme of the movie is how people react to death.* 사람들이 죽음에 어떻게 반응하는가가 그 영화의 주제이다. **2 theme music/song/tune** music or a song that is always played with a particular television or radio program ‖ 텔레비전이나 라디오의 특정한 프로그램에서 항상 연주되는 음악이나 노래. 주제곡. 주제가 **– thematic** /θi'mætɪk/ *adj*

theme park /'. ./ *n* an AMUSEMENT PARK that is based on one subject such as water or space travel ‖ 물이나 우주여행 등 한 가지 주제에 바탕을 둔 놀이동산. 테마 파크

them·selves /ðəm'sɛlvz, ðɛm-/ *pron* **1** the REFLEXIVE form of "they" ‖ "they"의 재귀형. 그들 자신[스스로]: *People usually like to talk about themselves.* 사람들은 보통 자신에 대해 말하기를 좋아한다. **2** the strong form of "they," used in order to emphasize the subject or object of a sentence ‖ 문장의 주어나 목적어를 강조하기 위해 쓰이는 "they"의 강조형: *Doctors themselves admit that the treatment does not always work.* 의사 자신들도 치료가 항상 효과적이 아니라는 것을 인정한다. **3 (all) by themselves**

a) without help ‖ 도움 없이. 자신들만의 힘으로: *The kids made cookies all by themselves.* 아이들은 스스로 과자를 만들었다. **b)** alone ‖ 홀로: *Many old people live by themselves.* 많은 노인들이 홀로 산다. **4 (all) to themselves** for their own use ‖ 그들 자신만이 쓰기 위해: *The kids had the pool to themselves today.* 아이들은 오늘 수영장을 자기 맘대로 쓸 수 있었다.

then' /ðen/ *adv* **1** after something has happened; next ‖ 무엇이 발생한 후에; 다음에: *We could have lunch and then go shopping.* 우리는 점심을 먹고 나서 쇼핑을 갈 수 있었다. **2** at a particular time in the past or future ‖ 과거나 미래의 특정 시점에. 그때에: *I'll have to leave by then.* 나는 그때까지 떠나야 한다. / *My family lived in New York back then.* 그 당시 나의 가족은 뉴욕에 살았다. **3** SPOKEN said in order to show that what you are saying is related in some way to what has been said before ‖ 현재 말하고 있는 것이 전에 말했던 것과 어떤 면에서 관련이 있다는 것을 나타내는 데에 쓰여. 그렇다면: *"He can't come on Friday." "Then how about Saturday?"* "그 사람 금요일에는 올 수 없어." "그러면 토요일은 어떻데?" / *So you're going into nursing then?* 그래 간호사가 된다고 그런데? **4** used in order to say that if one thing is true, the other thing is also true or should be the correct result ‖ 한가지 것이 사실이라면 다른 것 또한 사실이거나 마땅히 타당한 결과가 되야 한다고 말하는 데에 쓰여: *"I have to pick Bobby up at school." "Then you should leave by 2:30."* "나는 보비를 학교에서 데려 와야 해." "그러면 너는 2시 30분까지는 출발해야 해." **5** used in order to add something to what you have just said ‖ 방금 말한 것에 어떤 것을 덧붙이는 데에 쓰여. 게다가: *He's really busy at work, and then there's the new baby, too!* 그는 일하느라 정말 바쁜데 게다가 애까지 태어났어! **6 then and there** immediately ‖ 즉시. 곧장: *I would have given up then and there if my parents hadn't encouraged me.* 나의 부모님이 나를 격려해 주지 않았었다면 나는 바로 포기했었을 것이다. —see also **but then (again)**... (BUT'), **(every) now and then** (NOW')

then² *adj* at that time in the past ‖ 과거 그때의. 당시의: *the then President of the US* 미국의 당시 대통령

the·o·lo·gian /ˌθiə'loudʒən/ *n* someone who studies or writes about THEOLOGY ‖ 신학에 대한 연구를 하거나 집필을 하는 사람. 신학자

the·ol·o·gy /θi'ɑlədʒi/ *n* [U] the study of religion, religious beliefs, and God ‖ 종교·신앙·신에 대한 연구. 신학 – **theological** /ˌθiə'lɑdʒɪkəl/ *adj*

the·o·rem /'θiərəm, 'θɪrəm/ *n* TECHNICAL a statement that can be shown to be true, especially in mathematics ‖ 특히 수학에서 사실로 입증할 수 있는 명제. 정리(定理)

the·o·ret·i·cal /ˌθiə'rɛtɪkəl/ *adj* **1** relating to THEORY ‖ 이론에 관한. 이론의: *theoretical physics* 이론 물리학 **2** a theoretical situation or condition could exist but does not yet exist ‖ 상황이나 조건이 존재할 수는 있지만 아직은 존재하지 않는. 가정적인 – **theoretically** *adv*

the·o·rist /'θiərɪst/, **the·o·re·ti·cian** /ˌθiərə'tɪʃən/ *n* someone who develops ideas that explain why particular things happen or are true ‖ 특정한 일이 발생하거나 사실이 되는 까닭을 설명하는 개념을 전개하는 사람. 이론가

the·o·rize /'θiəˌraɪz/ *v* [I, T] to think of a possible explanation or reason for a particular event, fact etc. ‖ 특정한 사건·사실 등에 대한 가능한 설명이나 이유를 생각해 내다. 이론화하다. 이론을 세우다: *Doctors theorize that the infection is passed from animals to humans.* 의사들은 그 전염병이 동물로부터 사람에게 전염된다고 이론을 세웠다.

the·o·ry /'θiəri, 'θɪri/ *n* **1** an explanation for something that may be reasonable, but it has not yet been proven to be true ‖ 아직 사실로 입증되지는 않았지만 타당할지도 모르는 것에 대한 설명. 가설: *Darwin's theory of evolution* 다윈의 진화설 / *a theory that light is made up of waves* 빛이 파동으로 이루어진다는 학설 **2 in theory** something that is true in theory is supposed to be true but may not be true ‖ 사실이 아닐 수도 있지만 사실이라고 가정하여. 이론상으로: *In theory, the crime rate should decrease as employment increases.* 이론상으로는 취업률이 높아지면 범죄율은 감소해야 한다. **3** [U] the general principles or ideas of a subject such as science or music ‖ 과학이나 음악 등의 과목의 일반적 원리나 개념. 이론: *studying music theory* 음악 이론에 대한 연구

ther·a·peu·tic /ˌθɛrə'pyutɪk/ *adj* **1** relating to the treatment or cure of a disease ‖ 질병의 처치나 치료에 관한. 치료의: *therapeutic drugs* 치료제 **2** making you feel calm and relaxed ‖ 안정되고 긴장이 풀리는 느낌이 들게 하는. 건

강에 도움이 되는: *Long walks can be therapeutic.* 오랫동안 산책하는 것은 건강에 도움이 될 수 있다.

ther·a·py /'θɛrəpi/ *n* [C, U] the treatment of an illness or injury, or of a mental or emotional problem, especially without using drugs or SURGERY ‖ 특히 약이나 수술 없이 병이나 부상, 또는 정신적이거나 정서적인 문제를 치료함. 요법. 치료: *Ted's having physical therapy for his back.* 테드는 등에 물리 치료를 받고 있다. / *He's been in therapy for years.* 그는 수년간 치료를 받았다. **– therapist** *n*

there¹ /ðɛr/ *pron* used as the subject of a sentence in order to say that something exists or happens ‖ 무엇이 존재하거나 발생한다는 것을 말하기 위한 문장의 주어로 쓰여: *There were several people hurt in the accident.* 그 사고로 몇 사람이 다쳤다. / *Suddenly, there was a loud crash.* 갑자기, 꽝со리 났다. / *Are there any questions?* (무엇이든) 질문 있습니까?

there² *adv* **1** in or to a particular place that is not where you are or near you ‖ 현재 있는 장소나 근처가 아닌 특정한 장소에 또는 장소로. 그곳에서. 그곳으로: *Would you hand me that glass over there?* 거기 그 컵을 저에게 건네주시겠어요? / *He was just sitting there.* 그는 거기에 그냥 앉아 있었다. / *The party was almost over by the time I got there.* (=arrived) 내가 거기에 도착했을 때 파티는 거의 끝났다. —compare HERE¹ **2** at a particular point in time, in a story etc. ‖ 시간·이야기 등의 특정 부분에서. 그곳에서: *I'll read this chapter and stop there.* 내가 이 장을 읽다가 거기서 멈출게. **3 be there (for sb)** if someone is there for you, s/he will always help and support you when you have problems ‖ 문제가 있을 때 어떤 사람이 항상 도와주고 지지하다. (…의 곁에) 있다. (…을) 후원하다: *My folks are great – they're always there for me.* 내 가족들은 훌륭해. 그들은 항상 나를 도와줘.

--- SPOKEN PHRASES ---

4 there (you go) INFORMAL **a)** used when giving something to someone or when you have done something for someone ‖ 남에게 무엇을 줄 때나 남을 위해 무엇을 했을 때 쓰여. 자 여기 있어. 자 봐라: *Come on Aaron, let's get you your bottle – there you go.* 자 아론, 한 잔 더 하자. 자 여기. **b)** used in order to encourage someone ‖ 남을 격

려하는 데에 쓰여. 그래, 그거야: *Just one more situp, there.* 딱 한 번만 더 일어나 봐, 그렇지. **5 there** used when you have finished something ‖ 무엇을 끝마쳤을 때 쓰여. 자: *There, that's the last piece of the puzzle.* 자, 저게 마지막 퍼즐 조각이다. **6 there's...** said in order to make someone look at or pay attention to someone or something ‖ 남이 사람이나 사물을 보게 하거나 관심을 갖게 하는 데에 쓰여: *There's that restaurant I was telling you about.* 저기가 내가 말한 식당이야. **7 hello/hi there** used when greeting someone, especially when you have just noticed him/her ‖ 특히 남을 아는 체하며 인사할 때 쓰여. 야!(안녕!): *Hi there. You must be Liane.* 야, 너 라이언 맞지. **8 there, there** used in order to comfort a child ‖ 아이를 달래는 데에 쓰여. 자, 어서: *There, there, it's all right.* 그래, 그래, 괜찮아.

—see also **then and there** (THEN¹)

there·a·bouts /ˌðɛrə'baʊts, 'ðɛrə,-baʊts/ *adv* near a particular number, amount, time etc. ‖ 특정한 수·양·시간 등에 가깝게. …쯤[정도]: *The chair costs $50 or thereabouts.* 그 의자는 50달러 정도 한다.

there·af·ter /ðɛr'æftɚ/ *adv* FORMAL after a particular event or time; AFTERWARDS ‖ 특정한 사건이나 시간 이후에. 그 후에, ⑫ afterwards: *The store caught fire and closed shortly thereafter.* 그 상점은 불이 난 후 바로 문을 닫았다.

there·by /ðɛr'baɪ, 'ðɛrbaɪ/ *adv* FORMAL with the result that ‖ 그 결과로. 그것에 의하여: *Expenses were cut 12%, thereby increasing efficiency.* 효율을 높여 그 결과 경비가 12% 줄었다.

there·fore /'ðɛrfɔr/ *adv* FORMAL for the reason that has just been mentioned ‖ 방금 언급했던 그 이유로. 그러므로: *His health continued to decline, and therefore he retired from his job.* 그는 건강이 계속 악화되어서 직장에서 퇴직했다.

there·in /ðɛr'ɪn/ *adv* FORMAL **1** in that place, or in that piece of writing ‖ 그 장소에 또는 그 글에서. 거기에: *the contract and all the rules therein* 계약과 거기의 모든 조항 **2 therein lies** used in order to state the cause of something ‖ 무엇의 근거를 말하는 데에 쓰여. 그 점에 …이 있다: *He speaks the truth, and therein lies his power.* 그가 진실을 말하는 점에서 그에게 권위가 있다.

there·of /ðɛr'ʌv/ *adv* FORMAL relating to something that has just been mentioned ‖ 방금 언급된 것에 관하여. 그것에 관하여: *insurance for the home and the contents thereof* 주택 보험과 그것에 관한 내용

there·up·on /'ðɛrə,pɑn, ,ðɛrə'pɑn/ *adv* FORMAL ⇨ THEREFORE

ther·mal /'θɚməl/ *adj* relating to or caused by heat ‖ 열에 관한, 열에 의한: *thermal underwear* 방한용 내의 / *thermal energy* 열에너지

ther·mom·e·ter /θɚ'mɑmətɚ/ *n* a piece of equipment that measures the temperature of the air, your body etc. ‖ 공기·신체 등의 온도를 재는 기구. 온도계

ther·mo·nu·cle·ar /,θɚmou'nukliɚ/ *adj* relating to a NUCLEAR reaction caused by very high heat ‖ 아주 높은 열에 의해 일어나는 핵반응에 관한. 열핵반응

Ther·mos /'θɚməs/, **Thermos bot·tle** /'.. ,../ *n* TRADEMARK a special container like a bottle that keeps hot drinks hot or cold drinks cold ‖ 뜨거운 음료는 뜨겁게, 찬 음료는 차게 보관하는 병 모양의 특수 용기. 보온병

ther·mo·stat /'θɚmə,stæt/ *n* an instrument that controls the temperature of a room, machine etc. ‖ 방·기계 등의 온도를 조절하는 기구. 온도 조절기

the·sau·rus /θɪ'sɔrəs/ *n, plural* **thesauruses** *or* **thesauri** /-'sɔraɪ/ a book in which words are put into groups with other words that have a similar meaning ‖ 비슷한 의미를 갖는 단어들끼리 그룹지어 놓은 책. 동의어집

these /ðiz/ *determiner, pronoun* the plural form of THIS ‖ this의 복수형

the·sis /'θisɪs/ *n, plural* **theses** /'θisiz/ **1** a long piece of writing about a particular subject that you do for a university degree ‖ 대학 학위를 받기 위해 특정 주제에 대해 쓴 장편의 글. 논문: *She's writing her thesis on Victorian women criminals.* 그녀는 빅토리아 여왕 시대의 여성 범죄자들에 대한 논문을 쓰고 있다. **2** FORMAL an idea or statement that tries to explain why something happens ‖ 무엇이 발생하는 이유를 설명하려는 개념이나 주장. 논제. 명제

they /ðeɪ/ *pron* **1** the people, animals, or things that have been mentioned or are known about ‖ 언급되거나 알고 있는 사람[동물, 사물]. 그(것)들: *Ken gave me flowers, aren't they beautiful?* 켄이 내게 꽃을 주었는데 아름답지 않니? / *I stopped at Doris and Ed's place, but they weren't home.* 나는 도리스와 에드네 집에 들렀지만 그들은 집에 없었다. / *They're (=they are) not coming until 9:00.* 그들은 9시까지 오지 않을 겁니다. **2 a** particular group or organization, or the people involved in it ‖ 특정 집단이나 조직, 또는 관련된 사람들: *They sell all different kinds of candles.* 그 상인들은 모든 종류의 초를 판다. / *They took my appendix out last year.* 그 의사들은 작년에 내 맹장을 제거했다. / *They're going to build a new road.* 당국은 새로운 도로를 놓을 예정이다. **3** used in order to say what people in general believe, think, are saying etc. ‖ 사람들이 일반적으로 믿고 생각하며 말하는 것 등을 이르는 데에 쓰여. 전하기를: *They say it's bad luck to spill salt.* 소금을 쏟으면 재수가 없다고들 한다. **4** NONSTANDARD used instead of "he" or "she" after words such as someone, anyone, everyone etc. ‖ someone·anyone·everyone 등의 단어 뒤에서 "he" 또는 "she" 대신에 쓰여: *Somebody at work said that they had known you in college.* 회사의 어떤 사람이 당신을 대학 시절부터 알아왔다고 했습니다.

they'd /ðeɪd/ **1** the short form of "they had" ‖ "they had"의 단축형: *They'd had a lot to drink.* 그들은 술을 많이 마셨다. **2** the short form of "they would" ‖ "they would"의 단축형: *They'd like to visit us soon.* 그들은 빨리 우리를 방문하고 싶어한다.

they'll /ðeɪl, ðɛl/ the short form of "they will" ‖ "they will"의 단축형: *They'll have to wait.* 그들은 기다려야 할 거야.

they're /ðɚ; *strong* ðɛr/ the short form of "they are" ‖ "they are"의 단축형: *They're very nice people.* 그들은 정말 좋은 사람들이다.

they've /ðeɪv/ the short form of "they have" ‖ "they have"의 단축형: *They've been here before.* 그들은 전에 여기 살았다.

thick

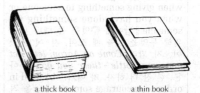

a thick book   a thin book

thick¹ /θɪk/ *adj* **1** measuring a large distance, or a larger distance than usual, between two opposite sides or surfaces ‖ 마주하는 양측이나 양면 사이의 두께가 넓게 측정되거나 보통보다 넓은. 두꺼운: *a nice thick piece of bread* 적당히 두꺼운 빵 조각 / *The clouds were getting thicker.* 구름이 점점 짙어지고 있다. —opposite THIN¹ **2** used in order to describe the distance between two opposite sides or surfaces ‖ 마주하는 양측이나 양면 사이의 두께를 표현하는 데에 쓰여: *The ice is two feet/five inches thick on the lake.* 호수에 2피트[5인치] 두께의 얼음이 얼었다. **3** a substance that is thick has very little water in it ‖ 물질이 물을 거의 함유하지 않은. 걸쭉한: *thick soup* 진한 수프 **4** filled with smoke, fog, etc., and difficult to see through or breathe in ‖ 연기·안개 등으로 차 있고 뚫어 보거나 숨을 들이쉬기 힘든. 가득 찬. 자욱한: *The air was thick with smoke from the fire.* 대기는 화재로 인한 연기로 자욱했다. **5** growing very close together with not much space in between ‖ 사이에 공간이 많지 않고 서로 매우 가까이 자라는. 빽빽한 / *He has thick black hair.* 그는 숱이 많고 까만 머리카락을 갖고 있다 –**thickly** *adv* – **thick** *adv* NONSTANDARD

thick² *n* **1 be in the thick of sth** to be involved in the most active, dangerous etc. part of a situation ‖ 가장 격하고 위험한 상황에 있다. …이 한창이다: *US troops are right in the thick of the action.* 미군은 치열한 교전 상태에 있다. **2 through thick and thin** in spite of any difficulties or problems ‖ 어떤 어려움이나 문제에도 불구하고: *They stayed married through thick and thin.* 그들은 온갖 어려움에도 불구하고 결혼생활을 지속했다.

thick·en /ˈθɪkən/ *v* [I, T] to become thick, or make something thick ‖ 진하게 되거나 무엇을 진하게 하다. 진해지다. 진하게 하다: *Thicken the soup with flour.* 밀가루로 수프를 걸쭉하게 만들어라.

thick·et /ˈθɪkɪt/ *n* a group of bushes and small trees ‖ 일단의 덤불과 작은 나무. 덤불. 잡목림

thick·ness /ˈθɪknɪs/ *n* [C, U] how thick something is ‖ 무엇의 두꺼운 정도. 두꺼움. 두께: *Roll out the dough to a thickness of 1 inch.* 1인치 두께로 반죽을 밀어라.

thick·set /ˌθɪkˈsɛt/ *adj* having a body that is wide and strong ‖ 몸이 뚱뚱하고

단단한. 땅딸막한

thick-skinned /ˌ. ˈ./ *adj* not being offended if people criticize you or do not like you ‖ 사람들이 비난하거나 좋아하지 않아도 화내지 않는. 무딘. 무감각한

thief /θif/ *n, plural* **thieves** /θivz/ someone who steals things ‖ 물건을 훔치는 사람. 도둑: *a car thief* 차 도둑

USAGE NOTE thief, shoplifter, pickpocket, mugger, burglar, and robber

All of these words mean "someone who takes things that do not belong to him/her." A **thief** is a general word for someone who steals. Someone who takes things from stores without paying for them is a **shoplifter**. Someone who takes things from the pockets of other people in the street, on a bus etc. is a **pickpocket**. A **mugger** is someone who uses violence when taking things from people, usually in a public place. A **burglar** takes things from houses, usually at night. A **robber** takes money from banks, people etc. and often uses violence.

이 단어들은 모두 "자신의 소유가 아닌 물건을 훔치는 사람"을 뜻한다. **thief**는 도둑질하는 사람을 뜻하는 일반적인 단어이다. **shoplifter**는 상점에서 값을 지불하지 않고 물건을 훔치는 도둑이다. **pickpocket**은 거리·버스 등에서 남의 호주머니의 물건을 훔치는 도둑이다. **mugger**는 공공장소에서 남의 물건을 빼앗기 위해 폭력을 쓰는 사람이다. **burglar**는 보통 밤에 남의 집에서 물건을 훔친다. **robber**는 종종 폭력을 써서 은행·사람들에게서 돈을 빼앗는다.

---

thigh /θaɪ/ *n* the top part of your leg between your knee and your HIP ‖ 무릎과 엉덩이 사이의 다리 윗부분. 넓적다리 —see picture at BODY

thim·ble /ˈθɪmbəl/ *n* a small hard cap that you put over the end of your finger to protect it when you are sewing ‖ 바느질할 때 손가락을 보호하기 위해 손가락 끝에 끼는 작고 딱딱한 덮개. 골무

thin¹ /θɪn/ *adj* **thinner, thinnest 1** measuring a small distance, or a smaller distance than usual, between two opposite sides or surfaces ‖ 마주하는 양측이나 양면 사이의 두께가 좁게 측정되거나 보통보다 좁은. 얇은: *a thin slice of cheese* 얇게 자른 치즈 / *a wire as thin as a human hair* 사람의 머리카락만큼 가는 전선 / *The walls here are* *paper-thin*. (=very thin) 이곳의 벽은 종잇장처럼 얇다. —opposite THICK¹ **2** having little fat on your body ∥ 몸에 살이 거의 없는. 마른: *He's tall, very thin, and has dark hair.* 그는 키가 크고 매우 마르고 머리카락은 검다. **3** air that is thin is difficult to breathe because there is not much OXYGEN in it ∥ 산소가 많이 들어 있지 않아 공기가 숨쉬기 곤란한. 산소가 희박한 **4** not close together, and with spaces in between ∥ 사이에 틈이 있어서 서로 붙어 있지 않은. 드문드문한: *His hair is very thin on top.* 그의 머리는 윗부분이 아주 성기다. **5** a substance that is thin has a lot of water in it ∥ 물질이 물을 많이 함유하고 있는. 묽은: *thin broth* 묽은 수프 – **thinness** n [U] – **thin** adv NONSTANDARD —see also thinly

---

USAGE NOTE thin

Thin is a general word that describes people who do not have much fat on their bodies. If someone is thin in a way that is attractive, use **slim** or **slender**. **Skinny** is an INFORMAL word that means that someone is too thin. **Underweight** means that someone does not weigh enough, and is often used by doctors or people who are worried about their weight. **Emaciated** means that someone is extremely thin in a way that is dangerous to his/her health.

thin은 몸에 지방이 많지 않은 사람을 묘사하는 일반적인 단어이다. 만약 사람이 매력적으로 말랐다면 **slim**이나 **slender**를 쓴다. **skinny**는 비격식적인 단어로 너무 마른 사람을 뜻한다. **underweight**는 몸무게 미달인 사람을 뜻하며 의사나 그들의 몸무게를 걱정하는 사람들이 사용한다. **emaciated**는 건강에 위험할 정도로 심하게 마른 사람을 의미한다.

---

thin² v **-nned, -nning** [T] to make something thinner or to become thinner ∥ 어떤 것을 더 얇게 하거나 얇아지다. 가늘게[묽게] 하다. 가늘어[묽어]지다: *his thinning hair* 그의 점차 빠져가는 머리털 / *paint thinned with water* 물로 묽게 만든 페인트

thin out phr v [I] if a crowd thins out, people gradually leave so there are fewer of them ∥ 사람들이 점차 빠져나가 수가 적어지다. 드문드문 해지다

thing /θɪŋ/ n **1** a fact, idea, statement, action, or event ∥ 사실[생각, 진술, 행위, 사건]. 것: *A funny thing happened last week.* 지난주에 재미있는 사건이 발생했다. / *I said the first thing that came into my mind.* 나는 제일 먼저 머릿속에 떠오른 생각을 말했다. / *I have better things to do with my time.* 나는 내 시간에 해야 할 더 나은 것이 있어. / *One thing is certain: we'll never go there again!* 한 가지는 확실해. 우리는 다시는 거기에 안 가! **2** an object ∥ 물건: *Do you know how to turn this thing off?* 이거 끄는 법 아니? / *The box had all sorts of things in it.* 그 상자에는 다양한 종류의 물건이 들어 있었다. / *I don't have a thing to wear!* 나는 입을 만한 것이 없어! **3 not know/feel/see etc. a thing** to know, feel, see etc. nothing ∥ 아무것도 모르거나 느끼지 못하거나 볼 수 없다: *He doesn't know a thing about fixing a car.* 그는 차 수리에 대해서는 아무것도 모른다. / *Sarah's leaving you, and you can't do a thing about it.* 사라가 너를 떠날 텐데 너는 아무것도 할 수가 없구나. **4 there's no such thing (as sth)** used in order to emphasize that someone or something does not exist or does not happen ∥ 사람이나 사물이 존재하지 않거나 발생하지 않는다는 것을 강조하는 데에 쓰여. (…같은) 그런 것은 없다: *There's no such thing as Santa Claus!* 산타클로스 같은 것은 없어! **5 be seeing/hearing things** to believe that you are seeing or hearing something that is not really there ∥ 실제로 거기에 없는 것을 보거나 듣는 것으로 여기다. 헛것[헛소리]을 보다[듣다] **6 the last thing sb wants/expects etc.** something that someone does not want, expect etc. at all ∥ 누군가가 전혀 바라고 기대하지 않는 것: *The last thing we wanted was to start a fight.* 싸우는 것은 우리가 가장 최후에 하길 바라는 것이다. **7 do your own thing** INFORMAL to do what you want, and not what someone else wants you to do ∥ 남이 원하는 것을 해주는 게 아니라. 자신이 원하는 것을 하다. 자신이 하고 싶은 [좋은] 일을 하다.

SPOKEN PHRASES

8 the thing is said when explaining a problem or the reason for something ∥ 어떤 것에 대한 문제나 이유를 설명하는 데에 쓰여. 문제는 …이다: *We want to come, but the thing is we can't find a babysitter.* 우리도 가고 싶지만 아이를 돌봐줄 사람을 구할 수 없다는 것이 문제이다. **9 for one thing** said when giving a reason for something ∥ 어떤 것에 대한 이유를 제시하는 데에 쓰여.

(첫째) 이유로는: *I don't think she'll get the part - for one thing she can't sing!* 나는 그녀가 그 역할을 맡을 거라고 생각지 않는다. 왜냐하면 그녀는 노래를 못하거든! **10 it's a good thing (that)** used in order to say that it is lucky or good that something happened ‖ 어떤 것의 발생이 운이 좋거나 잘된 일이라고 말하는 데에 쓰여. (…이어서) 다행이다: *It's a good thing the drug store's open late.* 약국이 늦게까지 열어서 다행이다. **11 first thing** at the beginning of the day or morning ‖ 하루나 아침의 초기에. 우선: *I'll call you first thing tomorrow, OK?* 내일 내가 가장 먼저 너한테 전화할게, 알겠지? **12 (it's) just one of those things** used in order to say that something that has happened is not someone's fault or could not have been avoided ‖ 일어난 일이 누구의 잘못도 아니거나 피할 수 없었을 것이라고 말하는 데에 쓰여. (그것은) 어쩌다 그렇게 된 일(이다) **13 it's (just) one thing after another** said when a lot of unpleasant things happen to you ‖ 불쾌한 사건들이 자신에게 많이 일어날 경우에 쓰여. 거듭해서 곤욕을 치르다

—see also THINGS

thing·a·ma·jig /'θɪŋəmə,dʒɪg/ *n* SPOKEN said when you cannot remember the real name of the thing you want to mention ‖ 말하고 싶은 것의 실제 이름이 생각나지 않을 때 쓰여. 거시기: *Where's the thingamajig for the garlic?* 마늘용 거시기 어디 있지?

things /θɪŋz/ *n* [plural] **1** life in general and the way it affects someone ‖ 일반적인 생활 및 남에게 영향을 주는 모양. 상황. 형편: *How are things with you?* 형편이 어떤가? / *Things couldn't be better.* 상황이 더 이상 좋을 수는 없다[최고의 상태다]. / *I know things can be very hard at times.* 나는 상황이 때때로 매우 힘들 거라는 것을 안다. **2** the things you own or the things you are carrying ‖ 소유하는 것이나 가지고 다니는 것. 소지품. 휴대품: *Just put your things there.* 너의 소지품을 거기에 놓아라.

think /θɪŋk/ *thought, thought, thinking* *v* [T] to have an opinion or belief about something ‖ 어떤 것에 대한 의견이나 신념을 갖다. 생각하다: *Fred thought (that) it was a good idea.* 프레드는 그것이 좋은 생각이라고 생각했다. / *So, what do you think about/of my new car?* 그렇다면, 내 새 차에 대해 어떻게 생

각하니? / *I didn't think you liked mayonnaise.* (=I believed you did not like it) 나는 네가 마요네즈를 좋아하지 않는다고 생각했다. **2** [I] to use your mind to decide something, solve problems, have ideas etc. ‖ 어떤 것을 결정하고 문제를 풀고 생각하려고 머리를 쓰다. 생각하다: *She lay awake thinking about the money.* 그녀는 누워서 자지 않고 돈에 관해 생각했다. / *Just a second, I'm thinking.* 잠깐만, 나 생각 중이야. **3 think about/of doing sth** to consider the possibility of doing something ‖ 어떤 것을 하는 가능성을 고려하다: *I'm thinking about moving to Albuquerque.* 나는 앨버커키로 이사 가는 것에 대해 생각 중이다. **4 think better of sth** to decide not to do something that you had intended to do, especially something bad or that could cause problems ‖ 하려고 했던 특히 나쁘거나 문제가 야기될 수 있는 것을 하지 않기로 결심하다. …을 다시 생각하여 그만두다: *He reached for a cigar, but then thought better of it.* 그는 손을 뻗어 시가를 집었지만 생각을 고쳐먹고 그만두었다. **5 think nothing of (doing sth)** to do something easily that other people consider to be difficult or unusual ‖ 다른 사람들은 어렵거나 특별하게 여기는 것을 쉽게 하다. (…하는 것을) 아무렇지 않게 여기다: *Purdey thinks nothing of driving two hours to work every day.* 퍼디는 매일 출근하기 위해 2시간 동안 운전하는 것을 아무렇지 않게 생각한다. **6 think twice** to consider a decision very carefully before you decide if you will do it or not ‖ 할지 안 할지 결정하기 전에 매우 신중히 생각하다. 숙고하다: *You should think twice about/before getting involved with a married man.* 너는 결혼한 남자와 깊이 사귀기 전에 다시 신중하게 생각해야 한다. **7 who would have thought?** used in order to say that something is very surprising ‖ 어떤 것이 매우 놀랍다는 것을 말하는 데에 쓰여. 누가 상상인들 했겠니?: *Who'd have thought being a mother would make you so happy?* 엄마가 된다는 것이 너를 그렇게 행복하게 해줄 거라고 누가 상상인들 했겠니? **8 think well/highly of** to admire or approve of someone or his/her work ‖ 사람에 대해 또는 사람이 한 일을 감탄하거나 인정하다. …을 좋게 생각하다/존중하다: *People had always thought highly of her grandmother.* 사람들은 항상 그녀의 할머니를 존중했다. **9 think positively** to believe that you are going to be successful or that a situation is going to have a good result ‖ 성공할 것이라고 믿거나 상황이 좋은 결과를 가져올 것이라고 믿다. 긍정적으로 생각하다

SPOKEN PHRASES

---

10 I think said when you believe something is true but you are not sure ‖ 확신하지는 않지만 어떤 것이 사실이라고 믿는 경우에 쓰여. …이라고 생각해요: *Quiet! I think I heard a burglar.* 쉿! 도둑이 들어온 것 같아. **11 I think so/I don't think so** used when answering a question to say that you do or do not believe something is true ‖ 질문에 대한 대답으로 어떤 것을 사실로 여기거나 사실로 여기지 않는다고 말하는 데에 쓰여. 나도 그렇게 생각해/나는 그렇게 생각하지 않아: *"Will she be back on Friday?" "I think so."* "그녀가 금요일에 돌아올까?" "그럴 것 같은데." **12 I think I'll/I thought I'd** said when telling someone what you will probably do ‖ 자신이 할 가능성이 있는 것을 남에게 말하는 데에 쓰여. 나는 … 할 생각이다/…할 생각이었다: *I think I'll stay with my parents through Christmas.* 저는 크리스마스 동안 제 부모님과 함께 보낼 생각입니다. / *I thought I'd go jogging today.* 나는 오늘 조깅할 생각이었다. **13 I thought…** a) used in order to say what you believed was true, when you discover it is not true ‖ 사실로 믿었던 것이 사실이 아니라는 것을 알았을 때 그것을 말하는 데에 쓰여: *Oh, I thought you were Catholic.* 아, 나는 네가 가톨릭 신자라고 생각했어. b) used in order to report exactly what was in your mind ‖ 마음에 있던 것을 정확히 말하는 데에 쓰여: *And I thought, wow, I can't believe she's 15 already.* 생각해 보니, 어머나, 그녀가 벌써 15살이라니 믿을 수 없구나. **14 when you think about it** used in order to say that you realize something about the subject or fact that you are considering ‖ 생각하던 문제나 사실에 대한 어떤 것을 확실히 알았다고 말하는 데에 쓰여: *It's a crazy price for a car when you think about it.* 곰곰이 생각해 보면 자동차 값이 너무 비싸다. **15 I'm thinking** NONSTANDARD used in order to tell someone your opinion or what you are considering ‖ 자신의 의견이나 생각하는 것을 남에게 말하는 데에 쓰여. 내가 생각하기에: *I'm thinking it's a bad time to go on vacation.* 내 생각으

로는 휴가를 가기에는 좋지 않은 시기야. **16 just think!** said when asking someone to imagine or consider something ‖ 남에게 무엇에 대해 상상하거나 생각해 보라고 청할 때 쓰여. 한번 생각해 봐!: *Just think – tomorrow we'll be in Hawaii!* 상상해 봐. 내일 우리는 하와이에 있을 거라구! **17 come to think of it** said when you have just remembered something that is related to your conversation ‖ 대화에 관련된 것을 막 기억해 냈을 때 쓰여. 생각해 보니: *Come to think of it, I did see Rita yesterday.* 생각해 보니까, 나는 어제 정말 리타를 봤어.

—see also unthinkable

think back *phr v* [I] to think about something that you remember from the past ‖ 과거의 일을 생각해 내다: *Think back to what we learned last week about the Constitution.* 지난주에 미국 헌법에 대해 우리가 배운 것을 생각해 봐.

think of sb/sth *phr v* [T] **1** to produce a new idea, suggestion etc. ‖ 새로운 아이디어·제안 등을 내다. …을 생각해 내다: *Can you think of anything better to do?* 할 만한 더 좋은 일 좀 생각나는 거 있어? **2** to remember a name or fact ‖ 이름이나 사실을 기억하다: *I can't think of his name now.* 나는 지금 그의 이름을 생각해 낼 수가 없다. **3** to show that you want to treat other people well ‖ 다른 사람들에게 친절히 대하고 싶어함을 보이다. 배려하다: *Bill's always thinking of others.* 빌은 항상 다른 사람들을 배려하고 있다.

think sth ↔ **out** *phr v* [T] to plan all the details of something very carefully ‖ 어떤 것의 모든 세부 사항들을 매우 꼼꼼히 계획하다. 곰곰 생각하여 안출하다: *Everything has been really well thought out.* 모든 것이 정말 잘 계획되었다.

think sth ↔ **over** *phr v* [T] to consider something carefully before making a decision ‖ 결정하기 전에 어떤 것을 신중히 생각하다. 숙고하다: *Take a few days to think over our offer.* 우리의 제안에 대해 며칠 간 생각해 봐.

think sth ↔ **through** *phr v* [T] to think carefully about the possible results of doing something ‖ 어떤 것을 하여 일어날 수 있는 결과에 대해 신중히 생각하다: *Give us time to think it through.* 우리에게 그것에 대해 곰곰이 생각할 시간을 주세요.

think sth ↔ **up** *phr v* [T] to produce an idea, plan etc. that is completely new ‖

완전히 새로운 아이디어·계획 등을 내다.
고안하다: *thinking up ways to get more
customers* 더 많은 소비자를 끌기 위한 방
법의 고안

think·ing /'θɪŋkɪŋ/ *n* [U] **1** an opinion
about something, or an attitude toward
something ‖ 어떤 것에 대한 의견이나 태
도. 견해. 사고 방식: *It is difficult to
know what the Democratic party's
thinking is on the issue.* 민주당의 의견은
무엇에 초점을 맞추고 있는지를 알기 어렵
다. **2** the activity of using your mind to
solve a problem, produce thoughts etc.
‖ 문제를 풀고 생각 등을 하기 위해 머리
를 쓰는 행위. 사고: *a situation that
requires careful thinking* 신중한 사고가
요구되는 상황

think tank /'. ./ *n* a committee of
people with experience in a particular
subject that an organization or
government establishes to produce
ideas and give advice ‖ 아이디어를 내고
조언을 하기 위해 조직이나 정부가 설립하
는, 특정 분야의 경험자들로 구성된 위원
회. 두뇌 집단: *a right-wing think tank* 우
파 두뇌 집단

thin·ly /'θɪnli/ *adv* **1** in a way that
leaves a very small distance between
two opposite sides or surfaces ‖ 마주하
는 양측이나 양면 사이의 거리를 매우 조
금 남겨서. 얇게: *a thinly sliced onion* 얇
게 썬 양파 **2** in a way that covers a
large area but leaves a lot of space in
between ‖ 넓은 지역에 퍼져 있지만 사이
의 공간을 많이 두어. 성기게: *a thinly
populated area* 인구가 희박한 지역

third /θɚd/ *number* **1** 3rd ‖ 셋째 **2** 1/3 ‖
3분의 1

third base /,. './ *n* [singular] in
baseball, the third place that a player
must touch before s/he can gain a point
‖ 야구에서 선수가 점수를 얻기 전에 반드
시 터치해야 하는 셋째 장소. 삼루 —see
picture on page 946

third de·gree /,. .'./ *n* **give sb the
third degree** INFORMAL to ask someone
a lot of questions in order to get
information from him/her ‖ 남에게 정보
를 얻기 위해 많은 질문을 하다. 엄하게
심문하다

third-de·gree burn /,. ... './ *n* a very
severe burn that goes through
someone's skin ‖ 피부에 입은 매우 심한
화상. 3도 화상

third per·son /,. '../ *n* [singular]
TECHNICAL in grammar, a form of a verb
or pronoun that you use to show the
person or thing that is being mentioned.

"He," "she," "it," and "they" are all
third person pronouns ‖ 문법에서 현재
언급되고 있는 사람이나 사물을 나타내기
위해 쓰는 동사나 대명사의 꼴. 삼인칭
(형). "he," "she," "it," 및 "they"는 모두
3인칭 대명사이다 —compare FIRST
PERSON, SECOND PERSON

third-rate /,. '../ *adj* of very bad
quality ‖ 질이 매우 좋지 않은. 하급의. 삼
류의

Third World /,. '../ *n* **the Third
World** a phrase meaning the poorer
countries of the world that do not have
developed industries, which some
people consider to be offensive ‖ 전 세계
에서 산업이 발달하지 않은 가난한 나라를
뜻하며 일부 사람들은 모욕적으로 여기는
표현. 발전 도상국. 제3세계 –**Third
World** /,. '../ *adj*

thirst /θɚst/ *n* **1** [singular] the feeling
of wanting to drink water ‖ 물을 마시고
싶은 느낌. 갈증: *a drink to quench your
thirst* (=get rid of it) 너의 갈증을 해소시
켜 줄 음료 ✗DON'T SAY "I have thirst."✗
"I have thirst."라고는 하지 않는다 **2** [U]
the state of not having enough to drink
‖ 물을 충분히 섭취하지 않은 상태. 수분
부족. 탈수 상태: *The cattle died of
thirst.* 소가 탈수증으로 죽었다. **3 a
thirst for sth** a strong desire for
something such as knowledge, power,
excitement etc. ‖ 지식·권력·흥미 등에 대
한 강렬한 욕망. 갈망. 열망

thirst·y /'θɚsti/ *adj* **1** feeling that you
want to drink something ‖ 무엇을 마시고
싶어하는. 목마른: *I'm thirsty – let's get
some beer.* 나 목말라. 맥주 좀 마시자. **2
thirsty for sth** LITERARY having a
strong desire for something ‖ 무엇에 대
한 강한 욕망이 있는. 갈망하는 –
thirstily *adv*

thir·teen /,θɚ'tin/ *number* 13 ‖ 숫자
13 –**thirteenth** /,θɚ'tinθ/ *number*

thir·ty /'θɚti/ *number* 1 30 ‖ 숫자 30 **2
the thirties a)** the years between 1930
and 1939 ‖ 1930년에서 1939년 사이의
시기. 30년대 **b)** the numbers between
30 and 39, especially when used for
measuring temperature ‖ 특히 온도를 측
정할 때 쓰이는 30에서 39 사이의 숫자.
30도대 –**thirtieth** /'θɚtiθ/ *number*

this¹ /ðɪs/ *determiner, pron, plural*
these 1 used when talking about
someone or something that is closer in
time, distance etc. than someone or
something else ‖ 어떤 사람이나 사물보다
시간·거리 등이 보다 가까운 사람이나 사
물을 언급할 때 쓰여. 이(것): *My mother*

gave me this necklace. (=the one I am wearing) 우리 엄마가 나한테 이 목걸이를 주셨어. / What should I do with this? (=something I am holding and showing you) 이걸로 내가 뭘 해야 돼? / We're driving up to the lake this Sunday. (=the Sunday that is coming) 우리는 이번 주 일요일에 차를 타고 호수에 갈 거야. —compare THAT¹ **2** used when talking about a person, thing etc. that has already been mentioned or that is already known about ‖ 이미 언급되었거나 또는 이미 알고 있는 사람·사물 등을 언급할 때 쓰여. 이(것): We took these photos on our vacation last summer. 우리는 지난 여름 휴가 때 이 사진들을 찍었다. / This is the third time he's been late this week. 금주에 그가 늦은 게 이번이 세 번째이다. **3** SPOKEN used in conversation to mention a particular person or thing ‖ 대화에서 특정한 사람이나 사물을 언급하기 위해 쓰여: This friend of mine said he could get us tickets. 나의 이 친구가 우리에게 표를 구해줄 수 있다고 했어. / We saw this really cool movie last night. 우리는 간밤에 정말 재미있는 이 영화를 봤어. **4 this is** SPOKEN used in order to introduce someone to someone else ‖ 누군가를 다른 사람에게 소개시키는 데에 쓰여. 이분은: Nancy, this is my wife, Elaine. 낸시, 이 쪽은 내 아내인 일레인이야. **5 this and that** various different things, subjects etc. ‖ 다양한 종류의 사물·주제 등. 이것저것: We just talked about guys and this and that. 우리는 단지 사람들 그리고 이것저것에 대해 이야기했다.

this² adv used when talking about the size, number, degree, or amount of something ‖ 어떤 것의 크기나 수효, 또는 정도나 양을 언급할 때 쓰여. 이만큼. 이렇게: I've never stayed up this late before. 나는 이전에 이렇게 늦게까지 자지 않은 적이 없었다. / Katie's about this tall now. (=said when using your hands to show a size) (손으로 나타내면서)케이티는 지금 한 이 정도로 커.

this·tle /ˈθɪsəl/ n a wild plant with purple flowers and leaves that have sharp points ‖ 자주색 꽃이 피고 날카로운 가시가 달린 잎을 가진 야생 식물. 엉겅퀴

thong /θɔŋ, θɑŋ/ n **1** a single string that forms part of a piece of clothing ‖ 옷의 일부를 이루는 한 개의 끈 **2** a long thin piece of leather used for fastening things or as part of a whip ‖ 물건을 묶기 위해 또는 채찍의 부분으로 쓰이는 길고 가는 가죽. 가죽끈 **3** [C usually plural] a pair of summer shoes, usually made of rubber, with only a v-shaped band across the front that fits between your toes to hold the shoes on ‖ 발가락 사이에 끼워 신도록 앞쪽에 v자 모양의 끈만 달린 보통 고무로 된 여름 신발. 고무 슬리퍼

thorn /θɔrn/ n **1** a sharp point that grows on a plant such as a rose ‖ 장미 등의 식물에 나는 끝이 뾰족한 것. 가시 **2 a thorn in your side** someone or something that annoys you or causes you problems over a long time ‖ 오랫동안 괴롭히거나 문제를 일으키는 사람이나 사물. 문제아. 두통거리

thorn·y /ˈθɔrni/ adj **1 thorny question/problem/issue etc.** a question, problem etc. that is very difficult to deal with ‖ 질문·문제 등이 다루기 힘든. 어려운[까다로운] 질문/문제/쟁점 **2** having a lot of THORNs ‖ 가시가 많은

thor·ough /ˈθɚou, ˈθʌrou/ adj **1** including every possible detail ‖ 있을 수 있는 세부 사항을 모두 포함하는. 철저한. 면밀한: The police conducted a thorough search of the property. 경찰은 재산을 철저히 수사했다. **2** careful to do everything that you should and avoid mistakes ‖ 해야 하는 모든 것에 신중을 기해 실수를 피하는. 꼼꼼한: As a scientist, Madison is methodical and thorough. 과학자로서 매디슨은 논리 정연하고 꼼꼼하다.

thor·ough·bred /ˈθɚəˌbrɛd, ˈθɚou-, ˈθʌr-/ n a horse that has parents of the same very good breed ‖ 부모의 혈통이 동일하며 매우 좋은 말. 순혈종 경주 말

thor·ough·fare /ˈθɚəˌfɛr, ˈθɚou-, ˈθʌr-/ n the main road through a city ‖ 도시로 통하는 주요 도로

thor·ough·ly /ˈθɚouli, ˈθʌr-/ adv **1** completely or very much ‖ 완전히, 대단히: Thanks for dinner; I thoroughly enjoyed it. 저녁 식사 감사합니다. 대단히 잘 먹었습니다. **2** carefully and completely ‖ 세심하면서 완벽하게. 철저히: Rinse the vegetables thoroughly. 야채를 속속들이 헹궈라.

those /ðouz/ determiner, pron the plural of THAT ‖ that의 복수형

though¹ /ðou/ conj **1** used in order to introduce a statement that is surprising, unexpected, or different from your other statements ‖ 놀랍거나 예기치 않은, 또는 자신이 한 여타의 말과 다른 말을 시작하는 데에 쓰여. …임에도 불구하고: Though Beattie is almost 40, she still plans to compete. 베티는 거의 40세임에

도 불구하고 그녀는 여전히 경기에 참가할 계획이다. / *I seem to keep gaining weight, even though I'm exercising regularly.* 나는 규칙적으로 운동을 하는 데도 계속 살이 찌는 것 같다. —compare ALTHOUGH **2** used like "but" in order to add a fact or opinion to what you have said ‖ 자신이 말한 것에 사실이나 의견을 덧붙이기 위해 "but"처럼 쓰여. 다만 …이지만 : *I bought it at one of the department stores, though it's probably cheaper at K-Mart.* K마트에서는 아마 더 싸겠지만 나는 그것을 백화점들 중 한 곳에서 샀다. **3 as though** used like "as if" in order to say how something seems or appears ‖ 어떤 것이 보이거나 드러나는 양상을 말하기 위해 "as if"처럼 쓰여. 마치 …인 것처럼: *She was staring at me as though she knew me.* 그녀는 마치 나를 알고 있다는 듯이 나를 뚫어져라 보고 있었다.

though² *adv* SPOKEN in spite of that ‖ 그것에도 불구하고. …이지만: *Raleigh's a nice city. Mark doesn't want to leave Georgia, though.* 롤리는 멋진 도시이지만 마크는 조지아 주를 떠나기 싫어한다.

thought¹ /θɔt/ *v* the past tense and PAST PARTICIPLE of THINK ‖ think의 과거·과거 분사형

thought² *n* **1** something that you think of, think about, or remember ‖ 떠오르거나 생각하는, 또는 기억나는 것. 생각: *Do you have any thoughts on the subject?* 그 주제에 대해 무슨 생각이라도 있는 거야? / *Even the thought of flying scares me.* 나는 비행하는 생각만으로도 무섭다. **2** [U] the act of thinking ‖ 생각하는 행위. 사색: *She sat at her desk, deep in thought.* (=thinking so much she did not notice anything else) 그녀는 책상에 앉아서 깊은 사색에 잠겼다. **3** [U] the act of considering something carefully and seriously ‖ 주의 깊고 진지하게 무엇을 고려하는 행위. 고찰: *You need to give the decision plenty of thought.* 너는 깊이 고찰하여 결론을 내려야 한다. **4 (it's) just a thought** SPOKEN said when you have made a suggestion and you have not thought about it very much ‖ 무엇에 대해 많이 생각하지 않고 제안했을 때 쓰여. 그냥 그렇다는 얘기야 **5** [C, U] a feeling of caring about someone ‖ 남을 염려하는 마음. 배려: *He had given no thought to the other passengers.* 그는 다른 승객들을 전혀 배려하지 않았다. **6** [C, U] an intention to do something ‖ 무엇을 하려는 의도. 의향. 작정: *We worked with no thought of making money.* 우리는 돈을

벌 생각도 없이 일을 했다.

thought·ful /ˈθɔtfəl/ *adj* **1** serious and quiet because you are thinking about something ‖ 무엇에 대해 생각하느라 진지하고 조용한. 생각에 잠긴: *a thoughtful expression on his face* 그의 얼굴에 나타난 생각에 잠긴 표정 **2** careful to do things to make other people happy or comfortable ‖ 다른 사람들을 행복하거나 편하게 하기 위해 조심스럽게 행동하는. 사려 깊은: *You have a very thoughtful husband.* 당신은 매우 사려 깊은 남편을 두셨네요. **- thoughtfully** *adv* **- thoughtfulness** *n* [U]

thought·less /ˈθɔtlɪs/ *adj* not thinking about the needs and feelings of other people ‖ 다른 사람들의 필요성과 감정에 대해 생각하지 않는. 인정이 없는: *a thoughtless remark/comment* 인정미가 없는 발언[논평]

thou·sand /ˈθaʊzənd/ *number* **1** 1000 ‖ 숫자 1000 **2 thousands of** INFORMAL a lot of ‖ 많은: *a cottage thousands of miles from anywhere* 그 어디에선가로부터 수천 마일 떨어져 있는 오두막 **- thousandth** *adj*

thrash /θræʃ/ *v* **1** [T] to hit someone violently, often as a punishment ‖ 종종 벌로 남을 호되게 때리다 **2** [I] to move from side to side in an uncontrolled way ‖ 아무렇게나 좌우로 움직이다. 뒹굴다. 몸부림치다: *a fish thrashing around on dry land* 마른 땅에서 팔딱거리는 물고기 **- thrashing** *n* [C, U]

thrash sth ↔ **out** *phr v* [T] to discuss a problem thoroughly until you find an answer ‖ 답을 알아낼 때까지 문제를 철저히 토의하다. 검토하다: *Officials are still trying to thrash out an agreement.* 담당자들은 여전히 합의안을 도출해 내려고 애쓰고 있다.

thread¹ /θrɛd/ *n* **1** [C, U] a long thin line of cotton, silk etc. that you use to sew cloth ‖ 직물을 꿰매기 위해 쓰는 무명·명주 등의 길고 가는 줄. 실: *a spool of thread* 실패 **2** [singular] the relation between different parts of a story, explanation etc. ‖ 이야기·설명 등에서 서로 다른 부분들 사이의 관계. 줄거리. 맥락: *He lost the thread* (=forgot the main part) *of his argument.* 그는 자기 주장의 주안점을 잊어 버렸다. **3** a raised line of metal that winds around the bottom part of a screw ‖ 나사의 몸통을 칭칭 감는 솟아나온 금속 선. 나사산

thread² *v* [T] **1** to put thread, string, rope etc. through a hole ‖ 구멍을 통해 실·끈·밧줄 등을 관통시키다. 꿰(뚫)다:

Will you thread the needle for me? 바늘에 실 좀 꿰어 줄래? **2 thread your way through/down etc.** to move through a place by carefully going around things that are in the way ‖ 방해가 되는 것들을 조심스레 우회하며 장소를 통과하다. …사이를 누비듯이 나아가다: *a biker threading his way through traffic* 자동차들 사이를 누비듯이 나아가는 자전거 탄 사람

thread·bare /ˈθrɛdbɛr/ *adj* clothes, CARPETs etc. that are threadbare are very thin because they have been used a lot ‖ 옷·양탄자 등이 많이 사용하여 매우 얇은. 올이 드러나게 낡은[닳아 빠진]

threat /θrɛt/ *n* **1** [C, U] a statement or warning that you will cause someone trouble, pain, or sadness ‖ 남에게 문제나 고통, 또는 슬픔을 일으키겠다는 말이나 경고. 위협. 협박: *He made a threat against my family.* 그는 내 가족을 협박했다. / *a death threat from the kidnappers* 유괴범의 죽이겠다는 협박 **2** [C usually singular] the possibility that something bad will happen ‖ 나쁜 일이 발생할 가능성. (위험의) 조짐: *a threat of rain* 비가 쏟아질 징조 **3** [C usually singular] someone or something that is a danger to something else ‖ 다른 것에 위험스러운 사람이나 사물: *a threat to national security* 국가 안보에 대한 위협

threat·en /ˈθrɛtˈn/ *v* **1** [T] to say that you will cause someone trouble, pain etc. if s/he does not do what you want ‖ 만일 자신이 바라는 것을 남이 하지 않을 경우, 문제를 일으키거나 고통스럽게 할 것이라고 말하다. 위협하다: *Sandra threatened to run away from home.* 산드라는 집에서 도망치겠다고 위협했다. / *Don't you threaten me!* 나를 협박하지 마! **2** [T] to be likely to harm or destroy something ‖ 무엇을 해치거나 파괴할 것 같다. …을 위태롭게 하다: *Pollution is threatening the historical buildings of Athens.* 오염으로 아테네의 역사적 건축물이 손상될 것 같다. **3** [I, T] if something unpleasant threatens to happen, it seems likely to happen ‖ 불쾌한 일이 발생할 것 같다. …의 조짐이 있다: *The fighting threatens to become a major war.* 그 전투는 큰 전쟁으로 비화될 위험이 있다.

threat·en·ing /ˈθrɛtˈn-ɪŋ/ *adj* making threats or intended to threaten someone ‖ 위협하거나 남을 협박하려는. 위협적인: *a threatening letter* 협박 편지

three /θri/ *number* **1** 3 ‖ 숫자 3 **2** three o'clock ‖ 3시: *I'll meet you at three.* 세

시에 만나자.

three-di·men·sion·al /ˌ. .ˈ.../, **3-D** /ˌθri ˈdi·/ *adj* having or seeming to have length, depth, and height ‖ 길이·깊이·높이가 있거나 있는 듯이 보이는. 삼차원의. 입체감이 있는: *a 3-D movie* 3차원 영화

thresh /θrɛʃ/ *v* [I, T] to separate the grain from corn, wheat etc. by beating it ‖ 옥수수·밀 등을 두드려서 낟알을 분리하다. 타작하다 – **thresher** *n*

thresh·old /ˈθrɛʃhould, -ʃould/ *n* **1 on the threshold of sth** at the beginning of a new and important event or development ‖ 새롭고 중요한 사건이나 개발의 시초에. 막 …하려는 시점에: *We're on the threshold of a new period in telecommunications.* 우리는 새로운 통신 시대의 출발점에 있다. **2** the level at which something begins to happen or have an effect on something ‖ 무엇이 발생하거나 무엇에 영향을 미치기 시작하는 단계. 기준점. 역치(閾値): *a plan to raise/lower the threshold for business tax* 영업세 한도를 높이려는[낮추려는] 계획 / *She has a high/low pain threshold.* 그녀는 고통을 잘 참는다[못 참는다]. **3** the entrance to a room, or the area of floor at the entrance ‖ 방의 입구나 출입구의 바닥 부분. 문지방. 문간

threw /θru/ *v* the past tense of THROW ‖ throw의 과거형

thrift /θrɪft/ *n* [U] OLD-FASHIONED wise and careful use of money ‖ 돈의 현명하고 신중한 사용. 검약. 절약 – **thrifty** *adj*

thrift store /ˈ. ./, **thrift shop** *n* a store that sells used goods, especially clothes, often in order to get money for a CHARITY ‖ 종종 자선을 위한 돈을 모으기 위해 특히 옷 등의 중고품을 파는 가게. 중고품점

thrill¹ /θrɪl/ *n* a strong feeling of excitement and pleasure, or the thing that makes you feel this ‖ 흥분·쾌감의 격한 느낌이나, 흥분·쾌감을 느끼게 하는 것. 전율. 스릴: *I'll never forget the thrill of my first parachute jump.* 나는 첫 낙하산 강하의 전율을 잊지 못할 것이다.

thrill² *v* [I, T] to feel strong excitement and pleasure, or make someone else feel this ‖ 격한 흥분과 쾌감을 느끼거나, 다른 사람을 이렇게 느끼게 하다. 설레다. 설레게 하다: *Manley thrilled us with stories from his travels.* 맨리는 그의 여행담으로 우리를 설레게 했다.

thrilled /θrɪld/ *adj* very excited, pleased, or happy ‖ 매우 흥분하거나 유쾌하거나 짜릿한: *I'm thrilled to finally* *have my own car.* 나는 마침내 내 소유의 차를 갖게 되어 짜릿했다.

thrill·er /'θrɪlə/ *n* a movie or book that tells an exciting story about murder, crime etc. ‖ 살인·범죄 등에 대한 흥미진진한 이야기를 전하는 영화나 책. 스릴러물. 추리 영화[소설]

thrill·ing /'θrɪlɪŋ/ *adj* exciting and interesting ‖ 자극적이며 흥미 있는. 오싹하게 하는: *a football game with a thrilling finish* 아슬아슬하게 끝난 미식축구 시합

thrive /θraɪv/ *v* **thrived** or **throve, thrived, thriving** [I] FORMAL to become very successful or very strong and healthy ‖ 상당히 성공하거나 매우 튼튼하고 건강해지다. 성공하다. 무럭무럭[무성하게] 자라다: *a plant that is able to thrive in dry conditions* 건조한 기후에서 잘 자라는 식물

thriv·ing /'θraɪvɪŋ/ *adj* very successful ‖ 매우 성공적인. 번성하는: *a thriving business* 매우 번창하는 사업

throat /θroʊt/ *n* **1** the passage from the back of your mouth down the inside of your neck ‖ 입의 뒷부분에서 목의 안쪽으로 내려가는 통로. 목구멍: *I have a sore throat.* 나는 목이 아프다. **2** the front of your neck ‖ 목의 앞쪽. 인후: *The attacker cut his throat with a razor.* 그 범인은 면도칼로 그의 목을 그었다. **3 force/ram sth down sb's throat** to force someone to accept your ideas or listen to your opinions when s/he does not want to ‖ 남에게 그 사람이 원하지 않는데도 자신의 생각을 받아들이거나 의견을 따르도록 강요하다. 남에게 억지로 밀어붙이다. 강요하다 **4 be at each other's throats** if two people are at each other throats, they are fighting or arguing with each other ‖ 두 사람이 서로 싸우거나 논쟁을 벌이다. 싸우고[다투고] 있다 —see also **clear your throat** (CLEAR²) **jump down sb's throat** (JUMP¹)

throat·y /'θroʊti/ *adj* making a low rough sound when you speak, sing, cough etc. ‖ 말할 때·노래할 때·기침할 때 등에 낮고 거친 소리를 내는. 쉰 목소리를 내는

throb¹ /θrɑb/ *v* **-bbed, -bbing** [I] **1** if a part of your body throbs, you get a regular feeling of pain in it ‖ 몸의 일부분에서 규칙적인 통증을 느끼다. 지근[욱신]거리다: *My head was throbbing with pain.* 머리가 통증으로 지근거리고 있었다. **2** to beat strongly and regularly ‖ 강하고 규칙적으로 고동치다. 두근거리다. 맥박치다

throb² *n* a strong regular beat ‖ 강하고 규칙적인 고동. 두근거림. 동계: *the low throb of the music* 여린 박자의 음악 — see also HEARTTHROB

throes /θroʊz/ *n* [plural] **in the throes of sth** in the middle of trying to deal with a very difficult situation ‖ 매우 어려운 상황을 처리하려고 애쓰는 중인. …이 한창인. 필사적으로 노력 중인: *a woman in the throes of childbirth* 출산의 고비에 이르러 있는 여자

throne /θroʊn/ *n* **1** the chair on which a king or queen sits ‖ 왕이나 여왕이 앉는 권좌. 옥좌. 왕좌 **2 the throne** the position and power of being king or queen ‖ 왕이나 여왕으로서의 지위와 권력. 왕위. 왕권

throng¹ /θrɔŋ, θrɑŋ/ *n* LITERARY ⇨ CROWD¹

throng² *v* [I, T] LITERARY if people throng a place, they go there in large numbers ‖ 많은 사람들이 떼지어 어떤 장소에 가다. 쇄도하다. 떼지어 모이다: *crowds thronging St. Peter's Square* 성 베드로 광장에 운집한 군중

throt·tle¹ /'θrɑtl/ *v* [T] ⇨ STRANGLE

throttle² *n* TECHNICAL a piece of equipment that controls the amount of gas going into an engine ‖ 엔진으로 들어가는 휘발유 양을 조절하는 장비. 스로틀

through¹ /θru/ *prep* **1** into one end of a passage, door etc. and out the other end or side ‖ 통로나 문 등의 한쪽 끝으로 들어가서 다른 쪽 끝이나 옆으로 나와. …을 통과하여: *He climbed in through the window.* 그는 창문을 통해 기어 들어갔다. */ a train going through a tunnel* 터널을 통과하는 기차 */ water flowing through a pipe* 파이프를 통해 흐르는 물 **2** going into an area, group etc. and moving across it or within it ‖ 어떤 지역·집단 등의 속으로 들어가서 가로지르거나 내부에서 움직여. …을 꿰뚫어. …을 두루: *He tried to push his way through the crowd.* 그는 군중 사이를 뚫고 지나가려 했다. */ a plane flying through the air* 공중을 가로지르며 나는 비행기 */ a trip through Europe* 유럽을 두루 구경하는 여행 **3** by means of, or because of someone or something ‖ 사람이나 사물에 의하여, 또는 사람이나 사물 때문에. …을 통해서: *They reached a settlement through negotiations.* 그들은 협상을 통해 합의에 이르렀다. **4** if you see or hear something through a window, wall etc., the window, wall etc. is between you and it ‖ 창문·벽 등이 사이에 있어 그를 통해 어떤 것을 보거나 듣는. …을 관통하

여[뚫고]: *I could see him through the window.* 나는 창문을 통해 그를 볼 수 있었다. / *music coming through the walls* 벽을 뚫고 흘러나오는 음악 **5** during and to the end of a period of time ‖ 일정 시간 동안과 끝까지. …동안 내내. 시종: *She slept calmly through the night.* 그녀는 밤새 고요히 잠잤다. **6** from one side of a thing or place to the other ‖ 어떤 사물이나 장소의 한 쪽에서 다른 쪽으로. …의 끝에서 끝까지: *We drove through a red light by accident.* 우리는 빨간불인지도 모르고 차로 지나쳐 갔다. / *A dog chewed through the rope.* 개가 밧줄을 통째로 씹어 놓았다. **7** Friday through Sunday/ through May 15th etc. from Friday until the end of Sunday, from Friday until the end of May 15th etc. ‖ 금요일부터 일요일까지/5월 15일까지: *The exhibit will be here through July 31st.* 전시회는 7월 31일까지 여기에서 개최됩니다. **8** look/search/go etc. through sth to look, search etc. among all the parts of something ‖ 어떤 것의 모든 부분들에 걸쳐서 보다·찾다 등. …을 샅샅이 찾다[뒤지다]: *I've searched through my files but I can't find the receipt.* 내 서류들을 샅샅이 찾아보았지만 그 영수증을 찾을 수가 없다. **9** get through sth to deal with a difficult situation successfully ‖ 어려운 상황을 성공적으로 처리하다. 해결하다. …을 극복해 나가다: *Janet needed a lot of support to get through the divorce.* 재닛의 이혼을 극복해 내기 위해서 많은 도움이 필요했다.

through² *adv* **1** from one end or side of something to the other ‖ 사물의 한 끝이나 면에서 다른 끝 쪽으로. …을 관통하여. 줄곧: *I held the door to let them through.* 나는 그들이 모두 지나가도록 문을 붙잡았다. / *He walked through to the library.* 그는 도서관까지 줄곧 걸었다. **2** read/think/study etc. sth through to read, think etc. about something very carefully from beginning to end ‖ 어떤 것에 대해 처음부터 끝까지 매우 주의 깊게 읽거나 생각하다. …을 자세히 읽다/생각하다/검토하다: *Read it through before signing it.* 그것에 서명하기 전에 자세히 읽어 봐라. **3** through and through completely ‖ 완전히. 송두리째. 속속들이: *He came in from the rain soaked through and through.* 그는 비에 흠뻑 젖은 채로 들어왔다. —see also **come through** (COME), **get through** (GET), **go through** (GO¹), **pull through** (PULL¹)

through³ *adj* be through (with sb/sth) INFORMAL **a)** to have finished using something, doing something etc. ‖ 어떤 것을 사용하거나 하는 것 등을 끝마쳤다. …하기를 끝내다. 다 쓰다: *I'm through with the phone now if you still need it.* 네가 아직도 필요하다면 이제 난 전화 다 썼어. **b)** to no longer have a romantic relationship with someone ‖ 남과 이제는 연애 관계를 가지지 않다. …과 헤어지다: *Steve and I are through!* 스티브와 나는 헤어졌어!

through·out /θru'aʊt/ *adv, prep* **1** in every part of a place ‖ 어떤 장소의 모든 부분에서. 도처에서. 구석구석: *Thanksgiving is celebrated throughout the US.* 추수 감사절은 미국 전역에서 기념된다. **2** during all of a particular time ‖ 특정한 시간 전부 동안. …동안 내내: *She was calm throughout the interview.* 그녀는 인터뷰하는 동안 내내 차분했다.

throve /θroʊv/ *v* a past tense of THRIVE ‖ thrive의 과거형

throw¹ /θroʊ/ *v* **threw**, **thrown**, **throwing**

throw away

1 ▶ THROW A BALL/STONE ETC. 공/돌을 던지다◀ [I, T] to make an object move quickly from your hand through the air by moving your arm ‖ 팔을 움직여서 물체를 손으로부터 공중을 가로질러 빠르게 움직이게 하다. 던지다: *It's Ted's turn to throw.* 이제 테드가 던질 차례다. / *Some kids are throwing bottles at the wall.* (=in order to hit it) 몇몇 아이들이 벽에 병을 던지고 있다. / *Throw the ball to Daddy.* 아빠에게 공을 던져라.

2 ▶PUT STH CARELESSLY 어떤 것을 부주의하게 놓다◀ [T] to put something somewhere quickly and carelessly ‖ 어떤 것을 어딘가에 급하고 부주의하게 놓다. 내던지다. 던져 놓다: *Just throw your coat on the bed.* 네 외투는 침대에 그냥 던져 놔.

3 ▶PUSH ROUGHLY 거칠게 밀다◀ [T] to push someone roughly toward a particular direction or position ‖ 남을 특정한 방향이나 위치로 거칠게 밀다. 팽개치다. 내동댕이치다: *Police threw the man to the ground and tied his hands.* 경찰은 그 남자를 땅바닥에 쓰러뜨리고 손을 묶었다.

4 throw yourself on/down etc. to move somewhere suddenly and with force ‖ 어딘가로 갑작스럽고 힘차게 움직

이다. 몸을 던지다. 심하게 움직이다:
Elise threw herself on the bed and started to cry. 엘리스는 침대에 몸을 던지더니 울기 시작했다.

5 ▶MAKE SB FALL 사람을 떨어지게 하다
◀ [T] if a horse throws its rider, it makes him/her fall off ‖ 말이 기수를 떨어뜨리다. 낙마시키다. 떨어뜨리다

6 ▶MOVE HANDS/HEAD ETC. 손/머리를 움직이다◀ [T] to suddenly move your hands, arms, head etc. in a particular direction ‖ 손·팔·머리 등을 특정한 방향으로 갑자기 움직이다. 심하게 움직이다:
Vic threw his head back and laughed. 빅은 머리를 뒤로 젖히면서 웃었다.

7 throw sb in jail INFORMAL to put someone in prison ‖ 남을 감옥에 집어넣다. 투옥[구속]시키다

8 throw sb SPOKEN to confuse or shock someone, especially by suddenly saying something ‖ 특히 어떤 것을 갑자기 말해서 남을 혼란스럽게 하거나 충격 받게 하다. 남을 어리둥절하게[대경실색케] 하다:
His reaction threw me for a loop. (=completely confused me) 그의 반응은 나를 완전히 어리둥절하게 했다.

9 throw a party to organize a party and invite people ‖ 파티를 준비해 사람들을 초대하다. 파티를 열다

10 throw your weight around to use your authority in an unreasonable way ‖ 불합리하게 권한을 사용하다. 권력을 휘두르다. 권한을 남용하다

11 throw the book at sb INFORMAL to punish someone as severely as possible ‖ 가능한 한 호되게 남을 처벌하다. …을 엄하게 벌하다[꾸짖다]

throw sth ↔ **away** *phr v* [T] **1** to get rid of something that you do not want or need ‖ 원하거나 필요하지 않은 것을 없애다. …을 버리다: *Do you still want the newspaper, or can I throw it away?* 너 아직도 이 신문 필요하냐? 아니면 갖다 버릴까? **2** to lose or waste a chance, advantage etc. ‖ 기회·이점 등을 잃거나 허비하다. …을 놓치다. 헛되이 보내다: *This is a good chance to study abroad; don't throw it away.* 이번이 해외에서 공부할 수 있는 좋은 기회다. 놓치지 마라. **throw in** *phr v* [T] **1** [**throw** sth ↔ **in**] to add something, especially to what you are selling ‖ 특히 팔고 있는 것에 어떤 것을 추가하다. …을 덤으로 주다. 끼워주다: *If you're really interested in the desk, we'll throw in the chair.* 정말 그 책상을 사실 의향이 있으시다면 의자는 끼워서 드리겠습니다. **2 throw in the towel** INFORMAL to admit that you have

been defeated ‖ 패배했음을 인정하다. 항복하다

throw sb/sth ↔ **off** *phr v* [T] **1** to take off a piece of clothing quickly and carelessly ‖ 옷을 급하고 부주의하게 벗다. …을 벗어 던지다 **2** to escape from someone ‖ 남에게서 도망치다. …을 따돌리다: *Somehow he managed to throw them off his trail.* 어쨌든 그는 그들의 추적을 가까스로 따돌렸다.

throw sth ↔ **on** *phr v* [T] to put on a piece of clothing quickly and carelessly ‖ 옷을 급히 부주의하게 입다. 급히 입다

throw out *phr v* [T] **1** [**throw** sth ↔ **out**] to get rid of something that you do not want or need ‖ 원하거나 필요하지 않은 것을 없애다. …을 버리다: *The meat smells funny - you'd better throw it out.* 그 고기는 냄새가 좀 이상해. 버리는 게 좋겠어. **2** [**throw** sb ↔ **out**] to make someone leave a place quickly because s/he has behaved badly ‖ 남이 행동을 잘못 해서 어떤 장소에서 서둘러 떠나게 하다. 쫓아내다: *Jim got thrown out of the Navy for taking drugs.* 짐은 마약을 복용해서 해군에서 쫓겨났다.

throw sth ↔ **together** *phr v* [T] to make something quickly and not very carefully ‖ 어떤 것을 급하고 그다지 정성들이지 않고 만들다. …을 서둘러 만들다: *How about throwing some sandwiches together for lunch?* 점심으로 샌드위치나 대충 만들어 먹는 게 어때?

throw up *phr v* [I, T] INFORMAL ⇨ VOMIT[1]

throw² *n* **1** an act of throwing something such as a ball ‖ 공 등의 것을 던지는 행위. 던지기. 투구: *The throw went right to first base.* 송구는 바로 1루로 갔다. **2** the distance that something is thrown ‖ 어떤 것이 던져진 거리. (던져서) 닿는 거리. 사정 거리: *a throw of 30 feet* 30피트 던지기

throw·a·way /ˈθroʊə,weɪ/ *adj* **1 throwaway remark/line etc.** a short remark that is said quickly and without thinking carefully ‖ 서둘러서 주의 깊게 생각하지 않고 말하는 짧은 발언. 즉흥적인 발언/대사 **2 throwaway society** a society that wastes things instead of caring about the environment ‖ 환경을 염려하지 않고 사물들을 내버리는 사회. 낭비 사회

throw·back /ˈθroʊbæk/ *n* something that is like something that existed in the past ‖ 과거에 존재했던 것과 유사한 것. 복고형: *His music is a throwback to the 1970s.* 그의 음악은 1970년대의 복고형

이다.

thrown /θroʊn/ v the PAST PARTICIPLE of THROW ‖ throw의 과거 분사형

thru /θru/ prep, adj, adv NONSTANDARD ➪ THROUGH¹

thrust¹ /θrʌst/ v thrust, thrust, thrusting [T] to push something somewhere with a sudden or violent movement ‖ 갑작스럽거나 격렬한 동작으로 어떤 것을 어딘가로 밀다. 밀어붙이다. 밀치다: Dean thrust his hands in his pockets. 딘은 손을 호주머니에 쑤셔 넣다.

thrust² n 1 [C, U] a sudden strong movement that pushes something forward ‖ 어떤 것을 앞으로 미는 갑작스럽고 강한 동작. 밀어붙이기. 추진: the thrust of an airplane 비행기의 추진력 2 the thrust the main meaning or most important part of what someone says or does ‖ 남이 말하거나 행하는 것의 주된 의미나 가장 중요한 부분. 요점. 취지: The thrust of his argument is that all of life is political. 그의 주장의 요점은 생활의 모든 것이 정치적이라는 것이다.

thru·way /θruweɪ/ n a wide road for fast traffic ‖ 빠른 교통을 위한 넓은 길. 고속도로

thud /θʌd/ n the low sound that is made by a heavy object hitting something else ‖ 무거운 물체가 다른 것에 부딪혀 나는 낮은 소리. 쿵. 팡. 털썩: The box fell with a thud. 상자가 쿵 하고 떨어졌다. – thud v [I]

thug /θʌg/ n a violent person ‖ 폭력적인 사람. 흉한. 악당

thumb¹ /θʌm/ n 1 the thickest finger on your hand, that helps you hold things ‖ 사물을 잡을 때 돕는, 손에서 가장 굵은 손가락. 엄지손가락 —see picture at HAND¹ 2 be under sb's thumb to do everything that someone wants ‖ 남이 원하는 모든 것을 하다. 남에게 꼼짝 못하다. 남이 시키는 대로 하다 3 give sth the thumbs up/down to show that you approve or disapprove of something ‖ 어떤 것에 찬성하거나 찬성하지 않는다는 것을 나타내다. …을 칭찬[비난]하다: We give the movie a thumbs up! 우리는 그 영화에 찬사를 보낸다!

thumb² v 1 thumb a ride INFORMAL ➪ HITCHHIKE 2 thumb your nose at to show that you do not respect rules, laws, someone's opinion etc. ‖ 규칙·법률·남의 의견 등을 존중하지 않음을 나타내다. …을 경멸[무시]하다: The Senator is basically thumbing his nose at the state's voters. 그 상원 의원은 근본적으로 그 주의 유권자들을 무시하고 있다.

thumb through phr v [T] to look through a book, magazine etc. quickly ‖ 책·잡지 등을 빠르게 훑어보다. 대충 [휙] 훑어보다

thumb·nail¹ /θʌmneɪl/ adj thumbnail sketch/description a short description that gives only the main facts ‖ 단지 주요 사실들만을 제공해 주는 짧은 기술. 간단한 스케치/기술

thumbnail² n the nail on your thumb ‖ 엄지손가락의 손톱

thumb·tack /θʌmtæk/ n a short pin with a wide flat top, used for attaching papers to walls ‖ 벽에 종이를 부착할 때 사용하는 위가 넓고 납작한 짧은 핀. 압정

thump /θʌmp/ v 1 [I, T] to make a dull sound by beating or falling against a surface ‖ 표면에 부딪치거나 떨어져서 무딘 소리를 내다. 쿵 부딪치다. 탁 치다: a dog thumping his tail on the floor 바닥에 꼬리를 탁탁 치는 개 2 [I] if your heart thumps, it beats very quickly because you are frightened or excited ‖ 겁을 먹었거나 흥분되어서 심장이 매우 빠르게 뛰다. 두근거리다. 쿵쿵 고동치다 3 [T] INFORMAL to hit someone very hard with your hand closed ‖ 주먹을 쥐고서 남을 매우 세게 때리다. 주먹으로 강타하다: I'm going to thump you on the head if you don't stop talking! 입을 다물지 않으면 머리에 꿀밤을 줄 거야! – thump n

thun·der¹ /θʌndɚ/ n [U] the loud noise that you hear during a storm, usually after a flash of LIGHTNING ‖ 폭풍우 동안에 보통 번개가 번득인 후 들리는 시끄러운 소리. 천둥. 우레

thunder² v 1 it thunders if it thunders, a loud noise comes from the sky, usually after LIGHTNING ‖ 보통 번개가 친 후 하늘에서 굉음이 나다. 천둥이 치다 2 [I] to make a very loud noise ‖ 매우 큰 소음을 내다. 굉음을 내다: The kids came thundering downstairs. 아이들은 쿵쾅거리며 계단을 내려왔다.

thun·der·bolt /θʌndɚˌboʊlt/ n a flash of LIGHTNING that hits something ‖ 어떤 것을 내리치는 번개. 벼락. 낙뢰

thun·der·clap /θʌndɚˌklæp/ n a loud noise of THUNDER ‖ 천둥의 굉음. 우레 소리

thun·der·cloud /θʌndɚˌklaʊd/ n a large dark cloud in a storm ‖ 폭풍우의 잔뜩 낀 어두운 구름. 먹장구름. 뇌운

thun·der·ous /θʌndərəs/ adj extremely loud ‖ 매우 큰 소리의. 굉음의. 우레 같은: thunderous applause 우레 같은 박수갈채

thun·der·storm /θʌndɚˌstɔrm/ n a

storm with THUNDER and LIGHTNING ‖ 천
등과 번개를 동반한 폭풍우. 심한 뇌우

thun·der·struck /ˈθʌndə،strʌk/ *adj*
extremely surprised or shocked ‖ 매우
놀라거나 충격을 받은. 깜짝 놀란

Thurs·day /ˈθəˑzdi, -deɪ/ *written
abbreviation* **Thurs.** *n* the fifth day of
the week ‖ 주의 다섯 번째 날. 목요일. —
see usage note at SUNDAY

thus /ðʌs/ *adv* FORMAL **1** as a result of
something that you have just
mentioned; so ‖ 방금 언급한 것의 결과로
서. 그러므로. 따라서; 그래서: *Traffic
will become heavier, thus increasing
pollution.* 교통은 더 복잡해질 테고 따라
서 오염도 증가할 것이다. **2** in this way ‖
이렇게. 이와 같이: *The oil spill could
thus contaminate the water supply.* 기름
유출은 이와 같이 상수도를 오염시킬 수도
있었다. **3 thus far** until now ‖ 지금까지
는. 여기까지는: *We've received only one
offer thus far.* 우리는 지금까지 단 하나의
제안을 받았을 뿐이다.

thwart /θwɔrt/ *v* [T] to prevent
someone from doing what s/he is trying
to do ‖ 남이 하려고 하는 것을 하지 못하
게 막다. 훼방 놓다. 방해하다

thy·roid /ˈθaɪrɔɪd/, **thyroid gland**
/ˈ.. ../ *n* an organ in your neck that
produces HORMONEs (=substances that
affect the way you develop and behave)
‖ 호르몬을 분비하는 목에 있는 기관. 갑
상선

ti·a·ra /tiˈɑrə, tiˈɛrə/ *n* a piece of
jewelry like a small CROWN ‖ 작은 왕관
같은 장신구류. 여성용 작은 관

tic /tɪk/ *n* a sudden uncontrolled
movement of a muscle in your face,
usually because of being nervous ‖ 보통
긴장해서 생긴 얼굴 근육의 갑작스럽고 통
제할 수 없는 움직임. 안면 경련

tick¹ /tɪk/ *n* **1** the short repeated sound
that a clock or watch makes every
second ‖ 벽시계나 손목시계가 매초마다
내는 짧고 반복적인 소리. 똑딱 소리 **2** a
small creature with eight legs that
attaches itself to animals and sucks
their blood ‖ 동물에 붙어서 피를 빨아먹
는, 다리가 여덟 개인 작은 생물. 진드기

tick² *v* **1** [I] if a clock or watch ticks, it
makes a short sound every second ‖ 벽
시계나 손목시계가 매초마다 짧은 소리를
내다. 똑딱거리다 **2 what makes sb tick**
INFORMAL the reasons that someone
behaves in a particular way ‖ 사람이 특
정하게 행동하는 이유. 사람을 움직이게
하는 힘[원동력, 원리]: *I can't figure out
what makes him tick.* 나는 그가 왜 그렇

게 행동하는지 이해할 수가 없다.

tick sb ↔ **off** *phr v* [T] INFORMAL to
annoy someone ‖ 남을 화나게 하다. 화를
돋우다. 분개시키다: *She got ticked off
because she had to wait in line again.*
그녀는 다시 줄을 서서 기다려야 했기 때
문에 부아가 났다.

tick·et¹ /ˈtɪkɪt/ *n* **1** a printed piece of
paper that shows that you have paid for
a movie or to travel on a bus, plane etc.
‖ 영화를 보기 위해 또는 버스·비행기 등
으로 이동하기 위해 요금을 지불했다는 것
을 나타내는 인쇄된 종이 조각. 표: *cheap
tickets to the theater* 싼 극장표 */ a
plane ticket to Tampa* 탐파행 비행기표 **2**
a printed note saying that you must pay
money because you have done
something illegal, especially while
driving or parking your car ‖ 특히 차를
운전하거나 주차하는 중에 불법적인 일을
저질러서 돈을 내야 한다고 쓰여진 인쇄된
쪽지. 교통[주차] 위반 카드. 딱지: *a
speeding/parking ticket* 속도[주차] 위반
딱지 **3** a list of the people supported by
a particular political party in an election
‖ 선거에서 특정한 정당이 지지하는 사람
들의 명단. 공천 후보자 명단: *the
Democratic ticket* 민주당의 공천 후보자
명단

ticket² *v* [T] to give someone a ticket
for parking his/her car in the wrong
place or for driving too fast ‖ 차를 위반
장소에 주차했거나 너무 빨리 운전한 데에
대해 남에게 딱지를 끊다. …에게 딱지를
떼다

tick·le¹ /ˈtɪkəl/ *v* **1** [T] to move your
fingers lightly over someone's body in
order to make him/her laugh ‖ 남을 웃게
하려고 그 사람의 몸 위로 손가락을 가볍
게 움직이다. 간지럽히다 **2** [I, T] if
something touching your body tickles
you, it makes you want to rub your
body because it is uncomfortable ‖ 몸에
닿는 것이 불편해서 몸을 긁고 싶게 되
다. 근질거리게 하다. 근질거리다:
Mommy, this blanket tickles. 엄마, 이 담
요는 근질거려요. **3** [T] if a situation,
remark etc. tickles you, it amuses
or pleases you ‖ 상황·발언 등이 재미있거
나 기쁘게 하다. 즐겁게 하다: *Mom will
be tickled pink/tickled to death*
(=very pleased) *to know you're visiting.*
네가 방문한다는 것을 알면 엄마는 기쁨으
로 어쩔 줄 모르실 거야[까무러치실 거
야].

tickle² *n* a feeling in your throat that
makes you want to cough ‖ 기침을 하고
싶게 하는 목구멍 속의 느낌. 근질근질함

tick·lish /ˈtɪklɪʃ/ *adj* **1** someone who is ticklish is sensitive to tickling (TICKLE) ‖ 사람이 간지럼 태우는 것에 민감한. 간지럼을 잘 타는 **2** INFORMAL a ticklish situation or problem must be dealt with very carefully ‖ 상황이나 문제가 매우 주의 깊게 다루어져야 하는. 다루기 어려운. 까다로운

tic-tac-toe /ˌtɪk tæk ˈtoʊ/ *n* [U] a children's game in which two players draw the marks X and O in a pattern of nine squares ‖ 두 명이 9개의 정사각형 모양에 ×와 ○ 표시를 하는 어린이들의 놀이. 3목(目) 놀이

tid·al /ˈtaɪdl/ *adj* relating to the regular rising and falling of the sea ‖ 바닷물의 규칙적인 만조(滿潮)와 간조(干潮)에 관련되는. 조수의: *tidal pools* 썰물 때 생기는 물웅덩이

tidal wave /ˈ.. ./ *n* a very large ocean wave that flows over the land and destroys things ‖ 육지 위로 넘쳐흘러 사물을 파괴하는 매우 거대한 대양의 파도. 해일

tid·bit /ˈtɪdˌbɪt/ *n* **1** a small piece of food that tastes good ‖ 맛이 좋은 작은 음식 조각. 한 입의 진미 **2** a small piece of interesting information, news etc. ‖ 흥미로운 짤막한 정보·뉴스 등. 한 토막의 화제

tide¹ /taɪd/ *n* the regular rising and falling of the level of the ocean ‖ 해수면의 규칙적인 상승과 하락. 조수: *It's high/low tide.* (=the ocean is at a high or low level) 만조[간조]다.

tide² *v*

tide sb **over** *phr v* [T] to help someone deal with a difficult time ‖ 남이 어려운 시기를 대처하도록 돕다. 고난을 벗어나게 [극복하게] 해 주다: *Could you lend me $50 to tide me over until payday?* 월급날까지 버티게 50달러를 빌려줄래요?

ti·dy /ˈtaɪdi/ *adj* ⇨ NEAT

tie¹ /taɪ/ *v* **tied, tied, tying 1** [I, T] to fasten something or be fastened with a rope, string etc. ‖ 밧줄·끈 등으로 어떤 것을 묶거나 묶이다. …을 매다[매어지다]: *The dress ties in the back.* 그 드레스는 등에서 끈으로 묶는다. / *She tied the scarf loosely around her neck.* 그녀는 스카프를 목에 느슨하게 매었다. **2** [T] to make a knot in a rope, string etc. ‖ 밧줄·끈 등에 매듭을 만들다. …을 매다. 매듭을 짓다: *Can you*

tie your shoelaces yet? 벌써 신발 끈을 맬 줄 아니? **3** [I] also **be tied** to have the same number of points in a competition ‖ 시합에서 같은 점수를 가지다. 동점이다: *two teams that are tied for first place* 1등 자리를 놓고 동점인 두 팀 / *The score is tied.* 점수는 동점이다.

tie sb **down** *phr v* [T] to stop someone from being free to do what s/he wants to do ‖ 남이 하고 싶은 것을 자유롭게 하지 못하게 하다. …을 구속[속박]하다: *Neil doesn't like feeling tied down.* 닐은 구속받는 것을 싫어한다.

tie in *phr v* [I] if one idea or statement ties in with another one, it helps to prove the same thing ‖ 하나의 생각이나 진술이 다른 것과 연결되어 서로 같음을 입증하도록 돕다. 상호간에 관련이 있다. 일치하다: *This data ties right in with ours.* 이 자료는 우리의 자료와 완전히 일치한다.

tie up *phr v* [T] **1** [**tie** sb ↔ **up**] to tie someone's arms, legs etc. so that s/he cannot move ‖ 움직이지 못하게 남의 팔·다리 등을 결박하다. 남을 단단히 결박하다: *They tied Davis up and took his money.* 그들은 데이비스를 묶은 다음 돈을 빼앗았다. **2** [**tie** sth ↔ **up**] to fasten something together by using string or rope ‖ 끈이나 밧줄을 이용해서 어떤 것을 함께 묶다. …을 동여매다: *a package tied up with heavy string* 굵은 끈으로 동여매진 소포 **3** [**tie** sth ↔ **up**] to prevent something from moving ‖ 어떤 것이 움직이지 못하게 하다. 꼼짝 못하게 하다: *Sorry I'm late—I got tied up in traffic.* 늦어서 미안해. 교통 때문에 꼼짝 못했어. **4 be tied up** a) to be very busy ‖ 몹시 바쁘다. 전념[몰두]하고 있다: *I'm kind of tied up these days.* 난 요즘 몹시 바쁜 편이야. **b)** if your money is tied up in something, it is all being used for that thing ‖ 모든 돈이 어떤 것을 위해 쓰여지고 있다. …에 (투자로) 묶여 있다: *Our money's tied up in a long-term savings plan.* 우리 돈은 장기 저축 계획에 투자되어 있다.

tie² *n* **1** a long narrow piece of cloth that men wear around their neck, tied in a knot outside their shirts ‖ 남자의 셔츠 밖에 매듭으로 묶어 목에 매는 길고 가는 천 조각. 넥타이 **2** a relationship between two people, groups, or countries ‖ 두 사람[집단, 국가] 사이의 관계. 연대[유대] 관계: *close family ties* 가족 간의 긴밀한 유대 관계 **3** a piece of string, wire etc. used in order to fasten or close something such as a bag ‖ 가방 등의 것

을 묶거나 조이는 데에 쓰이는 끈·철사
등. 끈. 매듭 **4** the result of a game,
competition, or election in which two or
more people get the same number of
points, votes etc. ∥ 둘 이상의 사람들이
같은 점수·득표수 등을 얻는 놀이[시합,
선거]의 결과. 동점: *The game ended in
a tie.* 그 경기는 동점으로 끝났다.

tie·break·er /'taɪˌbreɪkɚ/ *n* an
additional question or point that decides
the winner when two people or teams
have the same number of points in a
competition ∥ 두 사람이나 팀이 시합에서
같은 점수를 가졌을 때 승자를 결정짓는
추가 질문이나 점수. 동점 결승전

tier /tɪr/ *n* **1** a row of seats that has
other rows above or below it ∥ 위나 아래
에 다른 줄을 가지는 한 줄의 좌석. 좌석의
한 줄[열, 단] **2** one of several levels in
an organization or system ∥ 조직이나 제
도에서의 몇 가지 단계들 중의 하나. 계
층. 단계: *a company with four tiers of
management* 4개의 관리 단계를 갖춘 회
사

tiff /tɪf/ *n* a slight argument between
friends ∥ 친구 간의 사소한 언쟁. 사소한
말다툼. 승강이

ti·ger /'taɪgɚ/ *n* a large strong wild cat
with yellow and black lines on its fur ∥
모피에 노랗고 검은 줄이 있는 크고 힘이
센 야생 고양잇과. 호랑이

tight¹ /taɪt/ *adj*
1 ▶CLOTHES 옷◀ fitting part of your
body very closely ∥ 몸의 일부에 아주 꼭
맞는. 꽉 끼는: *These shoes feel too tight.*
이 신발은 너무 꽉 낀다. / *tight jeans* 꽉
끼는 청바지
2 ▶FIRMLY PULLED 단단하게 당긴◀
pulled or stretched firmly so that it is
straight ∥ 곧게 펴지도록 단단히 당기거나
늘인. 팽팽한: *Pull the thread tight.* 실을
팽팽하게 당겨라.
3 ▶FIRMLY FIXED 단단하게 고정된◀
firmly fixed and difficult to move ∥ 단단
하게 고정되어서 움직이기 어려운. 단단히
맨[조인]: *Make sure the screws are
tight.* 나사들이 단단히 조여졌는지 확인하
라.
4 ▶FIRMLY CONTROLLED 엄격하게 통제
되는◀ controlled very strictly and firmly
∥ 매우 엄격하고 견고하게 통제되는. 엄
한. 엄격한: *Security is tight for the
President's visit.* 대통령의 방문 때문에
경비가 삼엄하다.
5 ▶MONEY 돈◀ **a)** INFORMAL if money
is tight, you do not have enough of it ∥
돈을 충분히 가지고 있지 않은. 빠듯한
b) someone who is tight tries hard to

avoid spending money ∥ 사람이 돈 쓰기
를 피하려고 아주 애쓰는. 인색한. 짠
6 ▶TIME 시간◀ if time is tight, it is
difficult for you to do the things you
need to do in the time you have ∥ 해야
하는 일들을 주어진 시간 내에 하기에는
어려운. 빡빡한: *It's a tight schedule, but
we can manage.* 일정은 빡빡하지만 간신
히 해낼 수 있다.
7 ▶PEOPLE 사람들◀ INFORMAL **a)** two
people who are tight have a close
friendship ∥ 두 사람이 친한 친구 관계인.
친밀한: *We're getting pretty tight.* 우리
는 아주 가까운 사이가 돼 가고 있다. **b)**
INFORMAL drunk ∥ 술 취한
8 in a tight spot INFORMAL in a difficult
situation ∥ 어려운 상황 속에. 곤경에 처하
여: *I'm in kind of a tight spot – could you
lend me $20?* 나는 지금 돈이 쪼들리는데
20달러만 빌려줄래? **– tightly** *adv*

tight² *adv* very firmly or closely; tightly
∥ 매우 단단하게 또는 바짝. 꽉; 단단히:
Hold tight and don't let go of my hand.
꽉 잡고 내 손을 놓으면 안 돼. / *Put the
lid on tight.* 뚜껑을 꽉 닫아라.

tight·en /'taɪt'n/ *v* **1** [T] to close or
fasten something firmly by turning it ∥
어떤 것을 돌려서 단단히 밀폐하거나 고정
시키다. 단단히 죄다: *You'd better tighten
the cap on the bottle.* 병 뚜껑은 단단히
조이는 게 좋아. **2** [T] to stretch
something as far as possible ∥ 어떤 것을
가능한 한 늘이다. 팽팽하게 하다: *The
rope tightened and Arnie gave the
climber some slack.* 밧줄이 팽팽해지자
아니는 등반가에게 밧줄을 약간 풀어줬다.
/ *Tighten your seat belt before we start.*
출발하기 전에 안전띠를 꽉 매라. **3** [T] to
make something fit as closely as
possible ∥ 어떤 것을 가능한 한 꼭 들어
맞게 하다. 꽉 끼이게 하다 **4** [I] to close
firmly around something ∥ 어떤 것 주위
를 단단하게 감다. 꽉 잡다. 단단히 죄다:
Richard's grip tightened on her arm. 리
차드의 손이 그녀의 팔을 꽉 잡았다. **5** [T]
to make a rule, law, or system more
strict ∥ 규칙[법, 제도]을 더 엄격하게 하
다. 엄하게 하다: *City Hall has decided to
tighten up on security.* 시청은 경비를
강화하기로 결정했다. **6 tighten your
belt** INFORMAL to try to spend less
money than you usually spend ∥ 평소 쓰
는 것보다 돈을 덜 쓰려고 애쓰다. 허리띠
를 졸라매다. 내핍하다

tight-fist·ed /ˌ. '../ *adj* INFORMAL not
generous with money; STINGY ∥ 돈에 있
어서 관대하지 않은. 인색한. 구두쇠의;
⊕ stingy

tight·rope /'taɪt˺roʊp/ *n* a rope or wire high above the ground that someone walks along in a circus‖ 서커스에서 사람이 걸어다니는 공중의 밧줄이나 철사. 줄타기용 밧줄

tights /taɪts/ *n* [plural] girls' or women's clothing that fits closely around the feet and legs and up to the waist, that is thick and colored‖ 발과 다리, 위로 허리까지 꼭 끼는 두껍고 색깔이 있는 소녀나 여자의 의류. 타이츠

tight·wad /'taɪt˺wɑd/ *n* INFORMAL DISAPPROVING someone who hates to spend or give money‖ 돈을 쓰거나 주기를 싫어하는 사람. 구두쇠. 노랑이

tile /taɪl/ *n* a thin square piece of baked clay or other material that is used for covering roofs, walls, or floors‖ 지붕 [벽, 바닥]을 덮는 데에 쓰이는 얇은 정사각형의 구운 점토나 다른 소재의 조각. 타일. 기와 **– tile** *v* [T]

till¹ /tɪl, tl/ *prep, conj* SPOKEN until‖ …까지: *I was up till 1:00 a.m. studying for my test.* 나는 새벽 1시까지 시험공부를 하며 자지 않았다.

till² *n* ⇨ CASH REGISTER

tilt /tɪlt/ *v* [I, T] to move into a position where one side is higher than the other, or to make something do this‖ 한쪽이 다른 쪽보다 더 높은 위치가 되게 움직이다, 또는 어떤 것이 이렇게 하게 하다. 기울다 [기울이다]: *Don't tilt so far back in your chair.* 의자에 앉아서 너무 뒤로 젖히지 마라. / *She tilted her head and looked at him.* 그녀는 고개를 갸웃하며 그를 쳐다봤다. **– tilt** *n* [C, U]

tim·ber /'tɪmbɚ/ *n* trees that are cut down and used for building or making things‖ 벌채되어서 사물을 짓거나 만드는 데에 사용되는 나무. 목재

time¹ /taɪm/ *n*

1 ▶MINUTES/HOURS ETC.◀ 분/시간◀ [U] something that is measured in minutes, hours, years etc. using clocks‖ 시계를 사용해 분[시간, 연] 등으로 측정되는 것. 시간: *Time goes by* (=passes) *so quickly these days.* 요즘은 시간이 아주 빨리 간다.

2 ▶ON THE CLOCK◀ 시계상에서◀ [singular] a particular point in time that is shown on a clock in hours and minutes‖ 시계에서 시와 분으로 나타나 있는 특정한 시점. 시각. 시간: *What time is it?* 몇 시냐? / *Do you have the time?* (=used in order to ask someone what time it is) 몇 시냐?

3 ▶OCCASION◀ 경우◀ an occasion when something happens or someone does something‖ 어떤 일이 일어나거나 사람이 어떤 것을 하는 때. 때. …번. …회: *We visit him two or three times a month.* 우리는 한 달에 두세 번 그를 방문한다. / *When was the last time you saw Kelly?* 네가 켈리를 마지막으로 본 게 언제였어? / *Every/each time I offer to cook, she says no.* 내가 요리를 하겠다고 할 때마다 언제나[매번] 그녀는 거절한다. / *The next time you come, we'll go to a show.* 다음번에 네가 올 때는 쇼를 보러 가자. / *One time* (=once) *we went to Florida for spring break.* 우리는 봄 휴가 차 플로리다에 한 번 갔었다. / *Smoking is not allowed at any time.* 흡연은 언제라도 허락되지 않는다.

4 ▶HOW OFTEN/HOW LONG◀ 얼마나 자주/오래◀ [singular, U] used when talking about how often something happens or how long it continues‖ 어떤 것이 얼마나 자주 발생하는지 또는 얼마나 오래 지속되는지에 대해서 말할 때 쓰여. 때. 기간. 동안: *I used to play tennis all the time.* (=often) 나는 예전에 자주 테니스를 쳤었다. / *Randy drives most of the time.* (=usually) 대개 랜디가 운전한다. / *Where's Mandy? She's been gone for a long time.* 맨디는 어디 있지? 오래 전에 가 버렸어. / *Patty whined the whole time.* (=during all of a period of time) 패티는 내내 푸념했다. / *These pictures were taken some time ago.* (=a fairly long time ago) 이 사진들은 상당히 오래 전에 찍었다.

5 ▶WHEN STH HAPPENS◀ 어떤 것이 발생할 때◀ [C, U] the particular minute, hour, day etc. when something happens or someone does something‖ 어떤 것이 발생하거나 사람이 어떤 것을 하는 특정한 분[시간, 날] 등. 시각. 시간: *an arrival/departure time* (=time when a plane, train etc. arrives or leaves) 도착[출발] 시각 / *The program's on at breakfast/supper time.* 그 프로그램은 아침[저녁] 식사 시간에 방송된다. / *I was really hungry by the time I got home.* 집에 왔을 때쯤에 나는 무척 배가 고팠다. / *We left the building at the same time.* 우리는 동시에 그 건물을 떠났다. —see usage note at WHEN: ✗DON'T SAY "in the same time."✗ "in the same time"이라고는 하지 않는다.

6 it's time… used in order to say when something should be done, should happen, or is expected to happen‖ 어떤 것이 행해지거나 일어나야 하는 때, 또는 일어날 것으로 예상되는 때라고 말하는 데에 쓰여. …할 때다: *It's time for dinner.*

저녁 먹을 시간이다. / *It's time to go.* 이제
갈 시간이다.

7 ▶TIME NEEDED 필요한 시간◀ the
amount of time that it takes to do
something, or that is needed to do
something ‖ 어떤 것을 하기 위해 걸리거
나 필요한 시간의 양. 여가. 틈. 충분한
시간: *Learning a language takes time.*
(=takes a long time) 언어를 배우는 데에
는 시간이 걸린다. / *I won't have time to
shop for a gift before Friday.* 나는 금요
일 전에는 선물을 살 틈이 없다. / *I've
spent a lot of time writing this paper.*
나는 이 논문을 쓰면서 많은 시간을 보냈
다. / *Come on – stop wasting time.* 제발
시간 낭비하는 짓 그만 해.

8 be on time to arrive or happen at the
correct time or the time that was
arranged ‖ 정확한 시간이나 정해진 시간
에 도착하거나 발생하다. 시간을 어기지
않다. 정각이다: *The buses are never on
time.* 그 버스는 제때 온 적이 한 번도 없
다. ✗DON'T SAY "be in time."✗ "be in
time"이라고는 하지 않는다.

9 in time early or soon enough to do
something ‖ 어떤 것을 하기에 충분할 만
큼 일찍 또는 곧. 늦지 않게. 꼭 맞춰서:
*We got there just in time to see the
clowns.* 우리는 그곳에 때맞춰 도착해서
광대들을 봤다. / *They arrived in time
for dinner.* 그들은 저녁 시간에 맞춰 도착
했다. ✗DON'T SAY "on time to" or "on
time for."✗ "on time to"나 "on time for"
라고는 하지 않는다.

10 ahead of time before an event or
before you need to do something, in
order to be prepared ‖ 준비를 하기 위해
서 행사 이전에 또는 어떤 것을 할 필요가
있기 전에. 미리 …에 앞서(서): *We need
to get there ahead of time to get a good
seat.* 좋은 좌석을 얻기 위해서 미리 그곳
에 가야 한다.

11 ▶GOOD/RIGHT TIME 알맞은/적절한
시간◀ [C, U] a suitable time for
something to happen or be done ‖ 어떤
것이 일어나거나 행해지기에 적합한 시간.
때. 기회. 적시: *You've caught me at a
bad time – can I call you back later?* 좋
지 않은 때에 내게 연락했군요. 내가 나중
에 다시 전화할 수 있을까요? / *This isn't
the right time to ask for a raise.* 지금은
임금 인상을 요구할 적절한 때가 아니다.

12 in no time soon or quickly ‖ 곧 또는
빨리. 즉시. 당장: *We'll be there in no
time.* 우리가 즉시 그곳에 갈게.

13 it's about time SPOKEN said when
you feel strongly that something should
happen soon or should already have

happened ‖ 어떤 것이 곧 발생해야 하거
나 이미 발생했어야 했다고 강하게 느낄
때 쓰여. …할[…했을] 때다: *It's about
time you got a job!* 이제 너도 일자리를
구할 때가 됐어!

14 when the time comes when
something that you expect to happen
actually happens, or when something
becomes necessary ‖ 일어날 것으로 예상
하는 것이 실제로 발생할 때, 또는 어떤 것
이 필요할 때. 때가 되면: *She'll make the
right choice when the time comes.* 그녀
는 때가 되면 옳은 선택을 할 것이다.

15 at this/that/the time now, or at a
particular moment in the past ‖ 현재 또
는 과거의 특정한 순간에. 지금은[당장은
는]/그때(는)/그 당시(에는): *We can't
give you an answer at this time.* 우리는
지금 당장 대답해 드릴 수가 없습니다. /
At that/the time (=then) *I was still
living in Phoenix.* 그 때[당시] 나는 여전
히 피닉스에 살고 있었다. —see usage
note at WHEN

16 one/two etc. at a time allowing
only a specific number of things to
happen or exist at the same time ‖ 오직
지정된 수의 일만이 동시에 발생하거나 존
재하도록 허락하는. 한 번에 하나/둘: *You
can borrow three books at a time from
the library.* 도서관에서는 한 번에 세 권
의 책을 빌릴 수 있다.

17 take your time to do something
slowly or carefully without hurrying ‖ 어
떤 것을 서두르지 않고 천천히 또는 주의
깊게 하다. 시간을 갖고[느긋하게] 하다:
Take your time – you don't have to rush.
천천히 해라. 서두를 것 없어.

18 for the time being for a short time
but not permanently ‖ 영구히가 아닌 짧
은 시간 동안. 당분간: *They'll let us live
here for the time being.* 그들은 우리를 이
곳에서 당분간 살게 해줄 거야.

19 good/bad/difficult etc. time a part
of your life when you have experiences
that are good, bad etc. ‖ 좋거나 나쁜 경
험을 하는 인생의 한 순간. 즐거운/안 좋
은/힘든 시기[시절]: *That was the
happiest time of my life.* 그때가 내 인생
에서 가장 행복한 순간이었다.

20 ▶IN HISTORY 역사에서◀ a
particular period in history ‖ 역사에서의
특정한 시기. 시대: *It happened in the
time of the Romans.* 그것은 로마 시대에
발생했다. —see also TIMES²

21 time's up SPOKEN said in order to tell
people to stop doing something because
there is no more time left ‖ 더 이상의 시
간이 남아 있지 않기 때문에 사람들에게

하던 일을 멈추라고 말하는 데에 쓰여. 시간 다 되다[끝나다]: *Okay, time's up. You'll have to get out of the pool.* 자, 시간 다 됐다. 수영장에서 나와라.
22 in time to sth if you do something in time to a piece of music, you do it using the same RHYTHM and speed as the music ‖ 음악과 같은 박자와 속도를 이용해서 어떤 것을 하여. …에 (박자를) 맞추어
23 do time INFORMAL to spend time in prison ‖ 교도소에서 시간을 보내다. 복역하다 —see also TIMES²

USAGE NOTE time

When talking about what people do with their time, use the verbs **spend**, **pass**, and **waste**. To **spend** time is to do something useful with your time: *We spent the day cleaning the house.* If you **pass** the time, you have a lot of time and not a lot of useful things to do with it: *How do you pass the time now that you're retired?* To **waste** time is to not use your time well: *I wasted an hour trying to find a parking space!* 사람들이 자신들의 시간을 가지고 무엇을 하는가에 대해서 말할 때는 동사 **spend·pass·waste**를 쓴다. 시간을 **spend**하는 것은 자기의 시간으로 유용한 일을 하는 것을 말한다: 우리는 집을 청소하면서 하루를 보냈다. 시간을 **pass**한다면 시간은 많지만 그 시간으로 할 유용할 일은 많지 않은 것을 말한다: 퇴직을 하셨는데 시간을 어떻게 보내고 계세요? 시간을 **waste**하는 것은 시간을 잘 사용하지 못하는 것을 말한다: 나는 주차할 곳을 찾느라고 한 시간을 허비했어!

---

time² v [T] **1** to do something or arrange for something to happen at a particular time ‖ 특정한 시간에 어떤 것을 하거나 어떤 것이 발생하도록 하다. 시간을 정하다[맞추다]: *The bomb was timed to go off at 5:00.* 그 폭탄은 5시에 폭발하도록 시간이 맞추어져 있었다. / *an ill-timed announcement* (=one that happens at a bad time) 시의 적절치 않은 발표 **2** to measure how fast someone or something is going, how long it takes to do something etc. ‖ 사람이나 사물이 얼마나 빨리 가고 있는지 또는 어떤 것을 하는 데에 얼마나 오래 걸리는지 등을 측정하다. 시간을 재다: *Christie was timed at 10.02 seconds.* 크리스티는 10.02초를 기록했다. / *Okay, time how long it takes*

me to finish. 좋아, 내가 얼마만에 끝내는지 시간을 재봐.

time and a half /ˌ. . . ˈ./ n [U] one and a half times the normal rate of pay ‖ 정상 임금률의 한 배 반. 50% 초과 근무 수당

time bomb /ˈ. ./ n **1** a situation that is likely to become a very serious problem ‖ 매우 심각한 문제가 될 것 같은 상황. 불안한 정세: *Unemployment has become a time bomb.* 실업은 이제 위험 수위에 이르렀다. **2** a bomb that is set to explode at a particular time ‖ 특정한 시간에 폭발하도록 맞춰진 폭탄. 시한폭탄

time card /ˈ. ./ n a card on which the hours you have worked are recorded by a machine ‖ 일한 시간이 기계로 기록되는 카드. 근무 시간 기록표

time-con·sum·ing /ˈ. .ˌ../ adj needing a long time to do ‖ 해내는 데 오랜 시간이 필요한. 시간이 걸리는[소모하는]: *time-consuming work* 시간을 소모하는 작업

time-hon·ored /ˈ. ˌ../ adj a time-honored method, custom etc. is one that has existed or worked well for a long time ‖ 방식·관습 등이 오랫동안 존재해 왔거나 잘 작용해 온. 유서 깊은. 전통 있는

time·keep·er /ˈtaɪmˌkipɚ/ n someone who officially records how long it takes to do something, especially at a sports event ‖ 특히 스포츠 행사에서 어떤 것을 하는 데 얼마나 오래 걸리는지를 공식적으로 기록하는 사람. 시간 기록원. 계시원 (計時員)

time·less /ˈtaɪmlɪs/ adj always remaining beautiful, attractive etc. ‖ 항상 아름다움·매력 등을 유지하는. 시대[시간]를 초월한: *the timeless beauty of the ocean* 바다의 시간을 초월한 아름다움

time lim·it /ˈ. ˌ../ n the longest time that you are allowed to do something in ‖ 그 안에 어떤 것을 하도록 허락된 가장 긴 시간. 제한 시간: *There's a three-year time limit for writing a thesis.* 논문을 쓰는 데는 3년의 제한 시간이 있다.

time·ly /ˈtaɪmli/ adj done or happening at exactly the right time ‖ 정확히 바로 그 시간에 하거나 발생하는. 시기적절한: *a timely decision* 시기적절한 결정 — opposite UNTIMELY

time off /ˌ. ˈ./ n [U] time when you are officially allowed not to be at work or studying ‖ 직장에 나가지 않거나 공부하지 않아도 되는 공식적으로 허락받은 시간. 휴가. 휴식 시간

time out /ˌ. ˈ./ n **1 take time out** to

rest or do something different from your usual job or activities ∥ 쉬거나 평소의 일이나 활동과 다른 것을 하다. 잠시 쉬다. 짬을 내다 **2 a** short time during a sports game when the teams can rest and get instructions from the COACH ∥ 팀이 쉬면서 감독에게서 지시를 받을 수 있는 스포츠 경기 동안의 짧은 시간. 타임 아웃

tim·er /'taɪmɚ/ *n* an instrument for measuring time, when you are doing something such as cooking ∥ 요리 등을 하고 있을 때 시간을 재는 기구. 타이머

times[1] /taɪmz/ *prep* multiplied by ∥ …으로 곱해진. …곱[배]: *two times two equals four* 2곱하기 2는 4이다

times[2] *n* [plural] the present time or a particular period in history, and the ways that people do or did things during that period ∥ 현재나 역사상의 특정한 시기, 그리고 그 시기 동안에 사람들이 생활하거나 생활했던 방식. 시대(상). 현대: *modern times* 현대 / *Their technology is 30 years behind the times.* 그들의 기술은 시대적으로 30년 뒤떨어졌다.

time·ta·ble /'taɪm,teɪbəl/ *n* **1 a** plan of events and activities, with their dates and times ∥ 날짜와 시간이 적힌 행사나 활동의 계획. 예정 **2 ⇨** SCHEDULE[1]

time warp /'. ./ *n* [singular] INFORMAL the feeling that you are in a different time in history or in the future, instead of in the present ∥ 현재 대신에 과거나 미래의 다른 시대에 있는 느낌. 시간 왜곡

time zone /'. ./ *n* one of the 24 areas the world is divided into, each of which has its own time ∥ 세계를 24구역으로 분할해서 각각이 그 자체 시간대를 갖는 구역의 하나. 표준 시간대

tim·id /'tɪmɪd/ *adj* not brave or confident ∥ 용감하거나 자신 있지 않은. 겁이 많은. 소심한: *a timid child* 소심한 어린이 **– timidly** *adv* **– timidity** /tə'mɪdəti/ *n* [U]

tim·ing /'taɪmɪŋ/ *n* [U] the ability to decide the right time to do something, or the act of deciding this ∥ 어떤 것을 할 적당한 시간을 결정하는 능력이나 이것을 결정하는 행위. 타이밍. 적시 선택: *It's bad timing, starting a diet before Christmas.* 성탄절 전에 다이어트를 시작하는 것은 시기가 적절하지 못하다.

tin /tɪn/ *n* [U] a soft white metal used for making cans, building materials etc ∥ 깡통·건축자재 등을 만드는 데 사용되는 연질의 하얀 금속. 주석. 양철: *a tin can* (통조림) 깡통

tin·der /'tɪndɚ/ *n* [U] material that burns easily, used for lighting fires ∥ 불

을 붙일 때 사용하는 쉽게 타는 재료. 부싯깃

tin·der·box /'tɪndɚ,bɑks/ *n* a place or situation that is dangerous because it is likely that there will be fighting ∥ 곧 싸움이 날 듯 해서 위험한 장소나 상황. 일촉즉발의 화약고[상태]

tine /taɪn/ *n* a pointed part of something that has several points, for example on a fork ∥ 예를 들면 포크처럼 몇 개의 뾰족한 끝이 있는 물건의 뾰족한 부분. 날카로운 갈래 **—compare** PRONG

tin·foil /'tɪnfɔɪl/ *n* [U] OLD-FASHIONED ⇨ FOIL

tinge /tɪndʒ/ *n* a very small amount of color or emotion ∥ 매우 희미한 색깔이나 감정. 엷은 색. 기미. 티: *a tinge of sadness in her voice* 그녀 목소리의 슬픈 기색 / *white paint with a yellow tinge* 엷은 노란색이 도는 흰 페인트 **– tinged** *adj* : *black hair tinged with gray* 흰머리가 약간 섞인 검은 머리

tin·gle /'tɪŋgəl/ *v* [I] to feel a slight sting on your skin ∥ 피부에 살짝 찌르는 아픔을 느끼다. 따끔거리다. 얼얼하다: *My fingers tingled with the cold.* 내 손가락이 추위 때문에 얼얼했다. **– tingle** *n*

tin·ker /'tɪŋkɚ/ *v* [I] INFORMAL to try to improve something by making small changes to it, but without having a careful plan ∥ 주의 깊은 계획 없이 어떤 것에 작은 변화를 만들어서 개선시키려 애쓰다. 서투르게 수선하다. 어설프게 만지다: *He's outside tinkering with his car again.* 그는 밖에서 차를 다시 만지작 거리고 있다.

tin·kle /'tɪŋkəl/ *v* **1** [I] to make high soft RINGing sounds ∥ 종이 높고 부드럽게 울리는 소리를 내다. 딸랑딸랑 울리다: *a tinkling bell* 딸랑거리는 종 **2** [I] a word meaning to URINATE, used when speaking to young children ∥ 어린 어린이들에게 말할 때 쓰는 오줌을 누다를 의미하는 단어. 쉬하다 **– tinkle** *n*

tin·ny /'tɪni/ *adj* a tinny sound is unpleasant to listen to, like small pieces of metal hitting each other ∥ 작은 금속 조각이 서로 부딪치는 것처럼 소리가 듣기에 불쾌한. 듣기 거북한. 금속성의: *tinny music* 듣기 싫은 소리가 나는 음악

tin·sel /'tɪnsəl/ *n* [U] thin pieces of shiny silver paper, used especially as Christmas decorations ∥ 특히 성탄절 장식품으로 사용하는 얇고 빛나는 은색 종이 조각. 은박지

tint[1] /tɪnt/ *n* a pale or light shade of a particular color ∥ 특정한 색깔의 엷거나 밝은 색조. 엷은 색. 엷은 색조: *The sky* *had a pink tint.* 하늘은 분홍빛이 돌았다.

tint² *v* [T] to give something, especially your hair, a TINT ‖ 특히 머리 등에 엷은 색조를 주다. 염색하다. 물들이다

ti·ny /'taɪni/ *adj* extremely small ‖ 아주 작은. 조그마한: *a tiny room* 아주 작은 방 / *thousands of tiny fish* 수천 마리의 조그마한 물고기들

tip¹ /tɪp/ *n* **1** the end of something, especially something pointed ‖ 특히 뾰족한 것의 끝. 끝. 첨단. 선단. 정첨: *the tip of your nose* 코끝 / *Provincetown, on the northern tip of Cape Cod* 케이프 코드 곶의 북단에 있는 프라빈스타운 **2** an additional amount of money that you give to someone such as a WAITER or taxi driver for his/her service ‖ 웨이터나 택시 운전사 등의 사람에게 서비스의 대가로 주는 추가 금액. 팁: *Did you leave a tip?* 팁은 남겨 놓고 왔니? **3** a helpful piece of advice ‖ 유용한 충고 한 마디. 조언. 비법. 비결: *He gave me some useful tips on how to take good pictures.* 그는 나에게 사진을 잘 찍는 법에 대한 상당히 유용한 조언을 해 주었다. **4 on the tip of your tongue** if a word, name etc. is on the tip of your tongue, you know it but cannot remember it immediately ‖ 어떤 단어·이름 등은 알지만 즉시 기억해 낼 수는 없어. 말이 입안에서만 맴돌아 **5 the tip of the iceberg** a small sign of a problem that is much larger ‖ 훨씬 더 큰 문제의 작은 징후. 빙산의 일각: *What we have seen so far is just the tip of the iceberg.* 지금까지 우리가 보아온 것은 그저 빙산의 일각일 뿐이다.

CULTURE NOTE tipping

In the US and Canada, TIPs are given for particular services. The amount of the tip usually depends on the type of service. For a HAIRCUT, 10% of the price is the usual amount, unless the person who cut your hair is the owner. In this case, you do not give a tip. Ten percent of the FARE is also the usual amount given to a taxi driver. In a restaurant, it is usually 15% of the check. If the service is not good, you can leave less. In a hotel, the tip is usually $1 – $2 for each bag that is carried to your room for you. 미국과 캐나다에서 팁은 특정한 서비스의 대가로 준다. 팁의 액수는 보통 서비스의 종류에 달려 있다. 이발의 경우 자신의 머리를 자른 사람이 주인이 아닌 한 이발 가격의 10%가 일반적인 액수

이다. 주인인 경우에는 팁을 주지 않는다. 택시 운전사에게도 또한 요금의 10%가 일반적인 액수이다. 식당에서는 보통 계산서의 15%다. 서비스가 좋지 못하면 덜 줄 수도 있다. 호텔에서는 손님의 객실까지 대신 가져다 주는 각 가방당 대체로 1-2달러의 팁을 준다.

---

tip² *v* **-pped, -pping** **1** [I, T] also **tip over** to fall or turn over, or to make something do this ‖ 넘어지거나 뒤집어지다, 또는 어떤 것이 이렇게 하게 하다. 뒤엎다[뒤집히다]. 전도[전복]되다: *The baby tipped the plant over.* 아기가 식물을 넘어뜨렸다. / *The ladder must have tipped over during the night.* 사다리는 밤 사이에 넘어진 게 분명하다. **2** [I, T] to lean at an angle, or to make something do this ‖ 경사지게 기대다, 또는 어떤 것이 이렇게 하게 하다. 기울다[기울이다]: *I tipped the bucket to pour out the water.* 나는 물을 따라내기 위해 양동이를 기울였다. / *a man with his hat tipped forward* 모자를 앞으로 기울여 쓴 남자 **3** [I, T] to give a TIP to a WAITER, taxi driver etc. for his/her service ‖ 웨이터·택시 운전사 등에게 서비스의 대가로 팁을 주다: *Did you remember to tip the waitress?* 웨이트리스에게 잊지 않고 팁을 주었니? —see culture note at TIP¹

tip *sb* ↔ **off** *phr v* [T] INFORMAL to give someone such as the police secret information about something illegal ‖ 경찰 등의 사람에게 불법적인 일에 대해서 비밀 정보를 주다. (비밀을) 귀띔하다. 밀고하다: *The police must have been tipped off about the robbery.* 경찰은 그 강도 사건에 대한 정보를 틀림없이 미리 귀띔 받았을 것이다.

ti·pi /'tipi/ *n* ⇨ TEPEE

tip-off /'. ./ *n* INFORMAL **1** a warning or message about something illegal that is given secretly to the police, a government etc. ‖ 경찰·정부 등에게 비밀리에 제공된 불법적인 일에 대한 경고나 전언. 귀띔. 밀고 **2** the beginning of a basketball game ‖ 농구 경기의 시작: *Tip-off is at 7:30 tonight in the Coliseum.* 경기 시작은 콜리세움에서 오늘 밤 7시 30분이다.

tip·per /'tɪpə/ *n* INFORMAL someone who TIPs a WAITER, taxi driver, etc. for his/her service ‖ 웨이터·택시 운전사 등에게 서비스의 대가로 팁을 주는 사람: *He's a good tipper.* (=someone who gives large tips) 그는 팁을 후하게 주는 사람이다.

tip·ster /'tɪpstə/ *n* someone who gives

the police, a REPORTER etc. secret
information about something that is
going to happen ‖ 경찰·기자 등에게 곧
발생할 일에 대한 비밀 정보를 제공하는
사람. 밀고자. 제보자

tip·sy /'tɪpsi/ *adj* INFORMAL slightly
drunk ‖ 약간 취한. 얼근하게 취한

tip·toe¹ /'tɪptoʊ/ *n* **on tiptoe** standing
on your toes, with the rest of your feet
off the ground ‖ 발의 나머지는 지면에서
떨어진 상태이면서, 발가락으로 서는. 발
끝으로: *Matt stood on tiptoe to look
over the wall.* 매트는 까치발을 하고서 담
장 너머를 쳐다봤다.

tiptoe² *v* [I] to walk on TIPTOE ‖ 발끝으
로 걷다. (까치발로) 살금살금 걷다: *They
tiptoed past the door.* 그들은 까치발을
하고서 그 문을 지났다.

ti·rade /'taɪreɪd/ *n* a long angry speech
criticizing someone or something ‖ 다른
사람이나 사물을 비판하여 화가 나서 길게
하는 연설. 장황한 열변. 길고 신랄한 비
난: *The senator launched into a tirade
against his critics.* 그 상원 의원은 자기
의 비판자들을 향해 분노의 열변을 토했
다.

tire¹ /taɪɚ/ *n* a thick round piece of
rubber that fits around the wheel of a
car, bicycle etc. ‖ 차·자전거 등의 바퀴
주위에 끼운 두껍고 둥근 고무 조각. 타이
어: *I had a flat tire* (=one that has lost
all its air) *on the way home.* 나는 집에
오는 도중에 차바퀴가 펑크 났다.

tire² *v* **1** [I, T] to become tired, or to
make someone feel tired ‖ 피곤해지거나
사람을 피곤하게 하다. 지치다. 녹초가 되
다: *Aunt Mary was beginning to tire.* 메
리 고모는 지치기 시작하고 있었다. /
Even short walks tire her. 그녀는 아주
조금만 걸어도 금세 피곤해 한다. **2 tire
of sth** to become bored with something
‖ 어떤 것에 지루해지다. …에 싫증나다
[질리다]: *Sooner or later he'll tire of
politics.* 그는 머지않아 정치에 싫증날 것
이다.

tire sb ↔ **out** *phr v* [T] to make
someone very tired ‖ 남을 매우 지치게
하다. …을 물리게[넌더리 나게] 하다:
Those kids have tired me out. 나는 그
아이들 때문에 녹초가 되었다.

tired /taɪrd/ *adj* **1** feeling that you
want to sleep or rest ‖ 자거나 쉬고 싶어
하는. 피곤한. 지친: *I'm really tired.* 난
정말로 피곤하다. / *Ben looks tired too.* 벤
도 역시 피곤해 보인다. / *We're all pretty
tired out* (=completely tired) *after the
long flight.* 우리 모두는 장시간 비행 후에
완전히 녹초가 되어 있다. **2** bored or

annoyed with something ‖ 어떤 것에 지
루하거나 짜증이 난. 싫증난. 질린: *I'm
tired of your stupid comments.* 나는 너
의 멍청한 말에 이제 질렸어.

tire·less /'taɪɚlɪs/ *adj* very determined
and never getting tired ‖ 매우 확고하고
결코 지치지 않는. 지칠 줄 모르는. 끈기
있는: *a tireless worker* 지칠 줄 모르는 근
로자 **- tirelessly** *adv*

tire·some /'taɪɚsəm/ *adj* annoying and
boring ‖ 짜증 나고 지루한. 지겨운. 진저
리가 나는: *The winter had been long
and tiresome.* 겨울은 길고 지겨웠다. —
compare TIRING

tir·ing /'taɪrɪŋ/ *adj* making you feel
tired ‖ 피곤하게 느끼게 하는. 피로하게
하는. 힘드는: *a tiring trip across the
country by train* 기차로 전국을 횡단하는
힘든 여행

tis·sue /'tɪʃu/ *n* **1** ⇨ KLEENEX **2** [U] the
parts of a plant, animal, or human such
as muscles, skin, leaves etc. that are
made up of groups of similar cells ‖ 비슷
한 세포의 무리들로 구성된 근육·피부·
잎 등의 식물이나 동물, 또는 사람의 부위.
조직: *damaged lung tissue* 손상을 입은
폐 조직

tit-for-tat /ˌtɪt fɚ 'tæt/ *adj* INFORMAL a
tit-for-tat crime or action is something
bad that has been done to someone
because s/he has done something
similar to you ‖ 범죄나 행위가 남이 자신
에게 나쁜 짓을 해서 남에게 비슷한 짓을
하는 것인. 보복[앙갚음]의: *a series of
tit-for-tat murders* 연쇄 보복 살인

titan, Titan /'taɪtn/ *n* [C] a strong or
important person; giant ‖ 힘있거나 중요
한 사람. 거물. 실력자; 거인

tit·il·late /'tɪtl̩eɪt/ *v* [T] to make
someone feel excited or interested,
especially sexually ‖ 어떤 사람을 특히 성
적으로 흥분되게 또는 흥미 있게 하다. 흥
분시키다. 자극하다: *a story to titillate
the readers* 독자들을 자극하는 이야기

ti·tle¹ /'taɪtl̩/ *n* **1** the name given to a
book, painting, play etc. ‖ 책·그림·연극
등에 부여된 이름. 제목. 표제: *"What's
the title of this play?" "Heroes."* "이 연
극의 제목이 뭐야?" "영웅들이야." **2** a
word such as "Mrs.," "Dr.," "Senator"
etc. that is used before someone's name
to show whether s/he is married or
what his/her rank or position is ‖ 어떤
사람의 이름 앞에서 결혼 여부[계급, 지
위]를 나타내기 위해 쓰이는 "여사" "박
사" "상원 의원" 등의 말. 칭호. 경칭 **3** a
word or name that describes someone's
rank or position ‖ 누군가의 계급이나 지

위를 설명하는 말이나 명칭. 직함: *Her official title is editorial manager.* 그녀의 공식 직함은 편집 부장이다. **4** [singular, U] TECHNICAL the legal right to own something ‖ 사물을 소유하는 법적인 권리. 소유권: *Who has the title to this land?* 누가 이 땅의 소유권을 갖고 있습니까? **5** the most important game in a sport, that shows who the best team or player is ‖ 스포츠에서 최고의 팀이나 선수를 증명해 보이는 가장 중요한 시합. 타이틀. 선수권: *Foreman first won his heavyweight title in 1974.* 포먼은 1974년에 그의 첫 헤비급 (권투) 선수권을 획득했다.

title² *v* [T] to give a name to a book, play etc. ‖ 책·연극 등에 이름을 붙이다. 표제[제목]를 달다: *a concert titled "Home for the Holidays"* "공휴일을 위한 집"이란 표제의 연주회

title role /ˌ.. ˈ./ *n* the main character in a play, after whom the play is named ‖ 그 이름을 따서 연극명이 지어지는 연극의 중심 등장인물. 주연 배역: *Elizabeth Taylor plays the title role in "Cleopatra."* 엘리자베스 테일러가 "클레오파트라"에서 주연 배역을 맡는다.

tit·ter /ˈtɪtɚ/ *v* [I] to laugh quietly, especially in a nervous way ‖ 조용히 특히 조심스럽게 웃다. 킥킥거리다. 소리죽여 웃다 – **titter** *n*

tiz·zy /ˈtɪzi/ *n* [singular] INFORMAL **in a tizzy** feeling nervous, upset, and sometimes confused ‖ 초조하고 심란하고 때로 혼란스럽게 느끼는. 흥분한. 이성을 잃은: *Mom's in a tizzy because everyone's late.* 모두가 늦어서 엄마는 화가 나 있으시다.

TLC *n* [U] INFORMAL tender loving care; kindness and love that you give to someone when s/he is sick or upset ‖ tender loving care(다정한 사랑의 보살핌)의 약어; 남이 아프거나 심란할 때 베푸는 친절과 사랑

TN the written abbreviation of Tennessee ‖ Tennessee(테네시 주)의 약어

TNT *n* [U] a powerful explosive ‖ 강력한 폭발물. 티엔티

to¹ /tə, *before vowels* tʊ; *strong* tu/ [used with the basic form of a verb to make the infinitive. 부정사를 만들기 위해 동사의 기본형과 함께 쓰여.] ✗DO NOT USE "to" with modal verbs.✗ "to"는 법조동사와는 함께 쓰지 않는다. **1** used after verbs ‖ 동사의 뒤에 쓰여: *I'd love to go!* 나는 정말 가고 싶다! / *She didn't want to bother you.* 그녀는 너를 방해하길 원치

않았다. / *The men were told to leave the bar.* 그 남자들은 술집을 떠나라고 지시 받았다. **2** used after "how," "where," "who," "whom," "whose," "which," "when," "what," or "whether" ‖ "how" "where" "who" "whom" "whose" "which" "when" "what" "whether" 뒤에 쓰여: *Can you show me how to do this?* 이거 어떻게 하는지 보여줄 수 있어? / *Maria didn't know whether to call Tim or not.* 마리아는 팀에게 전화를 해야 할지 어쩔지 몰랐다. **3** used after some nouns ‖ 어떤 명사들 뒤에 쓰여. …할. …하는: *If you get a chance to see the play, you should.* 만약 네가 연극을 볼 수 있는 기회가 생긴다면 꼭 봐라. / *He has no reason to believe that.* 그가 그것을 믿을 이유가 없다. **4** used after adjectives ‖ 형용사 뒤에 쓰여. …하기 위한: *Dad says he's not ready to retire yet.* 아빠는 아직 은퇴할 준비가 되어 있지 않다고 하신다. / *It's great to see you!* 만나서 반가워! **5** used in order to show the purpose of an action ‖ 행동의 목적을 보여주는 데에 쓰여. …을 위해서. …하도록: *He covered the child to keep her from getting cold.* 그는 여자 아이가 감기에 걸리지 않도록 덮어 주었다. **6** used after "too" and an adjective ‖ "too"와 형용사 뒤에 쓰여. 너무 …해서 …할 수 없다: *It's too cold to go outside.* 너무 추워서 외출할 수 없다. **7** used after an adjective and "enough" ‖ 형용사와 "enough" 뒤에 쓰여. …하기에 충분한. …할 만큼[정도로]: *Are you feeling well enough to go back to work?* 다시 일할 수 있을 만큼 건강 상태가 좋아졌습니까? **8** used after "there is" and a noun ‖ "there is"와 명사 뒤에 쓰여: *There's nothing to do here.* 여기서 할 것은 아무것도 없다.

USAGE NOTE to

In written English, you should try not to put a word between **to** and the verb that comes after it: *He tried quietly to play his guitar.* Sometimes, however, we separate **to** from the verb that comes after it in order to emphasize something or because the sentence is clearer: *Your job is to really help these children.* 문어체 영어에서는 **to**와 뒤에 오는 동사 사이에 단어는 가능가지 않게 해야 한다: 그는 자기 기타를 연주하려고 말없이 애썼다. 그러나 때때로 어떤 것을 강조하기 위해서 또는 문장이 보다 확실해지기 때문에 **to**를 뒤에 오는 동사와 떨

어뜨려 쓴다: 네 임무는 이 아이들을 실제로 돕는 것이다.

to² *prep* **1** in order to be in a particular place, event, state etc. ‖ 특정 장소·사건·상태 등이 되도록: *The drive to the city takes five hours.* 그 도시까지는 차로 5시간이 걸린다. / *I couldn't go to sleep last night.* 어젯밤 나는 잠들 수 없었다. / *Are you going to the wedding?* 결혼식에 가시겠습니까? **2** toward or in the direction of a place ‖ 어떤 장소 쪽으로 또는 쪽에: *She went to the door.* 그녀는 문 쪽으로 갔다. / *Throw the ball to me.* 공을 내게 던져라. **3** used in order to show the position of something, especially in relation to something else ‖ 특히 다른 것과 관련해서 사물의 위치를 나타내는 데에 쓰여. …에(이르기까지): *The water came up to our knees.* 물이 우리 무릎까지 올라왔다. / *a town 50 miles to the south of Indianapolis* 인디애나폴리스 남쪽으로 50마일 거리에 있는 소도시 / *My back was to the door.* (=facing the door) 나는 문을 등지고 있었다. **4** used in order to show who receives or owns something, or to whom speech is directed ‖ 무엇을 받거나 소유하는 사람 또는 담화의 대상이 되는 사람이 누구인지를 나타내는 데에 쓰여. …에게: *Angie said "hi" to me this morning.* 앤지가 오늘 아침 내게 "안녕" 하고 인사했다. / *The ring belongs to her mother.* 그 반지는 그녀의 어머니 것이다. **5** starting with one thing or in one place and ending with or in another ‖ 한 가지 일이나 한 장소에서 시작되어 다른 일이나 장소에서 끝나는. …까지: *A to Z* A부터 Z까지 / *Mom, I can count to 100.* 엄마, 나 백까지 셀 수 있어. / *It's 30 miles from here to Toronto.* 여기서 토론토까지는 30마일(거리)이다. **6** used when showing who or what is affected by an action or situation ‖ 동작이나 상황에 의해 영향을 받는 사람이나 사물을 나타낼 때에 쓰여. …에게 있어. …에 대하여: *Mr. Reger is nice to everyone.* 리저 씨는 모두에게 친절하다. / *The chemicals are a danger to ocean life.* 그 화학 제품은 해양 생물에게 위험한 것이다. **7** fitting or being part of a machine or piece of equipment ‖ 기계나 장비에 꼭 맞거나 그것의 일부분이 되는. …에 맞는[속하는]: *I have a key to the office.* 나는 사무실 열쇠를 가지고 있다. **8** used when comparing two numbers, things etc. ‖ 두 개의 숫자·사물 등을 비교할 때에 쓰여. …에 비하여[과 대비하여]. …대(對)…: *The Bears won, 27 to 10.* 베어스가 27대 10으로 이겼다. **9** used in order to mean "before" when you are giving the time ‖ 시간을 알릴 때 "이전(以前)"을 의미하는 데에 쓰여. …전(前): *It's ten to four.* 4시 10분 전이다.

to³ /tu/ *adv* ⇨ TO AND FRO **come to** (COME)

toad /toud/ *n* an animal like a large FROG but brown in color ‖ 큰 개구리와 비슷하지만 색깔이 갈색인 동물. 두꺼비

toad·stool /'toudstul/ *n* a plant that looks like a MUSHROOM, but is usually poisonous ‖ 버섯처럼 생겼지만 대개 독이 있는 식물. 독버섯

to and fro /,tu ən 'frou/ *adv* moving in one direction and then back again ‖ 한 방향으로 움직이고 나서 다시 역행하는. 이쪽저쪽으로. 앞뒤로. 왔다갔다: *walking to and fro* 왔다갔다 걸어다님

toast¹ /toust/ *n* **1** [U] bread that has been heated until it is brown and CRISP ‖ 갈색이 나고 바삭바삭할 때까지 구운 빵. 토스트: *Could I have some toast with my eggs, please?* 계란을 넣은 토스트를 좀 먹을 수 있을까요? **2** an occasion when you TOAST someone ‖ 다른 사람에게 축배하는 때. 건배[축배](의 인사): *I'd like to propose a toast to the happy couple.* 행복한 부부를 위한 축배를 제안하고 싶습니다. **3 be the toast of Broadway/Hollywood etc.** to be very popular and praised by many people in a particular place ‖ 특정 장소에서 매우 인기 있고 많은 사람들에게 칭찬받다. 브로드웨이/할리우드의 유명 인사가 되다

toast² *v* [T] **1** to ask people to drink something with you in order to thank someone, wish someone luck etc. ‖ 어떤 사람에게 감사하거나 행운 등을 빌어 주기 위해 사람들에게 무엇을 함께 마시자고 청하다. 건배[축배]하다: *We toasted our victory with champagne.* 우리는 샴페인으로 우리 승리에 축배를 들었다. **2** to make bread turn brown by heating it ‖ 빵에 열을 가해 갈색으로 굽다. 노르스름하게 굽다

toast·er /'toustɚ/ *n* a machine used for making TOAST ‖ 토스트를 만드는 데에 쓰이는 기계. 토스터기

toast·y /'tousti/ *adj* SPOKEN warm in a way that makes you feel comfortable ‖ 안락함을 느끼게 할 정도로 따뜻한. 따끈따끈한. 훈훈한

to·bac·co /tə'bækou/ *n* [U]·dried brown leaves that are smoked in cigarettes, CIGARS etc., or the plant that these come from ‖ 담배·시가 등으로 피우는 갈색의 건조된 잎 또는 이들이 산출되는 식물. 담

배(잎)

to·bac·co·nist /tə'bækənɪst/ n OLD-FASHIONED someone who owns a store that sells tobacco, cigarettes, etc. ‖ 담배·궐련 등을 파는 가게를 소유한 사람. 담배 가게 주인[장사]

to·bog·gan·ing /tə'bɑɡənɪŋ/ n [U] the sport of sliding down snow covered hills on a special wooden board that curves up at the front ‖ 앞부분을 위로 구부려 올린 특수 나무판을 타고 눈 덮인 언덕을 미끄러져 내리는 스포츠. 눈썰매[터보건] 타기 –**toboggan** n –**toboggan** v [I]

to·day¹ /tə'deɪ/ n 1 the day that is happening now ‖ 지금 진행되고 있는 날짜. 오늘. 금일: *Today is Wednesday.* 오늘은 수요일이다. 2 the present time ‖ 현재. 지금. 현대. 요즘: *Video games are the obsession of today's youth.* 비디오 게임은 요즘 젊은이들을 사로잡는 것이다.

today² adv 1 during the day that is happening now ‖ 지금 진행되고 있는 날짜 동안에. 오늘[금일] 중에: *Mom, can we go to the park today?* 엄마, 우리 오늘 공원에 갈 수 있어요? 2 in the present time ‖ 현재. 오늘날. 현대에. 요즘: *Today, cancer is the leading cause of death in women.* 오늘날 암은 여성 사망의 주요한 원인이다.

tod·dle /'tɑdl/ v [I] to walk with short unsteady steps, like a very young child does ‖ 아주 어린 아이들이 하는 것처럼 보폭이 짧고 불안정한 걸음을 걷다. 아장아장[되뚝되뚝] 걷다

tod·dler /'tɑdlɚ/ n a child between the ages of about 1 and 3 ‖ 약 한 살에서 3살 연령대 사이의 아이. 유아. 아장아장 걷는 아이

to-do /tə 'du/ n [singular] INFORMAL unnecessary excitement or angry feelings about something; FUSS ‖ 사물에 대한 불필요한 흥분이나 화난 감정. 법석; ㊟ fuss: *She's always making a big to-do over something.* 그녀는 무슨 일에나 늘 야단 법석을 떨고 있다.

toe¹ /toʊ/ n 1 one of the five separate parts at the end of your foot ‖ 발 끝에 다섯 개로 갈라진 부분 중의 하나. 발가락: *I hurt my big toe.* (=largest toe) 나는 엄지발가락을 다쳤다. 2 **on your toes** ready for anything that might happen ‖ 일어날지도 모르는 어떤 것에 대해 준비가 된. 빈틈없는. 매우 신중한: *Practicing every day really keeps you on your toes.* 매일 매일의 연습은 자신을 매우 빈틈없게 해 준다.

toe² v **toe the line** to do what you are told to do by people in authority ‖ 권위 있는 사람이 지시한 것을 하다. 명령[규칙]대로 하다: *I refuse to toe the line anymore!* 난 더 이상 명령대로는 하지 않겠어!

TOEFL /'toʊfəl/ n TRADEMARK Test of English as a Foreign Language; a test that students can take if their first language is not English, that proves that they can understand English ‖ Test of English as a Foreign Language(외국어로서의 영어 시험)의 약어; 모국어가 영어가 아닐 경우에 영어 이해 능력을 증명하려고 치르는 시험. 토플

toe·hold /'toʊhoʊld/ n [singular] a position you have just gained, from which you can increase your power or success ‖ 방금 획득해서 그로부터 힘을 기르거나 성공할 수 있는 위치. 발판. 디딤돌: *It took us five years to gain a toehold in the market.* 우리가 시장에 진출하는 발판을 마련하는 데 5년이 걸렸다.

toe·nail /'toʊneɪl/ n the hard flat part that covers the top end of your toe ‖ 발가락의 위쪽 끝을 덮고 있는 단단하고 편평한 부분. 발톱

toe-to-toe /ˌ. . '. ./ adj ⇨ HEAD-TO-HEAD

tof·fee /'tɔfi, 'tɑfi/ n [C, U] a sticky brown candy made from sugar and butter, or a piece of this ‖ 설탕과 버터로 만든 끈적끈적한 갈색의 사탕 또는 그 사탕 한 개. 토피

to·fu /'toʊfu/ n [U] a soft white food that is made from SOYBEANS ‖ 콩으로 만든 부드러운 흰 식품. 두부

to·ga /'toʊɡə/ n a long loose piece of clothing worn by people in ancient Greece and Rome ‖ 고대 그리스·로마 사람들이 입었던 길고 헐렁한 옷. 토가

to·geth·er¹ /tə'ɡɛðɚ/ adv 1 if two or more things are put together, they form a single subject, group, mixture, or object ‖ 둘 이상의 사물이 하나의 주제[집단, 혼합물, 물체]를 형성하여. 함께. 같이. 하나가 되어: *Add the numbers together.* 숫자들을 모두 더해라. *We put the puzzle together last night.* 우리는 어젯밤 퍼즐을 (합쳐서) 맞추었다. 2 with or next to each other ‖ 서로 함께 또는 나란히. 더불어. 서로. 같이: *Kevin and I went to school together.* 케빈과 나는 같이 학교에 다녔다. / *Together we can win.* 힘을 합치면 우리는 이길 수 있다. / *We were crowded/packed etc.* together *in one little room.* 우리는 좁은 방 하나에서 함께 북적거렸다. 3 at the same time ‖ 동시에. 한(꺼)번에. 일괄하여: *Why do all the bills seem to come together?* 왜

모든 청구서들은 한꺼번에 오는 것 같은
거지? —see also **get your act
together** (ACT²)

together² adj SPOKEN thinking clearly,
being very organized etc. ‖ 분명하게 생
각하고 아주 잘 정리된 등. 침착한. 안정
된: *Carla seems really together.* 칼라는
정말 침착해 보인다.

to·geth·er·ness /təˈgɛðənɪs/ n [U] a
feeling of having a close relationship
with other people ‖ 다른 사람들과 밀접한
관계를 갖고 있는 느낌. 단결. 연대감. 친
목

tog·gle /ˈtɑgəl/ n a piece of wood or
plastic like a short stick that is used as a
button on coats, bags etc. ‖ 코트·가방 등
에 단추로 사용되는 짧은 막대 같은 나무
나 플라스틱 조각. 토글. 막대 모양의 장
식 단추

togs /tɑgz, tɔgz/ n [plural] INFORMAL
clothes ‖ 옷

toil /tɔɪl/ v [I] LITERARY to work very
hard for a long period of time ‖ 장시간
동안 아주 열심히 일하다. 수고하다 –
toil n [U]

toi·let /ˈtɔɪlɪt/ n a large bowl that you
sit on to get rid of waste matter from
your body ‖ 앉아서 인체의 노폐물을 배설
하는 큰 수세식 변기

USAGE NOTE toilet

Do not use this word to talk about a
room that has a **toilet** in it. Use
bathroom for the room in a house
that has a toilet in it. Use **restroom,
ladies' room, women's room,** and
men's room to talk about a room in
a public place with one or more
toilets. On a plane, this room is called
a **lavatory**.
toilet이 있는 곳에 대해 이야기할 때는
이 말을 쓰지 않는다. 가정 내의 변기가
있는 곳에 대해서는 **bathroom**을 쓴
다. 하나 이상의 변기가 있는 공공 장소
를 말할 때는 **restroom, ladies'
room, women's room, men's
room**을 쓴다. 항공기 내에서는 이곳을
lavatory라고 부른다.

---

toi·let·ries /ˈtɔɪlətriz/ n [plural] things
such as soap and TOOTHPASTE that are
used for washing yourself ‖ 몸을 씻는 데
에 쓰이는 비누·치약 등의 물건. 세면[화
장]용품

to·ken¹ /ˈtoʊkən/ n **1** a piece of metal,
shaped like a coin, that you use instead
of money in some machines ‖ 어떤 기
계들에 돈 대신 사용하는 동전 모양의

금속 조각. 토큰. 보조[대용] 화폐 **2**
something that represents a feeling,
fact, event etc. ‖ 감정·사실·사건 등을 표
시하는 것. 표시. 상징. 증거: *He had
given her the ring as a token of his
love.* 그는 자신의 사랑의 징표로 그녀에게
반지를 주었다.

token² adj a token action, change etc.
is small and not very important, but
shows that you are dealing with a
problem or will keep a promise ‖ 활동·
변화 등이 작고 중요하지 않지만 문제를
다루고 있거나 약속을 지킬 것을 보여주
는. …의 표시가 되는. 이름[명색]뿐인:
He receives a token salary for his help.
그는 자신의 지원에 대해 명목상의 봉급을
받는다.

to·ken·ism /ˈtoʊkəˌnɪzəm/ n [U]
actions that are intended to make
people think that an organization deals
fairly with people or problems when in
fact it does not ‖ 한 조직이 사실과는 다르
게 사람들이나 문제점들을 정당하게 처리
한다고 사람들이 생각하게 하려는 행위.
명목주의

told /toʊld/ v the past tense and PAST
PARTICIPLE of TELL ‖ tell의 과거·과거 분사
형

tol·er·a·ble /ˈtɑlərəbəl/ adj something
that is tolerable is not very good but is
acceptable ‖ 사물이 썩 좋지는 않지만 용
인할 만한. 그런 대로 괜찮은: *The
temperature was a tolerable 90 degrees.*
기온은 90도로 참을만 했다.

tol·er·ance /ˈtɑlərəns/ n **1** [U]
willingness to allow people to do, say,
or believe what they want ‖ 사람들에게
기꺼이 그들이 원하는 것을 하거나 말하거
나, 또는 믿도록 허용하는 것. 관용: *He
had little tolerance for laziness in his
sons.* 그는 아들들의 나태에 대해서는 추
호도 용인하지 않았다. **2** [C, U] the
degree to which someone or something
can suffer pain, difficulty etc. without
being harmed ‖ 사람이나 사물이 해를 입
지 않고 고통·어려움 등을 견뎌낼 수 있는
정도. 인내(력). 내성(耐性): *These
plants have a very limited tolerance for
cold weather.* 이 식물들은 거의 추위를
견디지 못한다.

tol·er·ate /ˈtɑləˌreɪt/ v [T] to accept
something even though you do not like it
‖ 어떤 것을 좋아하지 않지만 받아들이다.
허용하다. 너그럽게 봐주다. 참다: *I
couldn't tolerate the working conditions.*
나는 그 작업 상황을 참을 수 없었다. /
learning to tolerate other people's views
다른 사람들의 견해 용인법의 습득 –

tolerant /'tɑlərənt/ *adj* —see usage note at BEAR¹

toll¹ /toul/ *n* **1** the number of people killed or injured at a particular time ‖ 특정 시간에 죽거나 부상당한 사람들의 숫자. 사상자 수: *The death toll has risen to 83.* 사망자 수가 83명으로 늘어났다. **2 take its toll (on)** to have a bad effect on someone or something over a long period of time ‖ 오랜 시간에 걸쳐 다른 사람이나 사물에 나쁜 영향을 끼치다. 손실을 초래하다: *Years of smoking have taken their toll on his health.* 수년간의 흡연이 그의 건강을 악화시켰다. **3** the money you have to pay to use a particular road, bridge etc. ‖ 특정 도로·다리 등을 이용하기 위해 지불해야 하는 돈. 통행료. 사용료

toll² *v* [I, T] if a bell tolls, or you toll it, it keeps ringing slowly ‖ 종이 계속해서 천천히 울리거나 울리게 하다

toll booth /'. ./ *n* a place where you pay to use a particular road, bridge etc. ‖ 특정 도로·다리 등을 이용하기 위해 돈을 지불하는 곳. 요금 징수소

toll-free /,. '. / *adj* a toll-free telephone call does not cost any money ‖ 전화 요금을 전혀 내지 않는. 무료 전화의: *Call our toll-free number now.* 지금 우리의 무료 전화번호로 전화하세요.

toll.gate /'toulgeɪt/ *n* a TOLL BOOTH with a gate that opens when you pay money ‖ 돈을 지불하면 열리는 문이 있는 요금 징수소. 통행료 징수소. 톨게이트

tom·a·hawk /'tɑmə,hɔk/ *n* a HATCHET (=type of weapon) used by some Native Americans in past times ‖ 과거에 아메리카 원주민이 쓴 무기용 도끼. 큰 도끼

to·ma·to /tə'meɪtoʊ/ *n, plural* **tomatoes** a soft round red fruit, eaten as a vegetable raw or cooked ‖ 채소로서 날로 또는 조리해서 먹는 말랑하며 동그란 붉은 과일. 토마토: *a tomato sauce* 토마토 소스 —see picture on page 944

tomb /tum/ *n* a grave, especially a large one above the ground ‖ 묘, 특히 지상 위로 쌓아올린 큰 것. 무덤. 봉분

tom·boy /'tɑmbɔɪ/ *n* a girl who likes to play the same games as boys ‖ 소년들과 똑같은 놀이 하는 것을 좋아하는 소녀. 말괄량이. 선머슴 같은 소녀

tomb·stone /'tumstoʊn/ *n* ⇨ GRAVESTONE

tom·cat /'tɑmkæt/ *n* a male cat ‖ 수고양이

tome /toʊm/ *n* FORMAL a large heavy book ‖ 크고 무거운 책

tom·fool·er·y /,tɑm'fuləri/ *n* [U] OLD-FASHIONED silly behavior ‖ 바보 같은 행위. 얼빠진 짓[언행]

to·mor·row¹ /tə'mɑroʊ, -'mɔr-/ *n* **1** the day after today ‖ 오늘의 다음날. 내일: *Tomorrow is Thursday.* 내일은 목요일이다. **2** the future, especially the near future ‖ 특히 가까운 장래: *the world of tomorrow* 미래의 세계 **3 do sth like there's no tomorrow** to do something without worrying about the future ‖ 장래에 대한 걱정 없이 무엇을 하다. 흥청망청[마음대로] 하다: *We're spending money like there's no tomorrow.* 우리는 돈을 흥청망청 쓰고 있다.

tomorrow² *adv* on or during the day after today ‖ 오늘의 다음 날이나 다음 날 중에. 내일의[중에]: *Are we playing football tomorrow?* 우리 내일 미식축구 할 건가요?

ton /tʌn/ *n* **1** a unit for measuring weight, equal to 2000 pounds ‖ 2천 파운드에 해당하는 중량 측정 단위. 톤 **2** INFORMAL a very large quantity or weight ‖ 매우 많은 양이나 무게. 다량. 상당한 무게: *Your suitcase weighs a ton!* (=is very heavy) 네 가방은 엄청나게 무겁구나! / *We ate tons of* (=a lot of) *food.* 우리는 음식을 엄청나게 먹었다. **3 like a ton of bricks** INFORMAL happening unexpectedly in a way that shocks you ‖ 충격적으로 예상치 않게 일어나는. 맹렬한 기세로: *I hadn't missed my family much until that day, but then it hit me like a ton of bricks.* 나는 그날까지는 가족을 그렇게 그리워하지 않았었다. 그런데 그때는 그리움이 무섭게 사무쳤다.

tone¹ /toʊn/ *n* **1** [C, U] the way your voice sounds that shows how you are feeling, or what you mean ‖ 자신이 어떻게 느끼는지 또는 무엇을 뜻하는 지를 나타내는 목소리를 내는 방식. 어조: *I don't like your tone of voice.* (=rude or angry way of speaking) 나는 네 말투가 맘에 들지 않는다. / *He spoke in a threatening tone.* 그는 위협적인 어조로 말했다. **2** [singular, U] the general feeling or attitude expressed in a piece of writing, activity etc. ‖ 문장·활동 등에 표현된 일반적인 감정이나 태도. 기질. 분위기: *The argument set the tone* (=began a feeling that continued) *for the evening.* 그 언쟁이 저녁 동안의 분위기를 결정지었다. **3** a sound made by a piece of electronic equipment ‖ 전자 장비에 의해 생긴 소리. 발신[신호]음: *Please leave a message after the tone.* 신호음이 들린 후에[삐 소리가 난 후에] 메시지를 남겨 주세요. **4** [U] the quality of a sound, especially the sound of a musical instrument or someone's voice ‖ 특히 악기 소리나 사람의 목소리의 특질. 음색 **5** [U] how strong and firm your muscles, skin etc. are ‖ 근육·피부 등이 얼마나 강하고 단단한가의 정도. 상태: *muscle tone* 근육의 상태 **6 a** SHADE of a particular color ‖ 특정한 색의 명암. 농담. 색조

tone², **tone up** *v* [T] to make your muscles, skin etc. feel healthier, stronger, firmer etc. ‖ 근육·피부 등을 더 건강하고 강하며 단단하게 느껴지도록 만들다. 튼튼하게 하다. 강화하다. 단련시키다: *I'm trying to tone up my stomach.* 나는 복부를 단련시키려고 합니다.

tone sth ↔ **down** *phr v* [T] to make something such as a speech or piece or writing less offensive, exciting etc. ‖ 연설·견해·문장 등이 보다 덜 공격적이고 자극적이게 하다. 부드럽게[순하게] 하다: *They toned down the words to the song so it could be played on the radio.* 그들은 그 노래의 노랫말을 순화시켜서 라디오에서 틀 수 있게 했다.

tone-deaf /'. ./ *adj* unable to hear the difference between different musical notes ‖ 서로 다른 음계들 사이의 차이를 알아들을 수 없는. 음치의

tongs /taŋz, tɔŋz/ *n* [plural] a tool for picking up objects, made of two movable bars that are attached at one end ‖ 한쪽 끝이 붙어 있는 두 개의 움직일 수 있는 막대로 된, 물체를 집어 올리는 연장. 집게

tongue /tʌŋ/ *n* **1** the soft movable part in your mouth that you use for tasting and speaking ‖ 맛보거나 말하는 데 쓰는 입안의 움직일 수 있는 부드러운 부분. 혀 **2 bite/hold your tongue** to stop yourself from saying something ‖ 무슨 말을 하는 것을 자제하다. 입을 다물다: *I wanted to argue but I had to bite my tongue.* 나는 반박하고 싶었지만 입을 다물어야만 했다. **3 mother/native tongue** the language you spoke when you first learned to speak ‖ 최초로 말을 배우면서 말했던 언어. 모국어/자국어 **4** the part of a shoe under the LACES (=strings that you tie them with) ‖ 신발의 끈 밑에 있는 부분. (신발의)혀 —see also **on the tip of your tongue** (TIP¹), **slip of the tongue** (SLIP²), **a sharp tongue** (SHARP¹)

tongue-in-cheek /,. . '. ./ *adv* said or done seriously, but meant as a joke ‖ 심각하게 말했거나 행했지만 농담으로 한. 반은 농담으로. 비꼬아서: *The show was done in a tongue-in-cheek style.* 그 쇼는

비꼬는 스타일로 끝났다.

tongue-tied /'. ./ *adj* unable to speak easily because you are nervous ‖ 긴장해서 쉽게 말할 수 없는. 입이 안 떨어지는 [얼어붙은]

tongue twist·er /'. ,../ *n* a word or phrase with many similar sounds that is difficult to say quickly ‖ 빨리 말하기 어려운 비슷한 소리가 많은 단어나 구절. 혀가 잘 안 도는[꼬이는] 말: *"She sells sea shells by the seashore" is a tongue twister.* "She sells sea shells by the seashore"는 혀가 잘 꼬이는 말이다.

ton·ic /'tanɪk/ *n* **1** [C, U] also **tonic water** /'.. ,../ a bitter-tasting drink with BUBBLEs, that is added to some alcoholic drinks ‖ 거품이 일며 몇몇 술에 첨가되는 쓴 맛이 나는 음료. 토닉(워터) **2** something, especially a medicine, that gives you more energy or strength ‖ 더 많은 에너지나 힘을 주는 것, 특히 약제. 강장제[약]

to·night¹ /tə'naɪt/ *adv* on or during the night of today ‖ 오늘밤에. 오늘 밤 동안에: *Do you want to go out tonight?* 오늘밤에 외출할래?

tonight² *n* the night of today ‖ 오늘 밤: *Tonight is a very special occasion.* 오늘 밤은 매우 특별한 때이다. / *tonight's news* 금일 저녁 뉴스

ton·nage /'tʌnɪdʒ/ *n* [U] **1** the number of TONs that something weighs, or the amount of something that there is, measured in tons ‖ 물체의 중량에 대한 톤수나 어떤 물체를 톤으로 측정한 양. 톤수. 총무게 **2** the size of a ship or the amount of goods it can carry, shown in tons ‖ 톤 단위로 나타낸 배의 크기나 운반하는 물자의 양. 배의 톤수. 적재량

ton·sil /'tansəl/ *n* one of two small organs at the sides of your throat near the back of your tongue ‖ 혀의 뒷뿌리 부근 목구멍 양쪽에 있는 두 개의 조그만 조직중 하나. 편도선

ton·sil·li·tis /,tansə'laɪtɪs/ *n* [U] an infection of the TONSILs ‖ 편도선의 감염. 편도선염

To·ny /'touni/ *n* a prize given each year to the best plays, actors etc. in New York's theaters ‖ 매년 뉴욕의 극장에서 최고의 연극·배우 등에게 주어지는 상. 토니상

too /tu/ *adv* **1** more than is needed, wanted, or possible ‖ 필요한 것[원하는 것, 가능한 것]보다 더 많이. 너무. 지나치게: *You're going too fast!* 너 너무 빨리 간다! / *This is too busy a road to let the kids play near it.* 이곳은 근처에서 아이

들을 놓게 하기에는 너무 번잡한 도로이다. ✗DON'T SAY "This is a too busy road."✗ "This is a too busy road."라고는 하지 않는다. **2** also ‖ 또한. 역시. …도: *Sheila wants to come too.* 실라도 오고 싶어한다. / *"I'm really hungry." "I am too!"* "나 정말 배고파." "나도 그래!" **3** very ‖ 매우. 아주. 몹시: *It shouldn't be too long until dinner's ready.* 저녁이 준비될 때까지 그리 오래 걸리지는 않는다.

USAGE NOTE too, very, and enough

Use **too** before an adjective or adverb in order to say that something is more than you need or more than is acceptable: *This shirt is too big for me.* Use **very** before an adjective or adverb in order to emphasize it: *This shirt is very big.* Use **enough** after an adjective or adverb in order to say that something has as much of a quality as it needs: *The shirt is big enough for me.*

too는 형용사나 부사 앞에서 사물이 필요하거나 수용할 수 있는 것보다 많다는 것을 말하는 데에 쓰인다: 이 셔츠는 내게 너무 크다. **very**는 형용사나 부사 앞에서 그것을 강조하는 데에 쓰인다: 이 셔츠는 매우 크다. **enough**는 사물이 필요한 만큼 많은 특성을 가지고 있음을 말하려는 데에 형용사나 부사 뒤에 쓰인다: 그 셔츠는 내게 맞을 만큼 크다.

---

took /tʊk/ *v* the past tense of TAKE ‖ take의 과거형

tool¹ /tul/ *n* **1** something such as a hammer, SCREWDRIVER etc. that you use to make or repair things ‖ 무엇을 만들거나 고칠 때 쓰는 망치나 (스크루) 드라이버 등의 것. 연장. 도구 **2** something such as a piece of equipment or a treatment that is useful for a particular purpose ‖ 특정한 목적에 유용한 장비나 취급법 따위의 것. 수단. 도구: *Can television be used as a tool for learning?* 텔레비전이 학습 수단으로 쓰일 수 있을까? —see usage note at MACHINE¹

tool² *v* to decorate leather with a special tool ‖ 특수한 연장으로 가죽을 장식하다. 세공하다. 다듬다

tool along/down *phr v* [I] INFORMAL to drive fast, especially for fun ‖ 특히 즐기기 위해 빨리 운전하다. 재미로 고속 주행하다: *tooling along at 90 miles an hour* 시속 90마일의 고속 주행

toot /tut/ *v* [I, T] if a horn toots, or if you toot it, it makes a short sound ‖ 나팔이 짧게 소리 나다[소리를 내다]. 뚜뚜

울리다 –**toot** *n*

tooth /tuθ/ *n, plural* **teeth** **1** one of the hard objects in your mouth that you use to bite and CHEW your food ‖ 음식을 물고 씹는 데 쓰이는 입안의 단단한 물체들 중의 하나. 이(빨). 치아: *Did you brush your teeth?* (=clean them) 이 닦았니? **2** one of the pointed parts that sticks out from a comb, SAW etc. ‖ 빗·톱 등에서 튀어 나온 뾰족한 부분 중의 하나. 이. 날. 아귀 **3 fight (sb/sth) tooth and nail** to work or fight as hard as you can to prevent something from happening or to achieve something ‖ 어떤 일이 벌어지는 것을 막거나 달성하기 위해 가능한 한 힘껏 일하거나 싸우다. 전력을 다해 …하다: *The residents intend to fight the proposed shopping mall tooth and nail.* 주민들은 건축이 계획된 쇼핑몰에 맞서 필사적으로 싸울 작정이다. —see also **have a sweet tooth** (SWEET)

tooth·ache /'tuθeɪk/ *n* [C] a pain in a tooth ‖ 이의 통증. 치통

tooth·brush /'tuθbrʌʃ/ *n* a small brush for cleaning your teeth ‖ 이를 깨끗이 하기 위한 작은 솔. 칫솔

tooth·paste /'tuθpeɪst/ *n* [U] a substance used for cleaning your teeth ‖ 이를 닦는 데 쓰이는 물질. 치약

tooth·pick /'tuθ,pɪk/ *n* a small pointed piece of wood for removing pieces of food from between your teeth ‖ 이 사이의 음식 찌꺼기를 없애기 위한 작고 뾰족한 나뭇조각. 이쑤시개

top¹ /tɑp/ *n*

1 ▶HIGHEST PART 최상부◀ the highest part of something ‖ 사물의 가장 높은 부분. 정상. 꼭대기: *Write your name at the top of the page.* 페이지 맨 위에 이름을 쓰시오. / *There was a flag on top of the tower.* 탑의 꼭대기에는 깃발이 있었다. —opposite BOTTOM¹

2 ▶UPPER SURFACE 윗면◀ the flat upper surface of an object ‖ 물건의 평평한 윗면. 거죽. 표면: *The table has a glass top.* 그 테이블은 표면이 유리로 되어 있다. / *the top of my desk* 내 책상 윗면

3 on top of a) in addition to ‖ 무엇에 더해서. …위에. 게다가: *On top of everything else, I need $700 to fix my car!* 다른 온갖 것 외에, 나는 차를 수리하는 데에 7백 달러가 필요하다! **b)** in control of a situation ‖ 상황을 장악하여. …에 통달하여. …에 정통한: *I'm on top of the problem.* 나는 그 문제에 통달해 있다.

4 the top the highest position in a

company, competition etc. ‖ 회사·경쟁 등에서 가장 높은 위치. 최고 극점. 절정: *The Rockets are at the top of the league.* 로케츠 팀이 리그전의 정상에 올랐다.

5 ▶COVER 덮개◀ a cover for a pen, container etc., especially something that you push or turn ‖ 특히 밀거나 돌리는 펜·용기 등의 덮개. 뚜껑. 마개: *I can't unscrew the top of this jar.* 이 단지 뚜껑을 돌려서 열지 못하겠다.

6 ▶CLOTHING 의류◀ clothing that you wear on the upper part of your body ‖ 상체에 입는 의복. 상의. 윗옷: *Is that a new top?* 그게 새 윗옷이냐?

7 off the top of your head INFORMAL said without checking the facts ‖ 사실 확인 없이 말하여. 깊이 생각하지 않고. 무턱대고. 즉석에서: *Off the top of my head I'd say there were about 50.* 얼추 생각해서 약 50명이 있었다고 할 수 있겠지요.

8 at the top of your voice/lungs shouted or sung as loudly as you can ‖ 가능한 크게 소리치거나 노래하여. 목소리가 올라가는 데까지/숨이 미치는 데까지: *I yelled at the top of my lungs, but he didn't hear.* 나는 최대한도로 크게 외쳤지만 그는 듣지 못했다.

9 ▶TOY 장난감◀ a toy that spins and balances on its point when you twist it ‖ 비틀었을 때 빙빙 돌다가 그 자리에서 균형을 잡는 장난감. 오뚝이

10 top-of-the-line the best or most expensive ‖ 최고이거나 가장 비싼. 최고 수준의. 최고급품의: *a top-of-the-line video system* 최고급품 비디오 기계

11 on top of the world INFORMAL extremely happy ‖ 최고로 행복하게. 행복에 겨워 —see also **blow your top/ stack** (BLOW¹)

top² adj 1 at the top; highest ‖ 맨 위의; 가장 높은: *the top button of my shirt* 내 셔츠의 맨 윗단추 —opposite BOTTOM² **2** best or most successful ‖ 최고의, 가장 성공적인. 최상의: *Carl is one of our top salesmen* 칼은 우리의 최고 영업 사원 중 한 명이다. **3 top dog** INFORMAL the person in the highest or most important position ‖ 최고위직이거나 가장 중요한 위치에 있는 사람. 최고위층, 최고 권위자: *Tony's top dog around here.* 토니가 이 주위에서 최고위직 인물이다.

top³ v -pped, -pping [T] **1** to be higher, better, or more than something ‖ 다른 것보다 더 높아[좋아, 많아]지다. 능가[상회]하다. …이상이다: *Their profits have topped $5,000,000 this year.* 그들의 수익은 올해 5백만 달러를

상회했다. **2** to form or be the top for something ‖ 사물의 맨 위를 이루거나 되다. 선두에 서다. 정상이 되다: *ice cream topped with maple syrup* 맨 위에 단풍 당밀을 얹은 아이스크림

top sth ↔ **off** *phr v* [T] **1 to top it (all) off** INFORMAL in addition to other bad things that have happened ‖ 일어난 다른 나쁜 일에 더해서. 게다가. 엎친 데 덮쳐서: *Then I lost my job, and to top it all off, my dog died.* 그때 나는 실직했고 엎친 데 덮쳐서 개까지 죽었다. **2** INFORMAL to do one final thing before finishing something ‖ 어떤 일을 끝내기 전에 최종적인 것을 하다. …으로 마무리짓다. …을 해서 끝내다: *We topped off the evening with a visit to a local bar.* 우리는 동네 술집에 가는 것으로 그 밤을 마무리했다. **3** to add the last part of something that is needed to complete or fill it ‖ 어떤 것을 완성하거나 채우기 위해 필요한 마지막 부분을 추가하다. 끝까지 채우다: *Can you top off the tank with unleaded gas, please?* 무연 휘발유로 가득 채워 주시겠어요?

top out *phr v* [I] if something that is increasing tops out, it reaches its highest point and stops rising ‖ 사물이 증가해서 최고점에 도달하여 증가를 멈추다. 피크[정점, 절정]에 이르다[…으로 끝나다]: *The Dow Jones average topped out at 5999.75 today.* 다우 존스 지수가 오늘 5999.75로 최고치를 기록했다.

top-class /ˌ. ˈ./ *adj* of very good quality or a very high standard ‖ 아주 좋은 특질의 또는 최고 수준의. 최고의. 일류의

top 40 /ˌtɑp ˈfɔrţi/ *n* **1** [U] music that is popular with young people, consisting of simple tunes with a strong beat ‖ 강한 박자와 단순한 곡조로 이루어져 젊은이들 사이에 유행하는 음악. 팝스. 대중음악: *I like top 40 better than hard rock.* 나는 하드 록 음악보다 대중음악이 좋다. **2 the top 40** the list of the 40 most popular records in a particular week ‖ 특정 주간에 가장 인기 있는 40개 음반 목록. 상위 40곡

top hat /ˈ. ˌ./ *n* a man's tall hat with a flat top, worn in past times ‖ 과거에 쓰던 윗부분이 납작한 남자용 높은 모자

top-heav·y /ˈ. ˌ./ *adj* **1** too heavy at the top and therefore likely to fall over ‖ 윗부분이 너무 무거워서 넘어질 것 같은. 위가 무거운 **2** a top-heavy organization has too many managers ‖ 조직이 너무 많은 관리자를 둔. 간부가 너무 많은

top·ic /'tɑpɪk/ *n* a subject that people talk or write about ‖ 사람들이 말하거나 글을 쓰는 대상. 화제. 논제. 이야깃거리: *a discussion on the topic of human rights* 인권을 주제로 한 토론 / *Jackie's engagement was the main topic of conversation.* (=what was talked about) 재키의 약혼이 대화의 주된 화제였다.

top·i·cal /'tɑpɪkəl/ *adj* relating to something that is important at the present time ‖ 현재 중요한 것에 관한. 시사 문제를 다룬. 현재 화제가 되는: *a new TV show dealing with topical issues* 시사 문제를 다루는 새 텔레비전 쇼

top·less /'tɑplɪs/ *adj* not wearing any clothes on the upper part of the body ‖ 상체에 아무 옷도 입지 않는. 가슴을 노출시킨

top·most /'tɑpmoʊst/ *adj* highest ‖ 가장 높은. 최고의: *the topmost branches of the tree* 나무의 가장 높은 가지

top·notch /,. '·/ *adj* INFORMAL having the highest quality or standard ‖ 질이나 수준이 최고인. 일류의. 제일급의: *top-notch schools* 명문 학교들

to·pog·ra·phy /tə'pɑgrəfi/ *n* [U] **1** the science of describing or making a map of an area of land ‖ 한 지역의 지도를 그리거나 제작하는 학문. 지형학 **2** the shape of an area of land, including its hills, valleys etc. ‖ 구릉·계곡 등을 포함한 한 지역의 형상. 지형[지세](도) – **topographer** *n* – **topographical** /,tɑpə'græfɪkəl/ *adj*

top·ping /'tɑpɪŋ/ *n* [C, U] food that you put on top of other food to make it taste or look better ‖ 맛을 내거나 더 좋아 보이게 하려고 다른 식품 위에 얹는 식품. 위에 추가하는 것. 토핑: *a pizza with five toppings* 5가지 토핑을 얹은 피자

top·ple /'tɑpəl/ *v* **1** [I, T] to fall over, or to make something do this ‖ 넘어지다, 또는 사물이 이렇게 되게 하다. 쓰러지다. 쓰러뜨리다: *Several trees toppled over in the storm.* 몇 그루의 나무들이 폭풍 속에서 쓰러졌다. **2** [T] to take power away from a leader or government ‖ 지배자나 정부로부터 권력을 빼앗다. 권좌에서 끌어내리다. 몰락시키다: *The scandal could topple the government.* 그 스캔들은 정부를 와해시킬 수 있었다.

top-se·cret /,. '··/ *adj* top-secret documents or information must be kept completely secret ‖ 문서나 정보가 철저히 비밀로 지켜져야 하는. 극비의. 최고 기밀인

top·sy-tur·vy /,tɑpsi 'təvi·/ *adj* INFORMAL completely disorganized and in a state of confusion ‖ 완전히 무질서하고 혼란 상태에 있는. 뒤죽박죽의. 엉망인

torch[1] /tɔrtʃ/ *n* a long stick that you burn at one end for light or as a symbol ‖ 빛이나 상징으로서 한쪽 끝에 불을 붙인 긴 막대. 횃불: *the Olympic torch* 올림픽 성화

torch[2] *v* [T] INFORMAL to start a fire deliberately in order to destroy something ‖ 고의로 어떤 것을 파괴하기 위해 불을 지르다. 방화하다: *Someone torched the old warehouse.* 누군가가 낡은 창고에 불을 질렀다.

tore /tɔr/ *v* the past tense of TEAR ‖ tear 의 과거형

tor·ment[1] /'tɔrmɛnt/ *n* [C, U] severe pain and suffering, or something that causes this ‖ 심한 아픔과 고통 또는 그것을 일으키는 것. 괴로움. 말썽거리: *The war left thousands of families in torment.* 전쟁은 수많은 가족들을 고통받게 했다.

tor·ment[2] /tɔr'mɛnt/ *v* [T] to make someone suffer a lot of mental or physical pain ‖ 어떤 사람에게 많은 정신적 또는 육체적 고통을 겪게 하다. 몹시 괴롭히다: *The cat's tormenting the birds again.* 고양이가 또 새들을 괴롭히고 있다. – **tormentor** *n*

torn /tɔrn/ *v* the PAST PARTICIPLE of TEAR ‖ tear 의 과거 분사형

tor·na·do /tɔr'neɪdoʊ/ *n* an extremely violent storm with air that spins very quickly in the shape of a FUNNEL ‖ 깔때기 모양으로 몹시 빠르게 회전하는 공기에 의해 발생하는 극히 격렬한 폭풍. 토네이도. 뇌우. 대선풍 —see usage note at WEATHER

tor·pe·do /tɔr'pidoʊ/ *n* a weapon that is fired under the surface of the ocean from one ship at another ‖ 한 척의 배에서 다른 배를 겨냥해 바다 속에서 발사하는 무기. 어뢰 – **torpedo** *v* [T]

tor·rent /'tɔrənt, 'tɑr-/ *n* **1 a torrent of sth** a lot of something ‖ 대량의 어떤 것. …의 속출[연발]: *a torrent of criticism* 빗발치는 비난 **2** a large amount of water moving very quickly in a particular direction ‖ 특정 방향으로 매우 빠르게 움직이는 많은 양의 물. 급류. 분류 – **torrential** /tə'rɛnʃəl, tɔ-/ *adj* : *torrential rain* 호우(豪雨)

tor·rid /'tɔrɪd, 'tɑr-/ *adj* **1** involving strong emotions, especially sexual excitement ‖ 강렬한 감정, 특히 성적 흥분을 포함하는. 열렬한. 불타는 듯한: *a torrid love affair* 열정적인 애정 행각 **2** extremely hot ‖ 극심하게 뜨거운. 작열하

는. 불볕의

tor·so /'tɔrsou/ n the main part of your body, not including your arms, legs, or head ‖ 팔이나 다리, 또는 머리가 포함되지 않은 신체의 주요부. 몸통. 동체. 토르소

tort /tɔrt/ n LAW an action that is wrong but not criminal and can be dealt with in a civil court of law ‖ 잘못된 것이지만 범죄는 아니어서 민사 법정에서 다룰 수 있는 행위. 불법 행위

tor·ti·lla /tɔr'tiyə/ n a thin flat Mexican bread made from CORNMEAL or flour ‖ 옥수수 가루나 밀가루로 만든 얇고 납작한 멕시코 빵. 토르티야

tor·toise /'tɔrtəs/ n a kind of TURTLE with a sharp nose, that lives on land ‖ 뾰족한 코가 있고 육지에 사는 거북이의 일종

tor·tu·ous /'tɔrtʃuəs/ adj 1 very complicated, long, and therefore confusing ‖ 매우 복잡하고 길어서 혼란스러운. 에두르는: a tortuous process 복잡한 과정 2 a tortuous road has a lot of turns and is difficult to travel on ‖ 도로가 구부러진 곳이 많아서 통행하기 어려운. 구불구불한

tor·ture¹ /'tɔrtʃər/ n [C, U] 1 the act of torturing (TORTURE) someone ‖ 사람에게 고통을 주는 행위. 고문 2 mental or physical suffering ‖ 정신적, 또는 육체적 고통. 고난: It was torture, watching her cry and not being able to help. 그녀가 우는 것을 지켜보며 도와줄 수 없는 것은 고통이었다.

tor·ture² v [T] to make someone suffer severe physical punishment in order to make him/her give information ‖ 정보를 제공하도록 사람에게 심한 체벌의 고통을 받게 하다. 고문하다. 고문하여 …하게 하다: He was tortured to death in prison. 그는 감옥에서 고문으로 죽었다.

toss /tɔs/ v 1 [T] to throw something without much force ‖ 많은 힘을 가하지 않고 물건을 던지다: Could you toss me my keys? 내 열쇠 좀 던져 주실래요? 2 **toss and turn** to change your position a lot in bed because you cannot sleep ‖ 잠들 수가 없어서 침대에서 자세를 많이 바꾸다. 엎치락뒤치락하다. 이리저리 뒤치며 자다 3 also **toss** sth ↔ **out** INFORMAL to get rid of something ‖ 물체를 없애다. 내버리다: "Where's the newspaper?" "I tossed it." "신문 어디 있어?" "내가 버렸어." 4 [T] to cover one food with another food by gently moving them with a spoon ‖ 한 가지 식품을 숟가락으로 살짝 뒤적여서 다른 식품으로 덮

다. 버무리다: Rinse the blueberries and toss them with sugar. 블루베리를 썻어서 설탕으로 버무려라. – **toss** n —see also **toss/flip a coin** (COIN¹)

toss-up /'. ./ n it's a toss-up SPOKEN said when you do not know which of two things will happen, or which of two things to choose ‖ 두 가지 중 어느 것이 일어날지, 또는 어느 쪽을 선택할지 모를 때 쓰여. 반반의 가능성: So far the election is still a toss-up. 지금까지 선거는 여전히 예측이 어려운 상태이다.

tot /tɑt/ n INFORMAL a small child ‖ 아주 어린아이

to·tal¹ /'toutl/ adj 1 affecting or including everything; complete ‖ 모든 것에 영향을 미치거나 포함하는. 전부의; 철저한: His farm has a total area of 100 acres. 그의 농장은 전체 면적이 1백 에이커이다. / the total absence of any sound 전혀 아무 소리도 없는 상태 2 **total number/amount/cost etc.** the number, amount etc. that you get when you add all the parts of something together ‖ 사물의 모든 부분들을 함께 더할 때 얻는 수나 양 등. 총계/총량/총비용: The total cost of the building will be $6 million. 그 건물의 총 가격은 6백만 달러가 될 것이다. 3 SPOKEN used in order to emphasize the degree of something ‖ 무엇의 정도를 강조하는 데 쓰여. 완전한. 절대적인: He's a total idiot! 그는 완전히 바보야!

total² n the final number, amount etc. of something after all the parts have been added together; SUM ‖ 모든 각 부분들이 함께 더해진 후의 최종적인 수·양 등. 총계. 합계; ☞ sum: The city spent a total of two million dollars on the library. 그 시는 도서관에 총 2백만 달러를 지출했다. / I was out of work for 34 days in total. 나는 총 34일 동안 쉬었다.

total³ v [T] 1 to add up to a particular amount ‖ 특정 양까지 더해가다. 합계해서 …이 되다: Prize money totaling $5000 will be awarded. 합계 5천 달러에 이르는 상금이 수여될 것이다. 2 INFORMAL to damage a car so badly that it cannot be repaired ‖ 차를 수리할 수 없을 정도로 심하게 손상시키다. 엉망으로 만들다. 박살내다

to·tal·i·tar·i·an /tou,tælə'tɛriən/ adj based on a political system in which people are completely controlled by the government ‖ 사람들이 철저히 정부의 통제를 받는 정치 체제에 기반을 둔. 전체주의의 – **totalitarianism** n [U]

to·tal·i·ty /tou'tæləti/ n [U] FORMAL the

whole of something ‖ 어떤 것의 전체. 전체(성)

to·tal·ly /'toʊtl-i/ *adv* completely ‖ 완전히. 전부: *I totally agree with you.* 나는 전적으로 네게 동의한다. / *The whole game was totally unfair.* 전(全) 경기가 모두 불공정했다.

tote /toʊt/ *v* [T] INFORMAL to carry something ‖ 무엇을 나르다. 운반하다

tote bag /'. ./ *n* a large bag in which you carry things ‖ 물건을 휴대하는 큰 가방. 대형 손가방

to·tem pole /'toʊtəm ‚poʊl/ *n* a tall wooden pole with images of animals or faces cut into it, made by some Native American tribes ‖ 몇몇 아메리카 원주민 종족이 만든 동물의 형상이나 얼굴이 새겨진 높은 나무 기둥. 토템 폴

tot·ter /'tɑtɚ/ *v* [I] to walk or move in an unsteady way as if you are about to fall down ‖ 넘어질 듯이 불안정하게 걷거나 움직이다. 뒤뚝뒤뚝 걷다: *a woman tottering around in high heels* 굽이 높은 신발을 신고 뒤뚝뒤뚝 돌아다니는 여성

tou·can /'tukæn, -kɑn/ *n* a tropical bird with bright feathers and a very large beak ‖ 밝은 색 깃털과 매우 큰 부리를 가진 열대 조류. 큰부리새

touch[1] /tʌtʃ/ *v* **1** [T] to put your finger, hand etc. on something or someone so you feel him, her, or it ‖ 감촉할 수 있게 물건이나 사람에 손가락·손 등을 대다. 만지다. 손대다: *Don't touch the paint – it's still wet!* 페인트를 만지지 마라. 아직 덜 말랐어! / *Can you touch your toes?* (=while standing up and without bending your knees) (서서 무릎을 굽히지 않고) 발가락에 손을 댈 수 있니? **2** [I, T] if two things are touching, there is no space in between them ‖ 두 물체 사이에 공간이 없다. 닿다. 접하다: *Make sure the wires aren't touching.* 반드시 전선들이 닿지 않게 하시오. **3 not touch sth a)** to not use or handle something ‖ 무엇을 사용하거나 다루지 않다. 손을 대지 않다: *My brother won't let me touch his bike.* 내 형은 자기 자전거를 내가 손도 대지 못하게 한다. **b)** to not eat or drink something ‖ 무엇을 먹거나 마시지 않다. 입을 대지 않다: *She didn't touch her breakfast.* 그녀는 아침 식사에 입도 대지 않았다. **4 not touch sb** to not hurt someone physically ‖ 누군가를 신체적으로 다치게 하지 않다: *I swear Mom, I didn't touch him!* 엄마 맹세해요, 나는 그에게 손도 대지 않았어요! **5** [T] to deal with or become involved in a particular situation or problem ‖ 특정한 상황 또는 문제를 다루거나 관련되다. 관계하다: *Clancy said he wouldn't touch the case.* 클랜시는 그 사건에 관여하지 않겠다고 말했다. **6 touch base** to talk for a short time with someone about something you are both working on in order to share information ‖ 정보를 공유하기 위해 함께 일하고 있는 사안에 대하여 다른 사람과 잠시 얘기하다. 협의하다: *I wanted to touch base with you before the meeting.* 나는 회의 전에 너와 협의하고 싶었다. **7** [T] to affect someone's emotions, especially by making him/her feel pity or sympathy ‖ 특히 어떤 사람에게 연민이나 동정심을 느끼게 해서 남의 감정에 영향을 미치다. 마음을 움직이게 하다. 감동[감격]시키다: *His speech touched everyone present.* 그의 연설은 참석한 모든 사람을 감동시켰다. —see also TOUCHED

touch down *phr v* [I] if an aircraft touches down, it lands on the ground ‖ 항공기가 지상에 착륙하다

touch sth ↔ **off** *phr v* [T] to cause a bad situation or violent event to begin ‖ 나쁜 상황이나 폭력적인 사건이 시작되게 하다. 유발하다. 일으키다: *The report touched off a fierce debate.* 그 보고서는 격렬한 논쟁을 유발했다.

touch on/upon sth *phr v* [T] to mention something when you are talking or writing ‖ 말하거나 글을 쓸 때 무엇을 언급하다. …에 관해 쓰다[말하다]. 다루다: *Her songs touch on social issues.* 그녀의 노래는 사회 문제를 다루고 있다.

touch sth ↔ **up** *phr v* [T] to improve something by making small changes to it ‖ 작은 변화를 주어서 무엇을 개선하다. 손질하다. 수정하다: *Norma touched up her makeup for the picture.* 노마는 사진 찍기 위해 자신의 화장을 고쳤다.

touch[2] *n* **1** the action of putting your finger, hand etc. on someone or something ‖ 사람이나 물건에 손가락·손 등을 대기. 만지기. 접촉: *Rita felt the touch of his hand on her arm.* 리타는 그의 손이 자신의 팔에 닿는 것을 느꼈다. **2 get in touch (with sb)** to communicate with someone by letter or telephone ‖ 편지나 전화로 누군가와 의사 소통을 하다. 연락을 취하다: *I've been trying to get in touch with you all morning.* 나는 아침 내내 너와 연락을 취하려고 애쓰고 있다. **3 a)** the state of speaking or writing to someone regularly ‖ 누군가에게 정기적으로 말하거나 글을 쓰고 있는 상태. 접촉. 교섭: *We try to stay in touch* *through e-mail.* 우리는 이메일을 통해 접촉을 유지하려 노력하고 있다. / *I've lost touch with my high school friends.* 나는 고등학교 친구들과 연락이 끊겼다. **b)** the state of having the best information or knowledge about a situation or subject ‖ 상황이나 주제에 대한 최고의 정보나 지식을 갖고 있는 상태. ···에 능통함: *I think he's out of touch with the American people.* 나는 그가 미국 국민들에 대해 잘 알지 못한다고 생각한다. **4** [U] the sense that you use in order to feel things, especially by putting your finger, hand etc. on something ‖ 특히 손가락·손 등을 물건에 갖다 대어 물건을 느끼기 위해 사용하는 감각. 촉감: *Her skin was cool to the touch.* 그녀의 피부는 감촉이 차갑다. **5 a touch of sth** a very small amount of something ‖ 사물의 아주 적은 양. 약간. 조금. 기미: *a touch of sadness in her voice* 그녀의 목소리에 담긴 슬픔의 기미 / *salad dressing with a touch of lemon juice* 레몬주스를 조금 친 샐러드드 레싱 **6** a small detail or change that improves something ‖ 무엇을 개선시키는 사소한 세부 사항이나 변화. 손질. 마무리: *Becky put the finishing touches on the cake.* 베키는 케이크에 마지막 손질을 했다. **7** [U] a particular way of doing something skillful ‖ 무엇을 능숙하게 하는 특정한 방법. 솜씨. 기량: *I must be losing my touch – I can't hit anything today.* 내 솜씨가 떨어졌음이 틀림없다. 오늘은 하나도 맞출 수가 없다.

touch-and-go /ˌ. . ˈ./ *adj* INFORMAL if a situation is touch-and-go, there is a risk that something bad could happen ‖ 상황이 잘못될 위험이 있는. 위험한. 아슬아슬한. 일촉즉발의: *After Dad's operation, it was touch-and-go for a while.* 아버지는 수술 후에 상태가 한동안 위태로웠다.

touch-down /ˈtʌtʃdaʊn/ *n* **1** the action in American football of moving the ball into the opponents' END ZONE in order to gain points ‖ 미식축구에서 점수를 얻기 위해 상대편의 엔드존으로 공을 가져가는 행위. 터치다운 **2** the moment that a space vehicle lands on the ground ‖ 우주선이 지상에 착륙하는 순간. 착륙. 접지

touched /tʌtʃt/ *adj* feeling happy and grateful because of what someone has done for you ‖ 누군가가 해준 것 때문에 행복하고 감사하게 느끼는. 감동한. 감격한: *We were touched by their concern.* 우리는 그들의 배려에 감격했다.

touch-ing /ˈtʌtʃɪŋ/ *adj* affecting your emotions, especially making you feel

pity, sympathy, sadness etc. ‖ 특히 연민과 동정 그리고 슬픔을 느끼게 하는 등 감정에 영향을 미치는. 마음을 움직이는. 감동[감격]적인: *a touching movie about a boy and his dog* 소년과 그의 개에 대한 감동적인 영화

touch·stone /ˈtʌtʃstoʊn/ *n* a standard used for measuring the quality of something ‖ 사물의 품질을 판정하는 데 쓰이는 표준. 기준. 시금석

touch·y /ˈtʌtʃi/ *adj* **1** easily offended or annoyed ‖ 쉽게 화가 나거나 짜증나는. 성미가 급한. 신경질적인: *You've been very touchy lately – what's wrong?* 너 요새 매우 신경질적이구나. 무슨 일이야? **2 touchy subject/question etc.** something that you have to be careful about saying, in order not to offend someone ‖ 누군가가 불쾌하지 않도록 말을 조심해야만 하는 것. 까다로운 주제/질문

tough¹ /tʌf/ *adj* **1** INFORMAL difficult and needing a lot of effort ‖ 어렵고 많은 노력을 필요로 하는. 어려운. 고된: *Working as a fireman is tough.* 소방수로 일하는 것은 고되다. / *a tough question on the test* 시험에 나온 어려운 문제 / *a tough choice/decision* 힘든 선택[결정] **2** very determined, and able to deal with difficult conditions ‖ 아주 단호하며 어려운 상황에 대처할 수 있는. 억척같은. 불굴의: *She's a tough businesswoman.* 그녀는 억척스런 여성 사업가이다. **3** very strict ‖ 매우 엄격한: *tough anti-smoking laws* 엄격한 금연법 **4** difficult to cut or eat ‖ 자르거나 먹기 힘든. 단단한. 질긴: *a tough steak* 질긴 스테이크 —opposite TENDER¹ **5 tough!/tough luck!** SPOKEN said when you do not have any sympathy for someone else's problems ‖ 누군가의 문제에 아무런 동정심도 갖지 않을 때 쓰여. 설마!/자업자득이야!: *"I'm freezing!" "Tough! You should have worn your coat."* "얼어 죽겠어요!" "설마! 코트를 입었어야 하는데." **6** a tough place, area etc. is likely to have a lot of violence and crime ‖ 지역·장소 등이 폭력·범죄의 발생 가능성이 많은. 우범 지역의. 범죄 다발의: *He grew up in a tough neighborhood.* 그는 우범 지역에서 성장했다. —**toughness** *n* [U]

tough² *v*

tough sth ↔ out *phr v* [T] to deal with a very difficult situation by being determined to continue ‖ 단호하게 계속해서 매우 어려운 상황에 대처하다. ···을 견디다. 참고 해내다: *He could've gone home, but he stayed and toughed it out.*

그는 집에 갈 수도 있었으나 남아서 해냈다.

tough·en /'tʌfən/, **toughen up** v [I, T] to become TOUGHer, or to make someone or something do this ‖ 더 강인해지다, 또는 사람이나 사물을 이렇게 되게 하다. 억세어지다[지게 하다]: *Hard work has toughened her up.* 힘든 일이 그녀를 강인해지게 했다.

tou·pee /tu'peɪ/ n a piece of artificial hair that a man can wear when he has no hair on part of his head ‖ 남성이 머리카락이 없을 때 쓸 수 있는 인조 머리카락류. 가발

tour¹ /tʊr/ n 1 a trip taken for pleasure, in which you visit several different places in a country, area etc. ‖ 한 나라나 지역 내의 여러 다른 곳을 방문하는, 재미로 하는 여행. 관광[유람] 여행: *a 14-day tour of Egypt.* 14일간의 이집트 여행 2 a short trip through a place in order to see the things in it ‖ 한 장소에 있는 것들을 보기 위한 잠간 들러 보기. 견학. 시찰: *We went on a tour through/of the Smithsonian.* 우리는 스미스소니언 박물관에 견학을 갔다. 3 a planned trip by a group of musicians, a sports team etc. in order to play in several places ‖ 여러 곳에서 공연이나 시합을 하려고 일단의 음악가·스포츠 팀 등이 계획한 여행. 순회. 원정: *The band goes on tour later this year.* 그 악단은 올 하반기에 순회 공연을 간다.

tour² v [I, T] to visit a place on a tour ‖ 여행 차 어떤 장소를 방문하다. 유람하다. 관광 여행하다: *We're going to tour New England this summer.* 우리는 올여름에 뉴잉글랜드에 관광하러 갈 것이다.

tour·ism /'tʊrɪzəm/ n [U] the business of providing things for people to do and places for them to stay while they are on vacation ‖ 사람들이 휴가 중에 할 것과 머물 장소들을 제공하는 사업. 관광업. 여행 안내업: *The island depends on tourism for most of its income.* 그 섬은 대부분의 소득을 관광사업에 의존하고 있다.

tour·ist /'tʊrɪst/ n someone who is traveling or visiting a place for pleasure ‖ 즐기기 위해 어떤 장소를 여행하거나 방문하는 사람. 여행자. 관광객

tour·na·ment /'tɜrnəmənt, 'tɚ-/ n a competition in which many players compete against each other until there is one winner ‖ 많은 선수들이 한 명의 우승자가 남을 때까지 서로 간에 시합하는 경기(방식). 승자 진출전. 토너먼트

tour·ni·quet /'tʊrnɪkɪt, 'tɚ-/ n a band of cloth that is twisted tightly around an injured arm or leg to make blood stop coming out ‖ 피가 나오는 것을 막기 위해 상처 입은 팔이나 다리 주위에 꽉 감는, 천으로 된 띠. 지혈대. 압박대

tou·sle /'taʊzəl, -səl/ v [T] to make someone's hair look messy ‖ 사람의 머리를 흐트러져 보이게 하다. 머리를 헝클다 **– tousled** *adj*

tout /taʊt/ v [T] to praise someone or something in order to persuade people that he, she, or it is important or worth a lot ‖ 남을 설득하기 위해 어떤 사람 또는 사물이 중요하거나 상당한 가치가 있다고 칭찬하다. 과대 선전[추천]하다: *Paul's band is being touted as the next big thing.* 폴의 악단이 두 번째로 큰 것으로 과대 선전되고 있다.

tow¹ /toʊ/ v [T] to pull a vehicle or ship using a rope, chain etc. ‖ 밧줄·쇠사슬 등을 이용해 자동차나 배를 끌다. 견인하다. 예인하다: *Our car had to be towed away.* 우리 차는 견인되어야 했다.

tow² n 1 an act of TOWing a vehicle or ship ‖ 자동차나 배를 끌기. 견인. 예인 2 **in tow** following closely behind someone or something ‖ 사람이나 사물의 뒤에서 바짝 붙어 따라가는. 거느리고. 대동하고. 이끌고: *Mattie arrived with all her children in tow.* 매티는 아이들을 모두 데리고 도착했다.

to·ward /tɔrd, tə'wɔrd/, **towards** *prep* 1 in a particular direction ‖ 특정 방향으로. …의 쪽에. …을 향하여: *traffic moving toward the coast* 해안 쪽으로 이동하고 있는 차량 / *I saw a man coming toward me.* 나는 한 남자가 나를 향해 오는 것을 봤다. ✗DON'T SAY "I saw a man coming to me."✗ "I saw a man coming to me."라고는 하지 않는다. 2 concerning someone or something ‖ 어떤 사람이나 사물에 관한. …에 대해[대한]: *How do you feel toward her?* 그녀를 어떻게 생각하니? / *different attitudes towards divorce* 이혼에 대한 상이한 태도 3 in order to achieve something ‖ 무엇을 달성하기 위해. …을 위한: *working towards world peace* 세계 평화를 위한 활동 4 just before a particular time ‖ 특정 시간 바로 전에. …경[무렵]: *I felt tired toward the end of the day.* 날이 저물 무렵에 나는 피곤함을 느꼈다. 5 near a particular place ‖ 특정 장소 근처에. …의 부근에. …쪽으로[향해서]: *We're building a pipeline down toward Abilene.* 우리는 아빌렌 쪽을 향해 송유관을 부설하고 있다.

tow·el¹ /'taʊəl/ n a piece of cloth used

for drying something ‖ 무엇을 말리는 데에 쓰는 천 조각. 수건. 타월: *a bath towel* (=for drying yourself) 목욕 수건 / *a dish towel* 행주

towel², **towel off/down** *v* [I, T] to dry your body using a TOWEL ‖ 수건을 써서 몸을 말리다

tow·er¹ /ˈtaʊəʳ/ *n* **1** a tall narrow part of a castle, church etc. ‖ 성·교회 등의 높고 좁은 부분. 탑. 망루 **2** a tall structure used for signaling or broadcasting ‖ 신호나 방송에 쓰이는 높은 구조물. 탑: *a radio/television tower* 라디오[텔레비전] 송출탑

tower² *v* to be much taller than the people or things around you ‖ 주변의 사람이나 물건보다 훨씬 키가 크다. 높이 솟다: *O'Neal towered over the other players on the court.* 오닐은 코트에서 다른 선수들보다 키가 훨씬 크다. – **towering** *adj*

town /taʊn/ *n* **1** a place with houses, stores, offices etc. where people live and work, that is smaller than a city ‖ 사람들이 살고 일하는 집·상점·사무실 등이 있는 도시보다 작은 장소. 읍. 도회지: *a little town on the coast* 해변의 작은 시 / *She's from out of town.* (=lives in a different town) 그녀는 다른 도시에서 왔다. / *I'm coming into town on the 5:30 flight from Dallas.* 나는 댈러스 발 5시 30분 비행기 편으로 도착할 예정이다. **2** [U] the business or shopping center of a town ‖ 도회지의 사업이나 쇼핑센터. 번화가. 시내: *"Where's Dad?" "He's gone into town."* "아빠는 어디 계시지?" "시내에 가셨어요." **3** [singular] all the people who live in a particular town ‖ 특정 읍에 사는 모든 사람들. 시민. 읍 주민: *The whole town got involved in the celebrations.* 모든 주민들이 축제에 참여했다. **4 go to town (on sth)** SPOKEN to do something eagerly and with a lot of energy ‖ 무엇을 열심히 활기차게 하다. 기세 좋게 하다: *Larry really went to town on those pancakes.* (=ate them quickly) 래리는 저 케이크들을 정말 순식간에 먹어 치웠다. **5 on the town** INFORMAL going to restaurants, theaters etc. for entertainment ‖ 즐기기 위해 레스토랑·극장 등에 가는. 흥청거리는: *Everyone went out for a night on the town.* 모든 사람들이 즐거운 밤을 보내기 위해 외출했다.

town hall /ˌ. ˈ./ *n* a public building used for a town's local government ‖ 도시의 지방 자치를 위해 쓰이는 공공건물. 동사무소. 공회당

town·house /ˈtaʊnhaʊs/ *n* a house in a group of houses that share one or more walls ‖ 한 개 이상의 담을 공유하고 있는 집단 가옥들 중의 한 집. 주택 단지 내의 집 한 채 —see picture on page 945

town·ship /ˈtaʊnʃɪp/ *n* an area where people live and work that is organized under a local government ‖ 지방 자치제 하에 조직되어 사람들이 거주하고 일하는 지역. 군구(郡區)

towns·peo·ple /ˈtaʊnzˌpipəl/, **towns·folk** /ˈtaʊnfoʊk/ *n* [plural] all the people who live in a particular town ‖ 특정 읍[도시]에 사는 모든 사람들. 읍민. 시민

tow truck /ˈ. ./ *n* a strong truck that is used for pulling vehicles that cannot move on their own ‖ 스스로 움직일 수 없는 차량을 끄는 데에 쓰는 강한 트럭. 견인차

tox·ic /ˈtɑksɪk/ *adj* poisonous, or containing poison ‖ 유독한. 독이 들어 있는: *toxic exhaust fumes* 유독성 배기가스 – **toxicity** /tɑkˈsɪsəti/ *n* [U]

tox·i·col·o·gy /ˌtɑksɪˈkɑlədʒi/ *n* [U] the study of poisons and their effects ‖ 독과 그 효능에 대한 연구. 독물학

toxic waste /ˌ. ˈ./ *n* [C, U] waste products from industry that are harmful to people, animals, or the environment ‖ 사람이나 동물, 또는 환경에 유해한 공장의 폐기물[노폐물]. 유독성 폐기물

tox·in /ˈtɑksɪn/ *n* a poisonous substance, especially one made by BACTERIA ‖ 특히 박테리아에 의해 만들어진 독성 물질. 독소

toy¹ /tɔɪ/ *n* an object for children to play with ‖ 아이들이 가지고 노는 물건. 장난감. 완구: *What kind of toys did you get for Christmas?* 크리스마스에 무슨 장난감 받았어?

toy² *v*

toy with sb/sth *phr v* [T] **1** [toy with sth] to think about an idea, plan etc. for a short time and not very seriously ‖ 구상·계획 등에 대해 잠시 동안 그리 심각하지 않게 생각하다. 얼핏[지나치듯이] 생각하다: *She had toyed with the idea of becoming an actress.* 그녀는 막연하게 여배우가 되는 생각을 해봤다. **2** [toy with sb/sth] INFORMAL to make someone think that you like or love him/her when you do not ‖ 누군가를 좋아하거나 사랑하지 않으면서 상대가 그렇게 생각하게 만들다. 우롱하다. 가지고 놀다

trace¹ /treɪs/ *v* [T] **1** to study or describe the history, development, or origin of something ‖ 사물의 역사나 발

전, 또는 기원을 연구하거나 설명하다. 역사를 더듬(어 올라가 조사하)다. 알아내다: *He traced his family history back to the 17th century.* 그는 가족 역사를 17세기까지 역으로 더듬어 올라가 조사했다. **2** to copy a drawing, map etc. by putting a piece of paper over it and drawing the lines that you can see through it ‖ 설계도·지도 등 위에 종이 조각을 놓고 비쳐 보이는 선들을 그려서 복사하다. 투사도를 그리다 **3** to find someone or something that has disappeared by searching carefully for him, her, or it ‖ 실종된 사람이나 물체를 주의 깊게 수색해서 찾다. …을 찾아내다: *Police are still trying to trace the missing child.* 경찰은 아직도 실종된 아이의 종적을 찾고 있다. **4** to find out where a telephone call is coming from using electronic equipment ‖ 전자 장비를 사용해서 전화가 걸려 오는 곳을 알아내다. 발신지를 추적하다 — **traceable** *adj*

trace^2 *n* **1** [C, U] a small sign that someone or something was present or existed ‖ 사람·사물이 현장에 있었거나 존재했던 미세한 표시. 흔적. 자취. 종적: *We found no trace of them on the island.* 우리는 그 섬에서 그들의 흔적을 전혀 찾지 못했다. / *He simply disappeared without a trace.* (=completely) 그는 종적도 없이 사라졌다. **2** a very small amount of a substance, quality, emotion etc. that is difficult to notice ‖ 물질·특성·감정 등의 알아보기 어려운 정도의 적은 양. 미량. 기미. 기색: *There was a trace of poison in the glass.* 유리잔에 독성분이 미량 들어 있었다. / *a trace of sorrow in his voice* 그의 목소리에 담긴 슬픔의 기미

trac·er /'treɪsə/ *n* a person whose job is the tracing of missing packages, persons, etc. ‖ 실종된 소포·사람 등을 추적하는 직업인. 수색[추적] 담당자

track^1 /træk/ *n*

1 ▶ROAD/PATH 길/통로◀ a narrow road or path with a rough uneven surface ‖ 표면이 울퉁불퉁하고 고르지 않은 좁은 길이나 통로. 비포장 길. 오솔길: *a dirt track through the woods* 숲을 지나는 흙길

2 keep/lose track of sth to pay attention to someone or something so that you know what is happening, or to fail to do this ‖ 무슨 일이 벌어지는지 알기 위해 사람이나 사물에 주의를 기울이다, 또는 이렇게 하는 데 실패하다. …을 놓치지 않다/…을 놓치다: *It's hard to keep track of everyone's birthdays.* 모든

사람들의 생일을 잊지 않고 챙기는 것은 힘들다.

3 be on the right/wrong track to be doing or thinking things that are likely to make you succeed or fail ‖ 성공하게 또는 실패하게 할 수 있는 일을 하거나 생각하다. 올바른/잘못된 길에 있다: *Keep going, you're on the right track* 계속해라, 너는 잘하고 있다.

4 be on/off track to be in a state or situation that will lead to success or failure ‖ 성공 또는 실패로 이어질 상태 또는 상황에 있다. 궤도에 오르다/궤도에서 벗어나다: *I feel that my career is back on track now.* 나는 내 직장생활이 지금 다시 궤도에 올랐다고 생각한다.

5 ▶SONG 노래◀ one of the songs or pieces of music on a record ‖ 음반에 들어 있는 노래들 중 한 곡이나 악곡. 녹음된 노래[곡]: *the best track on the album* 앨범 중의 최고의 곡

6 ▶RAILROAD 철도◀ the two metal lines along which a train travels ‖ 열차가 따라서 달리는 두 개의 금속 선. 철로 궤도: *railroad tracks* 철도 선로

7 ▶FOR RACING 경주용◀ a course with a special surface on which people, cars, horses etc. race ‖ 사람·자동차·말 등이 경주하는 특수한 지면의 코스. 경주로. 트랙

8 ▶SPORT 운동◀ [U] the sport of running on a track ‖ 트랙 위를 달리는 운동. 육상 경기. 트랙 경기: *He ran track in high school.* 그는 고등학교에서 육상 경기를 했다.

9 tracks a series of marks on the ground made by a moving animal, person, or vehicle ‖ 이동하는 동물·사람·차량에 의해 만들어진 땅 위의 연속된 자국. (발)자국. 항적: *We saw bear tracks in the mud.* 우리는 진흙 속에서 곰의 발자국을 보았다.

10 make tracks INFORMAL to hurry when going somewhere ‖ 어딘가로 서둘러서 가다: *Come on, we'd better make tracks.* 자, 우리 서두르는 게 좋겠다. — see also **off the beaten track/path** (BEATEN), ONE-TRACK MIND

track^2 *v* [T] **1** to search for a person or animal by following a smell or TRACKS on the ground ‖ 땅 위에 있는 냄새나 자국을 쫓아서 사람이나 동물을 수색하다. …의 (발)자취를 쫓다. 자취를 찾아 추적하다: *We tracked the moose for hours.* 우리는 무스(사슴)를 몇 시간 동안 추적했다. **2** to follow the movements of an aircraft, ship etc. using RADAR ‖ 레이더를 써서 항공기·배 등의 움직임을 쫓다.

관측[추적]하다 **3** to leave mud or dirt behind you when you walk ‖ 걸을 때 뒤에 진흙이나 흙을 남기다. (진)흙 자국을 내다: *Who tracked mud all over the floor?* 누가 온 바닥에 진흙 발자국을 냈느냐?

track sb/sth ↔ **down** *phr v* [T] to find someone or something by searching for a long time in different places ‖ 여러 장소에서 오랫동안 수색하여 사람이나 물체를 발견하다. …을 찾아내다. 철저히 수색하다: *We finally were able to track down her parents.* 우리는 마침내 그녀의 부모를 찾아낼 수 있었다.

track and field /, . . './ *n* [U] all the sports that involve running races, jumping, and throwing things ‖ 경주·높이뛰기·던지기를 포함하는 모든 운동. 육상 경기(종목)

track meet /'. ./ *n* a sports competition with a variety of running, jumping, and throwing events ‖ 달리기·높이뛰기·던지기의 다양한 스포츠 경연 대회. 육상 경기 대회

track rec·ord /'. ,../ *n* [singular] all the things that a person or organization has done in the past that show how good she, he, or it will be at doing similar things in the future ‖ 사람 또는 단체가 미래에 비슷한 것들을 얼마나 잘할 수 있을지 보여주는 과거에 했던 모든 것들. 업적. 전적: *Liz has a lousy track record in her relationships with men.* 리즈는 남자와의 관계에서 전력이 좋지 않다.

tract /trækt/ *n* **1 digestive/ respiratory/urinary etc. tract** a system of connected organs in your body that have one purpose ‖ 단일 목적을 가진 인체 내의 연결된 장기 체계. 소화/호흡/배뇨 기관 **2** a large area of land ‖ 대지의 큰 구역. 지역. 지방. 지대: *a tract of forest* 삼림 지역 **3** FORMAL a short piece of writing, especially on a religious or political subject ‖ 특히 종교나 정치적 주제에 대한 간단한 글. 소책자. 논문. 팸플릿

trac·tion /'trækʃən/ *n* [U] **1** the force that prevents a wheel from sliding on a road ‖ 바퀴가 도로에서 미끄러지는 것을 방지하는 힘. 정지 마찰력: *The car lost traction and ran off the road.* 차는 정지 마찰력을 잃고 도로에서 벗어났다. **2** a medical treatment in which an injured body part is gently pulled using weights ‖ 부상당한 신체 부위를 추를 써서 부드럽게 당기는 치료법. 견인[수축]요법

trac·tor /'træktɚ/ *n* a strong vehicle with large wheels, used for pulling farm equipment ‖ 농기구를 끄는 데에 쓰이는 큰 바퀴가 달린 튼튼한 차량. 트랙터

trade[1] /treɪd/ *n* **1** [U] the activity of buying, selling, or exchanging goods, especially between countries ‖ 특히 국가 간에 상품을 사고 팔거나 교환하는 활동. 무역. 통상: *the arms/drug/slave etc. trade* 무기[마약, 노예] 거래 **2** an exchange ‖ 교환: *Let's make a trade - my frisbee for your baseball.* 내 프리스비와 네 야구공을 맞바꾸자. **3** a particular job, especially one in which you work with your hands ‖ 특히 손으로 하는 특정한 일. 직업. 일: *Jerry's a plumber by trade.* 제리는 직업이 배관공이다. —see usage note at JOB

trade[2] *v* **1** [I, T] to buy, sell, or exchange goods, especially between countries ‖ 특히 국가간에 상품을 사거나 팔거나 교환하다. 교역[거래]하다: *Our company has a lot of experience trading in Asia.* 우리 회사는 아시아에서의 교역에 많은 경험이 있다. **2** to exchange one thing for another ‖ 한 가지를 다른 것으로 교환하다: *I'll trade my apple for your candy bar.* 내 사과를 네(막대) 사탕과 바꿔야겠다. **3 trade insults (with sb)** if two people trade insults, they insult each other ‖ 두 사람이 상호 모욕을 주고 받다. (누군가와) 서로 모욕하다

trade sth ↔ **in** *phr v* [T] to give something old that you own as part of the payment for something new ‖ 새것에 대한 변제의 일부로 소유하고 있는 낡은 것을 주다. 보상 구매하다: *I traded my Chevy in for a Honda.* 나는 쉐비 차로 혼다 차를 보상 구매했다.

trade on sth *phr v* to use a situation or someone's kindness in order to gain an advantage for yourself ‖ 자신의 이득을 얻기 위해 어떤 상황이나 다른 사람의 친절을 이용하다. …을 기화로 삼다. …을 팔아 이득을 챙기다: *She's trading on her father's fame to try to make it in the music business.* 그녀는 음악 사업에서 성공하려고 아버지의 명성을 팔았다.

trade up *phr v* [I, T] to sell something such as a car or house so you can buy a better car or house ‖ 더 좋은 차나 집을 살 수 있도록 가지고 있는 차나 집 등을 팔다

trade-in /'. ./ *n* a car, piece of equipment etc. that you give as part of the payment for the newer one that you are buying ‖ 사려고 하는 새것에 대한 변제의 일부로서 주는 차·장비류 등. 보상

구입의 차액으로 내놓는 물품

trade·mark /'treɪdmɑrk/ *n* a special name, mark, or word on a product that shows it is made by a particular company ‖ 특정 회사에서 제조한 것을 나타내는 제품상의 특수 명칭이나 표시, 또는 어구. 상표

trade-off /'. ./ *n* an acceptable balance between two opposing things ‖ 두 가지 상반된 것들 사이의 용인 가능한 균형. 타협, 상호 교환. (타협을 위한) 거래: *The boats are difficult to build, but the trade-off is that I get a good price for them.* 선박을 건조하기는 어렵지만 그 대가로 좋은 가격을 받는다.

trad·er /'treɪdɚ/ *someone* who buys and sells goods or STOCKs ‖ 상품이나 주식을 사고파는 사람. 상인. 거래상. 증권 매매업자

trade school /'. ./ *n* a VOCATIONAL school ‖ 직업 학교

trade se·cret /'. ,./ *n* a piece of secret information about a particular business, that is only known by the people who work there ‖ 오직 거기서 일하고 있는 사람들만이 아는 특정 기업에 대한 비밀 정보. 기업 비밀

tra·di·tion /trə'dɪʃən/ *n* [C, U] **1** a belief, custom, or way of doing something that has existed for a long time ‖ 오랫동안 존재해 온 신념이나 관습, 또는 일하는 방식. 전통. 인습. 관례: *a country steeped in* (=full of) *tradition* 인습에 빠져 있는 나라 / *an old family/Jewish tradition* 오래된 가문[유대인]의 전통 —see usage note at HABIT **2 (be) in the tradition of** to have many of the same features as something made or done in the past ‖ 과거에 만들어졌거나 행해진 것과 같은 특성이 많이 있다. …의 전통이 있다: *He was an entertainer in the great tradition of vaudeville.* 그는 보드 빌(희가극)의 위대한 전통을 따르는 연예인이었다.

tra·di·tion·al /trə'dɪʃənəl/ *adj* **1** relating to the TRADITIONs of a country, group of people etc. ‖ 나라·일단의 사람들의 전통에 관한. 전통의: *a traditional greeting* 전통적인 인사 / *traditional music* 전통 음악 **2** following ideas, methods etc. that have existed for a long time rather than doing something new or different ‖ 새롭고 상이한 것을 하기보다 오랫동안 존재해온 생각·방법 등을 따르는. 전통[인습]적인: *My father has very traditional ideas about marriage.* 내 아버지는 결혼에 대해 매우 구태의연한 생각을 가지고 있다. –**traditionally**

adv

tra·di·tion·al·ist /trə'dɪʃənl-ɪst/ *n* someone who likes traditional ideas but does not like new ones ‖ 전통적인 것은 좋아하지만 새것은 좋아하지 않는 사람. 전통주의자

traf·fic¹ /'træfɪk/ *n* [U] **1** the vehicles moving along a particular road ‖ 특정 도로를 따라 움직이는 차량들. 교통(량): *There was heavy traffic* (=a lot of traffic) *on the roads this morning.* 오늘 아침 도로에 교통량이 많았다. **2** the movement of aircraft, ships, trains etc. from one place to another ‖ 비행기·선박·열차 등의 한 곳에서 다른 곳으로의 이동. 왕래. 통행: *air/shipping traffic* 항공[선박] 교통

traf·fic² *v* **trafficked, trafficked, trafficking**

traffic in sth *phr v* [T] to buy and sell illegal goods ‖ 불법적 물건들을 사고팔다. 불법 거래하다: *He's accused of trafficking in cocaine.* 그는 코카인 불법 거래로 기소됐다. –**trafficker** *n*

traffic jam /'.. ,./ *n* a long line of vehicles on the road that cannot move, or that move very slowly ‖ 도로상에서 움직일 수 없거나 서행하는 차량들의 긴 줄. 교통 체증[정체, 지체]: *We were stuck in a traffic jam for two hours!* 우리는 두 시간 동안 교통 체증으로 꼼짝달싹 못했어!

traf·fick·ing /'træfɪkɪŋ/ *n* **drug/arms trafficking** the activity of buying and selling illegal drugs or weapons ‖ 불법적인 마약이나 무기들을 사고파는 행위. 마약/무기 밀매

traffic light /'.. ,./, **traffic sig·nal** /'.. ,./ *n* ⇨ LIGHT¹

trag·e·dy /'trædʒədi/ *n* [C, U] **1** an event that is extremely sad, especially one that involves death ‖ 특히 죽음을 포함하는 극도로 슬픈 사건. 비극적 사건: *They never recovered from the tragedy of their son's death.* 그들은 아들의 비극적인 죽음에서 결코 헤어나지 못했다. **2** a serious play that ends sadly, usually with the death of the main character, or this style of writing ‖ 보통 주인공의 죽음으로 슬프게 끝이 나는 진지한 연극, 또는 그런 스타일의 희곡. 비극: *Shakespeare's tragedies* 셰익스피어의 비극들

tra·gic /'trædʒɪk/ *adj* a tragic event or situation is very sad, often because it involves death ‖ 사건이나 상황이 종종 죽음을 포함하고 있어 매우 슬픈. 비극적인. 비통한: *a tragic car accident* 비극적인 교통사고 – **tragically** *adv*

trail¹ /treɪl/ *v* **1** [I, T] also **trail behind** to be losing a game, competition, election etc. ‖ 시합·경쟁·선거 등에 지고 있다. 뒤지다: *The Cowboys are trailing 21-14 in the third quarter.* 카우보이스 팀이 3쿼터에서 21대 14로 지고 있다. **2** [I, T] if you trail something or it trails behind you, it gets pulled behind you as you move along ‖ 물건이 사람이 움직이는 대로 뒤에서 끌리다 또는 끌다: *She walked outside, her skirt trailing on the ground.* 그녀는 치맛자락을 질질 끌면서 밖으로 걸어 나갔다. **3** [I] to follow a short distance behind someone ‖ 누군가를 짧은 거리를 두고 뒤에서 따라가다. 뒤를 쫓아가다: *The two mothers walked along with their kids trailing behind them.* 두 어머니들은 아이들을 뒤에 데리고 죽 걸어 갔다. **4** [T] to follow someone such as a criminal in order to try to catch him/her ‖ 범죄자 등을 잡으려고 따라가다. 뒤를 밟다. 미행하다. 추적하다

trail off *phr v* [I] if your voice or something you say trails off, it becomes quieter and quieter until it cannot be heard ‖ 목소리나 말하는 것이 들을 수 없을 정도까지 점점 더 작아지다. 서서히 사라지다[약해지다]: *Her words trailed off as Mrs. Hellman walked into the room.* 그녀의 말은 헬만 부인이 방으로 걸어들어 오자 점점 작아졌다.

trail² *n* **1** a path across open country or through the forest ‖ 확 트인 시골을 가로 지르거나 숲 속으로 통하는 길. 오솔길: *a hiking trail in the mountains* 산속의 하이킹 길 **2 trail of blood/clues/ destruction etc.** a series of marks or signs left behind by someone or something that is moving ‖ 사람이나 사물이 이동하며 뒤에 남긴 일련의 자국이나 흔적. 핏자국/단서/파괴의 흔적: *The wounded animal left a trail of blood behind it.* 부상당한 동물은 핏자국을 뒤에 남겼다. **3 be on the trail of** looking for a person or information that is difficult to find ‖ 찾기 어려운 사람이나 정보를 찾고 있다. 뒤를 밟고[추적하고] 있다: *a reporter on the trail of a big story* 큰 기삿감을 추적하고 있는 기자

trail·blaz·er /'treɪl,bleɪzɚ/ *n* INFORMAL someone who is the first to discover or develop new methods of doing something ‖ 어떤 일을 하는 새로운 방법을 발견하거나 개발한 최초의 사람. 개척자. 선구자: *a trailblazer in the field of medical research* 의학 연구 분야의 선구자

trail·er /'treɪlɚ/ *n* **1** a vehicle that can be pulled behind a car, used for living in during a vacation ‖ 차 뒤에 끌고 다닐 수 있고 휴가 동안 거주용으로 쓰이는 차량. 이동 주택 **2** a frame that is pulled behind a vehicle, on which you carry something large such as a boat ‖ 보트 등 대형 물건을 실어 운반하며 차 뒤로 견인되는 구조물. 트레일러 —see picture on page 943 **3** a short advertisement for a movie or television program ‖ 영화나 텔레비전 프로그램에 대한 짧은 광고. 예고편

trailer park /'.. ,./ *n* an area where TRAILERS are parked and used as people's homes ‖ 이동 주택이 주차되어 사람들의 집으로 사용되는 지역. 트레일러 전용 주차장

train¹ /treɪn/ *n* **1** a set of connected railroad cars pulled by an ENGINE ‖ 엔진으로 움직이는 일련의 연결된 철도 차량. 열차 **2 train of thought** a related series of thoughts in an argument or discussion ‖ 논쟁이나 토론에서 그에 관련된 일련의 생각들. 사고의 맥락[연속]: *Sorry, I've lost my train of thought.* 미안, 내가 말하려 한 것을 잊어 버렸어. **3** a long line of moving people or animals ‖ 이동하는 사람이나 동물의 긴 줄. 대열. 행렬: *a camel train* 낙타 대열 **4** a part of a dress that spreads out over the ground behind the person wearing it ‖ 입고 있는 사람의 뒤로 땅에 펼쳐지는 드레스 부분. 뒤에 끌리는 옷자락

train² *v* **1** [I, T] to teach someone or be taught the skills of a particular job or activity ‖ 특정 직업 또는 활동의 기술을 가르치거나 배우다. 훈련시키다. 훈련 받다: *Sally spent two years training as a nurse.* 샐리는 2년을 간호사로 수련하면서 지냈다. **2** [T] to teach an animal to do something or to behave correctly ‖ 동물에게 어떤 일을 하거나 제대로 행동하도록 가르치다. 길들이다. 훈련시키다: *I've trained the dog to sit.* 나는 개에게 앉는 훈련을 시켰다. **3** [I, T] to prepare for a sports event by exercising and practicing, or to make someone do this ‖ 운동하거나 연습하면서 스포츠 대회에 대비하다, 또는 어떤 사람을 이렇게 하게 하다. 연습하다. 단련[훈련]하다: *He is training for the Olympics.* 그는 올림픽을 위해 훈련하고 있다. **–trained** *adj* **–trainer** *n*

train·ee /treɪ'ni/ *n* someone who is being trained for a job ‖ 직업을 위해 훈련받고 있는 사람. 직업 훈련자. 견습생: *a trainee pilot/salesperson* 견습 비행사

[판매 사원]

train·ing /'treɪnɪŋ/ n [U] **1** the process of teaching or being taught skills for a particular job ‖ 특정 직업을 위한 기술을 가르치거나 교육받고 있는 과정. 훈련. 훈육: *Did you have any training on the computer?* 컴퓨터 교육은 받았습니까? **2** special physical exercises that you do to stay healthy or prepare for a sporting event ‖ 건강을 유지하거나 스포츠 대회를 준비하기 위해 하는 특별한 신체 운동. 단련. 훈련: *He injured his knee in training.* 그는 훈련하는 도중에 무릎을 다쳤다.

trait /treɪt/ n a particular quality in someone's character; CHARACTERISTIC ‖ 사람의 성격상의 특정한 속성. 특징. 특색. 특질; ㈜ characteristic: *His jealousy is one of his worst traits.* 그의 질투심은 그의 나쁜 특성 중 하나이다.

trai·tor /'treɪtɚ/ n someone who betrays his/her country, friends etc. ‖ 자신의 나라·친구 등을 배신하는 사람. 배신자. 역적

tra·jec·to·ry /trə'dʒɛktəri/ n TECHNICAL the curved path of an object that is fired or thrown through the air ‖ 공중으로 발사되거나 던져진 물체의 곡선 진로. 탄도. 궤적

tram /træm/ n ⇨ STREETCAR

tramp¹ /træmp/ n **1** ⇨ TRANSIENT² **2** OLD-FASHIONED a woman who has too many sexual partners ‖ 성교 상대가 너무 많은 여자. 방종한 여자. 매춘부

tramp² v [I, T] to walk somewhere with heavy steps ‖ 무거운 발걸음으로 어딘가를 걸어가다. 쿵쿵거리며 걷다. 터벅터벅 걷다: *kids tramping through the snow* 눈 속을 터벅터벅 걷고 있는 아이들

tram·ple /'træmpəl/ v [I, T] **1** to step on something heavily so that you crush it with your feet ‖ 어떤 것을 무겁게 밟아서 발로 찌부러뜨리다. 짓밟다. 밟아 뭉개다: *One woman was trampled to death by the crowd.* 여자 한 명이 군중들에게 밟혀 죽었다. **2** to ignore or not care about someone's rights, ideas, hopes etc. ‖ 다른 사람의 권리·생각·희망 등을 무시하거나 개의치 않다. 짓밟다. 유린하다: *a rule that tramples on people's right to free speech* 사람들의 언론의 자유를 유린하는 규정

tram·po·line /ˌtræmpə'lin, 'træmpə,lin/ n a piece of sports equipment that you jump up and down on, made of a sheet of material tightly stretched across a large frame ‖ 한 장의 천을 큰 틀에 가로질러 팽팽히 쳐서 만들어 그 위에서 뛰어 오르내리는 스포츠 장비. 트램펄링

trance /træns/ n a state in which you seem to be asleep but you are still able to hear and understand what is said to you ‖ 잠자는 것처럼 보이지만 말하는 것을 여전히 들을 수 있고 이해할 수 있는 상태. 비몽사몽. 꿈결

tran·quil /'træŋkwəl/ adj pleasantly calm, quiet, and peaceful ‖ 기분 좋게 고요하고 조용하며 평화로운. 평온한: *a tranquil spot for a picnic* 피크닉을 위한 조용한 장소 – **tranquility** /træŋ'kwɪləti/ n [U]

tran·qui·liz·er /'træŋkwə,laɪzɚ/ n a drug used in order to make a person or animal calm or unconscious ‖ 사람이나 동물을 진정시키거나 의식을 잃게 하는 데에 쓰이는 약. 진정제. 정신 안정제 – **tranquilize** v [T]

trans·act /træn'zækt/ v [I, T] FORMAL to do business ‖ 사업을 하다. 업무를 행하다. 거래하다

trans·ac·tion /træn'zækʃən/ n FORMAL a business deal ‖ 상거래. 매매: *The company keeps a report of all stock transactions.* 그 회사는 모든 주식 거래의 기록을 보관한다.

trans·at·lan·tic /ˌtrænzət'læntɪk/ adj crossing the Atlantic Ocean, or involving people on both sides of the Atlantic ‖ 대서양을 횡단하는, 또는 대서양 양안에 사는 사람을 포함하는: *a transatlantic flight* 대서양 횡단 비행 / *a transatlantic business deal* 대서양을 오가는 상거래

tran·scend /træn'sɛnd/ v [T] FORMAL to go above or beyond the limits of something ‖ 사물의 한계를 넘다. 초월하다: *The appeal of baseball transcends age and gender.* 야구의 매력은 시대와 성을 초월한다. – **transcendence** n [U]

tran·scen·den·tal /ˌtrænsɛn'dɛntl/ adj existing above or beyond human knowledge or understanding ‖ 인간의 지식이나 이해를 초월하여 존재하는. 초자연적인. 선험적인

trans·con·ti·nen·tal /ˌtrænskɑntən'ɛntl, ˌtrænz-/ adj crossing a CONTINENT ‖ 대륙 횡단의: *the first transcontinental railroad* 최초의 대륙 횡단 철도

tran·scribe /træn'skraɪb/ v [T] to change information from one form to another ‖ 정보를 한 형태에서 다른 형태로 바꾸다. 복각[전사]하다: *recordings being transcribed onto disk* 디스크로 복각 된 녹음본 – **transcription**

/træn'skrɪpʃən/ *n* [C, U]

tran·script /'træn,skrɪpt/ *n* **1** an exact written or printed copy of something that was said ‖ 말해진 것이 정확하게 필사되거나 인쇄된 사본. 필기본. 대본 원고: *a transcript of the witness's testimony* 목격자의 증언을 받아쓴 진술서 **2** an official document that has a list of the classes you took as a student and the grades you received ‖ 학생으로서 수강 신청한 과목의 목록과 받은 성적이 적힌 공식 문서. 성적 증명서

trans·fer[1] /'trænsfɚ, træns'fɚ/ *v* **-rred, -rring 1** [I, T] to move from one place, job, etc. to another, or to make someone or something do this ‖ 어떤 장소나 직업 등에서 다른 곳으로 옮기다, 또는 다른 사람이나 사물을 이렇게 되게 하다. 전거(轉居)[전학, 전근, 전임, 전과]하다[시키다]: *After his first year he transferred to UCLA.* 그는 첫 해를 보낸 후 UCLA로 전학을 했다. / *They're transferring him from accounts to the shipping department.* 그들은 그를 회계과에서 발송과로 전임시킬 예정이다. **2** [T] LAW to officially give property or money to someone else ‖ 남에게 공식적으로 재산이나 돈을 주다. 양도하다 – **transferable** /træns'fɚəbəl/ *adj*

trans·fer[2] /'trænsfɚ/ *n* [C, U] the process of TRANSFER*ring* someone or something ‖ 사람이나 사물을 옮기는 과정. 전학. 전근. 양도. 이전: *the transfer of funds between banks* 은행간의 자금 이전 / *a job transfer* 이직(移職)

trans·fixed /træns'fɪkst/ *adj* be transfixed to be unable to move because you are shocked, frightened etc. ‖ 충격을 받거나 겁에 질리거나 하여 움직일 수 없다. 꼼짝[옴쭉]못하다: *We were transfixed by the pictures of the storm on TV.* 우리는 텔레비전에서 폭풍의 모습을 보고 아연실색했다.

trans·form /træns'fɔrm/ *v* [T] to change the appearance, character etc. of someone or something completely ‖ 어떤 사람이나 사물의 모습·성격 등을 완전히 바꾸다. 변형시키다: *the Soviet Union's attempts to transform the country into a democracy* 국가를 민주주의로 전환시키려는 구소련의 시도

trans·for·ma·tion /,trænsfɚ'meɪʃən/ *n* [U] a complete change in the appearance, character etc. of someone or something ‖ 어떤 사람이나 사물의 모습·성격 등을 완전히 바꿈. 변화. 변형. 전환: *the transformation of the old house into a restaurant* 식당으로 바뀐

낡은 집

trans·form·er /træns'fɔrmɚ/ *n* a piece of electrical equipment that changes the electricity from one VOLTAGE to another ‖ 전압을 바꾸는 전기 기구. 변압기

trans·fu·sion /træns'fyuʒən/ *n* [C, U] FORMAL the process of putting new blood into someone's body ‖ 어떤 사람의 몸에 새로운 피를 넣는 과정. 수혈

trans·gen·der /,trænz'dʒɛndɚ/, **transgendered** *adj* a transgender person wants to be or look like a member of the opposite sex, especially by having a medical operation ‖ 특히 의학 수술을 받아 반대 성(性)의 사람이 되거나 그와 닮아 보이기를 원하는. 성전환(자)의 – **transgender** *n*

trans·gress /trænz'grɛs/ *v* [I, T] FORMAL to do something that is against the rules of a religion or society ‖ 종교나 사회의 규칙을 어기는 일을 하다. 어기다. 위반하다 – **transgression** /trænz'grɛʃən/ *n* [C, U]

tran·sient[1] /'trænʒənt/ *adj* FORMAL **1** continuing or existing for only a short time ‖ 단지 짧은 시간 동안만 계속되거나 존재하는. 일시적인. 순간적인 **2** passing quickly through a place, or staying there only a short time ‖ 어떤 장소를 빨리 지나가거나 단지 짧은 시간만 그곳에 머무는. 단기 체류의: *transient workers* 단기 체류 근로자

transient[2] *n* someone who has no home or job and moves from place to place, often asking people for money ‖ 집이나 직업이 없고 종종 사람에게 돈을 요구하며 여기저기로 이동하는 사람. 방랑자. 떠돌이

tran·sis·tor /træn'zɪstɚ/ *n* a piece of electronic equipment that controls the flow of electricity in radios, televisions etc. ‖ 라디오나 텔레비전 등에서 전기의 흐름을 제어하는 전자 장비. 트랜지스터

tran·sit /'trænzɪt/ *n* [U] the process of moving people, products etc. from one place to another ‖ 한 장소에서 다른 장소로 사람·제품 등을 이동시키는 일. 운송. 운반. 수송: *The shipment must have been lost in transit.* 그 발송 화물은 운송 중에 분실되었음이 틀림없다.

tran·si·tion /træn'zɪʃən/ *n* [C, U] FORMAL the process of changing from one form or condition to another ‖ 한 형태나 상태에서 다른 것으로 바뀌는 일. 변천. 변화. 이행: *The transition from a dictatorship to a democracy is difficult.* 독재 국가에서 민주 국가로의 이행은 어렵다.

tran·si·tion·al /træn'zɪʃənl/ *adj*
relating to a period of change from one
form or condition to another ‖ 하나의 형
태나 조건에서 다른 것으로의 전환기에 관
한. 과도기의: *transitional government/
housing* 과도 정부[임시 거처] / *a
transitional period between the two
projects* 두 사업 사이의 과도기

tran·si·tive verb /ˌtrænzətɪv 'vɜːb/ *n*
TECHNICAL in grammar, a transitive verb
has an object. In the sentence "She
makes her own clothes," "makes" is a
transitive verb ‖ 문법에서 목적어를 갖는
동사. 타동사. "She makes her own
clothes." 문장에서 "makes"는 타동사이
다 —compare INTRANSITIVE VERB —see
study note on page 942

tran·si·to·ry /'trænzəˌtɔri/ *adj* ⇨
TRANSIENT¹

trans·late /'trænzleɪt, ˌtrænz'leɪt/ *v* 1
[I, T] to change speech or writing from
one language to another ‖ 말이나 글을
한 언어에서 다른 언어로 바꾸다. 번역하
다: *I have to translate from German
into English* 나는 독일어를 영어로 번역
해야 한다. —compare INTERPRET 2
translate into sth if one thing
translates into another, the second
thing happens as a result of the first ‖ 두
번째 것이 첫 번째 것의 결과로서 일어나
다. 전환하다: *Will more investment
translate into more jobs?* 더 많이 투자하
면 더 많은 일자리가 창출될 것인가? -
translation /trænz'leɪʃən/ *n* [C, U]

trans·la·tor /'trænzˌleɪtər/ *n* someone
who changes writing or speech into a
different language ‖ 글이나 말을 다른 언
어로 바꾸는 사람. 번역가. 역자 —
compare INTERPRETER

trans·lu·cent /trænz'lusənt/ *adj* not
transparent, but clear enough for some
light to pass through ‖ 투명하지는 않으나
어느 정도의 빛이 통과할 만큼 맑은. 반투
명인 - **translucence** *n* [U]

trans·mis·sion /trænz'mɪʃən/ *n* 1 [C,
U] the process of sending out radio or
television signals, or the program itself
‖ 라디오나 텔레비전 전파를 내보내는 일,
또는 그 프로그램 자체. 송신. 방송 (프로
그램) 2 the part of a vehicle that uses
the power from the engine to turn the
wheels ‖ 바퀴를 돌리기 위해 엔진에서 나
오는 힘을 이용하는 차량의 부품. 변속기.
변속 장치 3 [U] FORMAL the process of
sending or passing something from one
place, person etc. to another ‖ 한 장소나
사람 등으로부터 다른 장소나 사람에게 어
떤 것을 보내거나 전하는 과정. 전달. 전

송(傳送): *the transmission of disease* 병
의 전염

trans·mit /trænz'mɪt/ *v* **-tted, -tting** 1
to send out electric signals for radio or
television; broadcast ‖ 라디오나 텔레비
전용의 전기 신호를 보내다. 송신하다; 방
송하다 2 [T] to send or pass something
from one place, person etc. to another
‖ 한 장소나 사람 등으로부터 다른 장소나
사람에게 어떤 것을 보내거나 전하다. 전
달[전송, 전염]하다: *The virus is
transmitted through the blood.* 그 바이
러스는 혈액을 통해 전염된다.

trans·mit·ter /trænz'mɪtər,
'trænzˌmɪtər/ *n* equipment that sends out
radio or television signals ‖ 라디오나 텔
레비전 전파를 보내는 장치. 송신기

trans·par·ent /træns'pærənt, -'pɛr-/
adj 1 clear and able to be seen through
‖ 선명해서 꿰뚫어볼 수 있는. 투명한. 비
치는: *transparent glass* 투명한 유리 2
easy to notice and not deceiving anyone;
OBVIOUS ‖ 알아차리기 쉬워서 아무도 속일
수 없는. 뻔한. ㊌ obvious: *a transparent
attempt to fool the voters* 유권자를 우롱
하는 뻔한 수작 - **transparency** *n* [U]
- **transparently** *adv*

tran·spire /træn'spaɪr/ *v* [T] FORMAL to
happen ‖ 일어나다. 생기다: *Nobody
knows what transpired that day.* 그 날
무슨 일이 일어났는지 아무도 모른다.

trans·plant¹ /træns'plænt/ *v* [T] 1 to
move a plant from one place and put it
in another ‖ 식물을 한 장소에서 옮겨 다
른 장소에 심다. 옮겨 심다 2 to move an
organ such as a heart from one person's
body to another ‖ 심장 등의 장기를 한 사
람의 몸에서 다른 사람의 몸으로 옮기다.
이식하다

trans·plant² /'trænsplænt/ *n* [C, U] the
medical operation of TRANSPLANT*ing* an
organ, or the organ itself ‖ 장기를 이식
하는 의학 수술, 또는 그 장기 자체. 이식
(장기): *a heart transplant* 심장 이식 (수
술) —compare IMPLANT²

trans·port /træns'pɔrt/ *v* [T] to move
or carry goods, people etc. from one
place to another in a vehicle ‖ 차량으로
한 장소에서 다른 장소로 물자나 사람 등
을 옮기거나 운반하다. 수송[운송]하다.
나르다: *using helicopters to transport
equipment* 장비 수송을 위한 헬리콥터의
사용

trans·por·ta·tion /ˌtrænspər'teɪʃən/ *n*
[U] the process or business of moving
goods, people etc. from one place to
another ‖ 물자·사람 등을 한 장소에서 다
른 장소로 옮기는 일이나 사업. 수송[운

송](업): *Buses are the main form of public transportation.* 버스는 대중교통의 주형태이다. / *Sunny Tours provides free transportation from/to the airport.* 서니 투어스는 공항까지는 왕복으로 무료 교통편을 제공한다.

USAGE NOTE transportation

Use **by** with types of transportation to say how you traveled somewhere: *We came by car/by bus/by bicycle/by boat/by plane.* For walking, use **on foot:** *Pioneers crossed the Rockies on foot.* Use the verb **get** with a preposition to say how you enter or leave a vehicle. You **get on** or **get off** a subway, train, bicycle, motorcycle, plane, or boat. You **get in** or **get into** and **get out of** a car or taxi. Use **take** to talk about traveling by public transportation: *I usually take the bus/train/subway to work.* Use **go** to talk about traveling in a private car or on a bicycle: *I go to work by car.*
사람이 다른 곳으로 어떻게 이동했는지 말하기 위해서는 교통의 종류와 함께 **by**를 쓴다: 우리는 차로/버스로/자전거로/배로/비행기로 왔다. 걷기에는 **on foot**을 쓴다: 개척자들은 도보로 로키 산맥을 넘었다. 사람이 어떻게 탈것을 타거나 내리는가를 말하기 위해서는 전치사와 함께 동사 **get**을 쓴다. 지하철[기차, 자전거, 오토바이, 비행기, 배]를 타고 내리는 것은 "**get on**" "**get off**"를 쓴다. 차나 택시를 타고 내리는 것은 "**get in**"이나 "**get into**"와 "**get out of**"를 쓴다. 대중교통 수단으로 이동하는 것에 대해 말하기 위해서는 **take**를 쓴다: 나는 보통 버스/기차/지하철을 타고 출근한다. 개인의 차나 자전거로 이동하는 것에 대해 말하는 데는 **go**를 쓴다: 나는 자가용으로 출근한다.

---

trans·pose /træns'pouz/ *v* [T] FORMAL to change the order or position of two or more words, letters etc. ‖ 둘 이상의 단어·글자 등의 순서나 위치를 바꾸다. 뒤바꾸다

trans·sex·u·al /trænz'sɛkʃuəl/ *n* someone who has had a medical operation to become a person of the opposite sex ‖ 반대 성(性)의 사람이 되기 위해 수술을 받은 사람. 성전환자

trans·ves·tite /trænz'vɛstaɪt/ *n* someone who enjoys dressing like a person of the opposite sex ‖ 반대 성(性)의 사람같이 옷을 입는 것을 즐기는 사람.

복장 도착자. 이성의 복장 착용자

trap¹ /træp/ *n* **1** a piece of equipment for catching animals ‖ 동물을 잡는 데 사용하는 장치. 올가미. 덫: *a mouse trap* 쥐덫 **2** an unpleasant situation from which it is difficult to escape ‖ 모면하기 어려운 불쾌한 상황. 질곡. 수렁: *the deadly trap of drug and alcohol addiction* 마약과 알코올 중독의 헤어날 수 없는 수렁 **3** a trick that is intended to catch someone or make him/her say or do something that s/he did not intend to ‖ 다른 사람을 붙잡거나 다른 사람이 의도하지 않은 말이나 행동을 하게 하는 계략. 함정. 속임수. 덫

trap² *v* **-pped, -pping** [T] **1** to force someone into a place from which s/he cannot escape ‖ 남을 도망칠 수 없는 곳에 강제로 집어넣다. 가두다: *Up to 25 people may be trapped in the burning building.* 최대 25명까지 불타는 건물에 갇혀 있는지도 모른다. **2** to prevent something such as water, dirt, heat etc. from escaping or spreading ‖ 물·먼지·열 등이 새거나 퍼져나가는 것을 막다. 가리다. 방지하다: *a filter that traps dust* 먼지를 막는 필터 **3** to trick someone so that s/he says or does something that s/he did not intend to ‖ 다른 사람으로 하여금 그가 의도하지 않은 말이나 행동을 하도록 속이다. 속여서 …시키다: *He says that the police trapped him into confessing.* 그는 경찰이 자기를 속여서 자백하게 했다고 말한다. **4 be trapped** to be in an unpleasant situation from which it is difficult to escape ‖ 빠져 나가기 어려운 불쾌한 상황에 처하다. …의 수렁에 빠지다. 꼼짝 못하게 되다: *She was trapped in a bad marriage.* 그녀는 불행한 결혼생활에서 헤어나지 못했다. **5** to catch an animal in a trap ‖ 덫으로 동물을 잡다

trap door /ˌ. './ *n* a small door that covers an opening in a floor or roof ‖ 마루나 지붕의 개구부(開口部)를 덮는 작은 문. 치켜 올리는 뚜껑 문

tra·peze /træ'piz/ *n* a short BAR hanging from two ropes high above the ground, used by ACROBATs ‖ 곡예사가 사용하는, 지상의 높은 곳에서 두 개의 밧줄로 드리워진 짧은 막대. 곡예용 그네

trap·per /'træpɚ/ *n* someone who traps wild animals for their fur ‖ 모피를 얻기 위해 야생 동물을 덫으로 잡는 사람. 덫사냥꾼

trap·pings /'træpɪŋz/ *n* [plural] clothes, possessions etc. that show someone's success, or his/her position in a particular job ‖ 사람의 성공이나 특정 직업에서의 지위를 나타내주는 옷·소지품 등. 장식(의상). 예복: *He has all the trappings of stardom.* 그는 스타로서의 상징물들을 모두 가지고 있다.

trash¹ /træʃ/ *n* [U] **1** waste material such as old food, dirty paper etc., or the container this is put in; GARBAGE ‖ 오래된 음식·더러운 종이 등의 폐기물, 또는 이것을 넣는 용기. 쓰레기(통); ㊤ garbage: *Just put it in the trash.* 그것은 그냥 쓰레기통에 넣어라. **2** INFORMAL something that is of very poor quality ‖ 저질인 것. 형편없는 것: *There's so much trash on TV these days.* 요즈음 텔레비전에는 저질인 것이 매우 많다.

trash² *v* [T] INFORMAL **1** to destroy something completely ‖ 어떤 것을 완전히 파괴하다. 엉망진창으로 만들다: *You can't have parties if your friends are going to trash the place.* 네 친구들이 집을 엉망진창으로 만들 거라면 너는 파티를 열지 못한다. **2** to criticize someone or something severely ‖ 사람이나 사물을 심하게 비평하다. 쓰레기 취급하다. 혹평하다: *Critics have trashed the movie.* 비평가들은 그 영화를 혹평했다.

trash can /'. ./ *n* ⇨ GARBAGE CAN

trash com·pact·or /'. .,../ *n* a machine used in the home for pressing TRASH into a small block so that it takes less space ‖ 공간을 덜 차지하도록 집에서 쓰레기를 작은 덩어리로 압축시키는 데 사용하는 기계. 쓰레기 압축기

trash·y /'træʃi/ *adj* of extremely bad quality, and often about sex ‖ 매우 저질이며 흔히 성에 관한. 쓰레기 같은. 시시한: *trashy novels* 쓰레기 같은 소설

trau·ma /'trɔmə, 'traumə/ *n* [U] a state of extreme shock that is caused by a very frightening or unpleasant experience, or the experience itself ‖ 매우 무섭거나 불쾌한 경험에서 생기는 극단적인 충격 상태, 또는 그 경험 자체. 충격. 외상. 쇼크: *Children have trouble coping with the trauma of divorce.* 아이들은 이혼의 정신적 충격을 극복하기가 어렵다. */ soldiers suffering from trauma* 정신적 충격에 시달리는 병사들

trau·mat·ic /trə'mætɪk, trɔ-/ *adj* shocking and upsetting ‖ 충격적이고 마음을 혼란시키는. 정신적 충격의: *a traumatic experience* 충격적인 체험

trau·ma·tize /'trɔmə,taɪz, 'trau-/ *v* [T] to shock someone so badly that s/he is unable to do things normally ‖ 남에게 심하게 충격을 주어서 정상적으로 생활을 할 수 없게 하다. 정신적 충격[쇼크]을 주다

trav·el¹ /'trævəl/ *v* **1** [I] to make a trip from one place to another, especially to distant places ‖ 한 장소에서 다른 장소로 특히 먼 곳으로 여행하다. 돌아다니다: *Rick's traveling across/through the US with a backpack.* 릭은 배낭을 메고 미국을 가로질러[관통하여] 여행하고 있다. / *We always travel light.* (=without taking many bags) 우리는 항상 짐 없이 가벼운 차림으로 여행한다. **2** [I] to move from one place or person to another ‖ 한 장소나 사람에게서 다른 장소나 사람에게로 이동하다. 전해지다: *News travels fast in a small town like this.* 이 같은 작은 읍에서는 소식이 빨리 퍼진다. **3** [I, T] to go a particular distance or at a particular speed ‖ 특정한 거리나 특정한 속도로 가다. 나아가다. 진행해 가다: *We traveled over 400 miles the first day of our trip.* 우리는 여행 첫 날에 400마일 이상 나아갔다. / *The bus was traveling at a high speed.* 버스는 고속으로 가고 있었다.

travel² *n* [U] the act or activity of traveling ‖ 여행(하기): *Heavy rain is making road travel difficult.* 비가 많이 와서 도로 통행이 어려워지고 있다.

USAGE NOTE travel

Although the verb "to travel" generally means "to go from one place to another," the nouns **travel** and **travels** are usually used about traveling for long distances and long periods of time: *Wade came home after years of foreign travel.* / *She wrote a book about her travels in South America.* A **trip** is the time spent and the distance traveled in going from one place to another: *The trip to work takes me about 25 minutes.* Use **journey** instead of **trip** for a trip that is a long distance or is very difficult: *It was an uncomfortable journey on a crowded train.* Use **voyage** to talk about traveling by sea or in a SPACECRAFT.

일반적으로 "여행하다"는 동사는 "한 장소에서 다른 장소를 가다"를 의미하지만 명사 **travel**과 **travels**는 보통 장거리와 장기간 여행에 대해 쓰인다: 웨이드는 수년간의 외국 여행을 마치고 집에 돌아왔다. / 그녀는 남아메리카 여행에 대한 책을 썼다. **trip**은 한 장소에서 다른 장소로 가는 데 소비된 시간과 여행한 거리이다: 직장까지 통근은 약 25분 걸린다. 먼 거리나 아주 어려운 여행에

는 **trip** 대신에 **journey**를 쓴다: 그것은 만원 열차를 타는 불편한 여행이었다. 배나 우주선을 타고 하는 여행을 말하는 데는 **voyage**를 쓴다.

travel a·gen·cy /'.. ,..../ *n* a business that arranges travel and vacations ‖ 여행과 휴가를 주선하는 사업. 여행사[업]

travel a·gent /'.. ,../ *n* someone who works in a TRAVEL AGENCY ‖ 여행사에서 일하는 사람. 여행사 직원. 여행 안내업자

trav·el·er /'trævələ/ *n* someone who is on a trip or who travels often ‖ 여행 중이거나 자주 여행하는 사람. 여행자. 여객

traveler's check /'... ,./ *n* a special check that can be exchanged for the money of a foreign country ‖ 외국돈으로 교환되는 특별한 수표. 여행자 수표

trav·els /'trævəlz/ *n* [plural] trips, especially to places that are far away ‖ 특히 멀리 떨어져 있는 장소로의 여행. (장기간의) 외국 여행: *Kim has lots of photos of her travels.* 킴은 자신의 여행에서 찍은 사진을 많이 가지고 있다. —see usage note at TRAVEL²

tra·verse /trə'vɚs/ *v* [T] FORMAL to move across, over, or through something ‖ 사물을 가로질러[넘어서, 통과하여] 움직이다. 횡단하다. 건너다

trav·es·ty /'trævɪsti/ *n* a very bad example of something, that gives a completely false idea of it ‖ 어떤 것에 대한 완전히 잘못된 개념을 주는 매우 나쁜 예. 우습게 한 것. 희화화한 것: *The trial was described as a travesty of justice.* 그 재판은 정의를 희화화한 것으로 묘사되었다.

trawl /trɔl/ *n* a wide net that is pulled along the bottom of the ocean to catch fish ‖ 물고기를 잡기 위해 바다의 밑바닥에서 끌려지는 넓은 그물. 저인망. 트롤망 – **trawl** *v* [I, T]

trawl·er /'trɔlɚ/ *n* a fishing boat that uses a TRAWL ‖ 저인망을 사용하는 어선. 트롤선. 저인망 어선

tray /treɪ/ *n* a flat piece of plastic, metal, or wood with raised edges, that is used for carrying things such as plates, food etc. ‖ 접시·음식 등을 운반하는 데 사용되는 가장자리를 높인 플라스틱[금속, 나무]으로 된 납작한 것. 쟁반

treach·er·ous /'trɛtʃərəs/ *adj* **1** someone who is treacherous cannot be trusted because s/he secretly intends to harm you ‖ 남이 은밀하게 자신을 해칠 의도를 가져서 믿을 수 없는. 배반[배신]하는. 딴마음을 먹은 **2** extremely dangerous because you cannot see the

dangers ‖ 위험을 알 수 없기 때문에 매우 위험한. 기만적인 (위험의): *Black ice on the roads is making driving treacherous.* 도로상의 살얼음은 운전을 매우 위험하게 하고 있다.

treach·er·y /'trɛtʃəri/ *n* [U] actions that are not loyal to someone who trusts you ‖ 자신을 신뢰하는 사람에게 충성하지 않는 행동. 배반[배신](행위)

tread¹ /trɛd/ *v* **trod, trodden, treading 1 tread carefully/lightly etc.** to be very careful about what you say or do in a difficult situation ‖ 어려운 상황에서 말하거나 행동하는 것에 대해 매우 조심하다. 신중하게 말하다[행동하다]: *It's best to tread lightly when the boss is in a bad mood.* 상사가 기분이 안 좋을 때는 매우 조심하는 것이 상책이다. **2 tread water** to stay floating upright in deep water by moving your legs as if you were riding a bicycle ‖ 마치 자전거를 타듯이 다리를 움직여서 깊은 물속에 똑바로 떠 있다. 서서 헤엄치다 **3** OLD-FASHIONED to walk or step on something ‖ 사물 위를 걷거나 밟다. 걸어지나가다

tread² *n* **1** [C, U] the pattern of thick deep lines on the part of a tire that touches the road ‖ 도로에 닿는 타이어 부분의 굵고 깊은 선의 문양. 접지면(의 홈) **2** the part of a stair or step that you put your foot on ‖ 발을 올려놓는 계단이나 발판의 부분. 디딤판 **3** [singular] the sound that someone makes when s/he walks ‖ 사람이 걸을 때 내는 소리. 발소리: *a heavy tread* 무거운 발소리

tread·mill /'trɛdmɪl/ *n* [singular] **1** work or a way of life that seems very boring because you always have to do the same things ‖ 항상 똑같은 일을 해야 하기 때문에 매우 지루하게 보이는 일이나 생활 방식. 단조로운[쳇바퀴 같은] 일 [삶]: *It's time for me to step off the treadmill and get a new job.* 이제 쳇바퀴 같은 일에서 벗어나 새 직업을 구할 때다. **2** a piece of exercise equipment that has a large belt around a set of wheels, that moves when you walk on it ‖ 한 세트의 바퀴 둘레에 넓은 벨트가 있어 그 위에서 걸을 때 움직이는 운동 기구. 러닝 머신

trea·son /'trizən/ *n* [U] the crime of being disloyal to your country or government, especially by helping its enemies ‖ 특히 적을 도움으로써 자신의 국가나 정부를 배반하는 범죄. 반역(죄)

treas·ure¹ /'trɛʒɚ/ *n* **1** [U] gold, silver, jewels etc. ‖ 금·은·보석 등. 보물. 보배: *a story about buried treasure* 묻혀진 보물에 대한 이야기 **2** a very valuable and important object such as a painting or ancient document ‖ 그림이나 고문서 등의 매우 가치 있고 중요한 물건. 귀중품: *the treasures of the Art Institute of Chicago* 시카고 미술관의 귀중품

treasure² *v* [T] to treat something or someone as very special, important, or valuable ‖ 사물이나 사람을 매우 특별하게[중요하게, 가치 있게] 다루다. 소중히 하다. 귀중하게 여기다: *I'll always treasure the memories of this day.* 나는 이 날의 기억을 항상 소중히 할 것이다.

treas·ur·er /'trɛʒərər/ *n* someone who takes care of the money for an organization ‖ 한 조직의 돈을 관리하는 사람. 회계 담당자. 출납 담당자

treas·ur·y /'trɛʒəri/ *n* **1** the money in an organization's accounts ‖ 한 조직의 장부상의 돈. 자금 **2** a government office that controls a country's money ‖ 나라의 돈을 통제하는 정부 부처. 재무부

treat¹ /trit/ *v* [T] **1** to behave toward someone in a particular way ‖ 남에 대해 특별하게 행동하다. 대우하다. 취급하다: *Why do you treat me like an idiot?* 왜 나를 바보 취급합니까? / *She treats children the same as adults.* 그녀는 어린이들을 어른과 똑같이 대한다. / *Mr. Parker treats everyone equally/fairly.* 파커 씨는 모든 사람을 똑같이[공평하게] 대우한다. **2** to consider something in a particular way ‖ 사물을 특정하게 여기다. …으로 간주하다: *You can treat these costs as business expenses.* 이들 비용은 사업 경비로 간주할 수 있다. **3** to give someone medical attention for a sickness or injury ‖ 병이나 부상에 대해 남을 치료해 주다. 치료[처치]하다: *Eleven people were treated for minor injuries.* 11명이 경상으로 치료받았다. **4** to buy or arrange something special for someone ‖ 남을 위해 특별한 것을 사거나 준비하다. 대접하다. 한턱 내다: *We're treating Mom to dinner for her birthday.* 우리는 엄마의 생신에 저녁을 대접할 거예요. **5** to put a special substance on something or use a chemical process in order to protect or clean it ‖ 보호하거나 깨끗하게 하기 위해 사물에 특수한 물질을 넣거나 화학 처리를 이용하다. 약품 처리하다. 가공하다: *The wood has been treated to make it waterproof.* 그 목재는 방수가 되도록 가공되었다.

treat² *n* **1** something special that you give someone or do for him/her ‖ 남에게 주거나 해주는 특별한 일. 대접. 향응: *If you're good, I'll buy you a treat.* 당신이

좋으면 내가 한턱 내겠다. **2** [singular] an unexpected event that gives you a lot of pleasure ‖ 많은 기쁨을 주는 예기치 않은 사건. 만족[즐거움]을 주는 것: *Getting your letter was a real treat.* 너의 편지를 받아서 굉장히 즐거웠다. **3 my treat** SPOKEN used in order to tell someone that you will pay for something ‖ 자신이 어떤 것에 돈을 지불하겠다고 남에게 말하는 데에 쓰여. 내가 (한턱) 낼게: *Put away your money – dinner's my treat.* 네 돈은 넣어 둬. 저녁은 내가 한 턱 내는 거야.

treat·a·ble /'tritəbəl/ *adj* able to be medically treated ‖ 의학적으로 치료될 수 있는. 치유 가능한: *The disease is treatable with antibiotics.* 그 병은 항생제로 치유할 수 있다.

trea·tise /'tritəs/ *n* a serious book or article about a particular subject ‖ 특정한 주제에 대한 딱딱한 책이나 글. 논문. 전문 서적: *a treatise on political philosophy* 정치 철학에 관한 논문

treat·ment /'tritʰmənt/ *n* **1** [C, U] a method that is intended to cure an injury or sickness ‖ 상처나 병을 치료하기 위한 방법. 치료법: *He's trying a new treatment for cancer.* 그는 새로운 암 치료법을 시도해 보고 있다. **2** [U] a particular way of behaving toward someone or of dealing with him/her ‖ 남에 대한 행동이나 대우의 특정한 방법. 특별대우. 우대: *He's not getting any special treatment even if he is the coach's son.* 그는 코치의 아들이지만 어떤 특별대우도 받지 않는다. **3** [C, U] a particular way of dealing with or talking about a subject ‖ 주제를 다루거나 이야기하는 특정한 방식. 논술[취급]법: *He gives a thoughtful treatment of the subject.* 그는 그 주제를 사려 깊게 취급한다. **4** [U] a process by which something is cleaned, protected etc. ‖ 사물이 정화되고 보호되는 등의 과정. 처리. 처치: *a waste treatment plant* 쓰레기 처리 공장

trea·ty /'triti/ *n* a formal written agreement between two or more countries ‖ 두 나라 이상이 정식으로 조인하는 협정. 조약: *a peace treaty* 평화 조약

tre·ble¹ /'trɛbəl/ *n* the upper half of the whole range of musical notes ‖ 전체 음역(音域)의 상위 절반. 고음부. 최고 성부

treble² *v* [I, T] ⇨ TRIPLE²

tree /tri/ *n* a very tall plant that has a TRUNK, branches, and leaves, and lives for many years ‖ 둥치·가지·잎이 있고 여러 해 동안 사는 매우 키 큰 식물. 나무:

an apple tree 사과나무

tree·top /'tritɑp/ *n* [C usually plural] the top branches of a tree ‖ 나무의 꼭대기 가지. 나무 꼭대기

trek¹ /trɛk/ *v* **-kked, -kking** to make a long and difficult trip on foot ‖ 도보로 길고 힘든 여행을 하다. 걸어서 가다: *trekking across the Rockies* 로키 산맥을 걸어서 넘기 – **trek** *n* : *a trek across the country* 국토 횡단 도보 여행 – **trekking** *n* [U]

trel·lis /'trɛlɪs/ *n* a wooden frame for supporting climbing plants ‖ 덩굴 식물을 지지하는 데 사용하는 나무로 만든 틀. 격자 시렁

trem·ble /'trɛmbəl/ *v* [I] to shake because you are upset, afraid, or excited ‖ 사람이 화나서[두려워서, 흥분해서] 떨다. 덜덜 떨다: *Her lip trembled as she spoke.* 그녀의 입술은 말할 때 떨렸다. / *Ray's voice was trembling with fear/anger.* 레이의 목소리는 두려움에[분노로] 떨고 있었다.

tre·men·dous /trɪ'mɛndəs/ *adj* **1** very great in amount, size, power etc. ‖ 양·크기·힘 등이 매우 큰. 엄청난. 무서운: *I have tremendous respect for her.* 나는 그녀를 크게 존경하고 있다. / *a runner with tremendous speed* 엄청난 속도로 달리는 주자 **2** very good or impressive ‖ 매우 좋거나 인상적인. 굉장히 좋은[멋진]: *a tremendous success* 대성공

trem·or /'trɛmɚ/ *n* **1** a small EARTHQUAKE ‖ 작은 지진. 미진 **2** a slight shaking movement that you cannot control ‖ 스스로 제어할 수 없는 약간의 떠는 동작. 미동. 떨림. 몸서리

trench /trɛntʃ/ *n* a long narrow hole that is dug along the ground ‖ 지면을 따라 판 길고 좁은 구멍. 참호

tren·chant /'trɛntʃənt/ *adj* expressed very strongly, effectively, and directly ‖ 매우 강력하게·효과적으로·직접적으로 표현한. 신랄한. 날카로운: *a trenchant critic of big business* 대기업에 대한 신랄한 비판가

trench coat /'. ./ *n* a type of RAINCOAT that is similar to a military coat, with pockets and a belt ‖ 주머니와 벨트가 있는 군복 외투 비슷한 비옷의 한 유형. 트렌치 코트. 바바리

trend /trɛnd/ *n* **1** the way a situation is generally developing or changing ‖ 상황이 일반적으로 전개되거나 변하는 방식. 경향. 대세. 추세: *There's a trend toward more part-time employment.* 임시직 고용이 더 늘어나는 추세다. / *a fashion trend* (=what is fashionable right now) 유행 경향 **2 set the trend** to start doing something that other people copy ‖ 다른 사람이 모방하는 일을 하기 시작하다. 유행을 창출하다. 선구가 되다

trend·y /'trɛndi/ *adj* INFORMAL modern and fashionable ‖ 최신식이고 멋진. (최신) 유행의: *a trendy bar* 최신 유행의 바

trep·i·da·tion /ˌtrɛpə'deɪʃən/ *n* [U] FORMAL a feeling of anxiety or fear about something that is going to happen ‖ 일어날 일에 대한 걱정이나 두려움의 감정. 전율. 공포

tres·pass /'trɛspæs/ *v* [I] to go onto someone's land without permission ‖ 허가 없이 남의 땅에 들어가다. 불법 침입하다 – **trespasser** *n*

tres·tle /'trɛsəl/ *n* a wooden support made of beams in an "A" shape under a table or bridge ‖ 탁자나 다리 밑에 "A" 모양의 들보로 형태를 갖춘 목재 지지물. 가대(架臺). 버팀다리

tri·al /'traɪəl/ *n* **1** [C, U] a legal process in which a court of law examines a case to decide whether someone is guilty of a crime ‖ 사람이 죄를 범했는지 결정하기 위해 법원이 사건을 심리하는 법률상의 과정. 재판. 공판: *a murder trial* 살인 재판 / *Holt is on trial for bank robbery.* (=being judged in a court of law) 홀트는 은행 강도죄로 재판을 받고 있다. **2** [C, U] a test to know if something works well and is safe ‖ 사물이 잘 작용하고 안전한지 알기 위한 시험. 실험: *clinical trials of a new drug* 신약의 임상 실험 **3** [C, U] a time during which you employ someone in order to know if s/he is satisfactory for a particular job ‖ 어떤 사람이 특정한 일에 적합한지 알기 위해 채용하는 기간. 수습 (기간): *Bonnie's been hired on a trial basis.* 보니는 수습사원으로 채용되었다. **4 trial and error** testing different ways of doing something in order to find the best one ‖ 최선의 것을 찾기 위해 일을 하는 여러 가지 방법을 시험하기. 시행착오: *I learned to cook by trial and error.* 나는 시행착오를 하며 요리하는 것을 배웠다. —see also TRIALS

trial run /ˌ. './ *n* an occasion when you test something new in order to see if it works ‖ 작동이 잘 되는지 알기 위해 새것을 시험하는 경우. 시운전. 시용(試用)

tri·als /'traɪəlz/ *n* [plural] **1** a sports competition that tests a player's ability ‖ 선수의 능력을 시험하는 스포츠 시합. 평가전. 예선: *the Olympic swimming trials* 올림픽 수영 예선 **2 trials and**

tribulations difficult experiences and troubles ‖ 어려운 경험과 곤란. 고난. 쓰라린 역경: *all the trials and tribulations of being a teenager* 십대의 모든 고난과 시련

tri·an·gle /'traɪˌæŋgəl/ *n* **1** a flat shape with three straight sides and three angles ‖ 3개의 곧은 변과 3개의 각이 있는 편평한 모양. 삼각형 —see picture at SHAPE **2** a small musical instrument shaped like a triangle, that you play by hitting it with a small metal BAR ‖ 작은 금속 막대로 때려서 연주하는 삼각형 모양을 한 작은 악기. 트라이앵글

tri·ath·lon /traɪ'æθlɑn, -lən/ *n* a sports competition in which you run, swim, and bicycle ‖ 달리고 수영하고 자전거를 타는 스포츠 경기. 3종 경기

tribe /traɪb/ *n* a social group that consists of people of the same race who have the same beliefs, customs, language etc. and live in one area ruled by a chief ‖ 같은 신앙·관습·언어 등을 가진 같은 인종의 사람으로 구성되고 추장이 다스리는 지역에 사는 사회 집단. 부족. 종족: *the tribes of the Amazon jungle* 아마존 정글의 부족들 **– tribal** *adj* : *tribal art* 부족 예술 / *tribal leaders* 부족 지도자들 —see usage note at RACE¹

trib·u·la·tion /ˌtrɪbyə'leɪʃən/ *n* [C, U] difficult experiences that you have to deal with ‖ 사람이 치러야 하는 어려운 경험. 시련. 간난 —see also **trials and tribulations** (TRIALS)

tri·bu·nal /traɪ'byunl, trɪ-/ *n* a type of court that has official authority to deal with a particular situation or problem ‖ 특정한 상황이나 문제를 다루는 공식 권한을 가진 법정의 한 형태. 재판소: *a war crimes tribunal* 전쟁 범죄 재판소

tri·bu·tar·y /'trɪbyəˌtɛri/ *n* a river or stream that flows into a larger river ‖ 큰 강으로 흘러드는 강이나 시내. 강의 지류

trib·ute /'trɪbyut/ *n* [C, U] something that you say, do, or give in order to express your respect or admiration for someone ‖ 남에 대한 존경이나 찬사를 표현하기 위해 말하는[하는, 주는] 것. 감사 표시: *The concert will be a tribute to Bob Dylan.* 그 콘서트는 밥 딜런에게 바쳐질 것이다. —see also **pay tribute to sb/sth** (PAY¹)

tri·ceps /'traɪsɛps/ *n* the large muscle at the back of your upper arm ‖ 위팔의 뒤쪽에 있는 큰 근육. 삼두근

trick¹ /trɪk/ *n* **1** something you do in order to deceive someone ‖ 남을 속이기 위해 하는 일. 계교. 책략. 속임수: *It was*

just a trick to get me to agree. 그것은 나의 동의를 얻으려는 계략에 불과하였다. **2** something you do to surprise someone and make other people laugh ‖ 어떤 사람을 놀라게 해서 다른 사람을 웃기는 일. 장난. 심술궂은 짓: *The kids like playing tricks on the grownups.* 아이들은 어른들에게 장난을 치기 좋아한다. **3 do the trick** SPOKEN if something does the trick, it solves a problem or achieves what you want ‖ 어떤 것이 문제를 해결하거나 원하는 것을 달성하게 하다. 목적을 달성하다. 도움이 되다: *A little salt should do the trick.* 소금을 약간 치면 될 것이다. **4** an effective way of doing something ‖ 일을 하는 효과적인 방법. 요령. 비결: *There's a trick to getting the audience's attention.* 청중의 관심을 끄는 비결이 있다. **5** a skillful set of actions that seem like magic, done in order to entertain people ‖ 사람을 즐겁게 하기 위해 행해진, 요술처럼 보이는 숙련된 일련의 동작. 묘기. 기술: *Mike's learning some new card tricks.* 마이크는 몇 가지의 최신 카드 묘기를 배우고 있다. **6 How's tricks?** SPOKEN used in order to greet someone in a friendly way ‖ 남에게 친숙하게 인사하는 데에 쓰여. 좀 어때? 잘 되나?: *Hi, Bill. How's tricks?* 안녕, 빌. 요즘 어때?

trick² *v* [T] to deceive someone in order to get something from him/her or make him/her do something ‖ 남에게서 어떤 것을 얻어내거나 어떤 일을 하도록 하기 위해 속이다. 기만하다. 협잡질하다: *Believe me, we're not trying to trick you.* 나를 믿어, 우리는 너를 속이려는 것이 아니야. / *Clients were tricked into believing he'd invest the money.* 고객들은 속아넘어가 그가 그 돈을 투자할 것으로 믿었다.

trick·er·y /'trɪkəri/ *n* [U] the use of tricks to deceive or cheat people ‖ 사람을 속이거나 기만하는 계략의 사용. 속임수. 사기. 책략

trick·le¹ /'trɪkəl/ *v* [I] **1** if liquid trickles somewhere, it flows slowly in drops or in a thin stream ‖ 액체가 방울로 또는 가느다란 흐름으로 천천히 어떤 곳에서 흐르다. 졸졸 흐르다. 똑똑 떨어지다: *Sweat trickled down his face.* 땀이 그의 얼굴을 흘러내렸다. **2** if people, vehicles, goods etc. trickle somewhere, they move there slowly in small groups or amounts ‖ 사람·차량·물자 등이 소집단이나 소량으로 천천히 어떤 곳으로 이동하다. 드문드문[조금씩] (들어)오다[흘러들다]: *cars trickling into the parking lot* 주차장으로 드문드문 들어오는 차들

trickle² *n* **1** a thin slow flow of liquid ‖

액체의 가늘고 느린 흐름. 똑똑 떨어지는 것. 졸졸 흐름 **2** a movement of people, vehicles, goods etc. into a place in very small numbers or amounts ‖ 아주 작은 숫자나 양으로 사람·차량·물자의 한 장소로의 이동. 조금씩[드문드문] 오기[가기]: *Higher prices have reduced the number of visitors to a trickle.* 높은 가격으로 방문자의 수가 눈곱만큼으로 줄어들었다.

trick or treat /ˌ. . ˈ./ *v* **1 go trick or treating** if children go trick or treating, they put on COSTUMEs and go from house to house on HALLOWEEN in order to get candy ‖ 아이들이 할로윈 때 사탕을 얻기 위해 의상을 입고 이집 저집으로 다닌다. 과자를 얻으러 다니다 **2** SPOKEN said to someone in order to get candy on Halloween ‖ 할로윈 때 사탕을 얻으려고 남에게 말해. 장난칠까요, 아니면 맛있는 것 줄래요.

trick·ster /ˈtrɪkstɚ/ *n* someone who deceives or cheats people ‖ 사람을 속이거나 기만하는 사람. 사기[협잡]꾼

trick·y /ˈtrɪki/ *adj* **1** a tricky job or situation is difficult to deal with ‖ 일이나 상황이 다루기 어려운. 신중을 요하는: *Finding out how the trouble started will be tricky.* 그 문제가 어떻게 시작되었는지 알아내기가 그리 간단하지는 않다. **2** a tricky person is likely to deceive you ‖ 사람이 속일 듯한. 교활한. 방심할 수 없는

tri·cy·cle /ˈtraɪsɪkəl/ *n* a small vehicle with one wheel at the front and two wheels at the back, that you ride by pushing the PEDALs with your feet ‖ 발로 페달을 밟아 타는, 앞에 바퀴 하나와 뒤에 바퀴 2개가 있는 작은 탈것. 세발자전거

tri·dent /ˈtraɪdnt/ *n* a weapon with three points that looks like a large fork ‖ 큰 포크처럼 생긴 3개의 갈래진 끝이 있는 무기. 삼지창(三枝槍)

tried¹ /traɪd/ *v* the past tense and PAST PARTICIPLE of TRY ‖ try의 과거·과거 분사형

USAGE NOTE try to do and try doing

Saying *Nick tried to climb the mountain* means that he tried but he could not climb it. Saying *Nick tried climbing the mountain* means that he climbed it in order to have the experience of climbing.

닉은 등산하려고 했다(tried to climb)라는 말은 시도했으나 등산할 수 없었다는 것을 의미한다. 닉은 등산을 해봤다(tried climbing)는 말은 등산 경험을 하려고 등산을 한 것을 의미한다.

---

tried² *adj* **tried and tested/true** used successfully many times ‖ 여러 번 성공적으로 사용된. (과거의 실적을 통해) 신뢰할 수 있는. 충분히 검증된: *tried and tested methods* 충분히 증명된 방법들

tri·fle¹ /ˈtraɪfəl/ *adj, adv* **a trifle** ... slightly ‖ 조금. 소량: *It's a trifle salty, but otherwise delicious.* 약간 짜긴 하지만 그것만 빼면 맛이 있다.

trifle² *n* something that has little value or importance ‖ 가치나 중요성이 거의 없는 것. 시시한[하찮은] 것[일]

trig·ger¹ /ˈtrɪgɚ/ *n* **1** the part of a gun that you press with your finger to fire it ‖ 발사하기 위해 손가락으로 당기는 총의 부분. 방아쇠: *Carter aimed and pulled/squeezed the trigger.* 카터는 조준을 하고 방아쇠를 당겼다. **2 be the trigger (for)** to be the thing that causes a serious problem ‖ 심각한 문제를 야기하는 것이 되다. 원인[도화선]이 되다: *The doctor thinks stress was the trigger for Ben's heart attack.* 의사는 스트레스가 벤의 심장 마비의 원인이었다고 생각한다.

trigger², **trigger off** *v* [T] to make something happen ‖ 어떤 일이 일어나게 하다. 일으키다. 유발하다: *Heavy rain may trigger mudslides.* 폭우는 진흙사태를 일으킬지도 모른다.

trigger hap·py /ˈ.. ˌ../ *adj* too willing to use weapons to solve disagreements ‖ 불화를 해결하기 위해 너무 무기를 사용하려 하는. 무모하고 호전적인

trig·o·nom·e·try /ˌtrɪgəˈnɑmətri/ *n* [U] the part of mathematics that is concerned with the relationship between the angles and sides of TRIANGLEs ‖ 삼각형의 각과 변들 사이의 관계를 다루는 수학의 한 분야. 삼각법

trike /traɪk/ *n* INFORMAL ⇨ TRICYCLE

tri·lat·er·al /ˌtraɪˈlæt̬ərəl./ *adj* including three groups or countries ‖ 세 집단이나 나라를 포함하는. 3자에 의한: *a trilateral agreement* 3자 협정

trill /trɪl/ *n* a musical sound made by quickly repeating two notes that are very similar ‖ 매우 비슷한 두 개의 음을 빠르게 반복해서 내는 소리. 트릴. 전음(顫音): *a bird's trill* 새의 떨리는 울음소리 **– trill** *v* [I, T]

tril·lion /ˈtrɪlyən/ *number* 1,000,000,000,000 ‖ 조(兆)

tril·o·gy /ˈtrɪlədʒi/ *n* a group of three books, plays, movies etc. that have the same subject or characters ‖ 같은 주제나 등장인물이 있는 세 권의 책·연극·영화 등의 묶음. 삼부작

trim¹ /trɪm/ *v* **-mmed, -mming** [T] **1** to make something look neater by cutting a small amount off it ‖ 어떤 것에서 작은 양을 깎아내서 더 말쑥하게 보이게 하다. 깎아 다듬다. 손질하다: *My hair needs to be trimmed.* 나는 머리를 손질해야 한다. **2** to reduce the size or amount of something in order to save money ‖ 돈을 절약하기 위해 사물의 크기나 양을 줄이다. 삭감하다: *plans to trim the city's budget* 시의 예산을 줄이는 계획 / *The industry intends to trim more workers.* 그 업계는 근로자를 더 줄일 작정이다. **3** to decorate something around its edges ‖ 어떤 것의 가장자리 둘레를 장식하다: *a beautifully trimmed Christmas tree* 아름답게 장식한 크리스마스트리 / *a coat trimmed with velvet* 벨벳으로 장식한 코트

trim sth ↔ **off** *phr v* [T] to cut small pieces from the end of something so that it looks neater ‖ 말쑥하게 보이도록 어떤 것의 끝에서 작은 조각을 제거하다. 잘라내다: *Trim off the stems before putting the roses in water.* 장미를 물에 넣기 전에 줄기를 잘라내라.

trim² *adj* thin and healthy looking ‖ 호리호리하고 건강해 보이는. 균형 잡힌. 날씬한: *a trim figure* 날씬한 몸매

trim³ *n* **1** [singular] an act of cutting something in order to make it look neater ‖ 더 말쑥하게 보이도록 사물을 자르기. 깎기: *Your beard needs a trim.* 너 턱수염을 깎아야겠다. **2** [singular, U] a decoration around the edges of a car, piece of clothing etc. ‖ 차나 옷 등의 가장자리 둘레의 장식: *a blue car with white trim* 하얀 테두리 장식을 한 청색 차

tri·mes·ter /'traɪmestɚ, traɪ'mestɚ/ *n* **1** one of three periods into which a year at school or college is divided ‖ 학교나 대학에서 1년을 나눈 3학기제의 한 학기 **2** one of the three-month periods of a woman's PREGNANCY ‖ 여성의 임신을 3개월씩 나눈 기간의 하나

trim·mings /'trɪmɪŋz/ *n* [plural] **1** material or objects used for decorating things such as clothes ‖ 옷 등을 장식하는 데 사용되는 재료나 물건. 장식[부속]품 **2** **all the trimmings** all the other types of food that are traditionally served with the main dish of a meal ‖ 식사의 주요한 요리와 함께 전통적으로 제공되는 그 밖의 다른 음식. 곁들여 나오는 음식: *a turkey dinner with all the trimmings* 온갖 곁들인 음식과 함께 나오는 칠면조 요리

trin·ket /'trɪŋkɪt/ *n* a piece of jewelry or a small pretty object that is not worth

much money ‖ 비싸지 않은 보석이나 작고 예쁜 물건. 값싼 보석. 작은 장신구

tri·o /'triou/ *n* a piece of music written for three performers ‖ 3명의 공연자를 위해 쓴 곡. 3중창[중주]곡

trip¹ /trɪp/ *n* **1** an occasion when you go from one place to another ‖ 한 장소에서 다른 장소로 가는 경우. 여행. 이동: *We're taking a trip to Florida.* 우리는 플로리다로 여행을 갈 거야. / *You'll have to make two trips – there's too much to carry.* 너는 두 번 다녀와야 해. 가지고 갈 것이 너무 많아. / *When are you going on your business trip?* 출장은 언제 가지요? —see usage note at TRAVEL² **2** SLANG the experiences someone has while s/he is taking illegal drugs ‖ 사람이 마약을 복용하는 동안 가지는 경험. 도취감. 환각 증상 **3** SLANG a person or experience that is amusing and different from normal ‖ 재미있으며 보통과는 다른 사람이나 경험. 재미있는[유쾌한] 사람[것]: *Yeah, she's a real trip.* 그래, 그녀는 정말 재미있는 사람이야.

trip² *v* **-pped, -pping** **1** [I] to hit something with your foot while you are walking or running so that you fall or almost fall ‖ 사람이 걷거나 달리는 동안 넘어지거나 넘어질 뻔할 정도로 발이 사물에 부딪치다. 걸려 넘

trip

어지다: *"How did you hurt your foot?" "I tripped on/over a cord."* "네 발은 어떻게 다쳤니?" "줄에 걸려 넘어졌어." **2** [T] also **trip up** to make someone fall by putting your foot in front of him/her when s/he is moving ‖ 다른 사람이 움직일 때 그 앞에 발을 놓아 넘어지게 하다. 발을 걸다[걸어 넘어뜨리다] **3** **trip a switch/wire** to accidentally make an electrical system operate by moving part of it ‖ 우연히 전기 장치의 일부를 움직여 작동시키다. 오작동시키다. 잘못 건드리다: *I tripped the switch accidentally and set off the alarm.* 나는 우연히 스위치를 잘못 건드려서 경보기를 울렸다. **4** [I] also **trip out** SLANG to experience the effects of illegal drugs ‖ 마약의 효과를 경험하다. 환각 체험을 하다

trip up *phr v* [I] to make a mistake ‖ 실수를 하다. …에서 잘못하다: *It's easy to trip up on some of the details.* 세부 사항의 몇 가지는 실수하기 쉽다.

tripe /traɪp/ *n* [U] the stomach of a cow or pig, used as food ‖ 식품으로 사용되는

소나 돼지의 위

tri·ple¹ /'trɪpəl/ *adj* having three parts, or involving three people or groups ‖ 세 부분으로 된, 또는 세 사람이나 집단을 포함하는. 3부로 된: *The skater fell while attempting a triple jump.* 그 스케이팅 선수는 3회전 뛰기를 시도하다가 넘어졌다.

triple² *v* [I, T] to become three times as much or as many, or to make something do this ‖ 수나 양이 3배가 되다, 또는 어떤 것이 이렇게 되게 하다. … 을 3배로 하다: *The population may triple in 20 years.* 인구가 20년 후에는 3배가 될지도 모른다.

tri·plet /'trɪplɪt/ *n* one of three children born at the same time to the same mother ‖ 한 어머니에게서 동시에 태어난 세 아이들 중의 한 사람. 세 쌍둥이 중 하나

trip·li·cate /'trɪpləkɪt/ *n* **in triplicate** if a document is written in triplicate, there are three copies of it ‖ 문서가 사본이 세 통이 되도록 쓰여진. 세 통[벌, 배]으로 작성된

tri·pod /'traɪpɑd/ *n* a support with three legs, used for a camera, TELESCOPE etc. ‖ 카메라·망원경 등에 사용되는 다리가 3개 있는 지지대. 삼각대

trite /traɪt/ *adj* a trite remark, idea etc. has been used so often that it seems boring and not sincere ‖ 말·생각 등이 너무 자주 쓰여서 따분하고 진실해 보이지 않는. 진부한. 낡아[흔해]빠진

tri·umph¹ /'traɪəmf/ *n* **1** an important success or victory, especially after a difficult struggle ‖ 특히 악전고투 끝의 중요한 성공이나 승리. 대성공. 위업: *Winning a gold medal was a personal triumph for Sylvie.* 금메달의 획득은 실비 개인으로서는 대성공이었다. / *San Francisco's triumph over Cincinnati in the Super Bowl* 슈퍼볼에서 신시내티를 누른 샌프란시스코의 승리 **2** a feeling of pleasure and satisfaction that you get from victory or success ‖ 승리나 성공으로부터 얻는 즐거움과 만족의 감정. 승리감: *shouts of triumph* 승리의 함성 –

triumphant /traɪ'ʌmfənt/ *adj* : *a triumphant army* 승리한 군대

triumph² *v* [I] to gain a victory or success, especially after a difficult struggle ‖ 특히 악전고투 끝에 승리나 성공을 얻다. 승리를 거두다: *Once again, good triumphs over evil.* 다시 한번 선이 악을 이긴다.

tri·um·phal /traɪ'ʌmfəl/ *adj* done or made in order to celebrate a victory or success ‖ 승리나 성공을 축하하기 위해 하거나 만들어진. 승리를 축하하는: *a triumphal march* (승리를 축하하는) 개선행진곡

triv·i·a /'trɪviə/ *n* [plural] **1** unimportant or useless details ‖ 중요하지 않거나 쓸데없는 내용. 사소한[하찮은] 일: *Don't waste my time with trivia.* 사소한 일로 내 시간을 빼앗지 마라. **2** detailed facts about past events, famous people, sports etc., used in QUIZ games ‖ 퀴즈 게임에서 사용되는 과거 사건·유명 인사·스포츠 등에 대한 세세한 사실. 잡학적 지식

triv·i·al /'trɪviəl/ *adj* unimportant or of little value ‖ 중요하지 않거나 가치가 거의 없는. 하찮은. 사소한: *We do not view the issue as a trivial matter.* 우리는 그 문제를 사소한 일로 보지 않는다.

triv·i·al·ize /'trɪviə,laɪz/ *v* [T] to make something important seem less important than it really is ‖ 중요한 일을 실제보다 덜 중요하게 보이게 하다. 시시하게[하찮게] 만들다: *The media tried to trivialize the court's decision.* 언론은 법원의 결정을 대수롭지 않게 취급하려 했다.

trod /trɑd/ *v* the past tense of TREAD ‖ tread의 과거형

trod·den /'trɑdn/ *v* the PAST PARTICIPLE of TREAD ‖ tread의 과거 분사형

troll /troʊl/ *n* an imaginary creature in ancient Scandinavian stories, like a very large or very small ugly person ‖ 매우 크거나 매우 작은 못생긴 사람 같은 고대 스칸디나비아인의 이야기 속의 상상의 괴물. 트롤

trol·ley /'trɑli/ *n* an electric vehicle for carrying passengers, that moves along the street on metal tracks ‖ 금속 궤도 위로 거리를 따라 움직이는, 승객을 나르는 전기 차량. 노면[시가] 전차

trom·bone /trɑm'boʊn/ *n* a metal musical instrument, that you play by blowing into it and moving a long sliding tube ‖ 숨을 불어넣으며 긴 활주관을 움직여 연주하는 금속 악기. 트롬본

tromp /trɑmp, trɔmp/ *v* [I, T] INFORMAL ⇨ TRAMP²

troop¹ /trup/ *n* **1** an organized group of people or animals ‖ 사람이나 동물의 조직화된 집단. 무리. 떼. 단(團). 대(隊): *a Girl Scout troop* 걸 스카우트 단 **2** a group of soldiers, especially on horses or in TANKs ‖ 특히 말을 타거나 탱크를 타는 군인의 집단. 기병[기갑] 중대[부대] —see also TROOPS

troop² *v* [I] INFORMAL to move together in a group ‖ 집단으로 함께 이동하다. 떼

를 짓다. 줄줄이 가다: *We parked our cars and trooped over the grass to the picnic area.* 우리는 차를 주차시키고 소풍 지역으로 가기 위해 잔디 위를 줄을 지어 갔다.

troop·er /'trupə/ *n* a member of a state police force in the US ‖ 미국 주 경찰의 일원. 주 경찰관

troops /trups/ *n* [plural] organized groups of soldiers ‖ 조직화된 군인 집단. 군대. 부대: *Troops were sent in to stop the riots.* 폭동을 막기 위해 군대가 투입됐다.

tro·phy /'troufi/ *n* a prize for winning a competition, especially a silver cup or a PLAQUE ‖ 시합에서 우승했을 때 주는 상, 특히 은제 컵이나 기념패. 우승컵[패]. 트로피: *the first-place trophy* 1등 트로피

trop·i·cal /'trɑpɪkəl/ *adj* 1 coming from or existing in the hottest and wettest parts of the world ‖ 세계의 가장 덥고 습한 지역에서 나오거나 존재하는. 열대 지방의. 열대성의: *tropical flowers* 열대성 화초 2 weather that is tropical is hot and the air seems wet ‖ 날씨가 몹시 뜨겁고 대기가 습한. 몹시 더운. 혹서(용)의

trop·ics /'trɑpɪks/ *n* **the tropics** the hottest and wettest parts of the world, between the Tropic of Cancer and the Tropic of Capricorn ‖ 북회귀선과 남회귀선 사이의 세계에서 가장 덥고 습한 지역. 열대(지방)

trot /trɑt/ *v* **-tted, -tting** [I] 1 if a horse trots, it moves with quick small steps ‖ 말이 속보로 달리다 2 to run fairly slowly with short steps ‖ 짧은 걸음으로 꽤 천천히 달리다. 빠른 걸음으로 가다. 뛰다시피 걷다: *Jimmy trotted along behind his parents.* 지미는 부모님의 뒤를 빠른 걸음으로 따라갔다. **– trot** *n*

trot sb/sth ↔ **out** *phr v* [T] INFORMAL to bring something or someone out to show other people ‖ 사물이나 사람을 다른 사람에게 내보이다. 자랑삼아 보이다: *The Reids like to trot out photos of their grandchildren.* 리드 씨네는 손자들 사진을 자랑삼아 보이기를 좋아한다.

trou·ba·dour /'trubə,dɔr/ *n* a singer and poet who traveled around in past times ‖ 옛날에 여행하며 돌아다니던 가수이자 시인. 음유 시인[악사]

trou·ble¹ /'trʌbəl/ *n*

1 ▶PROBLEMS 문제들◀ [C, U] problems that make something difficult, make you worry, spoil your plans etc. ‖ 일을 어렵게 하는·걱정하게 하는·계획을 망치는 문제들. 말썽[걱정](거리): *They're having some trouble with their new car.* 그들은

새 차에 문제가 좀 있다. / *a plane with engine trouble* 엔진에 문제가 있는 비행기 / *People often come to me with their troubles.* 사람들이 종종 문젯거리를 가지고 나에게 온다.

2 the trouble with SPOKEN used when explaining what is not satisfactory about something or someone ‖ 사물이나 사람에 대한 만족스럽지 않는 점을 설명할 때 쓰여. 고민[손해]이 되는 점. 단점: *The trouble with you is you don't listen.* 너의 문제는 귀를 기울이지 않는다는 거야.

3 ▶BAD SITUATION 나쁜 상황◀ [U] a difficult or dangerous situation ‖ 힘들거나 위험한 상황: *We're in big/real/deep trouble now!* 우리는 지금 곤란한 상황에 처했다! / *a call from a ship in trouble* 조난 중인 배로부터의 (구조)호출

4 ▶HEALTH 건강◀ [U] INFORMAL a problem that you have with your health ‖ 사람의 건강에 관계있는 문제. 병: *heart/back trouble* 심장병[허리병]

5 ▶EFFORT 노력◀ [U] an amount of effort and time that is needed to do something ‖ 일을 하는 데 필요한 노력과 시간의 양. 수고. 노고: *She took the trouble to explain it to us again.* 그녀는 우리에게 그것을 다시 설명하는 수고를 했다. / *I'm sorry to put you to so much trouble.* 당신에게 정말 많은 폐를 끼쳐서 죄송합니다. / *"Could you help me carry this?" "Sure, it's no trouble."* (=I am happy to help) "이것을 운반하는 것 좀 도와주시겠어요?" "예, 물론 그러지요."

6 ▶BLAME 비난◀ [U] a situation in which someone in authority is angry with you or is likely to punish you ‖ 권한 있는 사람이 화가 나 있거나 처벌하려 할 것 같은 상황. 곤란한[처벌, 체포된] 상황: *My daughter's gotten into trouble at school.* 내 딸은 학교에서 처벌을 당할 처지에 놓여 있다. / *Joe's in trouble with the police again.* 조는 또다시 경찰에 체포될 상황에 처해 있다.

7 be asking for trouble INFORMAL to take risks or do something stupid that is likely to cause problems ‖ 문제를 일으킬 것 같은 위험한 일을 하거나 어리석은 일을 하다. 재난을 자초하다. 자업자득을 초래하다: *You're asking for trouble if you don't get those brakes fixed.* 그 브레이크를 수리하지 않으면 너는 재난을 자초하는 거야.

8 ▶ARGUMENT/VIOLENCE 언쟁/폭력◀ a situation in which people quarrel or fight with each other ‖ 사람이 서로 말다툼하거나 싸우는 상황. 분쟁. 소동: *recent troubles on college campuses* 대학 캠퍼

스에서의 최근의 말썽

trouble² /trʌbəl/ v [T] FORMAL **1** to ask someone to do something for you when it is difficult for him/her ‖ 다른 사람에게 어려운 어떤 것을 해달라고 부탁하다. 폐[수고, 부담, 번거로움]를 끼쳐 …하게 하다. 괴롭히다: I won't trouble you again. 다시는 폐를 끼치지 않겠습니다. **2 May I trouble you for...?** used in order to ask for something extremely politely ‖ 극히 정중하게 어떤 것을 요청하는 데에 쓰여. 죄송합니다만 …에 폐 좀 끼쳐도 될까요?: May I trouble you for more wine? 죄송하지만 포도주를 더 주시겠어요?

trou·bled /'trʌbəld/ adj having many emotional problems ‖ 많은 정서적인 문제가 있는. 불안정한. 심한 괴로움을 겪는: a deeply troubled man 아주 불안정한 남자

trou·ble·mak·er /'trʌbəl,meɪkɚ/ n someone who deliberately causes problems ‖ 고의적으로 문제를 일으키는 사람. 말썽꾼

trou·ble·shoot·er /'trʌbəl,ʃutɚ/ n someone who is employed by a company to deal with its most serious problems ‖ 가장 심각한 문제를 해결하도록 회사에 채용된 사람. 문제 해결자 – **troubleshooting** n [U]

trou·ble·some /'trʌbəlsəm/ adj causing you trouble for a long time ‖ 오랫동안 사람에게 어려움을 주는. 귀찮은. 성가신: troublesome back pain 괴로운 허리 통증

trou·ble·spot /'trʌbəlspat/ n a place where there is trouble such as fighting, or where trouble may happen ‖ 싸움 등의 분쟁이 있는 곳, 또는 분쟁이 일어날 수도 있는 곳. 분쟁 위험[상존] 지역: Tourists have been warned to stay away from troublespots. 관광객들은 분쟁 위험 지역에 가지 말라고 경고 받았다.

trough /trɔf/ n a long narrow open container that holds water or food for animals ‖ 동물이 먹을 물이나 음식을 담는 좁고 긴 덮개 없는 용기. 구유. 여물통

trounce /traʊns/ v [T] to defeat someone completely ‖ 남을 완전히 패배시키다. 완패시키다. 혼내주다: Colorado trounced Minnesota 58-7 on Saturday. 콜로라도는 토요일에 미네소타를 58대 7로 완패시켰다.

troupe /trup/ n a group of singers, actors, dancers etc. who work together ‖ 함께 일하는 가수·배우·무용수의 단체. 일행. 일단

trou·sers /'traʊzɚz/ n [plural] ⇨

PANTS

trout /traʊt/ n [C, U] a common river fish, or the meat from this fish ‖ 흔한 강물고기, 또는 이 물고기의 살. 송어(살)

trove /troʊv/ n a place where a large number of special or valuable things can be found ‖ 다수의 특별하거나 가치 있는 것들이 발견될 수 있는 곳. 보고(寶庫): The house contains a treasure trove of antique furniture. 그 집은 고(古)가구들의 보고이다.

tru·ant /'truənt/ n a student who stays away from school without permission ‖ 허가 없이 학교를 결석하는 학생. 무단결석 학생 – **truancy** n [U]

truce /trus/ n an agreement between two enemies to stop fighting or arguing for a short time ‖ 짧은 시간 동안 싸움이나 논쟁을 중단하는 양 적대국[자] 사이의 협정. 휴전. 정전: The warring sides have declared a truce. 교전중인 양측은 휴전을 선언했다.

truck¹ /trʌk/ n a large road vehicle that is used for carrying heavy loads ‖ 무거운 짐을 운반하는 데 쓰이는 큰 도로 차. 트럭 —see picture on page 943

truck² v [T] to take something somewhere by truck ‖ 트럭으로 사물을 어떤 곳으로 가져가다. 트럭으로 운반[운송]하다: Food and medicine were trucked in to flood victims. 음식과 의약품이 수재민에게 트럭으로 운반되었다.

truck farm /'. ./ n a farm that grows vegetables and fruit for sale ‖ 판매용 야채와 과일을 재배하는 농장. 시판용 야채 재배 농장

truck·ing /'trʌkɪŋ/ n [U] the business of taking goods from place to place by truck ‖ 트럭으로 물건을 여기저기로 운반하는 사업. 트럭 운송업

truck·load /'trʌkloʊd/ n the amount of something that a truck can carry ‖ 한 트럭이 운반할 수 있는 물건의 양. 트럭 1대분(의 짐)

truck stop /'. ./ n a cheap place to eat and buy gas on a HIGHWAY, used especially by truck drivers ‖ 특히 트럭 운전자가 이용하는, 간선도로상에서 싸게 식사하고 휘발유를 사는 장소. 트럭 (기사) 휴게소

truc·u·lent /'trʌkyələnt/ adj FORMAL bad-tempered and always willing to argue with people ‖ 성질이 고약하고 항상 다른 사람들과 다투려 하는. 싸움투의. 호전적인. 반항적인

trudge /trʌdʒ/ v [I] to walk with slow heavy steps because you are tired or sad ‖ 피곤하고 울적해서 느리고 무거운

걸음으로 걷다. 터벅터벅 걷다: *trudging home from shopping* 쇼핑하고 나서 집으로 터벅터벅 걷기

true /tru/ *adj* 1 based on facts and not imagined or invented ‖ 상상하거나 꾸며 낸 것이 아니라 사실에 기반한. 사실의. 실제의: *Believe me, it's a true story.* 정말 이야, 그것은 실제 이야기이다. / *Is it true that you're moving to Denver?* 당신이 덴버로 이사 간다는 것이 사실입니까? / *Answer the questions True or False.* 질문에 맞는지 틀린지 대답하라. —opposite FALSE 2 SPOKEN used when admitting that something is a fact ‖ 어떤 것이 사실이라고 인정할 때에 쓰여. 진실한. 정말인: *True, he has a college degree, but he doesn't have enough job experience.* 그가 학위를 소지한 것은 사실이지만 근무 경험은 충분치 않다. 3 **true love/courage/friendship etc.** love, courage, etc. that is strong and has all the qualities that it should have ‖ 강하며 가져야 할 모든 특성을 가진 사랑·용기 등. 진짜[진실한] 사랑/용기/우정 4 **come true** if dreams, wishes etc. come true, they happen ‖ 꿈·소원 등이 사실이 되어 일어나다. 실현되다: *Their dream of owning a house in the mountains had finally come true.* 산속에 집을 갖겠다는 그들의 꿈이 마침내 실현되었다. 5 faithful and loyal to someone ‖ 남에게 성실하고 충직한. 충실한. 충성스러운: *She stayed true to her husband during the trial.* 그녀는 재판 중에도 자신의 남편에게 충실했다. 6 **true friend/believer etc.** someone who behaves in the way that a good friend, believer etc. should behave ‖ 좋은 친구나 굳은 믿음이 있는 사람 등이 처신해야 하는 방식으로 처신하는 사람. 진실한 친구/신실한 신앙인: *You know who your true friends are at a time like this.* 너는 이런 때에 너의 진정한 친구가 누구인지 안다.

true-life /ˌ. '../ *adj* based on what really happened, and not invented ‖ 꾸며낸 것이 아니고 실제 일어난 일을 바탕으로 한. 실제인. 실제로 있었던: *a true-life adventure* 실제로 있었던 모험

truf·fle /'trʌfəl/ *n* 1 a soft chocolate candy ‖ 부드러운 초콜릿 캔디 2 a FUNGUS you can eat that grows under the ground ‖ 땅 속에서 자라는 먹을 수 있는 균류. 송로버섯

tru·ism /'truɪzəm/ *n* a statement that is clearly true, so that there is no need to say it ‖ 말할 필요가 없을 정도로 명백하게 사실인 진술. 자명한 이치. 진부한 말 — compare CLICHÉ

tru·ly /'truli/ *adv* 1 used in order to emphasize that the way you are describing something is true; really ‖ 어떤 것을 표현하는 방식이 참된 것임을 강조하는 데에 쓰여. 참으로. 정말; 실로: *They're truly the best athletes I've seen.* 그들은 정말로 내가 본 최고의 운동선수들이다. / *a truly amazing story* 정말 놀랄 만한 이야기 2 in an exact or correct way ‖ 정확하고 올바르게. 사실대로. 틀림없이: *A spider can't truly be called an insect.* 거미는 정확히 곤충이라고 불릴 수 없다. —see also **yours (truly)** (YOURS)

trump¹ /trʌmp/ *n* 1 a SUIT or a playing card that is chosen to be of a higher value than the others in a particular card game ‖ 특정한 카드 게임에서 다른 패보다 더 높은 가치가 있는 것으로 뽑힌 카드 한 벌이나 이에 속한 카드패 한 장. 으뜸패 (한 벌) 2 **play your trump card** to use an advantage that you have kept hidden until now, in order to make sure that you get what you want ‖ 원하는 것을 확실히 얻어내기 위해 지금까지 숨겨 놓았던 이점을 쓰다. 비장의 수를 쓰다

trump² *v* [T] to play a TRUMP that beats someone else's card in a game ‖ 게임에서 다른 사람의 카드를 이기는 으뜸패를 내다. 으뜸패로 따다

trumped-up /ˌ. '../ *adj* **trumped-up charges/evidence etc.** false information that has been used in order to make someone seem guilty of a crime ‖ 어떤 사람이 죄를 범한 것처럼 보이도록 하는 데 이용된 허위 정보. 꾸며낸[날조된] 혐의/증거

trum·pet¹ /'trʌmpɪt/ *n* 1 a musical instrument that you blow into, that consists of a long bent metal tube that is wide at one end ‖ 한쪽 끝이 넓은 길게 구부러진 금속관으로 이루어진, 입으로 부는 악기. 트럼펫 2 the loud noise made by some animals, such as ELEPHANTs ‖ 코끼리 등 일부 동물들이 내는 큰 소리. (코끼리 등의) 날카로운 울음소리

trumpet² *v* [T] to tell as many people as you can about something you think is important or are proud of ‖ 중요하거나 자랑스럽게 생각하는 것에 대해 되도록 많은 사람에게 말하다. 떠들썩하게 퍼뜨리다: *another new wine being trumpeted by its makers* 제조업자에 의해 요란하게 광고되고 있는 또 하나의 새 포도주

trun·cat·ed /'trʌŋˌkeɪtɪd/ *adj* made short, or shorter than before ‖ 짧게 된, 또는 전보다 더 짧아진. 간추린. 단축된: *a truncated speech* 간략해진 연설

trun·dle /'trʌndl/ v [I, T] to move slowly on wheels, or to make something do this by pushing it or pulling it ‖ 바퀴로 천천히 움직이다, 또는 밀거나 끌어서 어떤 것이 이렇게 하게 하다. 구르다. 굴리다. 회전하다[시키다]

trunk /trʌŋk/ n **1** the thick central wooden stem of a tree that branches grow on ‖ 가지가 자라는 나무의 굵직한 중심부 목질 줄기. 나무의 몸통. 수간(樹幹) **2** an enclosed space in the back of a car where you can put large bags, tools etc. ‖ 큰 가방이나 연장 등을 넣을 수 있는 차의 뒤에 있는 둘러싸인 공간. 트렁크 — see picture on page 943 **3** the very long nose of an ELEPHANT ‖ 코끼리의 매우 긴 코 **4** a large box that you store clothes, books etc. in, often used when traveling ‖ 흔히 여행할 때 사용되는, 옷·책 등을 담는 큰 상자. 대형 여행 가방. 트렁크 **5** TECHNICAL the main part of your body, not including your head, arms, or legs ‖ 머리[팔, 다리]를 포함하지 않는 몸의 주요한 부분. 몸통 —compare TORSO

trunks /trʌŋks/ n [plural] very short pants that men wear when swimming ‖ 수영할 때 남자들이 입는 매우 짧은 바지. (수영) 팬츠. 트렁크스

trust¹ /trʌst/ v **1** [T] to believe that someone is honest and will not hurt you, cheat you, disobey you etc. ‖ 남이 정직하며 자기를 해치지·속이지·거역하지 않을 것이라고 믿다. 신뢰[신용]하다: *I've never trusted her.* 나는 결코 그녀를 신뢰하지 않았다. / *Can you trust him with your car?* (=believe he will not damage it) (안심하고) 그에게 차를 맡길 수 있느냐? **2** [T] to depend on something ‖ 어떤 것에 의지하다. 의존하다: *Trust your instincts.* 너의 직관을 믿고 따르라. **3 I trust** SPOKEN FORMAL used in order to say that you hope something is true ‖ 어떤 것이 사실이길 바란다고 말하는 데에 쓰여. …을 믿다[확신하다]: *I trust that you had a successful business trip.* 나는 당신이 출장을 잘 다녀왔을 것으로 믿습니다.

trust in sb/sth *phr v* [T] FORMAL to believe that you can depend on someone or something ‖ 다른 사람이나 사물을 의지할 수 있다고 믿다. 신뢰하다

trust² n **1** [U] the belief that you can trust someone ‖ 남을 신뢰할 수 있는 믿음. 신임. 신뢰: *It took three years to earn his trust.* 그의 신임을 얻는 데 3년이 걸렸다. —opposite DISTRUST¹ **2** [U] an arrangement in which someone legally controls your money or property,

usually until you are old enough to use it ‖ 보통 자신의 돈이나 재산을 사용할 수 있을 만한 나이가 될 때까지 다른 사람이 합법적으로 그 돈이나 재산을 관리하는 제도. 신탁(제도): *$100,000 is being held in trust for his daughter.* 10만 달러가 그의 딸을 위해서 신탁되어져 있다. **3** a group of companies that work together to reduce competition ‖ 경쟁을 줄이기 위해 서로 협조하는 기업들의 집단. 기업 합동. 트러스트

trust·ee /trʌ'sti/ n a person or company that legally controls someone else's property ‖ 법적으로 다른 사람의 재산을 관리하는 사람이나 회사. 피신탁인. 수탁자(受託者)

trust·ing /'trʌstɪŋ/, **trust·ful** /'trʌstfəl/ adj willing or too willing to trust someone ‖ 남을 쉽게 믿거나 너무 잘 믿는. 신용[신뢰]하는: *a trusting little child* 의심할 줄 모르는 어린아이

trust·wor·thy /'trʌst,wɚði/ adj able to be trusted or depended on ‖ 믿을 수 있거나 의존할 수 있는. 신뢰[신용, 의지]할 만한

trust·y /'trʌsti/ adj HUMOROUS a trusty weapon, horse, friend etc. is one you can depend on ‖ 무기[말, 친구] 등이 의지할 수 있는. 신뢰할 수 있는

truth /truθ/ n **1 the truth** the true facts about something ‖ 어떤 것에 대한 진실. 실상: *Do you think he's telling the truth?* 그가 진실을 말하고 있다고 생각하니? **2** [U] the state or quality of being true ‖ 진실인 상태나 특질. 진실성. 사실과의 일치: *There was no truth in what she said.* 그녀의 말에는 진실성이 없었다. / *a poem about truth and beauty* 진실과 아름다움에 대한 시 **3** FORMAL an important fact or idea that is accepted as being true ‖ 참된 것으로 인정되는 중요한 사실이나 생각. 진리. 명제: *scientific truths* 과학적인 진리들 **4 to tell (you) the truth** SPOKEN used when you admit something or tell someone your true opinion ‖ 어떤 것을 인정하거나 남에게 자신의 진실된 의견을 말할 때에 쓰여. 사실대로 말하면. 실은: *To tell you the truth, I don't care where she went.* 사실대로 말하면 그녀가 어디에 갔든 개의치 않아.

truth·ful /'truθfəl/ adj giving the true facts about something ‖ 어떤 것에 대해 참된 사실을 주는. 진실인. 옳은: *He swore his statement was truthful and accurate.* 그는 자기의 진술이 진실하고 정확하다고 맹세했다. – **truthfully** adv

try¹ /traɪ/ v **tried, tried, trying 1** [I, T]

to attempt to do something ‖ 어떤 것을 하기를 시도하다. …하려고 하다. 노력하다: *Please try to come early.* 부디 일찍 오도록 해봐. / *Greg tried hard not to laugh.* 그레그는 웃지 않으려고 애썼다. / *Just try your best – it doesn't matter if you win or lose.* 단지 최선을 다해 봐라. 이기느냐 지느냐 문제가 되지 않는다. **2** [T] to do something, test something, or go somewhere, in order to find out if it is useful or will be successful ‖ 어떤 것이 유용한지 또는 성공적일지 알아내기 위해 해보다[시험하다, 어떤 곳에 가다]. 시험삼아 해보다: *Try the other light switch.* 다른 전기 스위치를 켜 봐. / *"Where's Bob?" "Try the next room."* "밥은 어디 있지?" "옆방을 찾아봐." **3** [T] to do, use, or taste something in order to find out if it is suitable or good ‖ 어떤 것이 적합하거나 좋은지 알아내려고 해보다[써보다, 맛보다]. 착수[시용, 시식]해 보다: *Do they fit or do you want to try a bigger size?* 몸에 맞니, 아니면 더 큰 사이즈를 입어 볼래? / *Try some of this cake!* 이 케이크를 좀 먹어 봐라! **4** [T] to examine and judge a person or a legal case in a court of law ‖ 법정에서 사람이나 법률 사건을 심문하고 재판하다. 심리[재판]하다: *Three men were tried for murder.* 세 사람은 살인죄로 재판받았다. **5 try sb's patience/nerves/temper etc.** to make someone start to feel impatient, nervous, angry etc. ‖ 남이 조바심 나게·불안하게·화나게 느끼기 시작하게 만들다. 참기 어렵게 하다/불안을 금치 못하게 하다/성질을 돋우다

try sth ↔ **on** *phr v* [T] to put on a piece of clothing to find out if it fits or makes you look attractive ‖ 옷이 맞는지 또는 매력적으로 보이는지 알아보려고 옷을 입다. 입어 보다: *Would you like to try those jeans on?* 그 진 바지들을 입어 보겠습니까?

try sth ↔ **out** *phr v* [T] to attempt to use something in order to find out if it works or is good ‖ 제대로 작동하는지 또는 양호한지 확인하기 위해 어떤 것을 사용해 보다. 시험해 보다: *When are you going to try out your new software?* 너는 새 소프트웨어를 언제 시험해 볼 거냐?

try out for sth *phr v* [T] to be tested in order to become a member of a team, an actor in a play etc. ‖ 팀의 일원이나 연극 배우 등이 되기 위해 테스트를 받다. …자리를 얻으려고 겨루다[도전해 보다]: *Sandra's trying out for the girls' basketball team.* 산드라는 여자 농구팀 선수 자리에 도전해 보려 한다.

try² *n* [C usually singular] an attempt to do something ‖ 일을 하는 시도. 시험: *I've never skated before, but I'll give it a try.* 나는 스케이트를 타 본 적이 전혀 없지만, 한번 타 보겠다.

try·ing /'traɪ-ɪŋ/ *adj* difficult and unpleasant to deal with ‖ 다루기 어렵거나 불쾌한. 괴로운. 쓰라린: *It's been a very trying time for us all.* 그것은 우리 모두에게 매우 괴로운 시간이었다.

try·out /'traɪ-aʊt/ *n* an occasion when someone is tested to decide whether s/he is good enough to be on a sports team ‖ 어떤 사람이 스포츠 팀에 들어가도 좋겠는지 결정하기 위해 테스트 받는 경우. 선수 선발 테스트

tsar /zɑr, tsɑr/ *n* ⇨ CZAR

T-shirt /'ti ʃət/ *n* a soft cotton shirt, with short SLEEVEs and no collar ‖ 소매가 짧으며 깃이 없는 부드러운 무명 셔츠. 티셔츠

tsp. *n* the written abbreviation of TEASPOON ‖ teaspoon의 약어

tub /tʌb/ *n* **1** ⇨ BATHTUB **2** a plastic or paper container with a lid, that food is sold in ‖ 음식을 담아 파는 뚜껑이 달린 플라스틱이나 종이 용기. 소형 용기: *a tub of ice cream* 아이스크림 용기 **3** a large round container used for washing things, storing things etc. ‖ 물건을 씻거나 저장하는 등에 사용되는 크고 둥근 용기. 통

tu·ba /'tubə/ *n* a large metal musical instrument with a wide opening that points straight up, that you play by blowing ‖ 입으로 불어 연주하며 똑바로 위를 향한 넓은 개구부(開口部)가 있는 커다란 금관 악기. 튜바

tub·by /'tʌbi/ *adj* INFORMAL short and fat ‖ 키가 작고 뚱뚱한. 땅딸막한. 똥똥한

tu·be /tub/ *n* **1** a pipe made of metal, plastic, glass etc., especially one that liquids or gases go through ‖ 특히 액체나 기체가 통과하는, 금속·플라스틱·유리 등으로 만든 관. 통: *tubes coming out of the patient's nose and mouth* 환자의 코와 입에 연결되어 나오는 관 **2** a container for a soft substance, that you SQUEEZE to push the substance out ‖ 부드러운 물질을 밖으로 밀어서 짜는 용기. 튜브: *a tube of toothpaste* 치약 한 통 —see picture at CONTAINER **3** one of the parts inside the body shaped like a tube ‖ 튜브처럼 생긴 몸 안의 기관들 중의 하나. 관: *a fallopian tube* (=part of a woman's organs for having babies) 나팔관 **4 go down the tubes** if a situation goes down the tubes, it suddenly becomes bad‖상황이 갑자기 악화되다. 수포로 돌아가다. 헛일이 되다: *My career's going down the tubes.* 나의 경력이 수포로 돌아가게 생겼다. **5 the tube** SPOKEN the television‖텔레비전: *What's on the tube?* 텔레비전에서 무엇을 방영하느냐?

tu·ber·cu·lo·sis /tʊˌbɚkyəˈloʊsɪs/ *n* [U] a serious infectious disease that affects the lungs and other parts of the body‖폐와 몸의 다른 기관을 침범하는 심각한 전염병. 결핵

tub·ing /ˈtubɪŋ/ *n* [U] tubes, usually connected together in a system‖보통 한 시스템에 서로 연결된 관. 배관: *copper tubing* 구리 배관

tu·bu·lar /ˈtubyəlɚ/ *adj* made of tubes or shaped like a tube‖관으로 만든, 혹은 관 모양의. 관의

tuck[1] /tʌk/ *v* **1** [T] to push the edge of a cloth or piece of clothing into something so that it stays in place‖천이나 옷자락이 제대로 자리하도록 어떤 것 속으로 밀어 넣다. 쑤셔[말아, 끼워] 넣다: *He tucked in his shirt and combed his hair.* 그는 셔츠 자락을 집어 넣고 머리를 빗질했다. **2** to put something in a small space, or a safe place‖어떤 것을 작은 공간이나 안전한 장소에 넣어 두다. 치워[깊이 넣어, 감추어] 두다: *She tucked the money into her pocket.* 그녀는 그 돈을 호주머니 속에 깊이 찔러 넣었다. **3** to move the arms, legs, or head close to the body and keep it there‖팔[다리, 머리]을 몸통 가까이로 이동시켜 거기에 그대로 두다. 구부려서 당기다. 움츠리다: *The duck had its head tucked under its wing.* 오리는 머리를 날개 밑에 묻었다. **4 tucked away** in a safe or hidden place‖안전하거나 숨긴 장소에. 숨겨진. 눈에 띄지 않는: *a little cabin tucked away in the mountains* 산 속 깊이 자리한 작은 오두막집

tuck sb ↔ **in** *phr v* [T] to make a child feel comfortable in bed by tightly covering him/her with a BLANKET‖담요로 꼭 덮어서 어린애가 침대에서 포근하게 느끼게 하다. 감싸[덮어] 주다

tuck[2] *n* **1** a fold of cloth sewn flat in a piece of clothing‖의류에 편평하게 꿰매어 붙인 천의 접은 부분. 단 **2** a medical operation to make someone look thinner or younger‖사람이 보다 홀쭉하거나 젊어 보이게 하는 수술. 미용 성형 수술: *a tummy tuck* 복부 지방 제거 수술

Tues·day /ˈtuzdi, -deɪ/, *written abbreviation* **Tues.** *n* the third day of the week‖한 주의 세 번째 날. 화요일 — see usage note at SUNDAY

tuft /tʌft/ *n* a short thick group of hairs, feathers, grass etc.‖머리털·깃털·잔디 등의 짧고 무성한 뭉치. 다발. 술: *a tuft of hair* 한 뭉치의 머리카락 – **tufted** *adj*

tug[1] /tʌg/ *v* **-gged, -gging** [I, T] to pull something suddenly and hard‖물건을 갑자기 세게 당기다. 세게 잡아[끌어]당기다: *Alice tugged at my hand, saying "Let's go!"* 앨리스는 "가자!"라고 말하면서 내 손을 힘껏 잡아당겼다.

tug[2] *n* **1** also **tug boat** a small strong boat used for pulling ships‖배를 예인하는 데 사용되는 작고 힘이 센 배. 예인선 **2** a sudden strong pull‖갑자기 강하게 잡아당기기. 세게 잡아당기기

tug-of-war /ˌ. . . ˈ./ *n* a competition in which two teams pull on the opposite ends of a rope‖두 팀이 로프의 반대편 끝에서 끌어당기는 경기. 줄다리기

tu·i·tion /tuˈɪʃən/ *n* [U] **1** the money you pay for being taught‖배우는 대가로 지불하는 돈. 수업료: *Tuition went up to $3000 last semester.* 수업료는 지난 학기에 3천 달러까지 올랐다. **2** the act of teaching‖가르치는 행위. 교육. 교수: *Ben improved his grades under the tuition of Mr. Neals.* 벤은 닐스 씨의 지도로 성적을 올렸다.

tu·lip /ˈtulɪp/ *n* a tall brightly colored garden flower, shaped like a cup‖컵처럼 생긴, 키가 크고 밝은 색깔을 띤 정원용 꽃. 튤립

tum·ble /ˈtʌmbəl/ *v* [I] to fall or roll in a sudden uncontrolled way‖갑작스럽게 중심을 잃고 떨어지거나 구르다. 곤두박질치다. 굴러 떨어지다: *Losing her balance, she tumbled down the stairs.* 균형을 잃고 그녀는 계단에서 굴러 떨어졌다. / *They think California will tumble into the ocean one day.* 그들은 캘리포니아가 언젠가 대양 속으로 무너져 내릴 거라고 생각한다. – **tumble** *n*

tum·bler /ˈtʌmblɚ/ *n* a glass with a flat bottom and no handle‖바닥이 편평하고 손잡이가 없는 유리잔. 큰 컵. 텀블러

tum·my /ˈtʌmi/ *n* INFORMAL stomach‖배: *Mommy, I have a tummy ache.* 엄마, 배가 아파요.

tu·mor /ˈtumɚ/ *n* a group of cells in the body that grow too quickly and cause sickness or health problems‖너무 빨리 자라며 병이나 건강 문제를 일으키는 인체 내 세포 덩어리. 종양. 종기: *a brain tumor* 뇌종양

tu·mult /ˈtumʌlt/ *n* [C, U] FORMAL a state of confusion, excitement, or other strong emotions‖혼란[흥분, 여타 강렬한 감정]의 상태. 소란. 소동: *the tumult*

of civil war 격동의 내란 / *the tumult of angry thoughts in her head* 그녀의 머리 속에서 소용돌이치는 분한 생각 –
tumultuous /tʊˈmʌltʃuəs/ *adj*

tu·na /ˈtuːnə/ *n* [C, U] a large common ocean fish, or the meat from this fish, usually sold in cans || 보통 캔으로 (포장 해서) 파는 크고 흔한 바다 물고기, 또는 이 물고기의 살코기. 참치[다랑어](살)

tun·dra /ˈtʌndrə/ *n* [U] the large flat areas of land in northern areas where it is very cold and there are no trees || 날씨가 매우 춥고 나무가 없는 북쪽 지방의 크고 편평한 지대. 툰드라

tune¹ /tuːn/ *n* 1 a series of musical notes that are nice to listen to || 듣기가 좋은 연속된 곡조. 가락. 선율. 멜로디: *Jill was humming a little tune to herself.* 질은 약간의 가락을 흥얼거리고 있었다. 2 **in tune/out of tune** playing or singing the correct musical notes, or playing or singing notes that are slightly too high or low || 올바른 음조로 연주하거나 노래하는, 또는 다소 높거나 낮은 음조로 연주하거나 노래하는. 곡조가 맞는/틀리는: *My guitar's completely out of tune.* 내 기타는 음이 전혀 안 맞는다. 3 **be in tune with/be out of tune with** to understand what someone needs, thinks, and wants, or to not understand this || 남이 필요로 하는·생각하는·원하는 것을 이해하다, 또는 이해하지 않다. 조화[일치, 동감]하다/하지 않다: *We try to stay in tune with students' needs.* 우리는 학생들의 요구에 부응하려고 애쓰고 있다. 4 **change your tune** to suddenly have a different opinion about something || 어떤 일에 관해 갑자기 전혀 다른 의견을 가지다. 의견[태도]를 바꾸다

tune² *v* [T] 1 to make a small change to a musical instrument so that it plays the correct PITCH || 정확한 음높이를 연주하도록 악기에 작은 변화를 주다. 악기를 조율하다: *We need to have the piano tuned.* 우리는 피아노의 음을 조정해야 한다. 2 to make a television or radio receive broadcasts from a particular CHANNEL or STATION || 텔레비전이나 라디오를 특정한 채널이나 방송국의 방송(신호)을 수신하게 하다. 선국하다. 채널을 조정하다: *Stay tuned for more great music on KHPI, the city's best rock station.* 더 좋은 음악을 듣기 위해 시에서 최고의 록 방송국인 KHPI에 채널을 맞춰 주세요. 3 to make small changes to an engine so that it works better || 엔진이 더 잘 작동하도록 엔진에 작은 변화를 주다. 엔진을 정비[조정]하다

tune in *phr v* 1 [I,T **tune** sth ↔ **in**] to watch or listen to a particular television or radio program, or to make your television or radio receive that program || 특정한 텔레비전이나 라디오 프로그램을 시청하거나 듣다, 또는 텔레비전이나 라디오를 특정한 프로그램을 수신하게 하다: *Over 3 million viewers tune in to our show daily.* 3백만 이상의 시청자가 매일 우리 쇼를 시청한다. 2 **tuned in** INFORMAL knowing what is happening around you or what other people are thinking || 자기 주위에 일어나는 일이나 다른 사람이 생각하는 것을 알고 있는. 소식에 밝은[정통한]: *Jean's really tuned in to the local music scene.* 진은 정말 그 지역 음악계에 정통하다.

tune out *phr v* [I,T **tune** sb ↔ **out**] INFORMAL to ignore someone or something, or to stop listening to him, her, or it || 다른 사람이나 사물을 무시하다, 또는 다른 사람이나 사물의 말을 듣지 않다. 개의치 않다. 귀를 기울이지 않다: *It's hard to tune out the noise in the office sometimes.* 때때로 사무실에서 소음에 개의치 않기란 어렵다.

tune up *phr v* 1 [T **tune** sth ↔ **up**] to fix and clean a car's engine || 차의 엔진을 수리하고 청소하다. 엔진을 조정[정비]하다 2 [I, T **tune** sth ↔ **up**] to prepare a musical instrument so that it plays at the same PITCH as other instruments || 다른 악기와 똑같은 음높이에서 연주하도록 악기를 준비하다. 같은 음에 맞추다

tun·er /ˈtuːnɚ/ *n* a piece of electronic equipment that lets you choose which electrical signal your radio, television etc. receives || 라디오나 텔레비전 등이 어떤 전기 신호를 수신할지 선택하게 하는 전자 장비. 튜너. 채널 선택 장치

tune-up /ˈ. ./ *n* an occasion when someone fixes and cleans your car's engine, or the process of doing this || 다른 사람이 자동차의 엔진을 수리하고 깨끗이 하는 경우, 또는 이렇게 하는 과정. 엔진 정비[조정](과정)

tu·nic /ˈtuːnɪk/ *n* a long loose piece of clothing, usually without SLEEVEs, often worn with a belt || 보통 소매가 없고 종종 허리띠를 매서 입는 길고 헐렁한 옷가지. 튜닉

tun·nel¹ /ˈtʌnl/ *n* a passage that has been dug under the ground or through a mountain, usually for cars or trains || 보통 차나 기차용으로 지하나 산을 관통하여 파 놓은 통로. 터널. 지하도

tunnel² *v* [I] to dig a TUNNEL || 터널을 파다

tunnel vi·sion /'.. ,../ *n* **1** the tendency to think about only one subject, so that you forget other things that may be important too ‖ 오직 한 가지 주제에만 골몰하여 마찬가지로 중요할지 모르는 다른 것들을 잊어버리는 경향. 극단적으로 시야가 좁음. 편협 **2** a condition in which someone's eyes are damaged so that they can only see straight ahead ‖ 사람의 눈이 손상되어 곧장 앞으로만 볼 수 있는 상태. 시야 협착증

Tup·per·ware /'tʌpɚˌwɛr/ *n* [U] TRADEMARK a type of plastic container with a tight lid, used for storing food ‖ 음식 보관에 쓰이는, 밀폐 덮개가 있는 플라스틱 용기의 일종. 터퍼웨어

tur·ban /'tɚbən/ *n* a long piece of cloth that is worn twisted around the top of your head ‖ 머리 꼭대기에 감아 두르는 긴 천 조각. 터번

tur·bine /'tɚbaɪn, -bɪn/ *n* an engine that works when the pressure from liquid or steam moves a special wheel inside it ‖ 액체나 증기의 압력이 엔진 내부의 특수한 바퀴를 움직일 때 작동하는 엔진. 터빈

tur·bu·lence /'tɚbyələns/ *n* [U] **1** strong changing movements of air or water ‖ 공기나 물의 강하게 변화하는 움직임. 난(기)류: *There was a lot of turbulence during the flight.* 비행 중에 많은 난기류가 있었다. **2** a situation in which people's thoughts, actions, and emotions are always changing ‖ 사람의 생각·행동·감정이 항상 변화하고 있는 상황. 동요. 소란: *political turbulence* 정치적인 소요

tur·bu·lent /'tɚbyələnt/ *adj* **1** experiencing a lot of sudden changes and often wars or violence ‖ 갑자기 많은 변화와 종종 전쟁이나 폭동을 경험하는. 소란[불안]스런. 요동치는. 격변하는: *the turbulent years before the Revolution* 명예 혁명 전의 격동의 몇 해 **2** turbulent winds, oceans etc. are full of strong changing movements ‖ 바람·대양 등이 강하게 변화하는 움직임으로 가득한. 험악한. 악천후의

turd /tɚd/ *n* **1** INFORMAL an impolite word for a piece of solid waste passed from the body ‖ 신체에서 배출된 굳은 배설물 덩어리에 대한 비속어. (한 덩어리의) 똥 **2** SPOKEN a very impolite word for an unpleasant person ‖ 불쾌한 사람에 대한 아주 저속한 말. 인간쓰레기. 싫은 놈

tu·reen /tʊ'rin/ *n* a large dish with a lid, used especially for serving soup ‖ 특히 수프를 차려내기 위해 사용되는 뚜껑이 있는 큰 접시

turf /tɚf/ *n* **1** [U] grass and soil on the ground's surface, or an artificial substance made to look like this ‖ 땅 표면의 잔디와 토양, 또는 이렇게 보이게 만든 인공 물질. 잔디(밭). 인공 잔디: *thick moist turf* 무성하고 축축한 잔디 / *The game was played on artificial turf.* 경기는 인공 잔디에서 벌어졌다. **2** INFORMAL an area that someone knows well and feels that s/he controls or owns ‖ 어떤 사람이 잘 알며 자신이 지배하거나 소유한다고 느끼는 지역. 세력권. 전문[활동] 영역: *The gangs will not allow any non-members onto their turf.* 갱들은 자기네 세력권역에 어떤 침입자도 허용하지 않을 것이다.

tur·gid /'tɚdʒɪd/ *adj* **1** boring and difficult to understand ‖ 지겹고 이해하기가 어려운. 난해한: *turgid poetry* 난해한 시 **2** swollen, especially with liquid ‖ (특히 액체로) 부풀어 오른. 부은

tur·key /'tɚki/ *n* [C, U] a bird similar to a chicken but larger, or the meat from this bird ‖ 닭과 비슷하지만 보다 큰 조류(鳥類), 또는 이 새의 고기. 터키(의 살코기) —see also COLD TURKEY

tur·moil /'tɚmɔɪl/ *n* [singular, U] a state of confusion, excitement, and trouble ‖ 혼란·흥분·분쟁의 상태. 소란. 동요: *In 1967 the country was in racial turmoil.* 1967년에 그 나라는 인종 분규의 상태에 있었다.

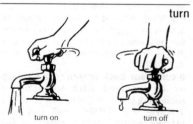

turn

turn on   turn off

turn¹ /tɚn/ *v*

1 ▸YOUR BODY 신체◂ [I] to move your body so that you are looking in a different direction ‖ 다른 방향을 보도록 신체를 움직이다. 돌리다. 향하다: *Alison turned towards us.* 앨리슨은 우리 쪽으로 몸을 돌렸다. / *Turn around so I can see the back of the dress.* 내가 드레스의 뒤쪽을 볼 수 있게 돌아봐라. / *He turned to look behind him.* 그는 뒤를 돌아다 보았다.

2 ▸OBJECT 물체◂ [T] to move an object

so that it is facing in a different direction ‖ 물체를 움직여서 다른 방향으로 향하게 하다. 뒤집다. 빙 돌리다: *She turned the box around/over to look at the label.* 그녀는 라벨을 보려고 상자를 빙 돌렸다[뒤집었다].

3 ▶DIRECTION 방향◀ [I] to go in a new direction when you are walking, driving etc. ‖ 걷거나 운전을 할 때 새로운 방향으로 나아가다. …의 진행 방향을 바꾸다: *Turn right at the next stop light.* 다음 신호등에서 우회전하세요.

4 ▶MOVE AROUND A CENTRAL POINT 중심점 주위를 움직이다◀ [I, T] to move around a central point that does not move ‖ 움직이지 않는 중심점 주위를 움직이다. 돌다. 회전하다: *The wheels turned slowly.* 바퀴가 천천히 돌았다.

5 ▶AGE 연령◀ [linking verb] to become a particular age ‖ 특정한 연령이 되다. …에 이르다: *Megan's just turned four.* 메간은 이제 막 4살이 되었다.

6 ▶COLOR 색깔◀ [linking verb] **a)** to become a different color ‖ 다른 색깔이 되다. …으로 변하다: *His hair is turning gray.* 그의 머리카락은 백발이 되어가고 있다. / *Helen turned bright red.* (=because she was embarrassed) 헬렌은 (당황해서)얼굴이 새빨개졌다.

7 ▶CHANGE 변화◀ [linking verb] to become different from before ‖ 이전과 다르게 되다. 바뀌다. 변하다: *The weather will turn colder.* 날씨가 더 추워질 것이다. / *The crowd turned violent when the soccer team lost.* 그 축구 팀이 패하자 군중들은 난폭해졌다.

8 ▶PAGE 페이지◀ [T] to move a page in a book or magazine so that you can see the next one ‖ 다음 페이지를 볼 수 있게 책이나 잡지의 페이지를 이동시키다. 페이지를 넘기다

9 turn your back (on) to refuse to help or be involved with someone or something ‖ 다른 사람이나 사물을 돕거나 관계하는 것을 거절하다. …에 등을 돌리다: *She wouldn't turn her back on her friends.* 그녀는 자신의 친구들에게 등을 돌리지는 않을 것이다.

10 turn your nose up at to refuse to accept something because you do not think it is good enough for you ‖ 자신에게 충분히 좋다고 생각하지 않기 때문에 어떤 것을 받아들이기를 거절하다. 우습게 보다. 깔보고 물리치다: *He won't turn his nose up at a $3000 pay raise.* 그는 3천 달러 임금 인상에는 코방귀를 뀌지는 않을 것이다.

11 turn over a new leaf to decide that you will change your behavior to make it better ‖ 자신의 행동을 더 좋아지게 바꿀 것을 결심하다. 마음[행실]을 고치다. 생활을 일신하다: *I'm going to turn over a new leaf and start exercising.* 나는 생활을 일신하고 운동을 시작하려고 한다.

12 turn a deaf ear/turn a blind eye to ignore what someone is saying or doing ‖ 남이 말하거나 하고 있는 것을 무시하다. …을 전혀 들으려고 하지 않다/…을 보고도 전혀 못 본 체하다: *The State has turned a deaf ear to the public's health needs.* 주 당국은 공중위생의 필요성에 전연 귀를 기울이려고 하지 않았다.

13 turn the tables (on sb) to become stronger or better than an opponent who has been stronger or better than you ‖ 지금까지 자신보다 더 강하거나 더 나았던 적수보다 더 강하거나 더 나아지다. 형세[국면]를 역전[전환]시키다. 주객을 전도시키다: *The team managed to turn the tables in the second half of the game.* 그 팀은 경기 후반전에서야 겨우 국면을 전환시켰다.

14 turn sb/sth loose to allow a person or animal to be free to do what she, he, or it wants ‖ 사람·동물을 자유롭게 해서 원하는 것을 하도록 허용하다. …을 풀어 주다. (감금 등에서) 해방시키다

15 turn a profit to make a profit ‖ 이익을 내다

turn sb against sb/sth *phr v* [T] to make someone stop liking or agreeing with someone or something ‖ 남이 다른 사람이나 사물을 좋아하거나 동의하는 것을 중단하게 만들다. 남을 …에 대해 거부[반대]하게 하다: *His experiences in Vietnam turned him against the war.* 그는 월남에서 겪은 경험 때문에 전쟁을 반대했다.

turn sth ↔ **around** *phr v* [T] **1** to complete the process of making a product or providing a service ‖ 제품 생산이나 서비스 제공 과정을 완료하다: *We can turn around 500 units by next week.* 우리는 다음 주까지는 500개를 생산 완료할 수 있다. **2** to make a plan, business etc. that was not working well begin to work ‖ 잘 운영되지 않았던 계획·사업 등을 가동되기 시작하게 하다. (나쁜 상황을) 호전[정상화]시키다: *It's taken four years, but we've turned the business around.* 4년이나 걸렸지만 우리는 사업을 호전시켰다.

turn away *phr v* **1** [T **turn** sb ↔ **away**] to refuse to let people into a theater, restaurant etc. because it is too full ‖ 만원이어서 극장·식당 등에 사람을 입장시키

기를 거절하다. …에서 되돌려 보내다: *By 6:00, we were turning people away.* 6시경에 우리는 사람들의 입장을 거절하는 상황이었다. **2** [I,T **turn** sb ↔ **away**] to refuse to give sympathy, help, or support ‖ 동정[원조, 지지]해 주기를 거절하다. 외면하다. 퇴짜놓다: *We never turn patients away, even if they don't have money.* 비록 환자가 돈이 없어도 우리는 결코 그들을 쫓아 내지 않는다. / *The US cannot just turn away from the world's problems.* 미국은 그저 세계 문제를 외면해 버릴 수만은 없다.

turn back *phr v* [I, T **turn** sb ↔ **back**] **1** to go in the opposite direction, or to tell someone to do this ‖ 반대 방향으로 가다, 또는 남에게 이렇게 하라고 말하다. 되돌아가다[가게 하다]: *Travelers had to turn back because of the snow.* 여행자들은 눈 때문에 되돌아가야 했다. / *The journalists were turned back at the border.* 기자들은 국경에서 되돌려 보내졌다. **2 turn back the clock** to try to do things the way they were done in the past ‖ 과거에 행해졌던 방식으로 일을 하려 하다. 예전으로 돌아가다

turn down *phr v* [T] **1** [**turn** sth ↔ **down**] to make a machine such as a television, OVEN etc. produce less sound, heat etc. ‖ 텔레비전·오븐 등의 기계가 소리·열 등을 덜 내게 하다. 약하게 하다. 줄이다. 낮추다: *Can you turn your radio down a little bit?* 라디오 소리를 조금 줄여 주겠니? **2** [**turn** sb/sth ↔ **down**] to refuse an offer, request, or invitation ‖ 제안[요청, 초청]을 거절하다. 물리치다. 각하하다: *If he asks me, I'll turn him down.* 만일 그가 나에게 요청한다면 나는 그의 요청을 거절할 것이다. / *Diane turned down the job offer.* 다이앤은 그 일자리 제안을 거부했다. —see usage note at REFUSE[1]

turn in *phr v* **1** [T **turn** sth ↔ **in**] to give something you find to someone in authority so that it can be returned to the owner ‖ 발견한 사물을 소유자에게 돌아갈 수 있게 당국자에게 주다. 돌려주다. 반환하다: *Luckily someone had turned my purse in.* 다행히도 누군가가 내 지갑을 돌려주었다. **2** [T **turn** sth ↔ **in**] to give work that you have done to the teacher to be given a grade ‖ 완료한 과제를 점수가 매겨지도록 선생님에게 주다. 제출하다: *Has everyone turned in last night's homework?* 어젯밤 숙제는 모두 제출했지요? **3** [T **turn** sb ↔ **in**] to tell the police where a criminal is ‖ 범인의 소재를 경찰에 알리다. 신고하다 **4** [I]

INFORMAL to go to bed ‖ 자러 가다. 잠자리에 들다: *I think I'll turn in.* 나 자러 가야겠어.

turn into sth *phr v* [T] [also **turn** sth **into** sth] to become something different, or to make someone or something do this ‖ 다른 사물이 되다, 또는 사람이나 사물이 이렇게 되게 하다. …을 …으로 바꾸다. 변하다. 변모되다: *The argument turned into a fight.* 논쟁이 싸움으로 바뀌었다. / *The witch turned the frog into a prince.* 마녀는 개구리를 왕자로 변신시켰다.

turn off *phr v* **1** [T **turn** sth ↔ **off**] to stop a supply of water, electricity etc., especially so that a machine stops working ‖ 기계의 작동을 멈추도록 물·전기 등의 공급을 중단하다. 잠그다. 끄다: *Turn off the television – it's dinner time.* 텔레비전을 꺼라. 저녁 식사 시간이다. / *Who turned the water off?* 누가 수돗물을 잠갔니? —see usage note at OPEN[2] **2** [I,T **turn off** sth] to drive off one road and onto another, often a smaller one ‖ 한 도로에서 벗어나 다른 도로, 종종 보다 작은 도로로 운전해 가다. (간선 도로에서) 샛길로 진입하다. …에서 다른 길로 빠져 나가다: *Make sure you turn off at the next exit.* 다음 출구에서 반드시 샛길로 진입하세요. / *We turned off the highway looking for a place to eat.* 우리는 식사할 곳을 찾아 고속도로에서 빠져 나갔다. **3** [T **turn** sb **off**] to make someone decide that s/he does not like someone or something, often in a sexual way ‖ 남에게 흔히 성적으로 다른 사람이나 사물을 좋아하지 않도록 결심하게 하다. (성적) 흥미를 잃게 하다: *I was turned off by the doctor's attitude – he just didn't care.* 나는 그 의사의 태도에 흥미를 잃어 버렸다. 그는 별로 관심이 없었다. / *She says skinny men turn her off.* 그녀는 말라빠진 남자에게서는 성적 매력을 느끼지 못한다고 말한다. —see also TURN-OFF

turn on *phr v* [T] **1** [**turn** sth ↔ **on**] to make the supply of water, electricity etc. begin to flow through a pipe, machine etc., so that it starts working ‖ 물·전기 등의 공급이 도관·기계 등을 통해 흐르기 시작하게 하여 그 작동을 시작하게 하다. 틀다. (텔레비전 등을) 켜다: *Could you turn on the dishwasher/TV?* 자동 식기 세척기[텔레비전]를 켜 주시겠어요? / *Has the gas company turned on the gas yet?* 가스 회사는 가스를 벌써 켰습니까? —see usage note at OPEN[2] **2** [**turn on** sb] to suddenly attack someone physically or using unpleasant words, after being nice to him/her ‖ 남에게 잘 대하다가 갑자기 신체적으로 또는 불쾌한 말을 쓰면서 공격하다. 돌변해서 대들다. 적대 관계를 취하다: *The dog turned on him and bit him.* 그 개가 그에게 덤벼들 더니 물어버렸다. **3 [turn sb on]** to make someone sexually excited ‖ 남을 성적으 로 흥분시키다

turn out *phr v* **1** [linking verb] to happen in a particular way, or to have a particular result ‖ 특정한 방식으로 발생 하다, 또는 특정한 결과를 얻다. …임이 드 러나다. 결국은 …으로 되다[판명되다]: *Are you happy with the way your essay turned out?* 너의 에세이가 그렇게 씌어 진 것에 만족하니? / *It turned out that he was married to someone else!* 그는 결 국 다른 사람과 결혼하고 말았어! **2** [T **turn** sth ↔ **out**] if you turn out a light, you push a button to stop the flow of electricity ‖ 전기의 흐름을 차단하기 위해 스위치를 누르다. (불·전기를) 끄다: *Don't forget to turn out the lights when you leave.* 나갈 때 불을 끄는 것을 잊지 마라. **3** [I] if people turn out for an event, they come to it ‖ 사람들이 행사에 (나)가다. 참석[출석]하다: *Only about 30 people turned out for the show.* 약 30명 만이 그 쇼에 참석했다. —see also TURNOUT **4** [T **turn** sth ↔ **out**] to produce or make something ‖ 사물을 생 산하거나 만들어내다. 배출하다: *Why do our high schools turn out students who can't read?* 왜 우리 고등학교는 문맹 학 생을 배출해 내지요? **5** [T **turn** sb **out**] to make someone leave his/her home ‖ 남을 그 사람의 집에서 떠나게 하다. 쫓아 내다

turn over *phr v* [T] **1** [turn sth ↔ **over to** sb] to give someone the right to own something such as a plan, business, piece of property, or to make him/her responsible for it ‖ 남에게 계획·사업·자 산 등을 소유할 권리를 주다, 또는 그에게 그 책임을 지게 하다. 양도하다. (책임 따 위를) 위임하다: *The industry is being turned over to private ownership.* 그 산 업은 민간 업체로 양도되는 중이다. **2** [turn sth ↔ **over**] to bring a criminal to the police or another official organization ‖ 범죄자를 경찰이나 다른 공 적인 기관에 데려다. (사람을 경찰에)건 네주다. 인도하다: *Benson was turned over to the FBI yesterday.* 벤슨은 어제 FBI에 인도되었다. **3** [turn over sth] if a business turns over a particular amount of money, it makes that amount during

a period of time ‖ 기업이 일정 시기 동안 에 특정 금액을 벌다. 매상을 올리다: *We turned over $5000 in our third month.* 우리는 3개월째에 5천 달러의 매출을 올 렸다. ⇨ TURNOVER

turn to *phr v* [T] **1** [turn to sb/sth] to try to get help from someone or by doing something ‖ 남으로부터 또는 어떤 것을 함으로써 도움을 받으려고 애쓰다. …을 구하려[얻으려] 찾다. …에 의지[의 존]하다: *He still turns to us for advice.* 그는 아직도 조언을 구하려 우리를 찾는 다. / *Some kids turn to selling drugs to get money.* 몇몇 아이들은 돈을 벌려고 마 약 판매에 의존한다 **2** [turn to sth] to go to a particular page in a book, magazine etc. ‖ 책·잡지 등의 특정한 페 이지로 가다. (페이지·기사 등을) 펴다. 참조하다: *Turn to page 45 in your math book.* 수학책 45쪽을 펴라. **3** [turn to sth] to begin thinking about or doing something new ‖ 새로운 일에 대해 생각 하거나 행위하기 시작하다. (일에) 착수하 다. …으로 돌아서다: *Bateman turned to politics after law school.* 베이트만은 로스쿨을 마치고 나서 정계에 입문했다.

turn up *phr v* **1** [T **turn** sth ↔ **up**] to make a machine such as a radio, OVEN etc. produce more sound, heat etc. ‖ 라 디오·오븐 등 기계가 소리·열을 더 많이 내게 하다. 높이다. 세게 하다: *Turn up the radio – I love this song.* 라디오(소리) 를 크게 해라. 나는 이 노래를 좋아한다. **2** [I] to be found after being searched for ‖ 탐색 후에 발견되다. 나타나다: *We looked for the ring for weeks, and then it turned up in my pocket.* 우리는 그 반 지를 수 주 동안 찾았는데 결국 내 주머니 에서 발견되었다. **3** to arrive ‖ 도착하다. …에 나타나다: *Danny turned up late as usual.* 대니는 평소처럼 늦게 도착했다. **4** [I] to happen, especially when you are not expecting it ‖ 특히 사람이 기대하지 않은 경우에 일어나다. (사물이 뜻밖에) 생기다: *Don't worry, a job will turn up soon.* 걱정 마라. 일자리는 곧 생길 것이 다. **5** [T **turn** sth ↔ **up**] to find something by searching for it thoroughly ‖ 철저하게 조사하여 사물을 발견하다. 찾아내다: *The police searched the house, but they didn't turn up anything.* 경찰은 그 집을 수색하였으나 아무것도 찾아내지 못했다.

turn² n

1 ▶CHANCE TO DO STH◀ 어떤 것을 할 기회◀ the time when it is your chance, duty, or right to do something that a group of people are doing, one after another ‖ 일단의 사람들이 잇따라 하고 있는 어떤 것을 할 자신의 기회[의무, 권리]가 된 때. 순번. 차례. 기회. 호기: *It's your turn to do the dishes tonight.* 오늘 저녁 설거지는 네 차례다. / *When do I get a turn?* 내 차례는 언제지?

2 take turns if a group of people take turns doing something, each of them has a chance or a duty to do it ‖ 일단의 사람들 각자가 어떤 것을 할 기회나 의무를 가지다. …을 번갈아(가며) 하다. 교대로 하다: *Why don't you take turns using the computer?* 컴퓨터를 교대로 사용하는 것이 어때? / *We agreed to take turns driving.* 우리는 교대로 운전하기로 했다.

3 in turn one after another ‖ 하나씩. 차례로: *He spoke to each of the students in turn.* 그는 차례로 학생들에게 개별적으로 말했다.

4 ▶CHANGE DIRECTION 방향 전환◀ a change in the direction you are moving in ‖ 사람이 움직이고 있는 방향의 전환. 진로 변경. 돌기: *Make a left/right turn at the stop sign.* 신호등에서 좌회전[우회전] 해라.

5 ▶MOVE STH 무엇을 움직이다◀ the act of turning something ‖ 사물을 돌리기. 회전: *Give the wheel another turn.* 그 바퀴를 한 번 더 돌려라.

6 ▶TWO ROADS JOIN 두 도로의 합류◀ a place where a road joins another road ‖ 어떤 도로가 다른 도로와 합류하는 장소. 합류[분기]점. 도는[바뀌는] 지점: *I think we missed our turn; we were supposed to go left on Holly St.* 우리는 도로 분기점을 지나친 것 같아. 홀리 스트리트에서 좌회전했어야 하는데.

7 the turn of the century the beginning of a century ‖ 세기의 시작. 세기의 전환기

8 take a turn for the better/worse to suddenly become better or worse ‖ 갑자기 더 좋아지거나 더 나빠지다. 급속히 호전되다/악화되다: *Her health took a turn for the worse.* 그녀의 건강은 갑자기 악화되었다.

9 turn of events an unexpected change in a situation ‖ 예상 밖의 상황 변화. 상황의 급전: *By some unfortunate turn of events, the documents were lost.* 몇몇 사태의 유감스러운 급변으로 그 문서들은 분실되었다.

10 do sb a good turn to help someone ‖ 남을 돕다

turn·a·round /ˈtɚnəˌraʊnd/ *n* an important and completely different change ‖ 중요하고 완전하게 다른 변경. 방향 전환. 전향. 전환: *The win was a*

turnaround for the team. 그 승리는 그 팀에게는 일대 전환점이 되었다.

turn·coat /ˈtɚnkoʊt/ *n* someone who stops supporting a political party or group and joins the opposite group ‖ 어떤 정당이나 정치 집단을 지지하는 것을 중단하고 반대 집단에 합류한 사람. 배신자. 변절자

turning point /ˈ.. ˌ./ *n* the time when an important change starts to happen ‖ 중요한 변화가 일어나기 시작하는 시기. 전환점. 전기: *Winning the race was a turning point in his athletic career.* 그 경주에서 우승한 것은 그의 운동 경력에서 일대 전기였다.

tur·nip /ˈtɚnɪp/ *n* [C, U] a large round pale yellow or white root, cooked and eaten as a vegetable ‖ 야채로 요리해서 먹는 크고 둥근 연노랑색이나 흰색의 뿌리. 순무

turn-off /ˈ../ *n* **1** a place where you can leave a main road to get onto another one. ‖ 주요 도로를 벗어나 다른 도로로 진입할 수 있는 장소. (고속도로 출구의) 램프. 분기점: *I think the turn-off was back there a few blocks.* 나는 고속도로 램프는 몇 블록 뒤에 있었다고 생각한다. **2** something that someone does that makes you dislike him/her, usually in a sexual way ‖ 보통 성적으로 싫증나게 하는 남이 하는 일. 흥미를 잃게 하는 것

turn·out /ˈtɚnaʊt/ *n* [singular] the number of people who go to an event such as a party, meeting, or election ‖ 파티[모임, 선거] 등의 행사에 가는 사람들의 수. 참석[참가]자수: *The voter turnout was 93%.* 투표율은 93%였다.

turn·o·ver /ˈtɚnˌoʊvɚ/ *n* **1** [singular] the amount of money a business earns in a particular period ‖ 특정 기간에 기업이 벌어들이는 금액. 영업상의 총매상(고): *an annual turnover of $35 million* 3천 5백만 달러의 연 총매출(고) **2** [U] the rate at which people leave an organization and are replaced by others ‖ 사람들이 조직을 떠나고 다른 사람으로 대체되는 비율. 이직률: *The company has a high rate of turnover.* 그 회사는 이직률이 높다. **3** a small fruit PIE ‖ 작은 과일 파이: *apple turnovers.* 반원형 사과 파이

turn·pike /ˈtɚnpaɪk/ *n* a main road that you have to pay a TOLL to use ‖ 이용 요금을 지불해야 하는 주요 도로. (특히) 유료 고속도로

turn sig·nal /ˈ. ˌ./ *n* one of the lights on a vehicle that is lit in order to show which direction the driver is turning, or the stick that you push up or down to turn on this light ‖ 어느 방향으로 운전자가 돌아가는지를 나타내기 위해 켜는 차량 등의 하나, 또는 이 등을 켜기 위해 위나 아래로 미는 막대. (차의) 방향 지시등(스위치) —see picture on page 943.

turn·stile /'tənstaɪl/ n a gate that only lets one person through at a time ‖ 한 번에 한 사람만을 통과시키는 문. 회전식 출입문[개찰구]

turn·ta·ble /'tən,teɪbəl/ n a piece of equipment used for playing RECORDs ‖ 음반을 재생하는 데 사용하는 장치. 레코드 플레이어의 회전반

tur·pen·tine /'təpən,taɪn/ n [U] a strong-smelling oil used for removing paint ‖ 페인트를 지우는 데 사용하는 강한 냄새가 나는 기름. 테레빈유(油)

tur·quoise /'təkwɔɪz, -kɔɪz/ n [U] a bright blue-green color ‖ 선명한 푸른 녹색. 청록색 **- turquoise** adj

tur·ret /'tət, 'tʌrɪt/ n a small tower on a large building, especially a CASTLE ‖ 큰 건물 특히 성의 작은 탑

tur·tle /'tətl/ n a REPTILE (=type of animal) that has four legs and a hard shell and lives mainly in water ‖ 네 개의 발과 딱딱한 껍질을 갖고 주로 물에서 사는 파충류. (바다)거북

tur·tle·neck /'tətl,nɛk/ n a type of shirt or SWEATER with a close-fitting collar that covers most of your neck ‖ 목의 대부분을 덮는 꼭 맞는 깃을 가진 셔츠나 스웨터 종류. 터틀넥

tush /tʊʃ/ n INFORMAL the part of your body that you sit on ‖ 앉는 신체 부위. 궁둥이

tusk /tʌsk/ n one of the two very long teeth that stick out of an animal's mouth, for example an ELEPHANT's ‖ 예컨대 코끼리의 경우 같이 동물의 입에서 툭 튀어나온 매우 긴 두 개의 이빨의 하나. 엄니. 뻐드렁니

tus·sle /'tʌsəl/ n a struggle or fight ‖ 다툼이나 싸움. 난투. 드잡이 **- tussle** v [I]

tu·tor /'tutə/ n someone who is paid to teach only one or a few students, especially students who are having difficulty with a subject ‖ 특히 어떤 과목에 어려움을 겪는 단 한 명이나 몇몇 학생들만 가르치고 대가를 받는 사람. 가정[과외] 교사: my French tutor 나의 프랑스어 가정교사 **- tutor** v [T]

tu·to·ri·al /tu'tɔriəl/ adj relating to a TUTOR or the teaching that s/he does ‖ 가정교사나 그 교습에 관한. 개별 지도의[교사에 의한]

tux·e·do /tʌk'sidoʊ/, **tux** /tʌks/ n a

man's suit, usually black, that is worn at formal occasions ‖ 공식 행사에 입는, 보통 흑색의 남자 예복. 남자 야회복. 턱시도

TV n [C, U] ⇨ TELEVISION : What's on TV? 텔레비전에 뭐가 방영되지? / Sue just bought a new TV. 수는 이제 막 새 텔레비전을 샀다.

TV din·ner /, . '. ./ n a frozen prepared meal you can buy from the store, that you heat up and eat at home ‖ 가게에서 구입해 집에서 데워 먹을 수 있도록 미리 요리된 냉동 식품

twang /twæŋ/ n 1 the quality of your voice when your speaking sounds come from your nose as well as your mouth ‖ 말하는 소리가 입과 동시에 코에서도 나오는 경우에 사람의 목소리의 특질. 새된 콧소리. 코맹맹이 말투. 비음 2 a short RINGing sound like the one made by quickly pulling a tight string ‖ 팽팽한 줄을 빠르게 당겨서 내는 것 같은 짧게 울리는 소리. (현악기가) 탕[윙] 하고 울리기[울리는 소리] **- twang** v [I, T]

twas /twʌz/ LITERARY a word meaning "it was," used in past times ‖ 옛날에 사용했던 "it was"를 의미하는 말

tweak /twik/ v [T] 1 to quickly pull or twist something ‖ 사물을 갑자기 당기거나 비틀다. …을 (집어)홱 잡아당기다[비틀다]: Grandpa tweaked my nose and laughed. 할아버지가 내 코를 홱 잡아당기고는 웃었다. 2 to make small changes to something in order to improve it ‖ 어떤 것을 개선하기 위해 약간 변경을 하다. (기계 등을) 미(微)조정하다

tweed /twid/ n [U] a rough wool cloth used especially for making JACKETs ‖ 특히 재킷을 만드는 데 사용되는 거친 모직 옷감. 트위드 천

tweet /twit/ v [I] to make a quick high sound like a small bird ‖ 작은 새처럼 빠르게 날카로운 소리를 내다. 지저귀다 **- tweet** n

tweez·ers /'twizəz/ n [plural] a small tool made from two thin pieces of metal joined at one end, used for example for pulling out single hairs ‖ 머리카락 한 개를 뽑아내는 경우 등에 쓰이는 한쪽 끝에서 접합한 두 개의 가는 금속 조각으로 만든 작은 도구. 핀셋. 족집게: a pair of tweezers 족집게 한 개

twelfth /twɛlfθ/ number 1 12th ‖ 열두 번째. 제12 2 1/12 ‖ 12분의 1

twelve /twɛlv/ number 1 12 ‖ 12 2 twelve o'clock ‖ 12시: I'm going to lunch at twelve. 나는 12시에 점심을 먹을 거야.

twen·ty¹ /'twɛnti/ number 1 20 ‖ 20 2

the twenties   **a)** the years between 1920 and 1929 ‖ 1920년과 1929년 사이의 연도. 20년대   **b)** the numbers between 20 and 29, especially when used for measuring temperature ‖ 특히 온도를 측정하는 데 사용하는 20과 29 사이의 수. 20도대   **– twentieth** /'twɛntiiθ/ *number*

twenty² *n* a piece of paper money worth $20 ‖ 20달러짜리 지폐

twenty-one /ˌ. '.ˌ/ *n* ⇨ BLACKJACK

twerp /twɚp/ *n* SPOKEN a stupid or annoying person ‖ 어리석거나 성가신 사람. 시시한[너절한] 놈

twice /twaɪs/ *adv* two times ‖ 두 번: *I've seen that movie twice already.* 나는 이미 그 영화를 두 번 보았다.

twid·dle /'twɪdl/ *v* [T] to move your fingers around, or to turn something with them many times, usually because you are bored ‖ 보통 지루해서 손가락을 이리저리 움직이다. 또는 손가락으로 어떤 것을 수없이 돌리다. …을 만지작거리다. 이리저리 비비 틀다[빙빙 돌리다]

twig /twɪg/ *n* a very thin branch that grows on a larger branch of a tree ‖ 나무의 큰 가지에서 자라는 매우 가는 가지. 어린[작은] 가지

twi·light /'twaɪlaɪt/ *n* [U] the time between day and night when the sky starts to become dark, or the pale light at this time ‖ 하늘이 어두워지기 시작할 때의 낮과 밤 사이의 시간, 또는 이 시간대의 희미한 빛. 어스름. 황혼. 여명. 땅거미

twin¹ /twɪn/ *n* one of two children who are born at the same time to the same mother ‖ 같은 어머니한테서 동시에 태어난 두 아이 중 한 명. 쌍둥이 중의 하나: *Jenny and Julie are identical twins.* (=twins who look exactly the same) 제니와 줄리는 일란성 쌍생아이다. / *I have a twin brother.* 나는 쌍둥이 형이 있다.

twin² *adj* like something else and considered with it as a pair ‖ 다른 것과 같아서 한 쌍으로 간주되는. 한 쌍의: *twin towers* 쌍둥이 고층 건물 / *twin cities* 쌍둥이 도시

twin bed /ˌ. './ *n* a bed for one person ‖ 1인용 침대. 트윈 베드. 한 쌍의 침대의 한쪽

twine¹ /twaɪn/ *n* [U] thick strong string ‖ 굵고 강한 줄. 삼끈. 꼰 실[끈]

twine² *v* [I, T] to twist something, or to twist around something ‖ 어떤 것을 비틀다, 또는 어떤 것을 감아 틀다. 꼬다. …을 (휘)감다: *The plant had twined around the fence.* 그 풀은 울타리를 휘감았다.

twinge /twɪndʒ/ *n* a sudden pain, or a sudden feeling of a bad emotion ‖ 갑작스런 아픔, 또는 갑작스런 좋지 않은 감정. 발작적인 날카로운 아픔. (정신적) 고통. (마음의) 아픔. 가책: *a twinge of guilt* 죄책감

twin·kle /'twɪŋkəl/ *v* **1** if a star or light twinkles, it continues to change from being bright to dark ‖ 별·빛 등이 밝아졌다가 어두워지는 변화를 계속하다. 반짝반짝 빛나다 **2** if someone's eyes twinkle, s/he has a happy expression ‖ (사람의 눈이) 행복한 표정을 짓다. (눈이 기쁨 등으로) 빛나다[반짝이다] **– twinkle** *n*

twin-size /ˌ. '.ˌ/ *adj* relating to a TWIN BED ‖ 트윈 침대에 관한. 트윈 사이즈의: *twin-size sheets* 트윈 사이즈의 침대보

twirl /twɚl/ *v* [I, T] to continue turning around quickly, or to make something do this ‖ 빠르게 계속 빙빙 돌다, 또는 어떤 것을 이렇게 하게 하다. 빙빙 돌리다. 휘두르다: *dancers leaping and twirling on stage* 무대에서 껑충껑충 뛰며 빙빙 돌고 있는 무용수들 **– twirl** *n*

twist¹ /twɪst/ *v* **1** [I, T] to continue to turn something, such as hair, wire, or cloth, several times with your hands ‖ 머리카락[철사, 옷감] 등을 손으로 여러 번 계속 돌리다. 꼬다. 틀다: *Her hair was twisted into a bun.* 그녀의 머리카락은 트레머리로 틀어졌다. / *Wash the green beans and twist off the stems.* (=remove them by twisting) 완두콩 풋꼬투리를 물로 씻은 다음 그 줄기를 비틀어 따라. **2** [I, T] to turn around or bend part of your body into another position ‖ 신체 부위를 다른 자세로 돌리거나 구부리다. 뒤틀리게 하다. 삐다. 접지르다: *She screamed, twisting in agony.* 그녀는 괴로움으로 몸을 뒤틀며 비명을 질렀다. / *I twisted my ankle playing soccer.* (=hurt it by turning in the wrong direction) 나는 축구를 하다가 발목을 삐었다. **3** [T] to change the true or intended meaning of someone's statement ‖ 남의 말의 진정한 또는 의도된 의미를 바꾸다. 곡해[왜곡]하다: *They twisted the story around and said we tried to cheat them.* 그들은 그 이야기를 곡해해서 우리가 그들을 속이려고 했다고 말했다. **4** [I] if a road, river etc. twists, it has a lot of curves in it ‖ 도로·강 등이 굽은 곳이 많다. 꼬불꼬불하다 **5 twist sb's arm** INFORMAL to persuade someone to do something that s/he does not want to do ‖ 하기 싫은 일을 하게 남을 설득하다. 남에게 강요[강제]하다: *I think she'll do it if we twist her arm a* *little.* 우리가 그녀에게 좀 강요하면 그녀는 그것을 할 것이라고 나는 생각한다.

twist² *n* **1** a shape made by twisting something, such as paper, rope, or hair ‖ 종이[밧줄, 머리카락] 등을 비틀어서 만든 모양. 비틀림. 꼬임: *pasta twists* 푸실리(파스타의 한 종류) **2** an unexpected change in a story or situation ‖ 이야기나 상황의 예상 밖의 변화. (사건·상황의) 의외의 급변: *Her disappearance added a new twist to the story.* 그녀가 자취를 감춘 사실은 그 이야기에 새로운 반전을 가져왔다. **3** a bend in a road, river etc. ‖ 도로·강 등의 굴곡

twist·ed /'twɪstɪd/ *adj* strange and slightly cruel ‖ 이상하고 약간 잔인한. (불쾌하게)이상한: *a twisted joke* 이상한 농담

twist·er /'twɪstɚ/ *n* INFORMAL ➪ TORNADO

twit /twɪt/ *n* SPOKEN a stupid or silly person ‖ 바보나 어리석은 사람. 멍청이

twitch /twɪtʃ/ *v* [I] if a part of your body twitches, it makes a sudden small uncontrolled movement ‖ 신체 부위가 갑자기 제멋대로 작은 움직임을 일으키다. (근육 등이) 실룩거리다. 경련하다: *The cat's tail twitched irritably.* 그 고양이는 신경질적으로 꼬리를 실룩실룩 거렸다. – **twitch** *n*

twit·ter /'twɪtɚ/ *v* [I] if a bird twitters, it makes a lot of short high sounds ‖ (새가)짧고 날카로운 소리를 많이 내다. 새가 지저귀다 – **twitter** *n* [singular]

two /tu/ *number* **1** 2 ‖ 2 **2** two o'clock ‖ 2시: *The game begins at two.* 그 경기는 2시에 시작된다. —compare SECOND²

two-bit /'. ./ *adj* SLANG not very good or important ‖ 매우 좋거나 중요하지 않은. 하찮은. 시시한: *a two-bit actor* 시시한 배우

two-by-four /'. . ,./ *n* a long piece of wood that is two inches thick and four inches wide ‖ 두께가 2인치이고 폭이 4인치인 긴 나무. (2×4인치 크기의) 각목

two-di·men·sion·al /,. .'../ *adj* flat ‖ 편평한. 이차원의: *a two-dimensional drawing* 평면 도면

two-faced /,. '../ *adj* INFORMAL saying different things about something to different people, in a way that is not honest or sincere ‖ 정직하거나 진지하지 않은 방식으로 사물에 대하여 다른 사람에게는 다른 것을 말하는. (사람·견해 등이)표리가 있는[양면의]. 위선적인

two-piece /,. '../ *adj* a two-piece suit has a coat and pants that match ‖ 정장이 조화되는 상의와 바지로 되어 있는

two·some /'tusəm/ *n* a group of two people ‖ 2명으로 된 조. 2인조

two-time /'. ./ *v* [T] INFORMAL to deceive your usual partner by having a secret sexual relationship with someone else ‖ 다른 사람과 몰래 성적 관계를 가져서 평소의 짝을 속이다. (애인·배우자를) 배반하다. 기만하다

two-tone /,. '../ *adj* having two different colors ‖ 두 가지의 다른 색깔을 가지는. 2색의: *two-tone shoes* 2색조의 구두

two-way /,. '../ *adj* **1** moving or allowing movement in both directions ‖ 양 방향으로 움직이거나 이동을 허용하는. 양면 교통의: *two-way traffic* 쌍방향 교통 **2** a two-way radio sends and receives messages ‖ (무전기가) 송수신 겸용의. 쌍방 통신의

TX the written abbreviation of Texas ‖ Texas(텍사스 주)의 약어

ty·coon /taɪ'kun/ *n* someone who is very successful in business and has a lot of money ‖ 사업으로 아주 성공하여 큰 돈을 번 사람. 거물. 거두: *an oil tycoon* 석유왕

ty·ing /'taɪ-ɪŋ/ *v* the PRESENT PARTICIPLE of TIE ‖ tie의 현재 분사형

tyke /taɪk/ *n* INFORMAL a small child ‖ 작은 아이. (남자) 아이

type¹ /taɪp/ *n* **1** a particular kind of person or thing, or a group of people or things that have similar features or qualities ‖ 특정한 종류의 사람이나 물건, 또는 유사한 모양이나 특질을 가진 일단의 사람이나 물건. (유)형: *What type of desserts do you have?* 어떤 종류의 디저트가 있어요? / *The least expensive model of this type sells for $400.* 이 유형의 최저 고가 모델은 400달러에 판매된다. **2** someone with particular qualities, interests, appearance etc. ‖ 특정한 성질·관심·외모 등을 가진 사람. …타입. 전형: *the athletic type* 운동선수 타입의 사람 **3** not be sb's type INFORMAL to not be the kind of person that someone is attracted to ‖ 누군가가 매력을 느끼는 그런 유형의 사람이 아니다. 좋아하는 타입이 아니다: *Alex is OK – but he's not really my type.* 알렉스는 괜찮아. 그러나 그는 실은 내가 좋아하는 타입이 아니다. **4** [U] printed letters ‖ 인쇄된 글자들. 활자(체): *italic type* 이탤릭체

type² *v* [I, T] to write something using a computer or TYPEWRITER ‖ 컴퓨터나 타자기를 써서 어떤 것을 쓰다. …을 타자하다. …으로 글자를 치다

type·cast /'taɪpkæst/ *v* **typecast,**

typecast, typecasting [T] to always give an actor the same type of character to play ‖ 배우에게 항상 동일한 배역을 주다. 틀에 박힌 역을 하게 하다: *He does not want to be typecast as a bad guy.* 그는 항상 악당의 배역으로 판박히는 것을 원하지 않는다.

type·face /'taɪpfeɪs/ *n* a group of letters, numbers etc. of the same style and size, used in printing ‖ 인쇄에 사용되는 같은 형과 크기의 일단의 글자·숫자. 활자면[체](의 모든 글자)

type·writ·er /'taɪpˌraɪtɚ/ *n* a machine that prints letters, numbers etc. onto paper ‖ 종이에 글자·숫자 등을 찍는 기계. 타자기 —compare PRINTER

type·writ·ten /'taɪpˌrɪtॣn/ *adj* written using a TYPEWRITER ‖ 타자기를 써서 쓴. 타자(打字)한: *a typewritten manuscript* 타자기로 친 원고

ty·phoid /'taɪfɔɪd/, **typhoid fe·ver** /ˌ.. '../ *n* [U] a serious infectious disease that is caused by BACTERIA in food or water ‖ 음식이나 물에 있는 박테리아에 의해 발생되는 위험한 전염병. 장티푸스

ty·phoon /taɪ'fun/ *n* a very strong tropical storm ‖ 매우 강한 열대성 폭풍. 태풍

ty·phus /'taɪfəs/ *n* [U] a serious infectious disease that is caused by the bite of an insect ‖ 곤충이 물어서 생기는 위험한 전염병. 발진티푸스

typ·i·cal /'tɪpɪkəl/ *adj* **1** having the usual features or qualities of a particular thing, person, or group ‖ 특정한 물건[사람, 집단]의 평소의 모습이나 성질을 가지는. 전형적인. 대표적인: *He looked like the typical tourist.* 그는 전형적인 여행자처럼 보였다. / *Cool weather is typical of early April.* 서늘한 날씨는 이른 4월의 특색이다. **2 typical!** SPOKEN said when you are annoyed that something bad has happened again ‖ 나쁜 일이 다시 발생한 것에 화가 났을 때에 쓰여. (어이없어) 여전하군. 노상 그 일이군: *The car won't start – typical!* 차가 시동이 안 걸려. 또야!

typ·i·cal·ly /'tɪpɪkli/ *adv* **1** in the way that something usually happens ‖ 어떤 것이 통상 발생하는 방식으로. 일반적으로: *Gasoline prices typically rise in the summer.* 유류 가격은 일반적으로 여름에 인상된다. **2** in the way that a person or group usually behaves ‖ 사람이나 집단이 보통 행동하는 방식으로. 전형적으로. 대표적으로: *Nothing is more typically American than hamburgers.* 햄버거 이상으로 미국다운 것은 없다.

typ·i·fy /'tɪpəˌfaɪ/ *v* [T] to be a typical example or feature of something ‖ 어떤 것의 전형적인 사례나 모습이 되다. …의 전형이 되다. …의 특징[특색]을 나타내다: *a dark painting that typifies her work* 그녀의 작품의 특징을 나타내는 어두운 그림[화법]

typ·ing /'taɪpɪŋ/ *n* [U] the activity of writing using a TYPEWRITER ‖ 타자기를 사용하여 글을 쓰기. 타자하기

typ·ist /'taɪpɪst/ *n* someone who uses a TYPEWRITER ‖ 타자기를 사용하는 사람. 타자수

ty·po /'taɪpoʊ/ *n* INFORMAL a mistake that you make when you write using a computer or TYPEWRITER ‖ 컴퓨터나 타자기를 써서 글을 쓸 때 하는 실수. 오식. 오타

ty·ran·ni·cal /tɪ'rænɪkəl/ *adj* behaving in an unfair or cruel way toward someone you have power over ‖ 다스리는 사람에 대해 불공정하거나 잔인하게 행동하는. 폭군적인. 전제적인: *a brutal and tyrannical government* 잔인하고 압제적인 정부 **– tyrannize** /'tɪrəˌnaɪz/ *v* [T]

tyr·an·ny /'tɪrəni/ *n* **1** [U] strict, unfair, and often cruel control over someone ‖ 다른 사람에 대한 엄격하고 불공하며 종종 잔인한 지배. 학정. 폭정: *the tyranny of poverty* 가혹한 빈곤 **2** [C, U] government by a cruel ruler who has complete power ‖ 완전한 권력을 가진 잔인한 통치자에 의한 정부. 전제 정치[국가]

ty·rant /'taɪrənt/ *n* someone, especially a ruler, who uses his/her power in an unfair or cruel way ‖ 불공정하거나 잔인한 방식으로 권력을 사용하는 사람, 특히 통치자. 폭군. 전제 군주: *Ginny sees her father as a harsh and selfish tyrant.* 지니는 자신의 아버지를 가혹하고 이기적인 폭군으로 여긴다.

tzar /zɑr, tsɑr/ *n* ⇨ CZAR

Uu

U, u /yu/ the twenty-first letter of the English alphabet ‖ 영어 알파벳의 스물한 째 자

u·biq·ui·tous /yuˈbɪkwətəs/ *adj* FORMAL seeming to be everywhere ‖ 도처에 있는 것처럼 보이는. 편재하는: *New York's ubiquitous yellow cabs* 여기저기 널려 있는 뉴욕의 노란 택시들 – **ubiquity** *n* [U]

ud·der /ˈʌdɚ/ *n* the part of a cow, goat etc. that produces milk ‖ 암소·염소 등의 젖을 만들어 내는 부분. 젖통

UFO *n* Unidentified Flying Object; a mysterious object in the sky, sometimes thought to be a space vehicle from another world ‖ Unidentified Flying Object (미확인 비행 물체)의 약어; 때때로 다른 세계에서 온 우주선으로 생각되는 하늘의 신비로운 물체

ugh /ʌg, ʌk, ʌh/ *interjection* used in order to show strong dislike ‖ 강한 혐오를 나타내는 데에 쓰여. 으. 으악. 으웩: *Ugh! That tastes terrible!* 윽! 맛이 정말 형편없네!

ug·ly /ˈʌgli/ *adj* **1** very unattractive or unpleasant to look at ‖ 쳐다보기에 매우 못생기거나 불쾌한. 추한: *an ugly face* 못생긴 얼굴 **2** very unpleasant or violent in a way that makes you feel frightened ‖ 겁에 질리도록 매우 불쾌하거나 폭력적인. 험악한: *an ugly scene at the bus stop* 버스 정류장에서의 험악한 광경 – **ugliness** *n* [U]

uh /ʌ/ *interjection* said when you are deciding what to say next ‖ 다음에 할 말을 결정할 때에 쓰여. 어. 에: *I, uh, I'm sorry I'm late.* 내가, 어, 늦어서 미안해.

UHF *n* [U] ultra-high frequency; a range of radio WAVES that produces very good sound quality ‖ ultra-high frequency(극초단파)의 약어; 매우 좋은 음질을 내는 전파 영역

uh huh /nˈhn, mˈhm, əˈhʌ/ *interjection* INFORMAL used in order to say yes or to show that you understand something ‖ 긍정의 대답을 말하거나 어떤 것을 이해한다는 것을 나타내는 데에 쓰여. 응. 그래: *"Is this the one you want?" "Uh huh."* "이것이 네가 원하는 거냐?" "그래."

uh oh /ˈʌ ˌoʊ/ *interjection* INFORMAL said when you have made a mistake or have realized that something bad has happened ‖ 실수를 했거나 안 좋은 일이 발생했다는 것을 깨달았을 때 쓰여. 이런. 아이고: *Uh oh, I think I forgot my keys.* 이런, 열쇠를 깜빡 잊고 두고 온 것 같아.

uh uh /ˈʌ n, ˈ m ˈm/ *interjection* INFORMAL used in order to say no ‖ 부정의 대답을 말하는 데에 쓰여. 아니: *"Did you go to Billy's game?" "Uh uh, I forgot."* "빌리의 경기에 갔었니?" "아니, 깜빡 했어."

ul·cer /ˈʌlsɚ/ *n* a sore area on your skin or inside your body, that may bleed ‖ 출혈가능성이 있는 피부나 신체 내부의 염증 부위. 궤양: *a stomach ulcer* 위궤양

ul·te·ri·or /ʌlˈtɪriɚ/ *adj* **ulterior motive/reason** a reason for doing something that you hide in order to get an advantage for yourself ‖ 자신에게 유리하도록 무엇인가를 숨기고 하는 이유. 숨겨진[이면의] 동기/이유: *Do you think she has an ulterior motive for helping us?* 그녀가 우리를 돕는 숨겨진 동기가 있다고 생각해?

ul·ti·mate¹ /ˈʌltəmɪt/ *adj* **1** better, bigger, worse etc. than others of the same kind ‖ 같은 종류의 다른 것보다 더 좋은[큰, 나쁜]. 최고[최악]의: *A Rolls Royce is the ultimate symbol of wealth.* 롤스로이스는 부(富)의 최고의 상징이다. / *the ultimate disgrace* 말로 다할 수 없는 치욕 **2** the ultimate purpose, aim, reason etc. is the final and most important one ‖ 목적[목표, 이유] 등이 최종적이며 가장 중요한. 최후의. 궁극의

ultimate² *n* **the ultimate in sth** the best example or highest level of something ‖ 어떤 것의 최상의 본보기나 최고의 수준. 궁극점. 결정판: *The Orient Express is the ultimate in rail travel.* 오리엔트 익스프레스는 철도 여행에서 단연 최고다.

ultimate fight·ing /ˌ…ˈ../ *n* [U] a competition, similar to BOXING, in which two people are allowed to hit or kick each other and in which there are almost no rules ‖ 두 사람이 서로 치고 발로 차는 것이 허용되는 거의 규칙 없는 권투와 비슷한 경기. 무한 격투기

ul·ti·mate·ly /ˈʌltəmɪtli/ *adv* in the end; FINALLY ‖ 결국. 최후로. 마침내; ⊞ finally: *Ultimately it's your decision.* 궁극적으로 네가 결정할 문제다.

ul·ti·ma·tum /ˌʌltəˈmeɪtəm/ *n* a

statement saying that if someone does not do what you want, s/he will be punished || 남에게 자신이 원하는 것을 하지 않으면 처벌을 받을 것이라고 말하는 성명. 최후통첩: *The government issued an ultimatum* (=gave an ultimatum) *to the rebels to surrender.* 정부는 반군에게 항복하라고 최후통첩을 보냈다.

ul·tra·son·ic /ˌʌltrəˈsɑnɪk-/ *adj* TECHNICAL ultrasonic sounds are too high for humans to hear || 소리가 너무 높아서 사람이 들을 수 없는. 초음파의

ul·tra·sound /ˈʌltrəˌsaʊnd/ *n* [C, U] a medical process that uses sound waves to produce images of the inside of your body || 인체 내부의 영상을 만들어 내기 위해 음파를 사용하는 의료 과정. 초음파 진단

ul·tra·vi·o·let /ˌʌltrəˈvaɪəlɪt-/ *adj* ultraviolet light is beyond the purple range of colors that humans can see || 빛이 사람이 볼 수 있는 보라색 영역을 넘어선. 자외선의 —compare INFRARED

um /m/ *interjection* said when you are deciding what to say next || 다음 할 말을 정하려 할 때 쓰여. 음. 어: *I can't – um, maybe I won't be able to come.* 나는 할 수 없어, 음, 어쩌면 오지 못할지도 몰라.

um·bil·i·cal cord /ʌmˈbɪlɪkəl ˌkɔrd/ *n* a tube of flesh that joins an unborn baby to its mother || 태아를 산모와 연결하는 관 모양의 살. 탯줄

um·brage /ˈʌmbrɪdʒ/ *n* **take umbrage (at sth)** FORMAL to be offended by something that someone has done or said || 남이 했거나 말한 것 때문에 기분이 상하다. …에 화내다. 불쾌하게 여기다: *Leiden took umbrage at O'Brian's comments.* 레이든은 오브라이언의 말에 화를 냈다.

um·brel·la /ʌmˈbrɛlə/ *n* **1** a thing that you hold above your head to protect you from the rain || 비를 막기 위해 머리 위로 들고 있는 것. 우산 **2 umbrella organization/group/agency** an organization that includes several smaller groups || 몇 개의 보다 작은 산하 집단들을 포함하는 조직. 상부 단체/집단/기관

umbrella

ump /ʌmp/ *n* INFORMAL ⇨ UMPIRE[1]

um·pire[1] /ˈʌmpaɪɚ/ *n* someone who makes sure that the rules are followed during a game in sports such as baseball and tennis || 야구와 테니스 등의

sports 경기 중에 규칙이 잘 지켜지는지 확인하는 사람. 심판. 주심 —see usage note at REFEREE —see picture on page 946

umpire[2] *v* [I, T] to be the UMPIRE for a game || 경기의 심판이 되다. …의 심판을 보다

ump·teenth /ˈʌmptinθ, ˌʌmˈtinθ/ *quantifier* INFORMAL a word used when you do not know a specific number, but want to say that the number is unreasonably large || 특정한 수는 모르지만 그 수가 터무니없이 많다고 말하고 싶을 때 쓰이는 단어. 수도 없는. 무수한: *They're showing "The Wizard of Oz" for the umpteenth time.* 그들은 "오즈의 마법사"를 수도 없이 방영하고 있다. – **umpteen** *quantifier*

UN *n* [U] the United Nations; an international organization that tries to find peaceful solutions to world problems || the United Nations (국제 연합)의 약어; 세계 문제에 대한 평화적인 해결책을 찾기 위해 노력하는 국제기구

un·a·bashed /ˌʌnəˈbæʃt/ *adj* not shy or embarrassed about something || 어떤 것에 대해 수줍어하거나 부끄러워하지 않는. 주저주저하지 않는. 태연한: *unabashed curiosity* 주저함이 없는 호기심

un·a·bat·ed /ˌʌnəˈbeɪtɪd/ *adj* continuing without becoming weaker or less forceful || 더 약해지거나 세력이 줄지 않고 지속되는. 줄어들지[감퇴되지] 않는: *The storm continued unabated.* 폭풍우는 약해지지 않고 계속됐다.

un·a·ble /ʌnˈeɪbəl/ *adj* not able to do something || 어떤 것을 할 수 없는: *He delivers food to people who are unable to leave their homes.* 그는 자신의 집을 떠날 수 없는 사람들에게 음식을 배달한다. —compare INABILITY

un·a·bridged /ˌʌnəˈbrɪdʒd-/ *adj* a book that is unabridged is complete || 책이 완전한. 생략[축약]되지 않은

un·ac·cept·a·ble /ˌʌnəkˈsɛptəbəl/ *adj* something that is unacceptable is so wrong or bad that it should not be allowed to continue || 어떤 것이 너무 잘못되거나 나빠서 계속되도록 허락되어서는 안 되는. 받아들일 수 없는. 용인할 수 없는: *Nancy's behavior is unacceptable.* 낸시의 행동은 용납할 수가 없다. – **unacceptably** *adv*

un·ac·count·a·ble /ˌʌnəˈkaʊntəbəl/ *adj* **1** not having to explain your actions or decisions to anyone else || 행동이나 결정을 다른 누구에게도 설명하지 않아도 되

는. 책임이 없는 **2** very surprising and difficult to explain ‖ 매우 놀랍고 설명하기 어려운. 설명할 수 없는. 영문 모를: *a product that flopped for unaccountable reasons* 영문 모를 이유 때문에 불량이 난 제품 - **unaccountably** *adv*

un·a·dul·ter·at·ed /ˌʌnəˈdʌltəˌreɪtɪd/ *adj* complete or pure, without having any other feelings, substances etc. mixed in ‖ 어떠한 다른 감정·물질 등도 섞이지 않고 완전하거나 순수한. 순전한: *unadulterated fun/evil* 순도 100%의 재미[악]

un·af·fect·ed /ˌʌnəˈfɛktɪd/ *adj* not changed or influenced by something ‖ 어떤 것에 의해 바뀌거나 영향을 받지 않는. 변함없는: *Parts of the city remained unaffected by the fire.* 도시의 일부분은 화재에도 불구하고 그대로 남았다.

un·aid·ed /ʌnˈeɪdɪd/ *adj* without help ‖ 도움 없이

un·A·mer·i·can /ˌʌn əˈmɛrɪkən/ *adj* not supporting or loyal to American customs, ideas etc. ‖ 미국의 관습·사고방식 등을 지지하거나 충실히 따르지 않는. 미국식이 아닌. 비미국적인

u·nan·i·mous /yuˈnænəməs/ *adj* a unanimous decision, vote etc. is one on which everyone agrees ‖ 결정·투표 등에 모든 사람이 동의하는. 만장일치의 – **unanimously** *adv* - **unanimity** /ˌyunəˈnɪməti/ *n* [U]

un·an·nounced /ˌʌnəˈnaʊnst/ *adj* happening without anyone knowing about it or expecting it ‖ 아무도 그것에 대해 알거나 예상하지 못한채 발생하는. 예고 없는: *Several people arrived unannounced.* 몇 명의 사람들이 예고도 없이 도착했다.

un·an·swered /ˌʌnˈænsəd/ *adj* an unanswered telephone, letter, question etc. has not been answered ‖ 전화·편지·질문 등이 응답되지 않은. 대답이 없는

un·armed /ˌʌnˈɑrmd/ *adj* not carrying any weapons ‖ 어떠한 무기도 지니지 않은. 무장하지 않은. 비무장의: *An officer shot an unarmed man.* 경찰관이 무장하지 않은 남자에게 총을 쐈다.

un·as·sum·ing /ˌʌnəˈsumɪŋ/ *adj* quiet and showing no desire for attention, or not attracting attention; MODEST ‖ 조용하며 주목을 끌고 싶지 않음을 나타내거나 주목을 끌지 않는. 젠 체하지 않는. 겸손한; ⓢ modest: *an unassuming friendly Italian restaurant* 요란하지 않으며 친절한 이탈리아 식당

un·at·tached /ˌʌnəˈtætʃt/ *adj* **1** not involved in a romantic relationship ‖ 연

애 관계에 관련되지 않은. 교제하지 않는 **2** not connected to anything ‖ 어떤 것에도 연결되지 않은. 붙어 있지 않은. 떨어져 있는

un·at·tend·ed /ˌʌnəˈtɛndɪd/ *adj* left alone without being watched ‖ 돌보지 않고 홀로 남겨진. 내버려 둔: *Small children should never be left unattended.* 작은 어린이들은 돌보지 않고 홀로 남겨 두어서는 안 된다.

un·at·trac·tive /ˌʌnəˈtræktɪv/ *adj* **1** not physically attractive or beautiful ‖ 육체적으로 매력적이거나 아름답지 않은. 관심을 끌지 못하는. 예쁘지 않은 **2** not good or desirable ‖ 좋거나 바람직하지 않은. 흥미 없는. 시시한: *High taxes make it an unattractive state in which to start a business.* 그 주는 높은 세금으로 사업을 시작하기에 매력적인 곳이 못 된다.

un·au·thor·ized /ˌʌnˈɔθəˌraɪzd/ *adj* without official approval or permission ‖ 공식적인 승인이나 허가가 없는. 권한이 없는. 비공인의: *an unauthorized biography of Marlon Brando* 말론 브란도의 비공인 자서전

un·a·vail·a·ble /ˌʌnəˈveɪləbəl/ *adj* **1** not able or willing to meet with someone ‖ 남을 만날 수 없거나 만날 의향이 없는. 부재의. 만나려 하지 않는: *Mr. Foster is unavailable for comment.* 포스터 씨는 논평에 응할 수 없습니다. **2** not able to be obtained ‖ 획득할 수 없는. 입수[이용]할 수 없는: *an album previously unavailable on CD* 이전에는 CD로 들을 수 없었던 앨범

un·a·void·a·ble /ˌʌnəˈvɔɪdəbəl/ *adj* if something is unavoidable, nothing can be done to prevent it ‖ 어떤 것을 막기 위해 아무것도 할 수 없는. 피할 수 없는. 불가피한: *an unavoidable delay* 부득이한 지연

un·a·ware /ˌʌnəˈwɛr/ *adj* not noticing or knowing about something ‖ 어떤 것에 대해서 알아채거나 알지 못하는. 눈치 채지[의식하지] 못하는: *He was unaware of his legal rights.* 그는 자신의 법적 권리를 알지 못했다.

un·a·wares /ˌʌnəˈwɛrz/ *adv* **catch/take sb unawares** to happen or do something to someone when s/he is not expecting it ‖ 누군가가 어떤 것을 예상하고 있지 않을 때 발생하거나 그 사람에게 그것을 하다. 남에게 기습을 가하다. 남의 허를 찌르다: *The events in the Middle East caught the CIA unawares.* 중동에서의 사건들은 CIA의 허를 찌른 것이었다.

un·bal·anced /ˌʌnˈbælənst/ *adj* **1**

slightly crazy ‖ 약간 미친. 이성을 잃은: *mentally unbalanced* 정신적으로 이상이 있는 **2** not balanced ‖ 균형이 잡히지 않은. 불안정한

un·bear·a·ble /ˌʌnˈbɛrəbəl/ *adj* too painful, unpleasant etc. for you to be able to deal with; INTOLERABLE ‖ 너무나 고통스럽거나 불쾌해서 대처할 수 없는. 참을[견딜] 수 없는; ⒮ intolerable: *Her pain had become unbearable.* 그녀의 고통은 참을 수 없을 지경이 되었다. – **unbearably** *adv*

un·beat·a·ble /ʌnˈbiṭəbəl/ *adj* someone or something that is unbeatable will always be better than any other person or thing ‖ 사람이나 사물이 항상 다른 어떤 사람이나 사물보다 더 나은. 패배시킬 수 없는: *We guarantee our prices are unbeatable!* 저희 가격이 타의 추종을 불허한다는 것을 보장합니다!

un·be·liev·a·ble /ˌʌnbɪˈlivəbəl/ *adj* extremely surprising ‖ 매우 놀라운. 믿을 수 없는. 놀랄 만한: *The tapes are tiny, but the sound quality is unbelievable.* 테이프는 작지만 음질은 믿을 수 없을 정도로 좋다. – **unbelievably** *adv*

un·born /ˌʌnˈbɔrn/ *adj* not yet born ‖ 아직 태어나지 않은. 태중에 있는: *an unborn child* 태아

un·bound·ed /ˌʌnˈbaʊndɪd/ *adj* FORMAL very great and seeming to have no limit ‖ 매우 광대하고 한계가 없는 것처럼 보이는. 끝없는. 무한한: *unbounded optimism* 끝없는 낙관주의

un·bri·dled /ˌʌnˈbraɪdld/ *adj* not controlled ‖ 통제되지 않는. 억제할 수 없는: *unbridled anger* 억제할 수 없는 분노

un·called-for /ʌnˈkɔld ˌfɔr/ *adj* behavior or remarks that are uncalled-for are unsuitable or rude ‖ 행동이나 말이 부적합하거나 무례한. 부적당한. 엉뚱한

un·can·ny /ʌnˈkæni/ *adj* very strange and difficult to explain ‖ 매우 이상하고 설명하기 어려운. 신비로운. 기괴한. 불가사의한: *He bears an uncanny resemblance to John Lennon.* 그는 존 레논과 묘하게 닮은 구석을 가지고 있다. – **uncannily** *adv*

un·cer·tain /ʌnˈsɚṭn/ *adj* **1** not sure or having doubts about something ‖ 어떤 것에 대해 확신이 없거나 의심을 가지고 있는. 자신이 없는. 망설이고 있는: *I'm uncertain about what to say to her.* 나는 그녀에게 무슨 말을 해야 할지 잘 모르겠다. **2** not known or not definite ‖ 알지 못하거나 분명하지 않은. 불확실한. 미정

의: *His future with the company is uncertain.* 그 회사에서의 그의 미래는 불확실하다. – **uncertainty** *n* [C, U] – **uncertainly** *adv*

un·chart·ed /ˌʌnˈtʃɑrṭɪd/ *adj* **uncharted territory/waters** a situation or activity that you have never experienced or tried before ‖ 이전에 한번도 경험하거나 시도해 보지 않은 상황이나 활동. 미지의 영역/수역

un·checked /ˌʌnˈtʃɛkt/ *adj* allowed to get worse because it is not controlled or stopped ‖ 통제되거나 중단되지 않아서 악화될 수 있는. 억제[저지]되지 않은: *Left unchecked, the disease will spread.* 억제하지 않고 방치하면 그 질병은 확산될 것이다.

un·cle /ˈʌŋkəl/ *n* the brother of your mother or father, or the husband of your AUNT ‖ 어머니나 아버지의 형제나 이모·고모의 남편. (외)삼촌. 큰[작은]아버지. 이모[고모]부 —see picture at FAMILY

un·clean /ˌʌnˈklin/ *adj* **1** dirty ‖ 더러운. 불결한 **2** not pure in a moral or religious way ‖ 도덕적으로나 종교적으로 순수하지 못한. 더럽혀진. 부정 탄

un·clear /ˌʌnˈklɪr/ *adj* difficult to understand or be sure about ‖ 어떤 것에 대해 이해하거나 확신하기 어려운. 확실하지 않은. 불명확한: *It is unclear whether the law covers this case.* 그 법이 이 사건에 적용되는지는 확실하지 않다.

Uncle Sam /ˌʌŋkəl ˈsæm/ *n* [singular] INFORMAL the US, or US government, represented by the figure of a tall man with a white BEARD and tall hat ‖ 흰 턱수염이 있고 높은 모자를 쓴 키가 큰 남자상으로 표현되는 미국이나 미국 정부. 미국. 미국 정부

Uncle Tom /ˌʌŋkəl ˈtɑm/ *n* DISAPPROVING a name for a Black person who is too friendly or respectful to white people ‖ 백인에게 지나치게 우호적이거나 존경심을 보이는 흑인의 이름. 엉클 톰

un·com·fort·a·ble /ʌnˈkʌmftəbəl, ʌnˈkʌmfɚṭəbəl/ *adj* **1** not feeling physically relaxed and satisfied, or not making someone feel this way ‖ 육체적으로 편안하고 만족스러운 기분이 들지 않는 또는 남을 이런 기분이 들게 하지 못하는. 불쾌한. 불편한: *The heat was making Irene uncomfortable.* 아이린은 더위에 시달리고 있었다./ *an uncomfortable chair* 불편한 의자 **2** unable to relax because you are embarrassed or worried ‖ 곤혹스럽거나 걱정이 되어서 긴장을 풀 수 없는. 초조하게 하는. 거북한: *I feel uncomfortable*

talking about sex education. 나는 성교육에 대해서 얘기할 때 거북하다. –
un·com·fort·ably *adv*
un·com·mon /ʌnˈkɑmən/ *adj* rare or unusual ‖ 드물거나 별난. 흔치 않은. 진기한: *It is not uncommon for children as young as ten to work in many countries.* (=it is fairly common) 열 살 정도의 어린 아이들이 일하는 것은 많은 나라들에서 흔히 볼 수 있는 일이다. –
uncommonly *adv*
un·com·pro·mis·ing /ʌnˈkɑmprə,-maɪzɪŋ/ *adj* determined not to change your opinions or intentions ‖ 단호하게 소신이나 태도를 바꾸려 하지 않는. 타협하지 않는. 강경한: *Grigson took an uncompromising position on gun control.* 그릭슨은 총기 규제에 대해 강경한 입장을 취했다.
un·con·cerned /ˌʌnkənˈsɝnd/ *adj* not anxious or worried about something ‖ 어떤 것에 대해서 근심하거나 걱정하지 않는. 태연한. 개의치 않는: *Americans cannot be unconcerned about the problem of the world's poor.* 미국인은 세계 빈곤 문제에 대해 무관심할 수 없다.
un·con·di·tion·al /ˌʌnkənˈdɪʃənəl/ *adj* not limited by or depending on any agreements or conditions ‖ 어떠한 협정이나 조건에 의해 제한받거나 그것에 의존하지 않는. 무조건의. 무제한의: *We are demanding the unconditional release of the hostages.* 우리는 인질의 무조건적인 석방을 요구하고 있다. – **unconditionally** *adv*
un·con·firmed /ˌʌnkənˈfɝmd/ *adj* not proved or supported by official information ‖ 공식적인 정보에 의해 입증되거나 뒷받침되지 않는. 미확인의. 확인되지 않은: *an unconfirmed report/rumor of a nuclear accident* 핵 사고에 대한 미확인 보도[소문]
un·con·scion·a·ble /ʌnˈkɑnʃənəbəl/ *adj* FORMAL morally wrong or unacceptable ‖ 도덕적으로 잘못이거나 받아들일 수 없는. 비양심적인
un·con·scious¹ /ˌʌnˈkɑnʃəs/ *adj* unable to see, move, feel etc. because you are not conscious ‖ 의식이 없어서 볼 수[움직일 수, 느낄 수] 없는. 의식을 잃은. 모르는: *The passenger was all right, but the driver was knocked unconscious.* 승객은 괜찮았지만 운전사는 의식을 잃고 쓰러졌다. – **unconsciously** *adv* – **unconsciousness** *n* [U]
unconscious² *n* **the/sb's unconscious** the part of your mind in which there are thoughts and feelings

that you do not realize that you have ‖ 자신은 가지고 있다는 것을 깨닫지 못하지만 생각과 감정이 있는 마음의 부분. 무의식
un·con·sti·tu·tion·al /ˌʌnkɑn-stəˈtuʃənəl/ *adj* not allowed by the rules that govern a country or organization ‖ 국가나 조직을 다스리는 법칙에 의해 허락되지 않는. 위헌의. 헌법에 위배되는
un·con·trol·la·ble /ˌʌnkənˈtroʊləbəl/ *adj* something that is uncontrollable cannot be controlled or stopped ‖ 어떤 것이 통제되거나 중단될 수 없는. 감당하기[다루기] 어려운. 억제할 수 없는: *uncontrollable rage/laughter* 억제할 수 없는 분노[웃음]
un·con·trolled /ˌʌnkənˈtroʊld/ *adj* **1** not controlled or stopped ‖ 통제되거나 중단되지 않은. 억제[규제]되지 않은: *the damage done by uncontrolled logging* 무분별한 벌목으로 입은 피해 **2** without rules or laws ‖ 규칙이나 법률 없이. 자유방임의: *a uncontrolled free market* 자유방임 시장
un·con·ven·tion·al /ˌʌnkənˈvɛnʃənəl/ *adj* very different from the way people usually behave, think, dress, or do things ‖ 사람들이 보통 행동하는[생각하는, 옷을 입는, 어떤 것을 하는] 방식과는 매우 다른. 관습[인습]에 얽매이지 않은. 틀에 박히지 않은
un·count·a·ble /ˌʌnˈkaʊntəbəl/ *adj* **uncountable noun** TECHNICAL in grammar, a noun that has no plural form, such as "water," "gold," or "furniture" ‖ 문법에서 "water", "gold", "furniture" 등 복수형을 가지지 않는 명사. 불가산 명사 —opposite COUNTABLE — see study note on page 940
un·couth /ʌnˈkuθ/ *adj* behaving or speaking in a way that is rude and unacceptable ‖ 무례하고 용인할 수 없게 행동하거나 말하는. 거친. 꼴불견의
un·cov·er /ʌnˈkʌvɚ/ *v* [T] **1** to discover something that had been kept secret or hidden ‖ 비밀로 해왔거나 숨겨져 있던 것을 발견하다. 폭로하다. 적발하다: *A search of their baggage uncovered two pistols.* 그들의 수하물에 대한 수색으로 권총 두 정을 적발했다. **2** to remove the cover from something ‖ 어떤 것에서 덮개를 제거하다. 뚜껑을 열다. …을 벗기다[드러내다]
un·cut /ˌʌnˈkʌt/ *adj* **1** a movie, book etc. that is uncut has not had violent or sexual scenes removed from it ‖ 영화·책 등에서 폭력적이거나 성적인 장면을 삭제하지 않은. 무삭제의. 완전판의 **2** an

uncut jewel has not yet been cut into a particular shape ‖ 보석을 아직 특정한 형상으로 자르지 않은. 아직 갈지[커트] 않은. 원형의

un·daunt·ed /ˌʌnˈdɔntɪd·, -ˈdɑn-/ *adj* not afraid to continue doing something in spite of difficulties or danger; DETERMINED ‖ 어려움이나 위험에도 불구하고 계속해서 어떤 것을 하기를 두려워하지 않는. 기가 꺾이지 않는. 불굴의; (유) determined: *Nelson was undaunted by the opposition to his plan.* 넬슨은 자신의 계획에 대한 반대에도 끄떡하지 않았다.

un·de·cid·ed /ˌʌndɪˈsaɪdɪd·/ *adj* not having made a decision about something ‖ 어떤 것에 대한 결정을 내리지 않은. 미결정의. 미해결의: *A majority of voters were undecided about which candidate to choose.* 대다수의 유권자들은 어떤 후보를 선택해야 할지 결정을 내리지 못했다.

un·de·ni·a·ble /ˌʌndɪˈnaɪəbəl·/ *adj* definitely true or certain ‖ 명확히 사실이거나 확실한. 부정할 수 없는. 틀림없는: *an undeniable fact* 부정할 수 없는 사실 – **undeniably** *adv*

un·der¹ /ˈʌndɚ/ *prep* **1** below something or covered by it ‖ 어떤 것의 아래에 또는 그것으로 덮여진. …의 밑에. …의 안(쪽)에: *He's hiding under the blanket.* 그는 담요 밑에 숨어 있다. / *a dog sleeping under the bed* 침대 밑에서 자고 있는 개 **2** less than a particular age, number, amount, or price ‖ 특정한 나이[수, 양, 가격] 이하의. …이하[미만]의: *I can't buy beer – I'm under age.* (=not old enough) 나는 맥주를 살 수 없어. 미성년자이거든. / *a ticket for under $10* 10달러 이하의 표 **3** controlled or governed by a particular leader, government, system etc. ‖ 특정한 지도자·정부·제도 등에 의해 통제되거나 통치되는. …하에. …아래: *a country under Marxist rule* 마르크스주의가 지배하는 국가 **4 be under discussion/construction/attack etc.** to be in the process of being discussed, built etc. ‖ 토론되는·건설되는 과정에 있다. 토론·공사/공격 중이다: *The new city library is still under construction.* 새로운 시 도서관은 아직 공사 중이다. **5 under way** happening or in the process of being done ‖ 일어나거나 행해지고 있는 과정에. 진행 중에: *Construction is already under way on the new library.* 새로운 도서관 건축 공사는 이미 진행 중이다. **6** affected by a particular influence, condition, or situation ‖ 특정한 작용[조건, 상황]에 영향을 받는. …을 받아: *She performs well under pressure.* 그녀는 압박감에도 불구하고 잘 한다. **7** if you are under someone at your job, you have a lower position of authority than s/he does ‖ 직장에서 남보다 낮은 권한의 지위를 가지고 있다. …보다 아래에. 하급(직)에 **8 be under the impression** to believe that something is true, especially something that is later proved to be untrue ‖ 특히 나중에 허위로 판명되는 어떤 것을 사실로 믿다. …이라고 믿다[인상을 받다, 착각하다]: *I was under the impression that she really liked me.* 나는 그녀가 정말로 나를 좋아한다고 착각했다. **9** according to a particular law, agreement etc. ‖ 특정한 법률·협정 등에 따라서. …에 의거하여: *Under section seven of the tax code, we are entitled to inspect your accounts.* 세법 7항에 의거하여, 우리는 당신의 장부를 조사할 권한이 있습니다. **10** in a particular part of a list, book, system etc. where you can find information ‖ 정보를 찾을 수 있는 목록·책·시스템 등의 특정한 부분에. …하에[속에]: *You'll find that topic under "Heart Disease" in the index.* 그 주제는 색인에서 "심장병" 항목을 보면 된다. — see also UNDERCOVER —compare BENEATH¹, OVER¹

under² *adv* **1** in or to a place that is below or covered by something ‖ 어떤 것의 아래나 그것으로 덮여진 장소에 또는 장소로. 밑에[으로]. 속에[으로]: *He pushed Lonnie's head under the water.* 그는 로니의 머리를 물 속으로 밀어 넣었다. **2** less than the age, number, or amount that is mentioned ‖ 언급된 나이[수, 양] 이하로. 이하로. 미만으로: *Children aged nine and under must be with a parent.* 9세 이하 어린이들은 부모와 함께 있어야 한다.

un·der·age /ˌʌndɚˈeɪdʒ/ *adj* too young to legally buy alcohol, drive a car etc. ‖ 너무 어려서 합법적으로 술을 사거나 차를 운전 할 수 없는. 미성년의: *a campaign to stop underage drinking* 미성년자 음주 방지 운동

un·der·class /ˈʌndɚˌklæs/ *n* [singular] the lowest social class, consisting of people who are very poor ‖ 매우 가난한 사람들로 구성되어 있는 가장 낮은 사회 계층. 하층민. 저소득층

un·der·cov·er /ˌʌndɚˈkʌvɚ·/ *adj* acting or done secretly in order to catch criminals or find out information ‖ 범인을 잡거나 정보를 알아내기 위해서 비밀리

에 행동하거나 수행된. 비밀의. 위장하는: *an undercover agent/cop* ‖ 비밀 요원[경찰]

un·der·cur·rent /'ʌndɚˌkɚənt, -ˌkʌr-/ *n* a feeling that someone does not express openly ‖ 사람이 공개적으로 표현하지 않은 감정. 내심. 저의: *There was an undercurrent of suspicion about the newcomers.* 새로 온 사람들에 대해서 의심의 눈초리가 있었다.

un·der·cut /ˌʌndɚˈkʌt, 'ʌndɚˌkʌt/ *v* [T] 1 to make someone's work, plans etc. not be successful or effective ‖ 남의 일·계획 등을 성공적이거나 효과적이지 못하게 하다. …을 약화시키다. 세력을 꺾다: *Such activity could undercut public confidence in Congress.* 그런 활동은 의회에 대한 대중의 신뢰를 약화시킬 수가 있다. 2 to sell something more cheaply than someone else ‖ 다른 사람보다 물건을 더 싸게 팔다. …보다 낮은 가격에 팔다: *Street vendors can undercut stores by up to 50%.* 노점상은 상점보다 50%까지 더 싸게 팔 수 있다.

un·der·dog /'ʌndɚˌdɔg/ *n* **the underdog** the person or team in a competition that is not expected to win ‖ 시합에서 이길 것으로 예상하지 않는 사람이나 팀. 약한[승산이 적은] 선수[팀]

un·der·es·ti·mate /ˌʌndɚˈɛstəˌmeɪt/ *v* 1 [I, T] to think that something is smaller, less expensive, or less important than it really is ‖ 어떤 것을 실제보다 더 작게[싸게, 중요하지 않게] 생각하다. 싸게 어림하다. 과소평가하다: *They underestimated the cost of the construction.* 그들은 공사비를 실제보다 낮게 잡았다. 2 [T] to think that someone is less skillful, intelligent etc. than s/he really is ‖ 남을 실제보다 솜씨가 떨어지며 똑똑하지 않다고 생각하다. 경시하다. 말보다 : *Don't underestimate Ronnie – he's very good at his job.* 로니를 과소평가하지 마라. 그는 자기 일을 아주 잘 한다. —opposite OVERESTIMATE

un·der·go /ˌʌndɚˈgoʊ/ *v* [T] if you undergo something unpleasant or hard to deal with, it happens to you or is done to you ‖ 불쾌하거나 다루기 힘든 일이 자신에게 일어나거나 행해지다. …을 경험하다[겪다]: *He'll have to undergo major heart surgery.* 그는 큰 심장 수술을 받아야 한다.

un·der·grad·u·ate /ˌʌndɚˈgrædʒuɪt/ *n* a student in the first four years of college ‖ 대학의 처음 4년 과정에 있는 학생. 학부생 — **undergraduate** *adj* — compare GRADUATE[1], POSTGRADUATE[1]

un·der·ground /'ʌndɚˌgraʊnd/ *adj, adv* 1 under the earth's surface ‖ 지표면 아래의. 지하의. 지하에(서): *an underground tunnel* 지하 터널 / *creatures that live underground* 땅 속에 사는 생물 2 secret, becoming secret, or done secretly ‖ 비밀인[비밀로 된, 비밀리에 행해진]. 비밀의. 지하(조직)의: *an underground rebellion* 지하 반군(조직) / *The Ukrainian church went underground during the Communist era.* 우크라이나 교회는 공산주의 치하에서 지하로 숨어들었다.

un·der·growth /'ʌndɚˌgroʊθ/ *n* [U] bushes, small trees etc. that grow around and under bigger trees ‖ 더 큰 나무들 주위와 아래에서 자라는 덤불·작은 나무 등. 나무 그늘[숲 속]의 관목

un·der·hand·ed /'ʌndɚˌhændɪd/ *adj* dishonest and done secretly ‖ 부정직하고 비밀리에 행한. 정정당당[공명정대]하지 못한. 은밀한: *an underhanded deal* 부정한 거래

un·der·line /'ʌndɚˌlaɪn, ˌʌndɚˈlaɪn/ *v* [T] 1 to draw a line under a word ‖ 단어 밑에 선을 긋다. …에 밑줄을 치다 2 to show that something is important ‖ 어떤 것이 중요하다는 것을 나타내다. …을 강조하다: *The rise in crime underlines the need for more jobs.* 범죄의 증가는 더 많은 일자리가 필요하다는 것을 잘 보여 준다.

un·der·ly·ing /'ʌndɚˌlaɪ-ɪŋ/ *adj* **underlying reason/cause/problem etc.** the reason, cause etc. that is most important but that is not easy to discover ‖ 가장 중요하지만 발견하기는 쉽지 않은 이유·원인 등. 근본적인 이유/원인/문제

un·der·mine /ˌʌndɚˈmaɪn, 'ʌndɚˌmaɪn/ *v* [T] to gradually make someone or something less strong or effective ‖ 점차적으로 사람이나 사물의 세기나 효과를 떨어지게 하다. …을 서서히 쇠퇴[약화]시키다: *He's trying to undermine Clinton's support in the South.* 그는 남부에서의 클린턴에 대한 지지를 약화시키려고 애쓰고 있다.

un·der·neath /ˌʌndɚˈniθ/ *prep, adv* directly below or under something ‖ 어떤 것의 바로 밑이나 아래에: *We turned some rocks over to see what was underneath.* 우리는 밑에 무엇이 있는지 보려고 몇 개의 돌을 뒤집었다. / *There's nice wood underneath all that paint.* 그 페인트를 한 꺼풀 벗겨내면 좋은 목재가 나온다. —compare BENEATH[1]

un·der·nour·ished /ˌʌndɚˈnɚɪʃt,

-'nʌriʃt/ *adj* not healthy because you have not eaten enough food || 충분한 음식을 먹지 못해서 건강하지 않은. 영양 불량[결핍]의

un·der·paid /ˌʌndəˈpeɪd/ *adj* earning less money than you deserve || 마땅히 받아야 하는 것보다 더 적은 돈을 버는. 저임금의. 박봉의 **– underpay** /ˌʌndəˈpeɪ/ *v* [I, T]

un·der·pants /ˈʌndəˌpænts/ *n* [plural] a short piece of underwear worn on the lower part of the body || 하체에 입는 짧은 속옷. 팬티

un·der·pass /ˈʌndəˌpæs/ *n* a road or path that goes under another road or path || 다른 도로나 길의 밑으로 뻗어 있는 도로나 길. 지하도

un·der·priv·i·leged /ˌʌndəˈprɪvlɪdʒd/ *adj* very poor and not having the advantages of most other people in society || 매우 가난하고 사회의 대부분의 다른 사람들이 가진 이점을 가지고 있지 않은. 기본권이 보장되지 않은. 불우한: *clothing for underprivileged children* 불우 아동을 위한 옷

un·der·rat·ed /ˌʌndəˈreɪtɪd/ *adj* if someone or something is underrated, people do not think he, she, or it is as good, effective etc. as he, she or it really is || 사람들이 어떤 사람이나 사물을 실제만큼 좋거나 효과적으로 생각하지 않는. 과소평가된: *He is underrated as an actor.* 그는 배우로서 과소평가되었다. **– underrate** *v* [T] **—opposite** OVERRATED

un·der·score /ˈʌndəˌskɔr/ *v* [T] to emphasize something so people pay attention to it || 사람들이 주목하도록 어떤 것을 강조하다. …을 강조[역설]하다: *The survey underscores the division between rich and poor in America.* 그 조사는 미국에서의 빈부의 괴리(乖離)를 역설하고 있다.

un·der·shirt /ˈʌndəˌʃət/ *n* a piece of underwear worn under a shirt || 셔츠 속에 입는 속옷가지. 메리야스

un·der·side /ˈʌndəˌsaɪd/ *n* **the underside of sth** the bottom side or surface of something || 어떤 것의 바닥 쪽이나 그 표면. 아래쪽. 밑바닥: *white spots on the underside of the leaves* 나뭇잎 밑면의 하얀 반점들

un·der·sized /ˌʌndəˈsaɪzd/ *adj* too small, or smaller than usual || 너무 작거나 보통보다 더 작은. 소형의

un·der·staffed /ˌʌndəˈstæft/ *adj* not having enough workers, or having fewer workers than usual || 근로자가 충분하지 않거나 정상보다 근로자가 더 적은. 직원[인원]이 부족한

un·der·stand /ˌʌndəˈstænd/ *v* **understood, understood, understanding 1** [I, T] to know the meaning of what someone is saying to you, or the language that s/he speaks || 남이 말하고 있는 것의 의미나 말하는 언어를 알다. (…을) 이해하다. 알아듣다: *Do you understand Spanish?* 너 스페인어 알아? / *I could barely understand what he was saying.* 나는 그가 무슨 말을 하고 있는지 거의 이해할 수가 없었다. ✗DON'T SAY "I am understanding."✗ "I am understanding."이라고는 하지 않는다 **2** [I, T] to know how someone feels and why s/he behaves the way s/he does || 남의 기분과 그렇게 행동하는 이유를 알다. (…을) 이해[파악]하다: *Believe me, John – I understand how you feel.* 존, 정말이야. 나도 네 기분 이해해. **3** [I, T] to know how or why a situation, event etc. happens, especially through learning or experience || 특히 학습이나 경험을 통해서 어떤 상황·사건 등이 어떻게 또는 왜 발생하는지 알다. …에 대한 지식이 있다. …을 알고 있다: *Do you understand how this works?* 너는 이것이 어떻게 작동하는지 아니? / *I don't understand why the experiment failed.* 나는 그 실험이 왜 실패했는지 모르겠어. **4 make yourself understood** to make what you say clear to other people || 자신이 말하는 것을 다른 사람에게 분명하게 하다. 자기 생각[말]을 남에게 이해시키다 **5 I understand (that)** SPOKEN used in order to say politely or formally that someone has already told you something || 남이 이미 어떤 것을 말해 주었다고 공손하게 또는 격식을 차려 말하는 데에 쓰여. …을 들어서 알고 있다: *I understand that you want to buy a painting.* 그림 한 점을 사고 싶으시다고요. **—compare** MISUNDERSTAND

un·der·stand·a·ble /ˌʌndəˈstændəbəl/ *adj* **1** understandable behavior, reactions etc. seem reasonable because of the situation you are in || 처한 상황 때문에 행동·반응 등이 합당해 보이는. 이해할 만한: *It's understandable that he's a little afraid – anyone would be.* 그가 조금 두려워하는 것도 이해할 만하다. 누군들 그렇지 않겠어. **2** able to be understood || 이해될 수 있는. 이해하기 쉬운: *legal documents written in understandable terms* 이해하기 쉬운 용어로 쓰여진 법률 서류

un·der·stand·ing[1] /ˌʌndəˈstændɪŋ/ *n* **1** [singular, U] knowledge about something, based on learning and experience || 학습과 경험에 근거한 어떤 것에 대한 지식. 이해. 숙지: *She has a basic understanding of computers.* 그녀는 컴퓨터에 대한 기본적인 지식이 있다. **2** [singular, U] sympathy toward someone's character and behavior || 남의 성격과 행동에 대한 공감. 이해심: *Harry thanked us for our understanding.* 해리는 우리가 이해해 준 것에 고마워했다. **3** an informal private agreement about something || 어떤 것에 대한 비공식적이며 사적인 동의. 합의. 일치: *I thought we had come to an understanding about the price.* 나는 가격에 대해서는 서로 합의를 본 것으로 생각했어요. **4** [U] the ability to know or learn; INTELLIGENCE || 알거나 배우는 능력. 이해력; ㉠ intelligence

understanding² *adj* showing sympathy and pity for other people's problems || 다른 사람의 문제에 동정과 연민을 보이는. 이해심 있는[많은]: *an understanding boss* 이해심이 많은 사장

un·der·state /ˌʌndəˈsteɪt/ *v* [T] to say that something is not as large or as important as it really is || 어떤 것이 실제만큼 크거나 중요하지 않다고 말하다. 줄여서 말하다: *The report understates the severity of the problem.* 그 보고서는 문제의 심각성을 축소하여 말하고 있다.

un·der·stat·ed /ˌʌndəˈsteɪtɪd/ *adj* done in a way that is not very noticeable or seems unimportant || 그다지 눈에 띄지 않거나 중요해 보이지 않게 행해진. 수수한. 삼가는: *the understated decoration of his office* 수수하게 꾸며진 그의 사무실

un·der·state·ment /ˈʌndəˌsteɪtmənt/ *n* a statement that is not strong enough to express how good, impressive, bad etc. something really is || 어떤 것이 실제로 얼마나 좋은지[인상적인지, 나쁜지] 등을 충분히 노골적으로 표현하지 않은 말. 줄여서[삼가서] 한 말: *To say that the effects of the earthquake were severe is an understatement.* 지진의 영향이 심했다고 말하는 것으로는 충분하지 않다.

un·der·stood /ˌʌndəˈstʊd/ *v* the past tense and PAST PARTICIPLE of UNDERSTAND || understand 의 과거·과거 분사형

un·der·stud·y /ˈʌndəˌstʌdi/ *n* an actor who learns a part in a play so that s/he can act if the usual actor cannot perform || 출연 배우가 공연할 수 없을 때 연기할 수 있도록 극의 역할을 익히고 있는 배우. 대역 배우

un·der·take /ˌʌndəˈteɪk/ *v* [T] FORMAL **1** to start to do a piece of work for which you are responsible || 자신이 책임을 지는 일을 하기 시작하다. …을 (떠)맡다. …할 의무를 지다: *Baker undertook the task of writing the annual report.* 베이커는 연례 보고서 작성 임무를 맡았다. **2 undertake to do sth** to promise to do something || 어떤 것을 하기로 약속하다. …임을 보증[보장]하다: *We undertook to publish within six months.* 우리는 6개월 내에 출판할 것을 보장했다.

un·der·tak·er /ˈʌndəˌteɪkə/ *n* someone whose job is to arrange funerals || 장례식을 준비하는 직업인. 장의사

un·der·tak·ing /ˈʌndəˌteɪkɪŋ/ *n* [C usually singular] an important job, piece of work etc. for which you are responsible || 책임을 지는 중요한 직무·일 등. 맡은 일. 사업: *Setting up the Summer Olympics was a massive undertaking.* 하계 올림픽을 준비하는 것은 대대적인 일이었다.

un·der·tone /ˈʌndəˌtoʊn/ *n* a feeling or quality that you notice even though it is difficult to see, hear, taste etc. || 비록 보고 듣고 맛보는 등을 하기가 어려움에도 불구하고 알아채는 느낌이나 특성. 기미. 기색: *an undertone of sadness in her voice* 그녀 목소리의 슬픈 음조

un·der·tow /ˈʌndəˌtoʊ/ *n* a strong current under the ocean's surface, that pulls water away from the shore || 해변에서 바닷물을 끌어당기는 해수면 아래의 강한 해류. 역류. 저류

un·der·wa·ter /ˌʌndəˈwɔtə, -ˈwɑ-/ *adj* below the surface of the water || 수면 아래의. 물 속[수중]의: *underwater photography* 수중 촬영 — **underwater** *adv*

underwater

un·der·wear /ˈʌndəˌwɛr/ *n* [U] clothes that you wear next to your body under your other clothes || 다른 옷 속에 몸에 바로 닿게 입는 옷. 속옷

un·der·weight /ˌʌndəˈweɪt/ *adj* weighing less than is expected or usual || 예상이나 보통보다 무게가 덜 나가는. 중량[체중] 미달인: *an underweight baby* 체중 미달인 아기 —opposite OVERWEIGHT —see usage note at THIN

un·der·world /ˈʌndəˌwəld/ *n* **1** [singular] the criminals in a particular place and the activities they are involved in ‖ 특정한 장소의 범죄자들과 그들이 개입된 활동들. 암흑가 **2 the place where the spirits of the dead live, especially in ancient Greek stories** ‖ 특히 고대 그리스 신화에서 죽은 자들의 영혼이 사는 장소. 저승. 황천

un·der·write /ˈʌndəˌraɪt, ˌʌndəˈraɪt/ v [T] FORMAL **to support an activity, business etc. with money** ‖ 활동·사업 등을 돈으로 지지하다. …에 기부를 승낙하다: *The project is underwritten by a National Science Foundation grant.* 전미 과학 재단이 그 프로젝트 비용의 지급을 승낙했다.

un·de·sir·a·ble /ˌʌndɪˈzaɪrəbəl/ adj FORMAL **bad and unpleasant, or not wanted because it may have a bad effect** ‖ 나쁜 영향을 미칠 수도 있어서 나쁘고 불쾌하거나 원하지 않는. 바람직하지 않은. 부적당한: *The treatment has no undesirable side effects.* 이 치료는 해로운 부작용이 없습니다.

un·de·ter·mined /ˌʌndɪˈtəmɪnd/ adj ⇨ INDETERMINATE

un·de·vel·oped /ˌʌndɪˈvɛləpt/ adj **undeveloped land has not been built on or used for a particular purpose** ‖ 토지가 그 위에 건물을 짓거나 특정한 목적에 사용되지 않은. 미개발의

un·dis·closed /ˌʌndɪsˈkloʊzd/ adj **not known publicly** ‖ 공개적으로 알려지지 않은. 공표[폭로]되지 않은: *Henderson was hired for an undisclosed amount/sum.* 헨더슨은 공표되지 않은 금액[총액]에 고용되었다.

un·dis·guised /ˌʌndɪsˈgaɪzd/ adj **clearly shown and not hidden** ‖ 분명하게 보이고 숨겨지지 않은. 숨김없는: *She looked at me with undisguised hatred.* 그녀는 나를 역력한 증오의 표정으로 쳐다봤다.

un·dis·put·ed /ˌʌndɪˈspyutɪd/ adj **undisputed leader/master/champion etc.** someone whom everyone agrees is the leader etc. ‖ 모든 사람이 지도자 등이라고 동의하는 사람. 논쟁의 여지가 없는 지도자/달인/챔피언

un·dis·turbed /ˌʌndɪˈstəbd/ adj, adv **not interrupted, moved, or changed** ‖ 방해받지[이동되지, 바뀌지] 않는: *They let her rest undisturbed.* 그들은 그녀를 방해받지 않고 쉬게 했다.

un·di·vid·ed /ˌʌndɪˈvaɪdɪd/ adj **complete** ‖ 완전한. 한눈팔지 않는. 전념[집중]한: *Please give me your undivided attention.* (=full attention) 제게 총집중해 주세요.

un·do /ʌnˈdu/ v [T] **1 to untie or open**

something that is tied or closed ‖ 묶이거나 잠겨진 것을 풀거나 열다. 끄르다. 벗기다: *I can't get the clasp on my necklace undone.* 나는 목걸이의 고리를 풀 수가 없다. **2 to try to remove the bad effects of something** ‖ 어떤 것의 나쁜 영향을 제거하려고 애쓰다. …을 제거[폐지]하다: *The courts have tried to undo the legal abuses of the past.* 법원은 과거의 법률 남용을 일소하려고 노력해 왔다.

un·do·ing /ʌnˈduɪŋ/ n **be sb's undoing to cause someone's failure, defeat, shame etc.** ‖ 어떤 사람에게 실패·패배·수치 등을 야기하다. …의 파멸[타락]의 원인이 되다: *Borrowing too much money proved to be his undoing.* 그는 너무 많은 돈을 빌려서 결국 파멸했다.

un·done /ʌnˈdʌn/ adj **1 not tied or closed** ‖ 묶이거나 잠겨지지 않은. 풀어진. 끌러진. 벗어진: *Your shirt button has come undone.* 너의 셔츠 단추가 풀렸다. **2 not finished or completed** ‖ 끝마치거나 완성되지 않은. 마무리짓지 않은. 미완성의: *Much of the work on the bridge has been left undone.* 다리 공사의 상당 부분이 마무리되지 않은 채 남겨졌다.

undone

un·doubt·ed·ly /ʌnˈdaʊtɪdli/ adv **used in order to emphasize that something is definitely true** ‖ 어떤 것이 확실히 사실이라는 것을 강조하는 데에 쓰여. 의심의 여지없이. 틀림없이: *He's undoubtedly one of the best guitar players of all time.* 그는 의심할 바 없이 역사상 가장 뛰어난 기타 연주자 중의 한 사람이다.

un·dress /ʌnˈdrɛs/ v [I, T] **to take your clothes off, or take someone else's clothes off** ‖ 옷을 벗다, 또는 다른 사람의 옷을 벗기다

un·dressed /ʌnˈdrɛst/ adj **not wearing any clothes, or wearing only PAJAMAS** ‖ 어떠한 옷도 입지 않은, 또는 잠옷만을 입은. 옷을 입지 않은. 잠옷 바람의: *Jessie got undressed quickly and snuggled into bed.* 제시는 서둘러 옷을 벗고는 침대 속으로 파고 들었다.

un·due /ʌnˈduʲ/ adj FORMAL **more than is reasonable, suitable, or necessary** ‖ 합당한[알맞은, 필요한] 것 이상의. 부당한. 과도한: *The tax creates an undue burden on farmers.* 그 세금은 농부들에게 과도한 짐을 지운다.

un·du·ly /ʌnˈduli/ adv FORMAL **much more than necessary, or much too**

extreme ‖ 필요한 것보다 훨씬 더 많은, 또는 너무 지나치게 극심한. 과도하게. 심하게: *unduly harsh punishment* 지나치게 가혹한 처벌

un·dy·ing /ʌnˈdaɪ-ɪŋ/ *adj* LITERARY continuing for ever ‖ 영원히 계속되는. 불멸의. 불후의: *undying love* 영원한 사랑

un·earth /ʌnˈəθ/ *v* [T] **1** to find something that was buried in the ground ‖ 땅 속에 묻힌 것을 찾다. …을 파 내다[발굴하다]: *Scientists have unearthed eight more skeletons at Pompeii.* 과학자들은 폼페이에서 유골 여덟 구를 더 발굴했다. **2** to find out the truth ‖ 진실을 찾아내다. 적발하다: *New evidence has been unearthed that connects them to the crime.* 그들을 범죄와 연관시키는 새로운 증거가 발견되었다.

un·earth·ly /ʌnˈəθli/ *adj* very strange and not seeming natural ‖ 매우 이상하고 자연스러워 보이지 않는. 이 세상의 것 같지 않은. 초자연적인: *an unearthly greenish light* 이 세상의 것 같지 않은 푸르스름한 빛

un·eas·y /ˌʌnˈizi/ *adj* not at all comfortable with what is happening in a situation ‖ 어떤 상황에서 벌어지고 있는 것에 전혀 편안하지 않은: *We felt uneasy about his decision.* 우리는 그의 결정에 대해서 마음이 편치 않았다. – **uneasiness** *n* [U] – **uneasily** *adv*

un·ed·u·cat·ed /ʌnˈɛdʒə‚keɪtɪd/ *adj* not having much education, or showing that someone is not well educated ‖ 교육을 많이 받지 않은, 또는 사람이 교육을 잘 받지 못한 것을 나타내는. 교육을 받지 않은. 교양 없는. 무식한

un·em·ployed /ˌʌnɪmˈplɔɪd/ *adj* **1** without a job ‖ 일자리가 없는. 실직한: *an unemployed teacher* 실직한 교사 **2 the unemployed** people who do not have jobs ‖ 일자리가 없는 사람들. 실업자

un·em·ploy·ment /ˌʌnɪmˈplɔɪmənt/ *n* [U] **1** the condition of not having a job, or the number of people who do not have a job ‖ 일자리가 없는 상태, 또는 일자리가 없는 사람들의 수. 실직(자수). 실업률: *There is high unemployment in the cities.* 도시에서는 실업률이 높다. **2** money that is paid regularly by the government to people who have no job ‖ 일자리가 없는 사람들에게 정부가 정기적으로 지급하는 돈. 실업 수당: *Bill's drawing unemployment.* (=receiving money) 빌은 실업 수당을 받고 있다.

un·e·qual /ʌnˈikwəl/ *adj* **1** not having the same rights, chances etc. as other people ‖ 다른 사람들과 동등한 권리·기회 등을 가지지 못하는. 불평등한. 불공평한: *the unequal treatment of minorities* 소수 인종에 대한 불공평한 대우 **2** not the same in size, amount, value, rank etc. ‖ 크기·양·가치·등급 등이 같지 않은. 동등하지 않은

un·e·quiv·o·cal /ˌʌnɪˈkwɪvəkəl/ *adj* FORMAL completely clear and definite with no doubts ‖ 의심의 여지없이 완전히 명확하고 분명한. 모호하지 않은. 명료한

un·er·ring /ʌnˈɛrɪŋ, ʌnˈərɪŋ/ *adj* always exactly correct ‖ 항상 정확히 옳은. 과오를 범하지 않는. 조금도 틀리지 않는: *Madsen's unerring judgment* 매드슨의 정확한 판단

un·eth·i·cal /ʌnˈɛθɪkəl/ *adj* considered to be morally wrong ‖ 도덕적으로 잘못된 것으로 간주되는. 비[반]윤리적인: *unethical behavior in business* 비윤리적인 상행위

un·e·ven /ʌnˈivən/ *adj* **1** not flat, smooth, or level ‖ 편평하지[매끄럽지, 수평하지] 않은. 고르지 않은. 울퉁불퉁한: *uneven ground* 울퉁불퉁한 땅 **2** not equal or balanced ‖ 동등하거나 균형이 잡히지 않은. 불평등한: *The racial mix of the school is uneven.* 그 학교의 인종 비율은 균등하지 않다. **3** good in some parts and bad in others ‖ 어떤 부분은 좋고 다른 부분은 나쁜. 불규칙한. 한결같지 않은: *a music album of uneven quality* 곡의 질이 고르지 못한 음악 앨범 – **unevenly** *adv*

un·ex·cused /ˌʌnɪkˈskuzd/ *adj* **unexcused absence** an occasion when you are away from school or work without permission ‖ 허가 없이 학교나 직장을 떠나 있는 경우. 무단결석[결근]

un·ex·pect·ed /ˌʌnɪkˈspɛktɪd/ *adj* surprising because of not being expected ‖ 예상을 하지 않았기 때문에 놀라운. 예기치 않은. 뜻밖의: *the unexpected death of his father* 그의 아버지의 예기치 못한 죽음 – **unexpectedly** *adv*

un·fail·ing /ʌnˈfeɪlɪŋ/ *adj* always happening or being shown, in spite of difficulties ‖ 어려움에도 불구하고 항상 발생하거나 나타나는. 기대에 어긋나지 않는. 틀림없는: *his unfailing kindness* 그의 변함없는 친절함

un·fair /ʌnˈfɛr/ *adj* not right or fair ‖ 옳거나 공정하지 않은. 불공정한. 부당한: *an unfair decision* 불공정한 결정 / *It's unfair to make her do most of the packing.* 그녀에게 대부분의 짐을 싸게 하는 것은 부당하다. – **unfairly** *adv* –

U

unfairness *n* [U]

un·faith·ful /ʌnˈfeɪθfəl/ *adj* someone who is unfaithful has sex with someone who is not his/her wife, husband, or usual partner ‖ 자기의 아내[남편, 평소의 짝]가 아닌 사람과 성관계를 하는. 바람을 피우는. 부정(不貞)한

un·fa·mil·iar /ˌʌnfəˈmɪlyɚ/ *adj* **1** not known to you ‖ 알지 못하는. 생소한. 낯선: *an unfamiliar face* 낯선 얼굴 **2** not knowing about something ‖ 어떤 것에 대해 알지 못하는. 잘 모르는: *I am unfamiliar with his books.* 나는 그의 책에 대해서는 잘 모른다. – **unfamiliarity** /ˌʌnfəˌmɪlˈyærəṭi/ *n* [U] —compare UNKNOWN[1]

un·fas·ten /ʌnˈfæsən/ *v* [T] ⇨ UNDO: *Lewis unfastened his seat belt and got out.* 루이스는 안전띠를 풀고 나왔다.

un·fa·vor·a·ble /ʌnˈfeɪvərəbəl/ *adj* **1** unfavorable conditions or events are not as good as you want them to be ‖ 상태나 사건이 바라는 만큼 좋지 않은. 형편이 나쁜. 불리한: *an unfavorable weather report* 좋지 못한 날씨 예보 **2** showing disapproval ‖ 불만을 나타내는. 호의적이 아닌. 반대하는: *an unfavorable review of the movie* 그 영화에 대한 호의적이지 못한 비평

un·feel·ing /ʌnˈfilɪŋ/ *adj* not showing sympathy or pity for others ‖ 다른 사람들에게 동정이나 연민을 나타내지 않는. 냉담한. 몰인정한

un·fet·tered /ʌnˈfɛṭɚd/ *adj* not restricted in any way ‖ 어떤 식으로든 제한받지 않는. 속박되지 않는. 자유로운: *the unfettered free-market system* 제한 없는 자유 시장 경제 체제

un·fit /ʌnˈfɪt/ *adj* not suitable or good enough to do something or to be used for something ‖ 어떤 것을 하거나 어떤 것에 쓰이기에는 충분히 알맞거나 좋지 않은. 부적당한. 부적합한: *That woman is unfit to raise a child!* 저 여자는 아이를 기를 자격이 없어! / *land unfit for cultivation* 경작에 부적합한 땅

un·fold /ʌnˈfoʊld/ *v* [I, T] **1** if a story, plan etc. unfolds, it becomes clearer and you understand it ‖ 이야기·계획 등이 더 명확해져서 이해하게 되다. (…을) 밝히다[털어놓다]: *The case began to slowly unfold in court.* 그 사건은 법정에서 서서히 밝혀지기 시작했다. **2** to open something that was folded ‖ 접혀진 것을 펴다. 펴다. 펼치다: *She unfolded the map.* 그녀는 지도를 펼쳤다.

un·fore·seen /ˌʌnfɔrˈsin, -fɚ-/ *adj* an unforeseen situation is one that you were not able to plan for because you did not expect it ‖ 상황을 예상하지 못해서 미리 대비하지 못한. 예기치 않은. 뜻밖의: *an unforeseen delay* 뜻밖의 지연

un·for·get·ta·ble /ˌʌnfɚˈgɛṭəbəl/ *adj* so beautiful, good, exciting etc. that you remember it for a long time ‖ 아주 아름답고 좋으며 흥미로와서 오랫동안 기억하는. 잊을 수 없는: *The ships, with their billowing sails, were an unforgettable sight.* 돛에 바람을 가득 싣고 나가는 배들은 잊을 수 없는 광경이었다.

un·for·tu·nate /ʌnˈfɔrtʃənɪt/ *adj* **1** happening because of bad luck ‖ 불운 때문에 발생하는. 불운한. 불행한: *an unfortunate accident* 불운한 사고 **2** unsuitable and causing embarrassment ‖ 부적합하며 당황하게 하는. 부적절한: *an unfortunate choice of words* 부적절한 말의 선택

un·for·tu·nate·ly /ʌnˈfɔrtʃənɪtli/ *adv* used when you are mentioning a fact that you wish were not true ‖ 진실이 아니었기를 바라는 사실을 언급할 때 쓰여. 불행하게도: *Unfortunately, your computer needs more memory to run this program.* 안됐지만, 네 컴퓨터는 이 프로그램을 실행하려면 메모리가 더 필요하다.

un·found·ed /ˌʌnˈfaʊndɪd/ *adj* not based on facts; wrong ‖ 사실에 근거하지 않은. 근거가 없는; 틀린: *The company insisted that our complaints were unfounded.* 회사는 우리의 불평이 근거가 없다고 주장했다.

un·furl /ʌnˈfɚl/ *v* [T] to unroll and open a flag, sail etc. ‖ 깃발·돛 등을 풀어서 펼치다. 펴다

un·gain·ly /ʌnˈgeɪnli/ *adj* awkward and not graceful ‖ 어색하며 보기 좋지 않은. 보기 흉한. 볼품없는: *an ungainly teenager* 꼴사나운 십대

un·gra·cious /ʌnˈgreɪʃəs/ *adj* not polite or friendly ‖ 공손하거나 친근하지 않는. 무뚝뚝한. 무례한: *She gave us an ungracious welcome.* 그녀는 우리를 쌀쌀맞게 맞이했다. – **ungraciously** *adv*

un·grate·ful /ʌnˈgreɪtfəl/ *adj* not thanking someone for something s/he has given to you or done for you ‖ 남이 주었거나 해 준 것에 대해 감사하지 않는. 감사할 줄 모르는. 배은망덕한

un·hap·py /ʌnˈhæpi/ *adj* **1** not happy ‖ 행복하지 않은. 불행한. 불우한: *He had a very unhappy childhood.* 그의 어린 시절은 매우 불우했다. **2** feeling worried or annoyed because you do not like what is happening ‖ 일어나고 있는 일을 좋아하

지 않아서 걱정이나 화가 나는. 기분이 안 좋은. 불만스러운: *Americans are deeply unhappy with the state of the nation.* 미국인은 국가의 현 상황에 대해서 매우 불만스러워 한다. – **unhappiness** *n* [U] – **unhappily** *adv*

un·health·y /ʌnˈhɛlθi/ *adj* **1** likely to make you ill ‖ 사람을 병들게 할 가능성이 있는. 몸에 나쁜. 유해한: *unhealthy city air* 유해한 도시 공기 **2** not physically healthy ‖ 육체적으로 건강하지 않은. 건강하지 못한. 병든: *an unhealthy baby that was born too early* 너무 일찍 태어난 건강하지 못한 아기 **3** not normal or natural and likely to cause harm ‖ 정상적이거나 자연스럽지 못하고 해를 끼칠 가능성이 있는. 불건전한. 위험한: *an unhealthy relationship* 불건전한 관계

un·heard-of /ʌnˈhɜd ˌʌv/ *adj* so unusual that it has never happened or been known before ‖ 아주 이상해서 한 번도 발생한 적이 없거나 이전에는 알려지지 않은. 전대미문의. 미증유의: *The opera raised the price of its seats to an unheard-of $100 each!* 그 오페라의 관람석 가격이 전례 없이 각 100달러로 오르다니!

un·ho·ly /ʌnˈhoʊli/ *adj* **1** INFORMAL unusual and offensive or upsetting ‖ 유별나고 기분을 상하게 하거나 화 나게 하는. 지독한. 터무니없는: *an unholy alliance between greed and politics* 탐욕과 정치간의 추악한 동맹 **2** not holy or not respecting what is holy ‖ 신성하지 않거나 신성한 것을 존중하지 않는. 부정한. 죄 많은. 사악한

un·hook /ʌnˈhʊk/ *v* [T] to unfasten or remove something from a hook ‖ 고리에서 사물을 풀거나 떼내다. …의 고리를 끄르다: *Can you help me unhook my necklace?* 내 목걸이 좀 풀어줄래?

UNICEF /ˈyunəˌsɛf/ *n* [U] the United Nations Children's Fund; an organization that helps children who suffer from disease, HUNGER etc. ‖ the United Nations Children's Fund (국제 연합 아동 기금)의 약어; 질병·굶주림 등으로 고통 받는 어린이들을 돕는 기구

u·ni·corn /ˈyunəˌkɔrn/ *n* an imaginary animal like a white horse with a long straight horn on its head ‖ 머리에 길고 곧은 뿔이 달린 백마처럼 생긴 상상의 동물. 일각수(一角獸)

un·i·den·ti·fied /ˌʌnaɪˈdɛntəˌfaɪd-, ˌʌnə-/ *adj* an unidentified person or thing is one that you do not recognize or know the name of ‖ 다른 사람이나 사물을 알아보지 못하거나 그 이름을 알지 못하는. 신원 미상의. 정체불명의: *An unidentified man was hit by a car.* 신원 미상의 남자가 차에 치었다.

u·ni·fi·ca·tion /ˌyunəfəˈkeɪʃən/ *n* [U] the act of combining two more groups, countries etc. to make a single group or country ‖ 두 개 이상의 집단·국가 등을 단일한 집단이나 국가로 만들기 위해 결합시키기. 통일. 통합: *the economic unification of Europe* 유럽의 경제 통합

u·ni·form¹ /ˈyunəˌfɔrm/ *n* **1** a particular type of clothing that the members of an organization wear to work ‖ 한 조직의 구성원들이 일할 때 입는 특정한 종류의 옷. 제복: *a blue police uniform* 푸른 경찰 제복 **2 be in uniform a)** to be wearing a uniform ‖ 제복을 입고 있다 **b)** to be in the army, navy etc. ‖ 육군·해군 등에 있다. 군복무 중이다. 군복을 입고 있다 – **uniformed** *adj*

uniform² *adj* a number of things that are a uniform size, weight etc. are all nearly the same size, weight etc. ‖ 많은 것들의 크기·무게 등이 거의 모두 같은. 동일한. 균일한 – **uniformly** *adv* – **uniformity** /ˌyunəˈfɔrməti/ *n* [U]

u·ni·fy /ˈyunəˌfaɪ/ *v* [T] **1** to combine the parts of a country, organization etc. to make a single unit ‖ 국가·조직 등의 부분들을 단일체로 만들려고 결합시키다. …을 통일[통합]하다: *Spain was unified in the 16th century.* 스페인은 16세기에 통일되었다. **2** to change a group of things so that they are all the same ‖ 모두 똑같게 하려고 일단의 것들을 바꾸다. 단일[일체]화하다: *a record that unifies different musical styles* 서로 다른 음악 양식을 단일화한 음반 – **unified** *adj*

u·ni·lat·er·al /ˌyunəˈlætərəl/ *adj* a unilateral action or decision is made by only one of the groups, organizations etc. that are involved in a situation ‖ 행동이나 결정이 상황에 개입한 집단·조직들 등 중에서 오직 한쪽에 의해서만 행해지는. 일방적인: *a unilateral ceasefire* 일방적인 전투 중지 —compare BILATERAL, MULTILATERAL

un·im·por·tant /ˌʌnɪmˈpɔrtnt-/ *adj* not important ‖ 중요하지 않은

un·in·sured /ˌʌnɪnˈʃʊrd-/ *adj* having no insurance ‖ 보험에 들지 않은. 무보험의: *uninsured drivers* 무보험 운전자들

un·in·tel·li·gi·ble /ˌʌnɪnˈtɛlədʒəbəl/ *adj* impossible to understand ‖ 이해하기 불가능한. 이해할 수 없는. 난해한: *Their radio transmissions were unintelligible.* 그들의 무선 송신은 해독할 수가 없었다.

un·in·ter·est·ed /ʌnˈɪntrɪstɪd,

-'ɪntərɛs-/ *adj* not interested ‖ 흥미가 없는. 무관심한 —compare DISINTERESTED

un·in·ter·rupt·ed /ˌʌnɪntə'rʌptɪd./ *adj* continuous, without being stopped ‖ 중단되지 않고 계속적인. 끊임없는. 연속적인 : *All I want is two hours of uninterrupted work.* 내가 오직 원하는 것은 두 시간동안 중단없이 일하는 것이다.

un·ion /'yunyən/ *n* **1** ⇨ LABOR UNION: *the auto workers' union* 자동차 노동자 노조 **2** a group of countries or states with the same central government ‖ 같은 중앙 정부를 가진 일단의 나라들이나 주(州)들. 연방 **3** [singular, U] FORMAL the act of joining two or more things together, or the state of being joined together ‖ 둘 이상의 것들을 함께 결합시키는 행위, 또는 함께 결합된 상태. 통합. 연합: *the union of East Germany with West Germany* 동독과 서독의 통합 **4** [singular, U] FORMAL the act of marriage, or the state of being married ‖ 결혼 행위나 결혼된 상태. 혼인 (관계)

un·ion·ized /'yunyə,naɪzd/ *adj* having formed a UNION, or belonging to one ‖ 노동조합을 결성한, 또는 노동조합에 소속한. 노동조합에 가입한 **– unionize** *v* [I, T]

u·nique /yu'nik/ *adj* **1** INFORMAL unusually good and special ‖ 대단히 좋고 특별한. 필적할[비길] 것이 없는. 무쌍의. 다시없는: *a unique opportunity to study with an artist* 예술가와 함께 공부할 수 있는 다시없는 기회 / *unique Christmas presents* 진기한 성탄절 선물들 **2** being the only one of its kind ‖ 그 종류 중에서 단 하나인. 유일(무이)한. 독특한: *a unique sculpture* 독특한 조각품 **– uniquely** *adv*

USAGE NOTE unique

Use this word in order to talk about something that is the only one of its kind: *Glenn Gould had a unique way of playing the piano.* You may sometimes hear people say "very unique," "more unique," "the most unique," etc. However, using **unique** in this way is nonstandard

이 단어는 그 종류 중에서 단 하나인 것에 대해서 말하는 데 쓴다: 글렌 굴드는 피아노를 독특한 방식으로 쳤다. 때때로 사람들이 "very unique" "more unique" "the most unique"등으로 말하는 것을 들을 수도 있다. 하지만 **unique**를 이런 식으로 사용하는 것은 비표준적 용법이다.

---

u·ni·sex /'yunə,sɛks/ *adj* suitable for both men and women ‖ 남자와 여자 둘 다에게 알맞은. 남녀 공통[공용]의: *a unisex jacket* 남녀 공용 재킷

u·ni·son /'yunəsən/ *n* **in unison a)** if people speak in unison, they say the same words at the same time ‖ 사람들이 동시에 같은 말을 하여. 일제히. 일치하여: *"Okay, Mom!" the twins said in unison.* "알았어요, 엄마!"라고 쌍둥이는 동시에 말했다. **b)** if people do something in unison, they do it together because they agree with each other ‖ 사람들이 서로 동의해서 어떤 것을 함께 하여. 일치[화합]하여: *Congress needs to act in unison on this issue.* 의회는 이 문제에 대해서 일치된 행동을 해야 한다.

u·nit /'yunɪt/ *n* **1** a person or thing that is one whole part of something larger ‖ 보다 큰 전체의 한 부분이 되는 사람이나 사물. 구성 단위: *The family is the smallest social unit.* 가족은 사회의 최소 단위이다. / *an eight-unit apartment building* (=it has 8 apartments) 여덟 가구수의 아파트 건물 **2** a group of people who work together as part of a larger group ‖ 더 큰 집단의 부분으로 함께 일하는 일단의 사람들. 한 부분[파트]: *the emergency unit of the hospital* 병원의 응급실 담당 파트 **3** an amount or quantity of something that is used as a standard of measurement ‖ 측정의 기준으로 사용되는 어떤 것의 양이나 수량. 단위: *The dollar is the basic unit of money in the US.* 달러는 미국에서 돈의 기본 단위이다. **4** a piece of furniture that can be fitted to others of the same type ‖ 같은 종류의 다른 가구들에 들어맞는 가구. 가구 세트: *a kitchen unit* 주방 가구 세트 **5** a piece of machinery that is part of a larger machine ‖ 더 큰 기계의 부분인 기계. (기계 등의) 구성 부품. …장치: *The cooling unit is broken.* 냉각 장치가 고장났다.

U·ni·tar·i·an /ˌyunə'tɛriən/ *adj* relating to a Protestant church whose members believe in religious freedom ‖ 신도들이 종교적 자유를 믿는 개신교에 관련된. 유니테리언교도의 **– Unitarian** *n*

u·nite /yu'naɪt/ *v* [I, T] to join together with other people or organizations and act as one group, or to make people join together in this way ‖ 다른 사람들이나 조직과 함께 결합해서 한 집단처럼 행동하다, 또는 이런 식으로 사람들을 함께 결합시키다. …을[…과] 연합[합체, 통일]하다 : *Congress united behind the President.* 의회는 대통령을 지지하며 단결했다. / *The deal would unite two of* *the country's oldest electronics firms.* 그 거래로 그 국가의 가장 오래된 전자 회사 두 개가 합병될 것이다.

u·nit·ed /yu'naɪtɪd/ *adj* **1** involving or done by everyone ‖ 모든 사람이 참여하거나 행하는. 합친. 결합[연합]한: *a united effort to clean up the environment* 환경을 정화하려는 일치단결된 노력 **2** closely related by sharing feelings, aims etc. ‖ 감정·목표 등을 공유함으로써 긴밀하게 연관되는. 협력[단결]한. 일심동체의. 뭉친: *a united community* 일치단결한 지역 사회

United Na·tions /.ˌ.. '../ *n* [singular] ⇨ UN

u·ni·ty /'yunəti/ *n* [singular, U] the state of being UNITED ‖ 결합된 상태. 통일(성). 단일체: *a new political unity among countries* 국가들 사이에 새로 형성된 정치적 단결[단일체]

u·ni·ver·sal /ˌyunə'vɚsəl/ *adj* **1** concerning all the members of a group or of the world ‖ 한 집단이나 세계의 모든 구성원들에 관한. 전체[만민]의: *universal voting rights* 인류 공통의 투표권 / *a universal health care program* 만민 의료 서비스 프로그램 **2** relating to everywhere in the world ‖ 세계의 모든 곳과 관련된. 전 세계적인: *universal environmental problems* 전 세계적인 환경 문제 **3** true or suitable in every situation ‖ 모든 상황에서 옳거나 적절한. 보편[일반]적인: *a universal truth* 보편적인 진리 – **universally** *adv*

u·ni·verse /'yunəˌvɚs/ *n* **the universe** all of space, including all the stars and PLANETS ‖ 모든 항성들과 행성들을 포함하는 모든 우주 공간. 우주

u·ni·ver·si·ty /ˌyunə'vɚsəti/ *n* [C, U] a school at the highest level, where you study for a DEGREE ‖ 학위를 얻기 위해 공부하는 최고 수준의 학교. 대학

un·just /ˌʌn'dʒʌst/ *adj* not fair or reasonable ‖ 공정하지 않거나 이치에 맞지 않은. 불공평한. 부당한: *unjust laws* 불공평한 법률

un·jus·ti·fied /ˌʌn'dʒʌstəˌfaɪd/ *adj* done without a good reason ‖ 타당한 이유 없이 행한. 적당하지 않은. 이치에 맞지 않는: *Experts think the fears about the economy are unjustified.* 전문가들은 경제에 대한 염려가 이치에 닿지 않는다고 생각한다. – **unjustifiable** *adj*

un·kempt /ˌʌn'kɛmpt/ *adj* not neat; messy ‖ 깔끔하지 않은. 단정치 못한. 어질러진; 엉망인: *Her hair was dirty and unkempt.* 그녀의 머리는 지저분하고 헝클어져 있었다.

un·kind /ˌʌn'kaɪnd/ *adj* nasty, unpleasant, or cruel ‖ 못된[불쾌한, 잔인한]. 불친절한. 몰인정한: *an unkind remark* 냉정한 말

un·know·ing·ly /ʌn'noʊɪŋli/ *adv* without realizing what you are doing or what is happening ‖ 하고 있는 일이나 발생하고 있는 일을 깨닫지 못하고. 모르고. 부지불식간에: *Millions of people may have been unknowingly infected.* 수백만 명의 사람들이 자기도 모르게 감염되었을지도 모른다.

un·known¹ /ˌʌn'noʊn/ *adj* **1** not known about by most people ‖ 대부분의 사람들이 알지 못하는. 알려지지 않은: *An unknown number of rebels are in hiding.* 알려지지 않은 많은 수의 반군이 숨어 있다. **2** not famous ‖ 유명하지 않은. 무명의: *an unknown musician* 무명의 음악가 **3 the unknown** things that you do not know about or understand ‖ 알거나 이해하지 못하는 것들. 미지의 세계[것]: *a fear of the unknown* 미지의 세계에 대한 두려움 —compare UNFAMILIAR

unknown² *n* someone who is not famous ‖ 유명하지 않은 사람. 무명인: *Early in her career, she was still an unknown.* 그녀도 데뷔 초기에는 무명인이었다.

un·law·ful /ʌn'lɔfəl/ *adj* not legal ‖ 합법적이 아닌. 불법의. 비합법적인

un·lead·ed /ˌʌn'lɛdɪd/ *n* [U] gas that does not contain any LEAD ‖ 납을 전혀 함유하지 않은 휘발유. 무연 휘발유 —compare REGULAR²

un·leash /ʌn'liʃ/ *v* [T] to suddenly let a strong force or feeling have its full effect ‖ 갑자기 강한 힘이나 감정이 그 효과를 완전히 발휘하게 하다. …의 속박[제어]를 풀다. …에게 폭발시키다: *The ceremony unleashed memories of the war.* 그 의식은 전쟁의 추억들을 한꺼번에 떠오르게 했다.

un·less /ən'lɛs, ʌn-/ *conjunction* used in order to say what will happen or be true if another thing does not happen or is not true ‖ 또다른 일이 발생하지 않거나 사실이 아닐 경우 무엇이 발생하거나 사실이 될거라고 말하는 데에 쓰여. …이 아닌 한. …하지 않는다면: *We can go in my car unless you want to walk.* 네가 걷겠다고 하지 않는 한 우리는 내 차로 가면 돼. / *He won't go to sleep unless you tell him a story.* 네가 그에게 이야기를 해 주지 않으면 그는 잠들지 않을 거야. ✗DON'T SAY "unless if."✗ "unless if."라고는 하지 않는다.

un·like¹ /ˌʌn'laɪk/ *prep* **1** completely different from another person or thing ‖

다른 사람이나 사물과는 완전히 다른. … 과는 다른. …과 닮지 않은: *Unlike most commercials, this one is educational.* 대부분의 광고와는 달리 이 광고는 교육적이다. **2** not typical of someone ‖ 어떤 사람의 전형적인 모습이 아닌. …답지 않게: *It's unlike Judy to leave without telling us.* 우리에게 말도 하지 않고 떠나다니 주디답지 않다.

unlike² *adj* different ‖ 다른. 같지[닮지] 않은: *I've never known two sisters so unlike.* 나는 두 자매가 그렇게 닮지 않은 것을 한 번도 보지 못했다.

un·like·ly /ˌʌnˈlaɪkli/ *adj* not likely to happen ‖ 일어날 것 같지 않은. 있을 법하지 않은. 의심스러운: *I'll try to get an earlier flight, but it's unlikely (that) I'll be able to.* 더 이른 비행기를 타려고 애써 보겠지만 탈 수 있을 것 같지는 않다. – **unlikelihood** *n* [U]

un·lim·it·ed /ˌʌnˈlɪmɪṭɪd/ *adj* without a fixed limit ‖ 정해진 한계가 없는. 무제한의: *unlimited mileage on the rental car* 렌터카의 제한 없는 주행 거리

un·list·ed /ˌʌnˈlɪstɪd/ *adj* an unlisted phone number is not in the list of numbers in the telephone book because someone does not want his/her number to be known ‖ 전화번호를 알리고 싶지 않아서 전화번호부 목록에 올리지 않은. 전화번호부에 실리지 않은

un·load /ʌnˈloʊd/ *v* **1** [I, T] to remove goods from a vehicle or large container, or to have them removed ‖ 차량이나 큰 컨테이너에서 물건을 치우거나 치워지게 하다. (…을) 내리다[부리다]: *unloading the dishwasher* 식기 세척기 내리기 / *The ship took a long time to unload.* 그 배는 짐을 부리는 데 오랜 시간이 걸렸다. **2** [T] INFORMAL to get rid of something by selling it quickly ‖ 어떤 것을 급하게 팔아서 없애다. 급하게 처분하다: *The warehouse is trying to unload a huge quantity of goods at discount prices.* 그 도매점은 할인 가격으로 대량의 물건을 처분하려고 애쓰고 있다. **3** [T] to get rid of work or a duty by giving it to someone else ‖ 다른 사람에게 일이나 임무를 맡겨 벗어나다. (싫은 일을) 없애다. …을 떠넘기다: *Don't let Donna unload those reports onto you.* 도나가 너에게 그 보고서들을 떠넘기게 하지 마라. **4** [I, T] to take film out of a camera or bullets out of a gun ‖ 사진기의 필름이나 총의 총알을 빼다. 장전물을 빼내다

un·lock /ʌnˈlɑk/ *v* [T] to undo the lock on a door, box etc. ‖ 문·상자 등의 자물쇠를 따다. 자물쇠를 열다: *I tried to*

---

unlock the door, but the key didn't fit. 나는 문의 자물쇠를 열려고 애썼지만 열쇠가 맞지 않았다.

un·luck·y /ˌʌnˈlʌki/ *adj* **1** having bad luck ‖ 운이 나쁜. 불운한. 불행한: *We were unlucky with the weather this weekend.* 운이 없게도 이번 주말의 날씨는 좋지 못했다. **2** happening as a result of bad luck ‖ 불운의 결과로서 발생하는. 공교로운. 게제가 나쁜: *It was unlucky for us that the bank closed just as we got there.* 우리가 그곳에 도착하자마자 공교롭게도 은행이 문을 닫았다. **3** causing bad luck ‖ 불운을 야기하는. 불길한. 재수 없는: *Some people think black cats are unlucky.* 일부 사람들은 검은 고양이가 불길하다고 생각한다.

un·marked /ˌʌnˈmɑrkt/ *adj* something that is unmarked has no words or signs on it ‖ 어떤 것이 그 위에 아무런 어구나 표지가 없는. 표시[표지]가 없는: *an unmarked police car* 아무런 표시가 없는 경찰차

un·mar·ried /ˌʌnˈmærid/ *adj* not married; SINGLE ‖ 결혼하지 않은. 미혼의. 독신의; ⑩ single

un·mask /ʌnˈmæsk/ *v* [T] to make a truth that has been hidden become known ‖ 숨겨진 진실이 알려지게 하다. 정체를 벗기다. 폭로하다: *He was unmasked as an enemy spy.* 그는 적의 첩자로 정체가 탄로났다.

un·mis·tak·a·ble /ˌʌnmɪˈsteɪkəbəl/ *adj* familiar and easy to recognize ‖ 친숙하고 쉽게 알아볼 수 있는. 틀릴[오해의] 여지가 없는. 틀림없는: *the unmistakable taste of garlic* 틀림없는 마늘 맛

un·mit·i·gat·ed /ˌʌnˈmɪṭəgeɪṭɪd/ *adj* **unmitigated disaster/failure etc.** something that is completely bad ‖ 완전히 나쁜 것. 복구 불능의[완전한] 재난/실패

un·moved /ˌʌnˈmuvd/ *adj* not worried, or not feeling pity ‖ 걱정하지 않거나 연민을 느끼지 않는. 마음이 흔들리지 않는. 냉정한: *The judge was unmoved by his excuses.* 그 판사는 그의 변명에 꿈쩍도 하지 않았다.

un·named /ˌʌnˈneɪmd/ *adj* an unnamed person, place, or thing is one whose name is not known publicly ‖ 사람[장소, 사물]의 이름이 공개적으로 알려지지 않은. 이름이 공표되지 않은: *a reporter's unnamed source* 이름이 알려지지 않은 기자의 취재원(取材源)

un·nat·u·ral /ˌʌnˈnætʃərəl/ *adj* **1** different from what you would normally expect ‖ 보통 기대하는 것과는 다른. 부자

연스러운. 비정상적인: *It's unnatural for a child to spend so much time alone.* 어린이가 혼자서 아주 많은 시간을 보내는 것은 비정상적이다. **2** different from what is produced in nature ‖ 자연적으로 생산되는 것과는 다른. 인위적인: *unnatural colors* 인위적인 색깔들 **3** different from normal human behavior in a way that seems morally wrong ‖ 도덕적으로 잘못돼 보이는 면에서 정상적인 인간의 행동과는 다른. 기괴망측한: *unnatural sexual practices* 기괴망측한 성행위

un·nec·es·sar·y /ˌʌnˈnɛsə,sɛri/ *adj* **1** not needed, or more than is needed ‖ 필요하지 않거나 필요 이상인. 불필요한. 쓸데없는: *The rule prevents unnecessary delays.* 그 규칙은 불필요한 지연을 막아 준다. **2** a remark or action that is unnecessary is unkind or unreasonable ‖ 말이나 행동이 불친절하거나 적절하지 않은 - **unnecessarily** *adv*

un·nerve /ʌnˈnɝv/ *v* [T] to upset or frighten someone so that s/he loses his/her confidence or ability to think clearly ‖ 남을 당황하게 하거나 겁을 주어 자신감이나 똑똑히 생각할 수 있는 능력을 잃게 하다. …을 무기력하게 하다: *Dave was completely unnerved by the argument with Terry.* 데이브는 테리와의 논쟁으로 완전히 자신을 잃었다. - **unnerving** *adj* : *She drove with unnerving speed up the dirt road.* 그녀는 비포장도로에서 무섭게 빠른 속도로 운전했다.

un·no·ticed /ˌʌnˈnoʊtɪst/ *adj* without anyone noticing someone or something ‖ 사람이나 사물에 주목하는 사람이 아무도 없는. 주목받지 않은: *She sat unnoticed at the back.* 그녀는 눈에 띄지 않게 뒤에 앉아 있었다.

un·ob·served /ˌʌnəbˈzɝvd/ *adj, adv* not seen, or without being seen ‖ 눈에 보이지 않거나 인식되지 않은[않게]. 관찰되지 않은[않게]. 알아채지 못한[못한 게]: *Bret left the meeting unobserved.* 브레트는 눈치 못 채게 회의장을 빠져나왔다.

un·ob·tru·sive /ˌʌnəbˈtrusɪv/ *adj* APPROVING not attracting attention and not likely to be noticed ‖ 주의를 끌지 않아 쉽게 눈에 띄지 않는. 나서지 않는. 삼가는: *an efficient unobtrusive waiter* 유능하며 겸손한 웨이터

un·oc·cu·pied /ʌnˈɑkyə,paɪd/ *adj* a seat, house, room etc. that is unoccupied has no one in it ‖ 좌석·집·방 등이 아무도 없는. 비어 있는

un·of·fi·cial /ˌʌnəˈfɪʃəl/ *adj* **1** without

approval or permission from someone in authority ‖ 권한이 있는 사람에게 승인이나 허가를 받지 않은. 공인되지 않은: *Unofficial reports say about 25 people are dead.* 비공인 보고서에는 약 25명이 사망했다고 나와 있다. **2** not made publicly known, or not done as part of official duties ‖ 공개적으로 알려지지 않거나 공무의 일부로서 수행되지 않은. 비공식적인 : *The President made an unofficial visit to a children's hospital.* 대통령은 아동 병원을 비공식적으로 방문했다. - **unofficially** *adv*

un·or·tho·dox /ʌnˈɔrθə,dɑks/ *adj* different from what is usual or accepted by most people ‖ 보편적이거나 대부분의 사람들이 받아들이는 것과 다른. 정통이 아닌. 이단(異端)의: *unorthodox behavior* 이단적인 행동

un·pack /ʌnˈpæk/ *v* [I, T] to take everything out of a box or SUITCASE and put it where it belongs ‖ 상자나 슈트케이스에서 모두 꺼내 원래 장소에 두다. 짐을 풀다

un·paid /ˌʌnˈpeɪd/ *adj* **1** an unpaid bill or debt has not been paid ‖ 청구서나 빚이 지불되지 않은. 미불의. 미납의 **2** done without getting any money ‖ 전혀 돈을 받지 않고 일하는. 무보수의: *unpaid work* 무보수 일

un·par·al·leled /ʌnˈpærə,lɛld/ *adj* FORMAL greater or better than all the others ‖ 다른 모든 것보다 더 훌륭하거나 나은. 비길 데 없는: *Those years were a time of unparalleled happiness in our lives.* 그 시기는 우리 삶에 있어 비할 데 없이 행복한 때였다.

un·pleas·ant /ʌnˈplɛzənt/ **1** not pleasant or enjoyable ‖ 유쾌하거나 즐겁지 않은. 불쾌한: *an unpleasant surprise* 불쾌한 뜻밖의 일 **2** not kind or friendly ‖ 친절하거나 호의적이지 않은. 불친절한: *unpleasant neighbors* 불친절한 이웃

un·plug /ʌnˈplʌɡ/ *v* **-gged, -gging** [T] to disconnect a piece of electrical equipment by taking its PLUG out of a SOCKET ‖ 소켓에서 플러그를 뽑아 전기 기구의 접속을 끊다. 플러그를 뽑다. 전원을 끊다

un·plugged /ʌnˈplʌɡd/ *adj* if a group of musicians performs unplugged, they perform without electric instruments ‖ 일단의 음악가들이 전기 악기로 공연하지 않는. (록음악이) 전기 악기를 사용하지 않는

un·pop·u·lar /ʌnˈpɑpyələr/ *adj* not liked by most people ‖ 대부분의 사람들이 좋아하지 않는. 인기가 없는: *an* *unpopular decision* 평판이 나쁜 결정

un·prec·e·dent·ed /ʌn'prɛsə,dɛntɪd/ *adj* never having happened before, or never having happened so much ‖ 전에 발생한 적이 전혀 없거나 많지 않은. 전례 없는: *The Steelers won an unprecedented four Super Bowls in six years.* 스틸러스는 6년간의 전미 프로 미식축구 선수권 대회에서 유례없는 네 번의 우승을 거두었다.

un·pre·dict·a·ble /ˌʌnprɪ'dɪktəbəl/ *adj* changing so much that you do not know what to expect ‖ 너무 많이 변해서 예측할 수 없는: *unpredictable weather* 예측할 수 없는 날씨

un·pre·pared /ˌʌnprɪ'pɛrd/ *adj* not ready to deal with something ‖ 무엇을 다룰 준비가 되지 않은. 준비가 안 된: *Their son seems unprepared for school.* 그들의 아들은 학교 갈 준비가 되지 않은 것 같다.

un·pre·pos·sess·ing /ˌʌnpripə'zɛsɪŋ/ *adj* not unusual, attractive, or interesting ‖ 특별하지[매력적이지, 흥미롭지] 않은. 호감을 주지 못하는. 붙임성 없는: *an unprepossessing girl of 14* 평범해 보이는 14살짜리 소녀

un·prin·ci·pled /ʌn'prɪnsəpəld/ *adj* FORMAL not caring about whether what you do is morally right or not ‖ 하는 일이 도덕적으로 옳은지 그른지에 대해 신경 쓰지 않는. 원칙이 없는. 부도덕한

un·print·a·ble /ʌn'prɪntəbəl/ *adj* words that are unprintable are rude or shocking ‖ 말들이 상스럽거나 충격적인. 인쇄에 부적합한

un·pro·duc·tive /ˌʌnprə'dʌktɪv/ *adj* not achieving any useful result ‖ 어떤 유익한 결과도 얻지 못하는. 비생산적인: *a totally unproductive meeting* 완전히 비생산적인 회의

un·pro·fes·sion·al /ˌʌnprə'fɛʃənəl/ *adj* not behaving according to the way that people in a particular profession or activity should behave ‖ 특정 직업이나 활동에 종사하는 사람들이 행동해야 하는 방식에 따라 행동하지 않는. 직업윤리에 어긋나는: *Osborn was fired for unprofessional conduct.* 오스본은 직업윤리에 어긋나는 행동으로 해고되었다.

un·prof·it·a·ble /ʌn'prɑfɪtəbəl/ *adj* 1 making no profit ‖ 수익이 나지 않는: *an unprofitable business* 벌이가 안 되는 사업 2 FORMAL bringing no advantage or gain ‖ 아무런 이익이나 보수가 없는. 무익한

un·pro·tect·ed /ˌʌnprə'tɛktɪd/ *adj* 1 something that is unprotected could

hurt someone or be damaged ‖ 무엇이나 사람을 해칠 수 있거나 피해를 입을 수 있는. 무방비의: *unprotected machinery* 방치된 기계 2 **unprotected sex** sex without a CONDOM ‖ 콘돔을 사용하지 않는 성관계

un·pro·voked /ˌʌnprə'voʊkt/ *adj* unprovoked anger, attacks, etc. are directed at someone who has not done anything to deserve them ‖ 분노·공격 등이 그것들을 당할 만한 어떤 짓도 하지 않은 사람을 향한. 정당한 이유가 없는. 까닭 없는

un·qual·i·fied /ʌn'kwɑlə,faɪd/ *adj* 1 not having the right knowledge, experience, or education to do something ‖ 무엇을 하기에 적절한 지식[경험, 교육]을 갖추지 않은. 자격이 없는: *The hospital was accused of hiring unqualified health workers.* 그 병원은 자격이 없는 간병인을 고용하여 기소 당했다. 2 complete ‖ 완전한: *The movie is an unqualified success.* 그 영화는 대성공이다.

un·ques·tion·a·bly /ʌn'kwɛstʃənəbli/ *adv* in a way that leaves no doubt ‖ 전혀 의심의 여지없이. 확실히: *This is unquestionably the coldest winter in years.* 올해는 두말할 것도 없이 수년래 가장 추운 겨울이다.

un·ques·tioned /ʌn'kwɛstʃənd/ *adj* accepted by everyone ‖ 모든 사람이 인정하는. 의심할 바 없는: *his unquestioned right to rule* 그의 명백한 통치권

un·quote /'ʌnkwoʊt/ *v* SPOKEN ⇨ **quote ... unquote** (QUOTE¹)

un·rav·el /ʌn'rævəl/ *v* 1 [I, T] if you unravel threads or if they unravel, they become separated ‖ 실을 분리하다, 또는 실이 분리되다. 풀다. 풀리다 2 [T] to understand or explain something that is very complicated ‖ 아주 복잡한 것을 이해하거나 해명하다.

un·real /ʌn'ril/ *adj* 1 an experience, situation etc. that is unreal seems so strange that you think you must be imagining it ‖ 경험·상황 등이 매우 이상하여 틀림없이 상상하고 있다고 여겨지는. 비현실적인. 상상의: *The trip took so long that it began to seem unreal.* 여행이 너무 오래 걸려서 비현실적인 것처럼 보이기 시작했다. 2 SPOKEN very exciting; excellent ‖ 매우 흥미로운. 환상적인; 훌륭한: *Some of the shots Magic Johnson made were unreal.* 매직 존슨이 던진 몇 개의 슛은 환상적이었다. 3 not relating to real things that happen ‖ 실제로 일어나는 것과 관계없는. 가공의: *Test* *questions often deal with unreal situations.* 시험의 질문은 종종 가공의 상황을 다룬다.

un·re·al·is·tic /ˌʌnriə'lɪstɪk/ *adj* unrealistic ideas are not based on fact ‖ 생각이 사실에 근거를 두지 않은. 비현실적인: *unrealistic job expectations* 비현실적인 취업 눈높이 / *You're being unrealistic – one new player is not going to change the way the whole team plays.* 너는 지금 현실적이지 않아. 한 명의 새로운 선수가 팀 전체가 경기하는 방식을 바꿀 수는 없어. / *It's unrealistic to expect her to be happy all the time.* 그녀가 항상 행복할 거라고 기대하는 것은 비현실적이다.

un·rea·son·a·ble /ʌn'rizənəbəl/ *adj* **1** wrong or unfair ‖ 잘못되거나 적절치 않은. 부당한. 불합리한: *It's unreasonable to give a 10-year-old so much responsibility.* 열 살짜리에게 그렇게 많은 책임을 부여하는 것은 불합리하다. **2** behaving in a way that is not pleasant, not sensible, and often silly ‖ 불쾌하고 분별없으며 종종 어리석게 행동하는: *He has a talent for dealing with the kids when they're being unreasonable.* 그는 아이들이 떼를 쓸 때 대처하는 능력이 있다. **3** unreasonable prices, costs etc. are too high ‖ 가격·비용 등이 매우 높은. 터무니없는

un·rec·og·niz·a·ble /ˌʌnrɛkəg'naɪzəbəl/ *adj* changed or damaged so much that you cannot recognize someone or something ‖ 너무 많이 변하거나 손상되어서 사람이나 사물을 인지할 수 없는. 알아볼 수 없는: *The downtown area is almost unrecognizable.* 시내 중심가는 거의 몰라볼 정도로 변했다.

un·rec·og·nized /ʌn'rɛkəgˌnaɪzd/ *adj* **1** not receiving the respect someone deserves ‖ 누군가가 받아야 할 존경을 받지 못한. 가치를 인정받지 못한: *an unrecognized jazz musician of the 1930s* 인정받지 못한 1930년대의 재즈 음악가 **2** not noticed or not thought to be important ‖ 인식되지 않거나 중요하게 생각되지 않는. 알아차리지 못한: *Violence in the home had gone unrecognized in the courts for years.* 가정 폭력은 오랫동안 법정에서 인정되지 않았다.

un·re·cord·ed /ˌʌnrɪ'kɔrdɪd/ *adj* not written down or recorded ‖ 적혀 있지 않거나 기록되지 않은: *an event unrecorded in history books* 역사책에 기록되지 않은 사건

un·re·fined /ˌʌnrɪ'faɪnd/ *adj* **1** an unrefined substance has not gone through the process of being separated from other substances that naturally combine with it ‖ 물질이 자연적으로 결합해 있는 다른 물질로부터 분리되는 과정을 거치지 않은. 정제되지 않은. 미가공의: *unrefined sugar* 정제되지 않은 설탕 **2** FORMAL not polite or educated ‖ 정중하지 않거나 교양 없는. 거친. 세련되지 않은

un·re·lat·ed /ˌʌnrɪ'leɪtɪd/ *adj* with no connection with something else ‖ 다른 것과 관계없는: *unrelated events* 서로 관련되지 않은 사건들

un·re·lent·ing /ˌʌnrɪ'lɛntɪŋ/ *adj* FORMAL an unpleasant situation that is unrelenting continues for a long time ‖ 불쾌한 상황이 오래 지속되는. 끊임없는: *two days of unrelenting rain* 이틀간 지겹게 계속 내리는 비

un·re·li·a·ble /ˌʌnrɪ'laɪəbəl/ *adj* unable to be trusted or depended on ‖ 신뢰하거나 의지할 수 없는: *unreliable information* 신뢰할 수 없는 정보 / *He was found to be an unreliable witness.* (=he did not tell the truth in a court) 그는 신뢰할 수 없는 증인으로 밝혀졌다.

un·re·lieved /ˌʌnrɪ'livd/ *adj* an unpleasant situation that is unrelieved continues for a long time because nothing happens to change it ‖ 변화시킬 아무런 일도 발생하지 않아서 불쾌한 상황이 오래 지속되는. 변함없는: *unrelieved pain* 완화되지 않는 고통

un·re·mit·ting /ˌʌnrɪ'mɪtɪŋ/ *adj* FORMAL something that is unremitting continues for a long time and probably will not stop ‖ 무엇이 멈추지 않을 것처럼 오랫동안 지속되는. 끊임없는: *unremitting pressure at work* 지속적인 업무상 압박감

un·re·quit·ed /ˌʌnrɪ'kwaɪtɪd/ *adj* **unrequited love** romantic love that you feel for someone who does not feel the same love for you ‖ 자신을 똑같이 사랑하지 않는 사람에게 느끼는 연애적인 사랑. 짝사랑

un·re·served /ˌʌnrɪ'zɜvd/ *adj* complete and without any doubts ‖ 어떤 의심의 여지없이 완전한. 무제한[무조건]의: *You have my unreserved support.* 나는 너를 전폭적으로 지지한다.

un·re·solved /ˌʌnrɪ'zɑlvd/ *adj* an unresolved problem or question has not been answered or solved ‖ 문제나 질문이 해결되지 않거나 답변되지 않은. 미해결의

un·re·spon·sive /ˌʌnrɪ'spɑnsɪv/ *adj* **1** not reacting to what people say to you ‖ 사람들이 말하는 것에 반응하지 않는. 둔감한: *The politicians seem to be* *unresponsive to the city's needs.* 정치인들은 시민의 요구에 반응하지 않는 것처럼 보인다. / *an unresponsive teenager* 무반응의 10대 **2** not affected by something ∥ 어떤 것의 영향을 받지 않는: *a disease that is unresponsive to drugs* 약에 반응하지 않는 질병

un·rest /ʌnˈrɛst/ *n* [U] a social or political situation in which people express their anger or dissatisfaction about something ∥ 사람들이 무엇에 대한 노여움이나 불만을 표현하는 사회적 또는 정치적 상황. 동요. 불안: *civil/political unrest in the former Soviet Union* 구 소련에서의 시민의[정치적] 동요

un·re·strained /ˌʌnrɪˈstreɪnd/ *adj* not controlled or limited ∥ 통제되거나 제한되지 않은. 거리낌 없는: *unrestrained laughter* 거리낌 없는 웃음

un·ri·valed /ʌnˈraɪvəld/ *adj* FORMAL better than any other ∥ 다른 어떤 것보다 나은. 무적의. 최상의: *an unrivaled collection of 19th century art* 19세기 최고의 미술 작품들

un·roll /ʌnˈroʊl/ *v* [T] to open something that was curled into the shape of a ball or tube, and make it flat ∥ 공이나 관 모양으로 말린 것을 펴서 평평하게 만들다. 풀다. 펼치다: *unrolling a sleeping bag* 침낭 펴기

un·ru·ly /ʌnˈruli/ *adj* **1** behaving in an uncontrolled or violent way ∥ 제멋대로 하거나 난폭하게 행동하는. 제어하기 어려운: *unruly children* 다루기 어려운 아이들 **2** unruly hair is messy ∥ 머리카락이 헝클어진

un·safe /ʌnˈseɪf/ *adj* **1** a building, machine etc. that is unsafe is dangerous ∥ 건물·기계 등이 위험한 **2** if you are unsafe, you are in danger of being hurt ∥ 다칠 위험이 있는. 안전하지 못한

un·said /ʌnˈsɛd/ *adj* **be left unsaid** if something is left unsaid, you do not say it although you think it ∥ 생각은 하지만 말하지 않다: *Some things are better left unsaid.* 말하지 않는 것이 더 나은 일도 있다.

un·san·i·tar·y /ʌnˈsænəˌtɛri/ *adj* very dirty and likely to cause disease ∥ 매우 더러워서 병을 일으킬 것 같은. 비위생적인: *unsanitary conditions* 비위생적인 상태

un·sat·is·fac·to·ry /ˌʌnsætɪsˈfæktəri/ *adj* not good enough ∥ 썩 좋지 않은. 불만스러운: *Your work is unsatisfactory.* 네 작업은 성에 차지 않는다.

un·sa·vor·y /ʌnˈseɪvəri/ *adj* unpleasant or morally unacceptable ∥ 불쾌하거나 도덕적으로 받아들일 수 없는. 불미스러운: *unsavory business deals* 불미스러운 사업 거래

un·scathed /ʌnˈskeɪðd/ *adj* not hurt by a bad or dangerous situation ∥ 나쁘거나 위험한 상황에 의해 상처받지 않은. 상처가 없는: *The driver came out of the crash unscathed.* 그 운전자는 상처없이 충돌 사고에서 빠져 나왔다.

un·screw /ʌnˈskru/ *v* [T] **1** to undo something by twisting it ∥ 어떤 것을 비틀어서 제거하다. 마개를 돌려서 빼다: *Turn off the light before unscrewing the bulb.* 전구를 돌려서 빼내기 전에 불을 꺼라. **2** to take the screws out of something ∥ 어떤 것에서 나사를 빼내다. 나사를 뽑다

un·scru·pu·lous /ʌnˈskrupyələs/ *adj* behaving in an unfair or dishonest way ∥ 불공정하거나 정직하지 않게 행동하는. 비양심적인: *an unscrupulous lawyer* 비양심적인 변호사

un·sea·son·a·ble /ʌnˈsizənəbəl/ *adj* unseasonable weather is unusual for the time of year ∥ 날씨가 연중의 시기에 이례적인. 시절에 맞지 않는. 때 아닌

un·seat /ʌnˈsit/ *v* [T] to remove someone from a position of power ∥ 누군가를 권력의 자리에서 쫓아버리다. 권좌에서 밀어내다: *Two candidates are trying to unseat the mayor.* 두 명의 후보가 시장을 밀어내려고 애쓰고 있다.

un·seem·ly /ʌnˈsimli/ *adj* FORMAL unseemly behavior is not polite or suitable ∥ 행동이 공손하거나 적절하지 않은. 보기 흉한: *an unseemly argument over money* 돈을 둘러싼 꼴사나운 논쟁

un·seen /ˌʌnˈsin/ *adj, adv* FORMAL not noticed or seen ∥ 눈치를 채거나 보이지 않는[않게]: *She left the office unseen.* 그녀는 눈치채지 못하게 사무실을 나갔다.

un·set·tled /ˌʌnˈsɛtld/ *adj* **1** an unsettled situation makes you feel unsure about what will happen ∥ 상황이 일어날 일에 대해 불확실한 느낌이 들게 하는. 불안정한: *Recent events have left the capital unsettled.* 최근의 사건들로 수도가 불안정해졌다. **2** worried or excited about something so that you feel upset or nervous ∥ 무엇에 대해 걱정되거나 흥분되어 심란하거나 신경질적인. 동요하는. 불안한: *The children are feeling unsettled by the divorce.* 아이들은 이혼으로 불안해 하고 있다. **3** an unsettled argument continues without reaching any agreement ∥ 논쟁이 어떤 합의에도 이르지 못하고 계속되는. 미해결인: *The issue remains unsettled.* 그 문제는 미해결인 채로 남아 있다. **4** weather that is unsettled changes a lot in a short time ‖ 날씨가 짧은 시간 동안 자주 변하는. 변하기 쉬운 **5** if your stomach is unsettled, you feel uncomfortable and a little sick ‖ 배가 편하지 않고 조금 아픈

un·set·tling /ʌnˈsɛtl-ɪŋ/ *adj* causing worry ‖ 걱정시키는. 동요시키는: *unsettling changes in the software industry* 소프트웨어 업계를 동요시키는 변화

un·sight·ly /ʌnˈsaɪtli/ *adj* unpleasant to look at ‖ 보기에 안 좋은. 보기 흉한. 볼품 없는: *unsightly office buildings* 보기 흉한 사무용 건물들

un·skilled /ˌʌnˈskɪld/ *adj* **1** not trained for a particular type of job ‖ 특정 종류의 일을 위한 훈련을 받지 않은. 숙련되지 않은: *unskilled workers* 미숙련 노동자 **2** unskilled work does not need people with special skills ‖ 일이 특별한 기술을 요하지 않는

un·so·phis·ti·cat·ed /ˌʌnsəˈfɪstə,-keɪt̬ɪd/ *adj* **1** having little knowledge or experience of new ideas and fashions, and showing this in your behavior ‖ 새로운 사조(思潮)와 패션에 대한 지식이나 경험이 거의 없으며 이것이 행동에 나타나는. 순진한. 세상 물정 모르는: *unsophisticated audiences* 순진한 관객 **2** unsophisticated tools, methods, or processes are simple or not very modern ‖ 도구[방법, 과정]이 단순하거나 최신식이 아닌. 복잡하지 않은

un·sound /ˌʌnˈsaʊnd/ *adj* **1** unsound arguments, methods etc. are not based on fact or reason ‖ 주장·방법 등이 사실이나 이성에 근거하지 않은. 논거가 희박한 **2** an unsound building or structure is in bad condition ‖ 건물이나 구조가 상태가 나쁜. 불량한

U **un·speak·a·ble** /ʌnˈspikəbəl/ *adj* extremely bad ‖ 극히 안 좋은. 지독한: *unspeakable crimes* 끔찍한 범죄

un·spe·ci·fied /ʌnˈspɛsə,faɪd/ *adj* not clearly or definitely stated ‖ 분명하거나 확실하게 언급되지 않은. 불특정한: *The ticket is valid for an unspecified period of time.* 그 표는 기한 없이 유효하다.

un·spo·ken /ʌnˈspoʊkən/ *adj* understood but not talked about ‖ 알고 있지만 얘기하진 않는. 입 밖에 내지 않는: *There was an unspoken agreement between us, that we would tell Dee.* 디에게 말해 주기로 우리 사이에 암묵적인 합의가 있었다.

un·sports·man·like /ʌnˈspɔrts-mən,laɪk/ *adj* not behaving in a fair honest way in playing sports ‖ 스포츠 경기에서 공정하고 정직하게 행동하지 않는. 스포츠맨답지 않은

un·sta·ble /ʌnˈsteɪbəl/ *adj* **1** likely to change suddenly, especially so that something difficult or dangerous happens ‖ 갑자기 변하여 특히 어렵거나 위험한 일이 발생할 것 같은. 불안정한: *an unstable economy* 불안정한 경제 / *unstable behavior* 정서적으로 불안정한 행동 **2** dangerous and likely to fall over ‖ 위험하고 곧 넘어질 것 같은. 쓰러지기 쉬운: *an unstable wall* 무너질 것 같은 벽

un·stead·y /ʌnˈstɛdi/ *adj* **1** shaking when you try to walk, hold something etc ‖ 걷거나 무엇을 잡으려 할 때 흔들리는. 비틀거리는: *I felt unsteady on my feet.* 나는 발걸음이 비틀거리는 것을 느꼈다. **2** not firm or likely to fall ‖ 견고하지 않거나 쉽게 쓰러질 것 같은: *The old bridge had become unsteady.* 그 오래된 다리는 흔들거리게 되었다. **3** an unsteady situation is likely to become worse ‖ 상황이 악화될 것 같은

un·stop·pa·ble /ʌnˈstɑpəbəl/ *adj* unable to be stopped ‖ 멈추게 할 수 없는. 막을 수 없는. 거침없는: *The team seems unstoppable this year.* 금년에 그 팀은 거칠 것이 없어 보인다.

un·suc·cess·ful /ˌʌnsəkˈsɛsfəl/ *adj* not achieving what you wanted to achieve ‖ 성취하길 바랐던 것을 성취하지 못한. 성공하지 못한: *an unsuccessful experiment/actor* 실패한 실험[배우] – **unsuccessfully** *adv* : *We tried, unsuccessfully, to convince Hererra of the truth.* 우리는 헤레라에게 진실을 깨닫게 하기 위해 애썼으나 실패했다.

un·suit·a·ble /ʌnˈsutəbəl/ *adj* not having the right qualities for a particular person, purpose, or situation ‖ 특정한 사람[목적, 상황]에 꼭 맞는 특성이 없는. 부적당한. 어울리지 않는: *This movie is unsuitable for young children.* 이 영화는 어린 아이들에게 적합하지 않다.

un·sung /ˌʌnˈsʌŋ/ *adj* not praised or famous for something you have done, although you deserve to be ‖ 그렇게 될 만한데도 자신이 한 일로 칭찬을 받거나 유명해지지 못한. 칭송받지 못한. 무명의: *the unsung heroes of the war against crime* 범죄와의 전쟁의 이름 없는 영웅들

un·sure /ˌʌnˈʃʊr/ *adj* **1** not certain about something or about what you have to do ‖ 무엇에 대해 또는 해야 할 것에 대해 확실하지 않은. 불확실한: *If you're unsure of the rules, ask the teacher.* 규칙을 잘 모르겠으면, 선생님께

여쭤봐라. **2 unsure of yourself** lacking confidence || 자신감이 부족한. 자신이 없는: *Clara seemed shy and unsure of herself.* 클라라는 수줍고 자신이 없는 것 같았다.

un·sus·pect·ing /ˌʌnsə'spɛktɪŋ/ *adj* not knowing that something bad is about to happen || 나쁜 일이 일어날 것을 알지 못하는. 의심하지 않는. 순진한: *Criminals can make easy money from mugging unsuspecting tourists.* 범죄자들은 순진한 관광객들에게 강도짓을 하여 쉽게 돈을 벌 수 있다.

un·swerv·ing /ʌn'swɚvɪŋ/ *adj* never changing in spite of difficulties || 어려움에도 불구하고 바꾸지 않는. 확고한. 변함없는: *unswerving loyalty* 변함없는 충성

un·tan·gle /ʌn'tæŋɡəl/ *v* [T] to make things straight that are twisted together || 서로 얽힌 것을 곧게 만들다. 엉킨 것을 풀다: *conditioner that helps untangle your hair* 머리카락이 엉키지 않게 해주는 린스

un·tapped /ˌʌn'tæpt‹/ *adj* an untapped RESOURCE, market etc. has not yet been used || 자원·시장 등이 아직 쓰이지 않은. 미개발의. 이용되지 않은

un·ten·a·ble /ʌn'tɛnəbəl/ *adj* an untenable argument, THEORY etc. is impossible to defend against criticism || 주장·이론 등이 비판에 대해 변호할 수 없는. 지지 받을 수 없는

un·think·a·ble /ʌn'θɪŋkəbəl/ *adj* impossible to accept or imagine || 인정하거나 상상할 수 없는. 생각할 수 없는: *It was unthinkable a few years ago for a woman to run for President.* 여성이 대통령에 출마한다는 것은 몇 년 전만 해도 생각조차 할 수도 없었다.

un·tie /ʌn'taɪ/ *v* [T] to undo the knots in something or undo something that has been tied || 어떤 것의 매듭이나 묶인 것을 풀다. 끄르다: *Mommy, can you untie my shoelaces?* 엄마, 내 신발 끈 좀 풀어 주실래요?

un·til /ən'tɪl, ʌn-/ *prep, conjunction* **1** used in order to say that something stops happening or being done at a particular time or when something else happens || 특정 시점이나 다른 일이 일어나는 경우에 어떤 것의 발생이나 수행이 그치는 것을 말하는 데에 쓰여. …까지: *I have classes until 7 p.m. today.* 나는 오늘 저녁 7시까지 수업이 있다. / *Debbie's on vacation until Monday.* 데비는 월요일까지 휴가다. **2 not until** used in order to say that something will not happen before a particular time || 어떤 일이 특정

시점 전에는 발생하지 않으리라는 것을 말하는 데에 쓰여. …할 때까지는: *The movie doesn't start until 8 p.m.* 그 영화는 8시가 되어서야 시작한다. / *The doctor's not available until tomorrow.* 그 의사는 내일이 되어서야 시간을 낼 수 있다.

un·time·ly /ʌn'taɪmli/ *adj* **1** happening earlier than it should or than you expected || 타당하거나 예상한 것보다 빨리 발생한. 때가 이른: *an untimely death* 요절 **2** not right for the occasion || 시기가 적절하지 않은: *an untimely show of anger* 때에 맞지 않게 부리는 화

un·tir·ing /ʌn'taɪərɪŋ/ *adj* never stopping while working or trying to do something || 일하거나 무엇을 하려고 애쓰면서 한 번도 멈추지 않는. 지칠 줄 모르는. 끈기 있는: *untiring efforts to help the homeless* 노숙자들을 돕기 위한 끊임없는 노력

un·told /ˌʌn'toʊld‹/ *adj* too much or too many to be counted || 양이나 수가 너무 많아서 셀 수 없는. 막대한: *Floods did untold damage to farmland.* 농지는 홍수로 막대한 피해를 입었다.

un·touch·a·ble /ʌn'tʌtʃəbəl/ *adj* someone who is untouchable is in such a strong position that s/he cannot be affected by, or punished for, anything || 사람이 어떤 것으로도 영향을 받거나 처벌 받지 않는 강력한 지위에 있는. 무적의: *These drug dealers think they're untouchable.* 이 마약 밀매자들은 자신들은 아무도 당할 수 없다고 생각한다.

un·to·ward /ˌʌn'tɔrd/ *adj* FORMAL unexpected, unusual, or not wanted || 예상치 못하거나 유별나거나 원하지 않은. 탐탁지 않은. 불미스러운: *Neighbors say that nothing untoward had happened on the night of the shooting.* 이웃들은 총격 사건이 있던 밤에 별다른 일은 발생하지 않았다고 한다.

un·tried /ˌʌn'traɪd‹/ *adj* new and not tested by being used || 새롭고 실제 사용으로 시험되지 않은. 시도되지 않은: *an untried theory* 검증되지 않은 이론

un·true /ʌn'tru/ *adj* a statement that is untrue does not give the right facts; false || 진술이 정확한 사실을 제공하지 않는; 허위의

un·truth·ful /ʌn'truθfəl/ *adj* dishonest or not true || 불성실하거나 사실이 아닌. 진실성이 없는

un·used[1] /ˌʌn'yuzd‹/ *adj* not being used, or never used || 쓰이지 않거나 사용된 적이 없는: *unused apartments* 비어 있는 아파트

un·used² /ʌnˈjust/ *adj* **unused to** not experienced in dealing with something ‖ 무엇을 다뤄본 경험이 없는: *She's unused to driving at night.* 그녀는 밤에 운전해본 경험이 없다.

un·u·su·al /ʌnˈjuʒuəl, -ʒəl/ *adj* **1** different from what is usual or ordinary ‖ 평범하거나 보통의 것과 다른. 보통이 아닌. 유별난: *Our team has an unusual number of talented players.* 우리 팀에는 능력 있는 선수들이 유별나게 많다. **2** interesting or attractive because of being different ‖ 다르기 때문에 흥미롭거나 매력적인. 독특한: *unusual clothes* 특이한 옷

un·u·su·al·ly /ʌnˈjuʒuəli, -ʒəli/ *adv* **1** **unusually hot/difficult etc.** more hot, difficult etc. than is usual ‖ 보통보다 더 뜨거운·어려운. 유난히 뜨거운/어려운: *an unusually rainy spring* 유별나게 비가 많이 내리는 봄 **2** in a way that is different from what is usual or ordinary ‖ 평소나 보통의 것과는 다르게. 특이하게: *houses painted unusually bright colors* 특이하게 밝은 색으로 페인트칠한 집들

un·veil /ʌnˈveɪl/ *v* [T] **1** to show or tell people something that was a secret ‖ 비밀이었던 것을 사람들에게 보여주거나 말하다. 밝히다: *The mayor will unveil plans for a new park.* 시장은 새로운 공원에 관한 계획을 공표할 것이다. **2** to remove the cover from something as part of a formal ceremony ‖ 공식 행사의 일부로서 어떤 것의 덮개를 벗기다. (동상 등의) 제막식을 거행하다

un·want·ed /ˌʌnˈwʌntɪd·, -ˈwɑn-, -ˈwɔn-/ *adj* not wanted or needed ‖ 바라지 않거나 필요가 없는: *unwanted visitors* 불청객들

un·war·rant·ed /ʌnˈwɔrəntɪd, -ˈwɑr-/ *adj* not done for any good reason ‖ 어떤 정당한 이유 없이 행해진. 정당화되지 않은: *The judge decided a delay in the case was unwarranted.* 판사는 그 사건의 지연은 이유 없다고 판결했다.

un·wel·come /ʌnˈwɛlkəm/ *adj* **1** not wanted, especially because it might cause embarrassment or problems ‖ 특히 난처하게 하거나 문제를 일으킬 수 있기 때문에 원치 않는. 달갑지 않은: *unwelcome sexual advances* 달갑지 않은 성적 접근 **2** **unwelcome guests, visitors** etc. are people that you do not want in your home ‖ 손님·방문객 등이 집에 들여놓고 싶지 않은. 환영받지 못하는

un·wield·y /ʌnˈwildi/ *adj* an unwieldy object is heavy and difficult to carry ‖ 물체가 무거워서 운반하기 힘든. 다루기 어

려운

un·will·ing /ʌnˈwɪlɪŋ/ *adj* **1** not wanting to do something and refusing to do it ‖ 무엇을 하고 싶지 않아서 하기를 거부하는. 반항적인: *He's unwilling to take responsibility.* 그는 책임지기를 싫어한다. **2** not wanting to do something, but doing it ‖ 무엇을 하고 싶지는 않지만 하는. 억지의. 마지못해 하는: *an unwilling helper* 억지로 도와주는 사람

un·wind /ʌnˈwaɪnd/ *v* **1** [I] to relax and stop feeling anxious ‖ 편안해지고 불안감을 느끼지 않다. 긴장이 풀리다: *Swimming helps me unwind.* 수영은 내가 긴장을 푸는 데 도움이 된다. **2** [I, T] to undo something that is wrapped or twisted around something else ‖ 다른 것 주위를 감싸거나 감은 것을 원상태로 돌리다. 풀다. 풀리다

un·wise /ˌʌnˈwaɪz/ *adj* likely to lead to a bad result ‖ 나쁜 결과를 초래할 것 같은. 어리석은: *an unwise decision* 어리석은 결정

un·wit·ting·ly /ʌnˈwɪtɪŋli/ *adv* without knowing or realizing something ‖ 무엇을 알거나 깨닫지 못하고. 무의식적으로: *Several employees unwittingly became involved in illegal activities.* 몇 명의 직원들은 뜻하지 않게 불법 행위에 가담하게 되었다. **– unwitting** *adj*

un·writ·ten /ˌʌnˈrɪtˈn·/ *adj* known about and understood by everyone but not written down ‖ 모든 사람에게 알려져서 이해되고 있지만 기록되어 있지 않은. 성문화되지 않은: *There was an unwritten rule in our family that nobody questioned my father.* 누구도 아버지의 말에 이의를 제기하지 않는다는 것이 우리 집안의 불문율이었다.

un·yield·ing /ʌnˈyildɪŋ/ *adj* not changed by other people's wishes ‖ 다른 사람들의 희망대로 바뀌지 않는. 완고한: *The terrorists are unyielding in their demands.* 테러범들은 그들의 요구를 굽히지 않고 있다.

un·zip /ʌnˈzɪp/ *v* **-pped, -pping** [T] **1** to unfasten the ZIPPER on a piece of clothing, bag etc. ‖ 옷·가방 등의 지퍼를 열다 **2** to change a computer FILE back to its normal size so that you can use it, after it has been made to take up less space ‖ 컴퓨터 파일을 공간을 덜 차지하게 만든 후에 다시 사용할 수 있도록 정상 크기로 되돌려 놓다. (압축된 파일을) 풀다

up¹ /ʌp/ *adv* **1** toward a higher position ‖ 더 높은 위치로. 위로: *Duncan climbed up into the tree.* 던컨은 나무 위로 올라갔

U

다. / *Put the picture up higher.* 그림을 더 높이 걸어라. / *Could you come up here and help us?* 위로 올라와서 우리 좀 도와 주시겠어요? **2** at or in a high position ∥ 높은 위치에서. 위에: *"Where's Dave?" "He's up in his room."* "데이브는 어디 있지?" "그는 자기 방에 올라가 있어." / *a balloon floating up above us* 우리 위로 떠올라 가는 풍선 **3** into an upright or raised position ∥ 똑바르거나 선 자세로: *The choir stood up to sing.* 성가대는 노래하기 위해 일어섰다. / *The hair on the dog's back was sticking up.* 개의 등에 난 털이 곤두서 있었다. **4** in or toward the North ∥ 북쪽에, 북쪽으로: *I'm driving up to see my parents.* 나는 부모님을 뵈러 북쪽으로 운전해 가고 있다. / *His relatives all live up North.* 그의 친척들은 모두 북쪽에 산다. **5** toward someone so that you are near him/her or in the place where s/he is ∥ 누군가가 있는 장소 가까이로. …쪽으로: *The cop came up to the car and asked Chad for his license.* 경찰은 차 쪽으로 다가가 채드에게 운전 면허증을 요구했다. **6** increasing in loudness, strength, heat, activity etc. ∥ 소리·강도·열·활동 등이 증가하여: *Turn up the TV.* TV 소리를 높여라. / *The level of violent crime was up by 3% this month.* 폭력 범죄의 비율이 이달에 3퍼센트 상승했다. **7** completely ∥ 완전히: *All the space in the basement is filled up.* 지하실의 공간 전체가 완전히 찼다. / *Eat up your dinner!* 저녁은 남기지 말고 다 먹어라! **8** broken or divided completely ∥ 완전히 부서지거나 나뉘어: *She tore the letter up into tiny pieces.* 그녀는 그 편지를 작은 조각들로 갈기갈기 찢었다. / *We'll split the money up evenly.* 우리는 돈을 균등하게 나눌 거야. **9** firmly fastened, covered, or joined ∥ 단단히 묶이거나 덮이거나 결합된. 꽉: *a box tied up with string* 끈으로 단단히 묶인 상자 / *Her dad covered her up and said goodnight.* 그녀의 아빠는 그녀에게 이불을 꼭 덮어주고 잘 자라고 말했다. **10** brought or gathered together in a group ∥ 한 무리로 불러모으거나 함께 모여. 합계하여: *Add up the following numbers…* 아래의 숫자들을 모두 합계하시오. / *He gathered up all the pens he could find.* 그는 찾을 수 있는 모든 펜을 그러모았다. **11** so as to receive attention ∥ 주목을 받으려고. 두드러져: *Payton brought that point up at the meeting.* 페이튼은 회의에서 그 점을 제기했다. **12** above and including a particular number or amount ∥ 특정한 수나 양 이상으로: *This movie is suitable for children aged 12 and up.* 이 영화는 12세 이상의 어린이에게 적합하다. **13 up and down** **a)** higher and lower ∥ 위 아래로: *kids jumping up and down* 펄쩍펄쩍 뛰는 아이들 **b)** to one end of something and then back again ∥ 무엇의 한쪽 끝으로 갔다가 다시 뒤로. 왔다갔다: *We walked up and down the street trying to find the house.* 우리는 그 집을 찾기 위해 그 거리를 왔다갔다 했다. **14 it's up to you** SPOKEN said to tell someone that you want him/her to make a decision ∥ 누군가에게 결정을 내리기 바란다고 말하는 데에 쓰여. 너에게 달려 있다: *"Do you think I should get the dress?" "It's up to you."* "내가 그 옷을 사야 한다고 생각하니?" "네 마음대로 해." **15 up close** very near someone or something ∥ 사람이나 사물의 매우 가까이: *If you look up close you can see the cracks.* 네가 만약 바로 곁에서 본다면 깨진 틈을 볼 수 있을 거야. **16 meet/see/know etc. up close** to experience something that you had previously only read or heard about, or to meet someone that you had only seen in newspapers, movies etc. ∥ 전에 단지 읽거나 듣기만 했던 것을 직접 경험하거나, 신문·영화 등에서만 보던 사람을 만나다. 바로 곁에서 만나다/보다/알다: *I was surprised by how short he was when I met him up close.* 내가 그를 바로 가까이 만났을 때 그의 키가 얼마나 작은지 깜짝 놀랐다. **17 up to** **a)** used in order to show the highest amount or level of something, or the latest time something can happen ∥ 무엇의 최대 양이나 수준 또는 무엇이 발생할 수 있는 최종 시기를 나타내는 데에 쓰여. …까지: *Up to 10 people are allowed in the elevator at one time.* 그 엘리베이터는 한번에 10명까지 수용할 수 있다. / *This offer is valid up to December 15.* 이 제안은 12월 15일까지 유효하다. **b)** good enough or well enough to do something ∥ 무엇을 하기에 충분히 좋은: *Do you feel up to a walk today?* 오늘 산책할 기분이 나니? / *The new machines aren't up to our usual standard.* 새로운 기계들은 우리의 평소 기준에 미치지 못한다. **c)** used in order to say or ask what someone is doing ∥ 누군가가 하는 일을 말하거나 묻는 데에 쓰여: *What have you been up to this week?* 이번 주에 뭘 했니? / *I'm sure Bob's up to something.* (=doing something secret). 나는 보브가 무슨 일을 꾸미고 있다고 확신한다.

up² adj 1 awake ∥ 깨어 있는: *"Sorry,*

were you in bed?" "No, I'm still up." "미
안해, 자는 중이었니?" "아니, 아직 안
자." **2 a computer system** that is up is
working ‖ 컴퓨터 시스템이 작동하고 있는
—opposite DOWN **3** a level, number, or
amount that is up is higher than before
‖ 수준[수, 양]이 전보다 높은. 상승한:
Profits were up by 4% this year. 올해 수
익이 4% 상승했다. —opposite DOWN **4
be up against** to have to deal with a
difficult situation or fight an opponent ‖
어려운 상황에 대처하거나 적과 싸워야만
하다: *We're up against some of the
biggest companies in the world.* 우리는
몇몇의 세계 최대 기업과 경쟁 중이다. **5
be up for a)** to be intended for a
particular purpose ‖ 특정한 목적에 쓸 작
정이다: *The house is up for sale.* 그 집은
팔려고 내놓았다. / *the topic up for
discussion at the meeting* 회의에서 토의
하기로 예정된 주제 **b)** SPOKEN to be
interested in something, or feeling well
enough to do something ‖ 무엇에 관심이
있거나 무엇을 할 만큼 충분히 컨디션이
좋다: *Is anybody up for a game of
tennis?* 누구 테니스 경기를 하고 싶은 사
람 없어요? **6 be up and running** if a
machine or process is up and running,
it is working correctly ‖ 기계나 공정이 정
상적으로 작동하고 있다: *The equipment
should be up and running in about three
weeks.* 장비가 약 3주 후에는 정상 가동되
어야 한다. **7 be up before** to be judged
in a court of law ‖ 법정에서 재판을 받게
되다: *He was up before the grand jury
on charges of fraud.* 그는 대배심 앞에서
사기 혐의로 재판을 받았다

SPOKEN PHRASES

8 What's up? used in order to greet
someone, or to ask if there is a
problem ‖ 남에게 인사하거나 문제가
있는지 묻는 데에 쓰여. 잘 지냈어? 무
슨 일 있어?: *Hey Mark! What's up?*
마크야! 잘 지냈어? / *What's up? Are
you OK?* 무슨 일 있어? 괜찮니? **9 be
up** if someone is up, s/he is happy ‖ 행
복하다: *Dario seemed really up for the
first time today.* 다리오는 오늘 처음으
로 정말 행복해 보였다. **10 be up on
(sth)** to know a lot about something
‖ 무엇에 대해 많이 알다: *I'm not
really up on the way things work
here.* 나는 이곳의 상황이 어떻게 돌아
가는지 정말 모르겠다.

---

up³ *prep* **1** toward or in a higher place ‖
더 높은 곳으로[에]: *Walk up the hill and

turn right.* 언덕을 걸어 올라가서 오른쪽
으로 돌아라. **2** toward or at the top or
far end of something ‖ 무엇의 꼭대기로
[에] 또는 무엇의 멀리 끝 쪽으로: *The
cat's up a tree.* 고양이가 나무 위에 있다.
/ *I'm going up the road to see Jill.* 나는
길을 곧장 따라가 질을 만날 작정이다. **3**
toward the place where a river starts ‖
강이 시작하는 곳으로. 강을 거슬러:
sailing up the river 배를 타고 강을 거슬
러 오르기

up⁴ *n* **ups and downs** the good things
and bad things that happen in a
particular situation ‖ 특정 상황에서 발생
하는 좋은 것과 나쁜 것. 오르막과 내리
막. 부침. 기복: *the ups and downs of
marriage* 결혼 생활의 기복

up⁵ *v* INFORMAL **1 -pped, -pping** [T] to
increase the amount or level of
something ‖ 무엇의 양이나 수준을 높이
다: *They've upped Don's salary by
$2500!* 그들은 돈의 봉급을 2500달러 올
려 줬어! **2 up and...** to suddenly start to
do something different or surprising ‖ 갑
자기 상이하거나 놀라운 것을 하기 시작하
다. 갑자기 …하기 시작하다: *...and then
Mike up and left, without telling
anybody.* 그리고 나서 마이크는 누구에게
도 말하지 않고 갑자기 떠났다.

up-and-com·ing /ˌ. . '../ *adj* likely to
be successful and popular ‖ 성공해서 인
기 있을 것 같은. 유망한: *an up-and-
coming actor* 유망한 배우

up·beat /ˈʌpˈbit/ *adj* cheerful and
making you feel that good things will
happen ‖ 유쾌하고 좋은 일이 발생할 것
같은 느낌을 갖게 하는. 즐거운. 행복한: *a
movie with an upbeat ending* 결말이 행
복한 영화

up·bring·ing /ˈʌpˌbrɪŋɪŋ/ *n* [singular]
the care and training that parents give
their children when they are growing up
‖ 아이들이 성장할 때 부모들이 쏟는 보살
핌과 훈육. 양육. 가정 교육: *a strict
upbringing* 엄한 가정 교육

up·chuck /ˈʌp-tʃʌk/ *v* [I] INFORMAL ⇨
VOMIT¹

up·com·ing /ˈʌpˌkʌmɪŋ/ *adj* happening
soon ‖ 곧 발생하는. 다가오는: *the
upcoming elections* 다가오는 선거

up·date¹ /ˈʌpdeɪt, ˌʌpˈdeɪt/ *v* [T] **1** to
add the most recent information to
something ‖ 무엇에 가장 최근의 정보를
추가하다. 최신의 것으로 만들다: *The
files need to be updated.* 그 파일은 최신
자료로 갱신되어야 한다. **2** to make
something more modern in the way it
looks or operates ‖ 무엇을 보다 현대적으

로 보이거나 작동하게 만들다. 새롭게 하다
**update² ** *n* the most recent news about
something ‖ 무엇에 대한 가장 최근의 소
식. 최신 정보: *an update on the
earthquake* 그 지진에 관한 최신 뉴스
up·end /ʌp'ɛnd/ *v* [T] to turn
something over so that it is standing
upside down ‖ 무엇을 거꾸로 서게 뒤집
다. …을 거꾸로 하다
up·front /ʌp'frʌnt/ *adj* **1 be upfront**
to talk or behave in a direct and honest
way ‖ 솔직하고 정직하게 말하거나 행동하
다: *Jill's always been upfront with him.*
질은 항상 그에게 솔직하다. **2** an upfront
payment, agreement etc. is done before
anything else ‖ 지불·동의 등이 다른 것보
다 앞서 행해진. 선금의. 선행의 –
upfront *adv* : *We'll need $300 upfront.*
우리는 선금으로 300달러가 필요할 것이
다.
up·grade /'ʌpgreɪd, ˌʌp'greɪd/ *v* [T] to
improve something, or to exchange
something for something better ‖ 무엇을
개선하거나 더 나은 것으로 바꾸다. 등급
을 올리다: *I was upgraded to first class
on the flight back.* 나는 돌아오는 비행편
에서는 1등석을 탔다. / *We need to
upgrade our computer.* 우리는 컴퓨터를
업그레이드해야 한다. – **upgrade** *n*
up·heav·al /ʌp'hivəl, 'ʌpˌhivəl/ *n* [C,
U] a very big change that often causes
problems ‖ 종종 문제를 야기하는 매우 큰
변동. 격변. 대변동: *political upheaval in
the former Soviet Union* 구소련의 정치적
격변
up·hill /ˌʌp'hɪl/ *adj, adv* **1** toward the
top of a hill ‖ 언덕 위의, 언덕 위로: *an
uphill climb* 오르막 등반 —opposite
DOWNHILL¹ **2** an uphill battle, job etc. is
very difficult and needs a lot of effort ‖
전투·일 등이 매우 힘들고 노력을 요하는.
고된. 어려운. 힘들여. 간신히
up·hold /ʌp'hoʊld/ *v* [T] **1** to defend or
support a law, system, or principle so
that it is not made weaker ‖ 약해지지 않
게 법률이나 체계, 또는 원칙을 옹호하거
나 지지하다. 후원하다. 격려하다: *They
want to uphold family values.* 그들은 가
족의 가치관을 유지하고 싶어한다. **2** if a
court upholds a decision that is made by
another court, it states that the decision
was correct ‖ 법원이 또 다른 법원에서 내
린 판결이 옳았음을 확인하다. 판결을 확
인[지지]하다
up·hol·ster /ə'poʊlstə, ʌp'hoʊl-/ *v* [T]
to cover a chair or SOFA with material ‖
의자나 소파를 천으로 씌우다. 천을 대다
– **upholstered** *adj*

up·hol·ster·y /ə'poʊlstəri/ *n* [U]
material that is used for covering chairs
and SOFAs, or the process of doing this ‖
의자·소파를 씌우기 위해 쓰이는 물질이
나, 또는 이렇게 하는 과정. (의자) 씌우개
[천갈이]
up·keep /'ʌpkip/ *n* [U] the care that is
needed to keep something in good
condition ‖ 무엇을 좋은 상태로 보존하기
위해 필요한 관심. 관리 유지: *the upkeep
of a big house* 큰 집의 관리 유지
up·lift·ing /ˌʌp'lɪftɪŋ/ *adj* making you
feel more cheerful ‖ 보다 활기차게 만드
는. 사기를 높이는: *uplifting music* 사기
를 북돋는 음악
up·load /'ʌploʊd/ *v* [I, T] if information, a computer PROGRAM etc.
uploads, or if you upload it, you move it
from a small computer to a computer
network so that many people can see it
or use it ‖ 많은 사람들이 보거나 이용할
수 있도록 정보나 컴퓨터 프로그램 등을
소형 컴퓨터에서 컴퓨터 네트워크로 옮기
다. 업로드하다
up·on /ə'pɑn, ə'pɔn/ *prep* FORMAL on ‖
위에: *We are completely dependent
upon your help.* 우리는 전적으로 너의 도
움에 의존하고 있다. / *sitting upon the
throne* 즉위(卽位)
up·per¹ /'ʌpɚ/ *adj* **1** in a higher
position than something else ‖ 다른 것보
다 더 높은 위치의. 더 위의: *the upper
jaw* 위턱 —opposite LOWER¹ **2** near or at
the top of something ‖ 무엇의 꼭대기 또
는 그 근처의: *the upper floors of the
building* 건물의 상층부 —opposite
LOWER¹ **3** more important or higher in
rank than other parts in an organization
‖ 조직에서 다른 부분보다 더 중요하거나
계급이 더 높은. 상급[상위]의: *the upper
grades in school.* 학교의 상급 학년 **4**
have/gain the upper hand to have
more power than someone else, so that
you are able to control a situation ‖ 상황
을 통제할 수 있을 정도로 다른 사람보다
더 많은 힘을 가지고 있다. 우세하다:
*Rebels have gained the upper hand in
some areas.* 반란군들은 몇몇 지역에서 우
위를 점하고 있다. **5 the upper limit** the
highest limit ‖ 가장 높은 한도. 최고 한
도: *sounds that are at the upper limit of
our hearing ability* 인간 청력의 최고 한
도에 있는 소리
upper² *n* the top part of a shoe ‖ 신발의
윗부분. 구두 갑피
uppercase /ˌ.. '../ *n* [U] letters
written in their large form, such as A,
B, C etc. ‖ A·B·C 등 큰 글자 자체(字體)로 씌

어진 글자. 대문자 —compare CAPITAL¹ , LOWERCASE

upper class /,.. '../ *n* **the upper class** the group of people who belong to the highest social class ‖ 가장 높은 사회 계층에 속하는 일단의 사람들. 상류 계급. 상류층 —see usage note at CLASS¹

up·per·most /'ʌpɚ,moust/ *adj* **1** most important ‖ 가장 중요한: *Environmental concerns should be uppermost.* 환경 문제가 가장 중요한 사안이 되어야 한다. / *It's your safety that's uppermost in my mind.* (=I think is most important) 너의 안전이 나의 최고의 관심사이다. **2** highest ‖ 가장 높은: *the uppermost branches of the tree* 나무 꼭대기의 가지

up·pi·ty /'ʌpəti/ *adj* SPOKEN thinking that you are better or more important than other people in your social class ‖ 자신의 사회 계층에서 다른 사람들보다 더 낫다거나 더 중요하다고 생각하는. 교만한. 주제넘은

up·right¹ /'ʌp-raɪt/ *adj* **1** standing straight up ‖ 똑바로 선 **2** always behaving in an honest way ‖ 항상 정직하게 행동하는. 정직한. 올바른: *upright citizens* 정직한 시민들

upright² *adv* **1** standing or sitting with your back straight ‖ 등을 곧추선 채로 서거나 앉아서. 꼿꼿이: *He sat bolt upright* (=completely upright), *terrified by the noise.* 그는 소음에 놀라 똑바로 앉았다. **2** made to stand straight up ‖ 똑바로 세워

up·ris·ing /'ʌp,raɪzɪŋ/ *n* an occasion when a group of people use violence to try to change the rules, laws etc. in an institution or country ‖ 협회나 국가의 규칙·법 등을 애써 바꾸려고 일단의 사람들이 폭력을 사용하는 상황. 폭동. 반란

up·riv·er /ʌp'rɪvɚ/ *adv* in the opposite direction from the way the water is flowing in a river ‖ 강에서 물이 흘러가는 방향과 반대로. 상류로

up·roar /'ʌp-rɔr/ *n* [singular, U] a lot of noise or angry protest about something ‖ 무엇에 대한 떠들썩한 소리나 분노의 항의. 소동. 소란: *His accusations against the country's Prime Minister caused an uproar in the foreign press.* 그가 국가의 수상을 고소한 사건은 외신을 떠들썩하게 했다.

up·root /,ʌp'rut/ *v* [T] **1** to pull a plant and its roots out of the ground ‖ 땅에서 식물과 그 뿌리를 잡아당기다. 뿌리째 뽑다 **2** to make someone leave his/her home for a new place, especially when this is difficult ‖ 특히 어려울 때, 누군가를 집을 떠나 새로운 장소로 향하게 하다.

이동시키다: *Steven's new job will mean uprooting the family.* 스티븐이 새로 얻은 직장은 가족의 이사를 의미하는 게 될 것이다.

up·scale /,ʌp'skeɪl/ *adj* relating to people from a high social class who have a lot of money ‖ 돈이 많은 상류층 사람들과 관계된. 부자의. 돈 많은: *upscale neighborhoods* 부자 동네

up·set¹ /,ʌp'sɛt/ *adj* **1** unhappy and worried because something unpleasant has happened ‖ 불쾌한 일이 발생하여 불만스럽고 걱정스러운. 심란한: *They're still upset about/over losing the money.* 그들은 돈을 잃어 여전히 기분이 상해 있다. / *Steve's upset that they forgot to make reservations.* 그들이 예약하는 것을 잊어버려서 스티브는 기분이 상해 있다. **2 an upset stomach/tummy** an illness that has an effect on the stomach and makes you sick ‖ 위에 영향을 주어 메스껍게 만드는 병. 탈이 난 위/배

up·set² /ʌp'sɛt/ *v* **upset**, **upset**, **upsetting** **1** [T] to make someone feel unhappy or worried ‖ 누군가를 불쾌한 기분이 들거나 걱정스럽게 만들다. 심란 [당황]하게 하다: *Kopp's comments upset many of his listeners.* 콥스의 논평은 그의 많은 청중들의 기분을 상하게 했다. **2 upset sb's stomach** to make someone feel sick ‖ 남을 아프게 하다. 배탈 나게 하다 **3** [T] to change a plan or situation in a way that causes problems ‖ 문제를 일으키게 계획이나 상황을 변화시키다. 엉망으로 만들다: *The ecological balance of the area has been upset.* 그 지역의 생태적 균형이 엉망이 되었다.

up·set³ /'ʌpsɛt/ *n* **1** an occasion when a person or team surprisingly beats a stronger opponent in a competition ‖ 사람이나 팀이 경기에서 놀랍게도 더 강한 상대를 이겼을 경우. 뜻밖의 승리 **2** an unexpected problem or difficulty ‖ 예상치 못한 문제나 어려움. 혼란: *upsets in sales and marketing* 판매와 마케팅의 혼란 상태

up·set·ting /ʌp'sɛtɪŋ/ *adj* making you feel upset ‖ 당혹스러운 기분이 들게 하는. 심란한: *I've just heard some very upsetting news.* 나는 방금 매우 당혹스러운 소식을 들었다.

up·shot /'ʌpʃat/ *n* **the upshot (of)** the final result of a situation ‖ 상황의 최종 결과. 결말: *The upshot is that she's moving to another department.* 결과는 그녀가 또 다른 부서로 옮긴다는 것이다.

up·side /'ʌpsaɪd/ *n* **the upside** the positive part of a situation ‖ 상황의 긍정

적 부분. 좋은 면: *The upside is that the problem is simple to prevent.* 문제를 예방하기 수월하다는 것은 그나마 좋은 점이다. —opposite DOWNSIDE

up·side down /ˌʌpsaɪd ˈdaʊn/ *adj, adv* 1 with the top at the bottom and the bottom at the top ‖ 위가 바닥이 되고 바닥이 위가 된. 거꾸로 된: *Isn't that picture upside down?* 저 그림 거꾸로 된 것 아니니? 2 disorganized and messy ‖ 무질서하고 엉망인. 난잡한: *We turned the house upside down looking for my keys.* 우리는 내 열쇠를 찾느라고 집을 엉망으로 만들었다.

up·stage /ˌʌpˈsteɪdʒ/ *v* [T] to do something that takes people's attention away from someone else who is more important ‖ 보다 중요한 인물에게서 사람들의 관심을 빼앗는 일을 하다. 인기를 가로채다

up·stairs¹ /ˌʌpˈstɛrz/ *adv* on or going toward a higher floor of a building, especially a house ‖ 건물, 특히 집의 위층에, 또는 위층으로 가는. 위층에[으로]: *Her office is upstairs on your right.* 그녀의 사무실은 네 오른쪽 위층에 있다. —opposite DOWNSTAIRS

upstairs

upstairs² *adj* 1 on the upper floor of a building ‖ 건물 위층의: *the upstairs bathroom* 위층의 화장실 2 **the upstairs** the rooms in the upper floors of a house ‖ 집의 위층에 있는 방. 윗방: *The upstairs has one very large bathroom.* 윗방에는 매우 큰 욕실 한 개가 있다.

up·start /ˈʌpstɑrt/ *n* someone who is new in his/her job and behaves as if s/he is more important than s/he is ‖ 일을 처음 하면서 실제보다 훌륭한 체 행동하는 사람. 잘난 체하는 사람

up·state /ˌʌpˈsteɪt/ *adj, adv* in or toward the northern part of a state ‖ 주의 북부 지역의[에], 또는 북부 지역을 향한[향해]: *She lives upstate, near the lake.* 그녀는 호수 근처의 주 북부에 산다. —compare DOWNSTATE

up·stream /ˌʌpˈstrim/ *adv* along a river, in the opposite direction from the way the water is flowing ‖ 강을 따라 물의 흐름과 반대 방향으로. 흐름을 거슬러 올라 – **upstream** /ˈ. ./ *adj* —compare DOWNSTREAM

up·surge /ˈʌpsɚdʒ/ *n* a sudden increase ‖ 갑작스런 증가. 급증: *a recent*

upsurge in car sales 최근의 자동차 판매의 급증

up·swing /ˈʌpswɪŋ/ *n* an improvement or increase in the level of something ‖ 어떤 것의 수준의 향상이나 증가. (…의) 급증. 급상승: *an upswing in the economy* 경제의 급성장

up·take /ˈʌpteɪk/ *n* **be slow/quick on the uptake** INFORMAL to be slow or fast at learning or understanding things ‖ 무엇을 배우거나 이해하는 것에 더디거나 빠르다

up·tight /ˌʌpˈtaɪt/ *adj* INFORMAL behaving in an annoyed way because you are feeling nervous and worried ‖ 초조하고 걱정스럽기 때문에 짜증스럽게 행동하는. 긴장한. 신경질적인

up-to-date /ˌ. . ˈ./ *adj* relating to or having the most recent knowledge, information etc. ‖ 가장 최근의 지식·정보 등에 관련되거나 그것들이 들어 있는. 최신의. 최신 정보를 포함한: *Our computer system is not up-to-date.* 우리 컴퓨터 시스템은 최신식이 아니다. / *Doctors must keep up-to-date with medical research.* 의사들은 최신의 의학 연구 결과를 잘 알고 있어야 한다. —see usage note at NEW

up·town /ˌʌpˈtaʊn/ *adv* to or in the northern area of a city or town, or the area where the richer people live ‖ 대도시나 소도시의 북쪽 지역으로[에], 또는 좀 더 부유한 사람들이 사는 지역으로[에]: *The Parkers live uptown.* 파커스 집안의 사람들은 부촌에 산다. — **uptown** /ˈ. ./ *adj* —compare DOWNTOWN²

up·turn /ˈʌptɚn/ *n* a time when business activity is increased and conditions improve ‖ 사업 활동이 증진되고 상황이 나아진 시기. (경기·물가 등의) 상승[호전](기): *an upturn in oil production* 석유 생산의 호전기 —compare DOWNTURN

up·turned /ˈʌptɚnd, ˌʌpˈtɚnd/ *adj* 1 turning upward at the end ‖ 끝이 위를 향한: *an upturned nose* 들창코 2 turned upside down ‖ 뒤집힌: *upturned boxes* 뒤집힌 상자

up·ward¹ /ˈʌpwɚd/ *adj* 1 moving or pointing toward a higher position ‖ 위쪽으로 움직이거나 향하는: *an upward movement of the hand* 손을 위로 뻗기 2 increasing to a higher level ‖ 더 높은 수준으로 올라가는. 상승하는: *the upward trend in house prices* 주택 가격의 상승 추세

upward², **upwards** *adv* 1 from a lower place or position to a higher one ‖ 보다 낮은 장소에서 높은 위치로. 위쪽

으로: *Billy pointed upward at the clouds*. 빌리는 구름을 향하여 위를 가리켰다. **2** increasing to a higher level ‖ 높은 수준으로 상승하여: *Salaries have been moving upwards*. 봉급이 계속 인상되어 오고 있다. —opposite DOWNWARD[1]

u·ra·ni·um /yʊˈreɪniəm/ *n* [U] a heavy RADIOACTIVE white metal that is used in producing nuclear energy and weapons ‖ 핵에너지와 핵무기의 제조에 쓰이는 방사능을 가진 백색의 중금속. 우라늄

U·ra·nus /yʊˈreɪnəs, ˈyʊrənəs/ *n* [singular] the seventh PLANET from the sun ‖ 태양에서 일곱 번째 행성. 천왕성

ur·ban /ˈɚbən/ *adj* relating to a town or city ‖ 소도시나 대도시에 관련된. 도시의: *the urban population* 도시의 인구 — compare RURAL

ur·bane /ɚˈbeɪn/ *adj* behaving in a relaxed and confident way in social situations ‖ 사교 장소에서 느긋하고 자신 있게 행동하는. 세련된. 우아한: *Jerome's urbane charm* 제롬의 세련미

urban re·new·al /ˌ.. ˈ.ˌ../ *n* [U] the process of improving poor city areas by building new houses, stores etc. ‖ 빈민가를 새로운 집·상점 등을 지어 개량하는 과정. 도시 재개발

urban sprawl /ˌ.. ˈ./ *n* [U] DISAPPROVING the spread of city buildings and houses into areas that were outside the city ‖ 도시의 외곽이었던 지역으로 건물과 집이 확산됨. 스프롤 현상

ur·chin /ˈɚtʃɪn/ *n* OLD-FASHIONED a small dirty child ‖ 단정치 못한 작은 아이. 개구쟁이

urge[1] /ɚdʒ/ *v* [T] **1** to strongly advise someone to do something ‖ 누군가에게 무엇을 하라고 강하게 권고하다. 재촉하다. 다그치다: *Cal's family urged him to find another job*. 칼의 가족은 그에게 다른 직업을 찾으라고 다그쳤다. / *I urge that you consider the problem carefully*. 저는 그 문제를 신중히 생각해 보기를 당신에게 촉구합니다. **2** FORMAL to strongly suggest that something should be done ‖ 어떤 것을 반드시 해야 한다고 강하게 제안하다. 주장하다. 역설하다: *Banks urged caution in raising interest rates*. 은행들은 이자율 인상에 대한 주의를 요망했다.

urge sb ↔ **on** *phr v* [T] to encourage a person or animal to work harder, go faster etc. ‖ 사람이나 동물이 더 열심히 일하고 더 빨리 달리도록 격려하다. 독려하다: *Lewis was urged on by the crowd*. 루이스는 군중들의 격려를 받았다.

urge[2] *n* a strong wish or need ‖ 강렬한

소망이나 욕구. 열망: *sexual urges* 성적 충동 / *I felt a sudden urge to hit him*. 나는 갑자기 그를 때리고 싶은 마음이 간절했다.

ur·gent /ˈɚdʒənt/ *adj* very important and needing to be dealt with immediately ‖ 매우 중요하고 즉시 처리되어야 할 필요가 있다. 다급한: *an urgent message* 긴급 전갈 / *She's in urgent need of medical attention*. 그녀는 응급 치료가 필요하다. —**urgency** /ˈɚdʒənsi/ *n* [U]

u·ri·nate /ˈyʊrəˌneɪt/ *v* [I] TECHNICAL to make URINE flow out of your body ‖ 몸 밖으로 소변을 배출하다. 방뇨하다. 오줌을 누다

u·rine /ˈyʊrɪn/ *n* [U] the liquid waste that comes out of your body when you go to the toilet ‖ 화장실에 가서 몸 밖으로 배출하는 액체 노폐물. 오줌. 소변

URL *n* uniform resource locator; a description of where a particular computer FILE can be found, especially on the Internet. Internet URLs usually begin with http:// ‖ uniform resource locator(인터넷상의 홈페이지 주소)의 약어; 특히 인터넷 상에서 특정 컴퓨터 파일을 찾아낼 수 있는 서술 형식

urn /ɚn/ *n* **1** a container that holds and pours a large amount of coffee or tea ‖ 많은 양의 커피나 차를 담거나 따르는 용기. 주전자 **2** a decorated container, especially one that is used for holding the ASHes of a dead body ‖ 특히 유골을 담는 데 쓰이는 장식된 용기. (유골) 단지

US *n* the abbreviation of the United States ‖ United States(미국)의 약어

us /əs; *strong* ʌs/ *pron* the object form of "we" ‖ "we"의 목적격. 우리를. 우리에게: *He walked by, but he didn't see us*. 그는 우리 곁으로 걸어갔지만, 우리를 보진 못했다. —see usage note at ME

us·age /ˈyusɪdʒ/ *n* **1** [C, U] the way that words are used in a language ‖ 한 언어에서 단어가 쓰이는 방식. 어법: *a book on modern English usage* 현대 영어의 관용법에 관한 책 **2** [U] the way in which something is used, or the amount of it that is used ‖ 무엇의 사용법이나 사용량: *plans to cut water usage* 절수를 위한 계획

use[1] /yuz/ *v* [T] **1** if you use a tool, method, service etc., you do something with it ‖ 도구·방법·서비스 등으로 무엇을 하다. …을 사용하다. 쓰다: *Use a food processor to grate the vegetables*. 야채를 가는 데에 식품 가공기를 써라. / *Can I* use your phone? 제가 전화를 좀 써도 되겠습니까? / *Most people use credit cards for shopping.* 대부분의 사람들이 쇼핑하는 데에 신용 카드를 사용한다. **2** to take something from a supply so that there is less left ‖ 공급량에서 무엇을 써서 남은 것이 적어지다. 소비하다: *These light bulbs use less electricity.* 이 백열전구들은 전기를 덜 소비한다. / *Our car's using too much oil.* 우리 차는 기름이 너무 많이 든다. **3** to make someone do something for you in a way that is not fair or honest ‖ 자신을 위해 남에게 부당하거나 정직하지 못하게 무엇을 시키다. 이용해 먹다: *They used her to smuggle drugs into the country.* 그들은 마약 밀반입에 그녀를 이용했다. **4** to say or write a particular word or phrase ‖ 특정 단어나 어구를 말하거나 쓰다: *I try not to use bad language around the kids.* 나는 아이들 앞에서 나쁜 말을 하지 않으려고 해. **5** to regularly take illegal drugs ‖ 마약을 상용하다

use sth ↔ **up** *phr v* [T] to use all of something ‖ 어떤 것을 모두 사용하다. 완전히 다 써버리다: *Who used up the toothpaste?* 누가 치약을 다 썼지?

use² /yus/ *n*

1 ▸ACT OF USING STH 사용◂ [singular, U] the act of using something or the amount that is used ‖ 어떤 것을 사용하는 행위나 사용량: *We've saved a lot of money through the use of energy-saving technology.* 우리는 에너지 절약 기술을 이용해서 많은 돈을 절약했다.

2 ▸WAY STH IS USED 사용법◂ a way in which something can be used, or the purpose for which it can be used ‖ 무엇이 쓰이는 방법이나 무엇이 쓰이는 목적. 사용법. 사용 목적: *educational uses for computers* 컴퓨터의 교육적인 효용

3 ▸RIGHT/ABILITY TO USE STH 사용권/사용 능력◂ the right or ability to use something ‖ 어떤 것을 사용하는 권리나 능력. 사용권. 활용력: *Joe's given me the use of his office.* 조는 내게 자신의 사무실을 이용할 수 있게 해주었다. / *Mr. Wayne doesn't have the use of his legs.* 웨인 씨는 다리를 쓰지 못한다.

4 be any use/be no use to be useful, or to not be useful ‖ 쓸모 있다, 쓸모없다: *Was that map any use?* 그 지도가 쓸모 있었나요? / *The information is of no use to us.* 그 정보는 우리에게 무익하다.

5 make use of to get an advantage from something ‖ 어떤 것에서 이익을 얻다. …을 이용하다: *We need to make use of the people we have available*

before we hire new ones. 우리는 새로운 사람들을 고용하기 전에는 있는 사람들을 활용해야 한다. / *I have to make better use of my time.* (=get more advantage from it) 나는 내 시간을 더 잘 활용해야 한다.

6 it's no use doing sth SPOKEN used in order to tell someone not to do something because it will have no effect ‖ 아무런 효과도 없을 것이기 때문에 무엇을 하지 말라고 말하는 데에 쓰여. …해 봐야 소용없다: *It's no use arguing with Kathy; she won't listen.* 캐시와 논쟁을 해 봐야 소용없어. 그 여자는 듣지 않을 거야.

7 put sth to (good) use to use knowledge, skills etc. for a particular purpose ‖ 지식·기술 등을 특정 목적을 위해 쓰다: *a chance to put your medical training to good use* 너의 의료 교육을 선용할 수 있는 기회

8 it's no use! SPOKEN used in order to say that you are going to stop doing something because you do not think it will be successful ‖ 성공하지 못하리라고 생각하기 때문에 무엇을 하는 것을 그만둔다고 말하는 데에 쓰여. 전혀 소용없다: *It's no use! I can't fix this.* 소용없어! 나는 이거 못 고쳐!

9 have no/little use for sb/sth to not like or respect someone or something ‖ 사람이나 사물을 좋아하거나 존중하지 않다. …을 질색[무시]하다: *Meisner has little use for rules about acting.* 마이스너는 연기 규칙을 거의 무시한다.

10 in use being used ‖ 사용 중인: *The computer room's in use all morning.* 컴퓨터실은 아침 내내 사용 중이다.

11 for the use of for a particular person or group to use ‖ 특정 사람이나 집단이 쓰도록. …용으로: *The gym is for the use of employees only.* 그 체육관은 직원들 전용이다.

12 ▸ WORDS 단어◂ one of the meanings of a word, or the way that a particular word is used ‖ 한 단어의 뜻 중 한 가지, 또는 특정 단어의 사용법

used¹ /yust/ *adj* be used to sth/be used to doing sth be familiar with something so that it no longer seems surprising, difficult etc. ‖ 무엇에 친숙해서 더 이상 놀랍거나 어려워 보이지 않다. 익숙하다: *Kathy is used to getting up early?* 캐시는 일찍 일어나는 데 익숙하니? / *He hasn't gotten used to the weather here yet.* 그는 아직도 여기 날씨에 익숙하지 않다. —opposite **unused to** (UNUSED²)

used² /yuzd/ *adj* **used cars/clothes etc.** cars, clothes etc. that have already had an owner; SECONDHAND ‖ 이미 주인이 있었던 차·옷 등. 중고차/옷; ㊤ secondhand

used to /'yustə; *final or before a vowel* 'yustu/ *modal v* if something used to happen, it happened often or regularly in the past but does not happen now ‖ 과거에는 자주 또는 규칙적으로 발생했지만 현재는 발생하지 않다. … 하곤 했다: *We used to go to the movies every week.* 우리는 매주 영화를 보러 가곤 했다. / *"Didn't you use to smoke?" "Yes, but I quit."* "담배를 피우지 않았었나요?" "네, 하지만 끊었어요."

USAGE NOTE used to, be used to, and get used to

Use **used to** to talk about something that someone did regularly in the past: *I used to play tennis twice a week, but I don't have time now.* Use **be used to** and **get used to** to talk about being or becoming more comfortable with a situation or activity, so that it does not seem strange or difficult: *Are you used to the cold winters yet? / I can't get used to living in a big city.*
used to는 어떤 사람이 과거에 규칙적으로 했던 것을 언급하는 데에 쓰인다: 나는 일주일에 두 번 테니스를 쳤는데, 지금은 할 시간이 없다. **be used to**와 **get used to**는 상황이나 행위가 보다 편해져서 낯설거나 어렵지 않은 상태를 언급하는 데에 쓰인다: 벌써 추운 겨울에 적응이 되었니?/ 나는 대도시에 사는 것에 익숙해지지가 않는다.

U

use·ful /'yusfəl/ *adj* helping you to do or to get what you want ‖ 원하는 것을 하거나 얻는 데 도움이 되는. 유익한: *useful information* 유익한 정보 / *a useful book for travelers* 여행자들에게 유용한 책 – **usefully** *adv* – **usefulness** *n* [U]

use·less /'yuslıs/ *adj* not useful ‖ 쓸모 없는 : *These scissors are completely/totally useless.* 이 가위는 전혀 쓸모없다. / *It's useless to complain.* 불평해 봤자 소용없어.

us·er /'yuzɚ/ *n* someone who uses a product, service etc. ‖ 제품·서비스 등을 이용하는 사람. 사용자: *computer users* 컴퓨터 사용자

us·er-friend·ly /ˌ..'../ *adj* well designed and easy to use ‖ 디자인이 잘 되어 사용하기 쉬운. 조작하기 쉬운

ush·er¹ /'ʌʃɚ/ *n* someone who shows people to their seats in a theater, wedding etc. ‖ 극장·예식장 등에서 사람들에게 좌석을 안내하는 사람. 안내원

usher² *v* [T] to help someone to get from one place to another by showing him/her the way ‖ 남에게 길을 안내해 주어 한 곳에서 다른 곳으로 가도록 도와주다. 안내하다: *The secretary ushered us into the office.* 비서는 사무실로 우리를 안내했다.

u·su·al /'yuʒuəl, -ʒəl/ *adj* **1** the same as what happens most of the time or in most situations ‖ 평소에 또는 대개의 상황에서 일어나는 것과 같은. 평상시의: *Let's meet at the usual place.* 평소 보던 데서 만나자. / *It's colder/warmer than usual for March.* 평년의 3월보다 춥다 [덥다]. **2 as usual** in the way that happens or exists most of the time ‖ 평소에 일어나거나 존재하는 식으로. 여느 때처럼: *They were late, as usual.* 그들은 평소처럼 지각했다.

u·su·al·ly /'yuʒuəli, -ʒəli/ *adv* used when describing what happens on most occasions or in most situations ‖ 대부분의 경우나 상황에서 일어나는 것을 서술할 때 쓰여. 보통은. 대개는: *We usually go out for dinner on Saturday.* 우리는 보통 토요일 저녁에 외식을 한다.

u·surp /yu'sɚp/ *v* [T] FORMAL to take someone else's power, position, job etc. ‖ 남의 권력·지위·일 등을 빼앗다. 강탈[찬탈]하다

UT the written abbreviation of Utah ‖ Utah(유타 주)의 약어

u·ten·sil /yu'tɛnsəl/ *n* a tool or object with a particular use ‖ 특정한 용도의 도구나 물건: *kitchen utensils* 주방용품

u·ter·us /'yutɚəs/ *n* TECHNICAL the organ in a woman or female MAMMAL where babies develop ‖ 아기가 자라는 여성이나 포유동물 암컷의 신체 기관. 자궁

u·til·i·ty /yu'tıləti/ *n* a service such as gas or electricity that is provided for people to use ‖ 사람들이 쓸 수 있게 가스나 전기가 공급되는 서비스. 공익사업: *Does the rent include utilities?* 집세에 공공요금이 포함됩니까?

u·til·ize /'yutlˌaız/ *v* [T] FORMAL to use something effectively ‖ 효율적으로 무엇을 이용하다. 활용하다: *You're not utilizing your skills in your job.* 너는 일하는 데 네 기술을 활용하지 못하고 있다. – **utilization** /ˌyutl-ə'zeıʃən/ *n* [U]

ut·most¹ /'ʌt'moust/ *adj* used in order to emphasize how important, strong, or serious something is ‖ 무엇의 중요성이나

강도, 또는 심각성을 강조하는 데에 쓰여. 극도의: *This is a matter of the utmost importance.* 이것이 가장 중요한 문제이다. / *He was treated with the utmost care and respect.* 그는 최고의 관심과 존경을 받았다.

utmost² *n* [singular] **1 to the utmost** to the highest limit, extent, degree etc. possible ‖ 가능한 한 최대의 한계·범위·정도 등으로. 최대한으로. 힘껏: *The piece challenges singers to the utmost.* 그 곡은 가수들의 능력을 최대한으로 시험한다.

2 do your utmost to try as hard as you can in order to achieve something ‖ 무엇을 이루려고 할 수 있는 만큼 열심히 하다. 최선을 다하다: *We've done our utmost to make them feel welcome.* 우리는 그들이 환영받는다는 느낌이 들도록 최선을 다했다.

u·to·pi·a /yuˈtoupiə/ *n* [C, U] an imaginary perfect world where everyone is happy ‖ 모든 사람들이 행복한 가상의 완벽한 세상. 유토피아. 이상향

ut·ter¹ /ˈʌtɚ/ *adj* complete or extreme ‖ 완전한, 극단적인: *We watched in utter amazement.* 우리는 매우 놀라서 쳐다봤다. **– utterly** *adv*

utter² *v* [T] FORMAL to say something ‖ 무엇을 말하다 **– utterance** *n*

U-turn /ˈyu tɚn/ *n* a turn that you make in a vehicle, so that you go back in the direction you came from ‖ 자동차의 방향을 돌려, 왔던 방향으로 되돌아가기. 유턴: *Shea made a U-turn on Oakland Road.* 시아는 오클랜드 로(路)에서 유턴을 했다.

Vv

V, v /vi/ **1** the twenty-second letter of the English alphabet ‖ 영어 알파벳의 스물두째 자 **2** the number 5 in the system of ROMAN NUMERALs ‖ 로마 숫자 체계에서 숫자 5

V *n* something that has a shape like the letter V ‖ 글자 V자처럼 생긴 것: *a dress with a V neck* 브이넥 드레스

VA the written abbreviation of Virginia ‖ Virginia(버지니아 주)의 약어

va·can·cy /ˈveɪkənsi/ *n* **1** a room or building that is not being used and is available for someone to stay in ‖ 사용되고 있지 않지만 사람이 거주에 쓸 수 있는 방이나 건물. 빈방. 빈 건물: *a motel sign saying "no vacancies"* "빈방 없음" 이라고 쓰인 모텔의 간판 **2** a job that is available for someone to start doing ‖ 사람이 일을 시작할 수 있는 일자리. 공석. 결원: *Are there any vacancies for cooks?* 요리사가 일할 빈자리가 있습니까?

va·cant /ˈveɪkənt/ *adj* **1** empty and available for someone to use ‖ 비어 있고 사람이 사용 가능한. 사용되지 않는. 입주자가 없는: *vacant apartments* 비어 있는 아파트 **2** a vacant job is available for someone to start doing ‖ 일자리가 어떤 사람이 일을 시작할 수 있는. 공석인. 결원인

va·cate /ˈveɪkeɪt/ *v* [T] FORMAL to leave a seat, room etc. so that someone else can use it ‖ 다른 사람이 사용할 수 있게 자리나 방을 떠나다. 비우다. (방을) 빼다: *Guests must vacate their rooms by noon.* 투숙객은 정오까지 방을 비워야 한다.

va·ca·tion /veɪˈkeɪʃən, və-/ *n* a time that is spent not working or not at school ‖ 근무나 수업을 하지 않고 보내는 때. 방학. 휴가: *They're on vacation for the next two weeks.* 그들은 다음 2주간 휴가 간다. / *the kids' summer vacation* 아이들의 여름 방학 / *We'd like to take a vacation in the Virgin Islands.* 우리는 버진 아일랜드에서 휴가를 보내고 싶다. – **vacation** *v* [I]

USAGE NOTE vacation

We use **vacation** to talk about time you spend away from school or work: *Where are you going on vacation this summer?* Use **break** to talk about a time that you stop working in order to rest, or about a short vacation from school: *You've been studying for hours; why don't you take a break? / We're going skiing during spring break.* Use **holiday** to talk about a day when no one officially has to go to work or school: *Christmas is my favorite holiday.* Use **leave** to talk about time when you are allowed not to work for a special reason: *Kate's on maternity leave for three months.*

vacation은 학교나 직장에서 떠나서 보내는 시간에 대해 말하기 위해 쓴다: 이번 여름휴가는 어디로 갈 거냐? **break** 는 휴식을 취하기 위해 일을 멈추는 시간이나 학교에서의 짧은 방학에 대해 말하기 위해 쓴다: 너는 여러 시간 동안 계속 공부해 오고 있는데, 잠깐 쉬는 게 어때? / 우리는 봄방학 동안 스키를 타러 간다. **holiday**는 모든 사람들이 공식적으로 직장이나 학교에 가지 않아도 되는 날에 대해 말하기 위해 쓴다: 크리스마스는 내가 가장 좋아하는 휴일이다. **leave**는 특별한 이유로 일하지 않도록 허용된 때에 대해 말하는 데 쓴다: 케이트는 3개월간 출산 휴가 중이다.

---

vac·ci·nate /ˈvæksəˌneɪt/ *v* [T] to protect someone from a disease by giving him/her a VACCINE ‖ 남에게 백신을 놓아 질병에서 보호하다. 예방 접종[주사]을 하다: *Have you been vaccinated against measles?* 홍역 예방 접종 맞았어요? – **vaccination** /ˌvæksəˈneɪʃən/ *n* [U]

vac·cine /vækˈsin/ *n* [C, U] a substance that contains a weak form of the virus that causes a disease and is used for protecting people from that disease ‖ 어떤 병을 일으키는 바이러스의 약한 형태를 가지고 있으며, 그 병으로부터 사람들을 보호하는 데 사용되는 물질. 백신: *polio vaccine* 소아마비 백신

vac·il·late /ˈvæsəˌleɪt/ *v* [I] FORMAL to continue to change your opinions, ideas etc. because you cannot decide between two choices ‖ 두 개의 선택안 사이에서 결정을 내릴 수 없어서 의견·생각 등을 계속 바꾸다. 동요하다. 흔들리다

vac·uum¹ /ˈvækyum/ *n* **1** ⇨ VACUUM

CLEANER **2** a space that is completely empty of all gas ‖ 모든 기체를 완전히 없앤 공간. 진공(공간) **3** [singular] a situation in which someone or something is missing or lacking ‖ 사람이나 사물이 빠지거나 결여된 상태. 공허. 공백: *Her husband's death left a vacuum in her life.* 남편의 죽음으로 그녀의 인생은 공허해졌다. **4 in a vacuum** if something happens in a vacuum, it happens without being influenced by anything ‖ 사물이 어떤 것에도 영향을 받지 않고 일어나는. 외부와 격리되어[고립되어]: *You can't make decisions in a vacuum.* 당신은 어떠한 것에도 영향을 받지 않고 혼자서 의사 결정을 내릴 수는 없다.

vacuum² *v* [I, T] to clean a place using a VACUUM CLEANER ‖ 진공 청소기로 어떤 장소를 청소하다

vacuum clean·er /'.. ,../ *n* a machine that cleans floors by sucking up the dirt from them ‖ 바닥에서 먼지를 빨아들여 청소하는 기계. 진공 청소기

vacuum-packed /'.. ,./ *adj* vacuum-packed food is packed in a container from which the air is removed, in order to keep the food fresh ‖ 식품을 신선하게 유지하기 위해 공기가 제거된 용기 속에 포장된. 진공 포장의

va·gi·na /vəˈdʒaɪnə/ *n* the passage from a woman's outer sexual organs to her UTERUS ‖ 여성의 외부 생식기에서 자궁까지의 통로. 질(膣) – **vaginal** /ˈvædʒənl/ *adj*

va·grant /ˈveɪɡrənt/ *n* FORMAL someone who has no home or work ‖ 집이나 일자리가 없는 사람. 부랑자. 거지

vague /veɪɡ/ *adj* **1** unclear because someone does not give enough details ‖ 충분한 세부 내용을 주지 않아서 분명치 않은. 불확실한. 확정되지 않은: *She's been vague about her plans for the summer.* 그녀의 여름철 계획은 아직 미정이다. **2 have a vague idea/feeling etc.** to think that something might be true or that you remember something, although you cannot be sure ‖ 비록 확신할 수는 없어도 어떤 것이 사실일지 모르거나 어떤 것을 기억한다고 생각하다. 막연한[모호한] 생각/감정 등을 갖다

vague·ly /ˈveɪɡli/ *adv* **1** slightly ‖ 약간. 조금. 다소: *She looked vaguely familiar.* 그녀는 어딘가 모르게 낯익어 보였다. **2** in a way that shows you are not thinking about what you are doing ‖ 현재 하고 있는 것에 대해 생각하고 있지 않음을 나타내듯이. 어렴풋이. 막연히: *He*

smiled vaguely. 그는 희미하게 미소를 지어 보였다.

vain /veɪn/ *adj* **1** full of pride in yourself, your appearance, and your abilities ‖ 자기 자신[외모, 능력]에 대한 자만심으로 가득 찬. 허영심이 강한. 뽐내는 **2 in vain** without success ‖ 성공 없이. 헛되이. 보람 없이: *I tried in vain to convince Paul to come.* 나는 폴이 오도록 설득했지만 허사였다. **3 vain attempt/hope etc.** an attempt, hope etc. that is not successful ‖ 성공하지 못한 시도·희망 등. 헛된 시도/희망 – **vainly** *adv*

val·en·tine /ˈvæləntaɪn/ *n* **1** a card given on Valentine's Day ‖ 밸런타인 데이에 보내는 카드 **2** a name for someone you love on VALENTINE'S DAY ‖ 밸런타인 데이에 자신이 사랑하는 사람에 대한 지칭. 애인: *Will you be my valentine?* (밸런타인 데이에) 내 애인이 되어줄래?

Valentine's Day /'... ./ *n* a holiday in some countries when people give special cards, candy, or flowers to people they love ‖ 사랑하는 사람에게 특별한 카드[사탕, 꽃]를 주는 몇몇 나라에서의 휴일. 성 밸런타인 데이

val·et /væˈleɪ, ˈvæleɪ/ *n* **1** someone who parks your car for you at a hotel or restaurant ‖ 호텔이나 식당에서 손님의 차를 대신 주차하는 사람. 주차 담당원 **2** a male servant who takes care of a man's clothes, serves his meals etc. ‖ 남자 주인의 옷을 관리하고 식사 준비 등의 일을 하는 남자 하인

val·iant /ˈvælyənt/ *adj* FORMAL very brave, especially in a difficult situation ‖ 특히 어려운 상황 속에서 매우 용감한. 씩씩한: *a valiant rescue attempt* 용감한 구출 시도

val·id /ˈvælɪd/ *adj* **1** a valid ticket, document, or agreement can be used legally or is officially acceptable ‖ 표[서류, 협정] 등이 법적으로 사용될 수 있거나 공식적으로 받아들여지는. 유효한. 효력 있는: *a valid passport* 유효한 여권 **2** based on strong reasons or facts ‖ 강력한 이유나 사실에 근거한. 정당한 근거가 있는. 타당한: *There is no valid data on the drug's safety.* 그 약의 안전성에 대해서는 확실한 자료가 없다. —opposite INVALID¹

val·i·date /ˈvæləˌdeɪt/ *v* [T] FORMAL to prove that something is true or correct, or to make a document or agreement officially and legally acceptable ‖ 어떤 것이 사실이거나 옳다고 증명하다, 또는 서류나 협정을 공식적이고 법적으로 받아

들일 수 있게 하다. 실증[확증]하다. …을 유효하게 하다 —opposite INVALIDATE

va·lid·i·ty /vəˈlɪdəti/ n [U] the state of being real, true, or based on facts ‖ 실제적인[진실된, 사실에 근거한] 상태. 정당[타당, 유효](성): *Scientists are questioning the validity of the experiment.* 과학자들은 그 실험의 타당성을 의문시하고 있다.

val·ley /ˈvæli/ n an area of lower land between two lines of hills or mountains ‖ 언덕이나 산의 두 능선 사이의 보다 낮은 지역. 계곡. 골짜기

val·or /ˈvælər/ n [U] LITERARY great courage, especially in war ‖ 특히 전쟁에서의 대단한 용기. 무용. 용맹성

val·u·a·ble /ˈvæljəbəl, -yuəbəl/ adj 1 worth a lot of money ‖ 많은 금전적 가치가 있는. 값비싼: *a valuable ring* 값비싼 반지 2 valuable help, advice etc. is very useful ‖ 도움·충고 등이 매우 유용한. 귀중한. 유익한 —compare INVALUABLE

val·u·a·bles /ˈvæljəbəlz/ n [plural] things that you own that are worth a lot of money, such as jewelry, cameras etc. ‖ 보석이나 카메라 등 많은 금전적 가치가 있는 소유물. 귀중품

val·ue¹ /ˈvælyu/ n 1 [C, U] the amount of money that something is worth ‖ 어떤 것의 가치를 나타내는 돈의 액수. 가격. 값: *Did the thieves take anything of value?* (=worth a lot of money) 그 도둑들이 어떤 값비싼 것들을 훔쳐갔나요? / *drugs with a street value of $50,000* (=the value of drugs when they are sold illegally) 암거래 가격 5만 달러 상당의 마약 2 [U] the importance or usefulness of something ‖ 어떤 것의 중요성이나 유용성. 가치. 값어치. 효용성: *His research was of great value to doctors working with this disease.* 그의 연구는 이 병을 치료하는 의사에게 대단히 중요한 것이었다. / *These earrings have sentimental value.* (=are important to you because they were a gift, remind you of someone etc.) 이 귀걸이는 나에게 의미있는 물건이다.

value² v [T] 1 to think that something is important to you ‖ 어떤 것이 자신에게 중요하다고 생각하다. …을 높이 평가하다. 중시하다: *I value your friendship.* 나에게 너의 우정은 소중하다. 2 to say how much something is worth ‖ 어떤 것이 얼마나 (많은) 값어치가 있는지 말하다. 평가하다. 견적하다: *a painting valued at $5 million* 5백만 달러로 감정된 그림

val·ues /ˈvælyuz/ n [plural] your principles about what is right and wrong, or your ideas about what is important ‖ 무엇이 옳고 그른지에 대한 자신의 원칙, 또는 무엇이 중요한지에 대한 자신의 생각. 가치관: *traditional family values* 전통적인 가정의 가치관

valve /vælv/ n a part of a tube or pipe that opens and closes like a door in order to control the flow of liquid, gas, air etc. passing through ‖ 통과하는 액체·가스·공기 등의 흐름을 통제하기 위해 문같이 열고 닫는 관이나 파이프의 한 부분. 밸브(장치)

vam·pire /ˈvæmpaɪər/ n an imaginary creature that looks like a person and sucks people's blood by biting their necks ‖ 사람 같은 모습에 사람들의 목을 물어 피를 빨아먹는다는 상상의 피조물. 흡혈귀

van /væn/ n 1 a TRUCK with an enclosed back, used for carrying goods ‖ 물건을 나르는 데 사용하는 후면 유개 트럭: *a moving van* 이사용 트럭 2 a large box-like car ‖ 큰 상자 같은 차. 승합차 —see picture on page 943

van·dal /ˈvændl/ n someone who VANDALIZES public property ‖ 공공물을 고의로 파괴[오손]하는 사람

van·dal·ism /ˈvændlˌɪzəm/ n [U] the crime of deliberately damaging things, especially public property ‖ 특히 공공물을 고의로 손상시키는 범죄. 공공시설 파손(행위)

van·dal·ize /ˈvændlˌaɪz/ v [T] to damage or destroy things deliberately, especially public property ‖ 특히 공공물을 고의로 손상시키거나 파괴하다

van·guard /ˈvængard/ n **in the vanguard** in the most advanced position of development ‖ 발전의 가장 앞선 위치에. 선봉에: *a group in the vanguard of political reform* 정치 개혁의 선봉에 서 있는 집단

va·nil·la /vəˈnɪlə/ n [U] a sweet-smelling liquid from the bean of a plant, that is added to particular foods ‖ 특정한 음식에 추가해 넣는, 식물의 열매로 만든 향긋한 냄새가 나는 액체. 바닐라 에센스: *vanilla ice cream* 바닐라 아이스크림

van·ish /ˈvænɪʃ/ v [I] to disappear suddenly, especially in a way that cannot be easily explained ‖ 특히 쉽게 설명될 수 없게 갑자기 사라지다. 자취를 감추다: *When I looked again, he'd vanished.* 내가 다시 보았을 때 그는 사라지고 없었다. / *Police say the suspect seems to have vanished without a trace.* (=disappeared so that no sign remains) 경찰은 용의자가 흔적 없이 사라

진 것 같다고 말한다. - **vanishing** *adj*

van·i·ty /'vænəti/ *n* [U] the quality of being too proud of yourself ‖ 자신을 너무 자랑스럽게 여기는 성질. 자만심

van·quish /'væŋkwɪʃ/ *v* [T] LITERARY to defeat someone or something completely ‖ 어떤 사람이나 사물을 완전히 패배시키다. …을 정복하다. 무찌르다

van·tage point /'væntɪdʒ ˌpɔɪnt/ *n* **1** a good position from which you can see something ‖ 어떤 것을 볼 수 있는 좋은 위치. 전망이 좋은 지점. 유리한 위치 **2** a way of thinking about things that comes from your own situation ‖ 자기 자신의 상황에서 기인한 사물에 대한 사고 방식. 입장: *Kopcek's ideas come from his vantage point as an immigrant.* 콥섹의 생각은 이민자라는 자신의 입장에서 나온 것이다.

va·por /'veɪpɚ/ *n* [C, U] many small drops of liquid that float in the air ‖ 대기에 떠다니는 수많은 작은 액체 방울. 증기: *water vapor* 수증기

va·por·ize /'veɪpəˌraɪz/ *v* [I, T] to be changed into a VAPOR, or change a liquid into a vapor ‖ 증기로 바뀌다, 또는 액체를 증기로 바꾸다. 증발[기화]되다[시키다]

var·i·able¹ /'vɛriəbəl, 'vær-/ *adj* **1** likely to change often ‖ 자주 변화하기 쉬운. 일정하지 않은. 변덕스러운: *the variable nature of the weather* 날씨의 변하기 쉬운 특성 **2** sometimes good and sometimes bad ‖ 때로는 좋고 때로는 나쁜. 가변적인. 일정하지 않은: *The group's performance has been variable lately.* 그 그룹의 공연의 질은 요즘 일정치 않다.

variable² *n* something that may be different in different situations ‖ 다른 상황에서는 달라질지도 모르는 것. 변수. 변하는[변하기 쉬운] 것: *cultural variables* 문화적 다양성

var·i·ance /'vɛriəns, 'vær-/ *n* [U] FORMAL **be at variance with** if two people or things are at variance with each other, they do not agree or are very different ‖ 두 사람이나 사물이 서로 일치하지 않거나 매우 차이가 나다. 서로 다투다. 불화하다

var·i·ant /'vɛriənt, 'vær-/ *n* something that is slightly different from the usual form of something ‖ 어떤 것의 보통의 형태에서 약간 다른 것. 변형. 별형. 이형(異型): *a spelling variant* (같은 낱말의) 다른 철자 - **variant** *adj*

var·i·a·tion /ˌvɛriˈeɪʃən, ˌvær-/ *n* [C, U] a difference or change from the usual

amount or form of something ‖ 어떤 것의 보통의 수량이나 형태에서의 차이나 변화. 변화량[률]. 변화의 정도: *variations in prices from store to store* 가게마다의 가격 차이

var·i·cose veins /ˌværəkoʊs 'veɪnz/ *n* [plural] a medical condition in which the VEINs in your leg become swollen and painful ‖ 다리의 정맥이 붓고 아픈 의학적인 상태. 정맥류

var·ied /'vɛrid, 'vær-/ *adj* consisting of or including many different types of things or people ‖ 많은 서로 다른 종류의 사물이나 사람으로 이루어지거나 포함하고 있는. 변화가 많은. 다양한. 갖가지의: *They make products as varied as ash trays and toys.* 그들은 재떨이와 장난감 같은 매우 다양한 제품을 만든다.

va·ri·e·ty /vəˈraɪəti/ *n* **1** [U] a lot of things of the same type that are different from each other in some way ‖ 같은 종류의 많은 사물들이 서로간에 약간 차이가 나는 것. 갖가지 다른 것. 여러 가지: *The data comes from a variety of sources.* 그 자료는 많은 출처에서 나온다. / *The variety that cable TV provides makes it very popular.* 케이블 텔레비전은 제공하는 프로그램의 다양성 때문에 인기가 매우 높다. **2** [U] the differences within a group, set of actions etc. that make it interesting ‖ 집단이나 일련의 행동 등 내에서 흥미 있게 만드는 차이(점). 변화(가 많음). 다양(성): *There isn't much she could do to add variety to her work.* 그녀가 자신의 작품에 다양성을 더하기 위해 할 수 있는 것은 많지 않다. **3** a type of something that is different from others in the same group ‖ 같은 집단 내의 다른 것들과는 차이가 나는 유형의 것. 종류. 품종: *a new variety of rose* 장미의 새 품종 / *To preserve the flavor of the cookies, store each variety in a separate container.* 쿠키의 맛을 보존하기 위해 각각의 용기에 각 종류별로 보관하시오.

variety show /.'... ˌ./ *n* a television or radio program or a play that consists of many different performances, especially funny ones ‖ 특히 오락물로서 많은 수의 상이한 공연물로 구성된 텔레비전이나 라디오의 프로그램이나 연극. 버라이어티 쇼

var·i·ous /'vɛriəs, 'vær-/ *adj* several different ‖ 여러 개의 서로 다른. 가지각색의. 여러 가지의. 다양한: *This coat comes in various colors.* 이 코트는 색깔별로 생산된다.

var·i·ous·ly /'vɛriəsli, 'vær-/ *adv* in many different ways ‖ 많은 상이한 방식

으로. 여러 가지로. 갖가지로: *He's been variously called a genius and a madman.* 그는 천재와 광인으로 다양하게 불려져 왔다.

var·nish¹ /ˈvɑːrnɪʃ/ *n* [C, U] a clear liquid that is painted onto things that are made of wood, to protect them and give them a shiny surface ‖ 나무로 만든 것들을 보호하고 표면에 광택을 내기 위해 칠하는 투명한 액체. 바니시. 니스

varnish² *v* [T] to paint something with VARNISH ‖ 니스로 어떤 것을 칠하다

var·si·ty /ˈvɑːrsəti/ *n* [C, U] the main team that represents a university, college, or school in sports ‖ 스포츠에서 대학[단과 대학, 각급 학교]을 대표하는 주요 팀. 대표팀: *the varsity basketball team* (그 대학의) 대표 농구팀

var·y /ˈvɛri, ˈværi/ *v* **1** [I] if several things of the same type vary, they are all different from each other ‖ 같은 종류의 여러 개의 것이 서로 모두 다르다. 갖가지[가지각색]이다: *Teaching methods vary greatly/enormously from school to school.* 가르치는 방법은 학교마다 크게 다르다. / *wines that vary in price/quality* 가격[질]이 다양한 포도주 **2** [I] to change often ‖ 자주 바뀌다. 변하다: *His moods seem to vary a lot.* 그의 기분은 심하게 바뀌는 것 같다. **3** [T] to regularly change what you do or the way that you do it ‖ 자신이 하고 있는 것이나 하는 방식을 규칙적으로 바꾸다. …을 (…과) 다르게 하다. …에 차이[변화]를 주다: *You need to vary your diet and get more exercise.* 당신은 식단에 변화를 주고 더 많은 운동을 하는 것이 필요하다.

var·y·ing /ˈvɛriɪŋ, ˈværiɪŋ/ *adj* changing or different ‖ 변화하고 있거나 차이가 있는. 갖가지[가지각색]의. 다양한: *Races are over varying distances.* 경주는 여러 구간에 걸쳐 벌어진다.

vase /veɪs, veɪz, vɑz/ *n* a container used for decoration or to put flowers in ‖ 장식용이나 꽃을 꽂는 데 쓰이는 용기. 꽃병. 화병

va·sec·to·my /vəˈsɛktəmi/ *n* [C, U] a medical operation to cut the small tube through which a man's SPERM passes, so that he is unable to produce children ‖ 아이를 낳을 수 없게 남성의 정자가 통과하는 작은 관을 자르는 의학적 수술. 정관절제술 —compare HYSTERECTOMY

vast /væst/ *adj* **1** extremely large ‖ 아주 넓은. 엄청나게 큰. 광대한: *vast deserts* 광대한 사막 **2 the vast majority of** almost all of a group of people or things ‖ 일단의 사람이나 사물

의 거의 대부분. 대다수

vast·ly /ˈvæstli/ *adv* very greatly ‖ 아주 대단하게. 매우. 굉장히: *vastly improved educational programs* 대단히 향상된 교육 프로그램

vat /væt/ *n* a very large container for keeping liquids in ‖ 액체를 담아두기 위한 매우 큰 통

vault¹ /vɔlt/ *n* **1** a room with thick walls and a strong door, where money, jewels etc. are kept safely ‖ 돈이나 보석 등이 안전하게 보관되는 두꺼운 벽과 강한 문으로 된 방. 귀중품 보관실 **2** a room where people from the same family are buried ‖ 동일 가계의 사람들이 묻혀 있는 방. 가족 납골당[매장실] **3** a jump over something ‖ 어떤 것 위로 뛰기. 도약

vault², vault over *v* [T] to jump over something in one movement, using your hands or a pole to help you ‖ 손이나 보조 장대를 이용해서 한 차례 움직여서 어떤 것을 뛰어넘다. 높이 뛰다. 도약하다: *He vaulted over the fence and ran off.* 그는 담을 훌쩍 뛰어넘어 달아났다.

V chip /ˈvi tʃɪp/ *n* a CHIP in a television that allows parents to prevent their children from watching programs that are violent or have sex in them ‖ 부모들에게 그 자녀들이 폭력물이나 에로물을 보는 것을 방지하게 하는 텔레비전 내의 소자[칩]. V칩

VCR *n* video cassette recorder; a machine that is used for recording television shows or watching VIDEOTAPES ‖ video cassette recorder(비디오 카세트 녹화기)의 약어;텔레비전 쇼를 녹화하거나 비디오테이프를 보기 위해 사용되는 기계

VD *n* [U] OLD-FASHIONED venereal disease; a disease that is passed from one person to another during sex ‖ venereal disease(성병)의 약어; 성교를 통해 한 사람에게서 다른 사람에게로 옮겨지는 병 —see also STD

VDU *n* visual display unit; a machine like a television that shows the information from a computer ‖ visual display unit((CRT를 사용한) 데이터 표시 장치)의 약어; 컴퓨터로부터 정보를 보여주는 텔레비전 같은 기계

-'ve /v, əv/ the short form of "have" ‖ "have"의 단축형: *I've/We've finished.* 나는[우리는] (일을) 끝냈다.

veal /vil/ *n* [U] the meat from a CALF (=young cow) ‖ 송아지의 고기 —see usage note at MEAT

veer /vɪr/ *v* [I] to change direction suddenly ‖ 갑자기 방향을 바꾸다: *The car veered sharply to the left.* 그 차는

왼쪽으로 방향을 휙 꺾었다.

veg /vɛdʒ/, **veg out** v [I] INFORMAL to relax and not do anything important ‖ 편히 쉬면서 중요한 것을 전혀 하지 않다. 아무 하는 일 없이 지내다: *I just want to veg out in front of the TV.* 나는 그저 하는 일없이 텔레비전이나 보고 싶을 뿐이다.

veg·e·ta·ble /'vɛdʒtəbəl/ n **1** a plant such as corn or potatoes, that is grown in order to be eaten ‖ 먹기 위해 재배되는 옥수수나 감자 등의 식물. 야채. 채소 **2** INFORMAL someone who cannot think or move because his/her brain has been damaged ‖ 뇌를 다쳐서 생각하거나 움직일 수 없는 사람. 식물 인간

veg·e·tar·i·an /,vɛdʒə'tɛriən/ n someone who does not eat meat or fish ‖ 고기나 생선을 먹지 않는 사람. 채식주의자 **– vegetarian** adj

veg·e·ta·tion /,vɛdʒə'teɪʃən/ n [U] plants in general, especially all the plants in one particular area ‖ 일반적인 식물, 특히 한 특정 지역의 모든 식물: *a meadow with thick vegetation* 초목이 무성한 초원

veg·gies /'vɛdʒiz/ n [plural] INFORMAL vegetables ‖ 야채 **– veggie** adj

ve·he·ment /'viəmənt/ adj showing very strong feelings or opinions ‖ 매우 강한 감정이나 의견을 나타내는. 열심인. 격렬한. 맹렬한: *vehement complaints* 격심한 불평 **– vehemently** adv

ve·hi·cle /'viikəl/ n FORMAL **1** a thing such as a car, bus etc. that is used for carrying people or things from one place to another ‖ 사람이나 사물을 한 장소에서 다른 장소로 수송하는 데 사용되는 자동차·버스 등의 것. 차량. 운반[운송] 수단. 탈것 **2** a vehicle for (doing) sth something that you use as a way of spreading your ideas, opinions, etc. ‖ 자신의 생각·의견 등을 전달하는 방법으로서 사용하는 것. 전달 수단. 매체 **– vehicular** /vi'hɪkyələ/ adj

veil[1] /veɪl/ n **1** a thin piece of material that women wear to cover their faces ‖ 여성이 자기의 얼굴을 가리기 위해 쓰는 얇은 천 조각. 베일. 면사포: *a bridal veil* 신부의 면사포 **2 a veil of secrecy/silence etc.** something that stops you knowing the full truth about a situation ‖ 어떤 상황에 대한 모든 사실을 아는 것을 막는 것. 비밀의/침묵의 장막: *A veil of mystery surrounded Gomez's death.* 고메즈의 죽음에는 의문의 베일이 쳐져 있었다.

veil[2] v [T] **1 be veiled in mystery/secrecy** if something is veiled in mystery, secrecy etc., very little is known about it ‖ 어떤 것이 의문·비밀 등에 싸여 있어 거의 알려지지 않다. 의문/비밀의 베일에 싸여 있다 **2** to cover something with a VEIL ‖ 어떤 것을 베일로 가리다. …에 베일을 치다

veiled /veɪld/ adj **veiled criticism/threats etc.** criticisms, threats etc. that are not said directly ‖ 직접적으로 말하지 않은 비판·위협 등. 드러내지 않은[은폐된] 비판/위협

vein /veɪn/ n **1** one of the tubes through which blood flows to your heart from other parts of your body ‖ 신체의 각 기관에서 심장으로 피가 흘러들어가는 관의 하나. 정맥 **—compare** ARTERY **2** one of the thin lines on a leaf or on the wing of an insect ‖ 잎이나 곤충의 날개 위의 잎맥이나 시맥(翅脈) **3** a thin layer of a valuable metal or mineral in rock ‖ 암석 속의 값어치 있는 금속이나 광물의 얇은 층. 광층. 광맥: *a rich vein of gold* 금의 풍부한 광맥 **4** a particular style of speaking or writing about something ‖ 어떤 것에 대해 말하거나 글을 쓰는 특정한 스타일. 수법. 기질. 성향: *Her speech continued in a similar/humorous vein.* 그녀의 연설은 시종 비슷한[해학적인] 스타일로 계속되었다.

Vel·cro /'vɛlkroʊ/ n [U] TRADEMARK a material used for fastening shoes, clothes etc., made from two special pieces of cloth that stick to each other ‖ 서로 들러 붙는 두 장의 특수 천 조각으로 만든, 신발·옷·등을 붙이는 데 쓰이는 소재. 벨크로. 매직 테이프

ve·loc·i·ty /və'lɑsəti/ n [C, U] TECHNICAL the speed at which something moves in a particular direction ‖ 어떤 것이 특정한 방향으로 움직이는 속도. 속력: *the velocity of light* 빛의 속도[광속]

ve·lour /və'lʊr/ n [U] heavy cloth that has a soft surface ‖ 표면이 부드러운 두꺼운 천. 벨루어

vel·vet /'vɛlvɪt/ n [U] cloth with a soft surface on one side ‖ 한쪽 면이 부드러운 표면인 천. 벨벳

vel·vet·y /'vɛlvɪti/ adj looking, feeling, tasting, or sounding smooth and soft ‖ 매끄럽고 부드럽게 보이는[느껴지는, 맛이 나는, 소리 나는]. 벨벳 같은 (촉감의): *a velvety voice* 부드러운 목소리

ven·det·ta /vɛn'dɛtə/ n a quarrel in which two families or groups try to harm each other over a long period of time ‖ 두 가족이나 집단이 오랜 기간 동안 서로 위해를 가하려고 애쓰는 싸움. 피의 보복. 원수 갚기. 뿌리깊은 반목

vend·ing ma·chine /'vendɪŋ mə,ʃin/ *n* a machine that you can get cigarettes, candy, drinks etc. from by putting in money ‖ 돈을 넣고 담배·사탕·음료수 등을 얻을 수 있는 기계. 자동판매기

ven·dor /'vɛndɚ/ *n* **1** someone who sells things, especially in the street ‖ 특히 길거리에서 물건을 파는 사람. 행상인: *That street vendor sells great hot dogs.* 그 길거리 행상인은 정말 맛있는 핫도그를 판다. **2** LAW someone who is selling something such as a house or land ‖ 집이나 땅 등을 파는 사람. 매각인

ve·neer /və'nɪr/ *n* **1** [C, U] a thin layer of good quality wood that covers the outside of a piece of furniture that is made of a cheaper material ‖ 값싼 제재로 만들어진 가구의 외장을 덮는, 질 좋은 목재의 얇은 판. 화장판. 단판(單板): *oak veneer* 오크 베니어판 **2** a veneer of FORMAL behavior that hides someone's real character or feelings ‖ 사람의 진짜 성격이나 감정을 숨기는 행동. 겉치레. 겉치장. 허식: *a veneer of politeness* 가식적인 정중함

ven·er·a·ble /'vɛnərəbəl/ *adj* FORMAL very old and respected because of age, experience, historical importance etc. ‖ 연륜·경험·역사적 중요성 때문에 매우 오래되고 존경받는. 존경할 만한. 유서 깊은. 오래된: *a venerable gentleman* 존경할 만한 신사

ven·er·ate /'vɛnə,reɪt/ *v* [T] FORMAL to treat someone or something with great respect, especially because she, he, or it is old ‖ 특히 사람이나 사물이 나이들었거나 오래 되어서 매우 존경심을 가지고 대하다. …을 존경하다. 경배하다: *The Chinese venerate their ancestors.* 중국인들은 자기들의 조상을 경배한다.

ve·ne·re·al dis·ease /və,nɪriəl dɪ'ziz/ *n* [C, U] ⇨ VD

Ve·ne·tian blind /və,niʃən 'blaɪnd/ *n* a set of long flat BARs used for covering a window, that can be raised or lowered to let in light ‖ 채광 조절을 위해 올렸다 내렸다 할 수 있게 한, 창문을 가리는 데 사용되는 한 조의 길고 납작한 막대기. 베니션 블라인드

venge·ance /'vɛndʒəns/ *n* **1** something violent or harmful that you do to someone in order to punish him/her for hurting you ‖ 자신을 해친 대가로 벌주기 위해 남에게 행하는 폭력이나 위해(危害). 복수. 원수 갚기. 앙갚음: *a desire for vengeance* 복수에 대한 열망 **2 with a vengeance** much more than is expected or normal ‖ 예상되거나 통상적인 것보다 훨씬 더. 세게. (극)심하게: *The music started up again with a vengeance.* 그 음악은 놀랄 정도로 크게 다시 시작되었다. —see also REVENGE, AVENGE

venge·ful /'vɛndʒfəl/ *adj* LITERARY very eager to punish someone who has hurt you ‖ 자신을 해친 사람을 몹시 응징하고 싶어 하는. 복수심에 불타는

ven·i·son /'vɛnəsən/ *n* [U] the meat of a DEER ‖ 사슴 고기

ven·om /'vɛnəm/ *n* [U] **1** a liquid poison that some snakes, insects etc. produce ‖ 몇몇 뱀·곤충 등이 만들어내는 독액 **2** extreme anger or hatred ‖ 매우 화내거나 미워함. 악의. 원한: *a speech full of venom* 악의로 가득 찬 연설

vent¹ /vɛnt/ *n* **1** a hole or pipe through which gases, smoke, or liquid can enter or go out ‖ 가스[연기, 액체]가 들어갔다 나왔다 할 수 있는 구멍이나 관. 배기관 [구멍]: *an air vent* 통풍구 **2 give vent to** FORMAL to do something to express a strong feeling ‖ 격한 감정을 표현하기 위해 어떤 것을 하다. 발산하다. 털어놓다

vent² *v* [T] to do something to express your feelings, often in a way that is unfair ‖ 종종 부당하게, 자신의 감정을 표현하기 위해 어떤 일을 하다. 배출[발산]하다. 터뜨리다: *Jay vented his anger on his family.* 제이는 자신의 가족에게 화풀이를 했다.

ven·ti·late /'vɛntl,eɪt/ *v* [T] to let fresh air into a room, building etc. ‖ 신선한 공기가 방·건물 등으로 들어오게 하다. 환기하다 **–ventilated** *adj* **–ventilation** /,vɛntl'eɪʃən/ *n* [U]

ven·ti·la·tor /'vɛntl,eɪtɚ/ *n* ⇨ RESPIRATOR

ven·tril·o·quism /vɛn'trɪlə,kwɪzəm/ *n* [U] the art of speaking without moving your lips, so that the sound seems to come from somewhere else ‖ 소리가 다른 곳에서 나는 것처럼 보이도록 입술을 움직이지 않고 말하는 기술. 복화술 **–ventriloquist** *n*

ven·ture¹ /'vɛntʃɚ/ *n* **1** a new business activity that involves taking risks ‖ 위험을 무릅써야 하는 새로운 사업 활동. 새로운 투자 사업. 벤처: *a new joint venture* (=an agreement between two companies to do something together) 새로운 합작 투자 사업 **2** a trip or attempt to do something that involves taking risks ‖ 위험을 무릅쓰고 어떤 것을 하려는 여행이나 시도. 모험

ven·ture² *v* FORMAL **1** [I] to risk going somewhere when it could be dangerous

‖ 위험성이 있을 때 어떤 곳에 가는 모험을 하다. 모험(길)에 나서다: *Several boats ventured out to sea, despite the weather.* 여러 배들이 날씨가 좋지 않음에도 불구하고 위험을 무릅쓰고 바다에 나갔다. **2** [T] to say something although you are afraid of how someone may react to it ‖ 비록 남이 어떻게 반응할지 걱정되더라도 어떤 것을 말하다. 감히 표명하다. 과감히 말하다: *Sandy shyly ventured a question.* 샌디는 수줍어 하면서도 과감히 질문을 했다. **3** [T] to take the risk of losing something ‖ 어떤 것을 잃어버릴 위험을 감수하다. …을 위험에 내맡기다. 모험적으로 …에 내걸다: *He ventured his savings on a new business.* 그는 새로운 사업에 자신의 저축금을 걸었다.

ven·ue /'vɛnyu/ *n* a place such as a theater, CLUB, or STADIUM where people go for an arranged activity ‖ 예정된 활동을 위해 가는 극장[클럽, 운동장] 등의 장소. 행위의 발생지. 행사장. 개최지: *a popular jazz venue* 대중 재즈 공연장

Ve·nus /'vinəs/ *n* [singular] a small PLANET, second from the sun ‖ 태양으로부터 두 번째의 작은 행성. 금성

ve·ran·da /və'rændə/ *n* ⇨ PORCH

verb /vəb/ *n* TECHNICAL in grammar, a word or group of words that is used in order to describe an action, experience, or state. In the sentence, "They arrived late," "arrived" is a verb ‖ 문법에서 행동[경험, 상태]을 설명하기 위해 사용되는 단어나 단어군들. 동사 "They arrived late." 문장에서 "arrived"는 동사이다 — see study note on page 942

ver·bal /'vəbəl/ *adj* **1** spoken ‖ 구두의: *a verbal agreement* 구두 계약 **2** relating to words or using words ‖ 말에 관계되거나 말을 사용하는. 말[언어]의. 말의 형태로: *verbal skill* 말하는 기술 – **verbally** *adv*

ver·ba·tim /və'beɪtɪm/ *adj, adv* repeating the actual words that were spoken or written ‖ 말해지거나 쓰여진 실제 언어를 되풀이하는. 똑같은 말로[의]. 정확히 말 그대로(의): *a verbatim report of our conversation* 우리의 대화를 그대로 옮긴 보고(서)

ver·bose /və'boʊs/ *adj* FORMAL using or containing too many words ‖ 너무 많은 말을 사용하거나 포함하고 있는. 말이 많은. 수다스러운. 장황한

ver·dict /'vədɪkt/ *n* **1** an official decision that is made by a JURY in a court of law about whether someone is guilty ‖ 사람이 죄가 있는지 없는지에 대해 법정에서 배심원단에 의해 내려지는 공식적인 결정. 평결: *Has the jury reached a verdict?* (=made a decision) 배심원단이 평결을 내렸느냐? **2** an official decision or opinion made by a person or group that has authority ‖ 권한을 가진 사람이나 단체에 의해 내려진 공식적인 결정이나 의견. 판정. 평가. 결론: *The panel will give their verdict tomorrow.* 위원회는 내일 판정을 내릴 것이다.

verge¹ /vədʒ/ *n* **be on the verge of** to be about to do something ‖ 바야흐로 어떤 것을 하려고 하다: *Andy was on the verge of tears.* 앤디는 막 눈물을 흘릴 듯 했다.

verge² *v*

verge on/upon sth *phr v* [T] to be very close to a harmful or extreme state ‖ 위험하거나 극단적인 상황에 매우 가까워지다. 근접하다. 금방 …하려고 하다: *Their behavior sometimes verges on insanity.* 그들의 행동은 때때로 무모함에 가깝다.

ver·i·fi·ca·tion /ˌvɛrəfə'keɪʃən/ *n* [U] proof that something is real, true, legal, or allowed ‖ 어떤 것이 실제적[사실적, 법적, 허용된 것]이란 증명. 입증. 검증. 실증. 확인: *Please send us written verification that you are a student.* 학생이라는 증명 서류를 우리에게 보내 주세요.

ver·i·fy /'vɛrəˌfaɪ/ *v* [T] **1** to find out if a fact, statement etc. is correct or true; CHECK ‖ 사실·말 등이 옳거나 진짜인지 알아내다. …이 진실임을 확인하다. 조회하다; 㜞 check: *This will have to be verified with the head office.* 이것은 본점에 확인해봐야 할 것이다. / *The bank will have to verify that you have an account.* 그 은행은 네가 계좌를 가지고 있다는 것을 조회해야 할 것이다. **2** to state that something is true ‖ 어떤 것이 사실이라고 진술하다. 진실성을 증명[선언]하다: *The suspect's statement was verified by a witness.* 피의자의 말은 목격자에 의해 사실임이 증명되었다.

ver·i·ta·ble /'vɛrətəbəl/ *adj* FORMAL used in order to emphasize a comparison that you think is correct ‖ 자신이 옳다고 생각하는 비교를 강조하는 데에 쓰여. 참다운. 진실한: *His paintings are a veritable feast of color.* 그의 그림은 정말 색깔의 향연이다.

ver·min /'vəmɪn/ *n* [plural] small animals, birds, or insects that destroy crops, spoil food, or cause other problems and are difficult to control ‖ 농작물을 해치거나 음식물을 못 쓰게 하거나 여타 문제를 야기하는 구제하

기 어려운 작은 동물[새, 곤충]. 해충. 해로운 짐승

ver·nac·u·lar /vɚˈnækyəlɚ/ *n* the language or DIALECT that people in a country or area speak, especially when this is not the official language ‖ 한 나라나 지역의 사람들이 쓰는, 특히 표준어가 아닌 언어나 방언. 지방어. 사투리. 자국어

ver·sa·tile /ˈvɚsətl/ *adj* **1** good at doing a lot of different things and able to learn new skills quickly and easily ‖ 여러 상이한 것을 하는 데 뛰어나며 새로운 기술을 빠르고 쉽게 배울 수 있는. 여러 방면에 능한. 다재다능한: *a versatile singer* 다재다능한 가수 **2** having many different uses ‖ 많은 다른 용도를 가진. 용도가 다양한: *Cotton is a versatile material.* 목화는 용도가 다양한 소재이다. **– versatility** /ˌvɚsəˈtɪləti/ *n* [U]

verse /vɚs/ *n* **1** a set of lines that forms one part of a poem or song, and that usually has a pattern that is repeated in other parts ‖ 시나 노래의 한 부분을 형성하며 보통 다른 부분에서 반복되는 일정 패턴을 가진 일련의 행. 절(節). 연(聯) **2** words arranged in the form of poetry ‖ 시의 형태로 배열된 말. 시. 운문: *a book of verse* 시집 **3** a sentence or group of sentences in the Bible that have a number ‖ 숫자가 붙여진 성경에서의 한 문장이나 일군의 문장들. 성경의 구절

versed /vɚst/ *adj* **be (well) versed in** to know a lot about a subject or to have a lot of skill in doing something ‖ 한 주제에 대해 많이 알거나 어떤 것을 하는 데 많은 기술을 가지다. …에 정통하다: *Tso is well versed in Navajo laws.* 초는 나바호 법에 정통하다.

ver·sion /ˈvɚʒən/ *n* **1** a copy of something that has been changed slightly ‖ 약간 바뀐 복사본. 형(型). 변형: *This is a simpler/later version of the camera.* 이것은 간편형[최신형] 카메라이다. **2** a description of an event that is given by one person ‖ 한 사람이 하는 사건에 대한 설명. 개인적 설명[의견, 견해]: *The two newspapers gave different versions of the accident.* 두 신문은 그 사고에 대해 상이한 기사를 실었다. **3** a play, movie etc. that is slightly different from the book, piece of music etc. on which it is based ‖ 기초로 삼은 원작의 책·악곡과 약간 다른 연극이나 영화 등. 각색. …판: *a shorter version of the book* 그 책의 축약판 **4** a TRANSLATION of a piece of writing ‖ 한 편의 글의 번역. 번역서[본, 판]: *an English version of an Italian poem* 이탈리아 시의 영역서

ver·sus /ˈvɚsəs/, *written abbreviation* **vs.** *prep* used in order to show that two people or teams are against each other in a game or a court case ‖ 두 사람이나 팀이 경기나 법정에서 서로 대항하고 있다는 것을 보이는 데에 쓰여. …대(對). …에 대한: *the Knicks versus the Lakers* 닉스 팀 대(對) 레이커스 팀

ver·te·bra /ˈvɚtəbrə/ *n, plural* **vertebrae** /-breɪ, -bri/ one of the small hollow bones down the center of your back ‖ 등의 중앙에서 내려오는 작고 속이 빈 뼈의 하나. 척추(골)

ver·ti·cal /ˈvɚtɪkəl/ *adj* pointing straight up and down in a line and forming an angle of 90 degrees with the ground or with another line ‖ 일직선으로 직상방과 하방을 가리키고 지면이나 또 다른 선과 90도 각도를 이루는. 수직의. 직립한: *a vertical rock face* 깎아지른 암벽 **– vertically** *adv* —compare HORIZONTAL

vertical

a vertical line / a diagonal line / a horizontal line

ver·ti·go /ˈvɚtɪˌgoʊ/ *n* [U] a sick DIZZY feeling that is caused by looking down from a very high place ‖ 매우 높은 곳에서 아래를 내려다봄으로써 생기는 아찔하고 어찔한 느낌. 현기증

verve /vɚv/ *n* [U] the quality of being cheerful and exciting ‖ 쾌활하고 열성적인 기질. 활기. 생기. 열정: *He plays the piano with great verve.* 그는 대단히 열정적으로 피아노를 연주한다.

ve·ry¹ /ˈvɛri/ *adv* **1** used in order to emphasize an adjective, adverb, or expression ‖ 형용사[부사, 표현]를 강조하는 데에 쓰여. 매우. 대단히: *We saw a very good movie the other night.* 우리는 요전날 밤에 매우 좋은 영화를 보았다. / *They only stay at the very best hotels.* 그들은 최고급 호텔에만 머문다. / *Sid gets embarrassed very easily.* 시드는 아주 쉽게 당황한다. / *We must understand the very real problems these people have.* 우리는 이들이 가지고 있는 매우 현실적인 문제를 이해해야 한다. **2 your very own** used in order to emphasize that something belongs to one particular person ‖ 어떤 것이 특정한 한 사람에게 속한다는 것을 강조하는 데에 쓰여. 자기만의 것(인…): *She's glad to have her very own room at last.* 그녀는 드디어 자기 자신만의 방을 가져서 기뻐한

다. **3 not very a)** used before a quality to mean exactly the opposite of that quality ‖ 어떤 특성에 정확히 반대되는 것을 의미하기 위해 그 특성 앞에 쓰여. 그다지. 별로: *She wasn't very happy about working overtime.* (=she was angry) 그녀는 초과 근무하는 것에 대해 몹시 못마땅해 했다. **b)** only slightly ‖ 단지. 약간: *"Was the game very exciting?" "Not very."* "그 경기가 매우 박진감 넘쳤니?" "별로." **4 very much** a lot ‖ 많이: *It didn't cost very much.* 비용이 많이 들지는 않았다. ✗DON'T SAY "It cost very much." SAY "It cost a lot."✗ "It cost very much."라고는 하지 않고 "It cost a lot."이라고 한다. / *I enjoyed my visit very much.* 방문해서 참 좋았었습니다. ✗DON'T SAY "I very much enjoyed my visit."✗ "I very much enjoyed my visit."라고는 하지 않는다. —see usage notes at MUCH¹, TOO

USAGE NOTE very

Use **very** in order to emphasize an adjective or adverb: *It's very cold outside. / She drives very fast.* Do not use **very** with adjectives that already have a strong meaning, such as "starving," "huge," "terrible" etc.: *By the time I got home, I was exhausted.* ✗DON'T SAY "very exhausted."✗ Do not use **very** in phrases that begin with "in," "on," "at" etc: *He was in love with Alice.* ✗DON'T SAY "very in love with."✗

very는 형용사나 부사를 강조하는 데에 쓰인다.: 바깥은 매우 춥다. / 그녀는 매우 빨리 운전한다. **very**는 이미 강한 의미를 가진 "starving," "huge," "terrible"등의 형용사와 함께 쓰지 않는다: 나는 집에 도착할 때쯤 녹초가 되어 있었다. "very exhausted"라고는 하지 않는다. **very**는 "in," "on," "at"등으로 시작되는 구에서는 쓰지 않는다: 그는 앨리스와 사랑에 빠졌다. "very in love with"라고는 하지 않는다.

very² *adj* used in order to emphasize a noun ‖ 명사를 강조하는 데에 쓰여. 꼭. 딱. 바로: *Start again from the very beginning.* 바로 처음부터 다시 시작해라. / *You come here this very minute!* (=now) 이 순간에 여기에 오다니! / *The very thought of food makes me feel sick.* (=just thinking about it) 음식 생각만 해도 나는 속이 울렁거린다.

very high fre·quen·cy /,.. . '.../ *n* [U] ⇨ VHF

ves·sel /'vɛsəl/ *n* FORMAL a ship or large boat ‖ 배나 큰 보트 —see also BLOOD VESSEL

vest /vɛst/ *n* **1** a piece of clothing without SLEEVEs that has buttons down the front, worn over a shirt ‖ 셔츠 위에 입는, 앞쪽 아래로 단추가 달린 소매 없는 옷. 조끼 **2** a piece of special clothing without SLEEVEs that is worn to protect your body ‖ 신체를 보호하기 위해 입는 소매 없는 특수한 옷가지. 방호용 조끼: *a bullet-proof vest* 방탄조끼

vest·ed in·terest /,.. '../ *n* a strong reason, especially a reason relating to money, for wanting something to happen ‖ 어떤 것이 일어나기를 원하는, 특히 돈과 관련된 강한 이유. 유인(誘因): *The company has a vested interest in attracting foreign trade.* 그 회사는 해외 거래를 트는 데에 강한 유인이 있다.

ves·ti·bule /'vɛstə,byul/ *n* FORMAL a wide passage or small room inside the front door of a public building ‖ 공공 건물의 정문 안의 넓은 통로나 작은 방. 문간방. 현관. 연결 통로

ves·tige /'vɛstɪdʒ/ *n* FORMAL a small part or amount of something that remains when most of it no longer exists ‖ 그 대부분이 더 이상 존재하지 않을 때 아직 남아 있는 어떤 것의 작은 부분이나 수량. 자취. 유물: *a policy that is one of the last vestiges of the Cold War* 냉전의 잔재 중의 하나인 정책

vet /vɛt/ *n* **1** the short form of VETERINARIAN; someone who is trained to give medical care and treatment to sick animals ‖ veterinarian의 단축형; 병든 동물에게 의학적인 치료를 해주기 위해 훈련받은 사람. 수의사 **2** INFORMAL the short form of VETERAN ‖ veteran의 단축형

vet·er·an /'vɛtərən/ *n* **1** someone who has been a soldier, sailor etc. in a war ‖ 전쟁에서 육군·해군 등의 군인이었던 사람. 재향[퇴역] 군인 **2** someone who has had a lot of experience in a particular activity ‖ 특정한 활동에서 많은 경험을 쌓은 사람. 고참. 베테랑: *a veteran traveler* 경험이 많은 여행가

vet·er·i·nar·i·an /,vɛtərə'nɛriən, ,vɛtrə-, ,vɛt⌐n-/ *n* ⇨ VET

vet·er·i·nar·y /'vɛtərə,nɛri, 'vɛtrə-/ *adj* TECHNICAL relating to the medical care and treatment of sick animals ‖ 병든 동물의 의학적인 치료에 관련된. 수의학(사)의

ve·to¹ /'vitoʊ/ *v* [T] **1** to officially refuse to allow something to happen, especially something that other people or organizations have agreed ‖ 특히 다

른 사람이나 조직이 동의한 어떤 것이 발생하도록 승인하기를 공식적으로 거절하다. (거부권을 사용해) 거부[부인]하다: *The UN Security Council vetoed the proposal.* 유엔 안전 보장 이사회는 그 동의안을 거부했다. **2** to refuse to accept a particular plan or suggestion ‖ 특정한 계획이나 제안을 받아들이기를 거절하다. 반대하다: *Sally wanted to invite 20 friends to her birthday party, but I vetoed that idea.* 샐리는 자신의 생일 파티에 스무 명의 친구들을 초대하고 싶어했지만 나는 그 생각에 반대했다.

veto² *n* [C, U] a refusal to give official permission for something, or the right to refuse to give such permission ‖ 어떤 것을 공식적으로 허가하는 것의 거절, 또는 그런 허가 부여를 거절하는 권리. 거부(권): *the governor's veto of a bill* 법안에 대한 주지사의 거부권

vex /vɛks/ *v* [T] OLD-FASHIONED to make someone feel annoyed or worried ‖ 남을 짜증나거나 걱정스럽게 느끼게 하다. 귀찮게 굴다. 화나게 하다: *vexing computer problems* 짜증나게 하는 컴퓨터 고장

VHF *n* [U] TECHNICAL very high frequency; radio waves that move very quickly and produce good sound quality ‖ very high frequency(초단파)의 약어; 매우 빨리 이동하고 양질의 소리를 내는 전파

VHS *n* [U] the type of VIDEOTAPE used by most people in the US ‖ 미국 내 대다수 사람들이 사용하는 비디오테이프 종류

vi·a /'vaɪə, 'viə/ *prep* **1** traveling through a place on the way to another place ‖ 다른 지역으로 가는 도중에 어떤 지역을 거쳐서 여행하는. …경유로. …을 지나서[거쳐]: *We're flying to Denver via Chicago.* 우리는 시카고를 경유하여 덴버로 가는 비행편을 이용할 거야. —see picture at DIRECT³ **2** using a particular person, machine etc. to send something ‖ 어떤 것을 보내기 위해 특정한 사람·기계 등을 사용하는. …을 통해. …매개로: *I sent a message to Jan via Ryan.* 나는 라이언을 통해 잰에게 메시지를 보냈다.

vi·a·ble /'vaɪəbəl/ *adj* able to succeed without any problems ‖ 아무런 문제없이 성공할 수 있는. 실행[실현] 가능한: *a viable plan/solution* 실행 가능한 계획[해결책] / *Solar energy is a viable alternative to coal or gas.* 태양 에너지는 석탄이나 가스를 대체할 수 있는 에너지 지원이다. / *The plan isn't economically/commercially viable.* 그 계획은 경제적[상업적]으로 실현 가능하지 않다.

vi·a·duct /'vaɪə,dʌkt/ *n* a long high bridge across a valley ‖ 계곡을 가로질러 높이 만든 긴 다리. 구름 다리

vi·al /'vaɪəl/ *n* a small bottle, especially for liquid medicines ‖ 특히 물약용의 작은 병

vibe /vaɪb/ *n* [C usually plural] INFORMAL the feelings that a particular person, group, or situation seems to produce and that you react to ‖ 특정한 사람[집단, 상황]이 조성할 것으로 여겨지는 느낌과 여기에 반응하는 느낌. 분위기. 감응: *I'm getting good/bad vibes from this guy.* 나는 이 사내에게서 좋은[좋지 않은] 인상을 받고 있다.

vi·brant /'vaɪbrənt/ *adj* **1** exciting, full of energy, and interesting ‖ 활기 차고 생기가 넘치며 흥미 있는. 활력 있는. 원기 왕성한: *a vibrant personality* 활발한 성격 **2** a vibrant color is bright and strong ‖ 색이 밝고 강렬한. 생생한. 자극적인

vi·brate /'vaɪbreɪt/ *v* [I, T] to shake continuously with small fast movements, or to make something do this ‖ 작고 빠른 움직임으로 계속해서 떨리다, 또는 어떤 것을 이렇게 하게 하다. 진동하다[시키다]: *The vocal chords vibrate as air passes over them.* 성대는 공기가 통과하면서 진동한다.

vi·bra·tion /vaɪ'breɪʃən/ *n* [C, U] a continuous slight shaking movement ‖ 계속해서 미약하게 떨리는 움직임. 진동: *the vibrations of the plane's engine* 비행기 엔진의 진동

vic·ar /'vɪkər/ *n* a religious leader in the Church of England ‖ 영국 국교회에서의 종교적 지도자. 교구 목사

vi·car·i·ous /vaɪ'kɛriəs/ *adj* experienced by watching or reading about someone else doing something ‖ 다른 사람이 어떤 것을 하는 것에 대해 보거나 읽어서 경험한. 추체험의. 대리 경험의: *Parents get vicarious pleasure/satisfaction from their children's success.* 부모들은 자녀의 성공으로부터 대리 즐거움[만족]을 느낀다.

vice /vaɪs/ *n* **1** [U] criminal activities that involve sex or drugs ‖ 성(性)이나 마약과 관련된 범죄 활동. 매춘. 마약 관련 범죄: *Police have smashed a vice ring in the city.* (=a group of criminals involved in vice) 경찰은 그 도시의 매춘 조직을 일망타진했다. **2** a bad habit ‖ 나쁜 습관. 악습. 나쁜 버릇: *Smoking is my only vice.* 흡연은 나의 유일한 악습이다. **3** a bad or immoral quality in someone's character ‖ 인간의 성격의 나쁘거나 부도덕한 특성. 나쁜 품성. 결함: *the vice of greed* 탐욕스런 품성

vice pres·i·dent /,. '.../ *n* **1** the person who is next in rank to the president of a country ‖ 한 나라의 대통령의 다음 직위에 있는 사람. 부통령 **2** someone who is responsible for a particular part of a company ‖ 회사의 특정 부문을 책임지고 있는 사람. 부사장: *the vice president of marketing* 마케팅 담당 부사장

vice squad /'. ./ *n* the part of the police force that deals with VICE ‖ 매춘·마약 등과 관련된 범죄를 다루는 경찰대. 풍기 법죄 단속반

vi·ce ver·sa /,vaɪs 'vɚsə, ,vaɪsə-/ *adv* used when the opposite of a situation you have just described is also true ‖ 자신이 방금 설명한 상황의 반대도 역시 사실이라고 말할 때에 쓰여. 반대의 경우도 마찬가지[사실]로: *Whatever Susie wants, James doesn't, and vice versa.* 수지가 원하는 것은 무엇이나 제임스는 원하지 않고, 반대도도 마찬가지다.

vi·cin·i·ty /və'sɪnəti/ *n* **in the vicinity (of)** in the area around a particular place ‖ 특정한 곳 주변 지역에. 근처에. 가까이에: *The car was found in the vicinity of the bus station.* 그 차는 버스 정류장 근처에서 발견되었다.

vi·cious /'vɪʃəs/ *adj* **1** violent and dangerous, and likely to hurt someone ‖ 폭력적이고 위험스러우며 다른 사람을 해칠 것 같은. 꽝포한. 사나운. 악독한: *a vicious dog* 사나운 개[맹견] **2** cruel and deliberately trying to upset someone ‖ 잔인하고 일부러 남의 기분을 상하게 하려고 하는. 악의 있는. 심술궂은: *Someone's spreading a vicious rumor about Stan.* 누군가가 스탠에 대한 나쁜 소문을 퍼뜨리고 있다. – **viciously** *adv*

vicious cir·cle /,.. '../ *n* [singular] a situation in which one problem causes another problem that then causes the first problem again ‖ 한 문제가 또 다른 문제를 일으키고 그런 다음 그것이 다시 처음 문제의 원인이 되는 상황. 악순환

vic·tim /'vɪktɪm/ *n* **1** someone who has been hurt or killed by someone or something or who has been affected by a bad situation ‖ 다른 사람이나 사물에 의해 다치거나 죽임을 당한, 또는 나쁜 상황의 영향을 받은 사람. 희생자. 피해자: *Eleven of the fire's 25 victims have died.* 그 화재로 인한 25명의 피해자 중 11명이 사망했다./ *an aid program for flood/earthquake victims* 홍수[지진] 피해자를 위한 원조 프로그램/ *An 18-year-old boy is the latest AIDS/polio victim.* 가장 최근의 에이즈[척수성 소아마비] 희생자는 18세의 소년이다. **2** something that is badly affected or destroyed by a situation or action ‖ 어떤 상황 또는 행동에 의해 심하게 해를 입거나 파괴되는 것. 제물. 희생(물): *Some small businesses have fallen victim to budget cuts.* 몇몇 영세기업이 예산 삭감의 희생물이 되었다.

vic·tim·ize /'vɪktə,maɪz/ *v* [T] to deliberately treat someone unfairly ‖ 다른 사람을 일부러 부당하게 대우하다. 괴롭히다. 희생시키다. 피해자로 만들다: *Some workers said they'd been victimized because of their political activity.* 몇몇 노동자들은 자신들의 정치적 활동 때문에 희생양이 되었다고 말했다.

vic·tor /'vɪktɚ/ *n* FORMAL the winner of a battle or competition ‖ 전투나 경쟁에서의 승리자. 전승자. 우승자

vic·to·ri·ous /vɪk'tɔriəs/ *adj* successful in a battle or competition ‖ 전투나 경쟁에서 이긴. 승리를 거둔

vic·to·ry /'vɪktəri/ *n* [C, U] the success you achieve by winning a battle or competition ‖ 전투나 시합에서 승리하여 얻는 성공. 전승. 우승: *the Lakers' victory over the Celtics* 셀틱스 팀에게 거둔 레이커스 팀의 승리/ *The Democrats easily won a victory at the polls.* 민주당은 그 선거에서 쉽게 승리를 거두었다. —opposite DEFEAT²

vid·e·o¹ /'vɪdioʊ/ *n* **1** a copy of a movie or television program that is recorded on VIDEOTAPE ‖ 비디오테이프에 녹화된 영화나 텔레비전 프로그램의 복사본. 비디오: *Let's rent a video tonight.* 오늘 밤 비디오 하나 빌려 보자. **2** [C, U] a VIDEOTAPE ‖ 비디오테이프: *Do we have a blank video?* 공 비디오 테이프가 우리에게 있을까? / *The movie "Toy Story" is now on video.* "Toy Story"란 영화는 지금 비디오테이프로 나와 있다. **3** [U] the process of recording and showing television programs, movies, real events etc. using video equipment ‖ 텔레비전 프로그램·영화·실제 사건 등을 비디오 장비를 사용해 기록하고 보여주는 과정. 비디오 촬영[녹화, 재생]: *Many teachers now use video in the classroom.* 지금은 많은 교사들이 교실에서 비디오를 이용한다.

video² *adj* relating to recording and broadcasting sound and pictures on a VIDEOTAPE ‖ 비디오테이프에 소리와 영상을 기록하고 방송하는 것과 관련된. 비디오 녹화[재생]의: *video equipment* 비디오(녹화) 장비 —compare AUDIO

vid·e·o·card /'vɪdioʊ,kɑrd/ *n* a CIRCUIT

BOARD (=piece of electronic equipment carrying electrical signals) that can be added to a computer so that it is able to show moving pictures ‖ 컴퓨터에 연결하여 동화상을 볼 수 있게 하는 회로판. 비디오 카드[보드]

video cas·sette re·cord·er /,... '. .,../ n ⇨ VCR

vid·e·o·disk /'vɪdioʊ,dɪsk/ n a round flat piece of plastic from which movies can be played in the same way as from a VIDEOTAPE ‖ 비디오테이프에서와 마찬가지로 영화가 재생 될 수 있는 둥글고 납작한 플라스틱 판. 비디오디스크

video game /'... ,./ n a game in which you move images on a screen by pressing electronic controls ‖ 전자 제어 장치를 눌러서 화면상의 영상을 움직이는 게임. 비디오 게임

vid·e·o·tape[1] /'vɪdioʊ,teɪp/ n a long narrow band of MAGNETIC material in a plastic container, on which movies, television programs etc. can be recorded ‖ 영화나 텔레비전 프로그램 등이 녹화될 수 있는, 플라스틱 용기 내의 길고 좁은 자기 물질의 띠. 비디오테이프

videotape[2] v [T] to record something on a VIDEOTAPE ‖ 어떤 것을 비디오테이프에 녹화하다: Detectives videotaped the interview with the suspect. 형사들은 용의자와의 인터뷰를 녹화했다.

vie /vaɪ/ v **vied, vied, vying** [I] to compete very hard with someone in order to get something ‖ 어떤 것을 얻기 위해 남과 심하게 경쟁하다. 겨루다. 싸우다: The two brothers vied for her attention. 그 두 형제는 그녀의 관심을 끌기 위해 경쟁했다.

view

From the window there was a beautiful view.

view[1] /vyu/ n **1** your belief or opinion about something ‖ 어떤 것에 대한 자신의 믿음이나 의견. 견해. 생각: I'd like to have your views on/about this issue. 이 문제에 대한 당신의 견해를 듣고 싶다. / In my/her/our view, the movie is too violent. 내[그녀의, 우리의] 관점에서 그 영화는 너무 폭력적이다. / What's your

point of view, Kate? 케이트, 네 생각은 어떠니? **2** a way of considering or understanding something ‖ 어떤 것을 생각하거나 이해하는 방식. 시각. 관점: The President's view of the situation wasn't discussed. 그 상황에 대한 대통령의 관점은 논의되지 않았다. / This book gives the artist's view of nature. 이 책은 자연을 보는 예술인의 관점을 보여 준다. / We have to consider religious/public/world views on the question. 우리는 그 문제를 종교적인[대중적인, 전 세계적인] 관점에서 고려해야 한다. **3** [C, U] what you are able to see or the possibility of seeing it ‖ 자신이 볼 수 있는 것이나 보게 될 가능성. 전망. 조망. 시야. 시계: From our window we have a beautiful/great view of the ocean. 우리 쪽 창문으로 보이는 바다의 전망은 아름답다[멋지다]. / The end of the tunnel finally came into view. (=began to be seen) 마침내 터널의 끝이 시계에 들어왔다. / I sat behind a tall guy who blocked my view. (=stopped me from seeing something) 나는 내 시야를 가리는 키 큰 사내의 뒤에 앉았다. **4** the whole area that you can see from somewhere ‖ 어떤 곳에서 볼 수 있는 전체 지역. 경관. 전경. 광경: a spectacular view of the mountains 그 산의 장관 / A new factory now spoils the view of the park. (=makes it look less beautiful) 새 공장이 지금은 공원의 경관을 망치고 있다. **5** a photograph or picture that shows a beautiful or interesting place ‖ 아름답거나 흥미 있는 장소를 보여 주는 사진이나 그림. 풍경화[사진]. 전망도: The postcards show scenic views of New York. 그 엽서들은 뉴욕의 멋진 전경을 보여 준다. **6 in view of** used in order to introduce the reason for your decision or action ‖ 자신의 결정이나 행동에 대한 이유를 소개하는 데에 쓰여. …때문에[탓으로]. …을 고려하여: In view of his unsportsman like behavior, Max has been suspended from the team. 맥스는 스포츠맨답지 않은 행동 때문에 그 팀에서 제명되었다.

USAGE NOTE view, opinion, and point of view

Use **view** and **opinion** to talk about what someone thinks or believes about something: There are different views on capital punishment. / I've always respected your opinion. Use **point of view** to talk about one part of a problem or situation: Try to see it from the landlord's point of view.

view와 **opinion**은 사람이 어떤 것에 대해 생각하거나 믿는 것을 말하는 데에 쓴다: 사형 제도에 대해서는 이견이 있다. / 나는 항상 당신의 의견을 존중했다. **point of view**는 문제나 상황의 한 부분에 대해 말하는 데에 사용한다: 집주인의 관점에서 그것을 보도록 해봐라.

Use all of these words as countable nouns in order to talk about things that you see. Use **view** to talk about what you can see from a window or a high place: *From my office window I have a good view of the park.* Use **sight** to talk about something that is unusual, beautiful, interesting etc.: *The Grand Canyon at dawn is a spectacular sight.* Use **scene** to talk about the place where something happened: *Police arrived within minutes at the scene of the accident.* Use **vision** to talk about an idea of what the future will be like: *He has a romantic vision of a world without war.* When **sight** and **vision** are used as uncountable nouns, they mean "the ability to see": *Dean lost his sight in a factory accident. / I've always had perfect vision.*

이 단어들은 모두 자신이 보는 것에 대해 말하기 위해 가산 명사로 쓴다: **view**는 창문이나 높은 곳에서 자신이 볼 수 있는 것에 대해 말하는 데에 쓴다: 내 사무실 창문에서는 공원이 잘 보인다. **sight**는 보통과 다르고 아름다우며 흥미로운 것을 말하는 데에 쓴다: 새벽에 보는 그랜드 캐니언은 장관이다. **scene**은 어떤 일이 일어난 곳에 대해 말하는 데에 쓴다: 경찰은 곧 사고 현장에 도착했다. **vision**은 미래가 어떻게 될 것인가의 생각에 대해 말하는 데 쓴다: 그는 전쟁 없는 세상이 될 거라는 낭만적인 이상을 가지고 있다. **sight**와 **vision**은 불가산 명사로 사용될 때 두 단어 모두 "볼 수 있는 능력"을 의미한다: 딘은 공장에서의 사고로 시력을 잃었다. / 나는 항상 완전한 시력을 가지고 있었다.

view² *v* **1** [T] FORMAL to look at something because you are interested ‖ 흥미가 있어서 어떤 것을 보다. 바라보다. 구경[견학]하다: *Many people came to view the fireworks.* 많은 사람들이 불꽃놀이를 보기 위해 왔다. **2** [T] to think of

something in a particular way ‖ 어떤 것을 특정한 방식으로 생각해 보다. …관점에서 보다. …이라고 간주하다: *Conflict is viewed as part of the child-parent relationship.* 갈등은 자녀와 부모 관계의 일부분으로 생각된다. / *I view the change as an adventure.* 나는 그 변화를 모험으로 생각한다. **3** [I, T] FORMAL to watch a television program, movie etc. ‖ 텔레비전 프로그램·영화 등을 보다: *a chance to view the movie before it opens in theaters* 그 영화가 극장에서 개봉되기 전에 볼 수 있는 기회

view·er /ˈvyuɚ/ *n* someone who watches television ‖ 텔레비전을 보는 사람. 시청자: *The series is watched by millions of viewers.* 수백만 명의 시청자가 그 시리즈물을 본다.

vig·il /ˈvɪdʒəl/ *n* [C, U] **1** a silent political protest in which people wait outside a building ‖ 사람들이 건물의 바깥에서 기다리는 침묵의 정치적인 항의. 농성(하기): *500 people held a vigil outside the embassy.* 500명의 사람들이 대사관 건물 바깥에서 농성을 벌였다. **2** a time, especially during the night, when you stay awake in order to pray or stay with someone who is ill ‖ 기도하거나 병든 사람과 함께 있기 위해 깨어 있는, 특히 밤 동안의 시간. 철야: *John's been keeping a vigil beside his son in the hospital.* 존은 병원에 있는 자신의 아들 옆에서 밤새워 간호해 오고 있다.

vig·i·lance /ˈvɪdʒələns/ *n* [U] careful attention that you give to what is happening ‖ 현재 일어나고 있는 일에 기울이는 조심스러운 주의. 경계. 조심

vig·i·lant /ˈvɪdʒələnt/ *adj* FORMAL giving careful attention to what is happening ‖ 현재 일어나고 있는 일에 조심스럽게 주의를 기울이는. 경계를 늦추지 않는. 방심하지 않는: *Health inspectors must be vigilant when examining restaurants.* 위생 조사관들은 식당을 조사할 때 철저히 살펴야 한다.

vig·i·lan·te /ˌvɪdʒəˈlænti/ *n* a member of an unofficial group of people who join together to catch or punish criminals ‖ 범죄자들을 잡거나 벌주기 위해 결성하는 비공식적 민간단체의 일원. 자경 단원

vig·or /ˈvɪgɚ/ *n* [U] physical and mental energy and determination ‖ 육체적·정신적인 기운과 결단력. 활기. 원기. 생기

vig·or·ous /ˈvɪgərəs/ *adj* **1** using a lot of energy and strength or determination ‖ 많은 기운과 힘 또는 결단력을 발휘하는. 원기 왕성한. 격렬한: *vigorous*

exercise 격렬한 운동 / *a vigorous debate on gun control* 총기 규제에 대한 활발한 논쟁 **2 vigorous opponent/defender etc.** someone who opposes or defends something strongly ‖ 어떤 것을 강하게 반대하거나 옹호하는 사람. 강력한 반대자 /옹호자: *a vigorous campaigner for human rights* 열성적인 인권 운동가 **3** strong and very healthy ‖ 강하고 매우 건강한. 강건한: *a vigorous young man* 매우 강건한 젊은 남성

vile /vaɪl/ *adj* **1** INFORMAL very unpleasant ‖ 매우 불쾌한. 몹시 나쁜[싫은]. 역겨운: *a vile temper* 성마른 성미 **2** evil ‖ 사악한. 야비한: *a vile book* 상스러운 책

vil·i·fy /ˈvɪlə,faɪ/ *v* [T] FORMAL to say bad things about someone in order to make other people have a bad opinion of him/her ‖ 다른 사람들이 어떤 사람에 대해 나쁜 견해를 갖도록 그 사람에 관한 나쁜 말을 하다. …을 욕하다[헐뜯다]. 비방하다

vil·la /ˈvɪlə/ *n* a big country house ‖ 큰 시골집. 대저택. 별장

vil·lage /ˈvɪlɪdʒ/ *n* **1** a very small town ‖ 매우 작은 읍. 마을. 촌락 **2 the village** the people who live in the village ‖ 마을에 사는 사람들. (거)주민: *The whole village came to the wedding.* 주민 모두가 그 결혼식에 왔다.

vil·lag·er /ˈvɪlɪdʒɚ/ *n* someone who lives in a village ‖ 마을에 사는 사람. 부락민. 마을 사람

vil·lain /ˈvɪlən/ *n* the main bad character in a movie, play, or story ‖ 영화[연극, 이야기]에서 악역의 주인공. 악한. 악당

vil·lain·y /ˈvɪləni/ *n* [U] evil or criminal behavior ‖ 사악하거나 범죄적인 행동. 악당의 소행. 극악(한 짓)

vin·di·cate /ˈvɪndə,keɪt/ *v* [T] FORMAL **1** to prove that someone or something is right or true ‖ 어떤 사람이나 사물이 옳거나 진실하다는 것을 증명하다. 옳음을 밝히다 **2** to prove that someone who has been blamed for something is not guilty ‖ 어떤 것으로 비난받아 온 사람이 죄가 없다고 밝히다. 비난·혐의를 풀다 – **vindication** /ˌvɪndəˈkeɪʃən/ *n* [U]

vin·dic·tive /vɪnˈdɪktɪv/ *adj* deliberately cruel and unfair ‖ 고의적으로 잔인하고 부당한. 원한[앙심]이 깊은: *He became bitter and vindictive after the divorce.* 그는 이혼하고 난 후 냉혹하고 앙심 깊은 사람이 되었다.

vine /vaɪn/ *n* a plant that grows long stems that attach themselves to other plants, trees, buildings etc. ‖ 다른 식물·나무·건물 등에 달라붙는, 줄기가 길게 자라는 식물. 덩굴(식물): *grape vines* 포도나무

vin·e·gar /ˈvɪnɪgɚ/ *n* [U] an acid-tasting liquid that is made from wine, used for improving the taste of food or preserving it ‖ 음식의 맛을 내거나 보존하는 데에 사용되는, 포도주로 만든 신맛이 나는 액체. 식초

vine·yard /ˈvɪnyɚd/ *n* a piece of land where GRAPES are grown in order to make wine ‖ 포도주 제조용의 포도가 재배되는 토지. 포도원[밭]

vin·tage¹ /ˈvɪntɪdʒ/ *adj* **1** vintage wine is good quality wine that is made in a particular year ‖ 포도주가 특정 연도에 만들어진 좋은 품질인. 연호가 적힌 포도주의 **2** old and showing high quality ‖ 오래되고 고급의 질을 나타내는. 유서 깊은 [깊어 가치 있는]: *a vintage car* 오래되어 값어치 있는 중고 자동차

vintage² *n* a particular year in which a wine is made ‖ 포도주가 만들어진 특정한 연도. …년도산(포도주)

vi·nyl /ˈvaɪnl/ *n* [U] a type of strong plastic ‖ 질긴 플라스틱의 일종. 비닐

vi·o·la /viˈoʊlə/ *n* a wooden musical instrument shaped like a VIOLIN but larger and with a lower sound ‖ 바이올린처럼 생겼지만 크기가 더 크고 낮은 소리를 내는 목제 악기. 비올라

vi·o·late /ˈvaɪə,leɪt/ *v* [T] **1** to disobey or do something against a law, agreement etc. ‖ 법·협정 등을 지키지 않거나 위반된 어떤 것을 하다. 위반하다. 어기다: *Killing the elephants violated international agreements.* 코끼리 살육은 국제 협정 위반이었다. **2** FORMAL to enter and spoil a place that should be respected ‖ 신성시되어야 하는 장소에 들어가서 더럽히다: *Vandals had violated the graveyard.* 예술·문화 파괴자들이 묘지를 더럽혔다.

vi·o·la·tion /ˌvaɪəˈleɪʃən/ *n* an action that breaks a law, agreement etc. ‖ 법·협정 등을 깨뜨리는 행위. 위반[위배] 행위: *human rights violations* 인권 침해 / *traffic violations* 교통 위반

vi·o·la·tor /ˈvaɪə,leɪtɚ/ *n* someone who has broken the law ‖ 법을 어긴 사람. 위반[침해]자

vi·o·lence /ˈvaɪələns/ *n* [U] **1** behavior that is intended to hurt other people physically ‖ 다른 사람을 신체적으로 해칠 의도의 행위. 폭력[난폭](행위): *Kids see too much violence on TV.* 아이들은 텔레비전에서 너무 많은 폭력 장면을 본다. /

acts of violence against the refugees 피난민들에 대한 폭력 행위 **2 an angry way of speaking or reacting** ‖ 화난 것 처럼 말하거나 반응함. 격렬함. 격분. 거침: *"What?" she said, with sudden violence.* 그녀는 갑자기 격렬하게 "뭐라고?"라고 말했다.

vi·o·lent /ˈvaɪələnt/ *adj* **1** violent actions are intended to hurt people ‖ 행동이 사람을 다치게 할 의도인. 난폭한. 폭력적인: *violent crimes such as murder and rape* 살인·강간과 같은 폭력적인 범죄 / *violent attacks* 난폭한 공격 **2** likely to hurt other people ‖ 다른 사람을 다치게 할 것 같은. 폭력적인: *a violent and dangerous criminal* 폭력적이고 위험한 범죄자 / *The demonstrators suddenly turned violent.* (=became violent) 시위대는 갑자기 폭력적으로 바뀌었다. **3** showing very strong angry emotions or opinions ‖ 매우 심하게 화내는 감정이나 의견을 보이는. 격한. 격렬한: *a violent argument* 매우 격렬한 논쟁 **4 violent movie/play etc.** a movie, play etc. that shows a lot of violent actions ‖ 폭력적인 행위가 많이 나오는 영화·연극 등. 폭력 장면이 많은 영화/연극 **5 violent storm/earthquake etc.** a storm, EARTHQUAKE etc. that happens with a lot of force ‖ 격렬하게 발생하는 폭풍우·지진. 맹렬한 폭풍/지진

vi·o·let /ˈvaɪəlɪt/ *n* a small sweet-smelling dark purple flower ‖ 향긋한 냄새가 나는 짙은 자주색의 작은 꽃. 제비꽃

vi·o·lin /ˌvaɪəˈlɪn/ *n* a small wooden musical instrument, that you play by pulling a special stick across wire strings ‖ 철사줄을 가로 지르며 특수한 활을 당겨서 연주하는 작은 목제 악기. 바이올린

VIP *n* a very important person; someone who is famous or powerful and is treated with respect ‖ very important person(매우 중요한 사람)의 약어; 유명하거나 세력이 있어서 정중하게 대우 받는 사람. 요인

vi·per /ˈvaɪpɚ/ *n* a small poisonous snake ‖ 독이 있는 작은 뱀. 북살무사

vi·ral /ˈvaɪrəl/ *adj* relating to or caused by a VIRUS ‖ 바이러스에 관련되거나 바이러스로 발생한. 바이러스의. 바이러스가 원인인: *viral pneumonia* 바이러스성 폐렴

vir·gin¹ /ˈvɚdʒɪn/ *n* someone who has never had sex ‖ 성교를 해 본 적이 없는 사람. 숫처녀[총각]. 동정녀[남]

virgin² *adj* **1 virgin land/forest etc.** land, forest etc. that is still in its natural state and has not been used or changed by people ‖ 아직 자연 그대로의 상태에 있고 사람들에 의해 사용되거나 변경되지 않은 토지·삼림. 처녀지/처녀림 **2** without sexual experience ‖ 성 경험이 없는. 처녀의. 동정의

vir·gin·i·ty /vɚˈdʒɪnəti/ *n* [U] the condition of never having had sex ‖ 성교를 해본 적이 없는 상태. 처녀. 동정: *He was 20 when he lost his virginity.* (=had sex for the first time) 그는 20세에 동정을 잃었다.

Virgin Mar·y /ˌvɚdʒɪn ˈmɛri/ *n* in the Christian religion, the mother of Jesus ‖ 크리스트교에서 예수의 어머니. 성모[동정녀] 마리아

Vir·go /ˈvɚgoʊ/ *n* [U] **1** the sixth sign of the ZODIAC, represented by a VIRGIN ‖ 처녀로 상징되는 황도 12궁의 여섯째 별자리. 처녀자리 **2** someone born between August 23 and September 22 ‖ 8월 23일부터 9월 22일 사이에 태어난 사람. 처녀좌 태생자

vir·ile /ˈvɪrəl/ *adj* having or showing traditionally male qualities such as strength and sexual attractiveness ‖ 힘과 성적 매력 등의 전통적인 남성적 특성을 갖거나 나타내는. 사내다운. 남성적인: *a young virile man* 젊고 사내다운 남자 **– virility** /vɚˈrɪləti/ *n* [U]

vir·tu·al /ˈvɚtʃuəl/ *adj* **1** almost or nearly something ‖ 어떤 것과 거의 또는 대략 같은. 사실상의. 실질상의: *He was a virtual prisoner in his own home.* 그는 사실상 집에 갇힌 죄수 신세였다. / *Most of the country lives in virtual poverty.* 그 나라의 대부분은 실제로 가난하게 산다. **2** relating to something that is made, done, seen etc. on a computer, rather than in the real world ‖ 실제 세계가 아닌 컴퓨터 상에서 만들어지거나 행해지거나 보여지는 등의 것에 관한. 가상(현실)의. 네트워크[인터넷]상의

vir·tu·al·ly /ˈvɚtʃuəli, -tʃəli/ *adv* **1** almost completely ‖ 거의 완전히. 사실상. 실질적으로: *He was virtually unknown until the elections.* 그는 선거 때까지는 사실상 알려지지 않았다. **2** on a computer, rather than in the real world ‖ 실제 세계에서가 아닌 컴퓨터로. 가상적으로

virtual re·al·i·ty /ˌ... .ˈ.../ *n* [U] an environment produced by a computer that surrounds the person looking at it and seems almost real ‖ 컴퓨터를 보고 있는 사람을 에워싸고 있어 거의 실제처럼 보이는 컴퓨터에 의해서 만들어진 환경. 가상 현실

vir·tue /ˈvɚtʃu/ *n* **1** [U] FORMAL moral goodness of character and behavior ‖ 성

격과 행동상의 도덕적 선량함. 덕. 선. 덕행. 선행: *a woman of the highest virtue* 고결한 여자 **2** a particular good quality in someone's character ‖ 성격상의 특징한 훌륭한 자질. 미덕: *Among his virtues are honesty and kindness.* 그의 미덕 가운데는 정직과 친절이 있다. **3** [C, U] an advantage that makes something better or more useful than something else ‖ 어떤 것을 다른 것보다 더 좋거나 더 유용하게 만드는 이점. 장점. 가치: *Free trade has its virtues.* 자유 무역은 장점이 있다. **4 by virtue of** FORMAL by means of or as a result of something ‖ 무엇에 의하여서 또는 무엇의 결과로. …의 힘[덕]으로. …덕분에: *He became chairman by virtue of hard work.* 그는 열심히 일한 덕분에 회장이 되었다.

vir·tu·o·so /ˌvɚtʃuˈoʊsoʊ/ *n* someone who is a very skillful performer, especially in music ‖ 특히 음악에서 아주 숙련된 연주자. (음악 분야의) 거장. 명인: *a piano virtuoso* 피아노의 거장 – **virtuoso** *adj*

vir·tu·ous /ˈvɚtʃuəs/ *adj* FORMAL behaving in a very honest and moral way ‖ 매우 정직하고 도덕적으로 행동하는. 덕 있는. 고결한

vir·u·lent /ˈvɪrələnt, ˈvɪryə-/ *adj* **1** FORMAL full of hatred ‖ 증오에 찬. 심술궂은: *virulent racism* 증오에 찬 인종 차별주의 **2** a poison, disease etc. that is virulent is very dangerous and affects people very quickly ‖ 독·질병 등이 매우 위험하고 사람들에게 매우 빠르게 영향을 미치는. 치명적인. 전염성이 강한

vi·rus /ˈvaɪrəs/ *n* **1** a very small living thing that causes infectious illnesses, or the illness caused by this ‖ 전염병을 일으키는 아주 작은 생물이나, 또는 이것으로 발생하는 질병. 바이러스(성 질병): *the common cold virus* 흔한 감기 바이러스 **2** a set of instructions secretly put into a computer, that can destroy information stored in the computer ‖ 컴퓨터에 저장된 정보를 파괴할 수 있는, 몰래 컴퓨터에 입력된 일련의 지시. 컴퓨터 바이러스 **3** a PROGRAM that sends a large number of annoying messages to many people's MOBILE PHONES in an uncontrolled way ‖ 많은 사람들의 휴대전화에 무제한적으로 다량의 성가신 메시지를 보내는 프로그램. 휴대폰 스팸 문자 프로그램

vi·sa /ˈvizə/ *n* an official mark that is put on your PASSPORT, that allows you to enter or leave another country ‖ 다른 나라에의 출입이 허용되는, 여권에 찍는 공적인 표시. 비자. 사증(查證): *She's here on a student visa.* 그녀는 학생 비자로 여기 와 있다.

vis·age /ˈvizɪdʒ/ *n* LITERARY a face ‖ 얼굴. 용모

vis-à-vis /ˌvizəˈvi/ *prep* FORMAL in relation to or in comparison with something or someone ‖ 사물이나 사람에 관련하여 또는 비교하여

vis·cous /ˈvɪskəs/ *adj* TECHNICAL a viscous liquid is thick and does not flow easily ‖ 액체가 진하고 쉽게 흐르지 않는. 점착력이 있는. 끈적끈적한 – **viscosity** /vɪsˈkasəti/ *n* [U]

vise /vaɪs/ *n* a tool that holds an object firmly so that you can work on it using both of your hands ‖ 양 손을 사용하여 작업을 할 수 있도록 물체를 단단히 죄는 공구. 바이스

vis·i·bil·i·ty /ˌvɪzəˈbɪləti/ *n* [U] the distance that it is possible to see at a particular time ‖ 특정한 시간에 볼 수 있는 거리. 시계(視界). 시정(視程): *There is poor visibility on the roads due to heavy fog.* 짙은 안개 때문에 도로상의 시계가 나쁘다.

vis·i·ble /ˈvɪzəbəl/ *adj* **1** something that is visible can be seen ‖ 어떤 것이 보이는. 가시(可視)의: *The mountains weren't visible because of the clouds.* 그 산들은 구름 때문에 보이지 않았다. — opposite INVISIBLE **2** an effect that is visible can be noticed ‖ 효과를 알아 챌 수 있는. 눈에 띄는: *a visible change in her attitude* 그녀의 태도상의 눈에 띄는 변화 – **visibly** *adv*

vi·sion /ˈvɪʒən/ *n* **1** [U] the ability to see ‖ 보는 능력. 시력: *Will the operation improve my vision?* 수술하면 내 시력이 좋아질까요? **2** a picture or idea in your mind of the way a situation could happen ‖ 일어날 수 있는 상황에 대한 마음속에 있는 그림이나 생각. 상상. 이상: *I have a vision of a better future for this city.* 나는 이 시에 대한 보다 나은 이상을 갖고 있다. **3** something you see in a dream as part of a religious experience ‖ 종교적인 경험의 일부로 꿈에서 보는 것. 환상. 환영: *The prophet Mohammed visited her in a vision.* 예언자 모하메드의 환영이 그녀에게 나타났다. **4** [U] the ability to make plans for the future with a clear purpose ‖ 분명한 목적으로 미래에 대한 계획을 세우는 능력. 선견지명. 통찰력: *We need a leader with vision.* 우리는 통찰력이 있는 지도자가 필요하다. —see usage note at VIEW²

vi·sion·ar·y /ˈvɪʒəˌnɛri/ *adj* having clear ideas of how the world can be better in the future ‖ 미래에 세계가 어떻게 더 좋아질 수 있는가에 대한 분명한 견해를 가진. 통찰력이 있는. 확실한 비전을 가진 - **visionary** n

vis·it¹ /'vɪzɪt/ v **1** to go and spend time with someone ‖ 누군가에게 가서 시간을 보내다. 방문하다: *My aunt is coming to visit next week.* 내 숙모는 내주에 방문차 오신다. **2** [I, T] to go and spend time in a place, especially as a tourist ‖ 특히 관광객으로 어떤 장소에 가서 시간을 보내다. 구경하러 가다: *We want to visit the Grand Canyon on our trip.* 우리는 여행 중에 그랜드캐니언에 가 보고 싶다. **3** [I] INFORMAL to talk socially with someone ‖ 남과 사교적으로 말하다. 이야기하다. 잡담하다: *We watched TV while Mom visited with Mrs. Levinson.* 엄마가 레빈슨 여사와 담소를 나누는 동안 우리는 텔레비전을 보았다.

visit² n **1** an occasion when someone visits a place or person ‖ 사람이 어떤 장소나 사람을 방문하는 경우. 방문: *When are you going to pay us a visit?* 너는 언제 우리를 방문할 거니? / *The Senator spoke to the girl during a visit to the hospital.* 그 상원 의원은 문병을 하는 동안 그 소녀와 이야기를 했다. / *We've just had a visit from the police.* 우리는 방금 경찰의 방문을 받았다. **2** INFORMAL an occasion when you talk socially with someone, or the time you spend doing this ‖ 남과 사교상의 대화를 하는 경우나 이렇게 하면서 보내는 시간. 이야기. 잡담: *Barbara and I had a nice long visit.* 바바라와 나는 오랫동안 즐겁게 이야기를 했다.

vis·it·a·tion /ˌvɪzəˈteɪʃən/, **visitation rights** n [U] LAW the right that a parent who is DIVORCEd has to see his/her children ‖ 이혼한 부모가 자녀를 만나는 권리. 자녀 방문권

vis·i·tor /'vɪzətɚ/ n someone who comes to visit a place or a person ‖ 어떤 장소나 사람을 방문하러 오는 사람. 방문자. 손님: *a guide book for visitors to Mexico City* 멕시코시티 방문객을 위한 여행 안내서 / *Let's not bother them now – they have visitors.* (=people are visiting them) 지금 그들을 성가시게 하지 말자. 그들은 손님을 맞이하고 있으니까.

vi·sor /'vaɪzɚ/ n **1** the curved part of a hat or HELMET that sticks out above your eyes, or a special hat that consists only of this ‖ 눈 위쪽으로 불쑥 튀어 나와 있는 모자나 헬멧의 휜 부분, 또는 이것만으로 된 특수 모자. 챙 **2** the part of a HELMET that can be lowered to protect your face

‖ 얼굴을 보호하기 위해 아래로 내릴 수 있는 헬멧의 부분. 면갑(面甲) **3** a flat piece of material in the front window of a car that you pull down to keep the sun out of your eyes ‖ 아래로 끌어내려 눈에 햇빛을 차단하는 자동차 앞유리창에 있는 편평한 물체. 선 바이저. 햇빛 가리개

vis·ta /'vɪstə/ n LITERARY a view, especially over a large area of land ‖ 특히 넓은 지역에 걸친 전망. 조망

vis·u·al /'vɪʒuəl/ adj relating to seeing or to your sight ‖ 보는 것이나 시력에 관한. 시각의. 시력의: *visual arts such as painting and sculpture* 그림·조각 등의 시각 예술 / *The movie has a strong visual impact.* 영화는 강한 시각 효과가 있다. - **visually** adv

visual aid /ˌ.. './ n something such as a map, picture, or movie that is used for helping people to learn ‖ 사람들의 학습을 돕기 위해 사용되는 지도 [그림, 영화]. 시각 교재

vis·u·al·ize /'vɪʒuəˌlaɪz/ v [T] to form a picture of someone or something in your mind; imagine ‖ 자신의 마음에 사람이나 사물의 그림을 형성하다. 떠올리다; 상상하다: *I tried to visualize the house as he described it.* 그가 그 집을 설명할 때 나는 상상해 보려고 애썼다.

vi·tal /'vaɪtl/ adj **1** extremely important or necessary ‖ 매우 중요하거나 필수적인. 불가결한. 긴요한: *These computer systems are vital to our business.* 이들 컴퓨터 시스템은 우리 사업에 불가결한 것이다. / *Are nuclear weapons vital for national security?* 핵무기는 국가 안보에 불가결한 것인가? **2** full of life and energy ‖ 생기와 기운이 가득한. 활기 있는. 기운 찬: *a vital person* 생기가 넘치는 사람

vi·tal·i·ty /vaɪˈtæləti/ n [U] life and energy ‖ 원기와 기운. 활력: *He has the vitality of a man half his age.* 그는 자기 나이의 절반 정도 되는 사람의 활력을 지니고 있다.

vi·tal·ly /'vaɪtl-i/ adv in an extremely important or necessary way ‖ 매우 중요하거나 필수적으로. 절대로. 참으로: *It's vitally important that you attend the meeting.* 네가 그 모임에 참석하는 것은 참으로 중요하다.

vital sta·tis·tics /ˌ.. '../ n [plural] facts about people such as their age, race, and whether they are married, especially in official records ‖ 특히 공식적인 기록상의 연령·인종·결혼 여부 등의 사람들에 대한 사실들. 인구 동태 통계

vi·ta·min /'vaɪtəmɪn/ n a chemical

substance found in food that is necessary for good health ‖ 음식에서 발견되는 건강에 필수적인 화학 물질. 비타민: *The doctor told me to get more vitamin A and vitamin C.* 그 의사는 나에게 비타민 A와 비타민 C를 더 많이 복용하라고 말했다.

vit·ri·ol·ic /ˌvɪtriˈɑlɪk/ *adj* something you say that is vitriolic is very cruel ‖ 하는 말이 매우 잔인한. 신랄한. 통렬한: *a vitriolic attack on homosexuals* 동성애자들에 대한 신랄한 공격

vi·va·cious /vɪˈveɪʃəs, vaɪ-/ *adj* someone, especially a woman, who is vivacious has a lot of energy and is fun to be with ‖ 특히 여성이 활기에 차고 같이 있으면 재미있는. 생기 넘치는. 쾌활한 - **vivaciously** *adv* - **vivacity** /vɪˈvæsəti/ *n* [U]

viv·id /ˈvɪvɪd/ *adj* 1 producing sharp clear pictures in your mind that makes something seem real ‖ 어떤 것을 사실처럼 보이게 마음속에서 뚜렷하고 명확한 모습을 그려내는. 생생한. 살아 있는 듯한: *a vivid description of the mountains* 그 산의 생생한 묘사 2 **vivid imagination.** the ability to imagine things so clearly that even unreal things may seem real ‖ 상상의 것일지라도 실재하는 것처럼 보이게 사물을 아주 분명하게 상상하는 능력. 생생하게 떠오르는 상상력: *Your daughter has a vivid imagination.* 네 딸은 생생한 상상력의 소유자이다. 3 vivid colors or patterns are very bright ‖ 색깔이나 무늬가 아주 밝은. 산뜻한 - **vividly** *adv*

viv·i·sec·tion /ˌvɪvəˈsɛkʃən/ *n* [U] the practice of operating on animals in order to do scientific tests on them ‖ 과학 실험을 하려고 동물에 시행하는 수술. 생체 해부

VJ, video jockey /ˈ... ˌ.ˌ./ *n* someone who introduces and plays VIDEOs of popular music on television ‖ 텔레비전에서 대중 음악의 비디오를 소개하고 틀어주는 사람. 비디오 자키

V-neck /ˈvi nɛk/ *n* a type of shirt or SWEATER with a collar that is shaped like the letter V ‖ 깃이 브이 자(字) 모양인 셔츠나 스웨터의 일종. V형의 깃

VOA *n* [U] Voice of America; a radio company that broadcasts American news and programs all over the world ‖ Voice of America(미국의 소리란 라디오 방송사)의 약어; 전 세계에 미국의 뉴스와 프로그램을 방송하는 라디오 방송사

vo·cab·u·lar·y /voʊˈkæbyəˌlɛri, və-/ *n* 1 [C, U] all the words that someone knows, learns, or uses ‖ 누군가가 알거나 배우거나, 또는 사용하는 모든 단어. 개인의 어휘: *He has a huge vocabulary for a five-year-old.* 그는 다섯 살배기로는 어휘를 많이 알고 있다. 2 [C, U] the words that are used when talking about a particular subject ‖ 특정 주제에 대하여 말할 때 사용되는 어휘들. 용어: *the vocabulary of doctors and scientists* 의사와 과학자들의 용어 3 all the words in a particular language ‖ 특정한 언어의 모든 어휘. 총어휘

vo·cal¹ /ˈvoʊkəl/ *adj* 1 relating to the voice ‖ 소리에 관련된. 음성의: *vocal music* 성악 2 INFORMAL expressing your opinion strongly or loudly ‖ 자신의 견해를 강하게 또는 크게 표현하는. 떠들썩한: *a vocal critic of the president* 대통령에 대한 떠들썩한 비평 - **vocally** *adv*

vocal² *n* [C usually plural] the part of a piece of music that is sung rather than played on an instrument ‖ 악기로 연주하는 것이 아니라 노래를 부르는 음악의 한 부분. 성악: *The song has Maria McKee on vocals.* 그 노래는 마리아 맥키가 성악으로 부른 것이 있다.

vocal cords /ˈ.. ˌ./ *n* [plural] thin pieces of muscle in your throat that produce sound when you speak or sing ‖ 말하거나 노래할 때 소리를 내는 목의 얇은 근육. 성대

vo·cal·ist /ˈvoʊkəlɪst/ *n* someone who sings, especially with a band ‖ 특히 악단과 함께 노래하는 사람. 가수. 보컬리스트

vo·ca·tion /voʊˈkeɪʃən/ *n* [C, U] the feeling that the purpose of your life is to do a particular job because it allows you to help other people, or the ability to do this job ‖ 다른 사람을 도울 수 있기 때문에 자신은 인생의 목표로 특정한 일을 하고 있다는 감정, 또는 이 일을 수행하는 능력. 소명. 천직: *Teaching isn't just a job to her - it's her vocation.* 교직은 그녀에게 단순한 직업이 아니다. 그것은 그녀의 천직이다.

vo·ca·tion·al /voʊˈkeɪʃənəl/ *adj* **vocational school/training/education etc.** a school or method of training that teaches you the skills you need to do a particular job ‖ 특정한 일을 하는 데 필요한 기술을 가르치는 학교나 훈련 방법. 직업 학교/훈련/교육

vo·cif·er·ous /voʊˈsɪfərəs/ *adj* FORMAL loud and determined in expressing your opinions ‖ 의견을 표현하는 데 크고 단호한. 큰 소리로 외치는. 떠들썩한: *vociferous complaints* 큰 소리로 외치는 불평 - **vociferously** *adv*

VOD *n* [U] video on demand; a special service that lets television viewers pay to watch particular films at whatever time they choose to watch them ‖ video on demand(주문형 TV프로그램)의 약어; 텔레비전 시청자가 돈을 지불하고 선택한 시청 시간에 특정 영화를 볼 수 있게 해주는 특수한 서비스

vod·ka /'vɑdkə/ *n* [U] a strong clear alcoholic drink, first made in Eastern Europe ‖ 동유럽에서 최초로 제조한 독하고 맑은 술. 보드카

vogue /voʊg/ *n* **be in vogue/be the vogue** to be fashionable and popular ‖ 유행하고 인기가 있다: *The preppy look was in vogue in the early 80s.* 프레피 룩은 80년대 초기에 유행했다.

voice¹ /vɔɪs/ *n* **1** [C, U] the sound you make when you speak or sing, or the ability to make this sound ‖ 말하거나 노래할 때 내는 소리, 또는 이러한 소리를 내는 능력. 목소리. 말하는 능력: *I thought I heard voices downstairs.* 나는 아래층에서 나는 목소리를 들은 것으로 생각했다. / *Andrea has a really beautiful voice.* (=singing voice) 안드레아는 목소리가 정말 아름답다. / *He's caught a bad cold and lost his voice.* (=cannot speak) 그는 지독한 감기에 걸려서 말을 할 수 없다. / *I can hear you – you don't have to raise your voice.* (=speak in a loud angry way) 나는 네 말이 들리거든. 그러니 목청을 높일 필요 없어. / *Keep your voice down,* (=speak more quietly) *it's supposed to be a surprise.* 목소리를 낮추어라. 깜짝 놀라게 해주어야 돼. / *"It won't work," he said in a loud/soft/worried/booming voice.* "잘되지 않을 거야."라고 그는 큰[부드러운, 걱정스러운, 낭랑한] 목소리로 말했다. ✗DON'T SAY "... with a loud/soft/worried/booming voice."✗ "…with a loud/soft/worried/booming voice."라고는 하지 않는다. **2 deep-voiced/husky-voiced etc.** having a voice that is deep and low etc. ‖ 굵고 낮은 목소리를 한. 굵은/쉰 목소리의 **3** [C, U] an opinion or wish that is expressed ‖ 표현된 견해나 바람. 의견. 희망: *Shouldn't parents have a voice in deciding how their children are educated?* 부모는 자신들의 자녀가 어떻게 교육을 받아야 하는지를 결정하는 데 발언권이 있어야 하는 것 아닙니까? **4** [singular] a person, organization, newspaper etc. that expresses the wishes or opinions of a group of people ‖ 일단의 사람들의 희망이나 의견을 표현하는 사람·조직·신문 등. 발표 기관. 표명

자. 대변자: *By the early 1960s, King had become the voice of the civil rights movement.* 1960년대 초까지 킹은 민권 운동의 대변자가 되었었다. **5 the voice of reason/experience etc.** someone who is sensible, has experience etc. especially in a situation where other people do not ‖ 특히 어떤 상황에서 다른 사람에게는 없는 분별력·경험 등을 가진 사람. 이성/경험의 목소리

voice² *v* [T] to tell people your opinions or feelings about a particular subject ‖ 특정한 주제에 대하여 사람들에게 자신의 의견이나 감정을 말하다. 표명하다: *We all voiced our concerns about the plan.* 우리 모두는 그 계획에 대해 우려를 표명했다.

voice mail /'. ./ *n* [U] a system, especially in a company, in which telephone calls are recorded so that someone can listen to them later ‖ 특히 회사에서 누군가가 나중에 들을 수 있도록 전화를 녹음하는 시스템. (전화의) 자동 응답 장치. 음성 우편

void¹ /vɔɪd/ *adj* **1** a contract or agreement that is void is officially no longer legal; INVALID¹ ‖ 계약이나 협정이 더이상 공식적으로 합법적이지 않은. 무효인; ㊐ invalid¹: *They were demanding that the elections be declared void.* 그들은 선거의 무효 선언을 요구하고 있었다. **2 be void of** to completely lack something ‖ 무엇이 완전히 결여되다: *Her eyes were void of all expression.* 그녀의 눈에는 아무런 표정도 없었다.

void² *n* **1** a feeling of great sadness that you have when someone you love dies or when something important is missing from your life ‖ 사랑하는 사람이 죽거나 자신의 인생에서 중요한 것을 상실했을 때 가지는 커다란 슬픈 감정. 상실감: *Their son's death left a painful void in their lives.* 아들의 죽음은 그들의 삶에 고통스런 상실감을 남겼다. **2** an empty space where nothing exists ‖ 아무것도 존재하지 않는 빈 공간. 진공. 공백 상태

void³ *v* [T] to make a contract or agreement VOID so that it has no legal effect ‖ 계약이나 협정 등을 법적 효력이 없게 만들다. 무효로 하다. 취소하다: *The cashier will void the sale.* 계산원은 그 판매를 취소할 것이다.

vol·a·tile /'vɑlətl/ *adj* **1** likely to change suddenly and become violent ‖ 갑자기 변해서 격해지기 쉬운. 변덕스러운: *He's a pretty volatile character.* 그는 아주 변덕스러운 성격의 소유자이다. / *a volatile situation* 폭발 직전의 상황 **2** a volatile liquid or substance changes easily into a gas ‖ 액체나 물질 등이 기체로 쉽게 변하는. 휘발성의 **- volatility** /ˌvɑləˈtɪləti/ n [U]

vol·ca·no /vɑlˈkeɪnoʊ/ n, plural **volcanoes** or **volcanos** a mountain with a large hole at the top out of which rocks, LAVA, and ASH sometimes explode ‖ 바위·용암·재를 때때로 분출하는, 정상에 큰 분화구가 있는 산. 화산: This island has several active volcanoes. (=volcanoes that may explode at any time) 이 섬에는 몇 개의 활화산이 있다. **- volcanic** /vɑlˈkænɪk/ adj : volcanic rocks 화산암

vo·li·tion /vəˈlɪʃən, voʊ-/ n [U] FORMAL of your own volition because you want to do something and not because you are forced to do it ‖ 무엇을 하라고 강요하기 때문이 아니라 하고 싶어서. 자진하여. 자유의사로: Robin left the company of her own volition. 로빈은 자진하여 회사를 떠났다.

vol·ley /ˈvɑli/ n 1 a large number of bullets, ARROWS, rocks etc. fired or thrown at the same time ‖ 동시에 발사되거나 투척된 다량의 탄환·화살·돌 등: a volley of shots 일제 사격 2 a lot of questions, insults, attacks etc. that are all said or made at the same time ‖ 동시에 모두 언급되거나 이뤄진 많은 질문·모욕·공격 등: a volley of abuse 빗발치는 독설

volleyball

vol·ley·ball /ˈvɑliˌbɔl/ n 1 [U] a game in which two teams hit a ball to each other across a net with their hands and try not to let it touch the ground ‖ 두 팀이 손으로 서로에게 공을 쳐서 네트를 넘기며 공이 땅에 닿지 않게 하려는 경기. 배구 2 the ball used in this game ‖ 이 경기에 사용되는 공. 배구공

volt /voʊlt/ n a unit for measuring the force of an electric current ‖ 전류의 세기를 측정하는 단위. 볼트

volt·age /ˈvoʊltɪdʒ/ n [C, U] the force of an electric current measured in VOLTs ‖ 볼트로 측정된 전류의 세기. 전압(량)

vol·ume /ˈvɑlyəm, -yum/ n 1 [U] the amount of sound produced by a television, radio etc. ‖ 텔레비전·라디오 등에서 나오는 소리의 양. 음량. 소리의 크기: I can't hear the TV; can you turn up the volume? 텔레비전 소리가 들리지 않는구나. 소리를 좀 크게 해 주겠니? 2 [U] the amount of space that a substance fills or an object contains ‖ 물질이 채우거나 물체가 수용되는 공간적인 양. 용적. 체적. 용량: Let the dough double in volume before you bake it. 굽기 전에 밀가루 반죽이 두 배로 부풀게 해라. 3 [C, U] the total amount of something ‖ 어떤 것의 총량. 총계: an increase in the volume of traffic 교통량의 증가 4 a book, especially one of the books into which a very long book is divided ‖ 책, 특히 내용이 매우 긴 책을 여러 권으로 분할한 책들 중의 하나. (전집의) 한 권: a 12-volume set of poetry 12권 세트 시집

vo·lu·mi·nous /vəˈlumənəs/ adj FORMAL 1 very large ‖ 매우 큰. 헐거운: a voluminous skirt 헐렁헐렁한 스커트 2 voluminous books, documents etc. are very long and contain a lot of information ‖ 책·문서 등이 (내용이) 매우 길고 많은 정보를 포함하는. 권수가 많은. 저작이 많은. 대작의

vol·un·tar·y /ˈvɑlənˌtɛri/ adj done willingly and without being forced or paid ‖ 강요받거나 대가 없이 기꺼이 한. 자발적인: voluntary work 자진하여 하는 일 / We're asking for people to help on a voluntary basis. (=without being paid) 우리는 사람들에게 자발적인 도움을 요청하고 있다. **- voluntarily** /ˌvɑlənˈtɛrəli/ adv

vol·un·teer¹ /ˌvɑlənˈtɪr/ v 1 [I, T] to offer to do something without expecting any reward ‖ 어떤 보상도 기대하지 않고 무엇을 할 것을 제의하다. 자진하여 …하다: Ernie volunteered to wash the dishes. 어니는 자발적으로 설거지를 했다. / I volunteered for the job. 나는 그 일에 자원했다. 2 [T] to tell someone something without being asked ‖ 부탁 받지 않고 무엇을 누군가에게 말하다. 자진하여 제공하다: Michael volunteered the information before I had a chance to say anything. 마이클은 내가 어떤 말도 하기 전에 정보를 자진하여 제공했다. 3 [I] to offer to join the army, navy etc. ‖ 육군·해군 등에 입대를 제의하다. 지원병이 되다: When the war began, my brother immediately volunteered. 전쟁이 시작되자 나의 동생은 곧 자원 입대했다.

volunteer² n **1** someone who offers to do something without expecting any reward or pay ‖ 어떤 보상이나 보수도 기대하지 않고 무엇을 하는 것을 제의하는 사람. 자원 봉사자 **2** someone who offers to join the army, navy etc. ‖ 육군·해군 등에 입대를 제의하는 사람. 지원병

vo·lup·tu·ous /vəˈlʌptʃuəs/ adj **1** a woman who is voluptuous has large breasts and a soft curved body, and is considered sexually attractive ‖ 여자가 풍만한 가슴과 부드럽게 만곡한 몸을 지녀 성적으로 매력적으로 여겨지는. 관능[육감]적인 **2** expressing or suggesting sexual pleasure ‖ 성적인 쾌락을 나타내거나 암시하는. 요염한: *a voluptuous gesture* 요염한 몸짓

vom·it¹ /ˈvɑmɪt/ v [I, T] FORMAL to bring food or drink up from the stomach and out through the mouth ‖ (먹은) 음식이나 음료를 위에서 입밖으로 내보내다. 토하다. 게우다

vomit² n [U] the food or drink that comes out when someone VOMITs ‖ 사람이 토할 때 나오는 음식이나 음료. 구토물

voo·doo /ˈvudu/ n [U] magical beliefs and practices used as a form of religion, especially in parts of Africa, Latin America, and the Caribbean ‖ 특히 아프리카·라틴 아메리카·카리브 해 지방에서 종교 형태로 사용된 주술적인 믿음과 관습. 부두교

vo·ra·cious /vəˈreɪʃəs, vɔ-/ adj FORMAL **1** eating or wanting large quantities of food ‖ 많은 양의 음식을 먹거나 원하는. 대식하는. 식욕이 왕성한: *The dog has a voracious appetite.* 그 개는 식욕이 왕성하다. **2** extremely eager to do something ‖ 무엇을 매우 열심히 하는. 매우 열심인. 정력적인: *a voracious reader* 탐독가 – **voracity** /vəˈræsəti/ n [U]

vor·tex /ˈvɔrtɛks/ n, plural **vortices** /ˈvɔrtəsiz/ LITERARY a large area of wind or water that spins rapidly and pulls things into its center ‖ 바람이나 물이 급하게 회전하면서 사물을 그 중심으로 끌어들이는 넓은 지역. 회오리바람. 소용돌이

vote¹ /voʊt/ v **1** [I, T] to mark a paper or raise your hand in order to show which person you want to elect, which plan you support, who you want to win a particular prize etc. ‖ 어떤 사람을 선출할 것인지·자신이 어떤 계획을 지지하는지·누가 특정한 상을 받기를 바라는지를 나타내려고 종이에 표시를 하거나 자신의 손을 들다. 투표하다: *He's too young to vote.* (=in an election) 그는 투표하기에는 너무 어리다. / *Who did you vote for?* 누

구에게 투표했니? / *If we can't agree, we'll have to vote on it.* 우리가 동의할 수 없다면 우리는 그것에 대해 투표를 해야 할 것이다. / *Congress voted to reduce taxes by 2%.* 의회는 2%의 조세 감세를 투표로 결정했다. / *85% of union members voted against going on strike.* 조합원의 85%가 파업 돌입에 반대 투표를 했다. **2** [T] to agree to provide something as the result of voting ‖ 투표의 결과로 무엇을 제공하는 데 동의하다. 투표로 의결하다: *Congress has voted an extra $20 million for road improvements.* 의회는 도로 개량에 2천만 달러를 추가 지원하기로 의결했다.

vote² n **1** a choice or decision that you make by voting ‖ 투표로 자신이 한 선택이나 결정. 투표: *He's certainly not going to get my vote!* 그는 분명히 내 표를 얻지 못해! / *There were 1079 votes for Mr. Swanson, and 766 for Mr. Reynolds.* 스완슨 씨는 1079표를 레이놀즈 씨는 766표를 얻었다. / *You have until 8:00 to cast your vote.* (=vote) 너는 8시까지 투표를 해야 한다. **2** an act of making a choice or decision by voting ‖ 투표로 선택이나 결정을 하는 행위. 표결: *We couldn't decide so we took a vote on it.* 결정할 수 없어서 우리는 그것을 표결에 부쳤다. / *Congress will put the bill to a vote tomorrow.* 의회는 내일 그 법안을 표결에 부칠 것이다. **3 the vote a)** the total number of votes made in an election or the total number of people who vote ‖ 선거에서 행사된 총투표수, 또는 총투표자수. 득표: *increasing our share of the vote* 우리쪽 득표수 높이기 / *efforts to win the African American/Irish/Jewish vote* (=all the votes of African Americans etc.) 아프리카계 [아일랜드계, 유대계] 미국인의 표를 얻기 위한 노력 **b)** the right to vote ‖ 투표권: *In France, women didn't get the vote until 1945.* 프랑스에서는 여자가 1945년까지 투표권이 없었다. **4 vote of confidence** the action of showing publicly that you support someone ‖ 남을 지지하는 것을 공개적으로 나타내는 행위. 지지, 신임 투표: *Darman got a vote of confidence from the committee and remained president.* 다만은 위원회로부터 신임을 얻어서 회장에 유임되었다.

vot·er /ˈvoʊtɚ/ n someone who votes or has the right to vote ‖ 투표를 하거나 투표권을 가진 사람. 투표자. 유권자: *The state decided to let the voters decide the issue.* 주 당국은 그 문제를 유권자들이 결정하도록 결의했다.

voting booth /'.. ˌ./ *n* an enclosed place where you can vote without being seen ‖ 보이지 않고 투표할 수 있게 둘러싸인 장소. 기표소

vouch /vautʃ/ *v*

vouch for sb/sth *phr v* [T] **1** to say that you have a firm belief that something is true or good because of your experience or knowledge of it ‖ 자신의 경험이나 지식으로 볼 때 어떤 것이 진실하거나 훌륭하다고 단언하다. 굳게 믿는다고 말하다: *I'll vouch for the accuracy of that report.* 나는 그 보고가 정확하다고 단언하겠다. **2** to say that you will be responsible for someone's behavior, actions etc. ‖ 누군가의 행실·행동 등에 대해 책임을 지겠다고 말하다. 보증하다: *I can vouch for my son, officer.* 경찰관님, 내가 내 아들을 보증할 수 있습니다.

vouch·er /'vautʃɚ/ *n* a kind of ticket that can be used for a particular purpose instead of money ‖ 돈을 대신하여 특정한 목적으로 사용될 수 있는 표의 일종. 상품 교환권. 쿠폰

vow¹ /vau/ *n* a serious promise ‖ 진지한 약속. 맹세. 서약: *She made a vow to herself that she would never tell anyone.* 그녀는 아무에게도 말하지 않겠다고 스스로 다짐했다. / *marriage vows* 결혼 서약

vow² *v* [T] to make a serious promise to yourself or someone else ‖ 자신이나 남에게 진지한 약속을 하다. 맹세하다: *He vowed to kill the man that destroyed his family.* 그는 자신의 가정을 파괴한 남자를 죽이기로 맹세했다. / *I vowed that I would never drink again.* 나는 다시는 술을 마시지 않겠다고 맹세했다.

vow·el /'vauəl/ *n* TECHNICAL the letter a, e, i, o, or u, and sometimes y ‖ 문자 a·e·i·o·u 및 때로는 y. 모음

voy·age /'vɔɪ-ɪdʒ/ *n* a long trip, especially in a ship or a space vehicle ‖ 특히 선박이나 우주선으로 하는 긴 여행. 배 여행. 우주 여행: *the voyage from England to America* 영국에서 미국까지의 선박 여행 – **voyage** *v* [I] LITERARY — see usage note at TRAVEL²

voy·eur /vɔɪ'ɚ/ *n* [U] someone who gets sexual pleasure from secretly watching other people's sexual activities ‖ 다른 사람들의 성행위를 몰래 보는 것에서 성적 쾌락을 얻는 사람. 관음증인 사람 – **voyeurism** /'vɔɪˌrɪzəm/ *n* [U] – **voyeuristic** /ˌvɔɪə'rɪstɪk/ *adj*

vs. /'vɚsəs/ the written abbreviation of VERSUS ‖ versus(…대(對))의 약어

VT the written abbreviation of Vermont ‖ Vermont(버몬트 주)의 약어

vul·gar /'vʌlgɚ/ *adj* very rude, offensive, and often relating to sex ‖ 매우 무례하고 불쾌감을 주며 흔히 성에 관련된. 상스러운. 외설적인: *vulgar language* 천한 말 – **vulgarity** /vəl'gærəti/ *n* [U]

vul·ner·a·ble /'vʌlnərəbəl/ *adj* easily harmed, hurt, or attacked ‖ 쉽게 해를 입거나 다치거나, 또는 공격 당하는. (사람·감정 등이) 상처받기 쉬운. (장소가) 공격받기 쉬운: *The army was in a vulnerable position.* 군대는 공격받기 쉬운 위치에 있었다. / *She looked so young and vulnerable.* 그녀는 아주 어리고 상처받기 쉬워 보였다. – **vulnerability** /ˌvʌlnrə'bɪləti/ *n* [U] —opposite INVULNERABLE

vul·ture /'vʌltʃɚ/ *n* **1** a large wild bird that eats dead animals ‖ 죽은 동물을 먹는, 몸집이 큰 야생의 새. 독수리. 콘도르 **2** someone who uses other people's troubles for his/her own advantage ‖ 다른 사람들의 곤경을 자신의 이익을 위해 이용하는 사람. 남을 등쳐먹는 사람

vy·ing /'vaɪ-ɪŋ/ *v* the PRESENT PARTICIPLE of VIE ‖ vie의 현재 분사형

V

Ww

W, w /'dʌbəl,yu, 'dʌbəyu/ the twenty-third letter of the English alphabet ‖ 영어 알파벳의 스물셋째 자

W 1 the written abbreviation of WEST or WESTERN ‖ west나 western의 약어 **2** the written abbreviation of WATT ‖ watt의 약어

WA the written abbreviation of Washington ‖ Washington(워싱턴 주)의 약어

wack·y /'wæki/ *adj* INFORMAL silly in an amusing way ‖ 우스꽝스럽게 엉뚱한. 별난. 터무니없는

wad¹ /wɑd/ *n* **1** a thick pile of thin sheets of something, especially money ‖ 물건, 특히 돈의 얇은 낱장을 두껍게 쌓은 것. 뭉치. 다발: *a wad of dollar bills* 달러 지폐 다발 **2** a thick soft mass of material that has been pressed together ‖ 부드러운 물질을 서로 압착시켜 두껍게 모아 놓은 것. 덩어리. 뭉치: *a wad of cotton* 솜뭉치

wad² *v* **-dded, -dding**

wad sth ↔ **up** *phr v* [T] INFORMAL to press something such as a piece of paper or cloth into a small tight ball ‖ 종이나 천의 조각 등을 단단하고 작고 둥글게 압착하다. (딴딴하게) 뭉치다: *Aaron wadded up the letter and threw it away.* 아론은 편지를 둘둘 뭉쳐서 던져 버렸다.

wad·dle /'wɑdl/ *v* [I] to walk with short steps, swinging from one side to another like a duck ‖ 짧은 걸음으로 오리처럼 이쪽저쪽으로 몸을 흔들며 걷다. 어기적어기적[뒤뚱뒤뚱] 걷다: *a fat man waddling along/up etc. the street* 뒤뚱거리며 거리를 죽 따라[올라]가는 뚱뚱한 남자 – **waddle** *n*

wade /weɪd/ *v* [I, T] to walk through water that is not deep ‖ 깊지 않은 물속을 걸어서 통과하다. 걸어서 건너다: *We waded across the stream.* 우리는 개울을 걸어서 건넜다.

wade through sth *phr v* [T] to read or deal with a lot of long and boring written work ‖ 길고 지루한 수많은 문서를 읽거나 취급하다. 간신히 읽다[독파하다]: *Preston was wading through a 500-page report.* 프레스톤은 5백 페이지짜리 보고서를 힘겹게 읽고 있었다.

wa·fer /'weɪfə/ *n* a very thin cookie ‖ 아주 얇은 과자. 웨이퍼

waf·fle¹ /'wɑfəl/ *n* a flat bread with a pattern of holes in it, often eaten for breakfast ‖ 종종 아침 식사로 먹는 안에 구멍 문양이 나 있는 납작한 빵. 와플

waf·fle² *v* [I] INFORMAL to be unable to decide what action to take ‖ 어떤 행동을 취할지 결정할 수 없다. 우물쭈물하다. 애매한 태도를 취하다: *He made his decision without waffling.* 그는 우물쭈물하지 않고 결정을 내렸다.

waft /wɑft, wæft/ *v* [I, T] to move gently through the air ‖ 공기 속으로 부드럽게 움직이다. 가볍게 떠돌다[떠돌게 하다]: *The smell of bacon wafted up from the kitchen.* 부엌에서 나는 베이컨 냄새가 공기 중에 감돌았다.

wag /wæg/ *v* **-gged, -gging** [I, T] **1** if a dog wags its tail, or the tail wags, it shakes from one side to another ‖ 개가 꼬리를 이쪽저쪽으로 흔들다. (꼬리를) 흔들다. (꼬리가) 흔들리다 **2** to shake your finger from one side to the other in order to tell someone not to do something ‖ 누군가에게 어떤 일을 하지 말라고 말하려고 손가락을 양옆으로 흔들다. 손가락을 흔들어 반대하다: *"Don't go back there again," she said, wagging her finger.* "다시는 거기 돌아가지 마라."라고 그녀는 손가락을 저으며 말했다. – **wag** *n*

wage¹ /weɪdʒ/ *n* [singular] the amount of money you earn, usually for each hour that you work ‖ 보통 일하는 매시간당 버는 돈의 액수. 임금. 급료. 삯: *The job's not very exciting, but he earns a good wage.* 그 일은 아주 재미있지는 않지만 그는 돈을 잘 벌고 있다. / *an hourly wage* 시간당 임금 ✗DON'T SAY "an annual wage." SAY "an annual salary."✗ "an annual wage"라고 하지 않고 "an annual salary"라고 한다. —see also WAGES — see usage note at PAY²

wage² *v* [T] to be involved in a war, struggle, or fight against someone or something ‖ 사람이나 사물에 대한 전쟁이나 투쟁, 또는 싸움에 관련되다. 싸우다. 치르다: *The police are waging a campaign/war against drug pushers.* 경찰은 마약 밀매자들에 대한 단속 운동[전쟁]을 벌이고 있다.

wa·ger¹ /'weɪdʒə/ *n* **1** an agreement to risk money on the result of a race, game etc. ‖ 경주·시합 등의 결과에 돈을

거는 약속. 내기(하기): *Higgins had a wager on the World Series.* 히긴스는 미 프로야구 월드 시리즈에 돈을 걸었다. **2** the money that you risk ‖ 내기에 건 돈. 판돈: *a $10 wager* 판돈 10달러

wager² *v* [T] to risk money on the result of a race, game etc. ‖ 경주·시합 등의 결과에 돈을 걸다: *Brad wagered $20 on the game.* 브래드는 그 시합에 20달러를 걸었다.

wag·es /'weɪdʒɪz/ *n* [plural] the money you get each day, week, or month, that is usually paid according to the number of hours that you work ‖ 보통 일한 시간 수에 따라 지불되는 매일[매주, 매달] 받는 돈. 임금. 급료 —compare SALARY

wag·on /'wægən/ *n* **1** a strong vehicle with four wheels, pulled by horses ‖ 말이 끄는 네 바퀴가 달린 튼튼한 탈 것. 짐마차 **2** a small CART with four wheels and a long handle in the front, used as a toy for children ‖ 네 바퀴와 앞쪽에 긴 손잡이가 달려 있어서 아이들의 장난감으로 쓰이는 작은 카트. 장난감차 **3** INFORMAL ⇨ STATION WAGON **4 be on the wagon** INFORMAL to no longer drink alcohol ‖ 더이상 술을 마시지 않다. 금주하다: *Harry's been on the wagon since he got married.* 해리는 결혼한 후 술을 끊어 왔다.

wagon train /'.. ,./ *n* a large group of WAGONs traveling together in past times ‖ 과거에 함께 여행하던 마차들의 대집단. 포장마차 대(열)

waif /weɪf/ *n* LITERARY a child or animal that is thin and unhealthy, and looks as if he, she, or it does not have a home ‖ 마르고 병약하고 집이 없는 것처럼 보이는 아이나 동물. 부랑아. 떠돌이

wail /weɪl/ *v* **1** [I] to make a long high sound with your voice because you are in pain or very sad, or to make a sound like this ‖ 고통에 처해 있거나 매우 슬퍼서 길고 높은 소리를 내거나 이렇게 소리를 내게 하다. 울부짖다. 구슬픈 소리를 내다: *women wailing with grief* 슬퍼서 울부짖는 여자들 / *sirens wailing in the distance* 멀리서 울어대는 사이렌 **2** [T] to say something in a loud, sad, and complaining way ‖ 크고 슬프며 불평하는 투로 어떤 말을 하다. 한탄[탄식]하다. 울부짖으며 말하다: *"My money's gone!" she wailed.* "내 돈이 없어졌어!"라고 그녀는 울부짖으며 말했다. –**wail** *n*

waist /weɪst/ *n* **1** the part in the middle of your body just above your HIPs ‖ 엉덩이 바로 위 신체 중앙의 부위. 허리: *She has a slim waist.* 그녀는 허리가 가늘다. —see picture at BODY **2** the part of a

piece of clothing that goes around your waist ‖ 의복의 허리둘레를 빙 도는 부위. 웨이스트: *These pants are too big in the waist.* 이 바지는 허리가 너무 크다.

waist·band /'weɪstbænd/ *n* the part of a skirt, pants etc. that fastens around your waist ‖ 치마·바지의 허리 둘레를 조여 주는 부분. 허리띠[끈]

waist·line /'weɪstlaɪn/ *n* **1** [singular] the measurement around your waist ‖ 허리 둘레의 측정치. 허리둘레 **2** the position of the waist of a piece of clothing ‖ 옷의 허리 위치. 허리(둘레)선

wait¹ /weɪt/ *v* **1** [I] to not do something until something else happens, someone arrives etc. ‖ 어떤 일이 일어나거나 누군가가 도착할 때까지 무엇을 하지 않다. 기다리다. 대기하다: *Hurry up! Everyone's waiting.* 서둘러! 모든 사람이 기다리고 있어. / *Wait right here until I come back.* 내가 돌아올 때까지 꼭 여기서 기다려라. / *We had to wait 45 minutes for a bus.* 우리는 45분간 버스를 기다려야 했다. / *Are you waiting to use the phone?* 전화를 쓰려고 기다리십니까? **2 wait tables** to serve food to people at their table in a restaurant ‖ 음식점에서 식탁에 앉은 사람들에게 음식을 제공하다. (식사) 시중을 들다. 웨이터로 일하다: *I waited tables to earn money in college.* 나는 대학 때 돈을 벌기 위해 식당에서 서빙을 했다.

SPOKEN PHRASES

3 wait a minute/second said in order to ask someone to wait for a short time ‖ 누군가에게 잠시 기다려 달라고 부탁하는 데에 쓰여. 잠깐만 기다려: *Wait a second, I'll get my coat and come with you.* 잠깐만 기다려, 내 코트 가져와서 너랑 같이 갈게. **4 I can't wait/I can hardly wait** said when you want to do something, go somewhere etc. very much ‖ 몹시 어떤 일을 하고 싶거나 어딘가 가고 싶을 때에 쓰여. 오래/거의 기다릴 [참을] 수 없다: *I can't wait to see the look on his face.* 나는 그의 얼굴 표정을 보고 싶어 못 견디겠다. **5 (just) you wait** said in order to warn or threaten someone ‖ 누군가에게 경고하거나 위협하는 데에 쓰여. 두고 봐: *I'll get you back for what you've done, just you wait.* 네가 한 짓에 대해 되갚아 줄 테니, 두고 봐.

---

wait around *phr v* [I] to do nothing while you are waiting for something to happen, someone to arrive etc. ‖ 어떤 일

이 일어나거나 누군가가 도착하기를 기다리는 동안 아무것도 하지 않다. 오로지 … 을 기다리다. 마냥[빈둥거리며] 기다리다: *We were waiting around for Dad's plane to come in.* 우리는 아버지의 비행기가 도착하기만 고대하고 있었다.

wait on sb *phr v* [T] **1** to serve food to someone at his/her table, especially in a restaurant ‖ 특히 음식점에서 테이블에 앉아 있는 사람에게 음식을 날라 주다. 식사 시중을 들다: *A very nice young woman waited on us at The Riverboat today.* 오늘 리버보트 레스토랑에서 매우 친절한 젊은 아가씨가 우리에게 서빙을 했다. **2 wait on** sb **hand and foot** OFTEN HUMOROUS to do everything for someone ‖ 누군가를 위해 모든 것을 다하다. …을 보살펴 주다. 수족이 되어 일해 주다

wait sth ↔ **out** *phr v* [T] to wait for something to finish ‖ 어떤 일이 끝나기를 기다리다. …이 지나가기[그치기]를 기다리다: *They found a place to wait out the storm.* 그들은 폭풍이 그치기를 기다릴 곳을 찾아냈다.

wait up *phr v* [I] **1** to wait for someone to return before you go to bed ‖ 잠자러 가기 전에 누군가가 돌아오기를 기다리다. …을 자지 않고 기다리다: *Please don't wait up for me.* 잠자지 않고 나를 기다리지 말아요. **2 Wait up!** SPOKEN used to tell someone to stop and wait for you ‖ 누군가에게 멈춰서 기다려 달라고 말하는 데에 쓰여. 기다려!: *Wait up you guys – I've dropped my wallet.* 얘들아 기다려. 내 지갑을 떨어뜨렸어.

USAGE NOTE wait and expect

Use **wait** to talk about staying somewhere until someone comes or something happens: *Please wait until Mr. Fletcher arrives. / She's been waiting all day for that phone to ring.* Use **expect** to say that you think something will probably happen, arrive etc., whether you want it to or not: *I didn't expect her to be so angry. / Were you expecting a phone call?* **wait** 는 누가 오거나 어떤 일이 일어날 때까지 어딘가에 머무는 것을 언급하는 데에 쓴다: 플레처 씨가 도착할 때까지 기다려 주세요. / 그녀는 그 전화가 울리기를 종일 기다리고 있다. **expect** 는 자신이 원하건 않건 간에 어떤 일이 아마 일어나거나 도래하리라고 생각한다고 말하는 데에 쓴다: 나는 그녀가 그렇게 화를 내리라고는 예상치 못했다. / 전화가 오리라고 기대하고 있었습니까?

---

wait² *n* [singular] a period of time in which you wait for something to happen, someone to arrive etc. ‖ 어떤 일이 일어나거나 누가 도착하기를 기다리는 시간. 대기 시간: *We had a three-hour wait for our flight.* 우리는 우리 비행기를 3시간 기다렸다. —see also **lie in wait (for sb/sth)** (LIE¹)

wait·er /ˈweɪtɚ/ *n* a man who serves food in a restaurant ‖ 음식점에서 음식 서빙을 하는 남자. 웨이터

waiting list /ˈ.. ./, **wait list** /ˈ. ./ *n* a list of people who have asked for something but who must wait before they can have it. ‖ 어떤 것을 청구했지만 그것을 갖기에 앞서 기다려야만 하는 사람들의 명단. 대기자 명단: *Over 500 students are on the waiting/wait list.* 5백 명 이상의 학생들이 대기자 명단에 올라 있다.

waiting room /ˈ.. ./ *n* a room for people to wait in, for example to see a doctor ‖ 사람들이 예를 들어 의사의 진찰을 받기 위해 그 안에서 기다리는 방. 대기실

wait·ress /ˈweɪtrɪs/ *n* a woman who serves food at the tables in a restaurant ‖ 음식점의 식탁에서 음식 서빙을 하는 여자. 웨이트리스

waive /weɪv/ *v* [T] to state officially that a right, rule etc. can be ignored ‖ 권리·규정 등이 묵살될 수 있다고 공식적으로 발언하다. …을 버리다. 포기하다: *She waived her right to a lawyer.* 그녀는 자신의 권리를 포기하고 변호사에게 넘겼다.

waiv·er /ˈweɪvɚ/ *n* an official statement saying that a right, rule etc. can be ignored ‖ 권리·규정 등이 무시될 수 있다고 말하는 공식적 발언. 권리 포기(의 의사 표시). (책임) 면제

wake¹ /weɪk/ *v* **woke, woken, waking** [I, T] also **wake up** to stop sleeping, or to make someone stop sleeping ‖ 깨어나다, 또는 사람을 깨우다. 일어나다[일어나게 하다]. 눈이 떠지다 [을 뜨게 하다]: *Try not to wake the baby.* 아기가 깨지 않게 해라. / *I woke up at 5:00 this morning.* 나는 오늘 아침 5시에 일어났다.

wake up *phr v* [I, T] to start to pay attention to something ‖ 어떤 것에 주의를 기울이기 시작하다. 정신을 차리다. 분발하다. 조심하다: *Hey! Wake up when I'm talking to you!* 이봐! 내가 네게 말하고 있을 때는 정신 차리고 들어!

wake up to *phr v* [T] to start to realize and understand a danger, an idea etc. ‖

W

위험·생각 등을 인식하고 이해하기 시작하다. 알아채다. 깨닫다. 직시하다: *You have to wake up to the fact that alcohol is killing you.* 너는 술이 네 자신을 죽이고 있다는 사실을 깨달아야 한다.

wake² *n* **1 in the wake of/in sth's wake** as a result of ‖ 무엇의 결과로: *Five members of the city council resigned in the wake of the scandal.* 다섯 명의 시의회 의원들이 그 추문의 여파로 사임했다. **2** the track or path made behind a car, boat etc. as it moves along ‖ 자동차·보트 등이 죽 나아갈 때 뒤에 만든 궤적이나 진로. 지나간 자국[흔적]: *The car left clouds of dust in its wake.* 차는 뒤로 먼지를 휘날리며 달렸다. **3** the time before a funeral when people meet to remember the dead person ‖ 사람들이 죽은 사람을 추모하기 위해 장례식 전에 만나는 시간. 철야 추도

wak·en /'weɪkən/ *v* [I, T] FORMAL to wake, or to wake someone ‖ 잠에서 깨다, 또는 남을 깨우다. 눈뜨다[눈을 뜨게 하다]. 일어나다[일어나게 하다]: *He was wakened by the sound of a car horn outside.* 그는 밖에서 들려오는 차 경적 소리에 깼다.

wake-up call /'.. ,./ *n* **1** an experience or event that shocks you and makes you realize that you must do something to change a situation ‖ 충격을 주어 상황을 변화시킬 무엇인가를 해야 한다고 깨닫게 하는 경험이나 사건. 주의[관심]을 환기하는 것 **2** a telephone call that someone makes to you, especially at a hotel, to wake you up in the morning ‖ 특히 호텔에서, 아침에 사람을 깨우려고 누군가가 해주는 전화. 모닝콜

wak·ing /'weɪkɪŋ/ *adj* **waking hours/moments etc.** all the time when you are awake ‖ 깨어 있는 모든 시간. 일어나 있는 시간/순간: *He spends every waking moment with that girl!* 그는 눈을 뜨고 있는 시간은 몽땅 그 소녀와 지내!

walk¹ /wɔk/ *v* **1** [I, T] to move along by putting one foot in front of the other ‖ 한 발을 다른 발 앞으로 놓아가며 나아가다. 걷다. 걸어가다: *We must have walked ten miles today.* 우리는 오늘 10마일을 걸은 게 틀림없다. / *Do you walk to work?* 당신은 직장까지 걸어가십니까? / *She walked up to him and kissed him.* 그녀는 그에게 걸어가서 키스했다. / *tourists walking around the downtown area* 번화가 지역을 돌아다니는 관광객들 —see picture on page 947 **2** [T] to walk through or across a particular area ‖ 특정 지역을 걸어서 통과하거나 가로지르다.

도보로 가다[통과하다, 건너다]: *walking the streets of Boston* 보스턴 거리를 도보로 걷기 **3 walk the dog** to take a dog outside to walk ‖ 개를 밖으로 데려가 걷게 하다 **4 walk sb somewhere** to walk somewhere with someone ‖ 누구와 함께 어떤 곳에 걸어가다. 수행[동반]하다. 걸려서 데려가다: *It's late – I'll walk you home.* 늦었으니 내가 집까지 데려다 줄게. **5 walk all over sb** INFORMAL to treat someone very badly ‖ 사람을 매우 나쁘게 대하다. 함부로 취급하다. 깔보다: *She lets those kids walk all over her.* 그녀는 그 아이들이 자신을 함부로 대하게 내버려 둔다. **6** [I] INFORMAL to leave a court of law without being punished or sent to prison ‖ 처벌 받거나 수감되지 않고 법정을 떠나다. 풀려나다. 석방되다: *I knew he'd walk – they didn't have enough evidence.* 나는 그가 풀려나리라는 것을 알았어. 그들은 충분한 증거를 가지고 있지 않았어.

walk away *phr v* [I] to leave a situation without caring what happens, even though you are responsible for it ‖ 비록 일어나는 일에 책임이 있어도 개의치 않고 어떤 상황을 방치하다. …에서 손을 떼다. 도망치다: *You can't just walk away from eight years of marriage!* 네 8년간의 결혼 생활을 그냥 팽개쳐 버릴 수는 없는 거야!

walk away with sth *phr v* [T] to win something easily ‖ 어떤 것을 쉽게 얻어내다. 상을 수월하게 타다: *Carrie walked away with the prize.* 캐리는 수월하게 그 상을 탔다.

walk in on sb *phr v* [T] to go into a place and interrupt someone whom you did not expect to be there ‖ 한 장소에 들어가 거기 있으리라고 예상하지 못한 사람을 방해하다. …과 마주치다. 현장을 목격하다: *I walked in on Terry and Lisa in bed.* 나는 우연히 테리와 리사가 침대에 있는 것을 목격했다.

walk into sth *phr v* [T] to become involved in a situation that is unpleasant or makes you look stupid without intending to ‖ 그럴 의도 없이 불쾌하거나 어리석어 보이게 하는 상황에 개입되다. 맞닥뜨리다. 빠지다: *You walked straight into that one!* 너 그것에 딱 걸렸구나!

walk sth **off** *phr v* [T] if you walk off an unpleasant feeling, you go for a walk to make it go away ‖ 불쾌한 감정을 없애기 위해 산책 가다. 걸어서 없애다: *If you get a cramp, just try to walk it off.* 만약 쥐가 나면 걸어서 풀어 봐라.

walk off with sth *phr v* to steal something, or to take something by mistake ‖ 어떤 것을 훔치거나 실수로 취하다. 슬쩍하다. 모르고 가져가다: *Someone walked off with my new jacket!* 누군가 내 새 재킷을 입고 가 버렸네!

walk out *phr v* [I] **1** to stop working as a protest ‖ 항의로서 일하기를 중단하다. 파업하다: *The electricians at the factory have walked out.* 공장의 전기공들이 파업에 들어갔다. **2** to leave your husband, wife etc. suddenly ‖ 남편·아내 등을 갑자기 떠나다. 버리다: *Mary just walked out on him one day.* 메리는 어느 날 그에게서 그대로 떠나 버렸다.

walk² *n* **1** the time you spend or the distance you travel when you are walking ‖ 걸을 때 소모한 시간이나 이동 거리. 보행 시간[거리]: *Would you like to go for a walk?* (=for pleasure) 산책하러 가시겠습니까? / *Let's take a walk after lunch.* 점심 먹고 산책합시다. / *It's only a ten minute/two mile walk from here.* 여기서 걸어서 불과 10분[2마일] 거리다. **2** a particular path or ROUTE for walking ‖ 걷기 위한 특별한 길이나 노선. 산책로. 걷는 길[코스]: *popular walks in Yellowstone National Park* 옐로스톤 국립공원의 인기 있는 산책로 **3** [U] the way someone walks ‖ 사람이 걸어가는 길. 노정. 도정 —see also WALK OF LIFE

walk·er /'wɔkɚ/ *n* **1** a metal frame that old or sick people use to help them walk ‖ 늙거나 아픈 사람들이 도움을 받아 걷는 데 쓰는 금속제 틀. 보행기 **2** someone who walks at a particular speed, in a particular place etc. ‖ 특정 속도로, 또는 특정 장소 등을 걷는 사람. 보행자: *A brisk walker can get there in 25 minutes.* 걸음이 빠른 사람은 25분이면 그곳에 도착할 수 있다.

walk·ie-talk·ie /ˌwɔki 'tɔki/ *n* a small radio that you can carry and use to speak to other people who have the same type of radio ‖ 가지고 다니며 같은 기종의 무전기를 가진 다른 사람에게 말하는 데 쓰는 작은 무전기. 휴대용 무전기. 워키토키

walk-in /'. ./ *adj* big enough for a person to walk inside ‖ 사람이 안에 걸어 들어갈 정도로 큰. 서서 들어갈 수 있는 크기의: *a walk-in closet* 선 채로 들어갈 수 있는 벽장

walking stick /'.. ,./ *n* a long thin stick, used to help support you when you walk ‖ 걸을 때 쓰러지지 않고 버티게 도와주는 길고 가는 막대기. 지팡이.

단장

Walk·man /'wɔkmən/ *n* TRADEMARK a small machine that plays TAPES and has HEADPHONES, that you carry with you to listen to music ‖ 테이프를 재생시키며 헤드폰이 달려 있고, 가지고 다니며 음악을 듣는 작은 기계. 워크맨

walk of life /ˌ. . '. ./ *n* the position in society that someone has ‖ 사람이 가진 사회적 지위. 계층: *The club has members from all walks of life.* 그 클럽은 사회의 모든 계층의 회원을 갖고 있다.

walk-on /'. ./ *n* a small acting part in a play or movie in which the actor has no words, or an actor who has this part ‖ 연극이나 영화에서 대사가 없는 작은 배역, 또는 이 역을 맡은 배우. 단역(배우) – **walk-on** *adj*

walk·out /'wɔk-aut/ *n* an occasion when people stop working or leave somewhere as a protest ‖ 사람들이 항의로서 작업을 중단하거나 어떤 곳을 떠나는 경우. 동맹 파업: *City employees staged a walkout in protest of the budget cuts.* 시공무원들은 예산 삭감에 대한 항의로 파업을 단행했다.

walk-up /'. ./ *n* INFORMAL an apartment that you have to walk up the stairs to, because there is no ELEVATOR in the building ‖ 건물에 엘리베이터가 없어서 계단을 걸어 올라가야 하는 아파트

walk·way /'wɔk-wei/ *n* a path, often above the ground, built to connect two parts of a building or two buildings ‖ 한 건물의 두 부분이나 두 건물을 연결하기 위해 종종 공중에 지어진 통로. 연결 통로

wall /wɔl/ *n* **1** one of the sides of a room or building ‖ 방이나 건물의 측면들 중 하나. 벽: *Hang that picture on the wall by the door.* 그 그림을 문 옆 벽에 걸어라. **2** an upright structure made of stone or brick, that divides one area from another ‖ 돌이나 벽돌로 만들어져 한 구역을 다른 곳과 나누는 수직 구조물. 담(장): *A brick wall surrounds the building.* 벽돌담이 그 건물을 에워싸고 있다. **3** the side of something hollow, such as a pipe or tube ‖ 파이프나 관 등 속이 빈 것의 벽면. 안벽. 내벽: *The walls of the blood vessels had been damaged.* 혈관벽이 손상됐다. **4** something that prevents you from doing something or going somewhere ‖ 무엇을 하거나 어딘가로 가는 것을 막는 것. 장벽. 장애: *A wall of people was blocking my view of the stage.* 사람들의 장벽에 가려 나는 무대 위가 보이지 않았다. – **walled** *adj* —see also **have your back to the wall**

(BACK¹)

wal·let /ˈwɑlɪt, ˈwɔ-/ *n* a small flat folding case for putting paper money in, usually made of leather ‖ 보통 가죽으로 만들어진, 지폐를 안에 넣기 위한 작고 납작한 접이식 케이스[갑]. 지갑

wal·lop /ˈwɑləp/ *v* [T] INFORMAL to hit someone or something very hard ‖ 사람이나 사물을 매우 세게 치다. 되게 때리[패]다. 강한 일격을 가하다

wal·low /ˈwɑlou/ *v* **1** DISAPPROVING to allow yourself to feel sad, upset, or full of pity, especially for too long a time ‖ 특히 너무 오랫동안 자신을 슬프거나 혼란스럽게, 또는 연민으로 가득하게 하다. …에서 헤어나지 못하다: *wallowing in self-pity/despair* 자기 연민[절망]에 빠짐 **2** [I] to roll around in mud, water etc. for pleasure ‖ 즐기기 위해 진흙탕·물속에서 이리저리 구르다. 뒹굴다: *pigs wallowing in the mud* 진흙탕에서 뒹굴고 있는 돼지들

wall·pa·per /ˈwɔlˌpeɪpɚ/ *n* [U] paper that you stick onto the walls of a room in order to decorate it ‖ 방의 벽면에 장식하기 위해 붙이는 종이. 벽지 – **wallpaper** *v* [T]

Wall Street /ˈ. ./ *n* **1** a street in New York City where the American STOCK EXCHANGE is ‖ 미국 증권 거래소가 있는 뉴욕 시의 거리. 월가 **2** the American STOCK EXCHANGE ‖ 미국 증권 거래소

wall-to-wall /ˌ. . ˈ./ *adj* covering the whole floor ‖ 바닥 전체를 덮는. 바닥 전체에 깔린: *wall-to-wall carpeting* 바닥 전체에 융단을 깔기

wal·nut /ˈwɔlnʌt/ *n* **1** a slightly bitter nut with a large light brown shell, or the tree on which this grows ‖ 연갈색의 큰 껍질을 가진 약간 쓴 견과, 또는 이것이 열리는 나무. 호두(나무) **2** [U] the dark brown wood of this tree ‖ 이 나무의 진갈색 목재. 호두나무 목재

wal·rus /ˈwɔlrəs, ˈwɑl-/ *n* a large sea animal similar to a SEAL with two long thick teeth ‖ 두 개의 길고 두툼한 이빨을 가진 물개와 유사한 큰 바다 동물. 바다코끼리

waltz¹ /wɔlts/ *n* a fairly slow dance with a RHYTHM consisting of patterns of three beats, or the music for this dance ‖ 3박자 형태로 된 리듬의 상당히 느린 춤, 또는 이 춤을 위한 음악. 왈츠(곡)

waltz² *v* [I] **1** to dance a WALTZ ‖ 왈츠를 추다 **2** INFORMAL to walk somewhere calmly and confidently ‖ 차분하고 자신 있게 어디로 걸어가다. 경쾌하게[춤추듯이] 걷다: *Jeff waltzed up to the bar and poured himself a drink.* 제프는 성큼성큼 바 쪽으로 다가가서는 자신의 잔에 술을 따랐다.

wan /wɑn/ *adj* looking pale, weak, or tired ‖ 창백하거나 약하거나 피로해 보이는. 파리한. 병약한. 힘없는: *a wan smile* 힘없는 웃음

wand /wɑnd/ *n* a thin stick you hold in your hand to do magic tricks ‖ 마술을 하기 위해 손에 쥐는 가는 막대. 요술 지팡이

wan·der /ˈwɑndɚ/ *v* **1** [I, T] to move or travel around an area without a clear direction or purpose ‖ 분명한 방향이나 목적 없이 한 지역을 돌아다니거나 왔다갔다 하다. 헤매다. 배회하다. 어슬렁거리다: *I'll just wander around the mall for a while.* 나는 쇼핑몰이나 그냥 잠시 둘러봐야겠다. / *wandering the streets* 거리를 배회하기 **2** [I] also **wander off** to move away from where you are supposed to stay ‖ 머물러 있기로 한 곳에서 벗어나다. 이탈하다: *Don't let her wander off.* 그녀를 이탈하지 못하게 해라. **3** [I] to start to talk or write about something not related to the main subject that you were talking or writing about before ‖ 전에 말하거나 글을 써 왔던 주된 주제와 관련되지 않는 것에 대해 말하거나 쓰기 시작하다. 주제에서 벗어나다[일탈하다]: *The book's plot wanders a little.* 그 책의 줄거리는 주제에서 약간 벗어나 있다. **4** [I] if your mind, thoughts etc. wander, you no longer pay attention to something ‖ 마음·생각 등이 더 이상 어떤 것에 주의를 쏟지 않다. 종잡지 못하다. 정신[넋]이 나가다: *She's getting old, and sometimes her mind wanders.* 그녀는 점점 나이가 들면서 때때로 정신이 나간다. – **wanderer** *n*

wane¹ /weɪn/ *v* [I] **1** if something such as power, influence, or a feeling wanes, it becomes gradually less strong or less important ‖ 세력[영향력, 감정]이 점차 약화되거나 중요하지 않게 되다. 약해지다. 쇠퇴하다: *My enthusiasm for the project was waning.* 그 프로젝트에 대한 내 열정은 식어 가고 있었다. **2** when the moon wanes, you gradually see less of it ‖ 달이 점차 줄어드는 것을 보게 되다. 이지러지다

wane² *n* **on the wane** becoming smaller, weaker, or less important ‖ 더 작아지게[약해지게, 중요하지 않게] 돼가는. 기울기[떨어지기] 시작하여. 종말에 가까워져: *The President's popularity seems to be on the wane.* 대통령의 인기도가 떨어지는 것 같다.

W

wan·gle /ˈwæŋɡəl/ v [T] INFORMAL to get something by persuading or tricking someone ‖ 사람을 설득하거나 속여서 어떤 것을 얻어내다. 감쪽같이 가로채다. 속여서 …시키다: *I managed to **wangle** an invitation out of George.* 나는 가까스로 조지로부터 초청장을 얻어냈다.

wan·na /ˈwʌnə, ˈwɑnə/ SPOKEN NONSTANDARD **1** a short form of "want to" ‖ "want to"의 단축형: *I don't **wanna** go.* 나는 가고 싶지 않아. **2** a short form of "want a" ‖ "want a"의 단축형: *Do you **wanna** sandwich?* 샌드위치 먹을래?

wan·na·be /ˈwɑnəˌbi/ n INFORMAL someone who tries to look or behave like a famous or popular person, or wants to become involved in a famous or popular group ‖ 유명하거나 인기 있는 사람처럼 보이거나 행동하려 하는, 또는 유명하거나 인기 있는 집단에 동참하기를 원하는 사람. …이 되고 싶은 사람. 지망자: *young **wanna-be** gang members* 조직 폭력배가 되고 싶어 하는 젊은이들

want¹ /wʌnt, wɑnt, wɔnt/ v [T] to have a desire or need for something ‖ 무엇에 대한 욕구나 필요성을 갖다. …을 원하다. 바라다. 갖고 싶어 하다: *What do you **want** for your birthday?* 네 생일에 갖고 싶은 것이 뭐냐? / *I don't **want** any more milk, thanks.* 고맙지만 우유는 더 이상 마시고 싶지 않아. / *They talked about moving, but Mark doesn't **want** to leave Iowa.* 그들은 이사에 대한 이야기를 했지만 마크는 아이오와를 떠나고 싶어 하지 않는다. / *Carlson **wants** him to take the work on vacation.* 칼슨은 휴가 때 그가 그 일을 맡아 주기를 원한다. / *I can pick it up on my way to work if you **want**.* (=if you would like that) 네가 원한다면 출근길에 받아서 갈게. —see usage note at DESIRE²

want for sth *phr v* [T] to not have something that you need ‖ 필요한 것이 없다. 부족하다. 모자라다: *Those kids have never **wanted for** anything.* 그 애들은 무엇 하나 부족한 것이 없었다.

want² n [C, U] something that you desire or need but do not have ‖ 원하거나 필요하지만 가지고 있지 않은 것. 결핍. 부족: *We watched television for **want** of anything better to do.* 우리는 할 만한 더 좋은 일이 없어서 TV를 봤다.

want ad /ˈ. ./ n a small advertisement that you put in a newspaper if you want to employ someone to do a job ‖ 일할 사람을 채용하고 싶을 때 신문에 게재하는 작은 광고. 구인 광고

want·ed /ˈwʌntɪd/ adj someone who is

wanted is being looked for by the police ‖ 사람이 경찰에 의해 수배중인: *The man is **wanted** for murder.* 그 남자는 살인 혐의로 수배중이다.

want·ing /ˈwʌntɪŋ/ adj proven to be not good enough ‖ 충분히 좋지 않은 것으로 판명된. 부족한. 모자라는. 없는: *Traditional solutions had been tried and found **wanting**.* 전통적인 해결책으로 시도해 봤지만 부족한 것으로 나타났다.

wan·ton /ˈwɑntˀn, ˈwɔn-/ adj **1** deliberately causing damage or harm for no reason ‖ 고의로 아무 이유 없이 손상이나 해를 끼치는. 고의에 의한. 의도적인: *wanton destruction* 고의적인 파괴 **2** OLD-FASHIONED a wanton woman is considered sexually immoral ‖ 여성이 성적으로 부도덕한 것으로 생각되는. 바람기 있는. 부정(不貞)한. 음탕한

war /wɔr/ n [C, U] **1** a time when two or more countries or opposing groups within a country fight each other with soldiers and weapons ‖ 두 개 이상의 나라들이나 한 국가 내의 대립하는 집단들이 병사와 무기로 서로 간에 싸우는 때. 전쟁. 교전. 무력 충돌: *In 1793 England was at war with/against France.* 1793년 영국은 프랑스와[에 대항해] 전쟁 중에 있었다. / *Was your dad in the war?* 네 아빠는 그 전쟁에 참전했니? / *What would happen if we lost this war?* 우리가 이 전쟁에서 진다면 어떻게 될까? / *the war between the states* 국가간의 전쟁 **2** a struggle to control or stop a bad or illegal activity ‖ 나쁘거나 불법적인 활동을 통제하거나 중지시키려는 투쟁. 근절[퇴치] 활동[전쟁]. 일제 단속: *the war on/against drugs* 마약과의[에 대한] 전쟁 **3** a situation in which a person or group is fighting for power, influence, or control ‖ 사람이나 집단이 세력[영향력, 지배력]을 위해 싸우는 상황. 싸움. 분쟁. 투쟁: *a trade war* 무역 전쟁 — **war** v [I]

war·ble /ˈwɔrbəl/ v [I, T] to sing with a high, continuous, but rapidly varying sound, the way a bird does ‖ 높고 지속적이지만 급속히 변하는 소리로 새들이 하듯이 노래하다. 목소리를 고음으로 떨면서 노래하다

war crime /ˈ. ./ n an illegal and cruel act done during a war ‖ 전쟁 중에 자행된 불법적이고 잔인한 행동. 전쟁 범죄 — **war criminal** /ˈ. ˌ.../ n

ward¹ /wɔrd/ n **1** a part of a hospital where people who need medical treatment stay ‖ 의학적 치료가 필요한 사

람들이 머무는 병원의 구역. 병동. 병실:
the maternity ward (=for women who
are having babies) 산부인과 병동 / *the
children's ward* 소아 병동 **2** LAW
someone, especially a child, who is
under the legal protection of another
person or of a law court ‖ 다른 사람이나
법원의 법적 보호 하에 있는 사람, 특히 어
린아이. 피후견인. 피보호자

ward² *v*

ward sth ↔ **off** *phr v* [T] to do
something to protect yourself from an
illness, danger, attack etc. ‖ 자신을 질
병·위험·공격 등으로부터 보호하기 위해
어떤 것을 하다. 피하다. 막아내다: *a
spray to ward off insects* 벌레를 퇴치하
는 (살충제) 분무기

war·den /'wɔrdn/ *n* the person in
charge of a prison ‖ 교도소를 책임 맡고
있는 사람. 교도소장

war·drobe /'wɔrdroʊb/ *n* the clothes
that someone has ‖ 사람이 갖고 있는 옷.
의상 (목록): *This skirt is the newest
addition to my wardrobe.* 이 치마는 내
의상(목록)에 가장 최근에 추가한 것이다
[산 것이다].

ware·house /'wɛrhaʊs/ *n* a large
building for storing large quantities of
goods ‖ 대량의 상품을 저장하기 위한 큰
건물. 창고

wares /wɛrz/ *n* [plural] LITERARY things
that are for sale, usually not in a store
‖ 보통 상점에 있는 것이 아닌 판매용 물
건들. 제품. 상품

war·fare /'wɔrfɛr/ *n* [U] a word
meaning the activity of fighting in a
war, used especially when talking about
particular methods of fighting ‖ 전쟁에서
전투 활동을 의미하는 말로 특히 특정한
전투 방법을 언급할 때 쓰여. …전(쟁):
chemical warfare 화학전

war game /'. ./ *n* an activity in which
soldiers fight an imaginary battle in
order to test military plans ‖ 군사 계획을
시험하기 위해 군인들이 가상의 전투를 하
는 활동. 도상 작전. 전쟁 게임

war·head /'wɔrhɛd/ *n* the explosive
part at the front of a MISSILE ‖ 미사일 앞
부분의 폭발하는 부분. 탄두

war·like /'wɔrlaɪk/ *adj* **1** threatening
war or attack ‖ 전쟁이나 공격의 조짐이
있는. 도발적인. 전쟁이 일어날 것 같은:
a warlike gesture 도발적인 몸짓 **2** liking
war and being good at it ‖ 전쟁을 좋아하
고 잘 하는. 호전적인: *a warlike
reputation* 호전적인 명성

war·lock /'wɔrlɑk/ *n* a man who is
supposed to have magic powers ‖

especially to do bad things ‖ 특히 좋지
않은 일들을 하기 위한 마력을 지닌 것으
로 생각되는 사람. 마법사. 마술사

war·lord /'wɔrlɔrd/ *n* a leader of a
military or fighting group, usually an
unofficial one ‖ 보통 비공식적인 군사나
전투 집단의 지도자. 장군. 군사령관

warm¹ /wɔrm/ *adj* **1** slightly hot,
especially pleasantly ‖ 특히 기분 좋게 약
간 뜨거운. 따뜻한. 훈훈한: *Are you
warm enough?* 꽤 따뜻합니까? / *I hope
we get some warmer weather soon.* 날씨
가 곧 조금 더 따뜻해졌으면 좋겠다. / *a
warm bath* 온(수)욕 —see usage note at
TEMPERATURE **2** able to keep in heat or
keep out cold ‖ 열을 지켜 주고 냉기를 막
을 수 있는. 따뜻한. 보온의: *warm
clothes* 보온 의류 **3** friendly ‖ 친절한. 마
음이 따뜻한. 진심어린: *a warm smile* 따
뜻한 미소 –**warmly** *adv*

warm² *v* [I, T] also **warm up** to
become warm or warmer, or to make
someone or something do this ‖ 따뜻해지
거나 점점 더 따뜻해지다, 또는 사람이나
사물을 이렇게 되게 하다. 녹다. 녹이다.
데우다: *Here, warm yourself by the fire.*
이봐, 불 옆에서 몸 좀 녹여라. / *There's
some soup warming up in the pot.* 냄비
에 데우고 있는 수프가 좀 있다.

warm to sb/sth *phr v* [T] also **warm up
to** to begin to like someone or
something ‖ 사람이나 사물을 좋아하기 시
작하다. 호의적으로 되다. 마음이 끌리다:
*Bruce didn't warm to him as he had to
Casey.* 브루스는 케이시에게 하듯이 그에
게는 호의적이지 않았다.

warm up *phr v* [I,T **warm** sb **up**] to do
gentle physical exercises to prepare
your body for exercise, singing, etc. ‖ 몸
을 운동·노래 등에 대비하도록 격하지 않
은 가벼운 운동을 하다. 준비 운동을 하
다: *warming up before the race* 경주 전
의 준비 운동

warm-blood·ed /ˌ. '../ *adj* having a
body temperature that remains fairly
high whether the temperature around it
is hot or cold ‖ 주위의 온도가 높든 낮
든 상당히 높은 체온을 유지하는. 정온(定
溫)의. 온혈의: *Mammals are warm-
blooded animals.* 포유동물은 온혈동물이
다. —compare COLD-BLOODED

warmed o·ver /ˌ. '../ *adj* **1** food that
is warmed over has been cooked before
and then heated again for eating ‖ 음식
이 이미 전에 조리되어 먹기 위해 다시 데
워진. 재가열의 **2** an idea or argument
that is warmed over has been used
before and is no longer interesting or

useful ‖ 생각이나 주장이 전에 이미 사용되어서 더 이상 흥미롭거나 유용하지 않은. 재탕의. 새로운 맛이 없는. 식상한

warm-heart·ed /ˌ ˈ ˌ / *adj* friendly and kind ‖ 다정하고 친절한. 마음이 따뜻한. 인정 많은: *a warm-hearted old lady* 인정 많은 노부인

war·mon·ger /ˈwɔr,mʌŋgə, -,mɑŋ-/ *n* someone who is eager to start a war ‖ 전쟁을 시작하기를 열망하는 사람. 전쟁 도발자. 주전론자 – **warmongering** *n* [U]

warmth /wɔrmθ/ *n* [U] **1** a feeling of being warm ‖ 따뜻한 느낌. 따뜻함. 온기: *the warmth of the sun* 햇볕의 온기 **2** friendliness ‖ 친절함. 온정. 마음의 따뜻함: *the warmth of her smile* 그녀의 다정한 미소

warm-up /ˈ. ./ *n* a set of gentle exercises that you do to prepare your body for exercise, dancing, singing etc. ‖ 운동·춤·노래 등을 하기 전에 신체를 대비시키기 위해 하는 일련의 가벼운 운동. 준비 운동. 워밍업

warn /wɔrn/ *v* [I, T] to tell someone that something bad or dangerous may happen, so that s/he can avoid it or prevent it ‖ 다른 사람에게 나쁜 또는 위험한 일이 일어날지 모른다고 말해 주어 피하거나 막을 수 있도록 하다. 경고하다. 주의를 환기하다: *Customers were warned of/about the risks involved.* 수반된 위험에 대해 고객들에게 주의를 시켰다. / *I warned you not to walk home alone.* 나는 네게 집에 혼자서 걸어가지 말라고 경고했다. / *We warned her that something like that might happen.* 우리는 그녀에게 그런 일이 일어날지 모른다고 경고했다.

warn·ing /ˈwɔrnɪŋ/ *n* [C, U] something that prepares you for something bad or dangerous that might happen ‖ 일어날지 모를 나쁘거나 위험한 일에 대비시키는 것. 경고. 주의. 경보: *The planes attacked without warning.* 항공기가 갑자기 공습했다. / *a warning to women over 50* 50세 이상 여성들에 대한 주의(사항) / *You've been given several warnings about this already.* 너는 이미 이에 대해 몇 차례의 경고를 받았다. / *Be aware of warning signs* (=pain etc. that shows that an illness is coming) *such as tiredness and headaches.* 피로와 두통 등 (질환이 진행되고 있음을 나타내는) 경고성 징후를 조심하시오.

warp /wɔrp/ *v* **1** [I, T] to become bent or twisted, or to make something do this ‖ 구부러지거나 비틀리다, 또는 사물이 이렇게 되게 하다. 휘어지다. 뒤틀리다. 휘게 하다. 뒤틀다: *The wet wood had warped in the heat.* 물기 있는 목재는 열을 받아 뒤틀렸다. **2** [T] to have a bad effect on someone so that they think strangely about things. ‖ 사물에 대하여 이상하게 생각하도록 남에게 나쁜 영향을 미치다. 빗나가게[비뚤어지게] 하다. 왜곡하다

war·path /ˈwɔrpæθ/ *n* **be on the warpath** HUMOROUS to be angry about something and want to punish someone for it ‖ 어떤 것에 화가 나서 누군가를 그에 대해 처벌하기를 원하다. 몹시 화가 나 있다. 시비조이다

warped /wɔrpt/ *adj* **1** having ideas or thoughts that most people think are not normal, or showing this quality ‖ 대다수 사람들이 정상이 아니라고 생각하는 아이디어나 생각을 갖는, 또는 이러한 특성을 보이는. 비뚤어진. 뒤틀린. 정상을 벗어난: *a warped sense of humor* 비뚤어진 유머 감각 **2** bent or twisted into the wrong shape ‖ 못쓰게 된 모양으로 구부러지거나 비틀린. 휜. 뒤틀린: *a warped cassette tape* 뒤틀린 카세트테이프

war·rant[1] /ˈwɔrənt, ˈwɑ-/ *v* [T] to be a good enough reason for something to happen or be done ‖ 어떤 일이 일어나거나 이뤄지기에 충분히 좋은 이유가 되다. …의 정당한 이유[근거]가 되다. …을 정당화하다: *The story doesn't really warrant the attention it's been given in the press.* 그 이야기는 실제로 언론에서 받아온 주목거리는 못 된다. —compare UNWARRANTED

war·rant[2] *n* an official paper that allows the police to do something ‖ 경찰이 어떤 일을 할 수 있게 허용하는 공식 문서. 영장: *The police have a warrant for Bryson's arrest.* 경찰은 브라이슨에 대한 체포 영장을 가지고 있다.

war·ran·ty /ˈwɔrənti, ˈwɑ-/ *n* [C, U] a written promise that a company will fix or replace something if it breaks after you have bought it ‖ 물건을 산 후에 고장 나면 회사가 고쳐 주거나 대체해 줄 거라는 문서로 된 약속. 보증(서): *The TV comes with a 3-year warranty.* 그 텔레비전은 3년 보증으로 판매한다.

war·ren /ˈwɔrən, ˈwɑ-/ *n* **1** a set of holes and passages under the ground that rabbits live in ‖ 토끼가 사는 땅 밑의 일련의 굴과 통로들. 토끼굴 **2** a lot of narrow passages in a building or between buildings ‖ 건물 안이나 사이의 많은 좁은 통로들. 미로. 거미줄 같은 통로: *a warren of alleyways and old*

tenement houses 미로 같은 뒷골목과 낡은 공동 주택들

war·ring /ˈwɔrɪŋ/ *adj* fighting in a war ‖ 전쟁에서 싸우는. 투쟁[교전] 중인. 서로 싸우는: *warring factions* 서로 싸우는 파벌들

war·ri·or /ˈwɔriəˌ ˈwɑ-/ *n* LITERARY a soldier, especially an experienced and skillful one ‖ 특히 경험 많고 솜씨가 좋은 병사. 군인. 노병

war·ship /ˈwɔrʃɪp/ *n* a navy ship with guns ‖ 대포를 갖춘 해군 군함. 전함

wart /wɔrt/ *n* a small hard raised spot on your skin caused by a VIRUS ‖ 바이러스에 의해 생긴 피부의 작고 단단하게 솟아오른 돌기. 혹. 사마귀

war·time /ˈwɔrtaɪm/ *n* [U] the time during which a war is happening ‖ 전쟁이 벌어지고 있는 동안의 시간. 전시(중): *a book about his wartime experiences* 그의 전시 중의 경험에 관한 책

war·y /ˈwɛri/ *adj* careful and worried about danger or problems ‖ 위험이나 문제들에 대해 조심하고 걱정하는. 신중한. 경계하고 있는: *Teach children to be wary of strangers.* 아이들에게 낯선 사람을 경계하라고 가르쳐라. **– warily** *adv*

was /wəz/ *strong* /wʌz, wɑz/ *v* the past tense of BE in the first and third person singular ‖ 일인칭·삼인칭 단수형에서 be의 과거형

wash¹ /waʃ, wɔʃ/ *v* **1** [T] to clean something with water ‖ 어떤 것을 물로 깨끗이 하다. 세탁하다. 빨다. 씻다: *These jeans need to be washed.* 이 진으로 된 옷들은 세탁해야 한다. / *Go wash your hands!* 가서 손을 씻어라! / *Wash the mud off the truck.* 트럭에서 진흙을 씻어내라. **2** [I] to clean your body with water ‖ 몸을 물로 깨끗이 하다. 몸을 씻다: *"I'm going upstairs to wash,"* *he called to Marge.* "나는 씻으러 위층에 올라간다."라고 그는 마지에게 소리쳤다 **3** [I, T] if water washes, it flows somewhere or makes something move somewhere ‖ 물이 어느 곳으로 흐르거나 어떤 것을 어딘가로 이동하게 하다. 씻어 내려가다. 휩쓸어 가다: *waves washing softly against the shore* 잔잔히 해변에 밀려오는 파도들 / *Floods washed much of the topsoil away.* 홍수가 많은 표토를 쓸고 내려갔다. / *Their boat washed up/ashore about five miles south.* 그들의 보트는 약 5마일 남쪽 해안으로 밀려

wash

왔다. **4 sth doesn't/won't wash** SPOKEN said when you do not believe someone or you think that other people will not believe him/her ‖ 다른 사람을 믿지 않을 때 또는 다른 사람들이 그 사람을 믿지 않을 거라고 생각할 때 쓰여. 곧이듣지 않다/않을 것이다: *His explanation just didn't wash.* 그의 설명은 그대로 곧이들리지 않았다. **5 wash your hands of sth** to refuse to be responsible for something ‖ 무엇에 대해 책임지기를 거부하다. …에서 손을 떼다: *They want to wash their hands of the whole thing.* 그들은 전체적인 일에서 손을 떼기를 원한다.

wash sth ↔ **down** *phr v* [T] **1** to drink something in order to help you swallow food or medicine ‖ 음식이나 약을 삼키는 것을 돕도록 무엇을 마시다. 삼키다. 삼켜 내리다: *He washed down a mouthful of toast with coffee.* 그는 한 입 가득한 토스트를 커피를 마셔 삼켰다. **2** to clean something using a lot of water ‖ 많은 물로 무엇을 깨끗이 하다. …을 씻어 내다[내리다]: *washing down the driveway* 진입로로 씻어내기

wash off *phr v* [I] if a substance washes off, you can remove it from the surface of something by washing ‖ 어떤 것의 표면을 물로 씻어서 물질을 제거하다. 씻어서 없애다[지우다]: *Will this paint wash off?* 이 페인트는 물로 씻어서 지워질까?

wash out *phr v* [I,T **wash** sth ↔ **out**] to remove dirt, a spot etc. by washing something, or to be removed in this way ‖ 어떤 것을 씻어서 먼지·얼룩 등을 제거하다, 또는 이렇게 제거되다. 씻어 없애다. 씻어 없어지다: *Will you wash out the cups?* 컵들을 씻어 줄래? / *I don't know if that ink will wash out.* 그 잉크가 씻어서 빠질지 나는 모르겠다.

wash up *phr v* [I] to wash your hands ‖ 손을 씻다: *Go wash up for supper* 저녁 먹게 가서 손을 씻어라.

wash² *n* **1** [C, U] clothing, sheets etc. that have been washed or that need washing ‖ 세탁된 또는 세탁이 필요한 옷·시트 등. 세탁(물). 빨래(감): *I did three loads of wash this morning.* 나는 오늘 아침 세 통분의 빨랫감을 세탁했다. / *Your socks are in the wash.* (=being washed or waiting to be washed) 네 양말은 (세탁 중이거나 세탁 할) 세탁물 속에 있어. **2 it will all come out in the wash** SPOKEN said when you think that a problem will be solved without you having to do anything about it ‖ 어떤 문

제에 대해 어떤것도 할 필요 없이 잘 해결
될 것으로 생각할 때 쓰여. 잘 되어 가다.
좋은 결과로 끝나다

wash·a·ble /'wɑʃəbəl/ *adj* able to be
washed without being damaged ‖ 손상
없이 세탁할 수 있는. 물빨래가 가능한: *a
machine washable sweater* 세탁기로 세
탁할 수 있는 스웨터

wash·bowl /'wɑʃboʊl/, **wash·ba·sin**
/'wɑʃ.beɪsən/ *n* ⇨ SINK

wash·cloth /'wɑʃklɔθ/ *n* a small
square piece of cloth that you use to
wash yourself ‖ 몸을 씻는 데 쓰는 작은
사각형의 천 조각. 목욕 수건

washed-out /ˌ. '../ *adj* very tired and
pale ‖ 매우 피곤하고 창백한. 지친 얼굴
의. 야윈: *My parents looked washed-out
after the long trip.* 내 부모님은 긴 여행
끝에 지친 표정이었다.

washed-up /ˌ. '../ *adj* INFORMAL
someone who is washed-up is no longer
successful ‖ 사람이 더 이상 성공적이지
못한. 완전히 실패한. 쓸모가 없는: *a
washed-up rock star* 한물 간 록 음악 가
수

wash·er /'wɑʃɚ/ *n* **1** a washing
machine ‖ 세탁기 **2** a small ring of
plastic or metal that you put between a
NUT and a BOLT, or between two pipes,
to make them fit together tightly ‖ 너트
와 볼트 사이, 또는 두 개의 파이프 사이에
서로 꼭 맞도록 넣는 플라스틱이나 금속제
의 작은 고리. 와셔. 자릿쇠

wash·ing /'wɑʃɪŋ/ *n* [U] clothes etc.
that need to be washed or have just
been washed ‖ 세탁해야 하거나 세탁이
막 끝난 의류 등. 세탁물. 빨래(감): *Hang
the washing on the line.* 빨래를 줄에 널
어라.

washing ma·chine /'.. ../ *n* a
machine that washes clothes ‖ 의류를 세
탁하는 기계. 세탁기

wash·out /'wɑʃ.aʊt/ *n* [singular]
INFORMAL a failure ‖ 실패: *Rosie's date
was a complete washout.* 로지의 데이트
는 완전한 실패였다.

wash·room /'wɑʃrum/ *n* OLD-FASHIONED
⇨ RESTROOM

wasn't /'wʌzənt, 'wazənt/ *v* the short
form of "was not" ‖ "was not"의 단축형:
He wasn't there. 그는 거기 없었다.

WASP, Wasp /wɑsp/ *n* White Anglo-
Saxon Protestant; a white American
whose religion is Protestant, and who is
often fairly rich ‖ White Anglo-Saxon
Protestant(앵글로색슨계 백인 신교도)의
약어; 종교는 프로테스탄트이고 종종 상당
히 부유한 미국 백인

wasp /wɑsp, wɔsp/ *n* a black and
yellow flying insect similar to a BEE, that
can sting you ‖ 벌과 유사하고 사람을 쏘
는 검고 노란 색의 날아다니는 곤충. 말
벌. 나나니벌

waste¹ /weɪst/ *n* **1** [singular, U] the use
of something in a way that is not useful
or sensible, or the act of using more
than you should of something ‖ 어떤 것
을 유익하거나 현명하지 못하게 사용하거
나 규정 이상으로 사용하기. 낭비. 허비:
*My father thought college would be a
complete waste of time/money.* 내 아버
지는 대학에 가는 것을 완전히 시간[돈]
낭비로 여겼다. / *A lot of the food ended
up going to waste.* 많은 음식이 허비되
어 버렸다. **2** [C, U] things that are left
after you have used something, or
things you no longer want ‖ 어떤 것을 사
용하고 난 뒤 남은 것들이나 더 이상 원하
지 않는 것들. 폐기물. 불필요한 것. 쓰레
기: *recycling household waste* 가정 쓰레
기의 재활용 / *laws on the safe disposal
of nuclear/toxic/hazardous wastes* 핵
[독성, 유해] 폐기물의 안전 처리에 관한
법

waste² *v* [T] **1** to use something in a
way that is not effective, or to use more
of it than you should ‖ 사물을 비효율적으
로 이용하거나 규정보다 더 많이 쓰다. …
을 허비[낭비]하다: *Turn off those lights,
you're wasting electricity!* 저 전등들을
꺼라, 전기를 낭비하고 있구나! / *They
wasted a lot of time trying to fix the
computer themselves.* 그들은 컴퓨터를
그들 스스로 고치려 하면서 많은 시간을
허비했다. —see usage note at TIME¹ **2 be
wasted on sb** if something is wasted on
someone, s/he does not understand it or
does not think it is worth anything ‖ 사
람이 어떤 것을 이해하지 못하거나 아무런
가치도 없다고 생각하다. 통하지 않다. 무
시되다. 소용없다: *All the romance in the
movie was wasted on him.* 영화의 모든
낭만적 사랑은 그에게는 통하지 않았다. **3**
SLANG to kill someone ‖ 누군가를 살해하
다. 죽이다 —see also **save your
breath/don't waste your breath**
(BREATH)

waste away *phr v* [I] to gradually
become thinner and weaker because
you are sick ‖ 병에 걸려서 점차 마르고
약해지다. 야위어가다. 초췌[쇠약]해지다:
He's wasting away to nothing. 그는 허깨
비같이 야위어 가고 있다.

waste³ *adj* not being used effectively or
no longer useful ‖ 효율적으로 이용되고
있지 않거나 더 이상 유용하지 않은. 낭비

[허비]되는. 쓸모없는. 폐기된: *waste paper* 폐지

waste·bas·ket /'weɪstˌbæskɪt/ *n* a container into which you put paper etc. that you want to get rid of ‖ 종이 등 버리고 싶은 것을 넣는 용기. 휴지통. 쓰레기통

wast·ed /'weɪstɪd/ *adj* **1** SPOKEN having drunk too much or taken drugs ‖ 너무 많이 술을 마시거나 마약으로 녹초가[인사불성이] 된. 피폐한: *Chuck got wasted at Bryan's party.* 척은 브라이언의 파티에서 인사불성이 되었다. **2** useless ‖ 쓸모없는. 무익한. 헛된: *It had been a wasted trip.* 그것은 무익한 여행이 되어 버렸다.

waste·ful /'weɪstfəl/ *adj* using more than is needed of something or using it badly, so that it is wasted ‖ 사물을 필요한 것보다 더 많이 사용하거나 함부로 사용해서 낭비가 된. 낭비가 많은. 소비적인. 황폐시키는: *wasteful packaging on groceries* 식료품의 필요 이상의 포장

waste·land /'weɪstlænd/ *n* [C, U] a place that is too dry to be used for anything ‖ 너무 건조해서 어느 것에도 이용될 수 없는 곳. 황무지. 불모지: *a wasteland unable to support human life* 사람이 살아갈 수 없는 불모지

waste·pa·per bas·ket /'weɪstˌpeɪpə ˌbæskɪt/ *n* ⇨ WASTEBASKET

watch

Lois is watching TV.

They are looking at the picture.

watch¹ /wɑtʃ, wɔtʃ/ *v* **1** [I, T] to look at and pay attention to something or someone ‖ 다른 사물이나 사람을 주의를 기울여 바라보다. 지켜보다. 주시하다. 관찰하다: *Harry was watching the game on TV.* 해리는 텔레비전으로 그 시합을 보고 있었다. / *I watched carefully for signs of emotion on her face.* 나는 그녀의 얼굴에 나타나는 기색을 주의 깊게 살폈다. **2** [T] to be careful about

something, or about how you use something ‖ 사물에 대해 또는 사물을 어떻게 사용할지에 대해 주의하다. 유의하다: *I should be watching my weight* (=being careful not to become fat). 나는 (뚱뚱해지지 않도록) 내 체중에 주의해야 한다. / *Billy, watch your language!* (=do not use rude words) 빌리, 말조심해라! / *Hey, watch it - you stepped on my toes.* 이봐, 조심해라. 내 발가락을 밟았어. **3** [T] to take care of someone or guard something ‖ 사람을 돌보거나 물건을 지키다. 경호하다. 감시하다. 망보다: *Could you watch the kids for me Saturday night?* 내 대신 토요일 밤에 아이들 좀 봐주시겠어요? —see usage note at SEE

watch for sth *phr v* [T] to look for something, so that you are ready to deal with it ‖ 무엇에 대처할 준비를 하려고 살펴보다. 관찰[주시]하다: *Doctors are watching for any change in his condition.* 의사들은 그의 상태에 어떠한 변화가 있는지 주시하고 있다.

watch out *phr v* [I] to pay attention to what you are doing and be careful about it ‖ 하고 있는 것에 주의를 기울이고 조심하다. 유의하다: *You can ride your bike here, but watch out for cars.* 자전거를 여기서 타도 좋은데 자동차를 조심해라. / *Watch out! You might cut yourself.* 조심해! 베일 수도 있으니.

watch over sth *phr v* [T] to take care of something or guard it ‖ 무엇을 돌보거나 지키다. 망보다. 감시[경계]하다: *The eldest child watches over the younger ones.* 가장 나이가 많은 아이가 더 어린 아이들을 돌보고 있다.

watch² *n* **1** [C] a small clock that you wear on your wrist or carry in your pocket ‖ 팔목에 차거나 주머니에 넣고 다니는 작은 시계. 손목[회중]시계: *My watch has stopped.* 내 시계는 섰다. **2** **keep a (close) watch on** to check a situation or a place carefully so that you always know what is happening and are ready to deal with it ‖ 항상 무엇이 일어나는지를 알고 그것을 처리할 준비를 하도록 상황 또는 장소를 주의 깊게 확인하다. …을 엄중히 감시하다: *Police kept a 24-hour watch on the house.* 경찰은 그 집을 24시간 엄중히 감시했다. / *Wall Street traders are keeping a close watch on gold prices.* 월 가의 증권 거래업자들은 금값을 예의 주시하고 있다. **3** **keep watch** to continue looking around an area in order to warn people of any danger ‖ 사람들에게 모든 위험을 경고하려고 일대를 계속 둘러 보다. 망을 보다:

W

Douglas kept watch while the others slept. 더글라스는 다른 사람들이 잠자는 동안에 망을 보았다. **4 keep a watch out for** to look carefully in order to try to find someone or something, while you are doing other things ‖ 자신이 다른 일을 하는 동안에 사람이나 사물을 찾아보기 위해 주의 깊게 보다: *When you vacuum, could you keep a watch out for my ring?* 진공청소기로 청소할 때 내 반지를 주의 깊게 찾아봐 주겠니? **5 be on the watch for** to be looking and waiting for something that might happen or someone you might see ‖ 발생 가능한 일 또는 만날지도 모를 사람을 찾아 기다리다. …을 빈틈없이 경계하고 있다. …을 지키고[기다리고] 있다: *Be on the watch for pickpockets around here.* 이 근처에서 소매치기를 경계해라. **6** [C, U] people employed to guard or protect someone or something, or the fixed period of the day or night when they do this ‖ 사람 또는 사물을 지키거나 보호하기 위해 고용된 사람, 또는 그들이 이런 일을 하는 낮 또는 밤의 고정된 기간. 감시인. 경비원. 당직[감시] 시간

watch·dog /'wɑtʃdɔg/ *n* **1** a person or group that makes sure other people follow rules ‖ 다른 사람이 규칙을 확실히 지키게 하는 사람 또는 그룹. 감시인. 파수꾼: *a US Department of Energy watchdog committee* 미국 에너지부 감시 위원회 **2** a dog that protects someone's property ‖ 사람의 재산을 지키는 개. 감시견

watch·ful /'wɑtʃfəl/ *adj* careful to notice what is happening, in order to prevent something bad happening ‖ 나쁜 일의 발생을 막으려고 무엇이 일어나는지를 조심스럽게 주시하는. 경계를 하는. 조심스러운: *keeping a watchful eye on the kids* 아이들을 예의 주시하기

watch·mak·er /'wɑtʃ,meɪkɚ/ *n* someone who makes and repairs watches and clocks ‖ 손목시계와 탁상시계를 제조하고 수리하는 사람. 시계 제조[수리]인

watch·man /'wɑtʃmən/ *n* someone whose job is to guard a building or area ‖ 건물·지역을 경비하는 직업인. 야경꾼. 경비원: *the night watchman* 야간 경비원

watch·word /'wɑtʃwɚd/ *n* [singular] the main principle or rule that you think about in a particular situation ‖ 특정한 상황에서 고려하는 주요 원칙 또는 규칙. 표어. 슬로건. 모토: *In the business of real estate, the watchword has been "buy" not "build."* 지금까지 부동산업계의

모토는 "건축" 아닌 "매입"이었다.

wa·ter¹ /'wɔtɚ, 'wɑ-/ *n* [U] **1** the clear colorless liquid that falls from the sky as rain, forms lakes, rivers, and oceans, and is necessary for life to exist ‖ 하늘에서 비로 떨어져 호수·강·대양을 형성하고, 생명이 존립하는 데 필요한 무색투명한 액체. 물: *Would you like a drink of water?* 물 한 잔 드릴까요? / *Ward waded out into the deepest water.* 워드는 가장 깊은 물속으로 걸어 들어갔다. / *floods left the entire area under water* 전 지역을 침수시킨 홍수 / *We sell only the finest fresh water* (=from a lake, river etc. not an ocean) *fish.* 우리는 가장 좋은 민물고기만을 판매한다. **2 in/into hot water** in a situation in which you have a lot of trouble ‖ 많은 분규가 있는 상황에. (…과) 곤경에 빠져: *My brother got into hot water borrowing all that money.* 내 동생은 그 모든 돈을 꾸면서 곤경에 빠졌다.

water² *v* **1** [T] to pour water on a plant or seeds in the ground to help them grow ‖ 성장을 도우려고 땅에 심은 식물·씨앗에 물을 붓다. 식물에 물을 주다: *I've had to water the lawn every day this week.* 나는 이번 주 매일 잔디에 물을 주어야 했다. **2** [I] if your eyes water, they fill with water because they hurt ‖ 눈이 아파서 눈물이 가득하다. 눈물을 흘리다: *The onions are making my eyes water.* 양파는 내 눈에 눈물이 나게 한다. **3** [I] if your mouth waters, it fills with water because you see something that looks good to eat ‖ 먹기에 좋아 보이는 것을 보아서 입에 침이 가득하다. 침을 흘리다

water sth ↔ **down** *phr v* [T] **1** to make something weaker by adding water ‖ 물을 추가해서 어떤 것을 약하게 만들다. 물을 타다. 희석하다: *The whiskey had been watered down.* 그 위스키는 물을 타서 묽게 되었다. **2** to make an idea, statement etc. less strong so that it does not offend or upset anyone ‖ 생각·말 등을 누구도 감정을 상하거나 심란하게 하지 않도록 덜 강하게 하다. 부드럽게 표현하다. 내용을 약화시키다: *We watered down the report a little for the broadcast.* 우리는 방송용으로 그 기사의 표현을 약하게 했다.

wa·ter·bed /'wɔtɚ,bɛd/ *n* a bed made of rubber or soft plastic and filled with water ‖ 고무 또는 부드러운 플라스틱으로 만들어 물을 채운 침대. 물침대

wa·ter·borne /'wɔtɚ,bɔrn/ *adj* carried by water ‖ 물에 의해 운반된. 선박[수상] 수송의. 물로 전염되는: *waterborne* *bacteria* 수인성(水因性) 박테리아

wa·ter·col·or /ˈwɔtəˌkʌlə/ *n* [C, U] a special paint mixed with water, or a painting made with these ‖ 물을 섞은 특수한 물감, 또는 이것으로 만든 그림. 수채화 (물감): *Most of her works are watercolors.* 대부분의 그녀의 작품은 수채화이다.

wa·tered-down /ˌ.. ˈ./ *adj* 1 a watered-down statement, plan etc. is not as strong or offensive as a previous one ‖ 말·계획 등이 이전의 것처럼 강하거나 공격적이지 않은. 싱거운. 김빠진: *watered-down versions of horror movies* 공포 영화의 완화판 2 a watered-down drink has been made weaker by having water added to it ‖ 마실 것 등이 물을 타서 약해진. 묽게 한

wa·ter·fall /ˈwɔtəˌfɔl/ *n* water that falls straight down over a rock or from the top of a mountain ‖ 바위 위에서 또는 산 정상에서 곧바로 떨어지는 물. 폭포

water foun·tain /ˈ.. ˌ../ *n* a piece of equipment in a public place that produces a stream of water that you can drink from; DRINKING FOUNTAIN ‖ 공공장소에 마실 수 있는 물줄기를 만드는 장치. 분수식 물 마시는 곳[음료수대]; 윤 drinking fountain

wa·ter·front /ˈwɔtəˌfrʌnt/ *n* [C] land at the edge of a lake, river etc. ‖ 호수·강 등의 가장자리에 있는 땅. 해변[강변]의 땅: *a new shopping center on the waterfront* 선창가의 신설 쇼핑센터

wa·ter·hole /ˈwɔtəˌhoʊl/ *n* a small area of water in a dry place where wild animals go to drink ‖ 야생 동물이 물 마시러 가는 건조 지대의 물이 있는 작은 장소. 물웅덩이

watering can /ˈ... ˌ./ *n* a container with a long hollow part on the front for pouring water on plants ‖ 식물에 물을 뿌리기 위해 앞쪽에 속이 빈 길쭉한 부분이 달린 통. 물뿌리개

wa·ter·ing hole /ˈ... ˌ./ *n* INFORMAL a place such as a club or BAR where people can buy drinks ‖ 술을 살 수 있는 클럽이나 술집 등의 장소: *the college students' favorite watering hole* 대학생들이 가장 좋아하는 바

wa·ter·logged /ˈwɔtəˌlɔgd, -ˌlɑgd/ *adj* land or an object that is waterlogged is so wet it cannot hold any more water ‖ 땅·물체 등이 물에 너무 젖어 더 이상의 물을 흡수할 수 없는. 물이 흥건한[밴]. 침수된

wa·ter·mark /ˈwɔtəˌmɑrk/ *n* 1 a special design on a piece of paper that

you can only see when it is held up to the light ‖ 빛에 비추어 볼 때에만 볼 수 있는 종이 조각 위의 특수한 무늬. 종이의 비침무늬 2 the mark showing the highest level of a lake, river etc. ‖ 호수·강의 가장 높은 수면을 나타내는 표시. 수위선[표]

wa·ter·mel·on /ˈwɔtəˌmɛlən/ *n* [C, U] a large round green fruit with juicy dark pink flesh and black seeds ‖ 즙이 많고 진한 핑크빛 과육(果肉)과 검은 씨가 있는 커다란 둥근 녹색 과일. 수박 —see picture on page 944

water po·lo /ˈ.. ˌ./ *n* [U] a game played in a swimming pool, in which two teams of players try to throw a ball into their opponents' GOAL ‖ 두 팀의 선수들이 상대방 골에 공을 던져 넣으려고 하는, 수영장 안에서 하는 경기. 수구

wa·ter·proof /ˈwɔtəˌpruf/ *adj* not allowing water to go through ‖ 물이 통과하는 것을 허용하지 않는. (완전) 방수의: *waterproof boots* 방수 (처리된) 부츠

water re·sis·tant /ˈ.. ˌ../ *adj* not letting water in easily, but not keeping all water out ‖ 물을 완전히 차단하지는 못하지만 물이 쉽게 들어오지 못하게 하는. (완전 방수가 아닌) 내수(耐水)의: *a water resistant watch* 내수 시계

wa·ters /ˈwɔtəz/ *n* [plural] 1 the part of the ocean near or belonging to a particular country ‖ 특정한 국가에 속하거나 근처에 있는 대양(大洋)의 일부. 근해. 영해. 수역: *fishing in Icelandic waters* 아이슬랜드 근해의 어업 2 the water in a particular lake, river etc. ‖ 특정한 호수·강 등의 물: *the point where the waters of the Amazon flow into the sea* 아마존 강의 물이 바다로 흘러들어가는 지점

wa·ter·shed /ˈwɔtəˌʃɛd/ *n* 1 [singular] the point at which an important change happens ‖ 중요한 변화가 발생하는 지점. 분기점. 분수령: *The beginning of television was a watershed in 20th century culture.* 텔레비전의 시작은 20세기 문화의 분수령이었다. 2 the high land separating two river systems ‖ 두 개의 하천 수계(水界)로 분기되는 높은 지대. 분수계(分水界)

wa·ter·side /ˈwɔtəˌsaɪd/ *adj* at the edge of a lake, river etc. ‖ 호수·강 등의 가장자리에. 물가의: *a waterside restaurant* 강변의 식당 –**waterside** *n* [singular]

water ski·ing /ˈ.. ˌ../ *n* [U] a sport in which someone is pulled along on skis over water by a boat ‖ 사람이 수상에서

보트가 끄는 스키를 타는 스포츠. 수상 스키: *Do you want to go water skiing?* 수상 스키하러 갈래? – **water ski** *v* [I] – **water skier** *n*

wa·ter·tight /'wɔtə,taɪt/ *adj* **1** not allowing water to get in ‖ 물이 들어오는 것을 허용하지 않는. 물이 스며들지 않는: *a watertight container* 물이 스미지 않는 용기 **2** having no mistakes or weaknesses ‖ 실수 또는 약점이 없는. 완벽한: *a watertight excuse/argument* 완벽한 변명/논의

wa·ter·way /'wɔtə,weɪ/ *n* an area of water, often part of a river, that ships can go through ‖ 선박이 통과할 수 있는, 종종 강의 일부인 수역. 운하. 수로

wa·ter·works /'wɔtə,wəks/ *n* [plural] buildings, pipes, and supplies of water forming a public water system ‖ 공공 용수 체계를 형성하는 건물·파이프·급수원. 급수 시설. 상수도

wa·ter·y /'wɔtəri/ *adj* containing too much water ‖ 너무 많은 물을 머금은. 축축한. 물기가 많은: *watery soup* 묽은 수프 / *watery eyes* 눈물을 머금은 눈

watt /wɑt/ *n* a unit for measuring electrical power ‖ 전력을 측정하는 단위. 와트: *a 100 watt light bulb* 100와트 백열전구

WAV *n* [U] TECHNICAL waveform audio; a type of computer FILE that contains sound ‖ waveform audio(windows 표준 음성 파일형식); 소리를 포함하는 컴퓨터 파일의 일종

wave¹ /weɪv/ *v*
waved, waving 1 [I, T] to move your hand, or something you hold in your hand, as a signal or greeting, or to express something ‖ 신호나 인사로, 또는 어떤 것을 표시하기 위해 손, 또는 손에 쥔 사물을 움직이다. 흔들다. 흔들어 인사[신호]하다: *demonstrators waving their signs* 구호 표지를 흔들고 있는 시위자들 / *Look! They're waving at us.* 봐라! 그들이 우리에게 손을 흔들고 있다. / *I waved goodbye as they pulled out of the driveway.* 나는 그들이 진입로를 빠져나갈 때 손을 흔들어 작별 인사를 했다. **2** [I] if a flag waves, it moves with the wind ‖ 깃발이 바람에 움직이다. 펄럭이다. 나부끼다. 물결치다

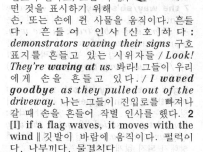
wave

wave sth ↔ **aside** *phr v* [T] to refuse to pay attention to a person or the things

s/he suggests, offers etc. ‖ 다른 사람이 제시·제안하는 사람이나 사물에 대해 주의를 기울이는 것을 거부하다. 퇴짜 놓다. 내치다: *"Not true!" she said, waving aside any further comments.* 더 이상의 언급을 거절하면서 그녀는 "진실이 아니야!"라고 말했다.

wave² *n* **1** an area of raised water that moves across the surface of a large area of water, especially the ocean ‖ 넓은 바다, 특히 대양의 수면을 가로질러 움직이는 솟아 오른 수역. 물마루. 파도. 물결: *Huge waves slammed onto the beach.* 거대한 파도가 해변에 부딪쳤다. **2** a sudden increase in a particular emotion, activity, number etc ‖ 특정한 감정·활동·숫자 등의 갑작스런 증가. 고조. 물결: *Police are trying to fight the recent crime wave in the suburbs.* 경찰은 최근 교외에서의 범죄 급증을 퇴치하려고 노력하고 있다. / *a wave of nostalgia for his childhood* 그의 어린 시절에 대한 밀려오는 향수 / *a huge wave of immigrants from Eastern Europe* 동유럽으로부터의 거대한 이민의 물결 **3** the movement you make when you wave your hand ‖ 손을 흔들 때 하는 동작. 흔들기: *The Governor gave a wave to the crowd.* 주지사는 군중들에게 손을 흔들어 주었다. **4** a part of your hair that curls slightly ‖ 약간 곱슬곱슬한 머리: *tight waves of hair* 아주 곱슬곱슬한 머리 **5** the form in which some types of energy move ‖ 몇몇 유형의 에너지가 움직이는 형상. (빛·소리 등의) 파동: *light/sound/radio waves* 광/음/전파 **6** **make waves** INFORMAL to cause problems ‖ 문제를 일으키다. 소동[풍파]을 일으키다: *We have a job to finish, so don't make waves, OK?* 우리는 일을 끝내야 하니까 문제를 일으키지 마라. 알았지? —see also HEAT WAVE

wave·length /'weɪvlɛŋkθ/ *n* **1** the size of a radio wave or the distance between two waves of energy such as sound or light ‖ 전파의 크기 또는 소리나 빛 등의 두 에너지파 사이의 거리. 주파수. 파장 **2** **be on the same wavelength** INFORMAL to think in the same way about something as someone else does ‖ 다른 사람이 하는 것과 같이 어떤 것에 대해 동일하게 생각하다. 생각이 같다

wa·ver /'weɪvə/ *v* [I] to be uncertain or unsteady ‖ 불확실하거나 불안정하다. 흔들리다. 비틀거리다. 주저하다: *Mrs. Shreve wavered as she took a step towards us.* 쉬레브 여사는 우리를 향해 한 걸음 내딛으며 비틀거렸다. / *The*

*president is **wavering between two** options.* 대통령은 두 가지 선택 사이에서 망설이고 있다.

wav·y /ˈweɪvi/ *adj* having waves (=even curved shapes) ‖ 웨이브를 가진. (머리털 등이) 물결치는. 물결처럼 곱슬거리는: *wavy hair* 찰랑거리는 머리

wax¹ /wæks/ *n* [U] a thick substance made of fats or oils, used for making things such as CANDLES ‖ 양초 등을 만드는 데 사용되는 지방이나 기름으로 만든 물질. 밀랍. 왁스

wax² *v* **1** [T] to put WAX on something, especially in order to polish it ‖ 특히 광을 내기 위해 물체에 왁스를 바르다. …을 왁스로 닦다[칠하다]: *The floors had been waxed recently.* 그 마루는 최근에 왁스로 닦았다. **2 wax romantic/ eloquent etc.** OFTEN HUMOROUS to talk eagerly about someone or something you admire, especially for a long time ‖ 자신이 숭배하는 사람이나 사물에 대해 특히 오랫동안 열심히 말하다. 낭만적으로/유창하게 묘사하다[찬양하다]: *Jamie sat at the bar, waxing poetical about Marcie.* 제이미는 술집에 앉아서 마시에 대해 시적으로 묘사했다. **3** [I] when the moon waxes, you gradually see more of it ‖ 달이 점점 더 많이 보이다. 달이 차다

waxed pa·per /ˌ. ˈ../, **wax paper** *n* [U] paper with a thin layer of WAX on it, used for wrapping food ‖ 얇은 왁스 층이 있는 음식을 포장하는 데 쓰이는 종이. 밀랍[파라핀] 종이

wax·y /ˈwæksi/ *adj* **1** made of WAX or covered in wax ‖ 왁스나 밀랍으로 만들었거나 덮인. 밀랍을 입힌: *apples with a waxy skin* 매끈한 껍질을 가진 사과 **2** looking or feeling like WAX ‖ 밀랍같이 보이는, 밀랍처럼 느껴지는: *vines with waxy leaves* 밀랍 같은 잎을 가진 포도덩굴 – **waxiness** *n* [U]

way¹ /weɪ/ *n*

1 ▶ROAD/PATH 도로/길◀ the road, path etc. that you have to follow in order to get to a particular place ‖ 특정한 장소에 도달하기 위해 따라가야 하는 도로·통로 등. 길: *Which way should we go?* 우리는 어느 길로 가야 하니? / *Can you mail this on your way downtown for me?* 시내[집]에 가는 길에 이 우편물을 부쳐 주겠니? / *Could you tell me the way to the police station from here?* 여기서 경찰서로 가는 길을 가르쳐 주시겠어요? / *I can give you a ride; it's on my/the way.* 내가 태워다 줄게, 가는 길이니까.

2 ▶DIRECTION 방향◀ a particular

direction ‖ 특정한 방향. 쪽. 방면: *Which way is north from here?* 여기서 북쪽은 어느 쪽이냐? / *Face this way, please.* 이쪽을 보세요. / *Move three steps this way.* 이쪽으로 세 걸음 옮기세요.

3 ▶METHOD 방법◀ [C] a manner or method of doing something or thinking about something ‖ 어떤 것을 하거나 생각하는 방식 또는 방법. 수단. 방책: *Nobody could figure out a way to solve the problem.* 아무도 그 문제를 해결할 방법을 생각해 낼 수 없었다. / *I'd like to tell her in my own way.* 나는 내 나름으로 그녀에게 말하고 싶다. / *Look at the way that guy's dressed!* 저 녀석이 옷 입은 꼴 좀 봐라! / *Ryan has a funny way of talking.* 라이언은 말투가 재미있다.

4 in a way/in some ways used in order to say that something is partly true ‖ 어떤 것이 부분적으로는 진실하다고 말하는 데에 쓰여. 그럭저럭. 얼마간. 어느 면에서는: *In a way, I like working alone better.* 어떤 면에서 나는 혼자 일하는 것을 더 좋아한다.

5 ▶ DISTANCE/TIME 거리/시간◀ [singular] also **ways** the distance or time between two places or events, especially if it is long ‖ 특히 멀리[길게] 떨어져 있는 두 장소나 사건 사이의 거리나 시간. 노정(路程): *a long way from home* 집에서 먼 거리 / *We have a ways to go yet before we're done.* 우리는 다하려면 아직 멀었다. / *Did he actually come all the way* (=the whole distance) *from Bali?* 그는 정말로 발리로부터 그 먼 길을 왔느냐?

6 have/get your way to do what you want even if someone else wants something different ‖ 남이 다른 것을 원할지라도 자신이 원하는 일을 하다. 제멋대로 하다: *They always let that kid get his own way.* 그들은 항상 그 아이가 제멋대로 하게 놔둔다.

7 the way/sb's way where someone wants to go ‖ 사람이 지나가기를 원하는 곳: *There was a big truck in the way.* (=preventing people from going past) 큰 트럭 한 대가 사람들의 통행을 막고 있다. / *Get out of my way!* (=move aside) (길을) 비켜!

8 get in the way of sth to prevent something from happening ‖ 어떤 것이 일어나는 것을 막다. …의 방해가 되다: *Don't let your social life get in the way of your studying.* 사교생활이 네 학업에 방해가 되지 않게 해라.

9 come a long way to have developed a lot ‖ 크게 발전하다. 많은 발전을 이루다:

Psychiatry has come a long way since the 1920s. 정신의학은 1920년대 이래 크게 발전했다.

10 a long way to go to need a lot of time to develop or reach a particular standard ‖ 특정한 수준에까지 발전하거나 도달하는 데 많은 시간이 필요하다. …까지 갈 길이 멀다: *There is a long way to go before democracy is accepted there.* 그곳에 민주주의가 받아들여지기까지는 갈 길이 멀다.

11 under way happening or moving ‖ 발생 또는 동작중인. 시작[진행]되어. 진척중인: *Building work is scheduled to get under way* (=start happening) *today.* 건축 공사가 오늘 착수하기로 예정되어 있다.

12 be on the way/its way/sb's way to be arriving soon ‖ 곧 도착하게 되다. … 도중이다. 진행[다가오는] 중이다: *The check is on its way.* 계산서를 가져오고 있습니다. / *Carla's already on her way here.* 칼라는 이미 이리 오고 있다.

13 way around a particular order or position that something should be in ‖ 사물이 있어야 할 특정한 순서나 위치. 제자리. 올바른 위치: *Which way around does this skirt go?* 이 스커트는 어느 쪽으로 입어야 하지? / *Make sure all the pictures are the right way around.* 모든 그림들이 올바른 위치에 있는지 확인해라.

14 give way to if one thing gives way to another thing, this other thing replaces it or controls it ‖ 다른 사물이 어떤 사물을 대체하거나 지배하다. 길을 내주다[양보하다]. 지다. 굴복하다: *fear gave way to anger* 분노로 바뀐 공포

15 go out of your way to do sth to do something that involves making a special effort, especially for someone else ‖ 특히 다른 사람을 위해 특별한 노력이 수반되는 어떤 일을 하다. 일부러 …하다: *Ben went out of his way to help us.* 벤은 우리를 일부러 도우려고 했다.

16 you can't have it both ways used in order to say that you cannot have the advantages of two different possible decisions ‖ 가능성 있는 두 가지의 서로 다른 결정으로 이득을 볼 수 없다는 것을 말하는 데에 쓰여

17 make way a) to move to one side so that someone or something can pass ‖ 사람 또는 사물이 지나갈 수 있게 한쪽 옆으로 움직이다. 길을 내주다 **b)** if one thing makes way for something else, this other thing replaces it ‖ 다른 물건이 어떤 물건을 대체하다. 양보하다. 물러나다: *Several houses were torn down to make way for a new fire station.* 새 소

방서를 짓기 위해 여러 채의 집이 철거되었다.

18 by the way said when you want to begin talking about a new subject that you have just remembered ‖ 자신이 방금 생각해 낸 새로운 주제에 대해 말을 시작하고자 할 때 쓰여. 그건 그렇고. 그런데: *Oh, by the way, I saw Marie yesterday.* 아, 그건 그렇고. 나는 어제 마리를 보았어.

19 no way! a) used in order to say that you will definitely not do or allow something ‖ 단연코 어떤 것을 하지 않거나 허용하지 않을 거라고 말하는 데 쓰여. 절대로 안돼. 천만의 말씀: *"Dad, can I have the car tonight?" "No way!"* "아버지, 오늘밤 자동차 좀 쓸 수 있어요?" "절대로 안돼!" **b)** used in order to say that you do not believe something or are surprised by it ‖ 어떤 것을 믿지 않거나 그것으로 인해 놀랐다고 말하는 데 쓰여. 말도 안돼: *She's 45? No way!* 그녀가 45살이라고? 말도 안돼!

20 way to go! used in order to tell someone that s/he has done something good, or done something very well ‖ 다른 사람에게 좋은 일을 했거나 어떤 일을 아주 잘했다고 말하는 데 쓰여. 잘 한다. 훌륭히 해냈어! — see also **out of the way** (OUT²)

───────────────────────────

USAGE NOTE on the way and in the way

Use **on the way** to talk about something you do while you are going somewhere, or a place that you will pass as you go there: *I'll get some gas on the way home. / The campground is on the way to the lake.* Use **in the way** to say that something is preventing you from getting to the place where you are going: *I can't get through the gate because your car is in the way.*

on the way는 어떤 곳에 가고 있는 도중에 하는 일, 또는 거기에 가면서 통과할 곳에 대해 말하는 데 쓴다: 집에 가는 도중에 기름 좀 넣겠다. / 야영장은 호수로 가는 길에 있다. **in the way**는 어떤 것이 가려고 하는 곳에 도달하는 것을 막고 있다고 말하는 데에 쓴다: 네 차가 가로막고 있어서 나는 출입문을 통과할 수 없다.

way² *adv* **1** long in distance or time ‖ 거

리가 멀거나 시간이 오래 전에. 먼 이전
에. 저 멀리에: *We took the boat way
out into the ocean.* 우리는 보트를 타고
바다 저 멀리 나갔다. / *a movie made
way back before they used sound* 음향
을 사용하기 훨씬 이전에 제작된 영화 **2
way more/bigger/longer etc.** SPOKEN
NONSTANDARD a lot more, bigger, longer
etc. ‖ 훨씬 많은/큰/긴: *This test was way
harder than the last one.* 이번 시험은 지
난 번 시험보다 훨씬 어려웠다.

way·lay /'weɪleɪ/ *v* [T] LITERARY to stop
someone so that you can talk to
him/her, or in order to harm or rob
him/her ‖ 사람이 말을 걸거나 해를 가하
거나 강탈하기 위해서 남을 불러 세우다.
잠복하여 습격하다. 길가에서 불러 세우
다

way of life /ˌ. . './ *n, plural* **ways of
life** the way someone lives, or the way
people in a society usually live ‖ 사람이
사는 방식, 또는 사회의 사람들이 보통 사
는 방식. 생활 방식: *the American way
of life* 미국인의 생활 방식

way·out /ˌ. '. / *adj* SPOKEN very modern
and strange ‖ 아주 현대적이고 이상한. 첨
단의. 전위적인: *I like jazz, but not the
way-out stuff.* 나는 재즈를 좋아한다. 그
렇지만 전위적인 것은 좋아하지 않는다.

way·side /'weɪsaɪd/ *n* **fall/go by the
wayside** to stop being successful,
important, popular etc. ‖ 성공하게, 중요
하게, 유명하게 되지 못하다. 중도에서 단
념하다. 보류되다: *With so many
domestic problems, foreign policy issues
fell by the wayside.* 너무 많은 국내 문제
들로 인해서 대외 정책의 쟁점은 밀려났
다.

way·ward /'weɪwərd/ *adj* not following
rules, and causing problems ‖ 규칙을 준
수하지 않고 문제를 일으키는. 제멋대로
인: *a wayward teenager* 제멋대로인 10
대

we /wi/ *pron* **1** the person who is
speaking and one or more other people
‖ 말하고 있는 사람과 한 사람 이상의 다
른 사람들. 우리: *We went to a bar that
night.* 우리는 그날 밤 술집에 갔다. / *We
live in Dallas.* 우리는 달라스에서 산다. **2**
people in general ‖ 일반적인 사람들. 우
리 인간[사람]: *We know almost nothing
about what causes the disease.* 우리는
그 병의 원인이 무엇인지에 대해서는 거의
아는 것이 없다. / *We all dream of being
rich one day.* 우리 모두는 어느날 부자가
되는 꿈을 꾼다.

weak /wik/ *adj* **1** not physically strong
‖ 육체적으로 강하지 않은. (허)약한:

Kate's still weak from her illness. 케이트
는 병으로 인해 아직 허약하다. / *a weak
heart* 약한 심장 **2** not strong in
character, and easily influenced ‖ 성격
이 강하지 않고 쉽게 영향을 받는. 의지가
약한. 심약한: *He's weak and afraid to
make decisions.* 그는 심약하여 결정내리
기를 두려워한다. **3** not having much
ability or skill in a particular activity or
subject ‖ 특정한 활동 또는 분야에서 많은
능력 또는 기량을 갖고 있지 않은. 모자라
는. 서투른: *I'm good at math, but weak
at/in science.* 나는 수학에는 강하지만 과
학에는 약하다. **4** not having much
power or influence ‖ 많은 힘 또는 영향력
이 없는. 미약한. 약화된. 힘이 없는: *a
very weak leader* 힘이 미약한 지도자 **5**
not being good enough to persuade or
influence people ‖ 사람들을 설득하거나
영향을 미치기에 충분하지 않은. 설득력이
약한. 별로 감명을 못 주는: *a weak
excuse* 설득력이 약한 변명 **6** containing
a lot of water or having little taste ‖ 물
을 많이 포함하거나 맛이 거의 없는.
묽은. 싱거운: *weak tea* 연하게 탄 차
– weakly *adv*

weak·en /'wikən/ *v* [I, T] **1** to become
less powerful or physically strong, or to
make someone or something do this ‖ 힘
이 약해지거나 육체적으로 더 약해지다.
또는 사람이나 사물을 이렇게 되게 하다.
약화되다[시키다]. 무력해지다[무력하게
만들다]: *The disease has weakened her
heart.* 그 질병은 그녀의 심장을 약화시켰
다. / *a country weakened by war* 전쟁으
로 무력해진 국가 **2** to become less
determined, or to make someone do this
‖ 단호함이 덜 해지다. 또는 남을 이렇게
되게 하다. 여려[물러]지다: *Nothing
could weaken her resolve.* 아무것도 그
녀의 결심을 흔들리게 할 수 없었다.

weak·ling /'wik-lɪŋ/ *n* DISAPPROVING
someone who is not physically strong ‖
육체적으로 강하지 않은 사람. 약골

weak·ness /'wiknɪs/ *n* **1** [U] the state
of lacking strength in your body or
character ‖ 신체 또는 성격에서 힘이 부
족한 상태. 허약. 심약: *weakness in the
muscles* 근육 쇠약 **2** a fault in
someone's character or in a system,
organization, design etc. ‖ 사람의 성격
[시스템, 조직, 디자인] 등에서의 결점. 약
점: *What do you think are your
strengths and weaknesses?* 너의 강점과
약점은 무엇이라고 생각하니? / *The cost
of the plan is its main weakness.* 계획의
비용이 그 주요 약점이다. **3 a weakness
for sth** if you have a weakness for

something, you like it very much even though it may not be good for you ‖ 자신에게 좋지 않을 수 있더라도 어떤 것을 매우 좋아함. …에 대한 지나친 기호[탐닉]: *She's always had a weakness for chocolate.* 그녀는 항상 초콜릿이라면 사족을 못 썼다.

wealth /wɛlθ/ *n* **1** [U] a large amount of money and possessions ‖ 대량의 돈과 재물. 재화. 부: *a family of great wealth* 엄청난 부(富)를 가진 가문 **2 a wealth of experience/choices etc.** a large amount of experience, a large number of choices etc. that can help you do something ‖ 어떤 것을 하는 데 도움을 줄 수 있는 많은 경험과 많은 선택의 기회 등. 풍부한 경험/선택: *the wealth of information that is available on the Internet* 인터넷상의 이용 가능한 풍부한 정보

wealth·y /'wɛlθi/ *adj* **1** having a lot of money or valuable possessions ‖ 많은 돈 또는 값비싼 재물을 갖고 있는. 부유한. 풍족한: *a very wealthy man* 매우 부유한 남자 **2 the wealthy** people who have a lot of money or valuable possessions ‖ 많은 돈 또는 값비싼 재물을 소유한 사람. 부자(들)

wean /win/ *v* [I, T] to gradually stop feeding a baby on his/her mother's milk and start giving him/her ordinary food ‖ 아기에게 모유 먹이기를 점차 중단하고 보통 음식을 주기 시작하다. 젖을 떼다. 이유시키다: *She was weaned at eight months.* 그녀는 8개월에 젖을 떼었다.

wean *sb* **off** *sth phr v* [T] to make someone gradually stop doing something you disapprove of ‖ 자기가 좋지 않다고 생각하는 것을 남으로 하여금 점차 중단하게 하다. 단념시키다. 멀리하게[버리게] 하다: *I'm still trying to wean my daughter off sugary snacks.* 나는 내 딸이 달콤한 스낵류를 먹지 못하게 하려고 아직도 애쓰고 있다.

wean *sb* **on** *sth phr v* [T] **be weaned on** INFORMAL to be influenced by something from a very early age ‖ 너무 이른 나이부터 어떤 것의 영향을 받다. …에 의해 키워지다: *young movie directors who were weaned on MTV videos* MTV 비디오를 보고 자란 젊은 영화감독

weap·on /'wɛpən/ *n* something that you use to fight with, especially a knife or gun ‖ 싸우는 데 사용하는 물건 특히 칼 또는 총. 무기 – **weaponry** *n* [U]

wear¹ /wɛr/ *v* **wore, worn, wearing 1** [T] to have something on your body, especially clothes or jewelry ‖ 몸에 특히

옷이나 보석을 착용하다. 입고[쓰고, 신고] 있다. 달고[차고, 끼고] 있다: *Why aren't you wearing your glasses?* 왜 안경을 끼고 있지 않니? / *I think I'll wear my black jeans to Pat's party.* 나는 팻의 파티에 검정 진 바지를 입을 생각이야. **2** [T] to have your hair in a particular style ‖ 특정한 스타일로 머리를 하다. …한 상태로 머리를 기르다: *Fay wore her hair in braids.* 페이는 머리를 땋아 늘였다. **3** [I, T] to become thinner, weaker etc. by continued use, or to make something do this ‖ 계속 사용하여 더 얇아지고 더 약해지다, 또는 물건을 이렇게 되게 하다. …을 해지게[닳게] 하다. 마멸되다: *The rug had worn in several places.* 그 양탄자는 여러 군데가 해졌다. / *He's worn a hole in his pants already.* 그의 바지는 닳아서 벌써 구멍이 뚫려 있다. **4** [T] to have a particular expression on your face ‖ 얼굴에 특별한 표정을 하다. (표정·모양·태도 등을) 띠고[나타내고] 있다: *wearing a smile* 미소 띠기 **5 wear well** to remain in good condition after a period of time ‖ 일정 기간 뒤에도 양호한 상태로 남아 있다. 오래 가다: *Expensive fabrics don't always wear well.* 값비싼 직물이 항상 오래 가는 것은 아니다. **6 sth is wearing thin** INFORMAL if an excuse, explanation, opinion etc. is wearing thin, it has been used so often that you no longer believe or accept it ‖ 변명·설명·견해 등이 너무 자주 쓰여서 더 이상 신뢰하거나 받아들이지 않다. 효과·믿음·재미가 줄어들다[다하다] **7 wear the pants** INFORMAL to be the person in a family who makes the decisions ‖ 집안에서 의사 결정을 하는 사람이 되다. (여자가) 집안 어른 노릇하다 —see usage note at DRESS¹

wear *sth* ↔ **away** *phr v* [I, T] to gradually become thinner, weaker etc., or to make something do this by using it, rubbing it etc. ‖ 점차로 더 얇아지고 약해지다. 또는 물건을 사용하고 문질러서 이렇게 되게 하다. 닳아 없애다. 마멸[침식]하다[시키다]: *Look at where the rocks have been worn away by the sea.* 바위가 바닷물에 의해 침식되어 온 것을 보아라.

wear down *phr v* **1** [I,T **wear** *sth* ↔ **down**] to gradually become smaller, or to make something do this by using it, rubbing it etc. ‖ 점차로 더 작아지다, 또는 물건을 사용하거나 문지르는 등으로 이렇게 되게 하다. 닳게 하다. 마멸[침식]해 가다[시키다]: *My shoes have worn down at the heel.* 내 구두는 뒤축이 닳아

서 없어졌다. **2 [T wear** sb ↔ **down]** to make someone physically weaker or less determined ‖ 사람을 육체적으로 더 약하게 하거나 결심이 해이해지게 하다. 지치게 하다. 기진맥진하게 하다: *He won simply by wearing down his opponent.* 그는 자신의 상대를 지치게 해서 간단히 이겼다.

wear off *phr v* [I] if pain or the effect of something wears off, it gradually stops ‖ 어떤 것의 아픔·효과 등이 점점 멈추다. 점점 약해지다[없어지다]: *The drug was starting to wear off.* 그 약은 효력이 점점 떨어지기 시작하고 있었다.

wear on *phr v* [I] if time wears on, it passes very slowly ‖ 시간이 매우 천천히 지나가다. 경과하다: *It became hotter as the day wore on.* 날이 갈수록 더워졌다.

wear out *phr v* [I, T] **1 [wear** sth ↔ **out]** to become weak, broken, or useless, or to make something do this by using it a lot or for a long time ‖ 약해지게[고장 나게, 쓸모없게] 되다, 또는 어떤 것을 많이 또는 오래 사용해서 이렇게 되게 하다. 너무 써서 쇠약하게[부서지게, 못 쓰게] 되다[되게 하다]. 다 써버리다: *I think these batteries have worn out.* 난 이 배터리들은 다 닳았다고 생각된다. **2 [wear** sb ↔ **out]** to feel extremely tired, or to make someone feel this way ‖ 너무나 피로하게 느끼다, 또는 남을 이렇게 느끼게 하다. 지치다[지치게 하다]: *You look really worn out.* 너는 정말 지친 것같이 보인다. **3 wear out your welcome** to stay at someone's house longer than s/he wants you to ‖ 어떤 사람의 집에 그 사람이 원하는 것보다 더 오래 머물게 나다. 미움을 받다

wear² *n* **1** [U] normal damage caused by continuous use over a long period ‖ 장기간 계속 사용하여 발생한 정상적인 손상. 마손. 마멸: *The tires are showing signs of wear and tear.* 그 타이어들은 마모의 흔적을 나타내고 있다. **2** [U] the amount of use you can expect to get from something ‖ 물건에서 얻기를 기대할 수 있는 사용량. 내구력. 예상 사용 수명: *You'll get a lot of wear out of a sweater like that.* 그런 스웨터는 오래 입을 수 있을 것이다. **3** clothes of a particular type, or worn for a particular activity ‖ 특정한 유형, 또는 특정 활동시 입는 옷: *evening wear* 야회복

wea·ri·some /'wɪrɪsəm/ *adj* FORMAL making you feel bored, tired, or annoyed ‖ 사람을 지루하게[피곤하게, 속 상하게] 느끼게 하는. 지치게 하는. 지겨

운: *a wearisome task* 지겨운 일

wea·ry¹ /'wɪri/ *adj* very tired ‖ 매우 피곤한: *weary of arguing* 말다툼에 진력이 난 / *The nation is weary of war and poverty.* 그 나라는 전쟁과 가난에 진저리가 나 있다. **– wearily** *adv* **– weariness** *n* [U]

weary² *v* [I, T] FORMAL to become very tired especially because you have been doing something for a long time, or to make someone feel this way ‖ 특히 오랫동안 어떤 것을 해서 매우 피곤해지다, 또는 사람을 이렇게 느끼게 하다. …으로 피곤해지다[싫증나다]. 남을 …으로 피곤하게[싫증나게] 하다: *Jacobs soon wearied of his job at the bank.* 제이콥스는 곧 자신의 은행 업무에 싫증이 났다.

wea·sel¹ /'wizəl/ *n* **1** an animal like a long thin rat that kills other small animals ‖ 다른 작은 동물을 죽이는 길고 홀쭉한 쥐처럼 생긴 동물. 족제비 **2** INFORMAL someone who has been disloyal to you or has deceived you ‖ 남에게 불성실하고 남을 속이는 사람. 교활하고 비열한 사람

weasel² *v*

weasel out of sth *phr v* [I] INFORMAL to avoid doing something you should do by using dishonest excuses or lies ‖ 정직하지 않은 변명이나 거짓말로 자신이 해야 할 일을 하는 것을 피하다. 책임을 회피하다. 약속을 어기다. 얼버무리다: *We made a deal, and you can't weasel out of it.* 우리는 약정을 했으니 너는 그것을 회피할 수 없다.

weath·er¹ /'wɛðɚ/ *n* **1** [singular, U] the temperature and other conditions such as sun, rain, and wind ‖ 기온과 태양·비·바람 등의 다른 조건들. 날씨: *What was the weather like on your vacation?* 휴가 중에 날씨는 어땠니? / *very dry/wet/hot/cold weather* 매우 건조한 [습한, 더운, 추운] 날씨 **2 under the weather** INFORMAL slightly sick ‖ 약간 아픈. 몸이 찌뿌드드한. 좀 기분이 나쁜: *I'm feeling a little under the weather.* 나는 몸이 좀 찌뿌드드하다.

USAGE NOTE weather

There are many words for talking about the weather. **Wind** is a general word for the air when it moves. A **breeze** is a pleasant, gentle wind. A **gust** is a sudden strong wind, and a **gale** is an extremely strong wind. **Rain** is water that falls from clouds. If it is raining hard, it is **pouring**. If it is raining a little, it is a **drizzle**. When rain lasts only a short time, it is a **shower**. When rain begins to freeze, it is **sleet**. Hard, frozen drops of rain are **hail**. Frozen **rain** that falls in soft white pieces is **snow**. A **storm** is a general word for bad, wet weather. A **hurricane** is a storm with an extremely strong wind, that usually moves over water. A **tornado** is a cloud that spins and can destroy things, that moves as part of a storm over land. Both hurricanes and tornados are types of **cyclone**, which is a strong wind that moves in a circle. A **blizzard** is a bad winter storm with a lot of wind and snow. A **drought** is a long period with no water. When a lot of water suddenly covers an area that is usually dry, it is a **flood**.

날씨에 대해서 말하는 데는 많은 어휘가 있다. **wind**는 공기가 움직이는 것에 대한 일반적인 말이다. **breeze**는 상쾌하고 산들산들 부는 미풍이다. **gust**는 갑작스레 이는 강한 돌풍이다. **gale**은 지극히 강한 강풍이다. **rain**은 구름에서 떨어지는 물이다. 비가 억수로 퍼붓는 것은 **pouring**이라 하고 비가 부슬부슬 약간 오는 것은 **drizzle**이라 한다. 비가 짧은 시간 동안만 지속하여 내리는 것은 **shower** (소나기)라 한다. 비가 얼기 시작하면 **sleet** (진눈깨비)라 한다. 딱딱하게 얼어붙은 빗방울은 **hail** (우박)이라 한다. 비가 얼어서 부드러운 하얀 조각으로 떨어지는 것은 **snow** (눈)라 한다. **storm**이란 비가 동반된 악천후이다. **hurricane**은 보통 바다 위에서 이동하는 아주 강한 바람을 동반한 폭풍이다. **tornado**는 폭풍의 일부로서 지상에서 이동하는 것으로 회오리쳐서 물건들을 파괴할 수 있는 구름이다. 허리케인과 토네이도는 모두 원을 그리며 움직이는 강한 바람인 **cyclone** 종류이다. **blizzard**는 많은 바람과 눈을 동반한 혹독한 겨울 폭풍이다. **drought**는 장기간 비가 없는 가뭄이다. 보통 건조한 지역을 갑자기 많은 비가 와서 쓸어버리는 경우를 **flood** (홍수)라 한다.

weather[2] *v* **1** [T] to come through a very difficult situation without failing ‖ 실패 없이 매우 어려운 상황을 뚫고 나가다. 극복하다: *Business was bad, but we knew we would weather the storm.* 사업은 어려웠지만 우리는 우리가 난관을 극복할 것을 알고 있었다. **2** [I, T] to change or be changed in color or shape

over a period of time because of sun, rain, wind etc. ‖ 태양·비·바람 등의 이유로 장기간 동안 색깔·형상을 변화하거나 변화되다. 변색하다[시키다]. 풍화하다[시키다]: *a weathered statue* 풍화된 조상 (彫像)

weather fore·cast /ˈ.. ˌ../ *n* a report saying what the weather is expected to be like in the near future ‖ 가까운 장래에 날씨가 어떻게 될 것인가 예상되는 것을 일러주는 보도. 일기 예보

weather fore·cast·er /ˈ.. ˌ.../ *n* someone on television or radio who tells you what the weather will be like ‖ 날씨가 어떠할 것이라고 텔레비전이나 라디오에서 말하는 사람. 일기 예보자

weath·er·man /ˈwɛðəˌmæn/ *n* a male WEATHER FORECASTER ‖ 남성 일기 예보자

weather vane /ˈwɛðə ˌveɪn/ *n* a metal object attached to the top of a building, that moves to show the direction the wind is blowing ‖ 바람이 부는 방향을 보여주며 움직이는, 건물의 꼭대기에 부착된 금속 물체. 풍향계

weave[1] /wiv/ *v* **wove** *or* **weaved**, **woven** *or* **weaved**, **weaving** **1** [I] to make threads into cloth by crossing them under and over each other on a special machine ‖ 특수한 기계에서 위아래로 실을 서로 가로질러서 옷감을 만들다. 실로 천을 짜다: *They weave beautiful cloths in Ireland.* 아일랜드 사람들은 아름다운 옷감을 짠다. **2** [T] to make something by weaving or by twisting pieces of things together ‖ 물체의 조각들을 서로 짜거나 꼬아서 어떤 것을 만들다. …을 엮어서[짜서] …으로 만들다: *weaving a basket* 바구니 짜기 **3** [I, T] to move somewhere by turning and changing direction a lot ‖ 방향을 자주 돌리거나 바꿔서 어떤 곳으로 이동하다. (길을) 누비며 나아가다: *The snake was weaving through the grass towards us.* 그 뱀은 풀밭을 요리조리 가르며 우리 쪽으로 다가왔다. – **weave** *n*

weave[2] *n* the way in which a material is woven, and the pattern formed by this ‖ 재료를 짜는 방식과 이렇게 짜서 생기는 무늬. 짜기. 엮기. 엮은[짠] 것: *a fine weave* 촘촘하게 짠 것

web /wɛb/ *n* **1** a net of sticky thin threads made by a SPIDER to catch insects ‖ 곤충을 잡으려고 거미가 만든 끈적끈적한 가는 실의 그물. 거미줄 **2 a web of sth** a closely related set of things that can be very complicated ‖ 매우 복잡해질 수 있는 긴밀히 연결된 것들. 얽히고 설킨[복잡한] 관계[정세]: *a web*

of lies 이리저리 꾸며낸 거짓말 **3 the Web** ⇨ WORLD WIDE WEB

webbed /wɛbd/ *adj* webbed feet or toes have skin between the toes ‖ 발이나 발가락 사이에 피부가 있는. 물갈퀴가 있는: *a duck's webbed feet* 오리의 물갈퀴를 가진 발

web·cast¹ /'webkæst/ *n* a programme that is broadcast on the Internet ‖ 인터넷 상에서 방송되는 프로그램. 인터넷 방송

web de·sign·er /'. .,../ *n* someone who designs WEBSITEs, especially websites for businesses or organizations ‖ 특히 사업체나 단체 등을 위한 웹사이트를 디자인하는 사람. 웹 디자이너

web-foot·ed /,. '../, **web-toed** '../ *adj* having toes that are joined by pieces of skin ‖ 피부의 일부분들로 연결된 발가락을 가진. 발에 물갈퀴가 있는

web·mast·er /'web,mæstə/ *n* someone who organizes a WEBSITE and makes sure it keeps working properly ‖ 웹사이트를 조직화하고 제대로 작동하도록 하는 사람. 웹 마스터

web·page /'webpeɪdʒ/ *n* all the information that you can see in one section of a website. You have to CLICK on a button to go to another webpage on the same website. ‖ 웹사이트에서 버튼을 눌러 페이지간 이동하며 그중 한 섹션에서 볼 수 있는 모든 정보. 웹페이지

web·site /'websaɪt/ *n* a program on a computer that is connected to the INTERNET and gives information about a particular subject or product ‖ 인터넷에 연결되어 특정한 주제나 제품에 대한 정보를 제공하는 컴퓨터 프로그램. 웹사이트

we'd /wid/ **1** the short form of "we had" ‖ "we had"의 단축형: *We'd better go now.* 우리는 지금 가는 것이 낫겠다. **2** the short form of "we would" ‖ "we would"의 단축형: *We'd rather stay.* 우리는 차라리 머물러 있겠다.

wed /wɛd/ *v* wed or wedded, wed or wedded, wedding **1** [I, T] LITERARY to marry someone ‖ (어떤 사람과) 결혼하다 **2 be wedded to sth** to be unable or unwilling to change a particular idea or way of doing things ‖ 특정한 생각이나 일을 하는 방식을 변경할 수 없거나 변경하는 것을 꺼리다. 집착[몰두]하고 있다: *Most California commuters are wedded to their cars* 대부분의 캘리포니아 통근자들은 자가운전을 고집한다.

wed·ding /'wɛdɪŋ/ *n* a marriage ceremony, especially one with a religious service ‖ 특히 종교적인 예식이 있는 결혼 의식. 결혼식: *Have you been invited to their wedding?* 너는 그들의 결혼식에 초대 받았니?

wedding ring /'.. ,../ *n* a ring worn to show that you are married, given to you on your wedding day ‖ 결혼식 날에 받는 것으로 결혼한 것을 나타내려고 끼는 반지. 결혼반지

wedge¹ /wɛdʒ/ *n* **1** a piece of wood, metal etc. that has one thick edge and one pointed edge, used for keeping a door open, splitting wood etc. ‖ 문을 열어 놓거나 나무를 쪼개는 데 등에 사용되는 것으로 한쪽 끝은 두껍고 한쪽은 뾰족한 나무·금속 등의 조각. 쐐기 **2** something shaped like a wedge ‖ 쐐기 모양의 사물: *a wedge of chocolate cake* 쐐기 모양의 초콜릿 케이크 / *shoes with wedge heels* 뒤축이 쐐기 모양인 구두

wedge² *v* [T] **1** to force something firmly into a narrow space ‖ 좁은 틈에 어떤 것을 억지로 꽉 밀어 넣다. 물건을 …에 억지로 쑤셔 넣다: *We wedged a towel **under** the door to keep the cold air out.* 우리는 찬바람이 못 들어오게 문 아래에 수건을 쑤셔 넣었다. **2 wedge sth open/shut** to put something under a door, window etc. to make it stay open or shut ‖ 문·창문 등이 열려 있거나 닫혀 있도록 그 아래에 어떤 것을 집어넣다. …을 쐐기로 고정시켜 열다/닫다

wed·lock /'wɛdlɑk/ *n* [U] OLD-FASHIONED **1 born out of wedlock** if a child is born out of wedlock, his/her parents are not married when s/he is born ‖ 아이가 결혼하지 않은 부모에게서 태어난. 사생아의. 서출의 **2 the state of being married** ‖ 결혼한 상태. 결혼 생활. 혼인

Wednes·day /'wɛnzdi, -deɪ/, *written abbreviation* **Wed.** *n* the fourth day of the week ‖ 주(週)의 네 번째 날. 수요일 —see usage note at SUNDAY

wee /wi/ *adj* **1** LITERARY very small ‖ 매우 작은. 조그마한: *a wee child* 조그마한 아이 **2 the wee hours** the early hours of the morning, just after MIDNIGHT ‖ 자정 직후의 이른 아침 시간. 꼭두새벽

weed¹ /wid/ *n* a wild plant that grows where you do not want it to grow ‖ 사람들이 원하지 않는 곳에서 자라는 야생 식물. 잡초

weed² *v* [I, T] to remove WEEDs from a place ‖ 어떤 장소에서 잡초를 제거하다. 잡초를 뽑다. 제초하다

weed sb/sth ↔ out *phr v* [T] to get rid of people or things that are not very good ‖ 그리 좋지 않은 사람이나 물건을 제거하다: *These tests are supposed to*

weed out unsuitable recruits. 이 테스트는 부적합한 입대자들을 제거하기 위한 것이다.

week /wik/ *n* **1** a period of time equal to seven days, beginning on Sunday and ending on Saturday ‖ 일요일에 시작하여 토요일에 끝나는 7일에 해당하는 시기. 주: *The movie starts this week.* 그 영화는 이번 주에 시작한다. / *last/next week* (=the week before or after this one) 지난[다음] 주 **2** any period of time equal to seven days and nights ‖ 7일의 낮과 밤에 해당하는 모든 기간. 한 주: *They spent three weeks in the tropics.* 그들은 열대지방에서 3주를 보냈다. / *In a week,* (=a week after today) *the guests will begin to arrive.* 1주일 후에 손님들은 도착하기 시작할 것이다. / *I'll be back a week from today/tomorrow/Friday.* (=a week after today etc.) 나는 오늘[내일, 금요일]부터 1주일 뒤에 돌아오겠다. / *Are you busy the week after next?* (=the week that follows next week) 너는 다다음주에 바쁘니? **3** also **work week** the part of the week when you go to work, usually from Monday to Friday ‖ 한 주 중 직장에 나가는 월요일에서 금요일까지의 날. 평일: *I don't see the kids much during the week.* 나는 평일에는 아이들을 많이 보지 못한다.

week·day /'wikdeɪ/ *n* any day of the week except Saturday and Sunday ‖ 주 중 토요일과 일요일을 제외한 모든 날. 평일

week·end /'wikɛnd/ *n* Saturday and Sunday ‖ 토요일과 일요일. 주말: *What are you doing this weekend?* (=the weekend that is coming) 너는 이번 주말에 뭐 할거니? / *last/next weekend* (=the weekend before or after this one) 지난[다음] 주말 / *over the weekend* (=during the weekend that is past or that is coming) 주말(중)에 —see usage note at WEEKNIGHT

week·ly /'wikli/ *adj* **1** happening or done every week ‖ 매주 발생하거나 행해지는. 매주의: *a weekly newspaper* 주간 신문 **2** relating to a single week ‖ 단 한 주에 관련되는. 한 주의[마다, 당]: *his weekly rate of pay* 그의 주급 —**weekly** *adv*

week·night /'wiknaɪt/ *n* any night except Saturday or Sunday ‖ 토요일이나 일요일을 제외한 모든 (날의) 밤. 평일 밤

---

beginning of the weekend because they do not have to go to school or work on Saturday. Sunday is part of the weekend, but people call it a **school night** because there is school on Monday.

금요일 밤은 실제로는 "**weeknignt** (평일 밤)"이지만 대부분의 사람들은 토요일에 학교나 직장에 갈 필요가 없기 때문에 주말의 시작으로 본다. 일요일은 주말의 일부분이지만 월요일에 수업이 있기 때문에 사람들은 "**school night** (수업 전날 밤)"이라고 부른다.

---

wee·nie /'wini/ *n* SPOKEN **1** ⇨ HOT DOG **2** a word meaning someone who is weak, afraid, or stupid, used especially by children ‖ 특히 어린이들이 사용하며, 약한[두려워하는, 멍청한] 사람을 의미하는 단어. 비실이. 겁보. 바보

weep /wip/ *v* **wept, wept, weeping** [I, T] to cry ‖ 울다. 흐느껴 울다. 눈물을 흘리다: *She wept as she described the man who had raped her.* 그녀는 자기를 강간한 남자를 묘사하면서 흐느껴 울었다.

weigh /weɪ/ *v* **1** [linking verb] to have a particular weight ‖ 특정한 무게를 가지다. (몸)무게가 …이다: *The baby weighs 12 pounds.* 그 아기는 몸무게가 12파운드 나간다. **2** [T] to use a machine to find out what something or someone weighs ‖ 물체나 사람의 무게가 얼마나 나가는지 알아내려고 기계를 사용하다. (몸)무게를 재다: *Have you weighed yourself lately?* 최근에 네 몸무게를 재봤니? **3** [T] to consider something carefully ‖ 어떤 것을 주의 깊게 고려하다. 신중히 숙고하다. …을 비교 검토하다: *I had to weigh the options pretty carefully.* 나는 선택 사항들을 아주 신중히 평가해 봐야 했다.

weigh down *phr v* [T] **1** [**weigh** sb/sth ↔ **down**] to make someone or something bend or feel heavy under a load ‖ 사람이나 물체를 하중으로 구부러지거나 무겁게 느끼게 하다. 무겁게[내리] 누르다. 짓누르다: *Sally was weighed down with shopping bags.* 샐리는 쇼핑백의 무게에 쳐였다. **2** [**weigh** sb ↔ **down**] to make someone feel worried ‖ 사람을 걱정하게 하다. 짓누르다. 압박하다: *a young man weighed down with responsibilities* 책임감으로 짓눌린 젊은이

weigh in *phr v* [I] **1** to have your weight tested before taking part in a BOXING fight or a horse race ‖ 권투 시합이나 경마에 참가하기 전에 몸무게를 재다. 체중을 재다. 계체하다 **2 weigh in**

(with) INFORMAL to add a remark to a discussion or an argument ‖ 토론이나 논쟁에 말을 덧붙이다. (의기양양하게) 의견을 내놓다[개진하다]: *Everyone at the meeting weighed in with his own opinion.* 그 회의의 모든 사람은 각자 자신의 의견을 앞다퉈 개진했다

weigh on sb *phr v* [T] to make someone feel worried ‖ 사람을 걱정하게 하다. 내리누르다. 괴롭히다: *The problem's been weighing on my mind for a long time.* 그 문제는 오랫동안 내 마음을 짓눌러 오고 있다.

weigh sth ↔ **out** *phr v* [T] to measure an amount of something by weighing it ‖ 무게를 재서 어떤 것의 양을 측정하다. 무게를 달다: *Could you weigh out half a pound of flour for me?* 밀가루 반 파운드만 달아 줄래요?

weight¹ /weɪt/ *n*

1 ▶WHAT SB/STH WEIGHS 사람/사물의 무게◀ [U] how heavy someone or something is, which can be shown when measured by a particular system ‖ 특정한 기구로 재었을 때 나타나는 사람이나 사물의 무게. (몸)무게. 체중: *She's been putting on weight/losing weight lately.* (=becoming heavier/lighter) 그녀는 최근에 살이 찌고[빠지고] 있다.

2 ▶HEAVINESS 무거움◀ [U] the fact of being heavy ‖ 무겁다는 사실. 무게. 중량: *The weight of her boots made it hard for her to run.* 그녀는 부츠의 무게 때문에 달리기가 힘들었다.

3 ▶ HEAVY THING 무거운 것◀ something that is heavy ‖ 무거운 것[짐]: *Omar can't lift heavy weights because he's hurt his back.* 오마는 허리를 다쳐서 무거운 것을 들 수 없다. / *The gym has a rowing machine, step machine, and weights.* 체육관에는 노 젓는 기구, 계단 오르는 기구, 중량 운동 기구들이 있다.

4 ▶FOR MEASURING QUANTITIES 양을 측정하기 위한◀ a piece of metal weighing a particular amount that is balanced against something else to measure what it weighs ‖ 무게를 재려고 다른 것과 대칭하여 균형을 잡는 특정한 양의 무게를 가진 금속 조각. 분동(分銅)

5 ▶RESPONSIBILITY/WORRY 책임감/걱정◀ something that makes you worry ‖ 사람을 걱정 시키는 것. 부담(감). 압박: *Selling the house was a great weight off my mind.* 집을 팔아서 내 마음이 아주 홀가분해졌다.

6 ▶IMPORTANCE 중요성◀ [U] value, influence, or importance ‖ 가치[영향력, 중요성]: *Tina's opinion doesn't carry much weight around here.* 티나의 의견은 이곳에서 별로 중요하게 여기지 않는다.

7 throw your weight around INFORMAL to use your position of authority to tell people what to do in an unpleasant and unreasonable way ‖ 사람들에게 불쾌하고 합당치 못하게 할 일을 지시하는 데 높은 지위를 휘두르다. 권력을 휘두르다. 거만하게 굴다: *Paul is the only manager here who doesn't throw his weight around and give orders to people.* 폴은 이곳에서 사람들에게 거만을 떨면서 명령하지 않는 유일한 지배인이다.

8 pull your weight INFORMAL to do all of the work that you are supposed to do ‖ 마땅히 해야 하는 모든 일을 하다. 자기 몫을 다하다: *If he's not pulling his weight, then talk to him about it!* 만약 그가 자기 몫을 다하지 못하면 바로 그에게 말해라!

weight², **weight down** *v* [T] to add something heavy to something or put a weight on it, especially in order to keep it in place ‖ 특히 어떤 것을 제자리에 고정시키기 위해서 무거운 것을 추가하거나 추를 달다. …에 무게를 더하다. …을 무겁게 하다: *fishing nets weighted with lead* 납으로 무겁게 한 어망

weight·ed /ˈweɪtɪd/ *adj* **weighted in favor/weighted against** producing conditions that are favorable or unfavorable to one particular group ‖ 특정한 집단 하나에 유리하거나 불리한 상황을 조성하는. …에게 유리한/불리한: *The system is weighted against middle-class taxpayers.* 이 제도는 중산층 납세자들에게 불리하다.

weight·less /ˈweɪtlɪs/ *adj* having no weight, especially when you are floating in space ‖ 특히 우주 공간에 떠 있을 때, 무게가 나가지 않는. 중량이 없는. 무중력의 – **weightlessness** *n* [U]

weight·lift·ing /ˈ. ˌ./ *n* [U] the sport of lifting specially shaped weights attached to the ends of a bar ‖ 봉의 끝에 부착된 특별한 모양의 중량 기구를 들어올리는 운동. 역도 – **weight-lifter** *n*

weight·y /ˈweɪti/ *adj* important and serious ‖ 중요하고 심각한. 중대한: *a weighty problem* 중대한 문제

weird /wɪrd/ *adj* INFORMAL unusual and strange ‖ 유별나고 이상한. 기묘한. 별난: *It's weird, but I don't like ice cream very much.* 이상하지만 나는 아이스크림을 별로 좋아하지 않는다.

weird·o /ˈwɪrdoʊ/ *n* SPOKEN someone who behaves strangely, wears unusual

W

clothes etc. ‖ 이상하게 행동하거나 별난 옷을 입거나 하는 사람. 괴짜. 기인

welch /wɛltʃ/ *v* [I] INFORMAL ⇨ WELSH

wel·come¹ /'wɛlkəm/ *interjection* said in order to greet someone who has just arrived ‖ 방금 도착한 사람을 반기는 데에 쓰여. 어서 오십시오. 환영합니다: *Welcome to Chicago!* 시카고에 오신 것을 환영합니다! / *Welcome back – it's good to see you again.* 잘 돌아왔어. 너를 다시 보니 기쁘다.

welcome² *adj* **1** someone who is welcome is accepted by people as being part of a group ‖ 어떤 사람을 한 집단의 일부로서 사람들이 받아들이는. 환영받는: *I had the feeling I wasn't really welcome.* 나는 내가 정말로 환영받지 못한다는 느낌을 받았다. **2** something that is welcome is something people are happy to receive or be given because it helps them ‖ 어떤 것이 도움이 되어서 사람들이 기쁘게 받거나 수용하는. 환영해야 할. 반가운: *a welcome suggestion* 반가운 제안 / *a welcome breeze on a hot day* 무더운 날의 고마운 산들 바람

SPOKEN PHRASES

3 you're welcome! said in order to reply politely to someone who has just thanked you for something ‖ 어떤 것에 대해 방금 감사를 표한 사람에게 공손하게 대답하는 데에 쓰여. 천만에요!: *"Thanks for the coffee." "You're welcome."* "커피 고맙습니다." "별말씀을요." **4 be welcome to sb/sth** used in order to say that someone can be with someone or have something if s/he wants to, because you do not want to ‖ 자신은 원하지 않기 때문에 다른 사람이 원하면 그와 함께 있을 수 있거나 어떤 것을 가질 수 있다고 말하는 데 쓰여. …에 대환영이다: *If Rob wants that job he's welcome to it!* 만약 로브가 그 일을 원하면 대환영이지! **5 be welcome to do sth** used in order say that someone can do something if s/he wants to ‖ 어떤 사람이 원하기만 하면 어떤 것을 할 수 있다고 말하는 데에 쓰여. 기꺼이 …해도 좋다: *You're welcome to stay for lunch.* 점심 식사를 위해 머물러도 좋습니다.

---

welcome³ *v* [T] **1** to say hello in a friendly way to someone who has just arrived ‖ 방금 도착한 사람에게 친밀하게 인사하다. 환영하다. (남을) 맞다: *Jill was welcoming guests at the door.* 질은 문에서 손님들을 맞이하고 있었다. **2** to

gladly accept an idea, suggestion etc. ‖ 생각·제안 등을 기쁘게 받아들이다. 기꺼이 받아들이다: *We would welcome a change in the law.* 우리는 그 법률의 개정을 기꺼이 받아들이겠다.

welcome⁴ *n* the greetings and acceptance you give to someone who has arrived as a guest ‖ 손님으로 도착한 사람에게 하는 인사와 응대(應待). 환영. 환대: *Thank you for your warm welcome.* 따뜻한 환대에 감사드립니다. —see also **wear out your welcome** (WEAR¹)

weld¹ /wɛld/ *v* [I, T] to attach metal objects to each other by melting their edges and pressing them together when they are hot, or to be attached in this way ‖ 금속 물체의 끄트머리를 녹여서 뜨거울 때 함께 눌러서 서로 붙이다, 또는 이런 방식으로 부착되다. …에 용접하다[되다] – **weld** *n* – **welder** *n*

wel·fare /'wɛlfɛr/ *n* [U] **1** also **Welfare** money paid by the government to people who are very poor, not working, sick etc. ‖ 매우 가난한[직장이 없는, 아픈] 사람들에게 정부가 지급하는 돈. 생활 보조금: *Most of my neighbors are on welfare.* 우리 이웃의 대부분은 생활 보호 대상자이다. **2** health, comfort, and happiness ‖ 건강·안락·행복. 복리. 복지: *We're only concerned with your welfare.* 우리는 오직 너의 행복만을 염려할 뿐이다.

we'll /wil; *strong* wil/ the short form of "we will" ‖ "we will"의 단축형: *We'll have to leave soon.* 우리는 곧 떠나야 할 것이다.

well¹ /wɛl/ *adv* **better, best 1** in a good or satisfactory way ‖ 좋거나 만족스럽게. 잘. 만족할 만큼: *Did you sleep well?* 잠은 잘 잤니? / *She doesn't hear very well.* 그녀는 아주 잘 듣지를 못한다. / *Is the business doing well?* (=successful) 사업은 잘 되고 있니? / *a well-dressed young man* 잘 차려입은 젊은이 **2** in a thorough way ‖ 철저하게. 완전히. 충분히: *I don't know her very well.* 나는 그녀를 아주 잘 알지는 못한다. / *Mix the flour and eggs well.* 밀가루와 달걀을 잘 섞어라. **3 as well as** in addition to something else ‖ 다른 것에 추가해서. …뿐만 아니라. …도 마찬가지로: *I'm learning French as well as Italian.* 나는 이탈리아어뿐만 아니라 프랑스어도 배우고 있다. **4 as well** also ‖ …도 또한. 게다가: *I'd like a cup of coffee please, and a piece of apple pie as well.* 커피 한 잔에다 애플파이도 한 조각 주세

요. **5 may/might/could well** used in order to say that something is likely to happen or is likely to be true ‖ 어떤 것이 발생할 것 같거나 사실일 것 같다고 말하는 데에 쓰여. 아마 …일 것이다. …일지 모른다: *What you say may well be true.* 네가 말한 것이 사실일지 모른다. **6 may/might as well do sth** INFORMAL **a)** used when you do not particularly want to do something but you still do it ‖ 어떤 것을 특별히 하고 싶어하지는 않지만 여전히 그것을 하고 있을 때 쓰여. …하는 편이 낫겠다/나았겠다: *We may as well get started.* 우리는 시작하는 편이 낫겠다. **b)** used in order to say that doing something else would have an equally good result ‖ 다른 일을 하는 것이 똑같이 좋은 결과를 얻을 수 있다는 것을 말하는 데 쓰여. …하는 것과 같다. …과 마찬가지이다: *That train was so slow, we might just as well have taken the bus.* 그 기차가 너무 느려서 우리는 버스를 타는 것과 마찬가지였다. **7** very much, or very long in time ‖ 매우 많은, 또는 매우 긴 시간의. 상당히. 꽤. 훨씬: *It was well after 2:00 by the time we finished.* 우리가 끝냈을 때는 2시가 훨씬 넘어서였다. / *I'm well aware of the problem.* 나는 그 문제를 아주 잘 알고 있다. —see usage note at GOOD¹

well² *adj* **better, best 1** healthy ‖ 건강한: *My mother's not very well.* 우리 어머니는 그다지 건강하지 않다. / *I'm feeling a lot better, thanks.* 나는 훨씬 좋아졌어요, 고맙습니다. **2 it's just as well (that)** SPOKEN used in order to say that things have happened in a way that is lucky or good, especially when they may have happened differently ‖ 특히 어떤 일이 다르게 발생할 수도 있었는데 운 좋게 또는 괜찮게 일어났다고 말하는 데에 쓰여. …했다는 것은 운이 좋다. 딱 좋게 되다: *It's just as well I couldn't go to the game, we lost anyhow.* 내가 그 경기를 보러갈 수 없었던 것은 잘된 일이었어. 어쨌든 우리가 졌으니까. **3 it's/that's all very well** SPOKEN used in order to say that you think something is not really good or satisfactory, even if someone else thinks it is ‖ 다른 사람은 어떤 것이 좋거나 만족스럽다고 생각하더라도 자신은 정말로 그렇게 생각하지 않는다고 말하는 데에 쓰여. …하면 능사[만능]다: *It's all very well for you to say you're sorry, but I've been waiting here for two hours!* 너는 미안하다고 말하면 다 되는 줄 알지만, 나는 여기서 두 시간이나 기다렸단 말이야!

well³ *interjection* **1** used in order to pause before saying something, to emphasize what you are saying, or to express surprise ‖ 어떤 것을 말하기 전에 멈추는 데[말하고 있는 것을 강조하는 데, 놀라움을 표시하는 데] 쓰여. 에. 저. 글쎄요. 자. 그건 그렇고: *Mary's been acting strangely and, well, I was worried she might do something stupid.* 메리는 이상하게 행동하고 있어요. 그래서 저, 나는 그녀가 어리석은 짓을 할까 봐 걱정했어요. / *Well, all I can say is it's a total waste of time!* 글쎄, 내가 할 수 있는 애기는, 그것은 전적으로 시간 낭비라는 것이다! / *Well, so Steve's a senior manager now is he?* 그건 그렇고, 스티브가 지금 수석 지배인이라는 말이지? **2** also **oh well** said in order to show that you accept a situation even though it is not a good one ‖ 상황이 썩 좋은 것은 아닐지라도 받아들인다는 것을 나타내는 데에 쓰여. 어쩔[하는] 수 없다: *Oh well, at least you did your best.* 하는 수 없지, 최소한 너는 최선을 다 했잖아. **3** said in order to connect two parts of a story that you are telling ‖ 자신이 말하고 있는 이야기의 두 부분을 연결하려는 데에 쓰여. 그런데. 그래서: *You know that guy I was telling you about? Well, he's been arrested!* 내가 너에게 말했던 그 남자 알지? 그런데 그 남자가 체포되었어!

well⁴ *n* **1** a deep hole in the ground from which water is taken ‖ 물을 퍼내는 지면에 있는 깊은 구멍. 우물 **2** a very deep hole in the ground from which oil is taken ‖ 석유를 채굴하는 지면에 있는 매우 깊은 구멍. 유정(油井)

well⁵, well up *v* [I] LITERARY **1** if liquids well or well up, they rise and start to flow ‖ 액체가 솟아올라 흐르기 시작하다. 분출하다. …을 내뿜다: *Tears began to well up in her eyes.* 그녀의 눈에 눈물이 솟아나기 시작했다. **2** if feelings well or well up, they start to get stronger ‖ 감정이 격해지기 시작하다. 솟구치다: *Anger welled up within him.* 그의 마음속에서 분노가 치밀어올랐다.

well-ad·just·ed /ˌ. .ˈ.-/ *adj* able to deal well with your emotions and with the problems of life ‖ 자신의 감정과 인생의 문제를 잘 처리할 수 있는. 사람이 사회 등에 잘 적응한. 정서적으로 안정된: *She seems pretty well-adjusted to me.* 그녀는 내가 보기에 정서적으로 아주 안정돼 보인다.

well-ad·vised /ˌ. .ˈ.-/ *adj* FORMAL **you would be well-advised to do sth** used when you are strongly advising

W

someone to do something ‖ 남에게 어떤 것을 하도록 강하게 충고할 때 쓰여. …하는 것이 현명한 처사다: *You would be well-advised to see a doctor about that mole.* 그 사마귀에 대해 의사의 진찰을 받는 것이 현명한 처사다.

well-be·ing /ˌ. '../ *n* [U] a feeling of being comfortable, healthy, and happy ‖ 안락하고 건강하며 행복한 감정. 행복. 안녕. 복지: *Regular exercise can improve your sense of well-being.* 규칙적인 운동은 너의 행복감을 향상시킬 것이다.

well-bred /ˌ. '../ *adj* OLD-FASHIONED very polite and knowing what to do in social situations ‖ 매우 예의 바르며 사교적 상황에서 무엇을 할지를 아는. 가정교육을 잘 받은. 품위 있는

well-de·fined /ˌ. '../ *adj* something that is well-defined is very clear and easy to see, recognize, or understand ‖ 어떤 것이 매우 분명하고, 알기[인식하기, 이해하기] 쉬운. 정의가 명확한. 분명하게 서술된: *well-defined muscles* 잘 발달된 근육 / *well-defined rules* 잘 정비된 규칙

well-done /ˌ. '../ *adj* meat that is well-done has been cooked thoroughly ‖ 고기가 완전히 익은. 잘 구워진: *He likes his steak well-done.* 그는 완전히 구워진 스테이크를 좋아한다.

well-groomed /ˌ. '../ *adj* someone who is well-groomed has a very neat and clean appearance ‖ 사람이 매우 말쑥하고 깨끗한 외모를 가진. 말끔한: *a well-groomed young man* 몸차림이 단정한 청년

well-heeled /ˌ. '../ *adj* rich ‖ 부유한: *a well-heeled family* 부유한 가족

well-in·ten·tioned /ˌ. '../ *adj* ⇨ WELL MEANING

well-known /ˌ. '../ *adj* known by a lot of people ‖ 많은 사람들에게 알려진. 주지의. 유명한: *a well-known artist and writer* 유명한 예술가이자 작가

well-mean·ing /ˌ. '../ *adj* intending or intended to be helpful, but often failing or making things worse ‖ 종종 잘못 되거나 사태를 악화시키지만, 도움을 줄 의도이거나 돕기 위해 의도된. 선의의[로 행한]: *well-meaning advice* 선의의 충고

well-off /ˌ. '../ *adj* having enough money to have a very good standard of living ‖ 높은 생활 수준을 유지하기에 충분한 돈을 가지고 있는. 부유한: *They're not extremely rich, but they're very well-off.* 그들은 대단한 부자는 아니지만 매우 부유하다.

well-read /ˌwɛl 'rɛd/ *adj* someone who is well-read has read many books and knows a lot about different subjects ‖ 사람이 많은 책을 읽어서 여러 가지 주제들에 대해서 많이 아는. 박학[박식]한

well-round·ed /ˌ. '../ *adj* **1** someone who is well-rounded has had a wide variety of experiences in life ‖ 사람이 인생에서 광범위하게 다양한 경험을 가진. 다방면의. 다재 다능한 **2** a well-rounded education or background is complete and gives you knowledge of a wide variety of subjects ‖ 교육이나 배경이 완전하며 광범위한 다양한 주제에 관한 지식을 제공해 주는. 폭넓은. 포괄적인

well-spo·ken /ˌ. '../ *adj* able to speak in a clear and polite way ‖ 명확하고 정중하게 말할 수 있는. 표현이 적절한. 말씨가 점잖은

well-thought-of /ˌ. '. ˌ. / *adj* liked and admired by other people ‖ 다른 사람들이 좋아하고 칭송하는. 평판이 좋은

well-timed /ˌ. '../ *adj* said or done at the most suitable moment ‖ 가장 적절한 순간에 말하거나 행한. 때를 잘 맞춘. 시의 적절한: *My arrival wasn't very well-timed.* 나는 때를 아주 잘못 맞추어 도착했다.

well-to-do /ˌ. . '../ *adj* rich ‖ 부유한: *a well-to-do family* 유복한 가정

well-wish·er /'. ˌ../ *n* someone who does something to show that s/he admires someone and wants him/her to succeed, be healthy etc. ‖ 남을 칭송하고 그 사람의 성공·건강 등을 원한다는 것을 나타내려고 어떤 것을 하는 사람. 남의 행복을 비는 사람. 지지자: *Hundreds of well-wishers waved as he climbed off the plane.* 그가 비행기에서 내려오자 수백 명의 지지자들이 손을 흔들었다.

Welsh /wɛlʃ/ *adj* relating to or coming from Wales ‖ 웨일스와 관련되거나 웨일스에서 나온. 웨일스의. 웨일스인의. 웨일스 산(産)의

welsh *v* [I] INFORMAL to not do something you have agreed to do ‖ 하기로 동의한 것을 하지 않다. 약속을 어기다: *He welshed on the deal.* 그는 그 거래를 이행하지 않았다.

welt /wɛlt/ *n* a raised mark on someone's skin where s/he has been hit ‖ 사람 피부에 맞아서 생긴 부은 자국. (매질 등으로) 부푼 자리

wel·ter /'wɛltɚ/ *n* FORMAL **a welter of** a large and confusing number of different details, emotions etc. ‖ 많고 혼란스런 여러 가지의 상이한 내용·감정 등. 혼란(상태). 뒤죽박죽: *a welter of*

information 혼란스런 정보

went /wɛnt/ *v* the past tense of GO ‖ go 의 과거형

wept /wɛpt/ *v* the past tense and PAST PARTICIPLE of WEEP ‖ weep의 과거·과거 분사형

we're /wɪr/ the short form of "we are" ‖ "we are"의 단축형: *We're going to the library.* 우리는 도서관에 갈 거야.

were /wɚ/ *v* the past tense of BE ‖ be의 과거형

weren't /wɚnt, 'wɚənt/ *v* the short form of "were not" ‖ "were not"의 단축형: *Why didn't you tell me that you weren't happy?* 행복하지 않다고 왜 말하지 않았어?

were·wolf /'wɛrwʊlf/ *n* a person in stories who changes into a WOLF ‖ 늑대로 변하는 이야기 속의 사람. 늑대 인간

west¹, West /wɛst/ *n* **1** [singular, U] the direction toward which the sun goes down ‖ 해가 지는 쪽 방향. 서쪽: *Which way is west?* 어느 길이 서쪽이냐? **2 the west** the western part of a country, state etc. ‖ 국가·주 등의 서쪽 부분. 서부 (지역): *Rain will spread to the west later today.* 비는 오늘 늦게 서부 지방까지 내립니다. **3 the West a)** the countries in North America and the western part of Europe ‖ 북미와 서부 유럽의 서부 지역 국가들. 서양. 서방. 서구 **b)** the part of the US west of the Mississippi River ‖ 미시시피강 서쪽의 미국 지역. 서부 **4 out West** in or to the west of the US ‖ 미국 서쪽에[으로]: *I've always wanted to travel out west.* 나는 항상 미국 서부를 여행해 보고 싶었다. —see usage note at NORTH³

west² *adj* **1** in, to, or facing the west ‖ 서쪽에[으로, 을 향한]: *four miles west of Toronto* 토론토 서쪽 4마일 / *the west coast of the island* 섬의 서해안 **2 west wind** a wind coming from the west ‖ 서쪽에서 불어오는 바람. 서풍

west³ *adv* toward the west ‖ 서쪽을 향해. 서쪽으로: *Go west on I-90 to Spokane.* I-90 고속도로를 타고 서쪽으로 스포케인까지 가시오. / *The window faces west.* 창문은 서쪽으로 나 있다.

west·bound /'wɛstbaʊnd/ *adj* traveling or leading toward the west ‖ 서쪽을 향해 이동하거나 이어진. 서쪽으로 가는. 서행(西行)의: *westbound traffic* 서쪽으로 가는 교통 / *the westbound lanes of the freeway* 고속도로의 서행 차선

west·er·ly /'wɛstɚli/ *adj* **1** in or toward the west ‖ 서쪽에[으로]: *sailing in a westerly direction* 서쪽 방향으로의 항해 **2** westerly winds come from the west ‖ 바람이 서쪽에서 불어오는. 서풍의

west·ern¹ /'wɛstɚn/ *adj* **1** in or from the west part of an area, country, state etc. ‖ 지역·국가·주 등의 서쪽 지역의[에서]. 서(부)의[에서]: *western Iowa* 서부 아이오와 **2 Western** in or from the countries in North America and the western part of Europe ‖ 북미와 유럽의 서부 지역 국가들의[에서]. 서방[서구, 서양]의: *Western technology* 서구의 기술 —see usage note at NORTH³

western² *n* a movie about life in the 19th century in the American West ‖ 19 세기 미국 서부의 생활에 대한 영화. 서부극

west·ern·er, Westerner /'wɛstɚnɚ/ *n* someone who comes from the WESTERN part of a country or the western HEMISPHERE ‖ 한 국가의 서부 지역이나 서반구출신의 사람. 서부인. 서양인

Western Eu·rope /ˌ.. ˈ../ *n* the western part of Europe, including places such as Great Britain and Italy ‖ 영국과 이탈리아 등지를 포함하는 유럽의 서부 지역. 서유럽 **— Western European** /ˌ.. ..ˈ../ *adj*

west·ern·ize /'wɛstɚˌnaɪz/ *v* [T] to bring ideas, types of behavior, business methods etc. that are typical of North America and western Europe to other countries ‖ 북미와 서유럽의 보편적인 사상·행동 양식·사업 방식 등을 다른 국가들에 가져오다. 서구화하다

west·ern·most /'wɛstɚnˌmoʊst/ *adj* farthest west ‖ 가장 서쪽의. 극서의: *The westernmost conflict of the American Civil War was fought in Arizona.* 미국 남북 전쟁 중 가장 서쪽의 전투는 애리조나에서 싸웠던 것이다.

west·ward /'wɛstwɚd/ *adj, adv* toward the west ‖ 서쪽을 향한. 서쪽으로(의)

wet¹ /wɛt/ *adj* **1** covered in or full of liquid ‖ 액체로 덮이거나 가득 찬. 젖은. 담근. 절인: *Try not to get your feet wet.* 발이 젖지 않도록 해라. / *a wet sponge* 물에 젖은 스펀지 **2 rainy** ‖ 비가 오는: *wet weather* 비 오는 날씨 **3 not yet dry** ‖ 아직 마르지 않은. 젖어 있는: *wet paint* 아직 마르지 않은 페인트 **4 wet behind the ears** INFORMAL very young and without much experience ‖ 아주 어리며 경험이 많지 않은. 미숙한 **—wetness** *n* [U]

wet² *v* wet *or* wetted, wet, wetting

[T] **1** to make something wet ∥ 어떤 것을 젖게 하다. …을 적시다. 축이다: *Wet this cloth and put it on her forehead.* 이 천을 적시어 그녀의 이마에 놓아라. **2 wet the bed/wet your pants** to make your bed or pants wet because you URINATE by accident ∥ 어쩌다가 오줌을 싸서 침대나 바지를 적시다. 이불/바지에 오줌을 싸다

wet blanket /ˌ. ˈ../ *n* [C] INFORMAL someone who tries to spoil other people's fun ∥ 다른 사람의 재미를 망치려고 하는 사람. 흥을 깨는 사람

wet suit /ˈwɛtsut/ *n* a thick piece of clothing, usually made of rubber, that swimmers wear to keep warm when they are in the water ∥ 수영하는 사람이 물속에서 (몸을) 따뜻하게 하려고 입는, 보통 고무로 만든 두꺼운 옷가지. 잠수복

we've /wiv/ the short form of "we have" ∥ "we have"의 단축형: *We've got to leave by 6:00.* 우리는 6시까지는 떠나야 해.

whack[1] /wæk/ *v* [T] INFORMAL to hit someone or something hard ∥ 사람이나 사물을 세게 치다. 세게 때리다: *I got whacked in the mouth by a baseball.* 나는 야구공에 입을 세게 맞았다.

whack[2] *n* **1** the act of hitting something hard, or the noise this makes ∥ 어떤 것을 세게 치는 행위나 이것이 내는 소리. 강타. 딱 소리 **2 out of whack** INFORMAL if a machine or system is out of whack, it is not working correctly ∥ 기계나 시스템이 제대로 작동하지 않는. 상태가 좋지 않은 **3 take a whack at** INFORMAL to try to do something ∥ 어떤 것을 하려고 시도하다: *I can't open this jar; do you want to take a whack at it?* 나는 이 단지를 열 수가 없어. 네가 한 번 해 볼래?

whacked /wækt/, **whacked out** *adj* SPOKEN **1** very tired ∥ 몹시 지친. 녹초가 된 **2** behaving in a very strange way ∥ 매우 이상하게 행동하는

whale[1] /weil/ *n* **1** a very large animal that swims in the ocean and breathes through a hole on the top of its head ∥ 바다에서 헤엄치며 머리끝에 난 구멍을 통해 숨을 쉬는 매우 큰 동물. 고래 **2 have a whale of a time** INFORMAL to enjoy yourself very much ∥ 대단히 즐기다

whale[2] *v*

whale on *sb/sth phr v* [T] SPOKEN to hit someone or something very hard ∥ 사람이나 물체를 매우 세게 치다. …을 심하게 때리다: *Three guys were just whaling on him.* 세 명이 그를 마구 심하게 때리고 있었다.

whal·er /ˈweilə/ *n* **1** someone who hunts whales ∥ 고래를 잡는 사람. 고래잡이 어부 **2** a boat used for hunting whales ∥ 고래 사냥에 사용되는 배. 포경선

whal·ing /ˈweilɪŋ/ *n* [U] the activity of hunting whales ∥ 고래를 잡는 활동. 고래잡이. 포경

wham[1] /wæm/ *interjection* **1** said when describing the sound of one thing hitting another thing very hard ∥ 한 물건이 다른 물건에 세게 부딪치는 소리를 묘사할 때 쓰여. 쾅: *The car went wham into the wall.* 차는 벽에 쾅 하고 부딪쳤다. **2** said in order to show that something very unexpected suddenly happens ∥ 매우 예기치 않은 일이 갑자기 일어난다는 것을 나타내는 데에 쓰여. 느닷없이: *Everything is going OK and then, wham, you lose your job.* 만사가 잘되어 가다가 느닷없이 일자리를 잃는다.

wham[2] *n* the sound made when something is hit very hard ∥ 사물이 세게 부딪칠 때 내는 소리. 쾅(소리): *a loud wham* 쾅 하는 커다란 소리

wharf /wɔrf/ *n*, *plural* **wharves** /wɔrvz/ a structure that is built out into the water so that boats can stop next to it; PIER ∥ 배가 옆에 붙어서 정박할 수 있도록 바다 쪽으로 세워진 구조물. 부두; (윤) pier

what /wʌt, wat; *weak* wət/ *determiner, pron* **1** used when asking about something that you do not know anything about ∥ 전혀 알지 못하는 어떤 것에 대해 물을 때 쓰여. 무엇. 무슨 일: *What are you doing?* (지금) 뭘 하고 있니? / *What did Ellen say?* 엘런이 뭐라고 말했니? / *What kind of dog is that?* 저 개는 무슨 종이지? / "*I didn't think it would be like this.*" "*What do you mean?*" "나는 이렇게 될 줄은 몰랐다" "무슨 뜻이니?" **2** used in order to talk about things or information, especially in questions that are not direct ∥ 특히 간접 의문문에서 사물이나 정보에 대해 말하는 데에 쓰여: *I'm not sure what you can do.* 나는 당신이 무슨 일을 할 수 있을지 모르겠다. / *I couldn't believe what he was saying.* 나는 그가 말하는 것을 믿을 수가 없었다. / *He showed us what he'd made.* 그는 자기가 만든 것을 우리에게 보여 주었다. **3 have what it takes** to have the ability or courage to do something ∥ 어떤 것을 할 능력이나 용기를 가지다. 필요한[불가결한] 것을 갖추다: *Whitman didn't have what it takes to do the job.* 휘트먼은 그 일을 하는 데

필요한 능력이 없었다.

SPOKEN PHRASES

4 a) said when you have not heard something that someone said ‖ 남이 한 말을 듣지 못했을 때 쓰여. 뭐라고: *"Do you want a fried egg?" "What?"* "계란 프라이를 원하니?" "뭐라고?" **b)** used in order to answer when someone calls your name ‖ 남이 자신의 이름을 부를 때 대답하는 데에 쓰여. 왜: *"Anita?" "What?" "Can you come here for a minute?"* "애니타?" "왜?" "잠시 이쪽으로 올 수 있니?" **5** used at the beginning of a sentence to emphasize what you are saying ‖ 자신이 하고 있는 말을 강조하기 위해 문장의 처음에 쓰여. 정말. 얼마나: *What an idiot!* 정말 바보구나! / *What a nice day.* 정말 날씨 좋다. **6 what about...?** **a)** used in order to make a suggestion ‖ 제안을 하는 데에 쓰여. …하는 건 어때?: *What about sending him an e-mail?* 그에게 이메일을 보내는 건 어때? **b)** used in order to introduce a new person or thing into the conversation ‖ 새로운 사람이나 사물을 대화에 소개하는 데 쓰여. …은 어때?: *What about the salad – should I throw it away?* 샐러드는 어떻게 해? 버려야 해? / *So, I've been enjoying work – what about you?* 그래서, 나는 일이 재미있는데. 너는 어때? **7 What's up?** **a)** used when saying hello to someone you know well ‖ 잘 아는 사람에게 인사할 때 쓰여. 어때? 잘 지내?: *"Hey Chris! What's up, buddy?" "Not a lot!"* "야 크리스! 잘 지내, 친구?" "그럭저럭!" **b)** used in order to ask what is wrong or what is happening ‖ 잘못된 것이나 현재 벌어지고 있는 것에 대해 묻는 데에 쓰여. 뭐야. 어떻게 된 거야: *What's up with this printer – does it work?* 이 프린터 어떻게 된 거야. 작동은 돼? **8 what's happening?** **a)** used in order to ask what people are doing or what a situation is ‖ 사람들이 현재 하고 있는 것이나 현재 상태를 묻는 데에 쓰여. 무슨 일이야[일이 벌어지고 있어]?: *What's happening? What's everyone staring at?* 무슨 일이야? 모두 무엇을 쳐다보고 있어? / *What's happening with your dad's business?* (=how is it?) 너의 아빠 사업은 어떻니? **b)** used when saying hello to someone you know well ‖ 잘 알고 있는 사람에게 안부 인사할 때 쓰여. 어떻게 지내: *Hi, Brad. What's happening, man?* 안녕,

브래드. 자네, 어떻게 지내? **9 what (...) for?** used in order to ask the reason for something or purpose of something 어떤 것에 대한 이유나 목적을 묻는 데에 쓰여. 무엇 때문에. 왜: *"Can I borrow your bike?" "What for?"* "네 자전거를 빌릴 수 있니?" "뭐 하려고?" / *What's this thing for?* 이건 무엇에 쓰는 물건이야? **10 what if...?** **a)** used in order to ask what will happen, especially when it could be something bad or frightening ‖ 특히 나쁘거나 겁나는 일일 수 있을 때 앞으로 무슨 일이 벌어질지 묻는 데에 쓰여. …하면 어떻게 될까?: *What if we get stuck out there in the snow?* 저 밖 눈 속에 우리가 갇히면 어떻게 될까? **b)** used when making a suggestion ‖ 제안할 때 쓰여. …이라면 어떨까?: *What if you just take that part out of the speech?* 연설의 그 부분을 그냥 없애면 어떨까? **11** said when you are very surprised ‖ 매우 놀랐을 때 쓰여. 뭐라고: *"They won't let Martin back into the country." "What?"* "그들은 마틴이 그 나라로 돌아가는 것을 허용하지 않아." "뭐라고?" **12 ... or what?** **a)** used in order to ask if there is another possibility ‖ 다른 가능성이 있는지 묻는 데에 쓰여. (그것) 아니면 무언데[어떻게 되는데]: *Are they doing that to save money, or what?* 그들은 돈을 절약하기 위해 그것을 하고 있는 거야 뭐야? **b)** used in order to show you are impatient when asking a question ‖ 질문을 할 때 조바심 내고 있음을 나타내는 데에 쓰여. 아니면 어떡할 거야?: *Are you coming now, or what?* 너 지금 올 거야, 아니면 말 거야. **13 what's with...?** used in order to ask why someone is behaving strangely or why something strange is happening ‖ 사람이 이상하게 행동하거나 이상한 일이 일어나는 이유를 묻는 데에 쓰여. 무슨 일이 있니? 어떻게 된 거야?: *What's with Nicky? He seems really mad.* 닉에게 무슨 일이 있니? 그는 정말 화난 것 같아.

—see also **guess what/you'll never guess** (GUESS¹), **so what?** (SO¹) —see also usage note at WHICH

USAGE NOTE what

When you are talking to someone and you do not understand what s/he says or you do not hear him/her clearly, it

is polite to say, "I'm sorry, I didn't hear you" or "I'm sorry, I don't understand you." It is not polite to just say, "What?"
남과 대화할 때 남이 말한 것을 이해하지 못하거나 남의 말을 분명하게 듣지 못할 때, "미안하지만 당신 말을 듣지 못했어요." 또는 "미안하지만 당신 말을 이해할 수 없어요."라고 말하는 것이 예의바르다. 단지 "뭐라고?" 말하는 것은 예의바르지 않다.

what·cha·ma·call·it /ˈwʌtʃəməˌkɔlɪt/ *n* SPOKEN a word you use when you cannot remember the name of something ‖ 어떤 것의 이름이 생각나지 않을 때 쓰는 단어. 거시기: *I've broken the whatchamacallit on my bag.* 내 가방의 거시기가 부서졌다.

what·ev·er¹ /wətˈɛvə/ *pron* **1** any or all of the things that are wanted, needed, or possible ‖ 원하는[필요한, 가능한] 것은 어떤 것이나 모두. 무엇이든: *Just take whatever you need.* 네가 필요한 것은 무엇이든 가져 가라. **2** used as a reply to mean that it does not matter what happens ‖ 무슨 일이 일어나든 중요하지 않다는 것을 의미하는 대답으로 쓰여. 아무래도 좋다: *"Do you want to go to the movies?" "Whatever."* "영화 보러 갈래?" "뭐 그러던가." **3** SPOKEN said when you do not know the exact name of someone or something ‖ 사람이나 사물의 정확한 이름을 모를 때 쓰여. 거 뭐더라: *Why don't you invite Steve, or whatever he's called, to supper?* 스티브인가 뭔가 하는 사람을 저녁 식사에 초대해보지 그래?

whatever² *determiner* **1** used in order to talk about anything or everything of a particular type ‖ 특정한 유형의 어느 것 또는 모든 것에 대해 이야기하는 데에 쓰여. 어떤[무슨] …일지라도: *Whatever faults he may have, I still like him.* 그에게 어떤 결점이 있을지라도 나는 여전히 그를 사랑한다. / *Whatever I suggest, she always disagrees.* 그녀는 항상 내가 제시하는 것은 무엇이나 반대한다. **2 whatever you say/want** used in order to agree with someone, when you do not want to argue ‖ 논쟁하고 싶지 않을 때 남에게 동의하는 데에 쓰여. 네가 뭘 말하든/원하든 (난 찬성이야): *"I want to go to Canada this year." "OK, whatever you want."* "나는 올해 캐나다에 가고 싶어." "그래, 너 좋을 대로 해."

whatever³, what·so·ev·er /ˌwʌtsoʊˈɛvə/ *adv* used in order to

emphasize a negative statement ‖ 부정적 진술[발언]을 강조하는 데에 쓰여. 전혀: *She had no money whatsoever.* 그녀는 돈이 전혀 없었다.

wheat /wit/ *n* [U] a plant that produces a grain, used for making flour and food such as bread ‖ 밀가루와 빵 등의 음식을 만드는 데 쓰이는 곡식을 산출하는 식물. 밀

whee·dle /ˈwidl/ *v* [I, T] to persuade someone to do something by saying pleasant things that you do not really mean ‖ 진심이 아닌 남이 듣기 좋은 말을 해서 그가 어떤 일을 하도록 설득하다. 남을 그럴듯한 말로 속이다. 남을 구슬려서 [감언으로 꾀어] …하게 하다: *He wheedled me into paying.* 그는 나를 꾀어서 돈을 지불하게 했다. / *She managed to wheedle $15 out of him.* 그녀는 그럴 듯한 말로 그를 구슬려서 15달러를 받아냈다.

wheel¹ /wil/ *n* **1** one of the round things under a car, bicycle etc. that turns and allows it to move ‖ 자동차나 자전거 등의 밑에서 회전하며 그것들을 움직이게 하는 둥근 물건 중의 하나. 바퀴. 차륜. **2** a flat round part in a machine that turns when the machine operates ‖ 기계가 작동할 때 도는 기계 내의 납작하고 둥근 부분. 바퀴 모양의 것 **3** ⇨ STEERING WHEEL **4 big wheel** INFORMAL an important person ‖ 중요한 사람. 실력자. 거물 —see also WHEELS

wheel² *v* **1** [T] to move something that has wheels ‖ 바퀴가 달린 것을 움직이다. 운전하다. 바퀴를 굴려 이동하다: *She wheeled her bike into the garage.* 그녀는 자전거를 밀어서 차고에 넣었다. **2** [I] to turn around suddenly ‖ 갑자기 빙글 돌다. 선회[회전]하다: *Anita wheeled around and started yelling at us.* 애니타는 빙 돌더니 우리를 보고 고함치기 시작했다. —see also **wheeling and dealing**

wheel·bar·row /ˈwilˌbæroʊ/ *n* a small CART with one wheel in the front and two long handles for pushing it, that you use outdoors to carry things ‖ 옥외에서 물건을 운반할 때 쓰는, 앞에 한 개의 바퀴가 있고 밀기 위한 두 개의 긴 손잡이가 있는 작은 손수레. 외바퀴 손수레

wheel·chair /ˈwilˌtʃɛr/ *n* a chair with wheels, used by people who cannot walk ‖ 걸을 수 없는 사람이 사용하는, 바퀴 달린 의자. 휠체어

wheel·ie /ˈwili/ *n* **do a wheelie** INFORMAL to balance on the back wheel of a bicycle or MOTORCYCLE that you are

riding ‖ 타고 있는 자전거나 오토바이의
뒷바퀴로 균형을 잡다. 뒷바퀴로 서기 묘
기를 하다

wheel·ing and deal·ing /,.. · '../ n
[U] activities that involve a lot of
complicated and sometimes dishonest
deals, especially in politics or business
‖ 특히 정치나 사업에서 복잡하고 때로 부
정한 거래를 많이 포함하는 활동. (수단
방법을 가리지 않고) 갖고 싶은 것을 얻
기 –**wheeler-dealer** /,.. '../ n

wheels /wilz/ n SPOKEN (**set of**)
wheels a car ‖ 자동차: *Wow! Nice
wheels!* 와! 자동차 멋진데!

wheeze /wiz/ v [I] to breathe with
difficulty, making a whistling sound in
your chest ‖ 가슴에서 색색 소리를 내며
어렵게 숨을 쉬다. 헐떡거리다. 씨근거리
다 –**wheezy** adj

when¹ /wɛn/ adv used when asking
what time something will happen ‖ 어떤
일이 몇 시에 일어날지를 물을 때에 쓰여.
언제: *When are we leaving?* 우리 언제
떠나지? / *When did you notice he was
gone?* 그가 없어진 것을 언제 알아차렸
니?

when² conjunction **1** used in order to
give a specific time ‖ 특정한 시간을 주는
데에 쓰여. …한 때: *When I was little, I
hated green beans.* 나는 어렸을 때 초록
깍지 강낭콩을 싫어했다. / *They look like
gold when the sun shines on them.* 그것
들에 햇빛이 비치면 금처럼 보인다. **2**
used in order to show what happens in
a particular situation ‖ 특정한 상황에서
무슨 일이 일어나는지를 보여 주는 데에
쓰여. …할 경우에: *When you think
about it, you'll see I'm right.* 그것에 대해
생각해 보면 내가 옳다는 것을 알 것이다.
3 even though or in spite of the fact that
something is true ‖ 어떤 것이 사실일지라
도 또는 사실임에도 불구하고. …인데도:
*Why do you want a new bike when this
one is perfectly good?* 이 자전거가 아주
좋은데 왜 새 자전거를 원하니? —see
also **since when** (SINCE²)

**USAGE NOTE when, at the time, by
the time, and by that time**

Use these phrases to talk about the
relationship between two events. Use
when at the beginning of a CLAUSE in
order to say what was happening at
the same time that another event
happened: *When the doorbell rang, I
was in the shower.* / *I was in the
shower when the doorbell rang.* Use
at the time to talk about a specific

time in the past when two things
happened at the same time: *I'm sorry
I couldn't see you this morning. I had
an appointment at the time.* / *At the
time, I had no idea what he was
talking about.* Use **by the time** to
say that one thing had already
happened when something else
happened, or that one thing will have
already happened when something
else happens. This phrase is used
with dependent clauses (=clauses
that cannot be used alone as
sentences): *By the time he decided to
go to the concert, there were no more
tickets.* / *By the time she graduates,
she will have lived in Boston for five
years.* **By that time** means the same
thing, but the phrase is used with
independent clauses (=clauses that
could be used alone as sentences):
*She said she'd phone us at 6:00, but
by that time we'd already left.* / *"I
can help you with the dishes in a few
minutes." "By that time, I'll have
finished washing them."*
이들 어구들은 두 사건 사이의 관계를
이야기하는 데 쓴다. **when**은 다른 사
건이 일어남과 동시에 일어난 일을 말하
기 위해 절의 시작부에 쓴다: 초인종이
울렸을 때, 나는 샤워 중이었다. **at the
time**은 두 가지 일이 동시에 일어난 과
거의 특정한 시간을 이야기하는 데 쓴
다: 오늘 아침에 당신을 볼 수 없게 돼
서 미안해요. 그 시간에 약속이 있었거
든요. / 그 당시 나는 그가 무슨 이야기
를 하는지 몰랐어요. **by the time**은
다른 일이 일어났을 때 한 가지 일이 벌
써 일어났거나 다른 일이 일어날 때는
한 가지 일이 이미 일어났을 것이라고
말하는 데 쓴다. 이 어구는 종속절과 함
께 쓰인다: 그가 콘서트에 가기로 결정
했을 때는 더 이상 표가 없었다. / 그녀
가 졸업할 때쯤이면 5년 동안 보스턴에
산 것이 될 것이다. **by that time** 은
마찬가지 의미이지만 이 어구는 독립절
과 함께 쓰인다: 그녀는 우리에게 6시에
전화하겠다고 말했으나 그 시간에 우리
는 이미 떠났었다. / "금방 접시 닦는 것
을 도와줄게." "그때는 이미 접시를 다
닦았을 거야."

---

when·ev·er /wɛ'nɛvɚ, wə-/ adv,
conjunction **1** every time ‖ 매번. …할 때
는 언제나. …할 때마다: *Whenever we
come here we see someone we know.* 여
기에 올 때마다 우리는 아는 사람을 만난
다. **2** at any time ‖ 언제라도. …했을 때

는 곧, 항상: *Come over whenever you want.* 원할 때는 언제나 오세요. **3** SPOKEN used in order to say that it does not matter when something happens ‖ 발생 시기는 문제가 되지 않는다고 말하는 데에 쓰여. 언제라도[든지]: *"Should I come over around six?" "Whenever."* "6시 경에 와야 해요?" "언제든지 괜찮아요."

where /wɛr/ *adv, conjunction* **1** used in order to ask or tell someone the place or position of something ‖ 남에게 사물의 장소나 위치를 묻거나 말하는 데에 쓰여. 어디에[로]: *Where do you live?* 너는 어디서 사니? / *Where did you park the car?* 자동차를 어디에 주차시켰니? / *I know where Ramon is.* 나는 레이몬이 어디 있는지 안다. **2** used in order to ask or talk about the situation or state of something ‖ 사물의 상황 또는 상태를 묻거나 이야기하는 데에 쓰여. 어떤 입장[상태]에: *Where do we go from here?* (=what do we do now?) 이제부터 어떻게 하지? / *I wish I knew where it will all end.* (=I wish I knew what will happen) 무슨 일이 일어날 것인지 [이 모든 것이 어디에서 끝날지] 알았으면 좋겠어.

where·a·bouts¹ /ˈwɛrəˌbaʊts, ˌwɛrəˈbaʊts/ *adv* SPOKEN used in questions when you are asking where a place is ‖ 어떤 장소의 위치를 묻고 있는 의문문에 쓰여. 어느 곳[언저리]에. 어디에[로]: *Whereabouts do you live?* 어디쯤에 살아요?

where·a·bouts² /ˈwɛrəˌbaʊts/ *n* [U] the place or area where someone or something is ‖ 사람이나 사물이 있는 장소 또는 지역. 소재. 위치. 행방: *His whereabouts are still a mystery.* 그의 행방은 아직도 묘연하다.

where·as /wɛrˈæz; *weak* wɛrəz/ *conjunction* used in order to say that although something is true of one thing, it is not true of another ‖ 어떤 일이 한 가지는 사실이지만 다른 것은 사실이 아니라고 말하는 데에 쓰여. …임에 비하여[반하여]: *They want a house, whereas we would rather live in an apartment.* 그들은 단독 주택을 원하는 반면에 우리는 아파트에서 살았으면 한다.

where·by /wɛrˈbaɪ/ *adv* FORMAL by means of which, or according to which ‖ 그것에 의해, 또는 그것에 따라: *a law whereby all children receive free education* 모든 어린이들이 무상 교육을 받게 하는 법률

where·in /wɛrˈɪn/ *adv, conjunction* FORMAL in what or in which ‖ 그 속에서. 거기서, 그 점에서: *a procedure wherein*

patients are given high doses of vitamin B 환자들에게 고단위의 비타민 B가 투여되는 치료 과정

where·u·pon /ˌwɛrəˈpɑn, ˈwɛrəˌpɑn/ *conjunction* FORMAL after which ‖ 그 후에. 그래서, 그 결과: *One of them said he was a liar, whereupon a fight broke out.* 그들 중의 하나가 그는 거짓말쟁이라고 말했다. 그래서 싸움이 일어났다.

wher·ev·er /wɛrˈɛvɚ/ *adv* **1** to or at any place ‖ 어떤 곳으로든지 또는 어떤 곳에나. 어디든지: *If you could go wherever you wanted to in the world, where would you go?* 세상에서 원하는 어디든지 갈 수 있다면 너는 어디로 가겠냐? / *Sit wherever you like.* 마음에 드는 곳 어디든지 앉으세요. **2** used at the beginning of a question to show surprise ‖ 놀라움을 나타내는 의문문의 문두에 쓰여. 도대체 어디서[로]: *Wherever did you find that old thing?* 그 오래된 물건을 도대체 어디서 발견했느냐?

where·with·al /ˈwɛrwɪˌðɔl, -ˌθɔl/ *n* **the wherewithal to do sth** the money or ability you need in order to do something ‖ 어떤 일을 하기 위해 필요한 돈이나 능력. 수단. 자금: *He just didn't have the wherewithal to do more with his life.* 그는 자기 생애를 더 잘 보낼 돈이 없었다.

whet /wɛt/ *v* **-tted, -tting** [T] **whet sb's appetite (for sth)** to make someone want more of something ‖ 다른 사람으로 하여금 어떤 것을 더 많이 원하게 하다. …에 대한 다른 사람의 욕구를 돋우다: *The trip to Paris has whetted my appetite for travel.* 파리 여행은 나의 여행 욕구를 돋우었다.

wheth·er /ˈwɛðɚ/ *conjunction* **1** used when talking about a choice between different possibilities ‖ 서로 다른 가능성 사이의 선택을 이야기할 때 쓰여. …인지 어떤지: *He asked me whether she was coming.* 그는 그녀가 오는지 아닌지를 내게 물었다. / *I couldn't decide whether or not I wanted to go.* 나는 내가 가기를 원하는지 아닌지를 판단할 수가 없었다. **2** used in order to say that something definitely will or will not happen in spite of what the situation is ‖ 상황에 상관 없이 어떤 일이 확실히 일어나거나 일어나지 않을 거라고 말하는 데에 쓰여. …이든 아니든: *Whether you like it or not, you're going to have to take that test.* 네가 좋아하든 싫어하든 상관없이 너는 그 시험을 치러야만 할 것이다.

whew /hwyu, hwu/ *interjection* ⇨ PHEW

which /wɪtʃ/ *determiner, pron* **1** used in order to ask or state what things you mean when a choice has to be made ‖ 선택을 내려야 할 때 어떤 것들을 말하는지를 묻거나 진술할 때 쓰여. 어느 쪽, 어느 것: *Which of these books is yours?* 이 책들 중 어느 것이 너의 것이냐? / *Ask him which one he wants.* 그에게 어느 쪽을 원하는지 물어봐라. **2** used in order to show what specific thing or things you mean ‖ 자신이 어떤 특정한 것이나 것들을 말하는지 보여주는 데에 쓰여. …한 것은: *The letters from fans, which have been coming every day, are mostly from teenagers.* 매일 오고 있는 팬들의 편지는 대부분 십대들에게서 온 것이다. **3** used in order to add more information about something, especially in written language after a COMMA ‖ 특히 문어(체)의 콤마 뒤에서, 어떤 것에 대한 추가 정보를 덧붙이는 데에 쓰여. (그리고[그러나]) 그것[그 일]은: *The train only takes two hours, which is quicker than the bus.* 기차는 단지 2시간 걸리는데 그것은 버스보다 더 빠른 것이다. —see also usage note at THAT¹

USAGE NOTE which and what

Use these words when asking a question about a choice you need to make. Use **what** when you make a choice from an unknown number of things or people: *What color would you like your room to be painted?* Use **which** when you make a choice from a limited number of things or people: *Which color would you like – blue or yellow?*
이 단어들은 선택이 필요한 질문을 할 때 쓴다. **what**은 불분명한 수의 사물이나 사람 중에서 선택을 할 때 쓴다: 당신 방을 어떤 색깔로 페인트칠하고 싶습니까? **which**는 제한된 수의 사물이나 사람 중에 선택을 할 때 쓴다: 청색이나 노란색 중에 어떤 색이 마음에 듭니까?

---

which·ev·er /wɪˈtʃɛvəˈ/ *determiner, pron* used in order to say that it does not matter what thing you choose, what you do etc. ‖ 사람이 어떤 물건을 선택하거나 어떤 일 등을 하든지 문제가 되지 않는다고 말하는 데에 쓰여. …하는 어느 것[쪽]이든: *You can have whichever you like best.* 네가 가장 좋아하는 것이면 어느 것이든 가져도 좋다. / *You get the same result whichever way you do it.* 네가 어떤 방법으로 하든 결과는 마찬가지이다.

whiff /wɪf/ *n* a smell of something that is not strong ‖ 어떤 것의 강하지 않은 냄새. 은은한[가볍게 풍기는] 향기: *As she walked past, I caught a whiff of* (=smelled) *her perfume.* 그녀가 걸어갔을 때 나는 은은한 그녀의 향수 냄새를 맡았다.

while¹ /waɪl/ *n* **a while** a period of time, especially a short one ‖ 특히 짧은 시간. 동안: *Can you wait a while or do you have to leave right now?* 잠깐 기다릴 수 있어, 아니면 당장 떠나야 돼? / *I've been alone for a while.* 나는 한동안 홀로 있었다. / *I'll be back in a little while.* 곧 돌아오겠다. —see also AWHILE, **worth your while** (WORTH¹)

while² *conjunction* **1** during the time that something is happening ‖ 어떤 일이 일어나고 있는 시간 동안에. …하는 동안에: *They arrived while we were having dinner.* 우리가 식사를 하는 중에 그들이 도착했다. / *I like to listen to music while I'm taking a bath.* 나는 목욕하면서 음악 듣기를 좋아한다. **2** in spite of the fact that; though ‖ 어떤 사실에도 불구하고. …인 데 대하여. …인데도; …임에도 불구하고: *While she is a likable woman she can be extremely difficult to work with.* 그녀는 좋아할 만한 여자인 반면에 같이 일하는 것은 극히 힘들 수 있다. **3** used in order to say that although something is true of one thing, it is not true of another ‖ 어떤 것이 한 가지는 사실이지만 다른 것은 사실이 아니라고 말하는 데에 쓰여. …임에 반하여. …하는 한편에: *That region has plenty of water, while this one has little.* 그 지역은 물이 많은 반면에 이 지역은 거의 없다.

while³ *v* **while away the hours/evening/days etc.** to spend time in a pleasant and lazy way ‖ 기분 좋고 느릿하게 시간을 보내다. 시간/밤/날들을 마음 편히 보내다: *We whiled away the summer evenings talking and drinking wine.* 우리는 이야기하고 포도주를 마시면서 여름밤을 보냈다.

whim /wɪm/ *n* a sudden desire to do or have something, especially when there is no good reason for it ‖ 특히 합당한 이유가 없을 때 어떤 일을 하거나 가지려는 갑작스러운 욕구. 변덕. 종잡을 수 없는 생각: *I went to visit her on a whim.* (=because of a whim) 나는 문득 그녀 생각이 나서 그녀를 방문하러 갔다.

whim·per /ˈwɪmpəˈ/ *v* [I] to make low crying sounds, or to speak in this way ‖ 낮게 우는 소리를 내다, 또는 이렇게 말하다. 흐느껴 울다. 우는 소리로 말하다: *A dog whimpered in the corner.* 개가 구석

에서 낑낑거렸다. / *"Don't hurt me," he whimpered.* "해치지 마세요!" 하며 그는 우는소리로 말했다. – **whimper** *n*

whim·si·cal /'wɪmzɪkəl/ *adj* unusual, but fun or showing that someone is having fun || 이상하지만 우스꽝스러운 또는 다른 사람이 재미있어 하는 것을 보여주는. 별난. 변덕스러운: *a whimsical smile* 묘한 미소

whine /waɪn/ *v* [I] **1** to complain about something in a sad annoying voice || 슬프고 짜증나는 목소리로 사물에 대해 불평하다. 우는소리를 하다: *Stop whining about everything!* 만사에 우는소리 하는 것 좀 그만둬! **2** to make a long high sound because you are in pain or unhappy || 아프거나 불행하기 때문에 길고 높은 소리를 내다. 애처롭게 울다. 낑낑거리다: *The dog was whining at the door.* 개는 문에서 낑낑거렸다. **3** if a machine whines, it makes a continuous high sound || 기계가 끊임없이 고음(高音)을 내다. 윙윙 소리를 계속 내다 – **whine** *n* – **whiner** *n*

whin·ny /'wɪni/ *v* [I] if a horse whinnies, it makes a quiet high sound || 말이 조용하게 높은 소리를 내다. 나직하게 히힝 울다 – **whinny** *n*

whip¹ /wɪp/ *n* a long thin piece of rope or leather with a handle, used for making animals move or for hitting people || 동물을 움직이게 하거나 사람을 때리는 데에 쓰이는, 손잡이가 달린 밧줄이나 가죽으로 만든 길고 가느다란 것. 채찍

whip² -**pped**, -**pping** *v* **1** [T] to hit someone with a whip || 채찍으로 남을 때리다. 채찍질하다. 매질하다 **2** [T] INFORMAL to defeat someone easily || 남을 쉽게 패배시키다. …에 이기다. 격파하다: *Smith ran for three touchdowns as the Hawks whipped the Huskies 42-3.* 호크스 팀이 허스키스 팀을 42대 3으로 대파할 때 스미스는 세 번의 터치다운을 기록했다. **3** [T] INFORMAL to move something with a quick sudden movement || 빠르고 갑작스러운 동작으로 어떤 것을 움직이다. 재빨리 움직이다: *He whipped out a gun.* 그는 재빨리 총을 꺼냈다. **4** [I] to move suddenly or violently || 갑자기 또는 격렬하게 움직이다. 휙 잡아당기다[밀다, 붙잡다, 던지다]: *The wind whipped across the plain.* 평원을 가로질러 바람이 휙 몰아쳤다. / *Bill whipped around to see what was happening.* 빌은 무슨 일이 일어나고 있는지 보기 위해 휙 뒤돌아봤다. **5 whip sb/sth into shape** INFORMAL to make a system, group of people etc. start to work in an organized way || 시스템·일단의 사람들 등이 조직적으로 작동하거나 일하기 시작하게 하다. …을 형체를 갖추게 하다. 강행하다 **6** [T] also **whip up** to continue to quickly mix something such as cream or the clear part of an egg very hard until it becomes stiff || 크림이나 계란 흰자 등이 빽빽해질 때까지 계속해서 빠르게 섞다. 거품이 일게 하다[휘젓다]

whip up *phr v* [T] **1 whip up support/enthusiasm etc.** to deliberately try to make people feel or react strongly || 일부러 다른 사람이 강한 감정을 느끼게 하거나 반응하게 하다. (흥분시켜)지지/열광을 유발하다 **2** [**whip sth ↔ up**] to quickly make something to eat || 먹을 것을 신속히 만들다. 재빨리 준비하다: *I could whip up a salad or something.* 샐러드나 그런 것들을 재빨리 준비할 수 있었다.

whip·lash /'wɪplæʃ/ *n* [U] a neck injury caused when your head moves forward and back again suddenly and violently, especially in a car accident || 특히 자동차 사고에서 고개가 갑작스럽고 격렬하게 앞뒤로 움직일 때 발생하는 목 부상. 편타성 상해

whip·ping /'wɪpɪŋ/ *n* a punishment given to someone by hitting him/her, especially with a whip || 특히 채찍으로 다른 사람을 때려서 가하는 벌. 채찍질. 태형

whir /wɚ/ *v* -**rred**, -**rring** [I] to make a fairly quiet regular sound, like the sound of something spinning or moving up and down in the air very quickly || 공중에서 매우 빠르게 빙빙 돌거나 위아래로 오르내리는 물체의 소리처럼 매우 조용하고 규칙적인 소리를 내다. 윙윙 소리 내어 움직이다[날다, 회전하다]: *Somewhere, an electric motor whirred.* 어딘가에서 전기 모터가 윙윙거리며 돌았다. – **whir** *n*

whirl¹ /wɚl/ *v* [I, T] to spin around very quickly, or to make something do this || 매우 빠르게 빙빙 돌다, 또는 어떤 것을 이렇게 하게 하다. 회전[선회]하다[시키다]: *The falling leaves whirled around her feet.* 떨어지는 잎들이 그녀의 발 주위를 빙빙 돌았다.

whirl² *n* **1 give sth a whirl** INFORMAL to try something that you are not sure you are going to like or be able to do || 좋아하게 될지 또는 할 수 있을지에 대한 확신 없이 어떤 것을 해보다. 시도하다. 시험 삼아 해보다 **2** [singular] a lot of activity of a particular kind || 특정한 종류의 많은 활동. 매우 빠르고 혼란스런 움직임[연속

활동]: *a whirl of social activity* 눈코 뜰 새 없는 사회 활동 **3 be in a whirl** to feel very excited or confused about something ‖ 어떤 것에 대해 매우 흥분되거나 혼란스럽게 느끼다. 혼란한 상태이다. 흥분해 있다: *Debbie's head was all in a whirl.* 데비의 머리는 매우 혼란스러웠다. **4** a spinning movement, or the shape of a substance that is spinning ‖ 회전 운동, 또는 회전하는 물질의 형상. 선회. 회오리: *a whirl of dust* 먼지의 회오리

whirl·pool /'wɚlpul/ *n* a powerful current of water that spins rapidly and pulls things down into it ‖ 빠르게 빙빙 돌고 물건을 끌어당겨 내리는 물살의 강력한 흐름. 소용돌이

whirl·wind /'wɚl,wɪnd/ *n* **1 a whirlwind romance/tour etc.** something that happens much more quickly than usual ‖ 평소보다 훨씬 더 빠르게 일어나는 것. 급히 서두른 사랑/여행 **2** an extremely strong wind that moves quickly with a circular movement, causing a lot of damage ‖ 원을 그리며 재빨리 움직이고 많은 피해를 주는 매우 강한 바람. 회오리바람 **3 a whirlwind of activity/emotions etc.** a situation in which you quickly experience a lot of different activities or emotions one after another ‖ 많은 상이한 활동이나 감정을 차례로 재빠르게 경험하는 상황. 활동/감정의 회오리

whisk¹ /wɪsk/ *v* [T] **1** to STIR liquids or soft food very quickly together ‖ 액체나 부드러운 음식을 매우 빨리 휘젓다. 거품 나게 하다: *Whisk the yolks and sugar in a bowl.* 사발에 있는 노른자와 설탕을 섞어 휘저어 거품을 내어라. **2** to quickly take something or someone somewhere ‖ 사물이나 사람을 어떤 곳으로 급히 데리고 가다. 잽싸게 나르다[숨기다]: *He whisked the letter away before I could read it.* 그는 내가 읽기도 전에 편지를 치워버렸다.

whisk² *n* a small kitchen tool made of curved pieces of wire, used for WHISKing eggs, cream etc. ‖ 계란·크림 등의 거품을 내는 데에 쓰이는 굽은 철사로 만든 작은 부엌 용구. 거품기

whisk·er /'wɪskɚ/ *n* one of the long stiff hairs that grow near the mouth of a cat, mouse etc. ‖ 고양이·쥐 등의 입 가까이에 자라는 길고 뻣뻣한 털의 하나. 고양이[쥐의] 수염

whisk·ers /'wɪskɚz/ *n* [plural] the hair that grows on a man's face ‖ 남자의 얼굴에 자라는 털. 구레나룻

whis·key /'wɪski/ *n, plural* **whiskeys** *or* **whiskies** [C, U] a strong alcoholic drink made from grain, or a glass of this drink ‖ 곡식으로 만든 독한 알코올 음료, 또는 이 음료 한 잔. 위스키(한 잔)

whis·per¹ /'wɪspɚ/ *v* **1** [I, T] to speak or say something very quietly, using your breath rather than your voice ‖ 목소리보다 호흡을 이용하여, 매우 조용하게 무엇을 말하다. 속삭이다: *What are you two whispering about over there?* 너희 둘은 거기서 무엇을 속삭이느냐? **2** [I] LITERARY to make a soft sound ‖ 부드러운 소리를 내다. 살랑거리다: *The wind whispered in the trees.* 바람이 나무에 살랑거리며 불었다.

whisper² *n* **1** a very quiet voice ‖ 매우 조용한 목소리. 속삭임. 속삭이는 소리: *"Quiet – they're coming!" he said in a whisper.* "조용히 해. 그들이 오고 있어!"라고 그는 속삭이는 소리로 말했다. **2** LITERARY a soft sound ‖ 부드러운 소리. 살랑거리는 소리: *the whisper of the meadow grasses* 목초 풀의 살랑거리는 소리

whis·tle¹ /'wɪsəl/ *v* **1** [I, T] to make a high or musical sound by blowing air out through your lips ‖ 입술 사이로 공기를 불어내어 높거나 음악적인 소리를 내다. 휘파람을 불다: *Adam whistled to/at me from across the street.* 아담은 거리 건너편에서 나에게 휘파람을 불었다. **2** [I] to make a high sound by blowing into a whistle ‖ 호각을 불어 높은 소리를 내다. 호각[피리]으로 신호하다: *The referee whistled and the game began.* 심판이 호각을 불었고 게임이 시작됐다. **3** [I] to move quickly with a high sound ‖ 높은 소리를 내며 빨리 움직이다. 핑 하고 날아가다: *Bullets were whistling through the air.* 탄환들이 공기를 가르며 핑핑 날고 있었다. **4** [I] to make a high sound when air or steam is forced through a small hole ‖ 공기나 스팀이 작은 구멍으로 억지로 통과될 때 높은 소리를 내다. 피리[기적, 경적]를 불다[울리다]: *a whistling kettle* 쉭쉭 끓고 있는 주전자

whistle² *n* **1** a small object that produces a high sound when you blow into it ‖ 안에 바람을 불어넣으면 높은 소리를 내는 작은 물건. 호각 **2** a high sound made by blowing air through a whistle, your lips etc. ‖ 호각·입술 사이로 공기를 불어서 내는 높은 소리. 경적. 휘파람 **3** a high sound made by something moving quickly ‖ 빠르게 움직이는 물체가 내는 높은 소리. (바람·탄환의) 휙휙 나는 소리: *the whistle of the wind* 휘잉하고

부는 바람 소리 —see also **blow the whistle (on sb)** (BLOW¹)

white¹ /waɪt/ *adj* **1** having a color that is lighter than every other color, like the color of snow or clouds ‖ 눈이나 구름의 색깔처럼 다른 모든 색깔보다 밝은 색깔을 가진. 흰. 순백의: *white paint* 흰색 페인트 **2** someone who is white has pale skin ‖ 사람의 피부가 흰. 백색 인종의. 백인의 – **whiteness** *n* [U]

white² *n* **1** [U] a white color ‖ 흰색 **2** also **White** someone who has pale skin ‖ 흰 피부를 가진 사람. 백인 **3** the white part of your eye ‖ 눈의 하얀 부분. 눈의 흰자위 **4** [C, U] the transparent part of the inside of an egg, that surrounds the yellow part and becomes white when cooked ‖ 노른자위를 둘러싸고 가열하면 하얗게 되는 계란 속의 투명한 부분. 계란의 흰자위

white-bread /ˌ. ˈ./ *adj* relating to people who are white and who have traditional American values, and who are often considered boring ‖ 백인이고 전통적인 미국적 가치관을 가지고 있으며, 종종 따분하다고 여겨지는 사람에 관한. 백인 중산 계급의: *a white-bread suburban family* 교외에 사는 백인 중산층 가족

white col·lar /ˌ. ˈ../ *adj* white collar workers do jobs in offices, banks etc., and often manage other workers ‖ 사무실·은행 등에서 일하고, 종종 다른 근로자들을 관리하는 근로자. 사무직[전문직]의. 화이트칼라의 —compare BLUE COLLAR — see usage note at CLASS¹

White House /ˈ. ./ *n* **1** [singular] the President of the US and the people who advise him/her ‖ 미국의 대통령과 그 조언자들. 백악관(당국). 미행정부: *an election that resulted in a Democratic White House* 민주당 집권으로 끝난 대선(大選) **2 the White House** the official home in Washington, D.C. of the President of the US ‖ 워싱턴 D.C에 있는 미국 대통령의 관저. 백악관. 화이트 하우스 – **White House** *adj*: *a White House spokesperson* 백악관 대변인

white lie /ˌ. ˈ./ *n* INFORMAL a lie that is not very important, especially one that you tell in order to avoid hurting someone's feelings ‖ 그다지 중요하지 않은 거짓말, 특히 남의 감정을 상하게 하지 않기 위해 말하는 것. 선의의[악의 없는] 거짓말

whit·en /ˈwaɪtʰn/ *v* [I, T] to become white, or to make something do this ‖ 희게 되다, 또는 어떤 것을 이렇게 되게 하

다. …을 희게 하다[칠하다]. 표백하다[시키다]: *It whitens your teeth and freshens your breath!* 그것은 네 이를 희게 하고 호흡을 상쾌하게 해줘!

white trash /ˌ. ˈ./ *n* [U] INFORMAL an insulting expression meaning white people who are poor and uneducated ‖ 가난하고 교육받지 않은 백인을 의미하는 모욕적인 표현. 백인쓰레기

white·wash /ˈwaɪtwɑʃ, -wɔʃ/ *n* **1** [C usually singular] an attempt to hide the true facts about a serious accident or illegal action ‖ 심각한 사고나 불법적인 행동에 대한 진실을 감추려는 시도. 잘못[과실]을 감추기[은폐]: *One magazine called the report a whitewash.* 한 잡지는 그 보고를 눈속임용이라고 평가했다. **2** [U] a white liquid mixture used for painting walls, fences etc. ‖ 벽이나 울타리 등을 칠하는 데에 쓰이는 흰색 액체 혼합물. 백색 도료. 회반죽 – **whitewash** *v* [T]

white·wa·ter /ˈwaɪtʰˌwɔtər, -ˌwɑ-/ *n* [U] a part of a river that looks white because the water is flowing very quickly over rocks ‖ 물이 바위 위로 매우 빠르게 흐르기 때문에 하얗게 보이는 강물의 부분. 급류. 분류

whit·tle /ˈwɪtl/ *v* [I, T] to cut a piece of wood into a particular shape by cutting off small pieces ‖ 나무를 조금씩 깎아서 특정한 모양을 만들다. 깎아내다

whittle sth ↔ **away** *phr v* [T] to gradually reduce the size, amount, or value of something ‖ 사물의 크기[양, 가치]를 점차 감소시키다. …을 점점 줄이다[깎다]: *The country is slowly whittling away at its huge trade imbalance.* 그 나라는 막대한 무역 불균형[적자]을 서서히 줄이고 있다.

whittle sth ↔ **down** *phr v* [T] to gradually make something smaller by taking parts away ‖ 부분적인 것들을 제거하여 점차 어떤 것을 더 작게 만들다. …을 잘라내다[줄이다]: *I've whittled down the list of guests from 30 to 16.* 손님 명단을 30명에서 16명으로 줄였다.

whiz¹ /wɪz/ *v* **-zzed, -zzing** [I] **1** INFORMAL to move very quickly, often making a sound like something rushing through the air ‖ 종종 공기를 급히 뚫고 나가는 것과 같은 소리를 내며 매우 빠르게 움직이다. 윙윙[핑핑] 하고 소리 나다. 쌕 지나가다: *Marty whizzed by us on his motorbike.* 마티는 오토바이를 타고 우리 옆을 쌕 지나갔다. **2** SLANG to URINATE

whiz² *n* **1** INFORMAL someone who is very fast, intelligent, or skilled in a particular activity, especially a young person ‖ 특히 나이 어린 사람으로 특정한 활동에 매우 빠른[총명한, 능숙한] 사람. 명수. 재주꾼: *a computer whiz kid* 컴퓨터 신동 **2** [singular] SLANG an act of urinating (URINATE) ‖ 소변보기

who /hu/ *pron* **1** used in order to ask about a person or group of people, or to make a statement about them ‖ 한 사람 또는 일단의 사람들에 대해 묻거나 그들에 대한 발언을 하는 데에 쓰여. 누구. 어느[어떤] 사람(들): *"Who is that?" "That's Amy's brother."* "저 사람은 누구지?" "그는 에이미의 동생이야." / *"Who told you about the fire?" "Mr. Garcia."* "그 화재에 대해 누가 네게 말해 줬지?" "가르시아씨야." / *I know who sent you that card.* 누가 너에게 그 카드를 보냈는지 나는 알아. / *The Wright brothers were the men who invented the airplane.* 라이트 형제는 비행기를 발명한 사람들이었다. **2** used in order to add more information about someone ‖ 남에 대한 더 많은 정보를 덧붙이는 데에 쓰여. 그리고[그렇다면, 그렇지만] 그 사람은: *She asked her English teacher, who had also studied Latin.* 그녀는 자기의 영어 선생한테 물었는데, 그도 또한 라틴어를 공부했었다. —see also usage note at THAT[1]

USAGE NOTE who and whom

In informal speech and writing, you can use **who** as an object, especially in questions: *Who did you see there?* In formal and written English, it is better to use **whom**: *Whom did you see there?*

who는 비격식 말과 글에서 특히 의문문에서 목적어로 쓸 수 있다: 그곳에서 너는 누구를 보았니? 격식적이고 문어체인 영어에서는 **whom**을 사용하는 것이 더 낫다: 그곳에서 너는 누구를 보았니?

---

whoa /wou, hwou, hou/ *interjection* a command given to a horse to make it stop ‖ 말을 멈추게 하기 위해 하는 명령. 우어. 워

who'd /hud/ **1** the short form of "who had" ‖ "who had"의 단축형: *a young girl who'd been attacked* (성)폭행 당한 어린 소녀 **2** the short form of "who would" ‖ "who would"의 단축형: *Who'd know where I can get tickets?* 어디서 표를 사는지 누구 아세요?

who·dun·it /hu'dʌnɪt/ *n* INFORMAL a book, movie etc. about a murder, in which you do not find out who the murderer is until the end ‖ 끝날 때까지 살인자가 누구인지 알 수 없는, 살인에 대한 책·영화 등. 추리[탐정] 소설[영화]

who·ev·er /hu'ɛvɚ/ *pron* **1** used in order to talk about someone when you do not know who s/he is ‖ 어떤 사람이 누구인지 모를 때 그 사람에 대해 이야기하는 데에 쓰여. …하는 사람은 누구나: *Whoever did this is in big trouble.* 이 일을 한 자가 누구이든 큰코 다칠 것이다. **2** used in order to show that it does not matter which person does something ‖ 누가 어떤 것을 하느냐는 중요하지 않다는 것을 나타내는 데에 쓰여. 누가 …이라도: *Whoever gets there first can find a table.* 그곳에 첫 번째로 도착한 사람은 누구든 테이블을 발견할 수 있다.

whole[1] /houl/ *n* **1 the whole of** all of something ‖ 어떤 것의 전부. 전체: *The whole of the morning was wasted.* 아침이 온통 허비됐다. **2 on the whole** used in order to say that something is generally true ‖ 어떤 것이 일반적으로 사실이라고 말하는 데에 쓰여. 대체로: *On the whole, life was much quieter after John left.* 대체로 존이 떠나간 후에 생활은 훨씬 조용해졌다. **3 as a whole** used in order to say that all the parts of something are being considered ‖ 어떤 것의 모든 부분이 고려되고 있다고 말하는 데에 쓰여. 전체적으로: *We must look at our educational system as a whole.* 우리는 우리의 교육 제도를 전체적으로 보아야 한다. **4** [C usually singular] something that consists of a number of parts, but is considered as a single unit ‖ 많은 부분들로 구성된 것이지만 한 단위로 간주되는 것. 완전체. 통일체: *Two halves make a whole.* 반쪽짜리 두개가 하나의 전체를 이룬다.

whole[2] *adj* all of something; ENTIRE ‖ 어떤 것 전부의. 모든. 전[총]…; ㈜ entire: *She drank a whole bottle of wine.* 그녀는 포도주 한 병을 다 마셨다. / *The whole thing* (=everything about a situation) *just makes me sick.* 그 모든 것들이 나를 구역질나게 한다. / *Barney spent the whole day in bed.* 바니는 하루 종일 침대에서 지냈다.

whole·heart·ed /ˌhoul'hɑrtɪd/ *adj* involving all your feelings, interest etc. ‖ 자신의 모든 감정·관심 등을 포함하는. 충심[진심]으로의: *You have our wholehearted support.* 너는 우리의 전폭적인 지지를 받고 있다. — **wholeheartedly** *adv*

whole·sale[1] /'houlseɪl/ *adj* **1** relating to the sale of goods in large quantities, usually at low prices to people or stores that then sell to other people ‖ 보통 다시 다른 사람에게 되파는 사람이나 가게에, 낮은 가격에 대량으로 상품을 판매하는 것에 관한. 도매의[로]: *a wholesale price* 도매가격 **2** affecting almost everything or everyone, and often done without any concern for the results ‖ 거의 모든 사물이나 사람에게 영향을 미치고, 종종 결과에 대한 어떤 염려도 없이 행해지는. 대규모의. 대량의: *wholesale destruction* 대규모의 파괴 **— wholesale** *adv*: *I can get it for you wholesale.* 내가 너에게 도매로 그것을 사줄 수 있다. **—compare** RETAIL

wholesale² *n* [U] the selling of goods in large quantities to RETAIL stores ‖ 소매상에게 대량으로 물건을 팔기. 도매: *goods bought at wholesale prices* 도매가격으로 산 물건 **—compare** RETAIL

whole·sal·er /'houl,seilə/ *n* a person or business that sells goods WHOLESALE ‖ 물건을 도매로 파는 사람이나 기업. 도매상인[업체]

whole·some /'houlsəm/ *adj* **1** likely to make you healthy ‖ 사람을 건강하게 할 것 같은. 건강(증진)에 좋은: *a good wholesome breakfast* 맛있고 건강에 좋은 아침식사 **2** considered to be morally good or acceptable ‖ 도덕적으로 좋거나 받아들일 만하다고 여겨지는. (도덕적으로) 건전한: *a nice clean wholesome kid* 귀엽고 순수하고 착실한 아이

whole wheat /,. '../ *adj* whole wheat flour or bread is made using every part of the WHEAT grain, including the outer layer ‖ 밀가루나 빵이 밀알의 외피층까지 포함한 모든 부분을 이용해서 만든. 통밀가루의. 완전 소맥분의

who'll /hul/ the short form of "who will" ‖ "who will"의 단축형: *This is Denise, who'll be your guide today.* 이쪽이 드니스이고, 오늘 네 안내자가 될 것이다.

whol·ly /'houli/ *adv* FORMAL completely ‖ 완전히. 전적으로. 아주: *The club is wholly responsible for the damage.* 그 클럽이 전적으로 손상에 대해 책임이 있다.

whom /hum/ *pron* the object form of "who," used especially in formal speech or writing ‖ 특히 격식적인 말이나 글에서 사용되는, "who"의 목적형. 누구를[에게]: *To whom am I speaking?* (전화 상대에게) 누구시죠? / *He spoke to a man with whom he used to work.* 그는 전에 함께 일했었던 사람에게 말했다. **—see** usage notes at THAT¹, WHO

whoop /hup, wup/ *v* [I] to shout loudly and happily ‖ 크고 행복하게 외치다. 큰 소리[환호성]를 지르다 **— whoop** *n*

whoops /wups/ *interjection* said when you make a small mistake, drop something, or fall ‖ 작은 실수를 하는 [물건을 떨어뜨리는, 넘어지는] 때에 쓰여. 이런. 아차. 아이코

whoosh /wuʃ, wuʃ/ *v* [I] INFORMAL to move very fast with a soft rushing sound ‖ 부드럽고 맹렬한 소리를 내며 매우 빠르게 움직이다. 휘익[쉬잇] 하고 지나가다[날다]: *cars whooshing past* 휙 하고 지나가는 차들 **— whoosh** *n*

whop·per /'wapə/ *n* INFORMAL **1** something that is unusually large ‖ 엄청나게 큰 것 **2** a lie ‖ 거짓말. 허풍

who're /'huə, hur/ the short form of "who are" ‖ "who are"의 단축형: *Who're those two guys?* 저 두 사람은 누구냐?

whore /hor/ *n* OFFENSIVE ⇨ PROSTITUTE¹

who's /huz/ **1** the short form of "who is" ‖ "who is"의 단축형: *Who's sitting next to Reggie?* 레기 옆에 앉아 있는 사람은 누구냐? **2** the short form of "who has" ‖ "who has"의 단축형: *That's Karl, the guy who's studied in Brazil.* 그 사람은 브라질에서 공부한 칼이다.

whose /huz/ *determiner, possessive pron* **1** used in order to ask which person or people a particular thing belongs to ‖ 특정한 사물이 어떤 한 사람이나 많은 사람들에게 속하는지 묻는 데에 쓰여. 누구의: *Whose jacket is this?* 이것은 누구의 재킷이지? **2** used in order to show the relationship between a person and something that belongs to that person ‖ 어떤 사람과 그 사람이 소유하는 사물과의 관계를 보여주는 데에 쓰여. (그 사람[것]의) …의[을] …한: *That's the man whose house burned down.* 집이 몽땅 타버린 사람이 저 사람이다.

who've /huv/ the short form of "who have" ‖ "who have"의 단축형: *There are a lot of people who've complained.* 불평해 온 사람들이 많다.

why /wai/ *adv, conjunction* **1** for what reason ‖ 무슨 이유로. 왜. 어째서: *Why are these books so cheap?* 이 책들은 왜 그렇게 싸냐? / *Why haven't you finished it yet?* 어째서 그것을 아직 끝내지 못했지? **2 why don't you/why doesn't he...etc.** SPOKEN used in order to make a suggestion ‖ 제안을 하는 데에 쓰여. …하면 어떤가: *Why don't you try this one?* 이쪽 것을 써 보시죠? **3 why not?** SPOKEN **a)** used in order to ask someone why s/he has not done something ‖ 남에

게 왜 어떤 것을 끝내지 않았는지 묻는 데에 쓰여. 어째서 안 되지[못하지]?: *"I haven't done my homework." "Why not?"* "나는 숙제를 하지 않았어." "왜 안 했니?" **b)** used in order to agree to do something ‖ 어떤 일을 하는 것에 동의하는 데에 쓰여. 좋지. 물론: *Do you want to come along?" "Yeah, why not?"* "함께 갈래?" "응, 좋고 말고."

WI the written abbreviation of Wisconsin ‖ Wisconsin(위스콘신 주)의 약어

wick /wɪk/ *n* the string on a CANDLE or in an oil lamp that is burned ‖ 양초나 석유램프의 연소되는 실. 심지. 등심

wick·ed /ˈwɪkɪd/ *adj* **1** morally bad; evil ‖ 도덕적으로 나쁜. 부도덕한; 사악한: *the wicked stepmother in "Cinderella"* "신데렐라" 동화의 사악한 계모 **2** bad in a way that seems harmless and amusing; MISCHIEVOUS ‖ 악의 없고 재미있어 보이는 짓궂은. 장난 잘 치는. 개구쟁이짓 하는; ⓟ mischievous: *a wicked grin* 장난스런 웃음 **3** SLANG very good ‖ 매우 좋은. 멋진. 훌륭한: *a wicked concert* 멋진 콘서트

wick·er /ˈwɪkɚ/ *adj* made from thin dry branches woven together ‖ 가늘고 마른 가지들을 함께 엮어 만든. 버들 고리로 만든: *a white wicker chair* 하얀 등의자

wick·et /ˈwɪkɪt/ *n* one of the curved wires used in CROQUET ‖ 크로케에서 사용되는 아치 모양의 철사 중의 하나. 주문 (柱門)

wide¹ /waɪd/ *adj* **1** measuring a large distance from one side to the other ‖ 한쪽에서 다른 쪽까지 거리가 넓게 측정되는. 폭이 넓은. 널따란: *a wide street* 폭이 넓은 거리 / *Jill has a wide mouth.* 질은 입이 크다. / *The quake was felt over a wide area.* 지진은 넓은 지역에서 감지됐다. —see picture at NARROW¹ **2** measuring a particular distance from one side to the other ‖ 한쪽에서 다른 쪽까지 특정한 거리가 측정되는. 폭[너비] …인: *The bathtub's three feet wide and five feet long.* 그 욕조는 너비 3피트, 길이 5피트이다. **3** including a large variety of different people, things, or situations ‖ 많은 종류의 다른 사람[사물, 상황]을 포함하는. 다양한. 각양각색의: *We offer a wider range of vegetarian dishes.* 우리는 보다 다양한 야채 요리를 제공한다. **4** from many people ‖ 많은 사람으로부터의. 광범위한: *The case has received wide attention.* 그 사건은 많은 주목을 받았다. **5 statewide/citywide/company-wide etc.** affecting all of a

place or all of the people in it ‖ 한 장소의 모든 곳이나 그 안의 모든 사람에게 영향을 미치는. 전주(全州)적/전시(全市)적/전사(全社)적인 **6 wide difference/gap etc.** a large and noticeable difference, GAP etc. ‖ 크고 주목할 만한 차이·격차 등. 동떨어진 차이/갭: *wide differences of opinion* 큰 의견 차이

wide² *adv* **1** used instead of "completely" ‖ "완전히" 대신에 쓰여. 크게 열어[뜨고], 넓게 벌려: *Somebody left the door wide open.* 누군가가 문을 활짝 열어 놓았다. / *wide open spaces* 완전히 개방된 공간 / *The guards stood with their legs wide apart.* 경비들이 다리를 넓게 벌리고 서 있었다. **2 wide open for/to sth** making it easy for people to do something ‖ 사람들이 어떤 것을 하기 쉽게 하는. …에[위해] 활짝 열린[개방된]: *She left herself wide open to criticism.* 그녀는 자신에 대한 비판에 무방비 상태였다. / *Siberia is wide open for investment.* 시베리아는 투자에 활짝 개방돼 있다. **3 wide awake** completely awake ‖ 완전히 잠이 깬 **4** away from the point that you were aiming at ‖ 목표로 해 왔던 지점에서 벗어나서. 표적을 빗나가서: *His shot went wide.* 그의 탄환은 표적을 빗나갔다.

wide-eyed /ˈ. ./ *adj, adv* **1** with your eyes wide open, especially because you are surprised or frightened ‖ 특히 놀라거나 두려워서 눈을 크게 뜬[떠]. 크게 뜬 눈의[으로]: *a wide-eyed stare* 눈을 크게 뜨고 응시하기 **2** too willing to believe, accept, or admire things because you do not have much experience of life ‖ 인생의 경험이 많지 않아서 어떤 것들을 너무 잘 믿는[받아들이는, 감탄하는]. 잘 속아 넘어가는. 순진한

wide·ly /ˈwaɪdli/ *adv* **1** in a lot of different places or by a lot of people ‖ 많은 다른 장소에 또는 많은 사람에 의해. 널리. 광범위하게: *products that are widely available* 도처에서 입수 가능한 제품 / *a widely read newspaper* 널리 읽히는 신문 **2** to a large degree; a lot ‖ 크게. 현저히; 많이: *Taxes vary widely from state to state.* 세금은 주마다 크게 다르다

wid·en /ˈwaɪdn/ *v* [I, T] **1** to become wider or to make something wider ‖ 넓어지다, 또는 어떤 것을 넓어지게 하다: *His eyes widened in fear.* 그의 눈은 두려움으로 크게 떠졌다. / *The old trail was widened into a road.* 오래된 오솔길이 도

로로 넓혀졌다. **2** to become greater or larger ‖ 더 거대해지거나 커지다. 확대되다: *The gap between low and high incomes began to widen after 1974.* 고소득과 저소득 사이의 격차는 1974년 이후에 커지기 시작했다.

wide·spread /ˌwaɪdˈsprɛd·/ *adj* happening in many places, among many people, or in many situations ‖ 많은 지역[사람사이, 상황]에서 일어나는. 광범위하게 퍼진. 보급된: *the widespread use of illegal drugs* 광범위하게 퍼진 불법 마약의 사용

wid·ow /ˈwɪdoʊ/ *n* a woman whose husband has died and who has not married again ‖ 남편이 죽고 재혼하지 않은 여성. 미망인. 과부

wid·owed /ˈwɪdoʊd/ *adj* having become a WIDOW or WIDOWER ‖ 미망인이나 홀아비가 된. 상배한. 외톨이가 된: *He was widowed three years ago.* 그는 3년 전에 홀아비가 되었다.

wid·ow·er /ˈwɪdoʊɚ/ *n* a man whose wife has died and who has not married again ‖ 아내가 죽고 재혼하지 않은 남성. 홀아비

width /wɪdθ, wɪtθ/ *n* [C, U] the distance from one side of something to the other ‖ 사물의 한 끝에서 다른 끝까지의 거리. 너비. 폭: *the width of the window* 창문의 너비 / *a width of 10 inches* 10인치의 폭 —see picture at HEIGHT

wield /wild/ *v* [T] **1 wield power/control/authority etc.** to have a lot of power, control etc. and be ready to use it ‖ 많은 권력·지배력 등을 갖고 사용할 준비가 되다. 권력을 휘두르다. 행사하다: *the influence wielded by the church* 교회가 행사하는 영향력 **2** to hold a weapon or tool and use it ‖ 무기나 도구를 잡고 사용하다. 휘두르다. 교묘하게 쓰다

wife /waɪf/ *n, plural* **wives** the woman that a man is married to ‖ 남자가 결혼한 여자. 아내. 처: *This is my wife, Elaine.* 이쪽이 제 아내 일레인입니다.

wig /wɪg/ *n* artificial hair that you wear to cover your head ‖ 머리를 덮기 위해 쓰는 인조 머리털. 가발: *a blond wig* 금발의 가발

wig

wig·gle /ˈwɪgəl/ *v* [I, T] to make small movements from side to side or up and down, or to make something move this way ‖ 작은 동작으로 좌우로 또는 위아래로 움직이다, 또는 사물을 이렇게 움직이게 하다. …을 흔든다. 옴질옴질[꿈틀꿈틀] 움직거리다: *Can you wiggle your ears?* 귀를 움직일 수 있니? – **wiggle** *n*

wig·wam /ˈwɪgwɑm/ *n* a type of tent that was used in past times by some Native Americans ‖ 몇몇 북미 인디언이 예전에 사용하던 텐트의 한 유형. 천막 오두막

wild¹ /waɪld/ *adj* **1** living or growing in a natural state, and not controlled by people ‖ 자연 상태에서 살거나 자라고, 사람에 의해 길들여지지 않은. 야생의: *wild horses* 야생마 / *wild flowers* 야생화 **2** showing strong uncontrolled emotions such as excitement, anger, or happiness ‖ 흥분[분노, 행복감] 등의 강하고 억제되지 않는 감정을 나타내는. 미친 듯이 …하는. 격정에 이끌린: *a wild look in her eyes* 그녀 눈의 격정적인 표정 / *wild applause from the audience* 청중으로부터의 열렬한 갈채 **3** SPOKEN exciting, interesting, unusual, or strange ‖ 흥분시키는, 재미있는, 유별난, 이상한: *Sarah's party was really wild.* 사라의 파티는 정말 신났었다. / *a wild haircut* 유별난 헤어스타일 / *"He's a year old and already saying words." "That's wild."* "그는 한 살인데 벌써 말을 하고 있어요." "그거 기가 찬데요." **4** done or said without knowing all the facts or thinking carefully about them ‖ 모든 사실을 알지 못하거나 그에 대해 주의 깊게 생각하지 않고 하거나 말해진. 엉뚱한. 무모한: *Take a wild guess.* (=guess without thinking carefully) 생각나는 대로 추측해 봐. **5 be wild about sth** SPOKEN to be very interested in or excited about something ‖ 어떤 것에 대해 매우 흥미를 느끼거나 흥분하다. 매우 좋아하다[열광하다]: *I'm not too wild about his movies.* 나는 그의 영화를 그렇게 좋아하지는 않는다. **6** a wild card in a game can represent any card that you want it to be ‖ 게임에서 카드패가 자신이 원하는 어떤 패든 대신할 수 있는. 점수를 마음대로 정하는

wild² *adv* **1 run wild** to behave in an uncontrolled way because you have no rules or people to control you ‖ 자신을 통제하는 규칙이나 사람들이 없기 때문에 무절제하게 행동하다. 제멋대로 굴다[행동하다] **2 go wild** to suddenly become very noisy and active because you are excited or angry ‖ 사람이 흥분하거나 화가 나서 갑자기 매우 소란해지고 활동적이 되다. 열광하다. 격노하다: *The crowd went wild when the Giants won.* 자이언

츠 팀이 이기자 관객은 흥분의 도가니에 빠졌다.

wild³ *n* **in the wild** in an area that is natural and not controlled or changed by people ‖ 자연적이고 사람에 의해 통제되거나 변화되지 않는 지역에서. 야생에서: *animals that live in the wild* 야생에서 사는 동물들 —compare CAPTIVITY

wil·der·ness /ˈwɪldənɪs/ *n* [singular, U] a large natural area of land that has never been farmed or built on ‖ 경작되거나 건물이 들어선 적이 없는 넓은 미개간 지역. 황야. 미개척지: *the Alaskan wilderness* 알래스카의 황무지

wild goose chase /ˌ. ˈ. ./ *n* [singular] a situation in which you waste a lot of time looking for something that cannot be found ‖ 밝혀낼 수 없는 것을 찾아 많은 시간을 허비하는 상황. 가망이 없는 탐구[기도]

wild·life /ˈwaɪldlaɪf/ *n* [U] animals and plants that live in natural conditions ‖ 자연 상태에서 사는 동물과 식물. 야생 생물: *the wildlife of the Rockies* 로키 산맥의 야생 생물

wiles /waɪlz/ *n* [plural] things you say or tricks you use in order to persuade someone to do what you want ‖ 남에게 자신이 원하는 것을 하도록 설득하기 위해서 말하는 것들이나 사용하는 속임수. 책략. 계략. 교묘한 수단

will¹ /wəl, əl, l; *strong* wɪl/ *modal v* **1** used in order to make the simple future tense ‖ 단순 미래 시제를 만드는 데에 쓰여. …일[할] 것이다: *Kathy will be there tomorrow.* 캐시는 내일 그곳에 갈 것이다. / *What time will she get here?* 그녀는 몇 시에 이곳에 도착할까? / *I'll* (=I will) *go shopping later.* 나는 나중에 쇼핑하러 가겠다. **2** used in order to say that you are ready or willing to do something ‖ 일을 할 준비가 되어 있거나 기꺼이 하겠다고 말하는 데에 쓰여. …하겠다. …할 작정이다: *I'll do whatever you say.* 나는 네가 말하는 것은 무엇이나 하겠다. / *Vern said he won't* (=will not) *work for Joe.* 번은 조를 위해 일하지 않겠다고 말했다. **3** used in order to ask someone to do something ‖ 남에게 어떤 것을 해 주기를 부탁하는 데에 쓰여. …하겠소? …하실 작정입니까?: *Will you do me a favor?* 부탁 좀 들어주시겠습니까? **4** used in conditional sentences that use the present tense ‖ 현재 시제를 사용하는 조건문에 쓰여: *If it rains, we'll have the barbecue in the clubhouse.* 만약 비가 오면 우리는 클럽 회관에서 바비큐 파티를 할 것이다. **5** used like "can" to show

what is possible ‖ 무엇이 가능한가를 보여 주기 위해 "can"처럼 쓰여: *This car will seat 5 people.* 이 차는 5명이 탑승할 수 있다. **6** used in order to say what always happens or what is generally true ‖ 항상 일어나는 것이나 일반적으로 사실인 것을 말하는 데에 쓰여: *Prices will always go up.* 가격은 항상 오른다. **7 Will you...** SPOKEN said when you are angrily telling someone to do something ‖ 남에게 어떤 것을 하라고 화를 내며 말할 때 쓰여. …(하도록) 해: *Will you shut up!* 조용히 해[입 다물어]! —see usage note at SHALL —see study note on page 932

will² *n* **1** [C, U] the determination to do what you have decided to do ‖ 하기로 결정했던 것을 하는 결단력. 의지. 결의: *He's lost the will to live.* 그는 삶의 의지를 상실했다. **2** a legal document that shows whom you want to give your money and property to after you die ‖ 죽은 후에 돈과 재산을 누구에게 주고 싶어 하는가를 보여 주는 법적인 문서. 유언. 유서: *Grandma Stacy left me $7000 in her will.* 스테이시 할머니는 유언으로 내게 7천 달러를 남기셨다. **3** [singular] what you decide should happen ‖ 일어나야 한다고 결정한 것. 뜻. 의사: *No one can force him to stay here against his will.* (=if he does not want to) 아무도 그의 생각을 꺾고 그를 여기에 머물게 할 수 없다. **4 at will** when or where you want, without any difficulty or opposition ‖ 어떤 어려움이나 반대 없이 원하는 때나 장소에. 뜻[마음]대로. 자유자재로: *They can just change their policies at will.* 그들은 자신들의 정책을 그저 마음대로 바꿀 수 있다. **5 where there's a will there's a way** SPOKEN used in order to say that if you are determined enough you will succeed ‖ 굳게 결심하면 성공할 것이라고 말하는 데에 쓰여. 뜻이 있는 곳에 길이 있다

will³ *v* [T] **1** to try to make something happen by thinking about it very hard ‖ 매우 열심히 생각하여 어떤 것이 일어나게 하다. …을 바라다. 원하다: *He shut his eyes, willing her to win.* 그는 그녀가 이기길 바라면서 자기의 눈을 감았다. **2** to give something to someone after you die ‖ 죽은 후에 남에게 어떤 것을 주다. 유증하다: *She willed the house to her son.* 그녀는 유언으로 자신의 아들에게 그 집을 물려줬다.

will·ful, wilful /ˈwɪlfəl/ *adj* deliberately doing what you want even though people tell you not to ‖ 사람들이

하지 말라고 함에도 자신이 원하는 것을 일부러 하는. 고집 센: *a willful child* 고집 센 아이 **– willfully** *adv*

will·ing /'wɪlɪŋ/ *adj* **1 be willing to do sth** able to be persuaded to do something ‖ 어떤 것을 하도록 설득될 수 있는. 기꺼이 …하다: *How much are they willing to pay?* 그들은 얼마를 지불하려고 할까? **2** eager or wanting to do something ‖ 어떤 것을 몹시 하고 싶어하거나 바라는. (사람·행위 등이) 자발적인: *willing helpers* 자발적으로 도와주는 사람들 **– willingness** *n* [U] **– willingly** *adv* —opposite UNWILLING

wil·low /'wɪloʊ/ *n* a tree with very long thin branches, that grows near water ‖ 물 가까이 자라는, 가지가 매우 길고 가느다란 나무. 버드나무

wil·low·y /'wɪloʊi/ *adj* tall, thin, and graceful ‖ 키가 크고 마르고 우아한. 날씬한

will·pow·er /'wɪl,paʊɚ/ *n* [U] the ability to control your thoughts and actions in order to achieve something ‖ 어떤 것을 성취하기 위해 자신의 생각과 행동을 조절하는 능력. 의지력. 자제력: *I don't have the willpower to diet.* 다이어트할 의지력이 없다.

wil·ly-nil·ly /,wɪli 'nɪli/ *adv* something that happens to you willy-nilly happens whether or not you want it to ‖ 자신이 어떤 것을 원하든 원치 않든 벌어지는. 싫든 좋든. 할 수 없이

wilt /wɪlt/ *v* [I] if a plant or flower wilts, it bends because it needs water or is old ‖ 식물이나 꽃이 물이 필요하거나 늙어서 이울다. (화초 등이) 시들다

wil·y /'waɪli/ *adj* good at using tricks in order to get something that you want ‖ 원하는 것을 얻어내기 위해 계교를 사용하는 데에 능숙한. 교활한. 잔꾀를 부리는: *a wily politician* 교활한 정치인

wimp /wɪmp/ *n* INFORMAL **1** someone who is afraid to do something difficult or unpleasant ‖ 어렵거나 불유쾌한 일을 하기 두려워하는 사람. 겁쟁이: *Don't be such a wimp!* 그렇게 겁내지 마! **2** a man who is small, weak, and not impressive ‖ 작고 허약하고 멋져 보이지 않은 사람. 약골 **– wimpy** *adj*

win¹ /wɪn/ *v* **won, won, winning 1** [I, T] to be the best or first in a competition, game, election etc. ‖ 시합·경기·선거 등에서 최고나 첫 번째가 되다. 이기다. 우승하다: *Who do you think will win the Super Bowl?* 슈퍼 볼에서 누가 우승하리라고 생각하느냐? / *Dad won at chess again.* 아빠가 체스에서 다시 이겼

다. / *Marcy's team is winning by 3 points.* 마시의 팀이 3점 차로 이기고 있다. **2** [T] to earn a prize at a competition or game ‖ 시합이나 게임에서 상을 획득하다. 상을 타다[받다]: *winning a gold medal* 금메달을 타기 / *I won $200 playing poker.* 포커를 하여 200달러를 땄다. **3** [T] to gain something good because of all your efforts and skill ‖ 온갖 노력이나 기술 덕분에 좋은 것을 얻다. …을 얻다: *Dr. Lee's work won her the admiration of scientists worldwide.* 이박사가 한 연구는 그녀에게 전 세계 과학자들의 찬사를 받게 해 주었다. —opposite LOSE —see usage note at GAIN¹

win out *phr v* [I] to succeed after being unsuccessful for a long time ‖ 오랫동안 실패한 후에 성공하다. 잘 되어 가다. 보답을 얻다: *Sooner or later good sense will win out.* 조만간 선의는 보답을 받게 된다.

win sb ↔ **over** *phr v* [T] to gain someone's support, friendship, trust etc. ‖ 남의 지지·우정·신뢰 등을 얻다. 설득하다: *She completely won him over that evening.* 그녀는 그 날 밤 그를 완전히 설득했다.

win² *n* a victory or success, especially in a sport ‖ 특히 스포츠에서의 승리나 성공: *a record of 7 wins and 6 losses* 7승 6패의 기록

wince /wɪns/ *v* [I] to react to something by looking upset or moving slightly, especially because you are in pain or embarrassed ‖ 특히 아프거나 당황해서 기분 나쁜 표정을 하거나 약간 움직여서 어떤 것에 반응하다. 얼굴을 찡그리다. 움츠러 들다: *I still wince at the memory of how badly I sang.* 나는 아직도 얼마나 노래를 못 했던지를 떠올리며 진저리 친다.

winch /wɪntʃ/ *n* a machine with a rope or chain used for lifting heavy objects ‖ 무거운 물체를 들어올리는 데에 사용하는 로프와 쇠사슬이 있는 기계. 윈치 **– winch** *v* [T]

wind¹ /wɪnd/ *n* **1** [C, U] the air outside when it moves with a lot of force ‖ 세차게 움직일 때의 대기. 바람: *Expect strong winds and rain tomorrow.* 내일 강한 바람과 비가 예상됩니다. / *The wind blew sand in my face.* 바람에 모래가 날려 얼굴을 때렸다. / *A cold east wind (=from the east) was blowing.* 찬 동풍이 불고 있었다. —see usage note at WEATHER **2 get wind of sth** to accidentally learn information that is private or secret ‖ 사적이거나 비밀인 정보를 우연히 알다 **3** your ability to breathe easily ‖ 쉽게 숨을

쉬는 능력. 숨. 호흡: *Rae got the wind knocked out of her.* (=was hit in the stomach and could not breathe for a short time) 레이는 배를 맞아서 잠시 동안 숨을 쉴 수 없었다. **4 the winds of change/freedom etc.** changes in people's ideas that will have important results ‖ 중요한 결과를 낳을 사람의 생각의 변화. 변화/자유에의 움직임 **5 be in the wind** to be likely to happen ‖ 일어날 것 같다. 임박해 있다: *Something was in the wind, something important.* 무언가 일어날 것 같았다, 무언가 중요한 일이. **6 take the wind out of sb's sails** INFORMAL to make someone less excited, or to make someone or something seem less important or impressive ‖ 사람을 덜 흥분되게 하다, 또는 사람이나 사물을 덜 중요하거나 덜 인상적으로 보이게 하다. 상대방의 자신감을 없애다. 김 빠지게 하다 **7 the winds** the people in an ORCHESTRA or band who play musical instruments that you blow into, such as the FLUTE ‖ 플루트 등 입으로 부는 악기를 연주하는 오케스트라나 밴드의 사람. 취주 악기[관악기]부

wind² /waɪnd/ *v* **wound, wound, winding 1** [I, T] to turn or twist something around and around, especially around something else ‖ 특히 다른 것 주위에 어떤 것을 여러 번 돌려 감거나 꼬다. (감아)싸다. 칭칭 감다: *Don't wind the cord around the iron.* 철 주위에 전기 코드를 감지 마세요./ *yarn wound into a ball* 둥글게 감은 실 — opposite UNWIND **2** [T] also **wind up** to make a machine, toy, clock etc. work by turning a small handle around and around ‖ 작은 손잡이를 빙빙 돌려서 기계·장난감·괘종 시계 등을 작동하게 하다. 태엽을 감다. 돌려서 가동시키다: *I forgot to wind my watch.* 나는 내 시계 태엽 감는 것을 잊어 버렸다. **3** [I] if a road, river etc. winds, it curves or bends many times ‖ 도로·강 등이 여러 번 굽어 지거나 구부러지다. 굴곡하다. 굽이치다

wind down *phr v* [I, T] to gradually become slower, less active etc., or to make an activity do this ‖ 점차 늦어지거나 덜 활동적 등이 되다, 또는 활동이 이렇게 하게 하다. 침체되다[시키다]. 점차 쇠 소되다[차분해지다]: *The party started winding down after midnight.* 그 파티는 자정 후에 서서히 끝나기 시작했다.

wind up *phr v* **1** [I] to do something, go somewhere, or become involved in something, without intending to ‖ 의도 없이 어떤 것을 하다[어떤 곳에 가다, 어

떤 것에 관련되다]. …으로 결말이 나다: *We always wind up doing what she wants to do.* 우리는 항상 그녀가 하고 싶은 일을 하면서 끝맺는다. / *Most of them wound up in prison.* 그들 대부분은 교도소에 갇힌 처지가 됐다. **2** [I,T **wind** sth ↔ **up**] to end an activity, meeting etc. ‖ 활동·모임 등을 끝내다. …에 결말을 내다. 마무리짓다: *It's almost 5:00 – we'd better wind things up.* 거의 5시가 되었어. 우리는 일을 마무리 짓는 것이 좋겠어.

wind·break·er /ˈwɪndˌbreɪkɚ/ *n* a type of coat made especially to protect you from the wind ‖ 특히 바람으로부터 보호하기 위해 만든 코트의 일종. 방풍용 점퍼

wind·chill fac·tor /ˈwɪndtʃɪl ˌfæktɚ/ *n* [U] the combination of cold weather and strong winds, that makes the temperature seem colder ‖ 온도를 더 추운 것으로 여기게 하는, 찬 날씨와 강한 바람의 결합. 체감 온도 지수. 풍속 냉각 지수

wind·ed /ˈwɪndɪd/ *adj* having difficulty breathing because you have exercised too much or have been hit in the stomach ‖ 너무 심하게 운동을 해 왔거나 배를 맞아서 호흡하기 힘든. 숨이 찬

wind·fall /ˈwɪndfɔl/ *n* an amount of money that you get unexpectedly ‖ 예상치 않게 얻은 돈의 액수. 뜻밖에 생긴 것. 횡재: *a windfall profit* 불로 소득

wind·ing /ˈwaɪndɪŋ/ *adj* curving or bending many times ‖ 여러 번 휘고 구부러진. 굽이치는. 구불구불한: *a long winding river* 길게 굽이치는 강

wind in·stru·ment /ˈwɪnd ˌɪn-strəmənt/ *n* a musical instrument such as the FLUTE that you play by blowing into it ‖ 불어서 연주하는 플루트 등 악기. 관악기

wind·mill /ˈwɪndˌmɪl/ *n* a building or structure with BLADES that the wind turns, used for producing electrical power or crushing grain ‖ 전력 생산이나 곡식 분쇄에 사용되는, 바람이 돌리는 날개를 가진 건물이나 구조물. 풍차

win·dow /ˈwɪndoʊ/ *n* **1** an opening with glass across it in the wall of a building, car etc., used for letting in air and light ‖ 공기와 빛을 들어오게 하는 데 쓰이는, 건물·차 등의 벽에 유리가 가로질러져 있는 구멍. 창문: *Can I open the window?* 창문 열어도 될까요? —see picture on page 945 **2** one of the areas on a computer screen where you can do different types of work ‖ 서로 다른 형태의 작업을 할 수 있는 컴퓨터 스크린 상의 구역 중 하나. 윈도

window dress·ing /ˈ.. ˌ../ *n* [U] **1** an

attempt to make something seem attractive when it is not ∥ 실제로 그렇지 않을 때 어떤 것을 매력적이게 보이게 하려는 시도. 겉치레하기 **2** the art of arranging things in a store window ∥ 가게의 진열창에 물건을 진열하는 기술. 진열창 장식법

win·dow·pane /'wɪndoʊ,peɪn/ *n* a whole piece of glass used in a window ∥ 창문에 사용되는 통으로 된 한 장의 유리. (끼워져 있는) 창유리

window shop·ping /'.. ,../ *n* [U] the activity of looking at goods in store windows without intending to buy them ∥ 사려는 의도 없이 가게의 진열창 속의 물건을 둘러보는 활동. 윈도 쇼핑

win·dow·sill /'wɪndoʊ,sɪl/ *n* a shelf that is attached to the bottom of a window ∥ 창문 밑에 붙어 있는 선반. 창턱

wind·pipe /'wɪndpaɪp/ *n* the tube through which air passes from your throat to your lungs ∥ 목에서 폐까지 공기가 통과하는 관. 기관(氣管)

wind·shield /'wɪndʃild/ *n* the large window at the front of a car, bus, plane etc. ∥ 자동차·버스·비행기 등의 앞부분의 큰 유리. 방풍 유리 —see picture on page 943

windshield wip·er /'.. ,../ *n* [C usually plural] a long thin piece of metal with a rubber edge, that moves across a WINDSHIELD to remove rain ∥ 빗물을 제거하기 위해 자동차의 앞 유리를 가로질러 움직이는, 고무 날을 가진 가늘고 긴 금속 조각. 와이퍼 —see picture on page 943

wind·surf·ing /'wɪnd,sɔfɪŋ/ *n* [U] the sport of sailing across water by standing on a special board and holding onto a large sail ∥ 특수한 판 위에 올라서고 큰 돛에 매달려서 물 위를 가로질러 항해하는 스포츠. 윈드서핑

wind·swept /'wɪndswɛpt/ *adj* **1** a place that is windswept is usually windy and has few trees, buildings etc. ∥ 한 장소가 보통 바람이 많이 불고 나무·건물 등이 거의 없는. 바람이 휘몰아친[쓸고 간] **2** made messy by the wind ∥ 바람에 의해 엉망이 된. (바람에) 흐트러진. 단정치 못한: *windswept hair* 바람을 맞아 헝클어진 머리

wind·y /'wɪndi/ *adj* with a lot of wind blowing, or getting a lot of wind ∥ 많은 바람이 부는, 또는 많은 바람을 받는. 바람을 맞는. 바람이 센[휘몰아치는]: *It's been windy all day.* 하루 종일 바람이 불었다. / *a windy beach* 바람이 많이 부는 해변

wine /waɪn/ *n* [C, U] an alcoholic drink made from GRAPEs or other fruit, or a particular type of this drink ∥ 포도나 다른 과일로 만든 알코올 음료, 또는 이 음료의 특정한 종류. 포도주. 과일주: *a glass of wine* 포도주 한 잔 / *a fine selection of wines* 정선된 포도주 (수집품)

wine·glass /'waɪnglæs/ *n* a glass for wine, with a base, a thin upright part, and a bowl-shaped top ∥ 받침·가늘게 수직으로 선 부분·사발 모양의 윗부분을 가진 포도주 잔. 와인글라스. 포도주용 유리잔

wing[1] /wɪŋ/ *n* **1** the part of a bird's or insect's body used for flying ∥ 나는 데 사용되는 새나 곤충의 몸의 한 부분. 날개: *ducks flapping their wings* 날개를 퍼더덕거리는 오리들 **2** one of the two flat parts that stick out of a plane's sides and help it stay in the air ∥ 비행기의 양 측면에서 튀어나오고 공중에 떠 있게 해주는 두 개의 평평한 부분 중 하나. 비행기의 날개 —see picture at AIRPLANE **3** one of the parts that a large building is divided into ∥ 큰 건물이 나뉘어진 부분들 중 하나. (중심 건물에서 옆으로 뻗은) 날개. 부속 건물: *the east wing of the library* 그 도서관의 동쪽(으로 뻗은) 부속 건물 **4** one of the groups that a political party is divided into, based on the members' opinions and aims ∥ 구성원들의 견해와 목표에 근거해서 분할되는 정당의 그룹들 중의 하나. 도당. 분파: *the conservative wing of the Democrats* 민주당의 보수파 —see also LEFT-WING, RIGHT-WING **5 take sb under your wing** to give advice, help, PROTECTION etc. to someone younger or less experienced than you ∥ 자신보다 나이가 어리거나 경험이 부족한 사람에게 충고·도움·보호 등을 주다. 남을 돌보다[보호하다]

wing[2] *v* **1 wing it** INFORMAL to do or say something without any planning or preparation; IMPROVISE ∥ 어떤 계획이나 준비 없이 어떤 것을 하거나 말하다. 즉석에서 …하다; 俞 improvise: *"I can't give a speech!" "Just wing it, you'll be fine!"* "연설하지 못하겠어!" "즉흥적으로 해 봐. 잘 할 거야!" **2** [I] LITERARY to fly ∥ 날다

winged /wɪŋd/ *adj* having wings ∥ 날개를 가진. 날개가 달린: *winged insects* 날개가 달린 곤충

wings /wɪŋz/ *n* [plural] **1 the wings** the side parts of a stage where actors are hidden from people watching the play ∥ 연극을 보고 있는 사람들로부터 배우들이 가려지는 무대의 양 측면 **2 waiting in the wings** ready to be used or ready to do something || 사용되거나 어떤 것을 할 준비가 된. …할 기회를 기다리는

wing·span /'wɪŋspæn/ *n* the distance from the end of one wing to the end of the other || 한쪽 날개의 끝에서 다른 쪽 날개 끝까지의 길이. 날개 길이. 익폭

wing·tip /'wɪŋtɪp/ *n* **1** the end of a wing || 날개 끝. 익단(翼端) **2** a type of shoe for men with a pattern of small holes on the toe || 앞부리에 작은 구멍의 무늬가 있는 남성용 구두의 일종. 윙팁

wink¹ /wɪŋk/ *v* [I] to open and close one eye quickly, usually to show that you are joking, being friendly, or telling a secret || 보통 농담하고 있다는[친근하다는, 비밀을 말한다는] 것을 보이기 위해 재빨리 한쪽 눈을 떴다 감았다 하다. 윙크하다: *And don't tell Mom," he said, winking at her.* 그는 그녀에게 윙크를 하며 "엄마에게 말하지 마."라고 말했다.

wink² *n* the action of winking, usually as a signal || 보통 신호로서 눈을 깜박이는 행동. 눈짓. 윙크: *He looked at Greta and gave her a wink.* 그는 그레타를 보면서 그녀에게 눈짓을 했다.

win·ner /'wɪnɚ/ *n* **1** someone who wins a competition, game, election etc. || 경기·시합·선거 등을 이긴 사람. 승리자. 수상자: *the winner of the poetry contest* 시 경연 대회의 수상자 **2** INFORMAL someone or something that is successful || 성공한 사람이나 성공할 만한 것

win·ning /'wɪnɪŋ/ *adj* **winning smile/charm/personality etc.** a feature you have that is so attractive that many people like you || 아주 매력적이어서 많은 사람들이 좋아하는 자신이 가진 특성. 사람을 끄는 미소/용모/성격

win·nings /'wɪnɪŋz/ *n* [plural] money that you win in a game or by GAMBLING || 게임에서 또는 도박으로 딴 돈. 상금

win·o /'waɪnoʊ/ *n* INFORMAL someone who drinks a lot of cheap wine and lives on the streets || 아주 싼 포도주를 마시고 길거리에서 사는 사람. 주정뱅이

win·some /'wɪnsəm/ *adj* LITERARY pleasant and attractive || 쾌활하고 매력적인. 사람을 끄는: *a winsome smile* 매력적인 미소

win·ter /'wɪntɚ/ *n* the season between fall and spring, when the weather is coldest || 날씨가 가장 추울 때인, 가을과 봄 사이의 계절. 겨울: *The park closes in (the) winter.* 그 공원은 겨울에 폐장한다. / *I hope it snows this winter.* 나는 이번 겨울에 눈이 오기를 바란다. / *last/next*

winter (=the winter before or after this one) 지난[다음] 겨울

win·ter·time /'wɪntɚˌtaɪm/ *n* [U] the time of year when it is winter || 한 해 중 기후가 겨울인 때. 겨울철

win·try /'wɪntri/ *adj* like winter, or typical of winter, especially because it is cold or snowing || 특히 춥거나 눈이 오기 때문에 겨울 같은, 또는 겨울의 특색을 잘 나타내는. 겨울의

win-win sit·u·a·tion /ˌ. ˌ. ..'../ *n* a situation that will end well for everyone involved in it || 관련된 모든 사람에게 유리하게 끝나는 상황. 쌍방[양측]이 유리한 [득을 보는] 상황

wipe /waɪp/ *v* [T] **1** to clean something by rubbing it with a cloth or against a soft surface || 천으로 문지르거나 부드러운 표면에 대고 문질러 어떤 것을 깨끗이 하다. 닦다. 닦아내다: *Could you wipe off the table for me?* 테이블 좀 닦아 주시겠어요? / *Wipe your feet before you come in.* 들어오기 전에 네 발을 닦아라. **2** to remove dirt, water etc. from something with a cloth or your hand || 천이나 손으로 어떤 것에서 먼지·물 등을 제거하다. 얼굴 등을 없애다. 훔치다: *He wiped the sweat from his face.* 그는 얼굴의 땀을 훔쳤다. / *wiping away her tears* 그녀의 눈물을 훔쳐 주기 **3** to remove all the information that is stored on a TAPE, VIDEO, or computer DISK || 테이프[비디오, 컴퓨터 디스켓]에 저장된 모든 정보를 없애다. 지우다

wipe out *phr v* **1** [T **wipe** sb/sth ↔ **out**] to completely remove, destroy, or defeat someone or something || 사람이나 사물을 완전히 없애다[파괴하다, 패배시키다]. …을 분쇄[말살, 일소]하다: *Fires wiped out half of the city.* 화재로 그 도시의 절반이 전소되었다. **2** [T **wipe** sb **out**] SPOKEN to make someone feel extremely tired || 남을 매우 피곤하게 느끼게 하다. 녹초가 되게 하다: *All that running has wiped me out.* 전력 질주로 인해 나는 녹초가 되었다. **3** [I] SPOKEN to fall down or hit something when driving a car, riding a bicycle etc. || 자동차를 운전할 때·자전거를 타고 갈 때 등에 넘어지거나 어떤 것을 치다. 떨어지다. 들이받고 자빠지다

wipe sth ↔ **up** *phr v* [T] to remove liquid from a surface using a cloth || 천을 사용해서 표면의 물기를 닦다. 훔쳐내다: *Quick! Get something to wipe up the mess!* 어서! 지저분한 것을 닦아낼 것 좀 갖다 줘!

wip·er /'waɪpɚ/ *n* [C usually plural] ➪

WINDSHIELD WIPER

wire¹ /waɪə/ *n* **1** [U] metal that is shaped like thick thread ‖ 굵은 실 같은 모양의 금속. 철사: *a wire fence* 철조망 울타리 **2** a piece of metal like this used for carrying electrical currents or sound waves ‖ 전류나 음파를 전송하는 데 쓰이는 이같은 금속 조각. 전선. 전화선: *a telephone wire* 전화선 **3** ⇨ TELEGRAM

wire² *v* [T] **1** also **wire up** to connect wires to something, usually in an electrical system ‖ 전기 시스템에서 어떤 것에 전선을 연결하다. 전선을 달다[끌다]: *I'm almost finished wiring up the alarm.* 나는 경보기 연결을 거의 끝냈다. **2** to fasten two or more things or parts together using wire ‖ 철사를 써서 두 개 이상의 물건이나 부분들을 고정시키다. 철사로 묶다[매다]: *Lila had to have her jaw wired.* 릴라는 자신의 턱을 철사로 고정시켜야 했다. **3** to send money electronically ‖ 전신으로 돈을 보내다. 전신환으로 송금하다 **4** to send a TELEGRAM ‖ 전보를 보내다. 전신으로 알리다

wired /waɪəd/ *adj* **1** a person, room etc. that is wired has a hidden piece of recording equipment attached to him, her, or it ‖ 사람·방 등이 숨겨진 녹음 장비가 부착되어 있는. 도청 장치가 된 **2** SPOKEN feeling very active, excited, and awake ‖ 매우 활동적이고 흥분되고 정신이 깨어 있게 느끼는. 긴장한. 신경이 곤두선

wireless com·mu·ni·ca·tions /ˌ... ...../ *n* [plural] a system of sending and receiving electronic signals that does not use electrical or telephone wires, for example the system used by MOBILE PHONEs ‖ 전선이나 전화선을 사용하지 않고 전자 신호를 송수신하는, 휴대용 단말기 시스템 등의 시스템. 무선 통신

wire·tap /ˈwaɪəˌtæp/ *v* **-pped, -pping** [I, T] to listen to or record someone's telephone conversations using electronic equipment ‖ 전자 장비를 써서 남의 전화를 듣거나 녹음하다. 전화 도청하다 **– wiretap** *n*

wir·ing /ˈwaɪərɪŋ/ *n* [U] the network of wires that form the electrical system in a building ‖ 건물 안의 전기적 시스템을 형성하는 전선망. 배선: *You'll have to replace the wiring.* 당신은 배선을 바꿔야만 할 것이다.

wir·y /ˈwaɪəri/ *adj* **1** someone who is wiry is thin but has strong muscles ‖ 사람이 말랐지만 근육이 강한. 강인한. 강단 있는 **2** wiry hair is stiff and curly ‖ 머리털이 뻣뻣하고 말린. 철사 같은

wis·dom /ˈwɪzdəm/ *n* [U] **1** good judgment and the ability to make wise decisions ‖ 좋은 판단과 현명한 결정을 내리는 능력. 지혜. 현명함 **2** knowledge gained through a lot of learning and experience over a long period of time ‖ 오랜 시간에 걸쳐 많은 학습과 경험을 거쳐 얻은 지식. 학문. 지식. 박식

wisdom tooth /ˈ... ../ *n* one of the four large teeth at the back of your mouth that do not grow until you are an adult ‖ 어른이 될 때까지 자라지 않는 입의 뒤쪽에 있는 네 개의 큰 이빨 중 하나. 사랑니

wise¹ /waɪz/ *adj* **1** based on good judgment and experience ‖ 좋은 판단과 경험에 근거한. 현명한: *It'd be wise to leave early.* 일찍 떠나는 것이 현명할 것이다. / *a wise decision* 현명한 결정 — opposite UNWISE **2** able to make good decisions and give good advice ‖ 훌륭한 결정을 내리고 좋은 충고를 줄 수 있는. 지혜로운: *a wise leader* 지혜로운 지도자 **3 be none the wiser** to not understand something even though it has been explained to you or to not know about something that someone has done ‖ 설명을 받았지만 어떤 것을 이해하지 못하다, 또는 남이 한 것에 대해 알지 못하다. 여전히 모르다: *They sent me on a training course, but I'm still none the wiser.* 그들은 나를 훈련 과정에 보냈지만 나는 여전히 알지 못하고 있다. **4 price-wise/time-wise etc.** SPOKEN when considering prices, time etc. ‖ 가격·시간 등을 고려하면: *It would have been a problem transportation-wise.* 운송 측면을 고려하면 문제가 되었을 것이다. **– wisely** *adv*

wise² *v*

wise up *phr v* [I] INFORMAL to begin to understand the situation that you are in and deal with it better ‖ 자신이 처해 있는 상황을 이해하고 더 잘 처리하기 시작하다. 알다. 알아차리다: *Corporations should wise up and realize that employees aren't machines.* 기업들은 종업원은 기계가 아니라는 것을 알고 자각해야 한다.

wise·crack /ˈwaɪzkræk/ *n* INFORMAL a quick funny, slightly unkind remark ‖ 즉각적으로 재미있고 약간 불친절한 말. 재치 있는 농담. 경구. 건방진 말

wise guy /ˈ. ./ *n* INFORMAL an annoying person who thinks that s/he knows more than someone else ‖ 자신이 다른 사람보다 더 많이 안다고 생각하는 짜증나게 하는 사람. 아는 체하는 녀석. 건방진 놈

wish¹ /wɪʃ/ *v* **1** [T] to hope that

something will happen or that you can do something, even though it is very unlikely ‖ 전혀 일어날 것 같지 않지만 어떤 것이 일어나기를 또는 자신이 어떤 것을 할 수 있기를 희망하다. 바라다: *I wish they'd hurry up!* 나는 그들이 서두르면 좋겠어! / *I wish (that) I could remember his name.* 나는 그의 이름을 기억할 수 있기를 바란다. **2** [I, T] FORMAL to want to do something ‖ 어떤 것을 하기 원하다. … 하고 싶다: *I wish to make a complaint.* 나는 항의하고 싶다. **3** [T] to say that you hope someone will be happy, successful, lucky etc. ‖ 남이 앞으로 행복하기·성공하기·운이 좋기를 자신이 바란다고 말하다. 남이 …하기를 바라다: *Wish me luck!* 내 행운을 빌어 줘! **4 I/you wish!** SPOKEN said when you do not think something is true or possible, but you want it to be ‖ 어떤 것이 사실이거나 가능하다고 생각지 않지만 자신은 그렇게 되기를 원할 때 쓰여. (…했으면 좋겠다고) 생각하다. 바라다. 빌다: *"I'm sure he likes you." "Yeah, I wish!"* "그가 나를 좋아한다고 나는 확신한다." "글쎄, 그랬으면 좋겠어." —see usage note at DESIRE²

wish for sth *phr v* [T] to express what you hope for or want, often silently ‖ 종종 조용히 자신이 바라거나 원하는 것을 표현하다. …을 갈망하다. 간절히 바라다: *If you could have anything, what would you wish for?* 무엇이라도 가질 수 있다면 너는 무엇을 원하니?

wish² *n* **1** the act of wishing for something that you want, or the thing that you wish for ‖ 원하는 것을 기원하는 행위, 또는 자신이 바라는 물건. 소원[소망](하는 것): *Close your eyes and make a wish!* 눈을 감고 소원을 빌어라! / *Did you get your wish?* 네가 소원하는 것을 얻었니? **2** FORMAL a desire to do something, or a hope that something will happen ‖ 어떤 것을 하려는 소망, 또는 어떤 것이 일어날 것이라는 희망. 기원. 바람: *I had no wish to see him.* 나는 그를 보고 싶은 바람은 없다. / *It was her wish that she be buried in Montana.* 몬태나에 묻히는 것이 그녀의 소망이었다. **3 best wishes** a phrase written in cards to say that you hope someone will be happy and successful ‖ 남이 행복하고 성공하기를 자신이 바란다고 말하기 위해 카드에 쓴 어구

wish·bone /ˈwɪʃboun/ *n* a Y-shaped chicken bone that two people pull apart in order to find out who will get his/her wish ‖ 누가 자신의 소망을 이룰 것인지를

알기 위해 두 사람이 잡아당겨 떼어 놓는 Y자형의 닭뼈 (긴 쪽을 차지하면 소원이 이루어진다고 함). 차골(叉骨)

wish·ful think·ing /ˌ.. ˈ../ *n* [U] the false belief that something will happen just because you want it to ‖ 단지 자신이 그것을 원하기 때문에 어떤 것이 일어날 것이란 잘못된 믿음. 희망적 관측[해설]. 부질없는 기대

wish·y-wash·y /ˈwɪʃi ˌwɑʃi, -ˌwɔʃi/ *adj* INFORMAL a wishy-washy person, question, idea etc. does not seem to have a definite aim or purpose ‖ (사람·질문·생각 등이) 명확한 목표 또는 목적을 가진 것처럼 보이지 않는. 흐리멍덩한. 알맹이가 없는

wisp /wɪsp/ *n* **1** a small thin amount of hair, grass etc. ‖ 머리털·풀 등의 작고 알파란 분량. 한 움큼. 작은 단[묶음]. 숱 **2** a small thin line of smoke, cloud etc. ‖ 연기·구름 등의 작고 얇은 분량. 한 줄기. 한 조각 – **wispy** *adj*

wist·ful /ˈwɪstfəl/ *adj* showing slight sadness because you know you cannot have something you want ‖ 자신이 원하는 것을 가질 수 없다는 것을 알고 있어서 약간의 슬픔을 나타내는. 간절한 마음의. 깊은 생각[수심]에 잠긴: *a wistful expression* 간절한 마음의 표현 – **wistfully** *adv*

wit /wɪt/ *n* **1** the ability to say things that are funny, intelligent, and interesting ‖ 재미있는[지적인, 흥미 있는] 일을 말하는 능력. 위트. 기지. 재치: *a writer famous for his wit* 위트 있는 표현으로 유명한 작가 **2** someone who has this ability ‖ 이 능력을 가진 사람. 재사. 재치[기지]가 풍부한 사람 —see also WITS

witch /wɪtʃ/ *n* a woman who is believed to have magic powers, especially ones that she uses for doing bad things ‖ 특히 나쁜 일을 하는 데 사용하는 마법의 힘을 가진 것으로 믿어지는 여자. 마녀. 여자 마법사 —compare WARLOCK

witch·craft /ˈwɪtʃkræft/ *n* [U] the use of magic in order to make strange things happen ‖ 이상한 일을 일어나게 하기 위한 마법의 사용. 마술

witch doc·tor /ˈ. ˌ../ *n* a man who is believed to be able to cure people using magic, especially in some parts of Africa ‖ 특히 아프리카의 일부 지역에서 마법을 이용하여 사람들을 치료할 수 있다고 믿어지는 사람. (미개 사회의) 주술사. 마법사

witch hunt /ˈ. ./ *n* DISAPPROVING an attempt to find and punish people whose opinions, political beliefs etc. are considered to be wrong or dangerous ‖ 의견·정치적 신념 등이 잘못됐거나 위험하다고 간주되는 사람들을 찾아서 처벌하려는 시도. 마녀 사냥

with /wɪθ, wɪð/ *prep* **1** used in order to show that two or more people or things are together or near each other ‖ 둘 이상의 사람이나 사물이 함께 있거나 서로 가까이 있다는 것을 나타내는 데에 쓰여. …과 함께: *She went to the beach with her friends.* 그녀는 친구들과 함께 해변에 갔다. / *Put this bag with the other ones.* 이 가방을 다른 가방들과 같이 놓아라. / *eggs mixed with milk* 우유가 섞인 계란 **2** having a particular condition, thing, quality, or feeling ‖ 특정한 조건[사물, 특성, 감정]을 가지고 있는. …을 가지고 있는. …이 있는: *a boy with a broken arm* 팔이 부러진 소년 / *Connie smiled with pride.* 코니는 자랑스러운 듯이 미소지었다. / *Where's the dish with the blue pattern?* 파란 무늬가 있는 접시가 어디 있니? **3** including ‖ …을 포함하여[합하여]: *Your dinner comes with fries.* 저녁은 감자 튀김이 같이 나옵니다. **4** using something ‖ 어떤 것을 사용하는. …으로: *Don't eat with your fingers!* 손으로 먹지 마! **5** because of something ‖ 어떤 것 때문에: *The room was bright with sunlight.* 그 방은 햇빛이 비쳐 밝았다. **6** used in order to say what covers or fills something ‖ 어떤 것을 덮거나 채우고 있는 것을 말하는 데에 쓰여. …으로: *a pillow filled with feathers* 깃털로 채워진 베개 / *His hands were covered with blood.* 그의 손은 피범벅이었다. **7** relating to something or someone ‖ 사물이나 사람과 관련되는. …에 관하여: *What's wrong with the radio?* 라디오가 왜 이러지? / *She's in love with you.* 그녀는 너를 사랑하고 있다. **8** supporting or liking someone ‖ 남을 지지하거나 좋아하는. …에게 동의[찬성]하는: *I agree with you.* 나는 너에게 동의한다. **9** against or opposing someone ‖ 남과 맞서거나 반대하는. …을 상대로: *He's always arguing with his son.* 그는 항상 아들과 다툰다. **10** at the same time or rate as something else ‖ 다른 것과 같은 시간이나 비율로. …에 따라[비례하여]: *The wine will get better with age.* 포도주는 묵을수록 더 좋아진다. **11 with it** SPOKEN thinking clearly and not tired ‖ 지치지 않고 명확하게 생각하는. 머리가 맑은. 잘 이해하는: *Sorry, I'm not very with it today.* 미안해, 오늘 내가 좀 머리가 안 돌아간다. **12 be with me/you** SPOKEN to

understand what someone is saying ‖ 어떤 사람이 말하고 있는 것을 이해하다. 말을 알아듣다: *Are you with me?* 내 말 알아듣겠니? **13** in the same direction as something ‖ 어떤 것과 같은 방향으로: *sailing with the wind* 바람을 타고 항해하기

with·draw /wɪθ'drɔ, wɪð-/ *v* **1** [T] to take money out of a bank account ‖ 은행 계좌에서 돈을 빼다. 인출하다: *He withdrew $200 from his savings account.* 그는 보통 예금 계좌에서 200달러를 인출했다. **2** [T] to stop giving something or stop making something available, especially because of an official decision ‖ 특히 공식적인 결정 때문에 어떤 것을 주거나 이용할 수 있게 하는 것을 중단하다. 철회[취소]하다: *Congress threatened to withdraw support for the space project.* 의회는 우주 계획에 대한 지지를 철회하겠지라고 위협했다. **3** [I, T] to stop being involved in something, or to make someone stop being involved ‖ 어떤 것에 개입하는 것을 중단하다, 또는 남이 개입하는 것을 중단하게 하다. 그만두다[두게 하다]: *She was withdrawn from Winston Academy.* 그녀는 윈스톤 학교를 그만두었다. / *The third candidate has withdrawn.* 제3의 후보는 물러났다. **4** [I, T] to move out of a place, or to make a person or group do this ‖ 어떤 장소에서 나오거나 사람이나 집단이 이렇게 하게 하다. 철수하다[시키다]: *American troops were gradually withdrawn.* 미군은 점진적으로 철수했다.

with·draw·al /wɪθ'drɔəl/ *n* **1** [C, U] the action of taking money out of a bank account, or the amount you take out ‖ 은행 계좌에서 돈을 빼는 행위나 뺀 액수. 인출(액): *I'd like to make a withdrawal, please.* 예금을 인출하고 싶습니다. **2** [C, U] the action of moving an army, its weapons etc. away from the area where it was fighting ‖ 군대·무기 등을 전투하고 있었던 지역에서 빼내는 행위. 철수: *the withdrawal of 1000 Russian tanks* 천 대의 러시아 탱크의 철수 **3** [C, U] the action of not continuing to give something or be involved in something ‖ 어떤 것을 주기를 계속하지 않거나 계속 개입하지 않는 행위. 철회. 정지: *the withdrawal of government aid* 정부 보조의 중단 / *Hanson's withdrawal from the competition surprised everyone.* 핸슨이 그 시합을 취소한 것은 모두를 놀라게 했다. **4** [U] the pain, bad feelings etc. that someone suffers when s/he stops regularly taking a drug ‖ 사람이 규칙적으로 약물을 복용하는 것을 중단할 때 겪는 고통·안 좋은 기분 등. 금단 증상

with·drawn /wɪθˈdrɔn/ *adj* quiet, thoughtful, and not willing to be around other people ‖ 조용하고 사색적이며 다른 사람들과 어울리려고 하지 않는. 집안에 틀어박힌. 내성적인

with·er /ˈwɪðər/ *v* [I] **1** also **wither away** if a plant withers, it starts to become drier and smaller because it is dying ‖ 식물이 죽어가고 있어서 더 마르고 작아지기 시작하다. 시들다 **2** to gradually become less in size, importance etc. ‖ 크기·중요성 등에서 점진적으로 작아지다. 쇠퇴[쇠약]하다: *Small towns are withering away as the young people leave for the cities.* 소도시들은 젊은이들이 대도시로 떠나면서 쇠퇴해지고 있다.

with·hold /wɪθˈhoʊld, wɪð-/ *v* [T] to refuse to give something to someone ‖ 남에게 어떤 것을 주기를 거절하다. 주지 않고 두다. 보류하다: *They said McShane had withheld information from Congress.* 그들은 맥쉐인이 의회에 정보를 일부러 제공하지 않았다고 말했다.

with·in /wɪˈðɪn, wɪˈθɪn/ *adv, prep* **1** during a particular period of time ‖ 특정한 기간 동안에. … 이내에: *The movie should start within the next 5 minutes.* 영화는 다음 5분 안에 시작할 것이다. / *Within a month of meeting him I knew I was in love.* 그를 만난 지 한 달도 못 되어서 나는 내 자신이 사랑에 빠진 것을 알았다. **2** inside a particular area or distance, and not beyond it ‖ 특정한 지역이나 거리를 넘지 않고 그 안쪽에. …내에: *We need a hotel within a mile of the airport.* 우리는 공항에서 1마일 내의 호텔이 필요하다. **3** inside an organization, society, or group of people ‖ 조직[사회], 사람 집단]의 내부에. …의 내부에: *They want to promote from within the department.* 그들은 부서 내부 사람을 승진시키고 싶어 한다. **4** obeying a particular set of rules, TRADITIONS, limits etc. ‖ 특정한 규정·전통·제한 등에 따르는. …의 범위[한계] 내에: *driving within the speed limit* 속도 제한 범위 안에서의 운전하기

with·out /wɪˈðaʊt, wɪˈθaʊt/ *adv, prep* **1** not having, not using, or not doing something ‖ 어떤 것을 가지고 있지[사용하지, 하고 있지] 않는. …없이: *I can't see anything without my glasses.* 나는 안경 없이는 아무것도 볼 수 없다. / *He left without saying goodbye.* 그는 작별 인사도 없이 떠났다. **2** not being with someone or not having someone to help you ‖ 남과 같이 있지 않거나 자기를 도울 사람이 없는. …없이: *Why did you leave without me?* 넌 왜 나를 두고 떠나 버렸니? / *We can't finish this job without Jake.* 우리는 제이크 없이는 이 일을 끝낼 수 없어. **3** **do/go without** to not have something that you really want or need, or to stop having it ‖ 정말로 원하거나 필요한 것을 갖지 않거나, 또는 가지는 것을 그만두다. …없이 지내다[견딘다]: *They went without food and water for 2 days.* 그들은 이틀간 음식과 물 없이 지냈다.

with·stand /wɪθˈstænd, wɪð-/ *v* [T] to be strong enough not to be harmed or changed by something ‖ 어떤 것에 의해 해를 입거나 바뀌지 않을 정도로 충분히 강하다. 잘 견디다[버티다]: *The buildings have withstood earthquakes since 1916.* 그 건물들은 1916년 이래로 지진을 잘 견디어 왔다.

wit·ness¹ /ˈwɪtnɪs/ *n* **1** someone who sees an accident or a crime and can describe what happened ‖ 사고나 범죄를 눈으로 보고 무슨 일이 일어났는지 진술할 수 있는 사람. 목격자: *Unfortunately there were no witnesses to the robbery.* 불행히도 그 강도 사건에는 목격자가 없었다. **2** someone who describes in a court of law what s/he has seen or what s/he knows about a crime ‖ 법정에서 범죄에 대해서 봤거나 아는 바를 진술하는 사람. 증인: *He asked the witness how well she knew the defendant.* 그는 증인에게 그녀가 피고인을 얼마나 잘 아는지 물었다. **3** someone who watches another person sign an official document, and then signs it also to prove this ‖ 다른 사람이 공식 문서에 서명하는 것을 지켜보고서 이것을 입증하기 위해 역시 서명하는 사람. 입회[부서]인

witness² *v* [T] **1** to see something happen, especially an accident or a crime ‖ 특히 사건이나 범죄가 발생하는 것을 보다. …을 목격하다: *Few people actually witnessed the event.* 그 사건을 실제로 목격한 사람은 거의 없었다. **2** to watch someone sign an official document, and then sign it also to prove this ‖ 남이 공식 문서에 서명하는 것을 지켜보고서 이것을 입증하기 위해 자기도 또 한 서명하다. …에 입회[부서]하다

witness stand /ˈ.. ./ *n* the raised area where WITNESSes sit when they are being questioned in a court of law ‖ 증인이 법정에서 신문을 받을 때 앉는 높은 장소. 증인석

wits /wɪts/ *n* [plural] **1 lose your wits** to lose your ability to think quickly and make good decisions ‖ 빠르게 생각하고 좋은 결정을 내리는 능력을 잃다. 제정신을 잃다 **2 be at your wits' end** to feel very annoyed, impatient, and upset because you do not know how to solve a problem ‖ 어떻게 문제를 풀어야 할지 몰라서 매우 짜증나고 조바심이 나며 속상해하다. 어찌할 바를 모르다 **3 keep/have your wits about you** to be ready to think quickly in order to deal with a problem ‖ 문제를 해결하기 위해 빠르게 생각할 준비가 되어 있다. 빈틈없이 머리를 쓰다 **4 scare sb out of his/her wits** to frighten someone so much that s/he cannot think clearly ‖ 남을 아주 많이 놀라게 해서 그 사람이 명확하게 생각할 수 없다. …을 기겁하게 하다. 얼이 빠지다

wit·ti·cism /ˈwɪtəˌsɪzəm/ *n* a quick, funny, and interesting remark ‖ 재빠르고 우습고 재미있는 말. 재치 있는 말. 재담

wit·ty /ˈwɪti/ *adj* using words in a funny, intelligent, and interesting way ‖ 말을 웃기고·총명하게·재미있게 사용하는. 재치[기지]가 있는: *a witty young man* 재치가 넘치는 젊은이 / *a witty response* 재치 있는 대답

wives /waɪvz/ *n* the plural of WIFE ‖ wife의 복수형

wiz·ard /ˈwɪzɚd/ *n* **1** a man who is believed to have special magic powers ‖ 특별한 마법의 힘을 가지고 있는 것으로 믿어지는 남자. 마법사 **2** also **wiz** INFORMAL someone who is very good at doing something or using something ‖ 어떤 것을 하거나 사용하는 데에 재주가 있는 사람. 귀재. 명수: *a computer wizard* 컴퓨터 도사

wiz·ened /ˈwɪzənd/ *adj* old and having dry skin with a lot of WRINKLEs (=lines) ‖ 늙고 주름이 많이 진 메마른 피부를 지닌. 쭈글쭈글한

wk. *n* the written abbreviation of WEEK ‖ week의 약어

wob·ble /ˈwɑbəl/ *v* [I] to move from side to side in an unsteady way ‖ 불안정하게 좌우로 움직이다. 비틀[흔들]거리다 **- wobbly** *adj* : *a wobbly chair* 덜거덕거리는 의자 **— wobble** *n*

woe /woʊ/ *n* [U] LITERARY great sadness ‖ 큰 슬픔. 비통. 비애 —see also WOES

woe·be·gone /ˈwoʊbɪˌgɔn, -ˌgɑn/ *adj* looking very sad ‖ 매우 슬퍼 보이는. 슬픔에 잠긴. 수심에 찬

woe·ful·ly /ˈwoʊfəli/ *adv* **1** deserving

to be criticized and pitied for being so bad ‖ 너무 형편없어서 비난받고 동정 받아 마땅하게. 한심하게도: *a woefully disappointing performance* 한심할 정도로 실망스러운 공연 **2** in a very sad way ‖ 매우 슬프게. 비통하게. 애처롭게: *He sighed and looked woefully around the room.* 그는 한숨을 쉬고 비통한 듯이 방을 둘러보았다.

woes /woʊz/ *n* [plural] FORMAL problems that are affecting someone greatly ‖ 어떤 사람에게 크게 영향을 미치고 있는 문제들. 고통[고민]의 원인. 재앙. 재난

wok /wɑk/ *n* a large wide pot, used especially to STIR-FRY meat and vegetables ‖ 특히 고기와 야채를 센 불에 재빨리 볶는 데에 쓰이는 크고 폭이 넓은 냄비. 중국 냄비 —see picture at PAN¹

woke /woʊk/ *v* the past tense of WAKE ‖ wake의 과거형

wo·ken /ˈwoʊkən/ *v* the PAST PARTICIPLE of WAKE ‖ wake의 과거 분사형

wolf¹ /wʊlf/, **wolf down** *v* [T] INFORMAL to eat something very quickly ‖ 어떤 것을 매우 빨리 먹다. 게걸스럽게 먹다: *She wolfed down a couple of hamburgers.* 그녀는 햄버거 몇 개를 걸신들린 듯이 먹어치웠다.

wolf² *n, plural* **wolves** /wʊlvz/ a wild animal similar to a dog ‖ 개와 비슷한 야생 동물. 늑대

wom·an /ˈwʊmən/ *n, plural* **women** **1** an adult female human ‖ 성인 여자. 여성: *the women I work with* 내가 함께 일하는 여자들 / *a woman doctor/lawyer/ politician* 여성 의사[변호사, 정치인] **2** women in general ‖ 일반적인 여자들. 여인: *It's not safe there for a woman traveling alone.* 그곳은 여성이 혼자 여행하기에는 안전하지 않다.

wom·an·hood /ˈwʊmənˌhʊd/ *n* [U] the state of being a woman, or the time when a female person is an adult ‖ 성인 여자인 상태나 여성이 성인이 되는 때. 성숙한 여성. 여자의 성년

wom·an·iz·er /ˈwʊməˌnaɪzɚ/ *n* a man who tries to have sexual relationships with many different women ‖ 다른 많은 여자들과 성관계를 가지려고 애쓰는 남자. 바람둥이. 호색한

wom·an·kind /ˈwʊmənˌkaɪnd/ *n* [U] women considered together as a group ‖ 한 집단으로 함께 간주되는 여자들. 여성. 여자들

womb /wum/ *n* ⇨ UTERUS

wom·en /ˈwɪmɪn/ *n* the plural of WOMAN ‖ woman의 복수형

won /wʌn/ *v* the past tense and PAST PARTICIPLE of WIN ‖ win의 과거·과거 분사형

won·der¹ /'wʌndər/ *v* [I, T] **1** to think about something and want to know what is true about it or what is happening or will happen ‖ 어떤 것에 대해 생각하며 그것에 대해서 무엇이 사실인지[무슨 일이 일어나고 있는지, 어떻게 될 것인지]를 알고 싶어 하다. 궁금하다. …을 궁금해 하다: *I wonder if she knows we're here.* 나는 그녀가 우리가 이곳에 있는 것을 아는지 궁금하다. / *I wonder how Wendy's feeling today.* 나는 오늘 웬디의 기분이 어떤지 궁금하다. / *We wondered where you'd gone.* 우리는 네가 어디 갔었는지 궁금했어. **2 I was wondering if/whether** SPOKEN **a)** used in order to offer a polite invitation ‖ 정중한 초대를 하는 데에 쓰여. …해 주지 않으시겠습니까?: *We were wondering whether you'd like to come with us.* 우리와 함께 가지 않으시겠습니까 **b)** used in order to politely ask for something ‖ …을 정중하게 요청하는 데에 쓰여. …했으면 합니다만: *I was wondering if I could use your phone.* 전화 좀 사용할 수 있을까요. **3** to have doubts about whether someone or something is true, good, normal etc. ‖ 사람이나 사물이 사실인지[좋은지, 정상인지] 등에 대해서 의심을 품다. 의심하다. 미심쩍게 여기다: *I began to wonder about this business of his.* 나는 그의 이 사업에 대해서 의심이 들기 시작했다. **4** to be surprised by something ‖ 어떤 것에 의해 놀라다. 불가사의하게[기이하게] 여기다: *I wonder why she didn't call the police.* 나는 그녀가 왜 경찰에 전화를 안 했는지 의아하다.

wonder² *n* **1** [U] a feeling of admiration and surprise ‖ 감탄과 놀라움의 감정. 경이. 경탄: *They listened to Lisa's story in/with wonder.* 그들은 리사의 이야기를 경탄하며 들었다. **2 no wonder** SPOKEN said when you are not surprised about something ‖ 어떤 것에 대해서 놀라지 않을 때에 쓰여. …은 조금도 놀랍지 않다: *No wonder you feel sick if you ate the whole pizza!* 피자 한 판을 다 먹었으니 토할 것 같은 것도 당연하지! **3** someone or something that makes you feel admiration and surprise ‖ 감탄과 놀라움을 느끼게 하는 사람이나 사물. 불가사의한[경이로운] 사람[것]: *the wonders of modern technology* 현대 과학 기술의 경이로움

wonder³ *adj* extremely good or effective ‖ 매우 좋거나 효과적인. 경이로

운. 특효의: *a new wonder drug* 새로 나온 특효약

won·der·ful /'wʌndərfəl/ *adj* extremely good ‖ 매우 좋은. 참으로 훌륭한. 대단한: *Congratulations! That's wonderful news!* 축하해! 그거 정말 대단한 소식이구나! **-wonderfully** *adv*

won't /wount/ *v* the short form of "will not" ‖ "will not"의 단축형: *Dad won't like it.* 아빠는 마음에 안 들어 하실 거야.

wont¹ /wɔnt, wount/ *adv* FORMAL **be wont to do sth** to have the habit of doing something ‖ 어떤 것을 하는 습성이 있다. …하는 것이 보통이다

wont² *n* FORMAL **as is sb's wont** used in order to say that it is someone's habit to do something ‖ 어떤 것을 하는 것이 어떤 사람의 습관이라고 말하는 데에 쓰여. 습관대로. 여느 때와 같이

woo /wu/ *v* [T] **1** to try to persuade someone to do something such as support you, vote for you, or buy something from you ‖ 남에게 자기를 지지하게[자기에게 투표하게, 자기에게서 물건을 사게] 하도록 설득하려고 애쓰다. 조르다. 간청하다: *Politicians were busy wooing voters.* 정치인들은 유권자들의 마음을 잡느라 여념이 없었다. **2** OLD-FASHIONED to be romantic in order to gain someone's love ‖ 남의 사랑을 얻으려고 낭만적이 되다. …에게 구애[구혼]하다

wood /wud/ *n* [C, U] the material that tree branches and TRUNKs are made of ‖ 나뭇가지와 나무 줄기로 만들어지는 물질. 나무. 목재: *polished wood floors* 윤을 낸 나무 바닥 / *a table made from three different types of wood* 세 가지의 다른 종류의 목재로 만든 탁자 —see also WOODS

wood·chuck /'wudtʃʌk/ *n* ⇨ GROUNDHOG

wood·ed /'wudɪd/ *adj* having WOODS or covered with trees ‖ 숲이 있거나 나무들로 뒤덮인. 나무가 무성한[우거진]

wood·en /'wudn/ *adj* **1** made from wood ‖ 나무로 만든. 목제[목조]의: *a wooden box* 나무 상자 **2** not showing enough expression, movement, or emotion ‖ 표정[움직임, 감정]을 충분히 나타내지 않는. 생기가 없는. 무표정한. 굳은: *a wooden performance* 딱딱한 공연

wood·land /'wudlənd, -lænd/ *n* [C, U] an area of land that is covered with trees ‖ 나무들로 뒤덮인 일정 지대. 삼림 지대

wood·peck·er /'wud,pɛkər/ *n* a bird with a long beak that it uses to make holes in trees ‖ 나무에 구멍을 내기 위해 사용하는 긴 부리가 있는 새. 딱따구리

woods /wʊdz/ *n* [plural] a small forest where a lot of trees grow ‖ 나무들이 많이 자라는 작은 삼림. 숲: *We live next to the woods.* 우리 숲 옆에 산다.

wood·wind /ˈwʊdˌwɪnd/ *n* **the woodwinds** the people in an ORCHESTRA or band who play musical instruments that you blow into, such as the CLARINET or FLUTE ‖ 관현악단이나 악단에서 클라리넷이나 플루트 등 입으로 부는 악기를 연주하는 사람들. 목관 악기부

wood·work /ˈwʊdwɚk/ *n* [U] **1** the parts of a building that are made of wood, usually for decoration ‖ 보통 장식을 위해, 나무로 만든 건물의 부분. 목조 부분 **2** the skill of making wooden objects ‖ 목제품을 만드는 기술. 목재 공예. 목세공

wood·y /ˈwʊdi/ *adj* looking, smelling, tasting, or feeling like wood ‖ 나무처럼 생긴[냄새가 나는, 맛이 나는, 느껴지는]. 나무 같은. 목질의: *woody plants* 나무 같은 식물

woof /wʊf/ *n* a word that represents the sound a dog makes ‖ 개가 내는 소리를 표현하는 단어. 멍멍

wool¹ /wʊl/ *n* [U] the soft thick hair of a sheep, used for making cloth and YARN ‖ 천과 털실을 만드는 데에 쓰이는 양의 부드럽고 숱이 많은 털. 양모. 양털

wool², **wool·en** /ˈwʊlən/ *adj* made from wool ‖ 양털로 만든. 양모(제)의: *a wool skirt* 양모 치마 / *wool blankets* 양모 담요

wool·ens /ˈwʊlənz/ *n* [plural] clothes that are made from wool ‖ 양털로 만든 옷. 모직 옷

wool·y /ˈwʊli/ *adj* looking or feeling like wool ‖ 양털처럼 생기거나 느껴지는. 양모 같은: *a wooly beard* 양털 같은 턱수염

woo·zy /ˈwuzi/ *adj* INFORMAL feeling weak and unsteady; DIZZY ‖ 약하고 불안정하게 느껴지는. 머리가 띵한[어지러운]; 윤 dizzy

word¹ /wɚd/ *n*

1 ▶LANGUAGE PART 언어 부분◀ the smallest unit of language used for making phrases and sentences, that usually represents an object, idea, action etc. ‖ 보통 사물/생각/동작 등을 표현하는 구절과 문장을 만들 때에 쓰이는 언어의 최소 단위. 낱말. 단어: *"Casa" is the Spanish word for "house."* "카사"는 "집"을 뜻하는 스페인어이다. / *Write a 500-word essay about your family.* 자기

의 가족에 대해서 500자 에세이를 쓰시오.

2 ▶STH SAID/WRITTEN 말해진/쓰인 것◀ something that you say or write ‖ 말하거나 쓴 것. 말. 글: *I didn't hear/understand a word you said.* 나는 네가 한 말을 알아듣지 못했다. / *Tell us what happened in your own words.* (=without being influenced by what others say) 네 입으로 직접 무슨 일이 일어났는지 말해 봐라. / *Promise you won't say a word about the accident to John.* 존에게 그 사고에 대해서 한 마디도 하지 않겠다고 약속해라.

3 ▶STATEMENT 말◀ a short important statement or discussion ‖ 짧고 중요한 말이나 논의. 말. 발언: *Mr. Gleeson like a word with you in his office.* 글리슨 씨가 사무실에서 당신과 얘기를 나누고 싶어 하십니다. / *a word of advice/warning/encouragement* 충고[경고, 격려] 한 마디

4 in other words used when you are repeating a statement in simpler, clearer, or more direct words ‖ 더 간단하거나 명확하거나 직접적인 말로 발언을 반복할 때에 쓰여. 바꾸어 말하면: *Some people aren't demonstrative. In other words, they don't express their feelings.* 어떤 사람들은 현시적이지 않다. 다시 말해서, 그들은 자신의 감정을 표현하지 않는다.

5 ▶NEWS 소식◀ [singular, U] information, news, or a message ‖ 정보[소식, 전갈]: *The word is the company's closing its offices in Boston.* 그 회사가 보스턴 지점을 폐쇄한다는 소식이 있다. / *Have you had any word from your lawyers yet?* 네 변호사들에게서 아직 아무런 말도 없니?

6 ▶PROMISE 약속◀ a promise ‖ 약속: *I give you my word: we'll take good care of him.* 내가 약속하지. 그는 우리가 잘 돌볼게. / *He's a man of his word.* (=does not break his promises) 그는 약속을 잘 지킨다.

7 swear/dirty/cuss word a word that is considered to be offensive or shocking by most people ‖ 대부분의 사람들이 기분이 상하거나 충격적으로 여기는 말. 욕설/상스러운 말/ 저주

8 word for word said, written, copied etc. with exactly the same words in exactly the same order ‖ 정확히 같은 어순으로 정확히 같은 단어로 말해진[쓰인, 인용한]. 말 그대로: *That's not what he said word for word, but it's close.* 그가 정확히 그렇게 말하지는 않았지만, 대충 비슷하다.

9 take sb's word for it to believe what

someone says even though s/he has no proof ‖ 남이 하는 말을 비록 그 사람이 증명하지 못하더라도 믿다. …의 말을 곧이 듣다: *Don't just take my word for it - ask them yourself!* 그냥 내 말만 그대로 믿지 말고 네가 직접 그 사람들에게 물어 봐라!

10 by word of mouth if information or news comes to you by word of mouth, someone tells you about it instead of you reading about it, seeing it on television etc. ‖ 정보나 소식에 대해 읽고 텔레비전에서 보는 대신에 남이 말해 주어. 구두[구전]로. 입소문으로

11 put in a good word for sb to talk about someone's valuable qualities with an important person ‖ 중요한 사람에게 남의 가치 있는 자질에 대해서 이야기하다. …을 칭찬[추천]하다: *Could you put in a good word for me with your boss?* 당신의 사장님께 저에 대해 말씀 좀 잘 해 주시겠습니까?

12 the last word the last statement in a discussion or argument ‖ 토론이나 논쟁에서의 마지막 말. 최종 결론: *She's not content unless she has the last word.* 그녀는 최종 결정을 듣지 않는 한 만족하지 않는다.

13 my word! SPOKEN OLD-FASHIONED said when you are very surprised ‖ 매우 놀랐을 때에 쓰여. 어머나! 이런!: *My word! Isn't he tall!* 놀라워라! 그는 정말 크지!

14 not in so many words not in a direct way ‖ 직접적이지 않은. 분명하지 [노골적이지, 확실하지] 않은: *"So Dad said he'd pay for it?" "Not in so many words."* "그래서 아빠가 그것을 사 주시겠다고 말씀하셨다고?" "확실하게 말씀하시지는 않았어."

15 give/say the word to tell someone to start doing something ‖ 남에게 어떤 것을 하기 시작하라고 말하다. 명령을 내리다: *Don't move until I give the word.* 내가 말할 때까지는 움직이지 마.

16 the final word the power to decide whether or how to do something ‖ 어떤 것을 할 것인지 또는 어떻게 할 것인지를 결정하는 힘. 최종 결정권: *My boss has the final word on hiring staff.* 사장님이 직원을 채용하는 최종 결정권을 가지고 있다.

word² *v* [T] to use particular words when saying or writing something ‖ 어떤 것을 말하거나 쓸 때 특정한 단어를 사용하다. 말을 골라 표현하다: *a carefully worded letter to the manager* 지배인에게 보내는 조심스러운 어투의 편지

word·ing /'wɚdɪŋ/ *n* [U] the words and

phrases used in order to express something ‖ 어떤 것을 표현하기 위해 사용하는 말과 구절. 말씨. 어법

word pro·cess·or /'. ,.../ *n* a small computer or a special computer program that you use for writing letters, reports etc. ‖ 편지·보고서 등을 쓸 때에 쓰이는 작은 컴퓨터나 특수한 컴퓨터 프로그램. 워드 프로세서 - **word pro·cessing** *n* [U]

word·y /'wɚdi/ *adj* using too many words ‖ 너무 말을 많이 하는. 말 많은. 장황한: *a long wordy explanation* 길고 장황한 설명

wore /wɔr/ *v* the past tense of WEAR ‖ wear의 과거형

work¹ /wɚk/ *v*

1 ▶DO A JOB 일을 하다◀ [I] to do a job in order to earn money, or to do the activities and duties that are part of your job ‖ 돈을 벌기 위해서 일을 하다, 또는 직업의 일부인 활동과 임무를 해내다. 일[근무]하다: *Heidi works for a law firm in Montreal.* 하이디는 몬트리올에 있는 법률 사무소에 근무한다. / *I used to work at Burger King.* 나는 예전에 버거킹에서 일했다. / *He's working with children who have learning difficulties.* 그는 학습 장애가 있는 어린이들을 대상으로 일을[연구를] 하고 있습니다.

2 ▶OPERATE 작동하다◀ [I] if a machine or piece of equipment works, it does what it has been designed to do ‖ 기계나 장비가 계획된 대로 일을 하다. 작동하다: *The CD player isn't working.* CD 플레이어가 작동하지 않는다.

3 ▶USE A MACHINE 기계를 사용하다◀ [T] to use a complicated machine or piece of equipment ‖ 복잡한 기계나 장비를 사용하다. …을 조작하다[작동시키다]: *Does any of you know how to work the printer?* 너희들 중 누가 이 프린터기를 작동시킬 수 있어?

4 ▶BE EFFECTIVE 효과적이다◀ [I] if something works, it is effective, successful, or gives you the results that you want ‖ 어떤 것이 효과적·성공적이거나 원하는 결과를 내다. 잘 되어 가다. 효과가 있다: *The glue didn't work, so I stapled it.* 접착제가 효과가 없어서 꺾쇠로 철했다. / *Did Gene's plan work?* 진의 계획 대로 됐니? / *I hope this cough medicine works.* 이 기침약이 잘 들었으면 좋겠다.

5 ▶DO AN ACTIVITY 활동을 하다◀ [I] to do an activity or a duty that involves a lot of time and effort ‖ 많은 시간과 노력이 수반되는 활동이나 임무를 수행하다.

종사하다. 작업하다: *I'd like you to work in small groups and discuss Chapter 7.* 나는 여러분들이 소집단으로 연구해서 7장을 토론하기 바랍니다.

6 work your way to move somewhere or achieve something gradually and with effort ‖ 점차적으로 그리고 열심히 어떤 곳으로 이동해 가거나 어떤 것을 성취하다. 노력하여 나아가다[얻다]: *Dave worked his way to the top of the firm.* 데이브는 열심히 일해서 회사의 최고 자리에 올랐다.

7 ▶MOVE SLOWLY 천천히 움직이다◀ [I, T] to move into a position slowly with many small movements, or to move something in this way ‖ 많은 작은 움직임으로 천천히 어떤 위치로 이동하다, 또는 어떤 것을 이렇게 이동하게 하다. 서서히 움직이다[움직이게 하다]: *The screw must have worked loose.* 나사가 헐거워졌던 게 틀림없다

8 work against sb to prevent someone from being successful or getting the result s/he wants ‖ 남이 성공하지 못하게 또는 원하는 결과를 얻지 못하게 막다. …에게 불리하게 작용하다: *Unfortunately her bad grades worked against her.* 불행히도 그녀의 나쁜 학점이 그녀에게 불리하게 작용했다.

9 work up an appetite/sweat to do so much exercise that you become very hungry or SWEATY ‖ 운동을 아주 많이 해서 매우 배가 고프거나 땀을 흘리게 되다. 운동을 해서 식욕/땀이 나게 하다

10 ▶SHAPE STH 어떤 것의 모양을 만들다◀ [T] if you work a material such as clay, leather, or metal, you bend it, shape it etc. in order to make something ‖ 어떤 것을 만들기 위해서 점토[가죽, 금속] 등의 재료를 구부리고 모양을 만들다. …을 제작하다[가공하다]

11 ▶LAND 땅◀ [T] if you work the land or the soil, you try to grow crops on it ‖ 땅이나 토지에서 농작물을 재배하려고 노력하다. …을 경작하다

12 ▶EXERCISE 운동◀ [T] if you work a muscle or part of your body, you are exercising it ‖ 근육이나 몸의 일부를 단련시키다. 운동하다

work on *phr v* [T] **1 [work on sth]** to try to repair something, complete something, or improve something ‖ 어떤 것을 수선[완성, 개선]하려고 애쓰다: *Dad's still working on the car.* 아빠는 아직도 차를 수리하고 계신다. / *Isn't Claire working on her Ph.D.?* 클레어는 박사 학위를 따려고 공부하고 있지 않니? / *I need to work on my essay.* 나는 에

세이를 써야 해. **2 [work on sb]** to try again and again to influence someone, so that s/he does what you want ‖ 남에게 영향을 주기 위해 자꾸만 노력하여 결국 자신이 원하는 것을 하게 하다. …을 계속 설득하다

work out *phr v* **1 [T work sth ↔ out]** to calculate an amount, price, or value ‖ 수량[가격, 가치]을 계산하다. …을 산정하다. 합계를 내다: *Have you worked out how much we owe them?* 너는 우리가 그들에게 얼마나 빚졌는지 계산해 봤니? **2 [I]** to cost a particular amount ‖ 특정한 액수의 비용이 들다. …을/에서 가격[비용]을 매기다: *The hotel works out to/at about $50 a night.* 그 호텔은 하룻밤 묵는데 대략 50달러 정도의 비용이 든다. **3 [T work sth ↔ out]** to think carefully in order to solve a problem or plan something ‖ 문제를 풀거나 어떤 것을 계획하기 위해서 주의 깊게 생각하다. …을 이끌어내다[인출하다]: *He still hasn't worked out which college he's going to.* 그는 아직도 어느 대학에 갈 것인지 결정하지 못했다. **4 [I]** if a problem or difficult situation works out, it gradually stops being a problem etc. ‖ 문제나 어려운 상황이 점차적으로 곤란한 것이 되지 않다. 잘 되어 가다. 풀리다: *Don't worry. I'm sure everything will work out fine.* 걱정하지 마. 나는 모든 것이 잘 풀릴 것으로 확신해. **5 [I]** to do a set of exercises regularly ‖ 규칙적으로 일련의 운동을 하다. 몸매·체력 관리 운동을 하다[단련하다]: *Sue works out in the gym twice a week.* 수는 체육관에서 일주일에 두 번 운동을 한다.

work up to sth *phr v* [T] to gradually prepare yourself to do something difficult ‖ 어려운 것을 할 수 있도록 스스로 조금씩 준비하다. …에 대비해 나가다: *I'm working up to being able to do 20 laps.* 나는 20바퀴를 돌 수 있도록 계속 준비하고 있다.

work² *n* **1** [U] a job you are paid to do, or the duties and activities that are a part of your job ‖ 돈을 받고 하는 일, 또는 직업의 일부인 임무와 활동. 일. 직업: *Her father's been out of work for a year.* 그녀의 아버지는 일 년째 실직 상태이다. / *Much of our work involves meeting clients.* 우리의 일은 대부분은 고객과 만나는 것이다. ✗DON'T SAY "I have a work." SAY "I have a job."✗ "I have a work."이라고는 하지 않고 "I have a job."이라고 한다. **2** [U] the place where you do your job, or the period during the day when you work ‖

일을 하는 장소, 또는 일하는 낮 동안의 기간. 직장. 업무 시간: *I'll see you at work on Monday.* 월요일에 회사에서 봐요. / *Do you want to go out to dinner after work?* 퇴근 후 저녁 식사하러 가겠어요? **3** [U] the act of doing something useful that involves a lot of effort and time, or the useful activities you do ‖ 많은 노력과 시간이 수반되는 유용한 일을 하는 행위, 또는 사람이 하는 유용한 활동. 생산 활동. 작업: *Hey! Stop talking and get to work!* (=start working) 이봐! 잡담은 그만하고 일을 해! / *Brenda and Lou have done a lot of work on their house.* 브렌다와 루는 집에 대대적인 공사를 했다. **4** [U] the things that you produce as a result of working, studying, or RESEARCH ‖ 작업[연구, 조사]의 결과로서 산출된 것. 작업 성과[산물]. 제작물: *We're pleased with your work.* 우리는 당신이 한 작업에 만족합니다. / *Einstein's work on nuclear physics* 핵물리학 분야의 아인슈타인의 업적 **5** [C, U] something that an artist makes, or the type of things s/he makes ‖ 예술가가 만드는 것이나 만드는 것의 유형. 작품: *great works of art* 대단한 예술 작품 / *I admire Degas' work.* 나는 드가의 작품을 높이 평가한다. —see also WORKS **6 at work** doing a job or an activity ‖ 일이나 활동을 하는. 일하고 있는. 작업 중인: *Crews were at work repairing the roads.* 인부들은 도로를 수리하는 작업 중이다. **7 work clothes** clothes you wear to work in ‖ 일하기 위해 입는 옷. 작업복 — see usage note at JOB

work·a·ble /ˈwɔkəbəl/ *adj* a workable plan, system, idea etc. can be used or done effectively ‖ 계획·체계·생각 등이 효과적으로 쓰이거나 행해질 수 있는. 실행[실현]할 수 있는: *a workable solution* 실행 가능한 해결책

work·a·hol·ic /ˌwɔkəˈhɔlɪk/ *n* INFORMAL someone who works much more than other people, and who does not have time and does not want to do anything else ‖ 다른 사람들보다 훨씬 더 많이 일하며 여가 시간이 없고 다른 어떤 것도 하고 싶어 하지 않는 사람. 일벌레[중독자]

work·bench /ˈwɔkbɛntʃ/ *n* a strong table with a hard surface, used when working with tools ‖ 연장으로 작업할 때에 쓰는, 표면이 단단한 강한 탁자. 작업대

worked up /ˌ ˈ / *adj* INFORMAL very upset or excited about something ‖ 어떤 것에 대해서 매우 화가 나거나 흥분한. 화가 난. 신경을 곤두세운: *Don't get so*

worked up about your daughter. 딸 때문에 너무 열 받지 마라.

work·er /ˈwɔkɚ/ *n* **1** someone who works for a company, organization etc., but is not a manager ‖ 회사·조직 등에서 일하지만 관리자는 아닌 사람. 근로자. 노동자: *Fifty workers lost their jobs.* 50명의 근로자가 일자리를 잃었다. / *a farm worker* 농장 인부 **2** someone who works well or quickly ‖ 일을 잘 하거나 빠르게 하는 사람. 일하는 사람: *Lisa's a good/hard/quick worker.* 리사는 일을 잘 한다[열심히 한다, 빨리 한다].

workers' com·pen·sa·tion /ˌ.. ..ˈ../ *n* [U] money that a company must pay to a worker who is injured or becomes ill as a result of his/her job ‖ 업무수행의 결과로서 부상을 당하거나 병이 든 근로자에게 회사가 지불해야 하는 돈. 산재 보상금

work·fare /ˈwɔkfɛr/ *n* [U] a system under which poor people must do some work, in exchange for the money that they are given by the government ‖ 정부가 주는 돈의 대가로써 가난한 사람들이 약간의 일을 해야 하는 제도. 취로 복지 제도

work·force /ˈwɔkfɔrs/ *n* [singular] all the people who work in a particular country, industry, or company ‖ 특정한 국가[산업, 회사]에서 일하는 모든 사람들. 노동 인구. 인력. 전 직원

work·ing /ˈwɔkɪŋ/ *adj* **1** having a job ‖ 직업이 있는. 일하는: *working parents* 일하는 부모 **2** relating to work, or used for work ‖ 일과 관련된, 또는 일할 때에 쓰는. 작업의: *bad working conditions* 나쁜 작업 환경 / *working clothes* 작업복 **3 be in working order** to be working well and not be broken or have problems ‖ 잘 작동하고 고장 나거나 문제가 없는. 순조롭게 사용[운전]되다: *My father's watch is still in good working order.* 아버지의 시계는 여전히 잘 가고 있다. **4 a working knowledge of sth** enough practical knowledge about something to use it effectively ‖ 효과적으로 사용할 수 있을 정도의 어떤 것에 대한 충분한 실질적인 지식. …의 실전[현장] 지식: *a working knowledge of Spanish* 실제 구사할 수 있는 스페인어 실력

working class /ˌ.. ˌ./ *n* **the working class** the social class that includes people who do not have much money or power and who usually do physical work ‖ 많은 돈이나 권력을 가지고 있지 않고 보통 육체노동을 하는 사람들을 포함하는 사회 계급. 노동자 계급 —

working-class *adj*

work·ings /'wɜːkɪŋz/ *n* [plural] the ways in which something works ‖ 어떤 것이 작동되는 방식. 활동. 작용. 운영: *the workings of government departments* 정부 부처의 활동

work·load /'wɜːkloʊd/ *n* the amount of work that a person or machine is expected to do ‖ 사람이나 기계가 할 수 있을 것으로 예상하는 작업량. (표준) 업무[작업]량: *a heavy workload* (=a lot of work) 과중한 업무량

work·man /'wɜːkmən/ *n* someone who does physical work such as building or repairing things ‖ 어떤 것을 짓거나 보수하는 등의 육체노동을 하는 사람. 직공. 숙련공. 노동자

work·man·like /'wɜːkmən,laɪk/ *adj* skillfully and carefully done ‖ 솜씨 있게 그리고 주의 깊게 한. 능숙한. 솜씨 좋은

work·man·ship /'wɜːkmən,ʃɪp/ *n* [U] skill in making things, or the quality of something that has been made ‖ 사물을 만드는 솜씨, 또는 만들어진 것의 품질. 솜씨. 기량. 만듦새: *the fine workmanship of this table* 만듦새가 훌륭한 이 테이블

work·out /'wɜːk-aʊt/ *n* a period when you do a lot of exercise, especially as training for a sport ‖ 특히 운동 경기를 위한 훈련으로써 많은 운동을 하는 기간. 연습 기간

works /wɜːks/ *n* **1** [plural] all of the writing, paintings etc. that a writer or artist has done ‖ 작가나 화가가 쓰고 그린 모든 글·그림 등. 전(全) 작품: *the complete works of Shakespeare* 셰익스피어 전집 **2 the works** SPOKEN everything ‖ 모든 것. 전부. 일체: *a hamburger with the works* (=with onions, cheese etc.) 모든 토핑이 들어간 햄버거 **3** OLD-FASHIONED a factory or industrial building ‖ 공장이나 산업 건물. 공장. 제작소: *a gas works* 가스 공장

work·sheet /'wɜːkʃiːt/ *n* a piece of paper with questions, exercises etc. for students ‖ 학생들을 위한 질문·연습 문제 등이 있는 종이 한 장. 연습 문제지

work·shop /'wɜːkʃɑp/ *n* **1** a room or building where tools and machines are used in order to make or repair things ‖ 물건들을 만들거나 보수하는 데에 쓰이는 도구와 기계들이 있는 실내나 건물. 작업장. 공장 **2** a meeting at which people try to improve their skills by discussing their experiences and doing practical exercises ‖ 사람들이 자신의 경험에 대해 토론하고 실습을 함으로써 솜씨를 향상시키려고 하는 모임. 연수[연구, 토론]회

work·sta·tion /'wɜːk,steɪʃən/ *n* the part of an office where you work, including your desk, computer etc. ‖ 책상·컴퓨터 등을 포함한 사무실 내의 개인이 일하는 부분. 워크스테이션

world /wɜːld/ *n* **the world** the PLANET we live on including all of the people, countries etc. on it; the Earth ‖ 모든 사람들·나라들 등을 포함한 우리가 살고 있는 행성. 세계. 세상; 현세: *Athletes from all over the world compete in the Olympics.* 전 세계에서 온 운동 선수들이 올림픽에서 경쟁한다. / *the world's longest river* 세계에서 가장 긴 강

1 ▶SOCIETY 사회◀ the society we live in, or a society that is based on a particular type of activity ‖ 우리가 살고 있는 사회 또는 특정 유형의 활동에 기초를 둔 사회. 사회. …계: *Modern technology is changing the world.* 현대의 과학 기술이 사회를 변화시키고 있다. / *the world of baseball* 야구계(界) / *the music world* 음악계

2 in the world SPOKEN used in order to emphasize something you are saying ‖ 말하고 있는 것을 강조하는 데에 쓰여. 도대체. 세상에서: *You're the best dad in the world.* 당신은 세상에서 가장 좋은 아빠입니다. / *Why in the world should I listen to you?* 도대체 왜 내가 네 말을 들어야 해?

3 ▶COUNTRIES 국가들◀ [singular] a group of countries or a part of the world ‖ 일단의 나라들이나 세계의 일부분. …세계: *the Western World* 서구 세계 / *the industrialized world* 선진 세계

4 ▶SB'S FEELINGS 사람의 감정◀ the set of feelings, experiences, thoughts etc. that someone has ‖ 사람이 가진 일련의 감정·경험·생각 등의 경향. 내면 세계. 정신 세계: *Ever since the accident she's been living in her own little world.* (=not noticing anything except her own thoughts etc.) 그 사건 이래 그녀는 자신만의 작은 세계 속에서 살아오고 있다.

5 the animal/plant/insect world animals etc. considered as a group ‖ 한 집단으로 간주되는 동물 등. 동물/식물/곤충계(界)

6 ▶ANOTHER WORLD 다른 세계◀ a PLANET in another part of the universe where other creatures might live ‖ 다른 생명체가 살지 모르는 우주의 다른 부분에 있는 행성. 외계(外界). 천체: *a strange world light years away from earth* 지구에서 수광년 떨어진 이상한 외계

7 a world of INFORMAL a lot of ‖ 많은. 무

수한: *A vacation would do you a world of good.* (=make you feel a lot better) 휴가를 갖고 나면 훨씬 기분 좋아질 거야.

8 be out of this world to be extremely good ‖ 매우 좋다. 월등히 좋다. 탁월하다: *Have you tried their ice cream? It's out of this world!* 너 그들의 아이스크림 먹어 봤어? 정말 환상적이야!

9 be/feel on top of the world to feel extremely happy ‖ 극도로 행복하게 느끼다. 의기양양하다. 좋아서 어쩔 줄 모르다

10 mean the world to sb to be the most important person or thing that someone cares about ‖ 누군가가 신경을 쓰는 가장 중요한 사람이나 사물이다. …에게 모두[전부]이다. 극히 소중하다

11 move/go up in the world to become richer, more important, more responsible etc. in society ‖ 사회에서 더 부유해지다[중요해지다, 책임이 많아지다]. 지위가 상승되다

12 have the best of both worlds to have the advantages of two completely different things ‖ 두 개의 완전히 다른 것들의 이점들을 가지다. 두 가지의 장점만 따다 —see usage note at EARTH

world-class /ˌ. './ *adj* among the best in the world ‖ 세계 최고의. 세계적인. 세계 일류의: *a world-class tennis player* 세계적인 테니스 선수

world·ly /'wɜːldli/ *adj* **1 sb's worldly goods/possessions** everything someone owns ‖ 어떤 사람이 소유하는 모든 것. …의 전 재산 **2** knowing a lot about people and society, based on experience ‖ 경험에 기초하여 사람과 사회에 대해 많이 알고 있는. 세상에 정통한. 처세에 뛰어난: *worldly young men* 처세에 뛰어난 젊은이들

world pow·er /ˌ. '../ *n* a powerful country whose trade, politics etc. affect other countries ‖ 무역·정치 등이 다른 나라들에게 영향을 주는 강력한 나라. 강대국

World Se·ries /ˌ. '../ *n* **the World Series** the last series of baseball games that is played each year in order to decide the best professional team in the US and Canada ‖ 미국과 캐나다의 최고의 프로 팀을 가리기 위해 매년 벌어지는 최종적인 일련의 야구 경기들. 월드 시리즈

world·wide /ˌwɜːld'waɪd./ *adj* everywhere in the world, or within the whole world ‖ 세계 도처에, 또는 전세계의. 세계적인. 전세계에 미치는: *worldwide fame* 세계적인 명성 / *The company employs 2000 people worldwide.* 그 회사는 전세계적으로 2천

명의 사람들을 고용하고 있다.

World Wide Web /ˌ. ˌ. './, written abbreviation **WWW** *n* [singular] **the World Wide Web** a popular system that makes it easier for people to see and use information on the INTERNET ‖ 사람들이 인터넷으로 정보를 찾아 활용하기 쉽게 해주는 널리 퍼진 망. 월드 와이드 웹 —see culture note at INTERNET

worm¹ /wɜːm/ *n* a small tube-shaped creature with a soft body and no legs that lives in the ground ‖ 물렁한 몸체에 다리는 없으며 땅 속에서 사는 작은 관 모양의 생명체. 지렁이 —see also **a (whole) can of worms** (CAN²)

worm² *v* **1 worm your way into sth** to move slowly through a small or crowded place ‖ 좁거나 밀집된 장소를 서서히 통과해 움직이다. 이리저리 뚫고[헤치고] 들어가다: *Reporters wormed their way into the court room.* 기자들은 이리저리 헤치고 법정으로 들어갔다. **2 worm sth out of sb** to get information from someone who does not want to give it ‖ 주고 싶어 하지 않는 사람에게서 정보를 얻어내다. 서서히[교묘하게] 알아내다

worn /wɜːn/ *v* the PAST PARTICIPLE of WEAR ‖ wear의 과거 분사형

worn out, worn-out /ˌ. '../ *adj* **1** very tired because you have been working too much ‖ 너무 많이 일해서 아주 피곤한. 지쳐 버린. 녹초가 된: *I'm all worn out.* 나는 완전히 녹초가 되었다. **2** too old or damaged to be used ‖ 너무 낡거나 손상돼서 사용할 수 없는. 닳아 해진. 낡아 빠진: *a pair of worn-out sneakers* 닳아빠진 운동화 한 켤레

wor·ried /'wɜːid, 'wʌrid/ *adj* unhappy or nervous because you are worrying about someone or something ‖ 어떤 사람이나 사물에 대해 걱정하고 있어서 기쁘지 않거나 불안한. 걱정스러운. 염려하고 있는: *We were really worried about you!* 우리는 정말 네가 걱정스러웠어! / *I got worried when you didn't call.* 나는 네가 전화하지 않아 걱정했다.

wor·ry¹ /'wɜːi, 'wʌri/ *v* **1** [I] to think about someone or something all the time, because you feel nervous or anxious about him, her, or it ‖ 어떤 사람이나 사물에 대해 불안하고 걱정스러워서 항상 생각하다. 걱정[염려]하다: *I worry about Dave – he doesn't eat right.* 나는 데이브가 걱정이 된다. 그는 잘 먹지 않는다. / *She's always worrying about her grades.* 그녀는 항상 자신의 점수에 대해 걱정하고 있다. **2 don't worry** SPOKEN **a)** said when you are trying to make someone feel less anxious ‖ 남을 덜 불안하게 하려고 할 때에 쓰여. 걱정 마, 안심해: *Don't worry, I'm sure they're both fine.* 걱정 마, 나는 둘 다 무사할 것으로 확신해. **b)** used in order to tell someone that s/he does not have to do something ‖ 어떤 사람에게 어떤 일을 할 필요가 없다고 말하는 데에 쓰여. 신경 쓰지 마. (내게) 맡겨: *Don't worry about the kids – I can drive them to school.* 아이들은 신경 쓰지 마. 내가 학교에 태워다 줄 수 있어. **3** [T] to make someone feel nervous, unhappy, or upset ‖ 어떤 사람을 불안하거나 불행하게, 또는 심란하게 하다. 걱정시키다. 속 타게 하다: *It worries me that she hasn't called yet.* 그녀가 아직 전화하지 않아서 나를 속 타게 한다.

worry² *n* **1** a problem or bad situation that makes you unhappy because you do not know how to solve it ‖ 해결 방법을 몰라서 불안하게 하는 문제나 나쁜 상황. 걱정[고민]거리: *My only worry is that the report won't be ready on time.* 내 유일한 걱정거리는 보고서가 제 시간에 준비되지 않을 거라는 것이다. **2** [U] the feeling of being anxious about something ‖ 사물에 대한 걱정스러운 감정. 근심. 불안. 염려

worse¹ /wɚs/ *adj* [the comparative of "bad" "bad"의 비교급] **1** not as good, more unpleasant, or having a lower quality ‖ 그다지 좋지 않은[더 불쾌한, 질이 더 낮은]. 더 나쁜. 열등한: *The play was worse than I expected.* 그 연극은 내가 기대했던 것보다 더 형편없었다. / *Traffic always gets worse after 4:30.* 교통은 항상 4시 30분 이후에 더 악화된다. **2** sicker or in a condition that is not as good ‖ 더 아프거나 상태가 그리 좋지 않은. 더 나빠진. 악화된: *If I feel any worse tomorrow I'll go see a doctor.* 내일 조금이라도 더 나빠지면 진찰 받으러 갈게. / *His hearing has gotten worse.* 그의 청력은 더 나빠졌다. —see study note on page 931

worse² *n* [U] **1** something worse ‖ 더 나쁜 것: *Moving from Georgia was a change for the worse.* 조지아 주에서 이사한 것은 잘못된 일이었어. / *"How was the opera?" "I've seen/heard worse."* (=not bad but not excellent) "오페라 어땠어?" "그저 그랬어." **2 go from bad to worse** to become even worse ‖ 더욱 나빠지다. 악화일로로 가다. 점점 더 악화되다: *Things went from bad to worse and finally we got divorced.* 사태는 점점 더

악화되어 결국 우리는 이혼했다.

worse³ *adv* **1** in a more severe or serious way than before ‖ 전보다 더 심하거나 심각하게. 더 나쁘게. 고약하게: *The pain hurts worse than yesterday.* 통증이 어제보다 더 심하다. **2** not as well, or less successfully ‖ 전혀 더 좋지 않게, 또는 더 성공적이지 않게. 더 나쁘게. 더욱 서투르게[형편없게]: *Margo sings even worse than I do!* 마고는 노래를 나보다 훨씬 더 못해!

wors·en /ˈwɚsən/ *v* [I, T] to become worse, or to make something become worse ‖ 악화되거나 사물이 악화되게 하다. 더 나쁘게[고약하게] 되다[만들다]: *If the weather worsens, the flight will be canceled.* 날씨가 더 악화되면 비행은 취소될 것이다.

worse off /ˌ. ˈ./ *adj* poorer, less successful, or having fewer advantages than you did before ‖ 전보다도 더 가난해진. 더 성공적이지 않은. 더 불리해진. 더 어려워진. 형편이 나빠진: *We're actually worse off than I thought.* 내가 생각했던 것보다 우리는 형편이 더 어렵다.

wor·ship /ˈwɚʃəp/ *v* **-ped**, **-ping** also **-pped**, **-pping** **1** [I, T] to show respect and love for a god, especially by praying in a church, TEMPLE etc. ‖ 특히 교회·절 등에서 기도함으로써 신에 대한 존경과 사랑을 나타내다. 찬양하다. 예배하다 **2** [T] to love and admire someone very much ‖ 누군가를 매우 사랑하고 존경하다. 숭배하다: *She absolutely worships her Grandpa Jim!* 그녀는 할아버지 짐을 절대적으로 존경해! **- worship** *n* [U]: *a house of worship* (=church or building where people can pray) 예배당 - **worshiper** *n*

worst¹ /wɚst/ *adj* [the superlative of "bad" "bad"의 최상급] worse than anything else of the same type ‖ 같은 종류의 어느 것보다 더 나쁜. 최악[최저]의: *It was the worst movie I've ever seen.* 그것은 내가 본 것 중 최악의 영화였다. / *the worst snowstorm in years* 수년 내 최악의 눈보라 —see study note on page 931

worst² *n* **1** also **the worst** someone or something that is worse than every other person, plan, quality, thing etc. ‖ 모든 다른 사람·계획·특성·것 등보다 더 나쁜 사람이나 사물. 가장 나쁜 사람[것]: *She was rude, but worst of all she wouldn't leave me alone.* 그녀는 무례했지만 가장 나쁜 것은 나를 홀로 내버려 두려 하지 않는 것이었다. / *This is the worst I've ever done on a test.* 이건 내가

시험을 본 것 중 최악이다. **2 the worst**
the worst possible result, experience, or
situation ‖ 최악으로 일어날 것 같은 결과
나 경험, 또는 상황. 최악의 사태[체험, 경
우]: *The worst of it is, he even took the
car!* 최악의 사태는 그가 차를 가져가
버렸다는 것이야! / *What's the worst
that can happen if we lose?* 우리가 지면
일어날 최악의 사태는 무엇일까? **3 at
worst** if a thing or situation is as bad as
it can be ‖ 일이나 상황이 있을 수 있는 한
에서 가장 나쁘다면. 최악의 경우에는[에
도]: *At worst the repairs will cost you
around $700.* 최악의 경우에는 수리비가
7백 달러 정도 들 것이다. **4 if (the)
worst comes to (the) worst** if the
worst possible thing happens ‖ 최악으로
일어날 수 있는 일이 일어난다면. 최악의
[만일의] 경우에는: *If worst comes to
worst, we'll have to sell the house.* 최악
의 경우에 우리는 집을 팔아야 할 것이다.

worst³ *adv* in the worst way or most
severely ‖ 최악으로 또는 가장 심하게. 가
장 나쁘게. 형편없이: *Their village was
worst affected by the war.* 그들의 마을이
전쟁으로 최악의 피해를 받았다.

worth¹ /wəθ/ *adj* **1 be worth sth** to
have a particular value, especially in
money ‖ 특히 돈으로 환산해 특정 가치를
가지다. …의 가치[값어치]가 있다. …에
상당한 가치가 있다: *Our house is worth
about $350,000.* 우리 집은 약 35만 달러
상당의 가치가 있다. / *Each question is
worth 4 points.* 각 문제는 4점짜리다. **2
be worth it/be worth doing** to be
helpful, valuable, or good for you ‖ 사람
에게 도움이 되거나 가치가 있거나, 또는
유용하다. (…할) 가치가 있다: *It might
be worth it to call them first.* 그들에게
먼저 전화하는 것은 그럴 만한 가치가 있
을지 모르겠다. / *It's worth a try.* (=you
might get what you want if you try
doing something) 그것은 해 볼 만하다
[가치가 있다]. / *Stop crying over him.
He's not worth it.* 그를 두고 울지 마라.
그는 그럴 가치가 없다. / *It's not worth
going if you get there late.* 네가 거기에
늦게 도착한다면 갈 필요가 없다. **3
worth your while** valuable to you
because you could gain something you
want or need ‖ 원하거나 필요한 것을 얻
을 수 있어서 가치 있는. 해 볼 만한 (가
치가 있는): *We can make it worth your
while to fly to Miami.* 저희는 여러분이
비행기를 타고 마이애미로 가는 것을 보람
있게 해 드릴 수 있습니다.

worth² *n* **1 … worth of sth** an amount
of something based on how much

money you spend, how much time you
use etc. ‖ 얼마나 많은 돈이나 시간 등을
들이는가에 기초한 사물의 양. …양의. …
(값)어치의. …상당의: *twenty dollars'
worth of gas* 20달러어치의 휘발유 / *a
year's worth of training* 1년 상당 기간의
훈련 / *three trucks' worth of supplies* 트
럭 세 대 분량의 보급품 **2 sb's worth**
how important someone is, and how
useful what s/he does is ‖ 어떤 사람의 중
요도 및 그 사람이 하는 일의 유용성의 정
도. …의 가치[진가, 유용성]: *You need
to let people know your real worth.* 너는
사람들이 너의 진가를 알게 해야 한다.

worth·less /'wəθlɪs/ *adj* **1** not
valuable, not important, or not useful ‖
가치 없는, 중요치 않은, 또는 쓸모없는:
*Are you saying the stocks are
worthless?* 그 주식이 가치가 없다는 말씀
입니까? / *I used to think studying was
worthless.* 나는 과거에 공부가 쓸모가 없
다고 생각하곤 했다. **2 a worthless**
person has no good qualities or useful
skills ‖ 사람이 좋은 특성이나 유용한 기술
을 갖지 않은. 쓸모없는, 별 볼일 없는

worth·while /,wəθ'waɪl/ *adj* worth all
of the time, effort, or money you have
used ‖ 소비해 온 모든 시간[노력, 돈]의
가치가 있는. …할 보람이 있는. 가치[값
어치] 있는: *All that work finally seemed
worthwhile.* 그 모든 일이 마침내 가치가
있게 여겨졌다.

wor·thy /'wəði/ *adj* **1** good enough to
deserve respect, admiration, or
attention ‖ 존경이나 감동, 또는 주목을 받
을 만큼 충분히 좋은. 가치가 있는. 훌륭
한: *a worthy opponent* 훌륭한 적수 /
worthy achievements 훌륭한 업적 **2 be
worthy of sth** FORMAL to deserve
something ‖ 무엇을 받을 만하다. …할 만
하다[가치가 있다]: *a leader who is
worthy of our trust* 우리의 신뢰를 받을
만한 지도자

would /wəd, əd, d; *strong* wʊd/ *modal
v* **1** used instead of "will" when
reporting what someone has said ‖ 누군
가가 한 말을 보고할 때 "will" 대신에 쓰
여. …이다[하다]고. …하겠다고: *Mr.
Thomas said it would be OK to go.* 토마
스 씨가 가도 좋다고 말했다. / *She told
me she wouldn't* (=would not) *come.* 그
녀는 오지 않겠다고 내게 말했다. **2** used
in CONDITIONAL sentences that use the
past tenses ‖ 과거 시제를 쓰는 조건문에
쓰여. …할[했을] 것이다. …할[했을] 텐
데: *Dad would be really mad if he knew.*
아빠가 알면 정말 화를 낼 텐데. / *You
know I would help you if I had time.* 정

말 내가 시간이 있으면 너를 도와줄 텐데. / *If you had listened to me, you wouldn't have gotten in trouble.* 네가 내 말을 들었다면 곤란해지지 않았을 것이다. **3** used in order to show that you expected something to happen or be true, but it did not or was not ‖ 어떤 것이 일어나거나 사실이기를 기대했지만 그렇게 되지 않았다는 것을 보여주는 데에 쓰여. …했을 것이다: *I thought Caroline would be happy, but she got really mad at me.* 나는 캐롤라인이 기뻐하리라고 생각했지만 그녀는 내게 정말 화가 나 있었다. **4** used in order to say that something happened regularly in the past ‖ 어떤 일이 과거에 정기적으로 일어났다는 것을 말하는 데에 쓰여. 으레[곧잘] …(하곤)했다. 때로 …하였었다: *Sometimes, Eva would come over and make dinner for the kids.* 때때로 에바가 건너와서 아이들에게 저녁을 해 주곤 했다. **5 would not/wouldn't** used in order to say that someone refused to do something ‖ 다른 사람이 어떤 일을 하기를 거부했다고 말하는 데에 쓰여. 기어이[한사코] …하지 않으려고 했다: *Blair wouldn't answer the question.* 블레어는 그 질문에 한사코 대답하지 않으려 했다. —see study note on page 933

SPOKEN PHRASES

6 would like/would love used in order to say that you want something ‖ 어떤 것을 원한다고 말하는 데에 쓰여. …하고 싶다: *I would love to see your new house!* 나는 네 새집을 보고 싶어! **7 Would you…?** said in order to ask for or offer something politely ‖ 어떤 것을 정중하게 요청하거나 제안하는 데에 쓰여. …해 주지 않겠습니까?: *Would you bring me that broom?* 저 빗자루 좀 갖다 주지 않겠습니까? / *Would you like some coffee or something?* 커피나 다른 것 좀 드시겠습니까? / *Would you mind waiting until tomorrow?* 내일까지 기다려도 괜찮으시겠습니까? **8 I would/I wouldn't** used in order to give advice ‖ 충고하는 데에 쓰여. 나라면 …하겠다/…하지 않겠다: *"What should I do?" "I would tell him you're sorry."* "내가 어떻게 해야지?" "나라면 그에게 미안하다고 하겠어." / *I'd (=I would) go if I were you.* 내가 너라면 가겠다. / *I wouldn't leave the car unlocked, if I were you.* 내가 너라면 자동차 문을 잠그지 않은 채 놔 두지 않겠다. **9** used before verbs that express what you

think, when you want to make an opinion less definite ‖ 의견을 덜 단정적으로 하고 싶을 때 생각하는 바를 표현하는 동사 앞에 쓰여. …입니다만[…일 텐데]: *I would guess the stores are closed by now.* 나는 가게가 지금쯤 문을 닫았으리라고 생각합니다만. / *I would have thought you'd be tired.* 당신이 피곤하리라 생각했습니다만. **10 would (just) as soon** used in order to say that you would prefer something to happen or be done ‖ 어떤 일이 일어나거나 이뤄지기를 선호한다고 말하는 데에 쓰여. 어느 쪽이냐 하면 …하고 싶다. …이기를 바라다: *I'd just as soon you didn't tell her.* 당신이 그녀에게 말하지 않았기를 바랍니다. **11 would rather** said when you prefer doing or having one thing instead of another ‖ 다른 것 대신에 한 가지를 하거나 갖기를 선호할 때 쓰여. …보다 오히려[차라리] …하고 싶다: *I would rather stay home alone than go out with those idiots.* 나는 저 멍청이들과 외출하기보다는 혼자 집에 남아 있고 싶다. **12** used in order to show you are annoyed about something that someone has done ‖ 누군가가 한 일에 대해 화가나 있음을 나타내는 데에 쓰여. …해 보려무나. …하다니: *You would go and tell the teacher!* 너는 어서 가서 선생님께 일러 봐!

would-be /ˈ. ./ *adj* **a would-be actor/robber etc.** someone who hopes to have a particular job or intends to do a particular thing ‖ 특정한 직업을 가지기를 바라거나 특정한 것을 하려고 하는 사람. 배우 지망생/강도 음모자

would·n't /ˈwʊdnt/ *v* the short form of "would not" ‖ "would not"의 단축형: *She wouldn't answer.* 그녀는 대답하지 않을 것이다.

would've /ˈwʊdəv/ *v* the short form of "would have" ‖ "would have"의 단축형: *You would've hated my old boyfriend.* 너는 내 옛 남자 친구를 미워했을 것이다.

wound¹ /wund/ *n* an injury, especially a deep cut made in your skin by a knife or bullet ‖ 부상, 특히 칼이나 탄환으로 피부에 생긴 깊은 상처. 외상. 열상: *gunshot wounds* 총상

wound² *v* [T] **1** to injure someone, especially with a knife or gun ‖ 특히 칼이나 총으로 누군가에게 상처를 입히다. 다치게 하다: *Two officers were badly wounded.* 두 명의 장교들이 심하게 부상당했다. **2 wound sb's pride** to upset

someone by criticizing him/her ‖ 누군가
를 비난해서 화가 나게 하다. …의 자존심
에 상처를 주다 – **wounded** *adj*

USAGE NOTE wounded, injured, and hurt

Use **wounded** when a part of the body is damaged by a weapon: *a wounded soldier.* Use **injured** when someone has been hurt in an accident or in an event such as an earthquake: *One passenger was killed and four were injured.* Use **hurt** to say that a part of your body feels pain: *My neck hurts.*

wounded는 신체의 일부분이 무기에
의해 손상당했을 때 쓴다: 부상당한 병
사. **injured**는 사람이 사고나 지진 등
의 사건에서 다쳤을 때 쓴다: 승객 한
명이 죽었고 네 명은 부상당했다. **hurt**
는 신체의 일부분이 통증을 느낀다고 말
하는 데에 쓴다: 내 목이 아프다.

---

wound³ /waʊnd/ *v* the past tense and PAST PARTICIPLE of WIND ‖ wind의 과거·과
거 분사형

wound up /ˌwaʊnd ˈʌp/ *adj* very angry, nervous, or excited ‖ 매우 화가
나거나 초조하거나, 또는 흥분한. 신경이
곤두선: *He got so wound up he couldn't sleep.* 그는 너무 흥분해서 잠을 이룰 수
없었다.

wove /woʊv/ *v* the past tense of WEAVE
‖ weave의 과거형

wo·ven /ˈwoʊvən/ *v* the PAST PARTICIPLE of WEAVE ‖ weave의 과거 분사형

wow /waʊ/ *interjection* said when you think something is impressive or surprising ‖ 사물이 감동적이거나 놀랍다
고 생각할 때 쓰여. 와. 야. 아이고. 저
런: *Wow! You look great!* 와! 너 정말 멋
있구나!

wran·gle /ˈræŋɡəl/ *v* [I] to argue with someone angrily for a long time ‖ 화나서
오랫동안 남과 다투다. 논쟁[언쟁]하다.
말다툼하다

wran·gler /ˈræŋɡlə/ *n* INFORMAL ⇨
COWBOY

wrap

---

wrap¹ /ræp/ *v* [T] **-pped, -pping 1** to fold cloth, paper etc. around something, especially in order to cover it ‖ 특히 무엇
을 싸기 위해 둘레를 천·종이 등으로 감
다. 포장하다. 감싸다. 두르다: *I haven't wrapped her present yet.* 나는 그녀의 선
물을 아직 포장하지 않았다. / *Wrap this blanket around you.* 이 담요를 몸에 둘러
라. **2 wrap your arms around** to hold someone or something by putting your arms around him, her, or it ‖ 팔을 사람
이나 사물의 주위에 둘러서 (끌어) 안다.
팔로 감싸 안다 **3 have sb wrapped around your finger** to be able to persuade someone to do whatever you want ‖ 원하는 것은 무엇이나 해 주도록
누군가를 설득할 수 있다. 손가락으로 부
리다. 좌지우지하다

wrap sth ↔ **up** *phr v* [T] **1** to completely cover something by folding paper, cloth etc. around it ‖ 종이·천 등
으로 무엇을 칭칭 감아서 완전히 덮다. 감
싸다. 포장하다: *sandwiches wrapped up in foil* 포일로 포장한 샌드위치 **2** to finish or complete a job, meeting etc. ‖
일·회의 등을 끝내거나 완수하다. …을 마
치다. 완료하다: *We should have the project wrapped up in a month.* 우리는
그 (사업) 계획을 한 달 이내에 끝내야 한
다. / *That just about wraps up our show for tonight.* 이것으로 오늘 밤 우리 쇼를
모두 마칩니다. **3 be wrapped up in your children/work etc.** to give too much attention to your children, work, etc. ‖ 아이들·일 등에 너무 많은 관심을
쏟다. 아이들/일에 푹 빠져 있다[몰두해
있다]

wrap² *n* OLD-FASHIONED ⇨ SHAWL

wrap·per /ˈræpə/ *n* the paper or plastic that covers a piece of food, especially candy ‖ 음식 조각 특히 사탕을
싸는 종이나 플라스틱. 포장지: *gum wrappers* 껌 포장지

wrapping pa·per /ˈ.. ˌ../ *n* [C, U] colored paper used for wrapping presents ‖ 선물을 싸는 데에 쓰이는 색종
이. 포장지

wrath /ræθ/ *n* [U] FORMAL very great anger ‖ 매우 심한 분노. 격노

wreak /rik/ *v* LITERARY **wreak havoc** to cause a lot of damage, problems, or suffering ‖ 많은 손해나 문제, 또는 고통을
초래하다. 폭행[파괴, 보복]을 하다

wreath /riθ/ *n* a decoration made from flowers and leaves arranged in a circle
‖ 꽃과 잎이 원형으로 배열되어 만들어진
장식물. 화환. 화관

wreck¹ /rɛk/ *v* [T] INFORMAL to

completely ruin, spoil, or destroy
something or someone ‖ 사물이나 사람을
완전히 파멸시키거나 못쓰게 만들거나, 또
는 파괴하다. 망가뜨리다. 해치다: *I hope
he doesn't wreck the car.* 나는 그가 차를
망가뜨리지 않기를 바란다. / *Her drinking
problem wrecked her marriage/health.*
그녀의 음주 문제는 결혼[건강]을 망쳐 놓
았다.

wreck² *n* **1** a car, plane, or ship that is
so damaged it cannot be repaired ‖ 심하
게 손상되어 수리할 수 없는 차나 비행기,
또는 배. 파괴된 것. 잔해 **2** INFORMAL
someone who is very nervous, tired, or
unhealthy ‖ 몹시 신경질적이거나 피로하
거나, 또는 병약한 사람. 정신[신체]적으로
영락한 사람. 폐인: *I feel like a wreck!* 나
는 완전히 폐인이 된 기분이야! **3** a bad
accident involving cars or planes ‖ 자동
차나 비행기가 관련된 심한 사고. (충돌
등의) 자동차 사고: *Only one person
survived the wreck.* 단 한 사람만이 그 자
동차 사고에서 살아남았다. **4** INFORMAL
something that is very messy and needs
a lot of repairs ‖ 엉망이 되어 많은 수리가
필요한 것. 고물. 폐물: *The house was a
wreck when we bought it.* 그 집은 우리가
샀을 때 폐가나 다름 없었다.

wreck·age /ˈrɛkɪdʒ/ *n* [U] the broken
parts of a car, plane, or building that
has been destroyed in an accident ‖ 사고
로 파괴된 차나 비행기, 또는 건물의 부서
진 부분. 잔해: *Ambulance crews
removed a man from the wreckage.* 구급
차 대원들이 사고 잔해에서 한 남자를 옮
겨갔다.

wren /rɛn/ *n* a very small brown bird
that sings ‖ 노래하는 매우 작은 갈색의
새. 굴뚝새

wrench¹ /rɛntʃ/ *v* [T] **1** to injure part of
your body by twisting it suddenly ‖ 신체
의 일부를 갑자기 비틀어서 상처를 입히
다. 삐다. 염좌하다: *Sam wrenched his
back lifting furniture.* 샘은 가구를 들다
가 허리를 삐었다. **2** to twist and pull
something from its position using force
‖ 어떤 것을 힘으로 그 위치에서 비틀어
당기다. 뽑아내다. 잡아떼다: *Prisoners
had even wrenched doors off their
hinges.* 죄수들은 심지어 문짝을 그 경첩
에서 잡아떼기조차 했다.

wrench² *n* **1** a metal tool with a round
end, used for turning NUTs ‖ 너트를 돌리
는 데에 쓰이는 끝이 둥근 연장. 렌치. 스
패너 **2** a strong feeling of sadness that
you get when you leave a person or
place that you love ‖ 사랑하는 사람이나
장소를 떠날 때 맛보는 격한 슬픈 감정. 비

통한 느낌: *It was a wrench to leave San
Diego.* 샌디에이고를 떠나는 것은 비통한
느낌이었다.

wrench·ing /ˈrɛntʃɪŋ/ *adj* extremely
difficult to deal with, and involving
strong emotions ‖ 다루기가 매우 어렵고
격한 감정을 포함하는. 강렬한 감동을 주는.
가슴이 미어지는 듯한: *a wrenching choice*
가슴 아픈 선택 / *a gut-wrenching/
heart-wrenching story* (=one that
makes you feel strong emotions) 창자가 뒤
틀리는[가슴이 미어지는] 이야기

wrest /rɛst/ *v* [T] FORMAL **wrest sth
from sb a)** to take away someone's
power or influence ‖ 누군가의 힘이나 영
향력을 빼앗다. 박탈하다. 탈취하다 **b)**
to violently pull something away from
someone ‖ 남에게서 어떤 것을 난폭하게
떼어놓다. 억지로 빼앗다. 잡아채다

wres·tle /ˈrɛsəl/ *v* **1** [I, T] to fight by
holding onto someone and trying to
push or pull him/her down ‖ 누군가를 꼭
잡고 밀거나 당겨 넘어뜨리려고 하면서 싸
우다. 씨름하다. 레슬링하다 **2** [I] to try
to deal with a difficult problem or
emotion ‖ 어려운 문제나 감정에 대처하려
고 애쓰다. 분투하다: *For weeks he
wrestled with his guilt.* 수 주일간 그는
죄책감과 씨름했다.

wres·tling /ˈrɛslɪŋ/ *n* [U] a sport in
which you try to throw your opponent to
the ground and hold him/her there ‖ 상
대를 땅에 쓰러뜨리고 거기서 제압하는 스
포츠. 레슬링 – **wrestler** /ˈrɛslɚ/ *n*

wretch /rɛtʃ/ *n* LITERARY someone
whom you pity ‖ 불쌍히 여겨지는 사람.
불행한[불쌍한, 불운한] 사람

wretch·ed /ˈrɛtʃɪd/ *adj* extremely
unhappy, especially because you are
lonely, sick, poor etc. ‖ 특히 외롭고 아프
고 가난하여 매우 불행한. 비참한. 불쌍한

wrig·gle /ˈrɪgəl/ *v* [I, T] to twist from
side to side with small quick
movements, or to move part of your
body this way ‖ 작고 빠른 동작으로 좌우
로 비틀거나 신체의 일부를 이렇게 움직이
다. 꿈틀거리다. 몸부림치다: *a worm
wriggling through the mud* 진흙속을 꿈
틀거리며 나아가는 지렁이 – **wriggle** *n*

wring /rɪŋ/ *v* **wrung, wrung,
wringing** [T] **1** also **wring out** to
tightly twist wet clothes, sheets etc. in
order to remove water from them ‖ 젖은
옷·시트 등에서 물기를 제거하기 위해 꽉
비틀다. 비틀어 짜다[짜내다] **2 wring
your hands** to rub and press your
hands together because you are nervous
or upset ‖ 초조하거나 심란하여 두 손을

서로 모아 비비고 누르다. 걱정하다. 불안해 하다 **3 wring sth's neck** to kill an animal or bird, such as a chicken, by twisting its neck ‖ 닭 등의 동물이나 새의 목을 비틀어 죽이다. 모가지를 비틀다

wring·er /'rɪŋɚ/ n **1 go through the wringer** INFORMAL to have an unpleasant or difficult experience ‖ 불쾌하거나 힘든 경험을 하다. 가혹한 시련을 겪다 **2** a machine used especially in past times for pressing water out of washed clothes ‖ 특히 예전에 세탁한 옷에서 물을 짜내는 데에 쓰인 기계. 탈수기

wrin·kle¹ /'rɪŋkəl/ n **1** a line on your face or skin that you get when you are old ‖ 늙었을 때 얼굴이나 피부에 생기는 선. 주름(살) **2** a line in cloth, paper etc. caused by crushing it or accidentally folding it ‖ 천이나 종이를 구기거나 우연히 접혀서 생기는 선. 주름. 구김: *wrinkles in his shirt* 그의 셔츠의 주름들 **3 iron out the wrinkles** to solve the last small problems that are preventing a plan, system, etc. from working ‖ 계획·시스템 등을 작동하지 못하게 하는 최종적인 사소한 문제들을 해결하다. 난점을 해결하다

wrinkle

His shirt is wrinkled.

wrin·kle² v [I, T] to form small folds in something such as clothes or skin, or to be shaped in these folds ‖ 옷이나 피부 등에 작은 주름을 형성하거나 이러한 주름이 형성되다. …에 주름을 잡다. 주름이 지다: *Oh no, I've wrinkled my dress.* 이런, 내 드레스를 구겼네. / *Her nose wrinkles when she smiles.* 그녀의 코는 웃을 때 주름이 진다. – **wrinkled** adj

wrist /rɪst/ n the joint between your hand and your arm ‖ 손과 팔 사이의 관절. 손목

wrist·watch /'rɪst-wɑtʃ/ n a watch that you wear on your wrist ‖ 손목에 차는 시계. 손목 시계

writ /rɪt/ n a legal document that orders someone to do something or not to do something ‖ 누군가에게 어떤 일을 하거나 하지 말라고 명령하는 법적인 문서. 영장

write /raɪt/ v **wrote, written, writing 1** [I, T] to produce a new book, story, song etc. ‖ 새 책·이야기·노래 등을 만들어 내다. 쓰다. 저술[저작·작곡]하다: *I'm writing about the Civil War for my history essay.* 나는 남북 전쟁에 대해 역사 소논문을 쓰고 있습니다. / *a poem*

written by Walt Whitman 월트 휘트먼이 쓴 시 / *a sign written in Spanish* 스페인어로 쓰인 표지판 **2** [I, T] to write a letter to someone ‖ 누군가에게 편지를 쓰다: *Have you written to Mom yet?* 엄마에게 벌써 편지를 썼느냐? / *He finally wrote me a letter.* 그는 마침내 내게 편지를 썼다. **3** [I, T] to form words, letters, or numbers with a pen or pencil ‖ 펜이나 연필로 단어나 문자, 또는 숫자를 만들어 내다. 글자를 쓰다[기입하다]: *We learned how to write in kindergarten.* 우리는 유치원에서 글 쓰는 법을 배웠다. / *Please write your name and address on the form.* 성명과 주소를 양식에 기입해 주세요. **4** [I, T] to write stories, plays, articles etc. to earn money ‖ 돈을 벌기 위해 소설·희곡·기사 등을 쓰다. 작품을 쓰다[기고하다]: *He writes for The Chronicle.* 그는 크로니클지에 기고한다.

write back phr v [I] to answer someone's letter by writing a letter and sending it to him/her ‖ 편지를 써 보내서 누군가의 편지에 답하다. 답장을 보내다: *Write back soon!* 빨리 답장 보내!

write sth ↔ **down** phr v [T] to write information, ideas etc. on a piece of paper so that you do not forget them ‖ 정보·생각 등을 잊지 않도록 종이조각에 써 놓다. …을 적어 두다. 기록하다: *Why didn't you write her address down?* 왜 그녀의 주소를 적어 두지 않았지?

write in phr v **1** [I] to write a letter to an organization in order to complain, ask for information, or give an opinion ‖ 불평을 하거나 정보를 요청하거나 의견을 말하려고 어떤 단체에 편지를 쓰다. 서면으로 보내다[전하다] **2** [T **write** sb ↔ **in**] to add someone's name to your ballot in order to vote for him/her ‖ 찬성 투표하기 위해 누군가의 이름을 투표용지에 기입하다. 기명 투표하다

write off phr v **1** [T **write** sb/sth ↔ **off**] to decide not to deal with someone or something any longer, because what you had hoped for did not succeed ‖ 바라던 것이 성공하지 못해서 어떤 사람이나 사물을 더 이상 상대하지 않기로 결정하다. …을 그만두다[포기하다]: *I didn't get the grades for the study abroad program, so I had to write it off.* 나는 해외 유학 프로그램에서 학점을 받지 못해서 그만두어야 했다. **2** [T **write** sth ↔ **off**] to decide that a debt will never be paid to you, and officially accept it as a loss ‖ 채무가 결코 변제되지 않으리라 보고 이를 공식적으로 손실로 받아들이기로

결정하다. 장부에서 지우다. 빚을 탕감하다: *The credit company must have written off ten percent as bad charges.* 그 신용 대출 회사는 10퍼센트를 악성 채권으로 장부에서 삭감했음이 틀림없다.

write sth ↔ **out** *phr v* [T] to write all the information that is needed for a list, report, check etc. ‖ 명단·보고서·수표 등에 필요한 모든 정보를 써 넣다. 기입하다. 상세히 쓰다: *Gina wrote out a check for $820.* 지나는 820달러짜리 수표를 (기입해서) 발행했다.

write sth ↔ **up** *phr v* [T] to write something such as a report, article etc. based on notes you made earlier ‖ 전에 작성한 메모를 토대로 보고서·기사 등을 쓰다. …을 상세히 쓰다. 정서하다: *Doug's writing up his review for the school paper.* 더그는 학교 신문에 실을 그의 논평을 작성하고 있다.

write-in /'. ./ *n* a vote for someone who is not on the BALLOT, that you can give by writing his/her name on it ‖ 투표 용지에 이름이 올라 있지 않은 후보의 이름을 기입하여 찬성하는 투표. 기명 투표

write-off /'. ./ *n* an amount of money that you lose from your income, for example because someone has not paid a debt ‖ 예를 들어 누군가가 부채를 지불하지 않아서 수입에서 누락되는 금액. 대손(상각)금. 회수 불능 채권액: *a $149 million write-off to pay for legal fees* 소송 비용을 지불하기 위한 1억 4천 9백만 달러의 손비 처리

writ·er /'raɪtɚ/ *n* someone who writes books, stories etc. in order to earn money ‖ 돈을 벌기 위해 책·소설 등을 쓰는 사람. 작가. 저술가. 문필가

write-up /'. ./ *n* an opinion that is written in a magazine or newspaper about a new book, play, product etc. ‖ 신간 서적·연극·제품 등에 대해 잡지나 신문에 게재된 의견. 기사. 보고. 평(評)

writhe /raɪð/ *v* [I] to twist your body because you are suffering pain ‖ 고통을 받고 있어서 몸을 비틀다. 몸을 뒤틀다. 몸부림치다: *writhing in agony* 괴로워서 몸부림치기

writ·ing /'raɪtɪŋ/ *n* [U] **1** words that are written or printed ‖ 쓰여지거나 인쇄된 말. 글. 글자로 씌어진 것: *I can't read her writing.* 나는 그녀의 글을 읽을 수 없다. **2 in writing** a promise, agreement etc. that is in writing has been written down, which proves that it is official ‖ 약속·협정 등이 공적임을 입증하는 문서로. 문장[서면, 증서]으로 **3** books, stories, and poems in general ‖ 책·소설·

시의 총칭. (문학) 작품. 저서: *We're studying European writing from the 1930s.* 우리는 1930년대부터의 유럽 (문학) 작품을 공부하고 있다. **4** the activity or job of writing books, stories etc. ‖ 책·소설 등을 쓰는 활동이나 직업. 저술[저작, 문필](업): *creative writing* 창의적 저술 활동

writ·ings /'raɪtɪŋz/ *n* [plural] the books, stories, poems etc. that a particular person writes ‖ 특정한 사람이 쓴 책·소설·시 등. 문학 작품. 저서: *Mark Twain's writings* 마크 트웨인의 저서

writ·ten /'rɪt̬n/ *v* the PAST PARTICIPLE of WRITE ‖ write의 과거 분사형

wrong¹ /rɔŋ/ *adj* **1** not correct, not the one you intended, or not the one you should use ‖ 올바르지 않은[의도한 것이 아닌, 또는 사용하기에 마땅한 것이 아닌]. 틀린. 빗나간. 부적당한: *Paul's wrong: Hilary's 17, not 18.* 폴이 틀려 힐러리는 18세가 아니라 17세야. / *I bought the wrong size.* 나는 맞지 않는 치수의 제품을 샀다. / *You must have dialed the wrong number.* (=not the telephone number you wanted) 다른 번호로 전화를 잘못 건 것 같습니다. —opposite RIGHT¹ **2** not morally right or acceptable; bad ‖ 도덕적으로 옳지 않거나 용인될 수 없는. 그릇된. 잘못된; 나쁜: *He didn't do anything wrong!* 그는 아무런 나쁜 짓을 하지 않았어! / *What's wrong with making a profit?* 이익을 내는 것이 뭐가 잘못이지? **3** not suitable ‖ 맞지 않는. 부적합한: *It's the wrong time of year to go skiing.* 스키를 타러 가기에는 맞지 않는 시기이다. / *I think they're wrong for each other.* 그들은 서로 어울리지 않는 것 같아. **4 what's wrong?** SPOKEN **a)** used in order to ask someone what problems s/he has, why s/he is unhappy etc. ‖ 누군가에게 갖고 있는 문제·즐겁지 않은 까닭 등을 물어보는 데에 쓰여. 무슨 문제라도 있어? 무슨 일인데? 뭐가 잘못 됐어?: *"What's wrong, Jenny?" "I miss Daddy."* "무슨 일이니, 제니야?" "아빠가 보고 싶어요." / *What's wrong with your shoulder?* 네 어깨에 무슨 문제라도 있어? **b)** used in order to ask why something is not working ‖ 어떤 것이 작동하지 않는 까닭을 묻는 데에 쓰여. 어떻게 된 거야? 왜 움직이지 않지?: *What's wrong with the phone?* 전화가 어떻게 된 거야? **5 be in the wrong place at the wrong time** to become involved in a bad situation without intending to ‖ 뜻밖에 나쁜 상황에 연관되다. 우연히 휘말리다 **6 get the**

wrong end of the stick INFORMAL to fail to understand the real meaning of something that someone says or does ‖ 어떤 사람이 하는 말이나 행동의 참뜻을 파악하지 못하다. 잘못 알아듣다[이해하다]. 엉뚱하게 받아들이다

wrong² *adv* **1** not done in the correct way ‖ 정확한 방법으로 하지 않아. 잘못하여. 틀리게: *You spelled my name wrong.* 너는 내 이름을 잘못 적었어. — opposite RIGHT² **2 go wrong** to develop problems and stop being good, successful, useful etc. ‖ 문제가 생겨서 양호하거나 성공적이 되거나 유용해지지 않게 되다. 고장 나다. 잘못되다: *Everything went wrong yesterday.* 어제는 모든 일이 순조롭지 못했어. / *If anything goes wrong with your car, we'll fix it for free.* 만약 당신 차가 조금이라도 고장 나면 저희가 무료로 수리해 드리죠. **3 get sth wrong** to remember or understand something incorrectly ‖ 어떤 것을 잘못 기억하거나 이해하다. 잘못 생각하다. 오해하다: *I got the answer wrong.* 나는 답을 잘못 생각했어. / *Don't get me wrong – I think it looks nice.* 나를 오해하지 마라. 내 생각엔 멋있게 보여.

wrong³ *n* **1** [U] behavior that is not morally correct ‖ 도덕적으로 올바르지 못한 행위. 악행: *He doesn't know the difference between right and wrong.* 그는 선악을 구별할 줄 모른다. **2** an action, decision, situation etc. that is not fair ‖ 정당하지 못한 행위·결정·상황 등. 부당한 것[대우]: *a chance to right the wrongs they suffered during the war* (=have a fair solution to an unfair situation) 전쟁 중에 그들이 겪었던 부당한 것들을 바로잡는 기회 **3 be in the wrong** to make a mistake or deserve the blame for something ‖ 잘못하거나 어떤 일로 비난을 받을 만하다 **4 sb can do no wrong** used in order to say that someone seems to be perfect ‖ 사람이 완벽해 보인

다고 말하는 데에 쓰여. …은 완벽한 인간이다: *That man seems to think he can do no wrong!* 저 사람은 자신을 완벽하다고 여기는 것 같아!

wrong⁴ *v* [T] FORMAL to treat someone unfairly or judge him/her unfairly ‖ 누군가를 불공정하게 대하거나 부당하게 평가하다. 학대하다. 오해하다

wrong·do·ing /ˈrɔŋˌduɪŋ/ *n* [C, U] FORMAL illegal actions or immoral behavior ‖ 불법 행위나 부도덕한 행동. 비행. 범죄 – **wrongdoer** *n*

wrong·ful·ly /ˈrɔŋfəli/ *adv* unfairly or illegally ‖ 부당하게. 불법적으로: *Tyrone was wrongfully accused of stealing.* 타이론은 절도 혐의로 부당하게 기소되었다.

wrong·head·ed /ˌrɔŋˈhɛdɪd/ *adj* based on or influenced by wrong ideas ‖ 잘못된 생각에 근거를 두거나 영향을 받은. 잘못 판단한

wrote /roʊt/ *v* the past tense of WRITE ‖ write의 과거형

wrought /rɔt/ *adj* LITERARY made or done ‖ 만들어진. 완성된

wrought i·ron /ˌ. ˈ.../ *n* [U] long thin pieces of iron formed into shapes ‖ 여러 가지 형태로 만들어지는 가늘고 긴 쇳조각. 단철(鍛鐵): *a wrought iron gate* 단철 문

wrung /rʌŋ/ *v* the past tense and PAST PARTICIPLE of WRING ‖ wring의 과거·과거분사형

wry /raɪ/ *adj* showing in a humorous way that you are not pleased by something ‖ 어떤 것 때문에 불쾌하다는 것을 익살스럽게 나타내는. 비꼬는: *a wry smile* 빈정대는 미소

WV the written abbreviation of West Virginia ‖ West Virginia(웨스트버지니아 주)의 약어

WWW *n* the written abbreviation of WORLD WIDE WEB ‖ world wide web(월드와이드 웹)의 약어

WY the written abbreviation of Wyoming ‖ Wyoming(와이오밍 주)의 약어

Xx

X, x /ɛks/ the twenty-fourth letter of the English alphabet ‖ 영어 알파벳의 스물넷째 자

X *adj* used in order to show that a movie has not been officially approved for anyone under the age of 18 ‖ 18세 미만의 사람에게는 공식적으로 허가되지 않은 영화라는 것을 나타내는 데에 쓰여. 미성년자 관람 금지의

X *n* a sign used in mathematics, representing a number or quantity that is not known but can be calculated ‖ 수학에서 밝혀지지는 않았지만 계산해 낼 수 있는 수나 양을 나타내는 데 쓰는 기호. 미지수: *If 3x = 6, then x = 2.* 3x가 6이면 x는 2이다.

xen·o·pho·bi·a /ˌzɛnəˈfoʊbiə/ *n* [U] an extreme fear or dislike of people from other countries ‖ 외국 사람들에 대한 심한 공포나 혐오감. 외국인 공포증

xe·rox, Xerox /ˈzɪrɑks, ˈzirɑks/ *n* TRADEMARK ⇨ PHOTOCOPY – **xerox** *v* [T]

X·mas /ˈkrɪsməs, ˈɛksməs/ *n* INFORMAL a written form of the word Christmas ‖ 크리스마스의 문어형. 크리스마스

XML *n* [U] TECHNICAL extensible markup language; a way of writing a document on a computer so that its structure is clear, and so that it can easily be read on a different computer system ‖ extensible markup language(확장 가능 마크업 언어)의 약어: 컴퓨터 상의 문서의 구조를 명확히 해서 다른 컴퓨터 시스템상에서 쉽게 읽힐 수 있도록 한 문서 작성 방식

x-ray¹ /ˈɛks reɪ/ *n* **1** a beam of RADIATION that can go through solid objects and is used for photographing the inside of the body ‖ 고체를 통과할 수 있어 신체 내부의 촬영에 쓰이는 방사선. 엑스선 **2** a photograph taken by doctors in order to search for broken bones, injuries etc. inside someone's body ‖ 신체 내부의 부러진 **뼈·부상** 등을 찾기 위해 의사들이 찍는 사진. 엑스선 사진

x-ray² *v* [T] to photograph part of someone's body using X-RAYS ‖ 엑스선을 이용해서 사람의 신체 부위의 사진을 찍다. 엑스선 사진을 찍다

xy·lo·phone /ˈzaɪləˌfoʊn/ *n* a musical instrument with flat metal BARs, that you play by hitting them with a stick ‖ 채로 두드려 연주하는, 납작한 금속 막대들로 되어 있는 악기. 실로폰

Y y

Y, y /waɪ/ the twenty-fifth letter of the English alphabet ‖ 영어 알파벳의 스물다섯째 자

ya /yʌ/ *pron* SPOKEN NONSTANDARD you ‖ 너: *See ya later!* 나중에 보자!

yacht /yɑt/ *n* a large expensive boat used for sailing, racing, and traveling for pleasure ‖ 항해·경기·유화에 쓰이는 대형 호화 선박. 유람선

yacht

yak¹ /yæk/ *n* a long-haired cow from central Asia ‖ 중앙 아시아산의 털이 긴 소. 야크

yak² *v* [I] **-kked, -kking** INFORMAL to talk continually about things that are not serious ‖ 심각하지 않은 것들에 대해 계속 이야기하다. 재잘거리다. 수다 떨다

y'all /yɔl/ *pron* SPOKEN a word meaning "you" or "all of you," used mainly in the southern US ‖ 주로 미국 남부에서 쓰이는 "당신"이나 "당신들 모두"를 뜻하는 단어. 여러분: *Will y'all be quiet for a minute?* 여러분 잠시만 조용히 해주겠어요?

yam /yæm/ *n* [C, U] ⇨ SWEET POTATO

yank /yæŋk/ *v* [I, T] to pull something quickly and with force ‖ 힘을 주어 어떤 것을 빠르게 잡아당기다: *Stop yanking on my hair!* 내 머리칼 좀 잡아당기지 마!

Yan·kee /'yæŋki/ *n* **1** someone who fought against the southern states in the American Civil War ‖ 미국 남북 전쟁 당시 남부 주에 대항해 싸운 사람. 북부인 **2** also **Yank** a word meaning a US citizen, often considered an insult when used by someone who is not American ‖ 미국인을 뜻하며 비미국인이 사용할 경우 종종 모욕적인 말로 여겨지는 단어. 양키

yap /yæp/ *v* **-pped, -pping** [I] if a small dog yaps, it BARKs in an excited way ‖ 작은 개가 흥분해서 짖다 **– yap** *n*

yard /yɑrd/ *n* **1** the land around a house, usually covered with grass ‖ 보통 잔디로 덮인 집 주위의 땅. 안뜰: *Somebody kicked a ball into our front yard.* 누군가가 우리집 앞뜰로 공을 차 넣었다. / *a swimming pool in the back yard* 뒤뜰의 수영장 **2** written abbreviation **yd.** a unit for measuring length, equal to 3 feet or 0.9144 meters ‖ 3피트나 0.9144미터에 상당하는 길이

측정 단위. 야드

yard sale /'. ./ *n* a sale of used clothes, furniture, toys etc., in someone's yard ‖ 누군가의 정원에서 하는 중고 의류·가구·장난감 등에 대한 판매. 야드 세일 —compare GARAGE SALE

yard·stick /'yɑrdˌstɪk/ *n* something that you compare another thing with, in order to judge how good or successful it is ‖ 우수함이나 성공의 정도를 판단하기 위해 다른 것과 비교하는 것. 기준. 척도: *He used Deborah's career as a yardstick for his own achievements.* 그는 데보라의 이력을 자신의 업적에 대한 기준으로 삼았다.

yar·mul·ke /'yɑmǝkǝ, 'yɑrmǝlkǝ/ *n* a small round cap worn by some Jewish men ‖ 일부 유대교 남자 신도가 쓰는 작고 둥근 모자. 야물커

yarn /yɑrn/ *n* **1** a thick wooly type of thread used for knitting (KNIT) ‖ 뜨개질용으로 쓰이는 두꺼운 털실의 일종 **2** INFORMAL a long story that is not completely true ‖ 모두 거짓인 장황한 이야기. 허풍

yawn¹ /yɔn/ *v* [I] **1** to open your mouth wide and breathe deeply, usually because you are tired or bored ‖ 보통 피곤하거나 지루하여 입을 크게 벌려 깊게 숨을 쉬다. 하품하다: *He looked at his watch and yawned.* 그는 자신의 시계를 보며 하품했다. **2** to be or become wide open ‖ 크게 벌어지다: *The ground shook and yawned under their feet.* 땅이 흔들리더니 그들의 발밑이 크게 벌어졌다.

yawn

yawn² *n* **1** an act of YAWNing ‖ 하품하는 행위. 하품하기 **2** SPOKEN said in order to show that you think something is not interesting or exciting ‖ 무엇이 흥미 있거나 감동적이지 않다는 생각을 나타내는 데에 쓰여. 지루한 것: *"We could go to Sherri's house." "Yawn!"* "우리는 쉐리의 집에 갈 수 있었어." "지겨워!"

yd. *n* the written abbreviation of YARD ‖ yard의 약어

yeah /yɛǝ/ *adv* SPOKEN yes ‖ 예, 그래 — see usage note at YES

year /yɪr/ written abbreviation **yr.** *n* **1**

also **calendar year** a period of time equal to about 365 days or 12 months, beginning on January 1 and ending on December 31 ‖ 1월 1일에 시작하여 12월 31일로 끝나는 약 365일이나 12개월에 해당하는 기간. 해. 역년: *Where are you spending Christmas this year?* 올해 크리스마스는 어디서 보낼 거니? / *last/next year* (=the year before or after this one) 작년[내년] **2** any period of time equal to about 365 days or 12 months ‖ 약 365일이나 12개월에 해당하는 기간. 1년: *Jenny is five years old.* 제니는 다섯 살이다. / *My passport expires in a year.* 내 여권은 1년이 만기이다. / *None of this will matter a year from now.* 이것은 지금부터 1년간 아무런 문제가 없을 것이다. / *The tax year begins in April.* 과세 연도는 4월에 시작된다. **3 years** INFORMAL many years ‖ 수 년: *It's been years since I played tag.* 나는 술래잡기 놀이를 한 지 오래되었다. / *I haven't seen her in/for years.* 나는 그녀를 몇 년간 만나지 못했다. **4 school/academic year** the period of time during a year when students are in school, college etc. ‖ 학생들이 학교·대학교 등에 다니는 1년간의 기간. 학년: *Final exams are near the end of the school year.* 기말 시험은 학년 말쯤에 있다. **5 all year round** during the whole year ‖ 1년 내내: *It's sunny there all year round.* 거기는 1년 내내 햇빛이 잘 든다.

year·book /ˈyɪrbʊk/ *n* a book printed once a year by a high school or college, about its students, sports events, clubs etc. during that year ‖ 고등학교나 대학교에서 당해 연도의 학생·스포츠 경기·클럽 등에 관해 1년에 한 번 발행되는 책. 학사 연보

year·ling /ˈyɪrlɪŋ/ *n* a young animal, especially a horse, between the ages of one and two ‖ 한 살에서 두 살 사이의 어린 동물, 특히 말

year·ly /ˈyɪrli/ *adj, adv* happening or done every year or once a year ‖ 매해 또는 1년에 한 번 발생하거나 수행되는. 연 1회의. 해마다: *our yearly trip to Florida* 1년에 한 번 있는 우리의 플로리다 여행 / *Investments are reviewed yearly.* 투자는 매년 재검토된다.

yearn /yɚn/ *v* [I] LITERARY to want something very much, especially something extremely difficult to get ‖ 특히 매우 얻기 어려운 것을 간절히 바라다. …을 갈망하다: *They yearned to go home.* 그들은 몹시 집에 가고 싶어했다. / *Trish yearns for affection.* 트리쉬는 애정을 갈망한다. – **yearning** *n* [U]

yeast /yist/ *n* [U] a substance used for making bread rise and for producing alcohol in beer or wine ‖ 빵을 부풀리거나 맥주나 포도주의 알코올 생성에 쓰는 물질. 이스트

yell /yɛl/ *v* [I, T] also **yell out** to shout or say something very loudly because you are angry, excited, or frightened ‖ 화가 나거나 흥분해서, 또는 놀라서 매우 크게 소리치거나 무엇이라고 말하다. 고함치다: *You didn't have to yell at me!* 너 나한테 고함칠 필요는 없었는데! – **yell** *n*

yel·low¹ /ˈyɛloʊ/ *adj* having the same color as LEMONs or butter ‖ 레몬이나 버터 같은 색을 가진. 노란색의

yellow² *n* [U] a yellow color ‖ 노란색 – **yellow** *v* [I, T]: *the yellowing pages of an old book* 낡은 책의 누런 책장들

Yellow Pag·es /ˌ.. ˈ../ *n* TRADEMARK **the Yellow Pages** a book that lists the telephone numbers and addresses of stores, restaurants, and businesses in a particular area ‖ 특정 지역 내의 상점·식당·기업의 전화번호와 주소가 기재된 책

yelp /yɛlp/ *v* [I] to make a short high cry like a dog makes, because of pain, excitement etc. ‖ 고통·흥분 등으로 개가 짖는 듯한 짧고 높은 울음소리를 내다. 캥캥 짖어대다. 비명을 지르다 – **yelp** *n*

yen /yɛn/ *n* **1** a standard unit of money used in Japan ‖ 일본에서 쓰이는 화폐의 기본 단위. 엔(円) **2** SINGULAR a strong desire ‖ 강한 욕망. 갈망: *a yen to travel* 여행에 대한 동경

yep /yɛp/ *adv* SPOKEN yes ‖ 예, 그래 — see usage note at YES

yes /yɛs/ *adv* SPOKEN **1** said in order to give a positive reply to a question, offer, or request ‖ 질문이나 제안, 또는 요청에 대한 긍정적 대답을 하는 데에 쓰여. 그래. 예: *"Is she back at college?" "Yes, she left two days ago."* "그녀가 대학으로 돌아갔니?" "응, 이틀 전에 떠났어." / *"Nancy, did you want some pie?" "Yes, please."* "낸시, 파이 먹고 싶었니?" "예, 주세요." / *"Antonio, will you come tomorrow?" "Yes, Becky, I will."* "안토니오, 내일 올래?" "응, 베키, 갈게." / *Why don't you ask Dad? I'm sure he'll say yes.* 아빠한테 물어 보는 게 어때? 아빠는 그러라고 하실 게 분명해. **2** said in order to agree with a statement ‖ 말한 것에 동의하는 데에 쓰여. 그래요: *"It's such a nice day." "Yes, it is."* "정말 날씨 좋구나." "정말 그래." / *"You're late again." "Yes, I'm sorry."* "너 또 늦었구나." "네, 죄송해요." **3** said in order to show that you do not completely agree with a statement ‖ 어떤 진술에 완전히 동의하지 않는다는 것을 나타내는 데에 쓰여. 그럴까. 설마: *"John doesn't like me anymore." "Yes he does!"* "존은 이제는 나를 좋아하지 않아." "설마 그럴려구!" / *"We need a vacation." "Yes, but we can't afford it."* "우리는 휴가가 필요해." "그래, 하지만 그럴 여유가 없어." **4** said when you have noticed that someone wants your attention ‖ 누군가가 주의를 끌고 싶어 하는 것을 알았을 때 쓰여. 왜요? 뭐지요?: *"Linda!" "Yes?"* "린다!" "왜 그러시죠?" / *Yes, sir, how may I help you?* 예, 선생님, 제가 어떻게 도와드릴까요? **5** said when you are very happy or excited ‖ 매우 행복하거나 흥분했을 때에 쓰여. 좋았어: *Yes! I got the job!* 좋았어! 나 취업했어!

USAGE NOTE yes

In informal speech, we use many different answers instead of **yes**. Some of these are **yeah, uh huh, yep, okay,** and **sure.**
비격식적인 대화에서, 우리는 **yes** 대신에 다양한 대답을 한다. 이러한 것들에는 **yeah, uh huh, yep, okay,** 그리고 **sure** 가 있다.

---

yes·ter·day /ˈyɛstɚdi, -ˌdeɪ/ *adv, n* **1** the day before today ‖ 오늘의 전날. 어제: *Yesterday was their tenth anniversary.* 어제가 그들의 10주년 기념일이었다. / *Did you go to the game yesterday?* 어제 시합에 갔었니? **2** the past, especially the recent past ‖ 과거, 특히 최근의 과거. 얼마 전. 요사이: *yesterday's fashions* 얼마 전의 유행

yet¹ /yɛt/ *adv* **1** a word meaning "at the present time" or "already," used in negative statements and questions ‖ 부정문과 의문문에 쓰여 "지금으로서는"이나 "이미"의 뜻을 지닌 단어. 아직. 벌써: *I don't think she's awake yet.* 그녀가 벌써 잠에서 깨어났다고 생각지 않아. / *Have you heard their new song yet?* 그들의 신곡을 벌써 들어봤니? **2** at some time in the future; still ‖ 미래의 어느 시점에. 언젠가는; 아직도: *She may change her mind yet.* 그녀는 언젠가는 생각을 바꿀지도 모른다. / *We have yet to hear from them.* (=we still have not heard) 우리는 아직도 그들에게서 소식을 듣지 못하고 있다. / *"Has Lori arrived?" "Not yet."* "로리가 도착했니?" "아직 안 왔어." **3** in addition to what you have already gotten, done etc. ‖ 이미 치르거나 행한 것

등에 덧붙여. 게다가: *yet another mistake* 또 다른 실수 / *I'm sorry to ask for help yet again.* (=one more time after many others) 또 다시 도와달래서 미안해. **4** in spite of something; but ‖ 무엇에도 불구하고; 그러나: *a quiet yet powerful leader* 조용하지만 능력 있는 지도자 —see usage notes at JUST¹, STILL¹

yet² *conjunction* in spite of something ‖ 무엇에도 불구하고: *The story's unbelievable, yet supposedly it's all true.* 그 이야기가 믿어지지 않지만 분명 모두 사실일 것이다.

yew /yu/ *n* a tree or bush with leaves that look like flat needles, or the heavy wood of this tree ‖ 납작한 바늘같이 생긴 잎이 있는 나무나 관목, 또는 이 나무의 큰 재목. 주목(朱木)(의 재목)

Yid·dish /ˈyɪdɪʃ/ *n* [U] a language similar to German, used in many places by Jewish people ‖ 여러 지역에서 유대인들이 쓰는 독일어와 유사한 언어. 이디시어 **–Yiddish** *adj*

yield /yild/ *v* **1** [T] to produce something ‖ 무엇을 생산하다. 산출하다: *Company investments yielded a profit of over $45,000.* 기업 투자가 45,000달러 이상의 수익을 산출했다. **2** [I, T] to allow yourself to be forced or persuaded to do something ‖ 무엇을 하기위한 강요나 설득에 자신을 허용하다. …을 포기하다. …에 응하다: *The city council yielded to the public's demands for better bus services.* 시의회는 더 나은 버스 서비스에 대한 대중의 요구에 응했다. / *a leader who will yield power to someone younger* 보다 젊은 사람에게 권력를 내어줄 지도자 **3** [I] to allow the traffic from a bigger road to go first ‖ 더 큰 도로 쪽에서 온 차량이 먼저 가도록 허용하다. 길을 양보하다 **4** [I] to move, bend, or break because of physical pressure ‖ 물리적 압력에 의해 움직이거나 구부러지거나 깨지다

yikes /yaɪks/ *interjection* INFORMAL said when you suddenly notice or realize something that is shocking or that means you must do something quickly ‖ 충격적이거나 빨리 무엇을 해야 한다는 것을 갑자기 알아채거나 깨달았을 때 쓰여. 이키. 으악: *Yikes! I'm late!* 이키! 늦었다.

yip·pee /ˈyɪpi/ *interjection* said when you are very happy or excited about something ‖ 무엇에 대해 매우 행복하거나 흥분했을 때 쓰여. 와. 만세

YMCA *n* Young Men's Christian Association; an organization that provides places to stay, sports centers, and training for young people, especially in large cities ‖ Young Men's Christian Association(기독교 청년회)의 약어; 특히 대도시에 있으며 젊은이들을 위한 숙소·스포츠 센터·훈련을 제공하는 단체 —see also YWCA

yo /youֿ/ *interjection* SLANG said in order to greet someone or get his/her attention, or as a reply when someone says your name ‖ 누군가를 반기거나 관심을 끌기 위해, 또는 누군가가 이름을 부를 때 그 대답으로 쓰여. 야

yo·del /'youdl/ *v* [I] to sing while changing your natural voice to a very high voice and back again many times ‖ 본래의 목소리와 가성을 여러 차례 왔다갔다 변화를 주며 노래하다. 요들조로 노래하다

yo·ga /'yougə/ *n* [U] a system of exercises in which you control your body and mind ‖ 몸과 마음을 조절하는 운동 방식. 요가

yo·gurt /'yougət/ *n* [C, U] a smooth, slightly sour, thick liquid food made from milk ‖ 부드럽고 약간 시큼하면서 걸쭉한 우유로 만든 식품. 요구르트

yoke /youk/ *n* a wooden bar used for joining together two animals, especially cattle, in order to pull heavy loads ‖ 무거운 짐을 끌도록 두 마리의 동물, 특히 소를 연결시키는 데 쓰는 나무 막대. 멍에 – **yoke** *v* [T]

yo·kel /'youkəl/ *n* HUMOROUS someone from the country who has not experienced living in modern society ‖ 현대 사회의 삶을 경험해 보지 않은 시골 사람. 시골뜨기. 촌놈

yolk /youk/ *n* [C, U] the yellow part in the center of an egg ‖ 계란 중앙의 노란 부분. 노른자위

yon·der /'yandə/ *adv, determiner* LITERARY over there ‖ 저쪽에

you /yə, yʊ; *strong* yu/ *pron* [used as a subject or object 주어나 목적어로 쓰여] 1 the person or people someone is speaking or writing to ‖ 누군가가 말이나 글로 언급하고 있는 사람이나 사람들. 당신(들): *You must be hungry.* 너는 배고픈 게 틀림없어. / *Do you want a cigarette?* 담배 피울래? / *I can't hear you.* 당신 말이 들리지 않아요. / *I hope you like the dress.* 나는 그 옷이 네 마음에 들었으면 좋겠다. / *Who made that for you?* 누가 너에게 저것을 만들어 줬니? 2 people in general ‖ 일반적인 사람들. 누구. 아무개: *You can't trust anybody these days.* 요새는 아무도 믿을 수 없다. / *You never know what Jim will say.* 누구도 짐이 무

슨 말을 할지 모른다. —compare ONE² 3 used with nouns or phrases when you are talking to or calling someone ‖ 누군가에게 말하거나 전화할 때 명사 및 구와 함께 쓰여: *You jerk!* 이 바보야! / *You kids be quiet!* 이 꼬맹이들아 조용히 해! 4 **you all** SPOKEN used instead of "you" when speaking to two or more people ‖ 두 명 이상의 사람들에게 말할 때 "you" 대신 쓰여. 자네들: *What do you all want to do tonight?* 너희들 오늘 저녁에 무엇을 하고 싶니?

you'd /yəd, yʊd; *strong* yud/ 1 the short form of "you would" ‖ "you would"의 단축형: *I didn't think you'd mind.* 나는 네가 싫어하지 않으리라고 생각했어. 2 the short form of "you had" ‖ "you had"의 단축형: *You'd better do what he says.* 너는 그가 말하는 것을 하는 편이 낫겠다.

you'll /yəl, yʊl; *strong* yul/ the short form of "you will" ‖ "you will"의 단축형: *You'll have to speak louder.* 너는 조금 더 크게 말해야 할 거야.

young¹ /yʌŋ/ *adj* 1 at an early stage of life or development; not old ‖ 인생이나 성장의 초기 단계인. 젊은. 어린. 늙지 않은: *young children* 어린아이들 / *I used to ski when I was young.* 나는 어렸을 때 스키를 타곤 했다. / *a young country* 신생국 2 seeming younger than you are, or looking younger than something is ‖ 자신보다 어려 보이거나 어떤 것보다 젊어 보이는: *a lotion for healthier younger skin* 보다 건강하고 젊어 보이는 피부를 위한 로션 3 designed or intended for young people ‖ 젊은 사람들을 위해 고안되거나 의도된: *Is this dress too young for me?* 이 옷은 내가 입기에 너무 젊은 스타일 아닌가요?

young² *n* 1 **the young** young people considered as a group ‖ 집합체로서의 젊은이들 2 [plural] young animals ‖ 동물의 새끼: *a turtle and her young* 거북이와 그 새끼

young·ster /'yʌŋstə/ *n* a young person ‖ 젊은이

your /yə; *strong* yʊr, yɔr/ *possessive adj* 1 belonging or relating to the person or people someone is speaking to ‖ 말하고 있는 상대나 상대들에 속하거나 관련된. 당신(들)의: *Is that your mother?* 저분이 너의 어머니시니? / *Your hair looks really nice.* 네 머릿결은 정말 좋아 보인다. / *Don't worry, it's not your fault.* 걱정하지 마, 그건 네 잘못이 아니야. 2 belonging to any person ‖ 어떤 사람에게 속한. 누구의. 아무의: *When*

times are bad you can rely on your friends. 힘든 시기에는 너의 친구들에게 의지할 수 있다.

you're /yər; *strong* yʊr, yɔr/ the short form of "you are" ‖ "you are"의 단축형: *You're bothering me.* 너는 나를 괴롭히는 구나.

yours /yʊrz, yɔrz/ *possessive pron* **1** the thing or things belonging to or relating to the person someone is speaking to ‖ 말하고 있는 상대에게 속하거나 관련된 사물이나 사물들. 너의 것: *Yours is the nicest car.* 네 차가 제일 멋지다. / *That bag is yours, isn't it?* 저 가방 네 것이지, 안 그래? / *Is he a friend of yours?* 그는 네 친구니? **2 yours (truly)** a phrase you write before you sign your name at the end of a letter ‖ 편지 끝에 서명하기 전에 쓰는 경구(敬具) **3 yours truly a)** HUMOROUS used instead of "I" ‖ "I" 대신 쓰여: *Yes, yours truly finally quit smoking.* 예, 제가 결국 담배를 끊었습니다.

your·self /yərˈsɛlf/ *pron, plural* **yourselves** /yərˈsɛlvz/ **1** the REFLEXIVE form of "you" ‖ "you"의 재귀형. 당신 자신: *Don't hurt yourself!* 스스로를 괴롭히지 마라! / *Make yourself a cup of coffee, if you want.* 커피 마시고 싶으면 손수 한 잔 타 드세요. **2** the strong form of "you," used in order to emphasize the subject or object of a sentence ‖ 문장에서 주어나 목적어를 강조하는 데에 쓰이는 "you"의 강조형. 당신 스스로: *Why don't you do it yourself?* 그것을 네 스스로 하는게 어때? **3 (all) by yourself a)** without help ‖ 도움 없이. 혼자 힘으로: *Did you move the sofa by yourself?* 너 혼자 소파 옮긴 거니? **b)** alone ‖ 홀로: *You're going to Ecuador by yourself?* 너 혼자 에콰도르에 갈 예정이니? **4 (all) to yourself** for your own use ‖ 자신이 쓰기 위해: *You'll have the house all to yourself this weekend.* 너는 이번 주말에 혼자 그 집을 독차지할 거야.

youth /yuθ/ *n* **1** [U] the period of time when someone is young, or the quality of being young ‖ 누군가의 어린 시절이나 젊음의 특성. 청춘기. 젊음: *During his youth he lived in France.* 그는 젊은 시절에 프랑스에서 살았다. **2** [U] young people in general ‖ 일반적인 젊은이들: *the youth of the 1960s* 1960년대의 젊은이들 / *a youth hostel* (=a cheap hotel for young people) (젊은이용의 저렴한)유스 호스텔. 청소년 간이 숙박소 **3** a boy or young man, especially a TEENAGER ‖ 특히 10대의 소년이나 젊은 남자. 젊은이: *A*

youth was arrested for stealing. 한 젊은이가 절도로 체포되었다.

youth·ful /ˈyuθfəl/ *adj* typical of young people, or seeming young ‖ 젊은이들 특유의, 또는 젊어 보이는: *his youthful strength* 그의 젊은이다운 체력 / *a youthful mother* 젊은 어머니

you've /yəv, yʊv; *strong* yuv/ the short form of "you have" ‖ "you have"의 단축형: *You've got to take care of yourself.* 스스로 몸조심해야 한다.

yo-yo /ˈyouyou/ *n* **1** a toy you hold in your hand that is made of two circular parts joined together that go up and down a string as you lift your hand up and down ‖ 손에 쥐고서 손을 오르락내리락하면 끈의 위아래로 왔다갔다 하는, 두 개의 연결된 원형 부분으로 이루어진 장난감. 요요 **2** SLANG someone who does stupid things ‖ 어리석은 짓을 하는 사람. 바보

yr. *n* the written abbreviation of YEAR ‖ year의 약어

yuck /yʌk/ *interjection* said when you think something is unpleasant ‖ 무엇이 불쾌하다고 생각할 때 쓰여. 체: *Yuck! This stuff tastes gross!* 체! 이 음식은 진짜 맛없다! –**yucky** *adj*

Yule /yul/ *n* LITERARY Christmas ‖ 크리스마스

Yule·tide /ˈyultaɪd/ *n* [U] LITERARY the period from just before Christmas until just after it ‖ 크리스마스 직전부터 크리스마스 직후까지의 기간. 크리스마스 시즌

yum /yʌm/ *interjection* said in order to emphasize that you think something tastes good ‖ 무엇이 맛있다는 것을 강조하는 데에 쓰여. 음. 맛있어: *Yum! Apple pie!* 음, 이 사과 파이 정말 맛있어!

yum·my /ˈyʌmi/ *adj* INFORMAL food that is yummy tastes very good ‖ 음식이 맛이 아주 좋은. 맛있는

yup·pie /ˈyʌpi/ *n* INFORMAL a young person who only seems interested in having a professional job, earning a lot of money, and buying expensive things ‖ 오직 전문 직업을 갖고 많은 돈을 벌고 값비싼 물건을 사는 데에만 관심이 있는 것처럼 보이는 젊은이. 여피(족)

YWCA *n* Young Women's Christian Association; an organization that provides places to stay, special help, and training for young women, especially in large cities ‖ Young Women's Christian Association(기독교여자 청년회)의 약어; 특히 대도시에서 젊은 여성들을 위한 숙소·특별한 도움·훈련을 제공하는 단체 —see also YMCA

Zz

Z, z /zi/ the last letter of the English alphabet ‖ 영어 알파벳의 마지막 자

za·ny /'zeɪni/ *adj* unusual in a way that is amusing and exciting ‖ 우습고 재미있는 면으로 보통은 아닌. 익살스러운: *a zany new TV comedy* 배꼽 빠지게 웃기는 새 텔레비전 코미디

zap /zæp/ *v* **-pped, -pping 1** [T] INFORMAL to kill, destroy, or attack something extremely quickly, especially by using electricity or a LASER beam ‖ 특히 전기나 레이저 광선으로 아주 재빠르게 어떤 것을 죽이거나 파괴하거나, 또는 공격하다. …을 단숨에 해치우다 **2** [I, T] to change the CHANNEL on a television, using a remote control (=something that allows you to control a television without touching it) ‖ 리모컨을 써서 텔레비전 채널을 바꾸다

zeal /zil/ *n* [U] great interest in something and eagerness to be involved in it ‖ 어떤 것에 대한 대단한 관심과 그것에 몰입하는 열의. 열중. 열정: *political zeal* 정치적 열정 **– zealous** *adj*

ze·bra /'zibrə/ *n* a wild African animal like a horse, that has black and white bands on its body ‖ 흑색과 백색의 줄무늬가 있는 아프리카산 야생 말. 얼룩말

ze·nith /'zinɪθ/ *n* [C usually singular] **1** the most successful point in the development of something ‖ 어떤 것의 발달 과정 중 가장 성공한 순간. 정상. 절정: *This album shows Simon at the zenith of his powers.* 이 앨범은 사이먼이 전성기에 있음을 보여준다. **2** the highest point that the sun or a star reaches in the sky ‖ 하늘로 뻗어 있는 해나 별의 최고점. 천정(天頂)

ze·ro¹ /'zɪroʊ, 'zɪrou/ *number* **1** 0 ‖ 숫자 0 **2** the point between − and + on a scale for measuring something, especially temperature ‖ 특히 온도를 측정하는 눈금에서 −와 + 사이의 점. 영도: *zero degrees Fahrenheit* 화씨 영도 **3** the temperature at which water freezes in the Celsius system of measuring temperature ‖ 섭씨 온도 측정 체계에서의 물이 어는 온도. 빙점(氷點): *20°C below zero* 섭씨 영하 20도

zero² *v*

zero in on sb/sth *phr v* [T] to aim at one thing or give special attention to one person or thing ‖ 어떤 것을 목표로 하거나 사람이나 사물에 특별한 관심을 쏟다. 목표를 겨냥하다. …에 주의를 집중시키다: *war planes zeroing in on a target* 목표물을 겨냥하고 있는 전투기

zero-sum game /ˌ...'./ *n* [singular] a situation in which you receive as much money or advantages as you give away ‖ 준 만큼 많은 돈이나 이득을 얻는 상황. 제로섬 게임

zest /zɛst/ *n* [U] a feeling of eagerness, excitement, and enjoyment ‖ 열의·흥미·즐거움의 감정. 흥취. 재미: *a zest for life* 삶에 대한 열정

zig·zag¹ /'zɪgzæg/ *n* a line that looks like a row of z's joined together ‖ 여러 개의 z자가 한 줄로 연결된 듯한 선. 지그재그

zigzag

zigzag² *v* **-gged, -gging** [I] to move forward by going to the left at an angle, and then to the right at an angle, and then to the left etc. ‖ 좌측으로 비스듬히 간 뒤 우측으로 비스듬히, 그리고 나서 좌측으로 등 앞으로 나아가다. 지그재그로 [좌우로 비스듬히 왔다갔다] 진행하다: *a path that zigzags across the mountain* 산을 가로질러 지그재그로 나 있는 오솔길

zil·lion /'zɪlyən/ *number* INFORMAL an extremely large number or amount ‖ 매우 큰 수나 양. 수천억(이라는 큰 수): *She asked a zillion questions.* 그녀는 매우 많은 질문을 했다.

zinc /zɪŋk/ *n* [U] a white metal that is an ELEMENT that is often used in order to produce other metals ‖ 종종 다른 합금을 만드는 데에 쓰이는 흰 금속. 아연

zip¹ /zɪp/ *v* **-pped, -pping 1** [T] also **zip up** to close or fasten something using a zipper ‖ 지퍼를 이용하여 무엇을 잠그거나 고정시키다. 지퍼로 잠그다: *Zip up your coat.* 코트 지퍼를 잠궈라. **—** opposite UNZIP **2** [I] to go somewhere or do something very quickly ‖ 재빨리 어딘가로 가거나 무엇을 하다. 쌩 하고 움직이다: *A few cars zipped past us.* 몇 대의 차량이 우리를 쌩 하고 지나갔다.

zip² *n* [U] SPOKEN **1** a short form of ZIP CODE ‖ zip code의 단축형 **2** none; zero ‖ 무(無); 영(零)

zip code /'. ./ *n* the number you write

below an address in the US on an envelope, that helps the post office deliver the mail more quickly ‖ 미국에서, 우체국이 우편물을 보다 신속히 배달할 수 있도록, 편지 봉투의 주소 아래에 적는 숫자. 우편 번호

zip file /'. ./ *n* TECHNICAL a computer file in which the information is COMPRESSed (=made smaller) so that it uses less space ‖ 정보가 압축되어 공간을 덜 차지하게 하는 컴퓨터 파일. 집[압축] 파일

zip·per /'zɪpɚ/ *n* an object for fastening clothes, bags etc., with two lines of small pieces of metal or plastic that slide together ‖ 두 줄의 작은 금속이나 플라스틱 조각들이 맞물리며 미끄러져 옷·가방 등을 잠그는 물건. 지퍼

zipper

zit /zɪt/ *n* SLANG ⇨ PIMPLE

zo·di·ac /'zoʊdiˌæk/ *n* **the zodiac** an imaginary circle in space that the sun, moon, and PLANETs follow as a path, which some people believe influences people's lives ‖ 일부 사람들이 사람들의 삶에 영향을 준다고 믿으며, 해·달·행성이 궤도를 이루며 움직인다는 가상의 천체 구대(球帶). 황도대(黃道帶)

zom·bie /'zambi/ *n* **1** INFORMAL someone who moves very slowly and cannot think clearly because s/he is very tired ‖ 매우 천천히 움직이며, 아주 피곤해서 제대로 생각할 수 없는 사람. 활기가 없는[멍청한] 사람 **2** a dead body that is made to move, walk etc. by magic ‖ 마력에 의해 움직이고 걸을 수 있게 된 시체. 되살아난 시체. 좀비

zone /zoʊn/ *n* part of an area that has a specific purpose or has a special quality ‖ 특별한 목적이나 특성이 있는 지역. 지대. 지구: *a no-parking zone* 주차 금지

지역 / *the war/battle/combat zone* 전쟁 [교전, 전투] 지구 —see also TIME ZONE

zon·ing /'zoʊnɪŋ/ *n* [U] a system of choosing areas to be used for particular purposes, such as building houses ‖ 집을 짓는 등의 특정한 목적에 쓰이도록 지역을 선정하는 제도. 지역[지구]제 –**zone** *v* [T]

zoo /zu/ *n* a place where many different types of animals are kept so that people can see them ‖ 사람들이 볼 수 있게 다양한 동물들을 가둬 둔 곳. 동물원

zo·ol·o·gy /zoʊˈɑlədʒi/ *n* [U] the scientific study of animals and their behavior ‖ 동물 및 그들의 행태에 관한 과학적 학문. 동물학 –**zoologist** *n* – **zoological** /ˌzoʊəˈlɑdʒɪkəl/ *adj*

zoom¹ /zum/ *v* [I] INFORMAL to travel very quickly ‖ 매우 빠르게 움직이다. 빨리 달리다: *We zoomed down the highway.* 우리는 고속도로를 질주했다.

zoom in/out *phr v* [I] if a camera zooms in or out, it makes the object it is photographing seem closer or farther away ‖ 카메라가 촬영 중인 피사체를 더 가까이 또는 더 멀리 보이게 하다. (줌 렌즈로) 화상을 확대/축소하다

zoom² *n* the sound an engine makes or the sound of something moving very quickly ‖ 엔진 소리나 어떤 것이 매우 빠르게 움직이는 소리. 붕 하는 소리

zoom lens /'. ./ *n* a camera LENS that moves in order to make the objects you are photographing seem closer and larger ‖ 촬영 중인 피사체를 더 가까이 그리고 더 크게 보이게 하기 위해 움직이는 카메라 렌즈. 줌렌즈

Zs, Z's /ziz/ *n* [plural] SPOKEN **catch/get some Zs** to sleep ‖ 자다

zuc·chi·ni /zuˈkini/ *n* [C, U] a long smooth dark green fruit, cooked and eaten as a vegetable ‖ 야채로 조리해서 먹는 길고 매끈한 진녹색의 과일. 주키니 (서양 호박 품종)

Zzz used in writing to represent sleep ‖ 잠자는 것을 글로 나타내는 데 쓰여. 쿨쿨

Z

Word Building (접사)

prefix (접두사)	meaning (의미)	example (예)
a-, an-	opposite; without; not	amoral, atypical, antonym
anti-	opposed to; against	antifreeze, antidote
audi-, audio-	relating to sound; relating to hearing	audiovisual, auditorium
auto-	of or by yourself	autobiography, automobile
bi-	two; twice	bilingual, biannual
bio-	relating to living things	biology, biochemistry
cent-, centi-	100; 100th part of something	centipede, centimeter
circum-	all the way around something	circumstance, circumference
co-, col-, com-, con-, cor-	with; together	coexist, collect, compassion, confederation, correlation
contra-	against	contraceptive
counter-	opposite; against	counterproductive
cyber-	relating to computers	cyberspace, cyberpunk
de-	to do or make the opposite of; remove from; reduce	decriminalize, decaffeinated, devalue
dis-	opposite	disapprove, dishonesty
down-	to a lower position; to or toward the bottom	downturn, downriver, downstairs
eco-	relating to the environment	ecological
electri-, electro-	relating to electricity	electrify, electrocute
em-, en-	to make something have a quality	empower, enlarge
ex-	no longer being or doing	ex-wife, ex-football player
ex-	out; from	exit, export
extra-	outside; beyond	extraterrestrial, extracurricular
geo-	relating to the earth	geology, geography
hydr-, hydro-	relating to or using water	hydroelectric, hydrant
il-, im-, in-, ir-	not	illogical, impossible, inconvenient, irrational
in-, im-	in; into	incoming, immerse
inter-, intro-, intra-	between; together; within	international, introduce, intravenous
mis-	bad; badly	misfortune, misbehave
mono-	one	monogram, monologue
multi-	many	multicolored, multicultural
non-	not	nonsmoking, nonstandard
over-	too much; beyond; outer; additional	overpopulate, overhang, overcoat, overtime
poly-	many	polygon
post-	later than; after	postgraduate, postpone
pre-	before	prewar, preview
pro-	in favor of	pro-American
re-	again	rewrite, redo, rewind
semi-	half; partly	semicircle, semiprecious
sub-	under; below; less important or powerful	subway, substandard, subcommittee
super-	larger; greater; more powerful	supermarket, superhuman, supervisor
sym-, syn-	with; together	sympathy, synthesis
tele-	at or over a long distance	telescope, television
theo-	relating to God or gods	theology
therm-, thermo-	relating to heat	thermostat, thermometer
trans-	on or to the far side of something; between two things	transatlantic, transportation
tri-	three	tricycle, triangle
ultra-	beyond; extremely	ultrasonic, ultramodern
un-	not; opposite	unhappy, unfair, undress
under-	too little	underdeveloped, underage
uni-	one	unilateral
vice-	next in rank below the most important person	Vice-President, vice-captain

suffix (접미사)	meaning (의미)	example (예)
-ability, -ibility	used in order to make nouns from adjectives that end in -able and -ible	accountability, flexibility
-able, -ible	capable of; having a particular quality	manageable, comfortable, reversible, responsible
al, -ial	relating to something; the act of doing something	coastal, electrical, financial, refusal, denial
-an, ian, -ean	from or relating to a place; someone who has a particular job or knows about a particular subject; relating to or similar to a time, thing, or person; someone who has a particular belief	American, suburban, librarian, historian, subterranean, Victorian, Christian
-ant, -ent	someone or something that does something	servant, disinfectant, resident, repellent
-ar	relating to something	muscular, stellar
-ary	relating to something	customary, planetary
-ation, -tion, -ion	the act of doing something; the state or result of doing something	examination, combination, completion, election
-cy	used in order to make nouns from adjectives	accuracy
-en	made of something; to make something have a particular quality	wooden, golden, darken, strengthen
-ence, -ance, -ency, -ancy	a state or quality; the act of doing something	intelligence, obedience, performance, tendency, presidency, pregnancy
-er, -or, -ar, -r	someone or something that does something	teacher, actor, beggar, writer, photocopier, accelerator
-ery, -ry	an act; a quality; a place where something is done or made	bribery, bravery, snobbery, distillery, bakery
-ful	full of	beauiful, harmful
-goer	someone who goes somewhere regularly	moviegoer, churchgoer
-graph, -graphy	something that is written or drawn	autograph, biography
-hood	the state or time of being something	childhood, manhood, womanhood
-ic, -ical	of; like; relating to a particular thing	photographic, historical
-ify	to affect in a particular way	purify, clarify, terrify
-ish	people or language; having a quality	Spanish, English, childish, selfish
-ism	a belief or set of ideas; the act of doing something	Buddhism, capitalism, criticism
-ist	relating to a political or religious belief	socialist, Methodist
-ity	having a particular quality	stupidity, regularity
-ive	having a particular quality	creative, descriptive
-ize	to make something have a quality; to change something into a different state	modernize, crystallize
-less	without something	childless, careless, endless
-logue, -log	relating to words	monologue, catalog
-ly	in a particular way; at regular times	slowly, quickly, hourly
-ment	the act or result of doing something	government, development
-ness	used in order to make nouns	happiness, softness
-ology	the study or science of something	geology, technology
-or	someone or something that does something	doctor, actor, inventor, radiator, incinerator, incubator
-ory	a place or thing used for doing something; having a particular quality	laboratory, satisfactory, obligatory
-ous, -ious	used in order to make adjectives from nouns	dangerous, furious
-proof	not allowing something to come in, come through, or destroy something	soundproof, waterproof, fireproof
-ship	having a particular position; an art or skill	membership, friendship, scholarship
-wear	clothes of a particular type	menswear, womenswear, sportswear
-y	full of or covered with something; tending to do something	hairy, fuzzy, sleepy, curly

Irregular Verbs (불규칙 동사)

아래의 표는 과거, 과거 분사, 또는 현재 분사가 불규칙한 형태를 갖는 동사를 나타낸 것이다. 두 가지 이상의 형태가 있는 것은 앞에 놓인 것이 가장 흔히 쓰는 형태이다.

verb (원형)	past tense (과거)	past participle (과거 분사)	present participle (현재 분사)
arise	arose	arisen	arising
awake	awoke	awoken	awaking
be	-see BE		
bear	bore	borne	bearing
beat	beat	beaten	beating
become	became	become	becoming
begin	began	begun	biginning
behold	beheld	beheld	beholding
bend	bent	bent	bending
bet	bet	bet	betting
bid²	bid	bid	bidding
bid³	bade or bid	bid or bidden	bidding
bind	bound	bound	binding
bite	bit	bitten	biting
bleed	bled	bled	bleeding
blow	blew	blown	blowing
break	broke	broken	breaking
breed	bred	bred	breeding
bring	brought	brought	bringing
broadcast	broadcast or broadcasted	broadcast or broadcasted	broadcasting
build	built	bulit	building
burn	burned	burned or burnt	burning
burst	burst	burst	bursting
buy	bought	bought	buying
cast	cast	cast	casting
catch	caught	caught	catching
choose	chose	chosen	choosing
cling	clung	clung	clinging
come	came	come	coming
cost²	cost	cost	costing
creep	crept	crept	creeping
cut	cut	cut	cutting
deal	dealt	dealt	dealing
dig	dug	dug	digging
dive	dived or dove	dived	diving
do	-see DO		
draw	drew	drawn	drawing
dream	dreamed or dreamt	dreamed or dreamt	dreaming
drink	drank	drunk	drinking
drive	drove	driven	driving
dwell	dwelled or dwelt	dwelled or dwelt	dwelling
eat	ate	eaten	eating
fall	fell	fallen	falling
feed	fed	fed	feeding
feel	felt	felt	feeling
fight	fought	fought	fighting
find	found	found	finding
fit	fit or fitted	fitted	fitting
flee	fled	fled	fleeing

verb (원형)	past tense (과거)	past participle (과거 분사)	present participle (현재 분사)
fling	flung	flung	flinging
fly	flew	flown	flying
forbid	forbade or forbid	forbid or forbidden	forbidding
forecast	forecast or forecasted	forecast or forecasted	forecasting
foresee	foresaw	foreseen	foreseeing
forget	forgot	forgotten	forgetting
forgive	forgave	forgiven	forgiving
freeze	froze	frozen	freezing
get	got	gotten	getting
give	gave	given	giving
go	went	gone	going
grind	ground	ground	grinding
grow	grew	grown	growing
hang¹	hung	hung	hanging
have	-see HAVE		
hear	heard	heard	hearing
hide	hid	hidden	hiding
hit	hit	hit	hitting
hold	held	held	holding
hurt	hurt	hurt	hurting
keep	kept	kept	keeping
kneel	knelt or kneeled	knelt or kneeled	kneeling
knit	knitted or knit	knitted or knit	knitting
know	knew	known	knowing
lay	laid	laid	laying
lead	led	led	leading
leap	leaped or leapt	leaped or leapt	leaping
leave	left	left	leaving
lend	lent	lent	lending
let	let	let	letting
lie¹	lay	lain	lying
lie²	lied	lied	lying
light	lit or lighted	lit or lighted	lighting
lose	lost	lost	losing
make	made	made	making
mean	meant	meant	meaning
meet	met	met	meeting
mislead	misled	misled	misleading
mistake	mistook	mistaken	mistaking
misunderstand	misunderstood	misunderstood	misunderstanding
outbid	outbid	outbid	outbidding
outdo	outdid	outdone	outdoing
overcome	overcame	overcome	overcoming
overdo	outdid	outdone	outdoing
overcome	overcame	overcome	overcoming
overdo	overdid	overdone	overdoing
overhang	overhung	overhung	overhanging
overhear	overheard	overheard	overhearing
override	overrode	overridden	overriding
overrun	overran	overrun	overrunning

verb (원형)	past tense (과거)	past participle (과거 분사)	present participle (현재 분사)
oversee	oversaw	overseen	overseeing
overtake	overtook	overtaken	overtaking
overthrow	overthrew	overthrown	overthrowing
pay	paid	paid	paying
prove	proved	proved *or* proven	proving
put	put	put	putting
read	read	read	reading
rebuild	rebuilt	rebuilt	rebuilding
redo	redid	redone	redoing
relay	relayed	relayed	relaying
repay	repaid	repaid	repaying
rewrite	rewrote	rewritten	rewriting
rid	rid	rid	ridding
ride	rode	ridden	riding
ring²	rang	rung	ringing
rise	rose	risen	rising
run	ran	run	running
saw	sawed	sawn *or* sawed	sawing
say	said	said	saying
see	saw	seen	seeing
seek	sought	sought	seeking
sell	sold	sold	selling
send	sent	sent	sending
set	set	set	setting
sew	sewed	sewn *or* sewed	sewing
shake	shook	shaken	shaking
shed	shed	shed	shedding
shine¹	shone	shone	shining
shrink	shrank	shrunk	shrinking
shut	shut	shut	shutting
sing	sang	sung	singing
sink	sank *or* sunk	sunk	sinking
sit	sat	sat	sitting
slay	slew	slain	slaying
sleep	slept	slept	sleeping
slide	slid	slid	sliding
sling	slung	slung	slinging
slit	slit	slit	slitting
sow	sowed	sown *or* sowed	sowing
speak	spoke	spoken	speaking
speed	sped *or* speeded	sped *or* speeded	speeding
spend	spent	spent	spending
spin	spun	spun	spinning
spit	spit *or* spat	spat	spitting
split	split	split	splitting
spread	spread	spread	spreading
spring	sprang	sprung	springing
stand	stood	stood	standing
steal	stole	stolen	stealing
stick	stuck	stuck	sticking

verb (원형)	past tense (과거)	past participle (과거 분사)	present participle (현재 분사)
sting	stung	stung	stinging
stink	stank or stunk	stunk	stinking
strew	strewed	strewn or strewed	strewing
stride	strode	stridden	striding
strike	struck	struck or stricken	striking
string	strung	strung	stringing
strive	strove or strived	striven or strived	striving
swear	swore	sworn	swearing
sweep	swept	swept	sweeping
swell	swelled	swollen	swelling
swim	swam	swum	swimming
swing	swung	swung	swinging
take	took	taken	taking
teach	taught	taught	teaching
tear	tore	torn	tearing
tell	told	told	telling
think	thought	thought	thinking
throw	threw	thrown	throwing
thrust	thrust	thrust	thrusting
tread	trod	trodden	treading
undergo	underwent	undergone	undergoing
understand	understood	understood	understanding
undertake	undertook	undertaken	undertaking
undo	undid	undone	undoing
unwind	unwound	unwound	unwinding
uphold	upheld	upheld	upholding
upset	upset	upset	upsetting
wake	woke	woken	waking
wear	wore	worn	wearing
weave	wove or weaved	woven or weaved	weaving
wed	wed or wedded	wed or wedded	wedding
weep	wept	wept	weeping
wet	wet or wetted	wet	wetting
win	won	won	winning
wind	wound	wound	winding
withdraw	withdrew	withdrawn	withdrawing
withhold	withheld	withheld	withholding
withstand	withstood	withstood	withstanding
wring	wrung	wrung	wringing
write	wrote	written	writing